Racehorse Record

FLAT 1998

Raceform's A-Z Guide to horses which ran during the 1998 Flat Season
(November 9th 1997 - November 7th 1998)

Sponsored by: Stan James Established 1973

Editor	Ashley Rumney
Editorial Director	David Dickinson
Production Editor	Steven Clarke
Comments by	Richard Lowther, David Bellingham, Andrew Ayres, Steven Clarke, Catherine Clarke, Nicky Bowen, Ashley Rumney
Production Assistants	Nicky Bowen, Louise Mackinlay, David Bellingham, Catherine Clarke,
Raceform Ratings	David Dickinson, Walter Glynn, Nicky Bowen
Colour Section	Liz Addison
Design	Daniel Di Pol, Ashley Rumney, Mike Shaw
Photographs	Martin Lynch

Typeset and Published by Raceform Ltd,
Compton, Newbury, Berkshire, RG20 6NL
Tel: 01635 578080
Fax: 01635 578101
Editorial: 01635 577643
Web http://www.raceform.co.uk
EMail: raceform@raceform.co.uk

Printed by BPC Information Ltd, Exeter

ISBN 1 901100 21 9

£22.00

CONTENTS

Full details of all Raceform services and publications are available from
Raceform, Compton, Newbury, Berkshire RG20 6NL.
Tel: 01635 578080 Fax: 01635 578101.
Web http://www.raceform.co.uk
EMail: raceform@raceform.co.uk

Cover Photo: Martin Lynch
High-Rise beats City Honours in the Vodafone Derby at Epsom

INTRODUCTION

WELCOME to *Racehorse Record Flat 1998*. Thank you to the many readers of the 1997 edition who gave us their enthusiastic support and in some cases constructive criticism.

Racehorse Record is now also incorporated as part of the *Raceform Weekly Form Book* subscription and we hope this will prove a popular addition to our subscribers' reference libraries. The book is designed not only as an historical reference, but also as a guide to the future.
As Flat racing becomes more global, it is also useful to have information on the top horses racing around the world and, to this end, we have included all horses trained abroad which appeared in *Raceform, The Form Book* and attained a rating of 90 or above.

The horses are listed in alphabetical order, together with their suffix. This is followed by the current *Raceform* Master Rating (RR) for the Flat (i.e. 74f), along with an All-Weather Master Rating if applicable (i.e. 65a). The figures after this are the Official BHB Ratings (Turf, and All-Weather where applicable) as at the end of the season (7th November), as long as the horse has been entered in a handicap during the season (otherwise a BHB Rating is not issued). It should be noted that BHB Handicappers officially rate no horse above 120 after September (100 for two-year-olds) in preparation for the International Classifications which assign a figure to all the best horses. These figures are released in January and appear in *Raceform Update*, and all other Trade publications.

The number to the far right is the number of the last race in the Form Book in which the horse competed, with finishing position. This allows the reader to refer quickly and easily to Racehorse Record's companion title, *Raceform Flat Annual For 1999*.

The second line displays the age, colour, sex and pedigree of the horse. The Sire's name and suffix is followed by the average winning distance of his progeny (excluding two-year-olds). This figure is the mean average winning distance of all wins by horses he has sired, displayed to the nearest tenth of a furlong. The number in **BOLD** type in parentheses which follows is the average highest winning rating of his progeny in the last 12 months. The same set of figures is given for the Grandsire (sire of dam), in his role as a Grandsire.

Full form figures are shown for the 1998 campaign, rather than just the last six runs, as trends often reveal themselves through the course of a season. For horses trained outside GB and Ireland, the figures relate only to races published in *Raceform, The Official Form Book* and *Computer Raceform*.

The win and total prizemoney is followed by the horse's win record, which displays the year, month, course, going, race type (H=Handicap, C=Claimer, S=Seller, L=listed, G1=Group One, G2=Group Two and G3=Group Three), distance to the nearest tenth of a furlong, BHB and *Raceform* Rating. Please note, the BHB Rating is the original mark of the horse at entry and NOT adjusted for such factors as overweight and penalties that may have been incurred. An Asterisk (*) at the start of the line indicates that the win was for the horse's current trainer, whilst an arrow at the end (<) indicates that it was the highest *Raceform* Rating gained thus far in its career.

The line directly above the narrative shows a breakdown of the runs in 1998 on Turf and All-Weather, listing the different distances and goings on which it raced, together with success rate.

The narrative itself produces an analysis of all the horse's runs and gives an assessment of physical attributes and ability. Distances at which the horse is effective, its optimum distance, going preferences, effectiveness in headgear, course preferences and best performance in the current season are all listed here. N.B. the going preferences shown are based on the *Raceform* going rather than the Official, as the latter is often called into question, whereas *Raceform's* is based on race times and takes into account other external influences. Where appropriate, the editorial also features an assessment of how the horse has run and views on its future prospects.

The final line details the trainer with wins-to-runs ratio in parentheses, followed by the owner's name. If the horse has been with more than one handler during its career, the previous trainer is shown, again with wins-to-runs ratio. N.B. National Hunt performances are included in the horse's total run figures for the trainer, for additional information.

ABBREVIATIONS AND THEIR MEANINGS

hvy	=	heavy	frm	=	firm
sft	=	soft	hrd	=	hard
g-s	=	good to soft	Equi	=	Equitrack All-Weather
gd	=	good	Fibr	=	Fibresand All-Weather
g-f	=	good to firm			

"acts on gd to frm, best on g-f" = horse is able to act effectively on any ground between good and firm, but is best when the ground is actually good to firm.

"Turf high" = this season's best performance rating

"AW high 68" = this season's performance rating if achieved on an All-Weather surface.

"(18 Aug Pont g-f RF 3637)" = the date, racecourse, going, and *Raceform* number in the Form Book where a horse achieved its highest rating.

"(1st run)" = indicates if a horse's rating was achieved on its first run on that surface.

"l.h. tracks" = courses with left-handed bends.

"r.h. tracks" = courses with right-handed bends.

"tight tracks" = courses with tight bends. (Raceform assess bend tightness, and these are not necessarily the tracks with the tightest circumference.

The tracks with the tightest bends are :-

Bath	Goodwood	Ripon
Catterick	Hamilton	Thirsk
Chester	Lingfield	Windsor
Epsom	Musselburgh	Wolverhampton
Folkestone	Redcar	Yarmouth

RACEFORM RATINGS

Raceform Ratings for each horse indicate the actual level of performance attained in that race. The figure shown after RR in the text represents the BEST public form that our Handicappers still believe each horse is capable of reproducing.

To use the ratings constructively in determining those horses best-in in future events, the following procedure should be followed:

(i) In races where all runners are the same age and are set to carry the same weight, no calculations are necessary. The horse with the highest rating is the horse best in.

(ii) In races where all runners are the same age but are set to carry different weights, add one point to the Raceform rating for every pound less than 10 stone to be carried, deduct one point for every pound more than 10 stone.

For example

Horse	Age & weight	Adjustment from 10 stone	RR base Rating	Adjusted Rating
Spotland	3-10-1	-1	78	77
Field Mill	3-9-13	+1	80	81
Moss Rose	3-9-7	+7	71	78
Oakwell	3-8-11	+17	60	77

Therefore Field Mill is top-rated (best-in)

(iii) In races concerning horses of different ages the procedure in example (ii) should again be followed, but reference must also be made to the Official Scale of Weight-For-Age (see page facing).

For example

12 furlongs July 20th

Horse	Age & weight	Adjust fr 10 st	RPH Rating	Adjust Rating	W-F-A deduct	Final Rating
Avocet	5-10-0	0	90	90	Nil	90
Sanderling	4-9-9	+5	83	88	Nil	88
Turnstone	3-9-4	+10	85	95	-12	83
Dunlin	4-8-7	+21	73	94	Nil	94

Therefore Dunlin is top-rated (best-in)

(A 3-y.o is deemed 12lb less mature than a 4-y.o or older horse on 20th July over 12f. Therefore, the deduction of 12 points is necessary).

The following symbols are used in conjunction with the ratings:

++ almost certain to prove better
+ likely to prove better
d disappointing (has run well below best recently)
? form hard to evaluate - rating may prove unreliable
t tentative rating based on race-time

Weight adjusted ratings for every race are published daily in Raceform Private Handicap. For subscription terms please contact the Subscription Department on 01635-578080.

THE OFFICIAL SCALE OF WEIGHT, AGE & DISTANCE (Flat)

The following scale of weight-for-age should be used only in conjunction with the Official ratings published in this book. Use of any other scale will introduce errors into calculations. The allowances are expressed as the number of pounds that is deemed the average horse in each group falls short of maturity at different dates and distances.

Distance Furlongs	Age	JAN		FEB		MARCH		APRIL		MAY		JUNE		JULY		AUGUST		SEPT		OCT		NOV		DEC	
		1/15	16/31	1/14	15/28	1/15	16/31	1/15	16/30	1/15	16/31	1/15	16/30	1/15	16/31	1/15	16/31	1/15	16/30	1/15	16/31	1/15	16/30	1/15	16/31
5	2	–	–	–	–	–	47	44	41	38	36	34	32	30	28	26	24	22	20	19	18	17	17	16	16
	3	15	15	14	14	13	12	11	10	9	8	7	6	5	4	3	2	1	1	–	–	–	–	–	–
6	2	–	–	–	–	–	–	–	–	44	41	38	36	33	31	28	26	24	22	21	20	19	18	17	17
	3	16	16	15	15	14	13	12	11	10	9	8	7	6	5	4	3	2	2	1	1	–	–	–	–
7	2	–	–	–	–	–	–	–	–	–	–	–	–	38	35	32	30	27	25	23	22	21	20	19	19
	3	18	18	17	17	16	15	14	13	12	11	10	9	8	7	6	5	4	3	2	2	1	1	–	–
8	2	–	–	–	–	–	–	–	–	–	–	–	–	–	–	37	34	31	28	26	24	23	22	21	20
	3	20	20	19	19	18	17	15	14	13	12	11	10	9	8	7	6	5	4	3	3	2	2	1	1
9	3	22	22	21	21	20	19	17	15	14	13	12	11	10	9	8	7	6	5	4	4	3	3	2	2
	4	1	1	–	–	–	–	–	–	–	–	–	–	–	–	–	–	–	–	–	–	–	–	–	–
10	3	23	23	22	22	21	20	19	17	15	14	13	12	11	10	9	8	7	6	5	5	4	4	3	3
	4	2	2	1	1	–	–	–	–	–	–	–	–	–	–	–	–	–	–	–	–	–	–	–	–
11	3	24	24	23	23	22	21	20	19	17	15	14	13	12	11	10	9	8	7	6	6	5	5	4	4
	4	3	3	2	2	1	1	–	–	–	–	–	–	–	–	–	–	–	–	–	–	–	–	–	–
12	3	25	25	24	24	23	22	21	20	19	17	15	14	13	12	11	10	9	8	7	7	6	6	5	5
	4	4	4	3	3	2	2	1	1	–	–	–	–	–	–	–	–	–	–	–	–	–	–	–	–
13	3	26	26	25	25	24	23	22	21	20	19	17	15	14	13	12	11	10	9	8	8	7	7	6	6
	4	5	5	4	4	3	3	2	1	–	–	–	–	–	–	–	–	–	–	–	–	–	–	–	–
14	3	27	27	26	26	25	24	23	22	21	20	19	17	15	14	13	12	11	10	9	9	8	8	7	7
	4	6	6	5	5	4	4	3	2	1	–	–	–	–	–	–	–	–	–	–	–	–	–	–	–
15	3	28	28	27	27	26	25	24	23	22	21	20	19	17	15	14	13	12	11	10	9	8	8	7	7
	4	6	6	5	5	4	4	3	3	2	1	–	–	–	–	–	–	–	–	–	–	–	–	–	–
16	3	29	29	28	28	27	26	25	24	23	22	21	20	19	17	15	14	13	12	11	10	9	9	8	8
	4	7	7	6	6	5	5	4	4	3	2	1	–	–	–	–	–	–	–	–	–	–	–	–	–
18	3	31	31	30	30	29	28	27	26	25	24	23	22	21	20	18	16	14	13	12	11	10	10	9	9
	4	8	8	7	7	6	6	5	5	4	3	2	1	–	–	–	–	–	–	–	–	–	–	–	–
20	3	33	33	32	32	31	30	29	28	27	26	25	24	23	22	20	18	16	14	13	12	11	11	10	10
	4	9	9	8	8	7	7	6	6	5	4	3	2	1	–	–	–	–	–	–	–	–	–	–	–

RACEFORM TOP RATED EUROPEAN THREE-YEAR-OLDS AND UPWARDS OF 1998

Horse	Rating
Intikhab (USA)	131
Desert Prince (IRE)	129
Dr Fong	128
Swain	127
Sagamix	127
Loup Sauvage (USA)	126
High-Rise (IRE)	126
Tiger Hill (IRE)	126
Croco Rouge (IRE)	125
Insatiable (IRE)	125
Elnadim (USA)	125
Royal Anthem	125
Fly To The Stars (GB)	125
Caitano (GB)	125
Jim And Tonic	124
Fragrant Mix	124
Leggera (IRE)	124
Dream Well	124
Astarabad (USA)	123
Marathon (USA)	123
Kayf Tara (GB)	123
Among Men	123

RACEFORM TOP RATED EUROPEAN TWO-YEAR-OLDS OF 1998

Horse	Rating
Lujain (USA)	120
Enrique	117
Mujahid (USA)	116
Aljabr (USA)	112
Auction House (USA)	111
Stravinsky (USA)	111
Bint Allayl	110
Commander Collins (IRE)	110
Show Me The Money (IRE)	108
Edabiya (IRE)	108
Orpen (USA)	107
Raise A Grand (IRE)	106
Josr Algarhoud (IRE)	106
Way of Light (USA)	106
Sheer Viking (IRE)	105
Red Sea (GB)	105
Smittenby (IRE)	105
Blue Melody (USA)	105
Bertolini (USA)	104
Wannabe Grand (IRE)	104
Pistachio	104
Sicnee (USA)	104
King Adam (IRE)	104

A. P. ASSAY (USA) RR 119a 5164a[5]
4 br f A P Indy (USA)
Form - 5
1998 AW 0-1: (6f) (Dirt)
Currently high-class filly.
**J Gonzalez in USA [0-1] Trudy McCaffery & John Toffan.*

AA-YOUKNOWNOTHING BHB 75f RR 80f 3757[13]
2 b c Superpower 6.6f **(58)** - Bad Payer (Tanfirion) 7f **(61)**
Form - 02116720
Record 1998 - 1st:2 2nd:2 3rd:0 Ran:8
Win Prizemoney £6,079 *Total Prizemoney* £8,038
Wins * **1998** May Thirsk (GD) 5f 68 <
* **1998** Apr Mussel (G-S) 5f 68 <
1998 Turf 2-8: (5f 2-7, 6f) (gd 2-6, g-f, frm)
Decent colt, effective 5f, acts on g-f, has worn blinkers. Turf high 80 - 2nd of 7 giving 7lb to Shirley Not (2 Aug Chester 5f g-f RF 3290). Got off the mark with a game victory in a maiden auction event at Musselburgh in April and showed progressive form in the first half of the campaign. Beaten in a hot seller on his final run, he was sold at Newmarket in October to Julie Craze for 4,000 gns. Takes his name from a remark made to Raceform's esteemed race-reader Alan Amies during the infamous Top Cees libel case.
**M W Easterby [2-8] Bodfari Stud Ltd.*

ABAJANY BHB 88f RR 89f 5078[19]
4 b g Akarad (FR) 9.7f **(73)** - Miss Ivory Coast (USA)(Sir Ivor) 10.2f **(70)**
Form - 4200401031204830
Record 1998 - 1st:2 2nd:2 3rd:2 Ran:16
Pre1998 - 1st:2 2nd:1 3rd:2 Ran:12
Win Prizemoney £18,444 *Total Prizemoney* £32,019
Wins * **1998** Aug Ayr (G-S) H 8f 78 85 <
* **1998** Jly Bath (GD) 10.2f 78
* 1997 Spt Sandow (G-F) H 8.1f 71 77
* 1997 Aug Leices (GD) H 8f 66 72
1998 Turf 2-16: (8f 1-8, 9f 2, 10f 1-6) (sft 2, g-s, gd 2-7, g-f 5, frm)
Useful gelding, effective 8 to 10f, best at 8f, acts on g-s to frm, likes left handed tracks. Turf high 89 - 2nd of 19 giving 2lb to Tonight's Prize (16 Aug Pontefract 8f frm RF 3673) - also 1st of 9 giving 7lb to Magic Mill (11 Aug Ayr RF 3520). Consistent. He had a very busy season, gaining his first success over ten furlongs at Bath in July, though he successfully dropped back to a mile at Ayr the following month. **M R Channon [4-32] John White and Partners.*

ABBAJABBA BHB 81f RR 83f 5068[4]
2 b c Barrys Gamble 7f **(50)** - Bo' Babbity (Strong Gale) 5.6f **(66)**
Form - 62054
Record 1998 - 1st:0 2nd:1 3rd:0 Ran:5
Win Prizemoney £0 *Total Prizemoney* £1,261
1998 Turf 0-5: (5f 3, 6f 2) (sft, gd 2, g-f 2)
Decent colt. Turf high 83 - 2nd of 6 getting 4lb from Mitchigan (3 Aug Ripon 6f gd RF 3313).
**C W Fairhurst [0-5] North Cheshire Trading & Storage Ltd.*

ABBATIALE (FR) RR 111f 1918a[2]
3 gr f Kaldoun (FR) 9.9f **(84)**
Form - 152
1998 Turf 1-3: (10f, 11f 1-2) (hvy 1-1, sft, gd)
Group-class filly. Turf high 111 - 2nd of 11 to Zainta (7 Jun Chantilly 11f sft RF 1918a) - also 1st of 7 from Welsh Autumn (14 Apr Saint-cloud RF 0832a). She looked promising when winning at Saint-Cloud in April, but her supporters lost faith after a below par effort on the same track the following month. Waiting tactics proved her downfall that day and, ridden more aggressively, she put up a much bolder display in the Prix de Diane Hermes, running Zainta to a short-head. Very tough, she relishes easy ground.
**D Sepulchre in FR [1-4] G Coude.*

ABBEYDORAN RR 11a 361[8]
7 ch m Gildoran 11.6f **(58)** - Royal Lace (Royal Palace) 9f **(56)**
Form - 8
Record 1998 - 1st:0 2nd:0 3rd:0 Ran:1
1998 AW 0-1: (8f) (Fibr)
Poor mare. **D Burchell [0-2] Mrs Iris Goode.*

ABBIE BLUEYES BHB 42f49a RR 45f 49a 4863[3]
2 b f Petong 7.6f **(58)** - Abalone (Abwah) 11.5f **(52)**
Form - 870003
Record 1998 - 1st:0 2nd:0 3rd:1 Ran:6
Win Prizemoney £0 *Total Prizemoney* £372
1998 Turf 0-4: (5f 2, 6f, 7f) (gd, frm 3) 1998 AW 0-2: (5f, 6f) (Fibr 2)
Moderate filly, has worn blinkers. Turf high 45. AW high 41.
**M W Easterby [0-6] T R Beston.*

ABE RR 90f 4950a[6]
2 ch c Barathea (IRE) - Patsy Western (Precocious) 8.6f **(62)**
Form - 1216
Record 1998 - 1st:2 2nd:1 3rd:0 Ran:4
Win Prizemoney £22,348 *Total Prizemoney* £23,588
Wins * **1998** Spt Cascin (SFT) L 7.5f 89+ <
1998 Jly San Si (HVY) 6f
1998 Turf 2-4: (6f 1-2, 8f 1-2) (hvy 1-1, sft 1-2, gd)
Useful colt. Turf high 90 (began Jly) - 2nd of 9 giving 2lb to Lough Swilly (12 Aug Nottingham 6f gd RF 3583) - also 1st of 8 from Chichicastenango (5 Spt Cascine RF 4216a). He has done most of his racing in Italy, and won two races, including a listed event.
**D T Thom [1-2] (from C Drew [1-2] Aug 1998).*

ABERFELDY BHB 68f RR 71f 4868[6]
2 b f Petong 7.6f **(58)** - Klewraye (Lord Gayle (USA)) 8.8f **(62)**
Form - 536
Record 1998 - 1st:0 2nd:0 3rd:1 Ran:3
Win Prizemoney £0 *Total Prizemoney* £487
1998 Turf 0-3: (5f, 6f 2) (gd, g-f 2)
Currently above-average filly. Turf high 71 (began Spt) - 3rd of 10 to Resalah (6 Oct Redcar 6f g-f RF 4673). **J Berry [0-3] J Berry.*

ABERKEEN BHB 55f RR 58f 3854[18]
3 ch g Keen 11.1f **(58)** - Miss Aboyne (Lochnager) 6f **(59)**
Form - 040073080
Record 1998 - 1st:0 2nd:0 3rd:1 Ran:9
Pre1998 - 1st:1 2nd:2 3rd:0 Ran:5
Win Prizemoney £3,243 *Total Prizemoney* £6,681
Wins * 1997 Jun Pontef (G-F) 6f 57 <
1998 Turf 0-9: (6f 2, 7f 5, 8f, 10f) (sft, g-s, gd 6, frm)
Workmanlike, fair gelding, effective 6f, acts on frm, has worn blinkers. Turf high 58. **M Dods [1-14] N A Riddell.*

ABFAB RR 4201[15]
6 b g Rabdan 10.1f **(42)** - Pas de Chat (Relko) 9.9f **(59)**
Form - 0
Record 1998 - 1st:0 2nd:0 3rd:0 Ran:1
1998 Turf 0-1: (8f) (gd)
Currently very poor gelding. **P J Hobbs [0-2] Winton Bloodstock Ltd.*

ABI BHB 79f RR 80f 4855[7]
3 ch f Chief's Crown (USA) 10.2f **(75)** - Carmelized (CAN) (Key To The Mint (USA)) 9.4f **(75)**
Form - 31407
Record 1998 - 1st:1 2nd:0 3rd:1 Ran:5
Win Prizemoney £3,436 *Total Prizemoney* £4,431
Wins * **1998** Jly Pontef (G-F) 10f 80 <
1998 Turf 1-5: (10f 1-3, 11f, 12f) (g-s, gd, frm 1-3)
Unfurnished, decent filly. Turf high 80 - 1st of 4 getting 5lb from King Tango (17 Jly Pontefract RF 2888).
**H R A Cecil [1-5] Old Road Securities Plc.*

ABISSINIA BHB 46f50a RR 28f 50a 2658[9]
2 b f Puissance 7.1f **(60)** - Amathus Glory (Mummy's Pet) 7.7f **(60)**
Form - 82730
Record 1998 - 1st:0 2nd:1 3rd:1 Ran:5
Win Prizemoney £0 *Total Prizemoney* £845
1998 Turf 0-2: (5f 2) (gd 2) 1998 AW 0-3: (5f 3) (Fibr 3)
Moderate filly. Turf high 28. AW high 46 (1st run) - 2nd of 11 getting 5lb from Shirley Not (27 Apr Southwell 5f Fibr RF 0888).
**N Tinkler [0-5] Mrs Christine Cawley.*

ABLA RR 52f 4135[10]
2 b f Robellino (USA) 9.5f **(68)** - Sans Blague (USA) (The Minstrel (CAN)) 10f **(72)**
Form - 0
Record 1998 - 1st:0 2nd:0 3rd:0 Ran:1
1998 Turf 0-1: (8f) (g-f)
Currently fair filly. **E A L Dunlop [0-1] Hamdan Al Maktoum.*

ABLE LASS (IRE) BHB 35f32a **RR 32f 32a** 2654[11]
4 ch f Classic Music (USA) 7.2f **(57)**-Miami Life(Miami Springs) 9.9f **(59)**
Form - 50
Record 1998 - 1st:0 2nd:0 3rd:0 Ran:1
Pre1998 - 1st:0 2nd:0 3rd:0 Ran:3
1998 AW 0-1: (8f) (Fibr)
Light-framed, very moderate filly. **R W Armstrong [0-4] Dr Cornel Li.*

ABLE PETE RR 65f 4928[11]
2 b c Formidable (USA) 7.8f **(60)** - An Empress (USA) (Affirmed (USA)) 9.3f **(79)**
Form - 70
Record 1998 - 1st:0 2nd:0 3rd:0 Ran:2
1998 Turf 0-2: (6f, 7f) (g-s, frm)
Currently average colt. Turf high 65 (1st run) - 7th of 15 giving 5lb to Golden Charm (15 May Nottingham 6f frm RF 1245).
**J L Dunlop [0-2] Paul Locke.*

ABOARD (FR) RR 107f 3054a[1]
3 b c Hero's Honor (USA) 9.2f **(76)** - Abordable (USA) (Formidable (USA)) 9.2f **(63)**
Form - 251
1998 Turf 1-3: (10f 1-2, 12f) (gd, g-f 1-2)
Currently Pattern-class colt. Turf high 107 - 1st of 12 getting 12lb from Triano (19 Jly Frankfurt RF 3054a). Demoted after winning a Group 3 in Frankfurt, he failed to stay a mile and a half in the German Derby, but returned to winning form over 10 furlongs in July. He has a bright turn-of-foot and should add to his reputation in 1999. **A Schutz in GER [1-3] H von Finck.*

ABOVE BOARD RR 40f 4256[11]
3 b g Night Shift (USA) 8.1f **(73)** - Bundled Up (USA) (Sharpen Up) 8.3f **(67)**
Form - 00800
Record 1998 - 1st:0 2nd:0 3rd:0 Ran:5
Pre1998 - 1st:0 2nd:0 3rd:1 Ran:2
Win Prizemoney £0 *Total Prizemoney* £514
1998 Turf 0-5: (5f, 7f 3, 8f) (gd 2, frm 3)
Scopey, moderate gelding, has worn blinkers. Turf high 40.
**J Hanson [0-5] J Hanson (from B W Hills [0-2] Jly 1997).*

A BREEZE BHB 42f47a **RR 38f 47a** 5079[23]
4 br g Precocious 7.2f **(54)** - Wasimah (Caerleon (USA)) 8.6f **(71)**
Form - 80556050
Record 1998 - 1st:0 2nd:0 3rd:0 Ran:8
Pre1998 - 1st:1 2nd:0 3rd:0 Ran:14
Win Prizemoney £4,162 *Total Prizemoney* £4,890
Wins * 1996 Aug Pontef (G-F) 5f 82 <
1998 Turf 0-7: (5f, 6f, 7f 2, 8f 3) (sft, gd, frm 5) 1998 AW 0-1: (6f) (Fibr)
Unfurnished, very moderate gelding, has worn blinkers. Turf high 50. Inconsistent. **D Morris [1-22] The A Breeze Fan Club.*

ABREEZE (USA) BHB 104f **RR 106df** 4315[5]
3 b c Danzig (USA) 8.1f **(88)** - Priceless Pearl (USA) (Alydar (USA)) 9.1f **(76)**
Form - 145
Record 1998 - 1st:1 2nd:0 3rd:0 Ran:3
Pre1998 - 1st:1 2nd:0 3rd:0 Ran:3
Win Prizemoney £11,298 *Total Prizemoney* £12,708
Wins * **1998** Jly Yarmou (G-F) H 6f 94 105+ <
* 1997 Spt Sandow (G-F) 7.1f 94++
1998 Turf 1-3: (6f 1-3) (gd, g-f 1-1, frm)
Well made, Pattern-class colt, effective 6f, acts on g-f, has worn blinkers. Turf high 106 (began Jly) - also 1st of 13 giving 14lb to Tattinger (21 Jly Yarmouth RF 2979). He looked a Group horse when winning on his reappearance at Yarmouth in July, but proved a costly failure on his two subsequent starts. It was a similar story during his juvenile campaign and he looks one who runs best when fresh. **S bin Suroor [2-6] Godolphin.*

ABSALOM'S LAD BHB 69f **RR 64f** 4498[10]
3 ch c Absalom 7.1f **(56)** - Rose Bouquet (General Assembly (USA)) 10f **(68)**
Form - 370
Record 1998 - 1st:0 2nd:0 3rd:1 Ran:3
Pre1998 - 1st:0 2nd:0 3rd:1 Ran:2
Win Prizemoney £0 *Total Prizemoney* £1,466
1998 Turf 0-3: (7f, 8f 2) (gd, g-f, frm)
Workmanlike, average colt. Turf high 64 (1st run) (began Spt) - 3rd of 8 giving 5lb to Queens Dagger (3 Spt York 8f g-f RF 4071).
**P W Harris [0-5] The Absolute Twelve.*

ABSENTEE BHB 57f **RR 59f** 4506[10]
3 br f Slip Anchor 12.7f **(75)** -Meliora (Crowned Prince (USA)) 10.1f **(67)**
Form - 4841750
Record 1998 - 1st:1 2nd:0 3rd:0 Ran:7
Pre1998 - 1st:0 2nd:0 3rd:0 Ran:1
Win Prizemoney £3,132 *Total Prizemoney* £3,342
Wins * **1998** Aug Nottin (G-F) H 14.1f 56 59 <
1998 Turf 1-6: (10f, 12f, 14f 1-3, 16f) (gd 2, g-f 1-2, frm 2) 1998 AW 0-1: (12f) (Fibr)
Leggy, fair filly, effective 14 to 16f, acts on gd to g-f. Turf high 59 - 1st of 7 getting 14lb from Netta Rufina (12 Aug Nottingham RF 3585). Consistent.
**J L Harris [1-5] J H Henderson (from W Jarvis [0-3] Jun 1998).*

ABSOLUTE BREEZE RR 7a 248[8]
4 gr f Absalom 7.1f **(56)** - Hosting (Thatching) 8f **(66)**
Form - 8
Record 1998 - 1st:0 2nd:0 3rd:0 Ran:1
1998 AW 0-1: (9f) (Fibr)
Light-framed, currently very poor filly. **Ian Williams [0-1] S F Turton.*

ABSOLUTE PERFORMER BHB 14f **RR** 2757[8]
3 ch f Theatrical Charmer 10.9f **(63)**-Absolutely Blue(Absalom) 7.2f **(58)**
Form - 8708
Record 1998 - 1st:0 2nd:0 3rd:0 Ran:4
1998 Turf 0-4: (6f, 7f, 10f, 11f) (gd 3, g-f)
Light-framed, formerly very poor filly, has worn blinkers - 8th of 8 getting 17lb from Diamond Crown (13 Jly Ayr 11f gd RF 2757).
**R M McKellar [0-4] Derek Fifer.*

ABSOLUTE RISK BHB 18f **RR 8f** 4401[22]
4 ch f Risk Me (FR) 8f **(53)** - Absent Lover (Nearly A Hand) 5.6f **(48)**
Form - 000
Record 1998 - 1st:0 2nd:0 3rd:0 Ran:3
1998 Turf 0-3: (6f, 10f, 11f) (frm 3)
Very poor filly. Turf high 8 (began Aug).
**W G M Turner [0-2] Oakford Horse Transport (from R Lee [0-1] Aug 1998).*

ABSOLUTE UTOPIA (USA) BHB 70f **RR 68f** 4480[4]
5 b g Mr Prospector (USA) 8.6f **(88)** - Magic Gleam (USA) (Danzig (USA)) 8.4f **(76)**
Form - 4025144
Record 1998 - 1st:1 2nd:1 3rd:0 Ran:7
Pre1998 - 1st:2 2nd:1 3rd:0 Ran:16
Win Prizemoney £10,619 *Total Prizemoney* £14,830
Wins * **1998** Aug Kempto (G-F) H 12f 63 67 <
* 1997 Oct Salisb (GD) H 10f 55 62
* 1997 Aug Bath (GD) H 8f 53 60
1998 Turf 1-7: (9f 2, 10f 2, 11f, 12f 1-2) (gd 2, g-f 3, frm 1-2)
Average gelding, effective 8 to 12f, best at 12f, acts on gd to frm, best on frm, likes right handed tracks, likes tight tracks, excels at Goodwood. Turf high 68 - 4th of 11 getting 3lb from Rainbow Ways (25 Spt Haydock 12f frm RF 4480) - also 1st of 8 giving 10lb to Duello (19 Aug Kempton RF 3737). Consistent. He got off the mark for the season when stepped up to twelve furlongs at Kempton in August.
**N E Berry [3-19] M T Lawrance (from E A L Dunlop [0-4] May 1996).*

ABSTONE QUEEN BHB 44f30a **RR 45f 30a** 2266[10]
4 b f Presidium 7.5f **(56)** - Heavenly Queen (Scottish Reel) 7f **(61)**
Form - 0000680
Record 1998 - 1st:0 2nd:0 3rd:0 Ran:4
Pre1998 - 1st:5 2nd:2 3rd:9 Ran:37
Win Prizemoney £15,834 *Total Prizemoney* £21,246
Wins * 1997 Mar Catter (GD) S 7f 56
* 1996 Oct Catter (GD) H 7f 61 66 <
* 1996 Aug Redcar (G-F) H 6f 57 49
* 1996 Aug Catter (G-F) S 7f 59+
* 1996 Aug Yarmou (GD) S 6f 55
1998 Turf 0-4: (7f 4) (gd 3, frm)
Light-framed, moderate filly, effective 7f, acts on gd to g-f, mostly

wears blinkers, likes left handed tracks, likes tight tracks. Turf high 45. Inconsistent. **P D Evans [5-42] J E Abbey.*

ABSTRACT (IRE) RR 64f 4400[20]
2 b f Perugino (USA) - Kalapa (FR) (Mouktar)
Form - 50540
Record 1998 - 1st:0 2nd:0 3rd:0 Ran:5
Win Prizemoney £0 *Total Prizemoney* £209
1998 Turf 0-5: (5f, 6f 4) (g-f, frm 4)
Average filly, has worn blinkers. Turf high 64 (began Jly).
**D J S Cosgrove [0-5] The Camelot Members.*

ABTAAL BHB 62f61a **RR 64f 61a** 4636[6]
8 b g Green Desert (USA) 7.8f **(78)** - Stufida (Bustino) 10.4f **(64)**
Form - 48031511726
Record 1998 - 1st:3 2nd:1 3rd:1 Ran:11
Pre1998 - 1st:2 2nd:2 3rd:2 Ran:27
Win Prizemoney £12,314 *Total Prizemoney* £18,860

Wins							
* 1998	*Aug*	*Southw*	*(STD)*	*C*	*7f*		*59+*
* 1998	Aug	Bright	(FRM)		7f		64
1998	Jly	Bright	(G-F)	C	7f		50
1997	Jun	Lingfi	(G-F)	SH	7f	49	48

1998 Turf 2-8: (6f 3, 7f 2-4, 8f) (gd 1-4, g-f 1-1, frm 3) 1998 AW 1-3: (7f 1-3) (Fibr 1-3)
Average gelding, effective 7f, acts on g-f - acts on Fibr, has worn blinkers (extremely effectively), prefers left handed tracks, likes tight tracks. Turf high 64 - 1st of 14 giving 12lb to Lady Yavanna (12 Aug Brighton RF 3574). AW high 62 (began Aug) - 2nd of 12 giving 11lb to Over The Moon (5 Spt Wolverhampton 7f Fibr RF 4117) - also 1st of 10 giving 1lb to Tayovullin (14 Aug Southwell RF 3639). A bit of a quirky customer, he did well during the summer with three wins, two at Brighton and one on the Southwell Fibresand. It seems as though seven furlongs is his best trip these days.
**Mrs N Macauley [2-6] G Wiltshire (from R J Hodges [2-25] Jly 1998).*

ABU CAMP BHB 60f **RR 66f** 4571[9]
3 b c Indian Ridge 7.6f **(74)** - Artistic Licence (High Top) 10.2f **(67)**
Form - 670370
Record 1998 - 1st:0 2nd:0 3rd:1 Ran:6
Pre1998 - 1st:0 2nd:0 3rd:0 Ran:1
Win Prizemoney £0 *Total Prizemoney* £474
1998 Turf 0-6: (6f, 8f 4, 10f) (gd, g-f 2, frm 3)
Workmanlike, average colt, has worn blinkers. Turf high 66 (began Jly). **M J Heaton-Ellis [0-7] John Manser.*

ABUHAIL (USA) BHB 85f **RR 84f** 4824[8]
3 b br c Silver Hawk (USA) 11.2f **(85)** - Bank Key (USA) (Key To The Mint (USA)) 9.4f **(75)**
Form - 45518
Record 1998 - 1st:1 2nd:0 3rd:0 Ran:5
Pre1998 - 1st:1 2nd:1 3rd:1 Ran:3
Win Prizemoney £11,573 *Total Prizemoney* £14,814

Wins								
* 1998	Oct	York	(GD)	H	10.4f	81	84	<
1997	Jly	Redcar	(G-F)		7f		74+	

1998 Turf 1-5: (8f, 10f 1-2, 11f, 12f) (g-f 1-2, frm 3)
Scopey, decent colt, effective 10f, acts on g-f. Turf high 84 - 1st of 15 giving 5lb to Puzzlement (7 Oct York RF 4698). Below-par on his early runs in 1998, but showed improved form after a break. He was sold for 34,000 guineas in October.
**P T Walwyn [1-5] Hamdan Al Maktoum (from D Morley [1-3] Oct 1997).*

ABULJJOOD (IRE) BHB 70f **RR 71f** 3047[5]
3 b c Marju (IRE) 9.2f **(76)** -Midway Lady(USA) (Alleged (USA)) 10f **(76)**
Form - 068635
Record 1998 - 1st:0 2nd:0 3rd:1 Ran:6
Win Prizemoney £0 *Total Prizemoney* £525
1998 Turf 0-6: (10f, 11f 2, 12f 2, 14f) (gd 2, g-f, frm 3)
Above-average colt, often wears blinkers. Turf high 87.
**B Hanbury [0-6] Hamdan Al Maktoum.*

ABUNDANCE BHB 51f **RR 60f** 4759[11]
3 b f Cadeaux Genereux 7.9f **(76)** - Flourishing (IRE) (Trojan Fen) 8.1f **(62)**
Form - 845034080
Record 1998 - 1st:0 2nd:0 3rd:1 Ran:9
Win Prizemoney £0 *Total Prizemoney* £686
1998 Turf 0-9: (6f, 7f 3, 8f 5) (g-s, gd 3, g-f, frm 4)
Scopey, average filly, effective 8f, acts on frm, has worn blinkers. Turf high 60 - 3rd of 11 getting 12lb from Mouche (5 Aug Leicester 8f frm RF 3379). **J G Smyth-Osbourne [0-9] P D Player.*

ABUSAMRAH (USA) BHB 72f **RR 70f** 2174[7]
3 b g Riverman (USA) 9.7f **(78)** - Azayim (Be My Guest (USA)) 9.3f **(67)**
Form - 5377
Record 1998 - 1st:0 2nd:0 3rd:1 Ran:4
Pre1998 - 1st:0 2nd:0 3rd:0 Ran:1
Win Prizemoney £0 *Total Prizemoney* £556
1998 Turf 0-4: (7f, 8f 2, 9f) (g-s, gd 2, g-f)
Workmanlike, above-average gelding. Turf high 70 (1st run) - 5th of 13 to Jalaab (4 May Doncaster 7f g-f RF 1010).
**R W Armstrong [0-5] Hamdan Al Maktoum.*

ABYAAN (IRE) RR 85f 1241[5]
3 b f Ela-Mana-Mou 12.7f **(72)** - Anna Comnena (IRE) (Shareef Dancer (USA)) 9.9f **(73)**
Form - 15
Record 1998 - 1st:1 2nd:0 3rd:0 Ran:2
Win Prizemoney £3,095 *Total Prizemoney* £3,095
Wins * 1998 Apr Bath (SFT) 10.2f 85 <
1998 Turf 1-2: (10f 1-2) (g-s 1-1, g-f)
Scopey, currently useful filly. Turf high 85 (1st run) - 1st of 11 getting 5lb from Red Ramona (28 Apr Bath RF 0897).
**J H M Gosden [1-2] Sheikh Ahmed Al Maktoum.*

ACADEMY (IRE) BHB 46f **RR 61f** 4961[15]
3 ch g Archway (IRE) 8.5f **(60)** - Dream Academy (Town And Country) 8.1f **(68)**
Form - 10067080
Record 1998 - 1st:1 2nd:0 3rd:0 Ran:8
Pre1998 - 1st:0 2nd:0 3rd:0 Ran:3
Win Prizemoney £2,428 *Total Prizemoney* £2,428
Wins * 1998 May Bright (FRM) 7f 65 <
1998 Turf 1-8: (7f 1-4, 8f 2, 10f, 12f) (gd, g-f 4, frm 1-3)
Workmanlike, average gelding, effective 7 to 8f, acts on frm. Turf high 65 (1st run) - 1st of 9 getting 11lb from Myttons Mistake (28 May Brighton RF 1549). Inconsistent.
**Andrew Turnell [1-11] Blenheim Thoroughbred Racing.*

ACADEMY STAR BHB 43f **RR 33f** 3379[11]
4 b f Royal Academy (USA) 7.8f **(77)** - Startino (Bustino) 10.4f **(64)**
Form - 0070
Record 1998 - 1st:0 2nd:0 3rd:0 Ran:4
Pre1998 - 1st:0 2nd:0 3rd:0 Ran:4
Win Prizemoney £0 *Total Prizemoney* £212
1998 Turf 0-4: (8f, 10f, 11f 2) (gd, g-f 2, frm)
Leggy, very moderate filly. Turf high 33. Becoming disappointing.
**J L Harris [0-4] Mrs James McAllister (from J R Fanshawe [0-4] Spt 1997).*

ACCELERATING (USA) BHB 79f **RR 71f** 4756[10]
2 b f Lear Fan (USA) 10.4f **(80)** - Fitzwilliam Place (Thatching) 8f **(66)**
Form - 342210
Record 1998 - 1st:1 2nd:2 3rd:1 Ran:6
Win Prizemoney £2,784 *Total Prizemoney* £6,080
Wins * 1998 Aug Ayr (G-S) 7f 70 <
1998 Turf 1-6: (6f 5, 7f 1-1) (sft, gd 1-2, g-f 2, hrd)
Above-average filly, effective 6 to 7f, acts on gd, has worn blinkers. Turf high 71. **J H M Gosden [1-6] George Strawbridge.*

ACCENTO RR 113f 2863a[3]
5 b h Midyan (USA) 9.9f **(64)** - Daleside Ladybird (Tolomeo) 5.6f **(60)**
Form - 3
1998 Turf 0-1: (8f) (gd)
Group-class colt. (1st run) - 3rd of 11 to Waky Nao (12 Jly Hoppegarten 8f gd RF 2863a). Thoroughly exposed, he seemed to run above himself at Hoppengarten in July, but was probably flattered to finish within a length and three-quarters of Lend A Hand.
**F Gang in GER [0-1] (from R Suerland in GER [1-7] Nov 1997).*

ACCESS ALL AREAS (IRE) RR 98+f 4039a[7]
2 b c Approach The Bench (IRE) - Adjalisa (IRE) (Darshaan) 9.9f **(84)**
Form - 711327

1998 Turf 2-6: (5f 1-2, 6f 1-4) (hvy, gd 2-4, frm)
Very useful colt, effective 6f, acts on gd to frm, best on gd. Turf high 98 - 3rd of 17 to Red Sea (16 Jun Ascot 6f gd RF 2013). This very useful juvenile was the narrow winner of a Curragh listed event before finishing fast into third in the Coventry after meeting with trouble in running, sustaining a badly-cut near-fore. He was runner-up in the Group One Phoenix Stakes before a useful effort from an unfavourable draw in a big field at the Curragh. He is sprint bred on his dam's side, and can make his mark over that sort of trip in 1999. **J E Mulhern in IRE [2-6] J E Mulhern.*

ACCOMMODATE YOU BHB 23f30a RR 12f 30a 3280[23]

5 br m Precocious 7.2f **(54)** - Time for Joy (Good Times (ITY)) 6.6f **(54)**
Form - 00000
Record 1998 - 1st:0 2nd:0 3rd:0 Ran:4
Pre1998 - 1st:0 2nd:0 3rd:0 Ran:3
1998 Turf 0-4: (6f 2, 7f 2) (gd 2, g-f 2)
Poor filly, has worn blinkers. Turf high 12.
**J M Bradley [0-7] Accomodation UK Ltd.*

ACCYSTAN BHB 65f69a RR 63f 69a 3095[3]

3 ch g Efisio 7.7f **(69)** - Amia (CAN) (Nijinsky (CAN)) 10.3f **(77)**
Form - 75613315433
Record 1998 - 1st:2 2nd:0 3rd:4 Ran:9
Pre1998 - 1st:0 2nd:0 3rd:0 Ran:3
Win Prizemoney £3,956 *Total Prizemoney* £5,806
Wins * 1998 *Feb Southw (STD) H 11f 60 67+* <
* 1998 *Jan Wolver (STD) C 9.4f 66*
1998 Turf 0-2: (12f 2) (gd 2) 1998 AW 2-7: (8f 2, 9f 1-2, 10f, 11f 1-2) (Equi, Fibr 2-6)
Strong, average gelding, effective 9 to 12f, acts on gd - acts on Fibr, favours tight tracks. Turf high 63. AW high 67 - 1st of 9 giving 8lb to Taylor's Pride (20 Feb Southwell RF 0321) - also 1st of 10 getting 8lb from Dancing Rio (10 Jan Wolverhampton RF 0065). He managed to win a couple of very poor events on Fibresand at the start of the year but is pretty modest, and a far from easy ride otherwise. **P C Haslam [2-12] Middleham Racing Bureau/G Heap.*

ACEBO LYONS (IRE) BHB 68f RR 72f 4351[5]

3 b f Waajib 8.9f **(67)** - Etage (Ile de Bourbon (USA)) 10.1f **(67)**
Form - 837105
Record 1998 - 1st:1 2nd:0 3rd:1 Ran:6
Pre1998 - 1st:0 2nd:1 3rd:0 Ran:4
Win Prizemoney £2,810 *Total Prizemoney* £4,676
Wins * **1998** Aug Haydoc (GD) 10.5f 70 <
1998 Turf 1-6: (9f, 10f 4, 11f 1-1) (sft, gd 2, g-f 1-3)
Leggy, above-average filly, effective 7 to 11f, acts on gd to g-f, best on gd. Turf high 72 - 3rd of 9 giving 2lb to My Pledge (15 Jun Windsor 10f gd RF 2006) - also 1st of 8 getting 13lb from Daniel Deronda (7 Aug Haydock RF 3436). Consistent. She has shown ability in handicap company, including winning at Haydock, but has swished her tail under pressure which is a slight worry.
**A P Jarvis [1-10] Terence Lyons II.*

ACE OF PARKES BHB 100f RR 98f 4857[5]

2 b c Teenoso (USA) 10.5f **(62)** - Summerhill Spruce (Windjammer (USA)) 7f **(59)**
Form - 4711135
Record 1998 - 1st:3 2nd:0 3rd:1 Ran:7
Win Prizemoney £16,831 *Total Prizemoney* £22,108
Wins * **1998** Aug Cheste (G-S) 6.1f 98 <
* **1998** Jly Cheste (G-F) 6.1f 98 <
* **1998** Jly Hamilt (FRM) 5f 91+
1998 Turf 3-7: (5f 1-2, 6f 2-5) (sft, gd 1-3, g-f, frm 2-2)
Very useful colt, effective 5 to 6f, best at 6f, acts on gd to frm, best on gd. Turf high 98 - 1st of 3 getting 3lb from Guinea Hunter (11 Jly Chester RF 2708) - also 1st of 4 giving 7lb to Saafend Rock (22 Aug Chester RF 3800). Comes from a family of prolific sprinting winners and completed a hat-trick before running creditably in a listed race. Ruined his chance on his second start by going far too freely to post. His limitations were exposed in better company later in the season, but his natural speed should enable him to win his share next season. **J Berry [3-7] Joseph Heler.*

ACE OF TRUMPS BHB 58f RR 68f 4671[6]

2 ch c First Trump - Elle Reef (Shareef Dancer (USA)) 9.9f **(73)**
Form - 65026212876
Record 1998 - 1st:1 2nd:3 3rd:0 Ran:11

Win Prizemoney £3,720 *Total Prizemoney* £6,625
Wins * **1998** Aug Newmar (FRM) S 7f 68 <
1998 Turf 1-11: (5f 3, 6f, 7f 1-5, 8f 2) (g-s, gd 3, g-f 3, frm 1-4)
Average colt, effective 6 to 7f, best at 7f, acts on g-f to frm, best on g-f, has worn blinkers. Turf high 68 - 2nd of 11 getting 4lb from Cosmo Jack (22 Aug Sandown 7f g-f RF 3818) - also 1st of 7 from Lost Spirit (7 Aug Newmarket RF 3438). Becoming disappointing. He had been tried with blinkers, but looked better off without them when landing a Newmarket seller in August
**W J Haggas [1-11] A A Goodman.*

ACERBUS DULCIS BHB 30f18a RR 25f 18a 1788[B]

7 ch g Hadeer 8.9f **(58)** - Current Pattie (USA) (Little Current (USA)) 9.6f **(75)**
Form - 767085B
Record 1998 - 1st:0 2nd:0 3rd:0 Ran:6
Pre1998 - 1st:1 2nd:1 3rd:2 Ran:23
Win Prizemoney £2,641 *Total Prizemoney* £4,714
Wins * 1997 Aug Yarmou (G-F) H 11.5f 29 31 <
1998 Turf 0-3: (10f 2, 12f) (frm 2, hrd)1998 AW 0-3: (8f, 11f,12f) (Fibr 3)
Little account gelding, effective 10 to 12f, acts on frm - acts on Fibr, has worn blinkers, favours left handed tracks, favours tight tracks. Turf high 25. AW high 14.
**M C Chapman [1-28] George Hooke (from J R Shaw [0-2] Apr 1994).*

ACHILLES BHB 92f RR 89f 5151[8]

3 ch c Deploy 11.4f **(67)** - Vatersay (USA) (Far North (CAN)) 9.7f **(75)**
Form - 1250668
Record 1998 - 1st:1 2nd:1 3rd:0 Ran:7
Pre1998 - 1st:0 2nd:2 3rd:2 Ran:4
Win Prizemoney £4,308 *Total Prizemoney* £12,417
Wins 1998 Mar Doncas (GD) 10.3f 97 <
1998 Turf 1-7: (10f 1-1, 11f 2, 12f 4) (sft, gd 1-3, g-f 2, frm)
Unfurnished, useful colt, effective 8 to 12f, acts on sft to frm, has worn blinkers, prefers left handed tracks. Turf high 97 - 2nd of 5 to The Glow-Worm (22 Apr Epsom 12f sft RF 0812) - also 1st of 11 from Spring Anchor (27 Mar Doncaster RF 0480). Consistent. Bolted up at Doncaster in March. Beaten by a fair sort at Epsom next time, he was not beaten far in the Lingfield Derby Trial but seemed to rather lose his way after transferring stables. However, he finished the season off with a good run in the November Handicap at Doncaster. He will be much stronger next year, and his shrewd trainer will find winning opportunities.
**K R Burke [0-4] Achilles International (from N P Littmoden [1-3] May 1998).*

ACHILLES SKY BHB 71f RR 78f 5146[7]

2 b c Hadeer 8.9f **(58)** - Diva Madonna (Chief Singer) 8.9f **(66)**
Form - 407
Record 1998 - 1st:0 2nd:0 3rd:0 Ran:3
Win Prizemoney £0 *Total Prizemoney* £257
1998 Turf 0-3: (8f 3) (gd 2, g-f)
Currently above-average colt. Turf high 78 (began Spt).
**K R Burke [0-3] Achilles International.*

ACHILLES STAR BHB 82f RR 80f 5148[10]

2 ch g Deploy 11.4f **(67)** - Norbella (Nordico (USA)) 6.5f **(62)**
Form - 15002100
Record 1998 - 1st:2 2nd:1 3rd:0 Ran:8
Win Prizemoney £11,143 *Total Prizemoney* £12,111
Wins * **1998** Oct York (GD) H 6f 76 80 <
1998 May Kempto (GD) 5f 80+
1998 Turf 2-8: (5f 1-2, 6f 1-3, 7f 3) (sft, gd 2-4, g-f 2, frm)
Decent gelding, effective 5 to 6f, best at 6f, acts on gd to g-f, best on gd. Turf high 80 - also 1st of 16 giving 6lb to Calcavella (7 Oct York RF 4703).
**K R Burke [1-6] Achilles International (from N P Littmoden [1-2] May 1998).*

ACICULA (IRE) BHB 93f RR 90f 4820[1]

2 b f Night Shift (USA) 8.1f **(73)** - Crystal City (Kris) 9.5f **(73)**
Form - 4252121
Record 1998 - 1st:2 2nd:3 3rd:0 Ran:7
Win Prizemoney £10,707 *Total Prizemoney* £14,914
Wins * **1998** Oct Newmar (GD) H 6f 89 90 <
* **1998** Spt Mussel (GD) 5f 85
1998 Turf 2-7: (5f 1-5, 6f 1-2) (sft, g-s, gd, g-f 1-2, frm 1-2)
Useful filly, effective 5 to 6f, best at 6f, acts on g-f to frm, best on

g-f. Turf high 90 - 1st of 15 giving 8lb to Mayaro Bay (15 Oct Newmarket RF 4820) - also 1st of 8 getting 5lb from Get Stuck In (27 Spt Musselburgh RF 4518). Showed promise in her early starts, but showed her best form in the autumn, winning a Musselburgh maiden and a Newmarket nursery under top weight.
**M Johnston [2-7] P D Savill.*

ACIDANTHERA BHB 78f **RR 77f** 2960[6]

3 b f Alzao (USA) 9.8f **(73)** - Amaranthus (Shirley Heights) 10.3f **(74)**
Form - 041036
Record 1998 - 1st:1 2nd:0 3rd:1 Ran:6
Win Prizemoney £3,626 *Total Prizemoney* £4,474
Wins * 1998 May Beverl (GD) 7.5f 70 <
1998 Turf 1-6: (7f 1-3, 8f 2, 9f) (sft, g-s, gd, frm 1-3)
Workmanlike, above-average filly, effective 7 to 8f, acts on frm. Turf high 77 - 3rd of 13 giving 14lb to Smarter Charter (8 Jly Kempton 8f frm RF 2633) - also 1st of 11 from Foxie Lady (19 May Beverley RF 1322). **J R Fanshawe [1-6] Lord Halifax.*

ACID TEST BHB 67f59a **RR 72f 59a** 4652[14]

3 ch c Sharpo 7.5f **(68)** - Clunk Click (Star Appeal) 9.6f **(65)**
Form - 007510000020
Record 1998 - 1st:1 2nd:1 3rd:0 Ran:12
Pre1998 - 1st:2 2nd:2 3rd:0 Ran:10
Win Prizemoney £9,736 *Total Prizemoney* £13,674
Wins * 1998 Jun Lingfi (GD) 7f 72 <
* 1997 Aug Newmar (G-F) H 7f 65 69
* 1997 Jly Lingfi (G-F) S 6f 63
1998 Turf 1-11: (6f, 7f 1-6, 8f 4) (gd 5, g-f 2, frm 1-4) 1998 AW 0-1: (8f) (Fibr)
Unfurnished, above-average colt, effective 6 to 8f, best at 7f, acts on gd to frm, likes left handed tracks, excels at Newbury and Lingfield. Turf high 72 - 1st of 9 giving 3lb to Morgan Le Fay (20 Jun Lingfield RF 2151). Twice a winner at two, he took his time finding his form last season, but landed a modest-looking classified stakes at Lingfield in June. Has lost his way subsequently.
**W R Muir [3-22] A J de V Patrick.*

ACQUITTAL (IRE) BHB 34f34a **RR 38f 34a** 3981[10]

6 b g Danehill (USA) 9.1f **(79)** -Perfect Alibi(Law Society(USA))9.9f **(70)**
Form - 62600
Record 1998 - 1st:0 2nd:1 3rd:0 Ran:5
Pre1998 - 1st:1 2nd:3 3rd:4 Ran:26
Win Prizemoney £2,668 *Total Prizemoney* £7,839
Wins 1995 Jun Mussel (G-F) H 11.1f 59 61 <
1998 Turf 0-5: (10f 4, 11f) (gd 2, g-f, frm 2)
Moderate gelding, effective 10f, acts on gd to g-f, best on gd, often wears blinkers (very effectively). Turf high 38 - 2nd of 18 getting 14lb from Ron's Round (17 Jun Nottingham 10f gd RF 2069).
**A Streeter [0-20] In The Clear Racing (from J Mackie [0-3] Jan 1996).*

ACRE BHB 67f **RR 68f** 4845[20]

2 b c Common Grounds 8.1f **(66)** - Realize **(77f)** (Al Nasr (FR)) 9.3f **(68)**
Form - 0470
Record 1998 - 1st:0 2nd:0 3rd:0 Ran:4
Win Prizemoney £0 *Total Prizemoney* £242
1998 Turf 0-4: (6f, 7f, 8f 2) (gd, g-f, frm 2)
Average colt. Turf high 68 (began Aug).
**W Jarvis [0-4] Lord Hartington.*

ACROSS THE WATER BHB 18f45a **RR 22f 45a** 2176[6]

4 b f Slip Anchor 12.7f **(75)** - Stara (Star Appeal) 9.6f **(65)**
Form - 50006
Record 1998 - 1st:0 2nd:0 3rd:0 Ran:5
Pre1998 - 1st:0 2nd:0 3rd:0 Ran:3
1998 Turf 0-3: (10f, 16f 2) (gd 3) 1998 AW 0-2: (12f, 16f) (Equi, Fibr)
Leggy, little account filly, has worn blinkers. Turf high 22. AW high 13. **C A Cyzer [0-8] R M Cyzer.*

ACT DEFIANT (USA) BHB 72f **RR 69f** 1929[8]

3 br c Nureyev (USA) 8.4f **(84)** -Alydariel (USA) (Alydar (USA)) 9.1f **(76)**
Form - 308
Record 1998 - 1st:0 2nd:0 3rd:1 Ran:3
Pre1998 - 1st:0 2nd:0 3rd:0 Ran:3
Win Prizemoney £0 *Total Prizemoney* £971
1998 Turf 0-3: (10f 2, 12f) (gd, frm 2)
Leggy, average colt, effective 8 to 12f, acts on frm. Turf high 68.
**P F I Cole [0-6] E J Hudson Jnr & W S Kilroy.*

ACTIONARY (IRE) **RR 69f** 2742[4]

2 b c Shalford (IRE) 7.8f **(63)** -Action Belle(Auction Ring(USA)) 8.6f **(65)**
Form - 4
Record 1998 - 1st:0 2nd:0 3rd:0 Ran:1
Win Prizemoney £0 *Total Prizemoney* £256
1998 Turf 0-1: (6f) (g-f)
Currently average colt. **J Berry [0-1] John Duffy.*

ACTION JACKSON BHB 41f50a **RR 47f 50a** 5038[5]

6 ch g Hadeer 8.9f **(58)** - Water Woo (USA) (Tom Rolfe) 9.4f **(75)**
Form - 8027784284265
Record 1998 - 1st:0 2nd:3 3rd:0 Ran:13
Pre1998 - 1st:2 2nd:6 3rd:2 Ran:31
Win Prizemoney £4,854 *Total Prizemoney* £12,571
Wins * 1996 Spt Pontef (GD) S 10f 45
* 1996 Jly Nottin (G-F) S 10f 55 <
1998 Turf 0-13: (10f 7, 11f, 12f, 14f 3, 16f) (sft, g-s, gd 4, g-f 3, frm 3, hrd)
Moderate gelding, effective 10 to 16f, best at 10f, acts on gd to frm, best on frm, favours tight tracks, excels at Nottingham. Turf high 50 - 2nd of 15 getting 7lb from Haroldon (22 May Nottingham 10f frm RF 1397).
**B J McMath [2-38] R G Levin (from G Rimmer [0-6] Jly 1995).*

ACT OF FOLLY **RR 59f** 3320[9]

3 b f Midyan (USA) 9.9f **(64)** -Height of Folly (Shirley Heights) 10.3f **(74)**
Form - 0
Record 1998 - 1st:0 2nd:0 3rd:0 Ran:1
Pre1998 - 1st:0 2nd:0 3rd:0 Ran:1
1998 Turf 0-1: (8f) (frm)
Scopey, currently fair filly. Related to middle-distance winners, one to watch for in handicaps in 1998.
**Lady Herries [0-2] Lady Herries.*

ACURIA (IRE) BHB 60f **RR 63f** 4651[7]

2 b f Contract Law (USA) 8.9f **(54)** - Curie Express (IRE) **(60f 48a)** (Fayruz)
Form - 532160387
Record 1998 - 1st:1 2nd:1 3rd:2 Ran:9
Win Prizemoney £2,843 *Total Prizemoney* £4,856
Wins * 1998 Jun Bath (G-S) 5.1f 63 <
1998 Turf 1-8: (5f 1-8) (gd 1-5, g-f, frm 2) 1998 AW 0-1: (5f) (Fibr)
Average filly, effective 5f, acts on gd to frm, best on gd. Turf high 63 - 1st of 8 getting 3lb from Zola Power (13 Jun Bath RF 1956).
**Mrs P N Dutfield [1-9] Mrs Jan Fuller.*

ADAMTON BHB 60f68a **RR 45f 68a** 305[5]

6 b g Domynsky 7.8f **(58)** - Berwyn (Sharpo) 7.7f **(59)**
Form - 05
Record 1998 - 1st:0 2nd:0 3rd:0 Ran:1
Pre1998 - 1st:3 2nd:1 3rd:0 Ran:10
Win Prizemoney £6,874 *Total Prizemoney* £7,731
Wins * 1996 *Dec Lingfi (STD) H 10f 66 69* <
* 1996 *Nov Lingfi (STD) H 10f 49 56*
* 1996 Oct Newcas (G-F) H 10.1f 45 45
1998 AW 0-1: (10f) (Equi)
Average gelding. Inconsistent. **Mrs J Cecil [3-11] Mrs J Cecil.*

A DAY ON THE DUB **RR 43f** 5060[4]

5 b g Presidium 7.5f **(56)** - Border Mouse (Border Chief)
Form - 4
Record 1998 - 1st:0 2nd:0 3rd:0 Ran:1
1998 Turf 0-1: (8f) (sft)
Moderate gelding. (1st run) - 4th of 15 getting 5lb from Scathebury (30 Oct Newcastle 8f sft RF 5060). **D Eddy [0-1] Revblayd.*

ADDITION BHB 64f **RR 69f** 4005[6]

2 b f Dilum (USA) 7.1f **(56)** - Cedar Lady (Telsmoss)
Form - 44366
Record 1998 - 1st:0 2nd:0 3rd:1 Ran:5
Win Prizemoney £0 *Total Prizemoney* £919
1998 Turf 0-5: (5f 3, 6f 2) (gd 2, g-f, frm 2)
Average filly. Turf high 69. **R J Hodges [0-5] David Mort.*

ADELPHI BOY (IRE) BHB 76f **RR 74f** 4413[4]
2 ch c Ballad Rock 7.2f **(63)** - Toda (Absalom) 7.2f **(58)**
Form - 0554
Record 1998 - 1st:0 2nd:0 3rd:0 Ran:4
Win Prizemoney £0 *Total Prizemoney* £183
1998 Turf 0-4: (5f, 6f, 7f 2) (gd 2, g-f, frm)
Above-average colt. Turf high 74 (began Spt) - 4th of 13 getting 3lb from Kangaroo Island (22 Spt Warwick 6f frm RF 4413).
**M C Chapman [0-4] Barry Brown.*

ADESTE FIDELES BHB 72f73a **RR 75f 73a** 4372[12]
3 b f Groom Dancer (USA) 9.5f **(75)** - Decided Air (IRE) (Sure Blade (USA)) 11.3f **(67)**
Form - 0414321830
Record 1998 - 1st:2 2nd:1 3rd:2 Ran:10
Pre1998 - 1st:1 2nd:0 3rd:1 Ran:3
Win Prizemoney £8,779 *Total Prizemoney* £11,377

Wins								
* **1998**	Jly	Catter	(G-F)	H	12f	70	75	<
* **1998**	May	Folkes	(G-F)		12f		70	
* 1997	*Oct*	*Wolver*	*(STD)*		*8.5f*		*61*	

1998 Turf 2-10: (10f, 12f 2-7, 13f, 14f) (g-s 2, gd 1-3, g-f, frm 1-4)
Workmanlike, above-average filly, effective 12f, acts on gd to frm, prefers tight tracks. Turf high 75 - 1st of 7 giving 5lb to Younico (15 Jly Catterick RF 2813) - also 1st of 8 getting 20lb from My Learned Friend (27 May Folkestone RF 1523). Very consistent, she twice won over twelve furlongs last term but did not seem to stay when tried over further. **M Bell [3-13] Capt B W Bell.*

ADIEU (GER) **RR 102f** 4077a[1]
3 Dashing Blade 7.9f **(80)** - Alabama (GER) (Surumu (GER)) 10f **(83)**
Form - 121
1998 Turf 2-3: (7f, 8f 2-2) (gd 2-3)
Currently very useful. Turf high 102 (began Jly) - 1st of 9 from Angel Heart (30 Aug Baden-Baden RF 4077a) - also 1st of 12 getting 4lb from Stanott (26 Jly San Siro RF 3228a). He developed into a useful three-year-old and is best employed over at least a mile.
**W Kujath in GER [2-3] W Frohlich.*

ADILOV BHB 40f23a **RR 47f 23a** 136[10]
6 b g Soviet Star (USA) 8.6f **(74)** - Volida (Posse (USA)) 8.9f **(61)**
Form - 00
Record 1998 - 1st:0 2nd:0 3rd:0 Ran:1
Pre1998 - 1st:0 2nd:0 3rd:1 Ran:17
Win Prizemoney £0 *Total Prizemoney* £656
1998 AW 0-1: (12f) (Equi)
Moderate gelding, has worn blinkers.
**J J Bridger [1-22] Trevor Mitchell (from K O Cunningham-Brown [0-5] Spt 1996).*

ADITO **RR 100f** 1227a[11]
3 b c Konigsstuhl (GER) 9f **(115)** - Arastou (GER) (Surumu (GER)) 10f **(83)**
Form - 20
1998 Turf 0-2: (8f 2) (sft, gd)
Currently very useful colt. Turf high 100 (1st run) - 2nd of 9 to Night Devil (19 Apr Hoppegarten 8f sft RF 0834a). He looked well worth his place in the German 2,000 Guineas, but ran poorly there and did not develop as anticipated. **H Blume in GER [0-2].*

ADJUTANT BHB 92f **RR 88f** 4498[1]
3 b c Batshoof 9.5f **(66)** -Indian Love Song(Be My Guest(USA))9.3f **(67)**
Form - 55210021
Record 1998 - 1st:2 2nd:2 3rd:0 Ran:8
Pre1998 - 1st:0 2nd:0 3rd:2 Ran:3
Win Prizemoney £13,555 *Total Prizemoney* £18,663

Wins								
* **1998**	Spt	Haydoc	(G-F)	H	7.1f	86	88	<
* **1998**	May	Goodwo	(G-F)	H	7f	83	88	<

1998 Turf 2-8: (7f 2-6, 8f 2) (g-s, gd 4, g-f 1-1, frm 1-2)
Workmanlike, useful colt, effective 7f, acts on gd to frm. Turf high 88 - 1st of 11 giving 1lb to Ariant (26 Spt Haydock RF 4498) - also 1st of 10 getting 4lb from Young Josh (19 May Goodwood RF 1324). Consistent. Suited by forcing tactics when runner-up in a Newmarket handicap in May before getting a Goodwood race courtesy of the Stewards, after being beaten a nose. Genuine sort, and has run creditably in valuable handicaps since.
**B J Meehan [2-11] J R Good.*

ADMIRALS FLAME (IRE) BHB 57f60a **RR 60f 60a** 4807[12]
7 b g Doulab (USA) 7.4f **(61)** - Fan The Flame (Grundy) 10.3f **(65)**
Form - 00001370380
Record 1998 - 1st:1 2nd:0 3rd:2 Ran:11
Pre1998 - 1st:4 2nd:3 3rd:2 Ran:35
Win Prizemoney £18,699 *Total Prizemoney* £27,133

Wins								
* **1998**	Jun	Windso	(SFT)	H	8.3f	55	60+	
* 1996	Aug	Windso	(G-F)	H	8.3f	74	80	<
* 1995	Jly	Kempto	(G-F)	H	8f	66	72+	
* 1995	Jun	Windso	(GD)	H	8.3f	60	64+	
* 1994	Mar	Leices	(SFT)	S	6f		56	

1998 Turf 1-11: (7f 2, 8f 1-9) (sft, g-s, gd 1-3, g-f 5, frm)
Average gelding. Turf high 60. Dropped right down the handicap due to some moderate efforts in the first half of this season, and this helped enable him to return. **C F Wall [5-46] Hintlesham Racing.*

ADMIRALS PLACE (IRE) **RR 47f** 2821[13]
2 ch c Perugino (USA) - Royal Daughter (High Top) 10.2f **(67)**
Form - 00
Record 1998 - 1st:0 2nd:0 3rd:0 Ran:2
1998 Turf 0-2: (6f 2) (g-f, frm)
Currently moderate colt. Turf high 47.
**R W Armstrong [0-2] C G Donovan.*

ADMIRALS SECRET (USA) BHB 61f56a **RR 68f 56a** 3855[4]
9 ch g Secreto (USA) 9.9f **(72)** - Noble Mistress (USA) (Vaguely Noble) 10.1f **(72)**
Form - 0127110044
Record 1998 - 1st:3 2nd:1 3rd:0 Ran:9
Pre1998 - 1st:6 2nd:6 3rd:4 Ran:53
Win Prizemoney £26,202 *Total Prizemoney* £35,812

Wins								
* **1998**	Jun	Lingfi	(GD)	H	11.5f	64	68	
* **1998**	Jun	Lingfi	(GD)	H	11.5f	62	61	
* **1998**	Apr	Bright	(GD)	H	11.9f	47	57	
* 1997	Jly	Windso	(G-F)	H	11.6f	50	53	
* 1995	Aug	Catter	(G-F)	H	13.8f	67	72	<
* 1995	Jun	Catter	(GD)	H	12f	62	65	
* 1995	May	Pontef	(GD)	H	12f	55	57	
* 1994	*Oct*	*Lingfi*	*(STD)*	*H*	*12f*	*54*	*64*	

1998 Turf 3-9: (11f 2-4, 12f 1-5) (gd 1-1, g-f 3, frm 2-5)
Average gelding, effective 11 to 12f, best at 11f, acts on frm, likes left handed tracks, favours tight tracks, excels at Lingfield. Turf high 68 - 1st of 10 giving 13lb to Iron Mountain (27 Jun Lingfield RF 2336) - also 1st of 16 giving 19lb to Fourdaned (20 Jun Lingfield RF 2148). This veteran has did well in modest middle-distance handicaps last season, winning three so far. He seems to be an ideal mount for an inexperienced rider.
**C F Wall [9-64] Mrs C A Wall.*

ADMIRAL WINGS (IRE) **RR 91f** 4296a[7]
4 bb g In The Wings 11.2f **(77)** - Folkboat (Kalaglow) 9.8f **(67)**
Form - 553177
1998 Turf 1-6: (12f 3, 14f 2, 16f 1-1) (hvy, g-s, gd 2, g-f, hrd 1-1)
Useful gelding, effective 12 to 16f, best at 12f, acts on sft to hrd, has worn blinkers, likes right handed tracks. Turf high 91 - 1st of 8 giving 22lb to Galletina (15 Aug Curragh RF 3718a). Decent handicapper, stays two miles. Best when held up and a good consistent sort. **J Oxx in IRE [4-16] A Gannon.*

ADMIRE BHB 48f **RR 43f** 3806[12]
3 b f Last Tycoon 9.4f **(73)** - Belle Isis (USA) (Sir Ivor) 10.2f **(70)**
Form - 80008R0
Record 1998 - 1st:0 2nd:0 3rd:0 Ran:7
Pre1998 - 1st:1 2nd:0 3rd:0 Ran:4
Win Prizemoney £3,350 *Total Prizemoney* £3,350

Wins								
* 1997	Aug	Chepst	(G-S)		8.1f		74+	<

1998 Turf 0-6:(7f 2, 8f 2,9f,12f)(hvy, gd 3, g-f 2)1998 AW 0-1:(8f) (Equi)
Neat, moderate filly, effective 8f, acts on gd, has worn blinkers. Turf high 47. Inconsistent. **Miss Gay Kelleway [1-8] Dorchester Racing Club (from Mrs N Macauley [0-3] Jly 1998).*

ADNAAN (IRE) BHB 100f **RR 93f** 5077[1]
2 ch c Nashwan (USA) 10.3f **(79)** - Whakilyric (USA) (Miswaki (USA)) 9f **(81)**
Form - 23211
Record 1998 - 1st:2 2nd:2 3rd:1 Ran:5
Win Prizemoney £14,604 *Total Prizemoney* £18,047

Wins * **1998** Oct Newmar (SFT) L 10f 93 <
* **1998** Oct Leices (G-S) 10f 86+
1998 Turf 2-5: (7f, 8f 2, 10f 2-2) (g-s 1-1, gd 1-2, g-f, frm)
Useful colt. Turf high 93 (began Aug) - 1st of 7 giving 3lb to Forest Shadow (31 Oct Newmarket RF 5077) - also 1st of 7 giving 3lb to Time Zone (12 Oct Leicester RF 4764). Improving as he steps up in trip, he comfortably won a Leicester conditions event over ten furlongs, and followed up in the Listed Zetland Stakes at Newmarket, both on soft ground. **J L Dunlop [2-5] Hamdan Al Maktoum.*

ADOBE BHB 50f **RR 41f** 3448[14]
3 b g Green Desert (USA) 7.8f **(78)** - Shamshir (Kris) 9.5f **(73)**
Form - 0080
Record 1998 - 1st:0 2nd:0 3rd:0 Ran:4
1998 Turf 0-4: (6f 3, 7f) (gd 3, frm)
Moderate gelding. Turf high 45.
**J H M Gosden [0-4] Sheikh Mohammed.*

ADORABLE **RR 32f** 4983[11]
2 b f Dalul - Helleborus (King of Spain) 7.8f **(52)**
Form - 00
Record 1998 - 1st:0 2nd:0 3rd:0 Ran:2
1998 Turf 0-2: (7f, 8f) (g-s, frm)
Currently very moderate filly. Turf high 32 (began Oct).
**S Dow [0-2] Ken Butler.*

ADORA'S DREAM (IRE) **RR 36f** 5145[7]
2 b c Mujtahid (USA) 7.4f **(69)** - Shady Bank (USA) **(42f)** (Alleged (USA)) 10f **(76)**
Form - 67
Record 1998 - 1st:0 2nd:0 3rd:0 Ran:2
1998 Turf 0-2: (8f 2) (sft, gd)
Currently very moderate colt, often wears blinkers. Turf high 36 (began Oct). **J W Hills [0-2] George Tong.*

ADRENALIN BHB 52f52a **RR 54df 52a** 5003[16]
3 ch g Risk Me (FR) 8f **(53)** -High Cairn (FR) (Ela-Mana-Mou) 10.1f **(70)**
Form - 510800
Record 1998 - 1st:1 2nd:0 3rd:0 Ran:6
Pre1998 - 1st:0 2nd:0 3rd:1 Ran:5
Win Prizemoney £2,085 *Total Prizemoney* £2,538
Wins * **1998** *Feb Southw (STD) 6f 59* <
1998 Turf 0-1: (6f) (sft) 1998 AW 1-5: (6f 1-4, 7f) (Equi, Fibr 1-4)
Scopey, fair gelding, effective 5 to 6f, acts on gd - acts on Fibr, has worn blinkers. AW high 59 - 1st of 7 giving 5lb to Stravsea (9 Feb Southwell RF 0255). Inconsistent. Showed only very modest form before getting off the mark in a bad maiden on the Southwell Fibresand in February.
**T T Clement [1-6] C Holcroft (from Mrs J R Ramsden [0-5] Jly 1997).*

ADULATION (USA) BHB 82f **RR 81f** 4527[3]
4 ch g Sheikh Albadou 9.2f **(75)** - Pedestal (High Line) 10.3f **(70)**
Form - 3223
Record 1998 - 1st:0 2nd:2 3rd:2 Ran:4
Win Prizemoney £0 *Total Prizemoney* £3,543
1998 Turf 0-4: (8f 3, 10f) (g-f, frm 3)
Workmanlike, decent gelding. Turf high 81 - 2nd of 9 giving 6lb to Cool Vibes (29 Aug Newmarket 8f frm RF 3954). Did not see a racecourse until he was four, and was off the track more than three months after his debut. Has shown promise in maidens.
**P W Chapple-Hyam [0-4] Chapple Hyam,Bloomsb Collins.*

ADVANCE EAST BHB 44f60a **RR 49f 60a** 4112[17]
6 b g Polish Precedent (USA) 9f **(73)** - Startino (Bustino) 10.4f **(64)**
Form - 1364560
Record 1998 - 1st:1 2nd:0 3rd:1 Ran:7
Pre1998 - 1st:0 2nd:3 3rd:2 Ran:27
Win Prizemoney £4,110 *Total Prizemoney* £9,816
Wins * **1998** Apr Pontef (G-S) H 10f 46 51 <
1998 Turf 1-7: (9f, 10f 1-3, 11f, 12f 2) (g-s 1-2, gd 2, frm 3)
Moderate gelding, effective 9 to 14f, best at 10f, acts on g-s to g-f, best on g-s, has worn blinkers. Turf high 51 (1st run) - 1st of 15 getting 7lb from Impetus (27 Apr Pontefract RF 0883).
**M Dods [2-27] A F Monk (from Mrs J R Ramsden [0-19] Spt 1996).*

AEGEAN BREEZE BHB 34f **RR 22f** 2761[10]
3 b g Pharly (FR) 11.5f **(64)** - Rich Pickings (Dominion) 8.5f **(63)**
Form - 053000
Record 1998 - 1st:0 2nd:0 3rd:1 Ran:6
Pre1998 - 1st:0 2nd:0 3rd:0 Ran:3
Win Prizemoney £0 *Total Prizemoney* £268
1998 Turf 0-6: (8f, 10f 3, 12f 2) (gd 2, g-f 2, frm 2)
Neat, little account gelding. Turf high 48. Inconsistent.
**R M Flower [0-6] Theobalds Stud (from Miss Gay Kelleway [0-3] Aug 1997).*

AEGEAN FLAME BHB 86f **RR 78f** 3151[3]
2 ch f Anshan 8.2f **(63)** - Dizzydaisy **(38f 52a)** (Sharpo) 7.7f **(59)**
Form - 72328113
Record 1998 - 1st:2 2nd:2 3rd:2 Ran:8
Win Prizemoney £9,309 *Total Prizemoney* £12,593
Wins * **1998** Jly Newbur (GD) 5.2f 78 <
* **1998** Jly Ripon (GD) 5f 77
1998 Turf 2-8: (5f 2-8) (hvy, sft, gd 2-4, g-f, frm)
Above-average filly, effective 5f, acts on gd to frm, best on gd. Turf high 78 - 3rd of 4 giving 2lb to Fadmoor (27 Jly Yarmouth 5f g-f RF 3151) - also 1st of 4 getting 3lb from Snap Cracker (12 Jly Newbury RF 2751). Improving. She had shown some ability before getting off the mark at Ripon in July. Stamina is obviously not a problem. Followed up at Newbury, before flopping on fast ground.
**K T Ivory [2-8] Theobalds Stud.*

AEGEAN GLORY **RR 29f** 4664[10]
2 b f Shareef Dancer (USA) 10.1f **(67)** - Sayulita (Habitat) 9.4f **(70)**
Form - 0
Record 1998 - 1st:0 2nd:0 3rd:0 Ran:1
1998 Turf 0-1: (8f) (g-s)
Currently little account filly. **C E Brittain [0-1] Theobalds Stud.*

AEOLINA (FR) BHB 52f54a **RR 55f 54a** 503[8]
4 b br f Kaldoun (FR) 9.9f **(84)** - Folia (Sadler's Wells (USA)) 10f **(76)**
Form - 1358
Record 1998 - 1st:0 2nd:0 3rd:1 Ran:3
Pre1998 - 1st:1 2nd:1 3rd:1 Ran:6
Win Prizemoney £2,294 *Total Prizemoney* £4,455
Wins * 1997 *Nov Southw (STD) 11f 54* <
1998 Turf 0-1: (11f) (sft) 1998 AW 0-2: (12f 2) (Fibr 2)
Workmanlike, fair filly, effective 11 to 14f, best at 11f, acts on g-s to frm - acts on Fibr, prefers left handed tracks. AW high 51.
**S E Kettlewell [1-9] J Tennant.*

AERAIOCHT (IRE) **RR 94f** 4794a[12]
2 b f Tenby 10.4f **(76)** - Direct Lady
Form - 3611200
1998 Turf 2-7: (5f, 6f 3, 7f 2-2, 8f) (sft, g-s 2-3, gd 3)
Useful filly, effective 6 to 7f, acts on g-s to gd. Turf high 94 - 2nd of 27 to Amazing Dream (29 Aug Curragh 6f gd RF 4039a) - also 1st of 12 from The Flying Pig (1 Aug Galway RF 3356a). Showed good form in the summer, taking two races before finishing runner-up in the Tattersalls Breeders' Stakes at the Curragh. She was below that form afterwards. **J S Bolger in IRE [2-7] D H W Dobson.*

AEROSMITH (NZ) **RR 112f** 5133a[3]
6 br g Indian Ore (USA) - Luna di Miele (NZ) (Barcas (NZ))
Form - 3
1998 Turf 0-1: (10f) (gd)
Currently Group-class gelding. (1st run) - 3rd of 11 giving 8lb to Champagne (31 Oct Flemington 10f gd RF 5133a).
**P Hurdle in NZ [0-1].*

AESOPS (USA) **RR 89f** 3819[2]
2 ch c Diesis 9f **(80)** -Affirmative Fable (USA) (Affirmed (USA)) 9.3f **(79)**
Form - 32
Record 1998 - 1st:0 2nd:1 3rd:1 Ran:2
Win Prizemoney £0 *Total Prizemoney* £2,226
1998 Turf 0-2: (7f, 8f) (g-f, frm)
Currently useful colt. Turf high 89 (began Jly) - 2nd of 5 getting 3lb from Fantastic Light (22 Aug Sandown 8f g-f RF 3819).
**J H M Gosden [0-2] Sheikh Mohammed.*

AFAAN (IRE) BHB 92f80a **RR 92f 80a** 4821[2]
5 ch h Cadeaux Genereux 7.9f **(76)** - Rawaabe (USA) (Nureyev (USA)) 8.7f **(78)**
Form - 21003112502

Record 1998 - 1st:2 2nd:2 3rd:1 Ran:9
Pre1998 - 1st:4 2nd:6 3rd:2 Ran:20
Win Prizemoney £21,548 *Total Prizemoney* £37,886
Wins * **1998** Jly Newmar (GD) H 5f 76 91+ <
* **1998** Jly Catter (FRM) H 5f 73 79
* 1997 *Dec Southw (STD) H 5f 65 72+*
* 1997 Nov Redcar (GD) 5f 79
* 1997 Oct Pontef (G-S) H 5f 62 67
* 1997 May Redcar (G-F) H 6f 56 64
1998 Turf 2-9: (5f 2-9) (sft, g-s, gd 2, g-f, frm 2-4)
Useful colt, effective 5f, acts on g-f to frm, best on frm, often wears blinkers (very effectively), excels at Redcar, does well at Newmarket. Turf high 92 - 2nd of 12 getting 6lb from Repertory (31 Aug Epsom 5f g-f RF 3983) - also 1st of 11 from Kilcullen Lad (18 Jly Newmarket RF 2920). A lightning-fast sprinter, he smashed the five-furlong track record at Newmarket in July. Held in warm company since, including the Prix de l'Abbaye. Given a sharp five and preferably a rail to run against, he can win nice races.
**R F Marvin [6-29] E Gray.*

AFARAD (IRE) RR 97f 4910a[4]
3 b c Slip Anchor 12.7f **(75)** - Afasara
Form - 14414
1998 Turf 2-5: (10f 1-1, 11f 1-2, 12f 2) (g-s 1-3, gd 1-2)
Very useful colt. Turf high 97 - 1st of 18 giving 18lb to Sunless (11 Oct Naas RF 4793a) - also 1st of 11 from Landing Slot (23 May Curragh RF 1508a). Fairly useful J.Oxx inmate, won his maiden at Curragh and handicap at Naas but has been well beaten since.
**J Oxx in IRE [2-5] H H Aga Khan.*

AFFIDAVIT RR 60f 4983[6]
2 b f Slip Anchor 12.7f **(75)** -Lady Barrister (Law Society(USA))9.9f **(70)**
Form - 56
Record 1998 - 1st:0 2nd:0 3rd:0 Ran:2
1998 Turf 0-2: (8f 2) (g-s, gd)
Currently average filly. Turf high 60 (began Oct).
**M Bell [0-2] Cheveley Park Stud.*

AFFIRMED SUCCESS (USA) RR 5164a[6]
4 b g Affirmed (USA) 10.3f **(75)**
Form - 6
1998 AW 0-1: (6f) (Dirt)
Currently very high-class gelding. Showed speed for a long way when sixth in the Breeders' Cup Sprint.
**R Schosberg in USA [0-1] A Fried Jnr.*

AFICIONADO (IRE) BHB 41f49a RR 54f 49a 4456[21]
4 b g Marju (IRE) 9.2f **(76)** - Haneena (Habitat) 9.4f **(70)**
Form - 20567070
Record 1998 - 1st:0 2nd:1 3rd:0 Ran:8
Pre1998 - 1st:1 2nd:2 3rd:3 Ran:16
Win Prizemoney £4,077 *Total Prizemoney* £7,950
Wins 1996 Nov Newmar (GD) S 8f 71 <
1998 Turf 0-8: (8f 5, 9f, 10f 2) (gd 4, g-f, frm 3)
Neat, fair gelding, effective 8 to 10f, acts on gd, has worn blinkers, favours tight tracks. Turf high 54. **R J Hodges [0-21] Miss R Dobson (from R F JohnsonHoughton [1-9] Nov 1996).*

AFON ALWEN BHB 62f RR 67f 1968[1]
5 ch m Henbit (USA) 10.2f **(46)** - Brenig (Horage) 10.3f **(61)**
Form - 1
Record 1998 - 1st:1 2nd:0 3rd:0 Ran:1
Pre1998 - 1st:1 2nd:1 3rd:4 Ran:9
Win Prizemoney £5,487 *Total Prizemoney* £7,740
Wins * **1998** Jun Lingfi (G-S) H 11.5f 60 67 <
1996 Spt Bright (FRM) 10f 51
1998 Turf 1-1: (11f 1-1) (gd 1-1)
Average filly, effective 11 to 14f, acts on gd to frm, best on gd. (1st run) - 1st of 11 giving 3lb to Eternity (13 Jun Lingfield RF 1968).
**P J Hobbs [3-5] Triple Two (from S C Williams [1-9] Spt 1997).*

AFRICAN-PARD (IRE) BHB 68f41a RR 69f 41a 347[6]
6 b g Don't Forget Me 9.5f **(66)** - Petite Realm (Realm) 8.1f **(65)**
Form - 04286
Record 1998 - 1st:0 2nd:1 3rd:0 Ran:3
Pre1998 - 1st:2 2nd:4 3rd:7 Ran:32
Win Prizemoney £6,366 *Total Prizemoney* £14,637
Wins * 1997 Aug Chepst (GD) H 10.2f 62 69 <
* 1997 Jly Nottin (G-F) H 10f 58 64
1998 AW 0-3: (11f 2, 12f) (Fibr 3)
Average gelding, effective 10f, acts on gd to frm, has worn blinkers, favours left handed tracks. AW high 42.
**D HaydnJones [2-35] J S Fox and Sons.*

AFRICAN SUN (IRE) BHB 37f29a RR 54f 29a 4698[15]
5 b g Mtoto 11.5f **(71)** - Nuit D'Ete (USA) (Super Concorde (USA)) 10.9f **(66)**
Form - 5006004080560
Record 1998 - 1st:0 2nd:0 3rd:0 Ran:13
Pre1998 - 1st:0 2nd:1 3rd:0 Ran:20
Win Prizemoney £0 *Total Prizemoney* £1,281
1998 Turf 0-10: (8f, 10f 7, 12f 2) (g-s, gd 2, g-f 5, hrd 2) 1998 AW 0-3: (12f 3) (Fibr 3)
Fair gelding, effective 10f, acts on gd, has worn blinkers. Turf high 58. AW high 26.
**M C Chapman [1-39] Noel Fletcher (from B Hanbury [0-7] Jun 1996).*

AFRICAN VISION BHB 55f RR 59f 4767[14]
2 b c Mtoto 11.5f **(71)** - Sibley (Northfields (USA)) 9f **(72)**
Form - 0080
Record 1998 - 1st:0 2nd:0 3rd:0 Ran:4
1998 Turf 0-4: (6f 3, 8f) (sft, gd, g-f, frm)
Fair colt. Turf high 59 (began Aug).
**Mrs J R Ramsden [0-4] Michael Payton.*

AFROSTAR (IRE) RR 81f 4567a[13]
4 b f Soviet Lad (USA) 9.4f **(63)** - Festival of Magic (USA) (Clever Trick (USA)) 6.6f **(77)**
Form - 103840
1998 Turf 1-6: (5f 1-2, 6f, 7f, 8f, 9f) (sft 1-1, g-s 2, gd 3)
Decent filly, effective 5 to 7f, acts on sft to g-s. Turf high 97 - 3rd of 9 to Diligent Dodger (9 Jly Tipperary 7f g-s RF 2792a) - also 1st of 4 getting 4lb from Aljjawarih (19 Jun Tipperary RF 2213a). Won on her debut but has shown little since.
**A Lee in IRE [1-6] Lisselan Farms Ltd.*

AFTER DAWN (IRE) BHB 32f35a RR 45f 35a 4777[8]
3 b f Brief Truce (USA) 9.1f **(73)** - Faakirah (Dragonara Palace (USA)) 6.1f **(55)**
Form - 357016008
Record 1998 - 1st:1 2nd:0 3rd:1 Ran:9
Pre1998 - 1st:0 2nd:0 3rd:0 Ran:7
Win Prizemoney £1,932 *Total Prizemoney* £2,307
Wins * **1998** Jly Folkes (G-F) S 9.7f 45 <
1998 Turf 1-7: (8f, 10f 1-4, 12f 2) (gd 3, g-f 1-1, frm 2, hrd) 1998 AW 0-2: (9f, 12f) (Fibr 2)
Light-framed, moderate filly. Turf high 45. AW high 37.
**Mrs P N Dutfield [1-17] One Over The Eight.*

AFTER EIGHT BHB 53f69a RR 53f 69a 4885[16]
3 b c Presidium 7.5f **(56)** - Vickenda (Giacometti) 11.2f **(56)**
Form - 351077020
Record 1998 - 1st:1 2nd:1 3rd:0 Ran:8
Pre1998 - 1st:0 2nd:0 3rd:1 Ran:5
Win Prizemoney £1,838 *Total Prizemoney* £2,938
Wins * **1998** *Feb Lingfi (STD) S 6f 63* <
1998 Turf 0-5: (6f 4, 7f) (g-s, gd 2, g-f, frm) 1998 AW 1-3: (6f 1-2, 8f) (Equi 1-2, Fibr)
Small, average colt, effective 6 to 7f, - acts on Equi, often wears blinkers, likes left handed tracks. Turf high 53. AW high 63 - 1st of 6 giving 5lb to Miss Skye (3 Feb Lingfield RF 0211). Inconsistent. Successfully dropped into selling company on the Lingfield Equitrack in February, beating a very poor field easily.
**M S Saunders [1-7] Peter Brazier (from R W Armstrong [0-6] Jan 1998).*

AGANON BHB 71f RR 71+f 1004[16]
3 b c Aragon 7.7f **(58)** - Plain Tree (Wolver Hollow) 8f **(56)**
Form - 0
Record 1998 - 1st:0 2nd:0 3rd:0 Ran:1
Pre1998 - 1st:0 2nd:0 3rd:0 Ran:3
1998 Turf 0-1: (6f) (gd)
Scopey, above-average colt. **M R Channon [0-4] Kingsdown Racing.*

AGENT LE BLANC (IRE) BHB 70f **RR 68f** 4150[5]
3 b g Kahyasi 12.9f **(74)** - White Witch (USA) (Nureyev (USA)) 8.7f **(78)**
Form - 725
Record 1998 - 1st:0 2nd:1 3rd:0 Ran:3
Win Prizemoney £0 *Total Prizemoney* £672
1998 Turf 0-3: (10f 2, 11f) (gd, g-f, frm)
Workmanlike, currently average gelding. Turf high 68 - 2nd of 9 to The Gamboller (16 Jly Leicester 10f frm RF 2852).
**T J Etherington [0-3] E Oliver.*

AGENT MULDER BHB 64f60a **RR 62f 60a** 5079[7]
4 b g Kylian (USA) 8.1f **(66)** - Precious Caroline (IRE) **(26a)** (The Noble Player (USA)) 6.5f **(67)**
Form - 032407117
Record 1998 - 1st:2 2nd:1 3rd:1 Ran:9
Pre1998 - 1st:1 2nd:1 3rd:0 Ran:6
Win Prizemoney £8,793 *Total Prizemoney* £11,656
Wins * **1998** Oct Nottin (SFT) 6.1f 58
* **1998** Oct Nottin (SFT) 6.1f 62 <
* 1997 Jun Windso (G-F) H 8.3f 55 61
1998 Turf 2-9: (6f 2-2, 7f, 8f 4, 9f, 10f) (sft, gd 2-6, g-f 2)
Scopey, average gelding, effective 6 to 8f, best at 8f, acts on gd to hrd, best on gd, has worn blinkers (very effectively), excels at Nottingham and Salisbury. Turf high 62 - 1st of 18 getting 3lb from Garnock Valley (6 Oct Nottingham RF 4669) - also 1st of 20 from Superbit (14 Oct Nottingham RF 4811). Consistent.
**P D Cundell [3-15] P D Cundell.*

AGGRESSIVE EYES (USA) RR 74?f 4842[3]
2 ch c Diesis 9f **(80)** - Jeldee (CAN) (Alysheba (USA)) 9f **(84)**
Form - 3
Record 1998 - 1st:0 2nd:0 3rd:1 Ran:1
Win Prizemoney £0 *Total Prizemoney* £1,088
1998 Turf 0-1: (7f) (g-f)
Currently above-average colt. Pulled too hard when third in the Houghton Stakes.
**Sir Michael Stoute [0-1] The Thoroughbred Corporation.*

AGINOR BHB 92f **RR 94f** 4487[1]
4 b g Slip Anchor 12.7f **(75)** - Fairy Feet (Sadler's Wells (USA)) 10f **(76)**
Form - 31231
Record 1998 - 1st:2 2nd:1 3rd:2 Ran:5
Win Prizemoney £8,590 *Total Prizemoney* £12,844
Wins * **1998** Spt Redcar (G-F) H 14.1f 90 93 <
* **1998** Jly Doncas (FRM) 12f 78
1998 Turf 2-5: (11f, 12f 1-2, 14f 1-1, 16f) (g-f, frm 2-4)
Workmanlike, useful gelding. Turf high 94 (began Jly) - 2nd of 6 getting 2lb from Mowelga (15 Aug Newbury 12f g-f RF 3654) - also 1st of 7 giving 13lb to Royal Castle (25 Spt Redcar RF 4487). He did not race at two and three-years-old, but justified connections' perseverance by winning twice and being placed in his other three runs. Inclined to carry his head high under pressure, he has not yet encountered soft ground, but his breeding suggests he should appreciate it. Val Ward paid 40,000 gns for him at Tattersalls Autumn Horses-in-Training Sale. **H R A Cecil [2-5] Mrs Irina Tsatsos.*

AGIOTAGE BHB 90f **RR 84+f** 5093[1]
2 br c Zafonic (USA) 9f **(83)** - Rakli **(85+f)** (Warning)
Form - 481
Record 1998 - 1st:1 2nd:0 3rd:0 Ran:3
Win Prizemoney £3,525 *Total Prizemoney* £3,737
Wins * **1998** Nov Redcar (G-S) 7f 84+ <
1998 Turf 1-3: (6f, 7f 1-2) (gd 1-3)
Currently decent colt. Turf high 84 (began Spt) - 1st of 11 from Desert Fruit (2 Nov Redcar RF 5093). Won a moderate maiden in decent style. **H R A Cecil [1-3] K Abdulla.*

AGREEABLE RR 93+f 1609[1]
2 ch c Zafonic (USA) 9f **(83)** - Princess Accord (USA) (D'Accord (USA)) 9f **(94)**
Form - 1
Record 1998 - 1st:1 2nd:0 3rd:0 Ran:1
Win Prizemoney £4,698 *Total Prizemoney* £4,698
Wins * **1998** May Newmar (G-F) 6f 93+ <
1998 Turf 1-1: (6f 1-1) (g-f 1-1)
Currently useful colt. (1st run) - 1st of 10 from Emily's Luck Charm (30 May Newmarket RF 1609). David Loder's first juvenile winner for Godolphin, he was the narrow winner of a useful maiden on his debut, but did not reappear. **D R Loder [1-1] Maktoum Al Maktoum.*

AHDAAB (USA) RR 55f 4595[17]
2 ch f Rahy (USA) 9.1f **(80)** - Dish Dash (Bustino) 10.4f **(64)**
Form - 0
Record 1998 - 1st:0 2nd:0 3rd:0 Ran:1
1998 Turf 0-1: (7f) (gd)
Currently fair filly. **R W Armstrong [0-1] Hamdan Al Maktoum.*

AHERNE BHB 45f **RR 44f** 1953[12]
3 b g Nalchik (USA) 12.6f **(44)** - Zoomar (Legend of France (USA)) 9.5f **(61)**
Form - 4470
Record 1998 - 1st:0 2nd:0 3rd:0 Ran:4
1998 Turf 0-2: (8f, 10f) (gd, frm) 1998 AW 0-2: (6f, 7f) (Fibr 2)
Moderate gelding. Turf high 44. AW high 46.
**B Palling [0-4] J Hamilton-Jones.*

AHLIYAT (USA) BHB 60a **RR 60a** 260[5]
4 ch f Irish River (FR) 9f **(77)** - Alimana (Akarad (FR)) 9f **(76)**
Form - 15
Record 1998 - 1st:0 2nd:0 3rd:0 Ran:1
Pre1998 - 1st:1 2nd:0 3rd:0 Ran:1
Win Prizemoney £3,306 *Total Prizemoney* £3,306
Wins * 1997 *Dec Wolver (STD) 8.5f 55* <
1998 AW 0-1: (10f) (Equi)
Currently fair filly. Got off the mark in a maiden on the Wolverhampton Fibresand in December, but was helped by running close to the inside rail all the way, a big plus at that particular meeting. She had an impossible task on her next start.
**J W Hills [1-2] Mrs Sonia Rogers.*

AIGLE D'ILLYRIA (FR) BHB 35f **RR 20f** 2510[20]
4 b f Subotica (FR) - Eagle's Nest (FR) (King Of Macedon) 8.1f **(59)**
Form - 00000
Record 1998 - 1st:0 2nd:0 3rd:0 Ran:5
1998 Turf 0-5: (6f, 8f 3, 10f) (gd 2, g-f 2, frm)
Little account filly. Turf high 24.
**K O Cunningham-Brown [0-5] A J Richards.*

AIM HIGH BHB 80f **RR 83f** 4705[3]
3 b c Sadler's Wells (USA) 11.3f **(87)** - Aim for the Top (USA) (Irish River (FR)) 8.6f **(78)**
Form - 6321323
Record 1998 - 1st:1 2nd:2 3rd:3 Ran:7
Win Prizemoney £3,436 *Total Prizemoney* £9,079
Wins * **1998** Jly Newcas (GD) 10.1f 77+ <
1998 Turf 1-7: (10f 1-5, 12f 2) (g-s, gd 1-2, g-f 2, frm 2)
Scopey, decent colt, effective 10 to 12f, best at 10f, acts on g-s to frm, has worn blinkers. Turf high 83 - 3rd of 15 giving 5lb to Zakuska (27 Jun Doncaster 10f gd RF 2332) - also 1st of 5 giving 5lb to Blow Me A Kiss (27 Jly Newcastle RF 3138). Sold for 40,000 gns in October to join Noel Meade's yard.
**Sir Michael Stoute [1-7] Cheveley Park Stud.*

AIR ATTACHE (USA) BHB 68f **RR 76f** 4883[8]
3 b c Sky Classic (CAN) 10f **(83)** - Diplomatic Cover (USA) (Roberto (USA)) 10f **(76)**
Form - 30302448
Record 1998 - 1st:0 2nd:1 3rd:2 Ran:8
Pre1998 - 1st:0 2nd:1 3rd:0 Ran:2
Win Prizemoney £0 *Total Prizemoney* £4,407
1998 Turf 0-8: (8f, 9f 2, 10f 2, 12f 2, 14f) (sft, g-s, gd 3, g-f 2, frm)
Workmanlike, above-average colt, effective 7 to 14f, acts on gd to frm, best on frm, has worn blinkers. Turf high 78.
**G Lewis [0-10] Khalifa Dasmal.*

AIR EXPRESS (IRE) BHB 120f **RR 122df** 2288a[4]
4 b c Salse (USA) 10.9f **(71)** - Ibtisamm (USA) (Caucasus (USA)) 8.2f **(74)**
Form - 74
Record 1998 - 1st:0 2nd:0 3rd:0 Ran:2
Pre1998 - 1st:4 2nd:2 3rd:3 Ran:13
Win Prizemoney £327,033 *Total Prizemoney* £405,609
Wins * 1997 Spt Ascot (GD) G1 8f 122 <
* 1997 May Cologn (SFT) G2 8f 108

* 1997 Apr Capann (GD) G2 8f 108
* 1996 Spt Yarmou (G-F) 6f 104
1998 Turf 0-2: (7f, 8f) (gd, frm)

Well made, very high-class colt, effective 8f, acts on gd to g-f, prefers right handed tracks. Turf high 109. He began the campaign a potential champion miler, but ran poorly on both his starts and was not the same horse as in 1997. He has been retired to the National Stud. **C E Brittain [4-15] Mohamed Obaida.*

AIR GROOVE (JPN) RR 120f — 2287a[2]

5 b m Tony Bin - Dyna Carle (JPN) (Northern Taste (CAN))
Form - 22
1998 Turf 0-1: (10f) (hvy)

Currently very high-class filly. (1st run) - 2nd of 14 to Sunrise Flag (21 Jun Hanshin 10f hvy RF 2287a). This mare ran a game race when second to Pilsudski in the 1997 Japan Cup, and filled the same position in another valuable event at Hanshin in June.
**Y Ito in JPN [0-2].*

AIR OF ESTEEM RR 54f — 1810[5]

2 b c Forzando 7.2f **(63)** - Shadow Bird (Martinmas) 7.6f **(59)**
Form - 5
Record 1998 - 1st:0 2nd:0 3rd:0 Ran:1
1998 Turf 0-1: (6f) (g-s)

Currently fair colt. **P C Haslam [0-1] Middleham Park Racing XV.*

AIRS IMAGE RR — 274[5]

3 ch f Bustino 11f **(64)** - Western Star (Alcide) 12.5f **(42)**
Form - 5
Record 1998 - 1st:0 2nd:0 3rd:0 Ran:1
1998 AW 0-1: (7f) (Equi)

Unfurnished, currently very poor filly. **D Morris [0-1] B McAllister.*

AISLO (IRE) RR 97f — 1195a[7]

3 b c Caerleon (USA) 10.9f **(79)** - Aisla (USA) (Miswaki (USA)) 9f **(81)**
Form - 117
1998 Turf 2-3: (9f 1-1, 10f 1-2) (hvy 1-1, sft 1-1, gd)

Very useful colt, effective 10f, acts on sft. Turf high 97 - 1st of 9 from Risk Material (19 Apr Leopardstown RF 0809a). Gutsy individual who put up an improved display to win the Ballysax Stakes at Leopardstown beating Risk Material. Subsequently beaten by that rival since on ground faster than he prefers.
**D Gillespie in IRE [2-3] Mrs A J F O'Reilly (from J G Burns in IRE [0-4] Oct 1997).*

AIX EN PROVENCE (USA) BHB 100f RR 95?f — 4233[6]

3 b c Geiger Counter (USA) 7.8f **(85)**-Low Hill(Rousillon (USA))8.2f **(74)**
Form - 6
Record 1998 - 1st:0 2nd:0 3rd:0 Ran:1
Pre1998 - 1st:2 2nd:0 3rd:1 Ran:6
Win Prizemoney £6,362 *Total Prizemoney* £8,720
Wins * 1997 Aug Ripon (G-F) 6f 84+
* 1997 Jun Ayr (GD) 6f 85+ <
1998 Turf 0-1: (7f) (gd)

Scopey, very useful colt, effective 6 to 7f, acts on gd to frm.
**M Johnston [2-7] Featherstone, Bird.*

AJANO (GER) RR 111f — 4219a[8]

4 b c Kings Lake (USA) 11.8f **(58)**-Anona(GER)(Arratos (FR))12.2f **(60)**
Form - 6478
1998 Turf 0-4: (10f, 12f 3) (sft 2, g-s, gd)

Group-class colt, effective 12f, acts on sft to gd. Turf high 111 - 4th of 10 giving 4lb to Ferrari (26 Apr Cologne 12f sft RF 0948a). He was awarded a Group race in 1997, but never threatened in that league last season.
**H J Groschel in GER [1-6] (from E Groschel in GER [0-1] Aug 1997).*

AJDAR BHB 34f51a RR 43f 51a — 3787[8]

7 b g Slip Anchor 12.7f **(75)** - Loucoum (FR) (Iron Duke (FR)) 8.8f **(60)**
Form - 62143645054788
Record 1998 - 1st:1 2nd:1 3rd:1 Ran:14
Pre1998 - 1st:1 2nd:2 3rd:0 Ran:17
Win Prizemoney £3,957 *Total Prizemoney* £6,935
Wins * **1998** *Jan Southw (STD) H 12f 44 46+* <
1996 Jan Southw (STD) H 11f 42 44
1998 Turf 0-7: (10f 3, 12f 4) (sft 2, g-s, gd 3, g-f) 1998 AW 1-7: (8f, 11f 2, 12f 1-3, 14f) (Fibr 1-7)

Fair gelding, effective 11 to 14f, - acts on Fibr, has worn blinkers, prefers left handed tracks, prefers tight tracks. Turf high 47. AW high 53 - also 1st of 13 getting 11lb from Blooming Amazing (30 Jan Southwell RF 0188). Becoming disappointing.
**Mrs S Lamyman [1-21] P Lamyman (from Miss Gay Kelleway [1-11] Jly 1996).*

AJIG DANCER BHB 69f RR 65f — 5007[6]

3 b f Niniski (USA) 13.2f **(67)** - Gloire (Thatching) 8f **(66)**
Form - 840360006
Record 1998 - 1st:0 2nd:0 3rd:1 Ran:9
Pre1998 - 1st:1 2nd:1 3rd:0 Ran:5
Win Prizemoney £3,034 *Total Prizemoney* £5,359
Wins * 1997 Spt Bath (GD) 5.1f 82+ <
1998 Turf 0-9: (5f 3, 6f 4, 7f, 8f) (hvy, sft 2, gd 4, g-f, frm)

Strong, average filly, effective 6f, acts on g-s. Turf high 78. Inconsistent. **M R Channon [1-14] Timberhill Racing Partnership.*

AJJAE (IRE) BHB 40f RR 38f — 5115[4]

2 b c High Estate 10.5f **(66)**-Lake Ormond(Kings Lake (USA)) 10.8f **(67)**
Form - 6804
Record 1998 - 1st:0 2nd:0 3rd:0 Ran:4
Win Prizemoney £0 *Total Prizemoney* £214
1998 Turf 0-4: (7f 3, 8f) (sft, gd 3)

Very moderate colt, mostly wears blinkers. Turf high 38 (began Aug). **I Semple [0-4] Andy Dickie.*

AJLAAN BHB 92f RR 94f — 2818[6]

5 b h Unfuwain (USA) 11.4f **(74)** - Shurooq (USA) (Affirmed (USA)) 9.3f **(79)**
Form - 366
Record 1998 - 1st:0 2nd:0 3rd:1 Ran:3
Win Prizemoney £0 *Total Prizemoney* £1,001
1998 Turf 0-3: (8f, 10f, 12f) (g-f 2, frm)

Useful colt. Turf high 94. A decent winner in Dubai, he ran well on his British debut but was well beaten in a listed race on rain-affected ground. (DEAD) **B W Hills [0-3] Hamdan Al Maktoum.*

AJNAD (IRE) BHB 57f60a RR 61f 60a — 4872[4]

4 b g Efisio 7.7f **(69)** - Lotte Lenta (Gorytus (USA)) 7.8f **(60)**
Form - 453030062807204
Record 1998 - 1st:0 2nd:2 3rd:2 Ran:15
Pre1998 - 1st:0 2nd:0 3rd:0 Ran:1
Win Prizemoney £0 *Total Prizemoney* £2,965
1998 Turf 0-10: (5f 6, 6f 3, 7f) (g-s, gd, g-f 2, frm 5, hrd) 1998 AW 0-5: (5f 2, 6f, 7f 2) (Fibr 5)

Workmanlike, average gelding, effective 5 to 6f, best at 5f, acts on frm - acts on Fibr, often wears blinkers (effectively). Turf high 61 - 2nd of 15 getting 7lb from Sue Me (15 Jly Doncaster 5f frm RF 2814). AW high 54 - 3rd of 14 giving 15lb to Erro Codigo (23 Feb Southwell 6f Fibr RF 0345). He has ability, but though making the frame in varied company, actually getting his head in front seems to be a real problem.
**R F Marvin [0-15] J Shine (from C J Benstead [0-1] Aug 1996).*

AKA LADY (FR) RR 99f — 5155a[2]

3 b f Sanglamore (USA) 12.9f **(67)** - Akadya (FR) (Akarad (FR)) 9f **(76)**
Form - 2
1998 Turf 0-1: (12f) (hvy)

Currently very useful filly. (1st run) - 2nd of 11 getting 16lb from Trait De Genie (2 Nov Nantes 12f hvy RF 5155a).
**D Sepulchre in FR [0-1].*

AKALIM BHB 62f55a RR 64f 55a — 5128[2]

5 b g Petong 7.6f **(58)** - Tiszta Sharok (Song) 7.2f **(61)**
Form - 420858122
Record 1998 - 1st:1 2nd:3 3rd:0 Ran:9
Pre1998 - 1st:2 2nd:0 3rd:3 Ran:18
Win Prizemoney £10,973 *Total Prizemoney* £14,405
Wins * **1998** Spt Chepst (G-S) H 7.1f 56 60
1995 Oct Nottin (G-F) H 6.1f 76 78 <
1995 Jly Newmar (GD) 6f 77
1998 Turf 1-7: (6f 3, 7f 1-4) (sft, g-s, gd 1-1, g-f 3, frm) 1998 AW 0-2: (7f, 8f) (Fibr 2)

Average gelding, effective 6 to 7f, best at 6f, acts on g-s to frm - acts on Equi, has worn blinkers, prefers left handed tracks, excels at Chepstow. Turf high 64 - 2nd of 16 giving 6lb to Indian Blaze (5

Nov Brighton 6f g-s RF 5128) - also 1st of 19 giving 3lb to Matoaka (10 Spt Chepstow RF 4202). AW high 55. Consistent.
**L G Cottrell [1-17] Mrs Lucy Halloran (from D Morley [2-10] Jly 1996).*

AKARITA (IRE) BHB 90f **RR 93f** 4496[12]

3 b f Akarad (FR) 9.7f **(73)** - Safita (Habitat) 9.4f **(70)**
Form - 25341420
Record 1998 - 1st:1 2nd:2 3rd:1 Ran:8
Pre1998 - 1st:0 2nd:0 3rd:1 Ran:3
Win Prizemoney £4,172 *Total Prizemoney* £13,779
Wins * 1998 Jly Cheste (G-F) 7.6f 68 <
1998 Turf 1-8: (7f, 8f 1-4, 10f 2, 11f) (sft, gd 2, g-f 4, frm 1-1)
Workmanlike, useful filly, effective 8f, acts on g-f. Turf high 93 - 4th of 12 giving 1lb to Fizzed (20 Jun Ascot 8f g-f RF 2135). A half-sister to the very useful miler Safawan, she showed ability in decent company before breaking her maiden at Chester. Decent runs in listed races since, but she will struggle to win in that class.
**B A McMahon [1-11] Barouche Stud Ltd.*

AKBAR (IRE) RR 90f 5108a[3]

2 bb c Doyoun 10.7f **(69)** - Akishka (Nishapour (FR)) 9.1f **(61)**
Form - 13
1998 Turf 1-2: (7f 1-2) (hvy 1-1, gd)
Currently useful colt. Turf high 90 (began Oct) - 3rd of 6 giving 3lb to Athlumney Lady (26 Oct Leopardstown 7f gd RF 5108a). A half-brother to Ribblesdale runner-up Akdariya, he won a maiden on his belated debut, and then found Athlumney Lady too quick at Leopardstown. He is likely to appreciate middle distances as a three-year-old. **J Oxx in IRE [1-2] H H Aga Khan.*

AKUNA BAY (USA) RR 90+f 4280a[1]

2 b f Mr Prospector (USA) 8.6f **(88)** - Dark Lomond (Lomond (USA)) 8.8f **(65)**
Form - 51
1998 Turf 1-2: (7f 1-2) (sft 1-1, frm)
Currently useful filly. Turf high 90 (began Aug) - 1st of 14 from Apparatchik (7 Spt Galway RF 4280a). Had two runs and one win, a decent Galway maiden that has thrown up a few winners. Prefers to get his toe in and an O'Brien inmate to keep an eye on.
**A P O'Brien in IRE [1-2] Mrs Barbara Murphy.*

ALAAMA (IRE) RR 81f 4411[4]

2 ch f Elmaamul (USA) 8.1f **(70)** - Rahik (Wassl) 9.7f **(62)**
Form - 4
Record 1998 - 1st:0 2nd:0 3rd:0 Ran:1
Win Prizemoney £0 *Total Prizemoney* £287
1998 Turf 0-1: (7f) (frm)
Currently decent filly. (1st run) - 4th of 17 to Kalidasa (22 Spt Warwick 7f frm RF 4411). **R W Armstrong [0-1] Hamdan Al Maktoum.*

ALABAQ (USA) BHB 100f **RR 84+f** 4514[4]

2 b br f Riverman (USA) 9.7f **(78)** - Salsabil (Sadler's Wells (USA)) 10f **(76)**
Form - 214
Record 1998 - 1st:1 2nd:1 3rd:0 Ran:3
Win Prizemoney £3,306 *Total Prizemoney* £13,551
Wins * 1998 Spt Lingfi (G-S) 7f 84+ <
1998 Turf 1-3: (6f, 7f 1-1, 8f) (gd 2, g-f 1-1)
Currently decent filly. Turf high 84 (began Aug) - 1st of 10 from Trump Street (8 Spt Lingfield RF 4144). A daughter of Salsabil, she made a most promising racecourse debut when chasing home Aidan O'Brien's Orpen in a newcomers' race at Goodwood, with the rest well beaten. Went one better at Lingfield, but was put in her place in the Fillies' Mile, beaten a long way by the principles. Lacks a bit of substance. **J L Dunlop [1-3] Hamdan Al Maktoum.*

ALAGNA BHB 44f43a **RR 47f 43a** 91[4]

4 b f Unfuwain (USA) 11.4f **(74)** - Spica (USA) (Diesis) 9.3f **(69)**
Form - 524
Record 1998 - 1st:0 2nd:1 3rd:0 Ran:3
Pre1998 - 1st:0 2nd:2 3rd:1 Ran:12
Win Prizemoney £0 *Total Prizemoney* £2,760
1998 AW 0-3: (12f 2, 13f) (Equi 2, Fibr)
Leggy, moderate filly, effective 12 to 15f, best at 12f, acts on gd to frm - acts on Fibr, has worn blinkers, favours tight tracks. AW high 45 - 2nd of 8 getting 9lb from State Approval (10 Jan Wolverhampton 12f Fibr RF 0068). Travels well through her races, but does not always put her best foot forward when push comes to shove. **S C Williams [0-15] W J de Ruiter.*

ALAKDAR (CAN) BHB 56f **RR 60f** 2839[11]

4 ch g Green Dancer (USA) 11.9f **(77)** - Population (General Assembly (USA)) 10f **(68)**
Form - 00
Record 1998 - 1st:0 2nd:0 3rd:0 Ran:2
Pre1998 - 1st:1 2nd:0 3rd:2 Ran:8
Win Prizemoney £2,784 *Total Prizemoney* £3,761
Wins 1997 Oct Catter (SFT) 12f 73 <
1998 Turf 0-2: (11f, 12f) (g-f 2)
Scopey, average gelding, effective 12 to 14f, acts on g-s to frm, favours tight tracks. Turf high 30. Inconsistent.
**R Champion [0-5] Mrs Judith Mendonca (from A C Stewart [1-7] Oct 1997).*

ALAMEIN (USA) BHB 70f75a **RR 69f 75a** 2524[8]

5 ch g Roi Danzig (USA) 10.5f **(62)** - Pollination (Pentotal) 7f **(53)**
Form - 100623368
Record 1998 - 1st:1 2nd:1 3rd:2 Ran:9
Pre1998 - 1st:2 2nd:1 3rd:4 Ran:15
Win Prizemoney £9,013 *Total Prizemoney* £17,083
Wins * 1998 *Mar Southw (STD) C 7f 72+*
1996 Jun Thirsk (FRM) 7f 78 <
1996 Jun Catter (GD) 7f 73
1998 Turf 0-7:(7f 3, 8f 4) (gd 4, frm 3)1998 AW 1-2: (7f 1-1, 8f)(Fibr 1-2)
Above-average gelding, effective 7f, acts on g-f, often wears blinkers. Turf high 70. AW high 72 (1st run). A fair handicapper for Willie Haggas, he made a successful debut for Dandy Nicholls on the Southwell Fibresand in March. His saddle slipped when he was favourite for the Doncaster Spring Mile a few days later, but he finished stone last in a handicap back at Southwell in April. Better efforts in modest company since.
**D Nicholls [1-9] R J H Ltd (from W J Haggas [2-11] Aug 1997).*

ALAMO BAY (USA) RR 108f 4947a[4]

5 b h Nureyev (USA) 8.4f **(84)**-Albertine (FR) (Irish River (FR)) 8.6f **(78)**
Form - 214
1998 Turf 1-3: (7f 1-3) (hvy, sft 1-1, gd)
Pattern-class colt. Turf high 108 - also 1st of 4 from Anntari (19 Spt Longchamp RF 4470g). A half-brother to Arcangues, he was not troubled to win a Listed event at Longchamp in September and could have followed up in the Group One Prix de la Foret had Olivier Peslier not set him a mountainous task. There is a Group race in this still unexposed horse. **A Fabre in FR [2-6].*

ALAMODE BHB 47f57a **RR 45f 57a** 4397[20]

4 b f Statoblest 6.4f **(63)** - Alo Ez (Alzao (USA)) 7.1f **(68)**
Form - 47000
Record 1998 - 1st:0 2nd:0 3rd:0 Ran:5
Pre1998 - 1st:1 2nd:0 3rd:0 Ran:3
Win Prizemoney £2,810 *Total Prizemoney* £2,810
Wins 1997 May Doncas (GD) 5f 48+ <
1998 Turf 0-4: (5f 2, 6f 2) (gd 2, frm 2) 1998 AW 0-1: (5f) (Fibr)
Scopey, fair filly, effective 5f, acts on frm. Turf high 45. Inconsistent.
**J Pearce [0-3] T H Rossiter (from J G Smyth-Osbourne [1-5] May 1998).*

ALANA'S CAVALIER (IRE) BHB 56f **RR 69f** 4934[3]

2 b c Forest Wind (USA) - Annais Nin (Dominion) 8.5f **(63)**
Form - 000033
Record 1998 - 1st:0 2nd:0 3rd:2 Ran:6
Win Prizemoney £0 *Total Prizemoney* £574
1998 Turf 0-6: (7f 3, 8f 2, 10f) (gd 2, g-f, frm 3)
Average colt, effective 8 to 10f, acts on gd. Turf high 69 (began Jly) - 3rd of 17 giving 5lb to Medelai (22 Oct Nottingham 8f gd RF 4934). **R Hollinshead [0-6] The Three R's.*

A LA PERRUCHE (IRE) BHB 33f **RR 21f** 4884[13]

2 b c Forest Wind (USA) - Pamiers (Huntercombe) 7.3f **(56)**
Form - 0000
Record 1998 - 1st:0 2nd:0 3rd:0 Ran:4
1998 Turf 0-4: (5f 2, 6f, 7f) (g-s, gd, frm 2)
Little account colt. Turf high 21. **R Curtis [0-4] Ivory & Ledoux Ltd.*

ALARICO (FR) BHB 64f72a **RR 66df 72a** 3299[11]
5 ch g Kadrou (FR) 10f **(74)** - Calabria (FR) (Vitiges (FR)) 8.2f **(59)**
Form - 0
Record 1998 - 1st:0 2nd:0 3rd:0 Ran:1
Pre1998 - 1st:1 2nd:1 3rd:2 Ran:9
Win Prizemoney £3,371 *Total Prizemoney* £5,538
Wins * 1997 *Jan Lingfi (STD) 10f 74 <*
1998 Turf 0-1: (14f) (gd)
Above-average gelding, effective 10 to 14f, best at 14f, acted on frm - acted on Equi. Inconsistent. (DEAD)
**Ian Williams [1-14] Hayman and Turton.*

ALARME BELLE RR 101f 4907a[3]
4 b f Warning 8.1f **(77)** -Dazzlingly Radiant(Try My Best(USA)) 7.6f **(67)**
Form - 28376583
1998 Turf 0-7: (6f 3, 7f 3, 8f) (hvy, sft 2, gd 4)
Very useful filly, effective 6 to 7f, acts on hvy to sft, often wears blinkers. Turf high 101. She struggled valiantly in decent company, running her best race in a Listed event at the Curragh in October, and will make a nice broodmare in due course.
**D K Weld in IRE [2-19] John Davis.*

ALASTAIR SMELLIE BHB 82f **RR 80f** 4820[3]
2 ch c Sabrehill (USA) 8.5f **(64)** - Reel Foyle (USA) (Irish River (FR)) 8.6f **(78)**
Form - 6783163
Record 1998 - 1st:1 2nd:0 3rd:2 Ran:7
Win Prizemoney £5,394 *Total Prizemoney* £7,196
Wins * **1998** Spt Ayr (G-S) H 6f 75 79 <
1998 Turf 1-7: (6f 1-4, 7f 2, 8f) (sft 1-1, gd, g-f 3, frm 2)
Decent colt, effective 6 to 7f, best at 6f, acts on sft to frm. Turf high 80 - 3rd of 15 getting 7lb from Acicula (15 Oct Newmarket 6f frm RF 4820) - also 1st of 16 giving 2lb to Never Can Tell (18 Spt Ayr RF 4349). **B W Hills [1-7] W J Gredley.*

AL AVA CONSONANT BHB 31f18a **RR 36f 18a** 207[7]
4 b f Reprimand 8.2f **(63)**-Dragonist (Dragonara Palace (USA)) 6.1f **(55)**
Form - 60007
Record 1998 - 1st:0 2nd:0 3rd:0 Ran:3
Pre1998 - 1st:0 2nd:0 3rd:1 Ran:14
Win Prizemoney £0 *Total Prizemoney* £359
1998 AW 0-3: (7f, 8f, 11f) (Fibr 3)
Scopey, very moderate filly, effective 8f, acts on gd, has worn blinkers, likes left handed tracks. Becoming disappointing.
**J D Bethell [0-17] The Dante Partnership.*

ALAZAN BHB 50f **RR 32f** 1598[4]
3 ch c Risk Me (FR) 8f **(53)** - Gunnard (Gunner B) 11.2f **(58)**
Form - 4
Record 1998 - 1st:0 2nd:0 3rd:0 Ran:1
Pre1998 - 1st:0 2nd:0 3rd:0 Ran:3
Win Prizemoney £0 *Total Prizemoney* £740
1998 Turf 0-1: (11f) (g-f)
Scopey, very moderate colt.
**D M Hyde [0-4] The Spanish Connection.*

ALAZIMA (USA) RR 65f 3896[6]
2 b br f Riverman (USA) 9.7f **(78)** - Manwah (USA) (Lyphard (USA)) 9.9f **(72)**
Form - 86
Record 1998 - 1st:0 2nd:0 3rd:0 Ran:2
1998 Turf 0-2: (7f 2) (gd 2)
Currently average filly. Turf high 65 (began Jly).
**M P Tregoning [0-2] Hamdan Al Maktoum.*

ALBAHA (USA) BHB 74f95a **RR 72f 95a** 217[1]
5 br g Woodman (USA) 9.7f **(77)** - Linda's Magic (USA) (Far North (CAN)) 9.7f **(75)**
Form - 1
Record 1998 - 1st:1 2nd:0 3rd:0 Ran:1
Pre1998 - 1st:3 2nd:2 3rd:3 Ran:21
Win Prizemoney £15,683 *Total Prizemoney* £26,049
Wins * **1998** *Feb Wolver (STD) H 12f 85 90 <*
* 1997 *Mar Wolver (STD) H 12f 80 82*
* 1997 *Jan Southw (STD) 12f 73*
* 1996 *Dec Southw (SLW) 12f 69+*
1998 AW 1-1: (12f 1-1) (Fibr 1-1)
Useful gelding, effective 12f, - acts on Fibr, has worn blinkers, prefers left handed tracks, prefers tight tracks. (1st run) - 1st of 6 giving 13lb to Greenspan (4 Feb Wolverhampton RF 0217). Inconsistent. Nothing special on turf, he is one of the best performers to have graced Fibresand in recent years. He came back to win a very competitive handicap at Wolverhampton in February in great style, making all, but opportunities for him on sand were very limited due to his high rating, and he has reportedly gone to America.
**J E Banks [4-14] UK Packaging Supplies Ltd (from R W Armstrong [0-11] Jly 1996).*

ALBARAHIN (USA) BHB 80f **RR 74f** 4968[4]
3 b c Silver Hawk (USA) 11.2f **(85)** - My Dear Lady (USA) (Mr Prospector (USA)) 8.8f **(78)**
Form - 34
Record 1998 - 1st:0 2nd:0 3rd:1 Ran:2
Pre1998 - 1st:0 2nd:2 3rd:0 Ran:2
Win Prizemoney £0 *Total Prizemoney* £5,383
1998 Turf 0-2: (10f 2) (sft, g-f)
Well made, above-average colt. Turf high 74 (began Oct). Fractured his near-fore in the spring and was found wanting in maidens. **S bin Suroor [0-4] Godolphin.*

ALBARAN (GER) RR 103f 4348a[3]
5 b h Sure Blade (USA) 10.6f **(66)** - Araqueen (GER) (Konigsstuhl (GER)) 11.2f **(76)**
Form - 13
1998 Turf 1-2: (12f 1-2) (sft 1-2)
Very useful colt. Turf high 103 (1st run) (began Aug) - 1st of 13 from Chirac (2 Aug Klampenborg RF 3422a). He claimed Taufan's Melody's scalp when winning the Scandinavian Open in August, but was found out in Group company the following month.
**Ms C Erichsen in NOR [1-2] (from NOR [0-1] Aug 1997).*

ALBEMINE (USA) BHB 60f54a **RR 54a** 338[6]
9 b g Al Nasr (FR) 9.9f **(72)** - Lady Be Mine (USA) (Sir Ivor) 10.2f **(70)**
Form - 56
Record 1998 - 1st:0 2nd:0 3rd:0 Ran:2
Pre1998 - 1st:1 2nd:0 3rd:2 Ran:8
Win Prizemoney £2,511 *Total Prizemoney* £4,430
1998 AW 0-2: (12f, 16f) (Fibr 2)
Fair gelding. AW high 50. Consistent.
**R T Juckes [1-6] A C W Price (from Mrs J Cecil [4-12] Spt 1993).*

ALBERICH (IRE) BHB 90f **RR 89f** 4226[4]
3 b c Night Shift (USA) 8.1f **(73)** - Tetradonna (IRE) (Teenoso (USA)) 9.9f **(72)**
Form - 14
Record 1998 - 1st:1 2nd:0 3rd:0 Ran:2
Pre1998 - 1st:1 2nd:0 3rd:1 Ran:3
Win Prizemoney £17,244 *Total Prizemoney* £18,395
Wins * **1998** Spt York (GD) H 11.9f 86 89 <
* 1997 Aug Beverl (GD) 8.5f 80+
1998 Turf 1-2: (12f 1-2) (g-f 1-2)
Strong, useful colt. Turf high 89 (began Spt) - 4th of 17 getting 4lb from Jazil (11 Spt Doncaster 12f g-f RF 4226) - also 1st of 9 getting 7lb from Murghem (3 Spt York RF 4069). Game winner of a valuable handicap on his belated return, but was held on faster ground at Doncaster. **M Johnston [2-5] David Abell.*

ALBERKINNIE BHB 43f **RR 44f** 5070[5]
3 b f Ron's Victory (USA) 9.2f **(52)** - Trojan Desert (Troy) 10.4f **(68)**
Form - 48776U065
Record 1998 - 1st:0 2nd:0 3rd:0 Ran:9
Win Prizemoney £0 *Total Prizemoney* £252
1998 Turf 0-7: (7f, 8f 3, 9f 2, 10f) (g-s, gd 2, g-f 2, frm 2) 1998 AW 0-2: (7f, 8f) (Fibr 2)
Workmanlike, moderate filly, effective 7f, acts on g-f, likes tight tracks. Turf high 44. AW high 35. Inconsistent.
**J L Harris [0-9] Paddy Barrett.*

ALBERT THE BEAR BHB 75f80a **RR 81df 80a** 4365[11]
5 b g Puissance 7.1f **(60)** - Florentynna Bay (Aragon) 8.1f **(60)**
Form - 0D056300
Record 1998 - 1st:0 2nd:0 3rd:1 Ran:8
Pre1998 - 1st:6 2nd:5 3rd:2 Ran:31

Win Prizemoney £30,854 *Total Prizemoney* £42,981

Wins	* 1997	Jun	Cheste	(G-F)	H	7f	84	87	<
	* 1997	May	Cheste	(HVY)	H	7.6f	78	87	<
	* 1996	Jun	Cheste	(G-F)	H	7f	77	77	
	* 1995	Aug	Catter	(G-F)	H	6f	61	65	
	* 1995	Aug	Bath	(HRD)	H	5.7f	61	65	
	* 1995	Jun	Carlis	(FRM)	S	5f		60	

1998 Turf 0-8: (6f 3, 7f 2, 8f 3) (sft, gd 3, g-f 3, frm)

Decent gelding, effective 6 to 8f, best at 7f, acts on hvy to frm, has worn blinkers, and excels at Lingfield. Turf high 84. Consistent handicapper who has a real liking for Chester, winning there for the third time in June '97, and running a blinder at the big meeting last season to finish third, though later demoted for interference. The extended seven at Chester looks to be the very limit of his stamina. **J Berry [6-39] Chris & Antonia Deuters.*

ALBOOSTAN BHB 110f **RR 107f** 2949[4]

3 b c Sabrehill (USA) 8.5f **(64)** - Russian Countess (USA) (Nureyev (USA)) 8.7f **(78)**

Form - 244

Record	**1998 -**	1st:0	2nd:1	3rd:0	Ran:3
	Pre1998 -	1st:2	2nd:1	3rd:1	Ran:4

Win Prizemoney £17,029 *Total Prizemoney* £48,952

Wins	1997	Spt	Goodwo	(GD)	L	8f		101	<
	1997	Jly	Beverl	(GD)		7.5f		86+	

1998 Turf 0-3: (9f, 10f, 11f) (gd 2, g-f)

Pattern-class colt, effective 8 to 9f, acts on gd. Turf high 107 (1st run) - 2nd of 6 giving 3lb to Border Arrow (16 Apr Newmarket 9f gd RF 0709). Very good-looking, he went into plenty of notebooks when running Border Arrow to a neck at Newmarket in April. Supplemented for the Derby at a cost of £8,000, he was scrubbed from the Epsom Classic after running poorly at Lingfield, and fared little better at Ayr in July. We have not seen the last or best of this colt, and he remains an interesting prospect over a mile and a quarter.

**B W Hills [0-3] Hamdan Al Maktoum (from D Morley [2-4] Oct 1997).*

ALBORADA BHB 121f **RR 122f** 4852[1]

3 gr f Alzao (USA) 9.8f **(73)** - Alouette (Darshaan) 9.9f **(84)**

Form - 1121

Record	**1998 -**	1st:3	2nd:1	3rd:0	Ran:4
	Pre1998 -	1st:2	2nd:0	3rd:2	Ran:4

Win Prizemoney £329,624 *Total Prizemoney* £369,651

Wins	* **1998**	Oct	Newmar	(GD)	G1	10f		122	<
	* **1998**	Aug	Goodwo	(GD)	G2	9.9f		116	
	* **1998**	Jun	Currag	(SFT)	G2	10f		104	
	* 1997	Oct	Currag	(G-S)	G3	7f		101	
	* 1997	Spt	Beverl	(G-F)		7.5f		77+	

1998 Turf 3-4: (10f 3-4) (sft 1-1, gd 2-3)

Light-framed, very high-class filly, effective 10f, acts on gd, excels at Curragh. Turf high 122 - 1st of 10 getting 8lb from Insatiable (17 Oct Newmarket RF 4852) - also 1st of 9 giving 3lb to Digitalize (1 Aug Goodwood RF 3256). Improving. Took a Group Three in Ireland on her final start of the 1997 season, and though it did not look as if she had beaten anything special at the time, the race subsequently threw up two Oaks winners. She was slow to come to hand this year, but landed the Pretty Polly at the Curragh in tidy style on her return, and put up a brave performance to follow up in Goodwood's Nassau Stakes. Although she appeared flattered to run Swain to half a length in the Irish Champion Stakes, she subsequently beat a field including the Eclipse and Juddmonte International winners in the English version. A thoroughly game and genuine filly, she is yet another example of her trainer's supreme skill in placing his horses.

**Sir Mark Prescott [5-8] Miss K Rausing.*

ALBRIGHTON BHB 55f **RR 58f** 3969[3]

3 b g Terimon 8.7f **(58)** - Bright-One (Electric) 10.1f **(61)**

Form - 871603

Record	**1998 -**	1st:1	2nd:0	3rd:1	Ran:6
	Pre1998 -	1st:0	2nd:0	3rd:0	Ran:2

Win Prizemoney £2,442 *Total Prizemoney* £2,862

Wins	* **1998**	Jly	Beverl	(G-F)	H	16.2f	53	58	<

1998 Turf 1-6: (7f, 11f, 14f, 16f 1-1, 17f 2) (gd, g-f 2, frm 1-3)

Strong, fair gelding, effective 14 to 16f, acts on g-f to frm, prefers tight tracks. Turf high 58 - 3rd of 6 getting 9lb from Generous Ways (29 Aug Redcar 14f g-f RF 3969) - also 1st of 11 getting 5lb from Rabea (20 Jly Beverley RF 2952).

**C W Thornton [1-6] Peter Rawson (from B S Rothwell [0-2] Nov 1997).*

ALCADIA (IRE) **RR 96f** 3541a[1]

3 ch f Thatching 7.8f **(69)** - Soltura

Form - 631

1998 Turf 1-3: (5f, 7f 1-2) (g-s 1-1, gd, hrd)

Currently very useful filly. Turf high 96 - 3rd of 8 to Mempari (22 Jly Naas 5f gd RF 3178a) - also 1st of 14 getting 5lb from Quinstars (4 Aug Roscommon RF 3541a). Won her maiden well after a couple of promising efforts beforehand. Looks useful.

**C O'Brien in IRE [1-3] Mrs M V O'Brien.*

ALCALALI (USA) BHB 78f **RR 75df** 1982[13]

4 ch f Septieme Ciel (USA) - Princess Verna (USA) (Al Hattab (USA)) 9.3f **(74)**

Form - 0

Record	**1998 -**	1st:0	2nd:0	3rd:0	Ran:1
	Pre1998 -	1st:0	2nd:1	3rd:0	Ran:11

Win Prizemoney £0 *Total Prizemoney* £8,011

1998 Turf 0-1: (12f) (g-s)

Above-average filly.

**M D Hammond [1-6] Steve Semple (from P A Kelleway [0-11] Oct 1997).*

ALCAYDE BHB 80f **RR 80f** 4973[5]

3 ch c Alhijaz 7.7f **(57)** - Lucky Flinders (Free State) 8.7f **(61)**

Form - 2321425

Record	**1998 -**	1st:1	2nd:3	3rd:1	Ran:7
	Pre1998 -	1st:0	2nd:0	3rd:0	Ran:1

Win Prizemoney £3,420 *Total Prizemoney* £7,790

Wins	* **1998**	Jly	Newcas	(G-F)	H	10.1f	77	77	<

1998 Turf 1-7: (8f 2, 10f 1-3, 12f 2) (sft, g-s 3, gd 1-2, g-f)

Neat, decent colt, effective 8 to 12f, best at 10f, acts on g-s to g-f, excels at Newcastle. Turf high 80 - 2nd of 9 to Kimberley (17 Oct Redcar 10f g-s RF 4855) - also 1st of 4 getting 10lb from Pension Fund (25 Jly Newcastle RF 3116). Consistent. He got off the mark in a modest four-runner handicap at Newcastle, but has looked decidedly one-paced otherwise and does not seem to be one of the stable stars. **J L Dunlop [1-8] Lady Cohen.*

ALCAZAR (IRE) BHB 110f **RR 105f** 5149[1]

3 b g Alzao (USA) 9.8f **(73)** - Sahara Breeze (Ela-Mana-Mou) 10.1f **(70)**

Form - 51741411

Record	**1998 -**	1st:4	2nd:0	3rd:0	Ran:8

Win Prizemoney £28,194 *Total Prizemoney* £31,877

Wins	* **1998**	Nov	Doncas	(SFT)	L	12f		105	<
	* **1998**	Oct	Haydoc	(SFT)		11.9f		103	
	* **1998**	Spt	Haydoc	(GD)	H	11.9f	100	103	
	* **1998**	Jun	Ripon	(SFT)		8f		92+	

1998 Turf 4-8: (8f 1-2, 10f, 11f, 12f 3-4) (sft 1-1, gd 2-3, g-f 3, frm 1-1)

Workmanlike, Pattern-class gelding, effective 11 to 12f, best at 12f, acts on sft to frm. Turf high 105 - 1st of 6 getting 6lb from Prince of Denial (7 Nov Doncaster RF 5149) - also 1st of 6 giving 2lb to Wales (14 Oct Haydock RF 4798). Consistent. He looked as weak as a kitten when unplaced at Sandown in July, but improved significantly in the second half of the season. Successful in a handicap and conditions event at Haydock, he capped a grand campaign by landing a Listed event at Doncaster in November. The ground was soft that day and, according to Pat Eddery, that is just what this colt requires. Sure to stay beyond middle-distances, he responds well to pressure and is an interesting prospect for next year. **J L Dunlop [4-8] JRepard,FMelrose,OPawle,MStokes,RBlack.*

ALCONLEIGH BHB 92f **RR 92f** 4467[10]

3 ch c Pursuit of Love 9.5f **(69)** - Serotina (IRE) (Mtoto)

Form - 040

Record	**1998 -**	1st:0	2nd:0	3rd:0	Ran:3
	Pre1998 -	1st:2	2nd:4	3rd:1	Ran:9

Win Prizemoney £8,600 *Total Prizemoney* £18,092

Wins	* 1997	Jly	Thirsk	(GD)		7f		90	<
	* 1997	May	Ripon	(G-S)		6f		77	

1998 Turf 0-3: (8f, 10f 2) (gd, g-f, frm)

Scopey, useful colt, effective 6 to 10f, best at 7f, acts on sft to g-f, excels at Doncaster. Turf high 92 - 4th of 20 giving 2lb to Himself (12 Spt Doncaster 10f g-f RF 4241). Inconsistent. A winner twice as a juvenile, he is perhaps a little too high in the weights as a result. However, he ran an encouraging race after a four-month break at the St Leger meeting. **M Johnston [2-12] David Abell.*

ALDINO (GER) RR 107f 4470h7

4 b c Dashing Blade 7.9f **(80)** -Alabama (GER)(Surumu (GER)) 10f **(83)**

Form - 27

1998 Turf 0-2: (10f 2) (sft, gd)

Currently Pattern-class colt. Turf high 107 (1st run) (began Aug) - 2nd of 16 to Happy Change (28 Aug Baden-Baden 10f sft RF 4074a). He could not catch Happy Change at Baden-Baden in August and was again given plenty to do at Franfurt the following month. A change in tactics would help his cause.

**In GER [0-1] (from W Kujath in GER [0-2] Aug 1998).*

ALDWYCH ARROW (IRE) BHB 60f65a **RR 66f 65a** 51185

3 ch g Rainbows For Life (CAN) 9.3f **(64)** - Shygate (Shy Groom (USA)) 10f **(66)**

Form - 322402211273835

Record	**1998** -	1st:2	2nd:5	3rd:3	Ran:15
	Pre1998 -	1st:0	2nd:0	3rd:0	Ran:5

Win Prizemoney £6,470 *Total Prizemoney* £12,903

Wins	**1998**	Jun	Mussel	(SFT)	H	14f	63	66	
	1998	Jun	Ayr	(GD)	H	13.1f	60	67	<

1998 Turf 2-11: (12f 2, 13f 1-1, 14f 1-2, 16f 6) (g-s, gd 2-4, g-f 4, frm 2)

1998 AW 0-4: (11f, 12f 3) (Equi, Fibr 3)

Average gelding, effective 11 to 16f, acts on g-s to g-f - acts on Fibr, prefers tight tracks. Turf high 68 - 2nd of 4 getting 18lb from Corniche (10 Jly Chepstow 16f g-f RF 2670) - also 1st of 7 getting 10lb from Mannequin (19 Jun Ayr RF 2116). AW high 63 - 2nd of 12 getting 3lb from Bustopher Jones (11 Mar Southwell 11f Fibr RF 0418). A likeable stayer, he was sold for 11,000 gns in the autumn, to join Mark Buckley's yard.

**M A Buckley [0-1] M A Buckley (from M Bell [2-19] Spt 1998).*

ALEANBH (IRE) RR 76f 4818

3 ch c Classic Secret (USA) 8.8f **(56)** - Highdrive (Ballymore) 7.3f **(64)**

Form - 8

Record	**1998** -	1st:0	2nd:0	3rd:0	Ran:1

1998 Turf 0-1: (7f) (gd)

Rangy, currently above-average colt.

**Miss Gay Kelleway [0-1] Tommy Staunton.*

ALEGRIA RR 84f 27661

2 b f Night Shift (USA) 8.1f **(73)** - High Habit (Slip Anchor) 9.8f **(73)**

Form - 51

Record	**1998** -	1st:1	2nd:0	3rd:0	Ran:2

Win Prizemoney £3,436 *Total Prizemoney* £3,436

Wins	* **1998**	Jly	Windso	(GD)	6f	84	<

1998 Turf 1-2: (6f 1-2) (frm 1-2)

Currently decent filly. Turf high 84 (began Jly) - 1st of 20 from Deviletta (13 Jly Windsor RF 2766). **J M P Eustace [1-2] J C Smith.*

ALEXANDER BHB 60f **RR 64f** 48607

2 b c Be My Chief (USA) 10.2f **(62)** - Arminda (Blakeney) 10.5f **(64)**

Form - 757

Record	**1998** -	1st:0	2nd:0	3rd:0	Ran:3

1998 Turf 0-3: (7f 2, 8f) (sft, gd 2)

Currently average colt. Turf high 64 (began Jly).

**C W Thornton [0-3] Guy Reed.*

ALEXFIELD (USA) RR 94f 5108a4

2 ch c Housebuster (USA) 7f **(81)** - Delagating (CAN)

Form - 174

1998 Turf 1-3: (6f 1-2, 7f) (g-s, gd 1-2)

Currently useful colt. Turf high 94 (began Spt) - also 1st of 13 giving 5lb to Timote (19 Spt Curragh RF 4429a). Won on his Curragh debut but has been well beaten since in Group and Listed company. Probably needs a drop in class.

**A P O'Brien in IRE [1-3] Y H Yue.*

ALEZAL BHB 105f **RR 109f** 17765

4 b c Anshan 8.2f **(63)** - Dance On The Stage (Dancing Brave (USA)) 8.4f **(76)**

Form - 335

Record	**1998** -	1st:0	2nd:0	3rd:2	Ran:3
	Pre1998 -	1st:3	2nd:3	3rd:0	Ran:7

Win Prizemoney £36,760 *Total Prizemoney* £46,434

Wins	* 1997	Oct	Ascot	(HVY)	H	10f	100	102	<
	* 1997	May	Haydoc	(G-S)	H	8.1f	90	94+	
	* 1997	May	Hamilt	(SFT)		8.3f		82+	

1998 Turf 0-3: (9f 2, 10f) (sft, gd, g-f)

Scopey, Pattern-class colt, effective 9 to 10f, best at 10f, acts on sft to g-f, best on sft, excels at Newmarket. Turf high 109 (1st run) - 3rd of 7 to Apprehension (15 Apr Newmarket 9f sft RF 0696). He struggled to make the transition from handicaps to Group races, but ran well when third in the Earl of Sefton Stakes at Newmarket in April. Lightly tried thereafter, he stays 10 furlongs and is best when ridden aggressively. **W Jarvis [3-10] Howard Spooner.*

ALFAHAAL (IRE) BHB 59f56a **RR 63f 56a** 54810

5 b h Green Desert (USA) 7.8f **(78)** - Fair of the Furze (Ela-Mana-Mou) 10.1f **(70)**

Form - 488300

Record	**1998** -	1st:0	2nd:0	3rd:1	Ran:4
	Pre1998 -	1st:2	2nd:1	3rd:1	Ran:17

Win Prizemoney £7,065 *Total Prizemoney* £9,166

Wins	1997	Oct	Leices	(SFT)		8f		63	<
	1997	Jly	Doncas	(GD)	H	8f	52	56	

1998 Turf 0-1: (7f) (sft) 1998 AW 0-3: (7f, 8f 2) (Equi 2, Fibr)

Average colt, effective 7 to 8f, best at 8f, acts on g-s to frm - acts on Equi, excels at Leicester. AW high 58.

**C A Dwyer [0-7] M M Foulger (from R F JohnsonHoughton [2-11] Oct 1997).*

AL FAHDA BHB 100f **RR 84f** 39223

2 b f Be My Chief (USA) 10.2f **(62)** - Fleetwood Fancy (Taufan (USA)) 7f **(57)**

Form - 7121353

Record	**1998** -	1st:2	2nd:1	3rd:2	Ran:7

Win Prizemoney £6,705 *Total Prizemoney* £15,316

Wins	* **1998**	Jun	Warwic	(G-S)	7f	84	<
	* **1998**	May	Leices	(GD)	6f	73	

1998 Turf 2-7: (5f, 6f 1-2, 7f 1-4) (gd, g-f 2-4, frm 2)

Decent filly, effective 6 to 7f, best at 7f, acts on gd to g-f, best on g-f. Turf high 84 - 3rd of 9 to Circle of Gold (28 Aug Goodwood 7f g-f RF 3922) - also 1st of 8 from Bathwick (24 Jun Warwick RF 2257). **R Hannon [2-7] Hassan Ahmadi.*

ALFANNAN BHB 80f **RR 71f** 29474

4 b c Lear Fan (USA) 10.4f **(80)** - Connecting Link (USA) (Linkage (USA)) 9.1f **(82)**

Form - 374

Record	**1998** -	1st:0	2nd:0	3rd:1	Ran:3
	Pre1998 -	1st:0	2nd:0	3rd:0	Ran:1

Win Prizemoney £0 *Total Prizemoney* £769

1998 Turf 0-3: (10f 3) (gd 2, g-f)

Above-average colt. Turf high 71 (1st run) - 3rd of 11 giving 14lb to Dynamism (27 May Ripon 10f g-f RF 1535).

**J H M Gosden [0-4] Sheikh Ahmed Al Maktoum.*

AL-FATEH (IRE) BHB 85f **RR 79f** 49738

3 b c Caerleon (USA) 10.9f **(79)** - Filia Ardross (Ardross) 10.6f **(68)**

Form - 178

Record	**1998** -	1st:1	2nd:0	3rd:0	Ran:3
	Pre1998 -	1st:0	2nd:0	3rd:1	Ran:2

Win Prizemoney £3,631 *Total Prizemoney* £4,200

Wins	* **1998**	May	Newcas	(G-S)	10.1f	79	<

1998 Turf 1-3: (10f 1-1, 12f 2) (sft, gd 1-2)

Workmanlike, above-average colt. Turf high 79 (1st run) - 1st of 9 giving 5lb to Raqqasa (4 May Newcastle RF 1024).

**J L Dunlop [1-5] A Bahbahani.*

ALFRESCO RR 52+f 12733

3 b f Alzao (USA) 9.8f **(73)** - Shadywood (Habitat) 9.4f **(70)**

Form - 3

Record	**1998** -	1st:0	2nd:0	3rd:1	Ran:1

Win Prizemoney £0 *Total Prizemoney* £512

1998 Turf 0-1: (12f) (g-f)

Workmanlike, fair filly. (1st run) - 3rd of 6 to Rafting (16 May Thirsk 12f g-f RF 1273). (DEAD) **H R A Cecil [0-1] Cliveden Stud.*

ALHARIR (USA) BHB 90f **RR 88f** 34266

3 b br f Zafonic (USA) 9f **(83)** - Thawakib (IRE) (Sadler's Wells (USA)) 10f **(76)**

Form - 726

Record	**1998** -	1st:0	2nd:1	3rd:0	Ran:3
	Pre1998 -	1st:1	2nd:0	3rd:1	Ran:3

Win Prizemoney £3,671 *Total Prizemoney* £6,410

Wins * 1997 Aug Redcar (G-F) 7f 92+ <
1998 Turf 0-3: (8f, 10f 2) (hvy, g-f 2)
Scopey, useful filly, effective 7f, acts on frm. Turf high 88. A daughter of Ribblesdale winner Thawakib, she slammed the opposition by fifteen lengths in an ordinary Redcar maiden on her second start at two, but has not progressed from that since.
**J L Dunlop [1-6] Hamdan Al Maktoum.*

ALHASAD (USA) BHB 80f **RR 84df** 4820[7]
2 b c Sheikh Albadou 9.2f **(75)** - Valley Prospector (USA) (Northern Prospect (USA)) 9.5f **(71)**
Form - 2537
Record 1998 - 1st:0 2nd:1 3rd:1 Ran:4
Win Prizemoney £0 *Total Prizemoney* £1,404
1998 Turf 0-4: (5f, 6f 3) (gd, frm 3)
Decent colt. Turf high 84 (1st run) (began Aug) - 2nd of 21 giving 5lb to Ras Shaikh (5 Aug Leicester 6f frm RF 3377).
**A C Stewart [0-4] Hamdan Al Maktoum.*

ALHAWA (USA) BHB 64f **RR 64f** 5119[6]
5 ch g Mt Livermore (USA) 7.7f **(90)** - Petrava (NZ) (Imposing (AUS)) 7.7f **(74)**
Form - 0057500536
Record 1998 - 1st:0 2nd:0 3rd:1 Ran:10
Pre1998 - 1st:2 2nd:0 3rd:1 Ran:12
Win Prizemoney £7,667 *Total Prizemoney* £10,857
Wins 1996 May Lingfi (G-F) 7.6f 81 <
1995 Oct Lingfi (GD) 7f 78
1998 Turf 0-10: (7f, 8f 4, 9f, 10f 3, 12f) (g-s, gd 4, g-f 2, frm 2, hrd)
Average gelding, effective 8 to 9f, best at 8f, acts on gd to frm, best on gd, has worn blinkers. Turf high 75 - 5th of 20 giving 3lb to Mount Holly (7 Jly Newmarket 8f frm RF 2579). Consistent. Proving hard to win with, but has run some fair races, including when keeping on really well over a mile at Newmarket in July.
**Mrs J R Ramsden [0-10] DGH Partnership (from R Akehurst [0-4] Jly 1997).*

ALHESN (USA) BHB 50f **RR 60f** 4816[4]
3 b br c Woodman (USA) 9.7f **(77)** - Deceit Princess (CAN) (Vice Regent (CAN)) 8.7f **(74)**
Form - 032454
Record 1998 - 1st:0 2nd:1 3rd:1 Ran:6
Win Prizemoney £0 *Total Prizemoney* £1,940
1998 Turf 0-6: (10f, 12f 3, 14f, 16f) (gd, g-f 2, frm 3)
Average colt, effective 10 to 14f, acts on g-f to frm. Turf high 60 (began Jly) - 4th of 6 getting 6lb from Generous Ways (29 Aug Redcar 14f g-f RF 3969). **C N Allen [0-6] J T B Racing.*

ALHOSAAM BHB 69f **RR 78f** 4850[19]
4 b g Belmez (USA) 11.4f **(65)** - Leipzig (Relkino) 8.9f **(65)**
Form - 500
Record 1998 - 1st:0 2nd:0 3rd:0 Ran:3
Pre1998 - 1st:1 2nd:0 3rd:1 Ran:6
Win Prizemoney £3,777 *Total Prizemoney* £4,599
Wins 1997 Spt Kempto (GD) H 12f 73 78 <
1998 Turf 0-3: (12f, 13f, 18f) (gd 2, g-f)
Scopey, above-average gelding, effective 12 to 16f, best at 12f, acts on g-s to frm, prefers tight tracks. Turf high 67 (began Spt).
**G L Moore [0-7] Nick Clark (from Major W R Hern [1-6] Spt 1997).*

ALIABAD (IRE) BHB 72f **RR 71df** 4521[5]
3 b br c Doyoun 10.7f **(69)** - Alannya (FR) (Relko) 9.9f **(59)**
Form - 02285
Record 1998 - 1st:0 2nd:2 3rd:0 Ran:5
Win Prizemoney £0 *Total Prizemoney* £2,320
1998 Turf 0-5: (8f, 11f, 12f 2, 16f) (gd 2, g-f 2, frm)
Scopey, above-average colt, has worn blinkers. Turf high 71 - 2nd of 9 to Grimshaw (22 May Brighton 12f frm RF 1386).
**Sir Michael Stoute [0-5] H H Aga Khan.*

ALIGN RR 57f 5071[9]
2 gr f Petong 7.6f **(58)** - Affirmation (Tina's Pet) 6.8f **(59)**
Form - 0
Record 1998 - 1st:0 2nd:0 3rd:0 Ran:1
1998 Turf 0-1: (7f) (gd)
Currently fair filly. **J W Hills [0-1] Wyck Hall Stud.*

ALIGNMENT (IRE) BHB 104f **RR 103?f** 1166[4]
3 b f Alzao (USA) 9.8f **(73)** - Scots Lass (Shirley Heights) 10.3f **(74)**
Form - 4
Record 1998 - 1st:0 2nd:0 3rd:0 Ran:1
Pre1998 - 1st:0 2nd:2 3rd:0 Ran:3
Win Prizemoney £0 *Total Prizemoney* £11,375
1998 Turf 0-1: (10f) (gd)
Workmanlike, very useful filly. Runner-up on her Sandown debut in 1997, she failed by the narrowest margin in the Group Three Prestige Stakes next time. She finished last of four in the Musidora on her only appearance in 1998.
**Sir Michael Stoute [0-4] Lord Weinstock.*

ALIPS (FR) RR 96f 3915a[3]
4 ch f Beaudelaire (USA) - New Miss (FR) (New Chapter) 8f **(57)**
Form - 3
1998 Turf 0-1: (10f) (sft)
Currently very useful filly. (1st run) - 3rd of 7 to Saafeya (22 Aug Deauville 10f sft RF 3915a). ** P Bary in FR [1-2]*

ALISADARA BHB 24f **RR 28f** 2111[F]
4 b f Nomination 7.3f **(57)** - Nishara (Nishapour (FR)) 9.1f **(61)**
Form - 4F
Record 1998 - 1st:0 2nd:0 3rd:0 Ran:2
Pre1998 - 1st:0 2nd:0 3rd:0 Ran:19
Win Prizemoney £0 *Total Prizemoney* £460
1998 Turf 0-2: (8f 2) (g-s, gd)
Neat, little account filly, had worn blinkers. Turf high 24. (DEAD)
**N Bycroft [0-21] G J Allison.*

ALIWAIYN (IRE) RR 92f 3550a[5]
4 b c Shernazar 11.8f **(71)** - Aleema (Red God) 8.5f **(65)**
Form - 2321075
1998 Turf 1-7: (10f 1-3, 11f, 12f 3) (hvy 2, g-s 2, gd 1-2, g-f)
Useful colt, effective 10 to 12f, acts on g-s to gd, often wears blinkers. Turf high 92 - 1st of 10 from Lawz (21 Jun Clonmel RF 2222a). Made a promising start and was blinkered when winning at Clonmel. Has been clobbered by the handicapper since and does not seem to have his mind on the job.
**E Lynam in IRE [1-7] Brig Gen J Beary.*

ALJABR (USA) RR 112f 4470f[1]
2 gr c Storm Cat (USA) 7f **(86)** - Sierra Madre (FR) **(111+f)** (Baillamont (USA)) 7f **(78)**
Form - 111
Record 1998 - 1st:3 2nd:0 3rd:0 Ran:3
Win Prizemoney £69,828 *Total Prizemoney* £69,828
Wins * **1998** Spt Longch (SFT) G1 7f 112 <
* **1998** Jly Goodwo (GD) G3 7f 98+
* **1998** Jly Sandow (GD) 7.1f 90+
1998 Turf 3-3: (7f 3-3) (sft 1-1, gd 2-2)
Currently Group-class colt. Turf high 112 (began Jly) - 1st of 6 from Kingsalsa (19 Spt Longchamp RF 4470f). He looked a class act from day one and was never headed in three outings. He got into a lather before the Group Three Lanson Champagne Vintage Stakes at Glorious Goodwood, but that did not hinder his performance in the slightest, as he ran right away from Raise A Grand in the final quarter mile. Connections did not duck a challenge from Stravinsky in the Group One Prix de la Salamandre at Longchamp in September and, under a fine ride from Frankie Dettori, Aljabr made all at a sensible gallop, holding enough in reserve to quicken inside the last and win by a decisive half-length. Out of a mare who won the Prix Marcel Boussac and Prix Vermeille, he will stay a mile and a quarter and has a favourite's chance of winning the 2000 Guineas. He will winter in Dubai. **S bin Suroor [3-3] Godolphin.*

ALJAZ BHB 58f70a **RR 17f 70a** 2967[2]
8 b g Al Nasr (FR) 9.9f **(72)** - Santa Linda (USA) (Sir Ivor) 10.2f **(70)**
Form - 221123722024212
Record 1998 - 1st:3 2nd:7 3rd:1 Ran:14
Pre1998 - 1st:3 2nd:5 3rd:5 Ran:41
Win Prizemoney £17,475 *Total Prizemoney* £29,388
Wins * **1998** *Jun Wolver (STD) H 6f 62 67* <
1998 *Jan Wolver (STD) C 5f 52*
1998 *Jan Wolver (STD) H 5f 52 52*
1996 *Aug Wolver (STD) H 5f 42 43*
1995 Mar Hamilt (HVY) H 6f 60 62

1998 Turf 0-1: (5f) (frm) 1998 AW 3-13: (5f 2-10, 6f 1-3) (Equi, Fibr 3-12)

Average gelding, effective 5 to 6f, best at 6f, - acts on Fibr, has worn blinkers, prefers left handed tracks, prefers tight tracks, excels at Wolverhampton. AW high 68 - 2nd of 11 giving 10lb to Grand Chapeau (20 Jly Wolverhampton 6f Fibr RF 2967) - also 1st of 12 getting 2lb from Royal Cascade (26 Jun Wolverhampton RF 2323). Consistent. A fair sprinter on sand on his day, he has finished runner-up more often than is probably desirable, but he started off '98 in good form with two victories over the minimum at Wolverhampton, his optimum conditions. He was claimed after the second win, and has run with credit for Norma Macauley.

**Mrs N Macauley [1-10] G Wiltshire (from R J O'Sullivan [0-1] Jan 1998).*

ALJJAWARIH (USA) RR 98f — 4439a[8]

3 b c Nureyev (USA) 8.4f **(84)** - Alghuzaylah (Habitat) 9.4f **(70)**
Form - 120882638
1998 Turf 1-9: (5f 1-5, 6f 4) (sft 2, gd 4, g-f 1-2, hrd)

Very useful colt, effective 5 to 6f, best at 5f, acts on sft to g-f, has worn blinkers. Turf high 107 (1st run) - 1st of 7 giving 5lb to Festival Song (21 May Tipperary RF 1495a). The handicapper was hard on him after he won a maiden at Tipperary in May, but he came back to run some fair races in late summer. He is worth another try over six furlongs.

**D K Weld in IRE [1-14] Hamdan Al Maktoum.*

ALKATEB BHB 86f RR 87f — 5151[11]

6 ch g Rock City 8.8f **(62)** - Corley Moor (Habitat) 9.4f **(70)**
Form - 0333700820
Record 1998 - 1st:0 2nd:1 3rd:3 Ran:10
Pre1998 - 1st:2 2nd:1 3rd:2 Ran:7
Win Prizemoney £10,017 *Total Prizemoney* £22,126
Wins * 1995 Aug Sandow (G-F) H 8.1f 87 87 <
* 1995 Jun Goodwo (G-F) 9f 82
1998 Turf 0-10: (9f, 10f 8, 12f) (sft, g-s, gd 2, g-f 5, frm)

Useful gelding, effective 10f, acts on sft to frm, best on g-f, has worn blinkers, excels at Sandown. Turf high 90 (began Jly) - 3rd of 8 giving 25lb to Bold Faith (17 Jly Newmarket 10f frm RF 2881). Ran just once in '96 and missed the whole of the following season with leg problems. He ran quite well without receiving much reward in 1998, but his consistency prevents any leniency from the Handicapper. **Miss Gay Kelleway [2-17] Brian Eastick.*

ALLATON (IRE) BHB 51f42a RR 59f 42a — 4550[16]

3 ch g Shalford (IRE) 7.8f **(63)** - Confirmed Friend (Wolverlife) 9.3f **(54)**
Form - 8000
Record 1998 - 1st:0 2nd:0 3rd:0 Ran:4
Pre1998 - 1st:0 2nd:0 3rd:0 Ran:3
1998 Turf 0-2: (8f, 10f) (g-f, frm) 1998 AW 0-2: (6f, 8f) (Fibr 2)

Strong, fair gelding. Turf high 50. AW high 14.

**M E Sowersby [0-2] A Milner (from Mrs P Sly [0-6] Jun 1998).*

ALLEGIANCE RR 44f — 4002[6]

3 b g Rock Hopper 10.6f **(54)** - So Precise (FR) (Balidar) 7.9f **(63)**
Form - 86
Record 1998 - 1st:0 2nd:0 3rd:0 Ran:2
1998 Turf 0-2: (9f, 11f) (g-f, frm)

Unfurnished, moderate gelding, often wears blinkers. Turf high 44 (began Aug). **G M McCourt [0-2] Christopher Shankland.*

ALLEMANDE (IRE) BHB 50f RR 5f — 238[6]

6 b h Nashwan (USA) 10.3f **(79)** - Dance Festival (Nureyev (USA)) 8.7f **(78)**
Form - 6
Record 1998 - 1st:0 2nd:0 3rd:0 Ran:1
Pre1998 - 1st:2 2nd:0 3rd:0 Ran:3
Win Prizemoney £9,434 *Total Prizemoney* £9,434
Wins 1995 Jly Newbur (GD) 7.3f 103 <
1995 *Mar Wolver (STD) 8.5f 71*
1998 AW 0-1: (12f) (Fibr)

Poor horse.

**Ronald Thompson [0-2] Stephen Jones (from J H M Gosden [2-2] Jly 1995).*

ALL GIRLS FORGET BHB 23f RR 30f — 4254[14]

4 ch f Rock Hopper 10.6f **(54)** - Happydrome (Ahonoora) 8.1f **(73)**
Form - 65380
Record 1998 - 1st:0 2nd:0 3rd:1 Ran:5
Pre1998 - 1st:0 2nd:0 3rd:0 Ran:3
Win Prizemoney £0 *Total Prizemoney* £402
1998 Turf 0-5: (12f, 14f, 16f 3) (g-s, gd, frm 3)

Very moderate filly, effective 16f, acts on frm, likes left handed tracks. Turf high 30 (began Jly). Inconsistent.

**J D Bethell [0-8] Robert Gibbons.*

ALLGRIT (USA) RR 80f — 4480[5]

3 b c Shadeed (USA) 7.7f **(72)**-Arsaan (USA) (Nureyev (USA)) 8.7f **(78)**
Form - 33041275
Record 1998 - 1st:1 2nd:1 3rd:2 Ran:8
Pre1998 - 1st:0 2nd:0 3rd:0 Ran:3
Win Prizemoney £3,626 *Total Prizemoney* £8,158
Wins * **1998** Jly Redcar (G-F) H 10f 74 79 <
1998 Turf 1-8: (8f 3, 9f, 10f 1-2, 11f, 12f) (g-s, gd 2, frm 4, hrd 1-1)

Rangy, decent colt, effective 8 to 12f, acts on g-s to hrd, has worn blinkers, prefers tight tracks. Turf high 80 - 2nd of 5 getting 4lb from Sick As A Parrot (9 Aug Redcar 11f frm RF 3489) - also 1st of 9 giving 3lb to Godabi (25 Jly Redcar RF 3124). Consistent. Got off the mark when stepped up in trip, and nearly scored next time, despite hanging in behind the winner. Seems best suited by a positive ride. Sold for 47,000 gns at Tattersalls autumn sales.

**E A L Dunlop [1-11] Maktoum Al Maktoum.*

ALLIED ACADEMY BHB 41f49a RR 40f 49a — 1969[9]

4 ch g Royal Academy (USA) 7.8f **(77)** - Tsungani (Cure The Blues (USA)) 9.5f **(63)**
Form - 070
Record 1998 - 1st:0 2nd:0 3rd:0 Ran:3
Pre1998 - 1st:0 2nd:0 3rd:0 Ran:6
1998 Turf 0-3: (8f, 10f, 12f) (g-s, gd, g-f)

Scopey, fair gelding, has worn blinkers. Turf high 40. Inconsistent.

**S C Williams [0-9] I A Southcott.*

ALLIED FORCES (USA) BHB 120f RR 120f — 4076a[4]

5 ch h Miswaki (USA) 8.1f **(81)** - Mangala (USA) (Sharpen Up) 8.3f **(67)**
Form - 454
Record 1998 - 1st:0 2nd:0 3rd:0 Ran:3
Pre1998 - 1st:3 2nd:1 3rd:1 Ran:9
Win Prizemoney £80,788 *Total Prizemoney* £204,309
Wins * 1997 Jun Ascot (GD) G2 8f 120 <
1995 Jly Newmar (G-F) L 7f 96+
1995 May York (GD) 6f 96+
1998 Turf 0-3: (7f, 8f 2) (hvy, gd, frm)

Very high-class colt, effective 7 to 10f, best at 8f, acts on gd to frm, best on g-f. Turf high 116 (1st run) - 4th of 16 to Taiki Shuttle (16 May Fuchu 7f frm RF 1378a). He has been globetrotting since the middle of 1997, and twice finished behind Taiki Shuttle in the middle of last season. That horse's subsequent exploits show just what he was up against. Retired to stud in Kentucky.

**S bin Suroor [1-7] Godolphin (from S bin Suroor in UAE [0-1] Jun 1998).*

ALLINSON'S MATE (IRE) BHB 45f43a RR 47f 43a — 4919[10]

10 b g Fayruz 6.6f **(63)** - Piney Pass (Persian Bold) 9.3f **(66)**
Form - 30577620620071070
Record 1998 - 1st:1 2nd:2 3rd:1 Ran:17
Pre1998 - 1st:17 2nd:12 3rd:10 Ran:119
Win Prizemoney £63,044 *Total Prizemoney* £93,640
Wins * **1998** Jly Doncas (G-F) H 7f 44 47
* 1997 May Doncas (GD) H 7f 58 64
* 1997 May Carlis (G-S) C 6.9f 59
* 1996 Oct Catter (GD) H 7f 56 61
* 1996 Jly Mussel (GD) H 7.1f 55 57
* 1995 Jly York (G-F) H 7f 71 73
* 1995 Jun Doncas (GD) H 7f 68 71
* 1995 Apr Carlis (GD) C 6.9f 69
* 1994 Jly Ayr (G-F) H 7f 67 67
* 1994 Apr Newcas (GD) H 7f 69 63
* 1994 *Mar Southw (STD) H 7f 70 74*
1998 Turf 1-11: (7f 1-8, 8f 3) (g-s 2, gd 5, g-f 1-3, frm) 1998 AW 0-6: (7f 4, 8f 2) (Equi, Fibr 5)

Fair gelding, effective 7f, acts on gd to frm, best on frm, has worn blinkers (effectively), likes right handed tracks, excels at Carlisle and Doncaster. Turf high 55. AW high 53. Still capable of winning his share of modest handicaps, he goes especially well for girl

apprentices. Difficult to predict these days, he will come up trumps when he wants to.
**T D Barron [18-136] Harrowgate Bloodstock Ltd.*

ALL MADE UP (USA) BHB 80f **RR 70f** 1393[3]

3 b c Sheikh Albadou 9.2f **(75)** - Mascara Miss (USA) (Fio Rito (USA)) 12.4f **(70)**
Form - 2133
Record 1998 - 1st:1 2nd:1 3rd:2 Ran:4
Pre1998 - 1st:0 2nd:0 3rd:0 Ran:2
Win Prizemoney £3,420 *Total Prizemoney* £5,808
Wins * 1998 Apr Newcas (SFT) 12.4f 70 <
1998 Turf 1-4: (11f, 12f 1-2, 14f) (sft 1-2, g-s, gd)
Scopey, above-average colt, effective 11 to 12f, acts on sft. Turf high 70 (1st run) - 2nd of 7 to Touchez du Bois (4 Apr Hamilton 11f sft RF 0561) - also 1st of 5 getting 21lb from Mr Lurpak (13 Apr Newcastle RF 0664). He only just failed to get up in a heavy-ground Hamilton maiden on his reappearance, and landed a soft-ground Newcastle maiden next time. Readily held at Ripon in similar conditions under a penalty. **M Bell [1-6] Nasser Abdullah.*

ALLMAITES BHB 65f63a **RR 71f 63a** 4837[15]

3 b g Komaite (USA) 6.9f **(61)** - Darling Miss Daisy (Tina's Pet) 6.8f **(59)**
Form - 3536202040
Record 1998 - 1st:0 2nd:2 3rd:2 Ran:10
Pre1998 - 1st:0 2nd:0 3rd:1 Ran:5
Win Prizemoney £0 *Total Prizemoney* £4,468
1998 Turf 0-8: (5f 7, 6f) (g-s, gd 2, g-f 3, frm, hrd) 1998 AW 0-2: (5f, 6f) (Fibr 2)
Scopey, above-average gelding, effective 5f, acts on g-f - acts on Fibr, has worn blinkers. Turf high 73 - 2nd of 10 to Dil (23 May Doncaster 5f g-f RF 1415). AW high 64 (1st run) - 3rd of 7 giving 17lb to Dahlidya (18 Feb Wolverhampton 5f Fibr RF 0310). Becoming disappointing. He has run some creditable races, but is finding it hard to get his head in front where it matters.
**S R Bowring [0-1] R J H Ltd (from D Nicholls [0-14] Jly 1998).*

ALL ON BHB 56f62a **RR 58f 62a** 1065[2]

7 ch m Dunbeath (USA) 9.9f **(53)** - Fresh Line (High Line) 10.3f **(70)**
Form - 32322
Record 1998 - 1st:0 2nd:3 3rd:2 Ran:5
Pre1998 - 1st:5 2nd:3 3rd:6 Ran:28
Win Prizemoney £14,423 *Total Prizemoney* £24,377
Wins * 1997 May Carlis (G-S) H 14.1f 39 55
* 1997 May Mussel (G-F) H 12f 39 47
* 1997 Apr Pontef (GD) H 21.6f 39 51
* 1996 *Oct Wolver (STD) H 12f 43 55++*
* 1995 *Jan Southw (STD) 12f 57+* <
1998 Turf 0-2: (16f, 22f) (g-s, gd) 1998 AW 0-3: (12f, 16f 2) (Fibr 3)
Average mare, effective 12 to 22f, best at 16f, acts on g-s to frm - acts on Fibr, likes Pontefract and Musselburgh. Turf high 58 - 2nd of 13 giving 19lb to Dally Boy (6 May Musselburgh 16f gd RF 1065). AW high 64 - 2nd of 9 getting 10lb from Noufari (2 Feb Southwell 16f Fibr RF 0200). Running well at Southwell early in 1998.
**J Hetherton [8-49] N Hetherton.*

ALLONES GIGANTES **RR 93?f** 4722a[8]

3 b c Perpendicular - Gitee (FR) (Carwhite) 7.2f **(61)**
Form - 88
Record 1998 - 1st:0 2nd:0 3rd:0 Ran:2
1998 Turf 0-2: (9f, 10f) (hvy, g-f)
Scopey, currently useful colt. Turf high 93 (began Jly). A winner in Italy, showed little in two runs in 1998. **H Akbary [0-2].*

ALL OUR BLESSINGS (IRE) BHB 35f31a **RR 28f 31a** 4927[12]

3 b f Statoblest 6.4f **(63)** - Zenga (Try My Best (USA)) 7.6f **(67)**
Form - 0700
Record 1998 - 1st:0 2nd:0 3rd:0 Ran:4
Pre1998 - 1st:0 2nd:0 3rd:0 Ran:3
1998 Turf 0-2: (7f, 10f) (g-s, g-f) 1998 AW 0-2: (7f 2) (Equi, Fibr)
Lengthy, little account filly, has worn blinkers. Turf high 28 (began Oct).
**Mrs A Swinbank [0-2] Middleham Park Racing And Breeding (from P C Haslam [0-5] Jan 1998).*

ALL OUR HOPE (USA) **RR 77+f** 2882[3]

2 b f Gulch (USA) 9.6f **(79)**-Knoosh (USA)(Storm Bird (CAN)) 10.3f **(74)**
Form - 3
Record 1998 - 1st:0 2nd:0 3rd:1 Ran:1
Win Prizemoney £0 *Total Prizemoney* £642
1998 Turf 0-1: (7f) (frm)
Currently above-average filly. (1st run) - 3rd of 7 to Kareymah (17 Jly Newmarket 7f frm RF 2882). Out of a very useful winner at up to a mile and a half, she finished nicely into third on her debut and should win races. **Sir Michael Stoute [0-1] Maktoum Al Maktoum.*

ALLRIGHTHEN BHB 57f **RR 59f** 4479[6]

2 b g Sizzling Melody 6.3f **(49)** - Luckifosome (Smackover) 6f **(52)**
Form - 070086
Record 1998 - 1st:0 2nd:0 3rd:0 Ran:6
1998 Turf 0-6: (5f, 6f 4, 7f) (gd, g-f 2, frm 3)
Fair gelding. Turf high 59 (began Jly). **T Wall [0-6] L R Perry.*

ALLSTARS DANCER BHB 37f35a **RR 38f 35a** 3749[1]

5 b m Primo Dominie 7.2f **(67)** - Danzig Harbour (USA) (Private Account (USA)) 8.5f **(74)**
Form - 6325358051
Record 1998 - 1st:1 2nd:1 3rd:2 Ran:9
Pre1998 - 1st:0 2nd:2 3rd:0 Ran:16
Win Prizemoney £2,999 *Total Prizemoney* £6,180
Wins * 1998 Aug Mussel (G-F) H 5f 24 38 <
1998 Turf 1-3: (5f 1-1, 6f, 7f) (sft, gd 1-1, frm) 1998 AW 0-6: (6f 4, 7f 2) (Equi 5, Fibr)
Very moderate filly, effective 5 to 7f, best at 5f, acts on gd - acts on Equi, has worn blinkers (extremely effectively). Turf high 38 - 1st of 16 getting 26lb from Miss Hit (19 Aug Musselburgh RF 3749). AW high 39. Despite often making the frame, it took her a very long time getting off the mark, and when she did, it was against a field of similarly disappointing types in a Musselburgh maiden handicap. **T J Naughton [1-25] T J Naughton.*

ALL THE WAY (IRE) **RR 79f** 3959[3]

2 b c Shirley Heights 12.1f **(76)** - Future Past (USA) (Super Concorde (USA)) 10.9f **(66)**
Form - 3
Record 1998 - 1st:0 2nd:0 3rd:1 Ran:1
Win Prizemoney £0 *Total Prizemoney* £564
1998 Turf 0-1: (8f) (g-f)
Currently above-average colt. (1st run) - 3rd of 8 to Pulau Tioman (29 Aug Nottingham 8f g-f RF 3959).
**T G Mills [0-1] John Humphreys (Turf Accountants) Ltd.*

ALLY (FR) BHB 86f **RR 85f** 5078[16]

3 b g Zilzal (USA) 8.5f **(79)** -Holy Tobin (USA)(J O Tobin(USA))9.4f **(67)**
Form - 5210
Record 1998 - 1st:1 2nd:1 3rd:0 Ran:4
Win Prizemoney £3,882 *Total Prizemoney* £4,802
Wins * 1998 Oct Yarmou (G-S) 7f 73+ <
1998 Turf 1-4: (7f 1-2, 8f 2) (sft, gd 1-3)
Tall, useful gelding. Turf high 85 - 2nd of 11 giving 5lb to Zante (23 May Kempton 8f gd RF 1423). Promising efforts in maidens early in the season, and overcame a five-month layoff to win a modest event at Yarmouth without too much bother. Never in the hunt in a huge field at Newmarket.
**Sir Michael Stoute [1-4] H R H Prince Fahd Salman.*

ALMA ALEGRE (IRE) **RR 96f** 4600a[10]

3 b f Lahib (USA) 8f **(69)** -Nimble Nova(USA)(Northern Dancer)9.6f **(80)**
Form - 30
1998 Turf 0-2: (10f, 11f) (hvy 2)
Currently very useful filly. Turf high 96 (1st run) - 3rd of 9 to Zomaradah (24 May San Siro 11f hvy RF 1558a).
**G Botti in ITY [0-2].*

AL MABROOK (IRE) BHB 69f **RR 76df** 4822[21]

3 b c Rainbows For Life (CAN) 9.3f **(64)** - Sky Lover (Ela-Mana-Mou) 10.1f **(70)**
Form - 763000
Record 1998 - 1st:0 2nd:0 3rd:1 Ran:6
Pre1998 - 1st:0 2nd:1 3rd:0 Ran:4
Win Prizemoney £0 *Total Prizemoney* £1,502
1998 Turf 0-6: (6f, 7f 2, 8f 2, 10f) (gd 5, frm)
Unfurnished, above-average colt, effective 5 to 6f, acts on gd to frm. Turf high 76. Becoming disappointing. He showed bits and

pieces of form in maiden company, and was set some stiff tasks in handicaps, but he did not get off the mark until winning on the Lingfield Equitrack in November. **K Mahdi [0-10] Hamad Al-Mutawa.*

AL MAJD BARHAN (IRE) RR 53f
3598[9]

3 b c Fairy King (USA) 7.7f **(75)**-North Kildare(USA)(Northjet) 10.3f **(74)**
Form - 0
Record 1998 - 1st:0 2nd:0 3rd:0 Ran:1
1998 Turf 0-1: (10f) (frm)
Scopey, currently fair colt. **E A L Dunlop [0-1] Jaber Abdullah.*

ALMANDAB (IRE) BHB 103f RR 116?f
2818[4]

3 b br c Last Tycoon 9.4f **(73)** - Fortune Teller (Troy) 10.4f **(68)**
Form - 54574
Record 1998 - 1st:0 2nd:0 3rd:0 Ran:5
Pre1998 - 1st:1 2nd:0 3rd:0 Ran:2
Win Prizemoney £3,460 *Total Prizemoney* £5,042
Wins * 1997 Oct Nottin (GD) 8.2f 96+ <
1998 Turf 0-5: (8f 2, 9f, 10f 2) (gd 4, frm)
High-class colt, effective 9f, acts on gd. Turf high 116 - 5th of 6 to Almutawakel (31 May Chantilly 9f gd RF 1736a). An able but somewhat disappointing type, he ran his best race of 1998 when a close fifth in a Group One at Longchamp, but was not seen after July.
**J H M Gosden [1-7] Sheikh Ahmed Al Maktoum.*

ALMASI (IRE) BHB 80f RR 79f
4365[18]

6 b m Petorius 8f **(66)** - Best Niece (Vaigly Great) 7f **(58)**
Form - 5508740
Record 1998 - 1st:0 2nd:0 3rd:0 Ran:7
Pre1998 - 1st:7 2nd:6 3rd:6 Ran:39
Win Prizemoney £25,417 *Total Prizemoney* £40,256
Wins * 1997 Spt Haydoc (G-S) 6f 88 <
* 1997 Aug Newbur (G-F) H 6f 77 82
* 1997 Jun Salisb (SFT) H 6f 68 72
* 1997 Jun Doncas (GD) H 6f 62 67
* 1996 Jun Doncas (GD) H 6f 62 64
* 1996 Apr Nottin (G-F) H 6.1f 54 56
* 1994 Aug Windso (GD) 6f 57
1998 Turf 0-7: (6f 7) (sft, gd 2, g-f 3, frm)
Above-average mare, effective 6f, acts on gd to frm, best on gd. Turf high 79. She showed progressive form in '97, winning four times and being placed on several other occasions, including when second in the Ayr Silver Cup. Failed to fire in 1998.
**C F Wall [7-46] The Equema Partnership.*

ALMATY (IRE) BHB 109f RR 110f
4821[1]

5 b h Dancing Dissident (USA) 6.8f **(65)** - Almaaseh (IRE) (Dancing Brave (USA)) 8.4f **(76)**
Form - 230027121
Record 1998 - 1st:2 2nd:3 3rd:1 Ran:9
Pre1998 - 1st:3 2nd:1 3rd:2 Ran:14
Win Prizemoney £60,802 *Total Prizemoney* £89,198
Wins * **1998** Oct Newmar (GD) H 5f 105 107
* **1998** Spt Beverl (G-F) 5f 97
1997 May Kempto (G-F) L 5f 108+
1995 Jly Goodwo (GD) G3 5f 111 <
1995 Jly Currag (SFT) G3 5f 100
1998 Turf 2-9: (5f 2-9) (gd 3, g-f 1-2, frm 1-4)
Group-class colt, effective 5f, acts on gd to frm, best on frm, has worn blinkers, excels at Beverley, does well at Newmarket. Turf high 113 (1st run) - 2nd of 6 giving 12lb to Bolshoi (9 May Beverley 5f frm RF 1118) - also 1st of 18 giving 14lb to Afaan (15 Oct Newmarket RF 4821). Another horse who thrived under the tutelage of William Muir, he ran much more consistently last season, winning twice over five furlongs at the back-end. At his very best on fast ground, he can win a Group race on the continent.
**W R Muir [2-10] Mrs H Levy (from J H M Gosden [1-7] Spt 1997).*

ALMAYMONA (IRE) BHB 57f RR 59f
4400[15]

2 ch f Pips Pride 6.7f **(70)** - Suppression (Kind of Hush) 10.1f **(62)**
Form - 506640
Record 1998 - 1st:0 2nd:0 3rd:0 Ran:6
1998 Turf 0-6: (5f, 6f 3, 7f 2) (gd, g-f, frm 4)
Fair filly, effective 6 to 7f, acts on gd to frm. Turf high 59.
**S Mellor [0-6] Shaikh Al Fairuz.*

ALMAZHAR (IRE) BHB 65f RR 57f
2456[8]

3 b c Last Tycoon 9.4f **(73)** -Mosaique Bleue(Shirley Heights) 10.3f **(74)**
Form - 488
Record 1998 - 1st:0 2nd:0 3rd:0 Ran:3
Pre1998 - 1st:0 2nd:0 3rd:0 Ran:1
Win Prizemoney £0 *Total Prizemoney* £234
1998 Turf 0-3: (7f, 8f 2) (gd 2, frm)
Scopey, fair colt, has worn blinkers. Turf high 57.
**E A L Dunlop [0-4] Hamdan Al Maktoum.*

ALMAZIONA BHB 53f RR 50f
2840[11]

2 ch f Formidable (USA) 7.8f **(60)**-Flying Amy (Norwick (USA)) 7.2f **(56)**
Form - 000
Record 1998 - 1st:0 2nd:0 3rd:0 Ran:3
1998 Turf 0-2: (5f, 6f) (gd, g-f) 1998 AW 0-1: (5f) (Fibr)
Currently fair filly. Turf high 50. **S Mellor [0-3] Shaikh Al Fairuz.*

ALMINSTAR RR 38f
4758[16]

2 b f Minshaanshu Amad (USA) 11.3f **(53)** - Joytime (John de Coombe) 7.9f **(40)**
Form - 0
Record 1998 - 1st:0 2nd:0 3rd:0 Ran:1
1998 Turf 0-1: (7f) (gd)
Currently very moderate filly. **C A Cyzer [0-1] Mrs G M Gooderham.*

ALMOHAD BHB 54f52a RR 53f 52a
4996[13]

3 ch c Belmez (USA) 11.4f **(65)** - Anna Paola (GER) (Prince Ippi (GER)) 10.4f **(68)**
Form - 5500
Record 1998 - 1st:0 2nd:0 3rd:0 Ran:4
Win Prizemoney £0 *Total Prizemoney* £344
1998 Turf 0-3: (8f 2, 9f) (g-s, g-f 2) 1998 AW 0-1: (10f) (Equi)
Workmanlike, fair colt, has worn blinkers. Turf high 53 (began Spt). **Dr J D Scargill [0-4] Mrs Janet Mudd.*

ALMOND ROCK BHB 99f RR 99f
4631[14]

6 b g Soviet Star (USA) 8.6f **(74)** - Banket (Glint of Gold) 9.3f **(66)**
Form - 263504210150
Record 1998 - 1st:2 2nd:2 3rd:1 Ran:12
Pre1998 - 1st:3 2nd:3 3rd:3 Ran:19
Win Prizemoney £38,610 *Total Prizemoney* £63,920
Wins * **1998** Aug Ripon (G-F) H 8f 94 99 <
* **1998** Jly Windso (GD) H 10f 93 97
* 1996 Aug Ripon (G-S) H 8f 94 99 <
* 1995 Spt Newbur (G-S) H 8f 79 88
* 1995 Jly Salisb (GD) H 8f 67 76
1998 Turf 2-12: (8f 1-4, 9f, 10f 1-7) (hvy, sft, gd 1-4, g-f 1-6)
Very useful gelding, effective 8 to 10f, best at 8f, acts on hvy to g-f, best on gd, likes left handed tracks, likes tight tracks, excels at Chester. Turf high 99 - 1st of 10 giving 27lb to Bollin Frank (31 Aug Ripon RF 3997) - also 1st of 6 giving 4lb to Kewarra (13 Jly Windsor RF 2767). Failed to make much impact in '97, but appreciates soft ground and ran well in some tough handicaps during the spring of 1998. Finally got his reward at Windsor, and added a valuable affair at Ripon in fluent style. Excellent effort at Ascot, after meeting trouble in running. He should be able to land a decent handicap next term. Was not disgraced in the Cambridgeshire and was sold for 31,000 guineas in October.
**J R Fanshawe [5-35] C I T Racing Ltd.*

ALMOST AMBER (USA) BHB 88f RR 86f
4269[10]

2 ch f Mt Livermore (USA) 7.7f **(90)** - Kelly Amber (USA) (Highland Park (USA))
Form - 5120
Record 1998 - 1st:1 2nd:1 3rd:0 Ran:4
Win Prizemoney £3,538 *Total Prizemoney* £5,204
Wins * **1998** Jun Salisb (G-F) 5f 76+ <
1998 Turf 1-4: (5f 1-4) (gd 2, g-f, frm 1-1)
Useful filly. Turf high 86 - 2nd of 6 to Angie Baby (26 Aug Lingfield 5f g-f RF 3893). **J H M Gosden [1-4] Sheikh Mohammed.*

ALMOST GOT IT RR 44f
1371[6]

3 ch f St Ninian - Star Leader (Kafu) 6f **(47)**
Form - 26
Record 1998 - 1st:0 2nd:1 3rd:0 Ran:2
Win Prizemoney £0 *Total Prizemoney* £675
1998 Turf 0-2: (10f 2) (g-f, frm)

Unfurnished, currently moderate filly. Turf high 44 (1st run) - 2nd of 14 getting 5lb from Opportune (9 May Beverley 10f frm RF 1115).
**J Parkes [0-2] C W Moore.*

AL MUALLIM (USA) BHB 98f **RR 99f** 4675[2]

4 b c Theatrical 11.5f **(78)** - Gerri N Jo Go (USA) (Top Command (USA)) 10f **(77)**
Form - 7232

Record	**1998** -	1st:0	2nd:2	3rd:1	Ran:4
	Pre1998 -	1st:3	2nd:1	3rd:1	Ran:7

Win Prizemoney £15,261 *Total Prizemoney* £31,583

Wins	Year	Month	Course	Going		Dist			
	* 1997	Oct	Newmar	(G-F)	H	7f	88	94	<
	* 1997	Aug	Lingfi	(G-F)	H	6f	80	87	
	* 1996	Oct	Catter	(GD)		6f		78	

1998 Turf 0-4: (7f 4) (g-s, gd, g-f 2)
Workmanlike, very useful colt, effective 7f, acts on g-s to frm. Turf high 99 (began Aug) - 2nd of 9 getting 5lb from Warningford (12 Spt Goodwood 7f g-s RF 4244). Consistent. Absent until August for each of the last two seasons, he has plenty of ability but is obviously difficult to train. Caught the eye on his '98 bow, and finished runner-up at Goodwood next time. Has continued to run well in useful company without getting his reward.
**J W Payne [3-11] Al Muallim Partnership.*

ALMUHIMM (USA) BHB 86f **RR 87+f** 4854[18]

6 b g Diesis 9f **(80)** - Abeesh (USA) (Nijinsky (CAN)) 10.3f **(77)**
Form - 0520611860

Record	**1998** -	1st:2	2nd:1	3rd:0	Ran:10
	Pre1998 -	1st:3	2nd:1	3rd:2	Ran:19

Win Prizemoney £39,367 *Total Prizemoney* £45,774

Wins	Year	Month	Course	Going		Dist			
	* **1998**	Aug	Beverl	(G-F)		7.5f		85+	
	* **1998**	Aug	Newbur	(GD)	H	7.3f	81	87+	<
	1997	Jly	Ayr	(G-F)	H	7f	81	85	
	* 1996	Jun	Newcas	(FRM)	H	7f	82	87	
	* 1996	Jun	Newmar	(G-F)	H	7f	79	84	

1998 Turf 2-10: (7f 2-9, 8f) (gd 5, g-f 2-3, frm 2)
Useful gelding, effective 7f, acts on gd to frm, best on g-f, likes tight tracks, excels at Ayr and Ascot. Turf high 87 - 1st of 9 giving 5lb to Blakeset (15 Aug Newbury RF 3650) - also 1st of 4 from Cybertechnology (24 Aug Beverley RF 3835). Mixed form last year, making a winning debut for Ed Dunlop in a Newbury rated stakes in August. Followed up in a weak race at Beverley. He is very much a seven-furlong specialist who needs everything to go his way, but is useful on his day. Sold for 38,000 gns in the autumn to race in America.
**E A L Dunlop [4-18] Burke's 5th Family Settlement (from M W Easterby [0-6] Jly 1998).*

ALMUROOJ BHB 57f **RR 59f** 4304[5]

3 b f Zafonic (USA) 9f **(83)** - Al Bahathri (USA) (Blushing Groom (FR)) 10.3f **(76)**
Form - 445

Record	**1998** -	1st:0	2nd:0	3rd:0	Ran:3
	Pre1998 -	1st:0	2nd:0	3rd:0	Ran:1

Win Prizemoney £0 *Total Prizemoney* £466

1998 Turf 0-3: (5f 2, 6f) (gd, g-f, hrd)
Neat, fair filly. Turf high 59 (began Aug). Bred in the purple, but has shown only a little so far. **B W Hills [0-4] Hamdan Al Maktoum.*

ALMUSHTARAK (IRE) BHB 118f **RR 121f** 4852[8]

5 b h Fairy King (USA) 7.7f **(75)** - Exciting (Mill Reef (USA)) 10.5f **(78)**
Form - 21534282668

Record	**1998** -	1st:1	2nd:3	3rd:1	Ran:11
	Pre1998 -	1st:4	2nd:2	3rd:2	Ran:19

Win Prizemoney £78,369 *Total Prizemoney* £166,875

Wins	Year	Month	Course	Going		Dist			
	* **1998**	Apr	Sandow	(SFT)	G2	8.1f		116	<
	* 1997	Spt	Doncas	(G-F)	G3	8f		114	
	1996	Jly	Lingfi	(G-F)	LH	7.6f	105	107	
	1996	Jun	Kempto	(G-F)	H	7f	85	90	
	1995	Spt	Bright	(GD)		6f		86?	

1998 Turf 1-11: (8f 1-7, 9f 2, 10f 2) (sft 1-3, gd 4, g-f 3, frm)
Very high-class colt, effective 8 to 10f, best at 8f, acts on sft to frm, prefers right handed tracks, likes tight tracks, excels at Goodwood. Turf high 121 - 2nd of 9 giving 9lb to Muhtathir (29 Aug Goodwood 8f g-f RF 3948) - also 1st of 9 getting 4lb from Crystal Hearted (24 Apr Sandown RF 0848). Consistent. A tough and useful performer who has helped put his Kuwaiti trainer Kamil Mahdi on the map, he was a fluent winner of the Group Two Sandown Mile on ground softer than he would normally like and has continued to give a good account on most starts, especially when runner-up in the Sussex Stakes and the Celebration Mile. He does seem to find true Group One company too much for him however, as his most recent runs testify.
**K Mahdi [2-21] Hamad Al-Mutawa (from Miss Gay Kelleway [3-9] Jly 1996).*

ALMUTAWAKEL BHB 117f **RR 120f** 4718a[8]

3 b c Machiavellian (USA) 9.8f **(83)** - Elfaslah (IRE) (Green Desert (USA)) 8.6f **(78)**
Form - 7128

Record	**1998** -	1st:1	2nd:1	3rd:0	Ran:4
	Pre1998 -	1st:2	2nd:1	3rd:0	Ran:4

Win Prizemoney £50,414 *Total Prizemoney* £102,854

Wins	Year	Month	Course	Going		Dist			
	* **1998**	May	Chanti	(GD)	G1	9f		117	<
	* 1997	Aug	Newmar	(GD)		7f		101+	
	* 1997	Jly	Sandow	(G-S)		7.1f		85+	

1998 Turf 1-4: (8f, 9f 1-1, 10f 2) (sft, gd 1-3)
Scopey, very high-class colt, effective 9 to 10f, acts on gd. Turf high 120 - 2nd of 7 to Limpid (21 Jun Longchamp 10f gd RF 2290a) - also 1st of 6 from Gold Away (31 May Chantilly RF 1736a). A useful juvenile, he was seventh in the 2000 Guineas on his reappearance. Earned Group One honours in the Prix Jean Prat at Longchamp, and went down by only a neck to Limpid in the Grand Prix de Paris. He was not seen after that until finishing unplaced in the Prix Dollar at the Arc meeting, where the ground was probably against him. **S bin Suroor [3-8] Godolphin.*

AL NABA (USA) **RR 88+f** 4846[1]

2 ch c Mr Prospector (USA) 8.6f **(88)** - Forest Flower (USA) (Green Forest (USA)) 9.9f **(68)**
Form - 21

Record	**1998** -	1st:1	2nd:1	3rd:0	Ran:2

Win Prizemoney £6,072 *Total Prizemoney* £7,276

Wins	Year	Month	Course	Going	Dist		
	* **1998**	Oct	Newmar	(GD)	6f	88+	<

1998 Turf 1-2: (6f 1-2) (g-f 1-2)
Currently useful colt. Turf high 88 (began Spt) - 1st of 19 from Sea Mark (16 Oct Newmarket RF 4846). A $300,000 son of an Irish 1000 Guineas winner, he beat a big field on his second start despite hanging right. A useful prospect at around a mile.
**E A L Dunlop [1-2] Hamdan Al Maktoum.*

ALNAJASHEE **RR 57f** 4806[6]

2 b c Generous (IRE) 11.5f **(82)** - Tahdid (Mtoto)
Form - 86

Record	**1998** -	1st:0	2nd:0	3rd:0	Ran:2

1998 Turf 0-2: (8f 2) (gd 2)
Currently fair colt. Turf high 57 (began Spt).
**P T Walwyn [0-2] Hamdan Al Maktoum.*

AL NAKHLAH (USA) **RR 22f** 5072[14]

2 b f Sheikh Albadou 9.2f **(75)** - Magic Slipper (Habitat) 9.4f **(70)**
Form - 0

Record	**1998** -	1st:0	2nd:0	3rd:0	Ran:1

1998 Turf 0-1: (7f) (gd)
Currently little account filly. **P T Walwyn [0-1] Hamdan Al Maktoum.*

ALOHA DANCER (IRE) BHB 83f **RR 88f** 4621[5]

3 b f Danehill (USA) 9.1f **(79)** - Spire (Shirley Heights) 10.3f **(74)**
Form - 2215705

Record	**1998** -	1st:1	2nd:2	3rd:0	Ran:7

Win Prizemoney £3,817 *Total Prizemoney* £7,437

Wins	Year	Month	Course	Going	Dist		
	* **1998**	May	Warwic	(G-F)	7f	78	<

1998 Turf 1-7: (7f 1-5, 8f 2) (sft, gd 4, g-f, frm 1-1)
Scopey, useful filly, effective 7f, acts on gd to g-f. Turf high 89 - 2nd of 8 to Enchant (6 May Chester 7f g-f RF 1061). She showed ability when finishing runner-up in her first two starts, and got off the mark with a victory at Warwick, though she had to work much harder than was probably expected. Not disgraced in a listed race over seven, she looks to need a mile at least.
**B W Hills [1-7] J R Fleming.*

ALONSA (IRE) **RR 56f** 4579[9]

2 b f Trempolino (USA) 11.9f **(77)** - Alimana (Akarad (FR)) 9f **(76)**
Form - 80

Record	**1998** -	1st:0	2nd:0	3rd:0	Ran:2

1998 Turf 0-2: (6f 2) (gd, g-f)
Currently fair filly. Turf high 56 (began Spt).
**C E Brittain [0-2] Saeed Manana.*

ALONZO (IRE) RR 99f 1507a[9]
3 b c Alzao (USA) 9.8f**(73)**-Rosa Mundi (USA)(Secretariat (USA))9f **(79)**
Form - 130
1998 Turf 1-3: (7f 1-3) (gd 2, hrd 1-1)
Very useful colt. Turf high 99 (1st run) - 1st of 9 from Amazink (3 May Gowran Park RF 1053a). Has produced some good runs behind useful rivals such as Sunshine Street and Shahtoush. Not quite in that class though. **C O'Brien in IRE [1-5] Mrs M V O'Brien.*

ALOYSIA (USA) RR 30f 4389[13]
2 ch f Diesis 9f **(80)** - Alyanaabi (USA) (Roberto (USA)) 10f **(76)**
Form - 0
Record 1998 - 1st:0 2nd:0 3rd:0 Ran:1
1998 Turf 0-1: (7f) (frm)
Currently very moderate filly.
**J H M Gosden [0-1] Sheikh Mohammed.*

ALPEN WOLF (IRE) BHB 72f **RR 68f** 4854[25]
3 ch g Wolfhound (USA) 7.3f **(71)** - Oatfield (Great Nephew) 9.9f **(64)**
Form - 843504811110
Record 1998 - 1st:4 2nd:0 3rd:1 Ran:12
Pre1998 - 1st:0 2nd:0 3rd:1 Ran:8
Win Prizemoney £9,058 *Total Prizemoney* £10,231
Wins * **1998** Spt Bright (FRM) 7f 68 <
* **1998** Aug Folkes (G-F) 6f 68 <
* **1998** Aug Bright (G-F) H 6f 56 64
* **1998** Aug Bright (FRM) S 6f 41
1998 Turf 4-12: (5f 3, 6f 3-7, 7f 1-2) (gd 3, g-f 1-3, frm 3-6)
Average gelding, effective 6 to 7f, best at 6f, acts on g-f to frm, best on frm, has worn blinkers, prefers left handed tracks. Turf high 68 - 1st of 12 giving 9lb to Krisamba (2 Spt Brighton RF 4048) - also 1st of 12 giving 3lb to Henry The Proud (27 Aug Folkestone RF 3901). Inconsistent. It took him sixteen attempts to get off the mark but, once he did, he went on to complete a fine four-timer with three wins coming at Brighton. They were only modest events, the first was a seller, and they were all gained narrowly, but his trainer deserves credit for some fine placement.
**W R Muir [4-20] R Haim.*

ALPHA RR 81df 4969[10]
2 b c Primo Dominie 7.2f **(67)** - Preening (Persian Bold) 9.3f **(66)**
Form - 14600
Record 1998 - 1st:1 2nd:0 3rd:0 Ran:5
Win Prizemoney £3,523 *Total Prizemoney* £3,746
Wins * **1998** Jly Beverl (GD) 5f 77+ <
1998 Turf 1-5: (5f 1-2, 6f 2, 7f) (g-s, gd 2, g-f 1-1, frm)
Decent colt. Turf high 81 (began Jly) - 4th of 5 getting 2lb from Henry Hall (15 Jly Doncaster 5f frm RF 2817) - also 1st of 10 from Hyperactive (3 Jly Beverley RF 2490).
**C W Thornton [1-5] Guy Reed and Mrs Ailsa Daniels.*

ALPINE HIDEAWAY (IRE) BHB 72f65a **RR 72f 65a** 1268[4]
5 b g Tirol 8.1f **(64)** - Arbour (USA) (Graustark) 10.1f **(70)**
Form - 0024
Record 1998 - 1st:0 2nd:1 3rd:0 Ran:4
Pre1998 - 1st:3 2nd:5 3rd:5 Ran:28
Win Prizemoney £7,279 *Total Prizemoney* £16,326
Wins 1997 Aug Ripon (G-F) C 8f 61
1997 *Jly Southw (STD) C 7f 66*
1996 Oct Leices (G-F) 7f 71 <
1998 Turf 0-3: (8f 3) (gd 2, frm) 1998 AW 0-1: (8f) (Fibr)
Above-average gelding, effective 7 to 8f, best at 8f, acts on gd to frm - acts on Fibr, has worn blinkers, excels at Redcar. Turf high 72 - 2nd of 14 giving 11lb to Pine Ridge Lad (11 May Redcar 8f gd RF 1148).
**M W Easterby [1-15] Easterby Trailers (from B Hanbury [3-23] Aug 1997).*

ALPINE LADY (IRE) RR 4415[13]
3 b f Tirol 8.1f **(64)** - Nonnita (Welsh Saint) 7.6f **(64)**
Form - 00
Record 1998 - 1st:0 2nd:0 3rd:0 Ran:2
1998 Turf 0-2: (8f, 10f) (gd, frm)
Light-framed, currently very poor filly. (began Spt).
**N A Callaghan [0-2] J Biggane.*

ALPINE MUSIC (IRE) BHB 35f37a **RR 25f 37a** 273[3]
4 b g Tirol 8.1f **(64)** - Holy Devotion (Commanche Run) 8.5f **(58)**
Form - 53
Record 1998 - 1st:0 2nd:0 3rd:1 Ran:2
Pre1998 - 1st:0 2nd:0 3rd:0 Ran:8
Win Prizemoney £0 *Total Prizemoney* £257
1998 AW 0-2: (10f, 16f) (Equi 2)
Workmanlike, moderate gelding, has worn blinkers. AW high 44.
**J W Mullins [0-4] Mrs Sally Mullins (from J M Bradley [0-8] Jly 1997).*

ALPINE PANTHER (IRE) BHB 58f **RR 62f** 4938[8]
5 b g Tirol 8.1f **(64)** - Kentucky Wildcat (Be My Guest (USA)) 9.3f **(67)**
Form - 1368
Record 1998 - 1st:1 2nd:0 3rd:1 Ran:4
Pre1998 - 1st:0 2nd:1 3rd:2 Ran:12
Win Prizemoney £3,074 *Total Prizemoney* £5,540
Wins * **1998** Mar Nottin (G-S) H 14.1f 55 63 <
1998 Turf 1-4: (14f 1-3, 16f) (g-s 1-1, gd 2, g-f)
Average gelding, effective 10 to 14f, best at 14f, acts on g-s to g-f, best on g-f, likes left handed tracks, favours tight tracks. Turf high 63 (1st run) - 1st of 14 getting 6lb from Smart Boy (31 Mar Nottingham RF 0521).
**Mrs M Reveley [3-16] P D Savill (from W Jarvis [0-5] May 1996).*

ALRABYAH (IRE) BHB 52f **RR 66f** 3745[10]
3 br c Brief Truce (USA) 9.1f **(73)** - Bean Siamsa (Solinus) 9f **(71)**
Form - 58600
Record 1998 - 1st:0 2nd:0 3rd:0 Ran:5
Pre1998 - 1st:0 2nd:0 3rd:0 Ran:2
1998 Turf 0-5: (8f 3, 10f, 12f) (gd, g-f, frm 2, hrd)
Tall, average colt. Turf high 66.
**K A Morgan [0-2] J A Outwin (from P T Walwyn [0-5] Jly 1998).*

ALRAHAAL (USA) RR 64f 4662[5]
3 b br c Diesis 9f **(80)** - Solar Star (USA) (Lear Fan (USA)) 8.5f **(73)**
Form - 05
Record 1998 - 1st:0 2nd:0 3rd:0 Ran:2
1998 Turf 0-2: (8f 2) (gd, g-f)
Scopey, currently average colt. Turf high 64 (began Spt).
**J H M Gosden [0-2] Hamdan Al Maktoum.*

ALRASSAAM RR 66f 4595[12]
2 b c Zafonic (USA) 9f **(83)** - Lady Blackfoot (Prince Tenderfoot (USA)) 9f **(61)**
Form - 0
Record 1998 - 1st:0 2nd:0 3rd:0 Ran:1
1998 Turf 0-1: (7f) (gd)
Currently average colt. **M A Jarvis [0-1] Sheikh Ahmed Al Maktoum.*

AL REET (IRE) BHB 51f40a **RR 54f 40a** 2335[5]
7 b m Alzao (USA) 9.8f **(73)** - Reet Petite (Thatching) 8f **(66)**
Form - 054242255
Record 1998 - 1st:0 2nd:3 3rd:0 Ran:7
Pre1998 - 1st:1 2nd:1 3rd:2 Ran:23
Win Prizemoney £3,356 *Total Prizemoney* £9,098
Wins * 1997 Jun Doncas (G-S) H 7f 50 53 <
1998 Turf 0-7: (6f, 7f 4, 8f 2) (g-s 2, gd 4, g-f)
Fair mare, effective 6 to 8f, acts on g-s to frm - acts on Fibr, has worn blinkers, likes left handed tracks, likes tight tracks, excels at Pontefract, does well at Doncaster. Turf high 54 - 2nd of 12 getting 12lb from Kass Alhawa (3 Jun Beverley 7f gd RF 1675). Consistent.
**S R Bowring [1-24] Mark Kilner (from M D Hammond [0-6] Nov 1996).*

ALRIGHT POPS BHB 50f **RR 43df** 4868[15]
2 b f Rock Hopper 10.6f **(54)** - Sea Aura (Roi Soleil) 8.7f **(57)**
Form - 006000
Record 1998 - 1st:0 2nd:0 3rd:0 Ran:6
1998 Turf 0-6: (5f 2, 6f 2, 7f, 8f) (gd, g-f 2, frm 3)
Moderate filly. Turf high 43. **R Dickin [0-6] Mrs C M Dickin.*

ALSAHIB (USA) BHB 45f76a **RR 51f 76a** 5081[1]
5 b g Slew O' Gold (USA) 10.2f **(73)** - Khwlah (USA) (Best Turn (USA)) 10.2f **(78)**
Form - 8231058040001

Record 1998 - 1st:2 2nd:0 3rd:1 Ran:11
Pre1998 - 1st:1 2nd:2 3rd:1 Ran:17
Win Prizemoney £11,727 *Total Prizemoney* £17,384
Wins * **1998** *Oct Wolver (STD) C 12f 81* <
* **1998** *Jan Southw (STD) H 11f 76 80*
* 1997 *Jun Wolver (STD) H 9.4f 64 76*
1998 Turf 0-6: (8f, 9f, 10f 3, 12f) (gd 3, g-f 2, frm) 1998 AW 2-5: (11f 1-2, 12f 1-3) (Fibr 2-5)
Decent gelding, effective 9 to 12f, best at 12f, - acts on Fibr, has worn blinkers, likes left handed tracks, likes tight tracks. Turf high 51 (began Jly). AW high 81 - 1st of 11 giving 12lb to Noukari (31 Oct Wolverhampton RF 5081) - also 1st of 12 giving 5lb to China Castle (12 Jan Southwell RF 0075). A very effective performer over middle distances on Fibresand, he had the distinction of managing to beat China Castle in the month of January, and not many achieve that. Below form on turf and sand after that, but returned to something like his best by winning a Wolverhampton claimer in October very easily.
**W R Muir [3-25] S Channing-Williams (from H ThomsonJones [0-4] Jun 1996).*

AL'S ALIBI BHB 75f RR 75f 3529[1]

5 b h Alzao (USA) 9.8f **(73)** - Lady Kris (IRE) (Kris) 9.5f **(73)**
Form - 71061
Record 1998 - 1st:2 2nd:0 3rd:0 Ran:5
Pre1998 - 1st:2 2nd:2 3rd:1 Ran:20
Win Prizemoney £17,757 *Total Prizemoney* £21,886
Wins * **1998** Aug Bath (FRM) H 11.7f 74 75
* **1998** May Newbur (GD) H 12f 72 75
* 1997 Aug Carlis (G-F) H 12f 72 76 <
* 1996 Apr Newbur (G-S) H 12f 72 75
1998 Turf 2-5: (12f 2-5) (gd, g-f 1-2, frm 1-2)
Above-average colt, effective 12f, acts on sft to frm, prefers tight tracks. Turf high 75 - 1st of 13 getting 15lb from Papua (15 May Newbury RF 1240) - also 1st of 7 getting 1lb from Fletcher (11 Aug Bath RF 3529). Quite a useful middle-distance handicapper, he managed victories at Newbury and Bath last season. Twelve furlongs and fast ground look to suit him best.
**W R Muir [4-25] J Haim.*

ALSAMEDAH (USA) RR 4983[14]

2 b f Shadeed (USA) 7.7f **(72)** - Alqwani (USA) (Mr Prospector (USA)) 8.8f **(78)**
Form - 0
Record 1998 - 1st:0 2nd:0 3rd:0 Ran:1
1998 Turf 0-1: (8f) (g-s)
Currently very poor filly. **J H M Gosden [0-1] Hamdan Al Maktoum.*

AL SAQIYA (USA) BHB 73f RR 73f 4856[13]

2 b f Woodman (USA) 9.7f **(77)** - Augusta Springs (USA) (Nijinsky (CAN)) 10.3f **(77)**
Form - 740
Record 1998 - 1st:0 2nd:0 3rd:0 Ran:3
Win Prizemoney £0 *Total Prizemoney* £262
1998 Turf 0-3: (7f 3) (sft, frm 2)
Currently above-average filly. Turf high 73 (began Aug).
**J L Dunlop [0-3] Hamdan Al Maktoum.*

AL'S FELLA (IRE) BHB 73f67a RR 69+f 67a 5095[1]

3 br g Alzao (USA) 9.8f **(73)** - Crystal Cross (USA) **(73f)** (Roberto (USA)) 10f **(76)**
Form - 63422001
Record 1998 - 1st:1 2nd:2 3rd:1 Ran:7
Pre1998 - 1st:0 2nd:1 3rd:1 Ran:8
Win Prizemoney £3,610 *Total Prizemoney* £7,443
Wins * **1998** Nov Redcar (G-S) H 11f 65 69+ <
1998 Turf 1-2: (9f, 11f 1-1) (gd 1-2) 1998 AW 0-5: (8f 3, 9f, 10f) (Equi, Fibr 4)
Neat, average gelding, effective 7 to 11f, acts on gd, has worn blinkers, likes tight tracks. Turf high 69 (began Oct) - 1st of 9 getting 10lb from First Master (2 Nov Redcar RF 5095). AW high 64.
**P F I Cole [1-15] Mrs Christopher Hanbury.*

ALTAWEELAH (IRE) BHB 104f RR 105f 5066[3]

3 b f Fairy King (USA) 7.7f **(75)** - Donya (Mill Reef (USA)) 10.5f **(78)**
Form - 8115243
Record 1998 - 1st:2 2nd:1 3rd:1 Ran:7
Win Prizemoney £10,340 *Total Prizemoney* £17,726
Wins * **1998** Jun York (G-S) 11.9f 94++ <
* **1998** May Haydoc (G-S) 10.5f 76
1998 Turf 2-7: (7f, 10f, 11f 1-1, 12f 1-4) (sft, g-s 1-1, gd 1-2, g-f 3)
Scopey, Pattern-class filly, effective 12f, acts on g-f. Turf high 105 - 2nd of 6 getting 5lb from Craigsteel (11 Spt Doncaster 12f g-f RF 4224). She looked a typical Luca Cumani improver when winning at Haydock and York, but failed to progress significantly on those performances. We may have seen the best of her.
**L M Cumani [2-7] Sheikh Ahmed Al Maktoum.*

ALTIBR (USA) RR 101++f 1230a[11]

3 ch c Diesis 9f **(80)** - Love's Reward (Nonoalco (USA)) 8.5f **(66)**
Form - 0
Record 1998 - 1st:0 2nd:0 3rd:0 Ran:1
Pre1998 - 1st:1 2nd:0 3rd:0 Ran:1
Win Prizemoney £3,782 *Total Prizemoney* £3,782
Wins * 1997 Oct Leices (GD) 7f 101++ <
1998 Turf 0-1: (8f) (gd)
Currently very useful colt. Showed little in the french 2000 guineas on his only start. **S bin Suroor [1-2] Godolphin.*

ALTICHIERO RR 71+f 4779[11]

2 b c Polish Precedent (USA) 9f **(73)** - Anna Matrushka (Mill Reef (USA)) 10.5f **(78)**
Form - 60
Record 1998 - 1st:0 2nd:0 3rd:0 Ran:2
1998 Turf 0-2: (7f, 8f) (gd, frm)
Currently above-average colt. Turf high 71 (began Spt). One to watch in handicaps. **Sir Michael Stoute [0-2] Sheikh Mohammed.*

ALTITUDE (IRE) BHB 74f RR 79f 3905[9]

3 b c Alzao (USA) 9.8f **(73)** - Elevate (Ela-Mana-Mou) 10.1f **(70)**
Form - 115420
Record 1998 - 1st:2 2nd:1 3rd:0 Ran:6
Pre1998 - 1st:0 2nd:0 3rd:0 Ran:3
Win Prizemoney £4,410 *Total Prizemoney* £5,942
Wins * **1998** Jun Bath (G-S) 11.7f 78+ <
* **1998** Jun Newcas (SFT) 12.4f 66
1998 Turf 2-6: (12f 2-4, 14f, 16f) (g-s 1-2, gd 1-2, g-f 2)
Well made, above-average colt, effective 12 to 16f, best at 12f, acts on gd to g-f, best on gd, likes tight tracks. Turf high 79 - 2nd of 5 giving 10lb to Lady Rachel (3 Aug Carlisle 12f gd RF 3306) - also 1st of 8 giving 2lb to Dancing Dervish (13 Jun Bath RF 1957). Completed a quick double in June, albeit in moderate company, but ran inexplicably poorly next time. Two miles looked just too far for him at Chepstow. Sold for 15,000 gns at Tattersalls Autumn Horses-in-Training Sales. **Sir Mark Prescott [2-9] Mrs F R Watts.*

AL WAFFI BHB 100f RR 96f 4950a[3]

2 b c Fairy King (USA) 7.7f **(75)** - Darrery **(98f)** (Darshaan) 9.9f **(84)**
Form - 21413
Record 1998 - 1st:2 2nd:1 3rd:1 Ran:5
Win Prizemoney £7,070 *Total Prizemoney* £32,324
Wins * **1998** Spt Leices (G-F) 7f 94 <
* **1998** Aug Salisb (G-F) 7f 77
1998 Turf 2-5: (7f 2-3, 8f 2) (sft 2, gd, g-f 1-1, frm 1-1)
Very useful colt. Turf high 96 (began Jly) - 3rd of 9 giving 3lb to Noble Pearl (18 Oct San Siro 8f sft RF 4950a) - also 1st of 5 from Red Delirium (21 Spt Leicester RF 4398). Beaten at odds on in a Newcastle maiden on his debut, he went one better at Salisbury next time and ran with credit for the rest of the season. He takes time getting going, but is genuine and looks a useful prospect.
**D R Loder [2-5].*

ALWAYS ALIGHT BHB 99f RR 102f 5152[10]

4 ch g Never so Bold 7.1f **(62)** - Fire Sprite (Mummy's Game) 8.2f **(60)**
Form - 14500001415730
Record 1998 - 1st:3 2nd:0 3rd:1 Ran:14
Pre1998 - 1st:3 2nd:3 3rd:5 Ran:21
Win Prizemoney £77,012 *Total Prizemoney* £87,619
Wins * **1998** Spt Ayr (G-S) H 6f 89 94 <
* **1998** Aug Ayr (G-S) 6f 87
* **1998** Mar Doncas (GD) H 6f 81 86
* 1997 Oct Newcas (G-F) H 6f 75 78
* 1997 Jun Goodwo (G-S) H 6f 72 74
* 1997 May Newbur (G-F) H 6f 62 69
1998 Turf 3-14: (6f 3-12, 7f 2) (sft 1-2, gd 2-9, g-f, frm 2)
Scopey, very useful gelding, effective 6f, acts on sft to g-f, has

worn blinkers, excels at Ayr. Turf high 102 - 7th of 16 giving 1lb to Bold Edge (16 Oct Newmarket 6f g-f RF 4844) - also 1st of 29 getting 3lb from Daring Destiny (19 Spt Ayr RF 4367). A horse with bags of character - he often plants himself and refuses to budge on the way to post - he is a game sprint handicapper, who swooped late to win Karl Burke his second Ayr Gold Cup. He will score again when the handicapper relents.

**K R Burke [6-35] M Nelmes-Crocker.*

ALWAYS LUCKY BHB 58f53a **RR 58f 53a** 569[3]

3 gr f Absalom 7.1f **(56)** - Petitesse (Petong) 6.6f **(58)**

Form - 00583

Record 1998 - 1st:0 2nd:0 3rd:1 Ran:5
Pre1998 - 1st:2 2nd:3 3rd:2 Ran:10

Win Prizemoney £4,923 *Total Prizemoney* £8,835

Wins 1997 *Jly Southw (STD) C 6f 65*
1997 *May Southw (STD) 5f 76 <*

1998 Turf 0-1: (8f) (g-s) 1998 AW 0-4: (6f 2, 7f, 9f) (Fibr 4)

Lengthy, fair filly, effective 5f, acts on g-f to frm - acts on Fibr. AW high 53. **J Pearce [0-5] G W Byrne (from J Berry [2-10] Oct 1997).*

ALWAYS ON MY MIND BHB 81f **RR 86df** 1948[6]

4 b f Distant Relative 7f **(69)** - Fleur Rouge (Pharly (FR)) 9.8f **(68)**

Form - 006

Record 1998 - 1st:0 2nd:0 3rd:0 Ran:3
Pre1998 - 1st:4 2nd:1 3rd:0 Ran:8

Win Prizemoney £17,302 *Total Prizemoney* £18,741

Wins * 1997 Nov Newmar (G-F) 6f 86
* 1997 Jly Doncas (GD) H 6f 80 88+ <
* 1997 Jly Newmar (G-S) H 6f 75 79
* 1997 Jly Warwic (SFT) 6f 73+

1998 Turf 0-3: (6f 3) (g-s, gd, g-f)

Scopey, useful filly, effective 6f, acts on gd to g-f, best on g-f. Turf high 67. **P J Makin [4-11] Mascalls Stud.*

ALWAYS TRYING BHB 52f49a **RR 46f 49a** 65[8]

3 b g Always Fair (USA) 14f **(61)** - Bassita (Bustino) 10.4f **(64)**

Form - 8

Record 1998 - 1st:0 2nd:0 3rd:0 Ran:1
Pre1998 - 1st:0 2nd:1 3rd:0 Ran:3

Win Prizemoney £0 *Total Prizemoney* £780

1998 AW 0-1: (9f) (Fibr)

Leggy, moderate gelding.

**M Johnston [0-4] Mark Johnston Racing Ltd.*

ALWENA RR 3f 4415[12]

3 ch f Henbit (USA) 10.2f **(46)** - Brenig (Horage) 10.3f **(61)**

Form - 0

Record 1998 - 1st:0 2nd:0 3rd:0 Ran:1

1998 Turf 0-1: (8f) (frm)

Lengthy, currently little account filly. **S C Williams [0-1] Edgar Lloyd.*

ALYA (USA) RR 52f 1593[14]

3 br f Deputy Minister (CAN) 9.2f **(71)** - Colonial Waters (USA) (Pleasant Colony (USA)) 7f **(70)**

Form - 50

Record 1998 - 1st:0 2nd:0 3rd:0 Ran:2

1998 Turf 0-2: (9f, 12f) (gd 2)

Light-framed, currently fair filly. Turf high 52.

**P F I Cole [0-2] H R H Prince Fahd Salman.*

ALYRIVA (USA) RR 92f 1029[1]

3 b c Alydeed (CAN) 8f **(81)** - Portio (USA) (Riva Ridge (USA)) 8.2f **(68)**

Form - 21

Record 1998 - 1st:1 2nd:1 3rd:0 Ran:2

Win Prizemoney £3,362 *Total Prizemoney* £5,084

Wins * **1998** May Warwic (GD) 8f 90 <

1998 Turf 1-2: (8f 1-2) (sft, g-f 1-1)

Well made, currently useful colt. Turf high 92 (1st run) - 2nd of 19 giving 5lb to The Sandfly (15 Apr Newmarket 8f sft RF 0701) - also 1st of 11 from Splendid Isolation (4 May Warwick RF 1029). This attractive colt beat all but one in the Wood Ditton and followed up by winning an ordinary maiden. However, he was not seen again.

**D R Loder [1-2] Sheikh Mohammed.*

ALY'S ALLEY (USA) RR 112a 5162a[2]

2 b c Alwuhush (USA) - Aly Capri (USA)

Form - 2

1998 AW 0-1: (9f) (Dirt)

Currently Group-class colt, always wears blinkers. (1st run) - 2nd of 14 to Answer Lively (7 Nov Churchill Downs 9f Dirt RF 5162a). Experienced American two-year-old, beaten a head in the Breeders' Cup Juvenile.

**J Tammaro III in USA [0-1] William Marquard.*

ALZAHRA BHB 60f **RR 64f** 1516[8]

3 ch f Interrex (CAN) 7.7f **(51)** - Flirty Lady (Never so Bold) 6.3f **(66)**

Form - 88

Record 1998 - 1st:0 2nd:0 3rd:0 Ran:2
Pre1998 - 1st:0 2nd:0 3rd:0 Ran:1

1998 Turf 0-2: (7f, 8f) (gd 2)

Unfurnished, average filly. Turf high 64. (DEAD)

**J G Smyth-Osbourne [0-3] Mrs J Harmsworth.*

ALZOTIC (IRE) BHB 31f31a **RR 36f 31a** 283[7]

5 b g Alzao (USA) 9.8f **(73)** - Exotic Bride (USA) (Blushing Groom (FR)) 10.3f **(76)**

Form - 8667

Record 1998 - 1st:0 2nd:0 3rd:0 Ran:4
Pre1998 - 1st:0 2nd:1 3rd:0 Ran:15

Win Prizemoney £0 *Total Prizemoney* £1,595

1998 AW 0-4: (16f 4) (Fibr 4)

Very moderate gelding, effective 14f, acts on g-f, has worn blinkers, likes left handed tracks. AW high 35.

**J Norton [0-18] Billy Parker (from S G Norton [0-6] Nov 1995).*

AMADOUR (IRE) BHB 58f75a **RR 51f 75a** 446[2]

5 b g Contract Law (USA) 8.9f **(54)** - Truly Flattering (Hard Fought) 8.8f **(62)**

Form - 182

Record 1998 - 1st:1 2nd:1 3rd:0 Ran:3
Pre1998 - 1st:2 2nd:2 3rd:1 Ran:12

Win Prizemoney £9,047 *Total Prizemoney* £12,182

Wins * **1998** *Jan Lingfi (STD) H 12f 70 73 <*
* 1997 *Feb Lingfi (STD) H 12f 65 66*
* 1996 Oct Bright (GD) H 11.9f 63 66

1998 AW 1-3: (12f 1-3) (Equi 1-2, Fibr)

Above-average gelding, effective 12f, - acts on Equi, prefers left handed tracks, favours tight tracks. AW high 73 - 2nd of 5 giving 2lb to Quiet Arch (19 Mar Lingfield 12f Equi RF 0446) - also 1st of 6 giving 3lb to Quiet Arch (29 Jan Lingfield RF 0181). Inconsistent. He won a modest apprentice handicap on the Lingfield Equitrack in February '97, but did not show much else after and was not seen out after June. However, he came back to beat a very good field in a handicap on the same surface in January. A decent piece of training. **P Mitchell [3-15] Lovine Partnership.*

AMALIA (IRE) RR 76f 4665[3]

2 b f Danehill (USA) 9.1f **(79)** - Cheviot Amble (IRE) **(97f)** (Pennine Walk) 8.5f **(61)**

Form - 63

Record 1998 - 1st:0 2nd:0 3rd:1 Ran:2

Win Prizemoney £0 *Total Prizemoney* £456

1998 Turf 0-2: (6f, 8f) (g-s, gd)

Currently above-average filly. Turf high 76 (began Spt) - 3rd of 11 to Magda (6 Oct Nottingham 8f g-s RF 4665).

**P W Harris [0-2] Mrs P W Harris.*

AMAL JUMAIRAH RR 66f 4930[5]

2 b c Barathea (IRE) - Fair Shirley (IRE) (Shirley Heights) 10.3f **(74)**

Form - 05

Record 1998 - 1st:0 2nd:0 3rd:0 Ran:2

1998 Turf 0-2: (7f, 8f) (g-s, frm)

Currently average colt. Turf high 66 (began Aug).

**M A Jarvis [0-2] Sheikh Ahmed Al Maktoum.*

AMARANTH (IRE) BHB 77f **RR 79f** 5011[1]

2 b c Mujadil (USA) 7.7f **(70)** - Zoes Delight (IRE) (Hatim (USA))

Form - 21

Record 1998 - 1st:1 2nd:1 3rd:0 Ran:2

Win Prizemoney £2,192 *Total Prizemoney* £2,879

Wins * **1998** Oct Redcar (SFT) 5f 79 <

1998 Turf 1-2: (5f 1-1, 6f) (gd 1-2)

Above-average colt. Turf high 79 (began Oct) - 1st of 6 giving 5lb

to Compton Amber (27 Oct Redcar RF 5011). (DEAD)
J L Eyre [1-2] M Gleason.

AMARETTO FLAME (IRE) RR 65f 4761[8]

2 ch f First Trump - Vestal Flame (Habitat) 9.4f **(70)**
Form - 8
Record 1998 - 1st:0 2nd:0 3rd:0 Ran:1
1998 Turf 0-1: (7f) (gd)
Currently average filly.
**B J Meehan [0-1] The Second Harlequin Partnership.*

AMARICE BHB 85f RR 89f 4991[8]

2 b f Suave Dancer (USA) 10.7f **(68)** - Almitra (Targowice (USA)) 11.4f **(70)**
Form - 3518
Record 1998 - 1st:1 2nd:0 3rd:1 Ran:4
Win Prizemoney £3,496 *Total Prizemoney* £4,094
Wins * **1998** Oct Ayr (G-S) 7f 89 <
1998 Turf 1-4: (6f 2, 7f 1-2) (sft 1-2, g-f, frm)
Useful filly. Turf high 89 (began Spt) - 1st of 14 getting 5lb from Mt Speculation (12 Oct Ayr RF 4752).
**M Johnston [1-4] Mrs S W O'Brien.*

AMAZING DREAM (IRE) BHB 100f RR 95f 4039a[1]

2 b f Thatching 7.8f **(69)** - Aunty Eileen (Ahonoora) 8.1f **(73)**
Form - 5401211
Record 1998 - 1st:3 2nd:1 3rd:0 Ran:7
Win Prizemoney £86,603 *Total Prizemoney* £96,343
Wins * **1998** Aug Currag (GD) 6f 95 <
* **1998** Aug Newbur (GD) L 5.2f 94
* **1998** Jly Windso (GD) 5f 84
1998 Turf 3-7: (5f 2-6, 6f 1-1) (gd 2-5, g-f 1-2)
Very useful filly, effective 5 to 6f, best at 5f, acts on gd. Turf high 95 - 1st of 27 from Aeraiocht (29 Aug Curragh RF 4039a) - also 1st of 7 from Crystal Charm (15 Aug Newbury RF 3651). She has been highly tried since her debut but, after a confidence-boosting win at Windsor, ran a blinder in the Molecomb and landed a Newbury Listed event. Also gave Richard Hannon his third successive win in the big Tattersalls Breeders Stakes at the Curragh. Hitting the front soon after halfway, she held off all challengers in the last two furlongs to score nicely. Never stopped improving through the season, and should make a very decent three-year-old.
**R Hannon [3-7] Mrs P & P Jubert.*

AMAZING FACT (USA) BHB 50f RR 60f 4883[14]

3 b g Known Fact (USA) 8.3f **(72)** - Itsamazing (USA) (The Minstrel (CAN)) 10f **(72)**
Form - 386000
Record 1998 - 1st:0 2nd:0 3rd:1 Ran:6
Win Prizemoney £0 *Total Prizemoney* £455
1998 Turf 0-6: (7f 3, 8f, 10f 2) (g-s 2, g-f, frm 3)
Scopey, average gelding. Turf high 75.
**Lady Herries [0-6] L G Lazarus.*

AMAZINK (IRE) RR 89f 2791a[6]

3 b c Green Desert (USA) 7.8f **(78)** - Alysardi (USA) (Alydar (USA)) 9.1f **(76)**
Form - 02346
1998 Turf 0-5: (6f 2, 7f, 8f, 9f) (sft, g-s 2, gd, hrd)
Useful colt, has worn blinkers. Turf high 98 - 2nd of 9 to Alonzo (3 May Gowran Park 7f hrd RF 1053a).
**J S Bolger in IRE [0-5] Anthony Paul Smurfit.*

AMAZON (IRE) RR 40f 3606[9]

2 b f Petorius 8f **(66)** - Sally Gone (IRE) (Last Tycoon) 8.5f **(62)**
Form - 550
Record 1998 - 1st:0 2nd:0 3rd:0 Ran:3
1998 Turf 0-3: (5f 2, 6f) (frm 3)
Currently moderate filly. Turf high 40 (began Jly).
**R Hannon [0-3] Antony Sofroniou.*

AMAZON EXPRESS BHB 50f RR 62f 1157[12]

9 b g Siberian Express (USA) 9f **(58)** - Thalestria (FR) (Mill Reef (USA)) 10.5f **(78)**
Form - 0
Record 1998 - 1st:0 2nd:0 3rd:0 Ran:1
Pre1998 - 1st:5 2nd:1 3rd:2 Ran:26
Win Prizemoney £12,201 *Total Prizemoney* £14,106
1998 AW 0-1: (14f) (Fibr)
Average gelding, has worn blinkers. Inconsistent.
**P Bowen [2-10] T M Morris (from R Akehurst [5-21] May 1994).*

AMAZONIAN BHB 39f46a RR 42f 46a 1547[9]

3 b c Formidable (USA) 7.8f **(60)**-Red Rose Garden (Electric) 10.1f **(61)**
Form - 80080
Record 1998 - 1st:0 2nd:0 3rd:0 Ran:3
Pre1998 - 1st:0 2nd:0 3rd:0 Ran:3
1998 Turf 0-3: (8f, 9f, 10f) (sft, gd, g-f)
Scopey, moderate colt. Turf high 19. **C W Thornton [0-6] Guy Reed.*

AMBER FORT BHB 79f70a RR 91?f 70a 4750[23]

5 gr g Indian Ridge 7.6f **(74)** - Lammastide (Martinmas) 7.6f **(59)**
Form - 0045117033350
Record 1998 - 1st:2 2nd:0 3rd:3 Ran:13
Pre1998 - 1st:3 2nd:4 3rd:3 Ran:26
Win Prizemoney £17,848 *Total Prizemoney* £29,606
Wins * **1998** Jly Kempto (G-S) H 7f 75 82 <
* **1998** Jun Goodwo (G-F) H 7f 75 81
* 1997 Jun Goodwo (G-S) H 7f 74 77
* 1996 Oct Newbur (SFT) H 7f 69 74
1996 *Jun Lingfi (STD) C 7f 60*
1998 Turf 2-13: (7f 2-7, 8f 6) (gd 2-5, g-f 6, frm 2)
Useful gelding, effective 7 to 8f, best at 7f, acts on gd to frm, best on gd, mostly wears blinkers (very effectively), prefers right handed tracks, likes tight tracks, excels at Goodwood. Turf high 91 - 3rd of 6 giving 15lb to Mihnah (24 Spt Goodwood 8f frm RF 4460) - also 1st of 14 giving 5lb to Mullitover (1 Jly Kempton RF 2446). Ran quite well in 1997, including a victory in a Goodwood apprentice handicap in June. Off the track for the best part of a year subsequently, he came back to form in the summer, winning a brace of seven-furlong handicaps. Ran well in September, appreciating a bit of cut, but perhaps needs to fall a few pounds in the weights.
**D R C Elsworth [4-27] The Caledonian Racing Society (from P F I Cole [1-12] Jun 1996).*

AMBER JASMINE (IRE) BHB 58f RR 70f 4813[7]

2 b g Petardia 8.2f **(58)** - Hollyberry (IRE) (Runnett) 7f **(59)**
Form - 5307
Record 1998 - 1st:0 2nd:0 3rd:1 Ran:4
Win Prizemoney £0 *Total Prizemoney* £465
1998 Turf 0-4: (5f 3, 6f) (gd 2, g-f 2)
Above-average gelding. Turf high 70.
**P C Haslam [0-4] Mrs E Chung.*

AMBER REGENT BHB 51f52a RR 56f 52a 4549[12]

3 ch g King's Signet (USA) 7f **(51)** - Silly Sally (Music Boy) 6.8f **(57)**
Form - 75341452704200
Record 1998 - 1st:1 2nd:2 3rd:1 Ran:13
Pre1998 - 1st:0 2nd:0 3rd:0 Ran:4
Win Prizemoney £3,436 *Total Prizemoney* £6,011
Wins 1998 *Feb Wolver (STD) H 7f 57 65* <
1998 Turf 0-4: (7f, 8f, 9f, 11f) (g-s, g-f, frm, hrd) 1998 AW 1-9: (6f, 7f 1-4, 8f, 9f 2, 11f) (Equi, Fibr 1-8)
Scopey, average gelding, effective 7f, - acts on AW, likes left handed tracks, likes tight tracks. Turf high 56. AW high 65 - 1st of 7 getting 13lb from I'm Tef (11 Feb Wolverhampton RF 0269). Inconsistent.
**Miss S J Wilton [0-2] John Pointon and Sons (from P C Haslam [1-15] Jly 1998).*

AMBER VALLEY (USA) BHB 35f RR 35f 3526[5]

7 ch g Bering 9.6f **(80)** - Olatha (USA) (Miswaki (USA)) 9f **(81)**
Form - 0455
Record 1998 - 1st:0 2nd:0 3rd:0 Ran:4
Pre1998 - 1st:1 2nd:4 3rd:0 Ran:17
Win Prizemoney £3,647 *Total Prizemoney* £10,085
1998 Turf 0-4: (10f, 12f 2, 17f) (gd, g-f, frm 2)
Very moderate gelding. Turf high 35 (began Jly). Only ran once on the Flat in 1997. A dual-purpose horse with some reasonable hurdling form, we have probably seen the best of his Flat days now.
**D L Williams [1-25] Berkshire Commercial Components Ltd (from J Hanson [1-15] Oct 1994).*

AMBIDEXTROUS (IRE) BHB 43f40a **RR 46f 40a** 5119[11]
6 b h Shareef Dancer (USA) 10.1f **(67)** - Amber Fizz (USA) (Effervescing (USA)) 8.1f **(79)**
Form - 56364573725303267400
Record 1998 - 1st:0 2nd:2 3rd:4 Ran:20
Pre1998 - 1st:4 2nd:3 3rd:7 Ran:37
Win Prizemoney £14,766 *Total Prizemoney* £26,701
Wins * 1997 Jly Cheste (G-F) H 10.3f 58 58 <
* 1997 Jun Mussel (GD) H 12f 45 53
* 1996 Jun Mussel (G-F) H 11.1f 43 48
* 1996 Jun Mussel (FRM) H 11.1f 43 48
1998 Turf 0-17: (10f 5, 11f 4, 12f 8) (sft, g-s, gd 5, g-f 7, frm 3) 1998 AW 0-3: (12f 3) (Fibr 3)
Moderate horse, effective 10 to 12f, acts on gd to frm, has worn blinkers, likes right handed tracks, excels at Musselburgh, likes Haydock and Chester. Turf high 55 - 3rd of 10 getting 6lb from Doc Ryan's (15 Jun Musselburgh 12f gd RF 1994). AW high 43. Inconsistent.
**E J Alston [6-68] Mrs Carol McPhail (from C E Brittain [0-4] Jly 1995).*

AMBIGUOUS BHB 87f88a **RR 87f 88a** 867[6]
3 ch c Arazi (USA) 9.2f **(74)** - Vaguely (Bold Lad (IRE)) 8.4f **(68)**
Form - 11616
Record 1998 - 1st:3 2nd:0 3rd:0 Ran:5
Pre1998 - 1st:0 2nd:0 3rd:0 Ran:3
Win Prizemoney £11,138 *Total Prizemoney* £11,312
Wins * **1998** Apr Ripon (SFT) H 8f 80 87 <
* **1998** *Mar Wolver (STD) 8.5f 81+*
* **1998** *Mar Wolver (STD) 8.5f 80*
1998 Turf 1-2: (8f 1-2) (sft, g-s 1-1) 1998 AW 2-3: (8f 2-2, 10f) (Equi, Fibr 2-2)
Well made, useful colt, effective 8f, acts on g-s - acts on Fibr, prefers tight tracks. Turf high 87 (1st run) - 1st of 11 giving 13lb to Prince Batshoof (16 Apr Ripon RF 0718). AW high 81 - 1st of 9 giving 6lb to Bint Nadia (7 Mar Wolverhampton RF 0405) - also 1st of 8 giving 5lb to Lady Rachel (4 Mar Wolverhampton RF 0397). Inconsistent. He made an immediate impact when tried on Fibresand with two wide-margin successes at Wolverhampton in the space of three days in March. He could only finish sixth in the Winter Derby on the Lingfield Equitrack after that, when the combination of a different surface and a step up in class and trip were all too much for him. Transferred his improvement to turf with a decisive win in soft at Ripon, but was well beaten in a Sandown handicap next time. He now looks a little high in the handicap on turf. **D R Loder [3-8] Abdullah Saeed Bul Hab.*

AMBITIOUS BHB 70f63a **RR 69?f 63a** 5097[8]
3 b f Ardkinglass 5f **(64)** - Ayodhya (IRE) (Astronef)
Form - 8
Record 1998 - 1st:0 2nd:0 3rd:0 Ran:1
Pre1998 - 1st:0 2nd:1 3rd:0 Ran:3
Win Prizemoney £0 *Total Prizemoney* £726
1998 Turf 0-1: (5f) (gd)
Unfurnished, average filly. **J R Fanshawe [0-4] Dr Catherine Wills.*

AMEENA (USA) BHB 65f **RR 67f** 4677[20]
3 b f Irish River (FR) 9f **(77)** - London Pride (USA) (Lear Fan (USA)) 8.5f **(73)**
Form - 384650
Record 1998 - 1st:0 2nd:0 3rd:1 Ran:6
Pre1998 - 1st:0 2nd:0 3rd:0 Ran:1
Win Prizemoney £0 *Total Prizemoney* £815
1998 Turf 0-6: (6f, 7f 3, 8f, 9f) (gd 2, g-f 2, frm 2)
Neat, average filly, effective 6f, acts on g-f. Turf high 67 - 4th of 21 giving 2lb to Haajra (1 Aug Thirsk 6f g-f RF 3281).
**R A Fahey [0-6] R Meredith (from P F I Cole [0-1] Spt 1997).*

AMELIA JANE BHB 24f **RR 14f** 350[8]
4 ch f Efisio 7.7f **(69)** - Blue Jane (Blue Cashmere) 6.4f **(54)**
Form - 6878
Record 1998 - 1st:0 2nd:0 3rd:0 Ran:2
Pre1998 - 1st:0 2nd:0 3rd:0 Ran:5
1998 AW 0-2: (6f, 10f) (Equi 2)
Small, little account filly, has worn blinkers.
**L MontagueHall [0-7] The Racing For Fun Partnership.*

AMENIXA (FR) BHB 64f **RR 59f** 2960[11]
4 gr f Linamix (FR) 8.2f **(64)** - Amen (USA) (Alydar (USA)) 9.1f **(76)**
Form - 15400
Record 1998 - 1st:1 2nd:0 3rd:0 Ran:5
Win Prizemoney £3,232 *Total Prizemoney* £3,643
Wins * **1998** Mar Nottin (G-S) 8.2f 75 <
1998 Turf 1-5: (8f 1-3, 10f, 12f) (g-s 1-1, gd, frm 3)
Fair filly, has worn blinkers. Turf high 75 (1st run) - 1st of 11 giving 12lb to Honest Borderer (31 Mar Nottingham RF 0517). Ex-French, she made a winning debut in this country at Nottingham in March.
**S P C Woods [1-5] Ian Deane.*

AMERICAN COUSIN BHB 53f69a **RR 58f 69a** 3886[15]
3 b g Distant Relative 7f **(69)** - Zelda (USA) (Sharpen Up) 8.3f **(67)**
Form - 082500
Record 1998 - 1st:0 2nd:1 3rd:0 Ran:6
Pre1998 - 1st:0 2nd:0 3rd:3 Ran:5
Win Prizemoney £0 *Total Prizemoney* £2,379
1998 Turf 0-6: (5f 4, 6f, 7f) (gd 3, g-f, frm 2)
Scopey, fair gelding, effective 5f, acts on frm, has worn blinkers. Turf high 58 - 2nd of 8 giving 12lb to Chakra (11 Jly Warwick 5f frm RF 2730).
**R F JohnsonHoughton [0-6] Middleham Park Racing XIV (from B J Meehan [0-5] Aug 1997).*

AMERICAN WHISPER BHB 97f **RR 93f** 1777[14]
4 b c Dixieland Band (USA) 10.1f **(80)** - Only A Rumour (Ela-Mana-Mou) 10.1f **(70)**
Form - 110
Record 1998 - 1st:2 2nd:0 3rd:0 Ran:3
Pre1998 - 1st:3 2nd:0 3rd:1 Ran:8
Win Prizemoney £45,361 *Total Prizemoney* £45,818
Wins * **1998** May Newmar (G-S) H 10f 90 93 <
* **1998** Apr Kempto (SFT) H 10f 83 88
* 1997 Oct Doncas (GD) H 10.3f 75 83
* 1997 Jun Yarmou (GD) H 10.1f 68 75
* 1997 Jun Goodwo (G-F) H 10f 64 67
1998 Turf 2-3: (10f 2-3) (hvy 1-1, gd 1-1, g-f)
Leggy, useful colt, effective 10f, acts on hvy to g-f. Turf high 93 - 1st of 14 getting 5lb from Future Perfect (2 May Newmarket RF 0973) - also 1st of 16 getting 10lb from Almond Rock (13 Apr Kempton RF 0659). He looked a progressive sort at the end of the 1997 season and confirmed that impression with victory in the Rosebery first time out, handling the soft ground well. He followed up with an equally game victory in a Newmarket rated stakes, but disappointed badly when last at Epsom and was not seen again. If he can put his problems behind him, he can win more handicaps in 1999. **P W Harris [5-11] The Confederates.*

AMEZOLA BHB 83f **RR 74f** 5009[1]
2 gr c Northern Park (USA) 10f **(57)** - Yamamah (Siberian Express (USA)) 8.8f **(65)**
Form - 81
Record 1998 - 1st:1 2nd:0 3rd:0 Ran:2
Win Prizemoney £2,479 *Total Prizemoney* £2,479
Wins * **1998** Oct Bath (HVY) 8f 74 <
1998 Turf 1-2: (7f, 8f 1-1) (sft 1-1, gd)
Currently above-average colt. Turf high 74 (began Jly) - 1st of 10 from Tiger Talk (27 Oct Bath RF 5009).
**Mrs A J Perrett [1-2] Bernard Keay.*

AMIARGE BHB 35f38a **RR 41df 38a** 4448[10]
8 b g Reference Point 12f **(66)** - Scotia Rose (Tap On Wood) 10.3f **(65)**
Form - 70000
Record 1998 - 1st:0 2nd:0 3rd:0 Ran:5
Pre1998 - 1st:4 2nd:4 3rd:4 Ran:49
Win Prizemoney £12,852 *Total Prizemoney* £20,645
Wins * 1997 Aug Ripon (G-F) H 16f 44 50
* 1997 Jun Doncas (G-S) H 14.6f 45 52 <
* 1996 Oct Nottin (GD) H 17.9f 44 49
* 1995 Aug Nottin (G-F) H 16f 31 37
1998 Turf 0-5: (16f 5) (g-s, gd 2, g-f, frm)
Moderate gelding, effective 15 to 16f, best at 16f, acts on g-s to frm, has worn blinkers (extremely effectively). Turf high 41. Becoming disappointing. **M Brittain [4-54] Miss Debi Woods.*

AMICO BHB 68a **RR 64f** 5061[8]
4 b g Efisio 7.7f **(69)** - Stormswept (USA) (Storm Bird (CAN)) 10.3f **(74)**
Form - 722200412206228

Record	**1998** -	1st:1	2nd:7	3rd:0	Ran:15
	Pre1998 -	1st:1	2nd:2	3rd:1	Ran:7

Win Prizemoney £4,758 *Total Prizemoney* £15,843

Wins	* **1998**	*Jly*	*Lingfi*	*(STD)*	*8f*	*67+*	<
	* 1997	*Feb*	*Lingfi*	*(STD)*	*8f*	*60*	

1998 Turf 0-8: (8f 3, 9f 2, 10f 3) (sft, g-s 2, gd 2, frm 3) 1998 AW 1-7: (8f 1-4, 9f 3) (Equi 1-3, Fibr 4)
Leggy, above-average gelding, effective 8 to 10f, acts on g-s - acts on AW, best on Equi, prefers left handed tracks, prefers tight tracks. Turf high 64 - 2nd of 16 giving 7lb to Slip Venture (21 Oct Nottingham 10f g-s RF 4927). AW high 73 - 2nd of 13 to Primary Colours (22 Aug Wolverhampton 9f Fibr RF 3826) - also 1st of 9 giving 8lb to Special Person (25 Jly Lingfield RF 3112). A fairly useful sort on sand, he won twice on Equitrack so far last season but is probably just as good on Fibresand. He has also finished runner-up more often than is ideal in the last couple of seasons, though in some cases he may have been just a little unfortunate.
**C W Thornton [2-22] Guy Reed.*

AMID THE STARS BHB 49f **RR 47f** 1480[16]
4 b f Midyan (USA) 9.9f **(64)** - Celebrity (Troy) 10.4f **(68)**
Form - 00

Record	**1998** -	1st:0	2nd:0	3rd:0	Ran:2
	Pre1998 -	1st:0	2nd:0	3rd:1	Ran:4

Win Prizemoney £0 *Total Prizemoney* £779
1998 Turf 0-2: (8f, 9f) (gd, g-f)
Leggy, moderate filly. Turf high 12.
**D W Barker [0-2] P Asquith (from M Johnston [0-2] Aug 1997).*

AMINGTON GIRL BHB 42f **RR 48f** 4350[7]
3 b f Tragic Role (USA) 9.4f **(63)** - Millfields House (Record Token) 6.3f **(53)**
Form - 02633214007

Record	**1998** -	1st:1	2nd:2	3rd:2	Ran:11
	Pre1998 -	1st:0	2nd:0	3rd:1	Ran:5

Win Prizemoney £2,637 *Total Prizemoney* £5,776

Wins	* **1998**	Jly	Nottin	(G-F)	C	8.2f	45	<

1998 Turf 1-10: (6f 2, 7f, 8f 1-6, 9f) (sft, g-s, gd 1-3, g-f 2, frm 3) 1998 AW 0-1: (6f) (Fibr)
Leggy, moderate filly, effective 6 to 8f, best at 8f, acts on gd to g-f - acts on Fibr, best on g-f, often wears blinkers (extremely effectively), prefers left handed tracks, prefers tight tracks. Turf high 48 - also 1st of 12 getting 13lb from Comeoutofthefog (18 Jly Nottingham RF 2926). (1st run) - 2nd of 11 giving 5lb to Tom Tun (9 Jly Southwell 6f Fibr RF 2656). She took her time getting off the mark, but managed it at Nottingham in July. She seemed to be suited by the mile there. **P D Evans [1-16] M J Higgins.*

AMISTAD RR 72f 2822[9]
2 ch c Mystiko (USA) 7.7f **(59)** - Ackcontent (USA) (Key To Content (USA)) 8f **(54)**
Form - 30

Record	**1998** -	1st:0	2nd:0	3rd:1	Ran:2

Win Prizemoney £0 *Total Prizemoney* £310
1998 Turf 0-2: (7f 2) (gd, frm)
Currently above-average colt. Turf high 72.
**C A Dwyer [0-2] Dr A Haloute.*

AMONG MEN (USA) BHB 120f **RR 123f** 5165a[11]
4 b c Zilzal (USA) 8.5f **(79)** - Questionablevirtue (USA) (Key To The Mint (USA)) 9.4f **(75)**
Form - 6211250

Record	**1998** -	1st:2	2nd:2	3rd:0	Ran:7
	Pre1998 -	1st:4	2nd:0	3rd:0	Ran:5

Win Prizemoney £198,534 *Total Prizemoney* £271,907

Wins	* **1998**	Jly	Goodwo	(GD)	G1	8f	123	<
	* **1998**	Jly	Yarmou	(GD)		7f	116	
	* 1997	Aug	Goodwo	(G-F)	G2	8f	115	
	* 1997	Jun	Ascot	(G-F)	G3	7f	112	
	* 1997	May	Kempto	(GD)	L	8f	100	
	* 1997	May	Newmar	(GD)		8f	87+	

1998 Turf 2-7: (7f 1-1, 8f 1-6) (gd 1-4, frm 2, hrd 1-1)
Very high-class colt, effective 7 to 8f, best at 8f, acts on gd to hrd, best on gd, prefers right handed tracks, excels at Goodwood. Turf high 123 - 1st of 10 from Almushtarak (29 Jly Goodwood RF 3205) - also 1st of 4 giving 5lb to Igreja (2 Jly Yarmouth RF 2475). Consistent. Unraced at two, he had a successful first season, but was disappointing on his reappearance in 1998. He has run in most of the top European mile races, and has usually been there or thereabouts, but his victory in a below-average quality field Sussex Stakes and a small race at Yarmouth have been his only victories. He looked to have had enough for the season when running moderately in the QE II, but he went to America for the Breeders' Cup Mile, and seemed to run much too freely in the early stages. **Sir Michael Stoute [6-12] M Tabor.*

AMOROSO (IRE) BHB 61f **RR 64f** 4925[6]
3 ch f Sharpo 7.5f **(68)** - Magical Spirit (Top Ville) 11.7f **(68)**
Form - 6668135026

Record	**1998** -	1st:1	2nd:1	3rd:1	Ran:10

Win Prizemoney £2,302 *Total Prizemoney* £3,637

Wins	* **1998**	Aug	Mussel	(G-F)	9f	55	<

1998 Turf 1-10: (6f 2, 7f 2, 8f 2, 9f 1-2, 10f 2) (g-s, gd 1-5, g-f 3, frm)
Leggy, average filly, effective 9 to 10f, best at 9f, acts on gd to g-f, best on gd, prefers tight tracks. Turf high 64 - 3rd of 18 to Elba Magic (31 Aug Ripon 10f gd RF 4001) - also 1st of 8 from Bolshoi Star (19 Aug Musselburgh RF 3750). Consistent. She got off the mark in a modest maiden over nine furlongs at Musselburgh in August. Not the easiest of rides. **C W Thornton [1-10] Guy Reed.*

AMRAVATI (IRE) RR 64f 4442a[14]
3 ch f Project Manager 7.2f **(47)**-Smaoineamh(Tap On Wood) 10.3f **(65)**
Form - 3700000
1998 Turf 0-7: (6f, 7f 2, 8f 3, 12f) (hvy, sft, gd 4, hrd)
Average filly, effective 7f, acts on g-s, has worn blinkers. Turf high 96. Becoming disappointing. Twice a winner at two, but she has been found out when tried in Pattern company.
**J S Bolger in IRE [2-11] D H W Dobson.*

AMRON BHB 49f **RR 48f** 5120[8]
11 b g Bold Owl 9.7f **(47)** - Sweet Minuet (Setay) 5.7f **(103)**
Form - 00848833718

Record	**1998** -	1st:1	2nd:0	3rd:2	Ran:11
	Pre1998 -	1st:12	2nd:8	3rd:5	Ran:93

Win Prizemoney £68,168 *Total Prizemoney* £86,039

Wins	* **1998**	Oct	Redcar	(SFT)	H	8f	45	48
	* 1997	Mar	Newcas	(GD)	H	5f	57	63
	* 1994	Mar	Doncas	(GD)		6f		98 <

1998 Turf 1-11: (5f, 6f 4, 7f 3, 8f 1-3) (sft, gd 1-7, g-f 3)
Moderate gelding, effective 5 to 6f, best at 6f, acts on gd. Turf high 48. A grand veteran, he wins very occasionally these days.
**J Berry [13-104] Roy Peebles.*

AMSARA (IRE) RR 54f 4389[11]
2 b f Taufan (USA) 8.3f **(65)** - Legend of Spain (USA) (Alleged (USA)) 10f **(76)**
Form - 70

Record	**1998** -	1st:0	2nd:0	3rd:0	Ran:2

1998 Turf 0-2: (7f, 8f) (gd, frm)
Currently fair filly. Turf high 54 (began Aug).
**M R Channon [0-2] Mrs A M Jones.*

AMUSING TIME (IRE) RR 99f 3051a[3]
-7521 b f Sadler's Wells (USA) 11.3f **(87)** - Ozone Friendly (USA) (Green Forest (USA)) 9.9f **(68)**
Form - 3
1998 Turf 0-1: (13f) (g-f)
Currently very useful filly. (1st run) - 3rd of 7 to Isle De France (14 Jly Deauville 13f g-f RF 3051a).
**Mme C Head in FR [0-1] Maktoum Al Maktoum.*

AMYAS (IRE) BHB 104f **RR 105f** 550a[6]
4 b c Waajib 8.9f **(67)** - Art Duo (Artaius (USA)) 9f **(69)**
Form - 6
1998 Turf 0-1: (12f) (g-f)
Scopey, Pattern-class colt, effective 10f, acts on gd to g-f. He could not hold a light to Group horses when transferred to Dubai.
**S bin Suroor in UAE [0-1] Godolphin (from B W Hills [4-11] Aug 1997).*

AMY LEIGH (IRE) BHB 34f37a **RR 40f 37a** 111[7]
5 b m Imperial Frontier (USA) 7f **(65)** -Hollyberry (IRE) (Runnett) 7f **(59)**
Form - 8007

Record 1998 - 1st:0 2nd:0 3rd:0 Ran:1
Pre1998 - 1st:3 2nd:3 3rd:2 Ran:32
Win Prizemoney £8,178 *Total Prizemoney* £12,235
Wins * 1997 *Mar Wolver (STD) SH 6f 51 50*
* 1997 *Jan Wolver (SLW) C 5f 41*
* 1995 *May Southw (STD) 5f 70+* <
1998 AW 0-1: (8f) (Fibr)
Moderate filly, effective 5 to 6f, - acts on Fibr, often wears blinkers (effectively), likes left handed tracks, likes tight tracks. She won a couple of small races on the sand at Wolverhampton early in '97, and if she is going to win again it is likely to be at Dunstall Park.
**Capt J Wilson [3-33] J P Hacking.*

ANAK-KU BHB 81f79a RR 76f 79a 5043[5]

5 ch g Efisio 7.7f **(69)** - City Link Lass (Double Jump) 9.4f **(58)**
Form - 100365
Record 1998 - 1st:1 2nd:0 3rd:1 Ran:6
Pre1998 - 1st:5 2nd:6 3rd:2 Ran:18
Win Prizemoney £22,277 *Total Prizemoney* £29,913
Wins * **1998** Jun Salisb (G-S) 9.9f 86 <
* 1997 Jly Windso (G-F) H 10f 75 79
* 1997 Jun Ripon (GD) 10f 75
* 1997 Jun Chepst (G-F) H 10.2f 65 72
* 1997 *Apr Lingfi (STD) H 10f 69 74*
* 1996 Jly Mussel (G-S) 8.1f 68
1998 Turf 1-6: (10f 1-6) (sft, gd 1-3, frm 2)
Above-average gelding, effective 10f, acts on gd to frm, best on frm, has worn blinkers, favours tight tracks, excels at Chepstow. Turf high 86 (1st run) - 1st of 7 giving 13lb to Indian Missile (9 Jun Salisbury RF 1834).
**Miss Gay Kelleway [6-24] H R H Sultan Ahmad Shah.*

ANCHOR VENTURE BHB 29f50a RR 33f 50a 4408[8]

5 b g Slip Anchor 12.7f **(75)** - Ski Michaela (USA) (Devil's Bag (USA)) 12.4f **(78)**
Form - 2077608078
Record 1998 - 1st:0 2nd:1 3rd:0 Ran:10
Pre1998 - 1st:1 2nd:0 3rd:4 Ran:14
Win Prizemoney £2,406 *Total Prizemoney* £5,197
Wins 1997 Jun Pontef (G-F) S 10f 45 <
1998 Turf 0-8: (8f 3, 10f 4, 12f) (sft, g-f 3, frm 4) 1998 AW 0-2: (8f 2) (Equi, Fibr)
Average gelding, effective 8f, - acts on Equi, likes left handed tracks, favours tight tracks. Turf high 44. AW high 62 (1st run) - 2nd of 12 giving 3lb to Roman Reel (19 Mar Lingfield 8f Equi RF 0441).
**D W Chapman [0-5] David Chapman (from S P C Woods [1-19] May 1998).*

ANDALISH BHB 75f RR 73f 4893[8]

3 b f Polish Precedent (USA) 9f **(73)** - Risanda (Kris) 9.5f **(73)**
Form - 522318
Record 1998 - 1st:1 2nd:2 3rd:1 Ran:6
Pre1998 - 1st:0 2nd:0 3rd:0 Ran:1
Win Prizemoney £3,517 *Total Prizemoney* £6,550
Wins * **1998** Spt Haydoc (G-F) 10.5f 73 <
1998 Turf 1-6: (10f 3, 11f 1-2, 12f) (gd, g-f 4, frm 1-1)
Scopey, above-average filly, effective 10 to 12f, acts on gd to frm, prefers tight tracks. Turf high 73 - 1st of 7 from Raqqasa (25 Spt Haydock RF 4478). **B W Hills [1-7] K Abdulla.*

ANDAMAN BHB 65f65a RR 72f 65a 4987[9]

4 b g Riverman (USA) 9.7f **(78)**-Balleta (USA) (Lyphard (USA)) 9.9f **(72)**
Form - 6422028600
Record 1998 - 1st:0 2nd:3 3rd:0 Ran:10
Win Prizemoney £0 *Total Prizemoney* £3,491
1998 Turf 0-7: (10f, 12f 3, 13f 3) (sft 2, g-s, gd 2, g-f, frm) 1998 AW 0-3: (9f, 10f, 12f) (Equi, Fibr 2)
Above-average gelding, effective 12 to 13f, best at 13f, acts on g-s to gd - acts on Fibr, prefers left handed tracks. Turf high 75 (1st run) - 2nd of 8 getting 4lb from Montecristo (28 Mar Warwick 13f g-s RF 0489). AW high 70 - 2nd of 6 to Russian Ruler (9 Mar Southwell 12f Fibr RF 0411). Becoming disappointing.
**D J G MurraySmith [0-10] Mrs Susan Nash.*

ANDITZ (IRE) BHB 38f RR 37f 5017[11]

3 b f Soviet Lad (USA) 9.4f **(63)** - Miss Fortunate (IRE) (Taufan (USA)) 7f **(57)**
Form - 00300
Record 1998 - 1st:0 2nd:0 3rd:1 Ran:5
Pre1998 - 1st:0 2nd:0 3rd:0 Ran:4
Win Prizemoney £0 *Total Prizemoney* £365
1998 Turf 0-5: (5f, 8f 3, 10f) (gd 2, g-f, frm 2)
Unfurnished, very moderate filly. Turf high 37.
**J L Eyre [0-9] Peter Watson.*

ANDREYEV (IRE) BHB 116f RR 119f 4947a[6]

4 ch c Presidium 7.5f **(56)** - Missish (Mummy's Pet) 7.7f **(60)**
Form - 1031341466
Record 1998 - 1st:3 2nd:0 3rd:2 Ran:10
Pre1998 - 1st:4 2nd:0 3rd:0 Ran:11
Win Prizemoney £65,780 *Total Prizemoney* £91,225
Wins * **1998** Aug Deauvi (GD) G3 6f 119 <
* **1998** Jun Newcas (SFT) L 6f 117
* **1998** Apr Kempto (SFT) 6f 107+
* 1997 May Newmar (GD) L 7f 100
* 1996 Oct Ascot (GD) 7f 102+
* 1996 Aug Cheste (G-S) 6.1f 104+
* 1996 Jun Windso (G-F) 5f 88
1998 Turf 3-10: (6f 3-8, 7f 2) (hvy, sft 2-2, g-s, gd 1-3, g-f, frm 2)
Workmanlike, high-class colt, effective 6f, acts on sft to gd. Turf high 119 - 1st of 9 from My Best Valentine (30 Aug Deauville RF 4081a) - also 1st of 8 getting 2lb from Cretan Gift (27 Jun Newcastle RF 2347). Consistent. A useful performer on his day, he just misses out on the highest class but still managed three victories last term, including a wide-margin victory in a Listed event at Newcastle. He seems ideally suited by a soft surface, though his win in the Prix de Meautry at Deauville came on faster ground.
**R Hannon [7-21] J Palmer-Brown.*

ANDY COIN BHB 20f RR 15f 3750[7]

7 ch m Andy Rew 6.7f **(41)** - Legal Coin (Official)
Form - 07
Record 1998 - 1st:0 2nd:0 3rd:0 Ran:2
Pre1998 - 1st:0 2nd:0 3rd:0 Ran:3
1998 Turf 0-2: (9f, 12f) (gd, g-f)
Poor mare. Turf high 15 (began Aug).
**W M Brisbourne [0-7] Bob Moseley.*

ANEMOS (IRE) BHB 75f RR 78f 4770[3]

3 ch c Be My Guest (USA) 10.2f **(66)** - Frendly Persuasion (General Assembly (USA)) 10f **(68)**
Form - 33723
Record 1998 - 1st:0 2nd:1 3rd:3 Ran:5
Pre1998 - 1st:0 2nd:0 3rd:1 Ran:2
Win Prizemoney £0 *Total Prizemoney* £3,108
1998 Turf 0-5: (8f 2, 10f 3) (sft 2, g-f 2, frm)
Scopey, above-average colt. Turf high 78. Lightly-raced, he has shown enough in maidens to suggest he can win races at around a mile.
**M A Jarvis [0-6] Andreas Michael (from M H Tompkins [0-1] Spt 1997).*

ANETTA BHB 42f RR 27f 2258[13]

4 ch f Aragon 7.7f **(58)** - Pronetta (USA) (Mr Prospector (USA)) 8.8f **(78)**
Form - 000500
Record 1998 - 1st:0 2nd:0 3rd:0 Ran:6
Pre1998 - 1st:1 2nd:0 3rd:1 Ran:10
Win Prizemoney £4,046 *Total Prizemoney* £4,418
Wins 1997 Jly Nottin (G-F) H 8.2f 51 52 <
1998 Turf 0-5: (5f, 6f 2, 7f 2) (gd 2, frm 3) 1998 AW 0-1: (8f) (Fibr)
Scopey, little account filly, effective 8f, acts on gd, has worn blinkers, likes left handed tracks, likes tight tracks. Turf high 27.
**John Harris [0-6] David Pettifor (from Miss S E Hall [1-10] Nov 1997).*

AN EXECUTIVE DO BHB 68f RR 65f 3252[1]

2 ch g Executive Man 8.9f **(52)** - Annacando (Derrylin) 8.8f **(54)**
Form - 41
Record 1998 - 1st:1 2nd:0 3rd:0 Ran:2
Win Prizemoney £2,740 *Total Prizemoney* £2,740
Wins * **1998** Jly Thirsk (GD) C 7f 65 <
1998 Turf 1-2: (5f, 7f 1-1) (g-f 1-2)
Currently average gelding. Turf high 65 - 1st of 14 giving 7lb to Miss Cody (31 Jly Thirsk RF 3252). **P C Haslam [1-2] Terry Rowley.*

ANGE D'HONOR (FR) RR 75f 4394[2]
3 b g Hero's Honor (USA) 9.2f **(76)** - Surfing Angel (FR) (Monseigneur (USA)) 7.7f **(63)**
Form - 2
Record 1998 - 1st:0 2nd:1 3rd:0 Ran:1
Win Prizemoney £0 *Total Prizemoney* £1,080
1998 Turf 0-1: (12f) (frm)
Workmanlike, currently above-average gelding. (1st run) - 2nd of 14 giving 5lb to Lear's Crown (21 Spt Kempton 12f frm RF 4394).
**S E H Sherwood [0-1] Uplands Bloodstock.*

ANGEL BORNE (USA) RR 83f 4309[5]
2 b f Exbourne (USA) - Secret Angel (Halo (USA)) 10.6f **(75)**
Form - 5
Record 1998 - 1st:0 2nd:0 3rd:0 Ran:1
1998 Turf 0-1: (8f) (g-f)
Currently decent filly. **B W Hills [0-1] K Abdulla.*

ANGEL EYES BHB 60f **RR 63f** 2557[9]
3 b f Batshoof 9.5f **(66)** - Fair and Wise (High Line) 10.3f **(70)**
Form - 050
Record 1998 - 1st:0 2nd:0 3rd:0 Ran:3
1998 Turf 0-3: (9f, 10f 2) (gd, g-f 2)
Scopey, currently average filly. Turf high 63.
**W R Muir [0-3] A J de V Patrick.*

ANGEL HEART (FR) RR 108f 4077a[2]
3 c Hero's Honor (USA) 9.2f **(76)**
Form - 732
1998 Turf 0-3: (8f 2, 10f) (sft, gd 2)
Currently Pattern-class colt. Turf high 108 - 3rd of 14 getting 13lb from Power Flame (2 Aug Cologne 8f sft RF 3419a).
**P Lautner in GER [0-3].*

ANGEL HILL BHB 73f **RR 75f** 3506[9]
3 ch f King's Signet (USA) 7f **(51)** - Tawny (Grey Ghost) 9.9f **(60)**
Form - 36270
Record 1998 - 1st:0 2nd:1 3rd:1 Ran:5
Pre1998 - 1st:1 2nd:1 3rd:2 Ran:8
Win Prizemoney £2,599 *Total Prizemoney* £9,858
Wins 1997 May Newcas (GD) 5f 63+ <
1998 Turf 0-5: (5f 2, 6f 3) (gd, g-f, frm 3)
Scopey, above-average filly, effective 5 to 6f, best at 5f, acts on g-f to frm, best on g-f. Turf high 75 - 2nd of 11 getting 2lb from Positive Air (29 Jun Pontefract 6f frm RF 2377).
**R A Fahey [0-5] K T D W Partnership (from T D Barron [1-8] Oct 1997).*

ANGELINA BHB 70a **RR 75f** 3376[14]
3 b f Most Welcome 8.6f **(66)** - Mystic Crystal (IRE) (Caerleon (USA)) 8.6f **(71)**
Form - 32335650
Record 1998 - 1st:0 2nd:1 3rd:3 Ran:8
Pre1998 - 1st:0 2nd:0 3rd:1 Ran:2
Win Prizemoney £0 *Total Prizemoney* £2,481
1998 Turf 0-6: (7f, 8f 2, 9f, 10f, 11f) (gd, g-f 2, frm 2, hrd) 1998 AW 0-2: (8f 2) (Fibr 2)
Scopey, above-average filly, effective 8 to 10f, acts on frm to hrd, prefers tight tracks. Turf high 77 - 3rd of 6 getting 3lb from Flow By (19 May Beverley 10f frm RF 1318). AW high 57.
**Mrs A E Johnson [0-7] A Foustok (from P Howling [0-3] Apr 1998).*

ANGELIQUE BHB 50f **RR 51df** 4302[18]
3 ch f Soviet Star (USA) 8.6f **(74)** - Lady Habitat (Habitat) 9.4f **(70)**
Form - 00
Record 1998 - 1st:0 2nd:0 3rd:0 Ran:2
Pre1998 - 1st:0 2nd:0 3rd:0 Ran:3
Win Prizemoney £0 *Total Prizemoney* £149
1998 Turf 0-2: (5f, 8f) (frm 2)
Workmanlike, fair filly. Turf high 12 (began Aug).
**D W Barker [0-2] Tom Carrick (from M J Haynes [0-3] Jun 1997).*

ANGELS VENTURE RR 84f 4823[4]
2 ch c Unfuwain (USA) 11.4f **(74)** - City of Angels (Woodman (USA)) 9f **(74)**
Form - 4
Record 1998 - 1st:0 2nd:0 3rd:0 Ran:1
Win Prizemoney £0 *Total Prizemoney* £504
1998 Turf 0-1: (8f) (frm)
Currently decent colt. **S P C Woods [0-1] Dr Frank Chao.*

ANGIE BABY BHB 89f **RR 87f** 3893[1]
2 b f Puissance 7.1f **(60)** - Hyde Princess (Touch Paper) 6.8f **(57)**
Form - 2114161
Record 1998 - 1st:4 2nd:1 3rd:0 Ran:7
Win Prizemoney £13,307 *Total Prizemoney* £14,263
Wins * **1998** Aug Lingfi (FRM) 5f 87 <
* **1998** Jly Hamilt (FRM) 5f 86+
* **1998** May Nottin (G-F) 5.1f 87 <
* **1998** Apr Redcar (SFT) 5f 60
1998 Turf 4-7: (5f 4-7) (sft 1-1, gd, g-f 1-3, frm 2-2)
Useful filly, effective 5f, acts on g-f to frm, best on frm. Turf high 87 - 1st of 6 from Almost Amber (26 Aug Lingfield RF 3893) - also 1st of 9 giving 6lb to Hasty Words (8 May Nottingham RF 1110).
**J Berry [4-7] The Cooper Group.*

ANGIE MARINIE RR 58f 4370[6]
2 b f Sabrehill (USA) 8.5f **(64)** - Lambast (Relkino) 8.9f **(65)**
Form - 6
Record 1998 - 1st:0 2nd:0 3rd:0 Ran:1
1998 Turf 0-1: (6f) (frm)
Currently fair filly. **R A Fahey [0-1] R A Fahey.*

ANGIE MINOR BHB 32f30a **RR 44f 30a** 4922[6]
3 b f Mazilier (USA) 8.5f **(56)**-Angelica Park(Simply Great(FR)) 8.2f **(65)**
Form - 0005700743686
Record 1998 - 1st:0 2nd:0 3rd:1 Ran:12
Pre1998 - 1st:0 2nd:0 3rd:0 Ran:4
Win Prizemoney £0 *Total Prizemoney* £318
1998 Turf 0-8: (8f 2, 10f 3, 11f, 14f 2) (g-s 2, gd 2, g-f, frm 3) 1998 AW 0-4: (7f, 8f 2, 11f) (Fibr 4)
Moderate filly, effective 8 to 10f, acts on frm - acts on Fibr, often wears blinkers (very effectively), likes tight tracks. Turf high 44 - 3rd of 10 getting 7lb from Tie Break (19 Aug Leicester 10f frm RF 3744). AW high 35 - 5th of 12 getting 25lb from Sharp Monkey (2 Feb Southwell 8f Fibr RF 0206). Inconsistent.
**J Wharton [0-16] Parkers of Peterborough Plc.*

ANGSTROM (IRE) BHB 86f **RR 81f** 2367[4]
3 b g Alzao (USA) 9.8f **(73)** - Anna Petrovna (FR) (Wassl) 9.7f **(62)**
Form - 3364
Record 1998 - 1st:0 2nd:0 3rd:2 Ran:4
Pre1998 - 1st:1 2nd:1 3rd:0 Ran:3
Win Prizemoney £3,614 *Total Prizemoney* £8,333
Wins * 1997 Oct Bright (G-F) 8f 84+ <
1998 Turf 0-4: (10f 2, 12f, 14f) (g-s, gd 3)
Scopey, decent gelding, effective 8f, acts on gd to g-f. Turf high 89. He managed to win a Brighton maiden in 1997, but also hung quite badly in his final start of the year. His efforts last season have shown him to be horribly one-paced, even when tried over fourteen furlongs, so further opportunities for him are going to be very difficult to find. **Sir Michael Stoute [1-7] Sheikh Mohammed.*

ANGUS-G BHB 95f **RR 93+f** 487[7]
6 br g Chief Singer 8.6f **(62)** - Horton Line (High Line) 10.3f **(70)**
Form - 7
Record 1998 - 1st:0 2nd:0 3rd:0 Ran:1
Pre1998 - 1st:4 2nd:2 3rd:3 Ran:13
Win Prizemoney £24,544 *Total Prizemoney* £45,535
Wins * 1997 May York (GD) H 11.9f 88 93 <
* 1997 Apr Newmar (GD) H 12f 82 87
* 1996 Aug Newmar (G-F) H 10f 73 78
* 1996 Jly Newmar (G-F) H 10f 71 74
1998 Turf 0-1: (12f) (gd)
Useful gelding. He gained fluent wins at Newmarket and York in 1997, but was not seen again until running at the Lincoln meeting in 1998. His problems must have recurred as that was all we saw of him. **Mrs M Reveley [4-14] W Ginzel.*

ANGUS THE BOLD RR 62f 476[2]
2 b g Puissance 7.1f **(60)** - Floral Spark **(61f 72a)** (Forzando) 7.6f **(59)**
Form - 2
Record 1998 - 1st:0 2nd:1 3rd:0 Ran:1
Win Prizemoney £0 *Total Prizemoney* £642

1998 Turf 0-1: (5f) (gd)
Currently average gelding. (1st run) - 2nd of 11 giving 5lb to Inya Lake (27 Mar Doncaster 5f gd RF 0476). Left Jack Berry's care after finishing runner-up in an early-season seller.
**J Berry [0-1] Chris & Antonia Deuters.*

ANITA AT DAWN (IRE) BHB 66f71a **RR 65f 71a** 4635[5]
3 br f Anita's Prince 6f **(62)** - Dawn is Breaking (Import) 6.6f **(68)**
Form - 00415
Record 1998 - 1st:1 2nd:0 3rd:0 Ran:5
Pre1998 - 1st:1 2nd:1 3rd:1 Ran:5
Win Prizemoney £7,067 *Total Prizemoney* £9,512
Wins * **1998** *Spt Southw (STD) H 7f 64 53*
* 1997 Jun Nottin (SFT) 6.1f 72 <
1998 Turf 0-2: (6f, 7f) (sft, frm) 1998 AW 1-3: (6f, 7f 1-2) (Fibr 1-3)
Light-framed, above-average filly, effective 6 to 7f, best at 6f, acts on sft to gd - acts on Fibr. Turf high 51. AW high 71 (began Spt) - 5th of 13 giving 6lb to Rum Lad (3 Oct Wolverhampton 6f Fibr RF 4635). **B Palling [2-10] D Brennan.*

ANITA MARIE (IRE) RR 35f 423[9]
3 b f Anita's Prince 6f **(62)**-Fandangerina(USA)(Grey Dawn II)11.1f **(72)**
Form - 0
Record 1998 - 1st:0 2nd:0 3rd:0 Ran:1
Pre1998 - 1st:0 2nd:0 3rd:0 Ran:1
1998 AW 0-1: (6f) (Fibr)
Tall, currently very moderate filly.
**M Johnston [0-2] Greenland Park Ltd.*

ANJOU BHB 50f60a **RR 55f 60a** 1430[12]
6 b g Saumarez 15.1f **(87)** - Bourbon Topsy (Ile de Bourbon (USA)) 10.1f **(67)**
Form - 23050
Record 1998 - 1st:0 2nd:0 3rd:0 Ran:3
Pre1998 - 1st:3 2nd:2 3rd:2 Ran:15
Win Prizemoney £7,588 *Total Prizemoney* £10,193
Wins * 1997 Oct Yarmou (GD) SH 11.5f 56 61
* 1995 *Dec Lingfi (STD) H 16f 60 69* <
* 1995 Oct Catter (G-F) 12f 69 <
1998 Turf 0-2: (12f 2) (sft, gd) 1998 AW 0-1: (16f) (Equi)
Fair gelding, effective 11 to 16f, acts on frm - acts on Equi. Turf high 51. **J Pearce [3-16] G H Tufts (from G Wragg [0-2] Feb 1995).*

ANKA LADY BHB 37f **RR 45f** 4409[17]
3 b f Precocious 7.2f **(54)** - Hicklam Millie (Absalom) 7.2f **(58)**
Form - 0
Record 1998 - 1st:0 2nd:0 3rd:0 Ran:1
Pre1998 - 1st:0 2nd:0 3rd:1 Ran:6
Win Prizemoney £0 *Total Prizemoney* £571
1998 Turf 0-1: (10f) (g-f)
Leggy, moderate filly.
**J J O'Neill [0-1] Fred Coulson (from D Moffatt [0-6] Nov 1997).*

ANLACE BHB 50f37a **RR 54f 37a** 31[10]
9 b m Sure Blade (USA) 10.6f **(66)** - Ascot Strike (USA) (Mr Prospector (USA)) 8.8f **(78)**
Form - 80
Record 1998 - 1st:0 2nd:0 3rd:0 Ran:1
Pre1998 - 1st:3 2nd:2 3rd:3 Ran:25
Win Prizemoney £8,267 *Total Prizemoney* £11,560
Wins * 1995 Jun Goodwo (G-F) H 9f 48 54
* 1994 Jun Chepst (FRM) H 8.1f 54 54
1998 AW 0-1: (13f) (Equi)
Fair mare, has worn blinkers.
**S Mellor [4-47] The Felix Bowness Partnership (from L M Cumani [1-4] Oct 1992).*

ANNA BHB 104f **RR 103?f** 1749[3]
3 b f Ela-Mana-Mou 12.7f **(72)** - Anna Rella (IRE) (Danehill (USA)) 10f **(72)**
Form - 3433
Record 1998 - 1st:0 2nd:0 3rd:3 Ran:4
Pre1998 - 1st:0 2nd:0 3rd:1 Ran:1
Win Prizemoney £0 *Total Prizemoney* £10,167
1998 Turf 0-4: (9f, 10f 3) (gd 4)
Scopey, very useful filly. Turf high 103 - 3rd of 4 to Bahr (12 May York 10f gd RF 1166). Placed behind Greek Dance, Midnight Line and Bahr, this filly should have won a race by now. It does not always pay to tilt at windmills and she would surely benefit from a drop in class before tackling Group company again. She looks to need ten furlongs. **C E Brittain [0-5] C E Brittain.*

ANNANDALE (IRE) BHB 55f **RR 55f** 4243[14]
2 ch f Balla Cove - Gruinard Bay (Doyoun) 9f **(69)**
Form - 6360
Record 1998 - 1st:0 2nd:0 3rd:1 Ran:4
Win Prizemoney £0 *Total Prizemoney* £402
1998 Turf 0-4: (5f 3, 6f) (gd 2, g-f, frm)
Fair filly. Turf high 55. **R A Fahey [0-4] C H McGhie.*

ANNAPURNA (IRE) RR 89f 4853[12]
2 b f Brief Truce (USA) 9.1f **(73)** - National Ballet (Shareef Dancer (USA)) 9.9f **(73)**
Form - 0210
Record 1998 - 1st:1 2nd:1 3rd:0 Ran:4
Win Prizemoney £4,413 *Total Prizemoney* £5,993
Wins * **1998** Spt Kempto (SFT) 7f 89 <
1998 Turf 1-4: (7f 1-4) (gd 1-2, g-f, frm)
Useful filly. Turf high 89 (began Aug) - 1st of 6 from Gracious Plenty (9 Spt Kempton RF 4191).
**B J Meehan [1-4] Thurloe Thoroughbreds.*

ANNELIINA BHB 83f **RR 79f** 4542[17]
2 b f Cadeaux Genereux 7.9f **(76)** - Blasted Heath (Thatching) 8f **(66)**
Form - 8450
Record 1998 - 1st:0 2nd:0 3rd:0 Ran:4
Win Prizemoney £0 *Total Prizemoney* £526
1998 Turf 0-4: (6f, 7f 3) (gd, frm 3)
Above-average filly. Turf high 79 (began Aug).
**C N Allen [0-4] Mrs K A Hyytiainen.*

ANNE THEATRE RR 34f 5138[13]
2 b f Saddlers' Hall (IRE) 10.5f **(65)**-Ballad Island (Ballad Rock)7.8f **(63)**
Form - 0
Record 1998 - 1st:0 2nd:0 3rd:0 Ran:1
1998 Turf 0-1: (7f) (gd)
Currently very moderate filly.
**T J Naughton [0-1] The Awayday Partnership.*

ANNIE APPLE (IRE) BHB 59f **RR 60f** 3897[1]
2 ch f Petardia 8.2f **(58)** - Art Duo (Artaius (USA)) 9f **(69)**
Form - 8751
Record 1998 - 1st:1 2nd:0 3rd:0 Ran:4
Win Prizemoney £1,725 *Total Prizemoney* £1,725
Wins * **1998** Aug Folkes (G-F) S 7f 60 <
1998 Turf 1-4: (6f 2, 7f 1-2) (gd 1-1, g-f, frm 2)
Average filly. Turf high 60 - 1st of 16 from Dream On Me (27 Aug Folkestone RF 3897). **R Hannon [1-4] David Allen.*

ANNIEMITCHELLSLASS BHB 27f **RR 25f** 4922[8]
3 b f Noble Patriarch 12.2f **(43)** - Fair Janet (Feelings (FR))
Form - 4058
Record 1998 - 1st:0 2nd:0 3rd:0 Ran:4
Pre1998 - 1st:0 2nd:1 3rd:0 Ran:3
Win Prizemoney £0 *Total Prizemoney* £852
1998 Turf 0-4: (10f, 12f, 14f 2) (g-s, gd, g-f, frm)
Light-framed, little account filly, has worn blinkers. Turf high 25 (began Aug). **D Moffatt [0-8] Die-Hard Racing Club.*

ANNIVERSARY DAY BHB 74f **RR 69f** 5093[8]
2 ch g Lion Cavern (USA) 7.5f **(74)** - Doyce **(72f)** (Formidable (USA)) 9.2f **(63)**
Form - 728
Record 1998 - 1st:0 2nd:1 3rd:0 Ran:3
Win Prizemoney £0 *Total Prizemoney* £1,050
1998 Turf 0-3: (6f, 7f, 8f) (g-s, gd 2)
Currently average gelding. Turf high 69 (began Spt) - 2nd of 12 to Triple Dash (21 Oct Newcastle 6f g-s RF 4915).
**W S Cunningham [0-3] Mrs Ann Bell.*

ANNO DOMINI BHB 97f **RR 92f** 3998[2]
2 b c Primo Dominie 7.2f **(67)** - Jalopy (Jalmood (USA)) 10.1f **(52)**
Form - 5152
Record 1998 - 1st:1 2nd:1 3rd:0 Ran:4

Win Prizemoney £3,907 *Total Prizemoney* £9,352
Wins * **1998** Jun Pontef (GD) 5f 81 <
1998 Turf 1-4: (5f 1-3, 6f) (gd 2, frm 1-2)
Useful colt. Turf high 92 - 2nd of 5 getting 3lb from Boldly Goes (31 Aug Ripon 6f gd RF 3998). After a promising debut when fifth behind some useful sorts in the Windsor Castle Stakes, he landed his maiden but failed to go the pace in a listed race over five furlongs on fast ground. Produced a better effort when second in a decent race at Ripon when stepped up to six furlongs, and may improve with age. **P F I Cole [1-4] P F I Cole Ltd.*

ANNOUNCING BHB 59f50a **RR 57f 50a** 3737[5]

4 b br g Old Vic 12.8f **(72)** - D'Azy (Persian Bold) 9.3f **(66)**
Form - 4455

Record	**1998** -	1st:0	2nd:0	3rd:0	Ran:4
	Pre1998 -	1st:0	2nd:1	3rd:1	Ran:6

Win Prizemoney £0 *Total Prizemoney* £1,816
1998 Turf 0-1: (12f) (frm) 1998 AW 0-3: (10f, 13f, 16f) (Equi 3)
Workmanlike, fair gelding, has worn blinkers. AW high 43. A half-brother to Presenting, he has been exposed as moderate.
**G L Moore [2-11] Miss Karen Shine (from J H M Gosden [0-6] Oct 1997).*

ANNTARI (IRE) **RR 103f** 4947a[8]

7 b h Shardari 12.1f **(59)**-Aneyza(USA)(Blushing Groom (FR))10.3f **(76)**
Form - 28
1998 Turf 0-2: (7f 2) (hvy, sft)
Currently very useful horse. Turf high 103 (1st run) (began Spt) - 2nd of 4 to Alamo Bay (19 Spt Longchamp 7f sft RF 4470g). This old-timer was asked some big questions and ran solidly before being out-classed behind Tomba in the Group One Prix de la Foret. **B Mohamed in FR [0-2].*

ANNUS MIRABILIS (FR) BHB 114f117a **RR 122f 117a** 5133a[4]

6 b h Warning 8.1f **(77)** - Anna Petrovna (FR) (Wassl) 9.7f **(62)**
Form - 712314

Record	**1998** -	1st:2	2nd:1	3rd:1	Ran:5
	Pre1998 -	1st:7	2nd:4	3rd:5	Ran:22

Win Prizemoney £647,426 *Total Prizemoney* £995,813

Wins							
* **1998**	Aug	Windso	(G-F)	G3	10f	115	
1998	*Mar*	*Nad Al*	*(FST)*		*10f*	*126*	<
* 1997	Aug	Windso	(GD)	G3	10f	122	
* 1997	Aug	Newmar	(G-F)		10f	107+	
* 1996	Oct	Fuchu	(FRM)	G2	9f	114	
* 1996	Aug	Windso	(G-F)	G3	10f	114	
1995	Spt	Ayr	(GD)	L	10.9f	89++	
1994	Spt	Newmar	(G-F)	L	7f	99+	
1994	Spt	Yarmou	(SFT)		7f	85+	

1998 Turf 1-4: (10f 1-4) (hvy, gd 2, g-f 1-1) 1998 AW 1-1: (10f 1-1) (Dirt 1-1)
Top-class horse, effective 10f, acts on hvy to g-f - acts on Dirt, has worn blinkers. Turf high 120 - 3rd of 14 giving 2lb to Sunrise Flag (21 Jun Hanshin 10f hvy RF 2287a). (1st run) - 1st of 10 from Intikhab (28 Mar Nad Al Sheba RF 0551a). A real flagbearer for Godolphin, he has been globetrotting for the last couple of years with a fair amount of success. Beat stablemate Intikhab six lengths in the Dubai Duty Free and won the Group Three Winter Hill Stakes at Windsor for the third year running on one of his rare appearances on home soil. Ran in Australia on his final start, and Frankie Dettori was panned for an 'ill-judged' ride.
**S bin Suroor [5-15] (from S bin Suroor in UAE [1-2] Mar 1998).*

ANOKATO BHB 56f61a **RR 52f 61a** 3366[11]

4 b g Tina's Pet 7.4f **(56)** - High Velocity (Frimley Park) 6.5f **(67)**
Form - 6371613020703400

Record	**1998** -	1st:2	2nd:1	3rd:2	Ran:13
	Pre1998 -	1st:3	2nd:0	3rd:7	Ran:30

Win Prizemoney £14,035 *Total Prizemoney* £20,587

Wins								
1998	*Jan*	*Lingfi*	*(STD)*	*C*	*5f*		*64*	
1998	*Jan*	*Lingfi*	*(STD)*	*C*	*5f*		*67*	
1997	*Nov*	*Lingfi*	*(STD)*	*H*	*5f*	*61*	*65*	
1997	May	Bright	(FRM)	H	5.3f	59	60	
1996	Spt	Folkes	(G-F)		5f		71	<

1998 Turf 0-8: (5f 4, 6f 4) (gd 2, g-f 2, frm 4) 1998 AW 2-5: (5f 2-4, 6f) (Equi 2-5)
Leggy, average gelding, effective 5 to 6f, best at 5f, acts on gd to frm - acts on Equi, mostly wears blinkers (extremely effectively), likes tight tracks, excels at Goodwood and does well at Brighton. Turf high 64 - 2nd of 17 giving 6lb to Step On Degas (22 May Brighton 6f frm RF 1389). AW high 67 (1st run) - 1st of 6 getting 4lb from Palacegate Jack (8 Jan Lingfield RF 0047) - also 1st of 4 giving 2lb to Aljaz (31 Jan Lingfield RF 0195). Really found his form with three wins over the minimum on the Lingfield Equitrack during the winter. Just touched off over six furlongs at Brighton in May, but usually well held on turf this year.
**T G Mills [0-10] Mrs Stephanie Merrydew (from K T Ivory [5-33] Jan 1998).*

ANONYM (IRE) BHB 45f53a **RR 39f 53a** 5079[18]

6 b g Nashamaa 8.1f **(58)** - Bonny Bertha (Capistrano) 9.4f **(64)**
Form - 1122486380

Record	**1998** -	1st:2	2nd:2	3rd:1	Ran:10
	Pre1998 -	1st:6	2nd:2	3rd:6	Ran:45

Win Prizemoney £22,308 *Total Prizemoney* £31,898

Wins								
1998	*Jan*	*Wolver*	*(STD)*	*S*	*8.5f*		*62*	
1998	*Jan*	*Wolver*	*(STD)*	*S*	*9.4f*		*59+*	
1997	*May*	*Wolver*	*(STD)*	*H*	*8.5f*	*68*	*74*	<
1997	*Jan*	*Wolver*	*(STD)*	*H*	*8.5f*	*63*	*68*	
1997	*Jan*	*Southw*	*(STD)*	*C*	*7f*		*71*	
1996	Jly	Mussel	(GD)	C	7.1f		55	
1995	Aug	Leices	(G-F)	H	8f	68	70	
1995	Jly	Doncas	(FRM)	H	7f	63	65	

1998 Turf 0-2: (7f 2) (sft, gd) 1998 AW 2-8: (7f, 8f 1-5, 9f 1-1, 10f) (Equi 4, Fibr 2-4)
Moderate gelding, effective 7 to 8f, best at 7f, acts on g-f - acts on AW, best on Fibr, often wears blinkers (very effectively), prefers left handed tracks, prefers tight tracks, excels at Wolverhampton. Turf high 34. AW high 67 - 2nd of 9 giving 6lb to Robellion (22 Jan Lingfield 8f Equi RF 0133). Consistent. He seems to be at his best during the winter, and he has won his first two starts of the year for each of the past two seasons. He looks better suited by Fibresand than by Equitrack, but is an effective sort in plating company on his favoured surface.
**C N Allen [0-8] J T B Racing (from J L Eyre [3-13] Jan 1998).*

ANOTHER BATCHWORTH BHB 55f53a **RR 60f 53a** 1365[7]

6 b m Beveled (USA) 6.9f **(64)** - Batchworth Dancer (Ballacashtal (CAN)) 5.3f **(50)**
Form - 073587

Record	**1998** -	1st:0	2nd:0	3rd:1	Ran:5
	Pre1998 -	1st:3	2nd:9	3rd:5	Ran:39

Win Prizemoney £9,024 *Total Prizemoney* £20,487

Wins								
* 1996	Oct	Redcar	(G-F)		5f		65	<
* 1996	Oct	Nottin	(GD)	H	5.1f	55	60	
1995	*Oct*	*Wolver*	*(STD)*	*H*	*6f*	*53*	*58+*	

1998 Turf 0-1: (5f) (g-f) 1998 AW 0-4: (5f 4) (Equi, Fibr 3)
Average mare, effective 5f, acts on gd to frm, best on frm, often wears blinkers (effectively). AW high 54. Pacey sprinter, she has given trouble before the start, but is capable of showing tremendous early pace. Barely stays five furlongs and really needs a very sharp track.
**E A Wheeler [2-30] M V Kirby (from S Mellor [1-14] Nov 1995).*

ANOTHER BEVELED BHB 50f **RR 65f** 2507[10]

3 ch c Beveled (USA) 6.9f **(64)** - Cotehele (Paddy's Stream)
Form - 550

Record	**1998** -	1st:0	2nd:0	3rd:0	Ran:3

1998 Turf 0-3: (10f 2, 14f) (g-s, gd, frm)
Unfurnished, average colt. Turf high 65. Winner over hurdles.
**A P Jones [0-3] The Eastbury Racing Club.*

ANOTHER DANCER (FR) **RR 115f** 3420a[6]

3 b f Groom Dancer (USA) 9.5f **(75)** - Green Light (FR) (Green Dancer (USA)) 10.3f **(74)**
Form - 2516
1998 Turf 1-4: (11f 2, 12f 1-1, 14f) (sft, gd 1-3)
High-class mare. Turf high 115 - 1st of 7 from Cantilever (21 Jun Longchamp RF 2289a). She looked a useful sort when winning at Longchamp in June, and seemed to be a much better horse on fast ground. It was therefore no surprise when she finished well beaten behind Leggera in soft ground at Deauville.
**D Sepulchre in FR [1-4] Julian Byng.*

ANOTHER EPISODE (IRE) BHB 27f70a **RR 38f 70a** 3332[15]

9 b g Drumalis 8.8f **(73)** - Pasadena Lady (Captain James) 5f **(59)**
Form - 066800477800

Record 1998 - 1st:0 2nd:0 3rd:0 Ran:12
Pre1998 - 1st:11 2nd:11 3rd:5 Ran:58
Win Prizemoney £42,433 *Total Prizemoney* £62,542
Wins 1994 Aug Warwic (G-F) C 5f 63
1994 Jun Goodwo (GF) C 5f 64
1994 May Southw (STD) H 5f 68 68
1998 Turf 0-12: (5f 11, 6f) (gd 7, g-f 3, frm 2)
Fair gelding, effective 5f, acts on g-s, has worn blinkers. Turf high 41. Inconsistent. Won plenty of races in his younger days for Jack Berry but is very moderate these days.
**Miss L A Perratt [0-23] Hay-Sutherland (from J Berry [11-47] May 1995).*

ANOTHER FANTASY (IRE) BHB 88f RR 97f 5050a[10]

3 b f Danehill (USA) 9.1f **(79)** - Ariadne (Bustino) 10.4f **(64)**
Form - 477563040
Record 1998 - 1st:0 2nd:0 3rd:1 Ran:9
Pre1998 - 1st:2 2nd:1 3rd:1 Ran:7
Win Prizemoney £76,838 *Total Prizemoney* £85,674
Wins 1997 Aug Currag (G-S) 6f 92 <
1997 May Kempto (GD) 5f 72
1998 Turf 0-9: (7f 2, 8f 2, 9f, 10f 4) (hvy, g-s, gd 4, g-f 2, frm)
Neat, very useful filly. Turf high 104. She had a tough season and never improved upon a creditable seventh place in the 1000 Guineas, and was again disappointing for Peter Chapple-Hyam in a Listed race at Deauville in October. Being a winner who has been placed in Listed company, she will make a decent broodmare.
**P W Chapple-Hyam [0-1] John Gunther (from R Hannon [2-15] Spt 1998).*

ANOTHER FIDDLE (IRE) BHB 20f40a RR 47f 40a 182[8]

8 b g Waajib 8.9f **(67)** - Elmar (Lord Gayle (USA)) 8.8f **(62)**
Form - 8
Record 1998 - 1st:0 2nd:0 3rd:0 Ran:1
Pre1998 - 1st:1 2nd:3 3rd:1 Ran:26
Win Prizemoney £4,659 *Total Prizemoney* £8,245
Wins 1994 Jly Epsom (G-F) H 7f 68 65 <
1998 AW 0-1: (10f) (Equi)
Moderate gelding, has worn blinkers.
**J E Long [0-11] Mrs D Crick (from B A Pearce [0-1] Nov 1996).*

ANOTHER LAURA RR 66f 513[5]

3 b f Puissance 7.1f **(60)** - Traumatic Laura (Pragmatic)
Form - 5
Record 1998 - 1st:0 2nd:0 3rd:0 Ran:1
1998 Turf 0-1: (7f) (gd)
Workmanlike, currently average filly.
**W McKeown [0-1] Miss Susan Blain.*

ANOTHER LOVER RR 26f 3837[6]

2 ch f Then Again 7.4f **(52)** - Love Street (Mummy's Pet) 7.7f **(60)**
Form - 46
Record 1998 - 1st:0 2nd:0 3rd:0 Ran:2
1998 Turf 0-2: (5f, 6f) (gd, frm)
Currently little account filly. Turf high 26.
**S G Knight [0-2] Mrs Ginny Withers.*

ANOTHER NIGHT (IRE) BHB 63f RR 68f 3762[11]

4 ch c Waajib 8.9f **(67)** - Little Me (Connaught) 7.7f **(63)**
Form - 56870
Record 1998 - 1st:0 2nd:0 3rd:0 Ran:5
Pre1998 - 1st:1 2nd:2 3rd:1 Ran:10
Win Prizemoney £3,647 *Total Prizemoney* £6,378
Wins 1997 Jun Haydoc (G-F) 8.1f 75+ <
1998 Turf 0-5: (12f, 13f, 14f 3) (g-s, gd, g-f 2, frm)
Scopey, average colt, effective 8 to 10f, acts on g-f. Turf high 72. Inconsistent. A half-brother to middle-distance claiming winner and hurdler Last Laugh, he looked to be an improving sort when winning at Haydock in June '97. He has not run as well since on the level, although he has won over timber.
**P G Murphy [1-13] Sunset Partnership (from R Hannon [1-10] Spt 1997).*

ANOTHER NIGHTMARE (IRE) BHB 37f43a RR 41f 43a 4771[16]

6 b m Treasure Kay 6.5f **(53)** - Carange (Known Fact (USA)) 7.4f **(67)**
Form - 005800257336006030
Record 1998 - 1st:0 2nd:1 3rd:3 Ran:18
Pre1998 - 1st:6 2nd:3 3rd:2 Ran:59
Win Prizemoney £16,551 *Total Prizemoney* £23,938
Wins 1997 Aug Thirsk (GD) SH 6f 44 50
1997 Jly Hamilt (SFT) H 5f 41 46
1997 Mar Wolver (STD) H 6f 41 42
1996 Aug Ripon (SFT) H 6f 47 53 <
1996 Aug Hamilt (G-F) H 6f 39 48
1994 Jly Hamilt (G-S) 5f 53
1998 Turf 0-17: (5f 7, 6f 10) (hvy, sft 2, g-s, gd 6, g-f 4, frm 3) 1998 AW 0-1: (7f) (Fibr)
Moderate mare, effective 5 to 6f, best at 6f, acts on gd to frm - acts on Fibr, best on gd, has worn blinkers. Turf high 41 - 2nd of 9 getting 32lb from Young Bigwig (10 Jun Hamilton 5f gd RF 1870). She is inconsistent, and is on a long losing run.
**D W Barker [0-2] GM Engineering (from R M McKellar [5-64] Aug 1998).*

ANOTHER RAINBOW (IRE) BHB 72f RR 65f 4650[2]

2 br f Rainbows For Life (CAN) 9.3f **(64)**-Phylella(Persian Bold)9.3f **(66)**
Form - 452
Record 1998 - 1st:0 2nd:1 3rd:0 Ran:3
Win Prizemoney £0 *Total Prizemoney* £1,256
1998 Turf 0-3: (5f, 6f 2) (g-f 2, frm)
Currently average filly. Turf high 65 (began Jly) - 2nd of 9 getting 5lb from Learned Friend (5 Oct Brighton 6f g-f RF 4650).
**Miss Gay Kelleway [0-3] Pot Of Gold Racing.*

ANOTHER TIME BHB 89f RR 93f 4631[20]

6 ch g Clantime 6.6f **(57)** - Another Move (Farm Walk) 11.6f **(55)**
Form - 08544103681000
Record 1998 - 1st:2 2nd:0 3rd:1 Ran:14
Pre1998 - 1st:7 2nd:3 3rd:1 Ran:32
Win Prizemoney £51,984 *Total Prizemoney* £76,415
Wins * **1998** Aug Lingfi (G-F) 10f 93 <
* **1998** Jun Ascot (G-S) H 10f 87 90
* 1997 Jly Newbur (G-F) H 9f 84 89
* 1997 Apr Pontef (G-F) H 8f 80 84
* 1996 Aug Lingfi (G-F) H 10f 70 77
* 1996 Jun Ripon (G-F) 10f 73
* 1995 Oct Redcar (FRM) 10f 72
* 1995 Spt Bright (GD) 8f 68
* 1995 Spt Thirsk (G-F) S 8f 58+
1998 Turf 2-14: (9f, 10f 2-13) (sft, gd 6, g-f 1-5, frm 1-2)
Useful gelding, effective 8 to 10f, best at 10f, acts on g-s to frm, likes left handed tracks, likes tight tracks, and likes Newbury. Turf high 93 - 1st of 4 giving 5lb to Ganga (16 Aug Lingfield RF 3668) - also 1st of 16 getting 17lb from Winter Romance (20 Jun Ascot RF 2138). A rather in-and-out handicapper, he was victorious in a valuable Ascot handicap in June, and also won a classified stakes in good style at Lingfield in August. Suited by coming off a fast pace, though he is not very consistent.
**S P C Woods [9-41] D Sullivan (from Miss S E Hall [0-5] May 1995).*

ANOTHER VICTIM RR 392[6]

4 ch g Beveled (USA) 6.9f **(64)** - Ragtime Rose (Ragstone) 9.6f **(59)**
Form - 6
Record 1998 - 1st:0 2nd:0 3rd:0 Ran:1
Pre1998 - 1st:0 2nd:0 3rd:0 Ran:1
1998 AW 0-1: (10f) (Equi)
Light-framed, currently very poor gelding.
**M R Bosley [0-1] John Hughes (from M Blanshard [0-1] May 1997).*

ANOTHER WYN-BANK BHB 36f RR 35f 4001[17]

3 b f Presidium 7.5f **(56)** - Wyn-Bank (Green God) 9.6f **(68)**
Form - 50870
Record 1998 - 1st:0 2nd:0 3rd:0 Ran:5
Pre1998 - 1st:0 2nd:0 3rd:0 Ran:4
1998 Turf 0-5: (8f, 10f 2, 11f, 12f) (gd 2, frm 2, hrd)
Workmanlike, very moderate filly, effective 7f, acts on gd. Turf high 44. **J G FitzGerald [0-9] Mrs Shirley France.*

ANSCHLUSS RR 79f 4800[3]

2 gr c Alzao (USA) 9.8f **(73)** - Avice Caro (USA) (Caro) 9.3f **(74)**
Form - 3
Record 1998 - 1st:0 2nd:0 3rd:1 Ran:1
Win Prizemoney £0 *Total Prizemoney* £457

1998 Turf 0-1: (7f) (sft)
Currently above-average colt. (1st run) - 3rd of 9 giving 5lb to Credit-A-Plenty (14 Oct Haydock 7f sft RF 4800).
**C E Brittain [0-1] Saeed Manana.*

ANSELLMAN BHB 83f78a **RR 85f 78a** 4741[13]

8 gr g Absalom 7.1f **(56)** - Grace Poole (Sallust) 8.4f **(63)**
Form - 85441232722300
Record 1998 - 1st:1 2nd:4 3rd:2 Ran:14
Pre1998 - 1st:8 2nd:11 3rd:7 Ran:72
Win Prizemoney £34,810 *Total Prizemoney* £89,094

Wins * **1998** May Redcar (GD) C 6f 84
* 1997 Spt Leices (G-F) H 5f 78 80
* 1997 Apr Ripon (G-F) C 5f 77
* 1996 Jly Chepst (G-F) H 5.1f 75 77
* 1996 Apr Bath (GD) H 5.1f 70 78
* 1995 Aug Catter (G-F) C 5f 74
* 1994 May Newmar (GS) H 5f 78 84

1998 Turf 1-13: (5f 7, 6f 1-6) (sft, g-s 2, gd 1-8, g-f 2) 1998 AW 0-1: (5f) (Fibr)
Useful gelding, effective 5 to 6f, best at 5f, acts on sft to frm - acts on Fibr, often wears blinkers (extremely effectively), excels at Haydock, does well at Newmarket. Turf high 85 - also 1st of 7 giving 10lb to Pierpoint (11 May Redcar RF 1147). Inconsistent. Running consistently well last term, he landed a Redcar claimer in May, and ran his socks off to finish runner-up in the Stewards' Cup. He can hardly be said to be improving, it was just a case of him running up to his very best on the day.
**J Berry [7-69] Ansells of Watford (from B Smart [0-3] Nov 1993).*

ANSELL'S EDITION (IRE) BHB 59f **RR 57f** 4997[8]

2 ch g Lahib (USA) 8f **(69)** - Anisimova (Kris) 9.5f **(73)**
Form - 808
Record 1998 - 1st:0 2nd:0 3rd:0 Ran:3
1998 Turf 0-3: (7f 2, 8f) (sft, gd, frm)
Currently fair gelding. Turf high 57 (began Jly).
**M J Haynes [0-3] Ansells of Watford.*

ANSTAND BHB 76f **RR 79f** 4751[1]

3 b g Anshan 8.2f **(63)** - Pussy Foot (Red Sunset) 8.2f **(63)**
Form - 05103704041
Record 1998 - 1st:2 2nd:0 3rd:1 Ran:11
Pre1998 - 1st:0 2nd:0 3rd:0 Ran:3
Win Prizemoney £10,209 *Total Prizemoney* £11,429

Wins * **1998** Oct York (GD) 6f 76
* **1998** May Ripon (GD) H 6f 66 86 <

1998 Turf 2-11: (5f, 6f 2-7, 7f 2, 8f) (g-s 2, gd 1-3, g-f 1-4, frm 2)
Light-framed, above-average gelding, effective 6f, acts on gd to g-f, best on gd, has worn blinkers. Turf high 86 - 1st of 19 giving 8lb to Pigeon (27 May Ripon RF 1532). Put up a stone after winning easily at Ripon in May, and was held subsequently until winning a classified stakes on his final start. Sold for 17,000 gns in October, reportedly to join Malcolm Saunders.
**Mrs J R Ramsden [2-14] Bernard Hathaway.*

ANSWER LIVELY (USA) **RR 112a** 5162a[1]

2 b c Lively One (USA) - Twosies Answer (USA)
Form - 1
1998 AW 1-1: (9f 1-1) (Dirt 1-1)
Currently Group-class colt. (1st run) - 1st of 14 from Aly's Alley (7 Nov Churchill Downs RF 5162a). Tough colt, narrow winner of the Breeders' Cup Juvenile. **B Barnett in USA [1-1] J A Franks.*

ANTAHKARANA (USA) **RR 95a** 5163a[6]

2 br f Dynaformer (USA) 12f **(82)** - Shivering Gal (USA)
Form - 6
1998 AW 0-1: (9f) (Dirt)
Currently very useful filly. **B Cecil in USA [0-1] L Schaffel.*

ANTARCTIC STORM BHB 65f **RR 68f** 4513[11]

5 b g Emarati (USA) 6.6f **(63)** - Katie Scarlett (Lochnager) 6f **(59)**
Form - 380480
Record 1998 - 1st:0 2nd:0 3rd:1 Ran:6
Pre1998 - 1st:4 2nd:1 3rd:2 Ran:20
Win Prizemoney £19,114 *Total Prizemoney* £25,478

Wins * 1997 Nov Mussel (G-S) H 8f 69 73 <
* 1997 Spt Hamilt (GD) H 8.3f 61 66
* 1997 Aug Ayr (G-F) H 8f 56 59
1996 Jun Windso (G-F) H 8.3f 60 62

1998 Turf 0-6: (8f 6) (sft, gd 2, g-f 2, frm)
Average gelding, effective 8f, acts on gd to g-f, best on gd, has worn blinkers, likes left handed tracks, prefers tight tracks. Turf high 68 - 4th of 10 getting 14lb from Wuxi Venture (7 Spt Hamilton 8f gd RF 4132).
**R A Fahey [3-22] Northumbria Leisure Ltd (from E A L Dunlop [1-5] Jun 1996).*

ANTARCTIQUE (IRE) **RR 105f** 5055a[4]

4 c Sadler's Wells (USA) 11.3f **(87)** - Arctique Royale (Royal And Regal (USA)) 9.5f **(60)**
Form - 44
1998 Turf 0-2: (16f, 20f) (hvy, sft)
Currently Pattern-class colt. Turf high 106 (began Oct) - 4th of 7 to Tiraaz (25 Oct Longchamp 16f hvy RF 5055a). He stays forever and ran above himself when finishing fourth in the Prix du Cadran.
**R Collet in FR [0-2] H Yokoyama.*

ANTHEM **RR 74f** 4745[4]

2 b c Saddlers' Hall (IRE) 10.5f **(65)** - Full Orchestra (Shirley Heights) 10.3f **(74)**
Form - 54
Record 1998 - 1st:0 2nd:0 3rd:0 Ran:2
Win Prizemoney £0 *Total Prizemoney* £474
1998 Turf 0-2: (8f 2) (gd 2)
Currently above-average colt. Turf high 74 (began Spt).
**M A Jarvis [0-2] Mohammed Bin Hendi.*

ANTHONY MON AMOUR (USA) BHB 64f **RR 74f** 3999[5]

3 b g Nicholas (USA) 6.1f **(63)** - Reine de La Ciel (USA) (Conquistador Cielo (USA)) 8.8f **(69)**
Form - 03441315
Record 1998 - 1st:2 2nd:0 3rd:2 Ran:8
Win Prizemoney £5,382 *Total Prizemoney* £6,469

Wins * **1998** *Jly Southw (STD) 6f 69*
* **1998** Jly Chepst (GD) H 6.1f 56 74 <

1998 Turf 1-5: (6f 1-3, 7f 2) (gd 1-4, g-f) 1998 AW 1-3: (6f 1-2, 8f) (Fibr 1-3)
Rangy, above-average gelding, effective 6f, acts on gd - acts on Fibr. Turf high 74 - 1st of 11 giving 9lb to Ready Fontaine (4 Jly Chepstow RF 2533). AW high 69 - 1st of 6 giving 3lb to Cameo (11 Jly Southwell RF 2724). Bolted up in a maiden handicap in July, looking one to follow, and has since added a handicap on the Fibresand. **W J Haggas [2-8] Henryk De Kwiatkowski.*

ANTINNAZ (IRE) **RR 90+f** 4686a[5]

2 ch f Thatching 7.8f **(69)** - Tootling
Form - 2125
1998 Turf 1-4: (5f 1-1, 6f 3) (g-s, gd 2, g-f 1-1)
Useful filly. Turf high 90 (1st run) (began Jly) - 2nd of 11 to Takariya (12 Jly Curragh 6f gd RF 2803a) - also 1st of 9 getting 5lb from Fanus (25 Jly Curragh RF 3184a). Decent filly by Thatching. Won her Curragh maiden and has been running well in top-class sprint company on last two starts. Should win more races next season. **T Stack in IRE [1-4] Mrs T Stack.*

ANTITHESIS (IRE) BHB 32f **RR 28f** 1890[6]

5 b m Fairy King (USA) 7.7f **(75)** - Music of The Night (USA) (Blushing Groom (FR)) 10.3f **(76)**
Form - 7076
Record 1998 - 1st:0 2nd:0 3rd:0 Ran:4
Pre1998 - 1st:1 2nd:1 3rd:2 Ran:19
Win Prizemoney £2,911 *Total Prizemoney* £4,116

Wins 1996 Aug Tipper (G-S) H 5f 65 66 <

1998 Turf 0-4: (5f 3, 6f) (g-s, gd, g-f 2)
Little account filly. Turf high 28.
**J S Haldane [0-12] G J Johnston (from T Stack in IRE [1-11] Oct 1996).*

ANTONIA'S CHOICE BHB 51f **RR 52df** 3938[7]

4 ch f Music Boy 6.5f **(56)** - Mainly Sunset (Red Sunset) 8.2f **(63)**
Form - 075604027
Record 1998 - 1st:0 2nd:1 3rd:0 Ran:9
Pre1998 - 1st:1 2nd:0 3rd:1 Ran:6
Win Prizemoney £6,976 *Total Prizemoney* £8,409

Wins * 1996 May Cheste (GD) 5.1f 72+ <
1998 Turf 0-8: (5f 8) (g-s, gd 3, g-f, frm 3) 1998 AW 0-1: (5f) (Fibr)
Fair filly, effective 5f, acts on gd, has worn blinkers (very effectively). Turf high 52 - 2nd of 10 giving 18lb to Lunar Music (12 Aug Nottingham 5f gd RF 3584). Best when allowed to dominate.
**J Berry [1-15] Chris & Antonia Deuters.*

ANTONIA'S DOUBLE BHB 62f **RR 61df** 4323[27]
3 ch f Primo Dominie 7.2f **(67)** - Mainly Sunset (Red Sunset) 8.2f **(63)**
Form - 58150
Record 1998 - 1st:1 2nd:0 3rd:0 Ran:5
Pre1998 - 1st:0 2nd:0 3rd:1 Ran:3
Win Prizemoney £3,387 *Total Prizemoney* £4,137
Wins * **1998** Jly Newcas (G-F) 5f 61 <
1998 Turf 1-5: (5f 1-4, 6f) (g-s, gd 1-1, g-f 2, frm)
Scopey, average filly, effective 5f, acts on gd. Turf high 61 (began Jly) - also 1st of 5 from Bollin Ann (27 Jly Newcastle RF 3139).
**J Berry [1-8] Chris & Antonia Deuters.*

ANTONIAS MELODY BHB 56f78a **RR 46f 78a** 4872[11]
5 b m Rambo Dancer (CAN) 8.4f **(59)** - Ayodessa (Lochnager) 6f **(59)**
Form - 004113334450
Record 1998 - 1st:2 2nd:0 3rd:3 Ran:10
Pre1998 - 1st:4 2nd:2 3rd:1 Ran:32
Win Prizemoney £19,347 *Total Prizemoney* £29,965
Wins * **1998** *Feb Southw (STD) H 7f 66 75+*
* **1998** *Feb Southw (STD) H 6f 66 68*
* 1997 *Feb Southw (STD) H 7f 64 77* <
* 1997 *Feb Southw (STD) H 6f 64 76*
* 1996 Apr Ripon (GD) H 6f 68 71
* 1995 Spt Nottin (G-S) H 6.1f 62 66
1998 Turf 0-6: (5f, 6f 2, 7f 2, 8f) (sft, g-s, gd 4) 1998 AW 2-4: (6f 1-2, 7f 1-1, 8f) (Fibr 2-4)
Above-average filly, effective 6 to 7f, best at 7f, - acts on Fibr, has worn blinkers, prefers left handed tracks, prefers tight tracks. Turf high 63. AW high 75 - 1st of 11 giving 37lb to Patina (23 Feb Southwell RF 0344) - also 1st of 7 giving 25lb to River Ensign (20 Feb Southwell RF 0327). Becoming disappointing. Scored two all-the-way victories on the Southwell Fibresand in February '97, and won the same two races this year, having done very little in between. Watch out for her in the same two races in 1999!
**S R Bowring [6-42] S R Bowring.*

ANTONIO JOLI BHB 40f **RR 49f** 1902[F]
3 b g Prince Sabo 6.6f **(64)** - Revisit (Busted) 10.2f **(61)**
Form - F
Record 1998 - 1st:0 2nd:0 3rd:0 Ran:1
Pre1998 - 1st:0 2nd:0 3rd:0 Ran:4
1998 Turf 0-1: (14f) (g-s)
Leggy, moderate gelding. (DEAD)
**P F I Cole [0-5] Richard Green (Fine Paintings).*

ANYAR REEM BHB 63f46a **RR 69f 46a** 3129[3]
7 b g Slip Anchor 12.7f **(75)** - Alruccaba (Crystal Palace (FR)) 12.5f **(76)**
Form - 03
Record 1998 - 1st:0 2nd:0 3rd:1 Ran:2
Pre1998 - 1st:1 2nd:4 3rd:1 Ran:9
Win Prizemoney £3,501 *Total Prizemoney* £8,091
Wins * 1997 Jun Doncas (G-S) H 10.3f 63 69 <
1998 AW 0-2: (11f, 12f) (Fibr 2)
Average gelding, often wears blinkers (effectively). AW high 43 (began Jly).
**D Shaw [1-5] Paul Murphy (from J H M Gosden [0-6] Aug 1994).*

ANY MOORE (IRE) BHB 68f **RR 68f** 3891[6]
2 b f Unblest - Collected (IRE) (Taufan (USA)) 7f **(57)**
Form - 748626
Record 1998 - 1st:0 2nd:1 3rd:0 Ran:6
Win Prizemoney £0 *Total Prizemoney* £1,602
1998 Turf 0-6: (5f, 6f 2, 7f 3) (gd 3, g-f 2, frm)
Average filly, effective 7f, acts on g-f. Turf high 68 - 2nd of 9 getting 2lb from Gino's Spirits (5 Aug Brighton 7f g-f RF 3362).
**J S Moore [0-6] Mrs Victoria Goodman.*

ANYTIME (IRE) **RR 76f** 996[8]
3 b c Fairy King (USA) 7.7f **(75)** - Alidiva (Chief Singer) 8.9f **(66)**
Form - 8
Record 1998 - 1st:0 2nd:0 3rd:0 Ran:1
1998 Turf 0-1: (8f) (gd)
Well made, currently above-average colt. A half-brother to Sleepytime, Ali-Royal and Taipan, all winners in the highest grade, he had a big home reputation prior to his debut in a Newmarket maiden, but could only finish eighth. Worth another chance.
**H R A Cecil [0-1] Greenbay Stables Ltd.*

ANZIO (IRE) BHB 109f95a **RR 105f 95a** 1911a[3]
7 b g Hatim (USA) 7.8f **(56)** - Highdrive (Ballymore) 7.3f **(64)**
Form - 3
1998 Turf 0-1: (6f) (sft)
Pattern-class gelding, often wears blinkers. (1st run) - 3rd of 13 giving 4lb to Hever Golf Rose (2 Jun Taby 6f sft RF 1911a). A once useful performer for Gay Kelleway, he is now trained in Norway. Ran well against Hever Golf Rose in June.
**A Lund in NOR [0-1] (from Miss Gay Kelleway [5-10] Dec 1996).*

AOIFE (IRE) BHB 67f **RR 65df** 5058[4]
3 ch f Thatching 7.8f **(69)** -Aunt Hester (IRE) (Caerleon (USA)) 8.6f **(71)**
Form - 224
Record 1998 - 1st:0 2nd:2 3rd:0 Ran:3
Win Prizemoney £0 *Total Prizemoney* £2,525
1998 Turf 0-3: (7f 3) (sft, gd, frm)
Workmanlike, currently average filly. Turf high 65 (began Spt) - 2nd of 6 getting 5lb from Ally (20 Oct Yarmouth 7f gd RF 4888).
**G Wragg [0-3] Kaniz Bloodstock Investments Ltd.*

APACHE RED (IRE) BHB 95f **RR 97f** 2650[13]
3 ch c Indian Ridge 7.6f **(74)** - Moonlight Partner (IRE) (Red Sunset) 8.2f **(63)**
Form - 6634100
Record 1998 - 1st:1 2nd:0 3rd:1 Ran:6
Pre1998 - 1st:1 2nd:0 3rd:1 Ran:8
Win Prizemoney £31,012 *Total Prizemoney* £35,819
Wins * **1998** Jun Epsom (GD) H 7f 92 97 <
1997 Oct Leopar (G-S) 8f 92
1998 Turf 1-6: (6f 3, 7f 1-3) (sft, gd 1-3, g-f, frm)
Very useful colt, effective 6 to 8f, acts on gd to g-f, best on gd, has worn blinkers. Turf high 97 - 1st of 17 giving 12lb to Bodfari Pride (5 Jun Epsom RF 1746). Trained in Ireland at two, he won a mile maiden at Leopardstown in October '97, but found Listed company too much for him. He finished last in the Greenham on his debut for his new stable, but after running well in a competitive sprint handicap on his third start, got up in the final stride to land an Epsom handicap over seven. Found things too quick for him in the Wokingham next time, and was drawn badly back at seven in the Bunbury Cup.
**D R C Elsworth [1-6] Mrs T Burns (from J S Bolger in IRE [1-8] Nov 1997).*

APARTMENTS ABROAD BHB 28f43a **RR 36f 43a** 2198[12]
5 b m Prince Sabo 6.6f **(64)**-La Graciosa (Comedy Star (USA)) 7.5f **(50)**
Form - 0
Record 1998 - 1st:0 2nd:0 3rd:0 Ran:1
Pre1998 - 1st:1 2nd:0 3rd:3 Ran:25
Win Prizemoney £2,981 *Total Prizemoney* £5,002
Wins 1995 *Dec Lingfi (STD) 8f 64* <
1998 Turf 0-1: (10f) (g-f)
Moderate filly, often wears blinkers. Becoming disappointing.
**Miss Z C Davison [0-1] Mrs J Irvine (from K McAuliffe [1-26] May 1997).*

APICULATE (IRE) BHB 15f **RR 10f** 616[14]
4 b g Exactly Sharp (USA) 8.4f **(66)** - Reine de Chypre (FR) (Habitat) 9.4f **(70)**
Form - 000
Record 1998 - 1st:0 2nd:0 3rd:0 Ran:3
Pre1998 - 1st:0 2nd:1 3rd:0 Ran:14
Win Prizemoney £0 *Total Prizemoney* £706
1998 Turf 0-1: (7f) (sft) 1998 AW 0-2: (8f, 12f) (Fibr 2)
Leggy, little account gelding, has worn blinkers. Becoming disappointing.
**S R Bowring [0-8] Ace Employment (from W T Kemp [0-10] Oct 1996).*

APOLLINAIRE BHB 54f52a **RR 63f 52a** 4818[12]
2 b c Midyan (USA) 9.9f **(64)** - Polly Worth (Wolver Hollow) 8f **(56)**

Form - 5280
Record 1998 - 1st:0 2nd:1 3rd:0 Ran:4
Win Prizemoney £0 *Total Prizemoney* £636
1998 Turf 0-3: (5f, 6f, 7f) (g-f, frm 2) 1998 AW 0-1: (7f) (Fibr)
Average colt. Turf high 63 - 2nd of 10 to Cosmo Jack (6 Jly Bath 5f g-f RF 2555). **W R Muir [0-4] M J Caddy.*

APOLLO RED BHB 68f87a **RR 72f 87a** 4649[10]

9 ch g Dominion 8.9f **(65)** - Woolpack (Golden Fleece (USA)) 7.9f **(74)**
Form - 10107050138500
Record 1998 - 1st:1 2nd:0 3rd:1 Ran:11
Pre1998 - 1st:11 2nd:7 3rd:16 Ran:73
Win Prizemoney £36,248 *Total Prizemoney* £51,408
Wins * **1998** Jly Bright (GD) H 7f 68 72
* 1997 *Dec Lingfi (STD) H 6f 85 87* <
* 1997 *Nov Lingfi (STD) H 6f 80 83*
* 1997 May Bright (G-F) H 7f 68 76
* 1997 *Apr Lingfi (STD) H 6f 72 79*
* 1997 *Feb Lingfi (STD) H 6f 60 65*
1996 *Dec Lingfi (STD) H 7f 58 62*
1996 *Nov Lingfi (STD) C 7f 59*
1996 May Lingfi (G-F) H 7f 54 57
1996 Apr Bright (FRM) H 5.3f 51 53
1994 Apr Bright (G-S) C 6f 45
1994 *Jan Lingfi (STD) H 7f 48 56*
1998 Turf 1-9: (5f, 6f 5, 7f 1-2, 8f) (g-s, gd 1-3, g-f 3, frm 2) 1998 AW 0-2: (6f, 7f) (Equi 2)
Useful gelding, effective 6f, - acts on Equi, has worn blinkers, likes left handed tracks, likes tight tracks. Turf high 72. AW high 73. A bit of a standing dish on the All-Weather at Lingfield, especially over six furlongs. He probably does not quite get a stiff seven on turf, though he has won over that trip on an easy track. He will continue to win his share under his optimum conditions, and he is particularly well ridden by Candy Morris.
**G L Moore [6-31] A Moore (from A Moore [6-42] Jan 1997).*

APOLLO WELLS **RR 103f** 1734a[8]

3 b c Sagal Wells - Sharrara (CAN) (Blushing Groom (FR)) 10.3f **(76)**
Form - 28
1998 Turf 0-1: (12f) (g-f)
Currently very useful colt. (1st run) - 8th of 16 to Central Park (31 May Capannelle 12f g-f RF 1734a). He was made to look moderate in the Italian Derby. **R Brogi in ITY [0-2].*

APPEARANCE MONEY (IRE) BHB 27f27a **RR 13f 27a** 1285[14]

7 b m Dancing Dissident (USA) 6.8f **(65)** - Fussy Budget (Wolver Hollow) 8f **(56)**
Form - 0
Record 1998 - 1st:0 2nd:0 3rd:0 Ran:1
Pre1998 - 1st:0 2nd:0 3rd:0 Ran:4
1998 Turf 0-1: (8f) (frm)
Poor mare. (DEAD) **F Murphy [1-27] Irish Festival Racing Club.*

APPIAN DAME (IRE) BHB 33a **RR 33a** 4788a[17]

3 b f Mukaddamah (USA) 7.6f **(74)** - Apapa Port (My Swanee) 7.6f **(52)**
Form - 676800
Record 1998 - 1st:0 2nd:0 3rd:0 Ran:4
Pre1998 - 1st:0 2nd:0 3rd:0 Ran:3
1998 Turf 0-1: (9f) (g-s) 1998 AW 0-3: (5f, 6f, 7f) (Fibr 3)
Leggy, very moderate filly, has worn blinkers. AW high 11.
**P J Flynn in IRE [0-1] D Twomey (from D J G MurraySmith [0-6] Mar 1998).*

APPLES AND PEARS (IRE) **RR 52f** 1474[11]

2 b f High Estate 10.5f **(66)** - Tiempo (King of Spain) 7.8f **(52)**
Form - 580
Record 1998 - 1st:0 2nd:0 3rd:0 Ran:3
1998 Turf 0-3: (5f 2, 6f) (g-f 2, frm)
Currently fair filly. Turf high 52.
**M H Tompkins [0-3] Mrs M H Tompkins.*

APPLE SAUCE BHB 63f **RR 63f** 4455[11]

3 b f Prince Sabo 6.6f **(64)** - Mrs Bacon (Balliol) 5f **(43)**
Form - 8521200
Record 1998 - 1st:1 2nd:2 3rd:0 Ran:7
Pre1998 - 1st:0 2nd:0 3rd:0 Ran:5
Win Prizemoney £3,582 *Total Prizemoney* £6,042
Wins * **1998** Aug Bath (GD) H 5.1f 55 58 <
1998 Turf 1-7: (5f 1-4, 6f 2, 7f) (gd 2, g-f 1-2, frm 3)
Scopey, average filly, effective 5 to 6f, best at 5f, acts on gd to g-f, best on gd. Turf high 63 - 2nd of 12 getting 10lb from Rififi (21 Aug Sandown 5f gd RF 3799) - also 1st of 9 getting 14lb from Levelled (4 Aug Bath RF 3323). Sprint-bred, she is a half-sister to the speedy Sizzling Melody. Generally progressive form in the middle of '98, including a victory in a Bath handicap, but ran moderately in her last two starts.
**L G Cottrell [1-7] Mrs B Skinner (from J R Arnold [0-5] Spt 1997).*

APPREHENSION BHB 105f **RR 112df** 3115[4]

4 b c In The Wings 11.2f **(77)** - First Kiss (Kris) 9.5f **(73)**
Form - 1574
Record 1998 - 1st:1 2nd:0 3rd:0 Ran:4
Pre1998 - 1st:1 2nd:0 3rd:1 Ran:5
Win Prizemoney £23,805 *Total Prizemoney* £30,584
Wins * **1998** Apr Newmar (SFT) G3 9f 112 <
* 1996 Spt Haydoc (G-F) 7.1f 84+
1998 Turf 1-4: (7f, 9f 1-1, 10f 2) (sft 1-2, gd, g-f)
Well made, Group-class colt, effective 9f, acts on sft, has worn blinkers. Turf high 112 (1st run) - 1st of 7 getting 3lb from Almushtarak (15 Apr Newmarket RF 0696). Stayed on well to land the Group Three Earl of Sefton first time out, but was last of five at Sandown next time. He does not look in love with the game and appears well named. **D R Loder [2-9] Sheikh Mohammed.*

APPROACHABLE (USA) BHB 50f **RR 47f** 4765[12]

3 b br c Known Fact (USA) 8.3f **(72)** - Western Approach (USA) (Gone West (USA)) 6.5f **(75)**
Form - 070
Record 1998 - 1st:0 2nd:0 3rd:0 Ran:3
1998 Turf 0-3: (7f, 8f 2) (gd, g-f 2)
Scopey, currently moderate colt, often wears blinkers. Turf high 47 (began Spt). **J H M Gosden [0-3] K Abdulla.*

APPROVANCE (USA) **RR 111f** 4443a[7]

6 gr g With Approval (CAN) 8.7f **(80)** - Anniversary Wish (USA) 00
Form - 1151447
1998 Turf 3-7: (8f 2-4, 9f 1-3) (sft 1-1, gd 2-4, g-f, hrd)
Group-class gelding, effective 8 to 9f, best at 9f, acts on sft to g-f, best on gd. Turf high 111 - 1st of 9 giving 8lb to Keriyoun (2 Aug Cork RF 3361a) - also 1st of 8 giving 20lb to Colombian Green (28 Jun Curragh RF 2434a). He improved dramatically for a horse of his age, putting up a career best performance to win a Listed race at Cork in August. He is unlikely to climb another rung of the ladder and will be pushed to equal last term's efforts.
**James Lenehan in IRE [3-7] Sheikh Mohammed (from J Oxx in IRE [0-1] Spt 1997).*

APPYABO BHB 47f48a **RR 22f 48a** 4996[6]

3 ch g Never so Bold 7.1f **(62)** - Cardinal Palace (Royal Palace) 9f **(56)**
Form - 222307000406
Record 1998 - 1st:0 2nd:2 3rd:1 Ran:11
Pre1998 - 1st:0 2nd:2 3rd:1 Ran:6
Win Prizemoney £0 *Total Prizemoney* £4,158
1998 Turf 0-6: (8f 2, 10f 2, 13f, 14f) (g-s 2, gd, g-f 2, frm) 1998 AW 0-5: (8f, 10f 3, 13f) (Equi 5)
Leggy, average gelding, effective 6 to 10f, acts on frm - acts on Equi, has worn blinkers. Turf high 48. AW high 68 - 2nd of 9 giving 6lb to Mystagogue (27 Jan Lingfield 10f Equi RF 0169). Inconsistent. He has made the frame often on turf and sand, but is thoroughly exposed.
**M Quinn [0-12] M Quinn (from M R Channon [0-5] Aug 1997).*

APRIL ACE BHB 72f73a **RR 82f 73a** 4924[6]

2 ch c First Trump - Champ d'Avril (Northfields (USA)) 9f **(72)**
Form - 741564406
Record 1998 - 1st:1 2nd:0 3rd:0 Ran:9
Win Prizemoney £2,969 *Total Prizemoney* £3,606
Wins * **1998** Jun Bath (G-S) 5.7f 70 <
1998 Turf 1-8: (6f 1-6, 7f 2) (sft, gd 1-5, frm 2) 1998 AW 0-1: (6f) (Fibr)
Decent colt. Turf high 82. **M Quinn [1-9] John Breslin.*

APRIL JACKSON BHB 30f25a **RR 24f 25a** 3462[12]

4 b f Petong 7.6f **(58)** - Raintree Venture (Good Times (ITY)) 6.6f **(54)**

Form - 70005000680
Record 1998 - 1st:0 2nd:0 3rd:0 Ran:11
Pre1998 - 1st:0 2nd:0 3rd:0 Ran:5
1998 Turf 0-5: (6f 2, 7f, 8f 2) (gd 2, g-f, frm, hrd) 1998 AW 0-6: (6f, 7f, 8f 2, 12f, 16f) (Fibr 6)
Workmanlike, little account filly. Turf high 24. AW high 24.
**P T Dalton [0-18] P T Dalton.*

APRIL SPIRIT RR 45f
4801[7]

3 b f Nomination 7.3f **(57)** - Seraphim (FR) (Lashkari) 9.8f **(67)**
Form - 67
Record 1998 - 1st:0 2nd:0 3rd:0 Ran:2
1998 Turf 0-2: (11f, 12f) (sft, frm)
Scopey, currently moderate filly. Turf high 45 (began Spt).
**R Hollinshead [0-2] Mrs B Ramsden.*

APRIL STOCK BHB 75f RR 76f
5150[3]

3 ch f Beveled (USA) 6.9f **(64)** - Stockline (Capricorn Line) 14.6f **(62)**
Form - 242233
Record 1998 - 1st:0 2nd:3 3rd:2 Ran:6
Win Prizemoney £0 *Total Prizemoney* £4,739
1998 Turf 0-6: (12f 3, 14f, 16f, 17f) (sft, gd 4, g-f)
Workmanlike, above-average filly, effective 12 to 17f, acts on sft to gd, best on gd. Turf high 76 - 3rd of 14 getting 12lb from Renzo (7 Nov Doncaster 17f gd RF 5150). Has done little wrong in defeat in staying events. **Miss Gay Kelleway [0-6] Mrs M Fairbairn.*

APRIL TREASURE BHB 43f RR 57f
4416[14]

3 b f Stani (USA) - Eleri (Rolfe (USA)) 12.1f **(65)**
Form - 68000
Record 1998 - 1st:0 2nd:0 3rd:0 Ran:5
1998 Turf 0-5: (11f 2, 12f 2, 13f) (gd 2, g-f, frm 2)
Light-framed, fair filly, has worn blinkers. Turf high 57.
**J L Spearing [0-5] W E Donohue.*

AQUAMARINA (IRE) BHB 36f RR 36f
4570[9]

2 b f Dolphin Street (FR) - Galapagos (Pitskelly) 8.5f **(53)**
Form - 0080
Record 1998 - 1st:0 2nd:0 3rd:0 Ran:4
1998 Turf 0-4: (6f 3, 7f) (g-f, frm 3)
Very moderate filly, often wears blinkers. Turf high 35 (began Jly).
**B J Meehan [0-4] Mrs D E Blackshaw.*

AQUATIC QUEEN BHB 38f38a RR 54f 38a
2688[10]

4 b f Rudimentary (USA) 8.2f **(66)** - Aquarula (Dominion) 8.5f **(63)**
Form - 00860
Record 1998 - 1st:0 2nd:0 3rd:0 Ran:4
Pre1998 - 1st:1 2nd:1 3rd:2 Ran:18
Win Prizemoney £3,210 *Total Prizemoney* £5,156
Wins * 1997 Jly Ripon (G-F) H 6f 50 55 <
1998 Turf 0-4: (5f, 6f 2, 7f) (g-s, g-f, frm 2)
Scopey, fair filly, effective 6f, acts on gd to frm, has worn blinkers. Turf high 37. Inconsistent. Helped by the draw when winning a maiden handicap on her first run for Chris Dwyer, and ran quite well either side of that win.
**C A Dwyer [1-10] J Johnston (from R J Weaver [0-12] Jun 1997).*

AQUAVITA BHB 32f52a RR 37f 52a
4588[5]

4 b gr f Kalaglow 11.2f **(67)**-Aigua Blava (USA) (Solford (USA))13f **(71)**
Form - 4205623702153705
Record 1998 - 1st:1 2nd:2 3rd:2 Ran:14
Pre1998 - 1st:0 2nd:1 3rd:0 Ran:9
Win Prizemoney £2,070 *Total Prizemoney* £5,274
Wins * **1998** *May Lingfi (STD) C 16f 54* <
1998 Turf 0-6: (10f, 12f, 14f 2, 15f, 17f) (gd 3, frm 3) 1998 AW 1-8: (12f 3, 13f, 16f 1-4) (Equi 1-7, Fibr)
Leggy, fair filly, effective 12 to 16f, best at 16f, acts on frm - acts on AW, best on Equi, prefers left handed tracks, prefers tight tracks, does well at Lingfield. Turf high 38. AW high 54 - 1st of 7 getting 10lb from Monaco Gold (13 May Lingfield RF 1199). Inconsistent.
**J S Moore [2-24] Ernie Houghton (from R Hannon [0-5] Jly 1997).*

ARAB GOLD BHB 65f RR 63df
2449[12]

3 b g Presidium 7.5f **(56)** - Parklands Belle (Stanford) 7.9f **(56)**
Form - 00
Record 1998 - 1st:0 2nd:0 3rd:0 Ran:2
Pre1998 - 1st:0 2nd:0 3rd:0 Ran:3
1998 Turf 0-2: (6f, 7f) (sft, gd)
Leggy, average gelding. **Miss S E Hall [0-5] C Platts.*

ARABIAN DESERT BHB 78f RR 77f
3166[13]

2 b c Tragic Role (USA) 9.4f **(63)** - Arabian Nymph (Sayf El Arab (USA)) 7.1f **(54)**
Form - 6140
Record 1998 - 1st:1 2nd:0 3rd:0 Ran:4
Win Prizemoney £2,700 *Total Prizemoney* £2,887
Wins * **1998** Jly Nottin (G-F) 5.1f 77 <
1998 Turf 1-4: (5f 1-1, 6f 3) (gd 3, g-f 1-1)
Above-average colt, has worn blinkers. Turf high 77 - 1st of 10 giving 5lb to Open Secret (4 Jly Nottingham RF 2543). He scored nicely at Nottingham in July but was disappointing subsequently.
**M Johnston [1-4] Ziad Galadari.*

ARABIAN MOON (IRE) RR 72f
4699[9]

2 ch c Barathea (IRE) -Excellent Alibi (USA) (Exceller (USA)) 12.5f **(74)**
Form - 70
Record 1998 - 1st:0 2nd:0 3rd:0 Ran:2
1998 Turf 0-2: (6f, 7f) (gd 2)
Currently above-average colt. Turf high 72 (began Spt).
**C E Brittain [0-2] Salem Suhail.*

ARAGROVE BHB 39f60a RR 40f 60a
3647[15]

8 b g Aragon 7.7f **(58)** - Grovehurst (Homing) 7.8f **(59)**
Form - 0000856800
Record 1998 - 1st:0 2nd:0 3rd:0 Ran:10
Pre1998 - 1st:8 2nd:4 3rd:4 Ran:41
Win Prizemoney £32,136 *Total Prizemoney* £40,696

Wins	1995	Jly	Goodwo	(G-F)	H	5f	77	80	<
	1995	Jun	Bright	(G-F)	H	6f	71	73	
	1995	Jun	Folkes	(GD)	H	6f	67	66	
	1995	May	Lingfi	(G-F)	H	5f	60	65	
	1995	Apr	Bright	(G-F)	H	5.3f	52	53	

1998 Turf 0-10: (5f 5, 6f 5) (gd 2, g-f 5, frm 2, hrd)
Moderate gelding, effective 5f, acts on frm, has worn blinkers. Turf high 40 - 6th of 10 getting 18lb from Sihafi (17 Jly Salisbury 5f frm RF 2890).
**M D I Usher [0-10] Bryan Fry (from J W Payne [5-22] Aug 1995).*

ARANTXA BHB 61f67a RR 67df 67a
4988[13]

4 b f Sharpo 7.5f **(68)** - Amalancher (USA) (Alleged (USA)) 10f **(76)**
Form - 510604000
Record 1998 - 1st:1 2nd:0 3rd:0 Ran:9
Pre1998 - 1st:1 2nd:0 3rd:0 Ran:3
Win Prizemoney £6,349 *Total Prizemoney* £6,590
Wins * **1998** Apr Hamilt (HVY) H 6f 70 73 <
* 1996 Nov Folkes (SFT) 6f 66+
1998 Turf 1-6: (6f 1-4, 7f, 8f) (sft 1-2, g-s 3, gd) 1998 AW 0-3: (6f, 7f, 8f) (Fibr 3)
Neat, above-average filly, effective 6 to 7f, best at 6f, acts on sft - acts on Fibr. Turf high 73 (1st run) - 1st of 12 getting 1lb from Nifty Norman (4 Apr Hamilton RF 0560). AW high 70 (1st run) - 5th of 8 giving 10lb to Mr Frosty (28 Mar Wolverhampton 7f Fibr RF 0495). Becoming disappointing.. **M Bell [2-12] Mrs Anne Yearley.*

ARARIBA BHB 30f RR 26f
3798[9]

3 b f Aragon 7.7f **(58)** - Free on Board (Free State) 8.7f **(61)**
Form - 0000
Record 1998 - 1st:0 2nd:0 3rd:0 Ran:4
1998 Turf 0-4: (6f, 8f, 9f, 10f) (gd 2, g-f, frm)
Light-framed, little account filly. Turf high 26.
**M Madgwick [0-4] D Knight.*

ARBENIG (IRE) BHB 50f60a RR 56f 60a
4885[4]

3 b f Anita's Prince 6f **(62)** - Out On Her Own (Superlative) 7.2f **(56)**
Form - 457513265377704
Record 1998 - 1st:1 2nd:1 3rd:2 Ran:13
Pre1998 - 1st:1 2nd:0 3rd:1 Ran:7
Win Prizemoney £4,617 *Total Prizemoney* £6,602
Wins * **1998** May Salisb (FRM) C 7f 60+
* *1997 Oct Wolver (STD) 6f 77* <
1998 Turf 1-11: (6f, 7f 1-10) (sft, g-s 2, gd 4, frm 1-4) 1998 AW 0-2: (7f 2) (Equi, Fibr)
Fair filly, effective 6f, acts on g-f - acts on Fibr. Turf high 60. AW

high 57. Consistent. **B Palling [2-20] A Smallwood & Alan Evans.*

ARBOR EALIS (IRE) BHB 66f68a **RR 73f 68a** 4230[11]
2 b f Woods of Windsor (USA) - North Lady (Northfields (USA)) 9f **(72)**

Form - 001038300
Record 1998 - 1st:1 2nd:0 3rd:2 Ran:9
Win Prizemoney £1,725 *Total Prizemoney* £3,254
Wins * **1998** *Jun Wolver (STD) S 5f 66 <*
1998 Turf 0-6: (5f 2, 6f 3, 7f) (g-s, gd 4, frm) 1998 AW 1-3: (5f 1-1, 6f 2) (Fibr 1-3)
Above-average filly, effective 5f, - acts on Fibr. Turf high 73. AW high 66 (1st run) - 1st of 7 getting 5lb from Five Ways Flyer (17 Jun Wolverhampton RF 2081). Inconsistent. She won a very bad seller on the Wolverhampton Fibresand in June, and will need to find an equally poor race in order to score again.
**H S Howe [1-9] Dr Ian Shenkin.*

ARC (IRE) BHB 56a **RR 51f** 4867[2]
4 b g Archway (IRE) 8.5f **(60)** - Columbian Sand (IRE) (Salmon Leap (USA)) 11f **(61)**
Form - 060662
Record 1998 - 1st:0 2nd:1 3rd:0 Ran:6
Pre1998 - 1st:0 2nd:0 3rd:2 Ran:10
Win Prizemoney £0 *Total Prizemoney* £1,371
1998 Turf 0-3: (5f, 6f, 7f) (frm 3) 1998 AW 0-3: (6f 2, 8f) (Fibr 3)
Average gelding, effective 5f, acts on gd, has worn blinkers. Turf high 51 (began Aug). AW high 59 (began Spt).
**F Jordan [0-5] Mrs A Roddis (from Mrs A Swinbank [0-4] Spt 1998).*

ARCADY BHB 58f62a **RR 60f 62a** 1120[7]
5 b m Slip Anchor 12.7f **(75)** - Elysian (Northfields (USA)) 9f **(72)**
Form - 407
Record 1998 - 1st:0 2nd:0 3rd:0 Ran:3
Pre1998 - 1st:4 2nd:4 3rd:6 Ran:29
Win Prizemoney £14,784 *Total Prizemoney* £25,683
Wins * 1997 Aug Newmar (G-F) H 16.1f 59 65 <
* 1997 May Sandow (G-F) H 14f 50 57
1996 *Nov Wolver (STD) H 14.8f 55 62*
1996 Spt Bath (G-F) H 13.1f 58 64
1998 Turf 0-3: (14f 2, 16f) (sft, g-s, frm)
Average filly, effective 14 to 20f, best at 16f, acts on g-f to frm, best on g-f, prefers right handed tracks. Turf high 60. Consistent.
**J L Harris [2-14] J H Henderson (from P T Walwyn [2-18] Nov 1996).*

ARCANE STAR (IRE) BHB 43f51a **RR 42f 51a** 4661[7]
3 b g Arcane (USA) 11.6f **(66)** - Chatsworth Bay (IRE) (Fairy King (USA)) 7.7f **(59)**
Form - 243320846007
Record 1998 - 1st:0 2nd:2 3rd:2 Ran:12
Pre1998 - 1st:0 2nd:0 3rd:0 Ran:6
Win Prizemoney £0 *Total Prizemoney* £1,913
1998 Turf 0-6: (5f, 6f 5) (g-s, gd 3, g-f, frm) 1998 AW 0-6: (5f, 6f 4, 7f) (Fibr 6)
Scopey, fair gelding, has worn blinkers. Turf high 47. AW high 50.
**A P Jarvis [0-18] B T G Partnership.*

ARCETTA (USA) RR 48f 4758[18]
2 b f Woodman (USA) 9.7f **(77)** - Dawn Deal (USA) (Grey Dawn II) 11.1f **(72)**
Form - 00
Record 1998 - 1st:0 2nd:0 3rd:0 Ran:2
1998 Turf 0-2: (6f, 7f) (gd, g-f)
Currently moderate filly. Turf high 48 (began Oct).
**C E Brittain [0-2] R A Pledger.*

ARCEVIA (IRE) BHB 72f **RR 66f** 4753[1]
3 b f Archway (IRE) 8.5f **(60)** - Estivalia (Persian Bold) 9.3f **(66)**
Form - 22631
Record 1998 - 1st:1 2nd:2 3rd:1 Ran:5
Win Prizemoney £2,745 *Total Prizemoney* £4,961
Wins * **1998** Oct Ayr (G-S) C 10.9f 66 <
1998 Turf 1-5: (9f, 10f 2, 11f 1-2) (sft 1-2, gd, g-f, frm)
Scopey, average filly. Turf high 82 (1st run) - 2nd of 10 to Putuna (22 Apr Epsom 9f sft RF 0815). She narrowly failed to make a winning debut at Epsom in April, but was well beaten in a listed race next time. Had to drop into claiming company to get off the mark.

**M R Channon [1-5] Kingsdown Racing.*

ARCH (USA) RR 102 5168a[9]
3 b c Kris S (USA) 9.3f **(76)**
Form - 0
1998 AW 0-1: (10f) (Dirt)
Currently very useful colt.
**F Brothers in USA [0-1] Claiborne Farm & Adele Dilschneider.*

ARCHELLO (IRE) BHB 44f **RR 47f** 4373[9]
4 b f Archway (IRE) 8.5f **(60)** - Golden Room (African Sky) 7.9f **(63)**
Form - 05058680
Record 1998 - 1st:0 2nd:0 3rd:0 Ran:8
Pre1998 - 1st:1 2nd:4 3rd:4 Ran:13
Win Prizemoney £3,452 *Total Prizemoney* £9,458
Wins * 1997 Aug Ripon (G-F) 5f 46+ <
1998 Turf 0-8: (5f, 6f 2, 7f 4, 8f) (gd 4, frm 4)
Leggy, moderate filly, effective 5 to 6f, acts on g-f to frm, has worn blinkers. Turf high 47. Consistent. Lacks a turn of foot.
**G R Oldroyd [1-21] E Gale.*

ARCHIE BABE (IRE) BHB 63f **RR 75f** 5148[13]
2 ch g Archway (IRE) 8.5f **(60)**-Frensham Manor(Le Johnstan) 7.4f **(55)**
Form - 36710060
Record 1998 - 1st:1 2nd:0 3rd:1 Ran:8
Win Prizemoney £2,512 *Total Prizemoney* £3,092
Wins * **1998** Spt Thirsk (GD) 7f 75 <
1998 Turf 1-8: (5f 2, 6f, 7f 1-3, 8f 2) (gd 2, g-f, frm 1-5)
Above-average gelding, effective 7f, acts on frm. Turf high 75 - 1st of 11 giving 4lb to Verposen (5 Spt Thirsk RF 4115).
**J J Quinn [1-8] Mrs K Mapp.*

ARCHITECT (IRE) RR 78f 5039[3]
2 b c Grand Lodge (USA) - Olean (Sadler's Wells (USA)) 10f **(76)**
Form - 43
Record 1998 - 1st:0 2nd:0 3rd:1 Ran:2
Win Prizemoney £0 *Total Prizemoney* £814
1998 Turf 0-2: (8f 2) (g-s, frm)
Currently above-average colt. Turf high 78 (began Spt). Has looked to require further than a mile.
**Sir Michael Stoute [0-2] Highclere Thoroughbred Racing Ltd.*

ARCHIVE FOOTAGE BHB 98f **RR 96f** 4793a[13]
6 b g Sadler's Wells (USA) 11.3f **(87)** - Trusted Partner (USA) (Affirmed (USA)) 9.3f **(79)**
Form - 111600
1998 Turf 3-6: (11f, 12f 1-3, 14f 2-2) (hvy 1-1, sft 1-1, g-s 1-2, gd, g-f)
Very useful gelding, effective 14f, acts on sft to g-s, often wears blinkers (extremely effectively). Turf high 116 - 1st of 7 giving 23lb to San Sebastian (13 Apr Cork RF 0796a) - also 1st of 9 giving 7lb to Blue Saddle (4 May Navan RF 1175a). Mixing hurdling with running on the Flat this year, he completed a hat-trick on soft ground in the spring, but his form tailed off afterwards.
**D K Weld in IRE [5-13] Michael Smurfit.*

ARCO COLORA BHB 55f **RR 61f** 1387[6]
4 b f Rainbow Quest (USA) 11.2f **(81)** - Bella Colora (Bellypha) 9.8f **(73)**
Form - 6
Record 1998 - 1st:0 2nd:0 3rd:0 Ran:1
Pre1998 - 1st:0 2nd:0 3rd:0 Ran:5
Win Prizemoney £0 *Total Prizemoney* £250
1998 Turf 0-1: (8f) (g-s)
Unfurnished, average filly. (1st run) - 6th of 13 giving 15lb to Miskin Heights (22 May Brighton 8f g-s RF 1387).
**D R C Elsworth [0-4] Helena Springfield Ltd (from Sir Michael Stoute [0-2] Jly 1997).*

ARCTIC AIR BHB 77f **RR 64f** 3935[8]
3 br f Polar Falcon (USA) 9f **(74)** - Breadcrumb (Final Straw) 7.9f **(64)**
Form - 7308
Record 1998 - 1st:0 2nd:0 3rd:1 Ran:4
Pre1998 - 1st:1 2nd:1 3rd:0 Ran:3
Win Prizemoney £4,536 *Total Prizemoney* £6,422
Wins * 1997 Spt Ayr (G-S) 7f 76 <
1998 Turf 0-4: (8f 3, 10f) (g-s, gd, g-f, frm)
Leggy, average filly, effective 7f, acts on gd, likes left handed tracks. Turf high 64. **E Weymes [1-7] T A Scothern.*

ARCTIC FANCY (USA) BHB 76f **RR 75f** 5126[6]

5 ch g Arctic Tern (USA) 12.2f **(71)** - Fit And Fancy (USA) (Vaguely Noble) 10.1f **(72)**

Form - 330271136

Record	**1998** -	1st:2	2nd:1	3rd:3	Ran:9
	Pre1998 -	1st:1	2nd:3	3rd:4	Ran:17

Win Prizemoney £8,849 *Total Prizemoney* £19,528

Wins								
* **1998**	Oct	Bright	(G-S)	H	11.9f	73	75	<
* **1998**	Spt	Newbur	(gd)	H	12f	69	70	
1996	Jun	Haydoc	(GD)		14f		73	

1998 Turf 2-9: (10f, 12f 2-3, 14f 4, 16f) (sft, g-s 1-3, gd 3, g-f, frm 1-1)

Above-average gelding, effective 12 to 14f, acts on g-s to frm, likes left handed tracks. Turf high 75 - 1st of 8 giving 15lb to Smart Boy (22 Oct Brighton RF 4932). Consistent.

**J G Smyth-Osbourne [2-9] The Cool Customers (from P W Harris [1-17] Spt 1997).*

ARCTIC OWL BHB 121f **RR 120f** 4632[1]

4 b g Most Welcome 8.6f **(66)** - Short Rations (Lorenzaccio) 10f **(64)**

Form - 11311

Record	**1998** -	1st:4	2nd:0	3rd:1	Ran:5
	Pre1998 -	1st:2	2nd:1	3rd:1	Ran:6

Win Prizemoney £88,917 *Total Prizemoney* £110,269

Wins								
* **1998**	Oct	Newmar	()	G3	16f		120	<
* **1998**	Aug	Deauvi	(SFT)	G2	15f		115	
* **1998**	Jun	York	(G-S)	H	13.9f	100	114	
* **1998**	May	Newmar	(GD)	H	12f	95	99	
* 1997	Spt	York	(SFT)	H	11.9f	88	95	
* 1997	Jun	Windso	(G-F)		10f		78	

1998 Turf 4-5: (12f 1-1, 14f 1-1, 15f 1-1, 16f 1-2) (sft 1-2, g-s 1-1, gd 1-1, g-f 1-1)

Scopey, very high-class gelding, effective 14 to 16f, acts on sft to g-f, excels at Newmarket and York. Turf high 120 - 1st of 7 getting 2lb from Celeric (3 Oct Newmarket RF 4632) - also 1st of 8 from Grey Shot (23 Aug Deauville RF 3917a). A progressive stayer, he was a good winner on his return at Newmarket, and won in great style at York next time. An unlucky third in the Northumberland Plate, he gained compensation when collaring Grey Shot in the Prix Kergorlay at Deauville. He followed-up with an emphatic victory in the Jockey Club Cup, and he looks likely to be one of the main contenders for the stayers' championship in 1999.

**J R Fanshawe [6-11] The Owl Society.*

Arctic Owl was a standard bearer for his in-form trainer

ARCTIC STAR BHB 48f59a **RR 40f 59a** 2229[12]

3 b g Polar Falcon (USA) 9f **(74)** - Three Stars (Star Appeal) 9.6f **(65)**

Form - 43574370

Record	**1998** -	1st:0	2nd:0	3rd:2	Ran:8
	Pre1998 -	1st:0	2nd:0	3rd:0	Ran:6

Win Prizemoney £0 *Total Prizemoney* £1,511

1998 Turf 0-5: (10f 2, 12f 2, 17f) (g-s, gd 4) 1998 AW 0-3: (9f, 10f, 12f) (Equi, Fibr 2)

Leggy, average gelding, effective 7f, acts on gd. Turf high 50. AW high 65. Inconsistent.

**V Thompson [0-3] Mrs V Thompson (from M R Channon [0-11] Apr 1998).*

ARCTIC THUNDER (USA) BHB 60f64a **RR 69f 64a** 4638[5]

7 b g Far North (CAN) 10.3f **(76)** - Flying Cloud (USA) (Roberto (USA)) 10f **(76)**

Form - 5854084005

Record	**1998** -	1st:0	2nd:0	3rd:0	Ran:9
	Pre1998 -	1st:3	2nd:3	3rd:2	Ran:19

Win Prizemoney £23,668 *Total Prizemoney* £38,623

Wins								
1995	May	York	(G-F)	H	11.9f	89	95	<
1994	Spt	York	(GD)	H	11.9f	87	89	
1994	Jly	Ayr	(GD)		10f		82	

1998 Turf 0-5:(12f, 14f 3, 16f)(sft, gd, g-f 3)1998 AW 0-4:(12f 4) (Fibr 4)

Average gelding, effective 12f, - acts on Fibr, likes left handed tracks, likes tight tracks. Turf high 69. AW high 66 - 5th of 12 getting 12lb from Primary Colours (3 Oct Wolverhampton 12f Fibr RF 4638). A useful handicapper in 1995, he has not shown his form for quite a while now.

**B Palling [0-13] Merthyr Motor Auctions (from Lady Herries [3-17] Jun 1996).*

ARDENT BHB 46f43a **RR 45f 43a** 4995[5]

4 b g Aragon 7.7f **(58)** - Forest of Arden (Tap On Wood) 10.3f **(65)**

Form - 6521770700235

Record	**1998** -	1st:1	2nd:2	3rd:1	Ran:13
	Pre1998 -	1st:0	2nd:0	3rd:0	Ran:7

Win Prizemoney £2,957 *Total Prizemoney* £5,159

Wins								
* **1998**	Apr	Bright	(GD)	H	8f	47	54	<

1998 Turf 1-10: (8f 1-8, 9f, 10f) (sft, g-s 1-1, gd 2, g-f 3, frm 3) 1998 AW 0-3: (8f 2, 10f) (Equi 3)

Moderate gelding, effective 8f, acts on g-s, has worn blinkers, likes left handed tracks. Turf high 54 (1st run) - 1st of 15 getting 9lb from Inclination (20 Apr Brighton RF 0766). AW high 43.

**C J Benstead [1-20] R Lamb.*

ARDLEIGH CHARMER BHB 65f **RR 68f** 4841[10]

3 ch c Theatrical Charmer 10.9f **(63)**-Miss Adventure(Adonijah) 10f **(61)**

Form - 66211511080580

Record	**1998** -	1st:4	2nd:1	3rd:0	Ran:14
	Pre1998 -	1st:0	2nd:0	3rd:0	Ran:2

Win Prizemoney £11,433 *Total Prizemoney* £12,177

Wins								
* **1998**	Jun	Ripon	(SFT)	H	12.3f	58	68	<
* **1998**	Jun	Sandow	(G-S)	H	11.4f	58	64	
* **1998**	May	Redcar	(GD)	H	10f	52	61	
* **1998**	Apr	Redcar	(SFT)	H	9f	46	52	

1998 Turf 4-13: (9f 1-1, 10f 1-2, 11f 1-2, 12f 1-4, 14f 3, 15f) (sft 1-2, g-s 1-1, gd 2-4, g-f 4, frm 2) 1998 AW 0-1: (8f) (Fibr)

Workmanlike, average colt, effective 10 to 14f, acts on g-s to g-f, has worn blinkers, likes left handed tracks, prefers tight tracks. Turf high 68 - 1st of 7 giving 11lb to Semi Circle (18 Jun Ripon RF 2094) - also 1st of 14 getting 2lb from Norski Lad (12 Jun Sandown RF 1938). In fine form early in the year, winning four times in modest company. Lost his way latterly. **C A Dwyer [4-16] Roalco Ltd.*

AREION (GER) **RR 108f** 4214a[1]

3 b c Big Shuffle (USA) - Aerleona (GER) (Caerleon (USA)) 8.6f **(71)**

Form - 11

1998 Turf 2-2: (6f 2-2) (sft 1-1, gd 1-1)

Currently Pattern-class colt. Turf high 108 (1st run) (began Jly) - 1st of 13 getting 6lb from Auenadler (4 Jly Hamburg RF 2664a) - also 1st of 9 getting 3lb from Auenadler (2 Spt Baden-Baden RF 4214a). He was beaten fair and square by Averti in a Group 2 at Baden-Baden and was fortunate to be gifted the race in the Stewards' room. He is, however, a useful and progressive young sprinter. **A Wohler in GER [2-2] Frau M Haller.*

AREISH (IRE) BHB 33f39a **RR 30f 39a** 4862^{7}

5 b m Keen 11.1f **(58)** - Cool Combination (Indian King (USA)) 7.4f **(64)**
Form - 444153651437
Record 1998 - 1st:2 2nd:0 3rd:2 Ran:10
Pre1998 - 1st:0 2nd:0 3rd:0 Ran:11
Win Prizemoney £4,451 *Total Prizemoney* £5,404
Wins 1998 *Spt Wolver (STD) SH 12f 39 41*
1998 *Jan Southw (STD) H 11f 38 43* <
1998 AW 2-10: (11f 1-3, 12f 1-6, 13f) (Equi 2, Fibr 2-8)
Moderate filly, effective 11 to 12f, best at 11f, - acts on AW, best on Fibr, has worn blinkers. AW high 43 - 1st of 8 getting 17lb from Broctune Line (26 Jan Southwell RF 0164) - also 1st of 12 getting 12lb from Bonne Ville (5 Spt Wolverhampton RF 4120). She has moved stables several times in her career, but has been successful in modest middle-distance events on Fibresand.
**J Balding [0-3] Mrs J Coghlan-Everitt (from M C Pipe [1-1] Spt 1998).*

ARE YER THERE BHB 34f **RR 12f** 3504^{10}

3 gr g Terimon 8.7f **(58)**-Indian Swallow(FR) (Shirley Heights) 10.3f **(74)**
Form - U0
Record 1998 - 1st:0 2nd:0 3rd:0 Ran:2
Pre1998 - 1st:0 2nd:0 3rd:0 Ran:6
1998 Turf 0-2: (12f, 16f) (g-f, frm)
Tall, poor gelding. (began Jly). **M W Easterby [0-9] T A Hughes.*

ARGUMENTATIVE BHB 42f **RR 40f** 4571^{11}

3 b g Mujadil (USA) 7.7f **(70)** - Dusky Nancy (Red Sunset) 8.2f **(63)**
Form - 050
Record 1998 - 1st:0 2nd:0 3rd:0 Ran:3
Pre1998 - 1st:0 2nd:0 3rd:0 Ran:7
Win Prizemoney £0 *Total Prizemoney* £231
1998 Turf 0-3: (7f, 8f, 10f) (sft, gd, g-f)
Workmanlike, moderate gelding, effective 7f, acts on g-f, likes tight tracks. Turf high 40. Inconsistent.
**T D McCarthy [0-1] David Horsman (from S Dow [0-9] Jun 1998).*

ARIAN DA BHB 54f76a **RR 41f 76a** 5121^{10}

3 ch f Superlative 8.8f **(57)** - Nell of The North (USA) (Canadian Gil (CAN)) 9.2f **(77)**
Form - 570087700080
Record 1998 - 1st:0 2nd:0 3rd:0 Ran:12
Pre1998 - 1st:1 2nd:5 3rd:2 Ran:12
Win Prizemoney £2,882 *Total Prizemoney* £8,970
Wins * 1997 Spt Sandow (G-F) 5f 75 <
1998 Turf 0-11: (5f 4, 6f 5, 7f 2) (g-s, gd 4, g-f 4, frm 2) 1998 AW 0-1: (6f) (Fibr)
Scopey, fair filly, effective 5f, acts on gd to frm, has worn blinkers. Turf high 78. Becoming disappointing.
**B Palling [1-24] J Hamilton-Jones.*

ARIAN SPIRIT (IRE) BHB 44f42a **RR 47f 42a** 1120^{14}

7 b m High Estate 10.5f **(66)** - Astral Way (Hotfoot) 10.5f **(59)**
Form - 00
Record 1998 - 1st:0 2nd:0 3rd:0 Ran:2
Pre1998 - 1st:9 2nd:8 3rd:6 Ran:57
Win Prizemoney £27,566 *Total Prizemoney* £36,928
Wins * 1997 Aug Ayr (G-F) H 15f 42 44
* 1997 Jly Beverl (G-F) H 16.2f 34 39
* 1996 Aug Ayr (GD) H 15f 51 57 <
* 1996 May Redcar (G-F) H 14.1f 47 53
* 1996 May Redcar (G-F) H 16f 45 50
* 1996 Mar Newcas (G-S) H 16.1f 37 46
* 1995 Oct Pontef (G-F) H 17.1f 33 42
* 1995 Jly Mussel (FRM) H 15.1f 30 38
1995 Jan Lingfi (STD) H 16f 36 38
1998 Turf 0-2: (16f 2) (gd, frm)
Moderate mare, effective 15 to 17f, best at 17f, acts on gd to frm - acts on Fibr, best on gd, has worn blinkers, excels at Ayr. Turf high 29. Becoming disappointing.
**J L Eyre [8-46] Martin West (from W J Musson [1-18] Jan 1995).*

ARIANT (USA) BHB 89f **RR 86f** 4707^{7}

3 ch c Mr Prospector (USA) 8.6f **(88)** - Six Months Long (USA) (Northern Dancer) 9.6f **(80)**
Form - 827
Record 1998 - 1st:0 2nd:1 3rd:0 Ran:3
Pre1998 - 1st:1 2nd:0 3rd:0 Ran:2
Win Prizemoney £3,863 *Total Prizemoney* £5,637
Wins * 1997 Jly Newbur (G-F) 6f 85+ <
1998 Turf 0-3: (7f 3) (frm 3)
Scopey, useful colt. Turf high 86 - 2nd of 11 getting 1lb from Adjutant (26 Spt Haydock 7f frm RF 4498). Decent efforts in seven-furlong handicaps. **J H M Gosden [1-5] Sheikh Mohammed.*

ARISAIG (IRE) BHB 53f **RR 54f** 2772^{9}

4 ch g Ela-Mana-Mou 12.7f **(72)** - Glasson Lady (GER) (Priamos (GER)) 11.1f **(61)**
Form - 268150
Record 1998 - 1st:1 2nd:1 3rd:0 Ran:6
Pre1998 - 1st:0 2nd:1 3rd:2 Ran:9
Win Prizemoney £4,045 *Total Prizemoney* £6,701
Wins * 1998 Jun Pontef (SFT) H 18f 52 54 <
1998 Turf 1-6: (16f 4, 18f 1-2) (g-s 1-1, gd 2, g-f, frm 2)
Scopey, fair gelding, effective 14 to 18f, best at 16f, acts on g-s to frm, has worn blinkers, prefers left handed tracks, excels at Nottingham. Turf high 57 (1st run) - 2nd of 15 getting 17lb from Outset (31 Mar Newcastle 16f gd RF 0514) - also 1st of 13 from Highfield Fizz (15 Jun Pontefract RF 2001). Consistent. Looks paceless and needs every yard of two miles, getting off the mark in quite a valuable handicap at Pontefract.
**P Calver [1-15] Mrs Janis MacPherson.*

ARJAN (IRE) BHB 76f **RR 69f** 5142^{21}

3 gr f Paris House 5.9f **(64)** - Forest Berries (IRE) (Thatching) 8f **(66)**
Form - 45106620070
Record 1998 - 1st:1 2nd:1 3rd:0 Ran:11
Pre1998 - 1st:1 2nd:0 3rd:0 Ran:4
Win Prizemoney £7,323 *Total Prizemoney* £10,117
Wins * 1998 May Catter (SFT) H 5f 73 81? <
* 1997 Oct Catter (SFT) 5f 75
1998 Turf 1-11: (5f 1-11) (sft 2, g-s 3, gd 1-4, g-f, frm)
Average filly, effective 5f, acts on gd. Turf high 84 - 2nd of 15 giving 1lb to Eastern Lyric (31 Jly Goodwood 5f gd RF 3235) - also 1st of 10 from Pleasure Time (29 May Catterick RF 1576).
**J Berry [2-15] W J Kelly.*

ARKADIAN HERO (USA) BHB 115f **RR 119f** 4105^{10}

3 ch c Trempolino (USA) 11.9f **(77)** - Careless Kitten (USA) (Caro) 9.3f **(74)**
Form - 402480
Record 1998 - 1st:0 2nd:1 3rd:0 Ran:6
Pre1998 - 1st:3 2nd:0 3rd:0 Ran:5
Win Prizemoney £53,663 *Total Prizemoney* £70,049
Wins * 1997 Spt Newbur (G-S) G2 6f 99
* 1997 Aug Ripon (G-F) L 6f 104+ <
* 1997 Jly Goodwo (G-F) 6f 102
1998 Turf 0-6: (5f, 6f 3, 7f, 8f) (sft, gd, g-f, frm 3)
High-class colt, effective 6f, acts on g-f to frm. Turf high 119 - 4th of 17 getting 6lb from Elnadim (9 Jly Newmarket 6f frm RF 2649). Very useful as a juvenile, he was taking on the best all season but did not manage a victory. He started off the season as a classic prospect, but made little impact in either the Free Handicap or the Guineas. Brought back to sprinting, he chased home Tamarisk at Lingfield, but was then found out in the top sprints for the rest of the season, his best effort being when fourth in the July Cup when not favourably drawn.
**L M Cumani [3-11] M Tabor & Mrs John Magnier.*

ARM AND A LEG (IRE) BHB 41f50a **RR 53f 50a** 4271^{7}

3 ch g Petardia 8.2f **(58)** - Ikala (Lashkari) 9.8f **(67)**
Form - 765867654U2087
Record 1998 - 1st:0 2nd:1 3rd:0 Ran:14
Pre1998 - 1st:1 2nd:1 3rd:2 Ran:12
Win Prizemoney £2,239 *Total Prizemoney* £5,102
Wins * 1997 May Yarmou (G-F) S 5.2f 61 <
1998 Turf 0-8: (8f 3, 10f 3, 11f, 12f) (g-s, gd, g-f 3, frm 3) 1998 AW 0-6: (6f, 7f, 8f, 10f 2, 12f) (Equi 2, Fibr 4)
Leggy, fair gelding, effective 5 to 9f, best at 7f, acts on gd to hrd, best on frm, has worn blinkers. Turf high 53. AW high 52.
**C A Dwyer [1-26] R West.*

ARMANDO CARPIO **RR 111f** $1380a^{3}$

5 b h Warning 8.1f **(77)** - Melodic (Song) 7.2f **(61)**
Form - 23
1998 Turf 0-1: (6f) (gd)

Group-class colt. He is capable of smart sprinting form, but was lightly tried last term. **A Renzoni in ITY [2-5] Scuderia Jerome.*

ARMIDALE (IRE) BHB 54f **RR 51f** 4803[6]
2 b c College Chapel - Bay Supreme (Martinmas) 7.6f **(59)**
Form - 006
Record 1998 - 1st:0 2nd:0 3rd:0 Ran:3
1998 Turf 0-3: (6f 2, 7f) (sft, gd 2)
Currently fair colt. Turf high 51 (began Spt).
**E A L Dunlop [0-3] Mrs John Dunlop.*

ARMILINA (FR) **RR 90f** 4724a[2]
3 gr f Linamix (FR) 8.2f **(64)** - Armarama (Persian Bold) 9.3f **(66)**
Form - 2
1998 Turf 0-1: (10f) (sft)
Currently useful filly. (1st run) - 2nd of 11 to Moteck (4 Oct Longchamp 10f sft RF 4724a). **S Wattel in FR [0-1] F Dufaut.*

ARMSTRONG (GER) **RR 103f** 3612b[3]
4 ch c Niniski (USA) 13.2f **(67)**-Arastou (GER) (Surumu (GER)) 10f **(83)**
Form - 3
1998 Turf 0-1: (13f) (gd)
Currently very useful colt. (1st run) - 3rd of 3 giving 12lb to Dark Moondancer (6 Aug Deauville 13f gd RF 3612b). He could not cope with Dark Moondancer at Deauville in August.
**H Blume in GER [0-1].*

ARNAQUEUR (USA) **RR 105f** 836a[4]
3 b c Miswaki (USA) 8.1f **(81)** - All Along (FR) (Targowice (USA)) 11.4f **(70)**
Form - 4
1998 Turf 0-1: (11f) (hvy)
Currently Pattern-class colt. **A Fabre in FR [0-2].*

ARNIE (IRE) BHB 36f22a **RR 42?f 22a** 131[11]
6 b g Double Schwartz 7f **(60)**-The Moneys Gone (Precocious) 8.6f **(62)**
Form - 0000
Record 1998 - 1st:0 2nd:0 3rd:0 Ran:2
Pre1998 - 1st:1 2nd:0 3rd:0 Ran:23
Win Prizemoney £4,012 *Total Prizemoney* £4,012
Wins * 1997 Jun Goodwo (SFT) H 6f 26 42 <
1998 AW 0-2: (7f, 10f) (Equi 2)
Moderate gelding, effective 6f, acts on gd, has worn blinkers (very effectively). AW high 5.
**J R Poulton [1-15] Mike Culling (from G L Moore [0-5] Nov 1995).*

AROUND THE WORLD (IRE) BHB 72f **RR 66f** 5137[4]
2 b f Thatching 7.8f **(69)** - Wild Applause (IRE) (Sadler's Wells (USA)) 10f **(76)**
Form - 544
Record 1998 - 1st:0 2nd:0 3rd:0 Ran:3
Win Prizemoney £0 *Total Prizemoney* £459
1998 Turf 0-3: (5f, 7f 2) (g-s, gd, frm)
Currently average filly. Turf high 66 (began Aug).
**M Johnston [0-3] The Walter S Partnership.*

ARPEGGIO BHB 75f **RR 79?f** 4633[7]
3 b c Polar Falcon (USA) 9f **(74)** - Hilly (Town Crier) 10.2f **(55)**
Form - 38047
Record 1998 - 1st:0 2nd:0 3rd:1 Ran:5
Pre1998 - 1st:0 2nd:2 3rd:0 Ran:3
Win Prizemoney £0 *Total Prizemoney* £3,979
1998 Turf 0-5: (7f 2, 8f 3) (sft, gd, g-f 2, frm)
Scopey, above-average colt, effective 5 to 7f, acts on gd to g-f, best on gd. Turf high 85 (1st run) - 3rd of 13 to Chattan (27 Mar Doncaster 7f gd RF 0481). Consistent.
**D Nicholls [0-2] Lhendup Dorji (from R Hannon [0-6] May 1998).*

ARRASAS LADY BHB 27f23a **RR 25f 23a** 3272[9]
8 ch m Arrasas (USA) 14.4f **(37)** - Sharelle (Relko) 9.9f **(59)**
Form - 044600070
Record 1998 - 1st:0 2nd:0 3rd:0 Ran:9
Pre1998 - 1st:0 2nd:1 3rd:4 Ran:29
Win Prizemoney £0 *Total Prizemoney* £2,385
1998 Turf 0-2: (9f, 10f) (gd, frm) 1998 AW 0-7: (7f, 8f 4, 10f 2) (Equi 3, Fibr 4)
Very moderate mare, effective 8f, - acts on Fibr, has worn blinkers. Turf high 20. AW high 30.
**J R Poulton [0-19] Miss E Thomas (from J E Long [0-15] May 1995).*

ARRIVING BHB 103f **RR 106f** 4630[2]
4 br f Most Welcome 8.6f **(66)** - Affirmation (Tina's Pet) 6.8f **(59)**
Form - 7152832
Record 1998 - 1st:1 2nd:2 3rd:1 Ran:7
Pre1998 - 1st:2 2nd:2 3rd:2 Ran:12
Win Prizemoney £30,433 *Total Prizemoney* £56,011
Wins * **1998** May York (GD) L 10.4f 102 <
* 1997 Spt Newbur (G-F) H 10f 65 71
* 1997 Jun Sandow (G-F) H 11.4f 60 64
1998 Turf 1-7: (10f 1-5, 11f 2) (sft, gd 1-4, g-f 2)
Workmanlike, Pattern-class filly, effective 10 to 11f, best at 10f, acts on sft to g-f, likes left handed tracks. Turf high 106 - also 1st of 7 from Star Precision (13 May York RF 1206). Inconsistent. She sprang a 33-1 shock when winning a Listed race at York in May, but showed that was no fluke when making the frame in two Group contests during the autumn. Only Arthur C. Clark can explain how she was beaten off a mark of 74 at Newmarket in May.
**J W Hills [3-19] Wyck Hall Stud.*

ARROYADA (GER) **RR 105f** 4342a[1]
3 b f Law Society (USA) 11.6f **(71)** - Alegria (Marduk (GER))
Form - 1
1998 Turf 1-1: (12f 1-1) (sft 1-1)
Currently Pattern-class filly. (1st run) - 1st of 9 from Golden Plate (13 Spt Hanover RF 4342a). She was ridden confidently when winning a Group Three at Hanover in September and is open to further improvement. **E Pils in GER [1-1] Grafin von Norman.*

ARRY MARTIN BHB 51f **RR 60f** 4961[14]
3 b c Aragon 7.7f **(58)** - Bells of St Martin (Martinmas) 7.6f **(59)**
Form - 48500030330
Record 1998 - 1st:0 2nd:0 3rd:3 Ran:11
Pre1998 - 1st:0 2nd:0 3rd:0 Ran:1
Win Prizemoney £0 *Total Prizemoney* £1,177
1998 Turf 0-9: (5f 2, 6f 5, 7f 2) (sft, g-s, gd, g-f 5, frm) 1998 AW 0-2: (6f, 8f) (Fibr 2)
Workmanlike, average colt, effective 6f, acts on g-f, has worn blinkers. Turf high 60 - 5th of 11 giving 4lb to Zeppo (23 Jun Lingfield 6f g-f RF 2201). AW high 46.
**W R Muir [0-12] Mrs Marion Wickham.*

ARTAN (IRE) **RR 119f** 3424a[2]
6 b h Be My Native (USA) 11.2f **(62)** - Cambridge Lodge (Tower Walk) 10f **(62)**
Form - 332
1998 Turf 0-3: (10f, 11f 2) (sft 2, gd)
High-class horse. Turf high 119 - 2nd of 7 giving 15lb to Elle Danzig (2 Aug Munich 10f sft RF 3424a). Consistent. A useful German-trained middle distance performer, he likes to make the running. Found Elle Danzig too strong for him twice during the summer.
**M Rolke in GER [3-12] Stall Brandenburg (from H-A Pantall in FR [1-1] Oct 1996).*

ARTERXERXES BHB 76f79a **RR 76f 79a** 4391[10]
5 b g Anshan 8.2f **(63)** - Hanglands (Bustino) 10.4f **(64)**
Form - 20000160
Record 1998 - 1st:1 2nd:1 3rd:0 Ran:8
Pre1998 - 1st:2 2nd:4 3rd:1 Ran:16
Win Prizemoney £9,840 *Total Prizemoney* £17,895
Wins * **1998** Aug Folkes (G-F) H 6.9f 73 76
* 1997 Aug Yarmou (G-F) H 7f 75 81 <
* 1996 Apr Folkes (FRM) 6.9f 71
1998 Turf 1-6: (7f 1-4, 8f 2) (gd, g-f 1-3, frm 2) 1998 AW 0-2: (7f, 8f) (Equi 2)
Above-average gelding, effective 7f, acts on gd to g-f - acts on Equi, has worn blinkers. Turf high 76 - 1st of 5 giving 7lb to Madame Claude (14 Aug Folkestone RF 3627). AW high 79 (1st run) - 2nd of 7 giving 11lb to Philistar (3 Apr Lingfield 7f Equi RF 0557). **M J Heaton-Ellis [3-24] P G Lowe & Partners.*

ARTFUL DANE (IRE) BHB 52f70a **RR 18f 70a** 4744[20]
6 b g Danehill (USA) 9.1f **(79)** - Art Age (Artaius (USA)) 9f **(69)**
Form - 00800000

Record 1998 - 1st:0 2nd:0 3rd:0 Ran:8
Pre1998 - 1st:4 2nd:3 3rd:3 Ran:33
Win Prizemoney £42,193 *Total Prizemoney* £54,329
Wins * 1997 Mar Doncas (G-F) H 8f 72 79 <
* 1996 Spt Newbur (G-F) H 8f 64 72
* 1996 Aug Bath (G-F) H 8f 62 66
* 1995 Jly Windso (G-F) 8.3f 74
1998 Turf 0-8: (8f 7, 10f) (sft, g-s, gd 3, g-f, frm 2)
Moderate gelding, effective 8f, acts on gd to frm, often wears blinkers (effectively). Turf high 65.
**M J Heaton-Ellis [4-41] S P Lansdown Racing.*

ARTHURS KINGDOM (IRE) BHB 69f **RR 70f** 4577[3]
2 b g Roi Danzig (USA) 10.5f **(62)** - Merrie Moment (IRE) (Taufan (USA)) 7f **(57)**
Form - 7053
Record 1998 - 1st:0 2nd:0 3rd:1 Ran:4
Win Prizemoney £0 *Total Prizemoney* £259
1998 Turf 0-4: (7f 4) (gd, g-f, frm 2)
Above-average gelding. Turf high 70 - 3rd of 12 to Dispol Rock (30 Spt Newcastle 7f g-f RF 4577). **A P Jarvis [0-4] Mrs Ann Jarvis.*

ARTIC COURIER BHB 59f69a **RR 65f 69a** 4252[8]
7 gr g Siberian Express (USA) 9f **(58)** - La Reine de France (Queen's Hussar) 11.6f **(58)**
Form - 4476533648
Record 1998 - 1st:0 2nd:0 3rd:2 Ran:10
Pre1998 - 1st:3 2nd:12 3rd:6 Ran:43
Win Prizemoney £13,240 *Total Prizemoney* £44,389
Wins * 1996 Jly Epsom (G-F) H 12f 80 85 <
* 1996 May Kempto (G-F) H 12f 76 80
* 1995 Jun Ripon (FRM) 12.3f 68
1998 Turf 0-8: (12f 6, 14f, 15f) (sft, gd 3, g-f 2, frm 2) 1998 AW 0-2: (12f 2) (Equi, Fibr)
Average gelding, effective 12f, acts on gd, has worn blinkers, likes left handed tracks, favours tight tracks. Turf high 67. AW high 64. Consistent. He has been sliding down the handicap over the past couple of seasons, but though making the frame from time to time, has not come any closer to actually winning.
**D J S Cosgrove [3-53] A D Hardy.*

ART OF VOICE (IRE) **RR 103f** 3424a[7]
4 ch c Sharp Victor (USA) 10f **(56)** - Ms Valerina (USA) (Miswaki (USA)) 9f **(81)**
Form - 37
1998 Turf 0-2: (10f 2) (sft, g-f)
Currently very useful colt. Turf high 103 (1st run) (began Jly) - 3rd of 12 giving 8lb to Aboard (19 Jly Frankfurt 10f g-f RF 3054a). He ran creditably in a Group Three at Frankfurt in July, but is no superstar. **M Trybuhl in GER [0-2] Stall Yellow.*

ART SOCIETY (IRE) BHB 40f **RR 19f** 4999[9]
2 ch c Perugino (USA) - Nisha Society (IRE) (Law Society (USA)) 9.9f **(70)**
Form - 000
Record 1998 - 1st:0 2nd:0 3rd:0 Ran:3
1998 Turf 0-3: (7f, 8f 2) (sft, gd, frm)
Currently poor colt. Turf high 19 (began Spt).
**J J Sheehan [0-3] P J Sheehan.*

ARZANI (USA) BHB 42f48a **RR 48f 48a** 3628[4]
7 ch h Shahrastani (USA) 11.5f **(69)** - Vie En Rose (USA) (Blushing Groom (FR)) 10.3f **(76)**
Form - 638505030404
Record 1998 - 1st:0 2nd:0 3rd:2 Ran:11
Pre1998 - 1st:4 2nd:2 3rd:2 Ran:31
Win Prizemoney £10,563 *Total Prizemoney* £13,925
Wins * 1997 Jly Warwic (G-F) SH 10.8f 54 59 <
* 1997 May Leices (GD) SH 10f 46 54
* 1996 *Nov Lingfi (STD) H 10f 45 52*
* 1996 *Nov Lingfi (STD) H 10f 50 53*
1998 Turf 0-8: (8f, 10f 3, 11f, 12f 3) (g-f 3, frm 4, hrd) 1998 AW 0-3: (10f 2, 12f) (Equi 2, Fibr)
Fair horse, effective 10 to 13f, acts on g-f - acts on Equi, has worn blinkers, likes left handed tracks, favours tight tracks, and excels at Warwick and Leicester. Turf high 55 - 5th of 18 giving 15lb to Rival Bid (25 May Leicester 10f g-f RF 1449). AW high 53 (1st run) - 3rd of 9 getting 6lb from Failed To Hit (24 Feb Lingfield 10f Equi RF 0350). **D J S Cosgrove [4-42] D J S Cosgrove.*

ARZILLO **RR 47f** 3143[14]
2 b c Forzando 7.2f **(63)** - Titania's Dance (IRE) **(49a)** (Fairy King (USA)) 7.7f **(59)**
Form - 070
Record 1998 - 1st:0 2nd:0 3rd:0 Ran:3
1998 Turf 0-3: (6f 3) (gd 2, frm)
Currently moderate colt. Turf high 47.
**S Dow [0-3] Brian Solomon and Miss Jo-Ann Wood.*

ASAALA (USA) **RR 73f** 5071[11]
2 ch f Slew O' Gold (USA) 10.2f **(73)** - Alghuzaylah (Habitat) 9.4f **(70)**
Form - 30
Record 1998 - 1st:0 2nd:0 3rd:1 Ran:2
Win Prizemoney £0 *Total Prizemoney* £430
1998 Turf 0-2: (7f 2) (gd 2)
Currently above-average filly. Turf high 73 (1st run) (began Oct) - 3rd of 9 to Sari (15 Oct Catterick 7f gd RF 4812).
**M P Tregoning [0-2] Hamdan Al Maktoum.*

ASA AVONMOUTH BHB 39f **RR 36df** 3245[18]
3 b f Ballacashtal (CAN) 7.9f **(51)** - Avonmouthsecretary (Town And Country) 8.1f **(68)**
Form - 000800
Record 1998 - 1st:0 2nd:0 3rd:0 Ran:6
1998 Turf 0-6: (6f 2, 7f, 8f 3) (gd 2, g-f 2, frm 2)
Workmanlike, very moderate filly. Turf high 36.
**Mrs P N Dutfield [0-6] John Tutton.*

ASAD BHB 105f **RR 102f** 1412[5]
3 ch c Lion Cavern (USA) 7.5f **(74)** - Negligent (Ahonoora) 8.1f **(73)**
Form - 15
Record 1998 - 1st:1 2nd:0 3rd:0 Ran:2
Pre1998 - 1st:1 2nd:0 3rd:0 Ran:1
Win Prizemoney £10,039 *Total Prizemoney* £10,039
Wins * **1998** May Doncas (G-F) 8f 102 <
* 1997 Oct Yarmou (FRM) 7f 89++
1998 Turf 1-2: (8f 1-1, 10f) (g-f 1-2)
Currently very useful colt. Turf high 102 (1st run) - 1st of 3 from Dower House (4 May Doncaster RF 1007). He beat Great Dane as a juvenile and created a favourable impression when following-up at Doncaster in May. Well beaten when returned to that track later in the month, he went on the missing list and has presumably had a problem. **S bin Suroor [2-3] Godolphin.*

ASCARI BHB 65f57a **RR 78f 57a** 5080[6]
2 br g Presidium 7.5f **(56)** - Ping Pong (Petong) 6.6f **(58)**
Form - 46406
Record 1998 - 1st:0 2nd:0 3rd:0 Ran:5
Win Prizemoney £0 *Total Prizemoney* £242
1998 Turf 0-4: (6f 2, 7f 2) (gd, g-f, frm 2) 1998 AW 0-1: (6f) (Fibr)
Above-average gelding, has worn blinkers. Turf high 78 (began Aug). **P W Harris [0-5] Bernstein, Shaw, Williams & Willis.*

ASCOT CYCLONE (USA) BHB 90f **RR 92f** 4707[13]
3 ch f Rahy (USA) 9.1f **(80)** - Dabaweyaa (Shareef Dancer (USA)) 9.9f **(73)**
Form - 031700
Record 1998 - 1st:1 2nd:0 3rd:1 Ran:6
Pre1998 - 1st:1 2nd:1 3rd:0 Ran:5
Win Prizemoney £24,021 *Total Prizemoney* £32,621
Wins * **1998** Jly Goodwo (G-S) H 7f 89 91 <
* 1997 May Bath (G-F) 5.7f 72+
1998 Turf 1-6: (7f 1-3, 8f 2, 10f) (gd 1-4, g-f, frm)
Scopey, useful filly, effective 7f, acts on gd to frm. Turf high 91 - 1st of 18 getting 3lb from Hujoom (31 Jly Goodwood RF 3229). A genuine sort who likes to make the running, she was a game winner of a keenly-contested handicap at Glorious Goodwood, but was put in her place in a conditions race next time.
**B W Hills [2-11] Salem Bel Obaida.*

ASEF ALHIND BHB 80f **RR 78f** 1922[3]
4 ch c Indian Ridge 7.6f **(74)** - Willowbed (Wollow) 8.2f **(61)**
Form - 0623
Record 1998 - 1st:0 2nd:1 3rd:1 Ran:4
Pre1998 - 1st:1 2nd:0 3rd:1 Ran:7

Win Prizemoney £3,457 *Total Prizemoney* £5,753
Wins * 1997 Jun Beverl (G-F) 8.5f 77 <
1998 Turf 0-4: (7f, 8f 3) (gd 2, g-f 2)
Workmanlike, above-average colt, has broken blood-vessels, effective 7 to 8f, best at 7f, acts on gd to frm, likes tight tracks. Turf high 78 - 3rd of 10 giving 29lb to Flying Pennant (12 Jun Chepstow 7f gd RF 1922). Consistent.
**B Hanbury [1-11] Hamdan Al Maktoum.*

ASFURAH (USA) BHB 110f **RR 103f** 1612[4]

3 b br f Dayjur (USA) 6.8f **(79)** - Mathkurh (USA) (Riverman (USA)) 9.1f **(76)**
Form - 4
Record 1998 - 1st:0 2nd:0 3rd:0 Ran:1
Pre1998 - 1st:2 2nd:2 3rd:0 Ran:4
Win Prizemoney £42,971 *Total Prizemoney* £73,820
Wins * 1997 Jly Newmar (GD) G2 6f 96 <
* 1997 Jun Ascot (GD) 5f 96 <
1998 Turf 0-1: (6f) (g-f)
Scopey, very useful filly. She finished in front of the subsequent Classic winner Tarascon in the Heinz 57 Phoenix Stakes as a juvenile after landing the Cherry Hinton, and looked to have done well over the winter when making her reappearance at Newmarket in May. A shade disappointing there, she went on the missing list and must have suffered a setback. **S bin Suroor [2-5] Godolphin.*

ASHANGEM BHB 33f **RR 20f** 768[10]

3 ch g Risk Me (FR) 8f **(53)** - Dancing Belle (Dance In Time (CAN)) 8.9f **(59)**
Form - 000
Record 1998 - 1st:0 2nd:0 3rd:0 Ran:3
Pre1998 - 1st:0 2nd:0 3rd:0 Ran:3
1998 Turf 0-2: (5f, 7f) (sft, g-s) 1998 AW 0-1: (11f) (Fibr)
Light-framed, little account gelding. Turf high 6.
**Bob Jones [0-6] Hobbs Racing Partnership.*

ASHBOURNE PAT BHB 85f **RR 77f** 4764[4]

2 b f Mtoto 11.5f **(71)** - Actraphane (Shareef Dancer (USA)) 9.9f **(73)**
Form - 14
Record 1998 - 1st:1 2nd:0 3rd:0 Ran:2
Win Prizemoney £3,947 *Total Prizemoney* £4,285
Wins * **1998** Spt Leices (G-S) 8f 77 <
1998 Turf 1-2: (8f 1-1, 10f) (gd, g-f 1-1)
Currently above-average filly. Turf high 77 (began Spt) - 4th of 7 getting 1lb from Adnaan (12 Oct Leicester 10f gd RF 4764) - also 1st of 13 from Rahayeb (8 Spt Leicester RF 4135).
**J Pearce [1-2] Hon Robert Acton.*

ASHBRITTLE LADY BHB 53f **RR 60f** 4524[11]

2 ch f King's Signet (USA) 7f **(51)** - Lady Longmead (Crimson Beau) 9.8f **(52)**
Form - 080
Record 1998 - 1st:0 2nd:0 3rd:0 Ran:3
1998 Turf 0-3: (6f 3) (gd, g-f 2)
Currently average filly. Turf high 60 (began Jly).
**L G Cottrell [0-3] Mrs Jenny Hopkins.*

ASHGORE BHB 32f35a **RR 41f 35a** 2965[7]

8 b g Efisio 7.7f **(69)** - Fair Atlanta (Tachypous) 8.6f **(55)**
Form - 8080007087
Record 1998 - 1st:0 2nd:0 3rd:0 Ran:8
Pre1998 - 1st:10 2nd:8 3rd:6 Ran:50
Win Prizemoney £37,210 *Total Prizemoney* £52,040
Wins 1996 *Jan Wolver (STD) H 7f 82 82* <
1995 *Aug Wolver (STD) C 7f 74*
1994 May Ayr (FRM) H 6f 77 74
1994 May Doncas (G-F) H 6f 73 73
1994 *Feb Wolver (STD) H 7f 79 78*
1994 *Jan Wolver (STD) H 6f 73 71*
1998 Turf 0-4: (7f 2, 8f 2)(gd 2, g-f, frm)1998 AW 0-4:(7f 2, 8f 2) (Fibr 4)
Moderate gelding, has worn blinkers. Turf high 41. AW high 29. He has had leg trouble, and has not shown his best form since leaving Mark Johnston.
**T H Caldwell [0-10] Harvey Ashworth (from J L Eyre [0-5] Jly 1997).*

ASHJAJON BHB 33f30a **RR 38f 30a** 384[9]

3 b f Lugana Beach 7f **(63)** - Dondale Rose (Nishapour (FR)) 9.1f **(61)**
Form - 500
Record 1998 - 1st:0 2nd:0 3rd:0 Ran:3
Pre1998 - 1st:0 2nd:0 3rd:0 Ran:2
1998 AW 0-3: (7f 2, 8f) (Equi 2, Fibr)
Workmanlike, very moderate filly. AW high 17.
**J Cullinan [0-3] Alan Spargo Ltd (from J White [0-2] May 1997).*

ASHKERNAZY (IRE) BHB 39f50a **RR 38f 50a** 3687[11]

7 ch m Salt Dome (USA) 6.5f **(59)** - Eskaroon (Artaius (USA)) 9f **(69)**
Form - 0400
Record 1998 - 1st:0 2nd:0 3rd:0 Ran:4
Pre1998 - 1st:4 2nd:4 3rd:3 Ran:35
Win Prizemoney £11,281 *Total Prizemoney* £17,227
Wins * 1997 Jly Chepst (G-F) H 5.1f 43 46
* 1996 Aug Windso (G-F) H 5f 43 41
* 1995 *Jly Wolver (STD) H 5f 43 44*
1998 Turf 0-4: (5f 3, 6f) (g-f, frm 2, hrd)
Very moderate mare, effective 5f, acts on g-f to frm, has worn blinkers. Turf high 38. Inconsistent.
**N E Berry [3-25] London Bridge II (from J G M O'Shea [0-8] Jly 1994).*

ASHLEIGH BAKER (IRE) BHB 55f **RR 38f** 5147[16]

3 b br f Don't Forget Me 9.5f **(66)** - Gayla Orchestra (Lord Gayle (USA)) 8.8f **(62)**
Form - 756710860700
Record 1998 - 1st:1 2nd:0 3rd:0 Ran:12
Win Prizemoney £2,851 *Total Prizemoney* £2,851
Wins * **1998** Jly Ayr (SFT) H 10.9f 60 66 <
1998 Turf 1-11: (7f, 8f 3, 9f, 10f 2, 11f 1-2, 13f, 16f) (sft 2, gd 1-7, g-f, frm) 1998 AW 0-1: (9f) (Fibr)
Light-framed, moderate filly, effective 10 to 11f, acts on gd, has worn blinkers, likes left handed tracks, favours tight tracks. Turf high 69 - 6th of 8 getting 25lb from Brave Reward (21 Aug Chester 10f gd RF 3792) - also 1st of 8 giving 15lb to Donna's Double (20 Jly Ayr RF 2948). **A Bailey [1-12] The David James Partnership.*

ASH MILLSHAW (IRE) BHB 62f **RR 63f** 5004[1]

2 gr g Archway (IRE) 8.5f **(60)** - Yalciyna (Nishapour (FR)) 9.1f **(61)**
Form - 70041
Record 1998 - 1st:1 2nd:0 3rd:0 Ran:5
Win Prizemoney £2,066 *Total Prizemoney* £2,066
Wins * **1998** Oct Bath (SFT) S 5.7f 63 <
1998 Turf 1-4: (6f 1-3, 7f) (sft 1-1, gd 2, frm) 1998 AW 0-1: (7f) (Fibr)
Average gelding. Turf high 63 (began Aug) - 1st of 19 from Risky Valentine (27 Oct Bath RF 5004).
**R Hollinshead [1-5] Clayton Bigley Partnership Ltd.*

ASHOVER BHB 46f57a **RR 49f 57a** 252[7]

8 gr g Petong 7.6f **(58)** - Shiny Kay (Star Appeal) 9.6f **(65)**
Form - 047
Record 1998 - 1st:0 2nd:0 3rd:0 Ran:3
Pre1998 - 1st:9 2nd:6 3rd:7 Ran:50
Win Prizemoney £30,965 *Total Prizemoney* £43,546
Wins * 1996 *Jan Southw (STD) H 11f 64 76* <
* 1995 Spt Beverl (GD) H 12f 55 63
* 1995 Jly Thirsk (GD) H 12f 53 63
* 1995 Jun Ripon (FRM) H 12.3f 49 55
* 1995 *Feb Southw (STD) 12f 68*
* 1995 *Feb Southw (STD) H 11f 60 60*
* 1994 Oct Pontef (SFT) H 12f 45 53
* 1994 Jly Beverl (G-F) H 9.9f 42 42
1998 AW 0-3: (11f 3) (Fibr 3)
Fair gelding, has worn blinkers. AW high 58. He was off the track for fifteen months after October '96, and has shown nothing since his return. **T D Barron [9-53] Timothy Cox.*

ASHOVER AMBER BHB 66f **RR 67f** 3933[13]

2 b f Green Desert (USA) 7.8f **(78)** - Zafaaf **(98df)** (Kris) 9.5f **(73)**
Form - 330
Record 1998 - 1st:0 2nd:0 3rd:2 Ran:3
Win Prizemoney £0 *Total Prizemoney* £947
1998 Turf 0-3: (5f, 6f 2) (gd, frm 2)
Currently average filly. Turf high 60 - 3rd of 7 to Unicamp (22 May Nottingham 6f frm RF 1400). **T D Barron [0-3] Timothy Cox.*

ASHRAAKAT (USA) BHB 107f **RR 106f** 4733[6]

3 b f Danzig (USA) 8.1f **(88)** - Elle Seule (USA) (Exclusive Native

(USA)) 9.1f **(81)**
Form - 20142516

Record	**1998** -	1st:2	2nd:2	3rd:0	Ran:8
	Pre1998 -	1st:1	2nd:1	3rd:0	Ran:3

Win Prizemoney £28,727 *Total Prizemoney* £45,907

Wins	* **1998**	Spt Doncas (GD)	L	7f	102	
	* **1998**	May Newmar (G-F)	L	6f	106	<
	* 1997	Aug Newmar (GD)		7f	94+	

1998 Turf 2-8: (6f 1-3, 7f 1-3, 8f 2) (g-s, gd 1-4, g-f 1-1, frm 2)
Scopey, Pattern-class filly, effective 6 to 8f, acts on gd to g-f, best on gd, excels at Newmarket. Turf high 106 - 2nd of 9 giving 3lb to Beraysim (30 Jly Goodwood 7f gd RF 3216) - also 1st of 6 from Desert Lady (30 May Newmarket RF 1612). She did not prove up to Classic standard and, like her brother Elnadim, was best over sprint distances. She made all to win Listed events at Newmarket and Doncaster and will make a top-class broodmare.
**J L Dunlop [3-11] Hamdan Al Maktoum.*

ASINBOX (IRE) BHB 53f49a **RR 54?f 49a** 2398[7]
3 ch g Persian Bold 10f **(69)** - Traveling Dancer (FR) (Lomond (USA)) 8.8f **(65)**
Form - 436447

Record	**1998** -	1st:0	2nd:0	3rd:1	Ran:6
	Pre1998 -	1st:0	2nd:0	3rd:0	Ran:3

Win Prizemoney £0 *Total Prizemoney* £802
1998 Turf 0-5: (10f, 13f, 14f 2, 18f) (g-s, gd, g-f 2, frm) 1998 AW 0-1: (15f) (Fibr)
Strong, fair gelding, effective 14f, acts on g-f, has worn blinkers, likes left handed tracks, likes tight tracks. Turf high 56. Consistent. **B J Meehan [0-9] Miss J Semple.*

AS-IS BHB 62f43a **RR 64f 43a** 2901[11]
4 b g Lomond (USA) 9.9f **(74)** - Capriati (USA) (Diesis) 9.3f **(69)**
Form - 700000

Ashraakat is a full-sister to July Cup winner Elnadim

ASIF RR 4666[16]
3 b c Mazaad 8.5f **(53)** - Venetian Joy (Windjammer (USA)) 7f **(59)**
Form - 00

Record	**1998** -	1st:0	2nd:0	3rd:0	Ran:2

1998 Turf 0-1: (8f) (g-s) 1998 AW 0-1: (7f) (Fibr)
Leggy, currently very poor colt, often wears blinkers - 16th of 17 giving 5lb to Lamanka Lass (6 Oct Nottingham 8f g-s RF 4666) - 11th of 11 getting 2lb from U-No-Harry (14 Aug Southwell 7f Fibr RF 3637). **R C Spicer [0-2] & Mrs L Kasparian.*

ASILANA (IRE) RR 11f 878[5]
2 b c College Chapel - Uninvited Guest (Be My Guest (USA)) 9.3f **(67)**
Form - 5

Record	**1998** -	1st:0	2nd:0	3rd:0	Ran:1

1998 Turf 0-1: (5f) (g-s)
Currently poor colt. **T D Easterby [0-1] C H Newton Jnr Ltd.*

Record	**1998** -	1st:0	2nd:0	3rd:0	Ran:4
	Pre1998 -	1st:4	2nd:4	3rd:0	Ran:18

Win Prizemoney £10,387 *Total Prizemoney* £13,766

Wins	1997	Apr Mussel	(G-F)	H	12f	60	62	
	1997	*Feb Lingfi*	*(STD)*	*C*	*12f*		*63*	<
	1997	*Feb Lingfi*	*(STD)*	*C*	*10f*		*51*	
	1997	*Jan Lingfi*	*(STD)*	*S*	*8f*		*58*	

1998 AW 0-4: (11f, 12f, 13f, 16f) (Equi 2, Fibr 2)
Neat, average gelding, effective 8 to 13f, best at 12f, acts on gd to frm - acts on AW, favours tight tracks, likes Lingfield. AW high 3. Becoming disappointing.
**K Bell [0-1] Mrs Joyce Wood (from M Johnston [4-21] Feb 1998).*

ASKERN BHB 62f **RR 63f** 1234[7]
7 gr g Sharrood (USA) 11.1f **(67)** - Silk Stocking (Pardao) 8.6f **(60)**
Form - 07

Record 1998 - 1st:0 2nd:0 3rd:0 Ran:2
Pre1998 - 1st:8 2nd:7 3rd:4 Ran:45
Win Prizemoney £31,664 *Total Prizemoney* £43,400
Wins * 1997 Jly Hamilt (G-F) H 9.2f 60 63
* 1996 Nov Redcar (G-F) H 10f 60 65
* 1996 Aug Hamilt (G-F) H 11.1f 65 75
* 1996 Aug Hamilt (G-F) H 11.1f 65 70
* 1995 Aug Haydoc (G-F) H 10.5f 66 75
* 1995 Jun Hamilt (FRM) S 9.2f 53+
1995 Jun Ayr (G-F) S 10f 65
1998 Turf 0-2: (8f 2) (hvy, gd)
Average gelding, effective 9 to 10f, acts on frm, has worn blinkers. Turf high 55.
**D HaydnJones [6-35] Hugh O'Donnell (from G M Moore [1-3] Jun 1995).*

ASLEY (IRE) BHB 91f **RR 89f** 4005[2]

2 b c Danehill (USA) 9.1f **(79)** - Ausherra (USA) (Diesis) 9.3f **(69)**
Form - 651312
Record 1998 - 1st:2 2nd:1 3rd:1 Ran:6
Win Prizemoney £6,619 *Total Prizemoney* £8,776
Wins * **1998** Aug Folkes (G-F) H 6.9f 82 80 <
* **1998** Jly Bright (GD) 6f 77
1998 Turf 2-6: (6f 1-5, 7f 1-1) (gd 1-4, g-f 1-1, frm)
Useful colt, effective 6 to 7f, acts on g-f to frm, mostly wears blinkers (extremely effectively). Turf high 89 - 2nd of 6 giving 19lb to Bundy (31 Aug Warwick 6f frm RF 4005) - also 1st of 11 giving 11lb to Juanita (14 Aug Folkestone RF 3626).
**M P Tregoning [2-6] Sheikh Ahmed Al Maktoum.*

ASOLO (GER) RR 110f 5055a[3]

4 b c Surumu (GER) - All Dancing (FR) (Fabulous Dancer (USA)) 9.4f **(70)**
Form - 32826383
1998 Turf 0-8: (12f 3, 15f 2, 16f 2, 20f) (hvy, sft 5, gd, g-f)
Group-class colt, effective 12 to 20f, best at 12f, acts on hvy to g-f, best on sft, prefers right handed tracks, does well at Chantilly, excels at Longchamp. Turf high 110 - 6th of 8 to Arctic Owl (23 Aug Deauville 15f sft RF 3917a). Consistent. He ran his heart out in smart company, but could not gain that all important big race win. There are plans to send him hurdling, and he would be hard to beat if taking to that game.
**J BertranDeBalanda in FR [0-1] Gestut Ammerland (from A Fabre in FR [0-4] Oct 1998).*

ASOOD RR 89+f 4892[1]

2 b c Machiavellian (USA) 9.8f **(83)** - Six Nations (USA) (Danzig (USA)) 8.4f **(76)**
Form - 1
Record 1998 - 1st:1 2nd:0 3rd:0 Ran:1
Win Prizemoney £3,542 *Total Prizemoney* £3,542
Wins * **1998** Oct Yarmou (G-S) 7f 89+ <
1998 Turf 1-1: (7f 1-1) (gd 1-1)
Currently useful colt. (1st run) - 1st of 5 from National Anthem (20 Oct Yarmouth RF 4892). **D R Loder [1-1] Sheikh Mohammed.*

ASPECTO LAD (IRE) BHB 50f56a **RR 36f 56a** 208[P]

4 ch g Imp Society (USA) 7.1f **(63)** - Thatcherite (Final Straw) 7.9f **(64)**
Form - P
Record 1998 - 1st:0 2nd:0 3rd:0 Ran:1
Pre1998 - 1st:1 2nd:4 3rd:2 Ran:14
Win Prizemoney £2,085 *Total Prizemoney* £6,445
Wins 1997 *Jan Southw (STD) S 8f 58* <
1998 AW 0-1: (8f) (Equi)
Workmanlike, average gelding, effective 8 to 12f, - acted on Equi to Fibr, best on Fibr, had worn blinkers. (DEAD)
**D L Williams [0-7] R J Matthews (from M Johnston [1-12] Mar 1997).*

ASPIRANT DANCER BHB 68f69a **RR 69f 69a** 4698[12]

3 b g Marju (IRE) 9.2f **(76)** - Fairy Ballerina (Fairy King (USA)) 7.7f **(59)**
Form - 211102400
Record 1998 - 1st:3 2nd:2 3rd:0 Ran:9
Pre1998 - 1st:0 2nd:0 3rd:0 Ran:3
Win Prizemoney £19,587 *Total Prizemoney* £21,796
Wins * **1998** May Haydoc (GD) H 10.5f 65 69 <
* **1998** Apr Folkes (SFT) H 9.7f 57 63
* **1998** *Apr Southw (STD) H 11f 49 63*
1998 Turf 2-7: (10f 1-4, 11f 1-2, 12f) (sft 1-1, gd 1-3, g-f 2, frm) 1998 AW 1-2: (9f, 11f 1-1) (Fibr 1-2)
Average gelding, effective 10 to 11f, best at 11f, acts on sft to g-f - acts on Fibr, likes left handed tracks, prefers tight tracks. Turf high 69 - 4th of 9 getting 10lb from Up At The Top (6 Aug Haydock 11f g-f RF 3407) - also 1st of 11 getting 17lb from Double Classic (10 May Haydock RF 1141). AW high 66 - also 1st of 10 giving 4lb to Cinder Hills (6 Apr Southwell RF 0576). Showed little at two, but after running a good second in a Folkestone handicap on his reappearance, completed a hat-trick of victories, the first of which was on Fibresand. He ran his first poor race of the year at the Epsom Derby meeting, and lost his way in he autumn.
**M Bell [3-12] Peter Coe.*

ASSAFIYAH (IRE) BHB 63f **RR 64f** 5098[17]

3 ch f Kris 10f **(75)** - Fayfa (IRE) (Slip Anchor) 9.8f **(73)**
Form - 0440
Record 1998 - 1st:0 2nd:0 3rd:0 Ran:4
Win Prizemoney £0 *Total Prizemoney* £490
1998 Turf 0-4: (10f 3, 12f) (g-s, gd, g-f, frm)
Unfurnished, average filly. Turf high 65.
**J L Dunlop [0-2] Prince A A Faisal (from H R A Cecil [0-2] Jly 1998).*

ASSET MANAGER BHB 85f **RR 88f** 3520[9]

3 b c Night Shift (USA) 8.1f **(73)** - Hud Hud (USA) (Alydar (USA)) 9.1f **(76)**
Form - 1018300
Record 1998 - 1st:2 2nd:0 3rd:1 Ran:7
Pre1998 - 1st:0 2nd:0 3rd:0 Ran:3
Win Prizemoney £12,567 *Total Prizemoney* £15,617
Wins * **1998** Jun Newcas (GD) H 8f 82 83 <
* **1998** May Sandow (GD) H 7.1f 74 78
1998 Turf 2-7: (7f 1-1, 8f 1-6) (g-s 1-1, gd 3, g-f 1-1, frm 2)
Lengthy, useful colt, effective 7 to 8f, best at 8f, acts on g-s to frm. Turf high 88 - 3rd of 10 getting 12lb from Florazi (18 Jly Newmarket 8f frm RF 2919) - also 1st of 12 getting 15lb from Celestial Key (26 Jun Newcastle RF 2308). Decent handicapper at around a mile who wore a tongue strap when scoring at Newmarket.
**M Johnston [2-10] Maktoum Al Maktoum.*

ASSOS (USA) RR 107f 2665a[3]

4 b c Alleged (USA) 11.8f **(81)** - Myth to Reality (FR) (Sadler's Wells (USA)) 10f **(76)**
Form - 23
1998 Turf 0-2: (13f, 16f) (sft 2)
Currently Pattern-class colt. Turf high 107 (1st run) - 2nd of 7 to Tajoun (6 Apr Maisons-laffitte 16f sft RF 0722a). He was half lengthed in a couple of Listed races and is capable of winning in that sphere. **D Sepulchre in FR [0-3] Niarchos Family*

ASSURED GAMBLE BHB 78f **RR 76f** 4241[12]

4 b g Rock Hopper 10.6f **(54)** - Willowbank (Gay Fandango (USA)) 8.5f **(59)**
Form - 187730
Record 1998 - 1st:1 2nd:0 3rd:1 Ran:6
Pre1998 - 1st:1 2nd:0 3rd:1 Ran:8
Win Prizemoney £11,882 *Total Prizemoney* £13,579
Wins * **1998** Apr Epsom (SFT) H 12f 77 80
* 1997 May Newmar (GD) 12f 82 <
1998 Turf 1-6: (10f 2, 12f 1-4) (sft 1-1, gd 2, g-f 3)
Scopey, above-average gelding, effective 12 to 14f, best at 12f, acts on sft to frm. Turf high 80 (1st run). Bounced back to form when making a winning reappearance in the Great Metropolitan Handicap at Epsom, and may well be the type who goes best fresh. **C E Brittain [2-14] Eddy Grimstead Honda.*

ASSURED MOVEMENTS (USA) RR 72f 2013[13]

2 b c Northern Flagship (USA) 12.2f **(72)** - Love At Dawn (USA) (Grey Dawn II) 11.1f **(72)**
Form - 750
Record 1998 - 1st:0 2nd:0 3rd:0 Ran:3
1998 Turf 0-3: (5f, 6f 2) (gd, g-f, frm)
Currently above-average colt. Turf high 72. Has shown ability in maidens, and had a very stiff task at Royal Ascot.
**C E Brittain [0-3] Peter Head.*

ASTARABAD (USA) RR 123f 4953a[5]

4 b c Alleged (USA) 11.8f **(81)** - Anaza (Darshaan) 9.9f **(84)**

Form - 6211265
1998 Turf 2-6: (9f, 10f 1-3, 11f 1-1, 12f) (sft 1-3, g-s 1-1, gd, frm)
Very high-class colt, effective 9 to 12f, acts on sft to g-f. Turf high 123 - 1st of 4 giving 3lb to Que Belle (26 Apr Longchamp RF 0950a) - also 1st of 6 getting 3lb from Majorien (5 Apr Longchamp RF 0635a). Consistent. Finished a good third in the 1997 Prix du Jockey-Club behind Peintre Celebre, but he twice found the top-class Loup Sauvage too good in the spring of 1998. However, this did not prevent him winning the Prix d'Harcourt and Prix Ganay in between. Failed to make a similar impact on his return from a summer break.
**J Canani in USA [0-1] (from A deRoyerDupre in FR [3-11] Oct 1998).*

ASTERLANE RR 29f — 3377[20]
2 b g Risk Me (FR) 8f **(53)** - Bernstein Bette **(35f 44a)** (Petong) 6.6f **(58)**
Form - 0
Record 1998 - 1st:0 2nd:0 3rd:0 Ran:1
1998 Turf 0-1: (6f) (frm)
Currently little account gelding. **W J Musson [0-1] Asterlane Ltd.*

ASTON EYRE RR 32f — 3606[10]
2 ch f Pharly (FR) 11.5f **(64)** - Lady Keyser (Le Johnstan) 7.4f **(55)**
Form - 700
Record 1998 - 1st:0 2nd:0 3rd:0 Ran:3
1998 Turf 0-3: (5f, 6f 2) (gd, g-f, frm)
Currently very moderate filly. Turf high 32 (began Jly).
**A G Juckes [0-3] Paul Sandy.*

ASTONISHED BHB 95f RR 89+f — 4857[6]
2 ch g Weldnaas (USA) 8.4f **(55)** - Indigo (Primo Dominie) 6.2f **(80)**
Form - 31136
Record 1998 - 1st:2 2nd:0 3rd:2 Ran:5
Win Prizemoney £8,233 *Total Prizemoney* £11,586
Wins * **1998** Spt Doncas (GD) H 6f 82 89+ <
* **1998** Aug Carlis (G-S) 5f 85++
1998 Turf 2-5: (5f 1-3, 6f 1-2) (sft, g-s, gd 1-1, g-f 1-1, frm)
Useful gelding. Turf high 89 (began Aug) - 1st of 22 giving 6lb to Flite of Life (12 Spt Doncaster RF 4243) - also 1st of 15 from Lucky Cove (26 Aug Carlisle RF 3882). From a prolific sprint family, he played his part with a cosy win in a Doncaster nursery, and lost little in defeat in a listed race. Remains a useful prospect.
**Mrs J R Ramsden [2-5] D R Brotherton.*

ASTON VILLA (GER) BHB 68f RR 64f — 4125[4]
4 ch f Master Willie 9.2f **(67)** - Askania Nova (Sharpen Up) 8.3f **(67)**
Form - 644
Record 1998 - 1st:0 2nd:0 3rd:0 Ran:3
Win Prizemoney £0 *Total Prizemoney* £495
1998 Turf 0-3: (10f, 12f, 14f) (gd, frm 2)
Scopey, currently average filly. Turf high 64 (began Jly) - 4th of 9 giving 9lb to Cuff (12 Aug Sandown 10f frm RF 3598). Does not look Premiership material. **D R C Elsworth [0-3] J Duffy.*

ASTORG (USA) RR 101f — 4470a[1]
3 f Lear Fan (USA) 10.4f **(80)** - Action Francaise (USA) (Nureyev (USA)) 8.7f **(78)**
Form - 01
1998 Turf 1-2: (8f 1-2) (sft 1-1, gd)
Currently very useful filly. Turf high 101 - 1st of 11 from Pan Galactic (4 Aug Deauville RF 4470a). She finished fast to mow down the useful Pan Galactic at Deauville in August and seems to enjoy easy ground. **A Fabre in FR [1-2] D Wildenstein.*

ASTRAC (IRE) BHB 99f88a RR 95f 88a — 4675[6]
7 b g Nordico (USA) 8.2f **(59)** -Shirleen (Daring Display (USA)) 6.9f **(69)**
Form - 0801500316
Record 1998 - 1st:2 2nd:0 3rd:1 Ran:9
Pre1998 - 1st:8 2nd:2 3rd:5 Ran:45
Win Prizemoney £101,908 *Total Prizemoney* £113,123

Wins								
* **1998**	Spt	Hamilt	(SFT)		6f		95	
* **1998**	May	Ayr	(GD)	H	6f	85	93	
1996	Nov	Evry	(SFT)	L	6f		113	<
1996	Nov	Doncas	(SFT)	L	6f		111	
1996	Oct	Nottin	(SFT)		6.1f		92+	
1995	Jun	Ascot	(FRM)	H	6f	89	96	
1994	Oct	York	(G-S)	H	6f	82	84	
1994	May	Lingfi	(GS)	H	7f	74	72	

1998 Turf 2-9: (5f, 6f 2-7, 7f) (sft, g-s 1-2, gd 1-4, g-f 2)
Very useful gelding, effective 5 to 7f, best at 6f, acts on g-s to g-f - acts on Fibr, has worn blinkers. Turf high 95 - 1st of 7 giving 5lb to Daring Destiny (28 Spt Hamilton RF 4534) - also 1st of 8 giving 14lb to Ryefield (29 May Ayr RF 1560). Inconsistent. Won at Ayr in May, but the handicapper took no chances with him and seemed to suffer as a result until winning at Hamilton in September. Best over six furlongs and with cut in the ground, he will win more races next term given those conditions.
**D Nicholls [2-9] T L Beecroft (from N Tinkler [0-8] Dec 1997).*

ASTRAKAN (IRE) BHB 85f RR 84f — 4834[1]
2 ch g Lycius (USA) 8.8f **(71)** - Star Ridge (USA) (Storm Bird (CAN)) 10.3f **(74)**
Form - 26421
Record 1998 - 1st:1 2nd:2 3rd:0 Ran:5
Win Prizemoney £4,016 *Total Prizemoney* £6,516
Wins * **1998** Oct Catter (sft) 5f 84 <
1998 Turf 1-5: (5f 1-4, 6f) (g-s 1-2, g-f, frm 2)
Decent gelding. Turf high 84 (began Jly) - 1st of 13 from Get Stuck In (16 Oct Catterick RF 4834). **W Jarvis [1-5] Buckram Oak Holdings.*

ASTRAL INVADER (IRE) BHB 37f38a RR 36f 38a — 461[6]
6 ch g Astronef 7.9f **(59)** - Numidia (Sallust) 8.4f **(63)**
Form - 8246
Record 1998 - 1st:0 2nd:1 3rd:0 Ran:3
Pre1998 - 1st:3 2nd:4 3rd:6 Ran:50
Win Prizemoney £7,253 *Total Prizemoney* £16,071
Wins * 1997 Mar Leices (G-F) S 7f 55 <
* 1994 Aug Lingfi (GD) C 6f 53
* 1994 Jly Lingfi (GF) S 5f 48
1998 AW 0-3: (6f 2, 7f) (Equi, Fibr 2)
Fair gelding, effective 7f, acts on frm - acts on Equi, has worn blinkers. AW high 52 (1st run) - 2nd of 9 giving 22lb to Miss Skye (24 Feb Lingfield 7f Equi RF 0351).
**M S Saunders [3-55] M S Saunders.*

ASTROLFELL (IRE) RR 40f — 3025[3]
3 ch f River Falls 8.2f **(56)** - Indian Starlight (Kafu) 6f **(47)**
Form - 3
Record 1998 - 1st:0 2nd:0 3rd:1 Ran:1
Pre1998 - 1st:0 2nd:0 3rd:0 Ran:1
Win Prizemoney £0 *Total Prizemoney* £288
1998 Turf 0-1: (8f) (frm)
Light-framed, currently moderate filly.
**J S Moore [0-2] Mrs P M Ratcliffe.*

ASTRO LINES (IRE) BHB 63f RR 62f — 2521[3]
4 ch g Classic Secret (USA) 8.8f **(56)** - Fado's Delight (Orchestra) 9.7f **(52)**
Form - 2263
Record 1998 - 1st:0 2nd:2 3rd:1 Ran:4
Pre1998 - 1st:0 2nd:1 3rd:1 Ran:9
Win Prizemoney £0 *Total Prizemoney* £3,274
1998 Turf 0-4: (14f, 16f 3) (gd, g-f 2, frm)
Average gelding, effective 10 to 16f, acts on gd to frm, best on gd, prefers right handed tracks. Turf high 62 - 2nd of 10 getting 15lb from Nigel's Lad (27 May Ripon 16f g-f RF 1534).
**F Murphy [1-6] K Lee and I Davies (from K Prendergast in IRE [1-12] Oct 1997).*

ASTROLOGER BHB 89f RR 92f — 2014[6]
3 b c Soviet Star (USA) 8.6f **(74)** - Taalif (Last Tycoon) 8.5f **(62)**
Form - 36
Record 1998 - 1st:0 2nd:0 3rd:1 Ran:2
Pre1998 - 1st:0 2nd:1 3rd:1 Ran:2
Win Prizemoney £0 *Total Prizemoney* £3,571
1998 Turf 0-2: (7f, 8f) (gd, g-f)
Scopey, useful colt. Turf high 92 - 6th of 31 getting 1lb from Plan-B (16 Jun Ascot 8f gd RF 2014). Has shown plenty of ability in maidens and when sixth in a huge field on his handicap debut, staying on well over a mile. Looked sure to win races, but was not seen again. **W R Muir [0-4] C L A Edginton.*

ASTRONOMER RR 74f — 4575[4]
2 br c Ardkinglass 5f **(64)** - Ayodhya (IRE) (Astronef)
Form - 034

Record 1998 - 1st:0 2nd:0 3rd:1 Ran:3
Win Prizemoney £0 *Total Prizemoney* £378
1998 Turf 0-3: (6f 2, 7f) (g-f 3)
Currently above-average colt. Turf high 74 (began Aug).
**J R Fanshawe [0-3] Dr Catherine Wills.*

ASYAAD (USA) BHB 59f **RR 58f** 4614[14]

3 b g Zilzal (USA) 8.5f **(79)** - Shihama (USA) (Shadeed (USA)) 8.2f **(70)**
Form - 0700
Record 1998 - 1st:0 2nd:0 3rd:0 Ran:4
Pre1998 - 1st:0 2nd:0 3rd:1 Ran:3
Win Prizemoney £0 *Total Prizemoney* £1,069
1998 Turf 0-4: (6f, 7f 2, 8f) (g-s, gd, frm 2)
Light-framed, fair gelding, effective 6f, acts on g-f. Turf high 58.
**Mrs L Stubbs [0-2] A P Griffin (from B W Hills [0-5] May 1998).*

ATHLUMNEY LADY RR 94+f 5108a[1]

2 br f Lycius (USA) 8.8f **(71)** - Simouna
Form - 51161
1998 Turf 3-5: (7f 2-4, 8f 1-1) (sft, gd 2-3, g-f 1-1)
Useful filly. Turf high 94 - 1st of 6 getting 3lb from Saffron Waldon (26 Oct Leopardstown RF 5108a) - also 1st of 10 giving 21lb to General Cloney (26 Aug Tralee RF 4024a). This Irish filly improved through maiden and nursery company before stealing a Group Three at Leopardstown. With the possible exception of the runner-up, who was making his debut, that did not look a great race, and she may struggle to find another Group event. However, she shows the right attitude. **J S Bolger in IRE [3-5] M J Smith.*

ATLANTA BHB 55f63a **RR 60f 63a** 4510[5]

3 b f Rock City 8.8f **(62)** - Olympic Run (Salse (USA)) 7.5f **(66)**
Form - 277004405
Record 1998 - 1st:0 2nd:0 3rd:0 Ran:7
Pre1998 - 1st:0 2nd:1 3rd:1 Ran:5
Win Prizemoney £0 *Total Prizemoney* £1,442
1998 Turf 0-7: (5f 2, 6f 4, 7f) (gd 3, g-f 3, frm)
Scopey, average filly, effective 5f, - acts on Fibr. Turf high 60.
**G Woodward [0-9] J Pownall (from J L Dunlop [0-3] Oct 1997).*

ATLANTIC DESIRE (IRE) BHB 82f **RR 86f** 4507[4]

4 b f Ela-Mana-Mou 12.7f **(72)** - Bold Miss (Bold Lad (IRE)) 8.4f **(68)**
Form - 7004
Record 1998 - 1st:0 2nd:0 3rd:0 Ran:4
Pre1998 - 1st:4 2nd:3 3rd:2 Ran:14
Win Prizemoney £18,829 *Total Prizemoney* £32,242

Wins							
* 1997	Aug	Salisb	(G-S)		8f		94 <
* 1997	Aug	Ripon	(G-F)	H	9f	90	92
* 1997	Jun	Newcas	(GD)		10.1f		90
* 1996	Spt	Epsom	(G-F)		8.5f		77+

1998 Turf 0-4: (8f, 10f 3) (gd 2, g-f 2)
Scopey, useful filly, effective 8 to 10f, acts on gd to frm, best on gd, likes right handed tracks, excels at Goodwood and Newcastle. Turf high 86. **M Johnston [4-18] Atlantic Racing Ltd.*

ATLANTIC DESTINY (IRE) BHB 100f **RR 99f** 4853[4]

2 b f Royal Academy (USA) 7.8f **(77)** - Respectfully (USA) (The Minstrel (CAN)) 10f **(72)**
Form - 1203154
Record 1998 - 1st:2 2nd:1 3rd:1 Ran:7
Win Prizemoney £16,463 *Total Prizemoney* £27,886

Wins						
* **1998**	Spt	Kempto	(G-S)	L	6f	93+ <
* **1998**	May	York	(GD)		6f	87+

1998 Turf 2-7: (5f 2, 6f 2-4, 7f) (g-s, gd 2-5, frm)
Very useful filly, effective 6 to 7f, best at 6f, acts on gd to frm, best on gd. Turf high 99 - 4th of 14 to Hula Angel (17 Oct Newmarket 7f gd RF 4853) - also 1st of 6 getting 5lb from Pistachio (9 Spt Kempton RF 4193). She looked smart when landing a York maiden on her debut, but did not seem to quite get home over an extra furlong at Epsom next time, having set a furious pace. Landed a listed race at Kempton in September before finishing a close fifth in the Group One Cheveley Park Stakes. Trying seven furlongs in the Rockfel Stakes on her final start, she performed with credit. Further success looks likely next term.
**M Johnston [2-7] Atlantic Racing Ltd.*

Atlantic Destiny wins first time out with Darryll Holland aboard

ATLANTIC MIST BHB 49f **RR 43f** 2303[9]
5 ch g Elmaamul (USA) 8.1f **(70)** - Overdue Reaction (Be My Guest (USA)) 9.3f **(67)**
Form - 42740
Record 1998 - 1st:0 2nd:1 3rd:0 Ran:5
Pre1998 - 1st:2 2nd:2 3rd:3 Ran:20
Win Prizemoney £7,156 *Total Prizemoney* £12,196
Wins * 1996 May Sandow (G-S) H 11.4f 59 63 <
* 1996 May Windso (G-F) H 11.6f 56 59
1998 Turf 0-5: (9f, 10f, 11f 2, 13f) (g-s, gd 2, g-f 2)
Moderate gelding, effective 10 to 12f, acts on gd to g-f, best on gd, has worn blinkers. Turf high 50 - 2nd of 18 getting 14lb from Pay Homage (4 May Warwick 11f g-f RF 1032). Consistent.
**B R Millman [3-30] The Wardour Partnership.*

ATLANTIC VIKING (IRE) BHB 81f **RR 91f** 4854[20]
3 b g Danehill (USA) 9.1f **(79)** - Hi Bettina (Henbit (USA)) 9f **(61)**
Form - 008305000
Record 1998 - 1st:0 2nd:0 3rd:1 Ran:9
Pre1998 - 1st:1 2nd:1 3rd:1 Ran:5
Win Prizemoney £3,067 *Total Prizemoney* £7,469
Wins * 1997 Jun Newcas (FRM) 5f 97+ <
1998 Turf 0-9: (5f 2, 6f 2, 7f 5) (g-s, gd 4, g-f 3, frm)
Scopey, useful gelding, effective 5 to 7f, best at 5f, acts on gd to frm. Turf high 91 - 3rd of 6 getting 14lb from Warningford (15 Jly Yarmouth 7f g-f RF 2838). Somewhat lost his way last term, but has reportedly joined David Nicholls' yard and is one to keep an eye on. **M Johnston [1-14] Atlantic Racing Ltd.*

AT LARGE (IRE) BHB 79f **RR 78f** 1885[3]
4 b g Night Shift (USA) 8.1f **(73)** - Lady Donna (Dominion) 8.5f **(63)**
Form - 23
Record 1998 - 1st:0 2nd:1 3rd:1 Ran:2
Pre1998 - 1st:1 2nd:2 3rd:2 Ran:8
Win Prizemoney £5,995 *Total Prizemoney* £12,138
Wins 1997 Oct Nottin (G-F) H 6.1f 74 77 <
1998 Turf 0-2: (5f 2) (gd, frm)
Lengthy, above-average gelding, effective 5 to 7f, acts on g-s to frm, best on gd. Turf high 77 (1st run) - 2nd of 5 to Mister Jolson (18 May Bath 5f frm RF 1296). Capable of finding a handicap at six or seven furlongs.
**J A R Toller [0-2] Duke of Devonshire (from J R Fanshawe [1-8] Oct 1997).*

AT MY COMMAND (IRE) BHB 69f **RR 65f** 4803[3]
2 ch f Barathea (IRE) - Fly Dont Run (USA) **(53f)** (Lear Fan (USA)) 8.5f **(73)**
Form - 503
Record 1998 - 1st:0 2nd:0 3rd:1 Ran:3
Win Prizemoney £0 *Total Prizemoney* £455
1998 Turf 0-3: (7f 3) (sft, g-f, frm)
Currently average filly. Turf high 65 (began Spt).
**W Jarvis [0-3] K P Seow.*

ATOMIC SHELL (CAN) BHB 55f **RR 67f** 1620[14]
5 ch g Geiger Counter (USA) 7.8f **(85)** - In Your Sights (USA) (Green Dancer (USA)) 10.3f **(74)**
Form - 080
Record 1998 - 1st:0 2nd:0 3rd:0 Ran:3
Pre1998 - 1st:0 2nd:0 3rd:0 Ran:4
Win Prizemoney £0 *Total Prizemoney* £257
1998 Turf 0-2: (6f, 8f) (hvy, g-f) 1998 AW 0-1: (8f) (Fibr)
Average gelding. Turf high 34.
**Mrs A Swinbank [0-3] Mrs Linda Corbett (from C F Wall [0-4] Jun 1997).*

ATOMIK BHB 33f **RR 40f** 4866[11]
2 b f Komaite (USA) 6.9f **(61)** - A Nymph Too Far (IRE) (Precocious) 8.6f **(62)**
Form - 07000
Record 1998 - 1st:0 2nd:0 3rd:0 Ran:5
1998 Turf 0-4: (5f 2, 6f, 7f) (gd, g-f 2, frm) 1998 AW 0-1: (8f) (Fibr)
Moderate filly. Turf high 40 (began Jly).
**Dr J D Scargill [0-5] Mrs Maureen Coppitters.*

A TOUCH OF FROST BHB 68f **RR 68f** 4332[11]
3 gr f Distant Relative 7f **(69)** - Pharland (FR) (Bellypha) 9.8f **(73)**
Form - 0180
Record 1998 - 1st:1 2nd:0 3rd:0 Ran:4
Win Prizemoney £3,746 *Total Prizemoney* £3,746
Wins * **1998** Aug Salisb (G-F) 8f 68 <
1998 Turf 1-4: (7f, 8f 1-2, 10f) (sft, g-f 2, frm 1-1)
Average filly. Turf high 68 - 1st of 14 from Silver Sun (7 Aug Salisbury RF 3443). **G G Margarson [1-4] Mrs Patricia Williams.*

ATTARIKH (IRE) BHB 34f **RR 46df** 4334[10]
5 b g Mujtahid (USA) 7.4f **(69)** - Silly Tune (IRE) (Coquelin (USA)) 8.4f **(58)**
Form - 06000
Record 1998 - 1st:0 2nd:0 3rd:0 Ran:5
Pre1998 - 1st:0 2nd:0 3rd:2 Ran:16
Win Prizemoney £0 *Total Prizemoney* £1,235
1998 Turf 0-4: (6f, 8f 3) (g-f 2, frm 2) 1998 AW 0-1: (7f) (Equi)
Moderate gelding, effective 8f, acts on gd, has worn blinkers, likes left handed tracks, likes tight tracks. Turf high 46 (began Jly). Becoming disappointing.
**Mrs A L M King [0-17] T P Hilliam (from J H M Gosden [0-5] Jly 1996).*

ATTRACTIVE CROWN (USA) **RR 109f** 2424a[2]
3 b f Chief's Crown (USA) 10.2f **(75)** - Attirance (FR) (Crowned Prince (USA)) 10.1f **(67)**
Form - 244012
1998 Turf 1-6: (8f 1-3, 10f 2, 11f) (hvy, sft 1-3, gd, g-f)
Pattern-class filly, effective 8 to 10f, acts on sft. Turf high 109 - 1st of 7 getting 5lb from Outspoken (17 Jun Naas RF 2208a). Her best performances have come on very soft ground. Fourth in the Cheshire Oaks, she is not really Group class and was flattered to get within two and a half lengths of Alborada at the Curragh in June. **K Prendergast in IRE [2-12] A D Brennan.*

AUBRIETA (USA) BHB 75f **RR 80f** 4796[12]
2 b f Dayjur (USA) 6.8f **(79)** - Fennel (Slew O' Gold (USA)) 8f **(75)**
Form - 6033030
Record 1998 - 1st:0 2nd:0 3rd:3 Ran:7
Win Prizemoney £0 *Total Prizemoney* £2,944
1998 Turf 0-7: (5f 4, 6f 2, 7f) (sft, gd 4, g-f 2)
Decent filly. Turf high 80. **C E Brittain [0-7] Ali Saeed.*

AUCTION HOUSE (USA) BHB 100f **RR 111f** 4851[2]
2 b c Exbourne (USA) - Fast Flow (USA) (Riverman (USA)) 9.1f **(76)**
Form - 41112
Record 1998 - 1st:3 2nd:1 3rd:0 Ran:5
Win Prizemoney £78,641 *Total Prizemoney* £129,516
Wins * **1998** Spt Doncas (GD) G2 7f 98
* **1998** Aug York (G-F) L 7f 101 <
* **1998** Jly Doncas (G-F) 7f 86+
1998 Turf 3-5: (7f 3-5) (g-s, gd, g-f 3-3)
Group-class colt. Turf high 111 - 2nd of 7 to Mujahid (17 Oct Newmarket 7f gd RF 4851). A punter's pal, this bonny colt tries his heart out and made all when gaining his three victories. Easily the pick of those efforts was his hard-fought win from Commander Collins in the Champagne Stakes at Doncaster in September, form that was boosted when the runner-up went on to land the Racing Post Trophy by seven lengths. Gallant in defeat when beaten by Mujahid in the Dewhurst Stakes on his final start, Auction House should stay a mile next term and will go into the 2,000 Guineas with a serious each-way chance. He is probably best on a fast surface. **B W Hills [3-5] K Abdulla.*

AUDACITY **RR 37f** 3377[17]
2 b c Minshaanshu Amad (USA) 11.3f **(53)** - Glory Isle (Hittite Glory) 8.7f **(50)**
Form - 000
Record 1998 - 1st:0 2nd:0 3rd:0 Ran:3
1998 Turf 0-3: (6f 3) (gd, frm 2)
Currently very moderate colt. Turf high 37.
**G Lewis [0-3] City Industrial Supplies Ltd.*

AUDEEN BHB 20f **RR 28f** 4399[14]
3 ch f Keen 11.1f **(58)** - Aude la Belle (FR) **(48f)** (Ela-Mana-Mou) 10.1f **(70)**
Form - 00070
Record 1998 - 1st:0 2nd:0 3rd:0 Ran:5
Pre1998 - 1st:0 2nd:0 3rd:0 Ran:1

1998 Turf 0-4: (7f, 8f, 10f, 12f) (gd, g-f, frm 2) 1998 AW 0-1: (13f) (Equi)
Neat, little account filly. Turf high 28.
**N A Callaghan [0-5] Mrs Val Rapkins (from S G Knight [0-1] Aug 1997).*

	1st	2nd	3rd	Ran
Pre1998 -	1st:0	2nd:1	3rd:0	Ran:3

Win Prizemoney £0 *Total Prizemoney* £675
1998 AW 0-1: (14f) (Fibr)
Leggy, fair filly.
**Mrs L Richards [0-6] Mrs L Richards(from BA McMahon[0-3] Jly 1997).*

Auction House (right) beating Commander Collins at Doncaster

AUENADLER (GER) RR 108f 4214a[2]
6 b h Big Shuffle (USA) - Auenmaid (Luciano) 11.2f **(65)**
Form - 212
1998 Turf 1-3: (6f 2, 7f 1-1) (sft, gd 1-2)
Pattern-class horse. Turf high 108 (began Jly) - 1st of 8 giving 6lb to Adieu (16 Aug Hoppegarten RF 3784a). A stalwart of German sprinting, he put the youngsters in their place at Hoppegarten in August and retains his form and enthusiasm.
**U Ostmann in GER [2-6].*

AUGUSTAN BHB 49f53a **RR 56f 53a** 4409[5]
7 b g Shareef Dancer (USA) 10.1f **(67)** - Krishnagar (Kris) 9.5f **(73)**
Form - 0444466226505

Record		1st	2nd	3rd	Ran
	1998 -	1st:0	2nd:2	3rd:0	Ran:13
	Pre1998 -	1st:5	2nd:6	3rd:13	Ran:65

Win Prizemoney £17,523 *Total Prizemoney* £34,489

Wins									
* 1997	Aug	Pontef	(G-F)	H	10f	55	60	
* 1997	May	Doncas	(GD)	H	12f	53	59	
* 1996	Jly	Chepst	(G-F)	H	12.1f	51	57	
* 1995	Jun	York	(G-F)	H	11.9f	60	65	<
1994	Jly	Windso	(G-F)	H	10f	57	58	

1998 Turf 0-13: (10f 3, 11f, 12f 8, 14f) (gd 2, g-f 6, frm 4, hrd)
Fair gelding, effective 10 to 12f, best at 10f, acts on gd to frm, best on frm, has worn blinkers, likes right handed tracks, prefers tight tracks, excels at Thirsk and Pontefract and Beverley. Turf high 56 - 2nd of 5 giving 3lb to Elusive Star (12 Aug Beverley 12f g-f RF 3568). Consistent. Lacks a real turn of foot but tries hard and usually runs his race.
**S Gollings [4-67] Robert Jones (from John Harris [1-8] Nov 1994).*

AUNT DAPHNE BHB 44f **RR 53f** 1941[9]
4 b f Damister (USA) 9.1f **(66)** - Forbearance (Bairn (USA)) 7.7f **(59)**
Form - 0
Record 1998 - 1st:0 2nd:0 3rd:0 Ran:1

AUNT FLO (IRE) BHB 95f **RR 88+f** 4061[4]
2 b f Royal Academy (USA) 7.8f **(77)** - Quinsigimond (Formidable (USA)) 9.2f **(63)**
Form - 220164
Record 1998 - 1st:1 2nd:2 3rd:0 Ran:6
Win Prizemoney £3,622 *Total Prizemoney* £9,829
Wins * 1998 Jly Nottin (G-F) 5.1f 88+ <
1998 Turf 1-6: (5f 1-2, 6f 4) (g-s, gd 2, g-f 1-2, frm)
Useful filly, effective 5 to 6f, acts on g-f. Turf high 88 - 4th of 4 giving 3lb to Imperial Beauty (3 Spt Salisbury 6f g-f RF 4061) - also 1st of 4 getting 5lb from Astrakan (24 Jly Nottingham RF 3080). Has faced some stiff tasks. **M Bell [1-6] Stamford Bridge Partnership.*

AUNTIE MAME (USA) RR 117f 4713a[1]
4 b f Theatrical 11.5f **(78)** - Lady Vixen (USA) (Sir Ivor) 10.2f **(70)**
Form - 1
1998 Turf 1-1: (10f 1-1) (frm 1-1)
Currently high-class filly. (1st run) - 1st of 5 giving 7lb to B A Valentine (3 Oct Belmont Park RF 4713a). A useful American-trained filly on turf, she landed the Grade One Flower Bowl Handicap at Belmont Park in October when Bahr was back in third.
**A Penna Jr in USA [1-2] Lazy Ranch*

AUNT SADIE BHB 75f **RR 69f** 682[14]
3 ch f Pursuit of Love 9.5f **(69)** - Piney River (Pharly (FR)) 9.8f **(68)**
Form - 0

Record		1st	2nd	3rd	Ran
	1998 -	1st:0	2nd:0	3rd:0	Ran:1
	Pre1998 -	1st:0	2nd:1	3rd:0	Ran:3

Win Prizemoney £0 *Total Prizemoney* £1,065
1998 Turf 0-1: (7f) (gd)
Workmanlike, average filly. **R Charlton [0-4] J R Boughey.*

AUNTY CATHERINE (IRE) RR 81f 5024a[7]
3 bb f Mujadil (USA) 7.7f **(70)** - Nation's Game (Mummy's Game) 8.2f

(60)
Form - 015780607
1998 Turf 1-9: (5f 3, 6f 1-2, 7f 3, 8f) (hvy, sft 2, g-s 2, gd 1-3, g-f)
Decent filly, effective 6f, acts on gd, has worn blinkers. Turf high 95 - 1st of 24 getting 5lb from Crystal Wind (11 Apr Naas RF 0689a). Inconsistent.
**Patrick Prendergast in IRE [1-9] Ms Maura Horan.*

AURIGNY BHB 87f RR 86f — 4140[6]
3 b f Timeless Times (USA) 6.1f **(56)**-Dear Glenda(Gold Song) 5.5f **(61)**
Form - 760076
Record 1998 - 1st:0 2nd:0 3rd:0 Ran:6
Pre1998 - 1st:2 2nd:1 3rd:4 Ran:9
Win Prizemoney £12,995 *Total Prizemoney* £34,824
Wins * 1997 Aug Newbur (G-F) L 5.2f 91 <
* 1997 May Bright (G-F) 5.3f 80+
1998 Turf 0-6: (5f 5, 6f) (gd 2, g-f 3, frm)
Workmanlike, useful filly, effective 5 to 6f, best at 5f, acts on sft to g-f. Turf high 92. Consistent. A very useful sprinting juvenile in 1997, a close second in the Prix Robert Papin and winner of a listed event at Newbury, she was well beaten on her return, although the stable was out of sorts at the time, and did not prove easy to place despite generally running well. **S Dow [2-15] J & S Kelly.*

AUSPICIOUS RR 84+f — 4514[5]
2 b f Shirley Heights 12.1f **(76)** - Blessed Event (Kings Lake (USA)) 10.8f **(67)**
Form - 25
Record 1998 - 1st:0 2nd:1 3rd:0 Ran:2
Win Prizemoney £0 *Total Prizemoney* £1,154
1998 Turf 0-2: (7f, 8f) (gd, frm)
Currently decent filly. Turf high 84 (1st run) (began Spt) - 2nd of 15 to Samut (16 Spt Beverley 7f frm RF 4299). A staying type, she showed plenty of promise on her debut. Tackled Group company in the Fillies' Mile last time out, but will win races at a slightly lower level. **Sir Michael Stoute [0-2] Cheveley Park Stud.*

AUTOCRAT BHB 83f RR 85f — 4969[9]
2 b c Polar Falcon (USA) 9f **(74)** - Dame Helene (USA) (Sir Ivor) 10.2f **(70)**
Form - 73802033611660
Record 1998 - 1st:2 2nd:1 3rd:3 Ran:14
Win Prizemoney £9,933 *Total Prizemoney* £12,830
Wins * **1998** Spt Mussel (GD) H 7.1f 75 82 <
* **1998** Spt Cheste (GD) H 7f 75 81
1998 Turf 2-14: (6f 3, 7f 2-8, 8f 3) (g-s 2, gd 1-4, g-f 1-4, frm 4)
Useful colt, effective 7 to 8f, best at 7f, acts on gd to frm, best on g-f. Turf high 85 - 6th of 20 getting 6lb from Fair Flight (16 Oct Newmarket 8f g-f RF 4845) - also 1st of 6 getting 1lb from Single Shot (27 Spt Musselburgh RF 4519). Took time getting off the mark, but hit form with a bang in September, winning nurseries at Chester and Musselburgh within the space of four days. Stays well. Sold for 20,000 gns at Tattersalls autumn sales.
**M R Channon [2-14] Kingsdown Racing.*

AUTOMATIC RR 79+f — 4579[4]
2 b c Clantime 6.6f **(57)** - Gentle Gypsy (Junius (USA)) 7.7f **(65)**
Form - 4
Record 1998 - 1st:0 2nd:0 3rd:0 Ran:1
Win Prizemoney £0 *Total Prizemoney* £236
1998 Turf 0-1: (6f) (g-f)
Currently above-average colt. **M Bell [0-1] Billy Maguire.*

AUTRICHE (IRE) RR 105f — 4602a[1]
4 b f Acatenango (GER) -Aminata (GER) (Local Suitor (USA)) 8.4f **(67)**
Form - 1
1998 Turf 1-1: (8f 1-1) (sft 1-1)
Currently Pattern-class filly. (1st run) - 1st of 12 giving 2lb to Gamberaia (27 Spt Cologne RF 4602a). She was not top-class last season and did well to win a Listed event at Cologne in September. **H Blume in GER [1-2] Gestut Zoppenbroiche.*

AUTUMN COVER BHB 69f60a RR 66f 60a — 4655[4]
6 gr g Nomination 7.3f **(57)** - Respray (Rusticaro (FR)) 8.2f **(65)**
Form - 100504
Record 1998 - 1st:1 2nd:0 3rd:0 Ran:6
Pre1998 - 1st:6 2nd:1 3rd:2 Ran:30
Win Prizemoney £56,269 *Total Prizemoney* £62,165
Wins * **1998** Apr Bright (GD) 8f 78
* 1997 May Kempto (GD) H 8f 75 79 <
* 1996 Spt Goodwo (G-F) H 9f 70 74
* 1996 Jly Goodwo (G-F) H 8f 64 70
* 1996 Jun Sandow (FRM) H 8.1f 55 58
1996 Apr Bright (FRM) H 8f 50 54
1996 Apr Bright (FRM) H 8f 43 51
1998 Turf 1-6: (8f 1-2, 9f, 10f 3) (gd 1-3, g-f 3)
Average gelding, effective 8f, acts on gd, has worn blinkers. Turf high 78 (1st run) - 1st of 4 giving 3lb to Rich In Love (30 Apr Brighton RF 0924). He started 1997 off by winning Kempton's Jubilee Handicap, despite being short of peak fitness according to his trainer, but was well beaten afterwards that season. He once again made a winning reappearance in '98, albeit narrowly, in a four runner event at Brighton, but has shown little since. He obviously goes well fresh.
**P R Hedger [5-22] G A Alexander (from R M Flower [2-15] May 1996).*

AUTUMN TIME (IRE) BHB 47f RR 48f — 2462[8]
4 b f Last Tycoon 9.4f **(73)** -Cochineal (USA) (Vaguely Noble) 10.1f **(72)**
Form - 658
Record 1998 - 1st:0 2nd:0 3rd:0 Ran:3
Pre1998 - 1st:0 2nd:1 3rd:0 Ran:5
Win Prizemoney £0 *Total Prizemoney* £1,356
1998 Turf 0-3: (12f, 16f 2) (g-s, frm 2)
Scopey, moderate filly, effective 12f, acts on g-f, has worn blinkers. Turf high 48. Inconsistent.
**H Alexander [0-3] Mrs K Craggs (from P W Chapple-Hyam [0-5] Oct 1997).*

AVANTI RR 53f — 3735[11]
2 gr c Reprimand 8.2f **(63)** - Dolly Bevan (Another Realm) 6.6f **(55)**
Form - 0
Record 1998 - 1st:0 2nd:0 3rd:0 Ran:1
1998 Turf 0-1: (6f) (frm)
Currently fair colt. **P J Makin [0-1] Skyline Racing Ltd.*

AVANTI BLUE BHB 31f36a RR 34f 36a — 5002[5]
4 b g Emarati (USA) 6.6f **(63)** - Dominion Blue (Dominion) 8.5f **(63)**
Form - 25138825605
Record 1998 - 1st:1 2nd:1 3rd:1 Ran:9
Pre1998 - 1st:0 2nd:2 3rd:1 Ran:11
Win Prizemoney £2,274 *Total Prizemoney* £4,929
Wins * **1998** *Jan Lingfi (STD) H 12f 48 52* <
1998 Turf 0-1: (12f) (sft) 1998 AW 1-8: (12f 1-7, 15f) (Equi 1-2, Fibr 6)
Workmanlike, fair gelding, effective 10 to 15f, best at 12f, - acts on AW, best on Fibr, has worn blinkers, favours left handed tracks, favours tight tracks. AW high 54 - 3rd of 10 getting 16lb from Petoskin (14 Jan Wolverhampton 15f Fibr RF 0087) - also 1st of 11 getting 8lb from Yet Again (1 Jan Lingfield RF 0006).
**K McAuliffe [1-20] Folly Road Racing Partners (1996).*

AVENGING ANGEL (IRE) RR 43f — 4465[12]
2 b f College Chapel - Dromacomer Lady (IRE) (Taufan (USA)) 7f **(57)**
Form - 60
Record 1998 - 1st:0 2nd:0 3rd:0 Ran:2
1998 Turf 0-2: (5f, 6f) (gd, frm)
Currently moderate filly. Turf high 43 (began Aug).
**N P Littmoden [0-2] Plyvine, Guy, Hart & Howells.*

AVERHAM STAR BHB 29f32a RR 13f 32a — 2965[12]
3 ch g Absalom 7.1f **(56)** - Upper Sister (Upper Case (USA)) 8.2f **(55)**
Form - 4546430500
Record 1998 - 1st:0 2nd:0 3rd:1 Ran:10
Pre1998 - 1st:0 2nd:0 3rd:0 Ran:4
Win Prizemoney £0 *Total Prizemoney* £619
1998 Turf 0-2: (6f, 8f) (g-f, frm) 1998 AW 0-8: (8f 5, 11f, 12f 2) (Equi, Fibr 7)
Strong, very moderate gelding, effective 8f, - acts on Fibr, often wears blinkers (effectively), likes left handed tracks, likes tight tracks. Turf high 13 (began Jly). AW high 38 - 4th of 12 getting 22lb from Sharp Monkey (2 Feb Southwell 8f Fibr RF 0206). Inconsistent. **D Shaw [0-14] Starburst Racing.*

AVERTI (IRE) BHB 114f RR 113f — 4726a[2]
7 b h Warning 8.1f **(77)** - Imperial Jade (Lochnager) 6f **(59)**

Form - 030007332

Record 1998 - 1st:0 2nd:1 3rd:3 Ran:9
Pre1998 - 1st:5 2nd:1 3rd:3 Ran:29

Win Prizemoney £47,269 *Total Prizemoney* £130,611

Wins * 1997 Jly Goodwo (G-F) G3 5f 107 <
* 1997 Apr Bath (G-F) 5.1f 106
* 1996 Jly Haydoc (GD) 6f 102

1998 Turf 0-9: (5f 6, 6f 3) (sft, gd 5, frm 3)

Group-class horse, effective 5 to 6f, best at 5f, acts on sft to frm, best on gd, excels at Longchamp. Turf high 113 - 2nd of 14 to My Best Valentine (4 Oct Longchamp 5f sft RF 4726a). Consistent. A marvellous servant to connections, this tough sprinter was ludicrously demoted after causing marginal interference at Baden-Baden in September. He ran the race of his life to finish second in the Prix de l'Abbaye at Longchamp the following month. Has been retired. **W R Muir [5-38] D J Deer.*

AVIVA LADY (IRE) BHB 40f33a RR 47f 33a 544[12]

3 ch f Mac's Imp (USA) 5.6f **(54)** - Flying Beauty (Super Concorde (USA)) 10.9f **(66)**

Form - 00

Record 1998 - 1st:0 2nd:0 3rd:0 Ran:2
Pre1998 - 1st:0 2nd:0 3rd:0 Ran:5

1998 Turf 0-1: (6f) (sft) 1998 AW 0-1: (5f) (Fibr)

Leggy, moderate filly. **C A Dwyer [0-7] R S G Jones.*

AVONDALE GIRL (IRE) BHB 72f RR 79+f 2740[3]

2 ch f Case Law 6f **(64)** - Battle Queen (Kind of Hush) 10.1f **(62)**

Form - 313

Record 1998 - 1st:1 2nd:0 3rd:2 Ran:3

Win Prizemoney £1,900 *Total Prizemoney* £3,420

Wins * **1998** Jun Yarmou (GD) S 5.2f 79+ <

1998 Turf 1-3: (5f 1-3) (gd 1-2, frm)

Currently above-average filly. Turf high 79 - 1st of 4 from Dream On Me (22 Jun Yarmouth RF 2187). She was beaten a fair way although third on her debut, but dropped into selling company, bolted up in a four-runner event at Yarmouth. Looked in need of six furlongs next time. **C A Dwyer [1-3] C A Lynch.*

AVRO ANSON BHB 60f RR 58f 478[4]

10 b g Ardross 12.4f **(67)** - Tremellick (Mummy's Pet) 7.7f **(60)**

Form - 4

Record 1998 - 1st:0 2nd:0 3rd:0 Ran:1
Pre1998 - 1st:3 2nd:1 3rd:0 Ran:11

Win Prizemoney £9,224 *Total Prizemoney* £11,050

1998 Turf 0-1: (18f) (gd)

Fair gelding. Consistent. A useful staying chaser, he makes infrequent appearances on the level.

**Miss J A Camacho [0-2] Axom (from M J Camacho [8-24] Oct 1994).*

AVRO AVIAN BHB 27f RR 40f 418[8]

4 b f Ardross 12.4f **(67)** - Tremellick (Mummy's Pet) 7.7f **(60)**

Form - 8

Record 1998 - 1st:0 2nd:0 3rd:0 Ran:1
Pre1998 - 1st:0 2nd:0 3rd:0 Ran:4

1998 AW 0-1: (11f) (Fibr)

Workmanlike, moderate filly.

**Miss J A Camacho [0-2] B P Skirton (from M J Camacho [0-4] Jly 1997).*

AWAFEH BHB 34f38a RR 42f 38a 245[9]

5 b g Green Desert (USA) 7.8f **(78)** - Three Piece (Jaazeiro (USA)) 9.2f **(54)**

Form - 150

Record 1998 - 1st:1 2nd:0 3rd:0 Ran:3
Pre1998 - 1st:0 2nd:2 3rd:0 Ran:14

Win Prizemoney £1,735 *Total Prizemoney* £3,467

Wins * **1998** *Jan Southw (STD) H 12f 34 35* <

1998 AW 1-3: (12f 1-3) (Fibr 1-3)

Moderate gelding, often wears blinkers (extremely effectively). AW high 35 (1st run) - 1st of 10 getting 3lb from Zesti (19 Jan Southwell RF 0113). He showed a bit of form on Fibresand in the middle of '96, but then seemed to lose his way. However, he bounced back to gain his first victory in a maiden handicap back on Fibresand in January, when stepped up dramatically in trip. It was a poor race however, and he will find it difficult to find another race on the Flat.

**S Mellor [1-11] Mrs S C Haine (from J W Payne [0-6] Nov 1995).*

AWARE RR 110f 4718a[9]

3 gr c Kenmare (FR) 9.6f **(76)**-Nesaah (USA) (Topsider (USA)) 8.3f **(71)**

Form - 320

1998 Turf 0-3: (10f 3) (sft 2, g-s)

Currently Group-class colt, has worn blinkers. Turf high 110 - 2nd of 4 getting 6lb from Dr Fong (19 Jly Maisons-Laffitte 10f sft RF 3056a). He finished like a rocket when short-headed by Dr Fong in a Group Two at Maisons-Laffitte in July, but that performance was starting to look like a flash in the pan by the autumn.

**P Bary in FR [0-3] K Abdulla.*

AWASH RR 57f 3387[8]

4 b g Reprimand 8.2f **(63)**-Wave Dancer(Dance In Time (CAN))8.9f **(59)**

Form - 8

Record 1998 - 1st:0 2nd:0 3rd:0 Ran:1
Pre1998 - 1st:0 2nd:0 3rd:0 Ran:1

1998 Turf 0-1: (8f) (frm)

Scopey, currently fair gelding.

**M D Hammond [0-1] Allerton Racing Club (from B W Hills [0-1] Nov 1996).*

AWASSI (IRE) BHB 60f RR 57f 519[12]

5 b h Fairy King (USA) 7.7f **(75)** - Phantom Row (Adonijah) 10f **(61)**

Form - 0

Record 1998 - 1st:0 2nd:0 3rd:0 Ran:1
Pre1998 - 1st:0 2nd:1 3rd:1 Ran:7

Win Prizemoney £0 *Total Prizemoney* £1,871

1998 Turf 0-1: (6f) (g-s)

Fair colt. Inconsistent. Has shown only a small amount of ability.

**K Mahdi [0-7] Hamad Al-Mutawa (from D K Weld in IRE [0-1] May 1996).*

AWESOME AGAIN (CAN) RR 129a 5168a[1]

4 b c Deputy Minister (CAN) 9.2f **(71)**

Form - 1

1998 AW 1-1: (10f 1-1) (Dirt 1-1)

Currently top-class colt. (1st run) - 1st of 10 from Silver Charm (7 Nov Churchill Downs RF 5168a). Unbeaten in six starts in 1998, culminating in a memorable victory in the Breeders' Cup Classic. Trained by English-born Pat Byrne, he has been retired to stud.

**P Byrne in USA [1-1] Stronach Stables Inc.*

AWESOME POWER BHB 40f50a RR 25f 50a 622[3]

12 b g Vision (USA) 10.4f **(57)**-Majestic Nurse (On Your Mark) 7.7f **(58)**

Form - 022233

Record 1998 - 1st:0 2nd:2 3rd:2 Ran:4
Pre1998 - 1st:10 2nd:26 3rd:9 Ran:78

Win Prizemoney £23,035 *Total Prizemoney* £49,802

Wins * 1997 *Mar Lingfi (STD) S 10f 45*
* 1996 *Nov Lingfi (STD) 10f 52*
* 1996 *Mar Lingfi (STD) S 10f 55*
* 1995 *Nov Lingfi (STD) S 10f 47*
* 1994 *May Lingfi (STD) C 10f 62*
* 1994 *Jan Lingfi (STD) C 10f 62*
* 1994 *Jan Lingfi (STD) 10f 67*

1998 AW 0-4: (10f 4) (Equi 4)

Average gelding, effective 10f, - acts on Equi. AW high 61 (1st run) - 2nd of 7 getting 6lb from Mazeed (1 Jan Lingfield 10f Equi RF 0003). He has been very successful over ten furlongs on the Lingfield Equitrack in modest company, having won ten times over course and distance. There are signs, however, that his best days are behind him.

**J W Hills [8-68] Garrett Freyne (from C R Nelson [2-12] Oct 1992).*

AWESOME VENTURE BHB 33f40a RR 33f 40a 1153[4]

8 b g Formidable (USA) 7.8f **(60)** - Pine Ridge (High Top) 10.2f **(67)**

Form - 3744534664453453004

Record 1998 - 1st:0 2nd:0 3rd:3 Ran:16
Pre1998 - 1st:4 2nd:15 3rd:6 Ran:81

Win Prizemoney £10,287 *Total Prizemoney* £27,684

Wins * 1996 *May Southw (STD) C 7f 73* <
* 1996 *Apr Southw (STD) C 8f 69*
* 1996 *Apr Southw (STD) H 8f 62 63*

1998 Turf 0-1: (6f) (g-s) 1998 AW 0-15: (6f 2, 7f 6, 8f 6, 11f) (Fibr 15)

Fair gelding, effective 6f, - acts on Fibr, has worn blinkers. AW high 54. A half-brother to In The Groove, he must be one of the busiest horses in training, and seems to have been running about

twice a week for a number of years. Despite some reasonable efforts on turf and sand, he is on a losing run stretching back to May '96.

**M C Chapman [3-92] Market Rasen Racing Club (from J A R Toller [1-9] Oct 1994).*

AWESOME WELLS (IRE) BHB 77f RR 73f 2699[6]

4 b c Sadler's Wells (USA) 11.3f **(87)** - Shadywood (Habitat) 9.4f **(70)**

Form - 76

Record 1998 - 1st:0 2nd:0 3rd:0 Ran:2
Pre1998 - 1st:1 2nd:3 3rd:0 Ran:6

Win Prizemoney £3,773 *Total Prizemoney* £7,192

Wins * 1997 Spt Lingfi (GD) 11.5f 78 <

1998 Turf 0-2: (12f 2) (g-f, frm)

Above-average colt, effective 11 to 14f, best at 11f, acts on g-f to frm, best on frm. Turf high 73. Consistent. Looked reluctant to race on his second start and is best avoided.

**H R A Cecil [1-8] Cliveden Stud.*

AWINITA RR 37f 5073[18]

2 b f Prince Sabo 6.6f **(64)** - Tsungani (Cure The Blues (USA)) 9.5f **(63)**

Form - 00

Record 1998 - 1st:0 2nd:0 3rd:0 Ran:2

1998 Turf 0-2: (7f, 8f) (gd 2)

Currently very moderate filly. Turf high 37 (began Oct).

**S C Williams [0-2] I A Southcott.*

AWWALIYA RR 80f 4812[2]

2 b f Distant Relative 7f **(69)** - El Rabab (USA) (Roberto (USA)) 10f **(76)**

Form - 42

Record 1998 - 1st:0 2nd:1 3rd:0 Ran:2

Win Prizemoney £0 *Total Prizemoney* £1,233

1998 Turf 0-2: (6f, 7f) (gd, g-f)

Currently decent filly. Turf high 80 (began Oct) - 2nd of 9 to Sari (15 Oct Catterick 7f gd RF 4812). Has run two promising races and should soon get off the mark.

**P T Walwyn [0-2] Hamdan Al Maktoum.*

AXEMAN (IRE) BHB 38f50a RR 42f 50a 650[8]

6 b g Reprimand 8.2f **(63)** - Minnie Tudor (Tudor Melody) 12.3f **(67)**

Form - 032743358

Record 1998 - 1st:0 2nd:1 3rd:3 Ran:9
Pre1998 - 1st:1 2nd:1 3rd:1 Ran:23

Win Prizemoney £3,663 *Total Prizemoney* £7,830

Wins 1994 Aug Ripon (G-F) 6f 79+

1998 AW 0-9: (6f 2, 7f 6, 8f) (Equi 3, Fibr 6)

Fair gelding, effective 6 to 7f, - acts on Fibr, has worn blinkers, likes left handed tracks, likes tight tracks. AW high 59 - 3rd of 11 getting 5lb from Elite Hope (4 Mar Wolverhampton 7f Fibr RF 0398).

**N P Littmoden [0-9] Tim Godkin (from Martyn Wane [0-7] Oct 1997).*

AZIHAAM (USA) RR 67f 4505[9]

2 ch f Cozzene (USA) 10.1f **(87)**-Tatwij (USA)(Topsider (USA)) 8.3f **(71)**

Form - 00

Record 1998 - 1st:0 2nd:0 3rd:0 Ran:2

1998 Turf 0-2: (7f, 8f) (gd 2)

Currently average filly. Turf high 67 (began Jly).

**M P Tregoning [0-2] Hamdan Al Maktoum.*

AZIZZI BHB 86f RR 97f 4586[11]

6 ch g Indian Ridge 7.6f **(74)** - Princess Silca Key (Grundy) 10.3f **(65)**

Form - 00

Record 1998 - 1st:0 2nd:0 3rd:0 Ran:2
Pre1998 - 1st:1 2nd:3 3rd:0 Ran:8

Win Prizemoney £3,239 *Total Prizemoney* £18,958

Wins * 1996 Apr Kempto (G-F) 7f 91 <

1998 Turf 0-2: (6f 2) (gd 2)

Very useful gelding, effective 6f, acts on gd to g-f. Turf high 45 (began Spt). Becoming disappointing.

**C R Egerton [1-10] Chris Brasher.*

AZOUZ PASHA (USA) RR 57+f 2748[7]

2 b c Lyphard (USA) 10.6f **(75)** - Empress Club (ARG) (Farnesio (ARG))

Form - 7

Record 1998 - 1st:0 2nd:0 3rd:0 Ran:1

1998 Turf 0-1: (7f) (gd)

Currently fair colt. **H R A Cecil [0-1] Wafic Said.*

AZTEC FLYER (USA) BHB 50f43a RR 52f 43a 4861[6]

5 b g Alwasmi (USA) 12.9f **(77)** - Jetta J (USA) (Super Concorde (USA)) 10.9f **(66)**

Form - 45504481576

Record 1998 - 1st:1 2nd:0 3rd:0 Ran:9
Pre1998 - 1st:3 2nd:0 3rd:2 Ran:20

Win Prizemoney £13,037 *Total Prizemoney* £15,338

Wins 1998 Aug Yarmou (FRM) H 14.1f 49 52
1997 Aug Warwic (SFT) H 16.1f 56 56 <
1997 Aug Nottin (G-F) H 16f 50 53
1997 Jly Yarmou (G-F) H 14.1f 45 56 <

1998 Turf 1-8: (12f, 14f 1-4, 16f 2, 17f) (g-s 2, gd, g-f 2, frm 1-3) 1998 AW 0-1: (16f) (Equi)

Fair gelding, effective 14 to 17f, acts on gd to frm - acts on Equi, often wears blinkers (extremely effectively), prefers left handed tracks, favours tight tracks, excels at Nottingham and Yarmouth. Turf high 52 - 1st of 9 getting 5lb from Saint Albert (20 Aug Yarmouth RF 3768). He scored a hat-trick in the middle of '97 following the application of blinkers. Like most from his stable, he did not shown his form last term though he did manage to win a ladies' race at Yarmouth in August.

**Mrs M Reveley [0-11] R Meredith (from C E Brittain [4-18] Spt 1998).*

AZULINO (IRE) BHB 50f RR 56f 2769[5]

3 gr f Bluebird (USA) 7.9f **(71)** - Page Blanche (USA) (Caro) 9.3f **(74)**

Form - 5005

Record 1998 - 1st:0 2nd:0 3rd:0 Ran:4
Pre1998 - 1st:0 2nd:0 3rd:0 Ran:2

1998 Turf 0-4: (7f 2, 8f, 10f) (gd, g-f, frm 2)

Leggy, fair filly, has worn blinkers. Turf high 56.

**J W Hills [0-6] K Y Lim.*

AZZAN (USA) BHB 77f RR 75+f 5139[5]

2 b br c Gulch (USA) 9.6f **(79)** - Dixieland Dream (USA) (Dixieland Band (USA)) 7f **(74)**

Form - 005

Record 1998 - 1st:0 2nd:0 3rd:0 Ran:3

1998 Turf 0-3: (6f 3) (g-s, gd, g-f)

Currently above-average colt. Turf high 75 (began Oct) - 5th of 22 to Mutaakkid (6 Nov Doncaster 6f gd RF 5139).

**J L Dunlop [0-3] Hamdan Al Maktoum.*

BAAJIL BHB 69f RR 57f 4765[5]

3 b g Marju (IRE) 9.2f **(76)**-Arctic River (FR)(Arctic Tern (USA))8.9f **(69)**

Form - 35

Record 1998 - 1st:0 2nd:0 3rd:1 Ran:2
Pre1998 - 1st:0 2nd:1 3rd:0 Ran:1

Win Prizemoney £0 *Total Prizemoney* £1,776

1998 Turf 0-2: (7f 2) (gd, frm)

Neat, currently fair gelding. Turf high 57 (began Spt).

**D J S Cosgrove [0-2] Crown Pkg & Mailing Svs Ltd (from L M Cumani [0-1] Oct 1997).*

BABA AU RHUM (IRE) BHB 67f RR 71f 3515[10]

6 b g Baba Karam 8.1f **(71)** - Spring About (Hard Fought) 8.8f **(62)**

Form - 4570

Record 1998 - 1st:0 2nd:0 3rd:0 Ran:4
Pre1998 - 1st:2 2nd:1 3rd:1 Ran:11

Win Prizemoney £6,726 *Total Prizemoney* £8,528

Wins * 1997 Aug Haydoc (G-F) H 8.1f 66 71 <
* 1997 Jun Sandow (G-F) H 8.1f 60 67

1998 Turf 0-4: (8f 4) (gd, g-f 2, hrd)

Above-average gelding, effective 8f, acts on gd to frm, best on g-f, favours tight tracks. Turf high 71 - 5th of 18 giving 22lb to Final Settlement (29 Jun Windsor 8f g-f RF 2387). Consistent.

**Ian Williams [3-20] & Mrs John Poynton.*

BABANINA BHB 60f56a RR 56f 56a 4640[11]

3 b f Night Shift (USA) 8.1f **(73)** - Babita (Habitat) 9.4f **(70)**

Form - 380

Record 1998 - 1st:0 2nd:0 3rd:1 Ran:3
Pre1998 - 1st:0 2nd:0 3rd:0 Ran:3

Win Prizemoney £0 *Total Prizemoney* £550

1998 Turf 0-2: (7f, 10f) (g-s, frm) 1998 AW 0-1: (9f) (Fibr)

Scopey, fair filly. Turf high 56.
**R T Phillips [0-1] Stephen Molloy (from C E Brittain [0-5] Jun 1998).*

BABA THONG (USA) RR 91f 184a[3]
6 b g Nureyev (USA) 8.4f **(84)** - Madame Premier (USA)
Form - 3
1998 Turf 0-1: (7f) (sft)
Currently useful gelding.
**In FR [0-1] (from Mme C Head in FR [1-2] Oct 1996).*

BABOLNA RR 35f 2443[7]
3 ch f Generous (IRE) 11.5f **(82)** - Spirit of The Wind (USA) (Little Current (USA)) 9.6f **(75)**
Form - 7
Record 1998 - 1st:0 2nd:0 3rd:0 Ran:1
1998 Turf 0-1: (10f) (gd)
Unfurnished, currently very moderate filly.
**B W Hills [0-1] H R H Princess Michael of Kent.*

BABY SPICE BHB 41f50a **RR 31f 50a** 4865[1]
3 ch f Then Again 7.4f **(52)** - Starawak (Star Appeal) 9.6f **(65)**
Form - 0000501
Record 1998 - 1st:1 2nd:0 3rd:0 Ran:7
Pre1998 - 1st:0 2nd:0 3rd:0 Ran:3
Win Prizemoney £2,553 *Total Prizemoney* £2,553
Wins * **1998** *Oct Wolver (STD) 7f 47* <
1998 Turf 0-5: (6f, 7f, 8f 2, 10f) (hvy, g-s, gd, frm 2) 1998 AW 1-2: (7f 1-1, 8f) (Fibr 1-2)
Leggy, moderate filly, effective 7f, - acts on Fibr, likes left handed tracks, likes tight tracks. Turf high 33. AW high 47 (began Jly) - 1st of 11 getting 5lb from Prodigal Son (17 Oct Wolverhampton RF 4865). Inconsistent. Showed nothing before getting off the mark in a maiden on the Wolverhampton Fibresand in October. It was a desperate race.
**R F JohnsonHoughton [1-1] W H Ponsonby (from M R Channon [0-9] Jly 1998).*

BACCHUS RR 64f 1254[22]
4 b g Prince Sabo 6.6f **(64)** - Bonica (Rousillon (USA)) 8.2f **(74)**
Form - 00
Record 1998 - 1st:0 2nd:0 3rd:0 Ran:2
Pre1998 - 1st:1 2nd:0 3rd:0 Ran:6
Win Prizemoney £3,913 *Total Prizemoney* £4,204
Wins 1997 Jly Newmar (G-S) 6f 80 <
1998 Turf 0-2: (6f 2) (gd, g-f)
Scopey, average gelding, effective 6f, acts on gd. Turf high 38.
**Miss J A Camacho [0-2] Ashley Carr Racing (from A C Stewart [1-6] Oct 1997).*

BACHELORS PAD BHB 67f **RR 79f** 4066[16]
4 b g Pursuit of Love 9.5f **(69)** - Note Book (Mummy's Pet) 7.7f **(60)**
Form - 005388420
Record 1998 - 1st:0 2nd:1 3rd:1 Ran:9
Pre1998 - 1st:1 2nd:1 3rd:1 Ran:9
Win Prizemoney £4,413 *Total Prizemoney* £9,936
Wins * 1996 Spt Goodwo (G-F) 6f 96+ <
1998 Turf 0-9: (7f 6, 8f 3) (sft, gd 2, g-f 4, hrd 2)
Leggy, above-average gelding, effective 7f, acts on gd, has worn blinkers, likes tight tracks. Turf high 79. Has ability, but was rather disappointing last season. Has reportedly joined David Nicholls.
**W Jarvis [1-18] Mrs Doris Allen.*

BACKCLOTH (IRE) RR 68f 5145[3]
2 b g Scenic 10.6f **(66)** - Traumerei (GER) (Surumu (GER)) 10f **(83)**
Form - 73
Record 1998 - 1st:0 2nd:0 3rd:1 Ran:2
Win Prizemoney £0 *Total Prizemoney* £485
1998 Turf 0-2: (7f, 8f) (gd 2)
Currently average gelding. Turf high 68 (began Oct).
**J L Dunlop [0-2] D Sieff.*

BACKHANDER (IRE) BHB 29f34a **RR 39tf 34a** 4201[14]
6 b g Cadeaux Genereux 7.9f **(76)** - Chevrefeuille (Ile de Bourbon (USA)) 10.1f **(67)**
Form - 2867064U00000
Record 1998 - 1st:0 2nd:1 3rd:0 Ran:13
Pre1998 - 1st:0 2nd:5 3rd:1 Ran:28
Win Prizemoney £0 *Total Prizemoney* £5,030
1998 Turf 0-8: (6f 3, 7f 4, 8f) (gd 4, g-f 2, frm 2) 1998 AW 0-5: (6f, 7f 3, 8f) (Fibr 5)
Very moderate gelding, effective 7f, acts on frm, has worn blinkers (effectively). Turf high 39. AW high 37. Becoming disappointing.
**M Waring [0-16] Lester Metcalf (from R T Phillips [0-10] Spt 1997).*

BACK LOG (IRE) RR 102f 3011a[7]
4 br f Bob Back (USA) 11.5f **(71)** - Postage Due (AUS) 00
Form - 73207
1998 Turf 0-5: (10f, 12f 2, 14f 2) (sft, gd 3, g-f)
Very useful filly, effective 12 to 14f, acts on sft to gd. Turf high 102 - 2nd of 8 giving 3lb to Bolino Star (19 Jun Tipperary 12f sft RF 2215a). She was set some stiff tasks in handicaps and fell short when tried in Listed events. **J S Bolger in IRE [1-10] J P M O'Connor.*

BACK ROW BHB 52f56a **RR 67?f 56a** 4769[5]
4 b f In The Wings 11.2f **(77)** - Temple Row (Ardross) 10.6f **(68)**
Form - 75756213258065
Record 1998 - 1st:1 2nd:2 3rd:1 Ran:14
Pre1998 - 1st:0 2nd:2 3rd:1 Ran:7
Win Prizemoney £2,770 *Total Prizemoney* £7,632
Wins * **1998** Jly Ayr (GD) 13.1f 67? <
1998 Turf 1-13: (11f, 12f, 13f 1-3, 14f 3, 15f, 16f 2, 17f 2) (sft 3, g-s 2, gd 1-5, g-f, frm 2) 1998 AW 0-1: (12f) (Fibr)
Neat, average filly, effective 12 to 14f, best at 12f, acts on gd to frm - acts on Fibr, best on gd, likes left handed tracks. Turf high 67 - 1st of 7 getting 5lb from Westminster (13 Jly Ayr RF 2753). (1st run) - 3rd of 11 giving 14lb to Silankka (25 Jly Southwell 12f Fibr RF 3125). Becoming disappointing. She has made the frame often, but has only a very narrow victory at Ayr to show for her pains. In truth, she looks slow.
**J Hetherton [1-16] C D Barber-Lomax (from L M Cumani [0-5] Oct 1997).*

BACKSCRATCHER RR 37f 3328[4]
4 b g Backchat (USA) 11.8f **(53)** - Tiernee Quintana (Artaius (USA)) 9f **(69)**
Form - 4
Record 1998 - 1st:0 2nd:0 3rd:0 Ran:1
1998 Turf 0-1: (16f) (gd)
Workmanlike, very moderate gelding.
**S Gollings [0-4] Mrs J M Barker.*

BACKVIEW BHB 38f43a **RR 34f 43a** 2325[5]
6 ch g Backchat (USA) 11.8f **(53)** - Book Review (Balidar) 7.9f **(63)**
Form - 85
Record 1998 - 1st:0 2nd:0 3rd:0 Ran:2
Pre1998 - 1st:3 2nd:1 3rd:4 Ran:25
Win Prizemoney £9,480 *Total Prizemoney* £13,130
Wins * 1996 *Mar Wolver (STD) H 14.8f 69 72* <
* 1996 *Feb Southw (STD) H 12f 60 67*
* 1995 *Jly Wolver (STD) 12f 67*
1998 Turf 0-2: (14f, 17f) (g-s, gd)
Above-average gelding, has worn blinkers. Turf high 34. Inconsistent. **B J Llewellyn [4-33] Eamonn O'Malley.*

BACKWOODS BHB 60f62a **RR 59f 62a** 1255[6]
5 ch g In The Wings 11.2f **(77)** - Kates Cabin (Habitat) 9.4f **(70)**
Form - 6
Record 1998 - 1st:0 2nd:0 3rd:0 Ran:1
Pre1998 - 1st:3 2nd:0 3rd:0 Ran:14
Win Prizemoney £10,160 *Total Prizemoney* £10,160
Wins * 1996 Oct Nottin (GD) H 16f 55 65 <
* 1996 Oct Catter (GD) H 15.8f 55 64
* 1996 *Aug Wolver (STD) H 14.8f 56 52*
1998 Turf 0-1: (16f) (gd)
Fair gelding. (1st run) - 6th of 9 to Unchanged (15 May Thirsk 16f gd RF 1255). Consistent.
**W M Brisbourne [3-14] P R Kirk (from G Wragg [0-1] Nov 1995).*

BADAGARA BHB 84f **RR 78f** 4772[5]
2 b g Warning 8.1f **(77)** - Badawi (USA) (Diesis) 9.3f **(69)**
Form - 235
Record 1998 - 1st:0 2nd:1 3rd:1 Ran:3
Win Prizemoney £0 *Total Prizemoney* £1,599
1998 Turf 0-3: (7f 3) (gd 2, g-f)

Currently above-average gelding. Turf high 78 (began Aug).
**C E Brittain [0-3] Sheikh Marwan Al Maktoum.*

BAD BERTRICH AGAIN (IRE) RR 110f 4603aP

5 b h Dowsing (USA) 7f **(61)**-Ajuga (USA) (The Minstrel (CAN)) 10f **(72)**
Form - 75P
1998 Turf 0-3: (12f 2, 13f) (sft 2, g-f)
Group-class colt, has broken blood-vessels, effective 11 to 13f, acts on sft to g-f, best on sft. Turf high 110 (1st run) - 7th of 10 to Ungaro (21 Jun San Siro 12f g-f RF 2293a). He is a tough old bird, but broke a blood vessel at Cologne in September and is not improving.
**F Gang in GER [0-3] (from A Lowe in GER [1-5] Aug 1997).*

BADDI QUEST BHB 30f60a RR 60a 3575[14]

6 b g Rainbow Quest (USA) 11.2f **(81)** - Baddi Baddi (USA) (Sharpen Up) 8.3f **(67)**
Form - 700
Record 1998 - 1st:0 2nd:0 3rd:0 Ran:3
Pre1998 - 1st:0 2nd:1 3rd:0 Ran:7
Win Prizemoney £0 *Total Prizemoney* £1,841
1998 Turf 0-3: (11f 2, 12f) (gd 2, g-f)
Fair gelding, has worn blinkers. Becoming disappointing.
**Martyn Wane [0-3] J P Slattery (from B Hanbury [0-7] Aug 1995).*

BADLESMERE (USA) BHB 95f RR 100f 4102[9]

4 b c Geiger Counter (USA) 7.8f **(85)** - Arising (USA) (Secreto (USA)) 8.7f **(72)**
Form - 3000
Record 1998 - 1st:0 2nd:0 3rd:1 Ran:4
Pre1998 - 1st:2 2nd:1 3rd:0 Ran:4
Win Prizemoney £8,622 *Total Prizemoney* £50,724
Wins * 1997 May Salisb (G-F) 12f 87 <
* 1997 May Kempto (GD) 8f 87 <
1998 Turf 0-4: (8f, 10f 2, 12f) (gd 2, frm 2)
Scopey, very useful colt, effective 8 to 12f, acts on gd to g-f, has worn blinkers. Turf high 100 (1st run) - 3rd of 10 giving 8lb to Soviet Bureau (28 Jun Goodwood 8f gd RF 2363). He was off for a long time after finishing fourth in last year's Italian Derby, but was absent until returning over an inadequate trip at Goodwood in June. He gave plenty of encouragement there, but has gone backwards since. **P F I Cole [2-8] Exors of the late Lord Sondes.*

BADRINATH (IRE) BHB 53f49a RR 53f 49a 4890[2]

4 b g Imperial Frontier (USA) 7f **(65)** - Badedra (Kings Lake (USA)) 10.8f **(67)**
Form - 231203817012
Record 1998 - 1st:3 2nd:2 3rd:1 Ran:10
Pre1998 - 1st:0 2nd:1 3rd:1 Ran:8
Win Prizemoney £9,566 *Total Prizemoney* £12,039
Wins * **1998** Spt Redcar (G-F) SH 10f 47 53
* **1998** Jun Newmar (GD) H 8f 40 48
* **1998** *Jan Lingfi (STD) 10f 55* <
1998 Turf 2-5: (7f, 8f 1-1, 10f 1-2, 11f) (gd, g-f 1-2, frm 1-2) 1998 AW 1-5: (7f, 8f, 10f 1-3) (Equi 1-3, Fibr 2)
Fair gelding, effective 8 to 11f, best at 10f, acts on g-f to frm - acts on AW, likes left handed tracks, likes tight tracks. Turf high 53 - 1st of 17 giving 8lb to Maradi (25 Spt Redcar RF 4486) - also 1st of 13 getting 30lb from Eurobox Boy (19 Jun Newmarket RF 2123). AW high 55 (1st run) - 1st of 14 from Sharbadarid (1 Jan Lingfield RF 0002). **H J Collingridge [3-18] D Burke.*

BAFFIN BAY BHB 89f RR 94f 4537[10]

3 b c Bustino 11f **(64)** - Surf Bird (Shareef Dancer (USA)) 9.9f **(73)**
Form - 415000
Record 1998 - 1st:1 2nd:0 3rd:0 Ran:6
Pre1998 - 1st:1 2nd:0 3rd:0 Ran:2
Win Prizemoney £8,651 *Total Prizemoney* £9,023
Wins * **1998** May Haydoc (GD) H 14f 85 91+ <
* 1997 Oct Leices (GD) 8f 76
1998 Turf 1-6: (12f 4, 14f 1-2) (gd 1-3, g-f 2, frm)
Well made, useful colt, effective 12 to 14f, acts on gd. Turf high 94 - 5th of 7 giving 9lb to Double Classic (3 Jun Goodwood 12f gd RF 1695) - also 1st of 3 giving 7lb to Bombastic (22 May Haydock RF 1393). Lightly raced, his win came in a three-horse affair at Haydock. Beaten when hampered at York in August, his first run for ten weeks, but was disappointing afterwards.
**H R A Cecil [2-8] L B Holliday.*

BAHAMIAN BANDIT RR 95+f 4146[1]

2 b c First Trump - Sound of the Sea (Windjammer (USA)) 7f **(59)**
Form - 51
Record 1998 - 1st:1 2nd:0 3rd:0 Ran:2
Win Prizemoney £2,826 *Total Prizemoney* £2,826
Wins * **1998** Spt Lingfi (G-S) 6f 95+ <
1998 Turf 1-2: (6f 1-2) (g-f 1-1, frm)
Currently very useful colt. Turf high 95 (began Jly) - 1st of 18 from Single Shot (8 Spt Lingfield RF 4146). After a fine debut run he scorched home in fine style at Lingfield on his final start, and though his winning margin was exaggerated by his having the plum stands'-rail draw, he was still impressive. He looks more than capable of making his mark next term.
**R Hannon [1-2] Lucayan Stud.*

BAHAMIAN PIRATE (USA) BHB 59f RR 65f 4304[6]

3 ch c Housebuster (USA) 7f **(81)** - Shining Through (USA) (Deputy Minister (CAN)) 7.4f **(80)**
Form - 50726
Record 1998 - 1st:0 2nd:1 3rd:0 Ran:5
Win Prizemoney £0 *Total Prizemoney* £1,392
1998 Turf 0-5: (5f 2, 6f, 7f, 8f) (gd, g-f, frm 2, hrd)
Average colt. Turf high 82.
**D Nicholls [0-3] Lucayan Stud (from C Collins in IRE [0-2] May 1998).*

BAHIA BLANCA SUN (IRE) BHB 52f RR 54f 4926[5]

3 b g Tirol 8.1f **(64)**-Wild Applause (IRE)(Sadler's Wells (USA)) 10f **(76)**
Form - 45
Record 1998 - 1st:0 2nd:0 3rd:0 Ran:2
Pre1998 - 1st:0 2nd:0 3rd:0 Ran:1
Win Prizemoney £0 *Total Prizemoney* £199
1998 Turf 0-2: (10f, 12f) (g-s, g-f)
Leggy, currently fair gelding. Turf high 54 (began Spt).
**J L Eyre [0-3] Tony Yates.*

Bahr; her unbeaten record continued at York in May.

BAHR BHB 117f RR 116f 4713a[3]

3 ch f Generous (IRE) 11.5f **(82)** - Lady of the Sea (Mill Reef (USA)) 10.5f **(78)**
Form - 121353
Record 1998 - 1st:2 2nd:1 3rd:2 Ran:6
Pre1998 - 1st:2 2nd:0 3rd:0 Ran:2
Win Prizemoney £111,995 *Total Prizemoney* £225,524
Wins * **1998** Jun Ascot (G-S) G2 12f 113 <
* **1998** May York (GD) G3 10.4f 110
1997 Aug Newbur (G-F) L 7f 97+

1997 Jun Doncas (G-S) 7f 97+
1998 Turf 2-6: (10f 1-2, 12f 1-4) (hvy, g-s 1-1, gd 1-3, frm)
Neat, high-class filly, effective 10 to 12f, best at 12f, acts on hvy to frm. Turf high 116 - 3rd of 5 getting 3lb from Auntie Mame (3 Oct Belmont Park 10f frm RF 4713a) - also 1st of 9 from Star Begonia (18 Jun Ascot RF 2083). Having moved to Godolphin, she put up a fine performance to win the Musidora on her return, but was just unable to cope with Shahtoush's turn of foot in the Oaks, despite battling on well. She made no mistake in the Ribblesdale, but she was a disappointment in the Irish Oaks, and did not seem to handle the very soft ground in the Vermeille. She ran no better than respectably in the States on her final start.
**S bin Suroor [2-6] Godolphin (from B W Hills [2-2] Aug 1997).*

BAHRAIN (IRE) RR 2f 4967[13]
2 ch c Lahib (USA) 8f **(69)** - Twin Island (IRE) (Standaan (FR)) 7f **(55)**
Form - 0
Record 1998 - 1st:0 2nd:0 3rd:0 Ran:1
1998 Turf 0-1: (6f) (sft)
Currently very poor colt.
**Sir Mark Prescott [0-1] H R H Prince Fahd Salman.*

BAILIEBOROUGH BOY (IRE) BHB 54f57a **RR 17f 57a** 3271[11]
4 ch g Shalford (IRE) 7.8f **(63)** - Salique (Sallust) 8.4f **(63)**
Form - 6000
Record 1998 - 1st:0 2nd:0 3rd:0 Ran:4
Pre1998 - 1st:3 2nd:2 3rd:3 Ran:12
Win Prizemoney £7,367 *Total Prizemoney* £10,024
Wins *1997 Feb Southw (STD) C 8f 67 <*
1997 Feb Wolver (STD) S 8.5f 65
1997 Feb Southw (STD) S 7f 57
1998 Turf 0-2: (8f, 11f) (g-f, frm) 1998 AW 0-2: (7f, 8f) (Equi, Fibr)
Workmanlike, poor gelding, effective 7 to 8f, best at 8f, - acts on AW, best on Fibr, often wears blinkers (extremely effectively), favours left handed tracks, favours tight tracks. Turf high 17. AW high 16. Becoming disappointing.
**D C O'Brien [0-5] Michael Gearon (from T D Barron [3-12] Mar 1997).*

BAIRN ATHOLL BHB 34f **RR 34f** 3367[12]
5 ch m Bairn (USA) 9.4f **(55)** - Noble Mistress (Lord Gayle (USA)) 8.8f **(62)**
Form - 020330
Record 1998 - 1st:0 2nd:1 3rd:2 Ran:6
Pre1998 - 1st:0 2nd:2 3rd:0 Ran:10
Win Prizemoney £0 *Total Prizemoney* £3,688
1998 Turf 0-6: (5f 2, 6f 3, 7f) (gd 3, g-f, frm 2)
Very moderate filly, effective 5 to 6f, best at 6f, acts on gd to frm, best on frm, likes left handed tracks. Turf high 34 - 3rd of 10 getting 6lb from Garbo (13 Jly Brighton 6f gd RF 2760).
**R J Hodges [0-16] D J F Phillips.*

BAISSE D'ARGENT (IRE) BHB 81f **RR 82f** 4251[1]
2 b c Common Grounds 8.1f **(66)** - Fabulous Pet (Somethingfabulous (USA)) 9.5f **(75)**
Form - 041
Record 1998 - 1st:1 2nd:0 3rd:0 Ran:3
Win Prizemoney £3,184 *Total Prizemoney* £3,447
Wins * **1998** Spt Mussel (GD) 8f 82 <
1998 Turf 1-3: (6f, 7f, 8f 1-1) (frm 1-3)
Currently decent colt. Turf high 82 (began Aug) - 1st of 6 giving 9lb to Super Forum (14 Spt Musselburgh RF 4251). Convincing winner of a Musselburgh maiden.
**D J S Cosgrove [1-3] Winning Circle Racing Club Ltd.*

BAJEES (USA) RR 72f 4104[4]
2 ch c Dehere (USA) - Intensive (USA) (Sir Wiggle (USA)) 9f **(70)**
Form - 4
Record 1998 - 1st:0 2nd:0 3rd:0 Ran:1
Win Prizemoney £0 *Total Prizemoney* £281
1998 Turf 0-1: (7f) (frm)
Currently above-average colt. **D R Loder [0-1] Maktoum Al Maktoum.*

BAKERS DAUGHTER BHB 56f44a **RR 57f 44a** 2119[9]
6 ch m Bairn (USA) 9.4f **(55)** - Tawnais (Artaius (USA)) 9f **(69)**
Form - 320
Record 1998 - 1st:0 2nd:1 3rd:1 Ran:3
Pre1998 - 1st:5 2nd:5 3rd:8 Ran:44
Win Prizemoney £13,896 *Total Prizemoney* £24,369
Wins * 1997 Jly Windso (G-F) H 10f 57 63 <
* *1996 Aug Lingfi (STD) H 10f 48 53*
* 1996 Jly Windso (GD) H 10f 47 53
* 1995 Jly Leices (GD) S 8f 53
* *1995 Feb Southw (STD) S 8f 49*
1998 Turf 0-2: (10f 2) (g-s, gd) 1998 AW 0-1: (10f) (Equi)
Fair mare, effective 10f, acts on g-s to frm, has worn blinkers, excels at Windsor. Turf high 57 (1st run) - 2nd of 9 giving 9lb to Flying Flip (28 Apr Nottingham 10f g-s RF 0903). A narrow winner at Windsor in July '97, she makes the frame regularly on turf and sand but is very difficult to win with.
**J R Arnold [5-47] Mrs Sue Baker.*

BALA BHB 52f **RR 34f** 4669[17]
3 ch f Casteddu 7.4f **(54)** - Baladee (Mummy's Pet) 7.7f **(60)**
Form - 80
Record 1998 - 1st:0 2nd:0 3rd:0 Ran:2
Pre1998 - 1st:0 2nd:0 3rd:1 Ran:5
Win Prizemoney £0 *Total Prizemoney* £760
1998 Turf 0-2: (6f 2) (gd 2)
Scopey, very moderate filly. Turf high 22 (began Spt).
**H Morrison [0-7] Lord Margadale.*

BALACLAVA (IRE) BHB 36f57a **RR 28f 57a** 3844[13]
3 b g Balla Cove - Little Cynthia (Wolver Hollow) 8f **(56)**
Form - 47508000
Record 1998 - 1st:0 2nd:0 3rd:0 Ran:8
Pre1998 - 1st:0 2nd:1 3rd:1 Ran:6
Win Prizemoney £0 *Total Prizemoney* £1,641
1998 Turf 0-5: (5f, 7f 2, 9f, 12f) (gd 3, g-f, frm) 1998 AW 0-3: (7f, 8f 2) (Fibr 3)
Leggy, fair gelding, effective 7f, acts on g-f, has worn blinkers. Turf high 37. AW high 59. Becoming disappointing.
**A J McNae [0-5] The Light Brigade (from I Semple [0-3] Feb 1998).*

BALANCE THE BOOKS BHB 45f **RR 51df** 4677[27]
3 b f Elmaamul (USA) 8.1f **(70)** - Psylla (Beldale Flutter (USA)) 9.7f **(71)**
Form - 040030000
Record 1998 - 1st:0 2nd:0 3rd:1 Ran:9
Pre1998 - 1st:1 2nd:0 3rd:0 Ran:6
Win Prizemoney £5,848 *Total Prizemoney* £6,182
Wins 1997 May York (GD) 5f 83 <
1998 Turf 0-8: (5f 2, 6f 2, 7f 3, 8f) (gd 2, g-f 2, frm 3, hrd) 1998 AW 0-1: (7f) (Fibr)
Scopey, fair filly, effective 5 to 7f, acts on gd to frm, has worn blinkers. Turf high 51. Becoming disappointing.
**J Parkes [0-9] Mrs E Comer (from R Hannon [1-6] Oct 1997).*

BALANITA (IRE) BHB 75f70a **RR 76f 70a** 4799[17]
3 b g Anita's Prince 6f **(62)** - Ballybannon (Ballymore) 7.3f **(64)**
Form - 40100
Record 1998 - 1st:1 2nd:0 3rd:0 Ran:4
Pre1998 - 1st:1 2nd:0 3rd:0 Ran:7
Win Prizemoney £6,353 *Total Prizemoney* £6,555
Wins * **1998** Jly Windso (GD) H 6f 67 76 <
* 1997 Oct Bright (G-F) H 7f 60 67
1998 Turf 1-4: (6f 1-3, 7f) (sft, g-f 1-2, frm)
Neat, above-average gelding, effective 6 to 7f, acts on g-f. Turf high 76 - 1st of 17 giving 15lb to Daynabee (6 Jly Windsor RF 2576). Inconsistent. **B Palling [2-11] Mrs Anita Quinn.*

BALI DANCE BHB 55f65a **RR 64f 65a** 4760[5]
3 br f Rambo Dancer (CAN) 8.4f **(59)** - Baliana **(47df)** (Midyan (USA)) 6f **(60)**
Form - 518604135465
Record 1998 - 1st:1 2nd:0 3rd:1 Ran:10
Pre1998 - 1st:1 2nd:0 3rd:4 Ran:12
Win Prizemoney £4,710 *Total Prizemoney* £8,273
Wins * **1998** Jun Carlis (G-S) 8f 60
* *1997 Dec Lingfi (STD) 7f 65 <*
1998 Turf 1-8: (7f 2, 8f 1-6) (gd 1-5, g-f 2, frm) 1998 AW 0-2: (7f, 8f) (Equi 2)
Neat, average filly, effective 6 to 8f, best at 7f, acts on sft to g-f - acts on Equi, has worn blinkers, likes left handed tracks, likes tight tracks, excels at Doncaster. Turf high 64 - 3rd of 8 getting 10lb from Scene (12 Jly Haydock 8f g-f RF 2741) - also 1st of 9 get-

ting 10lb from Gymcrak Flyer (25 Jun Carlisle RF 2267). AW high 53. **C B B Booth [2-22] J A Porteous.*

BALI-PET BHB 26f23a **RR 23f 23a** 71[12]

4 b g Tina's Pet 7.4f **(56)** - Baligay (Balidar) 7.9f **(63)**
Form - 8050
Record 1998 - 1st:0 2nd:0 3rd:0 Ran:2
Pre1998 - 1st:1 2nd:3 3rd:1 Ran:23
Win Prizemoney £1,735 *Total Prizemoney* £4,309
Wins 1996 *Nov Southw (STD) S 8f 56* <
1998 AW 0-2: (8f 2) (Fibr 2)
Lengthy, little account gelding, often wears blinkers. AW high 22.
**J Parkes [0-16] R Flegg (from W G M Turner [1-10] Jan 1997).*

BALISADA BHB 88f **RR 89f** 5000[1]

2 ch f Kris 10f **(75)** - Balnaha (Lomond (USA)) 8.8f **(65)**
Form - 231
Record 1998 - 1st:1 2nd:1 3rd:1 Ran:3
Win Prizemoney £3,622 *Total Prizemoney* £5,510
Wins * 1998 Oct Lingfi (HVY) 7f 89 <
1998 Turf 1-3: (6f 2, 7f 1-1) (sft 1-1, gd, g-f)
Currently useful filly. Turf high 89 (began Spt) - 1st of 10 from Heartwood (26 Oct Lingfield RF 5000).
**G Wragg [1-3] A E Oppenheimer.*

BALI TIMES RR 315[9]

4 b f Timeless Times (USA) 6.1f **(56)** - Bali Sunset (Balidar) 7.9f **(63)**
Form - 0
Record 1998 - 1st:0 2nd:0 3rd:0 Ran:1
1998 AW 0-1: (7f) (Equi)
Unfurnished, currently very poor filly.
**M J Haynes [0-1] Chris Buckerfield.*

BALLA D'AIRE (IRE) BHB 40f **RR 59f** 4338[9]

3 b br g Balla Cove - Silius (Junius (USA)) 7.7f **(65)**
Form - 047000
Record 1998 - 1st:0 2nd:0 3rd:0 Ran:6
Pre1998 - 1st:0 2nd:0 3rd:0 Ran:3
Win Prizemoney £0 *Total Prizemoney* £242
1998 Turf 0-6: (8f 2, 10f 2, 12f, 14f) (gd, g-f 2, frm 3)
Workmanlike, fair gelding, effective 6f, acts on gd. Turf high 59. Becoming disappointing.
**M Bell [0-6] Ms Lynn Bell (from R Boss [0-3] Oct 1997).*

BALLADONIA RR 82f 5071[2]

2 b f Primo Dominie 7.2f **(67)** - Susquehanna Days (USA) (Chief's Crown (USA)) 9.8f **(72)**
Form - 22
Record 1998 - 1st:0 2nd:2 3rd:0 Ran:2
Win Prizemoney £0 *Total Prizemoney* £2,340
1998 Turf 0-2: (7f 2) (gd 2)
Currently decent filly. Turf high 82 (began Oct) - 2nd of 16 to Noushkey (31 Oct Newmarket 7f gd RF 5071).
**Lady Herries [0-2] D K R & Mrs J B C Oliver.*

BALLANTRAE BOY BHB 50f **RR 53f** 1543[3]

4 ch g Safawan 6.6f **(60)** - Romany Home (Gabitat) 5f **(44)**
Form - 6121283
Record 1998 - 1st:2 2nd:2 3rd:1 Ran:7
Pre1998 - 1st:0 2nd:0 3rd:0 Ran:3
Win Prizemoney £5,568 *Total Prizemoney* £7,537
Wins * 1998 May Mussel (GD) H 5f 41 48 <
*** 1998** Apr Ripon (SFT) H 5f 23 38
1998 Turf 2-7: (5f 2-6, 6f) (sft, g-s 1-1, gd 1-3, g-f 2)
Fair gelding, effective 5f, acted on sft to g-f. Turf high 53 - 2nd of 11 giving 8lb to Henry the Hawk (7 May Hamilton 5f sft RF 1080) - also 1st of 8 getting 4lb from Bowcliffe Grange (6 May Musselburgh RF 1066). (DEAD)
**J S Goldie [2-9] J C McGee (from R M McKellar [0-1] Jun 1997).*

BALLARAT (IRE) RR 110f 2859a[3]

4 b c Sadler's Wells (USA) 11.3f **(87)** - Bex (USA) (Explodent (USA)) 9.4f **(87)**
Form - 3
1998 Turf 0-1: (15f) (gd)
Currently Group-class colt. (1st run) - 3rd of 5 to Palio Sky (6 Jly Chantilly 15f gd RF 2859a). He was outpaced by Palio Sky at Chantilly in June, and that horse is not a flying machine.
**A Fabre in FR [0-1].*

BALLARD LADY (IRE) BHB 40f50a **RR 40f 50a** 3576[9]

6 ch m Ballad Rock 7.2f **(63)** - First Blush (Ela-Mana-Mou) 10.1f **(70)**
Form - 07050006260
Record 1998 - 1st:0 2nd:1 3rd:0 Ran:11
Pre1998 - 1st:5 2nd:3 3rd:3 Ran:49
Win Prizemoney £18,999 *Total Prizemoney* £25,634
Wins * 1997 Aug Hamilt (GD) H 6f 39 45 <
* 1997 *Jan Southw (STD) H 6f 44 44*
* 1996 Aug Ayr (GD) H 6f 40 45 <
* 1996 Jly Haydoc (G-S) H 7.1f 33 40
* 1995 Jun Haydoc (G-S) H 8.1f 40 40
1998 Turf 0-11: (5f 2, 6f 5, 7f 3, 8f) (sft, g-s 2, gd 5, frm 3)
Moderate mare, effective 5 to 8f, best at 6f, acts on gd to frm - acts on Fibr, best on frm, has worn blinkers (effectively), excels at Newcastle. Turf high 40 - 2nd of 16 getting 29lb from Bintang Timor (16 Jly Leicester 6f frm RF 2857).
**J S Wainwright [5-61] Mrs P Wake.*

BALLASILLA BHB 46f53a **RR 47f 53a** 4865[6]

3 b f Puissance 7.1f **(60)** - Darussalam (Tina's Pet) 6.8f **(59)**
Form - 6006
Record 1998 - 1st:0 2nd:0 3rd:0 Ran:3
Pre1998 - 1st:0 2nd:0 3rd:0 Ran:5
1998 Turf 0-2: (6f, 8f) (g-f, frm) 1998 AW 0-1: (7f) (Fibr)
Workmanlike, fair filly. Turf high 13.
**B Palling [0-8] Merthyr Motor Auctions.*

BALLA SOLA (IRE) RR 97+f 5109a[4]

3 ch g Simply Great (FR) 11.9f **(61)** - Dance Alone (USA) (Monteverdi) 6.5f **(61)**
Form - 42801014
1998 Turf 2-8: (8f, 9f 2-2, 10f 3, 11f, 12f) (sft 1-3, g-s, gd 1-3, g-f)
Very useful gelding, effective 6 to 10f, acts on sft to gd, best on gd, likes Leopardstown and Gowran Park and Galway. Turf high 97 - 4th of 9 giving 4lb to Golden Rule (26 Oct Leopardstown 10f gd RF 5109a) - also 1st of 4 from Dual Star (16 Oct Gowran Park RF 4904a). Inconsistent. He took a while to find his form in Ireland as a two-year-old, but won his last two starts of the season and has won twice since stepping up in distance as a three-year-old. Used to run freely but is now held up. A tough, consistent sort.
**W P Mullins in IRE [4-16] Top Cat Syndicate.*

BALLET MASTER (USA) RR 104++f 5041[1]

2 ch c Kingmambo (USA) 10.9f **(85)** - Danse Royale (IRE) (Caerleon (USA)) 8.6f **(71)**
Form - 1
Record 1998 - 1st:1 2nd:0 3rd:0 Ran:1
Win Prizemoney £3,157 *Total Prizemoney* £3,157
Wins * 1998 Oct Yarmou (SFT) 7f 104++ <
1998 Turf 1-1: (7f 1-1) (sft 1-1)
Currently very useful colt. (1st run) - 1st of 10 giving 5lb to Umbrian Gold (28 Oct Yarmouth RF 5041). Lived up to his lofty home reputation when winning a back-end maiden by seven lengths. Out of a Group-winning half-sister to Salsabil and Marju, he is an exciting prospect and looks sure to make his mark in better company. **H R A Cecil [1-1] Tabor Mrs Magnier & Niarchos Family.*

BALLET RAMBERT BHB 50f **RR 35f** 3693[10]

3 b f Rambo Dancer (CAN) 8.4f **(59)** - Kind Thoughts (Kashmir II) 11.7f **(48)**
Form - 0700
Record 1998 - 1st:0 2nd:0 3rd:0 Ran:4
Pre1998 - 1st:1 2nd:0 3rd:0 Ran:9
Win Prizemoney £3,187 *Total Prizemoney* £3,515
Wins * 1997 Apr Bath (G-F) 5.1f 64 <
1998 Turf 0-4: (8f 2, 10f, 12f) (gd 2, g-f, frm)
Light-framed, very moderate filly, effective 5 to 8f, acts on gd to frm, has worn blinkers. Turf high 35. Becoming disappointing. Has not progressed since winning easily under a feather weight on her juvenile debut. **M J Heaton-Ellis [1-13] Mrs Janet Wain.*

BALLINA LAD (IRE) BHB 59f **RR 69f** 4376[8]

2 b c Mac's Imp (USA) 5.6f **(54)** - Nationalartgallery (IRE) (Tate Gallery (USA)) 7.4f **(67)**

Form - 1854808
Record 1998 - 1st:1 2nd:0 3rd:0 Ran:7
Win Prizemoney £1,945 *Total Prizemoney* £2,192
Wins * **1998** May Newcas (G-S) 5f 81+ <
1998 Turf 1-7: (5f 1-3, 6f 3, 7f) (gd 1-2, g-f 3, frm 2)
Average colt, effective 5f, acts on gd, has worn blinkers. Turf high 81 (1st run) - 1st of 10 giving 2lb to Callitwhatyouwant (4 May Newcastle RF 1019). **J G FitzGerald [1-7] Mike Browne.*

BALLYCROY RIVER BHB 40f RR 55f 4934[9]
2 b c Sizzling Melody 6.3f **(49)** - Little Tich (Great Nephew) 9.9f **(64)**
Form - 5000000
Record 1998 - 1st:0 2nd:0 3rd:0 Ran:7
1998 Turf 0-4:(7f 2, 8f, 10f)(gd 2, frm 2)1998 AW 0-3: (5f, 6f, 7f) (Fibr 3)
Fair colt, has worn blinkers. Turf high 55. AW high 38.
**B A McMahon [0-7] C G Conway.*

BALLYKEEFE BHB 42f RR 38f 5060[9]
3 ch g Elmaamul (USA) 8.1f **(70)** - Caviar Blini (What A Guest) 7f **(62)**
Form - 350000
Record 1998 - 1st:0 2nd:0 3rd:1 Ran:6
Win Prizemoney £0 *Total Prizemoney* £532
1998 Turf 0-5: (7f, 8f 3, 10f) (sft, g-s, gd, g-f, frm) 1998 AW 0-1: (8f) (Fibr)
Workmanlike, very moderate gelding, has worn blinkers. Turf high 56. **T J Etherington [0-6] B C B Partners.*

BALLYKISSANGEL BHB 25f18a RR 19f 18a 1307[8]
5 ro g Hadeer 8.9f **(58)** - April Wind (Windjammer (USA)) 7f **(59)**
Form - 003008
Record 1998 - 1st:0 2nd:0 3rd:1 Ran:6
Pre1998 - 1st:0 2nd:0 3rd:0 Ran:11
Win Prizemoney £0 *Total Prizemoney* £360
1998 Turf 0-1: (8f) (hvy) 1998 AW 0-5: (11f 3, 12f 2) (Fibr 5)
Poor gelding, has worn blinkers. AW high 19.
**N Bycroft [0-23] G J Allison.*

BALLYKISSANN BHB 40f RR 44f 3846[13]
3 ch g Ballacashtal (CAN) 7.9f **(51)** - Mybella Ann (Anfield) 8.5f **(59)**
Form - 00607730
Record 1998 - 1st:0 2nd:0 3rd:1 Ran:8
Pre1998 - 1st:0 2nd:0 3rd:0 Ran:2
Win Prizemoney £0 *Total Prizemoney* £336
1998 Turf 0-7: (8f 5, 9f, 10f) (sft, gd, g-f, frm 4) 1998 AW 0-1: (8f) (Equi)
Workmanlike, moderate gelding, has worn blinkers. Turf high 58.
**D J S ffrenchDavis [0-10] Paul De Weck.*

BALLYMORRIS BOY (IRE) RR 67f 4818[6]
2 b c Dolphin Street (FR) - Solas Abu (IRE) (Red Sunset) 8.2f **(63)**
Form - 6
Record 1998 - 1st:0 2nd:0 3rd:0 Ran:1
1998 Turf 0-1: (7f) (frm)
Currently average colt. **W R Muir [0-1] Mrs J M Muir.*

BALLYMOTE BHB 55f RR 71f 5173a[21]
4 b g Chilibang 7f **(55)** - Be My Honey (Bustino) 10.4f **(64)**
Form - 500855212140
Record 1998 - 1st:2 2nd:2 3rd:0 Ran:12
Pre1998 - 1st:2 2nd:2 3rd:0 Ran:14
Win Prizemoney £10,178 *Total Prizemoney* £15,624
Wins * **1998** Oct Punche (SFT) H 7.5f 71
* **1998** Spt Down R (GD) H 5f 65
1996 Spt Mussel (G-F) H 5f 73 73 <
1996 Jly Redcar (G-F) 5f 73 <
1998 Turf 2-12: (5f 1-6, 6f 3, 7f, 8f 1-2) (hvy, sft 1-2, g-s 3, gd 1-5, g-f)
Tall, above-average gelding, effective 5 to 8f, best at 5f, acts on sft to gd, best on gd. Turf high 71 - 2nd of 13 giving 4lb to Crown Point (26 Spt Listowel 6f gd RF 4566a) - also 1st of 18 giving 29lb to Gossie Madera (1 Oct Punchestown RF 4684a).
**M Halford in IRE [2-8] M Woods (from J Berry [2-18] Jun 1998).*

BALSOX RR 75f 4959[4]
2 b c Alzao (USA) 9.8f **(73)** - Bobbysoxer (Valiyar) 8.5f **(73)**
Form - 04
Record 1998 - 1st:0 2nd:0 3rd:0 Ran:2
Win Prizemoney £0 *Total Prizemoney* £315
1998 Turf 0-2: (6f, 7f) (g-f, frm)
Currently above-average colt. Turf high 75 (began Aug).
**J L Dunlop [0-2] Hesmonds Stud.*

BALTIC LOWLAND (USA) BHB 90f RR 87f 3957[3]
2 b c Gone West (USA) 7.8f **(82)** - Polish Style (USA) (Danzig (USA)) 8.4f **(76)**
Form - 23123
Record 1998 - 1st:1 2nd:2 3rd:2 Ran:5
Win Prizemoney £3,272 *Total Prizemoney* £8,887
Wins * **1998** Jly Yarmou (G-F) 5.2f 86+ <
1998 Turf 1-5: (5f 1-3, 6f 2) (gd, g-f 1-3, frm)
Useful colt, has worn blinkers. Turf high 87 - 3rd of 12 giving 9lb to Ingenious (29 Aug Newmarket 6f frm RF 3957) - also 1st of 5 giving 5lb to Bevelena (21 Jly Yarmouth RF 2980). Has plenty of ability, but his attitude is open to question.
**D R Loder [1-5] H E Sheikh Rashid Al Maktoum.*

BALTIC STATE (USA) BHB 103f RR 99f 3296[1]
3 b c Danzig (USA) 8.1f **(88)** - Kingscote (Kings Lake (USA)) 10.8f **(67)**
Form - 341
Record 1998 - 1st:1 2nd:0 3rd:1 Ran:3
Pre1998 - 1st:2 2nd:0 3rd:0 Ran:3
Win Prizemoney £19,394 *Total Prizemoney* £20,803
Wins * **1998** Aug Newcas (GD) 7f 99 <
* 1997 Jly Newmar (G-F) L 7f 98
* 1997 Jun Yarmou (FRM) 6f 77+
1998 Turf 1-3: (7f 1-3) (g-f 1-2, hrd)
Scopey, very useful colt, effective 7f, acts on g-f to frm, best on g-f. Turf high 99 (began Jly) - 1st of 4 from Dazilyn Lady (2 Aug Newcastle RF 3296). Not seen out after flopping at Goodwood on his third run at two, he ran respectably in his first two starts last term, and reversed Newbury running with Rainald when winning a four-runner conditions event at Newcastle in August. He was not seen out again and is obviously a hard horse to train, but is useful when right. **H R A Cecil [3-6] K Abdulla.*

BALWAT ALZAMAAN (IRE) RR 28f 1453[10]
2 ch f Lycius (USA) 8.8f **(71)** - Balwa (USA) (Danzig (USA)) 8.4f **(76)**
Form - 0
Record 1998 - 1st:0 2nd:0 3rd:0 Ran:1
1998 Turf 0-1: (6f) (g-f)
Currently little account filly.
**A C Stewart [0-1] Sheikh Ahmed Al Maktoum.*

BAMBOO GARDEN (USA) BHB 63f RR 68f 4773[6]
2 b c Desert Secret (IRE) - Miss Mischievous (USA) (Brazen Brother (USA))
Form - 606
Record 1998 - 1st:0 2nd:0 3rd:0 Ran:3
Win Prizemoney £0 *Total Prizemoney* £58
1998 Turf 0-3: (7f 2, 8f) (gd 2, g-f)
Currently average colt, has worn blinkers. Turf high 68 (began Spt). **G C H Chung [0-3] J Tse.*

BANBURY (USA) BHB 86f RR 79f 3106[8]
4 b c Silver Hawk (USA) 11.2f **(85)** - Sugar Hollow (USA) (Val de L'Orne (FR)) 12f **(75)**
Form - 78
Record 1998 - 1st:0 2nd:0 3rd:0 Ran:2
Pre1998 - 1st:1 2nd:0 3rd:2 Ran:5
Win Prizemoney £3,847 *Total Prizemoney* £4,879
Wins 1997 May Redcar (GD) 10f 94 <
1998 Turf 0-2: (12f 2) (g-f 2)
Light-framed, above-average colt, effective 10f, acts on frm. Turf high 79 (began Jly).
**M Johnston [0-2] Sheikh Mohammed (from J W Watts [1-5] Aug 1997).*

BANDBOX (IRE) BHB 67f RR 74f 4596[10]
3 ch c Imperial Frontier (USA) 7f **(65)** - Dublah (USA) (Private Account (USA)) 8.5f **(74)**
Form - 000027030260
Record 1998 - 1st:0 2nd:2 3rd:1 Ran:12
Pre1998 - 1st:1 2nd:5 3rd:1 Ran:11
Win Prizemoney £2,952 *Total Prizemoney* £10,205
Wins 1997 Oct Leices (GD) 6f 78 <
1998 Turf 0-12: (5f 4, 6f 7, 7f) (hvy, gd 5, g-f 3, frm 3)
Workmanlike, above-average colt, effective 5 to 6f, best at 6f, acts on gd to g-f, best on gd, has worn blinkers. Turf high 74.

**M Salaman [0-12] Falcon Boys Partnership (from S Mellor [1-11] Oct 1997).*

BAND ON THE RUN BHB 66f **RR 66f** 5147[1]

11 ch h Song 6.4f **(63)** - Sylvanecte (FR) (Silver Shark) 7.9f **(81)**
Form - 00044364530201
Record 1998 - 1st:1 2nd:1 3rd:2 Ran:14
Pre1998 - 1st:9 2nd:7 3rd:9 Ran:83
Win Prizemoney £97,806 *Total Prizemoney* £145,910
Wins * **1998** Nov Doncas (SFT) H 8f 62 66
* 1997 Jun Haydoc (G-F) H 8.1f 82 86
* 1995 Spt Doncas (G-S) H 8f 92 98 <
* 1995 Jly Haydoc (G-F) H 7.1f 86 89
* 1994 Spt Haydoc (GD) H 7.1f 84 85
* 1994 Apr Newmar (G-S) H 7f 85 90
1998 Turf 1-14: (8f 1-14) (sft, g-s, gd 1-7, g-f 2, frm 3)
Average horse, effective 8f, acts on g-f, has worn blinkers. Turf high 66. Ended an honourable career on a winning note.
**B A McMahon [10-97] D J Allen.*

BANGALORE RR 62f 5037[8]

2 ch c Sanglamore (USA) 12.9f **(67)** - Ajuga (USA) (The Minstrel (CAN)) 10f **(72)**
Form - 08
Record 1998 - 1st:0 2nd:0 3rd:0 Ran:2
1998 Turf 0-2: (7f 2) (g-s, g-f)
Currently average colt. Turf high 50 (began Spt).
**B W Hills [0-2] K Abdulla.*

BANKER DWERRY (FR) BHB 67f **RR 73f** 4572[1]

3 b c Unfuwain (USA) 11.4f **(74)** - Tartique Twist (USA) (Arctic Tern (USA)) 8.9f **(69)**
Form - 4368424031
Record 1998 - 1st:1 2nd:1 3rd:2 Ran:10
Pre1998 - 1st:0 2nd:1 3rd:0 Ran:2
Win Prizemoney £3,582 *Total Prizemoney* £7,635
Wins * **1998** Spt Bright (GD) 8f 70 <
1998 Turf 1-10: (8f 1-3, 9f 2, 10f, 11f, 12f 3) (gd 5, g-f 1-2, frm 3)
Above-average colt, effective 8 to 12f, best at 8f, acts on gd to frm, best on gd, likes tight tracks. Turf high 74 - 3rd of 11 giving 5lb to New Abbey (3 May Salisbury 12f gd RF 1001) - also 1st of 13 giving 5lb to Bint Kaldoun (30 Spt Brighton RF 4572).
**S P C Woods [1-12] Dr Frank Chao.*

BANKERS ORDER BHB 35f **RR 24f** 721[12]

4 b g Prince Sabo 6.6f **(64)** - Bad Payer (Tanfirion) 7f **(61)**
Form - 50
Record 1998 - 1st:0 2nd:0 3rd:0 Ran:2
Pre1998 - 1st:0 2nd:0 3rd:0 Ran:3
1998 Turf 0-1: (5f) (g-s) 1998 AW 0-1: (5f) (Fibr)
Light-framed, very moderate gelding.
**T D Easterby [0-5] Mrs Anne Henson.*

BANK HOUSE (IRE) BHB 42f **RR 50f** 4921[16]

3 ch g Zafonic (USA) 9f **(83)** - Shebasis (USA) (General Holme (USA)) 5.7f **(63)**
Form - 7830
Record 1998 - 1st:0 2nd:0 3rd:1 Ran:4
Win Prizemoney £0 *Total Prizemoney* £538
1998 Turf 0-4: (5f 2, 6f, 8f) (g-s, gd, frm 2)
Workmanlike, fair gelding. Turf high 50 (began Aug).
**G P Kelly [0-4] G P Kelly.*

BANK ON HER (USA) RR 72+f 4916[3]

2 ch f Rahy (USA) 9.1f **(80)** - Bank On Love (USA) (Gallant Romeo (USA)) 8.4f **(64)**
Form - 3
Record 1998 - 1st:0 2nd:0 3rd:1 Ran:1
Win Prizemoney £0 *Total Prizemoney* £492
1998 Turf 0-1: (7f) (g-s)
Currently above-average filly. **J H M Gosden [0-1] Mrs Shirley Taylor.*

BANK ON HIM BHB 45f69a **RR 43f 69a** 4996[2]

3 b g Elmaamul (USA) 8.1f **(70)** - Feather Flower (Relkino) 8.9f **(65)**
Form - 6632432412
Record 1998 - 1st:1 2nd:3 3rd:2 Ran:8
Pre1998 - 1st:0 2nd:0 3rd:0 Ran:3
Win Prizemoney £2,637 *Total Prizemoney* £5,897
Wins * **1998** *Spt Wolver (STD) H 8.5f 56 63* <
1998 Turf 0-2: (10f 2) (gd 2) 1998 AW 1-6: (7f, 8f 1-4, 10f) (Equi 3, Fibr 1-3)
Light-framed, average gelding, effective 8 to 10f, - acts on AW, likes left handed tracks, favours tight tracks. Turf high 40. AW high 66 - 2nd of 14 getting 3lb from Muyassir (26 Oct Lingfield 10f Equi RF 4996) - also 1st of 12 getting 9lb from Al's Fella (5 Spt Wolverhampton RF 4116). Fair form in modest company on turf and sand, he was becoming frustrating but managed to land a very modest maiden handicap on the Wolverhampton Fibresand in September. **G L Moore [1-11] Allen House Partnership.*

BANK ON MEE RR 58f 3831[2]

2 b f Weldnaas (USA) 8.4f **(55)** - Heemee (On Your Mark) 7.7f **(58)**
Form - 72
Record 1998 - 1st:0 2nd:1 3rd:0 Ran:2
Win Prizemoney £0 *Total Prizemoney* £580
1998 Turf 0-2: (5f, 7f) (g-f, frm)
Currently fair filly. Turf high 58 (began Aug) - 2nd of 16 to Sound's Ace (24 Aug Beverley 5f g-f RF 3831). **J J Quinn [0-2] B S Adamson.*

BANNERET (USA) BHB 55f61a **RR 59?f 61a** 5081[3]

5 b g Imperial Falcon (CAN) 9.2f **(72)** - Dashing Partner (Formidable (USA)) 9.2f **(63)**
Form - 1602113
Record 1998 - 1st:3 2nd:1 3rd:1 Ran:7
Pre1998 - 1st:0 2nd:0 3rd:0 Ran:7
Win Prizemoney £6,170 *Total Prizemoney* £7,067
Wins * **1998** *Jly Southw (STD) S 12f 64*
1998 *Jly Wolver (STD) S 12f 64*
1998 *Mar Wolver (STD) 9.4f 72+* <
1998 Turf 0-1: (10f) (g-f) 1998 AW 3-6: (9f 1-2, 12f 2-4) (Fibr 3-6)
Average gelding, effective 9 to 12f, best at 12f, - acts on Fibr, has worn blinkers, prefers left handed tracks, prefers tight tracks. AW high 72 (1st run) - 1st of 6 giving 19lb to Imperial Prince (21 Mar Wolverhampton RF 0457) - also 1st of 7 giving 17lb to Arm And A Leg (25 Jly Southwell RF 3129).
**Miss S J Wilton [1-2] John Pointon and Sons (from G Woodward [2-5] Jly 1998).*

BANNINGHAM BLADE BHB 76f **RR 83f** 4596[11]

3 b f Sure Blade (USA) 10.6f **(66)** -High Velocity (Frimley Park) 6.5f **(67)**
Form - 0607030070
Record 1998 - 1st:0 2nd:0 3rd:1 Ran:10
Pre1998 - 1st:4 2nd:2 3rd:3 Ran:17
Win Prizemoney £12,257 *Total Prizemoney* £41,242
Wins * 1997 May Windso (SFT) 5f 87 <
* 1997 Apr Bright (FRM) 5.3f 78
* 1997 Apr Bright (FRM) 5.3f 78
* 1997 Apr Lingfi (FRM) 5f 68
1998 Turf 0-10: (5f 8, 6f 2) (gd 5, g-f 2, frm 3)
Unfurnished, decent filly, effective 5f, acts on gd to g-f, best on gd, has worn blinkers, excels at Brighton. Turf high 83. A bragain buy, she did connections proud at two, but showed little in her second season. **K T Ivory [4-27] Crown Select.*

BANNINGHAM BREEZE BHB 59f **RR 68f** 4612[10]

2 br g Cyrano de Bergerac 7.3f **(58)** - Strapped **(55f)** (Reprimand)
Form - 0662344480810580
Record 1998 - 1st:1 2nd:1 3rd:1 Ran:16
Win Prizemoney £3,468 *Total Prizemoney* £6,073
Wins * **1998** Aug Goodwo (G-F) S 6f 66 <
1998 Turf 1-14: (5f 2, 6f 1-9, 7f, 8f 2) (g-s, gd 2, g-f 1-5, frm 5, hrd)
1998 AW 0-2: (6f 2) (Fibr 2)
Average gelding, effective 6f, acts on g-f, has worn blinkers. Turf high 68 - 2nd of 22 getting 5lb from Choral Express (8 Jun Windsor 6f g-f RF 1821) - also 1st of 7 giving 5lb to Compton Akka (28 Aug Goodwood RF 3924). AW high 68 (began Jly).
**K T Ivory [1-16] Crown Select.*

BANSHEE BREEZE (USA) RR 110 5166a[2]

3 b f Unbridled (USA)
Form - 2
1998 AW 0-1: (9f) (Dirt)
Currently Group-class filly. (1st run) - 2nd of 8 getting 3lb from Escena (7 Nov Churchill Downs 9f Dirt RF 5166a). Sent off at odds-on for the Breeders' Cup Distaff, following a brilliant victory in a

Grade One at Keeneland, but found Escena just too strong.
**C Nafzger in USA [0-1] J Tafel & Jayeff B Stables.*

BANZHAF (USA) BHB 72f85a **RR 72f 85a** 92[1]
5 ch g Rare Performer (USA) 7.6f **(82)** - Hang On For Effer (USA) (Effervescing (USA)) 8.1f **(79)**
Form - 3121
Record 1998 - 1st:1 2nd:1 3rd:0 Ran:2
Pre1998 - 1st:5 2nd:3 3rd:3 Ran:25
Win Prizemoney £19,600 *Total Prizemoney* £31,587
Wins * **1998** *Jan Lingfi (STD) C 8f 83*
* 1997 *Dec Lingfi (STD) H 8f 80 84* <
* 1997 Jly Sandow (G-F) C 7.1f 71
* 1996 *Jan Lingfi (STD) H 8f 77 79*
* 1996 *Jan Lingfi (STD) H 7f 70 75*
* 1995 *Nov Lingfi (STD) 7f 81*
1998 AW 1-2: (7f, 8f 1-1) (Equi 1-2)
Useful gelding, effective 7 to 8f, best at 8f, - acts on Equi, prefers left handed tracks, prefers tight tracks. AW high 86 (1st run) - 2nd of 8 giving 17lb to Redoubtable (3 Jan Lingfield 7f Equi RF 0022) - also 1st of 10 giving 18lb to Robellion (15 Jan Lingfield RF 0092). Very successful on Equitrack during the winter of '95/96, he had not shown much in '97 before a win in a Sandown claimer, his first turf victory. He regained winning form back on his favourite Equitrack in the winter with two victories, after which he was claimed to continue his career in Sweden.
**G L Moore [6-27] Bryan Pennick.*

BAPSFORD BHB 45f60a **RR 39f 60a** 4143[2]
4 b g Shalford (IRE) 7.8f **(63)** - Bap's Miracle (Track Spare) 8.8f **(62)**
Form - 5200834272
Record 1998 - 1st:0 2nd:2 3rd:1 Ran:8
Pre1998 - 1st:2 2nd:1 3rd:1 Ran:16
Win Prizemoney £3,642 *Total Prizemoney* £6,366
Wins 1997 *Spt Wolver (STD) C 8.5f 60* <
1997 *Aug Lingfi (STD) SH 10f 45 49*
1998 Turf 0-2: (8f, 10f) (gd, g-f) 1998 AW 0-6: (7f, 8f 3, 9f, 10f) (Equi 3, Fibr 3)
Neat, average gelding, effective 8 to 10f, best at 8f, - acts on AW, best on Equi, has worn blinkers, favours left handed tracks. Turf high 34. AW high 68 - 2nd of 8 getting 4lb from Sea Spouse (23 Jun Lingfield 8f Equi RF 2202). Inconsistent.
**M Waring [0-10] Dunstall Park Centre Ltd (from G L Moore [2-14] Spt 1997).*

BAPTISMAL ROCK (IRE) BHB 37f55a **RR 20f 55a** 3844[D]
4 ch g Ballad Rock 7.2f **(63)** - Flower From Heaven (Baptism) 10f **(59)**
Form - 7D
Record 1998 - 1st:0 2nd:0 3rd:0 Ran:2
Pre1998 - 1st:0 2nd:1 3rd:0 Ran:14
Win Prizemoney £0 *Total Prizemoney* £1,240
1998 Turf 0-2: (5f 2) (frm 2)
Little account gelding. Turf high 20 (began Jly).
**B J Curley [0-9] P Byrne (from T Stack in IRE [0-7] Oct 1996).*

BARABASCHI RR 87+f 4697[5]
2 b c Elmaamul (USA) 8.1f **(70)** - Hills' Presidium (Presidium)
Form - 35
Record 1998 - 1st:0 2nd:0 3rd:1 Ran:2
Win Prizemoney £0 *Total Prizemoney* £584
1998 Turf 0-2: (7f, 8f) (g-f, frm)
Currently useful colt. Turf high 87 (1st run) (began Spt) - 3rd of 14 to Serpentine (22 Spt Warwick 7f frm RF 4410).
**P W Chapple-Hyam [0-2] Dr Ornella Carlini Cozzi.*

BARAFAMY (IRE) BHB 100f **RR 92f** 4832a[1]
2 gr f Barathea (IRE) - Infamy (Shirley Heights) 10.3f **(74)**
Form - 22131
Record 1998 - 1st:2 2nd:2 3rd:1 Ran:5
Win Prizemoney £26,025 *Total Prizemoney* £31,622
Wins * **1998** Oct San Si (HLD) G3 8f 92 <
* **1998** Aug Newcas (GD) 7f 84
1998 Turf 2-5: (7f 1-3, 8f 1-2) (g-s 1-1, gd 2, g-f 1-1, frm)
Useful filly. Turf high 92 - 1st of 11 from Super Tassa (11 Oct San Siro RF 4832a) - also 1st of 5 getting 5lb from Just Name It (2 Aug Newcastle RF 3294). She came up against useful fillies in her first two runs, and had little to beat when landing a Newcastle maiden on her third start. She improved on that when third in the May Hill, and went to Italy to take a Group Three on her final outing. Out of a very useful middle-distance mare, she can win more good races in 1999.
**J L Dunlop [2-5] & Mrs G Pinchen.*

BARBASON BHB 71f71a **RR 75f 71a** 4933[6]
6 ch g Polish Precedent (USA) 9f **(73)** - Barada (USA) (Damascus (USA)) 8.9f **(71)**
Form - 335216235716822386
Record 1998 - 1st:2 2nd:4 3rd:2 Ran:15
Pre1998 - 1st:7 2nd:0 3rd:7 Ran:28
Win Prizemoney £29,081 *Total Prizemoney* £38,702
Wins * **1998** Jun Bright (FRM) H 8f 66 71
* **1998** *Jan Lingfi (STD) H 8f 69 72* <
* 1997 Jly Bright (FRM) H 7f 64 68
* 1997 Apr Bright (FRM) H 7f 59 67
* 1997 Apr Lingfi (FRM) H 7f 50 62
* 1997 *Mar Lingfi (STD) H 8f 57 68*
* 1997 *Mar Lingfi (STD) 7f 60*
* 1997 *Feb Lingfi (STD) H 7f 53 56*
1996 *Feb Lingfi (STD) 7f 52+*
1998 Turf 1-8: (8f 1-6, 9f 2) (g-s, gd 2, g-f 1-3, frm 2) 1998 AW 1-7: (7f 2, 8f 1-5) (Equi 1-7)
Above-average gelding, effective 7 to 8f, best at 8f, acts on gd to frm - acts on Equi, excels at Kempton and likes Brighton. Turf high 75 - 2nd of 12 giving 30lb to Clonoe (5 Aug Kempton 8f frm RF 3373) - also 1st of 5 getting 13lb from Asef Alhind (2 Jun Brighton RF 1641). AW high 72 - 1st of 10 giving 22lb to Fancy Design (17 Jan Lingfield RF 0109). Consistent. Seven furlongs on turf, or seven furlongs to a mile on sand seem to suit him best, and he is a great credit to his trainer and to Candy Morris, who rides him so well.
**G L Moore [8-30] A Moore (from A Moore [1-11] Jan 1997).*

BARBOLA (USA) RR 108f 4470e[2]
3 ch c Diesis 9f **(80)** - Barboukh (Night Shift (USA)) 7.2f **(69)**
Form - 2
1998 Turf 0-1: (10f) (sft)
Currently Pattern-class colt. (1st run) - 2nd of 4 to Quel Senor (19 Spt Longchamp 10f sft RF 4470e). He kept on well when finishing second in a Group Three at Longchamp in September, and stays in training as a four-year-old. There is a Group race with his name on it.
**J deRoualle in FR [0-1] R J McCreery.*

BARBRALLEN BHB 25f30a **RR 34f 30a** 2820[13]
6 b m Rambo Dancer (CAN) 8.4f **(59)** - Barrie Baby (Import) 6.6f **(68)**
Form - 8700
Record 1998 - 1st:0 2nd:0 3rd:0 Ran:4
Pre1998 - 1st:0 2nd:0 3rd:0 Ran:19
1998 Turf 0-4: (7f 3, 11f) (gd 3, frm)
Very moderate mare. Turf high 34.
**Mrs L C Jewell [0-17] Peter Allen (from D J S ffrenchDavis [0-8] Nov 1995).*

BARDONECCHIA (IRE) RR 108f 4729a[2]
3 ch f Indian Ridge 7.6f **(74)** - Rosa de Caerleon (Caerleon (USA)) 8.6f **(71)**
Form - 02172
1998 Turf 1-5: (8f, 9f, 10f 1-1, 11f, 12f) (hvy 2, sft 2, gd 1-1)
Pattern-class filly, effective 9 to 10f, acts on sft to gd. Turf high 108 - 2nd of 6 to Insight (4 Oct Longchamp 9f sft RF 4729a) - also 1st of 11 from Insight (8 Aug Deauville RF 3613a). Second in the Italian Oaks, she revelled in soft ground when winning a Group Three at Deauville in August. Never in the hunt when an unplaced outsider in the Prix Vermeille, she ran up to her best form when dropped back in trip for the Prix de l'Opera at Longchamp in October. Probably best when ridden up with the pace, she should win another Group event. **L Camici in ITY [1-7] Villa Dosia SRL.*

BARDON HILL BOY (IRE) BHB 69f77a **RR 81f 77a** 4958[5]
6 br g Be My Native (USA) 11.2f **(62)** - Star With A Glimer (Montekin) 11.1f **(55)**
Form - 3607646366512875
Record 1998 - 1st:1 2nd:1 3rd:2 Ran:16
Pre1998 - 1st:4 2nd:5 3rd:4 Ran:34
Win Prizemoney £24,200 *Total Prizemoney* £45,773
Wins * **1998** Aug Thirsk (G-F) H 16f 66 69
* 1996 Aug Newmar (GD) H 10f 87 91 <
* 1996 May Bath (G-F) H 10.2f 78 84

* 1995 May Wolver (STD) H 9.4f 74 75
* 1995 Jan Lingfi (STD) 10f 61+

1998 Turf 1-13: (10f 3, 12f 3, 14f 2, 15f, 16f 1-4) (sft, g-s, gd 6, g-f 2, frm 1-3) 1998 AW 0-3: (9f 2, 10f) (Equi, Fibr 2)

Decent gelding, effective 10 to 12f, best at 10f, acts on g-s to frm - acts on Equi, best on frm, excels at Chester. Turf high 81 - 4th of 7 giving 29lb to Vanadium Ore (3 Jun Chester 10f gd RF 1684). AW high 75. Has reportedly joined Philip Hobbs.

**B Hanbury [5-50] Miss Mary Breslin.*

BARGASH BHB 43f40a **RR 38f 40a** 2468[10]

6 ch g Sharpo 7.5f **(68)** - Anchor Inn (Be My Guest (USA)) 9.3f **(67)**

Form - 00

Record 1998 - 1st:0 2nd:0 3rd:0 Ran:2
Pre1998 - 1st:2 2nd:2 3rd:2 Ran:29

Win Prizemoney £5,871 *Total Prizemoney* £9,744

Wins 1996 Mar Catter (G-S) S 7f 57
1995 Jly Warwic (G-F) H 6f 65 71 <

1998 Turf 0-2: (6f, 7f) (frm 2)

Moderate gelding, has worn blinkers. Turf high 38.

**A Bailey [0-2] John Pugh (from P D Evans [2-29] Jan 1997).*

BARITONE BHB 53f **RR 51f** 4550[2]

4 b g Midyan (USA) 9.9f **(64)** - Zinzi (Song) 7.2f **(61)**

Form - 4355806037430032

Record 1998 - 1st:0 2nd:1 3rd:4 Ran:16
Pre1998 - 1st:0 2nd:1 3rd:3 Ran:11

Win Prizemoney £0 *Total Prizemoney* £4,812

1998 Turf 0-10: (6f, 7f 5, 8f 3, 9f) (sft, g-s, gd 3, frm 5) 1998 AW 0-6: (6f, 7f 4, 8f) (Equi, Fibr 5)

Fair gelding, effective 8f, acts on g-f, has worn blinkers, likes right handed tracks. Turf high 51. AW high 57. A half-brother to Ayr Gold Cup winner Sarcita, he has been placed often, but is finding winning beyond him, and is one to be wary of.

**S E Kettlewell [0-16] Hollinbridge Racing (from J W Watts [0-11] Jly 1997).*

BARNACLA (IRE) **RR 47f** 5064[12]

2 ch f Bluebird (USA) 7.9f **(71)** - Reticent Bride (IRE) (Shy Groom (USA)) 10f **(66)**

Form - 0

Record 1998 - 1st:0 2nd:0 3rd:0 Ran:1

1998 Turf 0-1: (6f) (g-f)

Currently moderate filly. **C F Wall [0-1] Zubieta Ltd.*

BARN OWL BHB 58f **RR 54f** 4697[19]

2 ch f Sabrehill (USA) 8.5f **(64)** - Ever Welcome (Be My Guest (USA)) 9.3f **(67)**

Form - 800

Record 1998 - 1st:0 2nd:0 3rd:0 Ran:3

1998 Turf 0-3: (7f 2, 8f) (g-f 2, frm)

Currently fair filly. Turf high 54 (began Spt).

**J L Dunlop [0-3] Sir Thomas Pilkington.*

BARON DE PICHON (IRE) BHB 58f **RR 52f** 4937[15]

2 b c Perugino (USA) - Ariadne (Bustino) 10.4f **(64)**

Form - 000

Record 1998 - 1st:0 2nd:0 3rd:0 Ran:3

1998 Turf 0-3: (5f 2, 6f) (gd 2, g-f)

Currently fair colt, has worn blinkers. Turf high 52.

**N P Littmoden [0-1] DGH Partnership (from Miss Gay Kelleway [0-2] Spt 1998).*

BARON LAZLO BHB 21f **RR 27f** 4371[9]

3 b g Sizzling Melody 6.3f **(49)** - Mrs Skinner (Electric) 10.1f **(61)**

Form - 8830

Record 1998 - 1st:0 2nd:0 3rd:1 Ran:4

Win Prizemoney £0 *Total Prizemoney* £298

1998 Turf 0-4: (10f 2, 14f 2) (g-s, g-f, frm 2)

Little account gelding, has worn blinkers. Turf high 27.

**R M Whitaker [0-4] Mrs Anna Fisher.*

BAROSSA VALLEY (IRE) BHB 44f58a **RR 40f 58a** 2202[7]

7 b g Alzao (USA) 9.8f **(73)** - Night of Wind (Tumble Wind (USA)) 7.5f **(57)**

Form - 7007

Record 1998 - 1st:0 2nd:0 3rd:0 Ran:4
Pre1998 - 1st:3 2nd:3 3rd:1 Ran:23

Win Prizemoney £10,200 *Total Prizemoney* £15,100

Wins * 1996 *Dec Lingfi (STD) H 10f 70 80*
* 1996 *Dec Lingfi (STD) C 10f 79*

1998 Turf 0-3: (7f 2, 8f) (sft, gd, g-f) 1998 AW 0-1: (8f) (Equi)

Fair gelding, has worn blinkers. Turf high 40. Inconsistent.

**P Butler [2-13] Christopher Wilson (from P W Chapple-Hyam [1-14] Aug 1995).*

BAROUD D'HONNEUR (FR) **RR 114f** 635a[5]

5 gr h Highest Honor (FR) 10.9f **(72)** - Petite Soeur (FR) (Lyphard (USA)) 9.9f **(72)**

Form - 5

1998 Turf 0-1: (10f) (g-s)

Group-class colt. (1st run) - 5th of 6 to Astarabad (5 Apr Longchamp 10f g-s RF 0635a). **J Bernard in FR [2-5].*

BARRANAK (IRE) BHB 60f59a **RR 65f 59a** 4004[7]

6 b g Cyrano de Bergerac 7.3f **(58)** - Saulonika (Saulingo) 6.2f **(53)**

Form - 668843120037

Record 1998 - 1st:1 2nd:1 3rd:2 Ran:12
Pre1998 - 1st:3 2nd:3 3rd:2 Ran:32

Win Prizemoney £13,217 *Total Prizemoney* £19,598

Wins * **1998** Jun Lingfi (GD) H 5f 52 56
* 1997 Jun Lingfi (GD) H 5f 60 59
* 1997 Jun Salisb (G-F) H 5f 52 56
* 1996 Aug Ripon (GD) 5f 64 <

1998 Turf 1-12: (5f 1-12) (hvy, gd 4, g-f, frm 1-5, hrd)

Average gelding, effective 5f, acts on g-s to hrd, best on frm, has worn blinkers, excels at Lingfield. Turf high 65 - 2nd of 15 giving 25lb to Windrush Boy (27 Jun Lingfield 5f frm RF 2339) - also 1st of 15 getting 15lb from Beau Venture (20 Jun Lingfield RF 2150). He was given some respite by the handicapper which enabled him to regain winning form back at Lingfield in June, but has gone back up the weights again. He has plenty of early speed which means that a sharp downhill five suits him best.

**G M McCourt [4-40] M MacCarthy (from Mrs M McCourt [0-4] Nov 1995).*

BARR BEACON **RR 54f** 1473[7]

2 br c Puissance 7.1f **(60)** - Lominda (IRE) (Lomond (USA)) 8.8f **(65)**

Form - 7

Record 1998 - 1st:0 2nd:0 3rd:0 Ran:1

1998 Turf 0-1: (5f) (g-f)

Currently fair colt. **T G Mills [0-1] Thorpe Vernon.*

BARRELBIO (IRE) BHB 51f **RR 50f** 4661[9]

3 b g Elbio 9f **(62)** - Esther (Persian Bold) 9.3f **(66)**

Form - 20000370

Record 1998 - 1st:0 2nd:1 3rd:1 Ran:8
Pre1998 - 1st:1 2nd:0 3rd:0 Ran:6

Win Prizemoney £3,395 *Total Prizemoney* £4,741

Wins * 1997 Nov Mussel (G-S) SH 5f 57 64 <

1998 Turf 0-7: (5f, 6f 5, 8f) (sft, gd 5, frm) 1998 AW 0-1: (6f) (Fibr)

Fair gelding, effective 5 to 6f, acts on sft to gd, has worn blinkers. Turf high 66 (1st run) - 2nd of 8 getting 3lb from Sorridar (30 Mar Hamilton 6f sft RF 0500). **J J O'Neill [1-14] A Sweeney.*

BARREN LANDS BHB 60f **RR 73f** 4957[6]

3 b g Green Desert (USA) 7.8f **(78)** - Current Raiser (Filiberto (USA)) 9.5f **(66)**

Form - 0852410006

Record 1998 - 1st:1 2nd:1 3rd:0 Ran:10

Win Prizemoney £3,376 *Total Prizemoney* £4,024

Wins * **1998** Jun Redcar (G-S) 6f 73 <

1998 Turf 1-10: (5f 2, 6f 1-3, 7f 4, 10f) (sft, gd 1-6, g-f 2, frm)

Strong, above-average gelding, effective 5 to 6f, best at 6f, acts on gd, has worn blinkers. Turf high 73 - 1st of 6 from Quiz Master (20 Jun Redcar RF 2159). Becoming disappointing. Got off the mark in a very weak Redcar maiden, looking to be suited by the easy ground. **R Guest [1-10] Matthews Breeding and Racing.*

BARRESBO BHB 56f47a **RR 63f 47a** 4936[9]

4 b g Barrys Gamble 7f **(50)** - Bo' Babbity (Strong Gale) 5.6f **(66)**

Form - 443248304640

Record 1998 - 1st:0 2nd:1 3rd:2 Ran:12
Pre1998 - 1st:1 2nd:2 3rd:1 Ran:19

Win Prizemoney £2,536 *Total Prizemoney* £7,741
Wins * 1997 Jly Newcas (GD) H 7f 60 67 <
1998 Turf 0-12: (7f 3, 8f 8, 9f) (g-s 3, gd 4, g-f, frm 4)
Workmanlike, average gelding, effective 7 to 9f, acts on gd to frm, best on g-f, has worn blinkers, prefers right handed tracks, excels at Beverley and Musselburgh. Turf high 65 - 2nd of 16 giving 21lb to Thatched (26 May Redcar 9f g-f RF 1480). Finds it difficult to win, although he generally ran well.
**C W Fairhurst [1-32] North Cheshire Trading & Storage Ltd.*

BARRIER RIDGE BHB 57f54a **RR 54f 54a** 5003^{9}

4 ch g Lycius (USA) 8.8f **(71)** - Star Ridge (USA) (Storm Bird (CAN)) 10.3f **(74)**
Form - 0560000000
Record 1998 - 1st:0 2nd:0 3rd:0 Ran:10
Pre1998 - 1st:1 2nd:1 3rd:1 Ran:3
Win Prizemoney £3,678 *Total Prizemoney* £5,594
Wins 1997 Jun Thirsk (FRM) 8f 59++ <
1998 Turf 0-5: (6f, 7f 3, 8f) (g-s 2, gd, g-f 2) 1998 AW 0-5: (7f 2, 8f 2, 9f) (Equi 3, Fibr 2)
Scopey, fair gelding, effective 8 to 9f, acts on gd, has worn blinkers, likes tight tracks. Turf high 54. AW high 52. He won a moderate-looking maiden at Thirsk in June '97 for Henry Cecil, but was not seen out after that until reappearing on sand at the start of '98 for Gary Moore. Yet to show much for his new trainer, but one to watch out for nonetheless.
**G L Moore [0-10] Miss C A Hockridge (from H R A Cecil [1-3] Jun 1997).*

BARROW CREEK BHB 58f56a **RR 61f 56a** 1302^{10}

4 ch c Cadeaux Genereux 7.9f **(76)** -Breadcrumb (Final Straw) 7.9f **(64)**
Form - 340
Record 1998 - 1st:0 2nd:0 3rd:1 Ran:3
Pre1998 - 1st:0 2nd:0 3rd:0 Ran:2
Win Prizemoney £0 *Total Prizemoney* £490
1998 Turf 0-2: (7f 2) (g-s, g-f) 1998 AW 0-1: (6f) (Equi)
Scopey, average colt. Turf high 60 (1st run) - 4th of 10 giving 13lb to Torso (18 Apr Thirsk 7f g-s RF 0754). (1st run) - 3rd of 7 giving 12lb to Hopeful Star (3 Apr Lingfield 6f Equi RF 0554).
**G Wragg [0-5] Baron G Von Ullmann.*

BARTHOLOMEW (IRE) BHB 68f **RR 63f** 5123^{2}

2 b c Second Set (IRE) 9.2f **(67)** - Why Not Glow (IRE) (Glow (USA)) 6.7f **(71)**
Form - 5252
Record 1998 - 1st:0 2nd:2 3rd:0 Ran:4
Win Prizemoney £0 *Total Prizemoney* £1,810
1998 Turf 0-4: (5f, 6f 2, 7f) (hvy, g-s 2, g-f)
Average colt. Turf high 63. **T J Naughton [0-4] E J Fenaroli.*

BASHER JACK RR 61f 4823^{17}

2 b c Suave Dancer (USA) 10.7f **(68)** - Possessive Lady (Dara Monarch) 8.8f **(59)**
Form - 0
Record 1998 - 1st:0 2nd:0 3rd:0 Ran:1
1998 Turf 0-1: (8f) (frm)
Currently average colt. **C N Allen [0-1] J T B Racing.*

BASHFUL BRAVE BHB 43f40a **RR 42f 40a** 4339^{17}

7 ch g Indian Ridge 7.6f **(74)** - Shy Dolly (Cajun) 5.2f **(54)**
Form - 570570000308200
Record 1998 - 1st:0 2nd:1 3rd:1 Ran:12
Pre1998 - 1st:6 2nd:5 3rd:3 Ran:41
Win Prizemoney £19,767 *Total Prizemoney* £27,778
Wins * 1997 Aug Ripon (G-F) SH 5f 48 51
1996 Apr Bright (FRM) H 6f 70 71 <
1995 Jly Warwic (FRM) H 5f 61 66
1995 Jun Folkes (FRM) H 5f 61 65
1995 May Folkes (G-F) H 5f 60 56
1995 Apr Folkes (G-F) 5f 54
1998 Turf 0-11: (5f 7, 6f 4) (gd, g-f 5, frm 5) 1998 AW 0-1: (6f) (Fibr)
Moderate gelding, effective 5f, acts on g-f to frm, has worn blinkers, likes left handed tracks, likes tight tracks. Turf high 42.
**B P J Baugh [1-27] W P Burnell (from J W Payne [5-18] Aug 1996).*

BASIC STYLE BHB 48f36a **RR 50f 36a** 2164^{6}

3 b g Alhijaz 7.7f **(57)** - Turbo Rose (Taufan (USA)) 7f **(57)**
Form - 088306
Record 1998 - 1st:0 2nd:0 3rd:1 Ran:5
Pre1998 - 1st:0 2nd:0 3rd:0 Ran:5
Win Prizemoney £0 *Total Prizemoney* £300
1998 Turf 0-2: (8f, 12f) (sft, frm) 1998 AW 0-3: (8f, 9f, 10f) (Equi, Fibr 2)
Neat, fair gelding, effective 8f, acts on sft, has worn blinkers, likes tight tracks. Turf high 48 (1st run) - 3rd of 6 to Top Floor (30 Mar Hamilton 8f sft RF 0502). AW high 30. Inconsistent.
**N A Callaghan [0-10] Martin Moore.*

BASMAN (IRE) BHB 90f **RR 93f** 5151^{22}

4 b c Persian Heights 10.5f **(61)** - Gepares (IRE) (Mashhor Dancer (USA)) 10f **(65)**
Form - 0040
Record 1998 - 1st:0 2nd:0 3rd:0 Ran:4
Pre1998 - 1st:1 2nd:2 3rd:1 Ran:7
Win Prizemoney £3,993 *Total Prizemoney* £12,401
Wins * 1997 Oct Nottin (SFT) 10f 101 <
1998 Turf 0-4: (10f 3, 12f) (sft, g-s, gd 2)
Leggy, useful colt, effective 10 to 12f, acts on g-s to gd, prefers left handed tracks, prefers tight tracks. Turf high 93 (began Jly). Inconsistent. Showed useful form in '97, but has had his training problems. Ran his best race at four when fourth at Leicester in October, and remains capable of better.
**B Smart [1-11] Nelson, Edmondson And Partners.*

BASSINELLO (USA) RR 71f 4495^{6}

2 ch f Nureyev (USA) 8.4f **(84)** - Feminine Wiles (IRE) (Ahonoora) 8.1f **(73)**
Form - 6
Record 1998 - 1st:0 2nd:0 3rd:0 Ran:1
Win Prizemoney £0 *Total Prizemoney* £225
1998 Turf 0-1: (7f) (gd)
Currently above-average filly.
**P W Chapple-Hyam [0-1] R E Sangster.*

BATALEUR BHB 50f47a **RR 49f 47a** 5059^{1}

5 b g Midyan (USA) 9.9f **(64)** - Tinkerbird (Music Boy) 6.8f **(57)**
Form - 05070581
Record 1998 - 1st:1 2nd:0 3rd:0 Ran:8
Pre1998 - 1st:1 2nd:0 3rd:2 Ran:12
Win Prizemoney £5,890 *Total Prizemoney* £6,937
Wins * **1998** Oct Newcas (SFT) H 6f 45 49
1996 Spt Hamilt (G-S) H 6f 55 56 <
1998 Turf 1-7: (6f 1-5, 7f 2) (sft 1-2, gd 2, g-f 2, frm) 1998 AW 0-1: (6f) (Fibr)
Moderate gelding, effective 5 to 6f, best at 6f, acts on sft to frm, has worn blinkers. Turf high 49 - 1st of 19 getting 11lb from Taffs Well (30 Oct Newcastle RF 5059).
**G Woodward [1-12] Michael Worth (from Miss J Bower [1-8] May 1997).*

BATCHWORTH BELLE BHB 88f75a **RR 87f 75a** 4821^{7}

3 b f Interrex (CAN) 7.7f **(51)** - Treasurebound (Beldale Flutter (USA)) 9.7f **(71)**
Form - 42123302835323811677
Record 1998 - 1st:2 2nd:2 3rd:4 Ran:15
Pre1998 - 1st:1 2nd:2 3rd:1 Ran:6
Win Prizemoney £12,667 *Total Prizemoney* £19,913
Wins * **1998** Spt Epsom (SFT) H 5f 77 80 <
* **1998** Aug Bright (G-F) H 5.3f 73 76
* 1997 *Dec Lingfi (G-S) 6f 66*
1998 Turf 2-15: (5f 2-11, 6f 4) (hvy, g-s, gd 1-3, g-f 3, frm 1-7)
Leggy, useful filly, effective 5f, acts on gd to frm, likes tight tracks. Turf high 87 - 7th of 18 getting 14lb from Almaty (15 Oct Newmarket 5f frm RF 4821) - also 1st of 9 giving 11lb to Mrs Malaprop (5 Spt Epsom RF 4097). She ran consistently well on Equitrack at the end of '97, including a victory over six furlongs, and though putting in some good efforts on turf this year, did not manage to win until getting up in the final stride at Brighton in August. She followed up in a better race at Epsom, again by the minimum margin, though the runner-up threw the race away.
**E A Wheeler [3-21] Mrs Diana Price.*

BATHE IN LIGHT (USA) BHB 63f65a **RR 66f 65a** 3636^{2}

4 ch f Sunshine Forever (USA) 13.2f **(76)** - Ice House (Northfields (USA)) 9f **(72)**
Form - 412134312

Record 1998 - 1st:3 2nd:2 3rd:2 Ran:9
Pre1998 - 1st:0 2nd:2 3rd:1 Ran:8
Win Prizemoney £11,223 *Total Prizemoney* £17,510
Wins * **1998** Aug Sandow (GD) H 14f 58 62
* **1998** *Mar Wolver (STD) H 12f 60 64 <*
* **1998** *Feb Wolver (STD) 12f 59+*
1998 Turf 1-5: (12f, 13f 2, 14f 1-2) (gd 1-2, g-f, frm 2) 1998 AW 2-4: (12f 2-4) (Equi, Fibr 2-3)
Scopey, average filly, effective 10 to 14f, acts on gd to frm - acts on Fibr, prefers left handed tracks, excels at Wolverhampton and Sandown. Turf high 66 - 2nd of 8 getting 9lb from Ormelie (14 Aug Newbury 13f g-f RF 3636) - also 1st of 11 getting 2lb from Back Row (2 Aug Sandown RF 3299). AW high 64 - 1st of 7 giving 24lb to Blue Hopper (4 Mar Wolverhampton RF 0402) - also 1st of 9 getting 8lb from Yaverland (11 Feb Wolverhampton RF 0264). Consistent. She showed some ability on turf in '97 without managing to score, but showed good form on Fibresand in the early part of the year, winning twice. She gained her first victory on turf at Sandown in August, having shown some fair form on that surface previously. **Lord Huntingdon [3-17] Coriolan Partnership.*

BATH KNIGHT BHB 25f32a **RR 15f 32a** 1551[7]

5 b g Full Extent (USA) 5.2f **(50)** - Mybella Ann (Anfield) 8.5f **(59)**
Form - 7
Record 1998 - 1st:0 2nd:0 3rd:0 Ran:1
Pre1998 - 1st:0 2nd:6 3rd:3 Ran:26
Win Prizemoney £0 *Total Prizemoney* £7,167
1998 Turf 0-1: (12f) (frm)
Poor gelding, has worn blinkers.
**G L Moore [0-2] Heart Of The South Racing (1) (from D J S ffrenchDavis [0-29] Jan 1997).*

BATHWICK (IRE) BHB 89f81a **RR 85f 81a** 4738[6]

2 b c Midyan (USA) 9.9f **(64)** - Dancing Heights (IRE) **(80f)** (High Estate)
Form - 212006116
Record 1998 - 1st:3 2nd:2 3rd:0 Ran:9
Win Prizemoney £14,358 *Total Prizemoney* £16,612
Wins * **1998** Spt Sandow (GD) 8.1f 85 <
* **1998** Spt Bath (GD) H 8f 83 85 <
* **1998** Jly Warwic (GD) 7f 83
1998 Turf 3-8: (7f 1-5, 8f 2-3) (g-s, gd 1-2, g-f 1-3, frm 1-2) 1998 AW 0-1: (6f) (Fibr)
Useful colt, effective 7 to 8f, best at 8f, acts on gd to frm, best on frm, has worn blinkers, prefers tight tracks. Turf high 85 - 1st of 7 giving 3lb to Biennale (15 Spt Sandown RF 4266) - also 1st of 16 getting 2lb from Joyeux Player (7 Spt Bath RF 4124). Showed plenty of ability in his first three starts, including a Warwick maiden victory, and his effort in a Goodwood nursery on his fourth start can be forgotten as he endured a nightmare passage. The step up to a mile brought two victories in September, but he was well held in better company on his final start. **B Smart [3-9] W Clifford.*

BATOUTOFTHEBLUE BHB 43f67a **RR 43f 67a** 4659[6]

5 br g Batshoof 9.5f **(66)** - Action Belle (Auction Ring (USA)) 8.6f **(65)**
Form - 24304616
Record 1998 - 1st:1 2nd:1 3rd:1 Ran:8
Pre1998 - 1st:2 2nd:1 3rd:1 Ran:17
Win Prizemoney £8,196 *Total Prizemoney* £11,463
Wins 1998 Aug Pontef (G-F) H 17.1f 39 43
1996 *Spt Wolver (STD) 14.8f 67 <*
1996 *Spt Southw (STD) H 14f 58 62*
1998 Turf 1-6: (14f, 16f 3, 17f 1-2) (gd 3, g-f 2, frm 1-1) 1998 AW 0-2: (14f, 15f) (Fibr 2)
Average gelding, effective 14 to 15f, best at 15f, - acts on Fibr, prefers left handed tracks, prefers tight tracks. Turf high 43. AW high 69 (1st run) - 2nd of 12 giving 32lb to Friendly Knight (11 May Southwell 14f Fibr RF 1157). He is a useful sort when given a distance of ground on Fibresand. Not so good on turf, though he won a modest handicap at Pontefract in August.
**J M Jefferson [0-1] Mrs I Gibson (from J Hetherton [1-7] Aug 1998).*

BATSMAN BHB 46f53a **RR 49f 53a** 4822[14]

4 b g Batshoof 9.5f **(66)** - Lady Bequick (Sharpen Up) 8.3f **(67)**
Form - 41264745020600
Record 1998 - 1st:1 2nd:2 3rd:0 Ran:14
Pre1998 - 1st:0 2nd:2 3rd:0 Ran:9
Win Prizemoney £2,398 *Total Prizemoney* £5,925
Wins * **1998** *Feb Wolver (STD) H 7f 48 50 <*
1998 Turf 0-9: (6f, 7f 6, 8f 2) (gd 4, g-f, frm 4) 1998 AW 1-5: (7f 1-3, 8f 2) (Equi 2, Fibr 1-3)
Leggy, fair gelding, effective 6 to 8f, acts on gd to frm - acts on AW, has worn blinkers, prefers left handed tracks, prefers tight tracks. Turf high 49 - 2nd of 19 getting 7lb from Celandine (18 Jly Warwick 7f frm RF 2940). AW high 55 - 2nd of 10 giving 18lb to Raased (13 Feb Southwell 8f Fibr RF 0286) - also 1st of 9 giving 1lb to Concer Arall (4 Feb Wolverhampton RF 0215). He got off the mark with a fluent win in a modest maiden handicap on the Wolverhampton Fibresand in February, but was beaten in a handicap at Southwell next time. Whether his rider dropping his whip at a crucial stage made any difference is a matter of conjecture. Modest efforts back on turf.
**W J Musson [1-23] Ex-Recession Partnership.*

BATSWING BHB 77f **RR 80f** 4098[9]

3 b c Batshoof 9.5f **(66)** - Magic Milly (Simply Great (FR)) 8.2f **(65)**
Form - 000
Record 1998 - 1st:0 2nd:0 3rd:0 Ran:3
Pre1998 - 1st:1 2nd:2 3rd:0 Ran:10
Win Prizemoney £3,315 *Total Prizemoney* £7,309
Wins 1997 Jun Lingfi (SFT) 5f 66+ <
1998 Turf 0-3: (7f, 10f 2) (gd 2, g-f)
Neat, decent colt, effective 7f, acts on sft, has worn blinkers (extremely effectively). Turf high 58 (began Jly).
**B R Millman [0-3] Richard Withers (from M Meade [1-10] Oct 1997).*

BATTLE GLEN (FR) **RR 46?f** 4935[11]

3 ch g Green Forest (USA) 7.4f **(73)** - Battle Quest (FR) (Noblequest (FR))
Form - 0
Record 1998 - 1st:0 2nd:0 3rd:0 Ran:1
1998 Turf 0-1: (8f) (gd)
Currently moderate gelding. **A Bailey [0-1] Bodfari Stud Ltd.*

BATTLE ON (USA) **RR 93f** 4900a[8]

3 ch c El Prado (IRE) 8f **(74)** - Proud Title (USA)
Form - 0022658
1998 Turf 0-7: (6f 2, 7f, 8f 2, 10f 2) (sft 2, g-s, gd 4)
Useful colt, effective 8 to 10f, acts on gd. Turf high 93 - 2nd of 11 getting 2lb from Foreign Love (22 Jly Naas 8f gd RF 3177a). Unraced at two, he ran up against a couple of useful sorts in the summer, but his form tailed off afterwards.
**F Ennis in IRE [0-7] Patrick Michael Hogg.*

BATTLE WARNING **RR 38f** 2329[9]

3 b g Warning 8.1f **(77)** - Royal Ballet (IRE) (Sadler's Wells (USA)) 10f **(76)**
Form - 0
Record 1998 - 1st:0 2nd:0 3rd:0 Ran:1
Pre1998 - 1st:0 2nd:0 3rd:0 Ran:1
1998 Turf 0-1: (12f) (gd)
Light-framed, currently very moderate gelding.
**H Candy [0-1] Mrs C M Poland (from H R A Cecil [0-1] Oct 1997).*

BAUBLE **RR 42f** 5008[8]

3 ch g Sanglamore (USA) 12.9f **(67)** - Princess Borghese (USA) (Nijinsky (CAN)) 10.3f **(77)**
Form - 8
Record 1998 - 1st:0 2nd:0 3rd:0 Ran:1
1998 Turf 0-1: (12f) (sft)
Currently moderate gelding. **G L Moore [0-1] Paul Chapman.*

B A VALENTINE (USA) **RR 118f** 5161a[1]

5 b m Apalachee (USA) 8.8f **(69)** - Bert's Valentine (USA) (Caracolero (USA)) 8.2f **(57)**
Form - 21
1998 Turf 1-2: (9f 1-1, 10f) (frm 1-2)
Currently high-class filly. Turf high 118 (began Oct) - 1st of 13 giving 3lb to Mingling Glances (7 Nov Churchill Downs RF 5161a). She split Auntie Mame and Bahr in the Grade One Flower Bowl Handicap at Belmont Park in October, and is obviously very smart.
**D Romans in USA [1-2] Alberta Butner.*

BAVARIO (USA) BHB 60f **RR 34f** 1901[5]

5 ch g Theatrical 11.5f **(78)** - Hawaiian Miss (USA) (Hawaii) 9.4f **(66)**

Form - 5
Record 1998 - 1st:0 2nd:0 3rd:0 Ran:1
Pre1998 - 1st:1 2nd:0 3rd:2 Ran:10
Win Prizemoney £4,110 *Total Prizemoney* £4,872
Wins 1996 Spt Leopar (GD) H 10f 73 61 <
1998 Turf 0-1: (10f) (g-s)
Very moderate gelding, effective 10 to 12f, acts on gd, often wears blinkers (very effectively). Becoming disappointing.
**D L Williams [0-2] Miss B W Palmer (from D K Weld in IRE [1-11] Aug 1997).*

BAWSIAN BHB 90f94a RR 96f 94a 4973[11]

3 b c Persian Bold 10f **(69)** - Bawaeth (USA) (Blushing Groom (FR)) 10.3f **(76)**
Form - 2111412506040
Record 1998 - 1st:4 2nd:1 3rd:0 Ran:12
Pre1998 - 1st:1 2nd:1 3rd:1 Ran:7
Win Prizemoney £30,734 *Total Prizemoney* £36,257
Wins * **1998** May York (GD) H 10.4f 90 96 <
* **1998** Mar Doncas (GD) H 10.3f 81 90
* **1998** *Jan Wolver (STD) H 8.5f 80 82*
* **1998** *Jan Wolver (STD) H 8.5f 75 77*
* 1997 Nov Redcar (GD) H 8f 65 72
1998 Turf 2-10: (10f 2-7, 11f, 12f 2) (sft, g-s 2, gd 2-2, g-f 3, frm 2) 1998 AW 2-2: (8f 2-2) (Fibr 2-2)
Very useful colt, effective 10 to 12f, best at 10f, acts on g-s to frm, excels at Wolverhampton, does well at York. Turf high 96 - 2nd of 6 giving 16lb to Mister Benjamin (6 Jun Haydock 11f frm RF 1782) - also 1st of 11 giving 7lb to Raffaello (12 May York RF 1165). AW high 82. Inconsistent. Improved on sand over the winter, gaining two very impressive victories over the extended mile at Wolverhampton in January. Back on turf, he added two more victories in the spring. Game and genuine, he ran with credit at the Ebor Meeting after a break but showed little after.
**J L Eyre [5-19] David Scott.*

BAYARD LADY BHB 55f RR 67f 4924[5]

2 b f Robellino (USA) 9.5f **(68)** - Lurking (Formidable (USA)) 9.2f **(63)**
Form - 37153005
Record 1998 - 1st:1 2nd:0 3rd:2 Ran:8
Win Prizemoney £3,074 *Total Prizemoney* £3,882
Wins * **1998** May Hamilt (GD) 5f 67 <
1998 Turf 1-8: (5f 1-4, 6f 4) (sft 3, g-s, gd 1-2, frm 2)
Average filly, effective 5f, acts on gd. Turf high 67 - 1st of 7 getting 5lb from Super Forum (15 May Hamilton RF 1233).
**D Moffatt [1-8] Bay Horse Racing Syndicate.*

BAYFORD GREEN (IRE) BHB 61f RR 60f 4622[8]

2 b f Distinctly North (USA) 7.4f **(63)** - Paddys Cocktail (IRE) (Tremblant)
Form - 0028
Record 1998 - 1st:0 2nd:1 3rd:0 Ran:4
Win Prizemoney £0 *Total Prizemoney* £860
1998 Turf 0-4: (5f 3, 6f) (gd, g-f 2, frm)
Average filly. Turf high 60 (began Aug) - 2nd of 10 to On Till Morning (14 Spt Musselburgh 5f frm RF 4250).
**J Berry [0-4] Mrs Jean Turner.*

BAYIN (USA) BHB 49f43a RR 55f 43a 4775[10]

9 b g Caro 9.6f **(78)** - Regatela (USA) (Dr Fager) 7f **(83)**
Form - 3006050083000
Record 1998 - 1st:0 2nd:0 3rd:2 Ran:13
Pre1998 - 1st:8 2nd:5 3rd:7 Ran:77
Win Prizemoney £32,178 *Total Prizemoney* £49,584
Wins * 1997 Jun Bath (GD) 5.7f 65
* 1996 Oct Leices (G-F) H 6f 68 72
* 1996 Jly Newbur (G-F) H 6f 72 77 <
* 1995 May Newbur (G-F) H 6f 64 66
* 1994 Apr Kempto (G-S) H 6f 57 59+
1998 Turf 0-12: (5f, 6f 9, 7f 2) (g-s, gd 4, g-f 3, frm 4) 1998 AW 0-1: (6f) (Fibr)
Fair gelding, effective 6f, acts on gd, has worn blinkers, likes left handed tracks. Turf high 57. Often slowly away and set too much to do, he is not one to rely on, but did manage to land a weak limited stakes at Bath in June '97. He will win another race or two, but it is difficult to say when.
**M D I Usher [8-88] Trevor Barker (from R W Armstrong [0-3] Spt 1992).*

BAYLEAF RR 105f 4844[9]

3 ch f Efisio 7.7f **(69)** - Bayonne (Bay Express) 7.1f **(60)**
Form - 50022320
Record 1998 - 1st:0 2nd:3 3rd:1 Ran:8
Pre1998 - 1st:1 2nd:0 3rd:0 Ran:2
Win Prizemoney £3,629 *Total Prizemoney* £19,787
Wins * 1997 Jly Newbur (G-F) 5.2f 77 <
1998 Turf 0-8: (5f 4, 6f 4) (g-s, gd 2, g-f 2, frm 3)
Strong, Pattern-class filly, effective 5 to 6f, best at 6f, acts on gd to frm, best on frm. Turf high 105 - 2nd of 7 to Zelanda (16 Aug Pontefract 6f frm RF 3672). She has never been able to add to her debut win, but ran some solid races in defeat last term. Unfortunately she will not be any easier to place in 1999.
**R F JohnsonHoughton [1-10] Lady Rothschild.*

BAYLHAM BHB 38f46a RR 51f 46a 4920[12]

3 b g Risk Me (FR) 8f **(53)** - So Beguiling (USA) (Woodman (USA)) 9f **(74)**
Form - 4440203777750
Record 1998 - 1st:0 2nd:1 3rd:1 Ran:13
Pre1998 - 1st:0 2nd:1 3rd:0 Ran:7
Win Prizemoney £0 *Total Prizemoney* £2,628
1998 Turf 0-12: (6f, 7f, 8f 7, 9f 2, 10f) (sft 2, g-s 2, gd 2, g-f 3, frm 2, hrd) 1998 AW 0-1: (8f) (Fibr)
Leggy, fair gelding, effective 6f, acts on frm, has worn blinkers. Turf high 51. **J S Goldie [0-22] Tough Construction Ltd.*

BAY OF BENGAL (IRE) BHB 43f RR 51f 4136[16]

2 ch f Persian Bold 10f **(69)** - Adjamiya (USA) (Shahrastani (USA)) 8.8f **(72)**
Form - 00300
Record 1998 - 1st:0 2nd:0 3rd:1 Ran:5
Win Prizemoney £0 *Total Prizemoney* £278
1998 Turf 0-5: (5f, 6f, 7f 2, 8f) (gd, g-f 3, frm)
Fair filly. Turf high 51 (began Jly). **H Alexander [0-5] Rosaly Racing.*

BAY OF DELIGHT BHB 68f RR 68f 4822[24]

3 ch f Cadeaux Genereux 7.9f **(76)** - Zawaahy (USA) (El Gran Senor (USA)) 9.6f **(76)**
Form - 56815520120
Record 1998 - 1st:2 2nd:2 3rd:0 Ran:11
Pre1998 - 1st:0 2nd:0 3rd:0 Ran:2
Win Prizemoney £6,732 *Total Prizemoney* £8,060
Wins * **1998** Spt Goodwo (G-F) H 7f 62 68 <
* **1998** Jly Beverl (G-F) H 8.5f 58 60
1998 Turf 2-11: (6f 3, 7f 1-3, 8f 1-4, 9f) (g-s, gd 2, g-f, frm 2-7)
Scopey, average filly, effective 7 to 9f, best at 7f, acts on gd to frm, best on frm, likes tight tracks. Turf high 68 - 1st of 18 getting 7lb from Great News (24 Spt Goodwood RF 4459) - also 1st of 15 giving 14lb to Buzz The Agent (14 Jly Beverley RF 2771).
**E A L Dunlop [2-13] Gainsborough Stud.*

BAY OF ISLANDS BHB 83f RR 88f 5151[9]

6 b g Jupiter Island 10.4f **(57)** - Lawyer's Wave (USA) (Advocator) 10.9f **(80)**
Form - 01238000
Record 1998 - 1st:1 2nd:1 3rd:1 Ran:8
Pre1998 - 1st:2 2nd:0 3rd:2 Ran:10
Win Prizemoney £14,809 *Total Prizemoney* £28,984
Wins * **1998** Jun Doncas (GD) H 12f 78 84 <
* 1997 Jun Cheste (G-F) H 10.3f 75 81
1995 Aug York (G-F) 10.4f 74
1998 Turf 1-8: (10f, 12f 1-5, 13f, 14f) (gd, g-f 1-4, frm 3)
Useful gelding, effective 10 to 14f, best at 12f, acts on gd to frm, best on frm, has worn blinkers, likes left handed tracks, excels at York. Turf high 89 - 3rd of 9 giving 1lb to Mowelga (5 Aug Pontefract 12f frm RF 3390) - also 1st of 11 getting 2lb from Invermark (6 Jun Doncaster RF 1772). Won a handicap in some style at Doncaster and ran well to chase home Perfect Paradigm at Haydock, but has been in the handicapper's grip since. The Morris stable had a poor season.
**D Morris [2-15] Bloomsbury Stud (from C E Brittain [1-3] Aug 1995).*

BAYONET BHB 72f RR 70f 2759[2]

2 b f Then Again 7.4f **(52)** - Lambay (Lorenzaccio) 10f **(64)**
Form - 422
Record 1998 - 1st:0 2nd:2 3rd:0 Ran:3

Win Prizemoney £0 *Total Prizemoney* £1,780
1998 Turf 0-3: (5f 3) (gd, g-f, frm)
Currently above-average filly. Turf high 70 - 2nd of 18 to Almost Amber (24 Jun Salisbury 5f frm RF 2249).
**R F JohnsonHoughton [0-3] Lady Rothschild.*

BAYOURIDA (USA) RR 110f 4343a[6]
3 f Slew O' Gold (USA) 10.2f **(73)** - Bellarida (FR)
Form - 526
1998 Turf 0-3: (10f, 12f 2) (hvy, sft, gd)
Currently Group-class filly. Turf high 110 - 6th of 11 to Leggera (13 Spt Longchamp 12f hvy RF 4343a). She was flattered to finish close-up behind Zainta at Deauville in August, and cut no ice in the Prix Vermeille. **C Laffon-Parias in FR [0-3] Wertheimer et Frere.*

BAY PRINCE (IRE) BHB 95f **RR 86f** 1981[20]
3 b c Mujadil (USA) 7.7f **(70)** - Kingston Rose (Tudor Music) 6.8f **(59)**
Form - 00
Record 1998 - 1st:0 2nd:0 3rd:0 Ran:2
Pre1998 - 1st:2 2nd:0 3rd:0 Ran:6
Win Prizemoney £16,245 *Total Prizemoney* £20,033
Wins * 1997 Aug York (GD) L 5f 95 <
* 1997 Aug Pontef (G-F) 5f 95 <
1998 Turf 0-2: (6f 2) (g-s, g-f)
Workmanlike, useful colt, effective 5 to 6f, best at 5f, acts on gd. Turf high 47. Inconsistent. Looked very speedy when landing a York listed race at two, but the fancied runners appeared to perform below-par, and he failed to live up to that performance. The saddle slipped first time out last term, and he was well beaten in a hot race off a stiff mark next time.
**M R Channon [2-8] D W Shepherd.*

BEACH BUOY (IRE) BHB 50f **RR 53f** 4540[17]
4 ch g Orchestra 7.5f **(44)** - Seapoint (Major Point) 10.5f **(70)**
Form - 130
Record 1998 - 1st:1 2nd:0 3rd:1 Ran:3
Pre1998 - 1st:0 2nd:1 3rd:1 Ran:6
Win Prizemoney £3,624 *Total Prizemoney* £6,152
Wins * **1998** Aug Haydoc (GD) H 10.5f 48 53 <
1998 Turf 1-3: (10f 2, 11f 1-1) (g-f 1-2, frm)
Workmanlike, fair gelding, effective 9 to 11f, acts on g-f to frm, favours tight tracks. Turf high 53 (1st run) (began Aug). He has shown a little ability, but looks as if twelve furlongs is his optimum trip.
**Mrs G S Rees [1-3] Mrs C J Black (from Capt J Wilson [0-6] Oct 1997).*

BEACON BLAZE BHB 78f80a **RR 69f 80a** 3128[10]
3 ch f Rudimentary (USA) 8.2f **(66)** - Beacon Hill (Bustino) 10.4f **(64)**
Form - 140
Record 1998 - 1st:1 2nd:0 3rd:0 Ran:3
Pre1998 - 1st:0 2nd:0 3rd:0 Ran:1
Win Prizemoney £3,028 *Total Prizemoney* £3,393
Wins * **1998** *Jun Southw (STD) 8f 84* <
1998 Turf 0-1: (10f) (g-f) 1998 AW 1-2: (7f, 8f 1-1) (Fibr 1-2)
Lengthy, decent filly. AW high 84 (1st run) - 1st of 11 getting 5lb from Goldfame (12 Jun Southwell RF 1943). Improved from her debut to win a very moderate maiden on the Southwell Fibresand. The form means little though she could do no more than win as easily as she did. Pulled rather hard on turf next time.
**R M H Cowell [1-3] Cheveley Park Stud (from D R Loder [0-1] Oct 1997).*

BEAMISH BOY (IRE) RR 95f 1345a[3]
4 b c Mujtahid (USA) 7.4f **(69)** - David's Star (Welsh Saint) 7.6f **(64)**
Form - 4343
1998 Turf 0-3: (7f, 8f, 10f) (sft, gd 2)
Very useful colt, effective 7 to 10f, best at 8f, acted on sft to gd, best on gd. Turf high 93 - 3rd of 8 giving 10lb to Canzona (16 May Cork 8f gd RF 1345a). (DEAD) **D Hanley in IRE [1-13] Mrs Vivien Cox.*

BEA'S RUBY (IRE) BHB 79f **RR 67df** 743[13]
4 b f Fairy King (USA) 7.7f **(75)** - Beautiful Secret (USA) (Secreto (USA)) 8.7f **(72)**
Form - 0
Record 1998 - 1st:0 2nd:0 3rd:0 Ran:1
Pre1998 - 1st:2 2nd:1 3rd:1 Ran:8
Win Prizemoney £10,513 *Total Prizemoney* £12,725
Wins * 1997 May Ayr (SFT) 8f 85 <
* 1997 May Cheste (SFT) 7f 67
1998 Turf 0-1: (8f) (sft)
Light-framed, average filly, effective 8f, acts on sft, has worn blinkers. Becoming disappointing.
**A Bailey [2-9] M Tabor & Mrs John Magnier.*

BEAT ALL (USA) RR 93f 4196[1]
2 b br c Dynaformer (USA) 12f **(82)** - Spirited Missus (USA) (Distinctive (USA)) 10.7f **(70)**
Form - 21
Record 1998 - 1st:1 2nd:1 3rd:0 Ran:2
Win Prizemoney £3,013 *Total Prizemoney* £4,095
Wins * **1998** Spt Chepst (G-S) 7.1f 93 <
1998 Turf 1-2: (7f 1-2) (gd 1-1, g-f)
Currently useful colt. Turf high 93 (began Jly) - 1st of 11 from Thrust (10 Spt Chepstow RF 4196). Was unlucky enough to run into Auction House on her debut, but got off the mark as expected next time. He can make up into a decent performer as a three-year-old. **Sir Michael Stoute [1-2] Saeed Suhail.*

BEAU BRUNO BHB 50f50a **RR 36f 50a** 1035[17]
5 b g Thatching 7.8f **(69)** - Lady Lorelei (Derring-Do) 11.1f **(64)**
Form - 00
Record 1998 - 1st:0 2nd:0 3rd:0 Ran:2
Pre1998 - 1st:0 2nd:1 3rd:2 Ran:8
Win Prizemoney £0 *Total Prizemoney* £1,270
1998 Turf 0-1: (10f) (gd) 1998 AW 0-1: (8f) (Fibr)
Very moderate gelding, has worn blinkers. Becoming disappointing. **D T Thom [0-2] D T Thom (from M Bell [0-8] Feb 1997).*

BEAUCATCHER (IRE) BHB 36f **RR 33f** 4123[9]
4 b f Thatching 7.8f **(69)** - Gale Warning (IRE) (Last Tycoon) 8.5f **(62)**
Form - 8500
Record 1998 - 1st:0 2nd:0 3rd:0 Ran:4
Pre1998 - 1st:0 2nd:0 3rd:0 Ran:5
1998 Turf 0-4: (7f, 8f 3) (gd, frm 3)
Lengthy, very moderate filly. Turf high 33 (began Jly).
**D R C Elsworth [0-4] Mrs R F Lowe (from M J Heaton-Ellis [0-5] Oct 1997).*

BEAUCHAMP KING BHB 102f **RR 108f** 4742[13]
5 gr h Nishapour (FR) 11.1f **(58)** - Afariya (FR) (Silver Shark) 7.9f **(81)**
Form - 10840
Record 1998 - 1st:1 2nd:0 3rd:0 Ran:5
Pre1998 - 1st:6 2nd:0 3rd:2 Ran:16
Win Prizemoney £146,988 *Total Prizemoney* £180,729
Wins * **1998** May Haydoc (G-S) LH 7.1f 104 108
1997 Jly Doncas (GD) 8f 96
1996 Apr Newmar (G-F) G3 8f 116
1995 Oct Doncas (G-F) G1 8f 116
1995 Oct Ascot (SFT) L 8f 117 <
1995 Spt Haydoc (GD) 8.1f 109+
1995 Aug Ayr (G-F) 7f 74+
1998 Turf 1-5: (7f 1-1, 8f 2, 9f, 10f) (g-s, gd 1-1, g-f, frm 2)
Pattern-class colt, effective 7f, acts on gd. Turf high 108 (1st run) - 1st of 11 getting 3lb from Ramooz (2 May Haydock RF 0966). He has never rediscovered the form of his juvenile days, and ran poorly after winning at Haydock on his reappearance. He is not one to rely upon, but is always capable of springing a surprise when fresh.
**G A Butler [1-5] E Penser (from J L Dunlop [6-16] Aug 1997).*

BEAUCHAMP KNIGHT BHB 30f **RR 19f** 1590[11]
5 ch g Chilibang 7f **(55)** - Beauchamp Cactus (Niniski (USA)) 10.6f **(65)**
Form - 000
Record 1998 - 1st:0 2nd:0 3rd:0 Ran:3
Pre1998 - 1st:0 2nd:0 3rd:0 Ran:5
1998 Turf 0-3: (9f, 10f, 12f) (sft, gd, frm)
Poor gelding, has worn blinkers. Turf high 19. Becoming disappointing. **H Candy [0-8] Henry Candy.*

BEAUCHAMP LION BHB 29f **RR 39f** 4588[14]
4 ch g Be My Chief (USA) 10.2f **(62)** - Beauchamp Cactus (Niniski (USA)) 10.6f **(65)**
Form - 0700
Record 1998 - 1st:0 2nd:0 3rd:0 Ran:4

Pre1998 - 1st:0 2nd:0 3rd:0 Ran:9
Win Prizemoney £0 *Total Prizemoney* £215
1998 Turf 0-4: (14f 2, 15f, 16f) (g-s, gd 2, frm)
Scopey, very moderate gelding, effective 12f, acts on g-f to frm, has worn blinkers. Turf high 39. Inconsistent. From a good family, he has proved rather disappointing.
**G A Butler [0-4] E Penser (from J L Dunlop [0-9] Oct 1997).*

BEAUCHAMP MAGIC BHB 65f **RR 68f** 4667[8]
3 b g Northern Park (USA) 10f **(57)** - Beauchamp Buzz (High Top) 10.2f **(67)**
Form - 032658
Record 1998 - 1st:0 2nd:1 3rd:1 Ran:6
Pre1998 - 1st:0 2nd:0 3rd:0 Ran:3
Win Prizemoney £0 *Total Prizemoney* £1,240
1998 Turf 0-6: (8f, 12f, 14f, 16f 3) (g-s 2, gd, g-f, frm 2)
Scopey, average gelding, effective 12 to 16f, acts on gd to frm, best on frm, has worn blinkers, prefers tight tracks. Turf high 68 - 5th of 16 giving 1lb to Duello (26 Spt Nottingham 14f gd RF 4506).
**G A Butler [0-6] E Penser (from J L Dunlop [0-3] Oct 1997).*

BEAUCHAMP NOBLE RR 66f 4930[6]
2 b c Northern Park (USA) 10f **(57)** - Beauchamp Cactus (Niniski (USA)) 10.6f **(65)**
Form - 56
Record 1998 - 1st:0 2nd:0 3rd:0 Ran:2
1998 Turf 0-2: (8f 2) (g-s, gd)
Currently average colt. Turf high 66 (began Oct).
**G A Butler [0-2] E Penser.*

BEAUCHAMP NYX RR 20f 5145[9]
2 b f Northern Park (USA) 10f **(57)** - Beauchamp Image (Midyan (USA)) 6f **(60)**
Form - 0
Record 1998 - 1st:0 2nd:0 3rd:0 Ran:1
1998 Turf 0-1: (8f) (gd)
Currently little account filly. **G A Butler [0-1] E Penser.*

BEAU CYRANO (IRE) BHB 32f **RR 44f** 4656[14]
6 b g Cyrano de Bergerac 7.3f **(58)** - Only Great (Simply Great (FR)) 8.2f **(65)**
Form - 047040
Record 1998 - 1st:0 2nd:0 3rd:0 Ran:6
Pre1998 - 1st:2 2nd:0 3rd:2 Ran:8
Win Prizemoney £4,452 *Total Prizemoney* £4,810

Wins	1996	May	Limeri	(GD)	H	8f	53	51	<
	1996	Apr	Tipper	(G-Y)	H	9f	47	48	

1998 Turf 0-5: (8f, 10f 2, 12f 2) (gd 2, g-f, frm, hrd) 1998 AW 0-1: (11f) (Fibr)
Moderate gelding, effective 10f, acts on g-f to frm. Turf high 44 (1st run) - 4th of 18 giving 3lb to Rival Bid (25 May Leicester 10f g-f RF 1449).
**D E Cantillon [0-11] Don Cantillon (from A Leahy in IRE [3-17] Apr 1997).*

BEAUMONT (IRE) BHB 74f57a **RR 75f 57a** 27[10]
8 br g Be My Native (USA) 11.2f **(62)** -Say Yes (Junius (USA)) 7.7f **(65)**
Form - 0
Record 1998 - 1st:0 2nd:0 3rd:0 Ran:1
Pre1998 - 1st:9 2nd:3 3rd:3 Ran:43
Win Prizemoney £38,396 *Total Prizemoney* £45,345

Wins	* 1997	Jly	Newmar	(GD)	H	14.8f	67	72	
	* 1996	Oct	York	(GD)	H	13.9f	61	69+	
	* 1996	Spt	Cheste	(GD)	H	15.9f	59	66	
	* 1996	*Jan*	*Wolver*	*(STD)*	*H*	*12f*	*56*	*66*	
	* 1995	*Dec*	*Southw*	*(STD)*	*H*	*11f*	*52*	*54*	
	1994	Jun	Ripon	(G-F)	H	10f	68	70	
	1994	Apr	Pontef	(SFT)	H	10f	66	77	<
	1994	Apr	Pontef	(G-S)	H	10f	57	59	

1998 AW 0-1: (16f) (Fibr)
Above-average gelding, effective 14 to 16f, acts on gd to g-f, best on g-f, has worn blinkers.
**J E Banks [5-29] P Cunningham (from J Pearce [4-23] Jun 1995).*

BEAU ROBERTO BHB 46f43a **RR 51f 43a** 4134[14]
4 b g Robellino (USA) 9.5f **(68)** - Night Jar (Night Shift (USA)) 7.2f **(69)**
Form - 334673843214413460
Record 1998 - 1st:2 2nd:1 3rd:5 Ran:18
Pre1998 - 1st:0 2nd:0 3rd:3 Ran:15
Win Prizemoney £5,479 *Total Prizemoney* £10,711

Wins	* 1998	Aug	Hamilt	(SFT)	H	11.1f	39	46+	<
	* 1998	Jly	Hamilt	(FRM)	H	11.1f	31	40	

1998 Turf 2-15: (6f, 8f 5, 9f, 10f 2, 11f 2-4, 12f 2) (sft, g-s 2, gd 1-7, g-f 3, frm 1-2) 1998 AW 0-3: (8f 2, 11f) (Fibr 3)
Strong, fair gelding, effective 7 to 11f, acts on gd to g-f, best on gd, has worn blinkers, likes tight tracks. Turf high 51 - 3rd of 7 getting 10lb from Manful (11 Aug Ayr 10f gd RF 3521) - also 1st of 8 getting 23lb from Manful (1 Aug Hamilton RF 3261). AW high 34.
**J S Goldie [2-26] J W Armstrong (from M Johnston [0-7] Jun 1997).*

BEAUTY GO LEOR (IRE) RR 92f 4781a[3]
2 gr c Cadeaux Genereux 7.9f **(76)** - Beautiful France (Sadler's Wells (USA)) 10f **(76)**
Form - 22613
1998 Turf 1-5: (6f 1-2, 7f 2, 8f) (g-s 1-2, gd 3)
Useful colt, mostly wears blinkers. Turf high 92 - 3rd of 16 giving 2lb to Ray Of Light (7 Oct Fairyhouse 7f g-s RF 4781a) - also 1st of 10 from Man Of The Sea (21 Spt Listowel RF 4551a). Useful sprinter. Scored at Listowel when dropped back from a mile and looks set for a decent three-year-old career.
**D K Weld in IRE [1-5] Moyglare Stud Farm.*

BEAU VENTURE (USA) BHB 51f54a **RR 65f 54a** 4311[12]
10 ch h Explodent (USA) 6.3f **(73)** - Old Westbury (USA) (Francis S) 5.1f **(92)**
Form - 8607472530000700
Record 1998 - 1st:0 2nd:1 3rd:1 Ran:15
Pre1998 - 1st:10 2nd:12 3rd:6 Ran:93
Win Prizemoney £47,642 *Total Prizemoney* £74,846

Wins	* 1997	Spt	Goodwo	(GD)	H	5f	65	69
	* 1997	Apr	Folkes	(G-F)		5f		67
	* 1996	Jun	Bath	(G-F)	H	5.7f	64	70
	1995	Jun	Ripon	(FRM)	H	5f	71	74
	1994	Aug	Haydoc	(GD)	H	5f	74	74

1998 Turf 0-15: (5f 13, 6f 2) (g-s, gd 2, g-f 3, frm 9)
Average horse, effective 5f, acts on gd to frm, best on g-f, has worn blinkers. Turf high 68.
**B Palling [3-44] Mrs A L Stacey (from F H Lee [7-64] May 1996).*

BEAU VIENNA BHB 35f45a **RR 45f 45a** 5120[7]
3 b f Superpower 6.6f **(58)** - Waltz on Air (Doc Marten)
Form - 8660507
Record 1998 - 1st:0 2nd:0 3rd:0 Ran:7
Pre1998 - 1st:0 2nd:0 3rd:0 Ran:1
Win Prizemoney £0 *Total Prizemoney* £211
1998 Turf 0-5: (8f 3, 9f, 11f) (g-s, gd, g-f 3) 1998 AW 0-2: (7f, 8f)(Fibr 2)
Neat, moderate filly. Turf high 45. AW high 34. Inconsistent.
**A R Dicken [0-8] The Forth Partnership.*

BEBE COSMONAUT RR 66f 4413[8]
2 ch f Cosmonaut - Bebe Altesse (GER)(Alpenkonig (GER)) 10.8f **(76)**
Form - 78
Record 1998 - 1st:0 2nd:0 3rd:0 Ran:2
1998 Turf 0-2: (6f, 7f) (frm 2)
Currently average filly. Turf high 66 (began Aug).
**A G Newcombe [0-2] D Bass.*

BE BRAVE BHB 45f45a **RR 45a** 2659[7]
8 b g Never so Bold 7.1f **(62)** - Boo (Bustino) 10.4f **(64)**
Form - 6467
Record 1998 - 1st:0 2nd:0 3rd:0 Ran:4
1998 AW 0-4: (11f, 14f 2, 16f) (Fibr 4)
Fair gelding. AW high 57.
**T J Etherington [1-26] Mrs Stephanie Parsons.*

BECKENHAM INSIGHT BHB 18f **RR** 2896[8]
4 b f Efisio 7.7f **(69)** - Capel Lass (The Brianstan) 5.9f **(55)**
Form - 0008
Record 1998 - 1st:0 2nd:0 3rd:0 Ran:4
Pre1998 - 1st:0 2nd:0 3rd:0 Ran:2
1998 Turf 0-2: (7f, 8f) (gd, frm) 1998 AW 0-2: (7f, 8f) (Equi, Fibr)
Neat, very poor filly, often wears blinkers.
**D C O'Brien [0-6] Mrs S Harris.*

BECKON BHB 58f **RR 61f** 4009[8]
2 ch f Beveled (USA) 6.9f **(64)** - Carolynchristensen (Sweet Revenge) 7.2f **(54)**
Form - 088
Record 1998 - 1st:0 2nd:0 3rd:0 Ran:3
1998 Turf 0-3: (5f 3) (gd, g-f, frm)
Currently average filly. Turf high 61 (began Jly).
**T D Barron [0-3] Lady Burnham.*

BEDAAYAT FARAH (USA) RR 90f 3511[1]
3 b c Clever Trick (USA) 7.6f **(69)** - Debutant Dancer (USA) (Noble Dancer) 7.8f **(101)**
Form - 21
Record 1998 - 1st:1 2nd:1 3rd:0 Ran:2
Win Prizemoney £3,805 *Total Prizemoney* £4,905
Wins * **1998** Aug Windso (G-F) 8.3f 72+ <
1998 Turf 1-2: (8f 1-2) (frm, hrd 1-1)
Scopey, useful colt. Turf high 90 (1st run) (began Jly) - 2nd of 15 giving 5lb to Keld (23 Jly Sandown 8f frm RF 3044). (DEAD)
**J H M Gosden [1-2] Sheikh Ahmed Al Maktoum.*

BEDAZZLE BHB 23f35a **RR 22f 35a** 3939[6]
7 b g Formidable (USA) 7.8f **(60)** - Wasimah (Caerleon (USA)) 8.6f **(71)**
Form - 006
Record 1998 - 1st:0 2nd:0 3rd:0 Ran:3
Pre1998 - 1st:1 2nd:8 3rd:4 Ran:50
Win Prizemoney £2,326 *Total Prizemoney* £10,671
Wins * 1996 Apr Mussel (GD) SH 8.1f 34 38 <
1998 Turf 0-3: (9f, 12f 2) (g-s, frm 2)
Little account gelding, effective 8 to 10f, best at 8f, acts on g-f to frm, best on frm, has worn blinkers, likes right handed tracks, favours tight tracks. Turf high 22 (began Jly).
**M Brittain [1-53] Northgate Lodge Racing Club.*

BEDEVILLED BHB 76f **RR 76f** 1466[8]
3 ch c Beveled (USA) 6.9f **(64)** - Putout (Dowsing (USA))
Form - 4458
Record 1998 - 1st:0 2nd:0 3rd:0 Ran:4
Pre1998 - 1st:0 2nd:1 3rd:1 Ran:2
Win Prizemoney £0 *Total Prizemoney* £2,235
1998 Turf 0-4: (5f, 6f 2, 7f) (g-s, gd, g-f, frm)
Neat, above-average colt, effective 6f, acts on gd. Turf high 76 - 4th of 18 to Point of Dispute (3 May Salisbury 6f gd RF 0998). Was flattered to get as close as he did to a very smart sort on his Nottingham debut at two, and put up a similar level of form on his second run. Despite some promise last season, he does not seem to have progressed. **M J Heaton-Ellis [0-6] David Caruth.*

BEDOUIN PRINCE (USA) BHB 36f39a **RR 39f 39a** 2922[9]
11 b g Danzig (USA) 8.1f **(88)**-Regal Heiress (English Prince) 10.1f **(61)**
Form - 0
Record 1998 - 1st:0 2nd:0 3rd:0 Ran:1
Pre1998 - 1st:4 2nd:9 3rd:11 Ran:53
Win Prizemoney £9,441 *Total Prizemoney* £19,628
Wins 1997 *Jun Lingfi (STD) SH 13f 36 46*
1998 Turf 0-1: (14f) (gd)
Moderate gelding, effective 12 to 13f, best at 12f, acts on g-f - acts on Equi, has worn blinkers (extremely effectively). Inconsistent.
**Miss M E Rowland [0-2] Tim Dean (from Mrs L Stubbs [1-10] Aug 1997).*

BEDTIME STORY RR 56[5]
3 b f Fairy King (USA)7.7f **(75)**-Prima Domina (FR) (Dominion) 8.5f **(63)**
Form - 55
Record 1998 - 1st:0 2nd:0 3rd:0 Ran:1
Pre1998 - 1st:0 2nd:0 3rd:0 Ran:1
1998 AW 0-1: (7f) (Fibr)
Unfurnished, currently moderate filly.
**R Guest [0-2] Matthews Breeding and Racing.*

BEEANTEE RR 16f 3097[11]
2 b f Gran Alba (USA) - Superb Lady (Marcus Superbus)
Form - 6570
Record 1998 - 1st:0 2nd:0 3rd:0 Ran:4
1998 Turf 0-2: (5f, 6f) (sft, frm) 1998 AW 0-2: (5f, 7f) (Fibr 2)
Poor filly. Turf high 16. AW high 12.
**W G M Turner [0-4] B & T Racing Club.*

BEE-CEE-JAY RR 1943[7]
3 gr f Absalom 7.1f **(56)** - Saltina (Bustino) 10.4f **(64)**
Form - 7
Record 1998 - 1st:0 2nd:0 3rd:0 Ran:1
1998 AW 0-1: (8f) (Fibr)
Lengthy, currently little account filly.
**Mrs A Swinbank [0-1] Middleham Park Racing VII.*

BEECHWOOD QUEST (IRE) BHB 60f49a **RR 50f 49a** 433[10]
3 b f River Falls 8.2f **(56)** - Egalite (IRE) (Fools Holme (USA))
Form - 8060
Record 1998 - 1st:0 2nd:0 3rd:0 Ran:4
Pre1998 - 1st:2 2nd:1 3rd:2 Ran:9
Win Prizemoney £3,969 *Total Prizemoney* £5,626
Wins * *1997 Aug Southw (STD) S 5f 62*
* *1997 Jly Southw (STD) S 5f 75* <
1998 AW 0-4: (5f 3, 6f) (Fibr 4)
Workmanlike, fair filly, effective 5f, - acts on Fibr, often wears blinkers (very effectively). AW high 44.
**B S Rothwell [2-13] B Valentine.*

BEE HEALTH BOY BHB 62f59a **RR 69f 59a** 4918[11]
5 b g Superpower 6.6f **(58)** - Rekindle (Relkino) 8.9f **(65)**
Form - 622562714000000
Record 1998 - 1st:1 2nd:3 3rd:0 Ran:15
Pre1998 - 1st:4 2nd:3 3rd:4 Ran:37
Win Prizemoney £22,420 *Total Prizemoney* £32,652
Wins * **1998** Jun Redcar (G-S) H 6f 65 69 <
* 1996 Aug Newmar (G-F) H 6f 66 68
* 1996 Aug Doncas (G-F) H 6f 62 65
* 1996 Jly Catter (G-S) H 6f 57 60
* 1995 Spt Haydoc (SFT) SH 6f 59 64
1998 Turf 1-15: (5f 2, 6f 1-13) (sft 3, g-s 5, gd 1-2, g-f, frm 4)
Average gelding, effective 5 to 6f, best at 6f, acts on sft to frm, best on gd, mostly wears blinkers (very effectively), excels at Ripon and Haydock, does well at Redcar. Turf high 69 - 1st of 8 getting 10lb from Young Bigwig (20 Jun Redcar RF 2158). He does not have a great strike-rate, despite often running well, but won well at Redcar in June when racing on his favoured soft ground.
**M W Easterby [5-52] Steve Ryan.*

BE GONE RR 89f 3383[1]
3 ch g Be My Chief (USA) 10.2f **(62)** - Hence (USA) (Mr Prospector (USA)) 8.8f **(78)**
Form - 51
Record 1998 - 1st:1 2nd:0 3rd:0 Ran:2
Win Prizemoney £3,452 *Total Prizemoney* £3,452
Wins * **1998** Aug Newcas (GD) 9f 89 <
1998 Turf 1-2: (8f, 9f 1-1) (g-f 1-1, frm)
Workmanlike, currently useful gelding. Turf high 89 (began Jly) - 1st of 6 from Pegnitz (5 Aug Newcastle RF 3383).
**H R A Cecil [1-2] Peter Burrell.*

BEGORRAT (IRE) BHB 65f **RR 65f** 4973[4]
4 ch g Ballad Rock 7.2f **(63)** - Hada Rani (Jaazeiro (USA)) 9.2f **(54)**
Form - 06420440414
Record 1998 - 1st:1 2nd:1 3rd:0 Ran:11
Pre1998 - 1st:2 2nd:0 3rd:1 Ran:13
Win Prizemoney £8,948 *Total Prizemoney* £14,610
Wins * **1998** Oct Ayr (G-S) H 10f 58 65
1997 Oct Ayr (SFT) C 10.9f 69 <
1997 Aug Haydoc (G-F) S 8.1f 68
1998 Turf 1-11: (10f 1-3, 11f 2, 12f 5, 13f) (sft 1-3, g-s, gd 6, frm)
Scopey, average gelding, effective 8 to 12f, acts on sft to g-f, often wears blinkers (very effectively), prefers left handed tracks, likes tight tracks, excels at Ayr. Turf high 68 - 4th of 13 getting 27lb from Largesse (12 May York 12f gd RF 1164) - also 1st of 8 getting 9lb from Shaffishayes (12 Oct Ayr RF 4754).
**J S Goldie [1-3] Mike Flynn (from D Moffatt [1-12] Aug 1998).*

BEGUILE RR 48a 554[7]
4 b g Most Welcome 8.6f **(66)** - Captivate (Mansingh (USA)) 7.4f **(55)**
Form - 7
Record 1998 - 1st:0 2nd:0 3rd:0 Ran:1
1998 AW 0-1: (6f) (Equi)
Currently moderate gelding. **R Ingram [0-1] D G Wheatley.*

BEHIND THE SCENES BHB 43f47a **RR 43f 47a** 5002[15]
4 ch g Kris 10f **(75)** - Free Guest (Be My Guest (USA)) 9.3f **(67)**
Form - 3075003400
Record 1998 - 1st:0 2nd:0 3rd:2 Ran:10
Pre1998 - 1st:1 2nd:1 3rd:0 Ran:8
Win Prizemoney £3,752 *Total Prizemoney* £5,639
Wins * 1997 May Goodwo (GD) 9f 65 <
1998 Turf 0-3: (12f 3) (gd 2, g-f) 1998 AW 0-7: (10f, 12f 2, 15f, 16f 3) (Equi 5, Fibr 2)
Well made, fair gelding, effective 9 to 16f, best at 16f, acts on gd - acts on AW, has worn blinkers, favours tight tracks. Turf high 43. AW high 63 (1st run) - 3rd of 13 giving 9lb to Signed And Sealed (18 Apr Wolverhampton 16f Fibr RF 0756). Inconsistent.
**C A Cyzer [1-18] R M Cyzer.*

BEHOLD BHB 85f **RR 86f** 2354[3]
3 ch f Prince Sabo 6.6f **(64)** - Be My Lass (IRE) (Be My Guest (USA)) 9.3f **(67)**
Form - 43
Record 1998 - 1st:0 2nd:0 3rd:1 Ran:2
Pre1998 - 1st:1 2nd:1 3rd:0 Ran:2
Win Prizemoney £3,015 *Total Prizemoney* £5,354
Wins * 1997 May Redcar (G-F) 6f 74+ <
1998 Turf 0-2: (6f, 8f) (gd, g-f)
Light-framed, useful filly. Turf high 86 - 3rd of 9 giving 10lb to Sweet Pea (27 Jun Newmarket 8f gd RF 2354). Ran well at Newmarket in June but refused to go in the stalls there next time.
**J R Fanshawe [1-4] Cheveley Park Stud.*

BEHRENS (USA) RR 100a 552a[5]
4
Form - 5
1998 AW 0-1: (10f) (Dirt)
Currently useful, often wears blinkers. He was put in his place behind Silver Charm and Swain in the Emirates Dubai World Cup.
**H J Bond in USA [0-2] W Clifton Jr & Rudlein Stable.*

BE IN LOVE (AUS) BHB 74f **RR 74+f** 4243[22]
2 b f Rivotious (USA) - I'm Alert (AUS) (Red Alert) 7.6f **(66)**
Form - 8650
Record 1998 - 1st:0 2nd:0 3rd:0 Ran:4
Win Prizemoney £0 *Total Prizemoney* £203
1998 Turf 0-4: (5f 2, 6f 2) (gd, g-f 2, frm)
Above-average filly. Turf high 74. **R Hannon [0-4] J E Baxter.*

BEJEWELLED (IRE) RR 33f 3510[8]
4 ch g Persian Bold 10f **(69)** - Anjuli (Northfields (USA)) 9f **(72)**
Form - 8
Record 1998 - 1st:0 2nd:0 3rd:0 Ran:1
1998 Turf 0-1: (12f) (hrd)
Currently very moderate gelding. **J R Poulton [0-1] Mrs J Druce.*

BELASCO (USA) BHB 100f **RR 99f** 4593[6]
2 ch c Gone West (USA) 7.8f **(82)** - Musicale (USA) (The Minstrel (CAN)) 10f **(72)**
Form - 2236
Record 1998 - 1st:0 2nd:2 3rd:1 Ran:4
Win Prizemoney £0 *Total Prizemoney* £10,389
1998 Turf 0-4: (6f 4) (gd 2, g-f, frm)
Very useful colt. Turf high 99 (began Jly). Came to his debut with a lofty home reputation, but did not get the clearest of passages and just failed to get up. Could not contain Threat at Goodwood, but had already run three furlongs after a false start. A close-up third in the Mill Reef Stakes, before running well in the Middle Park Stakes at Newmarket, he has reportedly joined Bill Mott in the United States. **P W Chapple-Hyam [0-4] R E Sangster.*

BELBAY STAR BHB 31f30a **RR 31f 30a** 172[9]
5 b m Belfort (FR) 6.7f **(53)** - Gavea (African Sky) 7.9f **(63)**
Form - 70
Record 1998 - 1st:0 2nd:0 3rd:0 Ran:1
Pre1998 - 1st:0 2nd:1 3rd:0 Ran:13
Win Prizemoney £0 *Total Prizemoney* £997
1998 AW 0-1: (7f) (Fibr)
Very moderate filly, effective 5f, acts on frm, has worn blinkers.
**J L Eyre [0-14] Miss Anne Simpson & Trevor Welbourn.*

BELCADE BHB 36f **RR 41f** 4574[15]
3 b g Belmez (USA) 11.4f **(65)** - Blue Brocade (Reform) 8.9f **(62)**
Form - 4480000
Record 1998 - 1st:0 2nd:0 3rd:0 Ran:7
Win Prizemoney £0 *Total Prizemoney* £628
1998 Turf 0-7: (8f, 9f, 10f 2, 11f, 12f 2) (hvy, sft, g-s, gd, g-f 2, frm)
Scopey, moderate gelding, mostly wears blinkers. Turf high 61.
**J R Poulton [0-1] Chris Steward (from D R C Elsworth [0-6] Jun 1998).*

BELDARIAN (IRE) RR 103+f 4913a[1]
3 b f Last Tycoon 9.4f **(73)** - Sorbus (Busted) 10.2f **(61)**
Form - 114281
1998 Turf 3-6: (10f 1-1, 12f 2-4, 15f) (sft 2-2, gd 1-4)
Very useful filly, effective 12f, acts on sft to gd, often wears blinkers. Turf high 103 - 1st of 13 getting 17lb from Gordi (17 Oct Down Royal RF 4913a). Stamina is the bottom line with this game filly. She has been found out in decent company thus far but, granted some give underfoot, is capable of winning a Listed event.
**J Oxx in IRE [3-7] Gerald Jennings.*

BELLA RR 13f 5138[18]
2 ch f Inchinor 8.9f **(64)** - Indian Jubilee (Indian King (USA)) 7.4f **(64)**
Form - 0
Record 1998 - 1st:0 2nd:0 3rd:0 Ran:1
1998 Turf 0-1: (7f) (gd)
Currently poor filly. **I A Balding [0-1] Lord Lloyd-Webber.*

BELLADERA (IRE) BHB 65f **RR 64f** 4406[15]
3 b f Alzao (USA) 9.8f **(73)** - Reality (Known Fact (USA)) 7.4f **(67)**
Form - 05580
Record 1998 - 1st:0 2nd:0 3rd:0 Ran:5
Pre1998 - 1st:1 2nd:1 3rd:0 Ran:5
Win Prizemoney £5,692 *Total Prizemoney* £7,466
Wins 1997 May York (GD) 6f 76 <
1998 Turf 0-5: (6f, 7f, 8f 2, 12f) (gd 3, g-f 2)
Light-framed, average filly, effective 6 to 7f, acts on gd to g-f. Turf high 64. Consistent.
**B J Meehan [0-2] Fieldspring Racing (from N Tinkler [1-8] Jun 1998).*

BELLAGRANA BHB 50f42a **RR 55f 42a** 177[7]
4 ch f Belmez (USA) 11.4f **(65)** -Nafis (USA) (Nodouble (USA)) 8.8f **(68)**
Form - 57
Record 1998 - 1st:0 2nd:0 3rd:0 Ran:2
Pre1998 - 1st:0 2nd:2 3rd:0 Ran:9
Win Prizemoney £0 *Total Prizemoney* £1,700
1998 AW 0-2: (10f, 13f) (Equi 2)
Scopey, fair filly, effective 10f, acts on gd to frm, likes left handed tracks, likes tight tracks. AW high 28. Becoming disappointing.
**M J Fetherston-Godley [0-11] M J Fetherston-Godley.*

BELLA LOUPA BHB 61f **RR 65f** 4929[8]
2 b f Wolfhound (USA) 7.3f **(71)** - Quay Line (High Line) 10.3f **(70)**
Form - 03688
Record 1998 - 1st:0 2nd:0 3rd:1 Ran:5
Win Prizemoney £0 *Total Prizemoney* £520
1998 Turf 0-5: (6f, 7f 4) (g-s 2, gd, g-f, frm)
Average filly. Turf high 65. **R Hannon [0-5] Major A M Everett.*

BELLAMONT FOREST (USA) RR 70f 4882[4]
2 br c Hermitage (USA) 8.6f **(84)** - Teresa's Spirit (USA) (Master Derby (USA)) 9.5f **(69)**
Form - 24
Record 1998 - 1st:0 2nd:1 3rd:0 Ran:2
Win Prizemoney £0 *Total Prizemoney* £702
1998 Turf 0-1: (6f) (g-s) 1998 AW 0-1: (6f) (Fibr)
Currently decent colt. (1st run) - 2nd of 11 giving 5lb to Nozomi (3 Oct Wolverhampton 6f Fibr RF 4637).
**P W Chapple-Hyam [0-2] Mrs J Magnier & R E Sangster.*

BELLARINA (IRE) RR 55f 4766[5]
2 b f Royal Academy (USA) 7.8f **(77)** - Spring Reel (Mill Reef (USA)) 10.5f **(78)**
Form - 85
Record 1998 - 1st:0 2nd:0 3rd:0 Ran:2
1998 Turf 0-2: (7f, 8f) (sft, frm)
Currently fair filly. Turf high 53 (began Spt).
**N Tinkler [0-2] Mrs D Wright.*

BELLAS GATE BOY BHB 50f40a **RR 45f 40a** 4321[4]
6 b g Doulab (USA) 7.4f **(61)** - Celestial Air (Rheingold) 10.4f **(62)**
Form - 014604
Record 1998 - 1st:1 2nd:0 3rd:0 Ran:6
Pre1998 - 1st:1 2nd:6 3rd:1 Ran:32
Win Prizemoney £5,801 *Total Prizemoney* £13,664
Wins * **1998** May Lingfi (GD) H 7f 46 52 <
* 1997 May Lingfi (G-F) H 7f 46 51
1998 Turf 1-6: (7f 1-1, 8f, 10f 2, 11f 2) (gd, g-f 1-1, frm 3, hrd)
Moderate gelding, effective 7 to 12f, best at 7f, acts on gd to frm, best on g-f, has worn blinkers. Turf high 52 - 1st of 14 getting 4lb from Carlton (30 May Lingfield RF 1601). He is not inconvenienced by carrying big weights, and goes well for an amateur, as he proved when scoring at Lingfield in May. Beaten over a variety of trips afterwards.
**J Pearce [2-26] Miss Ann Pauline Meadows (from G Lewis [0-3] Jly 1995).*

BELLA'S LEGACY BHB 33f30a **RR 33f 30a** 4201[8]
5 b m Thowra (FR) 11.2f **(47)** - Miss Lawsuit (Neltino) 7.6f **(54)**
Form - 258022008
Record 1998 - 1st:0 2nd:3 3rd:0 Ran:9
Pre1998 - 1st:0 2nd:1 3rd:2 Ran:15
Win Prizemoney £0 *Total Prizemoney* £4,028
1998 Turf 0-5: (6f 3, 8f 2) (g-s, gd 3, frm) 1998 AW 0-4: (7f 2, 8f 2) (Equi, Fibr 3)
Very moderate filly, effective 6 to 8f, acts on gd, likes left handed tracks, likes tight tracks. Turf high 48 - 2nd of 11 getting 3lb from Halmanerror (30 Apr Brighton 6f gd RF 0923). AW high 37.
**K R Burke [0-15] Vintage Services Ltd (from R J Hodges [0-9] Aug 1996).*

BELLATOR BHB 71f **RR 76f** 4958[4]
5 b g Simply Great (FR) 11.9f **(61)** - Jupiter's Message (Jupiter Island) 14f **(62)**
Form - 364
Record 1998 - 1st:0 2nd:0 3rd:1 Ran:3
Pre1998 - 1st:1 2nd:1 3rd:2 Ran:11
Win Prizemoney £4,653 *Total Prizemoney* £9,634
Wins * 1996 May Haydoc (G-S) H 14f 71 71 <
1998 Turf 0-3: (14f, 15f, 16f) (g-s, gd, frm)
Above-average gelding. Turf high 76 (1st run) - 3rd of 12 to Opaque (13 May York 14f gd RF 1210). Consistent. A useful hurdler on his day, he was a fair sort on the Flat in 1996. He needs easy ground in order to show his best. Better known as a hurdler nowadays. **G B Balding [4-23] Peter Richardson.*

BELLA WITH A ZEE (IRE) BHB 60f60a **RR 64f 60a** 3099[2]
3 b f Persian Bold 10f **(69)** - Verandah (Jaazeiro (USA)) 9.2f **(54)**
Form - 00172
Record 1998 - 1st:1 2nd:1 3rd:0 Ran:5
Pre1998 - 1st:0 2nd:0 3rd:0 Ran:3
Win Prizemoney £2,469 *Total Prizemoney* £2,992
Wins * **1998** Jun Pontef (SFT) S 10f 64 <
1998 Turf 1-4:(8f 2,10f 1-1, 11f)(sft, g-s 1-2, g-f)1998AW 0-1:(16f) (Fibr)
Average filly, effective 10 to 16f, acts on g-s - acts on Fibr, has worn blinkers. Turf high 64 - 1st of 9 getting 18lb from Grey Prospect (8 Jun Pontefract RF 1807). (1st run) - 2nd of 12 giving 8lb to Makati (24 Jly Wolverhampton 16f Fibr RF 3099). Inconsistent.
**N A Graham [1-3] E K Cleveland (from Ms J Morgan in IRE [0-5] May 1998).*

BELLE DE MONTFORT BHB 34f30a **RR 40f 30a** 3829[10]
3 b f Presidium 7.5f **(56)** - Judys Girl (IRE) (Simply Great (FR)) 8.2f **(65)**
Form - 030D00
Record 1998 - 1st:0 2nd:0 3rd:1 Ran:6
Pre1998 - 1st:0 2nd:0 3rd:0 Ran:3
Win Prizemoney £0 *Total Prizemoney* £303
1998 Turf 0-4: (8f, 11f 2,12f) (gd, g-f, frm 2) 1998 AW 0-2: (9f 2) (Fibr 2)
Light-framed, moderate filly, effective 11f, acts on frm, favours tight tracks. Turf high 40 - 3rd of 7 getting 3lb from Wedding Band (23 May Warwick 11f frm RF 1438). AW high 18 (began Jly).
**J L Spearing [0-10] Junior Nel Partnership.*

BELLE DE NUIT (IRE) BHB 72f **RR 77df** 5069[13]
3 b f Statoblest 6.4f **(63)** - Elminya (IRE) (Sure Blade (USA)) 11.3f **(67)**
Form - 0500470
Record 1998 - 1st:0 2nd:0 3rd:0 Ran:7
Pre1998 - 1st:2 2nd:1 3rd:0 Ran:7
Win Prizemoney £7,091 *Total Prizemoney* £13,109
Wins * 1997 Spt Yarmou (G-F) H 7f 72 73 <
* 1997 Aug Windso (GD) 6f 72
1998 Turf 0-7: (8f, 9f, 10f 3, 11f, 12f) (sft, gd 2, g-f 3, frm)
Leggy, above-average filly, effective 7 to 10f, acts on g-f, has worn blinkers. Turf high 81 (began Jly) - 5th of 12 giving 5lb to Scent of Success (29 Aug Windsor 8f g-f RF 3975). Inconsistent.
**B J Meehan [2-14] Richard Withers.*

BELLE MYSTERE RR 2155[7]
2 b f Mystiko (USA) 7.7f **(59)** - Maribella (Robellino (USA)) 7.6f **(80)**
Form - 7
Record 1998 - 1st:0 2nd:0 3rd:0 Ran:1
1998 Turf 0-1: (5f) (gd)
Currently very poor filly. **S Gollings [0-1] J D Chilton.*

BELLE OF HEARTS BHB 53f **RR 64f** 5012[7]
2 gr f Belfort (FR) 6.7f **(53)** - Three of Hearts **(56f 50a)** (Governor General)
Form - 823303007
Record 1998 - 1st:0 2nd:1 3rd:3 Ran:9
Win Prizemoney £0 *Total Prizemoney* £2,041
1998 Turf 0-9: (5f 4, 6f 5) (sft, gd 4, g-f 3, frm)
Average filly, effective 5 to 6f, acts on gd to frm. Turf high 64 - 2nd of 12 to Dispol Safa (16 Jun Thirsk 6f gd RF 2018). Becoming disappointing. She has shown ability in plating company, but also ran well in a Newcastle nursery, and should be capable of winning a small race.
**M A Peill [0-8] Mrs Valerie Dixon (from A B Mulholland [0-1] May 1998).*

BELLE'S BOY BHB 60f51a **RR 63f 51a** 432[3]
5 b g Nalchik (USA) 12.6f **(44)** - Ty-With-Belle (Pamroy) 12.5f **(55)**
Form - 433
Record 1998 - 1st:0 2nd:0 3rd:2 Ran:3
Pre1998 - 1st:2 2nd:1 3rd:0 Ran:10
Win Prizemoney £5,898 *Total Prizemoney* £7,641
Wins * 1996 Apr Warwic (GD) C 12.5f 63+
* 1995 *Dec Wolver (STD) 8.5f 69* <
1998 AW 0-3: (12f, 15f, 16f) (Fibr 3)
Average gelding, has worn blinkers. AW high 50. A winner at Warwick in '96, he was off the track for eighteen months before reappearing in February, but has run some sound races on sand since then. A small race over twelve furlongs could well come his way. **B Palling [2-13] Mrs M M Palling.*

BELLINO (GER) **RR 105f** 4603a[7]
3 c
Form - 6057
1998 Turf 0-4: (8f, 12f 3) (hvy, sft, gd 2)
Pattern-class colt. Turf high 105. He had little chance in Group One company. **D Ilic in GER [0-4].*

BELMARITA (IRE) BHB 61f **RR 63f** 4474[7]
5 ch m Belmez (USA) 11.4f **(65)** - Congress Lady (General Assembly (USA)) 10f **(68)**
Form - 7
Record 1998 - 1st:0 2nd:0 3rd:0 Ran:1
Pre1998 - 1st:0 2nd:3 3rd:2 Ran:14
Win Prizemoney £0 *Total Prizemoney* £5,183
1998 Turf 0-1: (15f) (g-f)
Average filly.
**G A Hubbard [4-16] G A Hubbard (from M H Tompkins [0-11] Oct 1996).*

BELSAZAR (USA) **RR 48f** 3988[4]
3 b c Miswaki (USA) 8.1f **(81)** - Blushing Redhead (USA) (Blushing Groom (FR)) 10.3f **(76)**
Form - 54
Record 1998 - 1st:0 2nd:0 3rd:0 Ran:2
Win Prizemoney £0 *Total Prizemoney* £236
1998 Turf 0-2: (7f, 8f) (g-f, frm)
Workmanlike, currently moderate colt. Turf high 48 (began Aug).
**G Wragg [0-2] Baron G Von Ullmann.*

BELTESHAZZAR (IRE) RR 33f 4572[11]
3 b g Un Desperado (FR) 9.3f **(42)** - Annalena (IRE) (Ela-Mana-Mou) 10.1f **(70)**
Form - 00
Record 1998 - 1st:0 2nd:0 3rd:0 Ran:2
1998 Turf 0-2: (7f, 8f) (g-f 2)
Neat, currently very moderate gelding. Turf high 33 (began Spt).
**B R Johnson [0-2] John Jess.*

BEMSHA SWING (IRE) BHB 100f **RR 101f** 1123[3]
3 b br c Night Shift (USA) 8.1f **(73)** - Move It Baby (IRE) (Thatching) 8f **(66)**
Form - 3
Record 1998 - 1st:0 2nd:0 3rd:1 Ran:1
Pre1998 - 1st:1 2nd:2 3rd:0 Ran:6
Win Prizemoney £4,163 *Total Prizemoney* £13,938
Wins * 1997 Aug Newmar (G-F) 6f 101 <
1998 Turf 0-1: (6f) (g-f)
Workmanlike, very useful colt, effective 6f, acts on g-f to frm, best on g-f. (1st run) - 3rd of 20 giving 8lb to Hill Magic (9 May Lingfield 6f g-f RF 1123). Ran an encouraging race on his reappearance but was not seen out again. Six furlongs on fast ground, together with forcing tactics seem to bring the best out of him.
**R Hannon [1-7] Michael Pescod.*

BEMUSE BHB 87f **RR 85f** 3651[6]
2 b f Forzando 7.2f **(63)** - Barsham (Be My Guest (USA)) 9.3f **(67)**
Form - 31136
Record 1998 - 1st:2 2nd:0 3rd:2 Ran:5
Win Prizemoney £6,912 *Total Prizemoney* £7,937
Wins * **1998** Jly Chepst (GD) 5.1f 85 <
* **1998** Jun Lingfi (GD) 5f 77+
1998 Turf 2-5: (5f 2-4, 6f) (gd 2, g-f 1-1, frm 1-2)
Useful filly, has worn blinkers. Turf high 85 - 3rd of 5 getting 1lb from Henry Hall (15 Jly Doncaster 5f frm RF 2817) - also 1st of 7 giving 1lb to Robber Red (10 Jly Chepstow RF 2668). Showed plenty of promise on her Newcastle debut, and strolled home at Lingfield next time. The opposition may not have been up to much but she looked speedy there, and she followed up with a fairly comfortable win at Chepstow. Rather disappointing last time, she may be better than that effort.
**Sir Mark Prescott [2-5] Cheveley Park Stud.*

BE MY WISH BHB 73f69a **RR 77f 69a** 4645[9]
3 b f Be My Chief (USA) 10.2f **(62)** - Spinner (Blue Cashmere) 6.4f **(54)**
Form - 0315650
Record 1998 - 1st:1 2nd:0 3rd:1 Ran:7
Pre1998 - 1st:0 2nd:0 3rd:1 Ran:4
Win Prizemoney £5,368 *Total Prizemoney* £7,737
Wins * **1998** Aug Ascot (G-F) 7f 77 <
1998 Turf 1-7: (7f 1-6, 8f) (gd 2, g-f 1-4, frm)
Well made, above-average filly, effective 7f, acts on gd to g-f, best on g-f. Turf high 77 - 1st of 7 getting 5lb from Fabrice (7 Aug Ascot RF 3428). **Miss Gay Kelleway [1-11] T Tran.*

BENATOM (USA) BHB 94f **RR 97f** 2737[6]
5 gr g Hawkster (USA) 12.4f **(71)** - Dance Til Two (USA) (Sovereign Dancer (USA)) 11.2f **(68)**
Form - 306
Record 1998 - 1st:0 2nd:0 3rd:1 Ran:3
Pre1998 - 1st:4 2nd:1 3rd:1 Ran:15
Win Prizemoney £32,405 *Total Prizemoney* £42,256
Wins 1997 Jly York (GD) LH 13.9f 90 97 <
1996 Aug Goodwo (G-F) H 14f 90 95
1996 Jly Newmar (GD) H 16.1f 85 90
1996 Apr Thirsk (G-F) 12f 76
1998 Turf 0-3: (12f, 14f 2) (g-f 2, frm)
Very useful gelding, effective 14f, acts on gd to frm, has worn blinkers. Turf high 97 (1st run) - 3rd of 7 giving 5lb to Henry Island (20 May Goodwood 14f g-f RF 1357).
**D R C Elsworth [1-7] Lordship Stud (from H R A Cecil [4-15] Jly 1997).*

BEND WAVY (IRE) BHB 76f80a **RR 76f 80a** 2949[7]
6 ch g Kefaah (USA) 11.2f **(64)** - Prosodie (FR) (Relko) 9.9f **(59)**
Form - 661618307
Record 1998 - 1st:2 2nd:0 3rd:1 Ran:9
Pre1998 - 1st:1 2nd:1 3rd:2 Ran:11
Win Prizemoney £11,600 *Total Prizemoney* £14,900
Wins * **1998** Jun Thirsk (SFT) H 12f 73 76
* **1998** Jun Haydoc (GD) H 10.5f 69 72
1996 Jly Beverl (G-F) H 8.5f 80 82 <
1998 Turf 2-9: (8f, 10f 4, 11f 1-2, 12f 1-2) (g-s, gd 1-5, g-f, frm 1-2)
Above-average gelding, effective 11 to 12f, best at 11f, acts on gd to frm, likes left handed tracks, likes tight tracks. Turf high 76 - 1st of 7 giving 3lb to Polar Champ (16 Jun Thirsk RF 2020) - also 1st of 16 giving 30lb to Saint Albert (5 Jun Haydock RF 1757). A disappointment in 1997 after a good season in '96, he did much better this season, winning twice. Ten furlongs looks to be his best trip.
**T H Caldwell [2-16] A J McDonald (from L M Cumani [1-6] Aug 1996).*

BENEVENTUS BHB 85f **RR 88f** 4619[4]
3 b c Most Welcome 8.6f **(66)** - Dara Dee (Dara Monarch) 8.8f **(59)**
Form - 310348034
Record 1998 - 1st:1 2nd:0 3rd:3 Ran:9
Pre1998 - 1st:0 2nd:0 3rd:1 Ran:3
Win Prizemoney £2,787 *Total Prizemoney* £6,900
Wins * **1998** May Newcas (G-F) 10.1f 83++ <
1998 Turf 1-9: (8f, 9f, 10f 1-7) (g-s, gd 6, g-f 1-2)
Workmanlike, useful colt, effective 8 to 10f, acts on gd to g-f, best on gd, has worn blinkers, prefers left handed tracks. Turf high 88 - 3rd of 10 getting 2lb from Shaska (9 Spt Doncaster 10f gd RF 4188) - also 1st of 6 giving 5lb to La Tiziana (21 May Newcastle RF 1371). Consistent. He was not beaten far in some good maidens at two, and scored with a ton in hand at Newcastle on his second start at three. He has struggled since however, and finds little off the bridle. Sold for 52,000 gns in October.
**J L Dunlop [1-9] R N Khan (from Major W R Hern [0-3] Spt 1997).*

BENFLEET BHB 50f75a **RR 51f 75a** 2497[6]
7 ch g Dominion 8.9f **(65)** - Penultimate (Final Straw) 7.9f **(64)**
Form - B366
Record 1998 - 1st:0 2nd:0 3rd:1 Ran:4
Pre1998 - 1st:7 2nd:7 3rd:4 Ran:51
Win Prizemoney £27,159 *Total Prizemoney* £49,518
Wins 1995 Apr Leices (GD) H 10f 74 79 <
1995 Jan Lingfi (STD) H 12f 75 76+
1995 Jan Lingfi (STD) H 12f 69 69
1994 May Leices (GD) H 8f 69 71
1994 May Windso (SFT) H 8.3f 69 70
1998 Turf 0-3: (12f 2, 14f) (g-s, gd, frm) 1998 AW 0-1: (16f) (Fibr)
Fair gelding. Turf high 51. Becoming disappointing.
**M C Pipe [0-8] Jim Ennis (from R W Armstrong [7-51] Oct 1996).*

BEN GUNN BHB 76f67a **RR 79f 67a** 4848[19]
6 b g Faustus (USA) 9.1f **(54)** - Pirate Maid (Auction Ring (USA)) 8.6f **(65)**
Form - 3026121036380
Record 1998 - 1st:2 2nd:2 3rd:3 Ran:13
Pre1998 - 1st:5 2nd:2 3rd:3 Ran:28
Win Prizemoney £29,408 *Total Prizemoney* £43,582
Wins * **1998** Jun Salisb (G-F) H 8f 73 78
* **1998** May Newmar (G-F) H 8f 70 75
* 1997 Jly Newmar (GD) H 8f 65 73
* 1997 May Salisb (G-F) H 7f 60 66
* 1995 Jly Windso (G-F) H 6f 67 68
* 1994 Oct Leices (G-S) 6f 79
* 1994 Oct Newmar (G-F) 7f 74+
1998 Turf 2-13: (7f 2, 8f 2-11) (sft, gd 3, g-f 1-6, frm 1-3)
Above-average gelding, effective 7 to 8f, best at 8f, acts on gd to frm, best on g-f, has worn blinkers, and excels at Salisbury. Turf high 79 - 3rd of 10 getting 8lb from Silk St John (29 Aug Windsor 8f g-f RF 3974) - also 1st of 7 getting 10lb from Therhea (24 Jun Salisbury RF 2251). Consistent. Ran a couple of fine races earlier in the season, and may have been unlucky not to have won at least one of them, but everything went right for him at Newmarket at the end of May. Has continued to run well. He does not look to be at his best on soft ground, and is suited by coming late off a fast pace. **P T Walwyn [7-41] Michael White.*

BENIN (USA) BHB 95f **RR 96f** 4619[6]
3 b c Sky Classic (CAN) 10f **(83)** - Battle Drum (USA) (Alydar (USA)) 9.1f **(76)**
Form - 42316
Record 1998 - 1st:1 2nd:1 3rd:1 Ran:5
Pre1998 - 1st:1 2nd:0 3rd:0 Ran:1

Win Prizemoney £10,484 *Total Prizemoney* £19,344
Wins * **1998** Aug Newbur (G-F) H 10f 91 96 <
* 1997 Oct Leices (G-F) 7f 89+
1998 Turf 1-5: (10f 1-4, 12f) (hvy, gd 3, g-f 1-1)
Light-framed, very useful colt, effective 7 to 12f, best at 10f, acts on gd to frm, best on gd. Turf high 96 - 1st of 9 giving 9lb to Chim Chiminey (14 Aug Newbury RF 3632). Ran too badly to be true in heavy ground on his reappearance, but has performed well since, third in a competitive handicap at Glorious Goodwood before winning at Newbury. Performed with credit on his final start, and looks capable of winning a nice handicap next term.
**H R A Cecil [2-6] Baron G Von Ullmann.*

BENJAMIN FRANK BHB 77f RR 80f 4054[10]

3 b g Tragic Role (USA) 9.4f **(63)** - Flower Princess (Slip Anchor) 9.8f **(73)**
Form - 2621230
Record 1998 - 1st:1 2nd:3 3rd:1 Ran:7
Pre1998 - 1st:0 2nd:0 3rd:0 Ran:1
Win Prizemoney £2,571 *Total Prizemoney* £6,493
Wins * **1998** Jun Bright (GD) 11.9f 62 <
1998 Turf 1-7: (10f, 11f 2, 12f 1-2, 14f 2) (hvy, gd 1-2, g-f, frm 3)
Workmanlike, decent gelding, effective 11 to 14f, acts on hvy to frm. Turf high 80 - 3rd of 5 getting 9lb from Wafir (2 Aug Newcastle 12f g-f RF 3295). Inconsistent. Simple task in a Brighton maiden, and has faced some stiff tasks since. **S P C Woods [1-8] B Lam.*

BENJAMINS LAW BHB 51f68a RR 54f 68a 9[2]

7 b or br g Mtoto 11.5f **(71)** - Absaloute Service (Absalom) 7.2f **(58)**
Form - 2
Record 1998 - 1st:0 2nd:1 3rd:0 Ran:1
Pre1998 - 1st:3 2nd:6 3rd:5 Ran:38
Win Prizemoney £7,844 *Total Prizemoney* £19,694
Wins * 1996 *Jan Southw (STD) H 8f 59 70+* <
* 1995 *Dec Wolver (STD) H 9.4f 56 61*
* 1995 *Nov Wolver (STD) H 9.4f 44 60*
1998 AW 0-1: (8f) (Fibr)
Above-average gelding, effective 8f, - acts on Fibr, likes left handed tracks, likes tight tracks. (1st run) - 2nd of 9 giving 22lb to Muara Bay (2 Jan Southwell 8f Fibr RF 0009).
**J A Pickering [3-39] D Lowe.*

BENROCK (IRE) BHB 29f46a RR 30f 46a 2811[11]

3 ch g Ballad Rock 7.2f **(63)** - Madame Champvert (IRE) (Cardinal Flower)
Form - 000600
Record 1998 - 1st:0 2nd:0 3rd:0 Ran:6
Pre1998 - 1st:0 2nd:0 3rd:0 Ran:3
1998 Turf 0-6: (6f 2, 7f, 8f 3) (gd, g-f, frm 4)
Very moderate gelding, has worn blinkers. Turf high 30. Inconsistent.
**Mrs G S Rees [0-6] J P Hacking (from Capt J Wilson [0-3] Oct 1997).*

BENS GIFT BHB 54f RR 57f 4338[16]

3 ch f Keen 11.1f **(58)** - Monstrosa (Monsanto (FR)) 6.5f **(59)**
Form - 68300
Record 1998 - 1st:0 2nd:0 3rd:1 Ran:5
Win Prizemoney £0 *Total Prizemoney* £321
1998 Turf 0-5: (8f 4, 10f) (g-f 2, frm 3)
Workmanlike, fair filly. Turf high 57.
**C F Wall [0-5] Mrs E M Bousquet-Payne.*

BENTICO BHB 47f53a RR 47f 53a 3092[6]

9 b g Nordico (USA) 8.2f **(59)** - Bentinck Hotel (Red God) 8.5f **(65)**
Form - 414856443046
Record 1998 - 1st:0 2nd:0 3rd:1 Ran:9
Pre1998 - 1st:16 2nd:14 3rd:11 Ran:105
Win Prizemoney £50,262 *Total Prizemoney* £71,447
Wins * 1997 *Dec Southw (STD) C 8f 63*
* 1997 *Jun Lingfi (STD) 8f 73* <
* 1997 *Jun Wolver (STD) C 7f 68*
* 1996 *Jun Wolver (STD) H 8.5f 68 69*
* 1995 Oct Leices (GD) 8f 70
* 1995 *Spt Wolver (STD) C 7f 72*
* 1995 *Feb Southw (STD) H 8f 67 71*
* 1994 *Dec Wolver (STD) H 9.4f 66 67*
* 1994 *Dec Southw (STD) H 8f 57 59*
* 1994 *Dec Wolver (STD) H 9.4f 57 57*
* 1994 Oct Leices (GD) 8f 58
1998 AW 0-9: (7f, 8f 8) (Fibr 9)
Fair gelding, effective 7 to 8f, best at 8f, - acts on AW, best on Fibr, often wears blinkers (effectively), favours left handed tracks, and excels at Lingfield. AW high 59. He is a tough sort who stands his racing well, but is not that easy to predict.
**Mrs N Macauley [11-86] Mrs N Macauley (from M A Jarvis [5-28] Spt 1994).*

BENZOE (IRE) BHB 72f RR 70f 5096[10]

8 b g Taufan (USA) 8.3f **(65)** - Saintly Guest (What A Guest) 7f **(62)**
Form - 0004157360022881530
Record 1998 - 1st:2 2nd:2 3rd:2 Ran:19
Pre1998 - 1st:7 2nd:7 3rd:8 Ran:70
Win Prizemoney £47,928 *Total Prizemoney* £78,504
Wins * **1998** Spt Redcar (G-F) H 6f 70 74
* **1998** May Thirsk (G-F) H 6f 68 73
* 1997 Jly Thirsk (GD) H 6f 73 77
* 1997 Jun Thirsk (G-F) H 5f 64 65
* 1996 Aug Thirsk (G-F) H 6f 77 81
* 1996 May Thirsk (G-F) H 6f 69 72
* 1995 May Thirsk (G-F) H 6f 66 71+
1998 Turf 2-19: (5f 6, 6f 2-12, 7f) (sft 2, g-s 4, gd 4, g-f 1-5, frm 1-4)
Above-average gelding, has broken blood-vessels, effective 5 to 6f, best at 6f, acts on gd to frm, has worn blinkers, does well at Thirsk, likes York. Turf high 74 - 1st of 23 getting 4lb from Redoubtable (25 Spt Redcar RF 4485) - also 1st of 11 getting 12lb from Tiler (16 May Thirsk RF 1277). Consistent. He is a useful performer if everything goes his way, although he is often slowly away, and goes well for Jimmy Fortune. Generally in good heart in 1998.
**Mrs J R Ramsden [7-64] Tony Fawcett (from M W Easterby [2-25] Oct 1994).*

BE PRACTICAL BHB 76f RR 82f 4446[10]

3 b f Tragic Role (USA) 9.4f **(63)** - Practical (Ballymore) 7.3f **(64)**
Form - 221200
Record 1998 - 1st:1 2nd:3 3rd:0 Ran:6
Win Prizemoney £2,814 *Total Prizemoney* £7,064
Wins * **1998** Jun Carlis (G-S) 5.9f 79 <
1998 Turf 1-6: (6f 1-2, 7f 4) (gd 1-5, frm)
Leggy, decent filly, effective 6 to 7f, acts on gd. Turf high 82 - 2nd of 6 getting 5lb from Captain Logan (19 Jun Ayr 7f gd RF 2115) - also 1st of 8 from Wyn (25 Jun Carlisle RF 2262).
**J Berry [1-6] T G & Mrs M E Holdcroft.*

BERAYSIM BHB 110f RR 111f 4849[9]

3 b f Lion Cavern (USA) 7.5f **(74)** - Silk Braid (USA) (Danzig (USA)) 8.4f **(76)**
Form - 2141520
Record 1998 - 1st:2 2nd:2 3rd:0 Ran:7
Win Prizemoney £27,931 *Total Prizemoney* £39,895
Wins * **1998** Jly Goodwo (G-S) L 7f 111+ <
* **1998** May Goodwo (G-F) 7f 86+
1998 Turf 2-7: (7f 2-6, 8f) (gd 1-3, g-f 1-2, frm 2)
Scopey, Group-class filly, effective 7f, acts on gd to frm. Turf high 111 - 1st of 9 getting 3lb from Ashraakat (30 Jly Goodwood RF 3216). She has trouble with her feet, but is very useful on her day and accelerated sharply when winning a Listed event at Glorious Goodwood. Half lengthed by Decorated Hero in a Group Three back there in September, she is capable of winning in that sphere.
**M A Jarvis [2-7] Sheikh Ahmed Al Maktoum.*

BERGAMO BHB 80f RR 78f 4764[7]

2 b c Robellino (USA) 9.5f **(68)** - Pretty Thing (Star Appeal) 9.6f **(65)**
Form - 553517
Record 1998 - 1st:1 2nd:0 3rd:1 Ran:6
Win Prizemoney £3,257 *Total Prizemoney* £3,757
Wins * **1998** Spt Bath (G-S) 10.2f 78 <
1998 Turf 1-6: (7f 2, 8f 2, 10f 1-2) (gd 2, g-f 1-3, frm)
Above-average colt, effective 8 to 10f, acts on gd to g-f. Turf high 78 (began Aug) - 1st of 11 from Son of Snurge (28 Spt Bath RF 4526). **J Noseda [1-6] Miss M Conti.*

BERGEN (IRE) BHB 81f RR 81f 4483[2]

3 b c Ballad Rock 7.2f **(63)** - Local Custom (IRE) (Be My Native (USA)) 10.2f **(71)**
Form - 77302

Record 1998 - 1st:0 2nd:1 3rd:1 Ran:5
Pre1998 - 1st:1 2nd:0 3rd:0 Ran:2
Win Prizemoney £3,485 *Total Prizemoney* £5,908
Wins * 1997 Jly Pontef (G-F) 6f 86+ <
1998 Turf 0-5: (7f, 8f 3, 9f) (sft, g-s, g-f, frm 2)
Light-framed, decent colt, effective 6 to 9f, acts on g-s to frm, best on frm, prefers left handed tracks. Turf high 81 - 2nd of 11 giving 6lb to Sualtach (25 Spt Haydock 8f frm RF 4483).
**J Hanson [1-7] J Hanson.*

BERING GIFTS (IRE) BHB 80f RR 83f 4933[4]
3 b g Bering 9.6f **(80)** - Bobbysoxer (Valiyar) 8.5f **(73)**
Form - 250211454
Record 1998 - 1st:2 2nd:2 3rd:0 Ran:9
Pre1998 - 1st:0 2nd:0 3rd:2 Ran:2
Win Prizemoney £11,080 *Total Prizemoney* £16,820
Wins * **1998** Aug Folkes (G-F) H 9.7f 78 83 <
* **1998** Aug Warwic (G-F) 8f 67
1998 Turf 2-9: (8f 1-4, 10f 1-3, 12f 2) (sft, g-s, gd, g-f 1-1, frm 1-5)
Well made, decent gelding, effective 10 to 12f, acts on g-f to frm, has worn blinkers, prefers tight tracks. Turf high 83 - 1st of 12 getting 1lb from Tequila (27 Aug Folkestone RF 3899). He is a very temperamental sort, and though he got off the mark in a Warwick maiden in August, he was long odds on to do so, and only won narrowly having looked none too keen. Followed up in a handicap despite flashing his tail. One to treat with caution.
**P F I Cole [2-11] GG Partnership.*

BERLIOZ RR 102f 4618[2]
2 b c Dolphin Street (FR) - Biraya (Valiyar) 8.5f **(73)**
Form - 12
Record 1998 - 1st:1 2nd:1 3rd:0 Ran:2
Win Prizemoney £11,576 *Total Prizemoney* £16,854
Wins * **1998** Spt Newbur (GD) 7f 87++ <
1998 Turf 1-2: (7f 1-2) (gd, g-f 1-1)
Currently very useful colt. Turf high 102 (began Spt). Backed as if defeat was out of the question when winning a Newbury maiden on his debut, he could not trouble Enrique when stepped-up a couple of grades on his only subsequent start. Given a moderate ride there - Enrique was allowed first run - he remains capable of better and can win a Group race in 1999.
**D R Loder [1-2] Hadi Masood.*

BERL'S GIFT BHB 45f RR 46f 4990[10]
3 b f Prince Sabo 6.6f **(64)** - Primitive Gift (Primitive Rising (USA))
Form - 35340
Record 1998 - 1st:0 2nd:0 3rd:2 Ran:5
Win Prizemoney £0 *Total Prizemoney* £741
1998 Turf 0-5: (7f, 8f 3, 10f) (sft 2, g-s, gd, hrd)
Unfurnished, moderate filly. Turf high 63 (1st run) - 3rd of 11 getting 5lb from Bodfari Pride (30 Apr Redcar 7f sft RF 0934).
**Mrs M Reveley [0-5] H Young.*

BERMUDA TRIANGLE (IRE) BHB 41f46a RR 31f 46a 2765[5]
3 b f Conquering Hero (USA) 10.6f **(50)** - Bermuda Princess (Lord Gayle (USA)) 8.8f **(62)**
Form - 6445075
Record 1998 - 1st:0 2nd:0 3rd:0 Ran:6
Pre1998 - 1st:1 2nd:2 3rd:0 Ran:9
Win Prizemoney £2,337 *Total Prizemoney* £4,122
Wins * 1997 Aug Lingfi (G-F) S 6f 50 <
1998 Turf 0-3: (7f, 12f 2) (gd, g-f 2) 1998 AW 0-3: (8f 2, 10f) (Equi 3)
Leggy, moderate filly, effective 6f, acts on gd to g-f. Turf high 31. AW high 44.
**M J Haynes [1-15] M J Haynes.*

BERNARDO BELLOTTO (IRE) BHB 61f76a RR 60f 76a 4961[7]
3 b g High Estate 10.5f **(66)**-Naivity (IRE)(Auction Ring (USA)) 8.6f **(65)**
Form - 00007
Record 1998 - 1st:0 2nd:0 3rd:0 Ran:5
Pre1998 - 1st:1 2nd:5 3rd:1 Ran:9
Win Prizemoney £3,468 *Total Prizemoney* £9,377
Wins * 1997 Aug Epsom (GD) 6f 78 <
1998 Turf 0-5: (7f 4, 9f) (sft, gd, frm 3)
Above-average gelding, effective 5 to 7f, best at 6f, acts on gd to g-f, best on gd, prefers tight tracks. Turf high 60 (began Aug).
**M Bell [1-14] Richard Green (Fine Paintings).*

BERNIE'S STAR (IRE) BHB 26f RR 27f 2659[11]
4 b br g Arcane (USA) 11.6f **(66)** - Abaca (USA) (Manila (USA)) 9.3f **(71)**
Form - 00
Record 1998 - 1st:0 2nd:0 3rd:0 Ran:2
Pre1998 - 1st:0 2nd:0 3rd:0 Ran:5
1998 Turf 0-1: (11f) (gd) 1998 AW 0-1: (14f) (Fibr)
Tall, little account gelding, has worn blinkers.
**N Bycroft [0-9] Bernard Rayner.*

BERSAGLIO BHB 74f RR 77f 4054[12]
3 ch c Rainbow Quest (USA) 11.2f **(81)** - Escrime (USA) (Sharpen Up) 8.3f **(67)**
Form - 06434830
Record 1998 - 1st:0 2nd:0 3rd:2 Ran:8
Win Prizemoney £0 *Total Prizemoney* £1,614
1998 Turf 0-8: (10f, 12f 2, 14f 4, 17f) (gd 2, g-f 3, frm 3)
Scopey, above-average colt, effective 12 to 14f, best at 14f, acts on g-f to frm, best on frm. Turf high 77 - 4th of 5 giving 5lb to In The Sun (23 Jly Sandown 14f frm RF 3047). Inconsistent.
**W Jarvis [0-8] Lord Howard de Walden.*

BERTOLINI (USA) BHB 100f RR 104f 4593[2]
2 b c Danzig (USA) 8.1f **(88)** - Aquilegia (USA) (Alydar (USA)) 9.1f **(76)**
Form - 2512472
Record 1998 - 1st:1 2nd:3 3rd:0 Ran:7
Win Prizemoney £18,260 *Total Prizemoney* £64,160
Wins * **1998** Jly Newmar (G-F) G3 6f 96+ <
1998 Turf 1-7: (6f 1-6, 7f) (gd 3, g-f 2, frm 1-2)
Very useful colt, effective 6f, acts on gd to frm, has worn blinkers. Turf high 104 - also 1st of 6 from El Tango (8 Jly Newmarket RF 2635). He was kept busy for a Group-class juvenile, gaining his sole win in the July Stakes at Newmarket. Firmly put in his place in decent company during the summer, he appreciated John Reid's positive ride in the Middle Park Stakes, running creditably to chase home the easy winner Lujain. He may not be easy to place next term. **J H M Gosden [1-7] Sheikh Mohammed.*

BERYL BHB 76f RR 78f 4767[4]
2 ch f Bering 9.6f **(80)** - Fayrooz (USA) **(81df)** (Gulch (USA)) 8f **(81)**
Form - 0224
Record 1998 - 1st:0 2nd:2 3rd:0 Ran:4
Win Prizemoney £0 *Total Prizemoney* £2,607
1998 Turf 0-4: (7f 2, 8f 2) (sft, gd, g-f, frm)
Above-average filly. Turf high 78 (began Aug).
**J L Dunlop [0-4] Capt J Macdonald-Buchanan.*

BERYL THE PERIL RR 9f 4152[6]
2 b f Presidium 7.5f **(56)** - Vague Reply (Vaigly Great) 7f **(58)**
Form - 56
Record 1998 - 1st:0 2nd:0 3rd:0 Ran:2
1998 Turf 0-2: (5f 2) (sft, frm)
Currently very poor filly. Turf high 9. **N Bycroft [0-2] C Lawson.*

BESCABY GIRL BHB 42f40a RR 34?f 40a 1441[P]
7 ch m Master Willie 9.2f **(67)** - Thatched Grove (Thatching) 8f **(66)**
Form - P
Record 1998 - 1st:0 2nd:0 3rd:0 Ran:1
Pre1998 - 1st:0 2nd:2 3rd:1 Ran:15
Win Prizemoney £0 *Total Prizemoney* £2,129
1998 Turf 0-1: (15f) (frm)
Very moderate mare, often wears blinkers.
**M Tate [0-1] R C Smith (from J S Wainwright [0-16] Jan 1995).*

BESEECHING (IRE) BHB 60f RR 54f 4888[5]
3 b br f Hamas (IRE) 8f **(72)** - Na-Ammah (IRE) **(84f)** (Ela-Mana-Mou) 10.1f **(70)**
Form - 745
Record 1998 - 1st:0 2nd:0 3rd:0 Ran:3
Win Prizemoney £0 *Total Prizemoney* £255
1998 Turf 0-3: (6f, 7f 2) (gd, frm 2)
Workmanlike, currently fair filly. Turf high 54 (began Aug).
**J A R Toller [0-3] P C J Dalby.*

BEST ATTEMPT RR 34f 2844[9]
3 ch g Beveled (USA) 6.9f **(64)** - Sheznice (IRE) (Try My Best (USA)) 7.6f **(67)**

Form - 0

Record	**1998** -	1st:0	2nd:0	3rd:0	Ran:1
	Pre1998 -	1st:0	2nd:0	3rd:0	Ran:1

1998 Turf 0-1: (5f) (gd)

Workmanlike, currently very moderate gelding.

**J Neville [0-2] J Neville.*

**D A Nolan [0-5] Mrs J McFadyen-Murray (from L J Barratt [0-7] Aug 1997).*

BEST OF ALL (IRE) BHB 79f70a RR 78f 70a 4522^{3}

6 b m Try My Best (USA) 7.8f **(68)**-Skisette (Malinowski (USA)) 10f **(56)**

Form - 00801711803

Bertolini wins the July Stakes from El Tango (far side)

BEST BEFORE DAWN (IRE) RR 95f $3863a^{2}$

7 b g Try My Best (USA) 7.8f **(68)** - Pistol Petal (Pitskelly) 8.5f **(53)**

Form - 475002

1998 Turf 0-6: (5f 2, 6f 4) (hvy, sft, gd 3, frm)

Very useful gelding, effective 5 to 6f, best at 6f, acts on g-s to frm, has worn blinkers. Turf high 95 - 2nd of 4 giving 12lb to Rhine Valley (20 Aug Tipperary 5f frm RF 3863a). Former useful Irish sprint handicapper, not the force of old but should still pick up a race or two. **A P O'Brien in IRE [8-33] Mrs E M Stockwell.*

BESTEMOR BHB 53f RR 56f 3679^{6}

4 b f Selkirk (USA) 7.9f **(76)** - Lillemor 00

Form - 6226

Record	**1998** -	1st:0	2nd:2	3rd:0	Ran:4
	Pre1998 -	1st:0	2nd:0	3rd:0	Ran:4

Win Prizemoney £0 *Total Prizemoney* £1,580

1998 Turf 0-4: (7f, 8f 3) (g-s, frm 3)

Scopey, fair filly, effective 8f, acts on gd to frm, best on frm. Turf high 56 (began Jly) - 2nd of 18 giving 4lb to Polonaise Prince (11 Aug Bath 8f frm RF 3524). **H Candy [0-8] M Berger.*

BEST KEPT SECRET BHB 24f32a RR 21f 32a 2682^{7}

7 b g Petong 7.6f **(58)** - Glenfield Portion (Mummy's Pet) 7.7f **(60)**

Form - 00007

Record	**1998** -	1st:0	2nd:0	3rd:0	Ran:5
	Pre1998 -	1st:6	2nd:9	3rd:13	Ran:64

Win Prizemoney £17,921 *Total Prizemoney* £33,410

Wins								
	1994	Jly	Hamilt	(FRM)	H	6f	70	70
	1994	Jly	Hamilt	(G-S)	S	6f		56
	1994	Jun	Hamilt	(GD)	S	5f		60

1998 Turf 0-5: (5f 2, 6f 3) (gd 2, g-f, frm 2)

Very moderate gelding, has worn blinkers. Turf high 23. Inconsistent.

Record	**1998** -	1st:3	2nd:0	3rd:1	Ran:11
	Pre1998 -	1st:5	2nd:4	3rd:3	Ran:35

Win Prizemoney £33,218 *Total Prizemoney* £39,902

Wins									
	* **1998**	Aug	Ripon	(G-F)	H	10f	75	77	<
	* **1998**	Jly	Goodwo	(G-S)	H	9f	68	72	
	* **1998**	Jly	Mussel	(GD)	H	9f	60	68	
	* 1997	Jun	Mussel	(GD)	H	8f	62	74	
	* 1997	Jun	Redcar	(FRM)	H	8f	62	67	
	* 1996	*Nov*	*Southw*	*(STD)*	*C*	*8f*		*61*	
	* 1995	Nov	Mussel	(SFT)	H	8.1f	67	72	
	* 1994	Jly	Ripon	(G-F)		5f		74+	

1998 Turf 3-11: (8f 4, 9f 2-3, 10f 1-4) (hvy, sft, g-s, gd 1-4, g-f 1-2, frm 1-2)

Above-average mare, effective 8 to 10f, best at 10f, acts on gd to frm, often wears blinkers (extremely effectively), likes right handed tracks, excels at Redcar and Musselburgh. Turf high 78 - 8th of 12 giving 8lb to Light Step (31 Aug Newcastle 10f frm RF 3992) - also 1st of 13 giving 8lb to Buzzy Bomb (15 Aug Ripon RF 3659). Inconsistent. A winning jumper, she stepped up on her previous form to win a fillies' handicap at Glorious Goodwood and followed up narrowly at Ripon. Effective coming off a strong pace.

**J Berry [11-56] Robert Aird.*

BEST OF OUR DAYS BHB 61f67a RR 66f 67a 4118^{12}

3 b c Clantime 6.6f **(57)** - Uptown Girl (Caruso) 5.8f **(63)**

Form - 211650570

Record	**1998** -	1st:2	2nd:0	3rd:0	Ran:8
	Pre1998 -	1st:0	2nd:1	3rd:0	Ran:3

Win Prizemoney £4,891 *Total Prizemoney* £5,535

Wins									
	* **1998**	*Jan*	*Lingfi*	*(STD)*	*H*	*5f*	*66*	*62*	
	* **1998**	*Jan*	*Lingfi*	*(STD)*		*5f*		*66*	<

1998 Turf 0-4: (5f 3, 7f) (gd, g-f 3) 1998 AW 2-4: (5f 2-3, 7f) (Equi 2-2, Fibr 2)

Average colt, effective 5f, acts on frm - acts on Equi, likes left handed tracks. Turf high 66. AW high 66 (1st run) - 1st of 7 giving 5lb to Miss Bananas (6 Jan Lingfield RF 0033) - also 1st of 5 giving 14lb to Leather And Scrim (22 Jan Lingfield RF 0132). Twice a winner at Lingfield in January, he looked a progressive and speedy sort over the minimum on Equitrack. Modest efforts on turf.

**C W Thornton [2-11] Guy Reed.*

BEST PORT (IRE) RR 31f 5137[15]

2 b g Be My Guest (USA) 10.2f **(66)** - Portree (Slip Anchor) 9.8f **(73)**
Form - 00
Record 1998 - 1st:0 2nd:0 3rd:0 Ran:2
1998 Turf 0-2: (7f, 8f) (gd, g-f)
Currently very moderate gelding. Turf high 31 (began Oct).

**M A Jarvis [0-2] Lord Harrington.*

BEST QUEST BHB 59f72a RR 60f 72a 4955[1]

3 b c Salse (USA) 10.9f **(71)** - Quest for the Best (Rainbow Quest (USA)) 10.4f **(75)**
Form - 2300201
Record 1998 - 1st:1 2nd:2 3rd:1 Ran:7
Pre1998 - 1st:0 2nd:0 3rd:0 Ran:3
Win Prizemoney £3,730 *Total Prizemoney* £6,024
Wins * **1998** Oct Doncas (SFT) C 7f 55 <
1998 Turf 1-5: (7f 1-4, 8f)(gd, g-f 2, frm 1-2)1998 AW 0-2: (7f 2) (Equi 2)
Workmanlike, above-average colt, effective 7f, - acts on Equi. Turf high 60. AW high 71.

**J H M Gosden [1-10] Exors of the late Herbert Allen.*

BE THANKFULL (IRE) RR 61f 4611[10]

2 gr f Linamix (FR) 8.2f **(64)** -Thank One's Stars (Alzao (USA)) 7.1f **(68)**
Form - 0
Record 1998 - 1st:0 2nd:0 3rd:0 Ran:1
1998 Turf 0-1: (6f) (g-s)
Currently average filly. **Major D N Chappell [0-1] Mrs G C Maxwell.*

BE THE CHIEF RR 100f 2013[2]

2 ch c Be My Chief (USA) 10.2f **(62)** - Blink Naskra (USA) (Naskra (USA)) 8.8f **(69)**
Form - 12
Record 1998 - 1st:1 2nd:1 3rd:0 Ran:2
Win Prizemoney £3,494 *Total Prizemoney* £14,769
Wins * **1998** May Doncas (GD) 6f 97+ <
1998 Turf 1-2: (6f 1-2) (gd, g-f 1-1)
Currently very useful colt. Turf high 100 - 2nd of 17 to Red Sea (16 Jun Ascot 6f gd RF 2013) - also 1st of 14 from Bertolini (23 May Doncaster RF 1410). It was hard to fault his early -form, which included a fine second place behind Red Sea in the Coventry Stakes at Royal Ascot. Kept off the track for the remainder of the season after injuring a pastern, he has made a full recovery and is being trained for the 2000 Guineas. Described as a 'sleeper' by connections, he is held in high regard and looks capable of winning a decent prize. **T G Mills [1-2] Mrs Stephanie Merrydew.*

BE TRUE BHB 49f40a RR 57f 40a 4654[5]

4 b g Robellino (USA) 9.5f **(68)** - Natchez Trace (Commanche Run) 8.5f **(58)**
Form - 756420805
Record 1998 - 1st:0 2nd:1 3rd:0 Ran:6
Pre1998 - 1st:2 2nd:0 3rd:2 Ran:16
Win Prizemoney £5,874 *Total Prizemoney* £7,628
Wins * 1997 Oct Bright (G-F) H 11.9f 45 56 <
* 1997 Oct Bright (FRM) H 11.9f 35 55+
1998 Turf 0-5: (10f, 12f 3, 15f) (g-f 3, frm 2) 1998 AW 0-1: (16f) (Equi)
Unfurnished, fair gelding, effective 12f, acts on g-f to frm, best on g-f, has worn blinkers. Turf high 57 - 2nd of 9 giving 5lb to Yet Again (2 Jun Brighton 12f g-f RF 1642).

**G L Moore [2-17] A Moore (from A Moore [0-5] Spt 1996).*

BETTER OFFER (IRE) BHB 94f RR 98?f 2058[6]

6 b g Waajib 8.9f **(67)** - Camden's Gift (Camden Town) 9.3f **(53)**
Form - 46
Record 1998 - 1st:0 2nd:0 3rd:0 Ran:2
Pre1998 - 1st:4 2nd:5 3rd:2 Ran:25
Win Prizemoney £62,634 *Total Prizemoney* £99,254
Wins 1996 Spt Ascot (GD) H 12f 98 105 <
1996 Jly Ascot (G-F) H 12f 93 96
1995 Aug Kempto (G-F) H 12f 85 91
1995 Jly Lingfi (G-F) H 10f 77 83
1998 Turf 0-2: (12f 2) (gd, g-f)
Very useful gelding, effective 12f, acts on g-f, likes right handed tracks. Turf high 89. Consistent. A pretty useful handicapper on his day, he has not had much success on the Flat since '96 but has shown some good form over hurdles. He is rather high in the handicap at present, and has consequently faced some stiff tasks in competitive events. He seems to reserve his best for Ascot.

**Mrs A J Perrett [2-15] Sir Eric Parker (from G Harwood [4-19] Nov 1996).*

BETTRON BHB 82f RR 79df 2531[12]

3 b g Alnasr Alwasheek 9.4f **(62)** - Aigua Blava (USA) (Solford (USA)) 13f **(71)**
Form - 4354410
Record 1998 - 1st:1 2nd:0 3rd:1 Ran:7
Pre1998 - 1st:1 2nd:1 3rd:1 Ran:5
Win Prizemoney £5,065 *Total Prizemoney* £8,891
Wins * **1998** Jun Sandow (G-S) C 10f 69+
* 1997 Jly Bright (FRM) C 7f 71+ <
1998 Turf 1-6: (7f, 8f 2, 9f, 10f 1-2) (hvy, g-s, gd 1-2, g-f 2) 1998 AW 0-1: (9f) (Fibr)
Unfurnished, above-average gelding, effective 7 to 9f, best at 7f, acts on g-s to g-f - acts on Fibr, likes tight tracks. Turf high 84 (1st run) - 3rd of 9 giving 14lb to Moon Gorge (28 Mar Warwick 8f g-s RF 0490). (1st run) - 4th of 7 getting 22lb from Diamond Flame (14 Mar Wolverhampton 9f Fibr RF 0429). Won a Sandown claimer with a ton in hand in June, but was well beaten next time. He is something of a character and does not find much off the bridle.

**R Hannon [2-12] R Gander.*

BE VALIANT BHB 45f RR 51f 4990[6]

4 gr g Petong 7.6f **(58)** - Fetlar (Pharly (FR)) 9.8f **(68)**
Form - 00612476
Record 1998 - 1st:1 2nd:1 3rd:0 Ran:8
Pre1998 - 1st:0 2nd:0 3rd:0 Ran:1
Win Prizemoney £2,295 *Total Prizemoney* £2,963
Wins 1998 Jly Ripon (GD) S 10f 50 <
1998 Turf 1-8: (8f 5, 10f 1-3) (sft, g-s, gd 2, g-f 1-2, frm 2)
Workmanlike, fair gelding, effective 10f, acts on gd to g-f, best on g-f, has worn blinkers, prefers tight tracks. Turf high 51 - also 1st of 13 from Diamond Crown (6 Jly Ripon RF 2566).

**Mrs N Macauley [0-2] G Wiltshire (from J R Fanshawe [1-7] Spt 1998).*

BEVELED HAWTHORN RR 24f 2273[10]

3 b f Beveled (USA) 6.9f **(64)** - Sideloader Special (Song) 7.2f **(61)**
Form - 00
Record 1998 - 1st:0 2nd:0 3rd:0 Ran:2
1998 Turf 0-2: (6f, 7f) (gd 2)
Leggy, currently little account filly. Turf high 24.

**M P Bielby [0-2] Mrs Margaret Dunning.*

BEVELENA BHB 74f RR 76f 3569[2]

2 ch f Beveled (USA) 6.9f **(64)** - Bella Helena (Balidar) 7.9f **(63)**
Form - 62212
Record 1998 - 1st:1 2nd:3 3rd:0 Ran:5
Win Prizemoney £3,037 *Total Prizemoney* £5,577
Wins * **1998** Aug Haydoc (G-S) H 5f 62 76 <
1998 Turf 1-4: (5f 1-4) (g-f 1-4) 1998 AW 0-1: (5f) (Fibr)
Above-average filly. Turf high 76 - 2nd of 4 getting 1lb from Key (12 Aug Brighton 5f g-f RF 3569) - also 1st of 9 getting 13lb from Ingenious (6 Aug Haydock RF 3405). She won a Haydock nursery in good style, seeming to appreciate the easier ground.

**P D Evans [1-5] Mrs F A Veasey.*

BEVERLEY MONKEY (IRE) BHB 64f71a RR 77f 71a 4183[15]

2 b f Fayruz 6.6f **(63)** - Godly Light (FR) (Vayrann) 9.7f **(74)**
Form - 411022660310
Record 1998 - 1st:3 2nd:2 3rd:1 Ran:12
Win Prizemoney £6,898 *Total Prizemoney* £9,226
Wins * **1998** Aug Lingfi (FRM) C 6f 66
* **1998** Jun Hamilt (GD) C 5f 71+
* **1998** May Newcas (G-F) C 6f 83+ <
1998 Turf 3-11: (5f 1-3, 6f 2-5, 7f 3) (hvy, g-s, gd 3, g-f 2-2, frm 1-4)
1998 AW 0-1: (6f) (Fibr)
Above-average filly, effective 6f, acts on frm, has worn blinkers. Turf high 83 - 1st of 9 giving 4lb to Cannylass (21 May Newcastle

RF 1367). Inconsistent. **J Berry [3-12] The Monkey Partnership.*

BEVIER BHB 60f **RR 60f** 1243[17]

4 b c Nashwan (USA) 10.3f **(79)** - Bevel (USA) (Mr Prospector (USA)) 8.8f **(78)**
Form - 0
Record 1998 - 1st:0 2nd:0 3rd:0 Ran:1
Pre1998 - 1st:1 2nd:0 3rd:0 Ran:7
Win Prizemoney £3,613 *Total Prizemoney* £3,661
Wins 1997 Jun Yarmou (FRM) 8f 69 <
1998 Turf 0-1: (10f) (g-f)
Tall, average colt, effective 8f, acts on frm.
**Mrs J Cecil [0-2] Mrs J Cecil (from C E Brittain [1-7] Oct 1997).*

BEWARE **RR 75f** 4354[12]

3 br g Warning 8.1f **(77)** - Dancing Spirit (IRE) (Ahonoora) 8.1f **(73)**
Form - 700230
Record 1998 - 1st:0 2nd:1 3rd:1 Ran:6
Pre1998 - 1st:1 2nd:1 3rd:2 Ran:8
Win Prizemoney £5,345 *Total Prizemoney* £9,319
Wins 1997 Oct Newbur (G-S) H 6f 81 84 <
1998 Turf 0-6: (5f, 6f 3, 7f 2) (hvy, sft, gd, g-f 2, frm)
Scopey, above-average gelding, effective 5 to 7f, best at 6f, acts on gd to frm. Turf high 75 - 3rd of 20 getting 6lb from Indian Spark (11 Spt Doncaster 5f g-f RF 4228). Inconsistent.
**D Nicholls [0-2] John Wilman (from R W Armstrong [1-12] Aug 1998).*

BE WARNED BHB 66f80a **RR 66f 80a** 5079[5]

7 b g Warning 8.1f **(77)** - Sagar (Habitat) 9.4f **(70)**
Form - 43022131711580354215
Record 1998 - 1st:5 2nd:2 3rd:2 Ran:16
Pre1998 - 1st:5 2nd:8 3rd:6 Ran:60
Win Prizemoney £40,380 *Total Prizemoney* £63,156
Wins * 1998 Oct Newbur (HVY) H 7f 56 66
* 1998 *Mar Southw (STD) H 8f 73 79* <
* 1998 *Mar Wolver (STD) H 9.4f 69 73*
* 1998 *Feb Wolver (STD) H 9.4f 62 69*
* 1998 *Jan Southw (STD) H 7f 55 55+*
* 1997 Spt Yarmou (FRM) H 6f 44 49
1995 *Nov Southw (STD) H 7f 75 76*
1995 Spt Yarmou (GD) H 6f 70 72
1994 Spt Haydoc (GD) H 6f 75 73
1994 Jun Kempto (G-F) H 7f 66 67
1998 Turf 1-5: (7f 1-4, 8f) (sft 1-2, g-f 2, frm) 1998 AW 4-11: (6f, 7f 1-2, 8f 1-4, 9f 2-3, 10f) (Equi 2, Fibr 4-9)
Above-average gelding, effective 8 to 9f, best at 9f, - acts on Fibr, mostly wears blinkers (effectively), and likes Wolverhampton. Turf high 66. AW high 79 - 1st of 12 giving 1lb to First Maite (17 Mar Southwell RF 0437) - also 1st of 13 giving 13lb to Dr Edgar (7 Mar Wolverhampton RF 0406). He managed just one win from umpteen efforts in 1997, which came over six furlongs at Yarmouth in September. However, he has really been in sparking form on Fibresand since the start of 1998, gaining four wins to date, and also bolted up in an apprentice handicap on heavy ground at Newbury in October. A mile at Southwell or the extended nine furlongs at Wolverhampton seem to bring out the best in him now.
**J Pearce [6-25] A J Thompson (from M Dods [0-13] Aug 1997).*

BEWITCHING LADY BHB 39f36a **RR 46f 36a** 2885[8]

4 ch f Primo Dominie 7.2f **(67)** - Spirit of India (Indian King (USA)) 7.4f **(64)**
Form - 608
Record 1998 - 1st:0 2nd:0 3rd:0 Ran:3
Pre1998 - 1st:1 2nd:2 3rd:2 Ran:17
Win Prizemoney £3,201 *Total Prizemoney* £6,491
Wins * 1997 Spt Yarmou (G-F) C 11.5f 51 <
1998 Turf 0-3: (12f 2, 13f) (frm 3)
Scopey, moderate filly, effective 11 to 13f, best at 11f, acts on frm, has worn blinkers, prefers left handed tracks, favours tight tracks. Turf high 46 (1st run) - 6th of 6 getting 11lb from Cheek To Cheek (18 May Bath 13f frm RF 1294). **D W P Arbuthnot [1-20] T S Redman.*

BEYOND CALCULATION (USA) BHB 54f **RR 64f** 4918[10]

4 ch g Geiger Counter (USA) 7.8f **(85)** -Placer Queen (Habitat) 9.4f **(70)**
Form - 0634857700
Record 1998 - 1st:0 2nd:0 3rd:1 Ran:10
Pre1998 - 1st:1 2nd:1 3rd:1 Ran:8
Win Prizemoney £3,525 *Total Prizemoney* £6,170
Wins 1997 Oct Redcar (G-F) 6f 74 <
1998 Turf 0-10: (6f 9, 7f) (g-s, gd 3, g-f 2, frm 4)
Scopey, average gelding, effective 6 to 7f, best at 7f, acts on g-f to frm - acts on Fibr, best on g-f. Turf high 64.
**J M Bradley [0-10] E A Hayward (from P W Harris [1-8] Oct 1997).*

BHAVNAGAR (IRE) BHB 29f **RR 10f** 4015[5]

7 gr g Darshaan 11.9f **(81)** - Banana Peel (Green Dancer (USA)) 10.3f **(74)**
Form - 05
Record 1998 - 1st:0 2nd:0 3rd:0 Ran:2
1998 Turf 0-2: (15f, 16f) (g-s, gd)
Poor gelding. Turf high 10 (began Aug). **B Ellison [1-9] E J Berry.*

BIANCONI (USA) **RR 119f** 4726a[12]

3 b c Danzig (USA) 8.1f **(88)** - Fall Aspen (USA) (Pretense (USA)) 6.3f **(88)**
Form - 1451210
1998 Turf 3-7: (5f, 6f 3-4, 7f, 8f) (sft, gd 2-4, g-f 1-1, frm)
High-class colt, effective 6f, acts on gd to frm. Turf high 119 - 1st of 9 getting 2lb from Russian Revival (26 Spt Ascot RF 4492) - also 1st of 6 giving 2lb to Remarkable Style (18 Jly Leopardstown RF 3010a). Inconsistent. He won a heavy-ground Navan maiden by a street on his reappearance, and ran a good fourth in the Irish Guineas. He was slightly disappointing when unplaced in the Jersey Stakes, but returned successfully to sprinting after that, winning at Leopardstown and gaining his biggest win to date in the Diadem. He was taken off his feet in the Abbaye and, despite his Navan win, he is probably better over six furlongs on a sound surface. **A P O'Brien in IRE [3-8] M Tabor & Mrs John Magnier.*

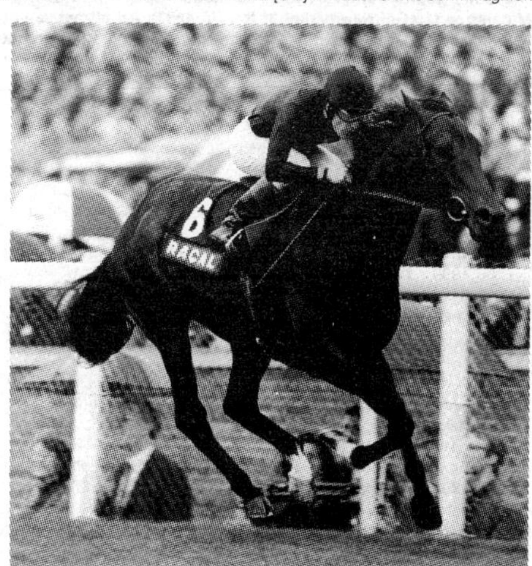

Bianconi lands his first Group success

BICTON PARK BHB 34f43a **RR 32f 43a** 2894[14]

4 b g Distant Relative 7f **(69)** - Merton Mill (Dominion) 8.5f **(63)**
Form - 080000
Record 1998 - 1st:0 2nd:0 3rd:0 Ran:6
Pre1998 - 1st:0 2nd:0 3rd:0 Ran:8
Win Prizemoney £0 *Total Prizemoney* £212
1998 Turf 0-5: (5f 3, 6f 2) (g-s, frm 4) 1998 AW 0-1: (5f) (Fibr)
Scopey, very moderate gelding, often wears blinkers. Turf high 47.
**K C Comerford [0-10] The Old Style Partnership (from D Morley [0-4] Nov 1996).*

BID ME WELCOME **RR 66f** 2902[4]

2 b c Alzao (USA) 9.8f **(73)** - Blushing Barada (USA) (Blushing Groom (FR)) 10.3f **(76)**
Form - 4
Record 1998 - 1st:0 2nd:0 3rd:0 Ran:1

Win Prizemoney £0 *Total Prizemoney* £247
1998 Turf 0-1: (6f) (gd)
Average colt. (DEAD) **M Johnston [0-1] Maktoum Al Maktoum.*

BIENAMADO (USA) RR 102+f 5134a[2]
2 ch c Bien Bien (USA) - Nakterjal (Vitiges (FR)) 8.2f **(59)**
Form - 112
Record 1998 - 1st:2 2nd:1 3rd:0 Ran:3
Win Prizemoney £27,131 *Total Prizemoney* £43,292
Wins * **1998** Oct Longch (SFT) G3 9f 102+ <
* **1998** Spt Haydoc (GD) 8.1f 82+
1998 Turf 2-3: (8f 1-1, 9f 1-1, 10f) (hvy, sft 1-1, frm 1-1)
Currently very useful colt. Turf high 102 (began Spt) - 1st of 5 from Persianlux (3 Oct Longchamp RF 4715a). He did exceptionally well for a relatively weak-looking juvenile, dead-heating at Haydock and then running out a most impressive winner of the Group Three Prix de Conde at Longchamp. Unable to cope with appalling ground when returned to France for the Group One Criterium de Saint-Cloud in November, he is being trained for the French Derby and should develop into a classy middle-distance three-year-old. **P W Chapple-Hyam [2-3] J Toffan & T McCaffery.*

BIENNALE (IRE) BHB 94f **RR 90f** 4823[2]
2 b c Caerleon (USA) 10.9f **(79)** - Malvern Beauty (Shirley Heights) 10.3f **(74)**
Form - 222
Record 1998 - 1st:0 2nd:3 3rd:0 Ran:3
Win Prizemoney £0 *Total Prizemoney* £5,677
1998 Turf 0-3: (8f 3) (gd, frm 2)
Currently useful colt. Turf high 90 (began Spt) - 2nd of 23 to Mutafaweq (15 Oct Newmarket 8f frm RF 4823). An attractive sort with middle-distance breeding, he was runner-up on all three outings. He will surely have little difficulty getting off the mark in 1999. **Sir Michael Stoute [0-3] M Tabor & Mrs John Magnier.*

BIFF-EM (IRE) BHB 42f **RR 38f** 5059[16]
4 ch g Durgam (USA) 12.3f **(53)** - Flash The Gold (Ahonoora) 8.1f **(73)**
Form - 383703534140755770
Record 1998 - 1st:1 2nd:0 3rd:4 Ran:18
Pre1998 - 1st:1 2nd:0 3rd:1 Ran:10
Win Prizemoney £6,707 *Total Prizemoney* £9,312
Wins * **1998** Jly Hamilt (FRM) H 6f 37 45
* 1996 Jun Hamilt (GD) 5f 61 <
1998 Turf 1-18: (5f 6, 6f 1-9, 7f 2, 8f) (sft 3, g-s, gd 9, g-f 2, frm 1-3)
Scopey, very moderate gelding. Turf high 46.
**Miss L A Perratt [2-28] Cree Lodge Racing Club.*

BIG AL (IRE) BHB 70f **RR 72f** 2904[6]
2 b c Shalford (IRE) 7.8f **(63)** - Our Pet (Mummy's Pet) 7.7f **(60)**
Form - 016
Record 1998 - 1st:1 2nd:0 3rd:0 Ran:3
Win Prizemoney £2,304 *Total Prizemoney* £2,304
Wins **1998** Jly Haydoc (G-S) S 6f 72 <
1998 Turf 1-3: (6f 1-2, 7f) (gd, frm 1-2)
Currently above-average colt. Turf high 72 - 1st of 9 from Hadeqa (2 Jly Haydock RF 2467).
**R A Fahey [0-1] J A Campbell (from R Hannon [1-2] Jly 1998).*

BIG BANG BHB 41f55a **RR 44f 55a** 617[10]
4 b g Superlative 8.8f **(57)**- Good Time Girl (Good Times(ITY)) 6.6f **(54)**
Form - 0435740
Record 1998 - 1st:0 2nd:0 3rd:1 Ran:6
Pre1998 - 1st:2 2nd:0 3rd:2 Ran:12
Win Prizemoney £4,857 *Total Prizemoney* £6,217
Wins * 1997 *Jun Southw (STD) H 12f 61 62*
* 1997 *Mar Wolver (STD) 9.4f 63* <
1998 Turf 0-1: (12f) (sft) 1998 AW 0-5: (11f, 12f 4) (Fibr 5)
Workmanlike, average gelding, effective 8 to 12f, best at 12f, - acts on Fibr, has worn blinkers, favours left handed tracks. AW high 61 - 3rd of 12 giving 15lb to Grovefair Lad (7 Feb Wolverhampton 12f Fibr RF 0245).
**M Blanshard [2-17] Gregory West (from M McCormack [0-1] Aug 1996).*

BIG BEN BHB 64a **RR 68f** 5003[8]
4 ch c Timeless Times (USA) 6.1f **(56)** - Belltina (Belfort (FR)) 6.8f **(63)**
Form - 13817087520738
Record 1998 - 1st:2 2nd:1 3rd:2 Ran:14
Pre1998 - 1st:4 2nd:0 3rd:3 Ran:18
Win Prizemoney £21,591 *Total Prizemoney* £26,631
Wins * **1998** May Newmar (G-F) 7f 77
* **1998** Apr Folkes (GD) H 6.9f 64 69
* 1997 *Jun Lingfi (STD) C 7f 61*
* 1997 Jun Goodwo (G-F) C 7f 71+
* 1996 Aug Lingfi (G-F) 5f 93+ <
* 1996 Jly Sandow (G-F) 5f 80
1998 Turf 2-12: (6f 2, 7f 2-10) (sft, gd 1-3, g-f 4, frm 1-4) 1998 AW 0-2: (6f, 7f) (Equi, Fibr)
Neat, average colt, effective 7f, acts on gd to frm, likes right handed tracks. Turf high 77 - 1st of 16 giving 3lb to Topton (16 May Newmarket RF 1270) - also 1st of 14 giving 26lb to Clonoe (1 Apr Folkestone RF 0540). AW high 63 (began Oct). Consistent.
**R Hannon [6-32] Lady Davis.*

BIG BUYER (USA) BHB 68f **RR 70f** 1625[6]
3 b f Quest for Fame 12.8f **(75)** - Royal Procession (USA) (Lyphard (USA)) 9.9f **(72)**
Form - 456
Record 1998 - 1st:0 2nd:0 3rd:0 Ran:3
Win Prizemoney £0 *Total Prizemoney* £260
1998 Turf 0-3: (8f, 10f, 12f) (sft, g-f, frm)
Scopey, currently above-average filly. Turf high 70.
**I A Balding [0-3] Robin Scully.*

BIG CHIEF RR 61tf 3927[20]
2 ch c Be My Chief (USA) 10.2f **(62)** - Grove Daffodil (IRE) (Salt Dome (USA))
Form - 670
Record 1998 - 1st:0 2nd:0 3rd:0 Ran:3
1998 Turf 0-3: (6f 2, 7f) (frm 3)
Currently average colt. Turf high 61 (began Jly).
**M H Tompkins [0-3] P H Betts (Holdings) Ltd.*

BIG OZ BHB 57f **RR 63f** 4732[12]
2 b g Kylian (USA) 8.1f **(66)** - Beau Dada (IRE) (Pine Circle (USA))
Form - 003660
Record 1998 - 1st:0 2nd:0 3rd:1 Ran:6
Win Prizemoney £0 *Total Prizemoney* £262
1998 Turf 0-6: (6f 2, 7f 4) (g-s, gd, g-f 2, frm 2)
Average gelding, effective 7f, acts on g-f, has worn blinkers. Turf high 63 - 3rd of 10 to Lokomotiv (21 Jly Yarmouth 7f g-f RF 2977).
**J Cullinan [0-6] Alan Spargo Ltd Toolmakers.*

BIG TARGET (IRE) BHB 60f **RR 65df** 1064[6]
4 b g Suave Dancer (USA) 10.7f **(68)** - Prima Domina (FR) (Dominion) 8.5f **(63)**
Form - 06
Record 1998 - 1st:0 2nd:0 3rd:0 Ran:2
Pre1998 - 1st:0 2nd:0 3rd:0 Ran:4
Win Prizemoney £0 *Total Prizemoney* £206
1998 Turf 0-2: (11f, 12f) (sft, gd)
Scopey, average gelding. Turf high 16.
**R Allan [0-5] Ian Dalgleish (from Sir Michael Stoute [0-4] Oct 1997).*

BIG WHEEL BHB 60f **RR 64f** 4804[14]
3 ch g Mujtahid (USA) 7.4f **(69)** - Numuthej (USA) (Nureyev (USA)) 8.7f **(78)**
Form - 2530
Record 1998 - 1st:0 2nd:1 3rd:1 Ran:4
Win Prizemoney £0 *Total Prizemoney* £1,500
1998 Turf 0-4: (8f 2, 9f, 10f) (gd 3, frm)
Light-framed, average gelding, mostly wears blinkers. Turf high 64 (1st run) - 2nd of 8 getting 6lb from I Can't Remember (24 Jun Chester 10f gd RF 2231). **M C Pipe [0-6] Jim Ennis.*

BILKO BHB 77f **RR 73f** 4582[2]
4 gr g Risk Me (FR) 8f **(53)** - Princess Tara (Prince Sabo) 7.2f **(62)**
Form - 081031322
Record 1998 - 1st:2 2nd:2 3rd:2 Ran:9
Pre1998 - 1st:1 2nd:1 3rd:0 Ran:5
Win Prizemoney £10,590 *Total Prizemoney* £15,940
Wins * **1998** Spt Ayr (G-S) H 5f 63 73 <
* **1998** Aug Catter (G-F) C 5f 59
1996 Apr Lingfi (G-S) 5f 64

1998 Turf 2-9: (5f 2-6, 6f 3) (g-s 1-1, gd 2, g-f 3, frm 1-3)
Strong, above-average gelding, has broken blood-vessels, effective 5 to 6f, best at 5f, acts on g-s to frm, best on g-f. Turf high 73 - 2nd of 16 giving 8lb to Royal Dome (30 Spt Newcastle 5f g-f RF 4582) - also 1st of 27 getting 22lb from Storyteller (17 Spt Ayr RF 4323). Formerly trained by Geoff Lewis, he had his problems, especially with broken blood-vessels, and was off the track for a year after June '97. Now with Dandy Nicholls, he was in cracking form in the autumn.
**D Nicholls [2-9] Promotions,I Blakey, Greaves (from G Lewis [1-5] Jun 1997).*

BILLADDIE BHB 72f58a **RR 70f 58a** 5126[5]
5 b g Touch of Grey 8.1f **(47)**-Young Lady (Young Generation) 7.7f **(63)**
Form - 8331333704213062212315
Record 1998 - 1st:4 2nd:4 3rd:5 Ran:19
Pre1998 - 1st:1 2nd:0 3rd:3 Ran:11
Win Prizemoney £20,975 *Total Prizemoney* £31,978
Wins * **1998** Oct Newbur (HVY) H 10f 66 70 <
* **1998** Spt Kempto (G-S) H 12f 58 61
* **1998** Jun Newmar (GD) H 12f 52 58
* **1998** *Jan Lingfi (STD) H 10f 51 61*
1996 *Jan Lingfi (STD) 8f 53*
1998 Turf 3-14: (8f, 10f 1-3, 11f 2, 12f 2-7, 14f) (sft 1-1, g-s 3, gd 1-2, g-f 1-5, frm 3) 1998 AW 1-5: (10f 1-5) (Equi 1-5)
Above-average gelding, effective 10 to 12f, best at 12f, acts on sft to frm - acts on Equi, likes right handed tracks. Turf high 70 - 1st of 15 getting 20lb from Alkateb (23 Oct Newbury RF 4966) - also 1st of 18 giving 4lb to Duello (9 Spt Kempton RF 4194). AW high 61 (1st run) - 1st of 7 giving 10lb to Four of Spades (8 Jan Lingfield RF 0049). Consistent. Did connections proud and always gave his best, but looked in the handicapper's grip on his final start.
**R M Flower [4-22] Richard Gurr (from R Boss [1-8] Mar 1997).*

BILLICHANG BHB 50f **RR 50f** 4546[7]
2 b c Chilibang 7f **(55)** - Swing O'The Kilt (Hotfoot) 10.5f **(59)**
Form - 7847
Record 1998 - 1st:0 2nd:0 3rd:0 Ran:4
Win Prizemoney £0 *Total Prizemoney* £240
1998 Turf 0-2: (6f, 7f) (frm 2) 1998 AW 0-2: (6f, 8f) (Fibr 2)
Fair colt. Turf high 50 (began Jly). AW high 50 (began Jly).
**P Howling [0-4] Paul Howling Racing Syndicate.*

BILLY BOX BHB 45f **RR 48f** 3070[19]
6 gr g Lord Bud 8.2f **(52)** - Counter Coup (Busted) 10.2f **(61)**
Form - 8070
Record 1998 - 1st:0 2nd:0 3rd:0 Ran:4
1998 Turf 0-4: (7f, 12f, 14f, 22f) (gd 2, g-f, frm)
Moderate gelding. Turf high 48.
**G M McCourt [2-11] Alec Tuckerman.*

BILLYCAN (IRE) BHB 25f **RR 7?f** 3431[18]
4 b g Mac's Imp (USA) 5.6f **(54)** - Sassalin (Sassafras (FR)) 9.6f **(69)**
Form - 00
Record 1998 - 1st:0 2nd:0 3rd:0 Ran:2
Pre1998 - 1st:0 2nd:0 3rd:0 Ran:7
1998 Turf 0-2: (7f, 12f) (g-f, hrd)
Unfurnished, little account gelding, has worn blinkers. (began Jly).
**B P J Baugh [0-9] Nigel Taylor.*

BILLY MCCAW BHB 84f **RR 85f** 3480[1]
2 b c Efisio 7.7f **(69)** - Thakhayr (Sadler's Wells (USA)) 10f **(76)**
Form - 4331
Record 1998 - 1st:1 2nd:0 3rd:2 Ran:4
Win Prizemoney £3,403 *Total Prizemoney* £4,797
Wins * **1998** Aug Epsom (G-F) 6f 85 <
1998 Turf 1-4: (6f 1-1, 7f 3) (gd 1-1, g-f 2, frm)
Useful colt. Turf high 85 - 1st of 7 giving 5lb to Brown's Flight (9 Aug Epsom RF 3480). **P F I Cole [1-4] Lord Lloyd-Webber.*

BILLY MOONSHINE BHB 54f **RR 63f** 4887[11]
6 ch g Nicholas Bill 9.8f **(56)** - Indian Moonshine (Warpath) 12.3f **(52)**
Form - 7500
Record 1998 - 1st:0 2nd:0 3rd:0 Ran:4
1998 Turf 0-4: (8f, 10f, 12f 2) (g-s, g-f 2, frm)
Average gelding. Turf high 63 (began Spt).
**G L Moore [0-4] Graham Haupt.*

BILLY NOMAITE BHB 53f **RR 65f** 4578[11]
4 ch g Komaite (USA) 6.9f **(61)** - Lucky Monashka (Lucky Wednesday) 8f **(50)**
Form - 502080
Record 1998 - 1st:0 2nd:1 3rd:0 Ran:6
Pre1998 - 1st:0 2nd:2 3rd:1 Ran:5
Win Prizemoney £0 *Total Prizemoney* £2,752
1998 Turf 0-6: (8f, 9f, 12f 4) (g-s 2, gd, g-f, frm 2)
Leggy, average gelding, effective 9 to 12f, acts on g-s to frm, likes right handed tracks. Turf high 65 - 2nd of 6 giving 15lb to Altitude (3 Jun Newcastle 12f g-s RF 1704). **Mrs S J Smith [0-11] R Preston.*

BIMBOLA (FR) **RR 117f** 5055a[6]
4 br f Bikala 12f **(79)** - Agnes Lily (USA) (Raise A Cup (USA)) 7.6f **(74)**
Form - 136
1998 Turf 1-3: (12f 1-1, 13f, 16f) (hvy, sft 1-2)
Currently high-class filly. Turf high 117 (began Spt) - 3rd of 7 to Lexa (3 Oct Longchamp 13f sft RF 4717a). A French Listed race winner in September courtesy of the stewards, she was subsequently found out in Group company.
**J BertranDeBalanda in FR [1-3] T Attias.*

BINA GARDENS BHB 97f **RR 97f** 1259[3]
4 b f Shirley Heights 12.1f **(76)** - Balabina (USA) (Nijinsky (CAN)) 10.3f **(77)**
Form - 3
Record 1998 - 1st:0 2nd:0 3rd:1 Ran:1
Pre1998 - 1st:2 2nd:0 3rd:0 Ran:5
Win Prizemoney £8,180 *Total Prizemoney* £10,700
Wins * 1997 Spt Chepst (GD) 10.2f 97 <
* 1997 Aug Ripon (GD) 10f 74
1998 Turf 0-1: (13f) (frm)
Workmanlike, very useful filly, effective 10 to 13f, acted on gd to frm. (1st run) - 3rd of 8 getting 5lb from Yorkshire (16 May Newbury 13f frm RF 1259). Third in a Listed race on her only run. (DEAD) **H R A Cecil [2-6] K Abdulla.*

BIN ALMOOJID RR 760[7]
2 b c Almoojid 7f **(36)** - Stella Royale (Astronef)
Form - 7
Record 1998 - 1st:0 2nd:0 3rd:0 Ran:1
1998 AW 0-1: (5f) (Fibr)
Currently very poor colt - 7th of 7 to Consultant (18 Apr Wolverhampton 5f Fibr RF 0760).
**Miss Kate Whitehouse [0-1] Duckhaven Stud.*

BIN FAA BHB 40f56a **RR 42f 56a** 2457[9]
3 b g Superlative 8.8f **(57)**-A Nymph Too Far (IRE)(Precocious)8.6f **(62)**
Form - 4645400460
Record 1998 - 1st:0 2nd:0 3rd:0 Ran:10
Win Prizemoney £0 *Total Prizemoney* £443
1998 Turf 0-5: (7f, 8f 3, 10f) (g-s, gd, g-f, frm 2) 1998 AW 0-5: (8f 2, 9f 2, 11f) (Equi 2, Fibr 3)
Workmanlike, fair gelding, effective 8f, acts on g-f, has worn blinkers (very effectively). Turf high 42 - 4th of 12 getting 1lb from Nouveau Cheval (26 May Leicester 8f g-f RF 1469). AW high 51.
**Dr J D Scargill [0-10] The Vibrations.*

BINT ALLAYL BHB 100f **RR 110+f** 3772[1]
2 b f Green Desert (USA) 7.8f **(78)** - Society Lady (USA) (Mr Prospector (USA)) 8.8f **(78)**
Form - 2111
Record 1998 - 1st:3 2nd:1 3rd:0 Ran:4
Win Prizemoney £84,767 *Total Prizemoney* £86,927
Wins * **1998** Aug York (G-F) G2 6f 110+ <
* **1998** Jun Ascot (GD) G3 5f 106+
* **1998** May Sandow (G-F) L 5f 99+
1998 Turf 3-4: (5f 2-3, 6f 1-1) (gd 2-3, frm 1-1)
Group-class filly. Turf high 110 - 1st of 10 getting 2lb from Wannabe Grand (20 Aug York RF 3772) - also 1st of 17 from Pipalong (17 Jun Ascot RF 2054). She was undoubtedly the best two-year-old filly in action last season, and would have been a short-priced favourite for the Cheveley Park Stakes had a hock injury not prevented her from running. The blistering turn-of-foot she unleashed when winning the Queen Mary and Lowther Stakes is a rare commodity, and leads to question marks about her staying a mile in the 1000 Guineas. A tendency to race keenly is not in

her favour, but her sheer natural ability makes her the one they will all have to beat at Newmarket in the spring. Remains with Mick Channon, who handled her so well.

**M R Channon [3-4] Sheikh Ahmed Al Maktoum.*

BINT KALDOUN (IRE) BHB 73f **RR 77f** 4854[30]

3 b f Kaldoun (FR) 9.9f **(84)** - Shy Danceuse (FR) (Groom Dancer (USA))

Form - 2686220

Bint Allayl is heading for the Guineas next May

BINTANG (IRE) BHB 105f **RR 99f** 1779[4]

3 ch c Soviet Star (USA) 8.6f **(74)** - Brush Away (Ahonoora) 8.1f **(73)**

Form - 54

Record **1998** - 1st:0 2nd:0 3rd:0 Ran:2
Pre1998 - 1st:2 2nd:1 3rd:0 Ran:3

Win Prizemoney £15,312 *Total Prizemoney* £20,310

Wins 1997 Spt Doncas (G-F) 6f 109 <
1997 Aug York (GD) 6f 104+

1998 Turf 0-2: (7f, 8f) (gd, g-f)

Scopey, very useful colt. Turf high 104. A useful juvenile, he has proved disappointing since joining the Godolphin team.

**S bin Suroor [0-2] Godolphin (from P F I Cole [2-3] Oct 1997).*

BINTANG TIMOR (USA) BHB 65f **RR 73f** 5079[20]

4 ch g Mt Livermore (USA) 7.7f **(90)** - Frisky Kitten (USA) (Isopach (USA)) 6f **(84)**

Form - 024280148268000

Record **1998** - 1st:1 2nd:3 3rd:0 Ran:15
Pre1998 - 1st:0 2nd:1 3rd:0 Ran:5

Win Prizemoney £3,246 *Total Prizemoney* £10,101

Wins *** 1998** Jly Leices (GD) H 6f 67 70 <

1998 Turf 1-15: (6f 1-9, 7f 6) (hvy, sft, gd 3, g-f 4, frm 1-6)

Scopey, above-average gelding, effective 6 to 7f, best at 6f, acts on g-f to frm, best on frm. Turf high 73 - 2nd of 13 giving 5lb to Stylish Ways (28 Aug Newmarket 6f frm RF 3928) - also 1st of 16 giving 29lb to Ballard Lady (16 Jly Leicester RF 2857). A somewhat disappointing sort, he is not a straightforward ride and is one to have reservations about.

**W J Musson [1-15] Lyons & Broughton (from P F I Cole [0-5] May 1997).*

Record **1998** - 1st:0 2nd:3 3rd:0 Ran:7
Pre1998 - 1st:0 2nd:0 3rd:0 Ran:1

Win Prizemoney £0 *Total Prizemoney* £3,631

1998 Turf 0-7: (7f 2, 8f 2, 10f 2, 12f) (g-s, gd 2, g-f 4)

Leggy, above-average filly, effective 7 to 12f, acts on g-s to g-f, has worn blinkers. Turf high 77 - 2nd of 12 giving 9lb to Forest Fire (16 Spt Sandown 8f g-f RF 4310).

**C E Brittain [0-6] Mohammed Jaber (from D R Loder [0-2] Apr 1998).*

BINT NADIA BHB 46f55a **RR 45f 55a** 4388[8]

3 b f Deploy 11.4f **(67)** - Faisalah (Gay Mecene (USA)) 8.6f **(69)**

Form - 3532158058

Record **1998** - 1st:1 2nd:1 3rd:2 Ran:10
Pre1998 - 1st:1 2nd:0 3rd:1 Ran:7

Win Prizemoney £5,114 *Total Prizemoney* £6,633

Wins *** 1998** *Apr Wolver (STD) H 9.4f 57 50*
1997 Aug Catter (G-F) S 7f 57 <

1998 Turf 0-2: (9f, 10f) (gd 2) 1998 AW 1-8: (8f 5, 9f 1-2, 12f) (Fibr 1-8)

Lengthy, average filly, effective 7 to 8f, best at 8f, acts on gd to g-f - acts on Fibr, prefers left handed tracks, prefers tight tracks. Turf high 39. AW high 61 (1st run) - 3rd of 12 giving 7lb to Sharp Monkey (26 Jan Southwell 8f Fibr RF 0160). She won a Catterick seller in August '97, and has shown some fair form on Fibresand since the start of 1998, including when winning a handicap at Wolverhampton in April. Now hurdling with Lord Tyrone.

**Miss J F Craze [1-10] T Marshall (from J D Bethell [1-7] Oct 1997).*

BINT ST JAMES BHB 54f53a **RR 63f 53a** 4544[7]

3 b f Shareef Dancer (USA) 10.1f **(67)** - St James's Antigua (IRE) (Law Society (USA)) 9.9f **(70)**

Form - 744340347

Record 1998 - 1st:0 2nd:0 3rd:2 Ran:9
Win Prizemoney £0 *Total Prizemoney* £1,849
1998 Turf 0-5: (12f 4, 16f) (gd 2, g-f, frm 2) 1998 AW 0-4: (7f, 8f, 12f, 14f) (Fibr 4)
Lengthy, average filly, effective 12f, acts on gd - acts on Fibr, prefers tight tracks. Turf high 63 - 4th of 6 giving 6lb to Semi Circle (6 Jly Ripon 12f gd RF 2568). AW high 58 - 3rd of 10 getting 17lb from Lucky Begonia (14 Aug Southwell 12f Fibr RF 3641). Consistent. **J D Bethell [0-9] Sheikh Amin Dahlawi.*

BIONIC RR 103++f 3220[1]

2 br f Zafonic (USA) 9f **(83)** - Bonash **(103f)** (Rainbow Quest (USA)) 10.4f **(75)**
Form - 1
Record 1998 - 1st:1 2nd:0 3rd:0 Ran:1
Win Prizemoney £10,455 *Total Prizemoney* £10,455
Wins * 1998 Jly Goodwo (G-S) 7f 103++ <
1998 Turf 1-1: (7f 1-1) (gd 1-1)
Currently very useful filly. (1st run) - 1st of 8 from Musical Treat (30 Jly Goodwood RF 3220). She was the talk of the town before her debut at Goodwood in July and duly won in sparkling fashion. The form of that race was boosted several times in the second half of the season and, while we did not have another opportunity to assess her - she bruised a foot - this filly is potentially top-class. Out of a middle-distance winner who finished fifth in the Oaks, she ought to stay at least a mile and a quarter, although we will know more about her after she has run in a 1000 Guineas trial. Her reappearance will be one of the early-season highlights.
**H R A Cecil [1-1] K Abdulla.*

BIRCHWOOD SUN BHB 52f54a RR 58f 54a 4275[7]

8 b g Bluebird (USA) 7.9f **(71)** - Shapely Test (USA) (Elocutionist (USA)) 8f **(77)**
Form - 22111063100087
Record 1998 - 1st:4 2nd:2 3rd:1 Ran:14
Pre1998 - 1st:8 2nd:8 3rd:7 Ran:80
Win Prizemoney £36,335 *Total Prizemoney* £49,387

Wins								
*	**1998**	Jun	Carlis	(G-S)	S	5.9f		58
*	**1998**	May	Newcas	(G-S)	C	7f		61
*	**1998**	Apr	Redcar	(SFT)	S	7f		62
*	**1998**	Apr	Carlis	(G-S)	H	5.9f	48	52
*	1997	May	Carlis	(G-S)	H	5.9f	49	59
*	1995	Spt	Newcas	(GD)	H	7f	61	69
*	1995	Jun	Carlis	(FRM)	H	5.9f	54	60
*	1995	Jun	Hamilt	(FRM)	H	6f	54	58
*	1994	May	Carlis	(HVY)	H	5.9f	56	50+

1998 Turf 4-14: (6f 2-7, 7f 2-5, 8f, 9f) (sft 1-2, g-s, gd 3-8, g-f, frm 2)
Fair gelding, effective 6 to 7f, best at 7f, acts on sft to gd, best on gd, mostly wears blinkers, likes right handed tracks, does well at Carlisle. Turf high 62 - 1st of 10 from Scathebury (30 Apr Redcar RF 0932) - also 1st of 11 getting 3lb from Mujova (4 May Newcastle RF 1022). Only won once in '97, but generally ran well in 1998, completing a hat-trick of victories early on and adding a Newcastle seller in June. A stiff six furlongs suits him best, though he has won over seven. He needs holding up until the last possible moment, and is not an ideal investment for anyone with a weak heart.
**M Dods [9-78] A G Watson (from R Hollinshead [3-16] May 1993).*

BIRD'S EMPIRE (GER) RR 55f 4984[8]

2 b f Doyoun 10.7f **(69)** - Bird's Wing (IRE) (Bluebird (USA)) 7.5f **(69)**
Form - 68
Record 1998 - 1st:0 2nd:0 3rd:0 Ran:2
1998 Turf 0-2: (6f, 7f) (g-s, gd)
Currently fair filly. Turf high 55 (began Spt).
**J L Dunlop [0-2] Mrs H Focke.*

BIRTHDAY VENTURE RR 53f 5058[3]

3 b f Soviet Star (USA) 8.6f **(74)** - Maestrale (Top Ville) 11.7f **(68)**
Form - 3
Record 1998 - 1st:0 2nd:0 3rd:1 Ran:1
Win Prizemoney £0 *Total Prizemoney* £515
1998 Turf 0-1: (7f) (sft)
Neat, currently fair filly. **S P C Woods [0-1] Dr Frank Chao.*

BIRTH OF THE BLUES BHB 70f RR 77f 4583[7]

2 ch c Efisio 7.7f **(69)** - Great Steps **(70f)** (Vaigly Great) 7f **(58)**
Form - 057
Record 1998 - 1st:0 2nd:0 3rd:0 Ran:3
1998 Turf 0-3: (7f, 8f 2) (gd, g-f, frm)
Currently above-average colt. Turf high 77 (began Jly).
**J L Dunlop [0-3] Bob Lalemant.*

BISHOPS COURT BHB 110f RR 116f 5054a[1]

4 ch g Clantime 6.6f **(57)** - Indigo (Primo Dominie) 6.2f **(80)**
Form - 8341722542311
Record 1998 - 1st:3 2nd:3 3rd:2 Ran:13
Pre1998 - 1st:2 2nd:3 3rd:5 Ran:12
Win Prizemoney £75,524 *Total Prizemoney* £130,795

Wins									
*	**1998**	Oct	Longch	(HVY)	G3	5f		115	
*	**1998**	Oct	Newmar	()	L	5f		116	<
*	**1998**	Jun	Epsom	(GD)	LH	5f	102	103	
*	1997	May	Cheste	(SFT)	H	6.1f	83	88++	
*	1996	Spt	Hamilt	(GD)		5f		78+	

1998 Turf 3-13: (5f 3-12, 6f) (hvy 1-1, g-s, gd 1-5, g-f 1-2, frm 4)
Strong, high-class gelding, effective 5f, acts on hvy to frm, best on gd, excels at Newmarket, does well at Chester. Turf high 116 - 1st of 6 giving 3lb to Almaty (1 Oct Newmarket RF 4594) - also 1st of 7 from Easycall (25 Oct Longchamp RF 5054a). Consistent. He is a very useful sprinter who needs to be delivered just at the right time, and gained just reward for his consistency when landing the Vodafone Dash on Derby day in a blanket finish. He was not disgraced in pattern company afterwards, but finished the season on a high by landing a Listed event at Newmarket, and gained his biggest win to date in the Group Three Prix du Petit Couvert. With his trainer retiring, he will be moving to France to be trained by John Hammond. **Mrs J R Ramsden [5-25] D R Brotherton.*

BISHOPSTONE POND (IRE) BHB 40f RR 42f 4413[11]

2 b f Persian Bold 10f **(69)**-Swift And Early (IRE)(Alzao (USA)) 7.1f **(68)**
Form - 0060
Record 1998 - 1st:0 2nd:0 3rd:0 Ran:4
1998 Turf 0-2: (6f 2) (g-f, frm) 1998 AW 0-2: (5f 2) (Fibr 2)
Moderate filly. Turf high 42 (began Jly).
**S Mellor [0-4] The Bishopstone Ducks.*

BIT OF A LAD BHB 38f32a RR 52f 32a 5070[17]

3 br c Touch of Grey 8.1f **(47)** - Lingfield Lass (USA) (Advocator) 10.9f **(80)**
Form - 806002680070
Record 1998 - 1st:0 2nd:1 3rd:0 Ran:10
Pre1998 - 1st:0 2nd:0 3rd:0 Ran:2
Win Prizemoney £0 *Total Prizemoney* £563
1998 Turf 0-8: (7f, 8f 6, 9f) (gd 2, g-f 4, frm 2) 1998 AW 0-2: (8f, 10f) (Equi 2)
Leggy, fair colt. Turf high 52. **R M Flower [0-12] Mrs H Kelleher.*

BIT ON THE SIDE (IRE) BHB 80f RR 82f 1240[12]

9 b m Vision (USA) 10.4f **(57)** - Mistress (USA) (Damascus (USA)) 8.9f **(71)**
Form - 0
Record 1998 - 1st:0 2nd:0 3rd:0 Ran:1
Pre1998 - 1st:7 2nd:5 3rd:3 Ran:43
Win Prizemoney £32,418 *Total Prizemoney* £45,868

Wins									
*	1996	Apr	Warwic	(G-S)	H	10.8f	76	79+	<
	1995	Spt	Doncas	(G-S)	H	12f	70	77	
	1994	May	Sandow	(GD)	H	14f	72	73	
	1994	Apr	Newmar	(G-S)	H	12f	67	74	

1998 Turf 0-1: (12f) (g-f)
Decent mare. Inconsistent.
**N E Berry [1-9] B Beale (from W J Musson [6-35] Oct 1995).*

BITTER SWEET RR 78f 5009[9]

2 gr f Deploy 11.4f **(67)** - Julia Flyte (Drone) 10.3f **(74)**
Form - 5554300
Record 1998 - 1st:0 2nd:0 3rd:1 Ran:7
Win Prizemoney £0 *Total Prizemoney* £531
1998 Turf 0-7: (6f, 7f 3, 8f 3) (sft, gd 2, g-f, frm 3)
Above-average filly, effective 8f, acts on g-f. Turf high 78.
**D R C Elsworth [0-7] J McGarry.*

BIYA (IRE) BHB 39f39a RR 41f 39a 4143[13]

6 ch g Shadeed (USA) 7.7f **(72)** - Rosie Potts (Shareef Dancer (USA)) 9.9f **(73)**
Form - 0D60

Record 1998 - 1st:0 2nd:0 3rd:0 Ran:4
Pre1998 - 1st:2 2nd:1 3rd:1 Ran:10
Win Prizemoney £6,276 *Total Prizemoney* £7,582
Wins * 1997 *Jan Lingfi (STD) H 10f 45 48*
1995 *Jan Lingfi (STD) 8f 56* <
1998 Turf 0-3: (10f 2, 11f) (g-f, frm 2) 1998 AW 0-1: (10f) (Equi)
Moderate gelding, effective 10f, - acts on Equi, has worn blinkers. Turf high 41 (began Jly).
**D McCain[1-25]Champ Chicken Co Ltd(fromMJohnston[1-4]Spt 1995).*

BLACK ARMY BHB 72f RR 68f 1253[10]

3 b c Aragon 7.7f **(58)** - Morgannwg (IRE) (Simply Great (FR)) 8.2f **(65)**
Form - 840
Record 1998 - 1st:0 2nd:0 3rd:0 Ran:3
Win Prizemoney £0 *Total Prizemoney* £217
1998 Turf 0-3: (6f 3) (gd 3)
Currently average colt. Turf high 68. **J M P Eustace [0-3] K J Mercer.*

Bishops Court; a last Group win for Lynda Ramsden

BIZZIE LIZZIE BHB 32f RR 33f 3888[P]

3 ro f Touch of Grey 8.1f **(47)** - Lovely Lizzie (Anax)
Form - 0565P
Record 1998 - 1st:0 2nd:0 3rd:0 Ran:5
1998 Turf 0-2: (10f, 12f) (gd, frm) 1998 AW 0-3: (12f, 14f, 16f) (Equi, Fibr 2)
Light-framed, very moderate filly. Turf high 33. AW high 31 (began Jly) - 5th of 15 getting 5lb from Happy Medium (14 Aug Southwell 14f Fibr RF 3638). (DEAD) **D T Thom [0-5] R Foulds.*

BLACK AMBER (IRE) RR 99f 3556a[4]

2 b c College Chapel - Flying Diva (Chief Singer) 8.9f **(66)**
Form - 1314
Record 1998 - 1st:2 2nd:0 3rd:1 Ran:4
Win Prizemoney £39,701 *Total Prizemoney* £47,921
Wins * **1998** Jly Maison (GD) G2 5.5f 99 <
* **1998** Jun Newmar (GD) 6f 82+
1998 Turf 2-4: (6f 2-4) (gd 1-1, g-f 1-1, frm 2)
Very useful colt. Turf high 99 - 1st of 4 from Bertolini (25 Jly Maisons-laffitte RF 3224a). Won a maiden on his debut, though it may not have been the strongest event of its type by Newmarket standards. He was unsuited by the steady gallop in the July Stakes but reversed the form with Bertolini in the Prix Robert Papin. Rather disappointing on his final start, but should be able to stay further in time and looks one to follow.
**N A Callaghan [2-4] Tabor/Mrs John Magnier.*

BLACKEYED BOY (IRE) BHB 41f RR 43f 4657[6]

2 ch g Forest Wind (USA) - Blackeye (Busted) 10.2f **(61)**
Form - 0006
Record 1998 - 1st:0 2nd:0 3rd:0 Ran:4
1998 Turf 0-4: (6f, 7f 2, 10f) (gd, g-f, frm 2)
Moderate gelding. Turf high 43 (began Jly).
**A Bailey [0-4] Mark Kilner.*

BLACK HAWK RR 111f 1378a[3]

4 b c Nureyev (USA) 8.4f **(84)** - Silver Lane (USA) (Silver Hawk (USA)) 8.6f **(70)**
Form - 3
1998 Turf 0-1: (7f) (frm)
Currently Group-class colt. (1st run) - 3rd of 16 getting 5lb from Taiki Shuttle (16 May Fuchu 7f frm RF 1378a). He ran well behind Taiki Shuttle at Fuchu in May and is a high-class performer.
**S Kunieda in JPN [0-1].*

BLACK ICE BOY (IRE) BHB 42f39a RR 44f 39a 4871[3]

7 b g Law Society (USA) 11.6f **(71)** - Hogan's Sister (USA) (Speak John) 10.7f **(72)**
Form - 410333
Record 1998 - 1st:1 2nd:0 3rd:3 Ran:6
Pre1998 - 1st:2 2nd:0 3rd:0 Ran:15
Win Prizemoney £8,926 *Total Prizemoney* £10,342
Wins * **1998** **Apr Pontef (G-S) H 21.6f 36 42** <
* **1997** **Jly Beverl (HVY) H 16.2f 32 37**
* **1997** **Jun Carlis (G-F) H 17.2f 28 31**

1998 Turf 1-6: (16f 2, 18f 3, 22f 1-1) (g-s 1-2, gd 3, frm)
Moderate gelding, effective 16 to 22f, best at 18f, acts on g-s to gd - acts on Fibr, best on g-s, often wears blinkers, likes Pontefract. Turf high 44 - 3rd of 13 getting 8lb from Arisaig (15 Jun Pontefract 18f g-s RF 2001) - also 1st of 15 getting 17lb from All On (27 Apr Pontefract RF 0880). Requires a real test of stamina.
**R Bastiman [3-27] Mrs Judith Marshall.*

BLACK ORPHEUS (IRE) BHB 50f **RR 60f** 4550[15]
3 b g Astronef 7.9f **(59)** - Cri Basque (Gay Fandango (USA)) 8.5f **(59)**
Form - 4056800
Record 1998 - 1st:0 2nd:0 3rd:0 Ran:7
Pre1998 - 1st:0 2nd:0 3rd:0 Ran:2
Win Prizemoney £0 *Total Prizemoney* £175
1998 Turf 0-6: (5f, 6f 3, 7f 2) (g-s 2, gd 2, frm, hrd) 1998 AW 0-1: (6f) (Fibr)
Average gelding. Turf high 83.
**P S Felgate [0-3] J M Flynn (from E J O'Grady in IRE [0-6] Jun 1998).*

BLACKPOOL ROCK BHB 85f **RR 75f** 4870[4]
2 b c Rock City 8.8f **(62)** - Latakia (Morston (FR)) 9.4f **(55)**
Form - 5330214
Record 1998 - 1st:1 2nd:1 3rd:2 Ran:7
Win Prizemoney £3,393 *Total Prizemoney* £5,948
Wins * 1998 Oct Nottin (G-S) H 10f 65 74+ <
1998 Turf 1-7: (6f, 7f 3, 8f 2, 10f 1-1) (g-s 1-1, gd 2, g-f, frm 3)
Above-average colt, effective 10f, acts on g-s, likes tight tracks. Turf high 75 - also 1st of 18 from Sunset Lady (6 Oct Nottingham RF 4663). **J J O'Neill [1-7] Clayton Bigley Partnership Ltd.*

BLACK ROCK DESERT (USA) **RR 95+f** 4687a[1]
2 b c Danzig (USA) 8.1f **(88)** - City Dance (USA) 00
Form - 1
1998 Turf 1-1: (6f 1-1) (g-s 1-1)
Currently very useful colt. (1st run) - 1st of 16 from Robzelda (3 Oct Curragh RF 4687a). Won his maiden at the Curragh and looks useful. One to watch out for. **A P O'Brien in IRE [1-1] Michael Tabor.*

BLACK ROCKET (IRE) **RR 69?f** 2910[16]
2 br f Perugino (USA) - Betelgeuse (Kalaglow) 9.8f **(67)**
Form - 67000
Record 1998 - 1st:0 2nd:0 3rd:0 Ran:5
1998 Turf 0-5: (5f 3, 6f 2) (gd 3, frm 2)
Average filly. Turf high 69. Has been way out of her depth on recent starts. **K Mahdi [0-5] Hamad Al-Mutawa.*

BLACK SILK BHB 77f **RR 78f** 4542[19]
2 b c Zafonic (USA) 9f **(83)** - Mademoiselle Chloe (Night Shift (USA)) 7.2f **(69)**
Form - 2340
Record 1998 - 1st:0 2nd:1 3rd:1 Ran:4
Win Prizemoney £0 *Total Prizemoney* £2,220
1998 Turf 0-4: (6f 3, 7f) (g-f, frm 3)
Above-average colt. Turf high 78. Son of a useful racemare, he belied his burly looks with a promising debut second. Failed to build on that, but should pay his way in 1999.
**C F Wall [0-4] S Fustok.*

BLACK WEASEL (IRE) BHB 60f **RR 69f** 4670[16]
3 b c Lahib (USA) 8f **(69)** - Glowlamp (IRE) (Glow (USA)) 6.7f **(71)**
Form - 80481000
Record 1998 - 1st:1 2nd:0 3rd:0 Ran:8
Pre1998 - 1st:0 2nd:0 3rd:1 Ran:1
Win Prizemoney £2,736 *Total Prizemoney* £5,297
Wins 1998 Jly Pontef (G-F) 10f 61 <
1998 Turf 1-8: (8f 2, 9f 4, 10f 1-2) (g-s 3, g-f, frm 1-4)
Average colt, effective 10f, acts on frm, often wears blinkers (very effectively), likes tight tracks. Turf high 69 - also 1st of 7 getting 11lb from Desert Fighter (7 Jly Pontefract RF 2591).
**Miss J F Craze [0-3] S A Pritchard (from J L Dunlop [1-6] Jly 1998).*

BLAKESET BHB 85f **RR 84f** 3956[2]
3 ch c Midyan (USA) 9.9f **(64)** - Penset (Red Sunset) 8.2f **(63)**
Form - 7775422
Record 1998 - 1st:0 2nd:2 3rd:0 Ran:7
Pre1998 - 1st:1 2nd:1 3rd:2 Ran:5
Win Prizemoney £4,347 *Total Prizemoney* £13,555
Wins * 1997 Apr Newmar (G-F) 5f 76 <
1998 Turf 0-7: (7f 6, 8f) (gd, g-f 2, frm 4)
Scopey, decent colt, effective 5 to 7f, best at 7f, acts on gd to frm, best on frm, excels at Newmarket. Turf high 84 - 2nd of 17 to Spanish Fern (29 Aug Newmarket 7f frm RF 3956). Consistent. He ran better as the season progressed, and twice finished runner-up in fair handicaps during August. Seven furlongs looks his trip. ** R Hannon [1-12] Mrs Caroline Parker.*

BLAKEY (IRE) **RR 34f** 3262[5]
2 b g Maledetto (IRE) - Villars (Home Guard (USA)) 9.3f **(66)**
Form - 885
Record 1998 - 1st:0 2nd:0 3rd:0 Ran:3
1998 Turf 0-3: (5f 2, 6f) (gd 2, frm)
Currently very moderate gelding. Turf high 34. **J Berry [0-3] J Berry.*

BLARNEY PARK BHB 37f **RR 41f** 4114[16]
3 b f Never so Bold 7.1f **(62)** -Walking Saint (Godswalk (USA)) 7.3f **(58)**
Form - 340200
Record 1998 - 1st:0 2nd:1 3rd:1 Ran:6
Pre1998 - 1st:0 2nd:0 3rd:2 Ran:9
Win Prizemoney £0 *Total Prizemoney* £2,001
1998 Turf 0-6: (5f 5, 6f) (g-f, frm 5)
Workmanlike, moderate filly, effective 5f, acts on frm, has worn blinkers. Turf high 44. Inconsistent.
**C A Dwyer [0-15] Blarney Park Racing Club.*

BLATANT OUTBURST BHB 57f52a **RR 60df 52a** 567[11]
8 b g War Hero - Miss Metro (Upper Case (USA)) 8.2f **(55)**
Form - 20
Record 1998 - 1st:0 2nd:1 3rd:0 Ran:2
Pre1998 - 1st:0 2nd:2 3rd:0 Ran:12
Win Prizemoney £0 *Total Prizemoney* £4,128
1998 AW 0-2: (16f 2) (Fibr 2)
Average gelding, has worn blinkers. AW high 41. Becoming disappointing.
**Miss S J Wilton [1-17] John Pointon and Sons (from G C Bravery [1-16] Oct 1996).*

BLAZE OF SONG BHB 50f54a **RR 48f 54a** 773[14]
6 ch g Jester 8.5f **(43)** - Intellect (Frimley Park) 6.5f **(67)**
Form - 0
Record 1998 - 1st:0 2nd:0 3rd:0 Ran:1
Pre1998 - 1st:3 2nd:4 3rd:1 Ran:25
Win Prizemoney £10,629 *Total Prizemoney* £16,827
Wins 1995 May Chepst (GD) 8.1f 82 <
1995 May Salisb (GD) H 8f 63 78
1995 May Doncas (G-F) 10.3f 61
1998 Turf 0-1: (14f) (sft)
Moderate gelding, has worn blinkers.
**D J Wintle [0-15] D Boocock (from R Hannon [3-25] Oct 1997).*

BLAZER'S BABY BHB 31f21a **RR 21f 21a** 3571[13]
4 ch f Norton Challenger 10f **(41)** - Qualitair Blazer (Blazing Saddles (AUS)) 6.7f **(46)**
Form - 7000
Record 1998 - 1st:0 2nd:0 3rd:0 Ran:3
Pre1998 - 1st:1 2nd:0 3rd:0 Ran:10
Win Prizemoney £1,984 *Total Prizemoney* £1,984
Wins 1997 Jly Nottin (G-F) S 10f 49 <
1998 Turf 0-1: (12f) (g-f) 1998 AW 0-2: (8f, 12f) (Fibr 2)
Unfurnished, little account filly, effective 10f, acts on frm, likes left handed tracks, likes tight tracks. AW high 9.
**Mrs N Macauley [0-11] G Wiltshire (from J R Fanshawe [1-5] Jly 1997).*

BLAZING BILLY BHB 34f **RR 24f** 4596[24]
3 ch g Anshan 8.2f **(63)** - Worthy Venture (Northfields (USA)) 9f **(72)**
Form - 460000
Record 1998 - 1st:0 2nd:0 3rd:0 Ran:6
Pre1998 - 1st:0 2nd:0 3rd:0 Ran:1
1998 Turf 0-4: (5f 2, 6f, 8f) (g-s, gd, frm 2) 1998 AW 0-2: (6f, 8f) (Equi, Fibr)
Leggy, little account gelding, has worn blinkers. Turf high 24. AW high 28. **C A Dwyer [0-7] R West.*

BLAZING FLAME RR 22f 4767[11]

2 br g Chaddleworth (IRE) - Blazing Sunset (Blazing Saddles (AUS)) 6.7f **(46)**
Form - 587000
Record 1998 - 1st:0 2nd:0 3rd:0 Ran:6
1998 Turf 0-4: (5f, 7f 2, 8f) (sft, gd, g-f 2) 1998 AW 0-2: (5f 2) (Fibr 2)
Moderate gelding. Turf high 22. AW high 40.
**J S Goldie [0-4] A Saccomando (from N P Littmoden [0-2] May 1998).*

BLAZING IMP (USA) BHB 48f RR 50f 3908[14]

5 ch g Imp Society (USA) 7.1f **(63)** - Marital (USA) (Marine Patrol (USA)) 5f **(52)**
Form - 07140540
Record 1998 - 1st:1 2nd:0 3rd:0 Ran:8
Pre1998 - 1st:1 2nd:0 3rd:1 Ran:14
Win Prizemoney £6,034 *Total Prizemoney* £6,618

Wins								
	* **1998**	Jly	Hamilt	(FRM)	S	5f	49	
	* 1997	Jun	Mussel	(G-S)		5f	52	<

1998 Turf 1-8: (5f 1-7, 6f) (gd 3, g-f 2, frm 1-3)
Fair gelding, effective 5f, acts on gd to frm. Turf high 50 - also 1st of 8 from Swan At Whalley (3 Jly Hamilton RF 2492).
**Mrs J Jordan [2-18] Forties Joint Venture (from W S Cunningham [0-4] Aug 1996).*

BLESS 'IM BHB 74f RR 82f 4381[14]

3 b c Presidium 7.5f **(56)** - Saint Systems (Uncle Pokey) 10.1f **(49)**
Form - 1254660
Record 1998 - 1st:1 2nd:1 3rd:0 Ran:7
Pre1998 - 1st:0 2nd:1 3rd:0 Ran:3
Win Prizemoney £2,595 *Total Prizemoney* £4,936

Wins							
	* **1998**	May	Leices	(GD)	8f	90	<

1998 Turf 1-7: (8f 1-5, 9f, 10f) (gd 3, g-f 1-4)
Light-framed, decent colt, effective 8f, acts on g-f. Turf high 90 (1st run) - 1st of 9 from Splendid Isolation (25 May Leicester RF 1451). Consistent. Has shown some form in handicaps, and seems to go well on any ground. He goes well fresh, but does not stay much further than a mile.
**R Hannon [1-10] J A Leek.*

BLESSINGINDISGUISE BHB 99f RR 100f 4516[9]

5 b g Kala Shikari 6f **(48)** - Blowing Bubbles (Native Admiral (USA)) 5f **(80)**
Form - 6011000
Record 1998 - 1st:2 2nd:0 3rd:0 Ran:7
Pre1998 - 1st:6 2nd:5 3rd:3 Ran:31
Win Prizemoney £57,793 *Total Prizemoney* £76,669

Wins									
	* **1998**	Jly	Ascot	(G-F)	H	5f	97	100	<
	* **1998**	Jly	York	(G-F)	H	5f	92	97	
	* 1997	Jly	Ascot	(GD)	H	5f	76	94	
	* 1997	Jly	Ayr	(G-F)	H	5f	76	80+	
	* 1997	Jly	Haydoc	(GD)	H	5f	70	71+	
	* 1997	Jun	Ripon	(GD)	H	5f	64	67	
	* 1997	May	Redcar	(G-F)	H	5f	58	61	
	* 1995	May	Newcas	(GD)		5f		58t	

1998 Turf 2-7: (5f 2-5, 6f 2) (gd 1-5, g-f, frm 1-1)
Very useful gelding, effective 5 to 6f, best at 5f, acts on gd to frm, best on gd, often wears blinkers (extremely effectively), excels at Haydock and likes Ascot. Turf high 100 - 1st of 13 giving 3lb to Bayleaf (24 Jly Ascot RF 3063) - also 1st of 8 giving 21lb to Polly Golightly (10 Jly York RF 2698). This popular five-furlong specialist hit form with a vengeance in July, winning valuable handicaps at York and Ascot within the space of a fortnight. He can be ridden forcefully or with restraint, wears a Monty Roberts blanket for stalls entry and usually takes a race or two to reach peak fitness.
**M W Easterby [8-38] A G Black.*

BLIND TRUST (IRE) RR 75f 3927[7]

2 b c Mtoto 11.5f **(71)** - Ancestry (Persepolis (FR)) 6.4f **(67)**
Form - 7
Record 1998 - 1st:0 2nd:0 3rd:0 Ran:1
1998 Turf 0-1: (7f) (frm)
Currently above-average colt. **C F Wall [0-1] N Ahamad.*

BLISS (IRE) BHB 63f RR 68f 4596[17]

3 b f Statoblest 6.4f **(63)** - Moira My Girl (Henbit (USA)) 9f **(61)**
Form - 0006082000

Blessingindisguise scores at Ascot

Record 1998 - 1st:0 2nd:1 3rd:0 Ran:10
Pre1998 - 1st:3 2nd:0 3rd:0 Ran:9
Win Prizemoney £13,901 *Total Prizemoney* £15,203
Wins * 1997 Oct Newmar (GD) H 5f 71 74 <
* 1997 Spt Sandow (GD) H 5f 63 70
* 1997 Spt Bright (G-F) H 5.3f 56 60
1998 Turf 0-9:(5f 6, 6f 3) (hvy, gd 2, g-f 2, frm 4)1998 AW 0-1:(5f) (Fibr)
Neat, average filly, effective 5 to 6f, best at 5f, acts on gd to frm. Turf high 68 - 2nd of 13 giving 13lb to Daynabee (27 Jly Windsor 6f frm RF 3145). **Mrs P N Dutfield [3-19] W A Harrison-Allan.*

BLIZZARD RR 42f 5123[7]

2 gr f Petong 7.6f **(58)** - Tempesta Rossa (IRE) (Persian Heights)
Form - 7
Record 1998 - 1st:0 2nd:0 3rd:0 Ran:1
1998 Turf 0-1: (6f) (g-s)
Currently moderate filly. **B Smart [0-1] The Dyball Partnership.*

BLOCKADE (USA) BHB 48f RR 55f 3949[7]

9 b g Imperial Falcon (CAN) 9.2f **(72)** - Stolen Date (USA) (Sadair) 9.1f **(68)**
Form - 033562047
Record 1998 - 1st:0 2nd:1 3rd:2 Ran:9
Pre1998 - 1st:17 2nd:5 3rd:5 Ran:61
Win Prizemoney £63,963 *Total Prizemoney* £78,329
Wins * 1997 Jun Nottin (G-F) 10f 55+
* 1997 May Yarmou (G-F) H 10.1f 55 57
* 1996 Jly Bright (FRM) C 7f 61
* 1996 Jly Yarmou (G-F) C 8f 61
* 1995 Aug Bright (FRM) C 8f 74
* 1995 Jly Yarmou (G-F) C 8f 74
* 1995 Jun Goodwo (FRM) C 9f 81 <
* 1995 May Newmar (GD) 7f 72
* 1994 Aug Newmar (GD) C 7f 74
* 1994 Jly Goodwo (FRM) C 8f 73
1998 Turf 0-9: (8f 2, 10f 7) (gd 3, g-f, frm 4, hrd)
Fair gelding, effective 10f, acts on g-f to hrd, best on g-f, likes left handed tracks, likes tight tracks. Turf high 58. He is still capable of winning in the right company, and is an ideal mount for an inexperienced rider. **M Bell [17-70] A M Warrender.*

BLONDANE BHB 21a RR 21a 215[5]

5 b g Danehill (USA) 9.1f **(79)** - Whos The Blonde (Cure The Blues (USA)) 9.5f **(63)**
Form - 765
Record 1998 - 1st:0 2nd:0 3rd:0 Ran:3
Pre1998 - 1st:0 2nd:0 3rd:0 Ran:4
1998 AW 0-3: (7f, 8f, 12f) (Fibr 3)
Little account gelding, has worn blinkers. AW high 23.
**S R Bowring [0-7] P A B S Racing.*

BLOOD ORANGE BHB 50a RR 30f 1475[14]

4 ch c Ron's Victory (USA) 9.2f **(52)** - Little Bittern (USA) (Riva Ridge (USA)) 8.2f **(68)**
Form - 060000
Record 1998 - 1st:0 2nd:0 3rd:0 Ran:4
Pre1998 - 1st:0 2nd:0 3rd:0 Ran:6
1998 Turf 0-2: (5f, 6f) (g-s, g-f) 1998 AW 0-2: (7f, 12f) (Equi, Fibr)
Scopey, fair colt. Turf high 30. AW high 32.
**G G Margarson [0-10] G G Margarson.*

BLOOMING AMAZING BHB 82f58a RR 85f 58a 4708[6]

4 b g Mazilier (USA) 8.5f **(56)** - Cornflower Blue (Tyrnavos) 10.1f **(55)**
Form - 6352243182411606
Record 1998 - 1st:3 2nd:3 3rd:2 Ran:15
Pre1998 - 1st:1 2nd:2 3rd:1 Ran:14
Win Prizemoney £16,396 *Total Prizemoney* £22,634
Wins * **1998** Aug Pontef (G-F) H 8f 78 85 <
* **1998** Aug Beverl (G-F) H 7.5f 78 76
* **1998** May Beverl (GD) H 7.5f 70 77
* 1997 Apr Beverl (G-F) H 8.5f 72 76
1998 Turf 3-9: (7f 2-2, 8f 1-5, 10f, 12f) (sft, gd 2, frm 3-6) 1998 AW 0-6: (7f, 8f 2, 9f, 12f 2) (Fibr 6)
Scopey, useful gelding, effective 7 to 8f, best at 8f, acts on gd to frm, best on frm, has worn blinkers, likes tight tracks, excels at Beverley. Turf high 85 - 1st of 12 giving 18lb to Goldfame (25 Aug Pontefract RF 3852) - also 1st of 17 giving 5lb to Gadge (9 May Beverley RF 1116). AW high 56. Running consistently well in '98, including winning at Beverley and Pontefract. He goes well on Fibresand too, and is a good ride for an amateur.
**J L Eyre [4-29] C H Stephenson & Partners.*

BLOSSOM DEARIE BHB 38f RR 34f 1475[10]

5 b m Landyap (USA) - Jose Collins (Singing Bede)
Form - 0700
Record 1998 - 1st:0 2nd:0 3rd:0 Ran:4
Pre1998 - 1st:0 2nd:0 3rd:0 Ran:5
Win Prizemoney £0 *Total Prizemoney* £213
1998 Turf 0-4: (5f, 6f 3) (sft, g-s, g-f 2)
Very moderate filly, has worn blinkers. Turf high 36. Consistent.
**R J Hodges [0-4] Miss Jacquie Tarr (from R G Frost [0-4] Jun 1996).*

BLOWING AWAY (IRE) BHB 44f RR 51f 4869[7]

4 b br f Last Tycoon 9.4f **(73)** - Taken By Force (Persian Bold) 9.3f **(66)**
Form - 432524733637
Record 1998 - 1st:0 2nd:2 3rd:4 Ran:12
Pre1998 - 1st:1 2nd:0 3rd:2 Ran:10
Win Prizemoney £2,868 *Total Prizemoney* £6,661
Wins * 1997 Oct Leices (GD) C 8f 54 <
1998 Turf 0-12: (8f, 9f 2, 10f 4, 11f 3, 12f 2) (gd 4, g-f 4, frm 4)
Unfurnished, fair filly, effective 8f, acts on hrd, has worn blinkers. Turf high 51. Consistent.
**M H Tompkins [2-25] Mark Tompkins Racing.*

BLOW ME A KISS BHB 65f RR 76f 4987[7]

3 ch f Kris 10f **(75)** - Lassoo (Caerleon (USA)) 8.6f **(71)**
Form - 30222327
Record 1998 - 1st:0 2nd:4 3rd:2 Ran:8
Win Prizemoney £0 *Total Prizemoney* £5,618
1998 Turf 0-8: (7f, 8f 2, 10f 4, 12f) (sft 2, gd 5, frm)
Tall, above-average filly, effective 8 to 10f, best at 10f, acts on gd. Turf high 76 - 2nd of 3 getting 5lb from Spring Fever (18 Jly Ayr 8f gd RF 2906). **C W Thornton [0-8] Guy Reed.*

BLU CARILLON (IRE) RR 107f 4730a[3]

3 ch c Love the Groom (USA) - Carillon Miss (USA) (The Minstrel (CAN)) 10f **(72)**
Form - 223
1998 Turf 0-3: (5f 2, 6f) (sft, gd 2)
Pattern-class colt. Turf high 101 - 2nd of 9 getting 5lb from Late Parade (19 Jly Agnano 5f gd RF 3057a). He ran well in Group Three company and acts on easy ground. **O Pessi in ITY [1-5].*

BLUE (IRE) BHB 89f RR 81f 4930[2]

2 b c Bluebird (USA) 7.9f **(71)** - Watership (USA) (Foolish Pleasure (USA)) 8.9f **(72)**
Form - 6622
Record 1998 - 1st:0 2nd:2 3rd:0 Ran:4
Win Prizemoney £0 *Total Prizemoney* £2,225
1998 Turf 0-4: (6f, 7f, 8f 2) (g-s, gd, g-f, frm)
Decent colt. Turf high 81 (began Aug) - 2nd of 11 to Nowhere To Exit (22 Oct Brighton 8f g-s RF 4930). A half-brother to Cesarewitch winner Captain's Guest, he will come into his own over a distance of ground. **Mrs A J Perrett [0-4] K J Buchanan.*

BLUE ANCHOR BHB 39f43a RR 43f 43a 4588[3]

3 b g Robellino (USA) 9.5f **(68)** - Fair Seas (General Assembly (USA)) 10f **(68)**
Form - 471673
Record 1998 - 1st:1 2nd:0 3rd:1 Ran:6
Pre1998 - 1st:0 2nd:0 3rd:0 Ran:5
Win Prizemoney £1,735 *Total Prizemoney* £2,264
Wins 1998 *Feb Southw (STD) H 11f 40 35 <*
1998 Turf 0-2: (11f, 14f) (gd 2) 1998 AW 1-4: (6f, 7f, 11f 1-2) (Fibr 1-4)
Moderate gelding, likes tight tracks. Turf high 37. AW high 35. Consistent. He got off the mark in a very bad handicap on the Southwell Fibresand in February when stepped up greatly in trip. He did show a tendency to idle in front.
**A W Carroll [0-1] D R Wellicome (from Mrs M Reveley [1-10] May 1998).*

BLUEBELLE BHB 80f RR 72f 3804[1]

3 b f Generous (IRE) 11.5f **(82)** - Hi Lass (Shirley Heights) 10.3f **(74)**
Form - 431
Record 1998 - 1st:1 2nd:0 3rd:1 Ran:3

Win Prizemoney £4,224 *Total Prizemoney* £5,004
Wins * **1998** Aug Cheste (G-S) 12.3f 72 <
1998 Turf 1-3: (8f, 10f, 12f 1-1) (gd 1-3)
Scopey, currently above-average filly. Turf high 72 - 1st of 5 from Andalish (22 Aug Chester RF 3804).
**Sir Mark Prescott [1-3] Faisal Salman & C M Budgett.*

BLUEBELL MISS BHB 50f55a **RR 46f 55a** 2231[7]
4 b f High Kicker (USA) 8.4f **(52)** - Mio Mementa (Streak) 10f **(58)**
Form - 007
Record **1998** - 1st:0 2nd:0 3rd:0 Ran:3
Pre1998 - 1st:2 2nd:2 3rd:2 Ran:11
Win Prizemoney £5,724 *Total Prizemoney* £7,404
Wins 1997 Jly Yarmou (GD) S 10.1f 60
1996 May Leices (G-S) 6f 71 <
1998 Turf 0-3: (10f 2, 11f) (gd, g-f 2)
Workmanlike, average filly, effective 10 to 12f, best at 10f, acts on g-f - acts on Fibr, favours tight tracks. Turf high 46. Becoming disappointing.
**A Streeter [0-3] Peter J Douglas Engineering (from M J Ryan [2-11] Jly 1997).*

BLUEBERRY PARKES BHB 67f **RR 61f** 1459[6]
3 b f Pursuit of Love 9.5f **(69)** - Summerhill Spruce (Windjammer (USA)) 7f **(59)**
Form - 276
Record **1998** - 1st:0 2nd:1 3rd:0 Ran:3
Win Prizemoney £0 *Total Prizemoney* £1,045
1998 Turf 0-3: (6f 2, 7f) (g-s, gd, g-f)
Workmanlike, currently average filly. Turf high 61 (1st run) - 2nd of 9 to Sarah Stokes (21 Apr Pontefract 6f g-s RF 0791).
**J Berry [0-3] Joseph Heler.*

BLUE BOMBER BHB 55f **RR 58?f** 1996[8]
7 b g Tina's Pet 7.4f **(56)** - Warm Wind (Tumble Wind (USA)) 7.5f **(57)**
Form - 8
Record **1998** - 1st:0 2nd:0 3rd:0 Ran:1
Pre1998 - 1st:6 2nd:1 3rd:1 Ran:24
Win Prizemoney £18,860 *Total Prizemoney* £20,990
Wins 1996 Aug Newcas (G-F) S 6f 58
1996 Jly Catter (G-F) C 7f 54
1996 Jly Catter (G-F) S 6f 63
1995 Oct Catter (G-F) H 7f 65 74
1998 Turf 0-1: (7f) (gd)
Fair gelding.
**V Thompson [0-2] L Ovenden (from G M Moore [1-1] Aug 1996).*

BLUE CALVINE BHB 30f **RR 25f** 46[14]
4 b g Silver Kite (USA) 10.2f **(51)** - Calvanne Miss (Martinmas) 7.6f **(59)**
Form - 0
Record **1998** - 1st:0 2nd:0 3rd:0 Ran:1
Pre1998 - 1st:0 2nd:0 3rd:0 Ran:4
1998 AW 0-1: (7f) (Equi)
Light-framed, little account gelding.
**W G M Turner [0-1] John Hill (from C J Hill [0-4] Spt 1997).*

BLUE CHEESE BHB 25f25a **RR 24f 25a** 1720[19]
4 gr f Mystiko (USA) 7.7f **(59)** - Legal Sound (Legal Eagle) 7.3f **(54)**
Form - 000
Record **1998** - 1st:0 2nd:0 3rd:0 Ran:3
Pre1998 - 1st:0 2nd:0 3rd:0 Ran:5
1998 Turf 0-3: (8f 2, 10f) (gd, frm 2)
Leggy, very moderate filly, has worn blinkers. Turf high 24. Inconsistent.
**J R Jenkins [0-8] The Cheese Gang (from Mrs N Macauley [0-4] Jly 1997).*

BLUE CHIEF (DEN) RR 108f 1912a[3]
6
Form - 3
1998 Turf 0-1: (10f) (sft)
Currently Pattern-class. (1st run) - 3rd of 13 to Galtee (2 Jun Taby 10f sft RF 1912a). He is not a Group horse and looks too long in the tooth to improve. **W Neuroth in NOR [0-2].*

BLUE CLOUD (IRE) RR 104f 4725a[3]
2 f Nashwan (USA) - Batave (Posse (USA)) 8.9f **(61)**
Form - 3
1998 Turf 0-1: (8f) (sft)
Currently very useful filly. (1st run) - 3rd of 11 to Juvenia (4 Oct Longchamp 8f sft RF 4725a). She looked a class act when winning at Longchamp in September, and was set to follow up in the Group One Prix Marcel Boussac before being reeled in close home and forced back to third spot. There was a lot to like about that performance and this daughter of Nashwan is an assured Group race winner, although she may not stay much beyond a mile.
**A Fabre in FR [0-1] D Wildenstein.*

BLUE DAWN (IRE) BHB 64f **RR 69f** 4748[26]
3 ch f Bluebird (USA) 7.9f **(71)** - Spring Carnival (USA) (Riverman (USA)) 9.1f **(76)**
Form - 0500
Record **1998** - 1st:0 2nd:0 3rd:0 Ran:4
Pre1998 - 1st:0 2nd:0 3rd:0 Ran:3
Win Prizemoney £0 *Total Prizemoney* £211
1998 Turf 0-4: (7f, 8f 2, 9f) (gd 2, g-f, frm)
Light-framed, average filly, effective 8f, acts on gd. Turf high 68 - 5th of 9 getting 6lb from Legal Issue (3 Jun Beverley 8f gd RF 1677). **E A L Dunlop [0-7] The Serendipity Partnership.*

BLUE DESERT BHB 65f56a **RR 53f 56a** 1892[12]
3 ch g Elmaamul (USA) 8.1f **(70)** - Shehana (USA) (The Minstrel (CAN)) 10f **(72)**
Form - 635715830
Record **1998** - 1st:1 2nd:0 3rd:1 Ran:7
Pre1998 - 1st:1 2nd:0 3rd:1 Ran:8
Win Prizemoney £4,147 *Total Prizemoney* £4,866
Wins **1998** Mar Nottin (G-S) S 8.2f 67
1997 Oct Nottin (GD) S 8.2f 85 <
1998 Turf 1-5: (8f 1-3, 9f, 10f) (sft, g-s 1-2, gd, frm) 1998 AW 0-2: (7f, 8f) (Fibr 2)
Light-framed, average gelding, effective 8f, acts on g-s, likes left handed tracks, likes tight tracks. Turf high 67 (1st run). AW high 54. Appreciated the drop in class and step up in trip to win a Nottingham seller by a street towards the end of 1997. After an All-Weather campaign with did not yield any further victories, he returned to Nottingham to win another seller in March. He obviously likes that track.
**D Nicholls [0-1] E W & M Tuer (from S R Bowring [1-6] May 1998).*

BLUE DIAMOND RR 19f 4671[19]
2 b f First Trump - Lammastide (Martinmas) 7.6f **(59)**
Form - 00
Record **1998** - 1st:0 2nd:0 3rd:0 Ran:2
1998 Turf 0-2: (6f, 7f) (g-f 2)
Currently poor filly. Turf high 19 (began Spt).
**M Bell [0-2] BillionMind Partnership.*

BLUE FLYER (IRE) BHB 65f57a **RR 68f 57a** 334[7]
5 b g Bluebird (USA) 7.9f **(71)**-Born to Fly (IRE) (Last Tycoon) 8.5f **(62)**
Form - 801467
Record **1998** - 1st:1 2nd:0 3rd:0 Ran:6
Pre1998 - 1st:4 2nd:3 3rd:4 Ran:32
Win Prizemoney £22,628 *Total Prizemoney* £28,544
Wins * **1998** *Jan Lingfi (STD) 7f 68*
* 1997 *Jan Lingfi (STD)* H *7f* 74 77 <
* 1996 Aug Salisb (G-F) H 7f 72 76
* 1996 *Feb Lingfi (STD) 8f* 72
* 1996 *Feb Lingfi (STD) 8f* 64
1998 AW 1-6: (7f 1-5, 8f) (Equi 1-6)
Average gelding, effective 7f, acts on gd - acts on Equi, often wears blinkers (extremely effectively). AW high 68 - 1st of 4 from Castle Ashby Jack (27 Jan Lingfield RF 0170). Won the valuable Ladbroke All-Weather Series Final at Lingfield in January '97, though he has not run up to that level since. His win in a limited stakes back at Lingfield in January came against three rivals with big questions marks against them.
**R Ingram [5-36] B Scott (from I A Balding [0-2] Spt 1995).*

BLUE GENTIAN (USA) BHB 88f **RR 85f** 1293[4]
3 b f Known Fact (USA) 8.3f **(72)** - Caithness (USA) (Roberto (USA)) 10f **(76)**
Form - 64
Record **1998** - 1st:0 2nd:0 3rd:0 Ran:2
Pre1998 - 1st:1 2nd:0 3rd:1 Ran:2

Win Prizemoney £3,213 *Total Prizemoney* £4,807
Wins * 1997 Spt Salisb (G-S) 7f 80+ <
1998 Turf 0-2: (10f 2) (gd, frm)
Scopey, useful filly. Turf high 85. **R Charlton [1-4] K Abdulla.*

BLUE GLASS BHB 58f **RR 30f** 4866[1]
2 b f Ardkinglass 5f **(64)** - Kajetana (FR) (Caro) 9.3f **(74)**
Form - 041
Record 1998 - 1st:1 2nd:0 3rd:0 Ran:3
Win Prizemoney £2,180 *Total Prizemoney* £2,389
Wins * **1998** *Oct Wolver (STD) S 8.5f 65* <
1998 Turf 0-1: (8f) (frm) 1998 AW 1-2: (8f 1-2) (Fibr 1-2)
Currently average filly. AW high 65 (began Spt) - 1st of 13 from Pride of Londubh (17 Oct Wolverhampton RF 4866). She got off the mark when holding on by the skin of her teeth in a seller on the Wolverhampton Fibresand in October.
**N P Littmoden [1-3] T Clarke.*

BLUE HOPPER BHB 30f32a **RR 35f 32a** 3677[14]
4 b f Rock Hopper 10.6f **(54)** - Kimble Blue (Blue Refrain)
Form - 846427800306763800
Record 1998 - 1st:0 2nd:1 3rd:2 Ran:17
Pre1998 - 1st:0 2nd:1 3rd:1 Ran:8
Win Prizemoney £0 *Total Prizemoney* £3,528
1998 Turf 0-10: (8f 4, 9f 2, 10f 3, 12f) (sft 2, g-s 2, gd, g-f 3, frm 2) 1998 AW 0-7: (8f, 9f, 12f 5) (Fibr 7)
Workmanlike, moderate filly, effective 8f, acts on frm, has worn blinkers (effectively), likes right handed tracks. Turf high 45 - 3rd of 18 giving 11lb to Jato Dancer (18 May Windsor 8f frm RF 1311). AW high 41.
**M Quinn [0-18] M Q Racing (from M R Channon [0-7] Jun 1997).*

BLUE KITE BHB 65f75a **RR 72f 75a** 4864[12]
3 ch c Silver Kite (USA) 10.2f **(51)** - Gold And Blue (IRE) (Bluebird (USA)) 7.5f **(69)**
Form - 54580220400
Record 1998 - 1st:0 2nd:2 3rd:0 Ran:11
Pre1998 - 1st:1 2nd:4 3rd:0 Ran:9
Win Prizemoney £2,277 *Total Prizemoney* £15,386
Wins * 1997 *Spt Wolver (STD) 5f 72* <
1998 Turf 0-7: (6f 7) (gd 3, g-f 4) 1998 AW 0-4: (5f 2, 6f, 7f) (Fibr 4)
Above-average colt, effective 5 to 7f, best at 6f, acts on gd to g-f - acts on Fibr, has worn blinkers, likes left handed tracks, likes tight tracks, excels at Wolverhampton. Turf high 77 - 8th of 20 getting 9lb from Hill Magic (9 May Lingfield 6f g-f RF 1123). AW high 77 - 2nd of 5 giving 5lb to Circuiteer (26 Jun Wolverhampton 7f Fibr RF 2321). Becoming disappointing. He showed a useful level of form on both Fibresand and turf as a juvenile, but though running creditably on both surfaces in '98, has not managed another victory.
**N P Littmoden [1-20] T Clarke.*

BLUE LAMP (USA) BHB 50f32a **RR 53f 32a** 330[9]
4 ch f Shadeed (USA) 7.7f **(72)** - Matter of Time (Habitat) 9.4f **(70)**
Form - 25637660
Record 1998 - 1st:0 2nd:0 3rd:1 Ran:5
Pre1998 - 1st:0 2nd:2 3rd:0 Ran:13
Win Prizemoney £0 *Total Prizemoney* £2,723
1998 AW 0-5: (6f, 7f, 8f, 10f, 13f) (Equi 4, Fibr)
Neat, fair filly, effective 5f, acts on frm, has worn blinkers. AW high 44. Becoming disappointing.
**R Ingram [0-6] B Scott (from M A Jarvis [0-12] Nov 1997).*

BLUE LASER (IRE) RR 65f 4235[7]
2 b c Mujtahid (USA) 7.4f **(69)** - Dazzling Fire (IRE) (Bluebird (USA)) 7.5f **(69)**
Form - 07
Record 1998 - 1st:0 2nd:0 3rd:0 Ran:2
1998 Turf 0-2: (5f, 6f) (gd, frm)
Currently average colt. Turf high 65 (began Spt).
**B J Meehan [0-2] Miss J Semple.*

BLUE LINE ANGEL BHB 52f **RR 43f** 4834[7]
2 b g Cyrano de Bergerac 7.3f **(58)** - Northern Line (Camden Town) 9.3f **(53)**
Form - 007
Record 1998 - 1st:0 2nd:0 3rd:0 Ran:3
1998 Turf 0-3: (5f 2, 6f) (g-s 2, gd)
Currently moderate gelding. Turf high 43.
**R A Fahey [0-3] Peter Tingey.*

BLUE LOTUS (IRE) RR 101f 4794a[10]
2 b c College Chapel - Priddy Blue (Blue Cashmere) 6.4f **(54)**
Form - 62424262140
1998 Turf 1-11: (5f 1-5, 6f 6) (g-s 5, gd 1-5, frm)
Very useful colt, effective 5 to 6f, best at 5f, acts on g-s to frm, best on gd. Turf high 101 - 2nd of 7 giving 23lb to Wish List (5 Spt Cork 5f gd RF 4172a) - also 1st of 10 giving 5lb to Dane's Lady (20 Spt Curragh RF 4438a). Consistent. He is not the most robust of individuals, but stood up well to a busy season and deserved greater reward for his efforts. He will be tough to place as a three-year-old, but will not fail through the lack of trying.
**A P O'Brien in IRE [1-11] Miss Katherine Magnier.*

BLUE LUGANA BHB 35f25a **RR 37tf 25a** 142[11]
6 b g Lugana Beach 7f **(63)** - Two Friendly (Be Friendly) 9.3f **(53)**
Form - 0
Record 1998 - 1st:0 2nd:0 3rd:0 Ran:1
Pre1998 - 1st:0 2nd:5 3rd:1 Ran:30
Win Prizemoney £0 *Total Prizemoney* £4,598
1998 AW 0-1: (7f) (Fibr)
Very moderate gelding, effective 6f, - acts on AW, best on Fibr, has worn blinkers. Inconsistent. **N Bycroft [0-34] J A Swinburne.*

BLUE MELODY (USA) BHB 100f **RR 105f** 4364[4]
2 b br f Dayjur (USA) 6.8f **(79)** - Blue Note (FR) (Habitat) 9.4f **(70)**
Form - 182224
Record 1998 - 1st:1 2nd:3 3rd:0 Ran:6
Win Prizemoney £3,600 *Total Prizemoney* £12,592
Wins * **1998** Jun Leices (GD) 5f 85++ <
1998 Turf 1-6: (5f 1-1, 6f 4, 7f) (sft, gd 2, frm 1-3)
Pattern-class filly, effective 7f, acts on gd. Turf high 105 - 2nd of 15 giving 3lb to Qhazeenah (9 Spt Doncaster 7f gd RF 4183). Closely related to top-class sprinters Zieten and Blue Duster, she is not as good as her superb pedigree suggests, and was well beaten in her forays into Listed and Group company. It would be interesting to see her forcing the pace in the same manner as her sire, Dayjur.
**D R Loder [1-6] Sheikh Mohammed.*

BLUE PERU (IRE) BHB 50f **RR 54f** 4301[9]
2 b f Perugino (USA) - Blue Czarina (Sandhurst Prince) 7.9f **(63)**
Form - 040
Record 1998 - 1st:0 2nd:0 3rd:0 Ran:3
1998 Turf 0-3: (6f, 7f 2) (gd, frm 2)
Currently fair filly. Turf high 54 (began Aug) - 4th of 16 to Annie Apple (27 Aug Folkestone 7f gd RF 3897).
**B Smart [0-3] The Dyball Partnership.*

BLUEPRINT (IRE) BHB 92f89a **RR 93f 89a** 5067[5]
3 b c Generous (IRE) 11.5f **(82)** - Highbrow (Shirley Heights) 10.3f **(74)**
Form - 411323185
Record 1998 - 1st:3 2nd:1 3rd:2 Ran:9
Pre1998 - 1st:0 2nd:0 3rd:0 Ran:2
Win Prizemoney £26,044 *Total Prizemoney* £36,538
Wins * **1998** Aug York (G-F) H 13.9f 89 93 <
* **1998** *May Lingfi (STD) H 12f 65 78+*
* **1998** *May Southw (STD) H 12f 65 69+*
1998 Turf 1-6: (12f 2, 14f 1-2, 15f, 16f) (sft, g-s, gd, g-f 1-2, frm) 1998 AW 2-3: (12f 2-3) (Equi 1-1, Fibr 1-2)
Scopey, useful colt, effective 12 to 14f, best at 14f, acts on g-s to frm, has worn blinkers (extremely effectively), excels at York. Turf high 93 - 1st of 12 getting 1lb from Murghem (18 Aug York RF 3698). AW high 78. He showed vastly improved form when tried on sand, winning at Southwell and Lingfield, but as maintained the improvement back on turf, finishing third at both Royal Ascot and Glorious Goodwood before winning York's Melrose Handicap. Well held when upped in class. **Lord Huntingdon [3-11] The Queen.*

BLUE ROCK LADY RR 19f 5041[10]
2 br f Rock City 8.8f **(62)** - Blues Player (Jaazeiro (USA)) 9.2f **(54)**
Form - 00
Record 1998 - 1st:0 2nd:0 3rd:0 Ran:2
1998 Turf 0-2: (6f, 7f) (sft, gd)
Currently poor filly. Turf high 19.
**C F Wall [0-2] Framlingham Racing Partners.*

BLUE SADDLE (IRE) RR 101f 1492a[4]

5 b h Sadler's Wells (USA) 11.3f **(87)** - Before Dawn (USA) 00

Form - 224

1998 Turf 0-3: (12f, 14f 2) (sft, g-s, g-f)

Currently very useful colt, always wears blinkers. Turf high 101 - 4th of 6 getting 1lb from French Ballerina (20 May Leopardstown 14f g-f RF 1492a). This ex-French horse is smart, but will be better employed in handicaps than Listed races.

**M J Grassick in IRE [0-3] Daniel Wildenstein.*

BLUE SHADOW BHB 68f80a **RR 67f 80a** 318[1]

3 gr c Pips Pride 6.7f **(70)** - Lingdale Lass (Petong) 6.6f **(58)**

Form - 4511231

Record	**1998 -**	1st:2	2nd:1	3rd:1	Ran:4
	Pre1998 -	1st:1	2nd:0	3rd:1	Ran:10

Win Prizemoney £9,621 *Total Prizemoney* £11,745

Wins								
	* **1998**	*Feb*	*Lingfi*	*(SLW)*	*H*	*7f*	*76*	*83* <
	* **1998**	*Jan*	*Lingfi*	*(STD)*	*H*	*7f*	*60*	*72*
	* 1997	*Dec*	*Lingfi*	*(STD)*	*H*	*6f*	*60*	*74*

1998 AW 2-4: (7f 2-2, 8f 2) (Equi 2-4)

Workmanlike, decent colt, effective 6 to 8f, - acts on Equi, has worn blinkers, prefers left handed tracks, prefers tight tracks. AW high 83 - 1st of 5 giving 10lb to Madman's Mirage (19 Feb Lingfield RF 0318). He showed much-improved form on the Lingfield Equitrack around new year, winning two handicaps. He may have been rather lucky to win the first one but there was no fluke about the second. He then twice had a rear view of Diamond Drill at Lingfield, and seemed to find a mile too far. Back to seven furlongs, he won again at Lingfield, but was very fortunate to keep the race as he badly hampered the third horse.

**R Hannon [3-14] J B R Leisure Ltd.*

BLUE SNAKE (USA) BHB 90f **RR 89f** 5039[9]

2 br c Gone West (USA) 7.8f **(82)** - Dabaweyaa (Shareef Dancer (USA)) 9.9f **(73)**

Form - 430

Record	**1998 -**	1st:0	2nd:0	3rd:1	Ran:3

Win Prizemoney £0 *Total Prizemoney* £1,294

1998 Turf 0-3: (6f, 8f 2) (g-s, g-f, frm)

Currently useful colt. Turf high 89 (began Jly) - 3rd of 19 to Timahs (29 Spt Newmarket 8f frm RF 4541). Out of a very useful mare, he showed plenty of promise on his first two runs, but failed to stay a mile in soft ground on his final start.

**S bin Suroor [0-3] Godolphin.*

BLUES OF THE NIGHT RR 44f 4577[8]

2 gr f Petong 7.6f **(58)** - Candane **(77f)** (Danehill (USA)) 10f **(72)**

Form - 08

Record	**1998 -**	1st:0	2nd:0	3rd:0	Ran:2

1998 Turf 0-2: (6f, 7f) (g-s, g-f)

Currently moderate filly. Turf high 44 (began Spt).

**N Tinkler [0-2] Mrs D E Sharp.*

BLUE STAR BHB 80f88a **RR 70f 88a** 4876[2]

2 b c Whittingham (IRE) -Gold And Blue (IRE)(Bluebird (USA)) 7.5f **(69)**

Form - 230182

Record	**1998 -**	1st:1	2nd:2	3rd:1	Ran:6

Win Prizemoney £18,990 *Total Prizemoney* £20,838

Wins							
	* **1998**	*Aug*	*Wolver*	*(STD)*	*6f*		*87* <

1998 Turf 0-2: (6f, 7f) (gd, frm) 1998 AW 1-4: (5f, 6f 1-3) (Fibr 1-4)

Useful colt, effective 6f, - acts on Fibr. Turf high 70 (began Aug). AW high 87 - 2nd of 13 giving 23lb to Indian Swinger (19 Oct Southwell 6f Fibr RF 4876) - also 1st of 13 from Jackie's Baby (22 Aug Wolverhampton RF 3827). Showed ability in Fibresand maidens before being way out of his depth in the Heinz 57 Phoenix Stakes. However, back on a more suitable surface, he landed the Weatherbys Dash at Wolverhampton. Difficult to know what his future may be as he has yet to show an aptitude for turf, and a transatlantic purchase may be his best chance in the long term.

**N P Littmoden [1-6] T Clarke.*

BLUEWAIN LADY BHB 70f **RR 73f** 5125[1]

3 b f Unfuwain (USA) 11.4f **(74)** - Blue Guitar (Cure The Blues (USA)) 9.5f **(63)**

Form - 75031

Record	**1998 -**	1st:1	2nd:0	3rd:1	Ran:5
	Pre1998 -	1st:0	2nd:0	3rd:1	Ran:3

Win Prizemoney £2,941 *Total Prizemoney* £4,780

Wins							
	* **1998**	Nov	Bright	(SFT)	11.9f	60	<

1998 Turf 1-5: (10f 2, 12f 1-2, 14f) (g-s 1-1, g-f, frm 3)

Scopey, above-average filly, effective 7f, acts on frm, has worn blinkers. Turf high 73 (began Jly). Consistent.

**P W Harris [1-8] The Blue Notes.*

BLUNDELL LANE (IRE) BHB 73f **RR 69f** 4128[17]

3 ch c Shalford (IRE) 7.8f **(63)** - Rathbawn Realm (Doulab (USA)) 9.8f **(65)**

Form - 301000000

Record	**1998 -**	1st:1	2nd:0	3rd:1	Ran:9
	Pre1998 -	1st:1	2nd:1	3rd:0	Ran:5

Win Prizemoney £14,037 *Total Prizemoney* £15,863

Wins									
	* **1998**	May	Cheste	(GD)	H	6.1f	75	86+	<
	* 1997	Oct	Redcar	(G-F)	H	6f	69	76	

1998 Turf 1-8:(5f, 6f 1-6, 7f)(gd 2, g-f 1-4, frm 2) 1998 AW 0-1:(6f) (Fibr)

Workmanlike, average colt, effective 6f, acts on g-f to frm, has worn blinkers. Turf high 86 - 1st of 16 getting 13lb from Marton Moss (6 May Chester RF 1057). Ran creditably on Fibresand on his reappearance, and bolted up from an ideal draw at Chester. However, he has shown nothing since and looks inconsistent.

**A P Jarvis [2-14] N Coverdale.*

BLUSHING GRENADIER (IRE) BHB 61f59a **RR 62f 59a** 5142[12]

6 ch g Salt Dome (USA) 6.5f **(59)** - La Duse (Junius (USA)) 7.7f **(65)**

Form - 21337102340173170

Record	**1998 -**	1st:4	2nd:2	3rd:4	Ran:17
	Pre1998 -	1st:2	2nd:2	3rd:2	Ran:35

Win Prizemoney £20,150 *Total Prizemoney* £25,735

Wins									
	* **1998**	Oct	Newcas	(SFT)	H	6f	56	62	<
	* **1998**	Spt	Haydoc	(GD)	SH	6f	50	55	
	1998	Jun	Warwic	(GD)	C	6f		47	
	1998	*Mar*	*Wolver*	*(STD)*	*S*	*6f*		*56*	
	1996	Jly	Windso	(GD)	H	6f	46	57?	
	1995	Jly	Doncas	(GD)	H	6f	50	52	

1998 Turf 3-10: (5f 5, 6f 3-5) (g-s 1-3, gd 1-4, g-f 2, frm 1-1) 1998 AW 1-7: (5f, 6f 1-4, 7f 2) (Equi, Fibr 1-6)

Average gelding, effective 5 to 8f, best at 6f, acts on g-s to frm - acts on AW, best on g-s, often wears blinkers (effectively), likes left handed tracks, likes tight tracks, excels at Wolverhampton. Turf high 62 - 1st of 20 getting 14lb from Mantles Pride (21 Oct Newcastle RF 4918) - also 1st of 24 getting 2lb from Sycamore Lodge (4 Spt Haydock RF 4093). AW high 56 - 1st of 8 getting 5lb from Bold Aristocrat (21 Mar Wolverhampton RF 0461). Consistent. Suited by soft ground and six furlongs, he has plenty of pace and enjoyed a good season.

**S R Bowring [2-11] Roland Wheatley (from M J Fetherston-Godley [4-40] Jun 1998).*

BLUSHING MELODY (IRE) RR 90+f 3016a[9]

3 ch f Never so Bold 7.1f **(62)** - Dime Bag (High Line) 10.3f **(70)**

Form - 2310

1998 Turf 1-4: (7f 1-2, 8f 2) (sft 1-3, g-s)

Useful filly. Turf high 90 (1st run) - 2nd of 13 getting 5lb from Playacting (2 May Curragh 8f sft RF 1051a) - also 1st of 12 giving 3lb to City Imp (19 Jun Tipperary RF 2217a). Won a Tipperary maiden on her third outing and only seen out once more after that, albeit well beaten. Looks moderate.

**J C Harley in IRE [1-4] Mrs D M Solomon.*

BLUSHING RISK (FR) RR 116f 4948a[1]

3 gr c Take Risks (FR) - Sea Goddess (Slip Anchor) 9.8f **(73)**

Form - 221

1998 Turf 1-3: (12f 1-1, 13f, 15f) (hvy 1-1, sft, gd)

Currently high-class colt, often wears blinkers. Turf high 116 - 1st of 5 getting 3lb from Saafeya (18 Oct Longchamp RF 4948a). A French-trained colt who ended the season on a high with an impressive victory in the Group Two Prix du Conseil de Paris. He will be back as a four-year-old and looks interesting.

**H-A Pantall in FR [1-3] Mme P Beck.*

BOATER BHB 64f73a **RR 70f 73a** 3523[7]

4 b g Batshoof 9.5f **(66)** - Velvet Beret (IRE) (Dominion) 8.5f **(63)**

Form - 23034707

Record	**1998 -**	1st:0	2nd:1	3rd:2	Ran:8
	Pre1998 -	1st:1	2nd:1	3rd:2	Ran:8

Win Prizemoney £3,044 *Total Prizemoney* £9,454
Wins 1997 Apr Bright (FRM) H 8f 69 71 <
1998 Turf 0-8: (7f 2, 8f 4, 9f, 10f) (sft, g-s, gd 3, g-f, frm 2)
Workmanlike, above-average gelding, effective 7 to 10f, best at 8f, acts on g-s to frm, has worn blinkers, likes tight tracks. Turf high 74 - 3rd of 12 giving 16lb to With A Will (30 May Kempton 9f gd RF 1590). Ran quite well in the early part of '98, although his high head carriage is a worry.
**R G Frost [0-3] Mrs C Loze (from B R Millman [0-7] Jly 1998).*

BOATMAN (USA) RR 86+f 4738[2]
2 ch c Irish River (FR) 9f **(77)**-Peplum (USA) (Nijinsky (CAN)) 10.3f **(77)**
Form - 12
Record 1998 - 1st:1 2nd:1 3rd:0 Ran:2
Win Prizemoney £9,223 *Total Prizemoney* £13,057
Wins * 1998 Spt Newbur (gd) 8f 86+ <
1998 Turf 1-2: (8f 1-2) (g-s, g-f 1-1)
Currently useful colt. Turf high 86 (1st run) (began Spt) - 1st of 6 from Entertainer (18 Spt Newbury RF 4359). Narrow winner of a warm conditions race on his debut, he was bogged down in the mud behind Daliapour at Ascot. **R Charlton [1-2] K Abdulla.*

BOBAKNOT BHB 40f RR 56f 5004[19]
2 b g Risk Me (FR) 8f **(53)** - Sporting Lass (Blakeney) 10.5f **(64)**
Form - 6800
Record 1998 - 1st:0 2nd:0 3rd:0 Ran:4
1998 Turf 0-3: (5f, 6f 2) (sft, gd, frm) 1998 AW 0-1: (5f) (Fibr)
Fair gelding. Turf high 56 (began Aug). **J S Moore [0-4] J S Moore.*

BOBBIE (IRE) RR 1317[10]
2 ch f Bob's Return (IRE) - Gazettalong (Taufan (USA)) 7f **(57)**
Form - 0
Record 1998 - 1st:0 2nd:0 3rd:0 Ran:1
1998 Turf 0-1: (5f) (frm)
Currently very poor filly. **M H Tompkins [0-1] Mark Tompkins Racing.*

BOBBYDAZZLE BHB 75f RR 82f 4645[7]
3 ch f Rock Hopper 10.6f **(54)** - Billie Blue (Ballad Rock) 7.8f **(63)**
Form - 7614787
Record 1998 - 1st:1 2nd:0 3rd:0 Ran:7
Pre1998 - 1st:1 2nd:1 3rd:0 Ran:6
Win Prizemoney £33,943 *Total Prizemoney* £35,383
Wins * 1998 Jun Newcas (SFT) H 8f 76 79+ <
* 1997 Aug Newcas (GD) H 8f 74 78
1998 Turf 1-7: (8f 1-5, 10f 2) (sft 2, gd 1-1, g-f 2, frm 2)
Light-framed, decent filly, effective 8f, acts on gd to g-f. Turf high 82 - also 1st of 4 giving 1lb to Shamwari Song (3 Jun Newcastle RF 1700). A half-sister to Tumbleweed Ridge and Tumbleweed Pearl, She returned to form when easily taking a four-runner handicap on soft ground over the same Newcastle straight mile on her third start of this season, but was well beaten afterwards.
**Dr J D Scargill [2-13] Mrs Bobby Cohen.*

BOBBY SWIFT BHB 25f RR 1481[12]
4 ch g Wing Park - Satin Box (Jukebox) 8.2f **(49)**
Form - 060
Record 1998 - 1st:0 2nd:0 3rd:0 Ran:3
1998 Turf 0-1: (8f) (gd) 1998 AW 0-2: (10f, 12f) (Equi, Fibr)
Currently very poor gelding. AW high 5.
**P Howling [0-3] Wing Park Progeny Syndicate.*

BOB KNOWS BHB 41f RR 51f 1764[10]
4 br g Robellino (USA) 9.5f **(68)** - Snowline (Bay Express) 7.1f **(60)**
Form - 00
Record 1998 - 1st:0 2nd:0 3rd:0 Ran:2
Pre1998 - 1st:0 2nd:0 3rd:0 Ran:4
1998 Turf 0-1: (12f) (frm) 1998 AW 0-1: (16f) (Fibr)
Lengthy, fair gelding.
**P W Hiatt [0-2] Anthony Harrison (from R F JohnsonHoughton [0-4] Oct 1997).*

BOB'S BUSTER BHB 63f RR 66f 4337[14]
2 b c Bob's Return (IRE) - Saltina (Bustino) 10.4f **(64)**
Form - 62000
Record 1998 - 1st:0 2nd:1 3rd:0 Ran:5
Win Prizemoney £0 *Total Prizemoney* £882
1998 Turf 0-5: (5f 2, 6f 2, 8f) (sft, gd, frm 3)
Average colt. Turf high 62. **J L Harris [0-5] Eric Atkinson.*

BOB'S PRINCESS BHB 75f RR 67f 4453[3]
2 b f Bob's Return (IRE) - Princess Rosananti (IRE) (Shareef Dancer (USA)) 9.9f **(73)**
Form - 13
Record 1998 - 1st:1 2nd:0 3rd:1 Ran:2
Win Prizemoney £2,224 *Total Prizemoney* £3,092
Wins * 1998 Aug Warwic (G-F) 7f 64 <
1998 Turf 1-2: (7f 1-2) (frm 1-2)
Currently average filly. Turf high 67 (began Aug) - also 1st of 12 from Sharoura (31 Aug Warwick RF 4006).
**P R Chamings [1-2] Mrs J E L Wright.*

BO DANCER (IRE) BHB 32f RR 24f 3331[6]
4 ch g Magical Wonder (USA) 7.2f **(60)** - Pitty Pal (USA) (Caracolero (USA)) 8.2f **(57)**
Form - 686
Record 1998 - 1st:0 2nd:0 3rd:0 Ran:3
1998 Turf 0-3: (12f, 14f 2) (gd 3)
Little account gelding. Turf high 24. **K W Hogg [0-5] K W Hogg.*

BODFARI ANNA BHB 62f58a RR 65f 58a 4623[5]
2 br f Casteddu 7.4f **(54)** - Lowrianna (IRE) (Cyrano de Bergerac) 6f **(68)**
Form - 05524272162445
Record 1998 - 1st:1 2nd:4 3rd:0 Ran:14
Win Prizemoney £2,110 *Total Prizemoney* £5,703
Wins * 1998 Aug Nottin (G-F) S 6.1f 64 <
1998 Turf 1-12: (5f 3, 6f 1-7, 7f 2) (g-s, gd 1-4, g-f 4, frm 3) 1998 AW 0-2: (5f 2) (Fibr 2)
Average filly, effective 6f, acts on gd to frm, mostly wears blinkers (extremely effectively). Turf high 65 - 2nd of 16 getting 1lb from Ticklish (1 Spt Ripon 6f gd RF 4013) - also 1st of 14 from Kissimmee Bay (12 Aug Nottingham RF 3581). AW high 55. Consistent. She showed better form when dropped into selling company, and though she should have won at Redcar in August, only to throw the race away, she did everything right when winning a similar event at Nottingham just four days later.
**M W Easterby [1-14] Bodfari Stud Ltd.*

BODFARIDISTINCTION (IRE) BHB 50f47a RR 52f 47a
4811[12]
3 b f Distinctly North (USA) 7.4f **(63)** - Brave Louise (Brave Shot) 10.3f **(54)**
Form - 020805370070
Record 1998 - 1st:0 2nd:1 3rd:1 Ran:12
Pre1998 - 1st:1 2nd:0 3rd:0 Ran:6
Win Prizemoney £6,970 *Total Prizemoney* £9,060
Wins * 1997 May Cheste (HVY) 5.1f 77 <
1998 Turf 0-10: (5f, 6f 4, 7f 4, 8f) (gd 7, g-f 2, frm) 1998 AW 0-2: (6f 2) (Fibr 2)
Lengthy, fair filly, effective 5 to 7f, acts on hvy to gd, has worn blinkers. Turf high 72 (1st run) - 2nd of 22 giving 2lb to Julies Jewel (28 Mar Doncaster 7f gd RF 0486). AW high 31. Becoming disappointing. **A Bailey [1-18] Bodfari Stud Ltd.*

BODFARI KOMAITE BHB 63f RR 68f 5144[11]
2 b c Komaite (USA) 6.9f **(61)** - Gypsy's Barn Rat (Balliol) 5f **(43)**
Form - 86631000
Record 1998 - 1st:1 2nd:0 3rd:1 Ran:8
Win Prizemoney £3,267 *Total Prizemoney* £3,715
Wins * 1998 Spt Redcar (G-F) H 5f 62 68 <
1998 Turf 1-8: (5f 1-7, 6f) (sft 2, gd 4, frm 1-2)
Average colt, effective 5f, acts on frm. Turf high 68 - 1st of 19 getting 7lb from Charlie Girl (25 Spt Redcar RF 4490).
**M W Easterby [1-8] Bodfari Stud Ltd.*

BODFARI MUKA (IRE) BHB 92f RR 89f 4447[4]
2 ch c Mukaddamah (USA) 7.6f **(74)** - Precious Egg (Home Guard (USA)) 9.3f **(66)**
Form - 2134054
Record 1998 - 1st:1 2nd:1 3rd:1 Ran:7
Win Prizemoney £6,885 *Total Prizemoney* £14,091
Wins * 1998 May Cheste (GD) 5.1f 82 <
1998 Turf 1-7: (5f 1-3, 6f 2, 7f 2) (g-s, gd 4, g-f 1-2)
Useful colt, effective 5f, acts on gd to g-f. Turf high 89 - also 1st of

10 from Conwy Lodge (6 May Chester RF 1058). Ran well on his Newmarket debut and got up close home to score at Chester. Has faced some difficult tasks since. Sold for 40,000 gns at Tattersalls Autumn Horses-in-Training Sales. **B W Hills [1-7] Bodfari Stud Ltd.*

BODFARI PRIDE (IRE) BHB 76f **RR 85df** 5096[19]
3 b g Pips Pride 6.7f **(70)** - Renata's Ring (IRE) (Auction Ring (USA)) 8.6f **(65)**
Form - 5115283500
Record 1998 - 1st:2 2nd:1 3rd:1 Ran:10
Pre1998 - 1st:0 2nd:0 3rd:1 Ran:2
Win Prizemoney £21,225 *Total Prizemoney* £31,264
Wins * 1998 May Cheste (GD) H 7.6f 68 76 <
*** 1998** Apr Redcar (SFT) 7f 76 <
1998 Turf 2-10: (6f 5, 7f 1-3, 8f 1-2) (sft 1-3, g-s 2, gd 3, g-f 1-2)
Useful gelding, effective 6 to 8f, best at 7f, acts on sft to g-f, best on gd, prefers tight tracks. Turf high 85 - 3rd of 11 getting 18lb from Superior Premium (24 Jun Chester 6f gd RF 2233) - also 1st of 11 from Pass The Rest (30 Apr Redcar RF 0934).
**A Bailey [2-12] Bodfari Stud Ltd.*

BODFARI QUARRY BHB 76f **RR 77f** 5148[3]
2 b f Efisio 7.7f **(69)** - Last Quarry **(44f)** (Handsome Sailor)
Form - 1303
Record 1998 - 1st:1 2nd:0 3rd:2 Ran:4
Win Prizemoney £3,782 *Total Prizemoney* £4,790
Wins * 1998 Aug Beverl (G-F) 5f 72+ <
1998 Turf 1-4: (5f 1-2, 6f, 7f) (sft, gd 1-2, g-f)
Above-average filly. Turf high 77 (began Aug) - also 1st of 13 from Lunar Prospector (13 Aug Beverley RF 3604). She made a winning debut when coming fast and late over the minimum at Beverley in August, and was her trainer's last runner when a creditable third in a Doncaster nursery. **Mrs J R Ramsden [1-4] Bodfari Stud Ltd.*

Bodfari Quarry was Lynda Ramsden's last runner

BODFARI SIGNET BHB 63f **RR 65f** 4835[2]
2 ch c King's Signet (USA) 7f **(51)** - Darakah **(37f 46a)** (Doulab (USA)) 9.8f **(65)**
Form - 080506572502
Record 1998 - 1st:0 2nd:2 3rd:0 Ran:12
Win Prizemoney £0 *Total Prizemoney* £1,734
1998 Turf 0-12: (5f 5, 6f 3, 7f 4) (sft, g-s, gd 5, g-f, frm 4)
Average colt, effective 7f, acts on g-s to frm, often wears blinkers (very effectively). Turf high 65 - 2nd of 15 getting 8lb from Itsanothergirl (16 Oct Catterick 7f g-s RF 4835).
**M W Easterby [0-12] Bodfari Stud Ltd.*

BODFARI STREET BHB 90f **RR 87f** 4185[5]
2 ch c Dolphin Street (FR) - As Sharp as **(61f)** (Handsome Sailor)
Form - 13405
Record 1998 - 1st:1 2nd:0 3rd:1 Ran:5
Win Prizemoney £3,530 *Total Prizemoney* £11,498
Wins * 1998 Jly Haydoc (GD) 6f 75 <
1998 Turf 1-5: (6f 1-5) (gd 2, g-f 1-1, frm 2)
Useful colt. Turf high 87 (began Jly). Looked worth a try over furlong when fifth to Boomerang Blade in a valuable sales race at Doncaster. Sold for 30,000 gns at Tattersalls in October.
**Mrs J R Ramsden [1-5] Bodfari Stud Ltd.*

BODFARI TIMES BHB 69f **RR 75f** 5042[6]
2 ch f Clantime 6.6f **(57)** - Tendency (Ballad Rock) 7.8f **(63)**
Form - 427756
Record 1998 - 1st:0 2nd:1 3rd:0 Ran:6
Win Prizemoney £0 *Total Prizemoney* £2,041
1998 Turf 0-6: (5f 6) (sft 2, gd, g-f 3)
Above-average filly, effective 5f, acts on g-f. Turf high 75 - 2nd of 4 getting 5lb from Choto Mate (19 May Goodwood 5f g-f RF 1327).
**A Bailey [0-6] Bodfari Stud Ltd.*

BODFARI WREN BHB 33f **RR 29f** 4535[14]
4 b f Handsome Sailor 6.6f **(53)** - My Valentine Card (USA) (Forli (ARG)) 9.6f **(67)**
Form - 660
Record 1998 - 1st:0 2nd:0 3rd:0 Ran:3
Pre1998 - 1st:0 2nd:0 3rd:0 Ran:2
Win Prizemoney £0 *Total Prizemoney* £242
1998 Turf 0-3: (7f 2, 8f) (g-s, gd, frm)
Little account filly. Turf high 29. (DEAD)
**A Bailey [0-5] Bodfari Stud Ltd.*

BODYGUARD BHB 98f **RR 97df** 1417[11]
3 ch c Zafonic (USA) 9f **(83)** - White Wisteria (Ahonoora) 8.1f **(73)**
Form - 760
Record 1998 - 1st:0 2nd:0 3rd:0 Ran:3
Pre1998 - 1st:3 2nd:0 3rd:1 Ran:5
Win Prizemoney £21,892 *Total Prizemoney* £28,547
Wins * 1997 Jly Sandow (G-S) L 5f 103 <
* 1997 May York (GD) 6f 87
* 1997 May Newmar (GD) 5f 85+
1998 Turf 0-3: (5f, 6f 2) (gd 2, g-f)
Very useful colt, effective 5f, acts on gd, has worn blinkers. Turf high 88. A very useful early two-year-old, who was Zafonic's first winner as a sire, he showed a smart turn of foot to win on his debut and later scored in listed company, but showed nothing at three. **P F I Cole [3-8] H R H Prince Fahd Salman.*

BOFFY (IRE) BHB 33f27a **RR 23f 27a** 1299[11]
5 ch h Mac's Imp (USA) 5.6f **(54)** - No Dowry (Shy Groom (USA)) 10f **(66)**
Form - 78400006586470
Record 1998 - 1st:0 2nd:0 3rd:0 Ran:14
Pre1998 - 1st:4 2nd:4 3rd:3 Ran:44
Win Prizemoney £11,507 *Total Prizemoney* £16,706
Wins * 1996 *Feb Southw (STD) S 5f 52*
* 1996 *Jan Wolver (STD) S 5f 73*
* 1995 Spt Haydoc (GD) C 6f 74 <
* 1995 Aug Leices (GD) S 5f 70
1998 Turf 0-1: (5f) (gd) 1998 AW 0-13: (5f 9, 6f 3, 7f) (Equi, Fibr 12)
Little account colt, effective 5f, - acts on Fibr, has worn blinkers. AW high 29. **B P J Baugh [4-58] Mrs J Gill.*

BOHEMIA BHB 70f **RR 66f** 4109[5]
2 b f Polish Precedent (USA) 9f **(73)** - Horseshoe Reef (Mill Reef (USA)) 10.5f **(78)**
Form - 045
Record 1998 - 1st:0 2nd:0 3rd:0 Ran:3
Win Prizemoney £0 *Total Prizemoney* £287
1998 Turf 0-3: (6f, 7f, 8f) (gd, frm 2)

Currently average filly. Turf high 66 (began Jly).
**J R Fanshawe [0-3] Lord Halifax.*

BOHEMIAN RR 37f 3897[11]

2 b br f Puissance 7.1f **(60)** - Monstrosa (Monsanto (FR)) 6.5f **(59)**
Form - 0

Record	**1998 -**	1st:0	2nd:0	3rd:0	Ran:1

1998 Turf 0-1: (7f) (gd)
Currently very moderate filly. **J S Moore [0-1] Western Solvents Ltd.*

BO'JUST RR 2[13]

6 b m Bold Fort 5.8f **(53)** - Just Blair (Prince Tenderfoot (USA)) 9f **(61)**
Form - 00

Record	**1998 -**	1st:0	2nd:0	3rd:0	Ran:1
	Pre1998 -	1st:0	2nd:0	3rd:0	Ran:1

1998 AW 0-1: (10f) (Equi)
Currently very poor mare. **P Hayward [0-2] P Hayward.*

BOLD AMUSEMENT BHB 59f74a RR 60f 74a 5098[1]

8 ch g Never so Bold 7.1f **(62)** - Hysterical (High Top) 10.2f **(67)**
Form - 0051

Record	**1998 -**	1st:1	2nd:0	3rd:0	Ran:4
	Pre1998 -	1st:3	2nd:5	3rd:1	Ran:29

Win Prizemoney £14,783 *Total Prizemoney* £22,840

Wins								
*	**1998**	Nov	Redcar	(G-S)	H	10f	55	60
*	1995	Jly	Beverl	(G-F)	H	8.5f	78	84
	1994	Jly	Doncas	(G-F)	H	10.3f	82	85 <

1998 Turf 1-4: (9f, 10f 1-2, 12f) (g-s 2, gd 1-1, frm)
Average gelding, has worn blinkers. Turf high 60 (began Spt). Inconsistent.
**W S Cunningham [2-26] Mrs Ann Bell (from Mrs M Reveley [2-12] Spt 1994).*

BOLD ARISTOCRAT (IRE) BHB 43f61a RR 41f 61a 1795[5]

7 b g Bold Arrangement 8.7f **(57)** - Wyn Mipet (Welsh Saint) 7.6f **(64)**
Form - 534536214112635

Record	**1998 -**	1st:3	2nd:2	3rd:2	Ran:11
	Pre1998 -	1st:6	2nd:6	3rd:14	Ran:81

Win Prizemoney £19,416 *Total Prizemoney* £30,806

Wins								
*	**1998**	*Mar*	*Southw*	*(STD)*	*S*	*6f*		*61*
*	**1998**	*Feb*	*Southw*	*(STD)*	*S*	*6f*		*60*
*	**1998**	*Feb*	*Southw*	*(STD)*	*S*	*6f*		*56*
*	1997	*Jun*	*Southw*	*(STD)*		*6f*		*68*
*	1997	*Feb*	*Southw*	*(STD)*	*SH*	*6f*	*60*	*60*
*	1996	*Feb*	*Southw*	*(STD)*	*SH*	*6f*	*50*	*46*
*	1996	*Jan*	*Southw*	*(STD)*	*C*	*6f*		*48*
*	1995	*Jly*	*Southw*	*(STD)*	*H*	*6f*	*45*	*47*

1998 AW 3-11: (6f 3-6, 7f 5) (Fibr 3-11)
Average gelding, effective 6 to 7f, best at 6f, - acts on Fibr, has worn blinkers, favours left handed tracks, favours tight tracks, and likes Southwell. AW high 61 - 1st of 11 from Elton Ledger (11 Mar Southwell RF 0423) - also 1st of 11 giving 5lb to Silk Cottage (23 Feb Southwell RF 0346). Runs almost every week, but pops up in modest company on Fibresand from time to time. In especially good form at the start of 1998, all of his recent victories have been over six furlongs at Southwell. **R Hollinshead [9-92] Mrs J Hughes.*

BOLD BRIEF BHB 47f RR 53f 845[17]

4 b g Tina's Pet 7.4f **(56)** - Immodest Miss (Daring Display (USA)) 6.9f **(69)**
Form - 0

Record	**1998 -**	1st:0	2nd:0	3rd:0	Ran:1
	Pre1998 -	1st:1	2nd:2	3rd:0	Ran:15

Win Prizemoney £2,584 *Total Prizemoney* £4,534

Wins								
*	1996	Jun	Ayr	(G-F)		5f		63 <

1998 Turf 0-1: (6f) (gd)
Scopey, fair gelding, effective 5 to 6f, best at 6f, acts on frm, has worn blinkers. Inconsistent. **Denys Smith [1-16] P & I Darling.*

BOLD BUSTER BHB 65f RR 73f 1037[14]

5 b g Bustino 11f **(64)** - Truly Bold (Bold Lad (IRE)) 8.4f **(68)**
Form - 70

Record	**1998 -**	1st:0	2nd:0	3rd:0	Ran:2
	Pre1998 -	1st:1	2nd:1	3rd:1	Ran:7

Win Prizemoney £3,836 *Total Prizemoney* £6,247

Wins								
*	1997	Aug	Lingfi	(G-S)	H	11.5f	64	67 <

1998 Turf 0-2: (12f 2) (sft, gd)
Above-average gelding, effective 11 to 16f, acts on g-s to gd, best on gd. Turf high 54. **I A Balding [1-13] Robert Hitchins.*

BOLD BYZANTIUM RR 34f 4673[9]

2 b f Bold Arrangement 8.7f **(57)** - Raunchy Rita (Brigadier Gerard) 9.3f **(58)**
Form - 0

Record	**1998 -**	1st:0	2nd:0	3rd:0	Ran:1

1998 Turf 0-1: (6f) (g-f)
Currently very moderate filly. **E J Alston [0-1] T A Couchman.*

BOLD CARDOWAN (IRE) RR 42f 4774[18]

2 br c Persian Bold 10f **(69)** - Moving Trend (IRE) (Be My Guest (USA)) 9.3f **(67)**
Form - 00

Record	**1998 -**	1st:0	2nd:0	3rd:0	Ran:2

1998 Turf 0-2: (6f, 7f) (gd, frm)
Currently moderate colt. Turf high 42 (began Spt).
**John Berry [0-2] J McCarthy.*

BOLD CONQUEROR BHB 45f RR 27f 4803[7]

2 br f Anshan 8.2f **(63)** - Freudenau (Wassl) 9.7f **(62)**
Form - 077

Record	**1998 -**	1st:0	2nd:0	3rd:0	Ran:3

1998 Turf 0-3: (5f, 6f, 7f) (sft, g-f, frm)
Currently little account filly. Turf high 27.
**J M Bradley [0-3] E A Hayward.*

BOLD EDGE BHB 110f RR 110f 4844[1]

3 ch c Beveled (USA) 6.9f **(64)** - Daring Ditty (Daring March) 7.1f **(61)**
Form - 11225251

Record	**1998 -**	1st:3	2nd:3	3rd:0	Ran:8
	Pre1998 -	1st:1	2nd:0	3rd:2	Ran:7

Win Prizemoney £30,764 *Total Prizemoney* £56,719

Wins								
*	**1998**	Oct	Newmar	(GD)	L	6f		108 <
*	**1998**	May	Newbur	(GD)		6f		107
*	**1998**	Apr	Leices	(SFT)		6f		100
*	1997	May	Newbur	(SFT)		6f		94+

1998 Turf 3-8: (6f 3-6, 7f, 8f) (sft 1-1, gd 4, g-f 2-2, frm)
Scopey, Group-class colt, effective 6 to 7f, best at 6f, acts on sft to frm, best on gd, excels at Newmarket, does well at Newbury. Turf high 110 - 2nd of 8 giving 5lb to Grazia (18 Jly Newbury 6f gd RF 2908) - also 1st of 16 getting 5lb from Tedburrow (16 Oct Newmarket RF 4844). Consistent. He had a profitable campaign and thoroughly deserved a Listed win at Newmarket during October. Suited by easy ground as are most Beveleds, he could do well in the better early-season sprints and will probably be aimed at the Duke Of York Stakes.
**R Hannon [4-15] Lady Whent and Friends.*

BOLD EFFORT (FR) BHB 90f96a RR 95f 96a 4965[10]

6 b g Bold Arrangement 8.7f **(57)** - Malham Tarn (Riverman (USA)) 9.1f **(76)**
Form - 06303168100050

Record	**1998 -**	1st:2	2nd:0	3rd:2	Ran:13
	Pre1998 -	1st:8	2nd:9	3rd:3	Ran:55

Win Prizemoney £110,614 *Total Prizemoney* £139,188

Wins								
*	**1998**	Jly	Sandow	(G-S)	H	5f	92	95 <
*	**1998**	May	Kempto	(G-F)	H	6f	89	91
*	1997	*May*	*Wolver*	*(STD)*	*H*	*6f*	*90*	*94*
*	1996	*Dec*	*Lingfi*	*(STD)*	*H*	*6f*	*82*	*89*
*	1996	Spt	Maison	(SFT)	H	6f		80
*	1996	Aug	Claire	(SFT)		8f		78
*	1995	Jun	York	(G-F)	H	6f	87	94
*	1995	May	Salisb	(G-F)	H	6f	74	82
*	1995	*Feb*	*Lingfi*	*(STD)*	*H*	*6f*	*72*	*74*
*	1995	*Jan*	*Lingfi*	*(STD)*		*6f*		*64*

1998 Turf 2-12: (5f 1-3, 6f 1-9) (sft, gd 1-7, g-f 2, frm 1-2) 1998 AW 0-1: (5f) (Fibr)
Very useful gelding, effective 5 to 7f, best at 6f, acts on gd to frm - acts on Fibr, often wears blinkers (very effectively), likes left handed tracks, excels at Doncaster, does well at Wolverhampton. Turf high 95 - 1st of 12 giving 12lb to Divine Miss-P (4 Jly Sandown RF 2552) - also 1st of 13 giving 19lb to White Emir (17 May Kempton RF 1281). He is a useful sprint handicapper on both turf and sand, and followed a good run in the Wokingham with a last-gasp victory at Sandown. Rather disappointing afterwards, but will win his usual handicap or two next term.

**K O Cunningham-Brown [10-68] A J Richards.*

BOLD FACT (USA) BHB 113f **RR 113f** 4461[3]
3 b c Known Fact (USA) 8.3f **(72)** - Sookera (USA) (Roberto (USA)) 10f **(76)**
Form - 10813

Record	**1998** -	1st:2	2nd:0	3rd:1	Ran:5
	Pre1998 -	1st:2	2nd:1	3rd:1	Ran:4

Win Prizemoney £49,328 *Total Prizemoney* £85,012

Wins						
* **1998**	Aug York	(FRM)	L	7f	111	
* **1998**	May Newmar	(G-F)	L	7f	115+	<
* 1997	Jly Newmar	(GD)	G3	6f	102	
* 1997	Jun Goodwo	(G-F)		6f	73+	

1998 Turf 2-5: (6f, 7f 2-4) (gd, frm 2-4)
Unfurnished, Group-class colt, effective 7f, acts on frm. Turf high 115 (1st run) - 1st of 7 giving 7lb to Daring Derek (16 May Newmarket RF 1267) - also 1st of 6 from Jo Mell (20 Aug York RF 3777). A brother to top-class sprinter So Factual, he looked a bit quirky on a couple of occasions at two. Made a winning reappearance in a Newmarket Listed event, but was very disappointing in the Jersey Stakes. Again well held in the July Cup, but regained winning form in a Listed race at York. He ended the season by finishing third to Decorated Hero in a Group Three at Goodwood.
**H R A Cecil [4-9] K Abdulla.*

(Fibr 1-3)
Average filly, effective 8 to 10f, best at 10f, acts on frm - acts on Fibr, prefers right handed tracks, excels at Newmarket, does well at Southwell. Turf high 68 - 1st of 9 getting 14lb from Muhtafel (1 Aug Newmarket RF 3276) - also 1st of 8 getting 25lb from Give Me A Ring (17 Jly Newmarket RF 2881). AW high 63 - 2nd of 11 giving 8lb to Green Bopper (9 Mar Southwell 8f Fibr RF 0414). In fine form in 1998, completing a four-timer with a win at Newmarket in August. Appreciates a bit of cut in the ground.
**W J Musson [6-15] Jumbo Ltd.*

BOLD FELICITER BHB 45f **RR 47f** 4530[7]
2 ch f Bold Arrangement 8.7f **(57)**-Jersey Maid (On Your Mark) 7.7f **(58)**
Form - 67086067

Record	**1998** -	1st:0	2nd:0	3rd:0	Ran:8

1998 Turf 0-8: (5f 2, 7f 3, 8f 3) (g-s, gd 4, g-f 2, frm)
Moderate filly. Turf high 47. **D Moffatt [0-8] Leslie Sloan.*

BOLD FRONTIER BHB 51f70a **RR 52f 70a** 4455[7]
6 gr g Chief Singer 8.6f **(62)** - Mumtaz Flyer (USA) (Al Hattab (USA)) 9.3f **(74)**
Form - 0001483107

Bold Fact seals a course record victory at York

BOLD FAITH BHB 72f70a **RR 68+f 70a** 3276[1]
5 b m Warning 8.1f **(77)** - Bold and Beautiful (Bold Lad (IRE)) 8.4f **(68)**
Form - 12001D11

Record	**1998** -	1st:4	2nd:1	3rd:0	Ran:8
	Pre1998 -	1st:2	2nd:0	3rd:0	Ran:7

Win Prizemoney £22,413 *Total Prizemoney* £23,854

Wins								
* **1998**	Aug Newmar	(G-F)	H	10f	65	68	<
* **1998**	Jly Newmar	(G-F)	H	10f	62	67	
* **1998**	May Leices	(GD)	H	10f	52	57	
* **1998**	*Feb Southw*	*(STD)*	*H*	*8f*	*51*	*56*	
* 1997	Nov Nottin	(GD)	H	8.2f	47	55	
* 1997	Jun Folkes	(SFT)	H	9.7f	45	51	

1998 Turf 3-5: (8f, 10f 3-4) (g-s, g-f 1-1, frm 2-3) 1998 AW 1-3: (8f 1-3)

Record	**1998** -	1st:2	2nd:0	3rd:1	Ran:10
	Pre1998 -	1st:4	2nd:4	3rd:2	Ran:20

Win Prizemoney £15,192 *Total Prizemoney* £21,314

Wins							
* **1998**	Aug Lingfi	(G-F)	SH	5f	47	52	
* **1998**	*Jly Lingfi*	*(STD)*	*C*	*5f*		*57*	
* 1997	*Mar Wolver*	*(STD)*	*H*	*5f*	*67*	*73*	<
* 1995	*Apr Wolver*	*(STD)*	*H*	*5f*	*62*	*70*	
* 1994	*Aug Southw*	*(STD)*	*S*	*5f*		*66+*	
* 1994	*Jly Southw*	*(STD)*	*S*	*5f*		*57*	

1998 Turf 1-8: (5f 1-7, 6f) (g-s, g-f, frm 1-5, hrd) 1998 AW 1-2: (5f 1-2) (Equi 1-1, Fibr)
Above-average gelding, effective 5 to 6f, best at 6f, - acts on Fibr,

mostly wears blinkers (effectively), prefers left handed tracks, prefers tight tracks. Turf high 52. AW high 68 (began Jly). He was in very good form on Fibresand at the start of '97, but was off the track for a year after winning at Wolverhampton in the March of that year. He was successful twice last season since coming back, once on Equitrack and once on turf, though at a much lower level.

**K T Ivory [6-30] K T Ivory.*

BOLD GAIT BHB 90f **RR 87f** 4850[13]

7 ch g Persian Bold 10f **(69)** - Miller's Gait (Mill Reef (USA)) 10.5f **(78)**

Form - 060

Record	**1998** -	1st:0	2nd:0	3rd:0	Ran:3
	Pre1998 -	1st:5	2nd:2	3rd:1	Ran:13

Win Prizemoney £88,683 *Total Prizemoney* £97,707

Wins								
• 1995	Jly	Newcas	(FRM)	H	16.1f	105	115	<
• 1995	Apr	Newbur	(G-F)	H	16f	95	102	
• 1994	Spt	Doncas	(GD)	H	14.6f	84	94	
• 1994	Jly	Newbur	(G-F)	H	13.3f	79	82	
• 1994	May	Warwic	(G-S)	H	10.8f	73	78	

1998 Turf 0-3: (13f, 15f, 18f) (gd 2, g-f)

Useful gelding. Turf high 87 (began Spt). Lightly-raced on the level these days, but won over hurdles in November.

**J R Fanshawe [5-20] Mrs I Phillips.*

BOLD HUNTER BHB 62f **RR 71f** 4670[8]

4 b g Polish Precedent (USA) 9f **(73)** - Pumpona (USA) (Sharpen Up) 8.3f **(67)**

Form - 00627035808

Record	**1998** -	1st:0	2nd:1	3rd:1	Ran:11
	Pre1998 -	1st:1	2nd:2	3rd:1	Ran:9

Win Prizemoney £2,740 *Total Prizemoney* £7,515

Wins 1997 Jun Sligo (FRM) 6.5f 77 <

1998 Turf 0-11: (6f 3, 7f 3, 8f 2, 9f, 10f 2) (g-s, gd 4, g-f 5, frm)

Above-average gelding, effective 7 to 9f, best at 7f, acts on gd to frm, often wears blinkers (very effectively), likes left handed tracks, likes tight tracks. Turf high 71 - 6th of 14 getting 3lb from Philistar (5 Jun Epsom 9f gd RF 1748). Inconsistent.

**Mrs P N Dutfield [0-11] The Carpetbaggers (from J S Bolger in IRE [1-9] Oct 1997).*

BOLD KING BHB 76f83a **RR 76f 83a** 4619[10]

3 br c Anshan 8.2f **(63)** - Spanish Heart (King of Spain) 7.8f **(52)**

Form - 1464530

Record	**1998** -	1st:1	2nd:0	3rd:1	Ran:7
	Pre1998 -	1st:0	2nd:3	3rd:0	Ran:4

Win Prizemoney £2,427 *Total Prizemoney* £7,904

Wins • **1998** *Apr Southw (STD) 8f 72+* <

1998 Turf 0-6: (7f, 8f 3, 10f 2) (gd 4, g-f, frm) 1998 AW 1-1: (8f 1-1) (Fibr 1-1)

Workmanlike, above-average colt, effective 8 to 10f, best at 8f, acts on gd to frm - acts on Fibr. Turf high 76 - 3rd of 20 getting 3lb from Quintus (23 Spt Goodwood 10f gd RF 4457). (1st run) - 1st of 8 giving 5lb to Angelina (27 Apr Southwell RF 0884). Consistent. Runner-up on his first three starts at two, he got off the mark by bolting up in a maiden on the Southwell Fibresand in April. Has been held in handicaps since, but is dropping to a decent mark.

**J W Hills [1-11] Avon Industries Ltd.*

BOLD LEGACY (IRE) BHB 32f45a **RR 18f 45a** 3944[19]

3 ch c Mujtahid (USA) 7.4f **(69)** - Lagrion (USA) (Diesis) 9.3f **(69)**

Form - 5748080

Record	**1998** -	1st:0	2nd:0	3rd:0	Ran:6
	Pre1998 -	1st:0	2nd:0	3rd:0	Ran:3

1998 Turf 0-5: (8f, 10f, 11f, 12f 2) (gd, frm 4) 1998 AW 0-1: (8f) (Equi)

Leggy, fair colt, has worn blinkers. Turf high 18 (began Jly).

**W R Muir [0-9] C L A Edginton.*

BOLDLY GOES BHB 100f **RR 98+f** 3998[1]

2 b c Bold Arrangement 8.7f **(57)** - Reine de Thebes (FR) (Darshaan) 9.9f **(84)**

Form - 11181

Record	**1998** -	1st:4	2nd:0	3rd:0	Ran:5

Win Prizemoney £24,947 *Total Prizemoney* £24,947

Wins								
• **1998**	Aug	Ripon	(G-F)	L	6f		98+	<
• **1998**	Jly	Thirsk	(FRM)		7f		88	
• **1998**	*Jun*	*Wolver*	*(STD)*		*6f*		*87*	
• **1998**	Apr	Pontef	(G-S)		5f		62	

1998 Turf 3-4: (5f 1-1, 6f 1-1, 7f 1-2) (g-s 1-1, gd 1-1, g-f, frm 1-1) 1998 AW 1-1: (6f 1-1) (Fibr 1-1)

Very useful colt. Turf high 98 - 1st of 5 giving 3lb to Anno Domini (31 Aug Ripon RF 3998). (1st run). He won his first three races in gritty style before finishing in midfield in a hot nursery, bounced back to form next time in a hot Listed race at Ripon. He is clearly useful and also impressed with his attitude at the business end of his races. Looks likely to have a successful campaign next term.

**C W Fairhurst [4-5] G H & S Leggott.*

BOLD ORIENTAL (IRE) BHB 70f **RR 72f** 4500[8]

4 b g Tirol 8.1f **(64)** - Miss Java (Persian Bold) 9.3f **(66)**

Form - 788

Record	**1998** -	1st:0	2nd:0	3rd:0	Ran:3
	Pre1998 -	1st:2	2nd:2	3rd:2	Ran:18

Win Prizemoney £7,684 *Total Prizemoney* £11,598

Wins								
1997	Apr	Bath	(G-F)	H	10.2f	79	81+	
1996	Spt	Goodwo	(G-F)	H	8f	72	83	<

1998 Turf 0-3: (9f, 12f, 14f) (g-f, frm 2)

Leggy, above-average gelding, effective 9 to 10f, best at 10f, acts on g-s to frm, has worn blinkers, prefers right handed tracks. Turf high 72 (began Aug).

**S E H Sherwood [0-3] Uplands Bloodstock (from N A Callaghan [2-18] Jly 1997).*

BOLD RAPAREE (IRE) **RR 101f** 4281a[6]

3 ch c Bob Back (USA) 11.5f **(71)** - Shagudine (USA)

Form - 71046

1998 Turf 1-4: (10f 1-2, 12f 2) (hvy, sft 1-1, g-f 2)

Very useful colt, effective 10f, acts on sft to g-f, has worn blinkers. Turf high 101 (1st run) - 1st of 5 giving 10lb to Miss Emer (4 May Navan RF 1173a). Inconsistent. He is not really Group or Listed class, but could do well over hurdles.

**D K Weld in IRE [2-9] A Castignani.*

BOLD SARAH BHB 34f **RR 49f** 4408[15]

4 ch f Bold Arrangement 8.7f **(57)** - Miss Sarajane (Skyliner) 7.3f **(53)**

Form - 0080800

Record	**1998** -	1st:0	2nd:0	3rd:0	Ran:7

1998 Turf 0-7: (5f, 6f, 7f, 8f 3, 10f) (g-s, gd 2, g-f 2, frm 2)

Scopey, moderate filly. Turf high 49. **R Hollinshead [0-7] J Smyth.*

BOLD SHADOW BHB 62f **RR 62?f** 3831[7]

2 gr f Never so Bold 7.1f **(62)** - Dangerous Shadow **(37f 47a)** (Absalom) 7.2f **(58)**

Form - 4437

Record	**1998** -	1st:0	2nd:0	3rd:1	Ran:4

Win Prizemoney £0 *Total Prizemoney* £881

1998 Turf 0-4: (5f 3, 6f) (gd, g-f 2, frm)

Average filly. Turf high 62. **R A Fahey [0-4] Prime Racing.*

BOLD SPRING (IRE) BHB 62f65a **RR 62f 65a** 4202[11]

4 b g Never so Bold 7.1f **(62)** - Oasis (Valiyar) 8.5f **(73)**

Form - 504810100

Record	**1998** -	1st:2	2nd:0	3rd:0	Ran:9
	Pre1998 -	1st:0	2nd:2	3rd:4	Ran:16

Win Prizemoney £6,364 *Total Prizemoney* £10,032

Wins								
• **1998**	Jly	Kempto	(G-F)	H	7f	58	62	<
• **1998**	Jun	Bright	(FRM)	H	7f	54	55	

1998 Turf 2-9: (6f 3, 7f 2-6) (sft, g-s, gd 2, g-f 1-3, frm 1-2)

Leggy, above-average gelding, effective 7f, acts on frm, has worn blinkers. Turf high 62 - 1st of 17 getting 2lb from Daryabad (8 Jly Kempton RF 2630). **R Hannon [2-25] J Newsome.*

BOLD TINA (IRE) BHB 62f62a **RR 68f 62a** 4962[18]

4 b f Persian Bold 10f **(69)** - Tinas Image (He Loves Me) 7.9f **(55)**

Form - 5322667214060

Record	**1998** -	1st:1	2nd:3	3rd:1	Ran:13
	Pre1998 -	1st:2	2nd:2	3rd:3	Ran:15

Win Prizemoney £9,067 *Total Prizemoney* £16,351

Wins								
• **1998**	Aug	Leices	(GD)		7f		67	<
• 1997	Oct	Lingfi	(FRM)	H	7f	60	64	
• 1997	Spt	Bright	(G-F)		7f		59	

1998 Turf 1-13: (6f, 7f 1-7, 8f 5) (sft, g-s, gd, g-f 7, frm 1-3)

Light-framed, average filly, effective 6 to 8f, best at 7f, acts on gd to frm, best on g-f, likes tight tracks, excels at Salisbury. Turf high 68 - 4th of 12 getting 2lb from Scent of Success (29 Aug Windsor 8f g-f RF 3975) - also 1st of 11 getting 3lb from Bubbly (19 Aug

Leicester RF 3740). **R Hannon [3-28] Mrs Chris Harrington.*

BOLD TOP BHB 36f37a RR 40f 37a 3939[10]

6 ch g Bold Owl 9.7f **(47)** - Whirlygigger (Taufan (USA)) 7f **(57)**
Form - 40360
Record 1998 - 1st:0 2nd:0 3rd:1 Ran:5
Pre1998 - 1st:1 2nd:4 3rd:7 Ran:37
Win Prizemoney £2,598 *Total Prizemoney* £9,381
Wins 1997 Aug Pontef (G-F) S 12f 46 <
1998 Turf 0-5: (10f 2, 12f 2, 16f) (g-f, frm 4)
Moderate gelding, effective 10 to 12f, best at 10f, acts on gd to frm, often wears blinkers (very effectively), likes left handed tracks. Turf high 40 (1st run) - 4th of 9 getting 1lb from Tapatch (29 Jun Pontefract 10f frm RF 2380).
**M E Sowersby [0-5] Racing Ladies (from B S Rothwell [1-41] Oct 1997).*

BOLD WELCOME BHB 65f RR 67?f 2520[6]

4 ch g Most Welcome 8.6f **(66)** - Song's Best (Never so Bold) 6.3f **(66)**
Form - 6
Record 1998 - 1st:0 2nd:0 3rd:0 Ran:1
Pre1998 - 1st:0 2nd:1 3rd:0 Ran:3
Win Prizemoney £0 *Total Prizemoney* £660
1998 Turf 0-1: (5f) (g-f)
Average gelding. (DEAD) **J Wharton [0-4] J M Berry.*

BOLD WORDS (CAN) RR 108f 3219[19]

4 ch c Bold Ruckus (USA) 7.5f **(83)** - Trillium Woods (CAN) (Briartic (CAN)) 9.5f **(84)**
Form - 5020
Record 1998 - 1st:0 2nd:1 3rd:0 Ran:4
Pre1998 - 1st:3 2nd:1 3rd:0 Ran:11
Win Prizemoney £14,355 *Total Prizemoney* £27,979
Wins * 1997 Apr Ripon (G-F) 9f 100 <
* 1996 Oct Newmar (GD) H 8f 85 91
* 1996 Oct Salisb (G-S) 8f 74
1998 Turf 0-4: (8f 4) (gd 3, frm)
Scopey, Pattern-class colt, effective 8f, acts on gd to frm, best on g-f, has worn blinkers. Turf high 108 (1st run) - 5th of 9 getting 1lb from Ramooz (13 May York 8f gd RF 1208). Inconsistent.
**E A L Dunlop [3-15] Maktoum Al Maktoum.*

BOLERO KID BHB 82f RR 86f 1223[12]

3 b g Rambo Dancer (CAN) 8.4f **(59)** - Barrie Baby (Import) 6.6f **(68)**
Form - 00
Record 1998 - 1st:0 2nd:0 3rd:0 Ran:2
Pre1998 - 1st:1 2nd:1 3rd:1 Ran:6
Win Prizemoney £3,834 *Total Prizemoney* £5,209
Wins * 1997 Jly Redcar (G-S) H 7f 77+ <
1998 Turf 0-2: (8f 2) (g-s, gd)
Scopey, useful gelding, effective 7f, acts on gd. Turf high 63. Appreciated the step up to seven and the softish ground to land a nursery at Redcar. Should continue to progress, although his initial effort of '98 was not encouraging.
**M W Easterby [1-8] Mybank Racing.*

BOLINO STAR (IRE) RR 100f 3351a[6]

7 b m Stalker 9.7f **(59)** - Gobolino (Don) 7.7f **(64)**
Form - 23241446
1998 Turf 1-7: (8f, 11f, 12f 1-4, 14f) (hvy 2, sft 1-2, g-s, gd, g-f)
Very useful mare, effective 12f, acts on sft, has worn blinkers, likes left handed tracks. Turf high 100 - 1st of 8 getting 3lb from Back Log (19 Jun Tipperary RF 2215a). She did well to finish third in the Irish Lincoln, but is better over middle-distances and put up a super effort to win a Listed race at Tipperary in June. A smart hurdler, she has given her connections tremendous value for money. **S J Treacy in IRE [5-33] Berkeley Syndicate.*

BOLLAN BHB 50f RR 55f 3838[6]

3 b g Democratic (USA) - Faustelerie (Faustus (USA)) 10f **(58)**
Form - 04U6
Record 1998 - 1st:0 2nd:0 3rd:0 Ran:4
Win Prizemoney £0 *Total Prizemoney* £255
1998 Turf 0-4: (8f, 9f, 10f 2) (g-f 2, frm 2)
Light-framed, fair gelding. Turf high 55 (began Jly).
**R Simpson [0-4] G Piper.*

BOLLERO (IRE) BHB 42f40a RR 44f 40a 841[4]

4 b f Topanoora 8.3f **(67)** - Charo (Mariacci (FR)) 8.8f **(70)**
Form - 05754
Record 1998 - 1st:0 2nd:0 3rd:0 Ran:5
Pre1998 - 1st:3 2nd:4 3rd:1 Ran:23
Win Prizemoney £8,575 *Total Prizemoney* £12,779
Wins * 1997 Jly Carlis (GD) C 6.9f 56
* 1997 Jly Chepst (G-S) S 8.1f 53
* 1996 Jun Hamilt (GD) 6f 62 <
1998 Turf 0-3: (7f 2, 8f) (gd 3) 1998 AW 0-2: (8f 2) (Fibr 2)
Scopey, moderate filly, effective 7 to 8f, best at 7f, acts on gd to frm, best on frm, has worn blinkers, likes right handed tracks. Turf high 44. AW high 36. **J Berry [3-34] Ian Bolland.*

BOLLIN ANN BHB 57f RR 64f 4582[13]

3 b f Anshan 8.2f **(63)** - Bollin Zola (Alzao (USA)) 7.1f **(68)**
Form - 00530221850
Record 1998 - 1st:1 2nd:2 3rd:1 Ran:11
Pre1998 - 1st:0 2nd:0 3rd:0 Ran:3
Win Prizemoney £3,436 *Total Prizemoney* £5,651
Wins * **1998** Aug Ripon (G-F) 5f 64 <
1998 Turf 1-11: (5f 1-3, 6f 7, 7f) (g-s, gd 5, g-f 1-5)
Light-framed, average filly, effective 5 to 6f, best at 6f, acts on gd to g-f, best on g-f. Turf high 64 - 1st of 9 getting 5lb from Tuscan Dream (15 Aug Ripon RF 3657). Narrow winner of a sprint maiden at Ripon, not scoring out of turn.
**T D Easterby [1-14] Lady Westbrook.*

BOLLIN ETHOS BHB 59f RR 60f 3410[9]

3 b c Precocious 7.2f **(54)** - Bollin Harriet (Lochnager) 6f **(59)**
Form - 076024100
Record 1998 - 1st:1 2nd:1 3rd:0 Ran:9
Pre1998 - 1st:0 2nd:0 3rd:0 Ran:1
Win Prizemoney £3,886 *Total Prizemoney* £4,987
Wins * **1998** Jly Catter (GD) H 7f 56 60 <
1998 Turf 1-9: (5f, 6f 3, 7f 1-5) (g-s, gd 4, g-f 2, frm 1-2)
Workmanlike, average colt, effective 7f, acts on gd to frm, best on gd. Turf high 60 - 2nd of 16 getting 12lb from Three Angels (4 Jun Haydock 7f gd RF 1712) - also 1st of 15 getting 3lb from Erro Codigo (2 Jly Catterick RF 2464).
**T D Easterby [1-10] Sir Neil Westbrook.*

BOLLIN FRANK BHB 67f RR 66f 4513[14]

6 b g Rambo Dancer (CAN) 8.4f **(59)** - Bollin Emily (Lochnager) 6f **(59)**
Form - 0514202020
Record 1998 - 1st:1 2nd:3 3rd:0 Ran:10
Pre1998 - 1st:3 2nd:6 3rd:3 Ran:35
Win Prizemoney £18,320 *Total Prizemoney* £38,765
Wins * **1998** May Nottin (FRM) 8.2f 62
* 1996 Jun Haydoc (G-S) H 8.1f 66 68 <
* 1996 May Haydoc (G-S) H 8.1f 62 64
1995 Jly Haydoc (G-F) H 8.1f 53 58
1998 Turf 1-10: (8f 1-10) (g-s, gd 3, g-f 3, frm 1-3)
Average gelding, effective 8f, acts on gd to frm, has worn blinkers, prefers right handed tracks, prefers tight tracks, excels at Haydock and Ripon. Turf high 66 - 2nd of 15 getting 7lb from Hurtleberry (6 Jun Haydock 8f frm RF 1784).
**T D Easterby [3-32] Sir Neil Westbrook (from M H Easterby [1-16] Oct 1995).*

BOLLIN JOANNE BHB 110f RR 106f 4330[8]

5 b m Damister (USA) 9.1f **(66)** - Bollin Zola (Alzao (USA)) 7.1f **(68)**
Form - 100048
Record 1998 - 1st:1 2nd:0 3rd:0 Ran:6
Pre1998 - 1st:5 2nd:7 3rd:3 Ran:18
Win Prizemoney £83,231 *Total Prizemoney* £118,511
Wins * **1998** May York (GD) G3 6f 116 <
* 1997 Spt Doncas (G-F) L 5f 109
* 1997 May York (GD) H 6f 95 99
* 1996 Oct York (GD) H 6f 87 94
* 1996 Aug Ripon (G-F) H 6f 80 89
* 1996 Jly Catter (GD) 6f 67
1998 Turf 1-6: (5f 4, 6f 1-2) (gd 1-3, g-f, frm 2)
Pattern-class filly, effective 5 to 6f, best at 6f, acts on gd to frm, best on frm, excels at York. Turf high 116 (1st run) - 1st of 10 getting 9lb from Elnadim (14 May York RF 1220). Consistent. She improved into a high-class sprinter in '97 and started 1998 in fine style with victory in the Group Three Duke of York Stakes.

However, she took on the very best sprinters after that and showed very little, apart from a fair fourth in a Doncaster Listed event.

**T D Easterby [6-23] Lady Westbrook (from M H Easterby [0-1] Jun 1995).*

BOLLIN RITA BHB 73f **RR 71f** 3601[4]

2 b f Rambo Dancer (CAN) 8.4f **(59)** - Bollin Harriet (Lochnager) 6f **(59)**

Form - 223424

Record 1998 - 1st:0 2nd:3 3rd:1 Ran:6

Win Prizemoney £0 *Total Prizemoney* £4,320

1998 Turf 0-6: (5f 2, 6f 3, 7f) (gd 2, frm 3, hrd)

Above-average filly, effective 5 to 6f, best at 6f, acts on gd to hrd, best on frm. Turf high 71. Sure to find an ordinary race.

**T D Easterby [0-6] Lady Westbrook.*

BOLLIN ROBERTA BHB 69f **RR 69f** 4261[2]

2 b f Bob's Return (IRE) - Bollin Emily (Lochnager) 6f **(59)**

Form - 352402

Record 1998 - 1st:0 2nd:2 3rd:1 Ran:6

Win Prizemoney £0 *Total Prizemoney* £2,481

1998 Turf 0-6: (5f, 6f 3, 7f 2) (gd, g-f 3, frm 2)

Average filly, effective 6f, acts on gd to g-f. Turf high 69 - 2nd of 19 giving 9lb to Clunie (14 Spt Nottingham 6f gd RF 4261).

**T D Easterby [0-6] Lady Westbrook.*

BOLLIN ROGER BHB 55f **RR 60tf** 4089[13]

2 b c Rock Hopper 10.6f **(54)** - Bollin Magdalene (Teenoso (USA)) 9.9f **(72)**

Form - 400

Record 1998 - 1st:0 2nd:0 3rd:0 Ran:3

Win Prizemoney £0 *Total Prizemoney* £223

1998 Turf 0-3: (7f 2, 8f) (gd, g-f, frm)

Currently average colt. Turf high 60 (began Jly).

**T D Easterby [0-3] Sir Neil Westbrook.*

BOLLIN TERRY BHB 81f **RR 83f** 4848[29]

4 b c Terimon 8.7f **(58)** - Bollin Zola (Alzao (USA)) 7.1f **(68)**

Form - 0033164320

Record	**1998** -	1st:1	2nd:1	3rd:3	Ran:10
	Pre1998 -	1st:1	2nd:1	3rd:1	Ran:8

Win Prizemoney £11,647 *Total Prizemoney* £26,967

Wins	* **1998**	Jly	Newcas (G-F)	H	8f	76	83	<
	* 1997	Jun	Newcas (FRM)	H	8f	72	79	

1998 Turf 1-10: (7f 2, 8f 1-7, 9f) (gd 1-6, g-f, frm 3)

Workmanlike, decent colt, effective 7 to 8f, best at 8f, acts on gd to frm, likes left handed tracks, excels at Newcastle and Pontefract. Turf high 83 - 1st of 12 from Captain Logan (25 Jly Newcastle RF 3118). Consistent. Sure to win a handicap or two over a mile on a sound surface. **T D Easterby [2-18] Sir Neil Westbrook.*

BOLSHAYA BHB 67f **RR 75df** 3999[16]

3 gr f Cadeaux Genereux 7.9f **(76)** -Mainly Dry (The Brianstan) 5.9f **(55)**

Form - 418160

Record	**1998** -	1st:2	2nd:0	3rd:0	Ran:6
	Pre1998 -	1st:0	2nd:0	3rd:0	Ran:3

Win Prizemoney £6,331 *Total Prizemoney* £6,331

Wins	* **1998**	Jly	Pontef (G-F)	6f	75	<
	* **1998**	Jun	Newcas (GD)	6f	66	

1998 Turf 2-6: (6f 2-6) (gd 1-2, g-f 2, frm 1-2)

Rangy, above-average filly, effective 6f, acts on gd to frm. Turf high 75 - 1st of 6 getting 2lb from Caution (17 Jly Pontefract RF 2889) - also 1st of 10 from Jocasta (25 Jun Newcastle RF 2273). Comes from a prolific sprinting family, being a half-sister to Bolshoi, Tod and Great Chaddington. Gave her paddock value a boost with victories at Newcastle and Pontefract.

**J Berry [2-9] Chris Deuters.*

BOLSHOI (IRE) BHB 115f **RR 120f** 5164a[7]

6 br g Royal Academy (USA) 7.8f **(77)** - Mainly Dry (The Brianstan) 5.9f **(55)**

Bolshoi; a job well done in the King's Stand at Royal Ascot

Form - 711174627
Record 1998 - 1st:3 2nd:1 3rd:0 Ran:9
Pre1998 - 1st:6 2nd:3 3rd:2 Ran:37
Win Prizemoney £166,604 *Total Prizemoney* £223,468
Wins * **1998** Jun Ascot (G-S) G2 5f 120 <
* **1998** May Sandow (G-F) G2 5f 118
* **1998** May Beverl (GD) 5f 101
* 1997 Apr Beverl (G-F) 5f 102
* 1996 Spt Ascot (GD) H 5f 88 94
* 1996 Jly Ascot (G-F) H 5f 83 89
* 1996 Jly Beverl (G-F) H 5f 73 80
* 1996 May Doncas (G-F) C 5f 68
* 1995 Apr Beverl (G-F) 5f 66
1998 Turf 3-8: (5f 3-5, 6f 3) (gd 2-3, g-f, frm 1-4) 1998 AW 0-1: (6f) (Dirt)
Very high-class gelding, effective 5 to 6f, best at 5f, acts on gd to frm, best on gd, mostly wears blinkers (very effectively). Turf high 120 - 1st of 19 giving 3lb to Lochangel (19 Jun Ascot RF 2108) - also 1st of 8 giving 3lb to Lochangel (25 May Sandown RF 1463). He was better than ever in 1998, completing a mid-season hat-trick including the Temple Stakes and the King's Stand at Ascot, proving on the last occasion that he does not require blinkers to be effective. Comes late from off the pace, and rather needs things to go his own way, but is a cracking sprinter when conditions are right. Stays six furlongs, as he showed when second behind Tamarisk in the Haydock Sprint Cup, and ran a creditable race in the Breeders' Cup Sprint. As a gelding he seems sure to be back among the top British sprinters in 1999. **J Berry [9-46] David Brown.*

BOLSHOI (POL) RR
2856[6]
5 b g All Hands On Deck (USA) - Becky Sharp (Sharpen Up) 8.3f **(67)**
Form - 6
Record 1998 - 1st:0 2nd:0 3rd:0 Ran:1
1998 Turf 0-1: (12f) (frm)
Currently very poor gelding - 6th of 7 giving 6lb to Gray Pastel (16 Jly Leicester 12f frm RF 2856). **M P Muggeridge [0-2] K H Eng.*

BOLSHOI STAR BHB 62f RR 68f
4383[R]
3 b f Soviet Star (USA) 8.6f **(74)** - Littlefield (Bay Express) 7.1f **(60)**
Form - 022442R
Record 1998 - 1st:0 2nd:3 3rd:0 Ran:7
Win Prizemoney £0 *Total Prizemoney* £3,196
1998 Turf 0-6: (8f 2, 9f 2, 10f 2) (gd 3, frm 2, hrd) 1998 AW 0-1: (8f) (Fibr)
Average filly. Turf high 68. She has shown some fair form in maiden company, but is not one to trust. **M Johnston [0-7] J M Cullinan.*

BOLT FROM THE BLUE RR 60f
3291[7]
2 b g Grand Lodge (USA) - Lightning Legacy (USA) (Super Concorde (USA)) 10.9f **(66)**
Form - 0047
Record 1998 - 1st:0 2nd:0 3rd:0 Ran:4
1998 Turf 0-4: (5f 3, 6f) (g-f, frm 3)
Average gelding. Turf high 60. **N Tinkler [0-4] A K Collins.*

BOMB ALASKA BHB 73f RR 81f
4995[2]
3 br g Polar Falcon (USA) 9f **(74)** - So True (So Blessed) 8.7f **(67)**
Form - 674226102
Record 1998 - 1st:1 2nd:3 3rd:0 Ran:9
Pre1998 - 1st:0 2nd:0 3rd:0 Ran:2
Win Prizemoney £3,766 *Total Prizemoney* £7,381
Wins * **1998** Spt Newbur (gd) 8f 81 <
1998 Turf 1-9: (7f 2, 8f 1-7) (sft, g-s, gd 2, g-f 1-3, frm 2)
Lengthy, decent gelding, effective 8f, acts on sft to g-f. Turf high 81 - 1st of 20 from Brilliant Corners (18 Spt Newbury RF 4356). Put his handicap experience to good use to beat a big field of maidens in September. **G B Balding [1-11] Miss B Swire.*

BOMBARD (USA) RR 87f
2301[1]
2 ch c Lord At War (ARG) 6.6f **(67)** - Mama Hawk (USA) (Silver Hawk (USA)) 8.6f **(70)**
Form - 21
Record 1998 - 1st:1 2nd:1 3rd:0 Ran:2
Win Prizemoney £4,386 *Total Prizemoney* £5,446
Wins * **1998** Jun Goodwo (G-F) 7f 81+ <
1998 Turf 1-2: (7f 1-2) (gd 1-2)
Currently useful colt. Turf high 87 (1st run) - 2nd of 7 to Distant Moon (12 Jun Sandown 7f gd RF 1934) - also 1st of 5 from Lots of Magic (26 Jun Goodwood RF 2301). Ran green when winning his maiden, and was not seen out again.
**P F I Cole [1-2] H R H Prince Fahd Salman.*

BOMBASTIC BHB 79f RR 79f
5008[9]
3 ch c Polish Precedent (USA) 9f **(73)** - Fur Hat (Habitat) 9.4f **(70)**
Form - 462820
Record 1998 - 1st:0 2nd:2 3rd:0 Ran:6
Pre1998 - 1st:0 2nd:2 3rd:0 Ran:3
Win Prizemoney £0 *Total Prizemoney* £5,297
1998 Turf 0-6: (10f, 12f 3, 13f, 14f) (sft 2, gd 2, g-f 2)
Scopey, above-average colt, effective 7 to 14f, acts on sft to gd, best on gd. Turf high 80. Consistent.
**B W Hills [0-9] H R H Prince Fahd Salman.*

BON AMI (IRE) BHB 95f RR 100f
4185[7]
2 b c Paris House 5.9f **(64)** - Felin Special (Lyphard's Special (USA)) 10.3f **(72)**
Form - 134222321127
Record 1998 - 1st:3 2nd:5 3rd:2 Ran:12
Win Prizemoney £10,612 *Total Prizemoney* £18,819
Wins * **1998** Aug Ripon (G-F) 6f 88
* **1998** Aug Newcas (GD) H 6f 100? <
* **1998** Apr Leices (SFT) 5f 77
1998 Turf 3-12: (5f 1-5, 6f 2-7) (sft 1-1, g-s 2, gd 2, g-f 2-4, frm 3)
Very useful colt, effective 6f, acts on g-f to frm. Turf high 100 - 1st of 9 giving 13lb to Peaceful (2 Aug Newcastle RF 3291). A typically tough Jack Berry juvenile, he only finished out of the frame once in 12 starts. He was shaping like a seven-furlong horse by the end of the campaign and should make a useful handicapper next term, although he probably needs to drop a few pounds before winning again. **J Berry [3-12] K T Ivory.*

BONANZA PEAK (USA) BHB 66f RR 68f
4670[11]
5 b h Houston (USA) 7.7f **(65)** - Bunnicula (USA) (Shadeed (USA)) 8.2f **(70)**
Form - 0
Record 1998 - 1st:0 2nd:0 3rd:0 Ran:1
Pre1998 - 1st:1 2nd:2 3rd:2 Ran:10
Win Prizemoney £2,708 *Total Prizemoney* £6,068
Wins * 1997 Aug Bath (GD) H 10.2f 61 66 <
1998 Turf 0-1: (10f) (g-s)
Average colt, effective 10f, acts on gd to frm, best on gd, likes left handed tracks. **Mrs J Cecil [1-11] Gavin Oram and Julie Cecil.*

BONAPARTISTE (FR) RR 109f
5167a[9]
4 b c Kendor - Fab's Melody (FR)
Form - 0
1998 Turf 0-1: (12f) (frm)
Pattern-class colt. Showed some useful form in '97, when racing in France. Moved to race in America and enjoyed a very successful campaign before finishing down the field in the Breeders' Cup Turf.
**R McAnally in USA [0-1] Ecurie Fabien Ouaki (from P Demercastel in FR [0-3] Oct 1997).*

BOND GIRL RR 28f
4868[12]
2 b f Magic Ring (IRE) 6.5f **(64)** - Whirling Words (Sparkler) 8.4f **(55)**
Form - 0
Record 1998 - 1st:0 2nd:0 3rd:0 Ran:1
1998 Turf 0-1: (6f) (gd)
Currently little account filly. **B Smart [0-1] R C Bond.*

BONELLI RR 57f
3362[9]
2 ch c Casteddu 7.4f **(54)** - Tawnais (Artaius (USA)) 9f **(69)**
Form - 50
Record 1998 - 1st:0 2nd:0 3rd:0 Ran:2
1998 Turf 0-2: (6f, 7f) (gd, g-f)
Currently fair colt. Turf high 57. **J R Arnold [0-2] Lofal Partnership.*

BONGO BHB 69a RR 65f 69a
2162[3]
4 b g Efisio 7.7f **(69)** - Boo Hoo (Mummy's Pet) 7.7f **(60)**
Form - 521015163
Record 1998 - 1st:3 2nd:1 3rd:1 Ran:8
Pre1998 - 1st:0 2nd:1 3rd:0 Ran:2
Win Prizemoney £5,725 *Total Prizemoney* £7,514
Wins * **1998** *May Wolver (STD) C 9.4f 67+*

* **1998** *Apr Wolver (STD) S 8.5f 68 <*
1998 *Feb Wolver (STD) S 9.4f 61*
1998 AW 3-8: (8f 1-3, 9f 2-5) (Fibr 3-8)
Leggy, average gelding, effective 6 to 9f, acts on g-f - acts on Fibr. AW high 68 - 1st of 9 giving 9lb to Patina (11 Apr Wolverhampton RF 0654) - also 1st of 13 getting 11lb from China Castle (29 May Wolverhampton RF 1578). Consistent.
**P D Evans [2-6] John Pugh (from C W Thornton [1-4] Feb 1998).*

BON GUEST (IRE) BHB 46f60a RR 56f 60a 1638[20]

4 ch g Kefaah (USA) 11.2f **(64)** - Uninvited Guest (Be My Guest (USA)) 9.3f **(67)**
Form - 132551050
Record 1998 - 1st:2 2nd:1 3rd:1 Ran:9
Pre1998 - 1st:1 2nd:3 3rd:4 Ran:23
Win Prizemoney £6,631 *Total Prizemoney* £10,963
Wins * **1998** *Feb Lingfi (SLW) C 12f 63 <*
* **1998** *Jan Lingfi (STD) H 10f 58 62*
1997 May Nottin (GD) H 8.2f 52 56
1998 Turf 0-1: (12f) (g-f) 1998 AW 2-8: (8f, 10f 1-3, 12f 1-2, 13f 2) (Equi 2-8)
Workmanlike, average gelding, effective 8 to 12f, acts on gd to frm - acts on AW, best on Equi, has worn blinkers, likes left handed tracks, favours tight tracks, excels at Nottingham and likes Wolverhampton. AW high 63 - 1st of 8 giving 3lb to Evezio Rufo (26 Feb Lingfield RF 0364) - also 1st of 8 giving 12lb to Badrinath (8 Jan Lingfield RF 0045). Becoming disappointing. A fair performer in modest company on turf and sand, his win at Nottingham in May '97 came in a particularly moderate apprentice handicap. He has either won or been placed on numerous occasions since, though one of his wins at Lingfield at the beginning of 1998 was due to a misdemeanour by the rider of the runner-up.
**Miss B Sanders [2-10] Mrs P J Sheen (from J G M O'Shea [0-4] Aug 1997).*

BON LUCK (IRE) BHB 57f RR 35f 3079[6]

6 ch g Waajib 8.9f **(67)** - Elle Va Bon (Tanfirion) 7f **(61)**
Form - 6
Record 1998 - 1st:0 2nd:0 3rd:0 Ran:1
Pre1998 - 1st:0 2nd:3 3rd:0 Ran:11
Win Prizemoney £0 *Total Prizemoney* £6,228
1998 Turf 0-1: (10f) (g-f)
Very moderate gelding. Becoming disappointing. An edgy sort, clearly suited by testing ground, he has two ways of running.
**B Preece [0-1] M Ephgrave (from J A Bennett [0-5] Jun 1997).*

BONNES NOUVELLES RR 77f 4998[5]

2 b f Shirley Heights 12.1f **(76)** - La Belle Creole (Rainbow Quest (USA)) 10.4f **(75)**
Form - 55
Record 1998 - 1st:0 2nd:0 3rd:0 Ran:2
1998 Turf 0-2: (7f 2) (sft, gd)
Currently above-average filly. Turf high 77 (1st run) (began Oct) - 5th of 20 to Hawriyah (12 Oct Leicester 7f gd RF 4758).
**J L Dunlop [0-2] Miss K Rausing.*

BONNE VILLE BHB 40f53a RR 34f 53a 4862[6]

4 gr f Good Times (ITY) 8.7f **(53)** - Ville Air (Town Crier) 10.2f **(55)**
Form - 207828236
Record 1998 - 1st:0 2nd:2 3rd:1 Ran:8
Pre1998 - 1st:1 2nd:3 3rd:1 Ran:15
Win Prizemoney £2,415 *Total Prizemoney* £5,916
Wins * 1996 *Oct Wolver (STD) S 8.5f 71 <*
1998 Turf 0-2: (11f, 15f) (g-f 2) 1998 AW 0-6: (12f 4, 14f, 15f) (Fibr 6)
Fair filly, effective 11 to 15f, - acts on Fibr, has worn blinkers, favours left handed tracks. Turf high 33. AW high 58 - 3rd of 12 giving 9lb to Operatic (19 Spt Wolverhampton 15f Fibr RF 4384).
**B Palling [1-23] Millbrook Associates.*

BONNIE DUNDEE RR 74+f 4881[8]

2 b f Rock City 8.8f **(62)** - Shy Dolly (Cajun) 5.2f **(54)**
Form - 6408
Record 1998 - 1st:0 2nd:0 3rd:0 Ran:4
Win Prizemoney £0 *Total Prizemoney* £212
1998 Turf 0-4: (5f 3, 6f) (g-s, gd, g-f 2)
Above-average filly. Turf high 74 (began Aug) - 4th of 14 to Diamond Geezer (15 Spt Sandown 5f gd RF 4264).
**M Kettle [0-4] Graham Racing.*

BON SIZZLE BHB 50f55a RR 46f 55a 2457[4]

3 b c Sizzling Melody 6.3f **(49)** - Bonne de Berry (Habitat) 9.4f **(70)**
Form - 052684
Record 1998 - 1st:0 2nd:1 3rd:0 Ran:6
Pre1998 - 1st:0 2nd:0 3rd:0 Ran:3
Win Prizemoney £0 *Total Prizemoney* £530
1998 Turf 0-4: (6f 3, 7f) (sft, g-s, gd, frm) 1998 AW 0-2: (6f 2) (Fibr 2)
Lengthy, fair colt, effective 6f, - acts on Fibr, has worn blinkers. Turf high 46. AW high 55 (1st run) - 2nd of 7 getting 15lb from Ice Age (7 May Southwell 6f Fibr RF 1085). Inconsistent.
**J R Fanshawe [0-9] Mrs Mary Watt.*

BON VOYAGE (USA) RR 46f 2841[2]

6 b g Riverman (USA) 9.7f **(78)** - Katsura (USA) (Northern Dancer) 9.6f **(80)**
Form - 2
Record 1998 - 1st:0 2nd:1 3rd:0 Ran:1
Win Prizemoney £0 *Total Prizemoney* £628
1998 Turf 0-1: (12f) (gd)
Moderate gelding, always wears blinkers. (1st run) - 2nd of 11 to Double Rush (16 Jly Bath 12f gd RF 2841).
**P J Hobbs [0-9] P J Hobbs.*

BONYALUA MILL BHB 38f38a RR 49f 38a 103[7]

4 gr f Chilibang 7f **(55)** - Candesco (Blushing Scribe (USA)) 6f **(45)**
Form - 047
Record 1998 - 1st:0 2nd:0 3rd:0 Ran:2
Pre1998 - 1st:1 2nd:0 3rd:0 Ran:5
Win Prizemoney £2,294 *Total Prizemoney* £2,487
Wins * 1997 *Mar Southw (STD) 6f 31 <*
1998 AW 0-2: (6f, 7f) (Fibr 2)
Leggy, moderate filly, often wears blinkers. AW high 34.
**A Streeter [1-7] Mrs Brenda Jeffery.*

BOOGY WOOGY BHB 71f RR 69f 5148[4]

2 ch g Rock Hopper 10.6f **(54)** - Primulette (Mummy's Pet) 7.7f **(60)**
Form - 460051014
Record 1998 - 1st:2 2nd:0 3rd:0 Ran:9
Win Prizemoney £8,589 *Total Prizemoney* £9,170
Wins * **1998** Oct Doncas (HVY) H 7f 64 68 <
* **1998** Oct Redcar (g-s) C 7f 66
1998 Turf 2-9: (6f 2, 7f 2-5, 8f 2) (g-s 1-2, gd 4, g-f 1-2, frm)
Average gelding, effective 6 to 7f, best at 7f, acts on g-s to frm, often wears blinkers (effectively). Turf high 69 - also 1st of 10 getting 25lb from Tough Guy (24 Oct Doncaster RF 4969). Inconsistent. **T D Easterby [2-9] Mrs P D Croft.*

BOOK AT BEDTIME (IRE) BHB 102f RR 91f 2536[6]

4 b f Mtoto 11.5f **(71)** - Akila (FR) (Top Ville) 11.7f **(68)**
Form - 7406
Record 1998 - 1st:0 2nd:0 3rd:0 Ran:4
Pre1998 - 1st:2 2nd:2 3rd:4 Ran:11
Win Prizemoney £23,533 *Total Prizemoney* £70,390
Wins * 1997 Spt Doncas (G-F) G3 14.6f 105 <
* 1997 Jly Sandow (G-S) 14f 72+
1998 Turf 0-4: (12f 2, 16f, 20f) (g-s, gd 2, g-f)
Strong, useful filly, effective 15 to 16f, best at 15f, acted on gd to frm, liked left handed tracks. Turf high 108 - 4th of 6 getting 3lb from Tajoun (17 May Longchamp 16f gd RF 1383a). Consistent. She did connections proud in '97, her finest hour coming with her victory in the Park Hill Stakes. She competed in the top staying races in '98, but failed to trouble the judge, and sadly died after sustaining a broken pelvis in August. (DEAD)
**C A Cyzer [2-15] R M Cyzer.*

BOOMERANG BLADE BHB 100f RR 99f 4628[6]

2 b f Sure Blade (USA) 10.6f **(66)** - Opuntia (Rousillon (USA)) 8.2f **(74)**
Form - 21316
Record 1998 - 1st:2 2nd:1 3rd:1 Ran:5
Win Prizemoney £182,161 *Total Prizemoney* £184,200
Wins * **1998** Spt Doncas (GD) 6f 97 <
* **1998** Jly Folkes (GD) 6f 73
1998 Turf 2-5: (6f 2-4, 7f) (gd 1-1, g-f 3, frm 1-1)
Very useful filly. Turf high 97 (began Jly) - also 1st of 22 getting 5lb from Flanders (9 Spt Doncaster RF 4185). Ran well on her debut and followed that with a smooth win next time, but was outclassed against the useful Mujahid at Salisbury. Put in an

improved effort to land the jackpot at Doncaster, in the St Leger Yearling Stakes with a very game display beating Flanders. Unlucky in running on her final start, the seven furlongs that day seemed no problem for her and she looks an interesting prospect for next term. **B Smart [2-5] John Ford.*

**I A Balding [2-5] R P B Michaelson & Wafic Said.*

BORDER FALCON BHB 62f **RR 61f** 3406[6]

4 ch g Polar Falcon (USA) 9f **(74)** - Tender Loving Care (Final Straw) 7.9f **(64)**

Boomerang Blade (second left) landing the richest two-year-old race of the season

BORANI BHB 82f **RR 80f** 4645[4]

3 b c Shirley Heights 12.1f **(76)** - Ower (IRE) (Lomond (USA)) 8.8f **(65)**

Form - 40724

Record	**1998 -**	1st:0	2nd:1	3rd:0	Ran:5
	Pre1998 -	1st:0	2nd:0	3rd:1	Ran:2

Win Prizemoney £0 *Total Prizemoney* £2,995

1998 Turf 0-5: (8f 2, 9f, 10f 2) (g-s, gd 2, g-f 2)

Lengthy, decent colt, effective 8 to 10f, best at 8f, acts on gd to g-f, best on gd, prefers tight tracks. Turf high 80 - 4th of 9 getting 9lb from Kayo (4 Oct Warwick 8f g-f RF 4645).

**I A Balding [0-7] Dr J A E Hobby.*

BORDER ARROW BHB 120f **RR 119f** 1778[3]

3 ch c Selkirk (USA) 7.9f **(76)** - Nibbs Point (IRE) (Sure Blade (USA)) 11.3f **(67)**

Form - 1333

Record	**1998 -**	1st:1	2nd:0	3rd:3	Ran:4
	Pre1998 -	1st:1	2nd:0	3rd:0	Ran:1

Win Prizemoney £19,503 *Total Prizemoney* £172,583

Wins	*** 1998**	Apr	Newmar (SFT)	L	9f	104+	<
	* 1997	Oct	Newmar (G-S)		8f	95++	

1998 Turf 1-4: (8f, 9f 1-1, 10f, 12f) (gd 1-3, g-f)

Neat, high-class colt. Turf high 119 - 3rd of 15 to High-Rise (6 Jun Epsom 12f g-f RF 1778). Created a very favourable impression when scoring at Newmarket as a two-year-old, and showed that he had trained on with a game victory in the Feilden Stakes on his return. He has had a touch of thirditis since then, filling that position in the Guineas, Dante, and the Derby itself. He gave the impression in each of those efforts that he needs a galloping track to be seen at his best, as he is a big, powerful galloper. His trainer thinks that he will not really come to himself until next season, which will be something to look forward to.

Form - 66

Record	**1998 -**	1st:0	2nd:0	3rd:0	Ran:2
	Pre1998 -	1st:0	2nd:0	3rd:0	Ran:1

1998 Turf 0-2: (8f, 11f) (g-f 2)

Scopey, currently average gelding. Turf high 61 (began Jly).

**M D Hammond [0-2] The Falconers (from I A Balding [0-1] Apr 1997).*

BORDER GLEN BHB 57f **RR 57f** 5068[8]

2 b c Selkirk (USA)7.9f**(76)**-Sulitelma(USA)(The Minstrel(CAN)) 10f **(72)**

Form - 00808

Record	**1998 -**	1st:0	2nd:0	3rd:0	Ran:5

1998 Turf 0-5: (5f 4, 6f) (g-s, gd 2, g-f 2)

Fair colt. Turf high 57 (began Aug).

**Sir Mark Prescott [0-5] L A Larratt.*

BORDER PRINCE RR 80f 4823[6]

2 ch c Selkirk (USA) 7.9f **(76)** - Princess Oberon (IRE) **(85f)** (Fairy King (USA)) 7.7f **(59)**

Form - 06

Record	**1998 -**	1st:0	2nd:0	3rd:0	Ran:2

1998 Turf 0-2: (7f, 8f) (g-f, frm)

Currently decent colt. Turf high 80 (began Spt).

**I A Balding [0-2] R P B Michaelson & D F Allport.*

BORDERS RR 70f 4611[8]

2 b c Selkirk (USA) 7.9f **(76)** - Pretty Poppy (Song) 7.2f **(61)**

Form - 88

Record	**1998 -**	1st:0	2nd:0	3rd:0	Ran:2

1998 Turf 0-2: (6f 2) (g-s, g-f)

Currently above-average colt. Turf high 70 (began Spt).

**H Candy [0-2] Mrs J E L Wright.*

Border Arrow was another string to Ian Balding's bow

BORDER STARLETTE (IRE) BHB 30f **RR 18f** 2952[6]
3 b f Ela-Mana-Mou 12.7f **(72)**-Fillette Lalo (FR)(Huntercombe) 7.3f **(56)**
Form - 080886
Record 1998 - 1st:0 2nd:0 3rd:0 Ran:6
1998 Turf 0-6: (7f, 8f 2, 11f, 14f, 16f) (sft, g-s, gd, g-f 2, frm)
Neat, poor filly. Turf high 28. *'Mrs M Reveley [0-6] D Young.*

BORDER TRADER (IRE) BHB 52f **RR 57f** 4927[7]
3 ch g Sharp Victor (USA) 10f **(56)** - Hi Dad (USA) (Verbatim (USA)) 8.5f **(64)**
Form - 040077
Record 1998 - 1st:0 2nd:0 3rd:0 Ran:6
Win Prizemoney £0 *Total Prizemoney* £253
1998 Turf 0-6: (10f 5, 12f) (g-s 2, gd, g-f 2, frm)
Workmanlike, fair gelding. Turf high 57.
'J S Moore [0-6] J Mulholland and Danny Hughes.

BOREAS BHB 85f **RR 85f** 4537[3]
3 b c In The Wings 11.2f **(77)** - Reamur (Top Ville) 11.7f **(68)**
Form - 55143
Record 1998 - 1st:1 2nd:0 3rd:1 Ran:5
Win Prizemoney £3,517 *Total Prizemoney* £6,013
Wins * 1998 Aug Ripon (G-F) 10f 84 <
1998 Turf 1-5: (10f 1-2, 12f 3) (g-f 1-2, frm 3)
Well made, useful colt. Turf high 85 (began Jly) - 4th of 9 getting 1lb from Alberich (3 Spt York 12f g-f RF 4069) - also 1st of 8 getting 8lb from Vicious Circle (22 Aug Ripon RF 3816).
'L M Cumani [1-5] Aston House Stud.

BOREAS HILL (IRE) BHB 37f **RR 36f** 1112[12]
3 b g Petardia 8.2f **(58)** - Salonniere (FR) (Bikala) 10.1f **(49)**
Form - 80
Record 1998 - 1st:0 2nd:0 3rd:0 Ran:2
Pre1998 - 1st:0 2nd:0 3rd:0 Ran:2
1998 Turf 0-1: (14f) (frm) 1998 AW 0-1: (8f) (Fibr)
Unfurnished, very moderate gelding, has worn blinkers.
'J R Arnold [0-4] P G Lowe.

BOREHILL JOKER BHB 43f45a **RR 39f 45a** 1767[6]
2 ch c Pure Melody (USA) - Queen Matilda (Castle Keep) 8.3f **(57)**
Form - 25446
Record 1998 - 1st:0 2nd:1 3rd:0 Ran:5
Win Prizemoney £0 *Total Prizemoney* £515
1998 Turf 0-2: (5f, 6f) (sft, frm) 1998 AW 0-3: (5f 2, 6f) (Fibr 3)
Moderate colt, has worn blinkers. Turf high 39. AW high 44.
'W G M Turner [0-5] O J Stokes.

BORGIA RR 71f 4763[1]
3 ch f Machiavellian (USA) 9.8f **(83)** - Cut Ahead (Kalaglow) 9.8f **(67)**
Form - 35U01
Record 1998 - 1st:1 2nd:0 3rd:1 Ran:5
Win Prizemoney £7,555 *Total Prizemoney* £8,118
Wins * 1998 Oct Leices (G-S) H 11.8f 66 71 <
1998 Turf 1-5: (10f 3, 11f, 12f 1-1) (gd 1-2, g-f 3)
Scopey, above-average filly. Turf high 71 (began Aug) - 1st of 13 getting 9lb from Classic Impact (12 Oct Leicester RF 4763).
'R Charlton [1-5] Lady Rothschild.

BORGIA (GER) RR 122f 5129a[2]
4 b f Acatenango (GER) - Britannia (GER) (Tarim)
Form - 82
1998 Turf 0-1: (11f) (g-s) 1998 AW 0-1: (10f) (Dirt)
Very high-class filly, effective 12f, acts on gd to hrd. A top-class German mare, a fine third in the Arc and close second in the Breeders' Cup Turf in 1997, she finished down the field in the Dubai World Cup on her return in March. She was injured shortly afterwards and her career put in doubt, and she was below her best when returning in the autumn.
'A Fabre in FR [0-1] Gestut Ammerland (from A Schutz in GER [0-1] Mar 1998).

BORIS THE COSSACK (IRE) RR 19f 2322[9]
2 ch c Soviet Lad (USA) 9.4f **(63)** - Mallee (Malinowski (USA)) 10f **(56)**
Form - 6050
Record 1998 - 1st:0 2nd:0 3rd:0 Ran:4
1998 Turf 0-2: (5f 2) (sft, frm) 1998 AW 0-2: (6f, 7f) (Fibr 2)
Little account colt. Turf high 19. AW high 28.
**H S Howe [0-4] Dr Ian Shenkin.*

BORN A LADY BHB 27f36a **RR 27f 36a** 4545[6]
5 ch m Komaite (USA) 6.9f **(61)** - Lucky Candy (Lucky Wednesday) 8f **(50)**
Form - 2406
Record 1998 - 1st:0 2nd:1 3rd:0 Ran:4
Pre1998 - 1st:1 2nd:1 3rd:6 Ran:36
Win Prizemoney £2,519 *Total Prizemoney* £7,873
Wins * 1995 *May Southw (STD) 5f 49* <
1998 Turf 0-2: (5f 2) (frm 2) 1998 AW 0-2: (5f, 11f) (Fibr 2)
Very moderate filly, often wears blinkers. Turf high 27 (began Jly). AW high 33 (began Aug).
**N P Littmoden [1-14] Paul Dixon (from Mrs V A Aconley [0-10] Aug 1997).*

BORN FREE RR 73+f 2442[2]
2 ch f Caerleon (USA) 10.9f **(79)** - Culture Vulture (USA) (Timeless Moment (USA)) 6f **(72)**
Form - 52
Record 1998 - 1st:0 2nd:1 3rd:0 Ran:2
Win Prizemoney £0 *Total Prizemoney* £1,065
1998 Turf 0-2: (6f, 7f) (gd 2)
Currently above-average filly. Turf high 73 - 2nd of 7 to Wince (1 Jly Kempton 7f gd RF 2442). Ran on nicely under sympathetic handling on her second start and is sure to win races.
**P F I Cole [0-2] H R H Prince Fahd Salman.*

BORN ON THE WILD BHB 29f **RR 24f** 3939[12]
5 b m Golden Lahab (USA) 14.4f **(32)** - First Born (Be My Native (USA)) 10.2f **(71)**
Form - 00
Record 1998 - 1st:0 2nd:0 3rd:0 Ran:2
Pre1998 - 1st:0 2nd:0 3rd:0 Ran:4
1998 Turf 0-2: (8f, 12f) (frm 2)
Little account filly. Turf high 24 (began Jly).
**N Tinkler [0-1] R Fenwick-Gibson (from D W Barker [0-1] Jly 1998).*

BORN WINNER RR 58f 971[6]
3 b c Rainbow Quest (USA) 11.2f **(81)** - Tinaca (USA) (Manila (USA)) 9.3f **(71)**
Form - 06
Record 1998 - 1st:0 2nd:0 3rd:0 Ran:2
Win Prizemoney £0 *Total Prizemoney* £55
1998 Turf 0-2: (10f, 12f) (gd 2)
Scopey, currently fair colt. Turf high 58.
**H R A Cecil [0-2] Wafic Said.*

BOROBUDUR (GER) RR 101f 4213a[3]
5 b g Mister Rock's (GER) - Bennetta (FR) (Top Ville) 11.7f **(68)**
Form - 3
1998 Turf 0-1: (16f) (gd)
Currently very useful gelding. (1st run) - 3rd of 8 to Taufan's Melody (2 Spt Baden-Baden 16f gd RF 4213a). He was only a length and three-quarters behind Taufan's Melody when finishing third at Baden-Baden and is a useful gelding.
**D Richardson in GER [0-1].*

BORRADOR BHB 32f **RR 27f** 2298[8]
4 b g Full Extent (USA) 5.2f **(50)** - Wild Jewel (Great Heron (USA)) 7.1f **(51)**
Form - 8
Record 1998 - 1st:0 2nd:0 3rd:0 Ran:1
Pre1998 - 1st:0 2nd:0 3rd:0 Ran:4
1998 Turf 0-1: (12f) (g-f)
Unfurnished, little account gelding. **R Curtis [0-7] Dr Patrick Walker.*

BORROMINI (USA) RR 103+f 4791a[1]
2 ch c Nureyev (USA) 8.4f **(84)** - Fine Spirit (USA) (Secretariat (USA)) 9f **(79)**
Form - 2241
1998 Turf 1-4: (5f 2, 6f 1-2) (g-s 1-1, gd, g-f, frm)
Very useful colt. Turf high 103 (began Aug) - 1st of 13 from Eternal Night (11 Oct Naas RF 4791a). Particularly attractive, he stepped-up considerably on his debut when chasing Sheer Viking home in the Group Two Flying Childers Stakes at Doncaster in September. Below par when refusing to settle in the Middle Park Stakes, he was allowed to race from the front when running away with a maiden at Naas in October and may be better ridden that way. Open to plenty of improvement, he should make a Group-class sprinter in 1999. **A P O'Brien in IRE [1-4] Mrs John Magnier.*

BOSOM PAL (IRE) BHB 28f **RR 22f** 2696[5]
4 b f Roi Danzig (USA) 10.5f **(62)** - Viceroy Express (Jalmood (USA)) 10.1f **(52)**
Form - 4575
Record 1998 - 1st:0 2nd:0 3rd:0 Ran:4
1998 Turf 0-1: (16f) (gd) 1998 AW 0-3: (12f 2, 14f) (Fibr 3)
Small, little account filly. AW high 27.
**N A Smith [0-6] Triumph International Ltd.*

BOUCCANEER (FR) RR 118f 5136a[3]
3 ch c Hero's Honor (USA) 9.2f **(76)** - Shahoune (FR) (Blushing Groom (FR)) 10.3f **(76)**
Form - 2223
1998 Turf 0-2: (8f, 9f) (sft, frm)
High-class colt. Turf high 118 - 3rd of 7 getting 2lb from Ladies Din (1 Nov Santa Anita 9f frm RF 5136a).
**R Frankel in USA [0-1] (from J-C Rouget in FR [0-1] Jun 1998).*

BOULEVARD ROUGE (USA) BHB 60f70a **RR 70f 70a** 4970[11]
3 b f Red Ransom (USA) 8.6f **(83)** - Beetwentysix (USA) (Buckaroo (USA))
Form - 7U3272300
Record 1998 - 1st:0 2nd:2 3rd:2 Ran:7
Pre1998 - 1st:0 2nd:1 3rd:2 Ran:8
Win Prizemoney £0 *Total Prizemoney* £4,810
1998 Turf 0-5: (8f, 10f 2, 11f 2) (sft, g-s, g-f, frm 2) 1998 AW 0-2: (8f 2) (Equi, Fibr)
Scopey, above-average filly, effective 6 to 11f, acts on g-f to frm, best on g-f. Turf high 70 (began Jly) - 2nd of 4 getting 2lb from Cage Aux Folles (18 Jly Redcar 11f frm RF 2933). AW high 64. Inconsistent.
**M W Easterby [0-2] K Hodgson & Mrs J Hodgson (from M Johnston [0-13] Spt 1998).*

BOUND FOR PLEASURE (IRE) BHB 85f **RR 82f** 4997[1]
2 gr c Barathea (IRE) -Dazzlingly Radiant (Try My Best (USA)) 7.6f **(67)**
Form - 021
Record 1998 - 1st:1 2nd:1 3rd:0 Ran:3
Win Prizemoney £3,525 *Total Prizemoney* £5,801
Wins * **1998** Oct Lingfi (HVY) 7f 82 <
1998 Turf 1-3: (7f 1-3) (sft 1-1, g-f 2)
Currently decent colt. Turf high 82 (began Spt) - 1st of 10 from Yakareem (26 Oct Lingfield RF 4997). Just learning the ropes on his debut, he ran well next time if no match for a Godolphin hot-pot, and was a workmanlike winner of a maiden on his final start. Open to further improvement when tackling a mile plus.
**G L Moore [1-3] Action.*

BOUNDLESS SHAPE (IRE) BHB 54f **RR 44f** 2123[13]
3 ch c Petardia 8.2f **(58)** - Burren Breeze (IRE) (Mazaad) 7.1f **(45)**
Form - 06000
Record 1998 - 1st:0 2nd:0 3rd:0 Ran:4
Pre1998 - 1st:0 2nd:0 3rd:0 Ran:1
1998 Turf 0-4: (6f, 7f 2, 8f) (gd 2, g-f 2)
Moderate colt. Turf high 44. **L M Cumani [0-5] Allevamento Gialloblu.*

BOUNTEOUS (IRE) RR 66f 2199[7]
3 b f Last Tycoon 9.4f **(73)**- Fair of the Furze (Ela-Mana-Mou) 10.1f **(70)**
Form - 27
Record 1998 - 1st:0 2nd:1 3rd:0 Ran:2
Win Prizemoney £0 *Total Prizemoney* £1,050
1998 Turf 0-2: (10f, 12f) (gd, g-f)
Workmanlike, currently average filly. Turf high 66 (1st run) - 2nd of 5 to Lucrezia (12 Jun Chepstow 12f gd RF 1923).
**P W Chapple-Hyam [0-2] M Tabor & Mrs John Magnier.*

BOUNTIFUL LADY (USA) RR 80+f 4916[1]

2 ch f Irish River (FR) 9f **(77)** - Bounding Away (CAN) (Vice Regent (CAN)) 8.7f **(74)**

Form - 1

Record 1998 - 1st:1 2nd:0 3rd:0 Ran:1

Win Prizemoney £3,338 *Total Prizemoney* £3,338

Wins * **1998** Oct Newcas (SFT) 7f 80+ <

1998 Turf 1-1: (7f 1-1) (g-s 1-1)

Currently decent filly. (1st run) - 1st of 10 from Height of Fantasy (21 Oct Newcastle RF 4916). A fluent winner on her debut, she is a decent prospect. **Sir Michael Stoute [1-1] Nasser Abdullah.*

BOW BELLS BHB 50f50a RR 40f 50a 2669[14]

3 b f Absalom 7.1f **(56)**-Dancing Chimes (London Bells (CAN)) 5.8f **(53)**

Form - 53657740

Record 1998 - 1st:0 2nd:0 3rd:1 Ran:7
Pre1998 - 1st:0 2nd:0 3rd:0 Ran:2

Win Prizemoney £0 *Total Prizemoney* £500

1998 Turf 0-5: (6f 3, 7f, 8f) (g-s, gd 2, g-f 2)1998 AW 0-2: (8f 2) (Equi 2)

Unfurnished, fair filly, effective 6f, acts on g-s, has worn blinkers. Turf high 58 (1st run) - 5th of 20 giving 10lb to River Ensign (28 Apr Nottingham 6f g-s RF 0899). AW high 38.

**C F Wall [0-9] Mrs R M S Neave.*

BOWCLIFFE BHB 67f73a RR 68f 73a 4848[18]

7 b g Petoski 10.4f **(56)** - Gwiffina (Welsh Saint) 7.6f **(64)**

Form - 14207456020532100

Record 1998 - 1st:2 2nd:3 3rd:1 Ran:17
Pre1998 - 1st:4 2nd:1 3rd:4 Ran:31

Win Prizemoney £35,088 *Total Prizemoney* £52,155

Wins * **1998** Spt Doncas (GD) H 8f 62 68 <
* ***1998*** *Jan Wolver (STD) H 9.4f 63 62+*
* 1997 Jly Carlis (GD) H 8f 51 62
* 1997 Jun Pontef (G-F) H 8f 46 54
1996 May Mussel (G-S) H 8.1f 44 50
1994 Aug Ripon (G-F) H 10f 58 58

1998 Turf 1-13: (8f 1-9, 9f 4) (g-s 2, gd 6, g-f 1-3, frm 2) 1998 AW 1-4: (8f 2, 9f 1-2) (Fibr 1-4)

Above-average gelding, effective 8 to 9f, best at 8f, acts on g-f to frm - acts on Fibr, has worn blinkers, likes left handed tracks, excels at Wolverhampton and Doncaster. Turf high 68 - 1st of 21 getting 18lb from Bollin Terry (12 Spt Doncaster RF 4238). AW high 73 - 2nd of 6 getting 1lb from Sualtach (21 Feb Wolverhampton 8f Fibr RF 0337). Much improved in '97, and continued the good work in a Fibresand campaign. His form since returning to turf has been rather in-an-out, but he landed a competitive handicap at Doncaster in September. Suited by a strongly-run race.

**E J Alston [4-31] Philip Davies (from Mrs A M Naughton [1-9] Nov 1996).*

BOWCLIFFE COURT (IRE) BHB 71f RR 74f 4963[5]

6 b g Slip Anchor 12.7f **(75)** - Res Nova (USA) (Blushing Groom (FR)) 10.3f **(76)**

Form - 0477261504525

Record 1998 - 1st:1 2nd:2 3rd:0 Ran:13
Pre1998 - 1st:3 2nd:3 3rd:3 Ran:22

Win Prizemoney £18,054 *Total Prizemoney* £31,591

Wins * **1998** Jly Newbur (G-F) H 16f 69 72
1997 Apr Warwic (G-F) H 14.9f 72 78 <
1996 Oct Newbur (SFT) H 16f 58 71
1995 Jun Beverl (GD) H 12f 55 62

1998 Turf 1-13: (15f 2, 16f 1-8, 17f, 18f, 20f) (sft 2, g-s 2, gd 5, g-f 1-3, frm)

Above-average gelding, effective 15 to 16f, best at 16f, acts on sft to g-f, best on g-s, excels at Newbury and Ascot. Turf high 74 - 2nd of 8 giving 9lb to Danegold (9 Oct Ascot 16f g-s RF 4737) - also 1st of 8 giving 1lb to Paradise Navy (17 Jly Newbury RF 2875). Not always the most resolute of battlers, he is not entirely consistent and has been largely disappointing of late, but was a narrow winner at Newbury in July.

**J Akehurst [1-17] A D Spence (from R Akehurst [2-9] Jly 1997).*

BOWCLIFFE GRANGE (IRE) BHB 36f44a RR 36f 44a 3908[4]

6 b g Dominion Royale 7.8f **(63)** - Cala-Vadella (Mummy's Pet) 7.7f **(60)**

Form - 823270504

Record 1998 - 1st:0 2nd:2 3rd:1 Ran:9
Pre1998 - 1st:4 2nd:1 3rd:5 Ran:34

Win Prizemoney £11,476 *Total Prizemoney* £17,299

Wins * 1996 Jly Doncas (G-F) H 5f 44 50 <
* 1996 Jly Windso (G-F) H 5f 44 50 <
* 1996 Jun Lingfi (FRM) H 5f 34 39
* 1996 Jun Beverl (G-F) H 5f 23 25

1998 Turf 0-7: (5f 7) (gd 3, g-f 2, frm 2) 1998 AW 0-2: (5f 2) (Fibr 2)

Moderate gelding, effective 5f, acts on gd to g-f - acts on AW, has worn blinkers. Turf high 48 - 2nd of 8 giving 4lb to Ballantrae Boy (6 May Musselburgh 5f gd RF 1066). AW high 45 - 2nd of 9 getting 19lb from Divine Miss-P (17 Mar Southwell 5f Fibr RF 0435). Inconsistent. In good form in the summer of '96, he has failed to win since and missed the break at Leicester in September, preventing him from doing his usual trailblazing.

**D W Chapman [4-42] David Chapman (from J Hanson [0-1] Oct 1994).*

BOWLED OVER BHB 43f58a RR 46f 58a 3797[10]

5 b g Batshoof 9.5f **(66)** - Swift Linnet (Wolver Hollow) 8f **(56)**

Form - 77858330

Record 1998 - 1st:0 2nd:0 3rd:2 Ran:6
Pre1998 - 1st:1 2nd:1 3rd:4 Ran:21

Win Prizemoney £4,230 *Total Prizemoney* £9,874

Wins * 1996 Jun York (GD) 11.9f 72 <

1998 Turf 0-6: (12f 2, 14f, 16f 2, 17f) (gd, g-f 2, frm 3)

Fair gelding, effective 12f, acts on gd, has worn blinkers, likes right handed tracks. Turf high 46. **C A Cyzer [1-27] R M Cyzer.*

BOWLERS BOY BHB 77f66a RR 77f 66a 5097[1]

5 ch g Risk Me (FR) 8f **(53)** - Snow Wonder (Music Boy) 6.8f **(57)**

Form - 078613000406121

Record 1998 - 1st:3 2nd:1 3rd:1 Ran:15
Pre1998 - 1st:4 2nd:7 3rd:3 Ran:33

Win Prizemoney £27,437 *Total Prizemoney* £39,062

Wins * **1998** Nov Redcar (G-S) 5f 65
* **1998** Oct Pontef (SFT) H 5f 68 74 <
* **1998** Jun Pontef (SFT) H 6f 68 70
* 1997 Aug Ripon (GD) H 6f 67 71
* 1997 Jly Beverl (HVY) H 5f 66 68
* 1996 Spt Pontef (G-F) H 5f 68 69
* 1996 Jly Pontef (G-F) 6f 64

1998 Turf 3-15: (5f 2-6, 6f 1-9) (sft 2, g-s 2, gd 3-7, g-f 2, frm 2)

Above-average gelding, effective 5 to 7f, best at 5f, acts on sft to g-f, and excels at Hamilton and Bath and Redcar. Turf high 77 - 2nd of 16 giving 19lb to Half Tone (27 Oct Bath 5f sft RF 5007) - also 1st of 16 getting 14lb from The Gay Fox (19 Oct Pontefract RF 4872). He has not always looked one to trust but has plenty of ability. Won at Ripon in August '97, and just failed to follow up at Hamilton three days later. He showed little this season until bouncing back to form with a victory at Pontefract in June.

**J J Quinn [7-48] Bowlers Racing.*

BOW PEEP (IRE) BHB 65f62a RR 66f 62a 4469[8]

3 b br f Shalford (IRE) 7.8f **(63)** - Gale Force Seven (Strong Gale) 5.6f **(66)**

Form - 7511048

Record 1998 - 1st:2 2nd:0 3rd:0 Ran:7
Pre1998 - 1st:0 2nd:0 3rd:0 Ran:4

Win Prizemoney £6,854 *Total Prizemoney* £7,100

Wins * **1998** Jly Nottin (G-F) 5.1f 63 <
* **1998** Jly Ripon (GD) H 6f 60 63 <

1998 Turf 2-7: (5f 1-3, 6f 1-4) (gd 1-3, g-f 1-1, frm 3)

Average filly, effective 5 to 6f, best at 6f, acts on gd to frm, has worn blinkers. Turf high 66 - 4th of 18 giving 8lb to King Uno (25 Aug Pontefract 6f frm RF 3854) - also 1st of 6 getting 7lb from Just Bob (24 Jly Nottingham RF 3081). Looks to need six furlongs.

**M W Easterby [2-11] Mrs Anne Jarvis.*

BRACKENTHWAITE BHB 50f58a RR 46f 58a 111[10]

8 ch g Faustus (USA) 9.1f **(54)** - Cosset (Comedy Star (USA)) 7.5f **(50)**

Form - 0

Record 1998 - 1st:0 2nd:0 3rd:0 Ran:1
Pre1998 - 1st:7 2nd:2 3rd:2 Ran:39

Win Prizemoney £23,256 *Total Prizemoney* £26,341

Wins 1994 *Mar Lingfi (STD) H 10f 65 77* <
1994 *Mar Wolver (STD) H 9.4f 65 67*

1998 AW 0-1: (8f) (Fibr)

Average gelding, has worn blinkers. Inconsistent.

**M A Peill [0-1] J B Slatcher (from L R Lloyd-James [0-11] Spt 1995).*

BRAITHWAITE BHB 80f **RR 81f** 4542[14]
2 ch c Arazi (USA) 9.2f **(74)** - Smarten Up (Sharpen Up) 8.3f **(67)**
Form - 0220
Record 1998 - 1st:0 2nd:2 3rd:0 Ran:4
Win Prizemoney £0 *Total Prizemoney* £1,959
1998 Turf 0-3: (7f 3) (g-f, frm 2) 1998 AW 0-1: (8f) (Fibr)
Decent colt. Turf high 81 (began Jly). (1st run) - 2nd of 7 to Deploy Venture (19 Spt Wolverhampton 8f Fibr RF 4386).
**P S McEntee [0-4] R B Collier.*

BRAMBLE BEAR BHB 65f **RR 71f** 4397[16]
4 b f Beveled (USA) 6.9f **(64)** - Supreme Rose (Frimley Park) 6.5f **(67)**
Form - 351452302800
Record 1998 - 1st:1 2nd:2 3rd:2 Ran:12
Pre1998 - 1st:3 2nd:1 3rd:1 Ran:18
Win Prizemoney £13,478 *Total Prizemoney* £18,818
Wins * **1998** May Lingfi (GD) H 5f 65 72 <
* 1997 May Catter (G-F) H 5f 62 67
* 1997 May Windso (SFT) H 5f 62 64
* 1996 Jly Bath (FRM) 5.1f 67
1998 Turf 1-12: (5f 1-11, 6f) (sft, g-s, gd, g-f 4, frm 1-5)
Light-framed, above-average filly, effective 5f, acts on gd to frm, best on frm. Turf high 72 - 1st of 19 from The Fugative (8 May Lingfield RF 1104).
**M Blanshard [4-30] Mrs Michael Hill & Mrs Heather Chakko.*

BRAMBLES WAY BHB 39f44a **RR 42f 44a** 4917[14]
9 ch g Clantime 6.6f **(57)** - Streets Ahead (Ovid) 10f **(32)**
Form - 7005250
Record 1998 - 1st:0 2nd:1 3rd:0 Ran:7
Pre1998 - 1st:3 2nd:3 3rd:4 Ran:39
Win Prizemoney £8,439 *Total Prizemoney* £12,888
Wins * 1997 Oct Newcas (G-F) H 10.1f 45 53
* 1997 Apr Beverl (G-F) H 9.9f 50 54 <
* 1996 Spt Redcar (FRM) SH 10f 41 49
1998 Turf 0-7: (8f, 9f 2, 10f 2, 11f, 12f) (g-s, gd 3, g-f 2, frm)
Moderate gelding, effective 10f, acts on gd to g-f, often wears blinkers (extremely effectively). Turf high 42. Consistent.
**Mrs M Reveley [9-39] Nigel Jones (from W L Barker [0-24] Jun 1996).*

BRANCASTER (USA) RR 104f 4964[1]
2 br c Riverman (USA) 9.7f **(78)** - Aseltine's Angels (USA) (Fappiano (USA)) 8.7f **(77)**
Form - 11
Record 1998 - 1st:2 2nd:0 3rd:0 Ran:2
Win Prizemoney £23,793 *Total Prizemoney* £23,793
Wins * **1998** Oct Newbur (HVY) G3 7.3f 104 <
* **1998** Spt Haydoc (G-F) 7.1f 97++
1998 Turf 2-2: (7f 2-2) (sft 1-1, frm 1-1)
Currently very useful colt. Turf high 104 (began Spt) - 1st of 6 from Sicnee (23 Oct Newbury RF 4964) - also 1st of 10 from Compensation (26 Spt Haydock RF 4503). Lived up to his tall home reputation despite showing signs of greenness, when slaughtering the opposition on his debut at Haydock. Only managed to scramble home by the skin of his teeth in the Horris Hill at Newbury, but coped well with the very testing conditions that day. He looks a useful prospect.
**P W Chapple-Hyam [2-2] The Royal Ascot Racing Club.*

BRAND NEW DANCE BHB 70f **RR 77df** 2830[9]
4 b g Gildoran 11.6f **(58)** - Starawak (Star Appeal) 9.6f **(65)**
Form - 40
Record 1998 - 1st:0 2nd:0 3rd:0 Ran:2
Pre1998 - 1st:1 2nd:1 3rd:0 Ran:6
Win Prizemoney £3,645 *Total Prizemoney* £5,210
Wins * 1997 *Apr Wolver (STD) 12f 65* <
1998 Turf 0-2: (14f 2) (g-s, g-f)
Scopey, above-average gelding, effective 13 to 14f, best at 14f, acts on g-f to frm, best on frm. Turf high 56.
**D W P Arbuthnot [1-8] J S Gutkin.*

BRANDON JACK BHB 82f **RR 86f** 4098[8]
4 ch g Cadeaux Genereux 7.9f **(76)** - Waitingformargaret (Kris) 9.5f **(73)**
Form - 0011108588
Record 1998 - 1st:3 2nd:0 3rd:0 Ran:10
Pre1998 - 1st:4 2nd:0 3rd:4 Ran:16
Win Prizemoney £25,981 *Total Prizemoney* £28,601
Wins * **1998** Jun Windso (GD) H 10f 76 86 <
* **1998** Jun Windso (G-F) H 10f 76 82
* **1998** May Windso (G-F) 10f 78
* 1997 Aug Sandow (G-F) 10f 76
* 1997 Jun Goodwo (G-S) H 9f 70 72
* 1996 Spt Goodwo (G-F) H 7f 78 78
* 1996 Aug Nottin (G-S) 6.1f 75
1998 Turf 3-10: (10f 3-10) (sft, gd 2, g-f 2-6, frm 1-1)
Scopey, useful gelding, effective 10f, acts on g-f to frm, best on g-f, prefers tight tracks. Turf high 86 - 1st of 12 giving 14lb to The Wild Widow (8 Jun Windsor RF 1820) - also 1st of 16 from Stone Ridge (1 Jun Windsor RF 1634). He was in fine form in the spring, completing a hat-trick of wins over Windsor's ten furlongs, but has been found out in much tougher company since.
**I A Balding [7-26] R P B Michaelson.*

BRANDONVILLE BHB 60f53a **RR 60f 53a** 591[11]
5 b h Never so Bold 7.1f **(62)** - Enduring (Sadler's Wells (USA)) 10f **(76)**
Form - 0
Record 1998 - 1st:0 2nd:0 3rd:0 Ran:1
Pre1998 - 1st:2 2nd:0 3rd:0 Ran:14
Win Prizemoney £6,113 *Total Prizemoney* £6,848
Wins * 1997 Jly Haydoc (G-S) H 7.1f 56 60 <
* 1997 May Ayr (SFT) H 7f 52 56
1998 Turf 0-1: (8f) (g-s)
Average colt, effective 7f, acts on sft to gd. Inconsistent.
**N Tinkler [2-12] Philip Grundy (from I A Balding [0-3] Oct 1995).*

BRANSTON BERRY (IRE) BHB 71f82a **RR 73f 82a** 4961[4]
3 ch f Mukaddamah (USA) 7.6f **(74)**-Food of Love (Music Boy) 6.8f **(57)**
Form - 522850014
Record 1998 - 1st:1 2nd:2 3rd:0 Ran:9
Pre1998 - 1st:2 2nd:3 3rd:2 Ran:10
Win Prizemoney £25,263 *Total Prizemoney* £31,504
Wins * **1998** Oct Catter (SFT) H 5f 66 73
* 1997 Spt Doncas (G-F) H 6.5f 74 72
* 1997 May Beverl (HVY) 5f 79 <
1998 Turf 1-6: (5f 1-2, 6f 2, 7f 2) (g-s 1-3, gd, g-f, frm) 1998 AW 0-3: (6f, 8f 2) (Fibr 3)
Workmanlike, above-average filly, effective 5 to 7f, best at 5f, acts on g-s to frm - acts on Fibr. Turf high 73 - 1st of 16 getting 9lb from Cauda Equina (16 Oct Catterick RF 4837). AW high 78 - 2nd of 13 giving 3lb to Magic Rainbow (20 Mar Southwell 6f Fibr RF 0452). Inconsistent. Gained a surprise win in a valuable nursery at Doncaster last September. After some reasonable efforts on Fibresand at the start of this season, she rather lost her way on turf, but she came back after a break to win at Catterick.
**J L Eyre [3-18] Diamond Racing Ltd (from M Johnston [0-1] Apr 1997).*

BRATBY (IRE) BHB 42f **RR 38f** 5123[10]
2 b c Distinctly North (USA) 7.4f **(63)** - Aridje (Mummy's Pet) 7.7f **(60)**
Form - 000
Record 1998 - 1st:0 2nd:0 3rd:0 Ran:3
1998 Turf 0-3: (5f, 6f, 7f) (g-s 2, gd)
Currently very moderate colt. Turf high 38 (began Oct).
**M Bell [0-3] C M Watt.*

BRAVACCIO (IRE) BHB 72f **RR 62f** 4743[5]
2 b c Petorius 8f **(66)** - So Stylish (Great Nephew) 9.9f **(64)**
Form - 005
Record 1998 - 1st:0 2nd:0 3rd:0 Ran:3
Win Prizemoney £0 *Total Prizemoney* £261
1998 Turf 0-3: (5f, 7f, 8f) (g-s, frm 2)
Currently average colt. Turf high 62. **P S McEntee [0-3] R B Collier.*

BRAVE CHARLIE RR 14f 3409[20]
2 b c Rudimentary (USA) 8.2f **(66)** - Besito (Wassl) 9.7f **(62)**
Form - 0
Record 1998 - 1st:0 2nd:0 3rd:0 Ran:1
1998 Turf 0-1: (6f) (g-f)
Currently poor colt. **N Bycroft [0-1] E D Atkinson.*

BRAVE EDGE BHB 99f **RR 100f** 4965[4]
7 b g Beveled (USA) 6.9f **(64)** - Daring Ditty (Daring March) 7.1f **(61)**
Form - 6428061086304
Record 1998 - 1st:1 2nd:1 3rd:1 Ran:13
Pre1998 - 1st:6 2nd:8 3rd:7 Ran:52

Win Prizemoney £58,267 *Total Prizemoney* £136,629

Wins * **1998** Jly Newbur (GD) H 6f 98 100
* 1997 Spt Hamilt (GD) 6f 90
* 1996 Jun Kempto (G-F) L 5f 107 <
* 1995 May York (GD) H 5f 90 92+
* 1995 Apr Sandow (GD) H 5f 86 83
* 1994 Apr Windso (GD) H 5f 80 84+

1998 Turf 1-13: (5f 5, 6f 1-8) (sft, gd 1-9, frm 3)

Very useful gelding, effective 5 to 6f, best at 5f, acts on gd to frm, best on gd, does well at Newbury. Turf high 102 - 2nd of 16 giving 20lb to Stuffed (13 May York 5f gd RF 1205) - also 1st of 15 giving 2lb to Return of Amin (12 Jly Newbury RF 2749). Consistent. He retains all his ability despite the passing of time, and paid for his keep by winning a valuable handicap at Newbury in July. Pat Eddery understands his quirks and is usually on top when he puts his best foot forward.

**R Hannon [7-65] Horris Vale Racing Partnership.*

BRAVE ENVOY BHB 60f **RR 61f** 4927[4]

4 b g High Estate 10.5f **(66)** - Restless Anna (Thatching) 8f **(66)**

Form - 0635240414

Record **1998** - 1st:1 2nd:1 3rd:1 Ran:10
Pre1998 - 1st:2 2nd:1 3rd:0 Ran:9

Win Prizemoney £9,659 *Total Prizemoney* £12,105

Wins * **1998** Oct Nottin (SFT) H 8.2f 58 61
* 1997 Oct Nottin (GD) H 8.2f 56 65 <
* 1997 Apr Leices (FRM) S 6f 56

1998 Turf 1-10: (8f 1-7, 10f 3) (g-s, gd 1-4, g-f 2, frm 3)

Scopey, average gelding, effective 6 to 10f, best at 8f, acts on g-s to g-f, best on gd, has worn blinkers, prefers left handed tracks, prefers tight tracks, excels at Nottingham. Turf high 61 - 1st of 17 giving 6lb to Czar Wars (14 Oct Nottingham RF 4807). Consistent.

**M J Heaton-Ellis [3-22] Tom Burge.*

BRAVE GIRL RR 662[6]

2 ch f Never so Bold 7.1f **(62)** - Polly Packer (Reform) 8.9f **(62)**

Form - 6

Record **1998** - 1st:0 2nd:0 3rd:0 Ran:1

1998 Turf 0-1: (5f) (sft)

Very poor filly. (DEAD) **M Brittain [0-1] Northgate Silver.*

BRAVEHEART (IRE) BHB 50f **RR 53f** 2574[14]

4 br g Mujadil (USA) 7.7f **(70)** - Salonniere (FR) (Bikala) 10.1f **(49)**

Form - 000770700

Record **1998** - 1st:0 2nd:0 3rd:0 Ran:9
Pre1998 - 1st:1 2nd:2 3rd:2 Ran:15

Win Prizemoney £3,367 *Total Prizemoney* £8,892

Wins * 1996 May Thirsk (G-F) 5f 64 <

1998 Turf 0-9: (6f, 7f 5, 8f 3) (sft, gd 3, g-f 2, frm 3)

Lengthy, fair gelding, effective 7f, acts on g-f to frm, has worn blinkers. Turf high 60. Consistent.

**M R Channon [1-24] W H Ponsonby.*

BRAVE KRIS (IRE) BHB 98f **RR 100f** 5076[7]

4 b f Kris 10f **(75)** - Famosa (Dancing Brave (USA)) 8.4f **(76)**

Form - 40620147

Record **1998** - 1st:1 2nd:1 3rd:0 Ran:8
Pre1998 - 1st:2 2nd:1 3rd:1 Ran:7

Win Prizemoney £44,684 *Total Prizemoney* £56,938

Wins * **1998** Spt San Si (HVY) L 8f 99 <
* 1997 Jun Ascot (SFT) LH 8f 90 96
* 1997 May Newmar (GD) H 8f 80 92

1998 Turf 1-8: (7f, 8f 1-5, 9f, 10f) (hvy 1-1, sft, g-s, gd 3, g-f, frm)

Scopey, very useful filly, effective 8 to 9f, best at 8f, acts on hvy to g-f, excels at Ascot and San Siro. Turf high 100 - 2nd of 8 giving 5lb to Kismah (7 Aug Ascot 8f g-f RF 3427) - also 1st of 11 giving 4lb to Dazilyn Lady (27 Spt San Siro RF 4607a). She had a hit and miss season, highlighted by a Listed win in Italy during September. She failed to stay when tried over an extended 10 furlongs at Newcastle and is better over a mile.

**L M Cumani [3-15] Robert Smith.*

BRAVE MAPLE BHB 32f **RR 29f** 4114[24]

3 b c Petong 7.6f **(58)** - Hazy Kay (IRE) (Treasure Kay)

Form - 747000

Record **1998** - 1st:0 2nd:0 3rd:0 Ran:6
Pre1998 - 1st:0 2nd:0 3rd:0 Ran:2

Win Prizemoney £0 *Total Prizemoney* £193

1998 Turf 0-5: (5f 4, 7f) (g-f 2, frm 3) 1998 AW 0-1: (7f) (Equi)

Strong, little account colt, effective 5f, acts on frm, has worn blinkers. Turf high 46 (1st run) - 4th of 9 getting 23lb from I Cried For You (22 May Brighton 5f frm RF 1388). Becoming disappointing.

**S C Williams [0-6] The Cherry Pickers Syndicate II (from J M P Eustace [0-2] Oct 1997).*

BRAVE MONTGOMERIE BHB 66f **RR 66f** 1617[4]

4 ch g Most Welcome 8.6f **(66)** - Just Precious (Ela-Mana-Mou) 10.1f **(70)**

Form - 02054

Record **1998** - 1st:0 2nd:1 3rd:0 Ran:5
Pre1998 - 1st:1 2nd:2 3rd:1 Ran:7

Win Prizemoney £4,581 *Total Prizemoney* £10,104

Wins * 1996 Spt Ayr (G-F) 7f 77 <

1998 Turf 0-5: (8f, 9f 2, 10f 2) (g-s 2, gd, g-f, frm)

Scopey, average gelding. Turf high 66. Consistent. Failed to strike form in a light season in 1997.

**Miss L A Perratt [1-12] C J C McLaren.*

BRAVE NOBLE (USA) BHB 81f **RR 85f** 4655[6]

3 ch c Woodman (USA) 9.7f **(77)** - Badge of Courage (USA) (Well Decorated (USA)) 7.6f **(64)**

Form - 08210728486

Record **1998** - 1st:1 2nd:2 3rd:0 Ran:11
Pre1998 - 1st:0 2nd:0 3rd:1 Ran:2

Win Prizemoney £3,590 *Total Prizemoney* £9,929

Wins * **1998** Jun Yarmou (G-F) H 11.5f 80 85 <

1998 Turf 1-11: (8f, 10f 3, 11f 1-2, 12f 5) (g-s, gd 2, g-f 3, frm 1-5)

Scopey, useful colt, effective 10 to 12f, acts on gd to frm, best on frm, prefers left handed tracks, prefers tight tracks. Turf high 85 - 1st of 8 giving 7lb to Benjamin Frank (4 Jun Yarmouth RF 1718).

**E A L Dunlop [1-13] Gainsborough Stud.*

BRAVE REWARD (USA) BHB 99f **RR 98f** 3792[1]

3 b c Lear Fan (USA) 10.4f **(80)** - A Tad Better (USA) (Northern Prospect (USA)) 9.5f **(71)**

Form - 537601

Record **1998** - 1st:1 2nd:0 3rd:1 Ran:6
Pre1998 - 1st:1 2nd:0 3rd:1 Ran:2

Win Prizemoney £8,951 *Total Prizemoney* £13,579

Wins * **1998** Aug Cheste (GD) H 10.3f 92 98 <
* 1997 Oct Leices (G-S) 7f 79+

1998 Turf 1-6: (7f 2, 8f 3, 10f 1-1) (gd 1-6)

Light-framed, very useful colt, effective 7 to 10f, acts on gd. Turf high 98 - 1st of 8 giving 8lb to Up At The Top (21 Aug Chester RF 3792). Consistent. No particular promise on his seasonal debut, then ran well in competitive handicaps until producing a disappointing effort in the William Hill Mile at Goodwood. Gained just reward for some promising performances when stepped up in trip to win on his final start at Chester in August. Over a distance of ten furlongs or more he can win a nice handicap.

**Sir Michael Stoute [2-8] Saeed Suhail.*

BRAVE SPY BHB 35f40a **RR 59f 40a** 3099[11]

7 b g Law Society (USA) 11.6f **(71)** - Contralto (Busted) 10.2f **(61)**

Form - 0

Record **1998** - 1st:0 2nd:0 3rd:0 Ran:1
Pre1998 - 1st:1 2nd:1 3rd:6 Ran:23

Win Prizemoney £2,560 *Total Prizemoney* £6,366

Wins 1995 *Jly Wolver (STD) H 14.8f 54 60* <

1998 AW 0-1: (16f) (Fibr)

Fair gelding. Becoming disappointing.

**A W Carroll [0-1] Simon Lewis (from C A Cyzer [1-23] Jan 1997).*

BRAVE TORNADO BHB 65f **RR 64f** 4963[4]

7 ch g Dominion 8.9f **(65)** - Accuracy (Gunner B) 11.2f **(58)**

Form - 54

Record **1998** - 1st:0 2nd:0 3rd:0 Ran:2
Pre1998 - 1st:2 2nd:0 3rd:0 Ran:7

Win Prizemoney £6,972 *Total Prizemoney* £7,390

Wins * 1994 Oct Warwic (SFT) H 16.1f 63 75 <
* 1994 Spt Haydoc (G-S) H 14f 59 64

1998 Turf 0-2: (16f 2) (sft, g-s)

Average gelding. Turf high 64 (began Oct). Consistent.

**G B Balding [7-20] Miss B Swire.*

BRAVE VISION BHB 61f **RR 61f** 4774[10]
2 b g Clantime 6.6f **(57)** - Kinlet Vision (IRE) (Vision (USA)) 9f **(64)**
Form - 000
Record 1998 - 1st:0 2nd:0 3rd:0 Ran:3
1998 Turf 0-3: (6f, 7f 2) (gd, g-f, frm)
Currently average gelding. Turf high 61 (began Aug).
**J R Arnold [0-3] J K Gale.*

BRAVO GORL (GER) RR 97f 4716a[9]
4 br f Tauchsport (GER) - Bravour (Ocos (GER))
Form - 30
1998 Turf 0-2: (16f, 20f) (sft, gd)
Currently very useful filly. Turf high 97 (1st run) - 3rd of 7 getting 4lb from Solo Mio (16 May Baden-Baden 16f gd RF 1376a).
**Uwe Stoltefuss in GER [0-2] G Nowack.*

BREAD WINNER RR 72f 2840[6]
2 b c Reprimand 8.2f **(63)** - Khubza (Green Desert (USA)) 8.6f **(78)**
Form - 46
Record 1998 - 1st:0 2nd:0 3rd:0 Ran:2
Win Prizemoney £0 *Total Prizemoney* £241
1998 Turf 0-2: (5f, 6f) (gd, g-f)
Currently above-average colt. Turf high 72.
**I A Balding [0-2] Al Muallim Partnership.*

BREAK FOR PEACE (IRE) BHB 61f **RR 65f** 3391[7]
3 b f Brief Truce (USA) 9.1f **(73)** - Run Bonnie (Runnett) 7f **(59)**
Form - 53267
Record 1998 - 1st:0 2nd:1 3rd:1 Ran:5
Pre1998 - 1st:0 2nd:0 3rd:0 Ran:1
Win Prizemoney £0 *Total Prizemoney* £1,256
1998 Turf 0-5: (5f 4, 6f) (gd, g-f 2, frm 2)
Leggy, average filly, effective 5f, acts on frm. Turf high 65.
**Sir Mark Prescott [0-6] Sharp But Fair Partnership.*

BREAKIN EVEN BHB 55f42a **RR 56f 42a** 3854[14]
3 ch g Chilibang 7f **(55)**-Bee Dee Dancer (Ballacashtal (CAN)) 5.3f **(50)**
Form - 8060180
Record 1998 - 1st:1 2nd:0 3rd:0 Ran:5
Pre1998 - 1st:0 2nd:0 3rd:0 Ran:4
Win Prizemoney £3,160 *Total Prizemoney* £3,160
Wins * **1998** May Haydoc (GD) H 6f 51 56 <
1998 Turf 1-4: (6f 1-3, 7f) (gd 1-3, frm) 1998 AW 0-1: (6f) (Fibr)
Workmanlike, fair gelding, effective 6f, acts on gd, mostly wears blinkers (effectively). Turf high 56 - 1st of 20 getting 14lb from Junior Muffin (22 May Haydock RF 1391). Inconsistent.
**J L Eyre [1-9] Mrs Frank Campbell.*

BREAK THE RULES BHB 72f65a **RR 74df 65a** 2231[4]
6 b g Dominion 8.9f **(65)** - Surf Bird (Shareef Dancer (USA)) 9.9f **(73)**
Form - 40830631034
Record 1998 - 1st:1 2nd:0 3rd:3 Ran:11
Pre1998 - 1st:7 2nd:5 3rd:3 Ran:34
Win Prizemoney £46,538 *Total Prizemoney* £57,166
Wins * **1998** May Cheste (GD) H 10.3f 66 71+
1997 Jun Cheste (SFT) C 10.3f 70
1997 May Cheste (SFT) H 10.3f 79 83 <
1997 Mar Doncas (G-F) H 10.3f 73 82
1996 Oct Doncas (GD) C 10.3f 79
1996 Jly Cheste (G-F) 12.3f 68+
1995 Aug Redcar (G-F) H 8f 71 75
1994 Apr Pontef (SFT) 5f 70+
1998 Turf 1-8: (10f 1-7, 11f) (sft 2, g-s, gd 3, g-f 1-1, frm) 1998 AW 0-3: (11f, 12f 2) (Fibr 3)
Above-average gelding, effective 9 to 12f, best at 10f, acts on gd to frm, best on gd, has worn blinkers, likes tight tracks, excels at Chester. Turf high 74 - 3rd of 7 giving 22lb to Vanadium Ore (3 Jun Chester 10f gd RF 1684). AW high 64. He was claimed to join Martin Pipe's string after winning on his final start of '96, and followed a successful hurdling campaign with three victories in '97 before he was claimed again, this time to join David Nicholls. He regained winning form at Chester in May, a track on which he thrives.
**D Nicholls [1-22] John Wilman (from M C Pipe [5-11] Jun 1997).*

BRECONGILL LAD BHB 59f **RR 55f** 5142[20]
6 b g Clantime 6.6f **(57)** - Chikala (Pitskelly) 8.5f **(53)**
Form - 2020306840
Record 1998 - 1st:0 2nd:2 3rd:1 Ran:10
Pre1998 - 1st:3 2nd:4 3rd:8 Ran:38
Win Prizemoney £14,274 *Total Prizemoney* £28,399
Wins 1996 Aug Beverl (GD) H 5f 65 67
1995 Aug Thirsk (G-F) H 5f 74 78 <
1995 Jun Newmar (GD) H 6f 65 69
1998 Turf 0-10: (5f 6, 6f 4) (g-s, gd 4, g-f 4, frm)
Fair gelding, effective 5 to 6f, best at 6f, acts on gd to frm, best on g-f, has worn blinkers, and excels at Pontefract. Turf high 68 - 2nd of 12 getting 3lb from Broadstairs Beauty (1 Jun Thirsk 5f g-f RF 1633). He has a lot more ability than he is prepared to show, and catching him on a going day is no easy task. Has plenty of toe.
**M D Hammond [0-10] P Davidson-Brown (from Miss S E Hall [3-38] Oct 1997).*

BREEDS HILL BHB 62f **RR 63f** 4006[6]
2 b f Chaddleworth (IRE) - Breed Reference (Reference Point) 6.8f **(70)**
Form - 766
Record 1998 - 1st:0 2nd:0 3rd:0 Ran:3
1998 Turf 0-3: (7f 3) (frm 3)
Currently average filly. Turf high 63 (began Jly).
**C F Wall [0-3] The Boadicea Partners.*

BREEZED WELL BHB 35f35a **RR 37f 35a** 3605[19]
12 b g Wolverlife 8.8f **(67)** - Precious Baby (African Sky) 7.9f **(63)**
Form - 8500860
Record 1998 - 1st:0 2nd:0 3rd:0 Ran:7
Pre1998 - 1st:2 2nd:3 3rd:11 Ran:91
Win Prizemoney £5,580 *Total Prizemoney* £22,551
Wins * 1997 Jly Beverl (HVY) H 9.9f 43 51 <
1994 Feb Wolver (STD) H 8.5f 47 49
1998 Turf 0-7: (7f 2, 8f, 10f 2, 11f 2) (g-f 2, frm 5)
Very moderate gelding, effective 8 to 10f, acts on g-s to g-f. Turf high 37.
**K G Wingrove [1-16] Mrs H Noonan (from B R Cambidge [1-42] Oct 1996).*

BRENDA DEE (IRE) BHB 67f **RR 65f** 4663[5]
2 br f Perugino (USA) - Children's Hour (Mummy's Pet) 7.7f **(60)**
Form - 24525
Record 1998 - 1st:0 2nd:2 3rd:0 Ran:5
Win Prizemoney £0 *Total Prizemoney* £3,161
1998 Turf 0-5: (6f 2, 7f, 8f, 10f) (g-s, gd, g-f, frm 2)
Average filly. Turf high 65. Capable of winning races at around a mile with cut in the ground. **A P Jarvis [0-5] Mrs Ann Jarvis.*

BREVITY RR 79f 2089[2]
3 b c Tenby 10.4f **(76)** - Rive (USA) (Riverman (USA)) 9.1f **(76)**
Form - 02
Record 1998 - 1st:0 2nd:1 3rd:0 Ran:2
Win Prizemoney £0 *Total Prizemoney* £790
1998 Turf 0-2: (8f, 10f) (sft, g-s)
Scopey, currently above-average colt. Turf high 79 - 2nd of 8 to General Monck (18 Jun Ripon 10f g-s RF 2089).
**J H M Gosden [0-2] K Abdulla.*

BREW BHB 75f **RR 63f** 4967[12]
2 b c Primo Dominie 7.2f **(67)** - Boozy (Absalom) 7.2f **(58)**
Form - 020
Record 1998 - 1st:0 2nd:1 3rd:0 Ran:3
Win Prizemoney £0 *Total Prizemoney* £1,070
1998 Turf 0-3: (5f, 6f 2) (sft, g-s, frm)
Currently average colt. Turf high 63.
**R Hannon [0-3] Mrs Robert Heathcote.*

BREYDON BHB 41f44a **RR 47df 44a** 4254[13]
5 ch g Be My Guest (USA)10.2f **(66)**-Palmella (USA)(Grundy) 10.3f **(65)**
Form - 6135533220
Record 1998 - 1st:1 2nd:2 3rd:3 Ran:10
Pre1998 - 1st:0 2nd:2 3rd:3 Ran:15
Win Prizemoney £2,346 *Total Prizemoney* £7,459
Wins * **1998** May Hamilt (SFT) SH 12.1f 26 32 <
1998 Turf 1-10: (8f, 11f 2, 12f 1-4, 16f 3) (hvy 1-1, gd 5, g-f 2, frm 2)
Moderate gelding, effective 11 to 16f, acts on gd to g-f, best on gd. Turf high 47 - 2nd of 8 to Diamond Crown (13 Jly Ayr 11f gd RF 2757).

**P Monteith [3-26] The Dregs Of Humanity (from M H Tompkins [0-8] Aug 1996).*

BRIAN'S BLUE (IRE) RR 335[8]
3 ch c Statoblest 6.4f **(63)** - Lamya (Hittite Glory) 8.7f **(50)**
Form - 08
Record 1998 - 1st:0 2nd:0 3rd:0 Ran:2
1998 AW 0-2: (6f, 9f) (Fibr 2)
Light-framed, currently poor colt. AW high 10.
**P Eccles [0-2] Brian A Lewendon & Mrs Carol Lewendon.*

BRIDAL WHITE BHB 70f **RR 71f** 4538[10]
2 b f Robellino (USA) 9.5f **(68)**-Alwatar (USA)(Caerleon (USA))8.6f **(71)**
Form - 43630
Record 1998 - 1st:0 2nd:0 3rd:2 Ran:5
Win Prizemoney £0 *Total Prizemoney* £1,265
1998 Turf 0-5: (6f 2, 7f 3) (gd, g-f, frm 3)
Above-average filly. Turf high 71 (began Aug) - 3rd of 20 getting 7lb from Central Coast (29 Aug Nottingham 6f g-f RF 3961).
**K G Wingrove [0-5] Peter Scott.*

BRIDE'S ANSWER BHB 80f **RR 80f** 4778[3]
3 ch f Anshan 8.2f **(63)** - Ivory Bride (Domynsky) 8f **(82)**
Form - 01333
Record 1998 - 1st:1 2nd:0 3rd:3 Ran:5
Win Prizemoney £3,793 *Total Prizemoney* £6,510
Wins * **1998** May Kempto (GD) 8f 80 <
1998 Turf 1-5: (8f 1-4, 10f) (sft, gd 1-2, g-f 2)
Decent filly. Turf high 80 - 1st of 13 from Marie Loup (4 May Kempton RF 1012). Improved from her debut to cause a surprise in a Kempton maiden, but has looked short of a turn of foot subsequently. **M R Channon [1-5] Mrs Jean Keegan.*

BRIDGE BHB 37f **RR 22f** 2771[13]
3 b f Batshoof 9.5f **(66)** - The Strid (IRE) (Persian Bold) 9.3f **(66)**
Form - 00
Record 1998 - 1st:0 2nd:0 3rd:0 Ran:2
Pre1998 - 1st:0 2nd:0 3rd:0 Ran:2
1998 Turf 0-2: (8f, 12f) (g-f, frm)
Scopey, little account filly, has worn blinkers. Turf high 15.
**S E Kettlewell [0-2] Don Chapman & Partners (from D Morley [0-2] Nov 1997).*

BRIDGEND BLUE (IRE) BHB 69f **RR 62f** 4377[13]
2 b g Up and At 'em - Sperrin Mist (Camden Town) 9.3f **(53)**
Form - 0650
Record 1998 - 1st:0 2nd:0 3rd:0 Ran:4
1998 Turf 0-4: (5f 2, 6f 2) (gd 2, g-f 2)
Average gelding, has worn blinkers. Turf high 62.
**M Bell [0-4] Ceredig, Dalton, Daw Mercer.*

BRIDIE'S PRIDE BHB 64f43a **RR 71f 43a** 5150[2]
7 b g Alleging (USA) 8.8f **(57)** - Miss Monte Carlo (Reform) 8.9f **(62)**
Form - 61220362
Record 1998 - 1st:1 2nd:3 3rd:1 Ran:8
Pre1998 - 1st:1 2nd:1 3rd:1 Ran:14
Win Prizemoney £8,575 *Total Prizemoney* £16,096
Wins * **1998** Jun Ascot (G-S) H 16.2f 50 57 <
* 1997 Jly Chepst (G-S) H 18f 46 50
1998 Turf 1-7: (16f 1-4, 17f, 18f 2) (g-s, gd 5, g-f 1-1) 1998 AW 0-1: (16f) (Fibr)
Above-average gelding, effective 17f, acts on gd, likes left handed tracks. Turf high 71. In fine form in the summer, including winning a competitive handicap at Ascot in June, and ran a cracker from out of the handicap in the Cesarewitch. Stays very well, and has a decent race in him. **G A Ham [2-29] K C White.*

BRIEF ENCOUNTA (FR) RR 80f 3912a[9]
2 ch c Brief Truce (USA) 9.1f **(73)** - Villa Blanca (SPA) (Rheffissimo (FR))
Form - 51440
Record 1998 - 1st:1 2nd:0 3rd:0 Ran:5
Win Prizemoney £8,081 *Total Prizemoney* £12,727
Wins * **1998** Jun Chanti (SFT) 6f 80? <
1998 Turf 1-5: (5f, 6f 1-1, 7f 2, 8f) (sft 1-2, gd, g-f, frm)
Decent colt. Turf high 80 - 1st of 10 from Campinas (11 Jun Chantilly RF 2102a). **B J Meehan [1-5].*

BRIEF ESCAPADE (IRE) BHB 95f **RR 96f** 4461[5]
3 ch f Brief Truce (USA) 9.1f **(73)**-Repetitious (Northfields (USA))9f **(72)**
Form - 1285
Record 1998 - 1st:1 2nd:1 3rd:0 Ran:4
Win Prizemoney £4,337 *Total Prizemoney* £6,547
Wins * **1998** Jly Warwic (GD) 8f 67 <
1998 Turf 1-4: (7f, 8f 1-3) (sft, g-f 1-1, frm 2)
Leggy, very useful filly. Turf high 96 (began Jly). Beat a moderate field of maidens with something in hand at Warwick, was not disgraced when running in better company afterwards.
**P W Chapple-Hyam [1-4] R Kaster & Cypress Farms.*

BRIEF SENTIMENT (IRE) RR 92f 3361a[9]
3 b f Brief Truce (USA) 9.1f **(73)** - Sentiment 00
Form - 342660
1998 Turf 0-6: (7f 2, 8f, 9f, 10f, 12f) (sft 4, gd 2)
Useful filly, effective 7 to 8f, best at 7f, acts on g-s to gd, best on gd. Turf high 98 - 2nd of 11 to Kitza (10 May Leopardstown 8f gd RF 1196a). **K Prendergast in IRE [1-9] Seamus Ross.*

BRIERY MEC BHB 46f **RR 53f** 1468[7]
3 b c Ron's Victory (USA) 9.2f **(52)** - Briery Fille (Sayyaf)
Form - 0877
Record 1998 - 1st:0 2nd:0 3rd:0 Ran:3
Pre1998 - 1st:0 2nd:0 3rd:0 Ran:2
1998 Turf 0-3: (8f, 10f, 12f) (g-s, gd, g-f)
Unfurnished, fair colt. Turf high 43. **H J Collingridge [0-5] C D Cole.*

BRIGADE CHARGE (USA) BHB 84f **RR 83f** 4069[7]
3 b c Affirmed (USA) 10.3f **(75)** - Fairy Footsteps (Mill Reef (USA)) 10.5f **(78)**
Form - 7217
Record 1998 - 1st:1 2nd:1 3rd:0 Ran:4
Win Prizemoney £3,598 *Total Prizemoney* £4,683
Wins * **1998** Jly Pontef (G-F) 12f 83 <
1998 Turf 1-4: (12f 1-4) (gd, g-f 2, frm 1-1)
Decent colt. Turf high 83 - 7th of 9 to Alberich (3 Spt York 12f g-f RF 4069) - also 1st of 8 from Profiler (7 Jly Pontefract RF 2589).
**L M Cumani [1-4] Robert Smith.*

BRIGHSTONE BHB 53f **RR 58f** 3838[8]
5 ch h Cadeaux Genereux 7.9f **(76)** - High Fountain (High Line) 10.3f **(70)**
Form - 522048
Record 1998 - 1st:0 2nd:2 3rd:0 Ran:6
Pre1998 - 1st:6 2nd:1 3rd:0 Ran:14
Win Prizemoney £21,369 *Total Prizemoney* £23,138
Wins * 1997 Oct Nottin (SFT) C 8.2f 60
* 1997 Spt York (SFT) C 8.9f 52+
* 1997 Aug Windso (G-F) S 11.6f 60
1997 Jun Bath (G-F) C 10.2f 72
1995 Nov Doncas (G-F) 8f 99+ <
1995 Oct Yarmou (FRM) 7f 72+
1998 Turf 0-6: (8f, 10f 2, 11f, 12f 2) (gd 2, g-f 3, frm)
Fair colt, effective 10f, acts on frm. Turf high 58. Becoming disappointing. Now tubed, he has found his level in sellers and claimers, but still throws in the odd stinker for good measure.
**M C Pipe [5-20] Richard Green (Fine Paintings) (from D R C Elsworth [1-2] Jun 1997).*

BRIGHT DESERT BHB 20f35a **RR 44f 35a** 2159[5]
5 b g Green Desert (USA) 7.8f **(78)** -Smarten Up (Sharpen Up) 8.3f **(67)**
Form - 0000800005
Record 1998 - 1st:0 2nd:0 3rd:0 Ran:9
Pre1998 - 1st:0 2nd:0 3rd:0 Ran:6
1998 Turf 0-4: (5f, 6f 2, 7f) (gd 3, g-f) 1998 AW 0-5: (5f, 6f 2, 7f, 8f) (Fibr 5)
Moderate gelding, has worn blinkers. Turf high 44. AW high 31. Inconsistent.
**Martyn Wane [0-12] William Graham (from R M McKellar [0-2] Mar 1997).*

BRIGHTER (USA) RR 76f 2882[4]
2 ch f Gone West (USA) 7.8f **(82)** - Top Trestle (USA) (Nijinsky (CAN)) 10.3f **(77)**
Form - 4
Record 1998 - 1st:0 2nd:0 3rd:0 Ran:1

Win Prizemoney £0 *Total Prizemoney* £291
1998 Turf 0-1: (7f) (frm)
Currently above-average filly. (1st run) - 4th of 7 to Kareymah (17 Jly Newmarket 7f frm RF 2882).
**H R A Cecil [0-1] H R H Prince Fahd Salman.*

BRIGHTER BYFAAH (IRE) BHB 43f46a **RR 50?f 46a** 4938[17]
5 ch g Kefaah (USA) 11.2f **(64)** - Bright Landing (Sun Prince) 12.4f **(52)**
Form - 0
Record 1998 - 1st:0 2nd:0 3rd:0 Ran:1
Pre1998 - 1st:2 2nd:0 3rd:0 Ran:10
Win Prizemoney £5,175 *Total Prizemoney* £5,175
Wins * 1997 Jly Bath (FRM) H 17.2f 42 50 <
* 1996 Jly Nottin (G-F) SH 14.1f 43 43
1998 Turf 0-1: (16f) (gd)
Fair gelding, has worn blinkers. **N A Graham [2-11] Paul Jacobs.*

BRIGHT EYES (IRE) BHB 25f **RR 23f** 4676[15]
5 b m Contract Law (USA) 8.9f **(54)** - Ferry Lane (Dom Racine (FR)) 9.2f **(62)**
Form - 8000
Record 1998 - 1st:0 2nd:0 3rd:0 Ran:4
1998 Turf 0-4: (5f, 6f 2, 10f) (gd, g-f 2, frm)
Little account filly. Turf high 23 (began Aug).
**J S Wainwright [0-4] J B Slatcher.*

BRIGHT FINISH (USA) RR 103f 4726a[11]
4 ch f Zilzal (USA) 8.5f **(79)** - Bialy (USA) (Alydar (USA)) 9.1f **(76)**
Form - 20
1998 Turf 0-2: (5f, 6f) (sft, gd)
Currently very useful filly. Turf high 103 (1st run) (began Spt) - 2nd of 3 getting 6lb from Keos (18 Spt Chantilly 6f gd RF 4470c). She has been dogged by injury (including a broken leg), but came back well in 1998, finishing second in a Group 3 at Chantilly in September. She looked out of her depth in the Prix de lÍAbbaye the following month, but may be worth keeping in training.
**Mme C Head in FR [0-2] Maktoum Al Maktoum.*

BRIGHT HOPE (IRE) RR 58f 4956[7]
2 b f Danehill (USA) 9.1f **(79)** - Crystal Cross (USA) **(73f)** (Roberto (USA)) 10f **(76)**
Form - 7
Record 1998 - 1st:0 2nd:0 3rd:0 Ran:1
1998 Turf 0-1: (8f) (frm)
Currently fair filly. **P W Harris [0-1] Mrs P W Harris.*

BRIGHT PARAGON (IRE) BHB 37f33a **RR 33f 33a** 2436[8]
9 b or br g Treasure Kay 6.5f **(53)** - Shining Bright (USA) (Bold Bidder) 8.8f **(67)**
Form - 200648
Record 1998 - 1st:0 2nd:1 3rd:0 Ran:6
Pre1998 - 1st:5 2nd:6 3rd:5 Ran:70
Win Prizemoney £14,948 *Total Prizemoney* £23,482
Wins * 1997 May Lingfi (GD) SH 5f 36 37
1994 Aug Sandow (GD) H 5f 46 45
1994 Jun Windso (G-F) H 6f 43 41
1998 Turf 0-6: (5f 6) (g-s, gd, frm 4)
Very moderate gelding, effective 5 to 6f, best at 5f, acts on gd to frm, best on frm, has worn blinkers, and excels at Yarmouth. Turf high 44 (1st run) - 2nd of 12 getting 21lb from Divine Miss-P (1 Apr Folkestone 5f gd RF 0536). Consistent.
**K T Ivory [1-24] D C G Cooper (from M C Chapman [0-2] Apr 1996).*

BRILLIANCE RR 74f 4925[1]
3 ch f Cadeaux Genereux 7.9f **(76)** - Rainbow's End (My Swallow) 9.2f **(71)**
Form - 47331
Record 1998 - 1st:1 2nd:0 3rd:2 Ran:5
Win Prizemoney £4,337 *Total Prizemoney* £5,511
Wins * 1998 Oct Nottin (SFT) H 8.2f 61 69 <
1998 Turf 1-5: (8f 1-5) (g-s 1-1, g-f 2, frm 2)
Well made, above-average filly, has worn blinkers. Turf high 74 (began Jly) - also 1st of 10 giving 2lb to Margaret's Dancer (21 Oct Nottingham RF 4925). **R Charlton [1-5] Lord Carnarvon.*

BRILLIANT CORNERS RR 81f 4666[2]
3 b c Royal Academy (USA) 7.8f **(77)** - Curie Point (USA) (Sharpen Up) 8.3f **(67)**
Form - 22
Record 1998 - 1st:0 2nd:2 3rd:0 Ran:2
Win Prizemoney £0 *Total Prizemoney* £2,388
1998 Turf 0-2: (8f 2) (g-s, g-f)
Scopey, currently decent colt. Turf high 81 (1st run) (began Spt) - 2nd of 20 to Bomb Alaska (18 Spt Newbury 8f g-f RF 4356). Runner-up in maidens, he was sold for 50,000 gns in the autumn.
**R Charlton [0-2] Michael Pescod.*

BRILLIANT RED BHB 94f93a **RR 95f 93a** 5078[9]
5 b g Royal Academy (USA) 7.8f **(77)** - Red Comes Up (USA) (Blushing Groom (FR)) 10.3f **(76)**
Form - 43110032100
Record 1998 - 1st:3 2nd:1 3rd:2 Ran:10
Pre1998 - 1st:2 2nd:2 3rd:4 Ran:17
Win Prizemoney £59,211 *Total Prizemoney* £76,046
Wins * **1998** Spt Newbur (GD) H 10f 92 95 <
* ***1998*** *Feb Lingfi (SLW) H 10f 85 92*
* ***1998*** *Feb Lingfi (SLW) H 10f 78 81*
* 1997 Jly Lingfi (G-F) 7.6f 83
1995 Aug Kempto (G-F) 7f 90+
1998 Turf 1-6: (8f 2, 9f, 10f 1-3) (sft, gd, g-f 1-2, frm 2) 1998 AW 2-4: (8f, 10f 2-3) (Equi 2-4)
Very useful gelding, effective 8 to 10f, best at 10f, acts on gd to frm - acts on Equi, best on g-f. Turf high 95 (began Jly) - 1st of 19 giving 12lb to Mister Benjamin (19 Spt Newbury RF 4379). AW high 92 - 1st of 8 giving 15lb to Chairmans Choice (17 Feb Lingfield RF 0305). Inconsistent. Gradually found his form on Equitrack at the beginning of '98, including two impressive victories in handicaps over ten furlongs in February, but cut little ice in the Winter Derby. First run since when down the field at Glorious Goodwood, having almost been brought down, and has run well since, including when landing the competitive Courage Handicap at Newbury. Ran with credit on final two starts of the season, and will win more handicaps next term.
**P R Hedger [4-21] Mrs M J George (from P F I Cole [1-8] Aug 1996).*

BRIMMING BHB 106f **RR 104f** 4481[1]
3 ch c Generous (IRE) 11.5f **(82)** - Rainbow Lake (Rainbow Quest (USA)) 10.4f **(75)**
Form - 2311021
Record 1998 - 1st:3 2nd:2 3rd:1 Ran:7
Pre1998 - 1st:0 2nd:1 3rd:1 Ran:2
Win Prizemoney £14,591 *Total Prizemoney* £23,681
Wins * **1998** Spt Haydoc (G-F) 14f 104 <
* **1998** Jly Newbur (G-F) H 13.3f 85 93
* **1998** Jun Haydoc (GD) 14f 70
1998 Turf 3-7: (12f 2, 13f 1-1, 14f 2-2, 15f, 16f) (g-s, gd 1-3, frm 2-3)
Neat, very useful colt, effective 14 to 15f, acts on gd to frm. Turf high 104 - 1st of 3 getting 5lb from Secret Archive (25 Spt Haydock RF 4481). He looked moderate in the spring, but improved as the season went on and beat the subsequent Cersarewitch hero Spirit Of Love in a conditions event at Haydock. He proved well served by waiting tactics that day and should make up into a smart staying four-year-old. **H R A Cecil [3-9] K Abdulla.*

BRIMMING OVER BHB 78f **RR 74f** 4928[3]
2 ch c Dashing Blade 7.9f **(80)** - Madam Trilby (Grundy) 10.3f **(65)**
Form - 646453
Record 1998 - 1st:0 2nd:0 3rd:1 Ran:6
Win Prizemoney £0 *Total Prizemoney* £1,209
1998 Turf 0-6: (5f, 7f 4, 10f) (g-s, gd 2, g-f 3)
Above-average colt, effective 7f, acts on g-s to g-f. Turf high 74 - 3rd of 14 to Pagan King (22 Oct Brighton 7f g-s RF 4928).
**R Hannon [0-6] J C Smith.*

BRIMSTONE (IRE) BHB 83f **RR 84f** 3235[15]
3 ch c Ballad Rock 7.2f **(63)** -Blazing Glory (IRE) (Glow (USA)) 6.7f **(71)**
Form - 240
Record 1998 - 1st:0 2nd:1 3rd:0 Ran:3
Pre1998 - 1st:1 2nd:1 3rd:0 Ran:4
Win Prizemoney £3,485 *Total Prizemoney* £6,276
Wins 1997 Jly Sandow (G-F) 5f 78 <
1998 Turf 0-3: (5f 2, 6f) (gd, g-f 2)
Well made, decent colt, effective 5 to 6f, best at 5f, acts on g-f to frm, best on frm. Turf high 84 (1st run) - 2nd of 8 giving 1lb to Gipsy Moth (26 Jun Newmarket 5f g-f RF 2316). Comfortable win-

ner of a maiden on his third start at two, he made an encouraging reappearance at Newmarket, despite losing a shoe during the race. Six furlongs looked to just stretch his stamina next time and he was poorly drawn on his third run of '98.

**R McGhin [0-3] Seymour Racing Partnership (from D R C Elsworth [1-4] Aug 1997).*

BRING SWEETS BHB 90f RR 87f 5143[1]

2 b c Sabrehill (USA) 8.5f **(64)** - Che Gambe (USA) (Lyphard (USA)) 9.9f **(72)**

Form - 8811

Record 1998 - 1st:2 2nd:0 3rd:0 Ran:4

Win Prizemoney £8,217 *Total Prizemoney* £8,217

Wins * **1998** Nov Doncas (SFT) 8f 87 <

* **1998** Oct Redcar (HVY) 8f 82

1998 Turf 2-4: (7f, 8f 2-3) (sft 1-1, gd 1-1, g-f 2)

Useful colt. Turf high 87 (began Spt) - 1st of 6 giving 2lb to Weet For Me (6 Nov Doncaster RF 5143) - also 1st of 9 from Single Shot (17 Oct Redcar RF 4860). Appreciated the ground when winning two backend events.

**B W Hills [2-4] H R H Prince Fahd Salman.*

BRISKA (IRE) BHB 25f47a RR 43f 47a 4654[7]

4 b f River Falls 8.2f **(56)** - Calash (Indian King (USA)) 7.4f **(64)**

Form - 0708007

Record 1998 - 1st:0 2nd:0 3rd:0 Ran:6

Pre1998 - 1st:1 2nd:0 3rd:1 Ran:10

Win Prizemoney £2,988 *Total Prizemoney* £3,426

Wins 1996 Jun Warwic (FRM) 7f 76 <

1998 Turf 0-6: (8f 4, 10f, 12f) (g-s, gd, g-f 3, frm)

Workmanlike, moderate filly. Turf high 43.

**J Akehurst [0-6] Robert Shafer (from R Akehurst [0-5] Nov 1997).*

BRISTOL CHANNEL BHB 108f RR 107f 4740[3]

3 b f Generous (IRE) 11.5f **(82)** - Shining Water (Kalaglow) 9.8f **(67)**

Form - 1213

Record 1998 - 1st:2 2nd:1 3rd:1 Ran:4

Pre1998 - 1st:1 2nd:0 3rd:0 Ran:2

Win Prizemoney £39,067 *Total Prizemoney* £51,112

Wins * **1998** Spt Ascot (SFT) L 12f 94+ <

* **1998** May Lingfi (GD) L 11.5f 94

* 1997 Spt Leices (G-F) 8f 84+

1998 Turf 2-4: (11f 1-1, 12f 1-3) (g-s, gd 1-1, g-f 1-1, frm)

Light-framed, Pattern-class filly, effective 12f, acts on frm. Turf high 107 - 2nd of 8 giving 6lb to Rambling Rose (20 Aug York 12f frm RF 3776). She had a hard race when winning the Listed Oaks Trial at Lingfield, and was rested for most of the summer. Second to Rambling Rose in the Galtres Stakes at York in August, she overcame appalling conditions to score at Ascot the following month. Tough and willing, she needs to improve to win in Group company. **B W Hills [3-6] K Abdulla.*

BRITANNIA MILLS BHB 20f20a RR 11f 20a 1953[11]

7 gr m Nordico (USA) 8.2f **(59)** - May Fox (Healaugh Fox) 10f **(46)**

Form - 0

Record 1998 - 1st:0 2nd:0 3rd:0 Ran:1

Pre1998 - 1st:1 2nd:1 3rd:1 Ran:35

Win Prizemoney £3,158 *Total Prizemoney* £4,426

Wins 1994 Aug Ripon (G-F) SH 10f 39 40 <

1998 Turf 0-1: (10f) (gd)

Poor mare.

**D J Wintle [0-1] A D Bennett (from M C Chapman [2-54] Jan 1997).*

BROADGATE FLYER (IRE) BHB 37f50a RR 12f 50a 4838[14]

4 b g Silver Kite (USA) 10.2f **(51)** - Fabulous Pet (Somethingfabulous (USA)) 9.5f **(75)**

Form - 00

Record 1998 - 1st:0 2nd:0 3rd:0 Ran:2

Pre1998 - 1st:0 2nd:2 3rd:1 Ran:13

Win Prizemoney £0 *Total Prizemoney* £1,987

1998 Turf 0-2: (7f, 12f) (g-s, frm)

Unfurnished, fair gelding, effective 7f, - acts on Equi, has worn blinkers, likes left handed tracks, favours tight tracks. Turf high 12 (began Spt).

**D A Lamb [1-10] D A Lamb (from Mrs L Stubbs [0-9] Jun 1997).*

BROADSTAIRS BEAUTY (IRE) BHB 86f82a RR 87f 82a 4502[18]

8 ch g Dominion Royale 7.8f **(63)** - Holy Water (Monseigneur (USA)) 7.7f **(63)**

Form - 341250110010000

Record 1998 - 1st:4 2nd:1 3rd:0 Ran:14

Pre1998 - 1st:8 2nd:12 3rd:7 Ran:55

Win Prizemoney £54,089 *Total Prizemoney* £73,327

Wins * **1998** Jun Doncas (GD) H 5f 84 87 <

* **1998** Jun Windso (GD) 5f 77

* **1998** Jun Thirsk (GD) H 5f 68 71

* **1998** *Jan Southw (STD) H 6f 74 76*

1995 *Nov Southw (STD) H 5f 75 77*

1995 Jly Newmar (G-F) H 5f 75 75

1995 May Ripon (GD) H 5f 70 71

1994 Spt Ayr (G-S) H 5f 55 56

1994 Aug Yarmou (G-S) H 7f 53 53

1994 *Jly Southw (STD) H 5f 68 69+*

1994 *May Southw (STD) H 5f 59 64+*

1998 Turf 3-11: (5f 3-7, 6f 4) (sft 2, g-s, gd 2, g-f 3-4, frm 2) 1998 AW 1-3: (6f 1-2, 7f) (Fibr 1-3)

Useful gelding, effective 5f, acts on g-f, often wears blinkers. Turf high 87 - 1st of 10 getting 8lb from Repertory (28 Jun Doncaster RF 2358). AW high 77. Able on both turf and Fibresand, he was running well at Southwell during the winter, and ended a long losing run when winning a handicap there in January. He won three times on turf in June before his form tailed off. Normally shows plenty of early pace.

**D Shaw [4-31] Mrs Judy Hunt (from P Howling [0-2] Jly 1996).*

BROADWAY MELODY BHB 53a RR 61?f 5007[16]

4 b f Beveled (USA) 6.9f **(64)** - Broadway Stomp (USA) (Broadway Forli (USA)) 5.8f **(46)**

Form - 488704620213420012530

Record 1998 - 1st:2 2nd:4 3rd:2 Ran:21

Pre1998 - 1st:1 2nd:0 3rd:0 Ran:6

Win Prizemoney £7,475 *Total Prizemoney* £11,930

Wins * **1998** Aug Warwic (G-F) C 5f 57 <

* **1998** Jly Bright (GD) H 5.3f 44 49

* 1997 *Jly Wolver (STD) 6f 55*

1998 Turf 2-17: (5f 2-10, 6f 7) (sft 2, gd 5, g-f, frm 2-8, hrd) 1998 AW 0-4: (5f, 6f 3) (Fibr 4)

Scopey, average filly, effective 5 to 6f, best at 6f, acts on gd to frm - acts on Fibr, has worn blinkers, likes left handed tracks. Turf high 61 - 2nd of 20 giving 1lb to Time To Tango (14 Spt Nottingham 6f gd RF 4260) - also 1st of 14 giving 6lb to Oare Kite (31 Aug Warwick RF 4004). AW high 45.

**A P Jarvis [3-27] Christopher Shankland.*

BROCKTON SAGA (IRE) BHB 62f RR 74df 4569[7]

2 b f Perugino (USA) - Danger Ahead (Mill Reef (USA)) 10.5f **(78)**

Form - 80851U07

Record 1998 - 1st:1 2nd:0 3rd:0 Ran:8

Win Prizemoney £2,814 *Total Prizemoney* £2,814

Wins * **1998** Spt Bath (GD) 5.1f 74 <

1998 Turf 1-8: (5f 1-7, 6f) (gd, g-f 2, frm 1-4, hrd)

Above-average filly, effective 5f, acts on frm. Turf high 74 (began Jly) - 1st of 14 giving 3lb to L'Agneau Noir (7 Spt Bath RF 4122).

**B J Meehan [1-8] Mrs La Trobe.*

BROCTUNE GOLD BHB 54f56a RR 43f 56a 5120[11]

7 b g Superpower 6.6f **(58)** - Golden Sunlight (Ile de Bourbon (USA)) 10.1f **(67)**

Form - 0001287100860

Record 1998 - 1st:2 2nd:1 3rd:0 Ran:13

Pre1998 - 1st:10 2nd:9 3rd:6 Ran:49

Win Prizemoney £32,883 *Total Prizemoney* £47,964

Wins * **1998** Aug Catter (GD) H 7f 58 59

* **1998** Jun Mussel (SFT) H 8f 54 57

* 1997 Jly Mussel (GD) C 7.1f 62

* 1997 Jun Mussel (GD) C 7.1f 56+

* 1996 Aug Beverl (GD) C 8.5f 64

* 1996 Jly Mussel (G-F) H 8.1f 60 68

* 1996 Jun Mussel (FRM) C 7.1f 61

* 1996 May Thirsk (G-F) S 7f 55

* 1995 May Redcar (FRM) C 6f 60+

* 1995 May Newcas (GD) C 7f 58

1998 Turf 2-13: (7f 1-7, 8f 1-5, 9f) (g-s 2, gd 2-5, g-f 2, frm 4)

Moderate gelding, effective 7 to 8f, best at 7f, acts on gd, prefers right handed tracks, favours tight tracks, excels at Musselburgh.

Turf high 59. Usually a front-runner, he is a completely different horse at Musselburgh where he has a tremendous record. He returned to winning form there in June, having not shown much up to that point, and also managed to pick up a very modest handicap at Catterick in August.
**Mrs M Reveley [12-61] Mrs M B Thwaites (from B W Hills [0-1] Aug 1997).*

BROCTUNE LINE BHB 38f56a **RR 38f 56a** 3396^{2}
4 ch g Safawan 6.6f **(60)** - Ra Ra (Lord Gayle (USA)) 8.8f **(62)**
Form - 020042
Record 1998 - 1st:0 2nd:2 3rd:0 Ran:6
Pre1998 - 1st:2 2nd:0 3rd:1 Ran:14
Win Prizemoney £5,208 *Total Prizemoney* £7,324
Wins * 1997 *Apr Southw (STD) H 11f 55 58* <
* 1997 *Jan Southw (STD) H 8f 45 46*
1998 Turf 0-4: (8f 2, 11f, 12f)(sft, gd, frm 2) 1998 AW 0-2:(11f 2)(Fibr 2)
Workmanlike, fair gelding, effective 11f, - acts on Fibr, has worn blinkers, prefers left handed tracks, prefers tight tracks. Turf high 38. AW high 58 - 2nd of 8 giving 17lb to Areish (26 Jan Southwell 11f Fibr RF 0164). Inconsistent. Twice a winner on sand at Southwell in '97, he looks quite a bit better on that surface than on turf. **Mrs M Reveley [2-25] Gerry Slater, Allen Evans & John Snaith.*

BRODESSA BHB 58f54a **RR 58f 54a** 5118^{6}
12 gr g Scallywag 15.1f **(43)** - Jeanne du Barry (Dubassoff (USA)) 14.2f **(55)**
Form - 175222115211106
Record 1998 - 1st:5 2nd:4 3rd:0 Ran:13
Pre1998 - 1st:11 2nd:11 3rd:7 Ran:47
Win Prizemoney £40,740 *Total Prizemoney* £55,437
Wins * **1998** Spt Mussel (GD) H 16f 55 58
* **1998** Aug Redcar (G-F) S 14.1f 56
* **1998** Aug Beverl (G-F) SH 16.2f 48 55
* **1998** Jly Catter (FRM) C 12f 49
* **1998** Jly Mussel (GD) C 16f 38
* 1997 *Nov Wolver (STD) C 14.8f 47*
* 1997 Jun Nottin (SFT) C 16f 48
* 1996 Aug Beverl (FRM) SH 16.2f 57 58
* 1996 Jun Nottin (G-F) C 16f 57
* 1995 Aug Redcar (G-F) S 14.1f 53+
* 1995 Aug Beverl (G-F) SH 16.2f 57 61
* 1995 Jun Redcar (FRM) C 14.1f 50+
* 1995 Jun Redcar (G-F) C 16f 51+
* 1994 Spt Mussel (G-F) C 15.1f 64
* 1994 Aug Mussel (G-F) C 15.1f 42
1998 Turf 5-12: (12f 1-1, 14f 1-5, 16f 3-5, 17f) (gd 4, g-f 1-3, frm 4-5)
1998 AW 0-1: (16f) (Fibr)
Fair gelding, effective 13 to 16f, best at 16f, acts on g-s to frm, best on gd, likes right handed tracks, favours tight tracks, excels at Nottingham, does well at Musselburgh and likes Beverley. Turf high 58 - 1st of 17 from Cut Diamond (14 Spt Musselburgh RF 4254) - also 1st of 4 from Good Hand (29 Aug Redcar RF 3966). Consistent. This popular veteran remains a money-spinner under both codes, and has winning five times in modest company in 1998. **Mrs M Reveley [19-67] The Mary Reveley Racing Club.*

BRONZINO BHB 58f **RR 57f** 5095^{3}
3 ch g Midyan (USA) 9.9f **(64)** - Indubitable (Sharpo) 7.7f **(59)**
Form - 306073
Record 1998 - 1st:0 2nd:0 3rd:2 Ran:6
Pre1998 - 1st:0 2nd:0 3rd:0 Ran:5
Win Prizemoney £0 *Total Prizemoney* £957
1998 Turf 0-6: (9f, 10f 2, 11f, 12f 2) (gd 3, g-f, frm 2)
Light-framed, fair gelding, effective 10f, acts on gd. Turf high 64 (1st run) (began Aug) - 3rd of 11 getting 6lb from Renown (12 Aug Salisbury 10f gd RF 3588). Consistent.
**G B Balding [0-11] Miss B Swire.*

BROOKHEAD BRANDY BHB 49f49a **RR 49f 49a** 5094^{17}
2 ch f Safawan 6.6f **(60)** - Purple Fan (Dalsaan) 9.8f **(64)**
Form - 085251040050
Record 1998 - 1st:1 2nd:1 3rd:0 Ran:12
Win Prizemoney £1,884 *Total Prizemoney* £2,411
Wins * **1998** Aug Leices (GD) SH 6f 57 62 <
1998 Turf 1-7: (5f, 6f 1-2, 7f 2, 8f 2) (gd 2, g-f 2, frm 1-3) 1998 AW 0-5: (5f, 7f 3, 8f) (Fibr 5)
Fair filly, effective 6 to 7f, acts on frm - acts on Fibr, often wears blinkers (very effectively). Turf high 62 - 1st of 8 getting 2lb from Gypsy Music (10 Aug Leicester RF 3499). AW high 59 - 2nd of 11 to March Party (24 Jly Wolverhampton 7f Fibr RF 3097).
**P D Evans [1-12] P D Evans.*

BROOKHOUSE LADY (IRE) BHB 55f46a **RR 56f 46a** 4957^{7}
3 b f Polish Patriot (USA) 7.8f **(70)** - Honagh Lee (Main Reef) 9.6f **(57)**
Form - 055721047
Record 1998 - 1st:1 2nd:1 3rd:0 Ran:9
Pre1998 - 1st:0 2nd:0 3rd:0 Ran:8
Win Prizemoney £3,095 *Total Prizemoney* £4,520
Wins * **1998** Spt Leices (G-S) H 10f 50 56 <
1998 Turf 1-8: (8f 2, 10f 1-3, 11f 2, 12f) (sft, gd, g-f 1-1, frm 5) 1998 AW 0-1: (9f) (Fibr)
Light-framed, fair filly, likes tight tracks. Turf high 56 (began Jly). Inconsistent.
**Ian Williams [1-9] & Mrs D J Smart (from R Hollinshead [0-8] Nov 1997).*

BROOKSIE BHB 60f **RR 55f** 902^{18}
3 b g Efisio 7.7f **(69)** - Elkie Brooks (Relkino) 8.9f **(65)**
Form - 0
Record 1998 - 1st:0 2nd:0 3rd:0 Ran:1
Pre1998 - 1st:0 2nd:0 3rd:0 Ran:3
1998 Turf 0-1: (8f) (g-s)
Scopey, fair gelding. **J W Hills [0-4] Mrs Shirley Trotman.*

BROTHER ROY BHB 40f45a **RR 64f 45a** 2566^{11}
5 b g Prince Sabo 6.6f **(64)** -Classic Heights (Shirley Heights) 10.3f **(74)**
Form - 0
Record 1998 - 1st:0 2nd:0 3rd:0 Ran:1
Pre1998 - 1st:0 2nd:0 3rd:0 Ran:8
1998 Turf 0-1: (10f) (g-f)
Average gelding. Becoming disappointing.
**T G Mills [0-9] T G Mills.*

BROUGHTON BELLE RR 13f 4668^{16}
2 b f Chaddleworth (IRE) - Broughtons Pet (IRE) (Cyrano de Bergerac) 6f **(68)**
Form - 0
Record 1998 - 1st:0 2nd:0 3rd:0 Ran:1
1998 Turf 0-1: (6f) (gd)
Currently poor filly. **W J Musson [0-1] Broughton Thermal Insulation.*

BROUGHTON MAGIC (IRE) BHB 38f **RR 39f** 5070^{21}
3 ch g Archway (IRE) 8.5f **(60)** - Magic Green (Magic Mirror)
Form - 000500
Record 1998 - 1st:0 2nd:0 3rd:0 Ran:6
1998 Turf 0-5: (6f 2, 7f, 8f, 9f) (g-s, g-f 4) 1998 AW 0-1: (6f) (Fibr)
Workmanlike, very moderate gelding. Turf high 39.
**W J Musson [0-6] Broughton Thermal Insulation.*

BROUGHTONS CHAMP BHB 26f **RR 31f** 3599^{2}
6 b g Dowsing (USA) 7f **(61)** - Knees Up (USA) (Dancing Champ (USA)) 8.8f **(80)**
Form - 0802
Record 1998 - 1st:0 2nd:1 3rd:0 Ran:4
Pre1998 - 1st:0 2nd:0 3rd:0 Ran:2
Win Prizemoney £0 *Total Prizemoney* £544
1998 Turf 0-4: (8f, 11f, 12f, 16f) (gd, frm 3)
Very moderate gelding. Turf high 31 - 2nd of 11 getting 22lb from Brodessa (13 Aug Beverley 16f frm RF 3599).
**W J Musson [0-6] Broughton Bloodstock.*

BROUGHTONS DIAMOND BHB 50f **RR 58f** 4939^{15}
3 ch g Weldnaas (USA) 8.4f **(55)** - Mona (Auction Ring (USA)) 8.6f **(65)**
Form - 0860
Record 1998 - 1st:0 2nd:0 3rd:0 Ran:4
1998 Turf 0-4: (8f, 10f 3) (gd 2, g-f 2)
Workmanlike, fair gelding, always wears blinkers. Turf high 58.
**W J Musson [0-4] Lyons & Broughton III.*

BROUGHTONS FORMULA BHB 39f47a **RR 37f 47a** 368^{3}
8 b g Night Shift (USA) 8.1f **(73)** - Forward Rally (Formidable (USA)) 9.2f **(63)**
Form - 73604123
Record 1998 - 1st:1 2nd:1 3rd:1 Ran:5

Pre1998 - 1st:16 2nd:9 3rd:8 Ran:86
Win Prizemoney £54,292 *Total Prizemoney* £69,748
Wins * **1998** *Jan Lingfi (STD) H 16f 43 45+*
* 1997 *Feb Lingfi (STD) H 16f 56 61*
* 1997 *Jan Lingfi (STD) H 16f 53 60*
* 1996 Oct Redcar (G-F) H 13.6f 41 46
* 1996 Spt Nottin (FRM) H 16f 34 38
* 1995 *Dec Lingfi (STD) H 13f 48 61*
* 1995 *Dec Lingfi (STD) H 13f 48 43*
* 1995 Aug Sandow (G-F) H 14f 48 53
* 1995 Aug Kempto (G-F) H 12f 47 54
* 1994 Mar Catter (GD) H 13.8f 54 59
* 1994 Mar Doncas (GD) H 12f 54 57
* 1994 *Feb Wolver (STD) H 14.8f 53 58*
1998 AW 1-5: (12f, 16f 1-4) (Equi 1-5)
Moderate gelding, effective 16f, - acts on Equi, mostly wears blinkers. AW high 48. Consistent. He gives his supporters a great deal of anxiety by tailing himself off in the early stages of his races, but is still capable of winning despite that, as long as the opposition are fairly modest. Two miles on the Lingfield Equitrack are his ideal conditions. **W J Musson [17-91] Crawford Gray & Aylett.*

BROUGHTON SIREN BHB 34f RR 33f 4955^{14}

3 b f Most Welcome 8.6f **(66)** -Royal Form (Formidable (USA)) 9.2f **(63)**
Form - 000
Record 1998 - 1st:0 2nd:0 3rd:0 Ran:3
1998 Turf 0-3: (7f 2, 8f) (frm 3)
Strong, currently very moderate filly. Turf high 33 (began Aug).
**W J Musson [0-3] Broughton Thermal Insulation.*

BROUGHTONS LURE (IRE) BHB 49f43a RR 50f 43a 4958^{14}

4 ch f Archway (IRE) 8.5f **(60)** - Vaal Salmon (IRE) (Salmon Leap (USA)) 11f **(61)**
Form - 2D66820
Record 1998 - 1st:0 2nd:2 3rd:0 Ran:7
Pre1998 - 1st:0 2nd:0 3rd:0 Ran:3
Win Prizemoney £0 *Total Prizemoney* £2,922
1998 Turf 0-6: (11f, 12f 2, 13f 2, 15f) (gd, g-f 2, frm 3) 1998 AW 0-1: (12f) (Fibr)
Workmanlike, fair filly, effective 11 to 13f, acts on g-f to frm, best on frm. Turf high 50 - 2nd of 22 getting 16lb from Lancer (8 Oct York 12f frm RF 4704). **W J Musson [0-10] Broughton Bloodstock.*

BROUGHTON'S PRIDE (IRE) BHB 50f39a RR 54f 39a 336^{12}

7 b m Superpower 6.6f **(58)** - French Quarter (Ile de Bourbon (USA)) 10.1f **(67)**
Form - 000
Record 1998 - 1st:0 2nd:0 3rd:0 Ran:2
Pre1998 - 1st:3 2nd:8 3rd:4 Ran:41
Win Prizemoney £6,128 *Total Prizemoney* £15,886
Wins 1997 *Feb Southw (STD) H 7f 48 53* <
1997 *Jan Southw (STD) H 8f 36 43*
1996 May Nottin (G-F) H 8.2f 47 52
1998 AW 0-2: (7f, 8f) (Fibr 2)
Fair mare, has broken blood-vessels, effective 7 to 8f, best at 8f, acts on g-s - acts on Fibr, has worn blinkers, favours tight tracks. Becoming disappointing.
**Ronald Thompson [0-3] Mrs Janet Morris (from J L Eyre [3-19] Jly 1997).*

BROUGHTONS SONG BHB 40f RR 45f 4122^{14}

2 b f Chaddleworth (IRE) - Princess Dancer (Alzao (USA)) 7.1f **(68)**
Form - 000
Record 1998 - 1st:0 2nd:0 3rd:0 Ran:3
1998 Turf 0-3: (5f 2, 6f) (gd, frm 2)
Currently moderate filly. Turf high 45 (began Aug).
**W J Musson [0-3] Lyons & Broughton II.*

BROUGHTONS TURMOIL BHB 72f73a RR 72f 73a 5040^{4}

9 b g Petorius 8f **(66)** - Rustic Stile (Rusticaro (FR)) 8.2f **(65)**
Form - 732517430654
Record 1998 - 1st:1 2nd:1 3rd:2 Ran:12
Pre1998 - 1st:6 2nd:6 3rd:6 Ran:44
Win Prizemoney £27,189 *Total Prizemoney* £51,349
Wins * **1998** *Jun Southw (STD) H 8f 67 72*
* 1997 Apr Ascot (G-F) H 8f 70 77 <
1996 Aug Kempto (GD) H 7f 66 70
1995 Aug Sandow (G-F) H 7.1f 60 66
1995 Jly Newmar (G-F) H 7f 52 63
1995 *Feb Lingfi (STD) SH 8f 55 54*
1995 *Jan Southw (STD) H 8f 49 62*
1998 Turf 0-11: (6f 5, 7f 3, 8f 3) (g-s 2, gd 5, g-f 2, frm 2) 1998 AW 1-1: (8f 1-1) (Fibr 1-1)
Above-average gelding, effective 6 to 8f, best at 8f, acts on gd to frm - acts on Fibr, best on g-f, likes left handed tracks, likes tight tracks, and does well at Goodwood. Turf high 76 - 3rd of 16 getting 12lb from Sugarfoot (25 Jly Ascot 8f g-f RF 3102). (1st run) - 1st of 14 giving 27lb to Kass Alhawa (18 Jun Southwell RF 2099). Consistent. He beat a huge field in an Ascot handicap in April '97, and though running well many times since, has not added another victory on turf. He did win on the Southwell Fibresand in June, but was well handicapped compared to his turf mark. Needs fast ground on turf.
**B R Millman [2-22] R Marlow (from W J Musson [5-34] Mar 1997).*

BROWNING BHB 58f64a RR 60f 64a 3513^{1}

3 b g Warrshan (USA) 9.7f **(59)** - Mossy Rose (King of Spain) 7.8f **(52)**
Form - 52220641
Record 1998 - 1st:1 2nd:3 3rd:0 Ran:7
Pre1998 - 1st:0 2nd:0 3rd:0 Ran:4
Win Prizemoney £3,013 *Total Prizemoney* £6,009
Wins * **1998** Aug Windso (G-F) H 11.6f 54 60 <
1998 Turf 1-4: (8f 2, 10f, 12f 1-1) (gd, g-f 2, hrd 1-1) 1998 AW 0-3: (8f 2, 10f) (Equi 2, Fibr)
Scopey, average gelding, effective 8 to 12f, best at 8f, acts on hrd - acts on AW, prefers tight tracks. Turf high 60 - 1st of 13 getting 7lb from Flying Bold (10 Aug Windsor RF 3513). AW high 63 - 2nd of 9 to Shaanxi Romance (4 Mar Wolverhampton 8f Fibr RF 0396). Consistent. Seemed to improve once put on to sand, but kept finding one too good. He eventually got off the mark back on turf in a Windsor handicap in August. **Lord Huntingdon [1-11] Stanley Sharp.*

BROWN'S FLIGHT BHB 75f RR 76f 4538^{11}

2 b f Jupiter Island 10.4f **(57)** - Fearless Princess (Tyrnavos) 10.1f **(55)**
Form - 534820
Record 1998 - 1st:0 2nd:1 3rd:1 Ran:6
Win Prizemoney £0 *Total Prizemoney* £1,792
1998 Turf 0-6: (6f 3, 7f 3) (gd 3, g-f 2, frm)
Above-average filly, effective 6 to 7f, best at 6f, acts on gd to g-f, best on gd. Turf high 76 - 2nd of 7 getting 5lb from Billy McCaw (9 Aug Epsom 6f gd RF 3480). She has shown ability but does not seem to get seven furlongs as yet. **S Dow [0-6] Cecil Brown.*

BROWN SUGAR RR 20f 2856^{5}

3 b f Reprimand 8.2f **(63)** - Secret Waters (Pharly (FR)) 9.8f **(68)**
Form - 705
Record 1998 - 1st:0 2nd:0 3rd:0 Ran:3
1998 Turf 0-3: (8f, 10f, 12f) (g-f 2, frm)
Light-framed, currently little account filly. Turf high 20.
**M Blanshard [0-3] David Sykes.*

BRUTAL FANTASY (IRE) BHB 68f68a RR 64f 68a 4121^{4}

4 b g Distinctly North (USA) 7.4f **(63)** - Flash Donna (USA) (Well Decorated (USA)) 7.6f **(64)**
Form - 064457000054
Record 1998 - 1st:0 2nd:0 3rd:0 Ran:12
Pre1998 - 1st:5 2nd:3 3rd:2 Ran:17
Win Prizemoney £16,812 *Total Prizemoney* £23,119
Wins * 1997 Apr Catter (GD) H 5f 78 83 <
* 1997 Mar Doncas (G-F) H 5f 72 78
* 1997 *Feb Wolver (STD) H 5f 72 72*
* 1997 *Jan Southw (STD) H 6f 65 74*
1996 May Mussel (G-S) S 5f 65+
1998 Turf 0-6: (5f 4, 6f 2) (g-s 2, gd 2, g-f, frm) 1998 AW 0-6: (5f, 6f 3, 7f, 8f) (Fibr 6)
Strong, average gelding, effective 5 to 6f, best at 5f, acts on gd - acts on Fibr, has worn blinkers. Turf high 78. AW high 67.
**J L Eyre [4-27] Diamond Racing Ltd (from N Tinkler [1-2] Jun 1996).*

BRYNKIR BHB 34f49a RR 41f 49a 4659^{7}

4 b g Batshoof 9.5f **(66)** - Felinwen (White Mill) 16.2f **(66)**
Form - 7415567
Record 1998 - 1st:1 2nd:0 3rd:0 Ran:7
Pre1998 - 1st:0 2nd:0 3rd:0 Ran:7
Win Prizemoney £2,085 *Total Prizemoney* £2,085
Wins * **1998** *Feb Wolver (STD) H 16.2f 44 53* <

1998 Turf 0-3: (16f 2, 17f) (gd 2, frm) 1998 AW 1-4: (12f, 16f 1-3) (Equi, Fibr 1-3)
Scopey, fair gelding, effective 16f, - acts on Fibr, favours left handed tracks, favours tight tracks. Turf high 41. AW high 53 - 1st of 9 giving 7lb to Drama King (21 Feb Wolverhampton RF 0338). He won a poor handicap over two miles on the Wolverhampton Fibresand in February, but is basically moderate.
**D J G MurraySmith [1-14] The 96 Partnership.*

BRYONY BRIND (IRE) BHB 98f **RR 105?f** 4740[4]
3 ch f Kris 10f **(75)** - Bayadere (USA) (Green Dancer (USA)) 10.3f **(74)**
Form - 1321154
Record 1998 - 1st:3 2nd:1 3rd:1 Ran:7
Pre1998 - 1st:0 2nd:0 3rd:0 Ran:1
Win Prizemoney £25,318 *Total Prizemoney* £29,348
Wins * **1998** Aug Deauvi (GD) L 12.5f 105 <
* **1998** Jly Haydoc (G-F) H 11.9f 86 87
* **1998** May Nottin (G-F) 8.2f 76
1998 Turf 3-7: (8f 1-1, 11f, 12f 1-3, 13f 1-1, 15f) (g-s, gd 1-4, g-f 1-1, frm 1-1)
Workmanlike, Pattern-class filly, effective 13f, acts on gd. Turf high 105 - 1st of 8 from Honeytrap (9 Aug Deauville RF 3615a). She surpassed her connections' expectations when running away with a Listed event at Deauville in August, and could not repeat the form on home ground. She will be hard pushed to win a Group race and is probably best retired to stud while her big-race victory is fresh in the memory. **J R Fanshawe [3-8] Mrs Denis Haynes.*

BUBBLY BHB 68f **RR 68f** 3740[2]
4 b g Rudimentary (USA) 8.2f **(66)** - Champagne Season (USA) (Vaguely Noble) 10.1f **(72)**
Form - 05422
Record 1998 - 1st:0 2nd:2 3rd:0 Ran:5
Pre1998 - 1st:1 2nd:1 3rd:0 Ran:9
Win Prizemoney £3,868 *Total Prizemoney* £7,207
Wins 1997 Apr Folkes (FRM) 6.9f 55+ <
1998 Turf 0-5: (6f 2, 7f 2, 8f) (sft, gd, g-f, frm 2)
Scopey, average gelding, effective 6 to 10f, best at 7f, acts on g-f to frm, best on frm. Turf high 68 - 2nd of 9 getting 17lb from Blooming Amazing (13 Aug Beverley 7f frm RF 3600).
**J Noseda [0-5] Christopher Ranson (from J L Dunlop [1-9] Oct 1997).*

BUCENTAURE **RR 40f** 4374[9]
3 ch f Ron's Victory (USA) 9.2f **(52)** - Gecko Rouge (Rousillon (USA)) 8.2f **(74)**
Form - 60
Record 1998 - 1st:0 2nd:0 3rd:0 Ran:2
1998 Turf 0-2: (7f, 8f) (frm 2)
Unfurnished, currently moderate filly. Turf high 40 (began Spt).
**Martyn Wane [0-2] J A Kavanagh.*

BUCKLE (IRE) **RR 82f** 4856[8]
2 b f Common Grounds 8.1f **(66)** - Maratona (Be My Guest (USA)) 9.3f **(67)**
Form - 38
Record 1998 - 1st:0 2nd:0 3rd:1 Ran:2
Win Prizemoney £0 *Total Prizemoney* £621
1998 Turf 0-2: (7f 2) (sft, frm)
Currently decent filly. Turf high 82 (1st run) (began Spt) - 3rd of 17 to Kalidasa (22 Spt Warwick 7f frm RF 4411).
**W Jarvis [0-2] Anthony Foster.*

BUCK'S BOY (USA) **RR 125f** 5167a[1]
5 b g Bucksplasher (USA) - Molly's Colleen (USA) (Verbatim(USA))
Form - 21
1998 Turf 1-2: (11f, 12f 1-1) (frm 1-2)
Currently top-class gelding. Turf high 125 (began Spt) - 1st of 13 from Yagli (7 Nov Churchill Downs RF 5167a). Adopted his usual front-running tactics to land the Breeders' Cup Turf at Churchill Downs. His earlier top-level form included a second to Daylami in the Man O'War Stakes at Belmont Park.
**N Hickey in USA [1-3] Quarter B Farm.*

BUCK TROUT (USA) **RR 93a** 5162a[7]
2 ch c Waqoit (USA) - Miss Buck Trout (USA)
Form - 7
1998 AW 0-1: (9f) (Dirt)
Currently useful colt. Put up a good display when seventh in the Breeders' Cup Juvenile at Churchill Downs in November.
**M Harrington in USA [0-1] Heinz Steinmann.*

BULLET BHB 76f **RR 76f** 4801[3]
3 b g Alhijaz 7.7f **(57)** - Beacon (High Top) 10.2f **(67)**
Form - 323
Record 1998 - 1st:0 2nd:1 3rd:2 Ran:3
Win Prizemoney £0 *Total Prizemoney* £2,140
1998 Turf 0-3: (10f, 12f 2) (sft, g-f, frm)
Tall, currently above-average gelding. Turf high 76 (1st run) (began Aug) - 3rd of 8 to Boreas (22 Aug Ripon 10f g-f RF 3816).
**W J Haggas [0-3] J W Bogie.*

BULLION BHB 75f **RR 82f** 4802[9]
3 b f Sabrehill (USA) 8.5f **(64)** - High and Bright (Shirley Heights) 10.3f **(74)**
Form - 0400
Record 1998 - 1st:0 2nd:0 3rd:0 Ran:4
Pre1998 - 1st:1 2nd:0 3rd:1 Ran:3
Win Prizemoney £3,074 *Total Prizemoney* £4,541
Wins 1997 Spt Haydoc (G-S) 8.1f 76+ <
1998 Turf 0-4: (7f, 10f 2, 11f) (sft, g-s, gd, frm)
Light-framed, decent filly, effective 8f, acts on gd. Turf high 74. Quickened away from some ordinary rivals when landing her maiden last year, but has been well beaten since.
**J Berry [0-2] T G & Mrs M E Holdcroft (from B W Hills [1-5] Jun 1998).*

BUMBLE BE BHB 34f **RR 25f** 3111[5]
3 b g Precocious 7.2f **(54)** - Lingering (Kind of Hush) 10.1f **(62)**
Form - 0005
Record 1998 - 1st:0 2nd:0 3rd:0 Ran:4
1998 Turf 0-4: (6f, 8f 2, 11f) (gd, g-f, frm 2)
Strong, little account gelding. Turf high 36.
**S Dow [0-4] J A Redmond.*

BUMPSE A DAISY BHB 55f **RR 52f** 2009[13]
4 b f Lord Bud 8.2f **(52)** - Zamina (The Brianstan) 5.9f **(55)**
Form - 060
Record 1998 - 1st:0 2nd:0 3rd:0 Ran:3
1998 Turf 0-3: (8f 2, 10f) (gd, frm 2)
Light-framed, fair filly. Turf high 52.
**D C O'Brien [0-4] Mrs V Costello.*

BUN ALLEY **RR 65f** 5064[7]
2 b c Be My Guest (USA) 10.2f **(66)** - Neptunalia **(66f)** (Slip Anchor) 9.8f **(73)**
Form - 07
Record 1998 - 1st:0 2nd:0 3rd:0 Ran:2
1998 Turf 0-2: (6f, 7f) (gd, g-f)
Currently average colt. Turf high 65 (began Aug). Capable of better in 1999. **J A R Toller [0-2] Lady Sophia Morrison.*

BUNDY BHB 70f67a **RR 71f 67a** 4658[7]
2 b c Ezzoud (IRE) - Sanctuary Cove (Habitat) 9.4f **(70)**
Form - 6307413187
Record 1998 - 1st:2 2nd:0 3rd:2 Ran:10
Win Prizemoney £5,483 *Total Prizemoney* £6,666
Wins * **1998** Aug Warwic (G-F) H 6f 69 71 <
1998 Jly Newcas (G-F) S 6f 68
1998 Turf 2-10: (5f 2, 6f 2-7, 7f) (sft, g-s, gd 1-3, g-f, frm 1-4)
Above-average colt, effective 5 to 6f, best at 6f, acts on gd to frm, best on frm. Turf high 71 - 3rd of 16 getting 1lb from Cashiki (25 Aug Pontefract 6f frm RF 3849) - also 1st of 6 getting 19lb from Asley (31 Aug Warwick RF 4005).
**M Dods [1-4] A J Henderson (from M R Channon [1-6] Jly 1998).*

BUNNIES OWN BHB 45f45a **RR 37f 45a** 5070[19]
3 b f Flockton's Own 7f **(42)** - Walsham Witch (Music Maestro) 7.7f **(66)**
Form - 345462148570
Record 1998 - 1st:1 2nd:1 3rd:0 Ran:10
Pre1998 - 1st:0 2nd:0 3rd:1 Ran:2
Win Prizemoney £1,738 *Total Prizemoney* £2,499
Wins * **1998** *Feb Southw (STD) S 7f 54 <*
1998 Turf 0-2: (7f, 9f) (gd, g-f) 1998 AW 1-8: (7f 1-2, 8f 3, 9f 2, 11f) (Fibr 1-8)
Unfurnished, very moderate filly, effective 7 to 8f, best at 7f, - acts

on Fibr, favours left handed tracks, favours tight tracks. Turf high 37. AW high 58 - 2nd of 9 to Honey Storm (16 Feb Southwell 8f Fibr RF 0299) - also 1st of 10 getting 12lb from Heathyards Sheik (27 Feb Southwell RF 0374). Becoming disappointing. She has shown her best form in selling company on sand, winning such a race on the Southwell Fibresand in February, though she was helped by the antics of the runner-up. **J L Harris [1-12] J Starbuck.*

BUNTY BHB 56f **RR 60f** 4243[20]
2 b f Presidium 7.5f **(56)** - Shirlstar Investor (Some Hand) 9f **(50)**
Form - 4374746850
Record 1998 - 1st:0 2nd:0 3rd:1 Ran:10
Win Prizemoney £0 *Total Prizemoney* £784
1998 Turf 0-10: (5f 5, 6f 4, 7f) (sft 2, gd 3, g-f 2, frm 2, hrd)
Average filly, effective 5 to 6f, best at 5f, acts on gd to hrd. Turf high 60 - 6th of 10 getting 23lb from Cubism (17 Aug Windsor 6f hrd RF 3685). Consistent. **C A Dwyer [0-10] John Purcell.*

BUONA SERA BHB 73f **RR 74f** 5146[9]
2 b c Marju (IRE) 9.2f **(76)** - Blueberry Walk (Green Desert (USA)) 8.6f **(78)**
Form - 340
Record 1998 - 1st:0 2nd:0 3rd:1 Ran:3
Win Prizemoney £0 *Total Prizemoney* £752
1998 Turf 0-3: (6f 2, 8f) (gd, g-f 2)
Currently above-average colt. Turf high 74 - 4th of 24 giving 5lb to Grey Princess (22 Jun Windsor 6f g-f RF 2182). In the frame in Windsor maidens, and appeals as the type for handicaps. **W R Muir [0-3] Fayzad Thoroughbred Ltd.*

to Tinker Amelia (17 Oct Curragh RF 4907a) - also 1st of 5 giving 7lb to Centre Stalls (12 Jly Curragh RF 2807a). He was once ran consistently well in 1998, winning four times in pattern company at distances from six furlongs to a mile. He is especially effective in soft ground.
**A P O'Brien in IRE [1-1] Michael Tabor (from C O'Brien in IRE [7-25] Aug 1998).*

BURLA (SPA) RR 41f 4762[8]
2 b f Aqueronte - Isla de Palma (SPA) (Palm Island)
Form - 8
Record 1998 - 1st:0 2nd:0 3rd:0 Ran:1
1998 Turf 0-1: (10f) (gd)
Currently moderate filly. **B Smart [0-1] Alvarez Cervera.*

BURLESQUE BHB 22f **RR 26f** 3887[4]
4 b g Old Vic 12.8f **(72)** - Late Matinee (Red Sunset) 8.2f **(63)**
Form - 030463344
Record 1998 - 1st:0 2nd:0 3rd:3 Ran:9
Pre1998 - 1st:0 2nd:0 3rd:0 Ran:6
Win Prizemoney £0 *Total Prizemoney* £1,261
1998 Turf 0-8: (12f 3, 13f, 15f, 16f, 17f 2) (hvy, sft 2, gd 3, g-f, frm) 1998 AW 0-1: (11f) (Fibr)
Scopey, little account gelding, has worn blinkers. Turf high 30.
**J D Bethell [0-15] The Gordon Partnership.*

BURMA BABY (USA) RR 57f 5139[14]
2 ch c Woodman (USA) 9.7f **(77)** - Rangoon Ruby (Sallust) 8.4f **(63)**
Form - 70

Burden Of Proof acquitted himself well

BURDEN OF PROOF (IRE) RR 116+f 4907a[1]
6 b h Fairy King (USA) 7.7f **(75)** - Belle Passe (Be My Guest (USA)) 9.3f **(67)**
Form - 41441131
1998 Turf 4-8: (6f 1-2, 7f 2, 8f 3-4) (hvy, sft 1-2, gd 3-4, hrd)
High-class horse, effective 6 to 8f, best at 8f, acts on sft to hrd, best on gd, and likes Curragh. Turf high 116 - 1st of 9 giving 12lb

Record 1998 - 1st:0 2nd:0 3rd:0 Ran:2
1998 Turf 0-2: (6f 2) (sft, gd)
Currently fair colt. Turf high 57 (began Oct).
**B W Hills [0-2] Maktoum Al Maktoum.*

BURNDEN DAYS (IRE) BHB 40f **RR 20f** 4114[23]
3 ch g Fayruz 6.6f **(63)** - Monaco Lady (Manado) 9.6f **(63)**

Form - 04500
Record 1998 - 1st:0 2nd:0 3rd:0 Ran:3
Pre1998 - 1st:0 2nd:0 3rd:0 Ran:4
1998 Turf 0-2: (5f 2) (frm 2) 1998 AW 0-1: (5f) (Equi)
Strong, fair gelding, has worn blinkers. (began Aug).
**Miss J F Craze [0-6] C D Barber-Lomax (from J Hetherton [0-1] Apr 1997).*

BURNING (USA) BHB 63f **RR 63f** 4672[8]

6 b g Bering 9.6f **(80)** - Larnica (USA) (Alydar (USA)) 9.1f **(76)**
Form - 463001208
Record 1998 - 1st:1 2nd:1 3rd:1 Ran:9
Pre1998 - 1st:1 2nd:1 3rd:1 Ran:19
Win Prizemoney £7,611 *Total Prizemoney* £13,569
Wins * 1998 Aug Bright (G-F) C 10f 63
1995 Apr Newmar (G-F) 10f 85 <
1998 Turf 1-6: (8f, 9f, 10f 1-3, 14f) (gd 2, g-f 2, frm 1-2) 1998 AW 0-3: (10f, 12f 2) (Equi, Fibr 2)
Average gelding, effective 11 to 12f, acts on g-f to frm, has worn blinkers, likes left handed tracks, favours tight tracks. Turf high 63. AW high 50. Suddenly struck form in August, winning easily over ten furlongs at Brighton and running well over a mile at the same track next time.
**N P Littmoden [1-9] T N Peters (from W J Haggas [0-4] Aug 1997).*

BURNING COST BHB 22f20a **RR 26f 20a** 361[10]

8 br m Lochnager 6.9f **(50)** - Sophie Avenue (Guillaume Tell (USA)) 13.2f **(54)**
Form - 000
Record 1998 - 1st:0 2nd:0 3rd:0 Ran:2
Pre1998 - 1st:0 2nd:0 3rd:0 Ran:22
1998 AW 0-2: (8f, 10f) (Equi, Fibr)
Little account mare, has worn blinkers. AW high 7.
**R E Peacock [0-16] R E Peacock (from G A Pritchard-Gordon [0-8] Jly 1993).*

BURNING LOVE BHB 34f **RR 27f** 2370[7]

3 b f Forzando 7.2f **(63)** - Latest Flame (IRE) (Last Tycoon) 8.5f **(62)**
Form - 0007
Record 1998 - 1st:0 2nd:0 3rd:0 Ran:4
Pre1998 - 1st:0 2nd:0 3rd:0 Ran:3
1998 Turf 0-4: (5f 2, 6f, 8f) (gd 3, frm)
Lengthy, little account filly, has worn blinkers. Turf high 27.
**N Tinkler [0-4] Miss Juliet Reed (from J S Moore [0-3] Jun 1997).*

BURNING TRUTH (USA) BHB 68f **RR 71f** 5017[5]

4 ch g Known Fact (USA) 8.3f **(72)** - Galega (Sure Blade (USA)) 11.3f **(67)**
Form - 0782285
Record 1998 - 1st:0 2nd:2 3rd:0 Ran:7
Pre1998 - 1st:0 2nd:3 3rd:3 Ran:7
Win Prizemoney £0 *Total Prizemoney* £9,338
1998 Turf 0-7: (8f 3, 9f 2, 10f 2) (sft, gd 3, g-f, frm 2)
Scopey, above-average gelding, effective 8 to 10f, best at 8f, acts on gd to frm, best on frm, prefers left handed tracks, prefers tight tracks. Turf high 71 - 2nd of 9 to My Learned Friend (24 Spt Pontefract 10f frm RF 4470). Despite finishing in the frame in varied company, he looked very one-paced and has had plenty of chances.
**Mrs A Swinbank [0-7] Middleham Park Racing IV (from R Charlton [0-7] Spt 1997).*

BURTONS FOLLY BHB 50f **RR 49f** 4395[17]

2 b c Casteddu 7.4f **(54)** - Nelliellamay (Super Splash (USA)) 7.3f **(54)**
Form - 060
Record 1998 - 1st:0 2nd:0 3rd:0 Ran:3
Win Prizemoney £0 *Total Prizemoney* £81
1998 Turf 0-3: (7f, 8f 2) (gd, g-f, frm)
Currently moderate colt. Turf high 49 (began Aug).
**R Ingram [0-3] Christopher Burton & Roger Ingram.*

BURUNDI (IRE) BHB 65f75a **RR 69f 75a** 4958[2]

4 b g Danehill (USA) 9.1f **(79)** - Sofala (Home Guard (USA)) 9.3f **(66)**
Form - 1224572
Record 1998 - 1st:0 2nd:3 3rd:0 Ran:6
Pre1998 - 1st:1 2nd:1 3rd:0 Ran:8
Win Prizemoney £1,998 *Total Prizemoney* £6,874
Wins * 1997 *Nov Southw (STD) S 11f 64* <
1998 Turf 0-6: (10f, 14f 3, 15f, 16f) (g-s, gd 2, g-f, frm 2)
Scopey, average gelding, effective 7 to 16f, best at 14f, acts on g-s to frm - acts on Fibr, has worn blinkers, prefers right handed tracks, excels at Sandown and Kempton. Turf high 69 - 2nd of 9 giving 4lb to Turgenev (13 Jun Sandown 14f g-s RF 1976). Consistent. a trip to Portman Square. Two creditable efforts on turf this year.
**A W Carroll [1-8] Gary Roberts (from P W Chapple-Hyam [0-6] Jly 1997).*

BUSHWHACKER BHB 70f **RR 81f** 1253[7]

4 b g Green Desert (USA) 7.8f **(78)** -Missed Again (High Top) 10.2f **(67)**
Form - 27
Record 1998 - 1st:0 2nd:1 3rd:0 Ran:2
Pre1998 - 1st:0 2nd:0 3rd:0 Ran:1
Win Prizemoney £0 *Total Prizemoney* £1,432
1998 Turf 0-2: (6f, 7f) (hvy, gd)
Workmanlike, currently decent gelding. Turf high 81 (1st run) - 2nd of 12 giving 19lb to Queen of Scotland (13 Apr Kempton 7f hvy RF 0656). **C R Egerton [0-3] The Bushwacker Partnership.*

BUSINESS WOMAN **RR 27f** 3409[17]

2 b f Primo Dominie 7.2f **(67)** - Golden Cay (Habitat) 9.4f **(70)**
Form - 000
Record 1998 - 1st:0 2nd:0 3rd:0 Ran:3
1998 Turf 0-2: (5f, 6f) (gd, g-f) 1998 AW 0-1: (6f) (Fibr)
Currently little account filly. Turf high 27 (began Jly).
**M W Easterby [0-3] Stephen Curtis.*

BUSTLING RIO (IRE) BHB 55f **RR 51f** 3933[12]

2 b g Up and At 'em - Une Venitienne (FR) (Green Dancer (USA)) 10.3f **(74)**
Form - 00
Record 1998 - 1st:0 2nd:0 3rd:0 Ran:2
1998 Turf 0-1: (6f) (frm) 1998 AW 0-1: (7f) (Fibr)
Currently fair gelding.
**P C Haslam [0-2] Rio Stainless Engineering Ltd/R Tutton.*

BUSTOPHER JONES BHB 49f49a **RR 41f 49a** 418[1]

4 b g Robellino (USA) 9.5f **(68)** - Catkin (USA) (Sir Ivor) 10.2f **(70)**
Form - 1
Record 1998 - 1st:1 2nd:0 3rd:0 Ran:1
Pre1998 - 1st:0 2nd:0 3rd:0 Ran:3
Win Prizemoney £2,463 *Total Prizemoney* £2,463
Wins * 1998 *Mar Southw (STD) H 11f 45 46* <
1998 AW 1-1: (11f 1-1) (Fibr 1-1)
Rangy, moderate gelding. (1st run) - 1st of 12 giving 3lb to Aldwych Arrow (11 Mar Southwell RF 0418). He managed to win a very poor maiden handicap on the Southwell Fibresand in March.
**C R Egerton [1-4] Chris Brasher.*

BUSY FLIGHT BHB 118f **RR 119f** 4632[5]

5 br h Pharly (FR) 11.5f **(64)** - Bustling Nelly (Bustino) 10.4f **(64)**
Form - 2125
Record 1998 - 1st:1 2nd:2 3rd:0 Ran:4
Pre1998 - 1st:5 2nd:3 3rd:2 Ran:15
Win Prizemoney £106,281 *Total Prizemoney* £155,623
Wins * 1998 May York (GD) G2 13.9f 114
* 1997 Spt Doncas (G-F) L 12f 115+ <
* 1997 Aug Newbur (G-F) 12f 107
* 1996 Oct Newmar (G-F) L 12f 115
* 1996 Spt Doncas (G-F) L 12f 113
* 1996 Aug Ripon (G-S) 12.3f 89+
1998 Turf 1-4: (14f 1-1, 16f 2, 18f) (gd 1-3, g-f)
High-class colt, effective 12 to 18f, acts on g-s to frm, best on gd, prefers left handed tracks, does well at Doncaster and Newmarket and Newbury. Turf high 119 - 2nd of 6 to Double Trigger (10 Spt Doncaster 18f gd RF 4206) - also 1st of 6 from Strategic Choice (14 May York RF 1221). Consistent. A good second to Persian Punch in the relocated Sagaro Stakes at Newmarket on his reappearance, he landed the Yorkshire Cup over two furlongs shorter next time. Unable to get past Double Trigger in the Doncaster Cup after travelling well, he ended the season with a modest effort in the Jockey Club Cup. **B W Hills [6-19] Exors of the late S WingfieldDigby.*

Busy Flight going to post before the Yorkshire Cup

BUTRINTO BHB 68f70a **RR 71f 70a** 4923[6]

4 ch g Anshan 8.2f **(63)** - Bay Bay (Bay Express) 7.1f **(60)**

Form - 0017058076

Record 1998 - 1st:1 2nd:0 3rd:0 Ran:10

Pre1998 - 1st:1 2nd:0 3rd:1 Ran:7

Win Prizemoney £7,356 *Total Prizemoney* £8,553

Wins * **1998** May Newbur (GD) H 6f 71 74 <

1997 Aug Salisb (G-F) 6f 69

1998 Turf 1-10: (5f, 6f 1-7, 7f 2) (hvy, sft, gd 3, g-f 1-1, frm 4)

Tall, above-average gelding, effective 5 to 6f, best at 6f, acts on sft to frm, has worn blinkers, excels at York and Salisbury. Turf high 74 - 1st of 16 giving 3lb to Bintang Timor (27 May Newbury RF 1526). Won at Newbury in May and ran very well in a hot race at Goodwood next time. Well held since, including when stepped up to seven furlongs.

**J Pearce [1-10] Michael Whatley (from Major W R Hern [1-7] Spt 1997).*

BUTTERSCOTCH BHB 66f **RR 67f** 4857[13]

2 b c Aragon 7.7f **(58)** - Gwiffina (Welsh Saint) 7.6f **(64)**

Form - 00300

Record 1998 - 1st:0 2nd:0 3rd:1 Ran:5

Win Prizemoney £0 *Total Prizemoney* £444

1998 Turf 0-5: (6f 2, 7f 2, 8f) (sft, g-f, frm 3)

Average colt. Turf high 65 (began Aug).

**J L Eyre [0-5] Sunpak Potatoes.*

BUTTERWOOD (USA) BHB 70f **RR 70f** 4524[9]

2 b f Woodman (USA) 9.7f **(77)** - Routilante (Rousillon (USA)) 8.2f **(74)**

Form - 4860

Record 1998 - 1st:0 2nd:0 3rd:0 Ran:4

Win Prizemoney £0 *Total Prizemoney* £354

1998 Turf 0-4: (6f 4) (gd, g-f 2, frm)

Above-average filly. Turf high 70.

**I A Balding [0-4] George Strawbridge.*

BUZZ BHB 82f **RR 87f** 4705[2]

3 b c Anshan 8.2f **(63)** - Ryewater Dream (Touching Wood (USA)) 8.2f **(55)**

Form - 62055321802

Record 1998 - 1st:1 2nd:3 3rd:1 Ran:11

Pre1998 - 1st:1 2nd:0 3rd:0 Ran:6

Win Prizemoney £8,235 *Total Prizemoney* £16,103

Wins * **1998** Aug Ripon (GD) H 9f 79 87 <

* 1997 Jun Mussel (G-S) 7.1f 77+

1998 Turf 1-11: (6f 4, 7f 2, 9f 1-2, 10f, 12f 2) (g-s, gd 1-7, g-f 2, frm)

Workmanlike, useful colt, effective 6 to 12f, best at 9f, acts on g-s to frm, best on gd, excels at York and Hamilton. Turf high 87 - 1st of 4 giving 9lb to Simply Super (3 Aug Ripon RF 3311). Consistent. He got off the mark for the season in a four-runner handicap at Ripon in August. He seems a much better horse with give in the ground. **C W Thornton [2-17] Guy Reed.*

BUZZING (IRE) BHB 63f **RR 60f** 1878[5]

3 ch c Ballad Rock 7.2f **(63)** - Buzzing Around (Prince Bee) 12f **(46)**

Form - 6545
Record 1998 - 1st:0 2nd:0 3rd:0 Ran:4
Pre1998 - 1st:0 2nd:0 3rd:0 Ran:1
Win Prizemoney £0 *Total Prizemoney* £242
1998 Turf 0-4: (6f 2, 7f 2) (hvy, gd 2, g-f)
Workmanlike, average colt. Turf high 60.
**R Hannon [0-5] Mrs P Jubert.*

BUZZ THE AGENT BHB 53f **RR 56f** 4869[18]
3 b g Prince Sabo 6.6f **(64)** - Chess Mistress (USA) (Run The Gantlet (USA)) 12.1f **(59)**
Form - 007237271000
Record 1998 - 1st:1 2nd:2 3rd:1 Ran:12
Pre1998 - 1st:0 2nd:0 3rd:0 Ran:4
Win Prizemoney £3,036 *Total Prizemoney* £5,094
Wins * 1998 Spt Beverl (G-F) H 12f 51 56 <
1998 Turf 1-12: (6f 2, 8f, 10f 4, 12f 1-5) (sft, gd 3, g-f 4, frm 1-4)
Workmanlike, fair gelding, effective 8 to 12f, best at 12f, acts on g-f to frm, best on g-f, often wears blinkers (extremely effectively), prefers right handed tracks, prefers tight tracks. Turf high 56 - 1st of 15 getting 17lb from Mark of Prophet (16 Spt Beverley RF 4305). Becoming disappointing. **M W Easterby [1-16] Alan Black & Co.*

BUZZY BOMB (IRE) BHB 97f **RR 78f** 4470k[1]
3 b f Tenby 10.4f **(76)** - Buz Kashi (Bold Lad (IRE)) 8.4f **(68)**
Form - 305121
Record 1998 - 1st:2 2nd:1 3rd:1 Ran:6
Win Prizemoney £46,030 *Total Prizemoney* £51,078
Wins * 1998 Spt San Si (GD) 12f 78 <
*** 1998** Jly Ripon (G-F) 9f 75
1998 Turf 2-6: (8f 2, 9f 1-1, 10f 2, 12f 1-1) (hvy, gd 1-3, g-f 1-2)
Above-average filly, effective 9 to 12f, acts on gd to g-f, best on g-f. Turf high 78 - 1st of 3 getting 4lb from Calci (20 Spt San Siro RF 4470k) - also 1st of 8 getting 5lb from Savile Row (18 Jly Ripon RF 2938). Winner of a valuable race in Milan, she was sold in the autumn for 68,000 gns. **L M Cumani [2-6] Miss Gatto Roissard.*

BY CHARLIE ALLEN (IRE) RR 84f 213a[2]
5 b h In The Wings 11.2f **(77)** - Simply Unique (USA)
Form - 832
1998 Turf 0-2: (10f, 11f) (gd 2)
Decent colt, effective 8 to 10f, acts on gd. Turf high 91. Consistent.
**P J Flynn in IRE [3-14] S Muduroglu.*

BY JAY (IRE) BHB 33f33a **RR 23f 33a** 2899[7]
4 b f Last Tycoon 9.4f **(73)** - Tomona (Linacre) 6.7f **(40)**
Form - 03277
Record 1998 - 1st:0 2nd:1 3rd:1 Ran:4
Pre1998 - 1st:0 2nd:0 3rd:0 Ran:15
Win Prizemoney £0 *Total Prizemoney* £1,694
1998 Turf 0-1: (13f) (g-f) 1998 AW 0-3: (8f, 12f, 14f) (Fibr 3)
Very moderate filly. AW high 33. Inconsistent.
**B J Curley [0-8] P Byrne (from A Leahy in IRE [0-11] Jun 1997).*

BY THE GLASS BHB 67f **RR 73f** 4643[7]
2 b c Ardkinglass 5f **(64)** - Mia Fillia (Formidable (USA)) 9.2f **(63)**
Form - 51435607
Record 1998 - 1st:1 2nd:0 3rd:1 Ran:8
Win Prizemoney £2,721 *Total Prizemoney* £3,222
Wins * 1998 May Leices (GD) 5f 73 <
1998 Turf 1-7: (5f 1-1, 6f 3, 7f 2, 8f) (gd, g-f 1-4, frm 2) 1998 AW 0-1: (5f) (Fibr)
Above-average colt, effective 5 to 7f, acts on g-f, has worn blinkers. Turf high 73 (1st run) - 1st of 14 from Heathyards Jake (26 May Leicester RF 1473). **P T Walwyn [1-8] C F Colquhoun.*

BYZANTIUM RR 67f 4744[17]
4 b c Shirley Heights 12.1f **(76)** - Dulceata (IRE) (Rousillon (USA)) 8.2f **(74)**
Form - 80700
Record 1998 - 1st:0 2nd:0 3rd:0 Ran:5
Pre1998 - 1st:1 2nd:0 3rd:0 Ran:4
Win Prizemoney £2,997 *Total Prizemoney* £3,066
Wins * 1997 May Kempto (GD) 8f 78 <
1998 Turf 0-5: (8f 2, 10f, 12f 2) (g-s, g-f, frm 3)
Workmanlike, average colt, effective 8f, acts on g-f. Turf high 67 (began Jly). Becoming disappointing. Won a maiden at Kempton on his debut in May '97, but has been very disappointing since.
**Lord Huntingdon [1-9] R Van Gelder.*

CABALLERO RR 100f 4242[4]
2 b c Cadeaux Genereux 7.9f **(76)** - On Tiptoes (Shareef Dancer (USA)) 9.9f **(73)**
Form - 420104
Record 1998 - 1st:1 2nd:1 3rd:0 Ran:6
Win Prizemoney £4,675 *Total Prizemoney* £8,454
Wins * 1998 Aug Windso (G-F) 6f 87+ <
1998 Turf 1-6: (5f, 6f 1-5) (sft, gd 2, g-f, frm, hrd 1-1)
Very useful colt, effective 5f, acts on g-f. Turf high 100 - 4th of 13 to Sheer Viking (12 Spt Doncaster 5f g-f RF 4242). He sweated up badly before getting off the mark in a Windsor conditions stakes in August, and has run well in useful company since.
**C E Brittain [1-6] Sheikh Marwan Al Maktoum.*

CABARET QUEST BHB 69f **RR 67f** 3735[7]
2 ch c Pursuit of Love 9.5f **(69)** - Cabaret Artiste (Shareef Dancer (USA)) 9.9f **(73)**
Form - 087
Record 1998 - 1st:0 2nd:0 3rd:0 Ran:3
1998 Turf 0-3: (6f, 7f 2) (gd, g-f, frm)
Currently average colt. Turf high 67 (began Jly).
**R Hannon [0-3] Thurloe Thoroughbreds III.*

CABBAGE CRUSADER RR 27f 5004[10]
2 b f Mon Tresor 7.9f **(60)** - Edith Piaf (Thatch (USA)) 9.8f **(62)**
Form - 00
Record 1998 - 1st:0 2nd:0 3rd:0 Ran:2
1998 Turf 0-2: (5f, 6f) (sft, gd)
Currently little account filly. Turf high 27 (began Spt).
**P L Gilligan [0-2] The Great Leap Forward Partnership.*

CABCHARGE BLUE BHB 46f34a **RR 52f 34a** 4655[8]
6 b m Midyan (USA) 9.9f **(64)** - Mashobra (Vision (USA)) 9f **(64)**
Form - 738226686728
Record 1998 - 1st:0 2nd:3 3rd:1 Ran:11
Pre1998 - 1st:7 2nd:2 3rd:4 Ran:38
Win Prizemoney £17,374 *Total Prizemoney* £25,346

Wins	* 1997	Oct	Bright	(G-F)	SH	10f	36	48
	* 1996	*Jan*	*Southw*	*(STD)*	*H*	*8f*	*48*	*52*
	* 1994	Spt	Nottin	(GS)	H	6.1f	69	67
	1994	Spt	Folkes	(G-S)	C	6f		50+
	1994	Jly	Nottin	(G-F)	C	5.1f		67
	1994	Jun	Lingfi	(GF)	S	6f		52+
	1994	Jun	Yarmou	(G-F)	S	5.2f		56

1998 Turf 0-9: (8f 5, 10f 3, 11f) (g-s 2, gd 2, g-f 2, frm 3) 1998 AW 0-2: (8f, 12f) (Fibr 2)
Fair mare, effective 8 to 11f, best at 8f, acts on g-s to frm, best on g-f, prefers right handed tracks. Turf high 52 - 6th of 12 getting 19lb from Scent of Success (29 Aug Windsor 8f g-f RF 3975). AW high 25. Benefited from being dropped into selling company when winning at Brighton in October '97, and despite some creditable efforts otherwise, that looks her level.
**T J Naughton [3-40] J J Wise (from M H Tompkins [4-10] Spt 1994).*

CABCHARGE GEMINI RR 3f 3331[9]
4 b g High Kicker (USA) 8.4f **(52)** - Miss Noname (High Top) 10.2f **(67)**
Form - 0
Record 1998 - 1st:0 2nd:0 3rd:0 Ran:1
Pre1998 - 1st:0 2nd:0 3rd:0 Ran:1
1998 Turf 0-1: (12f) (gd)
Leggy, currently very poor gelding, often wears blinkers.
**G G Margarson [0-2] Computer Cab Racing Club.*

CABCHARGE GLORY BHB 32f30a **RR 28f 30a** 436[7]
4 ch f Executive Man 8.9f **(52)** - Clipsall (Petitioner)
Form - 34887
Record 1998 - 1st:0 2nd:0 3rd:1 Ran:5
Pre1998 - 1st:0 2nd:0 3rd:0 Ran:5
Win Prizemoney £0 *Total Prizemoney* £725
1998 AW 0-5: (12f, 13f, 14f, 16f 2) (Equi 3, Fibr 2)
Leggy, moderate filly, effective 13f, - acts on Equi, has worn blinkers, likes left handed tracks, favours tight tracks. AW high 41 (1st run) - 3rd of 10 to Divinity (10 Jan Lingfield 13f Equi RF 0058).
**T T Clement [0-5] Glyn Lewis (from G G Margarson [0-5] Jly 1997).*

CABLE MEDIA BOY (IRE) BHB 57f63a **RR 66f 63a** 4548[6]
2 b c Great Commotion (USA) 9.2f **(80)** - Lady Fleetsin (IRE) (Double Schwartz) 7.9f **(55)**
Form - 10410666
Record 1998 - 1st:2 2nd:0 3rd:0 Ran:8
Win Prizemoney £5,382 *Total Prizemoney* £5,604
Wins * **1998** *Aug Wolver (STD) H 7f 56 70* <
* **1998** May Chepst (G-F) S 6.1f 55
1998 Turf 1-6:(6f 1-2, 7f 3, 8f)(g-f, frm 1-5)1998AW1-2:(7f 1-2)(Fibr 1-2)
Above-average colt, effective 7f, - acts on Fibr. Turf high 66. AW high 70 (1st run) (began Aug) - 1st of 9 getting 20lb from Heathyards Jake (7 Aug Wolverhampton RF 3450). It was only a seller he won on his Chepstow debut, but the nursery he won on his sand debut at Wolverhampton was a rather better affair, though he subsequently became very disappointing.
**S E Kettlewell [2-8] Cable Media Consultancy Ltd.*

CABLE MEDIA GIRL (IRE) BHB 41f **RR 54f** 5137[18]
2 b f River Falls 8.2f **(56)** - Brass Button (IRE) (Fools Holme (USA))
Form - 800
Record 1998 - 1st:0 2nd:0 3rd:0 Ran:3
1998 Turf 0-3: (6f, 7f 2) (g-s, gd, frm)
Currently fair filly. Turf high 54 (began Spt).
**S E Kettlewell [0-3] Cable Media Consultancy Ltd.*

CADEAUX CHER BHB 93f **RR 93f** 4821[17]
4 ch g Cadeaux Genereux 7.9f **(76)** - Home Truth (Known Fact (USA)) 7.4f **(67)**
Form - 0055006111001000
Record 1998 - 1st:4 2nd:0 3rd:0 Ran:16
Pre1998 - 1st:1 2nd:2 3rd:0 Ran:10
Win Prizemoney £57,456 *Total Prizemoney* £60,791
Wins * **1998** Spt Doncas (GD) H 5.6f 89 93 <
* **1998** Aug Ripon (G-F) H 6f 79 86
* **1998** Aug Leices (GD) 6f 76
* **1998** Jly Doncas (G-F) 6f 78?
* 1997 Mar Doncas (G-F) 6f 76
1998 Turf 4-16: (5f 2, 6f 4-13, 7f) (sft, gd 1-5, g-f 2-6, frm 1-4)
Scopey, useful gelding, effective 6f, acts on gd to g-f, has worn blinkers. Turf high 93 - 1st of 21 getting 6lb from Nuclear Debate (9 Spt Doncaster RF 4184) - also 1st of 22 getting 10lb from Emerging Market (15 Aug Ripon RF 3661). Generally well beaten in the first half of the season, but suddenly hit form in the late summer, completing his hat-trick in the valuable Great St Wilfrid Handicap at Ripon. Well beaten twice at York before bouncing back with a fluent victory in the Portland, having no problem with the rain-affected ground. He needs to come from behind and Ray Cochrane gets on very well with him. **B W Hills [5-26] N N Browne.*

Cadeaux Cher scored a summer hat-trick

CADETTE RR 89f 2850[1]
3 ch c Arazi (USA) 9.2f **(74)** - Carotene (CAN) (Great Nephew) 9.9f **(64)**
Form - 21
Record 1998 - 1st:1 2nd:1 3rd:0 Ran:2
Win Prizemoney £3,817 *Total Prizemoney* £5,157
Wins * **1998** Jly Doncas (FRM) 8f 80+ <
1998 Turf 1-2: (8f 1-2) (gd, frm 1-1)
Scopey, currently useful colt. Turf high 89 (1st run) - 2nd of 11 to Wealthy Star (22 Jun Nottingham 8f gd RF 2174) - also 1st of 9 from Singer Sargent (16 Jly Doncaster RF 2850).
**J H M Gosden [1-2] Sheikh Mohammed.*

CADILLAC JUKEBOX (USA) BHB 65f **RR 69f** 4838[5]
3 b br c Alleged (USA) 11.8f **(81)** - Symphonic Music (USA) (Al Nasr (FR)) 9.3f **(68)**
Form - 87375105
Record 1998 - 1st:1 2nd:0 3rd:1 Ran:8
Pre1998 - 1st:0 2nd:0 3rd:0 Ran:1
Win Prizemoney £2,140 *Total Prizemoney* £2,673
Wins * **1998** Aug Pontef (G-F) 12f 69 <
1998 Turf1-8:(8f, 10f 2, 11f 2, 12f 1-2,16f)(sft, g-s 2, gd 2, g-f 2, frm 1-1)
Unfurnished, average colt, effective 10 to 12f, acts on g-f to frm, has worn blinkers, likes left handed tracks, favours tight tracks. Turf high 69 - 1st of 4 getting 10lb from Once More for Luck (25 Aug Pontefract RF 3855). He got off the mark in a Pontefract classified stakes in first-time blinkers, though his rivals let him get away in front and the form may not amount to much.
**J W Hills [1-9] Freddy Bienstock.*

CADMAX (IRE) BHB 45f **RR 44f** 5062[3]
3 b g Second Set (IRE) 9.2f **(67)** - Stella Ann (Ahonoora) 8.1f **(73)**
Form - 3000023
Record 1998 - 1st:0 2nd:1 3rd:2 Ran:7
Pre1998 - 1st:0 2nd:0 3rd:0 Ran:1
Win Prizemoney £0 *Total Prizemoney* £1,664
1998 Turf 0-7: (8f 3, 11f, 12f 3) (hvy, sft, gd 3, g-f, frm)
Leggy, moderate gelding, effective 12f, acts on gd. Turf high 44 - 2nd of 15 to May King Mayhem (5 Oct Pontefract 12f gd RF 4656). Inconsistent. **K R Burke [0-8] A J Allright.*

CA'D'ORO BHB 62f **RR 63f** 5147[18]
5 ch g Cadeaux Genereux 7.9f **(76)** - Palace Street (USA) (Secreto (USA)) 8.7f **(72)**
Form - 33700002320210
Record 1998 - 1st:1 2nd:3 3rd:3 Ran:14
Pre1998 - 1st:4 2nd:1 3rd:2 Ran:24
Win Prizemoney £23,448 *Total Prizemoney* £30,466
Wins * **1998** Oct Nottin () H 8.2f 59 63
* 1997 Oct Nottin (G-S) H 8.2f 58 64 <
* 1997 Jun Goodwo (G-S) H 8f 53 59
* 1997 Jun Newbur (GD) H 8f 53 57
* 1996 Aug Bath (GD) H 8f 56 60
1998 Turf 1-14: (6f, 7f 5, 8f 1-8) (sft, gd 1-7, g-f 6)
Average gelding, effective 8f, acts on sft to g-f, likes left handed tracks, likes tight tracks, excels at Nottingham, does well at Goodwood. Turf high 66 - 3rd of 20 giving 14lb to Dancing Lawyer (4 May Warwick 8f g-f RF 1031) - also 1st of 18 getting 8lb from Scene (22 Oct Nottingham RF 4936). He looked in the handicapper's grip for the much of the season, but ran much better during the autumn, and finally won the race he had been threatening to win at Nottingham in October. A mile looks his trip now.
**G B Balding [5-38] Miss B Swire.*

CADW (IRE) BHB 71f **RR 73f** 5147[21]
3 b c Cadeaux Genereux7.9f **(76)** -Night Jar (Night Shift (USA))7.2f **(69)**
Form - 0440
Record 1998 - 1st:0 2nd:0 3rd:0 Ran:4
Win Prizemoney £0 *Total Prizemoney* £537
1998 Turf 0-4: (6f, 8f 3) (gd 3, g-f)
Scopey, above-average colt. Turf high 73.
**Lord Huntingdon [0-4] J T Thomas.*

CAERDYDD FACH BHB 53f48a **RR 57f 48a** 4800[8]
2 b f Bluebird (USA) 7.9f **(71)** - Waitingformargaret (Kris) 9.5f **(73)**
Form - 7350608
Record 1998 - 1st:0 2nd:0 3rd:1 Ran:7
Win Prizemoney £0 *Total Prizemoney* £245
1998 Turf 0-7: (6f 3, 7f 2, 8f 2) (sft, gd 2, g-f 3, frm)

Fair filly, effective 6f, acts on g-f. Turf high 57 (began Jly).
**K G Wingrove [0-4] Terry Connors (from J W Hills [0-3] Aug 1998).*

CAERFILLY DANCER BHB 68f **RR 64f** 4097[9]

4 ch f Caerleon (USA) 10.9f **(79)** - Darnelle (Shirley Heights) 10.3f **(74)**
Form - 50480
Record 1998 - 1st:0 2nd:0 3rd:0 Ran:5
Pre1998 - 1st:1 2nd:0 3rd:0 Ran:6
Win Prizemoney £5,472 *Total Prizemoney* £6,651
Wins 1996 Aug Ascot (G-F) 6f 77+ <
1998 Turf 0-5: (5f 3, 6f 2) (gd 2, g-f, frm 2)
Average filly. Turf high 64.
**R Guest [0-5] A P Davies (from R Akehurst [1-6] Jun 1997).*

CAERNARFON BAY (IRE) BHB 48f **RR 56f** 5006[14]

3 ch g Royal Academy (USA) 7.8f **(77)** - Bay Shade (USA) (Sharpen Up) 8.3f **(67)**
Form - 28050530
Record 1998 - 1st:0 2nd:1 3rd:1 Ran:8
Pre1998 - 1st:0 2nd:0 3rd:0 Ran:1
Win Prizemoney £0 *Total Prizemoney* £1,732
1998 Turf 0-6: (8f 2, 10f, 11f, 12f 2) (sft, g-s 2, gd, g-f 2) 1998 AW 0-2: (8f, 9f) (Equi, Fibr)
Workmanlike, average gelding, effective 9f, - acts on Fibr, has worn blinkers, likes left handed tracks, likes tight tracks. Turf high 56. AW high 62 (1st run) - 2nd of 10 giving 5lb to Feel Free (28 Mar Wolverhampton 9f Fibr RF 0496).
**P F I Cole [0-9] Sir George Meyrick.*

CAEROSA BHB 49f **RR 63f** 4677[13]

3 b f Caerleon (USA) 10.9f **(79)**-Famosa(Dancing Brave (USA))8.4f **(76)**
Form - 4570000
Record 1998 - 1st:0 2nd:0 3rd:0 Ran:7
Win Prizemoney £0 *Total Prizemoney* £242
1998 Turf 0-7: (7f 4, 8f 2, 10f) (gd 2, g-f 3, frm 2)
Scopey, average filly, effective 7f, acts on frm, likes tight tracks. Turf high 63 (1st run) - 4th of 11 to Acidanthera (19 May Beverley 7f frm RF 1322). **J G FitzGerald [0-7] & Mrs G Middlebrook.*

CAGE AUX FOLLES (IRE) BHB 70f **RR 73f** 3822[7]

3 b c Kenmare (FR) 9.6f **(76)** - Ivory Thread (USA) (Sir Ivor) 10.2f **(70)**
Form - 0201157
Record 1998 - 1st:2 2nd:1 3rd:0 Ran:7
Pre1998 - 1st:0 2nd:0 3rd:1 Ran:4
Win Prizemoney £7,354 *Total Prizemoney* £8,696
Wins * **1998** Jly Redcar (G-F) H 11f 70 73 <
* **1998** Jly Cheste (G-F) 12.3f 64
1998 Turf 2-7: (10f 2, 11f 1-1, 12f 1-3, 14f) (g-f 4, frm 2-3)
Workmanlike, above-average colt, effective 11 to 12f, best at 12f, acts on g-f to frm, best on frm, prefers tight tracks. Turf high 73 - 1st of 4 giving 2lb to Boulevard Rouge (18 Jly Redcar RF 2933) - also 1st of 5 getting 12lb from Hill Farm Dancer (10 Jly Chester RF 2675). Landed a couple of uncompetitive events in July.
**J W Hills [2-11] Christopher Wright.*

CAIRN DHU BHB 36f38a **RR 29f 38a** 3621[11]

4 ch g Presidium 7.5f **(56)** - My Precious Daisy (Sharpo) 7.7f **(59)**
Form - 05000
Record 1998 - 1st:0 2nd:0 3rd:0 Ran:4
Pre1998 - 1st:1 2nd:0 3rd:0 Ran:13
Win Prizemoney £1,634 *Total Prizemoney* £2,092
Wins 1997 Apr Nottin (G-F) S 6.1f 62+ <
1998 Turf 0-3: (5f, 6f, 7f) (gd, frm 2) 1998 AW 0-1: (6f) (Fibr)
Strong, little account gelding, effective 6f, acts on gd, has worn blinkers. Turf high 29 (began Aug).
**D W Barker [0-10] Mrs S J Barker (from Mrs J R Ramsden [1-8] May 1997).*

CAITANO **RR 125f** 5167a[8]

4 b c Niniski (USA) 13.2f **(67)** - Eversince (USA) (Foolish Pleasure (USA)) 8.9f **(72)**
Form - 403258
1998 Turf 0-5: (8f, 12f 4) (sft 2, gd, g-f, frm)
Top-class colt, effective 8 to 12f, best at 12f, acts on sft to g-f, prefers right handed tracks, likes San Siro. Turf high 125 - 5th of 14 giving 8lb to Sagamix (4 Oct Longchamp 12f sft RF 4727a). A high-class German-trained colt, successful twice at the top level in '97, he did not quite reach the same heights last term but ran well to finish fifth in the Arc, staying on well in the closing stages. He looks to need soft ground to show his best.
**A Schutz in GER [0-5] Gary Tanaka (from B Schutz in GER [3-7] Nov 1997).*

CALAMANDER (IRE) BHB 57f **RR 62f** 5174a[7]

4 b f Alzao (USA) 9.8f **(73)** - Local Custom (IRE) (Be My Native (USA)) 10.2f **(71)**
Form - 2642117
Record 1998 - 1st:2 2nd:2 3rd:0 Ran:7
Pre1998 - 1st:0 2nd:2 3rd:2 Ran:12
Win Prizemoney £8,250 *Total Prizemoney* £13,080
Wins * **1998** Oct Leopar (SFT) H 8f 60 62 <
* **1998** Oct Gowran (SFT) H 8f 55 61
1998 Turf 2-7: (7f, 8f 2-3, 9f 2, 10f) (sft, g-s 2, gd 2-3, frm)
Light-framed, average filly, effective 8 to 9f, best at 8f, acts on g-s to hrd, best on g-f, does well at Nottingham. Turf high 62 - 1st of 16 from Iftatah (26 Oct Leopardstown RF 5107a) - also 1st of 16 getting 8lb from No Animosity (16 Oct Gowran Park RF 4905a). Consistent.
**P J Flynn in IRE [2-6] H R D McCalmont (from W R Muir [0-9] May 1998).*

CALANDO (USA) BHB 100f **RR 98f** 4514[2]

2 b f Storm Cat (USA) 7f **(86)** - Diminuendo (USA) (Diesis) 9.3f **(69)**
Form - 5112
Record 1998 - 1st:2 2nd:1 3rd:0 Ran:4
Win Prizemoney £22,087 *Total Prizemoney* £60,887
Wins * **1998** Spt Doncas (GD) G3 8f 98+ <
* **1998** Jly Folkes (G-F) 7f 81++
1998 Turf 2-4: (5f, 7f 1-1, 8f 1-2) (g-s, gd 2-3)
Very useful filly. Turf high 98 - 2nd of 8 to Sunspangled (27 Spt Ascot 8f gd RF 4514) - also 1st of 10 from Kalidasa (10 Spt Doncaster RF 4207). Slightly disappointing on her debut, she won a Folkestone maiden with consummate ease, and followed up by landing the May Hill Stakes at the St Leger meeting. Good second to Sunspangled in Fillies' Mile at Ascot, after failing to obtain the clearest of passages she finished really well. Will be suited by middle distances next term, and looks a very useful prospect in the making. Is reportedly wintering in Dubai.
**D R Loder [2-4] Sheikh Mohammed.*

CALANDRELLA BHB 31f26a **RR 30f 26a** 2844[5]

5 b m Sizzling Melody 6.3f **(49)** - Maravilla (Mandrake Major) 7.6f **(53)**
Form - 00034600075
Record 1998 - 1st:0 2nd:0 3rd:1 Ran:11
Pre1998 - 1st:0 2nd:0 3rd:0 Ran:11
Win Prizemoney £0 *Total Prizemoney* £523
1998 Turf 0-8: (5f 6, 6f 2) (sft 2, g-s, gd 3, frm 2) 1998 AW 0-3: (5f, 6f, 7f) (Fibr 3)
Very moderate filly, effective 5f, acts on sft to g-s. Turf high 45 - 3rd of 8 getting 11lb from Montendre (20 Apr Nottingham 5f sft RF 0772). AW high 16. **G B Balding [0-23] M B Clemence.*

CALCAVELLA BHB 72f **RR 73f** 4703[2]

2 b f Pursuit of Love 9.5f **(69)** - Brightside (IRE) **(84f)** (Last Tycoon) 8.5f **(62)**
Form - 3022
Record 1998 - 1st:0 2nd:2 3rd:1 Ran:4
Win Prizemoney £0 *Total Prizemoney* £3,936
1998 Turf 0-4: (5f, 6f 3) (gd 3, frm)
Above-average filly. Turf high 73 (began Aug) - 2nd of 16 getting 6lb from Achilles Star (7 Oct York 6f gd RF 4703).
**M Kettle [0-4] Pillar To Post Racing.*

CALCHAS (IRE) BHB 94f **RR 93f** 3296[4]

3 b g Warning 8.1f **(77)** - Nassma (IRE) (Sadler's Wells (USA)) 10f **(76)**
Form - 554
Record 1998 - 1st:0 2nd:0 3rd:0 Ran:3
Pre1998 - 1st:2 2nd:1 3rd:1 Ran:5
Win Prizemoney £6,884 *Total Prizemoney* £10,009
Wins * 1997 Jun Epsom (G-S) 7f 81+
* 1997 *Jun Wolver (STD) 6f 88+* <
1998 Turf 0-3: (7f 2, 8f) (gd, g-f 2)
Workmanlike, useful gelding, effective 6 to 7f, best at 7f, acts on gd to frm - acts on Fibr. Turf high 93.
**Sir Mark Prescott [2-8] Sheikh Ahmed bin Saeed Al Maktoum.*

CALCI (USA) RR 107f 4470k[2]
3
Form - 462
1998 Turf 0-2: (12f 2) (gd, g-f)
Currently Pattern-class, has worn blinkers. Turf high 107 (1st run) - 6th of 16 to Central Park (31 May Capannelle 12f g-f RF 1734a).
**O Pessi in ITY [0-3].*

CALCUTTA BHB 83f **RR 80f** 2902[1]
2 b c Indian Ridge 7.6f **(74)** - Echoing (Formidable (USA)) 9.2f **(63)**
Form - 331
Record 1998 - 1st:1 2nd:0 3rd:2 Ran:3
Win Prizemoney £3,571 *Total Prizemoney* £5,310
Wins * 1998 Jly Ayr (GD) 6f 80 <
1998 Turf 1-3: (5f, 6f 1-2) (gd 1-3)
Currently decent colt. Turf high 80 - 1st of 7 from Pepperdine (18 Jly Ayr RF 2902). Narrow winner at Ayr on his third start having been placed in a couple of decent maidens.
**B W Hills [1-3] Mrs J M Corbett.*

CALCUTTA KING BHB 40f **RR 52f** 4818[24]
2 ch c Democratic (USA) - Calcutta Queen (Night Shift (USA)) 7.2f **(69)**
Form - 080
Record 1998 - 1st:0 2nd:0 3rd:0 Ran:3
1998 Turf 0-3: (5f, 7f 2) (gd, g-f, frm)
Currently fair colt. Turf high 52 (began Jly).
**R Simpson [0-3] Miss J Rumford.*

CALEDONIAN COLOURS (IRE) RR 87+f 4104[1]
2 ch c Indian Ridge 7.6f **(74)** - Unspoiled (Tina's Pet) 6.8f **(59)**
Form - 1
Record 1998 - 1st:1 2nd:0 3rd:0 Ran:1
Win Prizemoney £4,019 *Total Prizemoney* £4,019
Wins * 1998 Spt Haydoc (GD) 7.1f 87+ <
1998 Turf 1-1: (7f 1-1) (frm 1-1)
Currently useful colt. (1st run) - 1st of 12 from Entertainer (5 Spt Haydock RF 4104). Narrow winner of an ordinary Haydock maiden on his debut. **Sir Michael Stoute [1-1] Ivan Allan & Alex Ferguson.*

CALEDONIAN EXPRESS BHB 66f **RR 68f** 2572[8]
3 b f Northern Park(USA) 10f **(57)**- New Edition(Great Nephew)9.9f **(64)**
Form - 038
Record 1998 - 1st:0 2nd:0 3rd:1 Ran:3
Pre1998 - 1st:0 2nd:0 3rd:0 Ran:3
Win Prizemoney £0 *Total Prizemoney* £434
1998 Turf 0-3: (9f, 10f 2) (gd, g-f 2)
Scopey, average filly, effective 10f, acts on g-f. Turf high 68 - 3rd of 7 getting 1lb from Lady Rockstar (26 Jun Folkestone 10f g-f RF 2299). **J L Dunlop [0-6] R J McAulay.*

CALICO LADY BHB 47f **RR 57f** 3904[10]
2 ch f First Trump - Cottonwood (Teenoso (USA)) 9.9f **(72)**
Form - 6426777750
Record 1998 - 1st:0 2nd:1 3rd:0 Ran:10
Win Prizemoney £0 *Total Prizemoney* £1,376
1998 Turf 0-10: (5f 4, 6f 4, 7f 2) (hvy, g-s, gd 6, g-f 2)
Fair filly, effective 5f, acts on g-s. Turf high 57.
**W T Kemp [0-10] Drakemyre Racing.*

CALLDAT SEVENTEEN RR 51f 4745[9]
2 b c Komaite (USA) 6.9f **(61)** - Westminster Waltz (Dance In Time (CAN)) 8.9f **(59)**
Form - 0
Record 1998 - 1st:0 2nd:0 3rd:0 Ran:1
1998 Turf 0-1: (8f) (gd)
Currently fair colt. **P W D'Arcy [0-1] Exors of the late Derek Weeden.*

CALLIRAM BHB 41f43a **RR 35f 43a** 4624[10]
3 b f Petardia 8.2f **(58)** - Sheesha (USA) (Shadeed (USA)) 8.2f **(70)**
Form - 0000
Record 1998 - 1st:0 2nd:0 3rd:0 Ran:3
Pre1998 - 1st:0 2nd:0 3rd:3 Ran:11
Win Prizemoney £0 *Total Prizemoney* £806
1998 Turf 0-3: (5f, 6f 2) (gd, g-f, frm)
Small, very moderate filly, effective 6 to 7f, acts on g-f. Turf high 35 (began Aug). Inconsistent.
**A R Dicken [0-3] P F Chakko (from M Blanshard [0-11] Dec 1997).*

CALLITWHATYOUWANT BHB 65f **RR 71f** 2461[5]
2 b c Weldnaas (USA) 8.4f **(55)** - Alcassa (FR) (Satingo) 8.9f **(69)**
Form - 02255
Record 1998 - 1st:0 2nd:2 3rd:0 Ran:5
Win Prizemoney £0 *Total Prizemoney* £1,315
1998 Turf 0-5: (5f 5) (g-s, gd 3, frm)
Above-average colt. Turf high 71 - 2nd of 10 getting 2lb from Ballina Lad (4 May Newcastle 5f gd RF 1019).
**J J O'Neill [0-5] Clayton Bigley Partnership Ltd.*

CALL ME LUCKY BHB 65f **RR 71f** 4400[19]
2 b f Magic Ring (IRE) 6.5f **(64)** - Lucky Message (USA) **(59f)** (Phone Trick (USA))
Form - 5082310000
Record 1998 - 1st:1 2nd:1 3rd:1 Ran:10
Win Prizemoney £6,408 *Total Prizemoney* £7,950
Wins * 1998 Jly York (FRM) 6f 71 <
1998 Turf 1-10: (5f 5, 6f 1-5) (gd 4, g-f 2, frm 1-4)
Above-average filly, effective 5 to 6f, acts on frm. Turf high 71 - 1st of 17 getting 5lb from Pluralist (11 Jly York RF 2734). Got off the mark in a blanket finish at York, but it was a very moderate race for the track, and she has looked decidedly ordinary otherwise.
**M Brittain [1-10] Northgate Bronze.*

CALL ME SAM (FR) RR 101f 2283a[2]
4 gr c Kaldoun (FR) 9.9f **(84)** - Tkisan (FR) (Olantengy (FR))
Form - 2
1998 Turf 0-1: (12f) (sft)
Currently very useful colt. (1st run) - 2nd of 9 getting 3lb from Go Boldly (20 Jun Lyon Parilly 12f sft RF 2283a). He finished second in a run-of-the-mill Listed event in June and goes well on soft ground. **in FR [0-1].*

CALL ME VERA BHB 40f **RR 27f** 2760[9]
3 ch f Beveled (USA) 6.9f **(64)** - Cee Beat (Bairn (USA)) 7.7f **(59)**
Form - 0000
Record 1998 - 1st:0 2nd:0 3rd:0 Ran:4
Pre1998 - 1st:0 2nd:0 3rd:0 Ran:4
1998 Turf 0-4: (6f 2, 8f 2) (gd 2, g-f 2)
Light-framed, little account filly, has worn blinkers. Turf high 27.
**E A Wheeler [0-8] Austin Stroud & Co Ltd.*

CALL MY GUEST (IRE) BHB 31f31a **RR 24f 31a** 2673[8]
8 b g Be My Guest (USA) 10.2f **(66)** - Overcall (Bustino) 10.4f **(64)**
Form - 0778
Record 1998 - 1st:0 2nd:0 3rd:0 Ran:4
Pre1998 - 1st:0 2nd:0 3rd:0 Ran:5
1998 Turf 0-1: (12f) (g-f) 1998 AW 0-3: (12f 2, 16f) (Equi 2, Fibr)
Little account gelding. AW high 22. Becoming disappointing.
**R E Peacock [1-27] Derek D & Mrs Jean P Clee (from J G FitzGerald [0-6] Oct 1994).*

CALL THE BOSS (USA) RR 79+ 333[1]
3 b c Chief's Crown (USA) 10.2f **(75)** - Laz's Joy (USA) (Valdez (USA)) 10.7f **(70)**
Form - 1
Record 1998 - 1st:1 2nd:0 3rd:0 Ran:1
Win Prizemoney £3,436 *Total Prizemoney* £3,436
Wins * 1998 *Feb Lingfi (SLW) 8f 79* <
1998 AW 1-1: (8f 1-1) (Equi 1-1)
Workmanlike, currently above-average colt, always wears blinkers. (1st run) - 1st of 7 getting 19lb from Severity (21 Feb Lingfield RF 0333). He was part of his trainer's great start to his career when taking a maiden in good style on the Lingfield Equitrack in February. **J Noseda [1-1] Lady Sarah Barry.*

CALYPSO LADY (IRE) BHB 55f **RR 55f** 1692[9]
4 ch f Priolo (USA) 10.9f **(71)** - Taking Steps (Gay Fandango (USA)) 8.5f **(59)**
Form - 060
Record 1998 - 1st:0 2nd:0 3rd:0 Ran:3
Pre1998 - 1st:1 2nd:0 3rd:1 Ran:9
Win Prizemoney £3,095 *Total Prizemoney* £4,542
Wins * 1996 Spt Kempto (GD) 6f 77 <
1998 Turf 0-3: (8f, 10f 2) (gd, frm 2)
Scopey, fair filly. Turf high 55. **R Hannon [1-12] Mrs D M Wight.*

CAMARGO (IRE) RR 93f 4178a[12]
2 b f Brief Truce (USA) 9.1f **(73)** - You Make Me Real (USA) 00
Form - 21210
1998 Turf 2-5: (5f 1-2, 6f 1-2, 7f) (hvy, sft 2-2, gd, frm)
Useful filly. Turf high 93 - 1st of 5 getting 3lb from Namid (28 Jun Curragh RF 2431a) - also 1st of 8 getting 5lb from Flip The Switch (2 May Curragh RF 1046a). Useful sprinting juvenile, winner of the Group Three Railway Stakes. Probably found the seven furlongs of the Moyglare Stud Stakes too far.
**D K Weld in IRE [2-5] Edmund Gann.*

CAMBODIAN (USA) RR 84f 5109a[8]
4 b c Roanoke (USA) - September Kaper (USA) 00
Form - 431045078
1998 Turf 1-9: (7f, 8f 2, 9f 1-3, 10f 3)(hvy, sft 2, gd 2, g-f 2, frm 1-1, hrd)
Decent colt, effective 9f, acts on frm, has worn blinkers. Turf high 99 - 1st of 8 giving 21lb to Maytpleasethecourt (4 Jly Leopardstown RF 2611a). After a promising start, he became disappointing. **J S Bolger in IRE [2-13] Mrs Audrey O'Connor.*

CAMBRAI (IRE) RR 57f 5039[8]
2 b c Indian Ridge 7.6f **(74)** - Cambrel (IRE) **(78f)** (Soviet Star (USA))
Form - 8
Record 1998 - 1st:0 2nd:0 3rd:0 Ran:1
1998 Turf 0-1: (8f) (g-s)
Currently fair colt. **M P Tregoning [0-1] Sheikh Mohammed.*

CAMBRIDGE BLUE (USA) BHB 38f42a **RR 25f 42a** 1607[13]
4 gr g Sheikh Albadou 9.2f **(75)** - Fit And Ready (USA) (Fit To Fight (USA)) 9.7f **(45)**
Form - 07540070070
Record 1998 - 1st:0 2nd:0 3rd:0 Ran:9
Pre1998 - 1st:0 2nd:0 3rd:0 Ran:7
Win Prizemoney £0 *Total Prizemoney* £237
1998 Turf 0-6: (5f, 7f 2, 8f 2, 11f) (g-s, gd 5) 1998 AW 0-3: (7f, 8f, 9f) (Fibr 3)
Leggy, moderate gelding, often wears blinkers. Turf high 34. AW high 48.
**I Semple [0-11] The T B Consortium (from G Lewis [0-5] Jly 1997).*

CAMEO (IRE) BHB 53f56a **RR 58f 56a** 3840[7]
3 b g Statoblest 6.4f **(63)** - Centella (IRE) (Thatching) 8f **(66)**
Form - 87004025007
Record 1998 - 1st:0 2nd:1 3rd:0 Ran:11
Win Prizemoney £0 *Total Prizemoney* £834
1998 Turf 0-8: (5f 4, 6f 3, 7f) (hvy, g-s 4, gd 2, frm) 1998 AW 0-3: (5f, 6f 2) (Fibr 3)
Workmanlike, average gelding, effective 5 to 6f, acts on gd - acts on Fibr. Turf high 63. AW high 63 (1st run) (began Jly) - 2nd of 6 getting 3lb from Anthony Mon Amour (11 Jly Southwell 6f Fibr RF 2724). **M R Channon [0-11] Park Farm Racing.*

CAMERON JACK BHB 51f **RR 56f** 4957[5]
3 b g Elmaamul (USA) 8.1f **(70)** - Ile de Reine (Ile de Bourbon (USA)) 10.1f **(67)**
Form - 6844305
Record 1998 - 1st:0 2nd:0 3rd:1 Ran:7
Win Prizemoney £0 *Total Prizemoney* £903
1998 Turf 0-7: (10f 5, 12f 2) (gd 2, g-f, frm 4)
Light-framed, fair gelding, effective 12f, acts on frm. Turf high 56.
**J D Bethell [0-7] M W Territt.*

CAMIONNEUR (IRE) BHB 45f **RR 45f** 3567[13]
5 b g Cyrano de Bergerac 7.3f **(58)** - Fact of Time (Known Fact (USA)) 7.4f **(67)**
Form - 508600
Record 1998 - 1st:0 2nd:0 3rd:0 Ran:6
Pre1998 - 1st:2 2nd:8 3rd:4 Ran:50
Win Prizemoney £5,313 *Total Prizemoney* £20,939
Wins * 1997 Aug Redcar (G-F) H 6f 48 50 <
* 1996 Jly Ripon (G-F) H 6f 48 46
1998 Turf 0-6: (5f 3, 6f 3) (gd 4, g-f, frm)
Moderate gelding, effective 5 to 6f, best at 5f, acts on gd to frm, best on gd, mostly wears blinkers (very effectively). Turf high 45. Tends to forfeit ground at the start.
**T D Easterby [2-45] T E F Freight (Scarborough) Ltd (from M H Easterby [0-11] Nov 1995).*

CAMPARI (IRE) BHB 55f **RR 50f** 4990[4]
3 b f Distinctly North (USA) 7.4f **(63)** - Foolish Flight (IRE) (Fools Holme (USA))
Form - 804
Record 1998 - 1st:0 2nd:0 3rd:0 Ran:3
Pre1998 - 1st:0 2nd:0 3rd:2 Ran:5
Win Prizemoney £0 *Total Prizemoney* £1,561
1998 Turf 0-3: (8f 2, 10f) (sft, gd, g-f)
Unfurnished, fair filly. Turf high 50 (began Aug).
**J Pearce [0-1] Jack Fisher (from M A Jarvis [0-7] Aug 1998).*

CAMPASPE BHB 57f51a **RR 64f 51a** 4506[9]
6 b m Dominion 8.9f **(65)** - Lady River (FR) (Sir Gaylord) 10.6f **(64)**
Form - 203088440
Record 1998 - 1st:0 2nd:1 3rd:1 Ran:9
Pre1998 - 1st:6 2nd:5 3rd:4 Ran:24
Win Prizemoney £21,208 *Total Prizemoney* £31,702
Wins * 1997 Spt Beverl (G-F) H 12f 67 74 <
* 1997 Aug Mussel (GD) H 14f 61 67
* 1997 Aug Ripon (G-F) H 12.3f 58 64
* 1997 May Redcar (G-F) H 14.1f 54 58
* 1996 Spt Beverl (G-F) H 12f 42 53
* 1996 May Beverl (G-F) H 12f 37 42
1998 Turf 0-9: (12f, 14f 4, 15f, 16f 2, 17f) (sft, gd 5, frm 3)
Average mare, effective 12 to 15f, acts on gd to frm, has worn blinkers. Turf high 76 (1st run) - 2nd of 6 giving 16lb to Taufan Boy (2 May Haydock 14f gd RF 0969). Consistent.
**J G FitzGerald [6-33] J G FitzGerald.*

CAMPHAR BHB 28f37a **RR 14df 37a** 2117[14]
5 ch m Pharly (FR) 11.5f **(64)** - Camomilla (Targowice (USA)) 11.4f **(70)**
Form - 0
Record 1998 - 1st:0 2nd:0 3rd:0 Ran:1
Pre1998 - 1st:0 2nd:0 3rd:0 Ran:4
1998 Turf 0-1: (6f) (g-f)
Poor filly. (DEAD)
**J R Poulton [0-1] Miss Victoria Markowiak (from R M Flower [0-4] Jly 1997).*

CAMPIONE (IRE) BHB 44f **RR 25f** 5070[20]
3 b g Common Grounds 8.1f **(66)** - Kyrenia (Zino) 12.9f **(54)**
Form - 080000
Record 1998 - 1st:0 2nd:0 3rd:0 Ran:6
Pre1998 - 1st:0 2nd:0 3rd:0 Ran:3
1998 Turf 0-6: (5f, 6f 2, 7f, 9f, 10f) (gd 3, g-f, frm 2)
Leggy, little account gelding. Turf high 42.
**M H Tompkins [0-9] Mrs Patricia Kalman.*

CAMPO CATINO (IRE) RR 117f 3880a[5]
3 br c Woodman (USA) 9.7f **(77)** - Karri Valley (USA) (Storm Bird (CAN)) 10.3f **(74)**
Form - 311445
1998 Turf 2-6: (10f 1-2, 12f 1-3, 14f) (sft, g-s 1-1, gd 3, frm 1-1)
High-class colt, effective 12f, acts on sft. Turf high 117 - 4th of 10 to Dream Well (28 Jun Curragh 12f sft RF 2432a). He looked an improving sort when winning twice at Leopardstown in June, but was highly tried afterwards and did not show much, and his fourth place in the Irish Derby was very flattering.
**C O'Brien in IRE [2-7] Dr M V O'Brien.*

CAMPUS CROP (IRE) BHB 40f **RR 24f** 4762[18]
2 b f College Chapel - Meadow Grass (IRE) **(30f)** (Thatching) 8f **(66)**
Form - 000
Record 1998 - 1st:0 2nd:0 3rd:0 Ran:3
1998 Turf 0-3: (5f, 6f, 10f) (gd, g-f, frm)
Currently little account filly. Turf high 24 (began Jly).
**M J Fetherston-Godley [0-3] The Kennet House Partnership.*

CANADIAN APPROVAL (USA) BHB 77f **RR 82f** 4414[3]
2 ch f With Approval (CAN) 8.7f **(80)** - A Taste For Lace (USA) (Laomedonte (USA))
Form - 5133
Record 1998 - 1st:1 2nd:0 3rd:2 Ran:4
Win Prizemoney £2,098 *Total Prizemoney* £3,680
Wins * 1998 Aug Lingfi (FRM) 7.6f 82 <
1998 Turf 1-4: (7f 2, 8f 1-2) (gd, g-f 1-1, frm 2)
Decent filly. Turf high 82 (began Aug) - 1st of 10 getting 5lb from

Redouble (26 Aug Lingfield RF 3889).
**P W Harris [1-4] Ayton, Cordero, Rodway & Harris.*

CANADIAN FANTASY BHB 51f65a RR 57f 65a 3968[13]
4 b g Lear Fan (USA) 10.4f **(80)** - Florinda (CAN) (Vice Regent (CAN)) 8.7f **(74)**
Form - 840850
Record 1998 - 1st:0 2nd:0 3rd:0 Ran:6
Pre1998 - 1st:2 2nd:5 3rd:2 Ran:15
Win Prizemoney £6,506 *Total Prizemoney* £13,454
Wins 1997 Jly Hamilt (SFT) H 9.2f 74 76 <
1997 Jun Southw (STD) 8f 71
1998 Turf 0-6: (10f 2, 11f, 12f, 14f, 16f) (g-f 3, frm 3)
Leggy, above-average gelding, effective 8 to 9f, best at 9f, acts on gd - acts on Fibr, has worn blinkers. Turf high 57.
**Mrs V C Ward [0-13] Mrs R F Key & Mrs V C Ward (from M Johnston [2-15] Aug 1997).*

CANADIAN PUZZLER (USA) BHB 74f74a RR 76f 74a 3452[5]
3 gr c With Approval (CAN) 8.7f **(80)** - Puzzle Book (USA) (Text (USA))
Form - 6875
Record 1998 - 1st:0 2nd:0 3rd:0 Ran:4
Pre1998 - 1st:0 2nd:0 3rd:1 Ran:4
Win Prizemoney £0 *Total Prizemoney* £1,718
1998 Turf 0-3: (8f 2, 10f) (g-s, gd, frm) 1998 AW 0-1: (8f) (Fibr)
Strong, above-average colt, effective 8f, acts on gd. Turf high 76. Consistent. **P W Harris [0-8] The Maple Leafs.*

CANARY BLUE (IRE) BHB 22f20a RR 17f 20a 308[8]
7 b m Bluebird (USA) 7.9f**(71)** - Norfolk Bonnet (Morston (FR)) 9.4f **(55)**
Form - 08
Record 1998 - 1st:0 2nd:0 3rd:0 Ran:1
Pre1998 - 1st:0 2nd:0 3rd:0 Ran:13
Win Prizemoney £0 *Total Prizemoney* £233
1998 AW 0-1: (15f) (Fibr)
Poor mare, has worn blinkers.
**P W Hiatt [2-13] P W Hiatt (from P R Webber [0-2] Aug 1996).*

CANDELLINO BHB 60f RR 61f 4613[15]
2 b f Robellino (USA) 9.5f **(68)** - By Candlelight (IRE) **(80f)** (Roi Danzig (USA))
Form - 7080
Record 1998 - 1st:0 2nd:0 3rd:0 Ran:4
1998 Turf 0-4: (5f 2, 6f, 7f) (g-s, gd, g-f, hrd)
Average filly. Turf high 61 (began Aug).
**T R Watson [0-4] G H Dodsworth.*

CANDESCENT RR 45f 1836[11]
3 b f Machiavellian (USA) 9.8f **(83)** - Nearctic Flame (Sadler's Wells (USA)) 10f **(76)**
Form - 0
Record 1998 - 1st:0 2nd:0 3rd:0 Ran:1
1998 Turf 0-1: (8f) (gd)
Scopey, currently moderate filly.
**Sir Michael Stoute [0-1] Cheveley Park Stud.*

CANDLERIGGS (IRE) BHB 79f RR 74f 5064[2]
2 ch c Indian Ridge 7.6f**(74)** - Ridge Pool (IRE)(Bluebird (USA))7.5f **(69)**
Form - 052
Record 1998 - 1st:0 2nd:1 3rd:0 Ran:3
Win Prizemoney £0 *Total Prizemoney* £1,090
1998 Turf 0-3: (6f 2, 7f) (gd, g-f 2)
Currently above-average colt. Turf high 74 (began Spt).
**E A L Dunlop [0-3] The Right Angle Club.*

CANDLE SMILE (USA) BHB 85f RR 89f 4206[6]
6 b g Pleasant Colony (USA) 12.4f **(88)** - Silent Turn (USA) (Silent Cal (USA)) 14.5f **(91)**
Form - 86
Record 1998 - 1st:0 2nd:0 3rd:0 Ran:2
Pre1998 - 1st:2 2nd:3 3rd:2 Ran:12
Win Prizemoney £11,746 *Total Prizemoney* £23,998
Wins 1996 Spt Goodwo (G-F) H 16f 90 97 <
1996 May Ayr (GD) 13.1f 76
1998 Turf 0-2: (18f, 19f) (gd, g-f)
Useful gelding. Turf high 89 (1st run) - 8th of 18 giving 2lb to Silence in Court (6 May Chester 19f g-f RF 1059). Consistent. Missed the whole of 1997, changing stables in the interim, and sustained tendon injuries in a rough Chester Cup on his return.
**G Barnett [0-2] J C Bradbury (from Sir Michael Stoute [2-12] Oct 1996).*

CANDY'S DELIGHT BHB 30f28a RR 26f 28a 416[11]
5 b m Dunbeath (USA) 9.9f **(53)** - Simply Candy (IRE) (Simply Great (FR)) 8.2f **(65)**
Form - 0
Record 1998 - 1st:0 2nd:0 3rd:0 Ran:1
Pre1998 - 1st:0 2nd:0 3rd:0 Ran:7
1998 AW 0-1: (12f) (Fibr)
Little account filly. Becoming disappointing.
**J Norton [0-1] Jeff Slaney (from Mrs S J Smith [0-3] Oct 1996).*

CANDY TWIST BHB 34f RR 43f 4816[5]
3 b f Deploy 11.4f **(67)**- Simply Candy (IRE)(Simply Great (FR))8.2f **(65)**
Form - 648735
Record 1998 - 1st:0 2nd:0 3rd:1 Ran:6
Pre1998 - 1st:0 2nd:0 3rd:1 Ran:8
Win Prizemoney £0 *Total Prizemoney* £584
1998 Turf 0-6: (7f, 8f 3, 10f, 12f) (gd, g-f 3, frm 2)
Unfurnished, moderate filly, effective 6f, acts on frm. Turf high 43.
**Ronald Thompson [0-14] J Bradwell.*

CANNYLASS (IRE) BHB 44f RR 54f 4300[16]
2 b f Brief Truce (USA) 9.1f **(73)** - Starlust (Sallust) 8.4f **(63)**
Form - 026344500
Record 1998 - 1st:0 2nd:1 3rd:1 Ran:9
Win Prizemoney £0 *Total Prizemoney* £1,014
1998 Turf 0-9: (5f 2, 6f 5, 7f 2) (gd 5, g-f 2, frm 2)
Fair filly, effective 7f, acts on gd, often wears blinkers (effectively). Turf high 60. Becoming disappointing. **N Tinkler [0-9] Ian Blakey.*

CANONBIEBOTHERED RR 2097[9]
7 ch m Liberated - Play Mount (Spur On)
Form - 0
Record 1998 - 1st:0 2nd:0 3rd:0 Ran:1
1998 AW 0-1: (11f) (Fibr)
Formerly very poor mare. **M A Peill [0-5] A S McGimpsey.*

CANON CAN (USA) BHB 115f RR 116f 4716a[6]
5 ch g Green Dancer (USA) 11.9f **(77)** - Lady Argyle (USA) (Don B (USA)) 18f **(116)**
Form - 052436
Record 1998 - 1st:0 2nd:1 3rd:1 Ran:6
Pre1998 - 1st:5 2nd:1 3rd:2 Ran:14
Win Prizemoney £54,695 *Total Prizemoney* £91,898
Wins * 1997 Spt Doncas (G-F) G3 18f 114 <
* 1997 Jun Ascot (SFT) 22.2f 100
* 1997 Apr Newbur (G-F) H 16f 92 100
* 1996 Spt Pontef (GD) 18f 109
* 1996 Aug Newmar (G-F) H 16.1f 81 85
1998 Turf 0-6: (16f 3, 18f, 20f 2) (sft, g-s, gd 2, g-f 2)
High-class gelding, effective 16 to 20f, best at 18f, acts on g-s to frm, best on gd, excels at Ascot and Doncaster. Turf high 116 - 2nd of 9 getting 3lb from Double Trigger (30 Jly Goodwood 16f gd RF 3218). Consistent. He never really scaled the heights in 1998, despite making the frame in some of the top staying events, and his narrow defeat by Double Trigger in the Goodwood Cup was definitely his best effort. He is suited by a severe test of stamina.
**H R A Cecil [5-20] Canon (Anglia) O A Ltd.*

CANONIZE (IRE) BHB 64f RR 55f 3588[10]
3 b f Alzao (USA) 9.8f **(73)** - Cecina (Welsh Saint) 7.6f **(64)**
Form - 0
Record 1998 - 1st:0 2nd:0 3rd:0 Ran:1
Pre1998 - 1st:0 2nd:0 3rd:1 Ran:3
Win Prizemoney £0 *Total Prizemoney* £482
1998 Turf 0-1: (10f) (gd)
Workmanlike, fair filly. **J W Hills [0-4] George Tong.*

CANOVAS HEART BHB 85f70a RR 86df 70a 4975[9]
9 b g Balidar 6.5f **(58)** - Worthy Venture (Northfields (USA)) 9f **(72)**
Form - 6505100
Record 1998 - 1st:1 2nd:0 3rd:0 Ran:6
Pre1998 - 1st:9 2nd:2 3rd:3 Ran:32

Win Prizemoney £55,327 *Total Prizemoney* £59,386

Wins									
	* **1998**	Spt	Nottin	(G-F)	H	6.1f	82	86	<
	* 1997	Oct	York	(GD)	H	5f	79	86	<
	* 1997	May	Ripon	(G-S)	H	5f	78	84	
	* 1996	Spt	Yarmou	(GD)	H	5.2f	72	73	
	* 1996	Jun	York	(GD)	H	5f	70	71	
	* 1996	May	Folkes	(GD)	H	5f	65	68	
	* 1996	Apr	Warwic	(GD)	H	5f	60	66	
	* 1995	*Jun*	*Southw*	*(STD)*	*H*	*5f*	*49*	*53*	
	* 1995	Apr	Warwic	(G-S)	H	5f	53	54	
	* 1994	Oct	Warwic	(SFT)	H	5f	43	45	

1998 Turf 1-6: (5f 4, 6f 1-2) (sft, gd 1-4, frm)

Useful gelding, effective 5 to 6f, best at 5f, acts on gd. Turf high 86 - 1st of 20 getting 20lb from Nigrasine (26 Spt Nottingham RF 4508). Inconsistent. A pacey sprinter , he had done all his winning over five furlongs, until scoring at Nottingham. Unfamiliar hold-up tactics were employed there.

**Bob Jones [10-41] M J Osborne and Mrs J Woods.*

CAN SHE CAN CAN BHB 25f37a RR 6f 37a 3670[13]

6 b m Sulaafah (USA) 8.6f **(44)** - Dominance (Dominion) 8.5f **(63)**

Form - 0

Record 1998 - 1st:0 2nd:0 3rd:0 Ran:1
Pre1998 - 1st:1 2nd:4 3rd:3 Ran:22

Win Prizemoney £2,641 *Total Prizemoney* £7,402

Wins 1994 Aug Hamilt (FRM) C 6f 43

1998 Turf 0-1: (17f) (frm)

Very poor mare, has worn blinkers. Becoming disappointing.

**C Smith [0-24] The Hunting Ten Partnership (from M Johnston [1-13] Spt 1995).*

CANTA KE BRAVE (USA) BHB 93f RR 78f 4738[4]

2 ch c River Special (USA) - Stubborn Star (USA) (Star Choice (USA))

Form - 214

Record 1998 - 1st:1 2nd:1 3rd:0 Ran:3

Win Prizemoney £3,715 *Total Prizemoney* £5,420

Wins * **1998** Spt Goodwo (G-F) 8f 77 <

1998 Turf 1-3: (8f 1-3) (g-s, frm 1-2)

Currently above-average colt. Turf high 78 (began Spt) - also 1st of 6 from Home Office (23 Spt Goodwood RF 4452). Comfortable winner at Goodwood despite hanging left, but well-held in a Listed race in soft ground. **S P C Woods [1-3] Dwayne Woods.*

CANTGETYOURBREATH (IRE) BHB 66f RR 74f 4612[2]

2 ch g College Chapel - Cathy Garcia (IRE) (Be My Guest (USA)) 9.3f **(67)**

Form - 7362

Record 1998 - 1st:0 2nd:1 3rd:1 Ran:4

Win Prizemoney £0 *Total Prizemoney* £1,082

1998 Turf 0-4: (6f 4) (g-s, g-f 2, frm)

Above-average gelding. Turf high 74 (began Aug) - 2nd of 20 giving 7lb to Enthaisingh (2 Oct Lingfield 6f g-s RF 4612).

**B J Meehan [0-4] P Burdett.*

CANTILEVER RR 110f 4343a[8]

3 b f Sanglamore (USA) 12.9f **(67)** - Cantanta (Top Ville) 11.7f **(68)**

Form - 2128

1998 Turf 1-4: (11f, 12f 1-3) (hvy 2, gd 1-2)

Group-class filly. Turf high 110 - 2nd of 7 to Another Dancer (21 Jun Longchamp 12f gd RF 2289a) - also 1st of 6 from Fille du Lac (30 May Chantilly RF 1730a). She made all in a Group Three at Chantilly in May, but her opponents were wise to similar tactics when she was moved into the top class.

**Mme C Head in FR [1-4] K Abdulla.*

CANTINA BHB 78f RR 77f 4365[29]

4 b f Tina's Pet 7.4f**(56)** - Real Claire(Dreams to Reality(USA)) 6.4f **(73)**

Form - D001301300

Record 1998 - 1st:2 2nd:0 3rd:2 Ran:10
Pre1998 - 1st:1 2nd:0 3rd:1 Ran:4

Win Prizemoney £14,045 *Total Prizemoney* £16,067

Wins									
	* **1998**	Aug	Lingfi	(G-F)	H	7.6f	73	77	<
	* **1998**	Jly	Cheste	(G-F)	H	7.6f	69	72	
	* 1997	Spt	Catter	(G-F)		7f		62	

1998 Turf 2-10: (6f 3, 7f, 8f 2-6) (sft, gd 2, g-f 2, frm 2-5)

Light-framed, above-average filly, effective 8f, acts on gd to frm, best on frm. Turf high 77 - 1st of 12 getting 14lb from Consort (16 Aug Lingfield RF 3666) - also 1st of 14 giving 12lb to Knave's Ash (10 Jly Chester RF 2674). Inconsistent. Put up a fine performance to pass the post first in a very competitive Chester handicap on her seasonal debut, but was thrown out after having caused trouble when crossing over to the rail soon after the start. Put two poor runs behind her when making all back at Chester in July, and scored again at Lingfield the following month. Seven furlongs and fast ground suit her admirably. **A Bailey [3-14] B K Racing.*

CANTON VENTURE BHB 70f76a RR 65f 76a 1629[5]

6 ch g Arctic Tern (USA) 12.2f **(71)** - Ski Michaela (USA) (Devil's Bag (USA)) 12.4f **(78)**

Form - 035

Record 1998 - 1st:0 2nd:0 3rd:1 Ran:2
Pre1998 - 1st:10 2nd:5 3rd:1 Ran:31

Win Prizemoney £34,926 *Total Prizemoney* £41,179

Wins									
	* 1997	*May*	*Lingfi*	*(STD)*	*H*	*12f*	*74*	*79+*	<
	* 1996	Aug	Bright	(FRM)	H	11.9f	70	73	
	* 1996	Jly	Bright	(FRM)	H	11.9f	64	67	
	* 1996	Jun	Newcas	(FRM)	H	12.4f	60	63	
	* 1996	Jun	Thirsk	(FRM)	H	12f	51	61	
	* 1996	Jun	Warwic	(FRM)	H	12.5f	51	54	
	* 1996	May	Folkes	(GD)		12f		55	
	* 1996	*May*	*Southw*	*(STD)*	*H*	*11f*	*64*	*70*	
	* 1995	*Spt*	*Wolver*	*(STD)*	*H*	*12f*	*60*	*67*	
	* 1995	*Jly*	*Wolver*	*(STD)*	*H*	*12f*	*59*	*65+*	

1998 Turf 0-1: (12f) (g-f) 1998 AW 0-1: (12f) (Fibr)

Above-average gelding, effective 12f, acts on g-f to frm - acts on AW, has worn blinkers. (1st run) - 3rd of 5 giving 23lb to Evezio Rufo (7 Apr Wolverhampton 12f Fibr RF 0595).

**S P C Woods [14-44] Dr Frank Chao.*

CANYONLANDS RR 84f 4511[5]

2 b c Gulch(USA) 9.6f **(79)**-Queen's View (FR)(Lomond (USA))8.8f **(65)**

Form - 25

Record 1998 - 1st:0 2nd:1 3rd:0 Ran:2

Win Prizemoney £0 *Total Prizemoney* £3,950

1998 Turf 0-2: (7f 2) (gd, g-f)

Currently decent colt. Turf high 84 (began Spt). Should win races at around a mile. **Sir Michael Stoute [0-2] Sheikh Mohammed.*

CANYOUHEARME BHB 51f RR 58f 4473[5]

2 b f Sabrehill (USA) 8.5f **(64)** - Fiveofive (IRE) (Fairy King (USA)) 7.7f **(59)**

Form - 65855

Record 1998 - 1st:0 2nd:0 3rd:0 Ran:5

1998 Turf 0-5: (6f, 7f 3, 8f) (gd, g-f 3, frm)

Fair filly. Turf high 58 (began Jly) - 5th of 16 to Helen's Stardust (25 Spt Folkestone 6f g-f RF 4473).

**N A Callaghan [0-5] Mrs T A Foreman.*

CANZONA (IRE) RR 101f 1345a[1]

3 gr g Kenmare (FR) 9.6f **(76)** - Gay Nocturne

Form - 251

1998 Turf 1-3: (7f, 8f 1-1, 10f) (sft 2, gd 1-1)

Very useful gelding, has worn blinkers. Turf high 101 - 1st of 8 getting 9lb from Thats Logic (16 May Cork RF 1345a). He did not seem to stay when beaten over 10 furlongs and looked a better horse when dropped back to a mile. This lightly-raced colt has more to offer. **J Oxx in IRE [2-4] Lady Clague.*

CAPE CROSS (IRE) BHB 120f RR 121f 5165a[9]

4 b c Green Desert (USA) 7.8f **(78)** - Park Appeal (Ahonoora) 8.1f **(73)**

Form - 15340

Record 1998 - 1st:1 2nd:0 3rd:1 Ran:5
Pre1998 - 1st:2 2nd:2 3rd:1 Ran:8

Win Prizemoney £90,846 *Total Prizemoney* £133,455

Wins								
	* **1998**	May	Newbur	(G-F)	G1	8f	121	<
	1997	Aug	Goodwo	(G-F)		8f	107	
	1996	Spt	Doncas	(G-F)		8f	95+	

1998 Turf 1-5: (8f 1-5) (gd 3, frm 1-2)

Very high-class colt, effective 8f, acts on gd to frm, likes right handed tracks. Turf high 121 - also 1st of 10 from Poteen (16 May Newbury RF 1260). Consistent. Wintered in Dubai, and was beaten twice there before making all for a shock win in the Lockinge, a race in which he had been widely regarded as a pacemaker for Kahal. The softish ground was against him when he was a well-beaten fifth to stablemate Intikhab at Ascot, but he ran rather better to finish third in the Jacques le Marois and fourth in the QE II.

Ran well for a long way despite a slipping saddle in the Breeders' Cup Mile, and seems likely to race on in 1999.
**S bin Suroor [1-5] Godolphin (from J H M Gosden [2-8] Aug 1997).*

CAPE GRACE (IRE) BHB 100f **RR 92f** 4853[6]

2 b f Priolo (USA) 10.9f **(71)** - Saffron (FR) (Fabulous Dancer (USA)) 9.4f **(70)**
Form - 126
Record 1998 - 1st:1 2nd:1 3rd:0 Ran:3
Win Prizemoney £6,840 *Total Prizemoney* £9,361
Wins * 1998 Jly Ascot (G-F) 6f 86t <
1998 Turf 1-3: (6f 1-2, 7f) (gd 1-2, g-f)
Currently useful filly. Turf high 92 (began Jly) - 2nd of 4 giving 3lb to Imperial Beauty (3 Spt Salisbury 6f g-f RF 4061) - also 1st of 6 from Circle of Gold (24 Jly Ascot RF 3061). She caused a bit of a surprise when winning by the minimum margin on her Ascot debut. A physically imposing filly, she ran well at Salisbury when second to Imperial Beauty and was unfortunate at Newmarket on her final start when last leaving the stalls and having to make up ground. She has a bright future and she will stay much further than six furlongs. **R Hannon [1-3] S A Six.*

CAPE HOPE BHB 58f45a **RR 68df 45a** 2653[7]

3 b c Risk Me (FR) 8f **(53)** - Bernstein Bette **(35f 44a)** (Petong) 6.6f **(58)**
Form - 45415007
Record 1998 - 1st:1 2nd:0 3rd:0 Ran:7
Pre1998 - 1st:0 2nd:0 3rd:1 Ran:8
Win Prizemoney £2,490 *Total Prizemoney* £2,950
Wins * 1998 Apr Leices (SFT) S 6f 68 <
1998 Turf 1-3: (6f 1-3) (sft 1-1, g-s 2) 1998 AW 0-4: (6f, 7f 3) (Fibr 4)
Workmanlike, average colt, effective 6f, acts on sft. Turf high 68 (1st run) - 1st of 13 giving 5lb to Magni Momenti (2 Apr Leicester RF 0544). AW high 57. Becoming disappointing. He handled the soft ground well when winning a seller at Leicester in April.
**J Akehurst [1-7] Keith Sturgis (from R Boss [0-8] Nov 1997).*

CAPE PIGEON (USA) BHB 55f54a **RR 58f 54a** 2005[17]

13 ch g Storm Bird (CAN) 8.5f **(82)** - Someway Somehow (USA) (What Luck (USA)) 8.1f **(79)**
Form - 00
Record 1998 - 1st:0 2nd:0 3rd:0 Ran:2
Pre1998 - 1st:12 2nd:8 3rd:8 Ran:68
Win Prizemoney £39,196 *Total Prizemoney* £53,939
Wins * 1997 Jun Salisb (G-S) C 8f 66
* 1996 Jly Windso (GD) C 8.3f 65
* 1996 May Windso (GD) C 8.3f 59
* 1995 Jly Windso (GD) S 8.3f 68
* 1995 Jun Windso (GD) S 8.3f 57
* 1994 Oct Chepst (GD) S 8.1f 55
1998 Turf 0-2: (6f, 8f) (gd, g-f)
Fair gelding, effective 8f, acts on gd to hrd, has worn blinkers. Turf high 45. **L G Cottrell [12-70] E Gadsden.*

CAPE POINT **RR 69f** 3954[6]

4 ch f Indian Ridge 7.6f **(74)** - Long View (Persian Bold) 9.3f **(66)**
Form - 6
Record 1998 - 1st:0 2nd:0 3rd:0 Ran:1
1998 Turf 0-1: (8f) (frm)
Workmanlike, currently average filly.
**J H M Gosden [0-1] Sheikh Mohammed.*

CAPERCAILLIE BHB 50a **RR 41f** 4922[4]

3 ch g Deploy 11.4f **(67)** - Tee Gee Jay **(36f 36a)** (Northern Tempest (USA))
Form - 544600753334
Record 1998 - 1st:0 2nd:0 3rd:3 Ran:11
Pre1998 - 1st:0 2nd:0 3rd:0 Ran:2
Win Prizemoney £0 *Total Prizemoney* £1,209
1998 Turf 0-6: (8f 2, 10f 2, 14f 2) (g-s, gd, g-f 4) 1998 AW 0-5: (8f 2, 10f, 14f, 16f) (Equi 2, Fibr 3)
Workmanlike, fair gelding, effective 8f, - acts on Fibr, has worn blinkers, prefers left handed tracks, likes tight tracks. Turf high 41. AW high 55 - 4th of 9 getting 5lb from Emperor's Gold (12 Jan Southwell 8f Fibr RF 0076).
**D Morris [0-13] Future Electrical Services Ltd.*

CAPE SIREN BHB 23f **RR 15f** 2981[15]

4 b f Warning 8.1f **(77)** - Cape Race (USA) (Northern Dancer) 9.6f **(80)**
Form - 000080
Record 1998 - 1st:0 2nd:0 3rd:0 Ran:6
Pre1998 - 1st:0 2nd:0 3rd:0 Ran:3
1998 Turf 0-5: (10f, 11f, 13f, 14f 2) (gd, g-f 4) 1998 AW 0-1: (8f) (Fibr)
Neat, poor filly. Turf high 15. **M J Ryan [0-9] M J Ryan.*

CAPE VERDI (IRE) BHB 120f **RR 124+f** 1778[9]

3 b f Caerleon (USA) 10.9f **(79)** - Afrique Bleu Azur (USA) (Sagace (FR)) 8f **(124)**
Form - 10
Record 1998 - 1st:1 2nd:0 3rd:0 Ran:2
Pre1998 - 1st:2 2nd:1 3rd:0 Ran:4
Win Prizemoney £177,919 *Total Prizemoney* £190,385
Wins * 1998 May Newmar (GD) G1 8f 124+ <
1997 Aug York (GD) G2 6f 106
1997 May Newmar (G-F) 6f 94++
1998 Turf 1-2: (8f 1-1, 12f) (gd 1-1, g-f)
Well made, very high-class filly, effective 8f, acts on gd. Turf high 124 (1st run) - 1st of 16 from Shahtoush (3 May Newmarket RF 0993). A useful two-year-old for Peter Chapple-Hyam, she was a brilliant winner of the 1000 Guineas first time out this season for Godolphin, having wintered in Dubai. She was asked a big question when taking on the colts over the extra half-mile of the Derby, and in the event failed to shine in what turned out to be a rough race. She did not run again after the Derby, and has reportedly been retired to stud.
**S bin Suroor [1-2] Godolphin (from P W Chapple-Hyam [2-4] Spt 1997).*

CAPISTRANO DAY (USA) **RR 84f** 4856[1]

2 b f Diesis 9f **(80)** - Alcando (Alzao (USA)) 7.1f **(68)**
Form - 01
Record 1998 - 1st:1 2nd:0 3rd:0 Ran:2
Win Prizemoney £3,564 *Total Prizemoney* £3,564
Wins * 1998 Oct Redcar (HVY) 7f 84 <
1998 Turf 1-2: (6f, 7f 1-1) (sft 1-1, g-f)
Currently decent filly. Turf high 84 - 1st of 16 from Prosperous (17 Oct Redcar RF 4856). Out of Alcando who won the Prix de Psyche and a Grade One in America, this small, compact filly finished mid-division at Ascot in June. She was not seen out again until October, where on heavy ground, over an extra furlong, she lost her maiden tag. She will improve over the winter and is sure to stay further. **J H M Gosden [1-2] Anthony Speelman.*

CAPITALIST BHB 69f **RR 81+f** 4960[5]

2 br g Bigstone (IRE) - Pinkie Rose (FR) (Kenmare (FR)) 6.5f **(72)**
Form - 54437705
Record 1998 - 1st:0 2nd:0 3rd:1 Ran:8
Win Prizemoney £0 *Total Prizemoney* £1,099
1998 Turf 0-8: (5f 2, 6f, 7f 2, 8f 3) (gd 3, g-f, frm 4)
Decent gelding, effective 7 to 8f, best at 7f, acts on frm, has worn blinkers. Turf high 81 - 3rd of 7 getting 9lb from Minnesota (24 Jly Newmarket 7f frm RF 3077).
**Mrs J R Ramsden [0-8] Platinum Syndicate Ltd.*

CAPLAW SKEEN BHB 39f **RR 49f** 4768[2]

3 b g Sure Blade (USA) 10.6f **(66)** - Mary From Dunlow (Nicholas Bill) 10.1f **(56)**
Form - 2
Record 1998 - 1st:0 2nd:1 3rd:0 Ran:1
Pre1998 - 1st:0 2nd:0 3rd:0 Ran:2
Win Prizemoney £0 *Total Prizemoney* £695
1998 Turf 0-1: (9f) (sft)
Scopey, currently moderate gelding.
**J J O'Neill [0-1] J J Wright & G P Bernacchi (from J L Eyre [0-2] Nov 1997).*

CAPPELLA (IRE) BHB 75f **RR 73f** 4377[6]

2 br f College Chapel - Mavahra (Mummy's Pet) 7.7f **(60)**
Form - 32147106
Record 1998 - 1st:2 2nd:1 3rd:1 Ran:8
Win Prizemoney £6,789 *Total Prizemoney* £8,716
Wins * 1998 Aug Sandow (G-F) H 5f 74 73 <
*** 1998** Jun Salisb (G-S) 5f 73 <
1998 Turf 2-8: (5f 2-4, 6f 3, 7f) (gd 2-4, g-f 2, frm 2)

Above-average filly, effective 5 to 6f, best at 5f, acts on gd to g-f, best on gd. Turf high 73 - 1st of 4 from Lively Lady (10 Jun Salisbury RF 1882) - also 1st of 5 getting 3lb from Ingenious (21 Aug Sandown RF 3793). The winner of a Salisbury novice event and a Sandown nursery so far, she looks best suited by the minimum trip. **R Hannon [2-8] Thurloe Thoroughbreds III.*

his failure to get home in the Queen's Vase at Royal Ascot caused them to have a rethink. Dropped back to a mile and a half in the Group Three Cumberland Lodge Stakes in September, he put up a gritty performance to surge past the tough as teak Rabah. Unexposed over middle-distances, he will make a cracking four-year-old. **H R A Cecil [3-7] H R H Prince Fahd Salman.*

Cape Verdi, sadly retired after an injury in the Derby

CAPRI BHB 115f **RR 113f** 4491[1]

3 ch c Generous (IRE) 11.5f **(82)** - Island Jamboree (USA) (Explodent (USA)) 9.4f **(87)**

Form - 112321

Record	**1998** -	1st:3	2nd:2	3rd:1	Ran:6
	Pre1998 -	1st:0	2nd:1	3rd:0	Ran:1

Win Prizemoney £41,699 *Total Prizemoney* £57,518

Wins	*** 1998**	Spt	Ascot	(G-F)	G3	12f	113	<
	*** 1998**	May	Newmar	(G-S)		12f	99+	
	*** 1998**	Apr	Newmar	(G-S)		12f	93+	

1998 Turf 3-6: (10f, 12f 3-3, 15f, 16f) (gd 3-5, frm)

Scopey, Group-class colt, effective 12 to 16f, acts on gd. Turf high 113 - 1st of 9 getting 3lb from Rabah (26 Spt Ascot RF 4491). Connections seemed convinced he was an out-and-out stayer, but

CAPRIOARA BHB 30f **RR 45f** 4990[3]

3 b f Sharpo 7.5f **(68)** - Cominna (Dominion) 8.5f **(63)**

Form - 8000003

Record 1998 - 1st:0 2nd:0 3rd:1 Ran:7

Win Prizemoney £0 *Total Prizemoney* £360

1998 Turf 0-7: (5f, 7f 2, 8f 3, 10f) (sft, gd 4, frm 2)

Moderate filly. Turf high 45. **J L Harris [0-7] Mrs B Long.*

CAPRIOLO (IRE) BHB 88f **RR 89df** 4053[15]

2 ch c Priolo (USA) 10.9f **(71)** - Carroll's Canyon (IRE) (Hatim (USA))

Form - 3430

Record 1998 - 1st:0 2nd:0 3rd:2 Ran:4

Win Prizemoney £0 *Total Prizemoney* £2,643

1998 Turf 0-4: (6f 2, 7f, 8f) (g-f 2, frm 2)

Useful colt. Turf high 89 (1st run) - 3rd of 10 to Agreeable (30 May Newmarket 6f g-f RF 1609). **R Hannon [0-4] S L Partnership.*

CAPTAIN CARAT BHB 35f42a **RR 42f 42a** 4130[14]

7 gr g Handsome Sailor 6.6f **(53)** - Gem of Gold (Jellaby) 6.4f **(58)**
Form - 80860304400
Record 1998 - 1st:0 2nd:0 3rd:1 Ran:11
Pre1998 - 1st:6 2nd:9 3rd:10 Ran:80
Win Prizemoney £22,411 *Total Prizemoney* £40,337
Wins 1997 May Catter (G-F) C 5f 57
1996 May Newcas (GD) H 5f 62 65 <
1996 Apr Pontef (GD) H 5f 60 61
1995 May Doncas (G-F) H 6f 59 60
1994 Jly Nottin (G-F) H 6.1f 64 65 <
1994 Jun Doncas (G-F) H 6f 59 63
1998 Turf 0-8: (5f 3, 6f 5) (g-s, gd 2, frm 5) 1998 AW 0-3: (5f, 6f 2) (Equi, Fibr 2)
Moderate gelding, effective 5 to 6f, best at 6f, acts on gd to frm - acts on AW, has worn blinkers, likes left handed tracks, likes tight tracks. Turf high 42. AW high 32. He is not the easiest of rides, and performs best in blinkers. He requires luck in running and is capable of fair form when things go his way.
**D W Chapman [0-11] David Chapman (from Ronald Thompson [0-1] Nov 1997).*

CAPTAIN HARRY **RR 62f** 1298[11]

2 b g Safawan 6.6f **(60)** - Mrs Feathers (Pyjama Hunt) 11.1f **(38)**
Form - 200
Record 1998 - 1st:0 2nd:1 3rd:0 Ran:3
Win Prizemoney £0 *Total Prizemoney* £714
1998 Turf 0-3: (5f 3) (gd 3)
Currently average gelding. Turf high 62 (1st run) - 2nd of 10 getting 7lb from Diablo Dancer (7 Apr Nottingham 5f gd RF 0586). (DEAD) **Martyn Wane [0-3] Mrs C M Barlow.*

CAPTAIN JACK BHB 81f **RR 82f** 4850[10]

8 b g Salse (USA) 10.9f **(71)** - Sanctuary (Welsh Pageant) 10f **(65)**
Form - 450
Record 1998 - 1st:0 2nd:0 3rd:0 Ran:3
Pre1998 - 1st:5 2nd:2 3rd:0 Ran:17
Win Prizemoney £30,466 *Total Prizemoney* £33,486
Wins * 1997 Jly Newbur (G-F) H 16f 85 86
1994 Aug Newcas (FRM) H 16.1f 88 93 <
1994 Aug Newbur (GD) H 16f 81 83
1994 Jly Newbur (G-F) H 16f 73 73+
1994 Jun Yarmou (GD) H 14.1f 68 72
1998 Turf 0-3: (16f 2, 18f) (gd 3)
Decent gelding, has worn blinkers. Turf high 82 (began Jly). Consistent.
**M C Pipe [2-12] Clive Smith (from L M Cumani [4-13] Oct 1994).*

CAPTAIN JONES (IRE) BHB 38f **RR 9f** 4922[13]

3 ch g Imp Society (USA) 7.1f **(63)** - Thatcherite (Final Straw) 7.9f **(64)**
Form - 08000
Record 1998 - 1st:0 2nd:0 3rd:0 Ran:5
Pre1998 - 1st:0 2nd:0 3rd:1 Ran:4
Win Prizemoney £0 *Total Prizemoney* £540
1998 Turf 0-3: (7f, 8f, 14f) (g-s, gd, g-f) 1998 AW 0-2: (5f, 12f) (Fibr 2)
Workmanlike, very poor gelding, has worn blinkers. Turf high 9. AW high 7.
**A T Murphy [0-1] E H Jones (Paints) Ltd (from M A Buckley [0-4] Jly 1998).*

CAPTAIN LOGAN (IRE) BHB 84f **RR 91f** 4106[9]

3 b c Fairy King (USA) 7.7f **(75)** - Heaven High (High Line) 10.3f **(70)**
Form - 2120
Record 1998 - 1st:1 2nd:2 3rd:0 Ran:4
Pre1998 - 1st:0 2nd:0 3rd:0 Ran:2
Win Prizemoney £3,548 *Total Prizemoney* £6,594
Wins * 1998 Jun Ayr (GD) 7f 91 <
1998 Turf 1-4: (7f 1-3, 8f) (gd 1-3, frm)
Scopey, useful colt, effective 7 to 8f, best at 7f, acts on gd, has worn blinkers. Turf high 91 - 1st of 6 giving 5lb to Be Practical (19 Jun Ayr RF 2115). Has plenty of ability, and won an Ayr maiden quite nicely, although he does not look the sort to help his jockeys. **D R Loder [1-6] Lucayan Stud.*

CAPTAIN MCCLOY (USA) BHB 36f44a **RR 41f 44a** 4574[13]

3 ch g Lively One (USA) - Fly Me First (USA) (Herbager) 13f **(65)**
Form - 0783870
Record 1998 - 1st:0 2nd:0 3rd:1 Ran:7
Pre1998 - 1st:0 2nd:0 3rd:1 Ran:7
Win Prizemoney £0 *Total Prizemoney* £965
1998 Turf 0-6: (9f, 10f 2, 11f 2, 12f) (gd 2, g-f, frm 3) 1998 AW 0-1: (10f) (Equi)
Scopey, moderate gelding, effective 8f, acts on frm, has worn blinkers. Turf high 41. Consistent.
**N E Berry [0-7] D W Smith (from Mrs J R Ramsden [0-7] Oct 1997).*

CAPTAIN MILLER BHB 62f **RR 85f** 4835[4]

2 b c Batshoof 9.5f **(66)** - Miller's Gait (Mill Reef (USA)) 10.5f **(78)**
Form - 765210656564
Record 1998 - 1st:1 2nd:1 3rd:0 Ran:12
Win Prizemoney £2,070 *Total Prizemoney* £3,153
Wins * 1998 Jun Lingfi (G-S) 7f 82+ <
1998 Turf 1-12: (5f 3, 6f 2, 7f 1-7) (g-s 3, gd 1-3, g-f, frm 5)
Useful colt, effective 6 to 7f, acts on gd to frm. Turf high 85 - 2nd of 6 to Dillionaire (28 May Brighton 6f frm RF 1548) - also 1st of 10 giving 1lb to Jack Goodman (13 Jun Lingfield RF 1966).
**M R Channon [1-12] John Carey.*

CAPTAIN PICARD BHB 28f **RR** 2480a[7]

4 b g Today and Tomorrow 6.2f **(45)** - Nimble Dancer (Northern Wizard)
Form - 7
Record 1998 - 1st:0 2nd:0 3rd:0 Ran:1
Pre1998 - 1st:0 2nd:0 3rd:0 Ran:3
1998 Turf 0-1: (9f) (gd)
Leggy, very poor gelding - 7th of 8 giving 9lb to Keys Seminar (25 Jun Les Landes 9f gd RF 2480a).
**H J Manners [0-2] (from D C O'Brien [0-3] Jly 1997).*

CAPTAIN RON (IRE) **RR 42f** 4997[9]

2 b c Marju (IRE) 9.2f **(76)** - Callas Star (Chief Singer) 8.9f **(66)**
Form - 00
Record 1998 - 1st:0 2nd:0 3rd:0 Ran:2
1998 Turf 0-2: (7f 2) (sft, gd)
Currently moderate colt. Turf high 42 (began Oct).
**T J Naughton [0-2] The Awayday Partnership.*

CAPTAIN SCOTT (IRE) BHB 85f **RR 86f** 2738[6]

4 b g Polar Falcon (USA) 9f **(74)** - Camera Girl (Kalaglow) 9.8f **(67)**
Form - 63326
Record 1998 - 1st:0 2nd:1 3rd:2 Ran:5
Pre1998 - 1st:2 2nd:0 3rd:1 Ran:5
Win Prizemoney £6,970 *Total Prizemoney* £13,240
Wins * 1997 Jly Ayr (G-F) 10f 84 <
* 1997 *Mar Southw (STD) 8f 70+*
1998 Turf 0-5: (8f 2, 10f 3) (g-s, gd 3, frm)
Unfurnished, useful gelding, effective 8 to 10f, best at 8f, acts on gd to frm, best on gd, does well at York. Turf high 88 - 3rd of 18 giving 4lb to High Spirits (2 May Thirsk 8f gd RF 0981). Consistent. Progressive at three, he has been performing well in useful company of late, and was unlucky in running in the John Smith's Cup. Did not run again, but can win a nice handicap for his shrewd trainer. **J A Glover [2-10] The Write State Partnership.*

CAPTAIN'S DAY BHB 35f35a **RR 35f 35a** 1724a[6]

6 ch g Ballacashtal (CAN) 7.9f **(51)** - Seymour Ann (Krayyan) 8.5f **(49)**
Form - 6507766
Record 1998 - 1st:0 2nd:0 3rd:0 Ran:3
Pre1998 - 1st:4 2nd:2 3rd:3 Ran:40
Win Prizemoney £13,010 *Total Prizemoney* £18,755
Wins * 1997 *Mar Lingfi (STD) H 10f 40 48*
* 1997 *Feb Lingfi (STD) 10f 50*
1994 Spt Leices (GD) 7f 78
1994 Aug Salisb (G-F) C 7f 73
1998 Turf 0-1: (9f) (g-f) 1998 AW 0-2: (10f, 12f) (Equi 2)
Very moderate gelding, effective 8 to 10f, best at 10f, - acts on AW, best on Equi, has worn blinkers, favours left handed tracks, favours tight tracks. AW high 21.
**H J Collingridge [2-17] (from T G Mills [2-27] Spt 1996).*

CAPTAIN'S LOG BHB 78f **RR 83f** 4966[8]

3 b c Slip Anchor 12.7f **(75)** - Cradle of Love (USA) (Roberto (USA)) 10f **(76)**

Form - 671751624008
Record 1998 - 1st:2 2nd:1 3rd:0 Ran:12
Win Prizemoney £10,787 *Total Prizemoney* £15,687
Wins * **1998** Jun Newcas (GD) H 9f 73 76 <
* **1998** May Warwic (GD) 8f 74
1998 Turf 2-12: (8f 1-5, 9f 1-1, 10f 6) (sft 2, g-s 1-4, g-f 1-3, frm 3)
Light-framed, decent colt, effective 8 to 10f, best at 10f, acts on g-s to g-f, best on g-f, likes left handed tracks. Turf high 83 - 2nd of 10 getting 7lb from Himself (2 Aug Newcastle 10f g-f RF 3292) - also 1st of 13 giving 10lb to Saintes (26 Jun Newcastle RF 2309). Generally running well in 1998, although his come from behind style means he sometimes encounters trouble in running.
**M Bell [2-12] Christopher Wright.*

CAPTIVATING (IRE) BHB 35f60a **RR 36f 60a** 4001[10]

3 b f Wolfhound (USA) 7.3f **(71)** - Winning Appeal (FR) (Law Society (USA)) 9.9f **(70)**
Form - 700007000030
Record 1998 - 1st:0 2nd:0 3rd:1 Ran:12
Pre1998 - 1st:0 2nd:0 3rd:0 Ran:3
Win Prizemoney £0 *Total Prizemoney* £311
1998 Turf 0-10: (5f 4, 6f 3, 8f, 10f 2) (g-s, gd 3, g-f 3, frm 2, hrd) 1998 AW 0-2: (7f, 8f) (Equi, Fibr)
Light-framed, very moderate filly, has worn blinkers. Turf high 36. AW high 13.
**Mrs S Lamyman [0-9] John Purcell (from R Hannon [0-6] Mar 1998).*

CARABINE (USA) BHB 60f **RR 56f** 4668[14]

2 gr f Dehere (USA) - Caracciola (FR) (Zeddaan) 9f **(76)**
Form - 060
Record 1998 - 1st:0 2nd:0 3rd:0 Ran:3
1998 Turf 0-3: (6f 3) (gd 2, frm)
Currently fair filly. Turf high 56 (began Spt).
**Sir Mark Prescott [0-3] Miss K Rausing.*

CARADOC BHB 49f52a **RR 53f 52a** 1902[4]

3 ch c Bustino 11f **(64)** - Hathaway (Connaught) 7.7f **(63)**
Form - 7074
Record 1998 - 1st:0 2nd:0 3rd:0 Ran:3
Pre1998 - 1st:0 2nd:0 3rd:0 Ran:3
1998 Turf 0-3: (12f, 14f 2) (g-s, gd, g-f)
Leggy, fair colt. Turf high 53. **S C Williams [0-6] John Hurd.*

CARAMBO BHB 71f85a **RR 77f 85a** 4751[9]

3 b f Rambo Dancer (CAN) 8.4f **(59)** - Light the Way (Nicholas Bill) 10.1f **(56)**
Form - 36022604700
Record 1998 - 1st:0 2nd:2 3rd:1 Ran:11
Pre1998 - 1st:2 2nd:3 3rd:0 Ran:8
Win Prizemoney £6,218 *Total Prizemoney* £13,750
Wins * 1997 *Oct Wolver (STD) H* *7f* *82* *86* <
* 1997 *Jly Wolver (STD) H* *6f* *77*
1998 Turf 0-11: (6f 3, 7f 5, 8f 3) (sft, g-s 2, gd 4, g-f 2, frm, hrd)
Workmanlike, decent filly, effective 6 to 8f, best at 7f, acts on gd - acts on Fibr, prefers left handed tracks. Turf high 81 - 2nd of 16 getting 6lb from Tom Dougal (14 May York 8f gd RF 1223).
**J L Eyre [2-19] C H Stephenson & Partners.*

CARATI BHB 72f **RR 70f** 1614[7]

4 b f Selkirk (USA) 7.9f **(76)** - Clytie (USA) (El Gran Senor (USA)) 9.6f **(76)**
Form - 7
Record 1998 - 1st:0 2nd:0 3rd:0 Ran:1
Pre1998 - 1st:1 2nd:1 3rd:0 Ran:10
Win Prizemoney £2,761 *Total Prizemoney* £6,020
Wins 1996 Jly Nottin (G-F) 6.1f 76 <
1998 Turf 0-1: (8f) (g-f)
Leggy, above-average filly, has worn blinkers.
**C N Allen [0-1] Downhill Racing (from R Boss [1-10] Aug 1997).*

CARBON BHB 67f **RR 68f** 4459[15]

3 b g Batshoof 9.5f **(66)** - Reyah (Young Generation) 7.7f **(63)**
Form - 0670840
Record 1998 - 1st:0 2nd:0 3rd:0 Ran:7
Pre1998 - 1st:1 2nd:0 3rd:1 Ran:4
Win Prizemoney £4,260 *Total Prizemoney* £5,313
Wins 1997 Jun York (G-S) 6f 75+ <
1998 Turf 0-7: (6f 3, 7f 3, 8f) (gd 2, g-f 2, frm 3)
Scopey, average gelding, effective 6f, acts on frm. Turf high 68. Consistent. Not at his best this term.
**Lady Herries [0-7] I R Corke (from D Morley [1-4] Aug 1997).*

CARBURTON BHB 84f77a **RR 82f 77a** 4226[13]

5 b g Rock City 8.8f **(62)** - Arminda (Blakeney) 10.5f **(64)**
Form - 66115140
Record 1998 - 1st:3 2nd:0 3rd:0 Ran:8
Pre1998 - 1st:3 2nd:3 3rd:2 Ran:15
Win Prizemoney £29,566 *Total Prizemoney* £35,343
Wins * **1998** Jly Cheste (G-F) H 12.3f 81 82
* **1998** Jun Warwic (SFT) H 12.5f 70 76
* **1998** Jun Thirsk (GD) H 12f 70 75
* 1997 Jun Windso (G-F) H 10f 65 70
* 1995 Oct Doncas (G-F) H 7f 80 89 <
* 1995 Oct Haydoc (SFT) 7.1f 80+
1998 Turf 3-8: (10f 2, 12f 2-5, 13f 1-1) (g-s, gd 1-1, g-f 1-3, frm 1-3)
Decent gelding, effective 10 to 13f, acts on gd to frm, has worn blinkers, prefers tight tracks, excels at Windsor. Turf high 82 - 1st of 6 giving 4lb to Eagle's Cross (10 Jly Chester RF 2676) - also 1st of 5 giving 1lb to Andaman (8 Jun Warwick RF 1814). A handicapper with a turn of foot, he was in fine form in the summer, winning three times. According to his trainer, he will stay fourteen furlongs. **J A Glover [6-23] Bison Materials Handling.*

CARDIGAN BAY (IRE) BHB 94f **RR 96f** 5078[26]

4 b g Slip Anchor 12.7f **(75)** - Welsh Dancer (Welsh Saint) 7.6f **(64)**
Form - 4535350
Record 1998 - 1st:0 2nd:0 3rd:2 Ran:7
Pre1998 - 1st:1 2nd:0 3rd:1 Ran:2
Win Prizemoney £4,110 *Total Prizemoney* £22,877
Wins 1997 Aug Cork (SFT) 9f 87+ <
1998 Turf 0-7: (8f, 10f 5, 12f) (sft, g-s, g-f 4, frm)
Very useful gelding, effective 9 to 10f, best at 10f, acts on sft to frm, best on g-f. Turf high 96 - 3rd of 19 giving 2lb to Brilliant Red (19 Spt Newbury 10f g-f RF 4379). Consistent. A lightly-raced ex-Irish performer, he ran very well in a hot race at Ascot in June on his handicap debut before running a good third in the John Smith's Cup. Possibly still feeling the effects of that race when subsequently disappointing, he might not have stayed the twelve furlongs at Ascot, but is more than capable of winning handicaps at around ten furlongs next term.
**Lady Herries [0-7] E Reitel (from J Oxx in IRE [1-2] Aug 1997).*

CAREFUL TIMING BHB 96f **RR 83f** 4517[3]

3 b f Caerleon (USA) 10.9f **(79)** - By Charter (Shirley Heights) 10.3f **(74)**
Form - 3173
Record 1998 - 1st:1 2nd:0 3rd:2 Ran:4
Pre1998 - 1st:0 2nd:0 3rd:0 Ran:1
Win Prizemoney £4,503 *Total Prizemoney* £8,518
Wins * **1998** Jly Newmar (G-F) 12f 81 <
1998 Turf 1-4: (10f 2, 12f 1-2) (gd, g-f, frm 1-2)
Lengthy, decent filly. Turf high 83 - also 1st of 10 from Shalimar Garden (24 Jly Newmarket RF 3078).
**Sir Michael Stoute [1-5] R Barnett.*

CAREQUICK **RR 61f** 3505[12]

2 ch f Risk Me (FR) 8f **(53)** - Miss Serlby (Runnett) 7f **(59)**
Form - 08050
Record 1998 - 1st:0 2nd:0 3rd:0 Ran:5
1998 Turf 0-5: (5f 3, 6f 2) (gd 2, g-f, frm 2)
Average filly. Turf high 56. **A Bailey [0-5] Carequick Ltd.*

CARHUE LASS (IRE) **RR 94f** 4689a[7]

4 b f Common Grounds 8.1f **(66)** - Return Journey 00
Form - 272047
1998 Turf 0-6: (5f 6) (sft, g-s, gd 3, frm)
Useful filly, effective 5f, acts on sft. Turf high 110 (1st run) - 2nd of 5 giving 7lb to Lidanna (7 May Tipperary 5f sft RF 1180a). She could not repeat 1997's Listed win and is hard to place.
**P O'Leary in IRE [1-15] P O'Leary.*

CARIAD CYMRU BHB 52f **RR 52f** 1029[10]

4 b br g Welsh Captain 7.2f **(54)** - Daddy's Darling (Mummy's Pet) 7.7f **(60)**
Form - 70

Record **1998 -** 1st:0 2nd:0 3rd:0 Ran:2
Pre1998 - 1st:0 2nd:0 3rd:0 Ran:1
1998 Turf 0-2: (7f, 8f) (sft, g-f)
Light-framed, currently fair gelding. Turf high 52.
**J L Spearing [0-2] Mrs Richard Evans (from R Akehurst [0-1] May 1996).*

CARIBBEAN MONARCH (IRE) BHB 97f RR 100f 2014[4]

3 b c Fairy King (USA) 7.7f **(75)** - Whos The Blonde (Cure The Blues (USA)) 9.5f **(63)**
Form - 114
Record **1998 -** 1st:2 2nd:0 3rd:0 Ran:3
Pre1998 - 1st:0 2nd:0 3rd:0 Ran:1
Win Prizemoney £9,981 *Total Prizemoney* £12,081
Wins *** 1998** Jun Windso (G-F) 6f 93 <
*** 1998** Apr Newmar (G-S) 6f 83
1998 Turf 2-3: (6f 2-2, 8f) (gd 1-2, g-f 1-1)
Scopey, very useful colt. Turf high 100 - 4th of 31 giving 6lb to Plan-B (16 Jun Ascot 8f gd RF 2014) - also 1st of 8 from Tango (1 Jun Windsor RF 1636). He showed little on his sole outing as a juvenile, but improved markedly over the winter as he went on to win his first two starts in 1998. Both of those races were over six furlongs and, as expected, he showed improved form when stepped-up to a mile, finishing fourth in the ultra competitive Britannia Handicap at Royal Ascot. He went missing after that effort, but remains an interesting prospect and should do well as a four-year-old provided all is well. **Sir Michael Stoute [2-4] W H Scott.*

CARINO MIO (ITY) RR 95f 3057a[3]

3 ch c Nordance (USA) 7.4f **(69)** - Chalumeau (Relko) 9.9f **(59)**
Form - 3
1998 Turf 0-1: (5f) (gd)
Currently very useful colt. **A Manzi in ITY [0-1] Scuderia Green Star.*

CARINTHIA (IRE) BHB 72f RR 70f 4660[3]

3 br f Tirol 8.1f **(64)** - Hot Lavender (CAN) (Shadeed (USA)) 8.2f **(70)**
Form - 351043
Record **1998 -** 1st:1 2nd:0 3rd:2 Ran:6
Pre1998 - 1st:0 2nd:1 3rd:0 Ran:1
Win Prizemoney £2,981 *Total Prizemoney* £5,969
Wins *** 1998** Aug Salisb (G-F) H 6f 68 70 <
1998 Turf 1-6: (6f 1-2, 7f 3, 8f) (gd, frm 1-5)
Light-framed, above-average filly, effective 6f, acts on g-f to frm. Turf high 71 - also 1st of 9 giving 12lb to Broadway Melody (7 Aug Salisbury RF 3447). **C F Wall [1-7] Hintlesham Racing.*

CARLASANTA (IRE) BHB 27f33a RR 25f 33a 3638[4]

3 ch f Imp Society (USA) 7.1f **(63)** - Ski Slope (Niniski (USA)) 10.6f **(65)**
Form - 006844
Record **1998 -** 1st:0 2nd:0 3rd:0 Ran:6
Pre1998 - 1st:0 2nd:0 3rd:0 Ran:3
1998 Turf 0-4:(10f, 11f, 12f 2) (sft, frm 3)1998 AW 0-2:(12f, 14f) (Fibr 2)
Unfurnished, very moderate filly. Turf high 25. AW high 34 (began Jly). **A G Newcombe [0-9] Advanced Marketing Services Ltd.*

CARLTON (IRE) BHB 52a RR 69f 4988[8]

4 ch g Thatching 7.8f **(69)** - Hooray Lady (Ahonoora) 8.1f **(73)**
Form - 02502151232368
Record **1998 -** 1st:2 2nd:4 3rd:2 Ran:14
Pre1998 - 1st:1 2nd:0 3rd:1 Ran:11
Win Prizemoney £11,249 *Total Prizemoney* £19,031
Wins *** 1998** Jly Newbur (G-F) H 7f 60 62 <
*** 1998** Jun Windso (GD) H 6f 55 58
* 1997 May Beverl (GD) H 7.5f 53 60
1998 Turf 2-13: (6f 1-4, 7f 1-6, 8f 3) (sft, g-s 2, gd 4, g-f 2-4, frm 2) 1998 AW 0-1: (6f) (Fibr)
Scopey, average gelding, effective 6 to 8f, acts on g-s to frm, best on frm, has worn blinkers (extremely effectively), likes right handed tracks. Turf high 69 - 2nd of 21 getting 5lb from Peppiatt (12 Spt Goodwood 6f g-s RF 4246) - also 1st of 10 getting 12lb from Salty Jack (17 Jly Newbury RF 2877). Consistent. In good heart for most of the season, he only just stays seven furlongs.
**G Lewis [3-25] City Slickers.*

CARLYS QUEST BHB 84f80a RR 86f 80a 5151[2]

4 ch g Primo Dominie 7.2f **(67)** - Tuppy (USA) (Sharpen Up) 8.3f **(67)**
Form - 1315722322
Record **1998 -** 1st:2 2nd:4 3rd:2 Ran:10
Pre1998 - 1st:0 2nd:0 3rd:2 Ran:11
Win Prizemoney £10,673 *Total Prizemoney* £30,290
Wins *** 1998** May Warwic (G-F) H 10.8f 70 79 <
*** 1998** May Newmar (G-S) H 10f 64 70
1998 Turf2-10:(10f 1-4,11f 1-1, 12f 4,13f)(sft, g-s, gd 1-2, g-f 3, frm 1-3)
Strong, useful gelding, effective 11 to 12f, best at 12f, acts on sft to frm, often wears blinkers (extremely effectively). Turf high 86 - 2nd of 23 getting 26lb from Yavana's Pace (7 Nov Doncaster 12f gd RF 5151) - also 1st of 8 giving 9lb to Brave Noble (23 May Warwick RF 1437). Consistent. Beat a big field in a first-time visor at Newmarket on his reappearance and has generally run with credit since, ending his campaign with a second in the November Handicap. Doesn't do anything quickly, and is vulnerable to rivals with a turn of foot.
**J Neville [2-24] John Williams Transport (Newport) Ltd.*

CARMARTHEN (IRE) RR 74f 3624[9]

2 ch g Hamas (IRE) 8f **(72)** - Solar Attraction (IRE) (Salt Dome (USA))
Form - 2650
Record **1998 -** 1st:0 2nd:1 3rd:0 Ran:4
Win Prizemoney £0 *Total Prizemoney* £1,045
1998 Turf 0-4: (5f 4) (gd, g-f, frm 2)
Above-average gelding. Turf high 74.
**I A Balding [0-4] Elite Racing Club.*

CARMARTHEN BAY BHB 35f82a RR 40f 82a 4589[14]

5 ch h Prionsaa 8f **(48)** - Pattie's Grey (Valiyar) 8.5f **(73)**
Form - 008000
Record **1998 -** 1st:0 2nd:0 3rd:0 Ran:6
Pre1998 - 1st:2 2nd:2 3rd:1 Ran:14
Win Prizemoney £6,856 *Total Prizemoney* £10,086
Wins 1996 *Feb Lingfi (STD) H 8f 77 74*
1995 *Dec Lingfi (STD) 6f 81* <
1998 Turf 0-5: (7f, 8f, 10f 3) (g-s 2, gd 3) 1998 AW 0-1: (7f) (Fibr)
Moderate colt, has worn blinkers. Turf high 47.
**B J Llewellyn [0-8] D R W Jones (from G L Moore [2-13] Oct 1996).*

CARMINE LAKE (IRE) BHB 110f RR 112f 3164[13]

4 ch f Royal Academy (USA) 7.8f **(77)** - Castilian Queen (USA) (Diesis) 9.3f **(69)**
Form - 060
Record **1998 -** 1st:0 2nd:0 3rd:0 Ran:3
Pre1998 - 1st:3 2nd:0 3rd:2 Ran:8
Win Prizemoney £83,630 *Total Prizemoney* £91,209
Wins * 1997 Oct Longch (G-F) G1 5f 118 <
* 1996 Aug Goodwo (G-F) G3 5f 106
* 1996 Apr Newmar (G-F) 5f 79
1998 Turf 0-3: (5f 2, 6f) (gd 2, frm)
Group-class filly, effective 5f, acted on gd. Turf high 112. Consistent. Proved difficult to train at three due to an arthritic knee and did not make her reappearance until September 1997, but she made up for lost time by landing the Prix de l'Abbaye. She showed plenty of dash on her first two runs of this year and was obviously a top-class sprinter when right, but sadly was destroyed after a gallops accident in August. (DEAD)
**P W Chapple-Hyam [3-11] R E Sangster.*

CARNBREA FIRSTLOVE BHB 69f RR 74f 4676[1]

3 b g Pursuit of Love 9.5f **(69)** - Carnbrea Snip (Robellino (USA)) 7.6f **(80)**
Form - 62731
Record **1998 -** 1st:1 2nd:1 3rd:1 Ran:5
Win Prizemoney £3,629 *Total Prizemoney* £5,369
Wins *** 1998** Oct Redcar (G-S) 6f 50 <
1998 Turf 1-5: (6f 1-3, 7f 2) (gd, g-f 1-2, frm 2)
Strong, above-average gelding, has worn blinkers. Turf high 74 (began Aug) - 2nd of 12 giving 10lb to Discrimination (28 Aug Newmarket 7f frm RF 3931). **W J Haggas [1-5] Carnbrea Ltd.*

CAROL AGAIN BHB 25f43a RR 27f 43a 455[9]

6 b m Kind of Hush 9.6f **(50)** - Lady Carol (Lord Gayle (USA)) 8.8f **(62)**
Form - 881410
Record **1998 -** 1st:2 2nd:0 3rd:0 Ran:6
Pre1998 - 1st:3 2nd:5 3rd:2 Ran:37
Win Prizemoney £11,802 *Total Prizemoney* £16,707
Wins *** 1998** *Mar Southw (STD) H 14f 40 46*
*** 1998** *Feb Southw (STD) H 11f 35 38*

*1997 Feb Southw (STD) H 11f 39 43
*1996 Apr Southw (STD) H 12f 40 48+ <
*1996 Apr Southw (STD) H 11f 33 39
1998 AW 2-6: (11f 1-3, 12f 2, 14f 1-1) (Fibr 2-6)
Moderate mare, effective 11 to 14f, best at 12f, - acts on Fibr, has worn blinkers, prefers left handed tracks, excels at Southwell. AW high 46 - 1st of 14 getting 1lb from Dulas Bay (11 Mar Southwell RF 0422). Inconsistent. Not the most reliable of sorts these days, she pops up from time to time in modest company on sand, as when scoring at Southwell in February and March. Her recent victories have all been over middle distances on that track.
**N Bycroft [5-47] J G Lumsden.*

CAROL GRIMES BHB 42f **RR 40f** 4962[11]
3 b f Beveled (USA) 6.9f **(64)** - Come to Good (Swing Easy (USA)) 6.5f **(55)**
Form - 300600
Record 1998 - 1st:0 2nd:0 3rd:1 Ran:6
Pre1998 - 1st:0 2nd:0 3rd:1 Ran:2
Win Prizemoney £0 *Total Prizemoney* £562
1998 Turf 0-4: (6f 3, 7f) (sft, gd 2, frm) 1998 AW 0-2: (6f 2) (Fibr 2)
Unfurnished, moderate filly. Turf high 40. AW high 40 (began Jly).
**J S Moore [0-8] J K Grimes.*

CAROLINE'S PET (IRE) BHB 47f **RR 46f** 3434[8]
3 b f Contract Law (USA) 8.9f **(54)** - Princess Roxanne (Prince Tenderfoot (USA)) 9f **(61)**
Form - 048
Record 1998 - 1st:0 2nd:0 3rd:0 Ran:3
Pre1998 - 1st:0 2nd:0 3rd:0 Ran:4
Win Prizemoney £0 *Total Prizemoney* £236
1998 Turf 0-3: (6f, 10f, 11f) (gd 2, g-f)
Light-framed, moderate filly, has worn blinkers. Turf high 22.
**A Bailey [0-7] G J White.*

CAROL SINGER (USA) BHB 71f61a **RR 73df 61a** 717[6]
3 b f Geiger Counter (USA) 7.8f **(85)** - Wake Up Noel (USA) (Nureyev (USA)) 8.7f **(78)**
Form - 4066
Record 1998 - 1st:0 2nd:0 3rd:0 Ran:1
Pre1998 - 1st:0 2nd:2 3rd:2 Ran:9
Win Prizemoney £0 *Total Prizemoney* £2,852
1998 Turf 0-1: (5f) (g-s)
Lengthy, above-average filly, effective 5f, acts on frm.
**M Johnston [0-10] & Mrs G Middlebrook.*

CAROUSAL (IRE) BHB 44f **RR 52f** 4136[14]
2 b f Distinctly North (USA) 7.4f **(63)** - Mountain Hop (IRE) (Tirol)
Form - 06040
Record 1998 - 1st:0 2nd:0 3rd:0 Ran:5
1998 Turf 0-5: (5f, 6f 3, 8f) (g-f 4, frm)
Fair filly. Turf high 52. **R Hannon [0-5] T S M Cunningham.*

CAROUSE BHB 52f **RR 53df** 1115[7]
3 br g Petong 7.6f **(58)** - Merry Rous (Rousillon (USA)) 8.2f **(74)**
Form - 247
Record 1998 - 1st:0 2nd:1 3rd:0 Ran:3
Pre1998 - 1st:0 2nd:0 3rd:0 Ran:5
Win Prizemoney £0 *Total Prizemoney* £600
1998 Turf 0-3: (8f 2, 10f) (sft, g-s, frm)
Workmanlike, fair gelding. Turf high 53. He did not show much in '97, and after running well in a Nottingham seller on his reappearance, disappointed in heavy ground next time.
**M R Channon [0-8] John Carey.*

CARRADIUM BHB 67f **RR 62f** 3933[6]
2 b c Presidium 7.5f **(56)** - Carrapateira (Gunner B) 11.2f **(58)**
Form - 56556
Record 1998 - 1st:0 2nd:0 3rd:0 Ran:5
1998 Turf 0-5: (6f 2, 7f 3) (gd 2, frm 3)
Average colt. Turf high 62. **C W Fairhurst [0-5] R Shiels.*

CARRANITA (IRE) BHB 95f **RR 97f** 5152[9]
8 b m Anita's Prince 6f **(62)** - Take More (GER) (Frontal) 6.4f **(64)**
Form - 42215485624660
Record 1998 - 1st:1 2nd:3 3rd:0 Ran:14
Pre1998 - 1st:15 2nd:4 3rd:5 Ran:59
Win Prizemoney £100,096 *Total Prizemoney* £134,957
Wins *1998 May Haydoc (G-S) 6f 106
*1997 Oct Nottin (GD) 6.1f 96
*1996 Aug Newmar (G-F) L 6f 108 <
*1996 Jly York (GD) L 6f 107
*1996 Apr Thirsk (G-F) 6f 100
*1996 Mar Beverl (GD) L 5f 93
*1995 Nov Doncas (G-F) L 6f 104
*1995 Spt Yarmou (GD) 6f 103
*1994 Oct York (G-S) H 7f 100 94
*1994 Aug Chepst (GD) 7.1f 98
*1994 May Goodwo (SFT) H 6f 92 91
1998 Turf 1-14: (6f 1-12, 7f 2) (sft 2, g-s 2, gd 1-6, g-f 2, frm 2)
Very useful mare, effective 6 to 7f, best at 6f, acts on gd to frm, excels at Newmarket. Turf high 106 - 1st of 6 giving 5lb to Superior Premium (2 May Haydock RF 0967). They do not come much tougher than this popular mare, who is often at her best in the opening weeks of the season as she needs the ground on the easy side. Expect another early blitz if she stays in training.
**B Palling [16-73] Humphrey Okeke & Mrs Rena Davies.*

CARREAMIA BHB 45f49a **RR 41f 49a** 957[12]
5 b m Weldnaas (USA) 8.4f **(55)** - Carribean Tyme(Tyrnavos) 10.1f **(55)**
Form - 00
Record 1998 - 1st:0 2nd:0 3rd:0 Ran:2
Pre1998 - 1st:0 2nd:0 3rd:2 Ran:9
Win Prizemoney £0 *Total Prizemoney* £1,067
1998 Turf 0-1: (7f) (g-f) 1998 AW 0-1: (7f) (Fibr)
Moderate filly, effective 6f, acts on g-s to g-f.
**J L Eyre [0-11] J Ellis.*

CARRIE POOTER BHB 66f **RR 73f** 3937[11]
2 b f Tragic Role (USA) 9.4f **(63)** - Ginny Binny (Ahonoora) 8.1f **(73)**
Form - 05140
Record 1998 - 1st:1 2nd:0 3rd:0 Ran:5
Win Prizemoney £2,940 *Total Prizemoney* £2,940
Wins *1998 May Redcar (G-F) 6f 73 <
1998 Turf 1-5: (5f 2, 6f 1-3) (g-s, gd, g-f 1-1, frm 2)
Above-average filly. Turf high 73 - 1st of 14 from Midnight Orchid (26 May Redcar RF 1474). **T D Barron [1-5] Stephen Woodall.*

CARROLLS MARC (IRE) BHB 27f31a **RR 17f 31a** 2899[10]
10 b g Horage 11.4f **(58)** - Rare Find (Rarity) 10.1f **(60)**
Form - 073185642460
Record 1998 - 1st:1 2nd:1 3rd:1 Ran:12
Pre1998 - 1st:13 2nd:6 3rd:12 Ran:68
Win Prizemoney £33,929 *Total Prizemoney* £44,023
Wins **1998 Mar Wolver (STD) 16.2f 42*
1997 May Lingfi (STD) SH 16f 40 42
1997 Apr Southw (STD) C 12f 48
1996 Jan Lingfi (STD) 12f 55
1996 Jan Lingfi (STD) SH 12f 40 45
1994 Jly Wolver (STD) C 12f 59
1994 Mar Wolver (STD) C 12f 47
1994 Jan Wolver (STD) C 14.8f 61 <
1994 Jan Wolver (STD) H 14.8f 39 45+
1998 Turf 0-1: (15f) (sft) 1998 AW 1-11: (11f, 12f 4, 14f 2, 16f 1-4) (Equi 4, Fibr 1-7)
Moderate gelding, effective 11 to 16f, - acts on AW, best on Fibr, has worn blinkers, favours left handed tracks. AW high 42 - 2nd of 9 getting 12lb from Zorba (18 May Southwell 11f Fibr RF 1305) - also 1st of 4 from Blatant Outburst (21 Mar Wolverhampton RF 0460). He has won his share of All-Weather claimers and sellers over the years, but seems not to run two races alike these days.
**Pat Mitchell [1-12] Mrs G Dunlop (from C Murray [4-17] Jun 1997).*

CARRY THE FLAG BHB 94f **RR 101f** 2667a[2]
3 b c Tenby 10.4f **(76)** - Tamassos (Dance In Time (CAN)) 8.9f **(59)**
Form - 3062
Record 1998 - 1st:0 2nd:1 3rd:1 Ran:4
Pre1998 - 1st:2 2nd:0 3rd:0 Ran:4
Win Prizemoney £6,168 *Total Prizemoney* £19,968
Wins *1997 Oct Warwic (G-F) H 8f 84 91 <
*1997 Jun Thirsk (GD) 7f 62+
1998 Turf 0-4: (10f, 12f 3) (g-s, gd 2, g-f)
Neat, very useful colt, effective 8 to 12f, acts on gd to g-f, best on gd. Turf high 101 - 2nd of 9 to Clapham Common (5 Jly San Siro 12f gd RF 2667a). Inconsistent. A half-brother to Posidonas, he

looked an unlucky loser at York on his reappearance, but failed to progress as expected. He is worth another chance and probably has a decent handicap in him. **P F I Cole [2-8] Luciano Gaucci.*

CARTMEL PARK BHB 82f **RR 82f** 4322[12]

2 ch g Skyliner 6.8f **(51)** - Oh My Oh My (Ballacashtal (CAN)) 5.3f **(50)**
Form - 722212310
Record 1998 - 1st:2 2nd:4 3rd:1 Ran:9
Win Prizemoney £6,415 *Total Prizemoney* £10,711
Wins * **1998** Spt Newcas (GD) 5f 80+ <
* **1998** Jly Mussel (GD) 5f 69
1998 Turf 2-9: (5f 2-9) (g-s, gd 3, g-f, frm 2-4)
Decent gelding, effective 5f, acts on frm. Turf high 82 - 2nd of 5 getting 4lb from Henry Hall (15 Jly Doncaster 5f frm RF 2817) - also 1st of 6 getting 2lb from Shirley Not (8 Spt Newcastle RF 4152). Consistent. **J Berry [2-9] P G Airey & R R Whitton.*

CARVER DOONE BHB 46f43a **RR 59f 43a** 4996[11]

3 b g Tragic Role (USA) 9.4f **(63)** - Miss Milton (Young Christopher) 6f **(61)**
Form - 6020000
Record 1998 - 1st:0 2nd:1 3rd:0 Ran:7
Pre1998 - 1st:0 2nd:0 3rd:0 Ran:2
Win Prizemoney £0 *Total Prizemoney* £880
1998 Turf 0-6: (7f, 8f, 9f, 10f 2, 11f) (g-s, g-f 4, frm) 1998 AW 0-1: (10f) (Equi)
Workmanlike, fair gelding, effective 9f, acts on g-f, has worn blinkers, likes tight tracks. Turf high 59 (began Jly) - 2nd of 10 giving 1lb to Forest Fire (21 Aug Sandown 9f g-f RF 3798). Inconsistent.
**L A Dace [0-2] Trojan Racing (from Major D N Chappell [0-7] Spt 1998).*

CARVER JOHN BHB 35f30a **RR 30f 30a** 4865[11]

3 ch g Sure Blade (USA) 10.6f **(66)** - Dawn Ditty (Song) 7.2f **(61)**
Form - 00000
Record 1998 - 1st:0 2nd:0 3rd:0 Ran:5
Pre1998 - 1st:0 2nd:0 3rd:0 Ran:1
1998 Turf 0-4: (7f, 8f, 11f 2) (gd, g-f 2, frm) 1998 AW 0-1: (7f) (Fibr)
Light-framed, very moderate gelding, has worn blinkers. Turf high 17.
**A Barrow [0-6] Unity Farm Holiday Centre Ltd (from P D Cundell [0-1] May 1997).*

CASA ROSA BHB 38f **RR 39f** 4123[16]

3 b f Casteddu 7.4f **(54)** - Kasarose (Owen Dudley) 8.3f **(61)**
Form - 800
Record 1998 - 1st:0 2nd:0 3rd:0 Ran:3
Pre1998 - 1st:0 2nd:0 3rd:0 Ran:3
1998 Turf 0-2: (7f, 8f) (g-f, frm) 1998 AW 0-1: (7f) (Equi)
Workmanlike, very moderate filly. Turf high 39 (began Aug).
**G M McCourt [0-3] Graham McCourt (from R Hannon [0-3] Jun 1997).*

CASHIKI (IRE) BHB 72f **RR 73f** 4658[4]

2 ch f Case Law 6f **(64)** - Nishiki (USA) (Brogan (USA))
Form - 876211221354
Record 1998 - 1st:3 2nd:3 3rd:1 Ran:12
Win Prizemoney £7,395 *Total Prizemoney* £10,368
Wins * **1998** Aug Pontef (G-F) H 6f 70 73 <
* **1998** Jun Chepst (G-S) C 6.1f 61
* **1998** Jun Lingfi (GD) S 6f 58
1998 Turf 3-10: (5f, 6f 3-6, 7f 3) (g-s, gd 1-4, frm 2-4, hrd) 1998 AW 0-2: (5f 2) (Fibr 2)
Above-average filly, effective 6f, acts on gd to frm, best on frm, likes left handed tracks, likes tight tracks. Turf high 73 - 1st of 16 giving 5lb to Montague Tigg (25 Aug Pontefract RF 3849). AW high 34. Consistent. She gradually improved last season, winning in low grade at Lingfield and Chepstow, but then showing good form in nursery company, winning such an event at Pontefract. Very consistent, she should be able to win over seven.
**B Palling [3-12] The Valley Commandos.*

CASHMERE LADY BHB 70f90a **RR 72f 90a** 5147[5]

6 b m Hubbly Bubbly (USA) 9.5f **(43)** - Choir (High Top) 10.2f **(67)**
Form - 641177050227845
Record 1998 - 1st:2 2nd:2 3rd:0 Ran:14
Pre1998 - 1st:6 2nd:5 3rd:2 Ran:35
Win Prizemoney £30,672 *Total Prizemoney* £46,327
Wins * **1998** Apr Thirsk (G-S) H 8f 73 78
* **1998** *Mar Southw (STD) H 12f 87 89* <
* 1997 Aug Redcar (FRM) H 8f 72 78
* 1997 *Jun Wolver (STD) H 8.5f 76 89* <
* 1997 Jun Thirsk (GD) H 8f 65 70
* 1996 *Mar Wolver (STD) H 8.5f 72 77+*
* 1995 *Dec Wolver (STD) H 7f 65 66*
* 1995 *Nov Wolver (STD) 8.5f 64*
1998 Turf 1-12: (8f 1-2, 9f, 10f 7, 12f, 14f) (sft 2, g-s 1-2, gd 2, g-f 3, frm 2, hrd) 1998 AW 1-2: (9f, 12f 1-1) (Fibr 1-2)
Useful mare, effective 8 to 12f, - acts on Fibr, likes tight tracks. Turf high 78 (1st run). AW high 89 - 1st of 6 giving 12lb to Raed (23 Mar Southwell RF 0466). Best on the All-Weather, she scored on her second start of '98 on the Southwell Fibresand when stepped up to twelve furlongs, but the time of the race was not spectacular and she still has to prove conclusively that she stays. Followed up under a good ride at Thirsk, but held since.
**J L Eyre [8-49] Mrs Sybil Howe.*

CASIMIR (IRE) BHB 78f **RR 81+f** 4643[6]

2 b c Roi Danzig (USA) 10.5f **(62)** - Have A Cut (IRE) (Al Hareb (USA))
Form - 51206
Record 1998 - 1st:1 2nd:1 3rd:0 Ran:5
Win Prizemoney £3,120 *Total Prizemoney* £4,386
Wins * **1998** Jly Beverl (G-F) 5f 81+ <
1998 Turf 1-5: (5f 1-2, 6f 2, 7f) (gd 2, g-f, frm 1-2)
Decent colt. Turf high 81 (began Jly) - 1st of 14 giving 5lb to Cool Katie (14 Jly Beverley RF 2775).
**A C Stewart [1-5] P McGuinness & S J Hammond.*

CASINO CAPTIVE (USA) BHB 105f **RR 103f** 3162[5]

3 gr c Kenmare (FR) 9.6f **(76)**- Captive Island (Northfields(USA)) 9f **(72)**
Form - 11835
Record 1998 - 1st:2 2nd:0 3rd:1 Ran:5
Win Prizemoney £11,819 *Total Prizemoney* £15,304
Wins * **1998** May Chepst (G-F) 12.1f 92
* **1998** May Cheste (GD) 10.3f 99 <
1998 Turf 2-5: (10f 1-2, 12f 1-3) (gd 2, g-f 1-1, frm 1-2)
Light-framed, very useful colt. Turf high 103 - also 1st of 10 from Dancing Phantom (5 May Chester RF 1041). He refused to go in the stalls on his intended debut, but behaved impeccably and won well on his next two starts. Outclassed when tried in Group company, he ran a fine race behind Hitman in a valuable handicap at Newmarket's July Meeting. He is not the most impressive individual to look at, but can gallop and may improve again next term.
**P W Chapple-Hyam [2-5] R E Sangster.*

CASINO ROYALE (IRE) RR 71f 5137[3]

2 b c Royal Academy (USA) 7.8f **(77)** - Sharata (IRE) (Darshaan) 9.9f **(84)**
Form - 3
Record 1998 - 1st:0 2nd:0 3rd:1 Ran:1
Win Prizemoney £0 *Total Prizemoney* £497
1998 Turf 0-1: (7f) (gd)
Currently above-average colt. **J W Hills [0-1] Christopher Wright.*

CASSANDRA GO (IRE) RR 75f 4542[16]

2 gr f Indian Ridge 7.6f **(74)** - Rahaam (USA) (Secreto (USA)) 8.7f **(72)**
Form - 0
Record 1998 - 1st:0 2nd:0 3rd:0 Ran:1
1998 Turf 0-1: (7f) (frm)
Currently above-average filly. **G Wragg [0-1] Trevor Stewart.*

CASTANHAL (SWI) RR 4399[17]

3 b g Vision (USA) 10.4f **(57)** - Concisely (Connaught) 7.7f **(63)**
Form - 0
Record 1998 - 1st:0 2nd:0 3rd:0 Ran:1
1998 Turf 0-1: (10f) (frm)
Lengthy, currently very poor gelding.
**M Johnston [0-1] Markus Graff.*

CASTARA BEACH (IRE) BHB 73f **RR 67f** 4139[4]

2 b f Danehill (USA) 9.1f **(79)** - Sea Harrier (Grundy) 10.3f **(65)**
Form - 584
Record 1998 - 1st:0 2nd:0 3rd:0 Ran:3
Win Prizemoney £0 *Total Prizemoney* £217
1998 Turf 0-3: (5f, 7f 2) (gd, g-f, frm)

Currently average filly. Turf high 61 (began Jly).
**N A Callaghan [0-3] M Tabor & Mrs John Magnier.*

CASTAWAY PRINCESS BHB 30f **RR 40f** 3619[8]
2 b f Casteddu 7.4f **(54)** - Princess Dina (Huntercombe) 7.3f **(56)**
Form - 8008
Record 1998 - 1st:0 2nd:0 3rd:0 Ran:4
1998 Turf 0-4: (6f 2, 7f 2) (gd 2, g-f, frm)
Moderate filly. Turf high 40. **D W Barker [0-4] D W Barker.*

CASTILIAN (IRE) BHB 77f **RR 81f** 4657[2]
2 b g Priolo (USA) 10.9f **(71)** - Hertford Castle **(31f)** (Reference Point) 6.8f **(70)**
Form - 80702
Record 1998 - 1st:0 2nd:1 3rd:0 Ran:5
Win Prizemoney £0 *Total Prizemoney* £1,142
1998 Turf 0-5: (6f, 7f 3, 10f) (gd 3, frm 2)
Decent gelding. Turf high 81 (began Aug) - 2nd of 8 to Last Haven (5 Oct Pontefract 10f gd RF 4657). Steadily improving, although well beaten in a valuable sales race at Newmarket, he looks a stayer. **R Hannon [0-5] J C Smith.*

CASTLE ASHBY JACK BHB 38f49a **RR 42f 49a** 4867[7]
4 gr g Chilibang 7f **(55)** - Carly-B (IRE) (Commanche Run) 8.5f **(58)**
Form - 68273222135878005035O207
Record 1998 - 1st:1 2nd:4 3rd:3 Ran:21
Pre1998 - 1st:0 2nd:7 3rd:5 Ran:23
Win Prizemoney £3,403 *Total Prizemoney* £15,609
Wins * **1998** *Jan Lingfi (STD) 7f 59* <
1998 Turf 0-7: (6f 3, 7f 2, 8f 2) (gd 3, g-f, frm 3) 1998 AW 1-14: (6f, 7f 1-9, 8f 3, 10f) (Equi 1-12, Fibr 2)
Workmanlike, fair gelding, effective 6 to 7f, best at 7f, - acts on Equi, has worn blinkers, likes left handed tracks, likes tight tracks. Turf high 42. AW high 67 - 2nd of 4 to Blue Flyer (27 Jan Lingfield 7f Equi RF 0170) - also 1st of 7 giving 23lb to Mariana (31 Jan Lingfield RF 0197). He had numerous chances to get off the mark on turf and sand, but although runner-up on ten occasions, just could not get his head in front, though he never looked particularly ungenuine. However, he managed to break his duck at the twenty-ninth attempt in a maiden on the Lingfield Equitrack in January, though since then he has again shown his vulnerability to rivals with a turn of foot. **P Howling [1-44] Mrs J Lewis.*

CASTLE BEAU RR 2393[12]
3 ch c Safawan 6.6f **(60)** - Castle Maid **(28f)** (Castle Keep) 8.3f **(57)**
Form - 0
Record 1998 - 1st:0 2nd:0 3rd:0 Ran:1
1998 Turf 0-1: (8f) (gd)
Neat, currently very poor colt. **R J Hodges [0-1] R T Sercombe.*

CASTLE FRIEND BHB 54f **RR 55f** 3575[3]
3 b g Durgam (USA) 12.3f **(53)** - Furry Friend (USA) (Bold Bidder) 8.8f **(67)**
Form - 3263
Record 1998 - 1st:0 2nd:1 3rd:2 Ran:4
Pre1998 - 1st:0 2nd:0 3rd:0 Ran:4
Win Prizemoney £0 *Total Prizemoney* £1,657
1998 Turf 0-4: (9f, 10f 2, 11f) (sft, gd 3)
Scopey, fair gelding, effective 9 to 11f, acts on gd. Turf high 55 - 2nd of 16 to Celestial Welcome (24 Apr Carlisle 9f gd RF 0842). He is still a maiden, but has enough ability to be able to land a small race.
**M D Hammond [0-4] Middleham Racing Bureau/G Heap (from P C Haslam [0-4] Spt 1997).*

CASTLES BURNING (USA) BHB 55f60a **RR 59f 60a** 5003[4]
4 b br g Minshaanshu Amad (USA) 11.3f **(53)** - Major Overhaul (Known Fact (USA)) 7.4f **(67)**
Form - 046012754
Record 1998 - 1st:1 2nd:1 3rd:0 Ran:8
Pre1998 - 1st:3 2nd:2 3rd:4 Ran:25
Win Prizemoney £12,297 *Total Prizemoney* £18,233
Wins * **1998** Aug Bright (FRM) H 10f 50 56
* 1997 *Oct Lingfi (STD) H 10f 65 67*
* 1997 Aug Bright (FRM) H 11.9f 50 54
* 1997 *Mar Lingfi (STD) H 8f 69 78* <
1998 Turf 1-5: (10f 1-1, 11f, 12f 3) (gd, g-f 1-2, frm 2) 1998 AW 0-3: (7f, 10f, 12f) (Equi 3)
Scopey, average gelding, effective 8f, - acts on Equi, has worn blinkers, likes left handed tracks, favours tight tracks. Turf high 59 (began Jly). AW high 67. Inconsistent. He is probably a better horse on Equitrack, but has also shown a liking for the turf at Brighton, and it may well be that he just needs a sharp left-handed track. **C A Cyzer [4-33] R M Cyzer.*

CASTLE SECRET BHB 52f48a **RR 60f 48a** 154[8]
12 b g Castle Keep 10.5f **(58)** - Baffle (Petingo) 11f **(72)**
Form - 08
Record 1998 - 1st:0 2nd:0 3rd:0 Ran:1
Pre1998 - 1st:2 2nd:6 3rd:1 Ran:29
Win Prizemoney £12,226 *Total Prizemoney* £17,915
Wins * 1997 *May Wolver (STD) H 16.2f 47 52* <
1998 AW 0-1: (16f) (Fibr)
Average gelding, effective 16f, - acts on Fibr, has worn blinkers.
**D Burchell [8-57] Mrs Ruth Burchell (from J L Dunlop [1-5] Aug 1990).*

CASTLETOWN COUNT BHB 43f **RR 58f** 4627[11]
6 b g Then Again 7.4f **(52)** - Pepeke (Mummy's Pet) 7.7f **(60)**
Form - 0
Record 1998 - 1st:0 2nd:0 3rd:0 Ran:1
Pre1998 - 1st:1 2nd:1 3rd:0 Ran:13
Win Prizemoney £2,679 *Total Prizemoney* £3,426
Wins 1994 Jly Redcar (G-F) S 7f 59
1998 Turf 0-1: (16f) (g-f)
Fair gelding.
**M W Easterby [0-1] Abbots Salford Carav Park (from K W Hogg [1-13] Jun 1996).*

CATAPULT (IRE) RR 41f 4235[10]
2 ch c Catrail (USA) - Flimmering (Dancing Brave (USA)) 8.4f **(76)**
Form - 0
Record 1998 - 1st:0 2nd:0 3rd:0 Ran:1
1998 Turf 0-1: (6f) (gd)
Currently moderate colt. **J Noseda [0-1] Hesmonds Stud.*

CATCHASCATCHCAN BHB 114f **RR 115f** 3753[1]
3 b f Pursuit of Love 9.5f **(69)** - Catawba (Mill Reef (USA)) 10.5f **(78)**
Form - 1111
Record 1998 - 1st:4 2nd:0 3rd:0 Ran:4
Win Prizemoney £131,130 *Total Prizemoney* £131,130
Wins * **1998** Aug York (G-F) G1 11.9f 115 <
* **1998** Jly Newmar (GD) L 12f 106
* **1998** Jly Haydoc (G-F) G3 11.9f 110
* **1998** Jun Kempto (HVY) 12f 85+
1998 Turf 4-4: (12f 4-4) (g-s 1-1, g-f 1-1, frm 2-2)
Scopey, high-class filly. Turf high 115 - 1st of 7 from High And Low (19 Aug York RF 3753) - also 1st of 6 from Rambling Rose (4 Jly Haydock RF 2536). She earned Group One honours in the Yorkshire Oaks, admittedly a weak renewal, maintaining her unbeaten record in the process, but unfortunately suffered a minor injury there and was promptly retired. Henry Cecil had been bemoaning the fact that lack of suitable races forced him to run this maiden winner in the Group Three Lancashire Oaks on only her second start, but he had the last laugh as the filly ran out a useful winner. She followed up at Newmarket before beating High And Low at York. **H R A Cecil [4-4] Lord Howard de Walden.*

CATCH BALL BHB 54f **RR 56f** 3027[12]
2 ch f Prince Sabo 6.6f **(64)** - Canoodle (Warpath) 12.3f **(52)**
Form - 800
Record 1998 - 1st:0 2nd:0 3rd:0 Ran:3
1998 Turf 0-3: (6f, 7f 2) (gd, g-f, frm)
Currently fair filly. Turf high 56. **T R Watson [0-3] Newitt and Co Ltd.*

CATCH ME BHB 75f **RR 78f** 4709[13]
2 b f Rudimentary (USA) 8.2f **(66)** - Fast Chick (Henbit (USA)) 9f **(61)**
Form - 7112700
Record 1998 - 1st:2 2nd:1 3rd:0 Ran:7
Win Prizemoney £5,972 *Total Prizemoney* £6,980
Wins * **1998** Jly Cheste (G-F) H 7f 65
* **1998** Jun Beverl (GD) 7.5f 67 <
1998 Turf 2-7: (6f, 7f 2-5, 8f) (gd 2, g-f 2, frm 2-3)
Above-average filly, effective 7f, acts on gd to g-f. Turf high 78 - 2nd of 10 giving 2lb to Dandy Dancer (22 Jly Catterick 7f g-f RF

3020). **The winner of a Beverley maiden and a Chester nursery, she has performed with credit since.**

**T D Easterby [2-7] Mrs J B Mountifield.*

1998 Turf 0-1: (6f) (g-f)

Currently moderate gelding.

**E A Wheeler [0-1] The Over The Bridge Partnership.*

Catchascatchcan retired unbeaten after the Yorkshire Oaks

CATCHMENT BHB 31f **RR 38f** 5002[7]

4 ch g Persian Bold 10f **(69)** - Cachou (USA) (Roberto (USA)) 10f **(76)**

Form - 8707

Record					
1998 -	1st:0	2nd:0	3rd:0	Ran:4
Pre1998 -	1st:0	2nd:0	3rd:0	Ran:3

1998 Turf 0-3: (12f 2, 13f) (g-f, frm, hrd) 1998 AW 0-1: (12f) (Equi)

Scopey, very moderate gelding. Turf high 38.

**Mrs A J Perrett [0-7] Mrs Amanda Perrett.*

CATCHTHEBATCH RR 49f 4641[7]

2 b g Beveled (USA) 6.9f **(64)** - Batchworth Dancer (Ballacashtal (CAN)) 5.3f **(50)**

Form - 7

Record 1998 - 1st:0 2nd:0 3rd:0 Ran:1

CATCH THE DRAGON (IRE) RR 100+f 5109a[2]

3 b c Sharp Victor (USA) 10f **(56)** - Roblanna (Roberto (USA)) 10f **(76)**

Form - 212

1998 Turf 1-3: (7f 1-1, 8f, 10f) (sft 1-2, gd)

Very useful colt. Turf high 100 (began Oct) - 2nd of 9 to Golden Rule (26 Oct Leopardstown 10f gd RF 5109a).

**L Browne in IRE [1-5] Mrs P K Cooper.*

CATERINA SFORZA RR 91f 4600a[11]

3 f

Form - 70

1998 Turf 0-2: (10f, 11f) (hvy 2)

Currently useful filly, often wears blinkers. Turf high 91. Is not up to group class and her sights must be lowered for her to have a chance. **G Botti in ITY [0-2].*

CATFOOT LANE BHB 44f44a **RR 60f 44a** 4919[9]

3 b f Batshoof 9.5f **(66)** -T Catty (USA)(Sensitive Prince (USA))9.1f **(60)**
Form - 07410000
Record 1998 - 1st:1 2nd:0 3rd:0 Ran:8
Pre1998 - 1st:0 2nd:0 3rd:0 Ran:4
Win Prizemoney £2,136 *Total Prizemoney* £2,136
Wins * **1998** Jly Leices (GD) S 8f 60 <
1998 Turf 1-6: (7f, 8f 1-5) (g-s, gd 2, frm 1-2, hrd) 1998 AW 0-2: (11f, 12f) (Fibr 2)
Light-framed, average filly, effective 8f, acts on frm. Turf high 60 - 1st of 14 getting 5lb from Crofters Edge (22 Jly Leicester RF 3025). AW high 19. **W G M Turner [1-12] T Lightbowne.*

CATHEDRAL (IRE) BHB 110f **RR 113f** 4330[1]

4 b g Prince Sabo 6.6f **(64)** - Choire Mhor (Dominion) 8.5f **(63)**
Form - 477481
Record 1998 - 1st:1 2nd:0 3rd:0 Ran:6
Pre1998 - 1st:1 2nd:3 3rd:2 Ran:7
Win Prizemoney £34,523 *Total Prizemoney* £56,295
Wins * **1998** Spt Newbur (GD) L 5.2f 113 <
* 1997 Apr Beverl (G-F) 5f 91+
1998 Turf 1-6: (5f 1-4, 6f 2) (gd 4, g-f 1-2)
Lengthy, Group-class gelding, effective 5f, acts on gd to g-f, best on g-f. Turf high 113 - 1st of 12 giving 1lb to Night Shot (17 Spt Newbury RF 4330). He has always been held in high regard and ran well last season, pouncing late to win a Listed event at Newbury in September. Five furlongs is his trip.
**B J Meehan [2-13] Kennet Valley Thoroughbreds.*

CATHEDRAL BELLE BHB 48f **RR 57f** 3887[7]

4 ch f Minster Son 10.9f **(56)** - Corn Lily (Aragon) 8.1f **(60)**
Form - 670047
Record 1998 - 1st:0 2nd:0 3rd:0 Ran:6
1998 Turf 0-6: (8f 3, 12f, 16f, 17f) (sft, g-s, gd 2, frm 2)
Light-framed, fair filly. Turf high 57.
**Mrs M Reveley [1-9] Mrs Susan McDonald.*

CATRIONA **RR 73f** 5071[4]

2 b f Bustino 11f **(64)** - Nadia Nerina (CAN) (Northern Dancer) 9.6f **(80)**
Form - 4
Record 1998 - 1st:0 2nd:0 3rd:0 Ran:1
Win Prizemoney £0 *Total Prizemoney* £277
1998 Turf 0-1: (7f) (gd)
Currently above-average filly. **J Noseda [0-1] B E Nielsen.*

CATS BOTTOM BHB 38f50a **RR 38f 50a** 2099[7]

6 ch m Primo Dominie 7.2f **(67)** - Purple Fan (Dalsaan) 9.8f **(64)**
Form - 00431027
Record 1998 - 1st:1 2nd:1 3rd:1 Ran:7
Pre1998 - 1st:3 2nd:5 3rd:2 Ran:46
Win Prizemoney £11,021 *Total Prizemoney* £20,038
Wins * **1998** *Feb Southw (STD) H 8f 37 43*
* 1997 *Mar Southw (STD) H 8f 52 59*
* 1996 *Dec Southw (SLW) H 8f 47 51*
1994 Jun Pontef (FRM) 5f 76+
1998 AW 1-7: (7f 2, 8f 1-5) (Fibr 1-7)
Fair mare, effective 7 to 9f, - acts on Fibr, has worn blinkers, likes left handed tracks, favours tight tracks. AW high 50 - 2nd of 16 getting 9lb from Desert Invader (12 Jun Southwell 7f Fibr RF 1945). Inconsistent. Ended a long losing run when winning a fillies' handicap on the Southwell Fibresand in February. A mile at that track seems to suit her best.
**A G Newcombe [3-35] Advanced Marketing Services Ltd (from D J S Cosgrove [1-18] Spt 1995).*

CAT THIEF (USA) **RR 110** 5162a[3]

2 ch c Storm Cat (USA) 7f **(86)** - Train Robbery (USA) 00
Form - 3
1998 AW 0-1: (9f) (Dirt)
Currently Group-class colt, always wears blinkers. (1st run) - 3rd of 14 to Answer Lively (7 Nov Churchill Downs 9f Dirt RF 5162a). Failed to steal the kitty in the Breeders' Cup Juvenile, but finished a close third to Answer Lively, whom he had beaten in a Keeneland Grade Two.
**D W Lukas in USA [0-1] Overbrook Farm et al.*

CATULLUS **RR 74f** 4835[11]

2 b c Prince Sabo 6.6f **(64)** - Rive-Jumelle (IRE) (M Double M (USA)) 14.1f **(52)**
Form - 44600
Record 1998 - 1st:0 2nd:0 3rd:0 Ran:5
Win Prizemoney £0 *Total Prizemoney* £512
1998 Turf 0-5: (6f, 7f 3, 8f) (g-s, g-f, frm 3)
Above-average colt. Turf high 74 (began Jly) - 4th of 11 giving 5lb to Lady Muck (29 Jly Epsom 7f g-f RF 3198).
**M Bell [0-5] M D F Racing Partnership.*

CAUDA EQUINA BHB 79f **RR 81f** 4918[3]

4 gr g Statoblest 6.4f **(63)** - Sea Fret (Habat) 7.6f **(61)**
Form - 05560705322535301621106223
Record 1998 - 1st:3 2nd:5 3rd:4 Ran:26
Pre1998 - 1st:3 2nd:0 3rd:1 Ran:13
Win Prizemoney £20,425 *Total Prizemoney* £30,604
Wins * **1998** Spt Bath (GD) H 5.7f 64 76 <
* **1998** Spt Salisb (GD) H 5f 62 67
* **1998** Aug Bath (GD) C 5.7f 64
* 1997 Jly Ripon (GD) H 6f 75 76 <
* 1997 May Bath (G-S) 5.1f 71
* 1997 Apr Bath (G-F) S 5.1f 63
1998 Turf 3-26: (5f 1-7, 6f 2-19) (sft 2, g-s 3, gd 5, g-f 2-7, frm 1-9)
Scopey, decent gelding, effective 5 to 6f, best at 6f, acts on g-s to frm, best on g-s, has worn blinkers, likes left handed tracks, excels at Bath. Turf high 81 - 2nd of 23 giving 7lb to Anstand (10 Oct York 6f gd RF 4751) - also 1st of 18 getting 7lb from Hard to Figure (7 Spt Bath RF 4128). **M R Channon [6-39] Michael Foy.*

CAUDILLO (IRE) BHB 53f58a **RR 54f 58a** 3242[5]

5 b m Nordico (USA) 8.2f **(59)** - Over Swing (FR) (Saint Cyrien (FR)) 8.4f **(80)**
Form - 18242742435
Record 1998 - 1st:0 2nd:3 3rd:1 Ran:9
Pre1998 - 1st:2 2nd:4 3rd:2 Ran:21
Win Prizemoney £7,424 *Total Prizemoney* £14,832
Wins 1997 *Nov Wolver (STD) H 7f 53 57*
1996 Aug Leopar (G-S) 8f 70 <
1998 Turf 0-5:(7f 3, 8f 2)(gd 2, g-f 2, frm)1998 AW 0-4: (7f 3, 8f) (Fibr 4)
Fair filly, effective 6 to 8f, acts on gd to frm - acts on Fibr, best on gd, likes left handed tracks, likes tight tracks, and excels at Wolverhampton. Turf high 54. AW high 59 (1st run) - 2nd of 11 getting 8lb from Elite Hope (4 Mar Wolverhampton 7f Fibr RF 0398). Consistent. Ex-Irish, she showed some ability on turf but had to wait until November '97 on the Wolverhampton Fibresand to get off the mark in this country, despite hanging quite badly right. She ran quite well after returning in March, twice being beaten by the minimum margin. She looks to need at least a mile.
**Miss Gay Kelleway [0-3] Stable Investments Ltd (from Mrs P N Dutfield [1-22] Jun 1998).*

CAUTION BHB 68f **RR 67f** 4858[1]

4 b f Warning 8.1f **(77)**- Fairy Flax (IRE)(Dancing Brave (USA))8.4f **(76)**
Form - 8527476230701
Record 1998 - 1st:1 2nd:2 3rd:1 Ran:13
Pre1998 - 1st:3 2nd:2 3rd:2 Ran:14
Win Prizemoney £13,910 *Total Prizemoney* £20,018
Wins * **1998** Oct Redcar (HVY) 5f 65
1997 Jly Beverl (G-F) C 7.5f 61+
1997 Jun Cheste (G-F) C 6.1f 70
1996 Spt Ayr (G-F) 6f 79 <
1998 Turf 1-13: (5f 1-6, 6f 5, 7f 2) (sft 1-1, g-s, gd, g-f 4, frm 6)
Neat, average filly, effective 5 to 7f, best at 6f, acts on sft to frm, has worn blinkers, likes left handed tracks, likes tight tracks, and excels at Chester. Turf high 67 - 2nd of 6 giving 2lb to Bolshaya (17 Jly Pontefract 6f frm RF 2889) - also 1st of 11 getting 3lb from State of Caution (17 Oct Redcar RF 4858).
**S Gollings [1-21] Ian & Mrs Irene Thomas (from Mrs J R Ramsden [3-6] Jly 1997).*

CAVALLINA (USA) **RR 90f** 5177a[4]

3 b f Theatrical 11.5f **(78)** - Sedulous (Tap On Wood) 10.3f **(65)**
Form - 3354
1998 Turf 0-4: (8f 2, 9f 2) (sft, g-s, gd 2)
Useful filly, has worn blinkers. Turf high 90. Showed enough in Irish maidens to suggest that she can win races.
**D K Weld in IRE [0-5] Thomas McDonogh.*

CAVERNISTA RR 72f 4800[5]
2 b f Lion Cavern (USA) 7.5f **(74)** - Princess Genista (Ile de Bourbon (USA)) 10.1f **(67)**
Form - 05
Record 1998 - 1st:0 2nd:0 3rd:0 Ran:2
1998 Turf 0-2: (7f 2) (sft, gd)
Currently above-average filly. Turf high 72 (began Oct). Should come into her own when tackling a mile plus.
**J L Dunlop [0-2] I H Stewart-Brown.*

CAVERSFIELD BHB 60f **RR 68f** 5127[3]
3 ch c Tina's Pet 7.4f **(56)** - Canoodle (Warpath) 12.3f **(52)**
Form - 0048360203003
Record 1998 - 1st:0 2nd:1 3rd:3 Ran:13
Pre1998 - 1st:2 2nd:1 3rd:0 Ran:6
Win Prizemoney £6,643 *Total Prizemoney* £10,590
Wins * 1997 Oct Leices (GD) H 7f 75 76 <
* 1997 Aug Windso (G-F) H 6f 72 76 <
1998 Turf 0-13: (7f 9, 8f 3, 10f) (g-s 2, gd 4, g-f, frm 6)
Leggy, average colt, effective 6 to 7f, best at 7f, acts on g-s to frm, has worn blinkers. Turf high 68. **R Hannon [2-19] William Kelly.*

CAVIAR ROYALE (IRE) BHB 85f **RR 73f** 1682[13]
4 ch g Royal Academy (USA) 7.8f **(77)** - Petite Liqueurelle (IRE) (Shernazar) 10.2f **(73)**
Form - 060
Record 1998 - 1st:0 2nd:0 3rd:0 Ran:3
Pre1998 - 1st:2 2nd:3 3rd:3 Ran:14
Win Prizemoney £10,827 *Total Prizemoney* £23,424
Wins 1997 Aug Thirsk (GD) H 8f 93 100 <
1996 May Lingfi (G-F) 5f 81+
1998 Turf 0-3: (7f 2, 10f) (gd 2, g-f)
Scopey, above-average gelding, effective 8f, acts on gd, likes left handed tracks. Turf high 69. Inconsistent.
**M W Easterby [0-3] Burke's 5th Family Settlement (from T D Barron [1-8] Aug 1997).*

CAYMAN KAI (IRE) BHB 82f **RR 75f** 2689[4]
5 ch h Imperial Frontier (USA) 7f **(65)** - Safiya (USA) (Riverman (USA)) 9.1f **(76)**
Form - 6475084
Record 1998 - 1st:0 2nd:0 3rd:0 Ran:7
Pre1998 - 1st:3 2nd:5 3rd:2 Ran:18
Win Prizemoney £49,622 *Total Prizemoney* £119,865
Wins * 1996 Apr Newmar (G-F) LH 7f 113 100
* 1995 Spt Doncas (G-S) G2 5f 108 <
* 1995 May Lingfi (G-F) 5f 78+
1998 Turf 0-7: (6f 2, 7f 3, 8f 2) (g-s 2, gd, g-f 2, frm 2)
Above-average colt, effective 6f, acts on gd. Turf high 91. Becoming disappointing. He struggled to recapture any of his previous form, and has been retired to stud.
**R Hannon [3-25] I A N Wight.*

CEAD MILE FAILTE BHB 33f38a **RR 26f 38a** 3809[10]
3 ch c Most Welcome 8.6f **(66)** - Avionne (Derrylin) 8.8f **(54)**
Form - 65083005070
Record 1998 - 1st:0 2nd:0 3rd:1 Ran:11
Win Prizemoney £0 *Total Prizemoney* £430
1998 Turf 0-8: (5f, 6f 5, 7f 2) (gd 3, g-f 2, frm 3) 1998 AW 0-3: (7f, 8f, 10f) (Equi 3)
Workmanlike, fair colt, effective 6f, acts on frm, likes left handed tracks, likes tight tracks. Turf high 47 - 3rd of 17 getting 19lb from Step On Degas (22 May Brighton 6f frm RF 1389). AW high 52.
**R J O'Sullivan [0-4] Eddie Gleeson (from R Ingram [0-7] Jun 1998).*

CEDAR GIRL BHB 30f38a **RR 27f 38a** 2278[11]
6 b m Then Again 7.4f **(52)** - Classic Times (Dominion) 8.5f **(63)**
Form - 00
Record 1998 - 1st:0 2nd:0 3rd:0 Ran:2
Pre1998 - 1st:1 2nd:1 3rd:2 Ran:22
Win Prizemoney £2,563 *Total Prizemoney* £4,392
Wins * 1994 Jun Haydoc (G-F) S 6f 56
1998 Turf 0-2: (6f, 8f) (gd, frm)
Very moderate mare. Turf high 27.
**R J Hodges [1-22] Mrs Anna Sanders (from Mrs N Macauley [0-2] Feb 1996).*

CEDAR WELLS (USA) BHB 64f **RR 71f** 4929[11]
2 b c Desert Secret (IRE) - Sans Sorrow (USA) (Barachois (CAN)) 8.3f **(63)**
Form - 4400
Record 1998 - 1st:0 2nd:0 3rd:0 Ran:4
Win Prizemoney £0 *Total Prizemoney* £698
1998 Turf 0-4: (5f, 6f 2, 7f) (g-s, gd 2, g-f)
Above-average colt, has broken blood-vessels. Turf high 71 (began Jly). **G Lewis [0-4] & Mrs Kantis.*

CEE-N-K (IRE) BHB 37f49a **RR 50f 49a** 4486[9]
4 b c Thatching 7.8f **(69)** - Valois (Lyphard (USA)) 9.9f **(72)**
Form - 8628000030000
Record 1998 - 1st:0 2nd:1 3rd:1 Ran:11
Pre1998 - 1st:2 2nd:3 3rd:0 Ran:21
Win Prizemoney £8,746 *Total Prizemoney* £13,529
Wins 1997 Jly Beverl (G-F) H 7.5f 69 75
1996 Dec Lingfi (STD) H 8f 73 76 <
1998 Turf 0-9: (7f 2, 8f 5, 10f 2) (g-s, gd 2, g-f 3, frm 3) 1998 AW 0-2: (8f, 9f) (Fibr 2)
Strong, fair colt, effective 7 to 8f, best at 7f, acts on g-f to frm, best on frm, has worn blinkers, likes right handed tracks. Turf high 50. AW high 52. He is a fair performer on turf and sand when on song, but only shows his best form occasionally these days.
**E J Alston [0-10] North West Racing Club - Owners Group (from M Johnston [2-22] Jan 1998).*

CELANDINE BHB 63f65a **RR 61f 65a** 4962[12]
5 b m Warning 8.1f **(77)** - Silly Bold (Rousillon (USA)) 8.2f **(74)**
Form - 820104150
Record 1998 - 1st:2 2nd:1 3rd:0 Ran:9
Pre1998 - 1st:1 2nd:1 3rd:4 Ran:16
Win Prizemoney £9,709 *Total Prizemoney* £13,975
Wins * **1998** Spt Catter (G-F) H 7f 56 61
* **1998** Jly Warwic (G-F) H 7f 51 57
1995 Spt Bath (G-F) 5.7f 83 <
1998 Turf 2-9: (6f, 7f 2-8) (sft, g-s, g-f 4, frm 2-3)
Average filly, effective 7f, acts on g-f to frm, best on frm, prefers left handed tracks, prefers tight tracks. Turf high 61 - 1st of 17 giving 4lb to Miss Vivien (19 Spt Catterick RF 4373) - also 1st of 19 giving 7lb to Batsman (18 Jly Warwick RF 2940).
**Andrew Turnell [2-17] Dr John Hollowood (from J L Eyre [0-4] Jun 1996).*

CELEBRATE (IRE) RR 52f 1278[6]
2 ch f Generous (IRE) 11.5f **(82)** - Bright Generation (IRE) (Rainbow Quest (USA)) 10.4f **(75)**
Form - 6
Record 1998 - 1st:0 2nd:0 3rd:0 Ran:1
1998 Turf 0-1: (6f) (frm)
Currently fair filly. **P F I Cole [0-1] H R H Prince Fahd Salman.*

CELEBRATION BHB 63f **RR 59f** 2254[7]
3 br f Selkirk (USA) 7.9f **(76)** - No Restraint (Habitat) 9.4f **(70)**
Form - 087
Record 1998 - 1st:0 2nd:0 3rd:0 Ran:3
Pre1998 - 1st:0 2nd:0 3rd:0 Ran:1
1998 Turf 0-3: (7f 2, 8f) (gd, g-f, frm)
Workmanlike, fair filly. Turf high 59. **I A Balding [0-4] The Queen.*

CELEBRATION CAKE (IRE) BHB 45f **RR 39f** 5060[13]
6 b g Mister Majestic 9.9f **(56)** - My Louise (Manado) 9.6f **(63)**
Form - 3540140060
Record 1998 - 1st:1 2nd:0 3rd:1 Ran:10
Pre1998 - 1st:4 2nd:2 3rd:3 Ran:28
Win Prizemoney £22,756 *Total Prizemoney* £27,118
Wins * **1998** Aug Hamilt (SFT) C 9.2f 46
* 1996 Spt Ayr (G-F) H 7f 70 76 <
* 1996 Aug Haydoc (G-F) H 8.1f 58 73
* 1996 Aug Hamilt (G-F) H 8.3f 58 67
* 1995 Jun Ayr (G-F) H 8f 56 55
1998 Turf 1-10: (8f 3, 9f 1-6, 11f) (sft 3, g-s 2, gd 1-3, frm 2)
Very moderate gelding, effective 8f, acts on gd to frm, has worn blinkers, likes right handed tracks, favours tight tracks. Turf high 56. **Miss L A Perratt [5-40] Lightbody Celebration Cakes Ltd.*

CELERIC BHB 121f **RR 121f** 4632[2]

6 b g Mtoto 11.5f **(71)** - Hot Spice (Hotfoot) 10.5f **(59)**

Form - 868322

Record	**1998 -**	1st:0	2nd:2	3rd:1	Ran:6
	Pre1998 -	1st:11	2nd:5	3rd:1	Ran:26

Win Prizemoney £306,547 *Total Prizemoney* £383,672

Wins									
	1997	Jun	Ascot	(GD)	G1	20f		121	<
	1997	May	York	(GD)	G2	13.9f		115	
	1996	Oct	Newmar	(G-F)	G3	16f		112	
	1996	Aug	York	(GD)	L	15.9f		113+	
	1996	Jly	York	(GD)	LH	13.9f	102	104	
	1996	Jun	Newcas	(FRM)	H	16.1f	96	100	
	1996	May	York	(G-F)	H	13.9f	90	94+	
	1995	Aug	York	(G-F)	H	13.9f	87	93	
	1995	Jly	Newbur	(GD)	H	13.3f	83	91	
	1995	May	Nottin	(GD)	H	14.1f	79	81	
	1995	May	Warwic	(FRM)	H	12.5f	75	81	

1998 Turf 0-6: (12f, 14f, 16f 3, 20f) (g-s, gd 3, g-f 2)

Very high-class gelding, effective 14 to 20f, best at 16f, acts on gd to g-f, best on g-f, likes York. Turf high 121 - 2nd of 7 giving 2lb to Arctic Owl (3 Oct Newmarket 16f g-f RF 4632). This most likeable of racehorses progressed to the top of the staying tree in 1997, utilising his fine turn of foot to take the Yorkshire Cup and, under a superb ride from Eddery, the Gold Cup. After the death of his previous trainer David Morley, he took time to find his form for John Dunlop. However, he ran a lot better at Goodwood on ground softer than ideal, and lost out by inches in the Lonsdale Stakes at York. He gave the up-and-coming Arctic Owl a good race in the Jockey Club Cup, and will no doubt be one of that horse's main rivals next season.

**J L Dunlop [0-6] Christopher Spence (from D Morley [11-26] Oct 1997).*

CELESTIAL BAY (IRE) BHB 51f45a **RR 70f 45a** 4765[4]

3 b f Star de Naskra (USA) 8.8f **(63)** - Kandara (FR) (Dalsaan) 9.8f **(64)**

Form - 000003504

Record	**1998 -**	1st:0	2nd:0	3rd:1	Ran:9
	Pre1998 -	1st:0	2nd:0	3rd:2	Ran:4

Win Prizemoney £0 *Total Prizemoney* £2,377

1998 Turf 0-8: (5f 2, 6f 2, 7f 2, 8f 2) (g-s, gd, g-f 2, frm 4) 1998 AW 0-1: (6f) (Fibr)

Leggy, above-average filly, effective 6 to 7f, best at 6f, acts on g-f to frm, best on g-f. Turf high 70 - 3rd of 8 getting 5lb from Eljjanah (25 Aug Lingfield 6f frm RF 3845).

**E A Wheeler [0-9] Benham Racing (from A G Foster [0-4] Aug 1997).*

CELESTIAL CHOIR BHB 86f87a **RR 90f 87a** 1164[10]

8 b m Celestial Storm (USA) 11.8f **(58)** - Choir (High Top) 10.2f **(67)**

Form - 0

Record	**1998 -**	1st:0	2nd:0	3rd:0	Ran:1
	Pre1998 -	1st:12	2nd:11	3rd:6	Ran:76

Win Prizemoney £84,126 *Total Prizemoney* £114,678

Wins									
	*1997	Oct	York	(SFT)		11.9f		90	
	*1997	Aug	Pontef	(G-F)	H	12f	83	91	
	*1996	Aug	York	(GD)	H	11.9f	86	93	<
	*1996	Jly	Doncas	(G-F)	H	10.3f	83	85	
	*1996	*Jan*	*Southw*	*(STD)*		*12f*		*83*	
	*1996	*Jan*	*Lingfi*	*(STD)*	*H*	*10f*	*75*	*83*	
	*1995	Aug	Pontef	(G-F)	H	8f	78	84	
	*1994	Spt	Haydoc	(G-S)	H	8.1f	76	83+	
	*1994	Spt	Doncas	(GD)	H	8f	71	71	
	*1994	Aug	Ripon	(G-F)	H	8f	66	68	
	*1994	Jly	Pontef	(G-F)	H	8f	54	64	
	*1994	*Jan*	*Wolver*	*(STD)*	*H*	*7f*	*50*	*51*	

1998 Turf 0-1: (12f) (gd)

Useful mare, effective 9 to 12f, best at 12f, acts on g-s to frm - acts on Fibr, has worn blinkers, favours left handed tracks. Becoming disappointing. **J L Eyre [18-90] Mrs Carole Sykes.*

CELESTIAL FIRE BHB 32f **RR 18f** 2673[12]

6 gr g Celestial Storm (USA) 11.8f **(58)** - Fiery Gal (CAN) (Explodent (USA)) 9.4f **(87)**

Form - 00

Record	**1998 -**	1st:0	2nd:0	3rd:0	Ran:2
	Pre1998 -	1st:0	2nd:0	3rd:0	Ran:4

1998 Turf 0-2: (8f, 12f) (gd, g-f)

Poor gelding, has worn blinkers. Turf high 18.

**O O'Neill [0-6] James Atkin (from J White [1-5] Jly 1996).*

CELESTIAL KEY (USA) BHB 87f **RR 89f** 5078[14]

8 br g Star de Naskra (USA) 8.8f **(63)** - Casa Key (USA) (Cormorant (USA)) 8.2f **(104)**

Form - 3682602180

Record	**1998 -**	1st:1	2nd:2	3rd:1	Ran:10
	Pre1998 -	1st:10	2nd:5	3rd:6	Ran:65

Win Prizemoney £72,444 *Total Prizemoney* £106,789

Wins									
	***1998**	Aug	Dielsd	(GD)		9f		89	
	*1997	Spt	Dielsd	(GD)		8f		96	
	*1997	Aug	Dielsd	(GD)		8f		89	
	*1995	Oct	Newmar	(G-F)	L	8f		105	<
	*1995	Jun	Newbur	(G-F)	H	7f	93	99	
	*1995	Jun	Haydoc	(GD)	H	8.1f	93	97	
	*1995	May	Thirsk	(FRM)	H	7f	90	95	

1998 Turf 1-10: (7f 2, 8f 5, 9f 1-3) (sft, g-s, gd 1-5, g-f 2, frm)

Useful gelding, effective 8 to 9f, best at 8f, acts on g-s to g-f, best on gd, has worn blinkers, prefers left handed tracks. Turf high 89 - 1st of 8 giving 2lb to Mill King (23 Aug Dielsdorf RF 3918a). A versatile performer, he showed he retains plenty of ability when narrowly beaten by a stablemate at Newcastle in June, but looks a bit high in the weights in this country, and his wins in recent seasons have only been at Dielsdorf in Switzerland.

**M Johnston [7-48] Markus Graff (from S G Norton [4-28] Spt 1994).*

CELESTIAL WELCOME BHB 71f **RR 74df** 5095[6]

3 b f Most Welcome 8.6f **(66)** - Choral Sundown (Night Shift (USA)) 7.2f **(69)**

Form - 1111006

Record	**1998 -**	1st:4	2nd:0	3rd:0	Ran:7
	Pre1998 -	1st:0	2nd:0	3rd:0	Ran:4

Win Prizemoney £15,960 *Total Prizemoney* £15,960

Wins									
	***1998**	May	Redcar	(GD)	H	7f	62	74	<
	***1998**	May	Newcas	(G-S)	H	8f	62	65	
	***1998**	Apr	Carlis	(G-S)	H	9.3f	54	56	
	***1998**	Apr	Hamilt	(HVY)		8.3f		52	

1998 Turf 4-7: (7f 1-1, 8f 2-4, 9f 1-1, 11f) (sft 1-1, gd 3-6)

Scopey, above-average filly, effective 7 to 8f, acts on gd. Turf high 74 - 1st of 11 giving 11lb to Al Reet (11 May Redcar RF 1149) - also 1st of 10 getting 10lb from Piped Aboard (4 May Newcastle RF 1023). Completed a four-timer in the spring before the Handicapper took her measure.

**Mrs M Reveley [4-11] The Welcome Alliance.*

CELLINI BHB 75f **RR 70f** 4394[4]

3 br c Caerleon (USA) 10.9f **(79)** - Souk (IRE) (Ahonoora) 8.1f **(73)**

Form - 8024

Record	**1998 -**	1st:0	2nd:1	3rd:0	Ran:4

Win Prizemoney £0 *Total Prizemoney* £2,259

1998 Turf 0-4: (8f, 10f 2, 12f) (gd 2, g-f, frm)

Workmanlike, above-average colt. Turf high 70 - 4th of 14 giving 5lb to Lear's Crown (21 Spt Kempton 12f frm RF 4394).

**L M Cumani [0-4] Sheikh Mohammed.*

CELTIC COMFORT BHB 69f67a **RR 72f 67a** 389[3]

3 ch g Executive Man 8.9f **(52)** - Annacando (Derrylin) 8.8f **(54)**

Form - 83523

Record	**1998 -**	1st:0	2nd:1	3rd:2	Ran:4
	Pre1998 -	1st:1	2nd:1	3rd:1	Ran:7

Win Prizemoney £2,752 *Total Prizemoney* £5,398

Wins									
	*1997	Jly	Carlis	(GD)		5.9f		72	<

1998 AW 0-4: (8f, 10f, 11f, 12f) (Equi 2, Fibr 2)

Workmanlike, above-average gelding, effective 6 to 7f, best at 7f, acts on gd to frm - acts on Fibr, has worn blinkers. AW high 62.

**P C Haslam [1-11] Ray Tutton.*

CELTIC SEAL BHB 61f64a **RR 59f 64a** 4622[9]

2 br f Lugana Beach 7f **(63)** - Celtic Bird (Celtic Cone) 9.8f **(43)**

Form - 050

Record	**1998 -**	1st:0	2nd:0	3rd:0	Ran:3

1998 Turf 0-3: (5f 3) (gd, g-f, frm)

Currently average filly. Turf high 59 (began Aug).

**J Balding [0-3] Mrs Paula Haigh.*

CENSOR BHB 46f **RR 67f** 4768[14]

5 b g Kris 10f **(75)** - Mixed Applause (USA) (Nijinsky (CAN)) 10.3f **(77)**

Form - 88000

Record	**1998 -**	1st:0	2nd:0	3rd:0	Ran:5

Pre1998 - 1st:1 2nd:0 3rd:1 Ran:12
Win Prizemoney £3,492 *Total Prizemoney* £5,472
Wins 1995 Oct Nottin (G-F) 8.2f 83 <
1998 Turf 0-3: (7f, 8f, 9f) (sft, g-f, frm) 1998 AW 0-2: (6f, 11f) (Fibr 2)
Average gelding, has worn blinkers. Turf high 33 (began Spt). AW high 46. Becoming disappointing. He is a half-brother to multiple All-Weather winners Tempering and Claque and might be worth trying again on that surface, as he is not in the same league as his other close relatives Shavian and Paean.
**D Nicholls [0-13] G H Leatham (from H R A Cecil [1-6] Aug 1996).*

CENTRAL COAST (IRE) BHB 86f **RR 82f** 4857[14]
2 b c Hamas (IRE) 8f **(72)** - Clairification (IRE) **(56f 58a)** (Shernazar) 10.2f **(73)**
Form - 210
Record 1998 - 1st:1 2nd:1 3rd:0 Ran:3
Win Prizemoney £3,506 *Total Prizemoney* £4,556
Wins * 1998 Aug Nottin (G-F) 6.1f 82 <
1998 Turf 1-3: (6f 1-3) (sft, g-f 1-1, frm)
Currently decent colt. Turf high 82 (began Jly) - 1st of 20 giving 2lb to Cohiba Esplendidos (29 Aug Nottingham RF 3961). Won his maiden well despite appearing to dislike the fast ground.
**J M P Eustace [1-3] R Carstairs.*

CENTRAL COMMITTEE (IRE) BHB 77f **RR 80f** 4540[16]
3 ch g Royal Academy (USA) 7.8f **(77)** - Idle Chat (USA) (Assert) 10.6f **(85)**
Form - 7010400
Record 1998 - 1st:1 2nd:0 3rd:0 Ran:7
Pre1998 - 1st:1 2nd:0 3rd:0 Ran:2
Win Prizemoney £7,747 *Total Prizemoney* £8,602
Wins * 1998 Jly Warwic (G-F) H 10.8f 76 78
* 1997 Spt Beverl (G-F) 7.5f 88+ <
1998 Turf 1-7: (9f, 10f 2, 11f 1-1, 12f 2, 14f) (sft, g-s, gd, g-f, frm 1-3)
Scopey, decent gelding, effective 7 to 12f, acts on g-f to frm, best on frm. Turf high 80 - 4th of 10 getting 6lb from Karasi (15 Aug Ripon 12f g-f RF 3662). Has joined Charlie Egerton.
**P W Chapple-Hyam [2-9] R E Sangster.*

CENTRAL LOBBY (IRE) RR 103f 3225a[2]
3 ch c Kenmare (FR) 9.6f **(76)** - Style Of Life (USA) (The Minstrel (CAN)) 10f **(72)**
Form - 2
1998 Turf 0-1: (9f) (gd)
Currently very useful colt. (1st run) - 2nd of 7 to Kabool (25 Jly Maisons-laffitte 9f gd RF 3225a). He looked as if he needed further than nine furlongs when finishing second in a Group Three at Maisons-Laffitte in July. **A Fabre in FR [0-1] K Abdulla.*

CENTRAL PARK (IRE) BHB 113f **RR 113f** 4345a[5]
3 ch c In The Wings 11.2f **(77)** - Park Special (Relkino) 8.9f **(65)**
Form - 014315
Record 1998 - 1st:2 2nd:0 3rd:1 Ran:6
Pre1998 - 1st:3 2nd:0 3rd:0 Ran:5
Win Prizemoney £266,060 *Total Prizemoney* £298,779
Wins * 1998 Aug Hoppeg (GD) G2 12f 112 <
*** 1998** May Capann (G-F) G1 12f 111
1997 Jly Goodwo (G-F) G3 7f 111+
1997 Jun Ascot (GD) L 7f 103
1997 Jun Haydoc (G-F) 6f 92+
1998 Turf 2-6: (8f, 10f, 12f 2-4) (hvy, gd 1-4, g-f 1-1)
Scopey, Group-class colt, effective 7 to 12f, best at 12f, acts on gd to g-f, best on g-f, likes right handed tracks. Turf high 113 - also 1st of 6 from Hamond (16 Aug Hoppegarten RF 3785a). Consistent. A very smart juvenile for Paul Cole, he was transferred to the Godolphin team and made his reappearance in the Guineas, where he never really threatened to take hand in the finish. He beat a sub-standard field to win the Italian Derby in May, but was out of his depth for much of the remainder of the campaign and, though not officially a pacemaker, he did a good job of it in the Eclipse, ultimately finishing third to Daylami. A drop in class helped him land a German Group Two in August, but he will always struggle against the best middle-distance horses. Connections would be well advised to step him up in trip.
**S bin Suroor [2-6] Godolphin (from P F I Cole [3-5] Oct 1997).*

CENTRE COURT BHB 62f **RR 67f** 3398[5]
3 ch f Second Set (IRE) 9.2f **(67)** - Raffle (Balidar) 7.9f **(63)**
Form - 060555
Record 1998 - 1st:0 2nd:0 3rd:0 Ran:6
Pre1998 - 1st:1 2nd:0 3rd:0 Ran:4
Win Prizemoney £3,436 *Total Prizemoney* £3,651
Wins * 1997 Jly Windso (GD) 5f 76+ <
1998 Turf 0-6: (5f 3, 6f 2, 7f) (gd, g-f, frm 4)
Neat, average filly, effective 5f, acts on g-f, has worn blinkers. Turf high 67. **R Hannon [1-10] Bloomsbury Stud.*

CENTRE STALLS (IRE) BHB 111f **RR 113df** 4068[9]
5 b h In The Wings 11.2f **(77)** - Lora's Guest (Be My Guest (USA)) 9.3f **(67)**
Form - 7362520
Record 1998 - 1st:0 2nd:2 3rd:1 Ran:6
Pre1998 - 1st:4 2nd:2 3rd:2 Ran:15
Win Prizemoney £35,093 *Total Prizemoney* £97,209
Wins * 1997 May York (GD) LH 7.9f 110 117 <
* 1996 Spt Kempto (GD) L 8f 115
* 1996 Aug Sandow (G-F) 8.1f 100
* 1995 Spt Salisb (G-S) 7f 89+
1998 Turf 0-6: (8f 5, 9f) (gd 3, g-f, frm, hrd)
Group-class colt, effective 7 to 8f, best at 8f, acts on gd to frm. Turf high 115 (1st run) - 3rd of 10 to Cape Cross (16 May Newbury 8f frm RF 1260). Useful on his day, he was third in a below-average Lockinge on his seasonal debut but never really performed any better than that throughout the season. He twice finished second in Group Threes at the Curragh, and his other efforts were modest.
**R F JohnsonHoughton [4-21] Anthony Pye-Jeary.*

CERBERA BHB 32f28a **RR 28a** 757[9]
9 b g Caruso - Sealed Contract (Runnymede) 9.3f **(50)**
Form - 0
Record 1998 - 1st:0 2nd:0 3rd:0 Ran:1
Pre1998 - 1st:0 2nd:0 3rd:0 Ran:11
1998 AW 0-1: (7f) (Fibr)
Very moderate gelding, has worn blinkers. Becoming disappointing. **J P Smith [0-13] P R Wheeler.*

CERTAIN DANGER (IRE) BHB 43f **RR 49f** 3395[7]
3 b f Warning 8.1f **(77)**- Please Believe Me(Try My Best (USA))7.6f **(67)**
Form - 054057
Record 1998 - 1st:0 2nd:0 3rd:0 Ran:6
Pre1998 - 1st:0 2nd:0 3rd:0 Ran:1
1998 Turf 0-6: (7f 2, 8f, 10f 3) (gd 2, g-f 2, frm 2)
Light-framed, moderate filly, effective 8f, acts on g-f. Turf high 49 - 4th of 12 getting 20lb from Migrate (15 Jly Yarmouth 8f g-f RF 2835).
**N A Callaghan [0-6] Paul & Jenny Green (from R Hannon [0-1] Nov 1997).*

CERTAIN SURPRISE BHB 38f31a **RR 60f 31a** 1199[6]
4 b f Grey Desire 9.3f **(49)** - Richesse (FR) (Faraway Son (USA)) 10.3f **(55)**
Form - 766
Record 1998 - 1st:0 2nd:0 3rd:0 Ran:3
Pre1998 - 1st:0 2nd:0 3rd:0 Ran:4
1998 AW 0-3: (10f, 12f, 16f) (Equi 3)
Scopey, average filly, has worn blinkers. AW high 18.
**M Madgwick [0-12] Mrs H Veal.*

CERULEAN SKY (IRE) RR 102f 4725a[6]
2 f
Form - 6
1998 Turf 0-1: (8f) (sft)
Currently very useful filly. (1st run) - 6th of 11 to Juvenia (4 Oct Longchamp 8f sft RF 4725a). She made all to win on her debut, and was only beaten a length and a quarter when finishing sixth in the Prix Marcel Boussac. She did not enjoy much luck in running that day and could still make her mark in Group company.
**R Collet in FR [0-1] R C Strauss.*

CETEWAYO (USA) RR 109f 5167a[6]
4 b c His Majesty (USA) 10.6f **(69)**- Aletta Maria (USA)(Diesis) 9.3f **(69)**
Form - 6
1998 Turf 0-1: (12f) (frm)
Currently Pattern-class colt, always wears blinkers. Trained by Michael Dickinson, he did not run at all badly when sixth in the

Breeders' Cup Turf. **M W Dickinson in USA [0-1] J Chandler.*

CHABROL (CAN) BHB 48f62a **RR 55df 62a** 3586[4]
5 b h El Gran Senor (USA) 8.9f **(85)** - Off The Record (USA) (Chas Conerly (USA)) 10.1f **(76)**
Form - 20504
Record **1998** - 1st:0 2nd:1 3rd:0 Ran:5
Pre1998 - 1st:1 2nd:2 3rd:2 Ran:18
Win Prizemoney £2,945 *Total Prizemoney* £7,089
Wins 1996 Aug Yarmou (G-F) C 10.1f 61 <
1998 Turf 0-4: (14f, 15f, 16f 2) (gd, g-f, frm, hrd) 1998 AW 0-1: (16f) (Fibr)
Fair colt, effective 12 to 16f, best at 14f, acts on gd to frm - acts on Fibr, best on gd, prefers left handed tracks, prefers tight tracks, likes Nottingham. Turf high 55. (1st run) - 2nd of 9 giving 11lb to Swing West (2 Feb Southwell 16f Fibr RF 0202). Inconsistent. Without a win on the Flat since August '96, he has been placed several times since, and was runner-up on his sand debut at Southwell in February, though it was a very modest race.
**K G Wingrove [0-5] The Chabrol Partnership (from John Berry [1-7] Feb 1998).*

CHADLEIGH LANE (USA) BHB 49f47a **RR 43?f 47a** 2965[8]
6 ch g Imp Society (USA) 7.1f **(63)** - Beauty Hour (USA) (Bold Hour) 10f **(81)**
Form - 37428
Record **1998** - 1st:0 2nd:0 3rd:0 Ran:1
Pre1998 - 1st:7 2nd:5 3rd:7 Ran:49
Win Prizemoney £16,421 *Total Prizemoney* £24,460
Wins 1997 *Jan Southw (STD) H 8f 59 66*
1996 *Nov Southw (STD) C 8f 63*
1996 *Mar Wolver (STD) S 8.5f 64+*
1996 *Feb Southw (STD) H 7f 57 63*
1996 *Jan Southw (STD) C 8f 57*
1995 *Apr Wolver (STD) 7f 64*
1994 *Nov Southw (STD) 6f 70*
1998 AW 0-1: (8f) (Fibr)
Moderate gelding, effective 8 to 9f, - acts on Fibr, has worn blinkers, favours left handed tracks, favours tight tracks.
**K A Ryan [0-1] The Gloria Darley Racing Partnership (from A B Mulholland [0-13] Dec 1997).*

CHAHAYA TIMOR (IRE) BHB 60f70a **RR 66f 70a** 432[4]
6 b g Slip Anchor 12.7f **(75)** - Roxy Hart (High Top) 10.2f **(67)**
Form - 41164
Record **1998** - 1st:2 2nd:0 3rd:0 Ran:5
Pre1998 - 1st:1 2nd:1 3rd:1 Ran:7
Win Prizemoney £6,978 *Total Prizemoney* £8,891
Wins * **1998** *Feb Wolver (STD) S 16.2f 59++*
1998 *Jan Wolver (STD) S 14.8f 62*
1995 *Aug Wolver (STD) H 12f 66 67* <
1998 AW 2-5: (15f 1-2, 16f 1-3) (Equi, Fibr 2-4)
Average gelding. AW high 67. Lightly-raced of late, he won a very bad seller on the Wolverhampton Fibresand in January by a street, and was sold at the subsequent auction. He won a similarly poor race at the same track for his new stable by an equally emphatic margin, but has been a little fortunate to have found two such terrible events.
**Miss S J Wilton [1-3] John Pointon and Sons (from R Simpson [1-3] Jan 1998).*

CHAIRMANOFTHEBOARD (IRE) BHB 47f **RR 36f** 1475[17]
3 b g Mujadil (USA) 7.7f **(70)** - Leaps And Bounds (IRE) (Salmon Leap (USA)) 11f **(61)**
Form - 7700
Record **1998** - 1st:0 2nd:0 3rd:0 Ran:4
Pre1998 - 1st:0 2nd:0 3rd:0 Ran:1
1998 Turf 0-3: (6f, 7f, 8f) (sft 2, g-f) 1998 AW 0-1: (8f) (Fibr)
Very moderate gelding. Turf high 36.
**R Craggs [0-4] Ten For Sport Partnership (from J S Bolger in IRE [0-1] Jun 1997).*

CHAIRMANS CHOICE BHB 52f80a **RR 61f 80a** 3949[4]
8 ch g Executive Man 8.9f **(52)** - Revida Girl (Habat) 7.6f **(61)**
Form - 113220765514
Record **1998** - 1st:2 2nd:2 3rd:1 Ran:11
Pre1998 - 1st:6 2nd:3 3rd:8 Ran:35
Win Prizemoney £25,752 *Total Prizemoney* £38,242
Wins * **1998** Aug Bright (FRM) C 10f 61
* **1998** *Jan Lingfi (STD) C 10f 71*
* 1997 *Nov Lingfi (STD) S 10f 60+*
* 1996 Jun Bright (FRM) H 7f 56 66
* 1995 *Nov Wolver (STD) H 9.4f 65 77* <
* 1995 Aug York (G-F) H 7.9f 50 56
* 1995 Jly Ripon (G-F) H 8f 44 49
* 1994 *Jan Southw (STD) 8f 50+*
1998 Turf 1-7: (8f 4, 10f 1-3) (g-s, gd 2, g-f 1-2, frm 2) 1998 AW 1-4: (8f, 10f 1-3) (Equi 1-3, Fibr)
Above-average gelding, effective 8 to 10f, best at 10f, - acts on AW, best on Equi, prefers left handed tracks, prefers tight tracks, excels at Lingfield. Turf high 61. AW high 76 - 2nd of 11 getting 3lb from Herr Trigger (3 Mar Lingfield 10f Equi RF 0393) - also 1st of 7 getting 3lb from Joseph's Wine (10 Jan Lingfield RF 0061).
**A P Jarvis [8-47] Mrs D B Brazier.*

CHAI-YO BHB 80f **RR 75?f** 4744[13]
8 b g Rakaposhi King 9.3f **(55)** - Ballysax Lass (Main Reef) 9.6f **(57)**
Form - 0
Record **1998** - 1st:0 2nd:0 3rd:0 Ran:1
Pre1998 - 1st:0 2nd:1 3rd:0 Ran:4
Win Prizemoney £0 *Total Prizemoney* £1,938
1998 Turf 0-1: (8f) (g-s)
Above-average gelding. **J A B Old [5-22] Nick Viney.*

CHAKRA BHB 49f **RR 52f** 4649[6]
4 gr g Mystiko (USA) 7.7f **(59)** - Maracuja (USA) (Riverman (USA)) 9.1f **(76)**
Form - 0307101600536
Record **1998** - 1st:2 2nd:0 3rd:2 Ran:13
Pre1998 - 1st:1 2nd:0 3rd:0 Ran:9
Win Prizemoney £8,213 *Total Prizemoney* £9,245
Wins * **1998** Aug Warwic (G-F) H 5f 47 52 <
* **1998** Jly Warwic (G-F) H 5f 42 46
1997 Jly Bright (FRM) H 5.3f 45 48
1998 Turf 2-12: (5f 2-11, 6f) (gd 2, g-f 3, frm 1-6, hrd 1-1) 1998 AW 0-1: (6f) (Equi)
Strong, fair gelding, effective 5f, acts on frm to hrd, best on frm, prefers left handed tracks. Turf high 52 - 1st of 19 giving 1lb to Sotonian (14 Aug Warwick RF 3647) - also 1st of 8 getting 12lb from American Cousin (11 Jly Warwick RF 2730).
**J M Bradley [2-13] Clifton Hunt (from S Dow [1-9] Spt 1997).*

CHALCEDONY BHB 54f **RR 51f** 2224[10]
2 ch g Highest Honor (FR) 10.9f **(72)** - Sweet Holland (USA) (Alydar (USA)) 9.1f **(76)**
Form - 400
Record **1998** - 1st:0 2nd:0 3rd:0 Ran:3
Win Prizemoney £0 *Total Prizemoney* £221
1998 Turf 0-3: (5f, 6f 2) (gd 2, g-f)
Currently fair gelding. Turf high 51. **T D Barron [0-3] J Baggott.*

CHALKY DANCER BHB 27f29a **RR 17f 29a** 3412a[3]
6 br g Adbass (USA) 12.2f **(45)** - Tiny Feet (Music Maestro) 7.7f **(66)**
Form - 6803
Record **1998** - 1st:0 2nd:0 3rd:1 Ran:2
Pre1998 - 1st:0 2nd:4 3rd:1 Ran:26
Win Prizemoney £0 *Total Prizemoney* £4,380
1998 Turf 0-2: (7f 2) (g-f, frm)
Little account gelding, effective 8 to 10f, best at 8f, acts on gd to frm, has worn blinkers, prefers tight tracks. Turf high 14 (began Jly). **H J Collingridge [0-32].*

CHALLENGES (FR) **RR 84?f** 4211a[3]
2 b c Zieten (USA) - La Toscanella (FR) (Riverton (FR))
Form - 32533
Record **1998** - 1st:0 2nd:1 3rd:3 Ran:5
Win Prizemoney £0 *Total Prizemoney* £7,425
1998 Turf 0-5: (6f 2, 7f 2, 8f) (g-s, gd 4)
Decent colt. Turf high 84 - 3rd of 10 to Antinous (1 Spt Longchamp 8f gd RF 4211a). Caught the eye on his Newbury debut and ran in France for the remainder of the campaign. **B J Meehan [0-5].*

CHALOUPE BHB 61f **RR 59f** 4610[6]
2 b f College Chapel - Shallop **(44f 53a)** (Salse (USA)) 7.5f **(66)**
Form - 006

Record 1998 - 1st:0 2nd:0 3rd:0 Ran:3
1998 Turf 0-3: (5f, 6f 2) (g-s, gd, g-f)
Currently fair filly. Turf high 59. **H Candy [0-3] W M Lidsey.*

CHALUZ BHB 37f51a **RR 31f 51a** 1766[12]

4 b g Night Shift (USA) 8.1f **(73)** -Laluche (USA)(Alleged (USA))10f **(76)**
Form - 14531217440080
Record 1998 - 1st:2 2nd:1 3rd:0 Ran:10
Pre1998 - 1st:1 2nd:1 3rd:2 Ran:15
Win Prizemoney £6,113 *Total Prizemoney* £8,671
Wins * **1998** *Jan Southw (STD) H 7f 53 59 <*
* **1998** *Jan Southw (STD) H 8f 53 55*
* 1997 *Nov Southw (STD) H 7f 48 53*
1998 Turf 0-1: (8f) (frm) 1998 AW 2-9: (6f, 7f 1-4, 8f 1-4)(Equi, Fibr 2-8)
Strong, fair gelding, effective 7 to 8f, best at 8f, - acts on AW, best on Fibr, prefers left handed tracks, favours tight tracks, excels at Southwell. AW high 59 - 1st of 9 getting 2lb from Pleasure Trick (23 Jan Southwell RF 0143) - also 1st of 14 giving 2lb to Shontaine (12 Jan Southwell RF 0077). Becoming disappointing. A modest performer overall, he does win from time to time, and seems particularly well suited by seven furlongs to a mile at Southwell. He likes to race prominently.
**K R Burke [3-21] Nigel Shields (from M Johnston [0-4] Nov 1996).*

CHAMBRE SEPAREE (USA) **RR 77f** 5072[4]

2 ro f Cozzene (USA) 10.1f **(87)** - Ice House (Northfields (USA)) 9f **(72)**
Form - 74
Record 1998 - 1st:0 2nd:0 3rd:0 Ran:2
Win Prizemoney £0 *Total Prizemoney* £277
1998 Turf 0-2: (7f 2) (gd 2)
Currently above-average filly. Turf high 77 (began Oct) - 4th of 16 to Eden (31 Oct Newmarket 7f gd RF 5072).
**G Wragg [0-2] Miss K Rausing.*

CHAMELEON **RR 41f** 5064[14]

2 b f Green Desert (USA) 7.8f **(78)** - Old Domesday Book (High Top) 10.2f **(67)**
Form - 0
Record 1998 - 1st:0 2nd:0 3rd:0 Ran:1
1998 Turf 0-1: (6f) (g-f)
Currently moderate filly. **M Bell [0-1] Lordship Stud.*

CHAMELI BHB 51f59a **RR 61f 59a** 4535[9]

3 b f Nordico (USA) 8.2f **(59)** - Try Vickers (USA) (Fuzzbuster (USA)) 6.3f **(63)**
Form - 533070
Record 1998 - 1st:0 2nd:0 3rd:2 Ran:6
Pre1998 - 1st:0 2nd:0 3rd:0 Ran:2
Win Prizemoney £0 *Total Prizemoney* £1,097
1998 Turf 0-3:(7f, 8f, 12f)(g-s 2, frm)1998 AW 0-3: (8f, 10f, 12f) (Equi 3)
Lengthy, average filly, effective 8f, - acts on Equi, has worn blinkers, likes tight tracks. Turf high 51. AW high 57.
**J L Eyre [0-2] P Royle (from Mrs L Stubbs [0-6] Apr 1998).*

CHAMPAGNE (NZ) **RR 110f** 5153a[2]

4 b f Zabeel (AUS) - L'quiz (USA) (L'Enjoleur (CAN)) 8f **(65)**
Form - 12
1998 Turf 1-2: (10f 1-1, 16f) (gd 1-2)
Currently Group-class filly. Turf high 110 (began Oct) - 2nd of 24 to Jezabeel (3 Nov Flemington 16f gd RF 5153a) - also 1st of 11 getting 6lb from Northern Drake (31 Oct Flemington RF 5133a). Versatile New Zealand filly, just caught in the Melbourne Cup.
**L Laxon in NZ [1-2] R Emery.*

CHAMPAGNE AFFAIR **RR 10f** 5000[10]

2 b f Alnasr Alwasheek 9.4f **(62)** - Dewberry (Bay Express) 7.1f **(60)**
Form - 0
Record 1998 - 1st:0 2nd:0 3rd:0 Ran:1
1998 Turf 0-1: (7f) (sft)
Currently poor filly. **E A Wheeler [0-1] G Stafford & A J Claydon.*

CHAMPAGNE GOLD BHB 25f **RR 10f** 2176[9]

11 ch g Bairn (USA) 9.4f **(55)** - Halkissimo (Khalkis)
Form - 0
Record 1998 - 1st:0 2nd:0 3rd:0 Ran:1
Pre1998 - 1st:0 2nd:1 3rd:3 Ran:16
Win Prizemoney £0 *Total Prizemoney* £5,091
1998 Turf 0-1: (16f) (gd)
Poor gelding. Inconsistent.
**J C McConnochie [3-27] J C McConnochie (from Denys Smith [0-7] Oct 1990).*

CHAMPAGNE N DREAMS BHB 53f50a **RR 54f 50a** 4547[13]

6 b m Rambo Dancer(CAN) 8.4f **(59)**- Pink Sensation (Sagaro) 9.7f **(55)**
Form - 221030
Record 1998 - 1st:1 2nd:2 3rd:1 Ran:6
Pre1998 - 1st:1 2nd:0 3rd:4 Ran:27
Win Prizemoney £5,372 *Total Prizemoney* £10,239
Wins * **1998** Aug Chepst (G-F) H 8.1f 48 54
* 1995 May Mussel (GD) H 8.1f 53 58 <
1998 Turf 1-5: (7f, 8f 1-2, 10f 2) (g-f 2, frm 1-3) 1998 AW 0-1: (7f) (Fibr)
Fair mare, effective 7 to 10f, acts on g-f to frm, best on frm, has worn blinkers, likes tight tracks. Turf high 54 (began Jly) - 1st of 20 giving 13lb to Zahran (13 Aug Chepstow RF 3605).
**D Nicholls [2-36] G A Harker.*

CHAMPAGNE RIDER BHB 92f **RR 87f** 3221[5]

2 b c Presidium 7.5f **(56)** - Petitesse (Petong) 6.6f **(58)**
Form - 1310465
Record 1998 - 1st:2 2nd:0 3rd:1 Ran:7
Win Prizemoney £7,970 *Total Prizemoney* £11,113
Wins * **1998** May Kempto (GD) 6f 83 <
* **1998** Apr Kempto (HVY) 5f 74
1998 Turf 2-7: (5f 1-5, 6f 1-2) (hvy 1-1, g-s, gd 1-4, g-f)
Useful colt, effective 5 to 6f, acts on gd. Turf high 87 - 6th of 19 getting 1lb from Flanders (18 Jly Newbury 5f gd RF 2910) - also 1st of 7 giving 7lb to Pas de Probleme (23 May Kempton RF 1424). Out of a sister to Paris House, he was a useful two-year-old, a winner twice in the spring. Has run some creditable races in decent company, but is some way below top class.
**K McAuliffe [2-7] Highgrove Developments Ltd.*

CHANCANCOOK BHB 20f23a **RR 19f 23a** 13[8]

5 ch m Hubbly Bubbly (USA) 9.5f **(43)** - Majuba Road (Scottish Rifle) 10f **(55)**
Form - 8
Record 1998 - 1st:0 2nd:0 3rd:0 Ran:1
Pre1998 - 1st:0 2nd:0 3rd:0 Ran:7
1998 AW 0-1: (11f) (Fibr)
Poor filly. **J L Eyre [0-8] J Chan.*

CHANDLER'S HALL BHB 33f **RR 41f** 4506[15]

4 b c Saddlers' Hall (IRE) 10.5f **(65)** - Queen's Visit (Top Command (USA)) 10f **(77)**
Form - 855500
Record 1998 - 1st:0 2nd:0 3rd:0 Ran:6
Pre1998 - 1st:0 2nd:0 3rd:0 Ran:5
Win Prizemoney £0 *Total Prizemoney* £250
1998 Turf 0-5: (10f 2, 12f 2, 14f) (gd 3, g-f, frm) 1998 AW 0-1: (16f) (Equi)
Well made, moderate colt. Turf high 41 (began Jly). Inconsistent.
**M J Heaton-Ellis [0-11] Sir Peter Cazalet.*

CHANGED TO BAILEYS (IRE)BHB 51f47a **RR 52df 47a** 86[12]

4 b g Distinctly North (USA) 7.4f **(63)** - Blue Czarina (Sandhurst Prince) 7.9f **(63)**
Form - 0
Record 1998 - 1st:0 2nd:0 3rd:0 Ran:1
Pre1998 - 1st:0 2nd:0 3rd:2 Ran:8
Win Prizemoney £0 *Total Prizemoney* £1,036
1998 AW 0-1: (6f) (Fibr)
Light-framed, fair gelding, has worn blinkers. Becoming disappointing. **R T Juckes [0-1] A C W Price (from J Berry [0-8] Jun 1997).*

CHANSON D'AMOUR (IRE) BHB 20f **RR 17f** 3887[11]

4 b f High Estate 10.5f **(66)** - Wind of Change (FR) (Sicyos (USA))
Form - 0
Record 1998 - 1st:0 2nd:0 3rd:0 Ran:1
Pre1998 - 1st:0 2nd:0 3rd:1 Ran:17
Win Prizemoney £0 *Total Prizemoney* £839
1998 Turf 0-1: (17f) (gd)
Scopey, poor filly, has worn blinkers.
**M D Hammond [0-1] R F Stewart (from Miss L A Perratt [0-17] Spt 1997).*

CHARGE BHB 80f **RR 66f** 2959[3]
2 gr c Petong 7.6f **(58)** - Madam Petoski (Petoski) 5.7f **(62)**
Form - 343
Record 1998 - 1st:0 2nd:0 3rd:2 Ran:3
Win Prizemoney £0 *Total Prizemoney* £1,074
1998 Turf 0-3: (5f, 6f 2) (gd, g-f, frm)
Currently average colt. Turf high 66. **B Smart [0-3] Lacey, Buckham.*

CHARGE D'AFFAIRES RR 117f 4947a[2]
3 b c Kendor - Lettre de Cachet (FR) (Secreto (USA)) 8.7f **(72)**
Form - 582
1998 Turf 0-3: (5f, 7f, 8f) (hvy, sft, gd)
High-class colt, effective 6 to 8f, acts on hvy to gd. Turf high 113 - 2nd of 9 getting 2lb from Tomba (18 Oct Longchamp 7f hvy RF 4947a). A high-class juvenile in '97, he beat Xaar in the Morny and chased home Second Empire in the Grand Criterium. Finished fifth to Victory Note in the French Guineas in May and, after a break, was beaten under five lengths in the l'Abbaye. Chased home Tomba in the Prix de la Foret on his final start, over seven furlongs, which may prove his optimum trip.
**A deRoyerDupre in FR [1-8] Marquesa de Moratalla.*

CHARISMATIQUE (GER) RR 94f 2284a[1]
3 f
Form - 1
1998 Turf 1-1: (9f 1-1) (gd 1-1)
Currently useful filly. (1st run) - 1st of 12 giving 7lb to Katah (21 Jun Dortmund RF 2284a). **A Schutz in GER [1-1] Stall Veria.*

CHARITA (IRE) RR 95f 4795a[1]
4 ch f Lycius (USA) 8.8f **(71)** - Seme de Lys (USA) (Slew O' Gold (USA)) 8f **(75)**
Form - 561
1998 Turf 1-3: (8f 1-1, 10f, 12f) (g-s, gd 1-2)
Very useful filly, effective 8 to 10f, acts on g-s to gd, has worn blinkers. Turf high 95 (began Spt) - 1st of 15 giving 3lb to Heed My Warning (11 Oct Naas RF 4795a). Improving filly now with Liam Browne. Has been running in Listed company and can go on to score again.
**L Browne in IRE [1-3] Mrs Jacqueline Alder (from J G Burns in IRE [1-9] Aug 1997).*

CHARITY CRUSADER BHB 54f **RR 53f** 4254[7]
7 b g Rousillon (USA) 10.4f **(69)** - Height of Folly (Shirley Heights) 10.3f **(74)**
Form - 6744232147
Record 1998 - 1st:1 2nd:2 3rd:1 Ran:10
Pre1998 - 1st:3 2nd:3 3rd:1 Ran:18
Win Prizemoney £16,535 *Total Prizemoney* £25,495
Wins * 1998 Aug Mussel (G-F) H 16f 48 51
*** 1997** Aug Redcar (G-F) C 14.1f 41
1998 Turf 1-10: (14f 3, 16f 1-7) (g-s, gd 1-6, frm 3)
Fair gelding, effective 14 to 16f, best at 16f, acts on g-s to frm, often wears blinkers (very effectively), likes right handed tracks, favours tight tracks, and likes Musselburgh. Turf high 53 - 4th of 11 giving 19lb to On The Mat (1 Spt Ripon 16f g-s RF 4015) - also 1st of 6 getting 7lb from Netta Rufina (19 Aug Musselburgh RF 3748). Consistent. He has managed to reach the frame in modest handicaps this term, and was awarded a Musselburgh handicap in August, but is somewhat one-paced and not the heartiest of battlers.
**Mrs M Reveley [5-27] The Mary Reveley Racing Club (from P W Chapple-Hyam [2-10] Jun 1995).*

CHARLENE LACY (IRE) BHB 81f **RR 74f** 2910[14]
2 ch f Pips Pride 6.7f **(70)** - Friendly Song (Song) 7.2f **(61)**
Form - 1840
Record 1998 - 1st:1 2nd:0 3rd:0 Ran:4
Win Prizemoney £5,598 *Total Prizemoney* £5,819
Wins * 1998 Mar Doncas (GD) 5f 72 <
1998 Turf 1-4: (5f 1-4) (g-s, gd 1-2, frm)
Above-average filly. Turf high 74 - 4th of 9 getting 6lb from Red Lion (29 Jun Windsor 5f frm RF 2388) - also 1st of 17 getting 5lb from Principality (26 Mar Doncaster RF 0470). Won the Brocklesby on her debut, but has been found wanting since.
**A P Jarvis [1-4] Mrs Ann Jarvis.*

CHARLES SPENCELAYH (IRE) BHB 95f **RR 94f** 4870[6]
2 b g Tenby 10.4f **(76)** - Legit (IRE) (Runnett) 7f **(59)**
Form - 3116
Record 1998 - 1st:2 2nd:0 3rd:1 Ran:4
Win Prizemoney £7,105 *Total Prizemoney* £7,720
Wins * 1998 Spt Salisb (HVY) 7f 94 <
** 1998 Aug Wolver (STD) 7f 83+*
1998 Turf 1-2: (7f 1-1, 8f) (gd 1-2) 1998 AW 1-2: (5f, 7f 1-1) (Equi, Fibr 1-1)
Useful gelding. Turf high 94 (1st run) (began Spt) - 1st of 4 giving 11lb to Cheshire Cat (30 Spt Salisbury RF 4587). AW high 83. He finished third in a maiden on the Lingfield Equitrack in March which, though it did not look a great race at the time, has in fact worked out particularly well. Given four months off, during which time he was gelded, he won a maiden on the Wolverhampton Fibresand with consummate ease, but disappointed last time out in a Listed race at Pontefract. This was not his true form and this useful colt will improve. Needs soft ground.
**P F I Cole [2-4] Richard Green (Fine Paintings).*

CHARLIE CHANG (IRE) BHB 39f39a **RR 37f 39a** 883[9]
5 b g Don't Forget Me 9.5f **(66)** - East River (FR) (Arctic Tern (USA)) 8.9f **(69)**
Form - 620
Record 1998 - 1st:0 2nd:1 3rd:0 Ran:3
Pre1998 - 1st:1 2nd:1 3rd:1 Ran:16
Win Prizemoney £3,095 *Total Prizemoney* £6,439
Wins 1995 *Nov Lingfi (STD) 8f 73* <
1998 Turf 0-1: (10f) (g-s) 1998 AW 0-2: (9f, 11f) (Fibr 2)
Very moderate gelding, has worn blinkers. AW high 31.
**B J Llewellyn [0-8] A P Gent (from D W Barker [0-3] Spt 1997).*

CHARLIE CHOOK BHB 34f **RR 47f** 3310[8]
4 ch g Precocious 7.2f **(54)**- Double Merit (IRE)(Doulab (USA)) 9.8f **(65)**
Form - 700P08
Record 1998 - 1st:0 2nd:0 3rd:0 Ran:6
1998 Turf 0-6: (7f, 8f, 10f, 12f, 13f, 16f) (gd 3, g-f 2, frm)
Unfurnished, moderate gelding, has worn blinkers. Turf high 47.
**M Mullineaux [0-6] Mrs C E Collinson.*

CHARLIE GIRL RR 73f 4836[3]
2 b f Puissance 7.1f **(60)** - Charolles (Ajdal (USA)) 9.2f **(89)**
Form - 013334223
Record 1998 - 1st:1 2nd:2 3rd:4 Ran:9
Win Prizemoney £2,757 *Total Prizemoney* £7,146
Wins * 1998 May Mussel (G-F) 5f 69 <
1998 Turf 1-9: (5f 1-8, 6f) (g-s, gd 1-5, frm 3)
Above-average filly, effective 5f, acts on gd to frm, best on frm, excels at Musselburgh. Turf high 73 - 4th of 8 giving 5lb to Class Wan (19 Aug Musselburgh 5f gd RF 3747) - also 1st of 13 getting 6lb from Callitwhatyouwant (18 May Musselburgh RF 1298). Consistent. **J Berry [1-9] T G & Mrs M E Holdcroft.*

CHARLIELPAGEO'S BHB 46f **RR 48f** 4866[3]
2 ch f Pharly (FR) 11.5f **(64)** - Cryptal (Persian Bold) 9.3f **(66)**
Form - 46663
Record 1998 - 1st:0 2nd:0 3rd:1 Ran:5
Win Prizemoney £0 *Total Prizemoney* £290
1998 Turf 0-2: (6f 2) (gd 2) 1998 AW 0-3: (6f, 7f, 8f) (Fibr 3)
Fair filly. Turf high 48. AW high 50 (began Jly).
**W G M Turner [0-5] A R Brown.*

CHARLIES BRIDE (IRE) BHB 62f **RR 73f** 4677[21]
3 b br f Rich Charlie 5.9f **(50)** - Nordic Bride (IRE) (Nordico (USA)) 6.5f **(62)**
Form - 1254078140
Record 1998 - 1st:2 2nd:1 3rd:0 Ran:10
Win Prizemoney £5,158 *Total Prizemoney* £6,122
Wins * 1998 Aug Carlis (G-S) 6.9f 73 <
*** 1998** Apr Pontef (G-S) S 6f 52
1998 Turf 2-10: (5f, 6f 1-3, 7f 1-4, 8f 2) (g-s 1-2, gd 1-5, g-f 2, frm)
Above-average filly, effective 7f, acts on gd, has worn blinkers, likes tight tracks. Turf high 73 - 1st of 15 getting 2lb from Palo Blanco (26 Aug Carlisle RF 3883).
**J J O'Neill [2-10] Pointerfarm Racing Partnership.*

CHARLIE'S GOLD BHB 49f49a **RR 35f 49a** 3811[7]
3 b g Shalford (IRE) 7.8f **(63)** - Ballet (Sharrood (USA)) 10.5f **(72)**
Form - 70017
Record 1998 - 1st:1 2nd:0 3rd:0 Ran:5
Pre1998 - 1st:0 2nd:0 3rd:0 Ran:2
Win Prizemoney £1,966 *Total Prizemoney* £1,966
Wins • **1998** *Aug Wolver (STD) H 14.8f 46 51* <
1998 Turf 0-2: (6f, 7f) (sft, frm) 1998 AW 1-3: (6f, 15f 1-1, 16f) (Equi, Fibr 1-2)
Light-framed, fair gelding, effective 15f, - acts on Fibr, often wears blinkers. Turf high 35. AW high 51 - 1st of 12 getting 13lb from Makati (7 Aug Wolverhampton RF 3454). He caused something of a surprise when winning an apprentice handicap on the Wolverhampton Fibresand in August, but he had won impressively over hurdles just six days earlier, so was obviously in form.
•A Kelleway [2-7] Classic Gold (from I Campbell [0-2] Nov 1997).

CHARLIE SIDDLE BHB 40f **RR 47f** 3270[4]
4 b g Thowra (FR) 11.2f **(47)** - Figrant (USA) (L'Emigrant (USA)) 10.5f **(62)**
Form - 8874
Record 1998 - 1st:0 2nd:0 3rd:0 Ran:4
1998 Turf 0-3: (12f, 14f 2) (gd 2, frm) 1998 AW 0-1: (16f) (Equi)
Moderate gelding. Turf high 47. *•R Simpson [0-4] C B Siddle.*

CHARLTON SPRING (IRE) BHB 38f **RR 43f** 5173a[1]
4 ch f Masterclass (USA) 5.9f **(63)** - Relankina (IRE) (Broken Hearted)
Form - 58041
Record 1998 - 1st:1 2nd:0 3rd:0 Ran:5
Pre1998 - 1st:1 2nd:2 3rd:0 Ran:12
Win Prizemoney £6,922 *Total Prizemoney* £8,466
Wins • **1998** Nov Currag (SFT) H 7f 38 43
1996 Aug Windso (GD) H 6f 70 64 <
1998 Turf 1-5: (6f, 7f 1-1, 8f, 9f, 10f) (sft 1-1, g-s 2, frm 2)
Leggy, moderate filly, effective 7f, acts on sft. Turf high 43 - 1st of 23 getting 15lb from Three Musketeers (6 Nov Curragh RF 5173a). Showed little at three.
•P Martin in IRE [1-2] Impact II Racing Syndicate (from R J Hodges [1-15] Jun 1998).

CHARMED EXISTENCE (IRE) RR 66f 1793[9]
3 b f Sadler's Wells (USA) 11.3f **(87)** - Broadway Joan (USA) (Bold Arian (USA)) 10f **(97)**
Form - 0
Record 1998 - 1st:0 2nd:0 3rd:0 Ran:1
1998 Turf 0-1: (10f) (hrd)
Scopey, currently average filly.
•Sir Michael Stoute [0-1] M Tabor & Mrs John Magnier.

CHARMES (USA) BHB 100f **RR 95+f** 3912a[1]
2 b br c Personal Hope (USA) - Double The Charm (USA) (Nodouble (USA)) 8.8f **(68)**
Form - 3111
Record 1998 - 1st:3 2nd:0 3rd:1 Ran:4
Win Prizemoney £50,983 *Total Prizemoney* £51,500
Wins • **1998** Aug Deauvi (SFT) L 8f 95 <
• **1998** Jly Doncas (G-F) 7f 95+
• **1998** Jly Newbur (GD) 7.3f 92+
1998 Turf 3-4: (7f 2-3, 8f 1-1) (sft 1-1, gd 1-2, g-f 1-1)
Very useful colt. Turf high 95 - 1st of 11 getting 5lb from Franc (22 Aug Deauville RF 3912a) - also 1st of 4 giving 8lb to Courtesan (30 Jly Doncaster RF 3211). Ran with credit on his debut and then progressed into a useful performer, notching up a hat-trick of victories. Winning a Listed race at Deauville over a mile on his final start was the pick of his triumphs. Looks likely to improve again from two to three, and is an interesting prospect.
•J H M Gosden [3-4] Sheikh Mohammed.

CHARMING ADMIRAL (IRE) BHB 50f53a **RR 61f 53a** 1120[8]
5 b g Shareef Dancer (USA) 10.1f **(67)**- Lilac Charm (Bustino)10.4f **(64)**
Form - 38
Record 1998 - 1st:0 2nd:0 3rd:1 Ran:2
Pre1998 - 1st:0 2nd:3 3rd:1 Ran:10
Win Prizemoney £0 *Total Prizemoney* £4,246
1998 Turf 0-1: (16f) (frm) 1998 AW 0-1: (14f) (Fibr)
Average gelding. (1st run) - 3rd of 14 giving 14lb to Carol Again (11 Mar Southwell 14f Fibr RF 0422).
•Mrs A Swinbank [2-10] Mrs Linda Corbett (from C F Wall [0-9] Jly 1997).

CHARNWOOD JACK (USA) BHB 54f **RR 48f** 2263[15]
5 ch g Sanglamore (USA) 12.9f **(67)** - Hyroglyph (USA) (Northern Dancer) 9.6f **(80)**
Form - 03000
Record 1998 - 1st:0 2nd:0 3rd:0 Ran:3
Pre1998 - 1st:1 2nd:1 3rd:1 Ran:12
Win Prizemoney £2,392 *Total Prizemoney* £4,177
Wins 1997 Jun Yarmou (FRM) 14.1f 66 <
1998 Turf 0-3: (12f, 14f, 16f) (gd 3)
Average gelding, effective 12 to 14f, best at 14f, acts on gd to frm - acts on Fibr, best on gd, likes left handed tracks. Turf high 48. Becoming disappointing.
•Martin Todhunter [1-6] Leeds Plywood and Doors Ltd (from I Campbell [1-9] Dec 1997).

CHARROUX (IRE) BHB 72f **RR 68f** 2634[8]
3 b f Darshaan 11.9f **(81)** - Durtal (Lyphard (USA)) 9.9f **(72)**
Form - 348
Record 1998 - 1st:0 2nd:0 3rd:1 Ran:3
Win Prizemoney £0 *Total Prizemoney* £1,447
1998 Turf 0-3: (10f 3) (sft, g-s, frm)
Scopey, currently average filly. Turf high 68 (1st run) - 3rd of 6 getting 4lb from Mondschein (24 Apr Sandown 10f sft RF 0850). Third in a soft-ground maiden on her debut, this beautifully-bred filly has not gone on from that. *•P W Chapple-Hyam [0-3] R E Sangster.*

C-HARRY (IRE) BHB 55f50a **RR 53f 50a** 4636[12]
4 ch c Imperial Frontier (USA) 7f **(65)** - Desert Gale (Taufan (USA)) 7f **(57)**
Form - 07535623535727330344O
Record 1998 - 1st:0 2nd:2 3rd:6 Ran:20
Pre1998 - 1st:5 2nd:6 3rd:3 Ran:27
Win Prizemoney £13,569 *Total Prizemoney* £24,041
Wins • 1997 Jly Ayr (G-F) H 7f 60 64
• 1997 *Mar Wolver (STD) H 6f 68 67* <
• 1997 *Feb Wolver (STD) H 7f 64 64*
• 1996 May Haydoc (G-S) S 5f 51
• 1996 *May Wolver (STD) S 6f 51*
1998 Turf 0-6: (6f 3, 7f 3) (gd 3, g-f 2, frm) 1998 AW 0-14: (6f 4, 7f 9, 8f) (Fibr 14)
Strong, fair colt, effective 6 to 7f, best at 6f, acts on g-f - acts on Fibr, has worn blinkers, likes left handed tracks, likes tight tracks. Turf high 58. AW high 60. A fair sort in modest company on Fibresand, he has mainly been running over six and seven furlongs on that surface recently, but was on a long losing run until winning a seller at Wolverhampton in November. Not very consistent these days. *•R Hollinshead [5-47] D Coppenhall.*

CHARTER BHB 43f55a **RR 47f 55a** 4627[9]
7 b g Reference Point 12f **(66)**- Winter Queen (Welsh Pageant) 10f **(65)**
Form - 0053820
Record 1998 - 1st:0 2nd:1 3rd:1 Ran:7
Pre1998 - 1st:0 2nd:3 3rd:0 Ran:15
Win Prizemoney £0 *Total Prizemoney* £5,863
1998 Turf 0-7: (14f, 16f 5, 17f) (gd, g-f, frm 4, hrd)
Moderate gelding, effective 15 to 17f, acts on g-s to frm, has worn blinkers, likes left handed tracks. Turf high 47.
•W Storey [0-21] Victor Chandler (Equus) Ltd (from T J Naughton [0-2] Feb 1997).

CHARTER FLIGHT RR 42f 4880[8]
2 b c Cosmonaut - Irene's Charter (Persian Bold) 9.3f **(66)**
Form - 8
Record 1998 - 1st:0 2nd:0 3rd:0 Ran:1
1998 Turf 0-1: (7f) (g-s)
Currently fair colt. *•A G Newcombe [0-1] D Bass.*

CHASETOWN CAILIN BHB 55f **RR 52f** 3500[7]
3 b f Suave Dancer (USA) 10.7f **(68)** - Kilvarnet (Furry Glen) 8.9f **(63)**
Form - 5047
Record 1998 - 1st:0 2nd:0 3rd:0 Ran:4
Pre1998 - 1st:0 2nd:0 3rd:0 Ran:2
1998 Turf 0-4: (8f 2, 10f, 11f) (gd, g-f, frm 2)

Light-framed, fair filly. Turf high 60.
**R Hollinshead [0-6] Chasetown Civil Engineering Ltd.*

CHASETOWN FLYER (USA) BHB 47f48a **RR 39f 48a** 3112[8]
4 b c Thorn Dance (USA) 8.2f **(77)** - Thought Provoker (USA) (Exceller (USA)) 12.5f **(74)**
Form - 00608
Record 1998 - 1st:0 2nd:0 3rd:0 Ran:5
Pre1998 - 1st:2 2nd:2 3rd:2 Ran:21
Win Prizemoney £6,464 *Total Prizemoney* £8,475
Wins * 1997 Jun Windso (G-F) H 8.3f 52 64 <
* 1997 Jun Salisb (G-F) H 8f 52 54
1998 Turf 0-4: (8f 3, 9f) (gd, g-f 2, frm) 1998 AW 0-1: (8f) (Equi)
Very moderate colt, effective 7 to 8f, best at 8f, acts on gd to hrd - acts on Equi, likes right handed tracks. Turf high 51. Consistent.
**N E Berry [2-15] D W Smith (from R Hollinshead [0-11] Jan 1997).*

CHASKA BHB 54f53a **RR 44f 53a** 4302[16]
3 b f Reprimand 8.2f **(63)** - Royal Passion (Ahonoora) 8.1f **(73)**
Form - 70
Record 1998 - 1st:0 2nd:0 3rd:0 Ran:2
Pre1998 - 1st:1 2nd:0 3rd:0 Ran:7
Win Prizemoney £2,598 *Total Prizemoney* £2,851
Wins 1997 Aug Hamilt (G-F) C 6f 68 <
1998 Turf 0-1: (8f) (frm) 1998 AW 0-1: (8f) (Fibr)
Lengthy, moderate filly, effective 6f, acts on frm, has worn blinkers. **A Bailey [0-5] J B Wilcox (from M Johnston [1-4] Aug 1997).*

CHATEAU ROYAL (USA) **RR 106f** 3555a[7]
3 ch c Personal Hope (USA) - Petroleuse (Habitat) 9.4f **(70)**
Form - 222264347
1998 Turf 0-9: (7f 2, 8f 4, 9f, 12f, 14f) (hvy, sft 3, gd 4, g-f)
Pattern-class colt, effective 7 to 14f, acts on hvy to g-f, has worn blinkers, prefers left handed tracks, excels at Leopardstown. Turf high 107 (1st run) - 2nd of 8 getting 17lb from Muchea (5 Apr Curragh 7f hvy RF 0605a). Consistent. Won a maiden on heavy ground easily in 1997, but was beaten at odds-on in a Group Three at the back-end. Seemed to lose his way during a busy campaign in 1998 and was even beaten over hurdles in September.
**A P O'Brien in IRE [1-13] Mrs John Magnier.*

CHATTAN BHB 78f **RR 87f** 2819[9]
3 b c Lycius (USA) 8.8f **(71)** - Chanzi (USA) (El Gran Senor (USA)) 9.6f **(76)**
Form - 1000
Record 1998 - 1st:1 2nd:0 3rd:0 Ran:4
Pre1998 - 1st:0 2nd:1 3rd:1 Ran:2
Win Prizemoney £3,785 *Total Prizemoney* £5,220
Wins * **1998** Mar Doncas (GD) 7f 87 <
1998 Turf 1-4: (7f 1-2, 8f 2) (gd 1-3, frm)
Scopey, useful colt, effective 7f, acts on gd to frm. Turf high 87 (1st run) - 1st of 13 from Waiting Knight (27 Mar Doncaster RF 0481). Narrow winner of a Doncaster maiden on his reappearance despite proving easy to back. He was well beaten in handicap company. **B W Hills [1-6] Abdullah Saeed Bul Hab.*

CHATTING (USA) BHB 100f **RR 92f** 4797[1]
2 b c Exbourne (USA) - Non Stop Talker (USA) (Arctic Tern (USA)) 8.9f **(69)**
Form - 511
Record 1998 - 1st:2 2nd:0 3rd:0 Ran:3
Win Prizemoney £7,741 *Total Prizemoney* £7,908
Wins * **1998** Oct Haydoc (SFT) 8.1f 92+ <
* **1998** Spt Chepst (G-S) 7.1f 92
1998 Turf 2-3: (7f 1-2, 8f 1-1) (sft 1-1, gd 1-1, frm)
Currently useful colt. Turf high 92 (began Aug) - 1st of 4 from Forest Shadow (14 Oct Haydock RF 4797) - also 1st of 10 from Mt Speculation (10 Spt Chepstow RF 4197). Made a promising start to his racing career winning at Chepstow and Haydock. Handles soft ground and, with stamina his strong suit, he will certainly stay and is open to improvement next season.
**Sir Michael Stoute [2-3] The Thoroughbred Corporation.*

CHAUNCY LANE (IRE) **RR 93f** 4793a[16]
4 b f Sadler's Wells (USA) 11.3f **(87)** - Broadway Joan (USA) (Bold Arian (USA)) 10f **(97)**
Form - 160
1998 Turf 1-3: (11f 1-2, 14f) (g-s, gd 1-1, g-f)
Useful filly, effective 11f, acts on gd. Turf high 93 (1st run) - 1st of 12 giving 9lb to Hazarama (17 May Naas RF 1352a). Won her first race of the season, but was not so effective when upped in class.
**M J P O'Brien in IRE [2-8] Richard Bomze.*

CHAYANEE'S ARENA (IRE) BHB 46f **RR 45f** 3949[21]
3 b f High Estate 10.5f **(66)** - Arena (Sallust) 8.4f **(63)**
Form - 00
Record 1998 - 1st:0 2nd:0 3rd:0 Ran:2
Pre1998 - 1st:0 2nd:0 3rd:0 Ran:4
1998 Turf 0-2: (8f, 10f) (gd, frm)
Light-framed, moderate filly. Turf high 6.
**A G Newcombe [0-6] N W Lake.*

CHEEK TO CHEEK BHB 63f65a **RR 63f 65a** 3592[7]
4 b f Shavian 7.7f **(67)** - Intoxication (Great Nephew) 9.9f **(64)**
Form - 118107
Record 1998 - 1st:3 2nd:0 3rd:0 Ran:6
Pre1998 - 1st:0 2nd:2 3rd:1 Ran:9
Win Prizemoney £14,150 *Total Prizemoney* £16,120
Wins * **1998** Jly Yarmou (GD) H 14.1f 60 63 <
* **1998** May Bath (FRM) H 13.1f 59 63 <
* **1998** *Apr Wolver (STD) 12f 63* <
1998 Turf 2-5: (12f 2, 13f 1-1, 14f 1-2) (g-f, frm 2-4) 1998 AW 1-1: (12f 1-1) (Fibr 1-1)
Scopey, average filly, effective 10 to 14f, acts on g-f to frm - acts on Fibr, best on frm, prefers left handed tracks, excels at Yarmouth and Brighton. Turf high 63 (1st run) - 1st of 6 getting 13lb from Shalateeno (18 May Bath RF 1294) - also 1st of 5 from Benjamin Frank (1 Jly Yarmouth RF 2460). (1st run) - 1st of 11 getting 6lb from Spartan Heartbeat (18 Apr Wolverhampton RF 0759). She showed some fair form in middle-distance handicaps in '97, but it was not until she made her debut on the Wolverhampton Fibresand in April that she got off the mark. She has added two victories on turf since. **C A Cyzer [3-15] R M Cyzer.*

CHEEKY MONKEY (USA) **RR 58f** 4663[17]
2 ch f Beau Genius (CAN) - Crystal Lake (IRE) **(88+f)** (Shirley Heights) 10.3f **(74)**
Form - 0050
Record 1998 - 1st:0 2nd:0 3rd:0 Ran:4
1998 Turf 0-4: (6f 2, 8f, 10f) (g-s, g-f, frm 2)
Fair filly. Turf high 58 (began Jly). **J Noseda [0-4] North and South.*

CHEERFUL GROOM (IRE) BHB 36f60a **RR 34f 60a** 2964[8]
7 ch g Shy Groom(USA)8.2f **(59)**-Carange (Known Fact(USA)) 7.4f **(67)**
Form - 3446322626401041318
Record 1998 - 1st:3 2nd:3 3rd:3 Ran:19
Pre1998 - 1st:2 2nd:4 3rd:7 Ran:55
Win Prizemoney £14,961 *Total Prizemoney* £23,787
Wins * **1998** *Jly Wolver (STD) H 8.5f 56 59* <
* **1998** *Jun Wolver (STD) H 8.5f 51 52*
* **1998** *May Wolver (STD) H 8.5f 41 50*
1996 May Doncas (G-F) H 7f 36 42
1994 May Carlis (FRM) H 6.9f 53 49
1998 Turf 0-2: (8f 2) (gd, frm) 1998 AW 3-17: (6f 2, 7f 5, 8f 3-8, 9f 2) (Equi, Fibr 3-16)
Fair gelding, effective 8f, - acts on Fibr, has worn blinkers, favours left handed tracks, favours tight tracks. Turf high 33. AW high 59 - 1st of 5 getting 14lb from Sea Spouse (10 Jly Wolverhampton RF 2694) - also 1st of 13 getting 11lb from Waikiki Beach (26 Jun Wolverhampton RF 2318). His win at Wolverhampton in May ended a losing run stretching back to May '96. He looks best on Fibresand these days.
**D Shaw [3-29] Bill Cahill (from S R Bowring [1-9] Jly 1996).*

CHELSEA BARRACKS BHB 85f **RR 84f** 5146[1]
2 b g Deploy 11.4f **(67)** - Hymne D'Amour (USA) (Dixieland Band (USA)) 7f **(74)**
Form - 421
Record 1998 - 1st:1 2nd:1 3rd:0 Ran:3
Win Prizemoney £3,395 *Total Prizemoney* £4,736
Wins * **1998** Nov Doncas (SFT) 8f 84 <
1998 Turf 1-3: (8f 1-3) (gd 1-3)
Currently decent gelding. Turf high 84 (began Spt) - 1st of 13 giving 5lb to Spoonful of Sugar (7 Nov Doncaster RF 5146).
**J L Dunlop [1-3] The Earl Cadogan.*

CHEMCAST BHB 45f55a **RR 38f 55a** 4921[8]
5 ch g Chilibang 7f **(55)** - Golden October (Young Generation) 7.7f **(63)**
Form - 635330344000508
Record 1998 - 1st:0 2nd:0 3rd:4 Ran:15
Pre1998 - 1st:7 2nd:4 3rd:2 Ran:42
Win Prizemoney £22,129 *Total Prizemoney* £29,496
Wins * 1997 Mar Mussel (SFT) H 5f 68 68? <
* *1996 Nov Lingfi (STD) H 5f 63 64*
1996 Jun Mussel (FRM) H 5f 65 66
1996 Jan Lingfi (STD) C 5f 65
1996 Jan Lingfi (STD) H 5f 55 62
1995 Spt Folkes (G-F) H 5f 66 68
1995 Aug Goodwo (G-F) CH 5f 63 61
1998 Turf 0-8: (5f 7, 6f)(g-s 2, gd 2, g-f 4) 1998 AW 0-7:(5f 6, 6f)(Fibr 7)
Average gelding, effective 5f, acts on gd - acts on Fibr, often wears blinkers, likes left handed tracks, likes tight tracks. Turf high 55. AW high 65. Readily beatable nowadays, he recorded all his wins on turf when sporting blinkers.
**J L Eyre [2-32] Clayton Bigley Partnership Ltd (from D Nicholls [3-14] Aug 1996).*

CHENNELL'S HILL RR 47f 4155[11]
3 ch f Hubbly Bubbly(USA) 9.5f**(43)**-Oakhurst(Mandrake Major)7.6f **(53)**
Form - 40
Record 1998 - 1st:0 2nd:0 3rd:0 Ran:2
Win Prizemoney £0 *Total Prizemoney* £241
1998 Turf 0-2: (8f, 10f) (gd, frm)
Workmanlike, currently moderate filly. Turf high 47 (began Jly).
**A Bailey [0-2] Chennell's Syndicate.*

CHERISHED (IRE) BHB 50f52a **RR 53f 52a** 4759[20]
3 b f Distinctly North (USA) 7.4f **(63)** - Key Partner (Law Society (USA)) 9.9f **(70)**
Form - 052135420
Record 1998 - 1st:1 2nd:2 3rd:1 Ran:9
Pre1998 - 1st:0 2nd:0 3rd:2 Ran:9
Win Prizemoney £3,915 *Total Prizemoney* £7,430
Wins 1998 Jun Newmar (GD) S 8f 53 <
1998 Turf 1-9: (7f, 8f 1-6, 10f 2) (g-s, gd 2, g-f 3, frm 2, hrd 1-1)
Light-framed, fair filly, effective 8f, acts on g-f to hrd - acts on Fibr, often wears blinkers, likes tight tracks. Turf high 53 - 1st of 11 from Cry For Freedom (6 Jun Newmarket RF 1789).
**J E Banks [0-4] Giles Pritchard-Gordon (from N Tinkler [1-9] Jun 1998).*

CHEROKEE BAND (USA) BHB 57f **RR 44f** 1985[16]
3 b br c Dixieland Band (USA) 10.1f **(80)** - Cherokee Darling (USA) (Alydar (USA)) 9.1f **(76)**
Form - 080
Record 1998 - 1st:0 2nd:0 3rd:0 Ran:3
Pre1998 - 1st:0 2nd:0 3rd:0 Ran:2
1998 Turf 0-3: (7f, 8f, 10f) (gd 2, frm)
Scopey, moderate colt. Turf high 44.
**B W Hills [0-5] Maktoum Al Maktoum.*

CHEROKEE CHARLIE BHB 41f42a **RR 30f 42a** 4486[11]
3 ch g Interrex (CAN) 7.7f **(51)** - Valentine Song (Pas de Seul) 9.1f **(67)**
Form - 0070
Record 1998 - 1st:0 2nd:0 3rd:0 Ran:4
Pre1998 - 1st:0 2nd:0 3rd:0 Ran:3
1998 Turf 0-2: (10f, 14f) (frm 2) 1998 AW 0-2: (8f, 11f) (Fibr 2)
Very moderate gelding. Turf high 30 (began Spt). AW high 13.
**R Craggs [0-7] Ray Craggs.*

CHEROKEE FLIGHT BHB 62f61a **RR 64f 61a** 3981[1]
4 b g Green Desert (USA) 7.8f **(78)** - Totham (Shernazar) 10.2f **(73)**
Form - 5006000251
Record 1998 - 1st:1 2nd:1 3rd:0 Ran:8
Pre1998 - 1st:3 2nd:1 3rd:2 Ran:19
Win Prizemoney £12,703 *Total Prizemoney* £16,608
Wins * **1998** Aug Chepst (G-F) H 10.2f 59 63
* *1997 Aug Wolver (STD) H 9.4f 61 64* <
* *1997 Jly Wolver (STD) H 9.4f 55 60*
1996 Jly Nottin (G-F) 5.1f 63
1998 Turf 1-8: (8f, 10f 1-7) (gd 2, g-f 3, frm 1-3)
Strong, average gelding, effective 7 to 10f, acts on g-f to frm - acts on Fibr, best on g-f, has worn blinkers, likes right handed tracks, prefers tight tracks, does well at Sandown, likes Wolverhampton. Turf high 64.
**S Mellor [3-23] Silver Knight Exhibitions Ltd (from Mrs J R Ramsden [1-6] Spt 1996).*

CHEROKEE RIDGE (IRE) RR 37tf 1321[10]
3 b g Indian Ridge 7.6f **(74)** - Arab Art (Artaius (USA)) 9f **(69)**
Form - 00
Record 1998 - 1st:0 2nd:0 3rd:0 Ran:2
1998 Turf 0-2: (10f 2) (g-s, frm)
Workmanlike, currently very moderate gelding. Turf high 37.
**P W Harris [0-2] Twelve Artisans.*

CHERRY GARDEN (IRE) BHB 32f48a **RR 36f 48a** 4120[7]
5 b g Treasure Kay 6.5f **(53)** - Door To Door (USA) (Nureyev (USA)) 8.7f **(78)**
Form - 067
Record 1998 - 1st:0 2nd:0 3rd:0 Ran:3
Pre1998 - 1st:0 2nd:1 3rd:4 Ran:14
Win Prizemoney £0 *Total Prizemoney* £2,803
1998 Turf 0-2: (10f 2) (g-f, frm) 1998 AW 0-1: (12f) (Fibr)
Moderate gelding, has worn blinkers. Turf high 36 (began Aug).
**T J Naughton [0-17] T J Naughton.*

CHERRYMENTARY BHB 32a **RR 32a** 133[9]
4 b f Rudimentary (USA) 8.2f **(66)** - Beaute Fatale (Hello Gorgeous (USA)) 9.7f **(63)**
Form - 80
Record 1998 - 1st:0 2nd:0 3rd:0 Ran:2
Pre1998 - 1st:0 2nd:0 3rd:0 Ran:2
1998 AW 0-2: (8f 2) (Equi 2)
Light-framed, little account filly. AW high 29.
**K O Cunningham-Brown [0-4] Danebury Racing Stables Ltd.*

CHESHIRE CAT (IRE) BHB 82f **RR 81f** 4761[4]
2 b f Ezzoud (IRE) - Riyda (Be My Guest (USA)) 9.3f **(67)**
Form - 324
Record 1998 - 1st:0 2nd:1 3rd:1 Ran:3
Win Prizemoney £0 *Total Prizemoney* £1,736
1998 Turf 0-3: (6f, 7f 2) (gd 3)
Currently decent filly. Turf high 81 (began Spt) - 4th of 18 to Ski Lodge (12 Oct Leicester 7f gd RF 4761).
**B W Hills [0-3] Christopher Wright.*

CHESTER HOUSE (USA) BHB 119f **RR 121f** 4852[6]
3 b c Mr Prospector (USA) 8.6f **(88)** - Toussaud (USA) (El Gran Senor (USA)) 9.6f **(76)**
Form - 4121326
Record 1998 - 1st:2 2nd:2 3rd:1 Ran:7
Pre1998 - 1st:1 2nd:1 3rd:0 Ran:2
Win Prizemoney £29,765 *Total Prizemoney* £102,302
Wins * **1998** Jly Newbur (G-F) L 10f 116+ <
* **1998** May Doncas (G-F) 10.3f 104
* 1997 Aug Goodwo (G-F) 7f 81+
1998 Turf 2-7: (8f, 10f 2-6) (hvy, gd 1-4, g-f 1-2)
Scopey, very high-class colt, effective 10f, acts on gd to g-f, best on gd. Turf high 121 - 3rd of 8 getting 5lb from One So Wonderful (18 Aug York 10f g-f RF 3696) - also 1st of 5 getting 10lb from Labeq (18 Jly Newbury RF 2912). He took time to live up to his early reputation and finished tailed off in heavy ground at Kempton on his reappearance, but ran a cracker in defeat in the Prince of Wales's Stakes. Cantered home in a listed race before losing out by two short heads in a desperate finish to the Juddmonte International, hanging left under strong pressure. Might have felt that race's effects when beaten in a listed event at Goodwood, although that was run at a crawl, and looked over the top when unplaced in the Dubai Champion Stakes.
**H R A Cecil [3-9] K Abdulla.*

CHESTER WREN RR 717[8]
4 b f Handsome Sailor 6.6f **(53)** - Chester Belle (Ballacashtal (CAN)) 5.3f **(50)**
Form - 08
Record 1998 - 1st:0 2nd:0 3rd:0 Ran:2
1998 Turf 0-1: (5f) (g-s) 1998 AW 0-1: (8f) (Fibr)
Currently very poor filly, often wears blinkers.
**M Mullineaux [0-3] Michael Mullineaux.*

Chester House gains a Listed victory

CHETANI'S MOVE BHB 23f **RR 16f** 3121[11]

3 ch f Golden Lahab(USA) 14.4f **(32)** -Megan's Move(Move Off)15f **(41)**

Form - 8000

Record 1998 - 1st:0 2nd:0 3rd:0 Ran:4

1998 Turf 0-4: (7f, 8f, 11f, 12f) (sft, gd, frm, hrd)

Light-framed, poor filly. Turf high 16. **W Storey [0-4] H S Hutchinson.*

CHEWIT BHB 88f105a **RR 92f 105a** 4985[6]

6 gr g Beveled (USA) 6.9f **(64)** - Sylvan Song (Song) 7.2f **(61)**

Form - 3114814520706

Record	**1998 -**	1st:2	2nd:1	3rd:0	Ran:11
	Pre1998 -	1st:7	2nd:7	3rd:4	Ran:35

Win Prizemoney £48,433 *Total Prizemoney* £70,761

Wins	*** 1998**	May	Goodwo	(G-F)	H	7f	84	90	
	*** 1998**	*Mar*	*Wolver*	*(STD)*		*7f*		*89*	
	* 1997	*Dec*	*Wolver*	*(STD)*	*H*	*7f*	*99*	*102*	<
	* 1997	Aug	Ascot	(GD)	H	7f	82	83	
	1996	Spt	Lingfi	(FRM)		7.6f		79+	
	1996	Spt	Lingfi	(G-F)	H	7f	77	75	
	1996	*Feb*	*Lingfi*	*(STD)*	*H*	*6f*	*90*	*88*	
	1996	*Jan*	*Lingfi*	*(STD)*	*H*	*6f*	*80*	*88+*	
	1995	*Mar*	*Lingfi*	*(STD)*	*H*	*6f*	*73*	*74*	

1998 Turf 1-9: (6f, 7f 1-7, 8f) (g-s, gd 3, g-f 1-3, frm 2) 1998 AW 1-2: (7f 1-1, 10f) (Equi, Fibr 1-1)

Very useful gelding, effective 7 to 8f, best at 7f, - acts on AW, best on Fibr, has worn blinkers, prefers left handed tracks, prefers tight tracks, excels at Wolverhampton. Turf high 92. AW high 89 (1st run). He had another profitable campaign and must be the best seven-furlong horse running regularly on the All-Weather. He is not quite as effective on turf, but is always a threat in top handicap company and ran a cracking race to finish fourth in the Wokingham at Royal Ascot. Take note if he turns out on the dirt this winter.

**G L Moore [4-22] Ballard (1834) Ltd (from A Moore [5-24] Dec 1996).*

CHEYENNE GOLD (IRE) BHB 100f **RR 93?f** 4746[7]

2 b c Anita's Prince 6f **(62)**- Gentle Papoose(Commanche Run)8.5f **(58)**

Form - 113017

Record 1998 - 1st:3 2nd:0 3rd:1 Ran:6

Win Prizemoney £10,108 *Total Prizemoney* £10,576

Wins	*** 1998**	Aug	Windso	(G-F)	6f	93	<
	*** 1998**	Jun	Windso	(G-F)	5f	84	
	*** 1998**	May	Haydoc	(GD)	5f	93+	

1998 Turf 3-6: (5f 2-4, 6f 1-2) (gd 1-3, g-f 1-1, frm 1-2)

Useful colt, effective 5 to 6f, best at 5f, acts on gd to frm, best on frm. Turf high 93 - 1st of 11 giving 6lb to Mujadene (29 Aug Windsor RF 3971) - also 1st of 18 giving 8lb to Courtesan (22 May Haydock RF 1390). Won his first two starts in good style, but disappointed at Windsor and failed to land a blow in the Super Sprint. He returned to winning ways at Windsor the following month under a hard ride, but was outclassed in a Listed race at York on his final outing. Fairly speedy, he is unlikely to stay further than six furlongs and might be hard to place. Led out unsold at 68,000 gns at Tattersalls in October.

**R Hannon [3-6] The Gold Buster Syndicate (2).*

CHEZ CATALAN BHB 23f23a **RR 26f 23a** 2541[14]

7 b g Niniski (USA) 13.2f **(67)** - Miss Saint-Cloud (Nonoalco (USA)) 8.5f **(66)**

Form - 0680

Record	**1998 -**	1st:0	2nd:0	3rd:0	Ran:4
	Pre1998 -	1st:2	2nd:4	3rd:4	Ran:26

Win Prizemoney £5,777 *Total Prizemoney* £11,449

Wins	1994	Jly	Mussel	(GD)	H	15.1f	52	56	<
	1994	Jun	Hamilt	(GD)	H	13f	48	55	

1998 Turf 0-2: (12f, 14f) (g-f, frm) 1998 AW 0-2: (13f, 14f) (Equi, Fibr)

Little account gelding, mostly wears blinkers. AW high 10.

**Mrs L C Jewell [0-4] R B Morton (from R Akehurst [0-19] Spt 1997).*

CHICAGO BEAR (IRE) BHB 68f **RR 70f** 4999[6]

2 ch c Night Shift (USA) 8.1f **(73)** - Last Drama (IRE) (Last Tycoon) 8.5f **(62)**

Form - 006

Record 1998 - 1st:0 2nd:0 3rd:0 Ran:3

1998 Turf 0-3: (6f, 7f 2) (sft, g-s, gd)

Currently above-average colt. Turf high 70 (began Oct).

**P F I Cole [0-3] Christopher Wright.*

CHICA HOLLY RR 36f 4014[11]
3 b f Bold Fox - Chica Mia (Camden Town) 9.3f **(53)**
Form - 70
Record 1998 - 1st:0 2nd:0 3rd:0 Ran:2
1998 Turf 0-2: (8f 2) (g-s, frm)
Unfurnished, currently very moderate filly. Turf high 36 (began Aug). **J L Eyre [0-2] R S Wood.*

CHICKAWICKA (IRE) BHB 73f68a **RR 73f 68a** 4985[17]
7 b h Dance of Life (USA) 9.3f **(69)** - Shabby Doll (Northfields (USA)) 9f **(72)**
Form - 0700
Record 1998 - 1st:0 2nd:0 3rd:0 Ran:4
Pre1998 - 1st:4 2nd:6 3rd:3 Ran:53
Win Prizemoney £20,706 *Total Prizemoney* £46,805
Wins * 1997 Apr Newmar (GD) H 7f 85 92 <
* 1996 Jly Epsom (G-F) H 7f 82 85
1995 Jly Cheste (GD) C 7f 86
1998 Turf 0-4: (7f 3, 8f) (g-s, gd 2, g-f)
Above-average horse, effective 7f, acts on gd, has worn blinkers. Turf high 73 (began Aug).
**B Palling [3-30] Merthyr Motor Auctions (from M C Pipe [1-13] Oct 1995).*

CHICODOVE BHB 75f **RR 72f** 3977[4]
2 b f In The Wings 11.2f **(77)**-Chicobin (USA)(J O Tobin (USA))9.4f **(67)**
Form - 434
Record 1998 - 1st:0 2nd:0 3rd:1 Ran:3
Win Prizemoney £0 *Total Prizemoney* £973
1998 Turf 0-2: (7f, 8f) (gd, frm) 1998 AW 0-1: (7f) (Fibr)
Currently above-average filly. Turf high 72 (began Aug). She has run green in her early races and needs time and experience.
**Sir Mark Prescott [0-3] Hesmonds Stud.*

CHIEF ABBA BHB 65f **RR 68f** 4145[17]
2 ch c Be My Chief (USA) 10.2f **(62)** - Themeda (Sure Blade (USA)) 11.3f **(67)**
Form - 0050
Record 1998 - 1st:0 2nd:0 3rd:0 Ran:4
1998 Turf 0-4: (6f, 7f 3) (gd, g-f 3)
Average colt. Turf high 58. **R Hannon [0-4] Buddy Hackett.*

CHIEF BEARHART (CAN) RR 123f 5167a[4]
5 ch h Chief's Crown (USA) 10.2f **(75)** - Amelia Beaarhart (CAN) (Bold Hour) 10f **(81)**
Form - 24
1998 Turf 0-2: (12f 2) (frm 2)
Very high-class colt, has worn blinkers. Turf high 122 (1st run) (began Oct) - 2nd of 8 giving 7lb to Royal Anthem (18 Oct Woodbine 12f frm RF 4953a). He ended the 1997 season in fine style, winning the Canadian International and the Breeders' Cup Turf. However, he could not emulate that in 1998, finishing runner-up to Royal Anthem at Woodbine, and a fast-finishing fourth in the Breeders' Cup Turf, having been held up off a steady pace.
**M Frostad in CAN [2-6] Sam-Son Farm.*

CHIEF BLADE BHB 51f **RR 50f** 3644[3]
3 ch g Be My Chief (USA) 10.2f **(62)** - Nagida **(69f)** (Skyliner) 7.3f **(53)**
Form - 0007343
Record 1998 - 1st:0 2nd:0 3rd:2 Ran:7
Pre1998 - 1st:1 2nd:0 3rd:0 Ran:5
Win Prizemoney £3,486 *Total Prizemoney* £4,206
Wins 1997 Spt Folkes (GD) H 6.9f 65 65 <
1998 Turf 0-7: (7f 3, 8f 2, 9f, 10f) (gd 4, g-f, frm 2)
Workmanlike, fair gelding, effective 7f, acts on g-f. Turf high 50. Consistent.
**Miss Gay Kelleway [0-7] DGH Partnership (from R Akehurst [1-5] Oct 1997).*

CHIEF CASHIER BHB 75f **RR 75f** 4763[6]
3 b g Persian Bold 10f **(69)** - Kentfield (Busted) 10.2f **(61)**
Form - 284164146
Record 1998 - 1st:2 2nd:1 3rd:0 Ran:9
Pre1998 - 1st:0 2nd:0 3rd:1 Ran:4
Win Prizemoney £6,369 *Total Prizemoney* £9,055
Wins * **1998** Spt Epsom (SFT) H 10.1f 71 75 <
* **1998** Jly Epsom (G-F) H 10.1f 69 72
1998 Turf 2-9: (8f 2, 9f, 10f 2-4, 11f, 12f) (g-s, gd 1-3, g-f 1-2, frm 3)
Workmanlike, above-average gelding, effective 7 to 10f, acts on gd to frm, best on gd, likes tight tracks, excels at Chepstow and Epsom. Turf high 75 (1st run) - 2nd of 6 getting 12lb from Silk St John (25 May Chepstow 8f frm RF 1442) - also 1st of 10 getting 11lb from Edan Heights (5 Spt Epsom RF 4098).
**G B Balding [2-13] Surgical Spirits.*

CHIEF MONARCH BHB 82f **RR 86f** 2056[23]
4 b c Be My Chief (USA) 10.2f **(62)** - American Beauty (Mill Reef (USA)) 10.5f **(78)**
Form - 0640
Record 1998 - 1st:0 2nd:0 3rd:0 Ran:4
Pre1998 - 1st:1 2nd:1 3rd:1 Ran:8
Win Prizemoney £3,517 *Total Prizemoney* £6,285
Wins 1997 Jly Sandow (G-F) 8.1f 75 <
1998 Turf 0-4: (7f, 8f, 9f, 10f) (gd 4)
Scopey, useful colt, effective 8 to 10f, acts on gd to g-f, best on gd, likes tight tracks. Turf high 86 - 4th of 14 giving 7lb to Philistar (5 Jun Epsom 9f gd RF 1748).
**R A Fahey [0-4] Tommy Staunton (from B Smart [1-8] Spt 1997).*

CHIEF REBEL (USA) BHB 98f **RR 94f** 4746[9]
2 b c Chief's Crown (USA) 10.2f **(75)** - Robellino Miss (USA) (Robellino (USA)) 7.6f **(80)**
Form - 120
Record 1998 - 1st:1 2nd:1 3rd:0 Ran:3
Win Prizemoney £4,230 *Total Prizemoney* £5,890
Wins * **1998** Aug Newmar (G-F) 6f 79 <
1998 Turf 1-3: (6f 1-2, 7f) (gd 2, frm 1-1)
Currently useful colt. Turf high 94 (began Aug). Narrow winner of what looked a moderate July Course maiden on his debut, he came on for the run and finished second to Desaru at Doncaster. Disappointing on his final outing at York where he was very free to post. He has potential, but probably wants further.
**G Wragg [1-3] The Eclipse Partnership.*

CHIEF'S SONG BHB 34f **RR 38f** 3797[4]
8 b g Chief Singer 8.6f **(62)** - Tizzy (Formidable (USA)) 9.2f **(63)**
Form - 4
Record 1998 - 1st:0 2nd:0 3rd:0 Ran:1
Pre1998 - 1st:0 2nd:2 3rd:1 Ran:19
Win Prizemoney £0 *Total Prizemoney* £3,069
1998 Turf 0-1: (16f) (g-f)
Very moderate gelding, has worn blinkers. Becoming disappointing. Better known as a chaser these days.
**S Dow [9-47] Mrs Anne Devine (from B W Hills [0-5] Oct 1993).*

CHIEF'S SPIRIT BHB 40f37a **RR 2f 37a** 931[15]
4 b g Inca Chief (USA) 5.6f **(45)** - Country Spirit (Sayf El Arab (USA)) 7.1f **(54)**
Form - 0000
Record 1998 - 1st:0 2nd:0 3rd:0 Ran:4
Pre1998 - 1st:0 2nd:1 3rd:0 Ran:3
Win Prizemoney £0 *Total Prizemoney* £699
1998 Turf 0-2: (7f, 9f) (sft, gd) 1998 AW 0-2: (7f 2) (Fibr 2)
Leggy, little account gelding, effective 6f, acts on frm, has worn blinkers. AW high 24.
**S E Kettlewell [0-4] Alan Thompson (from G M Moore [0-3] Aug 1997).*

CHIEFTAIN (IRE) RR 80f 2513[2]
3 b c Indian Ridge 7.6f **(74)** - Legit (IRE) (Runnett) 7f **(59)**
Form - 640232
Record 1998 - 1st:0 2nd:2 3rd:1 Ran:6
Pre1998 - 1st:0 2nd:1 3rd:1 Ran:4
Win Prizemoney £0 *Total Prizemoney* £9,719
1998 Turf 0-6: (5f 2, 6f 4) (g-s, gd, g-f 3, frm)
Well made, decent colt, effective 5f, acts on gd. Turf high 80. Consistent. He ran fair races in some decent events at two, but has become disappointing.
**N A Callaghan [0-10] M Tabor & Mrs John Magnier.*

CHIKAL BHB 46f45a **RR 40f 45a** 2546[8]
3 b g Nalchik (USA) 12.6f **(44)** - Ty-With-Belle (Pamroy) 12.5f **(55)**
Form - 35088
Record 1998 - 1st:0 2nd:0 3rd:1 Ran:5
Pre1998 - 1st:0 2nd:0 3rd:0 Ran:4

Win Prizemoney £0 *Total Prizemoney* £297
1998 Turf 0-4: (10f 4) (sft, g-s, gd, g-f) 1998 AW 0-1: (9f) (Fibr)
Unfurnished, moderate gelding. Turf high 53. He has shown some ability in selling company, and looks capable of landing a race of that type. **B Palling [0-9] Mrs M M Palling.*

CHIKAPENNY BHB 48f49a **RR 60f 49a** 4311[9]
3 b f Mon Tresor 7.9f **(60)** - Arabian Nymph (Sayf El Arab (USA)) 7.1f **(54)**
Form - 63333530060
Record 1998 - 1st:0 2nd:0 3rd:5 Ran:10
Pre1998 - 1st:0 2nd:0 3rd:5 Ran:10
Win Prizemoney £0 *Total Prizemoney* £3,881
1998 Turf 0-5: (5f 5) (gd 3, frm 2) 1998 AW 0-5: (5f 3, 6f 2) (Equi 5)
Average filly, effective 5 to 6f, best at 5f, acts on gd to g-f, best on gd, mostly wears blinkers (effectively). Turf high 60 (1st run) - 3rd of 12 giving 15lb to Super Geil (29 Jun Musselburgh 5f gd RF 2370). AW high 56. If there was a prize for the horse who most often finishes third, she would win it.
**Mrs L Stubbs [0-20] Maurice Parker.*

CHIKA SHAN (IRE) BHB 34f39a **RR 15f 39a** 3280[22]
3 ch c Archway (IRE) 8.5f **(60)** - Judy's Pinch (Ballymore) 7.3f **(64)**
Form - 8876800
Record 1998 - 1st:0 2nd:0 3rd:0 Ran:6
Pre1998 - 1st:0 2nd:0 3rd:0 Ran:5
1998 Turf 0-2: (6f, 8f) (gd, g-f) 1998 AW 0-4: (8f 2, 9f, 12f) (Fibr 4)
Unfurnished, very moderate colt, often wears blinkers. Turf high 15. AW high 39. Becoming disappointing.
**S Mellor [0-7] Jafeica Partnership (from B Smart [0-4] Jly 1997).*

CHILDREN'S CHOICE (IRE) BHB 53f50a **RR 54f 50a** 5069[1]
7 b m Taufan (USA) 8.3f **(65)**- Alice Brackloon(USA)(Melyno) 10.4f **(55)**
Form - 77270841
Record 1998 - 1st:1 2nd:1 3rd:0 Ran:8
Pre1998 - 1st:6 2nd:5 3rd:2 Ran:42
Win Prizemoney £27,982 *Total Prizemoney* £36,706
Wins * **1998** Oct Newmar (G-S) H 12f 50 54
1997 Oct Nottin (G-F) H 14.1f 50 57
1997 Jly Yarmou (G-F) H 16f 49 51
1996 Aug Yarmou (G-F) H 14.1f 52 56
1995 Mar Doncas (GD) H 10.3f 53 60 <
1994 Spt Newbur (SFT) H 10f 50 48
1994 May Folkes (SFT) C 9.7f 46
1998 Turf 1-8: (12f 1-3, 14f 2, 15f, 16f 2) (gd, g-f 1-3, frm 4)
Fair mare, effective 12 to 16f, best at 16f, acts on gd to frm, best on g-f, has worn blinkers, likes left handed tracks, does well at Yarmouth and Nottingham, likes Newmarket. Turf high 54 (began Jly) - 2nd of 5 giving 12lb to Old Red (12 Aug Nottingham 16f g-f RF 3586) - also 1st of 13 getting 2lb from Dalwhinnie (30 Oct Newmarket RF 5069).
**D Morris [1-8] Mrs A V Totman (from W J Musson [2-12] Nov 1997).*

CHILI BOUCHIER (USA) BHB 35f **RR 37f** 3838[4]
4 br f Stop The Music (USA) 5f **(57)** - Low Approach (Artaius (USA)) 9f **(69)**
Form - 704
Record 1998 - 1st:0 2nd:0 3rd:0 Ran:3
Pre1998 - 1st:0 2nd:0 3rd:0 Ran:5
Win Prizemoney £0 *Total Prizemoney* £571
1998 Turf 0-3: (10f 2, 12f) (gd, frm 2)
Workmanlike, very moderate filly. Turf high 37. Inconsistent.
**D Marks [0-8] P J Pearson.*

CHI-LIN BHB 50f42a **RR 54df 42a** 5128[8]
3 b f Precocious 7.2f **(54)** - Cool Combination (Indian King (USA)) 7.4f **(64)**
Form - 53402408
Record 1998 - 1st:0 2nd:1 3rd:0 Ran:6
Pre1998 - 1st:0 2nd:0 3rd:1 Ran:3
Win Prizemoney £0 *Total Prizemoney* £1,067
1998 Turf 0-4: (6f 3, 8f) (sft, g-s 2, frm) 1998 AW 0-2: (7f 2) (Equi 2)
Workmanlike, fair filly, effective 6f, acts on sft. Turf high 54 (1st run) - 2nd of 15 getting 5lb from Henry The Proud (20 Apr Nottingham 6f sft RF 0770). AW high 25.
**P Butler [0-6] Mrs Janet Coleman (from J Ffitch-Heyes [0-3] Nov 1997).*

CHILLIAN BHB 49f **RR 60f** 4490[18]
2 b c Chilibang 7f **(55)** - Five Islands (Bairn (USA)) 7.7f **(59)**
Form - 75500
Record 1998 - 1st:0 2nd:0 3rd:0 Ran:5
1998 Turf 0-5: (5f 5) (gd 4, frm)
Average colt. Turf high 60. **M Brittain [0-5] Mel Brittain.*

CHILLING BHB 50f38a **RR 60f 38a** 4170a[1]
4 gr f Chilibang 7f **(55)** - Appealing (Star Appeal) 9.6f **(65)**
Form - 000006003650151
Record 1998 - 1st:2 2nd:0 3rd:1 Ran:10
Pre1998 - 1st:3 2nd:1 3rd:2 Ran:25
Win Prizemoney £11,568 *Total Prizemoney* £13,837
Wins * **1998** Spt Clonme (G-F) H 10f 60
* **1998** Aug Tramor (G-F) H 9f 56
1997 May Southw (STD) S 6f 62 <
1997 Feb Wolver (STD) SH 5f 60 59
1997 Jan Wolver (STD) S 6f 57
1998 Turf 2-8: (7f, 8f 2, 9f 1-3, 10f 1-2) (g-s 2, gd 3, g-f 2-3) 1998 AW 0-2: (6f, 7f) (Fibr 2)
Unfurnished, average filly, effective 5 to 10f, acts on gd to g-f - acts on Fibr, has worn blinkers. Turf high 60 - 1st of 14 giving 17lb to Liffeydale (3 Spt Clonmel RF 4170a) - also 1st of 15 giving 26lb to Sarahs Crusader (14 Aug Tramore RF 3715a). AW high 16. Inconsistent.
**Miss Frances Crowley in IRE [2-8] H J Muldoon (from J Woods in IRE [0-1] May 1998).*

CHILTERN EMERALD BHB 35f **RR 13f** 1765[11]
3 b f Thowra (FR) 11.2f **(47)** - Treasure Time (IRE) (Treasure Kay)
Form - 0
Record 1998 - 1st:0 2nd:0 3rd:0 Ran:1
Pre1998 - 1st:0 2nd:0 3rd:0 Ran:4
1998 AW 0-1: (8f) (Fibr)
Lengthy, poor filly.
**K C Comerford [0-1] Emerald Associates (from K R Burke [0-2] Aug 1997).*

CHIM CHIMINEY BHB 76f **RR 84f** 4619[14]
3 b f Sabrehill (USA) 8.5f **(64)** - William's Bird (USA) (Master Willie) 7f **(70)**
Form - 302870
Record 1998 - 1st:0 2nd:1 3rd:1 Ran:6
Pre1998 - 1st:1 2nd:0 3rd:0 Ran:4
Win Prizemoney £6,524 *Total Prizemoney* £9,728
Wins * 1997 Oct York (SFT) 7.9f 86 <
1998 Turf 0-6: (8f, 10f 5) (g-s, gd 2, g-f 3)
Neat, decent filly, effective 8 to 10f, acts on g-s to g-f, prefers left handed tracks. Turf high 85. Ran well in a ten-furlong handicap at Newbury in August, having shown her best form previously over a mile on an easier surface. Beaten off similar marks since.
**B W Hills [1-10] W J Gredley.*

CHIMES OF PEACE BHB 56f **RR 61f** 4408[4]
3 b f Magic Ring (IRE) 6.5f **(64)** - Leprechaun Lady (Royal Blend) 11.9f **(58)**
Form - 715532744
Record 1998 - 1st:1 2nd:1 3rd:1 Ran:9
Pre1998 - 1st:0 2nd:0 3rd:0 Ran:4
Win Prizemoney £2,965 *Total Prizemoney* £4,798
Wins * **1998** May Mussel (GD) 8f 55 <
1998 Turf 1-9: (8f 1-3, 10f 5, 12f) (g-s, gd, g-f 1-6, frm)
Leggy, average filly, effective 8 to 12f, best at 10f, acts on g-s to frm, best on g-f, likes right handed tracks, likes tight tracks, excels at Pontefract and Beverley. Turf high 61 - 2nd of 9 to Marske Machine (12 Aug Beverley 10f g-f RF 3565) - also 1st of 10 from Pride of Bryn (1 May Musselburgh RF 0953). Consistent.
**J L Eyre [1-13] The Secret Seven Partnership.*

CHIMINAGE (USA) RR 61+f 4389[8]
2 ch f Woodman (USA) 9.7f **(77)** - Informatrice (USA) (Trempolino (USA)) 12f **(71)**
Form - 8
Record 1998 - 1st:0 2nd:0 3rd:0 Ran:1
1998 Turf 0-1: (7f) (frm)
Currently average filly. **Sir Michael Stoute [0-1] Sheikh Mohammed.*

CHINABERRY BHB 39f58a **RR 44f 58a** 4255[12]
4 b f Soviet Star (USA) 8.6f **(74)** - Crimson Conquest (USA) (Diesis) 9.3f **(69)**
Form - 080620000
Record **1998** - 1st:0 2nd:1 3rd:0 Ran:9
Pre1998 - 1st:0 2nd:0 3rd:0 Ran:4
Win Prizemoney £0 *Total Prizemoney* £1,393
1998 Turf 0-7: (6f, 7f 4, 8f 2) (g-s, gd, g-f 2, frm 3) 1998 AW 0-2: (8f 2) (Fibr 2)
Neat, fair filly, effective 8f, acts on frm - acts on Fibr, likes left handed tracks, likes tight tracks. Turf high 47. AW high 56 (began Jly) - 2nd of 8 to Swan Island (17 Jly Southwell 8f Fibr RF 2896). Inconsistent.
**M Brittain [0-9] Mel Brittain (from C E Brittain [0-4] Jly 1997).*

CHINA CASTLE BHB 60f76a **RR 54f 76a** 4638[9]
5 b g Sayf El Arab (USA) 8.2f **(57** - Honey Plum(Kind of Hush)10.1f **(62)**
Form - 077211532480
Record **1998** - 1st:2 2nd:2 3rd:1 Ran:9
Pre1998 - 1st:8 2nd:1 3rd:4 Ran:35
Win Prizemoney £33,442 *Total Prizemoney* £40,663

Wins								
*** 1998**	*Jan*	*Wolver*	*(STD)*	*H*	*12f*	*71*	*75*	
*** 1998**	*Jan*	*Southw*	*(STD)*		*12f*		*75*	
* 1997	*Jan*	*Southw*	*(STD)*	*H*	*12f*	*67*	*82+*	
* 1997	*Jan*	*Southw*	*(STD)*	*H*	*11f*	*67*	*87*	<
* 1997	*Jan*	*Southw*	*(STD)*	*H*	*11f*	*67*	*77*	
* 1996	*Feb*	*Southw*	*(STD)*	*C*	*11f*		*67+*	
* 1996	*Jan*	*Wolver*	*(STD)*	*H*	*8.5f*	*68*	*72*	
* 1996	*Jan*	*Lingfi*	*(STD)*	*H*	*10f*	*54*	*64*	
* 1996	*Jan*	*Southw*	*(STD)*	*H*	*7f*	*54*	*72*	
* 1995	*Aug*	*Southw*	*(STD)*	*S*	*6f*		*64+*	

1998 AW 2-9: (8f, 9f 2, 11f, 12f 2-5) (Equi, Fibr 2-8)
Above-average gelding, effective 8 to 12f, best at 11f, - acts on Fibr, and excels at Southwell. AW high 79 - 4th of 5 giving 13lb to Nominator Lad (20 Jun Wolverhampton 8f Fibr RF 2163). He is a very effective performer on Fibresand, but only shows his very best form in January, especially over middle distances at Southwell. He spends the rest of the year getting his handicap mark down.
**P C Haslam [10-47] J M Davis & Middleham Park Racing I.*

CHINAIDER (IRE) BHB 63f61a **RR 59f 61a** 4661[6]
3 b f Mujadil (USA) 7.7f **(70)** - We Two (Glenstal (USA)) 10.1f **(64)**
Form - 0005062036
Record **1998** - 1st:0 2nd:1 3rd:1 Ran:10
Pre1998 - 1st:3 2nd:1 3rd:1 Ran:7
Win Prizemoney £16,086 *Total Prizemoney* £18,583

Wins							
1997	Aug	York	(GD)	S	6f	73	<
1997	Aug	Redcar	(G-F)	S	6f	69	
1997	*Jun*	*Southw*	*(STD)*	*S*	*5f*	*65+*	

1998 Turf 0-9: (6f 4, 7f 3, 8f 2) (gd 4, g-f, frm 4) 1998 AW 0-1: (7f) (Fibr)
Scopey, average filly, effective 5 to 6f, best at 6f, acts on gd to frm - acts on Fibr, best on gd. Turf high 59.
**D Nicholls [0-12] Mark Leatham (from M C Pipe [1-2] Spt 1997).*

CHINA RED (USA) BHB 88f78a **RR 89f 78a** 4700[2]
4 br g Red Ransom (USA) 8.6f **(83)**- Akamare(FR)(Akarad (FR)) 9f **(76)**
Form - 5128162
Record **1998** - 1st:2 2nd:2 3rd:0 Ran:7
Pre1998 - 1st:1 2nd:1 3rd:0 Ran:8
Win Prizemoney £21,405 *Total Prizemoney* £28,793

Wins								
*** 1998**	Jly	Goodwo	(GD)	H	8f	82	85	<
*** 1998**	May	Goodwo	(G-F)	H	8f	78	82	
* 1997	Apr	Nottin	(G-F)		8.2f		85	<

1998 Turf 2-6: (8f 2-6) (gd 1-2, g-f 1-4) 1998 AW 0-1: (8f) (Equi)
Useful gelding, effective 8f, acts on gd to frm, best on gd, excels at Goodwood. Turf high 89 - 2nd of 7 getting 13lb from Sugarfoot (7 Oct York 8f g-f RF 4700) - also 1st of 19 giving 23lb to Naviasky (28 Jly Goodwood RF 3168). Best run for some time when awarded a Goodwood handicap in May and added another victory there at the big meeting. A front-runner, he was sold for 36,000 gns at Tattersalls in the autumn. **J W Hills [3-15] N N Browne And Partners.*

CHINE **RR 103f** 2289a[6]
3 b f Inchinor 8.9f **(64)** - Tweedling (USA) (Sir Ivor) 10.2f **(70)**
Form - 336
1998 Turf 0-3: (11f, 12f 2) (hvy, gd 2)
Currently very useful filly. Turf high 103 - 3rd of 6 to Cantilever (30 May Chantilly 12f gd RF 1730a). She runs well in minor Group company, but needs a drop in class to get her head in front.
**Mme M Bollack-Badel in FR [0-3] Mrs de Chatelperron.*

CHINGACHGOOK BHB 58f56a **RR 34f 56a** 364[3]
4 b g Superlative 8.8f **(57)** - Petomania (Petong) 6.6f **(58)**
Form - 3562413
Record **1998** - 1st:1 2nd:1 3rd:1 Ran:6
Pre1998 - 1st:0 2nd:1 3rd:1 Ran:11
Win Prizemoney £2,305 *Total Prizemoney* £5,031
Wins **1998** *Feb Lingfi (SLW) H 12f 49 59* <
1998 AW 1-6: (10f 2, 12f 1-4) (Equi 1-6)
Lengthy, fair gelding, effective 8 to 12f, acts on frm - acts on Equi, has worn blinkers, prefers tight tracks. AW high 59 - 1st of 11 giving 4lb to Zorro (17 Feb Lingfield RF 0306). Narrowly won a poor handicap on the Lingfield Equitrack in February, but the rest of his form is modest at best.
**M R Bosley [0-1] H J M Webb (from S Dow [1-6] Feb 1998).*

CHIPS (IRE) BHB 85f **RR 78f** 3471[12]
3 ch c Common Grounds 8.1f **(66)** - Inonder (Belfort (FR)) 6.8f **(63)**
Form - 000
Record **1998** - 1st:0 2nd:0 3rd:0 Ran:3
Pre1998 - 1st:3 2nd:1 3rd:2 Ran:9
Win Prizemoney £19,880 *Total Prizemoney* £23,357

Wins							
* 1997	Aug	Baden-	(GD)	L	7.5f	90+	
* 1997	May	Kempto	(GD)		6f	83+	
* 1997	May	Salisb	(G-F)		5f	93	<

1998 Turf 0-3: (6f, 7f 2) (gd, frm, hrd)
Scopey, above-average colt, effective 5 to 8f, best at 5f, acts on gd to g-f, best on gd, has worn blinkers. Turf high 78 (began Jly). A useful juvenile, a winner of a listed race in Germany, he showed little in handicap company lsat term.
**D R C Elsworth [3-12] Mrs Anne Coughlan.*

CHIPSTEAD BAY (IRE) BHB 58f63a **RR 43f 63a** 2390[8]
4 b g Ballad Rock 7.2f **(63)** - Express Account (Carr de Naskra (USA)) 6f **(59)**
Form - 1117788
Record **1998** - 1st:0 2nd:0 3rd:0 Ran:3
Pre1998 - 1st:3 2nd:0 3rd:1 Ran:14
Win Prizemoney £6,948 *Total Prizemoney* £7,520

Wins								
* 1997	*Dec*	*Lingfi*	*(STD)*	*H*	*5f*	*44*	*59+*	<
* 1997	*Dec*	*Lingfi*	*(STD)*	*H*	*7f*	*44*	*55+*	
* 1997	*Dec*	*Lingfi*	*(G-S)*	*H*	*6f*	*44*	*53*	

1998 Turf 0-1: (6f) (frm) 1998 AW 0-2: (6f, 7f) (Equi 2)
Fair gelding, effective 5 to 7f, - acted on Equi, had worn blinkers, preferred left handed tracks, preferred tight tracks. AW high 59. Ex-Irish, he was a revelation when tried on Equitrack, completing a hat-trick in December over distances ranging from five to seven furlongs. (DEAD)
**K T Ivory [3-7] Ian Turnbull (from J G Coogan in IRE [0-10] Spt 1997).*

CHIQUITA LINDA (IRE) **RR 94?f** 1733a[1]
2 b f Mujadil (USA) 7.7f **(70)** - Twany Angel (Double Form) 7.3f **(58)**
Form - 1
1998 Turf 1-1: (6f 1-1) (g-f 1-1)
Currently useful filly. (1st run) - 1st of 9 from Shenck (31 May Capannelle RF 1733a). Won a Listed race at Capannelle in May, but her form has dropped off since.
**L d'Auria in ITY [1-1] Scuderia La Pe Re Re Ca srl.*

CHIRAC **RR 103f** 3422a[2]
4 b c Belmez (USA) 11.4f **(65)** - Vivienda (Known Fact (USA)) 7.4f **(67)**
Form - 2
1998 Turf 0-1: (12f) (sft)
Currently very useful colt. (1st run) - 2nd of 13 to Albaran (2 Aug Klampenborg 12f sft RF 3422a). He finished in front of Taufan's Melody in a Listed race at Klampennorg and is a useful middle-distance performer. **W Neuroth in NOR [0-2].*

CHIST (USA) BHB 102f **RR 104f** 5149[3]
3 b br c Lear Fan (USA) 10.4f **(80)** - Morna (Blakeney) 10.5f **(64)**
Form - 123
Record **1998** - 1st:1 2nd:1 3rd:1 Ran:3
Pre1998 - 1st:0 2nd:0 3rd:0 Ran:1
Win Prizemoney £3,655 *Total Prizemoney* £7,342

Wins * **1998** Apr Leices (SFT) 10f 86+ <
1998 Turf 1-3: (10f 1-1, 12f 2) (sft 1-2, gd)
Leggy, very useful colt. Turf high 104 - 2nd of 3 giving 4lb to Mowbray (26 Oct Leicester 12f sft RF 4993). He looked a nice prospect when winning a soft-ground maiden at Leicester in April, but was off the track a long time subsequently. Decent effort on his return and followed that with a brave display on his final start in a Listed event at Doncaster. He was not disgraced, and looks open to further improvement. **M H Tompkins [1-4] Mrs Jane Bailey.*

CHLO-JO BHB 50f **RR 63f** 4198^{10}
3 b f Belmez (USA) 11.4f **(65)** - Shaadin (USA) (Sharpen Up) 8.3f **(67)**
Form - 04522175070
Record **1998** - 1st:1 2nd:2 3rd:0 Ran:11
Pre1998 - 1st:0 2nd:0 3rd:0 Ran:5
Win Prizemoney £5,299 *Total Prizemoney* £7,202
Wins * **1998** Jun Pontef (SFT) H 10f 55 63 <
1998 Turf 1-11: (8f 2, 10f 1-6, 12f 3) (sft, g-s 1-3, gd 3, g-f 2, frm 2)
Neat, average filly, effective 10f, acts on g-s, likes tight tracks. Turf high 63. She looked to be suited by ten furlongs and soft ground when winning at Pontefract in June.
**M Brittain [1-11] D H Armitage (from A G Foster [0-5] Nov 1997).*

CHOCOLATE BOX BHB 47f50a **RR 55f 50a** 5002^{11}
3 ch f Most Welcome 8.6f **(66)** - Short Rations (Lorenzaccio) 10f **(64)**
Form - 5422764160
Record **1998** - 1st:1 2nd:2 3rd:0 Ran:10
Pre1998 - 1st:0 2nd:0 3rd:1 Ran:2
Win Prizemoney £2,743 *Total Prizemoney* £5,162
Wins * **1998** *Oct Lingfi (STD) 13f 60* <
1998 Turf 0-7: (8f, 11f, 12f 2, 13f, 14f 2) (g-s, gd, g-f, frm 4) 1998 AW 1-3: (12f, 13f 1-1, 14f) (Equi 1-2, Fibr)
Workmanlike, average filly, effective 7f, acts on g-s, has worn blinkers (effectively). Turf high 55. AW high 60 (began Aug). Inconsistent. **W J Haggas [1-12] J M Greetham.*

CHOCOLATE SOUFFLE (IRE) RR 59f 1566^{3}
2 b f Magic Ring (IRE) 6.5f **(64)** - Buraida (Balidar) 7.9f **(63)**
Form - 3
Record **1998** - 1st:0 2nd:0 3rd:1 Ran:1
Win Prizemoney £0 *Total Prizemoney* £482
1998 Turf 0-1: (6f) (frm)
Currently fair filly. **P F I Cole [0-1] H R H Prince Fahd Salman.*

CHOIRGIRL BHB 100f **RR 87f** 4514^{7}
2 b f Unfuwain (USA) 11.4f **(74)** - Choir Mistress (Chief Singer) 8.9f **(66)**

Form - 44127
Record **1998** - 1st:1 2nd:1 3rd:0 Ran:5
Win Prizemoney £3,392 *Total Prizemoney* £12,278
Wins * **1998** Aug Redcar (G-F) 7f 87 <
1998 Turf 1-5: (6f 2, 7f 1-2, 8f) (gd, g-f 2, frm 1-2)
Useful filly. Turf high 87 - 2nd of 9 to Circle of Gold (28 Aug Goodwood 7f g-f RF 3922) - also 1st of 8 from Kalidasa (8 Aug Redcar RF 3474). She made all in a Redcar maiden on her third start, although it was not much of a race. Better form when making Circle of Gold work for victory in a Goodwood Group Three.
**J H M Gosden [1-5] Cheveley Park Stud.*

CHOK-DI BHB 52f **RR 57f** 4490^{7}
2 b g Beveled (USA) 6.9f **(64)** - Pendona (Blue Cashmere) 6.4f **(54)**
Form - 60507
Record **1998** - 1st:0 2nd:0 3rd:0 Ran:5
1998 Turf 0-5: (5f 5) (gd 3, frm 2)
Fair gelding. Turf high 53.
**Mrs M Reveley [0-5] The Desert Rats Racing Club.*

CHOMPER (IRE) BHB 92f **RR 91f** 4924^{4}
2 ch c Mujtahid (USA) 7.4f **(69)**- Maculatus (USA)Sharpen Up) 8.3f **(67)**
Form - 41250642022334
Record **1998** - 1st:1 2nd:4 3rd:2 Ran:14
Win Prizemoney £3,517 *Total Prizemoney* £12,867
Wins * **1998** May Haydoc (G-S) 5f 64 <
1998 Turf 1-14: (5f 1-2, 6f 10, 7f, 8f) (sft, g-s 2, gd 1-5, g-f 3, frm 3)
Useful colt, effective 6f, acts on g-s to frm. Turf high 91 - 3rd of 7 giving 2lb to Compton Arrow (9 Oct Ascot 6f g-s RF 4735). Had a tremendously busy season and this tough cookie proved sound and genuine throughout. Scored a narrow victory in a Haydock maiden on his second start, but the photo went against him at Pontefract next time. He bit off a bit more than he could chew in warm company afterwards, but put up some gritty displays to be in the frame towards the end of the season. A real money-spinner, who has done connections proud, he will stay seven furlongs and goes on any ground. Reported to have been sold to race in the United States. **M R Channon [1-14] M Channon.*

CHOPIN (IRE) BHB 41f37a **RR 44f 37a** 2944^{11}
4 b g Classic Music (USA) 7.2f **(57)** - La Toulzanie (FR) (Sanctus II) 11.5f **(65)**
Form - 00
Record **1998** - 1st:0 2nd:0 3rd:0 Ran:2
Pre1998 - 1st:0 2nd:0 3rd:1 Ran:12
Win Prizemoney £0 *Total Prizemoney* £293
1998 Turf 0-1: (13f) (frm) 1998 AW 0-1: (12f) (Equi)
Narrow, moderate gelding, effective 7 to 12f, acts on g-f to frm, often wears blinkers. Inconsistent.
**K G Wingrove [0-8] M M Foulger (from R F JohnsonHoughton [0-12] Aug 1997).*

CHORAL EXPRESS (IRE) BHB 74f **RR 77f** 4377^{7}
2 b c College Chapel - Trull **(100f)** (Lomond)
Form - 1062477
Record **1998** - 1st:1 2nd:1 3rd:0 Ran:7
Win Prizemoney £3,420 *Total Prizemoney* £4,496
Wins * **1998** Jun Windso (GD) 6f 74 <
1998 Turf 1-7: (5f 3, 6f 1-4) (gd 3, g-f 1-2, frm 2)
Above-average colt, effective 6f, acts on g-f to frm, has worn blinkers. Turf high 77 - 2nd of 6 giving 9lb to Entropy (11 Aug Bath 6f frm RF 3528) - also 1st of 22 giving 5lb to Banningham Breeze (8 Jun Windsor RF 1821). **W R Muir [1-7] Duncan Wiltshire.*

CHORUS OF APPROVAL BHB 55f **RR 62f** 4756^{9}
2 b g Clantime 6.6f **(57)** - Fyas (Sayf El Arab (USA)) 7.1f **(54)**
Form - 85670
Record **1998** - 1st:0 2nd:0 3rd:0 Ran:5
1998 Turf 0-5: (5f 2, 6f 3) (sft, g-s, g-f 2, frm)
Average gelding. Turf high 62. **Miss L A Perratt [0-5] Gordon Cowan.*

CHOTO MATE (IRE) BHB 90f **RR 85f** 4237^{6}
2 ch c Brief Truce (USA) 9.1f **(73)** - Greatest Pleasure (Be My Guest (USA)) 9.3f **(67)**
Form - 310046
Record **1998** - 1st:1 2nd:0 3rd:1 Ran:6
Win Prizemoney £4,889 *Total Prizemoney* £6,050
Wins * **1998** May Goodwo (G-F) 5f 85+ <
1998 Turf 1-6: (5f 1-5, 6f) (g-s, gd 2, g-f 1-2, frm)
Useful colt, effective 5f, acts on g-f to frm. Turf high 85 - 1st of 4 giving 5lb to Bodfari Times (19 May Goodwood RF 1327). Looked a good prospect when scoring at Goodwood on his second start, but has failed to figure when upped in class.
**R Hannon [1-6] Vernon Carl Matalon.*

CHRISMAS CAROL (IRE) RR 68f 4668^{9}
2 b f Common Grounds 8.1f **(66)** - Stockrose (FR) (Horage) 10.3f **(61)**
Form - 30
Record **1998** - 1st:0 2nd:0 3rd:1 Ran:2
Win Prizemoney £0 *Total Prizemoney* £680
1998 Turf 0-2: (6f 2) (gd 2)
Currently average filly. Turf high 68 (began Jly).
**P W Harris [0-2] Resplendent Racing Ltd.*

CHRISTIANSTED (IRE) RR 90f 4277a^{9}
3 ch g Soviet Lad (USA) 9.4f **(63)** - How True (Known Fact (USA)) 7.4f **(67)**
Form - 33610
1998 Turf 1-5: (9f 2, 10f, 12f 1-2) (hvy, sft 1-4)
Useful gelding. Turf high 90 - 1st of 9 getting 17lb from Dusky Lamp (12 May Killarney RF 1332a). Unraced as a juvenile, he got off the mark at the fourth attempt, and stays better than his breeding might suggest.
**Ms J Morgan in IRE [0-1] Christian Syndicate (from J C Harley in IRE [1-4] May 1998).*

CHRISTOPHER ROBIN (IRE) BHB 39f **RR 36f** 4622[15]
2 b g Mac's Imp (USA) 5.6f **(54)** - Miss Ming (Tender King) 6.8f **(54)**
Form - 000
Record 1998 - 1st:0 2nd:0 3rd:0 Ran:3
1998 Turf 0-3: (5f 2, 6f) (g-f 2, frm)
Currently very moderate gelding. Turf high 36 (began Aug).
**J J Quinn [0-3] Bowlers Racing.*

CHRYSALIS BHB 48f **RR 67f** 4547[9]
3 b f Soviet Star (USA) 8.6f **(74)**- Vivienda (Known Fact(USA)) 7.4f **(67)**
Form - 033606700
Record 1998 - 1st:0 2nd:0 3rd:2 Ran:9
Pre1998 - 1st:0 2nd:0 3rd:2 Ran:3
Win Prizemoney £0 *Total Prizemoney* £1,948
1998 Turf 0-8: (6f, 7f 4, 8f 2, 9f) (gd 3, g-f 3, frm 2) 1998 AW 0-1: (7f) (Fibr)
Workmanlike, average filly, effective 8f, acts on g-f, has worn blinkers, likes tight tracks. Turf high 67. Becoming disappointing.
**D W P Arbuthnot [0-9] Christopher Wright (from P F I Cole [0-3] May 1997).*

CHRYSOLITE (IRE) BHB 75f **RR 69f** 2849[8]
3 ch c Kris 10f **(75)** - Alamiya (IRE) (Doyoun) 9f **(69)**
Form - 01048
Record 1998 - 1st:1 2nd:0 3rd:0 Ran:5
Pre1998 - 1st:0 2nd:0 3rd:1 Ran:3
Win Prizemoney £5,711 *Total Prizemoney* £6,865
Wins * 1998 May Lingfi (GD) H 9f 74 78 <
1998 Turf 1-5: (8f, 9f 1-2, 10f 2) (hvy, gd, g-f 1-2, frm)
Workmanlike, average colt, effective 9f, acts on g-f. Turf high 78 - 1st of 10 giving 4lb to Mansa Musa (9 May Lingfield RF 1122).
**B W Hills [1-8] A D Shead.*

CHUNITO BHB 44f **RR 55f** 4529[9]
3 b g Beveled (USA) 6.9f **(64)** - Wasimah (Caerleon (USA)) 8.6f **(71)**
Form - 0636600
Record 1998 - 1st:0 2nd:0 3rd:1 Ran:7
Pre1998 - 1st:0 2nd:0 3rd:1 Ran:3
Win Prizemoney £0 *Total Prizemoney* £1,325
1998 Turf 0-7: (7f, 8f 6) (g-f 4, frm 3)
Light-framed, fair gelding, has worn blinkers. Turf high 55. Becoming disappointing.
**P J Hobbs [0-10] In Touch Racing Club (from P W Chapple-Hyam [0-3] May 1997).*

CHURCHILL'S SHADOW (IRE) BHB 50f56a **RR 49f 56a** 1409[1]
4 b c Polish Precedent (USA) 9f **(73)** - Shy Princess (USA) (Irish River (FR)) 8.6f **(78)**
Form - 11261
Record 1998 - 1st:1 2nd:0 3rd:0 Ran:2
Pre1998 - 1st:2 2nd:2 3rd:0 Ran:10
Win Prizemoney £7,492 *Total Prizemoney* £9,631
Wins * 1998 May Doncas (GD) H 7f 45 49
* *1997 Nov Lingfi (STD) H 7f 44 53* <
* *1997 Nov Lingfi (STD) H 7f 44 46*
1998 Turf 1-1: (7f 1-1) (g-f 1-1) 1998 AW 0-1: (8f) (Equi)
Fair colt, effective 7f, acts on g-f to frm - acts on Equi. (1st run) - 1st of 22 getting 4lb from Celandine (23 May Doncaster RF 1409). Consistent. Has a useful turn of foot, best employed late.
**B A Pearce [3-12] Richard Gray.*

CHURLISH CHARM BHB 102f **RR 104f** 4723a[9]
3 b c Niniski (USA) 13.2f **(67)** - Blushing Storm (USA) (Blushing Groom (FR)) 10.3f **(76)**
Form - 215110
Record 1998 - 1st:3 2nd:1 3rd:0 Ran:6
Pre1998 - 1st:0 2nd:0 3rd:0 Ran:1
Win Prizemoney £26,588 *Total Prizemoney* £27,653
Wins * 1998 Spt Newbur (GD) H 16f 99 104 <
*** 1998** Jun Goodwo (GD) 12f 95
*** 1998** May Newmar (G-F) 12f 81
1998 Turf 3-6: (12f 2-3, 14f, 16f 1-2) (sft, gd 1-3, g-f 1-1, frm 1-1)
Very useful colt, effective 12 to 16f, best at 16f, acts on gd to g-f, best on gd. Turf high 104 - 1st of 11 giving 4lb to Murghem (17 Spt Newbury RF 4331) - also 1st of 4 giving 2lb to Benin (28 Jun Goodwood RF 2367). This strapping individual progressed throughout the season and needed a test of stamina by the autumn. He could not cope with soft ground in a German Group race during October, but will return a bigger and better four-year-old.
**R Hannon [3-7].*

CICCIA BHB 30f **RR 26f** 5117[8]
2 b f Minshaanshu Amad (USA)11.3f **(53)** - Me Spede(Valiyar) 8.5f **(73)**
Form - 8008
Record 1998 - 1st:0 2nd:0 3rd:0 Ran:4
1998 Turf 0-4: (5f 3, 7f) (sft, gd 2, frm)
Little account filly, has worn blinkers. Turf high 26 (began Aug).
**Miss L A Perratt [0-4] Mrs Every Roosmalecocq.*

CICEROADVERTISING BHB 47f **RR 37f** 4410[12]
2 b c Greensmith - Bluebell Copse (Formidable (USA)) 9.2f **(63)**
Form - 000
Record 1998 - 1st:0 2nd:0 3rd:0 Ran:3
1998 Turf 0-3: (6f, 7f 2) (g-f 2, frm)
Currently very moderate colt. Turf high 37 (began Aug).
**M C Pipe [0-3] A J Lomas.*

CINDER HILLS BHB 67f60a **RR 70f 60a** 4817[7]
3 ch f Deploy 11.4f **(67)** - Dame du Moulin (Shiny Tenth) 9.2f **(56)**
Form - 062113247
Record 1998 - 1st:2 2nd:2 3rd:1 Ran:9
Pre1998 - 1st:0 2nd:0 3rd:0 Ran:3
Win Prizemoney £6,610 *Total Prizemoney* £9,865
Wins * 1998 Apr Ripon (SFT) H 12.3f 53 64 <
*** 1998** Apr Ripon (SFT) H 10f 53 60
1998 Turf 2-6: (10f 1-1, 12f 1-3, 14f, 16f) (sft 1-1, g-s 1-2, gd, g-f, frm)
1998 AW 0-3: (6f, 7f, 11f) (Fibr 3)
Leggy, above-average filly, effective 10 to 14f, best at 12f, acts on sft to frm, prefers tight tracks. Turf high 70 - 2nd of 10 getting 9lb from Pairumani Star (5 Jun Haydock 14f frm RF 1759) - also 1st of 10 getting 11lb from Pairumani Star (16 Apr Ripon RF 0719). AW high 56. She was well supported in the market when finishing runner-up in a handicap on the Southwell Fibresand in April, but made no mistake on soft ground at Ripon just two days later. Followed up at the same track over an extra two furlongs and ran well in defeat at Chester. The Handicapper might have her now.
**M W Easterby [2-12] I Bray.*

CINDESTI (IRE) **RR 38f** 4779[17]
2 b c Barathea (IRE) - Niamh Cinn Oir (IRE) (King of Clubs) 7.1f **(57)**
Form - 00
Record 1998 - 1st:0 2nd:0 3rd:0 Ran:2
1998 Turf 0-2: (7f, 8f) (gd, frm)
Currently very moderate colt. Turf high 38 (began Spt).
**L M Cumani [0-2] Sheikh Mohammed.*

CINNAMON LADY BHB 69f **RR 75f** 4884[2]
2 ch f Emarati (USA) 6.6f **(63)** - Nice Lady (Connaught) 7.7f **(63)**
Form - 0602
Record 1998 - 1st:0 2nd:1 3rd:0 Ran:4
Win Prizemoney £0 *Total Prizemoney* £958
1998 Turf 0-4: (6f, 7f 3) (g-s 2, g-f 2)
Above-average filly. Turf high 75 - 2nd of 13 getting 7lb from Spitzbergen (20 Oct Folkestone 7f g-s RF 4884).
**D Morris [0-4] Mason Racing Ltd.*

CINNAMON STICK (IRE) BHB 27f36a **RR 25f 36a** 1407[14]
5 ch g Don't Forget Me 9.5f **(66)** - Gothic Lady (Godswalk (USA)) 7.3f **(58)**
Form - 0
Record 1998 - 1st:0 2nd:0 3rd:0 Ran:1
Pre1998 - 1st:0 2nd:0 3rd:0 Ran:10
1998 Turf 0-1: (12f) (frm)
Very moderate gelding, has worn blinkers. Inconsistent.
**M E Sowersby [1-3] Michael Robson (from P S Felgate [0-7] May 1997).*

CIRCLE OF GOLD (IRE) BHB 100f **RR 99f** 4539[6]
2 ch f Royal Academy (USA) 7.8f **(77)** - Never so Fair (Never so Bold) 6.3f **(66)**
Form - 2116
Record 1998 - 1st:2 2nd:1 3rd:0 Ran:4
Win Prizemoney £25,915 *Total Prizemoney* £29,400

Wins * 1998 Aug Goodwo (G-F) G3 7f 89
* 1998 Aug Newbur (G-F) 6f 90 <
1998 Turf 2-4: (6f 1-3, 7f 1-1) (gd, g-f 2-2, frm)
Very useful filly. Turf high 99 (began Jly) - 6th of 9 to Wannabe Grand (29 Spt Newmarket 6f frm RF 4539) - also 1st of 17 from Imperial Beauty (14 Aug Newbury RF 3630). Failed to live up to her encouraging home reports when narrowly beaten on her debut, but went on to land her next two starts in good style. Ran well in the Cheveley Park Stakes, but could not prevent the leaders establishing their advantage into the Dip and, though rallying, was never able to get into the action. Ideally suited by coming off a strong gallop, she will win more races at around a mile next term.
**P W Chapple-Hyam [2-4] Mrs Sangster, B Sangster, Sangster.*

CIRCUITEER (IRE) BHB 79f78a RR 82f 78a 4238[20]

3 ch g Pips Pride 6.7f **(70)** - Day Dress (Ashmore (FR)) 8.5f **(65)**
Form - 2511316500
Record 1998 - 1st:3 2nd:1 3rd:1 Ran:10
Pre1998 - 1st:0 2nd:1 3rd:2 Ran:6
Win Prizemoney £10,235 *Total Prizemoney* £12,987
Wins ** 1998 Jun Wolver (STD) H 7f 72 75*
* **1998** May Pontef (G-F) H 8f 78 81
* **1998** May Mussel (GD) 7.1f 85 <
1998 Turf 2-8: (7f 1-3, 8f 1-5) (sft, gd 1-3, g-f 2, frm 1-2) 1998 AW 1-2: (6f, 7f 1-1) (Fibr 1-2)
Leggy, decent gelding, effective 7 to 8f, best at 7f, acts on gd to frm - acts on Fibr, best on gd, has worn blinkers, prefers tight tracks. Turf high 85 - 1st of 9 from Sleepy Baby (6 May Musselburgh RF 1067) - also 1st of 16 from Sharp Cracker (22 May Pontefract RF 1406). AW high 75. Inconsistent.
**J Berry [3-16] David Fish.*

CIRCUMNAVIGATE BHB 46a RR 46a 1[10]

3 b f Slip Anchor 12.7f **(75)** - Circe (Main Reef) 9.6f **(57)**
Form - 570
Record 1998 - 1st:0 2nd:0 3rd:0 Ran:1
Pre1998 - 1st:0 2nd:0 3rd:0 Ran:2
1998 AW 0-1: (8f) (Equi)
Leggy, currently moderate filly.
**M Johnston [0-3] Mark Johnston Racing Ltd.*

CIRCUS BHB 93f RR 98?f 4700[7]

3 b c Caerleon (USA) 10.9f **(79)** - Circo (High Top) 10.2f **(67)**
Form - 34021457
Record 1998 - 1st:1 2nd:1 3rd:1 Ran:8
Pre1998 - 1st:0 2nd:0 3rd:0 Ran:3
Win Prizemoney £3,582 *Total Prizemoney* £21,467
Wins * **1998** Aug Ripon (GD) 10f 82 <
1998 Turf 1-8: (8f 2, 9f, 10f 1-3, 12f 2) (sft, gd 1-4, g-f 2, frm)
Scopey, very useful colt, has worn blinkers (very effectively), likes right handed tracks. Turf high 110. Out of his depth for most of the season, he struggled to land the odds in a maiden at Ripon in August, but was immediately stepped straight back into Group class. He is not in that league on the balance of his form.
**C E Brittain [1-11] Saeed Manana.*

CIRO'S PEARL (IRE) BHB 53f RR 47f 5125[8]

4 b f Petorius 8f **(66)** - Cut it Fine (USA) (Big Spruce (USA)) 11f **(71)**
Form - 03670048
Record 1998 - 1st:0 2nd:0 3rd:1 Ran:8
Pre1998 - 1st:2 2nd:1 3rd:2 Ran:12
Win Prizemoney £8,067 *Total Prizemoney* £15,469
Wins * 1997 Jun Goodwo (GD) H 12f 77 79 <
* 1997 May Lingfi (G-F) H 10f 74 78
1998 Turf 0-8: (10f 4, 12f 3, 14f) (sft, g-s, gd 2, g-f 2, frm, hrd)
Scopey, moderate filly, effective 10 to 12f, best at 12f, acts on gd to hrd, best on gd, has worn blinkers, likes right handed tracks. Turf high 76 - 3rd of 6 giving 7lb to Field of Vision (10 May Beverley 12f hrd RF 1139). Inconsistent.
**M H Tompkins [2-20] J H Shannon.*

CITY GAMBLER BHB 66f64a RR 64f 64a 5069[5]

4 b f Rock City 8.8f **(62)** - Sun Street (Ile de Bourbon (USA)) 10.1f **(67)**
Form - 6740125834235
Record 1998 - 1st:1 2nd:2 3rd:2 Ran:13
Pre1998 - 1st:2 2nd:1 3rd:3 Ran:15
Win Prizemoney £9,463 *Total Prizemoney* £18,256
Wins * **1998** Aug Leices (GD) H 10f 57 62
* 1997 Aug Leices (GD) H 8f 67 73 <
* 1997 Aug Lingfi (G-F) 7.6f 57
1998 Turf 1-12: (7f, 8f, 10f 1-5, 11f, 12f 4) (g-s, gd, g-f 4, frm 1-6) 1998 AW 0-1: (8f) (Equi)
Workmanlike, average filly, effective 8 to 12f, best at 8f, acts on gd to frm, best on g-f, excels at Leicester and Kempton. Turf high 65 (began Jly) - 2nd of 7 getting 9lb from Mono Lady (19 Aug Leicester 12f frm RF 3743). Consistent. **G C Bravery [3-28] J J May.*

CITY GUILD BHB 62f RR 60f 4772[13]

2 b g Saddlers' Hall (IRE) 10.5f **(65)** - Indubitable (Sharpo) 7.7f **(59)**
Form - 400
Record 1998 - 1st:0 2nd:0 3rd:0 Ran:3
Win Prizemoney £0 *Total Prizemoney* £353
1998 Turf 0-3: (7f 2, 8f) (gd 2, frm)
Currently average gelding. Turf high 60 (began Spt).
**G B Balding [0-3] Miss B Swire.*

CITY HONOURS (USA) BHB 124f RR 122f 2432a[2]

3 b c Darshaan 11.9f **(81)**- Ikebana (IRE)(Sadler's Wells (USA))10f **(76)**
Form - 222
Record 1998 - 1st:0 2nd:3 3rd:0 Ran:3
Pre1998 - 1st:1 2nd:0 3rd:1 Ran:3
Win Prizemoney £3,200 *Total Prizemoney* £414,728
Wins 1997 Spt Doncas (G-F) 8f 103+ <
1998 Turf 0-3: (10f, 12f 2) (sft, gd, g-f)
Well made, very high-class colt, effective 10 to 12f, best at 12f, acts on sft to g-f. Turf high 122 - 2nd of 15 to High-Rise (6 Jun Epsom 12f g-f RF 1778). Winner of a Doncaster maiden and placed in the Royal Lodge as a juvenile for Peter Chapple-Hyam, he joined Godolphin over the winter. He ran a fine race when runner-up in the Dante, and ran the race of his life to go down by a head in the Blue Riband itself. He was the bridesmaid once again in the Irish Derby, and failed to reappear after that. If he does return in 1999, there are top-class races to be won.
**S bin Suroor [0-3] Godolphin (from P W Chapple-Hyam [1-3] Spt 1997).*

CITY OF GOLD (IRE) RR 76f 4998[1]

2 b f Sadler's Wells (USA) 11.3f **(87)** - Northern Script (USA) (Arts And Letters (USA)) 12.7f **(68)**
Form - 1
Record 1998 - 1st:1 2nd:0 3rd:0 Ran:1
Win Prizemoney £3,655 *Total Prizemoney* £3,655
Wins * **1998** Oct Lingfi (HVY) 7f 76 <
1998 Turf 1-1: (7f 1-1) (sft 1-1)
Currently above-average filly. (1st run) - 1st of 10 from Thermopylae (26 Oct Lingfield RF 4998). Narrow winner of a maiden at a time when Loder's two-year-olds could do no wrong.
**D R Loder [1-1] Sheikh Mohammed.*

CITY PURSUIT RR 60f 5145[12]

2 b c Pursuit of Love 9.5f **(69)** - Diabaig **(70f)** (Precocious) 8.6f **(62)**
Form - 40
Record 1998 - 1st:0 2nd:0 3rd:0 Ran:2
Win Prizemoney £0 *Total Prizemoney* £256
1998 Turf 0-2: (7f, 8f) (g-s, gd)
Currently average colt. Turf high 60 (began Oct).
**J Pearce [0-2] Harvey White Partnership II.*

CITY REACH RR 71f 4967[2]

2 b c Petong 7.6f **(58)** - Azola (IRE) (Alzao (USA)) 7.1f **(68)**
Form - 2
Record 1998 - 1st:0 2nd:1 3rd:0 Ran:1
Win Prizemoney £0 *Total Prizemoney* £1,288
1998 Turf 0-1: (6f) (sft)
Currently above-average colt.
**P J Makin [0-1] T W Wellard Partnership.*

CLADANTOM (IRE) RR 65f 4509[5]

2 b f High Estate 10.5f **(66)** - Riflebird (IRE) (Runnett) 7f **(59)**
Form - 45
Record 1998 - 1st:0 2nd:0 3rd:0 Ran:2
Win Prizemoney £0 *Total Prizemoney* £204
1998 Turf 0-2: (6f, 7f) (gd, frm)
Currently average filly. Turf high 65 (began Spt).
**Mrs J Cecil [0-2] P and C Ince Ltd.*

CLAIM GEBAL CLAIM BHB 58f51a **RR 66f 51a** 4878[7]
2 b c Ardkinglass 5f **(64)** - Infra Blue (IRE) **(35f)** (Bluebird (USA)) 7.5f **(69)**
Form - 03436307
Record 1998 - 1st:0 2nd:0 3rd:3 Ran:8
Win Prizemoney £0 *Total Prizemoney* £1,355
1998 Turf 0-7: (5f 5, 6f 2) (gd, g-f 3, frm 2, hrd) 1998 AW 0-1: (7f) (Fibr)
Average colt, effective 5 to 6f, acts on gd to g-f. Turf high 66. Inconsistent. **Mrs A Swinbank [0-8] Stan Moffat.*

CLAIRE'S FOLLY RR 49df 2261[6]
2 br f King's Signet (USA) 7f **(51)**- Armaiti(Sayf El Arab (USA)) 7.1f **(54)**
Form - 006776
Record 1998 - 1st:0 2nd:0 3rd:0 Ran:6
1998 Turf 0-6: (5f 4, 6f 2) (g-s, gd 3, g-f 2)
Moderate filly, has worn blinkers. Turf high 49.
**T D Easterby [0-6] Dr John Hollowood.*

CLANBLUE CHICK BHB 45f **RR 40f** 1606[7]
3 b f Clantime 6.6f **(57)** - Lavenham Blue (Streetfighter) 6f **(56)**
Form - 507
Record 1998 - 1st:0 2nd:0 3rd:0 Ran:2
Pre1998 - 1st:0 2nd:0 3rd:0 Ran:3
1998 Turf 0-1: (5f) (gd) 1998 AW 0-1: (5f) (Fibr)
Light-framed, moderate filly. **J Berry [0-5] Aled Griffiths.*

CLAN CHIEF BHB 65f **RR 75f** 4455[20]
5 b g Clantime 6.6f **(57)** - Mrs Meyrick (Owen Dudley) 8.3f **(61)**
Form - 334204000
Record 1998 - 1st:0 2nd:1 3rd:2 Ran:9
Pre1998 - 1st:4 2nd:5 3rd:2 Ran:18
Win Prizemoney £29,113 *Total Prizemoney* £43,435

Wins							
* 1996	Spt	Goodwo (GD)	H	6f	79	81	<
* 1996	Aug	Goodwo (G-F)	H	5f	63	75	
* 1996	Jly	Sandow (G-F)	H	5f	63	70	
* 1996	Jly	Sandow (G-F)	H	5f	58	60	

1998 Turf 0-9: (5f 7, 6f 2) (gd 3, g-f 4, frm 2)
Above-average gelding, effective 5 to 6f, acts on gd, has worn blinkers. Turf high 75 - 2nd of 11 giving 5lb to Deep Space (15 Jly Sandown 5f gd RF 2827). Enjoyed a great season in 1996, with four victories culminating in the valuable William Hill Sprint Cup at Goodwood. He has found life harder since, but ran some good races in 1998 and is weighted to win again.
**J R Arnold [4-27] P G Lowe.*

CLANTYRE BHB 48f **RR 45f** 5080[12]
2 b c Clantime 6.6f **(57)** - Tyrian Belle (Enchantment) 5.4f **(52)**
Form - 000
Record 1998 - 1st:0 2nd:0 3rd:0 Ran:3
1998 Turf 0-2: (5f 2) (g-s, g-f) 1998 AW 0-1: (6f) (Fibr)
Currently moderate colt. Turf high 45 (began Oct).
**M Johnston [0-3] The Mathieson Partnership.*

CLAPHAM COMMON (IRE) BHB 103f **RR 105f** 3162[6]
3 b c Common Grounds 8.1f **(66)**- West of Eden(Crofter(USA)) 8.4f **(56)**
Form - 41116
Record 1998 - 1st:3 2nd:0 3rd:0 Ran:5
Pre1998 - 1st:1 2nd:0 3rd:1 Ran:2
Win Prizemoney £64,446 *Total Prizemoney* £67,540

Wins						
* **1998**	Jly	San Si (GD)	L	12f	105+	<
* **1998**	May	San Si (HVY)	L	10f	90+	
* **1998**	Apr	Newbur (HVY)		10f	99	
* 1997	Spt	San Si (GD)		8f		

1998 Turf 3-5: (8f, 10f 2-2, 12f 1-2) (hvy 1-1, sft 1-1, g-s, gd 1-2)
Pattern-class colt, effective 10 to 12f, acts on sft to gd. Turf high 105 - 1st of 9 from Carry The Flag (5 Jly San Siro RF 2667a) - also 1st of 3 giving 2lb to Evening World (18 Apr Newbury RF 0746). He has earned more lira than pounds, and is probably best campaigned on the continent. Connections let him go for 72,000 guineas at the Tattersalls Autumn Horses In Training Sales.
**L M Cumani [4-7] Anglia Bloodstock Syndicate 1996.*

CLARA BLUE BHB 72f **RR 76f** 4881[1]
2 gr f Alhijaz 7.7f **(57)** - Hazy Kay (IRE) (Treasure Kay)
Form - 0006571
Record 1998 - 1st:1 2nd:0 3rd:0 Ran:7
Win Prizemoney £2,070 *Total Prizemoney* £2,070
Wins * **1998** Oct Folkes (G-S) 5f 76 <
1998 Turf 1-7: (5f 1-5, 6f 2) (g-s 1-2, g-f, frm 4)
Above-average filly, effective 5f, acts on g-s. Turf high 76 - 1st of 11 from Vintage Pride (20 Oct Folkestone RF 4881).
**T D McCarthy [1-7] Epsom Sporting Proposals Ltd.*

CLARANNA BHB 57f **RR 65f** 3020[9]
2 b f Local Suitor (USA) 9.7f **(58)** - Zolica (Beveled (USA)) 9f **(59)**
Form - 722310
Record 1998 - 1st:1 2nd:2 3rd:1 Ran:6
Win Prizemoney £4,992 *Total Prizemoney* £6,381
Wins * **1998** Jun Newcas (G-S) S 6f 65 <
1998 Turf 1-5: (5f, 6f 1-3, 7f) (g-s 1-1, gd 3, g-f) 1998 AW 0-1: (5f) (Fibr)
Average filly, effective 5 to 6f, best at 6f, acts on g-s to gd, best on gd. Turf high 65 - 1st of 14 getting 5lb from Dynamic Dancer (26 Jun Newcastle RF 2310). She has paid her way in the lowest class. Might stay seven furlongs. **R A Fahey [1-6] Miss M J Barber.*

CLARENDON (IRE) BHB 62f **RR 66f** 5094[9]
2 ch c Forest Wind (USA) - Sparkish (IRE) (Persian Bold) 9.3f **(66)**
Form - 44606470
Record 1998 - 1st:0 2nd:0 3rd:0 Ran:8
Win Prizemoney £0 *Total Prizemoney* £691
1998 Turf 0-8: (6f 2, 7f 2, 8f 4) (g-s, gd 5, g-f 2)
Average colt, has worn blinkers. Turf high 79.
**J D Bethell [0-8] Clarendon Thoroughbred Racing.*

CLARINCH CLAYMORE BHB 60f **RR 51f** 4697[15]
2 b g Sabrehill (USA) 8.5f **(64)** - Salu **(58f)** (Ardross) 10.6f **(68)**
Form - 7050
Record 1998 - 1st:0 2nd:0 3rd:0 Ran:4
1998 Turf 0-4: (6f, 7f, 8f 2) (g-s, g-f, frm 2)
Fair gelding. Turf high 51 (began Aug).
**J M Jefferson [0-4] John Donald.*

No lapse of judgement by Ffrench on Clapham Common in April

CLARITY (IRE) BHB 68a **RR 52f** 5038[6]
3 b f Scenic 10.6f **(66)** - Cristalga (High Top) 10.2f **(67)**
Form - 233566207646
Record 1998 - 1st:0 2nd:2 3rd:2 Ran:12
Pre1998 - 1st:0 2nd:0 3rd:1 Ran:5
Win Prizemoney £0 *Total Prizemoney* £4,940
1998 Turf 0-11: (10f, 11f 2, 12f 5, 14f 2, 17f) (sft, g-s 2, gd, g-f 5, frm 2)
1998 AW 0-1: (12f) (Fibr)

Scopey, average filly, effective 7 to 10f, acts on g-f to frm, has worn blinkers. Turf high 74 (1st run) - 2nd of 17 getting 2lb from Saligo (1 Jun Leicester 10f frm RF 1624).
**A P Jarvis [0-17] A L R Morton.*

CLASSIC AFFAIR (FR) RR 67f 5073[15]

2 b g Always Fair (USA) 14f **(61)** - Classic Storm (Belfort (FR)) 6.8f **(63)**
Form - 00070
Record 1998 - 1st:0 2nd:0 3rd:0 Ran:5
1998 Turf 0-5: (6f 2, 7f, 8f 2) (g-s, gd, g-f, frm 2)
Average gelding. Turf high 67 (began Spt).
**M R Channon [0-5] D and L Ayres.*

CLASSICAL DANCE (IRE) BHB 46f RR 40f 4861[11]

4 b g Classic Music (USA) 7.2f **(57)** - Eyre Square (IRE) (Flash of Steel) 7.2f **(53)**
Form - 22000
Record 1998 - 1st:0 2nd:2 3rd:0 Ran:5
Pre1998 - 1st:0 2nd:0 3rd:1 Ran:6
Win Prizemoney £0 *Total Prizemoney* £2,338
1998 Turf 0-5: (12f, 13f, 14f 2, 16f) (sft, g-s 2, gd, g-f)
Workmanlike, moderate gelding, effective 11 to 16f, acts on sft to g-f. Turf high 49 - 2nd of 11 getting 16lb from Field of Vision (3 May Hamilton 13f g-s RF 0985). Consistent.
**Mrs M Reveley [0-11] Mrs M I Jackson.*

CLASSIC CAT (USA) RR 115 1377a[3]

3 ch c Mountain Cat (USA) - Sahsie (USA)
Form - 3
1998 AW 0-1: (10f) (Dirt)
Currently high-class colt. Finished a fair third in this year's Preakness. **D Cross Jnr in USA [0-1] G Garber.*

CLASSIC COLOURS (USA) BHB 48f RR 55f 2280[13]

5 ch g Blushing John (USA) 8.9f **(75)** - All Agleam (USA) (Gleaming (USA)) 11.5f **(75)**
Form - 63650
Record 1998 - 1st:0 2nd:0 3rd:1 Ran:5
Pre1998 - 1st:0 2nd:2 3rd:1 Ran:13
Win Prizemoney £0 *Total Prizemoney* £3,786
1998 Turf 0-5: (8f 2, 10f 2, 11f) (g-s, gd 2, g-f, frm)
Fair gelding, effective 8 to 11f, acts on g-f to frm, has worn blinkers, prefers left handed tracks. Turf high 55 - 6th of 14 to Bollin Frank (15 May Nottingham 8f frm RF 1248).
**G H Yardley [0-10] Philip Jones (from R Harris [0-5] Spt 1996).*

CLASSIC CONKERS (IRE) BHB 49f RR 59f 5119[15]

4 b g Conquering Hero (USA) 10.6f **(50)** - Erck (Sun Prince) 12.4f **(52)**
Form - 8500665120
Record 1998 - 1st:1 2nd:1 3rd:0 Ran:10
Win Prizemoney £2,005 *Total Prizemoney* £2,575
Wins * 1998 Oct Yarmou (G-S) SH 11.5f 45 49 <
1998 Turf 1-10: (6f, 8f 4, 10f, 11f 1-2, 12f, 14f) (g-s, gd, g-f 1-2, frm 4, hrd 2)
Light-framed, fair gelding, effective 11 to 14f, acts on g-s to g-f, likes tight tracks. Turf high 59 (began Jly) - 2nd of 10 giving 13lb to Dalwhinnie (28 Oct Yarmouth 14f g-s RF 5038).
**Pat Mitchell [1-10] Classic Bloodstock Plc.*

CLASSIC DAME (FR) BHB 43f38a RR 47f 38a 2065[12]

5 gr m Highest Honor (FR) 10.9f **(72)** - Reem El Fala (FR) (Fabulous Dancer (USA)) 9.4f **(70)**
Form - 00040
Record 1998 - 1st:0 2nd:0 3rd:0 Ran:5
Pre1998 - 1st:0 2nd:0 3rd:2 Ran:8
Win Prizemoney £0 *Total Prizemoney* £1,347
1998 Turf 0-4: (8f, 10f, 14f, 15f) (gd, frm 3) 1998 AW 0-1: (14f) (Fibr)
Moderate filly, effective 12f, acts on g-f, has worn blinkers. Turf high 47. Inconsistent.
**Miss A Stokell [0-5] Benton, Jinks, Stoke Wall (from S Dow [0-4] Nov 1997).*

CLASSIC EXHIBIT BHB 26f28a RR 24f 28a 2922[5]

9 b g Tate Gallery (USA) 8.2f **(63)** - See The Tops (Cure The Blues (USA)) 9.5f **(63)**
Form - 5
Record 1998 - 1st:0 2nd:0 3rd:0 Ran:1
Pre1998 - 1st:0 2nd:0 3rd:0 Ran:11
1998 Turf 0-1: (14f) (gd)
Little account gelding, has worn blinkers.
**A Streeter [2-8] Principal Racing (from A L Forbes [1-13] Mar 1995).*

CLASSIC FIGHTER (IRE) RR 32f 4452[6]

2 ch c Up and At 'em - Classic Choice (Patch) 11.5f **(51)**
Form - 06
Record 1998 - 1st:0 2nd:0 3rd:0 Ran:2
1998 Turf 0-2: (6f, 8f) (gd, frm)
Currently very moderate colt. Turf high 32 (began Spt).
**J J Sheehan [0-2] P J Sheehan.*

CLASSIC FIND (USA) BHB 61f70a RR 66f 70a 4263[P]

5 b br g Lear Fan (USA) 10.4f **(80)** - Reve de Reine (USA) (Lyphard (USA)) 9.9f **(72)**
Form - 2123024566014P
Record 1998 - 1st:1 2nd:2 3rd:1 Ran:12
Pre1998 - 1st:2 2nd:2 3rd:3 Ran:14
Win Prizemoney £11,570 *Total Prizemoney* £17,513
Wins * 1998 Aug Newmar (G-F) H 10f 60 64
* 1997 *Dec Lingfi (STD) H 10f 65 69 <*
1996 May Redcar (G-F) 10f 67+
1998 Turf 1-9: (8f 3, 10f 1-6) (gd, g-f 2, frm 5, hrd 1-1) 1998 AW 0-3: (10f 3) (Equi 3)
Above-average gelding, effective 8 to 14f, best at 10f, acts on gd to hrd - acts on Equi, likes left handed tracks, likes tight tracks, excels at Redcar and likes Lingfield. Turf high 66 - 6th of 20 getting 6lb from Mount Holly (7 Jly Newmarket 8f frm RF 2579). AW high 74 (1st run) - 2nd of 8 giving 3lb to Sea Danzig (20 Jan Lingfield 10f Equi RF 0122). Won an essentially uncompetitive handicap at Newmarket in August and pulled up lame on his final start.
**Pat Mitchell [2-17] Classic Bloodstock Plc (from I Campbell [0-6] Jly 1997).*

CLASSIC IMPACT (IRE) BHB 78f RR 79f 4763[2]

3 ch g Generous (IRE) 11.5f **(82)** - Vaison la Romaine (Arctic Tern (USA)) 8.9f **(69)**
Form - 7512002
Record 1998 - 1st:1 2nd:2 3rd:0 Ran:7
Pre1998 - 1st:0 2nd:0 3rd:0 Ran:2
Win Prizemoney £3,571 *Total Prizemoney* £6,951
Wins * 1998 Jun Newbur (HVY) H 12f 70 72 <
1998 Turf 1-7: (8f, 11f, 12f 1-5) (sft, g-s 1-1, gd 3, frm 2)
Scopey, above-average gelding, effective 11 to 12f, best at 12f, acts on g-s to frm. Turf high 79 - 2nd of 13 giving 9lb to Borgia (12 Oct Leicester 12f gd RF 4763) - also 1st of 9 getting 3lb from Sherganzar (11 Jun Newbury RF 1899). Caught the eye in maidens before a game winner on his handicap debut in testing ground. Ran well next time but well beaten since. Has joined Pat Murphy.
**P W Chapple-Hyam [1-9] , Sangster.*

CLASSIC JENNY (IRE) BHB 66f72a RR 63f 72a 95[1]

5 b m Green Desert (USA) 7.8f **(78)** - Eileen Jenny (IRE) (Kris) 9.5f **(73)**
Form - 1
Record 1998 - 1st:1 2nd:0 3rd:0 Ran:1
Pre1998 - 1st:0 2nd:0 3rd:0 Ran:4
Win Prizemoney £3,338 *Total Prizemoney* £3,806
Wins * 1998 *Jan Lingfi (STD) 10f 64+ <*
1998 AW 1-1: (10f 1-1) (Equi 1-1)
Average filly. (1st run) - 1st of 7 getting 3lb from Mutabassir (15 Jan Lingfield RF 0095). She got off the mark when making her Equitrack debut at Lingfield in January. She won with a ton in hand, but was not seen again.
**M R Channon [1-1] Classic Bloodstock Plc (from I Campbell [0-5] Oct 1997).*

CLASSIC MANOEUVRE (USA) BHB 68f68a RR 79f 68a 4996[3]

3 ch c Sky Classic (CAN) 10f **(83)** - Maid of Honor (USA) (Blushing Groom (FR)) 10.3f **(76)**
Form - 43332003
Record 1998 - 1st:0 2nd:1 3rd:4 Ran:8
Pre1998 - 1st:0 2nd:1 3rd:0 Ran:4
Win Prizemoney £0 *Total Prizemoney* £7,317
1998 Turf 0-7: (10f 5, 11f, 12f) (gd 4, g-f 2, frm) 1998 AW 0-1: (10f) (Equi)

Neat, above-average colt, effective 10 to 11f, acts on gd, has worn blinkers, likes tight tracks. Turf high 83 (1st run) - 4th of 12 to Legal Lunch (23 May Haydock 11f gd RF 1419). He has ability, but lack of acceleration is always likely to prove his downfall.
**R Hannon [0-12] Paul & Jenny Green.*

CLASSIC MASQUERADE (CAN) BHB 52f **RR 57f** 3322[4]
3 b c Regal Classic (CAN) - Muskoka Command (USA) (Top Command (USA)) 10f **(77)**
Form - 445644
Record 1998 - 1st:0 2nd:0 3rd:0 Ran:6
Win Prizemoney £0 *Total Prizemoney* £696
1998 Turf 0-6: (10f, 12f 4, 17f) (gd, g-f 2, frm 3)
Scopey, fair colt. Turf high 62. **R Hannon [0-6] Paul & Jenny Green.*

CLASS WAN BHB 76f **RR 76f** 5144[8]
2 ch f Safawan 6.6f **(60)** - Ayr Classic (Local Suitor (USA)) 8.4f **(67)**
Form - 075541618
Record 1998 - 1st:2 2nd:0 3rd:0 Ran:9
Win Prizemoney £6,638 *Total Prizemoney* £6,830
Wins * **1998** Oct Ayr (G-S) H 6f 67 76 <
* **1998** Aug Mussel (G-F) H 5f 66 71
1998 Turf 2-9: (5f 1-5, 6f 1-4) (sft 1-2, gd 1-5, frm, hrd)
Above-average filly, effective 5 to 6f, acts on sft to gd. Turf high 76 - 1st of 11 giving 10lb to Tancred Arms (12 Oct Ayr RF 4756) - also 1st of 8 giving 9lb to Wind In Winnipeg (19 Aug Musselburgh RF 3747). **J S Goldie [2-9] The Jersey Syndicate.*

CLASSY ABSTONE BHB 56f **RR 48f** 1309[5]
2 br f Tragic Role (USA) 9.4f **(63)** -Grey Twig(Godswalk (USA))7.3f **(58)**
Form - 445
Record 1998 - 1st:0 2nd:0 3rd:0 Ran:3
Win Prizemoney £0 *Total Prizemoney* £218
1998 Turf 0-1: (5f) (g-s) 1998 AW 0-2: (5f, 6f) (Fibr 2)
Currently moderate filly. AW high 36. Showed ability when a keeping-on fourth on her debut. **P D Evans [0-3] Men Behaving Badly.*

CLASSY CLEO (IRE) BHB 95f100a **RR 93f 100a** 5096[1]
3 b f Mujadil (USA) 7.7f **(70)** - Sybaris(Crowned Prince (USA))10.1f **(67)**
Form - 112352004510801500022521
Record 1998 - 1st:3 2nd:4 3rd:1 Ran:21
Pre1998 - 1st:6 2nd:5 3rd:4 Ran:19
Win Prizemoney £40,484 *Total Prizemoney* £56,350
Wins * **1998** Nov Redcar (G-S) H 6f 90 93
* **1998** Jly Cheste (G-F) H 5.1f 85 88
* **1998** May Cheste (GD) H 5.1f 85 87
* 1997 *Nov Lingfi (STD) H 5f 87 105* <
* 1997 *Nov Southw (STD) H 6f 87 86*
* 1997 Oct Yarmou (FRM) H 5.2f 79 86
1997 Spt Haydoc (G-S) C 6f 68
1997 Apr Pontef (GD) 5f 79
1997 Apr Beverl (G-F) 5f 79
1998 Turf 3-17: (5f 2-10, 6f 1-7) (sft 2, g-s, gd 1-6, g-f 1-4, frm 1-4)
1998 AW 0-4: (5f 2, 6f, 7f) (Fibr 4)
Unfurnished, useful filly, effective 5f, - acts on Equi, likes left handed tracks, likes tight tracks, excels at Chester. Turf high 93. AW high 93. Like most of her trainer's horses, she has to sing for her supper. Better than ever at the end of a long campaign, she signed off with a win at Redcar in November and is a credit to her connections.
**P D Evans [6-30] J E Abbey (from R Hannon [3-10] Spt 1997).*

CLAUDIUS BHB 60f **RR 62f** 4490[16]
2 b c Clantime 6.6f **(57)** - Pokey's Pet (Uncle Pokey) 10.1f **(49)**
Form - 0040
Record 1998 - 1st:0 2nd:0 3rd:0 Ran:4
Win Prizemoney £0 *Total Prizemoney* £241
1998 Turf 0-4: (5f 4) (frm 4)
Average colt. Turf high 62. **R A Fahey [0-4] Mrs Rosie Richer.*

CLAXON BHB 92f **RR 82f** 4766[1]
2 b f Caerleon (USA) 10.9f **(79)** - Bulaxie **(103f)** (Bustino) 10.4f **(64)**
Form - 231
Record 1998 - 1st:1 2nd:1 3rd:1 Ran:3
Win Prizemoney £3,444 *Total Prizemoney* £8,134
Wins * **1998** Oct Ayr (SFT) 8f 82 <
1998 Turf 1-3: (7f 2, 8f 1-1) (sft 1-1, g-f 2)
Currently decent filly. Turf high 82 (began Aug) - 1st of 6 from Discerning Air (13 Oct Ayr RF 4766). The first foal of a very useful racemare, she was runner-up in a listed race on her debut and ran respectably in a conditions race on her second start. An easy winner on her final run, relishing the soft ground.
**J L Dunlop [1-3] Hesmonds Stud.*

CLEAR NIGHT BHB 82f **RR 74f** 4568[6]
2 b c Night Shift (USA) 8.1f **(73)** - Clarista (USA) (Riva Ridge (USA)) 8.2f **(68)**
Form - 4536
Record 1998 - 1st:0 2nd:0 3rd:1 Ran:4
Win Prizemoney £0 *Total Prizemoney* £830
1998 Turf 0-4: (5f, 6f 2, 7f) (gd 2, g-f 2)
Above-average colt. Turf high 74 - 3rd of 22 to Maple (19 Spt Newbury 6f g-f RF 4382). **R Hannon [0-4] J A Lazzari.*

CLEAR THE SMOKE BHB 39f **RR 7f** 4637[9]
2 ch c Mystiko (USA) 7.7f **(59)** - Zipperti Do (Precocious) 8.6f **(62)**
Form - 000
Record 1998 - 1st:0 2nd:0 3rd:0 Ran:3
1998 Turf 0-2: (5f 2) (gd, frm) 1998 AW 0-1: (6f) (Fibr)
Currently very poor colt, has worn blinkers. Turf high 7 (began Spt). **Mrs N Macauley [0-3] Andy Peake.*

CLEF OF SILVER BHB 87f **RR 86f** 4626[1]
3 b c Indian Ridge 7.6f **(74)** - Susquehanna Days (USA) (Chief's Crown (USA)) 9.8f **(72)**
Form - 7501
Record 1998 - 1st:1 2nd:0 3rd:0 Ran:4
Pre1998 - 1st:1 2nd:4 3rd:0 Ran:5
Win Prizemoney £5,266 *Total Prizemoney* £13,476
Wins * **1998** Oct Catter (gd,) 6f 86 <
* 1997 Aug Catter (G-F) H 6f 80 85
1998 Turf 1-4: (6f 1-4) (g-s, g-f 1-2, frm)
Workmanlike, useful colt, effective 5 to 6f, best at 6f, acts on gd to frm, best on g-f, excels at Catterick. Turf high 86 (began Jly) - 1st of 8 getting 3lb from Classy Cleo (3 Oct Catterick RF 4626). Consistent. Not an easy ride, he had been shaping well prior to his win at Catterick. **W Jarvis [2-9] Silver Clef Racing Venture.*

CLEMENCY (IRE) BHB 44f57a **RR 44f 57a** 2728[18]
6 ch m Kefaah (USA) 11.2f **(64)** - Supreme Crown (USA) (Chief's Crown (USA)) 9.8f **(72)**
Form - 0
Record 1998 - 1st:0 2nd:0 3rd:0 Ran:1
Pre1998 - 1st:0 2nd:1 3rd:0 Ran:9
Win Prizemoney £0 *Total Prizemoney* £1,173
1998 Turf 0-1: (11f) (frm)
Moderate mare, has worn blinkers.
**M Tate [0-3] M Tate (from T D Barron [0-7] Spt 1994).*

CLERKENWELL (USA) BHB 109f **RR 109f** 4616[6]
5 b h Sadler's Wells (USA) 11.3f **(87)** - Forlene (Forli (ARG)) 9.6f **(67)**
Form - 10346
Record 1998 - 1st:1 2nd:0 3rd:1 Ran:5
Pre1998 - 1st:3 2nd:2 3rd:1 Ran:10
Win Prizemoney £108,316 *Total Prizemoney* £116,946
Wins * **1998** Jun Cheste (GD) 12.3f 101
* 1997 Spt Salisb (G-S) 14f 115+ <
* 1996 Aug York (GD) H 13.9f 93 106
* 1996 Jly Sandow (GD) 14f 75+
1998 Turf 1-5: (12f 1-4, 20f) (g-s, gd 1-3, g-f)
Pattern-class colt, effective 12 to 14f, acts on gd. Turf high 109 - 4th of 9 giving 8lb to Capri (26 Spt Ascot 12f gd RF 4491). He is a touch soft and did not seem to be enjoying himself toward the end of the season. One to oppose in anything but a weak race.
**Sir Michael Stoute [4-15] Sheikh Mohammed.*

CLEY TOURIST BHB 22f **RR*** 3744[10]
3 b f Forzando 7.2f **(63)** - Scotch Thistle (Sassafras (FR)) 9.6f **(69)**
Form - 0000
Record 1998 - 1st:0 2nd:0 3rd:0 Ran:4
1998 Turf 0-3: (6f, 8f, 10f) (g-f, frm 2) 1998 AW 0-1: (6f) (Fibr)
Strong, poor filly, often wears blinkers. (began Jly).
**A W Carroll [0-4] J C Wilson.*

CLIBURNEL NEWS (IRE) BHB 59f49a **RR 58f 49a** 3330[1]
8 b m Horage 11.4f **(58)** - Dublin Millennium (Dalsaan) 9.8f **(64)**
Form - 0036001
Record 1998 - 1st:1 2nd:0 3rd:1 Ran:7
Pre1998 - 1st:10 2nd:6 3rd:7 Ran:58
Win Prizemoney £27,837 *Total Prizemoney* £36,492
Wins * **1998** Aug Catter (GD) H 13.8f 55 58
* 1997 Spt Nottin (G-F) H 16f 47 52
1995 May Leices (G-F) H 11.8f 55 61
1995 Apr Leices (GD) H 11.8f 53 57
1994 Aug Ayr (GD) S 13.1f 48
1994 Jly Mussel (G-F) C 15.1f 48
1998 Turf 1-6: (14f 1-3, 16f 2, 17f) (gd 1-4, g-f, frm) 1998 AW 0-1: (14f) (Fibr)
Fair mare, effective 14 to 16f, best at 16f, acts on gd to g-f, best on gd, has worn blinkers, favours left handed tracks. Turf high 58 - 1st of 10 getting 1lb from Eternity (4 Aug Catterick RF 3330). Inconsistent. A modest staying handicapper these days, she returned to winning form at Catterick in August, and may the type of mare who finds her form in the second half of the season.
**D Shaw [2-10] K Nicholls (from A Streeter [0-9] Jun 1996).*

CLIFTON WOOD (IRE) BHB 56f **RR 64f** 4397[17]
3 b c Paris House 5.9f **(64)** - Millie's Lady (IRE) (Common Grounds)
Form - 5600
Record 1998 - 1st:0 2nd:0 3rd:0 Ran:4
Pre1998 - 1st:0 2nd:0 3rd:0 Ran:1
1998 Turf 0-4: (5f, 6f, 7f 2) (gd, frm 3)
Workmanlike, average colt. Turf high 64 (began Jly).
**J A Glover [0-5] P and S Partnership.*

CLOAK OF DARKNESS (IRE) BHB 85f **RR 86f** 4392[3]
3 b c Thatching 7.8f **(69)** - Madame Nureyev (USA) (Nureyev (USA)) 8.7f **(78)**
Form - 105353
Record 1998 - 1st:1 2nd:0 3rd:2 Ran:6
Pre1998 - 1st:0 2nd:0 3rd:0 Ran:3
Win Prizemoney £3,980 *Total Prizemoney* £6,117
Wins * **1998** Jun Windso (G-F) 10f 83 <
1998 Turf 1-6: (8f, 10f 1-4, 12f) (gd 2, g-f 1-2, frm 2)
Workmanlike, useful colt, effective 10 to 12f, best at 10f, acts on g-f to frm, best on g-f. Turf high 86 - 3rd of 9 getting 7lb from Benin (14 Aug Newbury 10f g-f RF 3632) - also 1st of 25 giving 5lb to Mole Creek (1 Jun Windsor RF 1639). Made all to beat a big field in a Windsor maiden on his reappearance, but was never sighted next time. He has run well in competitive handicaps since, but looks short of toe and probably needs a trip beyond ten furlongs.
**R Hannon [1-9] Mohamed Suhail.*

CLOHAMON BHB 60f53a **RR 60f 53a** 2264[8]
3 b g Aragon 7.7f **(58)** - Almadaniyah (Dunbeath (USA)) 7.8f **(70)**
Form - 7458
Record 1998 - 1st:0 2nd:0 3rd:0 Ran:4
Win Prizemoney £0 *Total Prizemoney* £204
1998 Turf 0-4: (5f 3, 6f) (gd 2, g-f, hrd)
Leggy, average gelding. Turf high 60.
**S E Kettlewell [0-4] S E Kettlewell.*

CLONOE BHB 47f38a **RR 46f 38a** 4995[11]
4 b g Syrtos 8.1f **(57)** - Anytime Anywhere (Daring March) 7.1f **(61)**
Form - 436084233421028043715370
Record 1998 - 1st:2 2nd:3 3rd:4 Ran:20
Pre1998 - 1st:0 2nd:0 3rd:1 Ran:6
Win Prizemoney £5,455 *Total Prizemoney* £10,268
Wins * **1998** Aug Kempto (G-F) H 8f 43 46
* **1998** Apr Folkes (SFT) H 6f 36 47? <
1998 Turf 2-14: (6f 1-4, 7f 7, 8f 1-3) (sft 1-2, g-s, gd 3, g-f 5, frm 1-3)
1998 AW 0-6: (6f 2, 7f 3, 12f) (Equi 5, Fibr)
Workmanlike, moderate gelding, effective 6 to 8f, best at 6f, acts on sft to frm - acts on AW, has worn blinkers, excels at Folkestone. Turf high 47 - 1st of 14 getting 3lb from Stock Hill Dancer (7 Apr Folkestone RF 0577) - also 1st of 12 getting 30lb from Barbason (5 Aug Kempton RF 3373). AW high 39 - 2nd of 9 getting 10lb from Time of Night (4 Feb Wolverhampton 7f Fibr RF 0214). Bolted up in an apprentice event at Folkestone, having raced on much the faster side of the track. Generally modest form after, though he added a Kempton handicap when stepped up to a mile.
**R Ingram [2-26] McKernan O'Neill.*

CLOON CREE (IRE) RR 33f 2977[10]
2 b f River Falls 8.2f **(56)** - Texly (FR) (Lyphard (USA)) 9.9f **(72)**
Form - 0000
Record 1998 - 1st:0 2nd:0 3rd:0 Ran:4
1998 Turf 0-4: (5f, 6f 2, 7f) (g-f 4)
Very moderate filly, often wears blinkers. Turf high 33.
**D J S Cosgrove [0-4] W A Barrett.*

CLOSE SHAVE BHB 77f **RR 80f** 3298[6]
3 b c Warning 8.1f **(77** - La Barberina (USA) (Nijinsky (CAN)) 10.3f **(77)**
Form - 56
Record 1998 - 1st:0 2nd:0 3rd:0 Ran:2
Pre1998 - 1st:0 2nd:0 3rd:1 Ran:2
Win Prizemoney £0 *Total Prizemoney* £802
1998 Turf 0-2: (8f, 10f) (gd, frm)
Scopey, decent colt. Turf high 71 (began Jly). He looked as if he might be a cut above the rest at one stage in 1997, but last season's efforts hardly had connections bristling with confidence. **Sir Michael Stoute [0-4] Sheikh Mohammed.*

CLOSE UP (IRE) BHB 94f **RR 88f** 867[4]
3 ch c Cadeaux Genereux 7.9f **(76)** - Zoom Lens (IRE) (Caerleon (USA)) 8.6f **(71)**
Form - 4
Record 1998 - 1st:0 2nd:0 3rd:0 Ran:1
Pre1998 - 1st:2 2nd:1 3rd:0 Ran:5
Win Prizemoney £8,257 *Total Prizemoney* £10,344
Wins * 1997 Oct Haydoc (SFT) 8.1f 85 <
* 1997 Spt Pontef (G-F) 8f 76
1998 Turf 0-1: (8f) (sft)
Workmanlike, useful colt, effective 7 to 8f, acted on g-s to frm. Steadily improved at two, and ran with credit on his sole run last season. (DEAD) **J L Dunlop [2-6] Ian Cameron.*

Cloud Castle was highly tried all season

CLOUD CASTLE RR 115f 4852[9]
3 b f In The Wings 11.2f **(77)** - Lucayan Princess (High Line) 10.3f **(70)**
Form - 148473250
Record 1998 - 1st:1 2nd:1 3rd:1 Ran:9
Pre1998 - 1st:0 2nd:0 3rd:1 Ran:1
Win Prizemoney £20,000 *Total Prizemoney* £93,116
Wins * **1998** Apr Newmar (G-S) G3 7f 105 <
1998 Turf 1-9: (7f 1-1, 8f 2, 10f 2, 12f 3, 13f) (hvy, sft, gd 1-6, frm)
Strong, high-class filly, effective 7 to 12f, best at 12f, acts on hvy to frm. Turf high 115 - 2nd of 11 to Leggera (13 Spt Longchamp 12f

hvy RF 4343a). Consistent. She caused a real surprise by winning the Nell Gwyn at odds of 33/1 on her reappearance, and then ran in three classics, with her fourth place in the 1,000 Guineas being by far her best effort. Ran a fine second to Leggera in the Prix Vermeille in September, appearing to relish the soft ground, but was a little below-par on both a return visit to Paris and in the Champion Stakes. **C E Brittain [1-10] Saeed Manana.*

CLOUD INSPECTOR (IRE) BHB 82f **RR 84f** 3919a[9]

7 b g Persian Bold 10f **(69)** - Timbale d'Argent (Petingo) 11f **(72)**

Form - 200060

Record 1998 - 1st:0 2nd:1 3rd:0 Ran:6
Pre1998 - 1st:2 2nd:4 3rd:1 Ran:8

Win Prizemoney £20,936 *Total Prizemoney* £36,388

Wins * 1997 Aug Dielsd (GD) 15f 89+ <
* 1997 Jly Goodwo (G-F) H 20f 75 82

1998 Turf 0-6: (12f, 14f, 15f, 16f, 19f, 20f) (sft 2, gd 2, g-f 2)

Decent gelding, effective 12 to 15f, acts on gd. Turf high 89. Inconsistent. An Ex-German and Irish performer who won the Goodwood Handicap in 1997, he was beaten in Switzerland and in a couple of warm handicaps last term. **M Johnston [2-14].*

CLOUDS OF GLORY BHB 62f59a **RR 61f 59a** 2896[4]

3 b f Lycius (USA) 8.8f **(71)** - Dance a Jig (Dance In Time (CAN)) 8.9f **(59)**

Form - 00404

Record 1998 - 1st:0 2nd:0 3rd:0 Ran:5
Pre1998 - 1st:0 2nd:0 3rd:0 Ran:3

1998 Turf 0-4: (6f 2, 8f 2) (hvy, gd, frm 2) 1998 AW 0-1: (8f) (Fibr)

Average filly, effective 8f, acts on frm. Turf high 61 - 4th of 10 giving 19lb to Lycian (29 May Bath 8f frm RF 1570).

**R Charlton [0-8] N Bryce-Smith.*

CLOVER GIRL BHB 30f **RR 18f** 1096[9]

7 bl m Spin of a Coin 14.1f **(56)** - Byerley Rose (Rolfe (USA)) 12.1f **(65)**

Form - 0

Record 1998 - 1st:0 2nd:0 3rd:0 Ran:1
Pre1998 - 1st:0 2nd:0 3rd:0 Ran:2

1998 Turf 0-1: (7f) (gd)

Poor mare, often wears blinkers.

**B Ellison [2-22] The Couriers Syndicate.*

CLUED UP BHB 52f44a **RR 55f 44a** 5098[5]

5 b m Beveled (USA) 6.9f **(64)** - Scharade (Lombard (GER)) 10.5f **(66)**

Form - 72017164065075

Record 1998 - 1st:2 2nd:1 3rd:0 Ran:13
Pre1998 - 1st:3 2nd:1 3rd:2 Ran:27

Win Prizemoney £14,502 *Total Prizemoney* £18,056

Wins * **1998** Jly Haydoc (G-S) H 11.9f 52 61 <
* **1998** Jun Cheste (G-S) H 12.3f 52 55
* 1997 Jly Chepst (G-S) H 8.1f 50 57
* 1997 May Hamilt (SFT) H 8.3f 46 50
* 1996 Aug Redcar (G-F) C 10f 43

1998 Turf 2-13: (10f 4, 11f 2, 12f 2-6, 16f) (gd 1-7, frm 1-6)

Fair filly, effective 8 to 16f, best at 12f, acts on gd to frm, best on frm, mostly wears blinkers (very effectively), excels at Chester. Turf high 61 - 1st of 4 giving 1lb to Mannequin (2 Jly Haydock RF 2472) - also 1st of 6 getting 19lb from Mono Lady (24 Jun Chester RF 2232).

**P D Evans [5-37] Mrs E J Williams (from M H Easterby [0-3] Spt 1995).*

CLUNIE BHB 73f **RR 71f** 4820[8]

2 ch f Inchinor 8.9f **(64)** - Bonita **(60f)** (Primo Dominie) 6.2f **(80)**

Form - 011018

Record 1998 - 1st:3 2nd:0 3rd:0 Ran:6

Win Prizemoney £9,650 *Total Prizemoney* £9,650

Wins * **1998** Spt Haydoc (G-F) H 6f 58 71 <
* **1998** Spt Nottin (GD) H 6.1f 58 67
* **1998** Aug Windso (G-F) S 6f 59

1998 Turf 3-6: (6f 3-6) (gd 1-1, frm 2-5)

Above-average filly, effective 6f, acts on gd to frm. Turf high 71 (began Aug) - 1st of 13 getting 9lb from Santandre (25 Spt Haydock RF 4479) - also 1st of 19 getting 9lb from Bollin Roberta (14 Spt Nottingham RF 4261). **W J Haggas [3-6] Tony Hirschfeld.*

CLYTHA HILL LAD BHB 52f **RR 49f** 1480[14]

7 b g Domitor (USA) 7.6f **(56)** - Quae Supra (On Your Mark) 7.7f **(58)**

Form - 80

Record 1998 - 1st:0 2nd:0 3rd:0 Ran:2
Pre1998 - 1st:4 2nd:2 3rd:1 Ran:18

Win Prizemoney £11,045 *Total Prizemoney* £12,895

Wins * 1997 Aug Haydoc (G-F) H 8.1f 45 56 <
* 1997 Aug Redcar (FRM) H 7f 45 49
* 1997 Jly Chepst (G-F) H 7.1f 31 43
* 1997 Jly Redcar (G-F) H 8f 31 35

1998 Turf 0-2: (8f, 9f) (g-f, frm)

Moderate gelding, effective 7 to 8f, acts on g-f to frm. Turf high 49. Consistent. **J M Bradley [4-22] Mrs Marion Morgan.*

COALMINERSDAUGHTER (IRE) BHB 58f60a **RR 61f 60a** 4753[3]

3 b f Dynaformer (USA) 12f **(82)** - Sportin' Notion (USA) (Sportin' Life (USA)) 11.1f **(75)**

Form - 66011613

Record 1998 - 1st:3 2nd:0 3rd:1 Ran:8
Pre1998 - 1st:0 2nd:0 3rd:0 Ran:3

Win Prizemoney £7,012 *Total Prizemoney* £7,409

Wins * **1998** Spt Yarmou (G-S) C 11.5f 59
* **1998** Aug Yarmou (G-F) C 10.1f 61 <
* ***1998*** *Jly Lingfi (STD) H 10f 56 57*

1998 Turf 2-6: (10f 1-2, 11f 1-4) (sft, gd 1-2, g-f, frm 1-2) 1998 AW 1-2: (8f, 10f 1-1) (Equi 1-1, Fibr)

Average filly, effective 10 to 11f, best at 10f, acts on gd to frm - acts on Equi, prefers left handed tracks, prefers tight tracks. Turf high 61 - 1st of 10 giving 4lb to Spanish Eyes (5 Aug Yarmouth RF 3395) - also 1st of 12 from Mysterious Ecology (15 Spt Yarmouth RF 4271). AW high 57 - 1st of 9 from Waasef (25 Jly Lingfield RF 3107). **J W Hills [3-11] Freddy Bienstock.*

COASTAL BLUFF BHB 112f **RR 115f** 2108[11]

6 gr g Standaan (FR) 5.4f **(46)** - Combattente (Reform) 8.9f **(62)**

Form - 00

Record 1998 - 1st:0 2nd:0 3rd:0 Ran:2
Pre1998 - 1st:7 2nd:2 3rd:1 Ran:17

Win Prizemoney £185,821 *Total Prizemoney* £203,136

Wins * 1997 Aug York (GD) G1 5f 115 <
* 1997 Jly Newmar (G-F) 5f 108+
* 1996 Spt Ayr (G-F) H 6f 104 115+
* 1996 Aug Goodwo (G-F) H 6f 88 101+
* 1996 Jly York (GD) H 5f 88 91+
* 1995 Oct Ascot (SFT) H 5f 84 88
* 1995 Apr Nottin (G-F) 5.1f 79+

1998 Turf 0-2: (5f 2) (gd 2)

High-class gelding, effective 5f, acts on gd to frm. Turf high 106. This fine stamp of a gelding dead-heated with Ya Malak in a sensational Nunthorpe in 1997, with rider Kevin Darley performing miracles after the bit broke early on. He did not fire at all in 1998, but it was sad to see this old warrior go through the sales ring at Newmarket in October. He deserved better than that public humiliation and only made 17,000 guineas.

**T D Barron [7-19] Mrs D E Sharp.*

COASTGUARDS HERO BHB 28f37a **RR 26f 37a** 3571[6]

5 ch g Chilibang 7f **(55)** - Aldwick Colonnade **(43f 41a)** (Kind of Hush) 10.1f **(62)**

Form - 0831341607573715256

Record 1998 - 1st:3 2nd:1 3rd:3 Ran:17
Pre1998 - 1st:1 2nd:2 3rd:1 Ran:22

Win Prizemoney £8,279 *Total Prizemoney* £12,441

Wins * ***1998*** *Jun Lingfi (STD) SH 13f 30 36*
1998 *Feb Lingfi (SLW) SH 16f 35 36*
1998 *Jan Lingfi (STD) H 13f 30 35*
1996 Feb Southw (STD) 6f 45 <

1998 Turf 0-5: (12f 3, 14f, 16f) (g-s, gd 2, g-f 2) 1998 AW 3-12: (13f 2-4, 14f, 16f 1-7) (Equi 3-11, Fibr)

Moderate gelding, effective 13 to 16f, best at 16f, - acts on Equi, prefers left handed tracks, favours tight tracks, excels at Lingfield. Turf high 32. AW high 41 - also 1st of 9 getting 11lb from Rowlandsons Charm (12 Feb Lingfield RF 0273). Basically a plater nowadays, he found his form when faced with a longer trip on Equitrack at the start of '98, winning twice over thirteen furlongs and once over two miles.

**B A Pearce [1-13] D Newman (from M D I Usher [3-29] Feb 1998).*

COBLE BHB 34f **RR 44f** 609[15]
4 b g Slip Anchor 12.7f **(75)** - Main Sail (Blakeney) 10.5f **(64)**
Form - 500
Record 1998 - 1st:0 2nd:0 3rd:0 Ran:3
Pre1998 - 1st:0 2nd:0 3rd:0 Ran:7
Win Prizemoney £0 *Total Prizemoney* £261
1998 Turf 0-2: (12f 2) (sft, gd) 1998 AW 0-1: (12f) (Fibr)
Scopey, moderate gelding, has worn blinkers. Turf high 28.
**D McCain [0-9] D McCain (from B W Hills [0-7] Aug 1997).*

COBOURG LODGE (IRE) RR 95f 4964[3]
2 b c Unblest - Rachel Pringle (IRE) 00
Form - 18726313
1998 Turf 2-8: (5f 1-2, 6f 1-4, 7f, 8f) (sft 1-2, g-s 1-3, gd 2, hrd)
Very useful colt, effective 6f, acts on g-s. Turf high 95 - 1st of 15 giving 6lb to Wish List (11 Oct Naas RF 4794a). Fairly useful two-year-old who is best with some cut. Came over to Newbury without troubling the English juveniles too much when stepped up in distance. **J T Gorman in IRE [2-8] Andrews Syndicate.*

COBRA LADY (IRE) BHB 47f **RR 43f** 5002[18]
3 ch f Indian Ridge 7.6f **(74)** - Rum Cay (USA) (Our Native (USA)) 11.2f **(63)**
Form - 6800
Record 1998 - 1st:0 2nd:0 3rd:0 Ran:4
1998 Turf 0-3: (6f, 7f 2) (gd, g-f 2) 1998 AW 0-1: (12f) (Equi)
Scopey, moderate filly. Turf high 43. **C R Egerton [0-4] A Hayes.*

COCHISE RR 50f 3233[10]
2 ch c Cosmonaut - Paircullis (Tower Walk) 10f **(62)**
Form - 070
Record 1998 - 1st:0 2nd:0 3rd:0 Ran:3
1998 Turf 0-3: (6f, 7f 2) (gd, g-f, frm)
Currently fair colt. Turf high 50.
**Miss Gay Kelleway [0-3] Rainbow Racing UK Ltd.*

COCHITI BHB 30f23a **RR 40f 23a** 3830[5]
4 b f Kris 10f **(75)** - Sweet Jaffa (Never so Bold) 6.3f **(66)**
Form - 75
Record 1998 - 1st:0 2nd:0 3rd:0 Ran:2
Pre1998 - 1st:0 2nd:0 3rd:1 Ran:9
Win Prizemoney £0 *Total Prizemoney* £342
1998 AW 0-2: (12f, 16f) (Equi, Fibr)
Light-framed, moderate filly, effective 12f, acts on frm, often wears blinkers (effectively), likes tight tracks. AW high 19.
**P W Hiatt [0-15] The Equus Club (from C W Thornton [0-9] Spt 1997).*

COCKATRICE BHB 65f **RR 69f** 5148[20]
2 b f Petong 7.6f **(58)** - Noble Peregrine (Lomond)
Form - 70040
Record 1998 - 1st:0 2nd:0 3rd:0 Ran:5
1998 Turf 0-5: (6f 2, 7f 3) (g-s, gd 2, frm 2)
Average filly. Turf high 69 (began Jly).
**D Morris [0-5] Mrs David Sieff.*

COCKSURE (IRE) BHB 61f **RR 53f** 4432a[27]
3 b g Nomination 7.3f **(57)** - Hens Grove (Alias Smith (USA)) 9.8f **(58)**
Form - 60508500
Record 1998 - 1st:0 2nd:0 3rd:0 Ran:8
Pre1998 - 1st:0 2nd:0 3rd:0 Ran:2
1998 Turf 0-9: (5f, 6f, 7f 4, 8f, 12f, 17f) (hvy, sft 3, gd 2, g-f 2, frm)
Scopey, fair gelding. Turf high 59. Inconsistent.
**A J Martin in IRE [0-5] Patrick Mackin (from J M P Eustace [0-6] Jly 1998).*

COCOBAY RR 4144[10]
2 b f Runnett 6.7f **(56)** - Romantic Melody (Battle Hymn)
Form - 0
Record 1998 - 1st:0 2nd:0 3rd:0 Ran:1
1998 Turf 0-1: (7f) (g-f)
Currently very poor filly.
**G M McCourt [0-1] Mercaston Consultants Ltd.*

COCO GIRL RR 80f 4411[5]
2 ch f Mystiko (USA) 7.7f **(59)** -Cantico(Green Dancer (USA)) 10.3f **(74)**
Form - 75
Record 1998 - 1st:0 2nd:0 3rd:0 Ran:2
1998 Turf 0-2: (7f 2) (g-f, frm)
Currently decent filly. Turf high 80 (began Spt) - 5th of 17 to Kalidasa (22 Spt Warwick 7f frm RF 4411).
**I A Balding [0-2] J C Smith.*

COCONUT CREEK (IRE) RR 97?f 3536a[1]
3 b c Danehill (USA) 9.1f **(79)** - Societe Royale (Milford) 9f **(61)**
Form - 6315541
1998 Turf 2-7: (5f, 6f 2-3, 7f 2, 8f) (g-s, gd 2-4, g-f, hrd)
Very useful colt, effective 6 to 7f, best at 7f, acts on g-s to hrd. Turf high 97 - 3rd of 9 to Alonzo (3 May Gowran Park 7f hrd RF 1053a) - also 1st of 23 giving 5lb to Magical Peace (17 May Naas RF 1353a). Has enjoyed a better season as a three-year-old and prefers six furlongs on good ground. Well beaten in the Irish 2,000 Guineas.
**A P O'Brien in IRE [2-12] Mrs John Magnier.*

CODED MESSAGE (IRE) RR 46f 884[4]
3 b g Deploy 11.4f **(67)** - Princess Carmen (IRE) (Arokar (FR))
Form - 04
Record 1998 - 1st:0 2nd:0 3rd:0 Ran:2
Pre1998 - 1st:0 2nd:0 3rd:0 Ran:1
1998 Turf 0-1: (8f) (gd) 1998 AW 0-1: (8f) (Fibr)
Unfurnished, moderate gelding. (DEAD) **J A Glover [0-3] P A Deal.*

CODE OF HONOUR (USA) RR 97f 1049a[3]
4 b c El Gran Senor (USA) 8.9f **(85)** - Filibloom (SWE) 00
Form - 3
1998 Turf 0-1: (10f) (sft)
Very useful colt, effective 7 to 8f, best at 7f, acts on sft to gd, best on gd. **A P O'Brien in IRE [4-8] Mrs John Magnier.*

CODICIL BHB 62f **RR 72f** 5012[5]
2 ch f Then Again 7.4f **(52)** - Own Free Will (Nicholas Bill) 10.1f **(56)**
Form - 531486755
Record 1998 - 1st:1 2nd:0 3rd:1 Ran:9
Win Prizemoney £2,388 *Total Prizemoney* £3,718
Wins * 1998 Jly Redcar (G-S) 5f 72+ <
1998 Turf 1-9: (5f 1-1, 6f 4, 7f 2, 8f 2) (sft, g-s 2, gd 1-4, g-f, hrd)
Above-average filly, effective 5f, acts on gd. Turf high 72 - 1st of 12 getting 11lb from Northern Svengali (1 Jly Redcar RF 2448).
**Mrs J R Ramsden [1-9] Mark Houlston.*

COEUR DU LION RR 53f 2493[8]
2 b f Whittingham (IRE) - The Fernhill Flyer (IRE) **(21f 65a)** (Red Sunset) 8.2f **(63)**
Form - 588
Record 1998 - 1st:0 2nd:0 3rd:0 Ran:3
1998 Turf 0-3: (5f 3) (gd, frm 2)
Currently fair filly. Turf high 53.
**D Nicholls [0-3] Contrac Promotions Ltd*

COFFEE CREAM BHB 85f **RR 86f** 4628[10]
2 b f Common Grounds 8.1f **(66)** - Sugar Town (IRE) **(57f)** (Tate Gallery (USA)) 7.4f **(67)**
Form - 510
Record 1998 - 1st:1 2nd:0 3rd:0 Ran:3
Win Prizemoney £3,013 *Total Prizemoney* £3,013
Wins * 1998 Spt Kempto (GD) 7f 79 <
1998 Turf 1-3: (6f, 7f 1-2) (gd, g-f, frm 1-1)
Currently useful filly. Turf high 86 (began Spt) - also 1st of 14 from Trawling (21 Spt Kempton RF 4396). **B J Meehan [1-3] Lord Portman.*

COHIBA BHB 35f43a **RR 57f 43a** 4627[14]
5 b g Old Vic 12.8f **(72)** - Circus Ring (High Top) 10.2f **(67)**
Form - 1020700
Record 1998 - 1st:1 2nd:1 3rd:0 Ran:7
Pre1998 - 1st:1 2nd:0 3rd:0 Ran:15
Win Prizemoney £4,876 *Total Prizemoney* £6,311
Wins * 1998 May Bright (G-F) H 11.9f 38 44 <
* 1997 Jly Nottin (G-F) SH 14.1f 34 42
1998 Turf 1-7: (12f 1-4, 16f 3) (sft, g-s, gd 1-2, g-f 3)
Fair gelding, effective 12f, acts on sft. Turf high 57 - 2nd of 18 getting 7lb from Quinze (30 Jly Galway 12f sft RF 3348a). Inconsistent.
**B J Curley [2-16] Mrs B J Curley (from T Stack in IRE [0-6] Spt 1996).*

COHIBA ESPLENDIDOS (IRE) **RR 78f** 4710a[1]
2 b c Fayruz 6.6f **(63)** - Haanem (Mtoto)
Form - 201
Record 1998 - 1st:1 2nd:1 3rd:0 Ran:3
Win Prizemoney £6,876 *Total Prizemoney* £7,934
Wins * **1998** Spt San Si (HVY) 7f
1998 Turf 1-3: (6f 2, 7f 1-1) (hvy 1-1, gd, g-f)
Currently above-average colt. Turf high 78 (1st run) (began Aug) - 2nd of 20 getting 2lb from Central Coast (29 Aug Nottingham 6f g-f RF 3961). **H Akbary [1-3] G Santamaria.*

COH SHO NO BHB 43f37a **RR 42f 37a** 3243[3]
5 b m Old Vic 12.8f **(72)** - Castle Peak (Darshaan) 9.9f **(84)**
Form - 60424523
Record 1998 - 1st:0 2nd:2 3rd:1 Ran:8
Pre1998 - 1st:1 2nd:1 3rd:5 Ran:19
Win Prizemoney £2,888 *Total Prizemoney* £8,111
Wins * 1997 Apr Folkes (FRM) H 15.4f 54 62 <
1998 Turf 0-6: (12f 3, 14f, 15f, 16f) (sft, gd, g-f 2, frm 2) 1998 AW 0-2: (13f, 16f) (Equi 2)
Moderate filly, effective 14 to 17f, acts on gd to frm, best on frm, has worn blinkers. Turf high 42. AW high 24.
**S Dow [1-24] Harold Nass (from I A Balding [0-3] Aug 1996).*

COLD CLIMATE BHB 65f **RR 61f** 4390[15]
3 b g Pursuit of Love 9.5f **(69)** - Sharpthorne (USA) (Sharpen Up) 8.3f **(67)**
Form - 838000
Record 1998 - 1st:0 2nd:0 3rd:1 Ran:6
Win Prizemoney £0 *Total Prizemoney* £462
1998 Turf 0-6: (6f 4, 7f, 8f) (gd 2, g-f, frm 3)
Workmanlike, average gelding, effective 6f, acts on gd. Turf high 76 - 3rd of 18 to Point of Dispute (3 May Salisbury 6f gd RF 0998).
**Bob Jones [0-3] Sandbaggers Club (from R Charlton [0-3] May 1998).*

COLD FRONT BHB 50f **RR 51f** 3500[4]
3 br c Polar Falcon (USA) 9f **(74)** - Chandni (IRE) (Ahonoora) 8.1f **(73)**
Form - 00564
Record 1998 - 1st:0 2nd:0 3rd:0 Ran:5
Pre1998 - 1st:0 2nd:0 3rd:0 Ran:1
1998 Turf 0-5: (6f, 8f 3, 11f) (sft, gd, frm 3)
Scopey, fair colt. Turf high 51. **J W Hills [0-6] George Tong.*

COLD STEEL BHB 46f50a **RR 45f 50a** 4117[11]
4 b g Warrshan (USA) 9.7f **(59)** - Rengaine (FR) (Music Boy) 6.8f **(57)**
Form - 50000
Record 1998 - 1st:0 2nd:0 3rd:0 Ran:5
Pre1998 - 1st:1 2nd:0 3rd:1 Ran:8
Win Prizemoney £2,900 *Total Prizemoney* £3,445
Wins 1997 *Jan Wolver (STD) 7f 71+* <
1998 Turf 0-3: (6f, 7f 2) (gd 2, g-f) 1998 AW 0-2: (7f 2) (Fibr 2)
Lengthy, moderate gelding, effective 7f, - acts on Fibr, has worn blinkers, likes tight tracks. Turf high 45. AW high 10 (began Aug).
**K A Morgan [0-3] Exors of the late A A Penney (from W Jarvis [1-10] Jun 1998).*

COLERIDGE BHB 28f55a **RR 36f 55a** 4417[4]
10 gr g Bellypha 11.9f **(66)** - Quay Line (High Line) 10.3f **(70)**
Form - 2258764
Record 1998 - 1st:0 2nd:2 3rd:0 Ran:7
Pre1998 - 1st:9 2nd:10 3rd:7 Ran:73
Win Prizemoney £27,750 *Total Prizemoney* £46,619
Wins * 1997 *Feb Lingfi (STD) H 16f 51 55*
* 1996 May Bath (G-F) H 17.2f 47 56
* 1995 *Nov Lingfi (STD) H 16f 41 51*
* 1995 Oct Warwic (G-S) H 16.1f 39 49
1998 Turf 0-5: (16f 2, 17f 3) (gd, g-f, frm 3) 1998 AW 0-2: (16f 2) (Equi, Fibr)
Moderate gelding, effective 16f, - acts on AW, best on Equi, mostly wears blinkers, prefers left handed tracks, excels at Southwell and Lingfield. Turf high 43. AW high 59 (1st run) - 2nd of 6 getting 15lb from Sheriff (21 Feb Lingfield 16f Equi RF 0329). This veteran won his fair share of staying handicaps on the All-Weather, but was not without ability on turf as well. However, he started to look his age in '98.
**J J Sheehan [4-60] P J Sheehan (from D Shaw [4-17] Feb 1993).*

COLINS CHOICE BHB 44f42a **RR 46f 42a** 2318[9]
4 ch f Risk Me (FR) 8f **(53)** - Give Me a Day (Lucky Wednesday) 8f **(50)**
Form - 165004340
Record 1998 - 1st:0 2nd:0 3rd:1 Ran:8
Pre1998 - 1st:3 2nd:1 3rd:2 Ran:12
Win Prizemoney £5,878 *Total Prizemoney* £8,426
Wins * *1997 Dec Wolver (STD) H 9.4f 49 53* <
* *1997 Spt Wolver (STD) C 8.5f 49*
* *1997 Jly Wolver (STD) C 8.5f 51*
1998 Turf 0-2: (10f, 12f) (sft, g-s) 1998 AW 0-6: (8f 2, 9f 4) (Fibr 6)
Leggy, moderate filly, effective 8 to 12f, best at 8f, acts on sft to g-s - acts on Fibr. Turf high 46 (1st run) - 3rd of 16 getting 8lb from Mr Fortywinks (20 Apr Nottingham 10f sft RF 0775). AW high 42.
**J L Spearing [3-20] Colin Ross.*

COLISEUM (IRE) **RR 96+f** 4830a[4]
2 b c Sadler's Wells (USA) 11.3f **(87)** - Gravieres (FR) (Saint Estephe (FR)) 16.4f **(79)**
Form - 4224
1998 Turf 0-4: (7f 2, 8f 2) (g-s, gd, g-f 2)
Very useful colt. Turf high 96 (began Jly) - 2nd of 9 to Mus-If (20 Spt Curragh 8f gd RF 4440a). Appeared with a big reputation that he did not really live up to. Unlucky in the National Stakes with too much to do and running on ground that was too soft at Longchamp, he should not be over-looked next season.
**A P O'Brien in IRE [0-4].*

COLLACAR BHB 28f43a **RR 33f 43a** 4877[8]
3 b g Man Among Men (IRE) 8f **(47)** - Safety First (Wassl) 9.7f **(62)**
Form - 500030038
Record 1998 - 1st:0 2nd:0 3rd:2 Ran:9
Pre1998 - 1st:0 2nd:0 3rd:0 Ran:5
Win Prizemoney £0 *Total Prizemoney* £732
1998 Turf 0-7: (5f 5, 6f, 7f) (sft, gd 2, frm 3, hrd) 1998 AW 0-2: (5f, 6f) (Fibr 2)
Scopey, moderate gelding, often wears blinkers. Turf high 33. AW high 43. Inconsistent.
**S R Bowring [0-9] Collins Chauffeur Dr Cars (from D Shaw [0-4] Jun 1997).*

COLLEGE BLUE (IRE) BHB 77f **RR 71f** 1971[8]
2 b f College Chapel - Mitsubishi Centre (IRE) (Thatching) 8f **(66)**
Form - 228
Record 1998 - 1st:0 2nd:2 3rd:0 Ran:3
Win Prizemoney £0 *Total Prizemoney* £2,665
1998 Turf 0-3: (5f 3) (gd, g-f, frm)
Currently above-average filly. Turf high 71 - 2nd of 9 getting 9lb from Cheyenne Gold (1 Jun Windsor 5f g-f RF 1637).
**T G Mills [0-3] M J Legg.*

COLLEGE CLIPPER BHB 25f28a **RR 28a** 4549[15]
3 b g Sizzling Melody 6.3f **(49)** - Mawaddah (USA) (Topsider (USA)) 8.3f **(71)**
Form - 0400
Record 1998 - 1st:0 2nd:0 3rd:0 Ran:3
Pre1998 - 1st:0 2nd:0 3rd:0 Ran:2
1998 Turf 0-1: (8f) (frm) 1998 AW 0-2: (8f, 11f) (Fibr 2)
Scopey, very moderate gelding. AW high 34 (began Jly).
**J L Harris [0-3] J F Coupland (from M P Bielby [0-2] Dec 1997).*

COLLEGE DEAN (IRE) BHB 74f **RR 74f** 4533[6]
2 ch c College Chapel - Phyllode **(53f)** (Pharly (FR)) 9.8f **(68)**
Form - 4638106
Record 1998 - 1st:1 2nd:0 3rd:1 Ran:7
Win Prizemoney £3,192 *Total Prizemoney* £3,918
Wins * **1998** Aug Hamilt (SFT) H 6f 70 <
1998 Turf 1-7: (5f, 6f 1-5, 7f) (sft, g-s, gd 1-2, g-f 2, frm)
Above-average colt, effective 6f, acts on gd. Turf high 74 - also 1st of 7 giving 2lb to Highly Fancied (1 Aug Hamilton RF 3266).
**J J O'Neill [1-7] Clayton Bigley Partnership Ltd.*

COLLEGE MOUNT BHB 30f **RR 29f** 4138[15]
3 b g Merdon Melody 6.8f **(56)** - Young Whip (Bold Owl) 8.5f **(45)**
Form - 000
Record 1998 - 1st:0 2nd:0 3rd:0 Ran:3
Pre1998 - 1st:0 2nd:0 3rd:0 Ran:2
1998 Turf 0-3: (8f 2, 10f) (g-f, frm 2)

Well made, little account gelding. Turf high 12 (began Aug).
**Mrs S Lamyman [0-3] J F Coupland (from M P Bielby [0-2] Oct 1997).*

COLLEGE MUSIC (IRE) BHB 61f RR 74f 4479[11]

2 b br f College Chapel - Lute and Lyre (IRE) (The Noble Player (USA)) 6.5f **(67)**
Form - 2241034000
Record 1998 - 1st:1 2nd:2 3rd:1 Ran:10
Win Prizemoney £1,934 *Total Prizemoney* £5,171
Wins * **1998** May Newcas (G-S) 5f 74 <
1998 Turf 1-10: (5f 1-4, 6f 6) (sft 2, g-s, gd 1-2, g-f, frm 3, hrd)
Above-average filly, effective 5 to 6f, best at 5f, acts on sft to hrd. Turf high 74 (1st run) - 2nd of 10 getting 5lb from Perugino Bay (8 Apr Ripon 5f sft RF 0608) - also 1st of 11 getting 5lb from Custom House (4 May Newcastle RF 1020). Inconsistent.
**M Brittain [1-10] Mel Brittain.*

COLLEGE PRINCESS BHB 43f52a RR 32f 52a 3844[9]

4 b f Anshan 8.2f **(63)** - Tinkers Fairy (Myjinski (USA)) 9.5f **(54)**
Form - 38000
Record 1998 - 1st:0 2nd:0 3rd:1 Ran:5
Pre1998 - 1st:1 2nd:1 3rd:3 Ran:14
Win Prizemoney £2,337 *Total Prizemoney* £4,878
Wins * 1997 Jly Redcar (G-F) SH 5f 47 46 <
1998 Turf 0-5: (5f 5) (gd, g-f, frm 3)
Unfurnished, moderate filly, effective 5f, acts on gd to frm - acts on Fibr, best on frm. Turf high 46 (1st run) - 3rd of 11 giving 7lb to Sunset Harbour (21 May Newcastle 5f frm RF 1370).
**S C Williams [1-13] College Farm Thoroughbreds (from C A Dwyer [0-6] Apr 1997).*

COLLEGE ROSE BHB 39f RR 34f 3765[11]

3 b f Prince Sabo 6.6f **(64)** - Tinkers Fairy (Myjinski (USA)) 9.5f **(54)**
Form - 40
Record 1998 - 1st:0 2nd:0 3rd:0 Ran:2
Pre1998 - 1st:0 2nd:0 3rd:0 Ran:2
Win Prizemoney £0 *Total Prizemoney* £271
1998 Turf 0-2: (6f, 7f) (g-f, frm)
Light-framed, very moderate filly. Turf high 2 (began Aug).
**S C Williams [0-4] Mrs Christine Dunnett.*

COLLEVILLE BHB 89f RR 90f 5151[21]

3 gr f Pharly (FR) 11.5f **(64)** - Kibitka (FR) (Baby Turk) 11.3f **(90)**
Form - 4611360
Record 1998 - 1st:2 2nd:0 3rd:1 Ran:7
Pre1998 - 1st:1 2nd:0 3rd:2 Ran:4
Win Prizemoney £12,560 *Total Prizemoney* £16,141
Wins * **1998** Jly Leices (GD) H 11.8f 87 88 <
* **1998** Jun Warwic (GD) 10.8f 86
* 1997 Aug Leices (GD) 7f 86+
1998 Turf 2-7: (8f 2, 11f 1-2, 12f 1-3) (gd 1-4, g-f 2, frm 1-1)
Small, useful filly, effective 7 to 12f, best at 12f, acts on gd to frm, best on g-f, excels at Leicester. Turf high 90 - 3rd of 9 giving 9lb to Up At The Top (6 Aug Haydock 11f g-f RF 3407) - also 1st of 6 from Kinnescash (22 Jly Leicester RF 3028). Consistent. Had a good season, winning twice, but on several other occasions she was unlucky and had various reasons for her below-par efforts. She stays well, is genuine, and, although she will be hard to place, she has the right attitude and can win more races.
**M A Jarvis [3-11] K G Powter.*

COLONEL CUSTER BHB 60f63a RR 56f 63a 1028[5]

3 ch g Komaite (USA) 6.9f **(61)** - Mohican (Great Nephew) 9.9f **(64)**
Form - 3525
Record 1998 - 1st:0 2nd:1 3rd:1 Ran:4
Pre1998 - 1st:1 2nd:0 3rd:0 Ran:3
Win Prizemoney £2,277 *Total Prizemoney* £3,880
Wins * 1997 *Jly Southw (STD) 6f 61* <
1998 Turf 0-1: (7f) (g-f) 1998 AW 0-3: (7f 2, 8f) (Equi, Fibr 2)
Scopey, average gelding, effective 6 to 7f, - acts on Fibr, prefers left handed tracks. AW high 63 - 2nd of 6 getting 18lb from Darwell's Folly (21 Mar Wolverhampton 7f Fibr RF 0459).
**C W Thornton [1-7] Guy Reed.*

COLONEL MUSTARD BHB 81f RR 86f 4204[13]

2 ch c Keen 11.1f **(58)** - Juliet Bravo (Glow (USA)) 6.7f **(71)**
Form - 6810
Record 1998 - 1st:1 2nd:0 3rd:0 Ran:4
Win Prizemoney £2,077 *Total Prizemoney* £2,077
Wins * **1998** Aug Lingfi (FRM) 7.6f 86+ <
1998 Turf 1-4: (6f, 7f, 8f 1-2) (gd, g-f 1-1, frm 2)
Useful colt. Turf high 86 (began Jly) - 1st of 9 giving 5lb to Mouton (26 Aug Lingfield RF 3890). **J R Fanshawe [1-4] Mrs Jan Hopper.*

COLONEL NORTH (IRE) RR 49f 4928[12]

2 b c Distinctly North (USA) 7.4f **(63)** - Tricky (Song) 7.2f **(61)**
Form - 0
Record 1998 - 1st:0 2nd:0 3rd:0 Ran:1
1998 Turf 0-1: (7f) (g-s)
Currently moderate colt. **W R Muir [0-1] Dulverton Equine.*

COLONEL SAM BHB 66f RR 79f 3849[9]

2 b c Puissance 7.1f **(60)** -Indian Summer (Young Generation) 7.7f **(63)**
Form - 3550
Record 1998 - 1st:0 2nd:0 3rd:1 Ran:4
Win Prizemoney £0 *Total Prizemoney* £380
1998 Turf 0-4: (5f 3, 6f) (gd, g-f 2, frm)
Above-average colt. Turf high 79 (1st run) - 3rd of 10 getting 3lb from Kastaway (4 May Doncaster 5f g-f RF 1005).
**J A Glover [0-4] W I Derry.*

COLOUR COUNSELLOR BHB 35f33a RR 4f 33a 5125[12]

5 gr g Touch of Grey 8.1f **(47)** -Bourton Downs (Philip of Spain) 10f **(42)**
Form - 40800
Record 1998 - 1st:0 2nd:0 3rd:0 Ran:2
Pre1998 - 1st:3 2nd:1 3rd:5 Ran:38
Win Prizemoney £6,832 *Total Prizemoney* £10,055
Wins 1997 Aug Bright (GD) H 10f 35 45+
1996 Spt Bright (FRM) SH 11.9f 41 47 <
1996 May Bright (GD) SH 11.9f 40 47 <
1998 Turf 0-2: (12f 2) (sft, g-s)
Very moderate gelding, effective 10 to 12f, best at 10f, acts on g-s to frm, best on frm, mostly wears blinkers (effectively), favours left handed tracks. Turf high 4 (began Oct). Becoming disappointing.
**Miss A M Newton-Smith [0-3] Tony Hayward (from R M Flower [3-34] Dec 1997).*

COLOUR KEY (USA) BHB 55f RR 59f 4776[18]

4 b g Red Ransom (USA) 8.6f **(83)** - Trend (USA) (Ray's Word (USA))
Form - 0
Record 1998 - 1st:0 2nd:0 3rd:0 Ran:1
Pre1998 - 1st:0 2nd:0 3rd:0 Ran:3
1998 Turf 0-1: (10f) (gd)
Unfurnished, fair gelding.
**P Hayward [0-1] Michael Jackson Bloodstock Ltd (from D R C Elsworth [0-3] Jun 1997).*

COLOURS TO GOLD (IRE) BHB 47f RR 49f 3508[14]

3 ch f Rainbows For Life (CAN) 9.3f **(64)** - Brave Ivy (Decoy Boy) 6.7f **(56)**
Form - 0008370
Record 1998 - 1st:0 2nd:0 3rd:1 Ran:7
Pre1998 - 1st:0 2nd:0 3rd:0 Ran:2
Win Prizemoney £0 *Total Prizemoney* £345
1998 Turf 0-6: (6f 2, 8f 3, 9f) (gd 2, frm 4) 1998 AW 0-1: (8f) (Fibr)
Scopey, moderate filly, has worn blinkers. Turf high 49.
**R A Fahey [0-9] I Bray.*

COLUMNA RR 58f 3896[9]

2 gr f Deploy 11.4f **(67)** - Copper Trader (Faustus (USA)) 10f **(58)**
Form - 0
Record 1998 - 1st:0 2nd:0 3rd:0 Ran:1
1998 Turf 0-1: (7f) (gd)
Currently fair filly. **H Candy [0-1] Mrs David Blackburn.*

COLWAY RAKE BHB 48f66a RR 38f 66a 5059[13]

7 b g Salse (USA) 10.9f **(71)** - Barely Hot (Bold Lad (IRE)) 8.4f **(68)**
Form - 080
Record 1998 - 1st:0 2nd:0 3rd:0 Ran:3
Pre1998 - 1st:3 2nd:3 3rd:2 Ran:27
Win Prizemoney £10,935 *Total Prizemoney* £19,336
Wins 1995 May Hamilt (GD) H 6f 62 65
1994 *Jun Southw (STD) H 6f 70 68* <
1994 Apr Beverl (G-S) 5f 61+

1998 Turf 0-3: (5f, 6f 2) (sft, gd, frm)
Average gelding, often wears blinkers. Turf high 38.
**W Storey [0-3] R Coleman (from J W Watts [3-27] Jly 1996).*

COLWAY RITZ BHB 72f RR 75f 4855^{9}

4 b g Rudimentary (USA) 8.2f **(66)** - Million Heiress (Auction Ring (USA)) 8.6f **(65)**
Form - 0562148325030

Record	**1998** -	1st:1	2nd:2	3rd:2	Ran:13
	Pre1998 -	1st:1	2nd:1	3rd:3	Ran:12

Win Prizemoney £8,615 *Total Prizemoney* £19,818

Wins	* **1998**	Jly	Beverl	(GD)	H	8.5f	68	70	<
	1997	Oct	Doncas	(GD)	H	7f	65	69	

1998 Turf 1-13: (7f, 8f 1-4, 10f 4, 12f 4) (g-s 2, gd 4, g-f 1-3, frm 4)
Workmanlike, above-average gelding, effective 6 to 12f, best at 8f, acts on gd to frm, best on gd, has worn blinkers, excels at Ripon. Turf high 75 - 2nd of 10 getting 1lb from Karasi (15 Aug Ripon 12f g-f RF 3662) - also 1st of 9 getting 2lb from Lucky Archer (3 Jly Beverley RF 2487). He gradually found his form last season, eventually gaining victory in a handicap at Beverley in June. He has not been disgraced in some competitive handicaps since, but seems the sort to find trouble in running.
**W Storey [1-16] R Coleman (from J W Watts [1-12] Oct 1997).*

COL-WOODY BHB 70f66a RR 68f 66a 4352^{8}

2 ch g Safawan 6.6f **(60)** - Sky Fighter (Hard Fought) 8.8f **(62)**
Form - 44748

Record	**1998** -	1st:0	2nd:0	3rd:0	Ran:5

Win Prizemoney £0 *Total Prizemoney* £980
1998 Turf 0-5: (7f 3, 8f 2) (sft, gd, frm 3)
Average gelding. Turf high 68. **A P Jarvis [0-5] Mrs Ann Jarvis.*

COMANCHE COMPANION BHB 65f56a RR 66f 56a 109^{10}

8 b m Commanche Run 10.3f **(63)** - Constant Companion (Pas de Seul) 9.1f **(67)**
Form - 730

Record	**1998** -	1st:0	2nd:0	3rd:1	Ran:2
	Pre1998 -	1st:7	2nd:8	3rd:5	Ran:61

Win Prizemoney £39,344 *Total Prizemoney* £65,388

Wins	* 1997	Jly	Windso	(G-F)	H	8.3f	57	63	
	* 1995	Oct	York	(GD)	H	7f	77	82	<
	* 1995	Spt	Sandow	(G-S)	H	7.1f	68	78	
	* 1994	Aug	Pontef	(G-F)	H	8f	67	72	

1998 AW 0-2: (8f, 10f) (Equi 2)
Average mare, effective 8 to 10f, best at 8f, acts on g-s to frm - acts on Equi, likes tight tracks, excels at Windsor. AW high 60 (1st run) - 3rd of 7 getting 6lb from Mazeed (1 Jan Lingfield 10f Equi RF 0003). **T J Naughton [7-63] Hever Racing Club.*

COMBINED VENTURE (IRE) BHB 58f RR 70f 4352^{10}

2 b c Dolphin Street (FR) - Centinela **(47f)** (Caerleon (USA)) 8.6f **(71)**
Form - 532730

Record	**1998** -	1st:0	2nd:1	3rd:2	Ran:6

Win Prizemoney £0 *Total Prizemoney* £2,143
1998 Turf 0-6: (5f 3, 6f, 7f, 8f) (sft, gd 2, g-f 3)
Above-average colt. Turf high 70.
**E Weymes [0-6] C I North Racing Club.*

COMEOUTOFTHEFOG (IRE) BHB 50f61a RR 56f 61a 5003^{2}

3 b g Mujadil (USA) 7.7f **(70)** - Local Belle (Ballymore) 7.3f **(64)**
Form - 2342114772580302

Record	**1998** -	1st:2	2nd:3	3rd:2	Ran:15
	Pre1998 -	1st:0	2nd:1	3rd:0	Ran:7

Win Prizemoney £4,970 *Total Prizemoney* £8,732

Wins	**1998**	*Feb*	*Lingfi*	*(SLW)*	*C*	*8f*	*68*	<
	1998	*Feb*	*Lingfi*	*(SLW)*	*C*	*7f*	*61+*	

1998 Turf 0-6: (7f, 8f 3, 9f, 10f) (gd 3, g-f, frm 2) 1998 AW 2-9: (7f 1-4, 8f 1-4, 9f) (Equi 2-7, Fibr 2)
Average gelding, effective 7 to 8f, best at 7f, - acts on Equi, has worn blinkers, likes left handed tracks, likes tight tracks. Turf high 56 (began Jly). AW high 68 - 1st of 7 getting 4lb from Lobuche (28 Feb Lingfield RF 0376) - also 1st of 7 getting 5lb from Heavenly Abstone (14 Feb Lingfield RF 0289). He took his time getting off the mark, but improved gradually on Equitrack, culminating in two comfortable victories at Lingfield in February.
**A J McNae [0-4] T L Beecroft (from Mrs A L M King [1-7] Aug 1998).*

COME UP SMILING (USA) RR 73f 3251^{3}

3 b f Gone West (USA) 7.8f **(82)** - Encorelle (FR) (Arctic Tern (USA)) 8.9f **(69)**
Form - 633223

Record	**1998** -	1st:0	2nd:2	3rd:3	Ran:6

Win Prizemoney £0 *Total Prizemoney* £3,822
1998 Turf 0-6: (7f 2, 8f 3, 10f) (g-s, gd 2, g-f 2, frm)
Scopey, above-average filly, effective 7 to 10f, best at 8f, acts on g-s to frm, best on g-f. Turf high 73 - 2nd of 10 to Shimaal (6 Jly Windsor 8f g-f RF 2577). **E A L Dunlop [0-6] Maktoum Al Maktoum.*

COME WHAT MAY (IRE) BHB 97f RR 75f 5015^{1}

2 ch f Common Grounds 8.1f **(66)** - Poplina (USA) (Roberto (USA)) 10f **(76)**
Form - 511

Record	**1998** -	1st:2	2nd:0	3rd:0	Ran:3

Win Prizemoney £5,088 *Total Prizemoney* £5,088

Wins	* **1998**	Oct	Redcar	(SFT)	7f	75	<
	* **1998**	Spt	Newcas	(GD)	7f	75	<

1998 Turf 2-3: (7f 2-3) (gd 1-1, g-f 1-2)
Currently above-average filly. Turf high 75 (began Spt) - 1st of 5 getting 3lb from Mesozoic (27 Oct Redcar RF 5015) - also 1st of 13 from Trawling (30 Spt Newcastle RF 4575).
**S P C Woods [2-3] The Storm Again Syndicate.*

COMIC (IRE) RR 73f 4499^{5}

2 b f Be My Chief (USA) 10.2f **(62)** - Circus Act (Shirley Heights) 10.3f **(74)**
Form - 45

Record	**1998** -	1st:0	2nd:0	3rd:0	Ran:2

Win Prizemoney £0 *Total Prizemoney* £257
1998 Turf 0-2: (8f 2) (g-f, frm)
Currently above-average filly. Turf high 73 (began Spt).
**J H M Gosden [0-2] Lord Hartington.*

COMILLAS (FR) RR 107+f $5051a^{1}$

2 gr f Kaldoun (FR) 9.9f **(84)** - Rive Du Sud (USA) 00
Form - 1
1998 Turf 1-1: (8f 1-1) (hvy 1-1)
Currently Pattern-class filly. (1st run) - 1st of 6 from Tycoon's Dolce (20 Oct Deauville RF 5051a). This French-trained filly held her head high and ran green when taking the Prix des Reservoirs in the autumn, and will be trained for the Prix de Diane in 1999.
**J deRoualle in FR [1-1] Mrs G Cabrero.*

COMMANDER COLLINS (IRE) BHB 100f RR 110f 4972^{1}

2 b c Sadler's Wells (USA) 11.3f **(87)** - Kanmary (FR) (Kenmare (FR)) 6.5f **(72)**
Form - 121

Record	**1998** -	1st:2	2nd:1	3rd:0	Ran:3

Win Prizemoney £107,407 *Total Prizemoney* £128,415

Wins	* **1998**	Oct	Doncas	(HVY)	G1	8f	110	<
	* **1998**	Jly	Newmar	(FRM)	L	7f	91+	

1998 Turf 2-3: (7f 1-2, 8f 1-1) (sft 1-1, g-f, frm 1-1)
Currently Group-class colt. Turf high 110 (began Jly) - 1st of 6 from Magno (24 Oct Doncaster RF 4972). Stepped firmly into the Derby picture with a fluent victory in the Racing Post Trophy, but it should be emphasised that the opposition was weak and that he showed a wayward side to his make-up when running about in the closing stages. Closely related to the high-class Colonel Collins, he justified his lofty home reputation with victory in a listed race at Newmarket on his debut, despite running green, and went down narrowly under firm Fortune driving in the Champagne Stakes. Should make a very useful middle-distance colt, but a touch of caution is advised.
**P W Chapple-Hyam [2-3] R E Sangster & A K Collins.*

COMMANDER CONN BHB 30f35a RR 22f 35a 2438^{6}

3 b c Perpendicular - Bonny Bright Eyes (Rarity) 10.1f **(60)**
Form - 6666

Record	**1998** -	1st:0	2nd:0	3rd:0	Ran:4

1998 Turf 0-2: (10f, 12f) (gd, frm) 1998 AW 0-2: (10f 2) (Equi 2)
Scopey, moderate colt. Turf high 22. AW high 44.
**T M Jones [0-4] Richard Page.*

COMMENDATORE RR 4935^{15}

3 b g Magic Ring (IRE) 6.5f **(64)** - Miss Hocroft (Dominion) 8.5f **(63)**

Form - 0
Record 1998 - 1st:0 2nd:0 3rd:0 Ran:1
1998 Turf 0-1: (8f) (gd)
Currently very poor gelding. **G M McCourt [0-1] Alec Tuckerman.*

COMMON CONSENT (IRE) RR 21f 4998^{10}
2 b f Common Grounds 8.1f **(66)** - Santella Bell (Ballad Rock) 7.8f **(63)**
Form - 00
Record 1998 - 1st:0 2nd:0 3rd:0 Ran:2
1998 Turf 0-2: (5f, 7f) (sft, gd)
Currently little account filly. Turf high 21 (began Spt).
**S Woodman [0-2] Mrs Fiona Gordon.*

COMMON ROCK (IRE) BHB 39f33a RR 33a 1768^{15}
4 b f Common Grounds 8.1f **(66)** - Quatre Femme (Petorius) 7.3f **(61)**
Form - 00
Record 1998 - 1st:0 2nd:0 3rd:0 Ran:2
Pre1998 - 1st:1 2nd:0 3rd:0 Ran:4
Win Prizemoney £2,070 *Total Prizemoney* £2,070
Wins 1996 *Jly Southw (STD) S 7f 46* <
1998 Turf 0-1: (7f) (gd) 1998 AW 0-1: (5f) (Fibr)
Unfurnished, very poor filly, often wears blinkers.
**J R Turner [0-2] Mrs Sylvia Blakeley (from J Norton [1-4] Jan 1997).*

COMMON VIEW (IRE) BHB 32f RR 27f 2453^{12}
3 b g Scenic 10.6f **(66)** - Stony Ground (Relko) 9.9f **(59)**
Form - 0070
Record 1998 - 1st:0 2nd:0 3rd:0 Ran:4
Pre1998 - 1st:0 2nd:0 3rd:0 Ran:4
1998 Turf 0-4: (11f 2, 13f, 14f) (gd 3, frm)
Strong, little account gelding, has worn blinkers. Turf high 27. Becoming disappointing. **N Tinkler [0-8] Arthur Plant.*

COMMONWEALTH (IRE) RR 76f 3889^{6}
2 b c Common Grounds 8.1f **(66)** - Silver Slipper **(62f)** (Indian Ridge)
Form - 66
Record 1998 - 1st:0 2nd:0 3rd:0 Ran:2
1998 Turf 0-2: (7f, 8f) (g-f 2)
Currently above-average colt. Turf high 76 (began Jly). Highly regarded by his trainer, he finished lame on his second run.
**G Lewis [0-2] Highclere Thoroughbred Racing Ltd.*

COMPANYS GAMBLE BHB 39f29a RR 32f 29a 544^{13}
3 b f Barrys Gamble 7f **(50)** -Pleasant Company (Alzao (USA)) 7.1f **(68)**
Form - 000
Record 1998 - 1st:0 2nd:0 3rd:0 Ran:1
Pre1998 - 1st:0 2nd:0 3rd:0 Ran:5
1998 Turf 0-1: (6f) (sft)
Scopey, very moderate filly. **B P J Baugh [0-6] Mrs P Stevens.*

COMPASS POINTER BHB 52f54a RR 54f 54a 4384^{9}
5 gr g Mazilier (USA) 8.5f **(56)** - Woodleys (Tyrnavos) 10.1f **(55)**
Form - 830
Record 1998 - 1st:0 2nd:0 3rd:1 Ran:3
Pre1998 - 1st:2 2nd:3 3rd:1 Ran:22
Win Prizemoney £6,940 *Total Prizemoney* £11,757
Wins * 1997 Jly Yarmou (G-S) H 14.1f 50 54
* 1996 *Nov Southw (STD) H 14f 57 63* <
1998 Turf 0-2: (14f, 15f) (sft, gd) 1998 AW 0-1: (15f) (Fibr)
Fair gelding, effective 14 to 15f, best at 15f, acts on g-s to gd, best on gd, prefers left handed tracks. Turf high 54 - 3rd of 10 giving 23lb to Give An Inch (11 Aug Ayr 15f gd RF 3522). Consistent. Has been slow to strike form in '97, but narrowly came good on his favoured soft ground in a Yarmouth handicap in July.
**J M P Eustace [3-32] R Carstairs.*

COMPATRIOT (IRE) RR 94f 3273^{4}
2 b c Bigstone (IRE) - Campestral (USA) (Alleged (USA)) 10f **(76)**
Form - 0424
Record 1998 - 1st:0 2nd:1 3rd:0 Ran:4
Win Prizemoney £0 *Total Prizemoney* £1,977
1998 Turf 0-4: (6f 3, 7f) (g-f, frm 3)
Useful colt. Turf high 94 - 2nd of 5 to Haafiz (24 Jly Newmarket 6f frm RF 3074). Has only ever been seen out at Newmarket and has certainly improved on his debut where he finished eleventh of thirteen. He has shown signs of temperament, but seemed to be settling down when second to Haafiz on his third run. He was disappointing on his last outing, where he helped set too strong a pace and found little. He will be an interesting proposition next year when tried over further. **N A Callaghan [0-4] M Tabor.*

COMPENSATION (IRE) RR 82f 5148^{6}
2 gr g Turtle Island (IRE)- Fontenoy (USA)(Lyphard's Wish (FR)) 9f **(74)**
Form - 04246
Record 1998 - 1st:0 2nd:1 3rd:0 Ran:5
Win Prizemoney £0 *Total Prizemoney* £1,615
1998 Turf 0-5: (6f, 7f 4) (g-s, gd 3, frm)
Decent gelding. Turf high 82 (began Aug) - 4th of 8 to Pal of Mine (5 Spt Epsom 6f gd RF 4095). **M A Jarvis [0-5] Mrs G R Smith.*

COMPLIMENTARY BHB 45f RR 46f 4612^{15}
2 b g Superpower 6.6f **(58)** - Syke Lane (Clantime)
Form - 070
Record 1998 - 1st:0 2nd:0 3rd:0 Ran:3
1998 Turf 0-2: (6f, 7f) (g-s, frm) 1998 AW 0-1: (7f) (Fibr)
Currently fair gelding. Turf high 46 (began Aug).
**W J Haggas [0-3] The Sun Punters Club.*

COMPOSITION BHB 67f RR 54f 4751^{10}
3 ch f Wolfhound (USA) 7.3f **(71)** - Tricky Note (Song) 7.2f **(61)**
Form - 070
Record 1998 - 1st:0 2nd:0 3rd:0 Ran:3
Pre1998 - 1st:1 2nd:0 3rd:2 Ran:6
Win Prizemoney £3,535 *Total Prizemoney* £4,620
Wins 1997 Jly Pontef (GD) H 6f 83 <
1998 Turf 0-3: (6f 2, 7f) (gd 2, hrd)
Scopey, fair filly, effective 6f, acts on frm. Turf high 54. Consistent.
**J Berry [0-2] Chris & Antonia Deuters (from M A Jarvis [1-7] Jun 1998).*

COMPRADORE BHB 69f RR 77f 4886^{1}
3 b f Mujtahid (USA) 7.4f **(69)** - Keswa (Kings Lake (USA)) 10.8f **(67)**
Form - 88470040061
Record 1998 - 1st:1 2nd:0 3rd:0 Ran:11
Pre1998 - 1st:1 2nd:1 3rd:0 Ran:4
Win Prizemoney £6,819 *Total Prizemoney* £9,075
Wins * 1998 Oct Folkes (G-S) 6f 69
* 1997 May Newbur (G-F) 5.2f 82 <
1998 Turf 1-11: (5f 6, 6f 1-4, 7f) (g-s 1-1, gd 5, g-f 2, frm 3)
Unfurnished, above-average filly, effective 5f, acts on frm. Turf high 77. Flew too high at two, and generally struggled last season.
**M Blanshard [2-15] Mrs James Watkins.*

COMPREHENSION (USA) RR 70f 3429^{6}
2 b f Diesis 9f **(80)** - Je Comprend (USA) (Caerleon (USA)) 8.6f **(71)**
Form - 6
Record 1998 - 1st:0 2nd:0 3rd:0 Ran:1
1998 Turf 0-1: (6f) (g-f)
Currently above-average filly. **C E Brittain [0-1] Saeed Manana.*

COMPTON ACE BHB 70f RR 71f 4526^{4}
2 ch c Pharly (FR) 11.5f **(64)** - Mountain Lodge (Blakeney) 10.5f **(64)**
Form - 004
Record 1998 - 1st:0 2nd:0 3rd:0 Ran:3
Win Prizemoney £0 *Total Prizemoney* £227
1998 Turf 0-3: (7f 2, 10f) (gd, g-f, frm)
Currently above-average colt. Turf high 71 (began Aug) - 4th of 11 to Bergamo (28 Spt Bath 10f g-f RF 4526). **G A Butler [0-3] E Penser.*

COMPTON ADMIRAL BHB 100f RR 96f 3796^{2}
2 b c Suave Dancer (USA) 10.7f **(68)** - Sumoto (Mtoto)
Form - 2212
Record 1998 - 1st:1 2nd:3 3rd:0 Ran:4
Win Prizemoney £6,872 *Total Prizemoney* £21,816
Wins * 1998 Jly Ascot (G-F) 7f 96 <
1998 Turf 1-4: (6f, 7f 1-3) (g-s, gd 1-1, g-f, frm)
Very useful colt. Turf high 96 - 2nd of 7 to Raise A Grand (21 Aug Sandown 7f g-f RF 3796) - also 1st of 5 from Killer Instinct (24 Jly Ascot RF 3065). Showed distinct promise when runner-up on his Goodwood debut, but was most unfortunate not to go one better in the Chesham next time as he got no sort of a run, yet still went down by just a head. Justice was done when he took the scalp of talking horse Killer Instinct back at Ascot, and he ran a fine second in the Solario. Will be seen at his best over a mile and remains a decent prospect to follow. **G A Butler [1-4] E Penser.*

COMPTON AJAX (IRE) RR 47f 4511[9]
2 gr c Paris House 5.9f **(64)** - Fear Naught (Connaught) 7.7f **(63)**
Form - 0
Record 1998 - 1st:0 2nd:0 3rd:0 Ran:1
1998 Turf 0-1: (7f) (gd)
Currently moderate colt. **G A Butler [0-1] E Penser.*

COMPTON AKKA (IRE) BHB 57f **RR 58f** 4876[13]
2 b f Balla Cove - Adjanada (Nishapour (FR)) 9.1f **(61)**
Form - 702300
Record 1998 - 1st:0 2nd:1 3rd:1 Ran:6
Win Prizemoney £0 *Total Prizemoney* £1,562
1998 Turf 0-5: (5f, 6f 4) (gd, g-f 2, frm 2) 1998 AW 0-1: (6f) (Fibr)
Fair filly, effective 6f, acts on g-f, has worn blinkers. Turf high 58 (began Jly) - 2nd of 7 getting 5lb from Banningham Breeze (28 Aug Goodwood 6f g-f RF 3924). **G A Butler [0-6] E Penser.*

COMPTON AMBER BHB 81f **RR 83f** 5144[13]
2 b f Puissance 7.1f **(60)** - Amber Mill (Doulab (USA)) 9.8f **(65)**
Form - 84436020
Record 1998 - 1st:0 2nd:1 3rd:1 Ran:8
Win Prizemoney £0 *Total Prizemoney* £8,789
1998 Turf 0-8: (5f 3, 6f 4, 7f) (g-s, gd 4, g-f, frm, hrd)
Decent filly, has worn blinkers. Turf high 83.
**G A Butler [0-8] E Penser.*

COMPTON AMICA (IRE) BHB 64f **RR 58f** 4929[5]
2 gr f High Estate 10.5f **(66)** - Nephrite (Godswalk (USA)) 7.3f **(58)**
Form - 0075
Record 1998 - 1st:0 2nd:0 3rd:0 Ran:4
1998 Turf 0-4: (6f 2, 7f 2) (g-s, g-f 2, frm)
Fair filly. Turf high 57 (began Aug). **G A Butler [0-4] E Penser.*

COMPTON ANGEL (IRE) RR 75f 4668[4]
2 b f Fairy King (USA) 7.7f **(75)** - Embla (Dominion) 8.5f **(63)**
Form - 04
Record 1998 - 1st:0 2nd:0 3rd:0 Ran:2
Win Prizemoney £0 *Total Prizemoney* £281
1998 Turf 0-2: (6f 2) (gd, g-f)
Currently above-average filly. Turf high 75 (began Spt).
**G A Butler [0-2] E Penser.*

COMPTON ARROW (IRE) BHB 95f **RR 95f** 5074[4]
2 b c Petardia 8.2f **(58)** - Impressive Lady (Mr Fluorocarbon) 6f **(55)**
Form - 510314
Record 1998 - 1st:2 2nd:0 3rd:1 Ran:6
Win Prizemoney £10,452 *Total Prizemoney* £11,357
Wins * **1998** Oct Ascot (SFT) 6f 95 <
* **1998** Aug Haydoc (G-S) 6f 86+
1998 Turf 2-6: (6f 2-4, 7f 2) (g-s 1-2, gd 3, g-f 1-1)
Very useful colt, effective 6 to 7f, best at 6f, acts on g-s to g-f. Turf high 95 (began Jly) - also 1st of 7 from Mitcham (9 Oct Ascot RF 4735). Won a Haydock maiden and an Ascot conditions event, showing his battling qualities on the second occasion. He will be suited by seven furlongs or a mile, and seems best when allowed to be making or forcing the pace. **G A Butler [2-6] E Penser.*

COMPTON PLACE BHB 110f **RR 106f** 2649[14]
4 ch c Indian Ridge 7.6f **(74)** - Nosey (Nebbiolo) 8.1f **(75)**
Form - 600
Record 1998 - 1st:0 2nd:0 3rd:0 Ran:3
Pre1998 - 1st:3 2nd:4 3rd:0 Ran:9
Win Prizemoney £100,166 *Total Prizemoney* £141,621
Wins * 1997 Jly Newmar (GD) G1 6f 122 <
* 1996 Aug Salisb (G-F) 6f 96
* 1996 Jun Bath (G-F) 5.1f 73+
1998 Turf 0-3: (5f, 6f 2) (g-s, gd, frm)
Leggy, Pattern-class colt, effective 6f, acts on frm. Turf high 106. He will always be remembered for a blitzing win in the 1997 July Cup. Way below his best last term, he has been retired to stud and should produce some speedy juveniles.
**J A R Toller [3-12] Duke of Devonshire.*

COMTEC'S LEGEND BHB 38f35a **RR 37f 35a** 2922[1]
8 ch m Legend of France (USA) 11.4f **(58)** - Comtec Princess (Gulf Pearl) 12f **(54)**
Form - 0400011
Record 1998 -
Pre1998 -
Win Prizemoney £16,44…
Wins * **1998** Jly Nottin
* **1998** Jly Nottin (G…
1996 Apr Ripon (GD)
1995 Dec Wolver (STD) H Ran:7
1995 Jan Wolver (STD) H Ran:52
1994 Jan Southw (STD) C …£23,402
1998 Turf 2-6: (12f 4, 14f 2-2) (gd 1-1, g-f 1-3, frm, h…
(11f) (Fibr)
Very moderate mare, effective 12 to 14f, best at 14f, act… frm, best on g-f, likes left handed tracks, favours tight track… high 37 - 1st of 14 getting 12lb from Action Jackson (18 Jly Nottingham RF 2922) - also 1st of 14 getting 19lb from Sharaf (4 Jly Nottingham RF 2541). Inconsistent.
**J Pearce [2-11] Qualitair Holdings Ltd (from J F Bottomley [5-48] May 1996).*

CONCA PELIGNA RR 93f 833a[5]
3 f
Form - 5
1998 Turf 0-1: (8f) (sft)
Currently useful filly. **A Renzoni in ITY [0-1].*

CONCER ARALL BHB 44a **RR 44a** 370[13]
4 ch g Ron's Victory (USA) 9.2f **(52)** - Drudwen (Sayf El Arab (USA)) 7.1f **(54)**
Form - 26280
Record 1998 - 1st:0 2nd:1 3rd:0 Ran:3
Pre1998 - 1st:0 2nd:1 3rd:1 Ran:5
Win Prizemoney £0 *Total Prizemoney* £1,589
1998 AW 0-3: (7f 2, 8f) (Equi, Fibr 2)
Neat, very moderate gelding, effective 7f, - acts on Fibr. AW high 38. **S C Williams [0-8] J E Lloyd.*

CONCER UN BHB 87f85a **RR 87f 85a** 3219[13]
6 ch g Lord Bud 8.2f **(52)** - Drudwen (Sayf El Arab (USA)) 7.1f **(54)**
Form - 30000
Record 1998 - 1st:0 2nd:0 3rd:1 Ran:5
Pre1998 - 1st:10 2nd:6 3rd:4 Ran:39
Win Prizemoney £95,472 *Total Prizemoney* £109,342
Wins * 1997 Aug York (GD) H 7.9f 86 92
* 1996 Aug Cheste (GD) H 7f 90 98 <
* 1996 Aug York (GD) H 7.9f 90 97
* 1996 Jly Sandow (G-S) H 8.1f 87 89
* 1996 Jun Bath (FRM) H 8f 81 83+
* 1996 Jun Bath (G-F) H 8f 78 82
* 1995 Spt Kempto (GD) H 8f 72 78
* 1995 Aug Thirsk (G-F) H 8f 61 70
* 1995 Aug Bath (HRD) H 8f 61 65
* 1995 Mar Hamilt (HVY) 8.3f 56
1998 Turf 0-5: (7f, 8f 3, 9f) (gd 4, g-f)
Useful gelding, effective 7 to 8f, best at 7f, acts on g-s to gd, best on gd, likes left handed tracks. Turf high 87. Consistent. His best performance of '96 was his victory in the Bradford & Bingley Handicap at York, and it was a similar story in '97, bouncing back to form at York having dropped in the weights. Below form later, and sold for a bargain 9,500 guineas at Tattersalls in October, he ran well on his reappearance at Goodwood, and was not disgraced subsquently. **S C Williams [10-44] Edgar Lloyd.*

CONFIDANTE (USA) RR 91f 4700[5]
3 b f Dayjur (USA) 6.8f **(79)** - Won't She Tell (USA) (Banner Sport (USA)) 8.6f **(93)**
Form - 11767425
Record 1998 - 1st:2 2nd:1 3rd:0 Ran:8
Pre1998 - 1st:0 2nd:0 3rd:1 Ran:1
Win Prizemoney £11,298 *Total Prizemoney* £19,890
Wins * **1998** May Sandow (G-F) H 7.1f 84 91 <
* **1998** May Thirsk (GD) 7f 85
1998 Turf 2-8: (7f 2-3, 8f 4, 10f) (gd 1-3, g-f 1-4, frm)
Scopey, useful filly, effective 7 to 8f, best at 7f, acts on gd to frm, best on g-f. Turf high 91 - 1st of 10 giving 12lb to Bold Tina (25 May Sandown RF 1461) - also 1st of 11 getting 5lb from Tankersley (2 May Thirsk RF 0980). Consistent. Showed promise in her sole start at two, and won her first two starts of the season at Thirsk and at Sandown where she put up a gritty display against experi-

...gled a little in better company in her ...s a good second to Risque Lady on her ...ough failing to make an impression at York ...s and goes on any ground and, when she ...atings, should be back to winning ways.

Sir Michael Stoute [2-9] Cheveley Park Stud.

...ICT (FR) **RR 89f** 4773[1]

... Warning 8.1f **(77)** - La Dama Bonita (USA) (El Gran Senor (USA)) ...f **(76)**

Form - 71

Record 1998 - 1st:1 2nd:0 3rd:0 Ran:2

Win Prizemoney £4,906 *Total Prizemoney* £4,906

Wins * **1998** Oct Leices (G-S) 7f 89 <

1998 Turf 1-2: (6f, 7f 1-1) (gd 1-2)

Currently useful colt. Turf high 89 (began Spt) - 1st of 7 giving 2lb to Elm Dust (13 Oct Leicester RF 4773).

C E Brittain [1-2] Sheikh Marwan Al Maktoum.

CONFRONTER BHB 47f55a **RR 48f 55a** 3839[3]

9 ch g Bluebird (USA) 7.9f **(71)** - Grace Darling (USA) (Vaguely Noble) 10.1f **(72)**

Form - 51526004437506563

Record 1998 - 1st:0 2nd:0 3rd:2 Ran:13
Pre1998 - 1st:10 2nd:18 3rd:8 Ran:96

Win Prizemoney £35,659 *Total Prizemoney* £69,931

Wins * 1997 *Nov Lingfi (STD) H 10f 52 54*
* 1997 Jun Bath (G-F) H 8f 53 57
* 1995 Spt Bright (GD) H 8f 70 86 <
* 1995 Spt Yarmou (GD) H 8f 70 77
* 1995 Apr Bright (GD) H 8f 63 72
* 1995 Jan Cagnes (G-S) 8f
* 1994 Feb Cagnes (SFT) 7.5f

1998 Turf 0-12: (8f 7, 10f 5) (sft 2, g-s, gd 4, g-f 2, frm 3) 1998 AW 0-1: (10f) (Equi)

Moderate gelding, effective 8 to 10f, best at 8f, acts on sft to frm - acts on Equi, has worn blinkers, prefers tight tracks, excels at Bath and does well at Lingfield. Turf high 57 - 4th of 15 getting 4lb from Statajack (7 Apr Folkestone 10f sft RF 0584). Consistent.

S Dow [7-92] Hatfield Ltd (from P F I Cole [3-17] Spt 1992).

CONICAL **RR 61f** 1433[7]

3 b f Zafonic (USA) 9f **(83)** - De Stael (USA) (Nijinsky (CAN)) 10.3f **(77)**

Form - 7

Record 1998 - 1st:0 2nd:0 3rd:0 Ran:1
Pre1998 - 1st:0 2nd:0 3rd:0 Ran:1

1998 Turf 0-1: (10f) (frm)

Tall, currently average filly. *R Charlton [0-2] K Abdulla.*

CONIC HILL (IRE) BHB 26f17a **RR 36f 17a** 4590[14]

7 ch g Lomond (USA) 9.9f **(74)** - Krisalya (Kris) 9.5f **(73)**

Form - 80074263000

Record 1998 - 1st:0 2nd:1 3rd:1 Ran:11
Pre1998 - 1st:2 2nd:3 3rd:1 Ran:30

Win Prizemoney £7,702 *Total Prizemoney* £13,168

Wins * 1994 Aug Beverl (G-F) H 9.9f 73 73 <
1994 Jun Salisb (G-F) C 8f 73 <

1998 Turf 0-8: (8f, 10f 6, 12f) (gd 2, g-f 2, frm 4) 1998 AW 0-3: (8f, 12f, 16f) (Equi 2, Fibr)

Very moderate gelding, effective 8 to 10f, acts on gd to g-f, has worn blinkers, likes tight tracks. Turf high 36 - 3rd of 11 getting 22lb from Chief Cashier (29 Jly Epsom 10f g-f RF 3197). AW high 15. Becoming disappointing.

J Pearce [1-30] Jeff Pearce (from R J Baker [0-4] May 1995).

CONNOISSEUR BAY (USA) BHB 102f **RR 101f** 2661a[2]

3 b c Nureyev (USA) 8.4f **(84)** -Feminine Wile (IRE)(Ahonoora) 8.1f **(73)**

Form - 2122

Record 1998 - 1st:1 2nd:3 3rd:0 Ran:4
Pre1998 - 1st:0 2nd:1 3rd:0 Ran:1

Win Prizemoney £3,566 *Total Prizemoney* £14,195

Wins * **1998** May Bath (G-F) 10.2f 100++ <

1998 Turf 1-4: (8f, 9f, 10f 1-2) (g-s 2, g-f, frm 1-1)

Neat, very useful colt. Turf high 101 - 2nd of 9 to Makaruka (30 Jun Maisons-laffitte 10f g-s RF 2661a) - also 1st of 6 from Way Out Yonder (29 May Bath RF 1565). Facile winner of a maiden, he ran well in a Listed race on his final start. *P W Chapple-Hyam [1-5].*

CONSORT BHB 92f **RR 92f** 5078[13]

5 b h Groom Dancer (USA) 9.5f **(75)** - Darnelle (Shirley Heights) 10.3f **(74)**

Form - 060220020

Record 1998 - 1st:0 2nd:3 3rd:0 Ran:9
Pre1998 - 1st:2 2nd:2 3rd:2 Ran:12

Win Prizemoney £27,496 *Total Prizemoney* £68,325

Wins * 1997 Nov Newmar (G-F) H 8f 84 89 <
1996 Aug Salisb (G-F) 7f 74

1998 Turf 0-9: (7f 3, 8f 5, 9f) (sft, gd 4, g-f 2, frm, hrd)

Useful colt, effective 7 to 9f, acts on gd to hrd, best on g-f, excels at Newmarket. Turf high 92 - 2nd of 35 giving 2lb to Lear Spear (3 Oct Newmarket 9f g-f RF 4631). As a four-year-old, he beat a big field in the Ladbroke Autumn Handicap at Newmarket on his final start of the season. He had shown little last term until putting in a couple of good runs in August, and ran an absolute blinder to finish runner-up in the Cambridgeshire, but unfortunately put in a stinker at his supposedly favourite track an his final start. Suited by a straight track and a strong gallop, he should win his share next season.

Mrs A J Perrett [1-15] Mrs S L Whitehead (from G Harwood [1-6] Oct 1996).

CONSPICUOUS (IRE) BHB 88f86a **RR 89f 86a** 5126[1]

8 b g Alzao (USA) 9.8f **(73)** - Mystery Lady (USA) (Vaguely Noble) 10.1f **(72)**

Form - 5266440571

Record 1998 - 1st:1 2nd:1 3rd:0 Ran:10
Pre1998 - 1st:6 2nd:11 3rd:7 Ran:49

Win Prizemoney £47,122 *Total Prizemoney* £93,431

Wins * **1998** Nov Bright (SFT) H 10f 83 89
* 1997 Oct Newbur (GD) H 10f 86 91 <
* 1997 Aug Salisb (G-F) H 8f 82 89
* 1996 Aug Goodwo (GD) 9f 84
* 1995 Spt Goodwo (GD) H 9f 69 75
* 1995 Aug Kempto (G-F) H 10f 59 65

1998 Turf 1-10: (8f 3, 9f, 10f 1-6) (sft, g-s 1-2, gd 3, g-f 3, frm)

Useful gelding, effective 8 to 10f, best at 8f, acts on g-s to frm, has worn blinkers, likes left handed tracks, and does well at Ascot. Turf high 92 - 2nd of 12 giving 12lb to China Red (19 May Goodwood 8f g-f RF 1326) - also 1st of 19 giving 15lb to Grinkov (5 Nov Brighton RF 5126). A decent handicapper, he had a frustrating season as he likes to come from behind off a strongly-run pace and these tactics often get him into trouble. He finally came good at the end of the season when winning a showcase race at Brighton.

L G Cottrell [6-46] Mrs Jenny Hopkins (from P F I Cole [1-13] Jly 1993).

CONSULTANT BHB 67f78a **RR 67f 78a** 4820[14]

2 b g Man of May - Avenita Lady (Free State) 8.7f **(61)**

Form - 31204140

Record 1998 - 1st:2 2nd:1 3rd:1 Ran:8

Win Prizemoney £5,188 *Total Prizemoney* £7,853

Wins * **1998** *Spt Wolver (STD) 6f 82* <
* **1998** *Apr Wolver (STD) S 5f 60+*

1998 Turf 0-4: (5f 3, 6f)(g-f, frm 3)1998 AW 2-4:(5f 1-2, 6f 1-2)(Fibr 2-4)

Decent gelding, effective 6f, - acts on Fibr. Turf high 67. AW high 82 - 4th of 13 to Blue Star (22 Aug Wolverhampton 6f Fibr RF 3827) - also 1st of 11 giving 7lb to Crystal Lass (5 Spt Wolverhampton RF 4119). Inconsistent. Third in a seller on the Wolverhampton Fibresand on his debut, he reversed the form with the winner of that race in no uncertain terms next time. Fair form on turf after, but showed his best form back at Wolverhampton, running a fine race to finish fourth in the Weatherbys Dash and winning a novice event in fine style. Six furlongs on that track suits him admirably.

N P Littmoden [2-8] J W C Coxon.

CONTE GRIMALDI (IRE) **RR 109f** 4730a[1]

3 b g Astronef 7.9f **(59)** - Gay Apparel (CAN) (Up Spirits (USA))

Form - 1

1998 Turf 1-1: (5f 1-1) (sft 1-1)

Currently Pattern-class gelding. (1st run) - 1st of 8 getting 3lb from Tedburrow (4 Oct San Siro RF 4730a). *D Arienti in ITY [1-1].*

CONTENTMENT (IRE) BHB 60a **RR 67f** 4652[6]

4 b c Fairy King (USA) 7.7f **(75)** - Quality Of Life (Auction Ring (USA)) 8.6f **(65)**

Form - 0742706
Record 1998 - 1st:0 2nd:1 3rd:0 Ran:6
Pre1998 - 1st:1 2nd:1 3rd:1 Ran:13
Win Prizemoney £3,662 *Total Prizemoney* £6,505
Wins 1997 Jun Windso (G-F) H 10f 69 77 <
1998 Turf 0-5: (7f, 10f 3, 11f) (g-s, g-f 3, frm) 1998 AW 0-1: (10f) (Equi)
Unfurnished, average colt, effective 10f, acts on gd to frm, likes tight tracks. Turf high 67.
**Miss Gay Kelleway [0-4] The Oberons Partnership (from S Dow [0-3] Apr 1998).*

CONTINUOUS TIME (USA) BHB 65f RR 66f 4880[7]
2 b f Shadeed (USA) 7.7f **(72)** - Trattoria (USA) (Alphabatim (USA))
Form - 607
Record 1998 - 1st:0 2nd:0 3rd:0 Ran:3
1998 Turf 0-3: (6f, 7f 2) (g-s, frm 2)
Currently average filly. Turf high 66 (began Aug).
**J R Jenkins [0-3] Khalifa Dasmal.*

CONTRARY MARY BHB 72f68a RR 73f 68a 5127[17]
3 b f Mujadil (USA) 7.7f **(70)** - Love Street (Mummy's Pet) 7.7f **(60)**
Form - 002330104D80
Record 1998 - 1st:1 2nd:1 3rd:2 Ran:12
Pre1998 - 1st:1 2nd:1 3rd:0 Ran:6
Win Prizemoney £6,720 *Total Prizemoney* £9,906
Wins * **1998** Aug Lingfi (G-F) H 7f 65 71
1997 May Lingfi (G-F) 5f 82+ <
1998 Turf 1-10: (6f 3, 7f 1-7) (g-s, gd 4, g-f 1-3, frm 2) 1998 AW 0-2: (6f, 7f) (Equi, Fibr)
Tall, above-average filly, effective 5f, acts on gd to g-f. Turf high 73. AW high 53. Inconsistent.
**J Akehurst [1-9] I Wicks (from S P C Woods [0-3] May 1998).*

CONTRAVENE (IRE) BHB 41f47a RR 7f 47a 1586[13]
4 b f Contract Law (USA) 8.9f **(54)** - Vieux Carre (Pas de Seul) 9.1f **(67)**
Form - 00
Record 1998 - 1st:0 2nd:0 3rd:0 Ran:2
Pre1998 - 1st:3 2nd:2 3rd:2 Ran:18
Win Prizemoney £9,356 *Total Prizemoney* £11,816
Wins 1996 *Spt Wolver (STD) SH 7f 56 65*
1996 Aug Hamilt (G-F) C 6f 66 <
1996 Apr Beverl (G-F) S 5f 47
1998 Turf 0-2: (7f 2) (gd, g-f)
Light-framed, very moderate filly, has worn blinkers. Turf high 7.
**B Mactaggart [0-2] T K Easdon (from J Berry [3-18] Mar 1997).*

CONWY LODGE (IRE) BHB 76f RR 80df 4796[18]
2 b c Lahib (USA) 8f **(69)** - Alriyaah (Shareef Dancer (USA)) 9.9f **(73)**
Form - 2116770
Record 1998 - 1st:2 2nd:1 3rd:0 Ran:7
Win Prizemoney £8,523 *Total Prizemoney* £10,593
Wins * **1998** Jun Doncas (GD) 5f 79+
* **1998** May Ripon (GD) 5f 80+ <
1998 Turf 2-7: (5f 2-7) (sft, gd 1-2, g-f 1-3, frm)
Decent colt, effective 5f, acts on gd to g-f, best on g-f, has worn blinkers. Turf high 80 (1st run) - 2nd of 10 to Bodfari Muka (6 May Chester 5f g-f RF 1058) - also 1st of 10 from Princely Dream (27 May Ripon RF 1530). Ran inexplicably poorly on his nursery debut after wining two small races. Did not seem to be getting home latterly. **J Berry [2-7] Lord Mostyn.*

COOL EDGE (IRE) BHB 108f RR 114f 4849[7]
7 ch g Nashamaa 8.1f **(58)** - Mochara (Last Fandango) 7.8f **(61)**
Form - 4334537
Record 1998 - 1st:0 2nd:0 3rd:3 Ran:7
Pre1998 - 1st:6 2nd:7 3rd:5 Ran:32
Win Prizemoney £61,253 *Total Prizemoney* £106,740
Wins * 1997 Apr Currag (GD) G3 7f 106 <
* 1996 Aug Newbur (GD) H 7.3f 96 99
* 1996 May Haydoc (G-S) LH 7.1f 91 95
* 1996 Mar Doncas (G-S) H 8f 80 86
* 1995 May Hamilt (G-F) 5f 61
* 1994 May Nottin (FRM) H 6.1f 62 70+
1998 Turf 0-7: (7f 5, 8f, 9f) (hvy, gd 3, g-f 2, frm)
Group-class gelding, effective 7 to 9f, best at 7f, acts on gd to g-f, best on gd, has worn blinkers. Turf high 114 - 3rd of 10 to Muchea (27 Jun Newmarket 7f gd RF 2352). He has become somewhat disappointing since beating Desert King at the Curragh in '97, and though running the odd creditable race he does not look the same horse he once was and has started to run too freely in his races.
**M H Tompkins [6-40] Henry Chan.*

COOLING CASTLE (FR) BHB 64f RR 60f 4595[22]
2 ch g Sanglamore (USA) 12.9f **(67)** - Syphaly (USA) (Lyphard (USA)) 9.9f **(72)**
Form - 300
Record 1998 - 1st:0 2nd:0 3rd:1 Ran:3
Win Prizemoney £0 *Total Prizemoney* £474
1998 Turf 0-3: (6f, 7f 2) (gd, g-f, frm)
Currently average gelding. Turf high 60 (began Aug).
**B J Meehan [0-3] Mrs E A Lerpiniere.*

COOLIN RIVER (IRE) BHB 51f51a RR 60f 51a 4504[14]
3 b g River Falls 8.2f **(56)** - The Coolin (Don) 7.7f **(64)**
Form - 48833060
Record 1998 - 1st:0 2nd:0 3rd:2 Ran:8
Pre1998 - 1st:0 2nd:0 3rd:0 Ran:5
Win Prizemoney £0 *Total Prizemoney* £960
1998 Turf 0-6: (7f, 8f 5) (gd 2, g-f, frm 3) 1998 AW 0-2: (7f, 8f) (Equi, Fibr)
Workmanlike, average gelding, effective 8f, acts on gd to frm, has worn blinkers. Turf high 60 - 3rd of 12 giving 17lb to Amington Girl (18 Jly Nottingham 8f gd RF 2926). AW high 53. Becoming disappointing. **K R Burke [0-13] Kate Booth and Toby Wand.*

COOL KATIE BHB 56f RR 68f 4405[8]
2 b f Komaite (USA) 6.9f **(61)** - Pomade (Luthier) 9.8f **(71)**
Form - 244258
Record 1998 - 1st:0 2nd:2 3rd:0 Ran:6
Win Prizemoney £0 *Total Prizemoney* £1,863
1998 Turf 0-6: (5f 6) (gd, g-f 2, frm 3)
Average filly. Turf high 68 (began Jly).
**K A Ryan [0-6] Roses Racing Club.*

COOL MYSTERY BHB 47f RR 50f 2585[15]
3 ro g Mystiko (USA) 7.7f **(59)** - Romantic Saga (Prince Tenderfoot (USA)) 9f **(61)**
Form - 60
Record 1998 - 1st:0 2nd:0 3rd:0 Ran:2
Pre1998 - 1st:0 2nd:0 3rd:0 Ran:5
Win Prizemoney £0 *Total Prizemoney* £208
1998 Turf 0-2: (8f, 10f) (sft, frm)
Scopey, fair gelding. Turf high 26.
**K A Ryan [0-1] The Gloria Darley Racing Partnership (from A B Mulholland [0-6] Apr 1998).*

COOL PERFORMANCE (USA) BHB 43f RR 53f 4938[13]
3 b c Lear Fan (USA)10.4f **(80)** -Christchurch(FR)(So Blessed) 8.7f **(67)**
Form - 77400
Record 1998 - 1st:0 2nd:0 3rd:0 Ran:5
Win Prizemoney £0 *Total Prizemoney* £229
1998 Turf 0-4: (10f 2, 12f, 16f) (gd 2, g-f, frm) 1998 AW 0-1: (10f) (Equi)
Unfurnished, fair colt, mostly wears blinkers. Turf high 53 (began Aug). **Lord Huntingdon [0-5] The Queen.*

COOL PROSPECT BHB 60f65a RR 65df 65a 4840[12]
3 b c Mon Tresor 7.9f **(60)** - I Ran Lovely (Persian Bold) 9.3f **(66)**
Form - 024200320
Record 1998 - 1st:0 2nd:3 3rd:1 Ran:9
Pre1998 - 1st:0 2nd:1 3rd:1 Ran:5
Win Prizemoney £0 *Total Prizemoney* £5,221
1998 Turf 0-7: (6f 5, 7f 2) (g-s 2, gd 3, g-f, frm) 1998 AW 0-2: (6f 2) (Fibr 2)
Leggy, average colt, effective 5 to 6f, best at 6f, acts on gd to frm - acts on Fibr, has worn blinkers, excels at Wolverhampton. Turf high 65 - 2nd of 10 getting 10lb from Ray of Sunshine (1 Jly Redcar 6f gd RF 2450). AW high 64 (began Spt) - 2nd of 13 getting 2lb from Rum Lad (3 Oct Wolverhampton 6f Fibr RF 4635).
**K A Ryan [0-8] The Gloria Darley Racing Partnership (from A B Mulholland [0-6] Apr 1998).*

COOL SECRET BHB 75f RR 53f 4771[24]
3 gr g Petong 7.6f **(58)** - Cool Run (Deep Run) 18f **(46)**
Form - 0037040
Record 1998 - 1st:0 2nd:0 3rd:1 Ran:7

Pre1998 - 1st:1 2nd:0 3rd:0 Ran:8
Win Prizemoney £5,249 *Total Prizemoney* £6,643
Wins 1997 Aug Redcar (FRM) H 6f 70 80 <
1998 Turf 0-6: (6f 3, 7f 2, 8f) (sft, gd 2, g-f 3) 1998 AW 0-1: (6f) (Fibr)
Light-framed, average gelding, effective 6f, acts on frm. Turf high 53. Inconsistent.
**K A Ryan [0-6] The Gloria Darley Racing Partnership (from A B Mulholland [1-9] Mar 1998).*

COOL VIBES BHB 80f **RR 83df** 4755[3]
3 br g Rock City 8.8f **(62)** - Meet Again (Lomond (USA)) 8.8f **(65)**
Form - 153
Record 1998 - 1st:1 2nd:0 3rd:1 Ran:3
Win Prizemoney £4,737 *Total Prizemoney* £5,581
Wins * 1998 Aug Newmar (G-F) 8f 83 <
1998 Turf 1-3: (8f 1-2, 10f) (sft, g-f, frm 1-1)
Well made, currently decent gelding. Turf high 83 (1st run) (began Aug) - 1st of 9 getting 6lb from Adulation (29 Aug Newmarket RF 3954). Popped up at 50/1 on his belated debut in August. That was over a mile, but he is bred to stay further.
**J Pearce [1-3] James Furlong.*

COOL WATERS BHB 30f **RR 18f** 3320[12]
3 b f Puissance 7.1f **(60)** -Keep Cool (FR)(Northern Treat (USA)) 6f **(50)**
Form - 000
Record 1998 - 1st:0 2nd:0 3rd:0 Ran:3
Pre1998 - 1st:0 2nd:0 3rd:0 Ran:2
1998 Turf 0-3: (7f, 8f, 12f) (gd, g-f, frm)
Leggy, poor filly.
**L P Grassick [0-2] Mrs Susan Keable (from M Meade [0-1] Apr 1998).*

COOPER ISLAND RR 72f 4359[6]
2 ch c Generous (IRE) 11.5f **(82)** - Colza (USA) **(74f)** (Alleged (USA)) 10f **(76)**
Form - 66
Record 1998 - 1st:0 2nd:0 3rd:0 Ran:2
Win Prizemoney £0 *Total Prizemoney* £160
1998 Turf 0-2: (8f 2) (g-f 2)
Currently above-average colt. Turf high 72 (began Spt).
**B W Hills [0-2] K Abdulla.*

COPELAND RR 111+f 4073a[1]
3 b c Generous (IRE) 11.5f **(82)** - Whitehaven (Top Ville) 11.7f **(68)**
Form - 11
1998 Turf 2-2: (12f 2-2) (sft 1-1, g-f 1-1)
Currently Group-class colt. Turf high 111 - 1st of 8 giving 3lb to Dancer and Son (26 Aug Clairefontaine RF 4073a) - also 1st of 11 from Smart Squall (21 Jun Frauenfeld RF 2286a). He won the Swiss Derby, which probably equates to Listed form.
**H-A Pantall in FR [2-2] Sheikh Mohammed.*

COPERNICUS RR 77f 3682[2]
3 b c Polish Precedent (USA) 9f **(73)** - Oxslip (Owen Dudley) 8.3f **(61)**
Form - 2
Record 1998 - 1st:0 2nd:1 3rd:0 Ran:1
Pre1998 - 1st:0 2nd:1 3rd:0 Ran:2
Win Prizemoney £0 *Total Prizemoney* £2,156
1998 Turf 0-1: (10f) (g-f)
Scopey, currently above-average colt. (1st run) - 2nd of 12 to Pegnitz (17 Aug Windsor 10f g-f RF 3682). Had obviously had his training problems. **P F I Cole [0-3] Christopher Wright.*

COPPERBEECH (IRE) BHB 43f43a **RR 38f 43a** 3958[12]
4 ch f Common Grounds 8.1f **(66)** - Caimanite(Tap On Wood) 10.3f **(65)**
Form - 00
Record 1998 - 1st:0 2nd:0 3rd:0 Ran:2
Pre1998 - 1st:0 2nd:1 3rd:0 Ran:5
Win Prizemoney £0 *Total Prizemoney* £1,100
1998 Turf 0-1: (10f) (g-f) 1998 AW 0-1: (6f) (Fibr)
Light-framed, very moderate filly, has worn blinkers.
**R Simpson [0-1] James Owen (from K C Comerford [0-2] Jan 1998).*

COPPER COOKIE BHB 30f **RR 47?f** 4935[10]
3 ch f Selkirk (USA) 7.9f **(76)** - Festival Fanfare (Ile de Bourbon (USA)) 10.1f **(67)**
Form - 004000
Record 1998 - 1st:0 2nd:0 3rd:0 Ran:6
Win Prizemoney £0 *Total Prizemoney* £246
1998 Turf 0-6: (7f, 8f 3, 10f, 11f) (gd 2, g-f 2, frm 2)
Light-framed, moderate filly. Turf high 47.
**M J Polglase [0-6] The Silver and Blue Horse Racing Club.*

COPPER SHELL BHB 50f **RR 44?f** 4262[18]
4 ch g Beveled (USA) 6.9f **(64)** - Luly My Love (Hello Gorgeous (USA)) 9.7f **(63)**
Form - 0
Record 1998 - 1st:0 2nd:0 3rd:0 Ran:1
Pre1998 - 1st:0 2nd:0 3rd:0 Ran:6
Win Prizemoney £0 *Total Prizemoney* £258
1998 Turf 0-1: (16f) (gd)
Leggy, moderate gelding.
**Mrs L C Jewell [0-2] Gallagher Equine Ltd (from A P Jones [0-6] Oct 1997).*

COPPLESTONE (IRE) BHB 79f **RR 78f** 4386[3]
2 b c Second Set (IRE) 9.2f **(67)** - Queen of the Brush (Averof) 8.2f **(62)**
Form - 634343
Record 1998 - 1st:0 2nd:0 3rd:3 Ran:6
Win Prizemoney £0 *Total Prizemoney* £5,057
1998 Turf 0-5: (6f, 7f 3, 8f) (g-f 2, frm 2, hrd) 1998 AW 0-1: (8f) (Fibr)
Above-average colt, effective 7 to 8f, best at 8f, acts on g-f to hrd - acts on Fibr, best on g-f, has worn blinkers. Turf high 78 (began Jly) - 4th of 14 getting 1lb from Hoh Steamer (31 Aug Newcastle 8f hrd RF 3991). (1st run) - 3rd of 7 to Deploy Venture (19 Spt Wolverhampton 8f Fibr RF 4386). Ran very well in a first-time visor in a hot nursery at York. The visor was left off when he ran on Fibresand on his final start. **P W Harris [0-6] Mrs P W Harris.*

COPS (IRE) BHB 63f **RR 76f** 4818[2]
2 ch c Grand Lodge (USA) - Gentle Guest (IRE) (Be My Guest (USA)) 9.3f **(67)**
Form - 652
Record 1998 - 1st:0 2nd:1 3rd:0 Ran:3
Win Prizemoney £0 *Total Prizemoney* £1,820
1998 Turf 0-3: (6f, 7f, 8f) (g-f, frm 2)
Currently above-average colt, has worn blinkers. Turf high 76 - 2nd of 28 to L S Lowry (15 Oct Newmarket 7f frm RF 4818).
**E A L Dunlop [0-3] Abdullah Ali.*

COPYFORCE BOY RR 47f 3037[8]
2 ch g Mystiko (USA) 7.7f **(59)** - Surpassing (Superlative) 7.2f **(56)**
Form - 008
Record 1998 - 1st:0 2nd:0 3rd:0 Ran:3
1998 Turf 0-3: (6f, 7f 2) (gd, frm 2)
Currently moderate gelding. Turf high 47.
**Miss B Sanders [0-3] Copyforce Ltd.*

COPYFORCE GIRL BHB 77f72a **RR 82f 72a** 4389[3]
2 b f Elmaamul (USA) 8.1f **(70)** - Sabaya (USA) (Seattle Dancer (USA))
Form - 803
Record 1998 - 1st:0 2nd:0 3rd:1 Ran:3
Win Prizemoney £0 *Total Prizemoney* £445
1998 Turf 0-3: (6f, 7f 2) (g-f, frm 2)
Currently decent filly, has broken blood-vessels. Turf high 82 (began Jly) - 3rd of 16 to Morning Music (21 Spt Kempton 7f frm RF 4389). **Miss B Sanders [0-3] Copyforce Ltd.*

CORALITA (IRE) RR 90f 3556a[5]
2 b f Night Shift (USA) 8.1f **(73)** - Mumble Peg (General Assembly (USA)) 10f **(68)**
Form - 4213225
1998 Turf 1-7: (5f 1-5, 6f 2) (sft, g-s 1-1, gd 4, frm)
Useful filly, effective 5f, acts on g-s to gd, has worn blinkers. Turf high 90 - also 1st of 9 from Sparkling Outlook (13 Jun Cork RF 2042a). She showed gradually improving form in Ireland, getting off the mark at Cork, before finishing a fine third in the Queen Mary. She continued to run well in Pattern company afterwards, and should get further next season.
**A P O'Brien in IRE [1-7] Mrs John Magnier.*

CORAL REEF (IRE) RR 53f 3363[6]
2 ch f Karinga Bay - Mamara Reef **(57df)** (Salse (USA)) 7.5f **(66)**
Form - 00236

Record 1998 - 1st:0 2nd:1 3rd:1 Ran:5
Win Prizemoney £0 *Total Prizemoney* £980
1998 Turf 0-4: (6f, 7f 3) (gd 2, g-f, frm) 1998 AW 0-1: (7f) (Fibr)
Fair filly, often wears blinkers. Turf high 53 - 2nd of 8 getting 4lb from Karakul (14 Jly Brighton 7f gd RF 2778). (1st run) - 3rd of 11 to March Party (24 Jly Wolverhampton 7f Fibr RF 3097).
**W G M Turner [0-5] K B Racing.*

CORAL SEEKER RR 64f 1625[7]

3 ch c Rainbow Quest (USA) 11.2f **(81)** - Miss Kuta Beach (Bold Lad (IRE)) 8.4f **(68)**
Form - 67
Record 1998 - 1st:0 2nd:0 3rd:0 Ran:2
1998 Turf 0-2: (12f 2) (frm 2)
Workmanlike, currently average colt. Turf high 64.
**G Wragg [0-2] J L C Pearce.*

CORAL WATERS (IRE) BHB 68f RR 65f 4611[7]

2 b f College Chapel- Premier Leap (IRE)(Salmon Leap (USA)) 11f **(61)**
Form - 077
Record 1998 - 1st:0 2nd:0 3rd:0 Ran:3
1998 Turf 0-3: (6f 2, 7f) (g-s, g-f, frm)
Currently average filly. Turf high 65 (began Aug).
**C A Cyzer [0-3] R M Cyzer.*

CORDIAL KNIGHT (USA) BHB 60f RR 27f 2391[13]

5 b g Night Shift (USA) 8.1f **(73)** - Temperence Cordial (USA) (Temperence Hill (USA)) 11f **(58)**
Form - 0
Record 1998 - 1st:0 2nd:0 3rd:0 Ran:1
Pre1998 - 1st:0 2nd:1 3rd:1 Ran:13
Win Prizemoney £0 *Total Prizemoney* £925
1998 Turf 0-1: (12f) (g-f)
Little account gelding, effective 7f, acts on gd, often wears blinkers.
**C P Morlock [0-7] J P M & J W Cook (from D K Weld in IRE [0-13] May 1997).*

CORELLI BHB 80f RR 76f 3258[11]

3 b c Machiavellian (USA) 9.8f **(83)** - Musical Bliss (USA) (The Minstrel (CAN)) 10f **(72)**
Form - 023210
Record 1998 - 1st:1 2nd:2 3rd:1 Ran:6
Win Prizemoney £3,574 *Total Prizemoney* £6,377
Wins * 1998 Jly Catter (GD) 13.8f 48++ <
1998 Turf 1-6: (8f, 10f, 11f, 12f, 14f 1-2) (gd 4, g-f 1-1, frm)
Well made, above-average colt, effective 10 to 12f, acts on gd to frm, best on gd. Turf high 84 - 2nd of 12 to Legal Lunch (23 May Haydock 11f gd RF 1419). He showed ability in maidens before winning a bad one at Catterick, but was beaten out of sight at Glorious Goodwood. **Sir Michael Stoute [1-6] Sheikh Mohammed.*

CORNDAVON (USA) BHB 79f RR 80f 4820[4]

2 b f Sheikh Albadou 9.2f **(75)** - Ferber's Follies (USA) (Saratoga Six (USA)) 7f **(73)**
Form - 552324
Record 1998 - 1st:0 2nd:2 3rd:1 Ran:6
Win Prizemoney £0 *Total Prizemoney* £3,400
1998 Turf 0-6: (5f 5, 6f) (gd, g-f 2, frm 3)
Decent filly, effective 5 to 6f, acts on g-f to frm. Turf high 80 - 2nd of 13 getting 6lb from Sunley Sense (19 Spt Newbury 5f g-f RF 4377). **M J Fetherston-Godley [0-6] Mrs Julia Scott.*

CORNFLOWER FIELDS BHB 87f RR 88f 4460[5]

3 b f Cadeaux Genereux 7.9f **(76)**- Mithl Al Hawa(Salse (USA))7.5f **(66)**
Form - 51741435
Record 1998 - 1st:2 2nd:0 3rd:1 Ran:8
Win Prizemoney £6,432 *Total Prizemoney* £8,936
Wins * 1998 Jly Leices (GD) H 7f 78 85+ <
*** 1998** May Bath (G-F) 8f 74
1998 Turf 2-8: (6f, 7f 1-4, 8f 1-3) (g-f 4, frm 2-4)
Unfurnished, useful filly, effective 7 to 8f, best at 7f, acts on g-f to frm, best on frm. Turf high 88 - 3rd of 12 getting 2lb from Golden Fortune (3 Spt Salisbury 7f g-f RF 4062) - also 1st of 7 giving 13lb to Morgan Le Fay (22 Jly Leicester RF 3029). Ran well dropped to six furlongs at Haydock in July, but her two wins have been over further. Running well despite a rise in the weights.

**R Hannon [2-8] Salem Suhail.*

CORNICHE (IRE) RR 90f 4841[11]

3 b br c Marju (IRE) 9.2f **(76)** - Far But Near (USA) (Far North (CAN)) 9.7f **(75)**
Form - 32170
Record 1998 - 1st:1 2nd:1 3rd:1 Ran:5
Pre1998 - 1st:1 2nd:2 3rd:0 Ran:3
Win Prizemoney £10,755 *Total Prizemoney* £18,579
Wins * 1998 Jly Chepst (GD) H 16.2f 86 90 <
* 1997 Oct Nottin (SFT) 8.2f 85
1998 Turf 1-5: (12f 2, 14f, 15f, 16f 1-1) (g-s, gd 2, g-f 1-2)
Scopey, useful colt, effective 8 to 16f, acts on gd to frm, best on gd, favours left handed tracks. Turf high 90 - 2nd of 7 getting 8lb from Secret Saver (25 Jun Newcastle 12f gd RF 2269) - also 1st of 4 giving 18lb to Aldwych Arrow (10 Jly Chepstow RF 2670). Hit form in July when winning a four-runner handicap in July, beating Aldwych Arrow by four lengths. His form has tailed off rather since, but he does stay and if he is dropped a few pounds, he may well improve. **P F I Cole [2-8] H R H Prince Fahd Salman.*

CORNICHE QUEST (IRE) BHB 60f50a RR 63f 50a 26[5]

5 b m Salt Dome (USA) 6.5f **(59)** - Angel Divine (Ahonoora) 8.1f **(73)**
Form - 72675
Record 1998 - 1st:0 2nd:0 3rd:0 Ran:1
Pre1998 - 1st:6 2nd:5 3rd:8 Ran:54
Win Prizemoney £16,874 *Total Prizemoney* £25,695
Wins * 1997 Aug Pontef (G-F) H 5f 60 66
* 1997 May Nottin (GD) 6.1f 68 <
* 1997 May Carlis (G-S) 5f 63
* 1996 Oct Folkes (G-S) S 6.9f 53
* 1996 Spt Yarmou (G-F) H 6f 52 54
* 1996 May Bright (GD) 8f 55
1998 AW 0-1: (6f) (Fibr)
Average filly, effective 5 to 6f, best at 5f, acts on g-s to frm, excels at Brighton and Nottingham, does well at Pontefract. Needs a stiff test when tackling the minimum trip. **M R Channon [6-55] M Bishop.*

CORNISH RING RR 299[8]

3 ch f King's Signet (USA) 7f **(51)** - Trelissick (Electric) 10.1f **(61)**
Form - 8
Record 1998 - 1st:0 2nd:0 3rd:0 Ran:1
1998 AW 0-1: (8f) (Fibr)
Currently very poor filly.
**M Brittain [0-1] Northgate Lodge Partnerships.*

CORONA RR 1244[16]

4 ch c Cigar 6.3f **(43)** - Crowebrass (Crowned Prince (USA)) 10.1f **(67)**
Form - 0
Record 1998 - 1st:0 2nd:0 3rd:0 Ran:1
1998 Turf 0-1: (10f) (frm)
Leggy, currently very poor colt. **T T Bill [0-1] P Royle.*

CORONADO'S QUEST (USA) RR 126 5168a[5]

3 ch c Forty Niner (USA) 8.8f **(73)**
Form - 5
1998 AW 0-1: (10f) (Dirt)
Currently top-class colt. (1st run) - 5th of 10 getting 4lb from Awesome Again (7 Nov Churchill Downs 10f Dirt RF 5168a). High-class American colt, fifth in an excellent renewal of the Breeders' Cup Classic.
**C McGaughey in USA [0-1] S Janney III & Stonerside Farm.*

CORONET BHB 85f RR 83f 3699[15]

3 br f Be My Chief (USA) 10.2f **(62)**- Thorner Lane (Tina's Pet) 6.8f **(59)**
Form - 51520
Record 1998 - 1st:1 2nd:1 3rd:0 Ran:5
Win Prizemoney £3,313 *Total Prizemoney* £4,993
Wins * 1998 May Nottin (G-F) 6.1f 81+ <
1998 Turf 1-5: (6f 1-4, 7f) (gd, g-f 2, frm 1-2)
Leggy, decent filly. Turf high 83 - 2nd of 11 getting 4lb from Fredora (5 Aug Kempton 7f frm RF 3371) - also 1st of 15 from Tattinger (8 May Nottingham RF 1109).
**A C Stewart [1-5] Mrs A C Stewart.*

CORSECAN BHB 38f65a RR 41df 65a 3267[15]

3 ch g Phountzi (USA) 9.6f **(60)** - Sagareina (Sagaro) 9.7f **(55)**

Form - 5531005780
Record 1998 - 1st:1 2nd:0 3rd:1 Ran:10
Pre1998 - 1st:0 2nd:0 3rd:1 Ran:7
Win Prizemoney £1,850 *Total Prizemoney* £2,583
Wins * **1998** *Feb Lingfi (SLW) H 8f 50 67+* <
1998 Turf 0-6: (6f, 7f 2, 8f 3) (g-s, gd 2, g-f, frm 2) 1998 AW 1-4: (7f, 8f 1-2, 10f) (Equi 1-4)
Leggy, average gelding, effective 5 to 8f, acts on gd - acts on Equi. Turf high 41. AW high 67 - 1st of 8 getting 26lb from Gadge (26 Feb Lingfield RF 0365). Inconsistent. Took time getting it together but eventually showed some form on Equitrack, including when winning a modest handicap very easily in February. Little to enthuse about on Turf. **S Dow [1-17] Ken Butler.*

Pattern-class filly. Turf high 105 - 2nd of 14 to Zalaiyka (10 May Longchamp 8f gd RF 1229a) - also 1st of 7 from Uninhibited (10 Apr Maisons-laffitte RF 0725a). She was beaten for speed in the French 1,000 Guineas, and looked certain to improve when stepped-up in trip. Unfortunately she did not progress as anticipated. **Mme C Head in FR [1-4] G A Oldham.*

COSCOROBA (IRE) BHB 55f RR 47f 5119[13]

4 ch f Shalford (IRE) 7.8f **(63)** - Tameeza (USA) (Shahrastani (USA)) 8.8f **(72)**
Form - 312000
Record 1998 - 1st:1 2nd:1 3rd:1 Ran:6
Pre1998 - 1st:0 2nd:1 3rd:2 Ran:3

Cortachy Castle, pillar-to-post at Sandown

CORTACHY CASTLE (IRE) BHB 101f RR 104f 4821[10]

3 ch c Pips Pride 6.7f **(70)** - Maricica (Ahonoora) 8.1f **(73)**
Form - 3217160
Record 1998 - 1st:2 2nd:1 3rd:1 Ran:7
Pre1998 - 1st:1 2nd:2 3rd:0 Ran:6
Win Prizemoney £15,781 *Total Prizemoney* £38,122
Wins * **1998** Aug Sandow (G-F) H 5f 100 104 <
* **1998** Jun Sandow (SFT) 5f 93
* 1997 Jun Nottin (G-F) 5.1f 66+
1998 Turf 2-7: (5f 2-6, 6f) (g-s 1-1, gd 1-3, g-f, frm 2)
Leggy, very useful colt, effective 5f, acts on sft to frm, best on gd, excels at Sandown. Turf high 104 - 1st of 7 giving 14lb to Mister Jolson (22 Aug Sandown RF 3820). He appreciates a stiff track and gained both his wins over Sandown's tough five furlongs. Group races are a struggle, but he will always be a force to reckon with in a slightly lower grade, particularly on easy ground.
**B J Meehan [3-13] Mrs E A Lerpiniere.*

CORTONA (IRE) RR 105f 2637[12]

3 b f Caerleon (USA) 10.9f **(79)** - Olbia (Mill Reef (USA)) 10.5f **(78)**
Form - 120
1998 Turf 1-3: (7f 1-1, 8f 2) (hvy 1-1, gd, frm)

Win Prizemoney £3,566 *Total Prizemoney* £5,710
Wins * **1998** Jun Hamilt (SFT) S 9.2f 43 <
1998 Turf 1-6: (8f 3, 9f 1-2, 12f) (sft, g-s 1-1, gd 4)
Workmanlike, moderate filly, effective 7 to 8f, best at 8f, acts on gd, favours tight tracks. Turf high 60 - 2nd of 10 giving 27lb to Seconds Away (19 Jun Ayr 8f gd RF 2111).
**P Monteith [1-7] M G Davidson (from J Berry [0-3] May 1997).*

COSMIC ALTITUDE BHB 42f RR 44f 4639[13]

2 b c Cosmonaut - Elaine Ann (Garda's Revenge (USA)) 8.3f **(51)**
Form - 680
Record 1998 - 1st:0 2nd:0 3rd:0 Ran:3
1998 Turf 0-1: (5f) (g-f) 1998 AW 0-2: (5f 2) (Fibr 2)
Currently moderate colt. AW high 21. **A G Newcombe [0-3] M Patel.*

COSMIC CASE BHB 57f RR 59f 3509[4]

3 b f Casteddu 7.4f **(54)** - La Fontainova (IRE) (Lafontaine (USA)) 8.7f **(62)**
Form - 6731537004
Record 1998 - 1st:1 2nd:0 3rd:2 Ran:10
Pre1998 - 1st:0 2nd:0 3rd:3 Ran:11
Win Prizemoney £2,981 *Total Prizemoney* £6,064

Wins * **1998** May Mussel (G-F) H 8f 57 64 <
1998 Turf 1-10: (5f, 7f 2, 8f 1-4, 9f 3) (g-s, gd 4, g-f 1-3, frm 2)
Scopey, fair filly, effective 6 to 8f, best at 8f, acts on gd to g-f, best on g-f, has worn blinkers, likes right handed tracks, likes tight tracks. Turf high 64 - 1st of 14 giving 12lb to Amington Girl (18 May Musselburgh RF 1303).
**J S Goldie [1-21] Strathayr Publishing Ltd.*

COSMIC COUNTESS (IRE) BHB 58f RR 42f 5128[6]

3 b f Lahib (USA) 8f **(69)** - Windmill Princess (Gorytus (USA)) 7.8f **(60)**
Form - 0004605006
Record 1998 - 1st:0 2nd:0 3rd:0 Ran:10
Pre1998 - 1st:1 2nd:0 3rd:1 Ran:5
Win Prizemoney £4,970 *Total Prizemoney* £6,000
Wins * 1997 Spt Bright (FRM) 6f 72 <
1998 Turf 0-10: (5f, 6f 4, 7f 4, 8f) (g-s 3, gd 2, g-f 3, frm 2)
Moderate filly, effective 6 to 7f, acts on g-f to frm, has worn blinkers. Turf high 67. Becoming disappointing.
**M A Jarvis [1-15] Cosmic Greyhound Racing Partnership II.*

COSMIC GIRL BHB 47f RR 49f 3444[5]

3 gr f Wolfhound (USA) 7.3f **(71)** - Remany (Bellypha) 9.8f **(73)**
Form - 07005
Record 1998 - 1st:0 2nd:0 3rd:0 Ran:5
1998 Turf 0-5: (9f, 10f, 12f 3) (g-s, gd, frm 3)
Unfurnished, moderate filly. Turf high 49.
**Miss B Sanders [0-5] Mrs P J Sheen.*

COSMIC HOPE RR 5011[6]

2 ch f Cosmonaut - Hopea (USA) (Drone) 10.3f **(74)**
Form - 6
Record 1998 - 1st:0 2nd:0 3rd:0 Ran:1
1998 Turf 0-1: (5f) (gd)
Currently very poor filly. **G P Kelly [0-1] A M McArdle.*

COSMIC STAR BHB 32f RR 15f 2541[11]

8 gr m Siberian Express (USA) 9f **(58)** - Miss Bunty (Song) 7.2f **(61)**
Form - 00
Record 1998 - 1st:0 2nd:0 3rd:0 Ran:2
Pre1998 - 1st:2 2nd:0 3rd:1 Ran:11
Win Prizemoney £5,150 *Total Prizemoney* £5,483
1998 Turf 0-2: (11f, 14f) (g-f, frm)
Poor mare, often wears blinkers. Turf high 15. Inconsistent.
**P Winkworth [0-12] P Winkworth (from S P C Woods [2-11] Spt 1993).*

COSMO JACK (IRE) BHB 69f RR 75f 4929[15]

2 b g Balla Cove - Foolish Law (IRE) (Law Society (USA)) 9.9f **(70)**
Form - 3301425100
Record 1998 - 1st:2 2nd:1 3rd:2 Ran:10
Win Prizemoney £4,856 *Total Prizemoney* £6,184
Wins * **1998** Aug Sandow (G-F) SH 7.1f 68 75 <
1998 Jly Bath (GD) S 5.1f 68
1998 Turf 2-10: (5f 1-4, 6f 2, 7f 1-3, 8f) (g-s, gd 2, g-f 2-4, frm 3)
Above-average gelding, effective 5 to 7f, best at 7f, acts on g-f. Turf high 75 - 1st of 11 giving 4lb to Ace of Trumps (22 Aug Sandown RF 3818) - also 1st of 10 from Apollinaire (6 Jly Bath RF 2555). He is only a plater, but won two such races last term. Despite winning over five, he is better suited by further as he showed when winning over seven at Sandown.
**M C Pipe [1-4] Kammac Plc (from B J Meehan [1-6] Jly 1998).*

COSSACK COUNT BHB 80f85a RR 83f 85a 110[5]

5 ch h Nashwan (USA) 10.3f **(79)** - Russian Countess (USA) (Nureyev (USA)) 8.7f **(78)**
Form - 715
Record 1998 - 1st:0 2nd:0 3rd:0 Ran:1
Pre1998 - 1st:3 2nd:0 3rd:0 Ran:9
Win Prizemoney £11,826 *Total Prizemoney* £11,826
Wins * 1997 *Dec Lingfi (STD) H 7f 68 79+* <
1996 May Leopar (GD) H 6f 78
1996 Mar Naas (SFT) 6f 76
1998 AW 0-1: (7f) (Equi)
Useful colt. (1st run) - 5th of 16 giving 13lb to Fayik (17 Jan Lingfield 7f Equi RF 0110). Inconsistent. A winner in Ireland, he has shown little on turf in this country, but scored in good style on his second try on the Lingfield Equitrack in December '97.
**S Dow [1-5] Normandy Developments (London) (from M Kauntze in IRE [2-5] Jun 1996).*

COTTAGE MAID RR 34f 5145[6]

2 ch f Inchinor 8.9f **(64)** - Mossy Rose (King of Spain) 7.8f **(52)**
Form - 6
Record 1998 - 1st:0 2nd:0 3rd:0 Ran:1
1998 Turf 0-1: (8f) (gd)
Currently very moderate filly. **Lord Huntingdon [0-1] Stanley Sharp.*

COTTAGE PRINCE (IRE) BHB 46f RR 44f 3161[2]

5 b g Classic Secret (USA) 8.8f **(56)** - Susan's Blues (Cure The Blues (USA)) 9.5f **(63)**
Form - 00532
Record 1998 - 1st:0 2nd:1 3rd:1 Ran:5
Pre1998 - 1st:2 2nd:0 3rd:2 Ran:15
Win Prizemoney £5,679 *Total Prizemoney* £7,902
Wins * 1997 Jun Catter (GD) H 12f 46 49 <
* 1997 May Redcar (FRM) H 11f 41 47
1998 Turf 0-5: (9f 2, 11f, 12f 2) (gd, g-f 4)
Moderate gelding, effective 11 to 12f, best at 12f, acts on gd to hrd, prefers tight tracks. Turf high 44 - 2nd of 10 getting 10lb from Hasta la Vista (28 Jly Beverley 12f g-f RF 3161).
**J J Quinn [5-29] Mrs Kay Thomas.*

COUGHLAN'S GIFT BHB 58f RR 65f 5122[3]

2 ch f Alnasr Alwasheek 9.4f **(62)** - Superfrost (Tickled Pink) 6.5f **(59)**
Form - 063
Record 1998 - 1st:0 2nd:0 3rd:1 Ran:3
Win Prizemoney £0 *Total Prizemoney* £435
1998 Turf 0-3: (6f 2, 7f) (sft, g-s, gd)
Currently average filly. Turf high 65 (began Oct) - 3rd of 9 getting 5lb from Full Egalite (5 Nov Brighton 6f g-s RF 5122).
**J C Fox [0-3] Mrs J A Cleary.*

COUL BANK BHB 42f RR 43f 4868[14]

2 b c Robellino (USA) 9.5f **(68)** - Future Options **(56f)** (Lomond (USA)) 8.8f **(65)**
Form - 000
Record 1998 - 1st:0 2nd:0 3rd:0 Ran:3
1998 Turf 0-3: (6f 2, 7f) (g-s, gd, g-f)
Currently moderate colt. Turf high 43 (began Spt).
**P T Walwyn [0-3] Mrs Robert Bingley.*

COULTHARD (IRE) BHB 87f RR 87f 4631[31]

5 ch g Glenstal (USA) 10f **(59)** - Royal Aunt (Martinmas) 7.6f **(59)**
Form - 24160
Record 1998 - 1st:1 2nd:1 3rd:0 Ran:5
Pre1998 - 1st:0 2nd:0 3rd:0 Ran:2
Win Prizemoney £4,117 *Total Prizemoney* £5,599
Wins * **1998** Jun Windso (SFT) 10f 84 <
1998 Turf 1-5: (9f, 10f 1-4) (gd 1-1, g-f 4)
Useful gelding, effective 10f, acts on gd to g-f, has worn blinkers. Turf high 87 - also 1st of 21 giving 18lb to Reliably Won (15 Jun Windsor RF 2009).
**Mrs P Sly [2-6] R Brazier (from A Leahy in IRE [0-8] Aug 1997).*

COUNSEL BHB 60a RR 53f 4874[12]

3 ch g Most Welcome 8.6f **(66)** - My Polished Corner (IRE) (Tate Gallery (USA)) 7.4f **(67)**
Form - 26060526700000
Record 1998 - 1st:0 2nd:2 3rd:0 Ran:14
Pre1998 - 1st:0 2nd:1 3rd:0 Ran:6
Win Prizemoney £0 *Total Prizemoney* £2,558
1998 Turf 0-12: (7f, 8f 4, 10f 6, 12f) (gd 2, g-f 5, frm 5) 1998 AW 0-2: (8f, 10f) (Equi, Fibr)
Neat, average gelding, effective 6 to 10f, acts on frm - acts on Equi, likes left handed tracks, likes tight tracks. Turf high 57. AW high 64 (1st run) - 2nd of 10 getting 4lb from Danzino (28 Feb Lingfield 10f Equi RF 0381). Becoming disappointing.
**D W Chapman [0-8] Miss N F Thesiger (from K R Burke [0-6] Aug 1998).*

COUNT DE MONEY (IRE) BHB 36f44a RR 53f 44a 4879[3]

3 b g Last Tycoon 9.4f **(73)** - Menominee (Soviet Star (USA))
Form - 50663003
Record 1998 - 1st:0 2nd:0 3rd:2 Ran:8
Win Prizemoney £0 *Total Prizemoney* £777

1998 Turf 0-6: (12f 5, 17f) (g-s, gd 2, g-f, frm 2) 1998 AW 0-2: (14f 2) (Fibr 2)
Scopey, fair gelding, effective 14f, - acts on Fibr, prefers tight tracks. Turf high 53. AW high 48 (began Aug) - 3rd of 9 getting 23lb from Silent Warning (19 Oct Southwell 14f Fibr RF 4879).
**A P Jarvis [0-8] Mrs Ann Jarvis.*

COUNTERPLOT (IRE) RR 97f — 4600a[4]
4 f
Form - 4
1998 Turf 0-1: (10f) (hvy)
Currently very useful filly. **V S San Marzano in ITY [0-2] Locsot.*

COUNTER STRIKE BHB 54f RR 45f — 3841[4]
3 b c Beveled (USA) 6.9f **(64)** - Encore L'Amour (USA) (Monteverdi) 6.5f **(61)**
Form - 856704
Record 1998 - 1st:0 2nd:0 3rd:0 Ran:6
1998 Turf 0-6: (6f, 7f 3, 8f 2) (gd 2, g-f, frm 3)
Leggy, moderate colt. Turf high 48.
**R Hannon [0-6] Mahmood Al-Shuaibi.*

COUNT FREDERICK RR 53f — 4823[19]
2 b g Anshan 8.2f **(63)** - Minteen (Teenoso (USA)) 9.9f **(72)**
Form - 0
Record 1998 - 1st:0 2nd:0 3rd:0 Ran:1
1998 Turf 0-1: (8f) (frm)
Currently fair gelding. **J R Jenkins [0-1] Mrs Stella Peirce.*

COUNT OF FLANDERS (IRE) BHB 48f RR 52f — 2069[17]
8 b g Green Desert (USA) 7.8f **(78)** - Marie de Flandre (FR) (Crystal Palace (FR)) 12.5f **(76)**
Form - 30
Record 1998 - 1st:0 2nd:0 3rd:1 Ran:2
Pre1998 - 1st:1 2nd:0 3rd:0 Ran:4
Win Prizemoney £3,669 *Total Prizemoney* £4,432
1998 Turf 0-2: (10f 2) (gd, frm)
Fair gelding, has worn blinkers. Turf high 52.
**K A Morgan [1-13] K A Morgan (from Sir Michael Stoute [1-3] Oct 1993).*

COUNTRY BELLE (USA) RR 102f — 838a[3]
3 b f Seattle Slew (USA) 7.8f **(64)** - Balbonella (FR) (Gay Mecene (USA)) 8.6f **(69)**
Form - 3
1998 Turf 0-1: (8f) (hvy)
Currently very useful filly. (1st run) - 3rd of 5 to Zalaiyka (19 Apr Longchamp 8f hvy RF 0838a). In season when finishing third in a Group Three at Longchamp in April, she is a smart filly but did not progress as expected.
**Mme C Head in FR [0-1] Maktoum Al Maktoum.*

COUNTRY ORCHID RR 42f — 4488[6]
7 b m Town And Country 8.5f **(47)** - Star Flower (Star Appeal) 9.6f **(65)**
Form - 46
Record 1998 - 1st:0 2nd:0 3rd:0 Ran:2
Win Prizemoney £0 *Total Prizemoney* £123
1998 Turf 0-2: (7f, 8f) (frm 2)
Moderate mare. Turf high 42 (began Spt).
**Mrs M Reveley [5-19] Mrs J V Kehoe.*

COUNTRY THATCH BHB 30f RR 35f — 4931[15]
5 b g Thatching 7.8f **(69)** - Alencon (Northfields (USA)) 9f **(72)**
Form - 0008662060
Record 1998 - 1st:0 2nd:1 3rd:0 Ran:10
Pre1998 - 1st:1 2nd:0 3rd:2 Ran:15
Win Prizemoney £3,494 *Total Prizemoney* £4,774
Wins * 1997 Aug Folkes (G-F) H 9.7f 38 40 <
1998 Turf 0-10: (8f 2, 9f, 10f, 12f 5, 13f) (g-s, gd 2, g-f 4, frm 3)
Very moderate gelding, effective 10 to 12f, best at 10f, acts on g-f, has worn blinkers, prefers right handed tracks, likes tight tracks. Turf high 35. Inconsistent. **C A Horgan [1-25] Mrs B Sumner.*

COUNTY TIMES BHB 52f RR 61f — 4136[9]
2 br g Timeless Times (USA) 6.1f **(56)** - Misty Rocket (Roan Rocket) 7.8f **(57)**
Form - 3450770
Record 1998 - 1st:0 2nd:0 3rd:1 Ran:7
Win Prizemoney £0 *Total Prizemoney* £306
1998 Turf 0-7: (5f 3, 7f 2, 8f 2) (gd 3, g-f, frm 3)
Average gelding, has worn blinkers. Turf high 58.
**B S Rothwell [0-7] The Three County Partnership.*

COUPLED BHB 70f RR 78df — 4190[17]
3 ch f Wolfhound (USA) 7.3f **(71)** - Twice A Fool (USA) (Foolish Pleasure (USA)) 8.9f **(72)**
Form - 54270
Record 1998 - 1st:0 2nd:1 3rd:0 Ran:5
Win Prizemoney £0 *Total Prizemoney* £1,195
1998 Turf 0-4: (7f 3, 8f) (gd 3, g-f) 1998 AW 0-1: (7f) (Equi)
Scopey, above-average filly. Turf high 78 (1st run) - 4th of 13 getting 5lb from Chattan (27 Mar Doncaster 7f gd RF 0481).
**S C Williams [0-5] Mrs Celia Miller.*

COURAGEOUS (IRE) BHB 61f RR 65f — 3275[14]
3 ch c Generous (IRE) 11.5f **(82)** - Legend of Arabia (Great Nephew) 9.9f **(64)**
Form - 268430
Record 1998 - 1st:0 2nd:1 3rd:1 Ran:6
Pre1998 - 1st:0 2nd:0 3rd:1 Ran:2
Win Prizemoney £0 *Total Prizemoney* £2,728
1998 Turf 0-5: (10f, 12f 3, 14f) (gd, g-f, frm 3) 1998 AW 0-1: (12f) (Fibr)
Scopey, above-average colt, effective 12f, - acts on Fibr. Turf high 65. (1st run) - 2nd of 4 to Jonas Nightengale (4 Apr Wolverhampton 12f Fibr RF 0565). He has proved very disappointing, but made 23,000 gns at Tattersalls in October.
**P F I Cole [0-8] H R H Prince Fahd Salman.*

COURAGEOUS KNIGHT BHB 34f56a RR 17f 56a — 2391[11]
9 gr g Midyan (USA) 9.9f **(64)** - Little Mercy (No Mercy) 8f **(61)**
Form - U0
Record 1998 - 1st:0 2nd:0 3rd:0 Ran:2
Pre1998 - 1st:1 2nd:3 3rd:6 Ran:37
Win Prizemoney £1,932 *Total Prizemoney* £7,973
1998 Turf 0-2: (12f 2) (gd, g-f)
Fair gelding, effective 12 to 14f, best at 12f, acts on g-f to hrd, prefers right handed tracks. Turf high 9. Becoming disappointing.
**P Hayward [3-30] The Welsh Connection (from J M Bradley [0-12] Spt 1994).*

COURAGE UNDER FIRE BHB 53f51a RR 55f 51a — 4939[2]
3 b g Risk Me (FR) 8f **(53)** - Dreamtime Quest (Blakeney) 10.5f **(64)**
Form - 7630142302
Record 1998 - 1st:1 2nd:2 3rd:2 Ran:9
Pre1998 - 1st:0 2nd:0 3rd:0 Ran:2
Win Prizemoney £2,206 *Total Prizemoney* £4,747
Wins * 1998 *Jun Southw (STD) H 12f 44 45 <*
1998 Turf 0-6: (8f, 10f 3, 11f, 12f) (sft, gd 3, frm 2) 1998 AW 1-3: (9f, 12f 1-2) (Fibr 1-3)
Workmanlike, fair gelding, effective 10 to 12f, best at 10f, acts on gd to frm - acts on Fibr, best on frm, likes left handed tracks, favours tight tracks. Turf high 55 - 2nd of 15 giving 12lb to Dangerman (22 Oct Nottingham 10f gd RF 4939). AW high 45.
**D W P Arbuthnot [1-11] Mrs Adrian Ireland.*

COURSE FISHING BHB 34f39a RR 37f 39a — 322[10]
7 ch g Squill (USA) 9.4f **(47)** - Migoletty (Oats) 8.9f **(46)**
Form - 2280
Record 1998 - 1st:0 2nd:1 3rd:0 Ran:3
Pre1998 - 1st:3 2nd:3 3rd:1 Ran:32
Win Prizemoney £9,551 *Total Prizemoney* £13,440
Wins * 1996 Aug Ripon (G-F) H 12.3f 38 45
* 1995 Aug Chepst (G-F) H 10.2f 35 48 <
* 1995 Jly Warwic (FRM) H 10.8f 33 38
1998 AW 0-3: (16f 3) (Fibr 3)
Moderate gelding, effective 12 to 16f, best at 12f, acts on g-s to frm - acts on Fibr, favours left handed tracks, and excels at Catterick. AW high 41 (1st run) - 2nd of 12 getting 24lb from Noufari (5 Jan Southwell 16f Fibr RF 0027). **B A McMahon [3-35] G D Bull.*

COURT CHAMPAGNE RR 5f — 4761[18]
2 b f Batshoof 9.5f **(66)** - Fairfield's Breeze (Buckskin (FR))
Form - 80
Record 1998 - 1st:0 2nd:0 3rd:0 Ran:2

1998 Turf 0-2: (6f, 7f) (gd, g-f)
Currently very poor filly. Turf high 5 (began Oct).
**R Dickin [0-2] Derek & Cheryl Holder.*

COURTEOUS BHB 115f **RR 116f** 4727a[11]

3 b c Generous (IRE) 11.5f **(82)** - Dayanata (Shirley Heights) 10.3f **(74)**
Form - 10620

Record	**1998 -**	1st:1	2nd:1	3rd:0	Ran:5
	Pre1998 -	1st:1	2nd:0	3rd:0	Ran:2

Win Prizemoney £44,687 *Total Prizemoney* £48,254

Wins							
* **1998**	Apr	Sandow	(SFT)	G3	10f	107	<
* 1997	Oct	Salisb	(GD)		8f	84	

1998 Turf 1-5: (10f 1-1, 12f 4) (sft 1-2, gd, g-f 2)
Scopey, high-class colt, effective 10 to 12f, acts on sft to g-f. Turf high 116 - 2nd of 8 giving 3lb to Rabah (4 Jly Haydock 12f g-f RF 2538) - also 1st of 4 getting 2lb from Eco Friendly (25 Apr Sandown RF 0868). Caused something of a surprise when winning the Thresher Classic Trial on his reappearance, handling the very soft ground rather better than his rivals, but did not handle Epsom at all in the Derby, hanging badly and becoming unbalanced. Hampered in the King Edward VII at Royal Ascot, he could not peg back Rabah in a Listed race at Haydock in July, and showed little in the Arc.
**P F I Cole [2-7] F Salman.*

Decent filly. Turf high 82 - 1st of 15 from Saffron (6 Jun Doncaster RF 1769) - also 1st of 9 giving 2lb to Beverley Monkey (7 Jly Pontefract RF 2586). She was in fine form last term, winning three times in varied company, and has shown that she can battle if required to.
**Mrs J R Ramsden [3-5] Tony Fawcett.*

COURT EXPRESS **RR 58f** 4672[5]

4 b g Then Again 7.4f **(52)** - Moon Risk (Risk Me (FR)) 5.9f **(53)**
Form - 07477347085

Record	**1998 -**	1st:0	2nd:0	3rd:1	Ran:11
	Pre1998 -	1st:2	2nd:1	3rd:0	Ran:10

Win Prizemoney £5,675 *Total Prizemoney* £7,083

Wins								
1997	Jun	Carlis	(G-F)	H	5.9f	63	68	<
1997	Jun	Carlis	(FRM)		5.9f		61	

1998 Turf 0-11: (6f 4, 7f 2, 8f 3, 9f 2) (gd 3, g-f 4, frm 4)
Leggy, fair gelding, effective 6f, acts on frm, has worn blinkers, prefers right handed tracks. Turf high 58.
**J M Jefferson [0-3] Tim Hawkins (from T J Etherington [2-18] Aug 1998).*

COURT HOUSE BHB 32f30a **RR 45f 30a** 4869[17]

4 b g Reprimand 8.2f **(63)** - Chalet Girl (Double Form) 7.3f **(58)**
Form - 00005600

After a winning start, Courteous gave way to the season's best

COURTESAN BHB 87f **RR 82f** 3602[1]

2 b f Pursuit of Love 9.5f **(69)** - Case for the Crown (USA) (Bates Motel (USA)) 6.5f **(77)**
Form - 21121

Record	**1998 -**	1st:3	2nd:2	3rd:0	Ran:5

Win Prizemoney £9,690 *Total Prizemoney* £12,385

Wins							
* **1998**	Aug	Beverl	(G-F)		7.5f	81	
* **1998**	Jly	Pontef	(G-F)	H	6f	82	<
* **1998**	Jun	Doncas	(GD)		6f	82	<

1998 Turf 3-5: (5f, 6f 2-2, 7f 1-2) (gd, g-f 1-2, frm 2-2)

Record	**1998 -**	1st:0	2nd:0	3rd:0	Ran:7
	Pre1998 -	1st:1	2nd:0	3rd:0	Ran:12

Win Prizemoney £2,448 *Total Prizemoney* £2,448

Wins							
1997	Jun	Pontef	(GD)	S	8f	60	<

1998 Turf 0-6:(8f 3, 10f 2, 12f)(gd 2, g-f 2, frm 2)1998 AW 0-1:(8f) (Fibr)
Light-framed, moderate gelding, has broken blood-vessels, effective 6 to 8f, acts on gd to g-f, likes left handed tracks, likes tight tracks. Turf high 45. Inconsistent.
**M C Chapman [0-17] F J Mills & W Mills (from B A McMahon [1-6] Jun 1997).*

COURTLEDGE BHB 50f **RR 52f** 2727[6]
3 b g Unfuwain (USA) 11.4f **(74)** - Tremellick (Mummy's Pet) 7.7f **(60)**
Form - 0006
Record 1998 - 1st:0 2nd:0 3rd:0 Ran:4
1998 Turf 0-3: (7f, 10f 2) (gd 2, g-f) 1998 AW 0-1: (12f) (Fibr)
Strong, fair gelding. Turf high 52.
**Miss J A Camacho [0-4] B P Skirton.*

COURTLY TIMES RR 65f 4662[3]
3 ch f Machiavellian (USA) 9.8f **(83)** - Dancing Moon (IRE) (Dancing Brave (USA)) 8.4f **(76)**
Form - 3
Record 1998 - 1st:0 2nd:0 3rd:1 Ran:1
Pre1998 - 1st:0 2nd:0 3rd:0 Ran:1
Win Prizemoney £0 *Total Prizemoney* £787
1998 Turf 0-1: (8f) (gd)
Leggy, currently average filly.
**E A L Dunlop [0-2] Maktoum Al Maktoum.*

COURTNEY GYM (IRE) BHB 35f **RR 38f** 4885[7]
3 ch g Shalford (IRE) 7.8f **(63)** - Fair Or Foul (Patch) 11.5f **(51)**
Form - 000070807
Record 1998 - 1st:0 2nd:0 3rd:0 Ran:9
Pre1998 - 1st:0 2nd:2 3rd:0 Ran:5
Win Prizemoney £0 *Total Prizemoney* £1,182
1998 Turf 0-9: (6f 2, 7f 2, 8f 3, 9f, 10f) (g-s, gd 2, g-f 2, frm 4)
Very moderate gelding, effective 6f, acts on frm. Turf high 38.
**P Burgoyne [0-9] Meers-Smith Partnership (from M R Channon [0-5] Oct 1997).*

COURT SHAREEF BHB 70f **RR 75f** 3299[8]
3 b c Shareef Dancer (USA) 10.1f **(67)** - Fairfields Cone (Celtic Cone) 9.8f **(43)**
Form - 46113358
Record 1998 - 1st:2 2nd:0 3rd:2 Ran:8
Pre1998 - 1st:0 2nd:0 3rd:0 Ran:1
Win Prizemoney £6,110 *Total Prizemoney* £7,456
Wins * **1998** May Leices (GD) H 11.8f 66 75 <
* **1998** May Windso (G-F) H 11.6f 58 62
1998 Turf 2-8: (10f, 12f 2-6, 14f) (sft, g-s, gd 2, g-f 1-3, frm 1-1)
Neat, above-average colt, effective 12f, acts on gd to g-f, best on g-f, favours tight tracks. Turf high 75 - 3rd of 8 getting 10lb from Tough Act (19 Jun Goodwood 12f g-f RF 2120) - also 1st of 10 getting 3lb from Eastwell Hall (26 May Leicester RF 1468). Won two modest handicaps in the spring, but went up in the handicap and has struggled since. **R Dickin [2-9] Derek & Cheryl Holder.*

COURT THIRTEEN RR 57f 2929[7]
2 b c Petong 7.6f **(58)** - Madam Bold (Never so Bold) 6.3f **(66)**
Form - 07
Record 1998 - 1st:0 2nd:0 3rd:0 Ran:2
1998 Turf 0-2: (7f 2) (gd, frm)
Currently fair colt. Turf high 57. **T D Barron [0-2] P D Savill.*

COVALLA (IRE) BHB 50f **RR 52f** 3408[9]
3 b f Balla Cove - Persian Myth (Persian Bold) 9.3f **(66)**
Form - 0
Record 1998 - 1st:0 2nd:0 3rd:0 Ran:1
Pre1998 - 1st:0 2nd:0 3rd:0 Ran:6
Win Prizemoney £0 *Total Prizemoney* £218
1998 Turf 0-1: (8f) (g-f)
Fair filly.
**R A Fahey [0-1] R A Fahey (from P J Flynn in IRE [0-6] Oct 1997).*

COVER GIRL (IRE) BHB 84f **RR 86f** 4623[1]
2 ch f Common Grounds 8.1f **(66)** - Peace Carrier (IRE) (Doulab (USA)) 9.8f **(65)**
Form - 27171
Record 1998 - 1st:2 2nd:1 3rd:0 Ran:5
Win Prizemoney £7,461 *Total Prizemoney* £8,511
Wins * **1998** Oct Catter (gd,) H 7f 77 86 <
* **1998** Jly Yarmou (G-F) 6f 69
1998 Turf 2-5: (6f 1-3, 7f 1-2) (gd, g-f 2-4)
Useful filly. Turf high 86 - 1st of 10 giving 11lb to Golden Charm (3 Oct Catterick RF 4623). **Sir Mark Prescott [2-5] The Speculators.*

CRACKER BHB 40f **RR 45f** 4927[15]
4 br g Lugana Beach 7f **(63)** - Greta's Song (Faraway Times (USA)) 7.4f **(52)**
Form - 6700
Record 1998 - 1st:0 2nd:0 3rd:0 Ran:3
Pre1998 - 1st:0 2nd:0 3rd:0 Ran:1
1998 Turf 0-3: (5f, 7f, 10f) (g-s, gd, frm)
Unfurnished, moderate gelding. Turf high 45 (began Spt).
**A Senior [0-3] A Senior (from G Fierro [0-1] Nov 1997).*

CRACKLE BHB 79f **RR 77f** 5148[16]
2 gr f Anshan 8.2f **(63)** - Crackling **(31f 35a)** (Electric) 10.1f **(61)**
Form - 321274410
Record 1998 - 1st:2 2nd:2 3rd:1 Ran:9
Win Prizemoney £6,517 *Total Prizemoney* £10,723
Wins * **1998** Oct Doncas (SFT) H 8f 72 77 <
* **1998** Jly Bath (GD) 5.7f 75
1998 Turf 2-9: (5f, 6f 1-2, 7f 4, 8f 1-2) (g-s, gd 1-2, g-f, frm 1-4, hrd)
Above-average filly, effective 6 to 8f, acts on gd to frm, best on frm. Turf high 77 - 1st of 11 from Nathan's Boy (23 Oct Doncaster RF 4960) - also 1st of 15 from Patsy Stone (16 Jly Bath RF 2840). Consistent. **B W Hills [2-9] S P Tindall.*

CRAFT BOOK INGOT RR 1953[13]
5 b m Ardross 12.4f **(67)** - Coca (Levmoss) 11.4f **(66)**
Form - 0
Record 1998 - 1st:0 2nd:0 3rd:0 Ran:1
1998 Turf 0-1: (10f) (gd)
Currently very poor filly - 13th of 13 giving 3lb to Flying Eagle (13 Jun Bath 10f gd RF 1953). **J M Bradley [0-3] Craftbook Ltd.*

CRAFTBOOK MARCHESA (IRE) BHB 30f38a **RR 38a** 1541[12]
4 br f Un Desperado (FR) 9.3f **(42)** - Dushenka (Jalmood (USA)) 10.1f **(52)**
Form - 0400
Record 1998 - 1st:0 2nd:0 3rd:0 Ran:4
Win Prizemoney £0 *Total Prizemoney* £227
1998 Turf 0-1: (10f) (frm) 1998 AW 0-3: (8f, 9f 2) (Fibr 3)
Unfurnished, very moderate filly. AW high 35.
**J M Bradley [0-4] Craftbook Ltd.*

CRAFTBOOK PAY LODE (IRE) BHB 21f **RR 31df** 3611[6]
5 b m Un Desperado (FR) 9.3f **(42)** - Vein (Kalydon)
Form - 00576
Record 1998 - 1st:0 2nd:0 3rd:0 Ran:5
1998 Turf 0-5: (8f, 10f, 12f 3) (gd 2, frm 3)
Very moderate filly. Turf high 31. **J M Bradley [0-5] Craftbook Ltd.*

CRAIGIE BOY BHB 31f26a **RR 3f 26a** 2494[14]
8 b g Crofthall 8.6f **(54)** - Lady Carol (Lord Gayle (USA)) 8.8f **(62)**
Form - 00846006060
Record 1998 - 1st:0 2nd:0 3rd:0 Ran:11
Pre1998 - 1st:4 2nd:11 3rd:6 Ran:77
Win Prizemoney £14,703 *Total Prizemoney* £34,287
Wins * 1996 May Hamilt (HVY) H 6f 46 45
* 1994 Apr Hamilt (SFT) H 6f 52 55 <
1998 Turf 0-8: (5f, 6f 7) (hvy, sft 3, g-s, gd, g-f, frm) 1998 AW 0-3: (6f 3) (Fibr 3)
Very poor gelding, effective 6f, acts on sft to frm, often wears blinkers. Turf high 45. AW high 2. Becoming disappointing. He has failed to win since May 1996 despite umpteen efforts in the meantime. However, he often runs well at Hamilton, and if he is to gain another victory it is very likely to be there.
**N Bycroft [4-90] Bernard Rayner (from J P Leigh [0-4] May 1992).*

CRAIGIEVAR BHB 92f **RR 89f** 1900[11]
4 b c Mujadil (USA) 7.7f **(70)** - Sweet Home (Home Guard (USA)) 9.3f **(66)**
Form - 00
Record 1998 - 1st:0 2nd:0 3rd:0 Ran:2
Pre1998 - 1st:3 2nd:0 3rd:1 Ran:8
Win Prizemoney £18,242 *Total Prizemoney* £22,226
Wins * 1997 May Haydoc (SFT) LH 7.1f 95 93
* 1996 Oct Nottin (G-S) H 6.1f 84 97+ <
* 1996 Oct Warwic (FRM) 6f 89
1998 Turf 0-2: (7f 2) (sft, g-s)
Light-framed, useful colt, effective 7f, acts on g-s. Turf high 71.

Inconsistent. Rather disappointing after winning a listed handicap at Haydock in '97, although he was fourth in a French Group Three. No promise last term. **J R Fanshawe [3-10] D I Russell.*

CRAIGSTEEL BHB 111f RR 115f 5140[1]

3 b c Suave Dancer(USA)10.7f **(68)** Applecross(Glint of Gold) 9.3f **(66)**
Form - 141
Record 1998 - 1st:2 2nd:0 3rd:0 Ran:3
Pre1998 - 1st:1 2nd:1 3rd:0 Ran:4
Win Prizemoney £23,382 *Total Prizemoney* £33,005
Wins * **1998** Nov Doncas (SFT) 14.6f 115 <
* **1998** Spt Doncas (GD) L 12f 111
* 1997 Jly Newmar (GD) 7f 96
1998 Turf 2-3: (12f 1-1, 15f 1-1, 16f) (gd 1-1, g-f 1-2)
Leggy, high-class colt, effective 12 to 16f, acts on gd to g-f, best on g-f. Turf high 115 (began Spt) - 1st of 4 giving 4lb to Sweetness Herself (6 Nov Doncaster RF 5140) - also 1st of 6 giving 5lb to Altaweelah (11 Spt Doncaster RF 4224). A foot problem kept him off the track until Doncaster in September, where he looked better than ever in winning a Listed event. Two miles was just beyond him at Newmarket the following month, but he returned to winning ways on his final start and is one to watch in 1999. He could develop into a Cup horse. **H R A Cecil [3-7] Sir David Wills.*

Workmanlike, very useful filly, effective 5 to 8f, acts on gd to frm. Turf high 104 - 5th of 13 to Tarascon (24 May Curragh 8f gd RF 1513a). Consistent. She took a while to recover from her exertions over a mile, but was back on song over sprint distances in late summer. We may have seen the best of a filly who will be remembered for her exploits as a juvenile.
**D HaydnJones [1-14] Hugh O'Donnell.*

CRAZY CHIEF BHB 74f RR 78f 1634[15]

5 b h Indian Ridge 7.6f **(74)** - Bizarre Lady (Dalsaan) 9.8f **(64)**
Form - 00
Record 1998 - 1st:0 2nd:0 3rd:0 Ran:2
Pre1998 - 1st:1 2nd:4 3rd:2 Ran:12
Win Prizemoney £3,967 *Total Prizemoney* £12,459
Wins * 1996 May Windso (GD) 8.3f 74 <
1998 Turf 0-1: (10f) (g-f) 1998 AW 0-1: (8f) (Fibr)
Above-average colt. **P F I Cole [1-14] David Simpson.*

CREDENZA BHB 49f RR 49f 3499[4]

2 ch f Superlative 8.8f **(57)** - Carousel Music **(36f)** (On Your Mark) 7.7f **(58)**
Form - 42457304
Record 1998 - 1st:0 2nd:1 3rd:1 Ran:8

Craigsteel splits Altaweelah and Mutawwaj (far side) at Doncaster

Win Prizemoney £0 *Total Prizemoney* £781
1998 Turf 0-8: (5f 4, 6f 3, 7f) (sft, gd 3, g-f, frm 3)
Moderate filly, effective 5f, acts on frm. Turf high 49.
**R Hannon [0-8] Scott Hardy Partnership.*

CRASH CALL LADY BHB 39f45a RR 57f 45a 5073[11]

2 b f Batshoof 9.5f **(66)** - Petite Louie (Chilibang)
Form - 004437400
Record 1998 - 1st:0 2nd:0 3rd:1 Ran:9
Win Prizemoney £0 *Total Prizemoney* £270
1998 Turf 0-6: (5f, 7f 3, 8f, 10f) (gd 4, g-f 2) 1998 AW 0-3: (5f, 6f, 7f) (Fibr 3)
Fair filly, often wears blinkers. Turf high 57. AW high 35.
**C N Allen [0-9] Crash Call Ltd.*

CRAZEE MENTAL BHB 97f RR 98f 3777[4]

3 b f Magic Ring (IRE) 6.5f **(64)** - Corn Futures (Nomination) 7f **(60)**
Form - 705882344
Record 1998 - 1st:0 2nd:1 3rd:1 Ran:9
Pre1998 - 1st:1 2nd:4 3rd:0 Ran:5
Win Prizemoney £3,517 *Total Prizemoney* £56,519
Wins * 1997 Jun Hamilt (GD) 6f 70 <
1998 Turf 0-9: (6f 3, 7f 3, 8f 3) (sft, gd 4, g-f, frm 3)

CREDIT-A-PLENTY RR 81+f 4800[1]

2 ch f Generous (IRE) 11.5f **(82)** - On Credit (FR) (No Pass No Sale) 11.9f **(85)**
Form - 1
Record 1998 - 1st:1 2nd:0 3rd:0 Ran:1
Win Prizemoney £3,111 *Total Prizemoney* £3,111
Wins * **1998** Oct Haydoc (SFT) 7.1f 81+ <
1998 Turf 1-1: (7f 1-1) (sft 1-1)
Currently decent filly. (1st run) - 1st of 9 getting 5lb from Zanay (14 Oct Haydock RF 4800). **J L Dunlop [1-1] Hesmonds Stud.*

CREES SQAW BHB 30f RR 54?f 142[5]

6 b m Cree Song 6.9f **(54)** - Elsocko (Swing Easy (USA)) 6.5f **(55)**

Form - 075
Record 1998 - 1st:0 2nd:0 3rd:0 Ran:2
Pre1998 - 1st:0 2nd:0 3rd:0 Ran:4
1998 AW 0-2: (7f 2) (Fibr 2)
Fair mare. AW high 28. **B A McMahon [0-6] J C Fretwell.*

CREME CARAMEL (USA) RR 86f 4276[1]

2 b f Septieme Ciel (USA) - Vexation (USA) (Vice Regent (CAN)) 8.7f **(74)**
Form - 5421
Record 1998 - 1st:1 2nd:1 3rd:0 Ran:4
Win Prizemoney £3,452 *Total Prizemoney* £4,955
Wins * 1998 Spt Yarmou (G-S) H 7f 85 86 <
1998 Turf 1-4: (6f, 7f 1-3) (gd 1-1, g-f, frm 2)
Useful filly. Turf high 86 - 1st of 11 giving 9lb to Gino's Spirits (15 Spt Yarmouth RF 4276). **P W Chapple-Hyam [1-4] Mrs C A Waters.*

CREME DE CASSIS RR 57f 4928[7]

2 ch f Alhijaz 7.7f **(57)** - Lucky Flinders (Free State) 8.7f **(61)**
Form - 7
Record 1998 - 1st:0 2nd:0 3rd:0 Ran:1
1998 Turf 0-1: (7f) (g-s)
Currently fair filly.
**P J Makin [0-1] Mrs Pauline Smith & Four Seasons Racing.*

CREON BHB 81f RR 81f 4523[1]

3 b g Saddlers' Hall (IRE) 10.5f **(65)** - Creake (Derring-Do) 11.1f **(64)**
Form - 3334321
Record 1998 - 1st:1 2nd:1 3rd:4 Ran:7
Win Prizemoney £2,827 *Total Prizemoney* £6,182
Wins * 1998 Spt Mussel (GD) 12f 80+ <
1998 Turf 1-7: (10f 3, 12f 1-4) (g-s, gd, g-f 1-3, frm 2)
Scopey, decent gelding, effective 10 to 12f, best at 12f, acts on g-s to frm, best on g-f, does well at Windsor. Turf high 81 - 2nd of 19 giving 12lb to Norcroft Joy (4 Spt Haydock 12f frm RF 4092) - also 1st of 4 from Wave of Optimism (27 Spt Musselburgh RF 4523). Although often placed, he was becoming frustrating until found an easy opportunity at Musselburgh in September, though he hardly won with his head in his chest.
**L M Cumani [1-7] Mohammed Al Nabouda.*

CRETAN GIFT BHB 100f105a RR 114f 105a 4844[13]

7 ch g Cadeaux Genereux 7.9f **(76)** - Caro's Niece (USA) (Caro) 9.3f **(74)**
Form - 122652042060830
Record 1998 - 1st:1 2nd:4 3rd:1 Ran:15
Pre1998 - 1st:11 2nd:12 3rd:4 Ran:67
Win Prizemoney £81,322 *Total Prizemoney* £131,312
Wins ** **1998** Mar Wolver (STD) H 5f 98 103* <
* 1997 Aug Leopar (G-S) G3 6f 102
* 1997 Jun Newcas (HVY) H 6f 93 96
** 1997 Feb Southw (STD) H 6f 90 97*
* 1996 Nov Redcar (G-F) H 6f 73 81
* 1996 Spt Ayr (G-F) H 6f 68 70
* 1996 Spt Nottin (FRM) H 5.1f 66 69
** 1996 Jun Wolver (STD) H 6f 85 86*
** 1996 Apr Wolver (STD) C 5f 82*
** 1995 Oct Wolver (STD) H 6f 66 70*
** 1995 Spt Wolver (STD) H 6f 59 64*
** 1995 Apr Southw (STD) H 6f 54 56*
1998 Turf 0-14: (5f 2, 6f 10, 7f 2) (sft 2, g-s, gd 6, g-f 2, frm 3) 1998 AW 1-1: (5f 1-1) (Fibr 1-1)
Group-class gelding, effective 5 to 6f, best at 6f, acts on g-s to gd, best on gd, mostly wears blinkers (effectively), likes Newmarket. Turf high 114 - 4th of 12 to Tomba (18 Jun Ascot 6f g-s RF 2086). (1st run). He paid for his keep in the first half of the campaign and might have won the Group Two Cork And Orrery Stakes at Royal Ascot had he been able to start his run sooner. A touch disappointing in the autumn, he is very tough and should come back as good as new after a break. He did win particularly well on the All-Weather last March and that is where he might be seen in the early spring.
**N P Littmoden [12-75] T Clarke (from John Harris [0-4] Jun 1994).*

CRICKET'S SONG (IRE) BHB 46f RR 41f 3970[11]

2 b f College Chapel - The Multiyorker (IRE) **(68f)** (Digamist (USA))
Form - 0000
Record 1998 - 1st:0 2nd:0 3rd:0 Ran:4
1998 Turf 0-4: (5f, 6f 3) (g-f, frm 3)
Moderate filly, has worn blinkers. Turf high 41.
**B J Meehan [0-4] Kennet Valley Thoroughbreds III.*

CRIMSON GLORY RR 79f 4309[6]

2 ch f Lycius (USA)8.8f **(71)**- Crimson Conquest (USA)(Diesis) 9.3f **(69)**
Form - 46
Record 1998 - 1st:0 2nd:0 3rd:0 Ran:2
Win Prizemoney £0 *Total Prizemoney* £267
1998 Turf 0-2: (7f, 8f) (gd, g-f)
Currently above-average filly. Turf high 79 (began Aug).
**C E Brittain [0-2] Sheikh Marwan Al Maktoum.*

CRIMSON TIDE (IRE) BHB 114f RR 116f 4953a[7]

4 b c Sadler's Wells (USA) 11.3f **(87)** - Sharata (IRE) (Darshaan) 9.9f **(84)**
Form - 16633157
Record 1998 - 1st:1 2nd:0 3rd:2 Ran:7
Pre1998 - 1st:4 2nd:2 3rd:3 Ran:10
Win Prizemoney £110,575 *Total Prizemoney* £123,366
Wins * 1998 Spt Epsom (SFT) G3 12f 102
* 1997 Nov Capann (HVY) G2 8f 114 <
* 1997 Oct Dussel (SFT) G2 8.5f 109
* 1997 Spt Bath (G-F) 8f 100
* 1996 Oct Newmar (GD) 7f 92
1998 Turf 1-7: (8f 3, 10f, 12f 1-3) (sft, gd 1-3, g-f 2, frm)
Scopey, high-class colt, effective 8 to 12f, acts on hvy to g-f, likes tight tracks. Turf high 116 - 3rd of 9 giving 4lb to Annus Mirabilis (29 Aug Windsor 10f g-f RF 3973). He looked easily beatable once again last season, except for winning a weak Group Three at Epsom in September when the soft ground was in his favour.
**J W Hills [5-17].*

CRISOS IL MONACO (IRE) RR 107f 1734a[10]

3 b c Common Grounds 8.1f **(66)** - Gayshuka (Lord Gayle (USA)) 8.8f **(62)**
Form - 10
1998 Turf 1-2: (8f 1-1, 12f) (gd 1-1, g-f)
Currently Pattern-class colt. Turf high 107 (1st run) - 1st of 13 from Trans Island (26 Apr Capannelle RF 0947a). He was beaten fair and square by Trans Island in the Italian 2,000 Guineas, but was awarded the race after a stewards' enquiry. He failed to stay in the Italian Derby and will be best at up to a mile and a quarter.
**L Camici in ITY [1-2].*

CRITICAL AIR BHB 54f53a RR 55f 53a 4677[8]

3 b g Reprimand 8.2f **(63)** - Area Girl (Jareer (USA)) 5.9f **(75)**
Form - 3243470138
Record 1998 - 1st:1 2nd:0 3rd:2 Ran:8
Pre1998 - 1st:0 2nd:1 3rd:1 Ran:6
Win Prizemoney £3,077 *Total Prizemoney* £5,155
Wins * 1998 Aug Mussel (GD) H 7.1f 51 55 <
1998 Turf 1-5: (7f 1-4, 8f) (gd, g-f 1-3, frm) 1998 AW 0-3: (5f, 6f, 7f) (Fibr 3)
Scopey, fair gelding, has worn blinkers, likes tight tracks. Turf high 55. AW high 48. Consistent. **Sir Mark Prescott [1-14] Neil Greig.*

CROAGH PATRICK BHB 51f30a RR 38f 30a 328[10]

6 b g Faustus (USA) 9.1f **(54)** - Pink Pumpkin (Tickled Pink) 6.5f **(59)**
Form - 0
Record 1998 - 1st:0 2nd:0 3rd:0 Ran:1
Pre1998 - 1st:0 2nd:0 3rd:0 Ran:6
1998 AW 0-1: (8f) (Equi)
Very moderate gelding. **J C Fox [0-12] Mrs J A Cleary.*

CROCO ROUGE (IRE) RR 125f 4727a[4]

3 b c Rainbow Quest (USA) 11.2f **(81)** - Alligatrix (USA) (Alleged USA)) 10f **(76)**
Form - 112324
1998 Turf 2-6: (10f, 11f 2-2, 12f 3) (hvy 1-2, sft, gd 1-3)
Top-class colt, effective 12f, acts on hvy to gd, prefers right handed tracks. Turf high 125 - 4th of 14 to Sagamix (4 Oct Longchamp 12f sft RF 4727a). Emerged as a high-class colt with victories in the Greffulhe and the Lupin in the spring, but was set a lot to do in the French Derby and failed by a neck to peg back stablemate Dream Well. After a slightly lacklustre third in the Grand Prix de Paris, he came back after a break to split Sagamix and Dream Well

in the Prix Niel. Beaten less than two lengths in the Arc, but never looked like winning. **P Bary in FR [2-7] Wafic Said.*

CROFTERS EDGE BHB 46f46a **RR 44f 46a** 5006[3]

3 ch g Beveled (USA) 6.9f **(64)** - Zamindara (Crofter (USA)) 8.4f **(56)**
Form - 60700223603
Record 1998 - 1st:0 2nd:2 3rd:2 Ran:11
Pre1998 - 1st:0 2nd:0 3rd:0 Ran:2
Win Prizemoney £0 *Total Prizemoney* £1,903
1998 Turf 0-8: (6f, 7f 2, 8f 4, 10f) (sft, gd 2, g-f, frm 4) 1998 AW 0-3: (6f 2, 8f) (Fibr 3)
Scopey, moderate gelding, effective 8f, acts on frm, has worn blinkers, likes left handed tracks, likes tight tracks. Turf high 51 - 3rd of 14 giving 3lb to Lady Yavanna (18 Aug Brighton 8f frm RF 3690). AW high 42. **A P Jarvis [0-13] Crofter's Edge.*

CROFT REVEILLE BHB 37f **RR 24f** 4149[13]

4 ch g Crofthall 8.6f **(54)** - Sannavally (Sagaro) 9.7f **(55)**
Form - 600
Record 1998 - 1st:0 2nd:0 3rd:0 Ran:3
1998 Turf 0-3: (6f, 7f, 10f) (g-f, frm 2)
Currently little account gelding. Turf high 24 (began Jly).
**T D McCarthy [0-3] Miss Vivian Pratt.*

CROFT SANDS BHB 32f **RR 30f** 4234[11]

5 ch g Crofthall 8.6f **(54)** - Sannavally (Sagaro) 9.7f **(55)**
Form - 0000
Record 1998 - 1st:0 2nd:0 3rd:0 Ran:4
Pre1998 - 1st:0 2nd:0 3rd:0 Ran:3
1998 Turf 0-4: (6f, 7f 2, 8f) (gd, g-f 2, frm)
Very moderate gelding. Turf high 30.
**J Akehurst [0-4] Miss Vivian Pratt (from R Akehurst [0-3] Nov 1997).*

CROMAC (ITY) RR 90f 4600a[8]

3 f
Form - 8
1998 Turf 0-1: (10f) (hvy)
Currently useful filly. **in ITY [0-1].*

CROMER PIER BHB 46f42a **RR 62f 42a** 4777[3]

3 b g Reprimand 8.2f **(63)** - Fleur du Val (Valiyar) 8.5f **(73)**
Form - 0043025403
Record 1998 - 1st:0 2nd:1 3rd:2 Ran:10
Pre1998 - 1st:0 2nd:0 3rd:0 Ran:1
Win Prizemoney £0 *Total Prizemoney* £1,496
1998 Turf 0-9: (7f, 8f, 11f 2, 12f 3, 14f 2) (gd 5, g-f, frm 3) 1998 AW 0-1: (11f) (Fibr)
Workmanlike, average gelding, effective 12f, acts on gd to g-f, has worn blinkers (effectively), likes tight tracks. Turf high 62 - 4th of 13 giving 9lb to Tigullio (22 Jun Windsor 12f g-f RF 2183).
**M H Tompkins [0-11] Mrs P D Sealey.*

CROSBY DON RR 38f 736[6]

3 b g Alhijaz 7.7f **(57)** - Evening Star (Red Sunset) 8.2f **(63)**
Form - 6
Record 1998 - 1st:0 2nd:0 3rd:0 Ran:1
Pre1998 - 1st:0 2nd:0 3rd:0 Ran:3
1998 Turf 0-1: (12f) (g-s)
Scopey, very moderate gelding. **E Weymes [0-4] Don Raper.*

CROSS LUGANA RR 1212[16]

2 b f Lugana Beach 7f **(63)** - Cross Mags **(45f)** (Hasty Word)
Form - 0
Record 1998 - 1st:0 2nd:0 3rd:0 Ran:1
1998 Turf 0-1: (5f) (frm)
Currently very poor filly. **D Burchell [0-1] H K Strickland.*

CROWDED AVENUE BHB 92f **RR 92f** 4821[3]

6 b g Sizzling Melody 6.3f **(49)** - Lady Bequick (Sharpen Up) 8.3f **(67)**
Form - 45343
Record 1998 - 1st:0 2nd:0 3rd:2 Ran:5
Pre1998 - 1st:6 2nd:4 3rd:3 Ran:31
Win Prizemoney £39,805 *Total Prizemoney* £63,425

Wins	* 1996	Aug	Sandow	(GD)	H	5f	95	93	<
	* 1995	Spt	Epsom	(G-F)	H	5f	82	92	
	* 1995	Aug	Epsom	(G-F)	H	5f	82	83	
	* 1995	Jly	Goodwo	(GD)	H	5f	67	75	
	* 1995	Jun	Mussel	(G-F)	H	5f	56	57+	
	* 1995	Jun	Ayr	(G-F)	H	5f	48	49	

1998 Turf 0-5: (5f 5) (gd 3, g-f, frm)
Useful gelding, effective 5f, acts on g-f. Turf high 92. Consistent. Has not won for donkey's ages, but that has not stopped him putting in some creditable performances. He is particularly well handicapped and, providing things go his way, he should regain the winning thread in 1999. **P J Makin [6-36] T W Wellard.*

CROWN OF LIGHT BHB 110f **RR 113df** 3753[6]

4 b f Mtoto 11.5f **(71)** - Russian Countess (USA) (Nureyev (USA)) 8.7f **(78)**
Form - 6
Record 1998 - 1st:0 2nd:0 3rd:0 Ran:1
Pre1998 - 1st:2 2nd:0 3rd:3 Ran:7
Win Prizemoney £15,834 *Total Prizemoney* £79,986

Wins	1997	May	Lingfi	(SFT)	L	11.5f	94	<
	1996	Aug	Leices	(GD)		7f	72+	

1998 Turf 0-1: (12f) (frm)
Strong, Group-class filly, effective 12f, acts on gd to g-f. A high-class filly for Michael Stoute in '97, third in the Epsom Oaks, she has obviously had her problems and was making her belated debut for Godolphin when tailed off last in the Yorkshire Oaks.
**S bin Suroor [0-1] Godolphin (from Sir Michael Stoute [2-7] Spt 1997).*

CROWN OF TREES (USA) RR 79f 4103[3]

2 b c Chief's Crown (USA) 10.2f **(75)** - Ribbonwood (USA) (Diesis) 9.3f **(69)**
Form - 13
Record 1998 - 1st:1 2nd:0 3rd:1 Ran:2
Win Prizemoney £4,781 *Total Prizemoney* £5,938
Wins * **1998** Aug Kempto (G-F) 7f 73 <
1998 Turf 1-2: (7f 1-1, 8f) (frm 1-2)
Currently above-average colt. Turf high 79 (began Aug) - 3rd of 4 to Mixsterthetrixster (5 Spt Haydock 8f frm RF 4103) - also 1st of 5 getting 3lb from Secret's Out (19 Aug Kempton RF 3738). He showed the right attitude when making a winning debut at Kempton in August, but was last of three when upped in class.
**D R Loder [1-2] Sheikh Mohammed.*

CROWN SECRET BHB 70f **RR 65f** 4337[13]

2 b c Zafonic (USA) 9f **(83)** - Free City (USA) (Danzig (USA)) 8.4f **(76)**
Form - 4060
Record 1998 - 1st:0 2nd:0 3rd:0 Ran:4
Win Prizemoney £0 *Total Prizemoney* £236
1998 Turf 0-4: (7f 3, 8f) (gd, g-f, frm 2)
Average colt. Turf high 65 (began Jly).
**P W Harris [0-4] Lawrence, Merchack, Williams.*

CROW'S NEST BHB 62f **RR 60f** 4861[13]

3 b f Shirley Heights 12.1f **(76)** - Mountain Lodge (Blakeney) 10.5f **(64)**
Form - 0060
Record 1998 - 1st:0 2nd:0 3rd:0 Ran:4
1998 Turf 0-4: (8f, 10f, 12f, 14f) (g-s, g-f, frm 2)
Scopey, average filly. Turf high 60.
**Lord Huntingdon [0-4] Lord Halifax.*

CRUINN A BHORD BHB 85f **RR 85f** 3463[2]

3 b f Inchinor 8.9f **(64)** - Selection Board (Welsh Pageant) 10f **(65)**
Form - 212
Record 1998 - 1st:1 2nd:2 3rd:0 Ran:3
Pre1998 - 1st:0 2nd:0 3rd:0 Ran:1
Win Prizemoney £2,234 *Total Prizemoney* £5,378
Wins * **1998** Jly Catter (G-F) 7f 60+ <
1998 Turf 1-3: (7f 1-1, 8f 2) (gd 2, frm 1-1)
Scopey, useful filly. Turf high 85 - 2nd of 13 getting 2lb from Wuxi Venture (8 Aug Haydock 8f gd RF 3463).
**A C Stewart [1-4] Lord Derby.*

CRUMPTON HILL (IRE) BHB 92f **RR 94f** 5078[8]

6 b g Thatching 7.8f **(69)** - Senane (Vitiges (FR)) 8.2f **(59)**
Form - 031004588
Record 1998 - 1st:1 2nd:0 3rd:1 Ran:9
Pre1998 - 1st:3 2nd:1 3rd:6 Ran:20
Win Prizemoney £39,388 *Total Prizemoney* £89,266

Wins	* **1998**	May	Kempto	(G-F)		7f		95	<
	* 1996	Jly	Newmar	(GD)	H	7f	86	93	

* 1995 Apr Newbur (G-F) H 8f 75 75+
* 1994 Spt Newcas (GD) 8f 77

1998 Turf 1-9: (7f 1-5, 8f 4) (sft 2, gd 4, g-f 1-2, frm)

Useful gelding, effective 7 to 8f, best at 8f, acts on gd to frm, best on gd, has worn blinkers, and excels at Kempton. Turf high 96 - 3rd of 20 giving 25lb to Tertium (4 May Kempton 8f gd RF 1014) - also 1st of 5 giving 5lb to Reunion (17 May Kempton RF 1282). Regularly thereabouts in competitive handicaps, though he just cannot put his head in front where it matters in races of that type, and his only victory last season came narrowly in a Kempton conditions event. **N A Graham [4-29] T H Chadney.*

CRUSTY LILY RR 14f 4189[19]

2 gr f Whittingham (IRE) - Miss Crusty **(35df)** (Belfort (FR)) 6.8f **(63)**
Form - 0
Record 1998 - 1st:0 2nd:0 3rd:0 Ran:1
1998 Turf 0-1: (6f) (gd)
Currently poor filly. **L P Grassick [0-1] L H Ballinger.*

CRUZ SANTA BHB 30f27a **RR 30f 27a** 3562[16]

5 b m Lord Bud 8.2f **(52)** - Linpac Mapleleaf (Dominion) 8.5f **(63)**
Form - 000010884630000
Record 1998 - 1st:1 2nd:0 3rd:1 Ran:12
Pre1998 - 1st:0 2nd:1 3rd:0 Ran:11
Win Prizemoney £2,085 *Total Prizemoney* £3,358
Wins * **1998** *Jan Southw (STD) 11f 40* <
1998 Turf 0-5: (7f, 8f 3, 10f) (gd, g-f, frm 3) 1998 AW 1-7: (11f 1-5, 12f 2) (Fibr 1-7)

Moderate filly, effective 7 to 11f, acts on gd - acts on Fibr, likes left handed tracks, likes tight tracks. Turf high 44 (1st run) - 3rd of 16 getting 5lb from Fancy A Fortune (15 May Thirsk 7f gd RF 1250). AW high 40 - 1st of 10 from Posie Chain (5 Jan Southwell RF 0024). The maiden that she won on the Southwell Fibresand in January was awful, an impression confirmed by her form both before and since.
**M C Chapman [1-16] Mrs C Lund (from T D Barron [0-8] Jly 1997).*

CRY FOR FREEDOM BHB 53f51a **RR 53f 51a** 4931[1]

3 b f Komaite (USA) 6.9f **(61)** - Heresheis (Free State) 8.7f **(61)**
Form - 64206561
Record 1998 - 1st:1 2nd:1 3rd:0 Ran:8
Win Prizemoney £2,102 *Total Prizemoney* £3,272
Wins * **1998** Oct Bright (G-S) SH 10f 44 53 <
1998 Turf 1-8: (8f 4, 10f 1-3, 11f) (g-s 1-1, g-f 2, frm 4, hrd)

Scopey, fair filly, effective 8 to 10f, acts on g-s to hrd. Turf high 53 - 1st of 20 giving 7lb to Memory's Music (22 Oct Brighton RF 4931). **J Pearce [1-8] Michael Whatley.*

CRYHAVOC BHB 65f **RR 75f** 4864[11]

4 b g Polar Falcon (USA) 9f **(74)** - Sarabah (IRE) (Ela-Mana-Mou) 10.1f **(70)**
Form - 608000
Record 1998 - 1st:0 2nd:0 3rd:0 Ran:6
Pre1998 - 1st:2 2nd:1 3rd:1 Ran:10
Win Prizemoney £10,542 *Total Prizemoney* £16,263
Wins * 1996 Oct Newmar (G-F) H 6f 86 96 <
* 1996 Spt Epsom (G-F) 6f 83
1998 Turf 0-5: (6f 2, 7f 3) (gd 3, g-f 2) 1998 AW 0-1: (6f) (Fibr)

Workmanlike, above-average gelding, effective 6 to 7f, acts on g-f, has worn blinkers. Turf high 75. Becoming disappointing. Without a win since his two-year-old days, he has been tried in all sorts of company since and is proving very difficult to place.
**J R Arnold [2-16] A H Robinson.*

CRYSTAL CHARM (IRE) RR 92f 4193[3]

2 gr f Danehill (USA) 9.1f **(79)** - Chamonis (USA) (Affirmed (USA)) 9.3f **(79)**
Form - 23
Record 1998 - 1st:0 2nd:1 3rd:1 Ran:2
Win Prizemoney £0 *Total Prizemoney* £4,343
1998 Turf 0-2: (5f, 6f) (gd 2)

Currently useful filly. Turf high 92 (1st run) (began Aug) - 2nd of 7 to Amazing Dream (15 Aug Newbury 5f gd RF 3651). She was reportedly useful before making her debut at Newbury, where she was only running because her owners were in the country at the time. Despite the race being a Listed event and the minimum trip being much too short, she still ran well, and was being backed for the Guineas. She only ran once more, putting in a creditable performance when third to Atlantic Destiny in a Listed race at Kempton. She will stay further and is open to improvement, but whether she is good enough to win the Guineas, we will have to wait and see.
**P W Chapple-Hyam [0-2] I Allan, Ming Yi Chen & Hung Chao-Hong.*

CRYSTAL CRAZE BHB 39f **RR 32f** 4311[14]

3 b f Warrshan (USA) 9.7f **(59)** - Single Gal (Mansingh (USA)) 7.4f **(55)**
Form - 26000
Record 1998 - 1st:0 2nd:1 3rd:0 Ran:5
Pre1998 - 1st:0 2nd:0 3rd:0 Ran:1
Win Prizemoney £0 *Total Prizemoney* £570
1998 Turf 0-4: (5f, 8f 2, 12f) (g-s, gd, frm 2) 1998 AW 0-1: (8f) (Equi)
Light-framed, very moderate filly. Turf high 32.
**C A Cyzer [0-6] R M Cyzer.*

CRYSTAL CREEK (IRE) RR 71f 4772[10]

2 b c River Falls 8.2f **(56)** - Dazzling Maid (IRE) (Tate Gallery (USA)) 7.4f **(67)**
Form - 00
Record 1998 - 1st:0 2nd:0 3rd:0 Ran:2
1998 Turf 0-2: (7f 2) (gd, frm)
Currently above-average colt. Turf high 71 (began Jly).
**Mrs A J Perrett [0-2] Fred Cotton.*

CRYSTAL DOWNS (USA) RR 104+f 4897a[1]

2 b f Alleged (USA) 11.8f **(81)**- Gazayil (USA)(Irish River (FR)) 8.6f **(78)**
Form - 4321
1998 Turf 1-4: (7f 1-3, 8f) (sft 1-2, gd, hrd)

Very useful filly. Turf high 104 (began Aug) - 2nd of 11 to Juvenia (4 Oct Longchamp 8f sft RF 4725a). She had a highly encouraging first season, running super races to finish second in the Group One Moyglare Stud Stakes and Prix Marcel Boussac. Connections wisely allowed her a confident-boosting maiden race win before the end of the campaign and she will have gone into winter quarters on a high. By Alleged and out of a half-sister to the smart middle-distance horse Husyan, she will stay well beyond a mile and may develop into a leading Oaks contender.
**A P O'Brien in IRE [1-4] Mrs T Hyde.*

CRYSTAL FALLS (IRE) BHB 72f **RR 79f** 4372[3]

5 b g Alzao (USA) 9.8f **(73)** - Honourable Sheba (USA) (Roberto (USA)) 10f **(76)**
Form - 322245516203803
Record 1998 - 1st:1 2nd:4 3rd:3 Ran:15
Pre1998 - 1st:1 2nd:3 3rd:1 Ran:10
Win Prizemoney £10,004 *Total Prizemoney* £24,525
Wins * **1998** Jly Ripon (G-F) H 12.3f 74 77
1995 Oct Doncas (G-F) H 8f 77 79 <
1998 Turf 1-15: (10f 2, 12f 1-11, 14f 2) (g-s, gd 4, g-f 1-7, frm 3)

Above-average gelding, effective 10 to 14f, best at 12f, acts on g-s to frm, best on g-f, has worn blinkers, likes left handed tracks, likes tight tracks, and excels at Thirsk and Catterick. Turf high 79 - 2nd of 7 giving 7lb to Carburton (1 Jun Thirsk 12f g-f RF 1629) - also 1st of 5 giving 5lb to Dancing Rio (18 Jly Ripon RF 2937). Not an easy ride, but he generally performed with credit last term, including winning at Ripon.
**T D Easterby [1-15] C H Stevens (from J J O'Neill [1-10] Jun 1997).*

CRYSTAL HEARTED BHB 114f **RR 110f** 1260[10]

4 b c Broken Hearted 10.1f **(65)** - Crystal Fountain (Great Nephew) 9.9f **(64)**
Form - 20
Record 1998 - 1st:0 2nd:1 3rd:0 Ran:2
Pre1998 - 1st:4 2nd:2 3rd:0 Ran:9
Win Prizemoney £77,321 *Total Prizemoney* £106,858
Wins * 1997 Spt Frankf (GD) G2 10f 106 <
* 1997 Jly Ayr (G-F) G3 10f 106 <
* 1997 May Cheste (HVY) L 10.3f 104?
* 1996 Oct Warwic (FRM) 7f 84+
1998 Turf 0-2: (8f 2) (sft, frm)

Scopey, Group-class colt, effective 10f, acts on hvy to g-f, best on gd. Turf high 110. Consistent. He produced some excellent front-running displays in 1997, but was outpaced in two starts over a mile in the spring. **H Candy [4-11] Mrs C M Poland.*

CRYSTAL HEIGHTS (FR) BHB 48f71a **RR 55df 71a** 1436[20]

10 ch g Crystal Glitters (USA) 8f **(89)** - Fahrenheit (Mount Hagen (FR))

8.4f **(70)**
Form - 00
Record 1998 - 1st:0 2nd:0 3rd:0 Ran:2
Pre1998 - 1st:9 2nd:9 3rd:8 Ran:60
Win Prizemoney £27,203 *Total Prizemoney* £41,632
Wins 1996 Aug Bright (FRM) H 6f 67 70
1996 Jly Bright (FRM) 6f 68
1996 Jly Bright (FRM) H 7f 59 64
1996 Feb Lingfi (STD) H 7f 68 69
1995 Oct Bright (GD) 7f 71
1995 Jly Bright (FRM) C 7f 60
1995 Jan Lingfi (STD) H 6f 55 54
1998 Turf 0-2: (8f, 10f) (gd, frm)
Average gelding, effective 6 to 7f, best at 7f, acts on g-f to frm, best on frm, has worn blinkers. Becoming disappointing.
**B R Cambidge [0-2] Mrs H Noonan (from R J O'Sullivan [7-45] Oct 1997).*

CRYSTAL LASS BHB 61f61a RR 62f 61a 5080[4]

2 b f Ardkinglass 5f **(64)** - That's Rich (Hot Spark) 7.6f **(62)**
Form - 55827334
Record 1998 - 1st:0 2nd:1 3rd:2 Ran:8
Win Prizemoney £0 *Total Prizemoney* £1,651
1998 Turf 0-2: (6f 2) (g-f 2) 1998 AW 0-6: (5f 2, 6f 4) (Fibr 6)
Average filly, effective 6f, acts on g-f, often wears blinkers (very effectively). Turf high 62 (began Jly) - 7th of 22 getting 20lb from Astonished (12 Spt Doncaster 6f g-f RF 4243). AW high 65. She has shown ability on Fibresand without managing to put her head in front. Seven furlongs may bring about the desired effect.
**J Balding [0-8] White House Racing Club.*

CRYSTAL LOUGH (IRE) BHB 45f RR 28f 1137[13]

3 b f Maelstrom Lake 8.8f **(53)** - Holy Water (Monseigneur (USA)) 7.7f **(63)**
Form - 70
Record 1998 - 1st:0 2nd:0 3rd:0 Ran:2
Pre1998 - 1st:0 2nd:0 3rd:0 Ran:3
1998 Turf 0-2: (5f 2) (g-s, hrd)
Scopey, little account filly. Turf high 28.
**G R Oldroyd [0-5] W F Burton.*

CRYSTAL ROSIE BHB 58f50a RR 66f 50a 4878[14]

2 gr f Ardkinglass 5f **(64)** - Indian Crystal **(45f 42a)** (Petong) 6.6f **(58)**
Form - 300
Record 1998 - 1st:0 2nd:0 3rd:1 Ran:3
Win Prizemoney £0 *Total Prizemoney* £325
1998 Turf 0-2: (6f 2) (gd 2) 1998 AW 0-1: (7f) (Fibr)
Currently average filly. Turf high 66 (began Aug).
**Mrs A Swinbank [0-3] Starnotes Racing.*

CRYSTAL WATERS (IRE) BHB 26f RR 28f 4304[13]

3 b f River Falls 8.2f **(56)**- Annie's Glen (IRE)(Glenstal (USA)) 10.1f **(64)**
Form - 00000
Record 1998 - 1st:0 2nd:0 3rd:0 Ran:5
Pre1998 - 1st:0 2nd:0 3rd:0 Ran:2
1998 Turf 0-5: (5f, 6f, 7f, 8f, 10f) (g-s, gd, g-f 2, hrd)
Little account filly. Turf high 28. **G R Oldroyd [0-7] Robert Cook.*

CRYSTAL WIND (IRE) RR 87f 4040a[11]

3 b c Common Grounds 8.1f **(66)** - Windini (Windjammer (USA)) 7f **(59)**
Form - 332212446360
1998 Turf 1-11: (6f 2, 8f 1-4, 9f 2, 10f 3) (hvy, sft, g-s 1-1, gd 7, frm)
Useful colt, effective 6 to 10f, acts on hvy to gd, best on gd. Turf high 96 - 2nd of 10 getting 8lb from Royal Midyan (23 May Curragh 10f gd RF 1505a) - also 1st of 16 giving 5lb to Amharclann (8 May Dundalk RF 1186a). Consistent.
**K Prendergast in IRE [1-14] Mrs A J F O'Reilly.*

CUANDO (USA) RR 118f 5161a[3]

4 b f Lord At War (ARG) 6.6f **(67)** - Last Glance (USA)
Form - 3
1998 Turf 0-1: (9f) (frm)
Currently high-class filly. (1st run) - 3rd of 13 giving 1lb to B A Valentine (7 Nov Churchill Downs 9f frm RF 5161a). **in USA [0-1].*

CUBISM (USA) BHB 88f RR 89f 4591[5]

2 b c Miswaki (USA) 8.1f **(81)** - Seattle Kat (USA) (Seattle Song (USA)) 9f **(77)**
Form - 14105
Record 1998 - 1st:2 2nd:0 3rd:0 Ran:5
Win Prizemoney £10,543 *Total Prizemoney* £10,790
Wins * 1998 Aug Windso (G-F) H 6f 85 89 <
*** 1998** Jly Yarmou (GD) 6f 77+
1998 Turf 2-5: (5f, 6f 2-4) (gd, g-f, frm 1-2, hrd 1-1)
Useful colt. Turf high 89 (began Jly) - 1st of 10 giving 16lb to Lively Jacq (17 Aug Windsor RF 3685). He lacks size, but is a game sort.
**J W Hills [2-5] K Y Lim.*

CUE MAN (IRE) BHB 41f RR 43f 4877[11]

3 b g Dancing Dissident (USA) 6.8f **(65)** - Albona (Neltino) 7.6f **(54)**
Form - 5086470
Record 1998 - 1st:0 2nd:0 3rd:0 Ran:7
Pre1998 - 1st:0 2nd:0 3rd:0 Ran:1
1998 Turf 0-3: (5f, 6f 2) (sft 2, g-f) 1998 AW 0-4: (5f, 6f 3) (Fibr 4)
Neat, moderate gelding. Turf high 43. AW high 39.
**D Shaw [0-3] J Roundtree (from J L Eyre [0-5] Apr 1998).*

CUFF BHB 75f RR 70f 4501[7]

3 b f Warning 8.1f **(77)** - Gold Bracelet (Golden Fleece (USA)) 7.9f **(74)**
Form - 177
Record 1998 - 1st:1 2nd:0 3rd:0 Ran:3
Win Prizemoney £3,485 *Total Prizemoney* £3,485
Wins * 1998 Aug Sandow (G-F) 10f 70 <
1998 Turf 1-3: (10f 1-1, 11f, 12f) (gd, frm 1-2)
Workmanlike, currently above-average filly. Turf high 70 (1st run) (began Aug) - 1st of 9 from Key Academy (12 Aug Sandown RF 3598). Unraced at two, she made a winning debut in a Sandown maiden in August, but did not go on from there.
**J H M Gosden [1-3] Lord Hartington.*

CUGINA BHB 90f RR 95f 4742[11]

4 b f Distant Relative 7f **(69)** - Indubitable (Sharpo) 7.7f **(59)**
Form - 6571400
Record 1998 - 1st:1 2nd:0 3rd:0 Ran:7
Pre1998 - 1st:2 2nd:3 3rd:0 Ran:8
Win Prizemoney £15,619 *Total Prizemoney* £23,978
Wins * 1998 Jun Sandow (G-S) H 10f 89 95 <
* 1997 Aug Sandow (SFT) H 10f 78 84
* 1997 Jly Chepst (G-S) H 10.2f 73 75
1998 Turf 1-7: (9f, 10f 1-5, 12f) (hvy, g-s, gd 1-4, frm)
Scopey, very useful filly, effective 10f, acts on sft to gd, best on gd, excels at Sandown, does well at Chepstow. Turf high 95 - 1st of 8 giving 12lb to Secret Ballot (12 Jun Sandown RF 1935). She looked a useful filly with give underfoot, when scoring in fluent style at Sandown in June. Failed to go on from that, and was rather disappointing in her last couple of runs.
**G B Balding [3-15] Miss B Swire.*

CULCRAGGIE BHB 42f RR 60f 4133[6]

3 b g Weldnaas (USA) 8.4f **(55)** - Strathrusdale (Blazing Saddles (AUS)) 6.7f **(46)**
Form - 635006
Record 1998 - 1st:0 2nd:0 3rd:1 Ran:6
Pre1998 - 1st:0 2nd:0 3rd:0 Ran:2
Win Prizemoney £0 *Total Prizemoney* £530
1998 Turf 0-6: (8f 2, 9f, 10f, 11f, 12f) (g-s, gd 3, g-f 2)
Leggy, average gelding, effective 7f, acts on sft. Turf high 60.
**J L Eyre [0-8] The Haydock Badgeholders.*

CULTURAL ICON (USA) BHB 23f32a RR 18f 32a 3811[6]

6 b g Kris S (USA) 9.3f **(76)** - Sea Prospector (USA) (Mr Prospector (USA)) 8.8f **(78)**
Form - 0006
Record 1998 - 1st:0 2nd:0 3rd:0 Ran:4
Pre1998 - 1st:0 2nd:0 3rd:0 Ran:4
1998 Turf 0-3: (12f 2, 16f) (gd, frm 2) 1998 AW 0-1: (16f) (Equi)
Very moderate gelding. Turf high 18.
**P Mitchell [0-11] Mrs Patricia Mitchell.*

CULTURED KING (IRE) BHB 48f46a RR 52f 46a 4544[4]

3 b g Imp Society (USA) 7.1f **(63)** - Regina St Cyr (IRE) (Doulab (USA)) 9.8f **(65)**
Form - 000820534
Record 1998 - 1st:0 2nd:1 3rd:1 Ran:9

Pre1998 - 1st:0 2nd:0 3rd:0 Ran:3
Win Prizemoney £0 *Total Prizemoney* £915
1998 Turf 0-8: (8f, 11f, 12f 4, 13f, 17f) (g-s, gd 3, g-f, frm 3) 1998 AW 0-1: (14f) (Fibr)
Lengthy, fair gelding, often wears blinkers. Turf high 52. Consistent.
**M W Easterby [0-4] Silvano Scanu (from J G Smyth-Osbourne [0-8] Jly 1998).*

CULZEAN (IRE) RR 80+f 4266[7]
2 b c Machiavellian (USA) 9.8f **(83)** - Eileen Jenny (IRE) (Kris) 9.5f **(73)**
Form - 17
Record 1998 - 1st:1 2nd:0 3rd:0 Ran:2
Win Prizemoney £3,427 *Total Prizemoney* £3,427
Wins * **1998** Spt Leices (G-S) 7f 80+ <
1998 Turf 1-2: (7f 1-1, 8f) (gd, g-f 1-1)
Currently decent colt. Turf high 80 (1st run) (began Spt) - 1st of 15 from Lover's Leap (8 Spt Leicester RF 4139).
**R Hannon [1-2] Stonethorn Stud Farms Ltd.*

CUMBRIAN CADET BHB 55f RR 61df 4153[9]
3 br g Handsome Sailor 6.6f **(53)** - City Sound (On Your Mark) 7.7f **(58)**
Form - 06052846300
Record 1998 - 1st:0 2nd:1 3rd:1 Ran:11
Pre1998 - 1st:1 2nd:3 3rd:1 Ran:10
Win Prizemoney £2,671 *Total Prizemoney* £9,762
Wins * 1997 Aug Ripon (G-F) 5f 73 <
1998 Turf 0-11: (5f 4, 6f 7) (gd 6, g-f 3, frm 2)
Lengthy, average gelding, effective 5 to 6f, best at 5f, acts on gd to g-f, best on g-f, has worn blinkers. Turf high 66.
**T D Easterby [1-21] Cumbrian Industrials Ltd.*

CUMBRIAN CARUSO BHB 63f RR 64f 4799[7]
3 b g Primo Dominie 7.2f **(67)** - Conquista (Aragon) 8.1f **(60)**
Form - 00040883307
Record 1998 - 1st:0 2nd:0 3rd:2 Ran:11
Pre1998 - 1st:1 2nd:2 3rd:0 Ran:4
Win Prizemoney £3,338 *Total Prizemoney* £8,022
Wins * 1997 Jun Redcar (FRM) 6f 68 <
1998 Turf 0-11: (5f 6, 6f 3, 7f 2) (sft, g-s 2, gd 6, frm 2)
Workmanlike, average gelding, effective 6f, acts on g-s to frm, has worn blinkers. Turf high 64.
**T D Easterby [1-15] Cumbrian Industrials Ltd.*

CUMULATE (USA) RR 65f 5093[3]
2 br f Gone West (USA) 7.8f **(82)** - Honoria (USA) 0**0**
Form - 43
Record 1998 - 1st:0 2nd:0 3rd:1 Ran:2
Win Prizemoney £0 *Total Prizemoney* £832
1998 Turf 0-2: (6f, 7f) (gd 2)
Currently average filly. Turf high 65 (began Jly).
**D R Loder [0-2] Maktoum Al Maktoum.*

CUNNING KATE (IRE) BHB 57f RR 66df 2194[9]
3 b f Roi Danzig (USA) 10.5f **(62)** - Persian Empress (IRE) (Persian Bold) 9.3f **(66)**
Form - 0
Record 1998 - 1st:0 2nd:0 3rd:0 Ran:1
Pre1998 - 1st:0 2nd:0 3rd:1 Ran:5
Win Prizemoney £0 *Total Prizemoney* £350
1998 Turf 0-1: (10f) (frm)
Average filly.
**B S Rothwell [0-1] Jack Hamilton (from O Weldon in IRE [0-5] Nov 1997).*

CUPBOARD LOVER BHB 68f RR 73f 4197[5]
2 ch g Risk Me (FR) 8f **(53)** - Galejade **(50df 37a)** (Sharrood (USA)) 10.5f **(72)**
Form - 055
Record 1998 - 1st:0 2nd:0 3rd:0 Ran:3
1998 Turf 0-2: (7f 2) (gd, frm) 1998 AW 0-1: (7f) (Fibr)
Currently above-average gelding, has worn blinkers. Turf high 73 (began Aug). **D HaydnJones [0-3] Mrs Judy Mihalop.*

CUSIN BHB 77f RR 80f 4410[7]
2 ch c Arazi (USA) 9.2f **(74)** - Fairy Tern (Mill Reef (USA)) 10.5f **(78)**
Form - 227
Record 1998 - 1st:0 2nd:2 3rd:0 Ran:3
Win Prizemoney £0 *Total Prizemoney* £2,166
1998 Turf 0-3: (6f 2, 7f) (frm 3)
Currently decent colt. Turf high 80 - 2nd of 6 to Mutaahab (27 May Yarmouth 6f frm RF 1536). **Mrs J Cecil [0-3] Mrs M Slater.*

CUSTOM HOUSE (IRE) RR 78+f 1796[2]
2 b c Paris House 5.9f **(64)** - Silence To Silence (IRE) (Salmon Leap (USA)) 11f **(61)**
Form - 22
Record 1998 - 1st:0 2nd:2 3rd:0 Ran:2
Win Prizemoney £0 *Total Prizemoney* £1,395
1998 Turf 0-1: (5f) (gd) 1998 AW 0-1: (6f) (Fibr)
Above-average colt. (1st run) - 2nd of 11 giving 5lb to College Music (4 May Newcastle 5f gd RF 1020). (1st run) - 2nd of 6 getting 8lb from Boldly Goes (6 Jun Wolverhampton 6f Fibr RF 1796). He had ability, as he proved by finishing runner-up on his first two starts, but may not have helped his cause by being very coltish in the preliminaries. (DEAD) **P C Haslam [0-2] Tutton/Mrs Haslam.*

CUTAWAY RR 73f 5039[10]
2 ch f Kris 10f **(75)** - Licorne (Sadler's Wells (USA)) 10f **(76)**
Form - 60
Record 1998 - 1st:0 2nd:0 3rd:0 Ran:2
1998 Turf 0-2: (7f, 8f) (g-s, gd)
Currently above-average filly. Turf high 73 (began Oct).
**Mrs J Cecil [0-2] Lord Howard de Walden.*

CUT DIAMOND BHB 68f RR 68f 4667[5]
3 ch g Keen 11.1f **(58)** - Diamond Princess (Horage) 10.3f **(61)**
Form - 33116217625
Record 1998 - 1st:3 2nd:2 3rd:2 Ran:11
Pre1998 - 1st:0 2nd:0 3rd:0 Ran:3
Win Prizemoney £8,040 *Total Prizemoney* £10,895
Wins * **1998** Aug Bath (GD) H 17.2f 67 67 <
* **1998** Jun Folkes (GD) H 16.4f 60 67 <
* **1998** May Mussel (G-F) 14f 59
1998 Turf 3-11: (12f, 14f 1-2, 15f, 16f 1-6, 17f 1-1) (g-s, gd 1-2, g-f 2-6, frm 2)
Workmanlike, average gelding, effective 14 to 17f, best at 16f, acts on gd to frm, has worn blinkers, likes right handed tracks, prefers tight tracks. Turf high 68 - 2nd of 17 to Brodessa (14 Spt Musselburgh 16f frm RF 4254) - also 1st of 14 getting 1lb from Fast Forward Fred (3 Jun Folkestone RF 1690). Sold for 6,800 guineas in October.
**D W P Arbuthnot [3-11] Stephen Crown (from P F I Cole [0-3] Jun 1997).*

CUTE CAROLINE RR 53f 4110[9]
2 ch f First Trump - Hissma (Midyan (USA)) 6f **(60)**
Form - 0
Record 1998 - 1st:0 2nd:0 3rd:0 Ran:1
1998 Turf 0-1: (7f) (frm)
Currently fair filly. **G Holmes [0-1] Murray Grubb.*

CUT THE SPICE RR 61+f 3507[15]
2 b g Suave Dancer (USA) 10.7f **(68)** - No Chili (Glint of Gold) 9.3f **(66)**
Form - 40
Record 1998 - 1st:0 2nd:0 3rd:0 Ran:2
Win Prizemoney £0 *Total Prizemoney* £222
1998 Turf 0-2: (7f 2) (gd, frm)
Currently average gelding. Turf high 61 (began Aug).
**T D Easterby [0-2] M H Easterby.*

CUTTING ANSHAKE BHB 46f60a RR 54f 60a 4917[9]
3 gr g Anshan 8.2f **(63)** - Golden Scissors (Kalaglow) 9.8f **(67)**
Form - 41454630
Record 1998 - 1st:0 2nd:0 3rd:1 Ran:6
Pre1998 - 1st:1 2nd:0 3rd:0 Ran:4
Win Prizemoney £1,998 *Total Prizemoney* £2,687
Wins 1997 *Dec Southw (STD) S 8f 60* <
1998 Turf 0-6: (8f 2, 9f, 10f 2, 15f) (g-s 2, gd, g-f, frm, hrd)
Lengthy, average gelding, effective 8f, acts on hrd - acts on Fibr. Turf high 54 - 4th of 11 giving 5lb to Cherished (6 Jun Newmarket 8f hrd RF 1789).
**Martin Todhunter [2-8] UGM Racing Club (from M R Channon [1-7] Jun 1998).*

CYBERTECHNOLOGY BHB 78f **RR 78df** 4859^{7}
4 b c Environment Friend 7.5f **(67)** - Verchinina (Star Appeal) 9.6f **(65)**
Form - 010562580207
Record 1998 - 1st:1 2nd:2 3rd:0 Ran:12
Pre1998 - 1st:2 2nd:2 3rd:0 Ran:11
Win Prizemoney £16,448 *Total Prizemoney* £24,077
Wins * **1998** Jly Redcar (G-S) H 7f 80 82
1997 Aug Newmar (G-F) H 7f 77 80
1996 Oct York (GD) 7.9f 84 <
1998 Turf 1-12: (7f 1-8, 8f 3, 10f) (sft, gd 1-4, g-f 3, frm 4)
Scopey, above-average colt, effective 7 to 12f, acts on g-s to frm, has worn blinkers. Turf high 82 - 6th of 13 giving 4lb to Wuxi Venture (8 Aug Haydock 8f gd RF 3463) - also 1st of 10 giving 20lb to Rymer's Rascal (1 Jly Redcar RF 2454). Consistent.
**Mrs J Cecil [1-13] E Pick (from B W Hills [2-11] Oct 1997).*

CYBER WORLD (USA) BHB 90f **RR 92f** 4232^{13}
3 b br c Robin Des Pins (USA) 8f **(92)** - Strike Alight (USA) (Gulch (USA)) 8f **(81)**
Form - 4314030
Record 1998 - 1st:1 2nd:0 3rd:2 Ran:7
Win Prizemoney £3,046 *Total Prizemoney* £7,266
Wins * **1998** May Kempto (G-F) 8f 79 <
1998 Turf 1-7: (8f 1-4, 9f, 10f 2) (gd 1-5, frm 2)
Workmanlike, useful colt, effective 10f, acts on frm, has worn blinkers. Turf high 92. Needed every inch of the mile to win his maiden, and ran a cracker in a ten-furlong handicap at York in a first-time visor. He disappointed on his next and final start at Goodwood. He has ability, but looks something of an in-and-out character. **Mrs J Cecil [1-7] Niarchos Family.*

CYBINKA BHB 93f **RR 94f** 4628^{7}
2 ch f Selkirk (USA) 7.9f **(76)** - Sarmatia (USA) (Danzig (USA)) 8.4f **(76)**
Form - 617
Record 1998 - 1st:1 2nd:0 3rd:0 Ran:3
Win Prizemoney £5,251 *Total Prizemoney* £5,251
Wins * **1998** Spt Salisb (GD) 7f 78 <
1998 Turf 1-3: (6f, 7f 1-2) (g-f 1-3)
Currently useful filly. Turf high 94 (began Aug). Comes from a good family and showed promise on her debut before making all to score next time. Suited by cut in the ground. She ran well, but was not good enough when running in a Listed event at Newmarket against the likes of Smittenby and Pipalong. She is bred to stay further and should win races, most likely abroad.
**R Hannon [1-3] Lady Howard de Walden.*

CYCLONE FLYER BHB 72f **RR 69f** 4518^{3}
2 br f College Chapel - Mainly Dry (The Brianstan) 5.9f **(55)**
Form - 683
Record 1998 - 1st:0 2nd:0 3rd:1 Ran:3
Win Prizemoney £0 *Total Prizemoney* £542
1998 Turf 0-3: (5f 3) (g-f, frm 2)
Currently average filly. Turf high 69 (began Aug).
**J Berry [0-3] R Leah.*

CYMBAL MELODY BHB 44f **RR 40f** 5073^{8}
2 b f Merdon Melody 6.8f **(56)** - Cymbal (Ribero) 9.3f **(56)**
Form - 0708
Record 1998 - 1st:0 2nd:0 3rd:0 Ran:4
1998 Turf 0-4: (5f, 7f 2, 8f) (gd 2, frm 2)
Moderate filly. Turf high 39. **J R Jenkins [0-4] Norman Hill.*

CYMMERIAD O GYMRU BHB 60f **RR 67f** 5008^{11}
3 b g Sparky Lad- Fleur Power (IRE)(The Noble Player (USA)) 6.5f **(67)**
Form - 700
Record 1998 - 1st:0 2nd:0 3rd:0 Ran:3
1998 Turf 0-3: (6f 2, 12f) (sft, g-f, frm)
Workmanlike, currently average gelding. Turf high 67 (began Spt).
**B Palling [0-3] Davies and Bridgeman.*

CYNDERS WAY RR 12f 2539^{8}
2 b f Cyrano de Bergerac 7.3f **(58** - Steppey Lane (Tachypous) 8.6f **(55)**
Form - 8
Record 1998 - 1st:0 2nd:0 3rd:0 Ran:1
1998 Turf 0-1: (6f) (g-f)
Currently poor filly. **J Hetherton [0-1] The Highfield Five.*

CYQUINTA BHB 52f **RR 41f** 4612^{18}
2 b f Cyrano de Bergerac 7.3f **(58)** - Lady Quinta (IRE) **(50f 49a)** (Gallic League)
Form - 7060
Record 1998 - 1st:0 2nd:0 3rd:0 Ran:4
1998 Turf 0-4: (5f 3, 6f) (g-s 2, gd, frm)
Moderate filly. Turf high 41. **C A Dwyer [0-4] Cedar Lodge Syndicate.*

CYRANO'S LAD (IRE) BHB 85f **RR 84f** 3464^{8}
9 b or br g Cyrano de Bergerac 7.3f **(58)** - Patiala (Crocket) 6.5f **(112)**
Form - 8017368
Record 1998 - 1st:1 2nd:0 3rd:1 Ran:7
Pre1998 - 1st:6 2nd:3 3rd:3 Ran:31
Win Prizemoney £58,088 *Total Prizemoney* £79,035
Wins * **1998** Jun Sandow (G-S) C 5f 73
1997 May Lingfi (G-F) L 6f 108 <
1997 May Newmar (GD) H 6f 98 102
1996 Jun Cheste (G-F) H 6.1f 91 93
1996 Jun York (GD) H 6f 87 88
1995 Spt Newmar (GD) H 7f 89 94
1995 Jun Lingfi (GD) 7.6f 84
1998 Turf 1-7: (5f 1-4, 6f 3) (gd 1-4, g-f, frm 2)
Decent gelding, effective 5 to 6f, best at 6f, acts on gd to g-f, best on g-f. Turf high 84. Put in a career-best performance when fourth in the Nunthorpe in '97, before his form tailed off. Dropped into a claimer at Sandown for his first win since. Blessed with terrific early speed, it is remarkable to think that he began his racing career in a bumper.
**J E Banks [1-7] M M Foulger (from C A Dwyer [5-26] Spt 1997).*

CYRAN PARK BHB 69f **RR 74f** 4882^{15}
2 b c Cyrano de Bergerac 7.3f **(58)** - Kimberley Park (Try My Best (USA)) 7.6f **(67)**
Form - 060
Record 1998 - 1st:0 2nd:0 3rd:0 Ran:3
1998 Turf 0-3: (6f 3) (g-s, g-f, frm)
Currently above-average colt. Turf high 74 (began Spt) - 6th of 13 getting 1lb from Kangaroo Island (22 Spt Warwick 6f frm RF 4413).
**W Jarvis [0-3] J K Racing.*

CYRIAN (IRE) BHB 90f **RR 92f** 4331^{4}
4 b g Persian Bold 10f **(69)** - Regina St Cyr (IRE) (Doulab (USA)) 9.8f **(65)**
Form - 348104
Record 1998 - 1st:1 2nd:0 3rd:1 Ran:6
Pre1998 - 1st:2 2nd:1 3rd:0 Ran:6
Win Prizemoney £81,735 *Total Prizemoney* £87,892
Wins * **1998** Jun Newcas (SFT) H 16.1f 85 89 <
* 1997 May Newbur (SFT) H 12f 79 85
* 1997 *Mar Wolver (STD) 8.5f 66*
1998 Turf 1-6: (12f, 14f, 16f 1-2, 19f, 20f) (sft 1-2, gd, g-f 2, frm)
Workmanlike, useful gelding, effective 12 to 19f, best at 16f, acts on sft to g-f, best on g-f, prefers left handed tracks, excels at Newbury. Turf high 92 - 4th of 11 giving 3lb to Churlish Charm (17 Spt Newbury 16f g-f RF 4331) - also 1st of 20 giving 3lb to Rainbow Frontier (27 Jun Newcastle RF 2345). Consistent. A game sort, he was stepped up in trip last term and posted useful efforts in the Chester Cup and Ascot Stakes before landing the Northumberland Plate. Cut no ice in the Ebor next time and was done no favours by the winner when already held at Newbury. Likes soft ground and is suited by two miles. He has a bright future ahead hurdling and he is now in the hands of Martin Pipe.
**P F I Cole [3-12] Lord Donoughmore.*

CYRO BHB 59f **RR 72f** 4835^{7}
2 b g Cyrano de Bergerac 7.3f **(58)** - Odile (Green Dancer (USA)) 10.3f **(74)**
Form - 01666507
Record 1998 - 1st:1 2nd:0 3rd:0 Ran:8
Win Prizemoney £3,054 *Total Prizemoney* £3,054
Wins * **1998** Jun Nottin (GD) 5.1f 72 <
1998 Turf 1-7: (5f 1-3, 7f 3, 8f) (g-s, gd 1-1, g-f 2, frm 3) 1998 AW 0-1: (5f) (Fibr)
Above-average gelding, effective 5 to 7f, acts on gd to frm. Turf high 72 (1st run) - 1st of 9 from Luanshya (17 Jun Nottingham RF 2067). Inconsistent. **M A Jarvis [1-8] T G Warner.*

CZAR WARS BHB 56f **RR 57f** 5147[17]
3 b c Warrshan (USA) 9.7f **(59)** - Dutch Czarina (Prince Sabo) 7.2f **(62)**
Form - 00724040020
Record 1998 - 1st:0 2nd:2 3rd:0 Ran:11
Pre1998 - 1st:1 2nd:0 3rd:0 Ran:5
Win Prizemoney £2,319 *Total Prizemoney* £5,613
Wins * 1997 Aug Warwic (G-S) 7f 70 <
1998 Turf 0-11: (6f 4, 7f 4, 8f 3) (g-s, gd 5, g-f 3, frm 2)
Neat, fair colt, effective 7f, acts on g-f, likes left handed tracks, likes tight tracks. Turf high 57. **P T Dalton [1-16] Mrs Julie Martin.*

DAAWE (USA) BHB 78f77a **RR 81f 77a** 4228[12]
7 b h Danzig (USA) 8.1f **(88)** - Capo Di Monte (Final Straw) 7.9f **(64)**
Form - 13010002500
Record 1998 - 1st:2 2nd:1 3rd:1 Ran:11
Pre1998 - 1st:9 2nd:4 3rd:5 Ran:51
Win Prizemoney £45,805 *Total Prizemoney* £58,497
Wins * **1998** May Doncas (GD) 6f 84 <
* **1998** Apr Thirsk (G-S) 5f 77
1997 Jun Redcar (GD) H 6f 75 78
1997 Apr Southw (STD) H 5f 70 75
1996 Jun York (GD) H 6f 63 66
1996 May Southw (STD) H 5f 65 72
1996 May Doncas (G-F) H 6f 56 63
1996 Mar Southw (STD) H 6f 58 57
1996 Jan Southw (STD) H 6f 52 57
1994 Jly Ayr (GD) H 7f 82 83
1994 Jun Ayr (G-S) 7f 39++
1998 Turf 2-10: (5f 1-6, 6f 1-4) (g-s 1-2, gd, g-f 1-3, frm 4) 1998 AW 0-1: (5f) (Fibr)
Decent horse, effective 5 to 6f, best at 6f, acts on g-s to frm - acts on Fibr, best on g-f, often wears blinkers (extremely effectively), excels at Newmarket. Turf high 84 - 1st of 10 giving 15lb to Demolition Jo (23 May Doncaster RF 1411) - also 1st of 7 giving 3lb to Jennelle (17 Apr Thirsk RF 0738). Inconsistent. A very tough and genuine sprinter who races regularly, he is capable of showing plenty of early speed in his races, and made a winning debut for his new stable at Thirsk in May. Mixed form since. He is equally effective on both turf and Fibresand.
**J A Glover [2-14] Mrs Andrea Mallinson (from Mrs V A Aconley [7-41] Aug 1997).*

DABAYA (IRE) RR 113+f 3011a[2]
3 b f In The Wings 11.2f **(77)** - Dabiliya (Vayrann) 9.7f **(74)**
Form - 1252
1998 Turf 1-4: (10f 1-2, 12f, 14f) (g-s, gd 1-2, g-f)
Group-class filly. Turf high 113 (1st run) - 1st of 8 from Star Begonia (13 May Navan RF 1338a). She is extremely attractive and looked destined for the top after chasing Risk Material home in a Listed event at The Curragh in May. Disappointing on both her subsequent starts, she seemed to find the mile-and-a-half trip a bit too far in the Ribblesdale. She may have been weaker than paddock inspection suggested and can improve significantly over the winter. **J Oxx in IRE [1-4] H H Aga Khan.*

DA BOSS BHB 65f **RR 68f** 4150[4]
3 ch c Be My Chief (USA) 10.2f **(62)** - Lady Kris (IRE) (Kris) 9.5f **(73)**
Form - 833374
Record 1998 - 1st:0 2nd:0 3rd:3 Ran:6
Pre1998 - 1st:0 2nd:0 3rd:1 Ran:5
Win Prizemoney £0 *Total Prizemoney* £2,053
1998 Turf 0-6: (7f, 8f, 10f 2, 11f, 12f) (g-s, g-f 3, frm 2)
Scopey, average colt, effective 7 to 12f, acts on g-f to frm, best on frm. Turf high 68 - 3rd of 6 getting 2lb from Dancing Rio (17 May Ripon 12f frm RF 1289). Consistent. He ran a most promising race on his debut at Windsor, but was well beaten subsequently albeit against potentially smart opposition on one occasion.
**W R Muir [0-11] R Haim.*

DABUS BHB 97f **RR 84f** 3972[3]
3 b c Kris 10f **(75)** - Licorne (Sadler's Wells (USA)) 10f **(76)**
Form - 313
Record 1998 - 1st:1 2nd:0 3rd:2 Ran:3
Win Prizemoney £3,598 *Total Prizemoney* £5,210
Wins * **1998** Jly Sandow (G-F) 10f 84+ <
1998 Turf 1-3: (10f 1-2, 12f) (g-f, frm 1-2)
Well made, currently decent colt. Turf high 84 (began Jly) - 1st of 11 from Ionian Spring (22 Jly Sandown RF 3035). Promise in middle-distance maidens. **H R A Cecil [1-3] Lord Howard de Walden.*

DACHA (IRE) BHB 84f **RR 99?f** 5151[23]
6 b g Soviet Star (USA) 8.6f **(74)** - Shadywood (Habitat) 9.4f **(70)**
Form - 0
Record 1998 - 1st:0 2nd:0 3rd:0 Ran:1
Pre1998 - 1st:2 2nd:1 3rd:2 Ran:7
Win Prizemoney £11,911 *Total Prizemoney* £21,629
Wins 1996 Spt Haydoc (G-F) H 11.9f 91 95 <
1996 Jly Pontef (G-F) 12f 79
1998 Turf 0-1: (12f) (gd)
Very useful gelding. He has been very difficult to train and has appeared only once since 1996, when he showed useful form in handicap company.
**Miss M E Rowland [0-1] Mrs Nicky Chambers (from H R A Cecil [2-7] Spt 1996).*

DACIAN (USA) BHB 46f **RR 49f** 3690[11]
3 b f Diesis 9f **(80)** - Barb's Lass (USA) (Seattle Slew (USA)) 9.4f **(76)**
Form - 0000
Record 1998 - 1st:0 2nd:0 3rd:0 Ran:4
1998 Turf 0-4: (6f, 7f, 8f 2) (gd 2, frm 2)
Light-framed, moderate filly. Turf high 41.
**I A Balding [0-4] G D Hawkins and J J McEntee.*

DAD'S KEY BHB 52f **RR 50f** 4671[26]
2 b g Then Again 7.4f **(52)** - Silverdale Rose (Nomination) 7f **(60)**
Form - 0000
Record 1998 - 1st:0 2nd:0 3rd:0 Ran:4
1998 Turf 0-4: (5f 2, 7f 2) (gd, g-f 2, frm)
Fair gelding. Turf high 50 (began Spt).
**M W Easterby [0-4] M W Easterby.*

DAFFODIL EXPRESS (IRE) BHB 37f20a **RR 8f 20a** 249[8]
5 b m Skyliner 6.8f **(51)** - Miss Henry (Blue Cashmere) 6.4f **(54)**
Form - 08
Record 1998 - 1st:0 2nd:0 3rd:0 Ran:1
Pre1998 - 1st:0 2nd:0 3rd:0 Ran:14
Win Prizemoney £0 *Total Prizemoney* £485
1998 AW 0-1: (16f) (Fibr)
Very poor filly, has worn blinkers. **M J Ryan [0-19] M J Ryan.*

DAGGERS DRAWN (USA) BHB 116f **RR 113df** 974[18]
3 ch c Diesis 9f **(80)** - Sun and Shade (Ajdal (USA)) 9.2f **(89)**
Form - 50
Record 1998 - 1st:0 2nd:0 3rd:0 Ran:2
Pre1998 - 1st:3 2nd:0 3rd:0 Ran:4
Win Prizemoney £85,041 *Total Prizemoney* £87,295
Wins * 1997 Spt Doncas (G-F) G2 7f 113 <
* 1997 Jly Goodwo (G-F) G2 6f 110+
* 1997 Jly Newmar (GD) 6f 93++
1998 Turf 0-2: (8f 2) (gd 2)
Well made, Group-class colt, effective 6 to 7f, acts on gd. Turf high 107. He ran as though something was amiss in the Dewhurst Stakes on his final juvenile start, and showed nothing as a three-year-old. This looks a classic case of a horse who simply failed to train on. **H R A Cecil [3-6] Cliveden Stud.*

DAHABIAH BHB 57f **RR 60f** 2677[4]
4 ch f Soviet Star (USA) 8.6f **(74)**- Queen Midas (Glint of Gold) 9.3f **(66)**
Form - 474
Record 1998 - 1st:0 2nd:0 3rd:0 Ran:3
Win Prizemoney £0 *Total Prizemoney* £546
1998 Turf 0-3: (6f, 8f 2) (gd, frm 2)
Workmanlike, currently average filly. Turf high 60 - 4th of 6 giving 9lb to Akarita (10 Jly Chester 8f frm RF 2677).
**M Kettle [0-3] Umm Qarn Racing.*

DAHIYAH (USA) BHB 53f48a **RR 51f 48a** 114[12]
7 b g Ogygian (USA) 6.6f **(65)** - Sticky Prospect (USA) (Mr Prospector (USA)) 8.8f **(78)**
Form - 0
Record 1998 - 1st:0 2nd:0 3rd:0 Ran:1
Pre1998 - 1st:4 2nd:2 3rd:4 Ran:32
Win Prizemoney £12,418 *Total Prizemoney* £15,548
Wins * 1997 *Jan Southw (STD) C 7f 52*
1996 Jun Goodwo (G-F) SH 6f 60 64 <

1996 *Jan Lingfi (STD) H 6f 54 58*
1995 May Bright (FRM) H 6f 53 61
1998 AW 0-1: (7f) (Fibr)
Fair gelding, effective 7f, - acts on Fibr, mostly wears blinkers, prefers left handed tracks, prefers tight tracks. Consistent.
**B Smart [1-7] W Clifford (from D L Williams [0-4] Oct 1996).*

DAHLIDYA BHB 37f46a **RR 20f 46a** 5127[13]
3 b f Midyan (USA) 9.9f **(64)** -Dahlawise(IRE)(Caerleon (USA)) 8.6f **(71)**
Form - 741830500000
Record 1998 - 1st:1 2nd:0 3rd:1 Ran:12
Pre1998 - 1st:0 2nd:0 3rd:0 Ran:3
Win Prizemoney £3,387 *Total Prizemoney* £4,058
Wins * **1998** *Feb Wolver (STD) H 5f 39 52* <
1998 Turf 0-6: (5f, 6f 3, 7f, 8f) (g-s 2, gd, g-f, frm 2) 1998 AW 1-6: (5f 1-1, 6f 2, 7f 2, 8f) (Equi 3, Fibr 1-3)
Tall, fair filly, effective 5f, - acts on Fibr, likes tight tracks. Turf high 35. AW high 52 - 1st of 7 getting 14lb from Phantom Ring (18 Feb Wolverhampton RF 0310). Inconsistent. She caused an upset when winning a handicap on the Wolverhampton in February, but the rest of her form is modest.
**M J Polglase [1-15] Gen Sir Geoffrey Howlett.*

DAHOMEY (USA) BHB 80f **RR 69f** 1719[8]
3 b br c Dayjur (USA) 6.8f **(79)** - Dish Dash (Bustino) 10.4f **(64)**
Form - 38
Record 1998 - 1st:0 2nd:0 3rd:1 Ran:2
Pre1998 - 1st:0 2nd:0 3rd:0 Ran:1
Win Prizemoney £0 *Total Prizemoney* £1,674
1998 Turf 0-2: (8f 2) (hvy, frm)
Workmanlike, currently average colt. Turf high 69. He was a well-beaten third of four in heavy ground at Kempton on his reappearance. Sold for just 600 gns in the autumn.
**C E Brittain [0-3] Saeed Manana.*

DA HOSS (USA) RR 131f 5165a[1]
6 b g Gone West (USA) 7.8f **(82)** - Jolly Saint (USA)
Form - 1
1998 Turf 1-1: (8f 1-1) (frm 1-1)
Currently high-calibre gelding. (1st run) - 1st of 14 from Hawksley Hill (7 Nov Churchill Downs RF 5165a). Landed his second Breeders' Cup Mile, injury having restricted him to just one prep run since his victory at Woodbine. If any trainer deserves the epithet 'genius' it is Michael Dickinson.
**M W Dickinson in USA [2-3] Prestonwood Farm Inc.*

DAHSHAH BHB 82f **RR 78f** 4316[3]
2 ch f Mujtahid (USA) 7.4f **(69)** - Rawaabe (USA) (Nureyev (USA)) 8.7f **(78)**
Form - 623
Record 1998 - 1st:0 2nd:1 3rd:1 Ran:3
Win Prizemoney £0 *Total Prizemoney* £1,862
1998 Turf 0-3: (5f, 6f 2) (gd, frm 2)
Currently above-average filly. Turf high 78 (began Aug).
**B W Hills [0-3] Hamdan Al Maktoum.*

DAINTREE (IRE) BHB 58f45a **RR 59f 45a** 4760[7]
4 b f Tirol 8.1f **(64)** - Aunty Eileen (Ahonoora) 8.1f **(73)**
Form - 26602472122837
Record 1998 - 1st:1 2nd:4 3rd:1 Ran:12
Pre1998 - 1st:0 2nd:1 3rd:5 Ran:16
Win Prizemoney £3,062 *Total Prizemoney* £12,592
Wins * **1998** Aug Windso (G-F) H 8.3f 49 47 <
1998 Turf 1-12: (6f, 7f 4, 8f 1-7) (g-s, gd 3, g-f 4, frm 1-3, hrd)
Leggy, fair filly, effective 7 to 8f, best at 8f, acts on g-f to hrd, has worn blinkers, prefers right handed tracks, excels at Yarmouth and Windsor. Turf high 59 - 2nd of 12 getting 14lb from Scent of Success (29 Aug Windsor 8f g-f RF 3975).
**H J Collingridge [1-28] G B Amy.*

DAINTY DISH (IRE) BHB 37f **RR 53f** 5073[19]
2 ch f Nucleon (USA) - Thornhaven (IRE) (Doulab (USA)) 9.8f **(65)**
Form - 70070
Record 1998 - 1st:0 2nd:0 3rd:0 Ran:5
1998 Turf 0-4: (7f 2, 8f 2) (hvy, sft, gd, g-f) 1998 AW 0-1: (8f) (Fibr)
Fair filly. Turf high 53.
**P Eccles [0-2] M Sawers (from I Semple [0-1] Spt 1998).*

DAIRA BHB 46f **RR 49f** 2928[14]
5 br m Daring March 9f **(54)** - Ile de Reine (Ile de Bourbon (USA)) 10.1f **(67)**
Form - 0620
Record 1998 - 1st:0 2nd:1 3rd:0 Ran:4
Pre1998 - 1st:1 2nd:4 3rd:4 Ran:22
Win Prizemoney £2,658 *Total Prizemoney* £11,448
Wins 1996 May Catter (GD) 12f 50 <
1998 Turf 0-4: (8f, 9f, 10f, 12f) (g-s, gd, frm 2)
Moderate filly, effective 11 to 12f, best at 12f, acts on g-f to frm, best on frm, has worn blinkers, prefers left handed tracks. Turf high 49. Inconsistent.
**B Ellison [0-4] Ronald McCulloch (from J D Bethell [1-22] Oct 1997).*

DAISY FAY BHB 34f **RR 36f** 3402[10]
3 b f Broadsword (USA) - Lily of the West (True Song)
Form - 0000
Record 1998 - 1st:0 2nd:0 3rd:0 Ran:4
1998 Turf 0-4: (6f, 7f 2, 8f) (gd, frm 3)
Unfurnished, very moderate filly. Turf high 36.
**T D McCarthy [0-4] Mrs J H M Mackenzie.*

DALAAUNA RR 61+f 5064[6]
2 ch f Cadeaux Genereux 7.9f **(76)** - Gunner's Belle (Gunner B) 11.2f **(58)**
Form - 6
Record 1998 - 1st:0 2nd:0 3rd:0 Ran:1
1998 Turf 0-1: (6f) (g-f)
Currently average filly. **J H M Gosden [0-1] Nabil Mourad.*

DALBY OF YORK BHB 55f **RR 56f** 4663[15]
2 ch g Polar Falcon (USA) 9f **(74)** - Miller's Creek (USA) (Star de Naskra (USA)) 9.7f **(65)**
Form - 00040
Record 1998 - 1st:0 2nd:0 3rd:0 Ran:5
Win Prizemoney £0 *Total Prizemoney* £495
1998 Turf 0-5: (6f 3, 8f, 10f) (g-s, g-f, frm 3)
Fair gelding. Turf high 56 (began Jly).
**P F I Cole [0-5] Richard Green (Fine Paintings).*

DALE FOREST (IRE) RR 30f 3934[14]
2 ch f Forest Wind (USA) - Jolly Dale (IRE) (Huntingdale)
Form - 00
Record 1998 - 1st:0 2nd:0 3rd:0 Ran:2
1998 Turf 0-2: (7f 2) (g-f, frm)
Currently very moderate filly. Turf high 30 (began Jly).
**J Parkes [0-2] Mrs Lynn Parkes.*

DALERIVER BHB 37f45a **RR 34f 45a** 1397[P]
7 ch g Never so Bold 7.1f **(62)** - Omnia (Hill Clown (USA)) 9.3f **(67)**
Form - 0605P
Record 1998 - 1st:0 2nd:0 3rd:0 Ran:5
Pre1998 - 1st:0 2nd:1 3rd:1 Ran:8
Win Prizemoney £0 *Total Prizemoney* £2,280
1998 Turf 0-3: (7f, 9f, 10f) (sft, gd, frm) 1998 AW 0-2: (7f, 12f) (Fibr 2)
Very moderate gelding. Turf high 34. (DEAD)
**R Bastiman [0-5] I B Barker (from J Hanson [0-8] Jly 1994).*

DALI RR 64f 4992[4]
3 b g Rock City 8.8f **(62)** - Supreme Kingdom (Take A Reef) 7.5f **(59)**
Form - 34
Record 1998 - 1st:0 2nd:0 3rd:1 Ran:2
Win Prizemoney £0 *Total Prizemoney* £905
1998 Turf 0-2: (7f 2) (sft, frm)
Workmanlike, currently average gelding. Turf high 64 (began Spt).
**B J Meehan [0-2] J R Good.*

DALIAPOUR (IRE) BHB 100f **RR 98+f** 4738[1]
2 b c Sadler's Wells (USA) 11.3f **(87)** - Dalara (IRE) **(113f)** (Doyoun) 9f **(69)**
Form - 6131
Record 1998 - 1st:2 2nd:0 3rd:1 Ran:4
Win Prizemoney £16,050 *Total Prizemoney* £17,734
Wins * **1998** Oct Ascot (SFT) L 8f 98+ <
* **1998** Aug Chepst (G-F) 8.1f 76
1998 Turf 2-4: (7f, 8f 2-3) (g-s 1-1, gd 1-2, g-f)
Very useful colt. Turf high 98 (began Jly) - 1st of 7 from Boatman

(10 Oct Ascot RF 4738). A plain individual, without substance, he did not look fully wound up for his debut, and benefited from that run when scoring over a mile at Chepstow on his next start. Not disgraced at Newbury next time, he put up a tremendous display in gruelling conditions at Ascot on his final start, as he made virtually all and forged clear in the final quarter of a mile to win with plenty up his sleeve. He has a middle-distance pedigree, and will be suited by even further in time. Looks a useful prospect.
**L M Cumani [2-4] H H Aga Khan.*

DALLIMORE BANKES RR 5f 2294[7]

2 b g Keen 11.1f **(58)** - Run for Love (Runnett) 7f **(59)**
Form - 007
Record 1998 - 1st:0 2nd:0 3rd:0 Ran:3
1998 Turf 0-2: (5f 2) (g-f 2) 1998 AW 0-1: (5f) (Fibr)
Currently very moderate gelding. Turf high 5.
**W G M Turner [0-3] T Lightbowne.*

DALLY BOY BHB 44f45a RR 45f 45a 2899[2]

6 b g Efisio 7.7f **(69)** - Gay Hostess (FR) (Direct Flight) 13.1f **(51)**
Form - 5451261472
Record 1998 - 1st:2 2nd:2 3rd:0 Ran:10
Pre1998 - 1st:0 2nd:1 3rd:0 Ran:15
Win Prizemoney £5,295 *Total Prizemoney* £8,832
Wins * 1998 Jun Mussel (SFT) H 14f 40 45 <
*** 1998** May Mussel (GD) H 16f 35 39
1998 Turf 2-8: (14f 1-1, 16f 1-6, 22f) (g-s, gd 2-6, frm) 1998 AW 0-2: (14f 2) (Fibr 2)
Moderate gelding, effective 14 to 16f, best at 14f, acts on gd - acts on Fibr, has worn blinkers. Turf high 45 - 1st of 10 getting 3lb from Kilnamartyra Girl (15 Jun Musselburgh RF 1997) - also 1st of 13 getting 19lb from All On (6 May Musselburgh RF 1065). AW high 45 - 2nd of 10 giving 12lb to Makati (17 Jly Southwell 14f Fibr RF 2899).
**T D Easterby [3-30] T H Bennett (from M H Easterby [0-14] Nov 1995).*

DALWHINNIE BHB 54f50a RR 55f 50a 5069[2]

5 b m Persian Bold 10f **(69)** - Land Line (High Line) 10.3f **(70)**
Form - 02170012
Record 1998 - 1st:2 2nd:2 3rd:0 Ran:7
Pre1998 - 1st:0 2nd:1 3rd:2 Ran:16
Win Prizemoney £4,155 *Total Prizemoney* £9,587
Wins * 1998 Oct Yarmou (SFT) C 14.1f 47
*** 1998** *Jan Southw (STD) 12f 51+* <
1998 Turf 1-3: (12f 2, 14f 1-1) (g-s 1-1, gd, g-f) 1998 AW 1-4: (11f, 12f 1-2, 16f) (Fibr 1-4)
Fair filly, effective 12f, acts on gd to g-f, best on gd, has worn blinkers. Turf high 55 (began Oct) - 2nd of 13 giving 2lb to Children's Choice (30 Oct Newmarket 12f g-f RF 5069). AW high 51.
**J Wharton [2-13] Ibra Racing Company (from J W Hills [0-10] Nov 1996).*

DAMALIS (IRE) BHB 94f RR 86f 4322[6]

2 b f Mukaddamah (USA) 7.6f **(74)** - Art Age (Artaius (USA)) 9f **(69)**
Form - 321434166
Record 1998 - 1st:2 2nd:1 3rd:2 Ran:9
Win Prizemoney £11,775 *Total Prizemoney* £18,323
Wins * 1998 Spt Ripon (SFT) 5f 86 <
*** 1998** May Cheste (G-F) 5.1f 86 <
1998 Turf 2-9: (5f 2-8, 6f) (sft, g-s, gd 1-3, g-f 1-3, frm)
Useful filly, effective 5f, acts on sft to g-f. Turf high 86 - also 1st of 10 from Kalidasa (7 May Chester RF 1073). Consistent. She took a Chester maiden in game style at the big May meeting, but was just found out when taking on decent company.
**E J Alston [2-9] Liam Ferguson.*

DAME JUDE BHB 77f RR 78f 4857[18]

2 ch f Dilum (USA) 7.1f **(56)** - Three Lucky (IRE) (Final Straw) 7.9f **(64)**
Form - 5145741400
Record 1998 - 1st:2 2nd:0 3rd:0 Ran:10
Win Prizemoney £5,724 *Total Prizemoney* £6,976
Wins * 1998 Aug Sandow (G-F) 5f 78 <
*** 1998** Apr Bright (GD) 5.3f 67
1998 Turf 2-10: (5f 2-5, 6f 4, 7f) (sft, g-s 1-1, gd 5, g-f 1-1, frm 2)
Above-average filly, effective 5f, acts on g-f. Turf high 78 - 1st of 7 getting 5lb from Hyphen (12 Aug Sandown RF 3594). Inconsistent. She won an ordinary race at Brighton, but was then a little too highly tried before landing an auction event at Sandown.
**W R Muir [2-10] Stableside Racing Partnership.*

DANCE MELODY BHB 25f29a RR 28f 29a 1456[13]

4 b f Rambo Dancer (CAN) 8.4f **(59)** - Cateryne (Ballymoss) 8.5f **(55)**
Form - 0
Record 1998 - 1st:0 2nd:0 3rd:0 Ran:1
Pre1998 - 1st:0 2nd:0 3rd:0 Ran:11
1998 Turf 0-1: (7f) (gd)
Unfurnished, little account filly, has worn blinkers. Inconsistent.
**G R Oldroyd [0-15] C J Nunn.*

DANCER AND SON RR 107f 4073a[2]

3 b c Suave Dancer (USA) 10.7f **(68)** - Caraniya (Darshaan) 9.9f **(84)**
Form - 2
1998 Turf 0-1: (12f) (sft)
Currently Pattern-class colt. (1st run) - 2nd of 8 getting 3lb from Copeland (26 Aug Clairefontaine 12f sft RF 4073a). He is capable of winning a Listed race judged on his performance against Smart Squall at Clairefontaine in August. **in FR [0-1].*

DANCER SHAREEF RR 93f 1734a[14]

3 c
Form - 00
1998 Turf 0-2: (8f, 12f) (gd, g-f)
Currently useful colt. Turf high 91. **P Guarsegnati in ITY [0-2].*

DANCE SO SUITE BHB 96f80a RR 102f 80a 4688a[6]

6 b g Shareef Dancer (USA) 10.1f **(67)** - Three Piece (Jaazeiro (USA)) 9.2f **(54)**
Form - 56
1998 Turf 0-2: (12f, 16f) (g-s, gd)
Very useful gelding, effective 12f, acts on gd to g-f, best on gd. Turf high 102 (1st run) - 5th of 11 giving 10lb to Winged Hussar (24 May Curragh 12f gd RF 1514a).
**E J O'Grady in IRE [4-6] J S Gutkin (from P F I Cole [5-29] Oct 1997).*

DANCETHENIGHTAWAY BHB 97f RR 103f 4975[8]

4 gr f Efisio 7.7f **(69)** - Dancing Diana (Raga Navarro (ITY)) 8f **(64)**
Form - 84502005858
Record 1998 - 1st:0 2nd:1 3rd:0 Ran:11
Pre1998 - 1st:3 2nd:3 3rd:3 Ran:18
Win Prizemoney £29,070 *Total Prizemoney* £57,160
Wins * 1997 Oct Ascot (HVY) H 5f 89 93 <
* 1997 May Cheste (SFT) H 5.1f 84 90
* 1996 Aug Bath (GD) 5.1f 74
1998 Turf 0-11: (5f 7, 6f 4) (sft, g-s, gd 5, g-f 3, frm)
Light-framed, very useful filly, effective 5 to 6f, best at 6f, acts on sft to frm, has worn blinkers. Turf high 103 - 5th of 7 to Lidanna (1 Jun Leopardstown 5f frm RF 1839a). She can get on her toes in the preliminaries, but that trait did not prevent her from running an excellent second in the Wokingham Handicap at Royal Ascot. Very free in first-time blinkers at Newmarket in October, she seemed to resent the blinds at Doncaster later that month and may be best without them. **B J Meehan [3-29] G A Bosley.*

DANCE TO THE BEAT BHB 47f55a RR 40f 55a 2449[8]

3 b f Batshoof 9.5f **(66)** - Woodleys (Tyrnavos) 10.1f **(55)**
Form - 614702068
Record 1998 - 1st:0 2nd:1 3rd:0 Ran:6
Pre1998 - 1st:1 2nd:1 3rd:0 Ran:8
Win Prizemoney £1,998 *Total Prizemoney* £3,382
Wins * 1997 *Dec Wolver (STD) S 6f 60* <
1998 Turf 0-5: (6f, 7f 4) (gd 3, g-f, frm) 1998 AW 0-1: (7f) (Equi)
Workmanlike, average filly, effective 6 to 8f, - acts on Fibr, has worn blinkers, likes left handed tracks, likes tight tracks. Turf high 50. Inconsistent. **M Meade [1-14] The Country Life Partnership.*

DANCIN' DOLL BHB 65f RR 71f 4664[7]

2 ch f Grand Lodge (USA) - Tisza (Kris) 9.5f **(73)**
Form - 607
Record 1998 - 1st:0 2nd:0 3rd:0 Ran:3
1998 Turf 0-3: (7f, 8f 2) (g-s, gd, frm)
Currently above-average filly. Turf high 71 (began Spt).
**J J O'Neill [0-3] Clayton Bigley Partnership Ltd.*

DANCING AL BHB 36f **RR 39f** 3734[11]
3 br g Alnasr Alwasheek 9.4f **(62)** - Lyne Dancer (Be My Native (USA)) 10.2f **(71)**
Form - 600
Record 1998 - 1st:0 2nd:0 3rd:0 Ran:3
Pre1998 - 1st:0 2nd:0 3rd:0 Ran:4
1998 Turf 0-3: (8f 2, 9f) (g-f 2, frm)
Neat, very moderate gelding. Turf high 39 (began Jly).
**J S Moore [0-7] Miss L D Martin.*

DANCING-ALONE BHB 37f37a **RR 37a** 3830[3]
6 ch g Adbass (USA) 12.2f **(45)** - Lady Alone (Mr Fluorocarbon) 6f **(55)**
Form - 3
Record 1998 - 1st:0 2nd:0 3rd:1 Ran:1
Pre1998 - 1st:0 2nd:1 3rd:0 Ran:4
Win Prizemoney £0 *Total Prizemoney* £910
1998 AW 0-1: (12f) (Fibr)
Fair gelding. He has had his problems, but ran well on Fibresand at the start of '97 after two years off, and again in August of this year after eighteen months' absence. If he can be kept sound, there are middle-distance races to be won with him on sand during the winter.
**D Morris [0-1] Miss June Frankham (from R J R Williams [0-1] Feb 1997).*

DANCING CAVALIER BHB 62f54a **RR 59f 54a** 4987[3]
5 b g Nalchik (USA) 12.6f **(44)**- Miss Admington(Double Jump) 9.4f **(58)**
Form - 3
Record 1998 - 1st:0 2nd:0 3rd:1 Ran:1
Pre1998 - 1st:6 2nd:5 3rd:8 Ran:42
Win Prizemoney £18,627 *Total Prizemoney* £28,073
Wins * 1997 Jun Warwic (GD) H 14.9f 59 62
* 1997 Jun Nottin (GD) H 14.1f 59 65
* 1997 Apr Nottin (G-F) H 14.1f 65 74+ <
* 1997 Mar Catter (GD) H 13.8f 58 69
* 1996 *Feb Southw (STD) H 11f 59 61*
* 1996 *Jan Southw (STD) H 8f 52 61*
1998 Turf 0-1: (12f) (sft)
Average gelding, effective 14 to 16f, best at 14f, acts on gd to g-f, best on gd, has worn blinkers, prefers left handed tracks, excels at Catterick and Nottingham. **R Hollinshead [6-43] The Three R's.*

DANCING DERVISH BHB 73f **RR 59f** 4402[17]
3 b g Shareef Dancer (USA) 10.1f **(67)** - Taj Victory (Final Straw) 7.9f **(64)**
Form - 2007205310
Record 1998 - 1st:1 2nd:2 3rd:1 Ran:10
Pre1998 - 1st:0 2nd:0 3rd:0 Ran:2
Win Prizemoney £2,913 *Total Prizemoney* £5,122
Wins * **1998** Aug Bright (G-F) H 8f 55 59 <
1998 Turf 1-10: (7f 3, 8f 1-3, 10f 3, 12f) (g-s, gd 4, g-f, frm 1-4)
Workmanlike, fair gelding, effective 7f, acts on gd, has worn blinkers (effectively). Turf high 72 (1st run) - 2nd of 8 to Stanott (7 Apr Folkestone 7f gd RF 0581). He took a long time in getting off the mark, but whirled home in a Brighton handicap in August.
**I A Balding [1-12] Miss A V Hill.*

DANCING DESTINY BHB 41f45a **RR 40f 45a** 3968[7]
6 b m Dancing Brave (USA) 10.4f **(78)** - Tender Loving Care (Final Straw) 7.9f **(64)**
Form - 36214022787027
Record 1998 - 1st:1 2nd:4 3rd:0 Ran:12
Pre1998 - 1st:0 2nd:4 3rd:1 Ran:18
Win Prizemoney £3,035 *Total Prizemoney* £10,355
Wins * **1998** *Jan Southw (STD) H 8f 42 45* <
1998 Turf 0-6: (8f 2, 9f, 11f, 12f 2) (g-s 2, g-f 4) 1998 AW 1-6: (8f 1-6) (Fibr 1-6)
Moderate mare, effective 8 to 12f, best at 8f, acts on g-f - acts on Fibr, favours left handed tracks, favours tight tracks. Turf high 40. AW high 47 - 2nd of 10 getting 6lb from Lucky Begonia (23 Mar Southwell 8f Fibr RF 0463) - also 1st of 8 giving 18lb to Palacegate Jo (26 Jan Southwell RF 0161).
**R Bastiman [1-25] I B Barker (from J R Fanshawe [0-5] Jun 1995).*

DANCING EM BHB 52f43a **RR 55f 43a** 4373[14]
3 b f Rambo Dancer (CAN) 8.4f **(59)** - Militia Girl (Rarity) 10.1f **(60)**
Form - 0443025112000
Record 1998 - 1st:2 2nd:2 3rd:1 Ran:13
Pre1998 - 1st:0 2nd:0 3rd:1 Ran:6
Win Prizemoney £5,247 *Total Prizemoney* £8,264
Wins * **1998** Aug Carlis (G-S) 6.9f 50 <
* **1998** Jly Thirsk (FRM) SH 8f 42 47
1998 Turf 2-12: (6f, 7f 1-4, 8f 1-7) (gd 1-5, g-f 2, frm 1-5) 1998 AW 0-1: (8f) (Fibr)
Leggy, fair filly, effective 7 to 8f, best at 8f, acts on gd to frm, best on frm, has worn blinkers, likes left handed tracks, likes tight tracks. Turf high 55 - 2nd of 8 getting 14lb from Gaily Mill (10 Aug Thirsk 8f frm RF 3509) - also 1st of 14 getting 6lb from Sycamore Lodge (3 Aug Carlisle RF 3308). **T D Easterby [2-19] D B Lamplough.*

DANCING FEATHER BHB 60f53a **RR 60f 53a** 3316[P]
4 ch f Suave Dancer (USA) 10.7f **(68)** - English Spring (USA) (Grey Dawn II) 11.1f **(72)**
Form - 01365P
Record 1998 - 1st:1 2nd:0 3rd:1 Ran:5
Pre1998 - 1st:0 2nd:0 3rd:1 Ran:7
Win Prizemoney £2,374 *Total Prizemoney* £3,486
Wins * **1998** Jun Bath (G-S) H 8f 57 60 <
1998 Turf 1-4: (8f 1-3, 10f) (gd 1-2, frm 2) 1998 AW 0-1: (8f) (Fibr)
Scopey, average filly, effective 8f, acts on gd, has worn blinkers, likes left handed tracks. Turf high 60 (1st run) - 1st of 17 giving 5lb to Aficionado (13 Jun Bath RF 1952).
**B W Hills [1-12] Mrs H Theodorou.*

DANCING GISELLE (IRE) RR 41f 3642[9]
2 b f Dancing Dissident (USA) 6.8f **(65)** - Lady Bidder (Auction Ring (USA)) 8.6f **(65)**
Form - 0070
Record 1998 - 1st:0 2nd:0 3rd:0 Ran:4
1998 Turf 0-3: (6f 3) (g-f, frm 2) 1998 AW 0-1: (5f) (Fibr)
Moderate filly. Turf high 41. **M Blanshard [0-4] J J Amass.*

DANCING GREY BHB 36f **RR 36f** 1902[8]
3 gr g Petong 7.6f **(58)** - Mountain Harvest (FR) (Shirley Heights) 10.3f **(74)**
Form - 607008
Record 1998 - 1st:0 2nd:0 3rd:0 Ran:5
Pre1998 - 1st:0 2nd:0 3rd:0 Ran:2
1998 Turf 0-4: (12f 2, 14f 2) (g-s, gd, frm 2) 1998 AW 0-1: (8f) (Fibr)
Strong, fair gelding, often wears blinkers. Turf high 36.
**P W Harris [0-7] The Mountaineers.*

DANCING JACK BHB 37f30a **RR 44f 30a** 4455[6]
5 ch g Clantime 6.6f **(57)** - Sun Follower (Relkino) 8.9f **(65)**
Form - 0060506
Record 1998 - 1st:0 2nd:0 3rd:0 Ran:7
Pre1998 - 1st:1 2nd:3 3rd:3 Ran:33
Win Prizemoney £2,211 *Total Prizemoney* £7,038
Wins * 1995 *Nov Lingfi (STD) H 5f 49 53* <
1998 Turf 0-6: (5f 5, 6f) (g-f, frm 4, hrd) 1998 AW 0-1: (8f) (Equi)
Moderate gelding, effective 5f, acts on hrd, has worn blinkers. Turf high 44. **J J Bridger [1-40] Mrs J M Stamp.*

DANCING KING (IRE) RR 52f 5138[8]
2 b c Fairy King (USA) 7.7f **(75)** - Zariysha (IRE) (Darshaan) 9.9f **(84)**
Form - 8
Record 1998 - 1st:0 2nd:0 3rd:0 Ran:1
1998 Turf 0-1: (7f) (gd)
Currently fair colt. **L M Cumani [0-1] M J Dawson.*

DANCING KRIS RR 100f 1088a[7]
5
Form - 7
1998 Turf 0-1: (8f) (g-s)
Currently very useful. **Mme C Head in FR [0-1].*

DANCING LAWYER BHB 51f47a **RR 56f 47a** 4920[3]
7 b g Thowra (FR) 11.2f **(47)** - Miss Lawsuit (Neltino) 7.6f **(54)**
Form - 7112040403
Record 1998 - 1st:2 2nd:1 3rd:1 Ran:10
Pre1998 - 1st:5 2nd:5 3rd:8 Ran:58
Win Prizemoney £19,446 *Total Prizemoney* £35,350
Wins 1998 May Warwic (GD) H 8f 44 56
1998 Apr Bright (GD) H 8f 44 52

1996 *Jan Lingfi (STD) C 8f 81 <*
1995 *Nov Lingfi (STD) H 8f 73 78*
1994 *Dec Lingfi (STD) H 7f 69 71*
1994 May Bright (G-F) H 8f 70 73

1998 Turf 2-9: (7f, 8f 2-7, 9f) (g-s, gd 1-3, g-f 1-2, frm 3) 1998 AW 0-1: (8f) (Equi)

Fair gelding, effective 7 to 8f, best at 8f, acts on g-s to frm, has worn blinkers, likes left handed tracks, likes tight tracks, does well at Brighton. Turf high 59 - 2nd of 11 getting 4lb from Monica's Choice (8 May Carlisle 7f gd RF 1096) - also 1st of 20 getting 7lb from Simlet (4 May Warwick RF 1031).

**B Ellison [0-1] Brian Ellison Racing Club (from K R Burke [2-14] Spt 1998).*

DANCING MELODY BHB 39f RR 33f 4138[13]

3 b f Merdon Melody 6.8f **(56)** - Cymbal (Ribero) 9.3f **(56)**
Form - 670
Record 1998 - 1st:0 2nd:0 3rd:0 Ran:3

1998 Turf 0-3: (8f, 10f 2) (g-f 2, frm)

Light-framed, currently very moderate filly. Turf high 33 (began Aug). **J L Spearing [0-3] The McIntyre Woods Partnership.*

DANCING MYSTERY BHB 58f73a RR 56f 73a 4864[3]

4 b g Beveled (USA) 6.9f **(64)** - Batchworth Dancer (Ballacashtal (CAN)) 5.3f **(50)**
Form - 1600632100043213
Record 1998 - 1st:2 2nd:2 3rd:3 Ran:15
Pre1998 - 1st:2 2nd:2 3rd:0 Ran:15
Win Prizemoney £11,727 *Total Prizemoney* £16,151
Wins * 1998 Spt Goodwo (G-F) H 5f 51 56
*** 1998** Jly Windso (GD) H 5f 48 50
* 1997 *Nov Lingfi (STD) H 5f 65 67 <*
* 1997 *Oct Southw (STD) 6f 63*

1998 Turf 2-12: (5f 2-10, 6f 2) (g-s, gd, g-f 3, frm 2-6, hrd) 1998 AW 0-3: (6f 3) (Fibr 3)

Workmanlike, above-average gelding, effective 5 to 6f, best at 6f, - acts on AW, best on Fibr, has worn blinkers, likes left handed tracks, prefers tight tracks, excels at Wolverhampton. Turf high 56. AW high 73 (began Spt) - 2nd of 13 giving 14lb to Village Native (19 Spt Wolverhampton 6f Fibr RF 4385). Inconsistent. Best coming from behind over a fast-run five furlongs.

**E A Wheeler [4-30] Austin Stroud & Co Ltd.*

DANCING PHANTOM BHB 102f RR 99f 2105[7]

3 b c Darshaan 11.9f **(81)** - Dancing Prize (IRE) (Sadler's Wells (USA)) 10f **(76)**
Form - 217
Record 1998 - 1st:1 2nd:1 3rd:0 Ran:3
Pre1998 - 1st:0 2nd:1 3rd:0 Ran:1
Win Prizemoney £3,696 *Total Prizemoney* £7,158
Wins * 1998 May Sandow (G-S) 10f 91+ <

1998 Turf 1-3: (10f 1-2, 12f) (gd 1-2, g-f)

Workmanlike, very useful colt. Turf high 99 - also 1st of 16 from Edwardian (26 May Sandown RF 1486). Runner-up to Mutamam on his sole run in 97, made him a warm order in a decent Chester maiden on his three-year-old bow, but he could not match the winner's late surge that day. He was an impressive winner at Sandown next time, spread-eagling his field. That form took a few knocks thereafter, and he failed to handle the big step up to Group Two company next time. Not seen out afterwards, but should stay further than twelve furlongs.

**Sir Michael Stoute [1-4] H R H Prince Fahd Salman.*

DANCING QUEEN (IRE) BHB 48f56a RR 51f 56a 3330[6]

4 b f Sadler's Wells (USA) 11.3f **(87)** - Bay Shade (USA) (Sharpen Up) 8.3f **(67)**
Form - 736
Record 1998 - 1st:0 2nd:0 3rd:1 Ran:3
Pre1998 - 1st:0 2nd:0 3rd:3 Ran:9
Win Prizemoney £0 *Total Prizemoney* £2,318

1998 Turf 0-3: (11f, 14f 2) (gd, g-f 2)

Scopey, fair filly, effective 10f, acts on frm, likes left handed tracks, favours tight tracks. Turf high 51 (began Jly). Inconsistent. A half-sister to Abury, who won the Cheshire Oaks, she has not shown anything like the same ability. **M Bell [0-12] Lordship Stud.*

DANCING RIO (IRE) BHB 78f74a RR 83f 74a 4638[11]

3 ch g Roi Danzig(USA) 10.5f **(62)** -Tameen (FR)(Pharly (FR)) 9.8f **(68)**
Form - 0122111516120800
Record 1998 - 1st:6 2nd:3 3rd:0 Ran:15
Pre1998 - 1st:0 2nd:0 3rd:0 Ran:6
Win Prizemoney £18,016 *Total Prizemoney* £21,038
Wins * 1998 May Ripon (G-F) H 12.3f 74 78 <
*** 1998** Apr Beverl (SFT) C 9.9f 72
*** 1998** *Feb Southw (STD) C 12f 77*
*** 1998** *Feb Lingfi (SLW) C 10f 71*
*** 1998** *Feb Southw (STD) H 8f 68 73*
*** 1998** *Jan Southw (STD) H 8f 61 69*

1998 Turf 2-6: (10f 1-1, 12f 1-4, 15f) (g-s 1-1, g-f 2, frm 1-3) 1998 AW 4-9: (8f 2-3, 9f, 10f 1-2, 12f 1-3) (Equi 1-2, Fibr 3-7)

Decent gelding, effective 6 to 12f, best at 12f, acts on gd to frm - acts on Fibr, excels at Ripon, does well at Southwell. Turf high 83 - 2nd of 5 getting 5lb from Crystal Falls (18 Jly Ripon 12f g-f RF 2937) - also 1st of 6 giving 1lb to High And Mighty (17 May Ripon RF 1289). AW high 77 - 1st of 6 giving 4lb to Celtic Comfort (27 Feb Southwell RF 0371). He was in fine form on both All-Weather surfaces in the early part of the year, winning four races. He rose in the handicap as a result, but remained effective in claimers, and regained winning form when returning to claiming company on turf at Beverley in April. He caused something of a surprise when winning a Ripon handicap the following month. He lacks a turn of foot, but now seems suited by twelve furlongs, and is as honest as they come. **P C Haslam [6-21] Rio Stainless Engineering Ltd.*

DANCING WOLF (IRE) BHB 66f RR 67f 5114[5]

3 b f Wolfhound (USA) 7.3f **(71)** - Aigue (High Top) 10.2f **(67)**
Form - 5470525
Record 1998 - 1st:0 2nd:1 3rd:0 Ran:7
Pre1998 - 1st:0 2nd:0 3rd:1 Ran:4
Win Prizemoney £0 *Total Prizemoney* £3,851

1998 Turf 0-7: (7f 4, 8f 2, 9f) (g-s, gd, g-f 4, frm)

Leggy, average filly, effective 5 to 8f, acts on g-s to frm, best on frm. Turf high 73 (began Aug). Consistent.

**A J McNae [0-7] The Iona Stud (from Miss Gay Kelleway [0-4] Oct 1997).*

DANDE FLYER BHB 63f67a RR 65f 67a 5007[7]

5 b br g Clantime 6.6f **(57)** - Lyndseylee (Swing Easy (USA)) 6.5f **(55)**
Form - 41717008604767
Record 1998 - 1st:2 2nd:0 3rd:0 Ran:14
Pre1998 - 1st:3 2nd:3 3rd:5 Ran:39
Win Prizemoney £16,720 *Total Prizemoney* £25,833
Wins * 1998 Apr Bath (SFT) H 5.1f 56 67
*** 1998** Apr Bright (GD) H 5.3f 56 67
* 1995 Oct Newmar (G-F) H 5f 60 82+ <
* 1995 Oct Yarmou (FRM) H 5.2f 60 74
* 1995 Oct Folkes (GD) 5f 66

1998 Turf 2-14: (5f 2-13, 6f) (hvy, sft 2, g-s 2-3, gd 2, g-f, frm 5)

Average gelding, effective 5f, acts on g-s to frm - acts on Fibr, best on g-s, has worn blinkers, likes left handed tracks, likes tight tracks. Turf high 67 - 1st of 17 giving 24lb to Harvey's Future (28 Apr Bath RF 0894) - also 1st of 12 getting 10lb from Divine Miss-P (20 Apr Brighton RF 0768). Had been on a long losing run prior to a victory at Brighton in April, but added another victory at Bath. A useful sprint handicapper in modest grade. Sold for 4,500 guineas at October. **D W P Arbuthnot [5-53] Dandelion Distribution Ltd.*

DANDE TIMES BHB 51f58a RR 53f 58a 579[5]

3 ch g Timeless Times (USA) 6.1f **(56)** - Miss Merlin (Manacle) 7.8f **(56)**
Form - 74222515
Record 1998 - 1st:1 2nd:3 3rd:0 Ran:6
Pre1998 - 1st:0 2nd:0 3rd:2 Ran:9
Win Prizemoney £1,813 *Total Prizemoney* £5,014
Wins * 1998 *Mar Southw (STD) S 5f 58 <*

1998 Turf 0-1: (5f) (sft) 1998 AW 1-5: (5f 1-5) (Equi 3, Fibr 1-2)

Light-framed, fair gelding, effective 5 to 6f, best at 5f, acts on g-f - acts on AW, best on Fibr, often wears blinkers (extremely effectively), likes tight tracks. AW high 58 - 1st of 9 getting 6lb from Junior Muffin (23 Mar Southwell RF 0467). He had been placed many times, but took a while to get off the mark, finally achieving it in a seller over the minimum on the Southwell Fibresand in March. He has plenty of early speed which is well suited to the Southwell five.

**K T Ivory [1-12] Crown Select (from D W P Arbuthnot [0-3] Jly 1997).*

DANDY DANCER BHB 87f **RR 87f** 3991[3]
2 br c Shareef Dancer (USA) 10.1f **(67)** - Highest Ever (FR) (Highest Honor (FR))
Form - 8063123
Record 1998 - 1st:1 2nd:1 3rd:2 Ran:7
Win Prizemoney £3,366 *Total Prizemoney* £11,599
Wins * **1998** Jly Catter (GD) H 7f 77 <
1998 Turf 1-6: (5f, 6f, 7f 1-3, 8f) (gd 2, g-f 1-2, frm, hrd) 1998 AW 0-1: (6f) (Fibr)
Useful colt, effective 7 to 8f, acts on g-f to hrd, has worn blinkers. Turf high 87 - 3rd of 14 giving 3lb to Hoh Steamer (31 Aug Newcastle 8f hrd RF 3991). He seems to be gradually improving with racing, and has run some fine races in nurseries, winning one at Catterick and only going down narrowly in a competitive event at Goodwood. His grit and determination should ensure further success. **S C Williams [1-7] M C North.*

DANDY REGENT BHB 63f **RR 61f** 3471[15]
4 b g Green Desert (USA) 7.8f **(78)** - Tahilla (Moorestyle) 6.9f **(64)**
Form - 21308600
Record 1998 - 1st:1 2nd:1 3rd:1 Ran:8
Pre1998 - 1st:0 2nd:1 3rd:0 Ran:6
Win Prizemoney £3,582 *Total Prizemoney* £5,982
Wins * **1998** Apr Bright (GD) H 7f 65 73 <
1998 Turf 1-7: (7f 1-5, 8f 2) (g-s 1-1, gd 3, g-f 2, hrd) 1998 AW 0-1: (7f) (Equi)
Scopey, average gelding, effective 7 to 8f, best at 7f, acts on g-s to frm, likes left handed tracks, prefers tight tracks. Turf high 73 (1st run) - 1st of 16 getting 8lb from Super Monarch (20 Apr Brighton RF 0763). Consistent. **C A Cyzer [1-14] R M Cyzer.*

DANEGOLD (IRE) BHB 65f68a **RR 65f 68a** 4963[7]
6 b g Danehill (USA) 9.1f **(79)** - Cistus (Sun Prince) 12.4f **(52)**
Form - 03417411167
Record 1998 - 1st:4 2nd:0 3rd:1 Ran:11
Pre1998 - 1st:4 2nd:4 3rd:6 Ran:41
Win Prizemoney £33,867 *Total Prizemoney* £46,636
Wins * **1998** Oct Ascot (SFT) H 16.2f 58 65+
* **1998** Oct Catter (gd,) H 15.8f 58 58
* **1998** Spt Goodwo (G-F) H 16f 52 58
* **1998** Jly Yarmou (G-F) H 16f 50 52
* 1995 Spt Sandow (G-S) H 8.1f 78 81+ <
* 1995 Jun Goodwo (G-F) H 10f 73 81+ <
* 1995 Jun Bath (GD) H 8f 67 66+
* 1995 Apr Ripon (G-F) 8f 64
1998 Turf 4-11: (12f 2, 16f 4-8, 17f)(sft 2, g-s 1-1, gd 2, g-f 2-3, frm 1-3)
Average gelding, effective 10 to 16f, acts on g-s to frm, often wears blinkers (very effectively), prefers right handed tracks, likes tight tracks. Turf high 65 - 1st of 8 getting 9lb from Bowcliffe Court (9 Oct Ascot RF 4737). Won twice over hurdles in August and went on to complete a hat-trick on the Flat. Suited by patient tactics, he does not find much off the bridle.
**M R Channon [14-66] Circular Distributors Ltd (from J W Hills [0-5] Oct 1994).*

DANE RIVER (IRE) **RR 97f** 3870a[2]
3 b c Danehill (USA) 9.1f **(79)** - Allegheny River (USA) (Lear Fan (USA)) 8.5f **(73)**
Form - 52
1998 Turf 0-2: (6f, 8f) (g-f, hrd)
Very useful colt. Turf high 97 (began Aug).
**J S Bolger in IRE [1-4] T F Brennan.*

DANESMAN (IRE) BHB 69f **RR 66df** 5125[11]
5 b g Danehill (USA) 9.1f **(79)** - Vernonhills (Hard Fought) 8.8f **(62)**
Form - 2252560
Record 1998 - 1st:0 2nd:3 3rd:0 Ran:7
Pre1998 - 1st:1 2nd:1 3rd:0 Ran:4
Win Prizemoney £4,581 *Total Prizemoney* £8,831
Wins 1995 Spt Yarmou (GD) 8f 82 <
1998 Turf 0-7: (10f 2, 11f, 12f 4) (g-s 2, gd, g-f 2, frm 2)
Average gelding, effective 11f, acts on g-f, has worn blinkers, favours left handed tracks, favours tight tracks. Turf high 73 (began Jly) - 2nd of 14 giving 8lb to Joli's Son (1 Aug Lingfield 11f g-f RF 3271). He has gone close to winning a few times, but has not appeared to be putting it in at the end of his races, and should be treated with some caution.
**G L Moore [0-7] C F Sparrowhawk (from W R Muir [0-2] Jly 1998).*

DANETIME (IRE) BHB 116f **RR 120f** 3614a[5]
4 b c Danehill (USA) 9.1f **(79)** - Allegheny River (USA) (Lear Fan (USA)) 8.5f **(73)**
Form - 33535
Record 1998 - 1st:0 2nd:0 3rd:3 Ran:5
Pre1998 - 1st:3 2nd:2 3rd:1 Ran:10
Win Prizemoney £59,468 *Total Prizemoney* £115,686
Wins * 1997 Aug Goodwo (G-F) H 6f 97 111 <
* 1997 Jly Newmar (GD) H 6f 97 107+
* 1996 Oct Newcas (G-F) 6f 93
1998 Turf 0-5: (5f, 6f 3, 7f) (gd 4, frm)
Workmanlike, very high-class colt, effective 6 to 7f, best at 6f, acts on gd to frm, best on gd. Turf high 120 - 3rd of 17 to Elnadim (9 Jly Newmarket 6f frm RF 2649). Consistent. Won the Stewards' Cup and was in the frame in the Haydock Sprint Cup in 1997. He was a little disappointing in the Abernant on his return, but may not have handled the soft ground. Produced a sound effort at York, and kept on really well into third in the July Cup after an interrupted preparation. Not seen again after running a close fifth at Deauville, he gave the impression on occasions that seven furlongs may have suited. Retired to stud.
**N A Callaghan [3-15] M Tabor & Mrs John Magnier.*

DANGERMAN (IRE) BHB 42f **RR 43f** 4939[1]
3 ch g Pips Pride 6.7f **(70)** - Two Magpies (Doulab (USA)) 9.8f **(65)**
Form - 00007000501
Record 1998 - 1st:1 2nd:0 3rd:0 Ran:11
Pre1998 - 1st:0 2nd:1 3rd:0 Ran:3
Win Prizemoney £3,183 *Total Prizemoney* £4,381
Wins * **1998** Oct Nottin () H 10f 37 43 <
1998 Turf 1-10: (5f 6, 6f, 7f, 10f 1-2) (g-s, gd 1-5, g-f, frm 3) 1998 AW 0-1: (5f) (Fibr)
Rangy, moderate gelding. Turf high 51.
**M W Easterby [1-14] Stephen Curtis.*

DANGEROUS DANCER BHB 81f **RR 86f** 4185[17]
2 b f Warning 8.1f **(77)** - Silabteni (USA) (Nureyev (USA)) 8.7f **(78)**
Form - 2220
Record 1998 - 1st:0 2nd:3 3rd:0 Ran:4
Win Prizemoney £0 *Total Prizemoney* £3,023
1998 Turf 0-4: (5f 3, 6f) (gd, frm 2, hrd)
Useful filly. Turf high 81 (began Jly) - 2nd of 13 giving 7lb to Petrovna (17 Aug Windsor 5f hrd RF 3686).
**B W Hills [0-4] Stephen Crown.*

DANGEROUS WATERS BHB 20a **RR 4f 20a** 42[8]
5 b m Risk Me(FR) 8f **(53)**- Queen's Lake(Kings Lake (USA)) 10.8f **(67)**
Form - 88
Record 1998 - 1st:0 2nd:0 3rd:0 Ran:2
Pre1998 - 1st:0 2nd:0 3rd:0 Ran:3
1998 AW 0-2: (8f, 9f) (Fibr 2)
Little account filly.
**J Neville [0-2] J Neville (from P G Murphy [0-3] Dec 1995).*

DANGERUS PRECEDENT (IRE) BHB 63f63a **RR 46f 63a** 4544[2]
3 ch g Polish Precedent (USA) 9f **(73)** - Circus Feathers (Kris) 9.5f **(73)**
Form - 2
Record 1998 - 1st:0 2nd:1 3rd:0 Ran:1
Pre1998 - 1st:0 2nd:0 3rd:0 Ran:3
Win Prizemoney £0 *Total Prizemoney* £540
1998 AW 0-1: (14f) (Fibr)
Unfurnished, fair gelding. (1st run) - 2nd of 11 giving 12lb to Primaticcio (29 Spt Southwell 14f Fibr RF 4544).
**C R Egerton [0-4] Chris Brasher.*

DAN HOI (IRE) BHB 33f **RR 46df** 4271[12]
3 ch g Roi Danzig (USA) 10.5f **(62)** - Honorine (USA) (Blushing Groom (FR)) 10.3f **(76)**
Form - 05450
Record 1998 - 1st:0 2nd:0 3rd:0 Ran:5
1998 Turf 0-5: (10f 2, 11f, 12f, 14f) (g-s, gd, g-f, frm 2)
Scopey, moderate gelding, has worn blinkers. Turf high 46.
**B J McMath [0-5] Mrs Lisa Olley.*

DANIEL DERONDA BHB 68f **RR 71df** 3737[7]
4 b c Danehill (USA) 9.1f **(79)** - Kilvarnet (Furry Glen) 8.9f **(63)**

Form - 06027
Record 1998 - 1st:0 2nd:1 3rd:0 Ran:5
Pre1998 - 1st:0 2nd:1 3rd:0 Ran:1
Win Prizemoney £0 *Total Prizemoney* £1,705
1998 Turf 0-5: (10f 3, 11f, 12f) (gd, g-f, frm 3)
Scopey, above-average colt. Turf high 71 - 2nd of 8 giving 13lb to Acebo Lyons (7 Aug Haydock 11f g-f RF 3436).
**P W Harris [0-6] The Rainbow Partnership.*

DANIELLA RIDGE (IRE) RR 79f 5063[5]

2 b f Indian Ridge 7.6f **(74)** - Daniella Drive (USA) (Shelter Half (USA)) 7.9f **(79)**
Form - 35
Record 1998 - 1st:0 2nd:0 3rd:1 Ran:2
Win Prizemoney £0 *Total Prizemoney* £796
1998 Turf 0-2: (6f 2) (g-f 2)
Currently above-average filly. Turf high 79 (1st run) (began Aug) - 3rd of 6 to Itlak (7 Aug Ascot 6f g-f RF 3429). A full sister to the useful but ill-fated Blomberg, she showed plenty of promise and should come into her own next term.
**R Hannon [0-2] A F Harrington.*

DANIELLE'S LAD BHB 88f RR 84f 5144[1]

2 b c Emarati (USA) 6.6f **(63)** - Cactus Road (FR) (Iron Duke (FR)) 8.8f **(60)**
Form - 431031
Record 1998 - 1st:2 2nd:0 3rd:2 Ran:6
Win Prizemoney £7,216 *Total Prizemoney* £8,411
Wins * **1998** Nov Doncas (SFT) H 5f 81 84 <
* **1998** Aug Goodwo (G-F) 5f 77
1998 Turf 2-6: (5f 2-5, 6f) (sft, gd 1-2, g-f 1-1, frm 2)
Decent colt, effective 5f, acts on gd to g-f. Turf high 84 (began Jly) - 1st of 20 giving 13lb to Piggy Bank (6 Nov Doncaster RF 5144) - also 1st of 8 from Sunley Sense (28 Aug Goodwood RF 3925).
**B Palling [2-6] Mrs B J Harkins.*

DANIELLE'S LASS (IRE) BHB 49f RR 66f 4400[18]

2 b f Balla Cove - Sylvaner (IRE) (Montelimar (USA))
Form - 748360
Record 1998 - 1st:0 2nd:0 3rd:1 Ran:6
Win Prizemoney £0 *Total Prizemoney* £272
1998 Turf 0-6: (5f 4, 6f 2) (gd, g-f, frm 4)
Average filly, effective 6f, acts on frm. Turf high 66 - 3rd of 14 to Indian City (19 Aug Leicester 6f frm RF 3741).
**B Palling [0-6] Mrs B J Harkins.*

DANISH RHAPSODY (IRE) BHB 117f RR 115f 4843[10]

5 b g Danehill (USA) 9.1f **(79)**- Ardmelody(Law Society (USA)) 9.9f **(70)**
Form - 1003275160
Record 1998 - 1st:2 2nd:1 3rd:1 Ran:10
Pre1998 - 1st:5 2nd:2 3rd:1 Ran:11
Win Prizemoney £107,868 *Total Prizemoney* £126,554
Wins * **1998** Spt Goodwo (G-F) L 9.9f 101
* **1998** May Haydoc (GD) L 10.5f 110 <
* 1997 Spt Goodwo (G-F) L 10f 105
* 1997 Spt Goodwo (GD) H 9f 95 100
* 1997 Jly Goodwo (G-F) H 10f 90 95
* 1997 Jly Lingfi (G-F) 10f 96
* 1997 May Folkes (G-F) H 9.7f 80 85
1998 Turf 2-10: (7f 2, 8f 2, 9f, 10f 1-4, 11f 1-1) (sft, gd 2-6, g-f 3)
High-class gelding, effective 7 to 11f, acts on gd to frm, best on gd, prefers right handed tracks, prefers tight tracks, excels at Goodwood. Turf high 115 - 2nd of 9 giving 6lb to Muhtathir (14 Aug Newbury 7f g-f RF 3633) - also 1st of 5 getting 3lb from Lord of Men (10 May Haydock RF 1142). An incredible bargain buy at just 1,300 gns, he has been campaigned at home and abroad this year, but after winning on his Haydock reappearance his form became somewhat patchy. However, he did register another victory when taking the notable scalp of Chester House in a Listed event at Goodwood in September. He ideally needs fast ground.
**Lady Herries [7-21] Chris Hardy & Friends.*

DANKA BHB 48f49a RR 29f 49a 4867[13]

4 gr g Petong 7.6f **(58)**- Angel Drummer(Dance In Time (CAN))8.9f **(59)**
Form - 6448300
Record 1998 - 1st:0 2nd:0 3rd:1 Ran:4
Pre1998 - 1st:0 2nd:0 3rd:0 Ran:8
Win Prizemoney £0 *Total Prizemoney* £969
1998 Turf 0-1: (14f) (gd) 1998 AW 0-3: (8f, 12f 2) (Fibr 3)
Scopey, fair gelding, often wears blinkers. AW high 51.
**K C Comerford [0-4] S J V Construction (from P T Walwyn [0-8] Dec 1997).*

DAN LOOSE (IRE) BHB 77f RR 83?f 3935[7]

3 b f Danehill (USA) 9.1f **(79)** - Cut Loose (High Top) 10.2f **(67)**
Form - 2667
Record 1998 - 1st:0 2nd:1 3rd:0 Ran:4
Win Prizemoney £0 *Total Prizemoney* £2,364
1998 Turf 0-4: (6f 2, 7f, 8f) (g-f 2, frm 2)
Rangy, decent filly. Turf high 83 (began Jly).
**M Bell [0-4] Scuderia Blueberry.*

DANNI RR 939[7]

5 ch m Clantime 6.6f **(57)** - Kasu (Try My Best (USA)) 7.6f **(67)**
Form - 7
Record 1998 - 1st:0 2nd:0 3rd:0 Ran:1
1998 AW 0-1: (6f) (Fibr)
Currently poor filly. **J L Harris [0-2] Cleartherm Ltd.*

DANNISTAR BHB 34f32a RR 35f 32a 4408[5]

6 br m Puissance 7.1f **(60)** - Loadplan Lass (Nicholas Bill) 10.1f **(56)**
Form - 875
Record 1998 - 1st:0 2nd:0 3rd:0 Ran:3
Pre1998 - 1st:1 2nd:2 3rd:0 Ran:15
Win Prizemoney £2,187 *Total Prizemoney* £3,689
Wins 1995 *Nov Wolver (STD) C 9.4f 57 <*
1998 Turf 0-3: (8f, 10f, 11f) (g-f 2, frm)
Very moderate mare. Turf high 35. Consistent.
**W M Brisbourne [0-6] John Pugh (from P D Evans [1-12] May 1997).*

DANNY DEEVER BHB 58f RR 62f 4145[13]

2 b c Deploy 11.4f **(67)** - Yes (Blakeney) 10.5f **(64)**
Form - 87480
Record 1998 - 1st:0 2nd:0 3rd:0 Ran:5
Win Prizemoney £0 *Total Prizemoney* £241
1998 Turf 0-5: (6f, 7f 3, 8f) (gd, g-f 2, frm 2)
Average colt, often wears blinkers. Turf high 62 (began Jly) - 8th of 12 getting 19lb from Pilot's Harbour (28 Aug Newmarket 8f frm RF 3932). **D T Thom [0-5] D T Thom.*

DANSKER (IRE) BHB 70f72a RR 63f 72a 5124[5]

2 b c Darshaan 11.9f **(81)** -Nassma(IRE)(Sadler's Wells (USA)) 10f **(76)**
Form - 6205
Record 1998 - 1st:0 2nd:1 3rd:0 Ran:4
Win Prizemoney £0 *Total Prizemoney* £924
1998 Turf 0-3: (7f, 8f 2) (g-s 2, gd) 1998 AW 0-1: (7f) (Fibr)
Above-average colt. Turf high 63. (1st run) - 2nd of 6 to Minnesota (29 Jun Southwell 7f Fibr RF 2384).
**Sir Mark Prescott [0-4] Sheikh Ahmed bin Saeed Al Maktoum.*

DANTESQUE (IRE) BHB 95f RR 92f 4226[2]

5 b h Danehill (USA) 9.1f **(79)** - I Want My Say (USA) (Tilt Up (USA)) 9.8f **(55)**
Form - 672
Record 1998 - 1st:0 2nd:1 3rd:0 Ran:3
Pre1998 - 1st:3 2nd:3 3rd:0 Ran:10
Win Prizemoney £11,818 *Total Prizemoney* £16,655
Wins * 1997 Spt Doncas (G-F) H 12f 85 91 <
* 1997 Aug Yarmou (G-F) 10.1f 85
* 1997 Jly Newcas (GD) 10.1f 67+
1998 Turf 0-3: (12f 3) (gd 2, g-f)
Useful colt, effective 10 to 12f, best at 12f, acts on g-f to frm, best on g-f, prefers left handed tracks. Turf high 92 - 2nd of 17 giving 6lb to Jazil (11 Spt Doncaster 12f g-f RF 4226). Quite useful in 97, he failed to progress last season. His stable was under a cloud for most of the campaign, which might explain his poor shows in the early part, and he ran his best race of the year on his final start. Sold for 28,000 gns in October to race in the United States.
**G Wragg [3-13] Mollers Racing.*

DANZARI RR 102f 3916a[13]

2 ch f Arazi (USA) 9.2f **(74)** - Dangora (USA) (Sovereign Dancer (USA)) 11.2f **(68)**
Form - 10
1998 Turf 1-2: (5f 1-1, 6f) (sft, gd 1-1)

Currently very useful filly. Turf high 102 (1st run) (began Aug) - 1st of 15 from Stella Berine (19 Aug Deauville RF 3910a). Very impressive in a Listed race at Deauville in August, she was immediately supplemented for the Group One Prix Morny just four days later. Unfortunately she performed like a non-stayer there, finishing last after disputing the lead. Obviously held in high regard by Andre Fabre, she is worth another chance over the minimum trip.

**A Fabre in FR [1-2] K Abdulla.*

DANZAS BHB 46f **RR 50f** 3944[13]

4 b g Polish Precedent (USA) 9f **(73)** - Dancing Rocks (Green Dancer (USA)) 10.3f **(74)**

Form - 0770400

Record	**1998 -**	1st:0	2nd:0	3rd:0	Ran:7
	Pre1998 -	1st:0	2nd:0	3rd:3	Ran:6

Win Prizemoney £0 *Total Prizemoney* £1,777

1998 Turf 0-7: (7f, 8f 4, 10f 2) (sft, gd 3, g-f 2, frm)

Scopey, fair gelding, effective 8 to 10f, acts on gd to frm, likes tight tracks. Turf high 57. Inconsistent.

**J M Bradley [0-7] Martyn James (from R Charlton [0-6] Oct 1997).*

DANZIG FLYER (IRE) BHB 46f55a **RR 52f 55a** 5002[12]

3 b c Roi Danzig (USA) 10.5f **(62)** - Fenland Express (IRE) (Reasonable (FR))

Form - 000000

Record	**1998 -**	1st:0	2nd:0	3rd:0	Ran:6
	Pre1998 -	1st:0	2nd:1	3rd:1	Ran:7

Win Prizemoney £0 *Total Prizemoney* £1,365

1998 Turf 0-5: (8f 2, 9f, 12f 2) (g-f 3, frm 2) 1998 AW 0-1: (12f) (Equi)

Workmanlike, fair colt, effective 7f, acts on gd - acts on Equi, has worn blinkers, likes tight tracks. Turf high 52 (began Jly).

**P W Harris [0-13] Shamrock Four.*

DANZINO (IRE) BHB 45f89a **RR 43f 89a** 4339[14]

3 b g Roi Danzig (USA) 10.5f **(62)** - Luvi Ullmann (Thatching) 8f **(66)**

Form - 12102327100880

Record	**1998 -**	1st:3	2nd:3	3rd:1	Ran:14
	Pre1998 -	1st:0	2nd:0	3rd:0	Ran:5

Win Prizemoney £9,489 *Total Prizemoney* £14,905

Wins	*** 1998**	*Jun*	*Wolver*	*(STD)*	*H*	*9.4f*	*83*	*85*	*<*
	*** 1998**	*Feb*	*Lingfi*	*(SLW)*	*H*	*10f*	*64*	*72*	
	*** 1998**	*Jan*	*Southw*	*(STD)*		*8f*		*72*	

1998 Turf 0-7: (6f, 7f 2, 8f 2, 10f 2) (gd 4, g-f, frm 2) 1998 AW 3-7: (8f 1-4, 9f 1-2, 10f 1-1) (Equi 1-2, Fibr 2-5)

Useful gelding, effective 8 to 9f, best at 8f, - acts on AW, best on Fibr, often wears blinkers (very effectively), prefers left handed tracks, prefers tight tracks, excels at Wolverhampton and Lingfield and Southwell. Turf high 54. AW high 85 - 1st of 11 giving 13lb to Law Dancer (6 Jun Wolverhampton RF 1797). Inconsistent. He is a very decent sort on sand, winning on all three All-Weather tracks. He looks an awkward ride at times, as he needs plenty of rousting along and flashes his tail regularly. Pat McCabe gets on particularly well with him, and gave him very aggressive rides when gaining his victories. He looks very moderate on turf.

**Mrs N Macauley [3-14] Godfrey Horsford (from A P Jarvis [0-5] Oct 1997).*

DAPHNE'S DOLL (IRE) BHB 70f **RR 68f** 4935[3]

3 b f Polish Patriot (USA) 7.8f **(70)** - Helietta (Tyrnavos) 10.1f **(55)**

Form - 4503

Record	**1998 -**	1st:0	2nd:0	3rd:1	Ran:4

Win Prizemoney £0 *Total Prizemoney* £815

1998 Turf 0-4: (7f, 8f 2, 10f) (gd 2, g-f 2)

Scopey, average filly. Turf high 68 - 3rd of 15 to Maria Isabella (22 Oct Nottingham 8f gd RF 4935).

**Miss Gay Kelleway [0-4] Mrs Alan Gordon.*

DARAJAT (IRE) BHB 34f **RR 42f** 3609[P]

3 b g Imperial Frontier (USA) 7f **(65)** - Fantasy To Reality (IRE) (Jester)

Form - 0000P

Record	**1998 -**	1st:0	2nd:0	3rd:0	Ran:5

1998 Turf 0-5: (6f, 7f, 8f 3) (gd, g-f, frm 3)

Neat, moderate gelding. Turf high 42.

**J G Portman [0-5] Madhatter Racing.*

DARA KAY (IRE) BHB 38f **RR 30f** 1902[6]

3 bb g Treasure Kay 6.5f **(53)** - Share The Vision (Vision (USA)) 9f **(64)**

Form - 76

Record	**1998 -**	1st:0	2nd:0	3rd:0	Ran:2
	Pre1998 -	1st:0	2nd:0	3rd:0	Ran:3

1998 Turf 0-2: (12f, 14f) (g-s, gd)

Very moderate gelding. Turf high 30.

**D J S Cosgrove [0-2] W A Barrett (from E J O'Grady in IRE [0-3] Jly 1997).*

DARBY FLYER BHB 50f32a **RR 24f 32a** 363[8]

5 ch g Dominion Royale 7.8f **(63)** - Shining Wood (Touching Wood (USA)) 8.2f **(55)**

Form - 878

Record	**1998 -**	1st:0	2nd:0	3rd:0	Ran:3
	Pre1998 -	1st:0	2nd:0	3rd:1	Ran:4

Win Prizemoney £0 *Total Prizemoney* £507

1998 AW 0-3: (6f, 7f, 8f) (Equi 2, Fibr)

Little account gelding. AW high 1. **W R Muir [0-7] Jacklin Ltd.*

DARE BHB 50f **RR 38f** 3949[15]

3 b g Beveled (USA) 6.9f **(64)** - Run Amber Run (Run The Gantlet (USA)) 12.1f **(59)**

Form - 040000

Record	**1998 -**	1st:0	2nd:0	3rd:0	Ran:6
	Pre1998 -	1st:0	2nd:0	3rd:0	Ran:1

Win Prizemoney £0 *Total Prizemoney* £247

1998 Turf 0-6: (6f, 7f 3, 8f, 10f) (gd 2, g-f, frm 3)

Leggy, very moderate gelding. Turf high 63.

**E L James [0-6] Browne, Cowan, James (from C James [0-1] Spt 1997).*

DARGO BHB 47f40a **RR 47f 40a** 5119[4]

4 b g Formidable (USA) 7.8f **(60)** - Mountain Memory (High Top) 10.2f **(67)**

Form - 00027400234

Record	**1998 -**	1st:0	2nd:2	3rd:1	Ran:11
	Pre1998 -	1st:0	2nd:1	3rd:0	Ran:3

Win Prizemoney £0 *Total Prizemoney* £2,964

1998 Turf 0-8: (8f 2, 10f, 11f, 12f 3, 13f) (g-s 2, gd 4, g-f 2) 1998 AW 0-3: (7f, 9f, 11f) (Fibr 3)

Workmanlike, moderate gelding, effective 8 to 12f, acts on g-f, prefers right handed tracks, favours tight tracks. Turf high 60 - 2nd of 5 giving 11lb to Happy Wanderer (1 Jun Hamilton 8f g-f RF 1618). AW high 43. Consistent.

**C W Thornton [0-12] Ailsa Daniels & Guy Reed (from M Johnston [0-2] Aug 1996).*

DARINA (IRE) RR 99f 4910a[5]

3 b f Danehill (USA) 9.1f **(79)** - Sweet Justice 00

Form - 111222215

1998 Turf 4-9: (7f 1-1, 8f 2-3, 9f, 10f 1-3, 11f) (g-s 1-1, gd 2-7, g-f 1-1)

Very useful filly, effective 7 to 10f, acts on g-s to g-f, best on gd, and likes Gowran Park. Turf high 99 (began Jly) - 2nd of 7 to Tadwiga (6 Spt Curragh 8f gd RF 4179a) - also 1st of 9 from Geisha Girl (3 Oct Curragh RF 4691a). Consistent. Useful filly who won four races last season. She may not be top class but she is tough and should stay further. **J S Bolger in IRE [4-9] D H W Dobson.*

DARING DEREK (USA) BHB 106f **RR 103f** 2053[4]

3 ch c Naevus (USA) 7.2f **(86)** - Gatap (USA) (Buckfinder (USA)) 8.1f **(71)**

Form - 1024

Record	**1998 -**	1st:1	2nd:1	3rd:0	Ran:4
	Pre1998 -	1st:1	2nd:0	3rd:0	Ran:1

Win Prizemoney £10,054 *Total Prizemoney* £17,363

Wins	*** 1998**	Apr	Newmar	(G-S)	7f	98+	<
	* 1997	Oct	Lingfi	(FRM)	6f	74+	

1998 Turf 1-4: (7f 1-3, 8f) (gd 1-3, frm)

Scopey, very useful colt. Turf high 103 - 2nd of 7 getting 7lb from Bold Fact (16 May Newmarket 7f frm RF 1267) - also 1st of 3 from Mister Rambo (14 Apr Newmarket RF 0684). He won a soft race at Newmarket in the spring and struggled thereafter, running his best race when finishing fourth in the Jersey Stakes at Royal Ascot. He needs to find a few lengths to win a Group event.

**D R Loder [2-5] Lucayan Stud.*

DARING DESTINY BHB 102f **RR 98f** 4620[1]

7 b m Daring March 9f **(54)** - Raunchy Rita (Brigadier Gerard) 9.3f **(58)**

Form - 3467221
Record 1998 - 1st:1 2nd:2 3rd:1 Ran:7
Pre1998 - 1st:7 2nd:5 3rd:3 Ran:33
Win Prizemoney £159,826 *Total Prizemoney* £195,026
Wins * **1998** Oct Newmar (GD) H 6f 96 98
* 1996 Aug Baden- (GD) G2 6f 112 <
* 1996 Aug Leopar (G-S) G3 6f 104
* 1996 Jun Newmar (G-F) 6f 94
* 1995 May Lingfi (FRM) L 7f 97
* 1994 Spt Ayr (G-S) H 6f 89 85
* 1994 Jun Epsom (G-F) H 7f 78 81
1998 Turf 1-7: (6f 1-6, 8f) (sft, g-s 2, gd 1-1, g-f, frm 2)
Very useful mare, effective 6f, acts on sft to gd, best on gd, often wears blinkers (effectively). Turf high 98 - 1st of 8 giving 9lb to Faraway Lass (2 Oct Newmarket RF 4620). She is a classy mare at her best, and ran her best race for quite some time at York in September before running a blinder when going down in a photo to stable-companion Always Alight in the Ayr Gold Cup. Winner of a rated stakes at Newmarket in October, she needs holding up for as long as possible. **K R Burke [8-40] Nigel Shields.*

DARING FLIGHT (USA) BHB 53f58a RR 10f 58a 3609[10]
4 b c Danzig (USA) 8.1f **(88)** - Life At the Top (Habitat) 9.4f **(70)**
Form - P00
Record 1998 - 1st:0 2nd:0 3rd:0 Ran:3
Pre1998 - 1st:0 2nd:0 3rd:0 Ran:6
Win Prizemoney £0 *Total Prizemoney* £968
1998 Turf 0-2: (7f 2) (frm 2) 1998 AW 0-1: (7f) (Fibr)
Scopey, fair colt. Turf high 10. Becoming disappointing.
**Lord Huntingdon [0-9] Henryk De Kwiatkowski.*

DARING GENERAL (USA) RR 100 5162a[4]
2 br g General Meeting - Flying Belle
Form - 4
1998 AW 0-1: (9f) (Dirt)
Currently very useful gelding. Despite staying on well, couldn't reach the principals when finishing fourth in the Breeders' Cup Juvenile. **C Dollase in USA [0-1] Golden Eagle Farm.*

DARING NEWS BHB 39f RR 40f 2164[5]
3 b g Risk Me (FR) 8f **(53)** - Hot Sunday Sport (Star Appeal) 9.6f **(65)**
Form - 5085
Record 1998 - 1st:0 2nd:0 3rd:0 Ran:4
Pre1998 - 1st:0 2nd:0 3rd:0 Ran:5
Win Prizemoney £0 *Total Prizemoney* £352
1998 Turf 0-2: (10f, 12f) (gd, frm) 1998 AW 0-2: (8f, 9f) (Fibr 2)
Scopey, moderate gelding. Turf high 39. AW high 35. Consistent.
**O O'Neill [0-4] Frank Clarke (from R Hannon [0-5] Oct 1997).*

DARIUS THE GREAT (IRE) BHB 28f RR 26f 1941[7]
6 ch g Persian Heights 10.5f **(61)** - Derring Dee (Derrylin) 8.8f **(54)**
Form - 7
Record 1998 - 1st:0 2nd:0 3rd:0 Ran:1
Pre1998 - 1st:0 2nd:0 3rd:0 Ran:4
1998 AW 0-1: (14f) (Fibr)
Little account gelding. **D Marks [1-13] C R Buttery.*

DARK AGE (IRE) BHB 39f70a RR 37f 70a 3200[9]
5 b g Darshaan 11.9f **(81)** - Sarela (USA) (Danzig (USA)) 8.4f **(76)**
Form - 0760
Record 1998 - 1st:0 2nd:0 3rd:0 Ran:4
Pre1998 - 1st:0 2nd:0 3rd:0 Ran:9
Win Prizemoney £0 *Total Prizemoney* £231
1998 Turf 0-4: (7f 2, 8f, 10f) (gd 2, g-f 2)
Moderate gelding. Turf high 37.
**J Akehurst [0-4] A D Spence (from R Akehurst [0-10] Nov 1997).*

DARK ALBATROSS (USA) BHB 86f RR 81f 4845[15]
2 b f Sheikh Albadou 9.2f **(75)** - Rossard (DEN) (Glacial (DEN))
Form - 1230430
Record 1998 - 1st:1 2nd:1 3rd:2 Ran:7
Win Prizemoney £3,663 *Total Prizemoney* £7,046
Wins * **1998** May Kempto (G-F) 6f 63+ <
1998 Turf 1-7: (6f 1-3, 7f 3, 8f) (g-s, gd, g-f 3, frm 1-2)
Decent filly, effective 7f, acts on g-f to frm. Turf high 81 - 3rd of 12 giving 4lb to Parisien Star (18 Spt Newbury 7f frm RF 4357). Comfortable winner of her debut, her form has been somewhat regressive since. **J L Dunlop [1-7] Thorpe (Susan Abbot Racing).*

DARK GREEN (USA) BHB 80f RR 82f 1164[7]
4 ch c Green Dancer (USA) 11.9f **(77)** - Ardisia (USA) (Affirmed (USA)) 9.3f **(79)**
Form - 47
Record 1998 - 1st:0 2nd:0 3rd:0 Ran:2
Pre1998 - 1st:0 2nd:2 3rd:2 Ran:5
Win Prizemoney £0 *Total Prizemoney* £4,574
1998 Turf 0-2: (12f 2) (gd 2)
Scopey, decent colt. Turf high 82 (1st run) - 4th of 11 getting 13lb from Arctic Owl (3 May Newmarket 12f gd RF 0995). Rather disappointing in '97, but ran quite well on his return at Newmarket.
**P F I Cole [0-7] H R H Prince Fahd Salman.*

DARK MENACE BHB 42f39a RR 39f 39a 3267[9]
6 br g Beveled (USA) 6.9f **(64)** - Sweet and Sure (Known Fact (USA)) 7.4f **(67)**
Form - 4B080251560
Record 1998 - 1st:1 2nd:1 3rd:0 Ran:8
Pre1998 - 1st:2 2nd:1 3rd:3 Ran:35
Win Prizemoney £7,153 *Total Prizemoney* £10,472
Wins * **1998** *Jun Southw (STD) SH 7f 32 37*
* 1997 Jun Bright (FRM) H 7f 47 52 <
* 1996 Jly Bright (FRM) H 6f 45 47
1998 Turf 0-4: (7f 2, 8f 2) (gd, g-f 2, frm) 1998 AW 1-4: (6f, 7f 1-2, 8f) (Equi 2, Fibr 1-2)
Very moderate gelding, effective 6 to 8f, acts on g-f to frm, best on frm, often wears blinkers (very effectively), prefers tight tracks, excels at Brighton. Turf high 54 (1st run) - 2nd of 18 giving 17lb to Jato Dancer (18 May Windsor 8f frm RF 1311). AW high 37. Won at Brighton in 1997, and regained winning form in an apprentice seller on the Southwell Fibresand in June. That looks his level now, but he has a very poor wins-to-runs ratio.
**E A Wheeler [3-31] Benham Racing (from S Mellor [0-12] Spt 1995).*

DARK MOONDANCER BHB 112f RR 111f 5075[1]
3 b c Anshan 8.2f **(63)** -Oh So Well(IRE)(Sadler's Wells (USA)) 10f **(76)**
Form - 311461
Record 1998 - 1st:3 2nd:0 3rd:1 Ran:6
Pre1998 - 1st:1 2nd:2 3rd:1 Ran:4
Win Prizemoney £46,118 *Total Prizemoney* £56,810
Wins * **1998** Oct Newmar (SFT) G3 12f 111 <
* **1998** Aug Deauvi (SFT) L 12.5f 105
* **1998** Jun Ascot (G-S) 12f 104
* 1997 Oct Haydoc (HVY) 7.1f 83
1998 Turf 3-6: (9f, 12f 2-2, 13f 1-2, 15f) (g-s 1-1, gd 1-3, g-f 1-2)
Scopey, Group-class colt, effective 12 to 15f, acts on g-s to g-f, excels at Deauville. Turf high 111 - 1st of 5 getting 7lb from Delilah (31 Oct Newmarket RF 5075) - also 1st of 3 getting 1lb from Shadow Dance (6 Aug Deauville RF 3612b). Improving. His only poor performance came in the St Leger, where he moved poorly and probably found the ground a shade fast. Much happier on a soft surface at Newmarket in October, he out-stayed Delilah inside the final furlong and won going away. Certain to improve, he could do well if campaigned in France, where the going is usually to his liking. **P W Chapple-Hyam [4-10] Dr Anne J F Gillespie & John Wilson.*

DARK SHELL (IRE) BHB 107f RR 113f 4329[4]
3 b c Darshaan 11.9f **(81)** - Grecian Urn (Ela-Mana-Mou) 10.1f **(70)**
Form - 16424
Record 1998 - 1st:1 2nd:1 3rd:0 Ran:5
Win Prizemoney £3,777 *Total Prizemoney* £10,890
Wins * **1998** Jun Sandow (G-S) 10f 92 <
1998 Turf 1-5: (10f 1-2, 11f, 12f 2) (gd 1-2, g-f 3)
Scopey, Group-class colt. Turf high 113 - 4th of 7 to Scorned (17 Spt Newbury 11f g-f RF 4329). He found life tough after winning a maiden at Sandown in June, continually performing as if needing further than a mile and a half. He will surely be given a chance to prove that theory correct next term.
**Sir Michael Stoute [1-5] Lord Weinstock.*

DARLING CLOVER BHB 57f56a RR 60f 56a 4409[2]
6 ch m Minster Son10.9f **(56)**- Lady Clementine(He Loves Me) 7.9f **(55)**
Form - 041402
Record 1998 - 1st:1 2nd:1 3rd:0 Ran:6
Pre1998 - 1st:5 2nd:4 3rd:1 Ran:25
Win Prizemoney £21,876 *Total Prizemoney* £28,159

Wins * **1998** Jun Nottin (GD) 10f 60
1996 Spt York (GD) C 8.9f 72 <
1996 Jly Beverl (G-F) H 9.9f 65 68
1996 Jly Beverl (G-F) H 9.9f 60 65
1996 Apr Beverl (G-F) H 9.9f 53 59
1995 May Windso (G-F) H 11.6f 54 58
1998 Turf 1-6: (7f, 10f 1-5) (gd 1-3, g-f 2, frm)
Average mare, effective 7 to 10f, best at 10f, acts on gd to g-f, best on gd, favours tight tracks. Turf high 60 - 1st of 17 getting 5lb from Westminster (8 Jun Nottingham RF 1805).
**R Bastiman [1-15] P A Brigham (from D Morley [5-16] Spt 1996).*

DARNAWAY BHB 97f **RR 100f** 2056[29]

4 b c Green Desert (USA) 7.8f **(78)** - Reuval (Sharpen Up) 8.3f **(67)**
Form - 810
Record 1998 - 1st:1 2nd:0 3rd:0 Ran:3
Pre1998 - 1st:1 2nd:1 3rd:1 Ran:4
Win Prizemoney £12,095 *Total Prizemoney* £14,229
Wins * **1998** May Newmar (G-F) H 7f 94 100 <
* 1997 Spt Lingfi (GD) 7f 84+
1998 Turf 1-3: (7f 1-2, 8f) (sft, gd, frm 1-1)
Scopey, very useful colt, effective 7f, acts on frm. Turf high 100 - 1st of 6 giving 4lb to Plaisir d'Amour (16 May Newmarket RF 1265). Very lightly raced, he was well ridden by Kieren Fallon when making all to win at Newmarket in May. Connections let him go for 13,000 guineas at the Tattersalls Autumn Horses In Training Sales.
**H R A Cecil [2-7] Sir David Wills.*

DARRAS SKY BHB 60f **RR 72f** 4326[11]

2 ch c Clantime 6.6f **(57)** - Sky Music **(82f)** (Absalom) 7.2f **(58)**
Form - 3670
Record 1998 - 1st:0 2nd:0 3rd:1 Ran:4
Win Prizemoney £0 *Total Prizemoney* £263
1998 Turf 0-4: (5f 3, 6f) (g-s, gd 3)
Above-average colt, has worn blinkers. Turf high 72.
**Miss S E Hall [0-4] Skylark Partnership.*

DARWELL'S FOLLY (USA) BHB 70f89a **RR 61f 89a** 4925[8]

3 ch g Blushing John (USA) 8.9f **(75)** - Hispanolia (FR) (Kris) 9.5f **(73)**
Form - 11708
Record 1998 - 1st:2 2nd:0 3rd:0 Ran:5
Pre1998 - 1st:1 2nd:0 3rd:0 Ran:3
Win Prizemoney £10,240 *Total Prizemoney* £10,309
Wins * **1998** *Mar Wolver (STD) H 7f 83 87* <
* **1998** *Feb Wolver (STD) H 6f 77 82*
* 1997 Jly Newcas (GD) 6f 79
1998 Turf 0-3: (8f, 9f, 12f) (g-s, gd 2) 1998 AW 2-2: (6f 1-1, 7f 1-1) (Fibr 2-2)
Strong, useful gelding, effective 6 to 7f, best at 6f, acts on g-f - acts on Fibr. Turf high 61. AW high 87 - 1st of 6 giving 18lb to Colonel Custer (21 Mar Wolverhampton RF 0459) - also 1st of 6 giving 18lb to Rockswain (4 Feb Wolverhampton RF 0219). Becoming disappointing. Narrowly won a maiden auction on his Newcastle debut in July '97, but showed little else on turf. He was gelded afterwards, and came back to make a winning sand debut over six furlongs at Wolverhampton in February. He successfully followed up over an extra furlong at the same track in March and seemed to be improving. Well beaten on Turf.
**M Johnston [3-8] S & P Darwell Ltd.*

DARYABAD (IRE) BHB 62f47a **RR 64f 47a** 5079[21]

6 b g Thatching 7.8f **(69)** - Dayanata (Shirley Heights) 10.3f **(74)**
Form - 807123460
Record 1998 - 1st:1 2nd:1 3rd:1 Ran:9
Pre1998 - 1st:1 2nd:0 3rd:0 Ran:12
Win Prizemoney £6,128 *Total Prizemoney* £8,056
Wins * **1998** Jly Catter (GD) 7f 64
1996 Aug Redcar (G-F) H 7f 72 73 <
1998 Turf 1-8: (7f 1-6, 8f 2) (sft 2, g-s, g-f, frm 1-4) 1998 AW 0-1: (7f) (Fibr)
Average gelding, effective 7 to 8f, best at 7f, acts on g-f to frm, best on frm, has worn blinkers (extremely effectively). Turf high 64 - 1st of 8 getting 3lb from Finisterre (2 Jly Catterick RF 2463). Inconsistent.
**R McGhin [1-9] The C & M Racing Partnership (from T J Naughton [1-12] Feb 1997).*

DASHER AND STASHER (IRE) BHB 63f **RR 72f** 4767[8]

2 b br c Distinctly North (USA) 7.4f **(63)** - Jep Chapeau (Viking (USA)) 6.7f **(65)**
Form - 16008
Record 1998 - 1st:1 2nd:0 3rd:0 Ran:5
Win Prizemoney £2,804 *Total Prizemoney* £2,804
Wins * **1998** Jun Ayr (GD) 6f 72 <
1998 Turf 1-5: (6f 1-4, 8f) (sft, gd 1-2, frm 2)
Above-average colt, has worn blinkers. Turf high 72 (1st run) - 1st of 7 from Perigeux (19 Jun Ayr RF 2112).
**J J O'Neill [1-5] Clayton Bigley Partnership Ltd.*

DASHIBA BHB 85f **RR 86f** 4389[2]

2 gr f Dashing Blade 7.9f **(80)** - Alsiba (Northfields (USA)) 9f **(72)**
Form - 3343732
Record 1998 - 1st:0 2nd:1 3rd:4 Ran:7
Win Prizemoney £0 *Total Prizemoney* £6,956
1998 Turf 0-7: (5f, 6f 3, 7f 3) (g-s, gd 2, g-f 2, frm 2)
Useful filly, effective 6 to 7f, best at 7f, acts on g-s to frm. Turf high 86 - 2nd of 16 to Morning Music (21 Spt Kempton 7f frm RF 4389). Third in the Chesham at Ascot, she gave her rider all sorts of problems next time and ran no sort of race. Decent runs since, and should find a race. **D R C Elsworth [0-7] J C Smith.*

DASHING BLUE BHB 109f **RR 110f** 4594[3]

5 ch g Dashing Blade 7.9f **(80)** - Blubella (Balidar) 7.9f **(63)**
Form - 50473053303
Record 1998 - 1st:0 2nd:0 3rd:4 Ran:11
Pre1998 - 1st:6 2nd:6 3rd:4 Ran:25
Win Prizemoney £54,948 *Total Prizemoney* £121,485
Wins * 1997 Oct Newmar (GD) L 5f 108
* 1997 Spt Doncas (G-F) H 5.6f 105 111 <
* 1997 Jly York (GD) H 5f 99 103
* 1996 Apr Sandow (GD) H 5f 93 94
* 1995 Oct York (GD) H 6f 86 91
* 1995 Aug Ripon (G-F) 6f 85
1998 Turf 0-11: (5f 8, 6f 3) (gd 6, g-f 2, frm 3)
Group-class gelding, effective 5 to 6f, best at 6f, acts on gd to frm, best on gd, excels at Doncaster, does well at York. Turf high 110 - 3rd of 17 giving 3lb to Lochangel (20 Aug York 5f frm RF 3773). He was as good as ever in 1998, but failed to get his head in front despite giving his all on every occasion. It is hard to imagine him improving at six, but connections will surely be able to find a suitably soft Listed race on the continent.
**I A Balding [6-36] Mrs Duncan Allen.*

DASHING CHIEF (IRE) BHB 95f **RR 108df** 3985[5]

3 b c Darshaan 11.9f **(81)** - Calaloo Sioux (USA) (Our Native (USA)) 11.2f **(63)**
Form - 33085
Record 1998 - 1st:0 2nd:0 3rd:2 Ran:5
Pre1998 - 1st:1 2nd:0 3rd:0 Ran:5
Win Prizemoney £3,915 *Total Prizemoney* £11,508
Wins * 1997 Oct Pontef (G-F) 10f 87 <
1998 Turf 0-5: (10f, 11f, 12f 3) (sft, g-f 4)
Pattern-class colt, effective 11f, acts on g-f. Turf high 108 - 3rd of 6 to High-Rise (9 May Lingfield 11f g-f RF 1125). He lost the plot after finishing third in the Group Three Derby Trial at Lingfield.
**M A Jarvis [1-10] Antonio Balzarini.*

DATE RR 80+f 2578[3]

2 b c Cadeaux Genereux 7.9f**(76)** - Faribole(IRE)(Esprit du Nord (USA))
Form - 3
Record 1998 - 1st:0 2nd:0 3rd:1 Ran:1
Win Prizemoney £0 *Total Prizemoney* £756
1998 Turf 0-1: (7f) (frm)
Currently decent colt. (1st run) - 3rd of 9 to Nimello (7 Jly Newmarket 7f frm RF 2578). **E A L Dunlop [0-1] Abdullah Ali.*

DATO STAR (IRE) BHB 92f **RR 99f** 5151[3]

7 br g Accordion 11.3f **(75)** - Newgate Fairy (Flair Path) 7.8f **(79)**
Form - P0313
Record 1998 - 1st:1 2nd:0 3rd:2 Ran:5
Pre1998 - 1st:0 2nd:2 3rd:1 Ran:7
Win Prizemoney £5,468 *Total Prizemoney* £24,553
Wins * **1998** Oct Ayr (HVY) H 13.1f 85 99 <
1998 Turf 1-5: (12f, 13f 1-2, 14f, 19f) (sft 1-2, gd 2, g-f)

Very useful gelding. Turf high 99 - 1st of 6 giving 24lb to Rossel (13 Oct Ayr RF 4769). Inconsistent. A very smart hurdler, he was very useful in bumpers prior to that, but has been set some stiff tasks in his rare sorties on the Flat proper, and does not have much in the way of a turn of foot. Scored in testing ground at Ayr in October, and was placed for the third year running in the November Handicap at Doncaster. Finds twelve furlongs on the sharp side nowadays, but will win more races on the Flat.

**J M Jefferson [6-21] Kath Riley, Mrs M Guthrie & Joe Donald.*

DAUNTED (IRE) BHB 73f80a RR 69f 80a 5073[2]

2 b g Priolo (USA) 10.9f **(71)** - Dauntess (Formidable (USA)) 9.2f **(63)**

Form - 07002

Record 1998 - 1st:0 2nd:1 3rd:0 Ran:5

Win Prizemoney £0 *Total Prizemoney* £1,270

1998 Turf 0-5: (5f, 6f, 7f 2, 8f) (g-s, gd 3, frm)

Decent gelding, has worn blinkers. Turf high 68 (began Aug) - 2nd of 19 to Gold Honor (31 Oct Newmarket 8f gd RF 5073).

**G L Moore [0-5] Allen & Associates.*

DAUNTING (IRE) BHB 50f RR 54f 4708[11]

3 br f Formidable (USA) 7.8f **(60)** - Durun (Run The Gantlet (USA)) 12.1f **(59)**

Form - 78000

Record 1998 - 1st:0 2nd:0 3rd:0 Ran:5

1998 Turf 0-5: (8f, 10f 3, 11f) (g-f 2, frm 3)

Scopey, fair filly. Turf high 54 (began Jly).

**Lady Herries [0-5] Hesmonds Stud.*

DAUNTING ASSEMBLY RR 18f 4108[13]

3 ch f Presidium 7.5f **(56)** - Dauntless Flight (Golden Mallard) 5.7f **(38)**

Form - 00

Record 1998 - 1st:0 2nd:0 3rd:0 Ran:2

1998 Turf 0-2: (8f 2) (g-f, frm)

Leggy, currently poor filly. Turf high 18 (began Aug).

**B W Murray [0-2] Miss N A Harrod.*

Daunting Lady was unfazed by heavy going in April

DAUNTING LADY (IRE) BHB 100f RR 101f 4367[22]

3 b f Mujadil (USA) 7.7f **(70)** - Dauntess (Formidable (USA)) 9.2f **(63)**

Form - 16877800

Record 1998 - 1st:1 2nd:0 3rd:0 Ran:8
Pre1998 - 1st:2 2nd:1 3rd:2 Ran:6

Win Prizemoney £30,523 *Total Prizemoney* £58,275

Wins * **1998** Apr Newbur (HVY) G3 7.3f 108+ <
* 1997 May Cheste (SFT) 5.1f 97+
* 1997 Apr Sandow (G-F) 5f 78+

1998 Turf 1-8: (6f 2, 7f 1-4, 8f 2) (sft 1-3, gd 3, g-f, frm)

Unfurnished, very useful filly, effective 7 to 8f, acts on sft to gd, has worn blinkers. Turf high 108 (1st run) - 1st of 7 from Wenda (18 Apr Newbury RF 0744). She put up a sizzling display when winning the Group Three Fred Darling Stakes on her reappearance, but failed to make the frame in any of her subsequent outings. She made 50,000 guineas at the Tattersalls Autumn Horses In Training Sales and will make a smashing broodmare.

**R Hannon [3-14] E C Nagell-Erichsen & T J Dale.*

DAUPHIN (IRE) BHB 32f44a RR 41f 44a 4890[8]

5 b br g Astronef 7.9f **(59)** - Va Toujours (Alzao (USA)) 7.1f **(68)**

Form - 0864D8008

Record 1998 - 1st:0 2nd:0 3rd:0 Ran:9
Pre1998 - 1st:3 2nd:2 3rd:2 Ran:24

Win Prizemoney £10,961 *Total Prizemoney* £14,213

Wins * 1997 Oct Ascot (HVY) H 12f 42 52 <
* 1997 May Warwic (FRM) H 10.8f 41 44
* 1996 Spt Haydoc (GD) H 11.9f 34 43

1998 Turf 0-9: (10f, 11f 2, 12f 3, 14f 2, 16f) (g-s, gd 2, g-f 3, frm 3)

Moderate gelding, effective 10 to 12f, best at 12f, acts on g-s to hrd. Turf high 41. Inconsistent. **W J Musson [3-33] Mrs Rita Brown.*

DAVE THE BANK RR 62f 5008[10]

3 ch g Desert Dirham (USA) - L'Ancressaan (Dalsaan) 9.8f **(64)**

Form - 40

Record 1998 - 1st:0 2nd:0 3rd:0 Ran:2

Win Prizemoney £0 *Total Prizemoney* £232

1998 Turf 0-2: (10f, 12f) (sft 2)

Workmanlike, currently average gelding. Turf high 62 (began Oct).

**A Bailey [0-2] Denis Gallagher.*

DAVID BHB 61f RR 72f 5124[7]

2 ch g Risk Me (FR) 8f **(53)** - Capriati (USA) (Diesis) 9.3f **(69)**

Form - 531407

Record 1998 - 1st:1 2nd:0 3rd:1 Ran:6

Win Prizemoney £1,819 *Total Prizemoney* £2,081

Wins * **1998** Jun Bright (GD) S 6f 72+ <

1998 Turf 1-4: (6f 1-3, 8f) (g-s, gd 1-2, frm) 1998 AW 0-2: (5f 2) (Equi, Fibr)

Above-average gelding, effective 6f, acts on gd. Turf high 72 (1st run) - 1st of 8 from Lucky Red (15 Jun Brighton RF 1986). AW high 60. **Miss Gay Kelleway [1-6] Miss Gay Kelleway.*

DAVID JAMES' GIRL BHB 26f43a RR 30f 43a 201[5]

6 b m Faustus (USA) 9.1f **(54)** - Eagle's Quest (Legal Eagle) 7.3f **(54)**

Form - 5

Record 1998 - 1st:0 2nd:0 3rd:0 Ran:1
Pre1998 - 1st:5 2nd:5 3rd:7 Ran:49

Win Prizemoney £12,919 *Total Prizemoney* £19,116

Wins * 1996 *Jun Southw (STD) SH 7f 52 63*
* 1996 *Mar Southw (STD) S 8f 50*
* 1995 *Mar Wolver (STD) H 7f 58 67* <
* 1994 *Dec Wolver (STD) S 7f 66*
* 1994 Spt Ayr (G-S) S 5f 66

1998 AW 0-1: (8f) (Fibr)

Moderate mare, effective 8 to 9f, best at 8f, - acts on Fibr, has worn blinkers, favours left handed tracks. (1st run) - 5th of 10 getting 12lb from Inclination (2 Feb Southwell 8f Fibr RF 0201).

**A Bailey [5-50] One In Ten Racing Club.*

DAVIS ROCK BHB 42f65a RR 31f 65a 4955[9]

4 ch f Rock City 8.8f **(62)** - Sunny Davis (USA) (Alydar (USA)) 9.1f **(76)**

Form - 35313322200000

Record 1998 - 1st:1 2nd:3 3rd:2 Ran:11
Pre1998 - 1st:2 2nd:7 3rd:3 Ran:21

Win Prizemoney £8,183 *Total Prizemoney* £19,520

Wins * **1998** *Jan Lingfi (STD) H 7f 64 67*
* 1997 Oct Folkes (GD) S 6.9f 52
1996 *Oct Wolver (STD) 6f 69* <

1998 Turf 0-6: (6f, 7f 5) (g-s, gd 3, g-f, frm) 1998 AW 1-5: (7f 1-5) (Equi 1-3, Fibr 2)

Workmanlike, average filly, effective 6 to 7f, best at 7f, acts on g-s to frm - acts on AW, best on Fibr, does well at Wolverhampton and Lingfield. Turf high 58 (1st run) - 2nd of 15 getting 10lb from Night of Glass (17 Apr Thirsk 7f g-s RF 0735). AW high 67 (1st run) - 1st of 9 giving 30lb to Allstars Dancer (6 Jan Lingfield RF 0036). Becoming disappointing. She is a consistent sort over seven furlongs on sand.

**W R Muir [2-23] Gordon Cunningham (from R M McKellar [0-5] Aug 1998).*

DAWN PATROL BHB 52f **RR 54f** 2569[7]
3 ch f Weldnaas (USA) 8.4f **(55)** - Silverdale Rose (Nomination) 7f **(60)**
Form - 502157
Record **1998** - 1st:1 2nd:1 3rd:0 Ran:6
Pre1998 - 1st:0 2nd:0 3rd:0 Ran:8
Win Prizemoney £2,940 *Total Prizemoney* £4,229
Wins * **1998** Jun Mussel (SFT) H 5f 49 54 <
1998 Turf 1-6: (5f 1-3, 6f 3) (gd 1-5, frm)
Lengthy, fair filly, effective 5 to 6f, best at 5f, acts on gd to frm, best on gd. Turf high 54 - 1st of 10 getting 6lb from Double Power (15 Jun Musselburgh RF 1993). After seeming to have had too many chances, she suddenly found her form in June, including a game success in a soft-ground Musselburgh handicap.
**K W Hogg [1-14] Auldyn Stud Ltd.*

DAWN TREADER (USA) BHB 38f37a **RR 43f 37a** 4931[6]
3 gr g El Prado (IRE) 8f **(74)** - Marie de La Ferte (Amber Rama (USA)) 10.2f **(45)**
Form - 600276
Record **1998** - 1st:0 2nd:1 3rd:0 Ran:5
Pre1998 - 1st:0 2nd:0 3rd:0 Ran:6
Win Prizemoney £0 *Total Prizemoney* £624
1998 Turf 0-4: (10f 3, 12f) (sft, g-s, frm 2) 1998 AW 0-1: (11f) (Fibr)
Workmanlike, moderate gelding. Turf high 43.
**R Hannon [0-11] Miss L Regis.*

DAY-BOY BHB 83f **RR 77f** 4349[14]
2 b g Prince Sabo 6.6f **(64)** - Lady Day (FR) (Lightning (FR)) 7.9f **(74)**
Form - 140
Record **1998** - 1st:1 2nd:0 3rd:0 Ran:3
Win Prizemoney £2,804 *Total Prizemoney* £3,162
Wins * **1998** May Ayr (GD) 6f 70 <
1998 Turf 1-3: (6f 1-3) (sft, gd 1-1, g-f)
Currently above-average gelding. Turf high 77 - also 1st of 9 giving 5lb to Three Green Leaves (29 May Ayr RF 1559). Won nicely first time despite running green, but hung badly throughout next time.
**Denys Smith [1-3] Duke of Sutherland.*

DAY COURAGE (USA) BHB 71f **RR 69f** 4876[4]
2 b c Dayjur (USA) 6.8f **(79)** - Badge of Courage (USA) (Well Decorated (USA)) 7.6f **(64)**
Form - 87654
Record **1998** - 1st:0 2nd:0 3rd:0 Ran:5
1998 Turf 0-4: (5f 2, 6f 2) (gd 2, g-f, frm) 1998 AW 0-1: (6f) (Fibr)
Average colt, has worn blinkers. Turf high 69.
**P W Chapple-Hyam [0-5] Luciano Gaucci.*

DAYDREAMER (USA) **RR 52f** 95[7]
5 b g Alleged (USA) 11.8f **(81)** - Stardusk (USA) (Stage Door Johnny) 10.3f **(84)**
Form - 7
Record **1998** - 1st:0 2nd:0 3rd:0 Ran:1
Pre1998 - 1st:0 2nd:0 3rd:0 Ran:1
1998 AW 0-1: (10f) (Equi)
Fair gelding.
**G L Moore [0-1] Mrs Rita Bates (from J H M Gosden [0-1] Nov 1995).*

DAYLAMI (IRE) BHB 123f **RR 123f** 4852[3]
4 gr c Doyoun 10.7f **(69)** - Daltawa (IRE) (Miswaki (USA)) 9f **(81)**
Form - 131413
Record **1998** - 1st:3 2nd:0 3rd:2 Ran:6
Pre1998 - 1st:2 2nd:2 3rd:2 Ran:6
Win Prizemoney £479,615 *Total Prizemoney* £670,137
Wins * **1998** Spt Belmon (FRM) 11f 123 <
* **1998** Jly Sandow (GD) G1 10f 123 <
* **1998** May Currag (G-F) G2 10f 119+
1997 May Longch (SFT) G1 8f 118
1997 Apr Longch (GD) G3 8f 109
1998 Turf 3-6: (10f 2-4, 11f 1-1, 12f) (gd 2-4, g-f, frm 1-1)
Very high-class colt, effective 8 to 12f, acts on g-s to frm, and likes Longchamp. Turf high 123 - 1st of 7 from Faithful Son (4 Jly Sandown RF 2550) - also 1st of 9 from Buck's Boy (12 Spt Belmont Park RF 4341a). Consistent. One of the leading three-year-old milers of 1997, winner of the French Guineas, he joined the Godolphin team for this term and was the easy winner of a Curragh Group Two on his debut for them. Possibly unlucky when third to stable-companion Faithful Son at Ascot, he reversed the form with that rival on better terms in the Eclipse, coming out best in a driving finish. He ran well to be fourth in the King George, before landing the Grade One Man O'War Stakes over eleven furlongs on firm ground, which looks to be the limit of his stamina. He was a touch disappointing when only third in the Champion Stakes, though it may have been a little too soon after his trip abroad. He was due to run in the Breeders' Cup Turf, but missed the race due to an infection.
**S bin Suroor [3-6] Godolphin (from A deRoyerDupre in FR [2-6] Spt 1997).*

DAYLIGHT DREAMS BHB 45f51a **RR 42df 51a** 2474[12]
4 b f Indian Ridge 7.6f **(74)** - Singing Nelly (Pharly (FR)) 9.8f **(68)**
Form - 0000
Record **1998** - 1st:0 2nd:0 3rd:0 Ran:4
Pre1998 - 1st:1 2nd:0 3rd:0 Ran:12
Win Prizemoney £3,363 *Total Prizemoney* £3,603
Wins * 1996 Apr Ripon (GD) 5f 79 <
1998 Turf 0-3: (6f 2, 8f) (g-s, g-f, hrd) 1998 AW 0-1: (7f) (Fibr)
Unfurnished, fair filly, has broken blood-vessels, effective 8f, acts on frm, likes left handed tracks, likes tight tracks. Turf high 27. Becoming disappointing. **C A Cyzer [1-16] R M Cyzer.*

DAYMARTI (IRE) **RR 113f** 2290a[6]
3 b c Caerleon (USA) 10.9f **(79)** -Daltawa (IRE) (Miswaki (USA)) 9f **(81)**
Form - 206
1998 Turf 0-3: (10f, 11f, 12f) (gd 3)
Group-class colt, has worn blinkers. Turf high 113 (1st run) - 2nd of 5 to Croco Rouge (10 May Longchamp 11f gd RF 1231a). A half-brother to Daylami, he proved most disappointing after running Croco Rouge close in the Prix Lupin. Colty as a juvenile, he may not have the ideal temperament.
**A deRoyerDupre in FR [0-5] H H Aga Khan.*

DAYNABEE BHB 51f **RR 56f** 3960[11]
3 b f Common Grounds 8.1f **(66)** - Don't Wary (FR) (Lomond (USA)) 8.8f **(65)**
Form - 87002251560
Record **1998** - 1st:1 2nd:2 3rd:0 Ran:11
Pre1998 - 1st:3 2nd:2 3rd:2 Ran:13
Win Prizemoney £10,621 *Total Prizemoney* £14,830
Wins * **1998** Jly Windso (G-F) H 6f 52 56
1997 Aug Nottin (G-F) C 5.1f 64 <
1997 Jly Newcas (GD) S 6f 61
1997 Jly Leices (GD) S 5f 59
1998 Turf 1-11: (6f 1-9, 7f 2) (g-s 2, gd 2, g-f 4, frm 1-3)
Unfurnished, fair filly, effective 5 to 6f, best at 5f, acts on gd to frm - acts on Fibr. Turf high 56.
**A J McNae [1-7] T L Beecroft (from N Tinkler [3-17] May 1998).*

DAYRAVEN BHB 55f **RR 57f** 4997[10]
2 ch c Midyan (USA) 9.9f **(64)** - Aunt Judy (Great Nephew) 9.9f **(64)**
Form - 800
Record **1998** - 1st:0 2nd:0 3rd:0 Ran:3
1998 Turf 0-3: (7f 2, 8f) (sft, gd 2)
Currently fair colt. Turf high 57 (began Spt).
**I A Balding [0-3] T M Mason.*

DAYRELLA BHB 48f45a **RR 44f 45a** 2559[12]
4 ch f Beveled (USA) 6.9f **(64)** - Divissima (Music Boy) 6.8f **(57)**
Form - 7600040
Record **1998** - 1st:0 2nd:0 3rd:0 Ran:7
Pre1998 - 1st:2 2nd:0 3rd:2 Ran:14
Win Prizemoney £5,355 *Total Prizemoney* £6,224
Wins * 1997 Jun Windso (G-F) H 6f 49 51 <
* 1997 *May Lingfi (STD) H 6f 49 48*
1998 Turf 0-4: (5f, 6f 3) (g-f 2, frm 2) 1998 AW 0-3: (6f 2, 7f) (Equi 3)
Light-framed, fair filly, effective 6 to 7f, best at 6f, acts on g-f to frm - acts on AW, has worn blinkers. Turf high 44. AW high 41.
**W R Muir [2-21] Dulverton Equine.*

DAYS OF GRACE BHB 58f **RR 58f** 2450[10]
3 gr f Wolfhound (USA) 7.3f **(71)** - Inshirah (USA) (Caro) 9.3f **(74)**
Form - 0540
Record **1998** - 1st:0 2nd:0 3rd:0 Ran:4
Pre1998 - 1st:1 2nd:0 3rd:2 Ran:9
Win Prizemoney £2,898 *Total Prizemoney* £5,760

Wins * 1997 May Redcar (FRM) 5f 69 <
1998 Turf 0-4: (5f 2, 6f 2) (gd, g-f 2, frm)
Fair filly, effective 5f, acts on g-f to hrd. Turf high 58.
**M Meade [1-13] Stephen Bayless.*

Win Prizemoney £7,943 *Total Prizemoney* £17,564
Wins 1995 Apr Kempto (GD) H 9f 56 64 <
1995 *Apr Southw (STD) H 8f 56 56*
1998 Turf 0-1: (10f) (gd)

Daylami lands Frankie Dettori a first Coral-Eclipse

DAY STAR RR 55f 5137[7]

2 b f Dayjur (USA) 6.8f **(79)** - Krisalya (Kris) 9.5f **(73)**
Form - 7
Record 1998 - 1st:0 2nd:0 3rd:0 Ran:1
1998 Turf 0-1: (7f) (gd)
Currently fair filly. **C F Wall [0-1] A E Oppenheimer.*

DAYTIME RR 61f 3653[17]

2 b c Danehill (USA) 9.1f **(79)** - Zenith (Shirley Heights) 10.3f **(74)**
Form - 0
Record 1998 - 1st:0 2nd:0 3rd:0 Ran:1
1998 Turf 0-1: (7f) (gd)
Currently average colt. **Lord Huntingdon [0-1] The Queen.*

DAYTONA BEACH (IRE) BHB 38f65a RR 58f 65a 4589[15]

8 ch g Bluebird (USA) 7.9f **(71)** - Water Spirit (USA) (Riverman (USA)) 9.1f **(76)**
Form - 0
Record 1998 - 1st:0 2nd:0 3rd:0 Ran:1
Pre1998 - 1st:3 2nd:7 3rd:3 Ran:30

Average gelding, has worn blinkers. Becoming disappointing.
**J W Mullins [0-1] Beach Buddies (from D J S ffrenchDavis [1-6] Oct 1996).*

DAZILYN LADY (USA) BHB 95f RR 102f 4971[2]

3 ch f Zilzal (USA) 8.5f **(79)** - Jetbeeah (IRE) (Lomond (USA)) 8.8f **(65)**
Form - 2682062432
Record 1998 - 1st:0 2nd:4 3rd:1 Ran:10
Pre1998 - 1st:2 2nd:1 3rd:0 Ran:5
Win Prizemoney £10,365 *Total Prizemoney* £32,848
Wins * 1997 Spt Pontef (G-S) 6f 96 <
* 1997 Jly Nottin (G-F) 6.1f 79
1998 Turf 0-10: (7f 2, 8f 8) (hvy 2, sft 2, g-s, gd 2, g-f 2, frm)
Scopey, very useful filly, effective 6 to 8f, best at 8f, acts on hvy to g-f, does well at Doncaster. Turf high 102 - 6th of 6 getting 12lb from Handsome Ridge (10 Spt Doncaster 8f gd RF 4205). Like most of Zilzal's stock, she is a fidget. That is no reflection on her generosity, however, and she ran a series of fine races in Listed events without getting her head in front. She does not look an obvious improver.
**P W Harris [2-15] M Parker G Knight & Mrs G Godfrey.*

DAZZLING QUINTET BHB 73f **RR 78f** 4836[5]
2 ch f Superlative 8.8f **(57)** - Miss Display (Touch Paper) 6.8f **(57)**
Form - 087413435
Record 1998 - 1st:1 2nd:0 3rd:2 Ran:9
Win Prizemoney £2,477 *Total Prizemoney* £3,495
Wins * **1998** Jly Beverl (GD) 5f 78 <
1998 Turf 1-9: (5f 1-8, 6f) (g-s, gd 1-3, g-f 3, frm, hrd)
Above-average filly, effective 5 to 6f, best at 5f, acts on gd to g-f, best on gd. Turf high 78 - 3rd of 9 getting 7lb from Lough Swilly (12 Aug Nottingham 6f gd RF 3583) - also 1st of 17 from Saffron (28 Jly Beverley RF 3159). Inconsistent.
**C Smith [1-9] Roman Bath V.*

DAZZLING STONE BHB 44f **RR 51f** 4676[4]
4 b g Mujtahid (USA) 7.4f **(69)** - Lady In Green (Shareef Dancer (USA)) 9.9f **(73)**
Form - 53624
Record 1998 - 1st:0 2nd:1 3rd:1 Ran:5
Pre1998 - 1st:0 2nd:1 3rd:0 Ran:7
Win Prizemoney £0 *Total Prizemoney* £2,836
1998 Turf 0-5: (5f 2, 6f 2, 7f) (gd 2, g-f 2, frm)
Scopey, fair gelding, effective 6f, acts on g-f. Turf high 51 (began Jly).
**C W Fairhurst [0-5] David Bartlett (from Lady Herries [0-6] Oct 1997).*

DEAC'S PET BHB 65f **RR 67f** 5011[4]
2 b c Tina's Pet 7.4f **(56)** - Springhead **(56df)** (Komaite (USA))
Form - 404
Record 1998 - 1st:0 2nd:0 3rd:0 Ran:3
Win Prizemoney £0 *Total Prizemoney* £264
1998 Turf 0-3: (5f, 6f 2) (g-s, gd 2)
Currently average colt. Turf high 67 (began Oct).
**M Johnston [0-3] Robert Deacon Elliott.*

DEAD AIM (IRE) BHB 63f **RR 65df** 4470[9]
4 b g Sadler's Wells (USA)11.3f **(87)** - Dead Certain (Absalom) 7.2f **(58)**
Form - 03320770
Record 1998 - 1st:0 2nd:1 3rd:2 Ran:8
Pre1998 - 1st:1 2nd:1 3rd:2 Ran:8
Win Prizemoney £3,467 *Total Prizemoney* £7,889
Wins 1997 Aug Windso (G-F) H 11.6f 75 78 <
1998 Turf 0-8: (10f, 11f, 12f 4, 13f, 15f) (sft, gd 2, g-f, frm 4)
Average gelding, effective 9 to 13f, acts on gd to frm, best on g-f, has worn blinkers, prefers tight tracks. Turf high 79 - 3rd of 15 giving 23lb to Veronica Franco (14 May Salisbury 12f frm RF 1218). Inconsistent.
**Mrs J Brown [0-4] Mrs Karan Ridley (from I A Balding [1-12] May 1998).*

DEADLY NIGHTSHADE (IRE) RR 102f 4739[2]
2 b f Night Shift (USA) 8.1f **(73)** - Dead Certain (Absalom) 7.2f **(58)**
Form - 112
Record 1998 - 1st:2 2nd:1 3rd:0 Ran:3
Win Prizemoney £7,146 *Total Prizemoney* £16,171
Wins * **1998** Spt Goodwo (G-F) 6f 88+ <
* **1998** Aug Bath (FRM) 5.1f 74+
1998 Turf 2-3: (5f 1-2, 6f 1-1) (g-s, frm 2-2)
Currently very useful filly. Turf high 102 (began Aug) - 2nd of 12 to Show Me The Money (10 Oct Ascot 5f g-s RF 4739). Held in the highest regard by her trainer, this filly was sold privately to Michael Tabor after making a winning debut at Bath in August. That looked a shrewd purchase after she found a fifth gear to win at Goodwood in September, but she was gunned down by Show Me The Money in the Group Three Cornwallis Stakes at Ascot the following month. However, connections believe that her speed was blunted by soft ground that day and, granted faster conditions, she could be challenging for top sprint honours in 1999.
**D R C Elsworth [2-3] M Tabor & Mrs John Magnier.*

DEAL FAIR RR 86f 4583[1]
2 b c Grand Lodge (USA) - Darshay (FR) (Darshaan) 9.9f **(84)**
Form - 31
Record 1998 - 1st:1 2nd:0 3rd:1 Ran:2
Win Prizemoney £2,107 *Total Prizemoney* £2,587
Wins * **1998** Spt Salisb (HVY) 8f 86 <
1998 Turf 1-2: (7f, 8f 1-1) (gd 1-1, g-f)
Currently useful colt. Turf high 86 (began Spt) - 1st of 13 giving 5lb to Sabotiere (30 Spt Salisbury RF 4583).
**H R A Cecil [1-2] Baron G Von Ullmann.*

DEBAAJ BHB 75f **RR 67f** 4196[8]
2 ch c Indian Ridge 7.6f **(74)** - Gold Bracelet (Golden Fleece (USA)) 7.9f **(74)**
Form - 348
Record 1998 - 1st:0 2nd:0 3rd:1 Ran:3
Win Prizemoney £0 *Total Prizemoney* £1,243
1998 Turf 0-3: (6f 2, 7f) (gd 2, frm)
Currently average colt. Turf high 67 (began Aug).
**J L Dunlop [0-3] Kuwait Racing Syndicate.*

DE BALLIOL RR 83f 5039[11]
2 b c Sadler's Wells (USA) 11.3f **(87)** - Khalafiya (Darshaan) 9.9f **(84)**
Form - 60
Record 1998 - 1st:0 2nd:0 3rd:0 Ran:2
Win Prizemoney £0 *Total Prizemoney* £224
1998 Turf 0-2: (7f, 8f) (g-s, gd)
Currently decent colt. Turf high 83 (began Spt).
**B W Hills [0-2] Sheikh Mohammed.*

DEBBIE'S HOPE RR 51 1971[10]
2 ch f Be My Chief (USA) 10.2f **(62)** - Appleton Heights (Shirley Heights) 10.3f **(74)**
Form - 0
Record 1998 - 1st:0 2nd:0 3rd:0 Ran:1
1998 Turf 0-1: (5f) (gd)
Currently fair filly. **K Mahdi [0-1] Greenfield Stud.*

DEB'S DELIGHT BHB 50f **RR 54f** 4768[13]
3 ch f Most Welcome 8.6f **(66)** - Adana (FR) (Green Dancer (USA)) 10.3f **(74)**
Form - 7060
Record 1998 - 1st:0 2nd:0 3rd:0 Ran:4
1998 Turf 0-4: (8f 3, 9f) (sft 2, gd, frm)
Leggy, fair filly. Turf high 54. **C W Thornton [0-4] Guy Reed.*

DECISIVE ACTION (USA) RR 91?f 4329[7]
3 br c Alleged (USA) 11.8f **(81)** - Maria Balastiere (USA) (Majestic Light (USA)) 10.6f **(75)**
Form - 7
Record 1998 - 1st:0 2nd:0 3rd:0 Ran:1
Pre1998 - 1st:1 2nd:0 3rd:0 Ran:1
Win Prizemoney £4,045 *Total Prizemoney* £4,045
Wins * 1997 Oct Nottin (SFT) 8.2f 91+ <
1998 Turf 0-1: (11f) (g-f)
Strong, currently useful colt. Tailed off in a Listed race on his sole run. **P F I Cole [1-2] Christopher Wright.*

DECODED BHB 50f **RR 63f** 5094[20]
2 ch c Deploy 11.4f **(67)** - Golden Panda (Music Boy) 6.8f **(57)**
Form - 0845800
Record 1998 - 1st:0 2nd:0 3rd:0 Ran:7
Win Prizemoney £0 *Total Prizemoney* £236
1998 Turf 0-7: (7f 2, 8f 4, 10f) (g-s, gd 4, g-f 2)
Average colt, often wears blinkers. Turf high 63.
**J L Eyre [0-7] A G Watson.*

DECORATED HERO BHB 119f **RR 121f** 4849[1]
6 b g Warning 8.1f **(77)** - Bequeath (USA) (Lyphard (USA)) 9.9f **(72)**
Form - 6164131
Record 1998 - 1st:3 2nd:0 3rd:1 Ran:6
Pre1998 - 1st:11 2nd:6 3rd:3 Ran:26
Win Prizemoney £309,026 *Total Prizemoney* £465,421
Wins * **1998** Oct Newmar (GD) G2 7f 121 <
* **1998** Spt Goodwo (G-F) G3 7f 121 <
* **1998** Jly Newcas (G-F) G3 7f 121 <
* 1997 Oct Longch (G-F) G2 8f 111
* 1997 Spt Goodwo (GD) G3 7f 112
* 1997 Aug Newbur (G-F) G3 7.3f 111
* 1997 Jly Newbur (G-F) 7.3f 117
* 1997 Jun Haydoc (G-F) L 7.1f 112
* 1996 Oct Evry (G-S) L 8f 115
* 1996 Oct Longch (SFT) L 8f 115+
* 1996 Spt Ascot (G-F) H 7f 103 114
* 1996 Spt Doncas (G-F) H 8f 100 104

* 1995 Jly Doncas (G-F) 8f 91+
* 1995 May Lingfi (FRM) 7f 74

1998 Turf 3-6: (7f 3-4, 8f 2) (sft, gd 2-2, g-f 2, frm 1-1)

Very high-class gelding, effective 7 to 8f, best at 7f, acts on gd to hrd, and excels at Newmarket and Goodwood. Turf high 121 (began Jly) - 1st of 10 giving 5lb to Lovers Knot (17 Oct Newmarket RF 4849) - also 1st of 8 giving 13lb to Beraysim (24 Spt Goodwood RF 4461). Consistent. He had a wonderful 1997, his victories including the Hungerford at Newbury and the Prix du Rond-Point at Longchamp, and ran probably the best race of his career when third in the Breeders' Cup Mile. He narrowly beat Diktat in the Beeswing on his belated reappearance, and ran a fine race under top weight in the Tote International Handicap. A respectable fourth in the Celebration Mile, although the watered ground was not as fast as he would have liked, he won back at Goodwood before a good third in this year's Rond-Point. Finished the season with a last-gasp victory in the Challenge Stakes, and will no doubt prove tough to beat again next year.

**J H M Gosden [14-32] Exors of the late Herbert Allen.*

Win Prizemoney £3,687 *Total Prizemoney* £9,536
Wins * 1998 Mar Doncas (GD) 8f 87 <

1998 Turf 1-4: (8f 1-1, 10f 2, 12f) (gd 1-3, g-f)

Scopey, very useful colt. Turf high 102 - 2nd of 5 to Chester House (23 May Doncaster 10f g-f RF 1412). He was beaten by three good horses after making a winning debut at Doncaster. Handicaps are probably out of the question and he will be hard to place.

**P F I Cole [1-4] W S Farish III.*

DEE PEE TEE CEE (IRE) BHB 63f **RR 72f** 4578[10]

4 b g Tidaro (USA) 8.2f **(75)** - Silver Glimpse (Petingo) 11f **(72)**
Form - 000
Record 1998 - 1st:0 2nd:0 3rd:0 Ran:3
Pre1998 - 1st:6 2nd:0 3rd:1 Ran:19
Win Prizemoney £19,709 *Total Prizemoney* £21,048
Wins * 1997 Jly Mussel (GD) H 8f 62 74+ <
* 1997 Jly Beverl (HVY) H 8.5f 62 74
* 1997 Jun Carlis (GD) 8f 65
* 1997 Jun Redcar (GD) H 9f 54 58

Decorated Hero (nearest) gains a last-gasp win in the Challenge Stakes

* 1997 Jun Beverl (SFT) H 7.5f 46 54
* 1996 Jun Redcar (G-F) S 7f 59+

1998 Turf 0-3: (8f 2, 9f) (g-f 2, frm)

Scopey, above-average gelding, effective 8f, acts on g-s to frm, prefers right handed tracks, prefers tight tracks, excels at Beverley. Turf high 57 (began Aug). Becoming disappointing. Lightly raced in '98. **M W Easterby [6-22] Mrs M E Curtis.*

DEECEEBEE BHB 52f **RR 47f** 3814[8]

3 b g Rudimentary (USA) 8.2f **(66)** - Do Run Run (Commanche Run) 8.5f **(58)**
Form - 7068
Record 1998 - 1st:0 2nd:0 3rd:0 Ran:4
Pre1998 - 1st:1 2nd:0 3rd:1 Ran:9
Win Prizemoney £3,615 *Total Prizemoney* £4,105
Wins 1997 Jun Newcas (HVY) 6f 74 <

1998 Turf 0-4: (8f, 9f 2, 12f) (g-s, gd, g-f, frm)

Workmanlike, moderate gelding, effective 6f, acts on g-s, has worn blinkers. Turf high 47. Becoming disappointing.

**J L Eyre [0-4] D C Batey (from W Storey [1-9] Nov 1997).*

DEEP DIVE (USA) BHB 105f **RR 102f** 1963[2]

3 ch c Manila (USA) 10f **(81)** - Shamrock Boat (USA) (Sauce Boat (USA)) 8.3f **(79)**
Form - 1222
Record 1998 - 1st:1 2nd:3 3rd:0 Ran:4

DEEPLY VALE (IRE) BHB 60f57a **RR 63df 57a** 442[9]

7 b g Pennine Walk 8.9f **(64)** - Late Evening (USA) (Riverman (USA)) 9.1f **(76)**
Form - 800
Record 1998 - 1st:0 2nd:0 3rd:0 Ran:2
Pre1998 - 1st:5 2nd:3 3rd:5 Ran:41
Win Prizemoney £11,185 *Total Prizemoney* £17,033
Wins * 1997 *Aug Southw (STD) C 7f 63*
* 1996 *Nov Lingfi (STD) C 7f 62*
* 1996 Apr Folkes (G-F) H 6f 60 65

* 1996 *Mar Wolver (STD) H 6f 65 66*
* 1994 May Folkes (SFT) 6.9f 68+ <
1998 AW 0-2: (7f, 8f) (Equi 2)
Average gelding, effective 7f, acts on sft - acts on Fibr. AW high 46.
**G L Moore [5-37] Speedline Telecom (from P Butler [0-3] Mar 1997).*

DEEP SEA (ITY) RR 98f
833a2
3 b f Royal Academy (USA) 7.8f **(77)** - Khai Taus (USA) (Tank's Prospect (USA))
Form - 22
1998 Turf 0-2: (8f 2) (sft 2)
Currently very useful filly. Turf high 98 - 2nd of 16 to Sopran Londa (19 Apr Capannelle 8f sft RF 0833a).
**M Guarnieri in ITY [0-1] Scuderia Giacobbe (from ITY [0-1] Apr 1998).*

DEEP SPACE (IRE) BHB 84f RR 85f
45088
3 br c Green Desert (USA) 7.8f **(78)** - Dream Season (USA) (Mr Prospector (USA)) 8.8f **(78)**
Form - 247141608
Record 1998 - 1st:2 2nd:1 3rd:0 Ran:9
Pre1998 - 1st:0 2nd:0 3rd:0 Ran:2
Win Prizemoney £8,374 *Total Prizemoney* £10,328
Wins * **1998** Aug Newmar (FRM) H 6f 79 85 <
* **1998** Jly Sandow (GD) H 5f 73 79
1998 Turf 2-9: (5f 1-2, 6f 1-7) (gd 1-5, g-f 2, frm 1-2)
Scopey, useful colt, effective 5 to 6f, best at 5f, acts on gd to frm, best on frm. Turf high 85 - 1st of 10 getting 3lb from Daawe (7 Aug Newmarket RF 3439) - also 1st of 11 getting 5lb from Clan Chief (15 Jly Sandown RF 2827). He looks a progressive young sprinter who scored twice last term, and has some valid excuses for his defeats. Should continue to give a good account.
**E A L Dunlop [2-11] Maktoum Al Maktoum.*

DEERLY BHB 37f43a RR 35f 43a
2033
5 b m Hadeer 8.9f **(58)** - Grafitti Gal (USA) (Pronto) 10f **(59)**
Form - 2083
Record 1998 - 1st:0 2nd:0 3rd:1 Ran:1
Pre1998 - 1st:2 2nd:1 3rd:3 Ran:29
Win Prizemoney £6,340 *Total Prizemoney* £9,367
Wins * 1997 May Chepst (GD) H 6.1f 44 48
1995 May Leices (G-F) S 6f 67+ <
1998 AW 0-1: (6f) (Fibr)
Moderate filly, effective 6f, acts on gd - acts on Fibr, has worn blinkers, likes left handed tracks. Won over six furlongs at Chepstow in May '97, but good performances since have been very few and far between.
**R Dickin [1-14] Mrs Bobbie Mundy (from C A Smith [0-5] Spt 1996).*

DEFIANCE BHB 78f RR 75+f
12237
3 b c Warning 8.1f **(77)** - Princess Athena (Ahonoora) 8.1f **(73)**
Form - 7
Record 1998 - 1st:0 2nd:0 3rd:0 Ran:1
Pre1998 - 1st:0 2nd:0 3rd:2 Ran:3
Win Prizemoney £0 *Total Prizemoney* £1,032
1998 Turf 0-1: (8f) (gd)
Lengthy, above-average colt. **B W Hills [0-4] Ray Richards.*

DEFINED FEATURE (IRE) BHB 63f82a RR 59f 82a
17043
5 ch m Nabeel Dancer (USA) 6.1f **(65)** - Meissarah (USA) (Silver Hawk (USA)) 8.6f **(70)**
Form - 03
Record 1998 - 1st:0 2nd:0 3rd:1 Ran:2
Pre1998 - 1st:3 2nd:2 3rd:4 Ran:19
Win Prizemoney £13,311 *Total Prizemoney* £21,644
Wins 1995 Aug Pontef (G-F) 6f 87 <
1995 Aug Yarmou (G-F) H 6f 84 87 <
1995 Jly Chepst (G-F) 5.1f 73+
1998 Turf 0-2: (7f, 12f) (g-s, frm)
Decent filly, effective 7f, - acts on Fibr, has worn blinkers. Turf high 51.
**Dr J D Scargill [0-12] Derek Johnson (from Sir Michael Stoute [3-9] Oct 1996).*

DEHOUSH (USA) BHB 100f RR 91f
45429
2 ch c Diesis 9f **(80)** - Dream Play (USA) (Blushing Groom (FR)) 10.3f **(76)**
Form - 130
Record 1998 - 1st:1 2nd:0 3rd:1 Ran:3
Win Prizemoney £4,581 *Total Prizemoney* £6,262
Wins * **1998** Jun Newmar (GD) 6f 76+ <
1998 Turf 1-3: (6f 1-1, 7f 2) (g-f 1-1, frm 2)
Currently useful colt. Turf high 91. Looked a useful prospect when making a winning debut at Newmarket, and stepped up on that when third in a listed race. Should do even better over a mile or more. **A C Stewart [1-3] Sheikh Ahmed Al Maktoum.*

DEKELSMARY BHB 45f RR 46f
48775
3 b f Komaite (USA) 6.9f **(61)** - Final Call (Town Crier) 10.2f **(55)**
Form - 000630005
Record 1998 - 1st:0 2nd:0 3rd:1 Ran:9
Pre1998 - 1st:0 2nd:1 3rd:1 Ran:6
Win Prizemoney £0 *Total Prizemoney* £2,133
1998 Turf 0-6: (5f, 6f 4, 7f) (gd 3, g-f 3) 1998 AW 0-3: (6f 3) (Fibr 3)
Workmanlike, moderate filly, effective 6f, acts on gd to frm, has worn blinkers. Turf high 46. AW high 51 (began Jly).
**J Balding [0-15] Derrick Moss.*

DEKI (USA) BHB 76f RR 83f
4268P
3 b br c Mujtahid (USA) 7.4f **(69)** - Glamorous Bride (FR) (Baillamont (USA)) 7f **(78)**
Form - 407P
Record 1998 - 1st:0 2nd:0 3rd:0 Ran:4
Pre1998 - 1st:2 2nd:1 3rd:1 Ran:4
Win Prizemoney £7,263 *Total Prizemoney* £9,826
Wins 1997 Aug Beverl (G-S) H 7.5f 84 87 <
1997 May Lingfi (G-F) 6f 75+
1998 Turf 0-4: (8f 3, 10f) (gd 2, g-f 2)
Leggy, decent colt, effective 7f, acted on gd. Turf high 83. (DEAD)
**E A L Dunlop [0-4] Hadi Al-Tajir (from D Morley [2-4] Aug 1997).*

DE LA HAYE RR
192112
3 b f Puissance 7.1f **(60)** - Hibiscus Ivy (AUS) (Rancher (AUS))
Form - 00
Record 1998 - 1st:0 2nd:0 3rd:0 Ran:1
Pre1998 - 1st:0 2nd:0 3rd:0 Ran:1
1998 Turf 0-1: (7f) (gd)
Leggy, currently poor filly.
**R Simpson [0-2] Wendover Dean Racing Club.*

DELAYED REACTION BHB 51f RR 53f
30737
3 b g Theatrical Charmer 10.9f **(63)** - Pingin (Corvaro (USA)) 9f **(53)**
Form - 5517
Record 1998 - 1st:1 2nd:0 3rd:0 Ran:4
Pre1998 - 1st:0 2nd:0 3rd:0 Ran:3
Win Prizemoney £2,950 *Total Prizemoney* £2,950
Wins * **1998** Jly Folkes (G-F) H 12f 47 53 <
1998 Turf 1-4: (10f, 12f 1-2, 14f) (gd, frm 1-3)
Rangy, fair gelding, effective 12f, acts on frm. Turf high 53 - 1st of 5 giving 5lb to Primaticcio (15 Jly Folkestone RF 2825). He got off the mark in a Folkestone handicap in July when well backed to do so. **N A Callaghan [1-7] R E Sangster.*

DELCIANA (IRE) BHB 48f RR 48f
452912
3 b f Danehill (USA) 9.1f **(79)** - Delvecchia (Glint of Gold) 9.3f **(66)**
Form - 0003080
Record 1998 - 1st:0 2nd:0 3rd:1 Ran:7
Pre1998 - 1st:0 2nd:0 3rd:2 Ran:6
Win Prizemoney £0 *Total Prizemoney* £1,605
1998 Turf 0-7: (6f 2, 7f 2, 8f 3) (g-f 3, frm 4)
Neat, moderate filly, effective 6f, acts on gd to frm. Turf high 48 (began Jly). **P W Harris [0-13] The Delvecchian Dozen.*

DELEGATE RR 96f
41404
5 ch g Polish Precedent (USA) 9f **(73)** - Dangora (USA) (Sovereign Dancer (USA)) 11.2f **(68)**
Form - 4
Record 1998 - 1st:0 2nd:0 3rd:0 Ran:1
Pre1998 - 1st:0 2nd:1 3rd:0 Ran:1
Win Prizemoney £0 *Total Prizemoney* £6,683
1998 Turf 0-1: (5f) (g-f)
Currently very useful gelding. Runner-up in the Prix Djebel at Evry as a three-year-old for Andre Fabre, he obviously had his training problems and was bought for 14,000 guineas. He seemed to find

the trip inadequate at Leicester on his only start last term, but there are not many miles on the clock

**J E Banks [0-1] Mrs P Reditt (from A Fabre in FR [0-1] Apr 1996).*

DELIGHT OF DAWN BHB 54f43a RR 53f 43a 5079[19]

6 b m Never so Bold 7.1f **(62)** - Vogos Angel (Song) 7.2f **(61)**

Form - 1000404736410

Record	1998 -	1st:2	2nd:0	3rd:1	Ran:13
	Pre1998 -	1st:7	2nd:8	3rd:2	Ran:56

Win Prizemoney £31,930 *Total Prizemoney* £42,700

Wins								
	* 1998	Oct	Leices	(G-S)	H	8f	49	53
	* 1998	Mar	Warwic	(G-S)	H	7f	48	54
	1996	May	Windso	(G-F)	C	8.3f		57
	1995	Aug	Newmar	(G-F)	C	7f		67
	1995	Aug	Leices	(G-F)	C	7f		70
	1995	Jly	Newmar	(G-F)	C	7f		70
	1994	Aug	Pontef	(G-F)	H	6f	72	78
	1994	Jly	Pontef	(G-F)	C	6f		56
	1994	Jly	Yarmou	(GD)	S	7f		56

1998 Turf 2-13: (7f 1-7, 8f 1-6) (sft, g-s 1-2, gd 1-2, g-f 4, frm 4)

Fair mare, effective 7 to 8f, best at 7f, acts on g-s to g-f, has worn blinkers, prefers right handed tracks, does well at Windsor. Turf high 54 (1st run) - 1st of 15 getting 26lb from Sweet Wilhelmina (28 Mar Warwick RF 0491) - also 1st of 20 getting 12lb from Elba Magic (12 Oct Leicester RF 4759). Consistent.

**E A Wheeler [2-31] Diamant Precision Engineering Ltd (from R M Stronge [0-10] Oct 1996).*

DELILAH (IRE) BHB 112f RR 111f 5075[2]

4 b f Bluebird (USA) 7.9f **(71)** - Courtesane (USA) (Majestic Light (USA)) 10.6f **(75)**

Form - 5621322

Record	1998 -	1st:1	2nd:3	3rd:1	Ran:6
	Pre1998 -	1st:2	2nd:2	3rd:2	Ran:9

Win Prizemoney £58,104 *Total Prizemoney* £108,438

Wins								
	* 1998	Spt	Doncas	(GD)	G3	14.6f	111	<
	* 1997	Oct	Ascot	(HVY)	G3	12f	104	
	* 1997	Spt	York	(SFT)		10.4f	88+	

1998 Turf 1-6: (12f 3, 13f, 14f, 15f 1-1) (sft, g-s 2, gd 1-3)

Scopey, Group-class filly, effective 12 to 15f, best at 12f, acts on sft to gd, best on g-s, mostly wears blinkers (extremely effectively), likes left handed tracks, likes Ascot. Turf high 111 - 1st of 9 giving 15lb to Kadaka (9 Spt Doncaster RF 4186). Consistent. She benefited from a superb Richard Quinn ride when winning the Group Three Park Hill Stakes at Doncaster in September, being coaxed alongside Kadaka before nosing ahead close home. She was not entirely convincing on her next three starts and was sent to the sales in America.

**Sir Michael Stoute [3-15] Highclere Thoroughbred Racing Ltd.*

DELIRIOUS MOMENT (IRE) BHB 80f RR 81f 5078[4]

4 ch f Kris 10f **(75)** - Stay That Way (Be My Guest (USA)) 9.3f **(67)**

Form - 0018731054

Record	1998 -	1st:2	2nd:0	3rd:1	Ran:10
	Pre1998 -	1st:1	2nd:3	3rd:0	Ran:7

Win Prizemoney £12,697 *Total Prizemoney* £18,387

Wins									
	* 1998	Spt	Yarmou	(G-S)	H	8f	75	81	
	* 1998	Jly	Windso	(G-F)	H	8.3f	72	76	
	1997	Aug	Leopar	(G-S)		8f		86	<

1998 Turf 2-10: (7f 3, 8f 2-6, 9f) (sft, g-s, gd 1-4, g-f 2, frm 1-2)

Decent filly, effective 8 to 10f, best at 8f, acts on g-s to frm. Turf high 81 - 1st of 18 giving 15lb to Swinging The Blues (16 Spt Yarmouth RF 4319). Consistent.

**P R Webber [2-10] F M Alger (from D K Weld in IRE [1-7] Oct 1997).*

DELLUA (IRE) BHB 53f48a RR 60f 48a 5002[10]

4 b f Suave Dancer (USA) 10.7f **(68)** - Joma Kaanem (Double Form) 7.3f **(58)**

Form - 004600

Record	1998 -	1st:0	2nd:0	3rd:0	Ran:6
	Pre1998 -	1st:1	2nd:1	3rd:0	Ran:7

Win Prizemoney £4,123 *Total Prizemoney* £5,358

Wins								
	1997	Spt	Folkes	(FRM)		9.7f	62+	<

1998 Turf 0-5: (10f 4, 11f) (g-s, gd, frm 3) 1998 AW 0-1: (12f) (Equi)

Average filly, effective 10 to 13f, best at 10f, acts on gd to frm, best on gd, likes left handed tracks, prefers tight tracks. Turf high 60 - 4th of 15 giving 1lb to Cherokee Flight (31 Aug Chepstow 10f frm RF 3981). Inconsistent.

**J W Hills [0-6] Khalid Affara (from R Guest [1-7] Oct 1997).*

DELMO RR 38f 3408[6]

3 ch g Democratic (USA) - Charlotte Piaf (Morston (FR)) 9.4f **(55)**

Form - 06

Record	1998 -	1st:0	2nd:0	3rd:0	Ran:2

1998 Turf 0-2: (7f, 8f) (gd, g-f)

Workmanlike, currently very moderate gelding. Turf high 38 (began Jly). **R Simpson [0-2] D J Christopher.*

DELPHIC WAY BHB 50f RR 48f 4961[21]

3 b f Warning 8.1f **(77)** - Palace Street (USA) (Secreto (USA)) 8.7f **(72)**

Form - 6088000

Record	1998 -	1st:0	2nd:0	3rd:0	Ran:7
	Pre1998 -	1st:0	2nd:0	3rd:0	Ran:2

1998 Turf 0-7: (6f 3, 7f 3, 11f) (gd, frm 5, hrd)

Neat, moderate filly. Turf high 56. **G B Balding [0-9] Miss B Swire.*

DELRAY (IRE) RR 95f 4438a[4]

2 b c Wolfhound (USA) 7.3f **(71)** - Euromill (Shirley Heights) 10.3f **(74)**

Form - 02454

1998 Turf 0-5: (5f 2, 6f 3) (sft, gd 3, g-f)

Very useful colt. Turf high 95 - 2nd of 11 giving 5lb to Fear And Greed (27 Jun Curragh 6f sft RF 2423a).

**C Collins in IRE [0-5] Mrs L K McCreery.*

DELTA SOLEIL (USA) BHB 76f70a RR 85?f 70a 4246[20]

6 b h Riverman (USA) 9.7f **(78)** - Sunny Roberta (USA) (Robellino (USA)) 7.6f **(80)**

Form - 67070601012000

Record	1998 -	1st:2	2nd:1	3rd:0	Ran:13
	Pre1998 -	1st:1	2nd:2	3rd:1	Ran:22

Win Prizemoney £19,726 *Total Prizemoney* £30,779

Wins									
	* 1998	Jly	Newbur	(G-F)	H	6f	71	75	
	* 1998	Jun	Salisb	(G-S)	H	6f	65	71	
	1995	Aug	York	(G-F)		7.9f		86	<

1998 Turf 2-11: (6f 2-9, 7f 2) (sft, g-s 2, gd 1-3, g-f 1-3, frm 2) 1998 AW 0-2: (7f, 8f) (Equi, Fibr)

Useful horse, effective 6 to 7f, best at 6f, acts on gd to hrd, excels at Salisbury. Turf high 85 - 2nd of 9 giving 6lb to Present Chance (31 Jly Goodwood 6f gd RF 3234). AW high 59. Inconsistent. He had become disappointing before suddenly popping up in a Salisbury handicap in June. There seemed to be no apparent reason for his improvement, except that he looks much better suited by six furlongs than further these days. Won two races later at Newbury, his trainer reporting that he needs to dominate, and is inconsistent.

**V Soane [2-13] American Quartet (from P W Harris [1-22] Nov 1997).*

DELTA'S WAY (USA) RR 83f 4196[4]

2 b c Dayjur (USA) 6.8f **(79)** - Lyphard's Delta (USA) (Lyphard (USA)) 9.9f **(72)**

Form - 44

Record	1998 -	1st:0	2nd:0	3rd:0	Ran:2

Win Prizemoney £0 *Total Prizemoney* £490

1998 Turf 0-2: (7f 2) (gd 2)

Currently decent colt. Turf high 83 (began Aug). Out of a Nassau Stakes winner, he should stay a mile. **H R A Cecil [0-2] S Khaled.*

DE MILLE (USA) RR 85f 3794[1]

3 ch f Nureyev (USA) 8.4f **(84)** - Ghaiya (USA) (Alleged (USA)) 10f **(76)**

Form - 1

Record	1998 -	1st:1	2nd:0	3rd:0	Ran:1

Win Prizemoney £3,631 *Total Prizemoney* £3,631

Wins							
	* 1998	Aug	Sandow	(G-F)	10f	85	<

1998 Turf 1-1: (10f 1-1) (g-f 1-1)

Unfurnished, currently useful filly. (1st run) - 1st of 13 from Royal Fontaine (21 Aug Sandown RF 3794). Unraced at two, she made a belated winning debut at Sandown in August, but still looked weak and may be even better next year.

**J H M Gosden [1-1] Sheikh Mohammed.*

DEMO BOYS (IRE) RR 26tf 3105[8]

2 b c Be My Guest (USA) 10.2f **(66)** - Karine (Habitat) 9.4f **(70)**

Form - 8

Record	1998 -	1st:0	2nd:0	3rd:0	Ran:1

1998 Turf 0-1: (6f) (g-f)

Currently little account colt. **C N Allen [0-1] J T B Racing.*

DEMOCRACY (IRE) RR 80f 1524^{3}

2 ch c Common Grounds 8.1f **(66)** - Inonder (Belfort (FR)) 6.8f **(63)**
Form - 3
Record 1998 - 1st:0 2nd:0 3rd:1 Ran:1
Win Prizemoney £0 *Total Prizemoney* £512
1998 Turf 0-1: (5f) (g-f)
Currently decent colt.
**R Hannon [0-1] Highclere Thoroughbred Racing Ltd.*

DEMOLITION JO BHB 85f73a RR 82f 73a 5152^{6}

3 gr f Petong 7.6f **(58)** - Fire Sprite (Mummy's Game) 8.2f **(60)**
Form - 45082001052268070026
Record 1998 - 1st:1 2nd:4 3rd:0 Ran:19
Pre1998 - 1st:2 2nd:7 3rd:1 Ran:17
Win Prizemoney £13,160 *Total Prizemoney* £34,709
Wins * **1998** Jun Cheste (G-S) H 7f 69 71
* 1997 Oct Newmar (G-S) H 6f 77 81 <
* 1997 Aug Mussel (G-F) 7.1f 73
1998 Turf 1-17: (5f, 6f 12, 7f 1-3, 8f) (sft, g-s, gd 1-6, g-f 6, frm 3) 1998 AW 0-2: (6f 2) (Fibr 2)
Light-framed, decent filly, effective 5 to 6f, best at 6f, acts on gd to g-f, best on gd, mostly wears blinkers (effectively). Turf high 90. AW high 70. Inconsistent. Was kept very busy last year and ran some good races, but only manged to win one race at Chester. Looks happy racing over five furlongs as well as seven furlongs, and should win a couple of races next term.
**P D Evans [3-36] John Pugh.*

DEMON D'OR (IRE) RR 96f $278a^{2}$

6 b h Machiavellian (USA) 9.8f **(83)** - Kilmona (USA) (Bold Bidder) 8.8f **(67)**
Form - 2
1998 Turf 0-1: (11f) (gd)
Currently very useful horse. (1st run) - 2nd of 20 giving 4lb to Fier Danseur (8 Feb Cagnes-Sur-mer 11f gd RF 0278a).
**L Boulard in FR [0-1].*

DENBRAE (IRE) BHB 47f53a RR 60f 53a 4775^{9}

6 b g Sure Blade (USA) 10.6f **(66)** - Fencing (Viking (USA)) 6.7f **(65)**
Form - 345857403680560
Record 1998 - 1st:0 2nd:0 3rd:2 Ran:15
Pre1998 - 1st:4 2nd:3 3rd:5 Ran:34
Win Prizemoney £12,731 *Total Prizemoney* £23,063
Wins * 1997 Aug Leices (GD) 7f 68
* 1996 Jun Chepst (G-F) H 6.1f 68 69 <
* 1995 Apr Nottin (GD) H 6.1f 66 64
* 1995 *Feb Southw (STD) 6f 57*
1998 Turf 0-10: (6f, 7f 8, 8f) (sft, gd 6, g-f 2, frm) 1998 AW 0-5: (7f 3, 8f 2) (Fibr 5)
Average gelding, effective 6 to 7f, best at 6f, acts on gd to frm, best on g-f. Turf high 60. AW high 58. His wins to runs ratio is pretty poor these days, and connections seem unsure as to his best trip. A tricky ride. **D J G MurraySmith [4-49] Cardinal Racing.*

DENSBEN BHB 29f RR 23f 5017^{15}

14 b g Silly Prices 6.8f **(51)** - Eliza de Rich (Spanish Gold) 6f **(49)**
Form - 007786600
Record 1998 - 1st:0 2nd:0 3rd:0 Ran:9
Pre1998 - 1st:12 2nd:8 3rd:12 Ran:124
Win Prizemoney £52,352 *Total Prizemoney* £74,759
Wins * 1996 Spt Haydoc (GD) CH 6f 47 49
* 1995 Spt Haydoc (GD) CH 6f 48 51
* 1995 Spt Haydoc (GD) SH 6f 45 48
1998 Turf 0-9: (5f, 6f 5, 8f 3) (g-s 2, gd 4, g-f, frm 2)
Little account gelding, effective 6 to 7f, acts on frm, has worn blinkers. Turf high 23. Wonderful veteran, but age has finally caught up with him. **Denys Smith [12-133] Mrs Janet Pike.*

DENTARDIA (IRE) BHB 44f60a RR 31f 60a 4609^{8}

3 br g Petardia 8.2f **(58)** - Modena (Sassafras (FR)) 9.6f **(69)**
Form - 30327008
Record 1998 - 1st:0 2nd:1 3rd:2 Ran:8
Pre1998 - 1st:0 2nd:0 3rd:0 Ran:4
Win Prizemoney £0 *Total Prizemoney* £2,292
1998 Turf 0-5: (10f, 12f, 14f 3) (g-s, gd 2, g-f, frm) 1998 AW 0-3: (8f, 12f 2) (Equi, Fibr 2)
Average gelding, effective 12 to 14f, acts on g-f - acts on Fibr, likes tight tracks. Turf high 56 - 2nd of 6 to Cut Diamond (18 May Musselburgh 14f g-f RF 1300). AW high 64 - 3rd of 8 to Blueprint (7 May Southwell 12f Fibr RF 1081). Inconsistent.
**J M P Eustace [0-12] Charles Curtis.*

DEPLOY VENTURE BHB 83f RR 84f 4845^{4}

2 ch c Deploy 11.4f **(67)** -Tasseled (USA) (Tate Gallery (USA)) 7.4f **(67)**
Form - 322314
Record 1998 - 1st:1 2nd:2 3rd:2 Ran:6
Win Prizemoney £3,272 *Total Prizemoney* £6,987
Wins * **1998** *Spt Wolver (STD) 8.5f 77* <
1998 Turf 0-5: (7f 3, 8f 2) (gd 2, g-f 3) 1998 AW 1-1: (8f 1-1) (Fibr 1-1)
Decent colt, effective 7 to 8f, best at 8f, acts on gd to g-f - acts on Fibr, best on g-f. Turf high 84 (began Jly) - 4th of 20 getting 9lb from Fair Flight (16 Oct Newmarket 8f g-f RF 4845). (1st run) - 1st of 7 from Braithwaite (19 Spt Wolverhampton RF 4386). Showed ability in maidens on turf, but looked a little one-paced. Therefore, the extended mile on the Wolverhampton Fibresand ought to have suited, and so it proved. **S P C Woods [1-6] Dr Frank Chao.*

DEPRECIATE BHB 70f79a RR 67f 79a 512^{P}

5 ch h Beveled (USA) 6.9f **(64)** - Shiny Penny (Glint of Gold) 9.3f **(66)**
Form - 874114P
Record 1998 - 1st:2 2nd:0 3rd:0 Ran:5
Pre1998 - 1st:2 2nd:0 3rd:1 Ran:17
Win Prizemoney £15,581 *Total Prizemoney* £19,339
Wins * **1998** *Mar Southw (STD) H 5f 65 77*
* **1998** *Mar Southw (STD) H 6f 65 70*
1995 Jly Cheste (GD) 6.1f 82 <
1995 Jun Goodwo (GD) 6f 72?
1998 Turf 0-2: (5f 2) (gd 2) 1998 AW 2-3: (5f 1-1, 6f 1-2) (Fibr 2-3)
Above-average colt, effective 5 to 6f, - acted on Fibr, had worn blinkers. Turf high 67. AW high 77 - 1st of 10 giving 31lb to Hiltons Executive (17 Mar Southwell RF 0433) - also 1st of 10 getting 10lb from Ziggy's Dancer (9 Mar Southwell RF 0413). He returned to something like his best form when winning two handicaps on the Southwell Fibresand in March. He ran well on his first run back on turf, but tragically had to be put down after sustaining an injury at Newcastle next time. (DEAD)
**T D Barron [2-6] Ian Armitage (from E L James [0-1] Nov 1997).*

DEPUTISE (IRE) RR 53f 4959^{13}

2 b c Caerleon (USA) 10.9f **(79)** - Depaze (USA) (Deputy Minister (CAN)) 7.4f **(80)**
Form - 0
Record 1998 - 1st:0 2nd:0 3rd:0 Ran:1
1998 Turf 0-1: (7f) (frm)
Currently fair colt. **J H M Gosden [0-1] Sheikh Mohammed.*

DERBAAS RR 34f 4926^{6}

3 gr c Polish Precedent (USA) 9f **(73)** - Integrity (Reform) 8.9f **(62)**
Form - 06
Record 1998 - 1st:0 2nd:0 3rd:0 Ran:2
1998 Turf 0-2: (8f, 10f) (g-s, g-f)
Workmanlike, currently very moderate colt. Turf high 34 (began Spt). **B Hanbury [0-2] A Al-Rostamani.*

DERNIERE BICHE (IRE) BHB 19f RR 17f 4549^{14}

3 b f Last Tycoon 9.4f **(73)** - Habichess (Habitat) 9.4f **(70)**
Form - 7000
Record 1998 - 1st:0 2nd:0 3rd:0 Ran:4
1998 Turf 0-3: (7f, 11f, 12f) (gd, frm, hrd) 1998 AW 0-1: (11f) (Fibr)
Workmanlike, poor filly, has worn blinkers. Turf high 17 (began Jly). **Mrs A Swinbank [0-4] The Jolly Boys Partnership.*

DERRYQUIN BHB 69f RR 83f 4962^{13}

3 b g Lion Cavern (USA) 7.5f **(74)** - Top Berry (High Top) 10.2f **(67)**
Form - 405000
Record 1998 - 1st:0 2nd:0 3rd:0 Ran:6
Pre1998 - 1st:2 2nd:0 3rd:0 Ran:3
Win Prizemoney £7,571 *Total Prizemoney* £7,961
Wins * 1997 Nov Doncas (GD) 8f 95 <
* 1997 Oct Lingfi (GD) 7f 81
1998 Turf 0-6: (7f 3, 8f 2, 10f) (sft, g-s, gd, g-f 2, frm)
Light-framed, decent gelding, effective 8f, acts on gd. Turf high 83.

Becoming disappointing. Progressive at two, he showed very little last season. **R Charlton [2-9] Lady Bland.*

DESARU (USA) BHB 100f RR 99f 4512^{3}

2 br c Chief's Crown (USA) 10.2f **(75)** - Team Colors (USA) (Mr Prospector (USA)) 8.8f **(78)**
Form - 213
Record 1998 - 1st:1 2nd:1 3rd:1 Ran:3
Win Prizemoney £5,552 *Total Prizemoney* £19,882
Wins * 1998 Spt Doncas (GD) 7f 99+ <
1998 Turf 1-3: (7f 1-2, 8f) (gd 1-2, frm)
Currently very useful colt. Turf high 99 (began Aug) - 1st of 5 getting 4lb from Chief Rebel (9 Spt Doncaster RF 4182). Made a promising debut in a big field, and skated away from some decent sorts at Doncaster on his second run. Ran well when third in the Royal Lodge on softish ground, and may prefer it faster. A useful prospect. **J Noseda [1-3] K Y Lim.*

DESCANT (IRE) RR 58f 1313^{4}

2 b f Bluebird (USA) 7.9f **(71)** - Dubai Lady (Kris) 9.5f **(73)**
Form - 4
Record 1998 - 1st:0 2nd:0 3rd:0 Ran:1
Win Prizemoney £0 *Total Prizemoney* £354
1998 Turf 0-1: (5f) (frm)
Currently fair filly. (1st run) - 4th of 7 getting 6lb from Oh I Say (18 May Windsor 5f frm RF 1313).
**R Hannon [0-1] The Royal Ascot Racing Club.*

DESDEMONA (IRE) RR 84+f 4665^{7}

2 b f Lahib (USA) 8f **(69)** - Tragic Point (IRE) **(88f)** (Tragic Role (USA))
Form - 27
Record 1998 - 1st:0 2nd:1 3rd:0 Ran:2
Win Prizemoney £0 *Total Prizemoney* £1,072
1998 Turf 0-2: (6f, 8f) (g-s, frm)
Currently decent filly. Turf high 84 (1st run) (began Spt) - 2nd of 10 to Truly Bewitched (25 Spt Redcar 6f frm RF 4489).
**G Wragg [0-2] Cheveley Park Stud.*

DESERT ARROW (USA) BHB 45f RR 28f 1010^{12}

3 b c Gone West (USA) 7.8f **(82)**-Afaff (USA)(Nijinsky (CAN)) 10.3f **(77)**
Form - 00
Record 1998 - 1st:0 2nd:0 3rd:0 Ran:2
Pre1998 - 1st:0 2nd:0 3rd:0 Ran:1
1998 Turf 0-2: (7f, 9f) (sft, g-f)
Scopey, currently little account colt. Turf high 24.
**E A L Dunlop [0-2] Maktoum Al Maktoum (from S bin Suroor [0-1] Jly 1997).*

DESERT CAT (IRE) BHB 48f RR 49f 4919^{6}

5 b g Green Desert (USA) 7.8f **(78)** - Mahabba (USA) (Elocutionist (USA)) 8f **(77)**
Form - 365034044716
Record 1998 - 1st:1 2nd:0 3rd:2 Ran:12
Pre1998 - 1st:0 2nd:0 3rd:2 Ran:12
Win Prizemoney £2,425 *Total Prizemoney* £4,460
Wins * 1998 Spt Mussel (GD) H 7.1f 46 48 <
1998 Turf 1-12: (7f 1-2, 8f 9, 9f) (g-s 2, gd 3, g-f 3, frm 1-4)
Moderate gelding, effective 7 to 9f, acts on frm, has worn blinkers, likes left handed tracks. Turf high 49 (1st run) - 3rd of 15 getting 4lb from Lucky Archer (22 May Nottingham 8f frm RF 1402). Consistent.
**Martyn Wane [1-19] Mrs Linda Miller (from H ThomsonJones [0-5] Jun 1996).*

DESERT DARLING BHB 67f RR 68df 3843^{6}

2 b f Green Desert (USA) 7.8f **(78)** - Habibti (Habitat) 9.4f **(70)**
Form - 306
Record 1998 - 1st:0 2nd:0 3rd:1 Ran:3
Win Prizemoney £0 *Total Prizemoney* £453
1998 Turf 0-3: (5f 3) (gd, frm 2)
Currently average filly. Turf high 68 (1st run) - 3rd of 9 getting 5lb from Westminster City (8 May Lingfield 5f frm RF 1103).
**J Berry [0-3] The Sussex Stud Ltd.*

DESERT DRAMA (IRE) RR 107f $4726a^{6}$

3 f
Form - 306
1998 Turf 0-2: (5f, 8f) (sft, gd)
Pattern-class filly. Turf high 103. She ran well when finishing sixth in the Prix de l'Abbaye, but is not really Group One material. Six furlongs might prove her optimum. **R Collet in FR [0-5] R C Strauss.*

DESERT DUKE RR 82+f 4846^{3}

2 b c Green Desert (USA) 7.8f **(78)** - Guilty Secret (IRE) (Kris) 9.5f **(73)**
Form - 33
Record 1998 - 1st:0 2nd:0 3rd:2 Ran:2
Win Prizemoney £0 *Total Prizemoney* £1,871
1998 Turf 0-2: (6f 2) (gd, g-f)
Currently decent colt. Turf high 82 (began Oct) - 3rd of 19 to Al Naba (16 Oct Newmarket 6f g-f RF 4846).
**Sir Michael Stoute [0-2] Abdulla Al Khalifa.*

DESERT FIGHTER BHB 63f RR 71f 3787^{4}

7 b g Green Desert (USA) 7.8f **(78)** - Jungle Rose (Shirley Heights) 10.3f **(74)**
Form - 032732544
Record 1998 - 1st:0 2nd:2 3rd:2 Ran:9
Pre1998 - 1st:5 2nd:1 3rd:3 Ran:19
Win Prizemoney £18,244 *Total Prizemoney* £24,141
Wins * 1997 May Newcas (G-F) H 12.4f 68 75
* 1997 Apr Thirsk (G-F) 12f 76
1994 Aug Haydoc (GD) H 10.5f 78 89 <
1994 Jly Windso (G-F) H 10f 78 82
1994 Jun Redcar (G-F) 8f 70
1998 Turf 0-9: (9f, 10f 4, 12f 4) (g-s 2, gd 5, frm 2)
Above-average gelding, effective 10 to 12f, best at 12f, acts on g-s to g-f, best on g-f. Turf high 71 - 2nd of 9 to Mcgillycuddy Reeks (3 Jun Newcastle 10f g-s RF 1702).
**Mrs M Reveley [6-35] A Frame (from D Nicholson [0-5] May 1995).*

DESERT FOX RR 117f $2432a^{3}$

3 b c Sadler's Wells (USA) 11.3f **(87)** - Radiant (USA) (Foolish Pleasure (USA)) 8.9f **(72)**
Form - 531363113
1998 Turf 3-9: (8f, 9f 2-2, 10f 1-3, 12f 3) (hvy 1-1, sft 3, gd 1-3, g-f 1-1, hrd)
High-class colt, effective 12f, acts on sft, has worn blinkers (very effectively), prefers right handed tracks. Turf high 117 - 3rd of 10 to Dream Well (28 Jun Curragh 12f sft RF 2432a). He was very busy in the first half of the year, running nine times between March and June. He won three times in minor company, but seemed below top class, until running on into third in the Irish Derby. He was flattered by that though as he merely ran on past beaten horses, and that was that for the season.
**A P O'Brien in IRE [3-12] Mrs John Magnier.*

DESERT FRUIT (USA) RR 75f 5093^{2}

2 b c Red Ransom (USA) 8.6f **(83)** - Lemons To Lemonade (CAN) (Conquistador Cielo (USA)) 8.8f **(69)**
Form - 2
Record 1998 - 1st:0 2nd:1 3rd:0 Ran:1
Win Prizemoney £0 *Total Prizemoney* £1,064
1998 Turf 0-1: (7f) (gd)
Currently above-average colt. **D R Loder [0-1] Maktoum Al Maktoum.*

DESERT GREEN (FR) BHB 72f RR 62df 3609^{11}

9 b g Green Desert (USA) 7.8f **(78)** - Green Leaf (USA) (Alydar (USA)) 9.1f **(76)**
Form - 0
Record 1998 - 1st:0 2nd:0 3rd:0 Ran:1
Pre1998 - 1st:4 2nd:4 3rd:2 Ran:32
Win Prizemoney £54,408 *Total Prizemoney* £73,537
Wins 1996 May Kempto (G-F) H 8f 95 101 <
1995 May Kempto (G-F) H 8f 85 92
1994 Jly Goodwo (FRM) H 8f 74 83
1998 Turf 0-1: (7f) (frm)
Average gelding. Inconsistent. Won Kempton's Jubilee Handicap in 1996, but has been well below that form on the Flat subsequently. **R G Frost [0-2] Terry Sanders (from R Hannon [3-25] Spt 1997).*

DESERT HARVEST BHB 47f38a RR 45?f 38a 886^{15}

6 b g Green Desert (USA) 7.8f **(78)** - Mill on the Floss (Mill Reef (USA)) 10.5f **(78)**
Form - 00

Record **1998 -** 1st:0 2nd:0 3rd:0 Ran:2
Pre1998 - 1st:0 2nd:1 3rd:0 Ran:8
Win Prizemoney £0 *Total Prizemoney* £1,193
1998 AW 0-2: (8f, 13f) (Equi, Fibr)
Moderate gelding. Inconsistent.
**J Cullinan [0-3] Alan Spargo Ltd (from G M McCourt [0-2] May 1996).*

DESERT INVADER (IRE) BHB 35f58a RR 24f 58a 4543[6]

7 br g Lead on Time (USA) 7.5f **(69)** - Aljood (Kris) 9.5f **(73)**
Form - 64040243014155706
Record **1998 -** 1st:2 2nd:1 3rd:1 Ran:17
Pre1998 - 1st:7 2nd:11 3rd:11 Ran:76
Win Prizemoney £23,046 *Total Prizemoney* £37,620

Wins ** **1998** Jun Wolver (STD) H 6f 60 63*
** **1998** Jun Southw (STD) H 7f 55 60*
** 1997 Jun Wolver (STD) H 6f 63 70* <
** 1997 May Southw (STD) C 7f 63*
** 1997 May Wolver (STD) C 6f 56+*
** 1996 Feb Southw (STD) H 7f 57 61*
** 1995 Spt Wolver (STD) H 6f 62 61*
** 1995 Feb Southw (STD) H 8f 60 62*

1998 Turf 0-2:(5f 2)(g-s, gd)1998AW 2-15: (6f 1-8, 7f 1-6, 8f) (Fibr 2-15)
Average gelding, effective 6 to 8f, best at 6f, - acts on Fibr, has worn blinkers, favours left handed tracks, favours tight tracks, and does well at Wolverhampton. Turf high 22. AW high 63 - 1st of 12 giving 1lb to Pharaoh's Joy (20 Jun Wolverhampton RF 2161). He must be one of the busiest horses in training, though he races almost exclusively on Fibresand these days. His strike rate is not brilliant overall though he is perfectly capable of winning races over six or seven furlongs.
**D W Chapman [8-89] David Chapman (from A A Scott [1-4] Jly 1994).*

DESERT KINGDOM (USA) RR 39f 3980[7]

3 b c Sheikh Albadou 9.2f **(75)** - Halley's Comeback (USA) (Key to the Kingdom (USA)) 8.3f **(65)**
Form - 77
Record **1998 -** 1st:0 2nd:0 3rd:0 Ran:2
1998 Turf 0-2: (10f, 12f) (frm 2)
Rangy, currently very moderate colt. Turf high 39 (began Aug).
**R Charlton [0-2] George Ward.*

DESERT LADY (IRE) BHB 100f RR 103f 2908[3]

3 b f Danehill (USA) 9.1f **(79)** - Hooray Lady (Ahonoora) 8.1f **(73)**
Form - 223
Record **1998 -** 1st:0 2nd:2 3rd:1 Ran:3
Pre1998 - 1st:2 2nd:2 3rd:0 Ran:5
Win Prizemoney £8,280 *Total Prizemoney* £22,874

Wins * 1997 Jly Salisb (FRM) 5f 88 <
* 1997 Jun Salisb (G-F) 5f 81+

1998 Turf 0-3: (6f 3) (gd, g-f, frm)
Strong, very useful filly, effective 6f, acts on gd. Turf high 103 - 3rd of 8 to Grazia (18 Jly Newbury 6f gd RF 2908). She improved on her juvenile form, but could never find a knockout punch in Listed events. **R Charlton [2-8] The Thoroughbred Corporation.*

DESERT LORE BHB 32f35a RR 33f 35a 2682[4]

7 b g Green Desert (USA) 7.8f **(78)** - Chinese Justice (USA) (Diesis) 9.3f **(69)**
Form - 04
Record **1998 -** 1st:0 2nd:0 3rd:0 Ran:2
Pre1998 - 1st:1 2nd:1 3rd:2 Ran:16
Win Prizemoney £3,699 *Total Prizemoney* £7,753
1998 Turf 0-2: (6f 2) (gd, frm)
Very moderate gelding. Turf high 33. Inconsistent.
**D A Nolan [0-3] Mrs J McFadyen-Murray (from R M McKellar [0-2] Jan 1997).*

DESERT LYNX (IRE) BHB 47f RR 46f 4475[12]

5 b m Green Desert (USA) 7.8f **(78)** - Sweeping (Indian King (USA)) 7.4f **(64)**
Form - 088000080
Record **1998 -** 1st:0 2nd:0 3rd:0 Ran:9
Pre1998 - 1st:2 2nd:0 3rd:4 Ran:17
Win Prizemoney £6,721 *Total Prizemoney* £9,108

Wins * 1997 Jly Haydoc (G-S) H 6f 68 70 <
* 1996 May Newcas (GD) H 6f 60 67

1998 Turf 0-9: (6f 4, 7f 3, 8f, 10f) (sft 2, gd 2, g-f 3, frm 2)
Moderate filly, effective 6f, acts on gd to g-f, has worn blinkers. Turf high 62. **T R Watson [2-26] Mrs R T Watson.*

DESERT MIRAGE BHB 65f78a RR 62f 78a 4459[11]

3 b c Green Desert (USA) 7.8f **(78)** - Anodyne (Dominion) 8.5f **(63)**
Form - 318400
Record **1998 -** 1st:1 2nd:0 3rd:0 Ran:5
Pre1998 - 1st:0 2nd:0 3rd:1 Ran:2
Win Prizemoney £3,550 *Total Prizemoney* £4,288

Wins ** **1998** Mar Wolver (STD) 8.5f 75* <

1998 Turf 0-4: (7f 3, 8f) (g-s, g-f 2, frm) 1998 AW 1-1: (8f 1-1) (Fibr 1-1)
Leggy, above-average colt, effective 8f, - acts on Fibr. Turf high 62. (1st run) - 1st of 13 from Mandhar (14 Mar Wolverhampton RF 0427). Got off the mark in a maiden on the Wolverhampton Fibresand in March, but was made to look moderate on turf.
**P W Chapple-Hyam [1-7] The Countess of Derby.*

DESERT NATIVE BHB 47f44a RR 56f 44a 62[5]

3 b f Formidable (USA) 7.8f **(60)** - Desert Nomad (Green Desert (USA)) 8.6f **(78)**
Form - 065
Record **1998 -** 1st:0 2nd:0 3rd:0 Ran:2
Pre1998 - 1st:0 2nd:0 3rd:0 Ran:7
1998 AW 0-2: (7f, 8f) (Equi 2)
Fair filly, has worn blinkers. AW high 35.
**Mrs L Stubbs [0-3] O J Williams (from C F Wall [0-3] Spt 1997).*

DESERT POWER BHB 40f42a RR 56f 42a 4931[13]

9 b g Green Desert (USA) 7.8f **(78)** - Rivers Maid (Rarity) 10.1f **(60)**
Form - 24200
Record **1998 -** 1st:0 2nd:2 3rd:0 Ran:5
Pre1998 - 1st:3 2nd:2 3rd:1 Ran:21
Win Prizemoney £12,357 *Total Prizemoney* £18,823

Wins * 1995 Jly Chepst (G-F) H 10.2f 62 66 <
* 1994 Jun Chepst (G-F) H 10.2f 67 65

1998 Turf 0-5: (10f 4, 11f) (g-s, gd 2, frm 2)
Fair gelding. Turf high 56 (began Aug). Inconsistent.
**D Burchell [3-25] Mrs Lynda Williams (from M Meade [0-3] May 1995).*

DESERT PRINCE (IRE) BHB 128f RR 129f 5165a[14]

3 b c Green Desert (USA) 7.8f **(78)** - Flying Fairy (Bustino) 10.4f **(64)**
Form - 1312110
Record **1998 -** 1st:4 2nd:1 3rd:1 Ran:7
Pre1998 - 1st:1 2nd:1 3rd:0 Ran:4
Win Prizemoney £419,274 *Total Prizemoney* £510,487

Wins * **1998** Spt Ascot (GD) G1 8f 129 <
* **1998** Spt Longch (SFT) G1 8f 127
* **1998** May Currag (G-F) G1 8f 119
* **1998** Apr Newmar (SFT) LH 7f 110 114
* 1997 May Doncas (GD) 6f 80+

1998 Turf 4-7: (7f 1-1, 8f 3-6) (sft 2-2, gd 2-4, frm)
Scopey, top-class colt, effective 8f, acts on sft to gd, best on gd, likes Ascot. Turf high 129 - 1st of 7 from Dr Fong (26 Spt Ascot RF 4493) - also 1st of 7 from Gold Away (6 Spt Longchamp RF 4217a). A most attractive individual, he was a nice winner of the Free Handicap on his seasonal debut and was third in the French Guineas before landing the Irish version, although that was a somewhat unsatisfactory race. Worn down close home by Dr Fong in the St James's Palace, he came back fresh and well to put up a fine performance in winning the Prix du Moulin. Gained revenge over Dr Fong in the Queen Elizabeth II Stakes back at Ascot, thereby putting in a justifiable claim for the title of Champion European Miler, but his racecourse career ended with a disappointment in the Breeders' Cup Mile, in which he finished last after sustaining a gashed off-fore. **D R Loder [5-11] Lucayan Stud.*

DESERT RECRUIT RR 57f 4752[10]

2 b c Marju (IRE) 9.2f **(76)** - Storm Gayle (IRE) (Sadler's Wells (USA)) 10f **(76)**
Form - 0
Record **1998 -** 1st:0 2nd:0 3rd:0 Ran:1
1998 Turf 0-1: (7f) (sft)
Currently fair colt. **I Semple [0-1] David McKenzie.*

DESERT RHAPSODY BHB 36f RR 23f 3391[11]

3 ch f Desert Dirham (USA) - Knavesmire (Runnymede) 9.3f **(50)**
Form - 800
Record **1998 -** 1st:0 2nd:0 3rd:0 Ran:3

1998 Turf 0-3: (5f 3) (g-f, frm 2)
Unfurnished, currently little account filly. Turf high 23 (began Jly).
**M Brittain [0-3] Mel Brittain.*

Form - 37607810
Record 1998 - 1st:1 2nd:0 3rd:1 Ran:8
Pre1998 - 1st:0 2nd:0 3rd:0 Ran:3

Irish 2000 Guineas winner Desert Prince

DESERT SAND BHB 75f **RR 76?f** 4470[8]
3 b f Tragic Role (USA) 9.4f **(63)** - Miss Suntan (Bruni) 8.2f **(50)**
Form - 0518
Record 1998 - 1st:1 2nd:0 3rd:0 Ran:4
Pre1998 - 1st:1 2nd:0 3rd:0 Ran:3
Win Prizemoney £7,769 *Total Prizemoney* £7,769
Wins * **1998** Spt Ayr (G-S) C 9.1f 76+ <
1997 Spt Ayr (G-S) 6f 76
1998 Turf 1-4: (8f 2, 9f 1-1, 10f) (sft 1-1, frm 3)
Scopey, above-average filly, effective 6 to 9f, acts on sft to frm. Turf high 76 (began Aug) - 1st of 15 getting 5lb from Wellaki (18 Spt Ayr RF 4350).
**J Hanson [1-4] J Hanson (from Miss S E Hall [1-3] Oct 1997).*

DESERT SONG BHB 50f **RR 59f** 4648[13]
3 ch f Desert Dirham (USA) - Affaire de Coeur (Imperial Fling (USA)) 7.1f **(58)**
Form - 33300
Record 1998 - 1st:0 2nd:0 3rd:3 Ran:5
Win Prizemoney £0 *Total Prizemoney* £1,208
1998 Turf 0-5: (7f 3, 8f, 10f) (gd 2, g-f 2, frm)
Workmanlike, fair filly. Turf high 59 (began Jly).
**S Dow [0-5] D R Hunnisett.*

DESERT SPA (USA) BHB 50f54a **RR 60f 54a** 4887[12]
3 b c Sheikh Albadou 9.2f **(75)** - Healing Waters (USA) (Temperence Hill (USA)) 11f **(58)**
Win Prizemoney £2,402 *Total Prizemoney* £3,170
Wins * **1998** *Spt Wolver (STD) H 12f 51 55 <*
1998 Turf 0-7: (8f, 9f, 10f 3, 11f, 12f) (g-s 2, gd 2, frm 3) 1998 AW 1-1: (12f 1-1) (Fibr 1-1)
Scopey, average colt, effective 10 to 12f, acts on frm - acts on Fibr, has worn blinkers, likes tight tracks. Turf high 63. (1st run) - 1st of 12 getting 3lb from Makati (19 Spt Wolverhampton RF 4388). He looked one-paced on turf, so the step up in trip and racing on Fibresand for the first time worked wonders at Wolverhampton in September.
**P W Harris [1-11] The Chieftains.*

DESERT TIME BHB 42f **RR 55f** 4931[8]
8 b or br g Green Desert (USA) 7.8f **(78)** - Supper Time (Shantung) 9.8f **(64)**
Form - 524U0078
Record 1998 - 1st:0 2nd:1 3rd:0 Ran:8
Pre1998 - 1st:3 2nd:3 3rd:2 Ran:25
Win Prizemoney £13,584 *Total Prizemoney* £19,319
Wins * 1995 Jun Goodwo (G-F) H 8f 73 73+ <
* 1994 Aug Salisb (FRM) H 7f 70 70
* 1994 Jly Doncas (G-F) 6f 65
1998 Turf 0-8: (8f 4, 9f, 10f 3) (g-s, gd 3, frm 4)
Fair gelding, effective 8f, acts on frm, has worn blinkers, likes right handed tracks. Turf high 55.
**C A Horgan [3-25] Mrs L M Horgan (from M R Channon [0-4] Spt 1995).*

DESERT TRACK BHB 94f **RR 103f** 279a[1]
4 b c Green Desert (USA) 7.8f **(78)**-Mill Path (Mill Reef (USA))10.5f **(78)**
Form - 1
1998 Turf 1-1: (8f 1-1) (gd 1-1)
Unfurnished, very useful colt. (1st run) - 1st of 8 giving 3lb to Vision Of Spirit (8 Feb Saint-moritz RF 0279a). Formerly trained by John Gosden, he won a minor race at Saint-Moritz in February.
**M Weiss in SWI [1-1] Stall Sacohn (from J H M Gosden [2-5] Nov 1997).*

DESERT TYCOON (IRE) RR 66f 3317[10]
3 b c Last Tycoon 9.4f **(73)** - Point of Honour (Kris) 9.5f **(73)**
Form - 20
Record 1998 - 1st:0 2nd:1 3rd:0 Ran:2
Win Prizemoney £0 *Total Prizemoney* £1,060
1998 Turf 0-2: (10f, 11f) (g-f, frm)
Leggy, currently average colt. Turf high 66 (began Jly).
**J H M Gosden [0-2] Sheikh Ahmed Al Maktoum.*

DESERT VALENTINE BHB 56f **RR 60f** 5006[7]
3 b g Midyan (USA) 9.9f **(64)** - Mo Ceri (Kampala) 8.5f **(56)**
Form - 060167
Record 1998 - 1st:1 2nd:0 3rd:0 Ran:6
Pre1998 - 1st:0 2nd:0 3rd:0 Ran:2
Win Prizemoney £3,465 *Total Prizemoney* £3,465
Wins * 1998 Spt Goodwo (G-S) H 8f 55 60 <
1998 Turf 1-6: (6f, 8f 1-4, 9f) (sft, gd 1-3, frm 2)
Leggy, average gelding, effective 8f, acts on gd. Turf high 60 - 1st of 19 giving 2lb to Muara Bay (11 Spt Goodwood RF 4229).
**L G Cottrell [1-8] Mrs Lucy Halloran.*

DESERT WAR (IRE) RR 58[10]
7 ch m Military Attache (USA) - War Demon (Tug of War)
Form - 0
Record 1998 - 1st:0 2nd:0 3rd:0 Ran:1
1998 AW 0-1: (13f) (Equi)
Currently very poor mare, always wears blinkers - 10th of 10 giving 5lb to Divinity (10 Jan Lingfield 13f Equi RF 0058).
**R Ingram [0-1] Paul Naughton.*

DESERT WARRIOR (IRE) BHB 45f **RR 54f** 1708[13]
4 b c Fairy King (USA) 7.7f **(75)**-Highland Girl (USA) (Sir Ivor) 10.2f **(70)**
Form - 0000
Record 1998 - 1st:0 2nd:0 3rd:0 Ran:4
Pre1998 - 1st:0 2nd:0 3rd:0 Ran:3
1998 Turf 0-3: (6f 2, 7f) (sft, gd 2) 1998 AW 0-1: (8f) (Fibr)
Scopey, fair colt. Turf high 25.
**K Mahdi [0-6] Hamad Al-Mutawa (from Miss Gay Kelleway [0-1] Spt 1996).*

DESIGNER (USA) RR 100f 4315[4]
3 b c Danzig (USA) 8.1f **(88)** - Classy Women (USA) (Relaunch (USA)) 6f **(92)**
Form - 164
Record 1998 - 1st:1 2nd:0 3rd:0 Ran:3
Pre1998 - 1st:0 2nd:0 3rd:3 Ran:3
Win Prizemoney £3,525 *Total Prizemoney* £17,349
Wins * 1998 Aug Newmar (G-F) 6f 82+ <
1998 Turf 1-3: (5f, 6f 1-2) (gd, g-f, hrd 1-1)
Scopey, very useful colt, effective 6f, acts on gd to g-f. Turf high 98 (began Aug) - 4th of 7 giving 1lb to Kumait (16 Spt Yarmouth 6f gd RF 4315). A $550,000 yearling, he finished third in each of his three outings at two, the last of which was in the Middle Park. That was a poor renewal however, and he disappointed in '98 after winning his maiden, putting in some lacklustre performances.
**J H M Gosden [1-6] Sheikh Mohammed.*

DESIGNER LINES BHB 50f **RR 35f** 3980[9]
5 ch g Beveled (USA) 6.9f **(64)**-Parrot Fashion(Pieces of Eight)7.8f **(51)**
Form - 00
Record 1998 - 1st:0 2nd:0 3rd:0 Ran:2
Pre1998 - 1st:1 2nd:0 3rd:0 Ran:5
Win Prizemoney £2,904 *Total Prizemoney* £2,904
Wins 1996 Aug Lingfi (G-F) 7.6f 75 <
1998 Turf 0-2: (8f, 12f) (frm 2)
Very moderate gelding, has worn blinkers. Turf high 35 (began Aug). **E L James [0-8] R A Shaw (from C James [1-5] Oct 1997).*

DESIRE'S GOLD BHB 28f **RR 12f** 2246[11]
3 br g Grey Desire 9.3f **(49)** - Glory Gold (Hittite Glory) 8.7f **(50)**
Form - 0000
Record 1998 - 1st:0 2nd:0 3rd:0 Ran:4
Pre1998 - 1st:0 2nd:0 3rd:0 Ran:3
1998 Turf 0-4: (8f, 9f, 10f, 11f) (sft, g-f 2, frm)
Leggy, poor gelding. Turf high 12. **M Brittain [0-7] Mel Brittain.*

DESKAHEH (IRE) RR 91f 1382a[7]
3 b f Bluebird (USA) 7.9f **(71)** - Osmosi (USA) (Stay for Lunch (USA))
Form - 27
1998 Turf 0-2: (10f, 12f) (sft, gd)
Currently useful filly. Turf high 91 (1st run) - 2nd of 6 to Zainta (26 Apr Cologne 12f sft RF 0949a). **C Lerner in FR [0-2].*

DETACHMENT (USA) BHB 36f **RR 26f** 4529[16]
5 b g Night Shift (USA) 8.1f **(73)** - Mumble Peg (General Assembly (USA)) 10f **(68)**
Form - 0000
Record 1998 - 1st:0 2nd:0 3rd:0 Ran:4
Pre1998 - 1st:0 2nd:2 3rd:1 Ran:9
Win Prizemoney £0 *Total Prizemoney* £4,829
1998 Turf 0-4: (8f 4) (gd, g-f 2, frm)
Little account gelding, has worn blinkers. Turf high 26. Becoming disappointing.
**Miss Z C Davison [0-4] Miss Z C Davison (from P W Chapple-Hyam [0-9] Oct 1996).*

DETECTIVE RR 58f 4542[24]
2 ch c Wolfhound(USA) 7.3f **(71)** -Ivoronica(Targowice (USA))11.4f **(70)**
Form - 0
Record 1998 - 1st:0 2nd:0 3rd:0 Ran:1
1998 Turf 0-1: (7f) (frm)
Currently fair colt.
**J H M Gosden [0-1] Highclere Thoroughbred Racing Ltd.*

DETERRENT BHB 104f **RR 95f** 1267[6]
3 b c Warning 8.1f **(77)** - Delve (IRE) (Shernazar) 10.2f **(73)**
Form - 6
Record 1998 - 1st:0 2nd:0 3rd:0 Ran:1
Pre1998 - 1st:2 2nd:2 3rd:1 Ran:6
Win Prizemoney £8,926 *Total Prizemoney* £13,628
Wins * 1997 Oct Salisb (GD) 6f 92 <
* 1997 Spt Nottin (G-F) 6.1f 81+
1998 Turf 0-1: (7f) (frm)
Workmanlike, very useful colt, effective 6f, acts on gd.
**J H M Gosden [2-7] Sheikh Mohammed.*

DETROIT CITY (IRE) BHB 62f **RR 62f** 4840[13]
3 b g Distinctly North (USA) 7.4f **(63)** - Moyhora (IRE) (Nashamaa) 7.1f **(66)**
Form - 70711045520
Record 1998 - 1st:2 2nd:1 3rd:0 Ran:11
Pre1998 - 1st:0 2nd:0 3rd:0 Ran:4
Win Prizemoney £5,618 *Total Prizemoney* £6,416
Wins * 1998 Jly Beverl (G-F) C 7.5f 62 <
*** 1998** Jun Mussel (SFT) 7.1f 57
1998 Turf 2-10: (6f, 7f 2-7, 8f, 10f) (g-s 3, gd 1-3, g-f, frm 1-3) 1998 AW 0-1: (6f) (Fibr)
Light-framed, average gelding, effective 7f, acts on gd to frm, prefers right handed tracks, likes tight tracks. Turf high 62 - 5th of 14 giving 12lb to Critical Air (27 Aug Musselburgh 7f g-f RF 3906) - also 1st of 8 from Durham Flyer (14 Jly Beverley RF 2773).
**B S Rothwell [2-9] Norman Jackson (from J Berry [0-6] Apr 1998).*

DEVA LADY BHB 56f **RR 35f** 4822[22]
3 b f Prince Sabo 6.6f **(64)** - Known Line (Known Fact (USA)) 7.4f **(67)**
Form - 80
Record 1998 - 1st:0 2nd:0 3rd:0 Ran:2
Pre1998 - 1st:0 2nd:0 3rd:2 Ran:7
Win Prizemoney £0 *Total Prizemoney* £2,463
1998 Turf 0-2: (8f 2) (gd, frm)
Lengthy, very moderate filly, effective 6f, acts on gd to frm. Turf high 35. Becoming disappointing.
**C N Allen [0-4] Cliff Woof (from M R Channon [0-5] Aug 1997).*

DEVILETTA (USA) BHB 75f **RR 82df** 4915^{4}
2 ch f Trempolino (USA) 11.9f **(77)** - Polish Devil (USA) (Devil's Bag (USA)) 12.4f **(78)**
Form - 2204
Record 1998 - 1st:0 2nd:2 3rd:0 Ran:4
Win Prizemoney £0 *Total Prizemoney* £2,433
1998 Turf 0-4: (5f, 6f 3) (g-s, gd, frm 2)
Decent filly. Turf high 82 (1st run) (began Jly) - 2nd of 20 to Alegria (13 Jly Windsor 6f frm RF 2766).
**J H M Gosden [0-4] Sheikh Mohammed.*

DEVIL'S IMP (IRE) RR 70+f 4847^{1}
2 ch f Cadeaux Genereux 7.9f **(76)** - High Spirited (Shirley Heights) 10.3f **(74)**
Form - 1
Record 1998 - 1st:1 2nd:0 3rd:0 Ran:1
Wins * **1998** Oct Newmar (GD) 7f 70+ <
1998 Turf 1-1: (7f 1-1) (g-f 1-1)
Currently above-average filly. (1st run) - 1st of 2 getting 5lb from Hougoumont (16 Oct Newmarket RF 4847). She won the Newmarket Challenge Cup against just one rival, and would have exerted herself more going down to the start.
**E A L Dunlop [1-1] Maktoum Al Maktoum.*

DEVILS NIGHT RR 4877^{13}
3 b g Faustus (USA) 9.1f **(54)** - Up All Night **(6f)** (Green Desert (USA)) 8.6f **(78)**
Form - 0
Record 1998 - 1st:0 2nd:0 3rd:0 Ran:1
1998 AW 0-1: (6f) (Fibr)
Currently very poor gelding. **K Bell [0-1] Brian Footer.*

DEVON COURT (IRE) BHB 92f **RR 91f** 5001^{5}
2 ch c Mujtahid (USA) 7.4f **(69)** - Next Episode (USA) (Nijinsky (CAN)) 10.3f **(77)**
Form - 4120263405
Record 1998 - 1st:1 2nd:2 3rd:1 Ran:10
Win Prizemoney £1,760 *Total Prizemoney* £6,296
Wins * **1998** *May Taby (GD) 5f 68+* <
1998 Turf 0-9: (5f 8, 6f) (sft, g-s 4, gd 2, g-f, frm) 1998 AW 1-1: (5f 1-1) (Dirt 1-1)
Useful colt, effective 5f, acts on gd to frm, has worn blinkers (effectively). Turf high 91 - 2nd of 8 getting 5lb from Kastaway (15 Jun Windsor 5f gd RF 2008). (1st run). He probably achieved more in running Kastaway close at Windsor than he had done in winning his previous race at Taby. Disappointed slightly afterwards, but six furlongs should suit next term. Sold for 16,000 gns at Tattersalls in October.
**T J Naughton [1-10] The Awayday Partnership.*

DEVON DREAM (IRE) RR 52f 4868^{11}
2 b c Paris House 5.9f **(64)** - Share The Vision (Vision (USA)) 9f **(64)**
Form - 080
Record 1998 - 1st:0 2nd:0 3rd:0 Ran:3
1998 Turf 0-3: (6f 3) (gd, g-f 2)
Currently fair colt. Turf high 52 (began Jly).
**H S Howe [0-3] R J Parish.*

DE-WOLF BHB 60f57a **RR 63f 57a** 4669^{18}
3 gr f Petong 7.6f **(58)** - Doppio (Dublin Taxi) 6.4f **(55)**
Form - 4700
Record 1998 - 1st:0 2nd:0 3rd:0 Ran:4
Pre1998 - 1st:0 2nd:0 3rd:0 Ran:1
Win Prizemoney £0 *Total Prizemoney* £240
1998 Turf 0-4: (6f 3, 7f) (gd 3, g-f)
Leggy, average filly. Turf high 63.
**P J Makin [0-5] Barrie Whitehouse.*

DHIRINA (FR) BHB 71f **RR 73f** $5050a^{14}$
3 ch f Bering 9.6f **(80)** - Dixiella (FR) (Fabulous Dancer (USA)) 9.4f **(70)**
Form - 710
Record 1998 - 1st:1 2nd:0 3rd:0 Ran:3
Win Prizemoney £3,615 *Total Prizemoney* £3,615
Wins * **1998** Spt Haydoc (G-F) 7.1f 73 <
1998 Turf 1-3: (7f 1-3) (g-s, gd, frm 1-1)
Workmanlike, currently above-average filly. Turf high 73 - 1st of 10 from Penrose (25 Spt Haydock RF 4482). **W Jarvis [1-3] A G Foster.*

DIABLO DANCER (IRE) BHB 92f **RR 86f** 5077^{5}
2 b c Deploy 11.4f **(67)** - Scharade (Lombard (GER)) 10.5f **(66)**
Form - 1332145435
Record 1998 - 1st:2 2nd:1 3rd:3 Ran:10
Win Prizemoney £6,424 *Total Prizemoney* £13,392
Wins * **1998** Jly Lingfi (G-F) 7f 82 <
* **1998** Apr Nottin (G-S) 5.1f 75
1998 Turf 2-10: (5f 1-2, 6f, 7f 1-4, 8f, 10f 2) (g-s, gd 1-5, g-f, frm 1-3)
Useful colt, effective 7 to 10f, acts on gd to frm, best on frm. Turf high 86 - 3rd of 7 giving 4lb to Adnaan (12 Oct Leicester 10f gd RF 4764) - also 1st of 6 giving 7lb to Pinnacle (11 Jly Lingfield RF 2710). Consistent. **B R Millman [2-10] Kentisbeare Quartet.*

DIADOMENOS (GER) RR 96f $4470h^{8}$
3 c
Form - 08
1998 Turf 0-2: (10f, 12f) (hvy, gd)
Currently very useful colt, often wears blinkers. Turf high 96 (began Jly). **W Baltromei in GER [0-2].*

DIAGHILEF (IRE) BHB 80f **RR 86f** 5151^{13}
6 b g Royal Academy (USA) 7.8f **(77)** - Miss Audimar (USA) (Mr Leader (USA)) 9.8f **(66)**
Form - 6440
Record 1998 - 1st:0 2nd:0 3rd:0 Ran:4
Pre1998 - 1st:2 2nd:3 3rd:1 Ran:9
Win Prizemoney £30,036 *Total Prizemoney* £39,391
Wins 1995 Jun Ascot (G-F) H 12f 99 102 <
1995 May Newcas (GD) 10.1f 74
1998 Turf 0-4: (12f 2, 13f, 14f) (gd 4)
Useful gelding. Turf high 86. Becoming disappointing. The '96 King George VI Handicap winner, he missed the following year and showed nothing on his first two runs this term, but ran better at Newbury in July.
**M A Buckley [0-4] C C Buckley (from M Johnston [2-9] Aug 1995).*

DIAMOND ABI RR 2888^{4}
3 b f Primitive Rising (USA) 8.1f **(48)**-Chomolonga (High Top) 10.2f **(67)**
Form - 04
Record 1998 - 1st:0 2nd:0 3rd:0 Ran:2
Win Prizemoney £0 *Total Prizemoney* £241
1998 Turf 0-2: (7f, 10f) (frm 2)
Neat, currently very poor filly. (began Jly) - 4th of 4 to Abi (17 Jly Pontefract 10f frm RF 2888). **R E Barr [0-2] Gary King.*

DIAMOND BLUSH RR 15f 3525^{13}
2 ch f Sure Blade (USA) 10.6f **(66)** - Dawn Ditty (Song) 7.2f **(61)**
Form - 0
Record 1998 - 1st:0 2nd:0 3rd:0 Ran:1
1998 Turf 0-1: (5f) (frm)
Currently poor filly. **R J Hodges [0-1] Unity Farm Holiday Centre Ltd.*

DIAMOND CROWN (IRE) BHB 43f44a **RR 49f 44a** 4938^{6}
7 ch g Kris 10f **(75)** - State Treasure (USA) (Secretariat (USA)) 9f **(79)**
Form - 0338210173356206
Record 1998 - 1st:2 2nd:2 3rd:4 Ran:16
Pre1998 - 1st:4 2nd:4 3rd:8 Ran:50
Win Prizemoney £13,929 *Total Prizemoney* £23,189
Wins * **1998** Aug Newcas (GD) S 12.4f 47
* **1998** Jly Ayr (GD) S 10.9f 47
* 1997 Jun Nottin (GD) SH 10f 42 45
* 1996 Oct Newcas (G-F) CH 8f 44 44
* 1995 Aug Beverl (G-F) S 12f 56 <
* 1994 Aug Nottin (G-F) SH 10f 45 49
1998 Turf 2-16: (8f 2, 10f 6, 11f 1-1, 12f 1-2, 14f 2, 16f 3) (g-s, gd 1-5, g-f 1-7, frm 3)
Moderate gelding, effective 10 to 16f, best at 12f, acts on gd to g-f, best on g-f, has worn blinkers, likes Nottingham. Turf high 49 - 5th of 14 giving 5lb to Rusk (22 Spt Beverley 12f g-f RF 4403) - also 1st of 5 from Breydon (5 Aug Newcastle RF 3385). Not one to trust entirely.
**Martyn Wane [6-69] J M Pickup (from P F I Cole [0-2] Jly 1993).*

DIAMOND DECORUM (IRE) BHB 76f **RR 78f** 4643^{4}
2 ch g Fayruz 6.6f **(63)** - Astra Adastra (Mount Hagen (FR)) 8.4f **(70)**
Form - 0041654
Record 1998 - 1st:1 2nd:0 3rd:0 Ran:7

Win Prizemoney £3,324 *Total Prizemoney* £3,574
Wins * **1998** Aug Thirsk (G-F) 5f 77 <
1998 Turf 1-7: (5f 1-1, 6f 2, 7f 4) (g-f 3, frm 1-4)
Above-average gelding, effective 5 to 7f, acts on g-f to frm. Turf high 78 (began Jly) - 4th of 20 getting 4lb from Pepperdine (4 Oct Warwick 7f g-f RF 4643) - also 1st of 14 from Upper Chamber (10 Aug Thirsk RF 3505). **P D Evans [1-7] Diamond Racing Ltd.*

DIAMOND DRILL (USA) BHB 81f93a **RR 83f 93a** 4459[6]

3 b c Geiger Counter (USA) 7.8f **(85)** - Decollete (USA) (Al Nasr (FR)) 9.3f **(68)**
Form - 11104516
Record 1998 - 1st:3 2nd:0 3rd:0 Ran:7
Pre1998 - 1st:1 2nd:0 3rd:1 Ran:3
Win Prizemoney £12,951 *Total Prizemoney* £13,785
Wins * **1998** *Spt Wolver (STD) H 7f 85 89* <
* **1998** *Jan Lingfi (STD) H 8f 78 81*
* **1998** *Jan Lingfi (STD) H 8f 73 75*
* 1997 *Dec Lingfi (STD) 7f 70+*
1998 Turf 0-3: (7f 3) (gd 2, frm) 1998 AW 3-4: (7f 1-1, 8f 2-3) (Equi 2-3, Fibr 1-1)
Leggy, useful colt, effective 7 to 8f, - acts on AW, prefers left handed tracks, prefers tight tracks. Turf high 83. AW high 89 - 1st of 12 giving 13lb to Wilton (5 Spt Wolverhampton RF 4118) - also 1st of 6 giving 11lb to Boulevard Rouge (24 Jan Lingfield RF 0150). He got off the mark on his third start when winning a modest maiden very easily on the Equitrack in December, and confirmed his liking for that surface by completing a hat-trick in rather better company. He did not show much on turf until a promising effort at Kempton in May, and was given a four-month break before bouncing back to win a fair handicap under top weight on the Wolverhampton Fibresand. That was his best effort yet, and he looks as though he would be an ideal purchase for someone to continue his career on dirt in the States. **P J Makin [4-10] Mrs Tricia Mitchell.*

DIAMOND EYRE BHB 34f41a **RR 19f 41a** 3079[8]

4 ch f Then Again 7.4f **(52)** - Renira (Relkino) 8.9f **(65)**
Form - 0000068
Record 1998 - 1st:0 2nd:0 3rd:0 Ran:7
Pre1998 - 1st:1 2nd:1 3rd:1 Ran:11
Win Prizemoney £2,294 *Total Prizemoney* £3,397
Wins 1997 *Feb Wolver (STD) S 7f 47* <
1998 Turf 0-5: (8f 2, 10f, 11f, 13f) (gd, g-f 2, frm 2) 1998 AW 0-2: (7f 2) (Fibr 2)
Unfurnished, poor filly, effective 7 to 8f, - acts on Fibr, likes left handed tracks, favours tight tracks. Turf high 19. AW high 18. An All-Weather selling winner, she has not run as well on turf.
**J J Birkett [0-7] Keith Thomas (from J L Eyre [1-11] Jun 1997).*

DIAMOND FLAME BHB 75f90a **RR 79f 90a** 5126[11]

4 b c Suave Dancer (USA) 10.7f **(68)** - Eternal Flame (Primo Dominie) 6.2f **(80)**
Form - 1180858530
Record 1998 - 1st:2 2nd:0 3rd:1 Ran:10
Win Prizemoney £6,775 *Total Prizemoney* £7,365
Wins * **1998** *Mar Wolver (STD) 9.4f 87* <
* **1998** *Feb Lingfi (SLW) 10f 83+*
1998 Turf 0-7: (10f 5, 12f 2) (sft, g-s 3, gd, g-f, frm) 1998 AW 2-3: (9f 1-1, 10f 1-2) (Equi 1-2, Fibr 1-1)
Useful colt, effective 9 to 10f, best at 10f, acts on g-s - acts on AW, prefers left handed tracks. Turf high 82. AW high 87 - 1st of 7 giving 12lb to Gralmano (14 Mar Wolverhampton RF 0429) - also 1st of 5 giving 21lb to Narrogin (24 Feb Lingfield RF 0353). He rewarded his connections' patience with a very impressive winning debut on the Lingfield Equitrack in February. The opposition may have been negligible, but he went on to beat a rather better field on the Wolverhampton Fibresand next time. The Winter Derby at Lingfield proved too much for him, but he should have a future in less-exalted company. Failed to make an impression on Turf in 1998.
**P W Harris [2-10] The Dancing Dozen.*

DIAMOND GEEZER (IRE) BHB 65f **RR 80f** 4969[8]

2 br c Tenby 10.4f **(76)** - Unaria (Prince Tenderfoot (USA)) 9f **(61)**
Form - 87601058
Record 1998 - 1st:1 2nd:0 3rd:0 Ran:8
Win Prizemoney £2,996 *Total Prizemoney* £3,077
Wins * **1998** Spt Sandow (G-S) C 5f 80 <
1998 Turf 1-8: (5f 1-1, 6f 4, 7f 3) (g-s 2, gd 1-2, g-f, frm 2, hrd)
Decent colt, effective 5 to 7f, acts on gd to frm. Turf high 80 - 1st of 14 getting 5lb from Robber Red (15 Spt Sandown RF 4264). Inconsistent. **R Hannon [1-8] J B R Leisure Ltd.*

DIAMOND LAD (IRE) BHB 60f **RR 59f** 4053[16]

2 b c Namaqualand (USA) - Eight Mile Rock (Dominion) 8.5f **(63)**
Form - 07760
Record 1998 - 1st:0 2nd:0 3rd:0 Ran:5
1998 Turf 0-5: (5f, 6f, 7f 2, 8f) (gd 3, g-f, frm)
Fair colt. Turf high 59. **W T Kemp [0-5] Mrs M Irwin.*

DIAMOND MARKET BHB 30f39a **RR 16?f 39a** 2160[7]

6 gr g Absalom 7.1f **(56)** - The Victor Girls (Crofthall) 6.3f **(59)**
Form - 07
Record 1998 - 1st:0 2nd:0 3rd:0 Ran:2
Pre1998 - 1st:0 2nd:2 3rd:1 Ran:14
Win Prizemoney £0 *Total Prizemoney* £2,307
1998 Turf 0-1: (8f) (gd) 1998 AW 0-1: (11f) (Fibr)
Poor gelding. Becoming disappointing.
**B R Cambidge [0-4] G A Farndon (from R Hollinshead [0-10] Nov 1995).*

DIAMOND ROUGE BHB 54f **RR 52f** 4250[3]

2 b f Puissance 7.1f **(60)** - Maravilla (Mandrake Major) 7.6f **(53)**
Form - 053
Record 1998 - 1st:0 2nd:0 3rd:1 Ran:3
Win Prizemoney £0 *Total Prizemoney* £415
1998 Turf 0-2: (5f 2) (g-f, frm) 1998 AW 0-1: (5f) (Fibr)
Currently fair filly. Turf high 52 (began Aug).
**A Bailey [0-3] Diamond Racing Ltd.*

DIAMOND SNAKE (IRE) **RR 94f** 4220a[2]

3 b c Thatching 7.8f **(69)** -Dorothy Harding (ITY) (Chief Singer) 8.9f **(66)**
Form - 32
1998 Turf 0-2: (8f, 10f) (hvy, sft)
Useful colt. Turf high 94 - 2nd of 6 giving 8lb to Green Tea (6 Spt San Siro 8f sft RF 4220a). **G Colleo in ITY [0-4].*

DIAMOND STEALTH **RR 60f** 4916[5]

2 b f Ardkinglass 5f **(64)** - Alumia (Great Nephew) 9.9f **(64)**
Form - 5
Record 1998 - 1st:0 2nd:0 3rd:0 Ran:1
1998 Turf 0-1: (7f) (g-s)
Currently average filly. **J L Eyre [0-1] Diamond Racing Ltd.*

DIAMOND WHITE BHB 95f **RR 95f** 5141[1]

3 b f Robellino (USA) 9.5f **(68)** - Diamond Wedding (USA) (Diamond Shoal) 9.1f **(66)**
Form - 00451706036105331
Record 1998 - 1st:3 2nd:0 3rd:3 Ran:17
Pre1998 - 1st:1 2nd:1 3rd:2 Ran:7
Win Prizemoney £27,895 *Total Prizemoney* £42,036
Wins * **1998** Nov Doncas (SFT) 10.3f 91
* **1998** Spt Nottin (G-F) 10f 90
1998 Jun Folkes (G-F) H 7f 85 95+ <
1997 Aug Newmar (G-F) L 7f 85
1998 Turf 3-17: (7f 1-2, 8f 8, 9f, 10f 2-6) (sft 2, g-s, gd 3-6, g-f 4, frm 3, hrd)
Neat, very useful filly, effective 7 to 10f, best at 10f, acts on g-s to frm, best on gd, has worn blinkers. Turf high 95 - 3rd of 8 to Lady In Waiting (15 Oct Newmarket 10f frm RF 4819) - also 1st of 9 getting 2lb from Filfilah (26 Jun Folkestone RF 2296). Consistent. She was very busy in '98, including facing some very stiff tasks, but she did manage four victories, the last being right at the end of the turf season. A credit to all concerned and will certainly pay her way again next term.
**K G Wingrove [2-10] Peter Scott (from G C Bravery [2-14] Jly 1998).*

DIAMONIXA (FR) **RR 117f** 1372a[1]

3 gr f Linamix (FR) 8.2f **(64)** - Diamonaka (FR) (Akarad (FR)) 9f **(76)**
Form - 1
1998 Turf 1-1: (11f 1-1) (gd 1-1)
High-class filly. (1st run) - 1st of 7 from Another Dancer (12 May Saint-cloud RF 1372a). She was considered a major Prix de diance candidate until suffering an accident at home. (DEAD)
**A Fabre in FR [1-1] J-L Lagardere.*

DIAVOLETTO (IRE) BHB 52f **RR 63f** 4808[9]
2 b g Imp Society (USA) 7.1f **(63)** - Balela (African Sky) 7.9f **(63)**
Form - 000
Record 1998 - 1st:0 2nd:0 3rd:0 Ran:3
1998 Turf 0-3: (7f, 10f 2) (gd, g-f, frm)
Currently average gelding. Turf high 63 (began Aug).
**W R Muir [0-3] Villa D'Este Racing.*

DIBOLA BHB 32f **RR 43f** 4114[19]
3 ch g Dilum (USA) 7.1f **(56)** - Bella Bambola (IRE) **(7f)** (Tate Gallery (USA)) 7.4f **(67)**
Form - 00
Record 1998 - 1st:0 2nd:0 3rd:0 Ran:1
Pre1998 - 1st:0 2nd:0 3rd:0 Ran:8
1998 Turf 0-1: (5f) (frm)
Neat, moderate gelding, has worn blinkers. Inconsistent.
**J S Wainwright [0-9] S Pedersen.*

DICK'S AT HOME BHB 35f **RR 25f** 5004[16]
2 b g Whittingham (IRE) - Homemaker **(18f 38a)** (Homeboy) 6.6f **(55)**
Form - 800
Record 1998 - 1st:0 2nd:0 3rd:0 Ran:3
1998 Turf 0-3: (6f 3) (sft, gd, frm)
Currently little account gelding. Turf high 25 (began Jly).
**P G Murphy [0-3] Racecourse Farm Racing II.*

DICK TURPIN (USA) BHB 72f67a **RR 70f 67a** 226[6]
4 br g Red Ransom (USA) 8.6f **(83)** - Turn To Money (USA) (Turn To Mars (USA)) 10f **(83)**
Form - 2316
Record 1998 - 1st:1 2nd:1 3rd:1 Ran:4
Pre1998 - 1st:0 2nd:0 3rd:1 Ran:5
Win Prizemoney £3,403 *Total Prizemoney* £5,738
Wins * **1998** *Jan Lingfi (STD) 10f 65 <*
1998 AW 1-4: (10f 1-2, 11f, 12f) (Equi 1-2, Fibr 2)
Scopey, above-average gelding, has broken blood-vessels, effective 10 to 11f, best at 10f, acts on gd to frm - acts on AW, prefers tight tracks. AW high 65 - 1st of 9 giving 21lb to Some Might Say (27 Jan Lingfield RF 0168). He has shown good form on sand, getting off the mark in a maiden on the Lingfield Equitrack in January, but did not run well on his handicap debut on the same track.
**B Smart [1-4] The Dyball Partnership (from Lord Huntingdon [0-5] Oct 1997).*

DIDIFON BHB 90f **RR 86f** 2455[2]
3 b c Zafonic (USA) 9f **(83)** - Didicoy (USA) (Danzig (USA)) 8.4f **(76)**
Form - 7432
Record 1998 - 1st:0 2nd:1 3rd:1 Ran:4
Win Prizemoney £0 *Total Prizemoney* £2,067
1998 Turf 0-4: (8f, 10f 2, 11f) (sft, gd, g-f, frm)
Strong, useful colt. Turf high 86 - 2nd of 7 giving 5lb to Kadaka (1 Jly Yarmouth 11f frm RF 2455). Out of a half-sister to Xaar, he showed promise in maidens. He will not be easy to place in handicap company. **H R A Cecil [0-4] K Abdulla.*

DIESEL DAN (IRE) BHB 65f60a **RR 78f 60a** 348[8]
5 b g Mac's Imp (USA) 5.6f **(54)** - Elite Exhibition (Exhibitioner) 8.7f **(61)**
Form - 8406258
Record 1998 - 1st:0 2nd:1 3rd:0 Ran:7
Pre1998 - 1st:1 2nd:1 3rd:2 Ran:15
Win Prizemoney £2,740 *Total Prizemoney* £5,586
Wins 1997 Jly Down R (G-F) 7f 78 <
1998 AW 0-7: (7f 4, 8f 2, 11f) (Equi 2, Fibr 5)
Above-average gelding, effective 7f, acts on gd to g-f, best on g-f, has worn blinkers. AW high 59.
**J R Jenkins [0-11] M A Ward (from T Stack in IRE [1-15] Jly 1997).*

DIET BHB 25f **RR 29f** 2682[9]
12 b g Starch Reduced 5.9f **(46)** - Highland Rossie (Pablond) 5.9f **(42)**
Form - 05600
Record 1998 - 1st:0 2nd:0 3rd:0 Ran:5
Pre1998 - 1st:11 2nd:14 3rd:8 Ran:133
Win Prizemoney £31,064 *Total Prizemoney* £59,879

Wins							
* 1996	Apr	Mussel	(GD)	SH	7.1f	51	57
* 1995	Aug	Hamilt	(FRM)	H	6f	51	51
* 1995	Jly	Mussel	(FRM)	C	7.1f		57
* 1995	May	Hamilt	(G-F)	H	5f	43	43

1998 Turf 0-5: (6f 2, 7f 2, 8f) (gd 3, g-f, frm)
Little account gelding, effective 6f, acts on frm, mostly wears blinkers. Turf high 29. He has been a prolific winner in his time, usually north of the border, but is very moderate nowadays.
**Miss L A Perratt [8-112] Miss L A Perratt (from J S Wilson [3-26] Aug 1991).*

DIGGIT (IRE) BHB 98f **RR 86f** 4306[2]
2 b c Waajib 8.9f **(67)** - Esquire Lady (Be My Guest (USA)) 9.3f **(67)**
Form - 12222
Record 1998 - 1st:1 2nd:4 3rd:0 Ran:5
Win Prizemoney £3,420 *Total Prizemoney* £12,121
Wins * **1998** Jly Bath (GD) 5.7f 76 <
1998 Turf 1-5: (6f 1-2, 7f 3) (gd, g-f 1-2, frm, hrd)
Useful colt. Turf high 86 (began Jly) - 2nd of 4 giving 6lb to Smart Savannah (16 Spt Sandown 7f g-f RF 4306). Runner-up to some decent sorts after winning his maiden.
**M R Channon [1-5] Tim Corby.*

DIGITALIZE (USA) BHB 110f **RR 112f** 4630[3]
3 b br f Dayjur (USA) 6.8f **(79)** - Dancer's Candy (USA) (Noble Dancer) 7.8f **(101)**
Form - 112023
Record 1998 - 1st:2 2nd:2 3rd:1 Ran:6
Win Prizemoney £18,021 *Total Prizemoney* £45,541
Wins * **1998** May Goodwo (G-F) L 8f 99 <
* **1998** May Newmar (G-S) 7f 90
1998 Turf 2-6: (7f 1-1, 8f 1-3, 10f 2) (gd 1-3, g-f 1-2, frm)
Strong, Group-class filly, effective 8 to 10f, acts on gd. Turf high 112 - 2nd of 9 getting 3lb from Alborada (1 Aug Goodwood 10f gd RF 3256). She put up her best performance when running Alborada to half a length in the Group 2 Nassau Stakes at Goodwood in August. Well below that form when a distant third in the Sun Chariot Stakes in the autumn, she does not look a big improver and could struggle if kept in training.
**H R A Cecil [2-6] S Khaled.*

DIGPAST (IRE) BHB 33f73a **RR 39f 73a** 2572[17]
8 ch g Digamist (USA) 8.8f **(56)** - Starlit Way (Pall Mall) 9.6f **(68)**
Form - 6402003511470800
Record 1998 - 1st:2 2nd:1 3rd:1 Ran:13
Pre1998 - 1st:4 2nd:6 3rd:4 Ran:59
Win Prizemoney £19,759 *Total Prizemoney* £30,425

Wins								
* **1998**	*Mar*	*Lingfi*	*(STD)*		*7f*		*69*	
* **1998**	*Mar*	*Lingfi*	*(STD)*	*H*	*10f*	*65*	*66*	
1996	*Feb*	*Lingfi*	*(STD)*	*H*	*8f*	*67*	*74*	<
1995	*Mar*	*Lingfi*	*(STD)*	*H*	*7f*	*59*	*65*	
1995	*Feb*	*Lingfi*	*(STD)*	*H*	*7f*	*52*	*53*	
1994	*Dec*	*Lingfi*	*(STD)*	*H*	*7f*	*47*	*48*	

1998 Turf 0-5: (7f, 8f 2, 10f, 12f) (gd 2, g-f 2, hrd) 1998 AW 2-8: (7f 1-2, 8f 3, 10f 1-1, 13f 2) (Equi 2-8)
Average gelding, effective 7 to 10f, best at 7f, - acts on Equi, often wears blinkers (effectively), prefers left handed tracks, favours tight tracks, excels at Lingfield. Turf high 39. AW high 69 - 1st of 11 giving 2lb to Dandy Regent (30 Mar Lingfield RF 0509) - also 1st of 9 getting 17lb from Threadneedle (19 Mar Lingfield RF 0447). Becoming disappointing. Quite a useful performer on Equitrack at his best, he only shows his true ability these days when Gary Bardwell is aboard. He ran a blinder when runner-up in the All-Weather Trophy Final in January, and his two victories in March were completely down to his jockey.
**J J Bridger [2-26] Miss Sarah Jones (from M Madgwick [0-4] Apr 1997).*

DIKTAT BHB 117f **RR 118f** 3115[2]
3 br c Warning 8.1f **(77)** - Arvola (Sadler's Wells (USA)) 10f **(76)**
Form - 1112
Record 1998 - 1st:3 2nd:1 3rd:0 Ran:4
Pre1998 - 1st:0 2nd:0 3rd:0 Ran:1
Win Prizemoney £49,033 *Total Prizemoney* £55,879
Wins * **1998** Jun Ascot (GD) G3 7f 114
* **1998** May Leices (GD) 7f 115+ <
* **1998** Apr Newmar (SFT) 7f 90+
1998 Turf 3-4: (7f 3-4) (gd 2-3, g-f 1-1)
Scopey, high-class colt. Turf high 118 - 2nd of 4 getting 10lb from Decorated Hero (25 Jly Newcastle 7f gd RF 3115) - also 1st of 4 getting 5lb from Rabi (26 May Leicester RF 1470). Showed some ability in his only start at two, but developed into a very smart colt

last term. After two impressive victories, he was successfully stepped up in class to land the Jersey Stakes at Royal Ascot in fine style. He was just beaten by the battle-hardened Decorated Hero in the Beeswing, but unfortunately was not seen again.
**D R Loder [3-5] Sheikh Mohammed.*

Diktat will be in new hands next season

DIKTYS (GER) **RR 107f** 2660a[3]
6 b h Kamiros II - Danae (GER) (Nebos (GER)) 9f **(78)**
Form - 3
1998 Turf 0-1: (16f) (hvy)
Pattern-class horse. He has won on heavy ground before, but was well beaten on that surface in a Listed event at Hamburg in June.
**H Blume in GER [2-4].*

DIL BHB 83f **RR 82f** 4596[15]
3 b g Primo Dominie 7.2f **(67)** - Swellegant (Midyan (USA)) 6f **(60)**
Form - 30414107810
Record 1998 - 1st:3 2nd:0 3rd:1 Ran:11
Pre1998 - 1st:0 2nd:1 3rd:0 Ran:4
Win Prizemoney £11,417 *Total Prizemoney* £14,092
Wins * **1998** Spt Leices (G-F) H 5f 78 82 <
* **1998** Jly Doncas (G-F) H 6f 73 76
1998 May Doncas (GD) 5f 74
1998 Turf 3-11: (5f 2-5, 6f 1-6) (g-s, gd 4, g-f 2-2, frm 1-3, hrd)
Decent gelding, effective 5 to 6f, best at 6f, acts on gd to frm. Turf high 83 (1st run) - 3rd of 17 to Epsom Cyclone (28 Mar Doncaster 6f gd RF 0488) - also 1st of 20 giving 11lb to High Carry (21 Spt Leicester RF 4397).
**Mrs N Macauley [2-6] Mrs N Macauley (from B Hanbury [1-9] Jun 1998).*

DILEEP SINGH (IRE) BHB 56f **RR 50df** 2331[22]
3 b g Shalford (IRE) 7.8f **(63)** - Another Deb (African Sky) 7.9f **(63)**
Form - 8400
Record 1998 - 1st:0 2nd:0 3rd:0 Ran:4
Win Prizemoney £0 *Total Prizemoney* £252
1998 Turf 0-4: (6f 2, 7f, 8f) (g-s, gd 3)
Rangy, fair gelding, has worn blinkers. Turf high 50.
**T D Easterby [0-4] Simon Bhullar.*

DILETTO (IRE) BHB 68f **RR 72f** 4845[18]
2 b f Mujadil (USA) 7.7f **(70)** - Avidal Park (Horage) 10.3f **(61)**
Form - 603263448420
Record 1998 - 1st:0 2nd:2 3rd:2 Ran:12
Win Prizemoney £0 *Total Prizemoney* £4,037
1998 Turf 0-10: (5f 4, 6f 4, 7f, 8f) (g-s, gd 5, g-f, frm 3) 1998 AW 0-2: (5f 2) (Fibr 2)
Above-average filly, effective 5 to 7f, best at 5f, acts on gd to frm, best on gd. Turf high 72 - 2nd of 7 getting 5lb from Sailing Shoes (3 Jun Chester 5f gd RF 1681). AW high 64.

**E J Alston [0-12] Liam Ferguson.*

DILIGENCE (IRE) BHB 100f **RR 85f** 4140[8]
3 b c Dilum (USA) 7.1f **(56)** - Florinda (CAN) (Vice Regent (CAN)) 8.7f **(74)**
Form - 8
Record 1998 - 1st:0 2nd:0 3rd:0 Ran:1
Pre1998 - 1st:1 2nd:1 3rd:0 Ran:3
Win Prizemoney £4,889 *Total Prizemoney* £9,259
Wins * 1997 May Goodwo (G-S) 5f 82 <
1998 Turf 0-1: (5f) (g-f)
Strong, useful colt. **P F I Cole [1-4] Axom.*

DILIGENT DODGER (IRE) **RR 89f** 5169a[8]
7 b g Posen (USA) 8.6f **(59)** - Crannog (Habitat) 9.4f **(70)**
Form - 7375131464138
1998 Turf 3-13:(5f 2, 6f 7, 7f 3-4)(hvy 2, sft, g-s 1-1, gd 1-6, g-f 1-2, hrd)
Useful gelding, effective 7f, acts on g-s, has worn blinkers. Turf high 101 - 1st of 9 giving 25lb to Frisky (9 Jly Tipperary RF 2792a). Consistent. He had a busy campaign, gaining all his wins over seven furlongs. Best when held-up, he retains his enthusiasm and will continue to give the youngsters a run for their money.
**K Prendergast in IRE [5-40] Mrs D M Donohoe (from IRE [0-3] Spt 1994).*

DILKUSHA (IRE) BHB 73f **RR 75f** 4308[11]
3 b g Indian Ridge 7.6f **(74)** - Crimson Glen (Glenstal (USA)) 10.1f **(64)**
Form - 040856361520
Record 1998 - 1st:1 2nd:1 3rd:1 Ran:12
Pre1998 - 1st:0 2nd:0 3rd:0 Ran:2
Win Prizemoney £2,924 *Total Prizemoney* £5,214
Wins * **1998** Aug Bright (FRM) H 7f 67 72 <
1998 Turf 1-12: (7f 1-9, 8f 3) (gd 4, g-f 1-4, frm 4)
Leggy, above-average gelding, effective 7f, acts on gd to frm, best on g-f, has worn blinkers. Turf high 76 - also 1st of 9 giving 7lb to The Thruster (12 Aug Brighton RF 3570). Consistent.
**B J Meehan [1-14] Trevor Painting.*

DILLIONAIRE BHB 68f **RR 74f** 4845[9]
2 b c Dilum (USA) 7.1f **(56)** - Running Tycoon (IRE) **(42f)** (Last Tycoon) 8.5f **(62)**
Form - 71437600
Record 1998 - 1st:1 2nd:0 3rd:1 Ran:8
Win Prizemoney £2,846 *Total Prizemoney* £3,996
Wins * **1998** May Bright (FRM) 6f 86 <
1998 Turf 1-8: (5f 3, 6f 1-3, 7f, 8f) (hvy, g-s, gd 3, g-f 2, frm 1-1)
Above-average colt, effective 6f, acts on frm. Turf high 86 - 1st of 6 from Captain Miller (28 May Brighton RF 1548). Has twice run poorly in soft ground and has become somewhat disappointing. Sold for 16,000 gns in the autumn. **R Hannon [1-8] J C Smith.*

DILLUS BHB 50f **RR 58f** 4115[11]
2 b f Dilum (USA) 7.1f **(56)** - Lismore (Relkino) 8.9f **(65)**
Form - 02462640
Record 1998 - 1st:0 2nd:2 3rd:0 Ran:8
Win Prizemoney £0 *Total Prizemoney* £1,549
1998 Turf 0-8: (5f, 6f 4, 7f 3) (gd 3, g-f 2, frm 3)
Fair filly, effective 5 to 6f, acts on gd. Turf high 58 - 2nd of 11 getting 5lb from Bundy (25 Jly Newcastle 6f gd RF 3117). Inconsistent. **B S Rothwell [0-8] S P Hudson.*

DI MATTEO (IRE) BHB 73f80a **RR 75f 80a** 1078[4]
3 ch g Emarati (USA) 6.6f **(63)** - Piney Lake (Sassafras (FR)) 9.6f **(69)**
Form - 234
Record 1998 - 1st:0 2nd:1 3rd:1 Ran:3
Pre1998 - 1st:0 2nd:1 3rd:1 Ran:3
Win Prizemoney £0 *Total Prizemoney* £2,588
1998 Turf 0-2: (9f, 10f) (hvy, gd) 1998 AW 0-1: (8f) (Equi)
Workmanlike, decent gelding, effective 8 to 10f, acted on gd - acted on Equi. Turf high 75 (1st run) - 3rd of 15 getting 8lb from Bawsian (26 Mar Doncaster 10f gd RF 0471). (1st run) - 2nd of 9 to Libra Star (28 Feb Lingfield 8f Equi RF 0377). He showed plenty of ability in maidens on turf and sand, and ran a fine race on his handicap debut at Doncaster. (DEAD)
**B Hanbury [0-6] C Gordon-Watson.*

DIMINUTIVE (USA) BHB 74f **RR 77f** 4893[9]
5 b g Diesis 9f **(80)** - Graceful Darby (USA) (Darby Creek Road (USA)) 9.5f **(77)**
Form - 40217340
Record 1998 - 1st:1 2nd:1 3rd:1 Ran:8
Pre1998 - 1st:3 2nd:1 3rd:3 Ran:18
Win Prizemoney £18,453 *Total Prizemoney* £24,508
Wins * **1998** Jly Bath (GD) H 10.2f 71 75
* 1996 Aug Yarmou (G-F) 10.1f 85 <
* 1996 Jly Bath (FRM) 10.2f 75
* 1996 Jun Thirsk (FRM) 8f 66
1998 Turf 1-8: (10f 1-8) (gd, g-f 1-3, frm 4)
Above-average gelding, effective 10f, acts on gd to frm, best on frm, likes left handed tracks, prefers tight tracks. Turf high 77 - 4th of 11 getting 1lb from Vola Via (24 Spt Pontefract 10f frm RF 4467) - also 1st of 12 giving 7lb to Pistol (6 Jly Bath RF 2556).
**J W Hills [4-26] Gainsbury Partnership.*

DIM OFAN BHB 85f **RR 89?f** 4924[1]
2 b f Petong 7.6f **(58)** - Wilsonic (Damister (USA)) 9f **(73)**
Form - 65512251
Record 1998 - 1st:2 2nd:2 3rd:0 Ran:8
Win Prizemoney £6,151 *Total Prizemoney* £8,348
Wins * **1998** Oct Nottin (SFT) 6.1f 89? <
* **1998** Jly Chepst (GD) 6.1f 69
1998 Turf 2-8: (6f 2-8) (sft 1-1, g-s, gd 2, g-f 1-3, frm)
Useful filly, effective 6f, acts on sft. Turf high 89 - 1st of 8 giving 1lb to Seven Springs (21 Oct Nottingham RF 4924). Improving.
**B Palling [2-8] Mrs D J Hughes.*

DIM OTS BHB 83f **RR 86f** 4750[17]
3 b f Alhijaz 7.7f **(57)** - Placid Pet (Mummy's Pet) 7.7f **(60)**
Form - 17452800
Record 1998 - 1st:1 2nd:1 3rd:0 Ran:8
Pre1998 - 1st:2 2nd:2 3rd:1 Ran:6
Win Prizemoney £11,463 *Total Prizemoney* £15,220
Wins * **1998** Apr Kempto (HVY) H 6f 80 91 <
* 1997 May Bath (G-S) 5.1f 72
* 1997 Apr Nottin (G-F) 5.1f 72
1998 Turf 1-8: (6f 1-6, 7f 2) (hvy 1-1, sft, gd, g-f 4, frm)
Light-framed, useful filly, effective 6f, acts on hvy to g-f, best on g-f. Turf high 91 (1st run) - 1st of 19 getting 1lb from Robin Goodfellow (11 Apr Kempton RF 0645). Inconsistent. A winner twice over the minimum at two, she made a successful reappearance in bottomless ground at Kempton, winning by a street. Found out in conditions races since, but ran well in a handicap at Newbury in August. **B Palling [3-14] Mrs D J Hughes.*

DINA LINE (USA) BHB 45f53a **RR 44f 53a** 4547[8]
4 ch f Diesis 9f **(80)** - Lajna (Be My Guest (USA)) 9.3f **(67)**
Form - 30105525P8
Record 1998 - 1st:1 2nd:1 3rd:1 Ran:10
Pre1998 - 1st:0 2nd:0 3rd:0 Ran:3
Win Prizemoney £3,132 *Total Prizemoney* £4,992
Wins * **1998** *May Southw (STD) H 8f 53 57* <
1998 Turf 0-7: (7f 3, 8f 3, 10f) (sft, gd 2, g-f 3, frm) 1998 AW 1-3: (7f, 8f 1-2) (Fibr 1-3)
Scopey, fair filly, effective 8f, - acts on Fibr, prefers left handed tracks, likes tight tracks. Turf high 44. AW high 57 - 1st of 16 giving 11lb to Lady Jazz (11 May Southwell RF 1154).
**M Bell [1-13] Lordship Stud.*

DING DONG RR 3321[13]
2 b f Librate 10.4f **(37)** - Dawn Bell (Belfort (FR)) 6.8f **(63)**
Form - 60
Record 1998 - 1st:0 2nd:0 3rd:0 Ran:2
1998 Turf 0-2: (5f 2) (g-f 2)
Currently very poor filly. **J M Bradley [0-2] J M Bradley.*

DINO'S MISTRAL BHB 18f29a **RR 18f 29a** 3944[8]
5 b g Petong 7.6f **(58)** - Marquessa d'Howfen (Pitcairn) 9.5f **(60)**
Form - 08
Record 1998 - 1st:0 2nd:0 3rd:0 Ran:2
Pre1998 - 1st:0 2nd:0 3rd:0 Ran:16
Win Prizemoney £0 *Total Prizemoney* £197
1998 Turf 0-1: (10f) (frm) 1998 AW 0-1: (7f) (Fibr)
Poor gelding, has worn blinkers.

**K A Morgan [0-10] R G Marriott (from F H Lee [0-14] Jly 1997).*

DION DEE BHB 70f **RR 78f** 4389[10]
2 ch f Anshan 8.2f **(63)** - Jade Mistress (Damister (USA)) 9f **(73)**
Form - 370
Record 1998 - 1st:0 2nd:0 3rd:1 Ran:3
Win Prizemoney £0 *Total Prizemoney* £540
1998 Turf 0-3: (7f 2, 8f) (g-f, frm 2)
Currently above-average filly. Turf high 78 (began Aug).
**A P Jarvis [0-3] Mrs Ann Jarvis.*

DIPLOMAT BHB 78f **RR 79f** 4370[2]
2 b c Deploy 11.4f **(67)** - Affair of State (IRE) (Tate Gallery (USA)) 7.4f **(67)**
Form - 5422
Record 1998 - 1st:0 2nd:2 3rd:0 Ran:4
Win Prizemoney £0 *Total Prizemoney* £2,121
1998 Turf 0-4: (6f 2, 7f 2) (gd, g-f 2, frm)
Above-average colt. Turf high 79 (began Jly) - 2nd of 12 to Northern Svengali (19 Spt Catterick 6f frm RF 4370).
**M R Channon [0-4] Stephen Crown.*

DIPPLE BHB 84f **RR 82f** 4703[11]
2 b f Komaite (USA) 6.9f **(61)**-Rynavey **(60a)**(Rousillon (USA)) 8.2f **(74)**
Form - 1250
Record 1998 - 1st:1 2nd:1 3rd:0 Ran:4
Win Prizemoney £3,551 *Total Prizemoney* £6,358
Wins * **1998** Jly Ayr (GD) 6f 77+ <
1998 Turf 1-4: (6f 1-3, 7f) (sft, gd 1-3)
Decent filly. Turf high 82 (began Jly) - also 1st of 12 getting 5lb from Espada (13 Jly Ayr RF 2754). Won nicely on her Ayr debut, but ran poorly on her last two starts and was later sold for 8,000 gns. **Denys Smith [1-4] Duke of Sutherland.*

DIRECT DEAL RR 83f 4772[3]
2 b c Rainbow Quest (USA) 11.2f **(81)** - Al Najah (USA) (Topsider (USA)) 8.3f **(71)**
Form - 3
Record 1998 - 1st:0 2nd:0 3rd:1 Ran:1
Win Prizemoney £0 *Total Prizemoney* £478
1998 Turf 0-1: (7f) (gd)
Currently decent colt. (1st run) - 3rd of 17 to Senure (13 Oct Leicester 7f gd RF 4772). **E A L Dunlop [0-1] Maktoum Al Maktoum.*

DIRECT DIAL (USA) BHB 49f **RR 36f** 1751[11]
6 br g Phone Trick (USA) 7f **(62)** -Jig Jig (USA) (Never Bend) 13.1f **(70)**
Form - 0
Record 1998 - 1st:0 2nd:0 3rd:0 Ran:1
Pre1998 - 1st:0 2nd:0 3rd:1 Ran:5
Win Prizemoney £0 *Total Prizemoney* £579
1998 Turf 0-1: (9f) (frm)
Very moderate gelding. (DEAD)
**J A R Toller [0-5] J A R Toller (from Miss Gay Kelleway [0-1] Aug 1996).*

DISCERNING AIR BHB 78f **RR 64f** 5057[3]
2 b f Ezzoud (IRE) - Jhansi Ki Rani (USA) (Far North (CAN)) 9.7f **(75)**
Form - 423
Record 1998 - 1st:0 2nd:1 3rd:1 Ran:3
Win Prizemoney £0 *Total Prizemoney* £1,639
1998 Turf 0-3: (8f 2, 9f) (sft 2, frm)
Currently average filly. Turf high 64 (began Spt).
**E Weymes [0-3] T A Scothern.*

DISCO TEX BHB 43f49a **RR 49f 49a** 4627[10]
3 b g Rambo Dancer (CAN) 8.4f **(59)** - Andbracket (Import) 6.6f **(68)**
Form - 066031366530
Record 1998 - 1st:1 2nd:0 3rd:3 Ran:12
Pre1998 - 1st:0 2nd:0 3rd:0 Ran:5
Win Prizemoney £2,668 *Total Prizemoney* £3,869
Wins * **1998** Jly Hamilt (FRM) H 13f 43 49 <
1998 Turf 1-11: (9f, 10f, 11f, 12f 4, 13f 1-1, 14f, 16f 2) (gd 3, g-f 4, frm 1-4) 1998 AW 0-1: (12f) (Fibr)
Scopey, moderate gelding, effective 12 to 16f, acts on frm, often wears blinkers (extremely effectively), favours tight tracks. Turf high 49 - 1st of 8 getting 6lb from Marisol (10 Jly Hamilton RF 2685). Consistent. **M W Easterby [1-17] Mybank Racing.*

DISCRETION (IRE) BHB 45f **RR 56f** 4811[19]
3 b f Alzao (USA) 9.8f **(73)** - Sawaki (Song) 7.2f **(61)**
Form - 450000
Record 1998 - 1st:0 2nd:0 3rd:0 Ran:6
Win Prizemoney £0 *Total Prizemoney* £250
1998 Turf 0-6: (6f 2, 7f 3, 8f) (gd 3, g-f 2, frm)
Workmanlike, fair filly. Turf high 56.
**S Gollings [0-6] Mrs Dave Mager Sue Mager.*

DISCRIMINATION BHB 66f **RR 68f** 4633[22]
3 b f Efisio 7.7f **(69)** - Prejudice (Young Generation) 7.7f **(63)**
Form - 53301200
Record 1998 - 1st:1 2nd:1 3rd:2 Ran:8
Win Prizemoney £4,077 *Total Prizemoney* £6,864
Wins * **1998** Aug Newmar (G-F) C 7f 65 <
1998 Turf 1-8: (5f, 7f 1-6, 8f) (sft, gd 2, g-f, frm 1-4)
Workmanlike, average filly, effective 7 to 8f, best at 7f, acts on gd to frm, best on frm. Turf high 68 (began Jly) - 2nd of 18 getting 10lb from Queens Consul (5 Spt Thirsk 8f frm RF 4111) - also 1st of 12 getting 10lb from Carnbrea Firstlove (28 Aug Newmarket RF 3931). Showed the right attitude when winning a Newmarket claimer in August. **Mrs J R Ramsden [1-8] L C and A E Sigsworth.*

DISHABILLE RR 43f 3475[13]
2 b f Dilum (USA) 7.1f **(56)**-Swagger Lady (Tate Gallery(USA)) 7.4f **(67)**
Form - 66850
Record 1998 - 1st:0 2nd:0 3rd:0 Ran:5
1998 Turf 0-4: (5f, 6f 2, 7f) (gd, g-f, frm 2) 1998 AW 0-1: (6f) (Fibr)
Moderate filly. Turf high 43. **J D Bethell [0-5] R M Chetham.*

DISILLUSIONED RR 304[6]
4 ch g Shavian 7.7f **(67)** - Expensive Gift (Record Token) 6.3f **(53)**
Form - 6
Record 1998 - 1st:0 2nd:0 3rd:0 Ran:1
1998 AW 0-1: (10f) (Equi)
Formerly very poor gelding - 6th of 6 getting 15lb from Threadneedle (17 Feb Lingfield 10f Equi RF 0304).
**K G Wingrove [0-3] N J Hurrell.*

DISPOL CLAN BHB 62f63a **RR 69f 63a** 4863[4]
2 ch f Clantime 6.6f **(57)** - She's a Breeze (Crofthall) 6.3f **(59)**
Form - 122423714
Record 1998 - 1st:2 2nd:3 3rd:1 Ran:9
Win Prizemoney £4,638 *Total Prizemoney* £7,033
Wins * **1998** *Oct Wolver (sta) S 5f 67*
1998 Apr Nottin (SFT) 5.1f 69 <
1998 Turf 1-6: (5f 1-6) (g-s 1-1, gd 3, g-f 2) 1998 AW 1-3: (5f 1-2, 6f) (Fibr 1-3)
Average filly, effective 5f, acts on g-s to gd - acts on Fibr. Turf high 69 (1st run) - 1st of 8 getting 5lb from Golden Reef (28 Apr Nottingham RF 0900). AW high 67 (began Aug) - 1st of 13 getting 5lb from Legal Venture (3 Oct Wolverhampton RF 4639). Won in soft ground at Nottingham on her debut, and continued to run well in modest company afterwards, eventually adding a victory on the Wolverhampton Fibresand in October.
**D J G MurraySmith [1-2] Cardinal Racing (from J L Eyre [0-2] Aug 1998).*

DISPOL DIAMOND BHB 60f **RR 68f** 4936[12]
5 b m Sharpo 7.5f **(68)** - Fabulous Rina (FR) (Fabulous Dancer (USA)) 9.4f **(70)**
Form - 1103266000
Record 1998 - 1st:2 2nd:1 3rd:1 Ran:10
Pre1998 - 1st:1 2nd:1 3rd:4 Ran:22
Win Prizemoney £12,146 *Total Prizemoney* £20,424
Wins **1998** Apr Pontef (G-S) H 8f 58 63+ <
1998 Apr Nottin (G-S) H 8.2f 47 57+
1997 May Redcar (FRM) S 7f 44
1998 Turf 2-10: (8f 2-8, 9f 2) (g-s 2-3, gd 2, g-f 2, frm 2, hrd)
Average filly, effective 8 to 9f, best at 8f, acts on g-s to frm, excels at York. Turf high 68 - 2nd of 17 getting 17lb from Rapier (13 Jun York 9f g-s RF 1980) - also 1st of 15 getting 14lb from Taffs Well (21 Apr Pontefract RF 0789).
**N Tinkler [0-3] Mrs D Drewery (from G R Oldroyd [3-29] Jly 1998).*

DISPOL EMERALD BHB 48f38a **RR 51f 38a** 139[10]
3 b f Emarati (USA) 6.6f **(63)** - Double Touch (FR) (Nonoalco (USA)) 8.5f **(66)**
Form - 70
Record 1998 - 1st:0 2nd:0 3rd:0 Ran:2
Pre1998 - 1st:0 2nd:0 3rd:0 Ran:3
1998 AW 0-2: (6f 2) (Fibr 2)
Light-framed, fair filly. AW high 20.
**S E Kettlewell [0-5] S E Kettlewell.*

DISPOL GEM BHB 57f **RR 55f** 2171[8]
5 b m Rambo Dancer (CAN) 8.4f **(59)** - Andbracket (Import) 6.6f **(68)**
Form - 8
Record 1998 - 1st:0 2nd:0 3rd:0 Ran:1
Pre1998 - 1st:2 2nd:2 3rd:3 Ran:28
Win Prizemoney £6,209 *Total Prizemoney* £10,386
Wins 1997 Jly Ripon (GD) H 8f 64 68 <
1997 May Redcar (G-F) H 9f 58 56
1998 Turf 0-1: (12f) (frm)
Fair filly, effective 8 to 9f, best at 8f, acts on g-f to frm, best on frm, prefers left handed tracks. Inconsistent.
**A R Dicken [0-4] Beach Boys Partnership (from P Calver [2-15] Nov 1997).*

DISPOL PRESIDENT RR 65f 3505[7]
2 b c Presidium 7.5f **(56)** -Sister Hannah (Monseigneur (USA)) 7.7f **(63)**
Form - 067
Record 1998 - 1st:0 2nd:0 3rd:0 Ran:3
1998 Turf 0-3: (5f 3) (sft, gd, frm)
Currently average colt. Turf high 65. **P Calver [0-3] W B Imison.*

DISPOL PRINCE BHB 15f **RR** 609[18]
5 b g Risk Me (FR) 8f **(53)** - Gemma Kaye (Cure The Blues (USA)) 9.5f **(63)**
Form - 0
Record 1998 - 1st:0 2nd:0 3rd:0 Ran:1
Pre1998 - 1st:0 2nd:0 3rd:0 Ran:5
1998 Turf 0-1: (12f) (sft)
Formerly very poor gelding, effective 10 to 12f, acts on sft to gd - 18th of 20 getting 5lb from Lucy Tufty (8 Apr Ripon 12f sft RF 0609). **G R Oldroyd [0-9] Robert Cook.*

DISPOL ROCK (IRE) BHB 75f **RR 75f** 4577[1]
2 b g Ballad Rock 7.2f **(63)** - Havana Moon (Ela-Mana-Mou) 10.1f **(70)**
Form - 371
Record 1998 - 1st:1 2nd:0 3rd:1 Ran:3
Win Prizemoney £1,903 *Total Prizemoney* £2,410
Wins * **1998** Spt Newcas (GD) 7f 75 <
1998 Turf 1-3: (7f 1-3) (g-f 1-2, frm)
Currently above-average gelding. Turf high 75 (began Aug) - 1st of 12 giving 5lb to Swynford Pleasure (30 Spt Newcastle RF 4577).
**P Calver [1-3] W B Imison.*

DISPOL SAFA BHB 72f **RR 69f** 3996[3]
2 b f Safawan 6.6f **(60)**-Aimee Jane (USA) (Our Native (USA))11.2f **(63)**
Form - 2120313
Record 1998 - 1st:2 2nd:2 3rd:2 Ran:7
Win Prizemoney £5,324 *Total Prizemoney* £7,871
Wins * **1998** Aug Catter (G-F) H 6f 67 69 <
* **1998** Jun Thirsk (SFT) S 6f 67
1998 Turf 2-7: (5f, 6f 2-3, 7f 3) (g-s, gd 1-4, g-f, frm 1-1)
Average filly, effective 6 to 7f, best at 7f, acts on gd to frm, best on gd. Turf high 69 - 1st of 8 getting 1lb from Cashiki (14 Aug Catterick RF 3620) - also 1st of 12 from Belle of Hearts (16 Jun Thirsk RF 2018). She got off the mark in a Thirsk seller on her second start, looking to be suited by the extra furlong and softer ground. She ran well over seven subsequently, but regained winning form back over six in a Catterick nursery.
**P Calver [2-7] W B Imison.*

DISPOL TRUMP BHB 52f **RR 61f** 3475[17]
2 ch f Chilibang 7f **(55)** - Broken Silence (Busted) 10.2f **(61)**
Form - 8400
Record 1998 - 1st:0 2nd:0 3rd:0 Ran:4
1998 Turf 0-4: (5f 2, 6f 2) (g-s, gd, frm 2)
Average filly. Turf high 61. **P Calver [0-4] W B Imison.*

DISTANT DYNASTY BHB 20f21a **RR 14f 21a** 2150[15]
8 br g Another Realm 8.5f **(49)** - Jianna (Godswalk (USA)) 7.3f **(58)**

Form - 00000
Record 1998 - 1st:0 2nd:0 3rd:0 Ran:5
Pre1998 - 1st:3 2nd:10 3rd:5 Ran:67
Win Prizemoney £8,265 *Total Prizemoney* £19,446
Wins * 1994 *Nov Lingfi (STD) H 5f 49 52* <
* 1994 *Jly Wolver (STD) H 6f 48 46*
* 1994 May Lingfi (HVY) H 6f 49 47
1998 Turf 0-4: (5f 3, 6f) (g-s, frm 3) 1998 AW 0-1: (6f) (Equi)
Poor gelding, has worn blinkers. Turf high 14.
**B A Pearce [3-54] Martin Gibbs (from J E Long [0-15] May 1994).*

DISTANT KING BHB 45f RR 54f 4921[9]

5 b g Distant Relative 7f **(69)** - Lindfield Belle (IRE) (Fairy King (USA)) 7.7f **(59)**
Form - 007607073141170000070
Record 1998 - 1st:3 2nd:0 3rd:1 Ran:20
Pre1998 - 1st:0 2nd:0 3rd:0 Ran:6
Win Prizemoney £7,950 *Total Prizemoney* £8,409
Wins * **1998** Jly Beverl (G-F) H 5f 49 54 <
* **1998** Jly Carlis (G-F) H 5f 43 45
* **1998** Jun Beverl (GD) H 5f 31 43
1998 Turf 3-19: (5f 3-10, 6f 4, 7f 2, 8f, 9f, 10f) (hvy, sft, g-s 4, gd 3, g-f, frm 3-9) 1998 AW 0-1: (7f) (Fibr)
Fair gelding, effective 5f, acts on frm, has worn blinkers. Turf high 54 - 1st of 19 giving 22lb to Born A Lady (14 Jly Beverley RF 2776) - also 1st of 13 giving 2lb to Young Ben (4 Jly Carlisle RF 2527). Gave his trainer his first-ever Flat success after eleven years of trying when scoring at Beverley in June. Only moderate, but won twice more the following month before losing his form.
**G P Kelly [3-25] A Barrett (from S Coathup [0-1] Aug 1995).*

DISTANT MIRAGE (IRE) BHB 104f RR 107f 1734a[7]

3 b c Caerleon (USA) 10.9f **(79)** - Desert Bluebell (Kalaglow) 9.8f **(67)**
Form - 37
Record 1998 - 1st:0 2nd:0 3rd:1 Ran:2
Pre1998 - 1st:1 2nd:1 3rd:0 Ran:3
Win Prizemoney £4,501 *Total Prizemoney* £13,796
Wins * 1997 Oct Newbur (G-S) 8f 90 <
1998 Turf 0-2: (12f 2) (g-f 2)
Scopey, Pattern-class colt. Turf high 107 (1st run) - 3rd of 5 to Gulland (5 May Chester 12f g-f RF 1042). He finished unplaced when a surprise favourite for the Italian Derby and was not seen out again. He ought to stay well, but does not look a Group One horse.
**P W Chapple-Hyam [1-5].*

DISTANT MOON BHB 95f RR 89df 3819[5]

2 b c Distant Relative 7f **(69)** - Moon Carnival **(96f)** (Be My Guest (USA)) 9.3f **(67)**
Form - 125
Record 1998 - 1st:1 2nd:1 3rd:0 Ran:3
Win Prizemoney £3,501 *Total Prizemoney* £5,923
Wins * **1998** Jun Sandow (G-S) 7.1f 89+ <
1998 Turf 1-3: (7f 1-2, 8f) (gd 1-1, g-f, frm)
Currently useful colt. Turf high 89 - 2nd of 4 to Tayil (11 Jly York 7f frm RF 2735) - also 1st of 7 from Bombard (12 Jun Sandown RF 1934). Won nicely on his debut, and just failed at York, but ran inexplicably poorly on his final run. Bred to need middle-distances in time, being from the family of Moon Madness and Sheriff's Star.
**Lady Herries [1-3] George Ward.*

DISTANT STORM BHB 51f49a RR 53f 49a 904[3]

5 ch g Pharly (FR) 11.5f **(64)** - Candle in the Wind (Thatching) 8f **(66)**
Form - 323523
Record 1998 - 1st:0 2nd:2 3rd:3 Ran:6
Pre1998 - 1st:1 2nd:1 3rd:0 Ran:8
Win Prizemoney £2,243 *Total Prizemoney* £7,396
Wins 1995 Jly Bright (FRM) S 7f 66 <
1998 Turf 0-2: (14f 2) (sft, g-s) 1998 AW 0-4: (16f 4) (Equi 3, Fibr)
Fair gelding, effective 14 to 16f, best at 16f, acts on sft to g-s - acts on AW, mostly wears blinkers (extremely effectively). Turf high 53 (1st run) - 2nd of 16 getting 28lb from Forgie (20 Apr Nottingham 14f sft RF 0773). AW high 51 - 2nd of 8 giving 8lb to Broughtons Formula (20 Jan Lingfield 16f Equi RF 0124). He has shown some ability in staying events on both All-Weather surfaces, and can find a small race.
**B J Llewellyn [4-24] D H Driscoll (from M Bell [1-7] Aug 1996).*

DISTINCT FLYER (IRE) BHB 37f RR 45f 4625[6]

3 gr g Distinctly North (USA) 7.4f **(63)** - Sabev (USA) (Saber Thrust (CAN))
Form - 00006
Record 1998 - 1st:0 2nd:0 3rd:0 Ran:5
1998 Turf 0-5: (10f 3, 12f 2) (g-f 3, frm 2)
Workmanlike, moderate gelding. Turf high 49.
**Andrew Turnell [0-5] Blenheim Thoroughbred Racing.*

DISTINCTIVE DANCE (USA) BHB 89f RR 94f 2738[12]

3 b c Distinctive Pro (USA) 8f **(62)** - Allison's Dance (USA) (Storm Bird (CAN)) 10.3f **(74)**
Form - 100
Record 1998 - 1st:1 2nd:0 3rd:0 Ran:3
Pre1998 - 1st:0 2nd:1 3rd:0 Ran:2
Win Prizemoney £2,070 *Total Prizemoney* £3,533
Wins * **1998** *Mar Lingfi (STD) 8f 73++* <
1998 Turf 0-2: (8f, 10f) (gd, frm) 1998 AW 1-1: (8f 1-1) (Equi 1-1)
Useful colt. Turf high 91. (1st run). He showed some ability on turf in the autumn of 1997, and got off the mark in a four-runner maiden on the Lingfield Equitrack in March. It was not a great race, and he faced much stiffer tasks in hot handicaps afterwards without cutting much ice. (DEAD) **Lord Huntingdon [1-5] George Ward.*

DISTINCTIVE DREAM (IRE) BHB 78f68a RR 84f 68a 4209[8]

4 b g Distinctly North (USA) 7.4f **(63)** - Green Side (USA) (Green Dancer (USA)) 10.3f **(74)**
Form - 0220008
Record 1998 - 1st:0 2nd:2 3rd:0 Ran:7
Pre1998 - 1st:6 2nd:4 3rd:0 Ran:25
Win Prizemoney £19,388 *Total Prizemoney* £30,010
Wins 1997 Spt Kempto (G-F) H 6f 73 79 <
1997 Aug Windso (GD) H 5f 63 70
1997 *Jly Southw (STD) H 5f 56 66*
1997 Jly Windso (G-F) H 6f 49 61
1997 Jly Salisb (FRM) CH 6f 43 53
1997 Jly Windso (GD) H 6f 45 50
1998 Turf 0-7: (6f 5, 7f 2) (gd 7)
Workmanlike, decent gelding, effective 6f, acts on gd to frm, best on gd, mostly wears blinkers (extremely effectively), excels at Kempton and Salisbury and Windsor. Turf high 85 - 2nd of 13 giving 10lb to Supreme Angel (23 May Kempton 6f gd RF 1428). Rattled up a five-timer in the summer of '97 and won six times in all. He ran some good races last term but failed to win, and it looks very much as if the Handicapper has got hold of him.
**Lady Herries [0-7] R Bremner (from K T Ivory [6-25] Nov 1997).*

DISTINCT VINTAGE (IRE) BHB 86f RR 78+f 835a[5]

3 b c Distinctly North (USA) 7.4f **(63)** - Princess Raisa (Indian King (USA)) 7.4f **(64)**
Form - 5
Record 1998 - 1st:0 2nd:0 3rd:0 Ran:1
Pre1998 - 1st:1 2nd:0 3rd:0 Ran:4
Win Prizemoney £3,292 *Total Prizemoney* £5,565
Wins * 1997 Jly Bright (FRM) 6f 78+ <
1998 Turf 0-1: (7f) (sft)
Neat, above-average colt. **R Hannon [1-5] E C Nagell-Erichsen.*

DIVIDE AND RULE BHB 41f30a RR 42f 30a 4200[11]

4 b c Puissance 7.1f **(60)** - Indivisible (Remainder Man) 11.2f **(45)**
Form - 00008800
Record 1998 - 1st:0 2nd:0 3rd:0 Ran:5
Pre1998 - 1st:1 2nd:0 3rd:3 Ran:19
Win Prizemoney £3,028 *Total Prizemoney* £5,363
Wins * 1996 Jun Ripon (G-F) 5f 71 <
1998 Turf 0-3: (5f 3) (gd, frm 2) 1998 AW 0-2: (5f, 7f) (Fibr 2)
Scopey, moderate colt. Turf high 32 (began Jly). AW high 15.
**R Hollinshead [1-24] M Johnson.*

DIVINE LADY BHB 60f RR 64f 4818[9]

2 ch f Prince Sabo 6.6f **(64)** -Lady St Lawrence (USA) (Bering) 7.4f **(61)**
Form - 418074180
Record 1998 - 1st:2 2nd:0 3rd:0 Ran:9
Win Prizemoney £4,444 *Total Prizemoney* £4,853
Wins * **1998** Spt Bright (FRM) S 7f 64 <
* **1998** Jun Salisb (G-S) 6f 64 <
1998 Turf 2-9: (6f 1-5, 7f 1-4) (gd 1-3, g-f, frm 1-4, hrd)

Average filly, effective 6 to 7f, acts on gd to frm. Turf high 64 - also 1st of 13 from Dolly Day Dream (9 Jun Salisbury RF 1835). Inconsistent. She won a Salisbury maiden auction event on her second start, but the rest of her form suggests that is as good as she is. Her win was gained with cut in the ground and it may well be that those are the conditions she requires.
**A P Jarvis [2-9] Christopher Shankland.*

DIVINE MISS-P BHB 80f74a **RR 85f 74a** 4741[17]

5 ch m Safawan 6.6f **(60)** - Faw (Absalom) 7.2f **(58)**
Form - 13521162213851230000

Record	**1998 -**	1st:5	2nd:4	3rd:3	Ran:20
	Pre1998 -	1st:3	2nd:1	3rd:0	Ran:13

Win Prizemoney £30,440 *Total Prizemoney* £40,622

Wins								
	* **1998**	Jun	Chepst	(G-S)	H	5.1f	74	81 <
	* **1998**	May	Bath	(GD)	H	5.1f	69	71
	* **1998**	Apr	Folkes	(GD)	H	5f	60	67
	* **1998**	*Mar*	*Southw*	*(STD)*	*H*	*5f*	*63*	*69*
	1998	*Feb*	*Wolver*	*(STD)*	*C*	*6f*		*64*
	1997	Aug	Warwic	(G-S)	C	5f		59
	1997	Aug	Yarmou	(G-F)	H	5.2f	50	57
	1997	Apr	Thirsk	(G-F)		6f		64

1998 Turf 3-14: (5f 3-10, 6f 4) (g-s 2, gd 2-9, g-f, frm 1-2) 1998 AW 2-6: (5f 1-3, 6f 1-3) (Equi 2, Fibr 2-4)
Useful filly, effective 5f, acts on gd. Turf high 85 - 3rd of 13 getting 11lb from Blessingindisguise (24 Jly Ascot 5f gd RF 3063) - also 1st of 10 getting 16lb from Hopping Higgins (30 Jun Chepstow RF 2395). AW high 69. Effective on Fibresand or turf, she paid her way again last term. She is normally very quick into her stride and possesses plenty of early speed, and though successful over six furlongs is probably better over five.
**J Cullinan [4-19] Alan Spargo Ltd Toolmakers (from A P Jarvis [4-14] Feb 1998).*

DIVING FOR PEARLS (IRE) BHB 35f **RR 12f** 3037[13]

2 ch c Petardia 8.2f **(58)** - Island Heather (IRE) (Salmon Leap (USA)) 11f **(61)**
Form - 000
Record 1998 - 1st:0 2nd:0 3rd:0 Ran:3
1998 Turf 0-3: (6f 2, 7f) (gd 2, g-f)
Currently poor colt. Turf high 12. **G Lewis [0-3] David Waters.*

DIVINITY BHB 62a **RR 64?f** 612[9]

4 ch f Lycius (USA) 8.8f **(71)** - Heavenly Abode (FR) (Habitat) 9.4f **(70)**
Form - 128860

Record	**1998 -**	1st:1	2nd:1	3rd:0	Ran:6
	Pre1998 -	1st:0	2nd:0	3rd:1	Ran:3

Win Prizemoney £3,436 *Total Prizemoney* £4,728
Wins * **1998** *Jan Lingfi (STD) 13f 47 <*
1998 Turf 0-2: (12f, 14f) (sft, g-s) 1998 AW 1-4: (13f 1-2, 15f, 16f) (Equi 1-3, Fibr)
Workmanlike, average filly, effective 13 to 14f, acts on g-f - acts on Equi, has worn blinkers, prefers left handed tracks. Turf high 43. AW high 60 - 2nd of 5 giving 12lb to Philosophic (31 Jan Lingfield 13f Equi RF 0199). She got off the mark when winning a very modest thirteen-furlong maiden on the Lingfield Equitrack in January, and was just caught in an equally modest handicap over the same course and distance later the same month. She has run poorly since. **S P C Woods [1-6] Ian Deane (from C E Brittain [0-3] Jly 1997).*

DIVORCE ACTION (IRE) BHB 65f **RR 66f** 4873[20]

2 b c Common Grounds 8.1f **(66)** - Overdue Reaction (Be My Guest (USA)) 9.3f **(67)**
Form - 5300
Record 1998 - 1st:0 2nd:0 3rd:1 Ran:4
Win Prizemoney £0 *Total Prizemoney* £484
1998 Turf 0-4: (6f, 7f 2, 8f) (gd 2, frm 2)
Average colt. Turf high 66 (began Jly). **P F I Cole [0-4] Frank Stella.*

DIVVINAYSHAN (IRE) BHB 65f **RR 78f** 4667[9]

3 b c Darshaan 11.9f **(81)** - Sharaniya (USA) (Alleged (USA)) 10f **(76)**
Form - 05500

Record	**1998 -**	1st:0	2nd:0	3rd:0	Ran:5
	Pre1998 -	1st:0	2nd:0	3rd:0	Ran:1

1998 Turf 0-5: (10f, 12f, 13f, 14f, 16f) (g-s 2, gd 2, g-f)
Leggy, above-average colt, has worn blinkers. Turf high 78.
**R W Armstrong [0-6] Ravi Tikkoo.*

DIXIE CROSSROADS BHB 48f38a **RR 55f 38a** 259[7]

3 b f Efisio 7.7f **(69)** - Moments Joy (Adonijah) 10f **(61)**
Form - 4567

Record	**1998 -**	1st:0	2nd:0	3rd:0	Ran:4
	Pre1998 -	1st:0	2nd:0	3rd:0	Ran:6

1998 AW 0-4: (6f, 7f, 8f, 10f) (Equi 4)
Lengthy, fair filly. AW high 37.
**S Dow [0-6] Eddie Davess (from R Hannon [0-4] Jun 1997).*

DIXIE D'OATS BHB 58f **RR 63f** 4573[8]

3 b f Alhijaz 7.7f **(57)** - Helsanon (Hello Gorgeous (USA)) 9.7f **(63)**
Form - 03358

Record	**1998 -**	1st:0	2nd:0	3rd:2	Ran:5
	Pre1998 -	1st:0	2nd:0	3rd:0	Ran:1

Win Prizemoney £0 *Total Prizemoney* £1,102
1998 Turf 0-5: (10f 3, 12f 2) (gd, g-f, frm 3)
Leggy, average filly, effective 10f, acts on frm. Turf high 63 (began Jly) - 3rd of 18 getting 5lb from Quintus (3 Aug Windsor 10f frm RF 3317). **E A L Dunlop [0-6] Downlands Racing.*

DIXIE JAZZ **RR 61f** 4856[9]

2 br f Mtoto 11.5f **(71)** -Dixie Favor (USA)(Dixieland Band (USA))7f **(74)**
Form - 60
Record 1998 - 1st:0 2nd:0 3rd:0 Ran:2
1998 Turf 0-2: (7f, 8f) (sft, frm)
Currently average filly. Turf high 61 (began Spt).
**Miss J A Camacho [0-2] Elite Racing Club.*

DIZZY TILLY BHB 51f **RR 64f** 4927[6]

4 b f Anshan 8.2f **(63)** - Nadema (Artaius (USA)) 9f **(69)**
Form - 70307005576

Record	**1998 -**	1st:0	2nd:0	3rd:1	Ran:10
	Pre1998 -	1st:2	2nd:1	3rd:2	Ran:15

Win Prizemoney £5,448 *Total Prizemoney* £8,221

Wins								
	* 1997	Jun	Windso	(G-S)		10f		66 <
	* 1997	Jun	Windso	(G-F)	H	11.6f	57	64+

1998 Turf 0-10: (10f 6, 11f 2, 12f, 14f) (g-s, gd 3, g-f 3, frm 3)
Scopey, average filly, effective 10 to 12f, best at 12f, acts on g-s to frm, best on g-f, excels at Windsor. Turf high 64 - 3rd of 12 getting 20lb from Brandon Jack (8 Jun Windsor 10f g-f RF 1820).
**T J Naughton [2-25] Mrs S Leech.*

D'MARTI BHB 66f **RR 58f** 5097[3]

3 b f Emarati (USA) 6.6f **(63)** - Hellene (Dominion) 8.5f **(63)**
Form - 033854210003

Record	**1998 -**	1st:1	2nd:1	3rd:3	Ran:12
	Pre1998 -	1st:0	2nd:1	3rd:2	Ran:4

Win Prizemoney £3,533 *Total Prizemoney* £8,930
Wins * **1998** Jly Sandow (G-S) H 5f 65 73 <
1998 Turf 1-12: (5f 1-10, 6f 2) (sft, g-s 1-2, gd 7, g-f, frm)
Scopey, fair filly, effective 5 to 6f, best at 5f, acts on sft to g-f, best on g-s. Turf high 73 - 1st of 13 getting 2lb from Poetry In Motion (3 Jly Sandown RF 2508). Broke her duck in an ordinary Sandown handicap over the minimum. **C B B Booth [1-16] Mrs Marian Rogers.*

DOATING (IRE) BHB 60f57a **RR 68f 57a** 3107[9]

3 b f Doyoun 10.7f **(69)** - Hayat (IRE) (Sadler's Wells (USA)) 10f **(76)**
Form - 460

Record	**1998 -**	1st:0	2nd:0	3rd:0	Ran:3
	Pre1998 -	1st:0	2nd:0	3rd:0	Ran:2

Win Prizemoney £0 *Total Prizemoney* £242
1998 Turf 0-1: (13f) (g-f) 1998 AW 0-2: (10f 2) (Equi 2)
Scopey, average filly. AW high 44. **J W Hills [0-5] J W Robb.*

DOBAANDI SECRET **RR 38f** 5146[10]

2 b g Reprimand 8.2f **(63)** -Secret Dance (Sadler's Wells(USA))10f **(76)**
Form - 00
Record 1998 - 1st:0 2nd:0 3rd:0 Ran:2
1998 Turf 0-2: (7f, 8f) (gd, frm)
Currently very moderate gelding. Turf high 38 (began Jly).
**P D Evans [0-1] Smiley Partnership (from N P Littmoden [0-1] Jly 1998).*

DOBERMAN (IRE) BHB 70f67a **RR 74f 67a** 4127[4]

3 br g Dilum (USA) 7.1f **(56)** - Switch Blade (IRE) (Robellino (USA)) 7.6f **(80)**
Form - 2254

Record 1998 - 1st:0 2nd:2 3rd:0 Ran:4
Win Prizemoney £0 *Total Prizemoney* £1,984
1998 Turf 0-4: (5f, 6f 2, 7f) (g-f, frm 2, hrd)
Workmanlike, above-average gelding. Turf high 74 (1st run) (began Jly) - 2nd of 9 giving 5lb to Uplifting (22 Jly Leicester 5f frm RF 3030). Has run well in maidens and may be able to pinch a race.
**B J Meehan [0-4] John Manley.*

DOCKLAND EXECUTIVE BHB 28f RR 32f 2833^{7}

3 b g Nomination 7.3f **(57)** - Khadino (Relkino) 8.9f **(65)**
Form - 00507
Record 1998 - 1st:0 2nd:0 3rd:0 Ran:5
Pre1998 - 1st:0 2nd:0 3rd:0 Ran:1
1998 Turf 0-5: (10f 5) (gd 2, g-f 2, frm)
Unfurnished, very moderate gelding. Turf high 32.
**B J McMath [0-5] Mrs Lisa Olley (from B Smart [0-1] Spt 1997).*

DOCKLANDS COURIER BHB 45f38a RR 44f 38a 364^{8}

6 b g Dominion 8.9f **(65)** - High Quail (USA) (Blushing Groom (FR)) 10.3f **(76)**
Form - 8
Record 1998 - 1st:0 2nd:0 3rd:0 Ran:1
Pre1998 - 1st:0 2nd:2 3rd:0 Ran:16
Win Prizemoney £0 *Total Prizemoney* £2,140
1998 AW 0-1: (12f) (Equi)
Moderate gelding.
**R T Phillips [0-4] Mrs Lisa Olley (from B J McMath [0-19] Jan 1997).*

DOCKLANDS LIMO BHB 86f70a RR 87f 70a 2138^{9}

5 b h Most Welcome 8.6f **(66)** - Bugle Sound (Bustino) 10.4f **(64)**
Form - 0330
Record 1998 - 1st:0 2nd:0 3rd:2 Ran:4
Pre1998 - 1st:3 2nd:1 3rd:2 Ran:14
Win Prizemoney £35,735 *Total Prizemoney* £44,363
Wins * 1997 Jly Down R (G-F) LH 12.3f 78+ <
* 1996 Apr Nottin (GD) 10f 74
* 1996 *Feb Lingfi (STD) 8f 59*
1998 Turf 0-4: (10f 3, 12f) (sft, gd, g-f 2)
Useful colt, effective 10 to 14f, best at 10f, acts on gd to g-f, best on gd. Turf high 87 - 3rd of 8 getting 2lb from Cugina (12 Jun Sandown 10f gd RF 1935). Running well in '98, but was not seen after June.
**B J McMath [3-18] Mrs Lisa Olley.*

DOCKLANDS MERC (IRE) RR 24f 1073^{10}

2 f Batshoof - Petite Louie (Chilibang)
Form - 0
Record 1998 - 1st:0 2nd:0 3rd:0 Ran:1
1998 Turf 0-1: (5f) (g-f)
Currently little account. **N Tinkler [0-1] Mrs Lisa Olley.*

DOCKSIDER (USA) RR 111f 3948^{9}

3 ch c Diesis 9f **(80)** - Pump (USA) (Forli (ARG)) 9.6f **(67)**
Form - 72710
Record 1998 - 1st:1 2nd:1 3rd:0 Ran:5
Pre1998 - 1st:1 2nd:2 3rd:0 Ran:4
Win Prizemoney £8,969 *Total Prizemoney* £63,640
Wins * **1998** Aug Sandow (G-F) 8.1f 111 <
* 1997 Jly Salisb (G-F) 7f 87
1998 Turf 1-5: (7f, 8f 1-4) (sft, gd 2, g-f, frm 1-1)
Scopey, Group-class colt, effective 7 to 8f, best at 8f, acts on gd to frm, best on gd. Turf high 111 - 2nd of 11 to Tiger Hill (10 May Cologne 8f gd RF 1227a) - also 1st of 4 getting 3lb from Haami (12 Aug Sandown RF 3596). Inconsistent. He bounces off fast ground and had perfect conditions when finishing second in the German 2,000 Guineas. Gifted a race against a sulky Haami at Sandown in August, he sweated-up and ran poorly in the Group Two Celebration Mile later that month. He will need to travel if he is to pay for his keep in 1999. **J W Hills [2-9] Freddy Bienstock.*

DOC RYAN'S BHB 63f64a RR 67f 64a 5119^{2}

4 b c Damister (USA) 9.1f **(66)** - Jolimo (Fortissimo) 11.8f **(61)**
Form - 568510002
Record 1998 - 1st:1 2nd:1 3rd:0 Ran:9
Pre1998 - 1st:1 2nd:1 3rd:4 Ran:13
Win Prizemoney £10,316 *Total Prizemoney* £14,645
Wins * **1998** Jun Mussel (SFT) H 12f 61 68 <
* 1997 Nov Mussel (G-S) H 12f 61 67
1998 Turf 1-9: (11f, 12f 1-6, 13f, 14f) (sft 2, g-s, gd 1-6)
Scopey, average colt, effective 8 to 12f, best at 12f, acts on gd, often wears blinkers (very effectively), likes right handed tracks. Turf high 68 - 1st of 10 giving 6lb to Kintavi (15 Jun Musselburgh RF 1994). Inconsistent. He is only very modest, but twelve furlongs on easy ground at Musselburgh seem to suit him well.
**M J Ryan [2-22] P J Flavin.*

DOCTOR BRAVIOUS (IRE) BHB 41f50a RR 41f 50a 2887^{9}

5 b g Priolo (USA) 10.9f **(71)** - Sharp Slipper (Sharpo) 7.7f **(59)**
Form - 0030620
Record 1998 - 1st:0 2nd:1 3rd:1 Ran:7
Pre1998 - 1st:1 2nd:0 3rd:1 Ran:14
Win Prizemoney £3,743 *Total Prizemoney* £6,800
Wins 1996 *Jan Wolver (STD) 8.5f 65* <
1998 Turf 0-7: (7f 2, 8f 4, 9f) (gd 4, g-f, frm 2)
Moderate gelding, effective 8f, acts on g-f, mostly wears blinkers (effectively). Turf high 41.
**B Ellison [0-15] Ms Glynis Purcell-Brydon (from M Bell [1-12] Jun 1997).*

DOCTOR KOOL BHB 74f RR 70f 4860^{4}

2 ch c Local Suitor (USA) 9.7f **(58)** - Hasty Sarah (Gone Native)
Form - 40474
Record 1998 - 1st:0 2nd:0 3rd:0 Ran:5
Win Prizemoney £0 *Total Prizemoney* £516
1998 Turf 0-5: (5f 2, 6f, 8f 2) (sft, gd 2, g-f, frm)
Above-average colt. Turf high 70. **T P Tate [0-5] The Ivy Syndicate.*

DOCTOR SPIN (IRE) BHB 99f RR 93+f 1595^{1}

2 b c Namaqualand (USA) - Madam Loving (Vaigly Great) 7f **(58)**
Form - 511
Record 1998 - 1st:2 2nd:0 3rd:0 Ran:3
Win Prizemoney £6,460 *Total Prizemoney* £6,460
Wins * **1998** May Lingfi (GD) 5f 93+ <
* **1998** May Windso (G-F) 5f 82
1998 Turf 2-3: (5f 2-3) (g-s, g-f 1-1, frm 1-1)
Currently useful colt. Turf high 93 - 1st of 7 giving 19lb to Lucy Mariella (30 May Lingfield RF 1595). He improved in each of his first three runs, winning nicely at Windsor despite becoming upset by the antics of a rival in the next stall, and following up at Lingfield. He tends to sweat up but it does not stop him winning. Will eventually be better over six or seven furlongs, and could be a very useful individual in the making.
**R F JohnsonHoughton [2-3] Anthony Pye-Jeary.*

DODO (IRE) BHB 82f RR 82f 5074^{6}

3 b f Alzao (USA) 9.8f **(73)** - Dead Certain (Absalom) 7.2f **(58)**
Form - 033300331336
Record 1998 - 1st:1 2nd:0 3rd:7 Ran:12
Pre1998 - 1st:0 2nd:2 3rd:0 Ran:5
Win Prizemoney £3,972 *Total Prizemoney* £15,366
Wins * **1998** Spt Kempto (GD) H 6f 72 78 <
1998 Turf 1-12: (6f 1-7, 7f 3, 8f 2) (g-s, gd 3, g-f 3, frm 1-5)
Scopey, decent filly, effective 6 to 8f, best at 6f, acts on gd to frm, best on gd, has worn blinkers, excels at Newmarket. Turf high 82 - 3rd of 23 getting 10lb from Primo Lara (10 Oct York 6f gd RF 4749) - also 1st of 26 giving 2lb to Fairy Prince (21 Spt Kempton RF 4390). A daughter of Dead Certain, she was in good form in the autumn, beating a huge field at Kempton.
**D R C Elsworth [1-17] D R C Elsworth.*

DOKOS (USA) BHB 98f RR 97f 5066^{4}

4 b c Nureyev (USA) 8.4f **(84)** - Pasadoble (USA) (Prove Out (USA)) 8f **(97)**
Form - 32404
Record 1998 - 1st:0 2nd:1 3rd:1 Ran:5
Pre1998 - 1st:1 2nd:1 3rd:0 Ran:2
Win Prizemoney £4,932 *Total Prizemoney* £10,816
Wins * 1997 Apr Newmar (GD) 8f 89 <
1998 Turf 0-5: (9f, 10f 4) (g-f 4, frm)
Scopey, very useful colt, effective 8 to 10f, best at 10f, acts on gd to frm, best on g-f. Turf high 97 (began Aug) - 4th of 5 giving 5lb to Marcus Maximus (11 Spt Doncaster 10f g-f RF 4223). He is a full brother to Miesque, and made a great start to his career by winning the '97 Wood Ditton Stakes at Newmarket in tremendous fashion. He was rather disappointing when beaten at odd-on next time, and was not seen again that season. Though placed in '98, it

is true to say he has not reached the heights that once seemed possible, and he finished last of 35 in the Cambridgeshire.
**H R A Cecil [1-7] Niarchos Family.*

DOLLAR LAW BHB 87f **RR 90f** 4779[1]
2 ch g Selkirk (USA) 7.9f **(76)** - Western Heights (Shirley Heights) 10.3f **(74)**
Form - 241
Record 1998 - 1st:1 2nd:1 3rd:0 Ran:3
Win Prizemoney £4,042 *Total Prizemoney* £5,321
Wins * 1998 Oct Leices (G-S) 8f 89 <
1998 Turf 1-3: (7f 2, 8f 1-1) (gd 1-1, g-f, frm)
Currently useful gelding. Turf high 90 (1st run) (began Spt) - 2nd of 14 to Mukhalif (8 Spt Leicester 7f g-f RF 4142) - also 1st of 20 from Mehmaas (13 Oct Leicester RF 4779). A half-brother to mile and a quarter winner Pinchincha, he had an extra furlong to contend with on his final start but, the further he went, the better he got. Will eventually be better over middle-distances, and hasn't stopped improving yet. **P F I Cole [1-3] N C Kersey.*

DOLLY DAY DREAM (IRE) BHB 68f68a **RR 62f 68a** 3514[2]
2 ch f Magic Ring (IRE) 6.5f **(64)** - Lariston Gale (Pas de Seul) 9.1f **(67)**
Form - 443450261522
Record 1998 - 1st:1 2nd:3 3rd:1 Ran:12
Win Prizemoney £1,882 *Total Prizemoney* £5,611
Wins * 1998 Jly Yarmou (GD) S 6f 62 <
1998 Turf 1-8: (5f 4, 6f 1-4) (g-s 2, gd 3, g-f, hrd 1-2) 1998 AW 0-4: (5f 3, 6f) (Equi 2, Fibr 2)
Above-average filly, effective 6f, - acts on Fibr, has worn blinkers. Turf high 62. AW high 75 - 2nd of 11 giving 6lb to Kilbowie Hill (24 Jly Wolverhampton 6f Fibr RF 3093). **K T Ivory [1-12] K T Ivory.*

DOLPHINELLE (IRE) BHB 69f **RR 75f** 5144[19]
2 b c Dolphin Street (FR) - Mamie's Joy(Prince Tenderfoot(USA))9f **(61)**
Form - 6770340
Record 1998 - 1st:0 2nd:0 3rd:1 Ran:7
Win Prizemoney £0 *Total Prizemoney* £624
1998 Turf 0-7: (5f 2, 6f 5) (gd, g-f, frm 5)
Above-average colt, effective 5f, acts on frm, often wears blinkers. Turf high 75. **R Hannon [0-7] Tommy Staunton.*

DOLPHIN FRIENDLY (IRE) BHB 57f **RR 62f** 4889[12]
2 b f Dolphin Street (FR) - Sound Performance (IRE) (Ahonoora) 8.1f **(73)**
Form - 0250
Record 1998 - 1st:0 2nd:1 3rd:0 Ran:4
Win Prizemoney £0 *Total Prizemoney* £690
1998 Turf 0-4: (6f, 7f 2, 8f) (gd 2, g-f 2)
Average filly. Turf high 62 (began Jly) - 2nd of 13 getting 5lb from Jack Goodman (15 Jly Folkestone 7f gd RF 2822).
**J W Payne [0-4] The Frankland Lodgers.*

DOMAPPEL BHB 76f **RR 79f** 4054[4]
6 b g Domynsky 7.8f **(58)** - Appelania (Star Appeal) 9.6f **(65)**
Form - 1222244
Record 1998 - 1st:1 2nd:4 3rd:0 Ran:7
Pre1998 - 1st:3 2nd:3 3rd:2 Ran:18
Win Prizemoney £22,163 *Total Prizemoney* £34,695
Wins * 1998 May Cheste (G-F) H 12.3f 70 72
* 1996 Jun Thirsk (FRM) H 12f 70 75 <
* 1995 Spt Yarmou (GD) H 10.1f 65 67
1994 Oct Newmar (G-S) S 8f 64
1998 Turf 1-7: (12f 1-3, 13f, 14f, 15f, 16f) (g-f 1-3, frm 4)
Above-average gelding, effective 12 to 16f, acts on g-f to frm, best on frm, prefers left handed tracks, does well at Chester. Turf high 79 - 2nd of 9 giving 20lb to Northern Motto (11 Jly Chester 16f frm RF 2705) - also 1st of 11 from Kinnescash (7 May Chester RF 1074). Consistent. Effective on the Flat and over hurdles, he got up right on the line to win a handicap at the big Chester meeting. Has regularly found one too good since. He is well suited by fast ground, and likes to dictate.
**Mrs J Cecil [6-31] M C Banks (from W Jarvis [1-1] Oct 1994).*

DOMINANT AIR BHB 77f79a **RR 74f 79a** 3234[9]
4 b g Primo Dominie 7.2f **(67)** - Area Girl (Jareer (USA)) 5.9f **(75)**
Form - 6040
Record 1998 - 1st:0 2nd:0 3rd:0 Ran:4
Pre1998 - 1st:5 2nd:2 3rd:2 Ran:14
Win Prizemoney £18,964 *Total Prizemoney* £22,359
Wins * 1997 Oct Newmar (GD) H 5f 77 84 <
* 1997 Jly Bath (G-F) H 5.1f 75 72
* 1997 *Jan Southw (STD) C 6f 72*
* 1996 *Dec Southw (SLW) H 5f 74 81*
* 1996 Oct Yarmou (GD) H 5.2f 72 75
1998 Turf 0-3: (5f 2, 6f) (gd 2, frm) 1998 AW 0-1: (5f) (Fibr)
Scopey, above-average gelding, effective 5 to 7f, acts on gd to frm, best on frm. Turf high 73. **Sir Mark Prescott [5-18] Neil Greig.*

DOMINANT DANCER BHB 93f **RR 85f** 4857[7]
2 ch f Primo Dominie 7.2f **(67)** - Footlight Fantasy (USA) **(66f)** (Nureyev (USA)) 8.7f **(78)**
Form - 40217
Record 1998 - 1st:1 2nd:1 3rd:0 Ran:5
Win Prizemoney £4,052 *Total Prizemoney* £5,449
Wins * 1998 Spt Pontef (G-F) 6f 81 <
1998 Turf 1-5: (5f, 6f 1-4) (sft, gd, g-f, frm 1-2)
Useful filly. Turf high 85 - 2nd of 19 to Frappe (9 Spt Kempton 6f gd RF 4189) - also 1st of 13 getting 5lb from Tomasean (24 Spt Pontefract RF 4465). Made all at Pontefract, despite sweating up profusely. **J W Hills [1-5] P F Warren.*

DOMINANT DUCHESS BHB 75f **RR 81f** 4850[12]
4 b f Old Vic 12.8f **(72)** -Andy's Find (USA) (Buckfinder (USA)) 8.1f **(71)**
Form - 64040
Record 1998 - 1st:0 2nd:0 3rd:0 Ran:5
Pre1998 - 1st:2 2nd:2 3rd:0 Ran:5
Win Prizemoney £5,828 *Total Prizemoney* £11,201
Wins * 1997 Apr Nottin (G-F) 10f 73+ <
* 1997 Mar Warwic (G-F) C 12.5f 61+
1998 Turf 0-5: (13f 2, 15f, 17f, 18f) (gd, g-f 3, frm)
Leggy, decent filly, effective 10 to 17f, acts on gd to frm, best on g-f, prefers tight tracks. Turf high 78 (began Aug) - 4th of 12 to Nanton Point (28 Spt Bath 17f g-f RF 4525). Consistent.
**J W Hills [2-10] Mrs Diana Patterson.*

DOMINELLE BHB 67f45a **RR 70f 45a** 4701[12]
6 b m Domynsky 7.8f **(58)** - Gymcrak Lovebird (Taufan (USA)) 7f **(57)**
Form - 052180343611816060
Record 1998 - 1st:4 2nd:1 3rd:2 Ran:18
Pre1998 - 1st:4 2nd:7 3rd:6 Ran:51
Win Prizemoney £27,551 *Total Prizemoney* £42,219
Wins * 1998 Aug Ripon (G-F) H 6f 65 67 <
* **1998** Aug Redcar (G-F) H 6f 53 63
* **1998** Aug Pontef (G-F) H 5f 54 58
* **1998** Jun Doncas (GD) H 6f 48 49
* 1996 Jun Beverl (G-F) H 5f 45 46
1995 Jly Carlis (FRM) H 5f 49 45
1995 Jun Carlis (FRM) H 5f 45 46
1994 Aug Ripon (G-F) S 6f 53+
1998 Turf 4-18: (5f 1-10, 6f 3-7, 7f) (gd 4, g-f 2-5, frm 2-9)
Above-average mare, effective 6f, acts on g-f to frm, best on g-f, has worn blinkers. Turf high 70 - 6th of 12 getting 5lb from Jocasta (29 Aug Nottingham 6f g-f RF 3960) - also 1st of 22 giving 3lb to Maiteamia (22 Aug Ripon RF 3817). A modest sprinter, her strike rate was not brilliant, but she did particularly well last term in winning four sprint handicaps. Six furlongs or a stiff five seem to suit her best.
**T D Easterby [5-47] Sandmoor Textiles Co Ltd (from M H Easterby [3-22] Oct 1995).*

DOMINO FLYER BHB 55f62a **RR 62f 62a** 4704[9]
5 b g Warrshan (USA) 9.7f **(59)** - Great Dilemma (Vaigly Great) 7f **(58)**
Form - 2540140
Record 1998 - 1st:1 2nd:1 3rd:0 Ran:7
Pre1998 - 1st:5 2nd:2 3rd:3 Ran:27
Win Prizemoney £14,785 *Total Prizemoney* £18,466
Wins * 1998 *Jun Southw (STD) H 8f 56 61*
* 1997 Mar Newcas (GD) H 10.1f 66 72 <
* 1997 *Jan Southw (STD) H 8f 58 56*
* 1996 *Nov Southw (STD) 8f 62*
* 1996 May Hamilt (SFT) 9.2f 63
* 1996 *Apr Southw (STD) H 7f 52 59*
1998 Turf 0-3: (8f 2, 12f) (g-s 2, frm) 1998 AW 1-4: (7f, 8f 1-2, 11f) (Fibr 1-4)
Average gelding, effective 8 to 10f, acts on gd - acts on Fibr,

favours left handed tracks. Turf high 62. AW high 62.
**Mrs A Swinbank [6-34] S Smith.*

DOM SHADEED BHB 72f RR 72df 3083[5]

3 b g Shadeed (USA) 7.7f **(72)** - Fair Dominion (Dominion) 8.5f **(63)**
Form - 755
Record 1998 - 1st:0 2nd:0 3rd:0 Ran:3
1998 Turf 0-3: (7f, 8f 2) (g-s, g-f 2)
Leggy, currently above-average gelding. Turf high 72 - 5th of 16 giving 5lb to Quiz Show (11 Jun Newbury 7f g-s RF 1897). Has shaped well in maidens, and handicaps over a mile plus look his mark. **Lord Huntingdon [0-3] David Shirley.*

DOMULLA BHB 63f RR 60df 4886[15]

8 br h Dominion 8.9f **(65)** - Ulla Laing (Mummy's Pet) 7.7f **(60)**
Form - 00000
Record 1998 - 1st:0 2nd:0 3rd:0 Ran:5
Pre1998 - 1st:5 2nd:3 3rd:1 Ran:25
Win Prizemoney £26,157 *Total Prizemoney* £30,844

Wins								
1995	Oct	Newbur	(G-S)	H	6f	88	96	<
1995	Apr	Haydoc	(GD)	H	6f	85	85	
1994	Apr	Leices	(SFT)	H	6f	81	83	
1994	Apr	Bright	(G-S)	H	6f	73	79	

1998 Turf 0-5: (6f 4, 7f) (g-s, gd 2, g-f 2)
Average horse. Turf high 77. Becoming disappointing. Once a useful sprint handicapper, he has been lightly raced in recent seasons and does not look anything like as good as he once was.
**T D McCarthy [0-5] A W Boon (from R Akehurst [5-25] Jly 1997).*

DONA FILIPA BHB 40f RR 41f 5059[14]

5 ch m Precocious 7.2f **(54)**-Quisissanno (Be My Guest (USA))9.3f **(67)**
Form - 0030352302100
Record 1998 - 1st:1 2nd:2 3rd:3 Ran:13
Pre1998 - 1st:1 2nd:0 3rd:2 Ran:26
Win Prizemoney £5,176 *Total Prizemoney* £8,743

Wins								
* 1998	Spt	Yarmou	(G-S)	H	6f	36	41	
* 1997	Aug	Mussel	(G-F)	H	5f	39	47	<

1998 Turf 1-10: (5f 7, 6f 1-3) (sft 2, gd 4, g-f, frm 1-3) 1998 AW 0-3: (5f 2, 6f) (Fibr 3)
Moderate filly, effective 5 to 6f, best at 5f, acts on gd to frm. Turf high 41 - 1st of 20 getting 9lb from Elton Ledger (17 Spt Yarmouth RF 4334). AW high 38 (began Jly). Inconsistent.
**Miss L C Siddall [2-39] A Emmerson.*

DON BOSCO (IRE) RR 64f 5064[8]

2 ch c Grand Lodge (USA) - Suyayeb (USA) (The Minstrel (CAN)) 10f **(72)**
Form - 08
Record 1998 - 1st:0 2nd:0 3rd:0 Ran:2
1998 Turf 0-2: (6f, 7f) (gd, g-f)
Currently average colt. Turf high 64 (began Oct).
**J E Banks [0-2] Mrs Patricia Cunningham.*

DONE AND DUSTED (IRE) BHB 54f57a RR 60f 57a 5080[3]

2 ch f Up and At 'em - Florentink (USA) (The Minstrel (CAN)) 10f **(72)**
Form - 50326843
Record 1998 - 1st:0 2nd:1 3rd:2 Ran:8
Win Prizemoney £0 *Total Prizemoney* £1,178
1998 Turf 0-6: (5f 3, 6f 3) (gd 3, g-f, frm 2) 1998 AW 0-2: (5f, 6f) (Fibr 2)
Average filly, effective 5f, acts on gd. Turf high 66. AW high 54 (began Oct). **J Berry [0-8] Chris & Antonia Deuters.*

DONE WELL (USA) BHB 50f RR 59f 4768[18]

6 b g Storm Bird (CAN) 8.5f **(82)** - Suspicious Toosome (USA) (Secretariat (USA)) 9f **(79)**
Form - 700
Record 1998 - 1st:0 2nd:0 3rd:0 Ran:3
Pre1998 - 1st:1 2nd:3 3rd:1 Ran:11
Win Prizemoney £4,557 *Total Prizemoney* £8,762
Wins 1994 Jly Newmar (GD) 7f 80
1998 Turf 0-3: (9f, 10f, 12f) (sft, gd, frm)
Fair gelding. Turf high 6 (began Aug). Becoming disappointing.
**P Monteith [2-18] Allan Melville (from E A L Dunlop [0-3] Jly 1995).*

DONKEY ENGINE (IRE) RR 110f 2288a[1]

4 b c Fairy King (USA) 7.7f **(75)** - City Ex (Ardross) 10.6f **(68)**
Form - 1
1998 Turf 1-1: (7f 1-1) (gd 1-1)
Currently Group-class colt. (1st run) - 1st of 5 from Alamo Bay (21 Jun Longchamp RF 2288a). He was given a super ride when winning a Group Three at Longchamp in June. A big race win beckoned, but he did not progress as expected.
**A deRoyerDupre in FR [1-1] Marquesa de Moratalla.*

DONNA GRAZIA BHB 51f RR 43f 1109[11]

3 ch f Sharpo 7.5f **(68)** - Little Change (Grundy) 10.3f **(65)**
Form - 800
Record 1998 - 1st:0 2nd:0 3rd:0 Ran:3
1998 Turf 0-2: (6f 2) (sft, frm) 1998 AW 0-1: (6f) (Fibr)
Lengthy, currently moderate filly. Turf high 43.
**M Bell [0-3] Cyril Humphris.*

DONNA'S DANCER (IRE) BHB 32f RR 31f 5060[8]

4 ch g Magical Wonder (USA) 7.2f **(60)** - Ice On Fire (Thatching) 8f **(66)**
Form - 04088
Record 1998 - 1st:0 2nd:0 3rd:0 Ran:5
Pre1998 - 1st:0 2nd:4 3rd:2 Ran:14
Win Prizemoney £0 *Total Prizemoney* £4,524
1998 Turf 0-5: (6f, 8f 2, 9f, 10f) (sft 2, frm 3)
Very moderate gelding, effective 6f, acts on frm, often wears blinkers. Turf high 47 (began Aug).
**Mrs A M Naughton [0-5] Steven Roper (from N Tinkler [0-7] Aug 1997).*

DONNA'S DOUBLE BHB 56f RR 54f 4807[7]

3 ch g Weldnaas (USA) 8.4f **(55)** - Shadha (Shirley Heights) 10.3f **(74)**
Form - 373342481137
Record 1998 - 1st:2 2nd:1 3rd:4 Ran:12
Pre1998 - 1st:0 2nd:0 3rd:0 Ran:4
Win Prizemoney £4,533 *Total Prizemoney* £7,504

Wins								
* 1998	Spt	Hamilt	(SFT)	H	8.3f	49	54	<
* 1998	Spt	Mussel	(GD)	H	7.1f	44	54	<

1998 Turf 2-12: (7f 1-2, 8f 1-4, 9f, 10f, 11f, 12f 3) (g-s 1-2, gd 6, g-f, frm 1-3)
Workmanlike, fair gelding, effective 7 to 12f, best at 7f, acts on g-s to frm, likes right handed tracks, excels at Hamilton. Turf high 54 - 1st of 14 getting 16lb from Technician (14 Spt Musselburgh RF 4256) - also 1st of 16 giving 6lb to Raased (28 Spt Hamilton RF 4536). Consistent.
**D Eddy [2-7] James Adams (from Don Enrico Incisa [0-5] Jun 1998).*

DON PEPE BHB 61f42a RR 61f 42a 4485[11]

7 br g Dowsing (USA) 7f **(61)** - Unique Treasure (Young Generation) 7.7f **(63)**
Form - 0550035314440
Record 1998 - 1st:1 2nd:0 3rd:2 Ran:13
Pre1998 - 1st:8 2nd:5 3rd:5 Ran:50
Win Prizemoney £30,907 *Total Prizemoney* £39,476

Wins								
* 1998	Jly	Yarmou	(G-F)	H	7f	55	58	
1997	Jun	Yarmou	(FRM)	H	6f	60	65	<
1996	Spt	Yarmou	(G-F)	H	7f	62	65	<
1996	Jun	Goodwo	(GD)	H	6f	56	61	
1995	Jun	Ayr	(G-F)	H	7f	67	65	<
1995	Apr	Mussel	(GD)	H	7.1f	64	65	<
1994	Spt	Goodwo	(GD)		7f		61	
1994	Aug	Mussel	(G-F)	H	7.1f	60	61	
1994	Jun	Mussel	(FRM)		7.1f		56	

1998 Turf 1-9: (6f 2, 7f 1-7) (gd 4, g-f 1-2, frm 3) 1998 AW 0-4: (6f, 7f 3) (Equi, Fibr 3)
Average gelding, effective 6 to 7f, best at 7f, acts on gd to frm, best on g-f, has worn blinkers, excels at Catterick and Yarmouth. Turf high 61 - 4th of 10 getting 10lb from Elbarree (20 Aug Yarmouth 7f frm RF 3767) - also 1st of 10 getting 9lb from Drive Assured (27 Jly Yarmouth RF 3153). AW high 48.
**D Nicholls [1-13] Mrs Elaine Aird (from R Boss [8-50] Oct 1997).*

DON QUIXOTE (IRE) RR 53f 4959[14]

2 b c Waajib 8.9f **(67)** - Maimiti (Goldhill) 8.5f **(55)**
Form - 0
Record 1998 - 1st:0 2nd:0 3rd:0 Ran:1
1998 Turf 0-1: (7f) (frm)
Currently fair colt. **L M Cumani [0-1] M Tabor & Mrs John Magnier.*

DON'T ASK RR 68f 4881[7]

2 b g Paris House 5.9f **(64)** - Glenfield Portion (Mummy's Pet) 7.7f **(60)**

Form - 47
Record 1998 - 1st:0 2nd:0 3rd:0 Ran:2
1998 Turf 0-2: (5f 2) (g-s, g-f)
Currently average gelding. Turf high 68 (1st run) (began Spt) - 4th of 14 to Ones Enough (25 Spt Folkestone 5f g-f RF 4471).
**D J G MurraySmith [0-2] Manny Bernstein (Racing) Ltd.*

DONTBETONME RR 56f
4309[10]
2 ch f Kris 10f **(75)** - Reveuse du Soir (Vision (USA)) 9f **(64)**
Form - 00
Record 1998 - 1st:0 2nd:0 3rd:0 Ran:2
1998 Turf 0-2: (7f, 8f) (g-f 2)
Currently fair filly. Turf high 56 (began Spt).
**M P Tregoning [0-2] Sheikh Ahmed Al Maktoum.*

DON'T DROP BOMBS (USA) BHB 30f37a RR 35f 37a
4050[5]
9 ch g Fighting Fit (USA) 7.9f **(70)** - Promised Star (USA) (Star de Naskra (USA)) 9.7f **(65)**
Form - 32332227300450305
Record 1998 - 1st:0 2nd:3 3rd:3 Ran:14
Pre1998 - 1st:8 2nd:12 3rd:14 Ran:83
Win Prizemoney £20,097 *Total Prizemoney* £37,986

Wins								
	1997	*Mar*	*Lingfi*	*(STD)*	*H*	*8f*	*33*	*39*
	1996	Spt	Bright	(FRM)	H	10f	39	43
	1996	Jly	Yarmou	(G-F)	H	10.1f	35	34
	1996	*Feb*	*Lingfi*	*(STD)*	*H*	*8f*	*34*	*40*
	1995	Aug	Bright	(FRM)	H	10f	31	39
	1995	*Jan*	*Lingfi*	*(STD)*	*H*	*12f*	*29*	*37*
	1994	*Jan*	*Lingfi*	*(STD)*	*H*	*12f*	*35*	*39*

1998 Turf 0-4: (8f 2, 10f 2) (frm 4) 1998 AW 0-10: (7f 2, 8f 5, 10f, 12f, 13f) (Equi 5, Fibr 5)
Moderate gelding, effective 8 to 13f, best at 10f, - acts on AW, best on Equi, mostly wears blinkers (effectively), prefers left handed tracks, prefers tight tracks, excels at Lingfield. Turf high 34. AW high 44 - 2nd of 12 getting 4lb from Failed To Hit (3 Feb Lingfield 8f Equi RF 0208). He shows his best form in amateur riders' events on Equitrack when allowed to dominate.
**R McGhin [0-17] Miss J Feilden.*

DON'T WORRY MIKE BHB 36f38a RR 31f 38a
4545[9]
4 ch g Forzando 7.2f **(63)** - Hat Hill (Roan Rocket) 7.8f **(57)**
Form - 766040
Record 1998 - 1st:0 2nd:0 3rd:0 Ran:5
Pre1998 - 1st:0 2nd:4 3rd:1 Ran:19
Win Prizemoney £0 *Total Prizemoney* £3,189
1998 Turf 0-1: (10f) (frm) 1998 AW 0-4: (8f 2, 9f, 11f) (Fibr 4)
Workmanlike, very moderate gelding, effective 6 to 7f, acts on frm - acts on Fibr, has worn blinkers, favours tight tracks. AW high 39.
**K S Bridgwater [0-3] Miss E E Hill (from J L Spearing [0-13] May 1998).*

DOODLE RR 41f
4529[17]
3 b f Green Desert (USA) 7.8f **(78)** - Quillotern (USA) (Arctic Tern (USA)) 8.9f **(69)**
Form - 00
Record 1998 - 1st:0 2nd:0 3rd:0 Ran:2
Pre1998 - 1st:0 2nd:0 3rd:0 Ran:2
1998 Turf 0-2: (6f, 8f) (g-f, frm)
Neat, moderate filly. Turf high 35 (began Spt).
**W J Haggas [0-4] B Haggas.*

DOOMNA (IRE) BHB 95f RR 97f
5050a[7]
3 b f Machiavellian (USA) 9.8f **(83)** - Just a Mirage (Green Desert (USA)) 8.6f **(78)**
Form - 2147
Record 1998 - 1st:1 2nd:1 3rd:0 Ran:4
Pre1998 - 1st:0 2nd:1 3rd:0 Ran:1
Win Prizemoney £6,926 *Total Prizemoney* £11,770
Wins * 1998 Jly Yarmou (G-F) 7f 97+ <
1998 Turf 1-4: (7f 1-4) (g-s, gd, g-f 1-1, frm)
Neat, very useful filly. Turf high 97 - 1st of 3 from Dan Loose (15 Jly Yarmouth RF 2837). A sister to Kahal, she joined Godolphin for '98, getting off the mark in a small Yarmouth event. Was slightly disappointing in her subsequent races, but perhaps faster ground is the answer .
**S bin Suroor [1-4] Godolphin (from E A L Dunlop [0-1] Jly 1997).*

DORADO RR 76f
4220a[4]
3 c
Form - 4
Record 1998 - 1st:0 2nd:0 3rd:0 Ran:1
Win Prizemoney £0 *Total Prizemoney* £825
1998 Turf 0-1: (8f) (sft)
Currently above-average colt. **L M Cumani [0-1].*

DORAID (IRE) BHB 77f RR 82f
4149[2]
3 b c Danehill (USA) 9.1f **(79)** - Quiche (Formidable (USA)) 9.2f **(63)**
Form - 222
Record 1998 - 1st:0 2nd:3 3rd:0 Ran:3
Pre1998 - 1st:0 2nd:0 3rd:1 Ran:1
Win Prizemoney £0 *Total Prizemoney* £3,910
1998 Turf 0-3: (6f, 7f 2) (gd, g-f, frm)
Workmanlike, decent colt. Turf high 82 (began Aug) - 2nd of 8 to Eljjanah (25 Aug Lingfield 6f frm RF 3845). He deserves that elusive victory. **J H M Gosden [0-4] Sheikh Ahmed Al Maktoum.*

DORISSIO (IRE) RR
851[6]
2 b f Efisio 7.7f **(69)** - Floralia (Auction Ring (USA)) 8.6f **(65)**
Form - 6
Record 1998 - 1st:0 2nd:0 3rd:0 Ran:1
1998 Turf 0-1: (5f) (hvy)
Currently very poor filly. **I A Balding [0-1] Miss A V Hill.*

DORMSTON BOYO BHB 22f24a RR 4f 24a
3887[8]
8 b g Sula Bula - March at Dawn (Nishapour (FR)) 9.1f **(61)**
Form - 8
Record 1998 - 1st:0 2nd:0 3rd:0 Ran:1
Pre1998 - 1st:0 2nd:1 3rd:0 Ran:13
Win Prizemoney £0 *Total Prizemoney* £888
1998 Turf 0-1: (17f) (gd)
Very poor gelding, has worn blinkers. Becoming disappointing.
**T Wall [1-22] D B Roberts (from K White [0-12] May 1995).*

DOROTHY ALLEN RR 58f
5004[7]
2 b f Mon Tresor 7.9f **(60)** - Anytime Anywhere (Daring March) 7.1f **(61)**
Form - P37
Record 1998 - 1st:0 2nd:0 3rd:1 Ran:3
Win Prizemoney £0 *Total Prizemoney* £270
1998 Turf 0-3: (5f 2, 6f) (sft, g-s, g-f)
Currently fair filly. Turf high 58 (began Spt).
**M R Channon [0-3] Malcolm Allen.*

DORRINGTON BHB 52f RR 56df
3025[9]
3 b g Puissance 7.1f **(60)** - Prydwen (Hard Fought) 8.8f **(62)**
Form - 680
Record 1998 - 1st:0 2nd:0 3rd:0 Ran:3
1998 Turf 0-3: (7f 2, 8f) (frm 3)
Workmanlike, currently fair gelding. Turf high 56 (began Jly).
**M Johnston [0-3] John Hulme.*

DORTON GRANGE BHB 45f47a RR 48f 47a
3840[9]
3 ch f Absalom 7.1f **(56)** - Stranger to Fear (Never so Bold) 6.3f **(66)**
Form - 03070
Record 1998 - 1st:0 2nd:0 3rd:1 Ran:5
Pre1998 - 1st:0 2nd:0 3rd:0 Ran:5
Win Prizemoney £0 *Total Prizemoney* £413
1998 Turf 0-5: (5f, 6f 4) (gd, g-f, frm 3)
Light-framed, moderate filly. Turf high 48.
**N E Berry [0-5] Alan Bosley (from K C Comerford [0-3] Oct 1997).*

DOT BHB 45f RR 53df
3605[20]
3 b f Reprimand 8.2f **(63)** - Summer Eve (Hotfoot) 10.5f **(59)**
Form - 080
Record 1998 - 1st:0 2nd:0 3rd:0 Ran:3
Pre1998 - 1st:0 2nd:0 3rd:0 Ran:3
1998 Turf 0-3: (8f 3) (frm 3)
Small, fair filly. Turf high 53. **R Hannon [0-6] G H Peter-Hoblyn.*

DOUBLE ACTION BHB 83f RR 95f
4985[19]
4 br g Reprimand 8.2f **(63)** - Final Shot (Dalsaan) 9.8f **(64)**
Form - 53520000000
Record 1998 - 1st:0 2nd:1 3rd:1 Ran:11
Pre1998 - 1st:3 2nd:2 3rd:2 Ran:16

Win Prizemoney £27,190 *Total Prizemoney* £60,977

Wins * 1997 Spt York (SFT) H 6f 90 104 <
* 1997 Jun Ripon (GD) H 6f 86 88
* 1996 May Thirsk (G-F) 5f 71

1998 Turf 0-11: (6f 9, 7f 2) (sft, g-s 3, gd 4, g-f, frm 2)

Scopey, very useful gelding, effective 6f, acts on sft to gd, best on gd, has worn blinkers. Turf high 95 - 5th of 13 giving 2lb to World Premier (12 May York 6f gd RF 1167). Some creditable efforts in '98, but might still be a few pounds too high, although his poor run in the Wokingham can be disregarded as he boiled over at the start, and he was not particularly well drawn in the Stewards' Cup.

**T D Easterby [3-27] C H Stevens.*

DOUBLE APPEAL (IRE) BHB 38f33a RR 38f 33a 1115P

3 b f Waajib 8.9f **(67)** - Leaping Salmon (Salmon Leap (USA)) 11f **(61)**

Form - 7057P

Record 1998 - 1st:0 2nd:0 3rd:0 Ran:5
Pre1998 - 1st:0 2nd:0 3rd:0 Ran:5

1998 Turf 0-1: (10f) (frm) 1998 AW 0-4: (7f 2, 8f, 9f) (Fibr 4)

Very moderate filly, had worn blinkers. AW high 28. Inconsistent. (DEAD)

**Mrs G S Rees [0-5] J Thompson (from Capt J Wilson [0-5] Oct 1997).*

DOUBLE BAILEYS RR 71+f 4484[3]

2 b c Robellino (USA) 9.5f **(68)** - Thimblerigger (Sharpen Up) 8.3f **(67)**

Form - 3

Record 1998 - 1st:0 2nd:0 3rd:1 Ran:1

Win Prizemoney £0 *Total Prizemoney* £512

1998 Turf 0-1: (9f) (frm)

Currently above-average colt.

**M Johnston [0-1] The Double Baileys Partnership.*

DOUBLE BLADE BHB 65f RR 73f 4769[6]

3 b g Kris 10f **(75)** - Sesame (Derrylin) 8.8f **(54)**

Form - 32373056

Record 1998 - 1st:0 2nd:1 3rd:3 Ran:8
Pre1998 - 1st:0 2nd:1 3rd:0 Ran:2

Win Prizemoney £0 *Total Prizemoney* £4,079

1998 Turf 0-8: (9f, 12f 2, 13f, 14f 2, 15f, 16f) (sft, gd 2, g-f, frm 4)

Strong, above-average gelding, effective 9 to 12f, best at 9f, acts on gd to frm, best on frm, has worn blinkers, prefers tight tracks. Turf high 81 (1st run) - 3rd of 10 to Moratorium (17 May Ripon 9f frm RF 1290). Out of a prolific middle-distance winner, he looks to have his own ideas about the game.

**M Johnston [0-10] The 2nd Middleham Partnership.*

DOUBLE BOUNCE BHB 83f RR 82f 5096[15]

8 b g Interrex (CAN) 7.7f **(51)** - Double Gift (Cragador) 6f **(67)**

Form - 050

Record 1998 - 1st:0 2nd:0 3rd:0 Ran:3
Pre1998 - 1st:6 2nd:2 3rd:4 Ran:35

Win Prizemoney £45,874 *Total Prizemoney* £72,646

Wins 1996 Jun Newcas (FRM) H 6f 84 85 <
1995 Oct York (GD) H 6f 77 81
1995 Spt Haydoc (GD) H 6f 70 74
1995 Jly Nottin (G-F) H 6.1f 65 66
1994 Jly Bath (FRM) 5.7f 59

1998 Turf 0-3: (6f 3) (sft, g-s, gd)

Decent gelding, effective 6f, acts on gd to frm, best on gd, has worn blinkers. Turf high 82 (began Spt). He has had injury problems in the past, though he should not yet be written off.

**H Candy [0-3] Mrs P Scott-Dunn (from P J Makin [4-23] Nov 1997).*

DOUBLE BRANDY BHB 76f RR 79f 5079[17]

3 ch c Elmaamul (USA) 8.1f **(70)** - Brand (Shareef Dancer (USA)) 9.9f **(73)**

Form - 551000

Record 1998 - 1st:1 2nd:0 3rd:0 Ran:6
Pre1998 - 1st:0 2nd:1 3rd:0 Ran:3

Win Prizemoney £6,157 *Total Prizemoney* £6,979

Wins * **1998** May Newbur (G-F) H 6f 74 79 <

1998 Turf 1-6: (6f 1-3, 7f 3) (sft 2, gd 3, frm 1-1)

Unfurnished, above-average colt, effective 6f, acts on gd to frm. Turf high 79 - 1st of 13 getting 7lb from Masha-Il (16 May Newbury RF 1261). He got off the mark in a Newbury handicap in May, but was then well beaten in competitive handicaps. He has yet to prove that he stays seven furlongs.

**I A Balding [1-9] Queen Elizabeth.*

DOUBLE CHOICE (IRE) BHB 76f RR 71f 3221[1]

2 b f Doubletour (USA) 12f **(46)** - Virginia Cottage (Lomond (USA)) 8.8f **(65)**

Form - 44611

Record 1998 - 1st:2 2nd:0 3rd:0 Ran:5

Win Prizemoney £10,010 *Total Prizemoney* £10,504

Wins * **1998** Jly Goodwo (G-S) H 5f 71 <
* **1998** Jly Leices (GD) H 5f 70

1998 Turf 2-5: (5f 2-4, 6f) (hvy, gd 1-2, g-f, frm 1-1)

Above-average filly. Turf high 71 - 1st of 6 getting 5lb from Ingenious (30 Jly Goodwood RF 3221) - also 1st of 9 getting 22lb from Bon Ami (22 Jly Leicester RF 3026). Found her form in nurseries, wining twice in July including at Glorious Goodwood.

**R Hannon [2-5] S L Partnership.*

DOUBLE CLASSIC (USA) BHB 102f RR 104+f 2088[1]

3 br c Riverman (USA) 9.7f **(78)** - Adam's Angel (USA) (Halo (USA)) 10.6f **(75)**

Form - 1211

Record 1998 - 1st:3 2nd:1 3rd:0 Ran:4
Pre1998 - 1st:0 2nd:0 3rd:1 Ran:2

Win Prizemoney £40,617 *Total Prizemoney* £45,579

Wins * **1998** Jun Ascot (SFT) H 12f 94 104 <
* **1998** Jun Goodwo (GD) H 12f 86 93
* **1998** Apr Ripon (SFT) 8f 78

1998 Turf 3-4: (8f 1-1, 11f, 12f 2-2) (g-s 2-2, gd 1-2)

Workmanlike, very useful colt, effective 12f, acts on g-s. Turf high 104 - 1st of 17 giving 4lb to Emerald Heights (18 Jun Ascot RF 2088). He won three of his four starts last term, his most important success coming in the King George V Handicap at Royal Ascot. He had been most progressive up to that point, but missed the second half of the campaign. There are other big prizes to be won if he returns safe and sound as a four-year-old.

**Sir Michael Stoute [3-6] Maktoum Al Maktoum.*

DOUBLE DASH (IRE) BHB 55f RR 37f 4674[15]

5 gr g Darshaan 11.9f **(81)** - Safka (USA) (Irish River (FR)) 8.6f **(78)**

Form - 0

Record 1998 - 1st:0 2nd:0 3rd:0 Ran:1
Pre1998 - 1st:0 2nd:0 3rd:0 Ran:6

Win Prizemoney £0 *Total Prizemoney* £263

1998 Turf 0-1: (14f) (g-f)

Moderate gelding, often wears blinkers.

**D Moffatt [1-11] The Sheroot Partnership (from M Johnston [0-5] Jly 1996).*

DOUBLE ECHO (IRE) BHB 35f39a RR 38f 39a 5002[17]

10 br g Glow (USA) 10.2f **(61)** - Piculet (Morston (FR)) 9.4f **(55)**

Form - 0003111320475070

Record 1998 - 1st:3 2nd:1 3rd:2 Ran:13
Pre1998 - 1st:7 2nd:6 3rd:3 Ran:59

Win Prizemoney £35,964 *Total Prizemoney* £52,181

Wins * **1998** *Jan Southw (STD) H 11f 31 44*
* **1998** *Jan Southw (STD) H 12f 25 45*
* **1998** *Jan Southw (STD) H 11f 25 32*
* 1996 Spt Newbur (G-F) H 12f 46 51
* 1994 May Newcas (G-F) H 12.4f 56 60+

1998 Turf 0-3: (10f, 12f 2) (gd, g-f 2) 1998 AW 3-10: (11f 2-3, 12f 1-7) (Equi, Fibr 3-9)

Moderate gelding, effective 11 to 12f, best at 12f, - acts on Fibr, has worn blinkers, favours left handed tracks. Turf high 38. AW high 45 - 1st of 11 getting 24lb from Moonraking (23 Jan Southwell RF 0145) - also 1st of 9 getting 18lb from Dr Edgar (26 Jan Southwell RF 0158). Inconsistent. The old boy experienced something of an Indian Summer on the Southwell Fibresand at the beginning of '98, gaining three fine victories over middle-distances plus other creditable efforts, but has paid for it in the handicap.

**J D Bethell [10-72] Mrs John Lee.*

DOUBLE EDGED BHB 85f85a RR 87f 85a 4966[6]

3 ch c Sabrehill (USA) 8.5f **(64)** - Island Lake (Kalaglow) 9.8f **(67)**

Form - 151306

Record 1998 - 1st:1 2nd:0 3rd:1 Ran:5
Pre1998 - 1st:1 2nd:1 3rd:0 Ran:4

Win Prizemoney £6,054 *Total Prizemoney* £8,554

Wins * **1998** Spt Chepst (G-S) H 10.2f 80 84 <
* 1997 *Nov Southw (STD) 8f 74*

1998 Turf 1-5: (8f, 10f 1-4) (sft, gd 1-2, frm 2)

Workmanlike, useful colt, effective 8 to 10f, best at 10f, acts on sft to frm, likes left handed tracks. Turf high 87 (began Aug) - 3rd of 11 getting 1lb from Vola Via (24 Spt Pontefract 10f frm RF 4467) - also 1st of 13 giving 1lb to Quintus (10 Spt Chepstow RF 4198). Fair form in turf maidens in 1997, though he was not too impressive when long odds-on at Lingfield in November '97. He returned after a nine-month absence in August, and scored on easy ground at Chepstow the following month, before running reasonably on fast ground at Pontefract.

**M Johnston [2-9] The 2nd Middleham Partnership.*

Wins * **1998** Oct Nottin (SFT) H 6.1f 67 68 <
* **1998** Jun Windso (SFT) H 6f 56 58
* **1998** May Nottin (G-F) H 6.1f 50 53

1998 Turf 3-11: (5f, 6f 3-10) (sft 1-2, gd 1-3, g-f 3, frm 1-3)

Average gelding, effective 5 to 6f, best at 6f, acts on sft to g-f, excels at Windsor and Nottingham. Turf high 68 - 1st of 17 getting 8lb from Quiz Show (21 Oct Nottingham RF 4923). Consistent. He took his time getting off the mark, but was successful at Nottingham and Windsor last season.

**K T Ivory [3-15] Mrs P Scott-Dunn (from P R Webber [0-10] Jan 1997).*

Double Classic remained under wraps after his Royal Ascot victory

DOUBLE-E-I-B-A BHB 25f RR 39f 383[6]

4 br g Reprimand 8.2f **(63)** - Doppio (Dublin Taxi) 6.4f **(55)**

Form - 66

Record 1998 - 1st:0 2nd:0 3rd:0 Ran:2
Pre1998 - 1st:0 2nd:0 3rd:0 Ran:5

1998 AW 0-2: (12f, 16f) (Equi, Fibr)

Workmanlike, very moderate gelding, has worn blinkers.

**D J S Cosgrove [0-4] Camelot Racing (from C N Allen [0-3] Oct 1996).*

DOUBLE-J (IRE) BHB 52f RR 51df 4402[14]

4 b g Fayruz 6.6f **(63)**-Farriers Slipper (Prince Tenderfoot(USA)) 9f **(61)**

Form - 0400800

Record 1998 - 1st:0 2nd:0 3rd:0 Ran:7
Pre1998 - 1st:1 2nd:4 3rd:2 Ran:15

Win Prizemoney £3,059 *Total Prizemoney* £12,362

Wins 1996 Jly Beverl (G-F) 5f 83 <

1998 Turf 0-7: (6f, 7f, 8f 5) (sft, g-s, gd, g-f 2, frm 2)

Leggy, fair gelding, effective 6f, acts on g-s, has worn blinkers, likes left handed tracks. Turf high 58.

**M Brittain [0-7] D H Armitage (from K McAuliffe [1-15] Oct 1997).*

DOUBLE MARCH BHB 73f60a RR 68f 60a 4923[1]

5 b g Weldnaas (USA) 8.4f **(55)** - Double Gift (Cragador) 6f **(67)**

Form - 17314324401

Record 1998 - 1st:3 2nd:1 3rd:2 Ran:11
Pre1998 - 1st:0 2nd:1 3rd:1 Ran:14

Win Prizemoney £12,423 *Total Prizemoney* £18,775

DOUBLE MATT (IRE) BHB 49f RR 44f 2474[5]

6 b g Double Schwartz 7f **(60)** - Kasarose (Owen Dudley) 8.3f **(61)**

Form - 0565

Record 1998 - 1st:0 2nd:0 3rd:0 Ran:4
Pre1998 - 1st:1 2nd:0 3rd:3 Ran:16

Win Prizemoney £4,199 *Total Prizemoney* £6,929

Wins 1995 Spt Thirsk (G-F) 6f 78 <

1998 Turf 0-4: (6f 3, 8f) (gd 2, frm, hrd)

Moderate gelding, effective 6f, acts on gd. Turf high 44.

**Mrs P Sly [0-9] Mrs P M Sly (from R Hannon [1-11] May 1996).*

DOUBLE-O BHB 66f85a RR 59f 85a 5142[10]

4 b g Sharpo 7.5f **(68)** - Ktolo (Tolomeo) 5.6f **(60)**

Form - 001811P0

Record 1998 - 1st:2 2nd:0 3rd:0 Ran:5
Pre1998 - 1st:3 2nd:0 3rd:1 Ran:13

Win Prizemoney £20,385 *Total Prizemoney* £20,713

Wins * **1998** *Feb Wolver (STD) H 5f 79 85* <
* **1998** *Feb Wolver (STD) H 6f 74 75*
* 1997 *Dec Wolver (STD) H 6f 69 75*
* 1997 *Mar Southw (STD) H 6f 70 73*
* 1996 *Dec Wolver (STD) 6f 78*

1998 Turf 0-1: (5f) (gd) 1998 AW 2-4: (5f 1-2, 6f 1-2) (Fibr 2-4)

Scopey, useful gelding, effective 5 to 6f, best at 6f, - acts on Fibr, has worn blinkers, prefers left handed tracks, prefers tight tracks. AW high 85 - 1st of 8 from Time To Fly (25 Feb Wolverhampton RF 0360). Inconsistent. A son of decent hurdler Ktolo, he has shown

little on turf but is useful on Fibresand. He won three times at Wolverhampton last winter, including when dropped to the minimum trip and blinkered for the first time, but reportedly lost his action when pulled-up there in March. **W Jarvis [5-18] R K Bids Ltd.*

DOUBLE OSCAR (IRE) BHB 81f93a **RR 86f 93a** 4872[12]

5 ch g Royal Academy (USA) 7.8f **(77)** - Broadway Rosie (Absalom) 7.2f **(58)**

Form - 1223031407561 1300080

Record	**1998 -**	1st:4	2nd:2	3rd:3	Ran:20
	Pre1998 -	1st:6	2nd:5	3rd:7	Ran:44

Win Prizemoney £44,968 *Total Prizemoney* £62,317

Wins									
	*** 1998**	Aug	Ascot	(G-F)	H	5f	73	84+	
	*** 1998**	Jly	Goodwo	(G-S)	H	5f	73	80	
	*** 1998**	*Apr*	*Wolver*	*(STD)*	*H*	*5f*	*84*	*88*	<
	*** 1998**	*Jan*	*Lingfi*	*(STD)*	*C*	*6f*		*75+*	
	* 1997	Aug	Carlis	(FRM)	H	5f	75	80	
	* 1997	Aug	Pontef	(G-F)	H	5f	62	76	
	* 1997	Aug	Catter	(G-F)	H	5f	62	69	
	* 1997	Jly	Folkes	(G-F)	H	6f	48	61+	
	* 1997	Apr	Nottin	(G-F)	C	5.1f		53	
	1995	Jun	Ayr	(G-F)		6f		68	

1998 Turf 2-15: (5f 2-10, 6f 5) (sft, g-s, gd 1-4, g-f 1-6, frm 3) 1998 AW 2-5: (5f 1-3, 6f 1-2) (Equi 1-2, Fibr 1-3)

Useful gelding, effective 5 to 6f, best at 5f, acts on gd to frm - acts on AW, best on g-f, often wears blinkers (extremely effectively), likes left handed tracks, excels at Goodwood and likes Wolverhampton. Turf high 86 - 3rd of 22 giving 3lb to Cadeaux Cher (15 Aug Ripon 6f g-f RF 3661) - also 1st of 22 giving 18lb to High Carry (7 Aug Ascot RF 3425). AW high 88 - 1st of 13 getting 8lb from King of Peru (30 Apr Wolverhampton RF 0940). He was in fine form in '97, winning five times, and landing a gamble or two in the process. Won a minor handicap at Glorious Goodwood this year, but an administrative mix-up prevented him from running in the Stewards' Cup. Gained some compensation at Ascot and was a close third in the Great St Wilfrid at Ripon. He may well find six furlongs on a slow surface right on the edge of his stamina limitations. Likes to come late, so he needs to get the run of the race, but Alex Greaves rides him just right.

**D Nicholls [9-50] Trilby Racing (from M Johnston [1-14] Aug 1996).*

DOUBLE POWER BHB 54f **RR 59f** 3938[15]

3 ch f Superpower 6.6f **(58)** - Double Decree (Sayf El Arab (USA)) 7.1f **(54)**

Form - 012700

Record	**1998 -**	1st:1	2nd:1	3rd:0	Ran:6
	Pre1998 -	1st:0	2nd:0	3rd:1	Ran:4

Win Prizemoney £2,206 *Total Prizemoney* £3,585

Wins									
	*** 1998**	May	Mussel	(G-S)		5f		44	<

1998 Turf 1-6: (5f 1-4, 6f 2) (g-s, gd 1-3, frm 2)

Unfurnished, fair filly, effective 5f, acts on gd to g-f, has worn blinkers. Turf high 59 - 2nd of 10 giving 6lb to Dawn Patrol (15 Jun Musselburgh 5f gd RF 1993). She showed much-improved form when faced with easy ground.

**L R Lloyd-James [1-10] S F Stubbings.*

DOUBLE RUSH (IRE) BHB 40f63a **RR 50f 63a** 4931[19]

6 b g Doulab (USA) 7.4f **(61)** - Stanza Dancer (Stanford) 7.9f **(56)**

Form - 026650423150840

Record	**1998 -**	1st:1	2nd:2	3rd:1	Ran:14
	Pre1998 -	1st:6	2nd:1	3rd:1	Ran:32

Win Prizemoney £16,518 *Total Prizemoney* £20,862

Wins									
	*** 1998**	Jly	Bath	(GD)	S	11.7f		48	
	* 1996	*Nov*	*Lingfi*	*(STD)*	*H*	*10f*	*53*	*61*	<
	* 1996	*Nov*	*Lingfi*	*(STD)*		*10f*		*59+*	
	* 1996	Aug	Bright	(FRM)	H	10f	48	56	
	* 1996	Aug	Bright	(FRM)	H	10f	40	48+	
	* 1995	*Nov*	*Lingfi*	*(STD)*		*10f*		*59*	
	* 1995	Mar	Folkes	(GD)		6.9f		58	

1998 Turf 1-12: (8f, 10f 4, 11f 2, 12f 1-5) (g-s 2, gd 1-3, g-f 3, frm 4) 1998 AW 0-2: (10f 2) (Equi 2)

Average gelding, effective 10f, - acts on Equi, has worn blinkers, likes left handed tracks. Turf high 50. AW high 65 (1st run) - 2nd of 6 giving 16lb to Feel Free (13 May Lingfield 10f Equi RF 1200).

**T G Mills [7-46] Tony Murray.*

DOUBLE SPLENDOUR (IRE) BHB 87f72a **RR 68f 72a** 5096[14]

8 b g Double Schwartz 7f **(60)** - Princess Pamela (Dragonara Palace (USA)) 6.1f **(55)**

Form - 14524000000

Record	**1998 -**	1st:1	2nd:1	3rd:0	Ran:11
	Pre1998 -	1st:7	2nd:6	3rd:3	Ran:32

Win Prizemoney £35,459 *Total Prizemoney* £65,523

Wins									
	*** 1998**	May	Newmar	(GD)	H	6f	95	100	<
	* 1996	Jly	York	(GD)	H	6f	82	87	
	* 1996	Apr	Nottin	(G-F)	H	6.1f	70	83+	
	* 1995	Oct	Newcas	(G-F)	H	6f	66	70	
	* 1995	Oct	Haydoc	(G-S)	H	6f	60	64	
	* 1995	Spt	Yarmou	(GD)	H	6f	51	61+	
	* 1995	Apr	Nottin	(G-F)	H	6.1f	41	46	
	* 1994	*Dec*	*Lingfi*	*(STD)*	*H*	*6f*	*41*	*39*	

1998 Turf 1-11: (6f 1-10, 7f) (sft, gd 1-6, g-f 3, frm)

Average gelding, effective 6f, acts on gd to frm, best on gd. Turf high 101 - 4th of 13 giving 7lb to World Premier (12 May York 6f gd RF 1167) - also 1st of 8 from Kumait (3 May Newmarket RF 0994). Becoming disappointing. He looked ready to roll when winning at Newmarket in May, after a hobdaying operation in the winter, but lost his way in the second half of the campaign. He starts 1999 on a decent mark and, having scored first-time-out in three of the last four seasons, is one to note for an early success.

**P S Felgate [8-43] E Rollinson.*

DOUBLET BHB 68f **RR 71f** 4590[3]

3 ch g Bustino 11f **(64)** - Pas de Deux (Nijinsky (CAN)) 10.3f **(77)**

Form - 563

Record	**1998 -**	1st:0	2nd:0	3rd:1	Ran:3

Win Prizemoney £0 *Total Prizemoney* £590

1998 Turf 0-3: (10f, 12f 2) (gd 2, frm)

Scopey, currently above-average gelding. Turf high 71 - 3rd of 16 giving 8lb to King Priam (1 Oct Newmarket 12f gd RF 4590).

**I A Balding [0-3] The Queen.*

DOUBLE TRIGGER (IRE) BHB 119f **RR 120f** 4206[1]

7 ch h Ela-Mana-Mou 12.7f **(72)** - Solac (FR) (Gay Lussac (ITY)) 16.7f **(109)**

Form - 68211

Record	**1998 -**	1st:2	2nd:1	3rd:0	Ran:5
	Pre1998 -	1st:12	2nd:1	3rd:1	Ran:24

Win Prizemoney £428,349 *Total Prizemoney* £554,997

Wins									
	*** 1998**	Spt	Doncas	(GD)	G3	18f		120	
	*** 1998**	Jly	Goodwo	(G-S)	G2	16f		120	
	* 1997	Jly	Goodwo	(G-F)	G2	16f		120	
	* 1996	Spt	Doncas	(G-F)	G3	18f		122+	<
	* 1996	May	Sandow	(G-S)	G3	16.4f		122	
	* 1996	May	Ascot	(G-F)	G3	16.2f		119	
	* 1995	Spt	Doncas	(GD)	G3	18f		118+	
	* 1995	Jly	Goodwo	(FRM)	G2	16f		121	
	* 1995	Jun	Ascot	(G-F)	G1	20f		119	
	* 1995	May	Sandow	(GD)	G3	16.4f		112+	
	* 1995	May	Ascot	(G-F)	G3	16.2f		109	
	* 1994	Nov	Tesio	(HVY)	G3	14.5f		114	

1998 Turf 2-5: (16f 1-3, 18f 1-1, 20f) (g-s, gd 2-3, g-f)

Very high-class horse, effective 16 to 20f, best at 16f, acts on g-s to frm, best on gd, has worn blinkers, excels at Goodwood and Doncaster. Turf high 120 - 1st of 9 giving 3lb to Canon Can (30 Jly Goodwood RF 3218) - also 1st of 6 from Busy Flight (10 Spt Doncaster RF 4206). Consistent. This hugely popular stayer made a lot of the running on his reappearance at Newmarket, but slightly different tactics were tried at Sandown, unsuccessfully as it turned out. He reverted to his former front-running role in the Ascot Gold Cup and ran a blinder, only finding the progressive Kayf Tara too strong, but had that one behind when running out the winner of an emotional Goodwood Cup. This was his third victory in the race, and he went on to complete a hat trick in the Doncaster Cup. He retired after that race as the winner of 14 races in six seasons' racing, with his principal victory being the 1995 Ascot Gold Cup. Wonderfully game, he now has the chance to pass on his attributes at stud. **M Johnston [14-29] R W Huggins.*

DOUBLE TWO (IRE) BHB 56f **RR 69f** 4577[11]

2 br g Petardia 8.2f **(58)** - Reasonably French (Reasonable (FR))

Form - 48343000

Record	**1998 -**	1st:0	2nd:0	3rd:2	Ran:8

Win Prizemoney £0 *Total Prizemoney* £994

1998 Turf 0-8: (5f 4, 6f 2, 7f 2) (sft, gd 5, g-f, frm)

Average gelding, often wears blinkers. Turf high 69. Becoming dis-

appointing. *T D Easterby [0-8] C H Stevens.*

DOUBLIN' BAY (IRE) BHB 34f **RR 49f** 3888^{10}
3 b f Roi Danzig (USA) 10.5f **(62)** - Nizamiya (Darshaan) 9.9f **(84)**
Form - 000080
Record 1998 - 1st:0 2nd:0 3rd:0 Ran:6
1998 Turf 0-5: (8f, 10f 3, 14f) (g-f 4, frm) 1998 AW 0-1: (16f) (Equi)
Leggy, moderate filly. Turf high 49.
**Dr J D Scargill [0-6] The S P Partnership.*

Record 1998 - 1st:0 2nd:1 3rd:0 Ran:14
Pre1998 - 1st:3 2nd:0 3rd:1 Ran:18
Win Prizemoney £17,640 *Total Prizemoney* £21,086
Wins * 1995 Aug Cheste (G-F) 6.1f 95
* 1995 May York (GD) 6f 92
* 1995 May Haydoc (G-F) 5f 98t? <
1998 Turf 0-11: (6f, 7f 8, 8f 2) (g-s 2, gd 2, g-f 4, frm 3) 1998 AW 0-3: (7f 3) (Equi, Fibr 2)
Average gelding, effective 7f, acts on g-f to frm, has worn blinkers.

Double Trigger - a fairytale ending to a wonderful career

DOUBTFUL STEP BHB 35f **RR 50f** 3121^{5}
3 ch f Fearless Action (USA) 8f **(44)** - Tread Carefully (Sharpo) 7.7f **(59)**
Form - 007685
Record 1998 - 1st:0 2nd:0 3rd:0 Ran:6
1998 Turf 0-6: (7f, 8f 2, 11f 2, 16f) (gd 3, g-f, frm, hrd)
Neat, fair filly, has worn blinkers. Turf high 43.
**T D Easterby [0-6] Mrs Ian Wills.*

DOUGS DREAM (IRE) BHB 37f **RR 33f** 2495^{4}
3 ch f Mac's Imp (USA) 5.6f **(54)** - Lomond Heights (IRE) (Lomond (USA)) 8.8f **(65)**
Form - 64
Record 1998 - 1st:0 2nd:0 3rd:0 Ran:2
Pre1998 - 1st:0 2nd:0 3rd:0 Ran:5
1998 Turf 0-2: (7f, 9f) (frm, hrd)
Workmanlike, very moderate filly, has worn blinkers. Turf high 30.
**Mrs A Swinbank [0-7] Doug Marshall.*

DOVEBRACE BHB 44f47a **RR 61f 47a** 5040^{14}
5 b g Dowsing (USA) 7f **(61)** - Naufrage (Main Reef) 9.6f **(57)**
Form - 566870205000860

Turf high 61 - 5th of 14 giving 15lb to Oriole (9 Aug Redcar 7f frm RF 3488). AW high 41. Inconsistent.
**A Bailey [3-16] Dovebrace Ltd (from T D Barron [0-16] Aug 1998).*

DOVEDON STAR BHB 90f **RR 105f** 4206^{5}
4 b f Unfuwain (USA) 11.4f **(74)** - Whitstar (Whitstead) 11.5f **(63)**
Form - 5342001835
Record 1998 - 1st:1 2nd:1 3rd:2 Ran:9
Pre1998 - 1st:1 2nd:1 3rd:3 Ran:8
Win Prizemoney £25,732 *Total Prizemoney* £35,702
Wins * **1998** Jun Ascot (G-S) 22.2f 93? <
1997 Oct Newmar (G-S) H 14f 75 81
1998 Turf 1-9: (13f, 14f, 16f 2, 18f 2, 20f 2, 22f 1-1) (sft 3, gd 1-6)
Leggy, Pattern-class filly, effective 18f, acts on gd. Turf high 105 - 5th of 6 getting 8lb from Double Trigger (10 Spt Doncaster 18f gd RF 4206). She covered some five and a quarter miles at this year's Royal Ascot, and richly deserved her battling win in the Queen Alexandra Stakes. She ran creditably in the Northumberland Plate, but was out of her depth in the Doncaster Cup and is only a handicapper. **A Kelleway [1-10] Osvaldo Pedroni (from P A Kelleway [1-7] Oct 1997).*

Dovedon Star wins the Queen Alexandra at Royal Ascot

DOVER SOUL BHB 35f33a **RR 43f 33a** 3396[16]
3 ch f Absalom 7.1f **(56)** - Whirling Words (Sparkler) 8.4f **(55)**
Form - 0850005600
Record 1998 - 1st:0 2nd:0 3rd:0 Ran:9
Pre1998 - 1st:0 2nd:0 3rd:3 Ran:5
Win Prizemoney £0 *Total Prizemoney* £1,251
1998 Turf 0-6: (6f, 7f, 8f, 12f 2, 14f) (gd 2, g-f 2, frm 2) 1998 AW 0-3: (7f 2, 8f) (Equi 3)
Moderate filly, effective 5f, acts on frm, has worn blinkers. Turf high 43. AW high 45. Inconsistent.
**P Howling [0-7] Top Hat Racing (from P J Makin [0-7] Feb 1998).*

DOVER STRAITS (USA) RR 101f 550a[5]
7 b or br h Riverman (USA) 9.7f **(78)** - Sahsie (USA)
Form - 5
1998 Turf 0-1: (12f) (g-f)
Very useful horse. He was well beaten by Stowaway in Dubai.
**K P McLaughlin in USA [0-3] (from J H M Gosden [1-7] Spt 1994).*

DOVEY'S DESIRE RR 11f 2122[9]
9 gr m Grey Desire 9.3f **(49)** - Dovey (Welsh Pageant) 10f **(65)**
Form - 0
Record 1998 - 1st:0 2nd:0 3rd:0 Ran:1
1998 Turf 0-1: (9f) (g-f)
Currently poor mare. **L A Dace [0-1] T J Arnold.*

DOWER HOUSE BHB 101f **RR 101f** 2738[17]
3 ch c Groom Dancer (USA) 9.5f **(75)** - Rose Noble (USA) (Vaguely Noble) 10.1f **(72)**
Form - 23130
Record 1998 - 1st:1 2nd:1 3rd:2 Ran:5
Pre1998 - 1st:1 2nd:1 3rd:0 Ran:5
Win Prizemoney £21,505 *Total Prizemoney* £37,833
Wins * **1998** Jun Epsom (GD) H 10.1f 95 97 <
* 1997 Spt Yarmou (FRM) 8f 84+
1998 Turf 1-5: (8f, 10f 1-3, 12f) (gd 1-1, g-f 2, frm 2)
Scopey, very useful colt, effective 10 to 12f, best at 10f, acts on gd to frm. Turf high 101 - 3rd of 4 to Secret Archive (14 May Salisbury 12f frm RF 1214) - also 1st of 11 giving 23lb to Mansa Musa (5 Jun Epsom RF 1750). He has never quite lived up to his trainer's billing, but developed into a useful handicapper in 1998. Unlucky at Doncaster in June, he ran unaccountably badly in the John Smith's Cup the following month and was not seen again.
**W Jarvis [2-10] Lord Howard de Walden.*

DOWNCLOSE DUCHESS BHB 29f45a **RR 28f 45a** 5127[15]
3 ch f King's Signet (USA) 7f **(51)** - Lucky Love (Mummy's Pet) 7.7f **(60)**
Form - 08000
Record 1998 - 1st:0 2nd:0 3rd:0 Ran:5
Pre1998 - 1st:0 2nd:0 3rd:0 Ran:6
Win Prizemoney £0 *Total Prizemoney* £219
1998 Turf 0-5: (7f, 8f 2, 10f 2) (g-s, gd 3, g-f)
Small, little account filly. Turf high 34 (began Aug). Inconsistent.
**P Eccles [0-5] Robert & Cora Till (from M Blanshard [0-6] Spt 1997).*

DOWNLAND (IRE) RR 77f 5063[8]
2 b c Common Grounds 8.1f **(66)** - Boldabsa (Persian Bold) 9.3f **(66)**
Form - 8
Record 1998 - 1st:0 2nd:0 3rd:0 Ran:1
1998 Turf 0-1: (6f) (g-f)
Currently above-average colt. **G Wragg [0-1] Mollers Racing.*

DOWN THE YARD BHB 29f24a **RR 33f 24a** 4141[14]
5 b m Batshoof 9.5f **(66)** - Sequin Lady (Star Appeal) 9.6f **(65)**
Form - 64388750
Record 1998 - 1st:0 2nd:0 3rd:1 Ran:8
Pre1998 - 1st:2 2nd:1 3rd:4 Ran:37
Win Prizemoney £4,377 *Total Prizemoney* £7,302
Wins * 1997 *Jan Southw (STD) H 8f 31 36*
* 1995 Jly Yarmou (G-F) S 6f 56 <
1998 Turf 0-3: (10f 2, 12f) (gd 2, g-f) 1998 AW 0-5: (7f, 8f 4) (Fibr 5)
Very moderate filly, effective 8 to 12f, acts on gd - acts on Fibr, favours tight tracks. Turf high 32. AW high 26.
**M C Chapman [4-68] Geoff Whiting.*

DRAFT OF VINTAGE (IRE) RR 96f 5028a[5]
5 b g Imperial Frontier (USA) 7f **(65)** - Kelly's Vintage 00
Form - 1641870511505
1998 Turf 4-13: (7f, 8f, 9f 2-6, 10f 2-3, 11f 2) (hvy 1-3, sft 2, g-s, gd 3-5, g-f 2)
Very useful gelding, effective 9 to 10f, best at 9f, acts on gd, prefers right handed tracks. Turf high 96 - 5th of 7 getting 2lb from Risk Material (20 Spt Curragh 9f gd RF 4443a) - also 1st of 11 giving 4lb to Darina (29 Aug Curragh RF 4040a). Game, consistent handicapper. Seems to act on any ground
**J E Mulhern in IRE [5-22] J E Mulhern.*

DRAGONADA (USA) BHB 102f **RR 101f** 4598a[2]
4 b f Nureyev (USA) 8.4f **(84)** - Don't Sulk (USA) (Graustark) 10.1f **(70)**
Form - 22
1998 Turf 0-2: (10f 2) (sft, gd)
Scopey, very useful filly, effective 8 to 10f, best at 10f, acts on sft to g-f, best on gd. Turf high 101 (began Aug) - 2nd of 10 getting 6lb from Lord of Men (23 Spt Maisons-laffitte 10f gd RF 4598a). Consistent. She improved as a four-year-old and was only narrowly beaten in a Listed event at Deauville in August. Superbly bred, she will make a classy broodmare.
**P Bary in FR [0-2] Niarchos Family.*

DRAGON BOY BHB 45f **RR 32f** 3376[5]
3 b g Bustino 11f **(64)** - Safe House (Lyphard (USA)) 9.9f **(72)**
Form - 005
Record 1998 - 1st:0 2nd:0 3rd:0 Ran:3
Pre1998 - 1st:0 2nd:0 3rd:0 Ran:4
1998 Turf 0-3: (7f, 8f 2) (gd, g-f, frm)
Neat, very moderate gelding. Turf high 32.
**Ian Williams [0-7] Mrs Nichola Mathias.*

DRAGON'S BACK (IRE) BHB 43f **RR 31f** 1268[26]
5 ch g Digamist (USA) 8.8f **(56)** - Classic Choice (Patch) 11.5f **(51)**
Form - 0
Record 1998 - 1st:0 2nd:0 3rd:0 Ran:1
Pre1998 - 1st:0 2nd:0 3rd:3 Ran:11
Win Prizemoney £0 *Total Prizemoney* £1,855

1998 Turf 0-1: (8f) (frm)
Moderate gelding. Inconsistent.
**D C O'Brien [0-9] Mrs J Scudder (from Mrs J Cecil [0-7] Spt 1996).*

DRAGON TRIUMPH (IRE) RR 104f 4430a[6]

3 b c Alzao (USA) 9.8f **(73)** - Tir-An-Oir (Law Society (USA)) 9.9f **(70)**
Form - 1624156
1998 Turf 2-7: (10f 1-2, 12f 1-4, 14f) (hvy 1-1, sft, gd 3, g-f 1-1, hrd)
Very useful colt, effective 10 to 12f, best at 12f, acts on hvy to hrd, prefers right handed tracks. Turf high 104 - 1st of 14 getting 5lb from Renge (14 Jly Down Royal RF 2992a) - also 1st of 12 from Sunshine Street (5 Apr Curragh RF 0601a). He put up a useful performance when winning the Ulster Harp Derby Handicap, but was out of his league when asked to have a crack at the Irish St Leger. He can win again when dropped in class.
**J T Gorman in IRE [2-11] Timothy Beardson.*

DRAKENSBERG RR 59f 4356[11]

3 b g Bering 9.6f **(80)** - Theme (IRE) (Sadler's Wells (USA)) 10f **(76)**
Form - 0
Record 1998 - 1st:0 2nd:0 3rd:0 Ran:1
1998 Turf 0-1: (8f) (g-f)
Workmanlike, currently fair gelding.
**Lady Herries [0-1] Mrs Berta Lazarus.*

DRAMA KING BHB 36f31a RR 36f 31a 567[9]

6 b g Tragic Role (USA) 9.4f **(63)** - Consistent Queen (Queen's Hussar) 11.6f **(58)**
Form - 5747220
Record 1998 - 1st:0 2nd:2 3rd:0 Ran:6
Pre1998 - 1st:1 2nd:2 3rd:0 Ran:16
Win Prizemoney £2,484 *Total Prizemoney* £5,401
Wins 1996 *Aug Wolver (STD) H 12f 36 35 <*
1998 AW 0-6: (12f, 15f, 16f 4) (Equi, Fibr 5)
Very moderate gelding, effective 15 to 16f, best at 16f, acts on g-f - acts on Fibr, often wears blinkers (extremely effectively). AW high 35 - 2nd of 9 getting 7lb from Brynkir (21 Feb Wolverhampton 16f Fibr RF 0338). Inconsistent.
**B J Llewellyn [1-13] Mrs Vicki Guy (from S R Bowring [1-12] Nov 1996).*

DRAMATIC SCENES RR 39f 5009[6]

2 b f Deploy 11.4f **(67)** - Dramatic Mood (Jalmood (USA)) 10.1f **(52)**
Form - 6
Record 1998 - 1st:0 2nd:0 3rd:0 Ran:1
1998 Turf 0-1: (8f) (sft)
Currently very moderate filly. **J S Moore [0-1] P Henley.*

DRAMATIZE (IRE) BHB 90f RR 93f 4591[14]

2 ch g Great Commotion (USA) 9.2f **(80)** - Silk Cord (Sallust) 8.4f **(63)**
Form - 12061040
Record 1998 - 1st:2 2nd:1 3rd:0 Ran:8
Win Prizemoney £7,237 *Total Prizemoney* £8,379
Wins * 1998 Aug Bright (FRM) 5.3f 93 <
*** 1998** Jun Goodwo (GD) 5f 89
1998 Turf 2-8: (5f 2-6, 6f 2) (g-s, gd 1-4, g-f 2, frm 1-1)
Useful gelding, effective 5 to 6f, best at 5f, acts on gd to frm. Turf high 93 - 1st of 7 giving 3lb to Unicamp (18 Aug Brighton RF 3688) - also 1st of 11 from Sarson (3 Jun Goodwood RF 1698). Gelded before he ever ran, he won a modest maiden at Goodwood on his debut, but was then just beaten over an extra furlong in soft ground. Well beaten in decent company afterwards, he regained winning form in a modest event at Brighton. He is obviously suited by sharp, downhill tracks. Sold for 13,000 gns in the autumn.
**B J Meehan [2-8] N B Attenborough.*

DRAM TIME BHB 58f RR 68f 3381[9]

2 b g Clantime 6.6f **(57)** - Chablisse (Radetzky) 9.8f **(56)**
Form - 4600
Record 1998 - 1st:0 2nd:0 3rd:0 Ran:4
Win Prizemoney £0 *Total Prizemoney* £230
1998 Turf 0-4: (5f 3, 7f) (gd, g-f 3)
Average gelding. Turf high 68.
**T D Easterby [0-4] Mrs Jennifer Pallister.*

DRAWING ROOM (IRE) RR 61f 5071[14]

2 b f Grand Lodge (USA) - Wild Abandon (USA) (Graustark) 10.1f **(70)**
Form - 00
Record 1998 - 1st:0 2nd:0 3rd:0 Ran:2
1998 Turf 0-2: (7f 2) (gd 2)
Currently average filly. Turf high 61 (began Oct).
**R F JohnsonHoughton [0-2] Bob Lanigan.*

DREAM CARRIER (IRE) BHB 34f32a RR 40f 32a 2318[8]

10 b g Doulab (USA) 7.4f **(61)** - Dream Trader (Auction Ring (USA)) 8.6f **(65)**
Form - 08468088
Record 1998 - 1st:0 2nd:0 3rd:0 Ran:7
Pre1998 - 1st:11 2nd:13 3rd:13 Ran:114
Win Prizemoney £37,821 *Total Prizemoney* £59,439
Wins * 1997 *Jun Southw (STD) H 7f 39 45*
1995 *Jan Southw (STD) C 7f 69*
1994 *Oct Wolver (STD) H 7f 63 67*
1994 *Spt Wolver (STD) C 7f 56*
1994 *Jan Southw (STD) C 7f 68*
1998 AW 0-7: (7f 3, 8f 4) (Equi, Fibr 6)
Moderate gelding, effective 6 to 8f, best at 7f, acts on frm - acts on AW, best on Fibr, has worn blinkers, favours left handed tracks, favours tight tracks, and likes Lingfield. AW high 32.
**R E Peacock [1-36] R E Peacock (from J G M O'Shea [0-9] Jly 1995).*

DREAMING RR 81f 4479[8]

2 b f Polar Falcon (USA) 9f **(74)** - Dream Baby (Master Willie) 7f **(70)**
Form - 124778
Record 1998 - 1st:1 2nd:1 3rd:0 Ran:6
Win Prizemoney £3,187 *Total Prizemoney* £4,460
Wins * 1998 *Jun Wolver (STD) 6f 78++ <*
1998 Turf 0-5: (5f, 6f, 7f 3) (gd, g-f 2, frm 2) 1998 AW 1-1: (6f 1-1) (Fibr 1-1)
Decent filly, effective 5 to 7f, acts on g-f to frm - acts on Fibr. Turf high 81 (1st run) - 2nd of 6 getting 3lb from Light Fingered (24 Jun Epsom 7f g-f RF 2237). (1st run) - 1st of 9 getting 5lb from Fiori (17 Jun Wolverhampton RF 2079).
**Sir Mark Prescott [1-6] Cheveley Park Stud.*

DREAM OF NURMI BHB 94f RR 98f 4515[11]

4 ch g Pursuit of Love 9.5f **(69)** - Finlandaise (FR) (Arctic Tern (USA)) 8.9f **(69)**
Form - 725200
Record 1998 - 1st:0 2nd:2 3rd:0 Ran:6
Pre1998 - 1st:1 2nd:4 3rd:1 Ran:8
Win Prizemoney £9,942 *Total Prizemoney* £35,257
Wins 1997 Jly York (GD) H 11.9f 84 88 <
1998 Turf 0-6: (10f, 12f 3, 14f 2) (gd 3, g-f, frm 2)
Scopey, very useful gelding, effective 10 to 14f, acts on gd to frm, has worn blinkers. Turf high 98 - 2nd of 8 getting 7lb from Sheer Danzig (11 Jly York 14f frm RF 2737). Some encouraging efforts last season, especially at Goodwood and York, but went off too fast in the early stages of the Ebor. Makes the running. Sold for 22,000 gns at Tattersalls in October.
**A C Stewart [0-6] Chris Brasher (from D R Loder [1-8] Jly 1997).*

DREAM ON DEYA (IRE) RR 3889[10]

2 ch f Dolphin Street (FR) - Karamana (Habitat) 9.4f **(70)**
Form - 0
Record 1998 - 1st:0 2nd:0 3rd:0 Ran:1
1998 Turf 0-1: (8f) (g-f)
Currently very poor filly - 10th of 10 to Canadian Approval (26 Aug Lingfield 8f g-f RF 3889). **Dr J D Scargill [0-1] P A & D G Sakal.*

DREAM ON ME BHB 55f RR 62f 4934[4]

2 b f Prince Sabo 6.6f **(64)**-Helens Dreamgirl (Caerleon (USA)) 8.6f **(71)**
Form - 3224
Record 1998 - 1st:0 2nd:2 3rd:1 Ran:4
Win Prizemoney £0 *Total Prizemoney* £1,312
1998 Turf 0-4: (5f 2, 7f, 8f) (gd 4)
Average filly. Turf high 62 - 4th of 17 to Medelai (22 Oct Nottingham 8f gd RF 4934). **D Morris [0-4] Mrs James McAllister.*

DREAM POWER (IRE) BHB 89f RR 87f 3206[15]

3 ch c In The Wings 11.2f **(77)** - Gelder Shiel (Grundy) 10.3f **(65)**
Form - 82210
Record 1998 - 1st:1 2nd:2 3rd:0 Ran:5
Win Prizemoney £3,468 *Total Prizemoney* £5,648

Wins * **1998** Jly Newbur (GD) 12f 87 <
1998 Turf 1-5: (10f, 12f 1-3, 14f) (gd 1-3, g-f, frm)
Workmanlike, useful colt. Turf high 87 - 1st of 10 giving 5lb to April Stock (12 Jly Newbury RF 2752).
**M A Jarvis [1-5] Sheikh Ahmed Al Maktoum.*

DREAM PURSUIT (IRE) BHB 63f RR 65f 4968[10]

3 b f Caerleon (USA) 10.9f **(79)** - Heaven Only Knows (High Top) 10.2f **(67)**
Form - 660

Record	**1998** -	1st:0	2nd:0	3rd:0	Ran:3

1998 Turf 0-3: (10f 2, 12f) (sft 2, gd)
Scopey, currently average filly. Turf high 65 (began Spt).
**H R A Cecil [0-3] Lordship Stud.*

DREAMS END BHB 70f RR 55f 4631[27]

10 ch h Rainbow Quest (USA) 11.2f **(81)**-Be Easy (Be Friendly)9.3f **(53)**
Form - 000

Record	**1998** -	1st:0	2nd:0	3rd:0	Ran:3
	Pre1998 -	1st:6	2nd:4	3rd:3	Ran:45

Win Prizemoney £35,829 *Total Prizemoney* £62,825

Wins							
* 1997	Jun	York	(G-S)	H	8.9f	77	81
* 1996	Oct	York	(GD)	H	8.9f	70	75
1994	Apr	Kempto	(G-S)	H	12f	81	88

1998 Turf 0-3: (9f, 10f, 14f) (g-f 2, frm)
Fair horse, likes left handed tracks. Turf high 48 (began Aug). Becoming disappointing. Also a useful hurdler, he had a good season on the level in '97 but was off the track last year until finishing tailed off in the Ebor.
**P Bowen [5-37] T G Price (from J M Bradley [0-5] Nov 1995).*

10 from City Honours (28 Jun Curragh RF 2432a) - also 1st of 13 from Croco Rouge (31 May Chantilly RF 1737a). He improved considerably for the fitting of blinkers, and outbattled Croco Rouge to win the Prix du Jockey-Club. Followed up in fluent style in the Irish Derby, beating the Epsom runner-up City Honours, but in truth it was a very poor renewal off the Irish Classic. He took a midsummer break before returning in the Prix Niel, in which he was a lacklustre third to Sagamix. Although never in contention, he finished a close eighth behind the same horse in the Arc.
**P Bary in FR [3-5] Wertheimer Brothers.*

DR EDGAR BHB 52f60a RR 53f 60a 475[2]

6 b g Most Welcome 8.6f **(66)**-African Dancer (Nijinsky(CAN))10.3f **(77)**
Form - 32222

Record	**1998** -	1st:0	2nd:4	3rd:1	Ran:5
	Pre1998 -	1st:3	2nd:2	3rd:5	Ran:29

Win Prizemoney £13,287 *Total Prizemoney* £21,935

Wins								
1995	Oct	Folkes	(GD)	H	9.7f	64	72	<
1995	Jun	Windso	(GD)	H	10f	58	61	
1994	Jly	Windso	(G-F)		6f		68	

1998 Turf 0-1: (10f) (gd) 1998 AW 0-4: (9f, 11f 2, 12f) (Fibr 4)
Fair gelding, effective 9 to 12f, best at 12f, acts on gd - acts on AW, best on Fibr, has worn blinkers (very effectively), favours left handed tracks, and excels at Southwell and Wolverhampton. (1st run) - 2nd of 17 getting 13lb from No Cliches (26 Mar Doncaster 10f gd RF 0475). AW high 59 - 2nd of 7 getting 17lb from Tough Leader (17 Mar Southwell 12f Fibr RF 0440). Consistent. He has looked a tricky ride, but has shown ability on Fibresand over the past couple of years without managing to get his head in front.
**J L Eyre [0-5] A G Watson (from M Dods [0-22] Apr 1997).*

Dream Well indeed for Cash Asmussen and Pascal Bary

DREAM WELL (FR) RR 124f 4727a[8]

3 b c Sadler's Wells (USA) 11.3f **(87)** - Soul Dream (USA) (Alleged (USA)) 10f **(76)**
Form - 11138
1998 Turf 3-5: (12f 3-5) (hvy, sft 1-2, gd 2-2)
Very high-class colt, mostly wears blinkers. Turf high 124 - 1st of

DRESSING GOWN BHB 83f RR 72f 4382[14]

2 b f Night Shift (USA) 8.1f **(73)** - Kiya (USA) (Dominion) 8.5f **(63)**
Form - 720

Record	**1998** -	1st:0	2nd:1	3rd:0	Ran:3

Win Prizemoney £0 *Total Prizemoney* £1,040
1998 Turf 0-3: (6f 3) (g-f 3)

Currently above-average filly. Turf high 72 (began Aug) - 2nd of 7 getting 5lb from Tissifer (31 Aug Epsom 6f g-f RF 3987).
**Lord Huntingdon [0-3] Lord Carnarvon.*

DR FONG (USA) BHB 127f **RR 128f** 5136a[2]

3 ch c Kris S (USA) 9.3f **(76)**-Spring Flight (USA)(Miswaki (USA))9f **(81)**
Form - 1431122
1998 Turf 3-7: (8f 1-2, 9f 2, 10f 2-3) (sft 1-1, gd 2-5, frm)
Scopey, top-class colt, effective 8 to 9f, best at 8f, acts on gd to frm, best on gd, excels at Ascot. Turf high 128 - 2nd of 7 to Desert Prince (26 Spt Ascot 8f gd RF 4493) - also 1st of 8 from Desert Prince (16 Jun Ascot RF 2012). Landed a workmanlike victory in the Newmarket Stakes in May, but lost his unbeaten record when fourth, having held every chance, in the Dante. A good run at Chantilly followed before he ran out a game winner of the St James's Palace Stakes. He landed a Group Two at Maisons-Laffitte over ten furlongs in soft ground and, after a break, was just unable to peg back old foe Desert Prince in the QE II. Subsequently switched to Neil Drysdale's yard in the States, finishing second in the Oak Tree Derby at Santa Anita, he is a genuine and likeable colt. **N Drysdale in USA [0-1] (from H R A Cecil [5-8] Spt 1998).*

Form - 5

Record	**1998 -**	1st:0	2nd:0	3rd:0	Ran:1
	Pre1998 -	1st:2	2nd:0	3rd:0	Ran:15

Win Prizemoney £5,635 *Total Prizemoney* £5,635

Wins	* 1995	*Nov Southw (STD) H*	*14f*	*28*	*34*	
	* 1995	*Jun Southw (STD) C*	*16f*		*45*	<

1998 AW 0-1: (15f) (Fibr)
Little account gelding, has worn blinkers.
**K McAuliffe [2-14] K W J McAuliffe (from P F I Cole [0-2] Nov 1993).*

DRIVE ASSURED BHB 72f **RR 71f** 4822[27]

4 gr g Mystiko (USA) 7.7f **(59)** - Black Ivor (USA) (Sir Ivor) 10.2f **(70)**
Form - 000522053010

Record	**1998 -**	1st:1	2nd:2	3rd:1	Ran:12
	Pre1998 -	1st:0	2nd:0	3rd:3	Ran:7

Win Prizemoney £2,577 *Total Prizemoney* £7,407

Wins	* **1998**	Oct Bright (GD) H	8f	65	71+	<

1998 Turf 1-10: (7f 4, 8f 1-4, 10f 2) (sft, g-f 1-5, frm 4) 1998 AW 0-2: (8f, 10f) (Equi 2)
Leggy, above-average gelding, effective 7 to 8f, acts on g-f to frm, likes tight tracks. Turf high 71 - 1st of 15 giving 12lb to Junikay (5 Oct Brighton RF 4653). AW high 51. Has joined Kevin Morgan.
**C E Brittain [1-19] Peter Head Racing Ltd.*

Dr Fong (right) repeated the dose at Ascot

DRIFT BHB 56f48a **RR 57?f 48a** 5038[P]

4 b g Slip Anchor 12.7f **(75)** - Norgabie (Northfields (USA)) 9f **(72)**
Form - 03240P

Record	**1998 -**	1st:0	2nd:1	3rd:1	Ran:6
	Pre1998 -	1st:0	2nd:1	3rd:1	Ran:9

Win Prizemoney £0 *Total Prizemoney* £2,891
1998 Turf 0-6: (12f, 13f, 14f 2, 15f, 16f) (sft, g-s, gd, g-f, frm 2)
Leggy, fair gelding, effective 12 to 15f, acts on gd to frm, has worn blinkers. Turf high 60 - 2nd of 9 getting 3lb from Miss Pin Up (29 Aug Nottingham 14f g-f RF 3963). Inconsistent.
**D E Cantillon [0-8] G W Byrne (from Sir Mark Prescott [0-9] Oct 1997).*

DRIMARD (IRE) BHB 25f33a **RR 27f 33a** 175[5]

7 ch g Ela-Mana-Mou 12.7f **(72)** - Babilla (USA)

DR JOHNSON (USA) **RR 117f** 1510a[4]

4 ch c Woodman (USA) 9.7f **(77)** - Russian Ballet (USA)
Form - 4
1998 Turf 0-1: (10f) (gd)
High-class colt, effective 12f, acts on gd. Runner-up in the '97 Irish Derby, he had the Arc as his reported target, but he broke down at the Curragh in the Tattersalls Gold Cup and has been retired to stud. **C O'Brien in IRE [4-9] Dr M V O'Brien.*

DR MARTENS (IRE) BHB 77f **RR 84f** 3640[14]

4 b g Mtoto 11.5f **(71)** - Suyayeb (USA) (The Minstrel (CAN)) 10f **(72)**

Form - 70
Record 1998 - 1st:0 2nd:0 3rd:0 Ran:2
Pre1998 - 1st:1 2nd:1 3rd:0 Ran:4
Win Prizemoney £3,642 *Total Prizemoney* £4,832
Wins 1997 Aug Windso (G-F) 8.3f 84 <
1998 Turf 0-1: (8f) (gd) 1998 AW 0-1: (8f) (Fibr)
Scopey, decent gelding, effective 8f, acts on hrd.
**J A Glover [0-2] R Griggs Group Ltd (from L M Cumani [1-5] Apr 1998).*

DROWNED IN BUBBLY RR **40f** 1245^{9}
2 b c Tragic Role (USA) 9.4f **(63)** - Champenoise (Forzando) 7.6f **(59)**
Form - 00
Record 1998 - 1st:0 2nd:0 3rd:0 Ran:2
1998 Turf 0-2: (5f, 6f) (g-s, frm)
Currently moderate colt. Turf high 40.
**J L Eyre [0-2] Lovely Bubbly Racing.*

DRURIDGE BAY (IRE) BHB 56f51a **RR 71df 51a** 5124^{8}
2 b g Turtle Island (IRE) - Lady of Shalott (Kings Lake (USA)) 10.8f **(67)**
Form - 45048608828
Record 1998 - 1st:0 2nd:1 3rd:0 Ran:11
Win Prizemoney £0 *Total Prizemoney* £1,106
1998 Turf 0-11: (5f 3, 6f 2, 7f 3, 8f 3) (g-s, gd 2, g-f 3, frm 5)
Above-average gelding, effective 7 to 8f, acts on gd to frm. Turf high 71. Inconsistent. **M R Channon [0-11] M G St Quinton.*

DR WOODSTOCK BHB 38f **RR 39f** 4919^{8}
4 br g Rock City 8.8f **(62)** - Go Tally-Ho (Gorytus (USA)) 7.8f **(60)**
Form - 7434550258
Record 1998 - 1st:0 2nd:1 3rd:1 Ran:10
Pre1998 - 1st:0 2nd:1 3rd:1 Ran:11
Win Prizemoney £0 *Total Prizemoney* £2,334
1998 Turf 0-10: (7f 2, 8f 5, 10f 2, 11f) (g-s, gd 2, g-f 2, frm 5)
Leggy, very moderate gelding, effective 8f, acts on gd to g-f. Turf high 41 - 4th of 14 getting 7lb from Nkapen Rocks (30 May Musselburgh 8f gd RF 1607). Consistent.
**W Storey [0-14] D O Cremin (from M Meade [0-11] Spt 1997).*

DRYAD BHB 51f65a **RR 45f 65a** 3305^{13}
3 ch c Risk Me (FR) 8f **(53)** - Lizzy Cantle (Homing) 7.8f **(59)**
Form - 46430820520
Record 1998 - 1st:0 2nd:2 3rd:1 Ran:10
Pre1998 - 1st:0 2nd:0 3rd:0 Ran:1
Win Prizemoney £0 *Total Prizemoney* £2,785
1998 Turf 0-4: (6f 4) (gd 3, frm) 1998 AW 0-6: (6f 4, 7f 2) (Fibr 6)
Workmanlike, average colt, effective 6 to 7f, - acts on Fibr, likes left handed tracks, likes tight tracks. Turf high 45. AW high 66 - 3rd of 7 to Polar Mist (28 Jan Wolverhampton 6f Fibr RF 0171). Inconsistent. **N P Littmoden [0-11] Brian Cantle.*

DRY LIGHTNING BHB 55f46a **RR 63f 46a** 5070^{7}
3 b f Shareef Dancer (USA) 10.1f **(67)**-Valkyrie (Bold Lad(IRE))8.4f **(68)**
Form - 72054143567
Record 1998 - 1st:1 2nd:1 3rd:1 Ran:11
Pre1998 - 1st:0 2nd:0 3rd:0 Ran:2
Win Prizemoney £3,882 *Total Prizemoney* £5,650
Wins * **1998** Jun Newmar(GD) C 10f 63 <
1998 Turf 1-10: (5f, 7f, 8f, 9f, 10f 1-3, 11f, 12f 2) (g-s 4, g-f 1-4, frm 2)
1998 AW 0-1: (12f) (Fibr)
Neat, average filly, effective 7 to 12f, best at 10f, acts on g-s to frm, best on g-f, likes tight tracks. Turf high 63 - 3rd of 6 getting 25lb from Rakeeb (6 Aug Haydock 12f g-f RF 3411) - also 1st of 13 getting 7lb from King Priam (26 Jun Newmarket RF 2312).
**M Bell [1-13] A M Warrender.*

DUAL STAR (IRE) RR **93f** $5027a^{5}$
3 b c Warning 8.1f **(77)** - Sizes Vary (Be My Guest (USA)) 9.3f **(67)**
Form - 21325
1998 Turf 1-5: (8f 1-3, 9f 2) (hvy, sft, g-s, gd 1-2)
Useful colt, has worn blinkers. Turf high 97 - 1st of 5 giving 5lb to Star Quality (29 Jly Galway RF 3345a).
**D K Weld in IRE [1-5] Moyglare Stud Farm.*

DUBAI MILLENNIUM RR **89++f** 5039^{1}
2 b c Seeking the Gold (USA) 7.4f **(80)** - Colorado Dancer (Shareef Dancer (USA)) 9.9f **(73)**
Form - 1
Record 1998 - 1st:1 2nd:0 3rd:0 Ran:1
Win Prizemoney £3,960 *Total Prizemoney* £3,960
Wins * **1998** Oct Yarmou (SFT) 8f 89++ <
1998 Turf 1-1: (8f 1-1) (g-s 1-1)
Currently useful colt. (1st run) - 1st of 18 from Tabareeh (28 Oct Yarmouth RF 5039). Impressed all onlookers with a fluent debut win at the back-end. Likely to stay middle-distances, he looks a Derby prospect even at this early stage.
**D R Loder [1-1] Sheikh Mohammed.*

DUBAI NURSE BHB 50f **RR 55f** 5097^{2}
4 ch f Handsome Sailor 6.6f **(53)** - Lady Eccentric (IRE) (Magical Wonder (USA))
Form - 00020620720002
Record 1998 - 1st:0 2nd:4 3rd:0 Ran:14
Win Prizemoney £0 *Total Prizemoney* £3,126
1998 Turf 0-12: (5f 10, 6f 2) (g-s 3, gd 5, g-f 3, frm) 1998 AW 0-2: (6f, 7f) (Fibr 2)
Fair filly, effective 5f, acts on g-s to gd. Turf high 55 - 2nd of 11 getting 9lb from Bowlers Boy (2 Nov Redcar 5f gd RF 5097). AW high 19. **A R Dicken [0-16] John Smith.*

DUBELLE BHB 20f **RR 37f** 3592^{9}
8 b m Dubassoff (USA) - Flopsy Mopsy (Full of Hope) 8.5f **(64)**
Form - 000
Record 1998 - 1st:0 2nd:0 3rd:0 Ran:3
Pre1998 - 1st:0 2nd:0 3rd:0 Ran:1
1998 Turf 0-3: (8f, 12f, 14f) (gd, g-f 2)
Very moderate mare. Turf high 37 (began Jly).
**J S King [4-28] W J Lee.*

DUBLIVIA BHB 56f **RR 41f** 1539^{11}
3 b f Midyan (USA) 9.9f **(64)** - Port Isaac (USA) (Seattle Song (USA)) 9f **(77)**
Form - 00
Record 1998 - 1st:0 2nd:0 3rd:0 Ran:2
Pre1998 - 1st:0 2nd:0 3rd:0 Ran:3
1998 Turf 0-2: (7f, 8f) (gd, frm)
Scopey, moderate filly. Turf high 18.
**C A Dwyer [0-5] Mrs Suzanne Costello-Haloute.*

DUCHESS OF FERRARA (IRE) BHB 56f **RR 51f** 4613^{18}
2 b f Fairy King (USA) 7.7f **(75)** - Tryarra (IRE) (Persian Heights)
Form - 7070
Record 1998 - 1st:0 2nd:0 3rd:0 Ran:4
1998 Turf 0-4: (5f 2, 6f, 7f) (g-s, gd 2, frm)
Fair filly. Turf high 51 (began Aug).
**A J McNae [0-2] The Iona Stud (from Miss Gay Kelleway [0-2] Aug 1998).*

DUCK ROW (USA) BHB 112f **RR 114df** 4736^{3}
3 ch c Diesis 9f **(80)** - Sunny Moment (USA) (Roberto (USA)) 10f **(76)**
Form - 63373
Record 1998 - 1st:0 2nd:0 3rd:3 Ran:5
Pre1998 - 1st:1 2nd:0 3rd:0 Ran:2
Win Prizemoney £9,416 *Total Prizemoney* £38,436
Wins * 1997 Spt Newbur (SFT) 8f 100 <
1998 Turf 0-5: (7f, 8f 3, 10f) (g-s, gd 3, g-f)
Scopey, Group-class colt, effective 8f, acts on gd. Turf high 114. He became very frustrating, losing a race he should have doddled at Ascot in October. However, his stable did not have the best of seasons and he is certainly better than recent evidence suggests.
**J A R Toller [1-7] Duke of Devonshire.*

DUDEEN (IRE) RR **48f** 1596^{6}
3 br f Anshan 8.2f **(63)** - Pipers Pool (IRE) (Mtoto)
Form - 06
Record 1998 - 1st:0 2nd:0 3rd:0 Ran:2
Pre1998 - 1st:0 2nd:0 3rd:0 Ran:2
1998 Turf 0-2: (10f 2) (gd, g-f)
Moderate filly. Turf high 40.
**T P McGovern [0-2] N Boyle (from D K Weld in IRE [0-2] Aug 1997).*

DUDLEY ALLEN BHB 45f **RR 42f** 4488^{7}
3 ch g Superlative 8.8f **(57)** - Smooth Flight (Sandhurst Prince) 7.9f **(63)**
Form - 7000587

Record 1998 - 1st:0 2nd:0 3rd:0 Ran:7
Pre1998 - 1st:0 2nd:0 3rd:0 Ran:2
1998 Turf 0-7: (7f 3, 8f, 9f, 10f, 11f) (gd, frm 6)
Scopey, moderate gelding. Turf high 42. Inconsistent.
**T T Clement [0-9] Miss L Davies.*

DUEL ISLAND BHB 63f RR 66f 4125^{12}
3 b g Jupiter Island 10.4f **(57)** - Duellist (Town Crier) 10.2f **(55)**
Form - 24470
Record 1998 - 1st:0 2nd:1 3rd:0 Ran:5
Win Prizemoney £0 *Total Prizemoney* £1,353
1998 Turf 0-5: (10f 3, 12f 2) (g-f 2, frm 3)
Light-framed, average gelding. Turf high 66 (1st run) (began Jly) - 2nd of 11 to Zalal (6 Jly Bath 10f g-f RF 2557).
**J L Spearing [0-5] C J Hitchings.*

DUELLING GIRL (USA) RR 78+f 2766^{5}
2 b f Dayjur (USA) 6.8f **(79)** - Carduel (USA) (Buckpasser) 10.8f **(80)**
Form - 5
Record 1998 - 1st:0 2nd:0 3rd:0 Ran:1
1998 Turf 0-1: (6f) (frm)
Currently above-average filly. (1st run) - 5th of 20 to Alegria (13 Jly Windsor 6f frm RF 2766).
**Sir Michael Stoute [0-1] Maktoum Al Maktoum.*

DUELLO BHB 56f70a RR 59f 70a 4887^{6}
7 b g Sure Blade (USA) 10.6f **(66)** - Royal Loft (Homing) 7.8f **(59)**
Form - 07048435202166
Record 1998 - 1st:1 2nd:2 3rd:1 Ran:14
Pre1998 - 1st:3 2nd:9 3rd:7 Ran:62
Win Prizemoney £20,204 *Total Prizemoney* £41,735
Wins * **1998** Spt Nottin (G-F) H 14.1f 56 59
* 1996 Spt Newbur (G-F) H 7.3f 64 66 <
* 1996 May Newbur (SFT) H 7.3f 60 62
* 1995 Spt Epsom (G-S) H 8.5f 55 62
1998 Turf 1-14: (8f 3, 9f, 10f 3, 12f 5, 14f 1-2) (g-s, gd 1-7, g-f 2, frm 4)
Average gelding, effective 7 to 8f, best at 8f, acts on g-s to frm, has worn blinkers, likes left handed tracks. Turf high 59.
**M Blanshard [4-80] C McKenna.*

DUE SOUTH BHB 96f RR 101f 5151^{20}
3 b f Darshaan 11.9f **(81)** - Island Wedding (USA) (Blushing Groom (FR)) 10.3f **(76)**
Form - 3630
Record 1998 - 1st:0 2nd:0 3rd:2 Ran:4
Pre1998 - 1st:1 2nd:0 3rd:2 Ran:5
Win Prizemoney £3,912 *Total Prizemoney* £15,941
Wins * 1997 Aug Beverl (G-S) 7.5f 78 <
1998 Turf 0-4: (11f, 12f 3) (g-s, gd, g-f, frm)
Neat, very useful filly, effective 8 to 12f, best at 8f, acts on gd to frm, likes right handed tracks. Turf high 101. A smart two-year-old, she was lightly raced in 1998 and only showed her true form when finishing third in a handicap at Newmarket after a layoff. She was well beaten in the November Handicap and, although she is not very big, she may progress from three to four.
**E A L Dunlop [1-9] Maktoum Al Maktoum.*

DUGGAN BHB 20f22a RR 22a 1605^{11}
11 b g Dunbeath (USA) 9.9f **(53)** - Silka (ITY) (Lypheor) 12f **(71)**
Form - 0
Record 1998 - 1st:0 2nd:0 3rd:0 Ran:1
Pre1998 - 1st:9 2nd:2 3rd:9 Ran:61
Win Prizemoney £25,376 *Total Prizemoney* £31,020
Wins * 1995 Jly Mussel (G-F) H 12.1f 30 34
* 1995 Jun Bright (FRM) SH 11.9f 25 22
1998 Turf 0-1: (16f) (gd)
Very moderate gelding, has worn blinkers.
**P D Evans [3-32] P D Evans (from M Johnston [0-3] Nov 1994).*

DUKHAN (USA) BHB 68a RR 49f 5118^{16}
4 b c Silver Hawk (USA) 11.2f **(85)** - Azayim (Be My Guest (USA)) 9.3f **(67)**
Form - 66138375000
Record 1998 - 1st:1 2nd:0 3rd:2 Ran:11
Pre1998 - 1st:0 2nd:0 3rd:0 Ran:3
Win Prizemoney £2,085 *Total Prizemoney* £3,972
Wins * **1998** *Feb Southw (STD) 12f 65* <
1998 Turf 0-7: (11f, 12f 5, 16f) (sft, gd 2, g-f 2, frm 2) 1998 AW 1-4: (8f, 11f, 12f 1-2) (Fibr 1-4)
Leggy, average colt, effective 8 to 12f, best at 12f, acts on gd to hrd - acts on Fibr, likes left handed tracks. Turf high 74 - 3rd of 13 getting 22lb from Largesse (12 May York 12f gd RF 1164). AW high 67 - 3rd of 7 getting 9lb from Tough Leader (17 Mar Southwell 12f Fibr RF 0440). Becoming disappointing. Showed his first real sign of ability when winning a limited stakes on the Southwell Fibresand in February, despite hanging badly in the closing stages, and has shown some ability on turf since.
**E J Alston [1-11] Ms Jan Fletcher (from R W Armstrong [0-3] Spt 1997).*

DULAS BAY BHB 38f46a RR 50f 46a 4656^{12}
4 b g Selkirk (USA) 7.9f **(76)** - Ivory Gull (USA) (Storm Bird (CAN)) 10.3f **(74)**
Form - 2740
Record 1998 - 1st:0 2nd:1 3rd:0 Ran:4
Pre1998 - 1st:0 2nd:1 3rd:1 Ran:11
Win Prizemoney £0 *Total Prizemoney* £2,112
1998 Turf 0-2: (12f, 16f) (gd 2) 1998 AW 0-2: (14f, 16f) (Fibr 2)
Rangy, fair gelding, effective 10 to 16f, best at 14f, acts on g-f to frm - acts on Fibr, prefers left handed tracks, prefers tight tracks. Turf high 38. AW high 49 (1st run) - 2nd of 14 giving 1lb to Carol Again (11 Mar Southwell 14f Fibr RF 0422). He has looked moderate on the Flat, but has run some fair races over staying trips.
**M W Easterby [1-20] Bodfari Stud Ltd.*

DULFORD RR 60f 2717^{4}
2 b c Never so Bold 7.1f **(62)** - Cabra (Red Sunset) 8.2f **(63)**
Form - 34
Record 1998 - 1st:0 2nd:0 3rd:1 Ran:2
Win Prizemoney £0 *Total Prizemoney* £455
1998 Turf 0-2: (6f 2) (gd, frm)
Currently average colt. Turf high 60. **B R Millman [0-2] B R Millman.*

DULFORD LAD RR 109f $1912a^{2}$
7 b h In Fijar (USA) 7.4f **(63)** - Highsplasher (USA) (Bucksplasher (USA)) 10.3f **(75)**
Form - 2
1998 Turf 0-1: (10f) (sft)
Pattern-class horse. (1st run) - 2nd of 13 to Galtee (2 Jun Taby 10f sft RF 1912a). Inconsistent. Formerly trained in Britain, he is now one of the top horses in Scandinavia.
**J Fretheim in NOR [0-5] (from B R Millman [1-6] Oct 1993).*

DUNCOMBE HALL BHB 35f35a RR 34f 35a 3768^{3}
5 b g Salse (USA) 10.9f **(71)** - Springs Welcome (Blakeney) 10.5f **(64)**
Form - 65303
Record 1998 - 1st:0 2nd:0 3rd:2 Ran:5
Pre1998 - 1st:1 2nd:1 3rd:5 Ran:20
Win Prizemoney £2,277 *Total Prizemoney* £5,571
Wins * 1997 Spt Folkes (GD) H 16.4f 35 43 <
1998 Turf 0-4: (8f, 12f 2, 14f) (g-s, gd, frm 2) 1998 AW 0-1: (16f) (Equi)
Moderate gelding, effective 12 to 16f, best at 16f, acts on g-f to frm, best on g-f, favours tight tracks. Turf high 37.
**C A Cyzer [1-25] R M Cyzer.*

DUNE HILL RR 44f 1469^{11}
3 b f Desert Dirham (USA) - Plough Hill (North Briton)
Form - 70
Record 1998 - 1st:0 2nd:0 3rd:0 Ran:2
1998 Turf 0-2: (8f 2) (g-f, frm)
Workmanlike, currently moderate filly. Turf high 44.
**S C Williams [0-2] J W Orbell.*

DUNSTON DURGAM (IRE) BHB 27f29a RR 5f 29a 2148^{16}
4 b g Durgam (USA) 12.3f **(53)** - Blazing Sunset (Blazing Saddles (AUS)) 6.7f **(46)**
Form - 36F5880000
Record 1998 - 1st:0 2nd:0 3rd:1 Ran:10
Win Prizemoney £0 *Total Prizemoney* £285
1998 Turf 0-3: (8f, 11f 2) (frm 3) 1998 AW 0-7: (8f, 11f, 12f 3, 14f, 16f) (Fibr 7)
Little account gelding, effective 11f, - acts on Fibr, favours left handed tracks, favours tight tracks. Turf high 5. AW high 43 (1st run) - 3rd of 10 giving 2lb to Cruz Santa (5 Jan Southwell 11f Fibr

RF 0024). Inconsistent. **N P Littmoden [0-10] O A Gunter.*

DURABLE GEORGE BHB 32f50a **RR 24f 50a** 3448^{15}

4 ch g Durandal 6f **(35)** - Sun Follower (Relkino) 8.9f **(65)**
Form - 38851501080
Record 1998 - 1st:2 2nd:0 3rd:0 Ran:7
Pre1998 - 1st:0 2nd:0 3rd:1 Ran:12
Win Prizemoney £5,869 *Total Prizemoney* £6,183
Wins * **1998** *Mar Lingfi (STD) H 6f 43 49* <
* **1998** *Jan Lingfi (STD) H 6f 39 43*
1998 Turf 0-3: (6f 2, 7f) (gd, g-f, frm)1998 AW 2-4: (6f 2-3, 7f) (Equi 2-4)
Neat, moderate gelding, effective 6f, - acted on Equi, liked left handed tracks, liked tight tracks. Turf high 24. AW high 49 - 1st of 8 getting 28lb from Mystical (30 Mar Lingfield RF 0510) - also 1st of 8 getting 16lb from Songsheet (3 Jan Lingfield RF 0018). (DEAD)
**J J Bridger [2-21] Mrs J M Stamp.*

DURAID (IRE) BHB 67f **RR 73f** 3852^{10}

6 ch g Irish River (FR) 9f **(77)** - Fateful Princess (USA) (Vaguely Noble) 10.1f **(72)**
Form - 084650500
Record 1998 - 1st:0 2nd:0 3rd:0 Ran:9
Pre1998 - 1st:2 2nd:1 3rd:0 Ran:14
Win Prizemoney £11,251 *Total Prizemoney* £15,195
Wins * 1997 Spt Haydoc (GD) H 8.1f 76 82 <
* 1997 Jun Newcas (GD) H 8f 64 73
1998 Turf 0-9: (7f, 8f 8) (g-s, gd 3, g-f, frm 4)
Above-average gelding, effective 8 to 9f, best at 8f, acts on g-s to frm, best on g-f, has worn blinkers, prefers right handed tracks, likes tight tracks, excels at Beverley, likes Ripon and Newcastle. Turf high 77 - 4th of 8 giving 10lb to Sick As A Parrot (19 May Beverley 8f frm RF 1319). Consistent. **Denys Smith [6-29] A Suddes.*

DURANO BHB 53f **RR 50f** 1994^{9}

7 b g Dunbeath (USA) 9.9f **(53)** - Norapa (Ahonoora) 8.1f **(73)**
Form - 50
Record 1998 - 1st:0 2nd:0 3rd:0 Ran:2
Pre1998 - 1st:1 2nd:1 3rd:4 Ran:11
Win Prizemoney £3,814 *Total Prizemoney* £7,451
Wins 1995 Jly Redcar (FRM) H 10f 62 67 <
1998 Turf 0-2: (12f, 14f) (gd 2)
Average gelding, has worn blinkers. Turf high 50. Inconsistent.
**T D Easterby [2-22] C H Stevens (from M H Easterby [1-11] Aug 1995).*

DURGAMS DELIGHT (IRE) BHB 40f46a **RR 43f 46a** 2922^{7}

3 b f Durgam (USA) 12.3f **(53)** - Miromaid (Simply Great (FR)) 8.2f **(65)**
Form - 04532457
Record 1998 - 1st:0 2nd:1 3rd:1 Ran:8
Pre1998 - 1st:0 2nd:0 3rd:0 Ran:5
Win Prizemoney £0 *Total Prizemoney* £1,213
1998 Turf 0-5: (10f, 11f, 12f, 14f 2) (gd 2, g-f 2, frm) 1998 AW 0-3: (8f, 11f 2) (Fibr 3)
Leggy, moderate filly, effective 14f, acts on g-f, has worn blinkers, likes left handed tracks, likes tight tracks. Turf high 49 - 2nd of 16 giving 8lb to Musalse (26 May Redcar 14f g-f RF 1478). AW high 42. Consistent. **B W Murray [0-13] The First Thursday Club.*

DURGAMS FIRST (IRE) BHB 46f40a **RR 47f 40a** 2403^{2}

6 ch g Durgam (USA) 12.3f **(53)** -Miromaid (Simply Great(FR)) 8.2f **(65)**
Form - 55272
Record 1998 - 1st:0 2nd:2 3rd:0 Ran:5
Pre1998 - 1st:8 2nd:10 3rd:6 Ran:39
Win Prizemoney £21,355 *Total Prizemoney* £33,349
Wins * 1997 Aug Carlis (FRM) C 12f 52
* 1997 May Carlis (FRM) H 14.1f 42 47
* 1995 Spt Catter (GD) S 13.8f 45
* 1995 Jly Haydoc (G-F) C 11.9f 66
* 1995 Jun Carlis (GD) C 12f 62
* 1995 *Feb Southw (STD) C 8f 62*
* 1995 *Jan Southw (STD) S 8f 69* <
* 1994 Aug Catter (GD) S 7f 63
1998 Turf 0-3: (11f, 12f 2) (sft, gd 2) 1998 AW 0-2: (11f 2) (Fibr 2)
Moderate gelding, effective 12f, acts on g-f to frm, best on g-f, likes right handed tracks, excels at Carlisle. Turf high 47. AW high 46. Consistent. **Mrs M Reveley [8-44] The Mary Reveley Racing Club.*

DURHAM BHB 65f60a **RR 68f 60a** 4476^{3}

7 ch g Caerleon (USA) 10.9f **(79)** - Sanctuary (Welsh Pageant) 10f **(65)**
Form - 6536213043
Record 1998 - 1st:1 2nd:1 3rd:3 Ran:8
Pre1998 - 1st:5 2nd:8 3rd:5 Ran:38
Win Prizemoney £22,805 *Total Prizemoney* £36,081
Wins * **1998** Jly Sandow (G-F) H 14f 60 64
* 1997 Aug Yarmou (G-F) H 14.1f 59 64
1996 Spt Ayr (G-F) H 13.1f 60 68 <
1996 Spt Kempto (GD) H 14.4f 54 61
1996 Aug Lingfi (G-F) S 14f 55
1996 Jun Nottin (G-F) H 14.1f 48 56
1998 Turf 1-8: (11f, 12f, 14f 1-6) (gd, g-f 2, frm 1-5)
Average gelding, effective 12 to 14f, best at 14f, acts on g-f to frm, best on g-f, mostly wears blinkers (very effectively), prefers right handed tracks, prefers tight tracks, excels at Salisbury and Sandown. Turf high 68 - 3rd of 8 giving 5lb to Happy Go Lucky (25 Spt Folkestone 12f g-f RF 4476) - also 1st of 13 giving 5lb to Padauk (22 Jly Sandown RF 3034). Something of a character, he has been kept very busy of late but is a fair sort in modest staying handicaps. He got off the mark for the season under a typical Fallon ride at Sandown in July, but is not one totally to rely on.
**G L Moore [2-22] Matthew Thole (from H S Howe [2-4] Oct 1996).*

DURHAM DANDY **RR 63f** 3137^{11}

2 b c Inchinor 8.9f **(64)**-Disco Girl (FR) (Green Dancer (USA)) 10.3f **(74)**
Form - 6000
Record 1998 - 1st:0 2nd:0 3rd:0 Ran:4
1998 Turf 0-4: (5f, 6f 3) (gd, g-f 2, frm)
Average colt. Turf high 63. **T D Easterby [0-4] C H Stevens.*

DURHAM FLYER BHB 58f **RR 65f** 4919^{4}

3 b g Deploy 11.4f **(67)** - Hyde Princess (Touch Paper) 6.8f **(57)**
Form - 75036182015004
Record 1998 - 1st:2 2nd:1 3rd:1 Ran:14
Pre1998 - 1st:0 2nd:1 3rd:0 Ran:7
Win Prizemoney £7,050 *Total Prizemoney* £9,662
Wins * **1998** Aug Carlis (G-S) C 6.9f 65 <
* **1998** Jun Redcar (G-S) H 7f 60 61
1998 Turf 2-14: (6f 4, 7f 2-5, 8f 3, 10f 2) (sft, g-s, gd 2-8, g-f 2, frm 2)
Average gelding, effective 6 to 8f, best at 7f, acts on g-s to frm, best on gd, has worn blinkers (effectively), likes right handed tracks, excels at Redcar. Turf high 65 - 1st of 7 getting 4lb from Master Caster (3 Aug Carlisle RF 3307) - also 1st of 8 getting 3lb from King of Dance (20 Jun Redcar RF 2156).
**T D Easterby [2-21] C H Stevens.*

DURST BHB 43f **RR 36f** 2623^{4}

4 ch f Risk Me (FR) 8f **(53)** - Farras (Song) 7.2f **(61)**
Form - 584
Record 1998 - 1st:0 2nd:0 3rd:0 Ran:3
Win Prizemoney £0 *Total Prizemoney* £176
1998 Turf 0-1: (6f) (g-f) 1998 AW 0-2: (5f, 6f) (Equi, Fibr)
Workmanlike, currently very moderate filly. AW high 31.
**Lord Huntingdon [0-3] Lord Huntingdon.*

DUSHANBE (IRE) BHB 86f **RR 89f** 3260^{7}

3 b c Alzao (USA) 9.8f **(73)** - Atyaaf (USA) (Irish River (FR)) 8.6f **(78)**
Form - 137
Record 1998 - 1st:1 2nd:0 3rd:1 Ran:3
Win Prizemoney £3,715 *Total Prizemoney* £4,709
Wins * **1998** Jun Beverl (GD) 7.5f 83 <
1998 Turf 1-3: (7f 1-2, 8f) (gd 1-2, frm)
Strong, currently useful colt. Turf high 89 - 3rd of 5 to Temeraire (10 Jly Lingfield 8f frm RF 2689) - also 1st of 15 giving 5lb to Notley Park (10 Jun Beverley RF 1868). Unraced at two, he made a winning debut in a Beverley maiden in June but has been rather disappointing since. **L M Cumani [1-3] H R H Prince Fahd Salman.*

DUSHYANTOR (USA) BHB 120f **RR 121f** $5167a^{3}$

5 b h Sadler's Wells (USA) 11.3f **(87)** - Slightly Dangerous (USA) (Roberto (USA)) 10f **(76)**
Form - 3
1998 Turf 0-1: (12f) (frm)
Very high-class colt, effective 12 to 13f, best at 12f, acts on gd to frm. (1st run) - 3rd of 13 to Buck's Boy (7 Nov Churchill Downs 12f frm RF 5167a). Consistent. Last seen in this country in the autumn

of 1997, he is now trained in the USA, and put up a fine effort when placed in the 1998 Breeders' Cup Turf.
**R Frankel in USA [0-1] Juddmonte Farms (from H R A Cecil [4-13] Spt 1997).*

DUST BHB 55f58a **RR 56f 58a** 280[4]
4 b f Green Desert (USA) 7.8f **(78)** - Storm Warning (Tumble Wind (USA)) 7.5f **(57)**
Form - 1714
Record 1998 - 1st:1 2nd:0 3rd:0 Ran:3
Pre1998 - 1st:1 2nd:0 3rd:0 Ran:5
Win Prizemoney £4,027 *Total Prizemoney* £4,278
Wins * 1998 *Feb Southw (STD) H 8f 49 54+* <
* 1997 *Nov Southw (STD) 8f 54*
1998 AW 1-3: (7f, 8f 1-2) (Equi, Fibr 1-2)
Scopey, fair filly, effective 8f, - acts on Fibr. AW high 54 - 1st of 9 giving 4lb to Gipsy Princess (2 Feb Southwell RF 0207). Consistent. She showed an aptitude for the Southwell Fibresand when scoring on it at the first attempt in November. After a modest effort on Equitrack, she regained winning form with an easy success back at Southwell in February, but did not reproduce that effort after and may need things to go her own way.
**Lord Huntingdon [2-8] The Queen.*

DUST IN DHAHRAN (IRE) RR 4818[28]
2 ch f Desse Zenny (USA) 12f **(53)** - Magic Green (Magic Mirror)
Form - 00
Record 1998 - 1st:0 2nd:0 3rd:0 Ran:2
1998 Turf 0-2: (6f, 7f) (gd, frm)
Currently very poor filly.
**J S Wainwright [0-1] Rosaly Racing (from H Alexander [0-1] May 1998).*

DUSTY DANCER BHB 65f **RR 64f** 4307[11]
2 ch c Risk Me (FR) 8f **(53)** - Eternal Triangle (USA) (Barachois (CAN)) 8.3f **(63)**
Form - 0580
Record 1998 - 1st:0 2nd:0 3rd:0 Ran:4
Win Prizemoney £0 *Total Prizemoney* £157
1998 Turf 0-4: (5f 4) (gd 2, g-f, frm)
Average colt. Turf high 64. **Miss Gay Kelleway [0-4] T O C S Ltd.*

DUTCH DYANE BHB 36f28a **RR 39f 28a** 4938[2]
5 b m Midyan (USA) 9.9f **(64)** - Double Dutch (Nicholas Bill) 10.1f **(56)**
Form - 0032
Record 1998 - 1st:0 2nd:1 3rd:1 Ran:4
Pre1998 - 1st:0 2nd:1 3rd:0 Ran:6
Win Prizemoney £0 *Total Prizemoney* £1,948
1998 Turf 0-4: (13f, 15f, 16f 2) (sft, gd, g-f, frm)
Very moderate filly, effective 12 to 16f, acts on g-s to frm, favours tight tracks. Turf high 39 - 2nd of 17 giving 4lb to Spiral Flyer (22 Oct Nottingham 16f gd RF 4938). Inconsistent.
**G P Enright [0-18] Leonard Fuller.*

DUTCH LAD BHB 79f **RR 81f** 3028[5]
3 b c Alnasr Alwasheek 9.4f **(62)**-Double Dutch (Nicholas Bill) 10.1f **(56)**
Form - 2132025
Record 1998 - 1st:1 2nd:3 3rd:1 Ran:7
Pre1998 - 1st:0 2nd:1 3rd:1 Ran:5
Win Prizemoney £2,600 *Total Prizemoney* £10,156
Wins * 1998 Apr Mussel (G-S) 12f 68+ <
1998 Turf 1-7: (10f, 12f 1-6) (sft, g-s 2, gd 1-1, g-f 2, frm)
Workmanlike, decent colt, effective 8 to 12f, best at 12f, acts on g-s to g-f, best on g-f, prefers tight tracks. Turf high 81 - 2nd of 7 giving 3lb to Flow By (6 Jly Windsor 12f g-f RF 2573). Out of a mare who won the Cesarewitch, he found his feet in nurseries towards the end of '97, and made an encouraging reappearance at Leicester. He appeared to have a simple task in a four-runner maiden at Musselburgh next time and duly scored a facile victory. Fair efforts since. **M H Tompkins [1-12] S Dean.*

DUTCH NIGHTINGALE RR 35f 4150[10]
4 b f Warrshan (USA) 9.7f **(59)** - Double Dutch (Nicholas Bill) 10.1f **(56)**
Form - 00
Record 1998 - 1st:0 2nd:0 3rd:0 Ran:2
1998 Turf 0-2: (10f, 11f) (g-f, frm)
Scopey, currently very moderate filly. Turf high 35 (began Aug).
**G P Enright [0-3] Beagley Furneaux Mou Fuller.*

DYCE BHB 32f34a **RR 36f 34a** 3449[5]
4 b f Green Ruby (USA) 6.9f **(47)**- Miss Display (Touch Paper) 6.8f **(57)**
Form - 050105
Record 1998 - 1st:1 2nd:0 3rd:0 Ran:6
Pre1998 - 1st:0 2nd:0 3rd:0 Ran:2
Win Prizemoney £2,301 *Total Prizemoney* £2,301
Wins * 1998 *Jly Wolver (STD) H 5f 32 34* <
1998 Turf 0-4: (5f 3, 6f) (gd 4) 1998 AW 1-2: (5f 1-2) (Fibr 1-2)
Very moderate filly, effective 5f, - acts on Fibr, often wears blinkers (very effectively). Turf high 36. AW high 34 (1st run) (began Jly) - 1st of 7 getting 5lb from Dona Filipa (10 Jly Wolverhampton RF 2697). Inconsistent. **J Balding [1-8] Mrs Gillian Jones.*

DYESS BHB 25f **RR 27f** 2844[12]
3 ch f King's Signet (USA) 7f **(51)** - Lysithea (Imperial Fling (USA)) 7.1f **(58)**
Form - 070
Record 1998 - 1st:0 2nd:0 3rd:0 Ran:3
1998 Turf 0-3: (5f 2, 7f) (gd 2, frm)
Workmanlike, currently little account filly. Turf high 27.
**W G M Turner [0-3] Richard Hedditch.*

DYHIM DIAMOND (IRE) RR 117f 4214a[4]
4 ch c Night Shift (USA) 8.1f **(73)** - Happy Landing (FR) (Homing) 7.8f **(59)**
Form - 142244
1998 Turf 1-6: (5f, 6f 1-4, 7f) (g-s, gd 1-5)
High-class colt, effective 6 to 7f, best at 6f, acts on g-s to gd, best on gd. Turf high 117 (1st run) - 1st of 5 from Cretan Gift (22 May Baden-Baden RF 1555a). Consistent. Looked a useful sprinting prospect when winning a Group Three in May, on the second occasion beating good yardstick Cretan Gift. He showed that he could mix it with the best in this country when a most creditable second in the Cork And Orrery. **C Laffon-Parias in FR [3-12].*

DYNAMIC DANCER BHB 46f **RR 67f** 4136[19]
2 ch g King's Signet (USA) 7f **(51)** - Eleckydo (Electric) 10.1f **(61)**
Form - 33420670
Record 1998 - 1st:0 2nd:1 3rd:2 Ran:8
Win Prizemoney £0 *Total Prizemoney* £2,392
1998 Turf 0-8: (5f 2, 6f 2, 7f 3, 8f) (hvy, g-s, gd, g-f 4, frm)
Average gelding, effective 6f, acts on g-s. Turf high 67 - 2nd of 14 giving 5lb to Claranna (26 Jun Newcastle 6f g-s RF 2310). Inconsistent. **J J O'Neill [0-8] Clayton Bigley Partnership Ltd.*

DYNAMISM (FR) RR 78f 1535[1]
3 b c Caerleon (USA) 10.9f **(79)** - Fextal (USA) (Alleged (USA)) 10f **(76)**
Form - 61
Record 1998 - 1st:1 2nd:0 3rd:0 Ran:2
Win Prizemoney £3,582 *Total Prizemoney* £3,582
Wins * 1998 May Ripon (GD) 10f 77 <
1998 Turf 1-2: (10f 1-2) (g-f 1-1, frm)
Scopey, currently above-average colt. Turf high 78 - also 1st of 11 from Mawsoof (27 May Ripon RF 1535).
**H R A Cecil [1-2] Niarchos Family.*

EAGER HERO BHB 32f30a **RR 41f 30a** 4399[10]
3 ch c Keen 11.1f **(58)** - Honour and Glory (Hotfoot) 10.5f **(59)**
Form - 85688205440
Record 1998 - 1st:0 2nd:1 3rd:0 Ran:11
Pre1998 - 1st:0 2nd:0 3rd:0 Ran:3
Win Prizemoney £0 *Total Prizemoney* £811
1998 Turf 0-9: (7f, 10f 5, 12f 3) (g-s 2, gd, g-f 4, frm, hrd) 1998 AW 0-2: (11f, 12f) (Fibr 2)
Small, moderate colt, effective 10f, acts on g-f, likes tight tracks. Turf high 41 - 2nd of 9 getting 17lb from Prophits Pride (28 May Ayr 10f g-f RF 1546). AW high 14. **M Brittain [0-14] Mel Brittain.*

EAGLE'S CROSS (USA) BHB 84f **RR 88+f** 4963[6]
3 b c Trempolino (USA) 11.9f **(77)** - Shining Bright (Rainbow Quest (USA)) 10.4f **(75)**
Form - 120056
Record 1998 - 1st:1 2nd:1 3rd:0 Ran:6
Pre1998 - 1st:0 2nd:0 3rd:0 Ran:2
Win Prizemoney £3,550 *Total Prizemoney* £6,665

Wins * **1998** Jun Bath (G-S) 11.7f 88+ <
1998 Turf 1-6: (12f 1-4, 13f, 16f) (sft, gd 1-1, g-f 2, frm 2)
Unfurnished, useful colt, effective 7 to 13f, best at 12f, acts on gd to frm. Turf high 88 (1st run) - 1st of 11 from Kadir (27 Jun Bath RF 2329). Landed his maiden before a good effort on unsuitably fast ground on his handicap debut. Failed to stay two miles on his final start. **R Charlton [1-8] K Abdulla.*

EARLY MEMORY (USA) RR 90f
3186a[10]

3 ch f Devil's Bag (USA) 9.3f **(73)** - Grenzen (USA) (Grenfall (USA)) 7f **(82)**
Form - 14460
1998 Turf 1-5: (6f, 7f 1-4) (g-s 2, g-f 1-2, frm)
Useful filly, effective 6f, acts on frm, often wears blinkers. Turf high 90 - 4th of 8 giving 18lb to Sacrementum (4 Jly Leopardstown 6f frm RF 2610a). **D K Weld in IRE [1-7] Moyglare Stud Farm.*

EARLY PURPLE RR 9f
4304[17]

3 b f Keen 11.1f **(58)** - Beautiful Orchid (Hays)
Form - 00
Record 1998 - 1st:0 2nd:0 3rd:0 Ran:2
1998 Turf 0-2: (5f, 8f) (gd, frm)
Leggy, currently very poor filly. Turf high 9 (began Spt).
**J J O'Neill [0-2] E A Brook.*

EASAAR RR 91+f
4595[1]

2 b c Machiavellian (USA) 9.8f **(83)** -Matila (IRE)(Persian Bold) 9.3f **(66)**
Form - 21
Record 1998 - 1st:1 2nd:1 3rd:0 Ran:2
Win Prizemoney £8,217 *Total Prizemoney* £9,385
Wins * **1998** Oct Newmar () 7f 91+ <
1998 Turf 1-2: (7f 1-2) (gd 1-2)
Currently useful colt. Turf high 91 (began Spt) - 1st of 27 from Tobruk (1 Oct Newmarket RF 4595). Made up for his shock defeat on his debut with a very impressive all-the-way success at Yarmouth. Although he may not have had a lot to beat, he showed that he could be out of the top drawer and is very much one to follow. **S bin Suroor [1-2] Godolphin.*

EAST BARNS (IRE) BHB 34f31a RR 35f 31a
7[9]

10 gr g Godswalk (USA) 8.5f **(56)** - Rocket Lass (Touch Paper)6.8f **(57)**
Form - 0
Record 1998 - 1st:0 2nd:0 3rd:0 Ran:1
Pre1998 - 1st:7 2nd:5 3rd:7 Ran:76
Win Prizemoney £19,947 *Total Prizemoney* £27,439
Wins * 1995 May Nottin (GD) H 10f 44 46
* 1994 Spt Yarmou (SFT) H 7f 33 35
1998 AW 0-1: (8f) (Fibr)
Very moderate gelding, mostly wears blinkers. Inconsistent.
**S Gollings [2-27] Northern Bloodstock Racing (from T D Barron [3-25] May 1994).*

EASTERN LYRIC RR 90f
4090[2]

3 gr f Petong 7.6f **(58)** - Songlines (Night Shift (USA)) 7.2f **(69)**
Form - 704181182
Record 1998 - 1st:3 2nd:1 3rd:0 Ran:9
Pre1998 - 1st:1 2nd:0 3rd:1 Ran:9
Win Prizemoney £23,551 *Total Prizemoney* £27,261
Wins * **1998** Jly Goodwo (G-S) H 5f 80 85 <
* **1998** Jly Bath (GD) H 5.1f 75 79
* **1998** Jun Ayr (G-F) H 5f 70 73
* 1997 May Warwic (FRM) 5f 65
1998 Turf 3-9: (5f 3-8, 6f) (g-s, gd 2-2, g-f 1-3, frm 3)
Light-framed, useful filly, effective 5 to 6f, acts on gd to frm. Turf high 90 - 2nd of 8 giving 7lb to Faraway Lass (4 Spt Haydock 6f frm RF 4090) - also 1st of 15 getting 1lb from Arjan (31 Jly Goodwood RF 3235). Hit top form in the Summer, winning three races. Best over five furlongs, she ran a really game race over six furlongs to chase home Faraway Lass at Haydock on her final start. A tough and genuine sort, she is bound to win more races.
**J Berry [4-18] R Meredith.*

EASTERN PROPHETS BHB 67f62a RR 69f 62a
4886[6]

5 b g Emarati (USA) 6.6f **(63)** - Four Love (Pas de Seul) 9.1f **(67)**
Form - 265243336061450374042200б
Record 1998 - 1st:1 2nd:2 3rd:4 Ran:21
Pre1998 - 1st:4 2nd:5 3rd:2 Ran:34
Win Prizemoney £22,703 *Total Prizemoney* £42,536
Wins * **1998** May Doncas (G-F) C 6f 70
* 1997 Mar Kempto (G-F) H 6f 79 82
* 1995 Jun Beverl (G-S) 5f 86 <
* 1995 May Bath (G-F) 5.1f 76
* 1995 May Doncas (G-F) 5f 64
1998 Turf 1-15: (5f 7, 6f 1-8) (sft 2, g-s, gd 4, g-f 1-4, frm 4) 1998 AW 0-6: (6f 6) (Equi 3, Fibr 3)
Average gelding, effective 5 to 6f, acts on gd to g-f, has worn blinkers. Turf high 70. AW high 67.
**G Lewis [5-45] Mrs J M Purches (from T J Naughton [0-10] Nov 1996).*

EASTERN PURPLE (IRE) BHB 105f RR 106f
5152[11]

3 b c Petorius 8f **(66)** - Broadway Rosie (Absalom) 7.2f **(58)**
Form - 0107535760
Record 1998 - 1st:1 2nd:0 3rd:1 Ran:10
Pre1998 - 1st:1 2nd:0 3rd:0 Ran:5
Win Prizemoney £15,106 *Total Prizemoney* £27,063
Wins * **1998** May Haydoc (G-S) LH 6f 93 106 <
* 1997 Aug Newcas (G-F) 6f 71+
1998 Turf 1-10: (5f 2, 6f 1-7, 7f) (sft, g-s, gd 1-5, g-f, frm 2)
Pattern-class colt, effective 6 to 7f, best at 6f, acts on gd to frm, best on gd, has worn blinkers (very effectively). Turf high 106 - 5th of 6 to Bold Fact (20 Aug York 7f frm RF 3777) - also 1st of 11 getting 12lb from Jimmy Too (23 May Haydock RF 1417). He revelled in yielding conditions when strolling home by eight lengths at Haydock in May. The handicapper did not forget that effort and the rest of the season was an uphill struggle, although he did run a super race when finishing third behind his stable-mate Superior Premium in the Stewards' Cup. Badly drawn when a creditable sixth in the Ayr Gold Cup, he can win another valuable race on an easy surface. **R A Fahey [2-15] T C Chiang.*

EASTERN TRIBUTE (USA) RR 70f
5039[13]

2 b c Affirmed (USA) 10.3f **(75)** - Mia Duchessa (USA) (Nijinsky (CAN)) 10.3f **(77)**
Form - 60
Record 1998 - 1st:0 2nd:0 3rd:0 Ran:2
1998 Turf 0-2: (7f, 8f) (sft, g-s)
Currently above-average colt. Turf high 70 (began Oct).
**E A L Dunlop [0-2] Maktoum Al Maktoum.*

EASTERN TRUMPETER RR 77f
3321[2]

2 b c First Trump - Oriental Air (IRE) **(49f 48a)** (Taufan (USA)) 7f **(57)**
Form - 52
Record 1998 - 1st:0 2nd:1 3rd:0 Ran:2
Win Prizemoney £0 *Total Prizemoney* £652
1998 Turf 0-2: (5f 2) (gd, g-f)
Currently above-average colt. Turf high 77 - 2nd of 13 to Ivory's Promise (4 Aug Bath 5f g-f RF 3321). **G Lewis [0-2] G H P Pritchard.*

EASTER OGIL (IRE) BHB 82f RR 83f
4498[7]

3 ch g Pips Pride 6.7f **(70)** - Piney Pass (Persian Bold) 9.3f **(66)**
Form - 1802442317
Record 1998 - 1st:2 2nd:2 3rd:1 Ran:10
Pre1998 - 1st:0 2nd:1 3rd:0 Ran:2
Win Prizemoney £7,091 *Total Prizemoney* £14,166
Wins * **1998** Spt Sandow (GD) 7.1f 83 <
* **1998** Apr Beverl (SFT) 5f 83 <
1998 Turf 2-10: (5f 1-3, 6f 4, 7f 1-3) (g-s 1-1, gd 1-2, g-f 4, frm 3)
Workmanlike, decent gelding, effective 5 to 7f, acts on g-s to frm, often wears blinkers (effectively), does well at Lingfield. Turf high 83 - 1st of 11 from Hadith (15 Spt Sandown RF 4267) - also 1st of 10 giving 5lb to Yanomami (23 Apr Beverley RF 0824). Narrowly got off the mark in a Beverley maiden in April, though the stiff five on heavy ground nearly found him out. Creditable efforts in warm handicaps since. **I A Balding [2-12] G M Smart.*

EASTLEIGH BHB 27f28a RR 30f 28a
3414a[5]

9 b g Efisio 7.7f **(69)** - Blue Jane (Blue Cashmere) 6.4f **(54)**
Form - 888566565
Record 1998 - 1st:0 2nd:0 3rd:0 Ran:9
Pre1998 - 1st:9 2nd:15 3rd:9 Ran:125
Win Prizemoney £28,650 *Total Prizemoney* £47,093
Wins * *1997 Feb Lingfi (STD) H 8f 35 43*
* *1995 Mar Lingfi (STD) H 8f 50 52*
* *1995 Feb Lingfi (STD) SH 8f 46 47*
1998 Turf 0-1: (10f) (g-f) 1998 AW 0-8: (8f 6, 9f, 11f) (Equi 2, Fibr 6)

Very moderate gelding, effective 8 to 9f, best at 8f, - acts on AW, best on Equi, has worn blinkers, favours left handed tracks, favours tight tracks. AW high 32. He probably runs on sand more often than almost any other horse, and wins from time to time in modest company, but his strike rate is pretty moderate.

**R Hollinshead [9-134].*

EASTWELL HALL BHB 73f RR 75f 4525[3]

3 b g Saddlers' Hall (IRE) 10.5f **(65)** -Kinchenjunga (Darshaan)9.9f **(84)**

Form - 11122603

Record 1998 - 1st:3 2nd:2 3rd:1 Ran:8
Pre1998 - 1st:0 2nd:0 3rd:0 Ran:5

Win Prizemoney £10,519 *Total Prizemoney* £14,066

Wins * **1998** May Warwic (GD) H 12.5f 53 68
* **1998** Apr Bath (SFT) H 10.2f 53 70+ <
* **1998** Apr Folkes (GD) H 9.7f 47 52

1998 Turf 3-8: (10f 2-2, 12f 3, 13f 1-1, 16f, 17f) (g-s 1-1, gd 1-2, g-f 1-4, frm)

Leggy, above-average gelding, effective 10 to 17f, best at 12f, acts on g-s to g-f, best on g-f, prefers tight tracks, does well at Bath. Turf high 77 - 2nd of 10 giving 3lb to Court Shareef (26 May Leicester 12f g-f RF 1468) - also 1st of 13 getting 16lb from Fantasy Night (28 Apr Bath RF 0893). He showed nothing at two, but completed a hat-trick at the start of last season. He took a hike in the handicap as a result but has continued to run well.

**R Curtis [3-13] Eastwell Manor Racing.*

EASTWELL MINSTREL BHB 43f RR 41f 5127[18]

3 ch c Risk Me (FR) 8f **(53)** - Ramz (IRE) (The Minstrel (CAN)) 10f **(72)**

Form - 800

Record 1998 - 1st:0 2nd:0 3rd:0 Ran:3
Pre1998 - 1st:1 2nd:0 3rd:0 Ran:3

Win Prizemoney £1,984 *Total Prizemoney* £1,984

Wins 1997 Jly Folkes (SFT) S 5f 65 <

1998 Turf 0-2: (6f, 7f) (g-s, gd) 1998 AW 0-1: (7f) (Equi)

Workmanlike, moderate colt, effective 5f, acts on gd. Turf high 41 (began Oct). He won probably one of the worst races ever run when taking a Folkestone seller in July '97.

**K Mahdi [0-3] Kamil Mahdi (from R Curtis [1-3] Jly 1997).*

EASTWELL STAR RR 4880[13]

2 b f Saddlers' Hall (IRE) 10.5f **(65)** -Kinchenjunga (Darshaan) 9.9f **(84)**

Form - 0

Record 1998 - 1st:0 2nd:0 3rd:0 Ran:1

1998 Turf 0-1: (7f) (g-s)

Currently very poor filly. **R Curtis [0-1] Eastwell Manor Racing.*

EAST WINDS BHB 77f RR 80f 4446[11]

3 ch g Suave Dancer (USA) 10.7f **(68)** - Dominio (IRE) (Dominion) 8.5f **(63)**

Form - 7322100

Record 1998 - 1st:1 2nd:2 3rd:1 Ran:7

Win Prizemoney £3,980 *Total Prizemoney* £6,810

Wins * **1998** Jly Warwic (GD) 6f 80 <

1998 Turf 1-7: (5f, 6f 1-6) (gd 4, g-f 1-3)

Decent gelding, effective 5 to 6f, best at 6f, acts on gd to g-f, best on g-f. Turf high 80 - 2nd of 11 giving 5lb to Night Spirit (27 May Folkestone 6f gd RF 1517) - also 1st of 12 from Chieftain (3 Jly Warwick RF 2513). **P T Walwyn [1-7] R J McCreery.*

EASYCALL BHB 109f RR 115f 5054a[2]

4 b c Forzando 7.2f **(63)** - Up And Going (FR) (Never so Bold) 6.3f **(66)**

Form - 36302001152

Record 1998 - 1st:2 2nd:2 3rd:2 Ran:11
Pre1998 - 1st:5 2nd:1 3rd:0 Ran:14

Win Prizemoney £104,248 *Total Prizemoney* £129,623

Wins * **1998** Spt Doncas (GD) L 5f 112
* **1998** Spt Leices (G-S) 5f 110
* 1996 Oct Ascot (GD) G3 5f 122 <
* 1996 Spt Doncas (G-F) G2 5f 116
* 1996 Aug Goodwo (G-F) G2 6f 111
* 1996 Jly Newmar (G-F) 5f 96
* 1996 Jun Leices (GD) 5f 92+

1998 Turf 2-11: (5f 2-10, 6f) (hvy, sft, gd 1-5, g-f 1-1, frm 3)

Scopey, high-class colt, effective 5f, acts on hvy to frm, best on gd, has worn blinkers. Turf high 115 - 2nd of 7 to Bishops Court (25 Oct Longchamp 5f hvy RF 5054a) - also 1st of 8 getting 3lb from Bishops Court (10 Spt Doncaster RF 4203). He came good in the autumn, winning at Leicester and Doncaster before running

Easycall (right) did not always have things go that way

two excellent races in defeat at Longchamp. He stays in training and should win a Group race next term.
**B J Meehan [7-25] Easycall Partnership.*

EASY DOLLAR BHB 95f **RR 88f** 5152[12]
6 ch g Gabitat 8.5f **(44)** - Burglars Girl (Burglar) 7.2f **(49)**
Form - 00
Record 1998 - 1st:0 2nd:0 3rd:0 Ran:2
Pre1998 - 1st:2 2nd:6 3rd:5 Ran:30
Win Prizemoney £24,479 *Total Prizemoney* £55,037
Wins * 1995 Jly Goodwo (FRM) H 7f 78 89 <
* 1995 Jly Newmar (GD) 6f 83
1998 Turf 0-2: (6f 2) (gd, g-f)
Useful gelding, effective 6f, acts on gd to g-f, best on gd, mostly wears blinkers (effectively). Turf high 88 (began Oct). Becoming disappointing. **B Gubby [2-32] Brian Gubby Ltd.*

EASY VIRTUE RR 43f 1551[6]
3 b f Northern Park (USA) 10f **(57)** - Last Clear Chance (USA) (Alleged (USA)) 10f **(76)**
Form - 247066
Record 1998 - 1st:0 2nd:1 3rd:0 Ran:6
Win Prizemoney £0 *Total Prizemoney* £775
1998 Turf 0-3: (10f, 12f 2) (gd, frm 2) 1998 AW 0-3: (8f, 10f 2) (Equi 3)
Neat, moderate filly, effective 8f, - acts on Equi. Turf high 43. AW high 45 (1st run) - 2nd of 9 to Rockette (20 Jan Lingfield 8f Equi RF 0120). **G L Moore [0-6] A Moore.*

EATON SQUARE (USA) RR 107f 2581[7]
3 b c Nureyev (USA) 8.4f **(84)**- Jolypha (USA)(Lyphard (USA)) 9.9f **(72)**
Form - 117
Record 1998 - 1st:2 2nd:0 3rd:0 Ran:3
Win Prizemoney £8,068 *Total Prizemoney* £8,068
Wins * **1998** Jun Goodwo (GD) 9.9f 107 <
* **1998** May Newbur (GD) 8f 95
1998 Turf 2-3: (8f 1-1, 10f 1-1, 12f) (gd 1-1, g-f 1-1, frm)
Scopey, currently Pattern-class colt. Turf high 107 - 1st of 4 from Deep Dive (3 Jun Goodwood RF 1693). He is Group class judged on a decisive win from Deep Dive at Goodwood in June, but pulled hard and ran no sort of race when tried in that sphere at Newmarket the following month. Beautifully bred, he is well worth another chance. **H R A Cecil [2-3] K Abdulla.*

EBADIYLA (IRE) RR 117f 3880a[2]
4 b f Sadler's Wells (USA) 11.3f **(87)**-Ebaziya (IRE)(Darshaan) 9.9f **(84)**
Form - 532
1998 Turf 0-3: (10f, 12f, 14f) (gd 3)
High-class filly, effective 12 to 16f, best at 12f, acts on sft to gd, best on gd. Turf high 117 - 3rd of 7 getting 3lb from Silver Patriarch (5 Jun Epsom 12f gd RF 1745). She looked a top-class staying prospect when winning the Irish Oaks and Prix Royal-Oak in 1997, but had a difficult four-year-old campaign, the only highlight being her close third in the Coronation Cup. She bled from the nose when withdrawn before the Irish St Leger - where she had been heavily backed - and that casts a further doubt about her future. **J Oxx in IRE [3-9] H H Aga Khan.*

EBDAA RR 46f 2330[6]
2 ch f Nashwan (USA) 10.3f **(79)** - Al Theraab (USA) (Roberto (USA)) 10f **(76)**
Form - 6
Record 1998 - 1st:0 2nd:0 3rd:0 Ran:1
1998 Turf 0-1: (7f) (gd)
Currently moderate filly. **Mrs J Cecil [0-1] Hamdan Al Maktoum.*

EBINZAYD (IRE) BHB 85f **RR 78f** 4960[9]
2 b c Tenby 10.4f **(76)** - Sharakawa (IRE) (Darshaan) 9.9f **(84)**
Form - 4710
Record 1998 - 1st:1 2nd:0 3rd:0 Ran:4
Win Prizemoney £3,371 *Total Prizemoney* £3,633
Wins * **1998** Spt Newcas (GD) 8f 78 <
1998 Turf 1-4: (8f 1-4) (gd, g-f 1-2, frm)
Above-average colt. Turf high 78 (1st run) (began Aug) - 4th of 8 to Pulau Tioman (29 Aug Nottingham 8f g-f RF 3959) - also 1st of 7 from Secret's Out (30 Spt Newcastle RF 4576).
**E A L Dunlop [1-4] Hamdan Al Maktoum.*

EBISU (GER) RR 112f 5053a[3]
3 c
Form - 8733
1998 Turf 0-4: (12f 4) (hvy 2, sft, gd)
Group-class colt. Turf high 112 (began Jly) - 3rd of 9 getting 10lb from Taipan (27 Spt Cologne 12f sft RF 4603a). He was out of his depth when pitched-in against Group One horses.
**A Schutz in GER [0-4] Stall Helena.*

EBLANA (IRE) BHB 35f **RR 39f** 4762[10]
2 b f Maledetto (IRE) - Dublin Millennium (Dalsaan) 9.8f **(64)**
Form - 8000
Record 1998 - 1st:0 2nd:0 3rd:0 Ran:4
1998 Turf 0-4: (7f 2, 8f, 10f) (gd 3, g-f)
Very moderate filly, often wears blinkers. Turf high 39 (began Jly).
**M H Tompkins [0-4] Michael Keogh.*

EBONY BHB 56f50a **RR 62f 50a** 4818[13]
2 b f Mujtahid (USA) 7.4f **(69)** - Sharia (USA) (Irish River (FR)) 8.6f **(78)**
Form - 820
Record 1998 - 1st:0 2nd:1 3rd:0 Ran:3
Win Prizemoney £0 *Total Prizemoney* £548
1998 Turf 0-3: (5f, 6f, 7f) (g-f, frm 2)
Currently average filly. Turf high 62 (began Spt) - 2nd of 11 getting 5lb from Landican Lane (30 Spt Brighton 5f g-f RF 4569).
**B J McMath [0-1] The Happy Go Lucky Partnership (from R Guest [0-2] Spt 1998).*

EBONY BEAVER (IRE) RR 24f 3741[12]
2 b f Petardia 8.2f **(58)** - Conditional Sale (IRE) (Petorius) 7.3f **(61)**
Form - 000600
Record 1998 - 1st:0 2nd:0 3rd:0 Ran:6
1998 Turf 0-6: (5f 3, 6f 3) (gd 2, g-f, frm 3)
Little account filly, has worn blinkers. Turf high 24.
**E A Wheeler [0-6] Beaver Racing Partnership.*

EBONY HEIGHTS RR 65f 2512[10]
2 br c Polar Falcon (USA) 9f **(74)** - Maestrale (Top Ville) 11.7f **(68)**
Form - 0
Record 1998 - 1st:0 2nd:0 3rd:0 Ran:1
1998 Turf 0-1: (7f) (g-f)
Currently average colt.
**W R Muir [0-1] Mrs E Clowes And Mrs D Edginton.*

E B PEARL BHB 37f **RR 35f** 3934[10]
2 ch f Timeless Times (USA) 6.1f **(56)** - Petite Elite (Anfield) 8.5f **(59)**
Form - 700057780
Record 1998 - 1st:0 2nd:0 3rd:0 Ran:9
1998 Turf 0-7: (5f 2, 6f 3, 7f 2) (g-s, g-f 4, frm 2) 1998 AW 0-2: (5f, 6f) (Fibr 2)
Very moderate filly, has worn blinkers. Turf high 35. AW high 26 (began Jly). **N Bycroft [0-9] T Umpleby.*

ECHELLE MUSICALE BHB 78f **RR 85f** 2589[7]
3 b f Rainbow Quest (USA) 11.2f **(81)** - Water Splash (USA) (Little Current (USA)) 9.6f **(75)**
Form - 537
Record 1998 - 1st:0 2nd:0 3rd:1 Ran:3
Win Prizemoney £0 *Total Prizemoney* £502
1998 Turf 0-3: (8f, 12f 2) (gd 2, frm)
Leggy, currently useful filly. Turf high 85 - 3rd of 5 to Star Crystal (22 May Haydock 12f gd RF 1395).
**E A L Dunlop [0-3] Maktoum Al Maktoum.*

ECLECTIC RR 46f 4389[16]
2 b f Emarati (USA) 6.6f **(63)** - Great Aim (Great Nephew) 9.9f **(64)**
Form - 00
Record 1998 - 1st:0 2nd:0 3rd:0 Ran:2
1998 Turf 0-2: (6f, 7f) (frm 2)
Currently moderate filly. Turf high 46 (began Jly).
**S Dow [0-2] Harold Nass.*

ECO FRIENDLY BHB 112f **RR 115f** 4718a[3]
3 ch c Sabrehill (USA) 8.5f **(64)** - Flower Girl (Pharly (FR)) 9.8f **(68)**
Form - 12073
Record 1998 - 1st:0 2nd:1 3rd:1 Ran:4

	Pre1998 -	1st:2	2nd:2	3rd:0	Ran:5

Win Prizemoney £28,356 *Total Prizemoney* £51,600

Wins	* 1997	Nov	Saint-	(HVY)	G3	8f	99+	<
	* 1997	Nov	Doncas	(G-S)		8f	83	

1998 Turf 0-4: (10f 3, 15f) (sft 2, g-f 2)

High-class colt, effective 10 to 15f, acts on sft to g-f. Turf high 115 - 3rd of 10 getting 4lb from Insatiable (3 Oct Longchamp 10f sft RF 4718a). Improving. He ran creditably in the Thresher Classic Trial on his reappearance, but was off the track for four months afterwards. He showed little on his return, and was then outclassed in the St Leger. Fair effort in the Prix Dollar at Longchamp on his final start.

**B W Hills [2-7] W J Gredley (from J R Fanshawe [0-2] Spt 1997).*

ECUDAMAH (IRE) BHB 77f **RR 77+f** 5068[7]

2 ch c Mukaddamah (USA) 7.6f **(74)** - Great Land (USA) (Friend's Choice (USA)) 8.6f **(57)**

Form - 8525304227

Record	**1998** -	1st:0	2nd:3	3rd:1	Ran:10

Win Prizemoney £0 *Total Prizemoney* £3,731

1998 Turf 0-10: (5f 7, 6f 2, 7f) (sft, gd 2, g-f 4, frm 3)

Above-average colt, effective 5 to 6f, best at 5f, acts on sft to frm. Turf high 77 (began Jly) - 2nd of 18 giving 13lb to Piggy Bank (14 Oct Haydock 5f sft RF 4796). Consistent.

**R T Phillips [0-10] Sanford Racing.*

from Fear And Greed (6 Spt Curragh RF 4178a). This half-sister to Ebadiyla looked a top-class prospect when landing the Group One Moyglare Stud Stakes at the Curragh. Ran green there and may have come too soon when beaten in the Fillies' Mile at Ascot. She should have no trouble staying middle distances next season, and looks an Oaks filly in the making. **J Oxx in IRE [2-3] H H Aga Khan.*

EDAN HEIGHTS BHB 76f73a **RR 77df 73a** 4098[2]

6 b g Heights of Gold 11.2f **(62)** - Edna (Shiny Tenth) 9.2f **(56)**

Form - 324710502

Record	**1998** -	1st:1	2nd:1	3rd:0	Ran:7
	Pre1998 -	1st:4	2nd:5	3rd:4	Ran:34

Win Prizemoney £22,798 *Total Prizemoney* £35,692

Wins	* **1998**	Jun	Newmar	(GD)	H	10f	74	77	<
	* 1997	Spt	Leices	(G-F)	H	10f	71	75	
	* 1996	Oct	Newbur	(SFT)	H	10f	72	76	
	* 1996	Jly	Sandow	(G-S)	H	11.4f	65	71	
	* 1995	Spt	Folkes	(SFT)		12f		71	

1998 Turf 1-7: (10f 1-5, 11f, 12f) (g-s, gd 2, g-f 1-4)

Above-average gelding, effective 10 to 14f, best at 10f, acts on gd to frm - acts on AW, best on gd, has worn blinkers, likes left handed tracks, prefers tight tracks, excels at Lingfield. Turf high 77 - 1st of 6 giving 4lb to Mister Benjamin (26 Jun Newmarket RF 2315). He put some moderate efforts behind him when winning at Newmarket in June. **S Dow [5-41] S Dow.*

Edabiya looks an Oaks prospect for next year

EDABIYA (IRE) **RR 108+f** 4514[3]

2 ch f Rainbow Quest (USA) 11.2f **(81)** - Ebaziya (IRE) (Darshaan) 9.9f **(84)**

Form - 113

1998 Turf 2-3: (7f 2-2, 8f) (gd 2-3)

Currently Pattern-class filly. Turf high 108 (began Aug) - 1st of 13

EDDIE ROMBO BHB 39f **RR 28f** 3121[9]

3 b g Aragon 7.7f **(58)** - Jolimo (Fortissimo) 11.8f **(61)**

Form - 800

Record	**1998** -	1st:0	2nd:0	3rd:0	Ran:3
	Pre1998 -	1st:0	2nd:0	3rd:0	Ran:4

1998 Turf 0-3: (8f, 11f 2) (g-s, gd, hrd)

Scopey, little account gelding. Turf high 28.
**N Tinkler [0-7] The Rovers Club.*

EDEN (IRE) RR 81+f
5072[1]

2 b f Polish Precedent (USA) 9f **(73)** - Isle of Flame (Shirley Heights) 10.3f **(74)**
Form - 1
Record 1998 - 1st:1 2nd:0 3rd:0 Ran:1
Win Prizemoney £4,321 *Total Prizemoney* £4,321
Wins * **1998** Oct Newmar (SFT) 7f 81+ <
1998 Turf 1-1: (7f 1-1) (gd 1-1)
Currently decent filly. (1st run) - 1st of 16 from Sea Picture (31 Oct Newmarket RF 5072). **L M Cumani [1-1] L Marinopoulos.*

EDEN ROCK (GER) RR 112f
2863a[8]

4 b c Dashing Blade 7.9f **(80)** -Eriphyle (GER) (Surumu (GER)) 10f **(83)**
Form - 178
1998 Turf 1-3: (8f, 9f, 10f 1-1) (hvy 1-1, gd 2)
Group-class colt, effective 8 to 10f, best at 10f, acts on hvy to gd. Turf high 112 (1st run) - 1st of 10 giving 2lb to Sambakonig (5 Apr Gelsenkirchen-horst RF 0634a). He was the best juvenile in Germany back in 1996, but has never quite fulfilled the hopes held out for him. He goes well when fresh and won a Group Three on his reappearance, but found life tough thereafter.
**A Schutz in GER [1-3] May 1998).*

EDIFICE (JPN) RR 54f
4541[16]

2 ch c Carroll House - Moon Tosho (JPN) (Steel Heart) 8.3f **(58)**
Form - 0
Record 1998 - 1st:0 2nd:0 3rd:0 Ran:1
1998 Turf 0-1: (8f) (frm)
Currently fair colt. **A C Stewart [0-1] Teiji Takasaki.*

EDIPO RE BHB 74f RR 57tf
4734[11]

6 b h Slip Anchor 12.7f **(75)**-Lady Barrister (Law Society(USA))9.9f **(70)**
Form - 0
Record 1998 - 1st:0 2nd:0 3rd:0 Ran:1
Pre1998 - 1st:2 2nd:1 3rd:0 Ran:6
Win Prizemoney £22,701 *Total Prizemoney* £25,178
Wins 1994 Oct San Si (HVY) L 8f 86++
1994 Spt San Si (HVY) 8f
1998 Turf 0-1: (12f) (g-s)
Fair horse.
**P J Hobbs [0-6] Tony Eaves (from J L Dunlop [2-2] Oct 1994).*

EDMO HEIGHTS BHB 72f RR 75f
4845[14]

2 ch c Keen 11.1f **(58)** - Bodham (Bustino) 10.4f **(64)**
Form - 6522610
Record 1998 - 1st:1 2nd:2 3rd:0 Ran:7
Win Prizemoney £3,078 *Total Prizemoney* £4,569
Wins * **1998** Spt Beverl (G-F) 7.5f 73 <
1998 Turf 1-7: (6f 2, 7f 1-3, 8f 2) (g-f 3, frm 1-4)
Above-average colt, effective 7f, acts on frm. Turf high 75 - 2nd of 8 getting 7lb from Courtesan (13 Aug Beverley 7f frm RF 3602) - also 1st of 11 getting 2lb from Mice Ideas (16 Spt Beverley RF 4301). Progressive form in maidens, although he tended to hang fire when runner-up on his third start. Rather one-paced, he won a modest race at Beverley. **T D Easterby [1-7] Edmolift UK Ltd.*

EDRAAK (IRE) RR 84f
5065[3]

2 b c Shirley Heights 12.1f **(76)** - Sahara Star (Green Desert (USA)) 8.6f **(78)**
Form - 3
Record 1998 - 1st:0 2nd:0 3rd:1 Ran:1
Win Prizemoney £0 *Total Prizemoney* £1,013
1998 Turf 0-1: (8f) (g-f)
Currently decent colt. (1st run) - 3rd of 13 to Lightning Arrow (30 Oct Newmarket 8f g-f RF 5065). Sure to find an ordinary race over around a mile. **D R Loder [0-1] Maktoum Al Maktoum.*

ED'S FOLLY (IRE) BHB 27f32a RR 24df 32a
3573[5]

5 b g Fayruz 6.6f **(63)** - Tabriya (Nishapour (FR)) 9.1f **(61)**
Form - 750000805
Record 1998 - 1st:0 2nd:0 3rd:0 Ran:7
Pre1998 - 1st:0 2nd:2 3rd:5 Ran:23
Win Prizemoney £0 *Total Prizemoney* £4,348
1998 Turf 0-7: (8f 2, 10f 2, 12f 3) (g-s, gd 2, g-f 3, frm)
Moderate gelding, effective 6 to 7f, best at 6f, acts on gd to frm, best on g-f, has worn blinkers, excels at Leicester, does well at Brighton. Turf high 29. Becoming disappointing.
**L A Dace [0-4] Eddie Davess (from S Dow [0-26] May 1998).*

EDWARDIAN BHB 92f RR 88+f
5151[16]

3 ch c Sanglamore (USA) 12.9f **(67)** - Woodwardia (USA) (El Gran Senor (USA)) 9.6f **(76)**
Form - 25110
Record 1998 - 1st:2 2nd:1 3rd:0 Ran:5
Pre1998 - 1st:0 2nd:1 3rd:0 Ran:1
Win Prizemoney £10,562 *Total Prizemoney* £12,882
Wins * **1998** Spt Kempto (GD) 12f 88+ <
* **1998** Spt Goodwo (G-S) 9.9f 82
1998 Turf 2-5: (10f 1-3, 12f 1-2) (g-s 1-1, gd 3, frm 1-1)
Useful colt, effective 8 to 12f, acts on g-s to frm, best on gd. Turf high 88 - 1st of 6 getting 3lb from Shouk (21 Spt Kempton RF 4392) - also 1st of 11 giving 5lb to Silver Sun (12 Spt Goodwood RF 4249). Showed promise in maidens, and came good with two comfortable victories in September, looking a progressive colt, but made no show in the November Handicap.
**Mrs A J Perrett [2-6] K Abdulla.*

EFFANDEMM (IRE) RR
4104[12]

2 ch g Up and At 'em - Bermuda Princess (Lord Gayle (USA)) 8.8f **(62)**
Form - 00
Record 1998 - 1st:0 2nd:0 3rd:0 Ran:2
1998 Turf 0-2: (5f, 7f) (gd, frm)
Currently very poor gelding. **Miss L A Perratt [0-2] F Johnson.*

EFODOS RR 3f
699[15]

3 ch f Pursuit of Love 9.5f **(69)** - Sariza (Posse (USA)) 8.9f **(61)**
Form - 0
Record 1998 - 1st:0 2nd:0 3rd:0 Ran:1
Pre1998 - 1st:0 2nd:0 3rd:0 Ran:1
1998 Turf 0-1: (7f) (sft)
Unfurnished, currently very poor filly.
**G Wragg [0-2] L Marinopoulos.*

EGO NIGHT (IRE) BHB 78f RR 84f
4741[14]

3 c b Night Shift (USA) 8.1f **(73)** - Sharp Ego (USA) (Sharpen Up) 8.3f **(67)**
Form - 22312080
Record 1998 - 1st:1 2nd:3 3rd:1 Ran:8
Pre1998 - 1st:0 2nd:1 3rd:0 Ran:1
Win Prizemoney £4,077 *Total Prizemoney* £12,106
Wins * **1998** Jun Folkes (G-F) 6f 81 <
1998 Turf 1-7: (5f 2, 6f 1-3, 7f 2) (g-s, gd 2, g-f 1-2, frm 2) 1998 AW 0-1: (8f) (Fibr)
Decent, effective 6 to 7f, best at 6f, acts on gd to frm. Turf high 84 - 2nd of 8 giving 24lb to Scissor Ridge (15 Jly Folkestone 6f frm RF 2824) - also 1st of 11 from Great News (26 Jun Folkestone RF 2295). Dropped back in trip to break his duck in a Folkestone maiden. **M Bell [1-9] Luciano Gaucci.*

EIDER HILL BHB 34f RR 38f
4275[19]

4 b f Alawir (FR) - Matrah (Northfields (USA)) 9f **(72)**
Form - 00760
Record 1998 - 1st:0 2nd:0 3rd:0 Ran:5
Pre1998 - 1st:0 2nd:0 3rd:0 Ran:3
1998 Turf 0-5: (7f, 8f 3, 10f) (g-s, gd, frm 3)
Scopey, very moderate filly, has worn blinkers. Turf high 38. Inconsistent. **D Morris [0-8] W J Cornish.*

EI EI BHB 72f RR 80f
4822[17]

3 b c North Briton 8.2f **(53)** - Branitska (Mummy's Pet) 7.7f **(60)**
Form - 10600300
Record 1998 - 1st:1 2nd:0 3rd:1 Ran:8
Pre1998 - 1st:0 2nd:0 3rd:1 Ran:3
Win Prizemoney £1,720 *Total Prizemoney* £2,823
Wins * **1998** Apr Folkes (SFT) 7f 86 <
1998 Turf 1-8: (7f 1-3, 8f 5) (gd 1-5, g-f, frm 2)
Leggy, decent colt, effective 7 to 8f, best at 7f, acts on gd. Turf high 86 (1st run) - 1st of 10 from King of The River (21 Apr Folkestone RF 0779).
**B W Hills [1-10] W J Gredley (from C E Brittain [0-1] Jly 1997).*

EIFFEL TIGER (IRE) BHB 42f **RR 43f** 4504[10]
3 b br g Paris House 5.9f **(64)** - Rosa Bengala (Balidar) 7.9f **(63)**
Form - 0008450
Record 1998 - 1st:0 2nd:0 3rd:0 Ran:7
Pre1998 - 1st:0 2nd:0 3rd:0 Ran:3
1998 Turf 0-7: (6f, 7f, 8f 4, 9f) (gd 3, frm 4)
Neat, moderate gelding, has worn blinkers. Turf high 43. Inconsistent. *Bob Jones [0-10] Mrs Joan Marioni.*

EIGHT (IRE) RR 65f 4699[10]
2 ch c Thatching 7.8f **(69)** - Up To You (Sallust) 8.4f **(63)**
Form - 0
Record 1998 - 1st:0 2nd:0 3rd:0 Ran:1
1998 Turf 0-1: (6f) (gd)
Currently average colt. *M J Heaton-Ellis [0-1] Mrs Anthony Andrews.*

EILEAN SHONA BHB 82f **RR 75+f** 5077[6]
2 b f Suave Dancer (USA) 10.7f **(68)** - Moidart **(88f)** (Electric) 10.1f **(61)**
Form - 816
Record 1998 - 1st:1 2nd:0 3rd:0 Ran:3
Win Prizemoney £3,548 *Total Prizemoney* £3,659
Wins * **1998** Spt Redcar (G-F) 9f 75 <
1998 Turf 1-3: (7f, 9f 1-1, 10f) (g-s, frm 1-2)
Currently above-average filly. Turf high 75 (began Aug) - 1st of 5 getting 5lb from Gold Lodge (25 Spt Redcar RF 4484). Improved from her debut to win narrowly over nine furlongs at Redcar in October. The form of that race is difficult to evaluate, and she was never going on her final start.
J R Fanshawe [1-3] Dr Catherine Wills.

EILEEN'S LADY BHB 33f43a **RR 21f 43a** 3848[10]
4 b f Mtoto 11.5f **(71)** - Laughsome (Be My Guest (USA)) 9.3f **(67)**
Form - 737040
Record 1998 - 1st:0 2nd:0 3rd:1 Ran:6
Pre1998 - 1st:0 2nd:0 3rd:0 Ran:2
Win Prizemoney £0 *Total Prizemoney* £386
1998 Turf 0-3: (8f, 10f, 12f) (sft, g-f, frm) 1998 AW 0-3: (8f, 10f 2) (Equi 2, Fibr)
Leggy, moderate filly, effective 10f, - acts on Equi, likes left handed tracks. Turf high 21. AW high 44 (1st run) - 3rd of 8 getting 19lb from Tallulah Belle (8 May Lingfield 10f Equi RF 1102).
G G Margarson [0-8] John Guest.

EIRAWE (FR) RR 873[11]
5 b g Lashkari 13.1f **(52)** - Ederiya (FR) (Top Ville) 11.7f **(68)**
Form - 0
Record 1998 - 1st:0 2nd:0 3rd:0 Ran:1
1998 AW 0-1: (8f) (Fibr)
Formerly very poor gelding - 11th of 13 giving 18lb to Landrfun (25 Apr Wolverhampton 8f Fibr RF 0873).
Paddy Farrell [0-2] Mrs Suzanne Fletcher.

EKANS RR 20f 3044[14]
7 b m Hello Sonny - Snake (The Brianstan) 5.9f **(55)**
Form - 0
Record 1998 - 1st:0 2nd:0 3rd:0 Ran:1
1998 Turf 0-1: (8f) (frm)
Currently little account mare. *P Bowen [0-1] D R James.*

ELA AGAPI MOU (USA) BHB 58f50a **RR 62+f 50a** 1133[7]
5 b g Storm Bird (CAN) 8.5f **(82)** - Vaguar (USA) (Vaguely Noble) 10.1f **(72)**
Form - 17
Record 1998 - 1st:1 2nd:0 3rd:0 Ran:2
Pre1998 - 1st:0 2nd:1 3rd:1 Ran:10
Win Prizemoney £3,131 *Total Prizemoney* £4,012
Wins * **1998** Apr Folkes (SFT) H 15.4f 48 62+ <
1998 Turf 1-2: (15f 1-1, 17f) (sft 1-1, frm)
Average gelding. Turf high 62 (1st run) - 1st of 9 giving 5lb to Kingsfold Pet (21 Apr Folkestone RF 0781). A winning hurdler, he showed his first Flat form for quite a while when winning on heavy ground at Folkestone in April with a ton in hand. He can win again under those conditions.
G L Moore [6-17] Action II (from A Moore [0-3] Jan 1997).

ELA-ANDRULLA (IRE) BHB 46f **RR 41f** 5121[12]
3 b f Rainbows For Life (CAN) 9.3f **(64)** - Rep's Retton (USA) (J O Tobin (USA)) 9.4f **(67)**
Form - 50606070
Record 1998 - 1st:0 2nd:0 3rd:0 Ran:8
1998 Turf 0-8: (6f 2, 7f 5, 8f) (g-s, gd, g-f 4, frm 2)
Scopey, moderate filly. Turf high 55. Consistent.
G Lewis [0-8] Mrs Andry Muinos.

ELABELLOU (IRE) BHB 42f **RR 47f** 169[4]
3 b f Ela-Mana-Mou 12.7f **(72)** - Salabella (Sallust) 8.4f **(63)**
Form - 0664
Record 1998 - 1st:0 2nd:0 3rd:0 Ran:2
Pre1998 - 1st:0 2nd:0 3rd:0 Ran:3
1998 AW 0-2: (10f 2) (Equi 2)
Scopey, moderate filly. AW high 41.
M Johnston [0-5] Montagu Bloodstock Ltd.

ELANAAKA RR 102f 5050a[3]
3 ch f Lion Cavern (USA) 7.5f **(74)** - Mousaiha (USA) (Shadeed (USA)) 8.2f **(70)**
Form - 373
1998 Turf 0-3: (7f, 10f 2) (hvy, sft, g-s)
Tall, very useful filly. Turf high 102 (1st run) (began Aug) - 3rd of 5 to Zainta (22 Aug Deauville 10f sft RF 3913a). Trained by the late David Morley as a juvenile, she proved herself a useful performer in France, running her best race when finishing third in a Group Three at Deauville in August.
J E Hammond in FR [0-3] Sheikh Hamdan Al Maktoum (from D Morley [0-2] Spt 1997).

ELA-YIE-MOU (IRE) BHB 51f **RR 56df** 765[10]
5 ch g Kris 10f **(75)** - Green Lucia (Green Dancer (USA)) 10.3f **(74)**
Form - 0
Record 1998 - 1st:0 2nd:0 3rd:0 Ran:1
Pre1998 - 1st:1 2nd:0 3rd:3 Ran:18
Win Prizemoney £3,622 *Total Prizemoney* £5,720
Wins 1996 May Nottin (G-F) H 14.1f 73 76 <
1998 Turf 0-1: (12f) (g-s)
Fair gelding, effective 14 to 16f, best at 14f, acts on g-f to frm, best on frm. Inconsistent.
S Dow [0-17] Hatfield Ltd (from L M Cumani [1-9] Aug 1996).

EL BAILADOR (IRE) BHB 50f50a **RR 65?f 50a** 54[11]
7 b g Dance of Life (USA) 9.3f **(69)** - Sharp Ego (USA) (Sharpen Up) 8.3f **(67)**
Form - 00
Record 1998 - 1st:0 2nd:0 3rd:0 Ran:1
Pre1998 - 1st:3 2nd:3 3rd:1 Ran:23
Win Prizemoney £9,206 *Total Prizemoney* £15,090
Wins * 1996 *Feb Southw (STD)* *12f* *54*
* 1995 Aug Nottin (G-F) H 10f 58 65 <
* 1995 *Jun Lingfi (STD) H* *8f* *58 60*
1998 AW 0-1: (16f) (Fibr)
Average gelding, has worn blinkers. Becoming disappointing.
J D Bethell [3-24] Mrs John Lee.

ELBA MAGIC (IRE) BHB 64f63a **RR 66f 63a** 4996[10]
3 b f Faustus (USA) 9.1f **(54)** -Dependable (Formidable (USA)) 9.2f **(63)**
Form - 14233153180200
Record 1998 - 1st:3 2nd:2 3rd:3 Ran:14
Pre1998 - 1st:0 2nd:0 3rd:0 Ran:4
Win Prizemoney £7,521 *Total Prizemoney* £10,971
Wins * **1998** Aug Ripon (G-F) H 10f 63 66 <
* **1998** Jly Yarmou (GD) H 10.1f 60 63
* **1998** *Apr Southw (STD) H* *7f* *55 63*
1998 Turf 2-11: (8f 3, 9f, 10f 2-7) (g-s 2, gd 1-4, g-f, frm 3, hrd 1-1)
1998 AW 1-3: (7f 1-1, 8f, 10f) (Equi, Fibr 1-2)
Workmanlike, average filly, effective 7 to 10f, best at 8f, acts on gd to hrd - acts on Fibr, best on gd, likes left handed tracks, likes tight tracks, and excels at Southwell. Turf high 66 - 1st of 18 giving 22lb to Mrs Middle (31 Aug Ripon RF 4001) - also 1st of 8 getting 24lb from Polar Champ (2 Jly Yarmouth RF 2478). AW high 66 - 4th of 16 getting 2lb from Dina Line (11 May Southwell 8f Fibr RF 1154) - also 1st of 14 giving 11lb to Miss All Alone (27 Apr Southwell RF 0889). Showed little at two, but got off the mark in a very modest-looking fillies' handicap on the Southwell Fibresand on her return. Ran well on turf afterwards, including victories at Yarmouth and Ripon.
C A Dwyer [3-17] Graham Mitchell (from H J Collingridge [0-1] Jly 1997).

ELBARREE (IRE) BHB 82f **RR 81f** 3767[1]

3 b g Green Desert (USA) 7.8f **(78)** - Walimu (IRE) (Top Ville) 11.7f **(68)**

Form - 13037441

Record 1998 - 1st:2 2nd:0 3rd:2 Ran:8
Pre1998 - 1st:0 2nd:0 3rd:0 Ran:1

Win Prizemoney £6,920 *Total Prizemoney* £8,983

Wins * **1998** Aug Yarmou (FRM) H 7f 77 81 <
* **1998** Mar Nottin (G-S) 8.2f 74

1998 Turf 2-8: (7f 1-3, 8f 1-4, 9f) (sft, g-s 1-1, gd 2, g-f, frm 1-3)

Scopey, decent gelding, effective 7 to 8f, best at 7f, acts on g-s to frm, best on frm, has worn blinkers. Turf high 81 - 1st of 10 getting 6lb from Rich In Love (20 Aug Yarmouth RF 3767) - also 1st of 11 from Alcayde (31 Mar Nottingham RF 0516). He won at Nottingham on his reappearance, but then only showed modest form until scoring at Kempton in August, though he was disqualified for causing interference. He managed to win at Yarmouth next time, though his nearest rival was badly handicapped by a slipping saddle. **M A Jarvis [2-9] Sheikh Ahmed Al Maktoum.*

ELBAZ (USA) **RR 55f** 1705[7]

2 ch c Thorn Dance (USA) 8.2f **(77)** - Stuttering (USA) (Ack Ack (USA)) 12.7f **(82)**

Form - 7

Record 1998 - 1st:0 2nd:0 3rd:0 Ran:1

1998 Turf 0-1: (6f) (gd)

Currently fair colt. **E A L Dunlop [0-1] Jaber Abdullah.*

ELEANOR RIGBY (IRE) **RR 10f** 5015[5]

2 b f Turtle Island (IRE) - Eleanor Antoinette (IRE) (Double Schwartz) 7.9f **(55)**

Form - 5

Record 1998 - 1st:0 2nd:0 3rd:0 Ran:1

1998 Turf 0-1: (7f) (gd)

Currently poor filly. **M Johnston [0-1] Mark Johnston Racing Ltd.*

ELECTION PROMISE BHB 73f **RR 72f** 4070[5]

2 b c Mujtahid (USA) 7.4f **(69)**-Trystero (Shareef Dancer(USA))9.9f **(73)**

Form - 02565

Record 1998 - 1st:0 2nd:1 3rd:0 Ran:5

Win Prizemoney £0 *Total Prizemoney* £1,084

1998 Turf 0-5: (7f 4, 8f) (gd 3, g-f 2)

Above-average colt. Turf high 72 (began Jly) - 5th of 17 getting 2lb from Ice (3 Spt York 8f g-f RF 4070). (DEAD)
**E A L Dunlop [0-5] Maktoum Al Maktoum.*

ELEGANT DANCE BHB 62f **RR 62f** 4390[18]

4 ch f Statoblest 6.4f **(63)**-Furry Dance (USA) (Nureyev (USA)) 8.7f **(78)**

Form - 0261000

Record 1998 - 1st:1 2nd:1 3rd:0 Ran:7
Pre1998 - 1st:0 2nd:0 3rd:0 Ran:3

Win Prizemoney £3,096 *Total Prizemoney* £3,771

Wins * **1998** Jun Salisb (G-F) H 6f 61 62 <

1998 Turf 1-7: (6f 1-4, 7f 2, 8f) (sft, g-f 2, frm 1-4)

Average filly, effective 6f, acts on frm. Turf high 62 - 1st of 14 giving 15lb to Heavenly Miss (25 Jun Salisbury RF 2278).
**J J Sheehan [1-10] Mrs Christina Dowling.*

ELEGANT FAN (USA) BHB 49f **RR 52f** 4801[10]

3 b br c Lear Fan (USA) 10.4f **(80)** - Elegance (USA) (Providential) 10.2f **(72)**

Form - 0560

Record 1998 - 1st:0 2nd:0 3rd:0 Ran:4

1998 Turf 0-4: (8f 2, 11f, 12f) (sft 2, g-s, frm)

Fair colt. Turf high 52.
**C E Brittain [0-4] The Thoroughbred Corporation.*

ELEGANT HERO (IRE) BHB 44f55a **RR 37f 55a** 4917[17]

3 b g Common Grounds 8.1f **(66)** - Good Relations (Be My Guest (USA)) 9.3f **(67)**

Form - 5086600

Record 1998 - 1st:0 2nd:0 3rd:0 Ran:7

1998 Turf 0-6: (8f 4, 10f 2) (g-s 2, gd 2, g-f 2) 1998 AW 0-1: (8f) (Equi)

Workmanlike, very moderate gelding, has worn blinkers. Turf high 66. **D Nicholls [0-1] W G Swiers (from R Hannon [0-6] Jly 1998).*

ELEGANT LADY **RR 82f** 5068[2]

2 ch f Selkirk (USA) 7.9f **(76)** - Prompting (Primo Dominie) 6.2f **(80)**

Form - 6042

Record 1998 - 1st:0 2nd:1 3rd:0 Ran:4

Win Prizemoney £0 *Total Prizemoney* £1,746

1998 Turf 0-4: (5f, 6f 2, 7f) (gd, g-f 3)

Decent filly. Turf high 79 - 2nd of 10 giving 14lb to Sound's Ace (30 Oct Newmarket 5f g-f RF 5068).
**J H M Gosden [0-4] Platt Promotions Ltd.*

ELEGANT RIDGE (IRE) **RR 101f** 4607a[3]

3 b f Indian Ridge 7.6f **(74)**-Elegant Bloom(Be My Guest(USA))9.3f **(67)**

Form - 23

1998 Turf 0-2: (8f 2) (hvy, sft)

Currently very useful filly. Turf high 101 (1st run) - 2nd of 11 to Elle Danzig (3 May Dusseldorf 8f sft RF 1093a). She finished second in the German 1,000 Guineas and was far from disgraced in an Italian Listed race. **H Blume in GER [0-2].*

ELEVENTH DUKE (IRE) BHB 84f **RR 79f** 4741[4]

3 b c Imperial Frontier (USA) 7f **(65)** - Disregard That (IRE) (Don't Forget Me) 8.3f **(74)**

Form - 08200064

Record 1998 - 1st:0 2nd:1 3rd:0 Ran:8
Pre1998 - 1st:2 2nd:1 3rd:1 Ran:9

Win Prizemoney £6,170 *Total Prizemoney* £12,756

Wins 1997 Aug Chepst (GD) H 5.1f 85 89+ <
1997 Aug Bath (GD) H 5.7f 79 83

1998 Turf 0-8: (5f, 6f 6, 7f) (hvy, g-s, gd 3, g-f, frm 2)

Above-average colt, effective 5 to 6f, best at 5f, acts on gd to frm, best on gd. Turf high 85 - 2nd of 9 giving 4lb to Robin Goodfellow (3 May Salisbury 6f gd RF 1002). Sold for 14,500 gns after his final start. **J Noseda [0-4] Lucayan Stud (from R Hannon [2-13] May 1998).*

ELFINAUNT **RR 60f** 1129[6]

3 ch f Magic Ring (IRE) 6.5f **(64)** - Aunt Judy (Great Nephew) 9.9f **(64)**

Form - 6

Record 1998 - 1st:0 2nd:0 3rd:0 Ran:1

1998 Turf 0-1: (8f) (frm)

Scopey, currently average filly. **I A Balding [0-1] M E Wates.*

ELFLAND (IRE) BHB 84f **RR 85f** 2365[15]

7 b g Fairy King (USA) 7.7f **(75)** - Ridge The Times (USA) (Riva Ridge (USA)) 8.2f **(68)**

Form - 430

Record 1998 - 1st:0 2nd:0 3rd:1 Ran:3
Pre1998 - 1st:2 2nd:0 3rd:2 Ran:14

Win Prizemoney £13,951 *Total Prizemoney* £22,187

Wins * 1997 Jun Newmar (G-S) H 7f 81 84 <
* 1995 May Doncas (GD) H 7f 77 82

1998 Turf 0-3: (7f 2, 8f) (g-s, gd 2)

Useful gelding, has broken blood-vessels, effective 7f, acts on gd to frm. Turf high 85.
**Lady Herries [2-12] The High Flying Partnership (from J H M Gosden [0-5] Aug 1994).*

EL FUERTE BHB 45f **RR 54f** 4002[12]

3 b g Perpendicular - Sleekit (Blakeney) 10.5f **(64)**

Form - 00500

Record 1998 - 1st:0 2nd:0 3rd:0 Ran:5

1998 Turf 0-4: (10f 3, 11f) (gd 2, g-f, frm) 1998 AW 0-1: (14f) (Fibr)

Workmanlike, fair gelding. Turf high 54.
**P J Makin [0-5] R J K Roberts.*

EL GHAAZEE (USA) BHB 60f67a **RR 63f 67a** 2392[7]

3 ch c Arazi (USA) 9.2f **(74)** - Gesedeh (Ela-Mana-Mou) 10.1f **(70)**

Form - 42017

Record 1998 - 1st:1 2nd:1 3rd:0 Ran:5

Win Prizemoney £2,574 *Total Prizemoney* £3,844

Wins * **1998** *Jun Wolver (STD) H 9.4f 63 64* <

1998 Turf 0-4: (8f, 10f 2, 12f) (g-s, gd, g-f 2) 1998 AW 1-1: (9f 1-1) (Fibr 1-1)

Lengthy, average colt. Turf high 63. (1st run) - 1st of 10 giving 22lb to Saxon Victory (20 Jun Wolverhampton RF 2164). Got off the mark in a terrible maiden handicap on the Wolverhampton Fibresand in June. He will be fortunate to find another race as bad.
**M A Jarvis [1-5] Sheikh Ahmed Al Maktoum.*

ELHABUB BHB 70f **RR 75f** 5070[2]
3 b c Lion Cavern (USA) 7.5f **(74)** - Million Heiress (Auction Ring (USA)) 8.6f **(65)**
Form - 550422
Record 1998 - 1st:0 2nd:2 3rd:0 Ran:6
Pre1998 - 1st:0 2nd:3 3rd:0 Ran:3
Win Prizemoney £0 *Total Prizemoney* £8,888
1998 Turf 0-6: (6f, 7f, 8f 2, 9f, 10f) (sft, gd 2, g-f 3)
Scopey, above-average colt, effective 6 to 10f, best at 6f, acts on sft to gd, best on gd. Turf high 75 - 2nd of 12 to Shamawan (23 Oct Newbury 10f sft RF 4968). Consistent.
**Miss Gay Kelleway [0-3] Paul & Andrew Swaffield (from B W Hills [0-6] Jun 1998).*

ELHAYQ (IRE) BHB 94f **RR 95f** 4734[2]
3 b c Nashwan (USA) 10.3f **(79)**-Mahasin (USA)(Danzig(USA))8.4f **(76)**
Form - 2127642
Record 1998 - 1st:1 2nd:3 3rd:0 Ran:7
Pre1998 - 1st:0 2nd:0 3rd:1 Ran:2
Win Prizemoney £3,938 *Total Prizemoney* £12,840
Wins * **1998** Apr Thirsk (G-S) 12f 86 <
1998 Turf 1-7: (10f, 12f 1-3, 14f 2, 15f) (sft, g-s 1-2, gd 3, g-f)
Rangy, very useful colt, effective 12 to 15f, acts on g-s to g-f, best on gd. Turf high 95 - 2nd of 11 giving 11lb to Robin Lane (9 Oct Ascot 12f g-s RF 4734) - also 1st of 8 giving 5lb to Bint Kaldoun (17 Apr Thirsk RF 0736). Consistent. Easy winner of a soft-ground maiden, he has run respectably since in handicap company. Good second on final start at Ascot, rallying well after being headed.
**J L Dunlop [1-9] Hamdan Al Maktoum.*

ELHIDA (IRE) BHB 100f **RR 95f** 4242[13]
2 ch f Mujtahid (USA) 7.4f **(69)** - Nouvelle Star (AUS) (Luskin Star (AUS)) 6.3f **(71)**
Form - 210
Record 1998 - 1st:1 2nd:1 3rd:0 Ran:3
Win Prizemoney £6,937 *Total Prizemoney* £8,665
Wins * **1998** Jly Goodwo (GD) 6f 95+ <
1998 Turf 1-3: (5f, 6f 1-2) (gd 1-1, g-f, frm)
Currently very useful filly. Turf high 95 (began Jly) - 1st of 6 from Kalidasa (28 Jly Goodwood RF 3167). A sharp sort, she showed plenty of pace when runner-up at Newmarket on her debut. Looked very promising when easily landing the odds in a maiden at Goodwood, but finished last in a Group Two event at Doncaster. Clearly something was amiss that day, and she still remains a very useful filly in the making. **M P Tregoning [1-3] Hamdan Al Maktoum.*

ELITE HOPE (USA) BHB 57f65a **RR 47f 65a** 1795[2]
6 ch m Moment of Hope (USA) 6.9f **(80)** - Chervil (USA) (Greenough (USA)) 6.9f **(85)**
Form - 013214612102
Record 1998 - 1st:3 2nd:3 3rd:0 Ran:9
Pre1998 - 1st:5 2nd:4 3rd:2 Ran:32
Win Prizemoney £21,383 *Total Prizemoney* £29,172
Wins * **1998** *Apr Wolver (STD) C 7f 66*
* **1998** *Mar Wolver (STD) C 7f 67*
* **1998** *Jan Wolver (STD) C 7f 77*
* 1997 *Nov Wolver (STD) C 6f 60*
* 1997 *Jan Wolver (SLW) H 7f 67 71*
* 1996 *Dec Wolver (STD) H 7f 64 66*
* 1996 *Nov Wolver (STD) H 7f 52 60*
1994 Oct Yarmou (GD) 7f 85+
1998 Turf 0-1: (8f) (g-f) 1998 AW 3-8: (6f 3, 7f 3-5) (Fibr 3-8)
Above-average mare, effective 6 to 7f, best at 7f, - acts on Fibr, has worn blinkers, favours left handed tracks, excels at Wolverhampton. AW high 77 - 1st of 12 giving 1lb to Theatre Magic (28 Jan Wolverhampton RF 0172). Seven furlongs at Wolverhampton are her optimum conditions, especially in non-handicap company, though she can win over six if allowed to dominate.
**N Tinkler [7-25] Elite Racing Club (from C R Egerton [1-16] Spt 1996).*

ELIZA ACTON BHB 74f **RR 74f** 3659[12]
3 b f Shirley Heights 12.1f **(76)** - Sing Softly (Luthier) 9.8f **(71)**
Form - 00
Record 1998 - 1st:0 2nd:0 3rd:0 Ran:2
Pre1998 - 1st:1 2nd:0 3rd:0 Ran:2
Win Prizemoney £3,460 *Total Prizemoney* £3,460
Wins * 1997 Oct Nottin (GD) 8.2f 74 <
1998 Turf 0-2: (10f 2) (gd, g-f)
Workmanlike, above-average filly. Turf high 61. Got off the mark when coming out best in a blanket finish to a Nottingham maiden in October '97, but was off the track a long time after her debut this term and must have had a problem. She is bred to stay well.
**P W Harris [1-4] Mrs P W Harris.*

EL JAYTEE BHB 40f44a **RR 46f 44a** 4671[17]
2 b c Anshan 8.2f **(63)** - Better Still (IRE) (Glenstal (USA)) 10.1f **(64)**
Form - 480000
Record 1998 - 1st:0 2nd:0 3rd:0 Ran:6
1998 Turf 0-5: (5f, 6f 2, 7f 2) (g-s, g-f, frm 3) 1998 AW 0-1: (5f) (Fibr)
Moderate colt. Turf high 46. **M W Easterby [0-6] Mrs Jean Turpin.*

ELJJANAH (USA) BHB 79f **RR 82f** 3845[1]
3 b c Riverman (USA) 9.7f **(78)** - True Celebrity (USA) (Lyphard (USA)) 9.9f **(72)**
Form - 6351
Record 1998 - 1st:1 2nd:0 3rd:1 Ran:4
Pre1998 - 1st:0 2nd:1 3rd:1 Ran:3
Win Prizemoney £3,720 *Total Prizemoney* £5,958
Wins * **1998** Aug Lingfi (G-F) 6f 82 <
1998 Turf 1-4: (6f 1-2, 7f 2) (gd, g-f, frm 1-2)
Leggy, decent colt, effective 6 to 7f, acts on frm. Turf high 82 - 1st of 8 from Doraid (25 Aug Lingfield RF 3845).
**J L Dunlop [1-7] Hamdan Al Maktoum.*

EL KARIM (USA) RR 71f 3211[3]
2 ch c Storm Cat (USA) 7f **(86)** - Gmaasha (IRE) (Kris) 9.5f **(73)**
Form - 03
Record 1998 - 1st:0 2nd:0 3rd:1 Ran:2
Win Prizemoney £0 *Total Prizemoney* £807
1998 Turf 0-2: (6f, 7f) (g-f 2)
Currently above-average colt. Turf high 71 (began Jly). Needed the outing and met trouble in running on his debut, and still looked green second time. Should do better.
**J L Dunlop [0-2] Hamdan Al Maktoum.*

ELKEYVOR RR 55f 2332[14]
3 b g Elmaamul (USA) 8.1f **(70)** - Petonica (IRE) (Petoski) 5.7f **(62)**
Form - 80
Record 1998 - 1st:0 2nd:0 3rd:0 Ran:2
1998 Turf 0-2: (10f, 12f) (g-s, gd)
Workmanlike, currently fair gelding. Turf high 55.
**T D Easterby [0-2] H Key.*

ELLA FALLS (IRE) BHB 33f34a **RR 35f 34a** 4399[5]
3 ch f Dancing Dissident (USA) 6.8f **(65)** - Over Swing (FR) (Saint Cyrien (FR)) 8.4f **(80)**
Form - 0340P68658000055
Record 1998 - 1st:0 2nd:0 3rd:1 Ran:15
Pre1998 - 1st:0 2nd:0 3rd:0 Ran:4
Win Prizemoney £0 *Total Prizemoney* £442
1998 Turf 0-10: (6f 2, 7f, 8f 5, 10f 2) (g-s 2, gd 2, g-f, frm 5) 1998 AW 0-5: (7f, 8f 4) (Fibr 5)
Neat, fair filly, effective 6f, acts on frm, has worn blinkers. Turf high 52. AW high 51.
**Miss J F Craze [0-12] Chris Cockcroft (from D Nicholls [0-4] Feb 1998).*

ELLA LAMEES BHB 52f **RR 51f** 3739[4]
4 b f Statoblest 6.4f **(63)** - Lamees (USA) (Lomond (USA)) 8.8f **(65)**
Form - 00544
Record 1998 - 1st:0 2nd:0 3rd:0 Ran:5
Pre1998 - 1st:1 2nd:1 3rd:0 Ran:9
Win Prizemoney £3,759 *Total Prizemoney* £4,928
Wins * 1997 Jly Windso (G-F) H 6f 55 60 <
1998 Turf 0-5: (6f 3, 7f, 8f) (gd, g-f 2, frm 2)
Unfurnished, fair filly, effective 6 to 8f, best at 6f, acts on frm. Turf high 51 - 4th of 11 getting 13lb from Mouche (5 Aug Leicester 8f frm RF 3379). **W J Musson [1-14] Billings & Broughton.*

ELLAMINE BHB 38a **RR 38a** 312[5]
4 b f Warrshan (USA) 9.7f **(59)** - Anhaar (Ela-Mana-Mou) 10.1f **(70)**
Form - 16605
Record 1998 - 1st:0 2nd:0 3rd:0 Ran:4
Pre1998 - 1st:1 2nd:0 3rd:0 Ran:3

Win Prizemoney £1,738 *Total Prizemoney* £1,738
Wins * 1997 *Dec Wolver (STD) S 14.8f 40* <
1998 AW 0-4: (12f 2, 16f 2) (Equi 2, Fibr 2)
Light-framed, very moderate filly, effective 15f, - acts on Fibr, has worn blinkers. AW high 32. She won a very modest seller on the Wolverhampton Fibresand in December, and her subsequent performances have confirmed what a bad race that must have been.
**D HaydnJones [1-7] G J Hicks.*

ELLE DANZIG (GER) RR 113f 4714a[1]
3 b f Roi Danzig (USA) 10.5f **(62)** - Elegie (GER) (Teotepec (GER))
Form - 111141
1998 Turf 5-6: (8f 1-1, 10f 2-2, 11f 2-2, 12f) (sft 5-6)
Group-class filly, effective 8 to 12f, acts on sft. Turf high 113 - 1st of 7 getting 15lb from Artan (2 Aug Munich RF 3424a) - also 1st of 7 getting 22lb from Oxalagu (28 Jun Hamburg RF 2482a). She had a tremendous season, winning the German 1,000 Guineas and Oaks and only tasting defeat once from seven starts. She has proven herself against the best from every generation at home, and should extend her reputation when sent to race abroad. We look forward to seeing more of her in 1999.
**A Schutz in GER [5-6] Gestut Wittekindshof.*

ELLEGANT GENT RR 32f 926[11]
3 b c Pharly (FR) 11.5f **(64)** - Ellegant Model (Latest Model) 6f **(62)**
Form - 00
Record 1998 - 1st:0 2nd:0 3rd:0 Ran:2
1998 Turf 0-2: (10f 2) (gd 2)
Workmanlike, currently very moderate colt. Turf high 32.
**J Pearce [0-2] Hazzar Partnership.*

ELLENBER BHB 45f49a RR 49f 49a 4256[12]
3 ch g Risk Me (FR) 8f **(53)** - Brig of Ayr (Brigadier Gerard) 9.3f **(58)**
Form - 54502000
Record 1998 - 1st:0 2nd:1 3rd:0 Ran:8
Pre1998 - 1st:0 2nd:0 3rd:1 Ran:8
Win Prizemoney £0 *Total Prizemoney* £1,038
1998 Turf 0-8: (7f, 8f 5, 9f, 12f) (sft, g-s, gd 3, g-f, frm 2)
Workmanlike, fair gelding, effective 8f, acts on g-s to g-f, has worn blinkers, likes right handed tracks, prefers tight tracks. Turf high 49 - 2nd of 14 to Margaret's Dancer (15 Jun Pontefract 8f g-s RF 1999). Becoming disappointing.
**W McKeown [0-16] Mrs L E McKeown.*

ELLENBROOK (IRE) BHB 61f63a RR 53f 63a 1742[9]
3 b f Petorius 8f **(66)** - Short Stay (Be My Guest (USA)) 9.3f **(67)**
Form - 2740
Record 1998 - 1st:0 2nd:1 3rd:0 Ran:4
Pre1998 - 1st:4 2nd:4 3rd:2 Ran:12
Win Prizemoney £9,269 *Total Prizemoney* £13,630
Wins * 1997 Jun Mussel (G-S) C 5f 64
* 1997 Jun Hamilt (G-S) C 5f 65 <
* 1997 *May Wolver (STD) S 6f 65+*
* 1997 *May Southw (STD) S 5f 56*
1998 Turf 0-1: (5f) (gd) 1998 AW 0-3: (5f, 6f 2) (Fibr 3)
Scopey, average filly, effective 5 to 6f, best at 5f, acts on gd to frm - acts on Fibr, best on frm, mostly wears blinkers (effectively). AW high 63. **J Berry [4-16] J K Brown.*

ELLENICA (IRE) RR 101f 2292a[1]
3 f Tenby 10.4f **(76)** - Elevated (Shirley Heights) 10.3f **(74)**
Form - 41
1998 Turf 1-2: (11f, 12f 1-1) (hvy, g-f 1-1)
Currently very useful filly. Turf high 101 - 1st of 10 getting 13lb from Ridaiyma (21 Jun San Siro RF 2292a). Fourth in the Italian Oaks, she did well to catch Ridaiyma in a Group Three in June. That form is useful and she is capable of winning another decent prize. **M Guarnieri in ITY [1-2] Scuderia Cocky.*

ELLENS ACADEMY (IRE) BHB 59f RR 70f 4760[12]
3 b c Royal Academy (USA) 7.8f **(77)** - Lady Ellen (Horage) 10.3f **(61)**
Form - 43720
Record 1998 - 1st:0 2nd:1 3rd:1 Ran:5
Win Prizemoney £0 *Total Prizemoney* £1,388
1998 Turf 0-5: (7f, 8f 3, 10f) (gd 2, g-f, frm 2)
Above-average colt, has worn blinkers. Turf high 70.
**E J Alston [0-2] Mrs Chris Harrington (from D K Weld in IRE [0-3] Jly 1998).*

ELLENS LAD (IRE) BHB 86f RR 88f 4975[3]
4 b g Polish Patriot (USA) 7.8f **(70)** - Lady Ellen (Horage) 10.3f **(61)**
Form - 4601668063
Record 1998 - 1st:1 2nd:0 3rd:1 Ran:10
Pre1998 - 1st:2 2nd:1 3rd:1 Ran:13
Win Prizemoney £13,543 *Total Prizemoney* £18,356
Wins * **1998** Jly Newmar (G-F) H 5f 81 86 <
1996 Nov Newmar (GD) H 5f 77 86 <
1996 Spt Folkes (G-F) H 5f 72 76
1998 Turf 1-10: (5f 1-6, 6f 4) (sft 2, g-s, gd 4, g-f 2, frm 1-1)
Scopey, useful gelding, effective 5 to 6f, best at 5f, acts on sft to frm, best on gd, has worn blinkers. Turf high 88 - also 1st of 14 giving 17lb to Mousehole (7 Jly Newmarket RF 2584). High in the handicap at three, but bounced back to score at the July Meeting, relishing the fast conditions. Not at all disgraced after, he was sold for 20,000 gns in October and will join Willie Musson.
**E J Alston [1-10] Mrs Chris Harrington (from R Hannon [2-13] Jly 1997).*

ELLE QUESTRO BHB 40f RR 29f 4983[12]
2 b f Rainbow Quest (USA) 11.2f **(81)** - Lady Be Mine (USA) (Sir Ivor) 10.2f **(70)**
Form - 000
Record 1998 - 1st:0 2nd:0 3rd:0 Ran:3
1998 Turf 0-3: (7f, 8f 2) (g-s 2, frm)
Currently little account filly. Turf high 29 (began Spt).
**J L Dunlop [0-3] Mrs Mark Burrell.*

ELLERBECK BHB 48f RR 56f 4355[8]
3 b f Priolo (USA) 10.9f **(71)** - Cadisa (Top Ville) 11.7f **(68)**
Form - 704408
Record 1998 - 1st:0 2nd:0 3rd:0 Ran:6
Pre1998 - 1st:0 2nd:0 3rd:0 Ran:2
1998 Turf 0-6: (10f, 11f, 16f 2, 17f 2) (sft, gd, g-f, frm 3)
Leggy, fair filly. Turf high 64. Inconsistent.
**J M Jefferson [0-8] & Mrs J M Davenport.*

ELLEYSANTA BHB 43f40a RR 48f 40a 5006[15]
3 b f Warrshan (USA) 9.7f **(59)** - Sophisticated Baby (Bairn (USA)) 7.7f **(59)**
Form - 6000017300
Record 1998 - 1st:1 2nd:0 3rd:1 Ran:9
Pre1998 - 1st:0 2nd:0 3rd:0 Ran:8
Win Prizemoney £2,458 *Total Prizemoney* £3,261
Wins * **1998** Jly Salisb (G-F) C 6f 45 <
1998 Turf 1-8: (6f 1-1, 7f 2, 8f 4, 12f) (sft, g-f 1-4, frm 3) 1998 AW 0-1: (8f) (Fibr)
Leggy, moderate filly, effective 6f, acts on hrd, has worn blinkers. Turf high 48. **A G Newcombe [1-17] Advanced Marketing Services Ltd.*

ELLIE MAI RR 11f 2437[6]
2 b f Distant Relative 7f **(69)** - Nigel's Dream (Pyjama Hunt) 11.1f **(38)**
Form - 7486
Record 1998 - 1st:0 2nd:0 3rd:0 Ran:4
1998 Turf 0-3: (5f, 6f, 7f) (sft, frm 2) 1998 AW 0-1: (5f) (Equi)
Poor filly. Turf high 11. (DEAD) **W G M Turner [0-4] A Pryer.*

ELLOPASSOFF BHB 62f RR 64f 2303[15]
6 b m Librate 10.4f **(37)** - Elena Patino (Dubassoff (USA)) 14.2f **(55)**
Form - 0661170
Record 1998 - 1st:2 2nd:0 3rd:0 Ran:7
Win Prizemoney £5,943 *Total Prizemoney* £5,943
Wins * **1998** Jun Chepst (G-S) H 10.2f 59 64 <
* **1998** May Warwic (G-F) H 8f 55 58
1998 Turf 2-6: (8f 1-3, 9f, 10f 1-2) (gd 1-3, g-f, frm 1-2) 1998 AW 0-1: (9f) (Fibr)
Average mare, effective 8 to 10f, acts on gd to frm. Turf high 64 - 1st of 5 getting 4lb from Prizefighter (12 Jun Chepstow RF 1924) - also 1st of 20 getting 1lb from Roman Reel (23 May Warwick RF 1436). **J M Bradley [2-11] E R Griffiths.*

ELLWAY DANCER (IRE) RR 47f 5123[6]
2 b f Mujadil (USA) 7.7f **(70)** - Moonlight Partner (IRE) (Red Sunset) 8.2f **(63)**
Form - 06

Record 1998 - 1st:0 2nd:0 3rd:0 Ran:2
1998 Turf 0-2: (6f 2) (sft, g-s)
Currently moderate filly. Turf high 47 (began Oct).
**I A Balding [0-2] Ellway Racing.*

ELLWAY PRINCE BHB 55f68a **RR 57f 68a** 4877[2]
3 b g Prince Sabo 6.6f **(64)** - Star Arrangement (Star Appeal) 9.6f **(65)**
Form - 06084242
Record 1998 - 1st:0 2nd:2 3rd:0 Ran:8
Pre1998 - 1st:0 2nd:0 3rd:0 Ran:2
Win Prizemoney £0 *Total Prizemoney* £1,938
1998 Turf 0-6: (6f 2, 7f 3, 9f) (hvy, gd, g-f 3, frm) 1998 AW 0-2: (6f 2) (Fibr 2)
Workmanlike, average gelding, often wears blinkers. Turf high 57. AW high 60 (began Spt).
**Mrs N Macauley [0-2] Stephen Roots (from I A Balding [0-8] Spt 1998).*

ELLWAY STAR (IRE) RR 81+f 3843[1]
2 ch f Night Shift (USA) 8.1f **(73)** - Searching Star (Rainbow Quest (USA)) 10.4f **(75)**
Form - 1
Record 1998 - 1st:1 2nd:0 3rd:0 Ran:1
Win Prizemoney £3,850 *Total Prizemoney* £3,850
Wins * **1998** Aug Lingfi (G-F) 5f 81+ <
1998 Turf 1-1: (5f 1-1) (frm 1-1)
Currently decent filly. (1st run) - 1st of 13 from Deviletta (25 Aug Lingfield RF 3843). **B Hanbury [1-1] Ellway Racing.*

ELM DUST BHB 90f **RR 86f** 4773[2]
2 ch f Elmaamul (USA) 8.1f **(70)** - Galaxie Dust (USA) (Blushing Groom (FR)) 10.3f **(76)**
Form - 132
Record 1998 - 1st:1 2nd:1 3rd:1 Ran:3
Win Prizemoney £3,099 *Total Prizemoney* £5,725
Wins * **1998** Aug Leices (GD) 7f 82+ <
1998 Turf 1-3: (7f 1-3) (gd 2, frm 1-1)
Currently useful filly. Turf high 86 (began Aug) - 2nd of 7 getting 2lb from Conflict (13 Oct Leicester 7f gd RF 4773) - also 1st of 14 from Creme Caramel (10 Aug Leicester RF 3498).
**J L Dunlop [1-3] Hesmonds Stud.*

ELMHURST BOY RR 72f 4857[12]
2 b c Merdon Melody 6.8f **(56)** - Young Whip (Bold Owl) 8.5f **(45)**
Form - 30
Record 1998 - 1st:0 2nd:0 3rd:1 Ran:2
Win Prizemoney £0 *Total Prizemoney* £562
1998 Turf 0-2: (6f 2) (sft, frm)
Currently above-average colt. Turf high 72 (began Spt). Faced a stiff task behind Deadly Nightshade on his debut.
**S Dow [0-2] R E Anderson.*

ELMS SCHOOLGIRL BHB 71f68a **RR 70+f 68a** 2657[6]
2 ch f Emarati (USA) 6.6f **(63)** - Ascend (IRE) (Glint of Gold) 9.3f **(66)**
Form - 036
Record 1998 - 1st:0 2nd:0 3rd:1 Ran:3
Win Prizemoney £0 *Total Prizemoney* £520
1998 Turf 0-2: (5f, 6f) (g-f 2) 1998 AW 0-1: (6f) (Fibr)
Currently above-average filly. Turf high 70 - 3rd of 24 to Grey Princess (22 Jun Windsor 6f g-f RF 2182). Stepped on her debut with a good run next time, making a lot of the running and hampered close home, but for which she would have finished closer.
**J M P Eustace [0-3] Park Lodge Racing.*

ELMUTABAKI RR 64+f 5137[5]
2 b c Unfuwain (USA) 11.4f **(74)** - Bawaeth (USA) (Blushing Groom (FR)) 10.3f **(76)**
Form - 5
Record 1998 - 1st:0 2nd:0 3rd:0 Ran:1
1998 Turf 0-1: (7f) (gd)
Currently average colt. **B W Hills [0-1] Hamdan Al Maktoum.*

ELNADIM (USA) BHB 122f **RR 125f** 4105[12]
4 b br c Danzig (USA) 8.1f **(88)** - Elle Seule (USA) (Exclusive Native (USA)) 9.1f **(81)**
Form - 23100
Record 1998 - 1st:1 2nd:1 3rd:1 Ran:5
Pre1998 - 1st:4 2nd:2 3rd:0 Ran:8
Win Prizemoney £165,212 *Total Prizemoney* £192,294
Wins * **1998** Jly Newmar (FRM) G1 6f 125 <
* 1997 Spt Ascot (G-F) G2 6f 122++
* 1997 Aug Newmar (GD) L 6f 115
* 1997 Jly Yarmou (G-F) H 6f 94 102
* 1997 Jun Pontef (G-F) 6f 86
1998 Turf 1-5: (5f 2, 6f 1-3) (gd 2, frm 1-3)
Workmanlike, top-class colt, effective 6f, acts on gd to frm. Turf high 125 - 1st of 17 giving 6lb to Tamarisk (9 Jly Newmarket RF 2649). An outstanding performer on his day, he put up a brilliant performance to win the July Cup, breaking the track record in the process, but his reputation was subsequently dented. An interrupted preparation and the drop to five furlongs contributed to a poor showing in the Nunthorpe, and he could never land a blow in the Haydock Sprint Cup. He had run free and slightly below par on his first two runs this year, having established himself as a leading sprinter with a runaway success in the Diadem Stakes at Ascot in 1997. **J L Dunlop [5-13] Hamdan Al Maktoum.*

EL NAFIS (USA) BHB 82f **RR 80f** 4358[10]
2 b f Kingmambo (USA) 10.9f **(85)** - Ghashtah (USA) (Nijinsky (CAN)) 10.3f **(77)**
Form - 810
Record 1998 - 1st:1 2nd:0 3rd:0 Ran:3
Win Prizemoney £3,225 *Total Prizemoney* £3,225
Wins * **1998** Aug Chepst (G-F) 8.1f 80 <
1998 Turf 1-3: (7f 2, 8f 1-1) (gd 1-1, g-f, frm)
Currently decent filly. Turf high 80 (began Aug) - 1st of 7 from Summer Splendour (31 Aug Chepstow RF 3977).
**P T Walwyn [1-3] Hamdan Al Maktoum.*

EL NAHRAWAN (USA) RR 81f 3951[2]
2 br c Red Ransom (USA) 8.6f **(83)** - Woodja (USA) (Woodman (USA)) 9f **(74)**
Form - 42
Record 1998 - 1st:0 2nd:1 3rd:0 Ran:2
Win Prizemoney £0 *Total Prizemoney* £1,650
1998 Turf 0-2: (7f 2) (g-f, frm)
Currently decent colt. Turf high 81 (began Aug).
**M P Tregoning [0-2] Hamdan Al Maktoum.*

EL NIDO BHB 28f18a **RR 36f 18a** 1944[9]
10 ch g Adonijah 11.2f **(56)** - Seleter (Hotfoot) 10.5f **(59)**
Form - 00080
Record 1998 - 1st:0 2nd:0 3rd:0 Ran:3
Pre1998 - 1st:11 2nd:6 3rd:7 Ran:66
Win Prizemoney £27,497 *Total Prizemoney* £35,444
Wins * *1997 Feb Southw (STD) H 16f 58 61*
1997 Jan Southw (STD) C 16f 54
1995 Mar Southw (STD) C 14f 60
1995 Jan Southw (STD) C 16f 61
1994 Dec Southw (STD) H 14f 56 60
1994 Mar Southw (STD) H 12f 56 54
1998 AW 0-3: (11f, 14f 2) (Fibr 3)
Very moderate gelding, effective 12 to 16f, best at 16f, - acts on Fibr, has worn blinkers, likes left handed tracks. AW high 8.
**D W Chapman [1-22] David Chapman (from M J Camacho [10-47] Jan 1997).*

EL PICADOR RR 66f 4307[17]
2 b g Aragon 7.7f **(58)** - Hawaiian Bloom (USA) (Hawaii) 9.4f **(66)**
Form - 80
Record 1998 - 1st:0 2nd:0 3rd:0 Ran:2
1998 Turf 0-2: (5f 2) (gd, g-f)
Currently average gelding. Turf high 66.
**B J Meehan [0-2] Mario Lanfranchi.*

ELSA DAWN BHB 35f **RR 28f** 2451[6]
3 ch f Weldnaas (USA) 8.4f **(55)** -Agnes Jane (Sweet Monday) 8.3f **(25)**
Form - 8086
Record 1998 - 1st:0 2nd:0 3rd:0 Ran:4
1998 Turf 0-3: (6f, 7f, 10f) (gd 2, frm) 1998 AW 0-1: (8f) (Fibr)
Leggy, little account filly. Turf high 28.
**N Bycroft [0-4] Mrs Susan Diver.*

ELSHAMMS BHB 105f **RR 103f** 5074[3]
3 ch f Zafonic (USA) 9f **(83)** - Gharam (USA) (Green Dancer (USA))

10.3f **(74)**
Form - 4533
Record 1998 - 1st:0 2nd:0 3rd:2 Ran:4
Pre1998 - 1st:1 2nd:0 3rd:1 Ran:3
Win Prizemoney £4,175 *Total Prizemoney* £16,955
Wins * 1997 Aug Newmar (GD) 7f 77+ <
1998 Turf 0-4: (6f, 7f 2, 8f) (g-s, gd 2, g-f)
Well made, very useful filly, effective 7f, acts on gd to g-f, best on gd. Turf high 103 - 3rd of 11 getting 8lb from Russian Revival (17 Spt Newbury 7f g-f RF 4328). Like her half-brother Shaya, she has bags of ability but is slightly disappointing. Tried from six furlongs to a mile, she races freely but lacks a finishing kick.
**A C Stewart [1-7] Hamdan Al Maktoum.*

Fibresand and at Goodwood either side. Narrowly touched off in the July Stakes before finding Golden Silca too good for him in a listed race. Unproven on soft ground.
**B J Meehan [2-5] Mrs Sheila Tucker.*

ELTAWAASUL (USA) BHB 100f **RR 96f** 4618[3]

2 ch c Nureyev (USA) 8.4f **(84)** - Grand Falls (USA) (Ogygian (USA))
Form - 1133
Record 1998 - 1st:2 2nd:0 3rd:2 Ran:4
Win Prizemoney £7,392 *Total Prizemoney* £10,726
Wins * **1998** Jun Doncas (GD) 6f 83 <
* **1998** Jun Haydoc (GD) 6f 83+
1998 Turf 2-4: (6f 2-2, 7f 2) (gd 2, g-f 1-1, frm 1-1)

Elnadim, just one win for this top sprinter

ELSIE BAMFORD BHB 62f **RR 65f** 4009[7]

2 b f Tragic Role (USA) 9.4f **(63)** - Sara Sprint (Formidable (USA)) 9.2f **(63)**
Form - 6807
Record 1998 - 1st:0 2nd:0 3rd:0 Ran:4
1998 Turf 0-4: (5f 3, 6f) (gd 3, g-f)
Average filly. Turf high 65. **J Berry [0-4] Mrs Sheila Ramsden.*

EL TANGO BHB 100f **RR 95f** 2911[2]

2 ch g Risk Me (FR) 8f **(53)** - Princess Tara (Prince Sabo) 7.2f **(62)**
Form - 10122
Record 1998 - 1st:2 2nd:2 3rd:0 Ran:5
Win Prizemoney £7,073 *Total Prizemoney* £16,705
Wins * **1998** Jun Goodwo (GD) 6f 88 <
* **1998** *May Southw (STD) 5f 79+*
1998 Turf 1-4:(5f, 6f 1-3)(g-s, gd 1-2, frm)1998AW1-1:(5f 1-1) (Fibr 1-1)
Very useful gelding. Turf high 95 - 2nd of 5 giving 2lb to Golden Silca (18 Jly Newbury 6f gd RF 2911) - also 1st of 4 getting 4lb from Muqtarib (26 Jun Goodwood RF 2304). (1st run). Beaten out of sight in the Norfolk Stakes, but scored on the Southwell

Very useful colt. Turf high 96. Won twice in June, and stepped up on those efforts when third to Desaru in a decent race at the St Leger meeting. Ran well in Listed race at Newmarket on final start, and looks sure to stay further than a mile in time.
**J L Dunlop [2-4] Hamdan Al Maktoum.*

EL TINA RR 4832a[9]

2 ch f Unfuwain (USA) 11.4f **(74)** - Mashair (USA) (Diesis) 9.3f **(69)**
Form - 10
Record 1998 - 1st:1 2nd:0 3rd:0 Ran:2
Win Prizemoney £6,876 *Total Prizemoney* £6,876
Wins * **1998** Spt San Si (HVY) 7f
1998 Turf 1-2: (7f 1-1, 8f) (hvy 1-1, g-s)
Currently very poor filly. (began Spt) - 9th of 11 to Barafamy (11 Oct San Siro 8f g-s RF 4832a) - also 1st of 10 getting 4lb from Gold Valley Hope (29 Spt San Siro RF 4711a). **D T Thom [1-2].*

ELTON LEDGER (IRE) BHB 48f66a **RR 55f 66a** 4874[6]

9 b g Cyrano de Bergerac 7.3f **(58)** - Princess of Nashua (Crowned Prince (USA)) 10.1f **(67)**

Form - 442631422220327671044728732376
Record 1998 - 1st:2 2nd:8 3rd:4 Ran:32
Pre1998 - 1st:10 2nd:15 3rd:3 Ran:63
Win Prizemoney £28,827 *Total Prizemoney* £52,049
Wins *** 1998** *Jun Southw (STD)* *6f* *71* <
*** 1998** *Mar Southw (STD) SH* *6f* *58* *64*
* 1997 *Feb Southw (STD) S* *6f* *71* <
* 1997 *Jan Southw (STD) H* *6f* *70* *69*
* 1996 *Spt Southw (STD) C* *5f* *71* <
* 1996 *Jun Southw (STD) H* *5f* *63* *66*
* 1996 *Apr Southw (STD)* *7f* *45*
* 1996 *Mar Southw (STD) H* *6f* *55* *56*
* 1994 *Aug Southw (STD) H* *6f* *68* *65*
1994 *May Southw (STD) S* *6f* *60*
1998 Turf 0-13: (5f 3, 6f 8, 7f 2) (sft, g-s 2, gd 5, g-f 2, frm 3) 1998 AW 2-19: (5f, 6f 2-10, 7f 6, 8f 2) (Fibr 2-19)
Average gelding, effective 6 to 7f, best at 6f, - acts on Fibr, often wears blinkers (effectively), likes left handed tracks, likes tight tracks, does well at Southwell. Turf high 59. AW high 71 - 1st of 6 giving 6lb to Inflation (18 Jun Southwell RF 2096) - also 1st of 11 giving 17lb to Imp Express (2 Mar Southwell RF 0387). A grand old servant, he has been running, and winning, almost exclusively at Southwell for a couple of years now, and can still win in his grade. Six furlongs is his trip though he can win over five and seven, and he ran a couple of good races on turf in '98.
**Mrs N Macauley [9-68] The Posse (from A A Scott [2-17] May 1994).*

ELUSIVE STAR BHB 45f RR 50f 5098[6]

8 b m Ardross 12.4f **(67)** - Star Flower (Star Appeal) 9.6f **(65)**
Form - 45018066
Record 1998 - 1st:1 2nd:0 3rd:0 Ran:8
Pre1998 - 1st:0 2nd:0 3rd:0 Ran:1
Win Prizemoney £2,372 *Total Prizemoney* £2,626
Wins *** 1998** Aug Beverl (G-F) 12f 54 <
1998 Turf 1-8: (10f 2, 11f, 12f 1-5) (gd 3, g-f 1-3, frm 2)
Fair mare, effective 12f, acts on g-f, favours tight tracks. Turf high 63 (began Jly) - also 1st of 5 getting 3lb from Augustan (12 Aug Beverley RF 3568). She regained winning form in a modest classified stakes at Beverley in August.
**Mrs M Reveley [2-18] W Ginzel (from J White [0-12] Jan 1996).*

ELVIS REIGNS RR 93+f 4325[1]

2 b c Rock City 8.8f **(62)** - Free Rein (Sagaro) 9.7f **(55)**
Form - 31
Record 1998 - 1st:1 2nd:0 3rd:1 Ran:2
Win Prizemoney £3,860 *Total Prizemoney* £4,497
Wins * **1998** Spt Ayr (G-S) 7f 93+ <
1998 Turf 1-2: (6f, 7f 1-1) (gd 1-1, frm)
Currently useful colt. Turf high 93 (began Aug) - 1st of 7 giving 5lb to Weaver of Words (17 Spt Ayr RF 4325). Showed plenty of promise on his debut after a slow start and from a poor draw. Proved well suited by the step up in distance and easy ground next time, if he had not been eased he would had have at least eight lengths to spare. A progressive type, he has further improvement in him. Sold for 75,000 gns in October, reportedly to race in France. **Mrs J R Ramsden [1-2] Bernard Hathaway.*

EMALLEN (IRE) BHB 20f30a RR 30a 240[9]

10 b g Prince Regent (FR) 8f **(65)** - Peperonia (Prince Taj)
Form - 0
Record 1998 - 1st:0 2nd:0 3rd:0 Ran:1
Pre1998 - 1st:0 2nd:1 3rd:0 Ran:12
Win Prizemoney £0 *Total Prizemoney* £1,150
1998 AW 0-1: (13f) (Equi)
Very poor gelding, has worn blinkers.
**Mrs L C Jewell [1-29] Peter Allen (from D A Wilson [0-13] Spt 1991).*

EMANATING (USA) RR 5163a[5]

2 br f Cox's Ridge (USA) 9.4f **(72)** - Lead Kindly Light (USA) 00
Form - 5
1998 AW 0-1: (9f) (Dirt)
Currently very useful filly.
**C McGaughey in USA [0-1] Cynthia Phipps.*

EMARINA RR 21f 2324[12]

2 b f Emarati (USA) 6.6f **(63)** - Cushina (Sparkler) 8.4f **(55)**
Form - 0
Record 1998 - 1st:0 2nd:0 3rd:0 Ran:1
1998 Turf 0-1: (6f) (gd)
Currently little account filly. **J L Spearing [0-1] D A Dobson.*

EMBATTLE RR 60f 4697[10]

2 ch c Rock City 8.8f **(62)** - Sleepline Princess (Royal Palace) 9f **(56)**
Form - 0
Record 1998 - 1st:0 2nd:0 3rd:0 Ran:1
1998 Turf 0-1: (8f) (g-f)
Currently average colt. **M R Channon [0-1] G Z Mizel.*

EMBODY RR 92f 4833a[7]

3 b c Indian Ridge 7.6f **(74)** - Kamakha (ITY) (Natroun (FR))
Form - 7
1998 Turf 0-1: (8f) (g-s)
Currently useful colt. **B Grizzetti in ITY [0-2].*

EMBROIDERED BHB 33f25a RR 31f 25a 2890[5]

5 br m Charmer 9f **(59)** - Emblazon (Wolver Hollow) 8f **(56)**
Form - 05
Record 1998 - 1st:0 2nd:0 3rd:0 Ran:2
Pre1998 - 1st:0 2nd:0 3rd:1 Ran:14
Win Prizemoney £0 *Total Prizemoney* £453
1998 Turf 0-2: (5f 2) (frm 2)
Very moderate filly, has worn blinkers. Turf high 31 (began Jly). Inconsistent.
**S Dow [0-6] James Evans (from R M Flower [0-13] Feb 1997).*

EMBRYONIC (IRE) BHB 73f RR 71f 1534[5]

6 b g Prince Rupert (FR) 10.4f **(60)** - Belle Viking (FR) (Riverman (USA)) 9.1f **(76)**
Form - 785
Record 1998 - 1st:0 2nd:0 3rd:0 Ran:3
Pre1998 - 1st:4 2nd:6 3rd:4 Ran:24
Win Prizemoney £15,658 *Total Prizemoney* £35,307
Wins * 1997 Jun Newcas (FRM) H 16.1f 78 83 <
* 1997 May Doncas (GD) H 16.5f 76 81
1995 May Hamilt (GD) H 13f 70 78
1995 Apr Newcas (G-F) 12.4f 71
1998 Turf 0-3: (12f, 16f 2) (gd, g-f 2)
Above-average gelding, effective 14 to 17f, acts on gd to frm, best on g-f, prefers left handed tracks. Turf high 71. Consistent.
**Martin Todhunter [2-10] Mrs D Miller (from R F Fisher [2-17] Oct 1996).*

EMERALD CLUSTER RR 932[10]

4 b f Rock City 8.8f **(62)** - Tufty Lady (Riboboy (USA)) 14f **(54)**
Form - 0
Record 1998 - 1st:0 2nd:0 3rd:0 Ran:1
1998 Turf 0-1: (7f) (sft)
Workmanlike, currently very poor filly.
**A Smith [0-1] The Rufus Partnership.*

EMERALD HEIGHTS BHB 93f RR 99df 4069[9]

3 b c Shirley Heights 12.1f **(76)** - Lady In Green (Shareef Dancer (USA)) 9.9f **(73)**
Form - 43112000
Record 1998 - 1st:2 2nd:1 3rd:1 Ran:8
Pre1998 - 1st:0 2nd:0 3rd:0 Ran:1
Win Prizemoney £11,668 *Total Prizemoney* £21,503
Wins *** 1998** Jun Haydoc (GD) H 10.5f 84 88 <
*** 1998** May Doncas (G-F) H 12f 79 82
1998 Turf 2-8: (8f, 10f, 11f 1-1, 12f 1-4, 13f) (g-s 2, gd 1-3, g-f 1-2, frm)
Tall, very useful colt, effective 12f, acts on g-s. Turf high 99 - 2nd of 17 getting 4lb from Double Classic (18 Jun Ascot 12f g-s RF 2088). He has steadily progressed this term, winning competitive handicaps at Doncaster and Haydock, and was a fine runner-up in the King George V Handicap at Royal Ascot. Disappointing since, he goes on any ground, stays up to a mile-and-a-half, and, if everything goes his way, he can win again.
**J R Fanshawe [2-9] Peter and Noreen Hodgson.*

EMERALD HUNTER (USA) RR 63f 3598[5]

3 b br c Quest for Fame 12.8f **(75)** - In Jubilation (USA) (Isgala) 12.1f **(64)**
Form - 55
Record 1998 - 1st:0 2nd:0 3rd:0 Ran:2
1998 Turf 0-2: (10f 2) (frm 2)

Workmanlike, currently average colt. Turf high 63 (began Aug).
**J Noseda [0-2] Goncalo Borges Torrealba.*

EMERALD ISLE (IRE) BHB 68f **RR 66?f** 4765[16]
3 ch c Second Set (IRE) 9.2f **(67)**-Irish Kick (Windjammer(USA)) 7f **(59)**
Form - 640
Record 1998 - 1st:0 2nd:0 3rd:0 Ran:3
Win Prizemoney £0 *Total Prizemoney* £264
1998 Turf 0-3: (7f, 8f, 10f) (g-s, gd, frm)
Well made, currently average colt. Turf high 66 (began Aug).
**L M Cumani [0-3] Sheikh Mohammed.*

EMERALD PROJECT (IRE) RR 64f 4895a[10]
3 bb f Project Manager 7.2f **(47)** - Emerald Pendant (Nebos (GER)) 9f **(78)**
Form - 34052300
1998 Turf 0-8: (8f 2, 9f, 10f 4, 12f) (sft 2, g-s, gd 2, g-f 2, hrd)
Average filly. Turf high 94. Consistent.
**Michael Kelly in IRE [0-3] Michael Kelly (from J S Bolger in IRE [0-8] Spt 1998).*

EMERGING MARKET BHB 94f **RR 95f** 4494[23]
6 b g Emarati (USA) 6.6f **(63)** - Flitteriss Park (Beldale Flutter (USA)) 9.7f **(71)**
Form - 00200
Record 1998 - 1st:0 2nd:1 3rd:0 Ran:5
Pre1998 - 1st:3 2nd:5 3rd:2 Ran:29
Win Prizemoney £57,059 *Total Prizemoney* £85,054
Wins * 1996 Jun Ascot (G-F) H 6f 95 98 <
* 1995 Apr Folkes (G-F) 6f 78
* 1994 Jly York (G-F) 6f 74+
1998 Turf 0-5: (6f 3, 7f 2) (gd 3, g-f 2)
Very useful gelding, effective 6 to 7f, best at 6f, acts on gd to frm. Turf high 95 (began Jly) - 2nd of 22 giving 10lb to Cadeaux Cher (15 Aug Ripon 6f g-f RF 3661). Inconsistent. Ran well in the Great St Wilfrid Handicap in August when beaten a head by Cadeux Cher, and it looked like he might recover some of the form from his youth. Unfortunately, he was disappointing afterwards and looks a shadow of his former self.
**J L Dunlop [3-34] Philip Wroughton.*

EMILIO ROMANO (GER) RR 108f 2666a[14]
3 b c Law Society (USA) 11.6f **(71)** - Eriphyle (GER) (Surumu (GER)) 10f **(83)**
Form - 10
1998 Turf 1-2: (9f 1-1, 12f) (hvy, gd 1-1)
Currently Pattern-class colt. Turf high 108 (1st run) - 1st of 9 from Tertullian (21 Jun Dortmund RF 2285a). He is useful, but was way off the pace in the German Derby.
**A Schutz in GER [1-2] Frau M Herbert.*

EMILY'S LUCK CHARM (USA) BHB 100f **RR 96f** 4449[1]
2 b br c Lear Fan (USA) 10.4f **(80)** - Emily's Charm (CAN) (Dom Alaric (FR))
Form - 26181
Record 1998 - 1st:2 2nd:1 3rd:0 Ran:5
Win Prizemoney £10,130 *Total Prizemoney* £11,534
Wins * **1998** Spt Cheste (GD) 7.6f 95+ <
* **1998** Jly Doncas (G-F) 6f 88+
1998 Turf 2-5: (6f 1-4, 8f 1-1) (gd 1-2, g-f, frm 1-2)
Very useful colt. Turf high 96 - also 1st of 4 giving 8lb to Helvetius (23 Spt Chester RF 4449). Just failed in a decent maiden before finishing a respectable sixth in the Coventry, for which he was sent off favourite. Got off the mark in a minor event at Doncaster, wearing a tongue-strap for the first time, but finished last in the Gimcrack. Gained another victory in an easy conditions race at Chester and had no problems with the extended trip. He may be difficult to place next year, but does have some ability.
**Sir Michael Stoute [2-5] Maktoum Al Maktoum.*

EMINENCE GRISE (IRE) BHB 72f **RR 69f** 3467[2]
3 b c Sadler's Wells (USA) 11.3f **(87)** - Impatiente (USA) (Vaguely Noble) 10.1f **(72)**
Form - 5372
Record 1998 - 1st:0 2nd:1 3rd:1 Ran:4
Win Prizemoney £0 *Total Prizemoney* £1,847
1998 Turf 0-4: (12f 4) (gd, frm 2, hrd)
Well made, average colt. Turf high 69 - 2nd of 4 to Rainbow Ways (8 Aug Newmarket 12f hrd RF 3467). Looks one of the slowest inmates of the Cecil yard.
**H R A Cecil [0-4] Wafic Said.*

EMINENT BHB 79f82a **RR 67f 82a** 354[2]
3 ch c Alnasr Alwasheek 9.4f **(62)** - Vague Lass (Vaigly Great) 7f **(58)**
Form - 23122
Record 1998 - 1st:1 2nd:2 3rd:1 Ran:4
Pre1998 - 1st:0 2nd:1 3rd:0 Ran:3
Win Prizemoney £2,085 *Total Prizemoney* £5,369
Wins * **1998** *Feb Southw (STD) 7f 67+* <
1998 AW 1-4: (6f, 7f 1-2, 8f) (Equi 2, Fibr 1-2)
Rangy, decent colt, effective 6 to 8f, - acts on AW. AW high 82 - 2nd of 5 giving 10lb to Genius (24 Feb Lingfield 8f Equi RF 0354). Improving steadily, he got off the mark with an easy win in a seven-furlong maiden on the Southwell Fibresand in February, and was unlucky next time when dropped to six, missing the break and not getting a clear run. He was beaten by an improving sort on Equitrack afterwards, but will surely regain winning ways before long.
**Lord Huntingdon [1-7] J Rose.*

EMINENT BLAZE BHB 44f **RR 41f** 4303[19]
2 b c Presidium 7.5f **(56)** - Fair Madame (Monseigneur (USA)) 7.7f **(63)**
Form - 000
Record 1998 - 1st:0 2nd:0 3rd:0 Ran:3
1998 Turf 0-3: (5f, 6f 2) (gd 2, frm)
Currently moderate colt. Turf high 41 (began Aug).
**D Nicholls [0-3] The Eminent Partnership.*

EMMAJOUN BHB 64f **RR 66f** 4127[11]
3 b f Emarati (USA) 6.6f **(63)** - Parijoun (Manado) 9.6f **(63)**
Form - 504230
Record 1998 - 1st:0 2nd:1 3rd:1 Ran:6
Pre1998 - 1st:0 2nd:0 3rd:0 Ran:3
Win Prizemoney £0 *Total Prizemoney* £1,192
1998 Turf 0-6: (5f 3, 6f 3) (gd 2, frm 3, hrd)
Workmanlike, average filly, effective 6f, acts on gd to g-f, best on gd. Turf high 66 - 3rd of 13 getting 5lb from The Woodcock (12 Aug Nottingham 6f gd RF 3582).
**W G M Turner [0-6] P Nabavi (from A P Jarvis [0-3] Spt 1997).*

EMMA-LYNE BHB 70f **RR 64f** 4412[3]
2 b f Emarati (USA) 6.6f **(63)** - Moreton's Martha (Derrylin) 8.8f **(54)**
Form - 223
Record 1998 - 1st:0 2nd:2 3rd:1 Ran:3
Win Prizemoney £0 *Total Prizemoney* £2,104
1998 Turf 0-3: (6f 2, 7f) (g-f, frm 2)
Currently average filly. Turf high 64 (began Jly) - 3rd of 12 getting 11lb from Mitcham (22 Spt Warwick 6f frm RF 4412).
**A P Jarvis [0-3] Quadrillian Partnership.*

EMMA PEEL RR 91f 4891[2]
2 b f Emarati (USA) 6.6f **(63)** - Trigamy (Tribal Chief) 8.5f **(61)**
Form - 12
Record 1998 - 1st:1 2nd:1 3rd:0 Ran:2
Win Prizemoney £4,202 *Total Prizemoney* £5,979
Wins * **1998** Oct Nottin (SFT) 6.1f 91+ <
1998 Turf 1-2: (6f 1-2) (gd 1-2)
Currently useful filly. Turf high 91 (1st run) (began Oct) - 1st of 17 from Gracious Gift (6 Oct Nottingham RF 4668). A half-sister to numerous winners, she handled the soft ground well and sprang a surprise when winning on her debut. Ran well again next time and improvement looks likely.
**B J Meehan [1-2] Arthur Smith.*

EMMA'S RISK BHB 40f23a **RR 36f 23a** 1581[8]
4 b f Risk Me (FR) 8f **(53)** - Lana's Pet (Tina's Pet) 6.8f **(59)**
Form - 8
Record 1998 - 1st:0 2nd:0 3rd:0 Ran:1
Pre1998 - 1st:0 2nd:0 3rd:2 Ran:8
Win Prizemoney £0 *Total Prizemoney* £608
1998 AW 0-1: (12f) (Fibr)
Leggy, very moderate filly. Becoming disappointing.
**K G Wingrove [0-1] Mrs Michaela Todd (from R Harris [0-5] Jun 1997).*

EMMA'S SUNSET (IRE) RR 1f 2154[10]
2 ch f Red Sunset 9f **(57)** - Rose A Village (River Beauty) 8.6f **(77)**
Form - 00

Record 1998 - 1st:0 2nd:0 3rd:0 Ran:2
1998 Turf 0-2: (5f, 7f) (gd, frm)
Currently very poor filly. Turf high 1. **N Tinkler [0-2] J P Hardiman.*

EMPEROR NAHEEM (IRE) BHB 82f **RR 80f** 4097[4]

3 b g Imperial Frontier (USA) 7f **(65)**-Desert Gale (Taufan(USA)) 7f **(57)**
Form - 44882035761316314
Record 1998 - 1st:3 2nd:1 3rd:3 Ran:17
Pre1998 - 1st:0 2nd:1 3rd:0 Ran:6
Win Prizemoney £9,701 *Total Prizemoney* £16,924
Wins * **1998** Aug Newmar (G-F) H 5f 78 80 <
* **1998** Aug Pontef (G-F) C 5f 76
* **1998** Jly Sandow (G-F) H 5f 71 75
1998 Turf 3-17: (5f 3-13, 6f 3, 7f) (g-s, gd 5, g-f 4, frm 3-7)
Leggy, decent gelding, effective 5 to 6f, best at 5f, acts on gd to frm, best on frm, has worn blinkers. Turf high 80 - 1st of 11 giving 15lb to Squire Corrie (29 Aug Newmarket RF 3953) - also 1st of 11 giving 7lb to Mamma's Boy (5 Aug Pontefract RF 3391). Consistent. His trainer does not believe in letting the grass grow under his feet, though it took him an awfully long time to get off the mark. He managed it at the seventeenth attempt at Sandown in July, and has since added a Pontefract claimer and a Newmarket ladies' event, as well as running some fine races in useful handicap company. **B J Meehan [3-23] Mrs Eithne Meehan.*

EMPEROR'S GOLD BHB 45f52a **RR 34f 52a** 5070[13]

3 gr g Petong 7.6f **(58)** -Tarnside Rosal **(56f)**(Mummy's Game) 8.2f **(60)**
Form - 2132380700
Record 1998 - 1st:1 2nd:1 3rd:2 Ran:9
Pre1998 - 1st:1 2nd:1 3rd:2 Ran:8
Win Prizemoney £3,463 *Total Prizemoney* £6,085
Wins 1998 *Jan Southw (STD) S 8f 68+* <
1997 Nov Wolver (STD) SH 8.5f 58 64
1998 Turf 0-1: (9f) (g-f) 1998 AW 1-8: (8f 1-5, 9f, 10f 2)(Equi 3, Fibr 1-5)
Tall, average gelding, effective 8 to 10f, best at 10f, - acts on AW, best on Equi, has worn blinkers, prefers left handed tracks, prefers tight tracks. AW high 68 (1st run) - 1st of 9 giving 5lb to Mystery Man (12 Jan Southwell RF 0076). Inconsistent.
**M J Polglase [0-5] Emperor's Gold Partnership (from I Campbell [2-12] Feb 1998).*

EMPIRE GOLD (USA) BHB 64f **RR 64f** 3745[1]

3 ch g Strike The Gold (USA) 8f **(79)** - Careless Halo (USA) (Sunny's Halo (CAN)) 6.7f **(70)**
Form - 0578761
Record 1998 - 1st:1 2nd:0 3rd:0 Ran:7
Pre1998 - 1st:0 2nd:0 3rd:0 Ran:1
Win Prizemoney £3,330 *Total Prizemoney* £3,330
Wins * **1998** Aug Leices (GD) H 8f 59 64 <
1998 Turf 1-7: (6f, 7f, 8f 1-4, 10f) (g-s, gd, g-f, frm 1-4)
Light-framed, average gelding. Turf high 64. Consistent. He did not make the frame in his first seven outings, but then landed a Leicester handicap in August.
**Mrs J R Ramsden [1-7] Charlton Bloodstock Ltd (from H R A Cecil [0-1] Oct 1997).*

EMPIRE STATE (IRE) BHB 67f **RR 72f** 4961[8]

3 b g High Estate 10.5f **(66)** - Palm Dove (USA) (Storm Bird (CAN)) 10.3f **(74)**
Form - 304014150808
Record 1998 - 1st:2 2nd:0 3rd:1 Ran:12
Pre1998 - 1st:0 2nd:0 3rd:0 Ran:3
Win Prizemoney £6,074 *Total Prizemoney* £6,832
Wins * **1998** Jly Catter (GD) H 6f 63 72 <
* **1998** Jun Carlis (G-S) H 5.9f 63 68
1998 Turf 2-12: (6f 2-6, 7f 3, 8f 2, 10f) (sft, gd 1-5, g-f 2, frm 1-4)
Above-average gelding, effective 6 to 8f, best at 6f, acts on gd to frm, best on gd, has worn blinkers. Turf high 72 - 1st of 12 giving 18lb to Penniless (2 Jly Catterick RF 2466) - also 1st of 20 giving 11lb to Sea Fig (24 Jun Carlisle RF 2228). Has reportedly joined Paul Felgate. **M H Tompkins [2-15] Miss D J Merson.*

EMPIRICAL (USA) BHB 62f **RR 75df** 2576[10]

3 b f Miswaki (USA) 8.1f **(81)** - Louisville (FR) (Val de L'Orne (FR)) 12f **(75)**
Form - 580
Record 1998 - 1st:0 2nd:0 3rd:0 Ran:3
Pre1998 - 1st:0 2nd:0 3rd:1 Ran:2
Win Prizemoney £0 *Total Prizemoney* £572
1998 Turf 0-3: (6f 2, 7f) (gd, g-f, frm)
Above-average filly. Turf high 56. Two fair efforts in maidens.
**J H M Gosden [0-5] K Abdulla.*

EMPLANE (USA) BHB 99f **RR 99f** 3427[4]

3 b f Irish River (FR) 9f **(77)** - Peplum (USA) (Nijinsky (CAN)) 10.3f **(77)**
Form - 7214
Record 1998 - 1st:1 2nd:1 3rd:0 Ran:4
Win Prizemoney £4,581 *Total Prizemoney* £7,335
Wins * **1998** Jly Newmar (GD) 8f 87+ <
1998 Turf 1-4: (7f, 8f 1-2, 10f) (sft, g-f, frm 1-2)
Well made, very useful filly. Turf high 99. Out of a Cheshire Oaks winner, she showed promise on her debut in April and ran well when reappearing three months later. Dropped back to a mile when winning on her third start, and was not disgraced in a conditions race at Ascot. She has shown a tendency to hang and will be better suited by going left-handed. **H R A Cecil [1-4] K Abdulla.*

EMPYREAN BHB 63f **RR 71f** 3626[6]

2 b c Emarati (USA) 6.6f **(63)** - Winter Lightning (Dominion) 8.5f **(63)**
Form - 8406576
Record 1998 - 1st:0 2nd:0 3rd:0 Ran:7
1998 Turf 0-6: (5f 4, 6f, 7f) (gd 2, g-f 3, frm) 1998 AW 0-1: (6f) (Fibr)
Above-average colt, effective 5f, acts on gd, has worn blinkers. Turf high 71 - 4th of 13 giving 11lb to Charlie Girl (18 May Musselburgh 5f gd RF 1298). **J M P Eustace [0-7] Park Lane Racing.*

EMWILLGEO (IRE) BHB 46f **RR 40f** 3159[14]

2 b f Petardia 8.2f **(58)** - Lhotse (IRE) (Shernazar) 10.2f **(73)**
Form - 050
Record 1998 - 1st:0 2nd:0 3rd:0 Ran:3
1998 Turf 0-3: (5f 2, 6f) (gd 2, g-f)
Currently moderate filly. Turf high 40.
**P C Haslam [0-3] Cunningham/R Popely.*

ENABEG (IRE) BHB 41f **RR 51f** 3996[14]

2 b f Forest Wind (USA) - Saturne (Bellypha) 9.8f **(73)**
Form - 4560
Record 1998 - 1st:0 2nd:0 3rd:0 Ran:4
1998 Turf 0-4: (6f 3, 7f) (gd 4)
Fair filly, has worn blinkers. Turf high 51 - 5th of 10 to Fizzy Whizzy (20 Jun Redcar 7f gd RF 2154). **J Parkes [0-4] P J Sweeney.*

ENCHANT BHB 93f **RR 89f** 4208[10]

3 ch f Lion Cavern (USA) 7.5f **(74)** - Belle et Deluree (USA) (The Minstrel (CAN)) 10f **(72)**
Form - 1360
Record 1998 - 1st:1 2nd:0 3rd:1 Ran:4
Pre1998 - 1st:0 2nd:0 3rd:0 Ran:1
Win Prizemoney £6,930 *Total Prizemoney* £9,470
Wins * **1998** May Cheste (GD) 7f 89 <
1998 Turf 1-4: (7f 1-2, 9f, 10f) (gd 2, g-f 1-2)
Workmanlike, useful filly. Turf high 89 (1st run) - 1st of 8 from Aloha Dancer (6 May Chester RF 1061). Got up close home to win a Chester maiden on her reappearance, but has been found out in Listed company since. **Sir Michael Stoute [1-5] Cheveley Park Stud.*

ENCHANTED ISLE BHB 50f **RR 49f** 4337[11]

2 b f Mujtahid (USA) 7.4f **(69)** - Belle Ile (USA) **(52f)** (Diesis) 9.3f **(69)**
Form - 405700
Record 1998 - 1st:0 2nd:0 3rd:0 Ran:6
Win Prizemoney £0 *Total Prizemoney* £396
1998 Turf 0-6: (5f, 6f 2, 7f 2, 8f) (gd, g-f 2, frm 3)
Moderate filly, has worn blinkers. Turf high 49.
**C A Dwyer [0-6] D J Donner.*

ENCHANTING EVE BHB 34f35a **RR 44?f 35a** 4815[14]

4 ch f Risk Me (FR) 8f **(53)** - Red Sails (Town And Country) 8.1f **(68)**
Form - 5766660000
Record 1998 - 1st:0 2nd:0 3rd:0 Ran:8
Pre1998 - 1st:5 2nd:3 3rd:4 Ran:26
Win Prizemoney £11,771 *Total Prizemoney* £16,588
Wins * 1997 *Mar Lingfi (STD) C 8f 67*
* 1997 *Feb Lingfi (STD) C 7f 67*
* 1996 *Jun Wolver (STD) S 6f 70* <
* 1996 *Jun Southw (STD) S 6f 66*

* 1996 Mar Beverl (GD) 5f 66
1998 Turf 0-1: (12f) (gd) 1998 AW 0-7: (7f 3, 8f 2, 10f 2) (Equi 5, Fibr 2)
Leggy, fair filly, effective 7 to 10f, best at 7f, - acts on Equi, has worn blinkers, favours left handed tracks, favours tight tracks. AW high 59. Becoming disappointing.
C N Allen [5-34] Newmarket Connections Ltd.

ENCOUNTER BHB 62f RR 69f 4835[9]
2 br c Primo Dominie 7.2f **(67)**-Dancing Spirit (IRE)(Ahonoora) 8.1f **(73)**
Form - 03700
Record 1998 - 1st:0 2nd:0 3rd:1 Ran:5
Win Prizemoney £0 *Total Prizemoney* £517
1998 Turf 0-5: (5f, 6f, 7f 3) (g-s, gd 2, g-f 2)
Average colt. Turf high 69. *C E Brittain [0-5] Wyck Hall Stud.*

ENDAXI SAM BHB 24f RR 35f 1795[6]
5 b h St Enodoc - Stos (IRE) (Bluebird (USA)) 7.5f **(69)**
Form - 036
Record 1998 - 1st:0 2nd:0 3rd:1 Ran:3
Pre1998 - 1st:0 2nd:0 3rd:0 Ran:4
Win Prizemoney £0 *Total Prizemoney* £252
1998 AW 0-3: (6f, 7f, 11f) (Fibr 3)
Very moderate colt. AW high 31.
N P Littmoden [0-3] Stephen Fletcher (from R Ingram [0-4] Oct 1996).

ENDLESS HOURS BHB 50f51a RR 53f 51a 4256[14]
4 ch f Timeless Times (USA) 6.1f **(56)** - Lonely Lass (Headin' Up) 9.4f **(57)**
Form - 0460640
Record 1998 - 1st:0 2nd:0 3rd:0 Ran:7
Win Prizemoney £0 *Total Prizemoney* £242
1998 Turf 0-3: (6f 2, 7f) (hvy, gd, frm) 1998 AW 0-4: (6f 2, 7f 2) (Fibr 4)
Fair filly. Turf high 53. AW high 51.
J L Eyre [0-7] Miss Victoria Jones.

END OF STORY (IRE) RR 72f 4772[9]
2 b c Doubletour (USA) 12f **(46)** - Baliana (CAN) (Riverman (USA)) 9.1f **(76)**
Form - 0
Record 1998 - 1st:0 2nd:0 3rd:0 Ran:1
1998 Turf 0-1: (7f) (gd)
Currently above-average colt. *R Hannon [0-1] High Seas Leisure Ltd.*

ENDOWMENT BHB 50f66a RR 55?f 66a 2753[7]
6 ch g Cadeaux Genereux 7.9f **(76)** -Palm Springs (Top Ville) 11.7f **(68)**
Form - 7
Record 1998 - 1st:0 2nd:0 3rd:0 Ran:1
Pre1998 - 1st:2 2nd:0 3rd:0 Ran:8
Win Prizemoney £7,596 *Total Prizemoney* £8,049
Wins 1995 Aug Bath (HRD) H 11.7f 71 74 <
1995 May Bath (GD) 10.2f 70
1998 Turf 0-1: (13f) (gd)
Fair gelding, has worn blinkers. Inconsistent.
J J O'Neill [0-1] R Hilley (from Mrs M Reveley [0-2] Spt 1996).

ENEMY ACTION (USA) RR 99f 4178a[11]
2 b f Forty Niner (USA) 8.8f **(73)** -Sun and Shade(Ajdal (USA)) 9.2f **(89)**
Form - 1140
Record 1998 - 1st:2 2nd:0 3rd:0 Ran:4
Win Prizemoney £7,183 *Total Prizemoney* £10,558
Wins * 1998 Jly Doncas (FRM) 6f 92 <
* 1998 Jun Goodwo (GD) 6f 82+
1998 Turf 2-4: (6f 2-3, 7f) (gd 1-2, frm 1-2)
Very useful filly. Turf high 99 - 4th of 10 getting 3lb from Bint Allayl (20 Aug York 6f frm RF 3772) - also 1st of 3 from Blue Melody (16 Jly Doncaster RF 2846). A half-sister to Daggers Drawn, she started her career by winning a maiden at Goodwood and followed-up with a novice stakes at Doncaster. Not disgraced when upped in class in the Lowther Stakes, beaten two lengths by Bint Allayl, she ran poorly at the Curragh next time, but is still a very useful prospect as she has plenty of size and scope and will be suited by further. *H R A Cecil [2-4] Cliveden Stud.*

ENERGY MAN BHB 38f35a RR 17f 35a 144[6]
5 b g Hadeer 8.9f **(58)** - Cataclysmic (Ela-Mana-Mou) 10.1f **(70)**
Form - 6
Record 1998 - 1st:0 2nd:0 3rd:0 Ran:1
Pre1998 - 1st:0 2nd:0 3rd:0 Ran:13
Win Prizemoney £0 *Total Prizemoney* £248
1998 AW 0-1: (11f) (Fibr)
Poor gelding, effective 9f, acts on frm, has worn blinkers.
M Dods [0-13] A J Henderson (from J R Fanshawe [0-3] Oct 1995).

ENFILADE BHB 69f RR 74f 4463[7]
2 b c Deploy 11.4f **(67)** - Bargouzine (Hotfoot) 10.5f **(59)**
Form - 03557
Record 1998 - 1st:0 2nd:0 3rd:1 Ran:5
Win Prizemoney £0 *Total Prizemoney* £527
1998 Turf 0-5: (6f, 7f 3, 8f) (gd, g-f 2, frm 2)
Above-average colt, has worn blinkers. Turf high 74 (began Jly).
B Hanbury [0-5] H Channon.

EN GARDE (USA) BHB 89f RR 76f 4746[10]
2 ch f Irish River (FR) 9f **(77)** - Stellaria (USA) (Roberto (USA)) 10f **(76)**
Form - 510
Record 1998 - 1st:1 2nd:0 3rd:0 Ran:3
Win Prizemoney £3,485 *Total Prizemoney* £3,842
Wins * **1998** Spt Bath (GD) 5.7f 76+ <
1998 Turf 1-3: (6f 1-2, 7f) (gd, g-f 1-2)
Currently above-average filly. Turf high 76 (began Spt) - 1st of 14 getting 5lb from Northern Spring (28 Spt Bath RF 4524).
B W Hills [1-3] K Abdulla.

ENGLISH INVADER BHB 39f50a RR 41f 50a 4861[12]
7 b h Rainbow Quest (USA) 11.2f **(81)** - Modica (Persian Bold) 9.3f **(66)**
Form - 01228030862350700
Record 1998 - 1st:1 2nd:3 3rd:2 Ran:16
Pre1998 - 1st:4 2nd:2 3rd:0 Ran:27
Win Prizemoney £11,300 *Total Prizemoney* £18,493
Wins 1998 *Jan Lingfi (STD) SH 13f 55 61* <
1997 Spt Wolver (STD) H 12f 55 61 <
1997 Mar Wolver (STD) C 12f 57
1997 Mar Lingfi (STD) H 13f 54 59+
1997 Feb Lingfi (STD) SH 13f 48 50
1998 Turf 0-7: (10f 2, 11f 2, 12f, 13f, 14f) (sft, g-s, gd, g-f 2, frm 2) 1998 AW 1-9: (11f 2, 12f, 13f 1-4, 16f 2) (Equi 1-6, Fibr 3)
Average horse, effective 12 to 16f, best at 12f, - acted on Equi to Fibr, best on Fibr, had worn blinkers, preferred left handed tracks, favoured tight tracks, liked Wolverhampton, did well at Lingfield. Turf high 41. AW high 61 (1st run) - 1st of 10 giving 16lb to Krayyan Dawn (6 Jan Lingfield RF 0031). (DEAD)
R C Spicer [0-3] John Purcell (from C A Dwyer [4-34] Jly 1998).

ENGLISH LADY (IRE) BHB 50f RR 54df 4886[13]
3 b f Fayruz 6.6f **(63)** - Paradise Regained (North Stoke) 10.4f **(55)**
Form - 555000
Record 1998 - 1st:0 2nd:0 3rd:0 Ran:6
Pre1998 - 1st:0 2nd:1 3rd:0 Ran:3
Win Prizemoney £0 *Total Prizemoney* £1,195
1998 Turf 0-6: (5f 3, 6f 3) (g-s, gd, g-f, frm 3)
Unfurnished, fair filly. Turf high 59. Becoming disappointing.
M J Haynes [0-9] English Lady Classics Ltd.

EN GRISAILLE BHB 52f RR 67f 4136[8]
2 gr f Mystiko (USA) 7.7f **(59)** - Hickleton Lady (IRE) **(60f 60a)** (Kala Shikari) 8.4f **(54)**
Form - 041478
Record 1998 - 1st:1 2nd:0 3rd:0 Ran:6
Win Prizemoney £1,725 *Total Prizemoney* £1,725
Wins * **1998** Aug Folkes (G-F) S 6f 67 <
1998 Turf 1-5: (6f 1-1, 7f 3, 8f) (g-f 2, frm 1-3) 1998 AW 0-1: (7f) (Fibr)
Average filly, effective 6f, acts on frm. Turf high 67 (began Jly) - 1st of 10 from Whatta Madam (6 Aug Folkestone RF 3400).
Sir Mark Prescott [1-6] H R Moszkowicz.

ENNOBLE RR 60f 3032[11]
2 b c Highest Honor (FR) 10.9f **(72)** - Villella (Sadler's Wells (USA)) 10f **(76)**
Form - 700
Record 1998 - 1st:0 2nd:0 3rd:0 Ran:3
1998 Turf 0-3: (7f 3) (gd, g-f, frm)
Currently average colt. Turf high 60.
H Morrison [0-3] The Summerdown Partnership.

EN RETARD (IRE) **RR 98f** 4907a5

3 bb f Petardia 8.2f **(58)** - Regal Society 00

Form - 50713301115

1998 Turf 4-11: (5f 3-5, 6f 1-4, 7f, 8f) (sft 2, g-s 2-4, gd 2-4, g-f)

Very useful filly, effective 5 to 6f, acts on g-s to gd, has worn blinkers (extremely effectively). Turf high 98 - 5th of 9 getting 13lb from Burden Of Proof (17 Oct Curragh 6f gd RF 4907a) - also 1st of 10 giving 7lb to Tinker Amelia (3 Oct Curragh RF 4689a). Really found her form in the autumn when dropped to the minimum trip. Her four-year-old career is worth watching.

**Patrick Prendergast in IRE [4-19] Aidan Walsh.*

ENRICA (GER) **RR 106f** 4600a2

4 f

Form - 2

1998 Turf 0-1: (10f) (hvy)

Currently Pattern-class filly. (1st run) - 2nd of 13 to Lomita (27 Spt Capannelle 10f hvy RF 4600a). She was touched off in a Group Two in Rome during September, and goes very well on a testing surface. **H Blume in GER [0-2] Gestut Rottgen.*

ENRIQUE (GER) **RR 94f** 4723a7

3 c

Form - 7

1998 Turf 0-1: (14f) (sft)

Currently useful colt. **in GER [0-1].*

ENTERTAINER (IRE) BHB 96f **RR 86df** 48007

2 b c Be My Guest (USA) 10.2f **(66)** - Green Wings (General Assembly (USA)) 10f **(68)**

Form - 227

Record 1998 - 1st:0 2nd:2 3rd:0 Ran:3

Win Prizemoney £0 *Total Prizemoney* £4,664

1998 Turf 0-3: (7f 2, 8f) (sft, g-f, frm)

Currently useful colt. Turf high 86 (began Spt) - 2nd of 6 to Boatman (18 Spt Newbury 8f g-f RF 4359). Narrowly beaten on his first two runs, but went down at 1/4 in soft ground on his third run.

**P W Chapple-Hyam [0-3] The Royal Ascot Racing Club.*

ENTHAISINGH BHB 58f **RR 68f** 492917

2 gr f Petong 7.6f **(58)** - Proper Madam (Mummy's Pet) 7.7f **(60)**

Enrique won on his eagerly-awaited debut

ENRIQUE **RR 117f** 48514

2 b c Barathea (IRE) - Gwydion (USA) (Raise A Cup (USA)) 7.6f **(74)**

Form - 114

Record 1998 - 1st:2 2nd:0 3rd:0 Ran:3

Win Prizemoney £21,780 *Total Prizemoney* £31,880

Wins	* **1998**	Oct	Newmar (GD)	L	7f	117++	<
	* **1998**	Jly	Goodwo (G-S)		7f	94+	

1998 Turf 2-3: (7f 2-3) (gd 2-3)

Currently high-class colt. Turf high 117 (began Jly) - 1st of 5 from Berlioz (2 Oct Newmarket RF 4618). Highly regarded, he won a warm maiden on his debut at Glorious Goodwood before winning a Listed race at Newmarket in facile style. Well fancied for the Dewhurst, he was impeded in the closing stages but was a beaten horse by then. That effort has to go down as a disappointment though he may not have been suited by the softening ground. He still looks a useful prospect for next season, though he is out of a high-class sprinter and is unlikely to stay beyond a mile.

**H R A Cecil [2-3] Niarchos Family.*

Form - 156547350100

Record 1998 - 1st:2 2nd:0 3rd:1 Ran:12

Win Prizemoney £4,140 *Total Prizemoney* £4,557

Wins	* **1998**	Oct	Lingfi	(SFT)	C	6f	68	<
	* **1998**	Apr	Folkes	(GD)		5f	55	

1998 Turf 2-12: (5f 1-5, 6f 1-5, 7f 2) (g-s 1-2, gd 1-2, g-f 2, frm 6)

Average filly, effective 6f, acts on g-s to frm, often wears blinkers (very effectively). Turf high 68 - also 1st of 20 getting 7lb from Cantgetyourbreath (2 Oct Lingfield RF 4612). Inconsistent.

**C A Dwyer [2-12] Cedar Lodge Syndicate.*

ENTROPY **RR 76df** 418311

2 b f Brief Truce (USA) 9.1f **(73)** - Distant Isle (IRE) (Bluebird (USA)) 7.5f **(69)**

Form - 32335160

Record 1998 - 1st:1 2nd:1 3rd:3 Ran:8

Win Prizemoney £2,723 *Total Prizemoney* £5,620

Wins	* **1998**	Aug	Bath	(FRM)	H	5.7f	73	76+	<

1998 Turf 1-8: (5f 3, 6f 1-4, 7f) (gd 4, g-f 2, frm 1-2)
Above-average filly, effective 5 to 6f, acts on gd to frm. Turf high 76 - 1st of 6 getting 9lb from Choral Express (11 Aug Bath RF 3528). **R Hannon [1-8] T G Holdcroft.*

ENTWINE BHB 86f **RR 83+f** 4739[11]
2 b f Primo Dominie 7.2f **(67)** - Splice **(101f)** (Sharpo) 7.7f **(59)**
Form - 4110
Record 1998 - 1st:2 2nd:0 3rd:0 Ran:4
Win Prizemoney £12,052 *Total Prizemoney* £12,312
Wins * **1998** Oct Newmar (gd) H 5f 77 83+ <
* **1998** Spt Beverl (G-F) 5f 69+
1998 Turf 2-4: (5f 2-4) (g-s, gd 2-2, frm)
Decent filly. Turf high 83 (began Spt) - 1st of 16 getting 16lb from Sunley Sense (1 Oct Newmarket RF 4591). Narrow winner of a Beverley maiden on her second start, she followed up in a Newmarket nursery, but this speedy filly was never in the hunt in a Group Three on her last run.
**J R Fanshawe [2-4] Cheveley Park Stud.*

ENVOY RR 41f 4504[12]
3 b c Presidium 7.5f **(56)** - Chief Dancer (Chief Singer) 8.9f **(66)**
Form - 747800000
Record 1998 - 1st:0 2nd:0 3rd:0 Ran:9
Win Prizemoney £0 *Total Prizemoney* £236
1998 Turf 0-7: (6f 2, 7f 3, 8f 2) (gd 3, g-f, frm 3) 1998 AW 0-2: (6f, 8f) (Fibr 2)
Moderate colt. Turf high 59. AW high 23. Inconsistent.
**C W Thornton [0-9] Guy Reed.*

ENZELI (IRE) RR 109f 4430a[4]
3 b c Kahyasi 12.9f **(74)** - Ebaziya (IRE) (Darshaan) 9.9f **(84)**
Form - 51134
1998 Turf 2-5: (10f, 12f 1-2, 14f 1-2) (hvy, sft 1-1, gd 2, g-f 1-1)
Pattern-class colt. Turf high 109. A half-brother to Ebadiyla, he looked a potential Group horse when winning a maiden and minor event, but was soon cut down to size when tried in Listed and Group company. Connections wisely dropped him back in class, and he repaid them by putting up a fine performance to win a long-distance handicap at Leopardstown in November. There is much more to come from this likeable colt.
**J Oxx in IRE [2-5] H H Aga Khan.*

EPIDAURUS RR 64f 3511[2]
3 b f Royal Academy (USA) 7.8f **(77)** - Trikymia (Final Straw) 7.9f **(64)**
Form - 62
Record 1998 - 1st:0 2nd:1 3rd:0 Ran:2
Win Prizemoney £0 *Total Prizemoney* £1,150
1998 Turf 0-2: (8f 2) (frm, hrd)
Scopey, currently average filly. Turf high 64 (began Jly) - 2nd of 9 getting 5lb from Bedaayat Farah (10 Aug Windsor 8f hrd RF 3511).
**H R A Cecil [0-2] L Marinopoulos.*

EPISTOLAIRE (IRE) RR 114f 4345a[4]
3 b c Alzao (USA) 9.8f **(73)** - Epistolienne (Law Society (USA)) 9.9f **(70)**
Form - 21314
1998 Turf 2-5: (12f 2, 13f 2-3) (hvy, sft 1-2, gd 1-2)
Group-class colt. Turf high 114 - 1st of 8 getting 11lb from Sibling Rival (30 Aug Deauville RF 4079a). He proved himself a high-class middle-distance horse when running Dream Well to a length and a half at Longchamp in May, but had a hard race when winning a Group Two at Deauville in August and seemed to be feeling the effects of that effort when finishing a below-par fourth in the Prix Niel. Better than that form suggests, he is certain to win another big race. **A Fabre in FR [2-5] Baron Edouard de Rothschild.*

EPSOM CYCLONE (USA) BHB 92f **RR 89+f** 4741[18]
3 ch c Rahy (USA) 9.1f **(80)** - Aneesati (Kris) 9.5f **(73)**
Form - 120010
Record 1998 - 1st:2 2nd:1 3rd:0 Ran:6
Pre1998 - 1st:0 2nd:0 3rd:0 Ran:1
Win Prizemoney £11,642 *Total Prizemoney* £14,102
Wins * **1998** Spt Salisb (HVY) H 6f 87 89 <
* **1998** Mar Doncas (GD) 6f 84
1998 Turf 2-6: (5f, 6f 2-5) (g-s, gd 2-4, g-f)
Scopey, useful colt, effective 6f, acts on gd. Turf high 89 - 1st of 11 getting 11lb from Carranita (30 Spt Salisbury RF 4586) - also 1st of 17 from The Downtown Fox (28 Mar Doncaster RF 0488). Put up a good performance to win at Salisbury, but lost his action next time. **B W Hills [2-7] Salem Bel Obaida.*

EPWORTH BHB 37f **RR 51f** 4927[11]
4 b f Unfuwain (USA) 11.4f **(74)**-Positive Attitude (Red Sunset) 8.2f **(63)**
Form - 0508080
Record 1998 - 1st:0 2nd:0 3rd:0 Ran:7
Pre1998 - 1st:0 2nd:3 3rd:1 Ran:10
Win Prizemoney £0 *Total Prizemoney* £5,365
1998 Turf 0-6: (7f, 8f, 10f 2, 11f, 12f) (sft, g-s, frm 4) 1998 AW 0-1: (8f) (Fibr)
Scopey, fair filly, effective 9 to 10f, acts on sft to gd, has worn blinkers. Turf high 51 (began Jly).
**L J Barratt [0-7] Ray Bailey (from J A Glover [0-9] Oct 1997).*

EQUERRY BHB 50f59a **RR 21f 59a** 4014[10]
7 b g Midyan (USA) 9.9f **(64)**-Supreme Kingdom(Take A Reef) 7.5f **(59)**
Form - 000
Record 1998 - 1st:0 2nd:0 3rd:0 Ran:3
Pre1998 - 1st:7 2nd:8 3rd:4 Ran:34
Win Prizemoney £32,832 *Total Prizemoney* £43,372
Wins 1996 Spt Ayr (G-F) C 8f 70
1996 Jly Newcas (G-F) H 7f 81 82 <
1996 Jun Newcas (FRM) H 8f 79 82 <
1996 Jun Beverl (G-F) H 8.5f 75 79
1995 Jly Thirsk (FRM) H 8f 67 75
1995 Jly Wolver (STD) H 8.5f 58 62
1995 May Beverl (G-F) H 8.5f 60 65
1998 Turf 0-3: (7f, 8f 2) (g-s, gd, frm)
Fair gelding, has worn blinkers. Turf high 21 (began Aug). Becoming disappointing.
**M Dods [0-4] A G Watson (from M Johnston [7-21] Spt 1996).*

EQUINOX RR 420[5]
7 b g Chauve Souris - Contessa (HUN) (Peleid) 7.6f **(37)**
Form - 5
Record 1998 - 1st:0 2nd:0 3rd:0 Ran:1
1998 AW 0-1: (12f) (Fibr)
Formerly very poor gelding - 5th of 5 to Filial (11 Mar Southwell 12f Fibr RF 0420). **A P Jarvis [0-1] Mrs P Stroud.*

EQUITY PRINCESS BHB 104f **RR 109f** 4733[2]
3 b f Warning 8.1f **(77)** - Hawait Al Barr (Green Desert (USA)) 8.6f **(78)**
Form - 51252252
Record 1998 - 1st:1 2nd:4 3rd:0 Ran:8
Pre1998 - 1st:1 2nd:2 3rd:1 Ran:5
Win Prizemoney £10,547 *Total Prizemoney* £51,111
Wins * **1998** Jun Hamilt (SFT) 9.2f 103+ <
* 1997 Spt Ayr (GD) 8f 81
1998 Turf 1-8: (8f 6, 9f 1-1, 10f) (sft, g-s 1-2, gd 3, g-f, frm)
Pattern-class filly, effective 8 to 9f, best at 8f, acts on sft to g-f, likes Ascot. Turf high 109 - 2nd of 12 giving 14lb to Fizzed (20 Jun Ascot 8f g-f RF 2135) - also 1st of 5 getting 5lb from Connoisseur Bay (10 Jun Hamilton RF 1872). Consistent. She is as game as a pebble and was terribly unlucky not to win a Listed or Group race, being beaten by no more than a length on three occasions. Connections are quite rightly proud of her tremendous will to win.
**M Johnston [2-13] Maktoum Al Maktoum.*

ERIC THE KING BHB 43f **RR 49f** 2626[14]
7 ch g Seymour Hicks (FR) 9.6f **(51)** - Friendly Marina (Be Friendly) 9.3f **(53)**
Form - 080
Record 1998 - 1st:0 2nd:0 3rd:0 Ran:3
1998 Turf 0-3: (8f 2, 10f) (g-f, frm 2)
Moderate gelding, has worn blinkers. Turf high 49.
**R Simpson [0-3] Miss J Rumford.*

ERIKA'S YOUNG MAN BHB 33f **RR 14f** 3110[6]
3 b c Unfuwain (USA) 11.4f **(74)** - Tearful Reunion (Pas de Seul) 9.1f **(67)**
Form - 006
Record 1998 - 1st:0 2nd:0 3rd:0 Ran:3
Pre1998 - 1st:0 2nd:0 3rd:0 Ran:4
Win Prizemoney £0 *Total Prizemoney* £339
1998 Turf 0-2: (12f, 16f) (g-f, frm) 1998 AW 0-1: (10f) (Equi)

Unfurnished, poor colt, has worn blinkers.
**B A Pearce [0-3] Richard Gray (from M J Haynes [0-4] Spt 1997).*

ERINRINCA (IRE) BHB 42f31a **RR 37f 31a** 31[9]
4 ch f Waajib 8.9f **(67)** - Rivulet (USA) (Irish River (FR)) 8.6f **(78)**
Form - 0
Record 1998 - 1st:0 2nd:0 3rd:0 Ran:1
Pre1998 - 1st:0 2nd:0 3rd:0 Ran:5
Win Prizemoney £0 *Total Prizemoney* £497
1998 AW 0-1: (13f) (Equi)
Workmanlike, very moderate filly, has worn blinkers.
**J E Banks [0-6] J A Bianchi.*

ERINVALE BHB 68f60a **RR 71+f 60a** 4876[12]
2 ch g Mon Tresor 7.9f **(60)** - Honey Mill (Milford) 9f **(61)**
Form - 30400
Record 1998 - 1st:0 2nd:0 3rd:1 Ran:5
Win Prizemoney £0 *Total Prizemoney* £509
1998 Turf 0-2: (5f 2) (gd, g-f) 1998 AW 0-3: (5f, 6f 2) (Fibr 3)
Above-average gelding. Turf high 71 - 4th of 5 giving 7lb to Beverley Monkey (1 Jun Hamilton 5f g-f RF 1616). AW high 49.
**P C Haslam [0-5] Middleham Park Racing.*

ERITH'S CHILL WIND BHB 55f **RR 64f** 4145[14]
2 b f Be My Chief (USA) 10.2f **(62)** - William's Bird (USA) (Master Willie) 7f **(70)**
Form - 07630
Record 1998 - 1st:0 2nd:0 3rd:1 Ran:5
Win Prizemoney £0 *Total Prizemoney* £256
1998 Turf 0-5: (6f 3, 7f 2) (gd, g-f 3, frm)
Average filly. Turf high 64 (began Jly).
**S Dow [0-5] Advance Reprographic Printers.*

ERLKING (IRE) BHB 41f40a **RR 51df 40a** 756[10]
8 b g Fairy King (USA) 7.7f **(75)**-Cape of Storms(Fordham(USA))8f **(49)**
Form - 0
Record 1998 - 1st:0 2nd:0 3rd:0 Ran:1
Pre1998 - 1st:2 2nd:3 3rd:5 Ran:23
Win Prizemoney £6,258 *Total Prizemoney* £10,460
Wins * 1996 *Jan Lingfi (STD) H 12f 35 39*
1998 AW 0-1: (16f) (Fibr)
Fair gelding, has worn blinkers. Inconsistent.
**S Mellor [4-36] The Ridgeway Ramblers (from Lord Huntingdon [1-13] Aug 1993).*

ERMINE (IRE) RR 67f 4998[6]
2 ch f Cadeaux Genereux 7.9f **(76)** - Nibbs Point (IRE) (Sure Blade (USA)) 11.3f **(67)**
Form - 06
Record 1998 - 1st:0 2nd:0 3rd:0 Ran:2
1998 Turf 0-2: (7f 2) (sft, frm)
Currently average filly. Turf high 67 (began Spt).
**L M Cumani [0-2] Lady Halifax.*

ERRANT BHB 34f55a **RR 40f 55a** 4313[14]
6 b h Last Tycoon 9.4f **(73)** - Wayward Lass (USA) (Hail the Pirates (USA)) 11f **(78)**
Form - 434253201186800
Record 1998 - 1st:2 2nd:2 3rd:2 Ran:14
Pre1998 - 1st:2 2nd:2 3rd:2 Ran:22
Win Prizemoney £10,572 *Total Prizemoney* £15,506
Wins * **1998** *Jun Southw (STD) C 11f 59*
* **1998** *Jun Southw (STD) S 11f 59*
* 1996 *Mar Lingfi (STD) 10f 65* <
* 1996 *Feb Lingfi (STD) 8f 56*
1998 Turf 0-6: (8f, 10f 5) (gd 2, g-f 3, hrd) 1998 AW 2-8: (10f 3, 11f 2-4, 12f) (Equi 3, Fibr 2-5)
Fair horse, effective 10 to 11f, best at 11f, acts on gd - acts on Fibr, likes left handed tracks, favours tight tracks. Turf high 56 (1st run) - 3rd of 18 to Eurolink the Lad (5 May Brighton 10f gd RF 1035). AW high 59 - 1st of 10 getting 5lb from State Approval (12 Jun Southwell RF 1944) - also 1st of 9 getting 3lb from Filmore West (18 Jun Southwell RF 2097). Becoming disappointing. Often there or thereabouts in modest events on turf and sand, but was on a long losing run until landing a couple of races of that sort in June.
**D J S Cosgrove [4-35] L Conway (from J H M Gosden [0-1] Jun 1995).*

ERRO CODIGO BHB 63f70a **RR 62f 70a** 3506[5]
3 b g Formidable (USA) 7.8f **(60)** - Home Wrecker (DEN) (Affiliation Order (USA)) 6f **(70)**
Form - 6136500342355
Record 1998 - 1st:1 2nd:1 3rd:3 Ran:13
Pre1998 - 1st:0 2nd:3 3rd:1 Ran:7
Win Prizemoney £3,550 *Total Prizemoney* £10,675
Wins * **1998** *Feb Southw (STD) 6f 62* <
1998 Turf 0-9: (5f, 6f 3, 7f 5) (sft, gd 5, g-f, frm 2) 1998 AW 1-4: (6f 1-4) (Fibr 1-4)
Strong, above-average gelding, effective 5 to 7f, best at 6f, acts on gd to frm - acts on Fibr, has worn blinkers, prefers left handed tracks, prefers tight tracks, and does well at Catterick. Turf high 62 - 2nd of 15 giving 3lb to Bollin Ethos (2 Jly Catterick 7f frm RF 2464). AW high 70 - 3rd of 13 giving 11lb to Rockswain (7 Mar Wolverhampton 6f Fibr RF 0409) - also 1st of 14 giving 5lb to Scurrilous (23 Feb Southwell RF 0345). He changed stables before embarking on a sand campaign, and got off the mark for his new yard in a maiden in the Southwell Fibresand in February. Mixed form since.
**S E Kettlewell [1-13] D Neale (from Mrs J R Ramsden [0-7] Aug 1997).*

ERTLON BHB 65f68a **RR 68f 68a** 1687[4]
8 b g Shareef Dancer (USA) 10.1f **(67)**-Sharpina (Sharpen Up) 8.3f **(67)**
Form - 6374
Record 1998 - 1st:0 2nd:0 3rd:1 Ran:3
Pre1998 - 1st:5 2nd:10 3rd:7 Ran:74
Win Prizemoney £21,915 *Total Prizemoney* £45,901
Wins * 1997 *Mar Lingfi (STD) C 7f 76*
* 1995 Apr Bright (G-F) H 7f 75 86 <
* 1994 *Nov Lingfi (STD) H 8f 72 82+*
* 1994 Oct Yarmou (GD) H 7f 68 68
1998 Turf 0-1: (7f) (gd) 1998 AW 0-2: (8f 2) (Equi 2)
Average gelding, effective 7 to 8f, best at 7f, acts on g-f to hrd - acts on Equi, has worn blinkers, excels at Lingfield, does well at Yarmouth. AW high 68 (1st run) - 3rd of 10 getting 8lb from Banzhaf (15 Jan Lingfield 8f Equi RF 0092). Consistent.
**C E Brittain [5-77] C E Brittain.*

ERUDITE RR 109f 5055a[2]
3 ch f Generous (IRE) 11.5f **(82)** - Roupala (USA) (Vaguely Noble) 10.1f **(72)**
Form - 22
1998 Turf 0-2: (12f, 16f) (hvy, sft)
Currently Pattern-class filly. Turf high 109 (began Spt) - 2nd of 7 getting 12lb from Tiraaz (25 Oct Longchamp 16f hvy RF 5055a). This French-trained filly was disqualified after winning a listed race at Chantilly in September, but improved on that when running the useful four-year-old Tiraaz to a short head in the Prix Royal-Oak. She looks a useful stayer in the making, and is likely to be aimed at the Ascot Gold Cup in 1999. **M Zilber in FR [0-2] K Abdulla.*

ERUPT BHB 54f53a **RR 57f 53a** 4153[6]
5 b g Beveled (USA) 6.9f **(64)** - Sparklingsovereign (Sparkler) 8.4f **(55)**
Form - 701058006
Record 1998 - 1st:1 2nd:0 3rd:0 Ran:9
Pre1998 - 1st:1 2nd:3 3rd:1 Ran:22
Win Prizemoney £6,396 *Total Prizemoney* £10,722
Wins * **1998** May Mussel (GD) H 7.1f 56 62
1995 Oct Chepst (SFT) H 6.1f 66 73 <
1998 Turf 1-8: (6f 2, 7f 1-4, 8f 2) (g-s, gd 2, g-f 1-3, frm 2) 1998 AW 0-1: (7f) (Fibr)
Fair gelding, effective 6 to 7f, best at 6f, acts on g-f to frm, best on g-f, has worn blinkers. Turf high 62 - 1st of 13 getting 6lb from Skyers Flyer (1 May Musselburgh RF 0957). He caught the eye more than once in '97 without managing to win, but popped up at a big price at Musselburgh in May. He is not easy to predict and looks inconsistent.
**M Brittain [1-9] Sidney Eaton (from G B Balding [1-22] Spt 1997).*

ESCENA (USA) RR 5166a[1]
5 b m Strawberry Road (AUS) 14.5f **(57)** - Claxton's Slew (USA) (Seattle Slew (USA)) 9.4f **(76)**
Form - 1
1998 AW 1-1: (9f 1-1) (Dirt 1-1)
Currently Group-class filly. (1st run) - 1st of 8 giving 3lb to Banshee Breeze (7 Nov Churchill Downs RF 5166a). Narrowly held off the favourite to land the Breeders' Cup Distaff. She has been

retired. **W Mott in USA [1-2] Allen Paulson.*

ESCORT RR 74f 5145[1]

2 b g Most Welcome 8.6f **(66)** - Benazir (High Top) 10.2f **(67)**
Form - 001
Record 1998 - 1st:1 2nd:0 3rd:0 Ran:3
Win Prizemoney £3,427 *Total Prizemoney* £3,427
Wins * **1998** Nov Doncas (SFT) 8f 74 <
1998 Turf 1-3: (6f 2, 8f 1-1) (g-s, gd 1-1, frm)
Currently above-average gelding. Turf high 74 (began Aug) - 1st of 13 from Tiger Talk (7 Nov Doncaster RF 5145).
**W J Haggas [1-3] J M Greetham.*

ES GO BHB 45f **RR 47f** 5061[2]

5 ch g Dunbeath (USA) 9.9f **(53)** - Track Angel (Ardoon) 7.3f **(53)**
Form - 70302412
Record 1998 - 1st:1 2nd:2 3rd:1 Ran:7
Pre1998 - 1st:0 2nd:0 3rd:0 Ran:5
Win Prizemoney £2,610 *Total Prizemoney* £5,008
Wins * **1998** Oct Newcas (SFT) H 10.1f 36 47 <
1998 Turf 1-7: (10f 1-2, 12f, 13f, 14f, 16f 2) (sft, g-s 1-1, gd, g-f, frm 3)
Moderate gelding, effective 10f, acts on sft to g-s, has worn blinkers, likes left handed tracks. Turf high 47 - 1st of 20 getting 14lb from Miss Salsa Dancer (21 Oct Newcastle RF 4917).
**R Bastiman [1-14] Peter Beaton-Brown.*

ESHTIAAL (USA) BHB 99f **RR 99f** 1458[8]

4 b br c Riverman (USA) 9.7f **(78)** - Lady Cutlass (USA) (Cutlass (USA)) 8.5f **(76)**
Form - 8
Record 1998 - 1st:0 2nd:0 3rd:0 Ran:1
Pre1998 - 1st:4 2nd:1 3rd:2 Ran:8
Win Prizemoney £19,190 *Total Prizemoney* £21,236
Wins * 1997 Spt Pontef (G-F) H 10f 94 99 <
* 1997 Aug Beverl (G-S) H 9.9f 84 94
* 1997 Aug Haydoc (G-F) H 10.5f 84 94
* 1997 Jly Ayr (G-F) 10f 72+
1998 Turf 0-1: (10f) (gd)
Scopey, very useful colt, effective 10 to 11f, best at 10f, acts on gd to frm, often wears blinkers (extremely effectively), prefers tight tracks. Ran a stinker on his sole start of '98.
**J L Dunlop [4-9] Hamdan Al Maktoum.*

ESPADA (IRE) RR 79f 3660[1]

2 b c Mukaddamah (USA) 7.6f **(74)** - Folk Song (CAN) (The Minstrel (CAN)) 10f **(72)**
Form - 54221
Record 1998 - 1st:1 2nd:2 3rd:0 Ran:5
Win Prizemoney £4,299 *Total Prizemoney* £6,699
Wins * **1998** Aug Ripon (G-F) 6f 79 <
1998 Turf 1-5: (5f, 6f 1-4) (gd 4, g-f 1-1)
Above-average colt. Turf high 79 - 1st of 11 giving 2lb to James Dee (15 Aug Ripon RF 3660). **P Calver [1-5] Mrs Janis MacPherson.*

ESPERERO (USA) RR 102f 3778a[3]

3 b c Forty Niner (USA) 8.8f **(73)** - Hydro Calido (USA) (Nureyev (USA)) 8.7f **(78)**
Form - 3
1998 Turf 0-1: (8f) (gd)
Currently very useful colt. (1st run) - 3rd of 7 to Sand Falcon (11 Aug Deauville 8f gd RF 3778a). He finished behind Florazi in a Listed event at Deauville and is not a Group horse on that form.
**in FR [0-1].*

ESPERTO BHB 52f50a **RR 57f 50a** 1244[2]

5 b g Risk Me (FR) 8f **(53)** - Astrid Gilberto (Runnett) 7f **(59)**
Form - 322
Record 1998 - 1st:0 2nd:2 3rd:1 Ran:3
Pre1998 - 1st:2 2nd:2 3rd:2 Ran:12
Win Prizemoney £3,704 *Total Prizemoney* £7,138
Wins * 1997 May Nottin (GD) S 10f 53 <
* 1996 Apr Nottin (GD) SH 10f 40 44
1998 Turf 0-3: (10f 3) (sft, gd, frm)
Fair gelding, effective 10f, acts on sft to hrd, excels at Folkestone and Nottingham. Turf high 57 - 2nd of 18 to Eurolink the Lad (5 May Brighton 10f gd RF 1035). Consistent.
**J Pearce [2-15] Mrs Anne Holman-Chappell.*

ESPRESSO RR 35f 2541[13]

3 br g Faustus (USA) 9.1f **(54)** - Shikabell (Kala Shikari) 8.4f **(54)**
Form - 700
Record 1998 - 1st:0 2nd:0 3rd:0 Ran:3
Pre1998 - 1st:0 2nd:0 3rd:0 Ran:4
1998 Turf 0-3: (10f, 14f 2) (g-s, g-f 2)
Workmanlike, very moderate gelding, often wears blinkers. Turf high 35. **J W Hills [0-7] Espresso Racing.*

ESPRIT DU COEUR (IRE) RR 1f 3400[10]

2 ch f Up and At 'em - Cri Basque (Gay Fandango (USA)) 8.5f **(59)**
Form - 80
Record 1998 - 1st:0 2nd:0 3rd:0 Ran:2
1998 Turf 0-2: (5f, 6f) (frm 2)
Currently very poor filly. Turf high 1 (began Jly).
**A Kelleway [0-2] P A Kelleway.*

ESSANDESS (IRE) BHB 40f45a **RR 46f 45a** 4677[17]

3 b f Casteddu 7.4f **(54)** - Ra Ra (Lord Gayle (USA)) 8.8f **(62)**
Form - 3858000760
Record 1998 - 1st:0 2nd:0 3rd:0 Ran:9
Pre1998 - 1st:0 2nd:0 3rd:1 Ran:6
Win Prizemoney £0 *Total Prizemoney* £613
1998 Turf 0-5: (7f 3, 8f, 10f) (gd 2, g-f 2, frm) 1998 AW 0-4: (6f, 7f, 8f 2) (Fibr 4)
Light-framed, moderate filly, effective 7f, - acts on Fibr. Turf high 46. AW high 37. **J L Eyre [0-15] Mrs Sybil Howe.*

ESTACADO (IRE) BHB 57f **RR 58f** 4453[6]

2 b f Dolphin Street (FR) - Raubritter (Levmoss) 11.4f **(66)**
Form - 8006
Record 1998 - 1st:0 2nd:0 3rd:0 Ran:4
Win Prizemoney £0 *Total Prizemoney* £75
1998 Turf 0-4: (5f, 6f, 7f 2) (gd, frm 3)
Fair filly, often wears blinkers. Turf high 58.
**B Gubby [0-4] Brian Gubby Ltd.*

ESTERAAD (IRE) BHB 91f **RR 80f** 4306[3]

2 ch f Cadeaux Genereux 7.9f **(76)** - Eclipsing (IRE) (Baillamont (USA)) 7f **(78)**
Form - 513
Record 1998 - 1st:1 2nd:0 3rd:1 Ran:3
Win Prizemoney £4,695 *Total Prizemoney* £5,217
Wins * **1998** Jly Nottin (G-F) 6.1f 78+ <
1998 Turf 1-3: (6f 1-2, 7f) (gd 1-1, g-f 2)
Currently decent filly. Turf high 80 - also 1st of 9 from Accelerating (18 Jly Nottingham RF 2923). **J L Dunlop [1-3] Khalil Alsayegh.*

ESTERELLE (USA) BHB 29f **RR 34f** 2856[4]

3 ch f Trempolino (USA) 11.9f **(77)** - Duck Flighting (USA) (Far North (CAN)) 9.7f **(75)**
Form - 0R04
Record 1998 - 1st:0 2nd:0 3rd:0 Ran:4
1998 Turf 0-4: (8f, 10f, 12f, 16f) (g-f, frm 3)
Neat, very moderate filly. Turf high 34.
**P S McEntee [0-4] Mrs B A McEntee.*

ESTIME (FR) BHB 71f69a **RR 72f 69a** 4889[7]

2 b f Caerleon (USA) 10.9f **(79)** - Almuhtarama (IRE) (Rainbow Quest (USA)) 10.4f **(75)**
Form - 2547
Record 1998 - 1st:0 2nd:1 3rd:0 Ran:4
Win Prizemoney £0 *Total Prizemoney* £1,291
1998 Turf 0-4: (5f, 6f, 7f, 8f) (gd 3, g-f)
Above-average filly. Turf high 72 (began Jly).
**M A Jarvis [0-4] Sheikh Ahmed Al Maktoum.*

ESTOPPED (IRE) BHB 38f50a **RR 40f 50a** 1816[20]

3 b g Case Law 6f **(64)** - Action Belle (Auction Ring (USA)) 8.6f **(65)**
Form - 3047648400080
Record 1998 - 1st:0 2nd:0 3rd:1 Ran:13
Pre1998 - 1st:0 2nd:0 3rd:1 Ran:5
Win Prizemoney £0 *Total Prizemoney* £1,190
1998 Turf 0-5: (7f, 8f, 10f, 12f, 14f) (g-s, gd, g-f, frm 2) 1998 AW 0-8: (7f, 8f 2, 9f, 10f 3, 11f) (Equi 4, Fibr 4)
Light-framed, fair gelding, effective 6 to 10f, acts on gd - acts on Equi, has worn blinkers. Turf high 40. AW high 58 (1st run) - 3rd of

6 giving 5lb to Nisaba (3 Jan Lingfield 10f Equi RF 0017).
**M Quinn [0-13] Mrs S G Davies (from M R Channon [0-5] Jly 1997).*

ETERNAL NIGHT (FR) RR 92f 4791a[2]

2 b c Night Shift (USA) 8.1f **(73)** - Echoes Of Eternity (FR)
Form - 72
1998 Turf 0-2: (6f 2) (g-s, gd)
Currently useful colt. Turf high 92 (began Spt).
**N Meade in IRE [0-2] Mrs Patricia Hunt.*

ETERNITY BHB 54a RR 72f 5141[3]

4 b f Suave Dancer (USA) 10.7f **(68)** - Chellita (Habitat) 9.4f **(70)**
Form - 0124724153

Record					
	1998 -	1st:2	2nd:2	3rd:1	Ran:9
	Pre1998 -	1st:0	2nd:0	3rd:0	Ran:5

Win Prizemoney £5,208 *Total Prizemoney* £8,422

Wins								
* **1998**	Spt	Kempto	(GD)	H	11.1f	56	59	
* **1998**	May	Catter	(SFT)		12f		64	<

1998 Turf 2-9: (10f, 11f 1-2, 12f 1-3, 14f 3) (g-s, gd 1-4, g-f, frm 1-3)
Scopey, above-average filly, effective 11 to 12f, acts on gd, likes left handed tracks, prefers tight tracks. Turf high 72 - also 1st of 4 giving 14lb to Aldwych Arrow (29 May Catterick RF 1574). A tough stayer, she usually races prominently.
**J R Fanshawe [2-14] Dr Catherine Wills.*

ETHBAAT (USA) BHB 43f47a RR 48f 47a 4905a[9]

7 b or br g Chief's Crown (USA) 10.2f **(75)** - Alchaasibiyeh (USA) (Seattle Slew (USA)) 9.4f **(76)**
Form - 656138641050

Record					
	1998 -	1st:2	2nd:0	3rd:1	Ran:9
	Pre1998 -	1st:4	2nd:2	3rd:2	Ran:27

Win Prizemoney £18,596 *Total Prizemoney* £21,587

Wins								
* **1998**	Jly	Killar	(G-F)	H	8.5f	43	48	
1998	*Jan*	*Wolver*	*(STD)*	*S*	*9.4f*		*55*	
1996	*Jly*	*Wolver*	*(STD)*	*C*	*8.5f*		*71*	
1996	*Jly*	*Wolver*	*(STD)*	*C*	*8.5f*		*76*	
1994	Aug	Kempto	(G-F)	H	7f	88	88	<
1994	May	Haydoc	(G-F)		7.1f		88	<

1998 Turf 1-5: (7f, 8f 1-4) (g-s, gd 3, g-f 1-1) 1998 AW 1-4: (8f 2, 9f 1-1, 14f) (Fibr 1-4)
Fair gelding, effective 9f, - acts on Fibr, favours left handed tracks. Turf high 48 (began Jly). AW high 55 (1st run). Inconsistent.
**G Cully in IRE [1-6] Miss J Galvin (from R T Juckes [0-3] Mar 1998).*

ETHEREAL RR 87f 665[1]

3 b c Fairy King (USA) 7.7f **(75)** - Secret Seeker (USA) (Mr Prospector (USA)) 8.8f **(78)**
Form - 1

Record					
	1998 -	1st:1	2nd:0	3rd:0	Ran:1
	Pre1998 -	1st:0	2nd:0	3rd:0	Ran:1

Win Prizemoney £3,533 *Total Prizemoney* £3,533

Wins								
* **1998**	Apr	Newcas	(SFT)		8f		87	<

1998 Turf 1-1: (8f 1-1) (sft 1-1)
Scopey, currently useful colt. (1st run) - 1st of 8 giving 5lb to Pursuit Venture (13 Apr Newcastle RF 0665). He got off the mark with a comfortable win in a soft-ground Newcastle maiden in April.
**D R Loder [1-2] Sheikh Mohammed.*

ETISALAT (IRE) BHB 48f RR 54f 4666[11]

3 b c Lahib (USA) 8f **(69)** - Sweet Repose (High Top) 10.2f **(67)**
Form - 050

Record					
	1998 -	1st:0	2nd:0	3rd:0	Ran:3

1998 Turf 0-3: (7f, 8f 2) (g-s, g-f, frm)
Strong, currently fair colt. Turf high 54 (began Spt).
**R W Armstrong [0-3] Hamdan Al Maktoum.*

ETIZAAZ (USA) RR 91+f 3470[2]

2 b f Diesis 9f **(80)** - Alamosa (Alydar (USA)) 9.1f **(76)**
Form - 12

Record					
	1998 -	1st:1	2nd:1	3rd:0	Ran:2

Win Prizemoney £6,108 *Total Prizemoney* £9,555

Wins								
* **1998**	Jly	York	(G-F)		7f		91++	<

1998 Turf 1-2: (7f 1-2) (frm 1-1, hrd)
Currently useful filly. Turf high 91 (1st run) (began Jly) - 1st of 6 getting 5lb from Silver Apple (10 Jly York RF 2703). A $500,000 yearling, she was an impressive winner on her York debut. Narrowly beaten in a listed race next time, but the fast ground and slow pace were against her and she remains a very promising filly. Joined Godolphin at the end of the year.
**J L Dunlop [1-2] Hamdan Al Maktoum.*

ETMA ROSE (IRE) BHB 45f RR 35f 4643[20]

2 b f Fairy King (USA) 7.7f **(75)** - Lassalia (Sallust) 8.4f **(63)**
Form - 0080

Record					
	1998 -	1st:0	2nd:0	3rd:0	Ran:4

1998 Turf 0-4: (5f, 6f, 7f 2) (gd 2, g-f, frm)
Very moderate filly. Turf high 35 (began Jly).
**R Hollinshead [0-4] Mrs E Rose.*

ETOILE DANCER RR 661[6]

3 ch g Suave Dancer (USA) 10.7f **(68)** - Padelia (Thatching) 8f **(66)**
Form - 6

Record					
	1998 -	1st:0	2nd:0	3rd:0	Ran:1

1998 Turf 0-1: (11f) (hvy)
Workmanlike, currently very poor gelding - 6th of 6 to Raffaello (13 Apr Kempton 11f hvy RF 0661).
**T G Mills [0-1] Mrs Stephanie Merrydew.*

ETTERBY PARK (USA) BHB 91f77a RR 93f 77a 5150[5]

5 b g Silver Hawk (USA) 11.2f **(85)** - Bonita Francita (CAN) (Devil's Bag (USA)) 12.4f **(78)**
Form - 523412215

Record					
	1998 -	1st:2	2nd:3	3rd:1	Ran:9
	Pre1998 -	1st:6	2nd:5	3rd:7	Ran:33

Win Prizemoney £40,721 *Total Prizemoney* £93,653

Wins								
* **1998**	Oct	Newmar	(G-S)	LH	16f	85	93	<
* **1998**	Spt	Yarmou	(G-S)	H	18.2f	80	81	
* 1997	Apr	Sandow	(G-F)	H	16.4f	74	83	
* 1996	Spt	Ayr	(G-F)	H	15f	69	78+	
* 1996	*Jly*	*Wolver*	*(STD)*	*H*	*14.8f*	*51*	*67+*	
* 1996	*Jly*	*Wolver*	*(STD)*	*H*	*12f*	*51*	*65*	
* 1996	Jly	Catter	(G-F)	H	12f	51	60+	
* 1996	Jun	Carlis	(FRM)	H	12f	44	44+	

1998 Turf 2-8: (16f 1-4, 17f, 18f 1-2, 20f) (gd 4, g-f 1-1, frm 1-3) 1998 AW 0-1: (15f) (Fibr)
Useful gelding, effective 16 to 18f, acts on gd to g-f, best on gd, likes right handed tracks. Turf high 93 (began Jly) - 1st of 6 getting 5lb from Souffle (30 Oct Newmarket RF 5067). A tough stayer, suited by forcing tactics, he has been much better on turf than sand despite having won on the latter surface. Running well this term, chasing home stablemate Spirit of Love in the Cesarewitch before an easy victory in a listed race. On his final start he was 12lb higher than when runner-up in the Cesarewitch, and as he does not have the build to carry such big weights, ran well in the circumstances. Acts on any ground, and is tough and genuine.
**M Johnston [8-36] & Mrs G Middlebrook (from Mrs J R Ramsden [0-2] May 1996).*

ETTRICK RR 81f 5137[1]

2 b c Selkirk (USA) 7.9f **(76)** - Lucia Tarditi (FR) (Crystal Glitters (USA)) 11.3f **(79)**
Form - 01

Record					
	1998 -	1st:1	2nd:0	3rd:0	Ran:2

Win Prizemoney £3,486 *Total Prizemoney* £3,486

Wins								
* **1998**	Nov	Doncas	(SFT)		7f		81	<

1998 Turf 1-2: (7f 1-2) (gd 1-2)
Currently decent colt. Turf high 81 (began Oct) - 1st of 20 from Silver Robin (6 Nov Doncaster RF 5137).
**A C Stewart [1-2] Lord Hartington.*

ETTRICK (NZ) BHB 57f RR 56f 4406[17]

3 b c Hereward The Wake (USA) - Kardinia (NZ) (Creag-an-Sgor)
Form - 5400

Record					
	1998 -	1st:0	2nd:0	3rd:0	Ran:4

Win Prizemoney £0 *Total Prizemoney* £563
1998 Turf 0-4: (5f, 7f 2, 10f) (gd, g-f 3)
Fair colt, has worn blinkers. Turf high 56 (began Aug).
**Mrs Barbara Waring [0-4] Mrs J C Andrews.*

EUPHORIC ILLUSION BHB 28f RR 24f 2001[9]

7 ch g Rainbow Quest (USA) 11.2f **(81)** - High and Bright (Shirley Heights) 10.3f **(74)**
Form - 0

Record					
	1998 -	1st:0	2nd:0	3rd:0	Ran:1

Pre1998 - 1st:0 2nd:0 3rd:1 Ran:8
Win Prizemoney £0 *Total Prizemoney* £1,075
1998 Turf 0-1: (18f) (g-s)
Little account gelding, effective 18f, acted on gd, liked tight tracks. (DEAD) **Mrs S J Smith [2-16] Mrs S Smith.*

EUROBOX BOY BHB 72f53a **RR 74f 53a** 2123[2]
5 ch g Savahra Sound 7.8f **(55)** - Princess Poquito (Hard Fought) 8.8f **(62)**
Form - 464334038302
Record 1998 - 1st:0 2nd:1 3rd:4 Ran:11
Pre1998 - 1st:5 2nd:7 3rd:2 Ran:32
Win Prizemoney £14,349 *Total Prizemoney* £28,377
Wins * 1997 Aug Sandow (GD) H 8.1f 67 72 <
* 1997 Jly Salisb (FRM) H 8f 61 59
* 1997 Apr Nottin (G-F) H 8.2f 56 62
* 1996 Aug Leices (G-F) H 8f 51 59
* 1996 Jly Newmar (G-F) C 8f 55
1998 Turf 0-6: (8f 6) (g-s, gd 2, g-f 2, frm) 1998 AW 0-5: (8f, 9f 2, 10f, 11f) (Equi, Fibr 4)
Above-average gelding, effective 8f, acts on g-s to g-f, best on g-f, has worn blinkers, likes right handed tracks. Turf high 74 - 2nd of 13 giving 30lb to Badrinath (19 Jun Newmarket 8f g-f RF 2123). AW high 53. **A P Jarvis [5-45] N Coverdale.*

EUROFEN BHB 38f **RR 34f** 4255[14]
3 br g Goldneyev (USA) - Mineramare (IRE) (Kenmare (FR)) 6.5f **(72)**
Form - 80
Record 1998 - 1st:0 2nd:0 3rd:0 Ran:2
Pre1998 - 1st:0 2nd:1 3rd:0 Ran:9
Win Prizemoney £0 *Total Prizemoney* £619
1998 Turf 0-2: (5f, 7f) (gd, frm)
Light-framed, very moderate gelding, effective 5f, acts on hrd, often wears blinkers (effectively). Turf high 20. Inconsistent.
**A R Dicken [0-1] D W Shaw (from A Bailey [0-1] Jun 1998).*

EUROLINK APACHE (IRE) RR 79f 4000[2]
3 b g Be My Chief (USA) 10.2f **(62)** - Eurolink Dancer (Petoski) 5.7f **(62)**
Form - 2
Record 1998 - 1st:0 2nd:1 3rd:0 Ran:1
Win Prizemoney £0 *Total Prizemoney* £1,095
1998 Turf 0-1: (12f) (gd)
Workmanlike, currently above-average gelding. (1st run) - 2nd of 9 to Profiler (31 Aug Ripon 12f gd RF 4000).
**M Johnston [0-1] Eurolink Group Plc.*

EUROLINK GIORGIANO RR 52f 2850[5]
3 ch c Selkirk (USA) 7.9f **(76)** - Taiga (Northfields (USA)) 9f **(72)**
Form - 5
Record 1998 - 1st:0 2nd:0 3rd:0 Ran:1
1998 Turf 0-1: (8f) (frm)
Well made, currently fair colt. **H R A Cecil [0-1] Eurolink Group Plc.*

EUROLINK MOUSSAKA RR 68f 4149[5]
3 b g Superlative 8.8f **(57)** - Albiflora (USA) (Manila (USA)) 9.3f **(71)**
Form - 75
Record 1998 - 1st:0 2nd:0 3rd:0 Ran:2
1998 Turf 0-2: (6f, 7f) (gd, g-f)
Strong, currently average gelding. Turf high 68 (began Aug).
**C F Wall [0-2] Eurolink Group Plc.*

EUROLINK PROFILE BHB 46f **RR 60f** 4270[17]
4 b f Prince Sabo 6.6f **(64)** - Taiga (Northfields (USA)) 9f **(72)**
Form - 5060
Record 1998 - 1st:0 2nd:0 3rd:0 Ran:4
Pre1998 - 1st:1 2nd:0 3rd:0 Ran:6
Win Prizemoney £2,784 *Total Prizemoney* £3,284
Wins 1997 Jun Yarmou (FRM) 7f 64+ <
1998 Turf 0-4: (6f, 7f, 8f, 10f) (gd, g-f, frm, hrd)
Leggy, average filly, effective 7f, acts on frm. Turf high 34 (began Aug). Becoming disappointing. Won a maiden at three when trained by Cumani, but has shown little since.
**J G Portman [0-4] The Goose Partnership (from L M Cumani [1-6] Oct 1997).*

EUROLINK THE LAD BHB 52f56a **RR 57f 56a** 4648[14]
11 b g Burslem 9.4f **(56)** - Shoshoni Princess (Prince Tenderfoot (USA)) 9f **(61)**
Form - 10
Record 1998 - 1st:1 2nd:0 3rd:0 Ran:2
Pre1998 - 1st:4 2nd:3 3rd:1 Ran:15
Win Prizemoney £53,291 *Total Prizemoney* £56,881
Wins 1998 May Bright (G-F) S 10f 57
1997 Apr Wolver (STD) H 9.4f 48 53
1998 Turf 1-2: (8f, 10f 1-1) (gd 1-1, g-f)
Fair gelding. Turf high 57 (1st run). Inconsistent.
**T D McCarthy [0-1] Eurolink Group Plc (from D Burchell [2-11] May 1998).*

EUROQUEST BHB 32f39a **RR 31f 39a** 190[9]
4 b g Ron's Victory (USA) 9.2f **(52)** - Raaya (Be My Guest (USA)) 9.3f **(67)**
Form - 00780
Record 1998 - 1st:0 2nd:0 3rd:0 Ran:4
Pre1998 - 1st:1 2nd:0 3rd:1 Ran:10
Win Prizemoney £3,723 *Total Prizemoney* £4,219
Wins * *1997 Feb Southw (STD) 6f 43* <
1998 AW 0-4: (8f 3, 11f) (Fibr 4)
Scopey, very moderate gelding, effective 6f, - acts on Fibr, has worn blinkers, likes left handed tracks. AW high 35.
**D Nicholls [1-14] W G Swiers.*

EURO SCEPTIC (IRE) BHB 46f **RR 48f** 3600[3]
6 ch g Classic Secret (USA) 8.8f **(56)** - Very Seldom (Rarity) 10.1f **(60)**
Form - 4000603333
Record 1998 - 1st:0 2nd:0 3rd:4 Ran:10
Pre1998 - 1st:7 2nd:7 3rd:3 Ran:52
Win Prizemoney £22,847 *Total Prizemoney* £35,619
Wins * 1997 Spt Beverl (G-F) H 8.5f 51 57
* 1997 Aug Carlis (G-F) H 8f 44 50
* 1996 Aug Beverl (G-F) H 7.5f 55 58
* 1996 Aug Thirsk (GD) SH 8f 47 59 <
* 1996 May Beverl (G-F) H 8.5f 44 47
1995 Jun Beverl (GD) H 7.5f 45 46
1995 May Beverl (G-F) H 7.5f 41 42
1998 Turf 0-10: (7f 8, 8f 2) (gd 3, g-f 3, frm 4)
Moderate gelding, effective 7 to 8f, best at 8f, acts on g-f to frm, best on frm, mostly wears blinkers (effectively), favours tight tracks, likes Beverley. Turf high 50. Consistent.
**T D Easterby [5-44] C H Stevens (from M H Easterby [2-18] Oct 1995).*

EURO VENTURE BHB 63f75a **RR 70f 75a** 2228[8]
3 b g Prince Sabo 6.6f **(64)** - Brave Advance (USA) (Bold Laddie (USA)) 5.6f **(69)**
Form - 18848
Record 1998 - 1st:1 2nd:0 3rd:0 Ran:5
Pre1998 - 1st:0 2nd:0 3rd:1 Ran:4
Win Prizemoney £3,485 *Total Prizemoney* £4,426
Wins * **1998** *Jan Wolver (STD) 6f 75* <
1998 Turf 0-3: (5f, 6f 2) (gd, g-f 2) 1998 AW 1-2: (6f 1-2) (Fibr 1-2)
Scopey, above-average gelding, effective 5 to 6f, acts on gd - acts on Fibr. Turf high 63. AW high 75 (1st run) - 1st of 8 giving 5lb to Sea Fig (14 Jan Wolverhampton RF 0085). His shrewd trainer found the right opening for him on Fibresand at Wolverhampton in January. He has been below that form since, but hinted at better to come a couple of times in June. **D Nicholls [1-9] W G Swiers.*

EVANDER (IRE) BHB 86f **RR 79f** 2088[12]
3 ch c Indian Ridge 7.6f **(74)**-Heavenly Hope (Glenstal(USA)) 10.1f **(64)**
Form - 63130
Record 1998 - 1st:1 2nd:0 3rd:2 Ran:5
Pre1998 - 1st:0 2nd:1 3rd:0 Ran:1
Win Prizemoney £5,071 *Total Prizemoney* £8,520
Wins * **1998** May Goodwo (G-F) 8f 79 <
1998 Turf 1-5: (8f 1-2, 9f, 10f, 12f) (g-s, gd 3, g-f 1-1)
Scopey, above-average colt, effective 8f, acts on gd to g-f. Turf high 87 - also 1st of 5 from Murghem (19 May Goodwood RF 1323). Showed plenty of promise in decent maidens before getting off the mark at Goodwood. Not seen out after Royal Ascot.
**P F I Cole [1-6] Anthony Speelman.*

EVASIVE STEP BHB 70f72a **RR 71f 72a** 5115[3]
2 b f Batshoof 9.5f **(66)** - Tread Carefully (Sharpo) 7.7f **(59)**
Form - 3556723
Record 1998 - 1st:0 2nd:1 3rd:2 Ran:7

Win Prizemoney £0 *Total Prizemoney* £1,949
1998 Turf 0-6: (6f, 7f 4, 8f) (g-s, gd 2, frm 3) 1998 AW 0-1: (7f) (Fibr)
Above-average filly, effective 6 to 8f, acts on g-s to gd, prefers tight tracks. Turf high 71 (1st run) - 3rd of 10 getting 11lb from Island Hero (8 Jun Pontefract 6f g-s RF 1810).
**T D Easterby [0-7] Mrs Ian Wills.*

EVENING CHORUS (USA) RR 64f 4513^{24}

3 b c Shadeed (USA) 7.7f **(72)** - Evening Air (USA) (J O Tobin (USA)) 9.4f **(67)**
Form - 05604000

Record	**1998** -	1st:0	2nd:0	3rd:0	Ran:8

Win Prizemoney £0 *Total Prizemoney* £631
1998 Turf 0-8: (7f 3, 8f 4, 10f) (g-s, gd 4, g-f 2, frm)
Average colt. Turf high 71. Becoming disappointing. He has been hopelessly outclassed so far. **R Simpson [0-8] Miss J Rumford.*

EVENING PROMISE BHB 100f RR 99f 4364^{1}

2 b f Aragon 7.7f **(58)** - Rosy Sunset (IRE) (Red Sunset) 8.2f **(63)**
Form - 241541

Record	**1998** -	1st:2	2nd:1	3rd:0	Ran:6

Win Prizemoney £15,007 *Total Prizemoney* £18,332

Wins							
	*** 1998**	Spt	Ayr	(G-S)	L	6f	99 <
	*** 1998**	Jly	Nottin	(G-F)		6.1f	77

1998 Turf 2-6: (6f 2-6) (sft 1-1, g-f 1-3, frm 2)
Very useful filly, effective 6f, acts on sft. Turf high 99 - 1st of 10 getting 3lb from First Musical (19 Spt Ayr RF 4364). Ran out of her skin when fifth to Bint Allayl in the Lowther Stakes, having looked rather outclassed. She was a shade disappointing next time out, but bounced back in the Firth of Clyde Stakes. Soft ground, and waiting tactics seem to suit this progressive filly, and she should be seen winning over seven furlongs next year.
**B A McMahon [2-6] Mrs C P Lees-Jones.*

EVENING WORLD (FR) BHB 103f RR 104f 4843^{11}

3 ch c Bering 9.6f **(80)** - Pivoine (USA) (Nureyev (USA)) 8.7f **(78)**
Form - 241160

Record	**1998** -	1st:2	2nd:1	3rd:0	Ran:6
	Pre1998 -	1st:1	2nd:0	3rd:2	Ran:4

Win Prizemoney £23,266 *Total Prizemoney* £29,153

Wins									
	*** 1998**	Jun	York	(G-S)	H	10.4f	99	104	<
	*** 1998**	May	Lingfi	(GD)	H	10f	91	96	
	* 1997	Spt	York	(SFT)		7.9f		100+	

1998 Turf 2-6: (8f, 9f, 10f 2-4) (sft 2, g-s 1-1, gd, g-f 1-2)
Very useful colt, effective 8 to 10f, best at 10f, acts on sft to g-f, best on sft. Turf high 104 - 1st of 6 giving 17lb to Simply Gifted (13 Jun York RF 1983) - also 1st of 11 giving 4lb to Kim's Brave (30 May Lingfield RF 1597). He is lanky, keen, and not an easy ride. That said, he possess plenty of ability as was highlighted by fine front-running displays at Lingfield and York. He failed to produce his best in the autumn, but is better judged on earlier efforts and remains capable of winning a Listed event.
**P F I Cole [3-10] T M Hely-Hutchinson.*

EVENTUALITY RR 58f 5145^{4}

2 b f Petoski 10.4f **(56)** - Queen's Tickle (Tickled Pink) 6.5f **(59)**
Form - 34

Record	**1998** -	1st:0	2nd:0	3rd:1	Ran:2

Win Prizemoney £0 *Total Prizemoney* £554
1998 Turf 0-2: (8f 2) (sft, gd)
Currently fair filly. Turf high 58 (began Oct).
**R F JohnsonHoughton [0-2] Anthony Harrison.*

EVERGREEN VENTURE RR 67f 2915^{7}

2 b c Pursuit of Love 9.5f **(69)** - Georgica (USA) (Raise A Native) 11.2f **(69)**
Form - 7

Record	**1998** -	1st:0	2nd:0	3rd:0	Ran:1

1998 Turf 0-1: (6f) (frm)
Currently average colt. **S P C Woods [0-1] Dr Frank Chao.*

EVERY PENNY BHB 36f RR 50f 4415^{10}

3 b f Interrex (CAN) 7.7f **(51)** - Shiny Penny (Glint of Gold) 9.3f **(66)**
Form - 0

Record	**1998** -	1st:0	2nd:0	3rd:0	Ran:1
	Pre1998 -	1st:0	2nd:0	3rd:0	Ran:2

1998 Turf 0-1: (8f) (frm)
Leggy, currently fair filly.
**E L James [0-1] V R Bedley (from A P Jones [0-2] Spt 1997).*

EVEZIO RUFO BHB 39f43a RR 55f 43a 4777^{5}

6 b g Blakeney 11.9f **(53)** - Empress Corina (Free State) 8.7f **(61)**
Form - 68321163225221645034356745

Record	**1998** -	1st:3	2nd:5	3rd:4	Ran:25
	Pre1998 -	1st:2	2nd:1	3rd:2	Ran:24

Win Prizemoney £13,334 *Total Prizemoney* £18,829

Wins								
	*** 1998**	*Apr*	*Wolver*	*(STD)*	*H*	*12f*	*54*	*57*
	*** 1998**	*Feb*	*Southw*	*(STD)*	*H*	*12f*	*44*	*61*
	*** 1998**	*Jan*	*Lingfi*	*(STD)*	*SH*	*13f*	*44*	*47*
	* 1997	*May*	*Southw*	*(STD)*	*H*	*11f*	*45*	*50*
	1994	Nov	Folkes	(SFT)		9.7f		82

1998 Turf 0-4: (12f 4) (gd 3, g-f) 1998 AW 3-21: (11f 3, 12f 2-13, 13f 1-2, 14f, 15f, 16f) (Equi 1-3, Fibr 2-18)
Fair gelding, effective 12 to 13f, best at 12f, acts on gd - acts on AW, best on Fibr, mostly wears blinkers (very effectively), favours tight tracks, excels at Lingfield and likes Wolverhampton. Turf high 55. AW high 61 - 1st of 6 getting 8lb from Moonraking (6 Feb Southwell RF 0238) - also 1st of 5 getting 27lb from Jamaican Flight (7 Apr Wolverhampton RF 0595). He is quite a versatile character, mixing hurdling with Flat racing on sand and turf. He has shown consistent form in modest events over middle distances on sand since the start of the year, including victories on both types of surface. Twelve furlongs looks to be the limit of his stamina.
**N P Littmoden [5-62] T Clarke (from J L Dunlop [1-4] Apr 1995).*

EVIE HONE (IRE) BHB 78f RR 63f 4956^{4}

2 ch f Royal Academy (USA) 7.8f **(77)** - Tochar Ban (USA) (Assert) 10.6f **(85)**
Form - 004

Record	**1998** -	1st:0	2nd:0	3rd:0	Ran:3

Win Prizemoney £0 *Total Prizemoney* £270
1998 Turf 0-3: (7f 2, 8f) (gd, g-f, frm)
Currently average filly, often wears blinkers. Turf high 63 (began Spt). **B W Hills [0-3] Jeremy Gompertz.*

EWAR SUNRISE BHB 52f32a RR 46f 32a 398^{10}

5 ch m Shavian 7.7f **(67)** - Sunset Reef (Mill Reef (USA)) 10.5f **(78)**
Form - 0080

Record	**1998** -	1st:0	2nd:0	3rd:0	Ran:4
	Pre1998 -	1st:0	2nd:2	3rd:1	Ran:10

Win Prizemoney £0 *Total Prizemoney* £3,069
1998 AW 0-4: (6f, 7f, 8f 2) (Equi 2, Fibr 2)
Moderate filly, has worn blinkers. AW high 17. Becoming disappointing.
**K O Cunningham-Brown [0-6] A J Richards (from C E Brittain [0-8] Jun 1996).*

EWENNY BHB 75f RR 76f 1548^{3}

2 b f Warrshan (USA) 9.7f **(59)** - Laleston (Junius (USA)) 7.7f **(65)**
Form - 133

Record	**1998** -	1st:1	2nd:0	3rd:2	Ran:3

Win Prizemoney £3,731 *Total Prizemoney* £4,652

Wins							
	*** 1998**	May	Warwic	(GD)		5f	66 <

1998 Turf 1-3: (5f 1-2, 6f) (g-f 1-2, frm)
Currently above-average filly. Turf high 76.
**J M P Eustace [1-3] K J Mercer.*

EXACTLY A NESHAD (GER) RR 13f 3689^{11}

4 gr g Neshad (USA) 5.5f **(59)** - Exactly A Thousand (FR) (Mille Balles (FR))
Form - 0

Record	**1998** -	1st:0	2nd:0	3rd:0	Ran:1

1998 Turf 0-1: (6f) (frm)
Currently poor gelding. **G L Moore [0-1] Mrs J Moore.*

EXALT RR 2657^{13}

2 b c Puissance 7.1f **(60)** - Gild the Lily (Ile de Bourbon (USA)) 10.1f **(67)**
Form - 0

Record	**1998** -	1st:0	2nd:0	3rd:0	Ran:1

1998 AW 0-1: (6f) (Fibr)
Currently very poor colt. **J Balding [0-1] Mrs J Coghlan-Everitt.*

EXALTATION (USA) RR 99f 4348a[2]

3 b/ c Exbourne (USA) - Ardy Arnie (USA) (Hold Your Peace (USA)) 9f **(72)**

Form - 222

1998 Turf 0-3: (8f 2, 12f) (hvy, sft 2)

Currently very useful colt. Turf high 99 - 2nd of 11 getting 9lb from Inchrory (13 Spt Taby 12f sft RF 4348a). **W Neuroth in NOR [0-3].*

EXALTED (IRE) BHB 65f77a RR 73df 77a 1787[7]

5 b g High Estate 10.5f **(66)** - Heavenward (USA) (Conquistador Cielo (USA)) 8.8f **(69)**

Form - 7

Record	**1998 -**	1st:0	2nd:0	3rd:0	Ran:1
	Pre1998 -	1st:1	2nd:1	3rd:3	Ran:14

Win Prizemoney £3,940 *Total Prizemoney* £9,381

Wins 1995 Jly Thirsk (GD) 7f 67+ <

1998 Turf 0-1: (16f) (frm)

Above-average gelding.

**W Jenks [1-14] Mrs Bryan Jenks (from Sir Mark Prescott [1-14] Oct 1996).*

EXBOURNE'S WISH (USA) BHB 81f RR 92f 2860a[1]

3 b c Exbourne (USA) - Social Wish(USA)(Lyphard's Wish (FR)) 9f **(74)**

Form - 1

1998 Turf 1-1: (8f 1-1) (hvy 1-1)

Scopey, useful colt, effective 6 to 8f, acts on hvy to g-f. (1st run) - 1st of 9 from Exaltation (9 Jly Ovrevoll RF 2860a).

**A Lund in NOR [1-1] Stall Bonne Nuit (from B W Hills [1-7] Oct 1997).*

EXCELLENT MEETING (USA) RR 5163a[2]

2 b f General Meeting - Fitted Crown (USA)

Form - 2

1998 AW 0-1: (9f) (Dirt)

Currently Group-class filly. (1st run) - 2nd of 11 to Silverbulletday (7 Nov Churchill Downs 9f Dirt RF 5163a). A Grade One winner, she was runner-up to her stablemate in the Breeders' Cup Juvenile Fillies. **B Baffert in USA [0-1] Golden Eagle Farm.*

EXCLUSION BHB 30f30a RR 42f 30a 186[10]

9 ch g Ballad Rock 7.2f **(63)** - Great Exception (Grundy) 10.3f **(65)**

Form - 0

Record	**1998 -**	1st:0	2nd:0	3rd:0	Ran:1
	Pre1998 -	1st:2	2nd:2	3rd:3	Ran:30

Win Prizemoney £5,984 *Total Prizemoney* £10,687

Wins * 1995 Aug Hamilt (FRM) H 12.1f 38 42

1998 AW 0-1: (12f) (Fibr)

Moderate gelding, has worn blinkers.

**J Hetherton [3-37] James Byrne (from P C Haslam [0-6] Spt 1994).*

EXCLUSIVE BHB 114f RR 114f 3696[6]

3 ch f Polar Falcon (USA) 9f **(74)** - Exclusive Order (USA) (Exclusive Native (USA)) 9.1f **(81)**

Form - 5316

Record	**1998 -**	1st:1	2nd:0	3rd:1	Ran:4
	Pre1998 -	1st:1	2nd:0	3rd:1	Ran:2

Win Prizemoney £131,291 *Total Prizemoney* £172,696

Wins * **1998** Jun Ascot (GD) G1 8f 109 <

* 1997 Spt Kempto (GD) 7f 85+

1998 Turf 1-4: (7f, 8f 1-2, 10f) (gd 1-3, g-f)

Scopey, Group-class filly, effective 8 to 10f, best at 8f, acts on gd to g-f, best on g-f. Turf high 114 - also 1st of 9 from Zalaiyka (17 Jun Ascot RF 2055). A half-sister to Guineas winner Entrepreneur, she looked in tremendous shape when showing improved form to finish third in the 1,000 Guineas, and appreciated waiting tactics when slicing through the field to win the Group One Coronation Stakes at Royal Ascot. Connections felt sure she would stay 10 furlongs, but that did not look the case when she was beaten in the Juddmonte International at York.

**Sir Michael Stoute [2-6] Cheveley Park Stud.*

EXCLUSIVE ASSEMBLY BHB 36f49a RR 29?f 49a 4263[13]

6 ch g Weldnaas (USA) 8.4f **(55)** - Pretty Pollyanna (General Assembly (USA)) 10f **(68)**

Form - 000

Record	**1998 -**	1st:0	2nd:0	3rd:0	Ran:3

Exclusive proved herself just that at Royal Ascot

Pre1998 - 1st:1 2nd:1 3rd:4 Ran:22
Win Prizemoney £3,073 *Total Prizemoney* £5,745
Wins * 1995 *Apr Southw (STD) 7f 57* <
1998 Turf 0-3: (7f, 8f, 10f) (gd, g-f, frm)
Little account gelding. Turf high 16 (began Aug). Becoming disappointing. **A P James [1-27] The Good Judgement Partnership.*

EXCLUSIVELY BHB 45f RR 42f 1987^{4}

3 gr f Absalom 7.1f **(56)** - Peters Pleasure (Jimsun)
Form - 544
Record 1998 - 1st:0 2nd:0 3rd:0 Ran:3
1998 Turf 0-3: (12f 2, 16f) (sft, gd, frm)
Workmanlike, currently moderate filly. Turf high 45.
**J Pearce [0-3] Exclusive Three Partnership.*

EXEAT (USA) RR 103f $4470f^{4}$

2 b br c Dayjur (USA) 6.8f **(79)** - By Your Leave (USA) (Private Account (USA)) 8.5f **(74)**
Form - 2124
Record 1998 - 1st:1 2nd:2 3rd:0 Ran:4
Win Prizemoney £3,631 *Total Prizemoney* £41,094
Wins * **1998** Jly Haydoc (G-F) 6f 93+ <
1998 Turf 1-4: (6f 1-3, 7f) (sft 2, gd, g-f 1-1)
Very useful colt. Turf high 103 - 2nd of 13 to Orpen (23 Aug Deauville 6f sft RF 3916a). He is no Chippendale to look at, but connections know the time of day and he was restricted to French Group One events after running away with a maiden at Haydock. Slightly unlucky when finishing second in the Prix Morny - he was left to race alone on the stands'-side he returned lame after running modestly behind Aljabr in the Prix de la Salamandre. There is a Group race waiting for this colt.
**J H M Gosden [1-4] Lady Harrison.*

EXECUTIVE CHOICE (IRE) BHB 41f RR 52f 4768^{7}

4 b g Don't Forget Me 9.5f **(66)** -Shadia (USA) (Naskra (USA)) 8.8f **(69)**
Form - 078364847
Record 1998 - 1st:0 2nd:0 3rd:1 Ran:9
Pre1998 - 1st:0 2nd:0 3rd:0 Ran:6
Win Prizemoney £0 *Total Prizemoney* £219
1998 Turf 0-9: (7f, 8f 3, 9f 2, 10f 3) (sft, g-s 3, gd 3, frm 2)
Fair gelding, has worn blinkers. Turf high 52.
**B Ellison [0-4] The Couriers Syndicate (from M J Grassick in IRE [0-11] Jly 1998).*

EXECUTIVE EVENT RR 74df 1063^{4}

2 ch c Executive Man 8.9f **(52)** - Recent Events (Stanford) 7.9f **(56)**
Form - 8134
Record 1998 - 1st:1 2nd:0 3rd:1 Ran:4
Win Prizemoney £2,687 *Total Prizemoney* £3,439
Wins * **1998** Apr Thirsk (G-S) C 5f 74 <
1998 Turf 1-4: (5f 1-4) (g-s 1-2, gd 2)
Above-average colt. Turf high 74 - 1st of 9 giving 7lb to Mammas F-C (18 Apr Thirsk RF 0749). **P C Haslam [1-4] Terry Rowley.*

EXECUTIVE OFFICER BHB 22f23a RR 23f 23a 1969^{10}

5 b g Be My Chief (USA) 10.2f **(62)** -Caro's Niece (USA)(Caro) 9.3f **(74)**
Form - 07880
Record 1998 - 1st:0 2nd:0 3rd:0 Ran:2
Pre1998 - 1st:0 2nd:1 3rd:0 Ran:16
Win Prizemoney £0 *Total Prizemoney* £655
1998 Turf 0-1: (10f) (gd) 1998 AW 0-1: (13f) (Equi)
Little account gelding, effective 10f, - acts on Equi, often wears blinkers (effectively), likes left handed tracks. Inconsistent.
**R M Flower [0-21] B C Isitt.*

EXIT RR 54f 2882^{6}

2 b f Exbourne (USA) - Meteoric (High Line) 10.3f **(70)**
Form - 6
Record 1998 - 1st:0 2nd:0 3rd:0 Ran:1
1998 Turf 0-1: (7f) (frm)
Currently fair filly. **M Bell [0-1] Richard Green (Fine Paintings).*

EXIT TO SOMEWHERE (IRE) BHB 94f RR 89f 2311^{1}

3 b c Exit To Nowhere (USA) 8.7f **(77)** - Zivania (IRE) (Shernazar) 10.2f **(73)**
Form - 43101
Record 1998 - 1st:2 2nd:0 3rd:1 Ran:5
Pre1998 - 1st:0 2nd:1 3rd:0 Ran:2
Win Prizemoney £12,344 *Total Prizemoney* £14,886
Wins * **1998** Jun Newcas (G-S) 10.1f 89 <
* **1998** May Chepst (G-F) 8.1f 74+
1998 Turf 2-5: (8f 1-3, 10f 1-2) (g-s 1-2, gd 2, frm 1-1)
Useful colt, effective 7 to 10f, acts on g-s to frm. Turf high 89 - 1st of 4 giving 2lb to Gypsy Passion (26 Jun Newcastle RF 2311). A half-brother to Ivan Luis, his win came in a modest maiden but he had run well in a warm handicap the time before. Down the field at Royal Ascot before winning a minor event at Newcastle in game style. **H R A Cecil [2-7] The Thoroughbred Corporation.*

EXPECT TO SHINE BHB 99f RR 96df 2837^{3}

3 b f Fairy King (USA) 7.7f **(75)** - Anjaab (USA) (Alydar (USA)) 9.1f **(76)**
Form - 3
Record 1998 - 1st:0 2nd:0 3rd:1 Ran:1
Pre1998 - 1st:1 2nd:1 3rd:0 Ran:5
Win Prizemoney £7,067 *Total Prizemoney* £17,655
Wins * 1997 Jly Goodwo (G-F) 6f 85 <
1998 Turf 0-1: (7f) (g-f)
Neat, very useful filly. Finished well on her debut behind Embassy as a two-year-old and duly got off the mark at Goodwood, but her limitations were exposed in useful company after that. She looked thoroughly awkward on her belated reappearance in '98 and finished a tailed-off last of three. One to treat with caution.
**B W Hills [1-6] Maktoum Al Maktoum.*

EXPLOSIVE POWER BHB 44f48a RR 53f 48a 4654^{13}

7 br h Prince Sabo 6.6f **(64)** - Erwarton Seabreeze (Dunbeath (USA)) 7.8f **(70)**
Form - 700
Record 1998 - 1st:0 2nd:0 3rd:0 Ran:3
Pre1998 - 1st:3 2nd:2 3rd:3 Ran:29
Win Prizemoney £7,937 *Total Prizemoney* £10,466
Wins * 1996 *Mar Wolver (STD) H 9.4f 63 75* <
* 1996 *Jan Lingfi (STD) H 10f 54 55*
* 1994 *Nov Lingfi (STD) H 12f 47 48*
1998 Turf 0-1: (12f) (g-f) 1998 AW 0-2: (8f, 10f) (Equi, Fibr)
Fair horse, has worn blinkers. AW high 44. Inconsistent.
**G C Bravery [3-22] G C Bravery (from S P C Woods [0-10] Oct 1994).*

EXPRESS AGAIN RR 34f 2895^{10}

6 b g Then Again 7.4f **(52)** - Before Long (Longleat (USA))
Form - 0
Record 1998 - 1st:0 2nd:0 3rd:0 Ran:1
1998 Turf 0-1: (14f) (gd)
Very moderate gelding. (DEAD)
**R F JohnsonHoughton [0-8] R F JohnsonHoughton.*

EXTENDED APPLAUSE (USA) RR $5163a^{4}$

2 br f Exbourne (USA) - Vivid Concert (IRE) (Chief Singer) 8.9f **(66)**
Form - 4
1998 AW 0-1: (9f) (Dirt)
Currently Pattern-class filly, always wears blinkers. (1st run) - 4th of 11 to Silverbulletday (7 Nov Churchill Downs 9f Dirt RF 5163a). Made much of the running when a close fourth in the Breeders' Cup Juvenile Fillies in 1998.
**M Azpurua in USA [0-1] W Johnston & G Smith.*

EXTRAVAGANZA BHB 83f RR 88f 4763^{3}

3 ch c Rainbow Quest (USA) 11.2f **(81)** - Affection Affirmed (USA) (Affirmed (USA)) 9.3f **(79)**
Form - 14653
Record 1998 - 1st:1 2nd:0 3rd:1 Ran:5
Win Prizemoney £3,434 *Total Prizemoney* £4,979
Wins * **1998** Jun Cheste (G-S) 13.4f 74 <
1998 Turf 1-5: (10f, 12f 2, 13f 1-1, 16f) (gd 1-2, g-f, frm 2)
Scopey, useful colt. Turf high 88. Had a simple task in a maiden on his debut but was well beaten when upped in class on faster ground. **P F I Cole [1-5] H R H Prince Fahd Salman.*

EYEBALLS OUT BHB 72f70a RR 72f 70a 4611^{5}

2 b c Polar Falcon (USA) 9f **(74)** - Jacquelina (USA) **(70f)** (Private Account (USA)) 8.5f **(74)**
Form - 005
Record 1998 - 1st:0 2nd:0 3rd:0 Ran:3
1998 Turf 0-3: (6f 3) (g-s 2, frm)

Currently above-average colt. Turf high 72 (began Spt).
**Sir Mark Prescott [0-3] John Brown & Megan Dennis.*

EYMIR (IRE) RR 102f — 3877a[5]

3 ch c Polish Patriot (USA) 7.8f **(70)** - Eviyrna (USA) 0**0**
Form - 1245
1998 Turf 1-4: (7f, 8f 1-1, 9f, 10f) (gd 3, hrd 1-1)
Very useful colt, effective 7 to 9f, acts on gd to hrd, best on gd. Turf high 102 (1st run) - 1st of 8 giving 16lb to Rahika Rose (3 May Gowran Park RF 1055a). He was outpaced over seven furlongs and is probably best when adopting forcing tactics over a mile.
**J Oxx in IRE [1-8] H H Aga Khan.*

EZRALOW (ITY) RR 92f — 5135a[3]

7 b h Damister (USA) 9.1f **(66)** - Heil (Star Appeal) 9.6f **(65)**
Form - 13
1998 Turf 1-2: (12f 1-1, 15f) (sft 1-1, g-s)
Currently useful horse. Turf high 92 (began Oct) - 3rd of 7 giving 7lb to Rondan (31 Oct Tesio 15f g-s RF 5135a) - also 1st of 8 giving 6lb to Tipetto Ganzo (17 Oct San Siro RF 4944a).
**L Batzella in ITY [1-2].*

FABILLION BHB 68f RR 70f — 2551[6]

6 ch g Deploy 11.4f **(67)** - Kai (Kalamoun) 10.4f **(67)**
Form - 2266
Record 1998 - 1st:0 2nd:2 3rd:0 Ran:4
Pre1998 - 1st:1 2nd:3 3rd:0 Ran:15
Win Prizemoney £4,305 *Total Prizemoney* £13,960
Wins * 1996 Apr Nottin (GD) H 14.1f 61 70 <
1998 Turf 0-4: (16f 2, 18f, 20f) (hvy, gd 3)
Above-average gelding. Turf high 70 (1st run) - 2nd of 13 getting 17lb from Turnpole (27 Mar Doncaster 18f gd RF 0478). Consistent. Returned from a lay-off of twenty months to chase home Turnpole at Doncaster, and ran another fine race to finish runner-up on heavy ground in the Queen's Prize. A keeping-on sixth at Royal Ascot, he stays all day. **C A Smith [1-19] Bill Horton.*

FABLED LIGHT (IRE) BHB 87f RR 85f — 1425[5]

4 b c Alzao (USA) 9.8f **(73)** - Fabled Lifestyle (Kings Lake (USA)) 10.8f **(67)**
Form - 5
Record 1998 - 1st:0 2nd:0 3rd:0 Ran:1
Pre1998 - 1st:1 2nd:0 3rd:0 Ran:5
Win Prizemoney £4,201 *Total Prizemoney* £4,201
Wins * 1997 May Ripon (G-S) H 12.3f 80 83+ <
1998 Turf 0-1: (10f) (gd)
Strong, useful colt. (DEAD) **G Wragg [1-6] Mollers Racing.*

FABRICE BHB 73f RR 73f — 3954[8]

3 b g Pursuit of Love 9.5f **(69)** - Parfum D'Automne (FR) (Sharpen Up) 8.3f **(67)**
Form - 428
Record 1998 - 1st:0 2nd:1 3rd:0 Ran:3
Pre1998 - 1st:0 2nd:0 3rd:1 Ran:1
Win Prizemoney £0 *Total Prizemoney* £2,465
1998 Turf 0-3: (6f, 7f, 8f) (g-f 2, frm)
Above-average gelding. Turf high 73 (began Jly).
**H Candy [0-4] Girsonfield Ltd.*

FABULOUS MTOTO BHB 41f38a RR 51f 38a — 3838[7]

8 b h Mtoto 11.5f **(71)** - El Fabulous (FR) (Fabulous Dancer (USA)) 9.4f **(70)**
Form - 85700400547
Record 1998 - 1st:0 2nd:0 3rd:0 Ran:11
Pre1998 - 1st:4 2nd:5 3rd:1 Ran:38
Win Prizemoney £11,931 *Total Prizemoney* £18,417
Wins * 1997 *Jan Lingfi (STD) H 10f 30 34*
* 1996 Jly Pontef (G-F) H 12f 49 56
* 1996 Jun Windso (G-F) H 11.6f 41 50
1998 Turf 0-9: (10f 4, 12f 5) (gd 2, g-f 2, frm 4, hrd) 1998 AW 0-2: (10f, 12f) (Equi 2)
Fair horse, has broken blood-vessels, effective 12f, acts on g-f to frm, best on frm, has worn blinkers, favours tight tracks. Turf high 53 (1st run) - 7th of 15 to Veronica Franco (14 May Salisbury 12f frm RF 1218). AW high 35.
**M S Saunders [3-50] N R Pike (from D R C Elsworth [1-5] Jun 1993).*

FACE-OFF BHB 55f RR 59f — 4373[10]

3 b f Aragon 7.7f **(58)** - Rock Face (Ballad Rock) 7.8f **(63)**
Form - 85350
Record 1998 - 1st:0 2nd:0 3rd:1 Ran:5
Pre1998 - 1st:0 2nd:0 3rd:0 Ran:6
Win Prizemoney £0 *Total Prizemoney* £815
1998 Turf 0-5: (6f, 7f 3, 8f) (g-f, frm 4)
Unfurnished, fair filly, effective 6f, acts on frm, has worn blinkers. Turf high 59. Consistent.
**C F Wall [0-8] N Ahamad (from R Hannon [0-3] Jun 1997).*

FACE THE CLASS (IRE) RR 55f — 4983[7]

2 ch f Up and At 'em - Siva (FR) (Bellypha) 9.8f **(73)**
Form - 7
Record 1998 - 1st:0 2nd:0 3rd:0 Ran:1
1998 Turf 0-1: (8f) (g-s)
Currently fair filly. **A Kelleway [0-1] Mike Perkins.*

FACILE TIGRE BHB 69f RR 74f — 5121[1]

3 gr g Efisio 7.7f **(69)** - Dancing Diana (Raga Navarro (ITY)) 8f **(64)**
Form - 742214600076001
Record 1998 - 1st:2 2nd:2 3rd:0 Ran:15
Pre1998 - 1st:0 2nd:0 3rd:0 Ran:6
Win Prizemoney £4,650 *Total Prizemoney* £7,425
Wins * **1998** Nov Bright (SFT) H 6f 63 68
* **1998** Jun Bright (FRM) H 5.3f 67 74 <
1998 Turf 2-15: (5f 1-13, 6f 1-1, 7f) (g-s 1-2, gd 3, g-f 1-5, frm 4, hrd)
Workmanlike, above-average gelding, effective 5 to 6f, acts on g-s to g-f, likes left handed tracks, likes tight tracks. Turf high 74 - 1st of 7 giving 2lb to Majalis (2 Jun Brighton RF 1645).
**S Dow [2-21] D G Churston.*

FACSIMILE BHB 62f55a RR 65f 55a — 4877[3]

3 b f Superlative 8.8f **(57)** - Just Julia (Natroun (FR))
Form - 4243
Record 1998 - 1st:0 2nd:1 3rd:1 Ran:4
Pre1998 - 1st:0 2nd:1 3rd:0 Ran:1
Win Prizemoney £0 *Total Prizemoney* £1,839
1998 Turf 0-3: (7f 2, 8f) (g-f, frm 2) 1998 AW 0-1: (6f) (Fibr)
Light-framed, average filly. Turf high 65 (began Aug) - 4th of 18 getting 5lb from Thelonius (4 Oct Warwick 8f g-f RF 4644).
**John Berry [0-4] H R Moszkowicz (from Capt J Wilson [0-1] Jly 1997).*

FADMOOR (IRE) BHB 85f RR 82?f — 3512[3]

2 ch c Mujtahid (USA) 7.4f **(69)** - Gingerly (USA) (Ferdinand (USA))
Form - 60013
Record 1998 - 1st:1 2nd:0 3rd:1 Ran:5
Win Prizemoney £4,780 *Total Prizemoney* £5,634
Wins * **1998** Jly Yarmou (G-F) 5.2f 82? <
1998 Turf 1-5: (5f 1-1, 6f 4) (gd, g-f 1-2, frm, hrd)
Decent colt. Turf high 82 - 1st of 4 getting 3lb from Baltic Lowland (27 Jly Yarmouth RF 3151). **M H Tompkins [1-5] P J M M Racing.*

FADO (FR) RR 117f — 4940a[2]

5 b h Unfuwain (USA) 11.4f **(74)** - Lusitana (FR) (Tyrnavos) 10.1f **(55)**
Form - 32
1998 Turf 0-2: (10f 2) (sft, gd)
Currently high-class colt. Turf high 117 (began Spt) - 2nd of 7 giving 7lb to Great Dane (12 Oct Lyon Parilly 10f sft RF 4940a). He was inched out by Great Dane in a Group Three at Lyon Parilly in October, but is unlikely to improve.
**A deRoyerDupre in FR [0-2] E Fierro.*

FADWA RR 72f — 3807[3]

2 ch f Mizoram (USA) - Mey Madam (Song) 7.2f **(61)**
Form - 53
Record 1998 - 1st:0 2nd:0 3rd:1 Ran:2
Win Prizemoney £0 *Total Prizemoney* £327
1998 Turf 0-2: (6f 2) (g-f, frm)
Currently above-average filly. Turf high 72 (began Aug).
**J W Hills [0-2] Ziad Galadari.*

FA-EQ (IRE) BHB 111f RR 113f — 2012[5]

3 ch c Indian Ridge 7.6f **(74)** - Searching Star (Rainbow Quest (USA)) 10.4f **(75)**
Form - 125
Record 1998 - 1st:1 2nd:1 3rd:0 Ran:3

Pre1998 - 1st:0 2nd:1 3rd:0 Ran:1
Win Prizemoney £5,493 *Total Prizemoney* £45,481
Wins * 1998 May Newmar (GD) 8f 96+ <
1998 Turf 1-3: (8f 1-3) (gd 1-3)
Lengthy, Group-class colt. Turf high 113 - 2nd of 7 to Desert Prince (23 May Curragh 8f gd RF 1506a). He bolted up in a hot Newmarket maiden in May, and had his next start in the Irish 2,000 Guineas. Far from disgraced in second place behind Desert Prince there, he failed to handle easy ground in the St James's Palace Stakes at Royal Ascot and was not seen out again. He is certainly capable of winning a Group race over a mile.
**S bin Suroor [1-4] Godolphin.*

FAFESTA (IRE) RR 5160a[7]
2 f
Form - 7
Record 1998 - 1st:0 2nd:0 3rd:0 Ran:1
1998 Turf 0-1: (9f) (hvy)
Currently very poor filly - 7th of 9 getting 3lb from River Hill (7 Nov San Siro 9f hvy RF 5160a). **L M Cumani [0-1].*

FAHRIS (IRE) BHB 117f RR 119f 1484[8]
4 ch c Generous (IRE) 11.5f **(82)** - Janbiya (IRE) (Kris) 9.5f **(73)**
Form - 8
Record 1998 - 1st:0 2nd:0 3rd:0 Ran:1
Pre1998 - 1st:4 2nd:2 3rd:2 Ran:10
Win Prizemoney £47,967 *Total Prizemoney* £69,808
Wins 1997 Oct Newmar (G-S) L 9f 119 <
1997 Spt Goodwo (GD) G3 10f 113
1997 Apr Newmar (G-F) L 9f 109
1996 Aug Salisb (G-F) 7f 84
1998 Turf 0-1: (10f) (gd)
Scopey, high-class colt, effective 9 to 12f, acts on gd to g-f, best on gd. He looks like a world beater and joined the Godolphin team for 1998. Unfortunately his sole start resulted in a lack-lustre effort at Sandown in May.
**S bin Suroor [0-1] Godolphin (from B Hanbury [3-8] Oct 1997).*

FAHS (USA) BHB 73f RR 72f 5126[4]
6 b br g Riverman (USA) 9.7f **(78)** - Tanwi (Vision (USA)) 9f **(64)**
Form - 33363544737024
Record 1998 - 1st:0 2nd:1 3rd:5 Ran:14
Pre1998 - 1st:2 2nd:2 3rd:5 Ran:22
Win Prizemoney £7,659 *Total Prizemoney* £37,065
Wins 1997 Oct Yarmou (GD) H 10.1f 75 79
1997 May Sandow (G-F) H 10f 70 80 <
1998 Turf 0-14: (8f, 10f 6, 12f 6, 14f) (g-s 2, gd 5, g-f 5, frm 2)
Above-average gelding, effective 10 to 14f, best at 10f, acts on gd to frm, best on gd, prefers right handed tracks, likes tight tracks, excels at Goodwood and Sandown and does well at Yarmouth. Turf high 82 - 5th of 15 getting 1lb from Seignorial (28 Jly Goodwood 14f gd RF 3163).
**G Lewis [0-14] City Industrial Supplies Ltd (from R Akehurst [2-22] Nov 1997).*

FAILED TO HIT BHB 40f67a RR 40f 67a 5002[13]
5 b g Warrshan (USA) 9.7f **(59)** - Missed Again (High Top) 10.2f **(67)**
Form - 43704314110413430410
Record 1998 - 1st:5 2nd:0 3rd:3 Ran:16
Pre1998 - 1st:1 2nd:3 3rd:2 Ran:21
Win Prizemoney £13,501 *Total Prizemoney* £17,756
Wins * 1998 *Oct Lingfi (STD) 12f 65*
* 1998 *Mar Wolver (STD) H 9.4f 60 66*
* 1998 *Feb Lingfi (SLW) 10f 62*
* 1998 *Feb Wolver (STD) C 8.5f 65+*
* 1998 *Feb Lingfi (STD) H 8f 43 51*
1996 Aug Folkes (G-F) 6f 67 <
1998 Turf 0-2: (10f 2) (gd, frm) 1998 AW 5-14: (8f 2-8, 9f 1-2, 10f 1-1, 12f 1-3) (Equi 3-6, Fibr 2-8)
Average gelding, effective 8 to 12f, best at 8f - acts on AW, best on Fibr, mostly wears blinkers (very effectively), favours left handed tracks, favours tight tracks, and excels at Lingfield. Turf high 40 (began Aug). AW high 68 - 3rd of 13 giving 11lb to Green Bopper (28 Mar Wolverhampton 8f Fibr RF 0493) - also 1st of 8 giving 1lb to Amico (21 Mar Wolverhampton RF 0462). Inconsistent. He was on long losing run, but suddenly hit form with three victories on sand in February, making all each time, and added further victories in March and October. Although his victories were against modest opposition, he seems effective on both types of artificial surface.
**N P Littmoden [5-33] M C S D Racing (from Sir Mark Prescott [1-5] Oct 1996).*

FAIR CESTRIAN (IRE) BHB 60f RR 53f 4412[9]
2 b g Petardia 8.2f **(58)** - Fair Chance (Young Emperor) 10.1f **(63)**
Form - 7070
Record 1998 - 1st:0 2nd:0 3rd:0 Ran:4
1998 Turf 0-4: (5f, 6f 2, 7f) (gd, frm 3)
Fair gelding. Turf high 53. **J Berry [0-4] J R & J Littler.*

FAIRFIELD BAY RR 54f 3760[8]
2 b c Emarati (USA) 6.6f **(63)** - Navarino Bay (Averof) 8.2f **(62)**
Form - 08008
Record 1998 - 1st:0 2nd:0 3rd:0 Ran:5
1998 Turf 0-5: (5f 2, 6f 2, 7f) (gd, g-f 3, frm)
Fair colt. Turf high 54.
**Mrs P N Dutfield [0-5] The Fairfield Partnership.*

FAIR FINNISH (IRE) RR 313[5]
4 b g Commanche Run 10.3f **(63)** - Karelia (USA) (Sir Ivor) 10.2f **(70)**
Form - 5
Record 1998 - 1st:0 2nd:0 3rd:0 Ran:1
1998 AW 0-1: (12f) (Equi)
Neat, poor gelding. **Lord Huntingdon [0-1] Lord Weinstock.*

FAIR FLIGHT BHB 96f RR 94f 4845[1]
2 b c Green Desert (USA) 7.8f **(78)** - Barari (USA) (Blushing Groom (FR)) 10.3f **(76)**
Form - 0441201
Record 1998 - 1st:2 2nd:1 3rd:0 Ran:7
Win Prizemoney £18,371 *Total Prizemoney* £27,480
Wins * **1998** Oct Newmar (GD) H 8f 92 94 <
* **1998** Aug Goodwo (GD) H 7f 80
1998 Turf 2-7: (6f 2, 7f 1-2, 8f 1-3) (g-s, gd 1-2, g-f 1-1, frm, hrd 2)
Useful colt, effective 8f, acts on g-f to hrd. Turf high 94 - 1st of 20 giving 22lb to Makebelieve Island (16 Oct Newmarket RF 4845). Gradually improved with racing, he landed a competitive nursery at Glorious Goodwood on his fourth start and was just touched off in a similar event at Newcastle. Got worked up before the start and ran poorly next time, but bounced back to form on his final start at Newmarket to land a competitive Nursery, carrying topweight. Looks a useful mile prospect. **E A L Dunlop [2-7] Khalifa Sultan.*

FAIRLY GREY (FR) RR 108f 4081a[3]
3 gr f Linamix (FR) 8.2f **(64)** - Fairlee Wild (FR) (Wild Again (USA))
Form - 3
1998 Turf 0-1: (6f) (gd)
Currently Pattern-class filly. (1st run) - 3rd of 9 getting 7lb from Andreyev (30 Aug Deauville 6f gd RF 4081a). She split some smart English sprinters in the Prix de Meautry at Deauville in August, and is obviously a fast lady. **A Fabre in FR [0-2] J-L Lagardere.*

FAIRLY SHARP (IRE) BHB 49f RR 74?f 4393[15]
5 b m Glenstal (USA) 10f **(59)** - Bengala (FR) (Hard To Beat) 10.1f **(67)**
Form - 00
Record 1998 - 1st:0 2nd:0 3rd:0 Ran:2
Pre1998 - 1st:3 2nd:3 3rd:0 Ran:8
Win Prizemoney £6,678 *Total Prizemoney* £8,732
Wins 1996 Aug Wexfor (GD) C 13f 74 <
1996 Jun Clonme (GD) C 12f 72
1996 May Tramor (GD) 12f 48
1998 Turf 0-2: (11f, 12f) (frm 2)
Above-average filly. Turf high 24 (began Spt). Becoming disappointing.
**J Mackie [0-7] Ms Caroline Breay (from Graeme Roe [1-7] Jun 1997).*

FAIRLY SURE (IRE) BHB 30f RR 26f 4049[5]
5 b m Red Sunset 9f **(57)** - Mirabiliary (USA) (Crow (FR)) 7.4f **(75)**
Form - 8005
Record 1998 - 1st:0 2nd:0 3rd:0 Ran:4
Pre1998 - 1st:1 2nd:0 3rd:0 Ran:16
Win Prizemoney £2,095 *Total Prizemoney* £2,293
Wins * 1996 Aug Lingfi (G-F) H 7.6f 46 39 <
1998 Turf 0-2: (7f, 8f) (frm 2) 1998 AW 0-2: (6f, 8f) (Fibr 2)
Little account filly. Turf high 26 (began Jly). AW high 22.

**N E Berry [1-20] Norman Berry.*

FAIR PHOEBE BHB 43f **RR 39f** 4762[12]
2 b f Shareef Dancer (USA) 10.1f **(67)** - Couleur de Rose (Kalaglow) 9.8f **(67)**
Form - 000
Record 1998 - 1st:0 2nd:0 3rd:0 Ran:3
1998 Turf 0-3: (8f 2, 10f) (gd, frm 2)
Currently very moderate filly. Turf high 39 (began Spt).
**J R Fanshawe [0-3] J M Greetham.*

FAIRTOTO BHB 67f **RR 60f** 4541[13]
2 b g Mtoto 11.5f **(71)** - Fairy Feet (Sadler's Wells (USA)) 10f **(76)**
Form - 700
Record 1998 - 1st:0 2nd:0 3rd:0 Ran:3
1998 Turf 0-3: (8f 3) (gd, frm 2)
Currently average gelding. Turf high 60 (began Spt).
**Mrs J R Ramsden [0-3] Mrs Joan Egan.*

Form - 003600050000
Record 1998 - 1st:0 2nd:0 3rd:1 Ran:10
Pre1998 - 1st:1 2nd:0 3rd:2 Ran:6
Win Prizemoney £2,830 *Total Prizemoney* £3,890
Wins 1997 May Hamilt (SFT) 5f 63 <
1998 Turf 0-7: (5f 4, 6f 3) (sft, g-s, gd, g-f, frm 3) 1998 AW 0-3: (5f 2, 6f) (Equi 2, Fibr)
Neat, moderate filly, effective 5f, acts on gd to g-f, has worn blinkers. Turf high 46. AW high 47.
**M Quinn [0-12] R G Sturmey (from M R Channon [1-4] May 1997).*

FAIRY FINGERS BHB 40f **RR 36f** 37[9]
4 b f Treasure Kay 6.5f **(53)** - Nellie Moss (Le Moss)
Form - 50
Record 1998 - 1st:0 2nd:0 3rd:0 Ran:1
Pre1998 - 1st:0 2nd:0 3rd:0 Ran:2
1998 AW 0-1: (8f) (Fibr)
Leggy, very moderate filly. **J L Eyre [0-3] W A A Farrell.*

Faithful Son (right) in winning action at Ascot

FAIR WARNING (GER) RR 79+f 2915[3]
2 b c Warning 8.1f **(77)** - Fairy Bluebird (Be My Guest (USA)) 9.3f **(67)**
Form - 3
Record 1998 - 1st:0 2nd:0 3rd:1 Ran:1
Win Prizemoney £0 *Total Prizemoney* £678
1998 Turf 0-1: (6f) (frm)
Currently above-average colt. **J W Hills [0-1] Michael Wauchope.*

FAIR WEATHER (IRE) RR 100f 4949a[3]
3 f Marju (IRE) 9.2f **(76)** - Matahina (Moorestyle) 6.9f **(64)**
Form - 053
1998 Turf 0-3: (8f, 10f, 11f) (hvy 2, sft)
Currently very useful filly. Turf high 100 - 3rd of 9 getting 2lb from Miss Carolina (18 Oct San Siro 8f sft RF 4949a).
**V Caruso in ITY [0-3] Laghi SRL.*

FAIRY DOMINO BHB 42f43a **RR 46f 43a** 4923[17]
3 ch f Primo Dominie 7.2f **(67)** - Fairy Fortune (Rainbow Quest (USA)) 10.4f **(75)**

FAIRY KNIGHT BHB 64f67a **RR 66f 67a** 4731[12]
6 b h Fairy King (USA) 7.7f **(75)** - Vestal Flame (Habitat) 9.4f **(70)**
Form - 7811067400
Record 1998 - 1st:2 2nd:0 3rd:0 Ran:10
Pre1998 - 1st:5 2nd:6 3rd:0 Ran:41
Win Prizemoney £28,481 *Total Prizemoney* £40,138

Wins								
	* **1998**	May	Kempto	(GD)	H	12f	67	74 <
	* **1998**	Apr	Folkes	(G-S)	H	12f	63	68
	* 1997	May	Haydoc	(SFT)	H	11.9f	68	70
	* 1996	Oct	Leices	(GD)	H	10f	66	71
	* 1996	Oct	Ascot	(GD)	H	12f	63	68
	* 1995	Oct	Redcar	(FRM)	H	10f	69	74 <
	* 1995	Jun	Goodwo	(G-F)	H	10f	69	71

1998 Turf 2-10: (10f, 12f 2-9) (sft 1-2, g-s 2, gd 1-4, g-f, frm)
Average horse, effective 12f, acts on sft to g-f, has worn blinkers, likes tight tracks. Turf high 74 - 1st of 12 getting 3lb from My Learned Friend (4 May Kempton RF 1013) - also 1st of 14 giving 14lb to Rear Window (21 Apr Folkestone RF 0782). Inconsistent. Sold for 4,500 guineas in October, he has joined Kim Bailey,
**R Hannon [7-54] P & S Lever Partners.*

FAIRY LIGHTS (IRE) BHB 49f47a **RR 63f 47a** 5006[8]

3 b f Fairy King (USA) 7.7f **(75)** - Gay Fantastic (Ela-Mana-Mou) 10.1f **(70)**
Form - 04008
Record 1998 - 1st:0 2nd:0 3rd:0 Ran:5
Win Prizemoney £0 *Total Prizemoney* £275
1998 Turf 0-4: (7f, 8f 3) (sft, g-f 3) 1998 AW 0-1: (7f) (Fibr)
Workmanlike, average filly. Turf high 63 (began Jly).
**P J Makin [0-5] Dr Carlos Stelling.*

FAIRY PRINCE (IRE) BHB 70f **RR 70f** 4751[12]

5 b g Fairy King (USA) 7.7f **(75)** - Danger Ahead (Mill Reef (USA)) 10.5f **(78)**
Form - 020501274620
Record 1998 - 1st:1 2nd:3 3rd:0 Ran:12
Pre1998 - 1st:4 2nd:4 3rd:2 Ran:24
Win Prizemoney £14,337 *Total Prizemoney* £26,408
Wins * 1998 Jly Beverl (GD) 5f 67
* 1997 Jly Doncas (GD) 6f 72 <
* 1997 Jly Nottin (G-F) 5.1f 65
* 1997 Jly Pontef (G-F) 6f 67
* 1996 Jun Carlis (FRM) H 5.9f 54 54
1998 Turf 1-12: (5f 1-4, 6f 8) (gd 1-3, g-f 4, frm 5)
Above-average gelding, effective 5 to 6f, best at 6f, acts on gd to frm, best on gd, excels at Beverley, does well at Pontefract. Turf high 70 - 2nd of 15 getting 2lb from Goretski (12 Aug Beverley 5f gd RF 3567) - also 1st of 5 getting 3lb from Mousehole (28 Jly Beverley RF 3160). Consistent. **Mrs A L M King [5-36] Aiden Murphy.*

FAIRY QUEEN (IRE) **RR 95f** 3045[1]

2 b f Fairy King (USA) 7.7f **(75)** - Dedicated Lady (IRE) (Pennine Walk) 8.5f **(61)**
Form - 11
Record 1998 - 1st:2 2nd:0 3rd:0 Ran:2
Win Prizemoney £12,613 *Total Prizemoney* £12,613
Wins * 1998 Jly Sandow (G-F) L 7.1f 95 <
* 1998 Jun Doncas (GD) 7f 80+
1998 Turf 2-2: (7f 2-2) (gd 1-1, frm 1-1)
Currently very useful filly. Turf high 95 - 1st of 7 from Wince (23 Jly Sandown RF 3045). A lean, lightly-made filly, who certainly has an engine, she showed a tremendous attitude to racing when impressively winning both her starts as a two-year-old. A very exciting prospect for next season, she will be suited by a mile and is sure to improve over the winter.
**D R Loder [2-2] Mohammed Jaber.*

FAIRY RIDGE (IRE) BHB 90f **RR 103f** 3338a[15]

3 ch c Indian Ridge 7.6f **(74)**-Fairy Folk(IRE)(Fairy King (USA))7.7f **(59)**
Form - 433130
1998 Turf 1-6: (7f, 8f 3, 9f 1-2) (sft, g-s 1-1, gd 2, g-f, frm)
Very useful colt, effective 9f, acts on g-s, has worn blinkers. Turf high 103 - 1st of 11 giving 5lb to Hallucination (9 Jly Tipperary RF 2791a). He won on the Flat and over timber for Aidan O'Brien, but has now joined Jonjo OíNeill. His future lies over obstacles, where he ought to stay beyond two miles.
**A P O'Brien in IRE [1-6] John McManus.*

FAIRY RING (IRE) BHB 65a **RR 43f** 2095[7]

4 b f Fairy King (USA) 7.7f **(75)** - Emmuska (USA) (Roberto (USA)) 10f **(76)**
Form - 6007
Record 1998 - 1st:0 2nd:0 3rd:0 Ran:4
Pre1998 - 1st:0 2nd:1 3rd:0 Ran:2
Win Prizemoney £0 *Total Prizemoney* £1,100
1998 Turf 0-3: (7f 2, 10f) (g-s, gd 2) 1998 AW 0-1: (8f) (Fibr)
Neat, moderate filly, has worn blinkers. Turf high 43.
**R M Whitaker [0-6] Mrs Margaret Schofield.*

FAIRY ROCK (IRE) **RR 73f** 2529[P]

3 b f Fairy King (USA) 7.7f **(75)** - Safe Home (Home Guard (USA)) 9.3f **(66)**
Form - P
Record 1998 - 1st:0 2nd:0 3rd:0 Ran:1
Pre1998 - 1st:0 2nd:0 3rd:0 Ran:2
Win Prizemoney £0 *Total Prizemoney* £266
1998 Turf 0-1: (7f) (gd)
Scopey, currently above-average filly, has broken blood-vessels.
**B W Hills [0-3] John Grant.*

FAIRY THREE BHB 35f **RR 45f** 4939[13]

3 b f Vague Shot 11f **(53)** - Fairy Free (Rousillon (USA)) 8.2f **(74)**
Form - 000002480
Record 1998 - 1st:0 2nd:1 3rd:0 Ran:9
Win Prizemoney £0 *Total Prizemoney* £675
1998 Turf 0-9: (8f 2, 10f 5, 12f 2) (gd, g-f 3, frm 4, hrd)
Workmanlike, moderate filly, effective 10f, acts on g-f, likes tight tracks. Turf high 45. Inconsistent.
**K A Morgan [0-1] Mrs Celia Miller (from S C Williams [0-8] Spt 1998).*

FAIRYTIME **RR 66f** 4814[3]

2 b f Efisio 7.7f **(69)** - Fairy Flax (IRE) (Dancing Brave (USA)) 8.4f **(76)**
Form - 3
Record 1998 - 1st:0 2nd:0 3rd:1 Ran:1
Win Prizemoney £0 *Total Prizemoney* £568
1998 Turf 0-1: (6f) (gd)
Currently average filly. **J R Arnold [0-1] A H Robinson.*

FAIRY TREE (USA) **RR** 2235[5]

3 b f Rahy (USA) 9.1f **(80)** -Magic Gleam(USA)(Danzig (USA)) 8.4f **(76)**
Form - 5
Record 1998 - 1st:0 2nd:0 3rd:0 Ran:1
1998 Turf 0-1: (13f) (gd)
Currently very poor filly - 5th of 5 getting 5lb from Extravaganza (24 Jun Chester 13f gd RF 2235).
**M Johnston [0-1] Maktoum Al Maktoum.*

FAITH AGAIN (IRE) BHB 64f **RR 60f** 4337[10]

2 b f Namaqualand (USA) - Intricacy (Formidable (USA)) 9.2f **(63)**
Form - 5560
Record 1998 - 1st:0 2nd:0 3rd:0 Ran:4
1998 Turf 0-4: (5f, 6f, 7f, 8f) (gd, frm 3)
Average filly. Turf high 60. **C F Wall [0-4] Prudence Lady Salt.*

FAITHFUL SON (USA) BHB 122f **RR 122f** 5153a[7]

4 b g Zilzal (USA) 8.5f **(79)** - Carduel (USA) (Round Table) 9.5f **(81)**
Form - 112247
Record 1998 - 1st:2 2nd:2 3rd:0 Ran:6
Pre1998 - 1st:3 2nd:1 3rd:1 Ran:6
Win Prizemoney £102,116 *Total Prizemoney* £298,929
Wins * 1998 Jun Ascot (G-S) G2 10f 118 <
* 1998 May Goodwo (G-F) L 9.9f 104+
1997 Spt Doncas (G-F) 10.3f 109
1997 May Leices (G-F) 7f 106+
1997 May Newbur (G-S) 8f 91
1998 Turf 2-6: (10f 2-4, 12f, 16f) (gd 1-4, g-f 1-2)
Scopey, very high-class gelding, effective 8 to 12f, best at 10f, acts on gd to g-f, best on gd, excels at Ascot. Turf high 122 - 2nd of 7 to Daylami (4 Jly Sandown 10f gd RF 2550) - also 1st of 8 giving 12lb to Chester House (16 Jun Ascot RF 2011). He was an easy winner of a Listed race at Goodwood on his 1998 reappearance and debut for Godolphin, before showing an admirable attitude to beat his stable companion Daylami in the Prince of Wales's Stakes at the Royal Meeting. He was just unable to confirm the form with that rival on slightly worse terms in the Eclipse, but lost no caste in defeat, and went down by a hair's breadth in the Juddmonte International, rallying gamely. He campaigned in Australia in the autumn, and on the strength of a fast-finishing fourth in the Caulfield Cup he started favourite for the Melbourne Cup. However, after having every chance, he seemed not to stay the two miles in that event. if kept in training, he looks capable of winning a Group One event over middle distances.
**S bin Suroor [2-6] Godolphin (from Sir Michael Stoute [3-6] Spt 1997).*

FAKHR (USA) BHB 86f **RR 87f** 4824[6]

3 b br c Riverman (USA) 9.7f **(78)** - Roseate Tern (Blakeney) 10.5f **(64)**
Form - 35776
Record 1998 - 1st:0 2nd:0 3rd:1 Ran:5
Pre1998 - 1st:1 2nd:0 3rd:0 Ran:2
Win Prizemoney £3,405 *Total Prizemoney* £4,765
Wins * 1997 Jly Salisb (G-F) 7f 91++ <
1998 Turf 0-5: (10f, 12f 4) (gd 2, frm 3)
Scopey, useful colt, effective 7 to 12f, acts on frm, has worn blinkers. Turf high 93 (1st run) - 3rd of 4 to Success And Glory (18 May Bath 10f frm RF 1293). A son of a Yorkshire Oaks winner, he

showed a smart turn of foot to score on his Salisbury debut but was most disappointing when upped in class and on soft ground. Wintered in Dubai, he was something of a disappointment in '98.
**J L Dunlop [1-7] Hamdan Al Maktoum.*

FALAK (USA) BHB 115f **RR 108f** 550a[9]
4 b c Diesis 9f **(80)** - Tafrah (IRE) (Sadler's Wells (USA)) 10f **(76)**
Form - 0
1998 Turf 0-1: (12f) (g-f)
Scopey, Pattern-class colt. A useful three-year-old, he was acquired by Godolphin and, since a poor effort in the Turf Classic at Nad Al Sheba in March, little has been heard of him.
**in UAE [0-1] Hamdan Al Maktoum (from Major W R Hern [3-7] Jly 1997).*

FALCARRAGH (IRE) BHB 30a **RR 19f 30a** 188[7]
8 b g Common Grounds 8.1f **(66)** - Tatra (Niniski (USA)) 10.6f **(65)**
Form - 7
Record 1998 - 1st:0 2nd:0 3rd:0 Ran:1
Pre1998 - 1st:0 2nd:0 3rd:1 Ran:1
Win Prizemoney £0 *Total Prizemoney* £243
1998 AW 0-1: (12f) (Fibr)
Poor gelding.
**Miss M E Rowland [0-1] Miss M E Rowland (from A J Martin in IRE [1-11] Nov 1996).*

FALCON CREST BHB 59f **RR 64df** 3314[4]
3 ch g Polar Falcon (USA) 9f **(74)** - Glowing With Pride (Ile de Bourbon (USA)) 10.1f **(67)**
Form - 0404
Record 1998 - 1st:0 2nd:0 3rd:0 Ran:4
Win Prizemoney £0 *Total Prizemoney* £555
1998 Turf 0-4: (8f 2, 10f 2) (sft, gd, g-f, frm)
Workmanlike, average gelding. Turf high 64.
**N A Callaghan [0-4] M Tabor & Mrs John Magnier.*

FALCON SALE (FR) RR 2396[12]
3 b br g Passing Sale (FR) - Falcon Crest (FR) (Cadoudal (FR))
Form - 0
Record 1998 - 1st:0 2nd:0 3rd:0 Ran:1
1998 Turf 0-1: (10f) (gd)
Formerly very poor gelding, always wears blinkers - 12th of 12 to Time Loss (30 Jun Chepstow 10f gd RF 2396).
**M C Pipe [0-1] P M Cain.*

FALKENBERG (FR) BHB 35f38a **RR 44df 38a** 3895[8]
3 ch g Polish Precedent (USA) 9f **(73)** - Mithi Al Gamar (USA) **(60f)** (Blushing Groom (FR)) 10.3f **(76)**
Form - 46645700830737008
Record 1998 - 1st:0 2nd:0 3rd:2 Ran:17
Pre1998 - 1st:0 2nd:0 3rd:1 Ran:6
Win Prizemoney £0 *Total Prizemoney* £1,612
1998 Turf 0-6: (6f, 7f 3, 8f, 10f) (g-s, gd 2, g-f, frm 2) 1998 AW 0-11: (7f 6, 8f 3, 10f 2) (Equi 10, Fibr)
Fair gelding, has worn blinkers. Turf high 49. AW high 59. Inconsistent.
**B A Pearce [0-15] J Salter (from M Johnston [0-8] Jan 1998).*

FALLACHAN (USA) **RR 60f** 5039[18]
2 ch c Diesis 9f **(80)** - Afaff (USA) (Nijinsky (CAN)) 10.3f **(77)**
Form - 00
Record 1998 - 1st:0 2nd:0 3rd:0 Ran:2
1998 Turf 0-2: (8f 2) (g-s, frm)
Currently average colt. Turf high 60 (began Spt).
**M A Jarvis [0-2] & Mrs Raymond Anderson Green.*

FALLAH BHB 43f **RR 45f** 2928[12]
4 b g Salse (USA) 10.9f **(71)** - Alpine Sunset (Auction Ring (USA)) 8.6f **(65)**
Form - 7067000
Record 1998 - 1st:0 2nd:0 3rd:0 Ran:7
Pre1998 - 1st:0 2nd:0 3rd:0 Ran:2
1998 Turf 0-7: (8f 4, 9f, 10f 2) (sft, g-s, gd 2, g-f, frm 2)
Scopey, moderate gelding, has worn blinkers. Turf high 45. Consistent.
**Lady Herries [0-7] The High Flying Partnership (from Major W R Hern [0-2] Spt 1996).*

FALLS O'MONESS (IRE) BHB 55f41a **RR 57f 41a** 4759[15]
4 b f River Falls 8.2f **(56)** - Sevens Are Wild (Petorius) 7.3f **(61)**
Form - 7770480835613545130
Record 1998 - 1st:2 2nd:0 3rd:3 Ran:19
Pre1998 - 1st:1 2nd:3 3rd:3 Ran:23
Win Prizemoney £8,966 *Total Prizemoney* £18,071
Wins * 1998 Spt Hamilt (SFT) H 8.3f 48 50
*** 1998** Aug Thirsk (G-F) SH 8f 40 48
1997 Spt Ayr (G-S) C 9f 65 <
1998 Turf 2-16: (8f 2-9, 9f 5, 10f 2) (sft 2, g-s 1-5, gd 4, g-f, frm 1-4)
1998 AW 0-3: (8f, 9f, 10f) (Equi, Fibr 2)
Fair filly, effective 9 to 11f, acts on g-s to gd, best on gd, has worn blinkers, likes left handed tracks. Turf high 57. AW high 36. She has a poor strike rate, as her victory in a Thirsk seller in August was only her second in thirty-five starts.
**E J Alston [2-10] Piquet Opera House Partnership (from K R Burke [1-32] Jun 1998).*

FALSE DAWN BHB 38f **RR 34f** 4662[8]
3 b f Reprimand 8.2f **(63)** - Mardessa (Ardross) 10.6f **(68)**
Form - 708
Record 1998 - 1st:0 2nd:0 3rd:0 Ran:3
1998 Turf 0-3: (7f, 8f 2) (gd, g-f, frm)
Tall, currently very moderate filly. Turf high 34 (began Spt).
**M Mullineaux [0-3] F H Lee.*

FAMILY MAN BHB 81f **RR 81f** 4848[22]
5 ch g Indian Ridge 7.6f **(74)** - Auntie Gladys (Great Nephew) 9.9f **(64)**
Form - 0532741010
Record 1998 - 1st:2 2nd:1 3rd:1 Ran:10
Pre1998 - 1st:1 2nd:1 3rd:0 Ran:10
Win Prizemoney £20,184 *Total Prizemoney* £25,212
Wins * 1998 Oct Newmar () H 7f 76 81 <
*** 1998** Spt Lingfi (G-S) H 7f 69 77
* 1997 May Newmar (G-F) H 8f 72 78+
1998 Turf 2-10: (7f 2-2, 8f 4, 9f, 10f 3) (gd 2, g-f 2-6, frm 2)
Decent gelding, effective 7 to 8f, best at 7f, acts on g-f, has worn blinkers. Turf high 81 - 1st of 29 giving 4lb to Weetman's Weigh (3 Oct Newmarket RF 4633) - also 1st of 14 getting 1lb from Peppiatt (8 Spt Lingfield RF 4147). Won in ready style at Newmarket when the stable was enjoying a purple patch, but he is not particularly consistent and is one to be wary of.
**J R Fanshawe [3-23] Family Man Partnership.*

FAMILY TREE (IRE) BHB 64f59a **RR 64f 59a** 5094[16]
2 ch f Soviet Lad (USA) 9.4f **(63)** - The Woman in Red (Red Regent) 7.2f **(44)**
Form - 6400310
Record 1998 - 1st:1 2nd:0 3rd:1 Ran:7
Win Prizemoney £3,210 *Total Prizemoney* £3,863
Wins 1998 Spt Ayr (g-s) S 8f 62 <
1998 Turf 1-7: (6f 2, 7f 2, 8f 1-3) (gd 1-4, g-f 2, frm)
Average filly, effective 8f, acts on gd. Turf high 64 - also 1st of 16 getting 5lb from Blackpool Rock (17 Spt Ayr RF 4320).
**D W Chapman [0-1] Michael Hill (from B W Hills [1-6] Spt 1998).*

FAMOUS (FR) BHB 44f41a **RR 47f 41a** 5081[6]
5 b g Tropular - Famous Horse (FR) (Labus (FR)) 12.8f **(52)**
Form - 87640057630206
Record 1998 - 1st:0 2nd:1 3rd:1 Ran:14
Pre1998 - 1st:0 2nd:0 3rd:1 Ran:1
Win Prizemoney £0 *Total Prizemoney* £1,450
1998 Turf 0-13: (7f, 8f 8, 10f 4)(gd 8, g-f, frm 4)1998 AW 0-1:(12f) (Fibr)
Moderate gelding, effective 10f, acts on gd, has worn blinkers, likes right handed tracks, likes tight tracks. Turf high 47 - 2nd of 19 giving 2lb to Mary Culi (15 Spt Sandown 10f gd RF 4270).
**J J Bridger [0-13] Exors of the late M R Pascall (from G L Moore [0-1] May 1998).*

FANCY A FORTUNE (IRE) BHB 53f54a **RR 60f 54a** 4406[4]
4 b g Fools Holme (USA) 10.3f **(64)** - Fancy's Girl (FR) (Nadjar (FR)) 7.2f **(49)**
Form - 5001301834274
Record 1998 - 1st:2 2nd:1 3rd:2 Ran:13
Pre1998 - 1st:1 2nd:2 3rd:4 Ran:18
Win Prizemoney £7,907 *Total Prizemoney* £14,510
Wins * 1998 Jly Beverl (GD) SH 7.5f 52 60

* 1998 May Thirsk (GD) S 7f 56
* 1997 Aug Thirsk (GD) H 7f 60 64 <
1998 Turf 2-13: (7f 2-8, 8f 5) (g-s, gd 1-6, g-f 1-4, frm 2)
Workmanlike, average gelding, effective 7 to 9f, best at 8f, acts on gd to frm, best on g-f, has worn blinkers, likes tight tracks, excels at Thirsk, does well at Ripon. Turf high 60 - 1st of 16 giving 22lb to Dancing Em (3 Jly Beverley RF 2485) - also 1st of 16 from Allinson's Mate (15 May Thirsk RF 1250).
**D Nicholls [3-22] E W & M Tuer (from J Pearce [0-9] Oct 1996).*

FANCY DESIGN (IRE) BHB 39f39a **RR 46f 39a** 3975[9]

5 b m Cyrano de Bergerac 7.3f **(58)** - Crimson Robes (Artaius (USA)) 9f **(69)**
Form - 3520766567203000
Record 1998 - 1st:0 2nd:2 3rd:2 Ran:16
Pre1998 - 1st:0 2nd:2 3rd:0 Ran:28
Win Prizemoney £0 *Total Prizemoney* £5,008
1998 Turf 0-9: (8f 7, 9f, 10f) (gd 2, g-f 3, frm 4) 1998 AW 0-7: (7f, 8f 4, 10f 2) (Equi 7)
Moderate filly, effective 8f, acts on frm - acts on Equi, has worn blinkers, likes right handed tracks, favours tight tracks. Turf high 46. AW high 46 - 2nd of 10 getting 22lb from Barbason (17 Jan Lingfield 8f Equi RF 0109). **P Mitchell [0-44] Mrs V M Harris.*

FANCY MY CHANCE BHB 83f **RR 84f** 4889[1]

2 b c Rainbow Quest (USA) 11.2f **(81)** - Yazeanhaa (USA) (Zilzal (USA))
Form - 00401
Record 1998 - 1st:1 2nd:0 3rd:0 Ran:5
Win Prizemoney £3,183 *Total Prizemoney* £3,425
Wins * **1998** Oct Yarmou (G-S) H 8f 76 84 <
1998 Turf 1-5: (7f 2, 8f 1-3) (gd 1-2, frm 3)
Decent colt. Turf high 84 (began Aug) - 1st of 13 giving 11lb to Salford Flyer (20 Oct Yarmouth RF 4889).
**E A L Dunlop [1-5] Maktoum Al Maktoum.*

FANCY THAT (IRE) BHB 51f **RR 61f** 4623[3]

2 b f Shalford (IRE) 7.8f **(63)** - Clancy's Corner (IRE) (Auction Ring (USA)) 8.6f **(65)**
Form - 0004553
Record 1998 - 1st:0 2nd:0 3rd:1 Ran:7
Win Prizemoney £0 *Total Prizemoney* £556
1998 Turf 0-7: (5f 2, 6f 4, 7f) (gd, g-f 4, frm 2)
Average filly. Turf high 61. **B W Hills [0-7] Guy Reed.*

FANCY WRAP **RR 43f** 4809[7]

3 b f Kris 10f **(75)** - Gift Wrapped (Wolver Hollow) 8f **(56)**
Form - 07
Record 1998 - 1st:0 2nd:0 3rd:0 Ran:2
1998 Turf 0-2: (11f, 14f) (gd, g-f)
Lengthy, currently moderate filly. Turf high 43 (began Aug).
**J L Dunlop [0-2] The Sussex Stud Ltd.*

FANDANGO DREAM (IRE) **RR 45f** 5063[14]

2 ch c Magical Wonder (USA) 7.2f **(60)** - Fandikos (IRE) (Taufan (USA)) 7f **(57)**
Form - 0
Record 1998 - 1st:0 2nd:0 3rd:0 Ran:1
1998 Turf 0-1: (6f) (g-f)
Currently moderate colt. **M D I Usher [0-1] Midweek Racing.*

FANETTA (IRE) BHB 55f **RR 60f** 4400[14]

2 b f Taufan (USA) 8.3f **(65)** - Bold Fille (IRE) (Bold Arrangement)
Form - 4060
Record 1998 - 1st:0 2nd:0 3rd:0 Ran:4
1998 Turf 0-4: (6f 2, 7f 2) (g-f 2, frm 2)
Average filly. Turf high 60.
**M H Tompkins [0-4] Pamela, Lady Nelson of Stafford.*

FAN OF VENT-AXIA BHB 38f34a **RR 41f 34a** 111[5]

4 b c Puissance 7.1f **(60)** - Miss Milton (Young Christopher) 6f **(61)**
Form - 5
Record 1998 - 1st:0 2nd:0 3rd:0 Ran:1
Pre1998 - 1st:0 2nd:0 3rd:2 Ran:14
Win Prizemoney £0 *Total Prizemoney* £1,313
1998 AW 0-1: (8f) (Fibr)
Unfurnished, moderate colt, effective 7f, acts on frm, has worn blinkers, likes left handed tracks, likes tight tracks.
**D J S Cosgrove [0-7] Camelot Racing (from C N Allen [0-8] Oct 1996).*

FANTAIL BHB 83f **RR 84f** 5151[10]

4 b c Taufan (USA) 8.3f **(65)** - Eleganza (IRE) (Kings Lake (USA)) 10.8f **(67)**
Form - 48134076700
Record 1998 - 1st:1 2nd:0 3rd:1 Ran:11
Pre1998 - 1st:4 2nd:0 3rd:1 Ran:12
Win Prizemoney £21,759 *Total Prizemoney* £31,189
Wins * **1998** Jun Beverl (GD) H 12f 83 87 <
* 1997 Nov Redcar (GD) H 11f 78 84+
* 1997 Jly Redcar (G-S) H 10f 76 79
* 1997 Jun Hamilt (SFT) H 11.1f 73 77
* 1997 May Redcar (G-F) H 11f 67 77
1998 Turf 1-11: (10f, 11f, 12f 1-6, 13f, 14f 2) (sft, g-s, gd 3, g-f 2, frm 1-3, hrd)
Well made, decent colt, effective 11 to 14f, best at 12f, acts on gd to frm, has worn blinkers, likes right handed tracks, prefers tight tracks, excels at Redcar. Turf high 93 - 4th of 15 giving 9lb to Seignorial (28 Jly Goodwood 14f gd RF 3163) - also 1st of 4 giving 21lb to Sandbaggedagain (23 Jun Beverley RF 2193). Effective with cut in the ground, he won at Beverley in June before good runs in a couple of warm handicaps, but lost his way thereafter.
**M H Tompkins [5-23] Pamela, Lady Nelson of Stafford.*

FANTASTIC BELLE (IRE) **RR 58f** 4524[6]

2 b f Night Shift (USA) 8.1f **(73)** - Gay Fantastic (Ela-Mana-Mou) 10.1f **(70)**
Form - 06
Record 1998 - 1st:0 2nd:0 3rd:0 Ran:2
1998 Turf 0-2: (6f 2) (gd, g-f)
Currently fair filly. Turf high 58 (began Spt).
**P J Makin [0-2] Dr Carlos Stelling.*

FANTASTIC DANCE (USA) **RR 63f** 5122[4]

2 br f Imperial Ballet (IRE) - Fantastic Bid (USA) (Auction Ring (USA)) 8.6f **(65)**
Form - 4
Record 1998 - 1st:0 2nd:0 3rd:0 Ran:1
Win Prizemoney £0 *Total Prizemoney* £205
1998 Turf 0-1: (6f) (g-s)
Currently average filly. **P J Makin [0-1] Dr Carlos Stelling.*

FANTASTIC LIGHT (USA) **RR 93f** 4231[3]

2 b c Rahy (USA) 9.1f **(80)** - Jood (USA) (Nijinsky (CAN)) 10.3f **(77)**
Form - 113
Record 1998 - 1st:2 2nd:0 3rd:1 Ran:3
Win Prizemoney £8,382 *Total Prizemoney* £10,257
Wins * **1998** Aug Sandow (G-F) 8.1f 93 <
* **1998** Aug Sandow (GD) 7.1f 82+
1998 Turf 2-3: (7f 1-1, 8f 1-2) (gd 1-2, g-f 1-1)
Currently useful colt. Turf high 93 (began Aug) - 3rd of 3 to Mutaahab (11 Spt Goodwood 8f gd RF 4231) - also 1st of 5 giving 3lb to Aesops (22 Aug Sandown RF 3819). He put up a fine performance to beat three previous winners on his Sandown debut over seven, and seemed to relish the extra furlong when following up on the same track. Not disgraced on his final start in Listed event at Goodwood. Capable of better still, and will be seen in a greater light given a real test of stamina.
**Sir Michael Stoute [2-3] Maktoum Al Maktoum.*

FANTASY FLIGHT BHB 21f **RR 24f** 5060[15]

4 b f Forzando 7.2f **(63)** - Ryewater Dream (Touching Wood (USA)) 8.2f **(55)**
Form - 0000
Record 1998 - 1st:0 2nd:0 3rd:0 Ran:4
Pre1998 - 1st:0 2nd:0 3rd:0 Ran:4
1998 Turf 0-3: (8f 2, 10f) (sft, frm 2) 1998 AW 0-1: (6f) (Fibr)
Workmanlike, little account filly, has worn blinkers. Turf high 24. Inconsistent.
**M A Peill [0-8] Michael Ng (from Mrs J R Ramsden [0-1] Aug 1996).*

FANTASY HILL (IRE) BHB 83f **RR 77f** 3959[5]

2 b c Danehill (USA) 9.1f **(79)** - Gay Fantasy (Troy) 10.4f **(68)**
Form - 355
Record 1998 - 1st:0 2nd:0 3rd:1 Ran:3

Win Prizemoney £0 *Total Prizemoney* £624
1998 Turf 0-3: (7f 2, 8f) (gd, g-f, frm)
Currently above-average colt. Turf high 77 - 5th of 8 to Pulau Tioman (29 Aug Nottingham 8f g-f RF 3959).
**J L Dunlop [0-3] Windflower Overseas Holdings Inc.*

FANTASY NIGHT (IRE) BHB 71f **RR 75f** 4457[15]
3 b g Night Shift (USA) 8.1f **(73)** - Gay Fantasy (Troy) 10.4f **(68)**
Form - 2241440
Record 1998 - 1st:1 2nd:2 3rd:0 Ran:7
Pre1998 - 1st:0 2nd:0 3rd:1 Ran:3
Win Prizemoney £4,160 *Total Prizemoney* £7,867
Wins * 1998 Jly Thirsk (FRM) H 12f 73 75 <
1998 Turf 1-7: (10f 2, 11f, 12f 1-3, 14f) (g-s, gd 2, g-f, frm 1-3)
Well made, above-average gelding, effective 11 to 12f, best at 12f, acts on gd to frm, prefers tight tracks. Turf high 76 - 2nd of 9 getting 3lb from Winsome George (25 May Redcar 11f gd RF 1457) - also 1st of 4 getting 2lb from Air Attache (24 Jly Thirsk RF 3088). gs looks his trip, as he failed to stay when tried over further.
**J L Dunlop [1-10] Windflower Overseas Holdings Inc.*

FANTAZIA BHB 75f **RR 72f** 4766[6]
2 b f Zafonic (USA) 9f **(83)** - Trescalini (IRE) (Sadler's Wells (USA)) 10f **(76)**
Form - 366
Record 1998 - 1st:0 2nd:0 3rd:1 Ran:3
Win Prizemoney £0 *Total Prizemoney* £590
1998 Turf 0-3: (7f, 8f 2) (sft, frm 2)
Currently above-average filly. Turf high 72 (began Spt).
**M Johnston [0-3] Maktoum Al Maktoum.*

FAN-TC GEM BHB 54f **RR 41f** 4639[11]
2 b f Lugana Beach 7f **(63)** - Florac (IRE) **(27df 32a)** (Sayf El Arab (USA)) 7.1f **(54)**
Form - 00
Record 1998 - 1st:0 2nd:0 3rd:0 Ran:2
1998 Turf 0-1: (5f) (g-f) 1998 AW 0-1: (5f) (Fibr)
Currently fair filly. **J Balding [0-2] Spring Hill Syndicate.*

FARASAN (IRE) BHB 114f **RR 108f** 2281a[2]
5 b h Fairy King (USA) 7.7f **(75)** - Gracieuse Majeste (FR) (Saint Cyrien (FR)) 8.4f **(80)**
Form - 2
1998 Turf 0-1: (10f) (sft)
Pattern-class colt. (1st run) - 2nd of 11 to Public Purse (18 Jun Longchamp 10f sft RF 2281a). Just below Group class when trained by Henry Cecil, he did not seem to have improved much for his new connections in France.
**J deRoualle in FR [0-1] Prince A A Faisal (from H R A Cecil [2-7] Apr 1997).*

FARAWAY LASS BHB 90f **RR 90f** 5152[7]
5 b m Distant Relative 7f **(69)** - Vague Lass (Vaigly Great) 7f **(58)**
Form - 0821247
Record 1998 - 1st:1 2nd:2 3rd:0 Ran:7
Pre1998 - 1st:4 2nd:3 3rd:2 Ran:19
Win Prizemoney £25,778 *Total Prizemoney* £42,932
Wins * 1998 Spt Haydoc (GD) 6f 86 <
* 1997 Jly York (GD) H 6f 77 80
* 1996 Oct York (GD) 6f 76
* 1996 Jun Salisb (G-F) H 6f 67 77
* 1996 May Nottin (G-F) 6.1f 62
1998 Turf 1-7: (5f 2, 6f 1-5) (gd 3, g-f 2, frm 1-2)
Useful filly, effective 5 to 6f, best at 6f, acts on gd to frm, excels at Newmarket and Goodwood. Turf high 90 - also 1st of 8 getting 7lb from Eastern Lyric (4 Spt Haydock RF 4090). Consistent. Just touched off in a valuable handicap at Goodwood in August, she went one better at Haydock. Five furlongs looks a trip a little short for her, but she will win more races. **Lord Huntingdon [5-26] J Rose.*

FARAWAY MOON RR 56f 4882[6]
2 gr f Distant Relative 7f **(69)** - Moon Magic **(59f)** (Polish Precedent (USA)) 10.2f **(60)**
Form - 6
Record 1998 - 1st:0 2nd:0 3rd:0 Ran:1
1998 Turf 0-1: (6f) (g-s)
Currently fair filly. **Lady Herries [0-1] Angmering Park Stud.*

FAR CRY (IRE) BHB 62f57a **RR 63f 57a** 3582[5]
3 b g Pharly (FR) 11.5f **(64)** - Darabaka (IRE) (Doyoun) 9f **(69)**
Form - 075
Record 1998 - 1st:0 2nd:0 3rd:0 Ran:3
1998 Turf 0-2: (6f, 8f) (gd, g-f) 1998 AW 0-1: (6f) (Fibr)
Currently average gelding. Turf high 63 (began Aug).
**Sir Mark Prescott [0-3] W E Sturt.*

FARFRAE BHB 64f **RR 75df** 4703[16]
2 ch f Emarati (USA) 6.6f **(63)** - Hanglands (Bustino) 10.4f **(64)**
Form - 643600
Record 1998 - 1st:0 2nd:0 3rd:1 Ran:6
Win Prizemoney £0 *Total Prizemoney* £893
1998 Turf 0-6: (5f 5, 6f) (sft, gd 3, g-f, frm)
Above-average filly, effective 5f, acts on frm. Turf high 75.
**M J Heaton-Ellis [0-6] S P Tindall.*

FARMOST BHB 88f96a **RR 85f 96a** 456[14]
5 ch g Pharly (FR) 11.5f **(64)** - Dancing Meg (USA) (Marshua's Dancer (USA)) 8.6f **(75)**
Form - 110
Record 1998 - 1st:0 2nd:0 3rd:0 Ran:1
Pre1998 - 1st:11 2nd:5 3rd:0 Ran:23
Win Prizemoney £71,469 *Total Prizemoney* £76,334
Wins * *1997 Dec Wolver (STD) L 9.4f 100* <
* *1997 Nov Wolver (STD) H 8.5f 82 87*
* *1997 Spt Wolver (STD) H 9.4f 70 84*
* 1997 Spt Bright (FRM) H 10f 80 85
* 1997 Jly Bath (FRM) 10.2f 78
* *1996 Aug Wolver (STD) H 9.4f 66 71*
* 1996 Jly Bright (FRM) H 8f 75 79
* 1996 Jun Folkes (G-F) 6.9f 78
* 1996 May Bright (GD) 7f 76
* 1996 May Sandow (GD) H 7.1f 61 69
* *1996 Jan Wolver (STD) 6f 56*
1998 AW 0-1: (10f) (Equi)
Very useful gelding, effective 9f - acts on Fibr, prefers left handed tracks, favours tight tracks. His victories have been due in no small part to his trainer's skill in placing his horses. He put up a better performance than was apparent at the time when beating Running Stag in a Listed race on the dirt at Wolverhampton in December 1997. Disappointing behind that horse at Lingfield in March, he has obviously had a problem.
**Sir Mark Prescott [11-24] W E Sturt.*

FARNDON PRINCESS BHB 41f49a **RR 45f 49a** 3582[9]
3 b f Nomination 7.3f **(57)** - Ankara's Princess (USA) (Ankara (USA)) 8f **(71)**
Form - 73708000
Record 1998 - 1st:0 2nd:0 3rd:1 Ran:8
Pre1998 - 1st:0 2nd:0 3rd:1 Ran:3
Win Prizemoney £0 *Total Prizemoney* £1,054
1998 Turf 0-5: (6f 4, 8f) (sft, gd 3, g-f) 1998 AW 0-3: (6f 3) (Fibr 3)
Unfurnished, moderate filly. Turf high 45. AW high 49. Inconsistent. **R Hollinshead [0-11] J D Graham.*

FAR REMOVED (IRE) BHB 76f **RR 79f** 4925[4]
3 b g Distant Relative 7f **(69)** - Cormorant Creek (Gorytus (USA)) 7.8f **(60)**
Form - 0803210304
Record 1998 - 1st:1 2nd:1 3rd:2 Ran:10
Pre1998 - 1st:1 2nd:2 3rd:0 Ran:5
Win Prizemoney £9,312 *Total Prizemoney* £15,469
Wins * 1998 Aug Redcar (G-F) H 8f 75 79 <
1997 Spt Doncas (G-F) H 6f 72 79 <
1998 Turf 1-10: (6f, 7f 4, 8f 1-5) (g-s, gd 4, g-f 1-2, frm 3)
Workmanlike, above-average gelding, effective 5 to 8f, best at 8f, acts on g-s to frm, excels at Redcar, likes Thirsk. Turf high 79 - 1st of 11 giving 7lb to Moving Arrow (29 Aug Redcar RF 3965). Consistent.
**Mrs V C Ward [1-5] Mrs V C Ward (from Mrs J R Ramsden [1-10] Aug 1998).*

FARRIERS STEAL RR 2628[10]
4 ch g Beveled (USA) 6.9f **(64)** - Super Style (Artaius (USA)) 9f **(69)**
Form - 00
Record 1998 - 1st:0 2nd:0 3rd:0 Ran:2

1998 Turf 0-1: (6f) (frm) 1998 AW 0-1: (8f) (Fibr)
Currently very poor gelding. **G M McCourt [0-2] Alf Hall.*

FARRINGDON HILL BHB 66f **RR 64f** 1833[3]

7 b g Minster Son 10.9f **(56)** - Firgrove (Relkino) 8.9f **(65)**
Form - 53

Record	**1998 -**	1st:0	2nd:0	3rd:1	Ran:2
	Pre1998 -	1st:4	2nd:1	3rd:3	Ran:22

Win Prizemoney £13,320 *Total Prizemoney* £16,942

Wins	* 1997	Aug	Redcar	(FRM)	H	11f	69	72+	
	* 1997	Aug	Windso	(G-F)	H	11.6f	65	68	
	1996	Jun	Sandow	(FRM)	H	14f	71	77	
	1994	Jly	Leices	(G-F)	H	11.8f	74	81+	<

1998 Turf 0-2: (10f, 12f) (gd, hrd)
Average gelding, effective 11 to 12f, acts on g-f to hrd, often wears blinkers (effectively). Turf high 64.
**J H M Gosden [2-8] Christopher Ranson (from Major W R Hern [2-16] Spt 1996).*

FAR-SO-LA BHB 50f45a **RR 51f 45a** 4229[17]

3 b g Absalom 7.1f **(56)** - Fara (Castle Keep) 8.3f **(57)**
Form - 10240

Record	**1998 -**	1st:1	2nd:1	3rd:0	Ran:5
	Pre1998 -	1st:0	2nd:0	3rd:0	Ran:5

Win Prizemoney £2,119 *Total Prizemoney* £2,887

Wins	**1998**	Jly	Folkes	(GD)	C	7f		48	<

1998 Turf 1-5: (7f 1-3, 8f 2) (gd 1-3, g-f, frm)
Fair gelding, effective 7 to 8f, acts on gd to frm, has worn blinkers. Turf high 51 (began Jly) - 2nd of 13 giving 7lb to Magical Dancer (14 Aug Warwick 8f frm RF 3644) - also 1st of 14 getting 5lb from Fire Goddess (15 Jly Folkestone RF 2820). Inconsistent.
**B A Pearce [0-4] Steve Murrell (from R J O'Sullivan [1-1] Jly 1998).*

FASCINO (FR) **RR 95f** 2667a[3]

3 c Hero's Honor (USA) 9.2f **(76)** -Fracassina (Rusticaro (FR)) 8.2f **(65)**
Form - 3
1998 Turf 0-1: (12f) (gd)
Currently very useful colt. Was third in a Listed race at San Siro to Clapham Common and Carry The Flag.
**G Botti in ITY [0-1] Effevi Snc.*

FASHION VICTIM BHB 77f **RR 74?f** 4226[17]

3 b c High Estate 10.5f **(66)** - Kirkby Belle (Bay Express) 7.1f **(60)**
Form - 0

Record	**1998 -**	1st:0	2nd:0	3rd:0	Ran:1
	Pre1998 -	1st:2	2nd:0	3rd:0	Ran:9

Win Prizemoney £10,792 *Total Prizemoney* £11,042

Wins	* 1997	Spt	Ayr	(G-S)	H	8f	74	79	<
	* 1997	Jly	Beverl	(G-F)		5f		69	

1998 Turf 0-1: (12f) (g-f)
Workmanlike, above-average colt, effective 8f, acts on g-s to gd.
**T H Caldwell [2-10] R S G Jones.*

FAST AND NEAT (IRE) BHB 50f **RR 48f** 4663[16]

2 ch c Soviet Lad (USA) 9.4f **(63)** - Stop The Cavalry (Relko) 9.9f **(59)**
Form - 060000

Record	**1998 -**	1st:0	2nd:0	3rd:0	Ran:6

1998 Turf 0-6: (6f 3, 7f, 8f, 10f) (g-s 2, gd 2, g-f, frm)
Moderate colt. Turf high 48.
**G Lewis [0-6] The Bricklayers Partnership.*

FAST FORWARD FRED BHB 57f46a **RR 57f 46a** 4458[7]

7 gr g Sharrood (USA) 11.1f **(67)** - Sun Street (Ile de Bourbon (USA)) 10.1f **(67)**
Form - 5212117

Record	**1998 -**	1st:3	2nd:2	3rd:0	Ran:7
	Pre1998 -	1st:0	2nd:1	3rd:0	Ran:10

Win Prizemoney £9,697 *Total Prizemoney* £12,298

Wins	* **1998**	Aug	Sandow	(G-F)	H	16.4f	48	57	<
	* **1998**	Aug	Bath	(FRM)	H	17.2f	48	52	
	* **1998**	Jly	Chepst	(GD)	H	18f	43	49	

1998 Turf 3-6: (16f 1-3, 17f 1-2, 18f 1-1) (gd 1-3, g-f 1-1, frm 1-2) 1998 AW 0-1: (12f) (Equi)
Fair gelding, effective 16 to 18f, acts on gd to frm. Turf high 57 - 1st of 12 giving 4lb to Sharaf (21 Aug Sandown RF 3797) - also 1st of 5 getting 11lb from Shampooed (11 Aug Bath RF 3526). Consistent. He was in fine form in modest staying handicaps last season, winning such events at Chepstow, Bath and Sandown.
**L MontagueHall [3-16] The Straight Forward Partnership (from G Lewis [0-2] Oct 1994).*

FAST FRANC (IRE) BHB 53f80a **RR 50f 80a** 4614[17]

3 ch g Paris House 5.9f **(64)** - Elle Va Bon (Tanfirion) 7f **(61)**
Form - 5113115000000

Record	**1998 -**	1st:4	2nd:0	3rd:1	Ran:12
	Pre1998 -	1st:2	2nd:0	3rd:2	Ran:10

Win Prizemoney £14,583 *Total Prizemoney* £16,522

Wins	* **1998**	*Feb*	*Lingfi*	*(SLW)*	*H*	*6f*	*70*	*93*	<
	1998	*Feb*	*Lingfi*	*(SLW)*	*C*	*7f*		*64*	
	1998	*Jan*	*Southw*	*(STD)*	*H*	*6f*	*50*	*66*	
	1998	*Jan*	*Southw*	*(STD)*	*C*	*6f*		*66*	
	1997	Jly	Hamilt	(SFT)	S	6f		70+	
	1997	Jun	Folkes	(SFT)	S	5f		55+	

1998 Turf 0-7: (6f 4, 7f 3) (sft, g-s, gd, g-f 2, frm 2) 1998 AW 4-5: (6f 3-4, 7f 1-1) (Equi 2-2, Fibr 2-3)
Workmanlike, useful gelding, effective 6f - acts on Equi, has worn blinkers, excels at Southwell, does well at Lingfield. Turf high 50. AW high 93 - 1st of 5 giving 5lb to Treble Term (17 Feb Lingfield RF 0303). Found his form with a vengeance on sand at the start of '98, winning four times. He has shown little on turf since, but when on song is a difficult horse to catch if allowed to dominate.
**T J Naughton [1-8] & Mrs D J Flahive (from S C Williams [5-13] Feb 1998).*

FAST TO LIGHT **RR 46f** 2500[11]

2 ch f Pharly (FR) 11.5f **(64)** - Khadino (Relkino) 8.9f **(65)**
Form - 80

Record	**1998 -**	1st:0	2nd:0	3rd:0	Ran:2

1998 Turf 0-2: (6f, 7f) (g-f, frm)
Currently moderate filly. Turf high 46. **N Tinkler [0-2] Philip Grundy.*

FASTWAN BHB 45f **RR 35f** 5057[6]

2 ch c Nashwan (USA) 10.3f **(79)** - Jammaayil (IRE) (Lomond (USA)) 8.8f **(65)**
Form - 206

Record	**1998 -**	1st:0	2nd:1	3rd:0	Ran:3

Win Prizemoney £0 *Total Prizemoney* £1,232
1998 Turf 0-3: (7f, 8f 2) (sft 2, g-f)
Currently very moderate colt. Turf high 35 (began Spt).
**J S Goldie [0-3] Frank Brady.*

FATEHALKHAIR (IRE) BHB 34f34a **RR 35f 34a** 4134[2]

6 ch g Kris 10f **(75)** - Midway Lady (USA) (Alleged (USA)) 10f **(76)**
Form - 42

Record	**1998 -**	1st:0	2nd:1	3rd:0	Ran:2
	Pre1998 -	1st:0	2nd:1	3rd:1	Ran:12

Win Prizemoney £0 *Total Prizemoney* £2,182
1998 Turf 0-2: (10f, 12f) (gd 2)
Moderate gelding, has worn blinkers. Turf high 35 - 2nd of 18 getting 9lb from Uniform (7 Spt Hamilton 12f gd RF 4134).
**B Ellison [6-31] Brian Chicken.*

FATHER DAN (IRE) BHB 54f52a **RR 56f 52a** 475[8]

9 ch g Martin John 10.5f **(52)** - Sonia John (Main Reef) 9.6f **(57)**
Form - 4353378

Record	**1998 -**	1st:0	2nd:0	3rd:2	Ran:5
	Pre1998 -	1st:7	2nd:10	3rd:6	Ran:59

Win Prizemoney £20,357 *Total Prizemoney* £34,312

Wins	* 1997	Spt	Bright	(FRM)	C	11.9f		56	
	* 1996	*Dec*	*Lingfi*	*(STD)*	*H*	*10f*	*58*	*58*	
	* 1995	*Nov*	*Southw*	*(STD)*		*11f*		*66*	<
	* 1995	Aug	Windso	(G-F)	H	11.6f	50	58	
	* 1995	*Feb*	*Lingfi*	*(STD)*		*10f*		*56*	
	* 1994	Jun	Warwic	(FRM)	H	10.8f	47	50	
	* 1994	May	Warwic	(G-F)	H	10.8f	44	47	

1998 Turf 0-1: (10f) (gd) 1998 AW 0-4: (10f 2, 12f 2) (Equi 4)
Fair gelding, has broken blood-vessels, effective 8 to 12f, best at 10f, acts on frm - acts on Equi, has worn blinkers, likes left handed tracks, favours tight tracks. AW high 53.
**Miss Gay Kelleway [8-68] Miss Gay Kelleway (from D Moffatt [0-4] Nov 1992).*

FATHER EDDIE BHB 46f48a **RR 41f 48a** 1139[6]

4 b g Aragon 7.7f **(58)** - Lady Philippa (IRE) (Taufan (USA)) 7f **(57)**

Form - 6
Record 1998 - 1st:0 2nd:0 3rd:0 Ran:1
Pre1998 - 1st:1 2nd:0 3rd:0 Ran:11
Win Prizemoney £2,721 *Total Prizemoney* £2,721
Wins 1997 May Beverl (GD) S 9.9f 52 <
1998 Turf 0-1: (12f) (hrd)
Scopey, moderate gelding, effective 10f, acts on gd, has worn blinkers.
**M E Sowersby [0-7] The Southwold Set (from J J O'Neill [1-11] Jun 1997).*

FATHER KRISMAS BHB 76f RR 76f 4926[1]

3 ch g Kris 10f **(75)** - My Sister Ellen (Lyphard (USA)) 9.9f **(72)**
Form - 441
Record 1998 - 1st:1 2nd:0 3rd:0 Ran:3
Win Prizemoney £3,882 *Total Prizemoney* £4,564
Wins * 1998 Oct Nottin (SFT) 10f 76 <
1998 Turf 1-3: (10f 1-2, 12f) (sft, g-s 1-1, g-f)
Rangy, currently above-average gelding. Turf high 76 (began Oct) - 1st of 7 giving 5lb to Karefree Katie (21 Oct Nottingham RF 4926).
**P F I Cole [1-3] M Arbib.*

FATHER MULCAHY RR 4413[13]

2 b c Safawan 6.6f **(60)** - Constant Delight (Never so Bold) 6.3f **(66)**
Form - 0
Record 1998 - 1st:0 2nd:0 3rd:0 Ran:1
1998 Turf 0-1: (6f) (frm)
Currently very poor colt - 13th of 13 getting 1lb from Kangaroo Island (22 Spt Warwick 6f frm RF 4413).
**R J R Williams [0-1] Harry Ormesher.*

FATHER SKY BHB 70f RR 71f 478[10]

7 b g Dancing Brave (USA) 10.4f **(78)** - Flamenco Wave (USA) (Desert Wine (USA)) 9.7f **(80)**
Form - 30
Record 1998 - 1st:0 2nd:0 3rd:1 Ran:2
Pre1998 - 1st:1 2nd:0 3rd:0 Ran:2
Win Prizemoney £3,663 *Total Prizemoney* £4,478
Wins * 1997 Spt Goodwo (G-F) H 16f 63 71 <
1998 Turf 0-1: (18f) (gd) 1998 AW 0-1: (16f) (Fibr)
Above-average gelding, mostly wears blinkers.
**O Sherwood [10-31] Kenneth Kornfeld.*

FATINA RR 74+f 4956[1]

2 ch f Nashwan (USA) 10.3f **(79)** - Gharam (USA) (Green Dancer (USA)) 10.3f **(74)**
Form - 1
Record 1998 - 1st:1 2nd:0 3rd:0 Ran:1
Win Prizemoney £4,110 *Total Prizemoney* £4,110
Wins * 1998 Oct Doncas (SFT) 8f 74+ <
1998 Turf 1-1: (8f 1-1) (frm 1-1)
Currently above-average filly. (1st run) - 1st of 10 from Musical Tones (23 Oct Doncaster RF 4956). Reported to be among the Dubai-bound contingent after winning a late-season maiden.
**S bin Suroor [1-1] Godolphin.*

FAUTE DE MIEUX BHB 69f RR 65f 1989[6]

3 ch c Beveled (USA) 6.9f **(64)** - Supreme Rose (Frimley Park) 6.5f **(67)**
Form - 522006
Record 1998 - 1st:0 2nd:2 3rd:0 Ran:6
Win Prizemoney £0 *Total Prizemoney* £2,000
1998 Turf 0-6: (5f 2, 6f 4) (sft, g-s, gd 2, g-f, hrd)
Leggy, average colt, effective 5 to 6f, acts on sft to hrd. Turf high 74 - 2nd of 11 to Shanillo (21 Apr Folkestone 6f sft RF 0780). Has shown plenty of promise in sprint maidens but has been found wanting in handicaps. **A P Jones [0-6] Mrs V Youell.*

FAVORITE TRICK (USA) RR 115f 5165a[8]

3 b/br c Phone Trick (USA)7f **(62)** - Evil Elaine(USA) (Medieval Man (USA))
Form - 8
1998 Turf 0-1: (8f) (frm)
Currently high-class colt. The winner of the Breeders' Cup Juvenile last year, his form this term had been somewhat patchy and he showed little in the Breeders' Cup Mile on turf. Has been retired.
**W Mott in USA [0-1] Lacombe Stables (from P Byrne in USA [1-1] Nov 1997).*

FAVOURED RR 81f 4758[3]

2 ch f Chief's Crown (USA) 10.2f **(75)** - Barboukh (Night Shift (USA)) 7.2f **(69)**
Form - 3
Record 1998 - 1st:0 2nd:0 3rd:1 Ran:1
Win Prizemoney £0 *Total Prizemoney* £510
1998 Turf 0-1: (7f) (gd)
Currently decent filly. (1st run) - 3rd of 20 to Hawriyah (12 Oct Leicester 7f gd RF 4758). **J H M Gosden [0-1] Sheikh Mohammed.*

FAWNING BHB 50f RR 61f 4456[16]

3 b f Alnasr Alwasheek 9.4f **(62)** - Flattering (USA) (Nodouble (USA)) 8.8f **(68)**
Form - 420226355370
Record 1998 - 1st:0 2nd:3 3rd:2 Ran:12
Pre1998 - 1st:0 2nd:0 3rd:1 Ran:4
Win Prizemoney £0 *Total Prizemoney* £4,237
1998 Turf 0-12: (8f 7, 10f 4, 12f) (sft, g-s, gd 3, g-f 2, frm 5)
Leggy, average filly, effective 8 to 10f, best at 8f, acts on g-s to frm, best on frm, likes left handed tracks, likes tight tracks. Turf high 63 - 2nd of 18 getting 12lb from Sweet Dreams (28 Apr Nottingham 8f g-s RF 0902). Running well in minor handicaps over a mile in the first half of the season.
**M Blanshard [0-16] H C Promotions Ltd.*

FAYEZ BHB 48f RR 54f 4627[15]

3 ch g Interrex (CAN) 7.7f **(51)** -Forest Nymph (Native Bazaar) 6.9f **(62)**
Form - 7570
Record 1998 - 1st:0 2nd:0 3rd:0 Ran:3
Pre1998 - 1st:0 2nd:0 3rd:0 Ran:2
1998 Turf 0-1: (16f) (g-f) 1998 AW 0-2: (10f, 15f) (Equi, Fibr)
Leggy, fair gelding, has worn blinkers. AW high 39.
**K McAuliffe [0-5] A Ezen.*

FAYIK BHB 68f83a RR 67f 83a 2365[17]

4 ch c Arazi (USA) 9.2f **(74)** - Elfaslah (IRE) (Green Desert (USA)) 8.6f **(78)**
Form - 32341111362400
Record 1998 - 1st:4 2nd:1 3rd:1 Ran:10
Pre1998 - 1st:0 2nd:1 3rd:3 Ran:11
Win Prizemoney £36,474 *Total Prizemoney* £46,858
Wins * 1998 *Mar Wolver (STD) H 8.5f 81 85* <
*** 1998** *Jan Wolver (STD) H 8.5f 76 83*
*** 1998** *Jan Lingfi (STD) H 7f 72 78*
*** 1998** *Jan Southw (STD) H 7f 67 70*
1998 Turf 0-4: (7f, 8f 2, 9f) (g-s, gd, g-f, frm) 1998 AW 4-6: (7f 2-2, 8f 2-3, 10f) (Equi 1-2, Fibr 3-4)
Scopey, useful colt, effective 7 to 8f, best at 8f - acts on AW, best on Fibr, prefers left handed tracks, likes tight tracks. Turf high 72. AW high 87 - also 1st of 13 getting 7lb from Nomore Mr Niceguy (14 Mar Wolverhampton RF 0431). Becoming disappointing. He really found his form once switching to sand, winning a string of good handicaps including the Ladbroke All-Weather Trophy Final and the Lincoln Trial. Third in the Winter Derby, he ran a couple of good races on turf before losing his form.
**A G Newcombe [4-18] Chris Bradbury (from Sir Michael Stoute [0-2] Jun 1997).*

FAYM (IRE) BHB 49f51a RR 55f 51a 4547[16]

4 b f Fayruz 6.6f **(63)** - Lorme (Glenstal (USA)) 10.1f **(64)**
Form - 3247005740
Record 1998 - 1st:0 2nd:1 3rd:1 Ran:10
Pre1998 - 1st:0 2nd:2 3rd:2 Ran:10
Win Prizemoney £0 *Total Prizemoney* £4,653
1998 Turf 0-1: (6f) (g-f) 1998 AW 0-9: (6f, 7f 5, 8f 3) (Fibr 9)
Leggy, average filly, effective 7f - acts on Fibr, has worn blinkers, likes left handed tracks, likes tight tracks. AW high 62 - 2nd of 13 giving 17lb to Moon Gorge (13 Feb Southwell 7f Fibr RF 0281). Inconsistent. She has made the frame on quite a few occasions on sand, but is finding winning difficult. Showed very little when tried on turf. **J Wharton [0-20] John Wharton.*

FAYRUZAH (IRE) RR 78f 4673[2]

2 b f Fayruz 6.6f **(63)** - Fraudulent (Sexton Blake) 12f **(51)**
Form - 2

Record 1998 - 1st:0 2nd:1 3rd:0 Ran:1
Win Prizemoney £0 *Total Prizemoney* £1,004
1998 Turf 0-1: (6f) (g-f)
Currently above-average filly. (1st run) - 2nd of 10 to Resalah (6 Oct Redcar 6f g-f RF 4673). **K Mahdi [0-1] Kamil Mahdi.*

FEAR AND GREED (IRE) RR 105f 4725a[D]
2 b f Brief Truce (USA) 9.1f **(73)** - Zing Ping
Form - 162D
1998 Turf 1-4: (6f 1-2, 7f, 8f) (sft 1-2, gd, frm)
Pattern-class filly. Turf high 103 - 2nd of 13 to Edabiya (6 Spt Curragh 7f gd RF 4178a). She won her maiden in soft ground and was disappointing until encountering a testing surface again in the Group One Moyglare Stud Stakes. Second there to Edabiya, she can win a decent early-season contest if we have a wet spring.
**T Stack in IRE [1-4] M Begleys.*

FEARBY CROSS (IRE) BHB 91f RR 91f 4974[5]
2 b c Unblest - Two Magpies (Doulab (USA)) 9.8f **(65)**
Form - 3105
Record 1998 - 1st:1 2nd:0 3rd:1 Ran:4
Win Prizemoney £3,824 *Total Prizemoney* £4,206
Wins * 1998 Spt Ayr (G-S) 6f 91+ <
1998 Turf 1-4: (5f, 6f 1-3) (sft 2, g-s 1-1, gd)
Useful colt. Turf high 91 (began Aug) - 1st of 15 giving 7lb to Get Stuck In (17 Spt Ayr RF 4326). Confirmed debut promise when winning a Ayr maiden, and far from disgraced in better company thereafter. Likes soft ground and can progress further.
**J D Bethell [1-4] Clarendon Thoroughbred Racing.*

FEARLESS BHB 65a RR 42f 3042[7]
3 b f Groom Dancer (USA) 9.5f **(75)** - Fearless Revival (Cozzene (USA)) 6f **(93)**
Form - 2346427
Record 1998 - 1st:0 2nd:2 3rd:1 Ran:7
Win Prizemoney £0 *Total Prizemoney* £1,809
1998 Turf 0-3: (5f 2, 6f) (gd 3) 1998 AW 0-4: (6f 2, 7f 2) (Equi, Fibr 3)
Workmanlike, average filly. Turf high 42. AW high 63.
**Sir Mark Prescott [0-7] Cheveley Park Stud.*

FEARLESS BRAVE BHB 51f48a RR 57f 48a 5118[14]
3 b c Aragon 7.7f **(58)** - Siouan (So Blessed) 8.7f **(67)**
Form - 521540830
Record 1998 - 1st:1 2nd:1 3rd:1 Ran:8
Pre1998 - 1st:0 2nd:0 3rd:0 Ran:3
Win Prizemoney £2,784 *Total Prizemoney* £4,140
Wins * 1998 May Mussel (GD) 12f 65 <
1998 Turf 1-8: (12f 1-5, 14f 2, 16f) (g-s 2, gd 1-4, g-f, frm)
Lengthy, fair colt, effective 12 to 14f, best at 12f, acts on g-s to gd, best on gd, has worn blinkers, likes right handed tracks, prefers tight tracks. Turf high 66 (1st run) - 2nd of 4 to Dutch Lad (9 Apr Musselburgh 12f gd RF 0631) - also 1st of 6 getting 18lb from Summerhill Special (6 May Musselburgh RF 1064).
**C W Thornton [1-11] Guy Reed.*

FEARLESS LADY RR 26f 4047[7]
2 b f Cyrano de Bergerac 7.3f **(58)** - I Fear Nothing **(70df 50a)** (Kalaglow) 9.8f **(67)**
Form - 70707
Record 1998 - 1st:0 2nd:0 3rd:0 Ran:5
1998 Turf 0-5: (5f 2, 6f 2, 7f) (frm 5)
Little account filly. Turf high 26. **V Soane [0-5] Summerdown Set.*

FEAR NOT (IRE) BHB 61f65a RR 58f 65a 1758[14]
3 b f Alzao (USA) 9.8f **(73)** - Fear Naught (Connaught) 7.7f **(63)**
Form - 14330
Record 1998 - 1st:1 2nd:0 3rd:2 Ran:5
Pre1998 - 1st:0 2nd:0 3rd:0 Ran:2
Win Prizemoney £3,723 *Total Prizemoney* £4,891
Wins * 1998 *Feb Wolver (STD) 7f 58+* <
1998 Turf 0-3: (8f 3) (g-f, frm 2) 1998 AW 1-2: (7f 1-2) (Equi, Fibr 1-1)
Scopey, fair filly, effective 7f - acts on Fibr. Turf high 58. AW high 58 - also 1st of 8 from Lady Jazz (25 Feb Wolverhampton RF 0357).
**M Bell [1-7] Die-Hard Racing Club.*

FEATHER 'N LACE (IRE) RR 68f 1465[3]
2 b f Green Desert (USA) 7.8f **(78)** - Report 'em (USA) (Staff Writer (USA)) 10f **(54)**
Form - 33
Record 1998 - 1st:0 2nd:0 3rd:2 Ran:2
Win Prizemoney £0 *Total Prizemoney* £1,169
1998 Turf 0-2: (5f, 6f) (gd, frm)
Currently average filly. Turf high 68. **C A Cyzer [0-2] R M Cyzer.*

FEATHERSTONE LANE BHB 45f65a RR 53f 65a 2080[5]
7 b g Siberian Express (USA) 9f **(58)** - Try Gloria (Try My Best (USA)) 7.6f **(67)**
Form - 886423212331541170305
Record 1998 - 1st:4 2nd:3 3rd:4 Ran:17
Pre1998 - 1st:3 2nd:13 3rd:16 Ran:95
Win Prizemoney £16,716 *Total Prizemoney* £40,729
Wins * 1998 *Apr Wolver (STD) C 5f 67*
*** 1998** *Apr Wolver (STD) C 5f 65*
*** 1998** *Mar Wolver (STD) S 5f 60*
*** 1998** *Jan Wolver (STD) H 5f 49 51*
* 1997 *Aug Wolver (STD) S 5f 44*
* 1996 *Feb Wolver (STD) H 5f 64 65*
1998 Turf 0-3:(5f 3) (gd, g-f, frm)1998AW 4-14:(5f 4-12, 6f 2) (Fibr 4-14)
Average gelding, effective 5 to 6f, best at 5f - acts on Fibr, often wears blinkers (very effectively), likes left handed tracks, likes tight tracks, does well at Wolverhampton. Turf high 52. AW high 67 - 1st of 4 giving 13lb to Risky Whisky (11 Apr Wolverhampton RF 0651) - also 1st of 6 giving 13lb to Young Ibnr (4 Apr Wolverhampton RF 0566). Despite a moderate wins to runs ratio overall, he ran consistently well on Fibresand in '98, especially in modest company at Wolverhampton. He is suited by the minimum trip and needs to be brought with a late run.
**Miss L C Siddall [7-112] D Parker.*

FEEL A LINE BHB 50f RR 53df 1607[12]
4 b g Petong 7.6f **(58)** - Cat's Claw (USA) (Sharpen Up) 8.3f **(67)**
Form - 300
Record 1998 - 1st:0 2nd:0 3rd:1 Ran:3
Pre1998 - 1st:3 2nd:1 3rd:2 Ran:19
Win Prizemoney £8,231 *Total Prizemoney* £10,549
Wins 1997 Aug Ayr (G-F) SH 7f 46 50
1997 Jly Yarmou (G-S) S 7f 60 <
1997 Jun Bright (FRM) H 7f 43 48
1998 Turf 0-3: (8f 3) (gd 2, g-f)
Fair gelding, effective 7 to 8f, best at 7f, acts on gd to g-f, best on g-f, mostly wears blinkers (very effectively). Turf high 53 (1st run) - 3rd of 10 giving 16lb to Chimes of Peace (1 May Musselburgh 8f g-f RF 0953).
**M D Hammond [0-8] Punters Haven Racing Club (from B J Meehan [3-19] Aug 1997).*

FEEL FREE (IRE) BHB 80f76a RR 80f 76a 3923[1]
3 b f Generous (IRE) 11.5f **(82)**-As You Desire Me(Kalamoun)10.4f **(67)**
Form - 211851
Record 1998 - 1st:3 2nd:1 3rd:0 Ran:6
Pre1998 - 1st:0 2nd:0 3rd:0 Ran:1
Win Prizemoney £15,949 *Total Prizemoney* £16,979
Wins * 1998 Aug Goodwo (G-F) H 9f 69 80 <
*** 1998** *May Lingfi (STD) 10f 72*
*** 1998** *Mar Wolver (STD) 9.4f 63*
1998 Turf 1-3: (9f 1-1, 10f 2) (g-f 1-3) 1998 AW 2-3: (9f 1-1, 10f 1-2) (Equi 1-2, Fibr 1-1)
Workmanlike, decent filly, effective 9 to 10f, acts on g-f - acts on Equi, prefers tight tracks. Turf high 80 - 1st of 10 getting 13lb from Harmony (28 Aug Goodwood RF 3923). AW high 72 - 1st of 6 getting 16lb from Double Rush (13 May Lingfield RF 1200). Twice successful on sand in the spring, she gradually found her form on turf and won quite a valuable handicap at Goodwood in August very easily. **Lord Huntingdon [3-7] The Queen.*

FEEL NO FEAR BHB 56f45a RR 59f 45a 4760[13]
5 b m Fearless Action (USA) 8f **(44)**-Charm Bird(Daring March)7.1f **(61)**
Form - 60780U62516200
Record 1998 - 1st:1 2nd:2 3rd:0 Ran:11
Pre1998 - 1st:0 2nd:0 3rd:2 Ran:6
Win Prizemoney £3,687 *Total Prizemoney* £6,648
Wins * 1998 Jly Newmar (G-F) H 8f 50 55 <
1998 Turf 1-11: (7f 3, 8f 1-5, 10f, 11f, 12f) (gd 3, g-f 3, frm 1-3, hrd 2)
Fair filly, effective 7 to 8f, best at 8f, acts on gd to frm, best on frm. Turf high 59 - 2nd of 15 giving 7lb to Dancing Dervish (24 Aug

Brighton 8f frm RF 3839) - also 1st of 9 getting 20lb from Stoppes Brow (17 Jly Newmarket RF 2878).
**R Simpson [1-11] Miss S Davies (from W R Muir [0-6] Dec 1997).*

FEE MAIL RR 68f 4396[3]
2 b f Danehill (USA) 9.1f **(79)** - Wizardry (Shirley Heights) 10.3f **(74)**
Form - 83
Record 1998 - 1st:0 2nd:0 3rd:1 Ran:2
Win Prizemoney £0 *Total Prizemoney* £442
1998 Turf 0-2: (7f 2) (g-f, frm)
Currently average filly. Turf high 68 (began Spt).
**I A Balding [0-2] Gary Coull.*

FELONY (IRE) BHB 29f29a **RR 14f 29a** 3830[7]
3 ch c Pharly (FR) 11.5f **(64)** - Scales of Justice (Final Straw) 7.9f **(64)**
Form - 503334607
Record 1998 - 1st:0 2nd:0 3rd:3 Ran:9
Pre1998 - 1st:0 2nd:0 3rd:0 Ran:1
Win Prizemoney £0 *Total Prizemoney* £798
1998 AW 0-9: (9f, 10f, 11f 2, 12f 3, 14f, 16f) (Equi, Fibr 8)
Moderate colt. AW high 48.
**D J G MurraySmith [0-10] Ms Diana Wilder.*

FEN WARRIOR BHB 39f **RR 52f** 3025[12]
3 b g Pursuit of Love 9.5f **(69)** - Kennedys Prima (Primo Dominie) 6.2f **(80)**
Form - 70
Record 1998 - 1st:0 2nd:0 3rd:0 Ran:2
Pre1998 - 1st:0 2nd:0 3rd:0 Ran:1
1998 Turf 0-2: (7f, 8f) (frm 2)
Leggy, currently fair gelding, has worn blinkers. Turf high 33 (began Jly). **W J Haggas [0-3] Jolly Farmers Racing.*

FERGHANA MA BHB 56f **RR 57f** 3111[3]
3 br f Mtoto 11.5f **(71)** - Justine (GER) (Luciano) 11.2f **(65)**
Form - 77423
Record 1998 - 1st:0 2nd:1 3rd:1 Ran:4
Pre1998 - 1st:0 2nd:0 3rd:0 Ran:2
Win Prizemoney £0 *Total Prizemoney* £1,232
1998 Turf 0-4: (7f, 10f, 11f 2) (sft, g-s, g-f, frm)
Light-framed, fair filly, effective 11f, acts on g-f. Turf high 57 - 2nd of 19 giving 2lb to Rock Scene (3 Jly Warwick 11f g-f RF 2509).
**S C Williams [0-6] Dr Klaus Rohde.*

FERN'S GOVERNOR BHB 59f53a **RR 61f 53a** 1638[3]
6 b m Governor General 6.8f **(45)** - Sharp Venita (Sharp Edge) 10f **(56)**
Form - 83
Record 1998 - 1st:0 2nd:0 3rd:1 Ran:2
Pre1998 - 1st:3 2nd:1 3rd:3 Ran:26
Win Prizemoney £9,910 *Total Prizemoney* £13,745

Wins	1997	Aug	Windso	(GD)	H	8.3f	53	61	<
	1996	Spt	Nottin	(G-F)	H	10f	51	56+	
	1996	Aug	Windso	(GD)	H	11.6f	40	47+	

1998 Turf 0-1: (12f) (g-f) 1998 AW 0-1: (10f) (Equi)
Average mare, effective 8 to 10f, best at 10f, acts on gd to frm.
**J J Bridger [0-2] J J Bridger (from W J Musson [3-26] Spt 1997).*

FERNS MEMORY BHB 26f **RR 22f** 2349[12]
3 ch f Beveled (USA) 6.9f **(64)** - Sharp Venita (Sharp Edge) 10f **(56)**
Form - 000
Record 1998 - 1st:0 2nd:0 3rd:0 Ran:3
1998 Turf 0-3: (8f 3) (g-f, frm 2)
Light-framed, currently little account filly. Turf high 22.
**W J Musson [0-3] Fern Components Ltd.*

FERNY FACTORS BHB 56f **RR 57f** 4663[9]
2 ch c King Among Kings 7.4f **(49)** - Market Blues (Porto Bello) 8.9f **(43)**
Form - 0861650
Record 1998 - 1st:1 2nd:0 3rd:0 Ran:7
Win Prizemoney £2,477 *Total Prizemoney* £2,477

Wins	* **1998**	Jly	Beverl	(GD)	S	7.5f	57	<

1998 Turf 1-7: (5f, 6f, 7f 1-4, 10f) (g-s, gd, g-f 1-2, frm 2, hrd)
Fair colt, effective 7f, acts on g-f, often wears blinkers. Turf high 57 - 1st of 17 from Risky Way (4 Jly Beverley RF 2516).
**Ronald Thompson [1-7] B Bruce.*

FERNY HILL (IRE) BHB 103f **RR 91f** 4616[7]
4 b c Danehill (USA) 9.1f **(79)** - Miss Allowed (USA) (Alleged (USA)) 10f **(76)**
Form - 20137
Record 1998 - 1st:1 2nd:1 3rd:1 Ran:5
Pre1998 - 1st:3 2nd:2 3rd:1 Ran:8
Win Prizemoney £18,593 *Total Prizemoney* £29,011

Wins	* **1998**	Aug	Windso	(G-F)		11.6f		89	
	1997	Spt	Redcar	(FRM)	H	14.1f	84	89	
	1997	Spt	Kempto	(G-F)		12f		90	<
	1997	Aug	Newcas	(G-F)		12.4f		84	

1998 Turf 1-5: (12f 1-3, 13f, 16f) (gd 2, g-f 1-2, frm)
Scopey, useful colt, effective 13f, acts on frm. Turf high 102 (1st run) - 2nd of 8 to Yorkshire (16 May Newbury 13f frm RF 1259). Consistent. Few horses improve when they leave Sir Mark Prescott, but Willie Muir did well with this fellow, placing him to win a decent conditions race at Windsor and make the frame in a Group Three at Epsom. Best on fast ground, he is worth another try over two miles.
**W R Muir [1-5] Miss Monique Van Bakel (from Sir Mark Prescott [3-8] Spt 1997).*

FERRARI (GER) RR 114f 1556a[2]
4 b c Alkalde (GER) - 00
Form - 412
1998 Turf 1-3: (10f, 11f, 12f 1-1) (hvy, sft 1-1, gd)
Group-class colt, effective 11 to 12f, acts on sft to gd. Turf high 114 - 2nd of 9 to Steward (24 May Baden-Baden 11f gd RF 1556a) - also 1st of 10 from Asolo (26 Apr Cologne RF 0948a). He finished like a train to win a Group Two at Cologne in April, but similar tactics proved his downfall at Baden-Baden the following month, where he was left with too much to do. He should stay beyond middle-distances. **P Lautner in GER [1-6] Mrs G Poorten.*

FERRET EDDIE (IRE) RR 1f 1390[18]
2 ch g Be My Guest (USA) 10.2f **(66)** -Musical Essence (Song) 7.2f **(61)**
Form - 0
Record 1998 - 1st:0 2nd:0 3rd:0 Ran:1
1998 Turf 0-1: (5f) (gd)
Currently very poor gelding. **T P Tate [0-1] The Ivy Syndicate.*

FERRUFINO (IRE) BHB 45f **RR 28f** 4647[12]
10 b g Montekin 7f **(36)** - Fauchee (Busted) 10.2f **(61)**
Form - 00
Record 1998 - 1st:0 2nd:0 3rd:0 Ran:2
1998 Turf 0-2: (10f, 13f) (gd, g-f)
Little account gelding. Turf high 28. **P M Rich [3-27] P M Rich.*

FESTIVAL FLYER BHB 64f **RR 69f** 4776[7]
3 b g Alhijaz 7.7f **(57)** - Odilese (Mummy's Pet) 7.7f **(60)**
Form - 47
Record 1998 - 1st:0 2nd:0 3rd:0 Ran:2
Pre1998 - 1st:0 2nd:0 3rd:0 Ran:5
Win Prizemoney £0 *Total Prizemoney* £757
1998 Turf 0-2: (10f 2) (gd, g-f)
Average gelding, effective 8f, acts on frm. Turf high 69 (began Jly).
**R W Armstrong [0-2] Mrs Joan Root (from R Boss [0-5] Oct 1997).*

FESTIVAL SONG (USA) RR 93f 3758[14]
3 b f Irish River (FR) 9f **(77)** - Amirati (USA) (Danzig (USA)) 8.4f **(76)**
Form - 452150370
1998 Turf 1-9: (5f 1-8, 6f) (hvy, g-s 1-2, gd 3, g-f 2, frm)
Useful filly, effective 5 to 6f, best at 6f, acts on sft to gd, best on gd, has worn blinkers. Turf high 93 - 1st of 9 getting 5lb from George (4 Jun Tipperary RF 1847a).
**A P O'Brien in IRE [1-20] Mrs T E Hyde.*

FFESTINIOG (IRE) BHB 90f **RR 93f** 4778[1]
3 b f Efisio 7.7f **(69)** - Penny Fan **(34f)** (Nomination) 7f **(60)**
Form - 44042781
Record 1998 - 1st:1 2nd:1 3rd:0 Ran:8
Pre1998 - 1st:3 2nd:0 3rd:0 Ran:5
Win Prizemoney £24,588 *Total Prizemoney* £29,360

Wins	* **1998**	Oct	Leices	(G-S)		8f	93+	
	* 1997	Oct	Newbur	(G-S)	L	7.3f	94	<
	* 1997	Jun	Ascot	(SFT)		6f	81	
	* 1997	Jun	Folkes	(G-F)		6f	77	

1998 Turf 1-8: (6f, 7f 3, 8f 1-4) (sft, gd 1-3, g-f 2, frm 2)
Light-framed, useful filly, effective 7 to 8f, best at 8f, acts on gd to g-f, best on gd. Turf high 95 - 4th of 6 giving 3lb to Digitalize (21 May Goodwood 8f g-f RF 1364) - also 1st of 4 giving 3lb to Molakai (13 Oct Leicester RF 4778). She is suited by soft ground and likes to dominate, but lost her way rather last season, and could not live up to her juvenile form. Stays up to a mile, and finally came good at the end of the season in a conditions race at Leicester.
**P F I Cole [4-13] Elite Racing Club.*

FIAMETTA BHB 88f RR 89?f 1361[5]

4 ch f Primo Dominie 7.2f **(67)** - Monaiya (Shareef Dancer (USA)) 9.9f **(73)**
Form - 075
Record 1998 - 1st:0 2nd:0 3rd:0 Ran:3
Pre1998 - 1st:1 2nd:0 3rd:0 Ran:4
Win Prizemoney £3,785 *Total Prizemoney* £4,991
Wins * 1997 Jun Folkes (SFT) 6f 74 <
1998 Turf 0-3: (8f, 10f, 12f) (sft 2, g-f)
Leggy, useful filly, effective 8f, acts on g-s. Turf high 89. Faced stiff tasks in Group races in 1998. **C E Brittain [1-7] B H Voak.*

FIAMMA (IRE) BHB 95f RR 92f 2917[5]

3 b f Irish River (FR) 9f **(77)** - Florie (FR) (Gay Mecene (USA)) 8.6f **(69)**
Form - 355
Record 1998 - 1st:0 2nd:0 3rd:1 Ran:3
Pre1998 - 1st:1 2nd:0 3rd:0 Ran:2
Win Prizemoney £9,642 *Total Prizemoney* £11,951
Wins * 1997 Spt San Si (GD) 7f
1998 Turf 0-3: (10f, 11f, 12f) (hvy, gd, frm)
Useful filly. Turf high 93.
**J L Dunlop [1-5] George S and Kay A Hofmeister.*

FICTITIOUS RR 81f 4495[3]

2 ch f Machiavellian (USA) 9.8f **(83)** - Trying for Gold (USA) (Northern Baby (CAN)) 11.6f **(71)**
Form - 53
Record 1998 - 1st:0 2nd:0 3rd:1 Ran:2
Win Prizemoney £0 *Total Prizemoney* £2,287
1998 Turf 0-2: (7f 2) (gd, g-f)
Currently decent filly. Turf high 81 (began Spt). A sister to Phantom Gold, she will come into her own over middle distances in time. **Lord Huntingdon [0-2] The Queen.*

FIDDLER'S ROCK (IRE) RR 73f 4790a[6]

3 b g Ballad Rock 7.2f **(63)** - Rockbourne (Midyan (USA)) 6f **(60)**
Form - 51544750886
1998 Turf 1-11: (5f, 6f 1-5, 7f 2, 8f 2, 9f) (hvy 1-1, sft 2, g-s, gd 4, g-f 3)
Above-average gelding, effective 6f, acts on hvy, has worn blinkers. Turf high 108 - 1st of 4 giving 5lb to Dress Design (12 Apr Cork RF 0692a). Consistent. He gained his only win at Cork in April, and was out of his depth when asked to tackle Listed and Group class horses. **G M Lyons in IRE [2-14] Mrs Christina Gilsenan.*

FIELDGATE FLYER (IRE) RR 19f 3885[6]

3 b f Sabrehill (USA) 8.5f **(64)** - Orba Gold (USA) (Gold Crest (USA))
Form - 66
Record 1998 - 1st:0 2nd:0 3rd:0 Ran:2
1998 Turf 0-2: (8f, 12f) (gd 2)
Workmanlike, currently poor filly. Turf high 19.
**R Hollinshead [0-2] G A Farndon.*

FIELD OF HOPE (IRE) RR 114f 5158a[2]

3 ch f Selkirk (USA) 7.9f **(76)** - Fracci (Raise A Cup (USA)) 7.6f **(74)**
Form - 312
1998 Turf 1-3: (8f 1-3) (sft 1-2, g-s)
Currently Group-class filly. Turf high 114 - 1st of 8 giving 4lb to Pan Galactic (30 Spt Saint-cloud RF 4712a). She looked a shade unlucky in the Italian 1,000 Guineas, and showed improved form when transferred to France in the second half of the season, winning a Listed event and finishing second to Handsome Ridge in a Group Three. She can make further progress if kept in training.
**P Bary in FR [1-2] Grundy Bloodstock Ltd (from G Botti in ITY [0-1] Apr 1998).*

FIELD OF VISION (IRE) BHB 70f60a RR 69f 60a 2930[5]

8 b g Vision (USA) 10.4f **(57)** - Bold Meadows (Persian Bold) 9.3f **(66)**
Form - 0463824114585
Record 1998 - 1st:2 2nd:1 3rd:1 Ran:12
Pre1998 - 1st:7 2nd:9 3rd:7 Ran:51
Win Prizemoney £34,812 *Total Prizemoney* £53,781
Wins * **1998** May Beverl (G-F) H 12f 68 74 <
* **1998** May Hamilt (G-S) H 13f 65 66
1996 Apr Hamilt (G-S) C 9.2f 64
1996 Jan Wolver (STD) H 9.4f 63 72
1996 Jan Wolver (STD) H 9.4f 63 65
1998 Turf 2-5: (12f 1-2, 13f 1-2, 16f) (g-s 1-3, frm, hrd 1-1) 1998 AW 0-7: (11f 2, 12f 4, 14f) (Fibr 7)
Average gelding, effective 11 to 16f, best at 12f, acts on g-s to hrd - acts on Fibr, has worn blinkers, favours tight tracks. Turf high 74 - 1st of 6 getting 7lb from Jamaican Flight (10 May Beverley RF 1139) - also 1st of 11 giving 16lb to Classical Dance (3 May Hamilton RF 0985). AW high 67 - 2nd of 11 giving 17lb to Grovefair Lad (9 Mar Southwell 12f Fibr RF 0416). Consistent.
**Mrs A Swinbank [5-33] Ms J A Bostock (from M Johnston [7-40] Apr 1996).*

FIELDS OF OMAGH (USA) BHB 71f RR 71+f 4312[6]

3 b g Pleasant Tap (USA) 13.1f **(71)** - Brave And True (USA) (Fappiano (USA)) 8.7f **(77)**
Form - 755843616
Record 1998 - 1st:1 2nd:0 3rd:1 Ran:9
Pre1998 - 1st:0 2nd:0 3rd:0 Ran:2
Win Prizemoney £2,931 *Total Prizemoney* £3,594
Wins * **1998** Spt Bath (GD) H 13.1f 64 71+ <
1998 Turf 1-9: (8f, 10f 3, 12f 3, 13f 1-1, 14f) (g-s 2, gd, g-f 3, frm 1-3)
Scopey, above-average gelding, effective 10 to 13f, acts on g-f to frm, likes tight tracks. Turf high 71 - 1st of 15 getting 1lb from Saintly Thoughts (7 Spt Bath RF 4126).
**I A Balding [1-11] Paul Mellon.*

FIERCELY GINGER BHB 34f RR 19f 2669[18]

3 ch g Interrex (CAN) 7.7f **(51)** - Broadway Stomp (USA) (Broadway Forli (USA)) 5.8f **(46)**
Form - 00000
Record 1998 - 1st:0 2nd:0 3rd:0 Ran:5
Pre1998 - 1st:0 2nd:0 3rd:0 Ran:3
1998 Turf 0-5: (6f, 7f, 8f, 10f, 12f) (gd 2, g-f 2, frm)
Scopey, poor gelding, has worn blinkers. Turf high 42.
**E A Wheeler [0-8] The Ferry Boat Syndicate.*

FIER DANSEUR (FR) RR 100f 278a[1]

4
Form - 1
1998 Turf 1-1: (11f 1-1) (gd 1-1)
Currently very useful. (1st run) - 1st of 20 getting 4lb from Demon d'Or (8 Feb Cagnes-sur-mer RF 0278a). Was well beaten in the Hocquart and the French Derby as a three-year-old, but managed to win a moderate Amateur event at Cagnes-Sur-Mer last February.
**J Lesbordes in FR [1-3].*

FIFIRE (GER) RR 109f 4599a[3]

6 b h King Of Macedon
Form - 3353
1998 Turf 0-4: (6f 2, 7f, 8f) (sft 2, gd 2)
Pattern-class horse, effective 6 to 8f, acts on sft. Turf high 109 (began Jly) - 3rd of 9 getting 2lb from Power Flame (26 Spt Cologne 8f sft RF 4599a). Consistent. He ran well in smart company from six furlongs to a mile, but always appears one-paced when asked for a finishing kick.
**P Pietsch in GER [0-6] (from GER [0-1] Spt 1998).*

FIFTH EMERALD BHB 49f RR 50f 4190[13]

3 b f Formidable (USA) 7.8f **(60)** - Glossary (Reference Point) 6.8f **(70)**
Form - 800100
Record 1998 - 1st:1 2nd:0 3rd:0 Ran:5
Pre1998 - 1st:0 2nd:0 3rd:0 Ran:2
Win Prizemoney £3,184 *Total Prizemoney* £3,184
Wins * **1998** Jly Pontef (G-F) H 8f 44 50 <
1998 Turf 1-5: (8f 1-3, 9f, 10f) (gd 2, g-f, frm 1-2)
Lengthy, fair filly, effective 8f, acts on frm. Turf high 50 - 1st of 14 getting 31lb from Mouche (7 Jly Pontefract RF 2590).
**C F Wall [1-7] M Ng.*

FIGAWIN BHB 46f47a **RR 46f 47a** 3085[12]
3 b g Rudimentary (USA) 8.2f **(66)** - Dear Person (Rainbow Quest (USA)) 10.4f **(75)**
Form - 0054253647070400
Record **1998** - 1st:0 2nd:1 3rd:1 Ran:12
Pre1998 - 1st:1 2nd:0 3rd:1 Ran:11
Win Prizemoney £1,984 *Total Prizemoney* £3,341
Wins 1997 *Jun Southw (STD) S 6f 59* <
1998 Turf 0-5: (6f, 8f 3, 10f) (sft, g-s, gd, g-f, frm) 1998 AW 0-7: (7f 3, 8f 3, 10f) (Equi 4, Fibr 3)
Leggy, fair gelding, effective 6f, acts on frm - acts on Fibr, has worn blinkers. Turf high 46. AW high 52.
**Mrs H L Walton [0-6] Mrs Jenny Carrington (from S Dow [0-10] Mar 1998).*

FIGHTER SQUADRON BHB 21f33a **RR 25f 33a** 2386[10]
9 ch g Primo Dominie 7.2f **(67)** - Formidable Dancer (Formidable (USA)) 9.2f **(63)**
Form - 7000
Record **1998** - 1st:0 2nd:0 3rd:0 Ran:4
Pre1998 - 1st:4 2nd:5 3rd:8 Ran:68
Win Prizemoney £13,194 *Total Prizemoney* £20,653
Wins 1994 Spt Yarmou (SFT) H 6f 53 57
1998 Turf 0-1: (7f) (g-f) 1998 AW 0-3: (6f 3) (Fibr 3)
Little account gelding, mostly wears blinkers. AW high 7. Becoming disappointing.
**R E Peacock [0-19] R E Peacock (from J A Glover [4-53] Nov 1994).*

FIGHTING TIMES BHB 48f49a **RR 55f 49a** 4917[13]
6 b g Good Times (ITY) 8.7f **(53)** - Duellist (Town Crier) 10.2f **(55)**
Form - 0
Record **1998** - 1st:0 2nd:0 3rd:0 Ran:1
Pre1998 - 1st:2 2nd:3 3rd:0 Ran:21
Win Prizemoney £5,133 *Total Prizemoney* £8,636
Wins * 1997 Oct Warwic (G-F) CH 10.8f 47 52 <
* 1997 Spt Nottin (GD) SH 10f 39 46+
1998 Turf 0-1: (10f) (g-s)
Fair gelding, effective 10 to 11f, best at 10f, acts on gd to g-f, best on gd, has worn blinkers (extremely effectively), prefers left handed tracks. **C A Smith [3-27] Julian Graves Ltd.*

FIGURE IT OUT **RR 22f** 3246[11]
3 ch g Dilum (USA) 7.1f **(56)** - Count On Me (No Mercy) 8f **(61)**
Form - 00
Record **1998** - 1st:0 2nd:0 3rd:0 Ran:2
1998 Turf 0-2: (6f, 7f) (gd, g-f)
Leggy, currently little account gelding. Turf high 22.
**R J Hodges [0-2] David Mort.*

FILEY BRIGG BHB 60f **RR 50f** 5059[10]
3 b f Weldnaas (USA) 8.4f **(55)** - Dusty's Darling (Doyoun) 9f **(69)**
Form - 670505000
Record **1998** - 1st:0 2nd:0 3rd:0 Ran:9
Pre1998 - 1st:2 2nd:1 3rd:3 Ran:13
Win Prizemoney £11,833 *Total Prizemoney* £18,424
Wins * 1997 Jun Beverl (G-F) 5f 84 <
* 1997 Apr Hamilt (G-S) 5f 65
1998 Turf 0-9: (6f 4, 7f, 8f 4) (sft, g-s 3, gd 3, g-f, frm)
Leggy, fair filly, effective 5 to 6f, acts on gd to g-f. Turf high 68. Inconsistent. A snip at just 1,000 gns, she had a busy and effective campaign at two, but cut very little ice in 1998.
**W T Kemp [2-22] Drakemyre Racing.*

FILFILAH BHB 96f **RR 96f** 4620[4]
3 ch f Cadeaux Genereux 7.9f **(76)** - El Rabab (USA) (Roberto (USA)) 10f **(76)**
Form - 64216104
Record **1998** - 1st:2 2nd:1 3rd:0 Ran:8
Pre1998 - 1st:1 2nd:1 3rd:0 Ran:4
Win Prizemoney £18,762 *Total Prizemoney* £22,807
Wins * **1998** Aug Lingfi (G-F) H 6f 90 96 <
* **1998** Jly Newmar (G-F) H 7f 86 91
* 1997 Jun Goodwo (GD) 6f 71+
1998 Turf 2-8: (6f 1-2, 7f 1-5, 8f) (gd 5, g-f, frm 2-2)
Scopey, very useful filly, effective 6 to 7f, best at 7f, acts on g-f to frm, best on frm, often wears blinkers (effectively). Turf high 96 - 1st of 11 giving 10lb to Easter Ogil (16 Aug Lingfield RF 3665) - also 1st of 9 from Golden Fortune (7 Jly Newmarket RF 2583). Consistent. Benefited from a first-time visor when winning a seven-furlong rated stakes at the July Meeting, and scored over a furlong less at Lingfield. Was outclassed in a Listed race at Doncaster. Needs fast ground, and can win if kept at a realistic level. **P T Walwyn [3-12] Hamdan Al Maktoum.*

FILIAL (IRE) BHB 70f70a **RR 75f 70a** 5013[1]
5 b g Danehill (USA) 9.1f **(79)** - Sephira (Luthier) 9.8f **(71)**
Form - 27223121043127421
Record **1998** - 1st:4 2nd:5 3rd:2 Ran:15
Pre1998 - 1st:3 2nd:2 3rd:1 Ran:17
Win Prizemoney £17,844 *Total Prizemoney* £25,064
Wins * **1998** Oct Redcar (SFT) C 11f 70
* **1998** May Hamilt (GD) H 13f 68 73
* **1998** Apr Ripon (SFT) H 12.3f 60 66
* **1998** *Mar Southw (STD) C 12f 61*
* 1997 *Nov Wolver (STD) C 12f 72*
1996 *Dec Lingfi (STD) H 12f 80 86* <
1996 Aug Sandow (G-F) 10f 75
1998 Turf 3-11: (10f, 11f 1-1, 12f 1-6, 13f 1-3) (sft 1-2, g-s 3, gd 2-4, g-f, frm) 1998 AW 1-4: (12f 1-4) (Equi, Fibr 1-3)
Above-average gelding, effective 11 to 13f, best at 12f, acts on sft to gd - acts on AW, has worn blinkers, likes left handed tracks, prefers tight tracks. Turf high 75 - 2nd of 6 giving 11lb to Madame Chinnery (4 Jun Haydock 12f gd RF 1716) - also 1st of 8 giving 12lb to Tycoon Tina (15 May Hamilton RF 1237). AW high 65.
**J Pearce [5-18] D Leech (from B J Meehan [1-9] Oct 1997).*

FILLE DU LAC (FR) **RR 107f** 2289a[4]
3 ch f Lac Ouimet (USA) 8.1f **(76)** - Sectarine (FR) (Maelstrom Lake)
Form - 24
1998 Turf 0-2: (12f 2) (gd 2)
Currently Pattern-class filly. Turf high 107. She is not quite a Group class filly, but should be able to win a Listed event, possibly beyond a mile and a half.
**E Lellouche in FR [0-2] Ecurie Ferdante.*

FILL THE BILL (IRE) BHB 85f80a **RR 83f 80a** 2319[5]
6 b h Bob Back (USA) 11.5f **(71)** - Neat Dish (CAN) (Stalwart (USA)) 9.9f **(78)**
Form - 5
Record **1998** - 1st:0 2nd:0 3rd:0 Ran:1
Pre1998 - 1st:0 2nd:3 3rd:2 Ran:12
Win Prizemoney £0 *Total Prizemoney* £10,957
1998 AW 0-1: (12f) (Fibr)
Decent horse, has broken blood-vessels. Consistent.
**M C Pipe [1-9] Mrs P B Browne (from A P O'Brien in IRE [0-15] Oct 1997).*

FILMORE WEST BHB 49f46a **RR 59f 46a** 4545[2]
5 b g In The Wings 11.2f **(77)** - Sistabelle (Bellypha) 9.8f **(73)**
Form - 032382
Record **1998** - 1st:0 2nd:2 3rd:2 Ran:6
Pre1998 - 1st:1 2nd:1 3rd:1 Ran:5
Win Prizemoney £4,342 *Total Prizemoney* £8,581
Wins 1996 Spt Goodwo (G-F) 10f 77 <
1998 Turf 0-3: (12f 3) (g-f 2, frm) 1998 AW 0-3: (11f 2, 15f) (Fibr 3)
Average gelding. Turf high 59. AW high 61. Becoming disappointing. Has been lightly-raced in recent seasons, and is now basically a plater.
**D W P Arbuthnot [0-8] Christopher Wright (from P F I Cole [1-3] Spt 1996).*

FINAL CLAIM BHB 48f **RR 49f** 4919[17]
3 b g Absalom 7.1f **(56)** - For Gold (Tina's Pet) 6.8f **(59)**
Form - 4000482720
Record **1998** - 1st:0 2nd:2 3rd:0 Ran:10
Pre1998 - 1st:0 2nd:1 3rd:0 Ran:2
Win Prizemoney £0 *Total Prizemoney* £2,042
1998 Turf 0-8: (6f 2, 7f 2, 8f 4) (g-s, gd 3, g-f, frm 3) 1998 AW 0-2: (6f, 8f) (Fibr 2)
Workmanlike, moderate gelding, effective 6f, acts on g-f, likes left handed tracks, likes tight tracks. Turf high 49. AW high 40. Inconsistent. **J G FitzGerald [0-12] Mrs R A G Haggie.*

FINAL DIVIDEND (IRE) BHB 68f **RR 68f** 4357[7]
2 b c Second Set (IRE) 9.2f **(67)** - Prime Interest (IRE) (Kings Lake (USA)) 10.8f **(67)**
Form - 853857
Record 1998 - 1st:0 2nd:0 3rd:1 Ran:6
Win Prizemoney £0 *Total Prizemoney* £505
1998 Turf 0-6: (5f, 6f 4, 7f) (gd, g-f, frm 4)
Average colt, effective 6f, acts on g-f. Turf high 68 - 3rd of 12 to Diggit (6 Jly Bath 6f g-f RF 2554).
**M J Fetherston-Godley [0-6] The Kennet House Partnership.*

FINAL GLORY RR 457[5]
4 ch f Midyan (USA) 9.9f **(64)** - Lady Habitat (Habitat) 9.4f **(70)**
Form - 65
Record 1998 - 1st:0 2nd:0 3rd:0 Ran:1
Pre1998 - 1st:0 2nd:0 3rd:0 Ran:1
1998 AW 0-1: (9f) (Fibr)
Neat, currently poor filly. **Lord Huntingdon [0-2] Sir Gordon Brunton.*

FINAL SETTLEMENT (IRE) BHB 65f **RR 64f** 3111[1]
3 b g Soviet Lad (USA) 9.4f **(63)** - Tender Time (Tender King) 6.8f **(54)**
Form - 311
Record 1998 - 1st:2 2nd:0 3rd:1 Ran:3
Pre1998 - 1st:0 2nd:0 3rd:0 Ran:3
Win Prizemoney £6,242 *Total Prizemoney* £6,712
Wins * **1998** Jly Lingfi (G-F) H 11.5f 60 64 <
* **1998** Jun Windso (GD) H 8.3f 58 60
1998 Turf 2-3: (8f 1-2, 11f 1-1) (g-f 1-2, frm 1-1)
Leggy, average gelding, effective 8 to 11f, best at 8f, acts on g-f to frm, best on g-f. Turf high 64 - 1st of 5 getting 10lb from Tigullio (25 Jly Lingfield RF 3111) - also 1st of 18 giving 10lb to Fancy Design (29 Jun Windsor RF 2387).
**J R Jenkins [2-6] The Meek Partnership.*

FINAL STAB (IRE) BHB 49f65a **RR 51df 65a** 4640[10]
5 b g Kris 10f **(75)** - Premier Rose (Sharp Edge) 10f **(56)**
Form - 30850
Record 1998 - 1st:0 2nd:0 3rd:1 Ran:5
Pre1998 - 1st:2 2nd:0 3rd:0 Ran:9
Win Prizemoney £8,474 *Total Prizemoney* £8,731
Wins 1997 Aug Bath (GD) H 8f 69 74+ <
1995 Spt Salisb (G-S) 7f 74
1998 Turf 0-2: (8f, 10f) (g-f, frm) 1998 AW 0-3: (7f, 9f, 12f) (Fibr 3)
Fair gelding, effective 8f, acts on frm, likes left handed tracks, likes tight tracks. Turf high 37 (began Aug). AW high 53 (began Jly).
**Miss S J Wilton [0-5] John Pointon and Sons (from P W Harris [2-9] Oct 1997).*

FINAL TANGO BHB 92f **RR 95f** 2135[3]
3 b f Danehill (USA) 9.1f **(79)** - Sombre Lady (Sharpen Up) 8.3f **(67)**
Form - 23
Record 1998 - 1st:0 2nd:1 3rd:1 Ran:2
Pre1998 - 1st:1 2nd:2 3rd:0 Ran:3
Win Prizemoney £3,395 *Total Prizemoney* £9,719
Wins * 1997 Oct Redcar (G-F) 7f 86 <
1998 Turf 0-2: (7f, 8f) (g-f, frm)
Scopey, very useful filly. Turf high 95 - 3rd of 12 giving 2lb to Fizzed (20 Jun Ascot 8f g-f RF 2135). A useful filly, who put up two good efforts in decent handicaps in '98, notably first-time out when only narrowly beaten by Safio at Goodwood. She was particularly unlucky, as Dettori dropped his whip and was unable to ride her out, which probably cost her the race. She proved she stayed a mile next time out at Ascot when third to Fizzed, but was not seen out again. **J H M Gosden [1-5] Mrs C A Waters.*

FINAL TRIAL (IRE) BHB 62f **RR 60f** 4527[7]
4 b c Last Tycoon 9.4f **(73)** - Perfect Alibi (Law Society (USA)) 9.9f **(70)**
Form - 4007
Record 1998 - 1st:0 2nd:0 3rd:0 Ran:4
Pre1998 - 1st:0 2nd:0 3rd:1 Ran:3
Win Prizemoney £0 *Total Prizemoney* £988
1998 Turf 0-4: (10f 3, 12f) (gd 2, g-f 2)
Scopey, average colt. Turf high 60. **G Wragg [0-7] Mollers Racing.*

FINARTS BAY BHB 34f **RR 31f** 2760[10]
4 b f Aragon 7.7f **(58)** - Salinas (Bay Express) 7.1f **(60)**
Form - 70080
Record 1998 - 1st:0 2nd:0 3rd:0 Ran:4
Pre1998 - 1st:0 2nd:0 3rd:1 Ran:7
Win Prizemoney £0 *Total Prizemoney* £757
1998 Turf 0-4: (5f 2, 6f, 8f) (gd 3, frm)
Light-framed, very moderate filly, has worn blinkers. Turf high 31.
**P D Evans [0-4] Mrs F A Veasey (from Mrs J Cecil [0-7] Nov 1997).*

FINESTATETOBEIN BHB 28f24a **RR 55df 24a** 2685[6]
5 ch m Northern State (USA) 12.6f **(45)** - Haywain (Thatching) 8f **(66)**
Form - 56
Record 1998 - 1st:0 2nd:0 3rd:0 Ran:2
Pre1998 - 1st:0 2nd:0 3rd:1 Ran:14
Win Prizemoney £0 *Total Prizemoney* £438
1998 Turf 0-2: (13f, 14f) (gd, frm)
Fair filly, effective 14f, acts on g-s, has worn blinkers, likes left handed tracks. Turf high 26. **F Watson [0-16] F Watson.*

FINE TIMES BHB 24f50a **RR 27f 50a** 3119[7]
4 b g Timeless Times (USA) 6.1f **(56)** - Marfen (Lochnager) 6f **(59)**
Form - 70507
Record 1998 - 1st:0 2nd:0 3rd:0 Ran:5
Pre1998 - 1st:0 2nd:2 3rd:0 Ran:19
Win Prizemoney £0 *Total Prizemoney* £1,944
1998 Turf 0-5: (6f 3, 7f, 9f) (hvy, sft, g-f, frm, hrd)
Scopey, very moderate gelding, effective 6f, acts on frm, has worn blinkers (effectively). Turf high 27. Inconsistent.
**J S Haldane [0-5] G J Johnston (from C W Fairhurst [0-19] Oct 1997).*

FINISTERRE (IRE) BHB 68f48a **RR 67f 48a** 4936[6]
5 b g Salt Dome (USA) 6.5f **(59)** - Inisfail (Persian Bold) 9.3f **(66)**
Form - 28102632056
Record 1998 - 1st:1 2nd:3 3rd:1 Ran:11
Pre1998 - 1st:1 2nd:3 3rd:3 Ran:23
Win Prizemoney £5,725 *Total Prizemoney* £13,193
Wins * **1998** May Catter (G-S) 7f 63 <
* 1996 May Ripon (GD) H 6f 57 58
1998 Turf 1-11: (6f 2, 7f 1-7, 8f 2) (g-s 3, gd 1-2, g-f 3, frm 3)
Average gelding, effective 7f, acts on gd to frm, has worn blinkers, likes left handed tracks. Turf high 67 - 2nd of 11 giving 32lb to Komlucky (22 Jly Catterick 7f g-f RF 3024) - also 1st of 14 from Marylebone (30 May Catterick RF 1586).
**J J O'Neill [2-34] Les Femmes Fatales.*

FINSBURY FLYER (IRE) BHB 34f **RR 49f** 4416[15]
5 ch g Al Hareb (USA) 9.4f **(53)** - Jazirah (Main Reef) 9.6f **(57)**
Form - 31120080
Record 1998 - 1st:2 2nd:1 3rd:1 Ran:8
Pre1998 - 1st:2 2nd:0 3rd:2 Ran:12
Win Prizemoney £7,372 *Total Prizemoney* £9,147
Wins * **1998** Jly Les La (G-F) H 9f 48
* **1998** Jun Les La (GD) H 7f 48
1997 May Windso (SFT) C 8.3f 65 <
1996 Jun Chepst (GD) C 7.1f 62
1998 Turf 2-7: (7f 1-2, 9f 1-1, 10f, 11f, 12f 2) (gd 1-2, g-f 1-4, frm) 1998 AW 0-1: (12f) (Fibr)
Moderate gelding, effective 8f, acts on gd, likes left handed tracks. Turf high 49.
**H J Manners [2-7] H J Manners (from A J Chamberlain [0-1] Jun 1998).*

FIONA'S DREAM (IRE) RR 28f 2274[17]
2 b br f Soviet Lad (USA) 9.4f **(63)** - Woody's Colours (USA) (Caro) 9.3f **(74)**
Form - 00
Record 1998 - 1st:0 2nd:0 3rd:0 Ran:2
1998 Turf 0-2: (6f, 7f) (gd, frm)
Currently little account filly. Turf high 28.
**Miss Gay Kelleway [0-2] A P Griffin.*

FIONN DE COOL (IRE) BHB 58f **RR 58f** 5040[12]
7 b g Mazaad 8.5f **(53)** - Pink Fondant (Northfields (USA)) 9f **(72)**
Form - 607136080
Record 1998 - 1st:1 2nd:0 3rd:1 Ran:9
Pre1998 - 1st:2 2nd:4 3rd:3 Ran:29
Win Prizemoney £17,108 *Total Prizemoney* £27,473
Wins * **1998** Jly Chepst (GD) H 8.1f 58 63

1997 Aug Epsom (GD) H 8.5f 59 64
1995 Aug Salisb (FRM) H 8f 70 75 <

1998 Turf 1-9: (7f, 8f 1-8) (g-s 3, gd 1-4, g-f 2)

Fair gelding, effective 8 to 9f, best at 8f, acts on gd to g-f, best on gd, likes left handed tracks. Turf high 65 - 3rd of 13 giving 10lb to Rebel County (21 Jly Bath 8f gd RF 2972) - also 1st of 12 getting 11lb from Sweet Dreams (4 Jly Chepstow RF 2531). Becoming disappointing. Difficult to win with, but he got it right at Chepstow in July.
**J Akehurst [1-9] Canisbay Bloodstock Ltd (from R Akehurst [2-29] Spt 1997).*

FIORI BHB 84f75a RR 91f 75a 4835[3]

2 b c Anshan 8.2f **(63)** - Fen Princess (IRE) (Trojan Fen) 8.1f **(62)**
Form - 63242223
Record 1998 - 1st:0 2nd:4 3rd:2 Ran:8
Win Prizemoney £0 *Total Prizemoney* £13,021
1998 Turf 0-7: (6f 2, 7f 2, 8f 3) (g-s, gd 2, g-f, frm 3) 1998 AW 0-1: (6f) (Fibr)

Useful colt, effective 8f, acts on frm. Turf high 91 - 2nd of 19 getting 4lb from Ice (8 Oct York 8f frm RF 4709). Has shown progressive form and deserved to get off the mark. Gets a mile well, but has hung left at times. **P C Haslam [0-8] S A B Dinsmore.*

FIRE DOME (IRE) BHB 103f95a RR 109?f 95a 4055[13]

6 ch g Salt Dome (USA) 6.5f **(59)** - Penny Habit (Habitat) 9.4f **(70)**
Form - 66017751000
Record 1998 - 1st:2 2nd:0 3rd:0 Ran:11
Pre1998 - 1st:3 2nd:4 3rd:2 Ran:17
Win Prizemoney £46,440 *Total Prizemoney* £59,846
Wins * 1998 Jly Sandow (G-S) L 5f 109 <
*** 1998** Apr Thirsk (G-S) 6f 106
1996 Mar Doncas (SFT) L 6f 107
1994 Spt Ascot (GD) 5f 95
1994 Jly Yarmou (GD) 5.2f 74+
1998 Turf 2-9: (5f 1-2, 6f 1-6, 7f) (sft, g-s 1-1, gd 1-4, g-f, frm 2) 1998 AW 0-2: (5f, 6f) (Fibr 2)

Pattern-class gelding, effective 5 to 6f, acts on g-s to gd, has worn blinkers. Turf high 109 - 1st of 11 getting 4lb from Bishops Court (4 Jly Sandown RF 2549) - also 1st of 8 from Carranita (18 Apr Thirsk RF 0751). AW high 87. He underlined David Nicholls' skill in revitalising horses when winning a couple of decent conditions races, the latter a Listed event at Sandown. Not beaten far in valuable handicaps in the second half of the season, he needs a stiff track when racing over five furlongs.
**D Nicholls [2-11] J M Ranson (from R Hannon [1-10] May 1996).*

FIRE GODDESS BHB 50f RR 49f 4962[17]

3 ch f Magic Ring (IRE) 6.5f **(64)** - Into the Fire (Dominion) 8.5f **(63)**
Form - 000632763300
Record 1998 - 1st:0 2nd:1 3rd:3 Ran:12
Pre1998 - 1st:0 2nd:0 3rd:3 Ran:9
Win Prizemoney £0 *Total Prizemoney* £3,530
1998 Turf 0-12: (6f 5, 7f 6, 8f) (sft 2, gd 2, g-f 4, frm 4)

Unfurnished, moderate filly, effective 6f, acts on hrd, has worn blinkers. Turf high 49. **J S Moore [0-21] J S Moore.*

FIRST BALLOT (IRE) RR 43f 4884[9]

2 b c Perugino (USA) - Election Special **(62f)** (Chief Singer) 8.9f **(66)**
Form - 0
Record 1998 - 1st:0 2nd:0 3rd:0 Ran:1
1998 Turf 0-1: (7f) (g-s)

Currently moderate colt. **D R C Elsworth [0-1] J C Smith.*

FIRST CONSUL (USA) BHB 78a RR 70f 4268[11]

3 ch c Rubiano (USA) 7.1f **(87)** - Sunflower Fields (USA) (Fit To Fight (USA)) 9.7f **(45)**
Form - 615230
Record 1998 - 1st:1 2nd:1 3rd:1 Ran:6
Pre1998 - 1st:0 2nd:0 3rd:0 Ran:1
Win Prizemoney £3,882 *Total Prizemoney* £5,801
Wins * 1998 *Jun Wolver (STD) 7f 72* <
1998 Turf 0-2: (7f, 8f) (gd 2) 1998 AW 1-4: (7f 1-3, 8f) (Fibr 1-4)

Well made, above-average colt, effective 7 to 8f, best at 7f - acts on Fibr. Turf high 69. AW high 78 - 2nd of 11 giving 18lb to Kosevo (25 Jly Southwell 7f Fibr RF 3128) - also 1st of 7 from Dryad (6 Jun Wolverhampton RF 1794). Got off the mark with a workmanlike victory in a Wolverhampton Fibresand maiden, and despite some fair efforts since, was not one of the stable stars. He looks to need at least a mile now. **Sir Michael Stoute [1-7] Maktoum Al Maktoum.*

FIRST DANCE BHB 65f RR 70?f 3025[8]

3 b f Primo Dominie 7.2f **(67)** - Soviet Swan (USA) (Nureyev (USA)) 8.7f **(78)**
Form - 8
Record 1998 - 1st:0 2nd:0 3rd:0 Ran:1
Pre1998 - 1st:1 2nd:1 3rd:0 Ran:6
Win Prizemoney £3,582 *Total Prizemoney* £5,288
Wins 1997 Aug Goodwo (G-F) S 6f 70 <
1998 Turf 0-1: (8f) (frm)

Scopey, above-average filly, effective 6f, acts on gd to g-f, best on g-f. **Dr J D Scargill [0-1] A C Edwards (from R Hannon [1-6] Aug 1997).*

FIRST FANTASY RR 46f 5037[7]

2 b f Be My Chief (USA) 10.2f **(62)** - Dreams **(80df)** (Rainbow Quest (USA)) 10.4f **(75)**
Form - 7
Record 1998 - 1st:0 2nd:0 3rd:0 Ran:1
1998 Turf 0-1: (7f) (g-s)

Currently moderate filly. **J R Fanshawe [0-1] Aylesfield Farms Ltd.*

FIRST FORAY BHB 47f RR 37f 5123[9]

2 ch c Mazaad 8.5f **(53)** - Donalee (Don) 7.7f **(64)**
Form - 000
Record 1998 - 1st:0 2nd:0 3rd:0 Ran:3
1998 Turf 0-3: (6f 2, 7f) (g-s, frm 2)

Currently very moderate colt. Turf high 37 (began Aug).
**R P C Hoad [0-3] Foray Racing.*

FIRST FRAME BHB 57f RR 61f 4001[15]

3 b c Mukaddamah (USA) 7.6f **(74)** - Point of Law (Law Society (USA)) 9.9f **(70)**
Form - 3702000
Record 1998 - 1st:0 2nd:1 3rd:1 Ran:7
Pre1998 - 1st:0 2nd:0 3rd:0 Ran:1
Win Prizemoney £0 *Total Prizemoney* £2,832
1998 Turf 0-7: (6f 3, 8f 3, 10f) (g-s, gd 4, g-f, frm)

Leggy, average colt, effective 8f, acts on g-f, has worn blinkers. Turf high 61 - 2nd of 15 to Miss Salsa Dancer (16 May Thirsk 8f g-f RF 1274). **J L Eyre [0-8] J Roundtree.*

FIRST HUSSAR BHB 69f RR 68f 4139[9]

2 b c Primo Dominie 7.2f **(67)** - Third Movement (Music Boy) 6.8f **(57)**
Form - 400
Record 1998 - 1st:0 2nd:0 3rd:0 Ran:3
Win Prizemoney £0 *Total Prizemoney* £252
1998 Turf 0-3: (6f 2, 7f) (gd, g-f 2)

Currently average colt. Turf high 68.
**P Howling [0-3] Laci Nester-Smith.*

FIRST IDEA BHB 44a RR 47f 289[6]

3 b f Primo Dominie 7.2f **(67)** - Good Thinking (USA) (Raja Baba (USA)) 10f **(64)**
Form - 566
Record 1998 - 1st:0 2nd:0 3rd:0 Ran:3
Pre1998 - 1st:0 2nd:0 3rd:0 Ran:3
1998 AW 0-3: (7f 2, 8f) (Equi 3)

Leggy, moderate filly. AW high 37. **S Dow [0-6] Mrs A M Upsdell.*

FIRST IMPRESSION RR 68f 4968[7]

3 b c Saddlers' Hall (IRE) 10.5f **(65)** - First Sapphire (Simply Great (FR)) 8.2f **(65)**
Form - 607
Record 1998 - 1st:0 2nd:0 3rd:0 Ran:3
1998 Turf 0-3: (8f 2, 10f) (sft, g-f 2)

Workmanlike, currently average colt. Turf high 68 (began Spt).
**Lady Herries [0-3] Ms Elaine Reffo.*

FIRST LEGACY RR 56f 3686[12]

2 ch f First Trump - Loving Legacy **(62f)** (Caerleon (USA)) 8.6f **(71)**
Form - 600
Record 1998 - 1st:0 2nd:0 3rd:0 Ran:3
1998 Turf 0-3: (5f 3) (gd 2, hrd)

Currently fair filly, has worn blinkers. Turf high 56.
**M Brittain [0-3] Mel Brittain.*

FIRST MAITE BHB 92f85a **RR 93?f 85a** 5096[13]

5 b g Komaite (USA) 6.9f **(61)** - Marina Plata (Julio Mariner) 7.2f **(57)**

Form - 33262334212351400100

Record	**1998** -	1st:3	2nd:4	3rd:5	Ran:20
	Pre1998 -	1st:5	2nd:4	3rd:0	Ran:29

Win Prizemoney £45,880 *Total Prizemoney* £68,241

Wins								
	* **1998**	Oct	Ascot	(SFT)	H	5f	85	93 <
	* **1998**	*Jly*	*Southw*	*(STD)*	*H*	*7f*	*77*	*83*
	* **1998**	May	Ripon	(G-F)	H	5f	83	84
	* 1997	May	Beverl	(GD)	H	5f	72	75
	* 1997	*Apr*	*Wolver*	*(STD)*	*C*	*5f*		*67*
	* 1996	*Feb*	*Southw*	*(STD)*	*H*	*6f*	*70*	*77*
	* 1996	*Feb*	*Southw*	*(STD)*	*H*	*6f*	*70*	*78*
	* 1995	Spt	Beverl	(GD)		5f		70

1998 Turf 2-12: (5f 2-4, 6f 6, 7f 2) (sft, g-s 1-3, gd 5, g-f 2, frm 1-1) 1998 AW 1-8: (6f 4, 7f 1-1, 8f 3) (Fibr 1-8)

Useful gelding, effective 5 to 7f, best at 5f, acts on g-s to frm - acts on Fibr, mostly wears blinkers (effectively), excels at Ripon. Turf high 93 - 1st of 18 getting 4lb from Levelled (10 Oct Ascot RF 4741) - also 1st of 14 giving 20lb to Swan At Whalley (17 May Ripon RF 1288). AW high 83. Ran well on both Fibresand and turf last season, if a little inconsistent, and landed a valuable prize at Ascot in October. **S R Bowring [8-49] S R Bowring.*

**Miss Gay Kelleway [1-10] Three's Lucky Partnership.*

FIRST MISTRESS (FR) RR 53f 4009[P]

2 gr f First Trump - Mistress Gwyn **(64f)** (Night Shift (USA)) 7.2f **(69)**

Form - 00P

Record	**1998** -	1st:0	2nd:0	3rd:0	Ran:3

1998 Turf 0-3: (5f 2, 6f) (gd 2, g-f)

Currently fair filly. Turf high 53 (began Aug). (DEAD)

**M W Easterby [0-3] Stephen Curtis.*

FIRST MUSICAL BHB 100f **RR 92f** 4857[11]

2 ch f First Trump - Musical Sally (USA) (The Minstrel (CAN)) 10f **(72)**

Form - 22211114280

Record	**1998** -	1st:4	2nd:4	3rd:0	Ran:11

Win Prizemoney £14,771 *Total Prizemoney* £23,286

Wins							
	* **1998**	Jly	Windso	(GD)	6f	89+	<
	* **1998**	Jun	Pontef	(GD)	6f	89	
	* **1998**	Jun	Ayr	(G-F)	5f	83	
	* **1998**	Jun	Pontef	(G-S)	5f	74+	

1998 Turf 4-11: (5f 2-5, 6f 2-6) (sft 2, g-s 1-1, gd 3, g-f 1-1, frm 2-3, hrd)

Useful filly, effective 5 to 6f, best at 6f, acts on g-f to frm, best on frm. Turf high 91 - 4th of 7 giving 7lb to Saafend Rock (1 Aug Newmarket 6f frm RF 3277) - also 1st of 5 giving 6lb to Grey Princess (20 Jly Windsor RF 2961). She showed promise in her early races but then became something of a revelation, completing a fine four-timer. Her first two wins were in modest company, but she continued the winning run in much better class, and six furlongs proved well within her compass. Her form deteriorated afterwards, but she remains a credit to her trainer.

**M Brittain [4-11] Bob Abson BJK Partnership.*

First Maite let no-one down. He ran 20 times in all

FIRST MASTER BHB 75f78a **RR 77f 78a** 5095[2]

3 ch c Primo Dominie 7.2f **(67)** - Bodham (Bustino) 10.4f **(64)**

Form - 0230322

Record	**1998** -	1st:0	2nd:3	3rd:2	Ran:7
	Pre1998 -	1st:1	2nd:0	3rd:0	Ran:3

Win Prizemoney £3,167 *Total Prizemoney* £8,333

Wins	* 1997	Oct	Folkes	(GD)	6.9f	74 <

1998 Turf 0-7: (8f, 10f 3, 11f 2, 12f) (gd 3, g-f, frm 3)

Workmanlike, decent colt, effective 7 to 11f, acts on gd to frm, best on gd. Turf high 77 (began Jly) - 2nd of 7 giving 5lb to Panama House (23 Oct Doncaster 10f frm RF 4957). A consistent and honest sort, he lacks pace.

FIRST STEP (GER) RR 97f 2666a[18]

3 c

Form - 00

1998 Turf 0-2: (12f 2) (hvy, g-f)

Currently very useful colt. Turf high 97. Was outclassed and failed to stay in both the Italian and German Derbys.
**H Blume in GER [0-2] Gestut Ittlingen.*

FIRST VILLAGE (IRE) BHB 75f RR 63f 2121[11]

3 b f Danehill (USA) 9.1f **(79)** - L-Way First (IRE) (Vision (USA)) 9f **(64)**
Form - 000
Record 1998 - 1st:0 2nd:0 3rd:0 Ran:3
Pre1998 - 1st:1 2nd:0 3rd:1 Ran:7
Win Prizemoney £3,564 *Total Prizemoney* £4,538
Wins * 1997 Aug Bath (GD) 5.1f 80 <
1998 Turf 0-3: (5f, 7f 2) (g-f 3)
Scopey, average filly, effective 5f, acts on frm, has worn blinkers. Turf high 63. Inconsistent. **J Berry [1-10] Dr G W W Tsoi.*

FIT FOR BUSINESS RR 21f 4758[19]

2 b f Tina's Pet 7.4f **(56)** - Mills Amend (Milford) 9f **(61)**
Form - 0
Record 1998 - 1st:0 2nd:0 3rd:0 Ran:1
1998 Turf 0-1: (7f) (gd)
Currently little account filly. **R Hollinshead [0-1] J D Callow.*

FIVE OF SPADES (IRE) BHB 90f90a RR 88f 90a 2233[9]

3 b g Roi Danzig (USA) 10.5f **(62)** - Hellicroft (High Line) 10.3f **(70)**
Form - 740110
Record 1998 - 1st:2 2nd:0 3rd:0 Ran:6
Pre1998 - 1st:2 2nd:1 3rd:0 Ran:9
Win Prizemoney £18,235 *Total Prizemoney* £19,688
Wins * **1998** Jun Newcas (SFT) H 6f 77 88 <
* **1998** *May Wolver (STD) H 6f 77 85*
* 1997 Nov Nottin (GD) H 6.1f 77 79
* 1997 Spt Pontef (G-S) H 6f 68 78
1998 Turf 1-5: (6f 1-3, 7f 2) (sft, g-s, gd 1-2, g-f) 1998 AW 1-1: (6f 1-1) (Fibr 1-1)
Useful gelding, effective 6f, acts on gd to g-f - acts on Fibr, best on gd, likes tight tracks. Turf high 88 - 1st of 11 giving 9lb to Grand Estate (3 Jun Newcastle RF 1703). (1st run) - 1st of 12 getting 6lb from First Maite (29 May Wolverhampton RF 1579). Inconsistent.
**R A Fahey [4-11] B L Cassidy (from D Nicholls [0-4] Jun 1997).*

FIVE WAYS FLYER (IRE) BHB 56f RR 58f 5172a[10]

2 br f Perugino (USA) - Flutinoa (FR) (African Song)
Form - 1623532880
Record 1998 - 1st:1 2nd:2 3rd:2 Ran:10
Win Prizemoney £1,898 *Total Prizemoney* £3,563
Wins 1998 May Haydoc (GD) S 5f 58 <
1998 Turf 1-9: (5f 1-8, 7f) (sft, gd 1-2, g-f 4, frm 2) 1998 AW 0-1: (5f) (Fibr)
Fair filly, effective 5f, acts on gd to frm, best on frm, has worn blinkers. Turf high 58 - also 1st of 7 from Claranna (22 May Haydock RF 1394). Becoming disappointing.
**D Hassett in IRE [0-1] John Bernard O'Connor (from P D Evans [1-9] Aug 1998).*

FIZZED BHB 112f RR 105f 3421a[2]

3 ch f Efisio 7.7f **(69)** - Clicquot (Bold Lad (IRE)) 8.4f **(68)**
Form - 16112
Record 1998 - 1st:3 2nd:1 3rd:0 Ran:5
Pre1998 - 1st:1 2nd:0 3rd:0 Ran:3
Win Prizemoney £32,719 *Total Prizemoney* £45,338
Wins * **1998** Jly Lingfi (G-F) LH 7.6f 94 98 <
* **1998** Jun Ascot (G-S) LH 8f 90 96
* **1998** Apr Beverl (SFT) 7.5f 89
* 1997 Aug Beverl (G-S) 5f 84
1998 Turf 3-5: (6f, 7f 1-1, 8f 2-3) (g-s 1-1, gd 2, g-f 1-1, frm 1-1)
Workmanlike, Pattern-class filly, effective 8f, acts on gd to frm. Turf high 105 - 2nd of 8 to Miss Berbere (2 Aug Deauville 8f gd RF 3421a) - also 1st of 7 getting 5lb from Headhunter (11 Jly Lingfield RF 2712). Inconsistent. She had a super season, winning two Listed handicaps and finishing second in a Group Two at Deauville in August. She is well served by forcing tactics and can win a Group race next term. **M Johnston [4-8] Duke of Roxburghe.*

FIZZYGIG RR 62f 5139[7]

2 br f Efisio 7.7f **(69)** - Buzzbomb (Bustino) 10.4f **(64)**
Form - 7
Record 1998 - 1st:0 2nd:0 3rd:0 Ran:1
1998 Turf 0-1: (6f) (gd)
Currently average filly.
**R F JohnsonHoughton [0-1] T D Holland-Martin.*

FIZZY WHIZZY BHB 51f RR 57f 2154[1]

2 b f Rambo Dancer (CAN) 8.4f **(59)** - Hi-Hunsley (Swing Easy (USA)) 6.5f **(55)**
Form - 0381
Record 1998 - 1st:1 2nd:0 3rd:1 Ran:4
Win Prizemoney £1,940 *Total Prizemoney* £2,244
Wins * **1998** Jun Redcar (G-S) S 7f 57 <
1998 Turf 1-3: (6f 2, 7f 1-1) (gd 1-1, g-f, frm) 1998 AW 0-1: (5f) (Fibr)
Fair filly. Turf high 57 - 1st of 10 getting 5lb from The Donk (20 Jun Redcar RF 2154). She was awarded a seven furlong Redcar seller by the stewards, but it was an improved performance nonetheless, and she seemed suited by the softer ground.
**C B B Booth [1-4] J A Porteous.*

FLAG FEN (USA) BHB 65f53a RR 60f 53a 5151[17]

7 b br g Riverman (USA) 9.7f **(78)** - Damascus Flag (USA) (Damascus (USA)) 8.9f **(71)**
Form - 507154100
Record 1998 - 1st:2 2nd:0 3rd:0 Ran:9
Pre1998 - 1st:1 2nd:3 3rd:1 Ran:23
Win Prizemoney £12,401 *Total Prizemoney* £15,315
Wins * **1998** Spt Newmar (GD) H 10f 57 60+
* **1998** Jly Newmar (G-F) H 10f 54 60
1997 May Ripon (G-S) S 8f 65 <
1998 Turf 2-6: (8f, 9f, 10f 2-3, 12f) (gd 2, g-f 2, frm 2-2) 1998 AW 0-3: (11f 2, 12f) (Fibr 3)
Average gelding, effective 8 to 10f, best at 10f, acts on gd to frm - acts on Fibr, best on frm, has worn blinkers, prefers right handed tracks, excels at Newmarket, likes Ripon. Turf high 60 (began Jly) - 1st of 25 getting 21lb from Carlys Quest (29 Spt Newmarket RF 4540) - also 1st of 15 getting 9lb from Mutadarra (31 Jly Newmarket RF 3241). AW high 8. Inconsistent.
**H J Collingridge [2-6] Mrs Carol Dolan (from J Parkes [1-9] Feb 1998).*

FLAGSTAFF (USA) BHB 32a RR 47f 4549[13]

5 b g Personal Flag (USA) - Shuffle Up (USA) (Raja Baba (USA)) 10f **(64)**
Form - 2070
Record 1998 - 1st:0 2nd:1 3rd:0 Ran:4
Pre1998 - 1st:0 2nd:4 3rd:0 Ran:25
Win Prizemoney £0 *Total Prizemoney* £3,818
1998 Turf 0-2: (12f, 13f) (g-f 2) 1998 AW 0-2: (11f, 12f) (Fibr 2)
Moderate gelding, effective 8 to 12f, acts on g-f - acts on Fibr, has worn blinkers, favours tight tracks. Turf high 47 (1st run) - 2nd of 16 getting 6lb from Talib (8 Jun Windsor 12f g-f RF 1818). AW high 27. Inconsistent.
**A W Carroll [0-5] Dennis Deacon (from K R Burke [0-14] Aug 1997).*

FLAK JACKET BHB 85f RR 83f 2535[1]

3 b g Magic Ring (IRE) 6.5f **(64)** - Vaula (Henbit (USA)) 9f **(61)**
Form - 70311
Record 1998 - 1st:2 2nd:0 3rd:1 Ran:5
Win Prizemoney £9,135 *Total Prizemoney* £9,583
Wins * **1998** Jly Haydoc (G-F) H 6f 80 83 <
* **1998** Jun Kempto (HVY) H 6f 70 79
1998 Turf 2-5: (5f, 6f 2-4) (gd 1-2, g-f 1-2, frm)
Scopey, decent gelding. Turf high 83 - 1st of 10 getting 14lb from Marton Moss (4 Jly Haydock RF 2535) - also 1st of 10 getting 6lb from Blue Kite (10 Jun Kempton RF 1878). He got off the mark when making his handicap debut in very soft ground at Kempton, though he was racing very much on the favoured side of the track, leaving some questions over the reliability of the form. Followed up in ready fashion at Haydock.
**B J Meehan [2-5] Kennet Valley Thoroughbred II.*

FLAME OF GLORY RR 4572[13]

4 ch g Polish Precedent (USA) 9f **(73)** - Danishkada (Thatch (USA)) 9.8f **(62)**
Form - 0
Record 1998 - 1st:0 2nd:0 3rd:0 Ran:1
1998 Turf 0-1: (8f) (g-f)
Workmanlike, currently very poor gelding.
**Miss Z C Davison [0-3] Mrs J Irvine.*

FLAME TOWER (IRE) BHB 54f63a **RR 60f 63a** 4048[4]

3 ch c Archway (IRE) 8.5f **(60)** - Guantanamera (USA) (El Gran Senor (USA)) 9.6f **(76)**

Form - 436234854

Record	**1998 -**	1st:0	2nd:1	3rd:2	Ran:9
	Pre1998 -	1st:0	2nd:1	3rd:1	Ran:7

Win Prizemoney £0 *Total Prizemoney* £3,348

1998 Turf 0-7: (6f, 7f 4, 8f, 10f) (g-s, gd 3, g-f, frm 2) 1998 AW 0-2: (6f, 8f) (Equi 2)

Workmanlike, average colt, effective 6 to 8f, acts on gd to frm - acts on Fibr, best on gd. Turf high 67 - 2nd of 5 giving 5lb to Soft Touch (28 May Brighton 8f frm RF 1552). AW high 57.

**R Hannon [0-16] Mahmood Al-Shuaibi.*

FLAMING MIRACLE (IRE) BHB 32f45a **RR 32f 45a** 4384[7]

8 b g Vision (USA) 10.4f **(57)** - Red Realm (Realm) 8.1f **(65)**

Form - 37

Record	**1998 -**	1st:0	2nd:0	3rd:1	Ran:2
	Pre1998 -	1st:0	2nd:2	3rd:3	Ran:12

Win Prizemoney £0 *Total Prizemoney* £3,095

1998 Turf 0-1: (17f) (gd) 1998 AW 0-1: (15f) (Fibr)

Very moderate gelding, often wears blinkers. Consistent.

**G Barnett [3-22] J C Bradbury (from P F I Cole [0-9] Aug 1993).*

FLAMINGO PARADISE **RR 106f** 2660a[1]

7 ch h Rainbow Quest (USA) 11.2f **(81)** - Fabula Dancer (Northern Dancer) 9.6f **(80)**

Form - 1

1998 Turf 1-1: (16f 1-1) (hvy 1-1)

Pattern-class horse. (1st run) - 1st of 6 getting 5lb from Sweetness Herself (30 Jun Hamburg RF 2660a). He thrashed Sweetness Herself in a Listed race at Hamburg in June and is a useful stayer.

**W Figge in GER [1-1] H von Finck (from H Blume in GER [1-4] Oct 1996).*

FLANDERS (IRE) **RR 99f** 4539[7]

2 b f Common Grounds 8.1f **(66)** - Family At War (USA) (Explodent (USA)) 9.4f **(87)**

Form - 1111327

Record	**1998 -**	1st:4	2nd:1	3rd:1	Ran:7

Win Prizemoney £101,402 *Total Prizemoney* £179,777

Wins						
	* **1998**	Jly	Newbur	(G-F)	5.2f	94
	* **1998**	Jun	Ascot	(G-S)	5f	98+
	* **1998**	Jun	Beverl	(G-S)	5f	99++ <
	* **1998**	May	Beverl	(G-F)	5f	74+

1998 Turf 4-7: (5f 4-4, 6f 3) (gd 3-4, frm 2, hrd 1-1)

Very useful filly, effective 5 to 6f, best at 6f, acts on gd to frm, best on gd, does well at Beverley. Turf high 99 - 2nd of 22 giving 5lb to Boomerang Blade (9 Spt Doncaster 6f gd RF 4185) - also 1st of 4 getting 8lb from Kastaway (3 Jun Beverley RF 1676). A very speedy filly, she won the Hilary Needler at Beverley, the Windsor Castle Stakes and the Weatherbys Super Sprint in great style. She ran well in good company when stepped up in trip, but six furlongs might be stretching her stamina, and a return to five may see her at her most effective. However, such speedy and precocious fillies do not always train on.

**T D Easterby [4-7] Mrs Jean Connew.*

FLASHFEET BHB 38f38a **RR 34f 38a** 2900[13]

8 b g Rousillon (USA) 10.4f **(69)**-Miellita (King Emperor (USA)) 9.4f **(58)**

Form - 0

Record	**1998 -**	1st:0	2nd:0	3rd:0	Ran:1
	Pre1998 -	1st:1	2nd:4	3rd:7	Ran:34

Win Prizemoney £2,519 *Total Prizemoney* £10,127

Wins 1995 *Jun Wolver (STD) H 7f 53 47 <*

1998 AW 0-1: (7f) (Fibr)

Very moderate gelding, has worn blinkers.

**P D Purdy [0-1] P D Purdy (from K Bishop [1-14] May 1997).*

Flanders - a fast lady

FLASHMAN BHB 35f36a RR 33?f 36a 4810[8]
8 b g Flash of Steel 9.7f **(64)** - Proper Madam (Mummy's Pet) 7.7f **(60)**
Form - 08
Record 1998 - 1st:0 2nd:0 3rd:0 Ran:2
Pre1998 - 1st:2 2nd:5 3rd:4 Ran:36
Win Prizemoney £6,192 *Total Prizemoney* £13,342
Wins * 1995 Jun Pontef (G-F) H 18f 37 46 <
* 1995 *Feb Southw (STD) H 16f 30 33*
1998 Turf 0-2: (16f, 17f) (gd, frm)
Very moderate gelding, has worn blinkers. Turf high 13.
**B J Llewellyn [2-22] Ken Russell (from F H Lee [0-25] Aug 1994).*

FLASHTALKIN' FLOOD BHB 54f56a RR 43f 56a 4672[15]
4 ch g Then Again 7.4f **(52)** - Linguistic (Porto Bello) 8.9f **(43)**
Form - 0310000
Record 1998 - 1st:1 2nd:0 3rd:1 Ran:6
Pre1998 - 1st:1 2nd:0 3rd:1 Ran:9
Win Prizemoney £6,047 *Total Prizemoney* £6,874
Wins * **1998** May Hamilt (G-S) H 8.3f 59 63
1997 Jun Nottin (SFT) SH 8.2f 57 70+ <
1998 Turf 1-6: (8f 1-5, 9f) (sft, g-s 1-1, gd, g-f 2, frm)
Workmanlike, moderate gelding, effective 8f, acts on g-s to gd, likes tight tracks. Turf high 63 - 1st of 12 giving 16lb to Cabcharge Blue (3 May Hamilton RF 0989). Becoming disappointing.
**Mrs M Reveley [1-7] Wessex House Racing (from C A Dwyer [1-9] Dec 1997).*

FLAUNT (IRE) RR 90f 4906a[16]
6 bb g Persian Bold 10f **(69)** - Fuchsia Belle 00
Form - 663000
1998 Turf 0-5: (8f 4, 9f) (sft 3, g-s, gd)
Useful gelding, effective 8 to 9f, acts on sft to gd. Turf high 90 - 3rd of 9 giving 15lb to Bajan Queen (11 May Killarney 8f sft RF 1330a). Becoming disappointing.
**M J Grassick in IRE [2-21] Mrs Michael Watt.*

FLAVIAN RR 97f 5063[1]
2 b f Catrail (USA) - Fatah Flare (USA) (Alydar (USA)) 9.1f **(76)**
Form - 21
Record 1998 - 1st:1 2nd:1 3rd:0 Ran:2
Win Prizemoney £3,687 *Total Prizemoney* £5,269
Wins * **1998** Oct Newmar (G-S) 6f 97 <
1998 Turf 1-2: (6f 1-2) (g-f 1-2)
Currently very useful filly. Turf high 97 (began Oct) - 1st of 16 from Talah (30 Oct Newmarket RF 5063). Only had two runs towards the back-end, both being at Newmarket in hot maidens. She put up a good effort first time out and progressed nicely to lose her maiden tag in good style. She will be an interesting proposition next year. **H Candy [1-2] Major M G Wyatt.*

FLAWLESS BHB 106f RR 103f 5076[4]
3 b f Warning 8.1f **(77)** - Made of Pearl (USA) (Nureyev (USA)) 8.7f **(78)**
Form - 364
Record 1998 - 1st:0 2nd:0 3rd:1 Ran:3
Pre1998 - 1st:1 2nd:2 3rd:0 Ran:4
Win Prizemoney £3,213 *Total Prizemoney* £20,641
Wins * 1997 Spt Salisb (G-S) 7f 79+ <
1998 Turf 0-3: (8f 2, 9f) (sft, g-s, frm)
Workmanlike, very useful filly, effective 7 to 8f, best at 8f, acts on gd to frm, best on frm. Turf high 103 (1st run) (began Jly) - 3rd of 13 to Lovers Knot (8 Jly Newmarket 8f frm RF 2637). She was lightly raced and failed to improve on her juvenile form. Soft ground may have been against her at Chantilly and Newmarket and she is worth another chance on a sound surface.
**Sir Mark Prescott [1-7] Cheveley Park Stud.*

FLAXEN PRIDE (IRE) BHB 42f RR 42f 3749[4]
3 ch f Pips Pride 6.7f **(70)** - Fair Chance (Young Emperor) 10.1f **(63)**
Form - 070004
Record 1998 - 1st:0 2nd:0 3rd:0 Ran:6
Pre1998 - 1st:0 2nd:1 3rd:0 Ran:3
Win Prizemoney £0 *Total Prizemoney* £835
1998 Turf 0-6: (5f, 6f, 7f 3, 9f) (gd 5, frm)
Strong, moderate filly, effective 7f, acts on gd. Turf high 42. Inconsistent. **Mrs M Reveley [0-9] G Fawcett And Partners.*

FLEET LADY (IRE) BHB 28f RR 21f 2626[11]
3 b f Don't Forget Me 9.5f **(66)** - Yavarro (Raga Navarro (ITY)) 8f **(64)**
Form - 060
Record 1998 - 1st:0 2nd:0 3rd:0 Ran:3
Pre1998 - 1st:0 2nd:0 3rd:0 Ran:6
1998 Turf 0-3: (7f, 10f 2) (gd, g-f, frm)
Workmanlike, little account filly. Turf high 21.
**Mrs P N Dutfield [0-9] Harry Dutfield.*

FLETCHER BHB 77f RR 78f 5126[10]
4 b g Salse (USA) 10.9f **(71)** - Ballet Classique (USA) (Sadler's Wells (USA)) 10f **(76)**
Form - 40325265210
Record 1998 - 1st:1 2nd:3 3rd:1 Ran:11
Pre1998 - 1st:1 2nd:1 3rd:2 Ran:17
Win Prizemoney £8,943 *Total Prizemoney* £18,148
Wins * **1998** Oct Ascot (SFT) H 12f 74 78
1996 Apr Newmar (G-F) 5f 83+ <
1998 Turf 1-11: (10f 3, 12f 1-5, 14f, 16f, 20f) (g-s 1-2, gd 3, g-f, frm 5)
Workmanlike, above-average gelding, effective 16f, acts on g-f, has worn blinkers, likes right handed tracks. Turf high 78. A stayer, he finds little off the bridle.
**H Morrison [1-24] Lady Margadale (from P F I Cole [1-7] Oct 1996).*

FLEUR D'OR RR 47f 4526[10]
2 b f Alhijaz 7.7f **(57)** - Forever Shineing **(35f)** (Glint of Gold) 9.3f **(66)**
Form - 760000
Record 1998 - 1st:0 2nd:0 3rd:0 Ran:6
1998 Turf 0-4: (5f, 6f, 7f, 10f) (gd, g-f 2, frm)1998 AW 0-2: (6f 2) (Fibr 2)
Moderate filly. Turf high 47. AW high 22.
**M J Polglase [0-6] M J Polglase.*

FLEUVE D'OR (IRE) BHB 45f35a RR 33f 35a 2[11]
4 gr f Last Tycoon 9.4f **(73)** - Aldern Stream (Godswalk (USA)) 7.3f **(58)**
Form - 80
Record 1998 - 1st:0 2nd:0 3rd:0 Ran:1
Pre1998 - 1st:0 2nd:0 3rd:0 Ran:4
1998 AW 0-1: (10f) (Equi)
Leggy, very moderate filly. **D HaydnJones [0-5] Mrs Judy Mihalop.*

FLIBBERTIGIBBET RR 757[10]
3 b f Almoojid 7f **(36)** - Stella Royale (Astronef)
Form - 0
Record 1998 - 1st:0 2nd:0 3rd:0 Ran:1
Pre1998 - 1st:0 2nd:0 3rd:0 Ran:1
1998 AW 0-1: (7f) (Fibr)
Light-framed, currently very poor filly.
**Miss Kate Whitehouse [0-1] Duckhaven Stud (from C J Hill [0-1] May 1997).*

FLICKER BHB 50f41a RR 51f 41a 2654[12]
3 b f Unfuwain (USA) 11.4f **(74)** - Lovers Light (Grundy) 10.3f **(65)**
Form - 005030
Record 1998 - 1st:0 2nd:0 3rd:1 Ran:5
Pre1998 - 1st:0 2nd:0 3rd:0 Ran:3
Win Prizemoney £0 *Total Prizemoney* £449
1998 Turf 0-4: (10f, 11f, 12f 2) (g-s 2, gd, frm) 1998 AW 0-1: (8f) (Fibr)
Light-framed, fair filly, often wears blinkers. Turf high 51. Inconsistent. **Lord Huntingdon [0-8] The Hodcott Syndicate.*

FLIGHT BHB 80f RR 77+f 277a[5]
3 ch g Night Shift (USA) 8.1f **(73)** - Caspian Tern (USA) (Arctic Tern (USA)) 8.9f **(69)**
Form - 2115
Record 1998 - 1st:2 2nd:0 3rd:0 Ran:3
Pre1998 - 1st:0 2nd:1 3rd:1 Ran:4
Win Prizemoney £10,101 *Total Prizemoney* £12,599
Wins * **1998** Jan Cagnes (GD) 8f 77 <
* **1998** Jan Cagnes (SFT) 8f 77+
1998 Turf 2-3: (8f 2-2, 10f) (sft 1-1, gd 1-2)
Scopey, above-average gelding, effective 8f, acts on sft to gd - acts on Equi. Turf high 77 - 1st of 14 getting 4lb from Mazel-Trick (30 Jan Cagnes-sur-mer RF 0230a) - also 1st of 13 from Just An Oasis (18 Jan Cagnes-sur-mer RF 0138a).
**S Dow [2-4] Clear Height Racing (from L M Cumani [0-3] Aug 1997).*

FLIGHT FOR FREEDOM BHB 53f50a **RR 55f 50a** 4332[15]
3 b f Saddlers' Hall (IRE) 10.5f **(65)** - Anatroccolo (Ile de Bourbon (USA)) 10.1f **(67)**
Form - 606200
Record 1998 - 1st:0 2nd:1 3rd:0 Ran:6
Pre1998 - 1st:0 2nd:0 3rd:0 Ran:1
Win Prizemoney £0 *Total Prizemoney* £1,196
1998 Turf 0-5: (10f 4, 11f) (gd, g-f 3, frm) 1998 AW 0-1: (9f) (Fibr)
Scopey, fair filly. Turf high 55.
**F Murphy [1-8] Miss Samantha Dare (from J R Fanshawe [0-1] Spt 1997).*

FLINT KNAPPER BHB 89f **RR 90f** 2138[15]
4 ch c Kris 10f **(75)** - Circe's Isle (Be My Guest (USA)) 9.3f **(67)**
Form - 710
Record 1998 - 1st:1 2nd:0 3rd:0 Ran:3
Pre1998 - 1st:2 2nd:1 3rd:1 Ran:5
Win Prizemoney £17,121 *Total Prizemoney* £19,350
Wins * **1998** May Kempto (G-F) H 10f 83 90 <
* 1997 Spt Newmar (G-F) H 10f 80 83
* 1997 Aug Warwic (G-S) 8f 67
1998 Turf 1-3: (10f 1-3) (gd 1-1, g-f 2)
Workmanlike, useful colt, effective 10f, acts on gd to frm. Turf high 90 - 1st of 14 getting 6lb from Song of Freedom (23 May Kempton RF 1425). Showed little on his reappearance but won in taking style at Kempton and went off too fast on his only other run. He can add further successes provided he can be taught to settle.
**G Wragg [3-8] A E Oppenheimer.*

FLIRTINA BHB 37f35a **RR 40f 35a** 627[12]
3 b f Tina's Pet 7.4f **(56)**-Immodest Miss(Daring Display (USA))6.9f **(69)**
Form - 700
Record 1998 - 1st:0 2nd:0 3rd:0 Ran:3
Pre1998 - 1st:0 2nd:0 3rd:0 Ran:4
1998 Turf 0-1: (8f) (gd) 1998 AW 0-2: (6f, 7f) (Fibr 2)
Light-framed, moderate filly, has worn blinkers.
**P D Evans [0-7] W J Hamilton.*

FLIRTING AROUND (USA) BHB 67f **RR 57f** 4731[6]
4 b g Silver Hawk (USA) 11.2f **(85)** - Dancing Grass (USA) (Northern Dancer) 9.6f **(80)**
Form - 408066
Record 1998 - 1st:0 2nd:0 3rd:0 Ran:6
Pre1998 - 1st:1 2nd:2 3rd:0 Ran:9
Win Prizemoney £7,758 *Total Prizemoney* £13,992
Wins 1997 May York (GD) 13.9f 94 <
1998 Turf 0-6: (12f 2, 13f, 14f 2, 19f) (g-s, gd 3, g-f, frm)
Well made, fair gelding, effective 12 to 16f, acts on g-s to g-f, has worn blinkers. Turf high 85 (1st run) - 4th of 6 giving 5lb to Thornby Park (3 May Salisbury 14f gd RF 1003).
**R Simpson [0-7] G Piper (from Sir Michael Stoute [1-9] Aug 1997).*

FLITE OF LIFE BHB 79f **RR 80f** 4377[12]
2 gr c Forzando 7.2f **(63)** - Frighten The Life (Kings Lake (USA)) 10.8f **(67)**
Form - 404420
Record 1998 - 1st:0 2nd:1 3rd:0 Ran:6
Win Prizemoney £0 *Total Prizemoney* £2,470
1998 Turf 0-6: (5f, 6f 5) (gd, g-f 3, frm, hrd)
Decent colt, effective 6f, acts on g-f to frm. Turf high 80 - 2nd of 22 getting 6lb from Astonished (12 Spt Doncaster 6f g-f RF 4243).
**W R Muir [0-6] Mrs Irene White.*

FLOATING CHARGE RR 62f 4633[26]
4 b g Sharpo 7.5f **(68)** - Poyle Fizz (Damister (USA)) 9f **(73)**
Form - 5551060
Record 1998 - 1st:1 2nd:0 3rd:0 Ran:7
Pre1998 - 1st:0 2nd:1 3rd:0 Ran:2
Win Prizemoney £2,884 *Total Prizemoney* £4,089
Wins * **1998** Jly Redcar (G-F) 9f 62 <
1998 Turf 1-7: (6f, 7f, 8f 2, 9f 1-2, 10f) (g-s 2, g-f 3, frm 1-2)
Average gelding, effective 8 to 9f, best at 8f, acts on g-f to frm, best on frm, has worn blinkers. Turf high 67 - 5th of 18 giving 2lb to Star Invader (7 May Chester 8f g-f RF 1069) - also 1st of 5 from Burning Truth (18 Jly Redcar RF 2932). He got off the mark by bolting up in a Redcar handicap in July, but it was a moderate race.
**J R Fanshawe [1-9] The Leonard Curtis Partnership.*

FLOATING LINE BHB 59f **RR 58f** 2705[P]
10 ch g Bairn (USA) 9.4f **(55)** - County Line (High Line) 10.3f **(70)**
Form - 44P
Record 1998 - 1st:0 2nd:0 3rd:0 Ran:3
Pre1998 - 1st:7 2nd:12 3rd:3 Ran:54
Win Prizemoney £30,615 *Total Prizemoney* £53,557
Wins * 1996 Oct Newmar (G-F) H 14f 69 77 <
* 1995 Spt Newmar (GD) H 14f 61 68
* 1995 Jly Newmar (G-F) H 10f 58 63
1994 Spt Pontef (GS) 10f 64
1994 Aug Ripon (G-F) H 12.3f 52 57
1998 Turf 0-3: (12f, 14f, 16f) (gd, g-f, frm)
Fair gelding. Turf high 58. Consistent. Has returned to action after missing the whole of '97.
**E J Alston [3-25] G Lowe (from P Wigham [4-40] Jun 1995).*

FLOOD'S FANCY BHB 46f47a **RR 24f 47a** 2231[8]
5 b gr m Then Again 7.4f **(52)** - Port Na Blath (On Your Mark) 7.7f **(58)**
Form - 8
Record 1998 - 1st:0 2nd:0 3rd:0 Ran:1
Pre1998 - 1st:1 2nd:0 3rd:0 Ran:13
Win Prizemoney £2,773 *Total Prizemoney* £2,773
Wins 1995 Jly Haydoc (G-F) S 6f 60 <
1998 Turf 0-1: (10f) (gd)
Moderate filly, has worn blinkers. Becoming disappointing.
**L J Barratt [0-10] P L Loake (from A Bailey [0-6] Jan 1996).*

FLOOD'S HOT STUFF BHB 37f20a **RR 40f 20a** 308[5]
4 gr f Chilibang 7f **(55)** - Tiszta Sharok (Song) 7.2f **(61)**
Form - 8505
Record 1998 - 1st:0 2nd:0 3rd:0 Ran:3
Pre1998 - 1st:1 2nd:1 3rd:0 Ran:14
Win Prizemoney £2,277 *Total Prizemoney* £3,049
Wins 1997 Aug Bright (G-F) C 8f 40 <
1998 AW 0-3: (8f 2, 15f) (Fibr 3)
Scopey, moderate filly, effective 8f, acts on frm, has worn blinkers. AW high 13.
**M Quinn [0-2] Philip Kirby (from N P Littmoden [1-11] Jan 1998).*

FLORAL RAJ (IRE) RR 73f 4258[4]
2 ch c Indian Ridge 7.6f **(74)** - Spring Daffodil (Pharly (FR)) 9.8f **(68)**
Form - 04
Record 1998 - 1st:0 2nd:0 3rd:0 Ran:2
Win Prizemoney £0 *Total Prizemoney* £214
1998 Turf 0-2: (6f, 7f) (gd 2)
Currently above-average colt. Turf high 73 (began Aug). He is highly regarded, but has disappointed in maidens.
**Sir Michael Stoute [0-2] P S Partnership.*

FLORAZI BHB 103f **RR 103f** 3778a[2]
3 b c Arazi (USA) 9.2f **(74)** - Flo Russell (USA) (Round Table) 9.5f **(81)**
Form - 17012
Record 1998 - 1st:2 2nd:1 3rd:0 Ran:5
Pre1998 - 1st:2 2nd:0 3rd:0 Ran:4
Win Prizemoney £36,060 *Total Prizemoney* £40,908
Wins * **1998** Jly Newmar (GD) H 8f 97 103
* **1998** Apr Sandow (SFT) H 8.1f 91 104 <
* 1997 Oct Doncas (GD) H 7f 86 90
* 1997 Oct Leices (G-F) 7f 75
1998 Turf 2-5: (8f 2-5) (sft 1-1, gd 3, frm 1-1)
Scopey, very useful colt, effective 8f, acts on sft to frm. Turf high 104 (1st run) - 1st of 10 giving 4lb to Wuxi Venture (25 Apr Sandown RF 0867) - also 1st of 10 getting 2lb from Mubrik (18 Jly Newmarket RF 2919). He more than paid his way, winning valuable handicaps at Sandown and Newmarket before finishing second in a Listed event at Deauville. He can be ridden aggressively over a mile and should stay further. **J L Dunlop [4-9].*

FLORENCE ASHER RR 9f 2868[8]
3 b f Shardari 12.1f **(59)** - Filicaia (Sallust) 8.4f **(63)**
Form - 8
Record 1998 - 1st:0 2nd:0 3rd:0 Ran:1
Pre1998 - 1st:0 2nd:0 3rd:0 Ran:1
1998 Turf 0-1: (7f) (frm)
Light-framed, currently very poor filly.
**Don Enrico Incisa [0-2] Razza Dormello Olgiata.*

FLORENTINO (IRE) BHB 68f **RR 70f** 2175[9]
5 b br g Machiavellian (USA) 9.8f **(83)** - Helens Dreamgirl (Caerleon (USA)) 8.6f **(71)**
Form - 0
Record 1998 - 1st:0 2nd:0 3rd:0 Ran:1
Pre1998 - 1st:3 2nd:2 3rd:2 Ran:16
Win Prizemoney £9,952 *Total Prizemoney* £13,104
Wins 1997 Jly Pontef (GD) 10f 74 <
1996 Jly Bath (G-F) H 10.2f 68 74 <
1996 May Folkes (GD) H 9.7f 62 63
1998 Turf 0-1: (10f) (gd)
Above-average gelding, effective 10 to 13f, best at 10f, acts on gd to frm, best on frm, prefers left handed tracks, prefers tight tracks, excels at Pontefract. Consistent.
**Mrs V C Ward [0-4] David Ashbrook (from B W Hills [3-16] Oct 1997).*

FLORISMART BHB 20f45a **RR 25df 45a** 1621[12]
6 b g Never so Bold 7.1f **(62)** - Spoilt Again (Mummy's Pet) 7.7f **(60)**
Form - 000
Record 1998 - 1st:0 2nd:0 3rd:0 Ran:3
Pre1998 - 1st:0 2nd:0 3rd:0 Ran:10
Win Prizemoney £0 *Total Prizemoney* £342
1998 Turf 0-3: (8f, 12f 2) (hvy, sft, frm)
Little account gelding.
**B P J Baugh [0-11] Messrs Chrimes, Winn & Wilson (from J A R Toller [0-5] Spt 1995).*

FLORISTAN (IRE) BHB 73f **RR 67f** 613[3]
4 b c Fairy King (USA) 7.7f **(75)** - Le Melody (Levmoss) 11.4f **(66)**
Form - 3
Record 1998 - 1st:0 2nd:0 3rd:1 Ran:1
Pre1998 - 1st:0 2nd:0 3rd:1 Ran:2
Win Prizemoney £0 *Total Prizemoney* £1,409
1998 Turf 0-1: (8f) (sft)
Scopey, currently average colt.
**L M Cumani [0-3] Lord Alexander Hope.*

FLOTILLA BHB 35a **RR 55f** 436[4]
4 b g Saddlers' Hall (IRE) 10.5f **(65)** - Aim for the Top (USA) (Irish River (FR)) 8.6f **(78)**
Form - 0822644
Record 1998 - 1st:0 2nd:2 3rd:0 Ran:6
Pre1998 - 1st:0 2nd:2 3rd:0 Ran:13
Win Prizemoney £0 *Total Prizemoney* £3,313
1998 AW 0-6: (12f 3, 14f, 16f 2) (Fibr 6)
Scopey, fair gelding, effective 10f, acts on frm, has worn blinkers (very effectively), likes left handed tracks. AW high 45. A son of Aim For The Top, he is closely related to Dance To The Top, but is nothing like as good as they were.
**S Mellor [0-14] Silver Knight Exhibitions Ltd (from Sir Mark Prescott [0-6] Oct 1996).*

FLOW BY BHB 83f **RR 85f** 4487[3]
3 b f Formidable (USA) 7.8f **(60)** - Lobinda (Shareef Dancer (USA)) 9.9f **(73)**
Form - 6131413
Record 1998 - 1st:3 2nd:0 3rd:2 Ran:7
Pre1998 - 1st:1 2nd:1 3rd:1 Ran:6
Win Prizemoney £13,765 *Total Prizemoney* £17,386
Wins * **1998** Aug Haydoc (GD) H 14f 80 82
* **1998** Jly Windso (G-F) 11.6f 80
* **1998** May Beverl (GD) H 9.9f 77 83 <
* 1997 Jly Bright (FRM) 7f 73
1998 Turf 3-7: (8f, 10f 1-2, 12f 1-2, 14f 1-2)(g-s, gd 1-2, g-f 1-1, frm 1-3)
Scopey, useful filly, effective 7 to 14f, best at 14f, acts on g-s to frm, best on frm, likes tight tracks. Turf high 85 - 3rd of 7 getting 17lb from Aginor (25 Spt Redcar 14f frm RF 4487) - also 1st of 6 giving 7lb to Pixielated (19 May Beverley RF 1318). Consistent. She has been in fine form this season, winning three times, and showing on the third occasion that she stays well. She seems best suited by faster ground. **J L Dunlop [4-13] Hesmonds Stud.*

FLOWER O'CANNIE (IRE) BHB 80f **RR 81f** 5151[7]
3 b f Mujadil (USA) 7.7f **(70)** - Baby's Smile (Shirley Heights) 10.3f **(74)**
Form - 8022573117
Record 1998 - 1st:2 2nd:2 3rd:1 Ran:10
Pre1998 - 1st:2 2nd:1 3rd:4 Ran:12
Win Prizemoney £14,098 *Total Prizemoney* £22,488
Wins * **1998** Nov Mussel (SFT) H 12f 68 81
* **1998** Oct Newcas (SFT) H 12.4f 68 75
* 1997 Jly Beverl (HVY) 7.5f 89? <
* 1997 Jun Hamilt (SFT) 6f 69
1998 Turf 2-10: (8f 3, 10f 3, 12f 2-3, 14f) (sft 1-2, g-s 2, gd 1-5, frm)
Leggy, decent filly, effective 7 to 12f, best at 7f, acts on g-s to g-f, likes tight tracks, excels at Ayr. Turf high 81 - 1st of 16 giving 5lb to Doc Ryan's (4 Nov Musselburgh RF 5119).
**M W Easterby [4-22] Mrs E Rhind.*

FLOWERS COVE BHB 27f **RR 51f** 4922[11]
3 ch f Then Again 7.4f **(52)** - Lady St Lawrence (USA) (Bering) 7.4f **(61)**
Form - 0024680600
Record 1998 - 1st:0 2nd:1 3rd:0 Ran:10
Win Prizemoney £0 *Total Prizemoney* £738
1998 Turf 0-10: (8f 3, 10f 3, 11f, 12f 2, 14f) (g-s, gd 2, g-f 3, frm 4)
Workmanlike, fair filly. Turf high 51. Inconsistent.
**Mrs N Macauley [0-2] Miss S Rudge (from M Blanshard [0-8] Spt 1998).*

FLOWN SOUTH BHB 65f **RR 65f** 4807[17]
3 b c Robellino (USA) 9.5f **(68)** - Belle Danseuse (Bellypha) 9.8f **(73)**
Form - 4550
Record 1998 - 1st:0 2nd:0 3rd:0 Ran:4
Win Prizemoney £0 *Total Prizemoney* £220
1998 Turf 0-4: (6f, 7f 2, 8f) (gd 2, g-f, frm)
Unfurnished, average colt. Turf high 65.
**J L Dunlop [0-4] Peter Winfield.*

FLUSH (FR) BHB 63f **RR 73f** 5147[9]
3 b br f Warning 8.1f **(77)** - Garden Pink (FR) (Bellypha) 9.8f **(73)**
Form - 388603010
Record 1998 - 1st:1 2nd:0 3rd:2 Ran:9
Pre1998 - 1st:0 2nd:0 3rd:0 Ran:3
Win Prizemoney £2,700 *Total Prizemoney* £4,267
Wins 1998 Oct Leices (SFT) C 8f 73 <
1998 Turf 1-9: (7f 2, 8f 1-6, 10f) (sft 1-1, gd, g-f 4, frm 3)
Lengthy, above-average filly, effective 8f, acts on sft to frm. Turf high 73 - 1st of 14 giving 7lb to High Noon (26 Oct Leicester RF 4990). **M C Pipe [0-1] Jim Ennis (from J W Hills [1-11] Oct 1998).*

FLYAWAY HILL (FR) BHB 53f **RR 56f** 1243[18]
4 b f Danehill (USA) 9.1f **(79)** - Flyaway Bride (USA) (Blushing Groom (FR)) 10.3f **(76)**
Form - 00
Record 1998 - 1st:0 2nd:0 3rd:0 Ran:2
Pre1998 - 1st:0 2nd:0 3rd:1 Ran:5
Win Prizemoney £0 *Total Prizemoney* £354
1998 Turf 0-2: (10f, 11f) (g-f 2)
Leggy, fair filly, has worn blinkers. Turf high 35.
**P W Harris [0-7] Pendley Fliers.*

FLY HIGH BHB 28f **RR 46df** 4545[15]
4 b f Wing Park - Nahawand (High Top) 10.2f **(67)**
Form - 60
Record 1998 - 1st:0 2nd:0 3rd:0 Ran:2
Pre1998 - 1st:0 2nd:0 3rd:0 Ran:4
1998 AW 0-2: (10f, 11f) (Equi, Fibr)
Workmanlike, moderate filly. AW high 20 (began Aug).
**H J Collingridge [0-2] Mrs D Sawyer (from D Morris [0-4] Jly 1997).*

FLY HOME BHB 55f **RR 65df** 4117[12]
3 br f Skyliner 6.8f **(51)** - Fille de Phaeton (Sun Prince) 12.4f **(52)**
Form - 300
Record 1998 - 1st:0 2nd:0 3rd:1 Ran:3
Win Prizemoney £0 *Total Prizemoney* £497
1998 Turf 0-2: (7f, 9f) (gd, g-f) 1998 AW 0-1: (7f) (Fibr)
Unfurnished, currently average filly. Turf high 65 (began Aug).
**A J McNae [0-3] P D Cundell.*

FLYING BOLD (IRE) BHB 58f68a **RR 67f 68a** 4625[5]
3 ch c Persian Bold 10f **(69)** - Princess Reema (USA) (Affirmed (USA)) 9.3f **(79)**
Form - 00458213685
Record 1998 - 1st:1 2nd:1 3rd:1 Ran:11
Pre1998 - 1st:1 2nd:1 3rd:0 Ran:4

Win Prizemoney £5,816 *Total Prizemoney* £8,305
Wins *** 1998** Aug Lingfi (G-F) H 11.5f 61 62
* 1997 Oct Newbur (G-S) H 7.3f 63 71 <
1998 Turf 1-11: (8f 2, 10f 3, 11f 1-1, 12f 5) (gd 3, g-f 2, frm 1-5, hrd)
Scopey, average colt, effective 7 to 12f, acts on gd to hrd - acts on Fibr, likes tight tracks. Turf high 67 - 2nd of 13 giving 7lb to Browning (10 Aug Windsor 12f hrd RF 3513) - also 1st of 8 getting 6lb from Opera Buff (16 Aug Lingfield RF 3663). Consistent. He took time to find his form last term, running better at Windsor in August and winning an apprentice event at Lingfield just six days later. **W R Muir [2-15] Mrs H Levy.*

FLYING CLOUDS BHB 36f RR 44f 3585[5]

3 b f Batshoof 9.5f **(66)** - Fleeting Rainbow (Rainbow Quest (USA)) 10.4f **(75)**
Form - 7007455
Record 1998 - 1st:0 2nd:0 3rd:0 Ran:7
Pre1998 - 1st:0 2nd:0 3rd:0 Ran:2
1998 Turf 0-7: (8f, 10f, 12f 2, 14f 2, 16f) (g-f 5, frm 2)
Workmanlike, moderate filly. Turf high 52. Consistent.
**M Blanshard [0-9] Downclose Stud.*

FLYING COLOURS (IRE) BHB 54a RR 48f 5002[3]

4 b f Fairy King (USA) 7.7f **(75)** - Crazed Rainbow (USA) (Graustark) 10.1f **(70)**
Form - 51232080033
Record 1998 - 1st:0 2nd:1 3rd:3 Ran:8
Pre1998 - 1st:1 2nd:1 3rd:0 Ran:10
Win Prizemoney £1,944 *Total Prizemoney* £4,575
Wins * 1997 *Nov Lingfi (STD) H 16f 46 49* <
1998 Turf 0-6: (12f 3, 14f, 15f, 17f) (gd 2, g-f 3, frm) 1998 AW 0-2: (12f, 16f) (Equi 2)
Strong, fair filly, effective 15 to 16f, best at 16f, acts on g-f - acts on Equi, likes left handed tracks, likes tight tracks. Turf high 48. AW high 51. **C J Benstead [1-18] Mrs R W S Baker.*

FLYING EAGLE BHB 78f RR 82f 4850[29]

7 b g Shaadi (USA) 8.1f **(75)** - Fly Me (FR) (Luthier) 9.8f **(71)**
Form - 1011123116000
Record 1998 - 1st:6 2nd:1 3rd:1 Ran:13
Win Prizemoney £16,150 *Total Prizemoney* £17,380
Wins *** 1998** Jly Epsom (G-F) H 12f 74 82 <
*** 1998** Jly Nottin (G-F) H 10f 74 75
*** 1998** Jly Bright (GD) C 10f 69+
*** 1998** Jun Warwic (G-S) S 10.8f 65+
*** 1998** Jun Bath (G-S) C 10.2f 65
*** 1998** May Nottin (G-F) S 10f 57+
1998 Turf 6-13: (10f 4-6, 11f 1-1, 12f 1-5, 18f) (gd 1-5, g-f 3-3, frm 2-5)
Decent gelding, effective 10 to 12f, best at 10f, acts on g-f to frm, best on g-f, prefers left handed tracks, favours tight tracks, excels at Nottingham. Turf high 82 - 1st of 9 giving 6lb to Random Kindness (29 Jly Epsom RF 3199) - also 1st of 8 giving 31lb to Brambles Way (24 Jly Nottingham RF 3079). Becoming disappointing. He showed good, consistent form last term, winning six times in varied company. Obviously better than a plater, he is a credit to his trainer. **R Simpson [7-19] T F Maycock.*

FLYING FLIP BHB 50f47a RR 56f 47a 4938[10]

4 b f Rolfe (USA) 11.2f **(46)** - Needwood Sprite (Joshua) 10.5f **(58)**
Form - 15234450
Record 1998 - 1st:1 2nd:1 3rd:1 Ran:8
Pre1998 - 1st:0 2nd:0 3rd:0 Ran:7
Win Prizemoney £4,077 *Total Prizemoney* £5,634
Wins *** 1998** Apr Nottin (SFT) H 10f 48 56 <
1998 Turf 1-8: (10f 1-1, 12f 4, 14f 2, 16f) (g-s 1-1, gd 3, g-f, frm 2, hrd)
Scopey, fair filly, effective 10 to 14f, best at 12f, acts on g-s to frm, and excels at Leicester. Turf high 58 - 2nd of 16 giving 3lb to Lancer (25 May Leicester 12f g-f RF 1454) - also 1st of 9 getting 9lb from Bakers Daughter (28 Apr Nottingham RF 0903). Consistent.
**B C Morgan [1-15] Tim Leadbeater.*

FLYING HAROLD BHB 39f RR 40f 2441[9]

5 b g Gildoran 11.6f **(58)** - Anytime Anywhere (Daring March) 7.1f **(61)**
Form - 00600
Record 1998 - 1st:0 2nd:0 3rd:0 Ran:5
Pre1998 - 1st:1 2nd:5 3rd:1 Ran:27
Win Prizemoney £3,226 *Total Prizemoney* £8,883
Wins 1997 Jun Chepst (G-F) H 6.1f 42 48 <
1998 Turf 0-5: (5f 3, 6f 2) (g-s, g-f, frm 3)
Moderate gelding, effective 5 to 6f, best at 5f, acts on gd to frm, best on g-f, likes left handed tracks, excels at Chepstow and Bath and Goodwood. Turf high 40 - 6th of 17 getting 24lb from Longwick Lad (18 May Bath 6f frm RF 1297). Inconsistent.
**R Ingram [0-1] Malcolm Allen (from M R Channon [1-31] May 1998).*

FLYING HOME RR 2465[6]

3 b g Flying Tyke 7.2f **(42)** - Bellinote (FR) (Noir Et Or) 10f **(38)**
Form - 6
Record 1998 - 1st:0 2nd:0 3rd:0 Ran:1
1998 Turf 0-1: (14f) (frm)
Currently very poor gelding. **J L Eyre [0-1] Park Racing Partnership.*

FLYING MEMORY RR 40f 2004[9]

2 b f Greensmith - Flying (Head for Heights) 9.6f **(55)**
Form - 060
Record 1998 - 1st:0 2nd:0 3rd:0 Ran:3
1998 Turf 0-1: (5f) (gd) 1998 AW 0-2: (5f, 6f) (Fibr 2)
Currently moderate filly. AW high 34.
**W G M Turner [0-3] Mrs S Manning, D Russell & Partners.*

FLYING PENNANT (IRE) BHB 52f RR 56f 4317[10]

5 ch h Waajib 8.9f **(67)** - Flying Beckee(IRE)(Godswalk (USA)) 7.3f **(58)**
Form - 26313806380
Record 1998 - 1st:1 2nd:1 3rd:3 Ran:11
Pre1998 - 1st:1 2nd:2 3rd:1 Ran:18
Win Prizemoney £6,366 *Total Prizemoney* £11,793
Wins *** 1998** Jun Chepst (G-S) H 7.1f 50 54
1996 May Salisb (G-F) C 7f 63 <
1998 Turf 1-11: (7f 1-11) (gd 1-5, g-f 4, frm 2)
Fair colt, effective 7f, acts on gd to frm, best on gd, often wears blinkers (extremely effectively), prefers tight tracks, excels at Brighton. Turf high 56 - 3rd of 14 giving 9lb to Oriole (24 Jun Carlisle 7f gd RF 2226) - also 1st of 10 getting 18lb from Huntswood (12 Jun Chepstow RF 1922). Back to form when winning at Chepstow in June, and ran well from a 6lb higher mark next time.
**J M Bradley [1-19] E A Hayward (from R Hannon [1-10] Oct 1996).*

FLYING THE FLAG (IRE) BHB 80f RR 69f 4524[3]

2 b f Thatching 7.8f **(69)** - Flagpole (IRE) (Be My Guest (USA)) 9.3f **(67)**
Form - 6523
Record 1998 - 1st:0 2nd:1 3rd:1 Ran:4
Win Prizemoney £0 *Total Prizemoney* £1,690
1998 Turf 0-4: (5f 2, 6f 2) (gd 2, g-f, frm)
Average filly. Turf high 69 (began Aug) - 3rd of 14 to En Garde (28 Spt Bath 6f g-f RF 4524). **J J Quinn [0-4] Alan Lillingston.*

FLYING TOUCH BHB 26a RR 26a 497[6]

3 ch f Greensmith - Flying (Head for Heights) 9.6f **(55)**
Form - 786
Record 1998 - 1st:0 2nd:0 3rd:0 Ran:3
1998 AW 0-3: (5f 2, 6f) (Fibr 3)
Light-framed, currently poor filly. AW high 15.
**W G M Turner [0-3] Avon & West Racing Club Ltd.*

FLY LIKE A BIRD BHB 66f RR 63f 4663[3]

2 ch f Keen 11.1f **(58)** - Turtle Dove (Gyr (USA)) 9.5f **(65)**
Form - 8603
Record 1998 - 1st:0 2nd:0 3rd:1 Ran:4
Win Prizemoney £0 *Total Prizemoney* £452
1998 Turf 0-4: (7f 2, 8f, 10f) (g-s, gd, frm 2)
Average filly. Turf high 63 (began Jly).
**S P C Woods [0-4] One Dream Partnership.*

FLY TO THE STARS BHB 120f RR 125f 5165a[5]

4 b c Bluebird (USA) 7.9f **(71)**-Rise and Fall (Mill Reef (USA)) 10.5f **(78)**
Form - 232115
Record 1998 - 1st:2 2nd:2 3rd:1 Ran:6
Pre1998 - 1st:3 2nd:3 3rd:2 Ran:11
Win Prizemoney £145,206 *Total Prizemoney* £252,502
Wins *** 1998** Oct Longch (SFT) G2 8f 125 <
*** 1998** Jly Deauvi (G-S) G3 8f 120
1997 Jly Goodwo (G-F) H 8f 106 112
1997 Jun Ascot (GD) H 8f 100 105
1997 Mar Doncas (G-F) 8f 92+

1998 Turf 2-4: (8f 2-4) (sft 1-1, gd, g-f 1-1, frm) 1998 AW 0-2: (8f, 10f) (Dirt 2)
Scopey, top-class colt, effective 8f, acts on sft to g-f, likes right handed tracks, excels at Ascot. Turf high 125 - 1st of 7 giving 3lb to Gold Away (4 Oct Longchamp RF 4728a) - also 1st of 9 getting 4lb from Jim And Tonic (12 Jly Deauville RF 2862a). AW high 112. He was a useful handicapper for Mark Johnston in 1997, winning both the Britannia and Schweppes Golden Mile, and moved to Godolphin during the winter. After running well in good company in Dubai, he ran a fine second under a big weight in the Royal Hunt Cup, and went on to win twice in France. The second of those victories came in the Group Two Prix du Rond-Point, his biggest victory to date. A respectable fifth in the Breeders' Cup Mile, he is most effective on soft ground.
**S bin Suroor [2-4] Godolphin (from S bin Suroor in UAE [0-2] Mar 1998).*

FNAN BHB 76f RR 78f 5094[3]

2 b c Generous (IRE) 11.5f **(82)** - Rafha (Kris) 9.5f **(73)**
Form - 8733
Record 1998 - 1st:0 2nd:0 3rd:2 Ran:4
Win Prizemoney £0 *Total Prizemoney* £1,038
1998 Turf 0-4: (7f, 8f 3) (gd 2, g-f, frm)
Above-average colt. Turf high 78 (began Aug) - 3rd of 22 giving 6lb to Seren Hill (2 Nov Redcar 8f gd RF 5094).
**J L Dunlop [0-4] Prince A A Faisal.*

FOCUS BHB 88f RR 87f 2378[4]

2 b c First Trump - Glimpse **(68f)** (Night Shift (USA)) 7.2f **(69)**
Form - 514
Record 1998 - 1st:1 2nd:0 3rd:0 Ran:3
Win Prizemoney £4,221 *Total Prizemoney* £4,564
Wins * **1998** Jun York (G-S) 6f 87 <
1998 Turf 1-3: (5f, 6f 1-2) (g-s 1-1, gd, frm)
Currently useful colt. Turf high 87 - 1st of 9 from Princely Dream (13 Jun York RF 1979). Touched off after an epic duel on his second run, and was eventually awarded the race after an appeal. His third run might have come too soon. His heart is in the right place, but he might need time to get over his exertions.
**P F I Cole [1-3] Highclere Thoroughbred Racing Ltd.*

FOGGY DAY (FR) RR 107f 3415a[2]

4 ch c Pistolet Bleu (IRE) - Evanescente (FR) (Pharly (FR)) 9.8f **(68)**
Form - 2
1998 Turf 0-1: (10f) (g-s)
Currently Pattern-class colt. (1st run) - 2nd of 7 getting 6lb from Steward (29 Jly Vichy 10f g-s RF 3415a). He was caught close home at Vichy in July and is not quite Group class.
**Miss H Van Zuylen in FR [0-1] Baron Thierry Van Zuylen.*

FOIST BHB 58f60a RR 54f 60a 4988[6]

6 b g Efisio 7.7f **(69)** - When The Saints (Bay Express) 7.1f **(60)**
Form - 7115008776
Record 1998 - 1st:2 2nd:0 3rd:0 Ran:10
Pre1998 - 1st:6 2nd:1 3rd:3 Ran:29
Win Prizemoney £31,161 *Total Prizemoney* £35,156

Wins							
* **1998**	May Warwic	(GD)		6f		65	
* **1998**	May Hamilt	(G-S)	H	6f	56	61	
* 1997	May Hamilt	(SFT)	H	6f	59	68+	<
* 1997	Apr Hamilt	(G-S)	H	6f	50	64	
* 1997	Mar Catter	(GD)	H	7f	46	50	
* 1996	*Apr Southw*	*(STD)*	*H*	*6f*	*40*	*58*	
* 1996	*Apr Wolver*	*(STD)*	*H*	*6f*	*40*	*51+*	
* 1996	*Mar Southw*	*(STD)*	*H*	*6f*	*30*	*36*	

1998 Turf 2-10: (5f, 6f 2-8, 7f) (g-s 1-5, gd 2, g-f 1-1, frm 2)
Fair gelding, effective 6 to 7f, best at 6f, acts on g-s to g-f, has worn blinkers, likes left handed tracks, likes tight tracks, excels at Hamilton. Turf high 65 - 1st of 15 giving 3lb to Akalim (4 May Warwick RF 1027) - also 1st of 10 getting 12lb from Buzz (3 May Hamilton RF 0986). **M W Easterby [8-39] D F Spence.*

FOLEYS QUEST (IRE) BHB 39f33a RR 52f 33a 2558[7]

4 b f River Falls 8.2f **(56)** - Katie's Delight (Relko) 9.9f **(59)**
Form - 707
Record 1998 - 1st:0 2nd:0 3rd:0 Ran:3
Pre1998 - 1st:0 2nd:1 3rd:0 Ran:5
Win Prizemoney £0 *Total Prizemoney* £755
1998 Turf 0-1: (17f) (g-f) 1998 AW 0-2: (13f, 16f) (Equi 2)
Scopey, fair filly, effective 12f, acts on hrd, favours tight tracks. AW high 13. Inconsistent. **J S Moore [1-14] Ernie Houghton.*

FOLKLORE BHB 90f RR 93+f 5050a[1]

3 b f Fairy King (USA) 7.7f **(75)** - Falsoola (Kris) 9.5f **(73)**
Form - 1
1998 Turf 1-1: (7f 1-1) (g-s 1-1)
Scopey, useful filly, effective 5 to 7f, acts on g-s to g-f. (1st run) - 1st of 15 getting 4lb from Hoh Chi Min (19 Oct Deauville RF 5050a). Formerly trained by David Loder, she won a Listed event at Deauville in October.
**H-A Pantall in FR [1-1] Sheikh Mohammed Al Maktoum (from D R Loder [1-7] Oct 1997).*

FOLLOW ME RR 51f 4091[15]

2 ch c Keen 11.1f **(58)** - Fairlead **(57f)** (Slip Anchor) 9.8f **(73)**
Form - 000
Record 1998 - 1st:0 2nd:0 3rd:0 Ran:3
1998 Turf 0-3: (6f 3) (gd, frm 2)
Currently fair colt. Turf high 51 (began Aug).
**C W Thornton [0-3] Guy Reed.*

FOLLY FOOT FRED BHB 33f RR 30?f 4931[20]

4 b g Crisp - Wessex Kingdom (Vaigly Great) 7f **(58)**
Form - 0
Record 1998 - 1st:0 2nd:0 3rd:0 Ran:1
Pre1998 - 1st:1 2nd:0 3rd:0 Ran:10
Win Prizemoney £1,932 *Total Prizemoney* £2,429
Wins 1996 Apr Nottin (G-F) S 5.1f 50 <
1998 Turf 0-1: (10f) (g-s)
Strong, very moderate gelding. Consistent.
**A G Newcombe [0-1] Derek Dymond (from B R Millman [1-10] Jly 1997).*

FONZY BHB 34f50a RR 26df 50a 4486[17]

4 b g Phountzi (USA) 9.6f **(60)** - Diavalezza (Connaught) 7.7f **(63)**
Form - 00
Record 1998 - 1st:0 2nd:0 3rd:0 Ran:2
Pre1998 - 1st:4 2nd:1 3rd:1 Ran:11
Win Prizemoney £10,357 *Total Prizemoney* £11,690

Wins						
1996	Jly Mussel	(GD)	C	5f	70	<
1996	Jun Mussel	(G-F)	C	5f	70	<
1996	May Thirsk	(G-F)	C	5f	59	
1996	*May Southw*	*(STD)*		*5f*	*54*	

1998 Turf 0-2: (6f, 10f) (frm 2)
Neat, moderate gelding, often wears blinkers. (began Spt). Becoming disappointing. He failed to give his connections any happy days in 1998.
**G R Oldroyd [0-2] The West Riding Partnership (from Mrs S J Smith [0-4] Spt 1997).*

FOOLISH FLUTTER (IRE) BHB 33f37a RR 20f 37a 2069[9]

4 b br f Fools Holme (USA) 10.3f **(64)** - Thornbeam (Beldale Flutter (USA)) 9.7f **(71)**
Form - 650706780
Record 1998 - 1st:0 2nd:0 3rd:0 Ran:9
Pre1998 - 1st:1 2nd:2 3rd:2 Ran:16
Win Prizemoney £2,574 *Total Prizemoney* £4,751
Wins * 1997 Jly Beverl (GD) SH 12f 41 45 <
1998 Turf 0-5: (10f 3, 12f 2) (hvy, sft, g-s 2, gd) 1998 AW 0-4: (11f 2, 12f 2) (Fibr 4)
Neat, very moderate filly, effective 11 to 12f, best at 12f, acts on gd to frm - acts on Fibr, often wears blinkers. Turf high 31. AW high 37. Managed to win a poor seller at Beverley in July '97, but her form has been regressive since.
**R Bastiman [1-17] Trevor Swailes (from G R Oldroyd [0-8] Oct 1996).*

FORANTE (USA) BHB 95f RR 80f 4333[5]

2 ch f Forty Niner (USA) 8.8f **(73)** - Danzante (USA) (Danzig (USA)) 8.4f **(76)**
Form - 185
Record 1998 - 1st:1 2nd:0 3rd:0 Ran:3
Win Prizemoney £3,790 *Total Prizemoney* £3,920
Wins * **1998** Jun Nottin (G-F) 5.1f 80++ <
1998 Turf 1-3: (5f 1-2, 6f) (gd, g-f 1-1, frm)
Currently decent filly. Turf high 80 - 5th of 8 giving 2lb to Two Clubs (17 Spt Yarmouth 6f frm RF 4333) - also 1st of 10 from

Entropy (8 Jun Nottingham RF 1800). She won nicely on her Nottingham debut, but a slow start did not help her cause in the Queen Mary. Ran too freely to stay six furlongs on her last run.
**R Charlton [1-3] K Abdulla.*

FORBES PARK BHB 55f **RR 59f** 4126[12]
3 b c Alzao (USA) 9.8f **(73)** - Rose Alto (Adonijah) 10f **(61)**
Form - 77730
Record 1998 - 1st:0 2nd:0 3rd:1 Ran:5
Win Prizemoney £0 *Total Prizemoney* £562
1998 Turf 0-5: (8f, 9f, 10f, 12f, 13f) (gd, g-f, frm 3)
Workmanlike, fair colt. Turf high 59. **C A Horgan [0-5] B R Tantoco.*

FOREIGN EDITOR BHB 66f **RR 59f** 4834[5]
2 ch c Magic Ring (IRE) 6.5f **(64)** - True Precision **(61f 59a)** (Presidium)
Form - 375
Record 1998 - 1st:0 2nd:0 3rd:1 Ran:3
Win Prizemoney £0 *Total Prizemoney* £478
1998 Turf 0-3: (5f 3) (g-s, gd, frm)
Currently fair colt. Turf high 59.
**R A Fahey [0-3] Pride Of Yorkshire Racing Club.*

FOREIGN LOVE (USA) RR 95f 4016a[5]
3 ch f Gulch (USA) 9.6f **(79)** - Overseas Romance (USA) 00
Form - 1815
1998 Turf 2-4: (7f 1-3, 8f 1-1) (sft, gd 1-2, frm 1-1)
Very useful filly. Turf high 95 - 1st of 11 giving 2lb to Battle On (22 Jly Naas RF 3177a). A filly with potential who has scored over seven and when stepped up to a mile. She is one to watch.
**D K Weld in IRE [2-5] Moyglare Stud Farm.*

FOREIGN RULE (IRE) BHB 75f **RR 77f** 648[11]
4 b g Danehill (USA) 9.1f **(79)**-Guida Centrale(Teenoso (USA)) 9.9f **(72)**
Form - 0
Record 1998 - 1st:0 2nd:0 3rd:0 Ran:1
Pre1998 - 1st:1 2nd:2 3rd:1 Ran:7
Win Prizemoney £3,556 *Total Prizemoney* £6,300
Wins 1997 Jly Haydoc (G-S) H 14f 72 77 <
1998 Turf 0-1: (16f) (hvy)
Scopey, above-average gelding, effective 12 to 14f, acts on gd to frm, best on frm.
**J R Jenkins [1-8] Mrs Susan McCarthy (from P W Chapple-Hyam [1-6] Jly 1997).*

FOREST BOY BHB 60f70a **RR 67?f 70a** 816[6]
5 b g Komaite (USA) 6.9f **(61)** - Khadine (Astec) 8.6f **(66)**
Form - 6
Record 1998 - 1st:0 2nd:0 3rd:0 Ran:1
Pre1998 - 1st:4 2nd:1 3rd:0 Ran:12
Win Prizemoney £12,397 *Total Prizemoney* £13,333
Wins 1997 *Jan Wolver (STD) H 9.4f 70 70 <*
1996 May Hamilt (SFT) H 8.3f 62 70 <
1996 Apr Catter (GD) H 7f 62 68
1996 Apr Hamilt (G-S) 8.3f 60
1998 Turf 0-1: (9f) (sft)
Above-average gelding, often wears blinkers (extremely effectively). Inconsistent.
**M R Bosley [0-4] Marks (Banbury) (from J R Bosley [1-4] Jan 1997).*

FOREST BUCK (USA) BHB 107f **RR 108f** 3782a[4]
5 ch h Green Forest (USA) 7.4f **(73)** - Perlee (FR) (Margouillat (FR)) 10.2f **(76)**
Form - 454
1998 Turf 0-3: (8f, 10f 2) (sft, gd 2)
Pattern-class colt. Turf high 108.
**B Grizzetti in ITY [0-3] BuckramOakHoldings.*

FOREST CALL BHB 63f **RR 68df** 5079[25]
3 ch f Wolfhound (USA) 7.3f **(71)** - Balnaha (Lomond (USA)) 8.8f **(65)**
Form - 04250
Record 1998 - 1st:0 2nd:1 3rd:0 Ran:5
Win Prizemoney £0 *Total Prizemoney* £1,573
1998 Turf 0-5: (7f 3, 8f 2) (sft 2, gd 2, g-f)
Scopey, average filly. Turf high 68. **G Wragg [0-5] A E Oppenheimer.*

FOREST DREAM BHB 52f **RR 65f** 4867[4]
3 b f Warrshan (USA) 9.7f **(59)** - Sirenivo (USA) (Sir Ivor) 10.2f **(70)**
Form - 5036704
Record 1998 - 1st:0 2nd:0 3rd:1 Ran:7
Win Prizemoney £0 *Total Prizemoney* £503
1998 Turf 0-6: (8f 6) (gd, g-f 2, frm 3) 1998 AW 0-1: (8f) (Fibr)
Workmanlike, average filly. Turf high 65.
**Lady Herries [0-7] Lord Cowdrey.*

FOREST ENDING (USA) BHB 90f **RR 89f** 4380[11]
3 ch c Green Forest (USA) 7.4f **(73)** - Perlee (FR) (Margouillat (FR)) 10.2f **(76)**
Form - 615870
Record 1998 - 1st:1 2nd:0 3rd:0 Ran:6
Win Prizemoney £3,860 *Total Prizemoney* £3,860
Wins * **1998** May Beverl (GD) 9.9f 88+ <
1998 Turf 1-6: (8f, 10f 1-3, 12f, 13f) (gd 2, g-f 2, frm 1-2)
Scopey, useful colt, effective 10f, acts on frm. Turf high 89 - also 1st of 17 from Profiler (19 May Beverley RF 1321). Only respectable efforts in warm handicaps since winning his maiden.
**H R A Cecil [1-6] Buckram Oak Holdings.*

FOREST FIRE (SWE) BHB 78f **RR 69f** 4724a[6]
3 b f Never so Bold 7.1f **(62)** - Mango Sampaquita (SWE) (Colombian Friend (USA)) 8.5f **(64)**
Form - 033526116
Record 1998 - 1st:2 2nd:1 3rd:2 Ran:9
Pre1998 - 1st:0 2nd:0 3rd:0 Ran:1
Win Prizemoney £6,633 *Total Prizemoney* £8,302
Wins * **1998** Spt Sandow (GD) H 8.1f 65 69 <
* **1998** Aug Sandow (G-F) C 9f 58
1998 Turf 2-9: (8f 1-3, 9f 1-1, 10f, 11f, 12f 3) (sft, g-s, gd, g-f 2-4, frm 2)
Unfurnished, average filly, effective 8 to 11f, acts on g-f to frm, prefers tight tracks. Turf high 71 - also 1st of 12 getting 9lb from Bint Kaldoun (16 Spt Sandown RF 4310). Consistent.
**B Hanbury [2-9] Mrs M Campbell-Andenaes (from P Mooney [0-1] Oct 1997).*

FOREST GLADE (IRE) RR 48f 3619[10]
2 b f Forest Wind (USA) - Better Goods (IRE) (Glow (USA)) 6.7f **(71)**
Form - 060000
Record 1998 - 1st:0 2nd:0 3rd:0 Ran:6
1998 Turf 0-6: (6f 4, 7f 2) (gd, g-f 3, frm 2)
Moderate filly. Turf high 48. **M Brittain [0-6] D H Armitage.*

FOREST GREY BHB 50f **RR 47f** 1705[8]
2 gr c Petong 7.6f **(58)** - Holyrood Park (Sharrood (USA)) 10.5f **(72)**
Form - 008
Record 1998 - 1st:0 2nd:0 3rd:0 Ran:3
1998 Turf 0-3: (5f, 6f 2) (gd, frm 2)
Currently moderate colt, has worn blinkers. Turf high 47.
**K McAuliffe [0-3] E P Jameson.*

FOREST KING (IRE) RR 50f 3198[10]
2 b c Forest Wind (USA) - Paryiana (IRE) (Shernazar) 10.2f **(73)**
Form - 00
Record 1998 - 1st:0 2nd:0 3rd:0 Ran:2
1998 Turf 0-2: (7f 2) (g-f, frm)
Currently fair colt. Turf high 50 (began Jly).
**J W Hills [0-2] R J Styles & R J Tarring.*

FOREST ROBIN BHB 57f **RR 63+f** 4578[16]
5 ch g Formidable (USA) 7.8f **(60)** - Blush Rambler (IRE) (Blushing Groom (FR)) 10.3f **(76)**
Form - 2318412018070
Record 1998 - 1st:3 2nd:2 3rd:1 Ran:13
Pre1998 - 1st:0 2nd:3 3rd:7 Ran:35
Win Prizemoney £9,066 *Total Prizemoney* £23,368
Wins * **1998** Aug Newmar (G-F) H 8f 56 63+ <
* **1998** Jly Redcar (G-F) H 8f 48 52
* **1998** May Redcar (G-F) H 6f 42 50
1998 Turf 3-12: (6f 1-2, 7f 2, 8f 2-6, 9f, 10f) (g-f 1-6, frm 1-5, hrd 1-1)
1998 AW 0-1: (7f) (Fibr)
Average gelding, effective 7 to 8f, best at 7f, acts on g-f to hrd, has worn blinkers, excels at Redcar. Turf high 63 - 1st of 12 giving 10lb to Mutahadeth (8 Aug Newmarket RF 3469). In good heart last season, he is usually held up and is a good mount for an inexperienced rider. **Mrs J R Ramsden [3-33] Miss E L Ramsden (from R F JohnsonHoughton [0-15] Oct 1996).*

FOREST SHADOW (IRE) BHB 97f **RR 89f** 5077[2]
2 b c Sadler's Wells (USA) 11.3f **(87)** - Bay Shade (USA) (Sharpen Up) 8.3f **(67)**
Form - 0122
Record 1998 - 1st:1 2nd:2 3rd:0 Ran:4
Win Prizemoney £4,146 *Total Prizemoney* £9,475
Wins * **1998** Aug Newbur (GD) 7f 84 <
1998 Turf 1-4: (7f 1-2, 8f, 10f) (sft, g-s, gd 1-2)
Useful colt. Turf high 89 (began Jly) - 2nd of 7 getting 3lb from Adnaan (31 Oct Newmarket 10f g-s RF 5077) - also 1st of 21 giving 5lb to Hararah (15 Aug Newbury RF 3653). He caused a real surprise when landing a Newbury maiden at 33/1 on his second start, but was beaten a long way by the winner when stepped up to a mile in soft ground at Haydock next time. Ran a much better race at Newmarket on his final start, battling on well.
**P W Chapple-Hyam [1-4] R E Sangster.*

FORGET ABOUT IT (IRE) RR 91f 3338a[4]
3 b f Be My Guest (USA) 10.2f **(66)** - You Make Me Real (USA) 00
Form - 42114
1998 Turf 2-5: (7f 1-1, 8f 1-4) (sft 1-3, g-s, gd 1-1)
Useful filly, effective 7 to 8f, best at 8f, acts on sft to gd, best on sft. Turf high 91 - also 1st of 10 giving 8lb to The Realtour (27 Jun Curragh RF 2426a). **C Collins in IRE [2-7] John Perotta.*

FORGET PARIS (IRE) BHB 38f40a **RR 37f 40a** 161[8]
5 gr m Broken Hearted 10.1f **(65)** - Miss Deauville (Sovereign Path) 9.3f **(55)**
Form - 8
Record 1998 - 1st:0 2nd:0 3rd:0 Ran:1
Pre1998 - 1st:0 2nd:0 3rd:0 Ran:8
1998 AW 0-1: (8f) (Fibr)
Moderate filly, has worn blinkers.
**B S Rothwell [0-10] Brian Rothwell.*

FORGIE (IRE) BHB 79f **RR 80f** 4958[3]
5 b g Don't Forget Me 9.5f **(66)** - Damia (Vision (USA)) 9f **(64)**
Form - 104383423
Record 1998 - 1st:1 2nd:1 3rd:3 Ran:9
Pre1998 - 1st:5 2nd:3 3rd:2 Ran:24
Win Prizemoney £28,484 *Total Prizemoney* £38,135
Wins * **1998** Apr Nottin (SFT) H 14.1f 77 82 <
* 1997 Spt Cheste (GD) H 15.9f 70 75
* 1997 Spt York (SFT) H 13.9f 64 70
* 1997 Jun Mussel (G-S) H 14f 64 68
* 1997 Jun Mussel (GD) H 14f 58 64
* 1996 May Redcar (G-F) H 14.1f 53 56
1998 Turf 1-9: (14f 1-2, 15f 2, 16f 4, 19f) (sft 1-1, gd 2, g-f 3, frm 3)
Decent gelding, effective 14 to 16f, acts on sft to frm, best on frm, excels at Musselburgh and Haydock, likes Doncaster. Turf high 82 (1st run) - 1st of 16 giving 28lb to Distant Storm (20 Apr Nottingham RF 0773). Consistent. Suited by a real stamina test, although he was originally bought with the Ayr Gold Cup in mind! He made a successful reappearance in a fourteen-furlong handicap at Nottingham, and continues to run with credit, although he can be a tricky customer. **P Calver [6-33] Mrs Janis MacPherson.*

FORGIVEN RR 47f 1146[8]
2 b c Noble Patriarch 12.2f **(43)** - Sinners Reprieve **(75f)** (Reprimand)
Form - 8
Record 1998 - 1st:0 2nd:0 3rd:0 Ran:1
1998 Turf 0-1: (5f) (gd)
Currently moderate colt. **T D Easterby [0-1] Mrs J B Mountifield.*

FORGLORI BHB 42f **RR 36f** 4356[19]
3 b c Formidable (USA) 7.8f **(60)** - Glorietta (USA) (Shadeed (USA)) 8.2f **(70)**
Form - 0000
Record 1998 - 1st:0 2nd:0 3rd:0 Ran:4
1998 Turf 0-4: (7f 3, 8f) (g-s, gd, g-f 2)
Very moderate colt. Turf high 36. **C J Benstead [0-4] R Lamb.*

FORGOTTEN STAR (IRE) BHB 35f **RR 45f** 4544[11]
3 b br f Don't Forget Me 9.5f **(66)** - Sterna Star (Corvaro (USA)) 9f **(53)**
Form - 0700
Record 1998 - 1st:0 2nd:0 3rd:0 Ran:4
Pre1998 - 1st:0 2nd:0 3rd:1 Ran:5
Win Prizemoney £0 *Total Prizemoney* £936
1998 Turf 0-3: (8f, 10f, 12f) (g-f, frm 2) 1998 AW 0-1: (14f) (Fibr)
Lengthy, moderate filly, has worn blinkers. Turf high 44 (began Jly). Inconsistent. **R F JohnsonHoughton [0-9] R F JohnsonHoughton.*

FORGOTTEN TIMES (USA) BHB 46f71a **RR 52f 71a** 4649[5]
4 ch f Nabeel Dancer (USA) 6.1f **(65)** - Etoile D'Amore (USA) (The Minstrel (CAN)) 10f **(72)**
Form - 50817580D08005
Record 1998 - 1st:1 2nd:0 3rd:0 Ran:14
Pre1998 - 1st:2 2nd:3 3rd:2 Ran:17
Win Prizemoney £8,910 *Total Prizemoney* £13,290
Wins * **1998** *Feb Lingfi (SLW) H 6f 67 71* <
1997 Feb Lingfi (STD) H 6f 69 71 <
1997 Jan Lingfi (STD) 6f 59
1998 Turf 0-8:(5f 6, 6f 2)(g-f 5, frm 3)1998 AW 1-6: (6f 1-5, 7f)(Equi 1-6)
Workmanlike, above-average filly, effective 6f, acts on g-f - acts on Equi, has worn blinkers, likes left handed tracks, likes tight tracks, excels at Lingfield. Turf high 52. AW high 71 - 1st of 11 giving 17lb to Rise 'n Shine (24 Feb Lingfield RF 0355). She regained winning form back on Equitrack in February when getting the best of a three-way photo and ran the odd good race on turf afterwards.
**K T Ivory [1-14] John Crook (from T M Jones [2-15] Spt 1997).*

FORMAL JOY RR 4201[19]
3 b g Formidable (USA) 7.8f **(60)** - Joytime (John de Coombe) 7.9f **(40)**
Form - 8P0
Record 1998 - 1st:0 2nd:0 3rd:0 Ran:3
1998 Turf 0-2: (8f, 10f) (gd, frm) 1998 AW 0-1: (7f) (Equi)
Workmanlike, currently very moderate gelding. (began Aug).
**C A Cyzer [0-3] Mrs G M Gooderham.*

FORMATION DANCER BHB 65f **RR 61?f** 3847[7]
3 ch c Groom Dancer (USA) 9.5f **(75)** - Golden Form (Formidable (USA)) 9.2f **(63)**
Form - 57
Record 1998 - 1st:0 2nd:0 3rd:0 Ran:2
Pre1998 - 1st:0 2nd:0 3rd:0 Ran:1
1998 Turf 0-2: (8f, 9f) (frm, hrd)
Scopey, currently average colt. Turf high 61 (began Aug).
**P W Harris [0-3] M Winter & Mrs P W Harris.*

FORMENTIERE BHB 21f31a **RR 12f 31a** 2928[11]
5 gr m Sharrood (USA) 11.1f **(67)** - Me Spede (Valiyar) 8.5f **(73)**
Form - 7000
Record 1998 - 1st:0 2nd:0 3rd:0 Ran:4
Pre1998 - 1st:0 2nd:0 3rd:0 Ran:6
1998 Turf 0-4: (8f, 10f 2, 11f) (frm 4)
Poor filly, has worn blinkers. Turf high 42.
**J M Bradley [0-12] R Miles.*

FORMER LOVE (USA) BHB 65f **RR 56f** 3648[4]
3 b f Dynaformer (USA) 12f **(82)** - Love and Legend (USA) (Lyphard's Wish (FR)) 9f **(74)**
Form - 804
Record 1998 - 1st:0 2nd:0 3rd:0 Ran:3
Pre1998 - 1st:0 2nd:0 3rd:0 Ran:4
Win Prizemoney £0 *Total Prizemoney* £835
1998 Turf 0-3: (8f, 10f, 13f) (g-f, frm 2)
Unfurnished, fair filly, effective 7f, acts on gd. Turf high 56 (began Jly). **P R Webber [0-7] C N Weatherby.*

FORMIDABLE FLAME BHB 38f40a **RR 43f 40a** 4931[12]
5 ch g Formidable (USA) 7.8f **(60)** - Madiyla (Darshaan) 9.9f **(84)**
Form - 6377D380
Record 1998 - 1st:0 2nd:0 3rd:2 Ran:8
Pre1998 - 1st:0 2nd:0 3rd:0 Ran:8
Win Prizemoney £0 *Total Prizemoney* £763
1998 Turf 0-5: (10f 2, 11f 2, 12f) (g-s, gd, g-f, frm 2) 1998 AW 0-3: (7f, 9f, 12f) (Fibr 3)
Moderate gelding, effective 9 to 11f, acts on g-f - acts on Fibr, likes left handed tracks, likes tight tracks. Turf high 43. AW high 44 - 3rd of 8 getting 17lb from Failed To Hit (21 Mar Wolverhampton 9f Fibr RF 0462). This moderate performer is best remembered for running amok through the Southwell enclosures in 1997.
**G A Ham [0-1] R D Starke (from W J Musson [0-17] Jly 1998).*

FORMIDABLE SPIRIT BHB 25f31a RR 15f 31a — 5060[11]
4 ch g Formidable (USA) 7.8f **(60)** - Hicklam Millie (Absalom) 7.2f **(58)**
Form - 0
Record 1998 - 1st:0 2nd:0 3rd:0 Ran:1
Pre1998 - 1st:0 2nd:0 3rd:0 Ran:9
1998 Turf 0-1: (8f) (sft)
Leggy, little account gelding, often wears blinkers.
**B Mactaggart [0-1] Mrs Hilary MacTaggart (from M J Heaton-Ellis [0-9] Jly 1997).*

FORMIDABLE STAR BHB 69f73a RR 77?f 73a — 5042[7]
2 ch c Forzando 7.2f **(63)** - Sheppard's Cross **(83f)** (Soviet Star (USA))
Form - 73575507
Record 1998 - 1st:0 2nd:0 3rd:1 Ran:8
Win Prizemoney £0 *Total Prizemoney* £490
1998 Turf 0-7: (5f 6, 6f) (sft 2, gd 4, frm) 1998 AW 0-1: (5f) (Fibr)
Above-average colt. Turf high 77.
**N P Littmoden [0-8] Clayton Bigley Partnership Ltd.*

FOR THE PRESENT BHB 61f RR 69f — 3817[15]
8 b g Then Again 7.4f **(52)** - Axe Valley (Royben) 7.3f **(60)**
Form - 843246500
Record 1998 - 1st:0 2nd:1 3rd:1 Ran:9
Pre1998 - 1st:5 2nd:2 3rd:7 Ran:44
Win Prizemoney £69,035 *Total Prizemoney* £85,292
Wins * 1996 Jun Redcar (FRM) H 6f 79 80
* 1994 Jly Goodwo (FRM) H 6f 80 83 <
1998 Turf 0-9: (5f 2, 6f 7) (gd 4, g-f, frm 3, hrd)
Average gelding, effective 5 to 6f, acts on gd. Turf high 69. The winner of the '94 Stewards' Cup, he was out of form for a long time subsequently but generally ran well in 1998.
**T D Barron [5-53] Mrs J Hazell.*

FORT KNOX (IRE) BHB 37f47a RR 37f 47a — 3267[7]
7 b g Treasure Kay 6.5f **(53)** - Single Viking (Viking (USA)) 6.7f **(65)**
Form - 00005027
Record 1998 - 1st:0 2nd:1 3rd:0 Ran:5
Pre1998 - 1st:6 2nd:7 3rd:6 Ran:61
Win Prizemoney £17,084 *Total Prizemoney* £29,431
Wins * 1996 *Mar Lingfi (STD) 7f 66* <
* 1996 *Mar Lingfi (STD) H 8f 56 57*
* 1995 *Nov Lingfi (STD) H 7f 49 47*
* 1995 Aug Newmar (G-F) H 8f 49 55
* 1994 Aug Lingfi (GD) H 7.6f 57 60
* 1994 Aug Bright (FRM) H 7f 53 51
1998 Turf 0-5: (7f, 8f 3, 12f) (gd 2, g-f 2, frm)
Moderate gelding, effective 7f - acts on Equi, often wears blinkers. Turf high 37. He is a regular in amateur and ladies races and often runs well, but is without a win on the Flat since being victorious on the Equitrack in March '96. Has won over hurdles.
**R M Flower [7-65] Mrs D M Hickling (from R W Armstrong [0-6] Jan 1994).*

FORT MORGAN (USA) RR 101f — 1049a[2]
4 bb c Pleasant Colony (USA) 12.4f **(88)** - Colorado Dancer (Shareef Dancer (USA)) 9.9f **(73)**
Form - 22
1998 Turf 0-1: (10f) (sft)
Currently very useful colt. He is obviously not easy to train, but has above-average ability. **J Oxx in IRE [0-2] Sheikh Mohammed.*

FORT SUMTER (USA) RR 83f — 4468[2]
2 b c Sea Hero (USA) - Gray And Red (USA) (Wolf Power (SAF))
Form - 822
Record 1998 - 1st:0 2nd:2 3rd:0 Ran:3
Win Prizemoney £0 *Total Prizemoney* £2,056
1998 Turf 0-3: (7f, 8f, 9f) (gd, g-f, frm)
Currently decent colt. Turf high 83. **I A Balding [0-3] Paul Mellon.*

FORT WILLIAM RR 62f — 4410[14]
2 b c Ezzoud (IRE) - Lovely Noor (USA) (Fappiano (USA)) 8.7f **(77)**
Form - 60
Record 1998 - 1st:0 2nd:0 3rd:0 Ran:2
1998 Turf 0-2: (7f 2) (g-f, frm)
Currently average colt. Turf high 62 (began Spt).
**Sir Michael Stoute [0-2] The Royal Ascot Racing Club.*

FORTY LOVE (IRE) BHB 59a RR 52df — 3261[6]
3 b g Second Set (IRE) 9.2f **(67)** - Pharjoy (FR) (Pharly (FR)) 9.8f **(68)**
Form - 68226266
Record 1998 - 1st:0 2nd:3 3rd:0 Ran:8
Pre1998 - 1st:1 2nd:0 3rd:0 Ran:7
Win Prizemoney £2,635 *Total Prizemoney* £4,771
Wins 1997 Aug Ripon (G-F) S 6f 66 <
1998 Turf 0-8: (8f 2, 10f, 11f 3, 12f, 13f) (hvy, sft, g-s 2, gd 3, g-f)
Scopey, fair gelding, effective 6 to 12f, acts on hvy to gd, often wears blinkers. Turf high 58 - 2nd of 9 giving 8lb to Breydon (7 May Hamilton 12f hvy RF 1077).
**D Moffatt [0-8] Tayside Farming (from J E Banks [1-7] Oct 1997).*

FORUM RR 85f — 4528[4]
3 b f Lion Cavern (USA) 7.5f **(74)** - Top Society (High Top) 10.2f **(67)**
Form - 606054
Record 1998 - 1st:0 2nd:0 3rd:0 Ran:6
Pre1998 - 1st:1 2nd:1 3rd:1 Ran:5
Win Prizemoney £3,380 *Total Prizemoney* £7,291
Wins * 1997 Oct Bright (FRM) 7f 62 <
1998 Turf 0-6: (7f, 8f 3, 10f 2) (hvy, gd 3, g-f 2)
Scopey, useful filly, effective 7f, acts on frm, prefers tight tracks. Turf high 85. **C E Brittain [1-11] Wyck Hall Stud.*

FOR VALOUR (USA) RR 113f — 2483a[7]
5 b h Trempolino (USA) 11.9f **(77)** - Glitter (FR) (Reliance II) 9.9f **(58)**
Form - 2347
1998 Turf 0-4: (12f 4) (gd 3, g-f)
Group-class colt, effective 10 to 13f, acts on sft to g-f, best on gd, has worn blinkers, does well at Longchamp and Saint-cloud. Turf high 113. His early season form was excellent when trained by Andre Fabre, including finishing fourth behind Silver Patriarch and Swain in the Coronation Cup. Now trained by Ken Cunningham-Brown. **A Fabre in FR [1-7].*

FORWARD MISS BHB 13f RR 6f — 1035[18]
4 b f Bold Arrangement 8.7f **(57)**-Maiden Bidder (Shack(USA)) 5.8f **(53)**
Form - 50
Record 1998 - 1st:0 2nd:0 3rd:0 Ran:1
Pre1998 - 1st:0 2nd:0 3rd:0 Ran:8
1998 Turf 0-1: (10f) (gd)
Neat, poor filly.
**Mrs L C Jewell [0-2] J S S Hollins (from C J Benstead [0-7] Nov 1997).*

FOR YOUR EYES ONLY BHB 106f RR 108+f — 4631[6]
4 b g Pursuit of Love 9.5f **(69)** - Rivers Rhapsody (Dominion) 8.5f **(63)**
Form - 32101176
Record 1998 - 1st:3 2nd:1 3rd:1 Ran:8
Pre1998 - 1st:2 2nd:3 3rd:3 Ran:21
Win Prizemoney £103,641 *Total Prizemoney* £134,575
Wins * **1998** Jly Goodwo (G-S) H 8f 102 108 <
* **1998** Jly Sandow (GD) H 8.1f 97 103
* **1998** May Sandow (GD) H 8.1f 90 102
* 1996 Jun Beverl (G-F) 5f 91+
* 1996 May Ripon (GD) 6f 78
1998 Turf 3-8: (7f, 8f 3-4, 9f 2, 10f) (gd 2-5, g-f 1-3)
Scopey, Pattern-class gelding, effective 8f, acts on gd to g-f, best on gd, often wears blinkers (very effectively), prefers tight tracks. Turf high 108 - 1st of 22 giving 20lb to King Slayer (30 Jly Goodwood RF 3219) - also 1st of 13 giving 6lb to Almond Rock (4 Jly Sandown RF 2548). He is only slight, but has a heart as big as himself and enjoyed an excellent season, winning three valuable handicaps including the William Hill Mile at Glorious Goodwood. He is best with blinkers and is capable of winning a Listed contest.
**T D Easterby [5-29] H E Sheikh Rashid Al Maktoum.*

FORZAIR BHB 48f38a RR 53f 38a — 417[7]
6 b g Forzando 7.2f **(63)** - Persian Air (Persian Bold) 9.3f **(66)**
Form - 77
Record 1998 - 1st:0 2nd:0 3rd:0 Ran:1
Pre1998 - 1st:4 2nd:8 3rd:9 Ran:60
Win Prizemoney £8,914 *Total Prizemoney* £19,882
Wins * 1997 Aug Catter (G-F) S 15.8f 51
* 1997 *Feb Southw (STD) S 12f 56*
1996 *Apr Southw (STD) S 12f 67+* <
1996 *Jan Southw (STD) 12f 66+*
1998 AW 0-1: (12f) (Fibr)

Fair gelding, effective 11 to 13f, best at 12f, acts on g-s to gd - acts on Fibr, has worn blinkers, likes left handed tracks. Despite winning on turf, he is probably better on sand, and has been an effective sort in staying claimers and sellers on Fibresand, though he did not show much in two starts in '98.
**J J O'Neill [5-46] Clayton Bigley Partnership Ltd (from S R Bowring [2-10] Apr 1996).*

* 1995	Aug	Haydoc	(G-F)	H	14f	78	82 <
* 1994	Spt	Haydoc	(G-S)	H	11.9f	76	80
* 1994	May	Ayr	(FRM)		13.1f		62

1998 Turf 1-2: (14f 1-1, 15f) (gd 1-1, frm)
Above-average gelding. Turf high 75 (1st run) (began Oct). Consistent. **Mrs M Reveley [6-29] A Sharratt.*

For Your Eyes Only was noticed by many

FOUND AT LAST RR 54f 3409[8]
2 b c Aragon 7.7f **(58)** - Girton (Balidar) 7.9f **(63)**
Form - 8
Record 1998 - 1st:0 2nd:0 3rd:0 Ran:1
1998 Turf 0-1: (6f) (g-f)
Currently fair colt. **J Hanson [0-1] J Hanson.*

FOUND AT SEA RR 40f 2089[6]
3 ch f Handsome Sailor 6.6f **(53)** - Close Call (Nearly A Hand) 5.6f **(48)**
Form - 6
Record 1998 - 1st:0 2nd:0 3rd:0 Ran:1
1998 Turf 0-1: (10f) (g-s)
Scopey, currently moderate filly.
**J G Smyth-Osbourne [0-1] Mrs Patrick Campbell Fraser.*

FOUNDRY LANE BHB 74f **RR 75f** 4958[8]
7 b g Mtoto 11.5f **(71)** - Eider (Niniski (USA)) 10.6f **(65)**
Form - 18
Record 1998 - 1st:1 2nd:0 3rd:0 Ran:2
Pre1998 - 1st:3 2nd:3 3rd:4 Ran:22
Win Prizemoney £21,609 *Total Prizemoney* £47,313
Wins * 1998 Oct York (GD) H 13.9f 70 75

FOUNTAINS (USA) RR 3092[8]
4 b g Danzig (USA) 8.1f **(88)**-Coxwold (USA)(Cox's Ridge (USA))8f **(68)**
Form - 8
Record 1998 - 1st:0 2nd:0 3rd:0 Ran:1
1998 AW 0-1: (8f) (Fibr)
Very poor gelding, always wears blinkers.
**H S Howe [0-3] Mrs Maureen Shenkin.*

FOURDANED (IRE) BHB 43f48a **RR 44f 48a** 4609[4]
5 b g Danehill (USA) 9.1f **(79)** - Pro Patria (Petingo) 11f **(72)**
Form - 80706028074
Record 1998 - 1st:0 2nd:1 3rd:0 Ran:8
Pre1998 - 1st:0 2nd:2 3rd:1 Ran:19
Win Prizemoney £0 *Total Prizemoney* £3,431
1998 Turf 0-7: (10f, 11f, 12f 4, 15f) (sft, gd, g-f, frm 3, hrd) 1998 AW 0-1: (12f) (Equi)
Fair gelding, effective 12f, acts on gd to frm, best on frm, has worn blinkers, likes right handed tracks, likes tight tracks. Turf high 44.
**T D McCarthy [0-6] N A Bedward (from S Dow [0-13] Apr 1998).*

FOURGREYS BHB 62f **RR 51f** 4579[8]
2 gr c Paris House 5.9f **(64)** - Wild Moon (USA) (Arctic Tern (USA)) 8.9f **(69)**
Form - 008
Record 1998 - 1st:0 2nd:0 3rd:0 Ran:3
1998 Turf 0-3: (5f, 6f 2) (gd, g-f 2)
Currently fair colt. Turf high 51 (began Jly).
**Miss J A Camacho [0-3] Fourgreys Partnership.*

FOUR OF SPADES BHB 41f39a **RR 53f 39a** 350[6]
7 ch g Faustus (USA) 9.1f **(54)** - Fall To Pieces (USA) (Forli (ARG)) 9.6f **(67)**
Form - 8266
Record 1998 - 1st:0 2nd:1 3rd:0 Ran:3
Pre1998 - 1st:8 2nd:11 3rd:7 Ran:66
Win Prizemoney £22,741 *Total Prizemoney* £37,872

Wins								
1995	*Dec*	*Lingfi*	*(STD)*	*H*	*7f*	*70*	*69*	<
1995	*Aug*	*Wolver*	*(STD)*	*H*	*6f*	*68*	*67*	
1995	Jun	Mussel	(G-F)	C	7.1f		55	
1995	Jun	Lingfi	(G-F)	SH	7f	48	53	
1994	*Dec*	*Wolver*	*(STD)*	*H*	*6f*	*62*	*61*	
1994	*Dec*	*Wolver*	*(STD)*	*S*	*7f*		*61*	
1994	*Jan*	*Lingfi*	*(STD)*		*5f*		*65*	

1998 AW 0-3: (10f 3) (Equi 3)
Fair gelding, effective 10f - acts on Equi, mostly wears blinkers, likes left handed tracks. AW high 49 (1st run) - 2nd of 7 getting 10lb from Billaddie (8 Jan Lingfield 10f Equi RF 0049). Inconsistent.
**R J Hodges [0-7] Mrs Anna Sanders (from K R Burke [0-3] Jan 1998).*

FOURTH TIME LUCKY BHB 42f **RR 32f** 5117[9]
2 b c Timeless Times (USA) 6.1f **(56)** - Wych Willow (Hard Fought) 8.8f **(62)**
Form - 400000
Record 1998 - 1st:0 2nd:0 3rd:0 Ran:6
Win Prizemoney £0 *Total Prizemoney* £221
1998 Turf 0-6: (5f 3, 6f 2, 7f) (gd 3, g-f, frm 2)
Very moderate colt, has worn blinkers. Turf high 58.
**B W Murray [0-6] M E Foxton.*

FOXES TAIL BHB 46f **RR 55f** 4321[17]
4 gr g Batshoof 9.5f **(66)** - Secret Gill (Most Secret) 7.1f **(58)**
Form - 006524500
Record 1998 - 1st:0 2nd:1 3rd:0 Ran:9
Pre1998 - 1st:2 2nd:0 3rd:1 Ran:11
Win Prizemoney £10,472 *Total Prizemoney* £12,424
Wins * 1996 Spt Ayr (G-F) H 8f 72 77 <
* 1996 Jly Mussel (G-S) 7.1f 70
1998 Turf 0-9: (8f, 9f, 10f 4, 11f 2, 12f) (g-s, gd, g-f 6, frm)
Light-framed, fair gelding, has worn blinkers. Turf high 58.
**Miss S E Hall [2-20] Mrs Joan Hodgson.*

FOXIE LADY BHB 68f **RR 72f** 4888[6]
3 ch f Wolfhound (USA) 7.3f **(71)** - Final Thought (Final Straw) 7.9f **(64)**
Form - 222506
Record 1998 - 1st:0 2nd:3 3rd:0 Ran:6
Pre1998 - 1st:0 2nd:0 3rd:0 Ran:1
Win Prizemoney £0 *Total Prizemoney* £3,508
1998 Turf 0-6: (7f 4, 8f, 10f) (gd, g-f, frm 4)
Scopey, above-average filly, effective 7f, acts on g-f to frm. Turf high 72. She finished runner-up in her first three starts last season, though she looks totally genuine and has just been unlucky. Lacks pace, however.
**E A L Dunlop [0-7] John Brown & Megan Dennis.*

FRAGRANT MIX (FR) RR 124f 4727a[6]
4 gr c Linamix (FR) 8.2f **(64)** - Fragrant Hill (Shirley Heights) 10.3f **(74)**
Form - 441126
1998 Turf 2-6: (10f, 11f, 12f 2-4) (hvy, sft 1-3, g-s, gd 1-1)
Very high-class colt, effective 10 to 12f, best at 12f, acts on hvy to gd, best on sft, excels at Longchamp. Turf high 124 - 6th of 14 giving 8lb to Sagamix (4 Oct Longchamp 12f sft RF 4727a) - also 1st of 9 from Romanov (28 Jun Saint-cloud RF 2483a). After a good fourth in the French Derby, he missed the remainder of that season. After a couple of runs, he found his form when winning the Grands Prix at Chantilly and Saint-Cloud. He just needed the run after a break when second to Limnos in the Prix Foy, and was subsequently sixth in the Arc.
**A Fabre in FR [3-8] J-L Lagardere.*

FRAGRANT OASIS (USA) BHB 100f **RR 102f** 4853[11]
2 ch f Rahy (USA) 9.1f **(80)**-Raahia (CAN)(Vice Regent (CAN))8.7f **(74)**
Form - 4120
Record 1998 - 1st:1 2nd:1 3rd:0 Ran:4
Win Prizemoney £10,058 *Total Prizemoney* £14,072
Wins * **1998** Spt Newbur (gd) 7f 86 <
1998 Turf 1-4: (7f 1-4) (gd, g-f 1-2, frm)
Very useful filly. Turf high 102 (began Aug) - 2nd of 10 to Smittenby (3 Oct Newmarket 7f g-f RF 4628). She got first run on Smittenby when winning a conditions event at Newbury in September, but could not match that filly's finishing burst when they had a re-match at Newmarket the following month. Disappointing in the Group Two Rockfel Stakes on her final start, she does not look of Classic standard, but can win a Listed race.
**E A L Dunlop [1-4] Maktoum Al Maktoum.*

FRANC (USA) RR 100f 5134a[5]
2 b c Woodman (USA) 9.7f **(77)** - Adventurousdi (USA) (Private Account (USA)) 8.5f **(74)**
Form - 125
1998 Turf 1-3: (7f 1-1, 8f, 10f) (hvy, sft, g-f 1-1)
Currently very useful colt. Turf high 100 (began Jly) - 2nd of 11 giving 5lb to Charmes (22 Aug Deauville 8f sft RF 3912a) - also 1st of 6 giving 3lb to Stella Berine (14 Jly Deauville RF 3050a). Possibly unlucky when a fast-finishing second in a Listed race at Deauville in August, he did not appear to cope with heavy ground at Saint-Cloud in late October. He is better than that form suggests and can win a decent prize in 1999.
**Mme C Head in FR [1-3] G W Kelly.*

FRANCE LAMBERT (ITY) BHB 36f **RR 38f** 5094[21]
2 gr f Tirol 8.1f **(64)** - Filicaia (Sallust) 8.4f **(63)**
Form - 06000
Record 1998 - 1st:0 2nd:0 3rd:0 Ran:5
1998 Turf 0-5: (6f 4, 8f) (gd 2, g-f 2, hrd)
Very moderate filly. Turf high 38.
**Don Enrico Incisa [0-5] Razza Dormello Olgiata.*

FRANCESCA'S FOLLY BHB 43f **RR 52f** 4590[13]
3 b f Efisio 7.7f **(69)** - Nashville Blues (IRE) **(74f)** (Try My Best (USA)) 7.6f **(67)**
Form - 53562140
Record 1998 - 1st:1 2nd:1 3rd:1 Ran:8
Pre1998 - 1st:1 2nd:0 3rd:0 Ran:7
Win Prizemoney £4,862 *Total Prizemoney* £5,940
Wins **1998** Spt Yarmou (G-S) S 10.1f 44
1997 Spt Leices (G-F) SH 8f 49 55 <
1998 Turf 1-8: (10f 1-5, 11f, 12f 2) (gd 1-3, g-f 2, frm 3)
Small, fair filly, effective 7 to 10f, acts on gd to frm, best on frm, excels at Leicester. Turf high 52 (1st run) - 5th of 11 getting 11lb from Konker (27 May Newbury 10f g-f RF 1528).
**N A Callaghan [0-2] Gallagher Equine Ltd (from J W Hills [2-13] Spt 1998).*

FRANCO MINA (IRE) RR 72+f 1503a[9]
2 b c Lahib (USA) 8f **(69)**-Play The Queen (IRE)(King of Clubs)7.1f **(57)**
Form - 010
Record 1998 - 1st:1 2nd:0 3rd:0 Ran:3
Win Prizemoney £3,452 *Total Prizemoney* £3,452
Wins * **1998** May Salisb (FRM) 5f 72+ <
1998 Turf 1-3: (5f 1-3) (gd 2, frm 1-1)
Currently above-average colt. Turf high 72 - 1st of 16 from Carmarthen (14 May Salisbury RF 1212).
**M R Channon [1-3] & Mrs Gary Pinchen.*

FRANKIE RR 28f 2566[9]
4 b g Shalford (IRE) 7.8f **(63)** - Twilight Secret (Vaigly Great) 7f **(58)**
Form - 0600
Record 1998 - 1st:0 2nd:0 3rd:0 Ran:4
Pre1998 - 1st:0 2nd:0 3rd:0 Ran:5
Win Prizemoney £0 *Total Prizemoney* £193
1998 Turf 0-4: (10f, 12f 3) (sft 2, gd, g-f)
Scopey, little account gelding, has worn blinkers. Turf high 28.
**R D E Woodhouse [0-6] Mrs Lynda Binner (from M H Tompkins [0-5] Aug 1997).*

FRANKIE FAIR (IRE) BHB 69f65a **RR 71f 65a** 3895[6]

3 b f Red Sunset 9f **(57)** - Animate (IRE) (Tate Gallery (USA)) 7.4f **(67)**

Form - 00111306

Record 1998 - 1st:3 2nd:0 3rd:1 Ran:8
Pre1998 - 1st:0 2nd:0 3rd:2 Ran:6

Win Prizemoney £7,281 *Total Prizemoney* £8,739

Wins * **1998** Jly Folkes (G-F) H 7f 62 71 <
* **1998** Jun Bright (GD) H 8f 53 60
1998 May Folkes (G-F) C 6.9f 58

1998 Turf 3-7: (6f 2, 7f 2-3, 8f 1-2) (g-s, gd 3-4, frm 2) 1998 AW 0-1: (7f) (Equi)

Scopey, above-average filly, effective 7 to 8f, acts on gd, prefers tight tracks. Turf high 71 - 1st of 16 giving 12lb to Imperator (8 Jly Folkestone RF 2624). Inconsistent.

**G L Moore [2-5] Joe Bates (Bloodstock) Ltd (from M A Jarvis [1-9] May 1998).*

FRANKIE FERRARI (IRE) BHB 79f **RR 59f** 407[1]

3 b c Common Grounds 8.1f **(66)** - Miss Kelly (Pitskelly) 8.5f **(53)**

Form - 121

Record 1998 - 1st:2 2nd:1 3rd:0 Ran:3
Pre1998 - 1st:0 2nd:0 3rd:0 Ran:3

Win Prizemoney £6,888 *Total Prizemoney* £7,918

Wins * **1998** *Mar Wolver (STD) H 12f 75 77* <
* **1998** *Feb Lingfi (SLW) H 10f 60 74*

1998 AW 2-3: (10f 1-2, 12f 1-1) (Equi 1-2, Fibr 1-1)

Scopey, above-average colt, effective 10 to 12f, best at 10f - acts on AW, best on Equi, often wears blinkers. AW high 77 - 1st of 8 giving 18lb to Operatic (7 Mar Wolverhampton RF 0407) - also 1st of 6 getting 4lb from Genius (7 Feb Lingfield RF 0241). Showed nothing on turf, but got off the mark on his Equitrack debut in a handicap at Lingfield in February over ten furlongs. He found one too good over the same course and distance next time, but ran out the narrow winner of a handicap on the Wolverhampton Fibresand the following month. **D R Loder [2-6] Wafic Said.*

FRANKIE HARRY RR 249[6]

6 ch g Buckley - Dame Caroline (Wollow) 8.2f **(61)**

Form - 86

Record 1998 - 1st:0 2nd:0 3rd:0 Ran:2

1998 AW 0-2: (11f, 16f) (Fibr 2)

Poor gelding. AW high 14. **A W Carroll [0-9] Mrs Helen Hogben.*

FRANKINCENSE (IRE) RR 58f 5063[13]

2 gr c Paris House 5.9f **(64)** - Mistral Wood (USA) (Far North (CAN)) 9.7f **(75)**

Form - 0

Record 1998 - 1st:0 2nd:0 3rd:0 Ran:1

1998 Turf 0-1: (6f) (g-f)

Currently fair colt. **J A R Toller [0-1] G B Partnership.*

FRANK LEBOEUF (USA) BHB 71f **RR 70f** 4805[4]

2 ch c Rahy (USA) 9.1f **(80)** - So Romantic (USA) (El Gran Senor (USA)) 9.6f **(76)**

Form - 034

Record 1998 - 1st:0 2nd:0 3rd:1 Ran:3

Win Prizemoney £0 *Total Prizemoney* £784

1998 Turf 0-3: (7f, 8f 2) (gd, g-f, frm)

Currently above-average colt. Turf high 70 (began Spt) - 3rd of 6 to Canta Ke Brave (23 Spt Goodwood 8f frm RF 4452). Sold for 40,000 gns in the autumn to race in America.

**A C Stewart [0-3] Racing For Gold.*

FRANKLIN-D RR 58f 3146[11]

2 ch c Democratic (USA) - English Mint (Jalmood (USA)) 10.1f **(52)**

Form - 570

Record 1998 - 1st:0 2nd:0 3rd:0 Ran:3

1998 Turf 0-3: (5f 2, 6f) (g-f, frm 2)

Currently fair colt, has worn blinkers. Turf high 58.

**J R Jenkins [0-3] Mrs Stella Peirce.*

FRANKLIN LAKES BHB 37f **RR 41f** 3902[8]

3 ch c Sanglamore (USA) 12.9f **(67)** - Eclipsing (IRE) (Baillamont (USA)) 7f **(78)**

Form - 500848

Record 1998 - 1st:0 2nd:0 3rd:0 Ran:6
Pre1998 - 1st:0 2nd:0 3rd:0 Ran:2

Win Prizemoney £0 *Total Prizemoney* £200

1998 Turf 0-6: (9f, 11f, 12f 2, 16f 2) (gd, g-f 3, frm 2)

Moderate colt. Turf high 41. Consistent.

**C A Horgan [0-8] B R Tantoco.*

FRANKY FURBO (IRE) RR 94f 5134a[6]

2 ch c Suave Dancer (USA) 10.7f **(68)** - Eljazzi (Artaius (USA)) 9f **(69)**

Form - 36

1998 Turf 0-2: (9f, 10f) (hvy, sft)

Currently useful colt, always wears blinkers. Turf high 94 (1st run) (began Oct) - 3rd of 5 to Bienamado (3 Oct Longchamp 9f sft RF 4715a). **P Bary in FR [0-2] J-L Bouchard.*

FRAPPE (IRE) RR 88f 4495[7]

2 b f Inchinor 8.9f **(64)** - Glatisant **(95f)**(Rainbow Quest(USA))10.4f **(75)**

Form - 17

Record 1998 - 1st:1 2nd:0 3rd:0 Ran:2

Win Prizemoney £3,810 *Total Prizemoney* £3,810

Wins * **1998** Spt Kempto (SFT) 6f 88+ <

1998 Turf 1-2: (6f 1-1, 7f) (gd 1-2)

Currently useful filly. Turf high 88 (1st run) (began Spt) - 1st of 19 from Dominant Dancer (9 Spt Kempton RF 4189). Won nicely on her debut, but was disappointing when upped in class.

**G Wragg [1-2] A E Oppenheimer.*

FRAPPER LE OR (USA) RR 90f 5167a[13]

3 ch c Strike The Gold (USA) 8f **(79)**

Form - 0

1998 Turf 0-1: (12f) (frm)

Currently useful colt, always wears blinkers.

**R Vukelic in USA [0-1] Pine Hollow Stables.*

FRECKLES BHB 35f40a **RR 46f 40a** 4574[10]

3 b f High Kicker (USA) 8.4f **(52)** - Ship of Gold (Glint of Gold) 9.3f **(66)**

Form - 580410780000

Record 1998 - 1st:1 2nd:0 3rd:0 Ran:12
Pre1998 - 1st:0 2nd:0 3rd:0 Ran:4

Win Prizemoney £3,184 *Total Prizemoney* £3,184

Wins * **1998** Jun Bright (GD) H 7f 36 46 <

1998 Turf 1-11: (7f 1-3, 8f 6, 10f 2) (gd 1-7, g-f 2, frm 2) 1998 AW 0-1: (8f) (Fibr)

Neat, fair filly, effective 7f, acts on gd, often wears blinkers, likes left handed tracks, likes tight tracks. Turf high 46 - 1st of 18 getting 12lb from Samata One (15 Jun Brighton RF 1985). Becoming disappointing. **M J Ryan [1-17] P E Axon.*

FREDDIE MAC (IRE) BHB 34f **RR 39f** 2340[11]

3 b g River Falls 8.2f **(56)** - Golden Thread (Glint of Gold) 9.3f **(66)**

Form - 060

Record 1998 - 1st:0 2nd:0 3rd:0 Ran:3
Pre1998 - 1st:0 2nd:0 3rd:0 Ran:1

1998 Turf 0-2: (7f, 11f) (gd, frm) 1998 AW 0-1: (13f) (Equi)

Workmanlike, very moderate gelding. Turf high 38.

**G C Bravery [0-4] Bravery Racing.*

FREDORA BHB 88f **RR 89f** 4496[16]

3 ch f Inchinor 8.9f **(64)** - Ophrys (Nonoalco (USA)) 8.5f **(66)**

Form - 61022100

Record 1998 - 1st:2 2nd:2 3rd:0 Ran:8

Win Prizemoney £9,278 *Total Prizemoney* £13,019

Wins * **1998** Aug Kempto (G-F) H 7f 87 89 <
* **1998** May Kempto (GD) 7f 82

1998 Turf 2-8: (7f 2-5, 8f 3) (gd 1-3, g-f 2, frm 1-3)

Leggy, useful filly, effective 7f, acts on gd to frm, best on frm. Turf high 89 - 1st of 11 giving 4lb to Coronet (5 Aug Kempton RF 3371) - also 1st of 17 getting 5lb from Temeraire (30 May Kempton RF 1589). Inconsistent. Won an ordinary Kempton maiden on her second start, and was just collared at Sandown on her fourth run following a disappointing effort against older horses. She returned to winning form when landing a handicap back at Kempton, before finishing unplaced in two hot handicaps over a mile.

**M Blanshard [2-8] Peter Goldring.*

FREDRIK THE FIERCE (IRE) BHB 65f55a **RR 62f 55a** 3639[8]

4 b g Puissance 7.1f **(60)** - Hollia (Touch Boy) 5f **(66)**

Form - 67058

Record 1998 - 1st:0 2nd:0 3rd:0 Ran:5

Pre1998 - 1st:2 2nd:1 3rd:0 Ran:10
Win Prizemoney £11,264 *Total Prizemoney* £12,991
Wins * 1996 Aug Goodwo (G-F) H 5f 94 <
* 1996 Jun Cheste (G-F) 5.1f 76
1998 Turf 0-4: (5f 2, 6f 2) (gd, g-f 2, frm) 1998 AW 0-1: (7f) (Fibr)
Scopey, average gelding, has worn blinkers. Turf high 62.
**J Berry [2-15] Chris & Antonia Deuters.*

FREE BHB 53f RR 56df 3887[13]
3 ch g Gone West (USA) 7.8f **(82)** - Bemissed (USA) (Nijinsky (CAN)) 10.3f **(77)**
Form - 056470
Record 1998 - 1st:0 2nd:0 3rd:0 Ran:5
Pre1998 - 1st:0 2nd:0 3rd:0 Ran:3
Win Prizemoney £0 *Total Prizemoney* £318
1998 Turf 0-5: (10f, 12f 2, 14f, 17f) (gd 2, g-f, frm 2)
Scopey, fair gelding. Turf high 56 (began Jly). Inconsistent.
**Mrs M Reveley [0-6] P D Savill (from P F I Cole [0-2] Spt 1997).*

FREEDOM QUEST (IRE) BHB 72f RR 77f 4209[18]
3 b c Polish Patriot (USA) 7.8f **(70)** - Recherchee (Rainbow Quest (USA)) 10.4f **(75)**
Form - 24400
Record 1998 - 1st:0 2nd:0 3rd:0 Ran:4
Pre1998 - 1st:0 2nd:3 3rd:0 Ran:3
Win Prizemoney £0 *Total Prizemoney* £3,208
1998 Turf 0-4: (7f 2, 8f, 9f) (gd, g-f, frm 2)
Light-framed, decent colt, effective 7f, acts on gd - acts on Fibr, has worn blinkers, prefers left handed tracks. Turf high 77 (began Jly). **J M Jefferson [0-2] B Valentine (from J Hetherton [0-2] Aug 1998).*

FREE FINISH (IRE) RR 7f 1144[10]
2 b f Distinctly North (USA) 7.4f **(63)** - Brave Louise (Brave Shot) 10.3f **(54)**
Form - 00
Record 1998 - 1st:0 2nd:0 3rd:0 Ran:2
1998 Turf 0-2: (5f, 6f) (gd 2)
Currently very poor filly. Turf high 7. **N Tinkler [0-2] Philip Grundy.*

FREE OPTION (IRE) BHB 92f RR 94f 4467[2]
3 ch g Indian Ridge 7.6f **(74)** - Saneena (Kris) 9.5f **(73)**
Form - 4348123512
Record 1998 - 1st:2 2nd:2 3rd:2 Ran:10
Pre1998 - 1st:0 2nd:2 3rd:1 Ran:5
Win Prizemoney £11,340 *Total Prizemoney* £20,891
Wins * **1998** Spt Newbur (gd) H 7.3f 85 94 <
* **1998** Jly Lingfi (G-F) 7.6f 72+
1998 Turf 2-9: (7f 1-3, 8f 1-5, 10f) (g-s, gd, g-f 3, frm 2-4) 1998 AW 0-1: (10f) (Equi)
Workmanlike, useful gelding, effective 7 to 10f, best at 7f, acts on frm. Turf high 94 - 1st of 20 from Shadow Creek (18 Spt Newbury RF 4360). A very consistent performer from seven to ten furlongs. He won two races, and can repeat that next term in the right grade.
**B Hanbury [2-15] Ahmed Ali.*

FREE TO SPEAK (IRE) BHB 104f RR 100+f 5109a[3]
6 ch g Be My Guest (USA) 10.2f **(66)** - Love For Poetry (Lord Gayle (USA)) 8.8f **(62)**
Form - 623716033
1998 Turf 1-9: (8f 1-4, 9f 4, 10f) (sft 1-2, g-s, gd 4, g-f, frm)
Very useful gelding, effective 8 to 10f, acts on sft to frm, best on gd, often wears blinkers (extremely effectively), excels at Galway and likes Leopardstown. Turf high 100 - 3rd of 7 getting 2lb from Risk Material (20 Spt Curragh 9f gd RF 4443a) - also 1st of 17 giving 5lb to Thats Logic (28 Jly Galway RF 3338a). Consistent. He is a smashing old horse and got a dream run up the rails when winning a valuable handicap at Galway in July. He should pay his way again next term. **D K Weld in IRE [2-21] Moyglare Stud Farm.*

FRENCH BALLERINA (IRE) RR 107f 2085[P]
5 b m Sadler's Wells (USA) 11.3f **(87)** -Filia Ardross(Ardross) 10.6f **(68)**
Form - 11P
1998 Turf 1-2: (14f 1-1, 20f) (g-s, g-f 1-1)
Pattern-class filly, effective 10 to 14f, acted on hvy to g-f. Turf high 107 (1st run) - 1st of 6 getting 3lb from Gordi (20 May Leopardstown RF 1492a). A brilliant novice hurdler she met a tragic end in the Ascot Gold Cup, injuring herself leaving the stalls. (DEAD)
**P J Flynn in IRE [8-16] Mrs Magnier,R Sangster,M O'Brien.*

FRENCH CONNECTION RR 87f 4368[13]
3 b c Tirol 8.1f **(64)** - Heaven-Liegh-Grey (Grey Desire) 8.7f **(50)**
Form - 1124500
Record 1998 - 1st:2 2nd:1 3rd:0 Ran:7
Pre1998 - 1st:0 2nd:2 3rd:0 Ran:3
Win Prizemoney £24,491 *Total Prizemoney* £30,653
Wins * **1998** May Haydoc (G-S) H 8.1f 77 81 <
* **1998** May Hamilt (SFT) 9.2f 79
1998 Turf 2-7: (8f 1-3, 9f 1-1, 10f 3) (hvy 1-1, sft 2, gd 1-2, g-f, frm)
Useful colt, effective 8 to 10f, best at 10f, acts on hvy to frm, has worn blinkers. Turf high 87 - 4th of 10 getting 12lb from Florazi (18 Jly Newmarket 8f frm RF 2919) - also 1st of 11 getting 20lb from Lucayan Indian (23 May Haydock RF 1418). Game winner of the Tote Credit Silver Bowl, he ran poorly on his final two starts.
**J Berry [2-10] Peter Dodd.*

FRENCH GINGER BHB 30f25a RR 37f 25a 4545[14]
7 ch m Most Welcome 8.6f **(66)** - French Plait (Thatching) 8f **(66)**
Form - 00060800470
Record 1998 - 1st:0 2nd:0 3rd:0 Ran:9
Pre1998 - 1st:1 2nd:1 3rd:1 Ran:19
Win Prizemoney £2,752 *Total Prizemoney* £4,896
Wins 1997 Spt Mussel (G-F) H 7.1f 45 54 <
1998 Turf 0-8: (7f 2, 8f 5, 12f) (g-s, gd 2, g-f 4, frm) 1998 AW 0-1: (11f) (Fibr)
Very moderate mare, effective 7f, acts on g-f, has worn blinkers, likes right handed tracks. Turf high 37.
**Don Enrico Incisa [0-9] Don Enrico Incisa (from L R Lloyd-James [1-7] Nov 1997).*

FRENCH GRIT (IRE) BHB 54f RR 51f 4469[14]
6 b g Common Grounds 8.1f **(66)** - Charbatte (FR) (In Fijar (USA)) 7.5f **(70)**
Form - 0570300
Record 1998 - 1st:0 2nd:0 3rd:1 Ran:7
Pre1998 - 1st:4 2nd:5 3rd:3 Ran:40
Win Prizemoney £21,683 *Total Prizemoney* £37,274
Wins * 1997 Jun Pontef (G-F) H 6f 71 75
* 1997 Apr Ripon (G-F) H 6f 72 78
* 1995 May Doncas (G-F) 6f 85 <
* 1994 Aug Redcar (G-F) 5f 80
1998 Turf 0-7: (5f 2, 6f 5) (g-s, gd, g-f, frm 4)
Fair gelding, effective 6f, acts on g-f to frm, best on frm. Turf high 57. **M Dods [4-47] Michael Wilson.*

FRENCH PRIDE (IRE) BHB 36f RR 36f 5058[5]
3 b f Pips Pride 6.7f **(70)** - Reasonably French (Reasonable (FR))
Form - 0080345807565
Record 1998 - 1st:0 2nd:0 3rd:1 Ran:13
Pre1998 - 1st:0 2nd:0 3rd:0 Ran:1
Win Prizemoney £0 *Total Prizemoney* £444
1998 Turf 0-12: (5f, 6f 8, 7f 3) (sft, g-s, gd 4, g-f 2, frm 4) 1998 AW 0-1: (6f) (Fibr)
Scopey, very moderate filly, effective 6f, acts on gd, likes left handed tracks, likes tight tracks. Turf high 46.
**A R Dicken [0-14] A McKenzie.*

FRENCH WOOD (USA) RR 28f 664[5]
3 b br c Woodman (USA) 9.7f **(77)** - Je Comprend (USA) (Caerleon (USA)) 8.6f **(71)**
Form - 05
Record 1998 - 1st:0 2nd:0 3rd:0 Ran:2
1998 Turf 0-2: (10f, 12f) (sft, gd)
Lengthy, currently little account colt. Turf high 28.
**B Hanbury [0-2] Khalifa Sultan.*

FRESH FRUIT DAILY BHB 60f43a RR 69df 43a 91[5]
6 b m Reprimand 8.2f **(63)** - Dalmally (Sharpen Up) 8.3f **(67)**
Form - 5
Record 1998 - 1st:0 2nd:0 3rd:0 Ran:1
Pre1998 - 1st:3 2nd:3 3rd:3 Ran:29
Win Prizemoney £7,647 *Total Prizemoney* £13,783
Wins 1997 *May Wolver (STD) H 12f 49 52*
1997 Apr Folkes (FRM) H 9.7f 63 71 <

1997 *Jan Southw (STD) 11f 52*
1998 AW 0-1: (12f) (Equi)
Average mare, effective 10f, acts on gd. Inconsistent.
**A Kelleway [0-3] Kevin Hudson (from P A Kelleway [3-31] Spt 1997).*

FREYA (IRE) RR 24f
5139[17]
2 b f Fayruz 6.6f **(63)** - My Croft (Crofter (USA)) 8.4f **(56)**
Form - 0
Record 1998 - 1st:0 2nd:0 3rd:0 Ran:1
1998 Turf 0-1: (6f) (gd)
Currently little account filly. **A C Stewart [0-1] R L Axworthy.*

FRIAR TUCK BHB 96f RR 100f
4965[9]
3 ch g Inchinor 8.9f **(64)** - Jay Gee Ell (Vaigly Great) 7f **(58)**
Form - 201030
Record 1998 - 1st:1 2nd:1 3rd:1 Ran:6
Pre1998 - 1st:1 2nd:0 3rd:2 Ran:6
Win Prizemoney £40,967 *Total Prizemoney* £47,918
Wins * 1998 Jun York (G-S) H 6f 95 100 <
* 1997 Jly Ayr (G-F) 6f 81
1998 Turf 1-6: (5f 2, 6f 1-4) (sft 2, g-s 1-2, g-f 2)
Scopey, very useful gelding, effective 5 to 6f, acts on g-s to g-f. Turf high 100 - 1st of 22 giving 8lb to Marton Moss (13 Jun York RF 1981). Inconsistent. He regained the winning habit when springing a surprise in the valuable William Hill Trophy at York in June, but was fighting a losing battle with the handicapper thereafter. He goes well on soft ground and can win again when he has slipped back down to a realistic mark.
**Miss L A Perratt [2-12] Cree Lodge Racing Club.*

FRIENDLY ALLIANCE RR 49f
4999[7]
2 b g Shareef Dancer (USA) 10.1f **(67)** - Snow Huntress (Shirley Heights) 10.3f **(74)**
Form - P77
Record 1998 - 1st:0 2nd:0 3rd:0 Ran:3
1998 Turf 0-3: (7f 2, 8f) (sft, g-s, g-f)
Currently moderate gelding. Turf high 49 (began Spt).
**R M Flower [0-3] The Twitchell Partnership.*

FRIENDLY BRAVE (USA) BHB 45f57a RR 46f 57a
4543[4]
8 b g Well Decorated (USA) 6.3f **(53)** - Companionship (USA) (Princely Native (USA)) 8.6f **(81)**
Form - 6313424405577456274
Record 1998 - 1st:0 2nd:2 3rd:1 Ran:16
Pre1998 - 1st:8 2nd:8 3rd:12 Ran:86
Win Prizemoney £23,790 *Total Prizemoney* £42,875
Wins * 1997 *Dec Lingfi (STD) H 5f 59 60*
* 1996 Aug Bath (G-F) H 5.1f 73 73
* 1996 Jun Folkes (FRM) H 5f 70 70
* 1996 Jun Goodwo (GD) H 6f 67 69
* 1996 Apr Folkes (G-F) 5f 66
* 1995 *Nov Lingfi (STD) H 5f 60 67*
* 1995 *Nov Lingfi (STD) H 5f 60 61*
1994 Mar Folkes (G-S) H 6.9f 70 74 <
1998 Turf 0-10: (5f 7, 6f 3) (sft, g-f 2, frm 6, hrd) 1998 AW 0-6: (5f 4, 6f 2) (Equi 5, Fibr)
Average gelding, effective 5 to 6f, best at 5f, acts on gd to frm - acts on Equi, has worn blinkers, likes left handed tracks. Turf high 53. AW high 63 - 4th of 6 to Anokato (8 Jan Lingfield 5f Equi RF 0047). He enjoyed a highly successful 1996 campaign, but has only shown sporadic form since then. His form on sand has been rather better than on turf recently, though even there victories have become scarce.
**Miss Gay Kelleway [7-68] Tempus Fugit Partnership (from T G Mills [1-29] Jun 1995).*

FRIENDLY KNIGHT BHB 32f37a RR 26f 37a
1157[1]
8 b g Horage 11.4f **(58)** - Be A Dancer (Be Friendly) 9.3f **(53)**
Form - 3471
Record 1998 - 1st:1 2nd:0 3rd:1 Ran:4
Pre1998 - 1st:0 2nd:2 3rd:1 Ran:15
Win Prizemoney £2,427 *Total Prizemoney* £4,460
Wins * 1998 *May Southw (STD) H 14f 29 37* <
1998 Turf 0-1: (12f) (gd) 1998 AW 1-3: (11f, 12f, 14f 1-1) (Fibr 1-3)
Very moderate gelding. AW high 37 - 1st of 12 getting 32lb from Batoutoftheblue (11 May Southwell RF 1157).
**Mrs A E Johnson [2-7] Mark Johnson (from J S Haldane [2-36] May 1997).*

FRIENDLY WARNING BHB 74f RR 65f
5078[15]
3 b f Warning 8.1f **(77)** - Dedara (Head for Heights) 9.6f **(55)**
Form - 300
Record 1998 - 1st:0 2nd:0 3rd:1 Ran:3
Pre1998 - 1st:1 2nd:1 3rd:0 Ran:4
Win Prizemoney £7,856 *Total Prizemoney* £10,251
Wins * 1997 Aug Claire (HVY) 7f 77+ <
1998 Turf 0-3: (8f 3) (sft, g-s, frm)
Neat, average filly, effective 7f, acts on hvy to gd. Turf high 65.
**J E Banks [1-7] The Allez France Partnership.*

FRILLY FRONT BHB 80f RR 85f
5144[17]
2 ch f Aragon 7.7f **(58)** - So so **(56f)** (Then Again)
Form - 13434730
Record 1998 - 1st:1 2nd:0 3rd:3 Ran:8
Win Prizemoney £2,770 *Total Prizemoney* £5,085
Wins * 1998 Jun Mussel (SFT) 5f 84+ <
1998 Turf 1-8: (5f 1-8) (sft, gd 1-4, g-f 3)
Useful filly, effective 5f, acts on gd to g-f, best on gd. Turf high 85 - 3rd of 8 giving 16lb to Class Wan (19 Aug Musselburgh 5f gd RF 3747) - also 1st of 7 from Midnight Orchid (15 Jun Musselburgh RF 1991). The betting market suggested she was not fancied for her Musselburgh debut, but she scored very easily in the soft ground. Fair efforts since on a faster surface.
**T D Barron [1-8] Geoffrey Martin.*

FRISKY FOX RR 46f
3804[3]
4 b f Risk Me (FR) 8f **(53)** - Hill Vixen (Goldhill) 8.5f **(55)**
Form - 3
Record 1998 - 1st:0 2nd:0 3rd:1 Ran:1
Win Prizemoney £0 *Total Prizemoney* £616
1998 Turf 0-1: (12f) (gd)
Currently moderate filly. **R Hollinshead [0-1] Mrs J P Bissill.*

FRISKY LADY BHB 52f54a RR 49f 54a
2266[13]
3 b f Magic Ring (IRE) 6.5f **(64)** - Epithet (Mill Reef (USA)) 10.5f **(78)**
Form - 0070100
Record 1998 - 1st:1 2nd:0 3rd:0 Ran:7
Pre1998 - 1st:0 2nd:0 3rd:1 Ran:4
Win Prizemoney £1,815 *Total Prizemoney* £2,489
Wins * 1998 Jun Catter (G-S) 7f 49 <
1998 Turf 1-6: (7f 1-4, 8f 2) (g-s, gd 1-4, frm) 1998 AW 0-1: (7f) (Fibr)
Neat, fair filly, effective 7f, acts on gd, often wears blinkers (very effectively), likes left handed tracks, likes tight tracks. Turf high 49 - 1st of 6 getting 3lb from One To Go (5 Jun Catterick RF 1743). Inconsistent. **T D Easterby [1-11] C H Stevens.*

FRITTON (IRE) BHB 56f RR 56f
4402[9]
3 br g Petardia 8.2f **(58)** - Calash (Indian King (USA)) 7.4f **(64)**
Form - 005010450
Record 1998 - 1st:1 2nd:0 3rd:0 Ran:9
Pre1998 - 1st:0 2nd:0 3rd:0 Ran:3
Win Prizemoney £2,145 *Total Prizemoney* £2,412
Wins * 1998 Jly Yarmou (GD) S 7f 56 <
1998 Turf 1-9: (7f 1-3, 8f 3, 10f 2, 12f) (g-s, gd, g-f, frm 1-5, hrd)
Scopey, fair gelding, effective 7f, acted on gd to frm, had worn blinkers. Turf high 56 - 1st of 14 giving 5lb to Peaceful Sarah (1 Jly Yarmouth RF 2457). (DEAD) **M H Tompkins [1-13] P F Riseborough.*

FROLICKING BHB 45f37a RR 37f 37a
2173[12]
3 b f Mujtahid (USA) 7.4f **(69)** - Perfect Desire (USA) (Green Forest (USA)) 9.9f **(68)**
Form - 008480380
Record 1998 - 1st:0 2nd:0 3rd:1 Ran:8
Pre1998 - 1st:0 2nd:0 3rd:0 Ran:8
Win Prizemoney £0 *Total Prizemoney* £1,005
1998 Turf 0-3: (7f 2, 8f) (gd 3) 1998 AW 0-5: (6f, 7f, 8f, 9f 2) (Fibr 5)
Unfurnished, very moderate filly, has worn blinkers. Turf high 37. AW high 36.
**W G M Turner [0-4] Foley Steelstock (from N P Littmoden [0-5] Feb 1998).*

FRONT BENCH RR 103f
3225a[3]
3 ch g Arazi (USA) 9.2f **(74)** - Fetish (Dancing Brave (USA)) 8.4f **(76)**
Form - 3
1998 Turf 0-1: (9f) (gd)
Currently very useful gelding. (1st run) - 3rd of 7 to Kabool (25 Jly

Maisons-laffitte 9f gd RF 3225a). He finished fast when snatching third place in a Group Three at Maisons-Laffitte in July and can win a similar event. **Mme C Head in FR [0-1] K Abdulla.*

FROSTY (IRE) RR 32f 4089[15]

2 ch g Lahib (USA) 8f **(69)** - Chilblains (Hotfoot) 10.5f **(59)**
Form - 0
Record 1998 - 1st:0 2nd:0 3rd:0 Ran:1
1998 Turf 0-1: (8f) (frm)
Currently very moderate gelding. **T D Easterby [0-1] Peter Bourke.*

FRUGAL BHB 30f RR 34f 1675[11]

5 b g Dunbeath (USA) 9.9f **(53)** - Sum Music (Music Boy) 6.8f **(57)**
Form - 00
Record 1998 - 1st:0 2nd:0 3rd:0 Ran:2
Pre1998 - 1st:0 2nd:0 3rd:0 Ran:3
1998 Turf 0-2: (7f 2) (gd 2)
Very moderate gelding. Turf high 3.
**B W Murray [0-7] Fir Trading Ltd.*

FRUITS OF LOVE (USA) RR 115f 4948a[4]

3 b c Hansel (USA) 12.6f **(78)** - Vallee Secrete (USA) (Secretariat (USA)) 9f **(79)**
Form - 350213584
Record 1998 - 1st:1 2nd:1 3rd:2 Ran:9
Pre1998 - 1st:1 2nd:1 3rd:1 Ran:3
Win Prizemoney £35,031 *Total Prizemoney* £53,435
Wins * **1998** Jly Newmar (G-F) G2 12f 114 <
* 1997 Aug Newcas (G-F) 7f 85+
1998 Turf 1-9: (10f 4, 12f 1-4, 13f) (hvy, gd 6, g-f, frm 1-1)
Strong, high-class colt, effective 10 to 13f, best at 12f, acts on hvy to frm, has worn blinkers, prefers right handed tracks. Turf high 115 - 4th of 5 giving 4lb to Blushing Risk (18 Oct Longchamp 12f hvy RF 4948a) - also 1st of 7 getting 13lb from Multicoloured (7 Jly Newmarket RF 2581). Consistent. He looked set to justify Mark Johnston's rave reviews when winning the Group Two Princess Of Walesís Stakes. However, it was a below-par renewal of that race, and he did not make the expected progress despite running creditably, mostly abroad. He does remain something of an enigma.
**M Johnston [2-12].*

FUEGIAN BHB 54f RR 61f 4644[9]

3 ch g Arazi (USA) 9.2f **(74)** - Well Beyond (IRE) (Don't Forget Me) 8.3f **(74)**
Form - 070
Record 1998 - 1st:0 2nd:0 3rd:0 Ran:3
1998 Turf 0-3: (8f 2, 10f) (gd, g-f, frm)
Scopey, average gelding. Turf high 61.
**M Madgwick [0-1] D Knight (from R Charlton [0-2] Aug 1998).*

FULL EGALITE BHB 70f RR 78f 5122[1]

2 gr g Ezzoud (IRE) - Milva (Jellaby) 6.4f **(58)**
Form - 061
Record 1998 - 1st:1 2nd:0 3rd:0 Ran:3
Win Prizemoney £2,965 *Total Prizemoney* £2,965
Wins * **1998** Nov Bright (SFT) 6f 78 <
1998 Turf 1-3: (6f 1-3) (g-s 1-1, gd, g-f)
Currently above-average gelding. Turf high 78 (began Spt) - 1st of 9 from Uzy (5 Nov Brighton RF 5122).
**W J Haggas [1-3] S Hassiakos.*

FULL MOON BHB 40f RR 32f 220[5]

3 b g Almoojid 7f **(36)** - High Time (FR) (Adonijah) 10f **(61)**
Form - 5
Record 1998 - 1st:0 2nd:0 3rd:0 Ran:1
Pre1998 - 1st:0 2nd:0 3rd:0 Ran:2
1998 AW 0-1: (6f) (Fibr)
Unfurnished, currently very moderate gelding, often wears blinkers. **P D Evans [0-3] Mrs E A Dawson.*

FULLOPEP BHB 58f RR 54f 3618[4]

4 b g Dunbeath (USA) 9.9f **(53)** - Suggia (Alzao (USA)) 7.1f **(68)**
Form - 634
Record 1998 - 1st:0 2nd:0 3rd:1 Ran:3
Pre1998 - 1st:1 2nd:1 3rd:0 Ran:11
Win Prizemoney £2,617 *Total Prizemoney* £4,336
Wins * 1997 May Catter (G-F) 12f 57+ <
1998 Turf 0-3: (10f, 12f 2) (gd 2, frm)
Workmanlike, fair gelding, effective 12 to 16f, best at 12f, acts on gd to g-f, best on g-f, prefers left handed tracks, favours tight tracks. Turf high 54. **Mrs M Reveley [1-14] & Mrs W J Williams.*

Fruits of Love (right) scored only once

FULL SPATE RR 80f 2075[4]
3 ch c Unfuwain (USA) 11.4f **(74)** - Double River (USA) (Irish River (FR)) 8.6f **(78)**
Form - 234
Record 1998 - 1st:0 2nd:1 3rd:1 Ran:3
Win Prizemoney £0 *Total Prizemoney* £1,966
1998 Turf 0-3: (7f, 8f 2) (gd 3)
Scopey, currently decent colt. Turf high 80 - 3rd of 17 giving 5lb to Fredora (30 May Kempton 7f gd RF 1589).
**R Charlton [0-3] K Abdulla.*

FUNKY BHB 24f **RR 25?f** 2958[15]
5 ch m Classic Music (USA) 7.2f **(57)** - Foreno (Formidable (USA)) 9.2f **(63)**
Form - 00
Record 1998 - 1st:0 2nd:0 3rd:0 Ran:2
Pre1998 - 1st:0 2nd:1 3rd:1 Ran:11
Win Prizemoney £0 *Total Prizemoney* £1,645
1998 Turf 0-2: (11f, 12f) (frm 2)
Little account filly. Turf high 3 (began Jly).
**F Jordan [1-11] Manor House Partnership (from D Nicholls [0-9] Apr 1997).*

FUNNY HOWITHAPPENS RR 28[11]
3 b f Forzando 7.2f **(63)** - Girl's Brigade (Brigadier Gerard) 9.3f **(58)**
Form - 0
Record 1998 - 1st:0 2nd:0 3rd:0 Ran:1
Pre1998 - 1st:0 2nd:0 3rd:0 Ran:1
1998 AW 0-1: (8f) (Fibr)
Workmanlike, currently very poor filly.
**J W Payne [0-1] Sackville House Racing (from C Murray [0-1] May 1997).*

FURLOUGH (USA) RR 5164a[10]
4 b f Easy Goer (USA) 8.7f **(81)** - Blitey (USA) (Riva Ridge (USA)) 8.2f **(68)**
Form - 0
1998 AW 0-1: (6f) (Dirt)
Currently Pattern-class filly. **C McGaughey in USA [0-1] O Phipps.*

FURTHER FLIGHT BHB 85f **RR 98?f** 5067[4]
12 gr g Pharly (FR) 11.5f **(64)** - Flying Nelly (Nelcius) 14.9f **(115)**
Form - 164074
Record 1998 - 1st:1 2nd:0 3rd:0 Ran:6
Pre1998 - 1st:22 2nd:8 3rd:7 Ran:61
Win Prizemoney £406,263 *Total Prizemoney* £485,020

Wins								
*	**1998**	Apr	Nottin	(SFT)		14.1f		101+
*	1997	Aug	Cheste	(SFT)	LH	13.4f	104	114+
*	1996	Apr	Nottin	(G-F)		14.1f		110
*	1995	Spt	Newmar	(G-F)	G3	16f		114
*	1995	Jly	Doncas	(G-F)		14.6f		82
*	1995	Apr	Haydoc	(GD)		16.2f		88
*	1994	Oct	Newmar	(GD)	LH	16f	105	107
*	1994	Oct	Newmar	(GD)	G3	16f		100

1998 Turf 1-6: (13f, 14f 1-1, 16f 3, 22f) (sft 1-1, gd 2, g-f 3)
Very useful gelding, effective 13 to 18f, best at 13f, acts on hvy to frm, prefers left handed tracks, excels at Chester. Turf high 101 (1st run). Becoming disappointing. Unplaced in a seven-furlong minor event at Chepstow on his debut in 1988, he went on to become one of Flat racing's favourite sons. His 24 wins were highlighted by an unprecedented five successes in the Jockey Club Cup, a record which is unlikely to be broken. Given a heart-warming send off after his swan-song at Newmarket in October, he has earned every minute of his retirement and should enjoy his new job as lead horse to the yearlings at Barry Hills' yard. Needless to say, he was a credit to all concerned with his career.
**B W Hills [23-67] Exors of the late S WingfieldDigby.*

FURTHER OUTLOOK (USA) BHB 80f **RR 85f** 4933[2]
4 gr g Zilzal (USA) 8.5f **(79)** - Future Bright (USA) (Lyphard's Wish (FR)) 9f **(74)**
Form - 0703002
Record 1998 - 1st:0 2nd:1 3rd:1 Ran:7
Pre1998 - 1st:2 2nd:1 3rd:1 Ran:8
Win Prizemoney £8,511 *Total Prizemoney* £23,404

Wins							
	1996	Spt	Hamilt	(GD)	8.3f	96	<
	1996	Aug	Beverl	(GD)	7.5f	85+	

1998 Turf 0-7: (7f 3, 8f 4) (g-s, gd, g-f 2, frm 3)
Workmanlike, useful gelding, effective 8f, acts on g-s. Turf high 85. Stayed on strongly over seven furlongs at Newbury in September, he wins only rarely but is an able performer on song.
**Mrs A J Perrett [0-10] Lady Harrison (from Sir Michael Stoute [2-5] Oct 1996).*

FURTHER RISK BHB 28f **RR 17f** 4627[20]
3 ch g Risk Me (FR) 8f **(53)** - Farinara (Dragonara Palace (USA)) 6.1f **(55)**
Form - 0000
Record 1998 - 1st:0 2nd:0 3rd:0 Ran:4
1998 Turf 0-4: (10f, 12f, 14f, 16f) (gd 2, g-f, frm)
Workmanlike, poor gelding. Turf high 17.
**Mrs H L Walton [0-4] A E Walton.*

FUSTANELLA RR 73f 4309[7]
2 b f Mtoto 11.5f **(71)** - Grecian Slipper **(96f)** (Sadler's Wells (USA)) 10f **(76)**
Form - 7
Record 1998 - 1st:0 2nd:0 3rd:0 Ran:1
1998 Turf 0-1: (8f) (g-f)
Currently above-average filly.
**J H M Gosden [0-1] Sheikh Mohammed.*

FUSUL (USA) RR 73f 4699[7]
2 ch c Miswaki (USA) 8.1f **(81)** - Silent Turn (USA) (Silent Cal (USA)) 14.5f **(91)**
Form - 57
Record 1998 - 1st:0 2nd:0 3rd:0 Ran:2
1998 Turf 0-2: (6f, 7f) (gd, frm)
Currently above-average colt. Turf high 73 (began Spt).
**B Hanbury [0-2] Hamdan Al Maktoum.*

FUTURE PERFECT BHB 103f **RR 103f** 2445[5]
4 b g Efisio 7.7f **(69)** - True Ring (High Top) 10.2f **(67)**
Form - 2425
Record 1998 - 1st:0 2nd:2 3rd:0 Ran:4
Pre1998 - 1st:3 2nd:2 3rd:0 Ran:8
Win Prizemoney £41,428 *Total Prizemoney* £66,132

Wins									
*	1997	Aug	Goodwo	(G-F)	H	10f	88	91	<
*	1997	Apr	Pontef	(G-F)		8f		90	
	1996	Oct	Haydoc	(SFT)		7.1f		77	

1998 Turf 0-4: (10f 4) (gd 3, g-f)
Strong, very useful gelding, effective 10f, acts on gd to g-f, best on gd. Turf high 103 - 2nd of 14 giving 15lb to Shadoof (6 Jun Epsom 10f g-f RF 1777).
**P F I Cole [2-11] R O M Racing (from M W Easterby [1-1] Oct 1996).*

FUTURE PROSPECT (IRE) BHB 65f70a **RR 69df 70a** 5119[14]
4 b g Marju (IRE) 9.2f **(76)** - Phazania (Tap On Wood) 10.3f **(65)**
Form - 10024180300
Record 1998 - 1st:2 2nd:1 3rd:1 Ran:11
Pre1998 - 1st:1 2nd:1 3rd:0 Ran:5
Win Prizemoney £7,817 *Total Prizemoney* £10,986

Wins							
1998	*Jly*	*Wolver*	*(STD)*	C	*8.5f*	*70*	
1998	May	Pontef	(G-F)	C	8f	73	
1996	Jun	Haydoc	(G-S)		5f	81+	<

1998 Turf 1-9: (7f 3, 8f 1-4, 9f, 12f) (gd 3, g-f 4, frm 1-2) 1998 AW 1-2: (8f 1-1, 9f) (Fibr 1-2)
Workmanlike, above-average gelding, effective 7 to 8f, best at 8f, acts on gd to frm - acts on Fibr, best on frm, favours tight tracks. Turf high 73 (1st run) - 1st of 9 from Alamein (22 May Pontefract RF 1403). AW high 70 (1st run) (began Jly) - 1st of 9 giving 12lb to Hyperico (24 Jly Wolverhampton RF 3094). Inconsistent. He did not run at all in '97 due to a broken pedal bone, but came back to win over a mile at Pontefract on his return last season. Inconsistent afterwards, though he did win quite nicely on the Wolverhampton Fibresand in July.
**M A Buckley [0-1] C C Buckley (from M Johnston [3-15] Spt 1998).*

FUTURE'S TRADER BHB 40f **RR 42f** 514[14]
5 b g Alzao (USA) 9.8f **(73)** - Awatef (Ela-Mana-Mou) 10.1f **(70)**
Form - 0
Record 1998 - 1st:0 2nd:0 3rd:0 Ran:1
Pre1998 - 1st:0 2nd:0 3rd:0 Ran:5
1998 Turf 0-1: (16f) (gd)

Moderate gelding.
**M D Hammond [0-5] Miss Sharon Long (from R Hannon [0-5] Oct 1996).*

Win Prizemoney £11,332 *Total Prizemoney* £16,024
Wins * **1998** Aug Haydoc (GD) H 8.1f 50 52

Popular grey Further Flight retired after an eleven-season career

FUWALA BHB 50f **RR 47f** 828[7]
4 b f Unfuwain (USA) 11.4f **(74)** - Lobela (Lorenzaccio) 10f **(64)**
Form - 47
Record 1998 - 1st:0 2nd:0 3rd:0 Ran:2 -
Pre1998 - 1st:0 2nd:0 3rd:0 Ran:2
Win Prizemoney £0 *Total Prizemoney* £202
1998 Turf 0-2: (8f, 10f) (g-s 2)
Rangy, moderate filly. Turf high 47.
**T D Easterby [0-2] A M Wragg (from D Shaw [0-2] Spt 1997).*

FYRESDAL ROCKY RR 22f 4002[16]
3 b g Rock Hopper 10.6f **(54)** - Hachimitsu (Vaigly Great) 7f **(58)**
Form - 00
Record 1998 - 1st:0 2nd:0 3rd:0 Ran:2
1998 Turf 0-2: (7f, 11f) (frm 2)
Neat, currently little account gelding. Turf high 22 (began Aug).
**G M McCourt [0-2] Mrs B Taylor.*

GABLESEA BHB 56f52a **RR 58f 52a** 4874[2]
4 b g Beveled (USA) 6.9f **(64)** - Me Spede (Valiyar) 8.5f **(73)**
Form - 1604463735523110 7232
Record 1998 - 1st:2 2nd:3 3rd:4 Ran:15
Pre1998 - 1st:2 2nd:1 3rd:0 Ran:18

* **1998** Jly Chepst (GD) H 7.1f 44 48
** 1997 Nov Southw (STD) H 7f 49 56* <
** 1997 Spt Wolver (STD) H 8.5f 44 47*
1998 Turf 2-9: (7f 1-5, 8f 1-4) (gd, g-f 2-5, frm 3) 1998 AW 0-6: (6f, 7f, 8f 4) (Fibr 6)
Leggy, fair gelding, effective 7 to 9f, best at 8f, acts on g-f - acts on Fibr, likes left handed tracks, excels at Southwell, likes Wolverhampton. Turf high 58 - 2nd of 20 getting 10lb from Knave's Ash (30 Spt Newcastle 8f g-f RF 4578) - also 1st of 16 getting 16lb from Queens Consul (7 Aug Haydock RF 3435). AW high 54 - 3rd of 10 getting 8lb from Godmersham Park (19 Jan Southwell 8f Fibr RF 0112). Hit form with a brace of short-head victories in the summer. **B P J Baugh [4-33] Messrs Chrimes, Winn & Wilson.*

GADGE BHB 67f56a **RR 68f 56a** 4918[12]
7 br g Nomination 7.3f **(57)** - Queenstyle (Moorestyle) 6.9f **(64)**
Form - 82024770024800100
Record 1998 - 1st:1 2nd:3 3rd:0 Ran:16
Pre1998 - 1st:8 2nd:3 3rd:9 Ran:62
Win Prizemoney £70,169 *Total Prizemoney* £87,252
Wins * **1998** Oct Bright (GD) 7f 68
* 1997 May Ayr (G-F) H 6f 66 80+ <
* 1997 May Goodwo (G-S) H 7f 66 72
* 1997 May Bath (G-S) H 8f 61 66

* 1997 May Thirsk (G-F) H 8f 58 63
* 1997 Mar Newcas (G-F) SH 8f 50 59
* 1997 *Feb Lingfi (STD) SH 8f 40 44*
1994 Spt Newbur (SFT) H 8f 69 71

1998 Turf 1-12: (5f 3, 6f 5, 7f 1-4) (sft 2, g-s 2, gd 3, g-f 1-2, frm 3) 1998 AW 0-4: (6f 2, 7f, 8f) (Equi, Fibr 3)

Average gelding, effective 6 to 7f, best at 6f, acts on gd to g-f, best on g-f, has worn blinkers. Turf high 70. AW high 51. Nothing like as effective in '98 as he had been the previous season.

**A Bailey [7-46] J B Wilcox (from D Morris [1-22] Jun 1996).*

GADROON BHB 41f33a **RR 44f 33a** 2230[7]

4 ch g Cadeaux Genereux 7.9f **(76)** - Greensward Blaze (Sagaro) 9.7f **(55)**

Form - 064107

Record 1998 - 1st:1 2nd:0 3rd:0 Ran:6
Pre1998 - 1st:0 2nd:1 3rd:1 Ran:7

Win Prizemoney £2,276 *Total Prizemoney* £3,543

Wins 1998 May Hamilt (GD) SH 11.1f 40 44 <

1998 Turf 1-5: (9f 2, 11f 1-1, 12f, 14f) (sft 2, gd 1-3) 1998 AW 0-1: (8f) (Fibr)

Workmanlike, moderate gelding, effective 8 to 11f, acts on sft to gd, best on gd. Turf high 44 - 1st of 10 giving 3lb to Portite Sophie (15 May Hamilton RF 1235). Inconsistent.

**V Thompson [0-2] V Thompson (from P C Haslam [1-12] May 1998).*

GAELIC QUINIE (IRE) BHB 34f45a **RR 31f 45a** 3141[16]

3 b f River Falls 8.2f **(56)** -Eliza Wooding **(24f)** (Faustus (USA)) 10f **(58)**

Form - 000

Record 1998 - 1st:0 2nd:0 3rd:0 Ran:3
Pre1998 - 1st:0 2nd:0 3rd:0 Ran:4

1998 Turf 0-3: (7f 2, 8f) (gd 2, g-f)

Light-framed, very moderate filly, has worn blinkers. Turf high 17.

**G R Oldroyd [0-7] William Riddell.*

GAELIC STORM BHB 111f95a **RR 115?f 95a** 5152[3]

4 b g Shavian 7.7f **(67)** - Shannon Princess (Connaught) 7.7f **(63)**

Form - 0731102080113

Record 1998 - 1st:4 2nd:1 3rd:2 Ran:12
Pre1998 - 1st:4 2nd:0 3rd:2 Ran:15

Win Prizemoney £63,907 *Total Prizemoney* £99,899

Wins * 1998 Oct Newbur (HVY) H 6f 105 115 <
* **1998** Oct York (GD) H 7f 102 105
* **1998** Jun Newcas (SFT) H 6f 95 98
* **1998** Jun York (G-S) H 6f 86 94
* 1997 Spt Catter (GD) 6f 76+
* 1997 Aug Epsom (GD) H 5f 81 83
* 1997 Aug Thirsk (G-F) H 5f 75 78
* 1996 Spt Sandow (G-F) 5f 84

1998 Turf 4-12: (6f 3-8, 7f 1-4) (sft 1-2, g-s 2-3, gd 3, g-f 3, frm 1-1)

Workmanlike, high-class gelding, effective 6 to 7f, acts on sft to frm, excels at York. Turf high 115 - 1st of 11 giving 10lb to Jimmy Too (23 Oct Newbury RF 4965). He enjoyed a successful season with four victories. Two of them came in June, at York and at Newcastle, and in both cases there was cut in the ground. Disappointed in the Stewards' Cup when heavily backed, but showed that running to be all wrong with a fine second in the Tote International Handicap at Ascot, despite not enjoying a clear passage. Regained winning form at York in October, and followed up in emphatic style at Newbury. He was tried in Listed company for his final start, but could only manage third. Soft ground is the key to this colt. **M Johnston [8-27] H C Racing Club.*

GAELIC SYMPHONY (IRE) **RR 110f** 5132a[3]

5 b h Fayruz 6.6f **(63)** - Time Is Flying

Form - 223

1998 Turf 0-3: (5f, 7f 2) (sft 3)

Group-class colt, has worn blinkers. Turf high 110 (began Spt) - 2nd of 10 getting 4lb from Tomba (11 Oct Munich 7f sft RF 4831a). He was flattered to run Tomba close at Munich in October, but is a useful sprinter.

**M Hofer in GER [0-3] Frau E Leiner (from D K Weld in IRE [0-3] Oct 1996).*

GAILY MILL **RR 80f** 4848[6]

3 b f Keen 11.1f **(58)** - Island Mill (Mill Reef (USA)) 10.5f **(78)**

Form - 343215551126

Record 1998 - 1st:3 2nd:2 3rd:2 Ran:12
Pre1998 - 1st:0 2nd:0 3rd:0 Ran:3

Win Prizemoney £14,347 *Total Prizemoney* £21,082

Wins * 1998 Aug Epsom (G-F) H 8.5f 73 78 <
* **1998** Aug Thirsk (G-F) H 8f 68 71
* **1998** Jun Salisb (G-S) H 7f 64 71

1998 Turf 3-12: (6f 3, 7f 1-4, 8f 1-4, 9f 1-1) (g-s, gd 1-5, g-f 1-3, frm 1-3)

Lengthy, decent filly, effective 7 to 9f, best at 8f, acts on gd to frm, best on g-f. Turf high 80 - 6th of 30 giving 2lb to Silken Dalliance (17 Oct Newmarket 8f gd RF 4848) - also 1st of 12 getting 10lb from Philistar (31 Aug Epsom RF 3986). She managed three victories in handicap company in '98 despite having an aversion to the stalls.

**I A Balding [3-15] Rae Smith.*

GAIN LINE (USA) BHB 44f **RR 45f** 3303[5]

5 b g Dayjur (USA) 6.8f **(79)** - Safe Play (USA) (Sham (USA)) 9.5f **(68)**

Form - 505000435

Record 1998 - 1st:0 2nd:0 3rd:1 Ran:9
Pre1998 - 1st:1 2nd:1 3rd:1 Ran:13

Win Prizemoney £3,709 *Total Prizemoney* £6,509

Wins * 1997 Jly Yarmou (G-F) H 7f 51 56 <

1998 Turf 0-9: (7f 5, 8f 3, 10f) (gd 5, g-f 2, frm 2)

Moderate gelding, effective 7 to 8f, best at 7f, acts on gd to g-f, best on gd, has worn blinkers. Turf high 50 (1st run) - 5th of 14 getting 11lb from Big Ben (1 Apr Folkestone 7f gd RF 0540). Inconsistent.

**C A Dwyer [0-9] Legend Racing (from Bob Jones [1-11] Nov 1997).*

GAJAN (IRE) BHB 44f44a **RR 36f 44a** 1577[12]

4 b g Ela-Mana-Mou 12.7f **(72)** - Delightful Time (Manado) 9.6f **(63)**

Form - 600

Record 1998 - 1st:0 2nd:0 3rd:0 Ran:3
Pre1998 - 1st:0 2nd:0 3rd:0 Ran:3

1998 Turf 0-2: (8f, 10f) (g-s, frm) 1998 AW 0-1: (8f) (Fibr)

Lengthy, very moderate gelding. Turf high 15.

**B J Llewellyn [0-3] John Williams Transport (Newport) Ltd (from J Neville [0-3] Jly 1997).*

GALA MISS BHB 32f **RR 26f** 585[13]

3 b f Sizzling Melody 6.3f **(49)** - Luckifosome (Smackover) 6f **(52)**

Form - 0

Record 1998 - 1st:0 2nd:0 3rd:0 Ran:1
Pre1998 - 1st:0 2nd:0 3rd:0 Ran:3

1998 Turf 0-1: (10f) (g-s)

Unfurnished, little account filly, often wears blinkers.

**P D Evans [0-4] M Woodall.*

GALAPINO BHB 68f68a **RR 66f 68a** 5118[9]

5 b g Charmer 9f **(59)** - Carousella (Rousillon (USA)) 8.2f **(74)**

Form - 380744770172020

Record 1998 - 1st:1 2nd:2 3rd:1 Ran:15
Pre1998 - 1st:5 2nd:8 3rd:2 Ran:37

Win Prizemoney £22,033 *Total Prizemoney* £42,196

Wins * 1998 Aug Goodwo (G-F) CH 9.9f 60 64
1997 Jun Warwic (G-F) H 12.5f 59 58
1997 Mar Doncas (G-F) H 12f 48 53
1997 *Jan Wolver (STD) C 12f 66*
1996 *Feb Wolver (STD) H 9.4f 65 76+* <
1996 *Feb Lingfi (STD) H 10f 65 69*

1998 Turf 1-13: (10f 1-2, 12f 4, 14f, 16f 4, 20f 2) (sft, g-s, gd 1-9, g-f, frm) 1998 AW 0-2: (12f, 13f) (Equi 2)

Average gelding, effective 10 to 20f, acts on sft to frm - acts on AW, has worn blinkers, excels at Sandown, does well at Doncaster and Ascot. Turf high 70 - 4th of 29 getting 15lb from San Sebastian (16 Jun Ascot 20f gd RF 2015). AW high 63. He had a good time of it in '97, but took time to recapture his form last season. A good fourth in the Ascot Stakes was more encouraging, but he changed stables in July, and got off the mark for his new yard when dropped back to ten furlongs at Goodwood the following month.

**M R Channon [2-10] Glendale Partnership Ltd (from Miss Gay Kelleway [2-20] Jly 1998).*

GALI **RR 65f** 4880[4]

2 gr c Petong 7.6f **(58)** - Wasimah (Caerleon (USA)) 8.6f **(71)**

Form - 04

Record 1998 - 1st:0 2nd:0 3rd:0 Ran:2

Win Prizemoney £0 *Total Prizemoney* £207

1998 Turf 0-2: (5f, 7f) (g-s, g-f)

Currently average colt. Turf high 65 (began Spt).

C A Horgan [0-2] B R Tantoco.

GALINGAL (USA) RR 71f 1354[6]
3 b f Known Fact (USA) 8.3f **(72)**-Galega (Sure Blade (USA)) 11.3f **(67)**
Form - 46
Record 1998 - 1st:0 2nd:0 3rd:0 Ran:2
Win Prizemoney £0 *Total Prizemoney* £482
1998 Turf 0-2: (7f, 8f) (g-f, frm)
Scopey, currently above-average filly. Turf high 71 (1st run) - 4th of 8 to Yanabi (10 May Bath 8f frm RF 1129).
R Charlton [0-2] K Abdulla.

GALLAASH (USA) BHB 65f **RR 56f** 3484[5]
3 b g Gulch (USA) 9.6f **(79)** - In View (USA) (In Reality) 7.4f **(74)**
Form - 5
Record 1998 - 1st:0 2nd:0 3rd:0 Ran:1
Pre1998 - 1st:0 2nd:0 3rd:0 Ran:2
1998 Turf 0-1: (7f) (gd)
Scopey, currently fair gelding.
J H M Gosden [0-3] Sheikh Ahmed Al Maktoum.

GALLANT FELLOW (FR) BHB 54f51a **RR 63f 51a** 4304[9]
3 ch c Cadeaux Genereux 7.9f **(76)** - Hiwaayati (Shadeed (USA)) 8.2f **(70)**
Form - 000
Record 1998 - 1st:0 2nd:0 3rd:0 Ran:3
1998 Turf 0-3: (5f, 6f, 8f) (gd, frm 2)
Scopey, currently average colt. Turf high 63 (began Jly).
C R Egerton [0-3] P Cook.

GALLANT GLORY (USA) RR 69f 5065[9]
2 b c Dynaformer (USA) 12f **(82)** - Triomphe (CHI) (Nobloys (FR))
Form - 00
Record 1998 - 1st:0 2nd:0 3rd:0 Ran:2
1998 Turf 0-2: (8f 2) (g-f 2)
Currently average colt. Turf high 69 (began Spt).
J H M Gosden [0-2] Sheikh Mohammed.

GALLERY GOD (FR) RR 67f 5037[4]
2 ch c In The Wings 11.2f **(77)** - El Fabulous (FR) (Fabulous Dancer (USA)) 9.4f **(70)**
Form - 04
Record 1998 - 1st:0 2nd:0 3rd:0 Ran:2
Win Prizemoney £0 *Total Prizemoney* £202
1998 Turf 0-2: (6f, 7f) (g-s, g-f)
Currently average colt. Turf high 67 (began Oct).
G Wragg [0-2] Takashi Watanabe.

GALTEE (IRE) RR 112f 4605a[2]
6 b h Be My Guest (USA) 10.2f **(66)** - Gandria (Charlottown) 10.9f **(57)**
Form - 112
1998 Turf 2-3: (10f 1-1, 12f 1-2) (sft 2-2, gd)
Group-class horse. Turf high 112 - 1st of 13 from Dulford Lad (2 Jun Taby RF 1912a). A German colt, he won a valuable race in Switzerland and picked up further good prize money in other Group Three races in Italy and his home country. Tough and consistent, he should continue to run well in minor Group races on the continent. *Uwe Stoltefuss in GER [3-6].*

GAMBERAIA (IRE) RR 100f 4602a[2]
4 gr f Konigsstuhl (GER) 9f **(115)**-Graciosa (GER) (Pentathlon) 8.5f **(59)**
Form - 2
1998 Turf 0-1: (8f) (sft)
Currently very useful filly. (1st run) - 2nd of 12 getting 2lb from Autriche (27 Spt Cologne 8f sft RF 4602a). She ran well in a Listed event in September, but does not seem likely to make significant improvement. *H Remmert in GER [0-1].*

GAME BIRD BHB 35f43a **RR 38f 43a** 4661[12]
3 b f Absalom 7.1f **(56)** - Mistral's Dancer (Shareef Dancer (USA)) 9.9f **(73)**
Form - 04800
Record 1998 - 1st:0 2nd:0 3rd:0 Ran:5
Pre1998 - 1st:0 2nd:0 3rd:0 Ran:4
1998 Turf 0-3: (5f, 6f 2) (gd, frm, hrd) 1998 AW 0-2: (5f, 6f) (Fibr 2)
Unfurnished, very moderate filly, often wears blinkers. Turf high 24. AW high 34. *J L Spearing [0-9] Mrs Robert Heathcote.*

GAME DILEMMA RR 42f 2895[8]
7 b m Sulaafah (USA) 8.6f **(44)** - Stagbury (National Trust)
Form - 8
Record 1998 - 1st:0 2nd:0 3rd:0 Ran:1
1998 Turf 0-1: (14f) (gd)
Moderate mare. *J W Mullins [3-24] Ian McGready.*

GAMEKEEPER RR 62f 4806[4]
2 ch c Mujtahid (USA) 7.4f **(69)** - High Tern (High Line) 10.3f **(70)**
Form - 4
Record 1998 - 1st:0 2nd:0 3rd:0 Ran:1
Win Prizemoney £0 *Total Prizemoney* £242
1998 Turf 0-1: (8f) (gd)
Currently average colt.
C E Brittain [0-1] Sheikh Mohammed Obaid Al Maktoum.

GAME TUFTY BHB 68f **RR 69f** 4889[5]
2 b g Sirgame - Melancolia (Legend of France (USA)) 9.5f **(61)**
Form - 7305
Record 1998 - 1st:0 2nd:0 3rd:1 Ran:4
Win Prizemoney £0 *Total Prizemoney* £530
1998 Turf 0-4: (7f 2, 8f 2) (gd, g-f, frm 2)
Average gelding. Turf high 69 (began Spt). *J Pearce [0-4] G H Tufts.*

GANDOURA (USA) BHB 62f **RR 60f** 4676[9]
3 b f Sheikh Albadou 9.2f **(75)** - Alqwani (USA) (Mr Prospector (USA)) 8.8f **(78)**
Form - 207040
Record 1998 - 1st:0 2nd:1 3rd:0 Ran:6
Pre1998 - 1st:0 2nd:0 3rd:0 Ran:3
Win Prizemoney £0 *Total Prizemoney* £2,680
1998 Turf 0-6: (6f 2, 7f 3, 8f) (gd, g-f 3, frm, hrd)
Workmanlike, average filly, effective 7f, acts on hrd, often wears blinkers. Turf high 79 (1st run) - 2nd of 14 giving 10lb to Yulara (6 Jun Newmarket 7f hrd RF 1791).
J H M Gosden [0-9] Hamdan Al Maktoum.

GANGA (IRE) BHB 83f **RR 87f** 4819[8]
4 ch f Generous (IRE) 11.5f **(82)** - Congress Lady (General Assembly (USA)) 10f **(68)**
Form - 7302528
Record 1998 - 1st:0 2nd:2 3rd:1 Ran:7
Pre1998 - 1st:3 2nd:0 3rd:0 Ran:7
Win Prizemoney £12,578 *Total Prizemoney* £18,484
Wins * 1997 Oct Redcar (G-F) H 10f 83 86 <
* 1997 Aug Ripon (GD) H 10f 78 84
* 1997 Jun Newcas (HVY) 8f 75+
1998 Turf 0-7: (10f 6, 12f) (sft, gd 3, frm 3)
Useful filly, effective 10f, acts on gd to frm, excels at Newcastle. Turf high 87 - 2nd of 4 getting 5lb from Another Time (16 Aug Lingfield 10f frm RF 3668). Consistent.
W Jarvis [3-14] Cuadra Africa.

GAN SARU RR 92f 4025a[6]
5 ch g Never so Bold 7.1f **(62)** - Ravaro (Raga Navarro (ITY)) 8f **(64)**
Form - 76
1998 Turf 0-2: (12f, 14f) (gd 2)
Useful gelding, effective 12f, acts on gd. Turf high 92.
P J Flynn in IRE [5-17] John Joseph Flynn.

GAPTON BOB (IRE) RR 10f 1903[9]
2 b c Bob's Return (IRE) - Bradwell (IRE) **(49f 47a)** (Taufan (USA)) 7f **(57)**
Form - 0
Record 1998 - 1st:0 2nd:0 3rd:0 Ran:1
1998 Turf 0-1: (7f) (g-f)
Currently poor colt. *M H Tompkins [0-1] P F Riseborough.*

GARAJ BHB 30a **RR 30a** 569[6]
3 ch g Alhijaz 7.7f **(57)** - Sunley Stars (Sallust) 8.4f **(63)**
Form - 606
Record 1998 - 1st:0 2nd:0 3rd:0 Ran:3
1998 AW 0-3: (7f, 8f, 9f) (Fibr 3)
Neat, currently very poor gelding. AW high 3.
J G M O'Shea [0-3] Gary Roberts.

GARBO BHB 49f44a **RR 48f 44a** 4550[9]
3 b f Superlative 8.8f **(57)** - Valence (BEL) (Sarajevo (FR)) 6f **(48)**
Form - 0061800
Record 1998 - 1st:1 2nd:0 3rd:0 Ran:7
Win Prizemoney £2,788 *Total Prizemoney* £2,788
Wins * **1998** Jly Bright (GD) H 6f 47 48 <
1998 Turf 1-6: (6f 1-2, 7f 2, 8f 2) (gd 1-3, g-f 2, frm) 1998 AW 0-1: (6f) (Fibr)
Scopey, moderate filly, effective 6f, acts on gd. Turf high 48 - 1st of 10 getting 18lb from Emmajoun (13 Jly Brighton RF 2760).
**R Hannon [1-7] Nimrod Company.*

GARNOCK VALLEY BHB 58f63a **RR 58f 63a** 5059[17]
8 b g Dowsing (USA) 7f **(61)** - Sunley Sinner (Try My Best (USA)) 7.6f **(67)**
Form - 1306720020
Record 1998 - 1st:1 2nd:2 3rd:1 Ran:10
Pre1998 - 1st:6 2nd:4 3rd:7 Ran:59
Win Prizemoney £27,240 *Total Prizemoney* £41,717
Wins * **1998** Apr Mussel (G-S) H 5f 60 64
* 1996 Oct Haydoc (SFT) H 6f 74 88 <
* 1996 Jun Ayr (G-F) H 5f 71 74
* 1996 May Mussel (G-S) H 5f 65 70
* 1996 Apr Mussel (GD) 5f 62
1998 Turf 1-10: (5f 1-8, 6f 2) (sft, g-s, gd 1-7, g-f)
Average gelding, effective 6f, acts on sft, has worn blinkers. Turf high 64 (1st run). He was on a long losing run after winning at Haydock in October 1996, but dropped right down the handicap as a result, and regained winning form on his first start of this season at Musselburgh. Modest form since. He has won on fast ground but looks better suited by some cut. **J Berry [7-69] Robert Aird.*

GARUDA (IRE) BHB 113f **RR 119f** 4603a[2]
4 b c Danehill (USA) 9.1f **(79)**-Ardmelody (Law Society (USA)) 9.9f **(70)**
Form - 1225422
Record 1998 - 1st:1 2nd:4 3rd:0 Ran:7
Pre1998 - 1st:1 2nd:0 3rd:1 Ran:5
Win Prizemoney £15,285 *Total Prizemoney* £84,541
Wins * **1998** Apr Kempto (SFT) L 10f 113+ <
* 1997 May Newbur (SFT) 10f 84
1998 Turf 1-7: (10f 1-4, 12f 3) (hvy 1-1, sft 2, gd 2, g-f, frm)
Workmanlike, high-class colt, effective 10 to 12f, best at 10f, acts on hvy to frm, best on sft, prefers right handed tracks, excels at Sandown. Turf high 119 - 2nd of 9 to Taipan (27 Spt Cologne 12f sft RF 4603a) - also 1st of 6 giving 5lb to Ukraine Venture (13 Apr Kempton RF 0658). Consistent. A useful performer, he was a facile winner in soft ground of a Listed race on his reappearance, but then kept on finding one or two too good throughout the rest of the season. He just lacks that turn of foot which would have turned him from a good horse into a very good one. Suited by soft ground and needs to be held up off a fast pace.
**J L Dunlop [2-12] Bob Demuyser.*

GATECRASHER BHB 83f **RR 82f** 3407[2]
3 b c Suave Dancer (USA) 10.7f **(68)** - Benazir (High Top) 10.2f **(67)**
Form - 612
Record 1998 - 1st:1 2nd:1 3rd:0 Ran:3
Win Prizemoney £3,826 *Total Prizemoney* £6,036
Wins * **1998** May Kempto (GD) 8f 77 <
1998 Turf 1-3: (8f 1-2, 11f) (sft, gd 1-1, g-f)
Workmanlike, currently decent colt. Turf high 82 - 2nd of 9 giving 1lb to Up At The Top (6 Aug Haydock 11f g-f RF 3407) - also 1st of 15 from Full Spate (4 May Kempton RF 1018).
**J R Fanshawe [1-3] J M Greetham.*

GAUNTLET (IRE) BHB 84f **RR 91f** 4410[2]
2 ch c Suave Dancer (USA) 10.7f **(68)** - Be My Everything (IRE) (Be My Guest (USA)) 9.3f **(67)**
Form - 532
Record 1998 - 1st:0 2nd:1 3rd:1 Ran:3
Win Prizemoney £0 *Total Prizemoney* £1,769
1998 Turf 0-3: (6f, 7f 2) (g-f, frm, hrd)
Currently useful colt. Turf high 91 (began Aug) - 2nd of 14 to Serpentine (22 Spt Warwick 7f frm RF 4410).
**J Noseda [0-3] M Olden.*

GAY BREEZE BHB 76f **RR 78f** 4502[5]
5 b g Dominion 8.9f **(65)** - Judy's Dowry (Dragonara Palace (USA)) 6.1f **(55)**
Form - 11122005
Record 1998 - 1st:3 2nd:2 3rd:0 Ran:8
Pre1998 - 1st:2 2nd:3 3rd:1 Ran:11
Win Prizemoney £18,909 *Total Prizemoney* £28,586
Wins * **1998** Jun Haydoc (GD) H 5f 61 70+ <
* **1998** May Doncas (G-F) H 6f 56 60
* **1998** Apr Nottin (SFT) H 6.1f 49 56
* 1997 Spt Yarmou (FRM) H 6f 43 48
* 1997 Aug Leices (GD) H 5f 40 42
1998 Turf 3-8: (5f 1-6, 6f 2-2) (sft 1-1, gd 1-4, g-f 1-2, frm)
Above-average gelding, effective 5f, acts on gd to frm, excels at Haydock. Turf high 78 - 2nd of 10 giving 9lb to Ocker (12 Jly Haydock 5f g-f RF 2743) - also 1st of 11 getting 8lb from Ocker (4 Jun Haydock RF 1717). He started off last season in fine form, completing a hat-trick, and has run well in the main since then despite a big hike in the handicap. Has bags of toe, and will win again once the Handicapper relents.
**P S Felgate [5-19] J M Flynn.*

GAZELLE ROYALE (FR) **RR 112f** 5129a[3]
4 b f Garde Royale - Beautywal (FR) (Magwal (FR))
Form - 53423
1998 Turf 0-5: (11f, 12f 3, 13f) (sft 2, g-s, gd 2)
Group-class filly, effective 10 to 13f, best at 12f, acts on sft to g-f, best on gd, and does well at Saint-cloud. Turf high 112 - 3rd of 9 getting 3lb from Fragrant Mix (28 Jun Saint-cloud 12f gd RF 2483a). Consistent. Ran a cracker when second in the '97 Oaks. Found wanting subsequently, although runner-up in an ordinary renewal of the Prix Vermeille, she ran her best race last term when third to Fragrant Mix in the Grand Prix de Saint-Cloud. She is certainly worth trying beyond middle-distances.
**J E Hammond in FR [0-11] K Yoshida.*

GEDY RED (USA) BHB 65f **RR 69df** 5150[13]
3 b c Alleged (USA) 11.8f **(81)** - Rose Red (USA) (Northern Dancer) 9.6f **(80)**
Form - 222300
Record 1998 - 1st:0 2nd:3 3rd:1 Ran:6
Win Prizemoney £0 *Total Prizemoney* £4,360
1998 Turf 0-6: (10f, 12f 2, 14f 2, 17f) (g-s, gd 4, g-f)
Scopey, average colt, effective 14f, acts on gd. Turf high 83 (1st run) (began Jly) - 2nd of 11 giving 5lb to Ivory Crown (3 Jly Sandown 14f gd RF 2507). Decent placed form without getting his head in front. Lacks a turn of foot.
**R C Spicer [0-1] The Green And Gold Partnership (from H R A Cecil [0-5] Oct 1998).*

GEE BEE BOY BHB 60f **RR 62f** 5125[2]
4 ch g Beveled (USA) 6.9f **(64)** - Blue and White (Busted) 10.2f **(61)**
Form - 2023602
Record 1998 - 1st:0 2nd:3 3rd:1 Ran:7
Pre1998 - 1st:1 2nd:0 3rd:0 Ran:9
Win Prizemoney £2,448 *Total Prizemoney* £5,537
Wins 1997 Jun Redcar (GD) 11f 68 <
1998 Turf 0-7: (11f, 12f 4, 14f, 16f) (g-s, gd, g-f 4, frm)
Scopey, average gelding, effective 11 to 12f, best at 11f, acts on g-s to frm, best on g-f, favours tight tracks, excels at Windsor. Turf high 63 - 2nd of 13 giving 2lb to Thatchmaster (29 Jun Windsor 12f g-f RF 2391).
**G M McCourt [0-1] Daltagh Construction Ltd (from A P Jarvis [1-15] Aug 1998).*

GEE BEE DREAM BHB 73f **RR 77f** 2365[16]
4 ch f Beveled (USA) 6.9f **(64)** - Return to Tara (Homing) 7.8f **(59)**
Form - 16530
Record 1998 - 1st:1 2nd:0 3rd:1 Ran:5
Pre1998 - 1st:1 2nd:2 3rd:0 Ran:13
Win Prizemoney £7,384 *Total Prizemoney* £19,957
Wins * **1998** Apr Epsom (SFT) 8.5f 74 <
* 1997 May Lingfi (GD) H 7f 72 65+
1998 Turf 1-5: (8f 3, 9f 1-2) (sft 1-1, gd 2, g-f 2)
Workmanlike, above-average filly, effective 7 to 9f, best at 9f, acts on sft to g-f, likes tight tracks. Turf high 77 - 3rd of 14 getting 3lb from Philistar (5 Jun Epsom 9f gd RF 1748) - also 1st of 7 getting 3lb from Stoppes Brow (22 Apr Epsom RF 0816). Won well on her

seasonal reappearance just as she did in 1997. She has run well since, especially when a close third in a valuable handicap at Epsom, and looks the type who goes particularly well when fresh.
**A P Jarvis [2-18] Grant & Bowman Ltd.*

GEEFORCE (IRE) BHB 45f **RR 45f** 5012[13]

2 ch f Soviet Lad (USA) 9.4f **(63)** - Great Pleasure (GER) (Star Appeal) 9.6f **(65)**
Form - 86800
Record 1998 - 1st:0 2nd:0 3rd:0 Ran:5
1998 Turf 0-5: (6f, 7f 3, 8f) (gd 2, frm 3)
Moderate filly. Turf high 45 (began Aug).
**Miss J F Craze [0-1] Robert Cook (from G R Oldroyd [0-4] Spt 1998).*

GEEGEE EMMARR BHB 43f **RR 51f** 5040[3]

5 b m Rakaposhi King 9.3f **(55)** - Fair Sara (McIndoe) 13.8f **(32)**
Form - 70503
Record 1998 - 1st:0 2nd:0 3rd:1 Ran:5
Win Prizemoney £0 *Total Prizemoney* £1,240
1998 Turf 0-5: (5f, 6f, 7f 2, 8f) (g-s, g-f, frm 3)
Fair filly. Turf high 51 (began Aug).
**S Gollings [0-5] Mrs Stella Barclay.*

GEIMHRIUIL (IRE) BHB 87f **RR 85+f** 1167[7]

4 b c Distinctly North (USA) 7.4f **(63)** - Ventry (Stanford) 7.9f **(56)**
Form - 07

Record	**1998** -	1st:0	2nd:0	3rd:0	Ran:2
	Pre1998 -	1st:2	2nd:2	3rd:1	Ran:7

Win Prizemoney £9,594 *Total Prizemoney* £11,952

Wins	* 1997	Jly	Newmar (G-F)	H	6f	81	85+	<
	* 1997	Jun	Goodwo (GD)		7f		71+	

1998 Turf 0-2: (6f 2) (gd 2)
Useful colt, effective 6 to 7f, acts on gd to frm. Turf high 77.
**L M Cumani [2-6] M J Dawson (from P Henley in IRE [0-3] Spt 1996).*

GEISHA GIRL **RR 102f** 4691a[2]

3 b f Nashwan (USA) 10.3f **(79)** - Miznah (IRE) (Sadler's Wells (USA)) 10f **(76)**
Form - 43342
1998 Turf 0-5: (10f, 12f 2, 14f 2) (sft, g-s, gd 2, g-f)
Very useful filly, effective 10 to 14f, acts on sft to g-f, does well at Leopardstown. Turf high 102 - 3rd of 9 to Joleah (18 Jly Leopardstown 14f g-f RF 3011a). She won a decent maiden at two and was campaigned solely in Listed company throughout 1998. Surprisingly dropped back to 10 furlongs on her final outing, all she does is stay. **C O'Brien in IRE [1-7] M E Parrish.*

GEM BHB 46f **RR 46f** 5070[3]

3 b f Most Welcome 8.6f **(66)** - Miss Top Ville (FR) (Top Ville) 11.7f **(68)**
Form - 45053

Record	**1998** -	1st:0	2nd:0	3rd:1	Ran:5
	Pre1998 -	1st:0	2nd:0	3rd:0	Ran:2

Win Prizemoney £0 *Total Prizemoney* £560
1998 Turf 0-5: (7f, 8f 2, 9f, 10f) (gd 2, g-f 2, frm)
Neat, moderate filly. Turf high 52. **P J Makin [0-7] T G Warner.*

GEMOLLY (IRE) BHB 27f **RR 34f** 4375[15]

5 b m Be My Native (USA) 11.2f **(62)** - Hayhurst (Sandhurst Prince) 7.9f **(63)**
Form - 0

Record	**1998** -	1st:0	2nd:0	3rd:0	Ran:1
	Pre1998 -	1st:0	2nd:0	3rd:0	Ran:3

1998 Turf 0-1: (16f) (frm)
Very moderate filly.
**R E Barr [0-5] R E Barr (from M Meade [0-3] Spt 1997).*

GENERAL ASSEMBLY (IRE) BHB 73f **RR 74f** 3062[14]

6 b g Pharly (FR) 11.5f **(64)** - Hastening (Shirley Heights) 10.3f **(74)**
Form - 760660

Record	**1998** -	1st:0	2nd:0	3rd:0	Ran:6
	Pre1998 -	1st:1	2nd:1	3rd:1	Ran:8

Win Prizemoney £4,055 *Total Prizemoney* £7,225

Wins	1995	Spt	Cheste (G-S)		13.4f		82+	<

1998 Turf 0-6: (12f, 14f, 16f 3, 19f) (sft, g-s, gd 2, g-f, frm)
Above-average gelding, effective 12 to 19f, acts on g-f. Turf high 85 - 6th of 18 getting 4lb from Silence in Court (6 May Chester 19f g-f RF 1059). Inconsistent. He has become a very disappointing sort in the last couple of seasons.
**G G Margarson [0-12] The Craftsmen (from H R A Cecil [1-8] Jun 1997).*

GENERAL EQUATION BHB 39f40a **RR 18f 40a** 3449[7]

5 b g Governor General 6.8f **(45)** - Logarithm (King of Spain) 7.8f **(52)**
Form - 086143063048307

Record	**1998** -	1st:1	2nd:0	3rd:3	Ran:13
	Pre1998 -	1st:1	2nd:0	3rd:2	Ran:18

Win Prizemoney £5,033 *Total Prizemoney* £7,198

Wins	* **1998**	*Jan*	*Wolver (STD)*	*H*	*5f*	*33*	*44*	
	* 1996	*Mar*	*Southw (STD)*	*S*	*5f*		*67*	<

1998 Turf 0-1: (5f) (sft) 1998 AW 1-12: (5f 1-12) (Fibr 1-12)
Moderate gelding, effective 5f - acts on Fibr, has worn blinkers (very effectively), prefers left handed tracks, prefers tight tracks. AW high 44 - 1st of 12 getting 10lb from Featherstone Lane (10 Jan Wolverhampton RF 0064). He showed nothing after winning on the Southwell Fibresand in March '96, but made all at Wolverhampton in January when blinkers seemed to make the difference. He has run some fair races since, but needs to be able to dominate, and sometimes shows an awkward head carriage.
**J Balding [2-31] Make Our Day.*

GENERAL GLEESON (IRE) **RR 24f** 58[8]

6 ch g Jackson's Drift (USA) - Lady General (General Ironside)
Form - 8

Record	**1998** -	1st:0	2nd:0	3rd:0	Ran:1
	Pre1998 -	1st:0	2nd:0	3rd:0	Ran:1

1998 AW 0-1: (13f) (Equi)
Little account gelding.
**R Ingram [0-1] The Emerald Gang (from O Weldon in IRE [0-2] Aug 1997).*

GENERAL GLOW BHB 40f **RR 44f** 5002[6]

5 b g Presidium 7.5f **(56)** - Glow Again (The Brianstan) 5.9f **(55)**
Form - 52506

Record	**1998** -	1st:0	2nd:1	3rd:0	Ran:5
	Pre1998 -	1st:3	2nd:0	3rd:3	Ran:22

Win Prizemoney £9,486 *Total Prizemoney* £12,928

Wins	* 1996	Aug	Haydoc (G-F)	H	10.5f	44	55	
	* 1996	Aug	Bright (FRM)	H	11.9f	44	65+	<
	* 1996	Jly	Bright (FRM)	H	10f	40	42+	

1998 Turf 0-4: (12f, 14f 2, 16f) (gd, g-f 2, frm) 1998 AW 0-1: (12f) (Equi)
Moderate gelding, effective 12 to 14f, acts on g-f to hrd, has worn blinkers, favours tight tracks. Turf high 44 (began Aug) - 2nd of 12 getting 29lb from Silently (27 Aug Musselburgh 14f g-f RF 3905). Consistent.
**P D Evans [3-23] J G White (from N Bycroft [0-7] Jun 1996).*

GENERAL HASTIE BHB 38f **RR 33f** 2720[6]

4 b g Cadeaux Genereux 7.9f **(76)** - Fast Car (FR) (Carwhite) 7.2f **(61)**
Form - 0556

Record	**1998** -	1st:0	2nd:0	3rd:0	Ran:4
	Pre1998 -	1st:0	2nd:0	3rd:0	Ran:3

1998 Turf 0-3: (7f 2, 14f) (sft, gd, frm) 1998 AW 0-1: (5f) (Fibr)
Very moderate gelding. Turf high 33. (DEAD)
**C L Popham [0-1] Mrs C R Hayton (from C W Thornton [0-6] May 1998).*

GENERAL KLAIRE BHB 52f66a **RR 52f 66a** 4385[9]

3 b br f Presidium 7.5f **(56)** - Klairover (Smackover) 6f **(52)**
Form - 060761660

Record	**1998** -	1st:1	2nd:0	3rd:0	Ran:9
	Pre1998 -	1st:0	2nd:0	3rd:0	Ran:4

Win Prizemoney £2,304 *Total Prizemoney* £2,304

Wins	* **1998**	*Jly*	*Wolver (STD)*		*6f*		*70*	<

1998 Turf 0-6: (6f 2, 7f 3, 8f) (sft 2, g-s, g-f 3) 1998 AW 1-3: (6f 1-3) (Fibr 1-3)
Scopey, above-average filly, effective 6f - acts on Fibr, likes left handed tracks, likes tight tracks. Turf high 52. AW high 70 (1st run) (began Jly) - 1st of 13 getting 5lb from Dryad (24 Jly Wolverhampton RF 3098). She showed aptitude for Fibresand when winning a Wolverhampton maiden in fine style in July, but that performance was way in excess of anything she has shown on turf to date. **B A McMahon [1-13] Tommy Staunton.*

GENERAL MONCK BHB 65f70a **RR 80f 70a** 4532[14]

3 ch g Formidable (USA) 7.8f **(60)** - Merton Mill (Dominion) 8.5f **(63)**
Form - 001640470

Record	**1998 -**	1st:1	2nd:0	3rd:0	Ran:9
	Pre1998 -	1st:0	2nd:0	3rd:1	Ran:3

Win Prizemoney £2,815 *Total Prizemoney* £3,909

Wins * **1998** Jun Ripon (SFT) 10f 80 <

1998 Turf 1-8: (10f 1-2, 11f 2, 12f 3, 16f) (g-s 1-2, g-f 4, frm 2) 1998 AW 0-1: (12f) (Fibr)

Scopey, decent gelding, effective 8 to 10f, acts on g-s to gd, has worn blinkers, likes tight tracks. Turf high 80 - 1st of 8 from Brevity (18 Jun Ripon RF 2089). Inconsistent.

**B Hanbury [1-9] Lord Clinton (from D Morley [0-3] Oct 1997).*

GENERAL MONTY BHB 35f **RR 38f** 1430[14]

6 b g Vague Shot 11f **(53)** - State Free (Free State) 8.7f **(61)**
Form - 00

Record	**1998 -**	1st:0	2nd:0	3rd:0	Ran:2
	Pre1998 -	1st:0	2nd:0	3rd:0	Ran:7

Win Prizemoney £0 *Total Prizemoney* £246

1998 AW 0-2: (11f, 16f) (Equi, Fibr)

Very moderate gelding, has worn blinkers.

**Mrs A E Johnson [0-5] Mrs Patricia Appleby (from T D Barron [0-6] Aug 1997).*

GENERAL SIR PETER (IRE) BHB 50f63a **RR 45f 63a** 2492[6]

6 br g Last Tycoon 9.4f **(73)** - Nashya (Rousillon (USA)) 8.2f **(74)**
Form - 066

Record	**1998 -**	1st:0	2nd:0	3rd:0	Ran:3
	Pre1998 -	1st:5	2nd:1	3rd:1	Ran:20

Win Prizemoney £15,066 *Total Prizemoney* £16,499

Wins	1997	Spt	Chepst	(GD)	H	5.1f	46	51	
	1997	*Apr*	*Wolver*	*(STD)*	*C*	*5f*		*73*	
	1995	Spt	Doncas	(G-S)	H	5f	72	74	<
	1995	Jly	Doncas	(G-F)	H	5f	68	67	
	1995	Apr	Warwic	(G-S)		5f		64	

1998 Turf 0-3: (5f 2, 6f) (gd 2, frm)

Above-average gelding, effective 5f - acted on Fibr, had worn blinkers. Turf high 43. Tended to give away ground at the start. (DEAD)

**R J Hodges [0-3] Mrs Anna Sanders (from N A Callaghan [2-15] Nov 1997).*

GENERAL SONG (IRE) BHB 48f41a **RR 89?f 41a** 4777[15]

4 b g Fayruz 6.6f **(63)** - Daybreaker (Thatching) 8f **(66)**
Form - 0000

Record	**1998 -**	1st:0	2nd:0	3rd:0	Ran:4
	Pre1998 -	1st:1	2nd:0	3rd:0	Ran:5

Win Prizemoney £12,180 *Total Prizemoney* £12,448

Wins * 1996 Spt Capann (GD) 7.5f

1998 Turf 0-1: (12f) (gd) 1998 AW 0-3: (7f, 9f 2) (Equi, Fibr 2)

Useful gelding, has worn blinkers. AW high 40. Becoming disappointing. **K McAuliffe [1-9] K W J McAuliffe.*

GENEROSITY BHB 99f **RR 101f** 5135a[2]

3 ch c Generous (IRE) 11.5f **(82)** - Pageantry (Welsh Pageant) 10f **(65)**
Form - 1341312

Record	**1998 -**	1st:3	2nd:1	3rd:2	Ran:7
	Pre1998 -	1st:1	2nd:0	3rd:0	Ran:3

Win Prizemoney £34,219 *Total Prizemoney* £49,935

Wins	* **1998**	Oct	San Si	(HVY)	L	15f		101	<
	* **1998**	Aug	Goodwo	(GD)	H	14f	86	92	
	* **1998**	May	Sandow	(G-S)	H	11.4f	78	85	
	* 1997	Spt	Hamilt	(GD)		8.3f		69	

1998 Turf 3-7: (11f 1-1, 12f 2, 14f 1-2, 15f 1-2) (hvy 1-1, g-s, gd 2-3, g-f, frm)

Unfurnished, very useful colt, effective 14 to 15f, best at 15f, acts on hvy to g-f, likes right handed tracks. Turf high 101 - 2nd of 7 giving 3lb to Rondan (31 Oct Tesio 15f g-s RF 5135a) - also 1st of 8 getting 10lb from Pasolini (3 Oct San Siro RF 4721a). Improving. He had conditions in his favour when scoring first time up this year, and regained winning form at Glorious Goodwood when stepped up to fourteen furlongs. Previously a strong puller, he settled better during the autumn and won a 15-furlong Listed event at San Siro during October, although he was unable to reverse that form with the third on 3lb worse terms when second in the Italian St Leger. He enjoys coming off a strong pace and is open to further improvement. **P F I Cole [4-10].*

GENEROUS LADY **RR 100f** 3011a[5]

4 ch f Generous (IRE) 11.5f **(82)** - Northern Blossom (CAN) (Snow Knight) 10.3f **(88)**
Form - 0403135

1998 Turf 1-6: (12f 2, 14f 1-3, 16f) (sft 2, gd 1-3, g-f)

Very useful filly, effective 12 to 14f, best at 14f, acts on sft to g-f, has worn blinkers, prefers left handed tracks, likes Leopardstown. Turf high 100 - 5th of 9 giving 14lb to Joleah (18 Jly Leopardstown 14f g-f RF 3011a) - also 1st of 11 giving 9lb to Colm's Rock (1 Jly Bellewstown RF 2598a). Improving. She struggles in Listed events and gained her sole win under a big weight in a modest handicap. She seems best when allowed to bully inferior opposition.

**G A Cusack in IRE [1-6] John McKay (from D P Kelly in IRE [3-9] Nov 1997).*

GENEROUS LIBRA BHB 108f **RR 104f** 5076[1]

4 b g Generous (IRE) 11.5f **(82)** - Come on Rosi (Valiyar) 8.5f **(73)**
Form - 22004511821

Record	**1998 -**	1st:3	2nd:3	3rd:0	Ran:11
	Pre1998 -	1st:1	2nd:1	3rd:3	Ran:9

Win Prizemoney £27,467 *Total Prizemoney* £42,489

Wins	* **1998**	Oct	Newmar	(SFT)	L	8f		104	<
	* **1998**	Spt	Epsom	(GD)	H	10.1f	90	97+	
	* **1998**	Aug	Epsom	(G-F)		10.1f		99+	
	1997	Jun	Beverl	(G-F)		7.5f		88+	

1998 Turf 3-11: (8f 1-2, 10f 2-8, 12f) (g-s 1-2, gd 1-4, g-f 1-4, frm)

Well made, very useful gelding, effective 8 to 10f, best at 8f, acts on g-s to g-f, best on g-f, likes left handed tracks, prefers tight tracks, excels at Epsom, does well at Newmarket. Turf high 104 - 1st of 8 giving 2lb to Generous Rosi (31 Oct Newmarket RF 5076) - also 1st of 6 from Supply And Demand (31 Aug Epsom RF 3985). Consistent. It transpired that he was taking on something a bit tasty when beaten by High-Rise on his reappearance at Pontefract, but he did not find winning form until twice winning over ten furlongs at Epsom in the autumn. Finished the season off in grand style, winning over a mile and on soft ground. He has on occasions not helped his chances by starting slowly, and still looks something of a tricky ride like his half-brother Bin Rosie, but retains plenty of ability and hasn't stopped winning yet.

**J L Dunlop [3-11] Wafic Said (from D R Loder [1-9] Oct 1997).*

GENEROUS PRESENT BHB 24f **RR 28f** 1541[10]

5 ch g Cadeaux Genereux 7.9f **(76)** - Dance Move (Shareef Dancer (USA)) 9.9f **(73)**
Form - 0

Record	**1998 -**	1st:0	2nd:0	3rd:0	Ran:1
	Pre1998 -	1st:2	2nd:0	3rd:1	Ran:18

Win Prizemoney £7,084 *Total Prizemoney* £7,523

Wins	* 1996	Jly	Hamilt	(G-F)	H	8.3f	50	59	<
	* 1996	Jun	Carlis	(FRM)	H	8f	46	51	

1998 Turf 0-1: (10f) (frm)

Little account gelding, has worn blinkers.

**J W Payne [2-20] Mrs J W Payne.*

GENEROUS ROSI BHB 107f **RR 103f** 5076[2]

3 b c Generous (IRE) 11.5f **(82)** - Come on Rosi (Valiyar) 8.5f **(73)**
Form - 22212222

Record	**1998 -**	1st:1	2nd:7	3rd:0	Ran:8
	Pre1998 -	1st:0	2nd:0	3rd:0	Ran:1

Win Prizemoney £5,208 *Total Prizemoney* £38,827

Wins * **1998** Jly Newmar (G-F) 10f 90 <

1998 Turf 1-8: (8f 3, 10f 1-4, 12f) (g-s, gd 2, g-f, frm 1-4)

Very useful colt, effective 8 to 10f, best at 8f, acts on g-s to frm. Turf high 103 - 2nd of 8 getting 2lb from Generous Libra (31 Oct Newmarket 8f g-s RF 5076). Improving. Despite finishing second seven times from eight starts, he is genuine. Lack of finishing pace could be the problem and, with that in mind, it is surprising that connections opted to race him around a mile when his sole win came over 10 furlongs. Take note when he is asked to tackle longer trips.

**J L Dunlop [1-8] Wafic Said (from D R Loder [0-1] Oct 1997).*

GENEROUS TERMS BHB 104f **RR 104f** 3945[2]

3 ch c Generous (IRE) 11.5f **(82)** - Time Charter (Saritamer (USA)) 9.5f **(63)**
Form - 112

Record	**1998 -**	1st:2	2nd:1	3rd:0	Ran:3
	Pre1998 -	1st:0	2nd:0	3rd:0	Ran:1

Win Prizemoney £9,296 *Total Prizemoney* £13,744
Wins *** 1998** Jun Salisb (G-F) 14.1f 104 <
*** 1998** Jun Leices (GD) 11.8f 90
1998 Turf 2-3: (12f 1-1, 14f 1-2) (gd 1-1, g-f, frm 1-1)
Workmanlike, very useful colt. Turf high 104 - 1st of 4 getting 14lb from The Faraway Tree (25 Jun Salisbury RF 2275). Bred to be a top-class stayer, he won his first two starts through grit rather than acceleration. Never likely to be suited by a slow gallop when beaten by Ta-Lim in the March Stakes at Goodwood in August, he is open to a deal of improvement and has a decent race in him.
**H Candy [2-4] H R H Prince Fahd Salman.*

GENEROUS WAYS BHB 69f **RR 71f** 4674[9]
3 ch c Generous (IRE) 11.5f **(82)** - Clara Bow (USA) (Coastal (USA)) 11.5f **(72)**
Form - 0535130
Record 1998 - 1st:1 2nd:0 3rd:2 Ran:7
Win Prizemoney £3,120 *Total Prizemoney* £4,202
Wins * 1998 Aug Redcar (G-F) H 14.1f 65 70 <
1998 Turf 1-7: (8f, 9f, 10f, 12f, 14f 1-2, 16f) (gd 2, g-f 1-3, frm 2)
Workmanlike, above-average colt, effective 14f, acts on g-f. Turf high 71 - also 1st of 6 from Lady Rachel (29 Aug Redcar RF 3969). Has joined Eric Alston. **E A L Dunlop [1-7] Gainsborough Stud.*

GENESIS **RR 79f** 4983[2]
2 ch f Rainbow Quest (USA) 11.2f **(81)** - Talented **(108f)** (Bustino) 10.4f **(64)**
Form - 2
Record 1998 - 1st:0 2nd:1 3rd:0 Ran:1
Win Prizemoney £0 *Total Prizemoney* £1,140
1998 Turf 0-1: (8f) (g-s)
Currently above-average filly. **D R Loder [0-1] Maktoum Al Maktoum.*

GENETIC BHB 56f **RR 64f** 4126[13]
3 b c Syrtos 8.1f **(57)** - Abdera (Ahonoora) 8.1f **(73)**
Form - 067240
Record 1998 - 1st:0 2nd:1 3rd:0 Ran:6
Win Prizemoney £0 *Total Prizemoney* £648
1998 Turf 0-6: (10f 3, 12f 2, 13f) (gd 2, frm 4)
Rangy, average colt, effective 12f, acts on gd. Turf high 64.
**P T Walwyn [0-6] R P & M Berrow.*

GENIUS (IRE) BHB 45f70a **RR 65f 70a** 4574[18]
3 b c Lycius (USA) 8.8f **(71)** - Once in My Life (IRE) (Lomond (USA)) 8.8f **(65)**
Form - 402110405300560000
Record 1998 - 1st:2 2nd:1 3rd:1 Ran:17
Pre1998 - 1st:0 2nd:0 3rd:0 Ran:5
Win Prizemoney £6,238 *Total Prizemoney* £7,932
Wins * 1998 *Feb Lingfi (SLW) H 8f 69 73* <
*** 1998** *Feb Lingfi (SLW) H 8f 64 66*
1998 Turf 0-12: (7f 4, 8f 5, 9f, 10f, 12f) (sft, gd 4, g-f 5, frm 2) 1998 AW 2-5: (7f, 8f 2-3, 10f) (Equi 2-5)
Well made, above-average colt, effective 8f - acts on Equi, has worn blinkers, likes left handed tracks, likes tight tracks. Turf high 65. AW high 73 - 1st of 5 getting 10lb from Eminent (24 Feb Lingfield RF 0354) - also 1st of 12 giving 5lb to Browning (12 Feb Lingfield RF 0275). Improved once put on Equitrack, getting off the mark with an all-out victory in a handicap over a mile in February, and following up against better opposition over the same course and distance. Generally well beaten on turf.
**S Dow [2-18] Normandy Developments (London) (from P F I Cole [0-4] Oct 1997).*

GENOA BHB 85f **RR 79f** 4226[11]
3 b f Zafonic (USA) 9f **(83)**-Yawl **(93f)** (Rainbow Quest(USA)) 10.4f **(75)**
Form - 231800
Record 1998 - 1st:1 2nd:1 3rd:1 Ran:6
Pre1998 - 1st:0 2nd:0 3rd:0 Ran:1
Win Prizemoney £4,310 *Total Prizemoney* £8,735
Wins * 1998 Aug Yarmou (G-F) 11.5f 56++ <
1998 Turf 1-6: (10f 3, 11f 1-1, 12f 2) (gd, g-f 2, frm 1-3)
Scopey, above-average filly, effective 10f, acts on g-f. Turf high 88 (1st run) - 2nd of 5 to Jibe (15 May Newbury 10f g-f RF 1241). Out of a useful racemare, she won a non-event at Yarmouth and has been found wanting in listed company.
**B W Hills [1-7] R D Hollingsworth.*

GENSCHER **RR 30f** 5138[15]
2 b c Cadeaux Genereux 7.9f **(76)** -Marienbad (FR)(Darshaan) 9.9f **(84)**
Form - 00
Record 1998 - 1st:0 2nd:0 3rd:0 Ran:2
1998 Turf 0-2: (7f, 8f) (sft, gd)
Currently very moderate colt. Turf high 30 (began Oct).
**M A Jarvis [0-2] Saif Ali.*

GENTLEMEN (ARG) **RR 118f** 5168a[P]
6 ch h Robin Des Bois (USA) - Elegant Glance (USA) (Loose Cannon (IRE))
Form - 22P
1998 AW 0-3: (9f, 10f 2) (Dirt 3)
Top-class horse, has worn blinkers. AW high 125 (1st run) (began Spt) - 2nd of 3 to Skip Away (19 Spt Belmont Park 9f Dirt RF 4470d). Pulled up with a broken blood-vessel in the Breeders' Cup Classic, his star had begun to look a little on the wane.
**R Mandella in USA [0-4] R D Hubbard.*

GENUINE JOHN (IRE) BHB 51f42a **RR 59f 42a** 4920[9]
5 b g High Estate 10.5f **(66)** - Fiscal Folly (USA) (Foolish Pleasure (USA)) 8.9f **(72)**
Form - 0057332341155271573505O
Record 1998 - 1st:3 2nd:2 3rd:4 Ran:19
Pre1998 - 1st:1 2nd:4 3rd:7 Ran:37
Win Prizemoney £12,569 *Total Prizemoney* £20,732
Wins * 1998 Jly Ripon (G-F) S 8f 59
*** 1998** May Hamilt (GD) H 8.3f 40 50
*** 1998** May Mussel (GD) H 8f 40 48
* 1997 *Mar Southw (STD) H 7f 65 64* <
1998 Turf 3-11: (7f, 8f 3-8, 9f 2) (g-s 2, gd 2-2, g-f 1-5, frm 2) 1998 AW 0-8: (7f, 8f 6, 11f) (Equi, Fibr 7)
Fair gelding, effective 7 to 9f, best at 7f, acts on gd to frm - acts on Fibr, has worn blinkers, likes right handed tracks, and likes Beverley. Turf high 59 - 1st of 18 from Gymcrak Premiere (18 Jly Ripon RF 2934). AW high 43.
**J Parkes [4-44] Mrs G M Z Spink (from K Prendergast in IRE [0-13] Spt 1996).*

GEORDIE LAD BHB 35f22a **RR 33f 22a** 96[10]
4 ch g Tina's Pet 7.4f **(56)** - Edraianthus (Windjammer (USA)) 7f **(59)**
Form - 780
Record 1998 - 1st:0 2nd:0 3rd:0 Ran:2
Pre1998 - 1st:0 2nd:0 3rd:0 Ran:12
1998 AW 0-2: (6f, 7f) (Equi 2)
Light-framed, very moderate gelding, has worn blinkers. AW high 10. Becoming disappointing.
**J A Bennett [0-15] Miller Place Partnership.*

GEORGE (IRE) BHB 70f **RR 90f** 4645[8]
3 b g Distinctly North (USA) 7.4f **(63)** -Heather Lark (Red Alert) 7.6f **(66)**
Form - 75210008
Record 1998 - 1st:1 2nd:1 3rd:0 Ran:8
Pre1998 - 1st:0 2nd:2 3rd:0 Ran:4
Win Prizemoney £4,795 *Total Prizemoney* £6,810
Wins 1998 Jun Cork (G-S) H 6f 75 90 <
1998 Turf 1-8: (5f 2, 6f 1-3, 7f 2, 8f) (g-s 1-3, gd 2, g-f 2, frm)
Useful gelding, effective 5 to 6f, acts on g-s. Turf high 90 - 1st of 9 giving 10lb to Mr Mcken (13 Jun Cork RF 2043a). Becoming disappointing.
**P S Felgate [0-3] Wild Racing (from M Halford in IRE [1-9] Jun 1998).*

GEORGE DILLINGHAM BHB 60f **RR 70f** 4321[18]
8 b g Top Ville 11f **(71)** - Premier Rose (Sharp Edge) 10f **(56)**
Form - 37643D300
Record 1998 - 1st:0 2nd:0 3rd:3 Ran:9
Pre1998 - 1st:2 2nd:6 3rd:3 Ran:21
Win Prizemoney £7,192 *Total Prizemoney* £29,077
Wins 1994 Jly Haydoc (G-F) H 14f 83 85 <
1998 Turf 0-9: (11f, 12f 3, 13f 2, 14f 3) (g-s, gd 5, g-f 3)
Above-average gelding, effective 14f, acts on gd, has worn blinkers. Turf high 76 - 7th of 12 giving 6lb to Opaque (13 May York 14f gd RF 1210).
**Denys Smith [2-25] Jim Blair (from P W Harris [2-15] Oct 1994).*

GEORGETTE (USA) **RR 94f** 4891[1]
2 ch f Geiger Counter (USA) 7.8f **(85)** - Odori (USA) (The Minstrel

(CAN)) 10f **(72)**
Form - 711
Record 1998 - 1st:2 2nd:0 3rd:0 Ran:3
Win Prizemoney £10,100 *Total Prizemoney* £10,100
Wins * **1998** Oct Yarmou (G-S) 6f 94 <
* **1998** Oct Newmar () 6f 84
1998 Turf 2-3: (6f 2-2, 7f) (gd 1-1, g-f 1-2)
Currently useful filly. Turf high 94 (began Spt) - 1st of 6 from Emma Peel (20 Oct Yarmouth RF 4891). She ran over seven on her debut, but was then dropped back to six and won her final two starts at Newmarket and Yarmouth. She looks to have a nice attitude to racing. **J H M Gosden [2-3] Sheikh Mohammed.*

GEORGIA VENTURE BHB 74f RR 85f 4850[28]
4 b f Shirley Heights 12.1f **(76)** - Georgica (USA) (Raise A Native) 11.2f **(69)**
Form - 245050000
Record 1998 - 1st:0 2nd:1 3rd:0 Ran:9
Pre1998 - 1st:2 2nd:2 3rd:2 Ran:10
Win Prizemoney £14,970 *Total Prizemoney* £30,579
Wins * 1997 Spt Goodwo (G-F) H 16f 86 92 <
* 1997 Jly Sandow (G-F) H 14f 72 77
1998 Turf 0-9: (14f 3, 15f, 16f 3, 18f, 20f) (sft 2, gd 4, frm 3)
Neat, useful filly, effective 14 to 16f, acts on sft to frm, best on frm, likes right handed tracks, likes tight tracks. Turf high 95. Becoming disappointing. Twice a winner in staying events in '97, she was runner-up to Further Flight first time out this term, but has been somewhat disappointing since and has failed to make her mark this season. **S P C Woods [2-19] Ian Deane.*

GERMANO BHB 118f RR 121f 4079a[6]
5 b h Generous (IRE) 11.5f **(82)** - Gay Fantastic (Ela-Mana-Mou) 10.1f **(70)**
Form - 13236
Record 1998 - 1st:1 2nd:1 3rd:2 Ran:5
Pre1998 - 1st:3 2nd:3 3rd:0 Ran:11
Win Prizemoney £44,195 *Total Prizemoney* £106,237
Wins * **1998** Apr Sandow (SFT) G3 10f 120 <
* 1997 May Goodwo (GD) L 10f 112
* 1997 May Newmar (GD) 10f 106
* 1995 Oct Doncas (G-F) 7f 92
1998 Turf 1-5: (10f 1-2, 12f 2, 13f) (sft 1-1, gd 3, frm)
Very high-class colt, effective 10 to 12f, best at 10f, acts on sft to frm, excels at Newmarket. Turf high 121 - 2nd of 7 to Posidonas (19 Jun Ascot 12f gd RF 2106) - also 1st of 5 from Garuda (25 Apr Sandown RF 0869). Consistent. Made all to win the Gordon Richards Stakes on his debut, thriving in the very soft ground. Ran a fair race back at Sandown next time and proved he stays a mile and a half with a fine second in the Hardwicke at Ascot. Faster ground and a slow pace conspired against him at Newmarket's July Meeting, and he ran to a similar level of form in the Grand Prix de Deauville. He really needs to get his toe in to be at his best. **G Wragg [4-16] Baron G Von Ullmann.*

GERMIGNANA (ITY) RR 100f 4600a[9]
5 b m Miswaki Tern (USA) - Guida Centrale (Teenoso (USA)) 9.9f **(72)**
Form - 70
1998 Turf 0-2: (10f 2) (hvy, gd)
Very useful filly. Turf high 99. Has been totally outclassed in Group company. **L Camici in ITY [1-7].*

GET A LIFE BHB 25f RR 26f 4408[17]
5 gr m Old Vic 12.8f **(72)** - Sandstream (Sandford Lad) 7.8f **(54)**
Form - 80808572200
Record 1998 - 1st:0 2nd:2 3rd:0 Ran:11
Pre1998 - 1st:0 2nd:0 3rd:1 Ran:8
Win Prizemoney £0 *Total Prizemoney* £2,365
1998 Turf 0-10: (8f 4, 10f 4, 13f 2) (g-s 2, gd 3, g-f 2, frm 3) 1998 AW 0-1: (12f) (Fibr)
Little account filly, effective 12f, acts on g-f, has worn blinkers. Turf high 26.
**M Brittain [0-11] NAJ Racing (from J O'Reilly [0-5] Aug 1997).*

GET STUCK IN (IRE) BHB 82f RR 85f 4937[2]
2 b c Up and At 'em - Shoka (FR) (Kaldoun (FR)) 10.3f **(68)**
Form - 52325022222
Record 1998 - 1st:0 2nd:7 3rd:1 Ran:11
Win Prizemoney £0 *Total Prizemoney* £9,094
1998 Turf 0-11: (5f 7, 6f 4) (g-s 2, gd 5, g-f 3, frm)
Useful colt, effective 5 to 6f, best at 5f, acts on g-s to g-f, best on gd. Turf high 85 - 2nd of 6 giving 4lb to First Musical (20 Jun Ayr 5f g-f RF 2142). Consistent.
**Miss L A Perratt [0-11] Clayton Bigley Partnership Ltd.*

GET THE POINT BHB 55f RR 53f 4760[14]
4 b c Sadler's Wells (USA) 11.3f **(87)** - Tolmi (Great Nephew) 9.9f **(64)**
Form - 0
Record 1998 - 1st:0 2nd:0 3rd:0 Ran:1
Pre1998 - 1st:0 2nd:2 3rd:0 Ran:18
Win Prizemoney £0 *Total Prizemoney* £3,219
1998 Turf 0-1: (8f) (gd)
Strong, fair colt, effective 8f, acts on gd, likes right handed tracks.
**S Gollings [0-1] R L Houlton (from R Hollinshead [0-18] Spt 1997).*

GET TOUGH BHB 21f RR 29f 3939[15]
5 b g Petong 7.6f **(58)** - Mrs Waddilove (Bustino) 10.4f **(64)**
Form - 0000000
Record 1998 - 1st:0 2nd:0 3rd:0 Ran:7
Pre1998 - 1st:1 2nd:1 3rd:1 Ran:14
Win Prizemoney £6,230 *Total Prizemoney* £7,712
Wins 1996 Jun Goodwo (G-F) H 10f 57 60 <
1998 Turf 0-7: (9f, 10f, 11f, 12f 4) (gd, g-f 4, frm 2)
Little account gelding, has worn blinkers. Turf high 36. Inconsistent.
**E A Wheeler [0-8] Michael Merridew (from S Dow [1-14] Spt 1996).*

GEVITY RR 54f 5037[5]
2 b f Kris 10f **(75)** - Cephira (FR) (Abdos) 10f **(77)**
Form - 5
Record 1998 - 1st:0 2nd:0 3rd:0 Ran:1
1998 Turf 0-1: (7f) (g-s)
Currently fair filly. **Mrs J Cecil [0-1] Lord Howard de Walden.*

GHAAZI BHB 73f RR 76f 4845[13]
2 ch c Lahib (USA) 8f **(69)** - Shurooq (USA) (Affirmed (USA)) 9.3f **(79)**
Form - 0430
Record 1998 - 1st:0 2nd:0 3rd:1 Ran:4
Win Prizemoney £0 *Total Prizemoney* £572
1998 Turf 0-4: (7f 2, 8f 2) (g-f 2, frm 2)
Above-average colt. Turf high 76 (began Jly). Steady improvement in maidens. **E A L Dunlop [0-4] Hamdan Al Maktoum.*

GHALI (USA) BHB 65f RR 69f 4817[11]
3 b c Alleged (USA) 11.8f **(81)** - Kareema (USA) (Coastal (USA)) 11.5f **(72)**
Form - 4630
Record 1998 - 1st:0 2nd:0 3rd:1 Ran:4
Pre1998 - 1st:0 2nd:0 3rd:0 Ran:1
Win Prizemoney £0 *Total Prizemoney* £1,773
1998 Turf 0-4: (10f 2, 12f, 16f) (gd 2, g-f, frm)
Scopey, average colt. Turf high 69 (began Spt).
**J L Dunlop [0-5] S Khaled.*

GHALIB (IRE) BHB 99f RR 103f 4992[1]
4 ch c Soviet Star (USA) 8.6f **(74)** - Nafhaat (USA) (Roberto (USA)) 10f **(76)**
Form - 5521
Record 1998 - 1st:1 2nd:1 3rd:0 Ran:4
Pre1998 - 1st:2 2nd:0 3rd:1 Ran:3
Win Prizemoney £13,668 *Total Prizemoney* £18,635
Wins * **1998** Oct Leices (HVY) 7f 103 <
1997 Oct Ascot (HVY) 8f 84
1997 Spt Newbur (SFT) 8f 83
1998 Turf 1-4: (7f 1-2, 8f, 10f) (sft 1-1, g-s, gd, g-f)
Scopey, very useful colt, effective 7 to 10f, acts on sft to g-f. Turf high 103 - 1st of 5 getting 6lb from Wixim (26 Oct Leicester RF 4992). He won a moderate race at Leicester in October, but was difficult to place. Soft ground suits him ideally.
**M P Tregoning [1-4] Hamdan Al Maktoum (from Major W R Hern [2-3] Oct 1997).*

GHITA (IRE) BHB 72f RR 77f 4145[2]
2 ch f Zilzal (USA) 8.5f **(79)** - Sabria (USA) (Miswaki (USA)) 9f **(81)**
Form - 3442
Record 1998 - 1st:0 2nd:1 3rd:1 Ran:4

Win Prizemoney £0 *Total Prizemoney* £1,898
1998 Turf 0-4: (6f 3, 7f) (gd 2, g-f, frm)
Above-average filly. Turf high 77. **J L Dunlop [0-4] R J McAulay.*

GHOST DANCING RR 61+f 4389[9]

2 ch f Lion Cavern (USA) 7.5f **(74)** - Tenderetta (Tender King) 6.8f **(54)**
Form - 0
Record 1998 - 1st:0 2nd:0 3rd:0 Ran:1
1998 Turf 0-1: (7f) (frm)
Currently average filly. **P J Makin [0-1] Skyline Racing Ltd.*

GHOST PATH BHB 42f RR 24f 3394[2]

3 gr f Absalom 7.1f **(56)** - Glide Path (Sovereign Path) 9.3f **(55)**
Form - 802
Record 1998 - 1st:0 2nd:1 3rd:0 Ran:3
Win Prizemoney £0 *Total Prizemoney* £1,040
1998 Turf 0-3: (7f, 8f, 11f) (gd, g-f, frm)
Unfurnished, currently little account filly. Turf high 24.
**C E Brittain [0-3] Mrs R B Skepper.*

GHUROOB (IRE) RR 54f 4983[8]

2 ch f Arazi (USA) 9.2f **(74)** - Tablah (USA) **(77f)** (Silver Hawk (USA)) 8.6f **(70)**
Form - 8
Record 1998 - 1st:0 2nd:0 3rd:0 Ran:1
1998 Turf 0-1: (8f) (g-s)
Currently fair filly. **P T Walwyn [0-1] Hamdan Al Maktoum.*

GIBBON BOY BHB 29f RR 15f 2250[15]

6 ch g Clantime 6.6f **(57)** - Touch O' Spirit (Malt)
Form - 000
Record 1998 - 1st:0 2nd:0 3rd:0 Ran:3
1998 Turf 0-3: (6f, 8f, 10f) (gd 2, frm)
Poor gelding, always wears blinkers. Turf high 15.
**J Neville [0-6] J Neville.*

GI BLUES BHB 60f RR 65f 3317[8]

3 b g Democratic (USA) - My Pretty Niece (Great Nephew) 9.9f **(64)**
Form - 778
Record 1998 - 1st:0 2nd:0 3rd:0 Ran:3
1998 Turf 0-3: (8f 2, 10f) (frm 3)
Workmanlike, currently average gelding. Turf high 65 (began Jly).
**R Simpson [0-3] Antony Charles Brown.*

GIFFOINE BHB 78f RR 78f 4472[6]

2 b f Timeless Times (USA) 6.1f **(56)**-Dear Glenda(Gold Song) 5.5f **(61)**
Form - 41506
Record 1998 - 1st:1 2nd:0 3rd:0 Ran:5
Win Prizemoney £3,557 *Total Prizemoney* £3,802
Wins * **1998** Aug Folkes (G-F) 5f 78 <
1998 Turf 1-5: (5f 1-4, 6f) (gd 2, g-f, frm 1-2)
Above-average filly. Turf high 78 - 1st of 6 getting 7lb from Devon Court (6 Aug Folkestone RF 3399). **S Dow [1-5] J & S Kelly.*

GIFTBOX (USA) BHB 25f31a RR 29f 31a 504[6]

6 b g Halo (USA) 10.9f **(67)** - Arewehavingfunyet (USA) (Sham (USA)) 9.5f **(68)**
Form - 6866
Record 1998 - 1st:0 2nd:0 3rd:0 Ran:4
Pre1998 - 1st:2 2nd:2 3rd:2 Ran:22
Win Prizemoney £5,714 *Total Prizemoney* £9,402
Wins 1996 Jly Hamilt (GD) 8.3f 59 <
1996 May Hamilt (HVY) 9.2f 59 <
1998 Turf 0-1: (12f) (sft) 1998 AW 0-3: (12f 2, 16f) (Fibr 3)
Little account gelding, effective 11f, acted on frm, favoured tight tracks. AW high 29. (DEAD)
**N Bycroft [0-13] G J Allison (from Sir Mark Prescott [2-15] Oct 1996).*

GIFTED BAIRN (IRE) BHB 48f RR 31f 129[7]

3 b f Casteddu 7.4f **(54)** - Latin Mass (Music Boy) 6.8f **(57)**
Form - 067
Record 1998 - 1st:0 2nd:0 3rd:0 Ran:3
Pre1998 - 1st:0 2nd:1 3rd:0 Ran:6
Win Prizemoney £0 *Total Prizemoney* £547
1998 AW 0-3: (5f 2, 6f) (Equi, Fibr 2)
Workmanlike, fair filly, effective 5f - acts on Fibr. AW high 7. Becoming disappointing. **D Nicholls [0-9] J P Hames.*

GIFT OF GOLD BHB 79f72a RR 82f 72a 4985[4]

3 ch c Statoblest 6.4f **(63)** - Ellebanna (Tina's Pet) 6.8f **(59)**
Form - 2034013504
Record 1998 - 1st:1 2nd:1 3rd:2 Ran:10
Pre1998 - 1st:1 2nd:1 3rd:0 Ran:8
Win Prizemoney £9,462 *Total Prizemoney* £22,919
Wins 1998 Jly Lingfi (G-F) H 7f 77 80 <
1997 Nov Mussel (G-S) 7.1f 73
1998 Turf 1-10: (6f, 7f 1-8, 8f) (g-s, gd 5, g-f 2, frm 1-1, hrd)
Decent colt, effective 6 to 8f, best at 7f, acts on gd to frm, best on gd, prefers tight tracks. Turf high 82 - 3rd of 18 getting 8lb from Ascot Cyclone (31 Jly Goodwood 7f gd RF 3229) - also 1st of 11 giving 3lb to Three Angels (11 Jly Lingfield RF 2711). Generally running well last term, narrowly beaten at Glorious Goodwood following his win at Lingfield.
**A Bailey [0-2] Classic Gold (from A Kelleway [1-8] Aug 1998).*

GIFTO WE'RE GONZO BHB 50f53a RR 36f 53a 4387[10]

2 b c Minshaanshu Amad (USA) 11.3f **(53)** - Princess Lucianne (Stanford) 7.9f **(56)**
Form - 00485418860
Record 1998 - 1st:1 2nd:0 3rd:0 Ran:11
Win Prizemoney £1,861 *Total Prizemoney* £1,861
Wins * **1998** *Jly Wolver (STD) S 6f 63* <
1998 Turf 0-3: (5f 2, 7f) (gd, g-f, frm) 1998 AW 1-8: (5f 2, 6f 1-4, 7f 2) (Fibr 1-8)
Average colt, effective 6f - acts on Fibr, mostly wears blinkers (effectively), likes left handed tracks, likes tight tracks. Turf high 36. AW high 63 - 1st of 7 giving 5lb to Torpedo Ray (20 Jly Wolverhampton RF 2968). **Mrs N Macauley [1-11] Frank McEntee.*

GIFT TOKEN BHB 80f RR 83f 3430[S]

4 b f Batshoof 9.5f **(66)** - Visible Form (Formidable (USA)) 9.2f **(63)**
Form - 4136S
Record 1998 - 1st:1 2nd:0 3rd:1 Ran:5
Pre1998 - 1st:1 2nd:0 3rd:1 Ran:11
Win Prizemoney £7,833 *Total Prizemoney* £10,316
Wins * **1998** May Nottin (G-F) 10f 79
* 1997 Jun Salisb (G-F) 8f 80 <
1998 Turf 1-5: (10f 1-2, 11f, 12f 2) (gd 2, g-f 2, frm 1-1)
Scopey, decent filly, effective 8 to 12f, best at 10f, acts on g-s to hrd, best on gd, has worn blinkers, likes Newmarket. Turf high 83 (1st run) - 4th of 24 giving 16lb to Carlys Quest (1 May Newmarket 10f gd RF 0962) - also 1st of 6 getting 3lb from Northern Sun (8 May Nottingham RF 1113). Consistent.
**Major D N Chappell [2-16] Mrs D Ellis.*

GIKO BHB 71f60a RR 71f 60a 4848[2]

4 b g Arazi (USA) 9.2f **(74)** - Gayane (Nureyev (USA)) 8.7f **(78)**
Form - 48346131042
Record 1998 - 1st:2 2nd:1 3rd:2 Ran:9
Pre1998 - 1st:1 2nd:1 3rd:3 Ran:13
Win Prizemoney £12,940 *Total Prizemoney* £28,799
Wins * **1998** Jly Sandow (GD) H 8.1f 63 69
* **1998** Jun Goodwo (G-F) H 9f 55 60
* 1997 Aug Chepst (G-F) 7.1f 71 <
1998 Turf 2-9: (7f 3, 8f 1-5, 9f 1-1) (g-s, gd 1-5, g-f 1-3)
Workmanlike, above-average gelding, effective 7 to 8f, best at 7f, acts on gd to frm. Turf high 71 - 2nd of 30 getting 8lb from Silken Dalliance (17 Oct Newmarket 8f gd RF 4848) - also 1st of 14 getting 8lb from Piped Aboard (15 Jly Sandown RF 2831). He ran pretty well all season, winning handicaps at Goodwood and Sandown, and also ran a blinder when narrowly beaten in the Rothmans Royals Final.
**J R Poulton [3-21] V R V Partnership (from Miss Gay Kelleway [0-1] May 1997).*

GI LA HIGH BHB 59f46a RR 61f 46a 173[5]

5 gr m Rich Charlie 5.9f **(50)** - Gem of Gold (Jellaby) 6.4f **(58)**
Form - 00657685
Record 1998 - 1st:0 2nd:0 3rd:0 Ran:5
Pre1998 - 1st:6 2nd:7 3rd:5 Ran:38
Win Prizemoney £16,644 *Total Prizemoney* £24,610
Wins * 1997 *Mar Wolver (STD) H 5f 59 62* <
* 1997 *Jan Wolver (STD) H 5f 51 52*
1996 *Feb Wolver (STD) H 5f 58 56+*
1995 *Dec Lingfi (STD) C 5f 62* <
1995 *May Southw (STD) S 5f 58*

1995 *Apr Wolver (STD) S* 5f 50t
1998 AW 0-5: (5f 3, 6f 2) (Equi 2, Fibr 3)
Average filly, effective 5 to 6f, best at 5f, acts on gd to frm - acts on AW, has worn blinkers. AW high 42. She is at her best over the minimum on sand, but showed very little in '98.
**M Meade [2-24] Ladyswood Racing Club (from J Berry [4-19] Nov 1996).*

GILDERSLEVE BHB 42f57a **RR 44f 57a** 4048[8]
3 ch f Gildoran 11.6f **(58)** - Fragrant Hackette (Simply Great (FR)) 8.2f **(65)**
Form - 30700808
Record 1998 - 1st:0 2nd:0 3rd:1 Ran:8
Pre1998 - 1st:0 2nd:1 3rd:0 Ran:4
Win Prizemoney £0 *Total Prizemoney* £1,191
1998 Turf 0-6: (7f 3, 8f 3)(gd 2, g-f 2, frm 2)1998 AW 0-2:(7f, 8f) (Fibr 2)
Neat, moderate filly, effective 5f, acts on frm. Turf high 44. AW high 49.
**N E Berry [0-8] Lancing Racing Syndicate (from J W Watts [0-4] Spt 1997).*

GILLING DANCER (IRE) BHB 40f33a **RR 40f 33a** 2093[4]
5 b g Dancing Dissident (USA) 6.8f **(65)** - Rahwah (Northern Baby (CAN)) 11.6f **(71)**
Form - 8500524
Record 1998 - 1st:0 2nd:1 3rd:0 Ran:7
Pre1998 - 1st:1 2nd:0 3rd:0 Ran:19
Win Prizemoney £2,857 *Total Prizemoney* £3,948
Wins * 1996 Jly Carlis (FRM) H 8f 55 56 <
1998 Turf 0-5: (8f, 10f 2, 12f 2) (sft, g-s 2, frm 2) 1998 AW 0-2: (8f, 11f) (Fibr 2)
Moderate gelding, effective 8f, acts on frm, has worn blinkers, likes right handed tracks. Turf high 40. AW high 34.
**P Calver [1-29] Keith Middleton.*

GILLY WEET BHB 40f **RR 26f** 5146[11]
2 b f Almoojid 7f **(36)** - Sindos (Busted) 10.2f **(61)**
Form - 000
Record 1998 - 1st:0 2nd:0 3rd:0 Ran:3
1998 Turf 0-3: (8f 3) (gd, g-f, frm)
Currently little account filly. Turf high 26 (began Spt).
**R Hollinshead [0-3] Mrs G A Weetman.*

GILOU BHB 59f **RR 62f** 4466[5]
2 b f Midyan (USA) 9.9f **(64)** - Lunagraphe (USA) (Time For A Change (USA))
Form - 47405
Record 1998 - 1st:0 2nd:0 3rd:0 Ran:5
Win Prizemoney £0 *Total Prizemoney* £440
1998 Turf 0-4: (5f, 6f, 7f, 8f) (gd, g-f 2, frm) 1998 AW 0-1: (6f) (Fibr)
Average filly. Turf high 62. **C W Fairhurst [0-5] Richmond & Paxton.*

GINGER FLOWER BHB 35f **RR 36f** 434[9]
9 ch m Niniski (USA) 13.2f **(67)** - Monterana (Sallust) 8.4f **(63)**
Form - 0
Record 1998 - 1st:0 2nd:0 3rd:0 Ran:1
Pre1998 - 1st:1 2nd:2 3rd:0 Ran:7
Win Prizemoney £2,070 *Total Prizemoney* £3,382
1998 AW 0-1: (7f) (Fibr)
Fair mare, has worn blinkers. Becoming disappointing.
**G P Kelly [0-4] Miss Jayne Sunley (from N Tinkler [0-1] Jan 1994).*

GINISKI PARK RR 30f 5139[21]
2 b f Risk Me (FR) 8f **(53)** - Georgina Park (Silly Season) 9.7f **(56)**
Form - 00
Record 1998 - 1st:0 2nd:0 3rd:0 Ran:2
1998 Turf 0-2: (5f, 6f) (gd 2)
Currently very moderate filly. Turf high 30 (began Oct).
**J Wharton [0-2] Appleby Lodge Stud.*

GINNER MORRIS BHB 47f **RR 54f** 5098[4]
3 b g Emarati (USA) 6.6f **(63)** - Just Run (IRE) (Runnett) 7f **(59)**
Form - 777007424
Record 1998 - 1st:0 2nd:1 3rd:0 Ran:9
Pre1998 - 1st:0 2nd:0 3rd:0 Ran:1
Win Prizemoney £0 *Total Prizemoney* £666
1998 Turf 0-9: (6f, 7f 3, 8f 4, 10f) (sft, g-s, gd 4, g-f, frm 2)
Lengthy, fair gelding, effective 8f, acts on g-s. Turf high 62. Consistent. **C B B Booth [0-10] Mrs Marian Rogers.*

GINNIESHOPE BHB 32f **RR 22f** 1570[10]
3 ch f Never so Bold 7.1f **(62)** - Sweet Home (Home Guard (USA)) 9.3f **(66)**
Form - 80
Record 1998 - 1st:0 2nd:0 3rd:0 Ran:2
Pre1998 - 1st:0 2nd:0 3rd:0 Ran:3
1998 Turf 0-1: (8f) (frm) 1998 AW 0-1: (5f) (Fibr)
Workmanlike, little account filly. **S G Knight [0-5] Mrs Ginny Withers.*

GINO'S SPIRITS BHB 79f **RR 80f** 4845[5]
2 ch f Perugino (USA) - Rising Spirits (Cure The Blues (USA)) 9.5f **(63)**
Form - 04130255
Record 1998 - 1st:1 2nd:1 3rd:1 Ran:8
Win Prizemoney £2,827 *Total Prizemoney* £4,516
Wins * 1998 Aug Bright (FRM) 7f 73 <
1998 Turf 1-8: (5f 2, 7f 1-4, 8f 2) (gd, g-f 1-2, frm 5)
Decent filly, effective 7 to 8f, best at 7f, acts on gd to frm, best on g-f. Turf high 80 - 5th of 20 getting 13lb from Fair Flight (16 Oct Newmarket 8f g-f RF 4845) - also 1st of 9 giving 2lb to Any Moore (5 Aug Brighton RF 3362). She seemed to appreciate the longer trip when scoring over seven at Brighton in August. Fair efforts since. **C E Brittain [1-8] R N Khan.*

GINZBOURG BHB 51f **RR 53f** 4416[3]
4 b g Ferdinand (USA) 9.6f **(82)** - Last Request (Dancers Image (USA)) 9.3f **(71)**
Form - 600000883
Record 1998 - 1st:0 2nd:0 3rd:1 Ran:9
Pre1998 - 1st:1 2nd:1 3rd:0 Ran:7
Win Prizemoney £2,936 *Total Prizemoney* £4,914
Wins 1996 Oct Folkes (G-S) 6.9f 81 <
1998 Turf 0-9: (7f 2, 8f 2, 10f 4, 11f) (hvy, sft, gd 4, g-f 2, frm)
Scopey, fair gelding, effective 10f, acts on g-f, has worn blinkers. Turf high 75. Struggled in handicap company in '97, and over hurdles, but did run a creditable race in the Lincoln on his reappearance. He has disappointed since however.
**R J O'Sullivan [0-12] R O S Racing (from J L Dunlop [1-7] Jly 1997).*

GIPSY MOTH BHB 97f **RR 91df** 4826a[2]
3 b f Efisio 7.7f **(69)** - Rock the Boat (Slip Anchor) 9.8f **(73)**
Form - 050108512
Record 1998 - 1st:2 2nd:1 3rd:0 Ran:9
Pre1998 - 1st:2 2nd:0 3rd:0 Ran:8
Win Prizemoney £17,739 *Total Prizemoney* £24,496
Wins * 1998 Spt Cologn (SFT) L 5f 79?
*** 1998** Jun Newmar (GD) H 5f 84 91 <
* 1997 Aug Haydoc (G-F) H 5f 84 87
* 1997 Jly Yarmou (G-F) 5.2f 82+
1998 Turf 2-9: (5f 2-8, 6f) (sft 1-2, gd 2, g-f 1-3, frm 2)
Workmanlike, useful filly, effective 5f, acts on g-f to frm, best on g-f. Turf high 91 - 1st of 8 getting 1lb from Brimstone (26 Jun Newmarket RF 2316). Dropped in class to win at Newmarket in June, having been found out in better company. She won a Listed race in Germany in September, and was runner-up in a similar event, but they must have been modest events judging by his form in this country. **B J Meehan [4-17].*

GIPSY PRINCESS BHB 44f41a **RR 55f 41a** 899[13]
4 b f Prince Daniel (USA) 11.4f **(46)** - Gypsy's Barn Rat (Balliol) 5f **(43)**
Form - 620860
Record 1998 - 1st:0 2nd:1 3rd:0 Ran:6
Pre1998 - 1st:1 2nd:2 3rd:3 Ran:22
Win Prizemoney £3,444 *Total Prizemoney* £9,089
Wins * 1996 Spt Catter (G-F) H 7f 62 61 <
1998 Turf 0-1: (6f) (g-s) 1998 AW 0-5: (6f, 7f, 8f 3) (Fibr 5)
Leggy, fair filly, effective 6 to 8f, best at 7f, acts on gd to frm, often wears blinkers. AW high 37. **M W Easterby [1-28] T A Hughes.*

GIPSY ROSE LEE (IRE) BHB 100f **RR 96f** 3101[2]
2 b f Marju (IRE) 9.2f **(76)**-Rainstone (Rainbow Quest (USA)) 10.4f **(75)**
Form - 112
Record 1998 - 1st:2 2nd:1 3rd:0 Ran:3
Win Prizemoney £8,118 *Total Prizemoney* £17,118
Wins * 1998 Jun Windso (GD) 6f 84 <

* 1998 Jun Sandow (G-S) 5f 78
1998 Turf 2-3: (5f 1-1, 6f 1-2) (gd 1-1, g-f, frm 1-1)
Currently very useful filly. Turf high 96 - 2nd of 6 to Mythical Girl (25 Jly Ascot 6f g-f RF 3101). Narrow winner of what looked a fairly moderate maiden by Sandown standards, she again won narrowly on her second start though it looked a slightly better race at Windsor. A good second in the Princess Margaret, she obviously knows how to battle, but was not seen out again and is open to improvement next term. **B J Meehan [2-3] Mrs K J Crangle.*

GIPSY SPIRIT RR 29f 3961[19]

2 b f Alhijaz 7.7f **(57)** - What A Pet (Mummy's Pet) 7.7f **(60)**
Form - 0
Record 1998 - 1st:0 2nd:0 3rd:0 Ran:1
1998 Turf 0-1: (6f) (g-f)
Currently little account filly. **T W Donnelly [0-1] Mrs Dianne Abel.*

GIRL OF MY DREAMS (IRE) BHB 43f32a RR 42f 32a 2335[1]

5 b m Marju (IRE) 9.2f **(76)** - Stylish Girl (USA) (Star de Naskra (USA)) 9.7f **(65)**
Form - 51807600731
Record 1998 - 1st:1 2nd:0 3rd:1 Ran:8
Pre1998 - 1st:1 2nd:0 3rd:0 Ran:10
Win Prizemoney £5,607 *Total Prizemoney* £6,175
Wins * 1998 Jun Doncas (GD) H 7f 38 42 <
** 1997 Nov Wolver (STD) H 7f 35 42* <
1998 Turf 1-3:(7f 1-1, 8f 2)(gd 1-2, g-f)1998 AW 0-5:(7f, 8f 3, 9f) (Fibr 5)
Moderate filly, effective 7 to 8f, best at 7f, acts on gd - acts on Fibr. Turf high 42 - 3rd of 11 getting 20lb from Scene (16 Jun Thirsk 8f gd RF 2022) - also 1st of 19 giving 3lb to Serape (27 Jun Doncaster RF 2335). AW high 31. **M J Heaton-Ellis [2-18] Miss V H Owen.*

GIRTON'S PRIDE RR 46f 5073[7]

2 b g Superlative 8.8f **(57)** - Gay Twenties (Lord Gayle (USA)) 8.8f **(62)**
Form - 07
Record 1998 - 1st:0 2nd:0 3rd:0 Ran:2
1998 Turf 0-2: (8f 2) (gd 2)
Currently moderate gelding. Turf high 45 (began Oct).
**C Drew [0-2] Peter Gordon.*

GIVE AN INCH (IRE) BHB 59f RR 61f 4674[12]

3 b f Inchinor 8.9f **(64)** - Top Heights (High Top) 10.2f **(67)**
Form - 650803712182180
Record 1998 - 1st:3 2nd:2 3rd:1 Ran:15
Win Prizemoney £10,098 *Total Prizemoney* £12,256
Wins * 1998 Spt Ayr (G-S) H 17.5f 51 61 <
*** 1998** Aug Ayr (G-S) H 15f 44 53+
*** 1998** Jly Redcar (G-F) S 11f 45
1998 Turf 3-15: (6f, 7f 2, 8f 3, 9f, 11f 1-1, 12f, 14f 2, 15f 1-1, 16f 2, 17f 1-1) (sft 1-1, gd 1-8, g-f 3, frm 2, hrd 1-1)
Leggy, average filly, effective 12 to 17f, acts on sft to frm, prefers left handed tracks, likes tight tracks. Turf high 61 - 1st of 13 getting 14lb from Sharaf (18 Spt Ayr RF 4355) - also 1st of 10 getting 28lb from Northern Motto (11 Aug Ayr RF 3522).
**W Storey [3-15] Black Type Racing.*

GIVE ME A RING (IRE) BHB 89f86a RR 93f 86a 4102[7]

5 b g Be My Guest (USA) 10.2f **(66)** - Annsfield Lady (Red Sunset) 8.2f **(63)**
Form - 07020257
Record 1998 - 1st:0 2nd:2 3rd:0 Ran:8
Pre1998 - 1st:4 2nd:2 3rd:1 Ran:14
Win Prizemoney £26,413 *Total Prizemoney* £42,351
Wins * 1997 May York (GD) H 10.4f 86 94 <
* 1996 Aug Ripon (G-F) H 9f 77 80
* 1996 Jly York (GD) H 7.9f 70 76
* 1996 Jly Beverl (G-F) H 8.5f 70 70
1998 Turf 0-8: (8f, 10f 6, 12f) (gd 3, g-f, frm 4)
Useful gelding, effective 8 to 10f, best at 10f, acts on gd to frm, best on frm, has worn blinkers. Turf high 93 - 2nd of 12 getting 6lb from Supreme Sound (19 Aug York 10f frm RF 3752). A useful handicapper when on song, he ran well when allowed to bowl along in front at Newmarket in July and was a good second at York in August, but he did not manage to win a race and turned in some moderate performances too. **C W Thornton [4-22] Guy Reed.*

GLADY BEAUTY (GER) RR 101f 4602a[3]

3 b f Big Shuffle (USA) - Glady Sum (GER) (Surumu (GER)) 10f **(83)**
Form - 33
1998 Turf 0-2: (8f 2) (sft 2)
Currently very useful filly. Turf high 101 - 3rd of 12 getting 5lb from Autriche (27 Spt Cologne 8f sft RF 4602a). She finished a distant third in the German 1,000 Guineas, but could not get any closer in Listed company during the autumn. **U Ostmann in GER [0-2].*

GLAIZE (USA) BHB 77f RR 82f 2114[4]

3 b c Gilded Time (USA) 7f **(76)** - Courtly Native (USA) (Our Native (USA)) 11.2f **(63)**
Form - 614
Record 1998 - 1st:1 2nd:0 3rd:0 Ran:3
Win Prizemoney £3,704 *Total Prizemoney* £3,934
Wins * 1998 Jun Thirsk (GD) 8f 82 <
1998 Turf 1-3: (8f 1-2, 9f) (gd, g-f 1-1, frm)
Rangy, currently decent colt. Turf high 82 - 1st of 6 from Harmony (1 Jun Thirsk RF 1631). **E A L Dunlop [1-3] Maktoum Al Maktoum.*

GLAMIS (USA) RR 100f 4830a[3]

2 b c Silver Hawk (USA) 11.2f **(85)** - Glaze (USA) (Mr Prospector (USA)) 8.8f **(78)**
Form - 31223
Record 1998 - 1st:1 2nd:2 3rd:2 Ran:5
Win Prizemoney £4,381 *Total Prizemoney* £55,912
Wins * 1998 Aug Goodwo (G-F) 7f 92+ <
1998 Turf 1-5: (7f 1-2, 8f 3) (g-s, gd 3, g-f 1-1)
Very useful colt. Turf high 100 (began Aug) - 3rd of 7 to Way of Light (11 Oct Longchamp 8f g-s RF 4830a) - also 1st of 5 from El Nahrawan (29 Aug Goodwood RF 3951). He enjoyed a confidence-boosting win at Goodwood before getting involved in two terrific scraps with Mutaahab, both of which he lost by half a length. They finished clear of the remainder when dominating the Group Two Royal Lodge Stakes and, whereas the winner was put by for the season, Glamis was called into action again in the Grand Criterium at Longchamp. A battling third on heavy ground there, he is a notably tough individual and deserves to win a valuable prize.
**J H M Gosden [1-5] Sheikh Mohammed.*

GLAMORGAN (IRE) BHB 36f RR 44f 2727[3]

3 b g Petardia 8.2f **(58)** - Presentable (Sharpen Up) 8.3f **(67)**
Form - 000003
Record 1998 - 1st:0 2nd:0 3rd:1 Ran:6
Pre1998 - 1st:0 2nd:0 3rd:0 Ran:3
Win Prizemoney £0 *Total Prizemoney* £371
1998 Turf 0-5: (6f, 10f 2, 11f, 12f) (g-s, gd, g-f 2, frm) 1998 AW 0-1: (12f) (Fibr)
Leggy, moderate gelding. Turf high 44. Consistent.
**M C Pipe [0-5] Elite Racing Club (from C A Dwyer [0-4] Mar 1998).*

GLANCE (IRE) RR 84+f 2361[1]

3 b c Ela-Mana-Mou 12.7f **(72)** - Cursory Look (USA) (Nijinsky (CAN)) 10.3f **(77)**
Form - 41
Record 1998 - 1st:1 2nd:0 3rd:0 Ran:2
Win Prizemoney £3,582 *Total Prizemoney* £3,815
Wins * 1998 Jun Doncas (GD) 12f 84+ <
1998 Turf 1-2: (12f 1-2) (gd, g-f 1-1)
Scopey, currently decent colt. Turf high 84 - 1st of 10 from Brigade Charge (28 Jun Doncaster RF 2361).
**L M Cumani [1-2] Sheikh Mohammed.*

GLANWYDDEN (IRE) BHB 83f RR 81f 5015[3]

2 ch c Grand Lodge (USA) - Brush Away (Ahonoora) 8.1f **(73)**
Form - 61430333
Record 1998 - 1st:1 2nd:0 3rd:4 Ran:8
Win Prizemoney £3,296 *Total Prizemoney* £6,731
Wins * 1998 Jly Beverl (GD) 7.5f 81 <
1998 Turf 1-8: (5f, 7f 1-7) (sft, gd, g-f 1-2, frm 4)
Decent colt, effective 7f, acts on gd to frm. Turf high 81 - 1st of 6 giving 5lb to Bollin Roberta (4 Jly Beverley RF 2522). Consistent.
**J Berry [1-8] Lord Mostyn.*

GLASSHOUSE BHB 85a RR 75f 57[12]

4 b c Thatching 7.8f **(69)**- Isle Of Glass(USA) (Affirmed (USA)) 9.3f **(79)**
Form - 0

Record 1998 - 1st:0 2nd:0 3rd:0 Ran:1
Pre1998 - 1st:1 2nd:0 3rd:0 Ran:3
Win Prizemoney £4,110 *Total Prizemoney* £4,110
Wins 1997 May Naas (G-S) 6f 75 <
1998 AW 0-1: (7f) (Fibr)
Above-average colt, has worn blinkers.
**R D E Woodhouse [0-2] Miss C Foster (from J Oxx in IRE [1-3] Jun 1997).*

GLASS RIVER BHB 50f **RR 40f** 2370[9]
3 b c Ardkinglass 5f **(64)** - Rion River (IRE) (Taufan (USA)) 7f **(57)**
Form - 060
Record 1998 - 1st:0 2nd:0 3rd:0 Ran:2
Pre1998 - 1st:0 2nd:0 3rd:1 Ran:10
Win Prizemoney £0 *Total Prizemoney* £259
1998 Turf 0-2: (5f 2) (gd, frm)
Light-framed, moderate colt, effective 5f, acts on frm. Turf high 40. Becoming disappointing.
**P D Evans [0-12] Exors of the Late R F F Mason.*

GLASTONBURY (IRE) **RR 62f** 4991[3]
2 b g Common Grounds 8.1f **(66)** - Harmonious (Sharrood (USA)) 10.5f **(72)**
Form - 74306023
Record 1998 - 1st:0 2nd:1 3rd:2 Ran:8
Win Prizemoney £0 *Total Prizemoney* £2,741
1998 Turf 0-8: (5f 2, 6f 2, 7f 4) (sft, g-s 3, gd, g-f, frm 2)
Above-average gelding, effective 7f, acts on g-s. Turf high 62.
**M R Channon [0-8] P D Savill.*

GLEAMING HILL (USA) BHB 89f **RR 88f** 4507[3]
3 b c Marquetry (USA) 10f **(88)** - Mountain Sunshine (USA) (Vaguely Noble) 10.1f **(72)**
Form - 323113
Record 1998 - 1st:2 2nd:1 3rd:3 Ran:6
Pre1998 - 1st:0 2nd:0 3rd:1 Ran:1
Win Prizemoney £12,622 *Total Prizemoney* £17,010
Wins * 1998 Spt Yarmou (G-S) H 10.1f 77 88 <
*** 1998** Spt Leices (G-S) 10f 80
1998 Turf 2-6: (7f, 8f, 10f 2-4) (sft, gd 1-3, g-f 1-2)
Scopey, useful colt, effective 8 to 10f, best at 10f, acts on gd to g-f, best on gd. Turf high 88 - 3rd of 5 giving 6lb to Diamond White (26 Spt Nottingham 10f gd RF 4507) - also 1st of 17 giving 11lb to My Learned Friend (16 Spt Yarmouth RF 4314). In the frame in modest maidens, he found his form in the autumn, winning at Leicester and Yarmouth, and seems to be improving.
**Sir Michael Stoute [2-7] Maktoum Al Maktoum.*

GLENFIELD HEIGHTS **RR 57f** 1691[3]
3 b g Golden Heights 7.1f **(50)** - Cleeveland Lady (Turn Back The Time (USA))
Form - 53
Record 1998 - 1st:0 2nd:0 3rd:1 Ran:2
Win Prizemoney £0 *Total Prizemoney* £318
1998 Turf 0-2: (12f, 14f) (gd, g-f)
Leggy, currently fair gelding. Turf high 57.
**W G M Turner [0-2] Mrs Philomena Reich.*

GLENMEAD BHB 85f **RR 79f** 3460[1]
3 ch c Polish Precedent (USA) 9f **(73)** - Fair Country (Town And Country) 8.1f **(68)**
Form - 7331
Record 1998 - 1st:1 2nd:0 3rd:2 Ran:4
Win Prizemoney £5,420 *Total Prizemoney* £6,599
Wins * 1998 Aug Ascot (G-F) 12f 79 <
1998 Turf 1-4: (10f 2, 12f 1-2) (g-f 1-2, frm 2)
Leggy, above-average colt. Turf high 79 - 1st of 4 from Gedy Red (8 Aug Ascot RF 3460). He got off the mark by taking a four-runner event at Ascot in August, though it looked a poor race for that track.
**A C Stewart [1-4] Robin Paterson.*

GLEN OGIL BHB 40f **RR 41f** 3677[7]
4 ch g Thatching 7.8f **(69)** - Cormorant Bay (Don't Forget Me) 8.3f **(74)**
Form - 15073867
Record 1998 - 1st:1 2nd:0 3rd:1 Ran:8
Pre1998 - 1st:0 2nd:2 3rd:1 Ran:6
Win Prizemoney £2,539 *Total Prizemoney* £5,228
Wins * 1998 Apr Hamilt (HVY) H 8.3f 47 56 <
1998 Turf 1-8: (8f 1-6, 9f 2) (sft 1-1, g-s 3, gd 2, frm 2)
Workmanlike, moderate gelding, effective 6 to 9f, acted on sft to g-f, best on g-f. Turf high 56 (1st run) - 1st of 8 getting 11lb from Stormless (4 Apr Hamilton RF 0563). (DEAD)
**M R Channon [1-13] W A Harrison-Allan (from I A Balding [0-1] Aug 1997).*

GLEN PARKER (IRE) BHB 70f **RR 82f** 4708[13]
5 ch h Bluebird (USA) 7.9f **(71)** - Trina's Girl (Nonoalco (USA)) 8.5f **(66)**
Form - 57460
Record 1998 - 1st:0 2nd:0 3rd:0 Ran:5
Pre1998 - 1st:1 2nd:2 3rd:1 Ran:7
Win Prizemoney £3,647 *Total Prizemoney* £7,266
Wins * 1996 Aug Pontef (G-F) 8f 73 <
1998 Turf 0-5: (8f, 10f 4) (gd, g-f 2, frm 2)
Decent colt, effective 8 to 10f, acts on g-f, has worn blinkers. Turf high 82.
**H R A Cecil [1-12] Angus Dundee Plc.*

GLENSTAL LAD BHB 35f41a **RR 37f 41a** 4661[14]
3 b c Nomination 7.3f **(57)**- Glenstal Princess(Glenstal (USA))10.1f **(64)**
Form - 0665777400070
Record 1998 - 1st:0 2nd:0 3rd:0 Ran:12
Pre1998 - 1st:0 2nd:0 3rd:2 Ran:5
Win Prizemoney £0 *Total Prizemoney* £756
1998 Turf 0-9: (6f 7, 7f, 8f) (sft, gd 4, g-f 3, frm) 1998 AW 0-3: (5f, 6f 2) (Fibr 3)
Neat, very moderate colt. Turf high 52. AW high 38.
**R Hollinshead [0-17] J D Graham.*

GLIDE PATH (USA) BHB 46f **RR 7f** 2515[7]
9 ch g Stalwart (USA) 11.8f **(95)** - Jolly Polka (CAN) (Nice Dancer (CAN)) 11.5f **(85)**
Form - 0073566160807
Record 1998 - 1st:1 2nd:0 3rd:1 Ran:10
Pre1998 - 1st:9 2nd:6 3rd:3 Ran:55
Win Prizemoney £120,256 *Total Prizemoney* £134,944
Wins * 1998 *Feb Southw (STD) H 16f 42 51+*
1995 Aug Taby (GD) G3 12f 93
1994 Spt Haydoc (GD) H 11.9f 93 98 <
1994 Jly Ripon (G-F) H 12.3f 92 97
1994 Jly Haydoc (G-F) H 11.9f 85 91
1998 Turf 0-2: (11f, 13f) (g-f, frm) 1998 AW 1-8: (12f 4, 13f, 16f 1-3) (Equi 4, Fibr 1-4)
Fair gelding, effective 12 to 16f - acts on AW, has worn blinkers. Turf high 7. AW high 51 - 1st of 12 getting 5lb from Notation (13 Feb Southwell RF 0283). Becoming disappointing. He had been a fine servant to connections, but has turned into a bit of a monkey, especially when amateur-ridden. However, two miles on the Southwell Fibresand and Darryll Holland in the saddle brought about a complete transformation in a handicap there in February, as he cruised home to victory. The novelty did not last long however. **J R Jenkins [1-20] B Shirazi (from J W Hills [9-50] Spt 1996).*

GLIDER (IRE) BHB 69a **RR 49f** 1803[12]
3 b f Silver Kite (USA) 10.2f **(51)**-Song of The Glens (Horage) 10.3f **(61)**
Form - 4241340
Record 1998 - 1st:1 2nd:1 3rd:1 Ran:6
Pre1998 - 1st:0 2nd:0 3rd:0 Ran:1
Win Prizemoney £1,906 *Total Prizemoney* £3,384
Wins * 1998 *Jan Lingfi (STD) H 8f 61 65* <
1998 Turf 0-1: (8f) (gd) 1998 AW 1-5: (7f 2, 8f 1-2, 10f) (Equi 1-4, Fibr)
Light-framed, average filly, effective 8f - acts on Equi. AW high 69 - also 1st of 12 giving 4lb to Comeoutofthefog (31 Jan Lingfield RF 0194). She attracted the attention of the stewards when fourth in a maiden on the Lingfield Equitrack in January, as she appeared to be given a very easy time. She confirmed that impression when winning an apprentice handicap at the same track later that month over a mile, but may not have stayed ten furlongs next time.
**N P Littmoden [1-5] Paul Stringer (from C W Thornton [0-2] Jan 1998).*

GLIMMERING HOPE (IRE) BHB 32f22a **RR 26f 22a** 317[10]
4 b g Petorius 8f **(66)** - Angevin (English Prince) 10.1f **(61)**
Form - 0460
Record 1998 - 1st:0 2nd:0 3rd:0 Ran:4
Pre1998 - 1st:0 2nd:0 3rd:0 Ran:4
1998 AW 0-4: (5f 3, 6f) (Equi, Fibr 3)
Workmanlike, little account gelding. AW high 18.

**D Shaw [0-6] J S Lammiman (from Miss J F Craze [0-3] Mar 1997).*

GLITTER PRINCESS BHB 44f **RR 48f** 3840[8]

3 ch f Prince Sabo 6.6f **(64)** - Maritime Lady (USA) (Polish Navy (USA)) 8f **(67)**
Form - 07008

Record	**1998 -**	1st:0	2nd:0	3rd:0	Ran:5
	Pre1998 -	1st:0	2nd:0	3rd:0	Ran:4

Win Prizemoney £0 *Total Prizemoney* £495
1998 Turf 0-5: (5f 2, 6f 3) (g-f, frm 4)
Neat, moderate filly. Turf high 48. Becoming disappointing.
**N E Berry [0-5] Hampton Mix Racing Partnership (from Major D Chappell [0-4] Oct 1997).*

GLOBAL DRAW (IRE) RR 51f 5139[19]

2 ch c Be My Guest (USA) 10.2f **(66)** - Almost A Lady (IRE) (Entitled)
Form - 50

Record	**1998 -**	1st:0	2nd:0	3rd:0	Ran:2

1998 Turf 0-2: (6f, 7f) (g-s, gd)
Currently fair colt. Turf high 51 (began Oct).
**M A Jarvis [0-2] Mrs B Sadowska.*

GLOBE RAIDER BHB 40f **RR 25f** 2903[5]

3 b g Safawan 6.6f **(60)** - Polola (Aragon) 8.1f **(60)**
Form - 485

Record	**1998 -**	1st:0	2nd:0	3rd:0	Ran:3
	Pre1998 -	1st:0	2nd:0	3rd:0	Ran:2

1998 Turf 0-3: (5f, 7f, 8f) (gd 3)
Scopey, little account gelding. Turf high 25.
**J J O'Neill [0-5] G & P Barker Ltd/Globe Engineering.*

GLORIOUSA BHB 60f **RR 58f** 4761[17]

2 b f Minshaanshu Amad (USA) 11.3f **(53)** - Lahin (Rainbow Quest (USA)) 10.4f **(75)**
Form - 600

Record	**1998 -**	1st:0	2nd:0	3rd:0	Ran:3

1998 Turf 0-3: (7f 3) (gd, g-f 2)
Currently fair filly. Turf high 58 (began Spt).
**M D I Usher [0-3] Vernon D'Costa.*

GLOROSIA (FR) BHB 106f **RR 111f** 4199[2]

3 ch f Bering 9.6f **(80)** - Golden Sea (FR) (Saint Cyrien (FR)) 8.4f **(80)**
Form - 352

Record	**1998 -**	1st:0	2nd:1	3rd:1	Ran:3
	Pre1998 -	1st:2	2nd:0	3rd:1	Ran:3

Win Prizemoney £96,767 *Total Prizemoney* £107,368

Wins							
* 1997	Spt	Ascot	(G-F)	G1	8f	111	<
* 1997	Jly	Newmar	(G-S)		7f	76+	

1998 Turf 0-3: (10f, 12f 2) (gd 3)
Strong, Group-class filly, effective 8 to 12f, acts on gd to g-f, best on gd. Turf high 107 (1st run) - 3rd of 7 to Another Dancer (21 Jun Longchamp 12f gd RF 2289a). Winner of the Fillies' Mile at two, she missed the Oaks due to a training setback, but ran quite well in a Group Two at Longchamp on her return to action as a three-year-old. After a very poor run in the Irish Oaks, she has failed to live up to expectations and is one to file under 'disappointing'.
**L M Cumani [2-6] Robert Smith.*

GLORY OF GROSVENOR (IRE) BHB 72f **RR 65f** 4394[11]

3 ch g Caerleon (USA) 10.9f **(79)** - Abury (IRE) (Law Society (USA)) 9.9f **(70)**
Form - 600

Record	**1998 -**	1st:0	2nd:0	3rd:0	Ran:3
	Pre1998 -	1st:0	2nd:1	3rd:0	Ran:2

Win Prizemoney £0 *Total Prizemoney* £1,902
1998 Turf 0-3: (9f, 12f 2) (sft, g-f, frm)
Scopey, average gelding. Turf high 65.
**P W Chapple-Hyam [0-5] R E Sangster.*

GLOW RR 67f 4823[11]

2 br f Alzao (USA) 9.8f **(73)** - Shimmer (Bustino) 10.4f **(64)**
Form - 0

Record	**1998 -**	1st:0	2nd:0	3rd:0	Ran:1

1998 Turf 0-1: (8f) (frm)
Currently average filly. **Lord Huntingdon [0-1] The Queen.*

GLOW FORUM BHB 60f71a **RR 60f 71a** 5069[8]

7 b m Kalaglow 11.2f **(67)** - Beau's Delight (USA) (Lypheor) 12f **(71)**
Form - 660018

Record	**1998 -**	1st:1	2nd:0	3rd:0	Ran:5
	Pre1998 -	1st:12	2nd:5	3rd:7	Ran:50

Win Prizemoney £35,408 *Total Prizemoney* £43,405

Wins								
* **1998**	Oct	Folkes	(SFT)	H	12f	55	60	
* 1997	Oct	Folkes	(GD)	H	12f	56	60	
* 1997	Jly	Chepst	(G-F)	H	12.1f	56	59	
* 1997	Jun	Lingfi	(SFT)	H	11.5f	52	54	
* 1997	*May*	*Wolver*	*(STD)*	*H*	*12f*	*73*	*75*	<
* 1997	*Jan*	*Lingfi*	*(STD)*	*H*	*12f*	*70*	*74*	
* 1996	*Oct*	*Wolver*	*(STD)*	*H*	*12f*	*67*	*72*	
* 1996	*Spt*	*Wolver*	*(STD)*	*H*	*12f*	*56*	*62*	
* 1996	*Aug*	*Southw*	*(STD)*	*H*	*12f*	*48*	*53*	
* 1996	*Jly*	*Southw*	*(STD)*	*H*	*12f*	*39*	*49*	
* 1996	May	Salisb	(SFT)	CH	12f	34	43	
1995	Aug	Bright	(FRM)	SH	11.9f	29	34	
1995	*Jly*	*Lingfi*	*(STD)*	*SH*	*13f*	*26*	*29*	

1998 Turf 1-4: (11f, 12f 1-3) (g-s 1-1, gd 2, g-f)1998 AW 0-1:(12f) (Equi)
Above-average mare, effective 12f - acts on AW, best on Fibr, likes left handed tracks, prefers tight tracks, does well at Wolverhampton and Folkestone and Lingfield. Turf high 60. Inconsistent. At her best she has been most effective in twelve-furlong handicaps on the smaller southern tracks. She has been a credit to her trainer.
**L MontagueHall [11-31] Miss J D Anstee & Partners (from G L Moore [2-24] Dec 1995).*

GLOWING BHB 66f **RR 68f** 3898[1]

3 b f Chilibang 7f **(55)** - Juliet Bravo (Glow (USA)) 6.7f **(71)**
Form - 0324321

Record	**1998 -**	1st:1	2nd:2	3rd:2	Ran:7

Win Prizemoney £2,070 *Total Prizemoney* £4,835

Wins						
* **1998**	Aug	Folkes	(G-F)	6f	67	<

1998 Turf 1-7: (6f 1-7) (sft, gd, g-f 1-4, frm)
Scopey, average filly, effective 6f, acts on gd to frm, best on g-f. Turf high 68 - 2nd of 13 getting 5lb from The Woodcock (12 Aug Nottingham 6f gd RF 3582) - also 1st of 6 getting 5lb from Loch Laird (27 Aug Folkestone RF 3898).
**J R Fanshawe [1-7] Peters Friends.*

GLOWING PATH BHB 23f44a **RR 20f 44a** 3038[7]

8 b g Kalaglow 11.2f **(67)** - Top Tina (High Top) 10.2f **(67)**
Form - 0707

Record	**1998 -**	1st:0	2nd:0	3rd:0	Ran:4
	Pre1998 -	1st:2	2nd:2	3rd:0	Ran:19

Win Prizemoney £5,081 *Total Prizemoney* £6,491
1998 Turf 0-4: (8f, 10f, 12f, 17f) (gd 2, g-f, frm)
Moderate gelding, often wears blinkers. Turf high 32.
**R J Hodges [6-53] P Slade (from C J Hill [2-10] Aug 1993).*

GO BETWEEN (FR) RR 108f 1915a[3]

5 b h Highest Honor (FR) 10.9f **(72)** - Ruffle (FR) (High Line) 10.3f **(70)**
Form - 53
1998 Turf 0-2: (8f, 9f) (sft, gd)
Pattern-class colt. Turf high 108. He ran a super race in a Group Three at Maisons-Laffitte in June and obviously goes well on soft ground.
**F Piedois in FR [0-2] N Pharaon (from G Doleuze in FR [0-1] Apr 1996).*

GO BOLDLY (IRE) RR 106f 4074a[3]

4 b c Sadler's Wells (USA) 11.3f **(87)** - Daivolina (USA) (Lear Fan (USA)) 8.5f **(73)**
Form - 133
1998 Turf 1-3: (10f 2, 12f 1-1) (sft 1-2, g-s)
Currently Pattern-class colt. Turf high 106 - 3rd of 16 to Happy Change (28 Aug Baden-Baden 10f sft RF 4074a) - also 1st of 9 giving 3lb to Call Me Sam (20 Jun Lyon Parilly RF 2283a). A Listed winner for Andre Fabre, he changed hands for 105,000 guineas at the Tattersalls Autumn Horse In Training Sales, and will now race in the green and gold silks of J P McManus. Already described as 'the next Istabraq', he is certainly one to look out for over hurdles.
**A Fabre in FR [1-3] M Tabor.*

GOCHINOS BHB 60f **RR 71f** 4253[15]
2 b c Wolfhound (USA) 7.3f **(71)** - Reflection (Mill Reef (USA)) 10.5f **(78)**
Form - 553600
Record 1998 - 1st:0 2nd:0 3rd:1 Ran:6
Win Prizemoney £0 *Total Prizemoney* £515
1998 Turf 0-6: (5f 5, 7f) (g-f 4, frm 2)
Above-average colt. Turf high 71. **S C Williams [0-6] E Carter.*

GODABI (JPN) BHB 73f **RR 74f** 3483[3]
3 b f Dr Devious (IRE) 9.9f **(74)** - Asakusa Odoriko (JPN) (Pas de Seul) 9.1f **(67)**
Form - 16023
Record 1998 - 1st:1 2nd:1 3rd:1 Ran:5
Win Prizemoney £3,096 *Total Prizemoney* £4,799
Wins * **1998** May Salisb (FRM) 9.9f 67 <
1998 Turf 1-5: (8f, 10f 1-3, 12f) (gd 2, g-f, frm 1-1, hrd)
Leggy, above-average filly. Turf high 74 - 3rd of 8 giving 6lb to Hardy Dancer (9 Aug Epsom 10f gd RF 3483) - also 1st of 10 from Mole Creek (14 May Salisbury RF 1211).
**Sir Michael Stoute [1-5] Seisuke Hata.*

GODLEY (IRE) BHB 75f **RR 74f** 4070[4]
2 b c Fayruz 6.6f **(63)** - Divine Apsara (Godswalk (USA)) 7.3f **(58)**
Form - 0244624
Record 1998 - 1st:0 2nd:2 3rd:0 Ran:7
Win Prizemoney £0 *Total Prizemoney* £3,357
1998 Turf 0-7: (6f, 7f 4, 8f 2) (g-f 3, frm 4)
Above-average colt, effective 7 to 8f, best at 8f, acts on g-f to frm, best on frm, often wears blinkers. Turf high 74 - 4th of 17 getting 1lb from Ice (3 Spt York 8f g-f RF 4070). Ran a cracker when a narrow second in a Newmarket nursery in August, his first attempt at a mile. **M J Fetherston-Godley [0-7] The Kennet House Partnership.*

GODMERSHAM PARK BHB 47f72a **RR 52f 72a** 4636[4]
6 b g Warrshan (USA) 9.7f **(59)** - Brown Velvet (Mansingh (USA)) 7.4f **(55)**
Form - 1111131770000004
Record 1998 - 1st:4 2nd:0 3rd:1 Ran:14
Pre1998 - 1st:2 2nd:4 3rd:2 Ran:22
Win Prizemoney £14,414 *Total Prizemoney* £19,501

Wins							
* **1998**	*Feb*	*Wolver*	*(STD)*	*H*	*8.5f*	*68*	*73* <
* **1998**	*Jan*	*Southw*	*(STD)*	*H*	*8f*	*54*	*65*
* **1998**	*Jan*	*Southw*	*(STD)*	*H*	*8f*	*54*	*63*
* **1998**	*Jan*	*Southw*	*(STD)*	*H*	*7f*	*54*	*59*
* 1997	*Dec*	*Southw*	*(STD)*	*H*	*7f*	*50*	*54*
* 1997	*Nov*	*Southw*	*(STD)*	*H*	*8f*	*46*	*51*

1998 Turf 0-5: (7f, 8f 3, 10f) (gd 2, g-f 2, hrd) 1998 AW 4-9: (7f 1-4, 8f 3-4, 9f) (Fibr 4-9)
Above-average gelding, effective 8f, acts on g-f - acts on Fibr, has worn blinkers, prefers left handed tracks, favours tight tracks, excels at Southwell. Turf high 52. AW high 73 - 1st of 6 getting 16lb from Queen's Pageant (11 Feb Wolverhampton RF 0266) - also 1st of 10 giving 23lb to Principal Boy (19 Jan Southwell RF 0112). Inconsistent. He took a long time in getting off the mark, but made up for it by having a brilliant time on Fibresand in the winter of 1997/98, winning six times. His form tailed off afterwards and he made no impact on turf, but he did hint at a revival in October and may be set for another successful Fibresand campaign in the winter of 1998/99.
**P S Felgate [6-26] H R Hornby (from M J Heaton-Ellis [0-10] Oct 1996).*

GO FOR GREEN BHB 51f38a **RR 53f 38a** 350[9]
4 br f Petong 7.6f **(58)** - Guest List (Be My Guest (USA)) 9.3f **(67)**
Form - 830
Record 1998 - 1st:0 2nd:0 3rd:1 Ran:3
Pre1998 - 1st:0 2nd:1 3rd:1 Ran:11
Win Prizemoney £0 *Total Prizemoney* £1,908
1998 AW 0-3: (8f, 10f 2) (Equi 3)
Fair filly, effective 8 to 10f, acts on g-s to g-f, has worn blinkers. AW high 32. **Dr J D Scargill [0-14] Manor Farm Packers Ltd.*

GO HANA GO RR 42f 1939[6]
2 b f Doyoun 10.7f **(69)** - Murooj (USA) (Diesis) 9.3f **(69)**
Form - 6
Record 1998 - 1st:0 2nd:0 3rd:0 Ran:1
1998 Turf 0-1: (5f) (gd)
Currently moderate filly. **C E Brittain [0-1] A Merza.*

GOING PLACES BHB 45f **RR 50f** 4455[15]
3 b f Risk Me (FR) 8f **(53)**-Spring High**(37f 55a)**(Miami Springs)9.9f **(59)**
Form - 00036000
Record 1998 - 1st:0 2nd:0 3rd:1 Ran:8
Pre1998 - 1st:1 2nd:0 3rd:2 Ran:7
Win Prizemoney £4,470 *Total Prizemoney* £5,983
Wins * 1997 May Windso (SFT) 5f 70 <
1998 Turf 0-6:(5f 3, 6f 2, 7f)(gd, g-f 3, frm 2)1998 AW0-2:(5f, 7f) (Fibr 2)
Neat, fair filly, effective 5f, acts on gd, has worn blinkers. Turf high 50. AW high 44 (began Aug). Becoming disappointing.
**K T Ivory [1-15] K T Ivory.*

GOLCONDA (IRE) RR 72f 4495[8]
2 br f Lahib (USA) 8f **(69)** - David's Star (Welsh Saint) 7.6f **(64)**
Form - 38
Record 1998 - 1st:0 2nd:0 3rd:1 Ran:2
Win Prizemoney £0 *Total Prizemoney* £545
1998 Turf 0-2: (5f, 7f) (gd 2)
Currently above-average filly. Turf high 72 (1st run) (began Spt) - 3rd of 19 to La Paola (16 Spt Sandown 5f gd RF 4307).
**M Bell [0-2] Innlaw Racing.*

GOLD ACADEMY (IRE) BHB 100f **RR 88f** 4618[5]
2 b c Royal Academy (USA) 7.8f **(77)** - Soha (USA) (Dancing Brave (USA)) 8.4f **(76)**
Form - 435
Record 1998 - 1st:0 2nd:0 3rd:1 Ran:3
Win Prizemoney £0 *Total Prizemoney* £5,191
1998 Turf 0-3: (6f, 7f 2) (gd 3)
Currently useful colt. Turf high 88. Good effort when third to Aljabr in the Vintage Stakes on only his second run, despite not relishing the softish ground. **R Hannon [0-3] George Teo.*

GOLD AWAY (IRE) RR 121f 5158a[3]
3 ch c Goldneyev - Blushing Away(FR)(Blushing Groom(FR)) 10.3f **(76)**
Form - 12223
1998 Turf 1-5: (8f 3, 9f 1-2) (sft 2, g-s, gd 1-2)
Very high-class colt, effective 8 to 9f, best at 8f, acts on sft to gd, best on sft, has worn blinkers, and excels at Longchamp. Turf high 121 - 2nd of 7 to Desert Prince (6 Spt Longchamp 8f sft RF 4217a). Inconsistent. A useful two-year-old, he made a winning return in the Prix de Guiche. He followed that up with three second places, in the Grand Prix de Paris, after a break to Desert Prince in the Prix du Moulin, and in the Prix du Rond-Point. He can make a top miler in 1999. **Mme C Head in FR [2-8] Wertheimer Brothers.*

GOLD BLADE BHB 52f55a **RR 45f 55a** 3157[10]
9 ch g Rousillon (USA) 10.4f **(69)** -Sharp Girl(FR)(Sharpman) 11.3f **(66)**
Form - 0
Record 1998 - 1st:0 2nd:0 3rd:0 Ran:1
Pre1998 - 1st:12 2nd:12 3rd:7 Ran:70
Win Prizemoney £33,545 *Total Prizemoney* £48,137

Wins							
* 1996	Aug	Catter	(G-F)	H	12f	67	58+
* 1996	Jly	Beverl	(G-F)	H	9.9f	64	68
* 1996	Jly	Ayr	(G-F)	H	13.1f	60	61
* 1996	Jly	Hamilt	(G-F)	H	9.2f	49	60
* 1996	Jly	Pontef	(G-F)	H	10f	49	61+
* 1996	Apr	Nottin	(GD)	H	10f	44	48
* 1996	*Jan*	*Southw*	*(STD)*	*H*	*12f*	*60*	*67*
* 1995	Jly	Hamilt	(FRM)	H	11.1f	42	49
* 1995	*Jan*	*Wolver*	*(STD)*	*H*	*12f*	*57*	*63*

1998 Turf 0-1: (10f) (g-f)
Fair gelding, effective 9 to 10f, acts on g-s to frm, has worn blinkers, likes tight tracks. Becoming disappointing.
**J Pearce [9-39] Arthur Old (from N A Graham [3-32] Jly 1994).*

GOLD CHANCE (IRE) BHB 64f **RR 68f** 4376[15]
2 ch c Fayruz 6.6f **(63)** - Maura Paul (Bonne Noel) 10.7f **(71)**
Form - 04370
Record 1998 - 1st:0 2nd:0 3rd:1 Ran:5
Win Prizemoney £0 *Total Prizemoney* £936
1998 Turf 0-5: (5f, 6f 3, 7f) (gd, g-f 3, frm)
Average colt. Turf high 68. **G C H Chung [0-5] Ian Pattle.*

GOLD CLIPPER BHB 26f42a **RR 37f 42a** 4313[9]

4 b c High Kicker (USA) 8.4f **(52)** - Ship of Gold (Glint of Gold) 9.3f **(66)**
Form - 230001700050
Record 1998 - 1st:1 2nd:0 3rd:0 Ran:8
Pre1998 - 1st:0 2nd:2 3rd:1 Ran:14
Win Prizemoney £2,253 *Total Prizemoney* £4,154
Wins * **1998** *Mar Southw (STD) C 8f 50* <
1998 Turf 0-3: (8f 2, 10f) (gd 2, g-f) 1998 AW 1-5: (8f 1-3, 10f, 11f) (Equi 2, Fibr 1-3)
Leggy, fair colt, effective 8 to 10f, best at 10f - acts on AW, best on Equi, has worn blinkers, likes left handed tracks. Turf high 37. AW high 50 - 1st of 12 giving 9lb to Al's Fella (20 Mar Southwell RF 0451). It took him a long time to get off the mark, but he managed to narrowly win a very modest claiming limited stakes on the Southwell Fibresand in March. **M J Ryan [1-24] P E Axon.*

GOLD COAST RR 65f 3268[11]

2 b g Alhijaz 7.7f **(57)** - Odilese (Mummy's Pet) 7.7f **(60)**
Form - 0600
Record 1998 - 1st:0 2nd:0 3rd:0 Ran:4
1998 Turf 0-4: (5f, 6f 2, 7f) (gd, g-f 2, frm)
Average gelding. Turf high 65. **S Dow [0-4] G Steinberg.*

GOLD CRYSTAL (IRE) BHB 68f **RR 70f** 4881[6]

2 b c Fayruz 6.6f **(63)** - Lightning Laser (Monseigneur (USA)) 7.7f **(63)**
Form - 3826
Record 1998 - 1st:0 2nd:1 3rd:1 Ran:4
Win Prizemoney £0 *Total Prizemoney* £1,148
1998 Turf 0-4: (5f 4) (g-s, g-f 3)
Above-average colt. Turf high 70 (1st run) - 3rd of 14 to By The Glass (26 May Leicester 5f g-f RF 1473).
**W Jarvis [0-4] The Gold Crystal Partnership.*

GOLD EDGE BHB 43f **RR 34f** 5097[11]

4 ch f Beveled (USA) 6.9f **(64)** - Golden October (Young Generation) 7.7f **(63)**
Form - 00230844448000
Record 1998 - 1st:0 2nd:1 3rd:1 Ran:14
Pre1998 - 1st:1 2nd:4 3rd:4 Ran:21
Win Prizemoney £3,631 *Total Prizemoney* £11,335
Wins 1997 Aug Chepst (G-F) H 6.1f 50 59 <
1998 Turf 0-14: (5f 9, 6f 5) (sft, g-s, gd 6, g-f 4, frm 2)
Strong, very moderate filly, effective 5 to 6f, best at 6f, acts on sft to frm, best on g-f. Turf high 55 - 2nd of 6 getting 23lb from Jennelle (30 Apr Redcar 5f sft RF 0935).
**Don Enrico Incisa [0-14] Don Enrico Incisa (from M R Channon [1-21] Oct 1997).*

GOLDEN ACE (IRE) BHB 42f32a **RR 52f 32a** 4704[15]

5 ch g Archway (IRE) 8.5f **(60)** - Gobolino (Don) 7.7f **(64)**
Form - 00233383570625400
Record 1998 - 1st:0 2nd:2 3rd:4 Ran:17
Pre1998 - 1st:2 2nd:0 3rd:2 Ran:14
Win Prizemoney £7,277 *Total Prizemoney* £14,138
Wins 1997 Aug Newmar (GD) S 8f 42
1996 Apr Newbur (G-S) 8f 85 <
1998 Turf 0-14: (10f 7, 11f 2, 12f 5) (sft 3, g-s 2, gd 3, g-f 3, frm 3) 1998 AW 0-3: (8f, 11f, 12f) (Fibr 3)
Fair gelding. Turf high 53. AW high 14.
**R C Spicer [0-22] G D J Linder (from R Hannon [2-9] Aug 1997).*

GOLDENACRES BHB 39f **RR 44f** 3690[9]

3 b g Desert Splendour - Normanby Damsel (High Line) 10.3f **(70)**
Form - 0058470
Record 1998 - 1st:0 2nd:0 3rd:0 Ran:7
Pre1998 - 1st:0 2nd:0 3rd:0 Ran:5
1998 Turf 0-7: (5f, 7f 3, 8f 3) (gd 3, frm 4)
Neat, moderate gelding, has worn blinkers. Turf high 44.
**M P Muggeridge [0-2] Brian A Lewendon & Mrs Carol Lewendon (from J Neville [0-11] Jun 1998).*

GOLDEN ARROW (IRE) BHB 75f **RR 46f** 4963[8]

7 ch g Glint of Gold 10.8f **(61)** - Sheer Luck (Shergar) 10.4f **(66)**
Form - 8
Record 1998 - 1st:0 2nd:0 3rd:0 Ran:1
Pre1998 - 1st:2 2nd:6 3rd:2 Ran:23
Win Prizemoney £11,515 *Total Prizemoney* £25,221
Wins * 1996 Aug Warwic (GD) H 16.1f 78 84 <
1994 Spt Kempto (G-S) H 12f 79 82
1998 Turf 0-1: (16f) (sft)
Moderate gelding, has worn blinkers. Consistent.
**M C Pipe [1-7] The Spinach Partnership (from I A Balding [4-32] May 1996).*

GOLDEN BIFF (IRE) BHB 70f65a **RR 70f 65a** 5080[8]

2 ch c Shalford (IRE) 7.8f **(63)** - Capable Kate (IRE) (Alzao (USA)) 7.1f **(68)**
Form - 032208
Record 1998 - 1st:0 2nd:2 3rd:1 Ran:6
Win Prizemoney £0 *Total Prizemoney* £2,555
1998 Turf 0-5: (5f 3, 6f 2) (g-s, gd 3, frm) 1998 AW 0-1: (6f) (Fibr)
Above-average colt, effective 5 to 6f, acts on g-s to gd. Turf high 70 (began Jly) - 2nd of 7 giving 3lb to Open Secret (3 Aug Carlisle 5f gd RF 3304). **I Semple [0-6] Patersons of Greenoakhill.*

GOLDEN CAT (USA) RR 73f 4691a[3]

3 ch f Storm Cat (USA) 7f **(86)** - Eurobird (Ela-Mana-Mou) 10.1f **(70)**
Form - 143
1998 Turf 1-3: (8f 1-1, 9f, 10f) (sft 1-1, g-s, gd)
Currently above-average filly. Turf high 97 - 3rd of 9 to Darina (3 Oct Curragh 10f g-s RF 4691a). **J Oxx in IRE [1-3] Gerald Jennings.*

GOLDEN CHARM (IRE) BHB 67f **RR 69f** 4835[13]

2 b f Common Grounds 8.1f **(66)** - Credit Crunch (IRE) (Caerleon (USA)) 8.6f **(71)**
Form - 61547420
Record 1998 - 1st:1 2nd:1 3rd:0 Ran:8
Win Prizemoney £3,366 *Total Prizemoney* £4,981
Wins * **1998** May Nottin (G-F) 6.1f 67 <
1998 Turf 1-8: (5f, 6f 1-5, 7f 2) (g-s, gd 2, g-f 3, frm 1-2)
Average filly, effective 6 to 7f, acts on g-f to frm. Turf high 69 - also 1st of 15 from Crackle (15 May Nottingham RF 1245).
**J E Banks [1-8] Mutual Racing.*

GOLDEN DICE (USA) BHB 93f **RR 94f** 5076[8]

3 ch c Diesis 9f **(80)** - Fariedah (USA) (Topsider (USA)) 8.3f **(71)**
Form - 2308
Record 1998 - 1st:0 2nd:1 3rd:1 Ran:4
Pre1998 - 1st:1 2nd:1 3rd:0 Ran:4
Win Prizemoney £3,696 *Total Prizemoney* £11,293
Wins * 1997 Aug Newcas (GD) 7f 84 <
1998 Turf 0-4: (8f 4) (g-s, gd 2, g-f)
Scopey, useful colt, effective 7 to 8f, best at 8f, acts on gd to frm, best on gd. Turf high 97 (1st run) - 2nd of 6 to Speedfit Too (23 May Kempton 8f gd RF 1426). Lightly-raced, this small colt started the season well when second in a listed race at Kempton. Unfortunately, he did not progress and even three months off in the summer failed to inspire him. **H R A Cecil [1-8] S Khaled.*

GOLDEN FACT (USA) BHB 77f **RR 100f** 5028a[3]

4 b g Known Fact (USA) 8.3f **(72)** - Cosmic Sea Queen (USA) (Determined Cosmic (USA))
Form - 261171013
1998 Turf 4-9: (7f, 8f 4-6, 9f 2) (hvy 1-2, sft 2, gd 2-4, g-f 1-1)
Strong, very useful gelding, effective 8 to 9f, best at 8f, acts on hvy to gd, best on gd. Turf high 100 - 1st of 15 giving 28lb to Willyever (26 Spt Listowel RF 4567a). He had a tremendous season, improving 25lb in the ratings and winning four competitive handicaps. Best when held-up, he acts on most types of ground and can carry big weights.
**M McElhone in IRE [4-9] Golden Sands Syndicate (from R Hannon [0-10] Aug 1997).*

GOLDEN FORCE BHB 84f **RR 82f** 2884[3]

2 b c Forzando 7.2f **(63)** - Silverlocks **(82f)** (Sharrood (USA)) 10.5f **(72)**
Form - 033
Record 1998 - 1st:0 2nd:0 3rd:2 Ran:3
Win Prizemoney £0 *Total Prizemoney* £1,076
1998 Turf 0-3: (6f 3) (frm 3)
Currently decent colt. Turf high 82 - 3rd of 16 giving 9lb to Scoop (17 Jly Pontefract 6f frm RF 2884). **R Hannon [0-3] George Teo.*

GOLDEN FORTUNE BHB 97f **RR 93+f** 4496[3]

3 ch f Forzando 7.2f **(63)** - Short And Sharp (Sharpen Up) 8.3f **(67)**

Form - 2113

Record 1998 - 1st:2 2nd:1 3rd:1 Ran:4
Pre1998 - 1st:2 2nd:0 3rd:0 Ran:5

Win Prizemoney £39,801 *Total Prizemoney* £46,077

Wins							
* **1998**	Spt	Salisb	(GD)	H	7f	88	93+ <
* **1998**	Jly	Beverl	(G-F)	H	7.5f	78	90
* 1997	Spt	Newmar	(G-F)	H	7f	68	78
* 1997	Spt	Nottin	(G-F)	H	6.1f	63	68

1998 Turf 2-4: (7f 2-3, 8f) (gd, g-f 1-1, frm 1-2)

Workmanlike, useful filly, effective 7 to 8f, best at 7f, acts on gd to frm, excels at Newmarket. Turf high 93 (began Jly) - 3rd of 17 getting 3lb from Risque Lady (26 Spt Ascot 8f gd RF 4496) - also 1st of 12 giving 2lb to Rich In Love (3 Spt Salisbury RF 4062). Improving. Ran a cracker when just failing on her belated seasonal debut at the July Meeting, and duly won her next two starts. She did not quite get home when stepped up to a mile at Ascot on her final outing.
**D R Loder [4-9] Lucayan Stud.*

GOLDENGIRLMICHELLE (IRE) BHB 30f RR 50f 4545[7]

3 b f Project Manager 7.2f **(47)** - Arbour Day (Artaius (USA)) 9f **(69)**

Form - 545877

Record 1998 - 1st:0 2nd:0 3rd:0 Ran:6

1998 Turf 0-3: (11f, 12f 2) (g-f, frm 2) 1998 AW 0-3: (11f 2, 12f) (Fibr 3)

Fair filly, effective 11f, acts on g-f, has worn blinkers. Turf high 50 (1st run) - 4th of 13 getting 23lb from Flying Eagle (24 Jun Warwick 11f g-f RF 2255). AW high 23.
**R Craggs [0-6] Ten For Sport Partnership.*

* 1997	*Jan*	*Wolver*	*(STD)*	*H*	*14.8f*	*48*	*63+*
* 1997	*Jan*	*Southw*	*(STD)*	*H*	*16f*	*48*	*63+*
* 1996	*Nov*	*Southw*	*(STD)*	*H*	*14f*	*44*	*48*
1994	Mar	Folkes	(G-S)	H	12f	47	46

1998 Turf 0-8: (12f, 14f 3, 15f, 16f 2, 17f) (sft, gd 5, g-f, frm) 1998 AW 1-4: (14f 1-1, 16f 3) (Fibr 1-4)

Average horse, effective 14 to 16f, best at 16f - acts on Fibr, has worn blinkers, likes left handed tracks, favours tight tracks, excels at Wolverhampton, likes Southwell. Turf high 46. AW high 69 - 3rd of 9 to Mister Aspecto (16 Jan Southwell 16f Fibr RF 0100) - also 1st of 7 giving 25lb to Dally Boy (18 May Southwell RF 1306). Becoming disappointing. He has been a very effective performer on Fibresand over the past couple of years, and also had a good time of it on turf at the beginning of '97. After a disappointing spell, he bounced back to form with a victory at Southwell in May, having slipped down the weights.
**M J Ryan [9-44] Four Jays Racing Partnership (from R Harris [1-5] Mar 1994).*

GOLDEN HAWK (USA) BHB 65f RR 67f 4817[6]

3 ch c Silver Hawk (USA) 11.2f **(85)** - Crockadore (USA) (Nijinsky (CAN)) 10.3f **(77)**

Form - 7526

Record 1998 - 1st:0 2nd:1 3rd:0 Ran:4
Pre1998 - 1st:0 2nd:0 3rd:1 Ran:1

Win Prizemoney £0 *Total Prizemoney* £2,610

1998 Turf 0-4: (7f, 9f, 16f 2) (g-s 2, gd, frm)

Golden Silca (second left) takes the Mill Reef Stks

GOLDEN HADEER BHB 39f69a RR 46f 69a 4590[16]

7 ch h Hadeer 8.9f **(58)** - Verchinina (Star Appeal) 9.6f **(65)**

Form - 55037010403000

Record 1998 - 1st:1 2nd:0 3rd:2 Ran:12
Pre1998 - 1st:9 2nd:3 3rd:5 Ran:35

Win Prizemoney £30,870 *Total Prizemoney* £36,764

Wins							
* **1998**	*May*	*Southw*	*(STD)*	*H*	*14f*	*63*	*69*
* 1997	May	Warwic	(G-F)	H	14.9f	47	53
* 1997	May	Nottin	(GD)	H	16f	43	49+
* 1997	May	Hamilt	(SFT)	H	13f	34	44
* 1997	*Feb*	*Southw*	*(STD)*	*H*	*16f*	*65*	*77* <
* 1997	*Jan*	*Wolver*	*(STD)*	*H*	*16.2f*	*54*	*66+*

Leggy, average colt. Turf high 67 - 2nd of 9 getting 13lb from Paradise Soul (6 Oct Nottingham 16f g-s RF 4667).
**P F I Cole [0-5] H R H Prince Fahd Salman.*

GOLDEN LYRIC (IRE) BHB 42f RR 42f 4708[15]

3 ch c Lycius (USA) 8.8f **(71)** - Adjala (Northfields (USA)) 9f **(72)**

Form - 607004440

Record 1998 - 1st:0 2nd:0 3rd:0 Ran:9
Pre1998 - 1st:0 2nd:0 3rd:0 Ran:2

1998 Turf 0-9: (7f, 8f 5, 10f 3) (sft, gd 2, g-f 2, frm 4)

Scopey, moderate colt, effective 8 to 10f, best at 8f, acts on gd to frm, best on frm, has worn blinkers. Turf high 47.

**G Wragg [0-11] Mollers Racing.*

GOLDEN MELODY BHB 45f48a RR 43f 48a 2001[7]

4 b f Robellino (USA) 9.5f **(68)**-Rose Chanelle (Welsh Pageant) 10f **(65)**
Form - 2507

Record	**1998** -	1st:0	2nd:1	3rd:0	Ran:4
	Pre1998 -	1st:0	2nd:0	3rd:0	Ran:11

Win Prizemoney £0 *Total Prizemoney* £1,283
1998 Turf 0-4: (15f 2, 18f, 22f) (sft 2, g-s 2)
Leggy, moderate filly, effective 14 to 16f, acts on sft to frm, has worn blinkers. Turf high 53 (1st run) - 2nd of 11 getting 2lb from Jucinda (7 Apr Folkestone 15f sft RF 0582).
**M J Heaton-Ellis [1-13] Amity Finance Ltd (from R Hannon [0-4] Oct 1996).*

GOLDEN PLATE (GER) RR 104f 4723a[10]

3 b f Polish Precedent (USA) 9f **(73)** - Gondola (GER) (Nebos (GER)) 9f **(78)**
Form - 20
1998 Turf 0-2: (12f, 14f) (sft 2)
Currently very useful filly. Turf high 104 (1st run) (began Spt) - 2nd of 9 to Arroyada (13 Spt Hanover 12f sft RF 4342a). She shaped encouragingly in a Group Two at Hanover in September, but ran poorly in Dortmund the following month.
**H Remmert in GER [0-2] Spt 1998).*

GOLDEN POUND (USA) BHB 62f69a RR 39f 69a 5128[14]

6 b g Seeking the Gold (USA) 7.4f **(80)** - Coesse Express (USA) (Dewan (USA)) 7.4f **(65)**
Form - 800184584400000

Record	**1998** -	1st:1	2nd:0	3rd:0	Ran:14
	Pre1998 -	1st:3	2nd:5	3rd:5	Ran:35

Win Prizemoney £14,201 *Total Prizemoney* £26,379

Wins								
	1998	May	Leices	(GD)	H	6f	72	77
	1997	Aug	Bright	(GD)	H	6f	75	78
	1996	Jly	Epsom	(G-F)	H	6f	77	83 <
	1996	Apr	Thirsk	(G-F)		6f		75

1998 Turf 1-14: (5f 4, 6f 1-9, 7f) (sft 2, g-s 2, gd 3, g-f 1-5, frm 2)
Average gelding, effective 6f, acts on g-f to frm, best on g-f, has worn blinkers (very effectively), likes tight tracks. Turf high 77 - 4th of 9 giving 9lb to The Fugative (24 Jun Epsom 6f g-f RF 2242) - also 1st of 10 giving 7lb to Ocker (25 May Leicester RF 1448). Becoming disappointing.
**Mrs L Stubbs [0-4] A P Griffin (from Miss Gay Kelleway [4-41] Spt 1998).*

GOLDEN RAINBOW (IRE) RR 62f 4732[11]

2 b c Rainbows For Life (CAN) 9.3f **(64)** - Nawadder (Kris) 9.5f **(73)**
Form - 506200

Record	**1998** -	1st:0	2nd:1	3rd:0	Ran:6

Win Prizemoney £0 *Total Prizemoney* £1,045
1998 Turf 0-6: (5f, 6f 2, 7f 3) (sft, g-s, gd, g-f 2, frm)
Average colt, effective 6f, acts on gd. Turf high 62 - 2nd of 9 getting 14lb from Parisien Star (4 Spt Epsom 6f gd RF 4083).
**B R Millman [0-6] Golden Rainbow Partnership.*

GOLDEN REEF BHB 67f RR 74f 2847[5]

2 b c Puissance 7.1f **(60)** - Cloudy Reef (Cragador) 6f **(67)**
Form - 0225775

Record	**1998** -	1st:0	2nd:2	3rd:0	Ran:7

Win Prizemoney £0 *Total Prizemoney* £1,368
1998 Turf 0-7: (5f 4, 6f 3) (sft, g-s, gd 3, frm 2)
Above-average colt, effective 5f, acts on sft to g-s. Turf high 74 - 2nd of 8 giving 5lb to Dispol Clan (28 Apr Nottingham 5f g-s RF 0900). **R Hollinshead [0-7] M Johnson.*

GOLDEN REPRIMAND (IRE) BHB 65f RR 69f 4150[3]

3 b c Reprimand 8.2f **(63)** - Elabella (Ela-Mana-Mou) 10.1f **(70)**
Form - 003003

Record	**1998** -	1st:0	2nd:0	3rd:2	Ran:6
	Pre1998 -	1st:0	2nd:0	3rd:0	Ran:2

Win Prizemoney £0 *Total Prizemoney* £1,075
1998 Turf 0-6: (8f, 9f 2, 11f, 12f 2) (gd, g-f 3, frm 2)
Scopey, average colt, effective 6f, acted on gd. Turf high 69. Consistent. A half-brother to useful sprinter Espartero, he showed some ability in maiden company in his first three starts, but faced an impossible task on his handicap debut at Epsom in June.

(DEAD) **R Hannon [0-8] George Teo.*

GOLDEN RULE RR 100f 5109a[1]

3 b c Emarati (USA) 6.6f **(63)** - Sparklingsovereign (Sparkler) 8.4f **(55)**
Form - 311142221
1998 Turf 4-9: (9f 1-1, 10f 2-5, 11f 1-2, 12f) (hvy, sft 1-1, g-s 1-2, gd 2-4, g-f)
Very useful colt, effective 9 to 11f, best at 11f, acts on sft to gd, best on gd, likes Curragh. Turf high 100 - 1st of 9 from Catch The Dragon (26 Oct Leopardstown RF 5109a) - also 1st of 10 giving 10lb to King of Peace (5 Jly Naas RF 2619a). Consistent. A very consistent Irish colt, he won some nice races last season but probably his best performance was when beaten by Yavana's Pace at Galway. Finished the season off with a win, and looks to be improving all the time.
**Miss Frances Crowley in IRE [4-9] Crock of Gold Syndicate (from A P O'Brien in IRE [1-3] Jly 1997).*

GOLDEN SADDLE (IRE) BHB 36a RR 113[8]

4 b f Waajib 8.9f **(67)** - Flying Beckee (IRE) (Godswalk (USA)) 7.3f **(58)**
Form - 708

Record	**1998** -	1st:0	2nd:0	3rd:0	Ran:1
	Pre1998 -	1st:0	2nd:0	3rd:0	Ran:3

1998 AW 0-1: (12f) (Fibr)
Very moderate filly. **Miss L A Perratt [0-4] F Johnson.*

GOLDEN SADDLE (USA) BHB 52f RR 58f 249[7]

4 bb g Riverman (USA) 9.7f **(78)** - Rossard (DEN) (Glacial (DEN))
Form - 47

Record	**1998** -	1st:0	2nd:0	3rd:0	Ran:2
	Pre1998 -	1st:0	2nd:0	3rd:0	Ran:9

1998 AW 0-2: (15f, 16f) (Fibr 2)
Fair gelding, effective 10f, acts on g-f, has worn blinkers, likes tight tracks. AW high 23. Inconsistent.
**D J Wintle [0-4] Bit Of A Mix Partners (from P F I Cole [0-8] Aug 1997).*

GOLDEN SILCA BHB 100f RR 99f 4539[8]

2 ch f Inchinor 8.9f **(64)** - Silca-Cisa (Hallgate)
Form - 121163118

Record	**1998** -	1st:5	2nd:1	3rd:1	Ran:9

Win Prizemoney £84,415 *Total Prizemoney* £103,355

Wins							
	* **1998**	Spt	Newbur	(GD)	G2	6f	99 <
	* **1998**	Spt	Baden-	(SFT)	G2	6f	97
	* **1998**	Jly	Newbur	(G-F)	L	6f	97
	* **1998**	May	Newbur	(GD)		5.2f	84
	* **1998**	Apr	Newbur	(HVY)		5.2f	84+

1998 Turf 5-9: (5f 2-3, 6f 3-6) (sft 2-3, gd 1-1, g-f 2-4, frm)
Very useful filly, effective 6f, acts on sft to g-f, excels at Newbury. Turf high 99 - 1st of 5 from Indiana Legend (19 Spt Newbury RF 4378) - also 1st of 5 getting 2lb from El Tango (18 Jly Newbury RF 2911). A really genuine filly, who has had a hard season, winning five out of nine races, including a Group Two at Baden-Baden and put up a very game performance in the Prix Morny when third to Orpen. She loves Newbury and has won there four times, including the Mill Reef Stakes. She can be forgiven her rather poor display in the Cheveley Park as she had probably gone over the top. She goes on any ground, is as tough as old boots and as game as a pebble, and is certainly one to look out for in 1999.
**M R Channon [5-9] Aldridge Racing Ltd.*

GOLDEN SKY (IRE) BHB 50f RR 50f 4671[18]

2 b f Petardia 8.2f **(58)** - Oriental Splendour (Runnett) 7f **(59)**
Form - 0700

Record	**1998** -	1st:0	2nd:0	3rd:0	Ran:4

1998 Turf 0-4: (5f 2, 6f, 7f) (g-s, gd, g-f, frm)
Fair filly. Turf high 50.
**Don Enrico Incisa [0-2] Don Enrico Incisa (from N Tinkler [0-2] Apr 1998).*

GOLDEN SNAKE (USA) RR 85+f 4227[1]

2 b c Danzig (USA) 8.1f **(88)** - Dubian (High Line) 10.3f **(70)**
Form - 51

Record	**1998** -	1st:1	2nd:0	3rd:0	Ran:2

Win Prizemoney £3,840 *Total Prizemoney* £3,840

Wins					
	* **1998**	Spt	Doncas	(GD)	8f	85+ <

1998 Turf 1-2: (7f, 8f 1-1) (gd, g-f 1-1)
Currently useful colt. Turf high 85 (began Aug) - 1st of 16 from

Blue (11 Spt Doncaster RF 4227). A half-brother to 1000 Guineas winner Sayyedati, he showed a nice turn of foot when landing his maiden. **B W Hills [1-2] Mohamed Obaida.*

GOLDEN STATE (USA) BHB 40f **RR 56f** 4399[18]

3 b g Zilzal (USA) 8.5f **(79)** - Worood (USA) (Vaguely Noble) 10.1f **(72)**
Form - 07700
Record 1998 - 1st:0 2nd:0 3rd:0 Ran:5
1998 Turf 0-5: (10f 4, 12f) (gd, g-f, frm 3)
Rangy, fair gelding. Turf high 56.
**J G Portman [0-5] Only For Fun Partnership.*

GOLDEN SYRUP (IRE) BHB 63f **RR 63f** 4091[4]

2 b f Dolphin Street (FR) - Sprint For Gold (USA) (Slew O' Gold (USA)) 8f **(75)**
Form - 58404
Record 1998 - 1st:0 2nd:0 3rd:0 Ran:5
1998 Turf 0-5: (6f 4, 7f) (gd, g-f 3, frm)
Average filly. Turf high 63 (1st run) - 5th of 13 giving 4lb to Divine Lady (9 Jun Salisbury 6f gd RF 1835).
**R Hannon [0-5] Lord Carnarvon.*

GOLDEN THATCH (IRE) **RR 66f** 4846[10]

2 b g Thatching 7.8f **(69)** - Pollyfidra (USA) (In Fijar (USA)) 7.5f **(70)**
Form - 0
Record 1998 - 1st:0 2nd:0 3rd:0 Ran:1
1998 Turf 0-1: (6f) (g-f)
Currently average gelding. **W J Haggas [0-1] Dandy Racing Ltd.*

GOLDEN THUNDERBOLT (FR) BHB 60f **RR 65f** 3885[4]

5 b g Persian Bold 10f **(69)** - Carmita (Caerleon (USA)) 8.6f **(71)**
Form - 411624
Record 1998 - 1st:2 2nd:1 3rd:0 Ran:6
Pre1998 - 1st:1 2nd:4 3rd:3 Ran:20
Win Prizemoney £7,166 *Total Prizemoney* £14,214
Wins * **1998** Jun Beverl (GD) C 12f 65
* **1998** May Mussel (G-S) C 12f 51
* 1997 May Pontef (GD) C 8f 67 <
1998 Turf 2-6: (12f 2-6) (gd 1-3, g-f, frm 1-2)
Average gelding, effective 8 to 12f, best at 8f, acts on gd to frm, best on gd, has worn blinkers, prefers right handed tracks, prefers tight tracks, does well at Beverley. Turf high 65 - 1st of 5 getting 4lb from Noukari (23 Jun Beverley RF 2192). Consistent. In good form in claimers, he needs to come from behind.
**N Tinkler [3-22] The Penniless Partnership (from J H M Gosden [0-8] Oct 1996).*

GOLDFAME (IRE) BHB 64f81a **RR 71f 81a** 4744[16]

3 b g Shalford (IRE) 7.8f **(63)** - Une Venitienne (FR) (Green Dancer (USA)) 10.3f **(74)**
Form - 662513612000
Record 1998 - 1st:2 2nd:2 3rd:1 Ran:12
Win Prizemoney £6,852 *Total Prizemoney* £10,408
Wins * **1998** *Aug Southw (STD) H 8f 73 79 <*
* **1998** *Jly Southw (STD) 8f 73+*
1998 Turf 0-7: (7f, 8f 5, 10f) (g-s 2, gd, g-f, frm 3) 1998 AW 2-5: (7f, 8f 2-4) (Fibr 2-5)
Strong, above-average gelding, effective 7 to 8f, best at 8f, acts on frm - acts on Fibr, has worn blinkers, prefers left handed tracks, prefers tight tracks. Turf high 71 - 2nd of 12 getting 18lb from Blooming Amazing (25 Aug Pontefract 8f frm RF 3852). AW high 79 - 1st of 16 getting 12lb from Pass The Rest (14 Aug Southwell RF 3640) - also 1st of 7 from Hever Golf Machine (11 Jly Southwell RF 2722). A real Fibresand specialist, his only poor effort on that surface to date came at Wolverhampton, when he blew his chance by sweating up in the preliminaries. Twice an impressive winner over the Southwell mile, it would not be a great surprise to see him racing on the other side of the Atlantic at some point in the future.
**W A O'Gorman [2-12] N S Yong.*

GOLD HONOR (FR) BHB 70f **RR 73f** 5073[1]

2 gr g Highest Honor (FR) 10.9f **(72)** - Golden Sea (FR) (Saint Cyrien (FR)) 8.4f **(80)**
Form - 0304071
Record 1998 - 1st:1 2nd:0 3rd:1 Ran:7
Win Prizemoney £4,240 *Total Prizemoney* £5,175
Wins * **1998** Oct Newmar (SFT) S 8f 73 <
1998 Turf 1-6: (6f, 7f 3, 8f 1-2) (gd 1-3, g-f, frm 2) 1998 AW 0-1: (6f) (Fibr)
Above-average gelding, effective 8f, acts on gd, has worn blinkers. Turf high 81 - also 1st of 19 from Daunted (31 Oct Newmarket RF 5073). **B J Meehan [1-7] Mrs Susan Roy.*

GOLD LANCE (USA) BHB 55f39a **RR 60f 39a** 3667[6]

5 ch g Seeking the Gold (USA) 7.4f **(80)** - Lucky State (USA) (State Dinner (USA)) 9.4f **(74)**
Form - 006
Record 1998 - 1st:0 2nd:0 3rd:0 Ran:2
Pre1998 - 1st:4 2nd:1 3rd:3 Ran:17
Win Prizemoney £13,264 *Total Prizemoney* £15,548
Wins * 1997 Spt Goodwo (GD) H 8f 56 60 <
* 1997 Aug Windso (G-F) H 8.3f 53 57
* 1997 Jly Chepst (G-F) SH 8.1f 48 53
* 1997 Apr Pontef (G-F) SH 8f 45 53
1998 Turf 0-2: (10f 2) (g-f, frm)
Average gelding, effective 8f, acts on gd to hrd, has worn blinkers. Turf high 44 (began Aug).
**R J O'Sullivan [4-24] Mrs Barbara Marchant (from Sir Michael Stoute [0-2] Jun 1996).*

GOLD LAND (USA) **RR 91f** 5164a[4]

7 b h Gone West (USA) 7.8f **(82)** - Lajna (Be My Guest (USA)) 9.3f **(67)**
Form - 4
1998 AW 0-1: (6f) (Dirt)
Very high-class horse. Trained by Paul Cole in 1993/94, he has been racing in the USA since, and was a strong-finishing fourth in the Breeders' Cup Sprint in 1998.
**N Drysdale in USA [0-1] H R H Prince Fahd Salman (from P F I Cole [3-15] Oct 1994).*

GOLDLINER GOSSIP (IRE) BHB 37f **RR 43f** 4275[20]

3 b f Pips Pride 6.7f **(70)** - Swift And Early (IRE) (Alzao (USA)) 7.1f **(68)**
Form - 500
Record 1998 - 1st:0 2nd:0 3rd:0 Ran:3
1998 Turf 0-3: (7f, 8f 2) (g-s, gd, frm)
Light-framed, currently moderate filly. Turf high 43.
**Miss M E Rowland [0-3] Goldliner Racing Club.*

GOLD LODGE BHB 85f **RR 80f** 4484[2]

2 ch c Grand Lodge (USA) - Glimmering Girl (USA) (Spectacular Bid (USA)) 11.2f **(76)**
Form - 042
Record 1998 - 1st:0 2nd:1 3rd:0 Ran:3
Win Prizemoney £0 *Total Prizemoney* £1,281
1998 Turf 0-3: (7f, 8f, 9f) (g-f, frm 2)
Currently decent colt. Turf high 80 (began Jly) - 2nd of 5 giving 5lb to Eilean Shona (25 Spt Redcar 9f frm RF 4484).
**S C Williams [0-3] Livingston Trading Ltd.*

GOLDMAN (IRE) **RR 96f** 4904a[3]

3 br c Statoblest 6.4f **(63)** - Adamparais 00
Form - 711703
1998 Turf 2-5: (7f 1-1, 8f, 9f 1-3) (sft, gd 1-3, g-f 1-1)
Very useful colt, effective 7 to 9f, acts on sft to gd, has worn blinkers. Turf high 96 (began Aug) - 3rd of 4 giving 5lb to Balla Sola (16 Oct Gowran Park 9f sft RF 4904a) - also 1st of 12 giving 7lb to Hartstown Girl (29 Aug Curragh RF 4041a).
**Miss Frances Crowley in IRE [2-5] Crock of Gold Syndicate (from A P O'Brien in IRE [0-9] Nov 1997).*

GOLD MIST BHB 80f **RR 81f** 3457[3]

3 b f Darshaan 11.9f **(81)** - Lake Mist (Kings Lake (USA)) 10.8f **(67)**
Form - 0014413
Record 1998 - 1st:2 2nd:0 3rd:1 Ran:7
Win Prizemoney £7,052 *Total Prizemoney* £9,462
Wins * **1998** Jly Sandow (GD) H 14f 78 81 <
* **1998** May Redcar (GD) 10f 79
1998 Turf 2-7: (7f 2, 10f 1-1, 11f, 12f, 14f 1-1, 16f) (sft, gd 1-4, g-f 1-2)
Leggy, decent filly, effective 10 to 14f, acts on gd to g-f, best on gd. Turf high 81 - 1st of 11 getting 14lb from Tough Act (15 Jly Sandown RF 2830) - also 1st of 5 getting 5lb from El Ghaazee (11 May Redcar RF 1150). The winner of a Redcar maiden in May, she stepped up in trip to land a fourteen-furlong handicap at Sandown in July, but did not seem to quite get two miles at Ascot.

**R W Armstrong [2-7] Mrs Johnny Mckeever.*

GOLD OF ARABIA (USA) RR 68[6]
5 b g Seeking the Gold (USA) 7.4f **(80)** - Twitchet (USA) (Roberto (USA)) 10f **(76)**
Form - 6
Record 1998 - 1st:0 2nd:0 3rd:0 Ran:1
1998 AW 0-1: (12f) (Fibr)
Very moderate gelding, always wears blinkers.
**K A Morgan [0-5] W Tyler.*

GOLD PARK BHB 65f **RR 58** 3098[12]
3 b g Wing Park - Little Park (Cragador) 6f **(67)**
Form - 520
Record 1998 - 1st:0 2nd:1 3rd:0 Ran:3
Win Prizemoney £0 *Total Prizemoney* £639
1998 AW 0-3: (6f 2, 8f) (Equi, Fibr 2)
Workmanlike, fair gelding. AW high 58 - 2nd of 11 giving 5lb to Silken Dalliance (20 Mar Southwell 6f Fibr RF 0453). (DEAD)
**J E Banks [0-3] Roger Cole Shilton.*

GOLD RUSH (IRE) BHB 87f **RR 72f** 2503[2]
2 b c Namaqualand (USA) - Shillay (Lomond (USA)) 8.8f **(65)**
Form - 012
Record 1998 - 1st:1 2nd:1 3rd:0 Ran:3
Win Prizemoney £4,402 *Total Prizemoney* £6,640
Wins * 1998 Jun Ayr (G-F) 7f 68 <
1998 Turf 1-3: (6f, 7f 1-2) (gd, g-f 1-2)
Currently above-average colt. Turf high 72 - also 1st of 7 from High Regard (20 Jun Ayr RF 2144). Won a small race at Ayr but was no match for Menus at Sandown next time. Looks a stayer.
**B W Hills [1-3] Guy Reed.*

GOLD SPICE RR 63f 2865[2]
2 b f King's Signet (USA) 7f **(51)** - Calvanne Miss (Martinmas) 7.6f **(59)**
Form - 02
Record 1998 - 1st:0 2nd:1 3rd:0 Ran:2
Win Prizemoney £0 *Total Prizemoney* £824
1998 Turf 0-2: (5f, 6f) (gd, frm)
Average filly. Turf high 63. (DEAD)
**J Berry [0-2] John Milner & Stephen Milner.*

GOLDTUNE BHB 52f **RR 55f** 2312[3]
3 b f Damister (USA) 9.1f **(66)** - Tantalizing Song (CAN) (The Minstrel (CAN)) 10f **(72)**
Form - 35003
Record 1998 - 1st:0 2nd:0 3rd:2 Ran:5
Pre1998 - 1st:0 2nd:0 3rd:0 Ran:3
Win Prizemoney £0 *Total Prizemoney* £1,113
1998 Turf 0-5: (7f, 8f 2, 10f 2) (g-s, gd, g-f 2, frm)
Workmanlike, fair filly. Turf high 55. **M A Jarvis [0-8] N S Yong.*

GONDOLA (IRE) RR 64f 3832[12]
3 b g Caerleon (USA) 10.9f **(79)** - River Memories (USA) (Riverman (USA)) 9.1f **(76)**
Form - 5680
Record 1998 - 1st:0 2nd:0 3rd:0 Ran:4
1998 Turf 0-4: (10f, 11f 2, 12f) (g-f 3, frm)
Neat, average gelding, always wears blinkers. Turf high 64 (began Jly). **J H M Gosden [0-4] Sheikh Mohammed.*

GONE FOR A BURTON (IRE) BHB 70f **RR 71f** 4708[5]
8 ch g Bustino 11f **(64)** - Crimbourne (Mummy's Pet) 7.7f **(60)**
Form - 08355
Record 1998 - 1st:0 2nd:0 3rd:1 Ran:5
Pre1998 - 1st:3 2nd:4 3rd:4 Ran:27
Win Prizemoney £8,946 *Total Prizemoney* £26,678
Wins * 1995 Apr Warwic (G-S) H 10.8f 80 86 <
* 1994 Spt Ayr (G-S) 10.9f 80
1998 Turf 0-5: (10f 3, 11f, 12f) (gd 2, g-f, frm 2)
Above-average gelding, effective 10f, acts on gd, has worn blinkers. Turf high 71. Consistent. He does not look the horse he once was. **P J Makin [3-38] H P Carrington.*

GONLARGO (GER) RR 98f 4215a[2]
2 b c Big Shuffle (USA) - Gonfalon (Slip Anchor) 9.8f **(73)**
Form - 2
1998 Turf 0-1: (6f) (sft)
Currently very useful colt. (1st run) - 2nd of 9 giving 4lb to Golden Silca (4 Spt Baden-Baden 6f sft RF 4215a). Showed moderate form when second to Golden Silca at Baden-Baden.
**U Ostmann in GER [0-1].*

GONTCHAROVA (IRE) RR 94f 2289a[7]
3 f
Form - 7
1998 Turf 0-1: (12f) (gd)
Currently useful filly. **A Fabre in FR [0-1] Mme P de Moussac.*

GONZAGA (IRE) RR 105f 276a[2]
4 ro c Pistolet Bleu (IRE) - Gay Spring (FR) (Free Round (USA)) 11.7f **(70)**
Form - 2
1998 Turf 0-1: (13f) (gd)
Scopey, Pattern-class colt. (1st run) - 2nd of 10 getting 13lb from Irish Holmes (4 Feb Cagnes-sur-mer 13f gd RF 0276a). Now trained by John Hammond, previously having been with John Dunlop, he is useful and seems to stay well.
**J E Hammond in FR [0-1] (from J L Dunlop [2-3] May 1997).*

GOODBYE (IRE) BHB 78f **RR 68f** 3976[7]
2 b c Thatching 7.8f **(69)** - Itqan (IRE) (Sadler's Wells (USA)) 10f **(76)**
Form - 567
Record 1998 - 1st:0 2nd:0 3rd:0 Ran:3
1998 Turf 0-3: (7f 2, 8f) (gd 2, frm)
Currently average colt. Turf high 68.
**J L Dunlop [0-3] Philip Wroughton.*

GOODBYE GATEMEN (IRE) BHB 51f50a **RR 42f 50a** 928[9]
4 gr g Soviet Lad (USA) 9.4f **(63)** - Simple Love (Simply Great (FR)) 8.2f **(65)**
Form - 0526235455340
Record 1998 - 1st:0 2nd:1 3rd:2 Ran:10
Pre1998 - 1st:1 2nd:5 3rd:0 Ran:15
Win Prizemoney £2,469 *Total Prizemoney* £9,159
Wins * 1997 Jly Leices (GD) 5f 46 <
1998 Turf 0-1: (6f) (gd) 1998 AW 0-9: (5f 4, 6f 3, 7f 2) (Equi 9)
Unfurnished, fair gelding, effective 5 to 7f, best at 7f, acts on gd to frm - acts on Equi, has worn blinkers. AW high 56. Consistent. He possesses a fair amount of early speed, but is not the easiest of rides.
**B A Pearce [1-24] Mrs E N Nield (from M J Heaton-Ellis [0-1] Oct 1996).*

GOODBYE GOLDSTONE RR 63f 4999[3]
2 b c Mtoto 11.5f **(71)** - Shareehan (Dancing Brave (USA)) 8.4f **(76)**
Form - 3
Record 1998 - 1st:0 2nd:0 3rd:1 Ran:1
Win Prizemoney £0 *Total Prizemoney* £495
1998 Turf 0-1: (7f) (sft)
Currently average colt. **T J Naughton [0-1] Ashley Carr Racing 2.*

GOOD CATCH (IRE) BHB 71f **RR 66f** 3874a[5]
3 br f Last Tycoon 9.4f **(73)** - Good Reference (IRE) (Reference Point) 6.8f **(70)**
Form - 005
Record 1998 - 1st:0 2nd:0 3rd:0 Ran:3
Pre1998 - 1st:0 2nd:0 3rd:2 Ran:5
Win Prizemoney £0 *Total Prizemoney* £990
1998 Turf 0-3: (9f, 10f, 13f) (g-f 2, frm)
Light-framed, average filly, effective 6 to 7f, acts on frm, has worn blinkers. Turf high 66. Becoming disappointing.
**D Wachman in IRE [0-2] Fountain Syndicate (from P R Webber [0-6] Jun 1998).*

GOOD ENOUGH (FR) RR 109f 1918a[4]
3 gr f Mukaddamah (USA) 7.6f **(74)** - Viceroy Princess (Godswalk (USA)) 7.3f **(58)**
Form - 34
1998 Turf 0-2: (10f, 11f) (sft, gd)
Currently Pattern-class filly. Turf high 109 (1st run) - 3rd of 9 to Zainta (17 May Longchamp 10f gd RF 1382a).
**P Demercastel in FR [0-2] Ecurie Fabien Ouaki.*

GOODENOUGH GIRL RR 2f 2732[15]

2 b f Mac's Imp (USA) 5.6f **(54)** - Marton Maid (Silly Season) 9.7f **(56)**
Form - 000
Record 1998 - 1st:0 2nd:0 3rd:0 Ran:3
1998 Turf 0-3: (6f 2, 7f) (gd 2, frm)
Currently very poor filly. Turf high 2.
**E A Wheeler [0-3] D Goodenough Removals & Transport.*

GOOD FOR YOU BHB 30f RR 454[15]

3 ch g Ron's Victory (USA) 9.2f **(52)** - To Oneiro (Absalom) 7.2f **(58)**
Form - 000
Record 1998 - 1st:0 2nd:0 3rd:0 Ran:3
Pre1998 - 1st:0 2nd:0 3rd:0 Ran:2
1998 AW 0-3: (5f, 6f, 7f) (Fibr 3)
Unfurnished, poor gelding, has worn blinkers. AW high 11.
**D Moffatt [0-3] Uncle Jacks Pub (from S E Kettlewell [0-2] Aug 1997).*

GOOD HAND (USA) BHB 55f RR 56f 3966[2]

12 ch g Northjet 14.1f **(78)** - Ribonette (USA) (Ribot) 15.4f **(65)**
Form - 111142232
Record 1998 - 1st:4 2nd:3 3rd:1 Ran:9
Pre1998 - 1st:12 2nd:8 3rd:5 Ran:71
Win Prizemoney £72,325 *Total Prizemoney* £102,781

Wins								
	*** 1998**	Jun	Hamilt	(G-S)	C	12.1f		55
	*** 1998**	Jun	Nottin	(GD)	C	16f		56
	*** 1998**	Jun	Catter	(G-S)	C	13.8f		52+
	*** 1998**	May	Catter	(SFT)	S	13.8f		55+
	* 1997	Aug	Redcar	(FRM)	S	14.1f		42
	* 1996	Spt	Redcar	(FRM)	H	14.1f	69	75+
	* 1996	Spt	Ayr	(G-F)	H	17.5f	64	69
	1996	Jun	Redcar	(G-F)	C	16f		59
	1995	May	Newcas	(GD)	H	16.1f	73	78
	1994	May	Newcas	(FRM)	H	16.1f	76	82+

1998 Turf 4-9: (12f 1-3, 14f 2-4, 16f 1-2) (gd 3-4, g-f 1-2, frm 3)
Fair gelding, effective 12 to 16f, acts on gd to frm, best on gd, has worn blinkers, likes left handed tracks, and excels at Catterick. Turf high 56 - 3rd of 4 getting 2lb from Silently (8 Aug Redcar 14f frm RF 3477) - also 1st of 9 giving 3lb to Brodessa (22 Jun Nottingham RF 2176). Consistent. Made hay last term, winning another seller and three claimers. A credit to connections, he crossed swords with Brodessa six times during the season.
**S E Kettlewell [11-23] Uncle Jacks Pub (from J W Watts [9-62] Jun 1996).*

GOOD ON YER BHB 36f RR 22f 4535[16]

3 b f Reprimand 8.2f **(63)** - Princess Eurolink (Be My Guest (USA)) 9.3f **(67)**
Form - 00
Record 1998 - 1st:0 2nd:0 3rd:0 Ran:2
Pre1998 - 1st:0 2nd:0 3rd:1 Ran:5
Win Prizemoney £0 *Total Prizemoney* £387
1998 Turf 0-2: (8f 2) (g-s, frm)
Little account filly. Turf high 16 (began Aug).
**S E Kettlewell [0-7] Uncle Jacks Pub.*

GOOD TO TALK BHB 26f RR 38f 3280[14]

5 b g Weldnaas (USA) 8.4f **(55)** - Kimble Blue (Blue Refrain)
Form - 00
Record 1998 - 1st:0 2nd:0 3rd:0 Ran:2
Pre1998 - 1st:0 2nd:2 3rd:1 Ran:27
Win Prizemoney £0 *Total Prizemoney* £2,497
1998 Turf 0-2: (5f, 6f) (g-f, frm)
Very moderate gelding, effective 5f, acts on gd, has worn blinkers (effectively). Turf high 12 (began Jly). Inconsistent.
**T D Easterby [0-22] Mrs Kate Hall (from M H Easterby [0-7] Spt 1995).*

GOODWOOD CAVALIER BHB 88f RR 91f 1694[4]

3 b g Efisio 7.7f **(69)** - Brassy Nell (Dunbeath (USA)) 7.8f **(70)**
Form - 234
Record 1998 - 1st:0 2nd:1 3rd:1 Ran:3
Pre1998 - 1st:1 2nd:0 3rd:0 Ran:3
Win Prizemoney £3,379 *Total Prizemoney* £7,153
Wins * 1997 Oct Leices (G-S) 7f 86 <
1998 Turf 0-3: (7f, 8f, 9f) (sft, g-s, gd)
Unfurnished, useful gelding, effective 7 to 8f, best at 7f, acts on sft to gd. Turf high 91 (1st run) - 2nd of 11 giving 3lb to The Downtown Fox (9 Apr Leicester 7f sft RF 0619). He ran quite well to make the frame in soft ground in his first two starts, but ran poorly on faster ground on his third and final start.
**J L Dunlop [1-6] Goodwood Racehorse Owners Group (Three).*

GOODWOOD JAZZ (IRE) BHB 73f RR 77f 4613[11]

2 b f Night Shift (USA) 8.1f **(73)** - Wood Violet (USA) (Riverman (USA)) 9.1f **(76)**
Form - 032370
Record 1998 - 1st:0 2nd:1 3rd:2 Ran:6
Win Prizemoney £0 *Total Prizemoney* £1,909
1998 Turf 0-6: (6f 2, 7f 4) (g-s, gd 3, g-f, frm)
Above-average filly, effective 7f, acts on g-f to frm. Turf high 77 - 3rd of 9 giving 7lb to Gino's Spirits (5 Aug Brighton 7f g-f RF 3362). **J L Dunlop [0-6] Goodwood Racehorse Owners Group (Four).*

GO POSITIVE BHB 40f43a RR 43f 43a 4862[3]

3 b f Profilic - Rather Gorgeous (Billion (USA)) 12f **(43)**
Form - 440384526203
Record 1998 - 1st:0 2nd:2 3rd:2 Ran:12
Win Prizemoney £0 *Total Prizemoney* £2,469
1998 Turf 0-7: (11f, 12f 4, 16f 2) (g-s, gd 3, g-f 2, frm) 1998 AW 0-5: (12f 5) (Fibr 5)
Moderate filly, effective 12f, acts on frm - acts on Fibr, favours tight tracks. Turf high 54. AW high 46 - 2nd of 11 getting 10lb from Miss Vita (22 Aug Wolverhampton 12f Fibr RF 3830). Consistent.
**Mrs G S Rees [0-12] Tom Murray.*

GORDI (USA) BHB 100f RR 102f 4913a[2]

5 ch g Theatrical 11.5f **(78)**-Royal Alydar (USA) (Alydar (USA)) 9.1f **(76)**
Form - 4206702
1998 Turf 0-7: (12f 3, 14f 2, 16f, 20f) (sft, g-s 2, gd, g-f 2, frm)
Very useful gelding, effective 14f, acts on g-f to frm, has worn blinkers, prefers left handed tracks. Turf high 108 - 2nd of 6 giving 3lb to French Ballerina (20 May Leopardstown 14f g-f RF 1492a). Inconsistent. He is not the force of old, but ran a sound race when finishing seventh in the Tote Ebor at York. Handicaps, rather than Group races, would seem to be his favoured option.
**D K Weld in IRE [3-17] Michael Smurfit*

GORE HILL BHB 32f RR 40f 3848[14]

4 b f Be My Chief (USA) 10.2f **(62)** - Hollow Heart (Wolver Hollow) 8f **(56)**
Form - 40440
Record 1998 - 1st:0 2nd:0 3rd:0 Ran:5
Pre1998 - 1st:0 2nd:0 3rd:0 Ran:5
1998 Turf 0-5: (10f 3, 11f, 12f) (gd 2, frm 3)
Neat, moderate filly, effective 10 to 12f, acts on gd, prefers left handed tracks, favours tight tracks. Turf high 40 (1st run) - 4th of 18 getting 10lb from Ron's Round (17 Jun Nottingham 10f gd RF 2069). Inconsistent.
**M R Bosley [0-5] The Blowingstone Partnership (from M Blanshard [0-5] Jun 1997).*

GORETSKI (IRE) BHB 70f80a RR 69f 80a 5142[3]

5 b g Polish Patriot (USA) 7.8f **(70)** - Celestial Path (Godswalk (USA)) 7.3f **(58)**
Form - 0078810511210500083
Record 1998 - 1st:4 2nd:1 3rd:1 Ran:19
Pre1998 - 1st:8 2nd:6 3rd:0 Ran:35
Win Prizemoney £41,008 *Total Prizemoney* £49,935

Wins									
	*** 1998**	Aug	Beverl	(G-F)	H	5f	70	74	
	*** 1998**	*Jly*	*Southw*	*(STD)*	*H*	*5f*	*74*	*80*	<
	*** 1998**	*Jly*	*Southw*	*(STD)*	*H*	*5f*	*67*	*74*	
	*** 1998**	Jun	Pontef	(SFT)		5f		66	
	* 1997	Aug	Beverl	(G-S)	H	5f	71	78	
	* 1997	Jly	Catter	(G-F)	H	5f	60	63	
	* 1997	Jly	Bath	(GD)	H	5.1f	60	65+	
	* 1997	*Jun*	*Southw*	*(STD)*	*H*	*5f*	*59*	*67*	
	* 1997	*Jun*	*Southw*	*(STD)*	*H*	*5f*	*59*	*63*	
	* 1997	May	Hamilt	(SFT)	H	5f	54	59	
	* 1996	Apr	Catter	(GD)	H	5f	58	57+	
	* 1995	Aug	Redcar	(FRM)	S	6f		66+	

1998 Turf 2-17: (5f 2-15, 6f 2) (sft, g-s 2, gd 2-9, g-f 2, frm 3) 1998 AW 2-2: (5f 2-2) (Fibr 2-2)
Decent gelding, effective 5f, acts on gd to frm - acts on Fibr, has worn blinkers, excels at Southwell and Beverley and Pontefract. Turf high 75 - 5th of 20 getting 4lb from Indian Spark (11 Spt Doncaster 5f g-f RF 4228) - also 1st of 15 giving 2lb to Fairy Prince

(12 Aug Beverley RF 3567). AW high 80 (began Jly) - 1st of 13 giving 32lb to Harvey's Future (25 Jly Southwell RF 3130) - also 1st of 12 giving 30lb to Mukarrab (17 Jly Southwell RF 2898). He returned to his very best in the middle of the season, adding two more victories over the Southwell five, including a course record, and turf wins at Pontefract and Beverley. **N Tinkler [12-54] P D Savill.*

GORGEOUS BHB 50a **RR 36f** 4383[12]

3 b f Prince Sabo 6.6f **(64)** - Crackerjill (Sparkler) 8.4f **(55)**
Form - 00
Record 1998 - 1st:0 2nd:0 3rd:0 Ran:2
Pre1998 - 1st:0 2nd:0 3rd:0 Ran:4
1998 Turf 0-1: (8f) (gd) 1998 AW 0-1: (8f) (Fibr)
Light-framed, very moderate filly.
**M Waring [0-2] Dunstall Park Centre Ltd (from N P Littmoden [0-4] Aug 1997).*

GORGEOUS GUSSY (USA) BHB 48f **RR 52f** 3040[9]

3 b br f Quiet American (USA) 7.9f **(60)** - Bounding Away (CAN) (Vice Regent (CAN)) 8.7f **(74)**
Form - 505650
Record 1998 - 1st:0 2nd:0 3rd:0 Ran:6
1998 Turf 0-4: (10f 2, 11f, 12f) (gd 2, g-f 2) 1998 AW 0-2: (12f, 15f) (Fibr 2)
Leggy, fair filly, has worn blinkers. Turf high 52. AW high 42.
**M Bell [0-6] Nasser Abdullah.*

GORSE BHB 107f **RR 111f** 5152[1]

3 b c Sharpo 7.5f **(68)** - Pervenche (Latest Model) 6f **(62)**
Form - 124011
Record 1998 - 1st:3 2nd:1 3rd:0 Ran:6
Win Prizemoney £20,497 *Total Prizemoney* £23,818
Wins * **1998** Nov Doncas (SFT) L 6f 111 <
* **1998** Oct Newmar (SFT) 6f 98
* **1998** May Salisb (G-S) 6f 100+
1998 Turf 3-6: (6f 3-6) (g-s 1-1, gd 2-2, g-f 3)
Group-class colt, effective 6f, acts on gd. Turf high 111 - 1st of 12 getting 6lb from Yorkies Boy (7 Nov Doncaster RF 5152). Kept off the track by a stress fracture in 1997, he burst on the scene when winning a maiden by nine lengths at Salisbury in May. Badly ridden when beaten at Newbury on his next start, he needs soft ground and was rested during the summer months. Back to his best when winning at Newmarket in October, he finished with a flourish when landing a Listed event at Doncaster the following month, and promises to make an even better four-year-old, when the Duke Of York Stakes could be a suitable early season target. He seems to need a strong jockey. **H Candy [3-6] Girsonfield Ltd.*

GO SALLY GO (IRE) BHB 51f **RR 56f** 2853[9]

2 b f Elbio 9f **(62)** - Pollette (Stanford) 7.9f **(56)**
Form - 000730
Record 1998 - 1st:0 2nd:0 3rd:1 Ran:6
Win Prizemoney £0 *Total Prizemoney* £252
1998 Turf 0-3: (5f 3) (gd, frm 2) 1998 AW 0-3: (5f 3) (Fibr 3)
Fair filly, effective 5f, acts on frm. Turf high 56 - 3rd of 6 to Yorkshire Grit (2 Jly Catterick 5f frm RF 2461). AW high 45.
**R Craggs [0-6] Ten For Sport Partnership.*

GOTHENBERG (IRE) BHB 117f **RR 113f** 848[9]

5 b h Polish Patriot (USA) 7.8f **(70)**-Be Discreet (Junius (USA)) 7.7f **(65)**
Form - 20
Record 1998 - 1st:0 2nd:0 3rd:0 Ran:1
Pre1998 - 1st:7 2nd:4 3rd:4 Ran:35
Win Prizemoney £200,037 *Total Prizemoney* £314,764
Wins * 1997 Jly Hoppeg (GD) G2 8f 116
* 1997 Jun San Si (HVY) G2 8f 118
* 1996 Jun Currag (GD) G2 8f 119 <
* 1996 Apr Currag (G-S) G3 7f 105?
* 1995 Jun Epsom (G-F) L 6f 92+
* 1995 May Newcas (GD) 5f 82+
* 1995 May Hamilt (G-F) 5f 64+
1998 Turf 0-1: (8f) (sft)
Group-class colt, effective 8f, acts on hvy to gd, best on gd, prefers right handed tracks. A cracking soft ground miler at his best, he went AWOL in 1998 and obviously had a problem.
**M Johnston [7-36] Brian Yeardley Continental Ltd.*

GOWITHTHEFLOW (IRE) BHB 61f **RR 61df** 4658[15]

2 b g River Falls 8.2f **(56)** - Astral Way (Hotfoot) 10.5f **(59)**
Form - 53400
Record 1998 - 1st:0 2nd:0 3rd:1 Ran:5
Win Prizemoney £0 *Total Prizemoney* £458
1998 Turf 0-5: (5f 3, 6f 2) (gd 3, g-f 2)
Average gelding. Turf high 66. **B S Rothwell [0-5] Mrs H M Carr.*

GO WITH THE WIND BHB 51f **RR 48f** 2270[15]

5 b h Unfuwain (USA) 11.4f **(74)** - Cominna (Dominion) 8.5f **(63)**
Form - 340
Record 1998 - 1st:0 2nd:0 3rd:1 Ran:3
Pre1998 - 1st:1 2nd:3 3rd:2 Ran:16
Win Prizemoney £3,343 *Total Prizemoney* £9,520
Wins 1996 Spt Nottin (G-F) H 16f 60 67 <
1998 Turf 0-3: (13f, 15f, 16f) (g-s, gd, g-f)
Moderate colt, has worn blinkers. Turf high 48. Becoming disappointing. **J S Goldie [2-7] Alf Chadwick (from M Bell [1-14] Oct 1996).*

GRACE BHB 59a **RR 60f** 4988[5]

4 b f Buzzards Bay 8.9f **(44)** - Bingo Bongo (Petong) 6.6f **(58)**
Form - 427061200605
Record 1998 - 1st:1 2nd:2 3rd:0 Ran:12
Pre1998 - 1st:0 2nd:0 3rd:0 Ran:7
Win Prizemoney £3,048 *Total Prizemoney* £5,511
Wins * **1998** Jun Chepst (G-S) H 6.1f 50 60 <
1998 Turf 1-11: (5f, 6f 1-10) (sft 2, g-s 3, gd 1-3, g-f, frm 2) 1998 AW 0-1: (6f) (Fibr)
Leggy, average filly, effective 6f, acts on g-s to g-f. Turf high 60 - 1st of 15 giving 16lb to Bairn Atholl (12 Jun Chepstow RF 1926).
**J M Bradley [1-19] Treevale Syndicate.*

GRACE BROWNING BHB 64f **RR 61f** 4475[13]

3 b f Forzando 7.2f **(63)** - Queen Angel (Anfield) 8.5f **(59)**
Form - 0000
Record 1998 - 1st:0 2nd:0 3rd:0 Ran:4
Pre1998 - 1st:1 2nd:0 3rd:1 Ran:2
Win Prizemoney £3,382 *Total Prizemoney* £3,838
Wins * 1997 Oct Warwic (G-F) 6f 81+ <
1998 Turf 0-4: (6f, 7f 3) (gd 2, g-f 2)
Average filly, effective 6f, acts on g-f. Turf high 61.
**H Candy [1-6] Mrs Robert Langton.*

GRACEFUL LASS BHB 97f **RR 99f** 4716a[7]

4 b f Sadler's Wells (USA)11.3f **(87)**-Hi Lass (Shirley Heights) 10.3f **(74)**
Form - 27
1998 Turf 0-2: (16f, 20f) (sft, gd)
Workmanlike, very useful filly, effective 12 to 20f, acts on sft to g-f. Turf high 99 (began Spt) - 7th of 9 getting 4lb from Invermark (3 Oct Longchamp 20f sft RF 4716a). Formerly trained by David Loder, she was a creditable second to Taufan's Melody at Baden-Baden, but was well outclassed in the Prix du Cadran.
**J E Pease in FR [0-2] A M Budgett (from D R Loder [2-8] Oct 1997).*

GRACE MELBURY BHB 54f **RR 59f** 4612[13]

2 ch f Forzando 7.2f **(63)** - Figini (Glint of Gold) 9.3f **(66)**
Form - 7070000
Record 1998 - 1st:0 2nd:0 3rd:0 Ran:7
1998 Turf 0-7: (5f 3, 6f 3, 7f) (g-s, gd 2, g-f, frm 3)
Fair filly, has worn blinkers. Turf high 56.
**M Blanshard [0-7] S P Tindall.*

GRACIOUS GIFT **RR 84f** 4668[2]

2 ch f Cadeaux Genereux 7.9f **(76)** - Gentle Persuasion (Bustino) 10.4f **(64)**
Form - 62
Record 1998 - 1st:0 2nd:1 3rd:0 Ran:2
Win Prizemoney £0 *Total Prizemoney* £1,262
1998 Turf 0-2: (6f 2) (gd, g-f)
Currently decent filly. Turf high 84 (began Spt) - 2nd of 17 to Emma Peel (6 Oct Nottingham 6f gd RF 4668).
**Lord Huntingdon [0-2] The Queen.*

GRACIOUS PLENTY (IRE) BHB 91f **RR 87f** 4495[5]

2 ch f Generous (IRE) 11.5f **(82)** - Formide (USA) (Trempolino (USA)) 12f **(71)**
Form - 325

Record 1998 - 1st:0 2nd:1 3rd:1 Ran:3
Win Prizemoney £0 *Total Prizemoney* £2,684
1998 Turf 0-3: (7f 3) (gd 2, frm)
Currently useful filly. Turf high 87 (began Aug) - 2nd of 6 to Annapurna (9 Spt Kempton 7f gd RF 4191). Ran a fine race on her debut when third in a big field of maidens, but was slightly disappointing subsequently albeit in a decent race on her final start.
**B W Hills [0-3] E D Kessly.*

GRADUATED (IRE) RR 94f — 5027a6

6 b g Royal Academy (USA) 7.8f **(77)** - Saviour (USA) (Majestic Light (USA)) 10.6f **(75)**
Form - 3376
1998 Turf 0-3: (8f, 9f, 11f) (hvy, g-s, gd)
Useful gelding, effective 8 to 12f, best at 9f, acts on g-s to gd, best on gd, has worn blinkers. Turf high 94.
**J S Bolger in IRE [7-23] Michael Smurfit.*

GRAF PHILIPP (GER) RR 106f — 4723a3

3 c Acatenango (GER)
Form - 73
1998 Turf 0-2: (12f, 14f) (hvy, sft)
Currently Pattern-class colt. Turf high 106 (began Jly) - 3rd of 10 to Laveron (4 Oct Dortmund 14f sft RF 4723a). He acts on soft ground, but is unlikely to make any waves outside Germany.
**A Schutz in GER [0-2].*

GRALMANO (IRE) BHB 78f98a RR 81f 98a — 3298 5

3 b c Scenic 10.6f **(66)** - Llangollen (IRE) (Caerleon (USA)) 8.6f **(71)**
Form - 111328438535
Record 1998 - 1st:1 2nd:1 3rd:3 Ran:10
Pre1998 - 1st:2 2nd:2 3rd:1 Ran:9
Win Prizemoney £8,856 *Total Prizemoney* £15,201
Wins * **1998** *Feb Lingfi (SLW) 8f 91*
* 1997 *Dec Wolver (STD) 7f 94* <
* 1997 *Nov Wolver (STD) 8.5f 69*
1998 Turf 0-7: (9f 2, 10f 3, 11f, 12f) (g-s, gd 4, g-f, frm) 1998 AW 1-3: (8f 1-1, 9f, 10f) (Equi 1-2, Fibr)
Workmanlike, useful colt, effective 7 to 9f - acts on AW, best on Fibr, has worn blinkers, prefers left handed tracks, likes tight tracks. Turf high 82. AW high 94 - 2nd of 7 getting 12lb from Diamond Flame (14 Mar Wolverhampton 9f Fibr RF 0429) - also 1st of 7 getting 9lb from Barbason (5 Feb Lingfield RF 0224). He is a fair sort on turf but is a much better performer on sand, on which he completed a fine hat-trick at around new year. His subsequent turf form was nothing like as good.
**N P Littmoden [3-19] Coleorton Moor Racing.*

GRAND CHAPEAU (IRE) BHB 62f64a RR 62f 64a — 3854 7

6 b g Ballad Rock 7.2f **(63)** - All Hat (Double Form) 7.3f **(58)**
Form - 0500741847
Record 1998 - 1st:1 2nd:0 3rd:0 Ran:10
Pre1998 - 1st:4 2nd:3 3rd:1 Ran:34
Win Prizemoney £17,257 *Total Prizemoney* £24,211
Wins * **1998** *Jly Wolver (STD) H 6f 59 60*
* 1997 Aug Redcar (G-F) H 6f 61 63 <
* 1997 Aug Thirsk (GD) H 6f 50 57
* 1996 Spt Pontef (GD) H 6f 55 59
1995 Jly Windso (G-F) H 5f 59 58
1998 Turf 0-8: (5f 3, 6f 5) (g-s, gd, g-f, frm 5) 1998 AW 1-2: (5f, 6f 1-1) (Fibr 1-2)
Average gelding, effective 5 to 6f, best at 6f, acts on gd to frm - acts on Fibr, best on gd, likes left handed tracks, likes tight tracks, does well at Thirsk and Pontefract. Turf high 67 (1st run) - 5th of 23 giving 12lb to Mike's Double (15 May Thirsk 6f gd RF 1254). AW high 60 - 1st of 11 getting 10lb from Aljaz (20 Jly Wolverhampton RF 2967).
**D Nicholls [4-32] David Faulkner (from R Hannon [1-12] Oct 1995).*

GRAND CORONET RR 46f — 5072 11

2 b f Grand Lodge (USA) - Coronati (IRE) (Bluebird (USA)) 7.5f **(69)**
Form - 0
Record 1998 - 1st:0 2nd:0 3rd:0 Ran:1
1998 Turf 0-1: (7f) (gd)
Currently moderate filly. **T G Mills [0-1] T G Mills.*

GRAND CRU BHB 47f49a RR 59f 49a — 4875 8

7 ch g Kabour 6.1f **(36)** - Hydrangea (Warpath) 12.3f **(52)**
Form - 00048
Record 1998 - 1st:0 2nd:0 3rd:0 Ran:5
Pre1998 - 1st:3 2nd:0 3rd:2 Ran:9
Win Prizemoney £10,407 *Total Prizemoney* £11,765
Wins * 1997 May Newbur (SFT) H 16f 62 67 <
1997 *Apr Southw (STD) S 12f 67* <
1997 *Feb Southw (STD) C 14f 39*
1998 Turf 0-3: (12f 2, 14f) (gd 2, frm) 1998 AW 0-2: (12f, 15f) (Fibr 2)
Fair gelding, effective 12 to 16f, best at 16f, acts on gd to g-f - acts on Fibr, likes left handed tracks. Turf high 59 (began Spt). AW high 55. Inconsistent.
**J Cullinan [1-13] Alan Spargo Ltd Toolmakers (from R Craggs [1-2] Apr 1997).*

GRAND ESTATE BHB 70f RR 79f — 3999 10

3 b g Prince Sabo 6.6f **(64)** - Ultimate Dream (Kafu) 6f **(47)**
Form - 253760
Record 1998 - 1st:0 2nd:1 3rd:1 Ran:6
Pre1998 - 1st:1 2nd:0 3rd:1 Ran:7
Win Prizemoney £3,782 *Total Prizemoney* £7,604
Wins * 1997 Aug Thirsk (G-F) H 6f 69 75 <
1998 Turf 0-6: (5f 2, 6f 4) (g-s, gd 4, g-f)
Unfurnished, above-average gelding, effective 5 to 6f, best at 6f, acts on gd to frm, best on g-f, has worn blinkers. Turf high 79 (1st run) - 2nd of 11 getting 9lb from Five of Spades (3 Jun Newcastle 6f gd RF 1703). **T D Easterby [1-13] Ian Armitage.*

GRAND HOTEL (IRE) BHB 20f40a RR 29f 40a — 3579 13

4 ch g Be My Guest (USA) 10.2f **(66)** - State Treasure (USA) (Secretariat (USA)) 9f **(79)**
Form - 00005068000
Record 1998 - 1st:0 2nd:0 3rd:0 Ran:11
Pre1998 - 1st:1 2nd:1 3rd:0 Ran:8
Win Prizemoney £2,277 *Total Prizemoney* £3,194
Wins 1997 *Jun Wolver (STD) H 9.4f 47 47* <
1998 Turf 0-9: (8f 3, 9f, 11f, 12f, 13f, 14f, 16f) (hvy, sft, gd 4, g-f 2, frm) 1998 AW 0-2: (9f, 12f) (Fibr 2)
Scopey, fair gelding, effective 9f - acts on Fibr, often wears blinkers, likes left handed tracks, favours tight tracks. Turf high 29. Showed nothing on turf, but made a winning debut on sand at Wolverhampton in June. It was a very poor race however.
**R M McKellar [0-12] Gordon Cunningham (from P W Harris [1-8] Spt 1997).*

GRANDIOSO (IRE) RR 46f — 5116 6

2 b c High Estate 10.5f **(66)** - Palmyra (GER) (Arratos (FR)) 12.2f **(60)**
Form - 56
Record 1998 - 1st:0 2nd:0 3rd:0 Ran:2
1998 Turf 0-2: (6f, 8f) (g-s, gd)
Currently moderate colt. Turf high 46 (began Oct).
**C W Thornton [0-2] Guy Reed.*

GRAND MAITRE (USA) BHB 77f RR 77f — 4410 5

2 gr ro c Gone West (USA) 7.8f **(82)** - La Grande Epoque (USA) (Lyphard (USA)) 9.9f **(72)**
Form - 835
Record 1998 - 1st:0 2nd:0 3rd:1 Ran:3
Win Prizemoney £0 *Total Prizemoney* £593
1998 Turf 0-3: (7f 3) (frm 3)
Currently above-average colt. Turf high 77 (began Aug). Looked green in his first two runs, but has shown promise and should win races in time. **J L Dunlop [0-3] Robin Scully.*

GRAND MUSICA BHB 61f RR 66f — 4589 7

5 b g Puissance 7.1f **(60)** - Vera Musica (USA) (Stop The Music (USA)) 9.2f **(71)**
Form - 004140607
Record 1998 - 1st:1 2nd:0 3rd:0 Ran:9
Pre1998 - 1st:1 2nd:3 3rd:0 Ran:12
Win Prizemoney £6,490 *Total Prizemoney* £13,735
Wins * **1998** Jly Haydoc (G-F) H 10.5f 63 66
* 1996 Aug Epsom (GD) 7f 78 <
1998 Turf 1-9: (7f, 8f 2, 10f 5, 11f 1-1) (g-s, gd 3, g-f 1-4, frm)
Average gelding, effective 8 to 11f, acts on gd to g-f, has worn blinkers. Turf high 66. A facile winner at Sandown, he pulls tends

to pull hard, but the ability is there.

**I A Balding [2-21] Mach 3 Racing.*

GRAND OVATION (IRE) BHB 46f49a RR 58f 49a 4087[15]

4 b g Green Desert (USA) 7.8f **(78)** - Fitnah (Kris) 9.5f **(73)**
Form - 50050
Record 1998 - 1st:0 2nd:0 3rd:0 Ran:5
Pre1998 - 1st:0 2nd:0 3rd:0 Ran:1
1998 Turf 0-2: (7f, 8f) (g-s, gd) 1998 AW 0-3: (8f 3) (Equi 2, Fibr)
Scopey, fair gelding. Turf high 34. AW high 55.
**D J S Cosgrove [0-5] Derrick Yarwood (from B Hanbury [0-1] May 1997).*

GRAND ROYALE (USA) RR 69f 4492[9]

3 b c Danzig (USA) 8.1f **(88)** - Good Mood (USA) (Devil's Bag (USA)) 12.4f **(78)**
Form - 70
Record 1998 - 1st:0 2nd:0 3rd:0 Ran:2
1998 Turf 0-2: (6f, 7f) (gd 2)
Scopey, currently average colt. Turf high 69 (began Spt). An ex-American colt, he has been highly tried in this company.
**N A Callaghan [0-2] M Tabor & Mrs John Magnier.*

GRAND SLAM (IRE) BHB 73f RR 76f 4822[13]

3 b c Second Set (IRE) 9.2f **(67)** - Lady In The Park (IRE) (Last Tycoon) 8.5f **(62)**
Form - 2422410
Record 1998 - 1st:1 2nd:3 3rd:0 Ran:7
Pre1998 - 1st:0 2nd:0 3rd:0 Ran:2
Win Prizemoney £2,658 *Total Prizemoney* £6,647
Wins * 1998 Spt Warwic (G-F) 8f 76 <
1998 Turf 1-7: (7f 4, 8f 1-3) (gd 2, g-f, frm 1-4)
Strong, above-average colt, effective 7 to 8f, best at 7f, acts on gd to frm. Turf high 76 - 1st of 13 from Kennet (22 Spt Warwick RF 4415). **R Hannon [1-9] Mrs D M Wight.*

GRAND SLAM (USA) RR 122 5164a[2]

3 b c Gone West (USA) 7.8f **(82)**
Form - 2
1998 AW 0-1: (6f) (Dirt)
Currently very high-class colt. (1st run) - 2nd of 14 to Reraise (7 Nov Churchill Downs 6f Dirt RF 5164a). Well beaten in the Breeders' Cup Juvenile in 1997, he fared much better when a good second in the 1998 Breeders' Cup Sprint.
**D W Lukas in USA [0-2] R Baker & D Cornstein & W Mack.*

GRAND SONNET (IRE) RR 67f 4511[8]

2 b c Second Set (IRE) 9.2f **(67)** - Mali (USA) (Storm Bird (CAN)) 10.3f **(74)**
Form - 8
Record 1998 - 1st:0 2nd:0 3rd:0 Ran:1
1998 Turf 0-1: (7f) (gd)
Currently average colt.
**D R C Elsworth [0-1] Michael Jackson Bloodstock Ltd.*

GRAND VIEW BHB 61f RR 56f 4937[6]

2 ch c Grand Lodge (USA) - Hemline (Sharpo) 7.7f **(59)**
Form - 506
Record 1998 - 1st:0 2nd:0 3rd:0 Ran:3
1998 Turf 0-3: (5f, 6f 2) (gd 3)
Currently fair colt. Turf high 56 (began Jly).
**R Hannon [0-3] I A N Wight.*

GRANGEVILLE (USA) BHB 88f RR 89f 4854[4]

3 b g Gulch (USA) 9.6f **(79)** - Cor Anglais (USA) (Nijinsky (CAN)) 10.3f **(77)**
Form - 04352104
Record 1998 - 1st:1 2nd:1 3rd:1 Ran:8
Win Prizemoney £3,761 *Total Prizemoney* £6,161
Wins * 1998 Spt Sandow (GD) H 7.1f 77 84+ <
1998 Turf 1-8: (7f 1-3, 8f 5) (sft, gd, g-f 1-2, frm 4)
Workmanlike, useful gelding, effective 7f, acts on gd to g-f. Turf high 89 - 4th of 30 to Prince Babar (17 Oct Newmarket 7f gd RF 4854) - also 1st of 16 giving 15lb to Ca'd'oro (16 Spt Sandown RF 4308). **I A Balding [1-8] George Strawbridge.*

GRANNY HELEN BHB 47f RR 57f 4400[17]

2 b f Reprimand 8.2f **(63)** - Peak Squaw (USA) (Icecapade (USA)) 11f **(62)**
Form - 7353500
Record 1998 - 1st:0 2nd:0 3rd:2 Ran:7
Win Prizemoney £0 *Total Prizemoney* £723
1998 Turf 0-7: (5f 4, 6f 3) (g-s, gd 3, g-f, frm 2)
Fair filly, effective 5f, acts on gd to frm, has worn blinkers. Turf high 57 - 3rd of 10 to Poco (19 May Beverley 5f frm RF 1317).
**D Nicholls [0-2] Burke's 5th Family Settlement (from M W Easterby [0-5] May 1998).*

GRANNY'S PET BHB 100f RR 100f 4965[7]

4 ch g Selkirk (USA) 7.9f **(76)** - Patsy Western (Precocious) 8.6f **(62)**
Form - 0651027
Record 1998 - 1st:1 2nd:1 3rd:0 Ran:7
Pre1998 - 1st:1 2nd:3 3rd:2 Ran:14
Win Prizemoney £15,254 *Total Prizemoney* £37,904
Wins * 1998 Spt Haydoc (GD) H 7.1f 89 99 <
* 1996 Jun Epsom (GD) 5f 84
1998 Turf 1-7: (6f 2, 7f 1-4, 8f) (sft 2, gd 2, g-f, frm 1-2)
Scopey, very useful gelding, effective 6 to 7f, best at 7f, acts on gd to frm, best on frm, has worn blinkers. Turf high 100 - 2nd of 14 getting 3lb from Gaelic Storm (8 Oct York 7f frm RF 4707) - also 1st of 16 giving 9lb to Adjutant (5 Spt Haydock RF 4106). He looked thoroughly miserable in the spring, but came back refreshed after a mid-summer sabbatical and won unchallenged at Haydock in September. Far from disgraced in decent company thereafter, he has never been one for the mortgage and will probably continue to frustrate and enthuse in equal measures next season. Seven furlongs seems to be his optimum trip.
**P F I Cole [2-21] Mrs Denise Margot Arbib.*

GRANNYS RELUCTANCE (IRE) BHB 56f RR 58f 4796[9]

2 b br f Anita's Prince 6f **(62)** - Dawn is Breaking (Import) 6.6f **(68)**
Form - 6300
Record 1998 - 1st:0 2nd:0 3rd:1 Ran:4
Win Prizemoney £0 *Total Prizemoney* £474
1998 Turf 0-4: (5f 2, 6f 2) (sft, gd 2, frm)
Fair filly. Turf high 58.
**B Palling [0-4] Philip Reynolds & Mrs Anita Quinn.*

GRATE SPARK (IRE) BHB 35f RR 37f 5146[13]

2 b c Posen (USA) 8.6f **(59)** - Linda's Fantasy (Raga Navarro (ITY)) 8f **(64)**
Form - 000
Record 1998 - 1st:0 2nd:0 3rd:0 Ran:3
1998 Turf 0-3: (7f, 8f 2) (gd, g-f, frm)
Currently very moderate colt, has worn blinkers. Turf high 37 (began Oct). **E Weymes [0-3] Mrs M Ashby.*

GRAVY BOAT (IRE) RR 33f 3137[14]

2 b c River Falls 8.2f **(56)** - Newstreet Princess (Head for Heights) 9.6f **(55)**
Form - 000
Record 1998 - 1st:0 2nd:0 3rd:0 Ran:3
1998 Turf 0-3: (6f 3) (gd, g-f, frm)
Currently very moderate colt. Turf high 33.
**Miss S E Hall [0-3] Miss Betty Duxbury.*

GRAY PASTEL (IRE) BHB 52f RR 56f 4777[20]

4 gr g Ai Nasr (FR) 9.9f **(72)** - Gay Pastel (FR) (No Pass No Sale) 11.9f **(85)**
Form - 10
Record 1998 - 1st:1 2nd:0 3rd:0 Ran:2
Win Prizemoney £2,259 *Total Prizemoney* £2,259
Wins * 1998 Jly Leices (GD) C 11.8f 56 <
1998 Turf 1-2: (12f 1-2) (gd, frm 1-1)
Fair gelding. Turf high 56 (1st run) (began Jly) - 1st of 7 getting 10lb from Golden Thunderbolt (16 Jly Leicester RF 2856).
**M C Pipe [3-11] Harry Saunders.*

GRAZALEMA (USA) RR 90f 4830a[5]

2 b c Storm Bird (CAN) 8.5f **(82)** - Dellagrazia (USA) (Trempolino (USA)) 12f **(71)**
Form - 15
1998 Turf 1-2: (8f 1-2) (hvy 1-1, g-s)

Currently useful colt. Turf high 90 (1st run) (began Spt) - 1st of 4 from Way of Light (13 Spt Longchamp RF 4344a). He narrowly won a Group Three at Longchamp in September, but was comfortably held in the Grand Criterium. **A Fabre in FR [1-2].*

1998 Turf 0-6: (6f 2, 7f, 8f 2, 9f) (gd 2, g-f 3, frm) 1998 AW 0-3: (7f, 8f 2) (Equi, Fibr 2)

Moderate gelding, effective 7 to 9f, acts on gd to frm - acts on Equi, best on gd. Turf high 44 - 3rd of 8 giving 14lb to Keys

Great Dane will remain in training in 1999

GRAZIA RR 108+f 3614a[9]

3 b f Sharpo 7.5f **(68)**-Dance Machine (Green Dancer (USA)) 10.3f **(74)**

Form - 10

Record	**1998 -**	1st:1	2nd:0	3rd:0	Ran:2
	Pre1998 -	1st:1	2nd:1	3rd:0	Ran:2

Win Prizemoney £81,661 *Total Prizemoney* £83,215

Wins	* **1998**	Jly	Newbur (G-F)	L	6f	108+	<
	* 1997	Oct	Redcar (G-F)		6f	97+	

1998 Turf 1-2: (6f 1-1, 7f) (gd 1-2)

Scopey, Pattern-class filly. Turf high 108 (1st run) (began Jly) - 1st of 8 getting 5lb from Bold Edge (18 Jly Newbury RF 2908). She looked a contender for the sprinter's crown when winning on her belated seasonal reappearance at Newbury in July, but was not seen out after failing to quicken in the Prix Maurice de Gheest. It would be premature to write her off just yet and she looks sure to stay seven furlongs. **Sir Mark Prescott [2-4] Cyril Humphris.*

GREAT BEAR BHB 28f18a **RR 25f 18a** 187[13]

6 ch g Dominion 8.9f **(65)** - Bay Bay (Bay Express) 7.1f **(60)**

Form - 7800

Record	**1998 -**	1st:0	2nd:0	3rd:0	Ran:3
	Pre1998 -	1st:2	2nd:1	3rd:0	Ran:38

Win Prizemoney £7,031 *Total Prizemoney* £11,492

Wins	* 1996	Jly	Newcas (G-F)	H	8f	41	47
	1994	Jun	Haydoc (GD)		5f		74

1998 AW 0-3: (8f 2, 13f) (Equi, Fibr 2)

Little account gelding, has worn blinkers. AW high 2.

**D W Chapman [1-31] J M Chapman (from R F JohnsonHoughton [1-10] Jly 1995).*

GREAT CHIEF BHB 33f31a **RR 44f 31a** 3412a[2]

5 ch g Be My Chief (USA) 10.2f **(62)** - Padelia (Thatching) 8f **(66)**

Form - 45832000732

Record	**1998 -**	1st:0	2nd:2	3rd:2	Ran:9
	Pre1998 -	1st:0	2nd:0	3rd:1	Ran:12

Win Prizemoney £0 *Total Prizemoney* £1,557

Seminar (25 Jun Les Landes 9f gd RF 2480a). AW high 39 - 2nd of 9 getting 21lb from Without Friends (21 Feb Lingfield 8f Equi RF 0330). **J S O Arthur in JER [0-2] (from Bob Jones [0-15] Jun 1998).*

GREAT DANE (IRE) BHB 115f **RR 119f** 4940a[1]

3 b c Danehill (USA) 9.1f **(79)** - Itching (IRE) (Thatching) 8f **(66)**

Form - 1183111

Record	**1998 -**	1st:5	2nd:0	3rd:1	Ran:7
	Pre1998 -	1st:0	2nd:1	3rd:0	Ran:1

Win Prizemoney £66,844 *Total Prizemoney* £68,889

Wins	* **1998**	Oct	Lyon P (SFT)	G3	10f	115	
	* **1998**	Spt	York (GD)	L	8.9f	115	
	* **1998**	Aug	Goodwo (GD)	L	8f	118+	
	* **1998**	May	Haydoc (GD)		8.1f	119?	<
	* **1998**	May	Haydoc (GD)		8.1f	83+	

1998 Turf 5-7: (8f 3-4, 9f 1-1, 10f 1-2) (sft 1-1, gd 3-4, g-f 1-2)

Workmanlike, high-class colt, effective 8 to 10f, best at 8f, acts on sft to g-f, best on gd, excels at Haydock. Turf high 119 - 1st of 6 getting 9lb from Weet-A-Minute (22 May Haydock RF 1396) - also 1st of 8 giving 5lb to Equity Princess (1 Aug Goodwood RF 3255). He enjoyed a very fruitful season with five wins from seven outings. The first two were in minor company and he was then found out in Pattern race. However, he regained winning ways by landing Listed events at Goodwood and York, and ended the season by narrowly winning a Group Three in France.

**H R A Cecil [5-8] Greenbay Stables Ltd.*

GREAT EASEBY (IRE) BHB 54f **RR 56f** 3123[6]

8 ch g Caerleon (USA) 10.9f **(79)** - Kasala (USA) (Blushing Groom (FR)) 10.3f **(76)**

Form - 036

Record	**1998 -**	1st:0	2nd:0	3rd:1	Ran:3
	Pre1998 -	1st:1	2nd:4	3rd:3	Ran:14

Win Prizemoney £7,765 *Total Prizemoney* £16,812

Wins	* 1996	Spt	Goodwo (G-F)	H	16f	60	63	<

1998 Turf 0-3: (16f 3) (gd 2, hrd)

Fair gelding. Turf high 56. Consistent. **W Storey [7-42] D C Batey.*

GREAT MELODY (IRE) BHB 58f64a **RR 56f 64a** 4540[23]

3 ch g Pips Pride 6.7f **(70)** - Unbidden Melody (USA) (Chieftain II) 10.4f **(75)**

Form - 216208060

Record 1998 - 1st:1 2nd:2 3rd:0 Ran:9
Pre1998 - 1st:0 2nd:0 3rd:0 Ran:3

Win Prizemoney £3,371 *Total Prizemoney* £9,137

Wins * 1998 *Feb Lingfi (STD) 8f 64 <*

1998 Turf 0-7: (7f, 8f 4, 9f, 10f) (g-s, gd 4, frm 2) 1998 AW 1-2: (8f 1-2) (Equi 1-2)

Workmanlike, average gelding, effective 8f, acts on gd - acts on Equi, often wears blinkers. Turf high 74 - 2nd of 27 getting 10lb from Tom Dougal (3 May Newmarket 8f gd RF 0991). AW high 64. Gradually improved before getting off the mark in a maiden on the Lingfield Equitrack in February. However, the word dreadful would be an understatement for the quality of that race. Good second in a huge field at Newmarket in May, disappointing since.

**D J S Cosgrove [1-9] Crown Pkg & Mailing Svs Ltd (from J M P Eustace [0-3] Oct 1997).*

GREAT NEWS BHB 75f **RR 73f** 4614[1]

3 b g Elmaamul (USA) 8.1f **(70)** - Amina (Brigadier Gerard) 9.3f **(58)**

Form - 322321

Record 1998 - 1st:1 2nd:3 3rd:2 Ran:6

Win Prizemoney £3,701 *Total Prizemoney* £8,070

Wins * 1998 Oct Lingfi (SFT) H 7f 69 73 <

1998 Turf 1-6: (6f, 7f 1-4, 8f) (g-s 1-2, g-f 2, frm 2)

Scopey, above-average gelding, effective 6 to 8f, best at 7f, acts on g-s to frm, best on g-s. Turf high 73 - 1st of 17 giving 12lb to Miss Penton (2 Oct Lingfield RF 4614).

**I A Balding [1-6] Mrs C H Bothway.*

GREAT ORATION (IRE) BHB 60f47a **RR 61f 47a** 3670[12]

9 b or br g Simply Great (FR) 11.9f **(61)** - Spun Gold (Thatch (USA)) 9.8f **(62)**

Form - 05350

Record 1998 - 1st:0 2nd:0 3rd:1 Ran:5
Pre1998 - 1st:7 2nd:4 3rd:11 Ran:49

Win Prizemoney £25,560 *Total Prizemoney* £37,776

Wins
* 1997 Aug Pontef (G-F) H 17.1f 60 66 <
* 1997 Apr Pontef (G-F) H 17.1f 54 58
* 1996 Jly Cheste (G-F) H 15.9f 51 56
* 1996 Jun Pontef (G-F) H 18f 41 50
* 1995 Aug Pontef (G-F) H 17.1f 38 46
* 1994 Jun Catter (FRM) H 15.8f 30 42
* 1994 Jun Mussel (FRM) H 15.1f 30 34

1998 Turf 0-5: (16f 4, 17f) (gd, frm 4)

Average gelding, effective 16 to 19f, acts on gd to frm, has worn blinkers, favours left handed tracks. Turf high 61. Inconsistent.

**F Watson [7-52] M D Hetherington (Packaging) Ltd (from M Bell [0-2] Oct 1991).*

GREAT TERN BHB 51f44a **RR 57f 44a** 489[5]

6 b m Simply Great (FR) 11.9f **(61)** - La Neva (FR) (Arctic Tern (USA)) 8.9f **(69)**

Form - 5

Record 1998 - 1st:0 2nd:0 3rd:0 Ran:1
Pre1998 - 1st:2 2nd:0 3rd:0 Ran:11

Win Prizemoney £7,318 *Total Prizemoney* £7,848

Wins
* 1996 Oct Doncas (GD) H 14.6f 47 55 <
* 1996 Spt Haydoc (GD) H 14f 41 47

1998 Turf 0-1: (13f) (g-s)

Fair mare. **N M Babbage [2-12] John Cantrill.*

GRECIAN PRINCE BHB 57f **RR 57f** 884[6]

3 ch g Risk Me (FR) 8f **(53)** - Troyes (Troy) 10.4f **(68)**

Form - 6

Record 1998 - 1st:0 2nd:0 3rd:0 Ran:1
Pre1998 - 1st:0 2nd:0 3rd:0 Ran:3

1998 AW 0-1: (8f) (Fibr)

Scopey, fair gelding. **J G Smyth-Osbourne [0-4] Spice Partnership.*

GRECIAN TALE (IRE) BHB 69f **RR 68f** 4820[15]

2 b g Catrail (USA) - Athens Belle (IRE) (Groom Dancer (USA))

Form - 6308230

Record 1998 - 1st:0 2nd:1 3rd:2 Ran:7

Win Prizemoney £0 *Total Prizemoney* £1,906

1998 Turf 0-7: (5f, 6f 6) (sft, gd, g-f 2, frm 3)

Average gelding, effective 6f, acts on g-f to frm, best on frm. Turf high 77 - 3rd of 20 to Hard Lines (16 May Newbury 6f frm RF 1257).

**A P Jarvis [0-7] Ambrose Turnbull.*

GREEBA BHB 65f **RR 62f** 1004[12]

3 b f Fairy King (USA) 7.7f **(75)**-Guanhumara (Caerleon(USA)) 8.6f **(71)**

Form - 0

Record 1998 - 1st:0 2nd:0 3rd:0 Ran:1
Pre1998 - 1st:0 2nd:0 3rd:0 Ran:4

1998 Turf 0-1: (6f) (gd)

Average filly. Has shown ability in fair maidens.

**R Hannon [0-5] Barouche Stud Ltd.*

GREEK DANCE (IRE) BHB 117f **RR 114f** 1778[5]

3 b c Sadler's Wells (USA) 11.3f **(87)** - Hellenic (Darshaan) 9.9f **(84)**

Form - 115

Record 1998 - 1st:2 2nd:0 3rd:0 Ran:3
Pre1998 - 1st:0 2nd:1 3rd:0 Ran:1

Win Prizemoney £17,049 *Total Prizemoney* £38,542

Wins
* **1998** May York (GD) 10.4f 112++ <
* **1998** Apr Newmar (G-S) 10f 95+

1998 Turf 2-3: (10f 2-2, 12f) (gd 2-2, g-f)

Well made, Group-class colt. Turf high 114 - 5th of 15 to High-Rise (6 Jun Epsom 12f g-f RF 1778) - also 1st of 5 getting 5lb from Capri (14 May York RF 1222). He developed into a leading Derby fancy after winning the Glasgow Stakes at York. Considering his inexperience, fifth place at Epsom was far from a disgrace and it later transpired that he had injured himself quite badly in the race itself. Providing all is well physically after a lengthy absence, he is very much one to follow in 1999. **Sir Michael Stoute [2-4] Lord Weinstock.*

GREEK PALACE (IRE) BHB 110f **RR 109f** 3231[4]

4 b c Royal Academy (USA) 7.8f **(77)** - Grecian Sea (FR) (Homeric) 9.8f **(67)**

Form - 0134

Record 1998 - 1st:1 2nd:0 3rd:1 Ran:4
Pre1998 - 1st:1 2nd:0 3rd:2 Ran:3

Win Prizemoney £33,266 *Total Prizemoney* £47,165

Wins
* **1998** Jun Ascot (G-S) H 12f 98 109 <
* 1997 May Ripon (G-F) 10f 85+

1998 Turf 1-4: (10f 2, 12f 1-2) (gd 1-4)

Scopey, Pattern-class colt, effective 10 to 12f, best at 12f, acts on gd. Turf high 109 - 1st of 20 getting 3lb from Sabadilla (17 Jun Ascot RF 2058). Connections have been extremely patient with this good-looking bay, and he showed just why when running away with the Bessborough Handicap at Royal Ascot. He looked certain to make the jump into Group races after that impressive victory, but failed to progress as expected when found wanting under a penalty in the Hong Kong Trophy at Sandown. He should improve again as a five-year-old and can win a Listed race at least.

**Sir Michael Stoute [2-7] Lord Weinstock.*

GREENAWAY BAY (USA) BHB 59f **RR 61f** 4936[3]

4 ch g Green Dancer (USA) 11.9f **(77)** - Raise 'n Dance (USA) (Raise A Native) 11.2f **(69)**

Form - 4030384043

Record 1998 - 1st:0 2nd:0 3rd:3 Ran:10
Pre1998 - 1st:1 2nd:0 3rd:0 Ran:5

Win Prizemoney £2,965 *Total Prizemoney* £6,816

Wins 1997 Mar Kempto (G-F) 7f 80+ <

1998 Turf 0-9: (8f, 9f 2, 10f 6) (g-s, gd 3, g-f 2, frm 2, hrd) 1998 AW 0-1: (8f) (Fibr)

Scopey, average gelding, effective 7f, acts on g-f, likes right handed tracks. Turf high 61. Has regressed since winning a maiden as a three-year-old when with Geoff Wragg.

**W J Musson [0-10] Asterlane Ltd (from G Wragg [1-5] Jly 1997).*

GREEN BOPPER (USA) BHB 62f62a **RR 40f 62a** 3828[6]

5 b g Green Dancer (USA) 11.9f **(77)** - Wayage (USA) (Mr Prospector (USA)) 8.8f **(78)**

Form - 21110546

Record 1998 - 1st:3 2nd:1 3rd:0 Ran:8
Pre1998 - 1st:1 2nd:0 3rd:1 Ran:10

Win Prizemoney £10,888 *Total Prizemoney* £12,398

Wins * 1998 *Apr Wolver (STD) 8.5f 64*

* **1998** *Mar Wolver (STD) H 8.5f 54 62*
* **1998** *Mar Southw (STD) H 8f 47 56*
1996 Apr Newcas (GD) 8f 80 <
1998 Turf 0-1: (8f) (frm) 1998 AW 3-7: (7f, 8f 3-5, 9f) (Fibr 3-7)
Average gelding, effective 8f - acts on Fibr, has worn blinkers, prefers left handed tracks, prefers tight tracks. AW high 64 - 1st of 9 giving 5lb to Caudillo (7 Apr Wolverhampton RF 0593) - also 1st of 13 giving 1lb to Muara Bay (28 Mar Wolverhampton RF 0493). Consistent. Won at Newcastle in April '96 but showed nothing afterwards, including over hurdles, until finishing second on his sand debut in a Southwell seller in February. He exceeded that effort when winning a non-seller at the same track next time, and followed up with two wins at Wolverhampton, getting up in the last stride on the second occasion. He looks well suited by trips of around a mile on Fibresand.
**G Woodward [3-8] Wetherby Racing Bureau 35 (from C P Morlock [0-6] May 1997).*

GREEN CARD (USA) BHB 107f **RR 105f** 5076[6]
4 br c Green Dancer (USA) 11.9f **(77)** - Dunkellin (USA) (Irish River (FR)) 8.6f **(78)**
Form - 5012153446
Record 1998 - 1st:2 2nd:1 3rd:1 Ran:10
Pre1998 - 1st:1 2nd:1 3rd:2 Ran:8
Win Prizemoney £14,462 *Total Prizemoney* £35,383
Wins * **1998** Jly Doncas (G-F) 8f 110 <
* **1998** Jun Nottin (GD) 8.2f 98
* 1997 Apr Ripon (G-F) 8f 81+
1998 Turf 2-10: (8f 2-9, 9f) (sft 2, g-s, gd 1-6, frm 1-1)
Workmanlike, Pattern-class colt, effective 8 to 10f, best at 8f, acts on gd to frm, best on frm, has worn blinkers, excels at Doncaster. Turf high 110 - 1st of 8 giving 9lb to Teapot Row (15 Jly Doncaster RF 2818). A journeyman miler, he falls short of the top class but always runs a race. There must be a Group race waiting for him on the continent. **S P C Woods [3-18] P K L Chu.*

GREEN GINGER BHB 83f **RR 78f** 4509[4]
2 ch c Ardkinglass 5f **(64)** - Bella Maggio (Rakaposhi King)
Form - 874
Record 1998 - 1st:0 2nd:0 3rd:0 Ran:3
Win Prizemoney £0 *Total Prizemoney* £292
1998 Turf 0-3: (6f 3) (gd, frm 2)
Currently above-average colt. Turf high 78 (began Jly) - 4th of 16 to Habub (26 Spt Nottingham 6f gd RF 4509).
**A Streeter [0-3] B J Garrett.*

GREEN GOD (IRE) RR 54f 4699[12]
2 b c Common Grounds 8.1f **(66)** - Inanna (Persian Bold) 9.3f **(66)**
Form - 0
Record 1998 - 1st:0 2nd:0 3rd:0 Ran:1
1998 Turf 0-1: (6f) (gd)
Currently fair colt. **M J Heaton-Ellis [0-1] Mrs Caroline Parker.*

GREEN JACKET BHB 65f **RR 50f** 3109[5]
3 b g Green Desert (USA) 7.8f **(78)** - Select Sale (Auction Ring (USA)) 8.6f **(65)**
Form - 76005
Record 1998 - 1st:0 2nd:0 3rd:0 Ran:5
Pre1998 - 1st:0 2nd:1 3rd:1 Ran:5
Win Prizemoney £0 *Total Prizemoney* £456
1998 Turf 0-5: (8f, 9f 3, 10f) (hvy, gd, g-f, frm 2)
Scopey, fair gelding, effective 7 to 9f, best at 7f, acts on gd to g-f, best on gd, has worn blinkers. Turf high 77 - 6th of 10 giving 6lb to Chrysolite (9 May Lingfield 9f g-f RF 1122). Becoming disappointing. **J L Dunlop [0-10] Ian Cameron.*

GREENLANDER BHB 100f **RR 99f** 4222[5]
3 b c Green Desert (USA) 7.8f **(78)** - Pripet (USA) (Alleged (USA)) 10f **(76)**
Form - 305845
Record 1998 - 1st:0 2nd:0 3rd:1 Ran:6
Pre1998 - 1st:2 2nd:0 3rd:0 Ran:3
Win Prizemoney £43,025 *Total Prizemoney* £53,266
Wins * 1997 Jly Maison (SFT) G2 5.5f 95 <
* 1997 Jly Yarmou (G-S) 6f 84+
1998 Turf 0-6: (7f, 8f 3, 10f 2) (sft, gd 3, g-f 2)
Neat, very useful colt. Turf high 109. Consistent. Winner of the Prix Robert Papin as a juvenile, he was a fair third in the Free Handicap on his return but has been well beaten in high-class company since and will do better dropped in class and trip, or possibly export could be his quickest route back to the winners' enclosure.
**C E Brittain [2-9] Sheikh Marwan Al Maktoum.*

GREEN POWER BHB 53f **RR 62f** 4748[9]
4 b g Green Desert (USA) 7.8f **(78)**-Shaft of Sunlight (Sparkler)8.4f **(55)**
Form - 008008000
Record 1998 - 1st:0 2nd:0 3rd:0 Ran:9
Pre1998 - 1st:1 2nd:1 3rd:2 Ran:8
Win Prizemoney £3,779 *Total Prizemoney* £6,961
Wins 1997 May Windso (SFT) 8.3f 69 <
1998 Turf 0-9: (7f, 8f 7, 9f) (gd 3, g-f 3, frm 3)
Strong, average gelding, effective 8f, acts on frm, likes tight tracks. Turf high 62.
**N P Littmoden [0-8] Gemini Associates (from J R Fanshawe [1-13] May 1998).*

GREENSAND BHB 100f **RR 86f** 4193[6]
2 b f Green Desert (USA) 7.8f **(78)** - Totham (Shernazar) 10.2f **(73)**
Form - 7316
Record 1998 - 1st:1 2nd:0 3rd:1 Ran:4
Win Prizemoney £3,701 *Total Prizemoney* £4,255
Wins * **1998** Aug Salisb (G-F) 6f 86+ <
1998 Turf 1-4: (6f 1-4) (gd, g-f 1-1, frm 2)
Useful filly. Turf high 86 (began Jly) - 1st of 15 getting 5lb from Mutamayyaz (12 Aug Salisbury RF 3587). She got off the mark with a comfortable win in a Salisbury maiden in August, and looks sure to win again. **R Hannon [1-4] Lord Carnarvon.*

GREEN SNAKE BHB 85f **RR 79f** 4364[10]
2 ch f Royal Academy (USA) 7.8f **(77)** - Tigwa **(66f)** (Cadeaux Genereux)
Form - 10
Record 1998 - 1st:1 2nd:0 3rd:0 Ran:2
Win Prizemoney £3,624 *Total Prizemoney* £3,624
Wins * **1998** Aug Beverl (G-F) 7.5f 79 <
1998 Turf 1-2: (6f, 7f 1-1) (sft, frm 1-1)
Currently above-average filly. Turf high 79 (1st run) (began Aug) - 1st of 7 from Hishmah (29 Aug Beverley RF 3943).
**C E Brittain [1-2] Mohamed Obaida.*

GREENSPAN (IRE) BHB 70f75a **RR 72f 75a** 2319[1]
6 b g Be My Guest (USA) 10.2f **(66)** - Prima Ballerina (FR) (Nonoalco (USA)) 8.5f **(66)**
Form - 241112122331
Record 1998 - 1st:4 2nd:3 3rd:2 Ran:9
Pre1998 - 1st:8 2nd:3 3rd:3 Ran:28
Win Prizemoney £30,287 *Total Prizemoney* £39,936
Wins * **1998** *Jun Wolver (STD) C 12f 76* <
1998 *Feb Southw (STD) C 12f 75*
1998 *Jan Wolver (STD) C 12f 65*
1998 *Jan Southw (STD) C 12f 75*
1997 *Dec Southw (STD) C 14f 70*
1997 *Mar Southw (STD) C 12f 68+*
1997 *Feb Southw (STD) C 12f 64*
1997 *Feb Southw (STD) C 12f 71+*
1996 *Dec Wolver (STD) C 9.4f 72*
1996 *Nov Wolver (STD) S 12f 60+*
1996 *Apr Southw (STD) C 12f 74*
1996 *Feb Southw (STD) H 12f 73 72*
1998 AW 4-9: (12f 4-9) (Fibr 4-9)
Above-average gelding, effective 12 to 16f, best at 12f - acts on Fibr, and likes Wolverhampton. AW high 76 - 1st of 9 giving 4lb to Banneret (26 Jun Wolverhampton RF 2319) - also 1st of 5 giving 14lb to Pickens (9 Jan Southwell RF 0053). Consistent. He has a tremendous record in claimers over middle distances on Fibresand, especially at Southwell, but he just does not seem able to win a handicap, despite some fine efforts. He was never in better form than at the start of '98, but was claimed in April.
**Miss S J Wilton [1-1] John Pointon and Sons (from W R Muir [12-40] Apr 1998).*

GREENSTONE (IRE) BHB 91f **RR 81f** 4766[4]
2 b f Green Desert (USA) 7.8f **(78)** - Mahabba (USA) (Elocutionist (USA)) 8f **(77)**
Form - 0244
Record 1998 - 1st:0 2nd:1 3rd:0 Ran:4

Win Prizemoney £0 *Total Prizemoney* £2,610
1998 Turf 0-4: (6f, 7f 2, 8f) (sft, g-f 3)
Decent filly. Turf high 81 (began Aug) - 4th of 11 to Fragrant Oasis (18 Spt Newbury 7f g-f RF 4358). A narrow runner-up on her second start, she will stay a mile plus, but lacks a bit of substance.
**J W Hills [0-4] David Caruth.*

GREEN TEA (USA) RR 98f 4722a[1]

3 c Green Forest (USA) 7.4f **(73)**
Form - 511
1998 Turf 2-3: (8f 1-2, 9f 1-1) (hvy 1-1, sft 1-1, gd)
Currently very useful colt. Turf high 98 - also 1st of 12 from Priwings (3 Oct San Siro RF 4722a). Obviously likes give in the ground, but is not up to Group class.
**A Marcialis in ITY [2-2] L'Idea (from R Rossini in ITY [0-1] Apr 1998).*

GREENWICH FORE BHB 50f42a RR 69f 42a 622[6]

4 b g Formidable (USA) 7.8f **(60)** - What a Challenge (Sallust) 8.4f **(63)**
Form - 366
Record 1998 - 1st:0 2nd:0 3rd:1 Ran:3
Pre1998 - 1st:0 2nd:0 3rd:2 Ran:13
Win Prizemoney £0 *Total Prizemoney* £1,726
1998 AW 0-3: (10f, 12f, 14f) (Equi 2, Fibr)
Strong, average gelding, has worn blinkers. AW high 39. He has done the majority of his racing at Lingfield, but produced a good effort on the All-Weather at Wolverhampton.
**T G Mills [0-16] T G Mills.*

GREY BUTTONS BHB 46f RR 45f 2577[9]

3 gr f Norton Challenger 10f **(41)** - Albury Grey (Petong) 6.6f **(58)**
Form - 060
Record 1998 - 1st:0 2nd:0 3rd:0 Ran:3
1998 Turf 0-3: (8f 2, 9f) (g-f, frm, hrd)
Leggy, currently moderate filly. Turf high 45.
**K R Burke [0-3] K Powell.*

GREYFIELD (IRE) BHB 61f RR 60f 4873[4]

2 b c Persian Bold 10f **(69)** - Noble Dust (USA) (Dust Commander (USA)) 10.3f **(77)**
Form - 0005404
Record 1998 - 1st:0 2nd:0 3rd:0 Ran:7
Win Prizemoney £0 *Total Prizemoney* £215
1998 Turf 0-7: (6f, 7f 2, 8f 4) (gd 3, frm 4)
Average colt, effective 8f, acts on gd. Turf high 59 - 4th of 20 getting 2lb from Persian Waters (19 Oct Pontefract 8f gd RF 4873).
**M R Channon [0-7] Paulton Bloodstock.*

GREY KINGDOM BHB 80f33a RR 80f 33a 4918[14]

7 gr g Grey Desire 9.3f **(49)** - Miss Realm (Realm) 8.1f **(65)**
Form - 04360103051864000200
Record 1998 - 1st:2 2nd:1 3rd:2 Ran:20
Pre1998 - 1st:7 2nd:2 3rd:7 Ran:40
Win Prizemoney £42,623 *Total Prizemoney* £60,823

Wins									
	* **1998**	Jly	Ayr	(SFT)	H	7f	75	77	<
	* **1998**	Jun	York	(G-S)	H	6f	68	72	
	* 1997	Jly	Epsom	(SFT)	H	7f	69	72	
	* 1997	Jun	York	(G-S)	H	6f	62	67	
	* 1997	May	Mussel	(G-F)	H	7.1f	42	57	
	* 1997	Apr	Carlis	(GD)	H	5.9f	41	59	
	* 1997	Apr	Nottin	(G-F)	H	6.1f	41	52	
	* 1996	Aug	Doncas	(G-F)	H	7f	41	43	
	* 1996	Jun	Beverl	(G-F)	H	7.5f	34	39	

1998 Turf 2-20:(6f 1-7, 7f 1-9, 8f 4)(sft 3, g-s 1-4,gd1-6, g-f 2, frm4, hrd)
Decent gelding, effective 6 to 7f, best at 7f, acts on sft to hrd, and does well at Ayr and York. Turf high 80 - 2nd of 29 giving 3lb to Royal Result (19 Spt Ayr 6f sft RF 4365) - also 1st of 8 getting 10lb from Persian Fayre (20 Jly Ayr RF 2951). Inconsistent. Admirably tough, and a credit to connections, he beat a big field at York in June and scored at Ayr the following month. Will continue to perform with credit but the handicapper is making life hard for him.
**M Brittain [9-60] Mel Brittain.*

GREY MATTER RR 48f 2539[7]

2 gr f Tina's Pet 7.4f **(56)** - Phar Lapa (Grundy) 10.3f **(65)**
Form - 5007
Record 1998 - 1st:0 2nd:0 3rd:0 Ran:4
1998 Turf 0-4: (5f 3, 6f) (gd, g-f 3)
Moderate filly. Turf high 48. **T H Caldwell [0-4] R S G Jones.*

GREY PRINCESS (IRE) BHB 92f RR 92+f 4651[1]

2 gr f Common Grounds 8.1f **(66)** - Miss Goodbody (Castle Keep) 8.3f **(57)**
Form - 1128121
Record 1998 - 1st:4 2nd:2 3rd:0 Ran:7
Win Prizemoney £11,523 *Total Prizemoney* £14,405

Wins									
	* **1998**	Oct	Bright	(GD)	H	5.3f	85	92+	<
	* **1998**	Spt	Bright	(FRM)	H	5.3f	80	82	
	* **1998**	Jly	Salisb	(FRM)		6f		78	
	* **1998**	Jun	Windso	(G-F)		6f		75	

1998 Turf 4-7: (5f 2-3, 6f 2-4) (g-f 2-3, frm 2-3, hrd)
Useful filly, effective 5f, acts on g-f to frm. Turf high 92 - 1st of 8 giving 15lb to La Paola (5 Oct Brighton RF 4651). She won four times in her first season, a couple of auction events (one courtesy of the Stewards) and two nurseries in the autumn. She seems to like Brighton. **P W Harris [4-7] The Commitments.*

GREY PROSPECT BHB 37f RR 53f 3508[17]

4 b g Grey Desire 9.3f **(49)** - Nicky Mygirl (Chief Singer) 8.9f **(66)**
Form - 02050
Record 1998 - 1st:0 2nd:1 3rd:0 Ran:5
Pre1998 - 1st:0 2nd:0 3rd:0 Ran:2
Win Prizemoney £0 *Total Prizemoney* £684
1998 Turf 0-5: (7f, 8f 3, 10f) (g-s, gd 2, g-f, frm)
Neat, fair gelding, effective 8f, acts on g-f, likes tight tracks. Turf high 53. **M Brittain [0-7] Mel Brittain.*

GREY SHOT BHB 109f RR 113f 4632[6]

6 gr g Sharrood (USA) 11.1f **(67)** - Optaria (Song) 7.2f **(61)**
Form - 726
Record 1998 - 1st:0 2nd:1 3rd:0 Ran:3
Pre1998 - 1st:6 2nd:6 3rd:2 Ran:25
Win Prizemoney £113,173 *Total Prizemoney* £174,985

Wins									
	* 1997	Oct	Newmar	(G-F)	G3	16f		120	<
	* 1996	Aug	Goodwo	(G-F)	G2	16f		113	
	* 1995	Spt	Longch	(SFT)	G3	15f		112	
	* 1995	Spt	Doncas	(G-F)	H	14.6f	98	104	
	* 1995	Jly	Newmar	(G-F)	L	14.8f		96	
	* 1994	Oct	Doncas	(G-S)		7f		77+	

1998 Turf 0-3: (15f, 16f 2) (sft, gd, g-f)
Group-class gelding, effective 15 to 16f, best at 16f, acts on sft to frm, prefers right handed tracks. Turf high 113 (began Jly) - 2nd of 8 to Arctic Owl (23 Aug Deauville 15f sft RF 3917a). A fine stayer at his best, especially in 1997 when he gained a fine all-the-way win in the Jockey Club Cup, breaking the course record in the process. He was given a superb tactical ride by Richard Quinn when almost stealing the Prix Kergorlay in August, but just lacks the finishing kick to win Group races on the Flat these days. Hurdling looks his preferred option. **I A Balding [8-31] J C Smith.*

GREY STRIKE (IRE) BHB 57f57a RR 59f 57a 4814[6]

2 gr c Magical Strike (USA) 5.5f **(61)** - Narrow Band (IRE) (Standaan (FR)) 7f **(55)**
Form - 0024706
Record 1998 - 1st:0 2nd:1 3rd:0 Ran:7
Win Prizemoney £0 *Total Prizemoney* £530
1998 Turf 0-4: (6f 3, 7f) (gd, g-f, frm 2) 1998 AW 0-3: (5f, 6f, 7f) (Fibr 3)
Fair colt, effective 6f - acts on Fibr. Turf high 59. AW high 51 (1st run) (began Jly) - 2nd of 7 to Welsh Assembly (11 Jly Southwell 6f Fibr RF 2726). **J Berry [0-7] G L Tanner.*

GREYVEE BHB 51f RR 56f 2149[9]

2 gr c Mizoram (USA) - Ziggi's Girl (IRE) (Glenstal (USA)) 10.1f **(64)**
Form - 43730
Record 1998 - 1st:0 2nd:0 3rd:2 Ran:5
Win Prizemoney £0 *Total Prizemoney* £501
1998 Turf 0-5: (5f, 6f 3, 7f) (gd, g-f, frm 3)
Fair colt, has worn blinkers. Turf high 56.
**Mrs L Stubbs [0-5] R P Johns.*

GRIEF (IRE) BHB 86f RR 84f 1240[5]

5 ch g Broken Hearted 10.1f **(65)** - Crecora (Royal Captive) 10f **(50)**
Form - 805
Record 1998 - 1st:0 2nd:0 3rd:0 Ran:3
Pre1998 - 1st:2 2nd:4 3rd:1 Ran:14

Win Prizemoney £7,869 *Total Prizemoney* £13,372
Wins * 1997 Aug Epsom (GD) H 12f 82 87 <
1996 Aug Roscom (GD) 10f 79
1998 Turf 0-3: (10f 2, 12f) (hvy, gd, g-f)
Decent gelding, effective 10 to 12f, acts on gd to g-f. Turf high 82.
**D R C Elsworth [1-12] Mike Balcomb (from J Oxx in IRE [1-7] Oct 1996).*

GRIMSHAW (USA) BHB 86f RR 87df 3853[2]

3 ch c St Jovite (USA) 11.8f **(75)** - Loa (USA) (Hawaii) 9.4f **(66)**
Form - 61622
Record 1998 - 1st:1 2nd:2 3rd:0 Ran:5
Win Prizemoney £4,162 *Total Prizemoney* £7,654
Wins * **1998** May Bright (FRM) 11.9f 73 <
1998 Turf 1-5: (12f 1-3, 16f, 18f) (gd, g-f, frm 1-3)
Well made, useful colt. Turf high 87 - 2nd of 8 giving 7lb to Woody's Boy (7 Aug Newmarket 16f frm RF 3437). Won an ordinary Brighton maiden on his second start, and hung fire on his final two runs. Not the heartiest of battlers.
**H R A Cecil [1-5] H R H Prince Fahd Salman.*

GRINKOV (IRE) BHB 76f RR 78f 5126[2]

3 b br g Soviet Lad (USA) 9.4f **(63)** - Tallow Hill (Dunphy) 9.4f **(57)**
Form - 4811512
Record 1998 - 1st:3 2nd:1 3rd:0 Ran:7
Pre1998 - 1st:0 2nd:0 3rd:0 Ran:1
Win Prizemoney £15,113 *Total Prizemoney* £17,618
Wins * **1998** Oct Folkes (SFT) H 9.7f 66 70 <
* **1998** Jly Windso (GD) H 10f 61 63
* **1998** Jly Windso (G-F) H 10f 57 60
1998 Turf 3-7: (7f, 8f, 10f 3-5) (g-s 1-2, gd 2, g-f 1-2, frm 1-1)
Workmanlike, above-average gelding, effective 10f, acts on g-s, prefers tight tracks. Turf high 78 - 2nd of 19 getting 15lb from Conspicuous (5 Nov Brighton 10f g-s RF 5126) - also 1st of 14 giving 1lb to King Priam (20 Oct Folkestone RF 4883). Improving. Found his form lsat season when stepped up to ten furlongs, winning twice at Windsor in the summer and a fair handicap at Folkestone in October. **H Morrison [3-8] Rosanne Dobson & Partners.*

GRINLING GIBBONS BHB 63f RR 61f 4772[12]

2 ch c Woodman (USA) 9.7f **(77)** - Saddle Bow (Sadler's Wells (USA)) 10f **(76)**
Form - 000
Record 1998 - 1st:0 2nd:0 3rd:0 Ran:3
1998 Turf 0-3: (6f, 7f 2) (gd, g-f 2)
Currently average colt. Turf high 61 (began Aug).
**J L Dunlop [0-3] Peter Winfield.*

GRIP FAST BHB 55f RR 42f 4989[5]

2 b c Saddlers' Hall (IRE) 10.5f **(65)** - Comic Talent (Pharly (FR)) 9.8f **(68)**
Form - 85
Record 1998 - 1st:0 2nd:0 3rd:0 Ran:2
1998 Turf 0-2: (8f 2) (sft, gd)
Currently fair colt. Turf high 42 (began Oct).
**I A Balding [0-2] Lady Rothes.*

GRISELDA (USA) RR 106f 4954a[3]

3 gr f Red Ransom (USA) 8.6f **(83)** - Ruling Crown (USA) (Spectacular Bid (USA)) 11.2f **(76)**
Form - 3
1998 Turf 0-1: (10f) (frm)
Currently Pattern-class filly. (1st run) - 3rd of 8 to Zomaradah (18 Oct Woodbine 10f frm RF 4954a). **B Girault in USA [0-1].*

GRIZELDA (IRE) BHB 60f RR 58f 4937[4]

2 ro f Bluebird (USA) 7.9f **(71)** - Phazania (Tap On Wood) 10.3f **(65)**
Form - 774
Record 1998 - 1st:0 2nd:0 3rd:0 Ran:3
Win Prizemoney £0 *Total Prizemoney* £248
1998 Turf 0-3: (5f 2, 6f) (gd, g-f 2)
Currently fair filly. Turf high 58. **J D Bethell [0-3] Mrs J M Corbett.*

GROESFAEN LADY (IRE) RR 51f 5122[8]

2 b f Anita's Prince 6f **(62)** - Out On Her Own (Superlative) 7.2f **(56)**
Form - F08
Record 1998 - 1st:0 2nd:0 3rd:0 Ran:3
1998 Turf 0-3: (5f 2, 6f) (g-s, frm 2)
Currently fair filly. Turf high 51 (began Aug).
**B Palling [0-3] John Harris and Mrs Sian Harris.*

GROOMS GOLD (IRE) BHB 47f54a RR 52f 54a 4867[8]

6 ch g Groom Dancer (USA) 9.5f **(75)** - Gortynia (FR) (My Swallow) 9.2f **(71)**
Form - 2220328668
Record 1998 - 1st:0 2nd:2 3rd:1 Ran:8
Pre1998 - 1st:1 2nd:2 3rd:1 Ran:13
Win Prizemoney £3,280 *Total Prizemoney* £6,933
Wins * 1995 Jly Redcar (FRM) H 10f 63 67 <
1998 Turf 0-4: (8f 2, 10f 2) (gd, g-f, frm 2) 1998 AW 0-4: (8f 4) (Equi 2, Fibr 2)
Fair gelding, effective 8 to 10f, best at 8f, acts on gd to frm - acts on AW, best on Fibr, likes left handed tracks, and excels at Southwell. Turf high 52 (1st run) - 2nd of 28 giving 5lb to Talk Back (16 May Newmarket 8f frm RF 1268). AW high 55 (1st run) - 2nd of 8 giving 15lb to Mogin (6 Jan Lingfield 8f Equi RF 0035). Consistent. He has finished runner-up often enough, but winning seems to be beyond him at present.
**P W Harris [1-20] Mrs P W Harris (from P J Hobbs [0-3] Mar 1996).*

GROOM'S GORDON (FR) BHB 81f RR 80f 2126[7]

4 b g Groom Dancer (USA) 9.5f **(75)** - Sonoma (FR) (Habitat) 9.4f **(70)**
Form - 7857
Record 1998 - 1st:0 2nd:0 3rd:0 Ran:4
Pre1998 - 1st:2 2nd:2 3rd:0 Ran:12
Win Prizemoney £8,332 *Total Prizemoney* £15,387
Wins * 1996 Jly Sandow (GD) 7.1f 100 <
* 1996 Jun Nottin (G-F) 6.1f 66
1998 Turf 0-4: (7f, 8f, 10f 2) (sft, gd, g-f 2)
Light-framed, decent gelding, effective 8f, acts on g-f, has worn blinkers. Turf high 80. Consistent. **J L Dunlop [2-16] Mrs H Focke.*

GROSVENOR FLYER (IRE) RR 75f 4880[12]

2 ch c Dolphin Street (FR) - Kilcsem Eile (IRE) (Commanche Run) 8.5f **(58)**
Form - 70
Record 1998 - 1st:0 2nd:0 3rd:0 Ran:2
1998 Turf 0-2: (7f, 8f) (g-s, frm)
Currently above-average colt. Turf high 75 (began Spt).
**P W Chapple-Hyam [0-2] R E Sangster.*

GROSVENOR SPIRIT (IRE) BHB 67f65a RR 68f 65a 4198[5]

3 b br f Fairy King (USA) 7.7f **(75)** - La Koumia (FR) (Kaldoun (FR)) 10.3f **(68)**
Form - 08011165
Record 1998 - 1st:3 2nd:0 3rd:0 Ran:8
Pre1998 - 1st:0 2nd:0 3rd:0 Ran:2
Win Prizemoney £8,933 *Total Prizemoney* £8,933
Wins * **1998** Jly Thirsk (GD) H 12f 62 68 <
* **1998** *Jly Southw (STD) H 12f 53 59*
* **1998** Jly Nottin (G-F) 10f 61
1998 Turf 2-6: (5f, 9f, 10f 1-2, 12f 1-2) (g-s, gd 2, g-f 2-2, frm) 1998 AW 1-2: (8f, 12f 1-1) (Fibr 1-2)
Scopey, average filly, effective 10 to 12f, best at 12f, acted on g-f - acted on Fibr, preferred left handed tracks, preferred tight tracks. Turf high 68 - 1st of 10 giving 1lb to Wings Awarded (31 Jly Thirsk RF 3250) - also 1st of 17 from Flight For Freedom (4 Jly Nottingham RF 2546). AW high 59 - 1st of 8 from Premium Quest (11 Jly Southwell RF 2727). Inconsistent. (DEAD)
**P W Chapple-Hyam [3-10] R E Sangster.*

GROUCHO (USA) BHB 36f34a RR 33f 34a 3762[12]

4 b c Lyphard (USA) 10.6f **(75)** -Alvernia (USA) (Alydar (USA)) 9.1f **(76)**
Form - 67060
Record 1998 - 1st:0 2nd:0 3rd:0 Ran:5
Pre1998 - 1st:0 2nd:0 3rd:0 Ran:1
1998 Turf 0-3: (13f, 14f 2) (sft, gd, g-f) 1998 AW 0-2: (9f, 12f) (Fibr 2)
Very moderate colt. Turf high 33. AW high 36.
**N M Babbage [0-5] Provex Products Ltd (from R Charlton [0-1] Apr 1997).*

GROUTY RR 38f 4818[20]

2 gr g Norton Challenger 10f **(41)** - Qualitair Blazer (Blazing Saddles (AUS)) 6.7f **(46)**

Form - 00
Record 1998 - 1st:0 2nd:0 3rd:0 Ran:2
1998 Turf 0-2: (6f, 7f) (g-f, frm)
Currently very moderate gelding. Turf high 38 (began Spt).
**J R Fanshawe [0-2] K Brooke.*

GROVEFAIR LAD (IRE) BHB 30f51a **RR 32f 51a** 2585[4]

4 b g Silver Kite (USA) 10.2f **(51)** - Cienaga (Tarboosh (USA)) 10f **(55)**
Form - 5626118604
Record 1998 - 1st:2 2nd:0 3rd:0 Ran:7
Pre1998 - 1st:0 2nd:2 3rd:1 Ran:27
Win Prizemoney £3,977 *Total Prizemoney* £5,760
Wins * 1998 *Mar Southw (STD) H 12f 46 53* <
*** 1998** *Feb Wolver (STD) H 12f 45 47*
1998 Turf 0-3: (8f, 10f, 14f) (g-s, gd, frm) 1998 AW 2-4: (11f, 12f 2-3) (Fibr 2-4)
Fair gelding, effective 12f - acts on Fibr, has worn blinkers, likes left handed tracks. Turf high 32. AW high 53 - 1st of 11 getting 17lb from Field of Vision (9 Mar Southwell RF 0416) - also 1st of 12 getting 7lb from Zermatt (7 Feb Wolverhampton RF 0245). It took him a very long time to get off the mark, but he finally managed it at the twenty-ninth attempt when scoring in a handicap on the Wolverhampton Fibresand in February. It was a particularly poor race, but he managed to follow up against a rather better field at Southwell. No show on turf.
**S R Bowring [2-12] David Garner (from Martyn Wane [0-12] Aug 1997).*

GUARANTEED BHB 78f75a **RR 81f 75a** 2972[12]

3 b c Distant Relative 7f **(69)** - Pay the Bank (High Top) 10.2f **(67)**
Form - 102150
Record 1998 - 1st:2 2nd:1 3rd:0 Ran:6
Pre1998 - 1st:0 2nd:3 3rd:1 Ran:5
Win Prizemoney £6,239 *Total Prizemoney* £11,214
Wins 1998 Jun Newmar (GD) C 8f 81 <
1998 *Apr Southw (STD) 7f 68*
1998 Turf 1-4: (8f 1-3, 10f) (gd 3, g-f 1-1) 1998 AW 1-2: (7f 1-1, 8f) (Fibr 1-2)
Scopey, decent colt, effective 7 to 8f, best at 8f, acts on g-s to g-f - acts on Fibr, likes tight tracks, excels at Chester. Turf high 81 - 2nd of 3 giving 10lb to Sunley Seeker (12 Jun Goodwood 8f gd RF 1930) - also 1st of 11 giving 2lb to King of The River (19 Jun Newmarket RF 2127). AW high 68 (1st run). Inconsistent.
**Miss K M George [0-2] Exterior Profiles Ltd (from B W Hills [2-9] Jun 1998).*

GUDLAGE (USA) BHB 97f **RR 81f** 4512[5]

2 b c Gulch (USA) 9.6f **(79)**-Triple Kiss (Shareef Dancer(USA)) 9.9f **(73)**
Form - 215
Record 1998 - 1st:1 2nd:1 3rd:0 Ran:3
Win Prizemoney £4,659 *Total Prizemoney* £7,615
Wins * 1998 Jly Newmar (G-F) 7f 81 <
1998 Turf 1-3: (7f 1-2, 8f) (gd 2, frm 1-1)
Currently decent colt. Turf high 81 (began Jly) - 1st of 12 from Secret's Out (31 Jly Newmarket RF 3240). A promising second to a useful colt on his debut, he got off the mark next time, despite rearing in the stalls. Well held in a Group Two on his third run, but there should be more to come. **B Hanbury [1-3] Hilal Salem.*

GUESSTIMATION (USA) BHB 60f46a **RR 64f 46a** 4768[11]

9 b g Known Fact (USA) 8.3f **(72)** - Best Guess (USA) (Apalachee (USA)) 9.4f **(71)**
Form - 322434035613214300
Record 1998 - 1st:2 2nd:1 3rd:3 Ran:13
Pre1998 - 1st:14 2nd:16 3rd:11 Ran:87
Win Prizemoney £46,267 *Total Prizemoney* £66,956
Wins * 1998 Aug Nottin (G-F) SH 10f 56 62
*** 1998** Jly Yarmou (G-F) S 10.1f 50
* 1997 Aug Bright (G-F) C 10f 63
* 1997 Aug Warwic (SFT) S 10.8f 60
* 1997 Jly Ayr (G-F) S 10.9f 41
* 1997 Jun Warwic (GD) S 10.8f 55
* 1996 Aug Warwic (GD) S 10.8f 53
* 1996 Jly Sandow (G-F) H 10f 57 56
* 1995 Spt Newmar (GD) H 10f 62 67 <
* 1995 Aug Kempto (G-F) S 9f 64
* 1995 Jun Ripon (FRM) SH 8f 57 60
* 1995 May Folkes (G-F) C 9.7f 57
* 1994 Spt Folkes (G-S) C 9.7f 51
* 1994 Spt Yarmou (G-F) S 7f 53
1998 Turf 2-11: (8f, 9f 2, 10f 2-7, 11f) (sft, gd, g-f 2-4, frm 5) 1998 AW 0-2: (11f, 12f) (Equi, Fibr)
Average gelding, effective 10 to 11f, best at 10f, acts on gd to frm, best on g-f, has worn blinkers, prefers left handed tracks, prefers tight tracks, excels at Warwick and Brighton, likes Yarmouth. Turf high 64 - 3rd of 16 giving 18lb to Brookhouse Lady (8 Spt Leicester 10f g-f RF 4141) - also 1st of 18 giving 11lb to Be Valiant (29 Aug Nottingham RF 3958). AW high 46. He has now reached a century of races.
**J Pearce [16-98] The Exclusive Two Partnership (from J H M Gosden [0-2] Jun 1992).*

GUEST ALLIANCE (IRE) BHB 46f62a **RR 48f 62a** 124[4]

6 ch g Zaffaran (USA) 16f **(64)**-Alhargah (Be My Guest (USA)) 9.3f **(67)**
Form - 24
Record 1998 - 1st:0 2nd:1 3rd:0 Ran:2
Pre1998 - 1st:2 2nd:5 3rd:3 Ran:35
Win Prizemoney £5,124 *Total Prizemoney* £11,671
Wins 1996 *Nov Lingfi (STD) H 16f 55 63* <
1995 *Nov Lingfi (STD) 16f 62*
1998 AW 0-2: (16f 2) (Equi 2)
Average gelding, effective 16f - acts on Equi, prefers left handed tracks. AW high 63 (1st run) - 2nd of 7 getting 10lb from King of Sparta (10 Jan Lingfield 16f Equi RF 0063). Consistent. He is an effective sort in staying handicaps on the Lingfield Equitrack.
**G L Moore [1-9] Ballard (1834) Ltd (from A Moore [2-31] Jan 1997).*

GUEST ENVOY (IRE) BHB 42f40a **RR 34f 40a** 5121[5]

3 b f Paris House 5.9f **(64)** - Peace Mission (Dunbeath (USA)) 7.8f **(70)**
Form - 580687021000005
Record 1998 - 1st:1 2nd:1 3rd:0 Ran:15
Pre1998 - 1st:0 2nd:0 3rd:0 Ran:1
Win Prizemoney £3,745 *Total Prizemoney* £4,565
Wins * 1998 Aug Hamilt (SFT) H 6f 40 46 <
1998 Turf 1-14: (6f 1-6, 7f 6, 10f, 12f) (sft 2, g-s 3, gd 1-3, g-f, frm 4, hrd) 1998 AW 0-1: (7f) (Fibr)
Small, very moderate filly, effective 6f, acts on gd, has worn blinkers. Turf high 46 - 1st of 18 getting 20lb from Trojan Hero (12 Aug Hamilton RF 3576). **C N Allen [1-16] Newmarket Connections Ltd.*

GUEST OF HONOUR **RR 53f** 4846[15]

2 gr f Petong 7.6f **(58)** - Special Guest (Be My Guest (USA)) 9.3f **(67)**
Form - 000
Record 1998 - 1st:0 2nd:0 3rd:0 Ran:3
1998 Turf 0-3: (6f 3) (g-f 3)
Currently fair filly. Turf high 53 (began Spt).
**B W Hills [0-3] Major Christopher Hanbury.*

GUILDHALL BHB 74f **RR 78f** 1258[7]

3 b c Saddlers' Hall (IRE) 10.5f **(65)** - Queen's Visit (Top Command (USA)) 10f **(77)**
Form - 37
Record 1998 - 1st:0 2nd:0 3rd:1 Ran:2
Pre1998 - 1st:0 2nd:0 3rd:1 Ran:2
Win Prizemoney £0 *Total Prizemoney* £1,436
1998 Turf 0-2: (12f 2) (g-s, frm)
Scopey, above-average colt. Turf high 74 (1st run) - 3rd of 4 to Seignorial (23 Apr Beverley 12f g-s RF 0827).
**B J Meehan [0-4] Merlyn Racing.*

GUILSBOROUGH BHB 57f **RR 56f** 4990[13]

3 br g Northern Score (USA) - Super Sisters (AUS) (Call Report (USA))
Form - 600540
Record 1998 - 1st:0 2nd:0 3rd:0 Ran:6
Pre1998 - 1st:0 2nd:0 3rd:0 Ran:2
1998 Turf 0-6: (6f 2, 7f 2, 8f 2) (sft, g-f 3, frm 2)
Fair gelding, has worn blinkers. Turf high 56.
**D Morris [0-8] Mason Racing Ltd.*

GUINEA HUNTER (IRE) BHB 95f **RR 98f** 2708[2]

2 b c Pips Pride 6.7f **(70)** - Preponderance (IRE) (Cyrano de Bergerac) 6f **(68)**
Form - 212
Record 1998 - 1st:1 2nd:2 3rd:0 Ran:3

Win Prizemoney £3,582 *Total Prizemoney* £8,387
Wins *** 1998** Jun Carlis (G-S) 5.9f 80+ <
1998 Turf 1-3: (6f 1-3) (gd 1-2, frm)
Currently very useful colt. Turf high 98 - 2nd of 3 giving 3lb to Ace of Parkes (11 Jly Chester 6f frm RF 2708). Second to the speedy Atlantic Destiny first time out, he came on for that outing when decisively winning a maiden at Carlisle. He finished strongly, but was unable to collar Ace Of Parkes at Chester in a conditions race, where that rival broke the two-year-old course record. Whether the track did not suit or he just was not quite good enough remains to be seen as he was not seen out again.
**T D Easterby [1-3] M P Burke Developments Ltd.*

GULF SHAADI BHB 86f95a **RR 97f 95a** 5078[10]

6 b g Shaadi (USA) 8.1f **(75)** - Ela Meem (USA) (Kris) 9.5f **(73)**
Form - 610028288406000700
Record **1998** - 1st:1 2nd:2 3rd:0 Ran:18
Pre1998 - 1st:12 2nd:4 3rd:5 Ran:57
Win Prizemoney £104,604 *Total Prizemoney* £131,942
Wins *** 1998** *Mar Wolver (STD) H 9.4f 85 90* <
* 1997 Oct Newmar (GD) H 8f 82 90 <
* 1997 Spt Ascot (G-F) H 8f 74 81
* 1997 Aug Sandow (G-F) H 7.1f 66 71
* 1997 Apr Beverl (G-F) H 7.5f 59 62
* 1997 *Jan Southw (STD) H 8f 51 67*
* 1997 *Jan Southw (STD) H 8f 55 60*
1995 *May Wolver (STD) C 8.5f 81+*
1995 *Mar Lingfi (STD) C 7f 75*
1995 *Mar Lingfi (STD) C 8f 73*
1995 *Jan Wolver (STD) H 7f 78 79*
1995 *Jan Lingfi (STD) C 7f 68*
1994 *Dec Lingfi (STD) 7f 71*
1998 Turf 0-15: (7f 2, 8f 12, 9f) (sft 3, gd 7, g-f 2, frm 2, hrd) 1998 AW 1-3: (8f 2, 9f 1-1) (Fibr 1-3)
Very useful gelding, effective 7 to 9f, best at 8f, acts on sft to gd - acts on Fibr, best on gd, has worn blinkers, excels at Sandown and likes Southwell. Turf high 97 - 4th of 13 getting 1lb from For Your Eyes Only (4 Jly Sandown 8f gd RF 2548). AW high 90 - 1st of 9 from Yarob (4 Mar Wolverhampton RF 0400). Was disappointing in the Lincoln, but bounced back at Newmarket when a creditable second to Tumbleweed Ridge. Since then his form has tailed off dramatically on Turf, but hopefully he can bounce back on sand.
**E J Alston [7-54] The Bibby Halliday Partnership (from G Lewis [2-8] Jun 1995).*

GULLAND BHB 113f **RR 120+f** 1778[11]

3 b c Unfuwain (USA) 11.4f **(74)** - Spin (High Top) 10.2f **(67)**
Form - 210
Record **1998** - 1st:1 2nd:1 3rd:0 Ran:3
Pre1998 - 1st:1 2nd:1 3rd:0 Ran:3
Win Prizemoney £45,479 *Total Prizemoney* £54,850
Wins *** 1998** May Cheste (GD) G3 12.3f 112 <
* 1997 Oct Pontef (G-S) L 8f 102+
1998 Turf 1-3: (8f, 12f 1-2) (gd, g-f 1-2)
Scopey, very high-class colt, effective 8 to 12f, acts on gd to g-f. Turf high 120 (1st run) - 2nd of 6 getting 3lb from Xaar (16 Apr Newmarket 8f gd RF 0710) - also 1st of 5 from The Glow-Worm (5 May Chester RF 1042). He gave Xaar a good race in the Craven on his reappearance in what was a muddling affair, and only held on by the skin of his teeth in the Chester Vase, giving the impression that he may not have stayed. He ran poorly in the Derby, sustaining a suspensory injury to a foreleg which sidelined him for the rest of the season. Stays in training, and if he can overcome his problems he will make up into a decent four-year-old.
**G Wragg [2-6] Mollers Racing.*

GUNBOAT DIPLOMACY **RR 38f** 1706[8]

3 b br g Mtoto 11.5f **(71)** - Pepper Star (IRE) (Salt Dome (USA))
Form - 008
Record **1998** - 1st:0 2nd:0 3rd:0 Ran:3
Pre1998 - 1st:0 2nd:0 3rd:0 Ran:2
1998 Turf 0-3: (6f, 7f 2) (gd 2, frm)
Leggy, very moderate gelding, has worn blinkers. Turf high 38.
**M J Fetherston-Godley [0-5] Abigail Ltd.*

GUNMAKER BHB 20f33a **RR 18f 33a** 2534[5]

9 ch g Gunner B 11.2f **(45)** - Lucky Starkist (Lucky Wednesday) 8f **(50)**
Form - 05
Record **1998** - 1st:0 2nd:0 3rd:0 Ran:2
Pre1998 - 1st:0 2nd:2 3rd:2 Ran:20
Win Prizemoney £0 *Total Prizemoney* £2,204
1998 Turf 0-2: (18f, 22f) (g-s, gd)
Little account gelding, has worn blinkers. Turf high 18.
**B J Llewellyn [3-45] Ken Russell (from R J Holder [0-4] Jun 1992).*

GUNNER SAM BHB 78f **RR 73f** 4882[3]

2 ch c Emarati (USA) 6.6f **(63)** - Minne Love (Homeric) 9.8f **(67)**
Form - 063
Record **1998** - 1st:0 2nd:0 3rd:1 Ran:3
Win Prizemoney £0 *Total Prizemoney* £369
1998 Turf 0-3: (6f 3) (g-s, gd, g-f)
Currently above-average colt. Turf high 73 (began Spt).
**B W Hills [0-3] R W Miller.*

GUNNERS GLORY BHB 34f35a **RR 35f 35a** 3523[10]

4 b g Aragon 7.7f **(58)** - Massive Powder (Caerleon (USA)) 8.6f **(71)**
Form - 040080
Record **1998** - 1st:0 2nd:0 3rd:0 Ran:6
Pre1998 - 1st:1 2nd:3 3rd:3 Ran:18
Win Prizemoney £2,997 *Total Prizemoney* £6,379
Wins 1996 Jly Windso (G-F) 5f 73 <
1998 Turf 0-5: (7f 3, 8f 2) (gd 2, g-f, frm 2) 1998 AW 0-1: (7f) (Equi)
Workmanlike, very moderate gelding, effective 5 to 7f, acts on gd to frm, best on frm, often wears blinkers (effectively). Turf high 35. Inconsistent.
**Mrs L Stubbs [0-13] Mrs L Stubbs (from D Marks [0-1] Aug 1997).*

GURKHA BHB 77f **RR 88f** 4985[16]

3 b c Polish Precedent (USA) 9f **(73)** - Glendera (Glenstal (USA)) 10.1f **(64)**
Form - 2470000300
Record **1998** - 1st:0 2nd:1 3rd:1 Ran:10
Pre1998 - 1st:1 2nd:0 3rd:0 Ran:2
Win Prizemoney £6,212 *Total Prizemoney* £11,580
Wins * 1997 Spt York (SFT) 6f 91 <
1998 Turf 0-10: (6f 2, 7f 5, 8f 3) (hvy, sft, g-s, gd 5, frm 2)
Useful colt, effective 6f, acts on sft. Turf high 88. Got off the mark with a wide-margin success in a York maiden last season, handling the sticky ground better than his rivals, but was a well beaten runner-up in similar conditions at Kempton on his return. He was out of his depth in a Group Three at the Curragh, but ran a bit better in a competitive Epsom handicap.
**R Hannon [1-12] Russell, Aston House Withey.*

GUY'S GAMBLE BHB 25f22a **RR 33f 22a** 253[9]

5 ch g Mazilier (USA) 8.5f **(56)** - Deep Blue Sea (Gulf Pearl) 12f **(54)**
Form - 0
Record **1998** - 1st:0 2nd:0 3rd:0 Ran:1
Pre1998 - 1st:1 2nd:0 3rd:1 Ran:14
Win Prizemoney £2,607 *Total Prizemoney* £2,959
Wins * 1996 *Jan Southw (STD) S 7f 57* <
1998 AW 0-1: (7f) (Fibr)
Very moderate gelding, effective 6f - acts on Fibr, has worn blinkers, favours left handed tracks.
**J Wharton [1-17] Parkers of Peterborough Plc.*

GWESPYR BHB 34f43a **RR 68f 43a** 4626[7]

5 ch g Sharpo 7.5f **(68)** - Boozy (Absalom) 7.2f **(58)**
Form - 5650540757007
Record **1998** - 1st:0 2nd:0 3rd:0 Ran:10
Pre1998 - 1st:3 2nd:0 3rd:4 Ran:30
Win Prizemoney £8,919 *Total Prizemoney* £12,571
Wins 1996 Jly Nottin (G-F) 5.1f 61
1996 Jly Haydoc (GD) H 5f 58 61
1995 Apr Lingfi (GD) 5f 78t <
1998 Turf 0-9: (5f 4, 6f 5) (gd 5, g-f, frm 3) 1998 AW 0-1: (7f) (Fibr)
Average gelding, effective 7f, acts on frm, has worn blinkers. Turf high 68.
**Don Enrico Incisa [0-15] Don Enrico Incisa (from R Hannon [0-7] Aug 1997).*

GYMCRAK FLYER BHB 60f65a **RR 61f 65a** 4840[10]

7 b m Aragon 7.7f **(58)** - Intellect (Frimley Park) 6.5f **(67)**
Form - 67024563D0200
Record **1998** - 1st:0 2nd:2 3rd:1 Ran:13

Pre1998 - 1st:10 2nd:3 3rd:4 Ran:42
Win Prizemoney £34,867 *Total Prizemoney* £45,634
Wins * 1997 Spt Yarmou (FRM) H 8f 62 68
* 1997 May Redcar (GD) H 7f 60 63
* 1997 Apr Pontef (GD) 8f 62
* 1996 Jly Yarmou (FRM) H 7f 63 66
* 1996 Jly Redcar (G-F) H 7f 58 60
* 1996 Jun Carlis (FRM) 8f 61
* 1995 Spt Haydoc (GD) 8.1f 66
* 1995 Aug Newcas (FRM) H 7f 59 66
* 1994 Jly Leices (G-F) H 8f 72 69 <
* 1994 Jun Pontef (FRM) 6f 53+
1998 Turf 0-13: (7f 8, 8f 5) (g-s, gd 3, g-f 5, frm 4)
Average mare, effective 6 to 8f, best at 8f, acts on gd to frm, best on frm, has worn blinkers, likes left handed tracks, does well at Yarmouth, likes Redcar. Turf high 61 - 2nd of 24 getting 10lb from Royal Result (3 Spt York 7f g-f RF 4066). She likes fast ground, and regained winning form under a fine ride from 'Angel Jacobs' at Beverley in August. That race was taken away from her at the end of the year.
**G Holmes [10-55] The Gymcrak Thoroughbred Racing Club.*

GYMCRAK GORJOS BHB 33f RR 32f 2069[6]
4 b br f Rock Hopper 10.6f **(54)** - Bit O' May (Mummy's Pet) 7.7f **(60)**
Form - 5006
Record 1998 - 1st:0 2nd:0 3rd:0 Ran:4
Pre1998 - 1st:0 2nd:2 3rd:0 Ran:7
Win Prizemoney £0 *Total Prizemoney* £1,642
1998 Turf 0-4: (10f 2, 12f, 14f) (gd 3, frm)
Workmanlike, very moderate filly, effective 10f, acts on frm, often wears blinkers (effectively), likes tight tracks. Turf high 32.
**G Holmes [0-11] The Gymcrak Thoroughbred Racing Club.*

GYMCRAK MYSTERY BHB 39f43a RR 18f 43a 4543[12]
3 br f Ballacashtal (CAN) 7.9f **(51)** - Little Unknown (Known Fact (USA)) 7.4f **(67)**
Form - 74000
Record 1998 - 1st:0 2nd:0 3rd:0 Ran:5
Pre1998 - 1st:0 2nd:0 3rd:1 Ran:3
Win Prizemoney £0 *Total Prizemoney* £471
1998 Turf 0-2: (7f 2) (gd, frm) 1998 AW 0-3: (6f 2, 9f) (Fibr 3)
Unfurnished, moderate filly, effective 6f - acts on Fibr, prefers tight tracks. Turf high 18 (began Aug). AW high 46 - 4th of 11 giving 8lb to Tom Tun (9 Jly Southwell 6f Fibr RF 2656). Becoming disappointing. **G Holmes [0-8] The Gymcrak Thoroughbred Racing Club.*

GYMCRAK PREMIERE BHB 59f RR 61f 3562[1]
10 ch g Primo Dominie 7.2f **(67)** - Oraston (Morston (FR)) 9.4f **(55)**
Form - 20185231
Record 1998 - 1st:2 2nd:2 3rd:1 Ran:8
Pre1998 - 1st:8 2nd:9 3rd:7 Ran:73
Win Prizemoney £53,353 *Total Prizemoney* £102,910
Wins * **1998** Aug Beverl (G-F) C 8.5f 47
* **1998** May Ripon (G-F) S 8f 51
* 1997 Spt Yarmou (G-F) S 7f 69
* 1997 Apr Beverl (G-F) H 9.9f 73 79
* 1995 Aug Newbur (G-F) H 7.3f 83 88
* 1994 Jly Lingfi (GD) H 7.6f 90 89
1998 Turf 2-8: (7f 2, 8f 2-4, 9f, 10f) (gd 2, g-f 1-5, frm 1-1)
Average gelding, effective 7 to 10f, best at 10f, acts on frm, has worn blinkers (extremely effectively), likes right handed tracks, likes tight tracks. Turf high 68. Consistent.
**G Holmes [6-55] The Gymcrak Thoroughbred Racing Club (from M H Easterby [4-26] Jly 1993).*

GYMCRAK TIGER (IRE) BHB 56f RR 55f 3939[1]
8 b g Colmore Row 10f **(45)** - Gossip (Sharp Edge) 10f **(56)**
Form - 41
Record 1998 - 1st:1 2nd:0 3rd:0 Ran:2
Pre1998 - 1st:1 2nd:1 3rd:2 Ran:12
Win Prizemoney £5,486 *Total Prizemoney* £9,251
Wins * **1998** Aug Beverl (G-F) SH 12f 44 55
1998 Turf 1-2: (12f 1-1, 16f) (frm 1-2)
Fair gelding, effective 12f, acts on frm, has worn blinkers (very effectively). Turf high 55 (began Aug) - 1st of 15 giving 11lb to Skyers A Kite (29 Aug Beverley RF 3939). Consistent.
**G Holmes [3-24] The Gymcrak Thoroughbred Racing Club (from M H Easterby [1-6] Jun 1993).*

GYPSY (IRE) BHB 66f RR 74f 4889[6]
2 b c Distinctly North (USA) 7.4f **(63)** - Winscarlet North (Garland Knight)
Form - 73541856
Record 1998 - 1st:1 2nd:0 3rd:1 Ran:8
Win Prizemoney £3,002 *Total Prizemoney* £3,659
Wins * **1998** Jly Yarmou (G-F) 7f 74 <
1998 Turf 1-8: (6f, 7f 1-5, 8f 2) (gd 2, g-f 1-3, frm 2, hrd)
Above-average colt, effective 7f, acts on gd to g-f. Turf high 74 - 1st of 8 from Royal Fusilier (27 Jly Yarmouth RF 3152). Consistent.
**M H Tompkins [1-8] Richard Flatt.*

GYPSY HILL BHB 62f RR 73f 4198[9]
3 ch f Theatrical Charmer 10.9f **(63)**-Mirkan Honey (Ballymore) 7.3f **(64)**
Form - 845080
Record 1998 - 1st:0 2nd:0 3rd:0 Ran:6
Pre1998 - 1st:1 2nd:1 3rd:1 Ran:6
Win Prizemoney £2,869 *Total Prizemoney* £5,066
Wins * 1997 May Bath (G-S) 5.1f 78 <
1998 Turf 0-6: (8f 3, 10f 3) (gd 3, g-f 3)
Leggy, above-average filly, effective 5 to 8f, acts on gd. Turf high 73 - 4th of 9 getting 5lb from Shalad'or (27 Jun Bath 8f gd RF 2327). Often misses the break.
**D HaydnJones [1-12] Kevan Kynaston.*

GYPSY MUSIC (IRE) BHB 54f RR 56f 4575[6]
2 b f Treasure Kay 6.5f **(53)** - Mighty Special (IRE) (Head for Heights) 9.6f **(55)**
Form - 83467820606
Record 1998 - 1st:0 2nd:1 3rd:1 Ran:11
Win Prizemoney £0 *Total Prizemoney* £1,205
1998 Turf 0-11: (5f 5, 6f 2, 7f 4) (sft, g-s, gd, g-f 3, frm 4, hrd)
Fair filly, effective 6f, acts on frm, has worn blinkers. Turf high 56 - 2nd of 8 giving 2lb to Brookhead Brandy (10 Aug Leicester 6f frm RF 3499). **G R Oldroyd [0-11] A Goodings & K Cummins.*

GYPSY PASSION (IRE) BHB 98f RR 97f 3230[1]
3 ch c Woodman (USA) 9.7f **(77)** - Rua D'Oro (USA) (El Gran Senor (USA)) 9.6f **(76)**
Form - 32441
Record 1998 - 1st:1 2nd:1 3rd:1 Ran:5
Pre1998 - 1st:1 2nd:0 3rd:0 Ran:3
Win Prizemoney £41,543 *Total Prizemoney* £51,435
Wins * **1998** Jly Goodwo (G-S) H 9.9f 91 97 <
* 1997 Nov Redcar (GD) 7f 85+
1998 Turf 1-5: (8f, 10f 1-3, 12f) (g-s, gd 1-4)
Very useful colt, effective 10 to 12f, best at 10f, acts on gd, has worn blinkers. Turf high 97 - 1st of 10 getting 4lb from Generous Rosi (31 Jly Goodwood RF 3230). Improving. Probably needed his reappearance at Doncaster. Went down fighting next time after a three-month absence, and was a staying-on fourth to stable companion Yavana's Pace in a hot race at Sandown. Ran twice in three days at Glorious Goodwood, winning on the second occasion when equipped with blinkers and returning to ten furlongs. Has not been seen out since, but should be able to give a good account of himself next season. **M Johnston [2-8] P D Savill.*

HAAFIZ (IRE) BHB 100f RR 103f 4378[4]
2 b c Green Desert (USA) 7.8f **(78)** - Midway Lady (USA) (Alleged (USA)) 10f **(76)**
Form - 3114
Record 1998 - 1st:2 2nd:0 3rd:1 Ran:4
Win Prizemoney £11,181 *Total Prizemoney* £14,543
Wins * **1998** Aug Pontef (G-F) 6f 103+ <
* **1998** Jly Newmar (G-F) 6f 99
1998 Turf 2-4: (6f 2-4) (g-f, frm 2-3)
Very useful colt. Turf high 103 (began Jly) - 1st of 3 getting 2lb from Bon Ami (25 Aug Pontefract RF 3851) - also 1st of 5 from Compatriot (24 Jly Newmarket RF 3074). He ran a fine race when narrowly beaten by Mujahid and Belasco on his debut and, as that form entitled him to, he subsequently landed a couple of minor events. Easily brushed aside in the Group Two Mill Reef Stakes, he is out of the Oaks winner Midway Lady and needs further than six furlongs. **B Hanbury [2-4] Hamdan Al Maktoum.*

HAAJRA (IRE) BHB 71f RR 72?f 4751[17]
3 b f Polish Precedent (USA) 9f **(73)** - Hejraan (USA) (Alydar (USA))

9.1f **(76)**
Form - 0871800
Record 1998 - 1st:1 2nd:0 3rd:0 Ran:7
Win Prizemoney £4,193 *Total Prizemoney* £4,193
Wins * **1998** Aug Thirsk (GD) H 6f 68 72++ <
1998 Turf 1-7: (6f 1-4, 7f, 8f 2) (sft 2, g-s, gd, g-f 1-1, frm 2)
Workmanlike, above-average filly, effective 6f, acts on g-f. Turf high 72 - 1st of 21 giving 2lb to Cool Prospect (1 Aug Thirsk RF 3281). **M A Jarvis [1-7] Sheikh Ahmed Al Maktoum.*

HAAMI (USA) BHB 116f **RR 117f** 4843[1]

3 b c Nashwan (USA) 10.3f **(79)** - Oumaldaaya (USA) (Nureyev (USA)) 8.7f **(78)**
Form - 50221
Record 1998 - 1st:1 2nd:2 3rd:0 Ran:5
Pre1998 - 1st:3 2nd:0 3rd:1 Ran:4
Win Prizemoney £29,469 *Total Prizemoney* £43,016
Wins * **1998** Oct Newmar (GD) L 9f 114 <
* 1997 Oct Newmar (G-F) L 7f 102+
* 1997 Jly Doncas (GD) 7f 95+
* 1997 Jly Newmar (GD) 7f 90++
1998 Turf 1-5: (8f 2, 9f 1-2, 12f) (gd, g-f 1-2, frm 2)
Well made, high-class colt, effective 8 to 9f, acts on gd to g-f. Turf high 117 (1st run) - 5th of 18 to King Of Kings (2 May Newmarket 8f gd RF 0974) - also 1st of 13 from Mudeer (16 Oct Newmarket RF 4843). There was nothing wrong with his effort in the 2,000 Guineas on his reappearance, finishing a good fifth, but he beat only one home in the Derby and apparently suffered a breathing problem. He looked to have been found the ideal opportunity to get back on the winning trail in a Sandown conditions event in August, but failed to deliver, and again flattered to deceive next time. He ended the season by winning a Listed event at Newmarket when, interestingly, he was wearing a tongue-strap for the first time. **J L Dunlop [4-9] Hamdan Al Maktoum.*

HABIBI BHB 53f54a **RR 58f 54a** 3563[6]

2 b f Alhijaz 7.7f **(57)** - Balearica (Bustino) 10.4f **(64)**
Form - 21556
Record 1998 - 1st:1 2nd:1 3rd:0 Ran:5
Win Prizemoney £1,898 *Total Prizemoney* £2,373
Wins * **1998** May Catter (G-S) S 6f 58 <
1998 Turf 1-2: (5f, 6f 1-1) (gd 1-2) 1998 AW 0-3: (6f 3) (Fibr 3)
Fair filly. Turf high 58 (1st run) - 1st of 9 from Claranna (30 May Catterick RF 1583). AW high 57. **J Berry [1-5] W J Kelly.*

HABUB (USA) **RR 90f** 4509[1]

2 b br c Danzig (USA) 8.1f **(88)** - Cheval Volant (USA) (Kris S (USA)) 7.9f **(71)**
Form - 21
Record 1998 - 1st:1 2nd:1 3rd:0 Ran:2
Win Prizemoney £4,402 *Total Prizemoney* £5,397
Wins * **1998** Spt Nottin (G-F) 6.1f 84 <
1998 Turf 1-2: (6f 1-2) (gd 1-2)
Currently useful colt. Turf high 84 (began Spt) - 1st of 16 giving 5lb to Hawriyah (26 Spt Nottingham RF 4509). Progressive form in Nottingham maidens. **J H M Gosden [1-2] Hamdan Al Maktoum.*

HADAYIK BHB 76f **RR 77f** 4111[17]

3 b f Unfuwain (USA) 11.4f **(74)** - Almarai (USA) (Vaguely Noble) 10.1f **(72)**
Form - 2550380
Record 1998 - 1st:0 2nd:1 3rd:1 Ran:7
Pre1998 - 1st:1 2nd:0 3rd:0 Ran:3
Win Prizemoney £4,269 *Total Prizemoney* £8,267
Wins * 1997 Aug Goodwo (G-F) 7f 84 <
1998 Turf 0-7: (8f 3, 10f 2, 11f, 12f) (g-s, g-f 2, frm 4)
Workmanlike, above-average filly, effective 7 to 11f, acts on g-s to g-f, best on g-f, has worn blinkers, prefers tight tracks. Turf high 91 - 5th of 6 to Bristol Channel (9 May Lingfield 11f g-f RF 1124). Consistent. Beaten by Sadian in a four-runner conditions event at Bath on her reappearance, she was very disappointing afterwards and was too high in the handicap.
**P T Walwyn [1-10] Hamdan Al Maktoum.*

HADEQA BHB 67f **RR 76f** 4969[5]

2 ch g Hadeer 8.9f **(58)** - Heavenly Queen (Scottish Reel) 7f **(61)**
Form - 55026137253005
Record 1998 - 1st:1 2nd:2 3rd:2 Ran:14
Win Prizemoney £4,996 *Total Prizemoney* £8,527
Wins * **1998** Aug Redcar (G-F) H 6f 61 63 <
1998 Turf 1-13: (5f 2, 6f 1-7, 7f 4) (sft, g-s 2, gd 3, g-f 2, frm 1-5) 1998 AW 0-1: (5f) (Fibr)
Above-average gelding, effective 6 to 7f, best at 6f, acts on gd to frm, best on frm, always wears blinkers. Turf high 76 - 3rd of 19 to Red Charger (19 Aug York 6f frm RF 3757). Consistent. Has paid his way in modest company, winning a nursery at Chester and finishing third in a valuable York seller.
**P D Evans [1-14] Men Behaving Badly.*

HADITH BHB 80f **RR 82f** 4267[2]

3 ch c Nashwan (USA) 10.3f **(79)** - Azyaa (Kris) 9.5f **(73)**
Form - 30413502
Record 1998 - 1st:1 2nd:1 3rd:2 Ran:8
Pre1998 - 1st:0 2nd:3 3rd:0 Ran:3
Win Prizemoney £5,090 *Total Prizemoney* £11,481
Wins * **1998** Jly Beverl (GD) H 8.5f 77 80 <
1998 Turf 1-8: (7f, 8f 1-3, 9f 2, 10f 2) (g-s, gd 3, g-f 1-3, frm)
Lengthy, decent colt, effective 7 to 8f, best at 7f, acts on gd to frm, best on gd, has worn blinkers, excels at Nottingham and Beverley. Turf high 82 - 2nd of 11 to Easter Ogil (15 Spt Sandown 7f gd RF 4267) - also 1st of 7 getting 6lb from Mustique Dream (4 Jly Beverley RF 2518). Consistent. Held since his Beverley victory, softish ground and ten furlongs could pay dividends.
**P T Walwyn [1-8] Hamdan Al Maktoum (from D Morley [0-3] Oct 1997).*

HADITOVSKI **RR 59f** 3602[7]

2 b c Hatim (USA) 7.8f **(56)** - Grand Occasion (Great Nephew) 9.9f **(64)**
Form - 7
Record 1998 - 1st:0 2nd:0 3rd:0 Ran:1
1998 Turf 0-1: (7f) (frm)
Currently fair colt. **T P Tate [0-1] T P Tate.*

HADLEIGH (IRE) BHB 85f **RR 83f** 4773[4]

2 b c Perugino (USA) - Risacca (ITY) (Sir Gaylord) 10.6f **(64)**
Form - 53104
Record 1998 - 1st:1 2nd:0 3rd:1 Ran:5
Win Prizemoney £3,728 *Total Prizemoney* £4,549
Wins * **1998** Aug Kempto (G-F) 6f 83 <
1998 Turf 1-5: (6f 1-3, 7f 2) (gd, g-f, frm 1-3)
Decent colt. Turf high 83 - 1st of 18 from Maple (19 Aug Kempton RF 3735). He got off the mark in a Kempton maiden in August, but was beaten a long way in a valuable Newmarket nursery next time.
**R W Armstrong [1-5] C G Donovan.*

HADRA (USA) **RR 70f** 1676[4]

2 b f Dayjur (USA) 6.8f **(79)**-Trampoli (USA) (Trempolino(USA)) 12f **(71)**
Form - 24
Record 1998 - 1st:0 2nd:1 3rd:0 Ran:2
Win Prizemoney £0 *Total Prizemoney* £1,814
1998 Turf 0-2: (5f, 6f) (gd, g-f)
Currently above-average filly. Turf high 70. Has the ability to win races, but bolted before her intended third run and might have a temperament problem. **P F I Cole [0-2] H R H Prince Fahd Salman.*

HAJAL (IRE) **RR 24f** 1904[7]

3 b br f Mujtahid (USA) 7.4f **(69)** - Three For Fantasy (IRE) (Common Grounds)
Form - 7
Record 1998 - 1st:0 2nd:0 3rd:0 Ran:1
1998 Turf 0-1: (7f) (g-f)
Scopey, currently little account filly.
**R W Armstrong [0-1] Hamdan Al Maktoum.*

HAJR (IRE) BHB 95f **RR 93f** 2058[8]

4 b g Rainbow Quest (USA) 11.2f **(81)** - Dance by Night (Northfields (USA)) 9f **(72)**
Form - 884118
Record 1998 - 1st:2 2nd:0 3rd:0 Ran:6
Pre1998 - 1st:2 2nd:1 3rd:0 Ran:7
Win Prizemoney £41,565 *Total Prizemoney* £46,479
Wins * **1998** Jun Epsom (GD) H 12f 90 93 <
* **1998** May Goodwo (G-F) H 12f 85 87
* 1997 Aug Newmar (G-F) H 10f 82 86+
* 1997 Jun Newbur (GD) 7f 75
1998 Turf 2-6: (8f, 10f 2, 12f 2-3) (sft, gd 3, g-f 2-2)

Well made, useful gelding, effective 10 to 12f, best at 12f, acts on g-s to frm, best on g-f, excels at Newmarket. Turf high 93 - 1st of 15 getting 7lb from Sabadilla (6 Jun Epsom RF 1780) - also 1st of 8 getting 10lb from Dream of Nurmi (21 May Goodwood RF 1363). Creditable efforts early in the season when his stable was not firing, but then found his form with victory in a Goodwood maiden, and just held on to land a valuable rated stakes at Epsom. He was not seen again after running moderately at Royal Ascot.

**E A L Dunlop [4-13] Maktoum Al Maktoum.*

HAKEEM (IRE) BHB 63f RR 64f 4190[10]

3 ch g Kefaah (USA) 11.2f **(64)** - Masarrah (Formidable (USA)) 9.2f **(63)**

Form - 7008000

Record 1998 - 1st:0 2nd:0 3rd:0 Ran:7
Pre1998 - 1st:1 2nd:0 3rd:1 Ran:3

Win Prizemoney £2,389 *Total Prizemoney* £3,351

Wins * 1997 Spt Folkes (GD) 6f 78 <

1998 Turf 0-7: (6f, 7f 4, 8f 2) (gd 6, g-f)

Scopey, average gelding, effective 6f, acts on g-f, has worn blinkers. Turf high 74. Not entirely disgraced so far in '98, although he is yet to reach the frame. **R W Armstrong [1-10] Ahmed Al Shafar.*

HAKIKI (IRE) BHB 82f RR 106f 4347a[2]

6 b h Ballad Rock 7.2f **(63)** - Salvationist (Mill Reef (USA)) 10.5f **(78)**

Form - 2

1998 Turf 0-1: (6f) (sft)

Pattern-class horse. (1st run) - 2nd of 10 to Mortens Prospect (13 Spt Taby 6f sft RF 4347a).

**W Neuroth in NOR [0-6] (from P T Walwyn [1-10] Oct 1995).*

HALBERT BHB 29f40a RR 17f 40a 3689[10]

9 b g Song 6.4f **(63)** - Stoneydale (Tickled Pink) 6.5f **(59)**

Form - 00000

Record 1998 - 1st:0 2nd:0 3rd:0 Ran:5
Pre1998 - 1st:4 2nd:8 3rd:5 Ran:67

Win Prizemoney £11,572 *Total Prizemoney* £23,662

Wins * 1996 *Dec Lingfi (STD) H 6f 40 44*
1995 Aug Bright (FRM) H 5.3f 54 62 <
1995 Jly Mussel (G-F) SH 5f 49 51
1995 Jun Hamilt (FRM) SH 5f 41 49

1998 Turf 0-5: (5f 3, 6f 2) (gd 2, g-f, frm 2)

Moderate gelding, often wears blinkers. Turf high 17.

**P Burgoyne [1-28] Philip Saunders (from M D I Usher [0-4] May 1997).*

HALF A KNICKER BHB 56f RR 57f 2156[8]

3 b g Weldnaas (USA) 8.4f **(55)** - Queen of the Quorn **(51df 45a)** (Governor General)

Form - 408

Record 1998 - 1st:0 2nd:0 3rd:0 Ran:3
Pre1998 - 1st:0 2nd:0 3rd:1 Ran:4

Win Prizemoney £0 *Total Prizemoney* £414

1998 Turf 0-3: (7f, 8f, 10f) (gd, frm 2)

Scopey, fair gelding, effective 6f, acts on hrd, has worn blinkers. Turf high 57. **R A Fahey [0-7] J A Campbell.*

HALF-HITCH (USA) BHB 88f RR 84f 1201[6]

3 b f Diesis 9f **(80)** - Marling (IRE) (Lomond (USA)) 8.8f **(65)**

Form - 76

Record 1998 - 1st:0 2nd:0 3rd:0 Ran:2
Pre1998 - 1st:1 2nd:0 3rd:1 Ran:3

Win Prizemoney £3,715 *Total Prizemoney* £4,534

Wins * 1997 Jly Thirsk (GD) 6f 86 <

1998 Turf 0-2: (7f 2) (gd, frm)

Leggy, decent filly. Turf high 84. **D R Loder [1-5] E J Loder.*

HALF TIDE BHB 44f RR 48f 4529[11]

4 ch c Nashwan (USA) 10.3f **(79)** - Double River (USA) (Irish River (FR)) 8.6f **(78)**

Form - 0670

Record 1998 - 1st:0 2nd:0 3rd:0 Ran:4

1998 Turf 0-4: (6f, 7f 2, 8f) (gd, g-f 2, frm)

Workmanlike, moderate colt. Turf high 48 (began Jly).

**P Mitchell [0-4] The Fruit Cake Partnership.*

HALF TONE BHB 63f63a RR 64f 63a 5121[2]

6 gr h Touch of Grey 8.1f **(47)** - Demilinga (Nishapour (FR)) 9.1f **(61)**

Form - 5625323268375047433877170012

Record 1998 - 1st:2 2nd:4 3rd:5 Ran:26
Pre1998 - 1st:7 2nd:6 3rd:11 Ran:52

Win Prizemoney £28,612 *Total Prizemoney* £48,233

Wins * **1998** Oct Bath (HVY) H 5.1f 54 60
* **1998** Aug Sandow (G-F) H 5f 51 56
* 1997 Aug Sandow (GD) H 5f 56 60
* 1997 May Goodwo (G-S) H 5f 52 53
* 1996 Aug Sandow (G-F) H 5f 50 54
* 1996 *Feb Lingfi (STD) H 5f 64 65* <
* 1995 *Dec Lingfi (STD) H 5f 53 60*
* 1995 *Nov Lingfi (STD) H 5f 53 52*
* 1995 *Jan Wolver (STD) H 5f 48 54*

1998 Turf 2-17: (5f 2-16, 6f) (sft 1-1, g-s, gd 4, g-f 1-5, frm 6) 1998 AW 0-9: (5f 5, 6f 3, 7f) (Equi 9)

Average horse, effective 5 to 6f, best at 6f, acts on sft to g-f - acts on Equi, mostly wears blinkers (effectively), likes left handed tracks, likes tight tracks. Turf high 64 - 2nd of 16 getting 3lb from Facile Tigre (5 Nov Brighton 6f g-s RF 5121) - also 1st of 16 getting 19lb from Bowlers Boy (27 Oct Bath RF 5007). AW high 67 (1st run) - 2nd of 11 getting 5lb from Pageboy (1 Jan Lingfield 6f Equi RF 0004). Effective on turf as well as Equitrack, he manages to reach the frame regularly, but probably does not win as often as he should. Capable of a power-packed finish, he is most effective coming from off a strong pace, as he showed when regaining winning form at Sandown in August, a race in which he had registered his previous win the year before.

**R M Flower [9-78] Mrs G M Temmerman.*

HAL HOO YAROOM BHB 50f65a RR 50f 65a 2646[7]

5 b h Belmez (USA) 11.4f **(65)** - Princess Nawaal (USA) (Seattle Slew (USA)) 9.4f **(76)**

Form - 223637

Record 1998 - 1st:0 2nd:2 3rd:2 Ran:6
Pre1998 - 1st:2 2nd:0 3rd:1 Ran:12

Win Prizemoney £6,835 *Total Prizemoney* £9,772

Wins 1996 Jly Folkes (FRM) H 15.4f 67 82 <
1996 Jun Yarmou (FRM) 14.1f 67

1998 Turf 0-2: (14f, 16f) (gd, frm) 1998 AW 0-4: (13f, 16f 3) (Equi 3, Fibr)

Average colt, effective 13 to 16f, best at 16f - acts on AW, best on Equi, prefers left handed tracks, prefers tight tracks. Turf high 50. AW high 64 (1st run) - 2nd of 8 giving 30lb to Coastguards Hero (8 Jan Lingfield 13f Equi RF 0051). Without a win on the Flat since July '96 though a winner over hurdles, he made the frame on both sand surfaces at the start of '98, but will need to find a moderate event in order to score.

**J R Jenkins [0-12] Ellis & Partners (Stockbrokers) Ltd (from R Akehurst [0-4] Oct 1997).*

HALLOA BHB 96f RR 81f 4333[7]

2 ch f Wolfhound (USA) 7.3f **(71)** - Fairy Fortune (Rainbow Quest (USA)) 10.4f **(75)**

Form - 13367

Record 1998 - 1st:1 2nd:0 3rd:2 Ran:5

Win Prizemoney £4,012 *Total Prizemoney* £7,067

Wins * **1998** Jun Nottin (GD) 6.1f 81 <

1998 Turf 1-5: (6f 1-3, 7f 2) (gd 1-2, g-f, frm, hrd)

Decent filly. Turf high 81 (1st run) - 1st of 9 getting 5lb from Baltic Lowland (22 Jun Nottingham RF 2178). She held on to win by the skin of her teeth on her debut at Nottingham, and has run with credit in listed races since. **J R Fanshawe [1-5] T & J Vestey.*

HALLUCINATION (IRE) RR 94f 3859a[1]

3 b f Last Tycoon 9.4f **(73)** - Welsh Berry (USA) (Sir Ivor) 10.2f **(70)**

Form - 302351

1998 Turf 1-6: (8f 1-1, 9f 4, 10f) (g-s 3, gd, g-f 1-2)

Useful filly, effective 8 to 9f, best at 9f, acts on g-s to g-f, best on g-f. Turf high 94 (1st run) - 3rd of 4 getting 12lb from Desert Fox (21 May Tipperary 9f g-f RF 1496a) - also 1st of 9 from Bee Off (19 Aug Dundalk RF 3859a). Inconsistent.

**T Stack in IRE [1-9] Mrs John Magnier.*

HALMAHERA (IRE) BHB 95f RR 103f 4821[12]

3 b c Petardia 8.2f **(58)** - Champagne Girl (Robellino (USA)) 7.6f **(80)**

Form - 574455850

Record 1998 - 1st:0 2nd:0 3rd:0 Ran:9
Pre1998 - 1st:4 2nd:2 3rd:1 Ran:8

Win Prizemoney £43,839 *Total Prizemoney* £52,345

Wins	* 1997	Oct	Ascot	(HVY)	G3	5f	111?	<
	* 1997	Spt	Ayr	(G-S)	L	5f	96	
	* 1997	Jly	Goodwo	(G-F)	H	6f	89	
	* 1997	Jly	Chepst	(G-S)		6.1f	71	

1998 Turf 0-9: (5f 7, 6f 2) (sft, g-s, gd 5, g-f, frm)

Leggy, very useful colt, effective 5f, acts on g-s, has worn blinkers. Turf high 103. Consistent. A runaway winner of the Cornwallis Stakes on his final two-year-old start, he proved most disappointing in 1998. Soft ground has always been his ideal, but he is no better than a smart handicapper nowadays.

**I A Balding [4-17] Robert Hitchins.*

HALMANERROR BHB 57f **RR 59f** 3201[3]

8 gr g Lochnager 6.9f **(50)** - Counter Coup (Busted) 10.2f **(61)**

Form - 1023164743

Record	**1998 -**	1st:2	2nd:1	3rd:2	Ran:10
	Pre1998 -	1st:6	2nd:3	3rd:3	Ran:52

Win Prizemoney £39,365 *Total Prizemoney* £47,624

Wins	* **1998**	Jun	Salisb	(G-S)	CH	7f	53	59	
	* **1998**	Apr	Bright	(GD)	C	6f		51	
	1997	May	Doncas	(G-S)	H	6f	57	60	
	1996	Aug	Doncas	(G-F)		6f		65	
	1995	Aug	Pontef	(G-F)	H	6f	67	66	<
	1995	Jly	Pontef	(G-F)	H	6f	61	63	
	1994	Oct	York	(G-S)	H	7f	57	59	
	1994	Spt	Redcar	(GD)	H	7f	53	55	

1998 Turf 2-9: (6f 1-4, 7f 1-3, 8f 2) (gd 2-5, g-f, frm 3) 1998 AW 0-1: (7f) (Fibr)

Fair gelding, effective 6 to 7f, best at 6f, acts on g-s to frm, excels at Salisbury. Turf high 59 - 1st of 18 giving 2lb to Caudillo (9 Jun Salisbury RF 1831) - also 1st of 11 giving 3lb to Bella's Legacy (30 Apr Brighton RF 0923). Consistent. Ex-Lynda Ramsden, he did not look a natural when tried over hurdles, and may just have been a non-stayer, as he has looked best over seven furlongs on the Flat last season. He has been running well for his new trainer, including wins at Brighton and Salisbury.

**G M McCourt [2-16] Caulkheads Racing (from Mrs J R Ramsden [6-48] Oct 1997).*

HALSE COPSE BHB 49f **RR 65f** 4114[10]

3 b f Robellino (USA) 9.5f **(68)** - Rengaine (FR) (Music Boy) 6.8f **(57)**

Form - 06684000

Record	**1998 -**	1st:0	2nd:0	3rd:0	Ran:8

Win Prizemoney £0 *Total Prizemoney* £207

1998 Turf 0-8: (5f 5, 6f, 7f 2) (gd, g-f 5, frm 2)

Workmanlike, average filly. Turf high 65. Becoming disappointing.

**J G Smyth-Osbourne [0-8] Grafton Farmers.*

HAMERKOP BHB 26f **RR 20f** 4922[7]

3 br f Damister (USA) 9.1f **(66)** - Royal Scene (NZ) (Sovereign Edition)

Form - 700707

Record	**1998 -**	1st:0	2nd:0	3rd:0	Ran:6

1998 Turf 0-5:(6f 2, 10f 2, 14f)(sft, g-s, g-f, frm 2)1998AW 0-1:(8f) (Fibr)

Workmanlike, little account filly, often wears blinkers. Turf high 36.

**John Berry [0-6] John Berry.*

HAMILTON PRINCESS RR 1f 561[6]

6 b m Sharrood (USA) 11.1f **(67)** - Yankee Special (Bold Lad (IRE)) 8.4f **(68)**

Form - 6

Record	**1998 -**	1st:0	2nd:0	3rd:0	Ran:1

1998 Turf 0-1: (11f) (sft)

Very poor mare. **K W Hogg [0-5] K W Hogg.*

HAMLET (IRE) BHB 78f83a **RR 82?f 83a** 1425[11]

5 b g Danehill (USA) 9.1f **(79)** - Blasted Heath (Thatching) 8f **(66)**

Form - 0

Record	**1998 -**	1st:0	2nd:0	3rd:0	Ran:1
	Pre1998 -	1st:2	2nd:1	3rd:0	Ran:9

Win Prizemoney £14,167 *Total Prizemoney* £15,628

Wins	1996	Jun	Newcas	(FRM)	H	10.1f	80	82	<
	1996	May	Redcar	(G-F)	H	11f	72	78	

1998 Turf 0-1: (10f) (gd)

Decent gelding, has broken blood-vessels.

**Mrs J Cecil [0-1] M B Hawtin (from M Bell [2-9] Jly 1996).*

HAMOND (GER) RR 112f 4219a[6]

3 c Acatenango (GER) - Happy Gini (Ginistrelli (USA)) 5.6f **(66)**

Form - 526

1998 Turf 0-3: (12f 3) (hvy, sft, gd)

Currently Group-class colt. Turf high 112 (began Jly) - 2nd of 6 to Central Park (16 Aug Hoppegarten 12f gd RF 3785a). He ran a cracker when touched off by Central Park at Hoppegarten in August, and should land a Group race in 1999.

**A Wohler in GER [0-3].*

HANA'S PRIDE (IRE) RR 42f 3279[6]

2 gr f Pips Pride 6.7f **(70)** - Singhana (IRE) (Mouktar)

Form - 6

Record	**1998 -**	1st:0	2nd:0	3rd:0	Ran:1

1998 Turf 0-1: (5f) (g-f)

Currently moderate filly. **Mrs A Swinbank [0-1] Bill Martin.*

HANBY BHB 52f **RR 53f** 3576[P]

6 b g Most Welcome 8.6f **(66)** - My Princess (King Emperor (USA)) 9.4f **(58)**

Form - 840831080113P

Record	**1998 -**	1st:3	2nd:0	3rd:2	Ran:13
	Pre1998 -	1st:0	2nd:0	3rd:0	Ran:4

Win Prizemoney £8,997 *Total Prizemoney* £9,905

Wins	* **1998**	Aug	Thirsk	(GD)	SH	6f	46	49	<
	* **1998**	Jly	Ayr	(GD)	SH	5f	41	39	
	* **1998**	Jun	Hamilt	(G-S)	H	5f	38	41	

1998 Turf 3-13: (5f 2-4, 6f 1-6, 7f 2, 8f) (sft 2, gd 1-6, g-f 2-3, frm 2)

Fair gelding, effective 5 to 6f, acted on gd to g-f. Turf high 53 - 3rd of 23 giving 2lb to Superbit (3 Aug Ripon 5f gd RF 3309) - also 1st of 24 getting 1lb from Spotted Eagle (1 Aug Thirsk RF 3280). (DEAD) **J S Goldie [3-17] Patrick Marron.*

HANDSOME BEAU RR 38f 4374[6]

3 ch g Handsome Sailor 6.6f **(53)** - Chester Belle (Ballacashtal (CAN)) 5.3f **(50)**

Form - 66

Record	**1998 -**	1st:0	2nd:0	3rd:0	Ran:2

1998 Turf 0-2: (7f 2) (frm 2)

Unfurnished, currently very moderate gelding. Turf high 38 (began Aug). **A Bailey [0-2] Sandybrow Stables Ltd.*

HANDSOME RIDGE BHB 119f **RR 118+f** 5158a[1]

4 ch c Indian Ridge 7.6f **(74)** - Red Rose Garden (Electric) 10.1f **(61)**

Form - 3524121

Record	**1998 -**	1st:2	2nd:2	3rd:1	Ran:7
	Pre1998 -	1st:3	2nd:2	3rd:2	Ran:9

Win Prizemoney £85,625 *Total Prizemoney* £133,840

Wins	* **1998**	Nov	Saint-	(HLD)	G3	8f	118+	<
	* **1998**	Spt	Doncas	(GD)	G3	8f	116	
	* 1997	Jly	Maison	(SFT)	G3	9f	101	
	* 1997	Jun	Goodwo	(G-S)		9f	104	
	* 1996	Nov	Doncas	(SFT)		7f	91+	

1998 Turf 2-7: (8f 2-4, 10f 3) (sft 3, g-s 1-1, gd 1-3)

Workmanlike, high-class colt, effective 8 to 10f, best at 8f, acts on sft to gd, likes right handed tracks, does well at Longchamp. Turf high 118 - 1st of 7 giving 8lb to Field of Hope (7 Nov Saint-cloud RF 5158a) - also 1st of 6 giving 9lb to Princely Heir (10 Spt Doncaster RF 4205). Improving. He ran with great credit in 1998, finishing second in a San Siro Group Two in June and winning Doncaster's Park Stakes, although that was a sub-standard Group Three, and his best effort would have been his penultimate run when running Insatiable to half a length at Longchamp.

**J H M Gosden [5-16] Platt Promotions Ltd.*

HANIBEL LADY (IRE) BHB 52f50a **RR 51f 50a** 5080[9]

2 br f Mac's Imp (USA) 5.6f **(54)** - Fast Bay (Bay Express) 7.1f **(60)**

Form - 24000

Record	**1998 -**	1st:0	2nd:1	3rd:0	Ran:5

Win Prizemoney £0 *Total Prizemoney* £828

1998 Turf 0-4: (5f 4) (sft 2, gd, frm) 1998 AW 0-1: (6f) (Fibr)

Fair filly. Turf high 51 (1st run) - 2nd of 9 giving 1lb to Irish Cream (30 Mar Hamilton 5f sft RF 0499).

**N P Littmoden [0-2] Hanibel Racing Partnership (from P D Evans [0-3] Spt 1998).*

Handsome Ridge was a model of consistency

HANNAH PARK (IRE) RR 58f 4761[12]

2 b f Lycius (USA) 8.8f **(71)** - Wassl This Then (IRE) (Wassl) 9.7f **(62)**
Form - 0
Record 1998 - 1st:0 2nd:0 3rd:0 Ran:1
1998 Turf 0-1: (7f) (gd)
Currently fair filly. **M Bell [0-1] Miss Susannah Farr.*

HANNAH'S USHER BHB 52f57a RR 51f 57a 4921[4]

6 b g Marching On 5.7f **(43)** - La Pepper (Workboy) 7.3f **(46)**
Form - 24537017708774
Record 1998 - 1st:1 2nd:0 3rd:1 Ran:12
Pre1998 - 1st:8 2nd:7 3rd:7 Ran:48
Win Prizemoney £24,489 *Total Prizemoney* £34,215

Wins								
* **1998**	Apr	Ripon	(SFT)	C	5f		52	
1996	*Mar*	*Wolver*	*(STD)*	*C*	*6f*		*66*	
1995	*Feb*	*Wolver*	*(STD)*	*H*	*5f*	*79*	*77*	<
1994	*Nov*	*Southw*	*(STD)*	*H*	*5f*	*70*	*70*	
1994	Spt	Mussel	(G-F)	H	5f	67	67	
1994	Aug	Newcas	(FRM)	C	5f		69+	
1994	Jly	Mussel	(G-F)	S	5f		66	
1994	May	Thirsk	(FRM)	C	5f		51	
1994	Apr	Catter	(GD)	S	5f		46+	

1998 Turf 1-7: (5f 1-4, 6f 2, 7f) (sft, g-s 1-3, gd 2, frm) 1998 AW 0-5: (6f 4, 7f) (Fibr 5)
Fair gelding, effective 5 to 6f, best at 6f, acts on g-s - acts on Fibr, has worn blinkers, prefers left handed tracks, prefers tight tracks, does well at Southwell and Wolverhampton. Turf high 52 - also 1st of 8 getting 11lb from Stuffed (16 Apr Ripon RF 0717). AW high 58 - 3rd of 12 giving 16lb to Rude Awakening (13 Feb Southwell 6f Fibr RF 0284). He has shown fair form and made the frame on many occasions on Fibresand, but is without a win on that surface since March '96. Nowhere near as good on turf, but was awarded a weak claimer in April.
**B P J Baugh [1-8] R Rayner (from P S Felgate [0-4] Apr 1998).*

HANNIBAL LAD BHB 63f66a RR 79f 66a 5148[9]

2 ch g Rock City 8.8f **(62)** - Appealing (Star Appeal) 9.6f **(65)**
Form - 51350
Record 1998 - 1st:1 2nd:0 3rd:1 Ran:5
Win Prizemoney £2,302 *Total Prizemoney* £3,187
Wins * **1998** *Spt Southw (STD) S 7f 68* <
1998 Turf 0-3: (7f 3) (sft, gd, frm) 1998 AW 1-2: (6f, 7f 1-1) (Fibr 1-2)
Above-average gelding. Turf high 79 (1st run) (began Oct) - 3rd of 28 giving 5lb to L S Lowry (15 Oct Newmarket 7f frm RF 4818). AW high 68 (began Jly). **P D Evans [1-5] John Pugh.*

HAPPY CHANGE (GER) RR 108f 4603a[5]

4 ch c Surumu (GER) - Happy Gini (Ginistrelli (USA)) 5.6f **(66)**
Form - 0615
Record 1998 - 1st:1 2nd:0 3rd:0 Ran:4
Pre1998 - 1st:0 2nd:1 3rd:2 Ran:6
Win Prizemoney £25,338 *Total Prizemoney* £86,246
Wins 1998 Aug Baden- (SFT) G3 10f 108+ <
1998 Turf 1-4: (10f 1-1, 11f, 12f 2) (sft 1-3, gd)
Pattern-class colt, effective 10 to 12f, best at 12f, acts on sft to gd, best on gd. Turf high 108 - 6th of 9 getting 4lb from Steward (24 May Baden-Baden 11f gd RF 1556a) - also 1st of 16 from Aldino (28 Aug Baden-Baden RF 4074a). Third in the 1997 German Derby, he won a Group 3 at Baden-Baden in August and has since joined the leading National Hunt trainer Venetia Williams. He will be a useful tool over hurdles.
**Miss Venetia Williams [0-1] Winning Line Racing Ltd (from A Wohler in GER [1-9] Aug 1998).*

HAPPY DAYS BHB 49f RR 56f 4536[15]

3 b g Primitive Rising (USA) 8.1f **(48)**-Miami Dolphin (Derrylin) 8.8f **(54)**
Form - 80744600
Record 1998 - 1st:0 2nd:0 3rd:0 Ran:8
Pre1998 - 1st:0 2nd:3 3rd:1 Ran:8
Win Prizemoney £0 *Total Prizemoney* £4,831
1998 Turf 0-8: (5f, 7f 2, 8f 2, 9f, 10f 2) (g-s 3, gd 4, g-f)
Unfurnished, fair gelding, effective 5 to 6f, best at 5f, acts on gd to frm, best on gd, has worn blinkers. Turf high 61. Inconsistent.
**J Berry [0-2] J W Barrett (from D Moffatt [0-14] Jun 1998).*

HAPPY DAYS AGAIN (IRE) BHB 63f80a RR 72df 80a 5142[13]

3 b f Elbio 9f **(62)** - Tacheo (Tachypous) 8.6f **(55)**
Form - 68800647700
Record 1998 - 1st:0 2nd:0 3rd:0 Ran:10
Pre1998 - 1st:2 2nd:2 3rd:0 Ran:9
Win Prizemoney £6,318 *Total Prizemoney* £8,759

Wins								
* 1997	Oct	Newmar	(G-F)	H	5f	80	84	<
* 1997	Jly	Ripon	(GD)		5f		77	

1998 Turf 0-10: (5f 10) (g-s, gd 3, g-f 4, frm 2)
Scopey, above-average filly, effective 5f, acts on gd to frm, has worn blinkers (extremely effectively). Turf high 74. Inconsistent.
**J Wharton [2-19] Mrs S M Moore.*

HAPPY GO LUCKY BHB 67f RR 69f 4476[1]

4 ch f Teamster 11.4f **(22)** - Meritsu (IRE) (Lyphard's Special (USA)) 10.3f **(72)**
Form - 3332001
Record 1998 - 1st:1 2nd:1 3rd:3 Ran:7
Pre1998 - 1st:2 2nd:0 3rd:1 Ran:13
Win Prizemoney £10,149 *Total Prizemoney* £15,692

Wins							
* **1998**	Spt	Folkes	(G-F)	12f	68	
1997	Jun	Warwic	(FRM)	10.8f	78	<
1996	Aug	Sandow	(G-F)	8.1f	78	<

1998 Turf 1-7: (10f 2, 12f 1-4, 13f) (g-s, gd 3, g-f 1-1, frm 2)
Unfurnished, average filly, effective 10 to 13f, acts on g-s to frm, best on frm, prefers left handed tracks, prefers tight tracks, excels at Chepstow and Bath. Turf high 73 - 3rd of 6 giving 11lb to Cheek To Cheek (18 May Bath 13f frm RF 1294).
**M J Weeden [1-9] Peter Bolton (from R J O'Sullivan [2-13] Oct 1997).*

HAPPY LADY (FR) **RR 53+f** 5139[9]
2 b f Cadeaux Genereux 7.9f **(76)** - Siwaayib (Green Desert (USA)) 8.6f **(78)**
Form - 0
Record 1998 - 1st:0 2nd:0 3rd:0 Ran:1
1998 Turf 0-1: (6f) (gd)
Currently fair filly. *B W Hills [0-1] Maktoum Al Maktoum.*

HAPPY MEDIUM (IRE) BHB 31f31a **RR 11f 31a** 3638[1]
5 b g Fairy King (USA) 7.7f **(75)** - Belle Origine (USA) (Exclusive Native (USA)) 9.1f **(81)**
Form - 0001
Record 1998 - 1st:1 2nd:0 3rd:0 Ran:3
Pre1998 - 1st:0 2nd:0 3rd:1 Ran:7
Win Prizemoney £2,763 *Total Prizemoney* £3,503
Wins * **1998** *Aug Southw (STD) H 14f 30 31 <*
1998 Turf 0-2: (11f, 12f) (frm 2) 1998 AW 1-1: (14f 1-1) (Fibr 1-1)
Fair gelding, effective 12f - acts on Equi, prefers left handed tracks. Turf high 11. (1st run). Inconsistent. He had shown precious little before winning an extremely poor maiden handicap on the Southwell Fibresand in August. He will be fortunate to find another race as bad.
G P Enright [1-9] Dave Howe (from C O'Brien in IRE [0-2] Aug 1996).

HAPPY VALENTINE BHB 115f **RR 121f** 4852[7]
4 b c Rainbow Quest (USA) 11.2f **(81)** - Nearctic Flame (Sadler's Wells (USA)) 10f **(76)**
Form - 5717707
Record 1998 - 1st:1 2nd:0 3rd:0 Ran:7
Pre1998 - 1st:1 2nd:0 3rd:0 Ran:1
Win Prizemoney £15,353 *Total Prizemoney* £16,378
Wins * **1998** Jly Kempto (G-S) L 10f 108 <
* 1996 Oct Yarmou (GD) 7f 103++
1998 Turf 1-7: (10f 1-3, 12f 3, 13f) (sft, gd 1-4, g-f, frm)
Well made, very high-class colt, effective 12f, acts on sft. Turf high 121 - 10th of 14 giving 8lb to Sagamix (4 Oct Longchamp 12f sft RF 4727a). Romped home in his maiden at two and was touted as a Derby candidate, but had to miss the whole of 1997. Won in Dubai in March 1998 and, though not running badly in a Group Two at Newmarket in May, ran much too freely over thirteen furlongs at Newbury next time. Stepped down to ten furlongs, he settled much better when landing a Kempton Listed event in July. Has fulfilled the pacemaker's role for Swain and other Godolphin top-notchers in his latter races. *S bin Suroor [2-8] Godolphin.*

HAPPY WANDERER BHB 64f63a **RR 65f 63a** 1618[1]
3 ch g Clantime 6.6f **(57)** - Maha (Northfields (USA)) 9f **(72)**
Form - 336431
Record 1998 - 1st:1 2nd:0 3rd:3 Ran:6
Pre1998 - 1st:0 2nd:0 3rd:0 Ran:3
Win Prizemoney £2,206 *Total Prizemoney* £3,297
Wins * **1998** Jun Hamilt (GD) 8.3f 65 <
1998 Turf 1-3: (7f, 8f 1-1, 9f) (sft, g-s, g-f 1-1) 1998 AW 0-3: (7f, 8f, 10f) (Equi, Fibr 2)
Scopey, above-average gelding, effective 7 to 8f, acts on g-f - acts on Fibr, favours tight tracks. Turf high 65 - 1st of 5 getting 11lb from Dargo (1 Jun Hamilton RF 1618). AW high 69 (1st run) - 3rd of 13 giving 5lb to Pip's Addition (2 Jan Southwell 7f Fibr RF 0011).
P C Haslam [1-9] McMurdo/Tutton.

HARARAH **RR 76f** 3977[3]
2 ch f Barathea (IRE) - Taroob (IRE) (Roberto (USA)) 10f **(76)**
Form - 23
Record 1998 - 1st:0 2nd:1 3rd:1 Ran:2
Win Prizemoney £0 *Total Prizemoney* £1,723
1998 Turf 0-2: (7f, 8f) (gd 2)
Currently above-average filly. Turf high 76 (1st run) (began Aug) - 2nd of 21 getting 5lb from Forest Shadow (15 Aug Newbury 7f gd RF 3653). *J L Dunlop [0-2] Hamdan Al Maktoum.*

HARBIYA (IRE) BHB 50f **RR 58f** 4644[15]
3 gr f Salse (USA) 10.9f **(71)** - Spectacular Dawn (Spectacular Bid (USA)) 11.2f **(76)**
Form - 3380
Record 1998 - 1st:0 2nd:0 3rd:2 Ran:4
Win Prizemoney £0 *Total Prizemoney* £1,132
1998 Turf 0-4: (7f, 8f 2, 10f) (g-f 3, frm)
Lengthy, fair filly. Turf high 58 (began Aug) - 3rd of 6 getting 5lb from Bering Gifts (14 Aug Warwick 8f frm RF 3645).
B Hanbury [0-4] Hamdan Al Maktoum.

HARD LINES (USA) **RR 83+f** 1257[1]
2 b c Silver Hawk (USA) 11.2f **(85)** - Arctic Eclipse (USA) (Northern Dancer) 9.6f **(80)**
Form - 1
Record 1998 - 1st:1 2nd:0 3rd:0 Ran:1
Win Prizemoney £4,042 *Total Prizemoney* £4,042
Wins * **1998** May Newbur (G-F) 6f 83+ <
1998 Turf 1-1: (6f 1-1) (frm 1-1)
Currently decent colt. (1st run) - 1st of 20 from Cusin (16 May Newbury RF 1257). Beat a big field nicely on his debut, and can go on to better things. *I A Balding [1-1] Robin Scully.*

HARD TO FIGURE BHB 79f74a **RR 83f 74a** 4923[8]
12 gr g Telsmoss 6.7f **(73)** - Count On Me (No Mercy) 8f **(61)**
Form - 330303527023648
Record 1998 - 1st:0 2nd:2 3rd:5 Ran:15
Pre1998 - 1st:13 2nd:9 3rd:14 Ran:100
Win Prizemoney £136,041 *Total Prizemoney* £218,802
Wins * 1997 Aug Bath (GD) C 5.7f 60
* 1997 Jly Bath (FRM) H 5.7f 73 83
* 1997 Jly Bath (G-F) C 5.1f 57
* 1996 Apr Kempto (GD) 6f 107
* 1995 Jly Newbur (GD) L 6f 109 <
* 1994 May Lingfi (HVY) 6f 94
1998 Turf 0-15: (5f, 6f 13, 7f) (sft 3, g-s, gd 4, g-f 5, frm 2)
Decent gelding, effective 6 to 7f, best at 6f, acts on gd to frm, best on frm, likes left handed tracks, excels at Bath. Turf high 83 - 2nd of 18 giving 7lb to Cauda Equina (7 Spt Bath 6f frm RF 4128). Consistent. A drop to claiming company seemed to rejuvenate this much-loved veteran in '97, and he ran up a hat-trick before running third in the Ayr Silver Cup. Did not quite find his form last season. He likes to come with a late run.
R J Hodges [13-116] J W Mursell.

HARD TO FOLLOW **RR 24f** 3246[12]
3 b f Dilum (USA) 7.1f **(56)** - Cedar Lady (Telsmoss)
Form - 800
Record 1998 - 1st:0 2nd:0 3rd:0 Ran:3
1998 Turf 0-3: (5f, 6f, 10f) (gd, g-f 2)
Leggy, currently little account filly. Turf high 16.
R J Hodges [0-3] J W Mursell.

HARDWICK LODGE **RR 30f** 4884[10]
2 ch f Grand Lodge (USA) - Mrs Musgrove (Jalmood (USA)) 10.1f **(52)**
Form - 0
Record 1998 - 1st:0 2nd:0 3rd:0 Ran:1
1998 Turf 0-1: (7f) (g-s)
Currently very moderate filly. *M J Ryan [0-1] A J Hollis.*

HARDY DANCER BHB 63f88a **RR 65f 88a** 4232[4]
6 ch g Pharly (FR) 11.5f **(64)** - Handy Dancer (Green God) 9.6f **(68)**
Form - 00154
Record 1998 - 1st:1 2nd:0 3rd:0 Ran:5
Pre1998 - 1st:3 2nd:2 3rd:6 Ran:31
Win Prizemoney £19,162 *Total Prizemoney* £36,652
Wins * **1998** Aug Epsom (G-F) H 10.1f 59 65
* 1995 May Kempto (G-F) H 9f 79 79 <
* 1995 Apr Leices (G-F) H 8f 74 70
* 1994 Oct Catter (G-F) 6f 71
1998 Turf 1-5: (9f 2, 10f 1-3) (gd 1-2, g-f, frm 2)
Average gelding, effective 10f, acts on gd to g-f, has worn blinkers. Turf high 65 (began Jly). He failed to win last season, and showed nothing in his first two starts, but bounced back to form with a victory at Epsom in August. *G L Moore [4-36] Peter Higson.*

HARE PARK POLLY BHB 41f **RR 51f** 5070[12]
3 ch f Deploy 11.4f **(67)** - Gohar (USA) (Barachois (CAN)) 8.3f **(63)**
Form - 74700
Record 1998 - 1st:0 2nd:0 3rd:0 Ran:5
Win Prizemoney £0 *Total Prizemoney* £285
1998 Turf 0-5: (8f 2, 9f, 11f, 12f) (g-f 2, frm 2, hrd)
Workmanlike, fair filly. Turf high 51 (began Jly).
A W Carroll [0-5] Peter Charter.

HARIK BHB 65f72a **RR 51f 72a** 1013[8]
4 ch g Persian Bold 10f **(69)** - Yaqut (USA) (Northern Dancer) 9.6f **(80)**
Form - 12108
Record 1998 - 1st:2 2nd:1 3rd:0 Ran:5
Pre1998 - 1st:0 2nd:0 3rd:0 Ran:1
Win Prizemoney £6,391 *Total Prizemoney* £6,999
Wins * **1998** *Mar Lingfi (SLW) H 13f 65 73* <
* **1998** *Feb Lingfi (SLW) 12f 65*
1998 Turf 0-2: (12f 2) (sft, gd) 1998 AW 2-3:(12f 1-2, 13f 1-1) (Equi 2-3)
Scopey, above-average gelding. Turf high 51. AW high 73 - 1st of 15 giving 5lb to Evezio Rufo (3 Mar Lingfield RF 0390) - also 1st of 10 giving 21lb to New Yorker (12 Feb Lingfield RF 0271). Ran once for Ben Hanbury in October '96, but was not seen again until reappearing successfully for Gary Moore in a maiden on the Lingfield Equitrack in February. Scored again in an amateur riders' event at the same track, and seems to be well suited by staying trips on that surface.
**G L Moore [2-6] The Best Beech Partnership (from B Hanbury [0-1] Oct 1996).*

HARIYANA (IRE) RR 67f 4805[3]
2 br f Kahyasi 12.9f **(74)** - Harouniya (Siberian Express (USA)) 8.8f **(65)**
Form - 03
Record 1998 - 1st:0 2nd:0 3rd:1 Ran:2
Win Prizemoney £0 *Total Prizemoney* £535
1998 Turf 0-2: (7f, 8f) (gd 2)
Currently average filly. Turf high 67 (began Oct).
**L M Cumani [0-2] H H Aga Khan.*

HARLEQUIN WALK (IRE) BHB 50f49a **RR 49f 49a** 4456[15]
7 ch m Pennine Walk 8.9f **(64)** - Taniokey (Grundy) 10.3f **(65)**
Form - 303145720
Record 1998 - 1st:1 2nd:1 3rd:1 Ran:7
Pre1998 - 1st:8 2nd:6 3rd:3 Ran:43
Win Prizemoney £25,091 *Total Prizemoney* £33,489
Wins * **1998** *Jan Lingfi (STD) H 12f 45 49*
* 1997 Oct Bright (FRM) H 10f 34 48+
* 1997 Spt Goodwo (GD) CH 8f 34 41
* 1997 *Spt Lingfi (STD) SH 10f 43 48*
* 1997 *Feb Lingfi (STD) H 12f 43 49*
* 1996 Jly Folkes (GD) SH 9.7f 32 42
* 1996 *Feb Lingfi (STD) C 12f 52*
1995 *Feb Lingfi (STD) C 12f 47*
1995 *Feb Wolver (STD) 12f 65* <
1998 Turf 0-3: (8f, 10f, 11f) (g-f, frm 2) 1998 AW 1-4: (10f, 12f 1-3) (Equi 1-4)
Moderate mare, effective 8 to 13f, best at 12f, acts on frm - acts on Equi, has worn blinkers, prefers left handed tracks, excels at Lingfield. Turf high 49 (began Aug) - 2nd of 15 giving 3lb to Persian Sabre (25 Aug Lingfield 10f frm RF 3848). AW high 49 - 1st of 9 getting 8lb from Rehaab (24 Jan Lingfield RF 0151). She did well in '97, winning four times, twice on Equitrack and twice on turf, and returned to winning form on Equitrack in January. She is an effective sort in modest company over ten to twelve furlongs on that surface.
**R J O'Sullivan [9-44] Mrs R J Doorgachurn (from A Hide [2-2] Feb 1995).*

HARLESTONE LANE BHB 54f **RR 55f** 4927[10]
3 gr f Chilibang 7f **(55)** - Harlestone Lake (Riboboy (USA)) 14f **(54)**
Form - 4760
Record 1998 - 1st:0 2nd:0 3rd:0 Ran:4
1998 Turf 0-4: (7f, 9f, 10f 2) (g-s 3, gd)
Workmanlike, fair filly. Turf high 55. **J L Dunlop [0-4] J L Dunlop.*

HARMONIC WAY BHB 93f **RR 96f** 4617[3]
3 ch c Lion Cavern (USA) 7.5f **(74)** - Pineapple (Superlative) 7.2f **(56)**
Form - 62435743
Record 1998 - 1st:0 2nd:1 3rd:2 Ran:8
Pre1998 - 1st:1 2nd:0 3rd:0 Ran:3
Win Prizemoney £3,194 *Total Prizemoney* £17,161
Wins * 1997 Aug Salisb (G-F) 6f 80 <
1998 Turf 0-8: (6f 4, 7f 4) (g-s, gd 2, g-f 4, frm)
Scopey, very useful colt, effective 6 to 7f, best at 7f, acts on g-s to frm, excels at Newmarket. Turf high 96 - 3rd of 20 getting 8lb from Ho Leng (9 Jly Newmarket 7f frm RF 2650). Consistent. He ran well at three, without actually winning, but making the frame in some ultra-competitive handicaps, including fifth in the Stewards' Cup. He proved difficult to settle in his last outing at Newmarket and, provided he matures during the winter, there could be some improvement in him. **R Charlton [1-11] Mrs Alexandra Chandris.*

HARMONY BHB 83f **RR 86f** 3923[2]
3 b c Shareef Dancer (USA) 10.1f **(67)** - Almitra (Targowice (USA)) 11.4f **(70)**
Form - 0221752
Record 1998 - 1st:1 2nd:3 3rd:0 Ran:7
Win Prizemoney £3,465 *Total Prizemoney* £8,962
Wins * **1998** Jun Beverl (GD) 8.5f 84+ <
1998 Turf 1-7: (8f 1-4, 9f, 10f 2) (gd 3, g-f 2, frm 1-2)
Well made, useful colt, effective 8f, acts on g-f to frm, best on frm. Turf high 86 - 5th of 10 getting 12lb from Florazi (18 Jly Newmarket 8f frm RF 2919) - also 1st of 7 giving 5lb to Bolshoi Star (23 Jun Beverley RF 2195). Easy winner of an ordinary Beverley maiden, he looked the sort to go on from there but has been rather disappointing since, and looked a bit quirky on one occasion.
**L M Cumani [1-7] Sheikh Mohammed.*

HARMONY HALL BHB 67f **RR 72f** 3436[6]
4 ch g Music Boy 6.5f **(56)** - Fleeting Affair (Hotfoot) 10.5f **(59)**
Form - 2451536
Record 1998 - 1st:1 2nd:1 3rd:1 Ran:7
Pre1998 - 1st:0 2nd:1 3rd:1 Ran:11
Win Prizemoney £5,247 *Total Prizemoney* £9,665
Wins * **1998** Jly Nottin (G-F) H 10f 64 69 <
1998 Turf 1-7: (10f 1-5, 11f, 12f) (gd 2, g-f 1-2, frm 3)
Strong, above-average gelding, effective 10 to 14f, best at 10f, acts on gd to frm, has worn blinkers, prefers right handed tracks, excels at Salisbury, does well at Newmarket, likes Nottingham. Turf high 72 - 3rd of 15 giving 13lb to Flag Fen (31 Jly Newmarket 10f frm RF 3241) - also 1st of 14 giving 5lb to Include Me Out (4 Jly Nottingham RF 2545). **J R Fanshawe [1-21] Raymond Tooth.*

HARNAGE (IRE) BHB 32f **RR 32?f** 4885[13]
3 b g Mujadil (USA) 7.7f **(70)** - Wilderness (Martinmas) 7.6f **(59)**
Form - 000
Record 1998 - 1st:0 2nd:0 3rd:0 Ran:3
Pre1998 - 1st:0 2nd:0 3rd:1 Ran:5
Win Prizemoney £0 *Total Prizemoney* £259
1998 Turf 0-3: (7f, 8f 2) (g-s, gd, frm)
Light-framed, very moderate gelding, effective 6f, acts on gd. (began Spt). Becoming disappointing.
**P Burgoyne [0-3] Ice Cooling Ltd (from M R Channon [0-5] Jly 1997).*

HAROLDON (IRE) BHB 49f37a **RR 53f 37a** 4143[7]
9 ch g Heraldiste (USA) 8.9f **(54)** - Cordon (Morston (FR)) 9.4f **(55)**
Form - 87641655060037
Record 1998 - 1st:1 2nd:0 3rd:1 Ran:12
Pre1998 - 1st:6 2nd:5 3rd:3 Ran:55
Win Prizemoney £24,629 *Total Prizemoney* £33,412
Wins * **1998** May Nottin (FRM) SH 10f 52 57
* 1997 Jly Windso (GD) H 10f 65 68
* 1995 Spt Haydoc (GD) H 10.5f 72 76
* 1995 Jly Windso (GD) H 11.6f 68 67
* 1995 May Warwic (FRM) H 10.8f 56 61
1998 Turf 1-11: (10f 1-7, 11f 2, 12f 2) (gd 3, g-f 3, frm 1-5) 1998 AW 0-1: (10f) (Equi)
Fair gelding, effective 10f, acts on g-f, has worn blinkers. Turf high 57. Inconsistent. Rather unpredictable, he pays his way in low-grade company. **B Palling [8-72] Lamb Brook Associates.*

HARP PLAYER (IRE) BHB 54f **RR 50f** 4370[12]
2 ch g Pips Pride 6.7f **(70)** - Angelic Sounds (IRE) (The Noble Player (USA)) 6.5f **(67)**
Form - 000
Record 1998 - 1st:0 2nd:0 3rd:0 Ran:3
1998 Turf 0-3: (6f 3) (g-f, frm 2)
Currently fair gelding. Turf high 50 (began Spt).
**M Bell [0-3] Billy Maguire.*

HARQUEBUSIER BHB 54f **RR 58f** 4569[3]
2 ch f Keen 11.1f **(58)** - Mainly Me **(17f)** (Huntingdale)
Form - 46303
Record 1998 - 1st:0 2nd:0 3rd:2 Ran:5
Win Prizemoney £0 *Total Prizemoney* £546

1998 Turf 0-5: (5f 4, 6f) (g-f 3, frm 2)
Fair filly. Turf high 58 (began Jly) - 3rd of 11 getting 5lb from Landican Lane (30 Spt Brighton 5f g-f RF 4569).
**J Pearce [0-5] & Mrs J Matthews.*

HARRY WOLTON BHB 98f RR 106f 2879[5]

4 b c Distant Relative 7f **(69)** - Tashinsky (USA) (Nijinsky (CAN)) 10.3f **(77)**
Form - 85

Record	**1998** -	1st:0	2nd:0	3rd:0	Ran:2
	Pre1998 -	1st:2	2nd:2	3rd:2	Ran:8

Win Prizemoney £9,077 *Total Prizemoney* £18,623

Wins	* 1997	Jun	Nottin	(G-F)	8.2f	101	<
	* 1996	Spt	Yarmou	(G-F)	7f	82+	

1998 Turf 0-2: (10f, 12f) (gd, frm)
Scopey, Pattern-class colt, effective 8 to 10f, best at 10f, acts on gd to frm, has worn blinkers. Turf high 85. He generally ran well in 1997 in handicap company, but was well beaten in a couple of conditions races in 1998. Will not be easy to place.
**H R A Cecil [2-10] Old Road Securities Plc.*

HARTSTOWN GIRL (IRE) RR 82f 5170a[4]

3 ch f Common Grounds 8.1f **(66)** - Very Sophisticated (USA) 00
Form - 035102734
1998 Turf 1-9: (6f 1-2, 7f 4, 8f 3) (hvy, sft 1-4, gd 4)
Decent filly, effective 6 to 8f, acts on sft to gd, best on sft, has worn blinkers. Turf high 90 - 1st of 12 getting 5lb from Jacks Estate (21 Jly Ballinrobe RF 3174a). Inconsistent.
**E Lynam in IRE [1-9] Thomas Meagher.*

HARVEY'S FUTURE BHB 36f43a RR 42f 43a 5121[3]

4 b g Never so Bold 7.1f **(62)** - Orba Gold (USA) (Gold Crest (USA))
Form - 285042463

Record	**1998** -	1st:0	2nd:2	3rd:1	Ran:9
	Pre1998 -	1st:0	2nd:0	3rd:0	Ran:5

Win Prizemoney £0 *Total Prizemoney* £2,244
1998 Turf 0-7: (5f 4, 6f 3) (sft, g-s 2, gd, g-f 2, frm) 1998 AW 0-2: (5f 2) (Fibr 2)
Moderate gelding, effective 5f, acts on g-s - acts on Fibr. Turf high 42. AW high 44 - 2nd of 13 getting 32lb from Goretski (25 Jly Southwell 5f Fibr RF 3130).
**P L Gilligan [0-10] The Cavotoro Partnership (from T T Clement [0-4] Aug 1997).*

HARVEY WHITE (IRE) BHB 53f40a RR 53f 40a 4748[6]

6 b or br g Petorius 8f **(66)** - Walkyria (Lord Gayle (USA)) 8.8f **(62)**
Form - 836

Record	**1998** -	1st:0	2nd:0	3rd:1	Ran:2
	Pre1998 -	1st:4	2nd:3	3rd:7	Ran:44

Win Prizemoney £13,357 *Total Prizemoney* £22,778

Wins	* 1997	Jun	Lingfi	(GD)	H	9f	52	55	
	* 1996	Spt	Kempto	(GD)	H	10f	56	62	
	* 1996	May	Warwic	(FRM)	H	10.8f	53	62	
	* 1995	Aug	Epsom	(G-F)	C	10.1f		64	<

1998 Turf 0-2: (9f, 10f) (gd, frm)
Fair gelding, effective 9 to 11f, best at 9f, acts on gd to g-f, best on g-f, prefers left handed tracks. Turf high 53 (began Spt) - 6th of 26 getting 18lb from Saligo (10 Oct York 9f gd RF 4748). Inconsistent.
**J Pearce [4-46] B & G Racing.*

HASANAT RR 94f 4795a[6]

3 b f Night Shift (USA) 8.1f **(73)** - Eye Witness
Form - 01231370626
1998 Turf 2-11: (7f 1-5, 8f 4, 9f 1-2) (hvy, sft 2, g-s, gd 1-5, g-f 1-1, hrd)
Useful filly, effective 7 to 9f, acts on hvy to g-f, best on gd, likes left handed tracks, and does well at Curragh. Turf high 94 - 2nd of 6 getting 7lb from Two-Twenty-Two (4 Oct Tipperary 7f hvy RF 4695a) - also 1st of 12 getting 20lb from Pasternak (18 Jly Leopardstown RF 3012a). Consistent.
**K Prendergast in IRE [3-16] Hamdan Al Maktoum.*

HASTA LA VISTA BHB 59f53a RR 59f 53a 4861[5]

8 b g Superlative 8.8f **(57)** - Falcon Berry (FR) (Bustino) 10.4f **(64)**
Form - 5041181333005

Record	**1998** -	1st:3	2nd:0	3rd:3	Ran:13
	Pre1998 -	1st:11	2nd:8	3rd:7	Ran:70

Win Prizemoney £45,602 *Total Prizemoney* £61,665

Wins	* **1998**	Jly	Beverl	(GD)	H	12f	52	55	
	* **1998**	May	Catter	(G-S)	H	13.8f	47	51	
	* **1998**	May	Mussel	(G-F)	H	12f	44	47	
	* 1997	Aug	Ripon	(GD)	H	12.3f	55	60	
	* 1997	Aug	Catter	(G-F)	H	13.8f	50	55	
	* 1997	Jly	Catter	(SFT)	H	15.8f	52	55	
	* 1997	Jun	Hamilt	(G-S)	H	13f	47	54	
	* 1997	May	Mussel	(G-F)	H	16f	48	53	
	* 1996	Apr	Catter	(GD)	H	12f	50	54	
	* 1995	Aug	Ripon	(G-F)	H	12.3f	41	48	
	* 1994	*Feb*	*Southw*	*(STD)*	*H*	*16f*	*52*	*61*	<
	* 1994	*Feb*	*Southw*	*(STD)*	*H*	*12f*	*52*	*61+*	

1998 Turf 3-13:(12f 2-6, 14f 1-5, 16f 2)(g-s 2, gd 1-2, g-f 2-3, frm 5, hrd)
Fair gelding, effective 12 to 16f, best at 12f, acts on sft to frm, best on gd, mostly wears blinkers (very effectively), prefers right handed tracks, excels at Musselburgh and likes Thirsk. Turf high 59 - 3rd of 16 getting 8lb from Once More for Luck (14 Spt Musselburgh 12f frm RF 4252) - also 1st of 10 giving 10lb to Cottage Prince (28 Jly Beverley RF 3161). A tough and versatile stayer, he often makes the running.
**M W Easterby [14-86] K Hodgson & Mrs J Hodgson.*

HASTATE BHB 56f51a RR 56f 51a 3902[1]

3 b g Persian Bold 10f **(69)** - Gisarne (USA) (Diesis) 9.3f **(69)**
Form - 703201

Record	**1998** -	1st:1	2nd:1	3rd:1	Ran:6
	Pre1998 -	1st:0	2nd:0	3rd:0	Ran:3

Win Prizemoney £2,448 *Total Prizemoney* £4,304

Wins	* **1998**	Aug	Folkes	(G-F)	H	16.4f	54	56	<

1998 Turf 1-5: (8f, 9f, 12f, 13f, 16f 1-1) (gd 2, g-f 1-1, frm 2) 1998 AW 0-1: (12f) (Fibr)
Well made, fair gelding, effective 12 to 16f, acts on g-f to frm, best on frm. Turf high 56 - 1st of 9 giving 9lb to Wedding Band (27 Aug Folkestone RF 3902). **W Jarvis [1-9] Lord Howard de Walden.*

HASTY WORDS (IRE) BHB 100f RR 100f 4853[3]

2 b f Polish Patriot (USA) 7.8f **(70)** - Park Elect (Ahonoora) 8.1f **(73)**
Form - 217033

Record	**1998** -	1st:1	2nd:1	3rd:2	Ran:6

Win Prizemoney £3,566 *Total Prizemoney* £12,823

Wins	* **1998**	May	Sandow	(G-F)	5f	78+	<

1998 Turf 1-6: (5f 1-2, 6f, 7f 3) (gd 1-2, g-f, frm 3)
Very useful filly, effective 7f, acts on gd to frm. Turf high 100 - 3rd of 14 to Hula Angel (17 Oct Newmarket 7f gd RF 4853). She did her job in fine style, winning a maiden and picking up a big bonus when the first filly home in a valuable sales race at Newmarket in September. Badly drawn when making the frame in the Group Two Rockfel Stakes, she will stay at least a mile but needs to improve to win in the major league. **B W Hills [1-6] W J Gredley.*

HATTA SUNSHINE (USA) BHB 27f38a RR 29f 38a 209[6]

8 b g Dixieland Band (USA) 10.1f **(80)** - Mountain Sunshine (USA) (Vaguely Noble) 10.1f **(72)**
Form - 786

Record	**1998** -	1st:0	2nd:0	3rd:0	Ran:3
	Pre1998 -	1st:4	2nd:6	3rd:3	Ran:51

Win Prizemoney £10,636 *Total Prizemoney* £17,658

Wins	* 1997	*Jan*	*Lingfi*	*(STD)*	*C*	*8f*		*58*	<
	1996	*Feb*	*Lingfi*	*(STD)*	*H*	*8f*	*49*	*49*	
	1995	*Mar*	*Lingfi*	*(STD)*	*H*	*8f*	*48*	*47*	
	1994	*Mar*	*Lingfi*	*(STD)*		*10f*		*42*	

1998 AW 0-3: (10f 2, 13f) (Equi 3)
Moderate gelding, effective 8f - acts on Equi, has worn blinkers, likes left handed tracks, favours tight tracks. AW high 25.
**G L Moore [1-16] R Kiernan (from A Moore [3-37] Dec 1996).*

HAUGHTY LADY RR 24f 1806[9]

2 b f Sizzling Melody 6.3f **(49)** - Juris Prudence (IRE) (Law Society (USA)) 9.9f **(70)**
Form - 000

Record	**1998** -	1st:0	2nd:0	3rd:0	Ran:3

1998 Turf 0-3: (5f 3) (sft, g-s, gd)
Currently little account filly. Turf high 24.
**C W Fairhurst [0-3] Mrs P J Dobson.*

HAUTE COUTURE BHB 28f RR 1f 4777[19]

4 b f Teamster 11.4f **(22)** - Sheer Gold (Yankee Gold) 7.6f **(55)**
Form - 000

Record 1998 - 1st:0 2nd:0 3rd:0 Ran:3
1998 Turf 0-3: (11f, 12f 2) (gd, g-f, frm)
Currently very poor filly. Turf high 1 (began Aug).
**B P J Baugh [0-3] Mrs Sylvia Knobbs.*

HAVANA RESERVE RR 1944[8]

4 ch g Cigar 6.3f **(43)** - Shy Hiker (Netherkelly) 5.6f **(46)**
Form - 8
Record 1998 - 1st:0 2nd:0 3rd:0 Ran:1
Pre1998 - 1st:0 2nd:0 3rd:0 Ran:1
1998 AW 0-1: (11f) (Fibr)
Leggy, very poor gelding.
**J G Portman [0-1] J G B Portman (from R Hannon [0-1] Nov 1996).*

HAVE A BREAK BHB 44f RR 49f 4312[13]

3 b g Most Welcome 8.6f **(66)** - Miss Tealeaf (USA) (Lear Fan (USA)) 8.5f **(73)**
Form - 060
Record 1998 - 1st:0 2nd:0 3rd:0 Ran:3
Pre1998 - 1st:0 2nd:0 3rd:0 Ran:3
1998 Turf 0-3: (8f, 10f, 14f) (g-f 2, frm)
Lengthy, moderate gelding, has worn blinkers. Turf high 49.
**C R Egerton [0-6] Direct Salt Supplies Ltd.*

HAVE MERCI RR 77f 3187a[9]

3 b f High Estate 10.5f **(66)** - Icecapped (Caerleon (USA)) 8.6f **(71)**
Form - 55460
1998 Turf 0-4: (9f, 10f 2, 11f) (sft 2, gd, g-f)
Above-average filly, effective 9f, acts on sft. Turf high 99 - 4th of 6 giving 6lb to Short Shift (19 Jun Tipperary 9f sft RF 2216a). Consistent. **Mrs J Harrington in IRE [1-10] R Wood.*

HAVEN SUNRISE RR 16f 5122[9]

2 b f Chaddleworth (IRE) - Gaynor Goodman (IRE) **(41f)** (Fayruz)
Form - 00
Record 1998 - 1st:0 2nd:0 3rd:0 Ran:2
1998 Turf 0-2: (6f 2) (g-s 2)
Currently poor filly. Turf high 13 (began Oct).
**P R Hedger [0-2] Ian Hutchins.*

HAVERI BHB 40f RR 37f 4473[15]

2 ch f Elmaamul (USA) 8.1f **(70)** - Far Claim (USA) (Far North (CAN)) 9.7f **(75)**
Form - 0600
Record 1998 - 1st:0 2nd:0 3rd:0 Ran:4
1998 Turf 0-3: (6f 2, 7f) (gd, g-f, frm) 1998 AW 0-1: (6f) (Fibr)
Very moderate filly. Turf high 37. **J S Moore [0-4] Mrs Derek Strauss.*

HAWA AL NASAMAAT (USA) BHB 58f55a RR 51f 55a 2653[6]

6 b g Houston (USA) 7.7f **(65)** - Barrera Miss (USA) (Barrera (USA)) 7f **(84)**
Form - 600000056
Record 1998 - 1st:0 2nd:0 3rd:0 Ran:9
Pre1998 - 1st:2 2nd:2 3rd:3 Ran:16
Win Prizemoney £10,674 *Total Prizemoney* £16,050
Wins 1996 Aug Goodwo (G-F) 6f 76
1995 Jun Redcar (FRM) H 7f 77 81 <
1998 Turf 0-7: (5f, 6f 5, 7f) (g-s 2, gd 2, g-f 2, frm) 1998 AW 0-2: (6f, 7f) (Fibr 2)
Fair gelding. Turf high 71. AW high 54. Absent in '97, he showed plenty of dash on his reappearance but has run poorly since.
**M Brittain [0-9] Mel Brittain (from E A L Dunlop [2-13] Spt 1996).*

HAWADETH BHB 91f RR 92f 2251[4]

3 ch c Machiavellian (USA) 9.8f **(83)** - Ghzaalh (USA) (Northern Dancer) 9.6f **(80)**
Form - 23414
Record 1998 - 1st:1 2nd:1 3rd:1 Ran:5
Win Prizemoney £3,598 *Total Prizemoney* £7,004
Wins * 1998 Jun Haydoc (GD) 8.1f 82 <
1998 Turf 1-5: (8f 1-2, 10f 3) (gd, g-f, frm 1-3)
Useful colt. Turf high 92 - 3rd of 10 to Casino Captive (5 May Chester 10f g-f RF 1041). Unraced at two, he ran well in his first three starts before getting off the mark in a Haydock maiden in June. He was taking on much more experiences rivals when fourth in a Salisbury handicap on his only subsequent start.
**M P Tregoning [1-5] Hamdan Al Maktoum.*

HAWAII STORM (FR) BHB 40f45a RR 47f 45a 4049[7]

10 b g Plugged Nickle (USA) 7.4f **(70)** - Slewvindaloo (USA) (Seattle Slew (USA)) 9.4f **(76)**
Form - 507715572505747
Record 1998 - 1st:1 2nd:1 3rd:0 Ran:13
Pre1998 - 1st:10 2nd:10 3rd:11 Ran:103
Win Prizemoney £26,013 *Total Prizemoney* £41,191
Wins * 1998 *Jan Lingfi (STD) C 8f 52+*
* 1997 Jly Bright (FRM) S 8f 52?
** 1997 Feb Lingfi (STD) H 8f 52 55*
** 1997 Jan Lingfi (STD) S 7f 55*
** 1995 Dec Lingfi (STD) H 7f 59 58*
1994 Dec Lingfi (STD) H 8f 52 53
1998 Turf 0-3:(7f, 8f 2)(gd, frm 2)1998 AW 1-10:(7f 2, 8f 1-8)(Equi 1-10)
Fair gelding, effective 7 to 8f, best at 8f, acts on g-f - acts on Equi, has worn blinkers, favours left handed tracks, favours tight tracks, does well at Lingfield. Turf high 47 (began Jly). AW high 52 - 1st of 10 getting 12lb from Anonym (27 Jan Lingfield RF 0166). An Equitrack specialist, he did win a small race at Brighton in July '97 but is basically very moderate on turf. Tends to get outpaced early on in his races, but remains capable of winning on his favoured surface, as he showed when popping up at 20/1 in January. Not easy to predict these days, he may just find seven furlongs too sharp for him now.
**D J S ffrenchDavis [5-59] Ms Renee Wheeler (from Miss A J Whitfield [6-57] Jan 1995).*

HAWALA (IRE) RR 78f 4891[3]

2 b f Warning 8.1f **(77)** - Halawa (IRE) (Dancing Brave (USA)) 8.4f **(76)**
Form - 3
Record 1998 - 1st:0 2nd:0 3rd:1 Ran:1
Win Prizemoney £0 *Total Prizemoney* £852
1998 Turf 0-1: (6f) (gd)
Currently above-average filly. **Sir Michael Stoute [0-1] H H Aga Khan.*

HAWAS RR 90f 4567a[14]

3 ch f Mujtahid (USA) 7.4f **(69)** - Alyakkh (IRE) (Sadler's Wells (USA)) 10f **(76)**
Form - 14220
1998 Turf 1-5: (8f 1-4, 9f) (sft, gd 1-3, frm)
Useful filly, has worn blinkers. Turf high 90 (began Jly) - 2nd of 6 giving 11lb to Broken Promise (20 Aug Tipperary 9f frm RF 3866a) - also 1st of 3 from Maya (11 Jly Limerick RF 2800a).
**D K Weld in IRE [1-5] Hamdan Al Maktoum.*

HAWKSBILL HENRY (USA) BHB 48f55a RR 49f 55a 3605[3]

4 ch g Known Fact (USA) 8.3f **(72)** - Novel Approach (USA) (Codex (USA)) 8.6f **(73)**
Form - 36225143
Record 1998 - 1st:1 2nd:2 3rd:2 Ran:8
Pre1998 - 1st:0 2nd:0 3rd:0 Ran:6
Win Prizemoney £3,157 *Total Prizemoney* £6,445
Wins * 1998 *Jly Lingfi (STD) H 10f 48 54* <
1998 Turf 0-7:(8f, 9f 2, 10f 4)(gd, frm 6)1998AW 1-1:(10f 1-1) (Equi 1-1)
Workmanlike, fair gelding, effective 8 to 10f, acts on frm - acts on Equi, likes tight tracks. Turf high 49 - 2nd of 13 getting 12lb from With A Will (20 Jun Lingfield 9f frm RF 2152). (1st run) - 1st of 12 getting 5lb from Sweet Patoopie (10 Jly Lingfield RF 2691).
**Mrs A J Perrett [1-14] Mrs Amanda Perrett.*

HAWKSLEY HILL (IRE) BHB 106f62a RR 131f 62a 5165a[2]

5 ch g Rahy (USA) 9.1f **(80)** - Gaijin (Caerleon (USA)) 8.6f **(71)**
Form - 2
1998 Turf 0-1: (8f) (frm)
High-calibre gelding, effective 8f, acts on frm, has worn blinkers (effectively). (1st run) - 2nd of 14 to Da Hoss (7 Nov Churchill Downs 8f frm RF 5165a). Improving. A former high-class handicapper for Lynda Ramsden, he has developed into a leading miler in the States, landing valuable purses at Bay Meadows and Santa Anita in 1998 before failing narrowly in the Breeders' Cup Mile. Suited by exaggerated waiting tactics.
**N Drysdale in USA [0-2] Prestonwood Farm Inc (from Mrs J R Ramsden [8-23] Spt 1997).*

HAWRIYAH (USA) RR 84f 4758[1]

2 b br f Dayjur (USA) 6.8f **(79)** - Lady Cutlass (USA) (Cutlass (USA)) 8.5f **(76)**

Form - 21
Record 1998 - 1st:1 2nd:1 3rd:0 Ran:2
Win Prizemoney £3,535 *Total Prizemoney* £4,855
Wins * **1998** Oct Leices (G-S) 7f 84 <
1998 Turf 1-2: (6f, 7f 1-1) (gd 1-2)
Currently decent filly. Turf high 84 (began Spt) - 1st of 20 from Mrs Siddons (12 Oct Leicester RF 4758).
**J L Dunlop [1-2] Hamdan Al Maktoum.*

HAYA YA KEFAAH BHB 50f47a RR 52f 47a 3147^{13}

6 b g Kefaah (USA) 11.2f **(64)** - Hayat (IRE) (Sadler's Wells (USA)) 10f **(76)**
Form - 0640
Record 1998 - 1st:0 2nd:0 3rd:0 Ran:3
Pre1998 - 1st:3 2nd:2 3rd:0 Ran:13
Win Prizemoney £13,669 *Total Prizemoney* £16,152
Wins * 1996 Spt Haydoc (GD) H 11.9f 63 66 <
* 1996 May Doncas (G-F) H 12f 55 60
* 1996 Mar Doncas (GD) H 12f 33 55+
1998 Turf 0-3: (12f 2, 17f) (gd, frm 2)
Average gelding, has worn blinkers. Turf high 52.
**N M Babbage [3-15] Alan Craddock (from Sir Mark Prescott [0-4] Feb 1995).*

HAYBURNER BHB 43f42a RR 51f 42a 4114^{7}

3 b g Mujadil (USA) 7.7f **(70)** - Kotsina (Top Ville) 11.7f **(68)**
Form - 026337067
Record 1998 - 1st:0 2nd:1 3rd:2 Ran:9
Pre1998 - 1st:0 2nd:1 3rd:1 Ran:9
Win Prizemoney £0 *Total Prizemoney* £3,433
1998 Turf 0-6:(5f 2, 6f 4)(gd, g-f 2, frm 3)1998 AW 0-3: (5f, 6f 2) (Fibr 3)
Small, fair gelding, effective 5 to 6f, acts on g-f to frm, mostly wears blinkers (effectively). Turf high 55. AW high 42.
**M W Easterby [0-18] Stephen Curtis.*

HAYDN JAMES (USA) BHB 54f57a RR 57f 57a 4589^{12}

4 ch g Danzig Connection (USA) 8.2f **(75)** - Royal Fi Fi (USA) (Conquistador Cielo (USA)) 8.8f **(69)**
Form - 223414407100
Record 1998 - 1st:2 2nd:0 3rd:0 Ran:9
Pre1998 - 1st:0 2nd:2 3rd:1 Ran:11
Win Prizemoney £6,160 *Total Prizemoney* £8,005
Wins * **1998** Aug Windso (G-F) H 10f 54 57 <
* **1998** May Nottin (FRM) H 10f 51 53
1998 Turf 2-9: (8f, 10f 2-7, 12f) (gd 3, g-f 2, frm 1-3, hrd 1-1)
Scopey, fair gelding, effective 9 to 10f, best at 10f, acts on frm to hrd - acts on AW, often wears blinkers (extremely effectively), prefers left handed tracks, favours tight tracks, excels at Lingfield, does well at Nottingham. Turf high 57 - 1st of 5 getting 4lb from Iron Mountain (10 Aug Windsor RF 3516) - also 1st of 14 getting 7lb from Rear Window (22 May Nottingham RF 1398).
**P W Harris [2-20] Resplendent Racing Ltd.*

HAYES WAY (IRE) BHB 80f RR 51?f 4955^{15}

4 b c Lahib (USA) 8f **(69)** - Edgeaway (Ajdal (USA)) 9.2f **(89)**
Form - 0
Record 1998 - 1st:0 2nd:0 3rd:0 Ran:1
Pre1998 - 1st:2 2nd:0 3rd:0 Ran:6
Win Prizemoney £6,192 *Total Prizemoney* £6,632
Wins * 1997 *Feb Lingfi (STD) 8f 87* <
* 1996 *Nov Lingfi (STD) 8f 78*
1998 Turf 0-1: (7f) (frm)
Workmanlike, useful colt, effective 8f - acts on Equi.
**T G Mills [2-7] T G Mills.*

HAYIL (USA) BHB 114f RR 107f 3614a^{10}

3 b c Dayjur (USA) 6.8f **(79)** - Futuh (USA) (Diesis) 9.3f **(69)**
Form - 30
1998 Turf 0-2: (7f 2) (gd 2)
Scopey, Pattern-class colt, effective 6f, acts on gd to g-f, has worn blinkers. Turf high 107. Inconsistent. He won a weak Middle Park Stakes in 1997 and found life a lot tougher last season. We may have seen the best of him.
**F Head in FR [0-2] Hamdan Al Maktoum (from D Morley [2-6] Oct 1997).*

HAYMAKER (IRE) RR 2f 5145^{11}

2 b c Thatching 7.8f **(69)** - Susie Sunshine (IRE) (Waajib)
Form - 0
Record 1998 - 1st:0 2nd:0 3rd:0 Ran:1
1998 Turf 0-1: (8f) (gd)
Currently very poor colt. **I A Balding [0-1] Axom.*

HAYSTACKS (IRE) BHB 69f RR 65f 5115^{2}

2 b c Contract Law (USA) 8.9f **(54)** - Florissa (FR) (Persepolis (FR)) 6.4f **(67)**
Form - 636004052
Record 1998 - 1st:0 2nd:1 3rd:1 Ran:9
Win Prizemoney £0 *Total Prizemoney* £1,168
1998 Turf 0-9: (5f 2, 6f 4, 7f 3) (g-s, gd 6, g-f, frm)
Average colt, effective 7f, acts on gd, often wears blinkers (very effectively). Turf high 65 - 2nd of 5 to Single Shot (4 Nov Musselburgh 7f gd RF 5115). Consistent.
**D Moffatt [0-9] & Mrs A G Milligan.*

HAZAAF (USA) BHB 50f RR 24f 469^{14}

9 ch h Woodman (USA) 9.7f **(77)** - Solo Disco (USA) (Solo Landing) 12f **(71)**
Form - 0
Record 1998 - 1st:0 2nd:0 3rd:0 Ran:1
Pre1998 - 1st:1 2nd:1 3rd:0 Ran:9
Win Prizemoney £3,054 *Total Prizemoney* £3,822
1998 Turf 0-1: (12f) (gd)
Little account horse, has worn blinkers.
**M Kettle [0-2] J D Eggleton (from A A Scott [1-9] Spt 1992).*

HAZARAMA (IRE) RR 98f 1855a^{6}

3 b f Kahyasi 12.9f **(74)** - Hazaradjat (IRE) (Darshaan) 9.9f **(84)**
Form - 216
1998 Turf 1-3: (11f 2, 13f 1-1) (gd 1-3)
Very useful filly, effective 11 to 13f, acts on gd. Turf high 98 - 1st of 11 getting 5lb from Vagrant (29 May Wexford RF 1661a). Lightly-raced, improving filly, who has the ability to pick up a race or two next season. **J Oxx in IRE [1-6] H H Aga Khan.*

HAZARD A GUESS (IRE) BHB 79f RR 83f 1008^{10}

8 ch g Digamist (USA) 8.8f **(56)** - Guess Who (Be My Guest (USA)) 9.3f **(67)**
Form - 0
Record 1998 - 1st:0 2nd:0 3rd:0 Ran:1
Pre1998 - 1st:10 2nd:6 3rd:7 Ran:59
Win Prizemoney £50,868 *Total Prizemoney* £68,556
Wins 1996 Oct York (GD) C 10.4f 64
1996 Aug Newcas (G-F) H 10.1f 82 85 <
1996 Apr Kempto (GD) H 10f 76 81
1995 May Beverl (G-F) H 9.9f 72 77
1995 May Pontef (FRM) 10f 79
1994 Jun Sandow (GD) H 10f 68 73
1994 Mar Doncas (GD) H 10.3f 66 71
1998 Turf 0-1: (10f) (g-f)
Decent gelding, effective 10 to 12f, best at 10f, acts on gd to frm, best on gd.
**B S Rothwell [1-4] J M G Promotions Ltd (from D Nicholls [3-26] Aug 1997).*

HEAD GARDENER (IRE) BHB 31f36a RR 24f 36a 3454^{5}

4 b br g Be My Chief (USA) 10.2f **(62)** - Silk Petal (Petorius) 7.3f **(61)**
Form - 05342233480363336045755
Record 1998 - 1st:0 2nd:2 3rd:6 Ran:20
Pre1998 - 1st:1 2nd:0 3rd:1 Ran:11
Win Prizemoney £2,294 *Total Prizemoney* £5,738
Wins * 1997 *Jan Southw (STD) 11f 71* <
1998 Turf 0-2: (10f, 11f) (g-f, frm) 1998 AW 0-18: (8f 2, 9f, 11f 7, 12f 3, 13f 2, 14f, 15f, 16f) (Equi 2, Fibr 16)
Workmanlike, moderate gelding, effective 11f - acts on Fibr, often wears blinkers. Turf high 24. AW high 50. He got off the mark in a modest maiden on the Southwell Fibresand in January '97, and although placed many times since, has looked a very difficult ride.
**N P Littmoden [1-29] The Gardening Partnership (from J L Dunlop [0-3] Jly 1996).*

HEAD HONCHO BHB 78f RR 77f 4377^{8}

2 b c Primo Dominie 7.2f **(67)** - Ahonita (Ahonoora) 8.1f **(73)**

Form - 441058
Record 1998 - 1st:1 2nd:0 3rd:0 Ran:6
Win Prizemoney £3,468 *Total Prizemoney* £4,027
Wins * **1998** Jun Sandow (G-S) 5f 77 <
1998 Turf 1-6: (5f 1-6) (gd 1-4, g-f 2)
Above-average colt, effective 5f, acts on gd. Turf high 77 - 1st of 8 from Robber Red (12 Jun Sandown RF 1939). Comfortable winner of an ordinary Sandown maiden but finished last in the Windsor Castle. Looks to need six furlongs. **D R C Elsworth [1-6] J C Smith.*

HEADHUNTER (IRE) BHB 99f RR 98f 4461[6]

3 b c Last Tycoon 9.4f **(73)** - Erzsi (Caerleon (USA)) 8.6f **(71)**
Form - 362326
Record 1998 - 1st:0 2nd:2 3rd:2 Ran:6
Pre1998 - 1st:1 2nd:0 3rd:1 Ran:3
Win Prizemoney £3,273 *Total Prizemoney* £25,891
Wins * 1997 Jly Yarmou (GD) 6f 80+ <
1998 Turf 0-6: (7f 4, 8f 2) (sft, gd 2, frm 3)
Workmanlike, very useful colt, effective 7 to 8f, best at 7f, acts on sft to frm, has worn blinkers. Turf high 98 - 2nd of 7 giving 5lb to Fizzed (11 Jly Lingfield 8f frm RF 2712). Consistent. He ran some creditable races in decent company, but failed to get his head in front. Sold for 110,000 gns at the end of the season, reportedly to race abroad. **W J Haggas [1-9] Highclere Thoroughbred Racing Ltd.*

HEADMASTER RR 1250[16]

5 b g Kris 10f **(75)** - Ghislaine (USA) (Icecapade (USA)) 11f **(62)**
Form - 0
Record 1998 - 1st:0 2nd:0 3rd:0 Ran:1
1998 Turf 0-1: (7f) (gd)
Formerly very poor gelding. **F P Murtagh [0-4] Norman Park.*

HEART BHB 66f RR 82f 1886[7]

5 ch m Cadeaux Genereux 7.9f **(76)** - Recipe (Bustino) 10.4f **(64)**
Form - 7
Record 1998 - 1st:0 2nd:0 3rd:0 Ran:1
Pre1998 - 1st:0 2nd:2 3rd:0 Ran:7
Win Prizemoney £0 *Total Prizemoney* £3,055
1998 Turf 0-1: (12f) (gd)
Decent filly.
**Miss H C Knight [0-12] Christopher Shirley Brasher (from Sir Michael Stoute [0-7] Nov 1996).*

HEART FULL OF SOUL BHB 52f RR 62f 925[13]

4 ch g Primo Dominie 7.2f **(67)** - Scales of Justice(Final Straw) 7.9f **(64)**
Form - 0
Record 1998 - 1st:0 2nd:0 3rd:0 Ran:1
Pre1998 - 1st:1 2nd:1 3rd:2 Ran:14
Win Prizemoney £4,354 *Total Prizemoney* £6,186
Wins 1996 Oct Warwic (FRM) H 8f 70 76 <
1998 Turf 0-1: (12f) (gd)
Scopey, average gelding, often wears blinkers. Inconsistent.
**P Shakespeare [0-3] Ms Jan Procter (from P F I Cole [1-14] Oct 1997).*

HEART OF ARMOR BHB 77f RR 63f 995[5]

4 b g Tirol 8.1f **(64)** - Hemline (Sharpo) 7.7f **(59)**
Form - 55
Record 1998 - 1st:0 2nd:0 3rd:0 Ran:2
Pre1998 - 1st:1 2nd:3 3rd:2 Ran:13
Win Prizemoney £3,584 *Total Prizemoney* £9,509
Wins * 1997 May Windso (SFT) H 11.6f 77 81 <
1998 Turf 0-2: (12f 2) (sft, gd)
Scopey, average gelding, effective 12 to 14f, best at 12f, acts on gd to frm, prefers tight tracks. Turf high 63. Becoming disappointing. Won at Windsor in soft ground in May '97 and has run with credit subsequently, including his debut in 1998.
**P F I Cole [1-15] J S Gutkin.*

HEARTWOOD (USA) BHB 82f RR 82f 5000[2]

2 ch f Woodman (USA) 9.7f **(77)** - Good Example (FR) (Crystal Glitters (USA)) 11.3f **(79)**
Form - 432
Record 1998 - 1st:0 2nd:1 3rd:1 Ran:3
Win Prizemoney £0 *Total Prizemoney* £1,883
1998 Turf 0-3: (6f, 7f 2) (sft, gd, frm)
Currently decent filly. Turf high 82 (began Aug) - 2nd of 10 to Balisada (26 Oct Lingfield 7f sft RF 5000). Ran green on her debut, but showed promise and will improve. Should find a race over middle-distances. **Sir Michael Stoute [0-3] Sheikh Mohammed.*

HEATHMAN (IRE) RR 33f 4880[10]

2 b g Common Grounds 8.1f **(66)** - Dul Dul (USA) (Shadeed (USA)) 8.2f **(70)**
Form - 0
Record 1998 - 1st:0 2nd:0 3rd:0 Ran:1
1998 Turf 0-1: (7f) (g-s)
Currently very moderate gelding.
**G C Bravery [0-1] The TT Partnership.*

HEATHYARDS HERO BHB 20f RR 3f 3025[14]

3 b g Puissance 7.1f **(60)** - Heathyards Gem **(43f 45a)** (Governor General)
Form - 0060
Record 1998 - 1st:0 2nd:0 3rd:0 Ran:4
1998 Turf 0-3: (6f, 7f, 8f) (gd, frm 2) 1998 AW 0-1: (5f) (Fibr)
Light-framed, formerly very poor gelding, mostly wears blinkers.
**D McCain [0-4] L A Morgan.*

HEATHYARDS JAKE BHB 70f70a RR 71f 70a 4857[15]

2 b c Nomination 7.3f **(57)** - Safe Bid (Sure Blade (USA)) 11.3f **(67)**
Form - 4238332840
Record 1998 - 1st:0 2nd:2 3rd:3 Ran:10
Win Prizemoney £0 *Total Prizemoney* £3,274
1998 Turf 0-6: (5f 4, 6f 2) (sft, gd 3, g-f, frm) 1998 AW 0-4: (6f 3, 7f) (Fibr 4)
Decent colt, effective 6 to 7f - acts on Fibr. Turf high 71. AW high 83 (began Jly) - 2nd of 9 giving 20lb to Cable Media Boy (7 Aug Wolverhampton 7f Fibr RF 3450). **R Hollinshead [0-10] L A Morgan.*

HEATHYARDS SHEIK BHB 69f70a RR 75f 70a 2382[1]

3 b c Alnasr Alwasheek 9.4f **(62)** - Wilsonic (Damister (USA)) 9f **(73)**
Form - 35412801101
Record 1998 - 1st:4 2nd:1 3rd:0 Ran:10
Pre1998 - 1st:0 2nd:0 3rd:2 Ran:10
Win Prizemoney £7,245 *Total Prizemoney* £8,853
Wins * **1998** *Jun Southw (STD) C 11f 67* <
* **1998** *Apr Wolver (STD) S 9.4f 67+*
* **1998** *Apr Wolver (STD) S 9.4f 64*
* **1998** *Feb Southw (STD) S 7f 63*
1998 AW 4-10: (7f 1-3, 8f 2, 9f 2-4, 11f 1-1) (Fibr 4-10)
Above-average colt, effective 5 to 11f, acts on g-f - acts on Fibr, has worn blinkers, likes left handed tracks, likes tight tracks, and does well at Southwell. AW high 67 - 1st of 13 giving 10lb to Spring Beacon (30 Apr Wolverhampton RF 0941) - also 1st of 7 from Zuryaf (29 Jun Southwell RF 2382). He has had problems at the start in some of his races, giving away vast amounts of ground, but that quirk seems to have been ironed out. When he behaves himself, modest middle distance events on Fibresand are his for the taking, though he is not so effective in better class.
**R Hollinshead [4-20] L A Morgan.*

HEATHYARDS TIPPLE (IRE) BHB 64f52a RR 59f 52a 4866[6]

2 b f Marju (IRE) 9.2f **(76)** - Nikki's Groom (Shy Groom (USA)) 10f **(66)**
Form - 8340046
Record 1998 - 1st:0 2nd:0 3rd:1 Ran:7
Win Prizemoney £0 *Total Prizemoney* £825
1998 Turf 0-4: (5f, 7f 2, 8f) (gd, frm 3) 1998 AW 0-3: (6f, 7f, 8f) (Fibr 3)
Fair filly, effective 7f, acts on frm. Turf high 59 - 4th of 15 to Regal Fan (11 Jly Warwick 7f frm RF 2732). AW high 46.
**D McCain [0-7] L A Morgan.*

HEAVENLY ABSTONE BHB 59f63a RR 60f 63a 3886[13]

3 b f Interrex (CAN) 7.7f **(51)** - Heavenly Queen (Scottish Reel) 7f **(61)**
Form - 52064353773003400
Record 1998 - 1st:0 2nd:1 3rd:4 Ran:17
Pre1998 - 1st:2 2nd:6 3rd:2 Ran:14
Win Prizemoney £5,820 *Total Prizemoney* £21,669
Wins * 1997 May Ayr (SFT) 5f 78 <
* 1997 Apr Mussel (G-F) 5f 72
1998 Turf 0-10: (5f 5, 6f 5) (g-s, gd 6, g-f, frm 2) 1998 AW 0-7: (5f 2, 6f 3, 7f 2) (Equi 2, Fibr 5)
Scopey, average filly, effective 5 to 6f, best at 6f, acts on sft to frm, mostly wears blinkers, excels at Musselburgh and Chester. Turf high 61. AW high 62. **P D Evans [2-31] J E Abbey.*

HEAVENLY HAND BHB 28f20a **RR 20a** 91[11]
4 ch f Out of Hand - My Home (Homing) 7.8f **(59)**
Form - 0
Record **1998** - 1st:0 2nd:0 3rd:0 Ran:1
Pre1998 - 1st:0 2nd:0 3rd:0 Ran:3
1998 AW 0-1: (12f) (Equi)
Strong, poor filly.
**G L Moore [0-3] A Moore (from A Moore [0-2] Dec 1996).*

HEAVENLY MISS (IRE) BHB 48f64a **RR 55f 64a** 4775[18]
4 b f Anita's Prince 6f **(62)** - Heavenly Blessed (Monseigneur (USA)) 7.7f **(63)**
Form - 07720603388300
Record **1998** - 1st:0 2nd:1 3rd:3 Ran:14
Pre1998 - 1st:3 2nd:5 3rd:2 Ran:33
Win Prizemoney £7,666 *Total Prizemoney* £16,148
Wins * 1996 *Dec Lingfi (STD) C 5f 71*
1996 Spt Nottin (FRM) H 6.1f 64 77 <
1996 Aug Leices (G-F) S 6f 63+
1998 Turf 0-14: (5f 6, 6f 7, 7f) (gd 5, g-f 3, frm 6)
Unfurnished, average filly, effective 5f - acts on Equi, has worn blinkers, likes left handed tracks. Turf high 55.
**J J Bridger [1-39] Trevor Mitchell (from D Burchell [1-3] Oct 1996).*

HEAVENLY RAY (USA) BHB 92f **RR 97?f** 3260[1]
4 ch f Rahy (USA) 9.1f **(80)** - Highest Truth (USA) (Alydar (USA)) 9.1f **(76)**
Form - 451
Record **1998** - 1st:1 2nd:0 3rd:0 Ran:3
Pre1998 - 1st:1 2nd:1 3rd:0 Ran:5
Win Prizemoney £10,846 *Total Prizemoney* £13,783
Wins * **1998** Aug Goodwo (GD) 7f 94 <
* 1997 May Yarmou (G-F) 8f 72+
1998 Turf 1-3: (7f 1-1, 9f, 10f) (gd 1-3)
Leggy, very useful filly, effective 7 to 9f, acts on gd to g-f, best on gd. Turf high 95 (1st run) - 4th of 8 to Yabint El Sultan (1 May Newmarket 9f gd RF 0963) - also 1st of 9 getting 1lb from White Heart (1 Aug Goodwood RF 3260). Inconsistent. She was found out in Listed company, but returned to winning form in a classified event at Glorious Goodwood.
**J R Fanshawe [2-8] Cheveley Park Stud.*

HEAVEN'S ECHO (USA) **RR 57f** 5072[10]
2 ch f Woodman (USA) 9.7f **(77)** - Heaven's Mine (USA) (Graustark) 10.1f **(70)**
Form - 0
Record **1998** - 1st:0 2nd:0 3rd:0 Ran:1
1998 Turf 0-1: (7f) (gd)
Currently fair filly. **J H M Gosden [0-1] Sheikh Mohammed.*

HEBONY BHB 69f **RR 74f** 4677[1]
3 b f Sabrehill (USA) 8.5f **(64)** - Hebba (USA) (Nureyev (USA)) 8.7f **(78)**
Form - 722233041
Record **1998** - 1st:1 2nd:3 3rd:2 Ran:9
Win Prizemoney £3,876 *Total Prizemoney* £8,389
Wins * **1998** Oct Redcar (G-S) H 7f 65 68 <
1998 Turf 1-9: (7f 1-6, 8f 3) (gd 4, g-f 1-4, frm)
Neat, above-average filly, effective 7 to 8f, best at 7f, acts on gd to frm, best on gd, has worn blinkers. Turf high 74 - 2nd of 9 to Pagoda Tree (4 Jly Chepstow 7f gd RF 2529) - also 1st of 29 giving 18lb to Sand Hawk (6 Oct Redcar RF 4677). Consistent. Something of a character, she deserved her victory.
**J H M Gosden [1-9] Sheikh Mohammed.*

HECKLE BHB 56f **RR 54f** 4104[11]
2 ch f In The Wings 11.2f **(77)** - Valiant Cry (Town Crier) 10.2f **(55)**
Form - 540
Record **1998** - 1st:0 2nd:0 3rd:0 Ran:3
Win Prizemoney £0 *Total Prizemoney* £248
1998 Turf 0-3: (6f 2, 7f) (g-f, frm 2)
Currently fair filly. Turf high 54 (began Jly).
**T D Easterby [0-3] Aston House Stud.*

HEED MY WARNING (IRE) **RR 93f** 5027a[2]
3 b f Second Set (IRE) 9.2f **(67)** - Warning Sound (Red Alert) 7.6f **(66)**
Form - 3204523422
1998 Turf 0-10: (7f 3, 8f 6, 10f) (hvy 2, sft 2, gd 6)
Useful filly, effective 7 to 8f, best at 7f, acts on hvy to gd, best on gd, has worn blinkers, excels at Curragh. Turf high 105 - 2nd of 6 getting 5lb from Kincara Palace (2 May Curragh 7f sft RF 1052a). She is a tough filly who received precious little reward for her efforts in Group company. A willing attitude marks her down as a first-rate broodmare prospect. **C Collins in IRE [1-13] John Hurt.*

HEIGHTH OF FAME BHB 49f62a **RR 45f 62a** 422[8]
7 b g Shirley Heights 12.1f **(76)** - Land of Ivory (USA) (The Minstrel (CAN)) 10f **(72)**
Form - 628
Record **1998** - 1st:0 2nd:1 3rd:0 Ran:2
Pre1998 - 1st:4 2nd:7 3rd:5 Ran:34
Win Prizemoney £9,019 *Total Prizemoney* £16,429
Wins * 1997 *Jun Southw (STD) S 11f 64+*
1996 *Nov Lingfi (STD) H 13f 66 70* <
1996 *Spt Wolver (STD) SH 12f 55 63*
1996 *Feb Lingfi (STD) SH 13f 43 52*
1998 AW 0-2: (14f, 16f) (Equi, Fibr)
Average gelding, effective 11 to 16f, best at 11f - acts on AW, best on Fibr, likes left handed tracks. AW high 62 (1st run) - 2nd of 14 giving 2lb to Philosophic (3 Mar Lingfield 16f Equi RF 0394). He ran a blinder against an in-form rival on the Lingfield Equitrack in March, but subsequently disappointed.
**J Hetherton [1-20] Dr W D Mackenzie And Janet Elvans (from D Burchell [2-6] Feb 1997).*

HEIGHT OF FANTASY (IRE) **RR 72f** 4916[2]
2 b f Shirley Heights 12.1f **(76)**-Persian Fantasy (Persian Bold) 9.3f **(66)**
Form - 72
Record **1998** - 1st:0 2nd:1 3rd:0 Ran:2
Win Prizemoney £0 *Total Prizemoney* £1,010
1998 Turf 0-2: (7f 2) (g-s, g-f)
Currently above-average filly. Turf high 72 (began Spt) - 2nd of 10 to Bountiful Lady (21 Oct Newcastle 7f g-s RF 4916).
**J L Dunlop [0-2] Windflower Overseas Holdings Inc.*

HEIRESS OF MEATH (IRE) BHB 26f **RR 20f** 5178a[18]
3 ch f Imperial Frontier (USA) 7f **(65)** - Rich Heiress (IRE) (Last Tycoon) 8.5f **(62)**
Form - 00070000
Record **1998** - 1st:0 2nd:0 3rd:0 Ran:8
Pre1998 - 1st:0 2nd:0 3rd:0 Ran:3
1998 Turf 0-7: (5f, 7f 3, 8f, 10f, 12f) (sft, g-s, gd 3, frm 2) 1998 AW 0-1: (8f) (Equi)
Light-framed, little account filly. Turf high 34.
**E J Creighton in IRE [0-2] Dr Ian Shenkin (from M D I Usher [0-10] Jun 1998).*

HELENES HILL BHB 28f **RR 36f** 4399[16]
3 b f Sabrehill (USA) 8.5f **(64)** - Sea of Clouds **(74?f)** (Soviet Star (USA))
Form - 00
Record **1998** - 1st:0 2nd:0 3rd:0 Ran:2
Pre1998 - 1st:0 2nd:0 3rd:0 Ran:3
1998 Turf 0-2: (10f 2) (gd, frm)
Light-framed, very moderate filly. (began Aug).
**J L Harris [0-3] J Starbuck (from C Smith [0-2] Aug 1997).*

HELEN'S STARDUST BHB 57f **RR 65f** 4929[7]
2 br f Ballacashtal (CAN) 7.9f **(51)** - Legendary Lady (Reprimand)
Form - 017
Record **1998** - 1st:1 2nd:0 3rd:0 Ran:3
Win Prizemoney £2,973 *Total Prizemoney* £2,973
Wins * **1998** Spt Folkes (G-F) C 6f 65 <
1998 Turf 1-3: (6f 1-2, 7f) (g-s, gd, g-f 1-1)
Currently average filly. Turf high 65 (began Spt) - 1st of 16 getting 11lb from Prince Consort (25 Spt Folkestone RF 4473).
**W R Muir [1-3] John Mills.*

HELISMAD BHB 49f **RR 54f** 2632[7]
3 b g Thowra (FR) 11.2f **(47)** - Princess Mona (Prince Regent (FR)) 9.8f **(54)**
Form - 067
Record **1998** - 1st:0 2nd:0 3rd:0 Ran:3
1998 Turf 0-3: (10f, 12f 2) (g-s, g-f, frm)
Workmanlike, currently fair gelding. Turf high 54.

**M J Haynes [0-3] J P Saunders.*

HELLO GOODBYE (IRE) **RR** 5138[19]
2 b g Unblest - Sharp Goodbye (Sharpo) 7.7f **(59)**
Form - 00
Record 1998 - 1st:0 2nd:0 3rd:0 Ran:2
1998 Turf 0-2: (6f, 7f) (gd 2)
Currently very poor gelding, often wears blinkers. (began Oct).
**J A Glover [0-2] Countrywide Classics Ltd.*

HELLO MISTER BHB 78f85a **RR 87f 85a** 4749[22]
7 b h Efisio 7.7f **(69)** - Ginnies Petong (Petong) 6.6f **(58)**
Form - 70300070
Record 1998 - 1st:0 2nd:0 3rd:1 Ran:8
Pre1998 - 1st:6 2nd:3 3rd:8 Ran:69
Win Prizemoney £64,775 *Total Prizemoney* £89,317
Wins 1995 Spt Doncas (G-F) H 5.6f 92 101 <
1994 Spt Doncas (GD) H 5.6f 97 98
1994 Aug Goodwo (GD) H 6f 91 90
1994 Jun Newmar (G-F) H 5f 81 84
1994 May Bright (GD) H 5.3f 75 79+
1998 Turf 0-8: (5f 4, 6f 4) (gd 6, g-f 2)
Useful horse, effective 6f, acts on g-f, has worn blinkers. Turf high 87. Did not show much in 1998, but it would be no surprise if he bounces back to form next term.
**N P Littmoden [0-8] M C S D Racing (from T E Powell [0-22] Oct 1997).*

HELLO SOSO (IRE) **RR 95f** 4340a[3]
2 b c Alzao (USA) 9.8f **(73)** - Silver Echo (Caerleon (USA)) 8.6f **(71)**
Form - 13
1998 Turf 1-2: (7f 1-1, 8f) (sft, gd 1-1)
Currently very useful colt. Turf high 95 (1st run) (began Aug) - 1st of 6 from Markale (14 Aug Vichy RF 3780a). Third to Saytarra in a Group Three, looking likely to need middle-distances.
**J deRoualle in FR [1-2] J L Tepper.*

HELVETIUS **RR 70f** 4449[2]
2 b c In The Wings 11.2f **(77)** - Hejraan (USA) (Alydar (USA)) 9.1f **(76)**
Form - 2
Record 1998 - 1st:0 2nd:1 3rd:0 Ran:1
Win Prizemoney £0 *Total Prizemoney* £1,772
1998 Turf 0-1: (8f) (gd)
Currently above-average colt.
**C E Brittain [0-1] Sheikh Mohammed Obaid Al Maktoum.*

HENRIETTA HOLMES (IRE) BHB 59f **RR 56f** 4413[9]
2 gr f Persian Bold 10f **(69)**-Faakirah(Dragonara Palace (USA))6.1f **(55)**
Form - 750
Record 1998 - 1st:0 2nd:0 3rd:0 Ran:3
1998 Turf 0-3: (6f, 7f 2) (g-f, frm 2)
Currently fair filly. Turf high 56 (began Jly).
**J R Fanshawe [0-3] William McGregor & Georgia Fanshawe.*

HENRY HALL (IRE) BHB 98f **RR 91f** 4739[8]
2 b c Common Grounds 8.1f **(66)** - Sovereign Grace (IRE) (Standaan (FR)) 7f **(55)**
Form - 12311548
Record 1998 - 1st:3 2nd:1 3rd:1 Ran:8
Win Prizemoney £9,425 *Total Prizemoney* £11,689
Wins * **1998** Jly Doncas (G-F) 5f 90 <
* **1998** Jly Beverl (GD) 5f 90 <
* **1998** May Thirsk (G-F) C 5f 79
1998 Turf 3-8: (5f 3-8) (g-s, gd, g-f 2-4, frm 1-2)
Useful colt, effective 5f, acts on g-f to frm. Turf high 91 - also 1st of 5 giving 4lb to Cartmel Park (15 Jly Doncaster RF 2817). Consistent. A decent sprint juvenile, he won three times this season, but found Pattern company a bit too strong in his final three starts. He looks to need fast ground.
**N Tinkler [3-8] J M G Promotions Ltd.*

HENRY HEALD BHB 78f **RR 78f** 3841[1]
3 b br g Anshan 8.2f **(63)** - Zalfa (Luthier) 9.8f **(71)**
Form - 3221
Record 1998 - 1st:1 2nd:2 3rd:1 Ran:4
Win Prizemoney £2,211 *Total Prizemoney* £4,963
Wins * **1998** Aug Bright (G-F) 7f 67 <
1998 Turf 1-4: (7f 1-2, 8f, 10f) (g-f, frm 1-3)
Above-average gelding. Turf high 78 - 2nd of 17 to Temeraire (22 Jun Windsor 8f g-f RF 2184). He got off the mark in a very modest Brighton maiden in August, but was long odds-on to do so and made very hard work of it. He is probably a bit better than that.
**P J Makin [1-4] Miss H Joly.*

HENRY ISLAND (IRE) BHB 87f **RR 81f** 4521[4]
5 ch h Sharp Victor (USA) 10f **(56)** - Monterana (Sallust) 8.4f **(63)**
Form - 010084
Record 1998 - 1st:1 2nd:0 3rd:0 Ran:6
Pre1998 - 1st:2 2nd:2 3rd:1 Ran:10
Win Prizemoney £24,464 *Total Prizemoney* £30,602
Wins * **1998** May Goodwo (G-F) H 14f 90 93 <
* 1996 Oct Doncas (GD) H 12f 88 93 <
* 1996 May Leices (G-S) 8f 73++
1998 Turf 1-6: (12f 3, 14f 1-2, 16f) (sft, gd 2, g-f 1-3)
Decent colt, effective 14f, acts on g-f. Turf high 93 - 1st of 7 getting 1lb from Mawared (20 May Goodwood RF 1357). Consistent. Missed the whole of '97, but was successful on his second start back this season, just holding on by the narrowest of margins at Goodwood. That was very much the high point in an otherwise disappointing season. **G Wragg [3-16] H H Morriss.*

HENRY THE HAWK BHB 42f39a **RR 56f 39a** 4130[5]
7 b g Doulab (USA) 7.4f **(61)** - Plum Blossom (USA) (Gallant Romeo (USA)) 8.4f **(64)**
Form - 470312428865865
Record 1998 - 1st:1 2nd:2 3rd:1 Ran:15
Pre1998 - 1st:4 2nd:3 3rd:8 Ran:52
Win Prizemoney £13,040 *Total Prizemoney* £20,972
Wins * **1998** May Hamilt (SFT) H 5f 40 47
* 1997 Jun Hamilt (G-F) H 6f 42 46
* 1996 May Hamilt (SFT) H 5f 47 51 <
* 1996 Apr Carlis (G-S) H 5.9f 43 47
* 1995 Jun Beverl (G-S) H 5f 41 48
1998 Turf 1-11: (5f 1-8, 6f 3) (sft 1-1, g-s 2, gd 4, g-f, frm 3) 1998 AW 0-4: (5f, 6f 3) (Fibr 4)
Fair gelding, effective 5 to 6f, best at 5f, acts on sft to frm, often wears blinkers (extremely effectively). Turf high 56 - 2nd of 8 to Souperficial (17 Jun Hamilton 5f gd RF 2062) - also 1st of 11 getting 8lb from Ballantrae Boy (7 May Hamilton RF 1080). AW high 39. **M Dods [5-67] S Barras.*

HENRY THE PROUD (IRE) BHB 50f48a **RR 65f 48a** 4962[14]
3 ch g Shalford (IRE) 7.8f **(63)** - June Goddess (Junius (USA)) 7.7f **(65)**
Form - 1700255204200000
Record 1998 - 1st:1 2nd:3 3rd:0 Ran:16
Pre1998 - 1st:0 2nd:0 3rd:0 Ran:4
Win Prizemoney £2,197 *Total Prizemoney* £4,289
Wins 1998 Apr Nottin (SFT) S 6.1f 60 <
1998 Turf 1-16: (5f 3, 6f 1-11, 7f 2) (sft 1-2, gd 9, g-f 3, frm 2)
Neat, average gelding, effective 6f, acts on g-f, has worn blinkers. Turf high 65 - 2nd of 12 getting 3lb from Alpen Wolf (27 Aug Folkestone 6f g-f RF 3901). Becoming disappointing. His only win to date has been in selling company, and six furlongs on soft ground look to suit him best.
**V Soane [0-6] Breeze In/Breeze Out Club (from J Berry [1-14] Aug 1998).*

HERB OF GRACE BHB 92f **RR 93f** 4628[8]
2 ch f Rudimentary (USA) 8.2f **(66)** - Crymlyn (Welsh Pageant) 10f **(65)**
Form - 411028
Record 1998 - 1st:2 2nd:1 3rd:0 Ran:6
Win Prizemoney £8,077 *Total Prizemoney* £10,118
Wins * **1998** Aug Newmar (FRM) H 7f 83 88 <
* **1998** Jly Warwic (G-F) 7f 74+
1998 Turf 2-6: (7f 2-6) (g-f 3, frm 2-3)
Useful filly, effective 7f, acts on frm. Turf high 93 (began Jly) - also 1st of 9 getting 2lb from Morning Music (7 Aug Newmarket RF 3441). Improving steadily, she landed a Warwick maiden and a Newmarket nursery, but got no sort of a run when onto a hat-trick at York. She ran well when going down narrowly at Goodwood, but found Listed company too much for her on her final start.
**Mrs J Cecil [2-6] Major C R Philipson.*

HERBSHAN DANCER BHB 36f48a **RR 44f 48a** 4938[11]
4 b g Warrshan (USA) 9.7f **(59)** - Herbary (USA) (Herbager) 13f **(65)**

Form - 023385830
Record 1998 - 1st:0 2nd:1 3rd:3 Ran:9
Pre1998 - 1st:0 2nd:1 3rd:2 Ran:15
Win Prizemoney £0 *Total Prizemoney* £4,035
1998 Turf 0-9: (12f 4, 13f 2, 14f, 16f 2) (gd 3, g-f 3, frm 3)
Neat, moderate gelding, effective 12f, acts on gd to g-f, best on gd, has worn blinkers, favours tight tracks. Turf high 44.
**S Earle [0-9] The Kingtroll Racing Partnership (from B R Millman [0-15] Oct 1997).*

HERE AND NOW (USA) BHB 70f RR 72f 4701[19]

3 ch f Green Forest (USA) 7.4f **(73)** - All Present (USA) (Tom Rolfe) 9.4f **(75)**
Form - 0210
Record 1998 - 1st:1 2nd:1 3rd:0 Ran:4
Win Prizemoney £3,655 *Total Prizemoney* £4,760
Wins * 1998 Spt Yarmou (G-S) 6f 72 <
1998 Turf 1-4: (5f 2, 6f 1-1, 7f) (gd 1-2, g-f, frm)
Scopey, above-average filly. Turf high 72 - 1st of 5 getting 7lb from Indian Brave (15 Spt Yarmouth RF 4273). Outclassed in a listed race on her debut, she made all to land a maiden on her third run.
**C E Brittain [1-4] The Thoroughbred Corporation.*

HERE COMES HERBIE BHB 68f RR 70f 478[8]

6 ch g Golden Lahab (USA) 14.4f**(32)**-Megan's Move(Move Off)15f **(41)**
Form - 8
Record 1998 - 1st:0 2nd:0 3rd:0 Ran:1
Pre1998 - 1st:4 2nd:5 3rd:3 Ran:25
Win Prizemoney £15,482 *Total Prizemoney* £24,863
Wins * 1997 Jly Redcar (G-S) H 16f 62 68 <
* 1997 Apr Ripon (GD) H 16f 51 58
* 1997 Mar Mussel (SFT) H 16f 37 54?
* 1996 Jun Catter (G-F) H 12f 32 42
1998 Turf 0-1: (18f) (gd)
Above-average gelding, effective 16f, acts on g-s to frm, prefers tight tracks, excels at Redcar, likes Musselburgh. Consistent.
**W Storey [6-36] H S Hutchinson.*

HERETICAL MISS BHB 26f25a RR 31?f 25a 765[9]

8 br m Sayf El Arab (USA) 8.2f **(57)** - Silent Prayer (Queen's Hussar) 11.6f **(58)**
Form - 0
Record 1998 - 1st:0 2nd:0 3rd:0 Ran:1
Pre1998 - 1st:0 2nd:0 3rd:2 Ran:26
Win Prizemoney £0 *Total Prizemoney* £1,174
1998 Turf 0-1: (12f) (g-s)
Very moderate mare, has worn blinkers.
**J Ffitch-Heyes [1-21] John Ffitch-Heyes (from R Hannon [0-20] Oct 1993).*

HERMINIUS (IRE) BHB 79f RR 80f 1974[4]

3 b c Ballad Rock 7.2f **(63)** - Scotia Rose (Tap On Wood) 10.3f **(65)**
Form - 084
Record 1998 - 1st:0 2nd:0 3rd:0 Ran:3
Pre1998 - 1st:1 2nd:0 3rd:0 Ran:4
Win Prizemoney £3,073 *Total Prizemoney* £4,599
Wins * 1997 Oct Redcar (G-F) 8f 80 <
1998 Turf 0-3: (8f 2, 9f) (g-s, gd 2)
Workmanlike, decent colt, effective 8 to 9f, acts on g-s to g-f. Turf high 78 - 4th of 10 giving 4lb to Radar (13 Jun Sandown 9f g-s RF 1974). **J L Dunlop [1-7] D R Hunnisett.*

HERNIECE BHB 28f28a RR 28a 1115[13]

3 b f Weldnaas (USA) 8.4f **(55)** - Sizzling Sista (Sizzling Melody)
Form - 0070
Record 1998 - 1st:0 2nd:0 3rd:0 Ran:2
Pre1998 - 1st:0 2nd:0 3rd:0 Ran:2
1998 Turf 0-1: (10f) (frm) 1998 AW 0-1: (6f) (Fibr)
Unfurnished, very poor filly. **J L Harris [0-4] Mrs M Hills.*

HERONSHILL RR 3039[14]

6 b g Tacheron 6.8f **(79)** - Dip N Dot (Golden Dipper) 6.5f **(42)**
Form - 00
Record 1998 - 1st:0 2nd:0 3rd:0 Ran:2
1998 Turf 0-2: (7f, 8f) (gd 2)
Formerly very poor gelding. (began Jly).
**L A Dace [0-5] Harry Hawkins Partnership.*

HERR TRIGGER BHB 57f80a RR 64f 80a 4540[11]

7 gr g Sharrood (USA) 11.1f **(67)**-Four-Legged Friend(Aragon) 8.1f **(60)**
Form - 313504600
Record 1998 - 1st:1 2nd:0 3rd:2 Ran:9
Pre1998 - 1st:6 2nd:4 3rd:3 Ran:23
Win Prizemoney £27,978 *Total Prizemoney* £40,612
Wins * *1998 Mar Lingfi (SLW) H 10f 75 81* <
* 1995 Jun Newmar (G-F) H 10f 57 68+
* 1995 Jun Ripon (FRM) H 10f 57 61
* 1995 May Newmar (G-F) H 10f 53 60
* *1994 Feb Lingfi (STD) H 8f 70 71*
* *1994 Jan Lingfi (STD) S 8f 57*
1998 Turf 0-5: (10f 4, 12f) (gd, frm 3, hrd) 1998 AW 1-4: (10f 1-3, 12f) (Equi 1-4)
Decent gelding, effective 10f - acts on Equi, mostly wears blinkers, prefers left handed tracks, likes tight tracks. Turf high 64. AW high 81 - 1st of 11 giving 3lb to Chairmans Choice (3 Mar Lingfield RF 0393). Becoming disappointing.
**Dr J D Scargill [7-32] The Inn Crowd.*

HESITATION RR 81++f 5138[1]

2 b f Deploy 11.4f **(67)** -Questionable (Rainbow Quest (USA)) 10.4f **(75)**
Form - 1
Record 1998 - 1st:1 2nd:0 3rd:0 Ran:1
Win Prizemoney £3,486 *Total Prizemoney* £3,486
Wins * 1998 Nov Doncas (SFT) 7f 81++ <
1998 Turf 1-1: (7f 1-1) (gd 1-1)
Currently decent filly. (1st run) - 1st of 19 getting 5lb from Otahuna (6 Nov Doncaster RF 5138). A sister to In Question, she was a comfortable winner on her debut and is one to keep and eye on.
**B W Hills [1-1] K Abdulla.*

HETRA HAWK RR 47f 5073[10]

2 ch g Be My Guest (USA) 10.2f **(66)** - Silver Ore (FR) (Silver Hawk (USA)) 8.6f **(70)**
Form - 00
Record 1998 - 1st:0 2nd:0 3rd:0 Ran:2
1998 Turf 0-2: (7f, 8f) (gd, frm)
Currently moderate gelding. Turf high 47 (began Oct).
**W J Musson [0-2] B N Fulton.*

HETRA HEIGHTS (USA) BHB 47f RR 50f 5069[12]

3 b f Cox's Ridge (USA) 9.4f **(72)** - Top Hope (High Top) 10.2f **(67)**
Form - 0270
Record 1998 - 1st:0 2nd:1 3rd:0 Ran:4
Pre1998 - 1st:0 2nd:0 3rd:0 Ran:2
Win Prizemoney £0 *Total Prizemoney* £1,452
1998 Turf 0-4: (8f, 12f 3) (g-s, g-f, frm 2)
Scopey, fair filly, effective 12f, acts on frm. Turf high 50 - 2nd of 17 getting 3lb from Tui (1 Aug Newmarket 12f frm RF 3275).
**W J Musson [0-6] K L West.*

HEVER FEVER BHB 36f48a RR 48a 4922[12]

3 br f Machiavellian (USA) 9.8f **(83)** - Wanisa (USA) (Topsider (USA)) 8.3f **(71)**
Form - 4535204000
Record 1998 - 1st:0 2nd:1 3rd:1 Ran:10
Win Prizemoney £0 *Total Prizemoney* £1,720
1998 Turf 0-3: (10f 2, 14f) (sft, g-s, g-f) 1998 AW 0-7: (7f, 8f 2, 9f 2, 10f 2) (Equi 3, Fibr 3, Dirt)
Moderate filly, effective 9f - acts on Fibr, favours left handed tracks, favours tight tracks. AW high 45.
**T J Naughton [0-10] T J Naughton.*

HEVER GOLF CHARMER BHB 40f RR 38f 654[9]

4 b g Precocious 7.2f **(54)** - Callas Star (Chief Singer) 8.9f **(66)**
Form - 04000
Record 1998 - 1st:0 2nd:0 3rd:0 Ran:5
Pre1998 - 1st:0 2nd:0 3rd:1 Ran:7
Win Prizemoney £0 *Total Prizemoney* £347
1998 Turf 0-2: (12f, 16f) (sft, gd) 1998 AW 0-3: (8f 2, 11f) (Fibr 3)
Well made, very moderate gelding, effective 8f, acts on gd, has worn blinkers, likes tight tracks. Turf high 12. AW high 30. Becoming disappointing.
**B S Rothwell [0-10] The Action Racing Club Ltd (from T J Naughton [0-6] Jly 1997).*

HEVER GOLF CLASSIC BHB 55f30a **RR 48f 30a** 370^{5}

5 b br g Bustino 11f **(64)** - Explosiva (USA) (Explodent (USA)) 9.4f **(87)**

Form - 065
Record 1998 - 1st:0 2nd:0 3rd:0 Ran:3
Pre1998 - 1st:0 2nd:0 3rd:0 Ran:4
1998 AW 0-3: (8f, 10f, 13f) (Equi 2, Fibr)
Moderate gelding. AW high 25. **T J Naughton [0-7] T J Naughton.*

HEVER GOLF EAGLE BHB 39f48a **RR 52f 48a** 925^{8}

5 b g Aragon 7.7f **(58)** - Elkie Brooks (Relkino) 8.9f **(65)**
Form - 08
Record 1998 - 1st:0 2nd:0 3rd:0 Ran:2
Pre1998 - 1st:1 2nd:2 3rd:4 Ran:20
Win Prizemoney £2,100 *Total Prizemoney* £5,177
Wins *1997 Feb Lingfi (STD) 10f 54 <*
1998 Turf 0-1: (12f) (gd) 1998 AW 0-1: (12f) (Equi)
Fair gelding, effective 8 to 10f, acts on gd - acts on Equi, has worn blinkers. Inconsistent.
**G L Moore [0-4] Speedline Telecom (from T J Naughton [1-21] Jly 1997).*

HEVER GOLF GLORY BHB 53f70a **RR 46f 70a** 5040^{8}

4 b g Efisio 7.7f **(69)** - Zaius (Artaius (USA)) 9f **(69)**
Form - 457682000864008
Record 1998 - 1st:0 2nd:1 3rd:0 Ran:15
Pre1998 - 1st:1 2nd:1 3rd:1 Ran:7
Win Prizemoney £21,990 *Total Prizemoney* £29,636
Wins 1997 Jun Taby (GD) 8f 81 <
1998 Turf 0-11: (7f 2, 8f 9) (g-s 3, gd 2, g-f 2, frm 4) 1998 AW 0-4: (8f 2, 10f 2) (Equi 3, Fibr)
Scopey, decent gelding, effective 8f, acts on gd - acts on Fibr. Turf high 79. AW high 84 - 5th of 13 giving 2lb to Fayik (14 Mar Wolverhampton 8f Fibr RF 0431). Went globetrotting in '97, including winning in Sweden, but had a very busy 1998 and shown very little. The closest he came to winning was when beaten a neck in a Sandown claimer in May. He did not make much impression when tried in good company on sand.
**N P Littmoden [0-9] Gemini Associates (from T J Naughton [1-13] May 1998).*

HEVER GOLF MACHINE BHB 63f70a **RR 66f 70a** $3617a^{2}$

3 ch c Rudimentary (USA) 8.2f **(66)** - Stop Press (USA) (Sharpen Up) 8.3f **(67)**
Form - 73604212
Record 1998 - 1st:1 2nd:2 3rd:1 Ran:7
Pre1998 - 1st:0 2nd:0 3rd:1 Ran:3
Win Prizemoney £2,801 *Total Prizemoney* £14,164
Wins * 1998 *Jly Wolver (STD) H 9.4f 53 58 <*
1998 Turf 0-4: (6f 2, 7f, 8f) (sft, gd, g-f, frm) 1998 AW 1-3: (8f 2, 9f 1-1) (Fibr 1-2, Dirt)
Strong, average colt, effective 6 to 9f, acts on sft to frm - acts on Fibr to Dirt. Turf high 66 - 4th of 11 giving 3lb to Pride of My Heart (24 Jun Salisbury 7f frm RF 2254). AW high 66 (began Jly) - 2nd of 12 to Mr Carrera (9 Aug Jagersro 8f Dirt RF 3617a) - also 1st of 10 getting 16lb from Aspirant Dancer (24 Jly Wolverhampton RF 3095). He has started to show ability as he has gone up in trip. Seven furlongs to a mile may prove ideal. **T J Naughton [1-10].*

HEVER GOLF MAGIC (IRE) BHB 34f **RR 18f** 2823^{12}

4 ch f Ballad Rock 7.2f **(63)** - Track Twenty Nine (IRE) (Standaan (FR)) 7f **(55)**
Form - 000
Record 1998 - 1st:0 2nd:0 3rd:0 Ran:3
Pre1998 - 1st:0 2nd:0 3rd:0 Ran:4
Win Prizemoney £0 *Total Prizemoney* £205
1998 Turf 0-3: (7f 2, 8f) (gd 2, frm)
Scopey, poor filly. Turf high 18.
**T J Naughton [0-5] Hever Racing Club (from M Johnston [0-2] Nov 1996).*

HEVER GOLF MOVER BHB 54f60a **RR 47df 60a** 4652^{17}

4 ch f Efisio 7.7f **(69)** - Joyce's Best (Tolomeo) 5.6f **(60)**
Form - 76000
Record 1998 - 1st:0 2nd:0 3rd:0 Ran:5
Pre1998 - 1st:2 2nd:3 3rd:1 Ran:17
Win Prizemoney £5,001 *Total Prizemoney* £8,906
Wins * 1997 Aug Carlis (G-F) H 5.9f 58 65 <
* 1997 Apr Bright (FRM) 6f 53
1998 Turf 0-3: (6f, 7f 2) (gd, g-f, frm) 1998 AW 0-2: (6f, 7f) (Equi, Fibr)
Light-framed, moderate filly, effective 6 to 7f, best at 6f, acts on gd to frm, best on frm. Turf high 37 (began Aug). AW high 45. She won a limited stakes at Brighton and a Carlisle handicap in '97, but they were modest affairs and she is basically moderate. She did not show much when tried on sand.
**T J Naughton [2-22] Hever Racing Club.*

HEVER GOLF PASSION (IRE) BHB 69f72a **RR 75f 72a** 4351^{6}

3 b f Pips Pride 6.7f **(70)** - Base Camp (Derring-Do) 11.1f **(64)**
Form - 52243742506
Record 1998 - 1st:0 2nd:3 3rd:1 Ran:11
Pre1998 - 1st:0 2nd:0 3rd:1 Ran:2
Win Prizemoney £0 *Total Prizemoney* £10,789
1998 Turf 0-8: (8f 4, 9f, 10f 2, 12f) (hvy, sft 2, g-s, gd, g-f, frm 2) 1998 AW 0-3: (6f, 7f 2) (Fibr 3)
Leggy, above-average filly, effective 7 to 10f, acts on g-f - acts on Fibr, likes left handed tracks, likes tight tracks. Turf high 75 - 2nd of 10 to Passionate Pursuit (23 Jun Lingfield 10f g-f RF 2199). AW high 67 - 2nd of 12 getting 1lb from Pow Wow (7 Mar Wolverhampton 7f Fibr RF 0404). Inconsistent.
**T J Naughton [0-13] Hever Racing Club.*

HEVERGOLF PRINCESS (IRE) BHB 51f55a **RR 54f 55a** 3376^{7}

3 ch f Petardia 8.2f **(58)** - High Profile (High Top) 10.2f **(67)**
Form - 5213557
Record 1998 - 1st:1 2nd:1 3rd:1 Ran:6
Pre1998 - 1st:0 2nd:0 3rd:0 Ran:3
Win Prizemoney £2,190 *Total Prizemoney* £3,209
Wins * 1998 *Feb Lingfi (SLW) 7f 58 <*
1998 Turf 0-4: (8f 3, 10f)(gd, frm 2, hrd)1998 AW 1-2: (7f 1-2) (Equi 1-2)
Leggy, fair filly, effective 7 to 10f, acts on gd - acts on Equi, prefers tight tracks. Turf high 57 (1st run) - 3rd of 15 giving 11lb to Eastwell Hall (1 Apr Folkestone 10f gd RF 0541). AW high 58 - 1st of 5 from Pearly Queen (12 Feb Lingfield RF 0274).
**T J Naughton [1-9] Hever Racing Club.*

HEVER GOLF RANGER BHB 84f93a **RR 88f 93a** 3371^{10}

3 b c Efisio 7.7f **(69)** - Bold Green(FR) (Green Dancer (USA)) 10.3f **(74)**
Form - 6215400
Record 1998 - 1st:1 2nd:1 3rd:0 Ran:6
Pre1998 - 1st:0 2nd:1 3rd:1 Ran:4
Win Prizemoney £3,452 *Total Prizemoney* £12,184
Wins * 1998 *Jan Lingfi (STD) 7f 84? <*
1998 Turf 0-4: (7f 3, 8f) (sft, gd, g-f, frm) 1998 AW 1-2: (7f 1-2) (Equi 1-1, Fibr)
Scopey, useful colt, effective 7 to 8f, acts on sft - acts on Equi. Turf high 88. AW high 84 - 1st of 8 from Wild Eagle (22 Jan Lingfield RF 0134). He got off the mark in good style on the Lingfield Equitrack in January, having previously shown promise on turf and Fibresand. Promising return four months later, but well held on his lsat two starts. **T J Naughton [1-10] Hever Racing Club.*

HEVER GOLF ROCKET BHB 57f55a **RR 65f 55a** 4669^{10}

4 b g Efisio 7.7f **(69)** - Truly Bold (Bold Lad (IRE)) 8.4f **(68)**
Form - 600004070
Record 1998 - 1st:0 2nd:0 3rd:0 Ran:9
Pre1998 - 1st:1 2nd:0 3rd:2 Ran:5
Win Prizemoney £2,966 *Total Prizemoney* £4,324
Wins * 1997 Jly Folkes (GD) 6f 57 <
1998 Turf 0-8:(6f 4, 7f 4)(sft 2, gd 2, g-f 2, frm 2)1998AW 0-1: (6f) (Fibr)
Strong, average gelding, effective 6f, acts on g-f, has worn blinkers. Turf high 65. **T J Naughton [1-14] Hever Racing Club.*

HEVER GOLF ROSE BHB 100f **RR 110df** 2108^{13}

7 b m Efisio 7.7f **(69)** - Sweet Rosina (Sweet Revenge) 7.2f **(54)**
Form - 550610
Record 1998 - 1st:1 2nd:0 3rd:0 Ran:5
Pre1998 - 1st:16 2nd:11 3rd:10 Ran:62
Win Prizemoney £448,497 *Total Prizemoney* £671,895
Wins * 1998 Jun Taby (SFT) L 5.8f 94
* 1997 Oct Longch (SFT) G3 5f 110
* 1997 Jun Taby (GD) L 6f 98
* 1997 May Longch (SFT) G3 5f 102

* 1995	Oct	Longch	(SFT)	G1	5f		120	<
* 1995	Spt	Chanti	(SFT)	G3	6f		115	
* 1995	Aug	Baden-	(SFT)	G2	6f		114	
* 1995	Aug	Taby	(GD)	L	6f		94	
* 1995	Jly	Goodwo	(G-F)	G3	5f		112	
* 1995	Jly	Hambur	(G-F)	G3	6f		107+	
* 1995	Jun	Bremen	(SFT)	L	6f		104	
* 1995	May	Capann	(HVY)	G2	6f		110	
* 1994	Aug	York	(G-F)	H	6f	104	108	
* 1994	Aug	Gelsen	(GD)		7f		96	
* 1994	Jly	Newmar	(G-F)	H	7f	89	91	

1998 Turf 1-5: (5f 2, 6f 1-3) (sft 1-1, g-s, gd 2, frm)
Group-class mare, effective 5 to 6f, best at 5f, acts on sft to g-f, best on sft, does well at Taby and Longchamp. Turf high 96. A marvellous servant to connections over the years, she won a listed race in Sweden prior to finishing down the field at Royal Ascot on her final start. In foal to Danehill.
**T J Naughton [17-67] Hever Racing Club.*

HEVER ROSINA RR 56f — 4994[4]
2 b f Efisio 7.7f **(69)** - Truly Bold (Bold Lad (IRE)) 8.4f **(68)**
Form - 4
Record 1998 - 1st:0 2nd:0 3rd:0 Ran:1
1998 Turf 0-1: (6f) (sft)
Currently fair filly. **T J Naughton [0-1] The Awayday Partnership.*

HEY UP MATE (IRE) BHB 40f RR 42f — 2245[13]
3 b g River Falls 8.2f **(56)** - Damira (FR) (Pharly (FR)) 9.8f **(68)**
Form - 7487030
Record 1998 - 1st:0 2nd:0 3rd:1 Ran:7
Pre1998 - 1st:0 2nd:0 3rd:0 Ran:7
Win Prizemoney £0 *Total Prizemoney* £327
1998 Turf 0-7: (7f 3, 8f 3, 9f) (g-s 2, gd 2, g-f 2, hrd)
Light-framed, moderate gelding, has worn blinkers. Turf high 44.
**J Berry [0-14] W R Astbury.*

HIBAAT RR 71f — 4595[10]
2 ch c Zafonic (USA) 9f **(83)** - Realisatrice (USA) (Raja Baba (USA)) 10f **(64)**
Form - 0
Record 1998 - 1st:0 2nd:0 3rd:0 Ran:1
1998 Turf 0-1: (7f) (gd)
Currently above-average colt.
**P T Walwyn [0-1] Hamdan Al Maktoum.*

HIBERNIAN RHAPSODY (IRE) RR 102f — 3534a[4]
3 bb c Darshaan 11.9f **(81)** - Elegance in Design (Habitat) 9.4f **(70)**
Form - 43264
1998 Turf 0-5: (10f 3, 12f, 14f) (gd 4, g-f)
Very useful colt, effective 10 to 14f, best at 10f, acts on gd to g-f, best on gd, often wears blinkers. Turf high 102 - 3rd of 6 getting 3lb from Desert Fox (6 Jun Cork 10f gd RF 1858a). He had the Irish Derby as a target after his reappearance, but proved a disappointment and ended the campaign by finishing last of four in a minor heat at Leopardstown. **D K Weld in IRE [1-6] Moyglare Stud Farm.*

HICKORY (IRE) BHB 60f RR 63df — 537[9]
3 b g Fayruz 6.6f **(63)** - La Mortola (Bold Lad (IRE)) 8.4f **(68)**
Form - 0
Record 1998 - 1st:0 2nd:0 3rd:0 Ran:1
Pre1998 - 1st:0 2nd:0 3rd:0 Ran:4
Win Prizemoney £0 *Total Prizemoney* £226
1998 Turf 0-1: (7f) (gd)
Workmanlike, average gelding. **M J Haynes [0-5] G Steinberg.*

HIDDEN MAGIC RR 84+f — 4891[5]
2 b c Magic Ring (IRE) 6.5f **(64)** - Magic Milly (Simply Great (FR)) 8.2f **(65)**
Form - 15
Record 1998 - 1st:1 2nd:0 3rd:0 Ran:2
Win Prizemoney £3,912 *Total Prizemoney* £4,050
Wins * **1998** Oct Catter (G-S) 6f 84+ <
1998 Turf 1-2: (6f 1-2) (gd 1-2)
Currently decent colt. Turf high 84 (1st run) (began Oct) - 1st of 10 giving 5lb to Lady Caroline (15 Oct Catterick RF 4814).
**Sir Mark Prescott [1-2] Platinum Syndicate Ltd.*

HIDDEN MEADOW BHB 115f RR 115f — 2352[6]
4 b c Selkirk (USA) 7.9f **(76)**-Spurned (USA) (Robellino (USA)) 7.6f **(80)**
Form - 6126
Record 1998 - 1st:1 2nd:1 3rd:0 Ran:4
Pre1998 - 1st:4 2nd:1 3rd:1 Ran:11
Win Prizemoney £80,661 *Total Prizemoney* £109,603

Wins									
* **1998**	May	Longch	(GD)	G3	7f		119	<
* 1997	Aug	York	(GD)	L	7f		119	<
* 1997	Jun	Epsom	(GD)		7f		108+	
* 1997	Apr	Newmar	(GD)	LH	7f	108	111+	
* 1996	Oct	York	(GD)		7.9f		86	

1998 Turf 1-4: (7f 1-2, 8f, 9f) (gd 1-3, g-f)
Leggy, high-class colt, effective 7f, acts on gd. Turf high 119 - 1st of 6 getting 1lb from Pas De Reponse (26 May Longchamp RF 1728a). He has always looked a real seven-furlong specialist, despite winning over a mile at two, and was victorious again over that trip at Longchamp in May. Good effort over the extended mile of the Diomed, if beaten a long way by Intikhab, and found out by rain-softened ground at Newmarket in June in what was to be his final outing. **I A Balding [5-15] George Strawbridge.*

HIDING PLACE RR 60f — 4625[12]
3 b f Saddlers' Hall (IRE) 10.5f **(65)** - Sanctuary Cove (Habitat) 9.4f **(70)**
Form - 036P55000
Record 1998 - 1st:0 2nd:0 3rd:1 Ran:9
Pre1998 - 1st:1 2nd:0 3rd:0 Ran:6
Win Prizemoney £2,595 *Total Prizemoney* £3,585
Wins 1997 Oct Leices (SFT) S 10f 60 <
1998 Turf 0-9: (10f, 12f 6, 14f, 16f) (gd 5, g-f 2, frm 2)
Scopey, average filly, effective 10 to 12f, acts on gd, likes tight tracks. Turf high 60 - 3rd of 10 getting 10lb from House of Dreams (5 Jun Catterick 12f gd RF 1741).
**W Storey [0-10] Foster Watson (from M Bell [1-5] Oct 1997).*

HIGH AND LOW BHB 112f RR 114f — 4240[2]
3 b f Rainbow Quest (USA) 11.2f **(81)** - Cruising Height (Shirley Heights) 10.3f **(74)**
Form - 1722
Record 1998 - 1st:1 2nd:2 3rd:0 Ran:4
Pre1998 - 1st:0 2nd:1 3rd:0 Ran:1
Win Prizemoney £28,235 *Total Prizemoney* £139,879
Wins * **1998** May Cheste (GD) L 11.4f 104 <
1998 Turf 1-4: (11f 1-1, 12f 2, 15f) (gd, g-f 1-2, frm)
Strong, Group-class filly. Turf high 114 - 2nd of 9 getting 3lb from Nedawi (12 Spt Doncaster 15f g-f RF 4240). Reported to be the apple of Barry Hills' eye after winning at Chester, she ran too badly to be true in the Oaks and was promptly given a lengthy break. Only caught in the shadow of the post by Nedawi in the St Leger, she enjoys front-running and does not fold once headed. She has the scope to improve again at four and should gain that first, elusive, Group win. **B W Hills [1-5] K Abdulla.*

HIGH AND MIGHTY BHB 79f RR 81f — 3822[1]
3 b g Shirley Heights 12.1f **(76)** -Air Distingue (USA) (Sir Ivor) 10.2f **(70)**
Form - 812331
Record 1998 - 1st:2 2nd:1 3rd:2 Ran:6
Pre1998 - 1st:0 2nd:0 3rd:0 Ran:2
Win Prizemoney £11,774 *Total Prizemoney* £14,283

Wins									
* **1998**	Aug	Sandow	(G-F)	H	14f	76	81	<
* **1998**	May	Cheste	(GD)	H	12.3f	66	71+	

1998 Turf 2-6: (11f, 12f 1-3, 14f 1-2) (gd, g-f 2-2, frm 3)
Neat, decent gelding, effective 11 to 14f, acts on g-f to frm, best on frm, has worn blinkers. Turf high 81 - 1st of 8 getting 8lb from Veronica Franco (22 Aug Sandown RF 3822). Stepped up greatly on his form in maidens to take a Chester handicap in May. He continued to run well after, and showed battling qualities to score over one mile six at Sandown in August.
**J H M Gosden [2-8] Sheikh Mohammed.*

HIGHBORN (IRE) BHB 71f82a RR 70f 82a — 5147[14]
9 b or br g Double Schwartz 7f **(60)** - High State (Free State) 8.7f **(61)**
Form - 70600480700000
Record 1998 - 1st:0 2nd:0 3rd:0 Ran:14
Pre1998 - 1st:13 2nd:6 3rd:7 Ran:65
Win Prizemoney £68,049 *Total Prizemoney* £89,447

Wins									
* 1997	Aug	Cheste	(G-S)	H	7f	92	100	<
* 1997	Aug	Ripon	(G-F)	H	8f	92	94	
* 1996	Oct	Newmar	(G-F)	H	7f	89	92	

* 1996	May Cheste	(GD)	H	7.6f	83	88
* 1995	Oct Redcar	(FRM)		6f		81
* 1994	Spt Yarmou	(G-F)	H	6f	75	76
* 1994	Aug Cheste	(GD)	H	7f	70	71
* 1994	*Jun Wolver*	*(STD)*	*H*	*6f*	*80*	*77*
* 1994	*Jun Wolver*	*(STD)*	*H*	*6f*	*74*	*76*

1998 Turf 0-13: (7f 3, 8f 4, 9f 3, 10f 2, 11f) (sft 3, gd 7, g-f 2, frm) 1998 AW 0-1: (8f) (Fibr)

Above-average gelding, effective 7 to 8f, acts on g-s to gd, likes tight tracks. Turf high 87. An admirable veteran, he took time to recapture his best in '97 and did not do so last year. Possibly best in a fast-run race over a mile.

**P S Felgate [13-79] Yorkshire Racing Club Owners Group 1990.*

HIGHBURY LEGEND BHB 47f45a RR 49f 45a 3744^{4}

3 ch g Mazilier (USA) 8.5f **(56)** - Jans Contessa (Rabdan) 5.9f **(53)**

Form - 8570322788278134

Record 1998 - 1st:1 2nd:3 3rd:2 Ran:12

Pre1998 - 1st:0 2nd:0 3rd:0 Ran:7

Win Prizemoney £2,595 *Total Prizemoney* £5,200

Wins 1998 Jun Pontef (GD) SH 12f 44 49 <

1998 Turf 1-7: (10f, 11f, 12f 1-5) (gd 2, g-f, frm 1-4) 1998 AW 0-5: (10f, 11f 3, 12f) (Equi, Fibr 4)

Neat, fair gelding, effective 10 to 12f, best at 12f, acts on g-f to frm, best on frm, has worn blinkers, favours tight tracks. Turf high 52 - 2nd of 14 getting 7lb from Maiella (28 May Brighton 12f frm RF 1551) - also 1st of 18 from Sharp Shooter (29 Jun Pontefract RF 2376). AW high 50.

**M C Pipe [0-3] 405200 Racing (from Bob Jones [1-17] Jun 1998).*

HIGH CARRY BHB 69f RR 70f 4858^{5}

3 b f Forzando 7.2f **(63)**-Carn Maire (Northern Prospect(USA)) 9.5f **(71)**

Form - 06000008425002025

Record 1998 - 1st:0 2nd:3 3rd:0 Ran:17

Pre1998 - 1st:2 2nd:2 3rd:1 Ran:9

Win Prizemoney £6,388 *Total Prizemoney* £14,059

Wins * 1997 Aug Sandow (G-S) H 5f 71 87 <

1997 Jly Beverl (G-F) C 5f 71

1998 Turf 0-17: (5f 14, 6f 2, 7f) (hvy, sft 2, gd 4, g-f 6, frm 4)

Scopey, above-average filly, effective 5 to 6f, best at 5f, acts on g-s to g-f, has worn blinkers, excels at Sandown. Turf high 82 - 6th of 13 to Classy Cleo (5 May Chester 5f g-f RF 1045). She ran some fine races at two, including two victories over the minimum, but took a long time to show anything in 1998. However, she dropped 22lb in the process and ran some good races in the latter part of the season.

**N Tinkler [1-23] James Marshall & Mrs Susan Marshall (from J E Banks [1-3] Jly 1997).*

HIGH CATCH BHB 49f RR 52f 4653^{15}

3 b f Belmez (USA) 11.4f **(65)** - Trapezium **(79f)** (Soviet Star (USA))

Form - 4350

Record 1998 - 1st:0 2nd:0 3rd:1 Ran:4

Win Prizemoney £0 *Total Prizemoney* £560

1998 Turf 0-4: (7f 2, 8f 2) (gd, g-f, frm, hrd)

Workmanlike, fair filly. Turf high 52 (1st run) - 4th of 12 getting 4lb from L'Estable Fleurie (5 May Brighton 7f gd RF 1038).

**J E Banks [0-4] Giles Pritchard-Gordon.*

HIGH CLARITY (IRE) BHB 50f RR 53f 4762^{8}

2 ch g Bigstone (IRE) - Classic Opera (Lomond (USA)) 8.8f **(65)**

Form - 0008

Record 1998 - 1st:0 2nd:0 3rd:0 Ran:4

1998 Turf 0-4: (6f 2, 7f, 10f) (gd 4)

Fair gelding, has worn blinkers. Turf high 53.

**R F JohnsonHoughton [0-4] C W Sumner.*

HIGH DEMAND RR 57f 2361^{7}

3 b f Sabrehill (USA) 8.5f **(64)** - Tithing (USA) (Nureyev (USA)) 8.7f **(78)**

Form - 207

Record 1998 - 1st:0 2nd:1 3rd:0 Ran:3

1998 Turf 0-3: (8f 2, 12f) (gd 2, g-f)

Currently fair filly. Turf high 57. **B W Hills [0-3] W J Gredley.*

HIGH DOMAIN (IRE) BHB 39f66a RR 43f 66a 4200^{8}

7 b g Dominion Royale 7.8f **(63)** - Recline (Wollow) 8.2f **(61)**

Form - 03700608

Record 1998 - 1st:0 2nd:0 3rd:1 Ran:8

Pre1998 - 1st:5 2nd:1 3rd:4 Ran:46

Win Prizemoney £19,756 *Total Prizemoney* £25,026

Wins * 1996 Nov Doncas (SFT) H 5f 64 65

* 1996 Jun Haydoc (GD) H 6f 64 69

* 1996 May Salisb (SFT) H 5f 58 64

1998 Turf 0-8: (5f 8) (gd 2, g-f 2, frm 4)

Fair gelding, effective 5f, acts on frm, has worn blinkers. Turf high 43.

**J L Spearing [3-30] Stephen Borsberry (from T D Barron [0-12] Spt 1995).*

HIGHEST ACCOLADE RR 64f 4394^{5}

3 b f Shirley Heights 12.1f **(76)** - Victoress (USA) (Conquistador Cielo (USA)) 8.8f **(69)**

Form - 45

Record 1998 - 1st:0 2nd:0 3rd:0 Ran:2

Win Prizemoney £0 *Total Prizemoney* £277

1998 Turf 0-2: (10f, 12f) (g-f, frm)

Tall, currently average filly. Turf high 64 (began Spt).

**J H M Gosden [0-2] Sheikh Mohammed.*

HIGH ESTEEM BHB 56f RR 58f 4699^{15}

2 b c Common Grounds 8.1f **(66)** - Whittle Woods Girl **(74f 60a)** (Emarati (USA))

Form - 060

Record 1998 - 1st:0 2nd:0 3rd:0 Ran:3

1998 Turf 0-3: (5f, 6f 2) (gd 2, frm)

Currently fair colt. Turf high 58. **M A Buckley [0-3] C C Buckley.*

HIGHEST HIGH RR 99f $1554a^{6}$

4 c

Form - 6

1998 Turf 0-1: (9f) (gd)

Currently very useful colt. **Mme C Head in FR [0-1].*

HIGHEST PEAK (USA) RR 81f 4999^{1}

2 ch c Mt Livermore (USA) 7.7f **(90)** - Disconiz (USA) (Northern Dancer) 9.6f **(80)**

Form - 41

Record 1998 - 1st:1 2nd:0 3rd:0 Ran:2

Win Prizemoney £3,492 *Total Prizemoney* £3,711

Wins * **1998** Oct Lingfi (HVY) 7f 81 <

1998 Turf 1-2: (7f 1-2) (sft 1-1, gd)

Currently decent colt. Turf high 81 (began Oct) - 1st of 9 from Whitewater Boy (26 Oct Lingfield RF 4999).

**Sir Michael Stoute [1-2] Maktoum Al Maktoum.*

HIGH FASHION RR 4856^{16}

2 b f Puissance 7.1f **(60)** - Superb Fashion (USA) (Topsider (USA)) 8.3f **(71)**

Form - 0

Record 1998 - 1st:0 2nd:0 3rd:0 Ran:1

1998 Turf 0-1: (7f) (sft)

Currently very poor filly. **J S Haldane [0-1] G J Johnston.*

HIGHFIELDER (IRE) BHB 61f RR 69f 4650^{7}

2 br c Unblest - River Low (IRE) (Lafontaine (USA)) 8.7f **(62)**

Form - 707

Record 1998 - 1st:0 2nd:0 3rd:0 Ran:3

1998 Turf 0-3: (6f 2, 8f) (gd, g-f 2)

Currently average colt. Turf high 69 (began Aug).

**J S Moore [0-3] Mrs Angela Speyer.*

HIGHFIELD FIZZ BHB 45f44a RR 53f 44a 4015^{6}

6 b m Efisio 7.7f **(69)** - Jendor (Condorcet (FR)) 12.3f **(62)**

Form - 05170221367356

Record 1998 - 1st:2 2nd:2 3rd:2 Ran:14

Pre1998 - 1st:2 2nd:7 3rd:5 Ran:38

Win Prizemoney £13,795 *Total Prizemoney* £26,730

Wins * **1998** Jun Mussel (G-F) H 16f 50 53

* **1998** Apr Pontef (G-S) H 17.1f 45 50

* 1996 Oct Redcar (G-F) H 14.1f 36 44

* 1995 Spt Redcar (GD) S 11f 57 <

1998 Turf 2-14: (14f 2, 16f 1-9, 17f 1-1, 18f, 22f) (g-s 1-4, gd 5, g-f, frm 1-3, hrd)

Fair mare, effective 14 to 18f, acts on g-s to frm, does well at

Musselburgh and excels at Pontefract. Turf high 53 - 1st of 6 getting 25lb from Star Rage (22 Jun Musselburgh RF 2169) - also 1st of 5 getting 30lb from Jamaican Flight (21 Apr Pontefract RF 0790). Has ability, but has finished runner-up more times than is probably desirable. However, she won over the extended seventeen furlongs at Pontefract in April, when the test of stamina compensated for her lack of pace, and her attitude could not be faulted when she won at Musselburgh in June.

**C W Fairhurst [4-52] Mrs P J Taylor-Garthwaite.*

HIGH GAIN BHB 39f60a **RR 33f 60a** 4504[17]

3 b f Puissance 7.1f **(60)** - Femme Formidable (Formidable (USA)) 9.2f **(63)**

Form - 05080080

Record 1998 - 1st:0 2nd:0 3rd:0 Ran:8
Pre1998 - 1st:1 2nd:1 3rd:3 Ran:8

Win Prizemoney £2,277 *Total Prizemoney* £5,680

Wins * 1997 Jly Bright (FRM) 5.3f 72 <

1998 Turf 0-6:(6f 2, 7f 3, 8f)(gd 2, frm 4)1998 AW 0-2:(6f, 7f)(Equi, Fibr)

Workmanlike, moderate filly, effective 5f, acts on gd to frm, best on g-f, has worn blinkers. Turf high 33. AW high 46.

**P Howling [1-16] Red Kite Racing.*

HIGH INTRIGUE (IRE) BHB 80f **RR 84f** 2640[10]

4 b br c Shirley Heights 12.1f **(76)** - Mild Intrigue (USA) (Sir Ivor) 10.2f **(70)**

Form - 7500

Record 1998 - 1st:0 2nd:0 3rd:0 Ran:4
Pre1998 - 1st:3 2nd:0 3rd:0 Ran:6

Win Prizemoney £16,255 *Total Prizemoney* £16,505

Wins * 1997 Spt Goodwo (GD) H 16f 81 86 <
* 1997 Jly Sandow (G-F) H 14f 77 81
* 1997 Jun Cheste (HVY) 13.4f 62

1998 Turf 0-4: (12f, 16f 2, 19f) (gd 2, g-f, frm)

Light-framed, decent colt, effective 14 to 19f, best at 16f, acts on gd to frm, best on gd, has worn blinkers. Turf high 84 - 5th of 11 giving 1lb to Premier Night (23 May Kempton 16f gd RF 1427). His form last season was modest at best, and it seems likely that he will end up in another stable before long, possibly with a view to hurdling. **H R A Cecil [3-10] Lordship Stud.*

HIGH JINKS BHB 62f **RR 61f** 2729[1]

3 b g High Estate 10.5f **(66)** - Waffling (Lomond (USA)) 8.8f **(65)**

Form - 81

Record 1998 - 1st:1 2nd:0 3rd:0 Ran:2
Pre1998 - 1st:0 2nd:0 3rd:0 Ran:3

Win Prizemoney £2,950 *Total Prizemoney* £2,950

Wins * **1998** Jly Warwic (G-F) H 14.9f 60 61 <

1998 Turf 1-2: (10f, 15f 1-1) (gd, frm 1-1)

Scopey, average gelding. Turf high 61 - 1st of 8 giving 10lb to Tereyna (11 Jly Warwick RF 2729).

**B Preece [1-2] Mrs E Sharp (from B Smart [0-3] Oct 1997).*

HIGHLAND CRUMPET BHB 48f46a **RR 57f 46a** 4639[6]

2 ch f First Trump - Tarvie (Swing Easy (USA)) 6.5f **(55)**

Form - 70506

Record 1998 - 1st:0 2nd:0 3rd:0 Ran:5

1998 Turf 0-4: (5f, 6f 3) (g-s, g-f, frm 2) 1998 AW 0-1: (5f) (Fibr)

Fair filly. Turf high 57. Bred for speed, being a half-sister to Macfarlane and Stalker. Needed the experience on her debut.

**M J Fetherston-Godley [0-5] P Fetherston-Godley.*

HIGHLAND FLING (IRE) BHB 40a **RR 40a** 366[8]

3 b f Mtoto 11.5f **(71)** - Highland Ball (Bold Lad (IRE)) 8.4f **(68)**

Form - 048

Record 1998 - 1st:0 2nd:0 3rd:0 Ran:3

1998 AW 0-3: (9f, 10f, 11f) (Equi, Fibr 2)

Neat, currently very moderate filly. AW high 31.

**M Johnston [0-3] The Celtic Connection.*

HIGHLAND LORD BHB 33a **RR 6f 33a** 275[9]

3 b c Primo Dominie 7.2f **(67)** - Tarvie (Swing Easy (USA)) 6.5f **(55)**

Form - 770

Record 1998 - 1st:0 2nd:0 3rd:0 Ran:2
Pre1998 - 1st:0 2nd:0 3rd:0 Ran:3

1998 AW 0-2: (6f, 8f) (Equi 2)

Workmanlike, very moderate colt, has worn blinkers. AW high 7.

**M J Fetherston-Godley [0-5] P Fetherston-Godley.*

HIGHLAND TRACKER (IRE) **RR 44f** 1283[10]

3 ch g Indian Ridge 7.6f **(74)** - Track Twenty Nine (IRE) (Standaan (FR)) 7f **(55)**

Form - 0

Record 1998 - 1st:0 2nd:0 3rd:0 Ran:1

1998 Turf 0-1: (7f) (g-f)

Scopey, currently moderate gelding.

**R W Armstrong [0-1] Hugh Hart.*

HIGHLY FANCIED BHB 71f **RR 75f** 4756[4]

2 b f High Kicker (USA) 8.4f **(52)** - Angie's Darling (Milford) 9f **(61)**

Form - 320262344

Record 1998 - 1st:0 2nd:3 3rd:2 Ran:9

Win Prizemoney £0 *Total Prizemoney* £4,415

1998 Turf 0-9: (6f 7, 7f 2) (sft 2, g-s, gd 3, frm 3)

Above-average filly, effective 6 to 7f, best at 6f, acts on sft to frm. Turf high 75 - 4th of 13 giving 6lb to Red Amazon (28 Spt Hamilton 6f g-s RF 4533). **Miss L A Perratt [0-9] Mrs Anne Bell.*

HIGHLY PLEASED (USA) **RR 72f** 1323[3]

3 b c Hansel (USA) 12.6f **(78)** - Bint Alfalla (USA) (Nureyev (USA)) 8.7f **(78)**

Form - 23

Record 1998 - 1st:0 2nd:1 3rd:1 Ran:2
Pre1998 - 1st:0 2nd:0 3rd:1 Ran:2

Win Prizemoney £0 *Total Prizemoney* £1,751

1998 Turf 0-2: (7f, 8f) (g-f, frm)

Workmanlike, above-average colt. Turf high 72 - 3rd of 5 to Evander (19 May Goodwood 8f g-f RF 1323).

**E A L Dunlop [0-4] Maktoum Al Maktoum.*

HIGHLY PRIZED BHB 72f **RR 77f** 4525[8]

4 b g Shirley Heights 12.1f **(76)** - On The Tiles (Thatch (USA)) 9.8f **(62)**

Form - 238631468

Record 1998 - 1st:1 2nd:1 3rd:2 Ran:9
Pre1998 - 1st:0 2nd:1 3rd:0 Ran:5

Win Prizemoney £3,030 *Total Prizemoney* £6,838

Wins * **1998** Jly Salisb (G-F) H 14.1f 70 77 <

1998 Turf 1-9: (14f 1-6, 16f, 17f 2) (g-s 2, gd 1-3, g-f 3, frm)

Unfurnished, above-average gelding, effective 12 to 17f, best at 14f, acts on g-s to frm, prefers right handed tracks, prefers tight tracks, likes Salisbury. Turf high 77 - 1st of 11 giving 3lb to Arctic Fancy (31 Jly Salisbury RF 3243).

**J S King [1-13] Mrs Marygold O'Kelly (from I A Balding [0-5] Jun 1997).*

HIGH NOON BHB 52f47a **RR 60f 47a** 5070[9]

3 b c Shirley Heights 12.1f **(76)** - Hocus (High Top) 10.2f **(67)**

Form - 4600020

Record 1998 - 1st:0 2nd:1 3rd:0 Ran:7
Pre1998 - 1st:0 2nd:0 3rd:0 Ran:1

Win Prizemoney £0 *Total Prizemoney* £1,010

1998 Turf 0-6: (8f, 9f, 10f 2, 12f 2) (sft, gd 2, g-f 2, frm) 1998 AW 0-1: (12f) (Fibr)

Neat, average colt. Turf high 76.

**N P Littmoden [0-4] Supreme Racing Ltd (from L M Cumani [0-4] Jly 1998).*

HIGH ON LIFE BHB 38f **RR 46f** 4932[3]

4 b g Mazilier (USA) 8.5f **(56)** - Tina Rosa (Bustino) 10.4f **(64)**

Form - 0068503

Record 1998 - 1st:0 2nd:0 3rd:1 Ran:7
Pre1998 - 1st:0 2nd:3 3rd:2 Ran:8

Win Prizemoney £0 *Total Prizemoney* £3,132

1998 Turf 0-7: (11f, 12f 4, 13f, 17f) (sft, g-s, frm 5)

Scopey, moderate gelding, effective 10 to 12f, best at 12f, acts on gd to frm, best on frm, has worn blinkers. Turf high 58.

**J Akehurst [0-7] Canisbay Bloodstock Ltd (from A C Stewart [0-8] Spt 1997).*

HIGH POLICY (IRE) **RR 60f** 4959[10]

2 ch c Machiavellian (USA) 9.8f **(83)** - Road To The Top (Shirley Heights) 10.3f **(74)**

Form - 0

Record 1998 - 1st:0 2nd:0 3rd:0 Ran:1

1998 Turf 0-1: (7f) (frm)

Currently average colt. **Sir Michael Stoute [0-1] Lord Weinstock.*

HIGH PREMIUM BHB 61f67a **RR 67f 67a** 5147^{7}

10 b g Forzando 7.2f **(63)** - High Halo (High Top) 10.2f **(67)**
Form - 0105124136607

Record	**1998** -	1st:3	2nd:1	3rd:1	Ran:13
	Pre1998 -	1st:13	2nd:9	3rd:7	Ran:56

Win Prizemoney £110,392 *Total Prizemoney* £157,396

Wins									
	* **1998**	Jly	Carlis	(G-F)	C	6.9f		64	
	* **1998**	Jun	Leices	(GD)	C	8f		66	
	* **1998**	Apr	Carlis	(G-S)	C	6.9f		72	
	* 1997	May	Beverl	(GD)	H	8.5f	79	84	
	* 1997	Apr	Carlis	(GD)	C	6.9f		82	
	* 1997	Apr	Hamilt	(SFT)	C	9.2f		66	
	* 1996	Oct	Ascot	(GD)	H	8f	73	76	
	* 1996	Spt	Haydoc	(GD)	H	8.1f	68	74	
	* 1996	*Jun*	*Wolver*	*(STD)*	*C*	*7f*		*82*	
	* 1996	*Mar*	*Wolver*	*(STD)*	*H*	*7f*	*73*	*75*	
	* 1996	*Mar*	*Southw*	*(STD)*	*H*	*8f*	*69*	*71*	
	* 1995	Spt	Ayr	(GD)	C	8f		76	

1998 Turf 3-12: (7f 2-2, 8f 1-8, 9f 2) (sft, gd 1-7, frm 2-4) 1998 AW 0-1: (8f) (Fibr)
Average gelding, effective 7 to 9f, best at 8f, acts on gd to frm, best on gd, has worn blinkers, likes right handed tracks, excels at Beverley and Carlisle. Turf high 74. Reported to have been retired.
**R A Fahey [12-48] J C Parsons (from Mrs J R Ramsden [4-21] Jly 1993).*

HIGH PRIORITY (IRE) BHB 70f **RR 27f** 2390^{11}

5 b h Marju (IRE) 9.2f **(76)** - Blinding (IRE) (High Top) 10.2f **(67)**
Form - 0

Record	**1998** -	1st:0	2nd:0	3rd:0	Ran:1
	Pre1998 -	1st:1	2nd:2	3rd:1	Ran:12

Win Prizemoney £4,198 *Total Prizemoney* £13,254

Wins								
	1995	Jun	Bath	(G-F)	5.1f		77	<

1998 Turf 0-1: (6f) (frm)
Little account colt. Becoming disappointing.
**J J Sheehan [0-1] Mrs Eileen Sheehan (from M J Haynes [0-1] Oct 1997).*

HIGH REGARD (JPN) BHB 75f **RR 75f** 4070^{7}

2 b c Nashwan (USA) 10.3f **(79)** - Hebba (USA) (Nureyev (USA)) 8.7f **(78)**
Form - 23267

Record	**1998** -	1st:0	2nd:2	3rd:1	Ran:5

Win Prizemoney £0 *Total Prizemoney* £2,805
1998 Turf 0-5: (7f 3, 8f 2) (gd, g-f 3, frm)
Above-average colt. Turf high 75 - 6th of 12 getting 6lb from Pilot's Harbour (28 Aug Newmarket 8f frm RF 3932). Has ability, and got no sort of run in a nursery at Newmarket in August.
**D R Loder [0-5] Sheikh Mohammed.*

HIGH-RISE (IRE) BHB 127f **RR 126f** $4727a^{7}$

3 b c High Estate 10.5f **(66)** - High Tern (High Line) 10.3f **(70)**
Form - 11127

Record	**1998** -	1st:3	2nd:1	3rd:0	Ran:5
	Pre1998 -	1st:1	2nd:0	3rd:0	Ran:1

Win Prizemoney £639,160 *Total Prizemoney* £771,160

Wins								
	* **1998**	Jun	Epsom	(GD)	G1	12f	122	<
	* **1998**	May	Lingfi	(GD)	G3	11.5f	115	
	* **1998**	Apr	Pontef	(G-S)		10f	100+	
	* 1997	Nov	Doncas	(GD)		7f	83+	

1998 Turf 3-5: (10f 1-1, 11f 1-1, 12f 1-3) (sft, g-s 1-1, g-f 2-3)
Strong, top-class colt, effective 12f, acts on sft to g-f, best on g-f. Turf high 126 - 2nd of 8 getting 12lb from Swain (25 Jly Ascot 12f g-f RF 3103) - also 1st of 15 from City Honours (6 Jun Epsom RF 1778). Luca Cumani was preparing his Derby winner High-Rise for a crack at the Breeders' Cup Turf when word came through that the colt had joined the Godolphin operation and would be sent straight to Dubai, with the World Cup his target. He was by no means an outstanding Derby winner, but he should do well in the highest grade at four. A maiden winner at Doncaster on his only outing at two, he bolted up in a Pontefract limited stakes on his reappearance, and left that form well behind with a battling victory in the Lingfield Derby Trial, though it has to be said that at the time it did not look Derby-winning form. However, he was the one who produced the goods on the big day, showing a smart turn of foot and great courage to beat City Honours by a head to land the Blue Riband. With some of the leading players not running their races and others suffering injuries, the form was nothing special, but he confirmed himself a top-class colt when runner-up to Swain in the King George, having had an interrupted passage in the straight. Beaten just over three lengths into seventh in the Arc on his final start, again meeting trouble in running.
**L M Cumani [4-6] Sheikh Mohamed Obaid Al Maktoum.*

HIGH SHOT BHB 69f **RR 68f** 3241^{7}

8 b g Darshaan 11.9f **(81)** - Nollet (High Top) 10.2f **(67)**
Form - 5027

Record	**1998** -	1st:0	2nd:1	3rd:0	Ran:4
	Pre1998 -	1st:0	2nd:0	3rd:1	Ran:3

Win Prizemoney £0 *Total Prizemoney* £2,094
1998 Turf 0-4: (10f 4) (gd, g-f, frm 2)
Average gelding. Turf high 68 - 2nd of 17 giving 17lb to Grinkov (20 Jly Windsor 10f frm RF 2962).
**R Rowe [0-4] The Tuesday Syndicate (from G Lewis [0-3] Apr 1997).*

HIGHSPEED (IRE) BHB 33f **RR 43f** 4416^{9}

6 ch g Double Schwartz 7f **(60)** - High State (Free State) 8.7f **(61)**
Form - 750870

Record	**1998** -	1st:0	2nd:0	3rd:0	Ran:6
	Pre1998 -	1st:3	2nd:1	3rd:1	Ran:17

Win Prizemoney £9,204 *Total Prizemoney* £11,093

Wins									
	1996	May	Ayr	(GD)	H	8f	52	57	
	1996	May	Ayr	(G-S)	H	7f	49	58	<
	1995	Aug	Ayr	(FRM)		7f		51	

1998 Turf 0-6: (7f, 8f 3, 11f, 12f) (g-s, gd 2, frm 2, hrd)
Moderate gelding, effective 8f, acts on frm, has worn blinkers. Turf high 43.
**P S Felgate [0-6] David Wright (from S E Kettlewell [3-17] Aug 1997).*

HIGH SPIRITS (IRE) BHB 87f **RR 90f** 4700^{3}

4 b g Great Commotion (USA) 9.2f **(80)** - Spoilt Again (Mummy's Pet) 7.7f **(60)**
Form - 31350216603

Record	**1998** -	1st:2	2nd:1	3rd:3	Ran:11
	Pre1998 -	1st:5	2nd:1	3rd:3	Ran:19

Win Prizemoney £41,099 *Total Prizemoney* £51,055

Wins									
	* **1998**	Aug	Thirsk	(GD)	H	8f	83	90	<
	* **1998**	May	Thirsk	(GD)	H	8f	77	88	
	* 1997	Aug	Ripon	(G-F)	H	9f	69	75	
	* 1997	Aug	Newcas	(G-F)	H	8f	63	70	
	* 1997	Jly	Beverl	(G-F)	H	8.5f	59	65	
	* 1997	Jun	Mussel	(G-S)	H	7.1f	54	65	
	* 1997	Jun	Catter	(GD)		7f		55	

1998 Turf 2-11: (8f 2-9, 10f 2) (sft, g-s, gd 1-3, g-f 1-3, frm 2, hrd)
Scopey, useful gelding, effective 8 to 10f, best at 8f, acts on gd to hrd, best on g-f, mostly wears blinkers (extremely effectively), likes right handed tracks, likes tight tracks, excels at York and Beverley, likes Thirsk. Turf high 90 - 1st of 10 getting 4lb from Celestial Key (1 Aug Thirsk RF 3283) - also 1st of 18 getting 1lb from Refuse To Lose (2 May Thirsk RF 0981). After a promising reappearance effort, he showed very mixed form last term, and both of his wins came over the Thirsk mile. Goes well off a fast pace. **T D Easterby [7-30] Mrs J B Mountifield.*

HIGH STAKES **RR 92f** $4794a^{5}$

2 b c Bluebird (USA) 7.9f **(71)** - Abet (USA) (Alleged (USA)) 10f **(76)**
Form - 8342365
1998 Turf 0-7: (6f 3, 7f 3, 8f) (hvy, sft, g-s 2, gd 2, g-f)
Useful colt, effective 6 to 7f, acts on g-s to gd, often wears blinkers (extremely effectively). Turf high 92 - 6th of 7 to Immovable Option (3 Oct Curragh 6f g-s RF 4686a).
**C O'Brien in IRE [0-7] John McManus.*

HIGH SUN BHB 60f **RR 66f** 5039^{14}

2 b c High Estate 10.5f **(66)** - Clyde Goddess (IRE) **(69df)** (Scottish Reel) 7f **(61)**
Form - 550

Record	**1998** -	1st:0	2nd:0	3rd:0	Ran:3

1998 Turf 0-3: (8f 2, 10f) (sft, g-s, gd)
Currently average colt. Turf high 66 (began Oct).
**S Gollings [0-3] R L Houlton.*

High-Rise - minutes away from his place in history

HIGH TATRA (IRE) BHB 60f **RR 51f** 4336[9]
2 b c Polish Patriot (USA) 7.8f **(70)** - Bouffant (High Top) 10.2f **(67)**
Form - 000
Record 1998 - 1st:0 2nd:0 3rd:0 Ran:3
1998 Turf 0-3: (7f, 8f 2) (g-f 2, frm)
Currently fair colt. Turf high 51 (began Aug).
**S P C Woods [0-3] Rex Norton.*

HIGH TENSION (USA) RR 82f 3698[11]
3 b c Sadler's Wells (USA) 11.3f **(87)** - Very Confidential (USA) (Fappiano (USA)) 8.7f **(77)**
Form - 0210
Record 1998 - 1st:1 2nd:1 3rd:0 Ran:4
Pre1998 - 1st:0 2nd:0 3rd:1 Ran:2
Win Prizemoney £4,012 *Total Prizemoney* £5,866
Wins * **1998** May Nottin (FRM) H 14.1f 75 71+ <
1998 Turf 1-4: (8f, 12f, 14f 1-2) (gd, g-f, frm 1-2)
Scopey, decent colt, effective 12f, acts on frm. Turf high 82 - 2nd of 13 giving 3lb to Masamadas (18 May Windsor 12f frm RF 1314). He got off the mark on fast ground at Nottingham when stepped up to a staying trip, but was well beaten in a warm race at York.
**P F I Cole [1-6] H R H Prince Fahd Salman.*

HIGHWAY BHB 43f **RR 47f** 3887[10]
4 gr g Salse (USA) 10.9f **(71)** - Ivory Lane (USA) (Sir Ivor) 10.2f **(70)**
Form - 78570
Record 1998 - 1st:0 2nd:0 3rd:0 Ran:5
Pre1998 - 1st:0 2nd:0 3rd:0 Ran:2
Win Prizemoney £0 *Total Prizemoney* £265
1998 Turf 0-5: (8f, 9f, 11f, 15f, 17f) (sft, gd 4)
Light-framed, moderate gelding. Turf high 47.
**C W Thornton [0-5] Guy Reed (from B W Hills [0-2] Spt 1996).*

HIGHWAYMAN (IRE) RR 84f 4497[3]
3 b g Danehill (USA) 9.1f **(79)** - Millerette (Mill Reef (USA)) 10.5f **(78)**
Form - 5743123
Record 1998 - 1st:1 2nd:1 3rd:2 Ran:7
Pre1998 - 1st:0 2nd:0 3rd:1 Ran:3
Win Prizemoney £5,434 *Total Prizemoney* £11,124
Wins * **1998** Aug Sandow (G-F) H 14f 77 78 <
1998 Turf 1-7: (10f 3, 14f 1-2, 15f, 16f) (gd 5, frm 1-2)
Scopey, decent gelding, effective 8 to 16f, acts on gd to frm, best on frm. Turf high 84 - 3rd of 17 getting 3lb from Spunkie (26 Spt Ascot 16f gd RF 4497) - also 1st of 8 getting 16lb from Renzo (12 Aug Sandown RF 3595). Consistent. He seems to be getting better as he goes up in trip, and duly got off the mark over fourteen furlongs at Sandown in August. Possibly a nice little staying handicapper in the making; someone seems to think so as he was sold for 78,000 guineas in October to race for Dermot Weld.
**Sir Michael Stoute [1-10] Highclere Thoroughbred Racing Ltd.*

HI-JENNY (IRE) BHB 46f **RR 53f** 4623[9]
2 b f High Estate 10.5f **(66)** -Dream of Jenny (Caerleon (USA)) 8.6f **(71)**
Form - 6337560
Record 1998 - 1st:0 2nd:0 3rd:2 Ran:7
Win Prizemoney £0 *Total Prizemoney* £473

1998 Turf 0-5: (5f, 6f, 7f 3) (gd, g-f 2, frm 2) 1998 AW 0-2: (6f 2) (Fibr 2)
Fair filly, has worn blinkers. Turf high 53. AW high 54.
**W Storey [0-1] Tony Stafford (from W G M Turner [0-6] Spt 1998).*

HILL FARM BLUES BHB 54f55a **RR 56f 55a** 5118[8]

5 b m Mon Tresor 7.9f **(60)** - Loadplan Lass (Nicholas Bill) 10.1f **(56)**
Form - 6018

Record	**1998** -	1st:1	2nd:0	3rd:0	Ran:4
	Pre1998 -	1st:2	2nd:2	3rd:0	Ran:15

Win Prizemoney £9,605 *Total Prizemoney* £12,199

Wins								
	* **1998**	Oct	Nottin	(SFT)	H	16f	51	56
	* 1997	Jly	Bath	(GD)	H	10.2f	58	63 <
	* 1997	May	Nottin	(GD)	SH	10f	49	57

1998 Turf 1-4: (12f, 16f 1-3) (g-s, gd 1-3)
Fair filly, effective 10 to 16f, best at 10f, acts on sft to frm, prefers left handed tracks, prefers tight tracks, excels at Ayr and Nottingham. Turf high 56 (began Spt) - 1st of 8 getting 29lb from Little Acorn (14 Oct Nottingham RF 4810).
**W M Brisbourne [4-16] Dennis Newton (from J L Eyre [0-4] Spt 1996).*

HILL FARM DANCER BHB 39f57a **RR 57f 57a** 5081[8]

7 ch m Gunner B 11.2f **(45)** - Loadplan Lass (Nicholas Bill) 10.1f **(56)**
Form - 25201274506088

Record	**1998** -	1st:1	2nd:3	3rd:0	Ran:14
	Pre1998 -	1st:8	2nd:5	3rd:9	Ran:49

Win Prizemoney £25,566 *Total Prizemoney* £39,539

Wins								
	* **1998**	Jly	Mussel	(GD)	H	12f	45	49
	* 1997	*Jan*	*Wolver*	*(STD)*	*H*	*12f*	*68*	*76* <
	* 1996	*Nov*	*Wolver*	*(STD)*		*12f*		*70*
	* 1996	*Nov*	*Wolver*	*(STD)*	*H*	*12f*	*53*	*62*
	* 1996	*Mar*	*Wolver*	*(STD)*	*C*	*12f*		*57*
	* 1996	*Feb*	*Wolver*	*(STD)*	*H*	*12f*	*47*	*53*
	* 1995	May	Bath	(GD)	H	11.7f	50	
	* 1994	*Jun*	*Wolver*	*(STD)*	*H*	*12f*	*48*	*44*
	* 1994	May	Carlis	(FRM)	C	12f		52

1998 Turf 1-11: (11f, 12f 1-8, 13f, 14f) (g-s 2, gd 2, g-f, frm 1-6) 1998 AW 0-3: (9f, 12f 2) (Fibr 3)
Fair mare, effective 9 to 12f, best at 12f - acts on Fibr. Turf high 57. AW high 49 (began Aug). Quite useful over middle distances on Fibresand on her day, though she did manage to win on turf at Musselburgh in July, after which she seemed to lose her form on both turf and sand. Usually held up.
**W M Brisbourne [9-60] M E Hughes (from P D Evans [0-3] Jly 1993).*

HILLINSKI (IRE) BHB 41f **RR 29f** 3883[14]

4 b c Danehill (USA) 9.1f **(79)** - Llangollen (IRE) (Caerleon (USA)) 8.6f **(71)**
Form - 070000

Record	**1998** -	1st:0	2nd:0	3rd:0	Ran:6

1998 Turf 0-6: (5f, 6f, 7f 3, 12f) (gd 4, g-f, frm)
Little account colt, has worn blinkers. Turf high 34.
**M Mullineaux [0-6] Birch Vale Racing.*

HILL MAGIC BHB 92f **RR 94f** 2919[9]

3 br c Magic Ring (IRE) 6.5f **(64)** -Stock Hill Lass (Air Trooper) 9.1f **(63)**
Form - 521U060

Record	**1998** -	1st:1	2nd:1	3rd:0	Ran:7
	Pre1998 -	1st:1	2nd:1	3rd:1	Ran:7

Win Prizemoney £39,992 *Total Prizemoney* £49,797

Wins								
	* **1998**	May	Lingfi	(GD)	H	6f	89	94 <
	* 1997	Jly	Bath	(GD)		5.7f		77

1998 Turf 1-7: (6f 1-6, 8f) (hvy, gd 2, g-f 1-2, frm 2)
Scopey, useful colt, effective 6f, acts on gd to g-f. Turf high 94 - 1st of 20 giving 3lb to Nuclear Debate (9 May Lingfield RF 1123). Inconsistent. Ran a blinder in a competitive Newmarket handicap on his second start this season, only being caught in the final few strides, before beating a big field at Lingfield under a good ride from Neil Pollard. He did not manage to make the frame again during the season, and unshipped Pollard at Newmarket when the saddle slipped.
**D R C Elsworth [2-14] Michael Jackson Bloodstock Ltd.*

HILLS GAMBLE BHB 44f36a **RR 53f 36a** 3099[10]

8 b g Remezzo - Mayleader (Gilded Leader)
Form - 4655400780

Record	**1998** -	1st:0	2nd:0	3rd:0	Ran:10

Win Prizemoney £0 *Total Prizemoney* £243

1998 Turf 0-2: (11f 2) (sft, frm) 1998 AW 0-8: (8f 3, 9f, 11f, 12f, 15f, 16f) (Fibr 8)
Fair gelding, effective 11f, acts on sft, has worn blinkers. Turf high 53 (1st run) - 4th of 10 giving 3lb to Riccarton (30 Apr Redcar 11f sft RF 0933). AW high 54. Inconsistent. **P J Bevan [0-19] John Hill.*

HILL STORM (IRE) BHB 60f **RR 64f** 4145[16]

2 b c Mukaddamah (USA) 7.6f **(74)** - Brockley Hill Lass (IRE) (Alzao (USA)) 7.1f **(68)**
Form - 0760

Record	**1998** -	1st:0	2nd:0	3rd:0	Ran:4

1998 Turf 0-4: (6f 3, 7f) (g-f 3, frm)
Average colt. Turf high 64. **K McAuliffe [0-4] E D Kessly.*

HILLSWICK BHB 37f **RR 43f** 1567[2]

7 ch g Norwick (USA) 9.4f **(51)**-Quite Lucky (Precipice Wood) 17.2f **(38)**
Form - 2

Record	**1998** -	1st:0	2nd:1	3rd:0	Ran:1
	Pre1998 -	1st:1	2nd:2	3rd:1	Ran:18

Win Prizemoney £3,533 *Total Prizemoney* £7,180

Wins								
	* 1997	Aug	Bath	(GD)	H	17.2f	37	40 <

1998 Turf 0-1: (17f) (frm)
Moderate gelding, effective 15 to 17f, best at 16f, acts on gd to frm, excels at Bath. (1st run) - 2nd of 9 getting 17lb from Tasik Chini (29 May Bath 17f frm RF 1567). Consistent.
**J S King [3-27] M G A Court.*

HILLZAH (USA) BHB 47f47a **RR 50f 47a** 4938[4]

10 ch g Blushing Groom (FR) 10.2f **(80)** - Glamour Girl (ARG) (Mysolo) 11.9f **(95)**
Form - 70715034054

Record	**1998** -	1st:1	2nd:0	3rd:1	Ran:9
	Pre1998 -	1st:12	2nd:10	3rd:6	Ran:72

Win Prizemoney £49,193 *Total Prizemoney* £64,363

Wins								
	* **1998**	*Feb*	*Southw*	*(STD)*	*H*	*16f*	*50*	*55*
	* 1995	Jly	Haydoc	(G-F)	H	10.5f	75	78
	* 1995	Jun	Carlis	(GD)	H	14.1f	66	69
	* 1995	*Jan*	*Wolver*	*(STD)*	*H*	*12f*	*80*	*80*
	* 1994	Oct	Pontef	(G-S)	H	10f	62	66
	* 1994	*Jan*	*Wolver*	*(STD)*	*H*	*12f*	*73*	*79*
	* 1994	*Jan*	*Southw*	*(STD)*	*H*	*11f*	*63*	*72*
	* 1994	*Jan*	*Wolver*	*(STD)*		*12f*		*70+*

1998 Turf 0-5: (14f 3, 16f, 22f) (g-s 2, gd 2, g-f) 1998 AW 1-4: (16f 1-4) (Fibr 1-4)
Fair gelding, effective 16f - acts on Fibr, has worn blinkers. Turf high 50. AW high 55 - also 1st of 10 giving 4lb to Notation (20 Feb Southwell RF 0322). He had been out of form for quite a while before causing a real shock when landing a staying handicap on the Southwell Fibresand in February.
**R Bastiman [11-69] Robin Bastiman (from P T Walwyn [2-12] Oct 1991).*

HIL RHAPSODY BHB 40f49a **RR 40f 49a** 5128[7]

4 ch f Anshan 8.2f **(63)** - Heavenly Note (Chief Singer) 8.9f **(66)**
Form - 000045304087

Record	**1998** -	1st:0	2nd:0	3rd:1	Ran:12
	Pre1998 -	1st:1	2nd:0	3rd:2	Ran:9

Win Prizemoney £2,880 *Total Prizemoney* £5,372

Wins								
	* 1996	Apr	Leices	(GD)		5f		69+ <

1998 Turf 0-11: (5f 4, 6f 6, 7f) (sft, g-s, gd 3, g-f, frm 5) 1998 AW 0-1: (7f) (Fibr)
Leggy, moderate filly, effective 5f, acts on frm. Turf high 46 - 5th of 5 giving 1lb to Odette (18 Jly Warwick 5f frm RF 2945). Consistent.
**B Palling [1-21] Mrs B J Harkins.*

HILTONS EXECUTIVE (IRE) BHB 50f45a **RR 51f 45a** 4921[7]

4 b f Petorius 8f **(66)** - Theatral (Orchestra) 9.7f **(52)**
Form - 33221501225007

Record	**1998** -	1st:2	2nd:4	3rd:2	Ran:14
	Pre1998 -	1st:0	2nd:1	3rd:2	Ran:14

Win Prizemoney £5,456 *Total Prizemoney* £11,289

Wins								
	* **1998**	May	Ayr	(G-F)	H	5f	41	47 <
	* **1998**	*Apr*	*Wolver*	*(STD)*	*H*	*5f*	*40*	*42*

1998 Turf 1-9: (5f 1-9) (g-s 2, gd 3, g-f 1-3, frm) 1998 AW 1-5: (5f 1-5) (Fibr 1-5)
Leggy, fair filly, effective 5f, acts on gd to g-f - acts on Fibr, best on g-f. Turf high 51 - 2nd of 11 getting 16lb from Storyteller (3 Jly Haydock 5f g-f RF 2502) - also 1st of 13 getting 15lb from Storyteller (28 May Ayr RF 1543). AW high 42 - 1st of 10 getting

17lb from Aljaz (7 Apr Wolverhampton RF 0597).
**E J Alston [2-28] Derek Hilton.*

HIMALAYAN LILY RR
497[8]
4 ch f Handsome Sailor 6.6f **(53)** - Indian Flower (Mansingh (USA)) 7.4f **(55)**
Form - 88
Record 1998 - 1st:0 2nd:0 3rd:0 Ran:2
1998 AW 0-2: (5f, 8f) (Fibr 2)
Currently very poor filly. **J A Pickering [0-2] George Patching.*

HIMSELF (USA) RR 95f
4241[1]
3 b c El Gran Senor (USA) 8.9f **(85)** - Celtic Loot (USA) (Irish River (FR)) 8.6f **(78)**
Form - 66811
Record 1998 - 1st:2 2nd:0 3rd:0 Ran:5
Pre1998 - 1st:1 2nd:0 3rd:0 Ran:1
Win Prizemoney £35,371 *Total Prizemoney* £35,494
Wins * **1998** Spt Doncas (GD) H 10.3f 91 95 <
* **1998** Aug Newcas (GD) H 10.1f 87 90
* 1997 Oct Leices (GD) 8f 81+
1998 Turf 2-5: (8f, 9f, 10f 2-3) (gd, g-f 2-3, frm)
Scopey, very useful colt, effective 10f, acts on g-f. Turf high 95 - 1st of 20 giving 14lb to Shinerolla (12 Spt Doncaster RF 4241) - also 1st of 10 giving 7lb to Captain's Log (2 Aug Newcastle RF 3292). Made quite an impression when winning on his Leicester debut at two, but was disappointing in his first three starts of last season until narrowly winning a Newcastle handicap in August. Awarded a valuable prize at the St Leger meeting the following month, he is not an easy ride and needs a strong jockey.
**H R A Cecil [3-6] Scrope, Scott Partners.*

HI MUJTAHID (IRE) BHB 30f35a RR 27f 35a
4804[15]
4 ch g Mujtahid (USA) 7.4f **(69)** - High Tern (High Line) 10.3f **(70)**
Form - 70000000000
Record 1998 - 1st:0 2nd:0 3rd:0 Ran:11
Pre1998 - 1st:1 2nd:4 3rd:2 Ran:14
Win Prizemoney £2,883 *Total Prizemoney* £7,508
Wins 1997 Jly Ayr (G-F) H 7f 44 50 <
1998 Turf 0-9: (5f, 6f 2, 7f 2, 8f 2, 10f 2) (g-s, gd 5, g-f 3) 1998 AW 0-2: (6f, 8f) (Fibr 2)
Workmanlike, moderate gelding, effective 6 to 7f, best at 7f, acts on gd to frm, best on g-f, has worn blinkers (extremely effectively), likes tight tracks, excels at Ayr. Turf high 37. AW high 40. Showed very little in 1998, but earned some reflected glory as a half-brother to High Rise.
**Mrs H L Walton [0-3] A E Walton (from S E Kettlewell [1-19] Jun 1998).*

HI NICKY RR 60f
1264[1]
2 ch f High Kicker (USA) 8.4f **(52)** - Sharp Top (Sharpo) 7.7f **(59)**
Form - 1
Record 1998 - 1st:1 2nd:0 3rd:0 Ran:1
Win Prizemoney £4,503 *Total Prizemoney* £4,503
Wins * **1998** May Newmar (G-F) 6f 60 <
1998 Turf 1-1: (6f 1-1) (frm 1-1)
Currently average filly. (1st run) - 1st of 7 from Leave It To Me (16 May Newmarket RF 1264). **M J Ryan [1-1] D Bell.*

HI NOD BHB 75f RR 69?f
4052[15]
8 b h Valiyar 9.6f **(54)** - Vikris (Viking (USA)) 6.7f **(65)**
Form - 0700
Record 1998 - 1st:0 2nd:0 3rd:0 Ran:4
Pre1998 - 1st:13 2nd:9 3rd:4 Ran:51
Win Prizemoney £88,663 *Total Prizemoney* £125,491
Wins 1997 Aug Cheste (G-F) 7f 95
1996 May Doncas (GD) H 7f 96 99 <
1995 Oct York (G-F) H 7f 93 96
1995 Jly Newcas (G-F) H 7f 85 88
1995 Jun Ayr (FRM) H 7f 76 78
1994 May Thirsk (FRM) H 7f 84 87
1998 Turf 0-4: (7f, 8f 2, 9f) (g-f, frm 3)
Average horse, effective 7 to 8f, acts on g-f. Turf high 69. Inconsistent. An admirable veteran, he lost his form in '98 and has reportedly been retired.
**Miss J A Camacho [0-4] Brian Nordan (from M J Camacho [13-51] Oct 1997).*

HIPPIOS BHB 26f31a RR 38f 31a
3638[6]
4 b br g Formidable (USA) 7.8f **(60)** - Miss Doody (Gorytus (USA)) 7.8f **(60)**
Form - 3375086
Record 1998 - 1st:0 2nd:0 3rd:0 Ran:2
Pre1998 - 1st:0 2nd:0 3rd:2 Ran:16
Win Prizemoney £0 *Total Prizemoney* £530
1998 AW 0-2: (14f, 16f) (Fibr 2)
Strong, very moderate gelding, effective 15f - acts on Fibr, has worn blinkers. AW high 28 (began Jly). Consistent.
**S Dow [0-18] S Dow.*

HIRO DE CROSS (JPN) RR 109f
2104a[3]
6 h Tamamo Cross (JPN) - Sunset Girl (JPN) (Par Elite (JPN))
Form - 3
1998 Turf 0-1: (8f) (hvy)
Currently Pattern-class horse. He finished third to the top Japanese miler Taiki Shuttle in June and is obviously very useful.
**Y Okubo in JPN [0-1] A Ohara.*

HI RUDOLF RR 1f
4644[18]
3 b g Ballet Royal (USA) - Hi Darlin' (Prince de Galles)
Form - 0
Record 1998 - 1st:0 2nd:0 3rd:0 Ran:1
Pre1998 - 1st:0 2nd:0 3rd:0 Ran:1
1998 Turf 0-1: (8f) (g-f)
Unfurnished, currently very poor gelding.
**H J Manners [0-1] H J Manners (from A J Chamberlain [0-1] Jly 1997).*

HISHMAH BHB 84f RR 84?f
3943[2]
2 b f Nashwan (USA) 10.3f **(79)** - Na-Ayim (IRE) (Shirley Heights) 10.3f **(74)**
Form - 462
Record 1998 - 1st:0 2nd:1 3rd:0 Ran:3
Win Prizemoney £0 *Total Prizemoney* £1,397
1998 Turf 0-3: (6f, 7f 2) (g-s, g-f, frm)
Currently decent filly. Turf high 84 (1st run) - 4th of 10 getting 5lb from Agreeable (30 May Newmarket 6f g-f RF 1609).
**E A L Dunlop [0-3] Hamdan Al Maktoum.*

HITMAN (IRE) BHB 110f RR 112f
3697[6]
3 b c Contract Law (USA) 8.9f **(54)** - Loveville (USA) (Assert) 10.6f **(85)**
Form - 251136
Record 1998 - 1st:2 2nd:1 3rd:1 Ran:6
Win Prizemoney £22,987 *Total Prizemoney* £29,217
Wins * **1998** Jly Newmar (G-F) H 10f 98 102 <
* **1998** Jun Yarmou (G-F) 8f 89
1998 Turf 2-6: (8f 1-3, 10f 1-1, 12f 2) (sft, gd 2, g-f, frm 2-2)
Scopey, Group-class colt, effective 10 to 12f, acts on gd to frm. Turf high 112 - 3rd of 6 to Nedawi (28 Jly Goodwood 12f gd RF 3162). He wore more bandages than the Invisible Man, but suspect fore-legs did not prevent him from developing into a smart performer. He bolted up in a valuable ten-furlong handicap at the July Meeting, and was only a length and three-quarters behind the subsequent St Leger winner Nedawi at Goodwood in July. He went wrong with a tendon injury when unplaced behind the same colt in the Great Voltigeur at York the following month and faces a spell on the sidelines. In the long-term, a hurdling career beckons, under the capable handling of Mrs Pitman for this likeable individual. **H R A Cecil [2-6] The Paper Boys.*

HIT THE BEACH BHB 84f RR 86+f
3313[3]
2 b g Turtle Island (IRE) - Malacca (USA) (Danzig (USA)) 8.4f **(76)**
Form - 013
Record 1998 - 1st:1 2nd:0 3rd:1 Ran:3
Win Prizemoney £3,215 *Total Prizemoney* £3,688
Wins * **1998** Jly Ripon (G-F) 5f 86++ <
1998 Turf 1-3: (5f 1-2, 6f) (gd 2, g-f 1-1)
Currently useful gelding. Turf high 86 - 1st of 14 from Combined Venture (18 Jly Ripon RF 2935). **M W Easterby [1-3] I Bray.*

HIT THE SPOT (IRE) BHB 70f74a RR 71f 74a
4407[14]
3 b f Night Shift (USA) 8.1f **(73)** - Winning Feature (Red Alert) 7.6f **(66)**
Form - 20622122010
Record 1998 - 1st:2 2nd:4 3rd:0 Ran:10
Pre1998 - 1st:0 2nd:1 3rd:0 Ran:3
Win Prizemoney £6,344 *Total Prizemoney* £11,434

Wins * **1998** Spt Sandow (GD) H 8.1f 65 71
* **1998** *Jly Southw (STD) H 8f 64 73+* <
1998 Turf 1-7: (7f 2, 8f 1-5) (g-s, gd 1-3, g-f, frm 2) 1998 AW 1-3: (7f, 8f 1-2) (Fibr 1-3)
Above-average filly, effective 7 to 8f, best at 8f, acts on g-s to frm - acts on Fibr, prefers tight tracks, excels at Wolverhampton. Turf high 71 - 1st of 14 getting 4lb from Kennet (15 Spt Sandown RF 4268). AW high 73 (1st run) (began Jly) - 1st of 16 giving 14lb to Miss All Alone (9 Jly Southwell RF 2654).
**W J Haggas [2-13] M Tabor & Mrs John Magnier.*

HOH CHI MIN BHB 101f **RR 94f** 5050a[2]
3 ch f Efisio 7.7f **(69)** - Special Guest (Be My Guest (USA)) 9.3f **(67)**
Form - 3556552
Record **1998** - 1st:0 2nd:1 3rd:1 Ran:7
Pre1998 - 1st:3 2nd:1 3rd:2 Ran:7
Win Prizemoney £30,902 *Total Prizemoney* £48,473
Wins * 1997 Oct San Si (GD) L 6f 96 <
* 1997 Jun Windso (G-S) 6f 80
* 1997 May Haydoc (SFT) 5f 72
1998 Turf 0-7: (6f, 7f 4, 8f 2) (sft, g-s 2, gd 2, g-f 2)

Hitman put two good races in the bag mid-season

HOBART JUNCTION (IRE) BHB 65f **RR 69f** 2562[3]
3 ch c Classic Secret (USA) 8.8f **(56)** - Art Duo (Artaius (USA)) 9f **(69)**
Form - 6452013
Record **1998** - 1st:1 2nd:1 3rd:1 Ran:7
Pre1998 - 1st:0 2nd:0 3rd:0 Ran:3
Win Prizemoney £2,248 *Total Prizemoney* £3,617
Wins * **1998** Jly Hamilt (FRM) C 9.2f 69 <
1998 Turf 1-7: (8f 2, 9f 1-2, 10f 2, 12f) (sft, gd, g-f, frm 1-4)
Scopey, average colt, effective 9 to 10f, acts on frm, has worn blinkers. Turf high 69 - 1st of 6 getting 8lb from Ten Past Six (3 Jly Hamilton RF 2495). Consistent.
**S C Williams [1-10] Tom Ford & Tony Regan.*

HOGAIF (IRE) BHB 48f **RR 70df** 4765[14]
3 ch g Persian Bold 10f **(69)** - Camarat (Ahonoora) 8.1f **(73)**
Form - 0
Record **1998** - 1st:0 2nd:0 3rd:0 Ran:1
Pre1998 - 1st:0 2nd:1 3rd:0 Ran:2
Win Prizemoney £0 *Total Prizemoney* £1,102
1998 Turf 0-1: (7f) (gd)
Currently above-average gelding.
**D Shaw [0-1] J C Fretwell (from J H M Gosden [0-2] Jun 1997).*

Scopey, useful filly, effective 6 to 7f, best at 7f, acts on g-s to g-f, best on gd. Turf high 98 - 5th of 9 giving 4lb to Nanoushka (9 May Lingfield 7f g-f RF 1126). Consistent. She showed some good, consistent form in decent company at two, including three victories, but was a well-beaten third in the Fred Darling on her reappearance. Had a hard race that day, and was slightly disappointing in listed company subsequently. **M Bell [3-14] D F Allport.*

HOH EXPLORER (IRE) BHB 37f53a **RR 29f 53a** 4015[9]
4 ch g Shahrastani (USA) 11.5f **(69)** - Heart's Harmony (Blushing Groom (FR)) 10.3f **(76)**
Form - 870
Record **1998** - 1st:0 2nd:0 3rd:0 Ran:3
Pre1998 - 1st:0 2nd:0 3rd:1 Ran:7
Win Prizemoney £0 *Total Prizemoney* £604
1998 Turf 0-3: (12f, 14f, 16f) (sft, g-s, gd)
Workmanlike, little account gelding, has worn blinkers. Turf high 26. Becoming disappointing.
**D W Barker [0-15] Saltire Racing Syndicate (from I A Balding [0-2] May 1997).*

HOH EXPRESS BHB 82f **RR 85df** 4100[6]
6 b g Waajib 8.9f **(67)** - Tissue Paper (Touch Paper) 6.8f **(57)**
Form - 46306
Record 1998 - 1st:0 2nd:0 3rd:1 Ran:5
Pre1998 - 1st:3 2nd:5 3rd:7 Ran:35
Win Prizemoney £28,433 *Total Prizemoney* £67,502
Wins 1997 May Goodwo (GD) H 12f 85 88
1995 Aug Baden- (GD) L 8f 97 <
1995 May Newbur (GD) 8f 81
1998 Turf 0-5: (10f 2, 12f 2, 14f) (sft, gd 2, frm 2)
Useful gelding, effective 10 to 14f, best at 12f, acts on g-s to frm, best on gd. Turf high 85 - 6th of 12 giving 14lb to Opaque (13 May York 14f gd RF 1210). Better known as a jumper, he can win more races on the level granted a fast-run twelve furlongs.
**P R Webber [0-4] Mrs Joan Egan (from Mrs J R Ramsden [1-8] May 1998).*

HOH NAVIGATOR (IRE) BHB 68f **RR 77f** 5079[11]
3 ch g Common Grounds 8.1f **(66)** - Flying Diva (Chief Singer) 8.9f **(66)**
Form - 28344020
Record 1998 - 1st:0 2nd:2 3rd:1 Ran:8
Pre1998 - 1st:0 2nd:0 3rd:1 Ran:1
Win Prizemoney £0 *Total Prizemoney* £3,285
1998 Turf 0-8: (6f 4, 7f 3, 8f) (sft, g-s, gd, g-f 3, frm 2)
Workmanlike, above-average gelding, effective 5 to 6f, best at 6f, acts on gd to frm, has worn blinkers. Turf high 77 (1st run) (began Jly) - 2nd of 6 giving 5lb to Kayoko (17 Jly Newmarket 6f frm RF 2880). **D J S ffrenchDavis [0-1] A Rybak (from M Bell [0-8] Oct 1998).*

HOH NO BHB 77f **RR 75f** 4709[3]
2 b c Efisio 7.7f **(69)** - Primetta (Precocious) 8.6f **(62)**
Form - 800313
Record 1998 - 1st:1 2nd:0 3rd:2 Ran:6
Win Prizemoney £3,215 *Total Prizemoney* £5,611
Wins * **1998** Spt Goodwo (G-F) H 8f 68 75 <
1998 Turf 1-6: (6f 3, 8f 1-3) (g-f 2, frm 1-4)
Above-average colt, effective 8f, acts on g-f to frm. Turf high 75 (began Jly) - also 1st of 11 getting 9lb from Miss Rimex (24 Spt Goodwood RF 4463). **M Bell [1-6] D Allport & R B Michaelson.*

HOH STEAMER (IRE) BHB 92f **RR 86f** 4357[2]
2 br gr g Perugino (USA) - Dane's Lane (IRE) (Danehill (USA)) 10f **(72)**
Form - 76401112
Record 1998 - 1st:3 2nd:1 3rd:0 Ran:8
Win Prizemoney £46,455 *Total Prizemoney* £48,405
Wins * **1998** Aug Newcas (GD) H 8f 82 86 <
* **1998** Aug York (G-F) H 7f 70 77
* **1998** Aug Newbur (GD) H 7.3f 70 75
1998 Turf 3-8: (5f 2, 6f, 7f 2-4, 8f 1-1) (gd 4, g-f 2-2, frm, hrd 1-1)
Useful gelding, effective 7 to 8f, best at 7f, acts on g-f to hrd. Turf high 86 - 2nd of 12 giving 7lb to Parisien Star (18 Spt Newbury 7f frm RF 4357) - also 1st of 14 getting 6lb from Fair Flight (31 Aug Newcastle RF 3991). Hit form with a bang in August, winning well contested nurseries at Newbury and York, and landing a big pay-day by winning the Blaydon Nursery by the skin of his teeth. His winning run came to an end at Newbury, but he lost nothing in defeat. **M Bell [3-8] D F Allport.*

HOLDERNESS GIRL BHB 32f38a **RR 32f 38a** 1965[14]
5 b m Lapierre - Isobel's Choice (Green God) 9.6f **(68)**
Form - 75853080700
Record 1998 - 1st:0 2nd:0 3rd:1 Ran:10
Pre1998 - 1st:0 2nd:0 3rd:0 Ran:1
Win Prizemoney £0 *Total Prizemoney* £315
1998 Turf 0-5: (5f 2, 6f, 7f 2) (g-s, gd 2, g-f, frm) 1998 AW 0-5: (5f, 6f 2, 7f 2) (Equi 2, Fibr 3)
Moderate filly, effective 7f - acts on Fibr, likes left handed tracks, likes tight tracks. Turf high 32. AW high 45 - 3rd of 12 getting 5lb from Pow Wow (7 Mar Wolverhampton 7f Fibr RF 0404).
**Miss J F Craze [0-13] J Morris.*

HO LENG (IRE) BHB 106f **RR 105f** 4971[7]
3 ch g Statoblest 6.4f **(63)** - Indigo Blue (IRE) (Bluebird (USA)) 7.5f **(69)**
Form - 101047
Record 1998 - 1st:2 2nd:0 3rd:0 Ran:6
Pre1998 - 1st:1 2nd:1 3rd:0 Ran:3
Win Prizemoney £51,150 *Total Prizemoney* £56,146
Wins * **1998** Jly Newmar (FRM) H 7f 102 105 <
* **1998** May York (GD) H 7f 95 100
* 1997 Aug Hamilt (G-F) 6f 88+
1998 Turf 2-6: (6f 2, 7f 2-4) (sft 2, gd 1-2, g-f, frm 1-1)
Scopey, Pattern-class gelding, effective 6 to 7f, best at 7f, acts on gd to frm. Turf high 105 - 1st of 20 getting 2lb from Kumait (9 Jly Newmarket RF 2650) - also 1st of 19 giving 14lb to Kayo (14 May York RF 1219). A seven-furlong specialist, he won a very competitive handicap at York on his return, but found the step up to Pattern company too much for him at Ascot, where the soft ground was against him. He bounced back to win the Bunbury Cup at the July Meeting where he put up a sterling effort for a three-year-old when defying a big weight. Ran well in a Listed race in October and can win at that level on fast ground.
**Miss L A Perratt [3-9] Alan Guthrie.*

HOLLOWAY MELODY BHB 43f45a **RR 44f 45a** 4117[8]
5 ch m Cree Song 6.9f **(54)** - Holloway Wonder (Swing Easy (USA)) 6.5f **(55)**
Form - 7632755006383731146448
Record 1998 - 1st:2 2nd:1 3rd:4 Ran:21
Pre1998 - 1st:1 2nd:0 3rd:2 Ran:21
Win Prizemoney £6,746 *Total Prizemoney* £9,326
Wins * **1998** Jly Chepst (GD) SH 8.1f 35 44
* **1998** Jly Warwic (GD) SH 8f 35 44
* 1996 Oct Nottin (GD) C 8.2f 62 <
1998 Turf 2-8: (6f, 7f, 8f 2-5, 10f) (sft, g-s, gd 2, g-f 2-3, frm) 1998 AW 0-13: (7f 5, 8f 6, 9f 2) (Fibr 13)
Moderate filly, effective 7 to 8f, best at 8f, acts on g-f - acts on Fibr, has worn blinkers. Turf high 44 - 1st of 20 getting 19lb from Queen of Shannon (3 Jly Warwick RF 2510) - also 1st of 18 giving 11lb to Zahran (10 Jly Chepstow RF 2669). AW high 46 - 4th of 10 getting 5lb from Abtaal (14 Aug Southwell 7f Fibr RF 3639). Consistent. Won two big-field selling handicap in July, showing a turn of foot for that level. **B A McMahon [3-42] Mrs Rita Gibson.*

HOLLOW HAZE (USA) BHB 69f75a **RR 72f 75a** 4118[7]
3 b br f Woodman (USA) 9.7f **(77)** - Libeccio (NZ) (Danzatore (CAN)) 8.5f **(86)**
Form - 567717
Record 1998 - 1st:1 2nd:0 3rd:0 Ran:6
Pre1998 - 1st:0 2nd:1 3rd:0 Ran:2
Win Prizemoney £3,313 *Total Prizemoney* £5,624
Wins * **1998** *Aug Wolver (STD) H 8.5f 69 76* <
1998 Turf 0-4: (8f, 9f, 11f, 12f) (gd 3, frm) 1998 AW 1-2: (7f, 8f 1-1) (Fibr 1-2)
Scopey, above-average filly, effective 7 to 8f, acts on gd - acts on Fibr. Turf high 72. AW high 76 (1st run) (began Aug) - 1st of 13 getting 4lb from Italian Symphony (22 Aug Wolverhampton RF 3828). Has ability, but has been mainly disappointing. She made a successful debut on the Wolverhampton Fibresand in August, though she ran about in front and looks an awkward ride.
**P W Chapple-Hyam [1-8] R E Sangster.*

HOLLY BLUE BHB 79f **RR 79f** 4761[6]
2 ch f Bluebird (USA) 7.9f **(71)** - Nettle (Kris) 9.5f **(73)**
Form - 456
Record 1998 - 1st:0 2nd:0 3rd:0 Ran:3
Win Prizemoney £0 *Total Prizemoney* £367
1998 Turf 0-3: (7f 3) (gd, g-f, frm)
Currently above-average filly. Turf high 79 (began Spt) - 6th of 18 to Ski Lodge (12 Oct Leicester 7f gd RF 4761).
**R Charlton [0-3] The Queen.*

HOLY SMOKE BHB 62f58a **RR 63f 58a** 5120[1]
3 b f Statoblest 6.4f **(63)** - Native Flair (Be My Native (USA)) 10.2f **(71)**
Form - 531017501
Record 1998 - 1st:3 2nd:0 3rd:1 Ran:9
Pre1998 - 1st:0 2nd:0 3rd:0 Ran:3
Win Prizemoney £9,081 *Total Prizemoney* £9,629
Wins * **1998** Nov Mussel (SFT) H 8f 56 63 <
* **1998** Aug Carlis (G-S) H 8f 53 58
* **1998** *Jun Southw (STD) H 8f 53 56*
1998 Turf 2-7: (8f 2-7) (sft, gd 2-4, frm 2) 1998 AW 1-2: (7f, 8f 1-1) (Fibr 1-2)
Workmanlike, average filly, effective 8f, acts on gd to frm - acts on Fibr, best on gd, prefers tight tracks. Turf high 63 - 1st of 12 getting 14lb from Wilton (4 Nov Musselburgh RF 5120) - also 1st of 17

giving 3lb to Komlucky (26 Aug Carlisle RF 3884). AW high 56 - 1st of 13 giving 4lb to Misconduct (5 Jun Southwell RF 1765).
J L Eyre [3-12] John Roberts (Wakefield).

Pre1998 - 1st:0 2nd:0 3rd:0 Ran:2
Win Prizemoney £6,060 *Total Prizemoney* £8,382
Wins * **1998** Aug Ripon (G-F) H 9f 78 81 <

Hoh Steamer was hard to catch on his mid-season run

HOME OFFICE BHB 78f **RR 76f** 4823[8]
2 b c Danehill (USA) 9.1f **(79)** - Liaison (USA) (Blushing Groom (FR)) 10.3f **(76)**
Form - 328
Record 1998 - 1st:0 2nd:1 3rd:1 Ran:3
Win Prizemoney £0 *Total Prizemoney* £1,668
1998 Turf 0-3: (8f 3) (g-s, frm 2)
Currently above-average colt. Turf high 76 (began Spt).
**Mrs A J Perrett [0-3] K Abdulla.*

HOMESTEAD BHB 50f42a **RR 53f 42a** 356[4]
4 ch g Indian Ridge 7.6f **(74)** - Bertrade (Homeboy) 6.6f **(55)**
Form - 3454
Record 1998 - 1st:0 2nd:0 3rd:1 Ran:4
Pre1998 - 1st:2 2nd:1 3rd:1 Ran:17
Win Prizemoney £5,085 *Total Prizemoney* £7,413
Wins * 1997 Aug Bright (FRM) 8f 57 <
* 1997 Aug Bright (GD) H 7f 45 51
1998 AW 0-4: (8f 2, 10f 2) (Equi 4)
Scopey, fair gelding, effective 7 to 10f, best at 8f, acts on gd to frm, best on frm, prefers tight tracks. AW high 42. Won twice at Brighton in August '97, but has shown patchy form since.
**R Hannon [2-21] G H Shoemark.*

HONEST BORDERER BHB 82f **RR 81f** 4314[16]
3 b g Selkirk (USA) 7.9f **(76)** - Tell No Lies (High Line) 10.3f **(70)**
Form - 230410
Record 1998 - 1st:1 2nd:1 3rd:1 Ran:6

1998 Turf 1-6: (8f 3, 9f 1-1, 10f 2) (g-s, gd 2, g-f 1-1, frm 2)
Leggy, decent gelding, effective 8 to 10f, acts on g-s to frm. Turf high 81 - 1st of 17 giving 11lb to Bowcliffe (22 Aug Ripon RF 3815). Consistent. Took time to break his duck, but looks the type to do better at four. **J L Dunlop [1-8] Mrs A Johnstone.*

HONEY BEE RR 59f 3741[11]
2 b f Alnasr Alwasheek 9.4f **(62)** - Mirkan Honey (Ballymore) 7.3f **(64)**
Form - 07550
Record 1998 - 1st:0 2nd:0 3rd:0 Ran:5
1998 Turf 0-5: (5f 2, 6f, 7f 2) (gd, g-f, frm 3)
Fair filly. Turf high 59 - 5th of 15 giving 4lb to Regal Fan (11 Jly Warwick 7f frm RF 2732). **R Hannon [0-5] P T Tellwright.*

HONEYBIRD BHB 65f **RR 72f** 4332[14]
3 b f Batshoof 9.5f **(66)** - Ivor's Honey (Sir Ivor) 10.2f **(70)**
Form - 3510
Record 1998 - 1st:1 2nd:0 3rd:1 Ran:4
Win Prizemoney £2,070 *Total Prizemoney* £2,636
Wins * **1998** Aug Lingfi (G-F) 9f 68 <
1998 Turf 1-4: (8f 2, 9f 1-1, 10f) (gd, g-f 2, frm 1-1)
Workmanlike, above-average filly. Turf high 72 - also 1st of 7 from Seattle Ribbon (25 Aug Lingfield RF 3847). **W R Muir [1-4] D J Deer.*

HONEYSCHOICE (IRE) BHB 45f **RR 67f** 4108[16]
5 b g Distinctly North (USA) 7.4f **(63)** - Indian Honey (Indian King (USA)) 7.4f **(64)**
Form - 0

Record 1998 - 1st:0 2nd:0 3rd:0 Ran:1
Pre1998 - 1st:1 2nd:2 3rd:0 Ran:11
Win Prizemoney £2,226 *Total Prizemoney* £3,752
Wins 1996 Aug Dundal (FRM) 7.8f 67 <
1998 Turf 0-1: (8f) (frm)
Average gelding.
**M D Hammond [0-9] The Bee Keepers (from P McCreery in IRE [1-11] Oct 1996).*

HONEY STORM (IRE) BHB 65f60a **RR 80?f 60a** 4660[16]

3 b f Mujadil (USA) 7.7f **(70)** - Milk And Honey (So Blessed) 8.7f **(67)**
Form - 3100
Record 1998 - 1st:1 2nd:0 3rd:1 Ran:4
Pre1998 - 1st:0 2nd:1 3rd:2 Ran:5
Win Prizemoney £1,738 *Total Prizemoney* £4,893
Wins *** 1998** *Feb Southw (STD) S 8f 61* <
1998 Turf 0-2: (8f 2) (gd, g-f) 1998 AW 1-2: (8f 1-2) (Fibr 1-2)
Leggy, decent filly, effective 6 to 7f, acts on gd to g-f. Turf high 43 (began Spt). AW high 61. Showed ability in her maiden races, but had to be dropped into a weak seller on the Southwell Fibresand in February to get off the mark. **M R Channon [1-9] Mrs T Burns.*

HONEY SUCKLE BHB 42f **RR 41f** 5006[9]

3 br f Petong 7.6f **(58)** - May the Fourteenth (Thatching) 8f **(66)**
Form - 48050
Record 1998 - 1st:0 2nd:0 3rd:0 Ran:5
Pre1998 - 1st:0 2nd:0 3rd:0 Ran:1
Win Prizemoney £0 *Total Prizemoney* £236
1998 Turf 0-5: (7f 2, 8f 2, 10f) (sft, gd 2, g-f 2)
Unfurnished, moderate filly, has worn blinkers. Turf high 52 (began Aug). **Miss Gay Kelleway [0-6] Mrs C J Powell.*

HONEYTRAP (FR) **RR 99f** 3615a[2]

3 b f Primo Dominie 7.2f **(67)** - Singapore Girl (FR) (Lyphard (USA)) 9.9f **(72)**
Form - 2
1998 Turf 0-1: (13f) (gd)
Currently very useful filly. (1st run) - 2nd of 8 to Bryony Brind (9 Aug Deauville 13f gd RF 3615a). ** in FR [0-1].*

HONOLULU **RR 58f** 4856[11]

2 b f Robellino (USA) 9.5f **(68)** - Apache Squaw (Be My Guest (USA)) 9.3f **(67)**
Form - 80
Record 1998 - 1st:0 2nd:0 3rd:0 Ran:2
1998 Turf 0-2: (6f, 7f) (sft, g-f)
Currently fair filly. Turf high 58 (began Oct).
**C W Thornton [0-2] Guy Reed.*

HOPEFUL STAR (IRE) BHB 46f57a **RR 48f 57a** 4996[8]

3 ch g Pips Pride 6.7f **(70)** - Mijouter (IRE) (Coquelin (USA)) 8.4f **(58)**
Form - 363715760008
Record 1998 - 1st:1 2nd:0 3rd:1 Ran:10
Pre1998 - 1st:0 2nd:0 3rd:1 Ran:4
Win Prizemoney £3,460 *Total Prizemoney* £4,390
Wins *** 1998** *Apr Lingfi (STD) 6f 59* <
1998 Turf 0-5: (6f, 7f 3, 10f) (g-s, gd, g-f, frm 2) 1998 AW 1-5: (6f 1-1, 7f 2, 9f, 10f) (Equi 1-4, Fibr)
Workmanlike, fair gelding, effective 6f - acts on Equi. Turf high 51. AW high 59 - 1st of 7 getting 7lb from Sweet Patoopie (3 Apr Lingfield RF 0554). Becoming disappointing.
**Miss Gay Kelleway [1-14] The Hopeful Millionaires.*

HOPE VALUE BHB 47f43a **RR 32f 43a** 3832[11]

3 b g Rock City 8.8f **(62)** - Folle Idee (USA) (Foolish Pleasure (USA)) 8.9f **(72)**
Form - 00
Record 1998 - 1st:0 2nd:0 3rd:0 Ran:2
Pre1998 - 1st:0 2nd:0 3rd:1 Ran:4
Win Prizemoney £0 *Total Prizemoney* £346
1998 Turf 0-1: (12f) (g-f) 1998 AW 0-1: (11f) (Fibr)
Scopey, very moderate gelding, effective 6f, acts on gd, has worn blinkers. **T D Easterby [0-6] M H Easterby.*

HOPPING HIGGINS (IRE) BHB 86f **RR 92f** 4620[8]

3 b f Brief Truce (USA) 9.1f **(73)** - Yellow Creek (Sandy Creek) 8.9f **(59)**
Form - 4072673458
Record 1998 - 1st:0 2nd:1 3rd:1 Ran:10
Pre1998 - 1st:2 2nd:3 3rd:0 Ran:8
Win Prizemoney £14,027 *Total Prizemoney* £43,916
Wins 1997 Aug Leopar (GD) L 5f 95+ <
1997 May Tipper (G-Y) 5f 95
1998 Turf 0-10: (5f 7, 6f 3) (gd 4, frm 6)
Useful filly, effective 5 to 6f, best at 5f, acts on g-s to g-f, best on gd, has worn blinkers, excels at Leopardstown and Curragh. Turf high 92. Consistent. She scored twice at two for Aidan O'Brien, but is now with Richard Hannon and did not manage to get her head in front in handicap company last term.
**R Hannon [0-10] Patrick Kelly & Partners (from A P O'Brien in IRE [2-8] Oct 1997).*

HOPPIT BHB 30f **RR 40f** 4051[9]

3 b f Rock Hopper 10.6f **(54)** - Pellinora (USA) (King Pellinore (USA)) 8.2f **(68)**
Form - 860000
Record 1998 - 1st:0 2nd:0 3rd:0 Ran:6
1998 Turf 0-5: (8f 2, 9f, 12f 2) (gd, g-f, frm 3) 1998 AW 0-1: (8f) (Fibr)
Scopey, moderate filly. Turf high 40.
**P Howling [0-6] P A & M J Reditt.*

HORIZONTAL BHB 39a **RR 46f** 3641[10]

3 b f Perpendicular - Silly Games (Siliconn) 8.4f **(55)**
Form - 054P60
Record 1998 - 1st:0 2nd:0 3rd:0 Ran:6
Win Prizemoney £0 *Total Prizemoney* £237
1998 Turf 0-4: (7f, 12f, 14f, 16f) (gd 2, g-f, frm) 1998 AW 0-2: (12f, 16f) (Equi, Fibr)
Leggy, moderate filly, has worn blinkers. Turf high 46. (began Aug). **C E Brittain [0-6] A J Massingberd-Mundy.*

HORNBEAM **RR 107f** 4971[5]

4 b c Rich Charlie 5.9f **(50)** - Thinkluckybelucky (Maystreak) 8.7f **(53)**
Form - 1876305
Record 1998 - 1st:1 2nd:0 3rd:1 Ran:7
Pre1998 - 1st:1 2nd:0 3rd:1 Ran:5
Win Prizemoney £14,992 *Total Prizemoney* £26,330
Wins *** 1998** Mar Doncas (GD) L 8f 107 <
* 1997 May Newbur (SFT) 7.3f 86
1998 Turf 1-7: (7f 2, 8f 1-4, 9f) (sft, gd 1-4, g-f, frm)
Scopey, Pattern-class colt, effective 7 to 8f, best at 8f, acts on gd to g-f, best on gd. Turf high 108 - also 1st of 8 from Russian Music (26 Mar Doncaster RF 0473). Nowhere near as good as his illustrious namesake, he is talented nonetheless. He has won first time out for the past two seasons and obviously goes well fresh, as was the case when he won the listed Doncaster Mile after a nine-month absence. Though only seventh overall, he 'won' the race for the Royal Hunt Cup on the far side of the track quite convincingly, and should be given plenty of credit for that performance. Looks best when covered up. **J R Jenkins [2-12] K C Payne.*

HORTON LIGHTS **RR 43f** 4405[12]

2 b c Clantime 6.6f **(57)** - Blue Rhythm (Blue Cashmere) 6.4f **(54)**
Form - 00
Record 1998 - 1st:0 2nd:0 3rd:0 Ran:2
1998 Turf 0-2: (5f 2) (g-f, frm)
Currently moderate colt. Turf high 43 (began Spt).
**Mrs A Swinbank [0-2] Eddie Shotton.*

HOT LEGS BHB 50a **RR 36f 50a** 4937[8]

2 b f Sizzling Melody 6.3f **(49)** - Ra Ra Girl (Shack (USA)) 5.8f **(53)**
Form - 78
Record 1998 - 1st:0 2nd:0 3rd:0 Ran:2
1998 Turf 0-1: (5f) (gd) 1998 AW 0-1: (5f) (Fibr)
Currently moderate filly. **B A McMahon [0-2] D J Allen.*

HOT PASSION BHB 54f **RR 59f** 2473[4]

2 b c Keen 11.1f **(58)** - Love You Madly (IRE) (Bob Back (USA))
Form - 704
Record 1998 - 1st:0 2nd:0 3rd:0 Ran:3
1998 Turf 0-3: (6f 2, 7f) (g-f 2, hrd)
Currently fair colt. Turf high 59. **M Bell [0-3] Frank Farrant.*

HOT POTATO RR 39f 4937[10]
2 b c Roman Warrior - My Song of Songs **(7f)** (Norwick (USA)) 7.2f **(56)**
Form - 500
Record 1998 - 1st:0 2nd:0 3rd:0 Ran:3
Win Prizemoney £0 *Total Prizemoney* £155
1998 Turf 0-3: (5f 3) (gd 2, g-f)
Currently very moderate colt. Turf high 39 (began Spt).
**C Smith [0-3] Mrs S A Donald.*

HOUGOUMONT RR 64?f 4847[2]
2 b g Formidable (USA) 7.8f **(60)** - Sure Victory (IRE) (Stalker)
Form - 2
Record 1998 - 1st:0 2nd:1 3rd:0 Ran:1
1998 Turf 0-1: (7f) (g-f)
Currently average gelding. **P T Walwyn [0-1] P T Walwyn.*

Hula Angel finished on a high note at Newmarket

HOT SPOT BHB 68f **RR 68f** 3320[8]
3 ch g Bustino 11f **(64)** - Royal Seal (Privy Seal)
Form - 658
Record 1998 - 1st:0 2nd:0 3rd:0 Ran:3
Pre1998 - 1st:0 2nd:0 3rd:0 Ran:1
1998 Turf 0-3: (8f, 10f 2) (gd, g-f, frm)
Lengthy, average gelding. Turf high 68.
**I A Balding [0-4] Queen Elizabeth.*

HOT TOPIC (IRE) RR 31f 564[6]
3 ch f Desse Zenny (USA) 12f **(53)** - Sajanjal (Dance In Time (CAN)) 8.9f **(59)**
Form - 06
Record 1998 - 1st:0 2nd:0 3rd:0 Ran:1
Pre1998 - 1st:0 2nd:0 3rd:0 Ran:3
1998 Turf 0-1: (8f) (sft)
Neat, very moderate filly.
**A Kelleway [0-2] Osvaldo Pedroni (from P A Kelleway [0-2] Oct 1997).*

HOUDINI'S HONEY (USA) RR 78f 4629[5]
2 ch f Mr Prospector (USA) 8.6f **(88)** - Coup de Folie (USA) (Halo (USA)) 10.6f **(75)**
Form - 5
Record 1998 - 1st:0 2nd:0 3rd:0 Ran:1
1998 Turf 0-1: (6f) (g-f)
Currently above-average filly. (1st run) - 5th of 14 to Georgette (3 Oct Newmarket 6f g-f RF 4629).
**Sir Michael Stoute [0-1] Niarchos Family.*

HOUND VENTURE BHB 73f **RR 73f** 4465[10]
2 ch c Wolfhound (USA) 7.3f **(71)** - Relatively Sharp (Sharpen Up) 8.3f **(67)**
Form - 030
Record 1998 - 1st:0 2nd:0 3rd:1 Ran:3
Win Prizemoney £0 *Total Prizemoney* £700
1998 Turf 0-3: (5f, 6f 2) (gd, frm 2)
Currently above-average colt. Turf high 73 (began Spt).
**S P C Woods [0-3] Dr Frank Chao.*

HOUSEKEEPER (IRE) BHB 95f **RR 98f** 4496[10]
3 b f Common Grounds 8.1f **(66)** - Staff Approved (Teenoso (USA)) 9.9f **(72)**
Form - 410
Record 1998 - 1st:1 2nd:0 3rd:0 Ran:3
Pre1998 - 1st:1 2nd:0 3rd:0 Ran:1
Win Prizemoney £8,263 *Total Prizemoney* £9,030
Wins * 1998 Spt Doncas (GD) 8f 98 <
* 1997 Oct Lingfi (GD) 7f 85+
1998 Turf 1-3: (8f 1-2, 10f) (gd 2, g-f 1-1)
Leggy, very useful filly. Turf high 98 (began Aug) - 1st of 5 getting 5lb from Sunstreak (11 Spt Doncaster RF 4222). Lightly raced at three, winning a decent minor event at the St Leger meeting.
**R Charlton [2-4] Anglia Bloodstock Syndicate 1996.*

HOUSEMASTER (IRE) BHB 100f **RR 95f** 4972[3]
2 b c Rudimentary (USA) 8.2f **(66)** - Glenarff (USA) (Irish River (FR)) 8.6f **(78)**
Form - 15563

Record 1998 - 1st:1 2nd:0 3rd:1 Ran:5
Win Prizemoney £3,130 *Total Prizemoney* £21,808
Wins * **1998** Jun Yarmou (G-F) 6f 80 <
1998 Turf 1-5: (6f 1-2, 7f 2, 8f) (sft, g-s, gd, frm 1-2)
Very useful colt. Turf high 95. Ran his best race when third in the Racing Post Trophy, staying on in the testing ground, and looks likely to stay ten furlongs at three.
**M Bell [1-5] Highclere Thoroughbred Racing Ltd.*

HOUSE OF DREAMS BHB 66f RR 65f 4674[8]

6 b g Darshaan 11.9f **(81)** -Helens Dreamgirl (Caerleon (USA)) 8.6f **(71)**
Form - 13146178
Record 1998 - 1st:3 2nd:0 3rd:1 Ran:8
Pre1998 - 1st:0 2nd:1 3rd:2 Ran:11
Win Prizemoney £13,855 *Total Prizemoney* £18,574
Wins * **1998** Spt Thirsk (GD) H 12f 62 65 <
* **1998** Jly Carlis (G-F) H 14.1f 59 63
* **1998** Jun Catter (G-S) H 12f 54 56
1998 Turf 3-8: (12f 2-5, 14f 1-3) (gd 1-2, g-f 2, frm 2-4)
Average gelding, effective 12 to 14f, best at 12f, acts on gd to frm, best on frm. Turf high 65 - 1st of 17 getting 10lb from Cashmere Lady (5 Spt Thirsk RF 4112) - also 1st of 11 giving 1lb to Kings Cay (17 Jly Carlisle RF 2866).
**G M Moore [7-29] J & M Leisure / Unos Restaurant (from B W Hills [0-5] Oct 1995).*

HOUSE ON FIRE (IRE) BHB 43f52a RR 22f 52a 2331[20]

3 b g Paris House 5.9f **(64)** - La Fille de Feu (Never so Bold) 6.3f **(66)**
Form - 7453600000
Record 1998 - 1st:0 2nd:0 3rd:1 Ran:8
Pre1998 - 1st:0 2nd:0 3rd:0 Ran:5
Win Prizemoney £0 *Total Prizemoney* £238
1998 Turf 0-3: (6f 2, 8f) (g-s, gd 2) 1998 AW 0-5: (6f, 7f 3, 8f) (Fibr 5)
Light-framed, fair gelding, effective 7f - acts on Fibr, has worn blinkers, likes left handed tracks, likes tight tracks. Turf high 20. AW high 53 - 3rd of 9 giving 5lb to She's A Gem (9 Jan Southwell 7f Fibr RF 0056). Becoming disappointing.
**G Woodward [0-3] M S Moule (from J Berry [0-10] Mar 1998).*

HOUSTON TIME (USA) RR 101f 4542[2]

2 ch c Rahy (USA) 9.1f **(80)** - Band (USA) (Northern Dancer) 9.6f **(80)**
Form - 12
Record 1998 - 1st:1 2nd:1 3rd:0 Ran:2
Win Prizemoney £3,900 *Total Prizemoney* £13,137
Wins * **1998** Spt Yarmou (G-S) 7f 81+ <
1998 Turf 1-2: (7f 1-2) (gd 1-1, frm)
Currently very useful colt. Turf high 101 (began Spt) - 2nd of 26 to Maidaan (29 Spt Newmarket 7f frm RF 4542). A full-brother to the Cherry Hinton winner Applaud, he won a hot maiden on his debut and lost nothing in defeat when beaten by Maidaan in the valuable Tattersalls Houghton Sales Stakes. That form is verging on Group class and he will be an interesting contender in top races from a mile to 10 furlongs next term. **D R Loder [1-2] Jaber Abdullah.*

HOWAY THE LADS (IRE) BHB 35f RR 25f 4320[16]

2 br f Petardia 8.2f **(58)** - Pepilin (Coquelin (USA)) 8.4f **(58)**
Form - 7870
Record 1998 - 1st:0 2nd:0 3rd:0 Ran:4
1998 Turf 0-4: (5f, 6f 2, 8f) (gd 4)
Little account filly, has worn blinkers. Turf high 25.
**N Tinkler [0-4] J Parks.*

HOW HIGH BHB 48f RR 50f 3025[13]

3 b g Puissance 7.1f **(60)** - Lucky Starkist (Lucky Wednesday) 8f **(50)**
Form - 300
Record 1998 - 1st:0 2nd:0 3rd:1 Ran:3
Win Prizemoney £0 *Total Prizemoney* £327
1998 Turf 0-3: (8f 3) (gd, g-f, frm)
Workmanlike, currently fair gelding, has worn blinkers. Turf high 50 (1st run) - 3rd of 12 giving 3lb to Nouveau Cheval (26 May Leicester 8f g-f RF 1469).
**R Simpson [0-2] James Bradley (from J Neville [0-1] May 1998).*

HOWIES CHOICE (IRE) BHB 51f RR 63f 4578[17]

3 b g Petardia 8.2f **(58)** - Better Goods (IRE) (Glow (USA)) 6.7f **(71)**
Form - 43037000
Record 1998 - 1st:0 2nd:0 3rd:2 Ran:8
Pre1998 - 1st:0 2nd:0 3rd:0 Ran:4
Win Prizemoney £0 *Total Prizemoney* £1,487
1998 Turf 0-8: (7f 3, 8f 2, 10f 3) (gd 5, g-f 2, frm)
Light-framed, average gelding, has worn blinkers. Turf high 75. Becoming disappointing.
**M Brittain [0-8] Ronald Howe (from K McAuliffe [0-4] Oct 1997).*

HOYLAND COMMON (IRE) BHB 41f33a RR 29f 33a 2654[16]

3 ch f Common Grounds 8.1f **(66)** - Scoby Lass (Prominer) 5f **(40)**
Form - 600
Record 1998 - 1st:0 2nd:0 3rd:0 Ran:3
Pre1998 - 1st:0 2nd:0 3rd:0 Ran:5
1998 AW 0-3: (6f, 7f, 8f) (Fibr 3)
Very moderate filly, has worn blinkers. AW high 4. Becoming disappointing. **N Tinkler [0-8] J P Hardiman.*

HUGWITY BHB 73f68a RR 80f 68a 4848[20]

6 ch g Cadeaux Genereux 7.9f **(76)** - Nuit D'Ete (USA) (Super Concorde (USA)) 10.9f **(66)**
Form - 002410260200
Record 1998 - 1st:1 2nd:3 3rd:0 Ran:12
Pre1998 - 1st:3 2nd:0 3rd:0 Ran:8
Win Prizemoney £27,582 *Total Prizemoney* £30,784
Wins * **1998** Jly Yarmou (GD) H 8f 75 80
1996 May Goodwo (GD) H 8f 79 83 <
1996 May Cheste (GD) H 10.3f 75 80
1996 Apr Leices (GD) 10f 73
1998 Turf 1-12: (7f, 8f 1-9, 10f 2) (g-s, gd 3, g-f 3, frm 1-5)
Decent gelding, effective 8f, acts on gd to frm, best on frm. Turf high 80 - 1st of 9 giving 25lb to Shining Cloud (1 Jly Yarmouth RF 2456).
**G C Bravery [1-12] Michael Whatley (from B Hanbury [3-8] Jun 1996).*

HUJOOM (IRE) BHB 97f RR 103f 4992[3]

3 b c Fairy King (USA) 7.7f **(75)** - Maellen (River Beauty) 8.6f **(77)**
Form - 047213
Record 1998 - 1st:1 2nd:1 3rd:1 Ran:6
Pre1998 - 1st:2 2nd:1 3rd:1 Ran:6
Win Prizemoney £14,627 *Total Prizemoney* £26,710
Wins * **1998** Spt Goodwo (G-S) 7f 103 <
* 1997 Spt Ayr (GD) H 6f 87 91
* 1997 Jly Salisb (FRM) 7f 76
1998 Turf 1-6: (6f, 7f 1-5) (sft, g-s 2, gd 1-3)
Unfurnished, very useful colt, effective 7f, acts on gd. Turf high 103 - 1st of 7 giving 5lb to Mihnah (11 Spt Goodwood RF 4233). Inconsistent. Something of a twilight horse, he fought a losing battle with the handicapper before winning a conditions event at Goodwood. Connections let him go for 40,000 guineas at the Tattersalls Autumn Horses In Training Sales.
**J L Dunlop [3-12] Kuwait Racing Syndicate.*

HULA ANGEL (USA) BHB 100f RR 103f 4853[1]

2 b f Woodman (USA) 9.7f **(77)** - Jode (USA) (Danzig (USA)) 8.4f **(76)**
Form - 731831
Record 1998 - 1st:2 2nd:0 3rd:2 Ran:6
Win Prizemoney £26,497 *Total Prizemoney* £29,839
Wins * **1998** Oct Newmar (GD) G2 7f 103 <
* **1998** Aug Kempto (G-F) 7f 91
1998 Turf 2-6: (7f 2-6) (gd 1-4, g-f, frm 1-1)
Very useful filly, effective 7f, acts on gd to g-f. Turf high 103 (began Jly) - 1st of 14 from Valentine Waltz (17 Oct Newmarket RF 4853). Third to the leading Classic fancy Bionic at Goodwood in July, she contested top-class races in the second half of the campaign. Asked to make all when disappointing in the Moyglare Stud Stakes, she proved infinitely more effective with waiting tactics on her final two starts, winning the Group Two Rockfel Stakes at Newmarket in mid-October. She is to be trained for the 1000 Guineas and, while she has something to find on the best of her generation, her trainer is confident that she will run well.
**B W Hills [2-6] J R Fleming.*

HULLBANK BHB 65f62a RR 72f 62a 4879[6]

8 b g Uncle Pokey 10f **(43)** - Dubavarna (Dubassoff (USA)) 14.2f **(55)**
Form - 1163606
Record 1998 - 1st:2 2nd:0 3rd:1 Ran:7
Pre1998 - 1st:3 2nd:8 3rd:4 Ran:24
Win Prizemoney £16,532 *Total Prizemoney* £29,243
Wins 1998 Jly Redcar (G-F) H 16f 68 71 <

1998	*Jly*	*Southw*	*(STD)*	*H*	*14f*	*55*	*58*
1997	Jun	Beverl	(G-F)	H	16.2f	63	68
1996	Jly	Beverl	(G-F)	H	16.2f	55	60
1995	Jun	Redcar	(FRM)		14.1f		68

1998 Turf 1-5: (14f 2, 16f 1-2, 18f) (g-f, frm 3, hrd 1-1) 1998 AW 1-2: (14f 1-2) (Fibr 1-2)

Above-average gelding, effective 14 to 18f, best at 16f, acts on gd to hrd, best on frm, has worn blinkers, likes left handed tracks, favours tight tracks, excels at Redcar. Turf high 72 (began Jly) - 6th of 7 getting 17lb from Aginor (25 Spt Redcar 14f frm RF 4487) - also 1st of 9 getting 1lb from Salska (25 Jly Redcar RF 3123). AW high 58 (1st run) (began Jly). Inconsistent. Always to be feared on firm ground at his favourite track, Beverley.

**J M Jefferson [0-3] Mrs V Haigh (from J Hetherton [2-4] Aug 1998).*

HUNAN (IRE) RR 94f 4378[5]

2 ch c College Chapel - Foolish Fun

Form - 14105

1998 Turf 2-5: (6f 2-5) (sft, gd 1-2, g-f, frm 1-1)

Useful colt. Turf high 94 (1st run) (began Jly) - 1st of 8 giving 5lb to Pharmacist (4 Jly Leopardstown RF 2609a) - also 1st of 6 giving 3lb to Danzigaway (1 Aug Deauville RF 3417a). He won a Leopardstown maiden and a Group Three at Deauville before being held in the Prix Morny and the Mill Reef.

**A P O'Brien in IRE [2-5] P L Biancone.*

Hunters of Brora; a first win in three years in the Lincoln

HUNTERS OF BRORA (IRE) BHB 95f RR 95f 5076[5]

8 b m Sharpo 7.5f **(68)** - Nihad (Alleged (USA)) 10f **(76)**

Form - 156105405

Record 1998 - 1st:2 2nd:0 3rd:0 Ran:9

Pre1998 - 1st:4 2nd:4 3rd:5 Ran:35

Win Prizemoney £86,906 *Total Prizemoney* £153,867

Wins	*** 1998**	Jun	Newcas	(GD)		8f		97 <
	*** 1998**	Mar	Doncas	(GD)	H	8f	90	96
	* 1995	May	Beverl	(G-F)	H	8.5f	85	89
	* 1994	Aug	Ripon	(G-F)	H	8f	76	80

1998 Turf 2-9: (8f 2-6, 9f, 10f 2) (sft, g-s, gd 2-6, g-f)

Very useful mare, effective 8 to 10f, best at 8f, acts on sft to frm, best on gd. Turf high 97 - 1st of 7 getting 3lb from Digitalize (25 Jun Newcastle RF 2271) - also 1st of 24 giving 7lb to King of Tunes (28 Mar Doncaster RF 0484). This genuine mare finally gained reward for a string of good efforts in competitive handicaps by winning the Lincoln on her reappearance, and was also victorious in a valuable mares' conditions event at Newcastle. Fair efforts otherwise, if a little out of her depth in Listed and Group Three company. Best suited by coming late in a strongly-run race.

**J D Bethell [6-44] Robert Gibbons.*

HUNTERS TWEED RR 32f 5116[8]

2 ch c Nashwan (USA) 10.3f **(79)** - Zorette (USA) **(60f)** (Zilzal (USA))

Form - 8

Record 1998 - 1st:0 2nd:0 3rd:0 Ran:1

1998 Turf 0-1: (8f) (gd)

Currently very moderate colt. **J D Bethell [0-1] Robert Gibbons.*

HUNT HILL (IRE) BHB 65f65a RR 70f 65a 4578[14]

3 b g High Estate 10.5f **(66)** - Royaltess (Royal And Regal (USA)) 9.5f **(60)**

Form - 101130

Record 1998 - 1st:3 2nd:0 3rd:1 Ran:6

Pre1998 - 1st:0 2nd:0 3rd:0 Ran:3

Win Prizemoney £8,559 *Total Prizemoney* £9,087

Wins	**1998**	Aug	Leices	(GD)	H	10f	62	66 <
	1998	Jun	Bright	(GD)		10f		64
	1998	*Jun*	*Southw*	*(STD)*	*H*	*8f*	*54*	*58*

1998 Turf 2-5: (8f, 10f 2-3, 11f) (gd 1-2, g-f 2, frm 1-1) 1998 AW 1-1: (8f 1-1) (Fibr 1-1)

Workmanlike, above-average gelding, effective 10 to 11f, best at 10f, acts on gd to frm, likes left handed tracks, prefers tight tracks. Turf high 70 - 3rd of 9 giving 10lb to Beach Buoy (7 Aug Haydock 11f g-f RF 3434) - also 1st of 13 giving 14lb to Courage Under Fire (5 Aug Leicester RF 3375). (1st run). Showed nothing in three races at two, but was shrewdly placed to win three times last term, one on Fibresand when heavily backed.

**J J O'Neill [0-1] P Byrne (from Sir Mark Prescott [3-8] Aug 1998).*

HUNTING GROUND BHB 19f25a RR 35f 25a 4627[16]

10 b g Dancing Brave (USA) 10.4f **(78)** - Ack's Secret (USA) (Ack Ack (USA)) 12.7f **(82)**

Form - 05600

Record 1998 - 1st:0 2nd:0 3rd:0 Ran:5

Pre1998 - 1st:5 2nd:4 3rd:0 Ran:31

Win Prizemoney £15,481 *Total Prizemoney* £18,522

1998 Turf 0-5: (16f 5) (gd, g-f 2, frm 2)

Very moderate gelding, often wears blinkers. Turf high 35 (began Jly).

**M Mullineaux [0-5] Esprit de Corps Racing (from B P J Baugh [0-4] Jun 1997).*

HUNTSWOOD BHB 81f RR 82df 5043[6]

3 b c Warning 8.1f **(77)** - Clarista (USA) (Riva Ridge (USA)) 8.2f **(68)**

Form - 00025001250306

Record 1998 - 1st:1 2nd:2 3rd:1 Ran:14

Pre1998 - 1st:2 2nd:0 3rd:1 Ran:5

Win Prizemoney £12,215 *Total Prizemoney* £19,098

Wins	*** 1998**	Jly	Newmar	(GD)	H	7f	78	85+
	* 1997	Aug	Folkes	(G-F)		5f		86 <
	* 1997	Jly	Cheste	(G-F)		5.1f		80+

1998 Turf 1-14: (5f, 6f, 7f 1-9, 8f 2, 10f) (sft, gd 7, g-f 2, frm 1-4)

Decent colt, effective 5 to 8f, best at 7f, acts on gd to frm, best on gd, likes left handed tracks, prefers tight tracks, excels at Chester. Turf high 88 - 2nd of 5 giving 19lb to Samara Song (2 Aug Sandown 7f gd RF 3300) - also 1st of 11 giving 6lb to Redswan (18 Jly Newmarket RF 2916). Slow to find his form this term, but scored at Newmarket in July and was just touched off next time. Ran a good race over a mile at Warwick in October.

**R Hannon [3-19] Mrs D F Cock.*

HURGILL DANCER BHB 50f73a **RR 56f 73a** 4588[16]
4 b g Rambo Dancer (CAN) 8.4f **(59)** - Try Vickers (USA) (Fuzzbuster (USA)) 6.3f **(63)**
Form - 058300
Record 1998 - 1st:0 2nd:0 3rd:1 Ran:6
Pre1998 - 1st:1 2nd:1 3rd:2 Ran:10
Win Prizemoney £3,371 *Total Prizemoney* £6,293
Wins 1997 Apr Ripon (G-F) H 12.3f 65 68 <
1998 Turf 0-6: (12f 3, 14f, 16f, 17f) (gd 4, g-f, frm)
Neat, fair gelding, effective 12f, acts on g-f, favours tight tracks. Turf high 60. Inconsistent.
**R J O'Sullivan [0-2] R O S Racing (from J A R Toller [0-4] Aug 1998).*

HURGILL LADY BHB 47f49a **RR 41f 49a** 1475[12]
4 ch f Emarati (USA) 6.6f **(63)** - Gitee (FR) (Carwhite) 7.2f **(61)**
Form - 72220080
Record 1998 - 1st:0 2nd:3 3rd:0 Ran:8
Pre1998 - 1st:0 2nd:2 3rd:0 Ran:6
Win Prizemoney £0 *Total Prizemoney* £3,923
1998 Turf 0-3: (5f 2, 6f) (gd, g-f, frm) 1998 AW 0-5: (5f, 6f 4) (Fibr 5)
Scopey, moderate filly, effective 5 to 6f, best at 6f - acts on Fibr. Turf high 41. AW high 47 - 2nd of 9 giving 1lb to Featherstone Lane (28 Jan Wolverhampton 5f Fibr RF 0173). Inconsistent.
**D Nicholls [0-8] G A Harker (from J W Watts [0-6] Jun 1997).*

HURRICANE STATE (USA) BHB 87f **RR 86f** 3458[21]
4 ch c Miswaki (USA) 8.1f **(81)** - Regal State (USA) (Affirmed (USA)) 9.3f **(79)**
Form - 5580
Record 1998 - 1st:0 2nd:0 3rd:0 Ran:4
Pre1998 - 1st:2 2nd:1 3rd:1 Ran:7
Win Prizemoney £34,413 *Total Prizemoney* £45,018
Wins * 1996 Oct Deauvi (GD) G3 6.5f 108 <
* 1996 Spt Goodwo (GD) 6f 99
1998 Turf 0-4: (6f 2, 7f 2) (g-s, gd, g-f 2)
Useful colt, has worn blinkers. Turf high 86. A Group Three winner at Deauville as a juvenile, he stayed on to finish a respectable sixth in the Italian Two Thousand Guineas on his reappearance in '97 but found winning opportunities hard to come by. Did not shine in minor company in 1998. Sold for 20,000 guineas in October. **P W Chapple-Hyam [2-11] R E Sangster.*

HURTLEBERRY (IRE) BHB 80f74a **RR 80f 74a** 3610[6]
5 b m Tirol 8.1f **(64)** - Allberry (Alzao (USA)) 7.1f **(68)**
Form - 1686
Record 1998 - 1st:1 2nd:0 3rd:0 Ran:4
Pre1998 - 1st:3 2nd:1 3rd:1 Ran:11
Win Prizemoney £19,334 *Total Prizemoney* £20,852
Wins * **1998** Jun Haydoc (GD) H 8.1f 72 80 <
* 1997 May Goodwo (G-S) H 8f 70 69+
* *1997 Jan Lingfi (STD) 7f 71*
* 1995 Aug Salisb (FRM) 6f 77
1998 Turf 1-4: (8f 1-3, 10f) (gd 2, frm 1-2)
Decent filly, effective 7 to 8f, best at 8f, acts on gd to frm - acts on Equi, best on gd, likes tight tracks, excels at Goodwood. Turf high 80 (1st run) - 1st of 15 giving 7lb to Bollin Frank (6 Jun Haydock RF 1784). Came back from a seven-month break to win most impressively at Haydock in June. Finished lame on her final start.
**Lord Huntingdon [4-15] Mrs A F B Crawshaw.*

HUSBIRD RR 2856[R]
3 b c Guadalcanal (IRE) - Lady Loquacious (Mon Cheval)
Form - R
Record 1998 - 1st:0 2nd:0 3rd:0 Ran:1
1998 Turf 0-1: (12f) (frm)
Unfurnished, currently very poor colt - Rth of 7 getting 6lb from Gray Pastel (16 Jly Leicester 12f frm RF 2856).
**Mrs N Macauley [0-1] Timothy Nuttall.*

HUSH RR 1408[17]
3 b f Barrys Gamble 7f **(50)** - Keep Mum (Mummy's Pet) 7.7f **(60)**
Form - 0
Record 1998 - 1st:0 2nd:0 3rd:0 Ran:1
1998 Turf 0-1: (6f) (frm)
Leggy, currently very poor filly.
**L R Lloyd-James [0-1] Mrs Carol Lloyd James.*

HUSH MONEY BHB 63f **RR 64f** 4613[12]
2 b c Aragon 7.7f **(58)** - Penny Blessing (So Blessed) 8.7f **(67)**
Form - 4600
Record 1998 - 1st:0 2nd:0 3rd:0 Ran:4
Win Prizemoney £0 *Total Prizemoney* £230
1998 Turf 0-4: (5f 3, 7f) (g-s, gd, g-f, frm)
Average colt. Turf high 64 (began Aug).
**B W Hills [0-4] Kennet Valley Thoroughbreds III.*

HUSO BHB 37f **RR 39f** 3386[8]
10 ch g Sharpo 7.5f **(68)** - Husnah (USA) (Caro) 9.3f **(74)**
Form - 08
Record 1998 - 1st:0 2nd:0 3rd:0 Ran:2
Pre1998 - 1st:2 2nd:1 3rd:1 Ran:22
Win Prizemoney £6,145 *Total Prizemoney* £8,907
1998 Turf 0-2: (10f, 17f) (g-f, frm)
Very moderate gelding, has worn blinkers. Turf high 23 (began Jly). Becoming disappointing.
**P C Haslam [8-37] H A N Orde-Powlett (from C E Brittain [0-5] Oct 1990).*

HUSSAR (IRE) BHB 40f **RR 26f** 4255[11]
3 ch c Shalford (IRE) 7.8f **(63)** - How Gorgeous (Frimley Park) 6.5f **(67)**
Form - 8000000
Record 1998 - 1st:0 2nd:0 3rd:0 Ran:7
1998 Turf 0-7: (6f 4, 7f 3) (g-s, gd 3, g-f, frm 2)
Strong, little account colt. Turf high 50.
**C W Thornton [0-7] Guy Reed.*

HUSTLE AN BUSTLE (USA) BHB 46f **RR 54f** 904[14]
4 ch f Lomond (USA) 9.9f **(74)** - City Crowds (General Assembly (USA)) 10f **(68)**
Form - 00
Record 1998 - 1st:0 2nd:0 3rd:0 Ran:1
Pre1998 - 1st:0 2nd:0 3rd:1 Ran:8
Win Prizemoney £0 *Total Prizemoney* £503
1998 Turf 0-1: (14f) (g-s)
Fair filly, effective 7f, acts on gd. Becoming disappointing.
**G Fierro [0-7] Pete Daykin (from J Muldoon in IRE [0-6] Aug 1997).*

HUTCHIES LADY BHB 18f33a **RR 14f 33a** 1605[8]
6 b m Efisio 7.7f **(69)** - Keep Mum (Mummy's Pet) 7.7f **(60)**
Form - 460508
Record 1998 - 1st:0 2nd:0 3rd:0 Ran:6
Pre1998 - 1st:1 2nd:2 3rd:0 Ran:32
Win Prizemoney £3,595 *Total Prizemoney* £6,147
Wins * 1996 May Hamilt (HVY) H 8.3f 30 41 <
1998 Turf 0-6: (8f, 11f, 12f 2, 13f, 16f) (hvy, sft 2, g-s, gd 2)
Little account mare, effective 8f, acts on gd, has worn blinkers. Turf high 15. **R M McKellar [1-45] Waygateshaw Racing Club.*

HYDE PARK (IRE) BHB 72f73a **RR 70f 73a** 4807[15]
4 b c Alzao (USA) 9.8f **(73)** - Park Elect (Ahonoora) 8.1f **(73)**
Form - 0006112010
Record 1998 - 1st:3 2nd:1 3rd:0 Ran:10
Pre1998 - 1st:1 2nd:1 3rd:0 Ran:3
Win Prizemoney £18,275 *Total Prizemoney* £21,605
Wins * **1998** Oct Bright (GD) H 8f 67 70
* **1998** Aug Cheste (G-S) H 7.6f 60 62
* **1998** Jly Pontef (G-F) H 8f 55 59
* *1996 Nov Lingfi (STD) 5f 71* <
1998 Turf 3-10: (5f 2, 6f 2, 8f 3-5, 9f) (gd 4, g-f 2-4, frm 1-2)
Scopey, above-average colt, effective 8 to 9f, best at 8f, acts on gd to g-f, best on g-f. Turf high 70 - 1st of 15 getting 3lb from Stoppes Brow (5 Oct Brighton RF 4648) - also 1st of 17 getting 6lb from Bollin Frank (2 Aug Chester RF 3287). In fine form since stepping up from sprint distances, he managed three victories on turf last year, and performed pretty well on his Equitrack debut when chasing home the useful-looking Mutabassir. Sold for 16,000 guineas in October. **Sir Mark Prescott [4-13] Neil Greig.*

HYPERACTIVE (IRE) BHB 78f **RR 75f** 2959[7]
2 b c Perugino (USA) - Hyannis (FR) (Esprit du Nord (USA))
Form - 427
Record 1998 - 1st:0 2nd:1 3rd:0 Ran:3
Win Prizemoney £0 *Total Prizemoney* £1,336
1998 Turf 0-3: (5f 2, 6f) (g-f, frm 2)

Currently above-average colt. Turf high 75 - 2nd of 10 to Alpha (3 Jly Beverley 5f g-f RF 2490). **A C Stewart [0-3] Racing For Gold.*

HYPERICO (IRE) BHB 57f54a **RR 49f 54a** 3829[4]

4 b g Nordico (USA) 8.2f **(59)** - Hype (USA) (Hyperborean (USA))
Form - 024
Record 1998 - 1st:0 2nd:1 3rd:0 Ran:2
Pre1998 - 1st:0 2nd:0 3rd:1 Ran:9
Win Prizemoney £0 *Total Prizemoney* £1,186
1998 AW 0-2: (8f, 9f) (Fibr 2)
Fair gelding, has worn blinkers. AW high 55 (began Jly). Inconsistent.
**Miss S J Wilton [0-1] John Pointon and Sons (from G Barnett [0-1] Jly 1998).*

HYPERSPECTRA BHB 86f **RR 85f** 5149[6]

3 b f Rainbow Quest (USA) 11.2f **(81)** - Hyabella (Shirley Heights) 10.3f **(74)**
Form - 166
Record 1998 - 1st:1 2nd:0 3rd:0 Ran:3
Win Prizemoney £3,517 *Total Prizemoney* £3,635
Wins * **1998** Spt Bath (G-S) 10.2f 85 <
1998 Turf 1-3: (10f 1-2, 12f) (gd, g-f 1-1, frm)
Light-framed, currently useful filly. Turf high 85 (1st run) (began Spt) - 1st of 9 getting 5lb from Anemos (28 Spt Bath RF 4527). Bolted up in a maiden but was well held in listed races.
**J R Fanshawe [1-3] Helena Springfield Ltd.*

HYPE SUPERIOR (IRE) BHB 44f46a **RR 44f 46a** 1623[16]

4 ch g Mac's Imp (USA) 5.6f **(54)** - Katysue (King's Leap) 8.4f **(61)**
Form - 45800
Record 1998 - 1st:0 2nd:0 3rd:0 Ran:4
Pre1998 - 1st:0 2nd:1 3rd:0 Ran:10
Win Prizemoney £0 *Total Prizemoney* £1,465
1998 Turf 0-4: (5f 2, 6f, 7f) (sft, gd, g-f, frm)
Scopey, moderate gelding, has worn blinkers. Turf high 44.
**A Bailey [0-14] Sandybrow Stables Ltd.*

HYPHEN BHB 78f85a **RR 88f 85a** 4732[10]

2 ch c Most Welcome 8.6f **(66)** - Finlandaise (FR) (Arctic Tern (USA)) 8.9f **(69)**
Form - 2212420
Record 1998 - 1st:1 2nd:4 3rd:0 Ran:7
Win Prizemoney £2,368 *Total Prizemoney* £6,117
Wins * **1998** Aug Newcas (GD) 6f 88 <
1998 Turf 1-5: (5f 2, 6f 1-2, 7f) (g-s, gd 1-1, g-f, frm 2) 1998 AW 0-2: (6f, 8f) (Fibr 2)
Useful colt, effective 5 to 8f, acts on gd to g-f - acts on Fibr. Turf high 88 (began Jly) - 1st of 14 from Spy (5 Aug Newcastle RF 3380). AW high 82 (began Jly) - 2nd of 8 getting 4lb from Maybe Special (29 Spt Southwell 8f Fibr RF 4546). Was sold for 31,000 guineas at Tattersalls in October. **Sir Mark Prescott [1-7] B Haggas.*

IAMUS BHB 80f74a **RR 81f 74a** 2308[4]

5 ch g Most Welcome 8.6f **(66)** - Icefern (Moorestyle) 6.9f **(64)**
Form - 044
Record 1998 - 1st:0 2nd:0 3rd:0 Ran:3
Pre1998 - 1st:2 2nd:3 3rd:3 Ran:23
Win Prizemoney £7,985 *Total Prizemoney* £26,205
Wins * 1997 Jly Newcas (GD) H 8f 80 87 <
1996 Jun Nottin (G-F) 8.2f 62
1998 Turf 0-3: (8f 2, 9f) (g-s 2, g-f)
Decent gelding, effective 8 to 9f, best at 8f, acts on g-s to g-f, best on gd, has worn blinkers, excels at Newcastle. Turf high 81 - 4th of 17 getting 2lb from Rapier (13 Jun York 9f g-s RF 1980). Consistent. Back with Barron after a spell over hurdles with David Nicholson, he finds it hard to get his head in front under either code, but ran a couple of sound races in June.
**T D Barron [1-13] The Oakfield Nurseries Partnership (from P T Walwyn [1-13] Spt 1996).*

IBLIS (IRE) BHB 70f71a **RR 73df 71a** 1980[14]

6 b g Danehill (USA) 9.1f **(79)** - In Unison (Bellypha) 9.8f **(73)**
Form - 0
Record 1998 - 1st:0 2nd:0 3rd:0 Ran:1
Pre1998 - 1st:2 2nd:1 3rd:1 Ran:18
Win Prizemoney £11,020 *Total Prizemoney* £15,134
Wins * 1995 Apr Newmar (G-F) H 7f 80 88
* 1994 Spt York (GD) 6f 89
1998 Turf 0-1: (9f) (g-s)
Above-average gelding, has worn blinkers. Becoming disappointing. **G Wragg [2-19] G Wragg.*

I CAN'T REMEMBER BHB 59f65a **RR 60f 65a** 4970[5]

4 br g Petong 7.6f **(58)** - Glenfield Portion (Mummy's Pet) 7.7f **(60)**
Form - 640046051205
Record 1998 - 1st:1 2nd:1 3rd:0 Ran:12
Pre1998 - 1st:4 2nd:3 3rd:0 Ran:29
Win Prizemoney £19,888 *Total Prizemoney* £26,505
Wins **1998** Jun Cheste (G-S) C 10.3f 59
1996 Oct Doncas (GD) H 8f 77 80 <
1996 Aug Cheste (G-S) H 7f 74 79
1996 Aug Cheste (G-F) H 6.1f 70 67
1996 Jly Catter (G-S) S 5f 46
1998 Turf 1-12: (7f 2, 8f 6, 9f, 10f 1-3) (g-s 2, gd 1-4, g-f 3, frm 3)
Neat, average gelding, effective 8f, acts on gd, has worn blinkers, likes left handed tracks, likes tight tracks. Turf high 60.
**M C Pipe [0-3] Knight Hawks Partnership (from P D Evans [5-36] Jun 1998).*

ICE BHB 92f **RR 95f** 4709[1]

2 b c Polar Falcon (USA) 9f **(74)** - Sarabah (IRE) (Ela-Mana-Mou) 10.1f **(70)**
Form - 2431121
Record 1998 - 1st:3 2nd:2 3rd:1 Ran:7
Win Prizemoney £19,826 *Total Prizemoney* £23,343
Wins * **1998** Oct York (GD) H 7.9f 83 95 <
* **1998** Spt York (GD) H 7.9f 69 80
* **1998** Aug Mussel (GD) H 7.1f 69 74
1998 Turf 3-7: (6f 2, 7f 1-2, 8f 2-3) (sft, g-s, gd 2, g-f 2-2, frm 1-1)
Very useful colt, effective 8f, acts on frm, often wears blinkers (extremely effectively). Turf high 95 - 1st of 19 giving 4lb to Fiori (8 Oct York RF 4709). A useful performer in nurseries, he carries his head high and requires a certain degree of cajoling by his riders.
**M Johnston [3-7] David Abell.*

ICE AGE BHB 49f64a **RR 49f 64a** 2857[12]

4 gr c Chilibang 7f **(55)** - Mazarine Blue (Bellypha) 9.8f **(73)**
Form - 251043106410
Record 1998 - 1st:3 2nd:0 3rd:1 Ran:10
Pre1998 - 1st:1 2nd:1 3rd:1 Ran:18
Win Prizemoney £10,067 *Total Prizemoney* £11,961
Wins * **1998** Jly Yarmou (GD) H 6f 44 49
* **1998** *May Southw (STD) S 6f 61*
* **1998** *Jan Southw (STD) H 6f 54 59*
* 1996 May Doncas (G-F) 5f 80+ <
1998 Turf 1-4: (6f 1-4) (gd, frm 2, hrd 1-1) 1998 AW 2-6: (5f, 6f 2-5) (Fibr 2-6)
Average colt, effective 5 to 6f, best at 6f, acts on g-f to frm - acts on Fibr, often wears blinkers, excels at Southwell. Turf high 49. AW high 61 - 1st of 7 giving 15lb to Bon Sizzle (7 May Southwell RF 1085) - also 1st of 9 getting 4lb from Gadge (16 Jan Southwell RF 0098). He used his early pace to best advantage when winning twice on the Southwell Fibresand, and again on turf at Yarmouth, but has not run so well when unable to dominate.
**R J R Williams [4-27] Harry Ormesher (from J W Payne [0-1] Feb 1998).*

ICEBAND (USA) BHB 86f **RR 87f** 3665[5]

3 ch c Dixieland Band (USA) 10.1f **(80)** - Zero Minus (USA) (It's Freezing (USA)) 10f **(83)**
Form - 70025
Record 1998 - 1st:0 2nd:1 3rd:0 Ran:5
Pre1998 - 1st:1 2nd:1 3rd:0 Ran:3
Win Prizemoney £5,300 *Total Prizemoney* £8,480
Wins * 1997 Spt Goodwo (GD) 6f 98 <
1998 Turf 0-5: (6f 2, 7f 3) (gd, g-f 3, frm)
Well made, useful colt, effective 6f, acts on gd, has worn blinkers. Turf high 87. Comfortable winner at Goodwood in '97, but showed little at three apart from finishing runner-up in a four-runner event at Doncaster. **J H M Gosden [1-8] Sheikh Mohammed.*

ICEMOON (GER) **RR 107f** 2482a[5]

4 ch c Monsagem (USA) - Icena (Jimmy Reppin) 8.8f **(64)**
Form - 5

1998 Turf 0-1: (11f) (sft)
Pattern-class colt, effective 10 to 11f, acts on sft to gd. (1st run) - 5th of 7 giving 18lb to Elle Danzig (28 Jun Hamburg 11f sft RF 2482a). He is useful, but usually finds something to beat him in Group company. **H Blume in GER [0-6] Spt 1997).*

ICE PACK RR 50f 5009[7]
2 gr f Mukaddamah (USA) 7.6f **(74)** - Mrs Gray (Red Sunset) 8.2f **(63)**
Form - 07
Record 1998 - 1st:0 2nd:0 3rd:0 Ran:2
1998 Turf 0-2: (7f, 8f) (sft, frm)
Currently fair filly. Turf high 50 (began Aug).
**J W Hills [0-2] Inpacks Ltd (Chilled).*

I CRIED FOR YOU (IRE) BHB 65f RR 63f 4886[10]
3 b c Statoblest 6.4f **(63)** - Fall of The Hammer (IRE) (Auction Ring (USA)) 8.6f **(65)**
Form - 631300685000
Record 1998 - 1st:1 2nd:0 3rd:2 Ran:12
Pre1998 - 1st:0 2nd:0 3rd:2 Ran:5
Win Prizemoney £2,749 *Total Prizemoney* £4,763
Wins * **1998** May Bright (FRM) H 5.3f 68 72 <
1998 Turf 1-12: (5f 1-5, 6f 7) (sft, g-s 2, gd 3, g-f, frm 1-5)
Light-framed, average colt, effective 5 to 7f, best at 6f, acts on sft to frm, best on frm, has worn blinkers. Turf high 74 - 3rd of 11 giving 17lb to Sizzling (28 May Brighton 6f frm RF 1553) - also 1st of 9 getting 2lb from Batchworth Belle (22 May Brighton RF 1388). Consistent. **R Hannon [1-17] Bob Lalemant.*

IDA'S COTTAGE (IRE) RR 22f 4884[11]
2 b g Fayruz 6.6f **(63)** - Coral Pink (Miramar Reef)
Form - 0
Record 1998 - 1st:0 2nd:0 3rd:0 Ran:1
1998 Turf 0-1: (7f) (g-s)
Currently little account gelding.
**P R Chamings [0-1] Wai-Chong Lee.*

IDLE RICH (USA) RR 101f 3538a[9]
3 ch f Sky Classic (USA) - Idle Affair (USA)
Form - 1330
1998 Turf 1-4: (7f 1-1, 8f 2, 10f) (sft 1-2, gd 2)
Very useful filly. Turf high 101 (1st run) - 1st of 5 getting 3lb from Kitza (19 Apr Leopardstown RF 0807a). She looked very promising when winning a Listed race on her debut, but did not progress. We may have seen the best of this filly.
**D K Weld in IRE [1-4] John Gunther.*

IDMA BHB 62f RR 65f 5058[2]
3 b f Midyan (USA) 9.9f **(64)** - Garah (Ajdal (USA)) 9.2f **(89)**
Form - 362
Record 1998 - 1st:0 2nd:1 3rd:1 Ran:3
Win Prizemoney £0 *Total Prizemoney* £1,655
1998 Turf 0-3: (7f, 8f 2) (sft, g-s, gd)
Scopey, currently average filly. Turf high 65 (began Oct) - 2nd of 7 to Kingdom Ruby (30 Oct Newcastle 7f sft RF 5058).
**J L Dunlop [0-3] Prince A A Faisal.*

IFTITAH (USA) RR 91++f 4842[1]
2 ch c Gone West (USA) 7.8f **(82)** - Mur Taasha (USA) **(103f)** (Riverman (USA)) 9.1f **(76)**
Form - 1
Record 1998 - 1st:1 2nd:0 3rd:0 Ran:1
Win Prizemoney £6,326 *Total Prizemoney* £6,326
Wins * **1998** Oct Newmar (GD) 7f 91++ <
1998 Turf 1-1: (7f 1-1) (g-f 1-1)
Currently useful colt. (1st run) - 1st of 5 from Bound For Pleasure (16 Oct Newmarket RF 4842). Slammed four rivals to win Newmarket's Houghton Stakes on his sole start, and looks a bright prospect. Likely to prove best at around a mile.
**S bin Suroor [1-1] Godolphin.*

IGREJA (ARG) BHB 99f RR 107?f 4328[9]
4 b f Southern Halo (USA) - Heiress (USA) (Greinton)
Form - 230
Record 1998 - 1st:0 2nd:1 3rd:1 Ran:3
Win Prizemoney £0 *Total Prizemoney* £5,077
1998 Turf 0-3: (7f 3) (gd, g-f, hrd)
Well made, currently Pattern-class filly. Turf high 107 (1st run) (began Jly) - 2nd of 4 getting 5lb from Among Men (2 Jly Yarmouth 7f hrd RF 2475). Like Zola Budd, she arrived from South Africa with a big reputation and, although she ran well behind Among Men on her British debut, she has proved somewhat disappointing. **H R A Cecil [0-3] D I Scott.*

IHTIMAAM (FR) BHB 26f55a RR 35f 55a 4002[10]
6 b g Polish Precedent (USA) 9f **(73)** - Haebeh (USA) (Alydar (USA)) 9.1f **(76)**
Form - 2500
Record 1998 - 1st:0 2nd:1 3rd:0 Ran:4
Pre1998 - 1st:2 2nd:0 3rd:4 Ran:22
Win Prizemoney £4,116 *Total Prizemoney* £6,801
Wins 1996 *Nov Southw (STD) S 11f 63* <
1996 *Jly Southw (STD) C 11f 53*
1998 Turf 0-4: (8f, 11f 2, 12f) (gd, frm 3)
Average gelding, has worn blinkers. Turf high 35 (began Jly).
**H E Haynes [0-4] Mrs H E Haynes (from Mrs A Swinbank [2-24] Aug 1997).*

IHTIYATI (USA) BHB 100f RR 100f 550a[7]
4 ch c Chief's Crown (USA) 10.2f **(75)** - Native Twine (Be My Native (USA)) 10.2f **(71)**
Form - 7
1998 Turf 0-1: (12f) (g-f)
Scopey, very useful colt, effective 10 to 12f, acts on gd to g-f.
**in UAE [0-1] Hamdan Al Maktoum (from J L Dunlop [2-9] Oct 1997).*

IKHTEYAAR (USA) BHB 105f RR 103f 2271[7]
3 b br f Mr Prospector (USA) 8.6f **(88)** - Linda's Magic (USA) (Far North (CAN)) 9.7f **(75)**
Form - 257
Record 1998 - 1st:0 2nd:1 3rd:0 Ran:3
Pre1998 - 1st:2 2nd:2 3rd:0 Ran:4
Win Prizemoney £13,254 *Total Prizemoney* £19,762
Wins * 1997 Oct Doncas (GD) L 6f 91+ <
* 1997 Spt Nottin (G-F) 6.1f 89+
1998 Turf 0-3: (6f, 7f, 8f) (gd, g-f 2)
Scopey, very useful filly, effective 6 to 7f, best at 6f, acts on g-f to frm, best on frm. Turf high 103 (1st run) - 2nd of 9 giving 4lb to Nanoushka (9 May Lingfield 7f g-f RF 1126). A cracking good juvenile, she had a tough race on her reappearance at Lingfield and went backwards thereafter. There was a hint of temperament in her performance at Newcastle in June, and she is one to have reservations about. **R W Armstrong [2-7] Hamdan Al Maktoum.*

IKIS GIRL BHB 32f RR 31f 2590[10]
7 ch m Silver Hawk (USA) 11.2f **(85)** - Jealous One (USA) (Raise A Native) 11.2f **(69)**
Form - 020
Record 1998 - 1st:0 2nd:1 3rd:0 Ran:3
Pre1998 - 1st:0 2nd:2 3rd:1 Ran:17
Win Prizemoney £0 *Total Prizemoney* £3,546
1998 Turf 0-3: (8f 2, 12f) (gd, frm, hrd)
Very moderate mare, has worn blinkers. Turf high 31. Consistent.
**S Gollings [0-12] Ian Stewart (from M Bell [0-8] Spt 1994).*

IKRAM BOY (USA) BHB 43f46a RR 37f 46a 4768[15]
4 b g Salem Drive (USA) 10f **(83)** - Vast Domain (CAN) (Vice Regent (CAN)) 8.7f **(74)**
Form - 40500
Record 1998 - 1st:0 2nd:0 3rd:0 Ran:4
Pre1998 - 1st:0 2nd:0 3rd:0 Ran:5
Win Prizemoney £0 *Total Prizemoney* £483
1998 Turf 0-4: (7f, 9f, 11f 2) (sft, gd 2, frm)
Unfurnished, very moderate gelding, has worn blinkers. Turf high 37. **A Bailey [0-9] Sandybrow Stables Ltd.*

ILANDRA (IRE) BHB 24f24a RR 26f 24a 436[10]
6 b m Roi Danzig (USA) 10.5f **(62)** - Island Goddess (Godswalk (USA)) 7.3f **(58)**
Form - 005360
Record 1998 - 1st:0 2nd:0 3rd:1 Ran:4
Pre1998 - 1st:0 2nd:2 3rd:0 Ran:19
Win Prizemoney £0 *Total Prizemoney* £1,783
1998 AW 0-4: (12f, 13f, 14f, 16f) (Equi, Fibr 3)

Very moderate mare, effective 8f - acts on Fibr, has worn blinkers. AW high 32.
**C L Popham [0-6] Brewers Arms Racing Club (from G L Moore [0-7] Nov 1997).*

IL BAMBINO BHB 33f **RR** 1833[8]

10 ch g Bairn (USA) 9.4f **(55)** - Trapani (Ragusa) 10.7f **(51)**
Form - 8
Record 1998 - 1st:0 2nd:0 3rd:0 Ran:1
Pre1998 - 1st:1 2nd:1 3rd:3 Ran:11
Win Prizemoney £2,673 *Total Prizemoney* £4,639
1998 Turf 0-1: (12f) (gd)
Very poor gelding.
**A J Chamberlain [0-1] H J Manners (from P F I Cole [1-11] Aug 1991).*

IL DESTINO BHB 61f66a **RR 63f 66a** 4065[6]

3 b c Casteddu 7.4f **(54)** - At First Sight (He Loves Me) 7.9f **(55)**
Form - 127066
Record 1998 - 1st:0 2nd:0 3rd:0 Ran:4
Pre1998 - 1st:1 2nd:1 3rd:0 Ran:4
Win Prizemoney £2,294 *Total Prizemoney* £3,130
Wins * 1997 *Nov Lingfi (STD) 7f 62* <
1998 Turf 0-4: (8f 4) (g-f 3, frm)
Scopey, above-average colt, effective 7 to 8f - acts on Equi. Turf high 63. **P J Makin [1-8] Skyline Racing Ltd.*

ILE DE LIBRATE BHB 57f **RR 61f** 3062[15]

4 b g Librate 10.4f **(37)** - Little Missile (Ile de Bourbon (USA)) 10.1f **(67)**
Form - 250
Record 1998 - 1st:0 2nd:1 3rd:0 Ran:3
Pre1998 - 1st:0 2nd:0 3rd:0 Ran:3
Win Prizemoney £0 *Total Prizemoney* £1,060
1998 Turf 0-3: (16f 2, 17f) (gd 2, g-f)
Lengthy, average gelding, effective 16 to 17f, acts on gd to g-f. Turf high 61 (1st run) - 2nd of 4 getting 6lb from Veronica Franco (12 Jun Goodwood 16f gd RF 1927).
**R J O'Sullivan [1-17] Skampcargo Racing Partnership.*

ILE DISTINCT (IRE) BHB 68f **RR 74f** 4748[15]

4 b g Dancing Dissident (USA) 6.8f **(65)** - Golden Sunlight (Ile de Bourbon (USA)) 10.1f **(67)**
Form - 60
Record 1998 - 1st:0 2nd:0 3rd:0 Ran:2
Pre1998 - 1st:2 2nd:0 3rd:2 Ran:8
Win Prizemoney £5,030 *Total Prizemoney* £6,050
Wins * 1997 Spt Nottin (G-F) 10f 69 <
* 1997 Aug Mussel (G-F) 8f 54
1998 Turf 0-2: (8f, 9f) (gd 2)
Workmanlike, above-average gelding, effective 8 to 10f, best at 10f, acts on gd to frm. Turf high 72 (1st run) (began Jly) - 6th of 12 getting 4lb from Bollin Terry (25 Jly Newcastle 8f gd RF 3118).
**Mrs A Swinbank [2-10] Windsor Room Syndicate.*

ILLEGALLY YOURS BHB 33f29a **RR 30f 29a** 91[8]

5 br m Be My Chief (USA) 10.2f **(62)** - Legal Precedent (Star Appeal) 9.6f **(65)**
Form - 68
Record 1998 - 1st:0 2nd:0 3rd:0 Ran:1
Pre1998 - 1st:0 2nd:2 3rd:3 Ran:20
Win Prizemoney £0 *Total Prizemoney* £2,609
1998 AW 0-1: (12f) (Equi)
Very moderate filly, effective 13 to 16f - acts on Equi, has worn blinkers, favours left handed tracks.
**L MontagueHall [0-23] Mrs J Murray.*

ILLINEYLAD (IRE) BHB 22f **RR 20f** 1640[11]

4 b g Whitehall Bridge - Illiney Girl (Lochnager) 6f **(59)**
Form - 0
Record 1998 - 1st:0 2nd:0 3rd:0 Ran:1
Pre1998 - 1st:0 2nd:0 3rd:0 Ran:3
1998 Turf 0-1: (7f) (g-f)
Little account gelding, has worn blinkers.
**J Neville [0-5] Mrs Theresa O'Toole (from M Cunningham in IRE [0-3] Jly 1997).*

ILLUMINATE BHB 52f55a **RR 57f 55a** 2302[8]

5 b g Marju (IRE) 9.2f **(76)** - Light Bee (USA) (Majestic Light (USA)) 10.6f **(75)**
Form - 0288
Record 1998 - 1st:0 2nd:1 3rd:0 Ran:4
Pre1998 - 1st:1 2nd:0 3rd:1 Ran:10
Win Prizemoney £3,257 *Total Prizemoney* £5,349
Wins * 1997 *Feb Lingfi (STD) 12f 64* <
1998 Turf 0-4: (12f, 14f 2, 16f) (gd 3, frm)
Average gelding, effective 12 to 14f, acts on gd - acts on Equi, has worn blinkers. Turf high 57 - 2nd of 8 getting 4lb from Veronica Franco (26 May Sandown 14f gd RF 1485).
**D C O'Brien [1-17] J S Court (from Miss Gay Kelleway [0-2] Aug 1996).*

ILLUSION BHB 107f **RR 108f** 4843[3]

4 b c Green Desert (USA) 7.8f **(78)** - Time Charter (Saritamer (USA)) 9.5f **(63)**
Form - 833
Record 1998 - 1st:0 2nd:0 3rd:2 Ran:3
Pre1998 - 1st:1 2nd:2 3rd:0 Ran:4
Win Prizemoney £5,420 *Total Prizemoney* £11,828
Wins * 1997 Jun York (G-S) 7.9f 82+ <
1998 Turf 0-3: (8f 2, 9f) (sft, gd, g-f)
Scopey, Pattern-class colt, effective 8 to 9f, best at 8f, acts on gd to g-f, best on g-f. Turf high 108 - 3rd of 13 giving 4lb to Haami (16 Oct Newmarket 9f g-f RF 4843). The product of a pedigree of extremes (by Green Desert out of Time Charter), he races like a horse without a trip. Middle-distances could be the answer for this unexposed and useful colt, who was sold to David Nicholls for 25,000 guineas at the Tattersalls Autumn Horses In Training Sales.
**Sir Michael Stoute [1-7] Cheveley Park Stud.*

IL PRINCIPE (IRE) BHB 63f65a **RR 68f 65a** 5118[3]

4 b g Ela-Mana-Mou 12.7f **(72)** - Seattle Siren (USA) (Seattle Slew (USA)) 9.4f **(76)**
Form - 00005183
Record 1998 - 1st:1 2nd:0 3rd:1 Ran:8
Pre1998 - 1st:5 2nd:2 3rd:0 Ran:13
Win Prizemoney £17,777 *Total Prizemoney* £20,266
Wins * **1998** Oct Redcar (G-S) H 14.1f 58 60
* 1997 Spt Catter (G-F) H 15.8f 54 65 <
* 1997 Spt Mussel (G-F) H 16f 46 61
* 1997 *Spt Southw (STD) H 14f 50 59*
* 1997 Aug Mussel (G-F) H 12f 35 48
* 1997 Aug Hamilt (GD) H 11.1f 35 40
1998 Turf 1-8: (8f, 10f, 12f, 14f 1-1, 16f 2, 17f, 18f) (gd 4, g-f 1-3, frm)
Unfurnished, average gelding, effective 14 to 16f, best at 16f, acts on gd to g-f - acts on Fibr, best on g-f, has worn blinkers, favours tight tracks, excels at Musselburgh. Turf high 68 (began Jly) - also 1st of 15 giving 12lb to Joli Flyers (6 Oct Redcar RF 4674).
**John Berry [6-21] The 1997 Partnership.*

IMAD (USA) BHB 46f51a **RR 28f 51a** 4262[14]

8 b or br g Al Nasr (FR) 9.9f **(72)** - Blue Grass Field (Top Ville) 11.7f **(68)**
Form - 20
Record 1998 - 1st:0 2nd:1 3rd:0 Ran:2
Pre1998 - 1st:1 2nd:0 3rd:0 Ran:6
Win Prizemoney £12,427 *Total Prizemoney* £13,059
Wins 1995 Jly Goodwo (FRM) H 20f 60 64 <
1998 Turf 0-1: (16f) (gd) 1998 AW 0-1: (16f) (Fibr)
Moderate gelding, has worn blinkers. Becoming disappointing. He was fit from hurdling when a comfortably-beaten second in a poor handicap on the Wolverhampton Fibresand in April.
**K C Comerford [0-5] Alan Brackley (from J White [3-19] Jun 1996).*

IMANI BHB 61f **RR 65f** 4332[5]

3 b f Danehill (USA) 9.1f **(79)** - Santarem (USA) (El Gran Senor (USA)) 9.6f **(76)**
Form - 806515045
Record 1998 - 1st:1 2nd:0 3rd:0 Ran:9
Win Prizemoney £3,688 *Total Prizemoney* £3,939
Wins * **1998** Jly Newbur (G-F) H 10f 57 65 <
1998 Turf 1-9: (7f, 8f, 9f 2, 10f 1-4, 11f) (g-s, gd 2, g-f 1-3, frm 3)
Average filly, effective 9 to 10f, acts on gd to g-f, prefers left handed tracks. Turf high 65 - 1st of 10 getting 13lb from Jungle Story (17 Jly Newbury RF 2872). **G Lewis [1-9] R N Khan.*

IMBACKAGAIN (IRE) BHB 56f57a **RR 58f 57a** 4001[14]
3 b g Mujadil (USA) 7.7f **(70)** - Ballinclogher (IRE) (Creative Plan (USA)) 7.5f **(67)**
Form - 1685068420
Record 1998 - 1st:1 2nd:1 3rd:0 Ran:10
Pre1998 - 1st:0 2nd:0 3rd:0 Ran:3
Win Prizemoney £2,085 *Total Prizemoney* £3,116
Wins ***1998** *Jan Southw (STD) H 6f 60 64 <*
1998 Turf 0-5: (7f 2, 8f, 9f, 10f) (gd 2, g-f, frm 2) 1998 AW 1-5: (6f 1-1, 7f 3, 9f) (Fibr 1-5)
Tall, average gelding, effective 6 to 9f, acts on frm - acts on Fibr, likes tight tracks. Turf high 61 - 5th of 18 giving 6lb to Wings Awarded (11 May Windsor 8f frm RF 1158). AW high 64 (1st run) - 1st of 7 giving 3lb to Red Pepper (9 Jan Southwell RF 0055).
**N P Littmoden [1-10] M C S D Racing (from P C Haslam [0-3] Aug 1997).*

IMLAK (IRE) BHB 25f **RR 13f** 2229[11]
6 ch g Ela-Mana-Mou 12.7f **(72)** - Mashteen (USA) (Majestic Prince (USA)) 10f **(74)**
Form - 080
Record 1998 - 1st:0 2nd:0 3rd:0 Ran:3
Pre1998 - 1st:0 2nd:0 3rd:0 Ran:12
Win Prizemoney £0 *Total Prizemoney* £531
1998 Turf 0-2: (12f, 17f) (gd 2) 1998 AW 0-1: (11f) (Fibr)
Poor gelding, has broken blood-vessels. Turf high 13. Becoming disappointing.
**J L Harris [0-18] D Jackson (from D Morley [0-7] Oct 1995).*

IMMOVABLE OPTION (IRE) **RR 98f** 4686a[1]
2 b c Fairy King (USA) 7.7f **(75)** - Perfect Welcome
Form - 52131
1998 Turf 2-5: (6f 2-4, 7f) (g-s 1-1, gd 1-4)
Very useful colt. Turf high 98 (began Jly) - 1st of 7 getting 5lb from Rolo Tomasi (3 Oct Curragh RF 4686a). Won a decent listed race over six furlongs, looking likely to be suited by further.
**D K Weld in IRE [2-5] Moyglare Stud Farm.*

IMPELLING (IRE) BHB 65f **RR 65f** 2634[7]
3 ch g Imp Society (USA) 7.1f **(63)** - Real Stunner (Chief Singer) 8.9f **(66)**
Form - 877
Record 1998 - 1st:0 2nd:0 3rd:0 Ran:3
1998 Turf 0-3: (8f 2, 10f) (g-f, frm 2)
Scopey, currently average gelding. Turf high 65.
**K R Burke [0-3] D M Littlejohn and Partners.*

IMPERATOR (IRE) BHB 42f **RR 51f** 4677[18]
3 b g Mac's Imp (USA) 5.6f **(54)** - Secret Hideaway (USA) (Key To The Mint (USA)) 9.4f **(75)**
Form - 8020400
Record 1998 - 1st:0 2nd:1 3rd:0 Ran:7
Pre1998 - 1st:0 2nd:0 3rd:0 Ran:1
Win Prizemoney £0 *Total Prizemoney* £732
1998 Turf 0-7: (6f 2, 7f 4, 8f) (g-s, gd 2, g-f 3, frm)
Workmanlike, fair gelding, effective 7f, acts on gd. Turf high 51 - 2nd of 16 getting 12lb from Frankie Fair (8 Jly Folkestone 7f gd RF 2624). Inconsistent. **Lady Herries [0-8] Imperial Arms Partnership.*

IMPERFECT WORLD (USA) **RR 98+f** 3916a[8]
2 ch f Carson City (USA) - Mais Oui (USA) (Lyphard (USA)) 9.9f **(72)**
Form - 138
1998 Turf 1-3: (5f 1-1, 6f 2) (sft, gd 1-2)
Currently very useful filly. Turf high 98 (1st run) (began Jly) - 1st of 5 getting 3lb from Zirconi (4 Jly Deauville RF 2663a). Speedy French juvenile who looked best at the minimum trip.
**P Bary in FR [1-3] S Fradkoff.*

IMPERIAL BEAUTY (USA) BHB 100f **RR 103f** 4539[2]
2 b f Imperial Ballet (IRE) -Multimara (USA)(Arctic Tern (USA)) 8.9f **(69)**
Form - 212
Record 1998 - 1st:1 2nd:2 3rd:0 Ran:3
Win Prizemoney £6,491 *Total Prizemoney* £42,111
Wins ***1998** Spt Salisb (GD) 6f 90+ <
1998 Turf 1-3: (6f 1-3) (g-f 1-2, frm)
Currently very useful filly. Turf high 103 (began Aug) - 2nd of 9 to Wannabe Grand (29 Spt Newmarket 6f frm RF 4539). She made a bold bid to give her trainer his first Group One winner in a 30-year career when going down narrowly to Wannabe Grand in the Cheveley Park Stakes. She did not have the clearest passage that day, and connections are understandably keen to run her in the 1000 Guineas. Whether she will stay a mile must be open to debate, but she does seem a naturally gifted athlete.
**P J Makin [1-3] Dr Carlos Stelling.*

IMPERIAL COURT (IRE) BHB 27f **RR** 1921[11]
3 b c Imperial Frontier (USA) 7f **(65)** - Fandikos (IRE) (Taufan (USA)) 7f **(57)**
Form - 800
Record 1998 - 1st:0 2nd:0 3rd:0 Ran:3
Pre1998 - 1st:0 2nd:0 3rd:0 Ran:1
1998 Turf 0-2: (6f, 7f) (gd, frm) 1998 AW 0-1: (7f) (Fibr)
Workmanlike, formerly very poor colt, has worn blinkers.
**J G M O'Shea [0-4] M G Lilwall & Partners.*

IMPERIAL GLEN (IRE) BHB 43f40a **RR 44f 40a** 2298[5]
4 b f Imperial Frontier (USA) 7f **(65)** - Tribute to Viqueen (Furry Glen) 8.9f **(63)**
Form - 70185
Record 1998 - 1st:1 2nd:0 3rd:0 Ran:5
Pre1998 - 1st:0 2nd:0 3rd:1 Ran:6
Win Prizemoney £3,365 *Total Prizemoney* £3,728
Wins ***1998** Jun Warwic (SFT) H 10.8f 28 44 <
1998 Turf 1-3: (11f 1-1, 12f, 15f) (sft, gd 1-1, g-f) 1998 AW 0-2: (12f, 14f) (Fibr 2)
Workmanlike, moderate filly, effective 11 to 12f, acts on gd to g-f, has worn blinkers, favours tight tracks. Turf high 44 - 1st of 11 getting 4lb from English Invader (8 Jun Warwick RF 1812). AW high 5. She won a modest apprentice handicap in soft ground at Warwick in June, but the rest of her form is very moderate indeed.
**M D I Usher [1-11] G A Summers.*

IMPERIAL HONEY (IRE) BHB 46f **RR 50f** 4543[14]
3 b f Imperial Frontier (USA) 7f **(65)** - Indian Honey (Indian King (USA)) 7.4f **(64)**
Form - 80085500
Record 1998 - 1st:0 2nd:0 3rd:0 Ran:8
Pre1998 - 1st:0 2nd:1 3rd:0 Ran:5
Win Prizemoney £0 *Total Prizemoney* £792
1998 Turf 0-7: (5f 5, 6f 2) (gd 2, g-f 2, frm 3) 1998 AW 0-1: (6f) (Fibr)
Neat, fair filly, effective 5f, acts on frm. Turf high 57.
**Mrs A Swinbank [0-13] Eddie Shotton.*

IMPERIAL LINE (IRE) BHB 30f **RR 37f** 254[10]
4 ch g Mac's Imp (USA) 5.6f **(54)** - Ellaline (Corvaro (USA)) 9f **(53)**
Form - 5700
Record 1998 - 1st:0 2nd:0 3rd:0 Ran:3
Pre1998 - 1st:0 2nd:0 3rd:0 Ran:7
1998 AW 0-3: (8f 2, 11f) (Fibr 3)
Very moderate gelding, has worn blinkers. AW high 6.
**A B Mulholland [0-10] Hambleton Racing Partnership.*

IMPERIAL PRINCE BHB 62a **RR 79f** 2151[6]
3 b g Prince Sabo 6.6f **(64)** - Joli's Girl (Mansingh (USA)) 7.4f **(55)**
Form - 3225356
Record 1998 - 1st:0 2nd:2 3rd:2 Ran:7
Pre1998 - 1st:0 2nd:0 3rd:0 Ran:1
Win Prizemoney £0 *Total Prizemoney* £2,435
1998 Turf 0-4: (7f, 8f 2, 10f) (g-s, gd, frm 2) 1998 AW 0-3: (8f, 9f, 10f) (Equi, Fibr 2)
Light-framed, above-average gelding, effective 8 to 10f, acts on g-s - acts on AW, often wears blinkers. Turf high 66. AW high 65 - 2nd of 6 getting 19lb from Banneret (21 Mar Wolverhampton 9f Fibr RF 0457). **K McAuliffe [0-8] George Tong.*

IMPETUS BHB 53f **RR 51f** 2194[6]
4 b g Puissance 7.1f **(60)** - Cold Line (Exdirectory)
Form - 0320066
Record 1998 - 1st:0 2nd:1 3rd:1 Ran:7
Pre1998 - 1st:0 2nd:1 3rd:0 Ran:3
Win Prizemoney £0 *Total Prizemoney* £2,616
1998 Turf 0-6: (9f, 10f 3, 12f 2) (sft, g-s, gd 2, g-f, frm) 1998 AW 0-1: (12f) (Fibr)
Fair gelding, effective 10f, acts on g-s to frm. Turf high 57 - 2nd of

15 giving 7lb to Advance East (27 Apr Pontefract 10f g-s RF 0883). Inconsistent. **J Hetherton [0-10] N Hetherton.*

IMP EXPRESS (IRE) BHB 35f36a RR 41f 36a 3309[21]

5 b g Mac's Imp (USA) 5.6f **(54)** - Fair Chance (Young Emperor) 10.1f **(63)**
Form - 062154727060
Record 1998 - 1st:1 2nd:1 3rd:0 Ran:9
Pre1998 - 1st:2 2nd:3 3rd:4 Ran:39
Win Prizemoney £9,564 *Total Prizemoney* £14,694
Wins * 1998 *Jan Wolver (STD) H 5f 35 46*
1995 Jly Ayr (GD) H 5f 63+
1995 Jun Mussel (G-F) S 5f 64 <
1998 Turf 0-1: (5f) (gd) 1998 AW 1-8: (5f 1-6, 6f 2) (Equi, Fibr 1-7)
Moderate gelding, effective 5 to 6f, best at 5f, acts on gd to g-f - acts on Fibr, has worn blinkers. AW high 46 (1st run) - 1st of 12 getting 14lb from Aljaz (7 Jan Wolverhampton RF 0040). Almost exclusively campaigned at the minimum, he scored in good style at Wolverhampton in January. Despite the fact that he makes the frame from time to time, he does not win very often.
**P S Felgate [1-12] J M Flynn (from G M Moore [2-36] Aug 1997).*

IMPISH (IRE) BHB 26a RR 46f 494[9]

4 ch g Imp Society (USA) 7.1f **(63)** - Halimah (Be My Guest (USA)) 9.3f **(67)**
Form - 00077000
Record 1998 - 1st:0 2nd:0 3rd:0 Ran:5
Pre1998 - 1st:1 2nd:0 3rd:4 Ran:21
Win Prizemoney £2,908 *Total Prizemoney* £4,630
Wins * 1997 May Hamilt (SFT) H 5f 43 49 <
1998 AW 0-5: (6f 4, 7f) (Fibr 5)
Strong, moderate gelding, effective 5f, acts on gd, has worn blinkers. AW high 29. **T J Etherington [1-26] Tim Etherington.*

IMPRESSIONIST (IRE) RR 107f 2429a[2]

3 b c Royal Academy (USA) 7.8f **(77)** - Yashville (Top Ville) 11.7f **(68)**
Form - 2
1998 Turf 0-1: (8f) (sft)
Pattern-class colt. (1st run) - 2nd of 3 getting 10lb from Burden Of Proof (28 Jun Curragh 8f sft RF 2429a). A useful juvenile, who won the Group Three Futurity Stakes at the Curragh, before finishing third to Xaar in the Dewhurst, he failed to make the expected progress in 1998. **A P O'Brien in IRE [2-5] Mrs John Magnier.*

I'M PROPOSIN (IRE) BHB 110f RR 104f 4592[1]

3 b c Posen (USA) 8.6f **(59)** - Kitterland (Rheingold) 10.4f **(62)**
Form - 111
Record 1998 - 1st:3 2nd:0 3rd:0 Ran:3
Win Prizemoney £19,283 *Total Prizemoney* £19,283
Wins * 1998 Oct Newmar (gd) L 8f 104 <
*** 1998** Apr Sandow (SFT) 8.1f 95+
*** 1998** Apr Leices (SFT) 8f 83+
1998 Turf 3-3: (8f 3-3) (sft 2-2, gd 1-1)
Lengthy, currently very useful colt. Turf high 104 - 1st of 6 from Generous Rosi (1 Oct Newmarket RF 4592) - also 1st of 4 giving 4lb to Bering Gifts (24 Apr Sandown RF 0846). He caught connections unawares when beating Hitman on his debut at Leicester in April, but proved that was no fluke when following up at Sandown a fortnight later. Off the track for 160 days after suffering a setback, he was very much the stable second string when returned to action in a Listed race at Newmarket in October, but lengthened behind a strong gallop to win going away. Bought to go jumping - he is a big, raw-boned type - this unbeaten colt is open to a deal of improvement and worth a try in Group company.
**J L Dunlop [3-3] Nicholas & Philippa Cooper.*

IMPULSIF (USA) BHB 37f62a RR 35df 62a 4339[12]

4 ch g Diesis 9f **(80)** - High Sevens (Master Willie) 7f **(70)**
Form - 20000800
Record 1998 - 1st:0 2nd:0 3rd:0 Ran:7
Pre1998 - 1st:1 2nd:4 3rd:1 Ran:17
Win Prizemoney £3,479 *Total Prizemoney* £9,756
Wins 1996 Oct Bright (GD) H 7f 74 80 <
1998 Turf 0-7: (6f, 7f 3, 8f 3) (gd, g-f 2, frm 4)
Leggy, average gelding, effective 6 to 8f, acts on g-f to frm - acts on Equi, has worn blinkers. Turf high 35.
**Mrs A L M King [0-7] Mrs Mary Moloney (from D J S ffrenchDavis [1-17] Nov 1997).*

IMPULSIVE AIR (IRE) BHB 58f58a RR 68f 58a 4672[10]

6 b g Try My Best (USA) 7.8f **(68)** - Tracy's Sundown (Red Sunset) 8.2f **(63)**
Form - 211070350800
Record 1998 - 1st:2 2nd:1 3rd:1 Ran:12
Pre1998 - 1st:5 2nd:6 3rd:2 Ran:40
Win Prizemoney £27,487 *Total Prizemoney* £45,873
Wins * 1998 Jun Carlis (G-S) H 8f 65 68 <
*** 1998** May Ripon (GD) H 8f 59 65
* 1997 Aug Mussel (G-F) 7.1f 62
* 1997 Aug Redcar (FRM) 8f 63
* 1996 Aug Newcas (G-F) H 8f 60 64
* 1996 Jun Carlis (FRM) H 6.9f 58 57
* 1994 Apr Haydoc (GD) 5f 68
1998 Turf 2-12: (7f 2, 8f 2-8, 9f 2) (gd 6, g-f 2-5, frm)
Average gelding, effective 7 to 10f, best at 8f, acts on g-s to frm, best on g-f, has worn blinkers, likes right handed tracks, likes tight tracks, excels at Nottingham and does well at Musselburgh. Turf high 68 - 1st of 8 getting 8lb from Sualtach (11 Jun Carlisle RF 1891) - also 1st of 10 giving 2lb to Takhlid (27 May Ripon RF 1533).
**E Weymes [7-52] T A Scothern.*

IMPULSIVE DECISION (IRE) BHB 57f62a RR 63f 62a 4640[12]

3 gr f Nomination 7.3f **(57)** - Siva (FR) (Bellypha) 9.8f **(73)**
Form - 41255600
Record 1998 - 1st:1 2nd:1 3rd:0 Ran:7
Pre1998 - 1st:1 2nd:0 3rd:2 Ran:7
Win Prizemoney £5,573 *Total Prizemoney* £7,245
Wins 1998 *Jan Lingfi (STD) C 8f 60*
1997 Oct Folkes (GD) 6f 63 <
1998 Turf 0-2: (7f, 8f) (gd, frm) 1998 AW 1-5: (7f, 8f 1-3, 9f) (Equi 1-2, Fibr 3)
Light-framed, average filly, effective 6 to 8f, best at 6f, acts on gd to frm - acts on AW. Turf high 47. AW high 66 - 2nd of 5 getting 15lb from One Singer (10 Jan Wolverhampton 7f Fibr RF 0067). Inconsistent.
**A G Newcombe [0-2] B P Ryan (from M Meade [2-12] May 1998).*

IMSHISHWAY (IRE) BHB 59f RR 65f 5126[17]

3 b c Royal Academy (USA) 7.8f **(77)** - Mama Lucia (Workboy) 7.3f **(46)**

Form - 785800700
Record 1998 - 1st:0 2nd:0 3rd:0 Ran:9
Pre1998 - 1st:1 2nd:0 3rd:0 Ran:4
Win Prizemoney £4,802 *Total Prizemoney* £4,802
Wins 1997 Spt Goodwo (GD) 7f 83 <
1998 Turf 0-9: (7f, 8f, 10f 7) (g-s 4, gd 2, g-f 2, frm)
Scopey, average colt, effective 7 to 10f, acts on gd to frm, has worn blinkers, prefers tight tracks. Turf high 75 - 5th of 8 giving 3lb to Praetorian Gold (30 Jun Chepstow 10f gd RF 2397). Inconsistent. Showed very little in 1998.
**M C Pipe [0-2] A S Helaissi (from B J Meehan [1-11] Aug 1998).*

I'M SUPPOSIN (IRE) BHB 104f RR 107f 2085[11]

6 b h Posen (USA) 8.6f **(59)** - Robinia (USA) (Roberto (USA)) 10f **(76)**
Form - 4560
Record 1998 - 1st:0 2nd:0 3rd:0 Ran:4
Pre1998 - 1st:1 2nd:4 3rd:5 Ran:17
Win Prizemoney £32,500 *Total Prizemoney* £54,385
Wins 1996 Jly Down R (GD) H 12.3f 104 105 <
1998 Turf 0-4: (12f, 13f, 16f, 20f) (sft, g-s, gd, frm)
Pattern-class horse. Turf high 113 (1st run) - 4th of 12 to Posidonas (18 Apr Newbury 12f sft RF 0741). In good form over hurdles before reverting to the Flat, where he is still capable of useful form, as a fourth placing in the John Porter Stakes underlines. Over timber is where his future lies.
**R Rowe [1-11] Nicholas Cooper (from K Prendergast in IRE [1-17] Oct 1996).*

I'M TEF BHB 41f66a RR 30f 66a 5017[13]

3 b g Noble Patriarch 12.2f **(43)** - Who's That Lady (Nordance (USA)) 7.5f **(52)**
Form - 2123120000
Record 1998 - 1st:1 2nd:2 3rd:1 Ran:8
Pre1998 - 1st:1 2nd:2 3rd:0 Ran:11
Win Prizemoney £7,025 *Total Prizemoney* £10,807
Wins * 1998 *Jan Southw (STD) H 7f 63 73+* <
* 1997 *Dec Southw (STD) H 7f 54 64*

1998 Turf 0-3:(8f 2, 9f)(g-s, gd, frm)1998 AW 1-5: (6f 2, 7f 1-3)(Fibr 1-5)
Neat, above-average gelding, effective 6 to 7f, best at 7f - acts on Fibr, has worn blinkers, prefers left handed tracks, prefers tight tracks. Turf high 27. AW high 73 - 1st of 6 giving 3lb to Poetto (30 Jan Southwell RF 0193). Becoming disappointing. Showed little on turf during '97, and has since done better in modest company on Fibresand. He won at Southwell in December, but afterwards appeared to throw away a couple of races which he seemed to have in the bag. He looked an awkward ride, and having a senior jockey on him seemed to make a difference when he won back at Southwell in February. He seems best at that track.

**T D Easterby [2-19] T E F Freight (Scarborough) Ltd.*

Scopey, fair colt, effective 8f, acts on g-f. Turf high 68 - 3rd of 10 to Captain's Log (4 May Warwick 8f g-f RF 1030).

**B W Hills [0-6] A L R Morton.*

INCHAHOY BHB 38f **RR 43f** 4656[7]

3 ch f Inchinor 8.9f **(64)** - Ackcontent (USA) (Key To Content (USA)) 8f **(54)**

Form - 06763037

Record	**1998 -**	1st:0	2nd:0	3rd:2	Ran:8
	Pre1998 -	1st:0	2nd:0	3rd:0	Ran:1

Win Prizemoney £0 *Total Prizemoney* £739

1998 Turf 0-8: (8f, 10f 2, 11f 2, 12f 3) (g-s 3, gd 3, frm 2)

I'm Proposin (left) makes it three out of three

INCA TERN BHB 97f **RR 93f** 4739[4]

2 b f Polar Falcon (USA) 9f **(74)** - No Hard Feelings (IRE) (Alzao (USA)) 7.1f **(68)**

Form - 61010474

Record 1998 - 1st:2 2nd:0 3rd:0 Ran:8

Win Prizemoney £5,782 *Total Prizemoney* £8,769

Wins	*** 1998**	Aug Hamilt	(SFT)	5f	77+	<
	*** 1998**	May Bath	(FRM)	5.1f	71+	

1998 Turf 2-8: (5f 2-7, 6f) (g-s, gd 1-6, frm 1-1)

Useful filly, effective 6f, acts on gd. Turf high 93. She won twice in modest company, but faced some stiff tasks otherwise. Sold for 33,000 guineas in October, to race in California.

**G C Bravery [2-8] The TT Partnership.*

INCENTIVE **RR 46f** 4000[7]

3 b c Rainbow Quest (USA) 11.2f **(81)** - In the Groove (Night Shift (USA)) 7.2f **(69)**

Form - 7

Record 1998 - 1st:0 2nd:0 3rd:0 Ran:1

1998 Turf 0-1: (12f) (gd)

Light-framed, currently moderate colt.

**J H M Gosden [0-1] Sheikh Mohammed.*

INCEPTA BHB 57f **RR 56f** 3375[11]

3 b c Selkirk (USA) 7.9f **(76)** - Ringlet (USA) **(53f 54a)** (Secreto (USA)) 8.7f **(72)**

Form - 63040

Record	**1998 -**	1st:0	2nd:0	3rd:1	Ran:5
	Pre1998 -	1st:0	2nd:0	3rd:0	Ran:1

Win Prizemoney £0 *Total Prizemoney* £470

1998 Turf 0-5: (8f 2, 9f, 10f 2) (g-s, gd, g-f, frm 2)

Unfurnished, moderate filly, effective 11f, acts on gd. Turf high 50.

**Miss L A Perratt [0-4] A Doran (from J G Smyth-Osbourne [0-5] Jly 1998).*

INCHALONG BHB 73f **RR 50f** 5014[10]

3 b f Inchinor 8.9f **(64)** - Reshift (Night Shift (USA)) 7.2f **(69)**

Form - 0043440125010000

Record	**1998 -**	1st:2	2nd:1	3rd:1	Ran:16
	Pre1998 -	1st:2	2nd:6	3rd:8	Ran:24

Win Prizemoney £16,825 *Total Prizemoney* £33,997

Wins	*** 1998**	Aug Ripon	(G-F)	H	6f	72	75	<
	*** 1998**	Jly Windso	(GD)	H	6f	69	72	
	* 1997	Aug Mussel	(GD)	H	7.1f	64	70	
	* 1997	Jun Newcas	(GD)	S	6f		61	

1998 Turf 2-16: (5f, 6f 2-8, 7f 7) (gd 1-7, g-f 4, frm 1-4, hrd)

Light-framed, fair filly, effective 6 to 7f, best at 7f, acts on gd to hrd, has worn blinkers, likes tight tracks, excels at Newmarket, does well at Doncaster. Turf high 75 - 3rd of 6 getting 3lb from John Ferneley (1 Jun Thirsk 7f g-f RF 1632) - also 1st of 20 giving 11lb to Stately Princess (31 Aug Ripon RF 3999). Consistent. A tough and speedy sprint handicapper who will continue to win races in the right grade.

**M Brittain [4-40] Northgate Lodge Partnerships.*

INCH PERFECT **RR 77df** 3364[3]

3 b g Inchinor 8.9f **(64)** - Scarlet Veil (Tyrnavos) 10.1f **(55)**

Form - 43

Record 1998 - 1st:0 2nd:0 3rd:1 Ran:2

Win Prizemoney £0 *Total Prizemoney* £597

1998 Turf 0-2: (10f, 12f) (g-f 2)

Scopey, currently above-average gelding. Turf high 77.

**W G M Turner [0-2] Diamond Racing Ltd.*

INCHRORY BHB 108f **RR 107f** 4348a[1]
5 b h Midyan (USA) 9.9f **(64)** - Applecross (Glint of Gold) 9.3f **(66)**
Form - 1
1998 Turf 1-1: (12f 1-1) (sft 1-1)
Pattern-class colt. (1st run) - 1st of 11 giving 9lb to Exaltation (13 Spt Taby RF 4348a). Improving. He put up a dominant display when winning a Group Three at Taby in September and is no pushover.
**A Hyldmo in NOR [1-2] Stall M I (from H R A Cecil [3-6] Oct 1995).*

INCHTINA BHB 80f **RR 86f** 4966[10]
3 b f Inchinor 8.9f **(64)** - Nikitina (Nijinsky (CAN)) 10.3f **(77)**
Form - 1680
Record 1998 - 1st:1 2nd:0 3rd:0 Ran:4
Pre1998 - 1st:0 2nd:2 3rd:0 Ran:2
Win Prizemoney £4,467 *Total Prizemoney* £6,636
Wins * 1998 Apr Nottin (SFT) 8.2f 71 <
1998 Turf 1-4: (8f 1-1, 10f 3) (sft, g-s 1-1, g-f 2)
Light-framed, useful filly, effective 7f, acts on frm. Turf high 86. Landed her maiden at Nottingham but has been well held since.
**H Candy [1-6] Peter Stevenson.*

INCLINATION BHB 57a **RR 51f** 4931[14]
4 b f Beveled (USA) 6.9f **(64)** - Pallomere (Blue Cashmere) 6.4f **(54)**
Form - 5128247302753680
Record 1998 - 1st:1 2nd:3 3rd:2 Ran:16
Pre1998 - 1st:0 2nd:3 3rd:6 Ran:15
Win Prizemoney £2,083 *Total Prizemoney* £11,045
Wins 1998 *Feb Southw (STD) H 8f 56 57* <
1998 Turf 0-11: (7f 2, 8f 6, 10f 2, 12f) (g-s 4, gd 3, g-f 2, hrd 2) 1998 AW 1-5: (8f 1-3, 9f, 10f) (Equi, Fibr 1-4)
Scopey, fair filly, effective 7 to 10f, best at 7f, acts on sft to frm - acts on Fibr, best on g-f, and excels at Leicester. Turf high 57 (1st run) - 2nd of 15 giving 9lb to Ardent (20 Apr Brighton 8f g-s RF 0766). AW high 57 - 1st of 10 giving 19lb to Bella's Legacy (2 Feb Southwell RF 0201). It took her a devil of a long time to get off the mark, despite several placings, but managed to score narrowly in a handicap on the Southwell Fibresand in February. She will need to find another poor race in order to supplement that win however.
**Mrs L C Jewell [0-1] R B Morton (from M Blanshard [1-31] Aug 1998).*

INCLUDE ME OUT BHB 63f **RR 66f** 3770[5]
4 ch g Old Vic 12.8f **(72)** - Tafila (Adonijah) 10f **(61)**
Form - 002215
Record 1998 - 1st:1 2nd:2 3rd:0 Ran:6
Pre1998 - 1st:0 2nd:0 3rd:0 Ran:3
Win Prizemoney £3,964 *Total Prizemoney* £7,344
Wins * 1998 Aug Redcar (G-F) H 10f 62 66 <
1998 Turf 1-6: (9f, 10f 1-4, 14f) (gd 2, g-f 2, frm 1-2)
Well made, average gelding, effective 10f, acts on frm. Turf high 66. He gradually got it together as the season progressed, and after a couple of good efforts at Nottingham, scored in good style at Redcar. Ten furlongs on fast ground seems to suit him best.
**J Wharton [1-6] Mrs Davina Whiteman (from J R Fanshawe [0-3] Oct 1996).*

IN COMMAND (IRE) BHB 107f **RR 109?f** 473[8]
4 b c Sadler's Wells (USA) 11.3f **(87)** - Flying Melody (Auction Ring (USA)) 8.6f **(65)**
Form - 8
Record 1998 - 1st:0 2nd:0 3rd:0 Ran:1
Pre1998 - 1st:2 2nd:1 3rd:2 Ran:8
Win Prizemoney £90,505 *Total Prizemoney* £125,165
Wins * 1996 Oct Newmar (GD) G1 7f 116 <
* 1996 Jly Goodwo (G-F) 6f 98+
1998 Turf 0-1: (8f) (gd)
Well made, Pattern-class colt. Winner of the 1996 Dewhurst, he has had his problems. **B W Hills [2-9] Maktoum Al Maktoum.*

INDECISION **RR 56f** 2310[8]
2 b g Aragon 7.7f **(58)** - Top Cover (High Top) 10.2f **(67)**
Form - 7588
Record 1998 - 1st:0 2nd:0 3rd:0 Ran:4
1998 Turf 0-4: (5f 3, 6f) (g-s 2, gd 2)
Fair gelding, had worn blinkers. Turf high 56. (DEAD)

**T D Easterby [0-4] Peter Bourke.*

INDIA (IRE) **RR 63f** 2731[3]
3 b f Indian Ridge 7.6f **(74)** - Athens Belle (IRE) (Groom Dancer (USA))
Form - 43
Record 1998 - 1st:0 2nd:0 3rd:1 Ran:2
Win Prizemoney £0 *Total Prizemoney* £755
1998 Turf 0-2: (7f, 10f) (gd, frm)
Workmanlike, currently average filly. Turf high 63 - 3rd of 7 getting 5lb from Polish Spirit (11 Jly Warwick 7f frm RF 2731).
**L M Cumani [0-2] Fittocks Stud.*

INDIANA LEGEND (IRE) BHB 100f **RR 99f** 4746[2]
2 ch c Indian Ridge 7.6f **(74)** - Mardi Gras Belle (USA) (Masked Dancer (USA))
Form - 21422
Record 1998 - 1st:1 2nd:3 3rd:0 Ran:5
Win Prizemoney £3,468 *Total Prizemoney* £29,076
Wins * 1998 Jly Windso (G-F) 6f 85 <
1998 Turf 1-5: (6f 1-5) (sft, gd, g-f 2, frm 1-1)
Very useful colt. Turf high 99 (began Jly) - 2nd of 11 to Undeterred (10 Oct York 6f gd RF 4746). Fourth in the Prix Morny, he was caught on the line by Golden Silca in the Mile Reef Stakes and looked slightly over the top when a narrow second in a listed race on his final start. **B J Meehan [1-5] D B Johnston.*

INDIANA PRINCESS BHB 57f **RR 59?f** 3905[5]
5 b m Warrshan (USA) 9.7f **(59)** - Lovely Greek Lady (Ela-Mana-Mou) 10.1f **(70)**
Form - 14165
Record 1998 - 1st:2 2nd:0 3rd:0 Ran:5
Pre1998 - 1st:0 2nd:1 3rd:0 Ran:9
Win Prizemoney £6,394 *Total Prizemoney* £7,479
Wins * 1998 Jly Pontef (G-F) H 12f 49 59 <
*** 1998** May Pontef (G-F) H 12f 46 47
1998 Turf 2-5: (12f 2-3, 13f, 14f) (g-f 2, frm 2-3)
Fair filly, effective 12f, acts on frm, prefers left handed tracks, favours tight tracks. Turf high 59 - 1st of 11 getting 10lb from Ordained (17 Jly Pontefract RF 2885).
**Mrs M Reveley [4-19] Wentdale Racing Partnership.*

INDIAN BAZAAR (IRE) BHB 40f **RR 18f** 5139[18]
2 ch c Indian Ridge 7.6f **(74)**-Bazaar Promise (Native Bazaar) 6.9f **(62)**
Form - 000
Record 1998 - 1st:0 2nd:0 3rd:0 Ran:3
1998 Turf 0-3: (5f 2, 6f) (g-s, gd 2)
Currently poor colt. Turf high 18 (began Oct).
**Sir Mark Prescott [0-3] W E Sturt.*

INDIAN BLAZE BHB 61f **RR 62f** 5128[1]
4 ch g Indian Ridge 7.6f **(74)** - Odile (Green Dancer (USA)) 10.3f **(74)**
Form - 26P00041
Record 1998 - 1st:1 2nd:1 3rd:0 Ran:8
Pre1998 - 1st:0 2nd:2 3rd:0 Ran:10
Win Prizemoney £1,955 *Total Prizemoney* £4,948
Wins * 1998 Nov Bright (SFT) H 6f 55 62 <
1998 Turf 1-6: (6f 1-3, 7f 2, 8f) (g-s 1-3, gd, g-f, frm) 1998 AW 0-2: (9f 2) (Fibr 2)
Workmanlike, average gelding, effective 6 to 10f, acts on g-s to frm - acts on Fibr, has worn blinkers, prefers left handed tracks, prefers tight tracks. Turf high 62 - 1st of 16 getting 6lb from Akalim (5 Nov Brighton RF 5128). AW high 55 (1st run) - 2nd of 8 getting 7lb from Be Warned (7 Feb Wolverhampton 9f Fibr RF 0250). Inconsistent.
**D R C Elsworth [1-5] The Braves (from P W Harris [0-13] Apr 1998).*

INDIAN BRAVE BHB 71f **RR 73f** 4390[3]
4 b c Indian Ridge 7.6f **(74)** - Supreme Kingdom (Take A Reef) 7.5f **(59)**
Form - 258507523
Record 1998 - 1st:0 2nd:2 3rd:1 Ran:9
Pre1998 - 1st:0 2nd:1 3rd:1 Ran:4
Win Prizemoney £0 *Total Prizemoney* £5,743
1998 Turf 0-9: (6f 8, 7f) (sft, gd 4, frm 4)
Scopey, above-average colt, effective 6f, acts on gd, has worn blinkers. Turf high 80 (1st run) - 2nd of 22 getting 5lb from Always Alight (27 Mar Doncaster 6f gd RF 0477). Consistent. A maiden, he was a narrow second in a big field of sprint handicappers at

Doncaster in March having been off the track for nine months, and has put in some fair efforts since.
**B J Meehan [0-9] J R Good (from M Johnston [0-4] Jun 1997).*

INDIAN CHARLIE (USA) RR 119f 1090a[3]
3 b c In Excess - Soviet Sojourn (USA) (Leo Castelli (USA))
Form - 3
1998 Turf 0-1: (10f) (frm)
Currently high-class colt. (1st run) - 3rd of 15 to Real Quiet (2 May Churchill Downs 10f frm RF 1090a). **B Baffert in USA [0-1].*

INDIAN CITY BHB 61f RR 74f 3982[7]
2 ch f Lahib (USA) 8f **(69)** - Alencon (Northfields (USA)) 9f **(72)**
Form - 217
Record 1998 - 1st:1 2nd:1 3rd:0 Ran:3
Win Prizemoney £2,024 *Total Prizemoney* £2,542
Wins * 1998 Aug Leices (GD) S 6f 74 <
1998 Turf 1-3: (6f 1-1, 7f 2) (g-f 2, frm 1-1)
Currently above-average filly. Turf high 74 (began Aug) - 1st of 14 from Light On The Waves (19 Aug Leicester RF 3741).
**R Guest [1-3] Mrs P D Savill.*

INDIAN FLAG (IRE) BHB 48f RR 55f 2533[11]
3 ch f Indian Ridge 7.6f **(74)** - Flagpole (IRE) (Be My Guest (USA)) 9.3f **(67)**
Form - 0030
Record 1998 - 1st:0 2nd:0 3rd:1 Ran:4
Win Prizemoney £0 *Total Prizemoney* £560
1998 Turf 0-4: (6f 2, 7f, 8f) (gd 3, g-f)
Lengthy, fair filly. Turf high 55. **J J Bridger [0-4] P Sweeting.*

INDIAN LODGE (IRE) BHB 80f RR 92f 5039[6]
2 b c Grand Lodge (USA) - Repetitious (Northfields (USA)) 9f **(72)**
Form - 386
Record 1998 - 1st:0 2nd:0 3rd:1 Ran:3
Win Prizemoney £0 *Total Prizemoney* £485
1998 Turf 0-3: (7f 2, 8f) (g-s, g-f, frm)
Currently useful colt. Turf high 92 (began Spt).
**Mrs A J Perrett [0-3] Seymour Cohn.*

INDIAN MISSILE BHB 90f RR 93f 4742[14]
3 ch c Indian Ridge 7.6f **(74)** - Haitienne (FR) (Green Dancer (USA)) 10.3f **(74)**
Form - 033221300
Record 1998 - 1st:1 2nd:2 3rd:3 Ran:9
Pre1998 - 1st:1 2nd:2 3rd:1 Ran:5
Win Prizemoney £10,469 *Total Prizemoney* £22,444
Wins * 1998 Jun Salisb (G-F) H 12f 85 88+ <
1997 Jun Chepst (G-F) 6.1f 70
1998 Turf 1-9: (7f, 8f, 9f, 10f 2, 11f, 12f 1-3) (sft, g-s, gd 4, g-f, frm 1-2)
Workmanlike, useful colt, effective 7 to 12f, best at 12f, acts on sft to frm, best on frm, likes tight tracks, excels at Salisbury. Turf high 93 - 3rd of 7 getting 12lb from Tough Leader (10 Jly York 12f frm RF 2699) - also 1st of 7 giving 3lb to Yanabi (24 Jun Salisbury RF 2253). Fair efforts in handicaps for his new yard in 1998, often making the frame before stepping up in trip to win at Salisbury. Below form in his last two starts, he was sold for 25,000 at Tattersalls Autumn horses-in-training sale.
**Major D N Chappell [1-9] R C C Villers (from J L Dunlop [1-5] Oct 1997).*

INDIAN NECTAR BHB 40f51a RR 39f 51a 1134[11]
5 b m Indian Ridge 7.6f **(74)** - Sheer Nectar (Piaffer (USA))
Form - 0
Record 1998 - 1st:0 2nd:0 3rd:0 Ran:1
Pre1998 - 1st:0 2nd:0 3rd:0 Ran:10
Win Prizemoney £0 *Total Prizemoney* £507
1998 Turf 0-1: (8f) (hrd)
Very moderate filly, has worn blinkers.
**R Brotherton [0-13] Mrs Carol Newman (from G B Balding [0-8] Mar 1997).*

INDIANNIE (IRE) BHB 50f RR 54f 4915[10]
2 b f Anita's Prince 6f **(62)** - Regal Charmer (Royal And Regal (USA)) 9.5f **(60)**
Form - 780
Record 1998 - 1st:0 2nd:0 3rd:0 Ran:3
1998 Turf 0-3: (5f, 6f, 7f) (g-s, gd, g-f)
Currently fair filly. Turf high 54 (began Spt).
**M R Channon [0-3] Timberhill Racing Partnership.*

INDIAN PLUME BHB 85f RR 91f 4353[4]
2 b c Efisio 7.7f **(69)** - Boo Hoo (Mummy's Pet) 7.7f **(60)**
Form - 514
Record 1998 - 1st:1 2nd:0 3rd:0 Ran:3
Win Prizemoney £3,191 *Total Prizemoney* £3,555
Wins * 1998 Aug Pontef (G-F) 6f 77 <
1998 Turf 1-3: (6f 1-2, 7f) (sft, gd, frm 1-1)
Currently useful colt. Turf high 77 (began Jly) - 1st of 12 from Kinan (5 Aug Pontefract RF 3389). Improved from his debut to score in game style at Pontefract, and may be even better suited by a softer surface. Finished lame on his last start.
**C W Thornton [1-3] Guy Reed.*

INDIAN POINT (GER) RR 105f 4831a[3]
5 b h Indian Ridge 7.6f **(74)** - Trull **(100f)** (Lomond)
Form - 23
1998 Turf 0-2: (7f 2) (sft 2)
Currently Pattern-class colt. Turf high 105 (began Aug) - 3rd of 10 getting 4lb from Tomba (11 Oct Munich 7f sft RF 4831a). He is useful, but unlikely to improve further. **D Richardson in GER [0-2].*

INDIAN SILVER BHB 56f RR 56f 4202[18]
3 b f Indian Ridge 7.6f **(74)** - Ovideo **(58f)** (Domynsky) 8f **(82)**
Form - 0080470
Record 1998 - 1st:0 2nd:0 3rd:0 Ran:7
Pre1998 - 1st:0 2nd:2 3rd:0 Ran:4
Win Prizemoney £0 *Total Prizemoney* £2,754
1998 Turf 0-7: (5f 2, 6f 2, 7f 3) (gd 3, g-f, frm 2, hrd)
Unfurnished, fair filly, effective 5f, acts on gd. Turf high 56 (began Jly). **M R Channon [0-11] Anthony Andrews.*

INDIAN SPARK BHB 90f RR 87f 5096[18]
4 ch c Indian Ridge 7.6f **(74)** - Annes Gift (Ballymoss) 8.5f **(55)**
Form - 0006725421640100010
Record 1998 - 1st:3 2nd:2 3rd:0 Ran:19
Pre1998 - 1st:2 2nd:3 3rd:0 Ran:13
Win Prizemoney £29,926 *Total Prizemoney* £40,643
Wins * 1998 Oct Doncas (HVY) H 5f 84 87
*** 1998** Spt Doncas (GD) H 5f 80 84
*** 1998** Jly Thirsk (FRM) H 6f 76 82
1997 May Salisb (G-F) H 6f 98 99 <
1996 Mar Doncas (GD) 5f 85+
1998 Turf 3-19: (5f 2-8, 6f 1-10, 7f) (sft 1-2, g-s 2, gd 7, g-f 1-4, frm 1-4)
Workmanlike, useful colt, effective 6f, acts on gd to g-f, best on g-f, does well at Doncaster. Turf high 87.
**J S Goldie [3-21] Frank Brady (from W G M Turner [2-11] Spt 1997).*

INDIAN SPLENDOUR (IRE) BHB 50a RR 50a 572[6]
3 b f Second Set (IRE) 9.2f **(67)** - Clover Honey (King of Clubs) 7.1f **(57)**
Form - 48426
Record 1998 - 1st:0 2nd:1 3rd:0 Ran:3
Pre1998 - 1st:0 2nd:0 3rd:0 Ran:2
Win Prizemoney £0 *Total Prizemoney* £715
1998 AW 0-3: (5f 3) (Fibr 3)
Neat, moderate filly. AW high 48 (1st run) - 4th of 12 to Sing For Me (11 Feb Wolverhampton 5f Fibr RF 0268). **R Guest [0-5] Vijay Mallya.*

INDIAN SWINGER (IRE) BHB 66f70a RR 61f 70a 4876[1]
2 ch c Up and At 'em - Seanee Squaw (Indian Ridge)
Form - 4881
Record 1998 - 1st:1 2nd:0 3rd:0 Ran:4
Win Prizemoney £3,099 *Total Prizemoney* £3,331
Wins * 1998 *Oct Southw (STD) H 6f 62 69* <
1998 Turf 0-3: (5f 2, 6f) (gd, frm 2) 1998 AW 1-1: (6f 1-1) (Fibr 1-1)
Average colt. Turf high 61 (began Aug). (1st run) - 1st of 13 getting 23lb from Blue Star (19 Oct Southwell RF 4876).
**J M P Eustace [1-4] Kissing Tree Partnership.*

INDIAN WARRIOR BHB 88f RR 81f 3803[10]
2 b c Be My Chief (USA) 10.2f **(62)** - Wanton (Kris) 9.5f **(73)**
Form - 22310
Record 1998 - 1st:1 2nd:2 3rd:1 Ran:5

Win Prizemoney £3,444 *Total Prizemoney* £6,421
Wins * **1998** Aug Warwic (G-F) 7f 81 <
1998 Turf 1-5: (6f 3, 7f 1-2) (gd, frm 1-4)
Decent colt. Turf high 81 (began Jly) - also 1st of 12 from Mundahish (14 Aug Warwick RF 3646).
**J Noseda [1-5] Hesmonds Stud.*

INDIGHIRKA (FR) RR 104f 1226a[2]
4 b f Bering 9.6f **(80)** - Innisfree (FR) (Crystal Palace (FR)) 12.5f **(76)**
Form - 2
1998 Turf 0-1: (11f) (g-s)
Currently very useful filly. (1st run) - 2nd of 9 to Lexa (8 May Lyon Parilly 11f g-s RF 1226a). She ran a nailer when touched off by Lexa at Lyon Parilly. On that form she will win a Group race.
**L Boulard in FR [0-1] J C Seroul.*

INDIGO BAY (IRE) BHB 72f **RR 69f** 4806[7]
2 b c Royal Academy (USA) 7.8f **(77)** - Cape Heights (Shirley Heights) 10.3f **(74)**
Form - 007
Record 1998 - 1st:0 2nd:0 3rd:0 Ran:3
1998 Turf 0-3: (7f 2, 8f) (gd, frm 2)
Currently average colt. Turf high 69 (began Aug).
**A C Stewart [0-3] Clare Hall Racing Ltd.*

INDIGO BEACH (IRE) BHB 53f60a **RR 50f 60a** 5094[7]
2 b g Rainbows For Life (CAN) 9.3f **(64)** - Sandy Maid (Sandy Creek) 8.9f **(59)**
Form - 70607
Record 1998 - 1st:0 2nd:0 3rd:0 Ran:5
1998 Turf 0-4: (6f, 7f 2, 8f) (g-s, gd, frm 2) 1998 AW 0-1: (6f) (Fibr)
Average gelding. Turf high 50 (began Spt).
**Sir Mark Prescott [0-5] Thurcoe Partnership.*

INDIGO DAWN BHB 60f71a **RR 57f 71a** 4659[2]
4 b f Rainbow Quest (USA) 11.2f **(81)** - Dame Ashfield (Grundy) 10.3f **(65)**
Form - 1132002
Record 1998 - 1st:0 2nd:2 3rd:1 Ran:5
Pre1998 - 1st:5 2nd:2 3rd:4 Ran:15
Win Prizemoney £12,733 *Total Prizemoney* £18,180
Wins * 1997 *Dec Lingfi (STD) H 16f 65 71* <
* 1997 *Nov Lingfi (STD) H 16f 62 69*
* 1997 *Jly Southw (STD) H 14f 59 65*
* 1997 Jly Warwic (G-F) H 14.9f 55 59
* 1997 Jly Hamilt (G-S) H 13f 55 60
1998 Turf 0-3: (16f 2, 17f) (gd 2, frm) 1998 AW 0-2: (16f 2) (Fibr 2)
Workmanlike, above-average filly, effective 12 to 16f, best at 16f, acts on frm - acts on AW, best on Equi, often wears blinkers, likes left handed tracks, excels at Wolverhampton and Lingfield. Turf high 57 (began Spt). AW high 72 - 2nd of 6 giving 2lb to Shakiyr (10 Jan Wolverhampton 16f Fibr RF 0069). Inconsistent.
**M Johnston [5-20] Greenland Park Ltd.*

INDIKATOR (GER) RR 110f 4078a[1]
3 c Sillery (USA) - Indica (GER) 00
Form - 01
1998 Turf 1-2: (11f 1-1, 12f) (hvy, gd 1-1)
Currently Group-class colt. Turf high 110 (began Jly) - 1st of 8 from Scorned (30 Aug Baden-Baden RF 4078a). He put up a smart effort when winning a Group Three at Baden-Baden in August. That form was boosted when the placed horses went on to win in decent company and he will be a force to reckon with in 1999.
**A Wohler in GER [1-2] Turf Syndicat 97.*

INDIMAAJ BHB 84f **RR 90f** 4647[11]
3 b c Mtoto 11.5f **(71)** - Fairy Feet (Sadler's Wells (USA)) 10f **(76)**
Form - 18647280
Record 1998 - 1st:1 2nd:1 3rd:0 Ran:8
Pre1998 - 1st:0 2nd:1 3rd:2 Ran:3
Win Prizemoney £3,557 *Total Prizemoney* £8,981
Wins * **1998** Apr Leices (SFT) 11.8f 87+ <
1998 Turf 1-8: (12f 1-6, 13f, 14f) (sft 1-1, g-s, gd 2, g-f 4)
Workmanlike, useful colt, effective 12f, acts on sft to g-f, has worn blinkers, likes right handed tracks. Turf high 90 - 2nd of 6 getting 1lb from Rakeeb (6 Aug Haydock 12f g-f RF 3411) - also 1st of 8 from Dutch Lad (2 Apr Leicester RF 0546). From the family of Light Cavalry and Fairy Footsteps, he always looked as though he would be suited by middle distances. He duly won a twelve-furlong maiden in soft ground at Leicester on his reappearance, but did not manage to win again during the season, despite one or two fair efforts. **J L Dunlop [1-11] Kuwait Racing Syndicate.*

INDIUM BHB 76f64a **RR 77f 64a** 5078[7]
4 b g Groom Dancer (USA) 9.5f **(75)** - Gold Bracelet (Golden Fleece (USA)) 7.9f **(74)**
Form - 05037208D041007
Record 1998 - 1st:1 2nd:1 3rd:1 Ran:15
Pre1998 - 1st:0 2nd:0 3rd:2 Ran:5
Win Prizemoney £18,075 *Total Prizemoney* £21,359
Wins * **1998** Spt Newbur (GD) H 8f 71 77 <
1998 Turf 1-13: (7f, 8f 1-10, 10f 2) (sft, gd 4, g-f 1-3, frm 4, hrd) 1998 AW 0-2: (10f 2) (Equi 2)
Scopey, above-average gelding, effective 8f, acts on g-f to frm, best on frm, prefers left handed tracks, likes tight tracks. Turf high 77 - 1st of 20 getting 4lb from Gaily Mill (19 Spt Newbury RF 4381). AW high 26. Consistent. Inclined to blow a bit hot and cold, he is quite useful when on song. He won an amateurs' handicap on the July Course under 'Angel Jacobs', and caused a bit of a surprise by winning a valuable handicap at Newbury in September. Best coming from off a strong pace.
**W J Musson [1-15] Magnificent Seven (from J H M Gosden [0-5] Jun 1997).*

INDUCEMENT BHB 83f **RR 84f** 4709[6]
2 ch c Sabrehill (USA) 8.5f **(64)** - Verchinina (Star Appeal) 9.6f **(65)**
Form - 33146
Record 1998 - 1st:1 2nd:0 3rd:2 Ran:5
Win Prizemoney £3,250 *Total Prizemoney* £5,698
Wins * **1998** Aug Beverl (G-F) 8.5f 81 <
1998 Turf 1-5: (6f, 7f, 8f 1-3) (g-s, gd, g-f 1-2, frm)
Decent colt. Turf high 84 (1st run) - 3rd of 9 to Focus (13 Jun York 6f g-s RF 1979) - also 1st of 9 from Nowhere To Exit (24 Aug Beverley RF 3833). **B W Hills [1-5] W J Gredley.*

INDY KNIGHT (IRE) BHB 49f **RR 52f** 4529[15]
3 ch f Indian Ridge 7.6f **(74)** - Bag Lady (Be My Guest (USA)) 9.3f **(67)**
Form - 070
Record 1998 - 1st:0 2nd:0 3rd:0 Ran:3
Pre1998 - 1st:0 2nd:0 3rd:0 Ran:2
1998 Turf 0-3: (8f 2, 11f) (g-f, frm 2)
Leggy, fair filly. Turf high 52 (began Jly).
**M J Fetherston-Godley [0-2] Derek D & Mrs Jean P Clee (from M Meade [0-3] Jly 1998).*

INDY VIDUAL (USA) RR 117f 4341a[3]
4 b c A P Indy (USA) - I'm Splendid (USA)(Our Native (USA)) 11.2f **(63)**
Form - 3
1998 Turf 0-1: (11f) (frm)
Currently high-class colt. (1st run) - 3rd of 9 to Daylami (12 Spt Belmont Park 11f frm RF 4341a). **J Kimmel in USA [0-1].*

INFAMOUS (USA) BHB 70f75a **RR 75f 75a** 3984[7]
5 ch g Diesis 9f **(80)** - Name And Fame (USA) (Arts And Letters (USA)) 12.7f **(68)**
Form - 6247
Record 1998 - 1st:0 2nd:1 3rd:0 Ran:4
Pre1998 - 1st:1 2nd:3 3rd:2 Ran:13
Win Prizemoney £3,595 *Total Prizemoney* £10,351
Wins 1996 Mar Leices (SFT) 11.8f 79 <
1998 Turf 0-4: (12f 4) (g-f 4)
Above-average gelding, effective 12f, acts on g-f, has worn blinkers. Turf high 75 - 2nd of 8 to Tough Act (19 Jun Goodwood 12f g-f RF 2120).
**R J O'Sullivan [2-15] Mrs Barbara Marchant (from P F I Cole [1-11] Spt 1996).*

INFATUATION BHB 82f **RR 89f** 4986[6]
5 b g Music Boy 6.5f **(56)** - Fleeting Affair (Hotfoot) 10.5f **(59)**
Form - 467216536
Record 1998 - 1st:1 2nd:1 3rd:1 Ran:9
Pre1998 - 1st:2 2nd:2 3rd:2 Ran:11
Win Prizemoney £28,374 *Total Prizemoney* £37,794
Wins * **1998** Aug Newmar (G-F) H 10f 83 88 <

* 1997 Spt Doncas (G-F) H 10.3f 77 82
* 1997 Jun Beverl (SFT) H 12f 71 77

1998 Turf 1-9: (10f 1-7, 12f 2) (sft, g-s, gd, g-f, frm 1-5)

Useful gelding, effective 10 to 12f, best at 10f, acts on sft to frm. Turf high 89 - 3rd of 15 getting 7lb from Present Arms (10 Oct Ascot 10f g-s RF 4742) - also 1st of 12 getting 6lb from Brilliant Red (29 Aug Newmarket RF 3955). Consistent. Got off the mark in a small handicap at Beverley last season, and held his form well subsequently. He did not settle in either of his first two starts this season, and will be suited by a strongly-run race. He showed a return to form at Sandown latest, and this may be his time of year.

**Lady Herries [3-20] Lady Katharine Phillips.*

INFIRAAJ (USA) BHB 38f38a **RR 15f 38a** 1116[15]

6 b g Dayjur (USA) 6.8f **(79)** - Capricorn Belle (Nonoalco (USA)) 8.5f **(66)**

Form - 7480

Record 1998 - 1st:0 2nd:0 3rd:0 Ran:4
Pre1998 - 1st:0 2nd:0 3rd:0 Ran:4

Win Prizemoney £0 *Total Prizemoney* £256

1998 Turf 0-1: (7f) (frm) 1998 AW 0-3: (7f, 8f, 16f) (Fibr 3)

Moderate gelding, has worn blinkers. AW high 40 - 4th of 14 giving 7lb to Patina (27 Feb Southwell 8f Fibr RF 0370).

**S R Bowring [0-5] D J W Edmunds (from Mrs D Haine [0-4] Jun 1996).*

INFLATION BHB 57f51a **RR 64f 51a** 2724[6]

4 b f Primo Dominie 7.2f **(67)** - Fluctuate (Sharpen Up) 8.3f **(67)**

Form - 600206

Record 1998 - 1st:0 2nd:1 3rd:0 Ran:6
Pre1998 - 1st:0 2nd:1 3rd:1 Ran:3

Win Prizemoney £0 *Total Prizemoney* £2,211

1998 Turf 0-3: (6f 2, 7f) (g-s, gd, frm) 1998 AW 0-3: (6f 3) (Fibr 3)

Scopey, average filly, has worn blinkers. Turf high 64. AW high 56. Inconsistent.

**J P Leigh [0-6] J W Rowles (from R F JohnsonHoughton [0-3] May 1997).*

INFLITE **RR 84f** 1524[2]

2 b c Indian Ridge 7.6f **(74)** - Nightitude **(58f)** (Night Shift (USA)) 7.2f **(69)**

Form - 32

Record 1998 - 1st:0 2nd:1 3rd:1 Ran:2

Win Prizemoney £0 *Total Prizemoney* £1,586

1998 Turf 0-2: (5f, 6f) (gd, g-f)

Currently decent colt. Turf high 84 - 2nd of 11 to Kaamen (27 May Newbury 5f g-f RF 1524). (DEAD) **W R Muir [0-2] Mrs Vicki Fleet.*

INGENIOUS (IRE) BHB 77f **RR 82f** 3957[1]

2 b c Zieten (USA) - Siddon Pretty (IRE) (Darshaan) 9.9f **(84)**

Form - 6442221

Record 1998 - 1st:1 2nd:3 3rd:0 Ran:7

Win Prizemoney £15,580 *Total Prizemoney* £20,122

Wins * 1998 Aug Newmar (G-F) H 6f 79 82 <

1998 Turf 1-7: (5f 5, 6f 1-2) (hvy, gd 3, g-f, frm 1-2)

Decent colt, effective 5 to 6f, best at 5f, acts on gd to frm, best on gd. Turf high 82 - 1st of 12 giving 7lb to Lively Jacq (29 Aug Newmarket RF 3957). **W Jarvis [1-7] Noodles Racing.*

IN GOOD FAITH BHB 45f50a **RR 52f 50a** 88[7]

6 b g Beveled (USA) 6.9f **(64)** - Dulcidene (Behistoun) 14.1f **(45)**

Form - 7

Record 1998 - 1st:0 2nd:0 3rd:0 Ran:1
Pre1998 - 1st:3 2nd:1 3rd:3 Ran:24

Win Prizemoney £14,226 *Total Prizemoney* £16,448

Wins * 1994 Oct York (G-S) H 7.9f 76 87
* 1994 Spt Ayr (G-S) H 8f 69 79
1994 Jun Pontef (G-F) 5f 63

1998 AW 0-1: (9f) (Fibr)

Fair gelding, effective 8f - acts on Fibr, has worn blinkers.

**J J Quinn [3-33] Mrs S Quinn (from J F Bottomley [1-3] Jly 1994).*

INITIATIVE **RR 76+f** 3192[3]

2 ch c Arazi (USA) 9.2f **(74)** - Dance Quest (FR) (Green Dancer (USA)) 10.3f **(74)**

Form - 3

Record 1998 - 1st:0 2nd:0 3rd:1 Ran:1

Win Prizemoney £0 *Total Prizemoney* £518

1998 Turf 0-1: (7f) (g-f)

Currently above-average colt.

**H R A Cecil [0-1] Lord Howard de Walden.*

INKBERRY BHB 75f **RR 80f** 5068[9]

2 ch f Cadeaux Genereux 7.9f **(76)** - Chatterberry (Aragon) 8.1f **(60)**

Form - 85010

Record 1998 - 1st:1 2nd:0 3rd:0 Ran:5

Win Prizemoney £3,915 *Total Prizemoney* £3,915

Wins * 1998 Oct Lingfi (SFT) 5f 80 <

1998 Turf 1-5: (5f 1-5) (g-s 1-1, gd, g-f 2, frm)

Decent filly. Turf high 80 (began Jly) - 1st of 13 getting 5lb from Astrakan (2 Oct Lingfield RF 4610).

**J Noseda [1-5] M Tabor & Mrs John Magnier.*

INKWELL BHB 53f38a **RR 61f 38a** 5127[1]

4 b g Relief Pitcher 7.6f **(47)** - Fragrant Hackette (Simply Great (FR)) 8.2f **(65)**

Form - 30010483310051

Record 1998 - 1st:3 2nd:0 3rd:2 Ran:12
Pre1998 - 1st:0 2nd:1 3rd:3 Ran:14

Win Prizemoney £12,478 *Total Prizemoney* £14,816

Wins * **1998** Nov Bright (SFT) C 7f 61 <
* **1998** Aug Bath (GD) H 8f 38 41
* **1998** Apr Bright (GD) H 8f 34 43

1998 Turf 3-11: (7f 1-1, 8f 2-8, 10f 2) (g-s 1-1, gd 1-4, g-f 1-3, frm 2, hrd) 1998 AW 0-1: (10f) (Equi)

Workmanlike, average gelding, effective 7f, acts on g-s, has worn blinkers (very effectively), likes left handed tracks, likes tight tracks. Turf high 61 - 1st of 18 giving 3lb to Tayovullin (5 Nov Brighton RF 5127). Runs regularly, and though his strike-rate is pretty low he was successful three times in '98. He seems best suited by a turning left-handed track.

**G L Moore [3-17] Phil Collins (from A Hide [0-11] Oct 1997).*

INNER LIGHT **RR 65f** 4968[8]

3 b g Slip Anchor 12.7f **(75)** - Radiance (FR) (Blakeney) 10.5f **(64)**

Form - 58

Record 1998 - 1st:0 2nd:0 3rd:0 Ran:2

1998 Turf 0-2: (8f, 10f) (sft, g-f)

Leggy, currently average gelding. Turf high 65 (began Oct).

**B A Pearce [0-2] Mrs P Salter.*

INNES **RR 56f** 4752[9]

2 b f Inchinor 8.9f **(64)** - Trachelium **(44df)** (Formidable (USA)) 9.2f **(63)**

Form - 0

Record 1998 - 1st:0 2nd:0 3rd:0 Ran:1

1998 Turf 0-1: (7f) (sft)

Currently fair filly. **Miss S E Hall [0-1] C Platts.*

INN ON THE PARK BHB 52f **RR 38f** 1001[7]

3 b g Northern Park (USA) 10f **(57)** - Hotel California (IRE) (Last Tycoon) 8.5f **(62)**

Form - 7

Record 1998 - 1st:0 2nd:0 3rd:0 Ran:1
Pre1998 - 1st:0 2nd:0 3rd:0 Ran:3

1998 Turf 0-1: (12f) (gd)

Leggy, very moderate gelding. **S Dow [0-4] A N Solomons.*

INNUENDO (IRE) BHB 107f **RR 109f** 4616[1]

3 b f Caerleon (USA) 10.9f **(79)** - Infamy (Shirley Heights) 10.3f **(74)**

Form - 11221

Record 1998 - 1st:3 2nd:2 3rd:0 Ran:5

Win Prizemoney £21,320 *Total Prizemoney* £28,511

Wins * **1998** Oct Newmar (GD) L 12f 104 <
* **1998** Jly Salisb (GD) 9.9f 90+
* **1998** Jun Pontef (GD) 10f 70++

1998 Turf 3-5: (10f 2-4, 12f 1-1) (gd 2-4, frm 1-1)

Scopey, Pattern-class filly. Turf high 109 - 2nd of 6 getting 11lb from Saafeya (15 Spt Yarmouth 10f gd RF 4272) - also 1st of 8 getting 12lb from Ivan Luis (2 Oct Newmarket RF 4616). Like her dam, Infamy, this scopey filly improved throughout her three-year-old season. A shade unlucky when narrowly beaten in Listed races at Salisbury and Yarmouth, she proved well suited by a mile and a half at Newmarket in October and is open further progress. She may stay beyond middle-distances as a four-year-old.

**L M Cumani [3-5] Gerald Leigh.*

INPUT RR 587[7]

2 ch f Primo Dominie 7.2f **(67)** - Putout (Dowsing (USA))
Form - 7
Record 1998 - 1st:0 2nd:0 3rd:0 Ran:1
1998 Turf 0-1: (5f) (gd)
Currently very poor filly. **J Berry [0-1] Robert Aird.*

INSATIABLE (IRE) BHB 123f **RR 125f** 5167a[10]

5 b h Don't Forget Me 9.5f **(66)** - Petit Eclair (Major Portion) 6.8f **(75)**
Form - 1174120
Record 1998 - 1st:3 2nd:1 3rd:0 Ran:7
Pre1998 - 1st:2 2nd:1 3rd:2 Ran:6
Win Prizemoney £78,001 *Total Prizemoney* £185,329

Wins								
* **1998**	Oct	Longch	(SFT)	G2	9.8f		119	
* **1998**	May	Sandow	(G-S)	G3	10f		120	<
* **1998**	May	Newmar	(G-S)		10f		109	
* 1997	May	Sandow	(G-F)	H	8.1f	96	105	
* 1995	Spt	Newcas	(GD)		7f		78+	

1998 Turf 3-7: (10f 3-6, 12f) (sft 1-1, gd 2-5, frm)
Top-class colt, effective 10f, acts on sft to gd, best on gd. Turf high 125 - 2nd of 10 giving 8lb to Alborada (17 Oct Newmarket 10f gd RF 4852) - also 1st of 9 from Garuda (26 May Sandown RF 1484). A top-notch performer at his best, he made a winning come-back at Newmarket in May, albeit narrowly, before proving a revelation in the Group Three Brigadier Gerard at Sandown, appreciating the rain-softened ground and scoring in clear-cut fashion. Disappointing effort at Royal Ascot when conditions ought to have been ideal, and he did not get the best of runs in the Eclipse, though it is doubtful that it cost him a winning chance. Bounced back with victory in the Prix Dollar at Longchamp three months later, and was possibly unlucky not to win the Champion Stakes as he finished very strongly after meeting trouble in running. His running in the Breeders' Cup Turf can be forgotten.
**Sir Michael Stoute [5-13] Sir Evelyn De Rothschild.*

INSEPARABLE BHB 83f **RR 97f** 4496[15]

6 ch m Insan (USA) 10.5f **(58)** - Lady Gerardina (Levmoss) 11.4f **(66)**
Form - 33845360
Record 1998 - 1st:0 2nd:0 3rd:3 Ran:8
Win Prizemoney £0 *Total Prizemoney* £3,289
1998 Turf 0-8: (7f, 8f 3, 10f 4) (gd 5, g-f 3)
Very useful mare, effective 7 to 10f, acts on g-f. Turf high 97. Ex-French, she proved a little hard to place last year.
**Lady Herries [0-8] Mrs B V Chennells.*

INSHALLAH BHB 35f **RR 30f** 4919[16]

3 ch f Durgam (USA) 12.3f **(53)** - Kaliala (FR) (Pharly (FR)) 9.8f **(68)**
Form - 000
Record 1998 - 1st:0 2nd:0 3rd:0 Ran:3
Pre1998 - 1st:0 2nd:0 3rd:1 Ran:8
Win Prizemoney £0 *Total Prizemoney* £561
1998 Turf 0-3: (5f, 6f, 8f) (g-s, gd, frm)
Neat, very moderate filly. Turf high 21 (began Aug). Becoming disappointing. **M Dods [0-1] Three Lions (from J Berry [0-2] Spt 1998).*

INSIDER TRADER BHB 48f65a **RR 48f 65a** 3622[7]

7 b g Dowsing (USA) 7f **(61)** - Careless Whisper (Homing) 7.8f **(59)**
Form - 04347
Record 1998 - 1st:0 2nd:0 3rd:1 Ran:5
Pre1998 - 1st:6 2nd:6 3rd:7 Ran:67
Win Prizemoney £32,438 *Total Prizemoney* £49,753

Wins								
1996	Jun	Ripon	(G-F)	H	5f	73	74	
1995	Oct	Catter	(G-F)	H	5f	72	77	<
1994	Oct	Catter	(G-F)	H	5f	75	77	<
1994	Aug	York	(G-F)	H	5f	69	75	
1994	Jly	Cheste	(G-F)	H	5.1f	64	64	
1994	Jun	Catter	(GD)	H	5f	54	61	

1998 Turf 0-5: (5f 4, 6f) (g-s, gd 3, frm)
Fair gelding, effective 5f, acts on g-f, often wears blinkers. Turf high 48. He is on a long losing run, but ran some good races in '97 and can chalk up another win when conditions suit. His last win at Ripon in June '96 came when he was visored.
**B S Rothwell [0-7] Mrs H M Carr (from Mrs J R Ramsden [1-33] Aug 1997).*

INSIGHT (FR) RR 111f 4729a[1]

3 f Sadler's Wells (USA) 11.3f **(87)** - Or Vision (USA) (Irish River (FR)) 8.6f **(78)**
Form - 833221
1998 Turf 1-6: (8f 2, 9f 1-2, 10f, 11f) (sft 1-3, gd 3)
Group-class filly, effective 8 to 11f, acts on sft to gd, best on sft, has worn blinkers, does well at Deauville and Chantilly. Turf high 111 - 1st of 6 from Bardonecchia (4 Oct Longchamp RF 4729a). She ended a frustrating run when gaining a well deserved win in the Prix de LíOpera, where the application of blinkers seemed to help her home. That is not to doubt the fillyís courage, as she is a most genuine individual. **J E Hammond in FR [1-7] Niarchos Family.*

INTENSITY RR 66f 4325[5]

2 b c Bigstone (IRE) - Brillante (FR) (Green Dancer (USA)) 10.3f **(74)**
Form - 5
Record 1998 - 1st:0 2nd:0 3rd:0 Ran:1
1998 Turf 0-1: (7f) (gd)
Currently average colt. **M H Tompkins [0-1] Mrs A Lovat and J Lovat.*

INTERDREAM BHB 57f **RR 57f** 3197[4]

4 b g Interrex (CAN) 7.7f **(51)** - Dreamtime Quest (Blakeney) 10.5f **(64)**
Form - 000004
Record 1998 - 1st:0 2nd:0 3rd:0 Ran:6
Pre1998 - 1st:3 2nd:3 3rd:2 Ran:19
Win Prizemoney £8,191 *Total Prizemoney* £12,469

Wins								
* 1997	Aug	Kempto	(GD)	H	9f	70	74	<
* 1997	Jly	Bright	(FRM)	H	10f	60	62+	
* 1996	Spt	Bright	(FRM)		7f		69	

1998 Turf 0-6: (8f 4, 9f, 10f) (gd 2, g-f 2, frm 2)
Scopey, fair gelding, effective 8 to 9f, acts on g-f, likes tight tracks. Turf high 57. Inconsistent. Suited by a stiff mile, he was in good heart in the second half of '97 despite a hefty rise in the weights. Disqualified at Brighton after being first past the post, he won back at the same track next time. He ran a sound race in defeat at Haydock, and returned to winning ways in a Kempton apprentice handicap. **R Hannon [3-25] Charles Farr & Mark Heaton.*

INTERNAL AFFAIR (USA) RR 53f 4961[5]

3 b g Nicholas (USA) 6.1f **(63)** - Gdynia (USA) (Sir Ivor) 10.2f **(70)**
Form - 7180005
Record 1998 - 1st:1 2nd:0 3rd:0 Ran:7
Pre1998 - 1st:0 2nd:0 3rd:0 Ran:1
Win Prizemoney £2,406 *Total Prizemoney* £2,406
Wins * **1998** *Jun Wolver (STD) 5f 62* <
1998 Turf 0-6:(5f 2, 6f 2, 7f 2)(gd 3, frm 3)1998 AW1-1:(5f 1-1)(Fibr 1-1)
Scopey, average gelding, effective 5f - acts on Fibr. Turf high 58. (1st run) - 1st of 10 from Tuscan Dream (26 Jun Wolverhampton RF 2320). **W J Haggas [1-8] Henryk De Kwiatkowski.*

IN THE GENES BHB 58f53a **RR 58f 53a** 3830[8]

4 b g Syrtos 8.1f **(57)** - Ruby's Vision (Balinger)
Form - 8
Record 1998 - 1st:0 2nd:0 3rd:0 Ran:1
Pre1998 - 1st:0 2nd:0 3rd:2 Ran:7
Win Prizemoney £0 *Total Prizemoney* £1,056
1998 AW 0-1: (12f) (Fibr)
Strong, fair gelding. Consistent. (DEAD)
**Ian Williams [0-12] The Edmunds Family (from J L Eyre [0-4] Aug 1997).*

IN THE GODS (IRE) BHB 72f **RR 75f** 5148[17]

2 b c In The Wings 11.2f **(77)** - Icy Tundra (Shaadi (USA))
Form - 0030
Record 1998 - 1st:0 2nd:0 3rd:1 Ran:4
Win Prizemoney £0 *Total Prizemoney* £474
1998 Turf 0-4: (6f, 7f 3) (g-s, gd 2, frm)
Above-average colt. Turf high 75.
**R F JohnsonHoughton [0-4] C W Sumner.*

IN THE SKY (IRE) BHB 38f **RR 46f** 4270[16]

4 ch f Imp Society (USA) 7.1f **(63)** - Susan's Angel (Lord Gayle (USA)) 8.8f **(62)**
Form - 700
Record 1998 - 1st:0 2nd:0 3rd:0 Ran:3
Pre1998 - 1st:0 2nd:0 3rd:0 Ran:3
Win Prizemoney £0 *Total Prizemoney* £157
1998 Turf 0-3: (7f, 8f, 10f) (gd 2, g-f)
Moderate filly. Turf high 36 (began Jly).

D T Thom [0-1] Matthew Sharkey (from G A Cusack in IRE [0-5] Aug 1998).

Form - 0020844300
Record 1998 - 1st:0 2nd:1 3rd:1 Ran:10

Intikhab clocks up one more for Frankie et al, but is not seen again

IN THE STOCKS BHB 51f **RR 52f** 4759[8]
4 b f Reprimand 8.2f **(63)** - Stock Hill Lass (Air Trooper) 9.1f **(63)**
Form - 677007148
Record 1998 - 1st:1 2nd:0 3rd:0 Ran:9
Win Prizemoney £2,444 *Total Prizemoney* £2,720
Wins * **1998** Spt Bath (GD) SH 8f 47 52 <
1998 Turf 1-9: (7f, 8f 1-7, 10f) (gd, g-f 3, frm 1-5)
Light-framed, fair filly, effective 8f, acts on frm, favours tight tracks. Turf high 59 - also 1st of 18 getting 3lb from Madame Maxi (7 Spt Bath RF 4123). **L G Cottrell [1-9] E Gadsden.*

IN THE SUN (USA) BHB 75f **RR 76f** 3047[1]
3 b f Alleged (USA) 11.8f **(81)** - Pandysia (USA) (Storm Bird (CAN)) 10.3f **(74)**
Form - 5721
Record 1998 - 1st:1 2nd:1 3rd:0 Ran:4
Pre1998 - 1st:0 2nd:0 3rd:0 Ran:3
Win Prizemoney £5,321 *Total Prizemoney* £6,371
Wins * **1998** Jly Sandow (G-F) H 14f 74 76 <
1998 Turf 1-4: (9f, 11f 2, 14f 1-1) (gd 2, g-f, frm 1-1)
Workmanlike, above-average filly, effective 11 to 14f, acts on g-f to frm. Turf high 76 - 1st of 5 getting 7lb from Winsome George (23 Jly Sandown RF 3047).
**J L Dunlop [1-7] Sir Payne-Gallwey(Susan Racing).*

INTIAASH (IRE) BHB 57f55a **RR 61f 55a** 4202[15]
6 br m Shaadi (USA) 8.1f **(75)**-Funun (USA) (Fappiano (USA)) 8.7f **(77)**
Pre1998 - 1st:5 2nd:5 3rd:3 Ran:38
Win Prizemoney £16,894 *Total Prizemoney* £26,468
Wins * 1997 *Jly Lingfi (STD) C 5f 69*
* 1997 May Bath (G-S) H 5.1f 75 79 <
* 1997 Apr Bath (G-F) H 5.1f 68 74
* 1996 *May Wolver (STD) C 6f 75*
1995 Oct Redcar (FRM) 6f 72
1998 Turf 0-6: (5f 2, 6f 3, 7f) (gd 2, frm 4) 1998 AW 0-4: (6f 2, 7f 2) (Equi, Fibr 3)
Average mare, effective 5 to 6f, best at 5f, acts on gd - acts on Equi, has worn blinkers, likes left handed tracks. Turf high 62. AW high 47. Inconsistent. Able on both sand and turf, she was running well in '97, including two wins at Bath and one on the Lingfield Equitrack. She finished lame in August five days after finishing down the field in the Stewards' Cup, and has shown little since.
**D HaydnJones [4-37] Howard Thomas (from P T Walwyn [1-11] Oct 1995).*

INTIKHAB (USA) BHB 131f **RR 131+f** 2010[1]
4 b c Red Ransom (USA) 8.6f **(83)** - Crafty Example (USA) (Crafty Prospector (USA)) 8.2f **(104)**
Form - 211
Record 1998 - 1st:2 2nd:1 3rd:0 Ran:3
Pre1998 - 1st:5 2nd:4 3rd:0 Ran:9
Win Prizemoney £137,064 *Total Prizemoney* £222,520
Wins * **1998** Jun Ascot (G-S) G2 8f 131+ <
* **1998** Jun Epsom (GD) G3 8.5f 121+
1997 Oct Newmar (GD) L 8f 87

1997	Spt	Epsom (GD)	L	8.5f	108
1997	Jly	Doncas (GD)		8f	99
1996	Oct	Yarmou (G-F)		6f	87+
1996	Spt	Pontef (G-F)		6f	83+

1998 Turf 2-2: (8f 1-1, 9f 1-1) (gd 1-1, g-f 1-1) 1998 AW 0-1: (10f) (Dirt)

Scopey, high-calibre colt, effective 8 to 9f, acts on gd to g-f. Turf high 131 - 1st of 9 getting 3lb from Among Men (16 Jun Ascot RF 2010). The top mile events were poorer for the absence of Intikhab, sidelined through the recurrence of a splint injury following brilliant victories in the Diomed at Epsom and the Queen Anne at the Royal Meeting. He had wintered in Dubai, finishing six lengths second to Intikhab in the Dubai Duty Free. Sure to make his mark at Group One level if returning fit and well, although he is reported as better suited by a straight mile than by running round a bend.

**S bin Suroor [2-2] Godolphin (from S bin Suroor in UAE [0-1] Mar 1998).*

INTIMAA (IRE) BHB 100f RR 92f 4495[2]

2 b f Caerleon (USA) 10.9f **(79)** - Nahilah (Habitat) 9.4f **(70)**

Form - 132

Record 1998 - 1st:1 2nd:1 3rd:1 Ran:3

Win Prizemoney £2,393 *Total Prizemoney* £8,178

Wins * 1998 Aug Yarmou (FRM) 6f 64 <

1998 Turf 1-3: (6f 1-2, 7f) (gd, g-f, frm 1-1)

Currently useful filly. Turf high 92 (began Aug) - 2nd of 8 giving 3lb to Subito (26 Spt Ascot 7f gd RF 4495). Dead-heated in a moderate Yarmouth maiden on her debut, and ran well in two fair conditions events after that. **P T Walwyn [1-3] Hamdan Al Maktoum.*

IN TIME BHB 65f RR 69f 4466[3]

2 ch f Generous (IRE) 11.5f **(82)** - Affection Affirmed (USA) (Affirmed (USA)) 9.3f **(79)**

Form - 6403

Record 1998 - 1st:0 2nd:0 3rd:1 Ran:4

Win Prizemoney £0 *Total Prizemoney* £682

1998 Turf 0-4: (6f 3, 8f) (gd 2, frm 2)

Average filly. Turf high 69.

**P F I Cole [0-4] H R H Prince Fahd Salman.*

INTIZAA (USA) RR 70tf 4445[3]

2 b br f Mr Prospector (USA) 8.6f **(88)** - Oumaldaaya (USA) (Nureyev (USA)) 8.7f **(78)**

Form - 43

Record 1998 - 1st:0 2nd:0 3rd:1 Ran:2

Win Prizemoney £0 *Total Prizemoney* £975

1998 Turf 0-2: (6f, 7f) (gd 2)

Currently above-average filly. Turf high 70 (began Jly).

**J L Dunlop [0-2] Hamdan Al Maktoum.*

INTO DEBT BHB 27f25a RR 35f 25a 408[8]

5 b m Cigar 6.3f **(43)** - Serious Affair (Valiyar) 8.5f **(73)**

Form - 60708008

Record 1998 - 1st:0 2nd:0 3rd:0 Ran:4
Pre1998 - 1st:1 2nd:1 3rd:1 Ran:26

Win Prizemoney £2,078 *Total Prizemoney* £3,593

Wins * 1997 *Jan Lingfi (STD) H 7f 30 34* <

1998 AW 0-4: (5f, 6f, 7f 2) (Equi 3, Fibr)

Very moderate filly, effective 7f - acts on Equi, often wears blinkers (effectively), likes left handed tracks, likes tight tracks. AW high 30. **J R Poulton [1-30] Mrs J Druce.*

INTRUDER (IRE) RR 111f 4212a[3]

5 br h Polish Patriot (USA) 7.8f **(70)** - Sheer Innocence (Shirley Heights) 10.3f **(74)**

Form - 3

1998 Turf 0-1: (8f) (gd)

Currently Group-class colt. (1st run) - 3rd of 7 getting 2lb from Power Flame (1 Spt Baden-Baden 8f gd RF 4212a). He was beaten by a couple of useful milers at Baden-Baden in September and is a fair performer. **O Larsen in DEN [0-1] Mrs N Bispelund.*

INTUITION (GER) RR 103f 2481a[2]

3 b f Gold and Ivory (USA) - Inspiration (GER) (Alpenkonig (GER)) 10.8f **(76)**

Form - 2

1998 Turf 0-1: (11f) (gd)

Currently very useful filly. (1st run) - 2nd of 11 getting 13lb from Saperlipoupette (27 Jun Hamburg 11f gd RF 2481a). She is useful, but could not match an older rival at Hamburg in June.

**H Blume in GER [0-1].*

INTUITIVE BHB 30f RR 31f 2376[7]

3 b f Teenoso (USA) 10.5f **(62)** - Hasland (Aragon) 8.1f **(60)**

Form - 60067

Record 1998 - 1st:0 2nd:0 3rd:0 Ran:5
Pre1998 - 1st:0 2nd:0 3rd:0 Ran:3

1998 Turf 0-5: (7f, 8f, 9f 2, 12f) (sft, gd, g-f, frm, hrd)

Light-framed, very moderate filly. Turf high 40.

**J L Eyre [0-8] John Ashcroft.*

INVADER BHB 81f RR 77f 4892[4]

2 b c Danehill (USA) 9.1f **(79)** - Donya (Mill Reef (USA)) 10.5f **(78)**

Form - 0044

Record 1998 - 1st:0 2nd:0 3rd:0 Ran:4

Win Prizemoney £0 *Total Prizemoney* £487

1998 Turf 0-4: (7f 4) (gd 3, frm)

Above-average colt. Turf high 77 (began Aug).

**C E Brittain [0-4] Sheikh Mohammed Obaid Al Maktoum.*

INVERGORDON RR 399[3]

3 ch g Efisio 7.7f **(69)** - Kintail (Kris) 9.5f **(73)**

Form - 13

Record 1998 - 1st:1 2nd:0 3rd:1 Ran:2

Win Prizemoney £2,801 *Total Prizemoney* £3,698

Wins * 1998 *Feb Wolver (STD) 6f 83+* <

1998 AW 1-2: (6f 1-1, 7f) (Fibr 1-2)

Currently useful gelding. AW high 91 - 3rd of 7 getting 12lb from Chewit (4 Mar Wolverhampton 7f Fibr RF 0399) - also 1st of 9 giving 5lb to Silken Dalliance (21 Feb Wolverhampton RF 0335). He won a six-furlong maiden on the Wolverhampton Fibresand in February very easily, and was not disgraced in a much better race on the same track next time over an extra furlong, but that was the last that was seen of him.

**J M P Eustace [1-2] Kissing Tree Partnership.*

INVERMARK BHB 110f RR 109f 5055a[7]

4 b g Machiavellian (USA) 9.8f **(83)** -Applecross (Glint of Gold) 9.3f **(66)**

Form - 66211417

Record 1998 - 1st:3 2nd:1 3rd:0 Ran:8
Pre1998 - 1st:1 2nd:1 3rd:1 Ran:8

Win Prizemoney £76,181 *Total Prizemoney* £84,118

Wins							
*** 1998**	Oct	Longch (SFT)	G1	20f		109	<
*** 1998**	Aug	Cheste (G-S)	LH	13.4f	90	100	
*** 1998**	Jly	Haydoc (GD)	H	14f	82	88	
* 1997	Jly	Yarmou (G-F)		11.5f		78	

1998 Turf 3-8: (12f 2, 13f 1-1, 14f 1-1, 16f 3, 20f 1-1) (hvy, sft 1-4, gd 1-1, g-f, frm 1-1)

Pattern-class gelding, effective 13 to 20f, acts on sft to gd, best on sft, likes left handed tracks. Turf high 109 - 1st of 9 from Tiraaz (3 Oct Longchamp RF 4716a) - also 1st of 9 getting 8lb from Delilah (22 Aug Chester RF 3802). He began the season rated 85 and ended it by winning the Group 1 Prix Du Cadran. A grand stayer who enjoys easy ground and has a bright turn-of-foot, he is a credit to his trainer and will be a live contender for next yearís Ascot Gold Cup if we have a wet summer.

**J R Fanshawe [4-16] Sir David Wills.*

INVESTMENT HERO (IRE) BHB 64f RR 4387[1]

2 b c Imperial Frontier (USA) 7f **(65)** - Superb Investment (IRE) (Hatim (USA))

Form - 551

Record 1998 - 1st:1 2nd:0 3rd:0 Ran:3

Win Prizemoney £2,092 *Total Prizemoney* £2,092

Wins * 1998 *Spt Wolver (STD) S 7f 61* <

1998 Turf 0-1: (5f) (frm) 1998 AW 1-2: (5f, 7f 1-1) (Fibr 1-2)

Currently average colt. AW high 61 (began Jly) - 1st of 12 from Risky Valentine (19 Spt Wolverhampton RF 4387).

**M Johnston [1-3] Markus Graff.*

INVEST WISELY BHB 60f RR 67?f 2015[21]

6 ch g Dashing Blade 7.9f **(80)**-Saniette (Crystal Palace (FR)) 12.5f **(76)**

Form - 0

Record 1998 - 1st:0 2nd:0 3rd:0 Ran:1
Pre1998 - 1st:4 2nd:0 3rd:1 Ran:19

Win Prizemoney £19,814								*Total Prizemoney* £21,543
Wins	1995	Spt	Yarmou (GD)	H	18.2f	83	91	<
	1995	Aug	Redcar (G-F)	H	14.1f	80	85	
	1995	Aug	Yarmou (G-F)	H	14.1f	74	80	
	1995	Jly	Yarmou (GD)	H	14.1f	68	72	

1998 Turf 0-1: (20f) (gd)

Average gelding, has worn blinkers. A genuine if one-paced stayer, he was pulled up on his second run of 1997. Won twice over hurdles in March.#j#Running respectably in staying handicap hurdles, a game winner twice at Newcastle in March.

**M D Hammond [3-11] A G Chappell (from J Eustace [4-17] Aug 1996).*

INVIGILATE BHB 24f23a **RR 31f 23a** 316[9]

9 ch g Viking (USA) 8f **(49)** - Maria da Gloria (St Chad) 6.7f **(67)**

Form - 0000

Record	**1998 -**	1st:0	2nd:0	3rd:0	Ran:4
	Pre1998 -	1st:6	2nd:6	3rd:5	Ran:69

Win Prizemoney £16,629							*Total Prizemoney* £25,156
Wins	1996	Jun	Redcar (G-F)	H	6f	47	48
	1994	Aug	Epsom (G-F)	H	6f	49	51
	1994	Aug	Folkes (G-F)		6f		43

1998 AW 0-4: (6f 2, 7f, 8f) (Equi, Fibr 3)

Very moderate gelding, has worn blinkers. AW high 24. Becoming disappointing.

**M Quinn [0-4] M Quinn (from M R Channon [0-3] Jun 1997).*

Fair gelding, effective 6 to 8f, best at 8f - acts on Equi, has worn blinkers, likes left handed tracks, favours tight tracks, excels at Lingfield. AW high 57 - 3rd of 9 to Without Friends (14 Feb Lingfield 8f Equi RF 0290). Becoming disappointing. He has been a fine servant to connections over the years, especially on Equitrack, but apart from a victory in a modest four-runner event on that surface in July '97, his form has been on the decline.

**G L Moore [3-28] R Kiernan (from A Moore [6-93] Jan 1997).*

INYA LAKE BHB 100f **RR 97f** 4739[12]

2 b f Whittingham (IRE) - Special One (Aragon) 8.1f **(60)**

Form - 111743170

Record	**1998 -**	1st:4	2nd:0	3rd:1	Ran:9

Win Prizemoney £32,495							*Total Prizemoney* £35,909
Wins	*** 1998**	Jly	Goodwo (G-S)	G3	5f	97	<
	*** 1998**	Jun	Catter (G-S)		5f	76	
	*** 1998**	Apr	Hamilt (HVY)		5f	65	
	*** 1998**	Mar	Doncas (GD)	S	5f	65	

1998 Turf 4-9: (5f 4-9) (sft 1-1, g-s 2, gd 3-5, g-f)

Very useful filly, effective 5f, acts on gd. Turf high 97 - 1st of 9 from Amazing Dream (31 Jly Goodwood RF 3232). Knew her job when winning a seller at the first Doncaster meeting, and went on to prove herself in much better company, springing a 20/1 surprise in the Molecomb at Glorious Goodwood. Lacks a bit of scope and won't find things easy at three. **M R Channon [4-9] Barry Minty.*

Inya Lake wasted no time getting off the mark

INVOCATION BHB 33f37a **RR 39f 37a** 1965[8]

11 ch g Kris 10f **(75)** - Royal Saint (USA) (Crimson Satan) 8f **(67)**

Form - 306654347008

Record	**1998 -**	1st:0	2nd:0	3rd:1	Ran:9
	Pre1998 -	1st:9	2nd:14	3rd:11	Ran:111

Win Prizemoney £26,086								*Total Prizemoney* £52,392
Wins	* 1997	*Jly*	*Lingfi*	*(STD)*		*7f*		*61*
	* 1997	*Feb*	*Lingfi*	*(STD)*	*H*	*8f*	*63*	*64*
	* 1997	*Jan*	*Lingfi*	*(STD)*	*C*	*8f*		*64*
	1997	*Jan*	*Lingfi*	*(STD)*	*H*	*6f*	*58*	*59*
	1995	*Mar*	*Lingfi*	*(STD)*	*H*	*6f*	*63*	*54*
	1994	Jun	Goodwo	(GF)	H	6f	63	61

1998 Turf 0-1: (9f) (frm) 1998 AW 0-8: (7f 2, 8f 6) (Equi 7, Fibr)

IOMAROU (IRE) BHB 32f **RR 41f** 2164[9]

3 b c Reprimand 8.2f **(63)** - Shillay (Lomond (USA)) 8.8f **(65)**

Form - 84600

Record	**1998 -**	1st:0	2nd:0	3rd:0	Ran:5

1998 Turf 0-2: (7f, 8f) (gd, g-f) 1998 AW 0-3: (6f, 7f, 9f) (Fibr 3)

Rangy, moderate colt. Turf high 41. AW high 24.

**R Hollinshead [0-5] R Hollinshead.*

IONIAN SECRET **RR 54f** 2249[6]

2 b f Mystiko (USA) 7.7f **(59)** - Hearten (Hittite Glory) 8.7f **(50)**

Form - 6

Record	**1998 -**	1st:0	2nd:0	3rd:0	Ran:1

1998 Turf 0-1: (5f) (frm)

Currently fair filly. **M P Tregoning [0-1] The Emotional Partnership.*

IONIAN SPRING (IRE) BHB 79f85a **RR 84?f 85a** 3451[1]

3 b g Ela-Mana-Mou 12.7f **(72)** - Well Head (IRE) (Sadler's Wells (USA)) 10f **(76)**

Form - 3221

Record 1998 - 1st:1 2nd:2 3rd:1 Ran:4

Win Prizemoney £2,872 *Total Prizemoney* £5,587

Wins * **1998** *Aug Wolver (STD) 9.4f 83+* <

1998 Turf 0-3: (8f, 10f 2) (gd, g-f, frm) 1998 AW 1-1: (9f 1-1) (Fibr 1-1)

Unfurnished, decent gelding. Turf high 84 (1st run) - 3rd of 11 to Alyriva (4 May Warwick 8f g-f RF 1029). (1st run) - 1st of 6 from Monet (7 Aug Wolverhampton RF 3451). He got off the mark in a very modest maiden on the Wolverhampton Fibresand in August, but won in style and will definitely win more races on that surface if an opportunity can be found.

**Lord Huntingdon [1-4] Lord Weinstock.*

IPCRESS FILLY BHB 60f **RR 59+f** 4577[6]

2 b f Puissance 7.1f **(60)** - Daymer Bay (Lomond (USA)) 8.8f **(65)**

Form - 56306

Record 1998 - 1st:0 2nd:0 3rd:1 Ran:5

Win Prizemoney £0 *Total Prizemoney* £289

1998 Turf 0-5: (5f, 6f 2, 7f 2) (gd 2, g-f 2, frm)

Fair filly. Turf high 59 (began Jly).

**J M P Eustace [0-5] Mrs James Eustace.*

IPLEDGEALLEGIANCE (USA) **RR 83f** 4823[5]

2 b c Alleged (USA) 11.8f **(81)** - Yafill (USA) (Nureyev (USA)) 8.7f **(78)**

Form - 55

Record 1998 - 1st:0 2nd:0 3rd:0 Ran:2

1998 Turf 0-2: (7f, 8f) (gd, frm)

Currently decent colt. Turf high 83 (began Oct).

**E A L Dunlop [0-2] Maktoum Al Maktoum.*

IPPON (FR) **RR 111f** 1230a[6]

3 b c Pursuit of Love 9.5f **(69)**-Lady Reem (USA)(Al Nasr (FR))9.3f **(68)**

Form - 116

1998 Turf 1-2: (7f 1-1, 8f) (hvy 1-1, gd)

Currently Group-class colt. Turf high 111 (1st run) - 1st of 5 from Silic (10 Apr Maisons-laffitte RF 0724a). He won a Listed race at Maisons-Laffitte with some authority in the spring, but could not cut the mustard when stepped-up a grade. **J-C Rouget in FR [2-3].*

I RECALL (IRE) BHB 41f44a **RR 41f 44a** 2280[11]

7 b g Don't Forget Me 9.5f **(66)** - Sable Lake (Thatching) 8f **(66)**

Form - 030

Record 1998 - 1st:0 2nd:0 3rd:1 Ran:3

Pre1998 - 1st:0 2nd:1 3rd:1 Ran:10

Win Prizemoney £0 *Total Prizemoney* £2,249

1998 Turf 0-3: (8f 2, 10f) (gd 3)

Moderate gelding, often wears blinkers. Turf high 41. Inconsistent. Has shown improved form in 1997/98 and should pick up a small race, probably at around two miles.

**P Hayward [0-26] Mrs S A Coplestone (from P Hayward [0-1] May 1995).*

IRIE MON (IRE) BHB 33f50a **RR 30f 50a** 2066[10]

6 b g Waajib 8.9f **(67)** - Achafalaya (USA) (Apalachee (USA)) 9.4f **(71)**

Form - 0650

Record 1998 - 1st:0 2nd:0 3rd:0 Ran:4

Pre1998 - 1st:1 2nd:3 3rd:3 Ran:19

Win Prizemoney £2,663 *Total Prizemoney* £6,540

Wins 1995 *Feb Lingfi (STD) C 7f 56* <

1998 Turf 0-4: (7f 2, 8f, 12f) (gd 3, frm)

Moderate gelding. Turf high 30. (DEAD)

**Mrs S Lamyman [0-4] Sotby Farming Company Ltd (from M P Bielby [0-9] Jly 1996).*

IRISH CREAM (IRE) BHB 56f71a **RR 56f 71a** 4876[6]

2 b f Petong 7.6f **(58)** - Another Baileys **(49f 55a)** (Deploy)

Form - 18533150046

Record 1998 - 1st:2 2nd:0 3rd:2 Ran:11

Win Prizemoney £5,040 *Total Prizemoney* £6,495

Wins * **1998** *Jly Southw (STD) C 6f 67* <

* **1998** Mar Hamilt (HVY) 5f 55

1998 Turf 1-8: (5f 1-2, 6f 4, 7f 2) (sft 1-2, g-s, gd, g-f, frm 3) 1998 AW 1-3: (6f 1-3) (Fibr 1-3)

Average filly, effective 6f - acts on Fibr, has worn blinkers. Turf high 56. AW high 67 - 1st of 10 giving 4lb to Palace Green (25 Jly Southwell RF 3126). Consistent. **P D Evans [2-11] P D Evans.*

IRISH FIRE (IRE) **RR 107f** 4347a[3]

6 br h Sure Blade (USA) 10.6f **(66)** - Inka Lilie (USA) (Caro) 9.3f **(74)**

Form - 33

1998 Turf 0-2: (6f 2) (sft, gd)

Currently Pattern-class horse. Turf high 107. He is a good old stick, but will always be found wanting against decent opposition.

**Uwe Stoltefuss in GER [0-2].*

IRISH GROOM BHB 25f **RR 20?f** 2728[13]

11 b g Shy Groom (USA) 8.2f **(59)** - Romany Pageant (Welsh Pageant) 10f **(65)**

Form - 0

Record 1998 - 1st:0 2nd:0 3rd:0 Ran:1

Pre1998 - 1st:1 2nd:4 3rd:3 Ran:41

Win Prizemoney £1,413 *Total Prizemoney* £5,051

1998 Turf 0-1: (11f) (frm)

Very moderate gelding, often wears blinkers. Inconsistent.

**A Streeter [0-6] J T Stimpson (from J P Smith [1-39] Jan 1994).*

IRISH HOLMES (IRE) **RR 116f** 276a[1]

5 b g Be My Native (USA) 11.2f **(62)** - Avoca Holmes (Be My Guest (USA)) 9.3f **(67)**

Form - 311

1998 Turf 2-3: (10f 1-2, 13f 1-1) (sft, gd 2-2)

Currently high-class gelding. Turf high 116 - 1st of 10 giving 13lb to Gonzaga (4 Feb Cagnes-sur-mer RF 0276a).

**C Boutin in FR [2-3] Mlle Laurence Baudouin.*

IRISH KINSMAN BHB 32f **RR 32f** 1397[13]

5 b g Distant Relative 7f **(69)** - Inesdela (Wolver Hollow) 8f **(56)**

Form - 0

Record 1998 - 1st:0 2nd:0 3rd:0 Ran:1

Pre1998 - 1st:0 2nd:0 3rd:0 Ran:10

1998 Turf 0-1: (10f) (frm)

Very moderate gelding, has worn blinkers.

**G H Yardley [0-9] M P Aldersey (from P T Walwyn [0-6] Aug 1996).*

IRISH MELODY (IRE) **RR 33f** 2778[8]

2 ch f Mac's Imp (USA) 5.6f **(54)** - Musical Gem (USA) (The Minstrel (CAN)) 10f **(72)**

Form - 0758

Record 1998 - 1st:0 2nd:0 3rd:0 Ran:4

1998 Turf 0-4: (6f 3, 7f) (gd 3, frm)

Very moderate filly. Turf high 33. **B J Meehan [0-4] Mrs Ruth Egan.*

IRISH PRIZE (USA) **RR 99f** 4830a[6]

2 ch c Irish River (FR) 9f **(77)** - Cadeaux D'Amie (USA) (Lyphard (USA)) 9.9f **(72)**

Form - 26

1998 Turf 0-2: (8f 2) (g-s, gd)

Currently very useful colt. Turf high 99 (1st run) (began Spt) - 2nd of 6 to Slickly (22 Spt Chantilly 8f gd RF 4597a). Found wanting at the top level in the Grand Criterium. **Mme C Head in FR [0-2].*

IRISH STAMP (IRE) BHB 25f **RR 20f** 4254[6]

9 b g Niniski (USA) 13.2f **(67)** - Bayazida (Bustino) 10.4f **(64)**

Form - 6

Record 1998 - 1st:0 2nd:0 3rd:0 Ran:1

Pre1998 - 1st:1 2nd:2 3rd:0 Ran:12

Win Prizemoney £2,448 *Total Prizemoney* £4,791

1998 Turf 0-1: (16f) (frm)

Little account gelding. Becoming disappointing.

**F Murphy [2-24] Paddy O'Donnell (from J Pearce [1-9] Oct 1993).*

IRISH SUMMIT (IRE) **RR 97+f** 3722a[3]

3 b c Erins Isle 8.3f **(76)** - La Meilleure (Lord Gayle (USA)) 8.8f **(62)**

Form - 613

1998 Turf 1-3: (8f, 10f 1-1, 11f) (sft, g-f 1-1, hrd)

Very useful colt. Turf high 97 - 1st of 5 giving 5lb to Susun Kelapa (25 Jly Curragh RF 3190a). **J S Bolger in IRE [2-4] A G Moylan.*

IRIS MAY BHB 77f **RR 80f** 4246^{14}
3 b f Brief Truce (USA) 9.1f **(73)** - Choire Mhor (Dominion) 8.5f **(63)**
Form - 5132360
Record 1998 - 1st:1 2nd:1 3rd:2 Ran:7
Pre1998 - 1st:1 2nd:3 3rd:1 Ran:8
Win Prizemoney £7,205 *Total Prizemoney* £16,637
Wins * 1998 May Windso (G-F) H 5f 70 74 <
* 1997 Oct Lingfi (FRM) 5f 74 <
1998 Turf 1-7: (5f 1-6, 6f) (g-s, gd, g-f 2, frm 1-3)
Light-framed, decent filly, effective 5f, acts on gd to frm, has worn blinkers. Turf high 80 - 2nd of 16 getting 6lb from Classy Cleo (10 Jly Chester 5f frm RF 2678) - also 1st of 16 getting 11lb from Chieftain (18 May Windsor RF 1315). A useful sprint handicapper, she won at Windsor in May and has continued to run well after.
**J Berry [2-15] John Brown & Megan Dennis.*

IRON COUNTY XMAS (USA) RR 90f $5105a^{2}$
4 bb g Cox's Ridge (USA) 9.4f **(72)** - Christmas Bonus (USA) (Key To The Mint (USA)) 9.4f **(75)**
Form - 110642
1998 Turf 2-6: (12f 2-3, 14f, 16f 2) (hvy 1-2, sft, g-s 1-1, gd 2)
Useful gelding, effective 12 to 16f, acts on hvy to g-s, always wears blinkers. Turf high 90 - 2nd of 11 giving 6lb to Manhattan Castle (26 Oct Galway 16f hvy RF 5105a) - also 1st of 5 from Rainbow Warrior (10 May Killarney RF 1191a).
**D K Weld in IRE [4-11] Iron County Farms.*

IRON MOUNTAIN (IRE) BHB 70f **RR 69df** 5126^{14}
3 b g Scenic 10.6f **(66)** - Merlannah (IRE) (Shy Groom (USA)) 10f **(66)**
Form - 0705212315120507160
Record 1998 - 1st:4 2nd:3 3rd:1 Ran:19
Pre1998 - 1st:0 2nd:1 3rd:1 Ran:8
Win Prizemoney £17,355 *Total Prizemoney* £22,264
Wins * 1998 Oct Leices (G-S) H 10f 67 69 <
*** 1998** Jly Beverl (GD) H 9.9f 65 64
*** 1998** Jly Bright (GD) H 10f 63 67
*** 1998** Jun Yarmou (GD) H 10.1f 58 61
1998 Turf 4-19:(8f 2, 9f, 10f 4-15, 11f)(g-s 2, gd 2-9, g-f 2-2,frm 4,hrd 2)
Scopey, average gelding, effective 7 to 11f, best at 10f, acts on gd to hrd, has worn blinkers, prefers left handed tracks, prefers tight tracks, excels at Yarmouth. Turf high 69 - 2nd of 5 giving 4lb to Haydn James (10 Aug Windsor 10f hrd RF 3516) - also 1st of 19 getting 3lb from City Gambler (13 Oct Leicester RF 4776). He has had a very busy season and it took him a long time to get off the mark, but he has made up for it by winning four times to date. He is a much better horse running in modest handicaps rather than carrying a low weight against better company.
**N A Callaghan [4-27] Gallagher Equine Ltd.*

IRONSIDE PRINCESS BHB 28f **RR 36f** 4777^{17}
3 b f Rock City 8.8f **(62)** - One Degree (Crooner) 9.9f **(49)**
Form - 0850
Record 1998 - 1st:0 2nd:0 3rd:0 Ran:4
1998 Turf 0-4: (7f, 8f, 12f 2) (gd, frm 2, hrd)
Very moderate filly. Turf high 36 (began Jly).
**R Simpson [0-4] Sampower Racing Club.*

IRREPRESSIBLE (IRE) BHB 55f **RR 58f** 2300^{11}
7 b g Don't Forget Me 9.5f **(66)** - Lady of Shalott (Kings Lake (USA)) 10.8f **(67)**
Form - 0140
Record 1998 - 1st:1 2nd:0 3rd:0 Ran:4
Pre1998 - 1st:1 2nd:1 3rd:3 Ran:21
Win Prizemoney £4,525 *Total Prizemoney* £7,957
Wins * 1998 May Folkes (G-F) C 6.9f 58 <
* 1996 Jun Yarmou (FRM) SH 8f 33 42+
1998 Turf 1-4: (7f 1-3, 8f) (gd 1-3, g-f)
Fair gelding, has worn blinkers. Turf high 58 - 1st of 13 giving 4lb to Halmanerror (27 May Folkestone RF 1520).
**R J Hodges [2-14] R Callow (from K Bishop [0-2] Oct 1995).*

IRRITANCY BHB 49f **RR 48f** 3993^{5}
2 b c Tenby 10.4f **(76)** - Anonymous (Night Shift (USA)) 7.2f **(69)**
Form - 005
Record 1998 - 1st:0 2nd:0 3rd:0 Ran:3
1998 Turf 0-3: (7f 2, 8f) (g-f 2, frm)
Currently moderate colt. Turf high 48 (began Jly).
**J G FitzGerald [0-3] Marquesa de Moratalla.*

ISABELLA BHB 52f **RR 43f** 579^{6}
3 ch f Primo Dominie 7.2f **(67)**-Scossa (USA)(Shadeed (USA)) 8.2f **(70)**
Form - 6
Record 1998 - 1st:0 2nd:0 3rd:0 Ran:1
Pre1998 - 1st:0 2nd:0 3rd:0 Ran:3
1998 Turf 0-1: (5f) (sft)
Scopey, moderate filly.
**J Noseda [0-1] M Olden (from T Keddy [0-3] Aug 1997).*

ISABELLA GONZAGA BHB 63f62a **RR 60f 62a** 5002^{2}
4 b f Rock Hopper 10.6f **(54)** - Lawful (Law Society (USA)) 9.9f **(70)**
Form - 301350012
Record 1998 - 1st:2 2nd:1 3rd:2 Ran:9
Pre1998 - 1st:0 2nd:0 3rd:0 Ran:4
Win Prizemoney £5,866 *Total Prizemoney* £8,463
Wins * 1998 *Oct Wolver (STD) H 12f 57 60 <*
*** 1998** Jly Yarmou (G-F) H 10.1f 57 60 <
1998 Turf 1-7: (10f 1-4, 11f 3) (gd 2, g-f 1-3, frm 2) 1998 AW 1-2: (12f 1-2) (Equi, Fibr 1-1)
Scopey, average filly, effective 10 to 12f, best at 10f, acts on gd to g-f - acts on AW, best on g-f, favours tight tracks. Turf high 60 - 1st of 9 giving 12lb to Champagne N Dreams (27 Jly Yarmouth RF 3154). AW high 63 (began Oct) - also 1st of 12 getting 1lb from Operatic (17 Oct Wolverhampton RF 4862). Inconsistent. She won a small Yarmouth handicap in July and a similar event on the Wolverhampton Fibresand in October.
**R M H Cowell [2-9] John Waugh (from J L Dunlop [0-4] Oct 1997).*

ISCA MAIDEN BHB 32f **RR 37f** 2509^{18}
4 b f Full Extent (USA) 5.2f **(50)** - Sharp N' Easy (Swing Easy (USA)) 6.5f **(55)**
Form - 0480
Record 1998 - 1st:0 2nd:0 3rd:0 Ran:4
Pre1998 - 1st:0 2nd:0 3rd:0 Ran:8
1998 Turf 0-4: (7f, 10f, 11f 2) (g-s, g-f 3)
Neat, very moderate filly, effective 11f, acts on g-f, likes tight tracks. Turf high 37 - 4th of 18 getting 27lb from Pay Homage (4 May Warwick 11f g-f RF 1032). Inconsistent.
**P Hayward [0-12] Mrs C A Davies.*

ISCAN (IRE) BHB 95f **RR 93?f** 3995^{1}
2 b c Caerleon (USA) 10.9f **(79)** - Idraak (Kris) 9.5f **(73)**
Form - 331
Record 1998 - 1st:1 2nd:0 3rd:2 Ran:3
Win Prizemoney £3,745 *Total Prizemoney* £8,123
Wins * 1998 Aug Newcas (GD) 7f 80 <
1998 Turf 1-3: (7f 1-3) (gd, g-f, hrd 1-1)
Currently useful colt. Turf high 93 (1st run) (began Jly) - 3rd of 5 to Compton Admiral (24 Jly Ascot 7f gd RF 3065). Third in decent races at Ascot and York, he got off the mark at Newcastle on his third start, though he did not have much to spare. He will stay a mile plus. **Sir Michael Stoute [1-3] Sheikh Mohammed.*

I SEE YOU SYDNEY (AUS) BHB 39f30a **RR 47f 30a** 531^{19}
4 ch g Al Hareb (USA) 9.4f **(53)** - Sorrento (AUS) (Best Western (AUS))
Form - 80040000
Record 1998 - 1st:0 2nd:0 3rd:0 Ran:5
Pre1998 - 1st:0 2nd:0 3rd:0 Ran:6
Win Prizemoney £0 *Total Prizemoney* £241
1998 Turf 0-1: (7f) (gd) 1998 AW 0-4: (11f 2, 12f 2) (Equi, Fibr 3)
Moderate gelding, often wears blinkers. AW high 47.
**M J Polglase [0-12] K S Lee.*

ISHMAEL BHB 26a **RR 26a** 336^{13}
5 b g Prionsaa 8f **(48)** - Pert (Sayf El Arab (USA)) 7.1f **(54)**
Form - 0040
Record 1998 - 1st:0 2nd:0 3rd:0 Ran:4
Pre1998 - 1st:0 2nd:0 3rd:0 Ran:1
Win Prizemoney £0 *Total Prizemoney* £166
1998 AW 0-4: (5f, 7f 2, 8f) (Fibr 4)
Poor gelding, often wears blinkers. AW high 15.
**B J Llewellyn [0-4] D R W Jones (from G L Moore [0-1] Jun 1997).*

ISHTIHAR (USA) RR 90f 3217^{4}
2 ch c Woodman (USA) 9.7f **(77)** - Aljawza (USA) (Riverman (USA))

9.1f **(76)**
Form - 14
Record 1998 - 1st:1 2nd:0 3rd:0 Ran:2
Win Prizemoney £3,870 *Total Prizemoney* £5,695
Wins * 1998 Jly Lingfi (G-F) 6f 90+ <
1998 Turf 1-2: (6f 1-2) (gd, frm 1-1)
Currently useful colt. Turf high 90 (1st run) (began Jly) - 1st of 7 from Indian Warrior (10 Jly Lingfield RF 2687). Well beaten last of four in the Richmond Stakes, having previously won an ordinary Lingfield maiden. **S bin Suroor [1-2] Godolphin.*

ISIT IZZY BHB 41f36a RR 41f 36a 2654[14]

6 b m Crofthall 8.6f **(54)** - Angie's Girl (Dubassoff (USA)) 14.2f **(55)**
Form - 080360
Record 1998 - 1st:0 2nd:0 3rd:1 Ran:6
Pre1998 - 1st:0 2nd:0 3rd:0 Ran:3
Win Prizemoney £0 *Total Prizemoney* £698
1998 Turf 0-4: (8f, 10f 3) (g-s, gd, frm 2) 1998 AW 0-2: (8f 2) (Fibr 2)
Moderate mare, effective 8f, acts on gd, likes tight tracks. Turf high 41 - 3rd of 16 getting 6lb from Miskin Heights (3 Jun Warwick 8f gd RF 1709). AW high 34. **B A McMahon [0-9] Mrs Angela Beard.*

ISITOFF BHB 76f69a RR 79f 69a 3315[3]

5 b g Vague Shot 11f **(53)** - Plum Blossom (USA) (Gallant Romeo (USA)) 8.4f **(64)**
Form - 3
Record 1998 - 1st:0 2nd:0 3rd:1 Ran:1
Pre1998 - 1st:3 2nd:3 3rd:4 Ran:19
Win Prizemoney £12,244 *Total Prizemoney* £22,001
Wins 1997 Aug Ripon (G-F) H 10f 72 76 <
1997 May Folkes (G-F) 12f 74
1996 May Windso (GD) H 11.6f 66 70
1998 Turf 0-1: (12f) (frm)
Above-average gelding, effective 10 to 12f, best at 10f, acts on gd to frm. Benefited from experienced handling to score at Folkestone on his third start of '97. Creditable efforts after, including when getting up right on the line to win a Ripon handicap in August.
**P J Hobbs [1-3] C J Butler (from S C Williams [3-15] Spt 1997).*

ISLAND HERO (IRE) RR 82f 1810[1]

2 b c Polar Falcon (USA) 9f **(74)**-Mnaafa (IRE)**(64f)** (Darshaan)9.9f **(84)**
Form - 211
Record 1998 - 1st:2 2nd:1 3rd:0 Ran:3
Win Prizemoney £6,631 *Total Prizemoney* £7,721
Wins * 1998 Jun Pontef (HVY) 6f 82 <
*** 1998** May Lingfi (G-F) 6f 75
1998 Turf 2-3: (6f 2-3) (g-s 1-1, gd, frm 1-1)
Currently decent colt. Turf high 82 - 1st of 10 giving 4lb to Pet Express Flyer (8 Jun Pontefract RF 1810) - also 1st of 12 from Tammam (23 May Lingfield RF 1431). **J Noseda [2-3] Mrs J M Ryan.*

ISLAND HOUSE (IRE) RR 78+f 4058[4]

2 ch c Grand Lodge (USA) - Fortitude (IRE) (Last Tycoon) 8.5f **(62)**
Form - 04
Record 1998 - 1st:0 2nd:0 3rd:0 Ran:2
Win Prizemoney £0 *Total Prizemoney* £450
1998 Turf 0-2: (7f 2) (frm 2)
Currently above-average colt. Turf high 78 (began Aug) - 4th of 11 giving 5lb to Scarlet Raider (2 Spt York 7f frm RF 4058). His second run was a big improvement on his debut.
**G Wragg [0-2] Mollers Racing.*

ISLAND RACE BHB 91f RR 71f 4965[8]

3 b f Common Grounds 8.1f **(66)** - Lake Isle (IRE) (Caerleon (USA)) 8.6f **(71)**
Form - 110778
Record 1998 - 1st:2 2nd:0 3rd:0 Ran:6
Pre1998 - 1st:0 2nd:0 3rd:0 Ran:1
Win Prizemoney £9,281 *Total Prizemoney* £9,281
Wins * 1998 May Kempto (GD) 6f 93+ <
*** 1998** Apr Thirsk (G-S) 6f 86+
1998 Turf 2-6: (6f 2-6) (sft, g-s 1-1, gd 1-2, frm 2)
Workmanlike, above-average filly, effective 6f, acts on g-s to gd, has worn blinkers. Turf high 93 - 1st of 6 getting 4lb from Poly Blue (4 May Kempton RF 1015) - also 1st of 17 from Prime Hand (17 Apr Thirsk RF 0739). She looked an improving sort when winning her first two starts of the season, but was unable to handle Listed company in her next two starts, and fared little better in handicap company for her final two efforts.
**J R Fanshawe [2-7] Car Colston Hall Stud.*

ISLAND SANDS (IRE) RR 102+f 4585[1]

2 b br c Turtle Island (IRE)-Tiavanita (USA) (J O Tobin (USA)) 9.4f **(67)**
Form - 11
Record 1998 - 1st:2 2nd:0 3rd:0 Ran:2
Win Prizemoney £8,409 *Total Prizemoney* £8,409
Wins * 1998 Spt Salisb (HVY) 6f 102+ <
*** 1998** Aug Salisb (G-F) 6f 102+ <
1998 Turf 2-2: (6f 2-2) (gd 1-1, g-f 1-1)
Currently very useful colt. Turf high 102 (began Aug) - 1st of 5 getting 6lb from Locombe Hill (30 Spt Salisbury RF 4585) - also 1st of 14 giving 2lb to Victory Spin (20 Aug Salisbury RF 3760). He does not have the pedigree or looks of a top-class horse, but that does not matter a jot when the starter says go. Strongly supported when winning a maiden at Salisbury in August, he coped with heavy ground and stiffer opposition in a well contested minor event at the same track the following month. He has something to prove when pushed into Group company, but is unexposed and likely to improve. By the mud-lark Turtle Island, he will always be a threat on a sloppy track. Reported to have been sold at the end of the season to go to Dubai, presumably to Godolphin.
**D R C Elsworth [2-2] Mrs Michael Meredith.*

ISLAND SONG (IRE) RR 57f 5116[4]

2 b c Saddlers' Hall (IRE) 10.5f **(65)** - Island Lake (Kalaglow) 9.8f **(67)**
Form - 74
Record 1998 - 1st:0 2nd:0 3rd:0 Ran:2
Win Prizemoney £0 *Total Prizemoney* £242
1998 Turf 0-2: (8f 2) (sft, gd)
Currently fair colt. Turf high 57 (began Oct).
**M Johnston [0-2] The 3rd Middleham Partnership.*

ISLAND STORY BHB 85f RR 87f 4841[9]

3 b f Shirley Heights 12.1f **(76)** - Once Upon a Time (Teenoso (USA)) 9.9f **(72)**
Form - 331320
Record 1998 - 1st:1 2nd:1 3rd:3 Ran:6
Win Prizemoney £3,452 *Total Prizemoney* £8,196
Wins * 1998 Jun Epsom (GD) 10.1f 83 <
1998 Turf 1-6: (7f, 9f, 10f 1-1, 12f, 14f, 16f) (gd 2, g-f 1-4)
Workmanlike, useful filly, effective 9 to 16f, acts on gd to g-f, best on g-f. Turf high 87 - 2nd of 7 getting 1lb from Spirit of Love (8 Aug Ascot 16f g-f RF 3457) - also 1st of 5 getting 5lb from Quintus (24 Jun Epsom RF 2238). This half-sister to Arabian Story was a narrow winner of an Epsom maiden in May, and has gone on to run with credit in fair handicap company since. A tail-swisher, she looks suited by a staying trip. **Lord Huntingdon [1-6] The Queen.*

ISLAND VISION (IRE) BHB 45f RR 79[4]

8 b g Vision (USA) 10.4f **(57)** - Verandah (Jaazeiro (USA)) 9.2f **(54)**
Form - 4
Record 1998 - 1st:0 2nd:0 3rd:0 Ran:1
1998 AW 0-1: (13f) (Equi)
Very moderate gelding. **J G M O'Shea [1-11] Gary Roberts.*

ISLE DE FRANCE (USA) RR 109f 4343a[10]

3 b f Nureyev (USA)8.4f **(84)**-Stella Madrid (FR)(Alydar (USA)) 9.1f **(76)**
Form - 10
1998 Turf 1-2: (12f, 13f 1-1) (hvy, g-f 1-1)
Currently Pattern-class filly. Turf high 101 (1st run) (began Jly) - 1st of 7 from Minority (14 Jly Deauville RF 3051a). She took time to come to hand, but looked right back to her best when winning the Prix Minerve at Deauville in July. Unfortunately she could not maintain that level of performance in the Prix Vermeille.
**A Fabre in FR [1-3] M Tabor.*

ISLE OF SODOR BHB 67f RR 68f 4479[10]

2 b f Cyrano de Bergerac 7.3f **(58)** - Costa Verde **(40df)** (King of Spain) 7.8f **(52)**
Form - 6380310
Record 1998 - 1st:1 2nd:0 3rd:2 Ran:7
Win Prizemoney £3,687 *Total Prizemoney* £4,645
Wins * 1998 Spt Leices (G-F) H 6f 58 68 <
1998 Turf 1-7: (5f 4, 6f 1-2, 7f) (sft, gd 3, frm 1-3)

Average filly, effective 6f, acts on frm. Turf high 68 - 1st of 22 getting 13lb from Sari (21 Spt Leicester RF 4400).
**K W Hogg [1-7] Auldyn Stud Ltd.*

ISMAROS BHB 106f **RR 109f** 2879[2]
4 ch c Selkirk (USA) 7.9f **(76)** - Trikymia (Final Straw) 7.9f **(64)**
Form - 6152
Record 1998 - 1st:1 2nd:1 3rd:0 Ran:4
Pre1998 - 1st:1 2nd:0 3rd:0 Ran:2
Win Prizemoney £8,787 *Total Prizemoney* £11,424
Wins *** 1998** May Newcas (G-F) 12.4f 108 <
* 1997 Jun Windso (G-F) 10f 72
1998 Turf 1-4: (10f, 12f 1-3) (gd 2, g-f 1-1, frm)
Scopey, Pattern-class colt, effective 10 to 12f, acts on g-f. Turf high 109 - also 1st of 4 giving 4lb to Symonds Inn (21 May Newcastle RF 1369). Won in the style of a smart performer at Newcastle in May, but was most disappointing next time. Much better effort at Newmarket, although no match for Mutawwaj at the weights. He is a big, scopey individual and may improve further as he grows into his frame. **H R A Cecil [2-6] L Marinopoulos.*

IS TIROL (IRE) RR 107f 2863a[9]
4 b c Tirol 8.1f **(64)** - Islande (Gift Card (FR)) 8.6f **(61)**
Form - 0
1998 Turf 0-1: (8f) (gd)
Pattern-class colt, has worn blinkers. **M Hofer in GER [0-4].*

ITALIAN ROSE BHB 51f58a **RR 55f 58a** 4923[14]
3 ch f Aragon 7.7f **(58)** - Cayla (Tumble Wind (USA)) 7.5f **(57)**
Form - 020720
Record 1998 - 1st:0 2nd:2 3rd:0 Ran:5
Pre1998 - 1st:0 2nd:0 3rd:2 Ran:7
Win Prizemoney £0 *Total Prizemoney* £2,257
1998 Turf 0-5: (6f 2, 7f 3) (sft, gd, g-f 2, frm)
Leggy, fair filly, effective 5f, acts on frm, has worn blinkers. Turf high 55. Ran with plenty of promise on her debut, but was disappointing later.
**A W Carroll [0-5] Serafino Agodino (from W J Musson [0-7] Nov 1997).*

ITALIAN SYMPHONY (IRE) BHB 36f85a **RR 38f 85a** 5120[3]
4 b g Royal Academy (USA) 7.8f **(77)** -Terracotta Hut (Habitat) 9.4f **(70)**
Form - 471762113152118034310342211223
Record 1998 - 1st:8 2nd:5 3rd:5 Ran:24
Pre1998 - 1st:2 2nd:2 3rd:1 Ran:22
Win Prizemoney £22,696 *Total Prizemoney* £30,705
Wins *** 1998** *Oct Wolver (sta) C 7f 74* <
*** 1998** *Spt Wolver (STD) H 6f 69 74* <
*** 1998** *Jly Southw (STD) C 7f 73*
*** 1998** *May Southw (STD) C 7f 73*
*** 1998** *Apr Wolver (STD) C 6f 60*
*** 1998** *Feb Wolver (STD) C 7f 67*
*** 1998** *Feb Lingfi (SLW) H 7f 63 72*
*** 1998** *Feb Wolver (STD) C 6f 61*
* 1997 *Dec Lingfi (STD) H 7f 59 63*
* 1997 *Nov Wolver (STD) H 6f 55 60*
1998 Turf 0-6: (7f 4, 8f 2) (gd 2, g-f 2, frm 2) 1998 AW 8-18: (6f 3-5, 7f 5-10, 8f 3) (Equi 1-2, Fibr 7-16)
Decent gelding, effective 6 to 8f, best at 6f - acts on AW, best on Fibr, mostly wears blinkers (extremely effectively), prefers left handed tracks, favours tight tracks, excels at Wolverhampton, likes Southwell and Lingfield. Turf high 38. AW high 82 - 2nd of 13 giving 9lb to Sihafi (17 Oct Wolverhampton 6f Fibr RF 4864) - also 1st of 12 giving 4lb to Be Warned (3 Oct Wolverhampton RF 4636). He has become one of the most consistent and successful All-Weather performers around, and seems to handle both types of surface equally well. He is effective over both six and seven furlongs, though any further seems to stretch his stamina a bit.
**P D Evans [10-36] J E Abbey (from M Johnston [0-10] May 1997).*

ITCH BHB 65f **RR 54f** 2464[10]
3 b c Puissance 7.1f **(60)** -Panienka (POL) (Dom Racine (FR)) 9.2f **(62)**
Form - 00
Record 1998 - 1st:0 2nd:0 3rd:0 Ran:2
Pre1998 - 1st:1 2nd:0 3rd:0 Ran:3
Win Prizemoney £2,248 *Total Prizemoney* £2,248
Wins ***** 1997 Oct Pontef (G-S) 6f 75 <
1998 Turf 0-2: (6f, 7f) (g-f, frm)
Scopey, fair colt. Turf high 50.
**R Bastiman [1-5] Victor Chandler (Equus) Ltd.*

ITHADTOBEYOU BHB 81f92a **RR 65f 92a** 1002[8]
3 b c Prince Sabo 6.6f **(64)** - Secret Valentine (Wollow) 8.2f **(61)**
Form - 1468
Record 1998 - 1st:1 2nd:0 3rd:0 Ran:4
Win Prizemoney £3,420 *Total Prizemoney* £3,894
Wins *** 1998** *Feb Lingfi (SLW) 5f 75+* <
1998 Turf 0-2: (6f 2) (sft, gd) 1998 AW 1-2: (5f 1-1, 7f) (Equi 1-1, Fibr)
Leggy, decent colt. Turf high 65. AW high 80 - also 1st of 7 giving 5lb to Phantom Ring (14 Feb Lingfield RF 0292). Got off the mark on his debut over the minimum on the Lingfield Equitrack in February, but did not seem to stay the extra two furlongs in a hot race at Wolverhampton next time. Tailed off in a decent race in soft on his turf debut. **P F I Cole [1-4] Mrs M McMillan.*

ITLAK (USA) RR 80+f 4358[9]
2 b f A P Indy (USA) - Mashaarif (USA) (Mr Prospector (USA)) 8.8f **(78)**
Form - 10
Record 1998 - 1st:1 2nd:0 3rd:0 Ran:2
Win Prizemoney £5,394 *Total Prizemoney* £5,394
Wins *** 1998** Aug Ascot (G-F) 6f 80+ <
1998 Turf 1-2: (6f 1-1, 7f) (g-f 1-2)
Currently decent filly. Turf high 80 (1st run) (began Aug) - 1st of 6 from Tebyaan (7 Aug Ascot RF 3429). Won what looked an ordinary maiden by Ascot standards on her debut.
**S bin Suroor [1-2] Godolphin.*

ITSALLHAPPENING (IRE) BHB 64f **RR 67f** 4083[8]
2 b f Second Set (IRE) 9.2f **(67)** - Primo Stampari **(78?f)** (Primo Dominie) 6.2f **(80)**
Form - 00028
Record 1998 - 1st:0 2nd:1 3rd:0 Ran:5
Win Prizemoney £0 *Total Prizemoney* £542
1998 Turf 0-5: (5f, 6f 4) (gd, g-f 3, frm)
Average filly. Turf high 67 - 2nd of 5 getting 8lb from Robber Red (26 Aug Lingfield 6f g-f RF 3892).
**T J Naughton [0-5] The Awayday Partnership.*

ITS ALL RELATIVE BHB 82f **RR 89f** 4404[8]
3 gr f Distant Relative 7f **(69)** - Sharp Anne (Belfort (FR)) 6.8f **(63)**
Form - 37805008
Record 1998 - 1st:0 2nd:0 3rd:1 Ran:8
Pre1998 - 1st:2 2nd:1 3rd:0 Ran:6
Win Prizemoney £6,273 *Total Prizemoney* £12,274
Wins ***** 1997 Jly Bath (FRM) 5.1f 89+ <
* 1997 Jun Mussel (GD) 5f 75
1998 Turf 0-8: (5f 7, 6f) (g-s, gd 2, g-f 4, frm)
Rangy, useful filly, effective 5f, acts on gd to frm, has worn blinkers. Turf high 90. Becoming disappointing. Won twice as a juvenile when looking a speedy sort, but faced stiff tasks for the whole of this season. Her best effort came on her reappearance when third in a Haydock Listed event. **J Berry [2-14] R Leah.*

ITSANOTHERGIRL BHB 72f **RR 74f** 4969[4]
2 b f Reprimand 8.2f **(63)** - Tasmim (Be My Guest (USA)) 9.3f **(67)**
Form - 6354314
Record 1998 - 1st:1 2nd:0 3rd:2 Ran:7
Win Prizemoney £3,233 *Total Prizemoney* £4,739
Wins *** 1998** Oct Catter (SFT) H 7f 68 74 <
1998 Turf 1-7: (5f 2, 6f, 7f 1-2, 8f 2) (g-s 1-3, gd, frm 3)
Above-average filly, effective 5 to 8f, acts on g-s to frm. Turf high 74 (began Jly) - 1st of 15 giving 8lb to Bodfari Signet (16 Oct Catterick RF 4835). **M W Easterby [1-7] Miss V Foster.*

IT'S A POSSIBILITY RR 42f 4984[9]
2 b g Cosmonaut - Possibility **(51f 44a)** (Robellino (USA)) 7.6f **(80)**
Form - 80
Record 1998 - 1st:0 2nd:0 3rd:0 Ran:2
1998 Turf 0-2: (5f, 7f) (g-s, frm)
Currently moderate gelding. Turf high 42.
**B R Johnson [0-2] Miss Julie Reeves.*

ITSINTHEPOST BHB 40f51a **RR 42f 51a** 5127[9]
5 b m Risk Me (FR) 8f **(53)** - Where's the Money (Lochnager) 6f **(59)**
Form - 75000865570
Record 1998 - 1st:0 2nd:0 3rd:0 Ran:10

Pre1998 - 1st:4 2nd:2 3rd:4 Ran:23
Win Prizemoney £10,965 *Total Prizemoney* £14,334
Wins * 1997 *Jly Wolver (STD)* *7f* *64*
* 1997 Jly Folkes (SFT) H 6.9f 48 57
1995 *Nov Lingfi (STD) H* *6f 64 73* <
1995 *Jly Wolver (STD)* *6f* *66*
1998 Turf 0-6: (7f 3, 8f 3) (g-s, gd 2, g-f 2, frm) 1998 AW 0-4: (7f 3, 8f) (Equi 2, Fibr 2)
Average filly, effective 7f, acts on gd - acts on AW, has worn blinkers, likes tight tracks. Turf high 42. AW high 62 (1st run) - 5th of 9 giving 2lb to Davis Rock (6 Jan Lingfield 7f Equi RF 0036). Showed fair form on sand before scoring on soft ground at Folkestone, and followed up back on sand at Wolverhampton.
**V Soane [2-24] First Class (from M Johnston [2-9] Dec 1995).*

IT'S MAGIC BHB 65f **RR 61f** 4928[8]
2 b g Magic Ring (IRE) 6.5f **(64)** - Ryewater Dream (Touching Wood (USA)) 8.2f **(55)**
Form - 508
Record 1998 - 1st:0 2nd:0 3rd:0 Ran:3
1998 Turf 0-3: (7f, 8f 2) (g-s, gd, g-f)
Currently average gelding. Turf high 61 (began Aug).
**B Hanbury [0-3] Mrs Hazel Barber.*

ITS MY PLEASURE RR 30f 3487[3]
4 b f Rock Hopper 10.6f **(54)** - The Fink Sisters (Tap On Wood) 10.3f **(65)**
Form - 3
Record 1998 - 1st:0 2nd:0 3rd:1 Ran:1
Pre1998 - 1st:0 2nd:0 3rd:1 Ran:1
Win Prizemoney £0 *Total Prizemoney* £1,012
1998 Turf 0-1: (9f) (frm)
Tall, currently very moderate filly.
**W S Cunningham [0-2] Mrs Ann Bell.*

ITSNOTYETNAMED BHB 36f **RR 32f** 5058[7]
3 b c Kasakov - Wych Willow (Hard Fought) 8.8f **(62)**
Form - 0007
Record 1998 - 1st:0 2nd:0 3rd:0 Ran:4
Pre1998 - 1st:0 2nd:0 3rd:0 Ran:4
1998 Turf 0-4: (6f, 7f, 10f 2) (sft, g-s, gd, frm)
Leggy, very moderate colt. Turf high 32. Inconsistent.
**A Smith [0-8] Just For Fun Partnership.*

IT'S OUR SECRET (IRE) BHB 65f **RR 64f** 4752[8]
2 ch c Be My Guest (USA) 10.2f **(66)** - Lady Dulcinea (ARG) (General (FR))
Form - 758
Record 1998 - 1st:0 2nd:0 3rd:0 Ran:3
1998 Turf 0-3: (5f, 6f, 7f) (sft, g-f, frm)
Currently average colt. Turf high 64.
**M H Tompkins [0-3] Mrs M Barwell.*

IVAN LUIS (FR) BHB 109f **RR 111f** 4951a[5]
4 b c Lycius (USA) 8.8f **(71)** - Zivania (IRE) (Shernazar) 10.2f **(73)**
Form - 5364425
Record 1998 - 1st:0 2nd:1 3rd:1 Ran:7
Pre1998 - 1st:3 2nd:2 3rd:4 Ran:13
Win Prizemoney £22,960 *Total Prizemoney* £104,688
Wins * 1997 Jly Haydoc (GD) L 11.9f 101 <
* 1997 Apr Catter (GD) 12f 90+
* 1996 Spt Thirsk (G-F) 8f 92
1998 Turf 0-7: (10f 2, 12f 5) (sft 2, gd 4, g-f)
Leggy, Group-class colt, effective 10 to 12f, best at 12f, acts on gd to g-f, best on gd, likes right handed tracks, likes San Siro. Turf high 113 - 3rd of 7 to Polar Prince (17 May Capannelle 10f gd RF 1381a). Consistent. He is a rugged individual who tries hard but lacks a decisive turn-of-foot. He usually runs in Group 1 races when sent abroad and will fare better if dropped a grade.
**M Bell [3-20].*

IVOR'S DEED BHB 47f55a **RR 48f 55a** 4867[12]
5 b g Shadeed (USA) 7.7f **(72)** - Gena Ivor (USA) (Sir Ivor) 10.2f **(70)**
Form - 1357451467078606000
Record 1998 - 1st:1 2nd:0 3rd:0 Ran:17
Pre1998 - 1st:3 2nd:2 3rd:5 Ran:21
Win Prizemoney £7,885 *Total Prizemoney* £12,235
Wins 1998 *Feb Lingfi (SLW) C* *7f* *63* <
1997 *Nov Lingfi (STD) H* *7f 59 61*
1997 May Folkes (G-F) C 6.9f 51
1996 Jun Catter (G-F) 7f 59
1998 Turf 0-7: (7f 2, 8f 3, 9f 2) (sft, gd 2, g-f 4) 1998 AW 1-10: (6f 2, 7f 1-5, 8f 2, 9f) (Equi 1-8, Fibr 2)
Average gelding, effective 6 to 7f, best at 7f - acts on Equi, has worn blinkers, favours tight tracks. Turf high 48. AW high 65 - 4th of 14 getting 4lb from Just Loui (19 Mar Lingfield 7f Equi RF 0443) - also 1st of 9 giving 10lb to Blushing Grenadier (24 Feb Lingfield RF 0352). Becoming disappointing. He has a mind of his own, but is an effective sort over seven furlongs on Equitrack.
**P D Evans [0-5] D B Brocklesby (from Miss Gay Kelleway [2-17] Jly 1998).*

IVOR'S FLUTTER BHB 79f **RR 87f** 4850[24]
9 b g Beldale Flutter (USA) 10.2f **(62)** - Rich Line (High Line) 10.3f **(70)**
Form - 1107070
Record 1998 - 1st:2 2nd:0 3rd:0 Ran:7
Pre1998 - 1st:4 2nd:2 3rd:4 Ran:25
Win Prizemoney £29,925 *Total Prizemoney* £40,329
Wins * **1998** Apr Sandow (SFT) H 16.4f 83 86 <
* **1998** Apr Kempto (HVY) H 16f 77 84
* 1996 Aug Sandow (GD) H 14f 78 84
* 1994 Spt Bath (GD) H 17.2f 74 79
1998 Turf 2-7: (16f 2-4, 18f, 19f, 20f) (hvy 1-1, sft 1-1, gd 4, g-f)
Useful gelding, effective 16f, acts on hvy to gd, prefers right handed tracks. Turf high 87 - 7th of 11 giving 6lb to Premier Night (23 May Kempton 16f gd RF 1427) - also 1st of 8 giving 7lb to Dovedon Star (24 Apr Sandown RF 0849). Won over hurdles in the winter, and handled the heavy ground well when winning the Queen's Prize on his Flat reappearance, following up at Sandown under promising apprentice Neil Pollard. Well beaten since, however.
**D R C Elsworth [8-51] W I M Perry.*

IVOR'S INVESTMENT BHB 69f **RR 78f** 4183[8]
2 ch f Forzando 7.2f **(63)** - Abbotswood (Ahonoora) 8.1f **(73)**
Form - 644438
Record 1998 - 1st:0 2nd:0 3rd:1 Ran:6
Win Prizemoney £0 *Total Prizemoney* £1,268
1998 Turf 0-6: (5f 3, 6f 2, 7f) (g-s, gd 2, g-f, frm, hrd)
Above-average filly, effective 5 to 6f, acts on gd to hrd. Turf high 78 - 3rd of 8 getting 5lb from Pal of Mine (5 Spt Epsom 6f gd RF 4095). **D R C Elsworth [0-6] W I M Perry.*

IVORY CHARM BHB 26f **RR 30f** 4588[15]
3 b f Batshoof 9.5f **(66)** - Amazing Journey (USA) (Spectacular Bid (USA)) 11.2f **(76)**
Form - 007660
Record 1998 - 1st:0 2nd:0 3rd:0 Ran:6
Pre1998 - 1st:0 2nd:0 3rd:0 Ran:3
1998 Turf 0-4: (10f, 12f, 14f, 16f) (gd, g-f 2, frm) 1998 AW 0-2: (9f, 12f) (Fibr 2)
Workmanlike, very moderate filly, has worn blinkers. Turf high 30 (began Jly). AW high 21. **K T Ivory [0-9] Dean Ivory.*

IVORY CROWN (IRE) BHB 91f **RR 93f** 5067[3]
3 b f Chief's Crown (USA) 10.2f **(75)** - Royal Myth (USA) (Sir Ivor) 10.2f **(70)**
Form - 221375423
Record 1998 - 1st:1 2nd:3 3rd:2 Ran:9
Pre1998 - 1st:0 2nd:0 3rd:0 Ran:1
Win Prizemoney £3,485 *Total Prizemoney* £12,720
Wins * **1998** Jly Sandow (GD) 14f 79 <
1998 Turf 1-9: (10f, 12f, 13f, 14f 1-4, 15f, 16f) (g-s, gd 1-3, g-f 2, frm 3)
Neat, useful filly, effective 14 to 15f, best at 14f, acts on gd to frm, prefers right handed tracks. Turf high 95 - 3rd of 5 getting 5lb from Kahtan (9 Jly Newmarket 15f frm RF 2647). Appreciated the 14-furlong trip when winning an ordinary maiden at Sandown, and was tackling two miles by the end of the campaign, running third in a Newmarket listed race.
**E A L Dunlop [1-10] The Serendipity Partnership.*

IVORY DAWN RR 77f 4390[23]
4 b f Batshoof 9.5f **(66)** -Cradle of Love (USA) (Roberto (USA)) 10f **(76)**
Form - 5050651133402540
Record 1998 - 1st:2 2nd:1 3rd:2 Ran:16
Pre1998 - 1st:1 2nd:4 3rd:3 Ran:21
Win Prizemoney £10,334 *Total Prizemoney* £21,370

Wins * **1998** Jly Lingfi (G-F) H 6f 60 72 <
* **1998** Jly Bright (GD) H 6f 60 64
* 1997 Jun Goodwo (GD) H 6f 65 70

1998 Turf 2-16: (5f, 6f 2-15) (sft, g-s 2, gd 3, g-f 5, frm 2-5)
Workmanlike, above-average filly, effective 5 to 7f, best at 6f, acts on g-s to frm, has worn blinkers, excels at Lingfield and Brighton and likes Newmarket. Turf high 77 - 2nd of 12 to Levelled (22 Aug Lingfield 6f g-f RF 3808) - also 1st of 12 giving 1lb to Sally Green (10 Jly Lingfield RF 2688). Consistent. She seems to run her best races in the summer, and is ideally suited by a very sharp downhill track. **K T Ivory [3-37] Dean Ivory.*

IVORY GIRL (IRE) BHB 30a **RR 7f** 515[16]
3 ch f Sharp Victor (USA) 10f **(56)** - Nordic Dance (USA) (Graustark) 10.1f **(70)**
Form - 880
Record 1998 - 1st:0 2nd:0 3rd:0 Ran:3
Pre1998 - 1st:0 2nd:0 3rd:0 Ran:2
1998 Turf 0-1: (8f) (g-s) 1998 AW 0-2: (6f, 7f) (Fibr 2)
Workmanlike, very poor filly. AW high 2.
**K G Wingrove [0-5] J Salmon.*

IVORY LEAGUE BHB 45f **RR 46f** 2325[4]
3 b f Last Tycoon 9.4f **(73)** - Ivory Lane (USA) (Sir Ivor) 10.2f **(70)**
Form - 0004
Record 1998 - 1st:0 2nd:0 3rd:0 Ran:4
Pre1998 - 1st:0 2nd:0 3rd:0 Ran:3
1998 Turf 0-4: (8f, 10f, 11f, 17f) (g-s, gd 2, frm)
Scopey, moderate filly. Turf high 46. **G Lewis [0-7] R D Hubbard.*

IVORY'S GRAB HIRE BHB 55f54a **RR 58f 54a** 4811[11]
5 b g Shavian 7.7f **(67)** - Knees Up (USA) (Dancing Champ (USA)) 8.8f **(80)**
Form - 08444758310074605530007520
Record 1998 - 1st:1 2nd:1 3rd:2 Ran:25
Pre1998 - 1st:6 2nd:7 3rd:9 Ran:59
Win Prizemoney £21,691 *Total Prizemoney* £36,668
Wins * **1998** *Apr Wolver (STD) H 5f 47 52*
* 1997 Aug Bright (G-F) H 5.3f 62 70 <
* 1997 May Bright (FRM) H 6f 55 67
* 1997 May Bright (FRM) H 6f 55 59
* 1997 *Mar Lingfi (STD) H 5f 48 45*
* 1997 *Feb Lingfi (STD) H 5f 43 44*
* 1996 Jun Lingfi (FRM) H 7f 53 62

1998 Turf 0-15: (5f 7, 6f 7, 7f) (gd 9, g-f 2, frm 4) 1998 AW 1-10: (5f 1-7, 6f 2, 7f) (Equi 8, Fibr 1-2)
Fair gelding, effective 5 to 6f, best at 6f, acts on gd to frm, mostly wears blinkers (effectively), likes left handed tracks, likes tight tracks, and does well at Brighton. Turf high 61. AW high 52. Consistent. Able in his grade, he is an effective sort in minor sprints either on turf or Equitrack, but managed to score on his Fibresand debut at Wolverhampton in April. He is effective over five, but can stay six on a sharp track like Brighton, where he was successful three times in '97. Good third at Glorious Goodwood in a first-time visor. He was never going to win the Derby with a name like that. **K T Ivory [7-84] Dean Ivory.*

IVORY'S JOY BHB 66f **RR 64f** 5007[5]
3 b f Tina's Pet 7.4f **(56)** - Jacqui Joy (Music Boy) 6.8f **(57)**
Form - 0402303326707545
Record 1998 - 1st:0 2nd:2 3rd:3 Ran:16
Pre1998 - 1st:3 2nd:2 3rd:1 Ran:13
Win Prizemoney £13,615 *Total Prizemoney* £23,403
Wins * 1997 Spt Newbur (G-S) H 5.2f 70 73 <
* 1997 Jun Goodwo (SFT) S 6f 73 <
* 1997 Jun Goodwo (GD) S 5f 65

1998 Turf 0-16: (5f 11, 6f 5) (sft 2, g-s, gd 5, g-f 3, frm 5)
Workmanlike, average filly, effective 5 to 6f, best at 5f, acts on gd to frm, best on gd, has worn blinkers, excels at Goodwood. Turf high 77 - 2nd of 11 getting 2lb from Eastern Lyric (16 Jly Bath 5f gd RF 2843). Consistent. She won a couple of sellers early on at two, but proved better than that in nursery company. She has run quite well in handicap company this season without managing to win one. **K T Ivory [3-29] K T Ivory.*

IVORY'S PROMISE BHB 59f **RR 77df** 5004[18]
2 gr f Pursuit of Love 9.5f **(69)** - Cole Slaw (Absalom) 7.2f **(58)**
Form - 51504301744600
Record 1998 - 1st:2 2nd:0 3rd:1 Ran:14
Win Prizemoney £5,640 *Total Prizemoney* £6,996
Wins * **1998** Aug Bath (GD) S 5.1f 77 <
* **1998** May Bath (GD) 5.1f 73+

1998 Turf 2-14: (5f 2-7, 6f 6, 7f) (sft, gd 7, g-f 1-2, frm 1-4)
Above-average filly, effective 5 to 6f, best at 5f, acts on g-f to frm, best on frm, often wears blinkers. Turf high 77 - 1st of 13 from Eastern Trumpeter (4 Aug Bath RF 3321) - also 1st of 18 getting 7lb from Pisces Lad (10 May Bath RF 1128). Still showed signs of greenness when winning on her second start, but faced stiff tasks subsequently until regaining winning form in a seller.
**K T Ivory [2-14] Dean Ivory.*

IVY BIRD (IRE) BHB 27f35a **RR 7f 35a** 3040[14]
3 b f Contract Law (USA) 8.9f **(54)** - Hollyberry (IRE) (Runnett) 7f **(59)**
Form - 7060
Record 1998 - 1st:0 2nd:0 3rd:0 Ran:2
Pre1998 - 1st:0 2nd:0 3rd:0 Ran:3
1998 Turf 0-1: (10f) (gd) 1998 AW 0-1: (9f) (Fibr)
Light-framed, very moderate filly, has worn blinkers.
**W Jarvis [0-5] William Jarvis.*

I WISH YOU LOVE BHB 63f **RR 67f** 4765[2]
3 ch c Risk Me (FR) 8f **(53)** - Sports Delight (Star Appeal) 9.6f **(65)**
Form - 46552
Record 1998 - 1st:0 2nd:1 3rd:0 Ran:5
Win Prizemoney £0 *Total Prizemoney* £940
1998 Turf 0-5: (7f 2, 8f 2, 9f) (gd, g-f 3, frm)
Workmanlike, average colt. Turf high 67.
**R Hannon [0-5] Bob Lalemant.*

JAAZIM (USA) **RR 94f** 4226[3]
3 b c Silver Hawk (USA) 11.2f **(85)** - Alvear (USA) (Seattle Slew (USA)) 9.4f **(76)**
Form - 310523
Record 1998 - 1st:1 2nd:1 3rd:2 Ran:6
Pre1998 - 1st:0 2nd:1 3rd:0 Ran:3
Win Prizemoney £9,098 *Total Prizemoney* £17,533
Wins * **1998** May Newbur (G-F) H 12f 86 90 <
1998 Turf 1-6: (10f, 12f 1-5) (g-s 2, g-f 2, frm 1-2)
Scopey, useful colt, effective 12f, acts on g-f to frm, best on g-f, has worn blinkers, prefers left handed tracks. Turf high 94 - 3rd of 17 getting 1lb from Jazil (11 Spt Doncaster 12f g-f RF 4226) - also 1st of 7 giving 9lb to Jonas Nightengale (16 May Newbury RF 1258). An expensive yearling, he showed some form in maiden company, but got off the mark when making all in a handicap at Newbury in May. Fair efforts in handicap company after that.
**Sir Michael Stoute [1-9] Hamdan Al Maktoum.*

JABAL HADEED (IRE) **RR 30f** 4644[14]
3 b g Caerleon (USA) 10.9f **(79)** - Emilia Romagna (USA) (Forli (ARG)) 9.6f **(67)**
Form - 60
Record 1998 - 1st:0 2nd:0 3rd:0 Ran:2
1998 Turf 0-2: (8f 2) (g-s, g-f)
Unfurnished, currently very moderate gelding. Turf high 30.
**M A Jarvis [0-2] Sheikh Ahmed Al Maktoum.*

JABAROOT (IRE) BHB 20f **RR 15f** 2564[5]
7 b g Sadler's Wells (USA) 11.3f **(87)** - Arctic Heroine (USA) (Arctic Tern (USA)) 8.9f **(69)**
Form - 755
Record 1998 - 1st:0 2nd:0 3rd:0 Ran:3
Pre1998 - 1st:1 2nd:0 3rd:0 Ran:22
Win Prizemoney £8,500 *Total Prizemoney* £8,500
Wins 1994 May Cheste (G-F) H 12.3f 70 71 <
1998 Turf 0-3: (14f 2, 16f) (gd 2, frm)
Poor gelding, has worn blinkers. Turf high 15.
**Martyn Wane [0-3] J P Slattery (from R M McKellar [0-14] Apr 1997).*

JACALANS GIFT **RR** 5009[10]
2 b f Almoojid 7f **(36)** - Bold Reine (FR) **(23f)** (Policeman (FR)) 9.8f **(80)**
Form - 0
Record 1998 - 1st:0 2nd:0 3rd:0 Ran:1
1998 Turf 0-1: (8f) (sft)
Currently very poor filly - 10th of 10 getting 5lb from Amezola (27 Oct Bath 8f sft RF 5009). **A Barrow [0-1] A Barrow.*

JACK BUTTON (IRE) BHB 75f **RR 70f** 1787[6]
9 b g Kings Lake (USA) 11.8f **(58)** - Tallantire (USA) (Icecapade (USA)) 11f **(62)**
Form - 6
Record 1998 - 1st:0 2nd:0 3rd:0 Ran:1
Pre1998 - 1st:8 2nd:10 3rd:7 Ran:49
Win Prizemoney £30,700 *Total Prizemoney* £72,770
Wins * 1994 Aug Newmar (G-F) H 16f 80 90 <
1998 Turf 0-1: (16f) (frm)
Above-average gelding, has worn blinkers. Consistent. Has been lightly raced in recent seasons and did not reappear until February 1998 last term. Probably retains some ability judged on his seventh place in the Gold Card Final at the Festival. He could win a long distance hurdle if the Handicapper relents.
**Bob Jones [10-58] Barrie Frost.*

JACKERIN (IRE) BHB 66f **RR 66f** 4837[14]
3 b g Don't Forget Me 9.5f **(66)** - Meanz Beanz (High Top) 10.2f **(67)**
Form - 0002274734254410
Record 1998 - 1st:1 2nd:3 3rd:1 Ran:16
Pre1998 - 1st:2 2nd:1 3rd:1 Ran:7
Win Prizemoney £8,828 *Total Prizemoney* £16,517
Wins * **1998** Oct Ayr (G-S) H 5f 61 66
* 1997 May Doncas (GD) 5f 79 <
* 1997 Mar Doncas (G-F) S 5f 63
1998 Turf 1-16: (5f 1-13, 6f 3) (sft 1-1, g-s, gd 5, g-f 4, frm 5)
Lengthy, average gelding, effective 5f, acts on gd to g-f, often wears blinkers. Turf high 66. Consistent.
**B S Rothwell [3-23] J B Young.*

JACK FLUSH (IRE) BHB 39f **RR 46f** 4156[18]
4 b g Broken Hearted 10.1f **(65)** - Clubhouse Turn (IRE) (King of Clubs) 7.1f **(57)**
Form - 8005000
Record 1998 - 1st:0 2nd:0 3rd:0 Ran:7
Pre1998 - 1st:1 2nd:2 3rd:2 Ran:17
Win Prizemoney £7,512 *Total Prizemoney* £10,647
Wins * 1997 May Thirsk (G-S) H 8f 58 64 <
1998 Turf 0-6: (8f 5, 9f) (g-s 2, g-f 2, frm 2) 1998 AW 0-1: (8f) (Fibr)
Leggy, moderate gelding, effective 8f, acts on g-s to frm, best on frm, has worn blinkers, likes tight tracks. Turf high 46.
**B S Rothwell [1-25] Derek Smith.*

JACK GOODMAN (IRE) BHB 66f **RR 74f** 4145[9]
2 ch c Simply Great (FR) 11.9f **(61)** - Donna Katrina (Kings Lake (USA)) 10.8f **(67)**
Form - 826140
Record 1998 - 1st:1 2nd:1 3rd:0 Ran:6
Win Prizemoney £2,490 *Total Prizemoney* £3,570
Wins * **1998** Jly Folkes (GD) 7f 68 <
1998 Turf 1-6: (6f 2, 7f 1-4) (gd 1-2, g-f 3, frm)
Above-average colt, effective 7f, acts on gd to g-f, best on gd. Turf high 74 - 2nd of 10 getting 1lb from Captain Miller (13 Jun Lingfield 7f gd RF 1966) - also 1st of 13 giving 5lb to Dolphin Friendly (15 Jly Folkestone RF 2822). **J S Moore [1-6] Mrs Victoria Goodman.*

JACKIE'S BABY BHB 87f85a **RR 84f 85a** 3827[2]
2 b c Then Again 7.4f **(52)** - Guarded Expression **(45f)** (Siberian Express (USA)) 8.8f **(65)**
Form - 431315312
Record 1998 - 1st:3 2nd:1 3rd:3 Ran:9
Win Prizemoney £8,973 *Total Prizemoney* £17,366
Wins * **1998** Aug Folkes (G-F) H 5f 77 84 <
* **1998** *Jly Southw (STD) H 5f 76*
* **1998** *May Southw (STD) 5f 68*
1998 Turf 1-5: (5f 1-5) (g-s, gd, g-f 1-2, frm) 1998 AW 2-4: (5f 2-3, 6f) (Fibr 2-4)
Decent colt, effective 5 to 6f, best at 5f, acts on g-f to frm - acts on Fibr. Turf high 84 - 1st of 9 giving 12lb to Legal Venture (14 Aug Folkestone RF 3624). AW high 84 - 2nd of 13 to Blue Star (22 Aug Wolverhampton 6f Fibr RF 3827) - also 1st of 7 giving 6lb to Palace Green (11 Jly Southwell RF 2723). A winner three times to date, two of which were on Fibresand, he is all action from the stalls. He was only just touched off in the Weatherby's Dash over six, but his style of running means that he is more likely to enjoy further success back over the minimum. **W G M Turner [3-9] Mrs J Glover.*

JACKIES WEBB BHB 27f **RR 8f** 3689[13]
3 b f Selkirk (USA) 7.9f **(76)** - Hawayah (IRE) **(33f)** (Shareef Dancer (USA)) 9.9f **(73)**
Form - 0000
Record 1998 - 1st:0 2nd:0 3rd:0 Ran:4
Pre1998 - 1st:0 2nd:0 3rd:0 Ran:3
1998 Turf 0-4: (6f 2, 7f, 10f) (gd, g-f 2, frm)
Neat, very poor filly. Turf high 8. **B Smart [0-7] Norman Webb.*

JACKINTHEBOX (IRE) **RR 57f** 1889[14]
2 ch g Pips Pride 6.7f **(70)** - Petite Maxine **(63f)** (Sharpo) 7.7f **(59)**
Form - 700
Record 1998 - 1st:0 2nd:0 3rd:0 Ran:3
1998 Turf 0-3: (5f 2, 6f) (gd, g-f 2)
Currently fair gelding. Turf high 57. **N Tinkler [0-3] P D Savill.*

JACK REEF **RR 40f** 4865[10]
3 b g Mystiko (USA) 7.7f **(59)** - Lady Reef (Mill Reef (USA)) 10.5f **(78)**
Form - 80
Record 1998 - 1st:0 2nd:0 3rd:0 Ran:2
1998 Turf 0-1: (7f) (frm) 1998 AW 0-1: (7f) (Fibr)
Currently moderate gelding. **D McCain [0-2] L A Morgan.*

JACK RUBY BHB 50f57a **RR 48df 57a** 4270[18]
3 b c Risk Me (FR) 8f **(53)** - Atisayin (USA) (Al Nasr (FR)) 9.3f **(68)**
Form - 200434000
Record 1998 - 1st:0 2nd:1 3rd:1 Ran:9
Pre1998 - 1st:0 2nd:0 3rd:0 Ran:3
Win Prizemoney £0 *Total Prizemoney* £1,590
1998 Turf 0-3: (7f 2, 10f)(gd 3)1998 AW 0-6:(6f 3, 7f 2, 8f) (Equi, Fibr 5)
Unfurnished, average colt, effective 6f - acts on Fibr, has worn blinkers, likes left handed tracks, likes tight tracks. Turf high 48. AW high 65 (1st run) - 2nd of 14 getting 3lb from Kayo (27 Apr Southwell 6f Fibr RF 0887). Becoming disappointing.
**P L Gilligan [0-12] Ellis Stud Partnership.*

JACK SAYS BHB 35f44a **RR 29f 44a** 531[17]
4 b g Rambo Dancer (CAN) 8.4f **(59)**-Madam Cody (Hot Spark)7.6f **(62)**
Form - 0070
Record 1998 - 1st:0 2nd:0 3rd:0 Ran:2
Pre1998 - 1st:0 2nd:1 3rd:4 Ran:16
Win Prizemoney £0 *Total Prizemoney* £2,290
1998 Turf 0-1: (7f) (gd) 1998 AW 0-1: (12f) (Fibr)
Moderate gelding, has worn blinkers. Becoming disappointing.
**D Shaw [0-11] K Nicholls (from T D Easterby [0-7] Oct 1996).*

JACKS ESTATE (IRE) **RR 91f** 4421a[4]
3 b g High Estate 10.5f **(66)** - Lady Tristram
Form - 03R3204
1998 Turf 0-7: (5f 2, 6f 3, 7f 2) (sft, g-s, gd 3, g-f, frm)
Useful gelding, effective 6f, acts on sft. Turf high 93.
**K P Cotter in IRE [0-7] Pinheads Pizza Syndicate.*

JACK THE LAD (IRE) BHB 66f53a **RR 62f 53a** 1287[9]
4 b g Shalford (IRE) 7.8f **(63)**-Indian Honey (Indian King (USA))7.4f **(64)**
Form - 076080
Record 1998 - 1st:0 2nd:0 3rd:0 Ran:5
Pre1998 - 1st:4 2nd:2 3rd:2 Ran:25
Win Prizemoney £13,025 *Total Prizemoney* £17,100
Wins * 1997 May Beverl (G-S) H 8.5f 66 77 <
* 1997 May Redcar (GD) H 10f 66 77 <
* 1997 May Carlis (G-S) H 8f 55 61
* 1997 May Redcar (FRM) H 9f 58 69
1998 Turf 0-3: (8f, 10f, 12f) (gd 2, frm) 1998 AW 0-2: (12f 2) (Fibr 2)
Strong, average gelding, effective 8 to 10f, best at 10f, acts on gd to frm, best on frm, likes tight tracks. Turf high 62. AW high 38. He tries hard, and contributed to a cracking spell for the yard with four victories in May '97, but has shown nothing since, including on sand.
**J Hetherton [4-24] Keith West Partnership (from C Murray [0-6] Spt 1996).*

JACK TO A KING BHB 57f **RR 61f** 4374[8]
3 b g Nawwar - Rudda Flash (General David)
Form - 608
Record 1998 - 1st:0 2nd:0 3rd:0 Ran:3
1998 Turf 0-3: (6f, 7f, 8f) (frm 3)

Currently average gelding. Turf high 61 (began Aug).
**J Balding [0-3] J D and J R Evans.*

JACMAR (IRE) BHB 63f **RR 60f** 5114[9]
3 br g High Estate 10.5f **(66)** - Inseyab (Persian Bold) 9.3f **(66)**
Form - 40030000270
Record 1998 - 1st:0 2nd:1 3rd:1 Ran:11
Pre1998 - 1st:3 2nd:3 3rd:0 Ran:8
Win Prizemoney £14,104 *Total Prizemoney* £28,557
Wins * 1997 Spt Hamilt (GD) H 6f 90 93+ <
* 1997 Aug Hamilt (GD) H 6f 80 81
* 1997 Jun Hamilt (G-F) 6f 79
1998 Turf 0-11: (6f 2, 7f, 8f 7, 9f) (sft 2, g-s, gd 8)
Scopey, average gelding, effective 6f, acts on gd. Turf high 83. He He proved very difficult to place at three.
**Miss L A Perratt [3-19] Marett-Sutherland-Hay.*

JACOBINA BHB 63f **RR 63f** 3836[7]
3 b f Magic Ring (IRE) 6.5f **(64)**-Mistitled (USA) (Miswaki (USA)) 9f **(81)**
Form - 040022107
Record 1998 - 1st:1 2nd:2 3rd:0 Ran:9
Pre1998 - 1st:0 2nd:0 3rd:2 Ran:4
Win Prizemoney £3,160 *Total Prizemoney* £5,675
Wins * **1998** Aug Haydoc (G-S) H 7.1f 59 63 <
1998 Turf 1-9: (7f 1-6, 8f 3) (gd 4, g-f 1-2, frm 3)
Unfurnished, average filly, effective 7f, acts on gd to frm, likes left handed tracks. Turf high 63 - also 1st of 16 getting 6lb from Morgan Le Fay (6 Aug Haydock RF 3410). She got off the mark in a Haydock handicap having had plenty of chances previously, but does not look particularly consistent.
**B S Rothwell [1-9] J M Ranson (from T D Barron [0-4] Jly 1997).*

JADE CHEQUER RR 74f 1327[3]
2 b f Green Desert (USA) 7.8f **(78)** - Draft Board (Rainbow Quest (USA)) 10.4f **(75)**
Form - 3
Record 1998 - 1st:0 2nd:0 3rd:1 Ran:1
Win Prizemoney £0 *Total Prizemoney* £693
1998 Turf 0-1: (5f) (g-f)
Currently above-average filly. (1st run) - 3rd of 4 getting 5lb from Choto Mate (19 May Goodwood 5f g-f RF 1327).
**J H M Gosden [0-1] Mark Horton.*

JADE TIGER BHB 78f **RR 76f** 4889[10]
2 ch c Lion Cavern (USA) 7.5f **(74)** - Precious Jade (Northfields (USA)) 9f **(72)**
Form - 62630
Record 1998 - 1st:0 2nd:1 3rd:1 Ran:5
Win Prizemoney £0 *Total Prizemoney* £1,620
1998 Turf 0-5: (6f 2, 7f, 8f 2) (gd 3, g-f, frm)
Above-average colt, has worn blinkers. Turf high 76 - 3rd of 20 giving 5lb to Panzeer (17 Spt Yarmouth 8f frm RF 4337).
**B J Meehan [0-5] F C T Wilson.*

JAGO BHB 40f **RR 35f** 3504[7]
3 b g Salse (USA) 10.9f **(71)** - Wanda (Taufan (USA)) 7f **(57)**
Form - 0677
Record 1998 - 1st:0 2nd:0 3rd:0 Ran:4
Pre1998 - 1st:0 2nd:0 3rd:0 Ran:3
1998 Turf 0-4: (6f, 8f, 12f, 16f) (gd, g-f, frm 2)
Unfurnished, very moderate gelding. Turf high 35.
**M W Easterby [0-7] E J Mangan.*

JAGUAR BHB 81f **RR 76f** 4797[3]
2 b c Barathea (IRE) - Oasis (Valiyar) 8.5f **(73)**
Form - 0753
Record 1998 - 1st:0 2nd:0 3rd:1 Ran:4
Win Prizemoney £0 *Total Prizemoney* £805
1998 Turf 0-4: (6f, 7f 2, 8f) (sft, gd 2, frm)
Above-average colt. Turf high 76 - 5th of 11 giving 5lb to Scarlet Raider (2 Spt York 7f frm RF 4058). Needed the run when last in the Coventry Stakes on his debut, and has had his limitations exposed in decent maidens since.
**Miss Gay Kelleway [0-4] Adrian Fitzpatrick.*

JAHAAM (USA) RR 80++f 5037[1]
2 b c Danzig (USA) 8.1f **(88)** - Elizabeth Bay (USA) (Mr Prospector (USA)) 8.8f **(78)**
Form - 1
Record 1998 - 1st:1 2nd:0 3rd:0 Ran:1
Win Prizemoney £3,187 *Total Prizemoney* £3,187
Wins * **1998** Oct Yarmou (SFT) 7f 80++ <
1998 Turf 1-1: (7f 1-1) (g-s 1-1)
Currently decent colt. (1st run) - 1st of 11 from Waabl (28 Oct Yarmouth RF 5037). Made all at Yarmouth to put himself into the Guineas picture. The form looks nothing special, however.
**D R Loder [1-1] Sheikh Mohammed.*

JAHANARA RR 56f 3794[11]
3 ch f Selkirk (USA) 7.9f **(76)** - Little White Star (Mill Reef (USA)) 10.5f **(78)**
Form - 70
Record 1998 - 1st:0 2nd:0 3rd:0 Ran:2
1998 Turf 0-2: (10f, 12f) (g-f, frm)
Unfurnished, currently fair filly. Turf high 56 (began Jly).
**B Hanbury [0-2] Paul Jackson.*

JALAAB (IRE) BHB 100f **RR 101+f** 2053[8]
3 b c Green Desert (USA) 7.8f **(78)** - Stay Sharpe (USA) (Sharpen Up) 8.3f **(67)**
Form - 8118
Record 1998 - 1st:2 2nd:0 3rd:0 Ran:4
Win Prizemoney £7,927 *Total Prizemoney* £7,927
Wins * **1998** May Yarmou (FRM) 8f 101 <
* **1998** May Doncas (G-F) 7f 76
1998 Turf 2-4: (7f 1-3, 8f 1-1) (gd 2, g-f 1-1, frm 1-1)
Workmanlike, very useful colt. Turf high 101 - 1st of 4 from The Editor (27 May Yarmouth RF 1538). He squeezed home over a mile at Yarmouth in May, and connections promptly dropped him straight back to seven furlongs in the Group Three Jersey Stakes. That, though, was too stiff a test.
**R W Armstrong [2-4] Hamdan Al Maktoum.*

JALB (IRE) BHB 65f **RR 68f** 4776[4]
4 b g Robellino (USA) 9.5f **(68)**-Adjacent (IRE) (Doulab (USA)) 9.8f **(65)**
Form - 00114304
Record 1998 - 1st:2 2nd:0 3rd:1 Ran:8
Pre1998 - 1st:0 2nd:0 3rd:1 Ran:7
Win Prizemoney £6,041 *Total Prizemoney* £7,967
Wins * **1998** Jly Beverl (GD) H 12f 58 66 <
* **1998** Jun Warwic (G-S) H 12.5f 58 64
1998 Turf 2-8: (10f 2, 11f, 12f 1-2, 13f 1-2, 14f) (gd 2, g-f 2-5, frm)
Scopey, average gelding, effective 10 to 14f, best at 12f, acts on gd to frm, likes tight tracks. Turf high 68 - 3rd of 12 giving 7lb to Toi Toi (9 Spt Kempton 14f gd RF 4195) - also 1st of 9 giving 13lb to Our Way (3 Jly Beverley RF 2488).
**P G Murphy [2-9] Family And Friends (from A C Stewart [0-7] Jly 1997).*

JAMAICA BRIDGE BHB 18f52a **RR 28?f 52a** 103[11]
8 b g Doulab (USA) 7.4f **(61)** - Mill Hill (USA) (Riva Ridge (USA)) 8.2f **(68)**
Form - 00
Record 1998 - 1st:0 2nd:0 3rd:0 Ran:1
Pre1998 - 1st:2 2nd:3 3rd:2 Ran:30
Win Prizemoney £5,665 *Total Prizemoney* £8,600
Wins 1995 *Jan Southw (STD) S 6f 59* <
1994 *Feb Southw (STD) 8f 46*
1998 AW 0-1: (7f) (Fibr)
Moderate gelding. Becoming disappointing.
**Mrs A M Naughton [0-4] B Hough (from S G Norton [1-19] Oct 1995).*

JAMAICAN FLIGHT (USA) BHB 68f82a **RR 78df 82a** 4850[9]
5 b h Sunshine Forever (USA) 13.2f **(76)** - Kalamona (USA) (Hawaii) 9.4f **(66)**
Form - 3125222033331800
Record 1998 - 1st:2 2nd:4 3rd:5 Ran:16
Pre1998 - 1st:1 2nd:6 3rd:1 Ran:15
Win Prizemoney £16,077 *Total Prizemoney* £33,621
Wins * **1998** Aug Pontef (G-F) 18f 78
* **1998** *Feb Wolver (STD) H 12f 72 79* <
1996 Jly Beverl (G-F) 16.2f 57
1998 Turf 1-12: (12f, 15f, 16f 4, 17f, 18f 1-3, 19f, 20f) (g-s, gd 6, g-f 2, frm 1-2, hrd) 1998 AW 1-4: (11f, 12f 1-2, 15f) (Fibr 1-4)
Decent colt, effective 12 to 19f, best at 12f, acts on g-s to hrd - acts

on Fibr, likes left handed tracks, prefers tight tracks, excels at Wolverhampton and does well at Pontefract. Turf high 78 - 3rd of 4 getting 16lb from Mawared (2 Aug Chester 19f g-f RF 3288) - also 1st of 3 giving 20lb to Grimshaw (25 Aug Pontefract RF 3853). AW high 81 - 2nd of 9 giving 5lb to Noufari (14 Mar Wolverhampton 15f Fibr RF 0432) - also 1st of 8 giving 2lb to Greenspan (25 Feb Wolverhampton RF 0359). An improved hurdler in the spring of 1997, this front-running stayer ran some good races on the level in '98, winning on the Wolverhampton Fibresand in February and a three-runner event at Pontefract in August.

**Mrs S Lamyman [8-35] P Lamyman (from C Smith [0-2] May 1997).*

JAMAICAN LAW (IRE) RR 34f 2294[6]
2 ch f Case Law 6f **(64)** - Kingston Rose (Tudor Music) 6.8f **(59)**
Form - 0806
Record 1998 - 1st:0 2nd:0 3rd:0 Ran:4
1998 Turf 0-4: (5f 3, 6f) (gd 2, g-f 2)
Very moderate filly, has worn blinkers. Turf high 34.
**M R Channon [0-4] Mrs T Burns.*

JAMES DEE (IRE) BHB 68f RR 74f 4307[14]
2 b c Shalford (IRE) 7.8f **(63)** - Glendale Joy (IRE) (Glenstal (USA)) 10.1f **(64)**
Form - 725230
Record 1998 - 1st:0 2nd:2 3rd:1 Ran:6
Win Prizemoney £0 *Total Prizemoney* £2,420
1998 Turf 0-5: (5f 4, 6f) (g-s, gd 2, g-f 2) 1998 AW 0-1: (5f) (Fibr)
Above-average colt, effective 5 to 6f, acts on gd to g-f. Turf high 74. **A P Jarvis [0-6] Mrs Ann Jarvis.*

JAMIES FIRST (IRE) RR 237[13]
5 ch g Commanche Run 10.3f **(63)** - Avionne (Derrylin) 8.8f **(54)**
Form - 0
Record 1998 - 1st:0 2nd:0 3rd:0 Ran:1
1998 AW 0-1: (11f) (Fibr)
Formerly very poor gelding. **R Ingram [0-4] Roger Ingram.*

JAMORIN DANCER BHB 66f RR 72f 4748[22]
3 b g Charmer 9f **(59)** - Geryea (USA) (Desert Wine (USA)) 9.7f **(80)**
Form - 3564100
Record 1998 - 1st:1 2nd:0 3rd:1 Ran:7
Pre1998 - 1st:0 2nd:1 3rd:1 Ran:2
Win Prizemoney £2,406 *Total Prizemoney* £4,725
Wins * 1998 Jun Lingfi (GD) 9f 72 <
1998 Turf 1-7: (9f 1-2, 10f 3, 12f 2) (sft, g-s, gd 3, g-f, frm 1-1)
Workmanlike, above-average gelding, effective 9 to 10f, acts on gd to frm, prefers tight tracks. Turf high 72.
**M A Jarvis [1-9] Mrs McLardy Smith.*

JAMPET RR 3f 2532[16]
2 b c No Big Deal - Jealous Lover (Alias Smith (USA)) 9.8f **(58)**
Form - 0780
Record 1998 - 1st:0 2nd:0 3rd:0 Ran:4
1998 Turf 0-3: (5f, 6f 2) (gd, frm 2) 1998 AW 0-1: (6f) (Fibr)
Very poor colt. Turf high 3. **A Barrow [0-4] Don Hazzard.*

JANARA BHB 40f46a RR 48f 46a 584[15]
4 b f Aragon 7.7f **(58)**-Aimee Jane (USA) (Our Native (USA)) 11.2f **(63)**
Form - 570
Record 1998 - 1st:0 2nd:0 3rd:0 Ran:3
Pre1998 - 1st:0 2nd:0 3rd:0 Ran:1
1998 Turf 0-1: (10f) (sft) 1998 AW 0-2: (9f 2) (Fibr 2)
Workmanlike, moderate filly. AW high 36.
**J Pearce [0-3] Ryszard Varisella (from L M Cumani [0-1] Spt 1997).*

JANDAL BHB 52f RR 51?f 2714[4]
4 ch g Arazi (USA) 9.2f **(74)** - Littlefield (Bay Express) 7.1f **(60)**
Form - 44
Record 1998 - 1st:0 2nd:0 3rd:0 Ran:2
Pre1998 - 1st:0 2nd:0 3rd:0 Ran:1
Win Prizemoney £0 *Total Prizemoney* £230
1998 Turf 0-1: (14f) (frm) 1998 AW 0-1: (12f) (Equi)
Leggy, currently fair gelding, has worn blinkers.
**G L Moore [0-2] A Moore (from C J Benstead [0-1] Jun 1997).*

JANE ANN (IRE) BHB 58f52a RR 60f 52a 5073[9]
2 ch f Perugino (USA) - Height of Elegance (Shirley Heights) 10.3f **(74)**
Form - 700340
Record 1998 - 1st:0 2nd:0 3rd:1 Ran:6
Win Prizemoney £0 *Total Prizemoney* £330
1998 Turf 0-5: (7f 4, 8f) (gd 2, g-f, frm 2) 1998 AW 0-1: (8f) (Fibr)
Average filly, effective 7f, acts on gd. Turf high 60 - 3rd of 13 getting 8lb from Jack Goodman (15 Jly Folkestone 7f gd RF 2822).
**A P Jarvis [0-6] Mrs Ann Jarvis.*

JANE GREY BHB 66f RR 71f 4967[10]
2 br f Tragic Role (USA) 9.4f **(63)** -Kind of Shy (Kind of Hush) 10.1f **(62)**
Form - 450
Record 1998 - 1st:0 2nd:0 3rd:0 Ran:3
Win Prizemoney £0 *Total Prizemoney* £260
1998 Turf 0-3: (5f, 6f 2) (sft, gd 2)
Currently above-average filly. Turf high 71 (began Spt).
**M Salaman [0-3] J P M & J W Cook.*

JANE'S LOFT (IRE) RR 39f 4370[11]
2 b f Up and At 'em - Excitingly (USA) (Val de L'Orne (FR)) 12f **(75)**
Form - 00
Record 1998 - 1st:0 2nd:0 3rd:0 Ran:2
1998 Turf 0-2: (6f 2) (g-f, frm)
Currently very moderate filly. Turf high 39 (began Aug).
**J Berry [0-2] J Wilkins.*

JANET LINDUP BHB 49f RR 51f 4817[8]
3 b f Sabrehill (USA) 8.5f **(64)** - Tartan Pimpernel (Blakeney) 10.5f **(64)**
Form - 07036828
Record 1998 - 1st:0 2nd:1 3rd:1 Ran:8
Pre1998 - 1st:0 2nd:0 3rd:0 Ran:1
Win Prizemoney £0 *Total Prizemoney* £1,724
1998 Turf 0-8: (8f, 10f 2, 12f 3, 14f, 16f) (g-s, gd 3, g-f 3, frm)
Light-framed, fair filly, effective 10 to 14f, acts on gd to g-f, prefers tight tracks. Turf high 59. **B W Hills [0-9] W J Gredley.*

JANGLYNYVE BHB 52f46a RR 61df 46a 2335[19]
4 ch f Sharpo 7.5f **(68)** - Wollow Maid (Wollow) 8.2f **(61)**
Form - 000
Record 1998 - 1st:0 2nd:0 3rd:0 Ran:3
Pre1998 - 1st:3 2nd:1 3rd:1 Ran:11
Win Prizemoney £9,872 *Total Prizemoney* £11,850
Wins 1997 Jun Newmar (SFT) C 10f 61 <
1997 May Leices (G-F) C 8f 60
1997 May Newmar (GD) C 8f 59
1998 Turf 0-3: (7f, 10f 2) (g-s, gd, g-f)
Leggy, average filly, effective 8 to 10f, best at 8f, acts on g-s to g-f. Turf high 11. Becoming disappointing.
**Mrs Merrita Jones [1-6] F J Sainsbury (from S P C Woods [3-11] Jun 1997).*

JANIB (USA) BHB 95f RR 102?f 2749[15]
4 ch c Diesis 9f **(80)** - Shicklah (USA) (The Minstrel (CAN)) 10f **(72)**
Form - 0
Record 1998 - 1st:0 2nd:0 3rd:0 Ran:1
Pre1998 - 1st:2 2nd:0 3rd:0 Ran:4
Win Prizemoney £16,087 *Total Prizemoney* £16,882
Wins 1996 Aug York (GD) L 5f 108 <
1996 Aug Thirsk (G-F) 5f 79
1998 Turf 0-1: (6f) (gd)
Neat, very useful colt.
**M P Tregoning [0-1] Hamdan Al Maktoum (from H ThomsonJones [2-4] Spt 1996).*

JAQUENETTA BHB 66f RR 55f 2641[7]
2 b f Manila (USA) 10f **(81)** - Jadeeda (USA) (Silver Hawk (USA)) 8.6f **(70)**
Form - 027
Record 1998 - 1st:0 2nd:1 3rd:0 Ran:3
Win Prizemoney £0 *Total Prizemoney* £775
1998 Turf 0-3: (6f, 7f 2) (gd, g-f, frm)
Currently fair filly. Turf high 55. Although making the frame in modest company, she does not look to be amongst the stable's stars. **P F I Cole [0-3] Sir George Meyrick.*

JARAAB BHB 43f79a RR 33f 79a 2078[5]
7 b g Sure Blade (USA) 10.6f **(66)** - Ostora (USA) (Blushing Groom (FR)) 10.3f **(76)**

Form - 214275

Record	1998 -	1st:1	2nd:2	3rd:0	Ran:6
	Pre1998 -	1st:10	2nd:1	3rd:2	Ran:31

Win Prizemoney £32,798 *Total Prizemoney* £36,479

Wins								
	* **1998**	*Mar*	*Southw*	*(STD)*	*C*	*14f*		*71*
	* 1996	*May*	*Southw*	*(STD)*	*C*	*16f*		*67*
	* 1996	*Apr*	*Wolver*	*(STD)*	*H*	*14.8f*	*82*	*85* <
	1996	*Apr*	*Southw*	*(STD)*	*C*	*16f*		*79*
	1996	*Feb*	*Lingfi*	*(STD)*	*H*	*16f*	*70*	*73*
	1995	*Nov*	*Lingfi*	*(STD)*	*H*	*16f*	*58*	*73+*
	1995	*Nov*	*Lingfi*	*(STD)*	*H*	*16f*	*58*	*61*
	1995	*May*	*Wolver*	*(STD)*	*H*	*14.8f*	*58*	*69+*
	1995	*Apr*	*Wolver*	*(STD)*	*H*	*7f*	*51*	*59*
	1995	*Mar*	*Lingfi*	*(STD)*	*H*	*16f*	*41*	*51*
	1995	*Feb*	*Lingfi*	*(STD)*	*H*	*12f*	*41*	*43*

1998 AW 1-6: (14f 1-1, 15f 3, 16f 2) (Fibr 1-6)

Decent gelding, effective 15f - acts on Fibr, mostly wears blinkers (effectively). AW high 80 - 2nd of 6 giving 1lb to Star Rage (25 Apr Wolverhampton 15f Fibr RF 0874). A prolific All-Weather winner, he is possibly one to avoid on his infrequent turf sorties, but ran a blinder to finish runner-up at Wolverhampton in February after being off the track for twenty-one months. He reversed the form with the winner in a Southwell claimer next time, but his form has deteriorated a bit since.

**Miss S J Wilton [3-9] John Pointon and Sons (from G Lewis [8-25] Apr 1996).*

JARRAYAN BHB 49f58a RR 39f 58a 2544[8]

3 ch f Machiavellian (USA) 9.8f **(83)** - Badrah (USA) (Private Account (USA)) 8.5f **(74)**

Form - 0078

Record	1998 -	1st:0	2nd:0	3rd:0	Ran:4
	Pre1998 -	1st:0	2nd:0	3rd:0	Ran:2

Win Prizemoney £0 *Total Prizemoney* £251

1998 Turf 0-3: (8f 2, 10f) (gd, g-f 2) 1998 AW 0-1: (8f) (Fibr)

Unfurnished, very moderate filly. Turf high 39.

**S C Williams [0-4] The Cherry Pickers Syndicate II (from Major W R Hern [0-2] Aug 1997).*

JASEUR (USA) BHB 96f RR 95f 3754[4]

5 b g Lear Fan (USA) 10.4f **(80)** - Spur Wing (USA) (Storm Bird (CAN)) 10.3f **(74)**

Form - 8024

Record	1998 -	1st:0	2nd:1	3rd:0	Ran:4
	Pre1998 -	1st:3	2nd:1	3rd:0	Ran:8

Win Prizemoney £27,339 *Total Prizemoney* £38,469

Wins								
	* 1997	Oct	Ascot	(HVY)	H	16.2f	82	87+ <
	* 1997	Spt	Ascot	(GD)	H	16.2f	74	82+
	* 1997	Spt	Bath	(GD)	H	13.1f	69	77

1998 Turf 0-4: (12f, 14f, 16f 2) (sft, g-f, frm 2)

Very useful gelding, effective 14 to 16f, best at 16f, acts on g-s to frm, best on frm, mostly wears blinkers (extremely effectively), excels at Ascot. Turf high 95 - 4th of 21 giving 3lb to Tuning (19 Aug York 14f frm RF 3754). A progressive stayer in '97, he was below his best on his first two runs of last season but ran a lot better at the July Meeting and when fourth in the Ebor. He handles soft ground particularly well and has a good turn of foot if produced late, but just lacks resolution in a battle.

**J H M Gosden [3-12] Sheikh Mohammed.*

JASHIN (IRE) RR 110f 2863a[10]

5 h

Form - 30

1998 Turf 0-2: (8f 2) (gd 2)

Group-class colt. Turf high 110 (1st run) - 3rd of 11 getting 2lb from Waky Nao (17 May Baden-Baden 8f gd RF 1379a). He is useful, but will struggle to beat genuine Group horses.

**A Lowe in GER [0-4].*

JASMINE BHB 78f RR 77f 1773[1]

3 b f Thatching 7.8f **(69)** - Jadirah (USA) (Deputy Minister (CAN)) 7.4f **(80)**

Form - 51

Record	1998 -	1st:1	2nd:0	3rd:0	Ran:2

Win Prizemoney £3,785 *Total Prizemoney* £3,785

Wins							
	* **1998**	Jun	Doncas	(GD)	5f		77 <

1998 Turf 1-2: (5f 1-1, 6f) (g-f 1-1, frm)

Lengthy, currently above-average filly. Turf high 77 - 1st of 10 getting 5lb from East Winds (6 Jun Doncaster RF 1773).

**R Guest [1-2] Miss K Rausing.*

JASMINE TEA BHB 56f RR 45f 1786[6]

3 ch f Alhijaz 7.7f **(57)** - Come To Tea (IRE) (Be My Guest (USA)) 9.3f **(67)**

Form - 6

Record	1998 -	1st:0	2nd:0	3rd:0	Ran:1
	Pre1998 -	1st:0	2nd:0	3rd:0	Ran:2

1998 Turf 0-1: (8f) (frm)

Unfurnished, currently moderate filly.

**S A Brookshaw [0-1] Mrs S C Birchall (from M Meade [0-2] Jun 1997).*

JATO DANCER (IRE) BHB 39f39a RR 58df 39a 4393[17]

3 b f Mukaddamah (USA) 7.6f **(74)** - Que Tranquila (Dominion) 8.5f **(63)**

Form - 3787172000

Record	1998 -	1st:1	2nd:1	3rd:1	Ran:10
	Pre1998 -	1st:1	2nd:0	3rd:0	Ran:5

Win Prizemoney £4,750 *Total Prizemoney* £6,107

Wins								
	* **1998**	May	Windso	(G-F)	C	8.3f		49 <
	1997	Jly	Bright	(FRM)	S	7f		49 <

1998 Turf 1-6: (7f, 8f 1-3, 9f, 11f) (gd, g-f, frm 1-4) 1998 AW 0-4: (7f, 8f 2, 10f) (Equi 4)

Leggy, fair filly, effective 7 to 9f, best at 7f, acts on g-f to frm - acts on Equi, has worn blinkers, likes left handed tracks, prefers tight tracks. Turf high 58 - 2nd of 9 getting 21lb from Star Manager (24 Jun Epsom 9f g-f RF 2241) - also 1st of 18 getting 17lb from Dark Menace (18 May Windsor RF 1311). AW high 51 (1st run) - 3rd of 10 getting 10lb from Nautical Warning (20 Jan Lingfield 7f Equi RF 0119). Becoming disappointing.

**J R Arnold [1-12] Norman Hill (from M R Channon [1-3] Aug 1997).*

JAVA RED (IRE) BHB 53f RR 54f 1994[P]

6 b g Red Sunset 9f **(57)** - Coffee Bean (Doulab (USA)) 9.8f **(65)**

Form - 7P

Record	1998 -	1st:0	2nd:0	3rd:0	Ran:2
	Pre1998 -	1st:3	2nd:0	3rd:4	Ran:21

Win Prizemoney £8,737 *Total Prizemoney* £10,649

Wins								
	* 1997	Spt	Pontef	(G-S)	S	10f		58 <
	* 1997	Jun	Beverl	(G-F)	H	7.5f	44	43
	* 1995	May	Ripon	(GD)	S	8f		54

1998 Turf 0-2: (12f 2) (gd, frm)

Fair gelding, effective 8 to 10f, best at 10f, acted on g-f to frm, best on frm, had worn blinkers, liked right handed tracks. Turf high 33. (DEAD) **J G FitzGerald [3-26] Michael Ng.*

JAVA RUPIAH (IRE) RR 779[9]

3 b f Hamas (IRE) 8f **(72)** - Java Jive (Hotfoot) 10.5f **(59)**

Form - 0

Record	1998 -	1st:0	2nd:0	3rd:0	Ran:1

1998 Turf 0-1: (7f) (gd)

Workmanlike, currently very poor filly - 9th of 10 getting 5lb from Ei Ei (21 Apr Folkestone 7f gd RF 0779).

**M R Channon [0-1] M Channon.*

JAVA SHRINE (USA) BHB 57f64a RR 66f 64a 4638[3]

7 b g Java Gold (USA) 9.3f **(67)** - Ivory Idol (USA) (Alydar (USA)) 9.1f **(76)**

Form - 0512D03103

Record	1998 -	1st:2	2nd:1	3rd:2	Ran:10
	Pre1998 -	1st:1	2nd:1	3rd:1	Ran:13

Win Prizemoney £8,099 *Total Prizemoney* £11,051

Wins								
	* **1998**	*Spt*	*Lingfi*	*(STA)*	*SH*	*10f*	*60*	*68*
	* **1998**	Jly	Warwic	(G-F)	SH	10.8f	50	56
	1994	Jun	Pontef	(FRM)		10f		69++ <

1998 Turf 1-8: (10f, 11f 1-4, 12f, 13f, 14f) (gd 2, g-f, frm 1-5) 1998 AW 1-2: (10f 1-1, 12f) (Equi 1-1, Fibr)

Average gelding, effective 10 to 13f, acts on frm - acts on AW, has worn blinkers (extremely effectively), prefers left handed tracks, favours tight tracks. Turf high 66 - 2nd of 12 giving 15lb to Ronquista d'Or (18 Jly Warwick 13f frm RF 2944). AW high 68 (1st run) (began Spt) - 1st of 13 from Bapsford (8 Spt Lingfield RF 4143).

**P Eccles [2-10] Plough Twenty (Ashto Keynes) (from A J Chamberlain [0-4] Aug 1997).*

JAWAH (IRE) BHB 71f **RR 76f** 4674[3]

4 br g In The Wings 11.2f **(77)** - Saving Mercy (Lord Gayle (USA)) 8.8f **(62)**

Form - 0000450723

Record	**1998** -	1st:0	2nd:1	3rd:1	Ran:10
	Pre1998 -	1st:3	2nd:1	3rd:0	Ran:11

Win Prizemoney £11,350 *Total Prizemoney* £14,820

Wins								
* 1997	Oct	Nottin	(GD)	H	14.1f	70	81+	<
* 1997	Oct	Doncas	(GD)	H	14.6f	70	75	
1997	Jly	Bellew	(G-S)	H	14f	66	62	

1998 Turf 0-10: (12f 3, 14f 3, 16f 3, 20f) (sft 2, gd 2, g-f 5, frm)

Above-average gelding, effective 14 to 17f, acts on sft to g-f, has worn blinkers, prefers left handed tracks. Turf high 76. He has a turn of foot and is reported by his trainer to need covering up until as late as possible.

**K Mahdi [2-15] Hamad Al-Mutawa (from D K Weld in IRE [1-6] Jly 1997).*

JAWHARI BHB 62f **RR 67f** 4771[25]

4 b c Lahib (USA) 8f **(69)** - Lady of the Land (Wollow) 8.2f **(61)**

Form - 00002600

Record	**1998** -	1st:0	2nd:1	3rd:0	Ran:8
	Pre1998 -	1st:1	2nd:1	3rd:0	Ran:6

Win Prizemoney £4,110 *Total Prizemoney* £6,132

Wins								
1997	Jly	Lingfi	(G-F)		7.6f		80	<

1998 Turf 0-8: (5f, 6f 5, 7f, 8f) (sft, g-s 2, gd 3, g-f, frm)

Scopey, average colt, effective 8f, acts on g-f. Turf high 67. Inconsistent. Took time to show any form for his new yard, but ran well when runner-up at Carlisle in July.

**D Nicholls [0-8] Geoffrey Thompson (from J L Dunlop [1-6] Oct 1997).*

JAY AND-A (IRE) **RR 90f** 4912a[2]

3 br f Elbio 9f **(62)** - Maybird (Royalty) 11.4f **(49)**

Form - 431435832

1998 Turf 1-9: (6f 1-3, 7f 5, 8f) (sft 1-1, g-s 2, gd 5, hrd)

Useful filly, effective 6 to 8f, best at 6f, acts on sft to gd, best on gd, has worn blinkers. Turf high 98 - 1st of 11 getting 5lb from Sarigor (17 Jun Naas RF 2204a).

**M Halford in IRE [1-12] Mrs A Hughes.*

JAYANNPEE BHB 84f **RR 84f** 4508[17]

7 ch g Doulab (USA) 7.4f **(61)** - Amina (Brigadier Gerard) 9.3f **(58)**

Form - 000031003570

Record	**1998** -	1st:1	2nd:0	3rd:2	Ran:12
	Pre1998 -	1st:9	2nd:4	3rd:4	Ran:45

Win Prizemoney £113,054 *Total Prizemoney* £141,518

Wins								
* **1998**	Jun	Bath	(G-S)	H	5.7f	82	84	
* 1996	Spt	Taby	(GD)	L	6f		95	
* 1996	Jly	Newbur	(G-F)	L	6f		107	<
* 1996	May	York	(G-F)	H	6f	96	104	
* 1996	May	Newmar	(G-F)	H	6f	90	95	
* 1994	Aug	Sandow	(GD)	H	5f	88	90	
* 1994	Jly	Goodwo	(FRM)	H	5f	76	83	
* 1994	Jly	Bath	(FRM)	H	5.1f	76	76	
* 1994	May	Bath	(GD)		5.1f		78+	
* 1994	May	Bath	(G-F)	H	5.7f	60	70	

1998 Turf 1-12: (5f 3, 6f 1-9) (sft, gd 1-9, g-f 2)

Decent gelding, effective 6f, acts on gd. Turf high 84. Consistent. He failed to sparkle in '97, putting up his best display on his first outing. He dropped in the handicap as a result and has shown mixed form this year, winning a modest Bath handicap on ground which would not have been ideal. He really needs it fast.

**I A Balding [10-57] I A Balding.*

JAYBEE SILVER BHB 44f **RR 32f** 3682[10]

3 gr f Mystiko (USA) 7.7f **(59)** - Pipistrelle (Shareef Dancer (USA)) 9.9f **(73)**

Form - 0

Record	**1998** -	1st:0	2nd:0	3rd:0	Ran:1
	Pre1998 -	1st:0	2nd:1	3rd:0	Ran:7

Win Prizemoney £0 *Total Prizemoney* £642

1998 Turf 0-1: (10f) (g-f)

Light-framed, very moderate filly, effective 6f, acts on g-f, has worn blinkers.

**H S Howe [0-1] John Bull (from M H Tompkins [0-7] Spt 1997).*

JAYCEE SUPERSTAR BHB 54f **RR 48f** 3747[8]

2 b f Cyrano de Bergerac 7.3f **(58)** - Sunley Stars (Sallust) 8.4f **(63)**

Form - 8648

Record	**1998** -	1st:0	2nd:0	3rd:0	Ran:4

Win Prizemoney £0 *Total Prizemoney* £219

1998 Turf 0-4: (5f 4) (gd 4)

Moderate filly. Turf high 48. **P D Evans [0-4] J W D Campbell.*

JAYESS ELLE BHB 39f **RR 40f** 4920[8]

3 b f Sabrehill (USA) 8.5f **(64)** - Sorayah (Persian Bold) 9.3f **(66)**

Form - 06008

Record	**1998** -	1st:0	2nd:0	3rd:0	Ran:5
	Pre1998 -	1st:0	2nd:0	3rd:0	Ran:2

1998 Turf 0-5: (8f 4, 10f) (g-s 2, gd, g-f 2)

Neat, moderate filly. Turf high 48.

**J G FitzGerald [0-7] John Smith's Ltd.*

JAY GEE (IRE) **RR 90f** 4450[13]

3 b f Second Set (IRE) 9.2f **(67)** - Polynesian Goddess (IRE) (Salmon Leap (USA)) 11f **(61)**

Form - 07320000

Record	**1998** -	1st:0	2nd:1	3rd:1	Ran:8
	Pre1998 -	1st:2	2nd:0	3rd:1	Ran:8

Win Prizemoney £21,599 *Total Prizemoney* £27,495

Wins								
* 1997	Aug	Newmar	(GD)	H	6f	82	92	<
* 1997	Jly	Windso	(G-F)		6f		84	

1998 Turf 0-8: (5f 5, 6f, 7f, 8f) (gd 5, g-f, frm 2)

Unfurnished, useful filly, effective 5 to 6f, best at 6f, acts on gd to frm, has worn blinkers. Turf high 90 - 2nd of 16 getting 5lb from Night Shot (20 Jun Ascot 5f g-f RF 2136). Becoming disappointing. A winner at Windsor and of a valuable Newmarket nursery at two, she was highly tried for most of last season and mostly ran poorly, though she was only just touched off in a valuable handicap at Ascot in June. **G G Margarson [2-16] John Guest.*

JAYIR (IRE) BHB 36f **RR 35f** 4399[12]

3 b g Mujtahid (USA) 7.4f **(69)** - Arylh (USA) (Lyphard (USA)) 9.9f **(72)**

Form - 70600060

Record	**1998** -	1st:0	2nd:0	3rd:0	Ran:8
	Pre1998 -	1st:0	2nd:0	3rd:0	Ran:2

Win Prizemoney £0 *Total Prizemoney* £404

1998 Turf 0-8: (5f, 6f 2, 7f 2, 8f 2, 10f) (gd 4, frm 4)

Well made, very moderate gelding. Turf high 53. Inconsistent.

**D Nicholls [0-8] Coal Trade Partnership (from A C Stewart [0-2] Spt 1997).*

JAY-OWE-TWO (IRE) BHB 76f75a **RR 75f 75a** 4848[14]

4 b g Distinctly North (USA) 7.4f **(63)**-Fiery Song (Ballad Rock) 7.8f **(63)**

Form - 300060765643120

Record	**1998** -	1st:1	2nd:1	3rd:2	Ran:15
	Pre1998 -	1st:4	2nd:2	3rd:0	Ran:16

Win Prizemoney £28,363 *Total Prizemoney* £40,656

Wins								
* **1998**	Spt	Ayr	(G-S)	H	7f	66	70+	
* 1997	Oct	Newmar	(G-S)	H	8f	71	81	<
* 1997	Oct	Pontef	(G-F)	H	8f	71	77	
* 1997	Apr	Beverl	(G-F)	H	7.5f	75	81	<
* 1996	*Dec*	*Southw*	*(SLW)*		*6f*		*79+*	

1998 Turf 1-15: (7f 1-5, 8f 10) (sft 1-4, gd 4, g-f 3, frm 4)

Rangy, above-average gelding, effective 7 to 8f, best at 8f, acts on sft to frm, often wears blinkers, excels at Ayr. Turf high 79. Consistent. He seems something of an autumn horse. After some modest efforts, he showed better form later in the season, eventually winning at the Ayr Great Western meeting and running another blinder just twenty-four hours later.

**R M Whitaker [5-31] Country Lane Partnership.*

JAZA BHB 32f **RR 33f** 4931[10]

4 b g Pursuit of Love 9.5f **(69)** - Nordica (Northfields (USA)) 9f **(72)**

Form - 0030

Record	**1998** -	1st:0	2nd:0	3rd:1	Ran:4
	Pre1998 -	1st:0	2nd:0	3rd:0	Ran:3

Win Prizemoney £0 *Total Prizemoney* £298

1998 Turf 0-4: (9f, 10f 2, 12f) (g-s, gd, frm 2)

Scopey, very moderate gelding, has worn blinkers. Turf high 33.

**M C Pipe [0-3] Paul Jacobs (from N A Graham [0-6] Jun 1998).*

JAZIL BHB 104f **RR 103f** 4616[3]
3 b c Nashwan (USA) 10.3f **(79)** - Gracious Beauty (USA) (Nijinsky (CAN)) 10.3f **(77)**
Form - 621313
Record 1998 - 1st:2 2nd:1 3rd:2 Ran:6
Win Prizemoney £11,927 *Total Prizemoney* £16,347
Wins * **1998** Spt Doncas (GD) H 12f 95 98 <
* **1998** Jly Ascot (G-F) 10f 95+
1998 Turf 2-6: (10f 1-2, 11f 2, 12f 1-2) (gd 1-3, g-f 1-3)
Very useful colt, effective 10 to 12f, best at 12f, acts on gd to g-f, best on g-f, has worn blinkers. Turf high 103 - 3rd of 8 giving 5lb to Innuendo (2 Oct Newmarket 12f gd RF 4616) - also 1st of 17 getting 6lb from Dantesque (11 Spt Doncaster RF 4226). Big and imposing, he took a while to find his feet and appeared to be keeping something to himself when third at Newbury in August. A visor was introduced at Doncaster the following month and, ridden up with the pace, he kept on strongly to beat a decent field. Third in a Listed event at Newmarket in October, he is going the right way physically and mentally and is the type to do well next term.
**J H M Gosden [2-6] Hamdan Al Maktoum.*

JAZZ CLUB (USA) BHB 85f **RR 85f** 1746[12]
3 b c Dixieland Band (USA) 10.1f **(80)** - Hidden Garden (USA) (Mr Prospector (USA)) 8.8f **(78)**
Form - 000
Record 1998 - 1st:0 2nd:0 3rd:0 Ran:3
Pre1998 - 1st:1 2nd:0 3rd:0 Ran:3
Win Prizemoney £4,648 *Total Prizemoney* £5,070
Wins * 1997 Aug Haydoc (G-F) 6f 90+ <
1998 Turf 0-3: (7f, 8f 2) (gd 2, g-f)
Small, useful colt, effective 6f, acts on g-f, has worn blinkers. Turf high 85.
**P F I Cole [1-6] W S Farish III.*

JAZZNIC BHB 65f65a **RR 72f 65a** 4612[4]
2 b f Alhijaz 7.7f **(57)** - Irenic (Mummy's Pet) 7.7f **(60)**
Form - 7004
Record 1998 - 1st:0 2nd:0 3rd:0 Ran:4
1998 Turf 0-4: (5f, 6f 2, 7f) (g-s, gd, frm 2)
Above-average filly. Turf high 72 - 4th of 20 giving 10lb to Enthaisingh (2 Oct Lingfield 6f g-s RF 4612).
**P J Makin [0-4] Ten of Hearts.*

JAZZ TRACK (IRE) BHB 80f **RR 80f** 2015[15]
4 b g Sadler's Wells (USA) 11.3f **(87)** - Minnie Hauk (USA) (Sir Ivor) 10.2f **(70)**
Form - 0
Record 1998 - 1st:0 2nd:0 3rd:0 Ran:1
Pre1998 - 1st:1 2nd:1 3rd:2 Ran:6
Win Prizemoney £3,717 *Total Prizemoney* £5,883
Wins 1997 Oct Catter (SFT) H 15.8f 78 80 <
1998 Turf 0-1: (20f) (gd)
Workmanlike, decent gelding, effective 12 to 16f, best at 12f, acts on g-s to frm, has worn blinkers.
**M C Pipe [0-6] Malcolm Jones (from P W Chapple-Hyam [1-6] Oct 1997).*

JAZZY **RR 21f** 4478[7]
3 b f Alhijaz 7.7f **(57)** - Irenic (Mummy's Pet) 7.7f **(60)**
Form - 87
Record 1998 - 1st:0 2nd:0 3rd:0 Ran:2
1998 Turf 0-2: (8f, 11f) (g-s, frm)
Lengthy, currently little account filly. Turf high 21 (began Spt).
**J Norton [0-2] T Hurst.*

JEAN PIERRE BHB 40f **RR 45f** 4141[6]
5 b g Anshan 8.2f **(63)** - Astolat (Rusticaro (FR)) 8.2f **(65)**
Form - 86
Record 1998 - 1st:0 2nd:0 3rd:0 Ran:2
Pre1998 - 1st:0 2nd:4 3rd:2 Ran:16
Win Prizemoney £0 *Total Prizemoney* £4,115
1998 Turf 0-2: (10f 2) (g-f, frm)
Moderate gelding, effective 10 to 12f, best at 10f, acts on g-s to frm, favours tight tracks. Turf high 37 (began Aug).
**J Pearce [0-18] P D Burnett.*

JEANZI (FR) **RR 95f** 137a[3]
4 b c Fabulous Dancer (USA) 10.6f **(81)**-Tinderella (Hot Spark) 7.6f **(62)**
Form - 3
1998 Turf 0-1: (8f) (sft)
Currently very useful colt. (1st run) - 3rd of 19 getting 3lb from Joumart (14 Jan Cagnes-sur-mer 8f sft RF 0137a). **in FR [0-1].*

JEDI KNIGHT BHB 72f **RR 73f** 5061[6]
4 b g Emarati (USA) 6.6f **(63)** - Hannie Caulder (Workboy) 7.3f **(46)**
Form - 0063042424056
Record 1998 - 1st:0 2nd:2 3rd:1 Ran:13
Pre1998 - 1st:4 2nd:4 3rd:1 Ran:23
Win Prizemoney £15,246 *Total Prizemoney* £28,352
Wins * 1997 Nov Redcar (GD) H 10f 69 74 <
* 1997 Aug Thirsk (G-F) H 8f 67 70
* 1997 Jun Carlis (FRM) H 8f 55 62++
* 1997 Jun Doncas (GD) H 7f 55 62
1998 Turf 0-13: (8f 8, 9f, 10f 2, 11f, 12f) (sft 2, g-s 2, gd 3, g-f 3, frm 3)
Workmanlike, above-average gelding, effective 8 to 12f, best at 8f, acts on gd to frm, best on frm, has worn blinkers, likes right handed tracks, likes tight tracks, excels at Haydock and Redcar, does well at Beverley and Doncaster. Turf high 73 - 5th of 30 getting 5lb from Silken Dalliance (17 Oct Newmarket 8f gd RF 4848). Consistent. Able, but not easy to catch right, a fast-run ten furlongs could be his trip.
**M W Easterby [4-36] K Hodgson & Mrs J Hodgson.*

JEFFREY ANOTHERRED BHB 77f **RR 78f** 5096[7]
4 b g Emarati (USA) 6.6f **(63)** - First Pleasure (Dominion) 8.5f **(63)**
Form - 00002351014260047
Record 1998 - 1st:2 2nd:2 3rd:1 Ran:17
Pre1998 - 1st:3 2nd:2 3rd:3 Ran:19
Win Prizemoney £20,103 *Total Prizemoney* £34,791
Wins * **1998** Jly Ayr (SFT) H 6f 70 84
* **1998** Jly Carlis (G-F) 5.9f 70
1996 Nov Doncas (SFT) H 7f 86 96 <
1996 Spt Kempto (GD) H 6f 78 74
1996 Aug Hamilt (G-F) 5f 69
1998 Turf 2-17: (5f, 6f 2-12, 7f 3, 8f) (sft 2, g-s 2, gd 1-9, frm 1-3, hrd)
Above-average gelding, effective 6 to 8f, best at 6f, acts on gd to g-f, best on gd, has worn blinkers, likes left handed tracks, likes tight tracks. Turf high 84 - 1st of 10 getting 6lb from Indian Spark (20 Jly Ayr RF 2950). Consistent. Broke a long losing run on fast ground at Carlisle in July, and scored again under very different conditions at Ayr.
**M Dods [2-18] A G Watson (from K McAuliffe [3-18] Oct 1997).*

JELLYBEEN (IRE) BHB 62f **RR 65f** 4930[7]
2 ch f Petardia 8.2f **(58)** - Lux Aeterna (Sandhurst Prince) 7.9f **(63)**
Form - 007
Record 1998 - 1st:0 2nd:0 3rd:0 Ran:3
1998 Turf 0-3: (7f, 8f 2) (g-s, frm 2)
Currently average filly. Turf high 65 (began Spt).
**Miss Gay Kelleway [0-3] N Parker.*

JENNELLE BHB 91f **RR 91f** 4184[12]
4 b f Nomination 7.3f **(57)** - Its A Romp (Hotfoot) 10.5f **(59)**
Form - 42154030
Record 1998 - 1st:1 2nd:1 3rd:1 Ran:8
Pre1998 - 1st:4 2nd:2 3rd:1 Ran:17
Win Prizemoney £18,369 *Total Prizemoney* £35,383
Wins * **1998** Apr Redcar (SFT) H 5f 78 83
* 1996 Oct Lingfi (G-S) 5f 89 <
* 1996 Jly Folkes (GD) H 5f 89 <
* 1996 Apr Thirsk (G-F) 5f 73
* 1996 Mar Folkes (G-S) 5f 72
1998 Turf 1-8: (5f 1-5, 6f 3) (sft 1-1, g-s, gd 4, g-f, frm)
Neat, useful filly, effective 5 to 6f, acts on sft to frm. Turf high 91 - 3rd of 18 getting 4lb from Lone Piper (2 Spt York 6f frm RF 4055) - also 1st of 6 giving 23lb to Gold Edge (30 Apr Redcar RF 0935). Showed patchy form last season, and as in the past faced some very stiff tasks in decent company. Her only victory came in a soft-ground Redcar handicap in April.
**C A Dwyer [5-25] Mrs J A Cornwell.*

JEOPARDY (FR) **RR 104f** 1091a[6]
3 ch c Funambule (USA) - Tent Pole (High Top) 10.2f **(67)**
Form - 36
1998 Turf 0-2: (11f 2) (hvy, sft)
Currently very useful colt. Turf high 104 (1st run) - 3rd of 6 to

Special Quest (13 Apr Longchamp 11f hvy RF 0830a). He was done no favours when third at Longchamp in April, but disappointed at Chantilly the following month. **Mme P Barbe in FR [0-2].*

JESSIES JAMES BHB 36f **RR 60f** 4486[14]

3 ch g Past Glories - Princess Jestina (IRE) (Jester)
Form - 080850
Record 1998 - 1st:0 2nd:0 3rd:0 Ran:6
1998 Turf 0-6: (9f, 10f 5) (g-f 4, frm 2)
Light-framed, average gelding. Turf high 60.
**W S Cunningham [0-1] Invicta Bloodstock (from W R Muir [0-5] Aug 1998).*

JESSINCA BHB 47f **RR 48f** 5073[6]

2 b f Minshaanshu Amad (USA) 11.3f **(53)** - Noble Soul (Sayf El Arab (USA)) 7.1f **(54)**
Form - U05064706
Record 1998 - 1st:0 2nd:0 3rd:0 Ran:9
1998 Turf 0-9: (5f 4, 6f 2, 7f, 8f 2) (gd 2, g-f 5, frm 2)
Fair filly. Turf high 47. Inconsistent.
**A P Jones [0-9] The Lambourn Racing Club.*

JESTER MINUTE BHB 25f25a **RR 25a** 1035[15]

4 gr g Jester 8.5f **(43)** - Jealous Lover (Alias Smith (USA)) 9.8f **(58)**
Form - 070
Record 1998 - 1st:0 2nd:0 3rd:0 Ran:3
Pre1998 - 1st:0 2nd:0 3rd:0 Ran:1
1998 Turf 0-1: (10f) (gd) 1998 AW 0-2: (10f, 13f) (Equi 2)
Light-framed, poor gelding, often wears blinkers. AW high 12.
**B A Pearce [0-7] S B Components.*

JEWEL (IRE) BHB 57f **RR 49f** 518[5]

3 b f Cyrano de Bergerac 7.3f **(58)** - Renzola (Dragonara Palace (USA)) 6.1f **(55)**
Form - 5
Record 1998 - 1st:0 2nd:0 3rd:0 Ran:1
Pre1998 - 1st:0 2nd:0 3rd:0 Ran:4
1998 Turf 0-1: (6f) (g-s)
Unfurnished, moderate filly. **R Hannon [0-5] Lady Tennant.*

JEWEL FIGHTER BHB 40f **RR 47f** 4919[15]

4 br f Good Times (ITY) 8.7f **(53)** - Duellist (Town Crier) 10.2f **(55)**
Form - 70
Record 1998 - 1st:0 2nd:0 3rd:0 Ran:2
Pre1998 - 1st:0 2nd:0 3rd:0 Ran:2
1998 Turf 0-2: (8f 2) (g-s 2)
Workmanlike, moderate filly. Turf high 47 (began Oct).
**C A Smith [0-4] Weir Investments.*

JEZABEEL (NZ) RR 110f 5153a[1]

5 br m Zabeel (AUS) - Passefleur (NZ) (Vice Regal (NZ))
Form - 1
1998 Turf 1-1: (16f 1-1) (gd 1-1)
Currently Group-class mare. (1st run) - 1st of 24 from Champagne (3 Nov Flemington RF 5153a). Landed a gamble in the Melbourne Cup, having been badly hampered by the winner Taufan's Melody in the Caulfield Cup.
**B Jenkins in NZ [1-1] A Burr & B Jenkins & P Tatham.*

JIBE (USA) BHB 103f **RR 106f** 2083[4]

3 b f Danzig (USA) 8.1f **(88)** - Slightly Dangerous (USA) (Roberto (USA)) 10f **(76)**
Form - 3814
Record 1998 - 1st:1 2nd:0 3rd:1 Ran:4
Pre1998 - 1st:1 2nd:1 3rd:0 Ran:3
Win Prizemoney £14,658 *Total Prizemoney* £59,078
Wins * **1998** May Newbur (GD) L 10f 94 <
* 1997 Spt Lingfi (GD) 7f 92++
1998 Turf 1-4: (7f, 8f, 10f 1-1, 12f) (g-s, gd 2, g-f 1-1)
Pattern-class filly, effective 7 to 12f, acts on g-s to g-f. Turf high 106 - 4th of 9 to Bahr (18 Jun Ascot 12f g-s RF 2083). She looked a genuine Classic contender as a juvenile, but only won a weak Listed race at Newbury. Seemed not to stay twelve furlongs at Ascot. **H R A Cecil [2-7] K Abdulla.*

JIBEREEN BHB 48f73a **RR 55f 73a** 5079[4]

6 b g Lugana Beach 7f **(63)** - Fashion Lover (Shiny Tenth) 9.2f **(56)**
Form - 813666580004
Record 1998 - 1st:1 2nd:0 3rd:1 Ran:11
Pre1998 - 1st:9 2nd:2 3rd:0 Ran:34
Win Prizemoney £29,936 *Total Prizemoney* £34,389

Wins * **1998**	*Jan*	*Southw*	*(STD)*	*H*	*8f*	*72*	*78*	
* 1997	Jly	Newmar	(GD)	H	8f	56	62	
* 1997	Jun	Newmar	(SFT)	H	7f	53	56	
* 1997	*Apr*	*Southw*	*(STD)*	*H*	*8f*	*70*	*75*	
* 1997	*Jan*	*Wolver*	*(STD)*	*C*	*7f*		*73*	
* 1997	*Jan*	*Southw*	*(STD)*	*C*	*7f*		*73*	
* 1996	*Dec*	*Southw*	*(SLW)*	*H*	*6f*	*67*	*67*	
1995	Oct	Chepst	(G-S)	H	7.1f	69	77	
1994	Spt	Bright	(GD)		6f		85	
1994	Aug	Salisb	(G-S)		6f		75+	

1998 Turf 0-8: (7f 2, 8f 5, 9f) (sft, gd 3, g-f, frm 3) 1998 AW 1-3: (8f 1-3) (Fibr 1-3)
Above-average gelding, effective 7 to 8f, best at 8f - acts on Fibr, likes left handed tracks, likes tight tracks, excels at Wolverhampton and likes Southwell. Turf high 57. AW high 78 (1st run) - 1st of 10 giving 25lb to Time of Night (2 Jan Southwell RF 0007). Won twice at Newmarket in the middle of '97.
**P Howling [7-32] Liam Sheridan (from G Lewis [3-13] Apr 1996).*

JIG (IRE) RR 87df 3045[7]

2 b f Catrail (USA) - River Jig (USA) (Irish River (FR)) 8.6f **(78)**
Form - 17
Record 1998 - 1st:1 2nd:0 3rd:0 Ran:2
Win Prizemoney £4,230 *Total Prizemoney* £4,230
Wins * **1998** Apr Newmar (SFT) 5f 87 <
1998 Turf 1-2: (5f 1-1, 7f) (sft 1-1, frm)
Currently useful filly. Turf high 87 (1st run) - 1st of 7 from Damalis (15 Apr Newmarket RF 0700). She won a soft-ground Newmarket maiden over the minimum on her debut in April, and choked badly on her belated return. **P F I Cole [1-2] H R H Prince Fahd Salman.*

JILA (IRE) BHB 101f **RR 101f** 1267[3]

3 ch c Kris 10f **(75)** - Enaya (Caerleon (USA)) 8.6f **(71)**
Form - 113
Record 1998 - 1st:2 2nd:0 3rd:1 Ran:3
Pre1998 - 1st:1 2nd:1 3rd:1 Ran:3
Win Prizemoney £17,656 *Total Prizemoney* £21,535
Wins * **1998** May Newmar (G-S) H 7f 95 101 <
* **1998** Apr Newmar (G-S) H 7f 87 95+
* 1997 Oct Yarmou (GD) 7f 84
1998 Turf 2-3: (7f 2-3) (gd 2-2, frm)
Scopey, very useful colt, effective 7f, acts on gd. Turf high 101 - 1st of 14 giving 16lb to Adjutant (1 May Newmarket RF 0959) - also 1st of 21 giving 2lb to Lido (14 Apr Newmarket RF 0682). A progressive juvenile, he kept up the good work in three starts at Newmarket during the spring, winning two valuable handicaps before finishing third in a Listed contest. He moved poorly on the last of those outings and promptly went on the missing list. He may need easy ground. **R W Armstrong [3-6] Hamdan Al Maktoum.*

JILLY BEVELED BHB 38f31a **RR 49f 31a** 627[1]

6 b m Beveled (USA) 6.9f **(64)** - Karens Valentine (Daring March) 7.1f **(61)**
Form - 31
Record 1998 - 1st:1 2nd:0 3rd:1 Ran:2
Pre1998 - 1st:1 2nd:1 3rd:1 Ran:24
Win Prizemoney £4,231 *Total Prizemoney* £5,681
Wins * **1998** Apr Mussel (G-S) SH 8f 31 37 <
1997 Feb Wolver (STD) H 8.5f 35 31
1998 Turf 1-2: (7f, 8f 1-1) (gd 1-2)
Moderate mare, effective 7f, acts on gd, favours tight tracks. Turf high 49 (1st run) - 3rd of 19 getting 9lb from Scathebury (1 Apr Catterick 7f gd RF 0531). Inconsistent.
**B Ellison [1-7] C E Sherry (from Ronald Thompson [1-16] Aug 1997).*

JILLY WOO BHB 34f48a **RR 32f 48a** 4927[13]

4 gr f Environment Friend 7.5f **(67)** - William's Bird (USA) (Master Willie) 7f **(70)**
Form - 0457086770
Record 1998 - 1st:0 2nd:0 3rd:0 Ran:10
Pre1998 - 1st:0 2nd:0 3rd:2 Ran:15
Win Prizemoney £0 *Total Prizemoney* £1,833
1998 Turf 0-10: (7f, 10f 7, 11f, 12f) (sft, g-s 2, gd 2, g-f 4, frm)
Unfurnished, very moderate filly, has worn blinkers. Turf high 48.

Consistent.
**P Hayward [0-11] Mrs J Wotherspoon (from B A Pearce [0-1] Aug 1997).*

JIM AND TONIC (FR) RR 124f 3614a[2]

4 g c Double Bed (FR) 13.9f **(54)** - Jimka (FR) (Jim French (USA)) 10.3f **(71)**
Form - 22122
1998 Turf 1-5: (7f, 8f 1-3, 10f) (sft 1-2, g-s, gd, g-f)
Very high-class colt, effective 7 to 10f, best at 8f, acts on sft to g-f, best on sft. Turf high 124 - 2nd of 9 giving 4lb to Fly To The Stars (12 Jly Deauville 8f g-f RF 2862a) - also 1st of 6 giving 3lb to Kaldou Star (6 Jun Maisons-laffitte RF 1915a). He was in particularly good form in 1998, winning once and being placed in Group company from six and a half to ten furlongs in Europe. He subsequently finished placed in Grade One company in the United States. He is a credit to his trainer. **F Doumen in FR [2-6] J D Martin.*

JIM DORE (IRE) BHB 46f42a RR 46f 42a 4865[9]

3 b br g Mac's Imp (USA) 5.6f **(54)** - Secret Assignment (Vitiges (FR)) 8.2f **(59)**
Form - 008000
Record 1998 - 1st:0 2nd:0 3rd:0 Ran:6
Pre1998 - 1st:0 2nd:0 3rd:0 Ran:1
Win Prizemoney £0 *Total Prizemoney* £228
1998 Turf 0-5: (5f, 6f 2, 7f 2) (gd, g-f 3, frm) 1998 AW 0-1: (7f) (Fibr)
Workmanlike, moderate gelding. Turf high 49.
**A P Jarvis [0-7] Mrs Ann Jarvis.*

JIMJAREER (IRE) BHB 27f28a RR 29f 28a 117[4]

5 br g Jareer (USA) 10.2f **(54)** - Onthecomet (Chief Singer) 8.9f **(66)**
Form - 564
Record 1998 - 1st:0 2nd:0 3rd:0 Ran:2
Pre1998 - 1st:1 2nd:1 3rd:1 Ran:22
Win Prizemoney £2,519 *Total Prizemoney* £5,081
Wins * 1995 *Jun Southw (STD) 5f 50+* <
1998 AW 0-2: (11f, 12f) (Fibr 2)
Very moderate gelding, effective 11f, acts on g-f, likes left handed tracks. AW high 14. **Capt J Wilson [1-24] Mrs G S Rees.*

JIMMY-S (IRE) BHB 20a RR 20a 343[8]

5 b g Marju (IRE) 9.2f **(76)** - Amber Fizz (USA) (Effervescing (USA)) 8.1f **(79)**
Form - 8
Record 1998 - 1st:0 2nd:0 3rd:0 Ran:1
Pre1998 - 1st:0 2nd:0 3rd:0 Ran:2
1998 AW 0-1: (12f) (Fibr)
Formerly very poor gelding - 8th of 8 getting 2lb from Private Despatch (23 Feb Southwell 12f Fibr RF 0343).
**Martyn Wane [0-1] J P Slattery (from R M McKellar [0-2] Aug 1996).*

JIMMY THE GREEK (IRE) RR 95f 5169a[2]

3 b g Tenby 10.4f **(76)** - Some Fun (Wolverlife) 9.3f **(54)**
Form - 81U072
1998 Turf 1-6: (6f 1-3, 7f, 8f 2) (hvy, sft 1-2, gd 3)
Very useful gelding, effective 6 to 7f, best at 6f, acts on sft to gd, best on sft, has worn blinkers. Turf high 95 - 1st of 12 getting 10lb from One Won One (28 Jun Curragh RF 2430a). Useful Irish sprint handicapper, winner of a valuable race on Irish Derby day at the Curragh. **Patrick Prendergast in IRE [2-12] Ms Maura Horan.*

JIMMY TOO BHB 95f RR 96f 5152[5]

3 b br c Nomination 7.3f **(57)** - Cutlass Princess (USA) (Cutlass (USA)) 8.5f **(76)**
Form - 042034045025
Record 1998 - 1st:0 2nd:2 3rd:1 Ran:12
Pre1998 - 1st:2 2nd:1 3rd:2 Ran:5
Win Prizemoney £8,218 *Total Prizemoney* £33,152
Wins * 1997 Aug Cheste (SFT) 6.1f 93 <
* 1997 Jun Cheste (SFT) 5.1f 66
1998 Turf 0-12: (5f 2, 6f 9, 8f) (sft 2, g-s, gd 3, g-f 5, frm)
Scopey, very useful colt, effective 6f, acts on sft to frm, has worn blinkers. Turf high 99 - 4th of 18 giving 2lb to Lone Piper (2 Spt York 6f frm RF 4055). Consistent. A useful juvenile, beaten only a neck in the Mill Reef Stakes on his last start of the season, he found it hard to get his head in front in 1998 but ran consistently well. Loves cut in the ground. **B A McMahon [2-17] J D Graham.*

JINGLE (GER) RR 24f 3675[10]

4 ch f Suave Dancer (USA) 10.7f **(68)** - Jacqueline d'Or (Kris) 9.5f **(73)**
Form - 0
Record 1998 - 1st:0 2nd:0 3rd:0 Ran:1
1998 Turf 0-1: (8f) (frm)
Lengthy, currently little account filly.
**K A Ryan [0-1] Basheer Kielany.*

JINGOIST (IRE) BHB 40f40a RR 41f 40a 1788[F]

4 b f Polish Patriot (USA) 7.8f **(70)** - Hot Curry (USA) (Sharpen Up) 8.3f **(67)**
Form - 604F
Record 1998 - 1st:0 2nd:0 3rd:0 Ran:4
Pre1998 - 1st:1 2nd:4 3rd:0 Ran:15
Win Prizemoney £2,490 *Total Prizemoney* £5,265
Wins 1996 Aug Leices (GD) SH 6f 53 47 <
1998 Turf 0-2: (10f, 12f) (frm, hrd) 1998 AW 0-2: (7f, 8f) (Fibr 2)
Leggy, moderate filly, often wore blinkers. Turf high 41. AW high 38. Inconsistent. (DEAD)
**John Harris [0-4] David Pettifor (from J L Harris [1-12] Jly 1997).*

JINSIYAH (USA) BHB 98f RR 97f 2135[9]

3 b br f Housebuster (USA) 7f **(81)** - Minifah (USA) (Nureyev (USA)) 8.7f **(78)**
Form - 31320
Record 1998 - 1st:1 2nd:1 3rd:2 Ran:5
Win Prizemoney £4,980 *Total Prizemoney* £15,148
Wins * **1998** May Newmar (G-S) 7f 87 <
1998 Turf 1-5: (7f 1-2, 8f 2, 9f) (sft, gd 1-3, g-f)
Very useful filly. Turf high 97 - 2nd of 8 getting 12lb from Lilli Claire (5 Jun Epsom 9f gd RF 1749). Took a Newmarket maiden on her second start in the manner of a progressive filly, and has run creditably in Listed company since then.
**B Hanbury [1-5] Hamdan Al Maktoum.*

JIVING RR 66f 4641[3]

2 ch f Generous (IRE) 11.5f **(82)** - Kerali (High Line) 10.3f **(70)**
Form - 3
Record 1998 - 1st:0 2nd:0 3rd:1 Ran:1
Win Prizemoney £0 *Total Prizemoney* £447
1998 Turf 0-1: (6f) (g-f)
Currently average filly. **R Charlton [0-1] K Abdulla.*

J J'S DREAM (USA) RR 5164a[11]

5 gr m Glitterman (USA)
Form - 0
1998 AW 0-1: (6f) (Dirt)
Currently Pattern-class filly. **B Barnett in USA [0-1] J Franks.*

JOB RAGE (IRE) BHB 37f RR 51f 52[8]

4 b br g Yashgan 8f **(51)** - Snatchingly (Thatch (USA)) 9.8f **(62)**
Form - 8
Record 1998 - 1st:0 2nd:0 3rd:0 Ran:1
Pre1998 - 1st:0 2nd:0 3rd:0 Ran:3
1998 AW 0-1: (11f) (Fibr)
Leggy, fair gelding. **A Bailey [0-4] Sandybrow Stables Ltd.*

JOCASTA BHB 81f RR 82f 4854[24]

3 b f Warning 8.1f **(77)** - Breed Reference (Reference Point) 6.8f **(70)**
Form - 8212100
Record 1998 - 1st:2 2nd:2 3rd:0 Ran:7
Pre1998 - 1st:0 2nd:0 3rd:0 Ran:1
Win Prizemoney £8,207 *Total Prizemoney* £10,992
Wins * **1998** Aug Nottin (G-F) H 6.1f 78 82 <
* **1998** Jly Newmar (G-F) H 6f 70 75
1998 Turf 2-7: (6f 2-3, 7f 4) (gd 4, g-f 2-3)
Neat, decent filly, effective 6 to 7f, best at 6f, acts on g-f. Turf high 82 - 1st of 12 getting 8lb from Lamarita (29 Aug Nottingham RF 3960) - also 1st of 8 getting 3lb from Majalis (17 Jly Newmarket RF 2883). **C F Wall [2-8] C J A Hughes.*

JOCK'S DREAM RR 17[6]

3 b f Noble Patriarch 12.2f **(43)** - Bold Sophie (Bold Owl) 8.5f **(45)**
Form - 06
Record 1998 - 1st:0 2nd:0 3rd:0 Ran:1
Pre1998 - 1st:0 2nd:0 3rd:0 Ran:1
1998 AW 0-1: (10f) (Equi)

Currently poor filly.
**B J McMath [0-2] The Happy Go Lucky Partnership.*

JOCKWEILER (IRE) BHB 28f31a **RR 33f 31a** 3196[9]

3 b g Night Shift (USA) 8.1f **(73)** - Johara (USA) (Exclusive Native (USA)) 9.1f **(81)**
Form - 050308700080

Record	1998 -	1st:0	2nd:0	3rd:1	Ran:9
	Pre1998 -	1st:0	2nd:0	3rd:0	Ran:7

Win Prizemoney £0 *Total Prizemoney* £465
1998 Turf 0-5: (5f 2, 6f, 8f 2) (gd, g-f 2, frm 2) 1998 AW 0-4: (6f, 8f 3) (Fibr 4)
Neat, very moderate gelding, has worn blinkers. Turf high 33. AW high 32.
**D W Chapman [0-14] David Chapman (from Mrs J R Ramsden [0-2] Jly 1997).*

JOEL ASH RR 24f 3376[16]

3 b g Crofthall 8.6f **(54)** - Lady Carol (Lord Gayle (USA)) 8.8f **(62)**
Form - 00

Record	1998 -	1st:0	2nd:0	3rd:0	Ran:2

1998 Turf 0-2: (5f, 8f) (g-f, frm)
Leggy, currently little account gelding. Turf high 24 (began Jly).
**S R Bowring [0-2] Miss Julie Tomkins.*

JOHAN CRUYFF RR 108f 839a[3]

4 b c Danehill (USA) 9.1f **(79)** - Teslemi (USA) (Ogygian (USA))
Form - 3
1998 Turf 0-1: (10f) (g-f)
Pattern-class colt. (1st run) - 3rd of 11 giving 2lb to Oriental Express (19 Apr Sha Tin 10f g-f RF 0839a). A smart performer in Ireland, he looked to have retained all his ability when finishing third in the prestigious Queen Elizabeth II Cup at Sha-Tin.
**P L Biancone in HK [0-1] (from A P O'Brien in IRE [3-5] Jun 1997).*

JOHAYRO BHB 58f60a **RR 46f 60a** 5142[22]

5 ch g Clantime 6.6f **(57)** - Arroganza (Crofthall) 6.3f **(59)**
Form - 003542214400040000

Record	1998 -	1st:1	2nd:2	3rd:1	Ran:18
	Pre1998 -	1st:5	2nd:7	3rd:1	Ran:41

Win Prizemoney £21,787 *Total Prizemoney* £35,554

Wins									
	* **1998**	Jly	Ayr	(GD)	H	5f	60	65	
	* 1997	Spt	Redcar	(FRM)	H	6f	60	63	
	* 1997	Apr	Catter	(GD)		6f		54	
	* 1997	Apr	Ripon	(G-F)	H	5f	51	61	
	* 1997	Apr	Mussel	(G-F)		5f		59	
	1995	Oct	Catter	(G-F)		5f		73+	<

1998 Turf 1-18: (5f 1-9, 6f 8, 7f) (sft, g-s, gd 1-7, g-f 6, frm 3)
Average gelding, effective 5 to 7f, best at 5f, acts on gd to frm, has worn blinkers, excels at Redcar and likes Musselburgh. Turf high 69 - 4th of 6 giving 15lb to Swynford Dream (22 Jly Catterick 5f g-f RF 3021) - also 1st of 8 getting 17lb from Storyteller (13 Jly Ayr RF 2756).
**J S Goldie [5-45] Frank Brady (from W G M Turner [1-14] Jly 1996).*

JOHN BOWDLER MUSIC BHB 63f **RR 57f** 5121[6]

3 b g Soviet Star (USA) 8.6f **(74)** - Arianna Aldini (Habitat) 9.4f **(70)**
Form - 24706

Record	1998 -	1st:0	2nd:1	3rd:0	Ran:5
	Pre1998 -	1st:0	2nd:0	3rd:0	Ran:1

Win Prizemoney £0 *Total Prizemoney* £1,273
1998 Turf 0-5: (6f 2, 7f, 8f, 9f) (g-s 2, gd 2, frm)
Workmanlike, fair gelding, effective 9f, acts on gd, has worn blinkers. Turf high 69 (1st run) (began Spt) - 2nd of 6 to Silverado (4 Spt Epsom 9f gd RF 4086). **M Johnston [0-6] Paul Dean.*

JOHN FERNELEY BHB 84f **RR 84f** 3229[6]

3 b g Polar Falcon (USA) 9f **(74)** - I'll Try (Try My Best (USA)) 7.6f **(67)**
Form - 1116

Record	1998 -	1st:3	2nd:0	3rd:0	Ran:4
	Pre1998 -	1st:0	2nd:0	3rd:0	Ran:1

Win Prizemoney £10,374 *Total Prizemoney* £10,374

Wins									
	* **1998**	Jly	Sandow	(G-F)	H	7.1f	78	81+	<
	* **1998**	Jun	Thirsk	(GD)		7f		81	
	* **1998**	Apr	Folkes	(SFT)		7f		75	

1998 Turf 3-4: (7f 3-4) (gd 1-2, g-f 1-1, frm 1-1)
Scopey, decent gelding, has worn blinkers. Turf high 84 - 6th of 18 getting 5lb from Ascot Cyclone (31 Jly Goodwood 7f gd RF 3229) - also 1st of 12 getting 7lb from Fredora (22 Jly Sandown RF 3033). Not a straightforward ride, his run came to an end when he met trouble in running at Goodwood.
**P F I Cole [3-5] Richard Green (Fine Paintings).*

JOHNNIE THE JOKER BHB 45f58a **RR 50f 58a** 4875[4]

7 gr g Absalom 7.1f **(56)** - Magic Tower (Tower Walk) 10f **(62)**
Form - 76563044

Record	1998 -	1st:0	2nd:0	3rd:1	Ran:8
	Pre1998 -	1st:9	2nd:8	3rd:4	Ran:62

Win Prizemoney £28,174 *Total Prizemoney* £38,488

Wins									
	* 1997	*Jun*	*Wolver*	*(STD)*	*H*	*8.5f*	*61*	*71*	
	* 1997	*Jun*	*Southw*	*(STD)*	*H*	*8f*	*61*	*68*	
	* 1997	*May*	*Southw*	*(STD)*	*H*	*8f*	*57*	*61*	
	* 1996	*Jun*	*Wolver*	*(STD)*	*H*	*7f*	*70*	*73*	<
	* 1996	May	Doncas	(GD)	H	7f	46	48	
	* 1994	*Aug*	*Southw*	*(STD)*	*H*	*6f*	*69*	*73*	<
	* 1994	*Jly*	*Southw*	*(STD)*	*H*	*7f*	*62*	*63*	
	* 1994	*Jun*	*Southw*	*(STD)*	*H*	*7f*	*56*	*54*	

1998 Turf 0-1: (10f) (g-f) 1998 AW 0-7: (7f 2, 8f 2, 9f, 11f, 12f) (Fibr 7)
Fair gelding, effective 8f - acts on Fibr, mostly wears blinkers, favours left handed tracks. AW high 58.
**J P Leigh [9-70] Miss Carrington Smith.*

JOHNNY STACCATO BHB 62f51a **RR 51f 51a** 5127[5]

4 b g Statoblest 6.4f **(63)** - Frasquita (Song) 7.2f **(61)**
Form - 0000280057005

Record	1998 -	1st:0	2nd:1	3rd:0	Ran:10
	Pre1998 -	1st:2	2nd:0	3rd:2	Ran:16

Win Prizemoney £7,734 *Total Prizemoney* £11,517

Wins								
	1997	Jun	Sandow	(G-F)	5f		88	
	1996	Aug	Windso	(G-F)	6f		89+	<

1998 Turf 0-10: (5f, 6f 7, 7f 2) (hvy, sft, g-s 2, gd 3, g-f 2, frm)
Small, fair gelding, effective 5 to 6f, best at 6f, acts on sft to g-f, has worn blinkers. Turf high 83 - 2nd of 24 giving 9lb to Marsad (13 Apr Kempton 6f sft RF 0660). Inconsistent.
**R J O'Sullivan [0-13] R O S Racing (from J M P Eustace [2-13] Spt 1997).*

JOH'S BROTHER BHB 37f **RR 33f** 4813[11]

2 ch c Clantime 6.6f **(57)** - Arroganza (Crofthall) 6.3f **(59)**
Form - 07000

Record	1998 -	1st:0	2nd:0	3rd:0	Ran:5

1998 Turf 0-5: (5f 5) (sft, gd 2, frm 2)
Very moderate colt. Turf high 33. **J S Goldie [0-5] Frank Brady.*

JOINT REGENT (USA) BHB 80f **RR 77f** 679[3]

3 br c St Jovite (USA) 11.8f **(75)** - Ice Fantasy (USA) (It's Freezing (USA)) 10f **(83)**
Form - 3

Record	1998 -	1st:0	2nd:0	3rd:1	Ran:1
	Pre1998 -	1st:0	2nd:0	3rd:0	Ran:2

Win Prizemoney £0 *Total Prizemoney* £1,123
1998 Turf 0-1: (12f) (gd)
Scopey, currently above-average colt. Showed promise in two starts as a juvenile, looking a stayer, and though running a good third in a Newmarket maiden on his reappearance, even the twelve furlongs there looked barely far enough.
**B W Hills [0-3] Maktoum Al Maktoum.*

JOLEAH (IRE) RR 104f 4688a[11]

3 b f Ela-Mana-Mou 12.7f **(72)** - Alchiea (USA) 0**0**
Form - 641435616380
1998 Turf 2-11: (9f, 10f 1-2, 11f, 12f 3, 13f, 14f 1-2, 16f) (sft 1-3, g-s, gd 4, g-f 1-3)
Very useful filly, effective 14f, acts on g-f. Turf high 104 - 1st of 9 from Dabaya (18 Jly Leopardstown RF 3011a). Inconsistent. She thrived on hard work. Successful in a handicap off a mark of 69 in May, she improved significantly and landed a Listed contest 10 weeks later. Further success proved elusive, but her mission was already accomplished. **Mrs J Harrington in IRE [2-18] R Wood.*

JOLI FILLE BHB 40f36a **RR 40f 36a** 4371[P]

3 b f Merdon Melody 6.8f **(56)**-Thabeh (Shareef Dancer(USA)) 9.9f **(73)**
Form - 8760646583642P

Record	1998 -	1st:0	2nd:1	3rd:1	Ran:11
	Pre1998 -	1st:0	2nd:0	3rd:0	Ran:7

Win Prizemoney £0 *Total Prizemoney* £1,033
1998 Turf 0-10: (10f 3, 11f, 12f 4, 14f 2) (sft, g-s 2, gd, g-f 3, frm 3)
1998 AW 0-1: (9f) (Fibr)
Unfurnished, moderate filly. Turf high 43.
**J S Wainwright [0-18] Joli Fille Partnership.*

JOLI FLYERS BHB 49f **RR 48f** 4938[3]

4 gr c Joli Wasfi (USA) 11.7f **(57)** - Hagen's Bargain (Mount Hagen (FR)) 8.4f **(70)**
Form - 6548155623

Record	**1998 -**	1st:1	2nd:1	3rd:1	Ran:9
	Pre1998 -	1st:0	2nd:0	3rd:0	Ran:3

Win Prizemoney £4,416 *Total Prizemoney* £5,971

Wins	*** 1998**	Jun	Kempto	(HVY)	H	12f	44	47	<

1998 Turf 1-9: (10f, 12f 1-5, 14f 2, 16f) (sft 2, g-s 1-1, gd 2, g-f 3, frm)
Scopey, moderate colt, effective 10 to 14f, best at 12f, acts on sft to frm, prefers right handed tracks, favours tight tracks. Turf high 48 - 2nd of 15 getting 12lb from Il Principe (6 Oct Redcar 14f g-f RF 4674) - also 1st of 13 getting 5lb from Billaddie (10 Jun Kempton RF 1879). Consistent. He had shown some ability beforehand, but it was still something of a surprise when he won a Kempton handicap in June. He may just have handled the heavy ground better than his rivals. Held since, he likes to race prominently.
**M J Haynes [1-12] Joli Racing.*

JOLI'S SON BHB 61f **RR 66f** 4731[10]

5 gr h Joli Wasfi (USA) 11.7f **(57)** - Hagen's Bargain (Mount Hagen (FR)) 8.4f **(70)**
Form - 851500

Record	**1998 -**	1st:1	2nd:0	3rd:0	Ran:6
	Pre1998 -	1st:0	2nd:0	3rd:0	Ran:4

Win Prizemoney £3,054 *Total Prizemoney* £3,412

Wins	*** 1998**	Aug	Lingfi	(GD)	H	11.5f	62	66	<

1998 Turf 1-6: (10f, 11f 1-1, 12f 3, 16f) (g-s, gd 3, g-f 1-2)
Average colt, effective 11f, acts on g-f, likes tight tracks. Turf high 66 (began Jly) - 1st of 14 getting 8lb from Danesman (1 Aug Lingfield RF 3271). He put up a game performance to win a modest Lingfield handicap in August. **M J Haynes [1-10] Joli Racing.*

JOLLYHACK BHB 52f **RR 56df** 4388[10]

3 b c Mon Tresor 7.9f **(60)**-Spiritofaffection (Raga Navarro (ITY)) 8f **(64)**
Form - 30070

Record	**1998 -**	1st:0	2nd:0	3rd:1	Ran:5
	Pre1998 -	1st:0	2nd:0	3rd:0	Ran:3

Win Prizemoney £0 *Total Prizemoney* £332
1998 Turf 0-3: (8f 3) (g-f, frm 2) 1998 AW 0-2: (8f, 12f) (Fibr 2)
Unfurnished, fair colt, effective 8f, acts on frm, has worn blinkers. Turf high 56 (1st run) - 3rd of 14 to Storm Cry (18 May Bath 8f frm RF 1291). AW high 41 (began Spt). Becoming disappointing.
**J G M O'Shea [0-8] Bell, McDonald, McGowan.*

JOLLY HARBOUR BHB 51f47a **RR 48f 47a** 1154[15]

3 b f Rudimentary (USA) 8.2f **(66)** - Ask Mama (Mummy's Pet) 7.7f **(60)**
Form - 00

Record	**1998 -**	1st:0	2nd:0	3rd:0	Ran:1
	Pre1998 -	1st:0	2nd:0	3rd:0	Ran:3

1998 AW 0-1: (8f) (Fibr)
Light-framed, moderate filly. **W J Haggas [0-4] Mrs Henrietta Charlet.*

JOLTO BHB 47f38a **RR 53f 38a** 89[7]

9 b g Noalto 6.9f **(56)** - Joytime (John de Coombe) 7.9f **(40)**
Form - 7

Record	**1998 -**	1st:0	2nd:0	3rd:0	Ran:1
	Pre1998 -	1st:6	2nd:4	3rd:2	Ran:46

Win Prizemoney £21,948 *Total Prizemoney* £29,473

Wins	1995	Aug	Salisb	(G-F)	H	7f	72	76	<
	1995	Jun	Salisb	(G-F)	H	7f	68	71	
	1994	Nov	Doncas	(SFT)	H	7f	63	62	
	1994	Oct	Newbur	(GD)	H	7f	51	58	
	1994	Jun	Salisb	(GD)	H	7f	37	35	

1998 AW 0-1: (8f) (Fibr)
Fair gelding, has worn blinkers.
**W Jenks [0-3] Peter Barclay (from K McAuliffe [0-7] Oct 1996).*

JO MAXIMUS BHB 55f46a **RR 55f 46a** 4202[14]

6 b g Prince Sabo 6.6f **(64)** - Final Call (Town Crier) 10.2f **(55)**
Form - 00300

Record	**1998 -**	1st:0	2nd:0	3rd:1	Ran:5
	Pre1998 -	1st:3	2nd:4	3rd:7	Ran:36

Win Prizemoney £10,826 *Total Prizemoney* £19,205

Wins	1996	Spt	Bright	(FRM)	H	7f	70	70	
	1995	Spt	Bright	(GD)	H	7f	68	75	<
	1995	Jun	Bright	(G-F)		6f		70	

1998 Turf 0-4: (7f 4) (gd 2, g-f 2) 1998 AW 0-1: (7f) (Fibr)
Fair gelding, effective 7f, acts on g-f - acts on Equi, has worn blinkers. Turf high 55 - 3rd of 19 giving 13lb to Gablesea (24 Jly Chepstow 7f g-f RF 3070). Inconsistent. He has gained all three of his career victories at Brighton, though he has not won since September 1996.
**J G Smyth-Osbourne [0-8] J G Smyth-Osbourne (from S Dow [3-33] Apr 1997).*

JO MELL BHB 107f **RR 106f** 3777[2]

5 b g Efisio 7.7f **(69)** - Militia Girl (Rarity) 10.1f **(60)**
Form - 04823012

Record	**1998 -**	1st:1	2nd:2	3rd:1	Ran:8
	Pre1998 -	1st:6	2nd:2	3rd:4	Ran:27

Win Prizemoney £178,062 *Total Prizemoney* £206,487

Wins	*** 1998**	Aug	Ascot	(G-F)	H	7f	98	106	<
	* 1997	Oct	Doncas	(GD)		7f		104	
	* 1997	Spt	Ascot	(G-F)	H	7f	93	103	
	* 1997	Jly	York	(GD)	H	7.9f	80	92	
	* 1997	Jly	Haydoc	(GD)	H	7.1f	73	85	
	* 1997	Jun	Newcas	(HVY)	H	7f	73	80	
	1995	Spt	Ayr	(GD)		7f		85+	

1998 Turf 1-8: (6f, 7f 1-6, 8f) (sft 2, gd 2, g-f 1-1, frm 3)
Pattern-class gelding, effective 7f, acts on gd to frm, likes left handed tracks, and excels at Ascot and Haydock. Turf high 106 - 1st of 25 getting 4lb from Gaelic Storm (8 Aug Ascot RF 3458). Tim Easterby produced one of the training performances of the season when saddling this tough gelding to win the inaugural running of the Tote International Handicap at Ascot in August. That race had been his target from the start of the campaign and it would be no surprise if returned for another crack in 1999. He does not want much racing on fast ground.
**T D Easterby [6-31] C H Newton Jnr Ltd (from M H Easterby [1-4] Oct 1995).*

JONA HOLLEY BHB 55f55a **RR 54f 55a** 5114[6]

5 b g Sharpo 7.5f **(68)** - Spurned (USA) (Robellino (USA)) 7.6f **(80)**
Form - 0226

Record	**1998 -**	1st:0	2nd:2	3rd:0	Ran:4
	Pre1998 -	1st:2	2nd:3	3rd:0	Ran:17

Win Prizemoney £5,185 *Total Prizemoney* £11,069

Wins	1997	*Oct*	*Southw*	*(STD)*	*H*	*8f*	*47*	*52*	<
	1997	Jly	Folkes	(SFT)	H	9.7f	43	50	

1998 Turf 0-4: (8f 2, 9f, 11f) (sft, gd 2, g-f)
Fair gelding, effective 8 to 10f, acts on gd to g-f - acts on Fibr, best on g-f, likes right handed tracks, excels at Hamilton. Turf high 54 - 2nd of 15 giving 5lb to Genuine John (15 May Hamilton 8f gd RF 1234).
**M D Hammond [0-6] John Sinclair (Haulage) Ltd (from G L Moore [2-7] Oct 1997).*

JONAS NIGHTENGALE BHB 78f80a **RR 81f 80a** 1759[7]

3 b g Deploy 11.4f **(67)** - Springs Welcome (Blakeney) 10.5f **(64)**
Form - 1227

Record	**1998 -**	1st:1	2nd:2	3rd:0	Ran:4
	Pre1998 -	1st:0	2nd:0	3rd:1	Ran:5

Win Prizemoney £3,525 *Total Prizemoney* £8,480

Wins	*** 1998**	*Apr*	*Wolver*	*(STD)*		*12f*		*83?*	<

1998 Turf 0-3:(12f, 13f, 14f) (g-f, frm 2)1998 AW 1-1: (12f 1-1) (Fibr 1-1)
Decent gelding, effective 12 to 13f, best at 12f, acts on g-f to frm - acts on Fibr, prefers left handed tracks. Turf high 81 (1st run) - 2nd of 7 giving 14lb to Eastwell Hall (4 May Warwick 13f g-f RF 1033). (1st run) - 1st of 4 from Courageous (4 Apr Wolverhampton RF 0565). Bred for stamina, he got off the mark in a four-runner maiden on the Wolverhampton Fibresand in April. Good efforts on turf on his next two starts. **C A Cyzer [1-9] R M Cyzer.*

JORROCKS (USA) **RR 88f** 4528[3]

4 b g Rubiano (USA) 7.1f **(87)**-Perla Fina (USA)(Gallant Man) 10.2f **(68)**
Form - 4306030003

Record	**1998 -**	1st:0	2nd:0	3rd:3	Ran:10
	Pre1998 -	1st:3	2nd:2	3rd:1	Ran:8

Win Prizemoney £31,121 *Total Prizemoney* £38,878

Wins	* 1997	Spt	Newbur	(SFT)	H	7.3f	87	94	<
	* 1997	Aug	Goodwo	(G-F)	H	7f	74	85	
	* 1997	Jly	Sandow	(G-F)	H	7.1f	74	77	

1998 Turf 0-10: (7f 7, 8f 2, 9f) (sft, g-s, gd 3, g-f 2, frm 2, hrd)

Scopey, useful gelding, effective 7f, acts on sft to gd, best on gd, has worn blinkers. Turf high 93 - 3rd of 11 getting 11lb from Beauchamp King (2 May Haydock 7f gd RF 0966). A winner three times in '97, he had a fruitless campaign this time around though for most of the season he was too high in the handicap. He made the frame a few times, but was well held otherwise. Realised 15,000 gns at Tattersalls Autumn Horses In Training Sales.

**I A Balding [3-18] Paul Mellon.*

JOSEPH'S WINE (IRE) BHB 46f66a RR 48f 66a 1720[10]

9 b g Smile (USA) 9.8f **(80)** - Femme Gendarme (USA) (Policeman (FR)) 9.8f **(80)**

Form - 1323750

Record	**1998 -**	1st:0	2nd:1	3rd:2	Ran:6
	Pre1998 -	1st:13	2nd:1	3rd:2	Ran:39

Win Prizemoney £36,371 *Total Prizemoney* £39,351

Wins	* 1997	*Dec*	*Southw*	*(STD)*	*C*	*8f*		*69*	
	1997	*Feb*	*Lingfi*	*(STD)*	*C*	*10f*		*80+*	<
	1997	*Jan*	*Southw*	*(STD)*	*C*	*8f*		*66*	
	1995	*Jan*	*Southw*	*(STD)*	*H*	*11f*	*75*	*80*	
	1994	*Dec*	*Lingfi*	*(STD)*	*H*	*10f*	*61*	*67*	
	1994	*Dec*	*Southw*	*(STD)*	*H*	*11f*	*61*	*65+*	
	1994	*Nov*	*Southw*	*(STD)*	*H*	*11f*	*55*	*59*	
	1994	Jun	Ayr	(G-F)	H	10f	49	60++	
	1994	Jun	Pontef	(G-F)	H	10f	44	55+	
	1994	Jun	Beverl	(G-F)	H	9.9f	35	46	
	1994	May	Nottin	(GD)	SH	10f	35	43+	

1998 Turf 0-2: (8f, 10f) (frm 2) 1998 AW 0-4: (8f 3, 10f) (Equi, Fibr 3)

Average gelding, has broken blood-vessels, effective 10f - acts on Equi, often wears blinkers (effectively), favours left handed tracks, favours tight tracks. Turf high 48. AW high 66. Becoming disappointing. A regular winner for David Nicholls, he made a winning debut for John Wharton when winning on the Southwell Fibresand in December, and has mainly run creditably since, apart from when breaking a blood-vessel at the same track in February.

**J Wharton [1-7] Wetherby Racing Bureau 22 (from D Nicholls [10-24] Feb 1997).*

JO'S PRINCESS RR 3377[U]

2 b f Emarati (USA) 6.6f **(63)** - Daima (Dominion) 8.5f **(63)**

Form - U

Record	**1998 -**	1st:0	2nd:0	3rd:0	Ran:1

1998 Turf 0-1: (6f) (frm)

Currently very poor filly. **J R Jenkins [0-1] Miss J L Watson.*

JOSR ALGARHOUD (IRE) RR 106+f 3755[1]

2 b c Darshaan 11.9f **(81)** - Pont-Aven (Try My Best (USA)) 7.6f **(67)**

Form - 31

Record	**1998 -**	1st:1	2nd:0	3rd:1	Ran:2

Win Prizemoney £71,565 *Total Prizemoney* £72,565

Wins	*** 1998**	Aug	York	(G-F)	G2	6f	106+	<

1998 Turf 1-2: (6f 1-2) (g-f, frm 1-1)

Currently Pattern-class colt. Turf high 106 (began Jly) - 1st of 8 from Sailing Shoes (19 Aug York RF 3755). Mick Channon was mystified by his debut defeat at Ascot, and we saw why when he produced a telling burst to settle the Gimcrack Stakes in a matter of strides. Unraced since then, this handsome colt has more scope than most and should make great strides over the winter. By a French Derby winner and out of a classy sprinter who has already produced the lightening-fast Sainte Marine, he is not certain to stay beyond a mile, but has a relaxed manner and may well do so. He will race under the Godolphin banner in 1999 and looks certain to win a big race or two.

**M R Channon [1-2] Sheikh Ahmed Al Maktoum.*

JOUMART RR 99f 137a[1]

4 b/ c Kendor (FR) 12.2f **(66)** - Dinner Out (FR) (Al Nasr (FR)) 9.3f **(68)**

Form - 1

1998 Turf 1-1: (8f 1-1) (sft 1-1)

Currently very useful colt. (1st run) - 1st of 19 giving 3lb to Leonine (14 Jan Cagnes-sur-mer RF 0137a).

**J-C Rouget in FR [1-1] Ecurie des Mousequetaire.*

JOUST BHB 55f RR 60f 306[9]

4 b g Keen 11.1f **(58)** - Tudorealm (USA) (Palace Music (USA))

Form - 0

Record	**1998 -**	1st:0	2nd:0	3rd:0	Ran:1
	Pre1998 -	1st:0	2nd:0	3rd:0	Ran:3

1998 AW 0-1: (12f) (Equi)

Scopey, average gelding. **C E Brittain [0-4] C E Brittain.*

JOYEUX DANSEUR (USA) RR 118f 5165a[7]

5 b h Nureyev (USA) 8.4f **(84)** - Fabuleux Jane (USA) (Le Fabuleux) 11.4f **(76)**

Form - 7

1998 Turf 0-1: (8f) (frm)

Currently high-class colt. **A Stall Jnr in USA [0-1] B W Hughes.*

JOYEUX PLAYER (USA) BHB 94f RR 86f 4950a[7]

2 b c St Jovite (USA) 11.8f **(75)** - Play On And On (USA) (Stop The Music (USA)) 9.2f **(71)**

Form - 41217

Record	**1998 -**	1st:2	2nd:1	3rd:0	Ran:5

Win Prizemoney £7,801 *Total Prizemoney* £9,928

Wins	*** 1998**	Spt	Ayr	(G-S)	8f		85+	<
	*** 1998**	Aug	Haydoc	(GD)	7.1f		78	

1998 Turf 2-5: (7f 1-2, 8f 1-3) (sft 1-2, gd, g-f 1-1, frm)

Useful colt. Turf high 86 (began Jly) - 2nd of 16 giving 2lb to Bathwick (7 Spt Bath 8f frm RF 4124) - also 1st of 3 giving 6lb to Fastwan (19 Spt Ayr RF 4363). **J L Dunlop [2-5].*

JOYFUL JOY BHB 19f17a RR 32f 17a 1075[13]

4 b f River God (USA) 6f **(37)** - Joyfulness (FR) (Cure The Blues (USA)) 9.5f **(63)**

Form - 00

Record	**1998 -**	1st:0	2nd:0	3rd:0	Ran:2
	Pre1998 -	1st:0	2nd:0	3rd:0	Ran:19

1998 Turf 0-1: (6f) (hvy) 1998 AW 0-1: (8f) (Fibr)

Light-framed, very moderate filly. **B P J Baugh [0-22] E Bennion.*

JOYFUL WELD RR 4878[12]

2 ch f Weld - Joyfulness (FR) (Cure The Blues (USA)) 9.5f **(63)**

Form - 0

Record	**1998 -**	1st:0	2nd:0	3rd:0	Ran:1

1998 AW 0-1: (7f) (Fibr)

Currently little account filly. **B P J Baugh [0-1] E Bennion.*

J R STEVENSON (USA) RR 87+f 4445[1]

2 ch c Lyphard (USA) 10.6f **(75)** - While it Lasts (USA) (Foolish Pleasure (USA)) 8.9f **(72)**

Form - 1

Record	**1998 -**	1st:1	2nd:0	3rd:0	Ran:1

Win Prizemoney £3,355 *Total Prizemoney* £3,355

Wins	*** 1998**	Spt	Cheste	(GD)	7f	87+	<

1998 Turf 1-1: (7f 1-1) (gd 1-1)

Currently useful colt. (1st run) - 1st of 7 from Tanusius (23 Spt Chester RF 4445). Only lightly made, he needs to strengthen up over the winter.

**P W Chapple-Hyam [1-1] R E Sangster and B V Sangster.*

JUANITA BHB 69a RR 67f 4889[4]

2 b f Be My Chief (USA) 10.2f **(62)** - Dominio (IRE) (Dominion) 8.5f **(63)**

Form - 000226544

Record	**1998 -**	1st:0	2nd:2	3rd:0	Ran:9

Win Prizemoney £0 *Total Prizemoney* £1,527

1998 Turf 0-7: (5f 2, 6f, 7f 3, 8f) (gd 3, g-f 2, frm 2) 1998 AW 0-2: (7f, 8f) (Fibr 2)

Average filly, effective 7f, acts on g-f - acts on Fibr, has worn blinkers. Turf high 67 - 2nd of 11 getting 11lb from Asley (14 Aug Folkestone 7f g-f RF 3626). AW high 68 (1st run) (began Jly) - 2nd of 6 to Schnitzel (25 Jly Southwell 7f Fibr RF 3127).

**P T Walwyn [0-9] Major & Mrs Kennard and Partners.*

JUBILEE SCHOLAR (IRE) BHB 32f54a RR 32f 54a 4143[4]

5 b g Royal Academy (USA) 7.8f **(77)**-Jaljuli (Jalmood (USA)) 10.1f **(52)**

Form - 15233344108754

Record	**1998 -**	1st:1	2nd:0	3rd:3	Ran:11
	Pre1998 -	1st:1	2nd:2	3rd:0	Ran:22

Win Prizemoney £4,226 *Total Prizemoney* £6,284

Wins	*** 1998**	*Apr*	*Lingfi*	*(STD)*	*H*	*8f*	*45*	*51*	<

* 1997	Nov Lingfi	(STD)	H	10f	36	39?

1998 Turf 0-4: (8f 2, 10f 2) (g-f 2, frm 2) 1998 AW 1-7: (8f 1-1, 10f 4, 12f 2) (Equi 1-7)

Fair gelding, effective 8 to 12f, best at 10f - acts on Equi, often wears blinkers, favours left handed tracks. Turf high 32. AW high 56 - 4th of 13 getting 6lb from Java Shrine (8 Spt Lingfield 10f Equi RF 4143) - also 1st of 12 getting 13lb from Kafil (9 Apr Lingfield RF 0626). He scored on the Lingfield Equitrack in November '97, and though the event was marked by a stalls debacle, it was still a big improvement on his previous form. He continued to run well on that surface after, though he did not regain winning form until dropped to a mile in April.

**G L Moore [2-23] M V Johnston (from K McAuliffe [0-7] Apr 1997).*

frm, prefers left handed tracks. Turf high 55 (1st run) - 1st of 11 giving 2lb to Golden Melody (7 Apr Folkestone RF 0582).

**J Pearce [1-14] Mrs Samantha Watson.*

JUDDY BHB 34f **RR 33f** 4955[13]

4 ch g Clantime 6.6f **(57)** - Two's Up (Double Jump) 9.4f **(58)**

Form - 00000

Record	**1998 -**	1st:0	2nd:0	3rd:0	Ran:5
	Pre1998 -	1st:0	2nd:1	3rd:0	Ran:3

Win Prizemoney £0 *Total Prizemoney* £447

1998 Turf 0-5: (6f 4, 7f) (gd, g-f 2, frm 2)

Very moderate gelding, effective 6f, acts on gd. Turf high 33.

**G Woodward [0-5]Burntwood Sports Ltd(from JO'Reilly [0-1] Jly 1997).*

Gimcrack winner Josr Algarhoud has been lightly raced

JUBRAN (USA) BHB 24f **RR 33f** 4254[15]

12 b g Vaguely Noble 10.6f **(68)** - La Vue (USA) (Reviewer (USA)) 9.4f **(73)**

Form - 04700

Record	**1998 -**	1st:0	2nd:0	3rd:0	Ran:5
	Pre1998 -	1st:7	2nd:8	3rd:7	Ran:69

Win Prizemoney £29,891 *Total Prizemoney* £49,783

Wins	1994	Aug Ripon	(G-F)	H	10f	71	74
	1994	Jly Mussel	(GD)	H	11.1f	70	71

1998 Turf 0-5: (10f, 12f 2, 14f, 16f) (g-s, gd, g-f, frm 2)

Very moderate gelding, effective 12f, acts on gd, has worn blinkers, favours right handed tracks, favours tight tracks. Turf high 33 (began Jly) - 4th of 10 getting 22lb from Netta Rufina (3 Aug Ripon 12f gd RF 3310).

**Mrs A M Naughton [0-5] Mrs Elke Scullion (from J L Eyre [0-6] Aug 1997).*

JUCINDA BHB 52f47a **RR 55f 47a** 1120[15]

4 gr f Midyan (USA) 9.9f **(64)** - Catch The Sun (Kalaglow) 9.8f **(67)**

Form - 160

Record	**1998 -**	1st:1	2nd:0	3rd:0	Ran:3
	Pre1998 -	1st:0	2nd:2	3rd:0	Ran:11

Win Prizemoney £3,080 *Total Prizemoney* £5,140

Wins	*** 1998**	Apr Folkes	(SFT)	H	15.4f	51	55	<

1998 Turf 1-3: (15f 1-2, 16f) (sft 1-2, frm)

Light-framed, fair filly, effective 14 to 16f, best at 14f, acts on sft to

JUDICIAL SUPREMACY BHB 71f **RR 74f** 2579[17]

4 b c Warning 8.1f **(77)** - Song Test(USA) (The Minstrel (CAN)) 10f **(72)**

Form - 0536430

Record	**1998 -**	1st:0	2nd:0	3rd:2	Ran:7
	Pre1998 -	1st:0	2nd:1	3rd:0	Ran:5

Win Prizemoney £0 *Total Prizemoney* £4,017

1998 Turf 0-6: (8f 2, 10f 4) (g-s, gd 2, g-f, frm 2) 1998 AW 0-1: (8f) (Equi)

Scopey, above-average colt, effective 10f, acts on gd to g-f, best on gd. Turf high 80 - 3rd of 24 giving 11lb to Carlys Quest (1 May Newmarket 10f gd RF 0962). Consistent.

**B W Hills [0-7] W J Gredley (from J R Fanshawe [0-5] Jun 1997).*

JUHINA (IRE) **RR 101f** 4949a[2]

3 b f Marju (IRE) 9.2f **(76)** - Matahina (Moorestyle) 6.9f **(64)**

Form - 202

1998 Turf 0-3: (8f 2, 10f) (hvy 2, sft)

Currently very useful filly. Turf high 101 - 2nd of 9 getting 2lb from Miss Carolina (18 Oct San Siro 8f sft RF 4949a).

**B Grizzetti in ITY [0-3].*

JUKEBOX JIVE BHB 45f50a **RR 32f 50a** 1968[10]

4 ch f Scottish Reel 8.6f **(58)** - My Sweet Melody (Music Boy) 6.8f **(57)**

Form - 000

Record	**1998 -**	1st:0	2nd:0	3rd:0	Ran:3
	Pre1998 -	1st:1	2nd:1	3rd:0	Ran:10

Win Prizemoney £4,077 *Total Prizemoney* £5,327
Wins 1997 Jun Newmar (SFT) C 8f 58 <
1998 Turf 0-3: (8f, 10f, 11f) (g-s, gd 2)
Leggy, very moderate filly, effective 8f, acted on gd. Turf high 32. (DEAD) **C Drew [0-3] Matthew Sharkey (from H Akbary [0-1] Jly 1997).*

JULIES JEWEL (IRE) BHB 60f67a **RR 61f 67a** 5147[23]
3 ch g Simply Great (FR) 11.9f **(61)** - Melungeon (Ardoon) 7.3f **(53)**
Form - 65107445124200240007800040
Record 1998 - 1st:2 2nd:3 3rd:0 Ran:24
Pre1998 - 1st:0 2nd:1 3rd:0 Ran:9
Win Prizemoney £7,822 *Total Prizemoney* £16,796
Wins * 1998 Mar Doncas (GD) H 7f 68 73 <
*** 1998** *Jan Southw (STD) H 6f 66 70*
1998 Turf 1-18: (6f 5, 7f 1-8, 8f 3, 9f 2) (sft, g-s 3, gd 1-6, g-f 5, frm 3)
1998 AW 1-6: (5f, 6f 1-4, 7f) (Fibr 1-6)
Leggy, above-average gelding, effective 6 to 7f, best at 7f, acts on g-s to gd - acts on Fibr, best on g-s, likes left handed tracks, likes tight tracks. Turf high 77 - 2nd of 13 getting 11lb from Fizzed (23 Apr Beverley 7f g-s RF 0826) - also 1st of 22 getting 2lb from Bodfaridistinction (28 Mar Doncaster RF 0486). AW high 72 - 4th of 11 giving 5lb to Ok Babe (6 Feb Southwell 6f Fibr RF 0235) - also 1st of 11 getting 4lb from Just Another Time (2 Jan Southwell RF 0012). A Fibresand winner, he won at 33/1 back on turf at Doncaster in March, but he has shown that it was no fluke by producing some good efforts since.
**M C Chapman [2-33] Mrs Julie Lamming.*

JULMAT JOHN (IRE) BHB 42f55a **RR 41f 55a** 5059[9]
6 b g Conquering Hero (USA) 10.6f **(50)** - Ramich John (Kampala) 8.5f **(56)**
Form - 000608000
Record 1998 - 1st:0 2nd:0 3rd:0 Ran:9
Pre1998 - 1st:2 2nd:1 3rd:3 Ran:20
Win Prizemoney £8,220 *Total Prizemoney* £10,387
Wins 1997 Jun Naas (G-S) H 6f 62 64 <
1996 Jun Gowran (G-S) H 7f 62 56
1998 Turf 0-8: (6f 5, 7f, 8f 2) (sft, gd, g-f 3, frm 3) 1998 AW 0-1: (7f) (Fibr)
Moderate gelding, effective 6 to 7f, best at 7f, acts on g-s to gd, best on g-s, has worn blinkers. Turf high 49 (began Jly). Consistent.
**E J Alston [0-9] Lords Of The Manor (from K O'Sullivan in IRE [2-20] Spt 1997).*

JUNCTION CITY (USA) BHB 41f **RR 40f** 4123[5]
4 b g Forty Niner (USA) 8.8f **(73)** - Key Witness (USA) (Key To The Mint (USA)) 9.4f **(75)**
Form - 0800065
Record 1998 - 1st:0 2nd:0 3rd:0 Ran:7
Pre1998 - 1st:0 2nd:0 3rd:0 Ran:1
1998 Turf 0-7: (6f, 7f, 8f 5) (hvy, g-s, gd 2, frm 3)
Scopey, moderate gelding, effective 8f, acts on frm, often wears blinkers (very effectively), likes tight tracks. Turf high 42.
**I A Balding [0-9] Paul Mellon.*

JUNE BOUNTY (USA) BHB 36f50a **RR 45df 50a** 4838[8]
3 b f Red Ransom (USA) 8.6f **(83)** - June Bride (USA) (Riverman (USA)) 9.1f **(76)**
Form - 670008
Record 1998 - 1st:0 2nd:0 3rd:0 Ran:6
Pre1998 - 1st:0 2nd:0 3rd:0 Ran:1
1998 Turf 0-5: (7f, 8f 2, 10f, 12f) (g-s, gd, g-f 2, frm) 1998 AW 0-1: (8f) (Fibr)
Workmanlike, moderate filly, has worn blinkers. Turf high 45.
**R M H Cowell [0-6] Bottisham Heath Stud (from G Wragg [0-1] Nov 1997).*

JUNGLE FRESH BHB 29f **RR 29f** 3431[3]
5 b g Rambo Dancer (CAN) 8.4f **(59)** - Report 'em (USA) (Staff Writer (USA)) 10f **(54)**
Form - 58053
Record 1998 - 1st:0 2nd:0 3rd:1 Ran:5
Pre1998 - 1st:0 2nd:0 3rd:0 Ran:7
Win Prizemoney £0 *Total Prizemoney* £656
1998 Turf 0-5: (8f, 11f, 12f, 13f 2) (gd 2, g-f 3)
Little account gelding, effective 13f, acts on gd. Turf high 38 (1st run) - 5th of 8 getting 32lb from Filial (15 May Hamilton 13f gd RF 1237).
**J D Bethell [0-12] Robert Gibbons.*

JUNGLE STORY (IRE) BHB 64f59a **RR 72f 59a** 4332[9]
3 b f Alzao (USA) 9.8f **(73)** - Jungle Jezebel (Thatching) 8f **(66)**
Form - 0824600
Record 1998 - 1st:0 2nd:1 3rd:0 Ran:7
Pre1998 - 1st:1 2nd:1 3rd:0 Ran:5
Win Prizemoney £3,226 *Total Prizemoney* £6,161
Wins * 1997 Spt Catter (GD) H 7f 70 74 <
1998 Turf 0-7: (8f 2, 10f 3, 12f 2) (g-s, gd 2, g-f 3, frm)
Leggy, above-average filly, effective 7 to 12f, best at 7f, acts on gd to g-f, best on gd, prefers tight tracks. Turf high 72 - 2nd of 10 giving 13lb to Imani (17 Jly Newbury 10f g-f RF 2872).
**P T Walwyn [1-12] Major & Mrs Kennard and Partners.*

JUNIE (IRE) BHB 51f35a **RR 54f 35a** 509[10]
4 ch f Astronef 7.9f **(59)** - Numidia (Sallust) 8.4f **(63)**
Form - 40000
Record 1998 - 1st:0 2nd:0 3rd:0 Ran:4
Pre1998 - 1st:0 2nd:0 3rd:0 Ran:7
1998 AW 0-4: (5f, 6f 2, 7f) (Equi 4)
Leggy, fair filly, has worn blinkers. AW high 18. Inconsistent.
**B R Johnson [0-2] Paul Lewis Kevin Cos Reeves (from T G Mills [0-9] Feb 1998).*

JUNIKAY (IRE) BHB 53f52a **RR 58f 52a** 4822[9]
4 b g Treasure Kay 6.5f **(53)** - Junijo (Junius (USA)) 7.7f **(65)**
Form - 0081070660656320
Record 1998 - 1st:1 2nd:1 3rd:1 Ran:15
Pre1998 - 1st:1 2nd:1 3rd:1 Ran:16
Win Prizemoney £6,104 *Total Prizemoney* £9,374
Wins * 1998 May Bright (G-F) H 7f 53 58
1996 Jly Ballin (GD) 6f 73 <
1998 Turf 1-15: (7f 1-2, 8f 6, 9f 3, 10f 4) (sft, g-s, gd 1-6, g-f 3, frm 4)
Fair gelding, has worn blinkers. Turf high 58. His victory in a Brighton handicap in May was very much the exception rather than the rule, as he has mostly run poorly since arriving from Ireland in 1997, and has been tried over all sorts of trips.
**R Ingram [1-23] Ellangowan Racing Partners (from J S Bolger in IRE [1-9] Jun 1997).*

JUNIOR BEN (IRE) BHB 23f32a **RR 35f 32a** 3980[6]
6 b g Tirol 8.1f **(64)** - Piney Pass (Persian Bold) 9.3f **(66)**
Form - 0846
Record 1998 - 1st:0 2nd:0 3rd:0 Ran:4
Pre1998 - 1st:0 2nd:3 3rd:2 Ran:30
Win Prizemoney £0 *Total Prizemoney* £5,069
1998 Turf 0-2: (12f 2) (g-f, frm) 1998 AW 0-2: (7f, 11f) (Fibr 2)
Very moderate gelding, effective 10 to 12f, best at 12f, acts on g-s to g-f, has worn blinkers, prefers left handed tracks, favours tight tracks. Turf high 35 (began Aug). AW high 7.
**A G Juckes [0-2] Mrs Iris Goode (from M E Sowersby [0-12] Mar 1998).*

JUNIOR MUFFIN (IRE) BHB 52f65a **RR 65df 65a** 4811[20]
3 b g Paris House 5.9f **(64)** - Clodianus (Bay Express) 7.1f **(60)**
Form - 267113268000
Record 1998 - 1st:2 2nd:2 3rd:1 Ran:12
Pre1998 - 1st:2 2nd:0 3rd:1 Ran:8
Win Prizemoney £8,621 *Total Prizemoney* £11,216
Wins * 1998 *Apr Wolver (STD) C 6f 65*
*** 1998** Apr Nottin (SFT) S 6.1f 63
* 1997 Aug Newcas (GD) C 5f 73 <
* 1997 Aug Bath (GD) S 5.1f 61
1998 Turf 1-9: (5f 2, 6f 1-7) (sft, g-s 1-2, gd 4, frm 2) 1998 AW 1-3: (5f, 6f 1-2) (Fibr 1-3)
Scopey, average gelding, effective 5 to 6f, best at 5f, acts on g-s to g-f - acts on Fibr, best on gd. Turf high 65 - 2nd of 20 giving 14lb to Breakin Even (22 May Haydock 6f gd RF 1391). AW high 65 - 1st of 10 getting 5lb from Desert Invader (30 Apr Wolverhampton RF 0939). Becoming disappointing.
**J Berry [4-20] Chris & Antonia Deuters.*

JUNO MARLOWE (IRE) BHB 97f **RR 86f** 4364[5]
2 b f Danehill (USA) 9.1f **(79)**- Why so Silent (Mill Reef(USA)) 10.5f **(78)**
Form - 31485
Record 1998 - 1st:1 2nd:0 3rd:1 Ran:5

Win Prizemoney £3,696 *Total Prizemoney* £5,993
Wins * **1998** Aug Kempto (G-F) 7f 86 <
1998 Turf 1-5: (6f, 7f 1-3, 8f) (sft, gd 2, g-f, frm 1-1)
Useful filly. Turf high 86 - 1st of 17 getting 5lb from Kondoty (5 Aug Kempton RF 3369). She showed a little bit of temperament when winning a Kempton maiden on her second start, and then ran fairly well to finish fourth in the Solario. Found the drop to six furlongs against her on her final start.
**P W Harris [1-5] Mrs P W Harris.*

JUPITER (IRE) BHB 45f70a **RR 35f 70a** 3316[12]
4 b g Astronef 7.9f **(59)** - Native Flower (Tumble Wind (USA)) 7.5f **(57)**
Form - 000
Record 1998 - 1st:0 2nd:0 3rd:0 Ran:3
Pre1998 - 1st:1 2nd:0 3rd:0 Ran:11
Win Prizemoney £2,381 *Total Prizemoney* £2,602
Wins * 1996 *Jun Southw (STD) 5f 65+* <
1998 Turf 0-3: (7f 2, 8f) (gd, frm 2)
Tall, fair gelding, effective 7f, acts on g-f, has worn blinkers. Turf high 35 (began Jly). Inconsistent. **G C Bravery [1-14] G C Bravery.*

JUS'CHILLIN' (IRE) BHB 56f **RR 35f** 2265[7]
3 b f Elbio 9f **(62)** - Not Mistaken (USA) (Mill Reef (USA)) 10.5f **(78)**
Form - 0007
Record 1998 - 1st:0 2nd:0 3rd:0 Ran:4
Pre1998 - 1st:0 2nd:2 3rd:0 Ran:6
Win Prizemoney £0 *Total Prizemoney* £1,646
1998 Turf 0-4: (6f, 7f, 8f 2) (gd 3, g-f)
Workmanlike, very moderate filly, effective 6f, acts on gd, likes tight tracks. Turf high 49. **C A Dwyer [0-10] M A Scaife.*

JUST ANOTHER TIME BHB 70f68a **RR 67f 68a** 443[5]
3 ch c Mazilier (USA) 8.5f **(56)** - Entourage (Posse (USA)) 8.9f **(61)**
Form - 112335
Record 1998 - 1st:0 2nd:1 3rd:2 Ran:4
Pre1998 - 1st:2 2nd:3 3rd:1 Ran:10
Win Prizemoney £4,588 *Total Prizemoney* £9,288
Wins * 1997 *Dec Lingfi (STD) C 5f 73* <
* 1997 *Nov Lingfi (STD) C 6f 67*
1998 AW 0-4: (6f 3, 7f) (Equi 2, Fibr 2)
Scopey, above-average colt, effective 5 to 6f, best at 6f, acts on gd to frm - acts on AW, best on Equi, excels at Lingfield. AW high 73 (1st run) - 2nd of 11 giving 4lb to Julies Jewel (2 Jan Southwell 6f Fibr RF 0012). He had shown some signs of ability, but was becoming something of a professional loser until winning twice on the Lingfield Equitrack in November. He should have completed the hat-trick at Southwell next time but was given an over-confident ride, and although placed, has not quite run up to his best since. **J Berry [2-14] Miss Lilo Blum.*

JUST A SNACK (IRE) RR 54f 5116[9]
2 b c Tenby 10.4f **(76)** - Opening Day (Day Is Done) 6.3f **(67)**
Form - 400
Record 1998 - 1st:0 2nd:0 3rd:0 Ran:3
Win Prizemoney £0 *Total Prizemoney* £215
1998 Turf 0-3: (7f 2, 8f) (sft, g-s, gd)
Currently fair colt. Turf high 54 (began Oct).
**M A Buckley [0-3] Mrs N W Buckley.*

JUST BOB BHB 56f65a **RR 66f 65a** 4837[9]
9 b g Alleging (USA) 8.8f **(57)** - Diami (Swing Easy (USA)) 6.5f **(55)**
Form - 0300006441362000000
Record 1998 - 1st:1 2nd:1 3rd:2 Ran:19
Pre1998 - 1st:17 2nd:11 3rd:8 Ran:96
Win Prizemoney £57,437 *Total Prizemoney* £76,687
Wins * **1998** Jun Hamilt (G-S) 6f 66
* 1997 Oct Newcas (G-F) H 5f 72 76 <
* 1997 Spt Ayr (G-S) H 5f 57 67
* 1997 Spt Doncas (G-F) H 5f 57 62
* 1996 May Carlis (G-F) 5f 66
* 1996 May Ayr (G-S) H 5f 60 69
* 1996 May Hamilt (SFT) 5f 69?
* 1994 Aug Carlis (FRM) H 5f 76 75
* 1994 Jun Mussel (G-F) H 5f 69 66
* 1994 Jun Hamilt (G-F) H 5f 69 72+
* 1994 May Ayr (GF) H 5f 66 62
1998 Turf 1-19: (5f 16, 6f 1-3) (hvy, sft, g-s 2, gd 6, g-f 1-5, frm 4)
Average gelding, effective 5 to 6f, best at 5f, acts on gd to g-f, best on gd, has worn blinkers. Turf high 66.
**S E Kettlewell [18-115] J Fotherby.*

JUST DESERTS BHB 58f **RR 68df** 3375[9]
3 b f Alhijaz 7.7f **(57)** - What A Pet (Mummy's Pet) 7.7f **(60)**
Form - 750
Record 1998 - 1st:0 2nd:0 3rd:0 Ran:3
Pre1998 - 1st:0 2nd:0 3rd:0 Ran:1
1998 Turf 0-3: (8f 2, 10f) (gd 2, frm)
Leggy, average filly. Turf high 68. Half-sister to Petardia.
**P J Makin [0-4] David Gibson.*

JUST DESMOND RR 4654[11]
4 b g Picea 12.7f **(43)** - Edith Piaf (Thatch (USA)) 9.8f **(62)**
Form - 0
Record 1998 - 1st:0 2nd:0 3rd:0 Ran:1
1998 Turf 0-1: (12f) (g-f)
Light-framed, currently very poor gelding.
**R Simpson [0-3] Blues Connection.*

JUST DISSIDENT (IRE) BHB 49f53a **RR 46f 53a** 5097[7]
6 b g Dancing Dissident (USA) 6.8f **(65)** - Betty Bun (St Chad) 6.7f **(67)**
Form - 3213240400800087
Record 1998 - 1st:0 2nd:1 3rd:1 Ran:13
Pre1998 - 1st:5 2nd:4 3rd:6 Ran:55
Win Prizemoney £19,635 *Total Prizemoney* £28,538
Wins * 1997 *Dec Lingfi (STD) H 5f 52 56*
* 1997 Jly Pontef (G-F) H 5f 57 58
* 1996 Aug Carlis (FRM) H 5f 57 58
* 1996 Jly Pontef (G-F) H 5f 55 56
* 1995 Jun Redcar (FRM) 6f 69 <
1998 Turf 0-9: (5f 9) (sft, gd, g-f 2, frm 5) 1998 AW 0-4: (5f 2, 6f 2) (Equi 2, Fibr 2)
Fair gelding, effective 5 to 6f, best at 5f, acts on gd to frm - acts on Equi, has worn blinkers, prefers left handed tracks, prefers tight tracks, excels at Lingfield. Turf high 46. AW high 58 - 2nd of 10 giving 15lb to Rise 'n Shine (12 Feb Lingfield 5f Equi RF 0272).
**R M Whitaker [5-68] Mrs C A Hodgetts.*

JUST FOR TINA BHB 45a **RR 10f 45a** 192[8]
3 b f Presidium 7.5f **(56)** - Mushy Boff (Tina's Pet) 6.8f **(59)**
Form - 7368
Record 1998 - 1st:0 2nd:0 3rd:0 Ran:2
Pre1998 - 1st:0 2nd:0 3rd:1 Ran:3
Win Prizemoney £0 *Total Prizemoney* £314
1998 AW 0-2: (7f 2) (Fibr 2)
Workmanlike, moderate filly, has worn blinkers. AW high 42.
**W G M Turner [0-4] John Hill (from C J Hill [0-1] Jun 1997).*

JUST FOR YOU JANE (IRE) BHB 67f **RR 71f** 4612[7]
2 b f Petardia 8.2f **(58)** - Steffi (Precocious) 8.6f **(62)**
Form - 735423307
Record 1998 - 1st:0 2nd:1 3rd:3 Ran:9
Win Prizemoney £0 *Total Prizemoney* £2,240
1998 Turf 0-9: (6f 5, 7f 4) (sft, g-s 2, gd, g-f 2, frm 3)
Above-average filly, effective 6 to 7f, best at 7f, acts on g-f to frm, best on frm, often wears blinkers (effectively). Turf high 71 (began Jly). Consistent. **T J Naughton [0-9] The Awayday Partnership.*

JUST GIFTED RR 65f 4067[5]
2 b c Rudimentary (USA) 8.2f **(66)** - Parfait Amour **(48f)** (Clantime)
Form - 35
Record 1998 - 1st:0 2nd:0 3rd:1 Ran:2
Win Prizemoney £0 *Total Prizemoney* £824
1998 Turf 0-2: (5f, 6f) (g-f, frm)
Currently average colt. Turf high 63 (began Aug).
**R M Whitaker [0-2] Mrs C A Hodgetts.*

JUST GREY BHB 39f **RR 37f** 4250[8]
2 gr f Petong 7.6f **(58)** - Russell Creek (Sandy Creek) 8.9f **(59)**
Form - 808
Record 1998 - 1st:0 2nd:0 3rd:0 Ran:3
1998 Turf 0-3: (5f 2, 6f) (g-s, gd, frm)
Currently very moderate filly. Turf high 37 (began Aug).
**Miss L A Perratt [0-3] Clayton Bigley Partnership Ltd.*

JUST IN FUN (GER) RR 100f 5052a[1]
4 b/ f In The Wings 11.2f **(77)** - Just In Front (FR) (Alias Smith (USA)) 9.8f **(58)**
Form - 21
1998 Turf 1-1: (10f 1-1) (hvy 1-1)
Currently very useful filly. (1st run) - 1st of 11 giving 1lb to Naskhi (24 Oct Gelsenkirchen-Horst RF 5052a).
**H Blume in GER [1-2] Gestut Sommerberg.*

JUSTINIANUS (IRE) BHB 41f38a **RR 45f 38a** 5127[14]
6 ch h Try My Best (USA) 7.8f **(68)** - Justitia (Dunbeath (USA)) 7.8f **(70)**

Form - 550104404055070
Record 1998 - 1st:1 2nd:0 3rd:0 Ran:15
Pre1998 - 1st:1 2nd:3 3rd:8 Ran:44
Win Prizemoney £5,558 *Total Prizemoney* £12,638
Wins * 1998 Apr Bright (GD) H 6f 41 48 <
* 1997 *Feb Lingfi (STD) S 6f 44*
1998 Turf 1-12: (5f 2, 6f 1-8, 7f 2) (g-s 2, gd 1-4, g-f 2, frm 4) 1998 AW 0-3: (6f, 7f, 8f) (Equi 3)
Moderate horse, effective 6f, acts on gd to frm, has worn blinkers, likes left handed tracks, likes tight tracks. Turf high 49 - 4th of 17 getting 7lb from Step On Degas (22 May Brighton 6f frm RF 1389). AW high 36.
**J J Bridger [2-57] Exors of the late M R Pascall (from Andre Hermans in BEL [0-2] Jan 1996).*

JUST IN TIME BHB 89f **RR 85+f** 4515[P]
3 b c Night Shift (USA) 8.1f **(73)** - Future Past (USA) (Super Concorde (USA)) 10.9f **(66)**
Form - 0221P
Record 1998 - 1st:1 2nd:2 3rd:0 Ran:5
Pre1998 - 1st:0 2nd:1 3rd:0 Ran:1
Win Prizemoney £3,397 *Total Prizemoney* £8,823
Wins * 1998 Aug Goodwo (G-F) 9.9f 85+ <
1998 Turf 1-5: (8f, 9f, 10f 1-2, 12f) (gd 1-3, g-f, frm)
Scopey, useful colt, effective 7 to 10f, best at 10f, acts on gd to frm. Turf high 85 - 1st of 6 from Classic Manoeuvre (28 Aug Goodwood RF 3920). He showed ability in maidens, and hardly had to come off the bridle when getting off the mark at Goodwood in August. The saddle slipped on his last start.
**T G Mills [1-6] Mrs Pauline Merrick.*

JUST LOUI BHB 67f82a **RR 59f 82a** 495[7]
4 gr g Lugana Beach 7f **(63)** - Absaloui (Absalom) 7.2f **(58)**
Form - 46211017
Record 1998 - 1st:3 2nd:1 3rd:0 Ran:8
Pre1998 - 1st:5 2nd:4 3rd:1 Ran:27
Win Prizemoney £23,127 *Total Prizemoney* £28,520
Wins * 1998 *Mar Lingfi (STD) C 7f 77*
*** 1998** *Feb Lingfi (SLW) H 6f 72 82*
*** 1998** *Feb Lingfi (SLW) H 7f 68 81*
1997 *Jan Lingfi (STD) H 6f 78 83*
1996 *Dec Lingfi (STD) H 6f 78 89* <
1996 *Dec Wolver (STD) 7f 84*
1996 *Nov Lingfi (STD) C 6f 71*
1996 *May Wolver (STD) 5f 68*
1998 AW 3-8: (5f, 6f 1-2, 7f 2-4, 8f) (Equi 3-4, Fibr 4)
Unfurnished, decent gelding, effective 6 to 7f, best at 6f, acts on gd to g-f - acts on Equi, has worn blinkers (effectively), likes left handed tracks, excels at Lingfield. AW high 82 - 1st of 9 giving 3lb to Robo Magic (28 Feb Lingfield RF 0379) - also 1st of 10 giving 17lb to Mustang (26 Feb Lingfield RF 0369). He rather lost his way after winning at Lingfield in January '97. However, he rediscovered his best form in February this year with two good wins back on the Lingfield Equitrack within the space of three days. He did not seem to stay when tried over a mile at Wolverhampton, but successfully reverted to seven furlongs back at Lingfield. Effective when able to dominate.
**K R Burke [3-15] Nigel Shields (from W G M Turner [5-20] Jun 1997).*

JUST MAGIC BHB 42f **RR 36f** 3582[11]
3 b f Beveled (USA) 6.9f **(64)** - Kissimmee (FR) (Petingo) 11f **(72)**
Form - 750
Record 1998 - 1st:0 2nd:0 3rd:0 Ran:3
1998 Turf 0-3: (6f, 7f 2) (gd 3)
Light-framed, currently very moderate filly. Turf high 36 (began Jly). **M Blanshard [0-3] Mara Racing.*

JUST NAME IT (USA) BHB 82f **RR 78f** 4109[2]
2 b c Miswaki (USA) 8.1f **(81)** - Ibtikar (USA) (Private Account (USA)) 8.5f **(74)**
Form - 622
Record 1998 - 1st:0 2nd:2 3rd:0 Ran:3
Win Prizemoney £0 *Total Prizemoney* £2,260
1998 Turf 0-3: (6f, 7f, 8f) (g-f, frm 2)
Currently above-average colt. Turf high 78 (began Jly) - 2nd of 8 to Moutahddee (5 Spt Thirsk 8f frm RF 4109).
**Sir Michael Stoute [0-3] The Thoroughbred Corporation.*

JUST NOBBY BHB 40f **RR 45f** 5058[6]
3 b g Totem (USA) 5f **(38)** - Loving Doll (Godswalk (USA)) 7.3f **(58)**
Form - 07707406
Record 1998 - 1st:0 2nd:0 3rd:0 Ran:8
Pre1998 - 1st:0 2nd:0 3rd:0 Ran:5
Win Prizemoney £0 *Total Prizemoney* £250
1998 Turf 0-8: (6f, 7f 3, 8f 2, 9f, 11f) (sft, gd 2, g-f 2, frm 2, hrd)
Moderate gelding, has worn blinkers. Turf high 45. Inconsistent.
**Don Enrico Incisa [0-8] Don Enrico Incisa (from N Tinkler [0-5] Spt 1997).*

JUST ORANGE BHB 53f55a **RR 60f 55a** 3619[9]
2 ch gr g Never so Bold 7.1f **(62)** - Just Greenwich **(43f)** (Chilibang)
Form - 873540
Record 1998 - 1st:0 2nd:0 3rd:1 Ran:6
Win Prizemoney £0 *Total Prizemoney* £254
1998 Turf 0-4: (5f, 6f, 7f 2) (gd, g-f 2, frm) 1998 AW 0-2: (5f, 6f) (Fibr 2)
Average gelding, effective 6f, acts on gd. Turf high 60 - 3rd of 9 giving 5lb to Habibi (30 May Catterick 6f gd RF 1583). AW high 59.
**P D Evans [0-6] Mrs E A Dawson.*

JUST SIDIUM BHB 30f30a **RR 1f 30a** 103[8]
4 b f Nicholas (USA) 6.1f**(63)**-Frimley Dancer(Northern Tempest (USA))
Form - 78
Record 1998 - 1st:0 2nd:0 3rd:0 Ran:2
Pre1998 - 1st:0 2nd:0 3rd:1 Ran:2
Win Prizemoney £0 *Total Prizemoney* £297
1998 AW 0-2: (6f, 7f) (Equi, Fibr)
Unfurnished, very moderate filly. AW high 21.
**W G M Turner [0-2] John Hill (from C J Hill [0-2] Jun 1997).*

JUST SUNDAY BHB 47f **RR 46f** 2322[6]
2 ch f Then Again 7.4f **(52)** - Striking Image (IRE) (Flash of Steel) 7.2f **(53)**
Form - 505436
Record 1998 - 1st:0 2nd:0 3rd:1 Ran:6
Win Prizemoney £0 *Total Prizemoney* £225
1998 Turf 0-3: (5f 3) (g-s, gd, frm) 1998 AW 0-3: (5f 2, 7f) (Fibr 3)
Moderate filly. Turf high 46. AW high 49.
**W G M Turner [0-6] Woodmarsh Racing.*

JUST TESTING BHB 61f **RR 67f** 4450[6]
3 br f Sharpo 7.5f **(68)**-Antoinette Jane (Ile de Bourbon(USA))10.1f **(67)**
Form - 41006066
Record 1998 - 1st:1 2nd:0 3rd:0 Ran:8
Pre1998 - 1st:0 2nd:0 3rd:0 Ran:3
Win Prizemoney £3,450 *Total Prizemoney* £3,735
Wins * 1998 Jly Doncas (G-F) H 5f 58 67 <
1998 Turf 1-8: (5f 1-6, 6f 2) (g-s, gd 4, g-f 1-1, frm 2)
Neat, average filly, effective 5f, acts on gd to g-f. Turf high 67 - 1st of 18 from Wishbone Alley (29 Jly Doncaster RF 3196).
**J L Eyre [1-11] Clayton Bigley Partnership Ltd.*

JUSTUPYOURSTREET (IRE) BHB 75f **RR 72f** 4709[4]
2 b c Dolphin Street (FR) - Sure Flyer (IRE) (Sure Blade (USA)) 11.3f **(67)**
Form - 3873054
Record 1998 - 1st:0 2nd:0 3rd:2 Ran:7
Win Prizemoney £0 *Total Prizemoney* £2,083
1998 Turf 0-7: (5f, 6f, 7f 2, 8f 3) (sft, gd, g-f 2, frm 3)
Above-average colt, effective 8f, acts on frm. Turf high 72 (began Jly). **J J O'Neill [0-7] E A Brook.*

JUST VISITING BHB 57f **RR 61f** 755[14]
4 b f Superlative 8.8f **(57)** - Just Julia (Natroun (FR))
Form - 80

Record 1998 - 1st:0 2nd:0 3rd:0 Ran:2
Pre1998 - 1st:2 2nd:2 3rd:2 Ran:12
Win Prizemoney £6,170 *Total Prizemoney* £11,150
Wins 1996 Aug Ripon (GD) 6f 85 <
1996 *May Southw (STD) 5f 60*
1998 Turf 0-1: (8f) (g-s) 1998 AW 0-1: (5f) (Fibr)
Leggy, average filly. No form for a long time.
**B Hanbury [0-2] Mrs Rosemary Moszkowicz (from Capt J Wilson [2-12] Spt 1997).*

JUST WHISTLE BHB 40f44a **RR 40f 44a** 4375[17]
6 gr m Absalom 7.1f **(56)** - Aunt Blue (Blue Refrain)
Form - 0
Record 1998 - 1st:0 2nd:0 3rd:0 Ran:1
Pre1998 - 1st:0 2nd:1 3rd:0 Ran:8
Win Prizemoney £0 *Total Prizemoney* £1,204
1998 Turf 0-1: (16f) (frm)
Moderate mare.
**K A Ryan [0-1] J J H Walker (from Miss Kate Milligan [0-4] Jun 1997).*

JUST WIZ BHB 60f **RR 64tf** 5144[5]
2 b c Efisio 7.7f **(69)** - Jade Pet **(84df)** (Petong) 6.6f **(58)**
Form - 58005
Record 1998 - 1st:0 2nd:0 3rd:0 Ran:5
1998 Turf 0-5: (5f 2, 6f 2, 7f) (sft, gd 3, g-f)
Average colt, has worn blinkers. Turf high 64 (began Aug).
**Lord Huntingdon [0-5] Peter Crane.*

JUVENIA (USA) RR 104f 4725a[1]
2 br f Trempolino (USA) 11.9f **(77)** - Vintage (USA) (Foolish Pleasure (USA)) 8.9f **(72)**
Form - 21
1998 Turf 1-2: (8f 1-2) (sft 1-2)
Currently very useful filly. Turf high 104 (began Spt) - 1st of 11 from Crystal Downs (4 Oct Longchamp RF 4725a). She was comprehensively outpointed by Saytarra in the Prix d'Aumale, but capitalised on that filly's absence from the Prix Marcel Boussac, providing Criquette Head with her fourth winner in the last seven runnings of that Group One. Connections do not see her as a miler, and have mapped out a middle-distance campaign, comprising the Prix Vanteaux, Prix Saint-Alary and Prix de Diane. She is notably tough. **Mme C Head in FR [1-2] Wertheimer Brothers.*

JUWWI BHB 68f79a **RR 72f 79a** 5142[4]
4 ch g Mujtahid (USA) 7.4f **(69)** - Nouvelle Star (AUS) (Luskin Star (AUS)) 6.3f **(71)**
Form - 110000060353862824
Record 1998 - 1st:2 2nd:2 3rd:2 Ran:18
Pre1998 - 1st:1 2nd:2 3rd:0 Ran:5
Win Prizemoney £11,143 *Total Prizemoney* £23,737
Wins * 1998 *Apr Lingfi (STD) H 5f 70 80+* <
* 1998 *Mar Wolver (STD) S 5f 64+*
1996 Jun Newbur (G-F) 6f 79+
1998 Turf 0-15: (5f 3, 6f 8, 7f 4) (sft 2, g-s 2, gd 5, g-f 2, frm 4) 1998 AW 2-3: (5f 2-3) (Equi 1-1, Fibr 1-2)
Strong, decent gelding, effective 5f - acts on Equi, prefers left handed tracks. Turf high 72. AW high 80 - 1st of 8 giving 8lb to Nobalino (9 Apr Lingfield RF 0624). A useful two-year-old for Dick Hern, he changed hands for only 2,000 guineas afterwards, ending up with Milton Bradley, and made a successful debut for that stable in a five-furlong seller on the Wolverhampton Fibresand in March. He went on to win a much better race on the Lingfield Equitrack the following month, but has been held since.
**J M Bradley [2-18] J M Bradley (from Major W R Hern [1-5] Jly 1997).*

JUYUSH (USA) BHB 95f **RR 113f** 4798[5]
6 b h Silver Hawk (USA) 11.2f **(85)** - Silken Doll (USA) (Chieftain II) 10.4f **(75)**
Form - 5
Record 1998 - 1st:0 2nd:0 3rd:0 Ran:1
Pre1998 - 1st:4 2nd:2 3rd:4 Ran:15
Win Prizemoney £34,819 *Total Prizemoney* £70,795
Wins 1996 Mar Doncas (SFT) 12f 113 <
1995 Jun Ascot (FRM) 12f 93
1995 Mar Doncas (G-F) 8f 92+
1994 Jly Ascot (G-F) 7f 92+
1998 Turf 0-1: (12f) (sft)
Group-class horse.
**J A B Old [4-8] W E Sturt (from B W Hills [4-15] Jun 1996).*

KAAMEN (IRE) BHB 99f **RR 90f** 2084[6]
2 ch c Mujtahid (USA) 7.4f **(69)** - Zumurrudah (USA) (Spectacular Bid (USA)) 11.2f **(76)**
Form - 316
Record 1998 - 1st:1 2nd:0 3rd:1 Ran:3
Win Prizemoney £3,493 *Total Prizemoney* £3,968
Wins * **1998** May Newbur (GD) 5.2f 90 <
1998 Turf 1-3: (5f 1-3) (g-s, g-f 1-1, frm)
Currently useful colt. Turf high 90 - 1st of 11 from Inflite (27 May Newbury RF 1524). Won nicely at Newbury on his second start, but looked in need of another furlong when unplaced in the Norfolk. That proved to be that for the season.
**B Hanbury [1-3] Hamdan Al Maktoum.*

KABOOL RR 112f 3781a[1]
3 b c Groom Dancer (USA) 9.5f **(75)** - Sheroog (USA) (Shareef Dancer (USA)) 9.9f **(73)**
Form - 11
1998 Turf 2-2: (9f 1-1, 10f 1-1) (gd 2-2)
Currently Group-class colt. Turf high 112 (began Jly) - 1st of 6 from Xaar (15 Aug Deauville RF 3781a) - also 1st of 7 from Central Lobby (25 Jly Maisons-laffitte RF 3225a). He is most progressive and claimed a notable scalp when beating Xaar in Deauville. He can produce a smart turn-of-foot and is one to watch in 1999.
**N Clement in FR [2-2] Maktoum Al Maktoum.*

KABUKI (GER) RR 97f 2864a[1]
2 b f Dashing Blade 7.9f **(80)** - Kajaana (Esclavo (FR))
Form - 1
1998 Turf 1-1: (6f 1-1) (g-f 1-1)
Currently very useful filly. (1st run) - 1st of 9 getting 3lb from Solitary Dancer (12 Jly San Siro RF 2864a).
**H Blume in GER [1-1] F Steinebach.*

KADAKA (IRE) BHB 106f **RR 108f** 4186[2]
3 b f Sadler's Wells (USA) 11.3f **(87)** - Kadissya (USA) (Blushing Groom (FR)) 10.3f **(76)**
Form - 41232
Record 1998 - 1st:1 2nd:2 3rd:1 Ran:5
Win Prizemoney £3,720 *Total Prizemoney* £17,004
Wins * **1998** Jly Yarmou (GD) 11.5f 81 <
1998 Turf 1-5: (10f, 11f 1-1, 12f 2, 15f) (gd, g-f, frm 1-3)
Scopey, Pattern-class filly. Turf high 108 - 2nd of 9 getting 15lb from Delilah (9 Spt Doncaster 15f gd RF 4186). She does not have the ability of he half-brother, the 1988 Derby winner Kahyasi, but has inherited all of her family's will to win. Touched off after a battle royal in the Park Hill Stakes, she stays a mile and three-quarters, preferably on soft ground, and put up her best performance when ridden positively. **L M Cumani [1-5] H H Aga Khan.*

KADAMANN (IRE) BHB 65f **RR 65f** 4590[10]
6 b g Doyoun 10.7f **(69)** - Kadissya (USA) (Blushing Groom (FR)) 10.3f **(76)**
Form - 6470
Record 1998 - 1st:0 2nd:0 3rd:0 Ran:4
Pre1998 - 1st:0 2nd:0 3rd:0 Ran:2
Win Prizemoney £0 *Total Prizemoney* £294
1998 Turf 0-4: (10f 2, 11f, 12f) (gd, g-f, frm 2)
Average gelding. Turf high 65 (began Aug).
**Mrs A J Perrett [0-5] Sir Eric Parker (from R Akehurst [0-3] Jun 1996).*

KADIR RR 88f 3698[8]
3 b br c Unfuwain (USA) 11.4f **(74)** - Rafif (USA) (Riverman (USA)) 9.1f **(76)**
Form - 2228
Record 1998 - 1st:0 2nd:3 3rd:0 Ran:4
Pre1998 - 1st:0 2nd:0 3rd:0 Ran:1
Win Prizemoney £0 *Total Prizemoney* £5,831
1998 Turf 0-4: (12f 2, 14f 2) (gd 3, g-f)
Lengthy, useful colt. Turf high 88 - 2nd of 11 getting 1lb from Generosity (1 Aug Goodwood 14f gd RF 3258). He finished runner-up on three consecutive occasions in the summer, but he stays well and deserves to get his head in front.
**M P Tregoning [0-4] Hamdan Al Maktoum (from S bin Suroor [0-1] Oct 1997).*

KAFFIR (IRE) RR 92f 3059a[2]
4 b c Alzao (USA) 9.8f **(73)** - Kenitra (ITY) (Head for Heights) 9.6f **(55)**
Form - 2
1998 Turf 0-1: (8f) (g-f)
Currently useful colt. (1st run) - 2nd of 7 to Ravier (19 Jly San Siro 8f g-f RF 3059a). *G Verricelli in ITY [1-2].*

KAFHANEE (USA) RR 74f 5071[3]
2 ch f Seeking the Gold (USA) 7.4f **(80)** - Baya (USA) (Nureyev (USA)) 8.7f **(78)**
Form - 3
Record 1998 - 1st:0 2nd:0 3rd:1 Ran:1
Win Prizemoney £0 *Total Prizemoney* £614
1998 Turf 0-1: (7f) (gd)
Currently above-average filly. *D R Loder [0-1] Sheikh Mohammed.*

KAFI (USA) RR 59f 4541[12]
2 b c Gulch (USA) 9.6f **(79)** - Nonoalca (FR) (Nonoalco (USA)) 8.5f **(66)**
Form - 0
Record 1998 - 1st:0 2nd:0 3rd:0 Ran:1
1998 Turf 0-1: (8f) (frm)
Currently fair colt. *M P Tregoning [0-1] Hamdan Al Maktoum.*

KAFIL (USA) BHB 44f62a **RR 36f 62a** 5003[1]
4 b br g Housebuster (USA) 7f **(81)** - Alchaasibiyeh (USA) (Seattle Slew (USA)) 9.4f **(76)**
Form - 126658032760260001
Record 1998 - 1st:1 2nd:2 3rd:1 Ran:15
Pre1998 - 1st:1 2nd:3 3rd:1 Ran:12
Win Prizemoney £5,408 *Total Prizemoney* £9,757
Wins * **1998** *Oct Lingfi (STD) 7f 67*
1997 Nov Lingfi (STD) 8f 68 <
1998 Turf 0-4: (8f 2, 9f 2) (sft, gd, g-f, frm) 1998 AW 1-11: (7f 1-1, 8f 6, 10f, 12f 2, 13f) (Equi 1-11)
Scopey, average gelding, effective 7 to 10f, best at 8f, acts on frm - acts on Equi, likes left handed tracks, favours tight tracks. Turf high 36. AW high 67 - 1st of 16 giving 2lb to Comeoutofthefog (26 Oct Lingfield RF 5003). Inconsistent.
J J Bridger [1-16] Exors of the late M R Pascall (from G L Moore [1-8] Dec 1997).

KAGOSHIMA (IRE) RR 77f 3078[6]
3 b c Shirley Heights 12.1f **(76)** - Kashteh (IRE) (Green Desert (USA)) 8.6f **(78)**
Form - 6
Record 1998 - 1st:0 2nd:0 3rd:0 Ran:1
1998 Turf 0-1: (12f) (frm)
Well made, currently above-average colt.
L M Cumani [0-1] Abdullah Saeed Bul Hab.

KAGSI BHB 36f **RR 32f** 4200[19]
3 br f King's Signet (USA) 7f **(51)** - Azaiyma (Corvaro (USA)) 9f **(53)**
Form - 000
Record 1998 - 1st:0 2nd:0 3rd:0 Ran:3
Pre1998 - 1st:0 2nd:0 3rd:0 Ran:2
1998 Turf 0-3: (5f, 7f 2) (g-s, gd, frm)
Unfurnished, very moderate filly. Turf high 32.
D C O'Brien [0-5] Graham Pasquill.

KAHAL BHB 117f **RR 121f** 4849[3]
4 b c Machiavellian (USA) 9.8f **(83)** - Just a Mirage (Green Desert (USA)) 8.6f **(78)**
Form - 470623
Record 1998 - 1st:0 2nd:1 3rd:1 Ran:6
Pre1998 - 1st:3 2nd:2 3rd:0 Ran:8
Win Prizemoney £72,757 *Total Prizemoney* £122,910
Wins * 1997 Oct Newmar (GD) G2 7f 114 <
* 1997 Spt Goodwo (GD) 7f 101++
1996 Spt Ascot (GD) 7f 98+
1998 Turf 0-6: (6f 2, 7f 3, 8f) (g-s, gd 2, g-f, frm 2)
Strong, very high-class colt, effective 7 to 8f, best at 7f, acts on gd to frm. Turf high 121 - 3rd of 10 to Decorated Hero (17 Oct Newmarket 7f gd RF 4849). Consistent. A grand-looking individual, he failed to stay the mile in the Lockinge on his return, and was well beaten when dropped to six furlongs at Royal Ascot, where the soft ground was against him, in the July Cup and in France. He performed much better in the autumn back over seven furlongs, being just touched off in the Challenge Stakes. He has plenty of ability and, if the key can be found, he can put a slightly disappointing 1998 behind him.
S bin Suroor [2-11] Godolphin (from E A L Dunlop [1-3] Oct 1996).

KAHTAN BHB 105f **RR 103f** 5067[6]
3 b c Nashwan (USA) 10.3f **(79)** - Harmless Albatross (Pas de Seul) 9.1f **(67)**
Form - 23136
Record 1998 - 1st:1 2nd:1 3rd:2 Ran:5
Pre1998 - 1st:1 2nd:0 3rd:0 Ran:2
Win Prizemoney £14,206 *Total Prizemoney* £24,046
Wins * **1998** Jly Newmar (FRM) L 14.8f 103 <
* 1997 Oct Newcas (G-F) 8f 80+
1998 Turf 1-5: (12f 2, 15f 1-2, 16f) (gd, g-f 2, frm 1-2)
Workmanlike, very useful colt, effective 12 to 15f, best at 15f, acts on gd to frm. Turf high 103 - 3rd of 6 to Dark Moondancer (20 Jun Ascot 12f g-f RF 2137) - also 1st of 5 from Capri (9 Jly Newmarket RF 2647). He has a rounded action, but goes well on fast ground and put up a good performance to outstay Capri in a Listed event at Newmarket in July. He failed to repeat that form on his two subsequent starts, and may not be easy to place.
J L Dunlop [2-7] Hamdan Al Maktoum.

KAIBO BHB 81f **RR 80f** 4185[13]
2 ch c Safawan 6.6f **(60)** - Jay Gee Ell (Vaigly Great) 7f **(58)**
Form - 32110
Record 1998 - 1st:2 2nd:1 3rd:1 Ran:5
Win Prizemoney £7,424 *Total Prizemoney* £8,539
Wins * **1998** Aug Haydoc (GD) 6f 80 <
* **1998** Jly Bright (G-F) 7f 80 <
1998 Turf 2-5: (6f 1-2, 7f 1-3) (gd 1-2, g-f 1-1, frm 2)
Decent colt. Turf high 80 - 1st of 6 giving 6lb to Thrust (7 Aug Haydock RF 3433) - also 1st of 13 from Deploy Venture (23 Jly Brighton RF 3037). *R Hannon [2-5] Mrs D M Wight.*

KAID (IRE) BHB 60f **RR 61f** 4265[13]
3 b g Alzao (USA) 9.8f **(73)** - Very Charming (USA) (Vaguely Noble) 10.1f **(72)**
Form - 0430
Record 1998 - 1st:0 2nd:0 3rd:1 Ran:4
Win Prizemoney £0 *Total Prizemoney* £752
1998 Turf 0-4: (8f, 10f 3) (gd 2, g-f, frm)
Workmanlike, average gelding. Turf high 61.
Mrs Barbara Waring [0-1] Joy and Valentine Feerick (from E A L Dunlop [0-3] Jun 1998).

KAILEY GODDESS (USA) BHB 56f56a **RR 55f 56a** 4640[6]
5 b h Nureyev (USA) 8.4f **(84)** - Gay Senorita (USA) (Raise A Native) 11.2f **(69)**
Form - 04230335046
Record 1998 - 1st:0 2nd:1 3rd:3 Ran:11
Pre1998 - 1st:0 2nd:0 3rd:0 Ran:4
Win Prizemoney £0 *Total Prizemoney* £2,275
1998 Turf 0-2: (7f, 8f) (g-s, gd) 1998 AW 0-9: (7f 2, 8f 5, 9f, 11f) (Fibr 9)
Average colt, effective 7 to 8f, best at 8f - acts on Fibr, often wears blinkers (extremely effectively), favours left handed tracks. Turf high 24. AW high 64 - 3rd of 5 giving 8lb to Cheerful Groom (10 Jly Wolverhampton 8f Fibr RF 2694). Despite the name, he is an entire, and has become expensive to follow.
R W Armstrong [0-15] Po Shing Woo.

KALA BHB 47f **RR 50f** 5006[16]
3 b f Alhijaz 7.7f **(57)** - Flushing Meadow (USA) (Raise A Native) 11.2f **(69)**
Form - 54000
Record 1998 - 1st:0 2nd:0 3rd:0 Ran:5
Win Prizemoney £0 *Total Prizemoney* £259
1998 Turf 0-5: (8f 3, 9f, 10f) (sft, gd, g-f 2, frm)
Leggy, fair filly. Turf high 60. *V Soane [0-5] David Bayliss.*

KALAHARI FERRARI BHB 64f **RR 65f** 3680[6]
2 ch g Clantime 6.6f **(57)** - Royal Agnes (Royal Palace) 9f **(56)**
Form - 444006
Record 1998 - 1st:0 2nd:0 3rd:0 Ran:6
Win Prizemoney £0 *Total Prizemoney* £676
1998 Turf 0-6: (5f 2, 6f 4) (sft, g-s, gd 2, g-f, frm)

Average gelding. Turf high 65. **J Berry [0-6] Chris & Antonia Deuters.*

KALAHARI SUNSHINE (IRE) BHB 28f **RR 12f** 1300^{6}

3 b f Lashkari 13.1f **(52)** - Inneen Alainn (Prince Hansel)
Form - 406

Record	**1998** -	1st:0	2nd:0	3rd:0	Ran:3

1998 Turf 0-3: (11f, 12f, 14f) (g-s, gd, g-f)
Small, currently poor filly. Turf high 12.
**R M McKellar [0-3] Mrs S J Nicol.*

* 1995	Aug Catter	(G-F)	H	5f	42	43	
* 1995	*Mar Lingfi*	*(STD)*	*H*	*5f*	*63*	*65*	
* 1994	*Dec Southw*	*(STD)*	*H*	*5f*	*58*	*61*	
* 1994	*Mar Lingfi*	*(STD)*	*H*	*5f*	*54*	*52*	
* 1994	*Mar Lingfi*	*(STD)*	*H*	*5f*	*46*	*49*	

1998 Turf 0-3: (5f 3) (gd, frm 2) 1998 AW 0-1: (5f) (Fibr)
Little account gelding, effective 5 to 6f, best at 5f - acts on AW, best on Fibr, mostly wears blinkers, prefers left handed tracks, prefers tight tracks. Turf high 27 (began Aug). Inconsistent.
**D W Chapman [14-143] J M Chapman.*

Kahtan did well when stepped up in trip

KALAMATA BHB 43f65a **RR 40f 65a** 126^{5}

6 ch h Kalaglow 11.2f **(67)** - Good Try (Good Bond) 9.2f **(54)**
Form - 845

Record	**1998** -	1st:0	2nd:0	3rd:0	Ran:1
	Pre1998 -	1st:6	2nd:2	3rd:1	Ran:20

Win Prizemoney £13,994 *Total Prizemoney* £16,379

Wins								
* 1997	*Jun Southw*	*(STD)*	*C*	*14f*		*78*		
* 1997	*May Southw*	*(STD)*	*H*	*14f*	*54*	*79+*	<	
* 1997	*May Southw*	*(STD)*	*H*	*14f*	*54*	*66+*		
* 1997	*Apr Southw*	*(STD)*	*C*	*16f*		*53*		
* 1997	*Feb Southw*	*(STD)*		*12f*		*59*		
* 1995	*Nov Wolver*	*(STD)*		*12f*		*75*		

1998 AW 0-1: (12f) (Fibr)
Fair horse, effective 14f - acts on Fibr, favours tight tracks. Inconsistent. Has done very well on the All-Weather in '97, especially at Southwell. He is one of comparatively few horses to be truly effective over long distances on Fibresand, and as such, will continue to win races of that type. He is nowhere near as effective on turf. **J A Glover [6-17] B H Farr (from A C Stewart [0-4] Oct 1995).*

KALAR BHB 31f45a **RR 27f 45a** 3938^{13}

9 b g Kabour 6.1f **(36)** - Wind And Reign (Tumble Wind (USA)) 7.5f **(57)**
Form - 000670

Record	**1998** -	1st:0	2nd:0	3rd:0	Ran:4
	Pre1998 -	1st:14	2nd:24	3rd:12	Ran:139

Win Prizemoney £39,080 *Total Prizemoney* £67,811

Wins							
* 1997	*Feb Lingfi*	*(STD)*	*C*	*5f*		*67*	
* 1997	*Jan Wolver*	*(STD)*	*C*	*5f*		*60*	
* 1996	*Dec Southw*	*(SLW)*	*H*	*6f*	*70*	*69*	<
* 1996	*Nov Lingfi*	*(STD)*	*H*	*5f*	*61*	*63*	
* 1996	Aug Catter	(G-F)	H	5f	48	49	
* 1995	Aug Thirsk	(G-F)	H	5f	47	45	

KALA SUNRISE BHB 83f **RR 80f** 2365^{9}

5 ch h Kalaglow 11.2f **(67)** - Belle of the Dawn (Bellypha) 9.8f **(73)**
Form - 0650

Record	**1998** -	1st:0	2nd:0	3rd:0	Ran:4
	Pre1998 -	1st:2	2nd:3	3rd:2	Ran:30

Win Prizemoney £11,800 *Total Prizemoney* £25,030

Wins							
* 1996	Oct York	(GD)	H	7.9f	83	86	<
* 1995	Apr Pontef	(FRM)		5f		77t	

1998 Turf 0-4: (8f 4) (gd 2, frm 2)
Decent colt, effective 8f, acts on gd to g-f, best on gd, likes tight tracks. Turf high 80. Consistent. **C Smith [2-34] A E Needham.*

KALATOS (GER) RR 111f $4470h^{2}$

6 ch h Big Shuffle (USA) - Kardia (GER) (Mister Rock's (GER))
Form - 362
1998 Turf 0-3: (8f, 9f, 10f) (gd 3)
Group-class horse, effective 8 to 10f, acts on sft to gd, best on gd, and excels at Dortmund. Turf high 110 (1st run) - 3rd of 9 giving 15lb to Emilio Romano (21 Jun Dortmund 9f gd RF 2285a). He was well ridden when narrowly beaten at Frankfurt in September, but is finding life tough in Group races.
**A Wohler in GER [1-12] Frau R & D von Mitzlaff.*

KALDOU STAR RR 113f $1915a^{2}$

4 ch c Kaldoun (FR) 9.9f **(84)** - Loisaida (FR) (Sicyos (USA))
Form - 362
1998 Turf 0-3: (8f 3) (hvy, sft, g-s)
Group-class colt, effective 8f, acts on hvy to gd. Turf high 113 - 2nd of 6 getting 3lb from Jim And Tonic (6 Jun Maisons-laffitte 8f sft RF 1915a). Consistent. Game and genuine, he goes well from off a fast pace. **E Lellouche in FR [2-9] J C Seroul.*

KALIANA (IRE) BHB 113f **RR 114+f** 1961[4]
4 b f Slip Anchor 12.7f **(75)** - Kadissya (USA) (Blushing Groom (FR)) 10.3f **(76)**
Form - 4
Record 1998 - 1st:0 2nd:0 3rd:0 Ran:1
Pre1998 - 1st:3 2nd:1 3rd:0 Ran:5
Win Prizemoney £42,500 *Total Prizemoney* £46,796
Wins * 1997 Oct Newbur (G-S) G3 12f 114+ <
* 1997 Aug York (GD) L 11.9f 109
* 1997 Jly Chepst (G-S) 10.2f 81
1998 Turf 0-1: (12f) (gd)
Neat, Group-class filly, effective 12f, acts on gd to g-f, best on gd. A most progressive filly at three, winner of the St Simon Stakes at Newbury, she was a close fourth at Leicester on her return but failed to reappear. **L M Cumani [3-6] H H Aga Khan.*

KALIDASA (USA) BHB 100f **RR 93f** 4411[1]
2 b f Nureyev (USA) 8.4f **(84)** - Aunt Pearl (USA) (Seattle Slew (USA)) 9.4f **(76)**
Form - 262221
Record 1998 - 1st:1 2nd:4 3rd:0 Ran:6
Win Prizemoney £4,289 *Total Prizemoney* £16,505
Wins * **1998** Spt Warwic (G-F) 7f 84 <
1998 Turf 1-6: (5f, 6f 2, 7f 1-2, 8f) (gd 2, g-f, frm 1-3)
Useful filly, effective 5 to 8f, acts on gd to frm, best on gd. Turf high 93 - 2nd of 6 to Elhida (28 Jly Goodwood 6f gd RF 3167) - also 1st of 17 from Tattling (22 Spt Warwick RF 4411). She finished runner-up behind some useful sorts in four of her first five starts, including in the May Hill, but made hard work of landing the odds in a Warwick maiden on her final outing.
**P W Chapple-Hyam [1-6] R E Sangster.*

KALIMAT BHB 60f64a **RR 62f 64a** 109[4]
4 b f Be My Guest (USA) 10.2f **(66)** - Kantado (Saulingo) 6.2f **(53)**
Form - 144
Record 1998 - 1st:0 2nd:0 3rd:0 Ran:2
Pre1998 - 1st:1 2nd:5 3rd:1 Ran:12
Win Prizemoney £2,294 *Total Prizemoney* £7,455
Wins * 1997 *Dec Lingfi (STD) 8f 47+* <
1998 AW 0-2: (7f, 8f) (Equi 2)
Leggy, average filly, effective 7 to 8f, best at 8f, acts on gd to frm - acts on AW, has worn blinkers, favours tight tracks, and excels at Southwell. AW high 65 (1st run) - 4th of 9 giving 1lb to Davis Rock (6 Jan Lingfield 7f Equi RF 0036). Consistent.
**W Jarvis [1-14] A Foustok.*

KALININI (USA) BHB 66f **RR 67f** 4112[14]
4 ch g Seattle Dancer (USA) 10.1f **(74)** - Kaiserfahrt (GER) (Frontal) 6.4f **(64)**
Form - 57470
Record 1998 - 1st:0 2nd:0 3rd:0 Ran:5
Pre1998 - 1st:0 2nd:0 3rd:1 Ran:6
Win Prizemoney £0 *Total Prizemoney* £1,815
1998 Turf 0-5: (7f, 9f 2, 12f, 14f) (gd 2, g-f, frm 2)
Lengthy, average gelding, effective 9 to 14f, acts on gd to frm, favours tight tracks. Turf high 67 - 4th of 10 giving 5lb to Robin Lane (10 Jly Hamilton 9f frm RF 2683).
**R A Fahey [0-5] C H McGhie (from L M Cumani [0-6] Jly 1997).*

KALINKA (IRE) BHB 80f70a **RR 85f 70a** 226[7]
4 b f Soviet Star (USA) 8.6f **(74)** - Tralthee (USA) (Tromos) 11.3f **(72)**
Form - 7
Record 1998 - 1st:0 2nd:0 3rd:0 Ran:1
Pre1998 - 1st:1 2nd:1 3rd:1 Ran:9
Win Prizemoney £2,738 *Total Prizemoney* £8,629
Wins 1996 Jly Warwic (G-F) 7f 68+ <
1998 AW 0-1: (10f) (Equi)
Workmanlike, useful filly, effective 8 to 9f, acts on gd to g-f, has worn blinkers. Consistent.
**C R Egerton [0-3] Elite Racing Club (from P F I Cole [1-9] Spt 1997).*

KALUANA COURT RR 9f 4641[9]
2 b f Batshoof 9.5f **(66)** - Fairfields Cone (Celtic Cone) 9.8f **(43)**
Form - 0
Record 1998 - 1st:0 2nd:0 3rd:0 Ran:1
1998 Turf 0-1: (6f) (g-f)
Currently very poor filly. **R Dickin [0-1] Derek & Cheryl Holder.*

KAMEEZ (IRE) BHB 71f **RR 72df** 2675[4]
3 ch f Arazi (USA) 9.2f **(74)** - Kalikala (Darshaan) 9.9f **(84)**
Form - 314
Record 1998 - 1st:1 2nd:0 3rd:1 Ran:3
Pre1998 - 1st:0 2nd:0 3rd:1 Ran:2
Win Prizemoney £3,288 *Total Prizemoney* £4,571
Wins * **1998** Jly Redcar (G-S) H 11f 69 72 <
1998 Turf 1-2: (11f 1-1, 12f) (gd 1-1, frm) 1998 AW 0-1: (12f) (Fibr)
Unfurnished, above-average filly. Turf high 72 (1st run) (began Jly) - 1st of 14 giving 11lb to Smart Spirit (1 Jly Redcar RF 2453).
**M Johnston [1-5] Ali Saeed.*

KANAWA BHB 28f40a **RR 33f 40a** 4150[8]
4 b f Beveled (USA) 6.9f **(64)** - Kiri Te (Liboi (USA))
Form - 4808
Record 1998 - 1st:0 2nd:0 3rd:0 Ran:4
Pre1998 - 1st:0 2nd:0 3rd:0 Ran:8
1998 Turf 0-4: (10f 3, 11f) (g-f 2, frm 2)
Light-framed, very moderate filly. Turf high 33 (began Aug).
**A P Jones [0-12] The Lambourn Racing Club.*

KANGAROO ISLAND (IRE) BHB 86f **RR 79f** 5154a[6]
2 b c Turtle Island (IRE) - Duly Elected (Persian Bold) 9.3f **(66)**
Form - 88136
Record 1998 - 1st:1 2nd:0 3rd:1 Ran:5
Win Prizemoney £2,859 *Total Prizemoney* £3,391
Wins * **1998** Spt Warwic (G-F) 6f 79 <
1998 Turf 1-5: (6f 1-2, 7f 2, 8f) (hvy, sft, gd, frm 1-2)
Above-average colt. Turf high 79 (began Aug) - also 1st of 13 giving 1lb to Kee Ring (22 Spt Warwick RF 4413).
**P W Chapple-Hyam [1-5].*

KANTONE (IRE) BHB 42f30a **RR 43f 30a** 401[8]
3 ch g Petardia 8.2f **(58)** - Green Life (Green Desert (USA)) 8.6f **(78)**
Form - 8088048
Record 1998 - 1st:0 2nd:0 3rd:0 Ran:7
Pre1998 - 1st:0 2nd:0 3rd:0 Ran:5
Win Prizemoney £0 *Total Prizemoney* £261
1998 AW 0-7: (5f, 6f 2, 7f 2, 8f, 9f) (Equi 3, Fibr 4)
Strong, moderate gelding, often wears blinkers. AW high 20.
**P D Evans [0-4] B Scott (from R Ingram [0-3] Jan 1998).*

KANZ PRIDE (USA) BHB 52f **RR 63f** 4356[16]
3 ch f Lion Cavern (USA) 7.5f **(74)** - Kanz (USA) (The Minstrel (CAN)) 10f **(72)**
Form - 580
Record 1998 - 1st:0 2nd:0 3rd:0 Ran:3
1998 Turf 0-3: (8f 2, 10f) (g-f, frm 2)
Workmanlike, currently average filly. Turf high 63 (began Aug).
**B W Hills [0-3] D J Deer.*

KANZ WOOD (USA) BHB 71f **RR 75f** 4204[8]
2 ch c Woodman (USA) 9.7f **(77)** - Kanz (USA) (The Minstrel (CAN)) 10f **(72)**
Form - 53008
Record 1998 - 1st:0 2nd:0 3rd:1 Ran:5
Win Prizemoney £0 *Total Prizemoney* £887
1998 Turf 0-5: (6f, 7f 2, 8f 2) (g-s, gd, g-f, frm 2)
Above-average colt. Turf high 75 - 9th of 12 getting 5lb from Pilot's Harbour (28 Aug Newmarket 8f frm RF 3932). Last of five on his debut but stayed on nicely in a decent maiden next time. Rather disappointing since. **W R Muir [0-5] D J Deer.*

KARADENI (IRE) BHB 20f31a **RR 19f 31a** 3887[6]
4 gr g Linamix (FR) 8.2f **(64)** - Karaferya (USA) (Green Dancer (USA)) 10.3f **(74)**
Form - 86705070086
Record 1998 - 1st:0 2nd:0 3rd:0 Ran:11
1998 Turf 0-2: (17f, 18f) (gd 2) 1998 AW 0-9: (8f, 9f 2, 14f 3, 15f, 16f 2) (Fibr 9)
Moderate gelding. Turf high 19 (began Jly). AW high 45.
**R Hollinshead [0-12] Mrs Jane Galpin.*

KARAKIA (IRE) BHB 87f **RR 85f** 3992[2]
4 b f Sadler's Wells (USA) 11.3f **(87)** - Kissagram (USA) (Alysheba (USA)) 9f **(84)**
Form - 125442

Record 1998 - 1st:1 2nd:2 3rd:0 Ran:6
Pre1998 - 1st:1 2nd:2 3rd:1 Ran:5
Win Prizemoney £7,047 *Total Prizemoney* £19,375
Wins * **1998** Jun Beverl (G-S) H 9.9f 75 78 <
1997 Aug Redcar (FRM) 9f 73+
1998 Turf 1-6: (10f 1-4, 12f 2) (gd 1-1, g-f 2, frm 3)
Scopey, useful filly, effective 10 to 12f, best at 10f, acts on gd to frm, best on g-f. Turf high 85 - 2nd of 12 giving 8lb to Light Step (31 Aug Newcastle 10f frm RF 3992) - also 1st of 6 giving 28lb to Warning Reef (10 Jun Beverley RF 1869). Consistent. Formerly with Gosden, she defied 10st to win first time out at Beverley and lost little in defeat next time. A staying-on fifth in the John Smith's Cup at York, she was touched off in a Listed race on her final run.
**S P C Woods [1-6] Mrs Luciana Moretti (from J H M Gosden [1-5] Oct 1997).*

KARAKUL (IRE) BHB 52f RR 62f 4337[12]
2 ch f Persian Bold 10f **(69)** - Cindy's Baby (Bairn (USA)) 7.7f **(59)**
Form - 07031680
Record 1998 - 1st:1 2nd:0 3rd:1 Ran:8
Win Prizemoney £2,571 *Total Prizemoney* £2,883
Wins * **1998** Jly Bright (GD) C 7f 62 <
1998 Turf 1-8: (5f 2, 6f 2, 7f 1-3, 8f) (gd 1-2, g-f 3, frm 3)
Average filly, effective 7f, acts on gd. Turf high 62 - 1st of 8 giving 4lb to Coral Reef (14 Jly Brighton RF 2778).
**M J Fetherston-Godley [1-8] The Kennet House Partnership.*

KARAMEG (IRE) BHB 71f RR 71f 4856[12]
2 b f Danehill (USA) 9.1f **(79)** - House of Queens (IRE) (King of Clubs) 7.1f **(57)**
Form - 740
Record 1998 - 1st:0 2nd:0 3rd:0 Ran:3
Win Prizemoney £0 *Total Prizemoney* £228
1998 Turf 0-3: (6f 2, 7f) (sft, gd, g-f)
Currently above-average filly. Turf high 71 (began Spt) - 4th of 10 to Resalah (6 Oct Redcar 6f g-f RF 4673).
**P W Harris [0-3] and Mrs G Knight.*

KARASI (IRE) BHB 95f RR 92f 4841[5]
3 b c Kahyasi 12.9f **(74)** - Karamita (Shantung) 9.8f **(64)**
Form - 024711135
Record 1998 - 1st:3 2nd:1 3rd:1 Ran:9
Win Prizemoney £18,411 *Total Prizemoney* £22,799
Wins * **1998** Spt York (GD) H 13.9f 90 92 <
* **1998** Aug Ripon (G-F) H 12.3f 85 89
* **1998** Aug Bright (FRM) 11.9f 83
1998 Turf 3-9: (8f, 9f, 10f, 12f 2-3, 13f, 14f 1-2)(sft, g-s, g-f 2-5, frm 1-2)
Scopey, useful colt, effective 12 to 14f, best at 12f, acts on g-f to frm, best on g-f, often wears blinkers (extremely effectively). Turf high 92 - also 1st of 14 getting 1lb from Totem Dancer (2 Spt York RF 4054). Consistent. A half-brother to Kartajana and unraced at two, he showed ability in his early starts but did not get off the mark until landing a bad Brighton maiden by a distance. That win must have boosted his confidence, because he went on to complete a hat-trick in much better company before the Handicapper caught up with him. Sold for 95,000 gns in the autumn to race in Australia. **Sir Michael Stoute [3-9] H H Aga Khan.*

KAREFREE KATIE (USA) BHB 65f58a RR 67f 58a 5141[6]
3 b f Lac Ouimet (USA) 8.1f **(76)** - Dame Cecilia (USA) (Vaguely Noble) 10.1f **(72)**
Form - 26
Record 1998 - 1st:0 2nd:1 3rd:0 Ran:2
Win Prizemoney £0 *Total Prizemoney* £1,160
1998 Turf 0-2: (10f 2) (g-s, gd)
Scopey, currently average filly. Turf high 67 (1st run) (began Oct) - 2nd of 7 getting 5lb from Father Krismas (21 Oct Nottingham 10f g-s RF 4926). **M Johnston [0-2] Lucayan Stud.*

KARENARAGON BHB 35f40a RR 20f 40a 3408[10]
3 b f Aragon 7.7f **(58)** - Rosy Sunset (IRE) (Red Sunset) 8.2f **(63)**
Form - 70
Record 1998 - 1st:0 2nd:0 3rd:0 Ran:2
Pre1998 - 1st:0 2nd:0 3rd:1 Ran:5
Win Prizemoney £0 *Total Prizemoney* £259
1998 Turf 0-2: (7f, 8f) (g-f, frm)
Neat, very moderate filly, has worn blinkers. Turf high 20 (began Jly). **Ronald Thompson [0-7] Allan Howling.*

KAREYMAH RR 92+f 4080a[1]
2 ch f Zafonic (USA) 9f **(83)** - Pastorale (Nureyev (USA)) 8.7f **(78)**
Form - 111
Record 1998 - 1st:3 2nd:0 3rd:0 Ran:3
Win Prizemoney £36,303 *Total Prizemoney* £36,303
Wins * **1998** Aug Deauvi (GD) G3 7f 92+ <
* **1998** Aug Newmar (G-F) L 7f 87+
* **1998** Jly Newmar (G-F) 7f 81+
1998 Turf 3-3: (7f 3-3) (gd 1-1, frm 1-1, hrd 1-1)
Currently useful filly. Turf high 92 (began Jly) - 1st of 6 from Stella Berine (30 Aug Deauville RF 4080a) - also 1st of 5 from Etizaaz (8 Aug Newmarket RF 3470). Looked a smart filly in the making when winning a maiden on the July Course and followed up over course and distance in a Listed race. Confirmed herself a high-class performer when scoring in a Group Three at Deauville on her third start, and has genuine classic aspirations.
**D R Loder [3-3] Sheikh Ahmed Al Maktoum.*

KARINSKA BHB 39f53a RR 48f 53a 4656[13]
8 b m Master Willie 9.2f **(67)** - Kaiserchronik (GER) (Cortez (GER)) 8.6f **(75)**
Form - 0808000
Record 1998 - 1st:0 2nd:0 3rd:0 Ran:7
Pre1998 - 1st:10 2nd:6 3rd:7 Ran:82
Win Prizemoney £36,988 *Total Prizemoney* £50,001
Wins * 1997 Spt Nottin (GD) H 8.2f 57 63
* 1997 Jly Yarmou (G-F) H 10.1f 56 55
* 1997 Jly Yarmou (G-S) H 7f 51 49
* 1995 Jun Windso (GD) H 8.3f 59 60
* 1995 Jun Catter (GD) H 7f 54 56
* 1995 Apr Thirsk (GD) H 8f 50 53
1998 Turf 0-7: (7f 2, 8f, 10f 3, 12f) (g-s, gd 3, g-f 3)
Moderate mare, effective 8 to 10f, best at 8f, acts on gd to frm, likes left handed tracks. Turf high 48 (began Jly).
**M C Chapman [10-92] Geoff Whiting (from Sir Mark Prescott [1-6] Jun 1993).*

KARISAL (IRE) BHB 92f RR 77f 2054[7]
2 b f Persian Bold 10f **(69)** - Pasadena Lady (Captain James) 5f **(59)**
Form - 417
Record 1998 - 1st:1 2nd:0 3rd:0 Ran:3
Win Prizemoney £4,162 *Total Prizemoney* £4,675
Wins * **1998** May Haydoc (G-S) 5f 77 <
1998 Turf 1-3: (5f 1-3) (gd 1-2, g-f)
Currently above-average filly. Turf high 77 - 1st of 7 from Bollin Rita (23 May Haydock RF 1421). A half-sister to a host of Berry-trained speedsters, she made all on her second start, but showed little in the Queen Mary. **J Berry [1-3] Mrs J E M Hawkins.*

KARIVER (FR) RR 106f 276a[3]
7 b g River Mist (USA) - The Equal Skies (USA) (Sir Gaylord) 10.6f **(64)**
Form - 3
1998 Turf 0-1: (13f) (gd)
Currently Pattern-class gelding. (1st run) - 3rd of 10 getting 8lb from Irish Holmes (4 Feb Cagnes-sur-mer 13f gd RF 0276a). He is a run-of-the-mill performer judged on his running at Cagnes-Sur-Mer in February. **X Puleo in FR [0-2].*

KARIYADAN (IRE) RR 8f 5039[15]
2 b c Akarad (FR) 9.7f **(73)** - Kadissya (USA) (Blushing Groom (FR)) 10.3f **(76)**
Form - 0
Record 1998 - 1st:0 2nd:0 3rd:0 Ran:1
1998 Turf 0-1: (8f) (g-s)
Currently very poor colt. **L M Cumani [0-1] H H Aga Khan.*

KARIYH (USA) BHB 94f RR 93f 3230[5]
3 b f Shadeed (USA) 7.7f **(72)** - Katiba (USA) (Gulch (USA)) 8f **(81)**
Form - 421645
Record 1998 - 1st:1 2nd:1 3rd:0 Ran:6
Win Prizemoney £3,844 *Total Prizemoney* £7,370
Wins * **1998** Jun Salisb (G-S) 8f 83+ <
1998 Turf 1-6: (7f 2, 8f 1-2, 10f 2) (gd 1-4, g-f, frm)
Scopey, useful filly, effective 8 to 10f, best at 10f, acts on gd to frm, best on gd. Turf high 93 - 5th of 10 giving 4lb to Gypsy Passion (31 Jly Goodwood 10f gd RF 3230). Clearly held in high

regard, she improved steadily before bolting up in a Salisbury maiden in June. Her best effort in her three subsequent outings came when fourth in a good-quality handicap at the Newmarket July meeting, but she was not seen out after the end of that month. **J L Dunlop [1-6] Hamdan Al Maktoum.*

KAROWNA BHB 69f **RR 66f** 4299[8]

2 ch f Karinga Bay - Misowni (Niniski (USA)) 10.6f **(65)**
Form - 578
Record 1998 - 1st:0 2nd:0 3rd:0 Ran:3
1998 Turf 0-3: (7f 3) (g-f, frm 2)
Currently average filly. Turf high 66 (began Aug).
**B A McMahon [0-3] Holding Partnership.*

KASHAN (IRE) RR 30df 765[11]

10 b g Darshaan 11.9f **(81)** - Kamanika (FR) (Amber Rama (USA)) 10.2f **(45)**
Form - 0
Record 1998 - 1st:0 2nd:0 3rd:0 Ran:1
Pre1998 - 1st:0 2nd:1 3rd:0 Ran:13
Win Prizemoney £0 *Total Prizemoney* £1,103
1998 Turf 0-1: (12f) (g-s)
Very moderate gelding, has worn blinkers.
**P Hayward [0-15] Mrs Marilyn Mein (from J M Bradley [0-22] Jun 1994).*

KASHWAN (SPA) RR 111f 5155a[3]

4 b c Unfuwain (USA) 11.4f **(74)** - Kalawelsh (FR) (Kalaglow) 9.8f **(67)**
Form - 3326433
1998 Turf 0-7: (12f 7) (hvy 3, sft 2, g-s, gd)
Group-class colt, effective 12f, acts on hvy to gd, best on hvy. Turf high 112 - 2nd of 5 to Limnos (15 May Saint-cloud 12f gd RF 1375a). Consistent. Despite a string of placed efforts, he is extremely genuine. Consistently frustrated against Group class opposition, he could do with a confidence booster.
**E Lellouche in FR [0-10].*

KASS ALHAWA BHB 69f43a **RR 71f 43a** 4748[10]

5 b g Shirley Heights 12.1f **(76)** - Silver Braid (USA) (Miswaki (USA)) 9f **(81)**
Form - 7124584812366010230
Record 1998 - 1st:3 2nd:3 3rd:2 Ran:18
Pre1998 - 1st:2 2nd:4 3rd:2 Ran:27
Win Prizemoney £16,236 *Total Prizemoney* £25,452

Wins								
	* **1998**	Aug Beverl	(G-F)	H	7.5f	63	66	
	* **1998**	Jun Beverl	(G-S)	H	7.5f	63	68	<
	* **1998**	*Feb Southw*	*(STD)*	*H*	*6f*	*31*	*38*	
	* 1997	Aug Catter	(G-F)	H	7f	59	63	
	* 1997	Jun Redcar	(GD)	H	8f	53	58	

1998 Turf 2-12: (6f, 7f 2-6, 8f 3, 9f 2) (g-s, gd 1-2, g-f 6, frm 1-3) 1998 AW 1-6: (6f 1-2, 7f, 8f 3) (Equi, Fibr 1-5)
Above-average gelding, effective 7 to 10f, best at 7f, acts on g-s to frm, best on g-f, has worn blinkers, likes right handed tracks, and excels at Nottingham and Beverley. Turf high 71 - 3rd of 20 giving 3lb to Knave's Ash (30 Spt Newcastle 8f g-f RF 4578) - also 1st of 12 giving 12lb to Al Reet (3 Jun Beverley RF 1675). AW high 42.
**D W Chapman [5-42] J B Wilcox (from Sir Michael Stoute [0-3] May 1996).*

KASTAWAY BHB 83f **RR 88df** 4264[10]

2 b f Distant Relative 7f **(69)** - Flourishing (IRE) (Trojan Fen) 8.1f **(62)**
Form - 11122140
Record 1998 - 1st:4 2nd:2 3rd:0 Ran:8
Win Prizemoney £14,937 *Total Prizemoney* £20,577

Wins							
	* **1998**	Jun Windso	(SFT)	5f		88	<
	* **1998**	May Doncas	(G-F)	5f		86	
	* **1998**	Apr Thirsk	(G-S)	5f		86	
	* **1998**	*Mar Lingfi*	*(STD)*	*5f*		*86*	

1998 Turf 3-7: (5f 3-7) (g-s 1-1, gd 1-4, g-f 1-2) 1998 AW 1-1: (5f 1-1) (Equi 1-1)
Useful filly, effective 5f, acts on g-s to g-f - acts on Equi, best on g-f. Turf high 88 - also 1st of 8 giving 5lb to Devon Court (15 Jun Windsor RF 2008). (1st run) - 1st of 7 from Oh I Say (30 Mar Lingfield RF 0505). She was a typical Jack Berry juvenile, in that she knew her job from the start. The winner of four of her first six races, she ended the campaign with a comprehensive defeat in a claimer. **J Berry [4-8] David Winter.*

KATATONIC (IRE) BHB 34a **RR 34a** 264[3]

5 b g Waajib 8.9f **(67)** - Miss Kate (FR) (Nonoalco (USA)) 8.5f **(66)**
Form - 3
Record 1998 - 1st:0 2nd:0 3rd:1 Ran:1
Pre1998 - 1st:0 2nd:0 3rd:1 Ran:2
Win Prizemoney £0 *Total Prizemoney* £908
1998 AW 0-1: (12f) (Fibr)
Moderate gelding.
**R T Juckes [0-1] A C W Price (from J A R Toller [0-2] Dec 1996).*

KATELA (IRE) BHB 37f **RR 26f** 3317[15]

3 b f Indian Ridge 7.6f **(74)** - Virginia Cottage (Lomond (USA)) 8.8f **(65)**
Form - 000
Record 1998 - 1st:0 2nd:0 3rd:0 Ran:3
1998 Turf 0-3: (8f 2, 10f) (g-f, frm 2)
Unfurnished, currently little account filly. Turf high 26 (began Jly).
**P Mitchell [0-3] Mrs Fiona Reilly.*

KATE LANE (IRE) BHB 42f **RR 35f** 3690[10]

3 b f Petardia 8.2f **(58)** - Splendid Yankee (Yankee Gold) 7.6f **(55)**
Form - 07808500
Record 1998 - 1st:0 2nd:0 3rd:0 Ran:8
Pre1998 - 1st:0 2nd:0 3rd:0 Ran:4
1998 Turf 0-7: (6f 3, 7f 2, 8f 2) (gd, g-f, frm 5) 1998 AW 0-1: (6f) (Fibr)
Unfurnished, moderate filly, has worn blinkers. Turf high 50.
**Mrs P N Dutfield [0-12] Mrs Nerys Dutfield.*

KATHIES PET BHB 57f **RR 46f** 5007[11]

3 b f Tina's Pet 7.4f **(56)** - Unveiled **(54f 48a)** (Sayf El Arab (USA)) 7.1f **(54)**
Form - 6731501800000
Record 1998 - 1st:2 2nd:0 3rd:1 Ran:13
Pre1998 - 1st:0 2nd:2 3rd:0 Ran:6
Win Prizemoney £5,903 *Total Prizemoney* £7,634

Wins								
	* **1998**	Jun Windso	(GD)	H	6f	60	66	<
	* **1998**	May Bright	(G-F)	H	6f	56	61	

1998 Turf 2-13: (5f 3, 6f 2-8, 7f, 8f) (sft 3, g-s, gd 1-2, g-f 1-4, frm 3)
Workmanlike, moderate filly, effective 6f, acts on gd to g-f, best on gd. Turf high 66 - 1st of 18 giving 13lb to Tremonnow (8 Jun Windsor RF 1819) - also 1st of 16 giving 16lb to Ready Fontaine (5 May Brighton RF 1039). Consistent.
**R J Hodges [2-19] Mrs E A Tucker.*

KATHRYN'S PET BHB 66f **RR 68f** 5119[7]

5 b m Blakeney 11.9f **(53)** - Starky's Pet (Mummy's Pet) 7.7f **(60)**
Form - 1047
Record 1998 - 1st:1 2nd:0 3rd:0 Ran:4
Pre1998 - 1st:2 2nd:2 3rd:2 Ran:17
Win Prizemoney £9,534 *Total Prizemoney* £12,544

Wins								
	* **1998**	Apr Catter	(GD)	H	13.8f	61	67	<
	* 1997	Jun Cheste	(SFT)	H	12.3f	60	64	
	* 1997	Mar Mussel	(SFT)		12f		56	

1998 Turf 1-4: (10f, 12f 2, 14f 1-1) (sft, gd 1-2, frm)
Average filly, effective 10 to 14f, acts on g-s to frm, likes left handed tracks, favours tight tracks, does well at Pontefract and Musselburgh. Turf high 68 - 4th of 9 getting 1lb from My Learned Friend (24 Spt Pontefract 10f frm RF 4470) - also 1st of 9 getting 9lb from Onefourseven (1 Apr Catterick RF 0532). Inconsistent.
**Mrs M Reveley [5-27] Bill Brown.*

KATIE-B BHB 20f **RR 8f** 3322[7]

3 b f Nalchik (USA) 12.6f **(44)** - Princess of Alar (Bold Owl) 8.5f **(45)**
Form - 0087
Record 1998 - 1st:0 2nd:0 3rd:0 Ran:4
1998 Turf 0-3: (8f, 10f, 17f) (gd, g-f, frm) 1998 AW 0-1: (12f) (Fibr)
Workmanlike, very poor filly. Turf high 8 - 8th of 8 getting 23lb from Banneret (10 Jly Wolverhampton 12f Fibr RF 2696).
**D Burchell [0-4] Lyn Phillips.*

KATIE HAWK RR 4f 2841[9]

4 b f Buzzards Bay 8.9f **(44)** - Rayne Park (Julio Mariner) 7.2f **(57)**
Form - 00
Record 1998 - 1st:0 2nd:0 3rd:0 Ran:2
1998 Turf 0-2: (8f, 12f) (gd, frm)
Workmanlike, currently very poor filly. Turf high 4 (began Jly).
**J M Bradley [0-2] Mrs T D Watts.*

KATIE KOMAITE BHB 44f34a **RR 46f 34a** 5120[6]
5 b m Komaite (USA) 6.9f **(61)** - City to City (Windjammer (USA)) 7f **(59)**
Form - 8001640236
Record 1998 - 1st:1 2nd:1 3rd:1 Ran:10
Pre1998 - 1st:1 2nd:4 3rd:3 Ran:32
Win Prizemoney £6,267 *Total Prizemoney* £12,206
Wins * **1998** Jun Pontef (SFT) H 8f 39 43
1997 Oct Nottin (GD) H 8.2f 39 45 <
1998 Turf 1-10: (8f 1-7, 9f 3) (sft, g-s 1-4, gd 4, frm)
Moderate filly, effective 7 to 10f, best at 8f, acts on g-s to frm, best on g-s, often wears blinkers (extremely effectively), likes left handed tracks, and excels at Nottingham. Turf high 46 - also 1st of 9 getting 12lb from Al Reet (8 Jun Pontefract RF 1808). She is a difficult type to win with.
**Mrs G S Rees [1-10] Red Rose Partnership (from Capt J Wilson [1-32] Nov 1997).*

KATIE OLIVER BHB 58f53a **RR 70f 53a** 1430[13]
6 b m Squill (USA) 9.4f **(47)**-Shih Ching (USA)(Secreto (USA)) 8.7f **(72)**
Form - 0
Record 1998 - 1st:0 2nd:0 3rd:0 Ran:1
Pre1998 - 1st:0 2nd:1 3rd:0 Ran:4
Win Prizemoney £0 *Total Prizemoney* £889
1998 AW 0-1: (16f) (Equi)
Above-average mare.
**B J McMath [0-1] Mrs Lisa Olley (from B Smart [0-4] Jan 1996).*

KATIE'S CRACKER BHB 46f46a **RR 46f 46a** 4922[1]
3 b f Rambo Dancer (CAN) 8.4f **(59)** - Tea-Pot (Ragstone) 9.6f **(59)**
Form - 24633140732680001
Record 1998 - 1st:2 2nd:1 3rd:3 Ran:16
Pre1998 - 1st:0 2nd:4 3rd:1 Ran:8
Win Prizemoney £5,543 *Total Prizemoney* £10,766
Wins * **1998** Oct Nottin (SFT) SH 14.1f 37 46
* **1998** *Mar Southw (STD) H 11f 53 56+* <
1998 Turf 1-6: (12f 3, 14f 1-3) (g-s 1-1, gd 2, frm 3) 1998 AW 1-10: (8f 2, 9f, 10f, 11f 1-3, 12f 2, 16f) (Equi 2, Fibr 1-8)
Light-framed, fair filly, effective 6 to 14f, acts on g-s to frm - acts on AW, best on Fibr, likes left handed tracks, favours tight tracks, likes Southwell. Turf high 53 (1st run) - 3rd of 20 getting 5lb from Court Shareef (11 May Windsor 12f frm RF 1159). AW high 56 - 1st of 5 getting 23lb from Spirit of Love (2 Mar Southwell RF 0389). Inconsistent.
**M Quinn [2-17] J Miller (from M R Channon [0-7] Spt 1997).*

KATIE'S KITTY BHB 43f44a **RR 44a** 889[6]
3 b f Noble Patriarch 12.2f **(43)** - Catherines Well (Junius (USA)) 7.7f **(65)**
Form - 64766
Record 1998 - 1st:0 2nd:0 3rd:0 Ran:5
1998 Turf 0-1: (6f) (sft) 1998 AW 0-4: (6f 2, 7f 2) (Fibr 4)
Moderate filly. AW high 46.
**M W Easterby [0-5] K Hodgson & Mrs J Hodgson.*

KATIES TREAT (IRE) BHB 37f **RR 34f** 3396[18]
3 ch f Superpower 6.6f **(58)** - Fancied (Dominion) 8.5f **(63)**
Form - 00
Record 1998 - 1st:0 2nd:0 3rd:0 Ran:2
Pre1998 - 1st:0 2nd:0 3rd:0 Ran:7
1998 Turf 0-2: (8f 2) (g-f, frm)
Neat, very moderate filly, often wears blinkers. Turf high 10 (began Jly). **D T Thom [0-8] Mrs R Nash (from B A Pearce [0-1] Apr 1997).*

KATTEGAT BHB 83f **RR 81f** 4805[1]
2 b c Slip Anchor 12.7f **(75)** - Kirsten (Kris) 9.5f **(73)**
Form - 01
Record 1998 - 1st:1 2nd:0 3rd:0 Ran:2
Win Prizemoney £3,752 *Total Prizemoney* £3,752
Wins * **1998** Oct Nottin (SFT) 8.2f 81 <
1998 Turf 1-2: (8f 1-2) (gd 1-1, g-f)
Currently decent colt. Turf high 81 (began Spt) - 1st of 10 giving 5lb to Pipa (14 Oct Nottingham RF 4805). Improved quite a bit from his debut when winning a Nottingham maiden over a mile in soft ground on his second start, though the form may not amount to much. **W Jarvis [1-2] Lord Howard de Walden.*

KATYUSHKA (IRE) BHB 70f **RR 75f** 4459[12]
3 b f Soviet Star (USA) 8.6f **(74)** - Welsh Note (USA) (Sharpen Up) 8.3f **(67)**
Form - 664010
Record 1998 - 1st:1 2nd:0 3rd:0 Ran:6
Pre1998 - 1st:0 2nd:0 3rd:0 Ran:4
Win Prizemoney £4,175 *Total Prizemoney* £4,706
Wins * **1998** Spt Lingfi (G-S) 7f 75 <
1998 Turf 1-6: (5f, 6f, 7f 1-3, 8f) (gd 2, g-f 1-2, frm 2)
Neat, above-average filly, effective 7f, acts on g-f. Turf high 75 - 1st of 16 getting 5lb from Doraid (8 Spt Lingfield RF 4149). She appeared to have had more than enough chances before landing a Lingfield maiden in September, though a plum draw helped her there, and the quality of much of the opposition left plenty to be desired. **Major D N Chappell [1-10] Mrs B Woodford.*

KAURIS BHB 71f **RR 70f** 5069[9]
3 br f Acatenango (GER) - Buckwig (USA) (Buckfinder (USA)) 8.1f **(71)**
Form - 33350
Record 1998 - 1st:0 2nd:0 3rd:3 Ran:5
Win Prizemoney £0 *Total Prizemoney* £2,712
1998 Turf 0-5: (11f, 12f 3, 14f) (gd 2, g-f 2, frm)
Above-average filly. Turf high 79 (1st run) (began Jly) - 3rd of 9 getting 5lb from Sces (19 Jly San Siro 11f g-f RF 3060a).
**L M Cumani [0-5] Dr Saini Fasanotti.*

KAYAARA (IRE) RR 99f 4296a[R]
6 b g Kahyasi 12.9f **(74)** - Ilyaara (Huntercombe) 7.3f **(56)**
Form - 2R
1998 Turf 0-2: (12f, 14f) (gd 2)
Very useful gelding. Turf high 99 (1st run) - 2nd of 11 giving 2lb to Winged Hussar (24 May Curragh 12f gd RF 1514a).
**N Furlong in IRE [1-7] N Furlong.*

KAYF TARA BHB 120f **RR 123f** 4430a[1]
4 b c Sadler's Wells (USA) 11.3f **(87)** - Colorspin (FR) (High Top) 10.2f **(67)**
Form - 131541
Record 1998 - 1st:3 2nd:0 3rd:1 Ran:6
Pre1998 - 1st:1 2nd:1 3rd:0 Ran:2
Win Prizemoney £217,610 *Total Prizemoney* £227,665
Wins * **1998** Spt Currag (SFT) G1 14f 123 <
* **1998** Jun Ascot (SFT) G1 20f 118
* **1998** May Haydoc (GD) 11.9f 95+
1997 Jly Ascot (GD) 10f 91
1998 Turf 3-6: (12f 1-1, 14f 1-1, 15f, 16f 2, 20f 1-1) (sft, g-s 1-1, gd 2-3, g-f)
Scopey, very high-class colt, effective 14 to 20f, acts on sft to g-f, best on gd, prefers right handed tracks, likes Ascot. Turf high 123 - 1st of 7 from Silver Patriarch (19 Spt Curragh RF 4430a) - also 1st of 16 getting 2lb from Double Trigger (18 Jun Ascot RF 2085). Improving. A brother to Opera House, he was unraced at two, and very lightly raced as a three-year-old. Joining Godolphin at the end of 1997, he won at Haydock on his return, and was not beaten far in the Henry II Stakes. He really came into his own when stepped up another half-mile for the Ascot Gold Cup, gaining a battling victory over the rejuvenated Double Trigger. Things did not go his way in his next two starts but, given a decent gallop, he was able to outstay Silver Patriarch in the Irish St Leger. He seems to prefer to get his toe in and, in those conditions, he is likely to prove a tenacious defender of his Gold Cup crown.
**S bin Suroor [3-6] Godolphin (from Sir Michael Stoute [1-2] Jly 1997).*

KAYO BHB 93f78a **RR 92f 78a** 4985[13]
3 b g Superpower 6.6f **(58)** - Shiny Kay (Star Appeal) 9.6f **(65)**
Form - 11271267055100
Record 1998 - 1st:4 2nd:2 3rd:0 Ran:14
Pre1998 - 1st:2 2nd:0 3rd:0 Ran:7
Win Prizemoney £32,108 *Total Prizemoney* £42,925
Wins * **1998** Oct Warwic (GD) H 8f 91 92 <
* **1998** Jun Newbur (HVY) 7f 86
* **1998** *May Southw (STD) H 7f 73 78*
* **1998** *Apr Southw (STD) H 6f 67 72*
* 1997 Oct Ayr (SFT) H 8f 67 71
* 1997 Spt Mussel (G-F) C 8f 66
1998 Turf 2-10: (6f 2, 7f 1-5, 8f 1-3) (sft, g-s 1-3, gd, g-f 1-3, frm 2)
1998 AW 2-4: (6f 1-1, 7f 1-2, 8f) (Fibr 2-4)
Workmanlike, useful gelding, effective 7 to 8f, best at 8f, acts on g-

s to g-f, best on g-f. Turf high 92 - 2nd of 9 giving 11lb to Redoubtable (27 Jun Newcastle 7f g-s RF 2343) - also 1st of 9 giving 4lb to Mundo Raro (4 Oct Warwick RF 4645). AW high 78. Managed four victories in '97, the first two of which came on the Southwell Fibresand. He ran well on turf in the first half of the season, including gaining another victory in heavy ground at Newbury, and though his form in the second half of the season was nothing like as good, he did win a rated stakes at Warwick in October. **T J Etherington [6-21] David Abell.*

KAYO GEE RR 50+f 5123[5]

2 b f Komaite (USA) 6.9f **(61)** - Darling Miss Daisy (Tina's Pet) 6.8f **(59)**
Form - 85
Record 1998 - 1st:0 2nd:0 3rd:0 Ran:2
1998 Turf 0-2: (6f 2) (g-s 2)
Currently fair filly. Turf high 50 (began Oct).
**A J McNae [0-2] Mrs E N Nield.*

KAYOKO (IRE) BHB 68f RR 74df 3808[12]

3 b f Shalford (IRE) 7.8f **(63)** - Karamana (Habitat) 9.4f **(70)**
Form - 731000
Record 1998 - 1st:1 2nd:0 3rd:1 Ran:6
Win Prizemoney £3,557 *Total Prizemoney* £4,127
Wins * **1998** Jly Newmar (G-F) 6f 74 <
1998 Turf 1-6: (5f, 6f 1-5) (gd, g-f 3, frm 1-2)
Scopey, above-average filly, effective 6f, acts on frm, has worn blinkers. Turf high 74 - 1st of 6 getting 5lb from Hoh Navigator (17 Jly Newmarket RF 2880). A half-sister to useful sprinter Proud Native, she made all in a maiden at Newmarket in July, although it was not a great race, and she was beaten a long way in handicaps.
**A P Jarvis [1-6] Ambrose Turnbull.*

KAYVEE BHB 70f RR 76f 5079[3]

9 gr g Kaldoun (FR) 9.9f **(84)** - Secret Life (USA) (Elocutionist (USA)) 8f **(77)**
Form - 4000674803
Record 1998 - 1st:0 2nd:0 3rd:1 Ran:10
Pre1998 - 1st:6 2nd:14 3rd:10 Ran:74
Win Prizemoney £35,970 *Total Prizemoney* £139,961

Wins	1996	Aug	Nottin	(G-S)		8.2f		94	
	1995	Jly	Ascot	(G-F)	H	8f	98	102	<
	1994	Oct	Chepst	(GD)		8.1f		84+	
	1994	Oct	Ascot	(G-F)		8f		86+	

1998 Turf 0-10: (7f 2, 8f 6, 9f 2) (sft, gd 4, g-f 4, frm)
Above-average gelding, effective 7 to 9f, best at 8f, acts on gd to frm, best on g-f, has worn blinkers, likes left handed tracks. Turf high 86 (1st run) - 4th of 10 to Peartree House (8 May Lingfield 8f frm RF 1106). He continues to run his share of good races, especially at Ascot, but he has not won since August '96 and is not getting any younger.
**Mrs A J Perrett [0-23] J H Richmond-Watson (from G Harwood [6-61] Nov 1996).*

KAYZEE (IRE) BHB 46f36a RR 32f 36a 654[6]

4 b f River Falls 8.2f **(56)** - Northern Amber (Shack (USA)) 5.8f **(53)**
Form - 6
Record 1998 - 1st:0 2nd:0 3rd:0 Ran:1
Pre1998 - 1st:0 2nd:0 3rd:2 Ran:8
Win Prizemoney £0 *Total Prizemoney* £744
1998 AW 0-1: (8f) (Fibr)
Workmanlike, moderate filly, effective 9f - acts on Fibr, likes left handed tracks, likes tight tracks.
**D Burchell [0-5] Simon Lewis (from S Dow [0-5] Jun 1997).*

KAZZOUD (IRE) RR 26f 4148[8]

2 b f Ezzoud (IRE) - Kates Cabin (Habitat) 9.4f **(70)**
Form - 8
Record 1998 - 1st:0 2nd:0 3rd:0 Ran:1
1998 Turf 0-1: (7f) (g-f)
Currently little account filly. **S Dow [0-1] Mrs A M Upsdell.*

KEEN ALERT BHB 57f75a RR 31f 75a 881[12]

4 b g Keen 11.1f **(58)** - Miss Coco (Swing Easy (USA)) 6.5f **(55)**
Form - 0
Record 1998 - 1st:0 2nd:0 3rd:0 Ran:1
Pre1998 - 1st:1 2nd:0 3rd:0 Ran:4
Win Prizemoney £1,927 *Total Prizemoney* £1,927
Wins * 1997 *Apr Southw (STD) 8f 59 <*
1998 Turf 0-1: (8f) (g-s)
Strong, fair gelding, has worn blinkers.
**M Bell [1-5] Ms Dawn Stagg.*

KEEN COMPANION BHB 54f54a RR 38f 54a 3484[7]

5 b m Keen 11.1f **(58)** - Constant Companion (Pas de Seul) 9.1f **(67)**
Form - 7
Record 1998 - 1st:0 2nd:0 3rd:0 Ran:1
Pre1998 - 1st:0 2nd:0 3rd:2 Ran:6
Win Prizemoney £0 *Total Prizemoney* £901
1998 Turf 0-1: (7f) (gd)
Moderate filly. **T J Naughton [0-7] T J Naughton.*

KEEN DANCER BHB 56f58a RR 58f 58a 3326[7]

4 ch g Keen 11.1f **(58)** - Royal Shoe (Hotfoot) 10.5f **(59)**
Form - 6467
Record 1998 - 1st:0 2nd:0 3rd:0 Ran:4
Pre1998 - 1st:0 2nd:0 3rd:0 Ran:7
Win Prizemoney £0 *Total Prizemoney* £449
1998 Turf 0-4: (10f, 11f, 13f, 16f) (hvy, gd, g-f 2)
Scopey, fair gelding, effective 8 to 13f, acts on gd, prefers left handed tracks. Turf high 58 - 4th of 5 getting 14lb from Carburton (8 Jun Warwick 13f gd RF 1814).
**M C Pipe [1-7] Mrs Alison Farrant (from M Bell [0-7] Jun 1997).*

KEEN HANDS RR 4139[15]

2 ch c Keen 11.1f **(58)** -Broken Vow (IRE) (Local Suitor (USA)) 8.4f **(67)**
Form - 0
Record 1998 - 1st:0 2nd:0 3rd:0 Ran:1
1998 Turf 0-1: (7f) (g-f)
Currently very poor colt - 15th of 15 to Culzean (8 Spt Leicester 7f g-f RF 4139). **Mrs N Macauley [0-1] Andy Peake.*

KEEP BATTLING BHB 41f RR 43f 2562[R]

8 b g Hard Fought 8.9f **(51)** - Keep Mum (Mummy's Pet) 7.7f **(60)**
Form - 304470R
Record 1998 - 1st:0 2nd:0 3rd:1 Ran:7
Pre1998 - 1st:3 2nd:5 3rd:5 Ran:41
Win Prizemoney £14,323 *Total Prizemoney* £25,470

Wins	* 1996	Jun	Mussel	(FRM)	H	12.1f	43	47	<
	* 1995	Jun	Ayr	(G-F)	H	10f	38	42	
	* 1995	May	Ayr	(G-F)	H	10.9f	32	38	

1998 Turf 0-7: (9f 3, 10f, 11f 2, 12f) (g-s, gd 2, g-f 3, frm)
Moderate gelding, effective 8 to 10f, best at 10f, acts on gd to frm, has worn blinkers, likes left handed tracks. Turf high 44.
**J S Goldie [7-61] J S Goldie (from A Harrison [0-11] Aug 1994).*

KEEPER HILL (USA) RR 5166a[3]

3 b f Deputy Minister (CAN) 9.2f **(71)** - Fineza (USA)
Form - 3
1998 AW 0-1: (9f) (Dirt)
Currently very useful filly, always wears blinkers. A very consistent sort, she ran well but was no match for the principals in the Breeders' Cup Distaff.
**R Frankel in USA [0-1] Mill Ridge Farm & Audrey Otto.*

KEEPING THE FAITH (IRE) RR 90f 4793a[3]

4 b f Ajraas (USA) 7f **(53)** - Felicitas (Mr Fluorocarbon) 6f **(55)**
Form - 10336573
1998 Turf 1-8: (10f 1-4, 11f 2, 12f 2) (g-s 2, gd 1-4, g-f 2)
Useful filly, effective 10 to 12f, best at 10f, acts on gd to g-f, best on gd, has worn blinkers, likes right handed tracks. Turf high 90 - 3rd of 6 giving 14lb to Rose Petal (15 Jly Down Royal 10f g-f RF 3000a) - also 1st of 13 giving 3lb to Hayward (30 May Gowran Park RF 1665a). Consistent. **T Carmody in IRE [2-25] Donkey Ltd.*

KEEP PLAYING (FR) RR 107f 426a[1]

4 ch c Highest Honor (FR) 10.9f **(72)** - Playing for Keeps (FR) (Royal Match) 11.8f **(54)**
Form - 1
1998 Turf 1-1: (8f 1-1) (sft 1-1)
Currently Pattern-class colt. (1st run) - 1st of 8 giving 3lb to Punishment (3 Mar Maisons-laffitte RF 0426a). He was a progressive three-year-old and easily brushed Punishment aside at Maisons-Laffitte in March. He looked sure to win Group races, but went on the missing list. **J-C Rouget in FR [1-3] Ecurie I M Fares.*

KEEPSAKE (IRE) BHB 30f **RR 39f** 4417[3]
4 b f Distinctly North (USA) 7.4f **(63)** - Souveniers (Relko) 9.9f **(59)**
Form - 5540506044653
Record 1998 - 1st:0 2nd:0 3rd:1 Ran:13
Pre1998 - 1st:1 2nd:2 3rd:1 Ran:17
Win Prizemoney £3,073 *Total Prizemoney* £7,491
Wins * 1997 Aug Salisb (G-F) H 12f 49 54 <
1998 Turf 0-13: (12f 5, 13f, 14f 3, 15f, 16f 3) (g-s 2, gd 2, g-f 4, frm 5)
Workmanlike, very moderate filly, effective 11 to 16f, acts on g-s to frm, best on g-f, has worn blinkers, likes right handed tracks, excels at Sandown. Turf high 49 - 4th of 6 getting 11lb from Cheek To Cheek (18 May Bath 13f frm RF 1294). Consistent.
**M D I Usher [1-30] Trevor Barker.*

KEE RING RR 77f 4928[9]
2 ch c Keen 11.1f **(58)** - Rose And The Ring (Welsh Pageant) 10f **(65)**
Form - 20
Record 1998 - 1st:0 2nd:1 3rd:0 Ran:2
Win Prizemoney £0 *Total Prizemoney* £852
1998 Turf 0-2: (6f, 7f) (g-s, frm)
Currently above-average colt. Turf high 77 (1st run) (began Spt) - 2nd of 13 getting 1lb from Kangaroo Island (22 Spt Warwick 6f frm RF 4413). **P R Chamings [0-2] Mrs J E L Wright.*

KELD (IRE) BHB 88f **RR 92f** 4621[1]
3 b f Lion Cavern (USA) 7.5f **(74)** - Society Ball (Law Society (USA)) 9.9f **(70)**
Form - 011
Record 1998 - 1st:2 2nd:0 3rd:0 Ran:3
Win Prizemoney £11,012 *Total Prizemoney* £11,012
Wins * **1998** Oct Newmar (GD) 8f 92 <
* **1998** Jly Sandow (G-F) 8.1f 89
1998 Turf 2-3: (8f 2-3) (gd 1-2, frm 1-1)
Leggy, currently useful filly. Turf high 92 - 1st of 5 getting 7lb from Wuxi Venture (2 Oct Newmarket RF 4621) - also 1st of 15 getting 5lb from Bedaayat Farah (23 Jly Sandown RF 3044). Did not race at two, and after showing little on her debut she went on to make all in a Sandown maiden in July. She was then off the track for three months before landing a Newmarket classified stakes, and is worth watching out for as a four-year-old.
**J R Fanshawe [2-3] C I T Racing Ltd.*

KEMO SABO BHB 44f **RR 39f** 4919[14]
6 b g Prince Sabo 6.6f **(64)** - Canoodle (Warpath) 12.3f **(52)**
Form - 000
Record 1998 - 1st:0 2nd:0 3rd:0 Ran:3
Pre1998 - 1st:2 2nd:4 3rd:5 Ran:25
Win Prizemoney £8,623 *Total Prizemoney* £17,070
Wins 1995 Jly Ayr (GD) H 8f 72 81 <
1994 Spt Ayr (G-S) 6f 77+
1998 Turf 0-3: (7f, 8f 2) (g-s 2, g-f)
Very moderate gelding. Turf high 39 (began Aug). Becoming disappointing. Not easy to win with.
**C Parker [1-19] R Nichol (from Mrs J R Ramsden [2-21] Spt 1995).*

KENMIST BHB 100f **RR 104f** 1776[10]
4 gr f Kenmare (FR) 9.6f **(76)** - Mistral's Collette (Simply Great (FR)) 8.2f **(65)**
Form - 60
Record 1998 - 1st:0 2nd:0 3rd:0 Ran:2
Pre1998 - 1st:2 2nd:0 3rd:3 Ran:6
Win Prizemoney £24,549 *Total Prizemoney* £37,138
Wins * 1997 Spt Ascot (G-F) LH 8f 97 104 <
* 1997 Jun San Si (HVY) 10f 89
1998 Turf 0-2: (9f, 10f) (gd, g-f)
Very useful filly, effective 8f, acts on gd to g-f, best on g-f. Turf high 75. **L M Cumani [2-8] Dr Saini Fasanotti.*

KENNEMARA STAR (IRE) BHB 90f **RR 93f** 1014[9]
4 ch g Kenmare (FR) 9.6f **(76)** - Dawn Star (High Line) 10.3f **(70)**
Form - 20
Record 1998 - 1st:0 2nd:1 3rd:0 Ran:2
Pre1998 - 1st:2 2nd:1 3rd:0 Ran:9
Win Prizemoney £8,298 *Total Prizemoney* £16,428
Wins * 1997 Spt Pontef (G-S) H 8f 80 90 <
* 1997 Apr Leices (G-S) H 8f 70 74
1998 Turf 0-2: (8f 2) (sft, gd)
Unfurnished, useful gelding, effective 8f, acts on sft to frm. Turf high 93 (1st run) - 2nd of 15 giving 4lb to Yabint El Sultan (18 Apr Newbury 8f sft RF 0743). A half-brother to Dawning Street and Special Dawn, he was twice a winner in '97 but appeared to have two very contrasting ways of running. He ran a fine race to finish runner-up in the Spring Cup on his reappearance, but disappointed at Kempton on his only subsequent start.
**J L Dunlop [2-11] Windflower Overseas Holdings Inc.*

KENNET BHB 68f63a **RR 73f 63a** 5070[15]
3 b g Kylian (USA) 8.1f **(66)** - Marwell Mitzi **(29f)** (Interrex (CAN))
Form - 26322280
Record 1998 - 1st:0 2nd:4 3rd:1 Ran:8
Pre1998 - 1st:0 2nd:3 3rd:0 Ran:11
Win Prizemoney £0 *Total Prizemoney* £8,515
1998 Turf 0-7: (6f 2, 7f, 8f 3, 9f) (gd 2, g-f 3, frm 2) 1998 AW 0-1: (7f) (Fibr)
Neat, above-average gelding, effective 5 to 8f, acts on gd to frm, best on frm, likes tight tracks, excels at Warwick. Turf high 73 - 2nd of 13 to Grand Slam (22 Spt Warwick 8f frm RF 4415). He looks the type who will always find one or two too good.
**P D Cundell [0-19] Miss M C Fraser.*

KENSTOWN GIRL BHB 42f **RR 36f** 4568[8]
2 ch f Rock City 8.8f **(62)** - On to Glory (Welsh Pageant) 10f **(65)**
Form - 008
Record 1998 - 1st:0 2nd:0 3rd:0 Ran:3
1998 Turf 0-3: (6f, 7f 2) (gd, g-f, frm)
Currently very moderate filly, has worn blinkers. Turf high 36 (began Jly). **R Ingram [0-3] U M S.*

KENTAVRUS WAY (IRE) BHB 50f35a **RR 49f 35a** 126[6]
7 b g Thatching 7.8f **(69)** - Phantom Row (Adonijah) 10f **(61)**
Form - 6
Record 1998 - 1st:0 2nd:0 3rd:0 Ran:1
Pre1998 - 1st:1 2nd:0 3rd:3 Ran:23
Win Prizemoney £2,738 *Total Prizemoney* £4,206
Wins 1994 Jly Lingfi (GD) SH 10f 50 49 <
1998 AW 0-1: (12f) (Fibr)
Moderate gelding, has worn blinkers.
**R J Price [0-1] Mrs J M Kitson (from A Moore [1-28] Jan 1997).*

KENZO (GER) RR 113f 5053a[2]
7
Form - 2
1998 Turf 0-1: (12f) (hvy)
Currently Group-class, always wears blinkers. (1st run) - 2nd of 8 giving 12lb to Ocasa (25 Oct Dusseldorf 12f hvy RF 5053a).
**Frau E Mader in GER [0-1] Stall Simone.*

KEOS (USA) RR 118f 4947a[3]
4 dk c Riverman (USA) 9.7f **(78)** - Konafa (USA) (Damascus (USA)) 8.9f **(71)**
Form - 231713
1998 Turf 2-6: (6f 2-2, 7f 2, 8f 2) (hvy 2, g-s, gd 2-3)
High-class colt, effective 6 to 8f, acts on hvy to gd, and excels at Saint-cloud. Turf high 118 - 3rd of 8 to Marathon (1 May Saint-cloud 8f g-s RF 1088a) - also 1st of 9 getting 4lb from Dyhim Diamond (13 Jly Deauville RF 3049a). Consistent. Progressive French colt, he won a couple of Group Threes over six furlongs before finishing third to Tomba in the Prix de la Foret.
**J E Hammond in FR [2-9] Niarchos Family.*

KERALIA (IRE) RR 73f 4411[8]
2 b f Doyoun 10.7f **(69)** - Keraka (USA) (Storm Bird (CAN)) 10.3f **(74)**
Form - 68
Record 1998 - 1st:0 2nd:0 3rd:0 Ran:2
1998 Turf 0-2: (7f 2) (frm 2)
Currently above-average filly. Turf high 73 (began Aug).
**Sir Michael Stoute [0-2] H H Aga Khan.*

KERIALI (USA) RR 1581[6]
5 b g Irish River (FR) 9f **(77)** - Kerita (Formidable (USA)) 9.2f **(63)**
Form - 6
Record 1998 - 1st:0 2nd:0 3rd:0 Ran:1
1998 AW 0-1: (12f) (Fibr)
Very poor gelding, always wears blinkers.

*J G M O'Shea [0-4] Tony Usher.

KERIYOUN (IRE) RR 106f 4034a[7]
3 b c Storm Bird (CAN) 8.5f **(82)** - Kerita (Formidable (USA)) 9.2f **(63)**
Form - 221127
1998 Turf 2-6: (7f 1-2, 8f 1-3, 9f) (g-s, gd 1-3, frm 1-2)
Pattern-class colt, effective 7 to 9f, acts on g-s to frm, best on gd, often wears blinkers (very effectively). Turf high 106 - 1st of 4 from Razik (10 Jly Gowran Park RF 2793a) - also 1st of 8 giving 5lb to Maya (4 Jly Leopardstown RF 2614a). He showed useful form in minor events during the summer, but was found out when tried in Listed company. Connections let him go for 35,000 guineas at the Tattersalls Autumn Horses In Training Sales.
J Oxx in IRE [2-6] H H Aga Khan.

KERNOF (IRE) BHB 60f **RR 60f** 2930[7]
5 b g Rambo Dancer (CAN) 8.4f **(59)** - Empress Wu (High Line) 10.3f **(70)**
Form - 87
Record 1998 - 1st:0 2nd:0 3rd:0 Ran:2
Pre1998 - 1st:3 2nd:2 3rd:0 Ran:19
Win Prizemoney £8,308 *Total Prizemoney* £10,655
Wins * 1997 Jly Beverl (GD) H 12f 59 60 <
* 1997 Jun Mussel (G-S) H 12f 50 53
* 1996 Jly Pontef (G-F) H 10f 47 49
1998 Turf 0-2: (10f, 16f) (frm 2)
Average gelding, effective 12f, acts on gd to frm, best on frm, has worn blinkers, favours tight tracks. Turf high 35. Inconsistent.
M D Hammond [6-32] J M Gahan.

KESTRAL BHB 63f **RR 60f** 5148[18]
2 ch c Ardkinglass 5f **(64)** - Shiny Kay (Star Appeal) 9.6f **(65)**
Form - 7000
Record 1998 - 1st:0 2nd:0 3rd:0 Ran:4
1998 Turf 0-4: (6f, 7f, 8f 2) (gd 2, g-f, frm)
Average colt. Turf high 60 (began Aug).
T J Etherington [0-4] The R and R Partnership.

KETTLESING (IRE) BHB 48f **RR 49f** 5059[18]
3 b f Mujadil (USA) 7.7f **(70)** - Icefern (Moorestyle) 6.9f **(64)**
Form - 0005764300
Record 1998 - 1st:0 2nd:0 3rd:1 Ran:10
Pre1998 - 1st:2 2nd:1 3rd:0 Ran:9
Win Prizemoney £7,080 *Total Prizemoney* £8,875
Wins * 1997 Oct Nottin (G-F) H 5.1f 67 74 <
* 1997 Spt Ayr (G-S) S 5f 66
1998 Turf 0-9: (5f 5, 6f 4) (sft 2, g-s, gd 4, g-f, frm) 1998 AW 0-1: (5f) (Fibr)
Neat, moderate filly, effective 5 to 6f, best at 5f, acts on g-s to g-f, best on gd, mostly wears blinkers (very effectively). Turf high 50.
M W Easterby [2-19] Mrs Denise Shefras.

KEWARRA BHB 84f **RR 93f** 4966[9]
4 b g Distant Relative 7f **(69)** - Shalati (FR) (High Line) 10.3f **(70)**
Form - 100203300
Record 1998 - 1st:1 2nd:1 3rd:2 Ran:9
Pre1998 - 1st:3 2nd:1 3rd:3 Ran:17
Win Prizemoney £26,186 *Total Prizemoney* £33,966
Wins * **1998** Apr Epsom (SFT) H 10.1f 85 90 <
* 1997 Oct Newmar (G-F) H 10f 78 84
* 1997 Spt Chepst (GD) H 10.2f 74 78
* 1997 Aug Chepst (G-F) H 10.2f 70 75
1998 Turf 1-9: (10f 1-7, 12f 2) (sft 1-2, gd, g-f 4, frm 2)
Light-framed, useful gelding, effective 10 to 12f, best at 10f, acts on sft to frm, best on g-f, likes left handed tracks, prefers tight tracks, excels at Epsom and Chepstow. Turf high 93 - 2nd of 6 getting 4lb from Almond Rock (13 Jly Windsor 10f g-f RF 2767) - also 1st of 15 getting 12lb from Present Arms (22 Apr Epsom RF 0814). He made a winning reappearance in the City And Suburban Handicap at Epsom, but did not manage another victory, though he made the frame in fair handicaps on three occasions. Ten furlongs is his trip. *B R Millman [4-26] G Palmer.*

KEY BHB 69f **RR 78f** 5001[4]
2 b f Midyan (USA) 9.9f **(64)** - Diamond Park (IRE) **(60f)** (Alzao (USA)) 7.1f **(68)**
Form - 523010804
Record 1998 - 1st:1 2nd:1 3rd:1 Ran:9
Win Prizemoney £3,371 *Total Prizemoney* £5,265
Wins * **1998** Aug Bright (FRM) H 5.3f 70 78 <
1998 Turf 1-9: (5f 1-4, 6f 3, 7f 2) (sft, g-s, gd 2, g-f 1-2, frm 3)
Above-average filly, effective 5f, acts on g-f to frm. Turf high 78 - 1st of 4 giving 1lb to Bevelena (12 Aug Brighton RF 3569).
R Hannon [1-9] Wyck Hall Stud.

KEY ACADEMY BHB 80f **RR 81f** 5069[3]
3 b f Royal Academy (USA) 7.8f **(77)** - Santa Linda (USA) (Sir Ivor) 10.2f **(70)**
Form - 2213
Record 1998 - 1st:1 2nd:2 3rd:1 Ran:4
Win Prizemoney £3,550 *Total Prizemoney* £6,735
Wins * **1998** Spt Bath (GD) 11.7f 70 <
1998 Turf 1-4: (10f 2, 12f 1-2) (g-f 2, frm 1-2)
Scopey, decent filly. Turf high 81 (began Jly) - 3rd of 13 giving 22lb to Children's Choice (30 Oct Newmarket 12f g-f RF 5069).
C A Horgan [1-4] Mrs B Sumner.

KEY PROVIDER (IRE) RR 102f 4177a[16]
3 ch c Be My Guest (USA) 10.2f **(66)** - Certain Supremacy (USA) 00
Form - 1220
1998 Turf 1-4: (7f 1-2, 8f, 9f) (gd 1-2, frm 2)
Very useful colt, has worn blinkers. Turf high 102 - 2nd of 6 giving 2lb to Right Job (1 Jun Leopardstown 9f frm RF 1841a) - also 1st of 8 getting 5lb from Eymir (17 May Naas RF 1351a). He inched home at Naas in May, but proved disappointing in the second half of the season. *D K Weld in IRE [1-5] Moyglare Stud Farm.*

KEYSER SOZE BHB 35f **RR 36f** 3522[9]
3 b g Petong 7.6f **(58)** - Lamees (USA) (Lomond (USA)) 8.8f **(65)**
Form - 50040
Record 1998 - 1st:0 2nd:0 3rd:0 Ran:5
Pre1998 - 1st:0 2nd:0 3rd:0 Ran:1
1998 Turf 0-3: (12f, 13f, 15f) (gd, g-f, frm) 1998 AW 0-2: (6f, 9f) (Fibr 2)
Leggy, very moderate gelding, effective 13f, acts on frm. Turf high 36 - 4th of 8 getting 26lb from Silankka (3 Jly Hamilton 13f frm RF 2496). AW high 26. He is a half-brother to a couple of juvenile winners. *D HaydnJones [0-6] Hugh O'Donnell.*

KEY TO BHB 35f **RR 23f** 427[12]
4 b f Interrex (CAN) 7.7f **(51)** - Key to Enchantment (Key To Content (USA)) 8f **(54)**
Form - 0
Record 1998 - 1st:0 2nd:0 3rd:0 Ran:1
Pre1998 - 1st:0 2nd:0 3rd:0 Ran:2
1998 AW 0-1: (8f) (Fibr)
Leggy, little account filly.
G M McCourt [0-1] Mike Perkins (from A P Jarvis [0-2] Oct 1997).

KEY TO DOOKS (IRE) RR 31f 2754[11]
2 b g Up and At 'em - Global Princess (USA) (Transworld (USA))
Form - 000
Record 1998 - 1st:0 2nd:0 3rd:0 Ran:3
1998 Turf 0-3: (5f, 6f 2) (gd 2, g-f)
Currently very moderate gelding, has worn blinkers. Turf high 31.
J Berry [0-3] R Fabrizius.

KHAFAYA RR 70f 4770[5]
3 b f Unfuwain (USA) 11.4f **(74)** - Mahrah (USA) (Vaguely Noble) 10.1f **(72)**
Form - 25
Record 1998 - 1st:0 2nd:1 3rd:0 Ran:2
Win Prizemoney £0 *Total Prizemoney* £1,120
1998 Turf 0-2: (10f 2) (sft, gd)
Currently above-average filly. Turf high 70 (1st run) (began Spt) - 2nd of 13 to Royal Fontaine (15 Spt Sandown 10f gd RF 4265).
A C Stewart [0-2] Hamdan Al Maktoum.

KHAIRABAR (IRE) RR 97f 4027a[3]
4 gr g Shernazar 11.8f **(71)** - Khairkana
Form - 23
1998 Turf 0-2: (12f, 17f) (gd 2)
Very useful gelding, has worn blinkers. Turf high 92 (began Jly) - 3rd of 5 to Moscow Express (27 Aug Tralee 17f gd RF 4027a).
C Roche in IRE[1-8] John McManus (from J Oxx in IRE[1-5]Oct 1997).

KHALAS BHB 90f **RR 87f** 3801[10]
3 b c Wolfhound (USA) 7.3f **(71)**-Absaar (USA) (Alleged (USA)) 10f **(76)**
Form - 01010
Record 1998 - 1st:2 2nd:0 3rd:0 Ran:5
Pre1998 - 1st:1 2nd:2 3rd:0 Ran:4
Win Prizemoney £17,148 *Total Prizemoney* £19,210
Wins * **1998** Aug Salisb (G-F) 8f 87 <
* **1998** May Ayr (G-F) 8f 85
* 1997 Oct Lingfi (GD) 7f 78+
1998 Turf 2-5: (8f 2-4, 10f) (gd 3, g-f 1-1, frm 1-1)
Neat, useful colt, effective 7 to 8f, best at 8f, acts on gd to frm, best on g-f. Turf high 87 - 1st of 6 giving 3lb to Brief Escapade (7 Aug Salisbury RF 3445) - also 1st of 5 from Night Flyer (28 May Ayr RF 1544). Mixed form this term, winning an ordinary sort of handicap at Ayr and a Salisbury classified stakes.
**B W Hills [3-9] Hamdan Al Maktoum.*

KHALED (IRE) RR 75f 4008[1]
3 b c Petorius 8f **(66)** -Felin Special (Lyphard's Special (USA))10.3f **(72)**
Form - 031
Record 1998 - 1st:1 2nd:0 3rd:1 Ran:3
Win Prizemoney £3,980 *Total Prizemoney* £4,850
Wins * **1998** Aug Warwic (G-F) 8f 75 <
1998 Turf 1-3: (7f, 8f 1-2) (gd 2, frm 1-1)
Workmanlike, currently above-average colt. Turf high 75 - 1st of 10 giving 5lb to La Isla Bonita (31 Aug Warwick RF 4008).
**K Mahdi [1-3] Hamad Al-Mutawa.*

KHALIK (IRE) BHB 60f **RR 64f** 4060[14]
4 br g Lear Fan (USA) 10.4f **(80)** - Silver Dollar (Shirley Heights) 10.3f **(74)**
Form - 03437700
Record 1998 - 1st:0 2nd:0 3rd:2 Ran:8
Pre1998 - 1st:0 2nd:1 3rd:0 Ran:3
Win Prizemoney £0 *Total Prizemoney* £2,534
1998 Turf 0-8: (5f, 6f 6, 7f) (gd 3, g-f 2, frm 3)
Workmanlike, average gelding, effective 6f, acts on g-f, has worn blinkers. Turf high 76.
**Mrs L Stubbs [0-8] A P Griffin (from E A L Dunlop [0-3] Jun 1997).*

KHARTOUM (IRE) RR 63f 970[11]
2 ch c Common Grounds 8.1f **(66)** - Kayu (Tap On Wood) 10.3f **(65)**
Form - 30
Record 1998 - 1st:0 2nd:0 3rd:1 Ran:2
Win Prizemoney £0 *Total Prizemoney* £594
1998 Turf 0-2: (5f 2) (gd 2)
Currently average colt. Turf high 63.
**J H M Gosden [0-2] Sheikh Mohammed.*

KHATANI (IRE) RR 93f 2435a[4]
3 b c Kahyasi 12.9f **(74)** - Khanata (USA) (Riverman (USA)) 9.1f **(76)**
Form - 14
1998 Turf 1-2: (10f 1-1, 14f) (sft, g-f 1-1)
Useful colt. Turf high 93 (1st run) - 1st of 11 from Jimmy Swift (7 Jun Roscommon RF 1863a). **J Oxx in IRE [1-4] H H Aga Khan.*

KHATTAFF (IRE) BHB 46f **RR 49f** 4156[13]
3 ch c Hamas (IRE) 8f **(72)** - Coven (Sassafras (FR)) 9.6f **(69)**
Form - 680800
Record 1998 - 1st:0 2nd:0 3rd:0 Ran:6
Pre1998 - 1st:0 2nd:0 3rd:0 Ran:5
Win Prizemoney £0 *Total Prizemoney* £213
1998 Turf 0-6: (8f 3, 9f 2, 10f) (gd 2, g-f, frm 3)
Moderate colt, effective 7f, acts on g-f, has worn blinkers, likes left handed tracks, likes tight tracks. Turf high 67.
**M Brittain [0-6] Mel Brittain (from Major W R Hern [0-5] Spt 1997).*

KHAYID RR 67f 4336[5]
2 b c Mtoto 11.5f **(71)** - Ayah (USA) (Secreto (USA)) 8.7f **(72)**
Form - 5
Record 1998 - 1st:0 2nd:0 3rd:0 Ran:1
1998 Turf 0-1: (8f) (frm)
Currently average colt. **D R Loder [0-1] Sheikh Mohammed.*

KHEYRAH (USA) BHB 98f **RR 94f** 3216[7]
3 b br f Dayjur (USA) 6.8f **(79)** - Khwlah (USA) (Best Turn (USA)) 10.2f **(78)**
Form - 17
Record 1998 - 1st:1 2nd:0 3rd:0 Ran:2
Pre1998 - 1st:2 2nd:0 3rd:0 Ran:4
Win Prizemoney £12,123 *Total Prizemoney* £12,123
Wins * **1998** Jun Leices (GD) 7f 94 <
* 1997 Spt Haydoc (GD) H 6f 83 83
* 1997 Aug Yarmou (G-F) 6f 82+
1998 Turf 1-2: (7f 1-2) (gd, frm 1-1)
Workmanlike, useful filly, effective 7f, acts on frm. Turf high 94 (1st run) - 1st of 4 from Sapphire Ring (1 Jun Leicester RF 1622). She looked in need of the outing when just getting up to land a four-runner conditions event at Leicester on her reappearance, but ran moderately in a Goodwood Listed event next time and was not seen again. **E A L Dunlop [3-6] Hamdan Al Maktoum.*

KHIBRAH (IRE) RR 77f 4994[3]
2 br f Lahib (USA) 8f **(69)** - Sabayik (IRE) **(84f)** (Unfuwain (USA))
Form - 33
Record 1998 - 1st:0 2nd:0 3rd:2 Ran:2
Win Prizemoney £0 *Total Prizemoney* £962
1998 Turf 0-2: (6f 2) (sft, gd)
Currently above-average filly. Turf high 77 (began Oct).
**E A L Dunlop [0-2] Hamdan Al Maktoum.*

KHUDUD RR 61f 4610[12]
2 b f Green Desert (USA) 7.8f **(78)** - Braari (USA) **(100f)** (Gulch (USA)) 8f **(81)**
Form - 50
Record 1998 - 1st:0 2nd:0 3rd:0 Ran:2
1998 Turf 0-2: (5f 2) (g-s, gd)
Currently average filly. Turf high 61 (began Spt).
**B W Hills [0-2] Hamdan Al Maktoum.*

KHUMBA MELA (IRE) RR 109f 3421a[3]
3 f Chief III
Form - 613
1998 Turf 1-3: (8f 2, 9f 1-1) (sft 1-1, gd 2)
Pattern-class filly. Turf high 109 - 1st of 7 from Insight (17 Jly Chantilly RF 3053a). She was very impressive when winning at Chantilly in July and it came as something of a disappointment when she was beaten in the Group 2 Prix d'Astarte the following month. She probably needs further than a mile.
**A Fabre in FR [1-5] Mme P de Moussac.*

KI CHI SAGA (USA) BHB 35f63a **RR 31f 63a** 4931[4]
6 ch g Miswaki (USA) 8.1f **(81)** - Cedilla (USA) (Caro) 9.3f **(74)**
Form - 00051344811O4238024
Record 1998 - 1st:3 2nd:2 3rd:2 Ran:16
Pre1998 - 1st:1 2nd:2 3rd:0 Ran:23
Win Prizemoney £7,562 *Total Prizemoney* £10,610
Wins * **1998** *Apr Lingfi (STD) S 10f 64* <
* **1998** *Mar Lingfi (STD) H 8f 52 57*
* **1998** *Feb Lingfi (SLW) S 8f 51*
1997 *Mar Lingfi (STD) 8f 61*
1998 Turf 0-2: (8f, 10f) (g-s, gd) 1998 AW 3-14: (8f 2-7, 9f, 10f 1-4, 11f, 12f) (Equi 3-11, Fibr 3)
Average gelding, effective 10f - acts on Equi, has worn blinkers, favours left handed tracks, favours tight tracks. Turf high 31. AW high 74 - 2nd of 8 giving 20lb to Polo Venture (23 May Lingfield 10f Equi RF 1435). Inconsistent.
**G L Moore [3-19] Danny Bloor (from M Madgwick [1-14] Jun 1997).*

KICKONSUN (IRE) BHB 23f **RR 31f** 4627[13]
4 b g High Estate 10.5f **(66)** - Damezao (Alzao (USA)) 7.1f **(68)**
Form - 03443000
Record 1998 - 1st:0 2nd:0 3rd:2 Ran:8
Pre1998 - 1st:0 2nd:0 3rd:0 Ran:6
Win Prizemoney £0 *Total Prizemoney* £851
1998 Turf 0-7: (12f, 13f, 16f 4, 17f) (gd, g-f 2, frm 4) 1998 AW 0-1: (12f) (Fibr)
Unfurnished, very moderate gelding, effective 12 to 16f, acts on g-f to frm, best on frm, has worn blinkers (very effectively), favours tight tracks. Turf high 31 (1st run) (began Jly) - 3rd of 8 giving 3lb to Disco Tex (10 Jly Hamilton 13f frm RF 2685). Becoming disappointing.
**K A Ryan [0-7] The Gloria Darley Racing Partnership (from R A Fahey [0-7] Jan 1998).*

KIDNAPPED RR 33f 3377[16]

2 b c Emarati (USA) 6.6f **(63)** - Haddon Anna (Dragonara Palace (USA)) 6.1f **(55)**

Form - 00

Record 1998 - 1st:0 2nd:0 3rd:0 Ran:2

1998 Turf 0-2: (6f 2) (gd, frm)

Currently very moderate colt. Turf high 33 (began Jly).

**Mrs A L M King [0-2] Mrs A Martin.*

**M Johnston [0-2] W M Johnstone.*

KIERANS BRIDGE (IRE) BHB 58f74a **RR 62f 74a** 4580[7]

3 ch f Arcane (USA) 11.6f **(66)** - Rhein Valley (IRE) (Kings Lake (USA)) 10.8f **(67)**

Form - 12135587

Record 1998 - 1st:2 2nd:1 3rd:1 Ran:8
Pre1998 - 1st:0 2nd:0 3rd:0 Ran:3

Killer Instinct failed to live up to the hype

Win Prizemoney £5,229 *Total Prizemoney* £6,385

Wins * **1998** *Mar Wolver (STD) H* *12f* *67* *72* <
* **1998** *Mar Southw (STD)* *12f* *53+*

1998 Turf 0-4: (12f 3, 16f) (g-s, g-f, frm 2) 1998 AW 2-4: (12f 2-3, 15f) (Fibr 2-4)

Above-average filly, effective 12 to 15f, best at 12f - acts on Fibr, prefers left handed tracks, prefers tight tracks. Turf high 62. AW high 73 - 3rd of 6 getting 28lb from Noufari (11 Apr Wolverhampton 15f Fibr RF 0653) - also 1st of 11 getting 9lb from Evezio Rufo (28 Mar Wolverhampton RF 0498). **A P Jarvis [2-11] G S Bray.*

KID ORY BHB 29f37a **RR 23f 37a** 3643[15]

7 ch g Rich Charlie 5.9f **(50)** - Woomargama (Creetown) 6.9f **(50)**

Form - 108080060

Record 1998 - 1st:1 2nd:0 3rd:0 Ran:9
Pre1998 - 1st:2 2nd:5 3rd:10 Ran:54

Win Prizemoney £9,461 *Total Prizemoney* £20,679

Wins * **1998** *Jan Southw (STD) H* *6f* *37* *34*
1995 Spt Redcar (GD) H 7f 65 70 <
1994 May Ripon (GD) H 6f 69 69

1998 Turf 0-3:(5f 2, 6f)(sft, g-f, frm)1998 AW 1-6: (6f 1-4, 7f 2) (Fibr 1-6)

Very moderate gelding, effective 6 to 7f, best at 6f, acts on gd to frm, has worn blinkers (effectively), likes left handed tracks, likes tight tracks. Turf high 23. AW high 34 (1st run).

**D W Chapman [1-25] David Chapman (from P Calver [2-38] Spt 1996).*

KID'Z'PLAY (IRE) RR 61f 4518[8]

2 b g Rudimentary (USA) 8.2f **(66)**-Saka Saka (Camden Town)9.3f **(53)**

Form - 78

Record 1998 - 1st:0 2nd:0 3rd:0 Ran:2

1998 Turf 0-2: (5f 2) (gd, g-f)

Currently average gelding. Turf high 61 (began Spt).

KIERKEGAARD RR 119f 4833a[2]

5

Form - 702

1998 Turf 0-2: (8f 2) (sft, g-s)

High-class. Turf high 113 - 2nd of 8 to Waky Nao (11 Oct San Siro 8f g-s RF 4833a). He has been ridden with restraint and tried from the front, but usually finds something to beat him in Group events nowadays. **G Pucciatti in ITY [0-3].*

KIKA BHB 22f34a **RR 36f 34a** 5125[6]
5 gr m Niniski (USA) 13.2f **(67)** - Goeswell (Roan Rocket) 7.8f **(57)**
Form - 25014560458006066
Record 1998 - 1st:1 2nd:1 3rd:0 Ran:17
Pre1998 - 1st:1 2nd:0 3rd:2 Ran:6
Win Prizemoney £5,621 *Total Prizemoney* £7,200
Wins 1998 Apr Bright (GD) C 11.9f 44 <
1997 Jly Doncas (GD) S 12f 42
1998 Turf 1-14: (10f, 11f 2, 12f 1-10, 14f) (g-s 1-2, gd 5, g-f 2, frm 4, hrd) 1998 AW 0-3: (12f, 13f, 16f) (Equi 3)
Very moderate filly, effective 12 to 13f, best at 12f, acts on g-s to frm - acts on Equi, has worn blinkers, prefers left handed tracks. Turf high 44 (1st run) - 1st of 11 getting 13lb from Lancer (20 Apr Brighton RF 0765). AW high 36 (1st run) - 2nd of 10 getting 4lb from Rowlandsons Charm (7 Feb Lingfield 13f Equi RF 0240).
**J J Bridger [0-13] W Wood (from K R Burke [2-10] Apr 1998).*

KILBOWIE HILL BHB 56f70a **RR 68f 70a** 4796[11]
2 b f Never so Bold 7.1f **(62)** - Out of Hours (Lochnager) 6f **(59)**
Form - 0041163700
Record 1998 - 1st:2 2nd:0 3rd:1 Ran:10
Win Prizemoney £4,821 *Total Prizemoney* £5,251
Wins * 1998 *Jly Wolver (STD) H* *6f* *68* <
*** 1998** Jly Leices (GD) S 5f 68 <
1998 Turf 1-7: (5f 1-4, 6f 3) (sft, gd 2, g-f, frm 1-3) 1998 AW 1-3: (5f, 6f 1-2) (Fibr 1-3)
Above-average filly, effective 5 to 6f, acts on frm - acts on Fibr. Turf high 68 - 1st of 11 from Nicholas Mistress (16 Jly Leicester RF 2853). AW high 73 - also 1st of 11 getting 6lb from Dolly Day Dream (24 Jly Wolverhampton RF 3093). Becoming disappointing.
**D McCain [2-10] Clayton Bigley Partnership Ltd.*

KILCULLEN (IRE) BHB 74f **RR 82df** 1314[13]
3 b br g In The Wings 11.2f **(77)** - Liffey Lass (USA) (Irish River (FR)) 8.6f **(78)**
Form - 00
Record 1998 - 1st:0 2nd:0 3rd:0 Ran:2
Pre1998 - 1st:0 2nd:0 3rd:1 Ran:2
Win Prizemoney £0 *Total Prizemoney* £870
1998 Turf 0-2: (10f, 12f) (gd, frm)
Scopey, decent gelding, has worn blinkers. Turf high 42.
**J H M Gosden [0-4] Sheikh Mohammed.*

KILCULLEN LAD (IRE) BHB 78f73a **RR 83f 73a** 4837[4]
4 b g Fayruz 6.6f **(63)** - Royal Home (Royal Palace) 9f **(56)**
Form - 01008204504
Record 1998 - 1st:1 2nd:1 3rd:0 Ran:11
Pre1998 - 1st:5 2nd:5 3rd:0 Ran:21
Win Prizemoney £24,023 *Total Prizemoney* £32,323
Wins * 1998 May Redcar (G-F) H 5f 75 81 <
1997 May Lingfi (G-F) H 6f 67 74
1996 *Dec Lingfi (STD) H 6f 70 75*
1996 *Nov Lingfi (STD) H 5f 61 77*
1996 Spt Redcar (FRM) H 5f 56 53
1996 Jun Lingfi (FRM) S 6f 48
1998 Turf 1-11: (5f 1-10, 6f) (g-s, gd 4, g-f 1-4, frm 2)
Decent gelding, effective 5 to 6f, best at 5f, acts on g-f to frm, best on g-f, often wears blinkers, does well at Sandown. Turf high 83 - 2nd of 11 to Afaan (18 Jly Newmarket 5f frm RF 2920) - also 1st of 16 giving 15lb to Maiteamia (26 May Redcar RF 1477). Returned to winning ways at Redcar in May, and has not run badly in hot races since, though he had no chance from his draw in the Stewards' Cup. **K T Ivory [1-11] George Tobitt (from P Mooney [5-21] Spt 1997).*

KILDEE GEM RR 53f 5005[7]
2 b c Minshaanshu Amad (USA) 11.3f **(53)** - To The Point (Sharpen Up) 8.3f **(67)**
Form - 07
Record 1998 - 1st:0 2nd:0 3rd:0 Ran:2
1998 Turf 0-2: (6f, 8f) (sft, g-f)
Currently fair colt. Turf high 53 (began Spt).
**A P Jones [0-2] J F O'Donovan.*

KILDEE LAD BHB 50f70a **RR 50f 70a** 3605[10]
8 b g Presidium 7.5f **(56)** - National Time (USA) (Lord Avie (USA)) 5.3f **(61)**
Form - 00
Record 1998 - 1st:0 2nd:0 3rd:0 Ran:2
Pre1998 - 1st:6 2nd:9 3rd:8 Ran:66
Win Prizemoney £21,368 *Total Prizemoney* £37,004
Wins 1996 Jly Bath (FRM) H 5.7f 69 78 <
1996 Jly Leices (G-F) H 6f 69 70
1994 Oct Chepst (GD) H 5.1f 68 69
1994 Spt Goodwo (G-F) H 5f 65 65
1994 May Bath (GD) H 5.7f 62 62
1998 Turf 0-2: (5f, 8f) (g-f, frm)
Average gelding, effective 5 to 6f, acts on gd to g-f, has worn blinkers, likes left handed tracks. Turf high 40. Becoming disappointing.
**P Bowen [0-1] Greenacre Racing Partnership Ltd (from I Semple [0-1] May 1998).*

KILIMANJARO BHB 112f **RR 112f** 2105[2]
3 b c Shirley Heights 12.1f **(76)** - Darara (Top Ville) 11.7f **(68)**
Form - 22
Record 1998 - 1st:0 2nd:2 3rd:0 Ran:2
Pre1998 - 1st:1 2nd:0 3rd:0 Ran:4
Win Prizemoney £4,305 *Total Prizemoney* £43,581
Wins * 1997 Aug Sandow (SFT) 8.1f 104+ <
1998 Turf 0-2: (10f, 12f) (gd, hrd)
Group-class colt, effective 8 to 12f, acts on gd to hrd. Turf high 112 - 2nd of 10 to Royal Anthem (19 Jun Ascot 12f gd RF 2105). Bred to be a top-class middle-distance performer, his reputation preceded him at two but he ultimately proved disappointing. He came up against Royal Anthem on both his starts of '98, chasing him home at Newmarket and Royal Ascot, but suffered an injury in the latter race and was retired to stud.
**Sir Michael Stoute [1-6] Tabor Mrs Magnier Lord Lloyd Webber.*

KILLARNEY JAZZ BHB 68f76a **RR 58f 76a** 1213[13]
3 b c Alhijaz 7.7f **(57)** - Killarney Belle (USA) (Irish Castle (USA)) 11.2f **(75)**
Form - 0461110
Record 1998 - 1st:3 2nd:0 3rd:0 Ran:6
Pre1998 - 1st:0 2nd:1 3rd:0 Ran:3
Win Prizemoney £6,278 *Total Prizemoney* £7,270
Wins * 1998 *May Southw (STD) C 8f 71+* <
1998 *Mar Southw (STD) C 8f 69*
1998 *Feb Southw (STD) H 8f 59 62*
1998 Turf 0-1: (8f) (frm) 1998 AW 3-5: (6f 2, 8f 3-3) (Fibr 3-5)
Scopey, above-average colt, effective 6 to 8f, best at 8f - acts on Fibr, has worn blinkers, prefers left handed tracks, prefers tight tracks. AW high 71 - 1st of 8 giving 15lb to Spring Beacon (7 May Southwell RF 1082) - also 1st of 9 giving 2lb to Sharp Monkey (2 Mar Southwell RF 0384).
**N P Littmoden [1-2] M Barton (from J Wharton [2-7] Mar 1998).*

KILLER INSTINCT RR 94+f 3065[2]
2 b c Zafonic (USA) 9f **(83)** - Rappa Tap Tap (FR) (Tap On Wood) 10.3f **(65)**
Form - 2
Record 1998 - 1st:0 2nd:1 3rd:0 Ran:1
Win Prizemoney £0 *Total Prizemoney* £2,080
1998 Turf 0-1: (7f) (gd)
Currently useful colt. (1st run) - 2nd of 5 to Compton Admiral (24 Jly Ascot 7f gd RF 3065). The subject of a great deal of hype before his Ascot debut in July, he found the experienced Compton Admiral too strong. That turned out to be his only start of the season, and his reappearance at three is awaited with great interest.
**H R A Cecil [0-1] The Thoroughbred Corporation.*

KILLERNAN KILMAINE (IRE) BHB 44f **RR 45f** 3410[12]
3 b g Sure Blade (USA) 10.6f **(66)** - Rio Piedras (Kala Shikari) 8.4f **(54)**
Form - 600
Record 1998 - 1st:0 2nd:0 3rd:0 Ran:3
Pre1998 - 1st:0 2nd:0 3rd:0 Ran:1
1998 Turf 0-3: (7f, 10f, 11f) (g-f 2, frm)
Lengthy, moderate gelding. Turf high 45.
**A Bailey [0-4] The Ponte Club.*

KILMEENA LAD BHB 78f **RR 80f** 5144[15]
2 b c Minshaanshu Amad (USA) 11.3f **(53)** - Kilmeena Glen (Beveled (USA)) 9f **(59)**
Form - 0010
Record 1998 - 1st:1 2nd:0 3rd:0 Ran:4

Win Prizemoney £4,276 *Total Prizemoney* £4,276
Wins * **1998** Oct Newbur (HVY) 6f 80 <
1998 Turf 1-4: (5f, 6f 1-1, 7f, 8f) (sft 1-1, gd 3)
Decent colt. Turf high 80 (began Spt) - 1st of 15 from City Reach (23 Oct Newbury RF 4967). **E A Wheeler [1-4] Mrs J A Cleary.*

KILMEENA LADY BHB 32f27a **RR 38f 27a** 330[8]
4 b f Inca Chief (USA) 5.6f **(45)** -Kilmeena Glen (Beveled (USA)) 9f **(59)**
Form - 7678
Record 1998 - 1st:0 2nd:0 3rd:0 Ran:2
Pre1998 - 1st:0 2nd:0 3rd:0 Ran:8
1998 AW 0-2: (8f 2) (Equi 2)
Leggy, very moderate filly. AW high 29.
**J C Fox [0-10] Mrs J A Cleary.*

KILNAMARTYRA GIRL BHB 36f33a **RR 45f 33a** 4839[8]
8 b m Arkan 9.7f **(39)** - Star Cove (Porto Bello) 8.9f **(43)**
Form - 08150222457038
Record 1998 - 1st:1 2nd:3 3rd:1 Ran:14
Pre1998 - 1st:5 2nd:7 3rd:7 Ran:49
Win Prizemoney £16,491 *Total Prizemoney* £29,284
Wins * **1998** May Newcas (G-S) H 12.4f 38 44
* 1997 Jly Mussel (GD) H 12f 38 42
* 1997 *Jan Southw (STD) H 12f 41 45*
* 1995 Aug Beverl (G-F) H 7.5f 51 53 <
* 1995 Jly Beverl (GD) H 7.5f 44 52
* 1994 Jly Newcas (G-F) H 7f 44 41
1998 Turf 1-12: (10f, 12f 1-5, 14f 3, 16f 3) (g-s 2, gd 1-3, g-f, frm 6)
1998 AW 0-2: (12f, 14f) (Fibr 2)
Moderate mare, effective 10 to 16f, best at 12f, acts on gd to frm - acts on Fibr, has worn blinkers, and excels at Musselburgh. Turf high 45 - 3rd of 14 to Rusk (22 Spt Beverley 12f g-f RF 4403) - also 1st of 12 getting 20lb from Talib (4 May Newcastle RF 1025). AW high 16. She lacks the pace to take her chances.
**J Parkes [8-80] P J Cronin.*

KILTING RR 84++f 4959[1]
2 ch f Nashwan (USA) 10.3f **(79)** - Balliasta (USA) (Lyphard (USA)) 9.9f **(72)**
Form - 1
Record 1998 - 1st:1 2nd:0 3rd:0 Ran:1
Win Prizemoney £4,695 *Total Prizemoney* £4,695
Wins * **1998** Oct Doncas (SFT) 7f 84++ <
1998 Turf 1-1: (7f 1-1) (frm 1-1)
Currently decent filly. (1st run) - 1st of 16 getting 5lb from Tarawan (23 Oct Doncaster RF 4959). Quickened away to win a Doncaster maiden on her only start, and looks an intriguing middle-distance prospect. **B W Hills [1-1] K Abdulla.*

KIMBERLEY BHB 88f **RR 83f** 4855[1]
3 b c Shareef Dancer (USA) 10.1f **(67)** - Willowbank (Gay Fandango (USA)) 8.5f **(59)**
Form - 02644611
Record 1998 - 1st:2 2nd:1 3rd:0 Ran:8
Pre1998 - 1st:0 2nd:0 3rd:0 Ran:1
Win Prizemoney £10,446 *Total Prizemoney* £12,606
Wins * **1998** Oct Redcar (HVY) H 10f 80 83 <
* **1998** Oct York (GD) 10.4f 82
1998 Turf 2-8: (10f 2-3, 12f 3, 15f, 16f) (g-s 1-1, gd 2, g-f 1-2, frm 3)
Decent colt, effective 10 to 12f, best at 10f, acts on g-s to frm, has worn blinkers. Turf high 83 - 1st of 9 from Alcayde (17 Oct Redcar RF 4855) - also 1st of 5 giving 5lb to Raqqasa (7 Oct York RF 4702). Consistent. **G Wragg [2-9] Mrs John Van Geest.*

KIM'S BRAVE BHB 89f **RR 86f** 1597[2]
3 b g Deploy 11.4f **(67)** - Princess Dina (Huntercombe) 7.3f **(56)**
Form - 02
Record 1998 - 1st:0 2nd:1 3rd:0 Ran:2
Pre1998 - 1st:2 2nd:0 3rd:0 Ran:10
Win Prizemoney £7,484 *Total Prizemoney* £11,524
Wins * 1997 Spt Bath (GD) H 8f 80 89 <
* 1997 Jun Bright (FRM) S 6f 61
1998 Turf 0-2: (10f, 12f) (g-f 2)
Workmanlike, useful gelding, effective 8 to 10f, best at 10f, acts on gd to g-f, best on g-f, often wears blinkers (very effectively). Turf high 86 - 2nd of 11 getting 4lb from Evening World (30 May Lingfield 10f g-f RF 1597). He does not look a straightforward ride.
**B J Meehan [2-12] J K Sim.*

KIMU (IRE) RR 90f 4295a[7]
5 b g Ela-Mana-Mou 12.7f **(72)** - Kifenia
Form - 208467
1998 Turf 0-6: (8f, 9f 3, 10f, 11f) (sft 2, gd 4)
Useful gelding, effective 9f, acts on sft. Turf high 90 (1st run) - 2nd of 6 giving 7lb to Short Shift (19 Jun Tipperary 9f sft RF 2216a).
**C Collins in IRE [1-13] Danilo Corridoni.*

KINAN (USA) BHB 89f **RR 85f** 4258[1]
2 b c Dixieland Band (USA) 10.1f **(80)** - Alsharta (USA) (Mr Prospector (USA)) 8.8f **(78)**
Form - 6261
Record 1998 - 1st:1 2nd:1 3rd:0 Ran:4
Win Prizemoney £3,336 *Total Prizemoney* £4,304
Wins * **1998** Spt Nottin (GD) 6.1f 85 <
1998 Turf 1-4: (6f 1-4) (gd 1-1, g-f 2, frm)
Useful colt. Turf high 85 - 1st of 12 from Habub (14 Spt Nottingham RF 4258). **R W Armstrong [1-4] Hamdan Al Maktoum.*

KINCARA PALACE (IRE) RR 100f 3870a[7]
3 b f Fairy King (USA) 7.7f **(75)** - Haughty Manner (High Top) 10.2f **(67)**
Form - 10637
1998 Turf 1-5: (6f 2, 7f 1-1, 8f 2) (sft 1-1, gd 3, g-f)
Very useful filly, effective 5 to 7f, best at 7f, acts on sft to gd, best on gd. Turf high 110 (1st run) - 1st of 6 giving 5lb to Heed My Warning (2 May Curragh RF 1052a). Inconsistent. She put up a brave effort to win by a short-head on her reappearance, but was highly tried and struggled thereafter.
**A P O'Brien in IRE [4-11] Mrs John Magnier.*

KIND SIR RR 76f 4779[5]
2 b c Generous (IRE) 11.5f **(82)** - Noble Conquest (USA) (Vaguely Noble) 10.1f **(72)**
Form - 75
Record 1998 - 1st:0 2nd:0 3rd:0 Ran:2
1998 Turf 0-2: (8f 2) (gd, frm)
Currently above-average colt. Turf high 76 (began Spt).
**B W Hills [0-2] A D Shead.*

KING ADAM (IRE) BHB 97f **RR 104+f** 4248[1]
2 b c Fairy King (USA) 7.7f **(75)**-Sailor's Mate(Shirley Heights)10.3f **(74)**
Form - 221
Record 1998 - 1st:1 2nd:2 3rd:0 Ran:3
Win Prizemoney £4,018 *Total Prizemoney* £6,226
Wins * **1998** Spt Goodwo (G-S) 8f 104+ <
1998 Turf 1-3: (7f 2, 8f 1-1) (g-s 1-1, gd, frm)
Currently very useful colt. Turf high 104 (began Jly) - 1st of 4 from Zindabad (12 Spt Goodwood RF 4248). He took the eye in the paddock on his debut at Sandown, and did little wrong in the race itself, pushing the subsequent Group winner Saytarra hard after running green. Disappointing at Chester in August, he was very impressive at Goodwood the following month and looked worth his place in one of the big back-end races. However, he was put away by his shrewd connections and will doubtless come back a bigger and better three-year-old. He is one for the notebook.
**Sir Michael Stoute [1-3] Lord Weinstock.*

KING ALEX BHB 110f **RR 110f** 4843[8]
5 b h Rainbow Quest (USA) 11.2f **(81)** - Alexandrie (USA) (Val de L'Orne (FR)) 12f **(75)**
Form - 4338
Record 1998 - 1st:0 2nd:0 3rd:2 Ran:4
Pre1998 - 1st:3 2nd:2 3rd:0 Ran:6
Win Prizemoney £27,727 *Total Prizemoney* £40,776
Wins * 1997 Aug Currag (G-S) G3 10f 112 <
* 1997 May Bath (G-S) 11.7f 96+
* 1996 Apr Leices (GD) 10f 66++
1998 Turf 0-4: (9f 2, 10f 2) (gd 2, g-f, frm)
Group-class colt, effective 9 to 10f, best at 10f, acts on gd to frm, best on gd. Turf high 110 (1st run) (began Jly) - 4th of 10 giving 6lb to Happy Valentine (1 Jly Kempton 10f gd RF 2445). Consistent. Lightly raced over the years, he seemed to lose the plot somewhat in 1998. Connections will not find him easy to place. **R Charlton [3-10] Wafic Said.*

KINGCHIP BOY BHB 42f58a **RR 61f 58a** 5127[16]
9 b g Petong 7.6f **(58)** - Silk St James (Pas de Seul) 9.1f **(67)**
Form - 00001171463470484080085000

Record 1998 - 1st:3 2nd:0 3rd:1 Ran:24
Pre1998 - 1st:17 2nd:16 3rd:7 Ran:105
Win Prizemoney £61,221 *Total Prizemoney* £86,432
Wins * **1998** *Feb Southw (STD) C 7f 68+*
* **1998** *Feb Southw (STD) H 7f 65 71*
* **1998** *Jan Southw (STD) H 8f 56 61*
* 1997 *Feb Southw (STD) H 8f 71 79* <
* 1997 *Feb Southw (STD) H 8f 71 75*
* 1997 *Jan Southw (STD) H 7f 68 68*
* 1996 *Apr Southw (STD) H 8f 64 69*
* 1996 *Jan Southw (STD) H 8f 46 66+*
* 1996 *Jan Southw (STD) H 8f 46 67*
* 1996 *Jan Southw (STD) H 8f 49 57*
* 1995 May Goodwo (FRM) H 8f 72 74
* 1994 Spt Bright (GD) H 8f 69 74
* 1994 Aug Epsom (G-F) H 7f 64 65
1998 Turf 0-11: (7f 4, 8f 6, 10f) (sft, g-s 3, gd 5, frm 2) 1998 AW 3-13: (7f 2-6, 8f 1-7) (Fibr 3-13)
Above-average gelding, effective 7 to 8f, best at 8f - acts on Fibr, often wears blinkers (effectively), likes left handed tracks, favours tight tracks, excels at Southwell. Turf high 61. AW high 71 - 1st of 11 giving 13lb to Mr Frosty (9 Feb Southwell RF 0251). He just seems a totally different horse in the first two months of the year, and 1998 was no exception with another three victories. At his best over seven furlongs to a mile on the Southwell Fibresand, he is suited by forcing tactics. **M J Ryan [20-130] Doug Fleet.*

KING CURAN (USA) BHB 51f65a **RR 51f 65a** 2841[6]

7 b g Lear Fan (USA) 10.4f **(80)** - Runaway Lady (USA) (Caucasus (USA)) 8.2f **(74)**
Form - 076
Record 1998 - 1st:0 2nd:0 3rd:0 Ran:3
Pre1998 - 1st:8 2nd:1 3rd:3 Ran:40
Win Prizemoney £29,750 *Total Prizemoney* £33,683
Wins 1996 Spt Hamilt (GD) H 8.3f 60 70+
1996 Jly Ayr (GD) H 7f 52 60
1995 Jun Ayr (FRM) H 10f 61 64
1995 Jun Ayr (G-F) H 8f 60 59
1995 May Hamilt (G-F) H 8.3f 57 59
1994 Spt Hamilt (GD) C 8.3f 57
1998 Turf 0-3: (10f, 12f 2) (gd, g-f 2)
Fair gelding, often wears blinkers. Turf high 51 (began Jly). Inconsistent.
**P Bowen [1-11] Peter Bowling (from D HaydnJones [2-12] Oct 1996).*

KING DARIUS (IRE) BHB 80f **RR 84f** 4966[15]

3 ch c Persian Bold 10f **(69)** - Valiant Friend (USA) (Shahrastani (USA)) 8.8f **(72)**
Form - 13871500
Record 1998 - 1st:2 2nd:0 3rd:1 Ran:8
Pre1998 - 1st:1 2nd:0 3rd:1 Ran:8
Win Prizemoney £13,424 *Total Prizemoney* £17,335
Wins * **1998** Aug Windso (G-F) H 11.6f 79 84 <
* **1998** May Kempto (GD) H 9f 77 82
* 1997 Jly Chepst (G-S) C 6.1f 74
1998 Turf 2-8: (9f 1-1, 10f 5, 12f 1-2) (sft, gd 1-4, g-f 1-2, frm)
Neat, decent colt, effective 6 to 12f, best at 12f, acts on gd to frm, likes tight tracks. Turf high 84 - 1st of 13 giving 15lb to Silvertown (17 Aug Windsor RF 3683) - also 1st of 12 giving 8lb to Prince Batshoof (4 May Kempton RF 1017). **R Hannon [3-16] John Perry.*

KINGDOM QUEEN (IRE) BHB 53f55a **RR 63f 55a** 4875[5]

3 b f Night Shift (USA) 8.1f **(73)** - Yashina (FR) (Tennyson (FR)) 12.1f **(50)**
Form - 6441655205
Record 1998 - 1st:1 2nd:1 3rd:0 Ran:10
Pre1998 - 1st:0 2nd:0 3rd:1 Ran:2
Win Prizemoney £2,087 *Total Prizemoney* £3,561
Wins * **1998** Jly Beverl (G-F) 9.9f 63 <
1998 Turf 1-8: (8f, 10f 1-2, 11f, 12f 4) (g-s 2, g-f 4, frm 1-2) 1998 AW 0-2: (12f, 15f) (Fibr 2)
Leggy, average filly, effective 10 to 15f, acts on g-f to frm - acts on Fibr, favours tight tracks. Turf high 63 - 1st of 5 getting 12lb from Tallulah Belle (20 Jly Beverley RF 2957). AW high 61 (1st run) (began Spt) - 2nd of 12 to Operatic (19 Spt Wolverhampton 15f Fibr RF 4384).
**Miss J A Camacho [1-10] G B Turnbull Ltd (from M J Camacho [0-2] Spt 1997).*

KINGDOM RUBY (IRE) BHB 63f62a **RR 66f 62a** 5058[1]

3 ch f Bluebird (USA) 7.9f **(71)** - Tapestry (Tap On Wood) 10.3f **(65)**
Form - 65261
Record 1998 - 1st:1 2nd:1 3rd:0 Ran:5
Win Prizemoney £3,485 *Total Prizemoney* £4,581
Wins * **1998** Oct Newcas (SFT) 7f 66 <
1998 Turf 1-5: (6f 3, 7f 1-2) (sft 1-1, g-s, gd 2, g-f)
Average filly. Turf high 68 - also 1st of 7 from Idma (30 Oct Newcastle RF 5058). **Miss J A Camacho [1-5] G B Turnbull Ltd.*

KINGFISHER GOLD (IRE) RR 63f 4868[8]

2 b g Perugino (USA) - Cerosia (Pitskelly) 8.5f **(53)**
Form - 78
Record 1998 - 1st:0 2nd:0 3rd:0 Ran:2
1998 Turf 0-2: (5f, 6f) (gd, g-f)
Currently average gelding. Turf high 63 (began Spt).
**T P Tate [0-2] C E Whiteley.*

KINGFISHER MILL (USA) BHB 108f **RR 111f** 4491[9]

4 ch c Riverman (USA) 9.7f **(78)** - Charming Life (NZ) (Sir Tristram) 10.7f **(76)**
Form - 4050
Record 1998 - 1st:0 2nd:0 3rd:0 Ran:4
Pre1998 - 1st:3 2nd:0 3rd:1 Ran:7
Win Prizemoney £110,388 *Total Prizemoney* £129,007
Wins * 1997 Spt Ascot (GD) G3 12f 119 <
* 1997 Jun Ascot (SFT) G2 12f 117
* 1997 Apr Newmar (GD) 10f 91+
1998 Turf 0-4: (10f, 12f 3) (gd 3, g-f)
Strong, Group-class colt, effective 12f, acts on gd. Turf high 111. Consistent. He ran a promising race in the Jockey Club Stakes on his reappearance, but finished last on two of his three subsequent outings. It is a long time since he put up a barn-storming effort to win at Royal Ascot in 1997.
**Mrs J Cecil [3-11] Lord Howard de Walden.*

KINGFISHERS BONNET BHB 55f **RR 65f** 4994[7]

2 b f Hamas (IRE) 8f **(72)** - Mainmast (Bustino) 10.4f **(64)**
Form - 3300407
Record 1998 - 1st:0 2nd:0 3rd:2 Ran:7
Win Prizemoney £0 *Total Prizemoney* £1,320
1998 Turf 0-7: (5f, 6f 4, 7f 2) (hvy, sft, gd 2, g-f 2, frm)
Average filly, effective 6f, acts on frm. Turf high 65 - 3rd of 15 to Golden Charm (15 May Nottingham 6f frm RF 1245).
**S G Knight [0-7] P J Wightman.*

KING FLYER (IRE) BHB 60f **RR 69f** 4663[13]

2 b c Ezzoud (IRE) - Al Guswa (Shernazar) 10.2f **(73)**
Form - 5400
Record 1998 - 1st:0 2nd:0 3rd:0 Ran:4
Win Prizemoney £0 *Total Prizemoney* £239
1998 Turf 0-3: (6f, 7f, 10f) (g-s, g-f 2) 1998 AW 0-1: (7f) (Fibr)
Average colt, has worn blinkers. Turf high 69 (began Jly).
**B Hanbury [0-4] Abdullah Ali.*

KING FOLEY BHB 70f **RR 66f** 3688[5]

2 b c Petong 7.6f **(58)** - Salacious (Sallust) 8.4f **(63)**
Form - 0155645
Record 1998 - 1st:1 2nd:0 3rd:0 Ran:7
Win Prizemoney £3,485 *Total Prizemoney* £3,982
Wins * **1998** May Bright (G-F) 5.3f 60+ <
1998 Turf 1-7: (5f 1-5, 6f 2) (gd 1-3, g-f 2, frm 2)
Average colt, mostly wears blinkers (very effectively). Turf high 71. Won a small race at Brighton before failing to handle a rise in class. **W G M Turner [1-7] Foley Steelstock.*

KING FOR A DAY BHB 72f **RR 68f** 4967[3]

2 b c Machiavellian (USA) 9.8f **(83)** - Dizzy Heights (USA) (Danzig (USA)) 8.4f **(76)**
Form - 063
Record 1998 - 1st:0 2nd:0 3rd:1 Ran:3
Win Prizemoney £0 *Total Prizemoney* £624
1998 Turf 0-3: (6f, 7f 2) (sft, gd, frm)
Currently average colt. Turf high 68 (began Aug).
**B W Hills [0-3] Maktoum Al Maktoum.*

KING LION **RR 34f** 1977[10]
3 b c Lion Cavern (USA) 7.5f **(74)** - Alo Ez (Alzao (USA)) 7.1f **(68)**
Form - 00
Record 1998 - 1st:0 2nd:0 3rd:0 Ran:2
1998 Turf 0-2: (7f, 8f) (g-s, gd)
Workmanlike, currently very moderate colt. Turf high 34.
**R W Armstrong [0-2] R J Arculli.*

KING OBERON (IRE) **RR 81f** 3074[3]
2 b c Fairy King (USA) 7.7f **(75)** - Annenberg (Slip Anchor) 9.8f **(73)**
Form - 43
Record 1998 - 1st:0 2nd:0 3rd:1 Ran:2
Win Prizemoney £0 *Total Prizemoney* £890
1998 Turf 0-2: (5f, 6f) (frm 2)
Currently decent colt. Turf high 81 (began Jly). (DEAD)
**W J Haggas [0-2] Highclere Thoroughbred Racing Ltd.*

KING OF DANCE BHB 39f **RR 62f** 4677[26]
3 ch g King's Signet (USA) 7f **(51)** - Times (Junius (USA)) 7.7f **(65)**
Form - 2700000
Record 1998 - 1st:0 2nd:1 3rd:0 Ran:7
Pre1998 - 1st:0 2nd:0 3rd:0 Ran:4
Win Prizemoney £0 *Total Prizemoney* £1,400
1998 Turf 0-7: (7f 4, 8f 3) (gd, g-f 5, frm)
Strong, average gelding, effective 7f, acts on gd, has worn blinkers. Turf high 62 (1st run) - 2nd of 8 giving 3lb to Durham Flyer (20 Jun Redcar 7f gd RF 2156). Becoming disappointing.
**B S Rothwell [0-11] Mrs Sybil St Quinton.*

KING OF HONEY (IRE) **RR 40f** 1967[7]
4 b c Fairy King (USA) 7.7f **(75)** - Sable Lake (Thatching) 8f **(66)**
Form - 7
Record 1998 - 1st:0 2nd:0 3rd:0 Ran:1
1998 Turf 0-1: (6f) (gd)
Workmanlike, currently moderate colt.
**J H M Gosden [0-1] Dikidada Racing Partnership.*

Very high-class colt, effective 8f, acts on gd. Turf high 123 (1st run) - 1st of 18 from Lend A Hand (2 May Newmarket RF 0974). A half-brother to General Monash, he was a very impressive winner on his Curragh debut at two, and went on to win four of his five races, although his narrow defeat by Lady Alexander left some doubts in people's minds. He apparently thrived during the winter, and his trainer was very confident that he would run a big race in the 2000 Guineas at Newmarket. Run a big race he did for, after travelling very well through the race, he showed a smart turn of foot to settle the issue in the last furlong. He was then sent for the Derby, but it all went horribly wrong. After a difficult journey to the track, he went lame during the race and was subsequently retired. He would probably have taken all the beating in all the top races over a mile had he been kept to that trip, but now we will never know. **A P O'Brien in IRE [5-7] Mrs John Magnier & M Tabor.*

KING OF MOMMUR (IRE) BHB 79f **RR 76f** 3078[8]
3 b c Fairy King (USA) 7.7f **(75)** - Monoglow (Kalaglow) 9.8f **(67)**
Form - 003638
Record 1998 - 1st:0 2nd:0 3rd:2 Ran:6
Win Prizemoney £0 *Total Prizemoney* £1,022
1998 Turf 0-6: (8f, 10f, 12f 3, 14f) (sft, gd 2, frm 3)
Strong, above-average colt, effective 12f, acts on frm, has worn blinkers. Turf high 82 - 3rd of 6 getting 6lb from Casino Captive (25 May Chepstow 12f frm RF 1444).
**B J Meehan [0-6] The Three Bears Racing.*

KING OF PERU BHB 73f94a **RR 76f 94a** 4209[16]
5 b h Inca Chief (USA) 5.6f **(45)** - Julie's Star (IRE) (Thatching) 8f **(66)**
Form - 727384580
Record 1998 - 1st:0 2nd:1 3rd:1 Ran:9
Pre1998 - 1st:4 2nd:2 3rd:3 Ran:28
Win Prizemoney £27,974 *Total Prizemoney* £41,026

Wins	1996	May	Goodwo (GD)	H	7f	100	97 <
	1995	Spt	Newmar (G-F)	H	6f	86	93
	1995	Spt	Ayr (GD)	H	6f	77	86
	1995	Jly	Haydoc (G-F)		6f		75+

A short reign for King Of Kings

KING OF KINGS (IRE) **RR 123+f** 1778[15]
3 b c Sadler's Wells (USA) 11.3f **(87)** - Zummerudd (Habitat) 9.4f **(70)**
Form - 10
1998 Turf 1-2: (8f 1-1, 12f) (gd 1-1, g-f)

1998 Turf 0-7: (5f 2, 6f 4, 7f) (sft 2, gd 3, frm 2) 1998 AW 0-2: (5f, 6f) (Fibr 2)
Useful colt, effective 5 to 6f, acts on gd - acts on Fibr, has worn

blinkers. Turf high 77. AW high 92 (1st run) - 2nd of 13 giving 8lb to Double Oscar (30 Apr Wolverhampton 5f Fibr RF 0940). He did not manage to win during the season, despite gradually dropping down the handicap on turf. His two best efforts both came on the Wolverhampton Fibresand, but he is officially rated so highly in that sphere that he is handicapped out of all but a few races.
**N P Littmoden [0-15] M C S D Racing (from A P Jarvis [4-22] May 1997).*

KING OF SPARTA BHB 75f85a **RR 78f 85a** 257[1]

5 b g Kefaah (USA) 11.2f **(64)** - Khaizaraan (CAN) (Sham (USA)) 9.5f **(68)**
Form - 141
Record 1998 - 1st:2 2nd:0 3rd:0 Ran:3
Pre1998 - 1st:1 2nd:4 3rd:0 Ran:8
Win Prizemoney £7,288 *Total Prizemoney* £11,779
Wins * **1998** *Feb Southw (STD) H 16f 79 82* <
* **1998** *Jan Lingfi (STD) H 16f 70 75+*
1996 Aug Bright (FRM) 10f 65
1998 AW 2-3: (12f, 16f 2-2) (Equi 1-1, Fibr 1-2)
Decent gelding. AW high 82 - 1st of 9 giving 19lb to Time Can Tell (9 Feb Southwell RF 0257) - also 1st of 7 giving 10lb to Guest Alliance (10 Jan Lingfield RF 0063). A dodgy customer when last running on the Flat in the autumn of '96, he managed to win two modest amateur riders' events on sand early in the year, but how long the novelty will remain is anyone's guess.
**O Sherwood [5-10] Darren Mercer (from L M Cumani [1-8] Spt 1996).*

KING OF STYLE BHB 55f **RR 53tf** 2305[5]

3 ch c Elmaamul (USA) 8.1f **(70)** - Superb Fashion (USA) (Topsider (USA)) 8.3f **(71)**
Form - 605
Record 1998 - 1st:0 2nd:0 3rd:0 Ran:3
1998 Turf 0-3: (10f, 12f 2) (sft, g-s, gd)
Tall, currently fair colt. Turf high 53. (DEAD)
**J J Sheehan [0-3] John Sheehan.*

KING OF THE RIVER (USA) BHB 74f **RR 76f** 3140[14]

3 b c Kingmambo (USA) 10.9f **(85)** - La Favorita (FR) (Nikos) 7.1f **(78)**
Form - 02561230
Record 1998 - 1st:1 2nd:2 3rd:1 Ran:8
Pre1998 - 1st:0 2nd:0 3rd:1 Ran:2
Win Prizemoney £2,458 *Total Prizemoney* £6,147
Wins 1998 Jun Chepst (G-S) C 7.1f 74 <
1998 Turf 1-8: (6f 2, 7f 1-5, 8f) (gd 1-6, g-f, frm)
Workmanlike, above-average colt, effective 7 to 8f, best at 7f, acts on gd to g-f, best on gd. Turf high 76 - 2nd of 11 getting 2lb from Guaranteed (19 Jun Newmarket 8f g-f RF 2127) - also 1st of 12 giving 17lb to Arbenig (12 Jun Chepstow RF 1921). He had to be dropped into claiming company at Chepstow in order to get off the mark. Left Chapple-Hyam after his next run, and shaped well for rookie trainer Greg Chung at Sandown.
**G C H Chung [0-2] Bernard Butt (from P W Chapple-Hyam [1-8] Jun 1998).*

KING OF TUNES (FR) BHB 80f79a **RR 79f 79a** 4631[35]

6 b h Chief Singer 8.6f **(62)** - Marcotte (Nebos (GER)) 9f **(78)**
Form - 250840
Record 1998 - 1st:0 2nd:1 3rd:0 Ran:6
Pre1998 - 1st:3 2nd:3 3rd:1 Ran:16
Win Prizemoney £13,858 *Total Prizemoney* £37,341
Wins * 1997 Jun Newmar (GD) H 8f 77 84 <
* 1996 *Jan Lingfi (STD) H 10f 68 71*
* 1995 Oct Ascot (SFT) 8f 75
1998 Turf 0-6: (8f 4, 9f 2) (gd 3, g-f 2, frm)
Above-average horse, effective 8 to 10f, best at 8f, acts on g-s to g-f, best on gd, has worn blinkers, and likes Newmarket. Turf high 89 (1st run) - 2nd of 24 getting 7lb from Hunters of Brora (28 Mar Doncaster 8f gd RF 0484). He is a bit of an in-and-out performer, quite capable of putting in a bold show in decent handicap company, as he showed when narrowly beaten in the Lincoln on his reappearance. He is very difficult to predict however, though he does seem to go well after a layoff.
**J J Sheehan [3-18] Mrs Eileen Sheehan (from M J Haynes [0-4] Oct 1997).*

KING PARROT (IRE) BHB 39f47a **RR 29f 47a** 3448[13]

10 br g King of Spain 7.3f **(55)** - Red Lory (Bay Express) 7.1f **(60)**
Form - 050
Record 1998 - 1st:0 2nd:0 3rd:0 Ran:3
Pre1998 - 1st:7 2nd:2 3rd:2 Ran:29
Win Prizemoney £18,479 *Total Prizemoney* £21,856
Wins * 1996 Jly Chepst (G-F) H 7.1f 51 55
* 1996 Jun Lingfi (FRM) SH 7f 47 53
* 1996 May Salisb (G-F) H 7f 46 50
* 1996 *Jan Lingfi (STD) H 7f 51 57*
* 1995 *Jan Southw (STD) H 8f 51 57*
1998 Turf 0-1: (7f) (frm) 1998 AW 0-2: (7f, 8f) (Equi, Fibr)
Very moderate gelding, effective 8f, acts on frm, has worn blinkers. AW high 39. Inconsistent.
**Lord Huntingdon [7-32] Lord Huntingdon.*

KING PERI (IRE) BHB 57f **RR 54f** 4709[18]

2 b c Fairy King (USA) 7.7f **(75)** - Maria Roberta (USA) (Roberto (USA)) 10f **(76)**
Form - 004480
Record 1998 - 1st:0 2nd:0 3rd:0 Ran:6
Win Prizemoney £0 *Total Prizemoney* £407
1998 Turf 0-6: (5f 2, 7f 3, 8f) (g-s, gd 2, frm 2, hrd)
Fair colt. Turf high 54. **N Tinkler [0-6] Leeds Plywood and Doors Ltd.*

KING PRIAM (IRE) BHB 67f **RR 68f** 5095[5]

3 b g Priolo (USA) 10.9f **(71)** - Barinia (Corvaro (USA)) 9f **(53)**
Form - 45523731265
Record 1998 - 1st:1 2nd:2 3rd:2 Ran:11
Pre1998 - 1st:0 2nd:0 3rd:0 Ran:1
Win Prizemoney £4,110 *Total Prizemoney* £8,712
Wins 1998 Oct Newmar (gd) C 12f 66 <
1998 Turf 1-11: (8f 2, 9f, 10f 3, 11f, 12f 1-4)(sft, g-s, gd 1-3, g-f 4, frm 2)
Lengthy, average gelding, effective 8 to 12f, best at 10f, acts on g-s to frm, best on g-f, often wears blinkers (effectively), excels at Newmarket and Folkestone. Turf high 70 - 2nd of 13 giving 7lb to Dry Lightning (26 Jun Newmarket 10f g-f RF 2312) - also 1st of 16 getting 15lb from Fletcher (1 Oct Newmarket RF 4590).
**M J Polglase [0-3] Ian Puddle (from M C Pipe [1-5] Oct 1998).*

KINGRHUMBA (USA) **RR 56f** 4395[8]

2 b c Kingmambo (USA) 10.9f **(85)** - Lady Ice (CAN) (Vice Regent (CAN)) 8.7f **(74)**
Form - 88
Record 1998 - 1st:0 2nd:0 3rd:0 Ran:2
1998 Turf 0-2: (7f, 8f) (g-f, frm)
Currently fair colt. Turf high 56 (began Spt).
**J Noseda [0-2] K Y Lim.*

KING RUFUS BHB 50f67a **RR 55f 67a** 4672[14]

5 ch h No Evil - Djanila (Fabulous Dancer (USA)) 9.4f **(70)**
Form - 00500
Record 1998 - 1st:0 2nd:0 3rd:0 Ran:5
Pre1998 - 1st:0 2nd:0 3rd:0 Ran:5
Win Prizemoney £0 *Total Prizemoney* £237
1998 Turf 0-5: (7f, 8f, 9f 2, 10f) (g-f 3, frm 2)
Fair colt. Turf high 55. Inconsistent.
**J L Eyre [0-5] Mrs N A Madsen (from J R Arnold [0-5] Jly 1996).*

KINGSALSA (USA) **RR 102f** 4470f[2]

2 br c Kingmambo (USA) 10.9f **(85)** - Caretta (Caro) 9.3f **(74)**
Form - 2
1998 Turf 0-1: (7f) (sft)
Currently very useful colt. He could not get his head in front on his first three starts, but ran a tremendous race in the Group One Prix de la Salamandre, finishing third, promoted to second, behind Aljabr and Stravinsky. He is obviously no superstar, but stays well and should win a Group race as a three-year-old.
**P Demercastel in FR [0-1] M Debeusscher.*

KINGS ARROW (IRE) BHB 58f **RR 58f** 4390[25]

3 b c Mujadil (USA) 7.7f **(70)** - Great Leighs (Vaigly Great) 7f **(58)**
Form - 0507200
Record 1998 - 1st:0 2nd:1 3rd:0 Ran:7
Pre1998 - 1st:0 2nd:0 3rd:0 Ran:1
Win Prizemoney £0 *Total Prizemoney* £1,513
1998 Turf 0-7: (6f 3, 7f 2, 8f 2) (sft, gd 3, frm 2, hrd)
Light-framed, fair colt, effective 6f, acts on gd. Turf high 58 - 2nd of 22 getting 9lb from Mamma's Boy (27 Jun Doncaster 6f gd RF

2331). *P Howling [0-1] C Hammond (from M Bell [0-7] Jly 1998).

KINGS ASSEMBLY BHB 52f50a **RR 56f 50a** 4887[2]

6 b g Presidium 7.5f **(56)** - To The Point (Sharpen Up) 8.3f **(67)**
Form - 0054002
Record 1998 - 1st:0 2nd:1 3rd:0 Ran:7
Pre1998 - 1st:3 2nd:1 3rd:1 Ran:17
Win Prizemoney £9,841 *Total Prizemoney* £14,880
Wins 1996 Apr Nottin (G-F) H 10f 76 80 <
1995 Jun Leices (GD) H 10f 67 68
1994 Oct Pontef (G-S) 6f 54
1998 Turf 0-7: (10f 3, 12f 3, 14f) (g-s, g-f 3, frm 2, hrd)
Fair gelding, effective 10f, acts on frm, favours tight tracks. Turf high 56 - 5th of 13 giving 15lb to Vanborough Lad (27 Jly Windsor 10f frm RF 3144).
J G Smyth-Osbourne [0-7] The Everhopefuls I (from P W Harris [3-17] Oct 1997).

KINGS CAY (IRE) BHB 59f **RR 62f** 4747[16]

7 b g Taufan (USA) 8.3f **(65)**-Provocation (Kings Lake (USA)) 10.8f **(67)**
Form - 08263200
Record 1998 - 1st:0 2nd:2 3rd:1 Ran:8
Pre1998 - 1st:5 2nd:2 3rd:3 Ran:25
Win Prizemoney £17,405 *Total Prizemoney* £24,348
Wins * 1996 Jly Hamilt (GD) H 11.1f 51 59
* 1996 Jun Carlis (FRM) 12f 62
* 1996 Jun Ripon (G-F) H 12.3f 46 55
1994 Jun Salisb (G-F) H 12f 73 76 <
1994 Apr Beverl (G-S) 8.5f 66
1998 Turf 0-8: (10f, 12f 4, 13f, 14f 2) (g-s 2, gd 2, g-f 3, frm)
Average gelding, effective 12 to 14f, acts on g-f to frm, best on g-f, has worn blinkers, favours tight tracks. Turf high 62 - 2nd of 11 getting 1lb from House of Dreams (17 Jly Carlisle 14f frm RF 2866). Inconsistent.
T H Caldwell [3-29] R S G Jones (from D R Loder [2-6] Jun 1994).

KING'S CHAMBERS **RR 25f** 4258[11]

2 ch g Sabrehill (USA) 8.5f **(64)** - Flower Girl (Pharly (FR)) 9.8f **(68)**
Form - 0
Record 1998 - 1st:0 2nd:0 3rd:0 Ran:1
1998 Turf 0-1: (6f) (gd)
Currently little account gelding, always wears blinkers.
B W Hills [0-1] W J Gredley.

KINGS CHECK BHB 41f **RR 46f** 4917[18]

3 b g Komaite (USA) 6.9f **(61)** - Ski Baby (Petoski) 5.7f **(62)**
Form - 67603000
Record 1998 - 1st:0 2nd:0 3rd:1 Ran:8
Pre1998 - 1st:0 2nd:0 3rd:0 Ran:3
Win Prizemoney £0 *Total Prizemoney* £255
1998 Turf 0-8: (6f 2, 7f 3, 8f 2, 10f) (g-s 3, gd 3, g-f 2)
Moderate gelding, effective 7f, acts on gd, has worn blinkers. Turf high 50. Inconsistent. *Miss J F Craze [0-11] W Cooper.*

KING'S COLOURS (USA) **RR 35f** 149[1]

3 b c Gold Legend (USA) 8f **(76)** - Aly's Delight (USA) (Alydar (USA)) 9.1f **(76)**
Form - 1
Record 1998 - 1st:1 2nd:0 3rd:0 Ran:1
Pre1998 - 1st:0 2nd:0 3rd:0 Ran:1
Win Prizemoney £2,765 *Total Prizemoney* £2,765
Wins * 1998 *Jan Lingfi (STD) 8f 76* <
1998 AW 1-1: (8f 1-1) (Equi 1-1)
Currently above-average colt, often wears blinkers. (1st run) - 1st of 6 from Great Melody (24 Jan Lingfield RF 0149). He got off the mark with an easy success in a maiden on the Lingfield Equitrack in January, though it was a poor race.
J Noseda [1-1] Mrs J M Ryan (from J S Bolger in IRE [0-1] Spt 1997).

KINGSFOLD BLAZE BHB 58f **RR 60df** 4457[19]

3 b f Mazilier (USA) 8.5f **(56)** - Kingsfold Flame (No Loiterer)
Form - 06330
Record 1998 - 1st:0 2nd:0 3rd:2 Ran:5
Win Prizemoney £0 *Total Prizemoney* £970
1998 Turf 0-5: (7f, 8f 2, 9f, 10f) (g-s, gd 2, g-f, frm)
Leggy, average filly. Turf high 60 - 3rd of 6 getting 5lb from Silverado (4 Spt Epsom 9f gd RF 4086).

*M J Haynes [0-5] Mrs Pauline Oliver.

KINGSFOLD PET BHB 47f **RR 47f** 781[2]

9 b g Tina's Pet 7.4f **(56)** - Bella Lisa (River Chanter) 15.4f **(51)**
Form - 2
Record 1998 - 1st:0 2nd:1 3rd:0 Ran:1
Pre1998 - 1st:1 2nd:0 3rd:2 Ran:10
Win Prizemoney £3,080 *Total Prizemoney* £4,720
Wins * 1994 Apr Folkes (HVY) H 15.4f 42 55+ <
1998 Turf 0-1: (15f) (sft)
Moderate gelding. *M J Haynes [9-41] George Nye Partnership.*

KINGS HARMONY (IRE) BHB 50f62a **RR 61df 62a** 3042[9]

5 b g Nordico (USA) 8.2f **(59)** - Kingston Rose (Tudor Music) 6.8f **(59)**
Form - 71287005000
Record 1998 - 1st:1 2nd:1 3rd:0 Ran:10
Pre1998 - 1st:4 2nd:5 3rd:1 Ran:24
Win Prizemoney £13,790 *Total Prizemoney* £21,706
Wins 1998 *Feb Lingfi (SLW) C 7f 72* <
1997 Jly Bright (FRM) C 7f 63
1996 Aug Bright (FRM) H 7f 66 71
1996 Apr Bright (FRM) 6f 66
1995 *Nov Southw (STD) 6f 69*
1998 Turf 0-6: (6f 2, 7f 4) (g-s, gd 2, frm 3) 1998 AW 1-4: (6f, 7f 1-3) (Equi 1-4)
Average gelding, effective 6 to 7f, best at 7f, acts on gd to frm - acts on Equi, has worn blinkers. Turf high 61. AW high 72 (1st run) - 1st of 10 getting 7lb from Stoppes Brow (5 Feb Lingfield RF 0223). Seems to like Brighton where he has been successful three times since April '96, and scored in a claimer on the Lingfield Equitrack in February. Not an easy horse to predict, however.
B A Pearce [0-9] Gerry Boyer (from P J Makin [5-25] Feb 1998).

KING'S HUSSAR BHB 52f49a **RR 54f 49a** 2229[8]

3 b g Be My Chief (USA) 10.2f **(62)** - Croire (IRE) (Lomond (USA)) 8.8f **(65)**
Form - 62478
Record 1998 - 1st:0 2nd:1 3rd:0 Ran:5
Pre1998 - 1st:0 2nd:0 3rd:0 Ran:4
Win Prizemoney £0 *Total Prizemoney* £660
1998 Turf 0-4: (10f, 12f, 14f, 17f) (g-s, gd 2, frm) 1998 AW 0-1: (16f) (Equi)
Neat, fair gelding, effective 12f, acts on g-s, has worn blinkers, likes tight tracks. Turf high 54.
R F JohnsonHoughton [0-5] W H Ponsonby (from P F I Cole [0-4] Oct 1997).

KING SLAYER BHB 93f **RR 102f** 4379[11]

3 b c Batshoof 9.5f **(66)** - Top Sovereign (High Top) 10.2f **(67)**
Form - 132022270
Record 1998 - 1st:1 2nd:4 3rd:1 Ran:9
Pre1998 - 1st:0 2nd:0 3rd:1 Ran:1
Win Prizemoney £2,490 *Total Prizemoney* £30,078
Wins * 1998 Apr Folkes (GD) 7f 72 <
1998 Turf 1-9: (7f 1-3, 8f 5, 10f) (g-s, gd 1-3, g-f 3, frm 2)
Leggy, very useful colt, effective 7 to 8f, acts on gd to g-f. Turf high 102 - 2nd of 9 to Rainald (17 Jly Newbury 7f g-f RF 2874). He bolted up on his reappearance and went on to run a series of fine races, including when touched off in the William Hill Mile at Glorious Goodwood. His trainer expects him to stay beyond a mile and he ought to win a decent handicap in 1999.
B Smart [1-10] A Khaleq.

KINGSTON VENTURE BHB 74f **RR 71f** 4124[6]

2 b g Interrex (CAN) 7.7f **(51)** - Tricata (Electric) 10.1f **(61)**
Form - 4166
Record 1998 - 1st:1 2nd:0 3rd:0 Ran:4
Win Prizemoney £2,915 *Total Prizemoney* £3,258
Wins * 1998 Jun Salisb (G-F) 7f 66 <
1998 Turf 1-4: (6f, 7f 1-2, 8f) (g-f, frm 1-3)
Above-average gelding. Turf high 71 - 6th of 16 getting 6lb from Bathwick (7 Spt Bath 8f frm RF 4124) - also 1st of 18 from Godley (25 Jun Salisbury RF 2274).
W G M Turner [1-4] Miss Corinne Overton.

KINGSTREE **RR 60f** 5123[3]

2 b c Distant Relative 7f **(69)** - Sinking (Midyan (USA)) 6f **(60)**

Form - 03
Record 1998 - 1st:0 2nd:0 3rd:1 Ran:2
Win Prizemoney £0 *Total Prizemoney* £435
1998 Turf 0-2: (6f 2) (g-s, g-f)
Currently average colt. Turf high 60 (began Oct).
J H M Gosden [0-2] Sheikh Mohammed.

KING TANGO (USA) BHB 87f RR 89?f 3406[1]

3 b c Kingmambo (USA) 10.9f **(85)** - Vana Turns (USA) (Wavering Monarch (USA)) 10.4f **(94)**
Form - 2221
Record 1998 - 1st:1 2nd:3 3rd:0 Ran:4
Win Prizemoney £3,824 *Total Prizemoney* £7,089
Wins * **1998** Aug Haydoc (G-S) 10.5f 79 <
1998 Turf 1-4: (10f 3, 11f 1-1) (gd 2, g-f 1-1, frm)
Scopey, useful colt, has worn blinkers. Turf high 89 (1st run) - 2nd of 15 to Dark Shell (12 Jun Sandown 10f gd RF 1937). Apparently Cecil's second string when a good second on his debut, he won what looked a fairly ordinary Haydock maiden in August and his future may well lie over hurdles.
H R A Cecil [1-4] The Thoroughbred Corporation.

KING UNO BHB 66f RR 67f 5079[12]

4 b g Be My Chief (USA) 10.2f **(62)** - The Kings Daughter (Indian King (USA)) 7.4f **(64)**
Form - 0600510112440
Record 1998 - 1st:3 2nd:1 3rd:0 Ran:13
Pre1998 - 1st:2 2nd:1 3rd:3 Ran:18
Win Prizemoney £16,139 *Total Prizemoney* £22,416

Wins								
* **1998**	Spt	Leices	(G-S)	H	7f	59	62	<
* **1998**	Aug	Pontef	(G-F)	H	6f	54	58	
1998	Jun	Nottin	(GD)	H	6.1f	49	52	
1997	Spt	Haydoc	(G-S)	SH	6f	47	50	
1997	Jun	Pontef	(GD)	H	6f	43	46	

1998 Turf 3-13: (6f 2-7, 7f 1-5, 8f) (sft 2, g-s, gd 1-7, g-f 1-1, frm 1-2)
Scopey, average gelding, effective 6 to 8f, best at 7f, acts on gd to frm, best on gd, often wears blinkers, prefers left handed tracks, excels at Pontefract, does well at Nottingham. Turf high 67 - 4th of 24 getting 3lb from Queen's Pageant (10 Oct York 7f gd RF 4750) - also 1st of 18 giving 10lb to Petite Danseuse (8 Spt Leicester RF 4137).
E J Alston [2-7] The Pain And Heartache Partnership (from Mrs J R Ramsden [3-24] Jun 1998).

KINLANO BHB 68f RR 76+f 4703[5]

2 b c Cyrano de Bergerac 7.3f **(58)** - Kinlacey (Aragon) 8.1f **(60)**
Form - 56805
Record 1998 - 1st:0 2nd:0 3rd:0 Ran:5
1998 Turf 0-5: (6f 5) (gd 2, g-f, frm 2)
Above-average colt. Turf high 76 (began Jly).
Mrs J R Ramsden [0-5] Bernard Hathaway.

KINNESCASH (IRE) BHB 73f63a RR 75f 63a 3984[10]

5 ch g Persian Heights 10.5f **(61)** - Gayla Orchestra (Lord Gayle (USA)) 8.8f **(62)**
Form - 20250
Record 1998 - 1st:0 2nd:2 3rd:0 Ran:5
Pre1998 - 1st:4 2nd:2 3rd:3 Ran:23
Win Prizemoney £13,849 *Total Prizemoney* £21,210

Wins								
* 1997	Jun	Windso	(G-S)	H	11.6f	59	67	<
* 1997	Apr	Leices	(G-S)	H	10f	53	62	
1995	Spt	Nottin	(G-S)	H	10f	65	67	<
1995	Aug	Bath	(HRD)	S	5.7f		64?	

1998 Turf 0-5: (12f 4, 20f) (gd, g-f 2, frm 2)
Above-average gelding, effective 11 to 13f, best at 12f, acts on g-s to frm, best on frm, likes tight tracks, excels at Leicester. Turf high 75 - 2nd of 6 to Colleville (22 Jly Leicester 12f frm RF 3028). Able under both codes, he ran a good race in the Ascot Stakes but failed to see out the marathon trip.
P Bowen [7-29] D R James (from M S Saunders [1-12] Jun 1996).

KINNINO BHB 52f55a RR 61df 55a 5003[6]

4 b g Polish Precedent (USA) 9f **(73)** - On Tiptoes (Shareef Dancer (USA)) 9.9f **(73)**
Form - 0608056
Record 1998 - 1st:0 2nd:0 3rd:0 Ran:7
1998 Turf 0-6: (7f 2, 8f 3, 9f) (gd, g-f 2, frm 3) 1998 AW 0-1: (7f) (Equi)
Average gelding, effective 7f - acts on Equi, likes tight tracks. Turf high 61. (1st run) - 6th of 16 to Kafil (26 Oct Lingfield 7f Equi RF 5003).
G L Moore [0-7] A Moore.

KINOKO BHB 27f RR 33f 3670[11]

10 ch g Bairn (USA) 9.4f **(55)** - Octavia (Sallust) 8.4f **(63)**
Form - 864857550
Record 1998 - 1st:0 2nd:0 3rd:0 Ran:9
Pre1998 - 1st:10 2nd:9 3rd:7 Ran:73
Win Prizemoney £33,544 *Total Prizemoney* £47,150

Wins							
* 1997	Apr	Beverl	(G-F)	H	16.2f	41	45
* 1997	Mar	Newcas	(GD)	H	16.1f	30	40
* 1995	Jly	Beverl	(G-F)	H	12f	35	42
* 1994	Apr	Catter	(GD)	H	11.5f	51	55
* 1994	Mar	Catter	(GD)	H	11.5f	49	50

1998 Turf 0-9: (12f, 14f 2, 16f 4, 17f, 18f) (sft, g-s, gd 2, g-f, frm 4)
Very moderate gelding, effective 16f, acts on gd to frm. Turf high 33.
K W Hogg [12-75] Anthony White (from R Hollinshead [0-18] Jly 1991).

KINTAVI BHB 50f RR 57f 3790[7]

8 b g Efisio 7.7f **(69)** - Princess Tavi (Sea Hawk II) 10.8f **(63)**
Form - 041052037
Record 1998 - 1st:1 2nd:1 3rd:1 Ran:9
Pre1998 - 1st:2 2nd:3 3rd:2 Ran:15
Win Prizemoney £9,324 *Total Prizemoney* £16,506

Wins								
* **1998**	Apr	Leices	(SFT)	H	11.8f	52	58	<
* 1997	May	Hamilt	(SFT)	H	13f	46	53	
* 1995	Jun	Warwic	(FRM)	H	12.5f	36	40	

1998 Turf 1-9: (12f 1-4, 13f 2, 14f 2, 16f) (sft 1-2, gd 5, g-f 2)
Fair gelding, effective 12 to 13f, best at 12f, acts on sft to g-f, prefers right handed tracks, prefers tight tracks, excels at Leicester and Hamilton. Turf high 58 - 1st of 11 getting 3lb from Zermatt (9 Apr Leicester RF 0617).
T W Donnelly [6-30] S Taberner (from J Mackie [0-5] Aug 1993).

KIPPANOUR (USA) BHB 43f RR 43f 2176[5]

6 b g Alleged (USA) 11.8f **(81)** - Innsbruck (General Assembly (USA)) 10f **(68)**
Form - 45
Record 1998 - 1st:0 2nd:0 3rd:0 Ran:2
1998 Turf 0-1: (16f) (gd) 1998 AW 0-1: (11f) (Fibr)
Moderate gelding. *Mrs N Macauley [0-5] G Wiltshire.*

KIRA BHB 71f67a RR 56f 67a 5142[18]

8 b m Starry Night (USA) 5.2f **(54)** - Irish Limerick (Try My Best (USA)) 7.6f **(67)**
Form - 0177406430040
Record 1998 - 1st:1 2nd:0 3rd:1 Ran:13
Pre1998 - 1st:8 2nd:8 3rd:4 Ran:50
Win Prizemoney £34,910 *Total Prizemoney* £55,049

Wins								
* **1998**	May	Thirsk	(GD)	H	5f	78	84	<
* 1997	May	Redcar	(FRM)	H	5f	77	80	
* 1997	Mar	Doncas	(G-F)	H	6f	66	74+	
* 1996	Aug	Pontef	(G-F)	H	5f	63	65	
* 1996	Aug	Redcar	(FRM)	H	5f	58	60	
* 1996	Apr	Newcas	(GD)	H	5f	52	57	
* 1996	*Mar*	*Wolver*	*(STD)*	*H*	*5f*	*67*	*73*	
* 1996	*Feb*	*Southw*	*(STD)*	*H*	*5f*	*58*	*62+*	
* 1996	*Jan*	*Southw*	*(STD)*		*6f*		*54*	

1998 Turf 1-12: (5f 1-7, 6f 5) (g-s 2, gd 1-6, g-f 4) 1998 AW 0-1: (5f) (Fibr)
Average mare, effective 5 to 6f, best at 5f, acts on gd to hrd, best on gd. Turf high 84 (1st run) - 1st of 11 giving 25lb to Storyteller (15 May Thirsk RF 1256).
J L Eyre [9-55] J E Wilson (from Miss L C Siddall [0-8] Aug 1994).

KIRBY OPPORTUNITY BHB 38a RR 38a 91[9]

10 ch m Mummy's Game 9.2f **(56)** - Empress Catherine (Welsh Pageant) 10f **(65)**
Form - 60
Record 1998 - 1st:0 2nd:0 3rd:0 Ran:1
Pre1998 - 1st:7 2nd:7 3rd:5 Ran:39
Win Prizemoney £14,540 *Total Prizemoney* £20,725
1998 AW 0-1: (12f) (Equi)
Poor mare, has worn blinkers.
G A Ham [0-4] K C White (from P Leach [0-4] Feb 1994).

KIRBY PRINCESS BHB 49f **RR 50f** 3832[8]
3 ch f Weldnaas (USA) 8.4f **(55)** - Lovely Greek Lady (Ela-Mana-Mou) 10.1f **(70)**
Form - 77858
Record 1998 - 1st:0 2nd:0 3rd:0 Ran:5
1998 Turf 0-5: (6f, 7f, 10f, 12f 2) (gd, g-f 2, frm 2)
Leggy, fair filly. Turf high 50 - 8th of 12 getting 2lb from Norcroft Joy (24 Aug Beverley 12f g-f RF 3832).
**R A Fahey [0-5] Wentdale Const Ltd.*

KIRILOV (IRE) BHB 73f **RR 73f** 4314[15]
3 b c Roi Danzig (USA) 10.5f **(62)** - Ever so (Mummy's Pet) 7.7f **(60)**
Form - 6640
Record 1998 - 1st:0 2nd:0 3rd:0 Ran:4
Win Prizemoney £0 *Total Prizemoney* £254
1998 Turf 0-4: (9f, 10f 3) (gd, g-f, frm 2)
Workmanlike, above-average colt. Turf high 73 - 4th of 12 to Pegnitz (17 Aug Windsor 10f g-f RF 3682).
**R W Armstrong [0-4] R N Bracher.*

KISMAH RR 107+f 3427[1]
3 ch f Machiavellian (USA) 9.8f **(83)** - Thaidah (CAN) (Vice Regent (CAN)) 8.7f **(74)**
Form - 11
Record 1998 - 1st:2 2nd:0 3rd:0 Ran:2
Win Prizemoney £18,811 *Total Prizemoney* £18,811
Wins * 1998 Aug Ascot (G-F) 8f 107+ <
*** 1998** Jly Ripon (GD) 8f 73++
1998 Turf 2-2: (8f 2-2) (gd 1-1, g-f 1-1)
Unfurnished, currently Pattern-class filly. Turf high 107 (began Jly) - 1st of 8 getting 5lb from Brave Kris (7 Aug Ascot RF 3427). She looked a hot prospect when laughing at some decent fillies in a Listed event at Ascot in August, but blotted her copybook when refusing to enter the stalls at York the following month. Hopefully that was a one-off, because this filly is certainly capable of winning a Group race. **A C Stewart [2-2] Hamdan Al Maktoum.*

KISSED BY MOONLITE BHB 48f **RR 40f** 4882[11]
2 gr f Petong 7.6f **(58)** - Rose Bouquet (General Assembly (USA)) 10f **(68)**
Form - 000
Record 1998 - 1st:0 2nd:0 3rd:0 Ran:3
1998 Turf 0-3: (6f, 7f 2) (g-s, g-f, frm)
Currently moderate filly. Turf high 40 (began Spt).
**P W Harris [0-3] The Musketeers.*

KISSEL BHB 42f42a **RR 42f 42a** 4862[5]
6 b m Warning 8.1f **(77)**-Ice Chocolate (USA)(Icecapade (USA))11f **(62)**
Form - 035
Record 1998 - 1st:0 2nd:0 3rd:1 Ran:3
Pre1998 - 1st:0 2nd:0 3rd:1 Ran:10
Win Prizemoney £0 *Total Prizemoney* £970
1998 Turf 0-1: (8f) (gd) 1998 AW 0-2: (11f, 12f) (Fibr 2)
Moderate mare, effective 7 to 11f, acts on sft - acts on Fibr, prefers left handed tracks. AW high 43 (1st run) (began Spt) - 3rd of 16 giving 7lb to Sassy (29 Spt Southwell 11f Fibr RF 4545). Consistent.
**S E Kettlewell [0-12] J D Chilton (from A Harrison [0-4] Jly 1996).*

KISSIMMEE BAY (IRE) BHB 51f **RR 63f** 4796[16]
2 b f Brief Truce (USA) 9.1f **(73)** - Deer Emily (Alzao (USA)) 7.1f **(68)**
Form - 66028000
Record 1998 - 1st:0 2nd:1 3rd:0 Ran:8
Win Prizemoney £0 *Total Prizemoney* £585
1998 Turf 0-8: (5f 3, 6f 5) (sft, gd 4, g-f, frm 2)
Average filly, effective 6f, acts on gd, has worn blinkers. Turf high 63 - 2nd of 14 to Bodfari Anna (12 Aug Nottingham 6f gd RF 3581). Becoming disappointing. **N Tinkler [0-8] Speedlith Group.*

KISS ME GOODKNIGHT BHB 89f **RR 76f** 4542[21]
2 b f First Trump - Flitteriss Park (Beldale Flutter (USA)) 9.7f **(71)**
Form - 1780
Record 1998 - 1st:1 2nd:0 3rd:0 Ran:4
Win Prizemoney £3,081 *Total Prizemoney* £3,081
Wins * 1998 Jly Chepst (GD) 6.1f 76+ <
1998 Turf 1-4: (6f 1-2, 7f 2) (sft, gd 1-1, g-f, frm)
Above-average filly. Turf high 76 (1st run) (began Jly) - 1st of 16 getting 5lb from Light The Rocket (4 Jly Chepstow RF 2532). Comes from a useful family, and made a winning debut at Chepstow. Faced stiff tasks subsequently.
**P W Chapple-Hyam [1-4] Derek D & Mrs Jean P Clee.*

KISS ME KATE BHB 62f **RR 65f** 4767[5]
2 b f Aragon 7.7f **(58)** - Ingerence (FR) (Akarad (FR)) 9f **(76)**
Form - 06540465
Record 1998 - 1st:0 2nd:0 3rd:0 Ran:8
Win Prizemoney £0 *Total Prizemoney* £255
1998 Turf 0-8: (5f, 6f, 7f 4, 8f 2) (sft, gd 2, g-f, frm 4)
Average filly. Turf high 65.
**J W Hills [0-8] The Dan Abbott Racing Partnership.*

KISSOGRAM BHB 114f **RR 117+f** 4630[1]
3 b f Caerleon (USA) 10.9f **(79)**-Alligram(USA) (Alysheba (USA)) 9f **(84)**
Form - 1411
Record 1998 - 1st:3 2nd:0 3rd:0 Ran:4
Win Prizemoney £50,403 *Total Prizemoney* £53,453
Wins * 1998 Oct Newmar () G2 10f 117+ <
*** 1998** Aug Sandow (G-F) L 8.1f 101+
*** 1998** Jun Yarmou (GD) 8f 82+
1998 Turf 3-4: (8f 2-2, 10f 1-2) (gd 1-2, g-f 2-2)
Leggy, high-class filly. Turf high 117 - 1st of 5 getting 5lb from Arriving (3 Oct Newmarket RF 4630). A well-bred filly, she was unraced at two but showed the right kind of attitude to win on her Yarmouth debut, and did not fare too badly when taking a massive step up in class and a quarter-mile step up in trip in the Nassau. Back to a mile, she took a Sandown Listed event very easily on her third outing and finished off the season by winning a substandard Sun Chariot. She will be worth watching out for if returning at four. **L M Cumani [3-4] Helena Springfield Ltd.*

Kissogram - lightly exposed, but a class act

KITOPH (IRE) RR 44f 2469[9]
3 b f Night Shift (USA) 8.1f **(73)** - Soxoph (Hotfoot) 10.5f **(59)**
Form - 0
Record 1998 - 1st:0 2nd:0 3rd:0 Ran:1
Pre1998 - 1st:0 2nd:0 3rd:0 Ran:1
1998 Turf 0-1: (7f) (frm)
Unfurnished, currently moderate filly.
**E A L Dunlop [0-2] Mrs Edward Dunlop.*

KITZA (IRE) RR 116f 4795a[5]
3 b f Danehill (USA) 9.1f **(79)** - Pitmarie (Pitskelly) 8.5f **(53)**
Form - 21226465
1998 Turf 1-8: (7f, 8f 1-4, 10f 2, 12f) (sft, gd 1-6, g-f)
High-class filly, effective 8 to 10f, acts on gd to g-f, has worn blinkers. Turf high 116 - 4th of 8 getting 8lb from One So Wonderful (18 Aug York 10f g-f RF 3696). She was runner-up in the two Irish fillies' classics having previously won a Listed event at Leopardstown, but was disappointing in the Nassau. Not beaten far into fourth in the Juddmonte International, she then failed to make much impact in Pattern company back in Ireland. She had a hard season, and it is difficult to work out just what her class level really was. **A P O'Brien in IRE [2-14] Mrs E M Stockwell.*

KNAVE'S ASH (USA) BHB 67f **RR 68f** 4748[14]
7 ch g Miswaki (USA) 8.1f **(81)** - Quiet Rendezvous (USA) (Nureyev (USA)) 8.7f **(78)**
Form - 000261808230160

Record	**1998** -	1st:2	2nd:2	3rd:1	Ran:15
	Pre1998 -	1st:4	2nd:0	3rd:2	Ran:23

Win Prizemoney £49,352 *Total Prizemoney* £63,700

Wins								
* **1998**	Spt	Newcas	(GD)	H	8f	64	68	
* **1998**	Jly	Thirsk	(FRM)	H	8f	60	61	
1995	Spt	Pontef	(GD)	H	10f	94	98	<
1995	Jly	Doncas	(G-F)	H	10.3f	88	93	
1994	May	York	(FRM)	H	7f	77	82+	

1998 Turf 2-15: (6f, 7f 3, 8f 2-7, 9f 4) (g-s, gd 3, g-f 1-4, frm 1-6, hrd)
Average gelding, effective 8 to 9f, best at 9f, acts on g-f to frm, best on g-f, prefers left handed tracks. Turf high 68 - 1st of 20 giving 10lb to Gablesea (30 Spt Newcastle RF 4578).
**D Nicholls [2-22] J P Hames (from Sir Michael Stoute [4-16] Spt 1995).*

KNIFE EDGE (USA) BHB 80f **RR 78f** 2186[3]
3 b br c Kris S (USA) 9.3f **(76)** - My Turbulent Miss (USA) (My Dad George (USA))
Form - 33

Record	**1998** -	1st:0	2nd:0	3rd:2	Ran:2
	Pre1998 -	1st:0	2nd:0	3rd:0	Ran:1

Win Prizemoney £0 *Total Prizemoney* £1,067
1998 Turf 0-2: (12f, 14f) (g-s, g-f)
Light-framed, currently above-average colt. Turf high 78.
**Sir Michael Stoute [0-3] Sheikh Mohammed.*

KNIGHTCRACKER BHB 25f30a **RR 30a** 4201[18]
3 b f Cadeaux Genereux 7.9f **(76)** - Top Treat (USA) (Topsider (USA)) 8.3f **(71)**
Form - 8000

Record	**1998** -	1st:0	2nd:0	3rd:0	Ran:2
	Pre1998 -	1st:0	2nd:0	3rd:0	Ran:3

1998 Turf 0-2: (8f 2) (gd, frm)
Light-framed, poor filly. (began Aug).
**R E Peacock [0-5] Derek D & Mrs Jean P Clee.*

KNIGHTED BHB 78f **RR 73f** 4251[3]
2 b c Bigstone (IRE) - Missed Again (High Top) 10.2f **(67)**
Form - 363

Record	**1998** -	1st:0	2nd:0	3rd:2	Ran:3

Win Prizemoney £0 *Total Prizemoney* £928
1998 Turf 0-3: (7f 2, 8f) (gd, frm 2)
Currently above-average colt. Turf high 73 (began Jly). Looks a staying type. **N Tinkler [0-3] Elite Racing Club.*

KNOBBLEENEEZE BHB 60f69a **RR 69f 69a** 4391[14]
8 ch g Aragon 7.7f **(58)** - Proud Miss (USA) (Semi-Pro) 7.5f **(70)**
Form - 03501430075050

Record	**1998** -	1st:1	2nd:0	3rd:2	Ran:14
	Pre1998 -	1st:10	2nd:10	3rd:9	Ran:86

Win Prizemoney £49,283 *Total Prizemoney* £75,167

Wins								
* **1998**	May	Newbur	(GD)	H	7.3f	62	67	
* 1997	Spt	Ayr	(G-S)	H	7f	65	65	
* 1997	Apr	Ripon	(GD)	H	8f	65	78	<
* 1996	Jun	Cheste	(G-F)	H	7f	67	73	
* 1995	Spt	Goodwo	(GD)		7f		73	
* 1995	Spt	Doncas	(GD)	H	7f	70	76	
* 1994	Spt	Newbur	(SFT)	H	7.3f	70	71	
* 1994	May	Lingfi	(GD)		7.6f		73	
* 1994	Mar	Bright	(G-S)	H	8f	65	67	

1998 Turf 1-14: (7f 1-9, 8f 5) (sft, gd 6, g-f 1-5, frm 2)
Average gelding, effective 7 to 8f, best at 8f, acts on hvy to frm, best on gd, mostly wears blinkers, likes left handed tracks, likes tight tracks, likes Goodwood. Turf high 69 - 4th of 12 getting 9lb from Safio (5 Jun Goodwood 7f frm RF 1754). A genuine handicapper, he is kept very busy and is a very good mount for an inexperienced rider. **M R Channon [11-100] Anthony Andrews.*

KNOCKEMBACK NELLIE BHB 76f **RR 77?f** 4524[4]
2 b f Forzando 7.2f **(63)** - Sea Clover (IRE) (Ela-Mana-Mou) 10.1f **(70)**
Form - 768802024

Record	**1998** -	1st:0	2nd:2	3rd:0	Ran:9

Win Prizemoney £0 *Total Prizemoney* £1,645
1998 Turf 0-9: (5f 2, 6f 6, 7f) (gd 3, g-f 3, frm 3)
Above-average filly, effective 6f, acts on g-f to frm. Turf high 77 - 2nd of 8 giving 12lb to Beverley Monkey (26 Aug Lingfield 6f g-f RF 3891). **D R C Elsworth [0-9] Notaproperjob Partnership.*

KNOTTY HILL BHB 57f68a **RR 60f 68a** 4669[11]
6 b g Green Ruby (USA) 6.9f **(47)** - Esilam (Frimley Park) 6.5f **(67)**
Form - 540271200

Record	**1998** -	1st:1	2nd:2	3rd:0	Ran:9
	Pre1998 -	1st:1	2nd:3	3rd:3	Ran:19

Win Prizemoney £6,665 *Total Prizemoney* £14,664

Wins							
* **1998**	May	Hamilt	(SFT)		6f	59	
* *1997*	*Feb*	*Southw*	*(STD)*		*7f*	*79+*	<

1998 Turf 1-7: (5f 2, 6f 1-4, 7f) (hvy 1-1, sft, gd 2, g-f 2, frm) 1998 AW 0-2: (6f, 7f) (Fibr 2)
Average gelding, effective 6 to 7f, best at 7f, acts on gd - acts on Fibr, likes tight tracks. Turf high 60. AW high 68. Inconsistent.
**R Craggs [2-28] Ray Craggs.*

KNYSNA LILY (USA) RR 75+f 4227[3]
2 b f Kris S (USA) 9.3f **(76)** - Kerygma (USA) (Drone) 10.3f **(74)**
Form - 3

Record	**1998** -	1st:0	2nd:0	3rd:1	Ran:1

Win Prizemoney £0 *Total Prizemoney* £540
1998 Turf 0-1: (8f) (g-f)
Currently above-average filly. (1st run) - 3rd of 16 getting 5lb from Golden Snake (11 Spt Doncaster 8f g-f RF 4227).
**J H M Gosden [0-1] Sheikh Mohammed.*

KOLBY BHB 46f **RR 43f** 3518[6]
3 b g Superpower 6.6f **(58)** - Abrasive (Absalom) 7.2f **(58)**
Form - 180766

Record	**1998** -	1st:1	2nd:0	3rd:0	Ran:6
	Pre1998 -	1st:0	2nd:1	3rd:0	Ran:2

Win Prizemoney £2,355 *Total Prizemoney* £3,023

Wins							
* **1998**	May	Mussel	(G-F)	S	5f	57	<

1998 Turf 1-6: (5f 1-2, 6f, 7f 3) (gd 1-5, frm)
Workmanlike, moderate gelding, effective 5f, acts on gd, mostly wears blinkers (extremely effectively). Turf high 57 (1st run) - 1st of 11 getting 8lb from Pallium (18 May Musselburgh RF 1299). Inconsistent. **A Bailey [1-8] Sandybrow Stables Ltd.*

KOLI BHB 44f **RR 46df** 547[6]
5 b m Sayf El Arab (USA) 8.2f **(57)** - Miss Willow (Horage) 10.3f **(61)**
Form - 66

Record	**1998** -	1st:0	2nd:0	3rd:0	Ran:2
	Pre1998 -	1st:0	2nd:0	3rd:0	Ran:1

1998 Turf 0-1: (10f) (sft) 1998 AW 0-1: (11f) (Fibr)
Currently moderate filly.
**D J S Cosgrove [0-2] P J Byrnes (from H J Collingridge [0-1] Aug 1996).*

KOMAL BHB 45f **RR 59f** 4934[8]
2 b c Komaite (USA) 6.9f **(61)** - Malcesine (IRE) **(38f 31a)** (Auction Ring (USA)) 8.6f **(65)**
Form - 00775050008

Record	**1998** -	1st:0	2nd:0	3rd:0	Ran:11

1998 Turf 0-10: (5f 2, 6f 5, 7f, 8f, 10f) (g-s, gd 4, g-f 3, frm 2) 1998 AW 0-1: (7f) (Fibr)
Fair colt, has worn blinkers. Turf high 59.
**M Quinn [0-11] & Mrs Gary Pinchen.*

KOMASEPH BHB 50f56a **RR 52f 56a** 4550[8]
6 b g Komaite (USA) 6.9f **(61)** - Starkist (So Blessed) 8.7f **(67)**

Form - 1628108
Record 1998 - 1st:2 2nd:1 3rd:0 Ran:7
Pre1998 - 1st:0 2nd:1 3rd:0 Ran:6
Win Prizemoney £4,806 *Total Prizemoney* £6,181
Wins * **1998** *Aug Southw (STD) H 6f 53 58* <
* **1998** *Jan Southw (STD) 6f 51*
1998 AW 2-7: (6f 2-6, 7f) (Fibr 2-7)
Fair gelding, effective 6f - acts on Fibr, favours left handed tracks, favours tight tracks. AW high 58 - 1st of 15 getting 9lb from Elton Ledger (14 Aug Southwell RF 3643) - also 1st of 12 giving 3lb to Hurgill Lady (30 Jan Southwell RF 0191). He won twice over six on the Southwell Fibresand last season, and both victories came after a substantial layoff. That looks to be the key to him.
**R F Marvin [2-13] R W Jaines.*

KOMASTA BHB 38f42a RR 42f 42a 4955[6]

4 b g Komaite (USA) 6.9f **(61)** - Sky Fighter (Hard Fought) 8.8f **(62)**
Form - 0080207004006
Record 1998 - 1st:0 2nd:1 3rd:0 Ran:13
Pre1998 - 1st:1 2nd:2 3rd:2 Ran:13
Win Prizemoney £2,900 *Total Prizemoney* £6,179
Wins 1996 *Dec Wolver (STD) 7f 56* <
1998 Turf 0-5: (7f, 8f 3, 10f) (g-s, gd, g-f, frm 2) 1998 AW 0-8: (7f 2, 8f 5, 9f) (Fibr 8)
Lengthy, fair gelding, effective 7 to 8f - acts on Fibr, often wears blinkers, likes left handed tracks, favours tight tracks. Turf high 42. AW high 51.
**Mrs G S Rees [0-12] F Cunliffe (from Capt J Wilson [1-14] Jan 1998).*

KOMISTAR BHB 92f RR 93f 1464[8]

3 ch c Komaite (USA) 6.9f **(61)** - Rosie's Gold (Glint of Gold) 9.3f **(66)**
Form - 208
Record 1998 - 1st:0 2nd:1 3rd:0 Ran:3
Pre1998 - 1st:1 2nd:0 3rd:1 Ran:3
Win Prizemoney £3,819 *Total Prizemoney* £7,016
Wins * 1997 Oct Warwic (G-F) 7f 93+ <
1998 Turf 0-3: (8f 2, 10f) (g-s, gd, g-f)
Neat, useful colt, effective 7 to 8f, best at 8f, acts on g-s to g-f. Turf high 93 (1st run) - 2nd of 4 getting 2lb from Mushraaf (7 Apr Nottingham 8f g-s RF 0588). Finished runner-up in a four-runner Nottingham conditions event on his reappearance, but ran poorly in his two subsequent outings and was not seen out after May.
**P W Harris [1-6] Class Act.*

KOMLUCKY BHB 46f27a RR 46f 27a 4373[5]

6 b m Komaite (USA) 6.9f **(61)** - Sweet And Lucky (Lucky Wednesday) 8f **(50)**
Form - 60750700212725
Record 1998 - 1st:1 2nd:3 3rd:0 Ran:14
Pre1998 - 1st:3 2nd:5 3rd:3 Ran:42
Win Prizemoney £10,281 *Total Prizemoney* £18,462
Wins * **1998** Jly Catter (GD) H 7f 29 35
1997 May Thirsk (GD) S 7f 55
1996 Spt Catter (G-F) H 7f 48 51
1994 *Dec Wolver (STD) S 6f 59*
1998 Turf 1-9: (7f 1-7, 8f 2) (gd 2, g-f 1-3, frm 4) 1998 AW 0-5: (6f 2, 7f 3) (Fibr 5)
Moderate mare, effective 7 to 8f, best at 7f, acts on gd to g-f, best on gd, mostly wears blinkers (effectively), likes tight tracks. Turf high 46 - 2nd of 17 getting 3lb from Holy Smoke (26 Aug Carlisle 8f gd RF 3884). AW high 41.
**K A Ryan [1-8] Hambleton Lodge Equine Premix Ltd (from A B Mulholland [2-35] Apr 1998).*

KOMODO (USA) BHB 21f29a RR 27f 29a 352[5]

6 ch g Ferdinand (USA) 9.6f **(82)** - Platonic Interest (USA) (Drone) 10.3f **(74)**
Form - 65
Record 1998 - 1st:0 2nd:0 3rd:0 Ran:2
Pre1998 - 1st:0 2nd:5 3rd:1 Ran:31
Win Prizemoney £0 *Total Prizemoney* £5,283
1998 AW 0-2: (7f, 8f) (Equi 2)
Very moderate gelding, has worn blinkers. AW high 31.
**J E Long [0-12] Mrs A Warren (from K O Cunningham-Brown [0-10] Jun 1996).*

KOMPLETELY BHB 21f23a RR 23a 1575[9]

4 b f Komaite (USA) 6.9f **(61)** - Lucky Councillor (Lucky Wednesday) 8f **(50)**
Form - 80700
Record 1998 - 1st:0 2nd:0 3rd:0 Ran:3
Pre1998 - 1st:0 2nd:0 3rd:0 Ran:2
1998 Turf 0-1: (5f) (gd) 1998 AW 0-2: (6f, 12f) (Fibr 2)
Unfurnished, very poor filly, has worn blinkers. AW high 6.
**J Neville [0-5] Mrs P A Barratt.*

KOMREYEV DANCER BHB 60f57a RR 54f 57a 2255[6]

6 b g Komaite (USA) 6.9f **(61)** - L'Ancressaan (Dalsaan) 9.8f **(64)**
Form - 050554250806
Record 1998 - 1st:0 2nd:1 3rd:0 Ran:9
Pre1998 - 1st:4 2nd:8 3rd:5 Ran:43
Win Prizemoney £16,653 *Total Prizemoney* £33,725
Wins * 1996 May Ripon (GD) H 10f 71 75 <
* 1996 Apr Beverl (G-F) H 9.9f 65 70
* 1995 *Jan Wolver (STD) H 8f 75 74*
* 1994 *Dec Wolver (STD) 8.5f 74*
1998 Turf 0-5: (10f 2, 11f, 12f 2) (sft, gd, g-f 3) 1998 AW 0-4: (11f 2, 12f 2) (Fibr 4)
Fair gelding, effective 12f, acts on gd, has worn blinkers, likes left handed tracks. Turf high 71 (1st run) - 5th of 21 giving 1lb to Protocol (26 Mar Doncaster 12f gd RF 0469). AW high 56. Consistent.
**A Bailey [4-53] Denis Gallagher.*

KONA GOLD (USA) RR 5164a[3]

4 b c Java Gold (USA) 9.3f **(67)**
Form - 3
1998 AW 0-1: (6f) (Dirt)
Currently very high-class colt. (1st run) - 3rd of 14 giving 3lb to Reraise (7 Nov Churchill Downs 6f Dirt RF 5164a). Ran a fine race when third to Reraise in the Breeders' Cup Sprint.
**B Headley in CAN [0-1] B Headley & I & A Molasky.*

KONDOTY (USA) RR 90f 4196[3]

2 b c Mtoto 11.5f **(71)** - Princess Haifa (USA) (Mr Prospector (USA)) 8.8f **(78)**
Form - 23
Record 1998 - 1st:0 2nd:1 3rd:1 Ran:2
Win Prizemoney £0 *Total Prizemoney* £1,562
1998 Turf 0-2: (7f 2) (gd, frm)
Currently useful colt. Turf high 90 (1st run) (began Aug) - 2nd of 17 giving 5lb to Juno Marlowe (5 Aug Kempton 7f frm RF 3369). Showed ability in both of his maidens, and looks as though he will appreciate middle distances at three.
**M R Channon [0-2] Sheikh Ahmed Al Maktoum.*

KONKER BHB 62f RR 70f 5095[7]

3 ch g Selkirk (USA) 7.9f **(76)** - Helens Dreamgirl (Caerleon (USA)) 8.6f **(71)**
Form - 3351507
Record 1998 - 1st:1 2nd:0 3rd:2 Ran:7
Pre1998 - 1st:0 2nd:0 3rd:0 Ran:3
Win Prizemoney £3,168 *Total Prizemoney* £4,215
Wins 1998 May Newbur (GD) C 10f 69 <
1998 Turf 1-7: (8f, 9f, 10f 1-2, 11f 2, 12f) (hvy, g-s, gd 2, g-f 1-2, frm)
Scopey, above-average gelding, effective 9 to 10f, best at 10f, acts on hvy to g-f. Turf high 74 - also 1st of 11 giving 5lb to Tiye (27 May Newbury RF 1528).
**G M Moore [0-2] J & M Leisure / Unos Restaurant (from W J Haggas [1-8] Jun 1998).*

KORALOONA (IRE) BHB 60f RR 62f 4500[6]

5 b g Archway (IRE) 8.5f **(60)** - Polynesian Charm (USA) (What A Pleasure (USA)) 8.4f **(61)**
Form - 8443206
Record 1998 - 1st:0 2nd:1 3rd:1 Ran:7
Pre1998 - 1st:3 2nd:1 3rd:0 Ran:14
Win Prizemoney £12,879 *Total Prizemoney* £16,378
Wins * 1997 Aug Windso (GD) H 11.6f 57 60 <
* 1997 Jun Goodwo (G-S) H 12f 54 56
* 1997 Jun Goodwo (G-S) H 10f 49 52
1998 Turf 0-7: (12f 5, 14f 2) (g-s, gd, g-f 3, frm 2)
Average gelding, effective 10 to 12f, best at 12f, acts on g-s to frm, best on g-f, likes right handed tracks, favours tight tracks, does well at Windsor and Goodwood. Turf high 62 - 2nd of 11 giving 12lb to Premier League (3 Aug Windsor 12f frm RF 3315). A winner three times last season, he seems to go well at Goodwood and

Windsor, and was most unfortunate not to get the race in the stewards' room when runner-up in an amateur riders' event at the latter track in August. **G B Balding [3-21] Bernard Keay.*

KOSEVO (IRE) BHB 36f53a **RR 43f 53a** 4385[5]
4 b g Shareef Dancer (USA) 10.1f **(67)** - Kallista (Zeddaan) 9f **(76)**
Form - 50420211058285
Record 1998 - 1st:2 2nd:3 3rd:0 Ran:13
Pre1998 - 1st:0 2nd:0 3rd:0 Ran:7
Win Prizemoney £5,577 *Total Prizemoney* £7,669
Wins * **1998** *Jly Southw (STD) H 7f 50 54*
1998 *Jly Southw (STD) S 7f 58 <*
1998 Turf 0-7: (5f 2, 6f 2, 7f 2, 8f) (gd, g-f 2, frm 4) 1998 AW 2-6: (6f 2, 7f 2-4) (Equi, Fibr 2-5)
Lengthy, fair gelding, effective 6 to 7f, best at 7f - acts on Fibr, often wears blinkers (extremely effectively), prefers left handed tracks, prefers tight tracks. Turf high 43. AW high 59 - 2nd of 8 getting 14lb from Italian Symphony (9 Jly Southwell 7f Fibr RF 2655) - also 1st of 14 getting 6lb from Rock Island Line (17 Jly Southwell RF 2900). He showed much improved form on the Southwell Fibresand during the summer, winning a seller and a handicap over seven. He has run well over six on Fibresand since, but is probably more effective over the longer trip.
**D Shaw [1-7] K Nicholls (from A Kelleway [1-4] Jly 1998).*

KPOLO BHB 26f **RR 31f** 4544[8]
3 b g Polish Precedent (USA) 9f **(73)** - Ktolo (Tolomeo) 5.6f **(60)**
Form - 00008
Record 1998 - 1st:0 2nd:0 3rd:0 Ran:5
1998 Turf 0-4: (7f, 8f 2, 11f) (g-s, gd, g-f, hrd) 1998 AW 0-1: (14f) (Fibr)
Scopey, very moderate gelding. Turf high 31.
**W Jarvis [0-5] R K Bids Ltd.*

KRAM BHB 60f **RR 61f** 4669[14]
4 ch g Kris 10f **(75)** - Balenare (Pharly (FR)) 9.8f **(68)**
Form - 0636214305030
Record 1998 - 1st:1 2nd:1 3rd:3 Ran:13
Pre1998 - 1st:1 2nd:2 3rd:0 Ran:14
Win Prizemoney £6,996 *Total Prizemoney* £13,906
Wins * **1998** Jun Salisb (G-F) H 5f 57 58
1997 Aug Tralee (G-S) H 5f 61 <
1998 Turf 1-13: (5f 1-8, 6f 5) (sft, gd 4, g-f 4, frm 1-4)
Average gelding, effective 5 to 7f, best at 5f, acts on g-s to frm, excels at Salisbury. Turf high 61 - 3rd of 10 getting 2lb from Sihafi (17 Jly Salisbury 5f frm RF 2890) - also 1st of 6 getting 1lb from Maladerie (25 Jun Salisbury RF 2276). Consistent.
**Mrs P N Dutfield [1-16] Mrs C A Clarke (from Patrick Prendergast in IRE [1-11] Aug 1997).*

KRAYYAN DAWN BHB 33f39a **RR 36f 39a** 1430[2]
8 ch g Krayyan 7.1f **(46)** - Tana Mist (Homeboy) 6.6f **(55)**
Form - 522602
Record 1998 - 1st:0 2nd:3 3rd:0 Ran:6
Pre1998 - 1st:3 2nd:1 3rd:4 Ran:41
Win Prizemoney £9,051 *Total Prizemoney* £13,066
Wins 1995 May Folkes (G-F) 12f 46
1995 Apr Folkes (G-F) H 9.7f 46 47 <
1994 *Dec Lingfi (STD) 7f 44*
1998 Turf 0-1: (12f) (gd) 1998 AW 0-5: (12f 2, 13f 2, 16f) (Equi 5)
Moderate gelding, effective 12 to 16f - acted on Equi, had worn blinkers, preferred left handed tracks, favoured tight tracks. AW high 44 - 2nd of 14 getting 8lb from Monaco Gold (23 May Lingfield 16f Equi RF 1430). (DEAD)
**J Akehurst [0-12] R E Greatorex (from R Akehurst [3-11] Oct 1995).*

KRIKLES BHB 63f **RR 62f** 4997[5]
2 ch c Selkirk (USA) 7.9f **(76)** - Bumpkin (Free State) 8.7f **(61)**
Form - 005
Record 1998 - 1st:0 2nd:0 3rd:0 Ran:3
1998 Turf 0-3: (7f, 8f 2) (sft, frm 2)
Currently average colt. Turf high 62 (began Spt).
**C A Horgan [0-3] Mrs Mette Campbell.*

KRISALIGHT (USA) RR 49f 4823[18]
2 b br f Kris S (USA) 9.3f **(76)** - Dancing Grass (USA) (Northern Dancer) 9.6f **(80)**
Form - 0
Record 1998 - 1st:0 2nd:0 3rd:0 Ran:1
1998 Turf 0-1: (8f) (frm)
Currently moderate filly. **J L Dunlop [0-1] Hesmonds Stud.*

KRISAMBA BHB 60f **RR 72f** 4275[10]
3 ch c Kris 10f **(75)** - Lia's Dance (Lead on Time (USA)) 8f **(65)**
Form - 425377305200
Record 1998 - 1st:0 2nd:2 3rd:2 Ran:12
Pre1998 - 1st:0 2nd:0 3rd:1 Ran:3
Win Prizemoney £0 *Total Prizemoney* £3,589
1998 Turf 0-12: (7f 6, 8f 5, 9f) (sft 2, g-s, gd 3, g-f 2, frm 4)
Scopey, above-average colt, effective 7 to 8f, acts on g-s to gd, has worn blinkers. Turf high 74 - 2nd of 8 to Pelagos (20 Apr Brighton 8f g-s RF 0769). Inconsistent. Still a maiden, but has a race in him. **B J Meehan [0-15] B Schmidt-Bodner.*

KRISHAN FROLIC BHB 52f **RR 47f** 4671[25]
2 b f Tragic Role (USA) 9.4f **(63)** - Kiveton Komet (Precocious) 8.6f **(62)**
Form - 0000
Record 1998 - 1st:0 2nd:0 3rd:0 Ran:4
1998 Turf 0-3: (5f, 7f 2) (gd, g-f 2) 1998 AW 0-1: (5f) (Fibr)
Moderate filly. Turf high 47 (began Jly).
**M W Easterby [0-4] Justin Lloyd.*

KRISPY KNIGHT BHB 108f **RR 98f** 947a[6]
3 ch c Kris 10f **(75)** - Top Table (Shirley Heights) 10.3f **(74)**
Form - 16
Record 1998 - 1st:1 2nd:0 3rd:0 Ran:2
Pre1998 - 1st:1 2nd:0 3rd:2 Ran:4
Win Prizemoney £15,463 *Total Prizemoney* £16,819
Wins * **1998** Apr Kempto (HVY) L 8f 97+ <
* 1997 Jly Newmar (G-F) 6f 96
1998 Turf 1-2: (8f 1-2) (hvy 1-1, gd)
Scopey, very useful colt, effective 6 to 8f, acts on hvy to frm. Turf high 98 - also 1st of 4 from Gurkha (11 Apr Kempton RF 0647). Won at Newmarket at two, and made a successful reappearance in the four-runner Easter Stakes at Kempton. However, he seemed much better suited by the very testing conditions than his rivals, and looked in need of a longer trip when sixth in the Italian Guineas next time. **J W Hills [2-6] Derek Clee.*

KRISSY (USA) RR 53f 4956[8]
2 br f Kris S (USA) 9.3f **(76)** - Rascal Rascal (USA) (Ack Ack (USA)) 12.7f **(82)**
Form - 8
Record 1998 - 1st:0 2nd:0 3rd:0 Ran:1
1998 Turf 0-1: (8f) (frm)
Currently fair filly. **J H M Gosden [0-1] Landon Knight.*

KRISTA BHB 73f **RR 73f** 3824[1]
3 ch f Kris 10f **(75)** - Tura (Northfields (USA)) 9f **(72)**
Form - 3261
Record 1998 - 1st:1 2nd:1 3rd:1 Ran:4
Win Prizemoney £3,225 *Total Prizemoney* £4,834
Wins * **1998** Aug Sandow (G-F) 8.1f 69 <
1998 Turf 1-4: (8f 1-3, 10f) (gd 3, g-f 1-1)
Leggy, above-average filly. Turf high 73 (1st run) - 3rd of 11 to Zante (23 May Kempton 8f gd RF 1423) - also 1st of 5 from La Isla Bonita (22 Aug Sandown RF 3824). She had shown some ability in maiden company before battling home at Sandown in August. It did not look a particularly competitive race however.
**J A R Toller [1-4] C N Hart.*

KRISTINA RR 93+f 4664[1]
2 ch f Kris 10f **(75)** - Derniere Danse (Gay Mecene (USA)) 8.6f **(69)**
Form - 21
Record 1998 - 1st:1 2nd:1 3rd:0 Ran:2
Win Prizemoney £3,214 *Total Prizemoney* £4,279
Wins * **1998** Oct Nottin (G-S) 8.2f 90 <
1998 Turf 1-2: (8f 1-2) (g-s 1-1, g-f)
Currently useful filly. Turf high 93 (1st run) (began Spt) - 2nd of 10 to Social Scene (16 Spt Sandown 8f g-f RF 4309) - also 1st of 10 from Ratatuia (6 Oct Nottingham RF 4664). Showed ability on her debut, but made hard work of landing long odds-on at Nottingham next time. The very soft ground may not have helped.
**Sir Michael Stoute [1-2] J H Richmond-Watson.*

KRYSTAL DAVEY (IRE) BHB 61f51a **RR 50f 51a** 191[12]
4 b g Classic Music (USA) 7.2f **(57)** - Robin Red Breast (Red Alert) 7.6f **(66)**
Form - 0040
Record 1998 - 1st:0 2nd:0 3rd:0 Ran:3
Pre1998 - 1st:1 2nd:0 3rd:0 Ran:7
Win Prizemoney £3,322 *Total Prizemoney* £3,322
Wins 1997 *Jan Lingfi (STD) H 5f 58 56* <
1998 AW 0-3: (5f, 6f, 7f) (Fibr 3)
Scopey, fair gelding, effective 5 to 7f - acts on AW, has worn blinkers, prefers left handed tracks, prefers tight tracks. AW high 53 - 4th of 12 getting 2lb from Rock Island Line (19 Jan Southwell 7f Fibr RF 0114). Inconsistent.
**S R Bowring [0-4] Roland Wheatley (from T D Barron [1-6] Mar 1997).*

KRYSTAL MAX (IRE) BHB 69f80a **RR 69f 80a** 444[1]
5 b g Classic Music (USA) 7.2f **(57)** - Lake Isle (IRE) (Caerleon (USA)) 8.6f **(71)**
Form - 2111
Record 1998 - 1st:3 2nd:1 3rd:0 Ran:4
Pre1998 - 1st:6 2nd:1 3rd:2 Ran:25
Win Prizemoney £31,181 *Total Prizemoney* £34,487
Wins * 1998 *Mar Lingfi (STD) H 5f 70 79*
*** 1998** *Mar Southw (STD) H 5f 70 75*
*** 1998** *Feb Lingfi (SLW) H 6f 60 65*
* 1997 *Jan Lingfi (STD) C 5f 67*
* 1996 *Feb Lingfi (STD) C 7f 82*
* 1996 *Jan Lingfi (STD) H 5f 83 82*
* 1995 *Dec Lingfi (STD) H 6f 80 84* <
* 1995 *Dec Southw (STD) H 5f 74 84* <
* 1995 Jun Redcar (FRM) 5f 78+
1998 AW 3-4: (5f 2-2, 6f 1-2) (Equi 2-2, Fibr 1-2)
Above-average gelding, effective 5f - acts on AW, has worn blinkers. AW high 79 - 1st of 8 getting 1lb from Robo Magic (19 Mar Lingfield RF 0444) - also 1st of 14 giving 7lb to Divine Miss-P (11 Mar Southwell RF 0421). Inconsistent. A useful All-Weather sprinter on either surface, he came back from an eight-month break to show some fine form early in the year, winning well at both Lingfield and Southwell. Kimberley Hart gets on very well with him.
**T D Barron [9-23] The Oakfield Nurseries Partnership (from J Cullinan [0-6] Jun 1997).*

KUALA LIPIS (USA) BHB 84f86a **RR 82f 86a** 1935[8]
5 b h Lear Fan (USA) 10.4f **(80)** - Caerna (USA) (Caerleon (USA)) 8.6f **(71)**
Form - 8
Record 1998 - 1st:0 2nd:0 3rd:0 Ran:1
Pre1998 - 1st:2 2nd:1 3rd:0 Ran:16
Win Prizemoney £47,078 *Total Prizemoney* £53,427
Wins * 1997 Mar Doncas (G-F) H 8f 86 93 <
* 1996 Jun York (GD) 7.9f 81
1998 Turf 0-1: (10f) (gd)
Decent colt, effective 8 to 10f, acts on gd, has worn blinkers. Consistent. A game winner of the Lincoln in '97, he has shown mixed form since, including when tried over hurdles. Ran just one in '98 and was sold at Tattersalls Horses-in-Training Sale for just 600 gns. Remarkably, another former Lincoln winner, Roving Minstrel, made the same paltry sum at the same sale.
**P F I Cole [2-18] H R H Sultan Ahmad Shah.*

KUMAIT (USA) BHB 105f **RR 105f** 4675[4]
4 b br g Danzig (USA) 8.1f **(88)** - Colour Chart (USA) (Mr Prospector (USA)) 8.8f **(78)**
Form - 247203144
Record 1998 - 1st:1 2nd:2 3rd:1 Ran:9
Pre1998 - 1st:1 2nd:1 3rd:5 Ran:11
Win Prizemoney £9,323 *Total Prizemoney* £29,665
Wins * 1998 Spt Yarmou (G-S) 6f 102 <
1996 Nov Newmar (GD) 6f 94
1998 Turf 1-9: (6f 1-4, 7f 5) (gd 1-3, g-f 3, frm 3)
Scopey, Pattern-class gelding, effective 6 to 7f, best at 7f, acts on gd to frm, best on frm. Turf high 105 - also 1st of 7 from To the Roof (16 Spt Yarmouth RF 4315). This likeable individual ran creditably throughout a busy campaign, gaining a well deserved victory at Yarmouth in September. A free-runner who is extremely game in a finish, he is good enough to win a Listed event.
**EAL Dunlop[1-9]Maktoum Al Maktoum(from DR Loder[0-3] Spt 1997).*

KUMATOUR BHB 102f **RR 103f** 3230[4]
3 b c Batshoof 9.5f **(66)** - Runelia (Runnett) 7f **(59)**
Form - 2221124
Record 1998 - 1st:2 2nd:3 3rd:0 Ran:6
Pre1998 - 1st:0 2nd:1 3rd:0 Ran:1
Win Prizemoney £13,328 *Total Prizemoney* £28,351
Wins * 1998 Jun San Si (G-F) 10f 93 <
*** 1998** May Windso (G-F) 10f 86
1998 Turf 2-6: (8f 2, 10f 2-4) (g-s 2, gd, g-f 1-1, frm 1-2)
Very useful colt, effective 10f, acts on gd to frm. Turf high 103 - 4th of 10 giving 11lb to Gypsy Passion (31 Jly Goodwood 10f gd RF 3230). He ended a frustrating run when winning a maiden at Windsor and decent minor event in San Siro. He put up an improved performance when splitting Hitman and Casino Captive in a valuable handicap at Newmarket in July and ran with credit on his final start. **L M Cumani [2-7] Paolo Riccardi.*

KURSIANG BHB 59f **RR 62f** 4929[6]
2 gr f Petong 7.6f **(58)** - Bellyphax (Bellypha) 9.8f **(73)**
Form - 00847356
Record 1998 - 1st:0 2nd:0 3rd:1 Ran:8
Win Prizemoney £0 *Total Prizemoney* £691
1998 Turf 0-8: (5f, 6f 3, 7f 4) (g-s, gd 2, g-f 4, hrd)
Average filly, effective 6 to 7f, acts on g-f to hrd, has worn blinkers. Turf high 62 - 5th of 20 getting 19lb from Pepperdine (4 Oct Warwick 7f g-f RF 4643).
**B R Millman [0-4] C I T Racing Ltd (from M Meade [0-4] Jly 1998).*

KUSTER RR 66f 4774[8]
2 b c Indian Ridge 7.6f **(74)** - Ustka (Lomond (USA)) 8.8f **(65)**
Form - 8
Record 1998 - 1st:0 2nd:0 3rd:0 Ran:1
1998 Turf 0-1: (7f) (gd)
Currently average colt. **L M Cumani [0-1] Lord Vestey.*

KUSTOM KIT KATE BHB 63f57a **RR 64f 57a** 1572[11]
3 b f Tragic Role (USA) 9.4f **(63)** - Wing of Freedom (Troy) 10.4f **(68)**
Form - 231850
Record 1998 - 1st:1 2nd:1 3rd:1 Ran:6
Pre1998 - 1st:0 2nd:0 3rd:1 Ran:4
Win Prizemoney £3,446 *Total Prizemoney* £4,961
Wins * 1998 Mar Nottin (G-S) H 6.1f 58 64 <
1998 Turf 1-3: (6f 1-3) (sft, g-s 1-1, gd) 1998 AW 0-3: (7f 3) (Fibr 3)
Light-framed, average filly, effective 5 to 7f, acts on g-s to g-f - acts on Fibr, has worn blinkers. Turf high 64 (1st run) - 1st of 20 getting 2lb from Sky Mountain (31 Mar Nottingham RF 0518). AW high 60 (1st run) - 2nd of 9 getting 7lb from She's A Gem (11 Mar Southwell 7f Fibr RF 0424).
**S R Bowring [1-10] Charterhouse Holdings Plc.*

KUSTOM KIT KLASSIC BHB 48f36a **RR 28f 36a** 245[11]
4 b c Chilibang 7f **(55)** - Norvi (Viking (USA)) 6.7f **(65)**
Form - 00
Record 1998 - 1st:0 2nd:0 3rd:0 Ran:2
Pre1998 - 1st:0 2nd:0 3rd:2 Ran:8
Win Prizemoney £0 *Total Prizemoney* £743
1998 AW 0-2: (8f, 12f) (Fibr 2)
Workmanlike, very moderate colt, effective 12f - acts on Fibr, has worn blinkers, favours left handed tracks. AW high 22.
**S R Bowring [0-10] Charterhouse Holdings Plc.*

KUSTOM KIT XPRES BHB 36f25a **RR 35f 25a** 142[9]
4 gr f Absalom 7.1f **(56)** - Miss Serlby (Runnett) 7f **(59)**
Form - 570
Record 1998 - 1st:0 2nd:0 3rd:0 Ran:3
Pre1998 - 1st:0 2nd:1 3rd:0 Ran:12
Win Prizemoney £0 *Total Prizemoney* £1,310
1998 AW 0-3: (7f, 11f, 12f) (Fibr 3)
Unfurnished, very moderate filly, has worn blinkers. AW high 18.
**S R Bowring [0-12] Charterhouse Holdings Plc (from M McCormack [0-3] Jun 1996).*

KUWAIT DAWN (IRE) BHB 80f **RR 84+f** 4309[8]
2 b f Pips Pride 6.7f **(70)** - Red Note (Rusticaro (FR)) 8.2f **(65)**
Form - 24008
Record 1998 - 1st:0 2nd:1 3rd:0 Ran:5
Win Prizemoney £0 *Total Prizemoney* £2,541

1998 Turf 0-5: (6f 2, 7f 2, 8f) (gd, g-f, frm 2, hrd)
Decent filly. Turf high 84 (1st run) (began Aug) - 2nd of 5 getting 8lb from Tough Guy (1 Aug Newmarket 7f frm RF 3273).
**K Mahdi [0-5] Greenfield Stud.*

KUWAIT FLAVOUR (IRE) RR 57f 5123[4]

2 b c Bluebird (USA) 7.9f **(71)**-Plume Magique (Kenmare (FR)) 6.5f **(72)**
Form - 4
Record 1998 - 1st:0 2nd:0 3rd:0 Ran:1
Win Prizemoney £0 *Total Prizemoney* £205
1998 Turf 0-1: (6f) (g-s)
Currently fair colt. **K Mahdi [0-1] Greenfield Stud.*

KUWAIT THUNDER (IRE) BHB 79f RR 78f 5139[3]

2 ch c Mac's Imp (USA) 5.6f **(54)** - Romangoddess (IRE) (Rhoman Rule (USA))
Form - 3543
Record 1998 - 1st:0 2nd:0 3rd:2 Ran:4
Win Prizemoney £0 *Total Prizemoney* £1,600
1998 Turf 0-4: (6f 4) (gd, g-f, frm, hrd)
Above-average colt. Turf high 78 (began Aug) - 3rd of 22 to Mutaakkid (6 Nov Doncaster 6f gd RF 5139).
**K Mahdi [0-4] Greenfield Stud.*

KWEILO BHB 66f RR 63f 2630[3]

4 b g Mtoto 11.5f **(71)** - Hug Me (Shareef Dancer (USA)) 9.9f **(73)**
Form - 13513
Record 1998 - 1st:2 2nd:0 3rd:2 Ran:5
Pre1998 - 1st:0 2nd:0 3rd:0 Ran:7
Win Prizemoney £6,753 *Total Prizemoney* £7,689
Wins * 1998 Jun Epsom (GD) H 7f 60 63 <
*** 1998** May Redcar (G-F) S 7f 47
1998 Turf 2-5: (7f 2-4, 8f) (gd 1-3, g-f 1-1, frm)
Average gelding, effective 7 to 8f, best at 7f, acts on gd to frm. Turf high 63 - 1st of 11 getting 11lb from Bold Hunter (24 Jun Epsom RF 2240). **J W Payne [2-12] Marwan Tabsh.*

KWIKPOINT BHB 50f RR 53f 4153[19]

4 ch g Never so Bold 7.1f **(62)** - Try the Duchess (Try My Best (USA)) 7.6f **(67)**
Form - 80400
Record 1998 - 1st:0 2nd:0 3rd:0 Ran:5
Pre1998 - 1st:0 2nd:0 3rd:0 Ran:3
Win Prizemoney £0 *Total Prizemoney* £252
1998 Turf 0-5: (5f, 6f 2, 7f, 8f) (gd, g-f 2, frm 2)
Workmanlike, fair gelding, effective 6f, acts on g-f, has worn blinkers. Turf high 53 - 4th of 20 giving 17lb to Martindale (18 Jly Ripon 6f g-f RF 2939). **Martin Todhunter [0-9] R Garside.*

KYELID (IRE) RR 98f 4723a[6]

3 c
Form - 56
1998 Turf 0-2: (10f, 14f) (sft, g-s)
Currently very useful colt. Turf high 98. **F Gang in GER [0-2].*

KYOTO CITY (JPN) RR 552a[6]

7 b h Soccer Boy (JPN) - Mountain Queen (JPN) (Nizon (JPN))
Form - 6
1998 AW 0-1: (10f) (Dirt)
Currently useful horse. **K Nakao in JPN [0-1] Yushun Horse Club Co.*

LAABED BHB 88f RR 85f 3991[10]

2 b c Mizoram (USA) - Petite Butterfly (Absalom) 7.2f **(58)**
Form - 5451320
Record 1998 - 1st:1 2nd:1 3rd:1 Ran:7
Win Prizemoney £3,366 *Total Prizemoney* £8,126
Wins * 1998 Jly Catter (GD) 6f 84+ <
1998 Turf 1-7: (5f 2, 6f 1-2, 7f 2, 8f) (gd, g-f 1-3, frm 2, hrd)
Useful colt, effective 6 to 7f, best at 7f, acts on g-f to frm, best on g-f. Turf high 85 - 2nd of 20 giving 9lb to Hoh Steamer (18 Aug York 7f g-f RF 3700) - also 1st of 7 giving 5lb to Miss Grapette (22 Jly Catterick RF 3018). Useful nursery form since landing his maiden, runner-up at York in August.
**M Johnston [1-7] Ziad Galadari.*

LAA JADEED (IRE) BHB 49f44a RR 52f 44a 4939[5]

3 b g Petorius 8f **(66)** - Sea Mistress (Habitat) 9.4f **(70)**
Form - 6700065
Record 1998 - 1st:0 2nd:0 3rd:0 Ran:6
Pre1998 - 1st:0 2nd:0 3rd:0 Ran:2
1998 Turf 0-5: (6f, 7f, 8f 2, 10f) (gd 2, g-f, frm 2) 1998 AW 0-1: (8f) (Fibr)
Scopey, fair gelding. Turf high 52 (began Aug). Consistent.
**J A Glover [0-7] B Dixon (from A C Stewart [0-1] Oct 1997).*

LABEQ (IRE) BHB 100f RR 105df 4379[15]

4 b c Lycius (USA) 8.8f **(71)** - Ahbab (IRE) (Ajdal (USA)) 9.2f **(89)**
Form - 027512000
Record 1998 - 1st:1 2nd:2 3rd:0 Ran:9
Pre1998 - 1st:2 2nd:1 3rd:0 Ran:5
Win Prizemoney £28,891 *Total Prizemoney* £44,867
Wins * 1998 Jun Doncas (GD) H 10.3f 94 99 <
*** 1997** Aug Newmar (G-F) H 10f 85 89+
*** 1997** Jly Lingfi (G-F) 9f 85+
1998 Turf 1-9: (8f 5, 10f 1-4) (hvy, gd 4, g-f 1-3, frm)
Scopey, Pattern-class colt, effective 10f, acts on g-f. Turf high 105 - also 1st of 10 giving 15lb to Karakia (28 Jun Doncaster RF 2360). He put in some solid performances, including a most creditable fifth in the Royal Hunt Cup and a fluent victory in a good handicap at Doncaster. No match for Chester House at the weights in a listed race, and was hampered quite badly at Goodwood, but found nothing when let down at York in August. He needs to come down the ratings, as he is not quite up to Pattern races, or clock up some air miles.
**P T Walwyn [3-14] Hamdan Al Maktoum.*

LA CHATELAINE BHB 46a RR 45f 4362[12]

4 b f Then Again 7.4f **(52)** - La Domaine (Dominion) 8.5f **(63)**
Form - 0860641400660
Record 1998 - 1st:1 2nd:0 3rd:0 Ran:13
Pre1998 - 1st:1 2nd:2 3rd:0 Ran:11
Win Prizemoney £7,271 *Total Prizemoney* £9,796
Wins * 1998 Jun Epsom (GD) H 12f 39 45
1997 Aug Bright (G-F) H 7f 43 48 <
1998 Turf 1-11: (8f 2, 11f 4, 12f 1-4, 14f) (g-s, gd 2, g-f 1-5, frm 3) 1998 AW 0-2: (8f, 10f) (Equi 2)
Unfurnished, moderate filly, effective 7 to 12f, best at 7f, acts on gd to frm, has worn blinkers, likes left handed tracks, likes tight tracks. Turf high 45 - 1st of 11 getting 15lb from Phantom Waters (24 Jun Epsom RF 2239). AW high 9.
**Miss B Sanders [1-13] Blake Wales & Laycock (from G Lewis [1-11] Spt 1997).*

LACHESIS BHB 38f33a RR 40f 33a 4339[8]

5 ch m Lycius (USA) 8.8f **(71)** - Chance All (FR) (Glenstal (USA)) 10.1f **(64)**
Form - 086305008
Record 1998 - 1st:0 2nd:0 3rd:1 Ran:8
Pre1998 - 1st:1 2nd:0 3rd:3 Ran:26
Win Prizemoney £3,327 *Total Prizemoney* £6,210
Wins 1997 Jly Leices (GD) H 6f 42 45 <
1998 Turf 0-6: (5f 2, 6f 4) (g-f 2, frm 4) 1998 AW 0-2: (5f, 7f) (Fibr 2)
Moderate filly, effective 6f, acts on gd to frm, has worn blinkers. Turf high 44 (1st run) - 3rd of 17 getting 24lb from Longwick Lad (18 May Bath 6f frm RF 1297). AW high 42.
**R McGhin [0-8] The 1 2 3 Partnership (from Mrs S Lamyman [0-2] Nov 1997).*

LA CINECITTA (FR) BHB 60f RR 61f 4916[7]

2 ch f Dancing Spree (USA) 8f **(59)** - Cox's Feather (USA) (Cox's Ridge (USA)) 8f **(68)**
Form - 657
Record 1998 - 1st:0 2nd:0 3rd:0 Ran:3
1998 Turf 0-3: (6f 2, 7f) (g-s, gd, frm)
Currently average filly. Turf high 61 (began Aug).
**C B B Booth [0-3] David Hutchinson.*

LA DOYENNE (IRE) BHB 51f52a RR 53f 52a 4921[11]

4 ch f Masterclass (USA) 5.9f **(63)** - Sainthill (St Alphage) 6.6f **(60)**
Form - 014612460004110080
Record 1998 - 1st:3 2nd:1 3rd:0 Ran:15
Pre1998 - 1st:2 2nd:0 3rd:2 Ran:14
Win Prizemoney £12,901 *Total Prizemoney* £14,812
Wins * 1998 Spt Hamilt (SFT) H 5f 48 53
*** 1998** Aug Beverl (G-F) H 5f 36 48

* **1998** *Feb Lingfi (SLW) H 5f 48 49*
* 1997 *Dec Southw (STD) H 5f 32 41*
* 1997 Aug Bright (G-F) 7f 54 <

1998 Turf 2-9: (5f 2-9) (g-s, gd 1-4, g-f, frm 1-3) 1998 AW 1-6: (5f 1-5, 6f) (Equi 1-4, Fibr 2)

Neat, fair filly, effective 5 to 7f, best at 5f, acts on gd to frm - acts on Equi, best on gd, likes left handed tracks, likes tight tracks, excels at Lingfield. Turf high 53 - 1st of 18 giving 12lb to Dona Filipa (7 Spt Hamilton RF 4130) - also 1st of 15 getting 29lb from Sihafi (29 Aug Beverley RF 3941). AW high 55 - 2nd of 10 getting 9lb from Manolo (19 Feb Lingfield 5f Equi RF 0317) - also 1st of 10 giving 8lb to Rise 'n Shine (5 Feb Lingfield RF 0222).

**C B B Booth [5-29] Mrs J B Robinson.*

LADY ALEXANDER (IRE) RR 112f 4726a[13]

3 ch f Night Shift (USA) 8.1f **(73)** - Sandhurst Goddess (Sandhurst Prince) 7.9f **(63)**

Form - 2620

1998 Turf 0-4: (5f 3, 6f) (sft, gd 2, frm)

Group-class filly, effective 5 to 6f, acts on gd. Turf high 112 - 2nd of 15 to Land of Dreams (28 Jly Goodwood 5f gd RF 3164). A very smart juvenile, ran her best race at three when runner-up to Land Of Dreams in the King George Stakes at Goodwood. That should have been a springboard to success, but she disappointed on her only subsequent start. **C Collins in IRE [3-11] Mrs N O'Callaghan.*

LADY ALMITRA BHB 43f48a RR 55f 48a 4383[11]

3 b br f Presidium 7.5f **(56)** - Armaiti (Sayf El Arab (USA)) 7.1f **(54)**

Form - 00

Record 1998 - 1st:0 2nd:0 3rd:0 Ran:2
Pre1998 - 1st:0 2nd:0 3rd:1 Ran:3

Win Prizemoney £0 *Total Prizemoney* £379

1998 Turf 0-1: (6f) (frm) 1998 AW 0-1: (8f) (Fibr)

Unfurnished, fair filly.

**R J Hodges [0-2] John Hill (from C J Hill [0-3] Oct 1997).*

LADY ANGHARAD (IRE) BHB 100f RR 90f 4738[7]

2 b f Tenby 10.4f **(76)** - Lavezzola (IRE) (Salmon Leap (USA)) 11f **(61)**

Form - 4118577

Record 1998 - 1st:2 2nd:0 3rd:0 Ran:7

Win Prizemoney £26,713 *Total Prizemoney* £26,965

Wins * **1998** Jun Salisb (G-F) 7f 88 <
* **1998** Jun Epsom (GD) L 6f 88 <

1998 Turf 2-7: (5f, 6f 1-2, 7f 1-2, 8f 2) (g-s, gd 1-3, g-f, frm 1-2)

Useful filly, effective 6 to 7f, best at 7f, acts on gd to frm. Turf high 90 - also 1st of 7 getting 3lb from Atlantic Destiny (5 Jun Epsom RF 1744). After showing promise on her Sandown debut, she came late to beat five previous winners in an Epsom Listed event. Followed up in a valuable race at Salisbury, but was well held in Pattern company after that. **A P Jarvis [2-7] Ambrose Turnbull.*

LADY ANNABEL RR 60f 2742[7]

2 b f Alhijaz 7.7f **(57)** - Anna Rella (IRE) (Danehill (USA)) 10f **(72)**

Form - 07

Record 1998 - 1st:0 2nd:0 3rd:0 Ran:2

1998 Turf 0-2: (5f, 6f) (gd, g-f)

Currently average filly. Turf high 60 (began Jly).

**C W Fairhurst [0-2] M R Handy.*

LADY ANSHAN RR 3f 2516[17]

2 ch f Anshan 8.2f **(63)** - Lady Sabo **(37?f 42a)** (Prince Sabo) 7.2f **(62)**

Form - 050

Record 1998 - 1st:0 2nd:0 3rd:0 Ran:3

1998 Turf 0-3: (5f 2, 7f) (g-s, g-f 2)

Currently very poor filly. Turf high 3. **N Bycroft [0-3] Mrs N Bycroft.*

LADY ARDROSS RR 4935[13]

3 b f Flying Tyke 7.2f **(42)** - Hatshepsut (Ardross) 10.6f **(68)**

Form - 0

Record 1998 - 1st:0 2nd:0 3rd:0 Ran:1

1998 Turf 0-1: (8f) (gd)

Light-framed, currently very poor filly. **A Smith [0-1] Alfred Smith.*

LADY BENSON (IRE) BHB 29f RR 26f 5121[14]

5 b m Pennine Walk 8.9f **(64)** - Sit Elnaas (USA) (Sir Ivor) 10.2f **(70)**

Form - 058000

Record 1998 - 1st:0 2nd:0 3rd:0 Ran:6
Pre1998 - 1st:0 2nd:0 3rd:0 Ran:4

Win Prizemoney £0 *Total Prizemoney* £210

1998 Turf 0-6: (5f 4, 6f 2) (g-s, gd 2, frm 2, hrd)

Little account filly. Turf high 37 (began Aug).

**W M Brisbourne [0-7] B L Benson (from D J S Cosgrove [0-3] Aug 1996).*

LADY BEWARE BHB 63f RR 70f 4400[8]

2 b f Warning 8.1f **(77)** - Thewaari (USA) (Eskimo (USA))

Form - 04505358

Record 1998 - 1st:0 2nd:0 3rd:1 Ran:8

Win Prizemoney £0 *Total Prizemoney* £651

1998 Turf 0-8: (5f 3, 6f 4, 7f) (gd 3, g-f 3, frm 2)

Above-average filly, effective 5f, acts on frm. Turf high 70 - 3rd of 14 giving 2lb to Brockton Saga (7 Spt Bath 5f frm RF 4122).

**M R Channon [0-8] W H Ponsonby.*

LADY BOX RR 40f 3132[14]

2 b f Pursuit of Love 9.5f **(69)** - Island Ruler (Ile de Bourbon (USA)) 10.1f **(67)**

Form - 0

Record 1998 - 1st:0 2nd:0 3rd:0 Ran:1

1998 Turf 0-1: (7f) (gd)

Currently moderate filly. **P F I Cole [0-1] Black Run Racing Club.*

LADY BOXER BHB 70f RR 74f 4746[11]

2 b f Komaite (USA) 6.9f **(61)** - Lady Broker **(44a)** (Petorius) 7.3f **(61)**

Form - 13560

Record 1998 - 1st:1 2nd:0 3rd:1 Ran:5

Win Prizemoney £3,470 *Total Prizemoney* £4,070

Wins * **1998** Jun Leices (SFT) 6f 74+ <

1998 Turf 1-5: (6f 1-5) (gd 1-3, g-f 2)

Above-average filly. Turf high 74 - also 1st of 7 getting 5lb from Prince Prospect (13 Jun Leicester RF 1962). Her stable is not noted for sending out two-year-old winners and she started at 40/1 when winning at Leicester. Mixed form since.

**M Mullineaux [1-5] Esprit de Corps Racing.*

LADYCAKE (IRE) BHB 61f RR 67f 5117[6]

2 gr f Perugino (USA) - Olivia's Pride (IRE) (Digamist (USA))

Form - 186271206

Record 1998 - 1st:2 2nd:2 3rd:0 Ran:9

Win Prizemoney £5,392 *Total Prizemoney* £6,961

Wins * **1998** Aug Mussel (GD) S 5f 67 <
* **1998** May Mussel (GD) 5f 65+

1998 Turf 2-9: (5f 2-9) (gd 4, g-f 2-3, frm 2)

Average filly, effective 5f, acts on g-f to frm, best on g-f. Turf high 67 - 1st of 10 giving 5lb to Cool Katie (27 Aug Musselburgh RF 3903) - also 1st of 6 getting 5lb from Northern Svengali (1 May Musselburgh RF 0955). **J Berry [2-9] Comerford Brothers Ltd.*

LADY CARBRON (IRE) BHB 57f58a RR 58f 58a 5117[3]

2 br f Elbio 9f **(62)** - Smart Turn (His Turn)

Form - 712422403

Record 1998 - 1st:1 2nd:3 3rd:1 Ran:9

Win Prizemoney £1,865 *Total Prizemoney* £3,921

Wins * **1998** *Apr Wolver (STD) S 5f 56* <

1998 Turf 0-5: (5f 5) (sft, gd 2, g-f 2) 1998 AW 1-4: (5f 1-4) (Fibr 1-4)

Average filly, effective 5f, acts on gd - acts on Fibr. Turf high 68 - 2nd of 13 giving 5lb to Polly Mills (15 Jun Windsor 5f gd RF 2004). AW high 64 - 2nd of 7 giving 5lb to Lightning Blaze (6 Jun Wolverhampton 5f Fibr RF 1798). **J Berry [1-9] P Conroy.*

LADY CARLYON BHB 35f RR 42f 2653[9]

5 b m Common Grounds 8.1f **(66)** - Little Preston (IRE) (Pennine Walk) 8.5f **(61)**

Form - 348500

Record 1998 - 1st:0 2nd:0 3rd:1 Ran:6

Win Prizemoney £0 *Total Prizemoney* £510

1998 Turf 0-3: (6f, 8f, 10f) (g-s, gd, g-f) 1998 AW 0-3: (5f, 6f, 7f) (Fibr 3)

Moderate filly, effective 5f, - acts on Fibr, has worn blinkers. Turf high 42. AW high 42 (1st run) - 3rd of 10 giving 15lb to Stately Favour (6 Apr Southwell 5f Fibr RF 0572). She ran quite promisingly to finish third over the minimum trip when making a very belated racecourse debut on the Southwell Fibresand in April, but has shown little on turf. **N A Callaghan [0-6] J T Handman and A Allum.*

LADY CAROLINE (IRE) RR 72f 5144[18]
2 b f Hamas (IRE) 8f **(72)** - Pericolo (IRE) (Kris) 9.5f **(73)**
Form - 5270
Record 1998 - 1st:0 2nd:1 3rd:0 Ran:4
Win Prizemoney £0 *Total Prizemoney* £1,176
1998 Turf 0-4: (5f 2, 6f 2) (gd 3, g-f)
Above-average filly. Turf high 72 (began Spt) - 2nd of 10 getting 5lb from Hidden Magic (15 Oct Catterick 6f gd RF 4814).
**M Johnston [0-4] Hertford Offset Ltd.*

LADY CHARLOTTE RR 63f 4455[13]
3 b f Night Shift (USA) 8.1f **(73)** - Circulate (High Top) 10.2f **(67)**
Form - 7680070
Record 1998 - 1st:0 2nd:0 3rd:0 Ran:7
Pre1998 - 1st:1 2nd:0 3rd:0 Ran:4
Win Prizemoney £3,428 *Total Prizemoney* £3,428
Wins * 1997 Spt Bath (G-F) 5.7f 82 <
1998 Turf 0-7: (5f 2, 6f 5) (gd 2, g-f, frm 4)
Neat, average filly, effective 6f, acts on frm. Turf high 73.
**D R C Elsworth [1-11] C J Harper.*

LADY COLDUNELL RR 64f 5071[10]
2 b f Deploy 11.4f **(67)** - Beau's Delight (USA) (Lypheor) 12f **(71)**
Form - 00
Record 1998 - 1st:0 2nd:0 3rd:0 Ran:2
1998 Turf 0-2: (7f, 8f) (gd, frm)
Currently average filly. Turf high 64 (began Oct).
**N A Callaghan [0-2] John Dunsdon.*

LADY DEALER BHB 39f **RR 35f** 4527[9]
3 b f No Big Deal - Our Horizon (Skyliner) 7.3f **(53)**
Form - 700
Record 1998 - 1st:0 2nd:0 3rd:0 Ran:3
1998 Turf 0-3: (7f, 8f, 10f) (g-f 3)
Workmanlike, currently very moderate filly. Turf high 35 (began Aug). **M D I Usher [0-3] Mrs J Gawthorpe.*

LADY EIL BHB 46f48a **RR 51f 48a** 3829[5]
3 ch f Elmaamul (USA) 8.1f **(70)** - Oakbrook Tern (USA) (Arctic Tern (USA)) 8.9f **(69)**
Form - 147380262585
Record 1998 - 1st:0 2nd:2 3rd:1 Ran:9
Pre1998 - 1st:1 2nd:1 3rd:0 Ran:7
Win Prizemoney £1,998 *Total Prizemoney* £3,910
Wins * 1997 *Nov Southw (STD) S 8f 55* <
1998 Turf 0-2: (8f, 10f) (frm 2) 1998 AW 0-7: (7f, 8f 3, 9f 3) (Fibr 7)
Light-framed, fair filly, effective 8f, - acts on Fibr, prefers left handed tracks, favours tight tracks. Turf high 39. AW high 56 - 2nd of 12 getting 15lb from Other Club (20 Jun Wolverhampton 8f Fibr RF 2162). **B Smart [1-16] B Smart.*

LADY EIRWEN RR 3f 4382[22]
2 b f Prince Sabo 6.6f **(64)** - Eustatia (Top Ville) 11.7f **(68)**
Form - 0
Record 1998 - 1st:0 2nd:0 3rd:0 Ran:1
1998 Turf 0-1: (6f) (g-f)
Currently very poor filly. **J Cullinan [0-1] W H Joyce.*

LADY EMRAL BHB 34f **RR 21f** 268[10]
3 br f Handsome Sailor 6.6f **(53)** - Precious Jay (Hotfoot) 10.5f **(59)**
Form - 70
Record 1998 - 1st:0 2nd:0 3rd:0 Ran:2
Pre1998 - 1st:0 2nd:0 3rd:0 Ran:2
1998 AW 0-2: (5f, 6f) (Fibr 2)
Little account filly. AW high 14. **Miss J F Craze [0-4] Mrs N Pritchard.*

LADY FELIX BHB 42f38a **RR 44f 38a** 3969[6]
3 br f Batshoof 9.5f **(66)** - Volcalmeh (Lidhame) 9.2f **(50)**
Form - 06633146
Record 1998 - 1st:1 2nd:0 3rd:2 Ran:8
Pre1998 - 1st:0 2nd:0 3rd:0 Ran:4
Win Prizemoney £2,364 *Total Prizemoney* £3,160
Wins * **1998** Aug Folkes (G-F) H 16.4f 41 44 <
1998 Turf 1-7: (8f, 11f 2, 12f, 14f, 16f 1-1, 17f) (gd, g-f 1-4, frm 2) 1998 AW 0-1: (16f) (Equi)
Light-framed, moderate filly, effective 11 to 17f, acts on g-f to frm, best on g-f, has worn blinkers (extremely effectively), likes left handed tracks, prefers tight tracks. Turf high 44 - 1st of 6 giving 7lb to Mrs Pickles (14 Aug Folkestone RF 3629). Consistent.
**S Mellor [1-12] The Felix Bowness Partnership.*

LADY FROM LIMERICK (IRE) BHB 50f50a **RR 59df 50a** 1099[8]
3 ch f Rainbows For Life (CAN) 9.3f **(64)** - Coshlea (Red Alert) 7.6f **(66)**
Form - 7708
Record 1998 - 1st:0 2nd:0 3rd:0 Ran:4
Pre1998 - 1st:0 2nd:1 3rd:1 Ran:6
Win Prizemoney £0 *Total Prizemoney* £1,617
1998 Turf 0-2: (5f, 6f) (g-s, gd) 1998 AW 0-2: (5f, 6f) (Fibr 2)
Workmanlike, fair filly, has worn blinkers. Turf high 39. AW high 33. **J Berry [0-10] Thomas Doherty.*

LADY GEORGIA BHB 100f **RR 101f** 4853[5]
2 gr f Arazi (USA) 9.2f **(74)** - Petillante (Petong) 6.6f **(58)**
Form - 426234685
Record 1998 - 1st:0 2nd:2 3rd:1 Ran:9
Win Prizemoney £0 *Total Prizemoney* £6,945
1998 Turf 0-9: (5f 2, 6f, 7f 4, 8f 2) (sft, gd 6, g-f 2)
Very useful filly, effective 8f, acts on sft. Turf high 101 - 8th of 11 to Juvenia (4 Oct Longchamp 8f sft RF 4725a). How this filly failed to win is a mystery; she would surely have benefited from a confidence-boosting success in the midst of her failed attempts in Group company. Hopefully connections will find her a soft target to kick-off with in 1999, for she is thoroughly genuine and will only remain a maiden while raced against the best of her generation.
**C E Brittain [0-9] A J Richards.*

LADY GODIVA BHB 52f40a **RR 52f 40a** 25[8]
4 b f Keen 11.1f **(58)** -Festival Fanfare (Ile de Bourbon(USA)) 10.1f **(67)**
Form - 4578
Record 1998 - 1st:0 2nd:0 3rd:0 Ran:2
Pre1998 - 1st:1 2nd:2 3rd:1 Ran:16
Win Prizemoney £6,836 *Total Prizemoney* £14,058
Wins * 1996 Spt York (GD) 7.9f 72 <
1998 AW 0-2: (6f, 7f) (Equi, Fibr)
Unfurnished, fair filly, has worn blinkers. AW high 34.
**M J Polglase [1-18] Keen Racing.*

LADY IMZA BHB 58f **RR 54f** 4260[20]
3 b f Polar Falcon (USA) 9f **(74)** - Blade of Grass (Kris) 9.5f **(73)**
Form - 00
Record 1998 - 1st:0 2nd:0 3rd:0 Ran:2
Pre1998 - 1st:0 2nd:0 3rd:0 Ran:2
1998 Turf 0-2: (6f 2) (gd 2)
Fair filly. Turf high 54.
**A Bailey [0-2] Sandybrow Stables Ltd (from W J Haggas [0-2] Oct 1997).*

LADY IN WAITING BHB 107f **RR 109+f** 4819[1]
3 b f Kylian (USA) 8.1f **(66)** - High Savannah (Rousillon (USA)) 8.2f **(74)**
Form - 4744121
Record 1998 - 1st:2 2nd:1 3rd:0 Ran:7
Pre1998 - 1st:2 2nd:1 3rd:0 Ran:4
Win Prizemoney £29,496 *Total Prizemoney* £55,746
Wins * **1998** Oct Newmar (GD) L 10f 97
* **1998** Spt Chepst (G-S) 10.2f 109+ <
* 1997 Jun Newmar (SFT) L 6f 92
* 1997 Jun Leices (G-F) 5f 86
1998 Turf 2-7: (8f 2, 10f 2-3, 12f 2) (gd 1-3, g-f, frm 1-3)
Workmanlike, Pattern-class filly, effective 8 to 12f, acts on gd to frm, best on gd, likes Newmarket. Turf high 109 - 1st of 2 getting 3lb from Glorosia (10 Spt Chepstow RF 4199). She rediscovered her form toward the end of the campaign, winning a competitive Listed event at Newmarket in October. She made all for both her wins and may be best when ridden from the front.
**P F I Cole [4-11] Pegasus Racing Ltd.*

LADY IONA BHB 46f **RR 43f** 4136[6]
2 ch f Weldnaas (USA) 8.4f **(55)** - Shadha (Shirley Heights) 10.3f **(74)**
Form - 78576
Record 1998 - 1st:0 2nd:0 3rd:0 Ran:5
1998 Turf 0-5: (6f 2, 7f 2, 8f) (g-s, gd, g-f 2, frm)
Moderate filly. Turf high 43. **Martyn Wane [0-5] Mrs C M Barlow.*

LADY JANE (IRE) BHB 52f55a **RR 56f 55a** 4929[10]
2 b f Petardia 8.2f **(58)** - Lune de Miel (Kalamoun) 10.4f **(67)**
Form - 440680
Record 1998 - 1st:0 2nd:0 3rd:0 Ran:6
Win Prizemoney £0 *Total Prizemoney* £446
1998 Turf 0-5: (6f 3, 7f, 8f) (g-s 2, g-f, frm, hrd) 1998 AW 0-1: (5f) (Fibr)
Fair filly. Turf high 56. **W R Muir [0-6] Hollywood Robbie.*

LADY JAZZ BHB 53f55a **RR 46f 55a** 3402[4]
3 b f Night Shift (USA) 8.1f **(73)** - Penamint (Siberian Express (USA)) 8.8f **(65)**
Form - 4240204
Record 1998 - 1st:0 2nd:2 3rd:0 Ran:7
Win Prizemoney £0 *Total Prizemoney* £2,484
1998 Turf 0-2: (7f 2) (hvy, frm) 1998 AW 0-5: (7f 3, 8f 2) (Equi, Fibr 4)
Unfurnished, fair filly, effective 7 to 8f, - acts on Fibr. Turf high 46. AW high 58 - 2nd of 16 getting 11lb from Dina Line (11 May Southwell 8f Fibr RF 1154). **T J Naughton [0-7] Miss L A Elliott.*

LADY JO BHB 67f **RR 55f** 3896[11]
2 ch f Phountzi (USA) 9.6f **(60)** -Lady Kalliste (Another Realm) 6.6f **(55)**
Form - 070
Record 1998 - 1st:0 2nd:0 3rd:0 Ran:3
1998 Turf 0-3: (6f, 7f 2) (gd 2, frm)
Currently fair filly. Turf high 55 (began Jly). **S Dow [0-3] Ken Butler.*

LADY LAPHROAIG (FR) BHB 49f55a **RR 42f 55a** 4775[16]
3 ch f Elmaamul (USA) 8.1f **(70)** - Venerate (IRE) (Ahonoora) 8.1f **(73)**
Form - 32344570
Record 1998 - 1st:0 2nd:0 3rd:1 Ran:6
Pre1998 - 1st:0 2nd:1 3rd:1 Ran:5
Win Prizemoney £0 *Total Prizemoney* £1,127
1998 Turf 0-3: (6f, 7f 2) (gd, g-f, frm)1998 AW 0-3:(6f, 7f 2)(Equi 2, Fibr)
Workmanlike, moderate filly, effective 6 to 7f, acts on gd - acts on Fibr, likes left handed tracks, likes tight tracks. Turf high 42 (began Aug). AW high 39. Consistent.
**W R Muir [0-11] Friends of Laphroaig.*

LADY LAUREN BHB 67f **RR 74f** 5148[22]
2 b f Cyrano de Bergerac 7.3f **(58)** - Wandering Stranger (Petong) 6.6f **(58)**
Form - 333540
Record 1998 - 1st:0 2nd:0 3rd:3 Ran:6
Win Prizemoney £0 *Total Prizemoney* £1,295
1998 Turf 0-6: (5f 3, 6f 2, 7f) (gd 2, g-f 2, frm, hrd)
Above-average filly, effective 5 to 6f, best at 5f, acts on gd to hrd. Turf high 74. **G Woodward [0-6] Luke Devine.*

LADY LAZARUS BHB 65f **RR 76f** 4613[9]
2 ch f Beveled (USA) 6.9f **(64)** - Swilly Express (Ballacashtal (CAN)) 5.3f **(50)**
Form - 46300
Record 1998 - 1st:0 2nd:0 3rd:1 Ran:5
Win Prizemoney £0 *Total Prizemoney* £772
1998 Turf 0-5: (6f 3, 7f 2) (g-s, gd 2, frm 2)
Above-average filly. Turf high 76 (began Aug).
**M Blanshard [0-5] P J Doherty.*

LADY LEW (IRE) BHB 30f **RR 27f** 3025[10]
3 b f River Falls 8.2f **(56)** - Tropical Desert (IRE) (King Persian)
Form - 000
Record 1998 - 1st:0 2nd:0 3rd:0 Ran:3
1998 Turf 0-3: (7f, 8f, 10f) (g-f, frm 2)
Light-framed, currently little account filly. Turf high 27.
**J S Moore [0-3] Brian Lewendon.*

LADY MABEL BHB 36f44a **RR 39f 44a** 3085[6]
3 ch f Inchinor 8.9f **(64)** - Late Matinee (Red Sunset) 8.2f **(63)**
Form - 600005866
Record 1998 - 1st:0 2nd:0 3rd:0 Ran:9
1998 Turf 0-6: (6f 2, 7f 2, 8f 2) (g-s, gd, g-f 2, frm 2) 1998 AW 0-3: (6f, 7f 2) (Fibr 3)
Unfurnished, very moderate filly. Turf high 39. AW high 34.
**J D Bethell [0-9] N D Fisher.*

LADY MELBOURNE (IRE) BHB 68f **RR 78f** 5042[4]
2 b f Indian Ridge 7.6f **(74)** - Gayshuka (Lord Gayle (USA)) 8.8f **(62)**
Form - 8244
Record 1998 - 1st:0 2nd:1 3rd:0 Ran:4
Win Prizemoney £0 *Total Prizemoney* £1,290
1998 Turf 0-4: (5f 2, 6f 2) (sft, g-s, gd, frm)
Above-average filly. Turf high 78 (began Aug) - 2nd of 8 getting 5lb from Pal of Mine (5 Spt Epsom 6f gd RF 4095).
**M Johnston [0-4] Hertford Offset Ltd.*

LADY MOORINGS (IRE) RR 45f 3220[8]
2 b f Dolphin Street (FR) - Crimson Ring (Persian Bold) 9.3f **(66)**
Form - 808
Record 1998 - 1st:0 2nd:0 3rd:0 Ran:3
1998 Turf 0-3: (6f 2, 7f) (gd 2, g-f)
Currently moderate filly. Turf high 45.
**M Blanshard [0-3] David Sykes.*

LADY MUCK (IRE) BHB 71f **RR 72f** 4845[12]
2 b f Shalford (IRE) 7.8f **(63)** - Kept in Style (Castle Keep) 8.3f **(57)**
Form - 24821560
Record 1998 - 1st:1 2nd:2 3rd:0 Ran:8
Win Prizemoney £3,647 *Total Prizemoney* £5,617
Wins * **1998** Jly Epsom (G-F) 7f 72 <
1998 Turf 1-8: (6f 3, 7f 1-2, 8f 3) (g-s, gd, g-f 1-2, frm 4)
Above-average filly, effective 7 to 8f, acts on g-f to frm, has worn blinkers. Turf high 72 - 1st of 11 getting 5lb from Pluralist (29 Jly Epsom RF 3198). Consistent. Fair efforts since winning an Epsom maiden. **D J S ffrenchDavis [1-8] Mrs Patrick McCarthy.*

LADY NAIRN BHB 54f **RR 37f** 2734[14]
2 b f Mujadil (USA) 7.7f **(70)** - Animate (IRE) (Tate Gallery (USA)) 7.4f **(67)**
Form - 360
Record 1998 - 1st:0 2nd:0 3rd:1 Ran:3
Win Prizemoney £0 *Total Prizemoney* £444
1998 Turf 0-3: (5f 2, 6f) (sft, g-f, frm)
Currently very moderate filly. Turf high 37.
**J J Quinn [0-3] Murray Grubb.*

LADY ODDJOB (IRE) RR 50f 5071[12]
2 gr f Up and At 'em - Thalssa (Rusticaro (FR)) 8.2f **(65)**
Form - 0
Record 1998 - 1st:0 2nd:0 3rd:0 Ran:1
1998 Turf 0-1: (7f) (gd)
Currently fair filly. **K McAuliffe [0-1] S S M Partnership.*

LADY OF ARAGON BHB 66f **RR 69f** 4337[20]
2 b f Aragon 7.7f **(58)** - Gentle Stream (Sandy Creek) 8.9f **(59)**
Form - 86440
Record 1998 - 1st:0 2nd:0 3rd:0 Ran:5
Win Prizemoney £0 *Total Prizemoney* £199
1998 Turf 0-5: (6f 2, 7f 2, 8f) (gd, g-f, frm 3)
Average filly. Turf high 69. **M J Heaton-Ellis [0-5] P G Lowe.*

LADYOFDISTINCTION (IRE) BHB 31f **RR 22f** 3121[12]
3 b f Distinctly North (USA) 7.4f **(63)** - Lady Anna Livia (Ahonoora) 8.1f **(73)**
Form - 700
Record 1998 - 1st:0 2nd:0 3rd:0 Ran:3
Pre1998 - 1st:0 2nd:0 3rd:0 Ran:4
1998 Turf 0-3: (8f, 11f, 12f) (g-s, frm, hrd)
Little account filly, has worn blinkers. Turf high 22.
**J S Wainwright [0-7] L Mason.*

LADY OF LORIEN (IRE) BHB 43f **RR 38f** 2443[8]
3 b f Lahib (USA) 8f **(69)** - Gentle Guest (IRE) (Be My Guest (USA)) 9.3f **(67)**
Form - 888
Record 1998 - 1st:0 2nd:0 3rd:0 Ran:3
1998 Turf 0-3: (8f 2, 10f) (gd 3)
Workmanlike, currently very moderate filly. Turf high 38.
**B J McMath [0-3] M K Armitt.*

LADY OF SPAIN BHB 48f43a **RR 51f 43a** 4408[3]
3 ch f Aragon 7.7f **(58)** - Myth (Troy) 10.4f **(68)**

Form - 50730023
Record 1998 - 1st:0 2nd:1 3rd:2 Ran:8
Win Prizemoney £0 *Total Prizemoney* £1,324
1998 Turf 0-5: (8f, 10f 4) (g-s, g-f 2, frm 2) 1998 AW 0-3: (8f 2, 12f) (Fibr 3)
Light-framed, fair filly, effective 10f, acts on g-f to frm. Turf high 51. AW high 39. **J P Leigh [0-8] J W Rowles.*

LADY OF THE DANCE BHB 39f **RR 30f** 4615[5]

3 b f Tragic Role (USA) 9.4f **(63)** - Waltz (Jimmy Reppin) 8.8f **(64)**
Form - 45
Record 1998 - 1st:0 2nd:0 3rd:0 Ran:2
Pre1998 - 1st:0 2nd:0 3rd:0 Ran:2
1998 Turf 0-1: (12f) (g-f) 1998 AW 0-1: (13f) (Equi)
Workmanlike, moderate filly.
**M A Jarvis [0-4] T G & Mrs M E Holdcroft.*

LADY OF THE LUNE BHB 35f **RR 27f** 3846[16]

3 b f Skyliner 6.8f **(51)** - Hot Feet (Marching On) 6f **(60)**
Form - 0060
Record 1998 - 1st:0 2nd:0 3rd:0 Ran:4
1998 Turf 0-3: (6f, 8f 2) (gd, frm 2) 1998 AW 0-1: (9f) (Fibr)
Workmanlike, little account filly. Turf high 27.
**D HaydnJones [0-4] Mrs K Howells.*

LADY PEPPIATT (IRE) BHB 57f60a **RR 64f 60a** 4005[5]

2 b f Tirol 8.1f **(64)** - Kirsova (Absalom) 7.2f **(58)**
Form - 03134431455
Record 1998 - 1st:2 2nd:0 3rd:3 Ran:11
Win Prizemoney £4,232 *Total Prizemoney* £5,896

Wins								
	***1998**	*Jly*	*Southw*	*(STD)*	*C*	*6f*	*64*	<
	***1998**	*Jun*	*Southw*	*(STD)*	*S*	*6f*	*64*	<

1998 Turf 0-7: (5f, 6f 5, 7f) (g-s, gd, frm 4, hrd) 1998 AW 2-4: (5f, 6f 2-3) (Fibr 2-4)
Average filly, effective 5 to 6f, best at 6f, acts on gd to hrd - acts on Fibr. Turf high 64 - 4th of 13 giving 5lb to Polly Mills (15 Jun Windsor 5f gd RF 2004). AW high 64 - 1st of 8 giving 2lb to Millionformerthyr (17 Jly Southwell RF 2897) - also 1st of 7 from Super Strides (5 Jun Southwell RF 1767). Consistent. An exposed but able plater, she seems equally effective on turf or Fibresand.
**J S Moore [2-11] Kevin Reddington.*

LADY PETRA BHB 52f **RR 53f** 4761[15]

2 b f Petong 7.6f **(58)** - Miss Clarinet **(8f)** (Pharly (FR)) 9.8f **(68)**
Form - 000
Record 1998 - 1st:0 2nd:0 3rd:0 Ran:3
1998 Turf 0-3: (6f, 7f 2) (gd 2, frm)
Currently fair filly. Turf high 53 (began Spt).
**V Soane [0-3] Classic Four Partnership.*

LADY RACHEL (IRE) BHB 65f62a **RR 73f 62a** 4625[10]

3 b f Priolo (USA) 10.9f **(71)** - Alpine Spring (Head for Heights) 9.6f **(55)**
Form - 2336314F313220
Record 1998 - 1st:2 2nd:3 3rd:5 Ran:14
Pre1998 - 1st:0 2nd:0 3rd:1 Ran:3
Win Prizemoney £6,607 *Total Prizemoney* £14,483

Wins									
	***1998**	Aug	Carlis	(G-S)	H	12f	64	69	<
	***1998**	May	Pontef	(G-F)	H	10f	60	66	

1998 Turf 2-12: (10f 1-3, 11f, 12f 1-6, 14f, 15f) (sft, g-s, gd 1-4, g-f 3, frm 1-3) 1998 AW 0-2: (8f 2) (Fibr 2)
Neat, above-average filly, effective 10 to 15f, acts on gd to frm, best on gd, likes left handed tracks, favours tight tracks. Turf high 73 - 2nd of 7 getting 10lb from Yanabi (17 Spt Ayr 15f gd RF 4324) - also 1st of 5 getting 10lb from Altitude (3 Aug Carlisle RF 3306). AW high 61. **J L Eyre [2-17] Steve Macdonald.*

LADY RALPHINA BHB 34f38a **RR 19f 38a** 1432[10]

3 b f General Wade 5.5f **(40)** - Lady Regent (Wolver Hollow) 8f **(56)**
Form - 767000
Record 1998 - 1st:0 2nd:0 3rd:0 Ran:6
Pre1998 - 1st:0 2nd:0 3rd:0 Ran:8
Win Prizemoney £0 *Total Prizemoney* £74
1998 Turf 0-4: (5f 3, 6f) (sft, g-s, gd, frm) 1998 AW 0-2: (5f, 6f) (Equi 2)
Light-framed, little account filly. Turf high 19. AW high 29.
**J J Bridger [0-14] W Wood.*

LADY ROCKSTAR BHB 80f **RR 80f** 5126[7]

3 b f Rock Hopper 10.6f **(54)** - Silk St James (Pas de Seul) 9.1f **(67)**
Form - 0011111111030757
Record 1998 - 1st:8 2nd:0 3rd:1 Ran:16
Pre1998 - 1st:0 2nd:0 3rd:0 Ran:3
Win Prizemoney £24,088 *Total Prizemoney* £25,835

Wins									
	***1998**	Jun	Windso	(GD)		10f		86+	<
	***1998**	Jun	Folkes	(G-F)	H	9.7f	65	76+	
	***1998**	Jun	Windso	(GD)	H	10f	65	78	
	***1998**	Jun	Nottin	(G-S)	H	8.2f	56	75	
	***1998**	Jun	Yarmou	(SFT)	H	10.1f	47	61+	
	***1998**	Jun	Haydoc	(GD)	H	8.1f	40	55	
	***1998**	Jun	Folkes	(GD)	H	9.7f	40	53+	
	***1998**	May	Ayr	(G-F)	H	9.1f	40	48	

1998 Turf 8-16:(8f 2-2, 9f 1-2, 10f 5-12)(g-s 1-2, gd 2-6, g-f 4-6, frm 1-2)
Workmanlike, decent filly, effective 10f, acts on g-f, has worn blinkers, likes left handed tracks, prefers tight tracks, excels at Windsor, does well at Yarmouth, likes Folkestone. Turf high 87 - 3rd of 6 getting 10lb from Supreme Sound (9 Aug Yarmouth 10f g-f RF 3496) - also 1st of 12 giving 2lb to Twin Time (29 Jun Windsor RF 2392). Consistent. One of the success stories of the season, she racked up eight consecutive victories in little more than a month, despite going up a mile in the handicap. The run came to an end in unfortunate circumstances at Newmarket, when she was almost brought down, and she was held subsequently. Versatile when it comes to trip and ground, has a turn of foot, and is a credit to her trainer. **M J Ryan [8-19] The Five Star Partnership.*

LADY SHERIFF BHB 67f72a **RR 69f 72a** 4228[20]

7 b m Taufan (USA) 8.3f **(65)** - Midaan (Sallust) 8.4f **(63)**
Form - 00803623340
Record 1998 - 1st:0 2nd:1 3rd:3 Ran:11
Pre1998 - 1st:10 2nd:15 3rd:4 Ran:75
Win Prizemoney £42,534 *Total Prizemoney* £72,989

Wins									
	* 1997	Jly	Goodwo	(G-F)	H	5f	77	83	<
	* 1997	May	Newcas	(GD)	H	5f	68	69	
	* 1997	*May*	*Southw*	*(STD)*	*H*	*5f*	*63*	*64*	
	1996	*May*	*Wolver*	*(STD)*	*H*	*5f*	*62*	*59*	
	* 1995	Jly	York	(G-F)	H	5f	60	67+	
	* 1995	Jly	Catter	(G-F)	H	5f	60	62	
	* 1995	Jun	Thirsk	(GD)	H	5f	51	56+	
	* 1995	May	Thirsk	(G-F)	H	5f	44	43	

1998 Turf 0-11: (5f 11) (g-s, gd 4, g-f 3, frm 3)
Average mare, effective 5 to 6f, best at 5f, acts on g-s to frm, best on gd, often wears blinkers (effectively). Turf high 69. In fine form in 1997, she failed to return to her best form in 1998. Reportedly in foal.
**M W Easterby [9-67] E J Mangan (from R Hollinshead [1-19] Nov 1996).*

LADY SILK BHB 30f37a **RR 34f 37a** 112[7]

7 ch m Prince Sabo 6.6f **(64)** - Adduce (USA) (Alleged (USA)) 10f **(76)**
Form - 527
Record 1998 - 1st:0 2nd:1 3rd:0 Ran:2
Pre1998 - 1st:6 2nd:2 3rd:6 Ran:70
Win Prizemoney £18,031 *Total Prizemoney* £22,525

Wins									
	* 1997	*Jan*	*Southw*	*(STD)*	*H*	*6f*	*43*	*45+*	
	* 1996	*Jly*	*Southw*	*(STD)*	*H*	*6f*	*43*	*44*	
	1994	Aug	Newmar	(G-F)	H	6f	55	63	<
	1994	*Jly*	*Southw*	*(FRM)*	*H*	*6f*	*62*	*60*	
	1994	*Jly*	*Southw*	*(STD)*	*H*	*6f*	*50*	*53*	
	1994	Apr	Nottin	(G-S)	S	6.1f		50	

1998 AW 0-2: (8f 2) (Fibr 2)
Very moderate mare, effective 6f, - acts on Fibr, has worn blinkers. AW high 37.
**Miss J F Craze [2-45] Miss J F Craze (from J Hetherton [4-25] Aug 1995).*

LADY SO BOLD BHB 46f44a **RR 41f 44a** 3502[6]

3 ch f Bold Arrangement 8.7f **(57)** - Lady Blues Singer (Chief Singer) 8.9f **(66)**
Form - 0056
Record 1998 - 1st:0 2nd:0 3rd:0 Ran:4
Pre1998 - 1st:0 2nd:0 3rd:0 Ran:3
1998 Turf 0-3: (7f 2, 8f) (g-f, frm 2) 1998 AW 0-1: (8f) (Equi)
Leggy, moderate filly. Turf high 41. **Mrs L Stubbs [0-7] A P Griffin.*

LADY YAVANNA BHB 42f **RR 51f** 4885[8]
3 ch f Lycius (USA) 8.8f **(71)** - Isotonic (Absalom) 7.2f **(58)**
Form - 86668216088
Record 1998 - 1st:1 2nd:1 3rd:0 Ran:11
Pre1998 - 1st:0 2nd:0 3rd:0 Ran:5
Win Prizemoney £2,687 *Total Prizemoney* £3,695
Wins * **1998** Aug Bright (FRM) 8f 50 <
1998 Turf 1-9: (6f, 7f 6, 8f 1-1, 10f) (g-s, gd 3, g-f, frm 1-4) 1998 AW 0-2: (7f, 9f) (Fibr 2)
Workmanlike, fair filly, has worn blinkers, likes left handed tracks, likes tight tracks. Turf high 57. AW high 47 (began Jly). Inconsistent. She took her time in getting off the mark, but achieved it with a narrow victory in a very moderate Brighton claiming event in August.
**K McAuliffe [1-13] Mrs J Kersey (from P F I Cole [0-3] Jun 1998).*

LA-FAAH (IRE) BHB 106f **RR 107f** 4849[6]
3 ch c Lahib (USA) 8f **(69)** - Rawaabe (USA) (Nureyev (USA)) 8.7f **(78)**
Form - 245046
Record 1998 - 1st:0 2nd:1 3rd:0 Ran:6
Pre1998 - 1st:3 2nd:0 3rd:0 Ran:4
Win Prizemoney £33,973 *Total Prizemoney* £55,371
Wins * 1997 Oct Newbur (GD) G3 7.3f 108+ <
* 1997 Oct Ascot (HVY) 7f 87+
* 1997 Jly Ascot (SFT) 6f 80t
1998 Turf 0-6: (7f 5, 8f) (sft, gd 3, g-f 2)
Leggy, Pattern-class colt, effective 7f, acts on sft to g-f. Turf high 109. He regressed after running well in top company during the spring. He won over seven furlongs on heavy ground as a juvenile, so it might be worth giving him another try over a mile.
**B W Hills [3-10] Hamdan Al Maktoum.*

LAFFAH (USA) BHB 54f **RR 59f** 4939[8]
3 b g Silver Hawk (USA) 11.2f **(85)** - Sakiyah (USA) (Secretariat (USA)) 9f **(79)**
Form - 006448
Record 1998 - 1st:0 2nd:0 3rd:0 Ran:6
Pre1998 - 1st:0 2nd:0 3rd:0 Ran:2
1998 Turf 0-6: (10f 4, 12f 2) (g-s, gd 3, g-f, frm)
Well made, fair gelding, effective 10f, acts on gd, has worn blinkers, likes tight tracks. Turf high 59 - 4th of 9 getting 2lb from Hunt Hill (15 Jun Brighton 10f gd RF 1990).
**M C Pipe [0-1] Richard Green (Fine Paintings) (from J H M Gosden [0-7] Jun 1998).*

LA FIJA (USA) BHB 65f **RR 53f** 2189[6]
3 b f Dixieland Band (USA) 10.1f **(80)** -Turkstand (USA) (Turkoman (USA))
Form - 546
Record 1998 - 1st:0 2nd:0 3rd:0 Ran:3
Win Prizemoney £0 *Total Prizemoney* £230
1998 Turf 0-3: (7f 2, 8f) (gd 2, g-f)
Neat, currently fair filly. Turf high 53.
**H Akbary [0-3] Count Federico Zichy-Thyssen.*

LAFITE BHB 76f **RR 79f** 4752[3]
2 b f Robellino (USA) 9.5f **(68)** - Gorgeous Dancer (IRE) (Nordico (USA)) 6.5f **(62)**
Form - 043
Record 1998 - 1st:0 2nd:0 3rd:1 Ran:3
Win Prizemoney £0 *Total Prizemoney* £714
1998 Turf 0-3: (7f 3) (sft, g-f, frm)
Currently above-average filly. Turf high 79 (began Spt).
**J W Hills [0-3] Uplands Bloodstock.*

L'AGNEAU NOIR BHB 64f **RR 70f** 4882[7]
2 br f Rock City 8.8f **(62)** - Shernborne (Kalaglow) 9.8f **(67)**
Form - 207
Record 1998 - 1st:0 2nd:1 3rd:0 Ran:3
Win Prizemoney £0 *Total Prizemoney* £852
1998 Turf 0-3: (5f 2, 6f) (g-s, gd, frm)
Currently above-average filly. Turf high 66 (1st run) (began Spt) - 2nd of 14 getting 3lb from Brockton Saga (7 Spt Bath 5f frm RF 4122). **W R Muir [0-3] S Lamb.*

LAGO DI VARANO BHB 86f **RR 90f** 4975[6]
6 b g Clantime 6.6f **(57)** - On the Record (Record Token) 6.3f **(53)**
Form - 3684210462202003806
Record 1998 - 1st:1 2nd:4 3rd:2 Ran:19
Pre1998 - 1st:6 2nd:7 3rd:3 Ran:52
Win Prizemoney £31,623 *Total Prizemoney* £81,490
Wins * **1998** Jun Ripon (SFT) H 5f 80 84
* 1997 Jly Newcas (GD) H 5f 79 80
* 1996 Jun Doncas (G-F) H 5f 83 84
1996 Apr Ripon (G-F) C 5f 73
1994 Spt Ayr (G-S) L 5f 98
1994 Spt Chepst (G-S) 5.1f 93
1994 Apr Newcas (GD) 5f 71
1998 Turf 1-19: (5f 1-10, 6f 9) (sft 2, g-s 1-4, gd 7, g-f 4, frm 2)
Useful gelding, effective 5 to 6f, best at 6f, acts on sft to frm, mostly wears blinkers (effectively), and does well at Newcastle and Ripon. Turf high 90 - 3rd of 29 to Always Alight (19 Spt Ayr 6f sft RF 4367) - also 1st of 8 giving 15lb to Pleasure Time (18 Jun Ripon RF 2091). A useful sprint handicapper on his day, he had a very busy 1998, running nineteen times before the end of the turf season, but managing only a solitary victory at Ripon. He was always running his heart out however, and went very close to winning on a couple of other occasions. He has run well over six, but his winning has been over five.
**R M Whitaker [3-51] The PBT Group (from J Berry [4-20] Apr 1996).*

LAGUNA BAY (IRE) BHB 40f35a **RR 49f 35a** 2974[7]
4 b f Arcane (USA) 11.6f **(66)** - Meg Daughter (IRE) (Doulab (USA)) 9.8f **(65)**
Form - 007
Record 1998 - 1st:0 2nd:0 3rd:0 Ran:3
Pre1998 - 1st:1 2nd:2 3rd:0 Ran:13
Win Prizemoney £2,623 *Total Prizemoney* £5,157
Wins 1997 Aug Yarmou (G-F) C 10.1f 54 <
1998 Turf 0-2: (14f, 17f) (g-s, gd) 1998 AW 0-1: (12f) (Equi)
Scopey, moderate filly, effective 9 to 11f, best at 11f, acts on g-s to frm, best on frm, favours tight tracks. Turf high 21. Becoming disappointing.
**G M McCourt [1-8] Town and Country Tyre Services Ltd (from A P Jarvis [1-13] Oct 1997).*

LAHAB NASHWAN BHB 37f **RR 15f** 4451[12]
4 ch g Nashwan (USA) 10.3f **(79)** - Shadha (USA) (Devil's Bag (USA)) 12.4f **(78)**
Form - 0000
Record 1998 - 1st:0 2nd:0 3rd:0 Ran:4
Pre1998 - 1st:0 2nd:0 3rd:0 Ran:3
1998 Turf 0-4: (11f, 12f 3) (g-f, frm 3)
Lengthy, poor gelding, has worn blinkers. Turf high 14.
**R Curtis [0-8] Mrs R A Smith (from M R Channon [0-3] May 1997).*

LAILA MANJA (IRE) **RR 52f** 2442[7]
2 b f Diesis 9f **(80)** - London Pride (USA) (Lear Fan (USA)) 8.5f **(73)**
Form - 7
Record 1998 - 1st:0 2nd:0 3rd:0 Ran:1
1998 Turf 0-1: (7f) (gd)
Currently fair filly. **P F I Cole [0-1] H R H Sultan Ahmad Shah.*

LA ISLA BONITA BHB 64f **RR 68f** 4822[23]
3 ch f Lion Cavern (USA) 7.5f **(74)** - La Dama Bonita (USA) (El Gran Senor (USA)) 9.6f **(76)**
Form - 2432200
Record 1998 - 1st:0 2nd:3 3rd:1 Ran:7
Win Prizemoney £0 *Total Prizemoney* £4,153
1998 Turf 0-7: (8f 7) (gd, g-f, frm 5)
Leggy, average filly, effective 8f, acts on g-f to frm, best on frm. Turf high 68 - 2nd of 5 to Krista (22 Aug Sandown 8f g-f RF 3824).
**J W Hills [0-7] Christopher Wright.*

LAJADHAL (FR) BHB 14f15a **RR 15a** 2325[8]
9 gr g Bellypha 11.9f **(66)** -Rose d'Amour (USA) (Lines of Power (USA))
Form - 088
Record 1998 - 1st:0 2nd:0 3rd:0 Ran:3
Pre1998 - 1st:0 2nd:0 3rd:0 Ran:27
Win Prizemoney £0 *Total Prizemoney* £174
1998 Turf 0-2: (17f 2) (gd, frm) 1998 AW 0-1: (14f) (Fibr)
Very poor gelding, has worn blinkers. Becoming disappointing.
**P D Purdy [0-3] P D Purdy (from K Bishop [0-12] Aug 1995).*

LAKE ARIA BHB 16f26a **RR 24df 26a** 5060[14]
5 b m Rambo Dancer (CAN) 8.4f **(59)** - Hinge (Import) 6.6f **(68)**
Form - 7020060000
Record 1998 - 1st:0 2nd:1 3rd:0 Ran:9
Pre1998 - 1st:0 2nd:0 3rd:0 Ran:5
Win Prizemoney £0 *Total Prizemoney* £585
1998 Turf 0-5: (7f, 8f 2, 12f, 16f) (sft, gd, g-f, frm 2) 1998 AW 0-4: (7f, 11f, 12f 2) (Fibr 4)
Very moderate filly. Turf high 24. AW high 31. Inconsistent.
**J L Eyre [0-3] Mrs M P Neatby (from G Woodward [0-4] Jun 1998).*

LAKE CANNON RR 2769[7]
3 b g Alnasr Alwasheek 9.4f **(62)** - Bay Runner (Bay Express) 7.1f **(60)**
Form - 07
Record 1998 - 1st:0 2nd:0 3rd:0 Ran:2
1998 Turf 0-2: (9f, 10f) (g-f 2)
Workmanlike, currently very poor gelding - 7th of 7 giving 5lb to Peridot (13 Jly Windsor 10f g-f RF 2769).
**J J Bridger [0-2] Mrs Julie Lankshear.*

LAKE DOMINION BHB 30f34a **RR 33f 34a** 4384[10]
9 b g Primo Dominie 7.2f **(67)** - Piney Lake (Sassafras (FR)) 9.6f **(69)**
Form - 52380
Record 1998 - 1st:0 2nd:1 3rd:1 Ran:5
Pre1998 - 1st:1 2nd:0 3rd:3 Ran:19
Win Prizemoney £1,984 *Total Prizemoney* £4,512
Wins * 1997 *Jly Wolver (STD) H 16.2f 37 36 <*
1998 Turf 0-2: (14f, 17f) (gd 2) 1998 AW 0-3: (15f, 16f 2) (Equi, Fibr 2)
Moderate gelding, effective 16f, - acts on Fibr, has worn blinkers. Turf high 33. AW high 41 (1st run) (began Jly) - 3rd of 12 giving 5lb to Makati (24 Jly Wolverhampton 16f Fibr RF 3099).
**K C Comerford [1-9] Mrs Betty Bate and Mark Campbell (from J White [1-3] Jun 1994).*

LAKELAND PRIDE (IRE) BHB 48f **RR 45f** 2228[16]
3 gr g Pips Pride 6.7f **(70)** - Divine Apsara (Godswalk (USA)) 7.3f **(58)**
Form - 07580508060
Record 1998 - 1st:0 2nd:0 3rd:0 Ran:11
Pre1998 - 1st:0 2nd:0 3rd:3 Ran:9
Win Prizemoney £0 *Total Prizemoney* £1,993
1998 Turf 0-10: (5f 2, 6f 4, 7f, 8f 3) (gd 7, g-f 3) 1998 AW 0-1: (6f) (Fibr)
Scopey, moderate gelding, effective 6 to 7f, best at 6f, acts on gd to hrd, best on gd, has worn blinkers. Turf high 59. Inconsistent.
**D Nicholls [0-11] D Maloney (from P D Evans [0-9] Spt 1997).*

LAKE MEHRA RR 2575[12]
2 b c Superlative 8.8f **(57)** - Westering **(29f 38a)** (Auction Ring (USA)) 8.6f **(65)**
Form - 0
Record 1998 - 1st:0 2nd:0 3rd:0 Ran:1
1998 Turf 0-1: (5f) (g-f)
Currently very poor colt. **M H Tompkins [0-1] P J M M Racing.*

LAKE SUNBEAM RR 89f 4823[3]
2 b c Nashwan (USA) 10.3f **(79)** - Moon Drop (Dominion) 8.5f **(63)**
Form - 3
Record 1998 - 1st:0 2nd:0 3rd:1 Ran:1
Win Prizemoney £0 *Total Prizemoney* £1,098
1998 Turf 0-1: (8f) (frm)
Currently useful colt. (1st run) - 3rd of 23 to Mutafaweq (15 Oct Newmarket 8f frm RF 4823). This half-brother to four winners ran a cracker on his debut. **R Hannon [0-1] Mohamed Suhail.*

LAKE TAAL BHB 55f52a **RR 61f 52a** 4407[11]
3 ch f Prince Sabo 6.6f **(64)** - Calachuchi (Martinmas) 7.6f **(59)**
Form - 0300
Record 1998 - 1st:0 2nd:0 3rd:1 Ran:4
Pre1998 - 1st:0 2nd:0 3rd:0 Ran:2
Win Prizemoney £0 *Total Prizemoney* £604
1998 Turf 0-3: (6f, 8f 2) (gd, g-f 2) 1998 AW 0-1: (8f) (Fibr)
Leggy, average filly, effective 8f, acts on g-f. Turf high 59 - 3rd of 11 getting 18lb from Far Removed (29 Aug Redcar 8f g-f RF 3965).
**Miss J A Camacho [0-4] M Gleason (from M J Camacho [0-2] Oct 1997).*

LAKE WOBEGONE (IRE) BHB 25f **RR 10f** 2727[8]
3 ch g Inchinor 8.9f **(64)** - Westerlake (Blakeney) 10.5f **(64)**
Form - 0008
Record 1998 - 1st:0 2nd:0 3rd:0 Ran:4
Pre1998 - 1st:0 2nd:0 3rd:0 Ran:2
1998 Turf 0-3: (8f 2, 12f) (frm 2, hrd) 1998 AW 0-1: (12f) (Fibr)
Leggy, poor gelding, often wears blinkers. Turf high 10.
**John Berry [0-6] John Berry.*

LALINDI (IRE) BHB 57f70a **RR 55f 70a** 3787[7]
7 b m Cadeaux Genereux 7.9f **(76)** - Soemba (General Assembly (USA)) 10f **(68)**
Form - 055R057
Record 1998 - 1st:0 2nd:0 3rd:0 Ran:7
Pre1998 - 1st:7 2nd:6 3rd:3 Ran:38
Win Prizemoney £26,179 *Total Prizemoney* £39,796

Wins									
	1997	Jly	Beverl	(HVY)	H	12f	68	74?	
	1996	Jly	Haydoc	(G-S)	H	11.9f	72	72	
	1996	Jun	Lingfi	(FRM)	H	11.5f	66	73	
	1995	Jun	Warwic	(G-F)	H	16.1f	70	74	
	1995	Apr	Warwic	(G-S)	H	14.9f	64	77	<
	1994	*Spt*	*Southw*	*(STD)*	*H*	*12f*	*67*	*73+*	
	1994	*Spt*	*Wolver*	*(STD)*	*H*	*9.4f*	*62*	*65+*	

1998 Turf 0-7: (9f, 11f, 12f 4, 13f) (gd, g-f, frm 4, hrd)
Above-average mare, effective 12f, acts on sft, has worn blinkers. Turf high 55. Inconsistent.
**R Champion [0-8] Christopher Ranson (from A C Stewart [1-4] Jly 1997).*

LA LYONESSE BHB 56f51a **RR 59f 51a** 4996[4]
3 b f Lion Cavern (USA) 7.5f **(74)** - Princess Sioux (Commanche Run) 8.5f **(58)**
Form - 7563084
Record 1998 - 1st:0 2nd:0 3rd:1 Ran:7
Pre1998 - 1st:0 2nd:0 3rd:0 Ran:3
Win Prizemoney £0 *Total Prizemoney* £576
1998 Turf 0-5: (10f 3, 11f 2) (g-f, frm 4) 1998 AW 0-2: (10f, 15f) (Equi, Fibr)
Leggy, fair filly, effective 10 to 11f, best at 10f, acts on g-f to frm - acts on Equi, prefers tight tracks. Turf high 59 - 3rd of 10 getting 13lb from Include Me Out (8 Aug Redcar 10f frm RF 3478). AW high 50 (began Spt) - 4th of 14 getting 15lb from Muyassir (26 Oct Lingfield 10f Equi RF 4996).
**J W Hills [0-10] Racegoers Club Owners Group (1997).*

LAMANKA LASS (USA) BHB 72f **RR 77f** 4925[7]
3 ch f Woodman (USA) 9.7f **(77)** - Pattimech (USA) (Nureyev (USA)) 8.7f **(78)**
Form - 5417
Record 1998 - 1st:1 2nd:0 3rd:0 Ran:4
Win Prizemoney £4,175 *Total Prizemoney* £4,472
Wins * **1998** Oct Nottin (SFT) 8.2f 77 <
1998 Turf 1-4: (7f, 8f 1-3) (sft, g-s 1-3)
Neat, above-average filly. Turf high 77 - 1st of 17 getting 5lb from Brilliant Corners (6 Oct Nottingham RF 4666).
**H R A Cecil [1-4] D Buchanan.*

LAMARITA BHB 90f **RR 99f** 4844[12]
4 b f Emarati (USA) 6.6f **(63)** - Bentinck Hotel (Red God) 8.5f **(65)**
Form - 335000023040
Record 1998 - 1st:0 2nd:1 3rd:3 Ran:12
Pre1998 - 1st:2 2nd:2 3rd:2 Ran:10
Win Prizemoney £6,988 *Total Prizemoney* £18,434
Wins * 1997 Jun Nottin (G-F) H 5.1f 77 77+ <
* 1997 Apr Thirsk (G-F) 5f 76
1998 Turf 0-12: (5f 8, 6f 4) (g-s, gd 8, g-f 3)
Strong, very useful filly, has worn blinkers. Turf high 99. She looked a little unlucky on more than one occasion last term but has also shown a distinct tendency to hang left. If the steering can be sorted out then there is a nice sprint handicap to be won with her. **J M P Eustace [2-22] Park Lane Racing / Mrs D A La Trobe.*

LAMBRINI LAD (IRE) BHB 53f **RR 56f** 3408[3]
3 b g Shalford (IRE) 7.8f **(63)** - Swift Reply (He Loves Me) 7.9f **(55)**
Form - 88603
Record 1998 - 1st:0 2nd:0 3rd:1 Ran:5
Pre1998 - 1st:0 2nd:0 3rd:0 Ran:1
Win Prizemoney £0 *Total Prizemoney* £310
1998 Turf 0-5: (6f, 7f 3, 8f) (gd 2, g-f 3)
Scopey, fair gelding, has worn blinkers. Turf high 56.

**A Bailey [0-6] Halewood International Ltd.*

LAMBSON KATOOSHA RR 9f 4394[14]
3 b f Weldnaas(USA) 8.4f **(55)** -Lamsonetti **(9f)**(Never so Bold) 6.3f **(66)**
Form - 80
Record 1998 - 1st:0 2nd:0 3rd:0 Ran:2
1998 Turf 0-2: (8f, 12f) (g-f, frm)
Lengthy, currently very poor filly. Turf high 9 (began Spt).
**J Pearce [0-2] Ian Hall.*

LA MENORQUINA (USA) BHB 32f47a **RR 34?f 47a** 200[3]
8 b m Woodman (USA) 9.7f **(77)** - Hail The Lady (USA) (Hail the Pirates (USA)) 11f **(78)**
Form - 253
Record 1998 - 1st:0 2nd:0 3rd:1 Ran:2
Pre1998 - 1st:3 2nd:7 3rd:3 Ran:41
Win Prizemoney £7,698 *Total Prizemoney* £14,674
Wins * 1997 *Apr Wolver (STD) H 16.2f 44 51* <
* 1995 *May Southw (STD) H 16f 43 50*
* 1995 *Feb Southw (STD) H 16f 33 38*
1998 AW 0-2: (15f, 16f) (Fibr 2)
Moderate mare, effective 14 to 16f, best at 16f, - acts on Fibr, has worn blinkers, favours left handed tracks, and excels at Wolverhampton. AW high 49 (1st run) - 5th of 10 getting 12lb from Petoskin (14 Jan Wolverhampton 15f Fibr RF 0087). Consistent.
**D Marks [5-49] Joe Arden (from L M Cumani [0-10] Nov 1993).*

LAMENT BHB 62a **RR 65f** 4863[10]
2 b f Phountzi (USA) 9.6f **(60)** - Devils Dirge (Song) 7.2f **(61)**
Form - 8532215680
Record 1998 - 1st:1 2nd:2 3rd:1 Ran:10
Win Prizemoney £2,070 *Total Prizemoney* £3,441
Wins * **1998** Aug Lingfi (GD) C 6f 65 <
1998 Turf 1-9: (5f, 6f 1-5, 7f 3) (g-s, gd 2, g-f 1-4, frm 2) 1998 AW 0-1: (6f) (Fibr)
Average filly, effective 6f, acts on gd to frm. Turf high 65 - 1st of 13 getting 4lb from Magic Memories (1 Aug Lingfield RF 3268). Very consistent in her early races, she got off the mark in a Lingfield claimer in August.
**Mrs L Stubbs [1-6] A P Griffin (from J E Banks [0-4] Jun 1998).*

LA MODISTE BHB 77f70a **RR 82f 70a** 4933[5]
5 b m Most Welcome 8.6f **(66)** - Dismiss (Daring March) 7.1f **(61)**
Form - 70045102037075
Record 1998 - 1st:1 2nd:1 3rd:1 Ran:14
Pre1998 - 1st:6 2nd:3 3rd:3 Ran:27
Win Prizemoney £35,983 *Total Prizemoney* £51,957
Wins * **1998** Jun Doncas (GD) H 8f 76 82 <
* 1997 Spt Salisb (G-S) H 7f 70 80
* 1997 *Jly Lingfi (STD) H 10f 62 63*
* 1997 May Sandow (G-F) C 8.1f 66
* 1997 Apr Epsom (GD) 8.5f 66
1995 Spt Bath (HRD) 8f 77
1995 Aug Bright (FRM) 6f 66+
1998 Turf 1-13: (7f 4, 8f 1-8, 9f) (g-s 2, gd 5, g-f 1-4, frm 2) 1998 AW 0-1: (8f) (Equi)
Decent filly, effective 7 to 9f, best at 8f, acts on gd to frm, likes left handed tracks, likes tight tracks, excels at Epsom. Turf high 82 - 1st of 21 giving 16lb to Bowcliffe (28 Jun Doncaster RF 2359). Ran creditably in the Lincoln on her reappearance, but then lost her form as did many in the stable, before bouncing back with a fine victory at Doncaster in June. Generally ran well afterwards, meeting trouble in running more than once.
**Miss Gay Kelleway [5-25] The Winning Line (from S Dow [2-16] Feb 1997).*

LAMORNA BHB 46f45a **RR 47f 45a** 4995[10]
4 ch f Shavian 7.7f **(67)** - Malibasta (Auction Ring (USA)) 8.6f **(65)**
Form - 60016000
Record 1998 - 1st:1 2nd:0 3rd:0 Ran:8
Pre1998 - 1st:3 2nd:2 3rd:3 Ran:22
Win Prizemoney £20,554 *Total Prizemoney* £23,729
Wins * **1998** Aug Folkes (G-F) H 7f 43 47
1997 Spt Catter (G-F) H 7f 48 53
1996 Aug York (GD) S 6f 77 <
1996 Jun Warwic (FRM) 6f 64+
1998 Turf 1-7: (7f 1-4, 8f 3) (sft, gd, g-f 2, frm 1-3) 1998 AW 0-1: (7f) (Equi)
Scopey, moderate filly, effective 7f, acts on gd to frm, likes tight tracks. Turf high 47 - 1st of 13 getting 7lb from Matoaka (6 Aug Folkestone RF 3402). Inconsistent.
**D W P Arbuthnot [1-8] W H Ponsonby (from M R Channon [3-22] Oct 1997).*

LAMOURA BHB 20f **RR 40df** 3324[10]
3 ch f Executive Man 8.9f **(52)** - Armalou (Ardoon) 7.3f **(53)**
Form - 04000
Record 1998 - 1st:0 2nd:0 3rd:0 Ran:5
Pre1998 - 1st:0 2nd:0 3rd:0 Ran:4
1998 Turf 0-5: (5f, 6f 3, 8f) (g-s, g-f 2, frm 2)
Light-framed, moderate filly. Turf high 40.
**R Brotherton [0-9] Baskerville Racing Club.*

LAMZENA (IRE) RR 65+f 5064[3]
2 b f Fairy King (USA) 7.7f **(75)** - Ezana (Ela-Mana-Mou) 10.1f **(70)**
Form - 3
Record 1998 - 1st:0 2nd:0 3rd:1 Ran:1
Win Prizemoney £0 *Total Prizemoney* £520
1998 Turf 0-1: (6f) (g-f)
Currently average filly. **G Wragg [0-1] R N Bracher.*

LANCASHIRE LEGEND BHB 35f41a **RR 44f 41a** 2323[7]
5 gr g Belfort (FR) 6.7f **(53)** - Peters Pet Girl (Norwick (USA)) 7.2f **(56)**
Form - 57843452365007
Record 1998 - 1st:0 2nd:1 3rd:2 Ran:11
Pre1998 - 1st:1 2nd:3 3rd:4 Ran:31
Win Prizemoney £3,206 *Total Prizemoney* £8,988
Wins 1996 *Nov Lingfi (STD) 7f 62* <
1998 AW 0-11: (6f 3, 7f 6, 8f 2) (Equi 5, Fibr 6)
Moderate gelding, effective 7f, - acts on Equi, has worn blinkers, favours left handed tracks. AW high 55. He has been on a long losing run since winning on the Lingfield Equitrack in November 1996, and although he has run well on a few occasions, he is not one to trust nowadays.
**John Harris [0-6] David Pettifor (from S Dow [1-36] Feb 1998).*

LANCER (USA) BHB 72f58a **RR 71f 58a** 4704[1]
6 ch g Diesis 9f **(80)** - Last Bird (USA) (Sea Bird II) 9f **(71)**
Form - 2400225136125647221
Record 1998 - 1st:3 2nd:6 3rd:1 Ran:19
Pre1998 - 1st:1 2nd:0 3rd:1 Ran:8
Win Prizemoney £15,856 *Total Prizemoney* £23,503
Wins * **1998** Oct York (GD) H 11.9f 66 71 <
* **1998** Jun Folkes (G-F) H 12f 59 63
* **1998** May Leices (GD) H 11.8f 53 60
1994 Jly Beverl (G-F) 7.5f 64+
1998 Turf 3-16: (10f, 12f 3-13, 13f, 14f) (sft, g-s, gd 3, g-f 2-5, frm 1-5, hrd) 1998 AW 0-3: (14f, 15f, 16f) (Fibr 3)
Above-average gelding, effective 10 to 12f, best at 12f, acts on g-f to frm, best on frm, has worn blinkers (very effectively), prefers right handed tracks, excels at Folkestone. Turf high 71 - 1st of 22 giving 16lb to Broughtons Lure (8 Oct York RF 4704) - also 1st of 18 giving 19lb to Coh Sho No (26 Jun Folkestone RF 2298). AW high 31. Consistent.
**J Pearce [3-18] The Fijon Partnership (from R T Juckes [1-16] Feb 1998).*

LANCE'S PET BHB 42f **RR 37f** 1692[10]
4 b f Warning 8.1f **(77)** - Snub (Steel Heart) 8.3f **(58)**
Form - 600
Record 1998 - 1st:0 2nd:0 3rd:0 Ran:3
Pre1998 - 1st:0 2nd:0 3rd:0 Ran:1
1998 Turf 0-3: (10f 2, 12f) (sft, gd, frm)
Very moderate filly. Turf high 37. **D C O'Brien [0-4] Lance Lodge.*

LANDFORD LAD (IRE) BHB 69f **RR 70f** 5137[14]
2 ch c Mujtahid (USA) 7.4f **(69)** - Bold And Bright (FR) (Bold Lad (USA)) 10f **(65)**
Form - 460
Record 1998 - 1st:0 2nd:0 3rd:0 Ran:3
Win Prizemoney £0 *Total Prizemoney* £237
1998 Turf 0-3: (7f, 8f 2) (gd 3)
Currently above-average colt. Turf high 68 (began Aug).
**B Palling [0-3] J Hackett & D Brennan.*

LANDICAN LANE BHB 62f **RR 68f** 4569[1]
2 b g Handsome Sailor 6.6f **(53)** - Harifa (Local Suitor (USA)) 8.4f **(67)**
Form - 467001
Record 1998 - 1st:1 2nd:0 3rd:0 Ran:6
Win Prizemoney £1,955 *Total Prizemoney* £2,203
Wins * **1998** Spt Bright (GD) S 5.3f 68 <
1998 Turf 1-6: (5f 1-4, 6f 2) (gd 3, g-f 1-2, frm)
Average gelding, effective 5f, acts on g-f, has worn blinkers. Turf high 71 - also 1st of 11 giving 5lb to Ebony (30 Spt Brighton RF 4569). **R F JohnsonHoughton [1-6] Lord Leverhulme.*

LAND OF DREAMS BHB 112f **RR 114f** 4726a[10]
3 b f Cadeaux Genereux 7.9f **(76)** - Sahara Star (Green Desert (USA)) 8.6f **(78)**
Form - 401000
Record 1998 - 1st:1 2nd:0 3rd:0 Ran:6
Pre1998 - 1st:2 2nd:2 3rd:0 Ran:6
Win Prizemoney £57,783 *Total Prizemoney* £69,492
Wins * **1998** Jly Goodwo (GD) G3 5f 114 <
* 1997 Spt Doncas (G-F) G2 5f 98+
* 1997 Jun Pontef (G-F) 6f 88+
1998 Turf 1-6: (5f 1-5, 6f) (sft, gd 1-3, frm 2)
Strong, Group-class filly, effective 5f, acts on gd. Turf high 114 - 1st of 15 from Lady Alexander (28 Jly Goodwood RF 3164). Mark Johnston has always maintained that this filly is the fastest horse he has trained. She certainly looked smart when winning the King George Stakes at Glorious Goodwood, but she was well held in the Nunthorpe, in which she was poorly drawn, and in the Haydock Sprint Cup, where the sixth furlong stretched her stamina. She remains an interesting prospect for 1999 and the Godolphin team obviously agree, as they will be training her.
**M Johnston [3-12] Maktoum Al Maktoum.*

LANDRFUN BHB 40f52a **RR 44f 52a** 4867[6]
3 b c Lugana Beach 7f **(63)** - Basic Fun (Teenoso (USA)) 9.9f **(72)**
Form - 0076401360060086
Record 1998 - 1st:1 2nd:0 3rd:1 Ran:14
Pre1998 - 1st:0 2nd:0 3rd:0 Ran:2
Win Prizemoney £1,725 *Total Prizemoney* £2,405
Wins * **1998** *Apr Wolver (STD) C 8.5f 58* <
1998 Turf 0-8: (7f 3, 8f 5) (g-s, gd 3, frm 4) 1998 AW 1-6: (8f 1-3, 9f 3) (Fibr 1-6)
Workmanlike, fair colt, effective 8f, - acts on Fibr. Turf high 56. AW high 58 - 1st of 13 getting 14lb from Cheerful Groom (25 Apr Wolverhampton RF 0873).
**H J Collingridge [1-16] Group 1 Racing (1994) Ltd.*

LANGANS FIGURINE (IRE) BHB 63f **RR 64f** 3793[5]
2 b f Petardia 8.2f **(58)** - Cree's Figurine (Creetown) 6.9f **(50)**
Form - 3845
Record 1998 - 1st:0 2nd:0 3rd:1 Ran:4
Win Prizemoney £0 *Total Prizemoney* £468
1998 Turf 0-4: (5f 2, 6f 2) (gd 4)
Average filly, has worn blinkers. Turf high 62.
**M J Fetherston-Godley [0-4] R A Shepherd.*

LANIN BHB 47f **RR 50f** 2839[9]
3 b g Shirley Heights 12.1f **(76)** - Minute Waltz (Sadler's Wells (USA)) 10f **(76)**
Form - 06700
Record 1998 - 1st:0 2nd:0 3rd:0 Ran:5
1998 Turf 0-5: (7f 2, 8f, 10f, 11f) (g-s, g-f 3, frm)
Workmanlike, fair gelding. Turf high 50.
**D J S Cosgrove [0-5] Darren Croft.*

LA NUIT ROSE (FR) BHB 107f **RR 104f** 4272[3]
3 b f Rainbow Quest (USA) 11.2f **(81)** - Caerlina (IRE) (Caerleon (USA)) 8.6f **(71)**
Form - 33583
Record 1998 - 1st:0 2nd:0 3rd:3 Ran:5
Pre1998 - 1st:1 2nd:0 3rd:0 Ran:1
Win Prizemoney £3,223 *Total Prizemoney* £38,832
Wins * 1997 Oct Leices (SFT) 7f 89+ <
1998 Turf 0-5: (8f 4, 10f) (gd 4, frm)
Light-framed, very useful filly, effective 8f, acts on gd. Turf high 104 - 3rd of 13 to Tarascon (24 May Curragh 8f gd RF 1513a). Placed in the French and Irish 1000 Guineas on her first two starts, this filly looked a sure-fire big-race winner. Unfortunately she regressed as the season went on, putting too much effort into the first part of her races and failing to get home.
**S bin Suroor [1-6] Godolphin.*

LA PAOLA (IRE) BHB 72f **RR 72f** 4796[8]
2 ch f Common Grounds 8.1f **(66)** -Lotte Lenta(Gorytus (USA)) 7.8f **(60)**
Form - 00128
Record 1998 - 1st:1 2nd:1 3rd:0 Ran:5
Win Prizemoney £3,680 *Total Prizemoney* £4,470
Wins * **1998** Spt Sandow (G-S) 5f 72 <
1998 Turf 1-5: (5f 1-3, 6f 2) (sft, gd 1-1, g-f, frm 2)
Above-average filly. Turf high 72 (began Jly) - 2nd of 8 getting 15lb from Grey Princess (5 Oct Brighton 5f g-f RF 4651) - also 1st of 19 from Calcavella (16 Spt Sandown RF 4307).
**B J Meehan [1-5] G Battocchi.*

LA PETITE FLAMECHE BHB 67f **RR 66f** 4459[13]
3 b f Cigar 6.3f **(43)** - Little Missile (Ile de Bourbon (USA)) 10.1f **(67)**
Form - 0630
Record 1998 - 1st:0 2nd:0 3rd:1 Ran:4
Win Prizemoney £0 *Total Prizemoney* £575
1998 Turf 0-4: (6f 3, 7f) (gd 3, frm)
Light-framed, average filly. Turf high 66.
**R J O'Sullivan [0-4] M T Bevan.*

LA PETITE FUSEE BHB 63f62a **RR 72f 62a** 4653[11]
7 br m Cigar 6.3f **(43)** - Little Missile (Ile de Bourbon (USA)) 10.1f **(67)**
Form - 740274000
Record 1998 - 1st:0 2nd:1 3rd:0 Ran:6
Pre1998 - 1st:7 2nd:4 3rd:10 Ran:51
Win Prizemoney £24,196 *Total Prizemoney* £41,784
Wins * 1996 Aug Salisb (GD) H 6f 73 79 <
* 1996 Jly Chepst (G-F) 6.1f 74
* 1995 *Nov Wolver (STD) 7f 59+*
* 1995 *Nov Southw (STD) H 6f 60 72+*
* 1995 Jun Lingfi (GD) H 6f 64 66
* 1994 Spt Folkes (G-S) H 6f 55 55
* 1994 Jly Lingfi (GD) H 6f 47 48
1998 Turf 0-4: (6f 3, 8f) (g-s, g-f 2, frm) 1998 AW 0-2: (6f, 7f) (Fibr 2)
Above-average mare, has broken blood-vessels, effective 6 to 7f, best at 6f, acts on gd to frm, best on gd. Turf high 69 (began Jly). AW high 60. **R J O'Sullivan [7-57] P W Saunders.*

LAPIMI **RR** 299[9]
3 b f Lapierre - Miami Pride (Miami Springs) 9.9f **(59)**
Form - 0
Record 1998 - 1st:0 2nd:0 3rd:0 Ran:1
Pre1998 - 1st:0 2nd:0 3rd:0 Ran:1
1998 AW 0-1: (8f) (Fibr)
Light-framed, currently very poor filly.
**Mrs N Macauley [0-2] J Teasdale.*

L'APPASSIONATA (IRE) **RR** 4064[12]
2 ch f Shalford (IRE) 7.8f **(63)** - Gayla Orchestra (Lord Gayle (USA)) 8.8f **(62)**
Form - 0
Record 1998 - 1st:0 2nd:0 3rd:0 Ran:1
1998 Turf 0-1: (7f) (g-f)
Currently very poor filly. **M S Saunders [0-1] M S Saunders.*

LAPU-LAPU BHB 47f48a **RR 57f 48a** 4815[13]
5 b m Prince Sabo 6.6f **(64)** - Seleter (Hotfoot) 10.5f **(59)**
Form - 000
Record 1998 - 1st:0 2nd:0 3rd:0 Ran:2
Pre1998 - 1st:3 2nd:1 3rd:2 Ran:24
Win Prizemoney £8,353 *Total Prizemoney* £11,664
Wins 1997 Jly Hamilt (G-S) 8.3f 55
1996 Oct Newcas (G-F) H 10.1f 52 56 <
1996 Aug Pontef (G-F) H 8f 47 53
1998 Turf 0-2: (10f, 12f) (gd, g-f)
Fair filly, effective 8 to 10f, best at 10f, acts on gd to g-f, best on g-f. Turf high 22 (began Spt). Becoming disappointing.
**Miss J A Camacho [0-2] Dunstan French (from M J Camacho [3-24] Nov 1997).*

LARGESSE BHB 108f97a **RR 107f 97a** 5075[4]
4 b c Cadeaux Genereux 7.9f **(76)** - Vilanika (FR) (Top Ville) 11.7f **(68)**
Form - 6121641434
Record 1998 - 1st:3 2nd:1 3rd:1 Ran:9
Pre1998 - 1st:3 2nd:1 3rd:0 Ran:12
Win Prizemoney £35,818 *Total Prizemoney* £47,332
Wins * **1998** Spt Ayr (G-S) L 10.9f 107 <
* **1998** May York (GD) H 11.9f 94 98
* **1998** Mar Nottin (G-S) H 10f 82 87
* 1997 Spt Haydoc (GD) H 11.9f 73 77
* 1997 Spt Haydoc (G-S) H 10.5f 67 71
* 1996 Jly Pontef (G-F) 5f 84+
1998 Turf 3-9:(10f 1-1, 11f 1-2, 12f 1-5, 14f)(sft 1-2, g-s 1-2, gd 1-4, g-f)
Workmanlike, Pattern-class colt, effective 11 to 12f, best at 12f, acts on sft to gd, best on gd, has worn blinkers, prefers left handed tracks, likes tight tracks, likes Haydock. Turf high 107 - 1st of 6 from Salmon Ladder (19 Spt Ayr RF 4366) - also 1st of 13 giving 20lb to Crystal Falls (12 May York RF 1164). The star of John Berry's small stable, he is a very useful individual granted cut in the ground, as he showed when landing a Nottingham handicap on his reappearance and Ayr's Doonside Cup (listed) in September. Has a marked tendency to edge to his left, but is genuine and could go to the very top if tried over hurdles.
**John Berry [6-21] Mrs Rosemary Moszkowicz.*

LARIMAR BAY RR 65f 4967[4]
2 b c Puissance 7.1f **(60)** - Aryaf (CAN) (Vice Regent (CAN)) 8.7f **(74)**
Form - 04
Record 1998 - 1st:0 2nd:0 3rd:0 Ran:2
Win Prizemoney £0 *Total Prizemoney* £292
1998 Turf 0-2: (6f 2) (sft, g-f)
Currently average colt. Turf high 65 (began Oct).
**B J Meehan [0-2] B J Meehan.*

LARK'S RISE BHB 42f **RR 48?f** 3649[10]
4 b f Niniski (USA) 13.2f **(67)** - Line of Cards (High Line) 10.3f **(70)**
Form - 0
Record 1998 - 1st:0 2nd:0 3rd:0 Ran:1
Pre1998 - 1st:0 2nd:0 3rd:0 Ran:3
1998 Turf 0-1: (11f) (frm)
Light-framed, moderate filly.
**R J Price [0-1] E G Bevan (from H Candy [0-3] Oct 1997).*

LA ROCHELLE (IRE) BHB 78f **RR 81f** 3792[7]
3 b f Salse (USA) 10.9f **(71)** - Lagta (Kris) 9.5f **(73)**
Form - 517
Record 1998 - 1st:1 2nd:0 3rd:0 Ran:3
Pre1998 - 1st:0 2nd:0 3rd:0 Ran:1
Win Prizemoney £3,517 *Total Prizemoney* £3,517
Wins * **1998** Aug Pontef (G-F) 8f 81 <
1998 Turf 1-3: (8f 1-1, 10f 2) (sft, gd, frm 1-1)
Workmanlike, decent filly. Turf high 81 - 1st of 9 getting 5lb from Shogun (5 Aug Pontefract RF 3387).
**C E Brittain [1-4] Saeed Manana.*

LASER LIGHT LADY BHB 20a **RR 20a** 460[4]
6 b m Tragic Role (USA) 9.4f **(63)** - Raina Perera (Tyrnavos) 10.1f **(55)**
Form - 84
Record 1998 - 1st:0 2nd:0 3rd:0 Ran:2
Pre1998 - 1st:0 2nd:0 3rd:0 Ran:2
1998 AW 0-2: (9f, 16f) (Fibr 2)
Poor mare.
**M Waring [0-2] Dunstall Park Centre Ltd (from N P Littmoden [0-2] May 1996).*

LASHKARI GOLD (IRE) BHB 58f **RR 65f** 4671[11]
2 b g Lashkari 13.1f **(52)** -Filet Mignon (USA) (Topsider (USA)) 8.3f **(71)**
Form - 75082180
Record 1998 - 1st:1 2nd:1 3rd:0 Ran:8
Win Prizemoney £2,066 *Total Prizemoney* £2,630
Wins * **1998** Aug Catter (G-F) S 7f 65 <
1998 Turf 1-8: (5f 4, 7f 1-4) (gd, g-f 4, frm 1-3)
Average gelding, effective 7f, acts on g-f to frm. Turf high 65 - 2nd of 14 to Risky Way (22 Jly Catterick 7f g-f RF 3019) - also 1st of 13 from Rebel Tiger (14 Aug Catterick RF 3619). He was given a good ride when winning a Catterick seller in August, but was well held in better company otherwise.
**J Berry [1-8] John Milner & Stephen Milner.*

LA SOEUR D'ALBERT BHB 55f **RR 54f** 4326[7]
2 b f Puissance 7.1f **(60)** - Florentynna Bay (Aragon) 8.1f **(60)**
Form - 807
Record 1998 - 1st:0 2nd:0 3rd:0 Ran:3
1998 Turf 0-3: (5f 2, 6f) (g-s, gd, frm)
Currently fair filly. Turf high 54 (began Aug).
**J Berry [0-3] Chris & Antonia Deuters.*

LAST CHANCE BHB 41f44a **RR 46f 44a** 3479[23]
4 b g River Falls 8.2f **(56)** - Little Red Hut (Habitat) 9.4f **(70)**
Form - 5480
Record 1998 - 1st:0 2nd:0 3rd:0 Ran:4
Pre1998 - 1st:1 2nd:3 3rd:1 Ran:17
Win Prizemoney £2,973 *Total Prizemoney* £10,802
Wins 1996 Jun Bath (G-F) 5.1f 72 <
1998 Turf 0-4: (6f 2, 7f, 8f) (gd, frm 3)
Strong, moderate gelding, effective 7f, acts on frm, has worn blinkers. Turf high 46. Inconsistent.
**J S Wainwright [0-1] Darren Barratt (from D J S Cosgrove [0-12] Jly 1998).*

LAST CHRISTMAS BHB 85f **RR 89f** 3654[4]
3 b c Salse (USA) 10.9f **(71)** -State Ball (Dance In Time(CAN)) 8.9f **(59)**
Form - 2824
Record 1998 - 1st:0 2nd:2 3rd:0 Ran:4
Pre1998 - 1st:1 2nd:0 3rd:1 Ran:2
Win Prizemoney £3,582 *Total Prizemoney* £8,308
Wins * 1997 Spt Haydoc (GD) 7.1f 83 <
1998 Turf 0-4: (10f 2, 12f, 14f) (hvy, gd 2, g-f)
Leggy, useful colt, effective 7f, acts on g-f. Turf high 91. Decent effort in bottomless ground on his reappearance, but he did not progress from that in his three subsequent outings.
**B W Hills [1-6] A D Shead.*

LAST HAVEN (FR) BHB 84f **RR 87f** 5143[4]
2 b c Slip Anchor 12.7f **(75)** - Lady Norcliffe (USA) (Norcliffe (CAN)) 14f **(72)**
Form - 6814
Record 1998 - 1st:1 2nd:0 3rd:0 Ran:4
Win Prizemoney £3,779 *Total Prizemoney* £4,106
Wins * **1998** Oct Pontef (GD) 10f 87+ <
1998 Turf 1-4: (8f 3, 10f 1-1) (gd 1-2, g-f 2)
Useful colt. Turf high 87 (began Aug) - 1st of 8 from Castilian (5 Oct Pontefract RF 4657). **J G FitzGerald [1-4] Marquesa de Moratalla.*

LAST KNIGHT (IRE) BHB 55f53a **RR 54f 53a** 4887[16]
3 b g Distinctly North (USA) 7.4f **(63)** - Standing Ovation (Godswalk (USA)) 7.3f **(58)**
Form - 522446500
Record 1998 - 1st:0 2nd:2 3rd:0 Ran:9
Pre1998 - 1st:0 2nd:0 3rd:0 Ran:3
Win Prizemoney £0 *Total Prizemoney* £2,307
1998 Turf 0-7: (12f 5, 13f, 14f) (g-s 2, gd, g-f 2, frm 2) 1998 AW 0-2: (10f, 11f) (Equi, Fibr)
Fair gelding, effective 11 to 12f, acts on frm - acts on Fibr, likes tight tracks. Turf high 58. AW high 55 - 2nd of 13 getting 10lb from Nakhal (11 Mar Southwell 11f Fibr RF 0419). He does pull rather hard.
**D W P Arbuthnot [0-1] W H Ponsonby (from M R Channon [0-11] May 1998).*

LAST LAP BHB 44a **RR 50f** 4922[3]
3 b f Noble Patriarch 12.2f **(43)** - Warning Bell (Bustino) 10.4f **(64)**
Form - 248352771002043
Record 1998 - 1st:1 2nd:3 3rd:2 Ran:15
Pre1998 - 1st:0 2nd:0 3rd:1 Ran:5
Win Prizemoney £1,842 *Total Prizemoney* £5,010
Wins * **1998** Aug Catter (GD) S 15.8f 42 <
1998 Turf 1-13: (10f, 12f 3, 13f, 14f 3, 16f 1-4, 17f) (g-s 2, gd 1-3, g-f 3, frm 5) 1998 AW 0-2: (12f 2) (Fibr 2)
Leggy, fair filly, effective 12 to 14f, best at 14f, acts on gd to frm, often wears blinkers, prefers left handed tracks, likes tight tracks. Turf high 54 (1st run) - 2nd of 8 getting 10lb from Make Believe (1 Apr Catterick 12f gd RF 0530). AW high 34.
**T D Easterby [1-20] Mrs P E Needham.*

LAST LAUGH (IRE) BHB 60f **RR 63f** 4525[6]

6 b m Last Tycoon 9.4f **(73)** - Little Me (Connaught) 7.7f **(63)**

Form - 726

Record 1998 - 1st:0 2nd:1 3rd:0 Ran:3

Pre1998 - 1st:4 2nd:1 3rd:2 Ran:14

Win Prizemoney £12,330 *Total Prizemoney* £15,508

Wins 1997 Apr Bath (G-F) H 11.7f 56 62

1995 Aug Chepst (G-F) C 12.1f 63

1995 May Newbur (GD) C 12f 50

1994 Jly Salisb (G-F) 6f 66

1998 Turf 0-3: (14f 2, 17f) (gd 2, g-f)

Average mare. Turf high 63 (began Jly) - 2nd of 13 getting 7lb from Paradise Navy (20 Aug Salisbury 14f gd RF 3762). (DEAD)

**P J Hobbs [0-3] Charles Eden Ltd (from N M Babbage [1-1] Apr 1997).*

LASTMAN (USA) RR 65f 5008[4]

3 b br g Fabulous Dancer (USA) 10.6f **(81)** - Rivala (USA) (Riverman (USA)) 9.1f **(76)**

Form - 4

Record 1998 - 1st:0 2nd:0 3rd:0 Ran:1

Win Prizemoney £0 *Total Prizemoney* £252

1998 Turf 0-1: (12f) (sft)

Currently average gelding. **D Nicholson [0-1] Darren Mercer.*

LAST REPUTATION (IRE) BHB 73f78a **RR 73f 78a** 4854[7]

3 b f Zafonic (USA) 9f **(83)** - Reputation (Tower Walk) 10f **(62)**

Form - 455167

Record 1998 - 1st:1 2nd:0 3rd:0 Ran:6

Win Prizemoney £3,834 *Total Prizemoney* £4,173

Wins * **1998** Spt Catter (G-F) 7f 56 <

1998 Turf 1-6: (7f 1-5, 8f) (sft, gd 2, g-f, frm 1-2)

Scopey, above-average filly, effective 7 to 8f, best at 7f, acts on sft to frm. Turf high 73 - 5th of 9 getting 5lb from Cool Vibes (29 Aug Newmarket 8f frm RF 3954). **B W Hills [1-6] R E Sangster.*

LAST WARNING RR 46f 4336[11]

2 b c Warning 8.1f **(77)** - Dancing Crystal (Kris) 9.5f **(73)**

Form - 0

Record 1998 - 1st:0 2nd:0 3rd:0 Ran:1

1998 Turf 0-1: (8f) (frm)

Currently moderate colt. **E A L Dunlop [0-1] Mohammed Jaber.*

LAS VISTAS BHB 43f36a **RR 42f 36a** 4402[10]

4 b f Tina's Pet 7.4f **(56)** - Maravista (Swing Easy (USA)) 6.5f **(55)**

Form - 8603800

Record 1998 - 1st:0 2nd:0 3rd:1 Ran:6

Pre1998 - 1st:0 2nd:0 3rd:2 Ran:9

Win Prizemoney £0 *Total Prizemoney* £1,596

1998 Turf 0-6: (6f 4, 7f, 8f) (gd 2, frm 4)

Lengthy, moderate filly, effective 7f, acts on g-f. Turf high 50.

**H J Collingridge [0-15] R H Coombes.*

LA TACHE BHB 59f **RR 59f** 4613[13]

2 b f Namaqualand (USA) - Fabulous Deed (USA) (Shadeed (USA)) 8.2f **(70)**

Form - 577070

Record 1998 - 1st:0 2nd:0 3rd:0 Ran:6

1998 Turf 0-6: (7f 4, 8f 2) (sft, g-s, gd, g-f, frm 2)

Fair filly. Turf high 59 (began Jly). **G C Bravery [0-6] A L Burke.*

LATALOMNE (USA) BHB 92f **RR 96f** 2056[22]

4 ch g Zilzal (USA) 8.5f **(79)** - Sanctuary (Welsh Pageant) 10f **(65)**

Form - 40

Record 1998 - 1st:0 2nd:0 3rd:0 Ran:2

Pre1998 - 1st:1 2nd:2 3rd:0 Ran:4

Win Prizemoney £4,218 *Total Prizemoney* £9,122

Wins * 1997 Apr Nottin (G-F) 8.2f 88 <

1998 Turf 0-2: (7f, 8f) (gd, frm)

Rangy, very useful gelding, effective 7 to 8f, best at 7f, acts on gd to frm, best on frm. Turf high 95 (1st run) - 4th of 6 giving 1lb to Darnaway (16 May Newmarket 7f frm RF 1265).

**E A L Dunlop [1-6] Maktoum Al Maktoum.*

LA TAVERNETTA (IRE) BHB 62f65a **RR 60f 65a** 4671[3]

2 ch f Magical Wonder (USA) 7.2f **(60)** - Carolina Rua (USA) (L'Emigrant (USA)) 10.5f **(62)**

Form - 5142158043

Record 1998 - 1st:2 2nd:1 3rd:1 Ran:10

Win Prizemoney £3,596 *Total Prizemoney* £4,813

Wins * **1998** *Jun Wolver (STD) S 7f 70+* <

* **1998** May Bright (FRM) S 6f 60

1998 Turf 1-8: (5f, 6f 1-2, 7f 5) (gd 2, g-f 4, frm 1-2) 1998 AW 1-2: (7f 1-2) (Fibr 1-2)

Above-average filly, effective 6 to 7f, acts on frm - acts on Fibr, prefers left handed tracks, prefers tight tracks. Turf high 60. AW high 70 (1st run) - 1st of 9 from Miss Take (26 Jun Wolverhampton RF 2322). **B J Meehan [2-10] Mrs Sylvia Mead.*

LATCH LIFTER BHB 48f **RR 42f** 4639[10]

2 b c Prince Sabo 6.6f **(64)** - Thevetia (Mummy's Pet) 7.7f **(60)**

Form - 07700

Record 1998 - 1st:0 2nd:0 3rd:0 Ran:5

1998 Turf 0-4: (5f 3, 6f) (gd, g-f 2, frm) 1998 AW 0-1: (5f) (Fibr)

Moderate colt, has worn blinkers. Turf high 42.

**G Lewis [0-5] David Barker.*

LATEEN BHB 42f **RR 51f** 5038[7]

3 b f Midyan (USA) 9.9f **(64)** - Sail Loft (Shirley Heights) 10.3f **(74)**

Form - 80677

Record 1998 - 1st:0 2nd:0 3rd:0 Ran:5

1998 Turf 0-5: (10f 3, 12f, 14f) (g-s, gd, g-f, frm 2)

Leggy, fair filly. Turf high 51.

**Major D N Chappell [0-5] Major D N Chappell.*

LATE NIGHT LAD BHB 56f51a **RR 58f 51a** 4878[10]

2 b g Emarati (USA) 6.6f **(63)** - Beveled Edge **(36f 53a)** (Beveled (USA)) 9f **(59)**

Form - 23050

Record 1998 - 1st:0 2nd:1 3rd:1 Ran:5

Win Prizemoney £0 *Total Prizemoney* £921

1998 Turf 0-3: (5f 2, 8f) (gd 3) 1998 AW 0-2: (5f, 7f) (Fibr 2)

Fair gelding. Turf high 58 - 3rd of 9 giving 5lb to Lune Lass (25 Jun Carlisle 5f gd RF 2261). AW high 54 (began Oct).

**J J O'Neill [0-5] E A Brook.*

LATE NIGHT OUT BHB 99f **RR 94f** 4971[6]

3 b c Lahib (USA) 8f **(69)** - Chain Dance (Shareef Dancer (USA)) 9.9f **(73)**

Form - 53616

Record 1998 - 1st:1 2nd:0 3rd:1 Ran:4

Pre1998 - 1st:1 2nd:0 3rd:1 Ran:3

Win Prizemoney £8,781 *Total Prizemoney* £11,979

Wins * **1998** Oct Redcar (G-S) 7f 94 <

* 1997 Oct Nottin (GD) 6.1f 88+

1998 Turf 1-4: (6f, 7f 1-3) (sft 2, gd, g-f 1-1)

Workmanlike, useful colt, effective 6 to 7f, best at 6f, acts on hvy to g-f. Turf high 94 - 1st of 7 getting 2lb from Al Muallim (6 Oct Redcar RF 4675). Came back from five month's absence to score at Redcar, appreciating the cut in the ground, but heavy conditions have found him out on more than one occasion.

**W Jarvis [2-7] J M Greetham.*

LATIN BAY BHB 42f **RR 45f** 4574[9]

3 b c Superlative 8.8f **(57)** - Hugging (Beveled (USA)) 9f **(59)**

Form - 530001400

Record 1998 - 1st:1 2nd:0 3rd:1 Ran:9

Pre1998 - 1st:0 2nd:0 3rd:0 Ran:6

Win Prizemoney £2,733 *Total Prizemoney* £3,361

Wins * **1998** Aug Kempto (G-F) H 9f 42 45 <

1998 Turf 1-9: (8f 4, 9f 1-1, 10f, 11f 2, 12f) (gd 4, g-f 3, frm 1-2)

Light-framed, moderate colt, effective 9 to 11f, acts on gd to frm, likes tight tracks. Turf high 53 - 3rd of 9 getting 24lb from Winsome George (25 May Redcar 11f gd RF 1457) - also 1st of 14 getting 14lb from Imbackagain (19 Aug Kempton RF 3734). Inconsistent. Mainly out of form during the past couple of seasons, but he was given a most positive ride when landing an apprentice handicap at Kempton in August.

**P W Harris [1-15] Superlative Twelve.*

LATIN NEXUS (USA) BHB 63f **RR 68f** 2627[6]

3 b f Roman Diplomat (USA) - Miami Game (USA) (Crozier)

Form - 456

Record 1998 - 1st:0 2nd:0 3rd:0 Ran:3

Pre1998 - 1st:0 2nd:0 3rd:1 Ran:3

Win Prizemoney £0 *Total Prizemoney* £496
1998 Turf 0-3: (11f, 12f 2) (gd 2, g-f)
Light-framed, average filly, effective 6 to 11f, acts on gd to g-f. Turf high 68 (1st run) - 4th of 7 getting 5lb from Tory Boy (8 Jun Warwick 11f gd RF 1813). **P F I Cole [0-6] Frank Stella.*

LA TIZIANA BHB 78f **RR 77f** 4802[6]
3 b f Rudimentary (USA) 8.2f **(66)** - Tizona (Pharly (FR)) 9.8f **(68)**
Form - 3257126
Record 1998 - 1st:1 2nd:2 3rd:1 Ran:7
Pre1998 - 1st:0 2nd:0 3rd:1 Ran:2
Win Prizemoney £14,720 *Total Prizemoney* £19,868
Wins * **1998** Spt Newbur (GD) H 10f 72 77 <
1998 Turf 1-7: (8f, 10f 1-3, 11f 3) (sft, gd 2, g-f 1-3, frm)
Lengthy, above-average filly, effective 7 to 11f, best at 10f, acts on g-s to g-f, best on g-f, prefers left handed tracks. Turf high 77 - 1st of 15 getting 3lb from Mole Creek (17 Spt Newbury RF 4332). Consistent. Showed a commendable attitude when getting off the mark in a fillies' handicap at Newbury in September.
**W Jarvis [1-9] The Phantom House Partnership.*

L A TOUCH BHB 41f52a **RR 42f 52a** 4093[8]
5 b m Tina's Pet 7.4f **(56)** - Silvers Era (Balidar) 7.9f **(63)**
Form - 60030168
Record 1998 - 1st:1 2nd:0 3rd:1 Ran:8
Pre1998 - 1st:1 2nd:5 3rd:0 Ran:23
Win Prizemoney £5,804 *Total Prizemoney* £10,744
Wins * **1998** Aug Yarmou (FRM) H 6f 33 42
1995 Aug Leices (G-F) S 6f 61 <
1998 Turf 1-8: (5f 3, 6f 1-5) (sft, g-f 2, frm 1-5)
Moderate filly, effective 6f, acts on gd to frm. Turf high 42 - 1st of 12 getting 3lb from Make Ready (20 Aug Yarmouth RF 3765). She won a particularly poor fillies' handicap at Yarmouth in August, though she got the breaks in a rough race whilst several of her rivals did not.
**J J Quinn [1-16] C A Rosen (from C A Dwyer [1-11] Aug 1996).*

LATVIAN BHB 28f **RR 40f** 4838[11]
11 gr g Rousillon (USA) 10.4f **(69)**- Lorelene (FR)(Lorenzaccio) 10f **(64)**
Form - 552854580
Record 1998 - 1st:0 2nd:1 3rd:0 Ran:9
Pre1998 - 1st:11 2nd:12 3rd:12 Ran:63
Win Prizemoney £35,411 *Total Prizemoney* £59,072
Wins * 1997 May Mussel (G-F) C 12f 52
* 1996 Aug Carlis (FRM) C 12f 63
* 1996 May Newcas (GD) H 12.4f 62 67
* 1995 Aug Pontef (G-F) H 12f 68 75 <
* 1995 Jly Catter (G-F) C 12f 70+
1994 Jly Hamilt (FRM) H 13f 67 69
1994 Jun Mussel (FRM) H 11.1f 65 68
1998 Turf 0-9: (12f 5, 14f 2, 16f 2) (g-s, gd 5, g-f, frm 2)
Moderate gelding, effective 12f, acts on gd to frm, has worn blinkers, likes right handed tracks, favours tight tracks. Turf high 40. Not one to rely on but capable in the bottom grades on his day.
**R Allan [10-67] I Bell (from P Monteith [2-12] Spt 1994).*

LAUREL PRINCE BHB 51f **RR 58f** 4300[13]
2 b g Reprimand 8.2f **(63)** - Laurel Queen (IRE) (Viking (USA)) 6.7f **(65)**
Form - 6064650
Record 1998 - 1st:0 2nd:0 3rd:0 Ran:7
Win Prizemoney £0 *Total Prizemoney* £326
1998 Turf 0-7: (6f 2, 7f 5) (gd 2, g-f 2, frm 3)
Fair gelding. Turf high 58. **J Berry [0-7] Laurel (Leisure) Ltd.*

LAUREL SEEKER (USA) BHB 58f53a **RR 65?f 53a** 105[15]
4 b g Mining(USA) 7.8f **(78)** -L'On Vite (USA)(Secretariat (USA)) 9f **(79)**
Form - 10
Record 1998 - 1st:0 2nd:0 3rd:0 Ran:1
Pre1998 - 1st:1 2nd:0 3rd:1 Ran:6
Win Prizemoney £2,294 *Total Prizemoney* £2,816
Wins * 1997 *Dec Lingfi (STD) 12f 52* <
1998 AW 0-1: (12f) (Equi)
Scopey, average gelding, effective 11f, acts on frm, prefers left handed tracks. Gained his first win a modest amateur riders' event on the Lingfield Equitrack in December '97. Winning hurdler too.
**Mrs A J Perrett [1-8] G Harwood.*

LAUREN'S LAD BHB 51f57a **RR 53f 57a** 3605[18]
3 ch c Tachyon Park - Glory Isle (Hittite Glory) 8.7f **(50)**
Form - 5557280
Record 1998 - 1st:0 2nd:1 3rd:0 Ran:6
Pre1998 - 1st:1 2nd:0 3rd:0 Ran:7
Win Prizemoney £3,746 *Total Prizemoney* £4,542
Wins 1997 Oct Lingfi (FRM) H 7f 45 57+ <
1998 Turf 0-4: (8f 3, 10f) (gd, g-f, frm 2) 1998 AW 0-2: (8f 2) (Equi, Fibr)
Neat, average colt, often wears blinkers (effectively). Turf high 53. AW high 55.
**B J Llewellyn [0-1] David Lewis (from Lady Herries [0-2] Jly 1998).*

LAURENTIAN BHB 34f **RR 29f** 4885[14]
3 b f Shareef Dancer (USA) 10.1f **(67)** - Kiomi **(64f)** (Niniski (USA)) 10.6f **(65)**
Form - 08077850
Record 1998 - 1st:0 2nd:0 3rd:0 Ran:8
1998 Turf 0-7: (7f 4, 8f 2, 10f) (g-s, gd 3, frm 2, hrd) 1998 AW 0-1: (10f) (Equi)
Neat, little account filly. Turf high 44. **K R Burke [0-8] I Goldsmith.*

LAURENTIDE (USA) BHB 104f **RR 105f** 2057[2]
3 b c Pleasant Colony (USA) 12.4f **(88)** - Northern Sunset (USA) (Northfields (USA)) 9f **(72)**
Form - 212
Record 1998 - 1st:1 2nd:2 3rd:0 Ran:3
Win Prizemoney £4,476 *Total Prizemoney* £19,309
Wins * **1998** May Newmar (G-F) 14f 87 <
1998 Turf 1-3: (12f, 14f 1-1, 16f) (gd 2, g-f 1-1)
Workmanlike, currently Pattern-class colt. Turf high 105 - 2nd of 8 to Maridpour (17 Jun Ascot 16f gd RF 2057). A brother to St Jovite, he was Henry Cecil's third-string when short-headed in the Queen's Vase at Royal Ascot. That was a fine effort and it was disappointing that he was not seen afterwards. A scratchy mover, he will always be suited by easy ground.
**H R A Cecil [1-3] Mrs Virginia Kraft Payson.*

LAUTREC RR 71f 3152[3]
2 b c Shareef Dancer (USA) 10.1f **(67)** - Pride of Paris (Troy) 10.4f **(68)**
Form - 603
Record 1998 - 1st:0 2nd:0 3rd:1 Ran:3
Win Prizemoney £0 *Total Prizemoney* £397
1998 Turf 0-3: (7f 3) (gd, g-f 2)
Currently above-average colt. Turf high 71 (began Jly) - 3rd of 8 to Gypsy (27 Jly Yarmouth 7f g-f RF 3152).
**R J R Williams [0-3] Mrs S E Homewood.*

LAVACA RIVER RR 30f 1589[15]
3 b c Primo Dominie 7.2f **(67)** - Rose Music (Luthier) 9.8f **(71)**
Form - 00
Record 1998 - 1st:0 2nd:0 3rd:0 Ran:2
1998 Turf 0-2: (7f 2) (gd, g-f)
Strong, currently very moderate colt. Turf high 30.
**P Howling [0-2] King Size Racing.*

LAVERNOCK LADY BHB 26f **RR 28f** 4371[6]
3 b f Don't Forget Me 9.5f **(66)** -Danissa(Dancing Brave(USA)) 8.4f **(76)**
Form - 8456
Record 1998 - 1st:0 2nd:0 3rd:0 Ran:4
Pre1998 - 1st:0 2nd:0 3rd:0 Ran:3
1998 Turf 0-4: (10f, 11f, 14f, 16f) (g-f, frm 2, hrd)
Unfurnished, little account filly. Turf high 28 (began Jly).
**J J Quinn [0-7] The Home Countries.*

LAVERY (IRE) RR 100f 4225[5]
2 b c Royal Academy (USA) 7.8f **(77)** -Lady Donna (Dominion) 8.5f **(63)**
Form - 615
1998 Turf 1-3: (6f 1-2, 7f) (gd, g-f, frm 1-1)
Currently very useful colt. Turf high 100 (began Jly) - 1st of 11 from Access All Areas (9 Aug Leopardstown RF 3556a). It was from the ridiculous to the sublime for this colt, who finished unplaced in a maiden on his debut and won the Group One Heinz 57 Phoenix Stakes on his very next start. That was not the greatest Pattern race run in Europe last season, and he was firmly put in his place when finishing a well-beaten fifth behind Auction House at Doncaster on his final outing. He does not look one of Aidan O'Brien's best three-year-olds, but should win another Group race

in Ireland. *A P O'Brien in IRE [1-3] M Tabor & Mrs John Magnier.

Record 1998 - 1st:1 2nd:2 3rd:0 Ran:9

Lavery (left) whose form is hard to assess

LA VOLTA BHB 40f39a **RR 48f 39a** 4858[10]

5 b m Komaite (USA) 6.9f **(61)** - Khadino (Relkino) 8.9f **(65)**

Form - 0000000840

Record	**1998 -**	1st:0	2nd:0	3rd:0	Ran:10
	Pre1998 -	1st:3	2nd:1	3rd:0	Ran:19

Win Prizemoney £9,351 *Total Prizemoney* £11,520

Wins	* 1997	Spt	Nottin	(G-F)	H	6.1f	42	48	
	1995	Oct	Redcar	(FRM)		7f		81	<
	1995	May	Hamilt	(G-F)		5f		76+	

1998 Turf 0-9: (5f 2, 6f 6, 7f) (sft 2, gd 4, g-f, frm 2) 1998 AW 0-1: (5f) (Fibr)

Moderate filly, effective 6f, acts on gd, often wears blinkers. Turf high 48. Inconsistent.

**Miss J F Craze [1-15] Paul Byrne (from J G FitzGerald [2-14] Jun 1997).*

LAW COMMISSION BHB 86f **RR 84f** 3458[19]

8 ch g Ela-Mana-Mou 12.7f **(72)** - Adjala (Northfields (USA)) 9f **(72)**

Form - 00500050

Record	**1998 -**	1st:0	2nd:0	3rd:0	Ran:8
	Pre1998 -	1st:6	2nd:5	3rd:2	Ran:48

Win Prizemoney £35,103 *Total Prizemoney* £69,947

Wins	* 1997	Spt	Goodwo	(G-S)	H	7f	91	93	<
	* 1996	Aug	Ascot	(G-F)	H	7f	88	91	
	* 1996	Jly	Kempto	(GD)	C	6f		81	
	* 1996	Jun	Folkes	(G-F)	H	6f	79	81	
	* 1995	Aug	Salisb	(FRM)	H	6f	77	79	

1998 Turf 0-8: (6f 3, 7f 4, 8f) (sft, gd 4, g-f 2, frm)

Decent gelding, effective 7f, acts on gd. Turf high 96. Began the season on a lofty perch and the Handicapper relented only gradually. Not as good as he was. **D R C Elsworth [6-56] Raymond Tooth.*

LAW DANCER (IRE) BHB 44f57a **RR 31f 57a** 3483[7]

5 b g Alzao (USA) 9.8f **(73)**- Judicial (USA)(Law Society (USA))9.9f **(70)**

Form - 661722477

Pre1998 -	1st:2	2nd:4	3rd:1	Ran:27

Win Prizemoney £9,956 *Total Prizemoney* £17,109

Wins	* **1998**	*Apr*	*Wolver*	*(STD)*	*H*	*9.4f*	*53*	*56*	
	* 1996	*Apr*	*Wolver*	*(STD)*	*H*	*9.4f*	*68*	*74*	<
	* 1996	*Mar*	*Wolver*	*(STD)*	*H*	*9.4f*	*60*	*66*	

1998 Turf 0-1:(10f)(gd)1998AW1-8:(8f 2, 9f 1-4, 10f, 12f)(Equi, Fibr 1-7)

Fair gelding, effective 9 to 12f, best at 9f, - acts on Fibr, has worn blinkers, favours left handed tracks. AW high 59 - 2nd of 10 giving 16lb to Shanghai Lil (20 Jun Wolverhampton 12f Fibr RF 2166). Becoming disappointing. **T G Mills [3-36] T J Oswin.*

LAWFUL CONTRACT (IRE) BHB 37f45a **RR 32f 45a** 2173[15]

3 br g Contract Law (USA) 8.9f **(54)** - Lucciola (FR) (Auction Ring (USA)) 8.6f **(65)**

Form - 7500

Record	**1998 -**	1st:0	2nd:0	3rd:0	Ran:4
	Pre1998 -	1st:0	2nd:0	3rd:0	Ran:4

1998 Turf 0-2: (8f 2) (gd, g-f) 1998 AW 0-2: (6f, 8f) (Fibr 2)

Tall, moderate gelding. Turf high 4. AW high 41. Inconsistent.

**R Hollinshead [0-8] J Doxey.*

LAWLESS BRIDGET BHB 50f **RR 57f** 1888[12]

3 b f Alnasr Alwasheek 9.4f **(62)** - Geoffrey's Sister (Sparkler) 8.4f **(55)**

Form - 40600

Record	**1998 -**	1st:0	2nd:0	3rd:0	Ran:5
	Pre1998 -	1st:0	2nd:0	3rd:0	Ran:1

Win Prizemoney £0 *Total Prizemoney* £300

1998 Turf 0-5: (6f 2, 7f 2, 8f) (sft, g-s, gd 2, g-f)

Small, fair filly. Turf high 57. **M Meade [0-6] R M West.*

LAWNETT RR 60f 5022a[5]

2 b f Runnett 6.7f **(56)** - Polar Storm (IRE) **(69f)** (Law Society (USA)) 9.9f **(70)**

Form - 0806055

Record	**1998 -**	1st:0	2nd:0	3rd:0	Ran:7

1998 Turf 0-7: (6f 3, 8f 3, 9f) (hvy, sft, g-s, gd 3, g-f)

Average filly, effective 8f, acts on hvy, has worn blinkers. Turf high 60 - 5th of 18 getting 3lb from Mrs Evans (22 Oct Punchestown 8f hvy RF 5022a).

**D Gillespie in IRE [0-5] Duncan McGregor (from J L Dunlop [0-2] Jun 1998).*

LAW REVIEW (IRE) BHB 70f RR 63?f 3990[3]

3 ch f Case Law 6f **(64)** - Persian Polly (Persian Bold) 9.3f **(66)**

Form - 453

Record 1998 - 1st:0 2nd:0 3rd:1 Ran:3

Win Prizemoney £0 *Total Prizemoney* £851

1998 Turf 0-3: (5f, 6f, 8f) (gd, frm 2)

Workmanlike, currently average filly. Turf high 63 (began Jly).

**M Johnston [0-3] Mrs A M Burns.*

LAY THE BLAME BHB 65f RR 73df 5147[20]

5 b g Reprimand 8.2f **(63)** -Rose And The Ring(Welsh Pageant)10f **(65)**

Form - 0

Record 1998 - 1st:0 2nd:0 3rd:0 Ran:1
Pre1998 - 1st:2 2nd:1 3rd:2 Ran:16

Win Prizemoney £7,830 *Total Prizemoney* £10,024

Wins 1995 Oct Nottin (G-F) 6.1f 86 <
1995 Oct Warwic (G-S) 6f 73

1998 Turf 0-1: (8f) (gd)

Above-average gelding, effective 8 to 10f, best at 10f, acts on g-f to frm, best on frm. Inconsistent.

**M D Hammond [0-15] J D Gordon & E C Gordon (from W Jarvis [2-9] Aug 1996).*

LEADING NOTE (USA) BHB 62f RR 57f 4963[9]

4 ch f Blushing John (USA) 8.9f **(75)** - Beat (USA) (Nijinsky (CAN)) 10.3f **(77)**

Form - 70

Record 1998 - 1st:0 2nd:0 3rd:0 Ran:2
Pre1998 - 1st:0 2nd:0 3rd:3 Ran:6

Win Prizemoney £0 *Total Prizemoney* £1,826

1998 Turf 0-2: (13f, 16f) (sft, g-f)

Scopey, fair filly, effective 11f, acts on g-f. Turf high 57 (began Oct). Becoming disappointing.

**Miss H C Knight [0-5] The Leaders (from L M Cumani [0-6] Oct 1997).*

LEADING PRINCESS (IRE) BHB 31f47a RR 35df 47a 4130[16]

7 gr m Double Schwartz 7f **(60)** - Jenny Diver (USA) (Hatchet Man (USA)) 6.3f **(51)**

Form - 03000

Record 1998 - 1st:0 2nd:0 3rd:1 Ran:5
Pre1998 - 1st:7 2nd:4 3rd:7 Ran:67

Win Prizemoney £21,492 *Total Prizemoney* £29,981

Wins * 1997 May Hamilt (SFT) 5f 48
* 1996 Oct Newcas (G-F) H 6f 47 48
* 1996 Aug Hamilt (G-F) 6f 49 <
* 1996 Jun Carlis (FRM) H 5f 44 44
* 1995 Oct Newcas (G-F) H 5f 44 49 <
* 1995 Spt Hamilt (GD) H 6f 35 45
* 1994 Jly Ayr (GD) H 5f 37 39

1998 Turf 0-5: (5f 3, 6f 2) (gd 3, g-f, frm)

Very moderate mare, effective 5 to 6f, best at 6f, acts on g-s to frm, mostly wears blinkers. Turf high 35.

**Miss L A Perratt [7-72] Mrs Ruth Wyllie.*

LEADING PROSPECTOR (USA) RR 81f 5063[6]

2 b c Mr Prospector (USA) 8.6f **(88)** - Araadh (USA) **(64f)** (Blushing Groom (FR)) 10.3f **(76)**

Form - 6

Record 1998 - 1st:0 2nd:0 3rd:0 Ran:1

1998 Turf 0-1: (6f) (g-f)

Currently decent colt.

**C E Brittain [0-1] The Thoroughbred Corporation.*

LEADING SPIRIT (IRE) BHB 81f85a RR 76f 85a 5126[18]

6 b g Fairy King (USA) 7.7f **(75)** - Shopping (FR) (Sheshoon) 11.9f **(69)**

Form - 0302500

Record 1998 - 1st:0 2nd:1 3rd:1 Ran:7
Pre1998 - 1st:5 2nd:2 3rd:2 Ran:20

Win Prizemoney £22,873 *Total Prizemoney* £31,526

Wins 1997 *Feb Wolver (STD) H 12f 71 79+*
1996 Spt Kempto (GD) H 12f 83 87 <
1996 Jun Kempto (G-F) H 12f 73 83+
1995 Spt Hamilt (GD) H 12.1f 66 74
1995 Spt Sandow (G-S) H 11.4f 60 66

1998 Turf 0-7: (10f, 12f 4, 13f, 14f) (g-s, gd 4, g-f, frm)

Above-average gelding, effective 12f, acts on g-f - acts on Fibr, prefers left handed tracks. Turf high 86 - 3rd of 9 giving 23lb to Emerald Heights (23 May Doncaster 12f g-f RF 1414). Inconsistent. Lightly raced in recent seasons, he ran a better race at Newbury in July when stepped up to a mile and five.

**R Champion [0-1] Christopher Ranson (from C F Wall [5-28] Spt 1998).*

LEA GRANDE BHB 77f RR 80f 3794[4]

3 ch f Highest Honor (FR) 10.9f **(72)** - Lovely Rita (USA) (Topsider (USA)) 8.3f **(71)**

Form - 6244

Record 1998 - 1st:0 2nd:1 3rd:0 Ran:4
Pre1998 - 1st:0 2nd:0 3rd:1 Ran:2

Win Prizemoney £0 *Total Prizemoney* £7,617

1998 Turf 0-4: (8f 2, 9f, 10f) (gd, g-f, frm 2)

Decent filly, effective 7 to 8f, best at 8f, acts on g-f to frm, best on frm. Turf high 80 - 2nd of 13 to Sahara (1 Jly Brighton 8f frm RF 2440). **L M Cumani [0-6] Allevamento del Torrione.*

LEAPING CHARLIE BHB 67f RR 72f 5139[12]

2 b c Puissance 7.1f **(60)** - Impala Lass (Kampala) 8.5f **(56)**

Form - 8030

Record 1998 - 1st:0 2nd:0 3rd:1 Ran:4

Win Prizemoney £0 *Total Prizemoney* £296

1998 Turf 0-4: (5f, 6f 3) (gd 3, frm)

Above-average colt. Turf high 72 (began Spt) - 3rd of 6 to Amaranth (27 Oct Redcar 5f gd RF 5011).

**Mrs A Swinbank [0-4] Starnotes Racing.*

LEARNED FRIEND (IRE) BHB 85f RR 87f 4650[1]

2 ch c College Chapel - Caring (Crowned Prince (USA)) 10.1f **(67)**

Form - 3473431

Record 1998 - 1st:1 2nd:0 3rd:3 Ran:7

Win Prizemoney £3,355 *Total Prizemoney* £6,317

Wins * 1998 Oct Bright (GD) 6f 77+ <

1998 Turf 1-7: (6f 1-4, 7f 3) (gd 3, g-f 1-2, frm, hrd)

Useful colt, effective 6 to 7f, best at 7f, acts on gd to hrd. Turf high 87 - 3rd of 10 to Chatting (10 Spt Chepstow 7f gd RF 4197). Knocking on the dooor prior to his maiden win, he went for 16,000 guineas at Tattersall's Autumn Horses-in-Training sales

**R Hannon [1-7] J C Smith.*

LEAR'S CROWN (USA) BHB 78f RR 76f 4841[4]

3 b f Lear Fan (USA) 10.4f **(80)** - Crowning Ambition (USA) (Chief's Crown (USA)) 9.8f **(72)**

Form - 314

Record 1998 - 1st:1 2nd:0 3rd:1 Ran:3

Win Prizemoney £3,566 *Total Prizemoney* £4,559

Wins * 1998 Spt Kempto (GD) 12f 72 <

1998 Turf 1-3: (10f, 12f 1-1, 14f) (gd, g-f, frm 1-1)

Scopey, currently above-average filly. Turf high 76 (began Aug) - 4th of 11 giving 8lb to Mark of Prophet (16 Oct Newmarket 14f g-f RF 4841) - also 1st of 14 getting 5lb from Ange d'Honor (21 Spt Kempton RF 4394). **Mrs A J Perrett [1-3] K Abdulla.*

LEAR SPEAR (USA) BHB 106f RR 108f 4843[4]

3 b c Lear Fan (USA) 10.4f **(80)** - Golden Gorse (USA) (His Majesty (USA)) 10.9f **(82)**

Form - 0280313314

Record 1998 - 1st:2 2nd:1 3rd:3 Ran:10
Pre1998 - 1st:0 2nd:0 3rd:2 Ran:3

Win Prizemoney £55,921 *Total Prizemoney* £61,542

Wins * 1998 Oct Newmar () H 9f 90 96 <
*** 1998** Aug Sandow (GD) 8.1f 75

1998 Turf 2-10: (8f 1-6, 9f 1-2, 10f 2) (g-s, gd 1-3, g-f 1-5, frm)

Scopey, Pattern-class colt, effective 8 to 9f, acts on g-f. Turf high 108 - 4th of 13 to Haami (16 Oct Newmarket 9f g-f RF 4843). He was not the only one given a poor ride when beaten in a Sandown maiden during July, and connections did well to stick by young Neil Pollard. They were repaid when both horse and rider put up a personal best to win the Cambridgeshire, and better could follow next term. **D R C Elsworth [2-13] Raymond Tooth.*

LEATHER AND SCRIM (IRE) BHB 55f54a **RR 45f 54a** 132[2]
3 b f Imperial Frontier (USA) 7f **(65)** - Yola (IRE) (Last Tycoon) 8.5f **(62)**
Form - 02
Record 1998 - 1st:0 2nd:1 3rd:0 Ran:2
Pre1998 - 1st:0 2nd:0 3rd:0 Ran:4
Win Prizemoney £0 *Total Prizemoney* £761
1998 AW 0-2: (5f, 6f) (Equi, Fibr)
Workmanlike, moderate filly, effective 5f, - acts on Equi. AW high 46 - 2nd of 5 getting 14lb from Best of Our Days (22 Jan Lingfield 5f Equi RF 0132). **D Nicholls [0-6] First Past The Post.*

LEA VALLEY DANCER BHB 50f **RR 53f** 5141[8]
5 b m Niniski (USA) 13.2f **(67)** - Ivory Gull (USA) (Storm Bird (CAN)) 10.3f **(74)**
Form - 058
Record 1998 - 1st:0 2nd:0 3rd:0 Ran:3
Win Prizemoney £0 *Total Prizemoney* £150
1998 Turf 0-3: (7f, 8f, 10f) (sft, g-s, gd)
Fair filly. Turf high 53 (began Oct). **J R Jenkins [0-4] Lea Valley.*

LEAVE IT TO ME RR 57f 3514[5]
2 b f College Chapel - Enaam (Shirley Heights) 10.3f **(74)**
Form - 2775
Record 1998 - 1st:0 2nd:1 3rd:0 Ran:4
Win Prizemoney £0 *Total Prizemoney* £1,344
1998 Turf 0-4: (6f 4) (gd 2, frm, hrd)
Fair filly. Turf high 59 (1st run) - 2nd of 7 to Hi Nicky (16 May Newmarket 6f frm RF 1264).
**S P C Woods [0-4] Mrs Marian Borsberry.*

LEAVE IT TO RODNEY BHB 40f **RR 37f** 3647[16]
3 b g Tina's Pet 7.4f **(56)** -Fivesevenfiveo**(59df)**(Enchantment) 5.4f **(52)**
Form - 060880
Record 1998 - 1st:0 2nd:0 3rd:0 Ran:6
1998 Turf 0-6: (5f 4, 6f, 7f) (gd 2, g-f, frm 2, hrd)
Leggy, very moderate gelding, has worn blinkers. Turf high 46.
**R J Hodges [0-6] B Dennett.*

LE BAL BHB 30f22a **RR 38f 22a** 4549[16]
6 b m Rambo Dancer (CAN) 8.4f **(59)** - Skarberg (FR) (Noir Et Or) 10f **(38)**
Form - 00
Record 1998 - 1st:0 2nd:0 3rd:0 Ran:2
Pre1998 - 1st:0 2nd:1 3rd:1 Ran:17
Win Prizemoney £0 *Total Prizemoney* £1,654
1998 Turf 0-1: (10f) (gd) 1998 AW 0-1: (11f) (Fibr)
Very moderate mare, often wears blinkers.
**M A Peill [0-2] Mrs Valerie Dixon (from Miss J F Craze [0-4] Mar 1996).*

LEBASQUE RR 40f 1979[8]
2 gr c First Trump - Simply Sooty (Absalom) 7.2f **(58)**
Form - 8
Record 1998 - 1st:0 2nd:0 3rd:0 Ran:1
1998 Turf 0-1: (6f) (g-s)
Currently moderate colt. **J Berry [0-1] J Hanson.*

LEDGENDRY LINE BHB 68f **RR 72f** 562[2]
5 b g Mtoto 11.5f **(71)** - Eider (Niniski (USA)) 10.6f **(65)**
Form - 2
Record 1998 - 1st:0 2nd:1 3rd:0 Ran:1
Pre1998 - 1st:1 2nd:1 3rd:3 Ran:15
Win Prizemoney £2,956 *Total Prizemoney* £10,099
Wins * 1997 Jun Ayr (GD) H 13.1f 70 77 <
1998 Turf 0-1: (13f) (sft)
Above-average gelding, effective 12 to 13f, best at 13f, acts on sft to g-f, best on gd, likes tight tracks. (1st run) - 2nd of 7 giving 11lb to Rossel (4 Apr Hamilton 13f sft RF 0562). Consistent.
**Mrs M Reveley [3-20] The Home & Away Partnership.*

LEDHAM (USA) BHB 77f **RR 78f** 4984[3]
2 ch c Diesis 9f **(80)** - First Tracks (USA) (Alleged (USA)) 10f **(76)**
Form - 463
Record 1998 - 1st:0 2nd:0 3rd:1 Ran:3
Win Prizemoney £0 *Total Prizemoney* £767
1998 Turf 0-3: (7f 3) (g-s, gd, g-f)
Currently above-average colt. Turf high 78 (began Aug).
**Sir Michael Stoute [0-3] Saeed Suhail.*

LEGAL ISSUE (IRE) BHB 62f57a **RR 64f 57a** 5119[10]
6 b h Contract Law (USA) 8.9f **(54)** - Natuschka (Authi) 8.9f **(89)**
Form - 221312145058060
Record 1998 - 1st:2 2nd:1 3rd:1 Ran:12
Pre1998 - 1st:6 2nd:11 3rd:4 Ran:48
Win Prizemoney £23,287 *Total Prizemoney* £38,892
Wins 1998 Jun Beverl (G-S) H 8.5f 67 68
1998 Apr Pontef (G-S) 8f 67
1997 Dec Lingfi (STD) H 10f 55 59
1997 Aug Wolver (STD) H 8.5f 51 52
1996 Jly Catter (G-S) 7f 68
1996 Jun Doncas (GD) H 7f 56 59
1995 Aug Mussel (G-F) H 7.1f 62 69 <
1995 Jun Mussel (G-F) 7.1f 59
1998 Turf 2-10: (8f 2-3, 9f, 10f 4, 12f 2) (g-s 1-3, gd 1-5, g-f, hrd) 1998 AW 0-2: (8f 2) (Fibr 2)
Average horse, effective 8 to 12f, best at 8f, acts on g-s to hrd - acts on AW, has worn blinkers, prefers tight tracks, excels at Pontefract, does well at Beverley. Turf high 68 - 1st of 9 getting 10lb from Blooming Amazing (3 Jun Beverley RF 1677) - also 1st of 12 from White Settler (27 Apr Pontefract RF 0881). AW high 53 (began Aug).
**J M Jefferson [0-4] B Valentine (from J Hetherton [2-8] Aug 1998).*

LEGAL LARK (IRE) BHB 38f60a **RR 49f 60a** 4649[16]
3 ro g Case Law 6f **(64)** - Park Silver (Beldale Flutter (USA)) 9.7f **(71)**
Form - 6710050666080600
Record 1998 - 1st:1 2nd:0 3rd:0 Ran:15
Pre1998 - 1st:1 2nd:0 3rd:0 Ran:8
Win Prizemoney £6,242 *Total Prizemoney* £6,242
Wins * **1998** *Jan Lingfi (STD) H 6f 60 66*
* 1997 Spt Folkes (FRM) C 6f 68 <
1998 Turf 0-11: (5f 5, 6f 5, 7f) (g-s, g-f 3, frm 7) 1998 AW 1-4: (6f 1-3, 8f) (Equi 1-3, Fibr)
Workmanlike, average gelding, effective 6f, acts on g-f - acts on Equi, has worn blinkers. Turf high 52. AW high 66 - 1st of 4 getting 2lb from Treble Term (8 Jan Lingfield RF 0050).
**P Howling [2-23] C Hammond.*

LEGAL LUNCH (USA) BHB 87f **RR 88f** 4497[12]
3 b c Alleged (USA) 11.8f **(81)** - Dinner Surprise (USA) (Lyphard (USA)) 9.9f **(72)**
Form - 41050530
Record 1998 - 1st:1 2nd:0 3rd:1 Ran:8
Pre1998 - 1st:0 2nd:1 3rd:0 Ran:1
Win Prizemoney £3,680 *Total Prizemoney* £6,310
Wins * **1998** May Haydoc (G-S) 10.5f 90 <
1998 Turf 1-8: (10f, 11f 1-2, 12f 2, 14f, 16f 2) (g-s 2, gd 1-2, g-f 2, frm 2)
Scopey, useful colt, effective 7 to 16f, acts on g-s to frm. Turf high 90 - 1st of 12 from Corelli (23 May Haydock RF 1419). Consistent. Appreciated the cut in the ground when a comfortable winner of a Haydock maiden on his second start but has been found wanting in handicaps. He looked as though he would appreciate a step up trip, and may have been a bit unlucky when third over two miles at Goodwood in the autumn. **P W Harris [1-9] The Alleged Partnership.*

LEGAL SET (IRE) RR 80f 5063[7]
2 b br c Second Set (IRE) 9.2f **(67)** - Tiffany's Case (IRE) **(58f)** (Thatching) 8f **(66)**
Form - 07
Record 1998 - 1st:0 2nd:0 3rd:0 Ran:2
1998 Turf 0-2: (6f, 8f) (g-f, frm)
Currently decent colt. Turf high 80 (began Oct).
**C A Horgan [0-2] John Kelsey-Fry.*

LEGAL VENTURE (IRE) BHB 61f66a **RR 67f 66a** 5042[10]
2 ch g Case Law 6f **(64)** - We Two (Glenstal (USA)) 10.1f **(64)**
Form - 888413324520
Record 1998 - 1st:1 2nd:2 3rd:2 Ran:12
Win Prizemoney £1,725 *Total Prizemoney* £4,762
Wins 1998 Jly Lingfi (G-F) S 5f 64+ <
1998 Turf 1-11: (5f 1-11) (sft 2, g-s, gd 2, g-f 4, frm 1-2) 1998 AW 0-1: (5f) (Fibr)
Above-average gelding, effective 5f, acts on g-f to frm - acts on Fibr, best on g-f. Turf high 67 - 3rd of 4 getting 5lb from Key (12 Aug Brighton 5f g-f RF 3569) - also 1st of 8 getting 2lb from Five Ways Flyer (25 Jly Lingfield RF 3108). (1st run) - 2nd of 13 giving 5lb to Dispol Clan (3 Oct Wolverhampton 5f Fibr RF 4639).

**N P Littmoden [0-1] Hanibel Racing Partnership (from B J Meehan [1-11] Oct 1998).*

LEGEND RR 77f 5146[3]

2 b f Belmez (USA) 11.4f **(65)** - Once Upon a Time (Teenoso (USA)) 9.9f **(72)**

Form - 53

Record 1998 - 1st:0 2nd:0 3rd:1 Ran:2

Win Prizemoney £0 *Total Prizemoney* £480

1998 Turf 0-2: (8f 2) (gd, frm)

Currently above-average filly. Turf high 77 (began Oct) - 3rd of 13 getting 5lb from Chelsea Barracks (7 Nov Doncaster 8f gd RF 5146). **Lord Huntingdon [0-2] The Queen.*

LEGEND OF LOVE BHB 65f60a **RR 60+f 60a** 4817[1]

3 b g Pursuit of Love 9.5f **(69)** - Legendary Dancer (Shareef Dancer (USA)) 9.9f **(73)**

Form - 853486362531

Record 1998 - 1st:1 2nd:1 3rd:3 Ran:12
Pre1998 - 1st:0 2nd:0 3rd:1 Ran:5

Win Prizemoney £3,730 *Total Prizemoney* £7,375

Wins * **1998** Oct Catter (G-S) H 15.8f 48 60+ <

1998 Turf 1-10: (10f 2, 12f 2, 14f 3, 16f 1-3) (sft 2, g-s, gd 1-1, g-f 2, frm 4) 1998 AW 0-2: (12f, 14f) (Fibr 2)

Workmanlike, average gelding, has worn blinkers. Turf high 62. AW high 44.

**B J Llewellyn [1-3] David Lewis (from J A Glover [0-14] Spt 1998).*

LEGGERA (IRE) BHB 121f **RR 124f** 5167a[12]

3 b f Sadler's Wells (USA) 11.3f **(87)** - Lady Ambassador (General Assembly (USA)) 10f **(68)**

Form - 12241120

Record 1998 - 1st:2 2nd:3 3rd:0 Ran:7
Pre1998 - 1st:2 2nd:0 3rd:2 Ran:4

Win Prizemoney £130,406 *Total Prizemoney* £328,330

Wins * **1998** Spt Longch (SFT) G1 12f 116 <
* **1998** Aug Deauvi (SFT) G2 13.5f 112
* 1997 Nov Maison (HLD) L 8f 92
* 1997 Aug Sandow (G-F) 7.1f 92+

1998 Turf 2-7: (10f, 11f, 12f 1-4, 14f 1-1) (hvy 1-1, sft 2, gd 1-2, g-f, frm)

Scopey, very high-class filly, effective 12f, acts on hvy to sft, prefers right handed tracks. Turf high 124 - 2nd of 14 getting 3lb from Sagamix (4 Oct Longchamp 12f sft RF 4727a) - also 1st of 11 from Cloud Castle (13 Spt Longchamp RF 4343a). She ran creditably in her first three starts of the 1998 season, but really improved during the autumn. She landed a Group Two at Deauville before beating a good field in the Group One Prix Vermeille. She looked like winning the Arc at one point, but was just caught by Sagamix. She contested the Breeders' Cup Turf, but may have been over the top by then. Very much suited by soft ground.

**J L Dunlop [4-11] Mrs H Focke.*

LEGS BE FRENDLY (IRE) BHB 74f **RR 66f** 4988[18]

3 b c Fayruz 6.6f **(63)** - Thalssa (Rusticaro (FR)) 8.2f **(65)**

Form - 0000

Record 1998 - 1st:0 2nd:0 3rd:0 Ran:4
Pre1998 - 1st:1 2nd:6 3rd:1 Ran:10

Win Prizemoney £4,653 *Total Prizemoney* £14,429

Wins * 1997 Oct Lingfi (GD) 5f 64 <

1998 Turf 0-4: (6f 3, 7f) (hvy, g-s, gd, g-f)

Scopey, average colt, effective 6f, acts on g-f to frm, best on frm, has worn blinkers. Turf high 66. Inconsistent.

**K McAuliffe [1-14] BABK Racing.*

LEICESTER TIGER BHB 44f **RR 48df** 2154[9]

2 b c Presidium 7.5f **(56)** - Glenfield Greta **(46f 43a)** (Gabitat) 5f **(44)**

Form - 3080

Record 1998 - 1st:0 2nd:0 3rd:1 Ran:4

Win Prizemoney £0 *Total Prizemoney* £357

1998 Turf 0-3: (5f, 6f, 7f) (gd 2, g-f) 1998 AW 0-1: (5f) (Fibr)

Moderate colt, has worn blinkers. Turf high 48.

**T J Etherington [0-4] David Abell.*

LEIF THE LUCKY (USA) BHB 47f52a **RR 55?f 52a** 501[9]

9 ch g Lemhi Gold (USA) 8.2f **(71)** -Corvine (USA) (Crow (FR)) 7.4f **(75)**

Form - 0

Record 1998 - 1st:0 2nd:0 3rd:0 Ran:1
Pre1998 - 1st:5 2nd:4 3rd:5 Ran:47

Win Prizemoney £23,976 *Total Prizemoney* £39,825

Wins * 1994 Aug Ayr (G-S) H 8f 77 79 <
* 1994 May Carlis (HVY) H 8f 71 75

1998 Turf 0-1: (9f) (sft)

Fair gelding, effective 9 to 11f, acts on gd to frm, best on gd. Becoming disappointing.

**Miss S E Hall [4-43] Miss S E Hall (from W Jarvis [1-6] Oct 1992).*

LEIGH CROFTER BHB 47f56a **RR 55f 56a** 2100[2]

9 ch g Son of Shaka 6.2f **(29)** - Ganadora (Good Times (ITY)) 6.6f **(54)**

Form - 0737844325434455742

Record 1998 - 1st:0 2nd:2 3rd:3 Ran:17
Pre1998 - 1st:12 2nd:9 3rd:5 Ran:106

Win Prizemoney £39,723 *Total Prizemoney* £58,675

Wins *1997 Jan Wolver (SLW) H 7f 62 66*
1996 Dec Wolver (STD) H 7f 58 64
1996 Nov Southw (STD) H 7f 47 57
1996 Nov Wolver (STD) 7f 60
1995 Jan Wolver (STD) H 5f 70 72
1994 May Newbur (G-F) H 6f 75 77 <
1994 May Lingfi (GD) H 6f 72 71
1994 Apr Warwic (HVY) H 5f 68 65
1994 Mar Warwic (SFT) H 6f 63 64

1998 Turf 0-4: (6f 3, 7f) (hvy, g-s, gd, g-f) 1998 AW 0-13: (6f 3, 7f 7, 8f 3) (Fibr 13)

Fair gelding, effective 7f, - acts on Fibr, mostly wears blinkers, favours left handed tracks, favours tight tracks. Turf high 55. AW high 60 - 2nd of 8 getting 8lb from Alamein (23 Mar Southwell 7f Fibr RF 0464). Consistent. Now at the veteran stage but still racing regularly, mostly on Fibresand. He changed stables at the start of 1998 and has run creditably since, but is without a win since January 1997.

**John Harris [0-14] Mrs Annette Harris (from J L Harris [0-1] Mar 1998).*

LEMON BRIDGE (IRE) BHB 77f **RR 81f** 4532[12]

3 b c Shalford (IRE) 7.8f **(63)** - Sharply (Sharpman) 11.3f **(66)**

Form - 323135460

Record 1998 - 1st:1 2nd:1 3rd:3 Ran:9
Pre1998 - 1st:0 2nd:0 3rd:0 Ran:1

Win Prizemoney £3,850 *Total Prizemoney* £7,660

Wins * **1998** Jun Goodwo (G-F) 9.9f 79 <

1998 Turf 1-9: (7f, 9f, 10f 1-5, 12f 2) (hvy 2, g-s 2, gd 1-2, g-f 2, frm)

Light-framed, decent colt, effective 7 to 12f, best at 10f, acts on hvy to frm. Turf high 81 - 3rd of 6 getting 17lb from Evening World (13 Jun York 10f g-s RF 1983) - also 1st of 6 from Ionian Spring (26 Jun Goodwood RF 2305). He has been very consistent this season, including scoring at Goodwood, though ten furlongs looks to be the very limit of her stamina. **J W Hills [1-10] Martin Myers.*

LEMON STRIP BHB 35f **RR 21f** 4524[14]

2 ch f Emarati (USA) 6.6f **(63)** -Lon Isa **(39f 47a)** (Grey Desire) 8.7f **(50)**

Form - 000

Record 1998 - 1st:0 2nd:0 3rd:0 Ran:3

1998 Turf 0-3: (6f 3) (g-f 2, frm)

Currently little account filly. Turf high 21 (began Aug).

**B Palling [0-3] H Weeks.*

LEND A HAND BHB 119f **RR 121f** 3783a[6]

3 b c Great Commotion (USA) 9.2f **(80)** - Janaat (Kris) 9.5f **(73)**

Form - 2236

Record 1998 - 1st:0 2nd:2 3rd:1 Ran:4
Pre1998 - 1st:5 2nd:1 3rd:0 Ran:6

Win Prizemoney £102,221 *Total Prizemoney* £217,643

Wins * 1997 Oct San Si (GD) G1 8f 115+ <
* 1997 Spt Doncas (G-F) H 8f 94 103+
* 1997 Jly Beverl (G-F) 7.5f 90
* 1997 Jly Catter (G-F) 7f 94+
* 1997 Jly Epsom (G-S) 6f 75

1998 Turf 0-4: (8f 4) (gd 4)

Scopey, very high-class colt, effective 8f, acts on gd. Turf high 121 (1st run) - 2nd of 18 to King Of Kings (2 May Newmarket 8f gd RF 0974). Showed progressive form to win five in a row as a two-year-old in 1997, stepping up from a valuable nursery at the St Leger meeting to land the Gran Criterium in Milan. He seemed to improve over the winter, and ran a superb race to finish runner-up in the 2000 Guineas. Missed Ascot due to injury, and never really regained his sparkle. He was a little disappointing in Germany

before finishing third to two older horses in the Sussex Stakes. If he can recapture his form in 1999, when he will race for Godolphin, he will be a major contender for the top mile prizes, running in the Godolphin blue.
**M Johnston [5-10] Maktoum Al Maktoum.*

LENNOX **RR 78+f** 5145[5]
2 b c Bustino 11f **(64)** - Ivory Gull (USA) (Storm Bird (CAN)) 10.3f **(74)**
Form - 485
Record 1998 - 1st:0 2nd:0 3rd:0 Ran:3
Win Prizemoney £0 *Total Prizemoney* £247
1998 Turf 0-3: (7f, 8f 2) (gd, g-f, frm)
Currently above-average colt. Turf high 78 (1st run) (began Jly) - 4th of 9 giving 5lb to Penmayne (15 Jly Sandown 7f g-f RF 2828).
**P F I Cole [0-3] Sir George Meyrick.*

LENNOX LEWIS BHB 48f45a **RR 46f 45a** 566[6]
6 b g Superpower 6.6f **(58)** - Song's Best (Never so Bold) 6.3f **(66)**
Form - 06376
Record 1998 - 1st:0 2nd:0 3rd:1 Ran:4
Pre1998 - 1st:3 2nd:3 3rd:1 Ran:39
Win Prizemoney £15,398 *Total Prizemoney* £30,481
Wins 1994 Aug Kempto (G-F) 6f 84
1994 Jly Goodwo (GF) 6f 86
1994 Jly Ripon (G-F) 5f 84
1998 AW 0-4: (5f, 6f 3) (Fibr 4)
Moderate gelding, has worn blinkers. AW high 41. Consistent. He looks to be very much on the downgrade these days, but if anyone can get him back in the winner's enclosure, Dandy can.
**D Nicholls [0-11] P S Platt (from A P Jarvis [3-32] Mar 1997).*

LEOFRIC BHB 49f61a **RR 53f 61a** 4988[16]
3 b g Alhijaz 7.7f **(57)** - Wandering Stranger (Petong) 6.6f **(58)**
Form - 0054804380008800
Record 1998 - 1st:0 2nd:0 3rd:1 Ran:15
Pre1998 - 1st:0 2nd:0 3rd:5 Ran:11
Win Prizemoney £0 *Total Prizemoney* £4,126
1998 Turf 0-15: (5f 6, 6f 6, 7f 2, 8f) (g-s, gd 4, g-f 5, frm 5)
Scopey, fair gelding, effective 5 to 7f, acts on g-f to frm, best on frm, often wears blinkers. Turf high 57.
**M J Polglase [0-26] Keen Racing.*

LEONATO (FR) BHB 99f **RR 102f** 2345[12]
6 b g Law Society (USA)11.6f **(71)**-Gala Parade (Alydar(USA)) 9.1f **(76)**
Form - 4320
Record 1998 - 1st:0 2nd:1 3rd:1 Ran:4
Pre1998 - 1st:0 2nd:2 3rd:0 Ran:8
Win Prizemoney £0 *Total Prizemoney* £18,388
1998 Turf 0-4: (12f 2, 16f, 19f) (sft, gd 2, g-f)
Very useful gelding. Turf high 103 (1st run) - 4th of 8 getting 2lb from Poseidon (28 Mar Doncaster 12f gd RF 0487). Ex-French, he looked a touch unlucky in the Chester Cup in May, and was half-lengthed by Clerkenwell when sent back there for a conditions event the following month. Not seen out after finishing unplaced in the Northumberland Plate, he may have suffered a setback.
**P D Evans [0-12] Colin Booth.*

LER CRU (IRE) BHB 23f30a **RR 19?f 30a** 105[16]
9 b g Lafontaine (USA) 12.7f **(65)** - Kirsova (Absalom) 7.2f **(58)**
Form - 070
Record 1998 - 1st:0 2nd:0 3rd:0 Ran:2
Pre1998 - 1st:1 2nd:0 3rd:2 Ran:28
Win Prizemoney £2,782 *Total Prizemoney* £4,307
1998 AW 0-2: (12f, 16f) (Equi 2)
Very moderate gelding, had worn blinkers. (DEAD)
**G P Enright [0-3] Stephen Findlay & Mrs Medeana Findlay (from J Ffitch-Heyes [0-20] Aug 1995).*

LE SAUVAGE (IRE) BHB 39f **RR 60f** 4615[6]
3 b g Tirol 8.1f **(64)** - Cistus (Sun Prince) 12.4f **(52)**
Form - 086
Record 1998 - 1st:0 2nd:0 3rd:0 Ran:3
1998 Turf 0-2: (10f, 12f) (gd, frm) 1998 AW 0-1: (13f) (Equi)
Scopey, currently average gelding. Turf high 60 (began Spt).
**M R Channon [0-3] R M Brehaut.*

LE SHUTTLE BHB 27f34a **RR 25f 34a** 2335[17]
4 b f Presidium 7.5f **(56)** - Petitesse (Petong) 6.6f **(58)**
Form - 00600
Record 1998 - 1st:0 2nd:0 3rd:0 Ran:5
Pre1998 - 1st:0 2nd:2 3rd:3 Ran:16
Win Prizemoney £0 *Total Prizemoney* £2,600
1998 Turf 0-4: (5f, 6f 2, 7f) (g-s, gd 2, frm) 1998 AW 0-1: (5f) (Fibr)
Neat, very moderate filly, has worn blinkers. Turf high 25.
**P S McEntee [0-4] Mrs Bridget Blum (from P M McEntee [0-1] Apr 1998).*

LESLEY'S ADVENTURE (IRE) BHB 36f40a **RR 38f 40a** 3580[9]
3 b br f Petardia 8.2f **(58)** - Island Adventure (Touching Wood (USA)) 8.2f **(55)**
Form - 600550
Record 1998 - 1st:0 2nd:0 3rd:0 Ran:6
Pre1998 - 1st:0 2nd:0 3rd:0 Ran:3
1998 Turf 0-5: (6f, 8f 3, 10f) (sft, gd 2, frm 2) 1998 AW 0-1: (7f) (Fibr)
Light-framed, very moderate filly. Turf high 38.
**E J Alston [0-6] Tom Dearden (from Capt J Wilson [0-3] Aug 1997).*

L'ESTABLE FLEURIE (IRE) BHB 66f72a **RR 67f 72a** 4229[18]
3 b f Common Grounds 8.1f **(66)** - Dorado Llave (USA) (Well Decorated (USA)) 7.6f **(64)**
Form - 353151440
Record 1998 - 1st:2 2nd:0 3rd:2 Ran:9
Pre1998 - 1st:0 2nd:0 3rd:1 Ran:9
Win Prizemoney £5,135 *Total Prizemoney* £7,288
Wins **1998** *Jun Lingfi (STD) C 7f 78* <
1998 May Bright (G-F) C 7f 64
1998 Turf 1-4: (6f, 7f 1-1, 8f 2) (gd 1-2, frm 2) 1998 AW 1-5: (6f 2, 7f 1-2, 9f) (Equi 1-2, Fibr 3)
Above-average filly, has worn blinkers, likes left handed tracks, likes tight tracks. Turf high 67. AW high 78.
**B Smart [0-3] Miss N Jefford (from P J Makin [2-6] Jun 1998).*

LETHAL HOPE (IRE) BHB 77f **RR 67f** 4243[12]
2 b c Mujtahid(USA) 7.4f **(69)** -Vian (USA)(Far Out East (USA))8.4f **(65)**
Form - 3830
Record 1998 - 1st:0 2nd:0 3rd:2 Ran:4
Win Prizemoney £0 *Total Prizemoney* £1,024
1998 Turf 0-4: (6f 4) (gd, g-f 2, frm)
Average colt. Turf high 67.
**J Noseda [0-1] Saleh Al Homeizi (from R Hannon [0-3] Jly 1998).*

LEVEL HEADED BHB 40f **RR 38f** 5006[4]
3 b f Beveled (USA) 6.9f **(64)** - Snowline (Bay Express) 7.1f **(60)**
Form - 7064
Record 1998 - 1st:0 2nd:0 3rd:0 Ran:4
1998 Turf 0-4: (6f, 7f, 8f 2) (sft, gd 2, g-f)
Leggy, very moderate filly. Turf high 38 (began Spt).
**E A Wheeler [0-4] Anthony Harrison.*

LEVELLED BHB 90f **RR 87f** 5169a[5]
4 b g Beveled (USA) 6.9f **(64)** - Baino Charm (USA) (Diesis) 9.3f **(69)**
Form - 406060020217012134205
Record 1998 - 1st:3 2nd:4 3rd:1 Ran:21
Pre1998 - 1st:4 2nd:1 3rd:4 Ran:19
Win Prizemoney £28,216 *Total Prizemoney* £45,592
Wins * **1998** Spt Yarmou (G-S) H 5.2f 76 81 <
* **1998** Aug Lingfi (G-F) 6f 80
* **1998** Aug Bright (FRM) H 6f 67 71
* 1997 Spt Bright (FRM) H 5.3f 70 75
* 1997 Jun Bright (FRM) H 6f 68 69
* 1997 Apr Folkes (G-F) C 5f 65
* 1996 Aug Carlis (FRM) 5f 58
1998 Turf 3-21: (5f 1-12, 6f 2-9) (hvy, sft, g-s, gd 1-7, g-f 2-7, frm 4)
Unfurnished, useful gelding, effective 5 to 6f, best at 5f, acts on gd to g-f, best on gd, prefers left handed tracks, excels at Brighton. Turf high 90 - 3rd of 9 getting 11lb from To the Roof (27 Spt Ascot 5f gd RF 4516) - also 1st of 19 giving 9lb to Eastern Prophets (15 Spt Yarmouth RF 4274). Consistent. He had another very busy campaign, and showed his best form in the second half of the season. He won three handicaps, and ran several other good races despite going up in the weights, including missing out in three photos. **M R Channon [7-40] & Mrs Gary Pinchen.*

LEVITICUS (IRE) BHB 75f **RR 80df** 2747[11]
4 b g Law Society (USA) 11.6f **(71)** - Rubbiera (IRE) (Pitskelly) 8.5f **(53)**
Form - 00
Record 1998 - 1st:0 2nd:0 3rd:0 Ran:2
Pre1998 - 1st:1 2nd:1 3rd:3 Ran:12
Win Prizemoney £4,056 *Total Prizemoney* £7,953
Wins * 1997 Aug Thirsk (G-F) H 16f 73 80 <
1998 Turf 0-2: (16f, 20f) (gd 2)
Scopey, decent gelding, effective 10 to 16f, acts on gd to frm. Turf high 34. Much better over hurdles.
**T P Tate [4-19] Mrs S L Worthington.*

LIBERALIS BHB 20f **RR** 3523[11]
3 ch f Interrex (CAN) 7.7f **(51)** - Hello Lady (Wolverlife) 9.3f **(54)**
Form - 0
Record 1998 - 1st:0 2nd:0 3rd:0 Ran:1
Pre1998 - 1st:0 2nd:0 3rd:0 Ran:3
1998 Turf 0-1: (8f) (frm)
Unfurnished, formerly very poor filly.
**G F H Charles-Jones [0-4] V K Cox.*

LIBERTY LINES (USA) RR 78f 5139[2]
2 b c Zilzal (USA)8.5f **(79)** -Bold 'n Determined (USA) (Bold And Brave)
Form - 02
Record 1998 - 1st:0 2nd:1 3rd:0 Ran:2
Win Prizemoney £0 *Total Prizemoney* £1,251
1998 Turf 0-2: (6f, 7f) (gd, g-f)
Currently above-average colt. Turf high 78 (began Spt) - 2nd of 22 to Mutaakkid (6 Nov Doncaster 6f gd RF 5139).
**B W Hills [0-2] Maktoum Al Maktoum.*

LIBRA STAR (USA) BHB 84f84a **RR 88f 84a** 3311[4]
3 b c Hermitage (USA) 8.6f **(84)** - Aromalibra (USA) (Galaxy Libra) 8.1f **(82)**
Form - 21284
Record 1998 - 1st:1 2nd:2 3rd:0 Ran:5
Win Prizemoney £2,274 *Total Prizemoney* £5,233
Wins 1998 *Feb Lingfi (SLW) 8f 86* <
1998 Turf 0-3: (8f, 9f, 10f) (g-s, gd 2) 1998 AW 1-2: (8f 1-2) (Equi 1-1, Fibr)
Tall, useful colt. Turf high 88. AW high 86 - 1st of 9 from Di Matteo (28 Feb Lingfield RF 0377). Showed ability in his early starts on sand, including winning a Lingfield maiden. He then changed stables but, after running quite well on his Turf debut, disappointed badly afterwards.
**J G FitzGerald [0-3] Lord Lloyd-Webber (from D R Loder [1-2] Feb 1998).*

LIDANNA RR 109f 4431a[4]
5 b m Nicholas (USA) 6.1f **(63)** - Shapely Test (USA) (Elocutionist (USA)) 8f **(77)**
Form - 4131864
1998 Turf 2-7: (5f 2-5, 6f 2) (hvy, sft 1-1, gd 4, frm 1-1)
Pattern-class filly, effective 5f, acts on sft to frm. Turf high 109 - 1st of 7 giving 3lb to Strike Hard (1 Jun Leopardstown RF 1839a) - also 1st of 5 getting 7lb from Carhue Lass (7 May Tipperary RF 1180a). She finds life tough in handicaps and does all her winning in Listed or Group Three events. Three of her last four wins have been gained in photo-finishes and she seems best when held up for a last-gasp effort.
**D Hanley in IRE [4-12] McLoughlin Family Syndicate.*

LIDO (IRE) BHB 87f **RR 86f** 1219[9]
3 ch c Waajib 8.9f **(67)** - Licimba (GER) (Konigsstuhl (GER)) 11.2f **(76)**
Form - 20
Record 1998 - 1st:0 2nd:1 3rd:0 Ran:2
Pre1998 - 1st:1 2nd:2 3rd:1 Ran:7
Win Prizemoney £2,792 *Total Prizemoney* £8,703
Wins * 1997 Jly Bath (G-F) 5.7f 85+ <
1998 Turf 0-2: (7f 2) (gd 2)
Leggy, useful colt, effective 6 to 7f, best at 7f, acts on gd to frm, best on gd. Turf high 86 (1st run) - 2nd of 21 getting 2lb from Jila (14 Apr Newmarket 7f gd RF 0682). A winner at Bath at two, he ran a fine second in a competitive Newmarket handicap on his return, and met with an interrupted passage on his only start. One to watch if returning sound.
**B W Hills [1-9] Guy Reed.*

LIFE OF RILEY BHB 86f **RR 89f** 4850[26]
4 ch c Caerleon (USA) 10.9f **(79)** - Catina (Nureyev (USA)) 8.7f **(78)**
Form - 71221000
Record 1998 - 1st:2 2nd:2 3rd:0 Ran:8
Pre1998 - 1st:1 2nd:0 3rd:1 Ran:5
Win Prizemoney £12,913 *Total Prizemoney* £18,154
Wins * **1998** Jly Sandow (GD) H 16.4f 85 89 <
* **1998** May Kempto (G-F) H 14.4f 76 81
1997 Jun Pontef (G-F) 10f 74
1998 Turf 2-8: (12f, 14f 1-2, 16f 1-4, 18f) (gd 1-6, g-f 1-2)
Scopey, useful colt, effective 12 to 16f, best at 16f, acts on gd to g-f, best on gd, has worn blinkers, prefers right handed tracks, prefers tight tracks, does well at Kempton. Turf high 89 - 1st of 12 giving 32lb to Bridie's Pride (4 Jly Sandown RF 2551) - also 1st of 8 giving 1lb to Russian Rose (17 May Kempton RF 1280). Made all on his first attempt at fourteen furlongs, and stayed the two miles well when winning at Sandown. Lost his way afterwards.
**B J Meehan [2-8] John Manley (from G Lewis [1-5] Spt 1997).*

LIFT BOY (USA) BHB 35f37a **RR 47f 37a** 5127[7]
9 b g Fighting Fit (USA) 7.9f **(70)** - Pressure Seat (USA) (Ginistrelli (USA)) 5.6f **(66)**
Form - 80566334070706087
Record 1998 - 1st:0 2nd:0 3rd:2 Ran:15
Pre1998 - 1st:8 2nd:7 3rd:9 Ran:68
Win Prizemoney £20,846 *Total Prizemoney* £30,215
Wins * 1997 *Feb Lingfi (STD) H 7f 58 60*
1996 Jun Folkes (G-F) S 5f 50
1996 *Mar Wolver (STD) H 6f 61 66* <
1996 *Feb Lingfi (STD) C 5f 58*
1996 *Jan Lingfi (STD) C 5f 53*
1995 May Lingfi (G-F) SH 5f 42 44
1995 *Jan Wolver (STD) C 6f 60*
1998 Turf 0-7: (5f, 6f 2, 7f 3, 8f) (g-s, gd 2, g-f 2, frm 2) 1998 AW 0-8: (7f 4, 8f 3, 10f) (Equi 8)
Moderate gelding, effective 7f, - acts on Equi, has worn blinkers. Turf high 47. AW high 44. A multiple winner on Equitrack over the years, he has been below form of late.
**G L Moore [1-24] A Moore (from A Moore [6-41] Jan 1997).*

LIFT THE OFFER (IRE) BHB 58f82a **RR 69f 82a** 4927[5]
3 ch c Ballad Rock 7.2f **(63)** - Timissara (USA) (Shahrastani (USA)) 8.8f **(72)**
Form - 110377368685
Record 1998 - 1st:0 2nd:0 3rd:2 Ran:10
Pre1998 - 1st:2 2nd:1 3rd:1 Ran:7
Win Prizemoney £6,272 *Total Prizemoney* £9,220
Wins * 1997 *Nov Lingfi (STD) 7f 67+*
* 1997 *Nov Lingfi (STD) H 8f 68 77* <
1998 Turf 0-10: (7f, 8f 5, 9f, 10f 2, 11f) (g-s, gd 4, g-f 2, frm 3)
Scopey, above-average colt, effective 7 to 8f, best at 8f, acts on gd to frm - acts on Equi, has worn blinkers, likes left handed tracks. Turf high 71 - 3rd of 7 getting 8lb from Rachaels North (15 May Nottingham 8f frm RF 1249). Showed early promise, and thrived on the Lingfield Equitrack with two victories in November 1997. Fair form on turf last season, but would be interesting back on Equitrack.
**R Hannon [2-17] Broadgate II.*

LIGHT FINGERED (IRE) BHB 95f **RR 88f** 2378[3]
2 ch c Soviet Lad (USA) 9.4f **(63)** - Light Hand (Star Appeal) 9.6f **(65)**
Form - 6113
Record 1998 - 1st:2 2nd:0 3rd:1 Ran:4
Win Prizemoney £6,379 *Total Prizemoney* £7,176
Wins * **1998** Jun Epsom (GD) 7f 88 <
* **1998** Jun Carlis (G-S) 5f 76
1998 Turf 2-4: (5f 1-2, 6f, 7f 1-1) (g-f 2-3, frm)
Useful colt. Turf high 88 - also 1st of 6 giving 3lb to Dreaming (24 Jun Epsom RF 2237). Looked to need further when winning over the minimum at Carlisle, and appreciated the step up to seven when adding a victory at Epsom. The drop to six contributed to his defeat in a warm little conditions race next time.
**M H Tompkins [2-4] Robert Levitt.*

LIGHTNING ARROW (USA) BHB 100f **RR 90f** 5065[1]
2 br c Silver Hawk (USA) 11.2f **(85)** - Strait Lane (USA) (Chieftain II) 10.4f **(75)**
Form - 6221
Record 1998 - 1st:1 2nd:2 3rd:0 Ran:4

Win Prizemoney £5,643 *Total Prizemoney* £8,829
Wins * **1998** Oct Newmar (G-S) 8f 90 <
1998 Turf 1-4: (7f, 8f 1-3) (gd, g-f 1-1, frm 2)
Useful colt. Turf high 90 (began Aug) - 1st of 13 getting 2lb from Sossus Vlei (30 Oct Newmarket RF 5065). Narrow runner-up in two maidens before getting of the mark in a Newmarket conditions event. He should continue to progress when stepped up in trip next season. **J L Dunlop [1-4] Wafic Said.*

LIGHTNING BLAZE BHB 60f RR 74+f 4490[8]

2 ch f Cosmonaut - Royal Deed (USA) (Shadeed (USA)) 8.2f **(70)**
Form - 031012113708
Record 1998 - 1st:4 2nd:1 3rd:2 Ran:12
Win Prizemoney £8,524 *Total Prizemoney* £10,224
Wins 1998 Jly Folkes (G-F) C 5f 64
1998 Jly Beverl (G-F) C 5f 64
1998 Jun Folkes (G-F) S 5f 74+ <
1998 *Jun Wolver (STD) S 5f 62*
1998 Turf 3-11: (5f 3-10, 6f) (gd, g-f 1-5, frm 2-5) 1998 AW 1-1: (5f 1-1) (Fibr 1-1)
Above-average filly, effective 5f, acts on g-f to frm, best on frm. Turf high 74 - 1st of 8 from Polly Mills (26 Jun Folkestone RF 2294). (1st run). Paid her way in lowly company for first-season trainer Phil McEntee.
**J Pearce [0-2] Mrs K J Crangle (from P S McEntee [4-9] Aug 1998).*

LIGHTNING REBEL BHB 42f38a RR 45df 38a 925[18]

4 b g Rambo Dancer (CAN) 8.4f **(59)** - Ozra (Red Alert) 7.6f **(66)**
Form - 00
Record 1998 - 1st:0 2nd:0 3rd:0 Ran:2
Pre1998 - 1st:0 2nd:1 3rd:0 Ran:7
Win Prizemoney £0 *Total Prizemoney* £796
1998 Turf 0-1: (12f) (gd) 1998 AW 0-1: (9f) (Fibr)
Light-framed, moderate gelding. Becoming disappointing.
**P W Hiatt [0-2] P W Hiatt (from C W Thornton [0-7] Aug 1997).*

LIGHT ON THE WAVES RR 69f 3741[2]

2 b f Greensmith - Roof Dancer (Martinmas) 7.6f **(59)**
Form - 62
Record 1998 - 1st:0 2nd:1 3rd:0 Ran:2
Win Prizemoney £0 *Total Prizemoney* £564
1998 Turf 0-2: (6f 2) (gd, frm)
Currently average filly. Turf high 69 (began Aug) - 2nd of 14 to Indian City (19 Aug Leicester 6f frm RF 3741).
**M C Pipe [0-2] Paul Neczypir.*

LIGHT REFLECTIONS BHB 37f RR 29f 2969[7]

5 b g Rainbow Quest (USA) 11.2f **(81)** - Tajfah (USA) (Shadeed (USA)) 8.2f **(70)**
Form - 007
Record 1998 - 1st:0 2nd:0 3rd:0 Ran:3
Pre1998 - 1st:0 2nd:0 3rd:0 Ran:4
Win Prizemoney £0 *Total Prizemoney* £151
1998 Turf 0-2: (12f, 17f) (g-f, frm) 1998 AW 0-1: (15f) (Fibr)
Little account gelding. Turf high 29.
**P G Murphy [0-6] Miss J Collison (from B W Hills [0-1] Aug 1995).*

LIGHT SHIP BHB 63f58a RR 67f 58a 4996[12]

3 b f Warning 8.1f **(77)** - Bireme (Grundy) 10.3f **(65)**
Form - 4430
Record 1998 - 1st:0 2nd:0 3rd:1 Ran:4
Win Prizemoney £0 *Total Prizemoney* £1,058
1998 Turf 0-3: (8f 3) (g-f 2, frm) 1998 AW 0-1: (10f) (Equi)
Unfurnished, average filly. Turf high 67 (1st run) (began Aug) - 4th of 14 to A Touch of Frost (7 Aug Salisbury 8f frm RF 3443).
**M P Tregoning [0-4] R D Hollingsworth.*

LIGHTS OF HOME BHB 45f39a RR 48f 39a 1812[6]

4 b g Deploy 11.4f **(67)** - Dream Chaser (Record Token) 6.3f **(53)**
Form - 00636
Record 1998 - 1st:0 2nd:0 3rd:1 Ran:5
Pre1998 - 1st:0 2nd:0 3rd:0 Ran:5
Win Prizemoney £0 *Total Prizemoney* £453
1998 Turf 0-5: (5f, 6f, 10f 2, 11f) (g-s, gd, g-f 2, frm)
Workmanlike, moderate gelding. Turf high 48.
**Miss C Johnsey [0-8] T A Johnsey (from R Hannon [0-2] Nov 1996).*

LIGHT STEP (USA) BHB 88f RR 85f 4507[5]

3 b f Nureyev (USA) 8.4f **(84)** - Nimble Feet (USA) (Danzig (USA)) 8.4f **(76)**
Form - 22115
Record 1998 - 1st:2 2nd:2 3rd:0 Ran:5
Pre1998 - 1st:0 2nd:0 3rd:2 Ran:3
Win Prizemoney £16,187 *Total Prizemoney* £20,575
Wins * **1998** Aug Newcas (GD) LH 10.1f 81 85 <
* **1998** Aug Yarmou (FRM) 10.1f 58++
1998 Turf 2-5: (7f, 9f, 10f 2-3) (sft, gd 2, frm 2-2)
Neat, useful filly, effective 7 to 10f, acts on sft to frm. Turf high 85 - 1st of 12 getting 8lb from Karakia (31 Aug Newcastle RF 3992). She had shown plenty of ability in maiden and handicap company before gaining a confidence-boosting win in an awful Yarmouth maiden in August. Followed up in a valuable Newcastle handicap when she had to really battle, but did it well.
**H R A Cecil [2-8] K Abdulla.*

LIGHT THE ROCKET (IRE) BHB 100f RR 90f 4242[12]

2 ch c Pips Pride 6.7f **(70)** - Coolrain Lady (IRE) (Common Grounds)
Form - 7271140
Record 1998 - 1st:2 2nd:1 3rd:0 Ran:7
Win Prizemoney £10,457 *Total Prizemoney* £13,747
Wins * **1998** Aug Ascot (G-F) 5f 90 <
* **1998** Aug Sandow (GD) 5f 83+
1998 Turf 2-7: (5f 2-6, 6f) (gd 1-4, g-f 1-2, frm)
Useful colt, effective 5f, acts on gd to g-f, best on gd. Turf high 90 - 1st of 5 getting 6lb from Queensland Star (8 Aug Ascot RF 3456) - also 1st of 8 from Sunley Sense (2 Aug Sandown RF 3297). He looked an improving sort when putting up a convincing display in a Sandown maiden, and followed up in a better race at Ascot. However, he looked a bit out of his depth in a Listed race at Deauville and in the Flying Childers. **R Hannon [2-7] M Mulholland.*

LIGNE GAGNANTE (IRE) BHB 73f RR 69f 4732[8]

2 b c Turtle Island (IRE) - Lightino (Bustino) 10.4f **(64)**
Form - 7648
Record 1998 - 1st:0 2nd:0 3rd:0 Ran:4
Win Prizemoney £0 *Total Prizemoney* £241
1998 Turf 0-4: (6f 3, 7f) (g-s, g-f, frm 2)
Average colt. Turf high 69 (began Aug).
**W J Haggas [0-4] The Winning Line.*

LIKELY STORY (IRE) BHB 92f RR 85f 4844[16]

3 b f Night Shift (USA) 8.1f **(73)** - Perfect Alibi (Law Society (USA)) 9.9f **(70)**
Form - 010
Record 1998 - 1st:1 2nd:0 3rd:0 Ran:3
Pre1998 - 1st:1 2nd:2 3rd:1 Ran:7
Win Prizemoney £15,764 *Total Prizemoney* £19,175
Wins * **1998** Aug Cheste (G-S) L 6.1f 84 <
* 1997 Aug Epsom (GD) 6f 84 <
1998 Turf 1-3: (6f 1-3) (gd, g-f 1-2)
Unfurnished, useful filly, effective 6f, acts on gd to g-f, best on gd. Turf high 85 (began Jly) - also 1st of 6 from Demolition Jo (2 Aug Chester RF 3286). Consistent. Lightly raced in 1998, she got up on the line to win a weak listed race at Chester in August.
**J L Dunlop [2-10] Michael Page.*

LILANITA BHB 47f RR 45f 5006[5]

3 b f Anita's Prince 6f **(62)** - Jimlil (Nicholas Bill) 10.1f **(56)**
Form - 40012036005
Record 1998 - 1st:1 2nd:1 3rd:1 Ran:11
Pre1998 - 1st:0 2nd:0 3rd:0 Ran:2
Win Prizemoney £2,374 *Total Prizemoney* £3,539
Wins * **1998** Jun Chepst (G-S) S 8.1f 53 <
1998 Turf 1-11: (6f, 7f 2, 8f 1-6, 10f 2) (sft, gd 1-7, frm 3)
Neat, moderate filly, effective 8 to 10f, best at 8f, acts on gd to frm, best on gd. Turf high 61 - 2nd of 10 getting 5lb from Iron Mountain (13 Jly Brighton 10f gd RF 2762) - also 1st of 12 from Tui (30 Jun Chepstow RF 2393). Consistent. **B Palling [1-13] Mrs M M Palling.*

LILLI CLAIRE BHB 105f RR 107f 4733[1]

5 ch m Beveled (USA) 6.9f **(64)** - Lillicara (FR) (Caracolero (USA)) 8.2f **(57)**
Form - 661507018801
Record 1998 - 1st:3 2nd:0 3rd:0 Ran:12

Pre1998 - 1st:5 2nd:2 3rd:1 Ran:16
Win Prizemoney £77,584 *Total Prizemoney* £84,079

Wins								
* 1998	Oct	Ascot	(SFT)	L	8f		107	<
* 1998	Spt	Epsom	(GD)	L	8.5f		96	
* 1998	Jun	Epsom	(GD)	L	8.5f		99	
1997	May	Lingfi	(GD)		7.6f		92+	
1996	Jly	Newmar	(GD)	H	7f	85	87	
1996	May	Salisb	(G-F)	H	8f	74	77	
1995	Spt	Goodwo	(GD)	S	7f		72	
1995	Aug	Windso	(GD)	S	6f		64	

1998 Turf 3-12: (7f 4, 8f 1-6, 9f 2-2) (g-s 1-1, gd 2-6, g-f 4, frm)
Pattern-class filly, effective 8 to 9f, best at 8f, acts on g-s to gd, best on gd. Turf high 107 - 1st of 8 giving 6lb to Equity Princess (9 Oct Ascot RF 4733) - also 1st of 8 giving 12lb to Jinsiyah (5 Jun Epsom RF 1749). This smashing mare had a great season for her new trainer, winning three Listed races around a mile. Consistency is not her forte, but when everything slots into place she is useful and, like most Beveleds, she prefers some give underfoot.
**D R C Elsworth [3-12] C Leafe (from A G Foster [5-16] May 1997).*

LIMEHOUSE BLUES RR 5013[6]

3 b g Hamas (IRE) 8f **(72)** - Gertrude Lawrence (Ballymore) 7.3f **(64)**
Form - 6
Record 1998 - 1st:0 2nd:0 3rd:0 Ran:1
1998 Turf 0-1: (11f) (gd)
Leggy, currently very poor gelding - 6th of 6 getting 6lb from Filial (27 Oct Redcar 11f gd RF 5013). **R Ingram [0-1] Ms Ann Cully.*

LIMELIGHT BHB 43f52a RR 50f 52a 4458[10]

4 b f Old Vic 12.8f **(72)** - Nellie Dean (Song) 7.2f **(61)**
Form - 2588460
Record 1998 - 1st:0 2nd:1 3rd:0 Ran:7
Pre1998 - 1st:0 2nd:0 3rd:1 Ran:7
Win Prizemoney £0 *Total Prizemoney* £1,712
1998 Turf 0-7: (12f, 13f, 14f, 15f, 16f, 17f 2) (g-s, gd 2, g-f, frm 3)
Workmanlike, fair filly, effective 10 to 17f, acts on g-s to frm, has worn blinkers, prefers left handed tracks, favours tight tracks. Turf high 54 (1st run) - 2nd of 10 getting 7lb from Raspberry Sauce (28 Apr Bath 12f g-s RF 0896). Consistent.
**P G Murphy [1-12] SB Partners (from J A R Toller [0-7] Spt 1997).*

LIME STREET BLUES (IRE) BHB 51f65a RR 58f 65a 4506[13]

7 b g Digamist (USA) 8.8f **(56)** - Royal Daughter (High Top) 10.2f **(67)**
Form - 0
Record 1998 - 1st:0 2nd:0 3rd:0 Ran:1
Pre1998 - 1st:2 2nd:2 3rd:2 Ran:21
Win Prizemoney £9,316 *Total Prizemoney* £14,577
1998 Turf 0-1: (14f) (gd)
Fair gelding, effective 14f, acts on gd to frm, best on frm, favours tight tracks. Inconsistent.
**T Keddy [0-17] The Blues Partnership (from R Hannon [2-13] Aug 1994).*

LIMPID RR 120f 4727a[12]

3 b c Soviet Star (USA) 8.6f **(74)** - Isle Of Glass (USA) (Affirmed (USA)) 9.3f **(79)**
Form - 1150
1998 Turf 2-4: (7f 1-1, 10f 1-2, 12f) (sft 1-2, gd 1-1, g-f)
Very high-class colt. Turf high 120 - 1st of 7 from Almutawakel (21 Jun Longchamp RF 2290a). This French-trained colt met with trouble in running in the Juddmonte International at York, but was beaten only a length and a half into fifth. He had progressed steadily beforehand, relishing the ten furlongs on fast round when landing the Group One Grand Prix de Paris in June. He may not have got home when tried at twelve furlongs in the Arc, will race under the Godolphin banner in 1999.
**A Fabre in FR [2-4] Sheikh Mohammed.*

LINCOLN DEAN RR 68f 5037[10]

2 b c Mtoto 11.5f **(71)** - Play With Me (IRE) (Alzao (USA)) 7.1f **(68)**
Form - 80
Record 1998 - 1st:0 2nd:0 3rd:0 Ran:2
1998 Turf 0-2: (7f 2) (g-s, frm)
Currently average colt. Turf high 68 (began Oct).
**Sir Mark Prescott [0-2] Cyril Humphris.*

LINDAS GEM BHB 56f RR 55df 4569[11]

2 ch f Kasakov - Kabella (Kabour)
Form - 2040
Record 1998 - 1st:0 2nd:1 3rd:0 Ran:4
Win Prizemoney £0 *Total Prizemoney* £1,060
1998 Turf 0-4: (5f 4) (gd 3, g-f)
Fair filly. Turf high 64. **Mrs L Stubbs [0-4] D M Smith.*

LINDESBERG BHB 52f RR 58df 3488[14]

3 b f Doyoun 10.7f **(69)** - Be Discreet (Junius (USA)) 7.7f **(65)**
Form - 248000
Record 1998 - 1st:0 2nd:1 3rd:0 Ran:6
Pre1998 - 1st:0 2nd:1 3rd:1 Ran:3
Win Prizemoney £0 *Total Prizemoney* £3,031
1998 Turf 0-6: (6f, 7f 3, 8f 2) (sft, gd 3, frm 2)
Scopey, fair filly, effective 6f, acts on gd, has worn blinkers. Turf high 58. Becoming disappointing.
**M Johnston [0-9] Brian Yeardley Continental Ltd.*

LINDRICK LADY (IRE) BHB 37f RR 38f 1741[8]

4 b f Broken Hearted 10.1f **(65)** - Fiodoir (Weavers' Hall) 9.8f **(53)**
Form - 000808
Record 1998 - 1st:0 2nd:0 3rd:0 Ran:6
Pre1998 - 1st:3 2nd:1 3rd:0 Ran:11
Win Prizemoney £8,827 *Total Prizemoney* £9,784

Wins								
* 1997	Jly	Beverl	(HVY)	H	9.9f	67	69	<
* 1997	May	Beverl	(G-S)	H	12f	65	66	
* 1997	May	Beverl	(SFT)	C	7.5f		62	

1998 Turf 0-6: (8f 2, 10f 2, 12f 2) (sft, g-s, gd, frm 2, hrd)
Leggy, very moderate filly, effective 7 to 12f, acts on sft to gd, prefers right handed tracks, favours tight tracks. Turf high 38.
**B S Rothwell [3-17] S P Hudson.*

LINEA-G BHB 39f RR 41f 4409[9]

4 ch f Keen 11.1f **(58)** - Horton Line (High Line) 10.3f **(70)**
Form - 4700
Record 1998 - 1st:0 2nd:0 3rd:0 Ran:4
Pre1998 - 1st:0 2nd:0 3rd:0 Ran:3
1998 Turf 0-3: (10f 2, 11f) (g-f 2, frm) 1998 AW 0-1: (12f) (Fibr)
Rangy, moderate filly. Turf high 41 (began Aug). A half-sister to Angus-G, she is taking time to get the hang of things.
**Mrs M Reveley [0-10] W Ginzel.*

LINEAGE BHB 63f RR 66f 4415[5]

3 b f Distant Relative 7f **(69)** - Hymne D'Amour (USA) (Dixieland Band (USA)) 7f **(74)**
Form - 65535
Record 1998 - 1st:0 2nd:0 3rd:1 Ran:5
Pre1998 - 1st:0 2nd:0 3rd:0 Ran:1
Win Prizemoney £0 *Total Prizemoney* £421
1998 Turf 0-5: (8f 2, 10f 2, 12f) (g-s, gd, g-f 2, frm)
Scopey, average filly, effective 8f, acts on frm. Turf high 69.
**N A Graham [0-6] The Earl Cadogan.*

LINE CALL RR 75f 5138[4]

2 b c Second Set (IRE) 9.2f **(67)** - Misguided (Homing) 7.8f **(59)**
Form - 4
Record 1998 - 1st:0 2nd:0 3rd:0 Ran:1
Win Prizemoney £0 *Total Prizemoney* £225
1998 Turf 0-1: (7f) (gd)
Currently above-average colt.
**D W P Arbuthnot [0-1] T D Holland-Martin.*

LINGUISTIC DANCER BHB 29f RR 27f 4995[8]

3 ch f Aragon 7.7f **(58)** - Linguistic (Porto Bello) 8.9f **(43)**
Form - 0060008
Record 1998 - 1st:0 2nd:0 3rd:0 Ran:7
Pre1998 - 1st:0 2nd:0 3rd:0 Ran:1
1998 Turf 0-6: (7f 2, 8f 4) (sft, gd 2, g-f, frm 2) 1998 AW 0-1: (6f) (Fibr)
Light-framed, little account filly. Turf high 27.
**A G Newcombe [0-8] Panamarenko.M Ellis, Patel.*

LINK HILL RR 34f 5071[15]

2 ch f Generous (IRE) 11.5f **(82)** - Phaleria (USA) (Lyphard (USA)) 9.9f **(72)**
Form - 0
Record 1998 - 1st:0 2nd:0 3rd:0 Ran:1

1998 Turf 0-1: (7f) (gd)
Currently very moderate filly. **Mrs A J Perrett [0-1] K Abdulla.*

LINNETSONG BHB 35f34a RR 16f 34a 4485[22]

3 b f Rambo Dancer (CAN) 8.4f **(59)** - Blue Linnet (Habitat) 9.4f **(70)**
Form - 00070000000

Record					
	1998 -	1st:0	2nd:0	3rd:0	Ran:10
	Pre1998 -	1st:1	2nd:0	3rd:0	Ran:7

Win Prizemoney £2,272 *Total Prizemoney* £2,522
Wins 1997 Jun Redcar (GD) S 7f 62 <
1998 Turf 0-5: (6f 4, 7f) (g-s, gd, g-f, frm 2) 1998 AW 0-5: (5f, 6f, 7f 2, 8f) (Fibr 5)
Scopey, little account filly, effective 7f, acts on g-f, mostly wears blinkers. Turf high 16. AW high 26.
**D W Chapman [0-11] M J Cowie (from G R Oldroyd [1-6] Spt 1997).*

LION CUB (IRE) BHB 60f RR 58f 4814[7]

2 b g Catrail (USA) - Lightly Dancing (FR) (Groom Dancer (USA))
Form - 007
Record 1998 - 1st:0 2nd:0 3rd:0 Ran:3
1998 Turf 0-3: (6f, 7f, 8f) (gd 2, frm)
Currently fair gelding. Turf high 58 (began Spt).
**J E Banks [0-3] The Allez France 4.*

LIONHEARTED (IRE) RR 68f 5063[9]

2 b c Catrail (USA) - Quiche (Formidable (USA)) 9.2f **(63)**
Form - 0
Record 1998 - 1st:0 2nd:0 3rd:0 Ran:1
1998 Turf 0-1: (6f) (g-f)
Currently average colt. **J H M Gosden [0-1] Sheikh Mohammed.*

Pre1998 - 1st:4 2nd:0 3rd:0 Ran:10
Win Prizemoney £17,106 *Total Prizemoney* £17,638

Wins									
	* 1997	*Dec*	*Wolver*	*(STD)*	*H*	*8.5f*	*93*	*97*	<
	* 1997	*Dec*	*Lingfi*	*(G-S)*		*8f*		*87*	
	* 1997	Oct	Leices	(GD)	H	8f	80	84	
	1996	Apr	Newmar	(G-F)		7f		76	

1998 Turf 0-4: (8f 4) (gd 2, frm 2)
Very useful colt, effective 8f, - acts on AW, often wears blinkers (extremely effectively), likes left handed tracks. Turf high 83. In good heart on the sand during the winter, gaining impressive wins in a Lingfield conditions event and a Wolverhampton handicap. He did not shown the same level of form in warm handicaps on turf, but would be an ideal sort to continue his career on dirt in the States.
**Mrs J Cecil [3-9] Lord Howard de Walden (from P W Chapple-Hyam [1-5] May 1997).*

LISALA BHB 39f RR 55f 3897[15]

2 ch f Beveled (USA) 6.9f **(64)** - Super Style (Artaius (USA)) 9f **(69)**
Form - 3700
Record 1998 - 1st:0 2nd:0 3rd:1 Ran:4
Win Prizemoney £0 *Total Prizemoney* £260
1998 Turf 0-4: (7f 4) (gd 2, g-f, frm)
Fair filly. Turf high 55 (1st run) - 3rd of 10 to Fizzy Whizzy (20 Jun Redcar 7f gd RF 2154). **W G M Turner [0-4] Mrs L Wayne.*

LISA'S PRIDE (IRE) BHB 64f RR 56f 3447[7]

3 ch f Pips Pride 6.7f **(70)** - Brazilian Princess (Absalom) 7.2f **(58)**
Form - 07
Record 1998 - 1st:0 2nd:0 3rd:0 Ran:2

Literary Society hit form at the Ebor meeting

LIONIZE (USA) BHB 80f100a RR 83f 100a 2056[30]

5 ch h Storm Cat (USA) 7f **(86)** - Pedestal (High Line) 10.3f **(70)**
Form - 4110050
Record 1998 - 1st:0 2nd:0 3rd:0 Ran:4

Pre1998 - 1st:1 2nd:0 3rd:0 Ran:6
Win Prizemoney £2,581 *Total Prizemoney* £2,581
Wins 1997 Jun Salisb (G-F) 6f 73 <

1998 Turf 0-2: (6f, 10f) (sft, frm)
Workmanlike, fair filly, effective 6f, acts on hrd. Turf high 56. Inconsistent.
**Mrs L Stubbs [0-1] A P Griffin (from Miss Gay Kelleway [1-7] Apr 1998).*

LITERARY SOCIETY (USA) BHB 95f **RR 94f** 4821[16]
5 ch h Runaway Groom (CAN) 8.1f **(69)** - Dancing Gull (USA) (Northern Dancer) 9.6f **(80)**
Form - 115010
Record 1998 - 1st:3 2nd:0 3rd:0 Ran:6
Pre1998 - 1st:4 2nd:4 3rd:3 Ran:20
Win Prizemoney £48,171 *Total Prizemoney* £57,798
Wins * **1998** Aug York (G-F) H 6f 90 94 <
* **1998** Jun Yarmou (GD) 6f 91
* **1998** May Newmar (G-F) H 5f 83 86
* 1997 Jly Newbur (G-F) H 6f 77 77
* 1997 May Newmar (G-F) H 5f 71 74
* 1996 Aug Thirsk (GD) H 5f 66 67+
* 1996 Jly Bright (FRM) 5.3f 61
1998 Turf 3-6: (5f 1-3, 6f 2-3) (gd 1-3, g-f 2-2, frm)
Useful colt, effective 5 to 6f, best at 6f, acts on gd to g-f, best on gd. Turf high 94 - 1st of 23 giving 4lb to Lago Di Varano (18 Aug York RF 3699) - also 1st of 6 giving 3lb to Taoiste (22 Jun Yarmouth RF 2188). Consistent. Won his first two starts of the season, a Newmarket handicap and a Yarmouth classified event, and was not disgraced in a competitive Ascot handicap nor in the Stewards' Cup. Regained winning form in a hot sprint handicap at the Ebor meeting, and his only poor effort came at Newmarket on his final start. **J A R Toller [7-26] Lady Celina Carter.*

LITIGATE (USA) BHB 57f63a **RR 58f 63a** 4663[18]
2 b c Alydeed (CAN) 8f **(81)** - Saucy Action (USA) (Grand Central)
Form - 546480
Record 1998 - 1st:0 2nd:0 3rd:0 Ran:6
Win Prizemoney £0 *Total Prizemoney* £198
1998 Turf 0-4: (6f, 7f 2, 10f)(g-s, gd, g-f, frm) 1998 AW 0-2: 7f 2)(Fibr 2)
Above-average colt, has worn blinkers. Turf high 58. AW high 70.
**R Hannon [0-6] Highclere Thoroughbred Racing Ltd.*

LITTLE ACORN BHB 82f65a **RR 85f 65a** 4810[2]
4 b g Unfuwain (USA) 11.4f **(74)** - Plaything (High Top) 10.2f **(67)**
Form - 300708102
Record 1998 - 1st:1 2nd:1 3rd:1 Ran:9
Pre1998 - 1st:2 2nd:4 3rd:1 Ran:10
Win Prizemoney £14,472 *Total Prizemoney* £22,702
Wins * **1998** Spt Goodwo (G-S) H 16f 77 82 <
* 1997 Apr Carlis (GD) H 12f 74 76
* 1997 Mar Catter (GD) H 12f 65 66
1998 Turf 1-9: (14f, 16f 1-7, 20f) (hvy, sft, g-s 1-1, gd 6)
Workmanlike, useful gelding, effective 12 to 16f, best at 12f, acts on hvy to frm, has worn blinkers, prefers tight tracks. Turf high 85 - 2nd of 8 giving 29lb to Hill Farm Blues (14 Oct Nottingham 16f gd RF 4810) - also 1st of 8 giving 6lb to Bardon Hill Boy (12 Spt Goodwood RF 4247). A tail-swisher, he showed mixed form in staying handicaps. **S C Williams [3-19] Alasdair Simpson.*

LITTLE AMIN RR 80+f 5139[8]
2 b c Unfuwain (USA) 11.4f **(74)** - Ghassanah (Pas de Seul) 9.1f **(67)**
Form - 38
Record 1998 - 1st:0 2nd:0 3rd:1 Ran:2
Win Prizemoney £0 *Total Prizemoney* £497
1998 Turf 0-2: (6f 2) (gd, g-f)
Currently decent colt. Turf high 80 (1st run) (began Spt) - 3rd of 14 to Sir Jack (30 Spt Newcastle 6f g-f RF 4579).
**J D Bethell [0-2] Sheikh Amin Dahlawi.*

LITTLE BOY BLUE (IRE) RR 608[9]
2 br g Petardia 8.2f **(58)** - Bluebutton (Blue Cashmere) 6.4f **(54)**
Form - 0
Record 1998 - 1st:0 2nd:0 3rd:0 Ran:1
1998 Turf 0-1: (5f) (sft)
Currently very poor gelding.
**N Tinkler [0-1] Clayton Bigley Partnership Ltd.*

LITTLE BRAVE BHB 59f69a **RR 58f 69a** 5118[4]
3 b g Kahyasi 12.9f **(74)** - Littlemisstrouble (USA) (My Gallant (USA)) 9f **(71)**
Form - 108663224
Record 1998 - 1st:1 2nd:2 3rd:1 Ran:9
Pre1998 - 1st:0 2nd:0 3rd:0 Ran:2
Win Prizemoney £3,436 *Total Prizemoney* £6,365
Wins * **1998** *Mar Southw (STD)* *8f* *68* <
1998 Turf 0-8: (8f, 10f 2, 12f, 14f, 16f 3) (gd 3, g-f 3, frm 2) 1998 AW 1-1: (8f 1-1) (Fibr 1-1)
Workmanlike, average gelding, effective 8f, - acts on Fibr, likes left handed tracks, likes tight tracks. Turf high 61. (1st run) - 1st of 9 from Ego Night (23 Mar Southwell RF 0465).
**J M P Eustace [1-11] Brave Maple Partnership.*

LITTLE CAESAR BHB 40f **RR 38f** 4488[11]
4 ch g Keen 11.1f **(58)** - Loredana (Grange Melody) 7f **(59)**
Form - 440
Record 1998 - 1st:0 2nd:0 3rd:0 Ran:3
Win Prizemoney £0 *Total Prizemoney* £383
1998 Turf 0-1: (7f) (frm) 1998 AW 0-2: (12f 2) (Fibr 2)
Currently very moderate gelding. AW high 33.
**S C Williams [0-3] D A Shekells.*

LITTLE CHAPEL (IRE) BHB 69f **RR 65f** 4732[14]
2 b f College Chapel - Istaraka (IRE) (Darshaan) 9.9f **(84)**
Form - 023800
Record 1998 - 1st:0 2nd:1 3rd:1 Ran:6
Win Prizemoney £0 *Total Prizemoney* £1,684
1998 Turf 0-6: (5f 3, 6f 2, 7f) (g-s, gd 3, g-f, frm)
Average filly, effective 5f, acts on g-f. Turf high 65.
**D J S ffrenchDavis [0-6] North Social Racing Club.*

LITTLE CINNAMON BHB 70f **RR 67f** 5148[12]
2 ch c Timeless Times (USA) 6.1f **(56)** - Belltina (Belfort (FR)) 6.8f **(63)**
Form - 57640
Record 1998 - 1st:0 2nd:0 3rd:0 Ran:5
Win Prizemoney £0 *Total Prizemoney* £255
1998 Turf 0-5: (5f 4, 7f) (gd 3, g-f, frm)
Average colt. Turf high 67 (began Aug).
**J L Eyre [0-5] Ms Kim Jansen.*

LITTLE CRACKER BHB 49a **RR 55f** 3135[9]
3 ch f Tina's Pet 7.4f **(56)** - All That Crack (Stanford) 7.9f **(56)**
Form - 6236660
Record 1998 - 1st:0 2nd:1 3rd:1 Ran:6
Pre1998 - 1st:0 2nd:0 3rd:1 Ran:4
Win Prizemoney £0 *Total Prizemoney* £1,313
1998 Turf 0-5: (10f, 11f, 12f 3) (sft, g-s, gd, frm 2) 1998 AW 0-1: (14f) (Fibr)
Leggy, fair filly, effective 10 to 12f, acts on sft to g-s, favours tight tracks. Turf high 61 (1st run) - 2nd of 17 giving 6lb to Northern Lass (7 Apr Nottingham 10f g-s RF 0585). Inconsistent.
**A G Newcombe [0-10] McGlynn & Smith.*

LITTLE EM BHB 43f **RR 30f** 1921[10]
3 ch f Rock City 8.8f **(62)** - Sleepline Princess (Royal Palace) 9f **(56)**
Form - 000
Record 1998 - 1st:0 2nd:0 3rd:0 Ran:3
1998 Turf 0-3: (6f, 7f 2) (gd 2, frm)
Light-framed, currently very moderate filly. Turf high 30.
**R J Hodges [0-3] G Z Mizel.*

LITTLE EMILY BHB 49f55a **RR 10f 55a** 381[9]
3 gr f Zafonic (USA) 9f **(83)** - Petillante (Petong) 6.6f **(58)**
Form - 4000
Record 1998 - 1st:0 2nd:0 3rd:0 Ran:2
Pre1998 - 1st:0 2nd:0 3rd:0 Ran:3
Win Prizemoney £0 *Total Prizemoney* £217
1998 AW 0-2: (7f, 10f) (Equi 2)
Leggy, very moderate filly. AW high 36.
**C E Brittain [0-5] A J Richards.*

LITTLE GEM BHB 77f **RR 75f** 4414[5]
2 b f Night Shift (USA) 8.1f **(73)** -Um Lardaff (Mill Reef (USA))10.5f **(78)**
Form - 243415
Record 1998 - 1st:1 2nd:1 3rd:1 Ran:6
Win Prizemoney £3,436 *Total Prizemoney* £5,672
Wins * **1998** Spt Epsom (SFT) 8.5f 75 <
1998 Turf 1-6: (6f 2, 7f, 8f 2, 9f 1-1) (gd 1-1, g-f, frm 4)

Above-average filly, effective 7 to 9f, acts on gd to frm. Turf high 75 - 1st of 6 getting 5lb from Fort Sumter (5 Spt Epsom RF 4096). Game winner at Epsom in September, having been running well.
**R Hannon [1-6] Mohamed Suhail.*

LITTLE GREENBIRD BHB 49f RR 50f 4122[8]

2 b f Ardkinglass 5f **(64)** - Hot Money (Mummy's Pet) 7.7f **(60)**
Form - 088
Record 1998 - 1st:0 2nd:0 3rd:0 Ran:3
1998 Turf 0-2: (5f, 6f) (g-f, frm) 1998 AW 0-1: (5f) (Fibr)
Currently fair filly. Turf high 50. **W G M Turner [0-3] Mrs L P Green.*

LITTLE HENRY BHB 55f RR 62f 4934[10]

2 ch c My Generation 6.5f **(68)** - White African (Carwhite) 7.2f **(61)**
Form - 763436703530
Record 1998 - 1st:0 2nd:0 3rd:4 Ran:12
Win Prizemoney £0 *Total Prizemoney* £1,113
1998 Turf 0-11: (5f, 7f 6, 8f 3, 10f) (gd 5, g-f 3, frm 3) 1998 AW 0-1: (7f) (Fibr)
Average colt, effective 7 to 8f, acts on g-f, always wears blinkers. Turf high 62 - 3rd of 14 to Risky Way (22 Jly Catterick 7f g-f RF 3019). Consistent. **P D Evans [0-12] J G White.*

LITTLE IBNR BHB 54f38a RR 48f 38a 939[6]

7 b g Formidable (USA) 7.8f **(60)** - Zalatia (Music Boy) 6.8f **(57)**
Form - 070376646
Record 1998 - 1st:0 2nd:0 3rd:1 Ran:6
Pre1998 - 1st:12 2nd:9 3rd:9 Ran:78
Win Prizemoney £35,504 *Total Prizemoney* £49,494

Wins
* 1997 *Mar Wolver (STD) S 5f 58*
* 1997 *Jan Wolver (STD) 7f 63*
* 1996 *Apr Wolver (STD) H 6f 68 66*
* 1995 *Dec Wolver (STD) C 6f 79*
* 1995 Oct Nottin (G-F) 5.1f 62
* 1995 *Feb Wolver (STD) H 7f 80 81* <
* 1995 *Jan Southw (STD) H 6f 73 74*
* 1995 *Jan Wolver (STD) H 7f 67 73*
* 1994 *Dec Southw (STD) 6f 61*
* 1994 *Dec Wolver (STD) H 6f 60 61*

1998 AW 0-6: (5f, 6f 4, 7f) (Fibr 6)
Moderate gelding, effective 5 to 7f, best at 6f, - acts on Fibr, has worn blinkers, favours left handed tracks, favours tight tracks. AW high 35.
**P D Evans [10-62] Swinnerton Transport Ltd (from P D Cundell [0-9] Feb 1998).*

LITTLE IMP (IRE) BHB 37f RR 39f 3523[9]

3 b f Imp Society (USA) 7.1f **(63)** - Poka Poka (FR) (King Of Macedon) 8.1f **(59)**
Form - 770060
Record 1998 - 1st:0 2nd:0 3rd:0 Ran:6
1998 Turf 0-4:(6f, 7f, 8f 2)(g-s, gd, frm 2) 1998 AW 0-2:(7f 2)(Equi, Fibr)
Leggy, very moderate filly, has worn blinkers. Turf high 39. AW high 20. **K R Burke [0-6] The Ginge Racing Partnership.*

LITTLE INDIAN BHB 85f RR 93df 4460[6]

3 ch c Little Missouri (USA) 13.8f **(97)** - Both Sides Now (USA) (Topsider (USA)) 8.3f **(71)**
Form - 6063646
Record 1998 - 1st:0 2nd:0 3rd:1 Ran:7
Pre1998 - 1st:2 2nd:0 3rd:2 Ran:5
Win Prizemoney £22,964 *Total Prizemoney* £29,617

Wins
* 1997 Aug Sandow (G-S) G3 7.1f 102 <
* 1997 Jly Haydoc (GD) 6f 89

1998 Turf 0-7: (8f 3, 9f, 10f, 11f, 12f) (gd 4, g-f, frm 2)
Scopey, useful colt, effective 7f, acts on gd, has worn blinkers. Turf high 96. Consistent. Caused something of a surprise when winning the Solario at Sandown at two, but also ran well in other good races that season. However, he looked totally outclassed in his first three starts of 1998, and did not do a great deal better when dropped in class. Sold for 23,000 gns at Newmarket in the autumn. **S P C Woods [2-12] G V Wright.*

LITTLE ITALY (IRE) RR 47f 4868[13]

2 b f Common Grounds 8.1f **(66)** - Broken Romance (IRE) (Ela-Mana-Mou) 10.1f **(70)**
Form - 50
Record 1998 - 1st:0 2nd:0 3rd:0 Ran:2
1998 Turf 0-2: (6f, 7f) (gd, frm)
Currently moderate filly. Turf high 47 (began Jly).
**P F I Cole [0-2] Andrea Pecoraro.*

LITTLE JOHN BHB 78f RR 80f 4752[4]

2 b c Warrshan (USA) 9.7f **(59)** - Silver Venture (USA) (Silver Hawk (USA)) 8.6f **(70)**
Form - 444
Record 1998 - 1st:0 2nd:0 3rd:0 Ran:3
Win Prizemoney £0 *Total Prizemoney* £678
1998 Turf 0-3: (7f 3) (sft, gd 2)
Currently decent colt. Turf high 80 (began Aug).
**Miss L A Perratt [0-3] Mrs A E Robertson.*

LITTLE MERMAID (IRE) RR 5139[22]

2 b f Mac's Imp (USA) 5.6f **(54)** -Aegaen Lady **(42f)** (Lochnager) 6f **(59)**
Form - 0
Record 1998 - 1st:0 2nd:0 3rd:0 Ran:1
1998 Turf 0-1: (6f) (gd)
Currently very poor filly. **G Woodward [0-1] Burntwood Sports Ltd.*

LITTLE MISS HUFF (IRE) BHB 78f RR 73+f 2573[7]

3 b f Anita's Prince 6f **(62)** - Regal Charmer (Royal And Regal (USA)) 9.5f **(60)**
Form - 7
Record 1998 - 1st:0 2nd:0 3rd:0 Ran:1
Pre1998 - 1st:1 2nd:0 3rd:0 Ran:2
Win Prizemoney £2,342 *Total Prizemoney* £2,342

Wins * 1997 Aug Warwic (G-S) 7f 73+ <

1998 Turf 0-1: (12f) (g-f)
Leggy, currently above-average filly. **R Guest [1-3] M G Hill.*

LITTLE MISS RIBOT BHB 39f36a RR 40f 36a 3272[8]

8 b m Lighter 9.5f **(36)** - Little Missile (Ile de Bourbon (USA)) 10.1f **(67)**
Form - 85147328
Record 1998 - 1st:1 2nd:1 3rd:1 Ran:6
Pre1998 - 1st:3 2nd:3 3rd:2 Ran:29
Win Prizemoney £10,461 *Total Prizemoney* £15,826

Wins
* **1998** *Feb Lingfi (SLW) H 10f 31 37*
* 1995 *Feb Lingfi (STD) H 10f 28 31*
* 1995 *Jan Lingfi (STD) H 10f 33 32*
* 1994 Jun Bright (FRM) H 8f 38 38 <

1998 Turf 0-4: (8f, 9f, 10f 2) (g-s, gd 2, frm) 1998 AW 1-2: (10f 1-2) (Equi 1-2)
Moderate mare, effective 8 to 10f, acts on g-s to frm - acts on Equi, favours left handed tracks. Turf high 40 - 2nd of 13 getting 11lb from May Queen Megan (9 Jly Lingfield 9f frm RF 2645). AW high 37 (1st run) - 1st of 7 getting 30lb from Rehaab (19 Feb Lingfield RF 0314). Gradually improved on Equitrack during the winter, eventually winning a fillies' handicap at Lingfield in February. Better form on turf than on sand since.
**R J O'Sullivan [4-36] Mrs R J Doorgachurn.*

LITTLE MISS ROCKER BHB 42f RR 46f 4051[7]

4 b f Rock Hopper 10.6f **(54)** - Drama School (Young Generation) 7.7f **(63)**
Form - 038377
Record 1998 - 1st:0 2nd:0 3rd:2 Ran:6
Pre1998 - 1st:1 2nd:1 3rd:1 Ran:8
Win Prizemoney £2,277 *Total Prizemoney* £4,132

Wins 1997 Aug Bright (GD) 11.9f 61 <

1998 Turf 0-6: (12f 6) (gd 2, g-f 2, frm 2)
Neat, moderate filly, effective 10 to 12f, best at 12f, acts on g-f to frm, best on frm, has worn blinkers, prefers left handed tracks. Turf high 46.
**G L Moore [0-2] Phil Collins (from A R Dicken [1-9] Jly 1998).*

LITTLE MOVIE STAR BHB 93f RR 78f 2054[6]

2 ch f Risk Me (FR) 8f **(53)** - Yukosan (Absalom) 7.2f **(58)**
Form - 21736
Record 1998 - 1st:1 2nd:1 3rd:1 Ran:5
Win Prizemoney £2,532 *Total Prizemoney* £4,057

Wins * **1998** *May Southw (STD) 5f 80+* <

1998 Turf 0-3: (5f 3) (gd 2, g-f) 1998 AW 1-2: (5f 1-1, 6f) (Fibr 1-2)
Decent filly. Turf high 78. AW high 80 (1st run) - 1st of 16 giving 6lb to Sweet Compliance (11 May Southwell RF 1155). Her victory

came on the Southwell Fibresand on her second start, but she has been set some very difficult tasks on Turf since. She has not been entirely disgraced, but is unlikely to prove successful in Pattern company. She did not seem to stay when tried over six furlongs at Wolverhampton. **B J Meehan [1-5] Roldvale Ltd.*

LITTLE MUFFKINS BHB 49f RR 43f 4671[21]

2 b f Ardkinglass 5f **(64)** - Skelton (Derrylin) 8.8f **(54)**
Form - 0700
Record 1998 - 1st:0 2nd:0 3rd:0 Ran:4
1998 Turf 0-4: (5f, 6f, 7f 2) (gd, g-f 2, frm)
Moderate filly. Turf high 43. **M E Sowersby [0-4] T W Heseltine.*

LITTLE PILGRIM BHB 23f29a RR 28f 29a 364[6]

5 b g Precocious 7.2f **(54)** - Bonny Bright Eyes (Rarity) 10.1f **(60)**
Form - 84506
Record 1998 - 1st:0 2nd:0 3rd:0 Ran:4
Pre1998 - 1st:0 2nd:1 3rd:0 Ran:19
Win Prizemoney £0 *Total Prizemoney* £527
1998 AW 0-4: (7f 2, 8f, 12f) (Equi 4)
Very moderate gelding, effective 7f, acts on g-f. AW high 33.
**T M Jones [0-23] Richard Page.*

LITTLE PIPPIN BHB 80f RR 72f 4583[3]

2 ch f Rudimentary (USA) 8.2f **(66)** - Accuracy (Gunner B) 11.2f **(58)**
Form - 0673
Record 1998 - 1st:0 2nd:0 3rd:1 Ran:4
Win Prizemoney £0 *Total Prizemoney* £473
1998 Turf 0-4: (6f 2, 7f, 8f) (gd 2, g-f, frm)
Above-average filly. Turf high 72. **G B Balding [0-4] Miss B Swire.*

LITTLE PROGRESS BHB 25f20a RR 56f 20a 351[8]

4 b g Rock City 8.8f **(62)** - Petite Hester (Wollow) 8.2f **(61)**
Form - 8508
Record 1998 - 1st:0 2nd:0 3rd:0 Ran:3
Pre1998 - 1st:0 2nd:0 3rd:0 Ran:9
1998 AW 0-3: (6f 2, 7f) (Equi 3)
Workmanlike, fair gelding, has worn blinkers. AW high 16.
**T M Jones [0-12] T M Jones.*

LITTLE RISK BHB 36f RR 44f 2341[10]

3 b f Risk Me (FR) 8f **(53)** - Little Preston (IRE) (Pennine Walk) 8.5f **(61)**
Form - 0
Record 1998 - 1st:0 2nd:0 3rd:0 Ran:1
Pre1998 - 1st:0 2nd:0 3rd:0 Ran:4
1998 Turf 0-1: (9f) (frm)
Lengthy, moderate filly.
**Mrs L C Jewell [0-1] Gallagher Equine Ltd (from K McAuliffe [0-4] Oct 1997).*

LITTLE ROCK RR 86+f 4774[1]

2 b c Warning 8.1f **(77)** - Much Too Risky (Bustino) 10.4f **(64)**
Form - 1
Record 1998 - 1st:1 2nd:0 3rd:0 Ran:1
Win Prizemoney £3,301 *Total Prizemoney* £3,301
Wins * 1998 Oct Leices (G-S) 7f 86+ <
1998 Turf 1-1: (7f 1-1) (gd 1-1)
Currently useful colt. (1st run) - 1st of 18 from Nabonassar (13 Oct Leicester RF 4774). Looks an interesting prospect at around ten furlongs. **Sir Michael Stoute [1-1] J M Greetham.*

LITTLE TUMBLER (IRE) BHB 50f RR 56f 4614[8]

3 b f Cyrano de Bergerac 7.3f **(58)** - Glass Minnow (IRE) (Alzao (USA)) 7.1f **(68)**
Form - 1447708
Record 1998 - 1st:1 2nd:0 3rd:0 Ran:7
Pre1998 - 1st:0 2nd:2 3rd:0 Ran:6
Win Prizemoney £2,070 *Total Prizemoney* £3,643
Wins * 1998 May Lingfi (G-F) H 6f 55 61 <
1998 Turf 1-7: (6f 1-5, 7f 2) (g-s, gd, g-f 2, frm 1-3)
Neat, fair filly, effective 6 to 7f, best at 6f, acts on gd to frm, best on gd. Turf high 61 (1st run) - 1st of 20 getting 10lb from Madame Jones (13 May Lingfield RF 1202). Becoming disappointing.
**S Woodman [1-13] Mrs W Edgar.*

LIVELY JACQ (IRE) BHB 70f RR 72f 4820[6]

2 ch f Case Law 6f **(64)** - Nordic Living (IRE) (Nordico (USA)) 6.5f **(62)**
Form - 21122576
Record 1998 - 1st:2 2nd:3 3rd:0 Ran:8
Win Prizemoney £5,171 *Total Prizemoney* £12,561
Wins * 1998 Aug Yarmou (G-F) H 6f 62 60 <
*** 1998** Jly Yarmou (G-F) S 6f 60 <
1998 Turf 2-8: (6f 2-7, 7f) (gd, g-f 2-3, frm 2, hrd 2)
Above-average filly, effective 6f, acts on g-f to hrd, and excels at Newmarket. Turf high 72 (began Jly) - 2nd of 12 getting 7lb from Ingenious (29 Aug Newmarket 6f frm RF 3957). Consistent. Only small, this selling-race winner ran with credit in nursery company.
**C N Allen [2-8] J T B Racing.*

LIVELY LADY BHB 66f63a RR 67f 63a 5144[4]

2 b f Beveled (USA) 6.9f **(64)** - In the Papers (Aragon) 8.1f **(60)**
Form - 142036024
Record 1998 - 1st:1 2nd:2 3rd:1 Ran:9
Win Prizemoney £1,725 *Total Prizemoney* £4,199
Wins * 1998 Apr Folkes (SFT) S 5f 67+ <
1998 Turf 1-7: (5f 1-6, 6f) (sft 1-2, gd 2, g-f 2, frm) 1998 AW 0-2: (5f, 6f) (Fibr 2)
Average filly, effective 5f, acts on sft to gd, best on sft, has worn blinkers. Turf high 67 (1st run) - 1st of 6 from Credenza (21 Apr Folkestone RF 0777). AW high 59 (began Jly). She won a heavy-ground seller at Folkestone on her debut by a very wide margin, and has not been disgraced since. **J R Jenkins [1-9] S Powell.*

LIVELY PROJECT (IRE) BHB 50f RR 59df 4808[12]

2 b f Project Manager 7.2f **(47)** - Lovely Ali (IRE) (Dunbeath (USA)) 7.8f **(70)**
Form - 8470
Record 1998 - 1st:0 2nd:0 3rd:0 Ran:4
Win Prizemoney £0 *Total Prizemoney* £208
1998 Turf 0-4: (7f 2, 8f, 10f) (gd, g-f, frm 2)
Fair filly. Turf high 59 (began Spt).
**M Dods [0-4] Three Plus One Racing 98.*

LIVE PROJECT (IRE) BHB 43f66a RR 41f 66a 4874[3]

6 b g Project Manager 7.2f **(47)** - Saturday Live (Junius (USA)) 7.7f **(65)**
Form - 142118437483
Record 1998 - 1st:2 2nd:1 3rd:2 Ran:11
Pre1998 - 1st:3 2nd:3 3rd:1 Ran:24
Win Prizemoney £10,811 *Total Prizemoney* £15,515
Wins * 1998 *Mar Southw (STD) H 7f 59 68* <
*** 1998** *Feb Southw (STD) H 7f 54 59*
* 1997 *Dec Southw (STD) H 7f 50 52*
1997 *Mar Lingfi (STD) H 8f 55 57*
1997 *Feb Southw (STD) H 7f 50 54*
1998 Turf 0-5: (6f, 7f 2, 8f 2) (g-s, gd, g-f, frm 2) 1998 AW 2-6: (7f 2-2, 8f 4) (Fibr 2-6)
Average gelding, effective 7f, - acts on Fibr, likes left handed tracks, likes tight tracks. Turf high 41 (began Jly). AW high 68 - 1st of 11 giving 17lb to Forest Robin (2 Mar Southwell RF 0382) - also 1st of 11 giving 21lb to Cheerful Groom (9 Feb Southwell RF 0253). Seven furlongs at Southwell seems to be his optimum at the moment.
**R Craggs [3-16] Mrs Gillian Quinn (from M Johnston [2-19] Apr 1997).*

LIVIUS (IRE) BHB 77f RR 83f 4380[14]

4 b g Alzao (USA) 9.8f **(73)** - Marie de Beaujeu (FR) (Kenmare (FR)) 6.5f **(72)**
Form - 3442020
Record 1998 - 1st:0 2nd:2 3rd:1 Ran:7
Pre1998 - 1st:0 2nd:1 3rd:0 Ran:1
Win Prizemoney £0 *Total Prizemoney* £4,079
1998 Turf 0-7: (10f 4, 12f, 13f, 14f) (gd 3, g-f 2, frm 2)
Strong, decent gelding, effective 10 to 12f, best at 10f, acts on gd to frm, has worn blinkers. Turf high 83 - 4th of 8 giving 20lb to Bold Faith (17 Jly Newmarket 10f frm RF 2881). A half-brother to a German Derby winner, he has been difficult to train but ran a couple of fine races in maiden company. Failed to progress as anticipated in handicaps, and seems on a stiff mark for what he has achieved. He is blessed with stamina rather than speed, so forcing tactics might pay off. May be worth a try over hurdles.
**Major D N Chappell [0-8] Ms Liz Kilfeather.*

LIVNLETLIVE BHB 37f RR 28f 2516[13]

2 b g Cyrano de Bergerac 7.3f **(58)** - Woodleys (Tyrnavos) 10.1f **(55)**
Form - 05640
Record 1998 - 1st:0 2nd:0 3rd:0 Ran:5

1998 Turf 0-5: (5f 2, 6f, 7f 2) (gd 2, g-f 2, frm)
Little account gelding. Turf high 28. **C A Dwyer [0-5] Roalco Ltd.*

LOBUCHE (IRE) BHB 52f55a **RR 67f 55a** 4775^{19}

3 b c Petardia 8.2f **(58)** - Lhotse (IRE) (Shernazar) 10.2f **(73)**
Form - 528251374000000

Record					
1998 -	1st:1	2nd:2	3rd:1	Ran:15	
Pre1998 -	1st:0	2nd:1	3rd:0	Ran:8	

Win Prizemoney £3,054 *Total Prizemoney* £5,386
Wins * **1998** Jun Yarmou (SFT) H 6f 58 67 <
1998 Turf 1-9: (6f 1-5, 7f 2, 8f, 10f) (g-s, gd 3, g-f 1-3, frm, hrd) 1998 AW 0-6: (6f 2, 8f 3, 10f) (Equi 3, Fibr 3)
Average colt, effective 6 to 10f, best at 6f, acts on g-f to frm - acts on Equi, has worn blinkers, likes left handed tracks, likes tight tracks. Turf high 67 - 1st of 11 giving 4lb to Suite Factors (11 Jun Yarmouth RF 1906). AW high 64 - 2nd of 7 giving 4lb to Comeoutofthefog (28 Feb Lingfield 8f Equi RF 0376).
**M C Chapman [1-10] Geoff Whiting (from R Hannon [0-13] Apr 1998).*

a small race at Bath before finishing in the frame in three Group races at five furlongs, and then earned Group One honours by winning the Nunthorpe. Found the extra furlong beyond her at Haydock and did not handle the soft ground in the Abbaye. She should be back next year. **I A Balding [3-14] J C Smith.*

LOCH DANCER BHB 30f **RR 13f** 4149^{15}

5 br m Lochnager 6.9f **(50)** - Cute Dancer (Remainder Man) 11.2f **(45)**
Form - 080
Record 1998 - 1st:0 2nd:0 3rd:0 Ran:3
1998 Turf 0-3: (7f, 10f 2) (gd, g-f 2)
Poor filly. Turf high 13.
**D McCain [0-1] Mrs Elizabeth Crewe (from A G Newcombe [0-2] Jly 1998).*

LOCHDENE (IRE) BHB 60f **RR 69df** 4755^{4}

3 b c Robellino(USA) 9.5f **(68)** -Cat's Claw (USA)(Sharpen Up) 8.3f **(67)**
Form - 4

Lochangel- keeping it in the family

LOCHANGEL BHB 114f **RR 115f** $4726a^{6}$

4 ch f Night Shift (USA) 8.1f **(73)** - Peckitts Well (Lochnager) 6f **(59)**
Form - 21223166

Record				
1998 -	1st:2	2nd:3	3rd:1	Ran:8
Pre1998 -	1st:1	2nd:1	3rd:1	Ran:6

Win Prizemoney £101,505 *Total Prizemoney* £156,012

Wins							
* **1998**	Aug	York	(FRM)	G1	5f	115	<
* **1998**	May	Bath	(GD)	L	5.7f	108	
* 1996	Spt	Ascot	(G-F)		6f	91	

1998 Turf 2-8: (5f 1-6, 6f 1-2) (sft, g-s, gd 3, frm 2-3)
Scopey, high-class filly, effective 5 to 6f, best at 5f, acts on gd to frm, best on gd. Turf high 115 - 1st of 17 giving 2lb to Sainte Marine (20 Aug York RF 3773) - also 1st of 9 giving 10lb to Desert Lady (10 May Bath RF 1131). Consistent. A half-sister to Lochsong, she developed into a leading sprinter in 1998. She won

Record				
1998 -	1st:0	2nd:0	3rd:0	Ran:1
Pre1998 -	1st:0	2nd:0	3rd:0	Ran:2

Win Prizemoney £0 *Total Prizemoney* £556
1998 Turf 0-1: (8f) (sft)
Scopey, currently average colt. **M Johnston [0-3] J S Morrison.*

LOCH FYNE BHB 66f **RR 69f** 4524^{12}

2 b f Ardkinglass 5f **(64)** - Song's Best (Never so Bold) 6.3f **(66)**
Form - 5370
Record 1998 - 1st:0 2nd:0 3rd:1 Ran:4
Win Prizemoney £0 *Total Prizemoney* £519
1998 Turf 0-4: (5f 3, 6f) (gd, g-f 2, frm)
Average filly. Turf high 69 - 3rd of 18 to Almost Amber (24 Jun Salisbury 5f frm RF 2249). **W R Muir [0-4] D J Deer.*

LOCH-HURN LADY BHB 31f **RR 35f** 4401[19]
4 b f Lochnager 6.9f **(50)** - Knocksharry (Palm Track) 9.8f **(50)**
Form - 8060000
Record 1998 - 1st:0 2nd:0 3rd:0 Ran:7
Pre1998 - 1st:1 2nd:1 3rd:0 Ran:17
Win Prizemoney £2,511 *Total Prizemoney* £3,431
Wins * 1997 Mar Catter (GD) 5f 66 <
1998 Turf 0-7: (5f 5, 6f 2) (g-s, gd, g-f 2, frm 3)
Neat, very moderate filly, effective 5f, acts on sft. Turf high 35 (began Jly). **K W Hogg [1-26] Hurn Racing Club.*

LOCH LAIRD BHB 76f **RR 81f** 4459[7]
3 b g Beveled (USA) 6.9f **(64)** - Daisy Loch (Lochnager) 6f **(59)**
Form - 3227
Record 1998 - 1st:0 2nd:2 3rd:1 Ran:4
Pre1998 - 1st:0 2nd:2 3rd:1 Ran:3
Win Prizemoney £0 *Total Prizemoney* £4,645
1998 Turf 0-4: (6f 3, 7f) (g-f 2, frm 2)
Unfurnished, decent gelding, effective 5 to 6f, best at 6f, acts on g-f to frm, best on g-f. Turf high 81 (began Jly) - 2nd of 16 to Pursuit of Gold (7 Spt Bath 6f frm RF 4127).
**M Madgwick [0-7] Miss E M L Coller.*

LOCHLASS (IRE) BHB 39f33a **RR 45f 33a** 903[6]
4 b f Distinctly North (USA) 7.4f **(63)** - Littleton Song (Song) 7.2f **(61)**
Form - 7006
Record 1998 - 1st:0 2nd:0 3rd:0 Ran:4
Pre1998 - 1st:0 2nd:0 3rd:4 Ran:15
Win Prizemoney £0 *Total Prizemoney* £1,564
1998 Turf 0-1: (10f) (g-s) 1998 AW 0-3: (8f, 11f, 16f) (Fibr 3)
Neat, moderate filly, effective 8 to 10f, acts on frm, has worn blinkers (extremely effectively). AW high 9. Becoming disappointing.
**R J Price [0-5] My Left Foot Racing Syndicate (from S P C Woods [0-15] Oct 1997).*

LOCH PATRICK BHB 78f **RR 79?f** 3260[9]
8 b g Beveled (USA) 6.9f **(64)** - Daisy Loch (Lochnager) 6f **(59)**
Form - 00
Record 1998 - 1st:0 2nd:0 3rd:0 Ran:2
Pre1998 - 1st:6 2nd:1 3rd:2 Ran:32
Win Prizemoney £44,309 *Total Prizemoney* £51,508
Wins * 1996 May Goodwo (GD) 6f 100 <
1995 Jun Sandow (G-F) 5f 99
1994 Jly Ascot (G-F) H 5f 95 95
1994 Jun Chepst (FRM) H 5.1f 87 93+
1998 Turf 0-2: (7f 2) (g-s, gd)
Above-average gelding, has worn blinkers. Turf high 62. He was a useful sprinter, but has not shown his best form for a couple of seasons now. A step up in trip does not seem to have made much difference.
**M Madgwick [1-17] Miss E M L Coller (from L J Holt [5-17] Spt 1995).*

LOCH STYLE BHB 39f47a **RR 42f 47a** 3412a[4]
5 b g Lochnager 6.9f **(50)** - Simply Style (Bairn (USA)) 7.7f **(59)**
Form - 0632424870484
Record 1998 - 1st:0 2nd:2 3rd:1 Ran:11
Pre1998 - 1st:2 2nd:1 3rd:2 Ran:29
Win Prizemoney £5,091 *Total Prizemoney* £7,664
Wins * 1997 *Jan Wolver (STD) S 8.5f 53+*
* 1996 Jun Pontef (G-F) S 8f 55 <
1998 Turf 0-6: (7f 3, 8f 2, 9f) (gd 4, g-f, frm) 1998 AW 0-5: (8f 2, 9f 3) (Fibr 5)
Fair gelding, effective 7 to 8f, best at 8f, acts on gd - acts on Fibr, likes left handed tracks, favours tight tracks. Turf high 42. AW high 51 - 2nd of 7 getting 5lb from Anonym (14 Jan Wolverhampton 8f Fibr RF 0089). Tends to do a little bit better on sand than on turf, but has been on a long losing run since scoring at Wolverhampton in January 1997, and is basically moderate these days. **R Hollinshead [2-42].*

LOCOMBE HILL (IRE) BHB 100f **RR 103f** 4964[6]
2 b c Barathea (IRE) - Roberts Pride (Roberto (USA)) 10f **(76)**
Form - 11626
Record 1998 - 1st:2 2nd:1 3rd:0 Ran:5
Win Prizemoney £7,356 *Total Prizemoney* £9,043
Wins * **1998** Jly Newbur (G-F) 6f 95+ <
* **1998** Jun Newbur (SFT) 6f 85+
1998 Turf 2-5: (6f 2-3, 7f 2) (sft, g-s 1-1, gd, g-f 1-2)
Very useful colt. Turf high 103 - 2nd of 5 giving 6lb to Island Sands (30 Spt Salisbury 6f gd RF 4585) - also 1st of 4 giving 6lb to Indiana Legend (17 Jly Newbury RF 2871). He is as big as a bull and would carry condition if he spent all day on the gallops. The easy winner of a maiden and conditions event at Newbury on his first two starts, he only managed to beat two horses home in a couple of Group races, and is not in that league at present.
**M Blanshard [2-5] Stanley Hinton.*

LOGANLEA (IRE) BHB 53f **RR 52f** 4390[7]
4 br f Petong 7.6f **(58)** - White's Pet (Mummy's Pet) 7.7f **(60)**
Form - 307817
Record 1998 - 1st:1 2nd:0 3rd:1 Ran:6
Pre1998 - 1st:0 2nd:0 3rd:0 Ran:6
Win Prizemoney £2,455 *Total Prizemoney* £2,831
Wins * **1998** Spt Yarmou (G-S) H 6f 48 52 <
1998 Turf 1-6: (5f, 6f 1-4, 7f) (gd, g-f, frm 1-4)
Leggy, fair filly, effective 6f, acts on frm. Turf high 52 - 1st of 19 giving 9lb to Present 'n Correct (17 Spt Yarmouth RF 4339).
**W J Musson [1-12] Mrs P A Linton.*

LOGIE PERT LAD BHB 23f35a **RR 22f 35a** 391[6]
6 b g Green Ruby (USA) 6.9f **(47)** - Rhazya (Rousillon (USA)) 8.2f **(74)**
Form - 507440456
Record 1998 - 1st:0 2nd:0 3rd:0 Ran:6
Pre1998 - 1st:0 2nd:0 3rd:0 Ran:32
Win Prizemoney £0 *Total Prizemoney* £646
1998 AW 0-6: (5f 3, 6f 3) (Equi 6)
Moderate gelding, has worn blinkers. AW high 41.
**J J Bridger [0-38] Donald Smith.*

LOHAN (IRE) **RR 61f** 5122[7]
2 b c Perugino (USA) - Deep In September (IRE) (Common Grounds)
Form - 07
Record 1998 - 1st:0 2nd:0 3rd:0 Ran:2
1998 Turf 0-2: (6f, 7f) (g-s 2)
Currently average colt. Turf high 61 (began Oct).
**Miss Z C Davison [0-2] Mrs M Flannery.*

LOKOMOTIV BHB 73f **RR 67+f** 2977[1]
2 b c Salse (USA) 10.9f **(71)** - Rainbow's End (My Swallow) 9.2f **(71)**
Form - 061
Record 1998 - 1st:1 2nd:0 3rd:0 Ran:3
Win Prizemoney £1,987 *Total Prizemoney* £1,987
Wins * **1998** Jly Yarmou (G-F) S 7f 67+ <
1998 Turf 1-3: (7f 1-3) (gd, g-f 1-2)
Currently average colt. Turf high 67 - 1st of 10 getting 5lb from Cosmo Jack (21 Jly Yarmouth RF 2977).
**M R Channon [1-3] Allevamento La Nuova Sbarra SRL.*

LOLITA (FR) BHB 62a **RR 59?f** 4887[17]
4 b f Hellios (USA) - Silver Dime (FR) (Son of Silver)
Form - 55600
Record 1998 - 1st:0 2nd:0 3rd:0 Ran:5
Win Prizemoney £0 *Total Prizemoney* £329
1998 Turf 0-4: (6f, 10f, 12f 2) (g-s, g-f 2, frm) 1998 AW 0-1: (12f) (Fibr)
Fair filly. Turf high 59.
**J R Jenkins [0-9] Southern Counties Finance & Leasing.*

LONACH **RR 32f** 5008[13]
3 gr g Warning 8.1f **(77)** - Snowing (USA) (Icecapade (USA)) 11f **(62)**
Form - 000
Record 1998 - 1st:0 2nd:0 3rd:0 Ran:3
1998 Turf 0-3: (7f, 10f, 12f) (sft, g-s, g-f)
Scopey, currently very moderate gelding. Turf high 32.
**B R Johnson [0-1] Mrs S Scott (from J R Fanshawe [0-2] Jun 1998).*

LONDON BE GOOD (USA) BHB 74f **RR 75f** 4540[22]
3 ch f Storm Bird (CAN) 8.5f **(82)** - Dream Touch (USA) (Riverman (USA)) 9.1f **(76)**
Form - 503150
Record 1998 - 1st:1 2nd:0 3rd:1 Ran:6
Win Prizemoney £3,850 *Total Prizemoney* £4,395
Wins * **1998** Jly Doncas (G-F) H 8f 70 75 <
1998 Turf 1-6: (8f 1-3, 9f, 10f 2) (gd, g-f 1-1, frm 3, hrd)
Unfurnished, above-average filly, effective 8 to 9f, best at 8f, acts

on g-f to frm, best on frm. Turf high 75 - 1st of 7 getting 4lb from Minetta (29 Jly Doncaster RF 3194).
**J R Fanshawe [1-6] Joseph Allen.*

LONELY HEART BHB 95f **RR 96f** 2445[9]
4 b f Midyan (USA) 9.9f **(64)** - Take Heart (Electric) 10.1f **(61)**
Form - 310
Record 1998 - 1st:1 2nd:0 3rd:1 Ran:3
Pre1998 - 1st:1 2nd:2 3rd:1 Ran:13
Win Prizemoney £8,123 *Total Prizemoney* £13,511
Wins * 1998 Jun Windso (GD) 10f 96 <
* 1997 Aug Goodwo (G-F) 10f 82
1998 Turf 1-3: (10f 1-3) (gd, g-f 1-2)
Very useful filly, effective 10f, acts on g-f, has worn blinkers, prefers tight tracks. Turf high 96 - 1st of 6 giving 12lb to Alharir (22 Jun Windsor RF 2181). Inconsistent. Faced some tough tasks, but was a good third in a listed race in May before winning a minor event at Windsor. In foal to Magic Ring.
**D R C Elsworth [2-13] C J Harper (from Major D N Chappell [0-3] Oct 1996).*

LONE PIPER BHB 102f **RR 101?f** 4367[29]
3 b c Warning 8.1f **(77)** - Shamisen (Diesis) 9.3f **(69)**
Form - 5100710
Record 1998 - 1st:2 2nd:0 3rd:0 Ran:7
Pre1998 - 1st:0 2nd:0 3rd:1 Ran:3
Win Prizemoney £24,284 *Total Prizemoney* £24,814
Wins * 1998 Spt York (GD) H 6f 96 101 <
*** 1998** May Newmar (GD) 7f 99
1998 Turf 2-7: (6f 1-2, 7f 1-5) (sft 2, gd 1-3, frm 1-1, hrd)
Neat, very useful colt, effective 6 to 7f, best at 7f, acts on gd to frm, best on gd. Turf high 101 - 1st of 18 getting 8lb from Nigrasine (2 Spt York RF 4055) - also 1st of 6 getting 3lb from Quiet Assurance (3 May Newmarket RF 0990). Inconsistent. He put up his best performance when dropped back to six furlongs at York in September, turning a supposedly competitive handicap into a one-sided affair. Well fancied when finishing unplaced and lame in the Ayr Gold Cup, he is unexposed over sprint distances and could pick up another valuable prize next term.
**C E Brittain [2-10] Saeed Manana.*

LONESOME RR 48f 4805[7]
2 b f Night Shift (USA) 8.1f **(73)** - Pine Ridge (High Top) 10.2f **(67)**
Form - 7
Record 1998 - 1st:0 2nd:0 3rd:0 Ran:1
1998 Turf 0-1: (8f) (gd)
Currently moderate filly.
**Sir Michael Stoute [0-1] Capt J Macdonald-Buchanan.*

LONESOME DUDE (CAN) RR 98f 4379[6]
3 b c With Approval (CAN) 8.7f **(80)** - Local Lass (Local Suitor (USA)) 8.4f **(67)**
Form - 115426
Record 1998 - 1st:2 2nd:1 3rd:0 Ran:6
Pre1998 - 1st:0 2nd:1 3rd:0 Ran:1
Win Prizemoney £10,007 *Total Prizemoney* £17,148
Wins * 1998 Jun Goodwo (GD) 9f 94+ <
*** 1998** May Kempto (G-F) 7f 90
1998 Turf 2-6: (7f 1-1, 9f 1-3, 10f 2) (g-s, gd 1-2, g-f 1-2, frm)
Very useful colt, effective 7 to 10f, best at 10f, acts on g-s to frm, has worn blinkers. Turf high 98 - 2nd of 14 giving 13lb to Somayda (11 Spt Goodwood 9f gd RF 4232) - also 1st of 4 from Wuxi Venture (3 Jun Goodwood RF 1694).
**Sir Michael Stoute [2-7] Saeed Suhail.*

LONG BOND (IRE) BHB 65f **RR 81df** 2286a[11]
3 ch c Kris 10f **(75)** - Compton Lady (USA) (Sovereign Dancer (USA)) 11.2f **(68)**
Form - 4320
Record 1998 - 1st:0 2nd:1 3rd:1 Ran:4
Pre1998 - 1st:0 2nd:2 3rd:0 Ran:2
Win Prizemoney £0 *Total Prizemoney* £3,487
1998 Turf 0-3: (10f, 12f 2) (sft, gd, g-f) 1998 AW 0-1: (12f) (Fibr)
Decent colt, effective 7f, acts on gd to frm. Turf high 60.
**M Johnston [0-6].*

LONGBOWMAN BHB 40a **RR 29f 40a** 160[12]
3 ch g Prince Sabo 6.6f **(64)** - Nuit de Lune (FR) (Crystal Palace (FR)) 12.5f **(76)**
Form - 000
Record 1998 - 1st:0 2nd:0 3rd:0 Ran:2
Pre1998 - 1st:0 2nd:0 3rd:0 Ran:2
1998 AW 0-2: (8f 2) (Fibr 2)
Scopey, very moderate gelding, has worn blinkers. AW high 37.
**Mrs L Stubbs [0-4] Doug Kirk and Darren Kirk.*

LONG ISLAND BHB 61a **RR 68f** 4877[4]
3 ch g Elmaamul (USA) 8.1f **(70)** - Ginny Binny (Ahonoora) 8.1f **(73)**
Form - 60463836384
Record 1998 - 1st:0 2nd:0 3rd:3 Ran:10
Pre1998 - 1st:0 2nd:0 3rd:1 Ran:6
Win Prizemoney £0 *Total Prizemoney* £1,567
1998 Turf 0-8: (5f 3, 6f 2, 7f 2, 8f) (g-f 5, frm 3) 1998 AW 0-2: (6f 2) (Fibr 2)
Lengthy, average gelding, effective 5 to 7f, acts on g-f to frm, best on g-f, often wears blinkers (effectively). Turf high 68 - 4th of 9 to Acid Test (20 Jun Lingfield 7f frm RF 2151). AW high 56 (began Spt). Consistent.
**K T Ivory [0-10] Taker Bloodstock (from R Hannon [0-6] Nov 1997).*

LONG SIEGE (IRE) BHB 81f **RR 80f** 4508[18]
3 ch c Brief Truce (USA) 9.1f **(73)** - Sugarbird (Star Appeal) 9.6f **(65)**
Form - 1380
Record 1998 - 1st:1 2nd:0 3rd:1 Ran:4
Pre1998 - 1st:0 2nd:0 3rd:0 Ran:1
Win Prizemoney £3,688 *Total Prizemoney* £4,184
Wins * 1998 Jly Salisb (G-F) 6f 80 <
1998 Turf 1-4: (6f 1-4) (g-s, gd 2, g-f 1-1)
Decent colt. Turf high 80 (1st run) (began Jly) - 1st of 16 getting 5lb from Madmun (31 Jly Salisbury RF 3247).
**J H M Gosden [1-4] Mrs Diane Snowden (from D R Loder [0-1] Jly 1997).*

LONGWICK LAD BHB 60f **RR 66f** 4311[7]
5 ro h Chilibang 7f **(55)** - Bells of St Martin (Martinmas) 7.6f **(59)**
Form - 0610858050607
Record 1998 - 1st:1 2nd:0 3rd:0 Ran:13
Pre1998 - 1st:2 2nd:3 3rd:0 Ran:17
Win Prizemoney £11,695 *Total Prizemoney* £15,458
Wins * 1998 May Bath (FRM) H 5.7f 67 70
* 1997 May Thirsk (G-F) H 5f 72 73 <
* 1996 Spt Bath (G-F) H 5.7f 67 68
1998 Turf 1-13: (5f 9, 6f 1-4) (g-s, gd 3, g-f 3, frm 1-6)
Average colt, effective 5 to 6f, acts on gd to frm, has worn blinkers. Turf high 70 - 1st of 17 giving 7lb to Intiaash (18 May Bath RF 1297). Sold for 7,000 guineas at Tattersalls in October.
**W R Muir [3-30] Mrs Marion Wickham.*

LONGWOOD LADY BHB 62f **RR 59f** 3765[7]
3 b f Rudimentary (USA) 8.2f **(66)** - Brown Velvet (Mansingh (USA)) 7.4f **(55)**
Form - 3607
Record 1998 - 1st:0 2nd:0 3rd:1 Ran:4
Win Prizemoney £0 *Total Prizemoney* £510
1998 Turf 0-3: (6f, 7f, 8f) (g-f, frm 2) 1998 AW 0-1: (6f) (Fibr)
Tall, fair filly. Turf high 59. **S P C Woods [0-4] Longwood Partnership.*

LOOKINGFORLOVE DEL (IRE) BHB 35f **RR 38f** 585[7]
3 ch f Be My Guest (USA) 10.2f **(66)** - Debenham (Formidable (USA)) 9.2f **(63)**
Form - 07
Record 1998 - 1st:0 2nd:0 3rd:0 Ran:1
Pre1998 - 1st:0 2nd:0 3rd:0 Ran:4
1998 Turf 0-1: (10f) (g-s)
Workmanlike, very moderate filly, has worn blinkers.
**N A Callaghan [0-5] N A Callaghan.*

LOOK WHO'S CALLING (IRE) BHB 42f **RR 55f** 4120[3]
5 b g Al Hareb (USA) 9.4f **(53)** - House Call (Artaius (USA)) 9f **(69)**
Form - 050073443
Record 1998 - 1st:0 2nd:0 3rd:2 Ran:9
Pre1998 - 1st:0 2nd:1 3rd:2 Ran:12
Win Prizemoney £0 *Total Prizemoney* £3,037
1998 Turf 0-7: (6f, 7f 2, 8f 2, 10f 2) (gd 3, g-f 4) 1998 AW 0-2: (12f 2) (Fibr 2)

Fair gelding, effective 7f, acts on hrd, has worn blinkers. Turf high 55. AW high 46 (began Aug). **B A McMahon [0-21] S L Edwards.*

LOOP THE LOUP RR 77f 4989[3]

2 b g Petit Loup (USA) - Mithi Al Gamar (USA) **(60f)** (Blushing Groom (FR)) 10.3f **(76)**
Form - 73
Record 1998 - 1st:0 2nd:0 3rd:1 Ran:2
Win Prizemoney £0 *Total Prizemoney* £536
1998 Turf 0-2: (7f, 8f) (sft, gd)
Currently above-average gelding. Turf high 77 (began Oct) - 3rd of 11 to Mount Irish (26 Oct Leicester 8f sft RF 4989).
**J L Dunlop [0-2] D Sieff.*

LORD ADVOCATE BHB 41f38a RR 46?f 38a 4532[9]

10 br g Law Society (USA) 11.6f **(71)** - Kereolle (Riverman (USA)) 9.1f **(76)**
Form - 7666614442050
Record 1998 - 1st:1 2nd:1 3rd:0 Ran:13
Pre1998 - 1st:11 2nd:16 3rd:13 Ran:117
Win Prizemoney £36,549 *Total Prizemoney* £59,061

Wins							
* **1998**	Jun	Hamilt	(GD)	H	13f	40	44
* 1997	Jun	Hamilt	(GD)	H	13f	46	57
* 1996	Jun	Hamilt	(GD)	H	13f	45	53
* 1996	May	Mussel	(GD)	H	11.1f	42	47
* 1996	May	Hamilt	(SFT)	H	13f	32	43
* 1995	Aug	Mussel	(G-F)	H	12.1f	30	35
* 1995	Jun	Hamilt	(FRM)	H	13f	33	37
* 1995	May	Hamilt	(G-F)	SH	11.1f	26	36

1998 Turf 1-13: (11f 2, 12f 5, 13f 1-6) (sft 3, g-s 3, gd 3, g-f 1-3, frm)
Moderate gelding, effective 11 to 13f, acts on gd to frm, mostly wears blinkers, favours right handed tracks, excels at Hamilton. Turf high 46. All of his wins since 1992 have been in Scotland, and he is always capable of putting in a good effort at Hamilton or Musselburgh.
**D A Nolan [8-85] Mrs J McFadyen-Murray (from T Craig [1-5] Jly 1993).*

LORD BERGERAC BHB 85f RR 78+f 4585[5]

2 b c Cyrano de Bergerac 7.3f **(58)** - Vax Lady (Millfontaine)
Form - 165
Record 1998 - 1st:1 2nd:0 3rd:0 Ran:3
Win Prizemoney £3,582 *Total Prizemoney* £3,738
Wins * **1998** Aug Hamilt (SFT) 6f 78+ <
1998 Turf 1-3: (6f 1-3) (g-s 1-1, gd 2)
Currently above-average colt. Turf high 78 (1st run) (began Aug) - 1st of 11 from Golden Biff (17 Aug Hamilton RF 3680). He was up against several rivals with placed form when scoring on his Hamilton debut. Failed to handle a step up in class .
**J L Spearing [1-3] A J & Mrs L Brazier.*

LORD BUSTER RR 2841[10]

5 gr g Bustino 11f **(64)** - Crispahan (Critique (USA))
Form - 0
Record 1998 - 1st:0 2nd:0 3rd:0 Ran:1
1998 Turf 0-1: (12f) (gd)
Formerly very poor gelding - 10th of 11 to Double Rush (16 Jly Bath 12f gd RF 2841).
**G B Balding [0-3] Mrs David Russell & Partners.*

LORD CORNELIOUS BHB 20f RR 19f 1870[7]

5 b h Lochnager 6.9f **(50)** - Title (Brigadier Gerard) 9.3f **(58)**
Form - 67
Record 1998 - 1st:0 2nd:0 3rd:0 Ran:2
Pre1998 - 1st:0 2nd:0 3rd:0 Ran:14
Win Prizemoney £0 *Total Prizemoney* £238
1998 Turf 0-2: (5f 2) (gd 2)
Poor colt, has worn blinkers. Turf high 19.
**D A Nolan [0-17] Mrs J McFadyen-Murray.*

LORD ELLANGOWAN (IRE) BHB 34f26a RR 42f 26a 93[9]

5 ch g Astronef 7.9f **(59)** - Gossip (Sharp Edge) 10f **(56)**
Form - 0
Record 1998 - 1st:0 2nd:0 3rd:0 Ran:1
Pre1998 - 1st:0 2nd:2 3rd:0 Ran:15
Win Prizemoney £0 *Total Prizemoney* £1,973
1998 AW 0-1: (16f) (Equi)
Moderate gelding, often wears blinkers. Becoming disappointing.
**R Ingram [0-19] Ellangowan Racing Partners.*

LORD EUROLINK (IRE) BHB 90f RR 92f 1425[3]

4 b c Danehill (USA) 9.1f **(79)** - Lady Eurolink (Kala Shikari) 8.4f **(54)**
Form - 3
Record 1998 - 1st:0 2nd:0 3rd:1 Ran:1
Pre1998 - 1st:1 2nd:0 3rd:2 Ran:5
Win Prizemoney £4,435 *Total Prizemoney* £7,180
Wins * 1997 May Doncas (GD) 8f 83 <
1998 Turf 0-1: (10f) (gd)
Workmanlike, useful colt, effective 8 to 10f, best at 8f, acts on gd. (1st run) - 3rd of 14 giving 5lb to Flint Knapper (23 May Kempton 10f gd RF 1425). He ran well at Kempton on his reappearance, but that was to prove his only start of the season.
**J L Dunlop [1-6] Eurolink Group Plc.*

LORD HIGH ADMIRAL (CAN) BHB 71f RR 74f 5142[5]

10 b g Bering 9.6f **(80)** - Baltic Sea (CAN) (Danzig (USA)) 8.4f **(76)**
Form - 200022505
Record 1998 - 1st:0 2nd:3 3rd:0 Ran:9
Pre1998 - 1st:10 2nd:5 3rd:4 Ran:56
Win Prizemoney £46,616 *Total Prizemoney* £67,243

Wins								
* 1997	Spt	Salisb	(G-S)	H	5f	75	85+	
* 1996	Spt	Haydoc	(GD)	H	5f	82	87	
* 1996	Jly	Sandow	(G-S)	H	5f	82	86	
* 1996	Jun	Sandow	(G-F)	C	5f		70	
* 1995	Jun	Sandow	(G-F)	C	5f		78+	
* 1995	May	Haydoc	(G-S)	H	5f	86	89	<
* 1994	May	Haydoc	(G-F)	H	5f	87	81	

1998 Turf 0-9: (5f 8, 6f) (hvy, gd 7, g-f)
Above-average gelding, effective 5f, acts on gd, has worn blinkers. Turf high 82 (1st run) - 2nd of 18 getting 21lb from Proud Native (26 Mar Doncaster 5f gd RF 0472). Inconsistent. Seems best over a stiff five with cut in the ground, and when able to dominate.
**M J Heaton-Ellis [10-53] Elite Racing Club (from C R Egerton [0-3] Oct 1995).*

LORD JIM (IRE) BHB 91f93a RR 99f 93a 3203[4]

6 b g Kahyasi 12.9f **(74)** - Sarah Georgina (Persian Bold) 9.3f **(66)**
Form - 734
Record 1998 - 1st:0 2nd:0 3rd:1 Ran:3
Pre1998 - 1st:3 2nd:3 3rd:3 Ran:24
Win Prizemoney £18,172 *Total Prizemoney* £49,323

Wins							
* 1996	Aug	Leopar	(GD)	L	14f	97	<
* 1996	Jun	Salisb	(G-F)		14f	90	
1995	Mar	Leices	(SFT)		11.8f	72	

1998 Turf 0-3: (16f, 20f, 22f) (gd 2, g-f)
Very useful gelding, effective 16 to 22f, acts on g-s to gd, has worn blinkers. Turf high 99. He finds it hard to win on the Flat, although he was in good heart in staying novice hurdles through the winter of 1997/8. Third in the Queen Alexandra at Ascot before finishing fourth in the Goodwood Handicap.
**Lord Huntingdon [2-14] Mrs S Y Thomas (from Miss Gay Kelleway [1-9] Dec 1995).*

LORD KINTYRE BHB 105f RR 111f 4330[12]

3 b c Makbul - Highland Rowena (Royben) 7.3f **(60)**
Form - 2523030
Record 1998 - 1st:0 2nd:2 3rd:2 Ran:7
Pre1998 - 1st:2 2nd:2 3rd:0 Ran:7
Win Prizemoney £77,929 *Total Prizemoney* £123,079

Wins						
* 1997	Jly	Newbur	(G-F)	5.2f	98	<
* 1997	Jun	Windso	(G-F)	6f	80	

1998 Turf 0-7: (5f 5, 6f 2) (gd 4, g-f 2, frm)
Workmanlike, Group-class colt, effective 5 to 6f, best at 6f, acts on gd to g-f, best on gd. Turf high 111. He had a fine season at two, landing the Weatherbys Super Sprint as well as running other fine races in decent company. Generally ran well in 1998, although winning in Group company proved a step too far. This tough colt ran an admirable race to finish third in the King's Stand Stakes at Royal Ascot, where he was given a positive ride. He has yet to race on the continent and that may be his best option.
**B R Millman [2-14] M Calvert.*

LORD LAMB BHB 81f RR 69+f 4850[11]

6 gr g Dunbeath (USA) 9.9f **(53)** - Caroline Lamb (Hotfoot) 10.5f **(59)**
Form - 754310

Record 1998 - 1st:1 2nd:0 3rd:1 Ran:6
Win Prizemoney £7,262 *Total Prizemoney* £8,393
Wins * **1998** Spt Haydoc (G-F) H 14f 69 69+ <
1998 Turf 1-6: (8f, 10f, 11f, 14f 1-1, 15f, 18f) (gd 2, g-f, frm 1-3)
Average gelding, effective 14 to 15f, acts on frm. Turf high 69 (began Jly) - 1st of 8 getting 3lb from Spring Anchor (26 Spt Haydock RF 4500). A decent bumper performer, he showed improved form on the Flat in his first handicap, when stepped up markedly in trip, but was a little disappointing when well backed for the Cesarewitch. Was well fancied for the Cesarewitch, but sustained an injury. **Mrs M Reveley [3-9] A Sharratt & J Renton.*

LORD LIEUTENANT BHB 85f **RR 83f** 2136[15]

3 b g Primo Dominie 7.2f **(67)** - Danzig Harbour (USA) (Private Account (USA)) 8.5f **(74)**
Form - 3050
Record 1998 - 1st:0 2nd:0 3rd:1 Ran:4
Pre1998 - 1st:1 2nd:0 3rd:0 Ran:3
Win Prizemoney £4,034 *Total Prizemoney* £5,214
Wins * 1997 Spt Beverl (G-F) 5f 79 <
1998 Turf 0-4: (5f 2, 6f 2) (gd, g-f 3)
Lengthy, decent gelding, effective 5 to 6f, best at 5f, acts on gd to frm. Turf high 87 (1st run) - 3rd of 15 giving 17lb to Rioja (16 Apr Newmarket 6f gd RF 0711). Ran a fine race at Newmarket on his reappearance. There looks to be another race in him, but he is inconsistent. **M Bell [1-7] Highclere Thoroughbred Racing Ltd.*

LORD NITROGEN (USA) BHB 40f37a **RR 40f 37a** 87[P]

8 b or br g Greinton 15.8f **(75)** - Jibber Jabber (USA) (Jacinto) 9.9f **(79)**
Form - P
Record 1998 - 1st:0 2nd:0 3rd:0 Ran:1
Pre1998 - 1st:1 2nd:0 3rd:0 Ran:12
Win Prizemoney £3,483 *Total Prizemoney* £3,483
1998 AW 0-1: (15f) (Fibr)
Moderate gelding. Inconsistent.
**B J Llewellyn [3-22] B J Llewellyn (from R W Emery [0-5] Dec 1994).*

LORD OF LOVE BHB 48f **RR 55f** 2867[6]

3 b g Noble Patriarch 12.2f **(43)** - Gymcrak Lovebird (Taufan (USA)) 7f **(57)**
Form - 0644456
Record 1998 - 1st:0 2nd:0 3rd:0 Ran:7
Pre1998 - 1st:0 2nd:0 3rd:2 Ran:10
Win Prizemoney £0 *Total Prizemoney* £1,892
1998 Turf 0-7: (8f 3, 9f 3, 11f) (gd 6, frm)
Leggy, fair gelding, effective 6 to 7f, acts on g-f to frm, likes right handed tracks. Turf high 58.
**T D Easterby [0-17] Cumbrian Industrials Ltd.*

LORD OF MEN BHB 112f **RR 112f** 4598a[1]

5 ch h Groom Dancer (USA) 9.5f **(75)** - Upper Strata (Shirley Heights) 10.3f **(74)**
Form - 3215351
Record 1998 - 1st:2 2nd:1 3rd:1 Ran:6
Pre1998 - 1st:6 2nd:0 3rd:2 Ran:9
Win Prizemoney £128,969 *Total Prizemoney* £213,685
Wins * **1998** Spt Maison (GD) G3 10f 112 <
* **1998** Jly Cheste (G-F) 10.3f 107+
* 1997 Aug Deauvi (GD) G3 10f 107
* 1997 Jly Sandow (G-F) 10f 107
* 1997 Jun Doncas (G-S) 8f 99
* 1995 Spt Longch (SFT) G1 7f 108+
* 1995 Aug Lingfi (G-F) 7.6f 95+
* 1995 Aug Newmar (G-F) 7f 93+
1998 Turf 2-6: (10f 2-4, 11f, 12f) (gd 1-5, frm 1-1)
Group-class colt, effective 10 to 13f, acts on sft to frm, best on gd, has worn blinkers, excels at Deauville. Turf high 112 - 1st of 10 giving 6lb to Dragonada (23 Spt Maisons-laffitte RF 4598a) - also 1st of 2 giving 12lb to On The Ridge (10 Jly Chester RF 2679). Consistent. He was a revelation when tried in a visor at Maison-Laffitte in September, breaking a course record that had been set by Dr Fong earlier in the campaign. There are better prizes to be won if he can reproduce that effort. Easy ground and ten furlongs look his ideal conditions. **J H M Gosden [8-15] Sheikh Mohammed.*

LORD OLIVIER (IRE) BHB 60f **RR 66f** 3767[9]

8 b g The Noble Player (USA) 7.7f **(58)** - Burkina (African Sky) 7.9f **(63)**
Form - 5850840
Record 1998 - 1st:0 2nd:0 3rd:0 Ran:7
Pre1998 - 1st:8 2nd:8 3rd:3 Ran:54
Win Prizemoney £28,855 *Total Prizemoney* £55,543
Wins * 1997 Spt Bright (FRM) 7f 71
* 1997 Apr Epsom (GD) H 6f 75 81
* 1996 Aug Haydoc (G-F) C 6f 73
* 1996 Jly Epsom (GD) C 6f 65
* 1994 Apr Thirsk (GD) 6f 87
1998 Turf 0-7: (6f 4, 7f 3) (gd 2, g-f 2, frm 3)
Average gelding, effective 6 to 7f, best at 7f, acts on gd to frm, best on frm, has worn blinkers. Turf high 68. Veteran sprinter who was not at his best in '98. **W Jarvis [8-61] Miss V R Jarvis.*

LORD ROCHESTER BHB 69f **RR 61f** 4772[15]

2 b c Distant Relative 7f **(69)** - Kentfield (Busted) 10.2f **(61)**
Form - 850
Record 1998 - 1st:0 2nd:0 3rd:0 Ran:3
1998 Turf 0-3: (7f 2, 8f) (gd, g-f, frm)
Currently average colt. Turf high 61.
**B R Millman [0-3] Lewis, Gudge, Calver Geering.*

LORD SKY BHB 48f65a **RR 46f 65a** 651[4]

7 b g Emarati (USA) 6.6f **(63)** - Summer Sky (Skyliner) 7.3f **(53)**
Form - 44
Record 1998 - 1st:0 2nd:0 3rd:0 Ran:2
Pre1998 - 1st:5 2nd:5 3rd:4 Ran:54
Win Prizemoney £17,097 *Total Prizemoney* £27,172
Wins * 1997 *Mar Lingfi (STD) H 5f 68 65*
* 1997 *Jan Lingfi (STD) C 6f 61*
* 1995 *Feb Wolver (STD) H 5f 68 66*
1994 Aug Bath (G-F) C 5.7f 68
1998 AW 0-2: (5f 2) (Equi, Fibr)
Moderate gelding, effective 5 to 6f, best at 5f, - acts on Equi, has worn blinkers, prefers left handed tracks, prefers tight tracks. AW high 35. Inconsistent. A regular on sand in recent seasons, his best form has been over sprint trips on Equitrack, though he has not shown much since winning on that surface in March 1997. He is a little hard to predict nowadays.
**A Bailey [3-48] Ray Bailey (from P F I Cole [2-8] Aug 1994).*

LORD STROLLER BHB 63f **RR 67f** 4230[9]

2 b c Petong 7.6f **(58)** - Breakfast Boogie (Sizzling Melody)
Form - 06660
Record 1998 - 1st:0 2nd:0 3rd:0 Ran:5
1998 Turf 0-5: (5f 2, 6f 2, 7f) (g-s, gd 2, frm 2)
Average colt, has worn blinkers. Turf high 67 - 6th of 15 giving 5lb to Golden Charm (15 May Nottingham 6f frm RF 1245).
**B R Millman [0-5] Gudge, Calvert, Lewi Geering.*

LORD WARFORD BHB 57f **RR 62f** 4869[15]

3 b g Bustino 11f **(64)** - Jupiter's Message (Jupiter Island) 14f **(62)**
Form - 0460330
Record 1998 - 1st:0 2nd:0 3rd:2 Ran:7
Pre1998 - 1st:0 2nd:0 3rd:0 Ran:4
Win Prizemoney £0 *Total Prizemoney* £1,060
1998 Turf 0-7: (10f 4, 12f 3) (g-s, gd 3, g-f, frm 2)
Scopey, average gelding, effective 10f, acts on gd, likes tight tracks. Turf high 62 - 4th of 8 getting 11lb from Praetorian Gold (30 Jun Chepstow 10f gd RF 2397). **G B Balding [0-12] Peter Richardson.*

LORENZO (IRE) BHB 62f60a **RR 69f 60a** 5125[10]

3 b br c Distinctly North (USA) 7.4f **(63)** - Stephens Guest (IRE) (Don't Forget Me) 8.3f **(74)**
Form - 05060063470
Record 1998 - 1st:0 2nd:0 3rd:1 Ran:11
Win Prizemoney £0 *Total Prizemoney* £822
1998 Turf 0-10: (6f, 7f 4, 8f 4, 12f) (sft, g-s 2, gd 3, g-f 2, frm, hrd) 1998 AW 0-1: (10f) (Equi)
Workmanlike, average colt, effective 8f, acts on frm, likes tight tracks. Turf high 69 - 3rd of 10 to Khaled (31 Aug Warwick 8f frm RF 4008). **K Mahdi [0-11] Hamad Al-Mutawa.*

LORINER'S LASS **RR 49f** 4583[9]

2 b f Saddlers' Hall (IRE) 10.5f **(65)** - Sixslip (USA) (Diesis) 9.3f **(69)**
Form - 00
Record 1998 - 1st:0 2nd:0 3rd:0 Ran:2
1998 Turf 0-2: (7f, 8f) (gd, frm)

Currently moderate filly. Turf high 49 (began Spt).
**I A Balding [0-2] Summertree Stud.*

LOST IN LUCCA BHB 61f **RR 59+f** 4835[12]

2 b f Inchinor 8.9f **(64)** - Poyle Fizz (Damister (USA)) 9f **(73)**
Form - 4640
Record 1998 - 1st:0 2nd:0 3rd:0 Ran:4
Win Prizemoney £0 *Total Prizemoney* £183
1998 Turf 0-3: (6f, 7f 2) (g-s, gd, frm) 1998 AW 0-1: (7f) (Fibr)
Fair filly. Turf high 59 (1st run) (began Jly) - 4th of 13 getting 2lb from Jack Goodman (15 Jly Folkestone 7f gd RF 2822).
**J W Hills [0-4] The Jampot Partnership.*

LOST SPIRIT BHB 54f **RR 57df** 3924[6]

2 b g Strolling Along (USA) - Shoag (USA) (Affirmed (USA)) 9.3f **(79)**
Form - 026
Record 1998 - 1st:0 2nd:1 3rd:0 Ran:3
Win Prizemoney £0 *Total Prizemoney* £1,110
1998 Turf 0-3: (6f, 7f 2) (g-f, frm 2)
Currently fair gelding, often wears blinkers. Turf high 57 (began Jly). **B Hanbury [0-3] C H Bothway.*

LOTS OF MAGIC BHB 96f **RR 85f** 4306[4]

2 b c Magic Ring (IRE) 6.5f **(64)** - Pounelta (Tachypous) 8.6f **(55)**
Form - 22414
Record 1998 - 1st:1 2nd:2 3rd:0 Ran:5
Win Prizemoney £3,452 *Total Prizemoney* £8,273
Wins * 1998 Spt Epsom (GD) 7f 85 <
1998 Turf 1-5: (7f 1-5) (gd 1-4, g-f)
Useful colt. Turf high 85 - 1st of 9 from Maple (4 Spt Epsom RF 4082). Has twice finished behind Aljabr, fourth to him in a Group Three at Goodwood. Moderate effort on his final start.
**R Hannon [1-5] Peter Valentine.*

LOUBIN LANE BHB 47f **RR 31f** 2173[P]

3 b f Deploy 11.4f **(67)** - Another Lane (Tina's Pet) 6.8f **(59)**
Form - 00P
Record 1998 - 1st:0 2nd:0 3rd:0 Ran:3
Pre1998 - 1st:0 2nd:0 3rd:0 Ran:4
1998 Turf 0-3: (8f 2, 10f) (sft, gd, frm)
Workmanlike, very moderate filly, effective 8f, acted on gd. Turf high 31. (DEAD) **A G Newcombe [0-7] G E Harris.*

LOUGHANLEA (USA) BHB 61f **RR 57f** 4960[11]

2 b br g Salt Lake (USA) - Moment Of Flight (USA) (My Favorite Moment (USA))
Form - 0000
Record 1998 - 1st:0 2nd:0 3rd:0 Ran:4
1998 Turf 0-4: (5f, 6f, 7f, 8f) (gd 2, g-f, frm)
Fair gelding. Turf high 57.
**M A Jarvis [0-3] Burke's 5th Family Settlement (from M W Easterby [0-1] Apr 1998).*

LOUGH SWILLY (IRE) BHB 97f **RR 93f** 4738[5]

2 b c Mukaddamah (USA) 7.6f **(74)** - Flooding (USA) (Irish River (FR)) 8.6f **(78)**
Form - 41315
Record 1998 - 1st:2 2nd:0 3rd:1 Ran:5
Win Prizemoney £8,935 *Total Prizemoney* £10,014
Wins * 1998 Spt Goodwo (G-F) 7f 93 <
*** 1998** Aug Nottin (G-F) 6.1f 93+
1998 Turf 2-5: (6f 1-3, 7f 1-1, 8f) (g-s, gd 1-2, frm 1-2)
Useful colt. Turf high 93 (began Jly) - 1st of 9 getting 2lb from Abe (12 Aug Nottingham RF 3583) - also 1st of 8 giving 11lb to Herb of Grace (23 Spt Goodwood RF 4453). The winner of a Nottingham maiden and a Goodwood conditions event, he was stepped up in class and up to a mile at Ascot for his final start, but failed to handle the very soft ground and was well beaten.
**B W Hills [2-5] John Grant.*

LOUIS PHILIPPE (USA) BHB 75f **RR 82f** 4644[7]

3 b c El Gran Senor (USA) 8.9f **(85)** -Naqiyah(USA)(In Reality) 7.4f **(74)**
Form - 447
Record 1998 - 1st:0 2nd:0 3rd:0 Ran:3
Pre1998 - 1st:0 2nd:1 3rd:0 Ran:2
Win Prizemoney £0 *Total Prizemoney* £1,624
1998 Turf 0-3: (8f 2, 10f) (gd, g-f, frm)
Scopey, decent colt, has worn blinkers. Turf high 77 - 4th of 6 giving 5lb to Nasaayem (24 Spt Goodwood 10f gd RF 4464).
**J H M Gosden [0-5] P D Savill.*

LOVEABLE ROGUE **RR 42f** 4860[8]

2 b c Simply Great (FR) 11.9f **(61)** - Quick J (Jim J (USA))
Form - 8
Record 1998 - 1st:0 2nd:0 3rd:0 Ran:1
1998 Turf 0-1: (8f) (sft)
Currently moderate colt. **M A Peill [0-1] Geoff Bonson.*

LOVE ACADEMY BHB 55f68a **RR 56f 68a** 5114[3]

3 b g Royal Academy (USA) 7.8f **(77)** - Quiet Week-End (Town And Country) 8.1f **(68)**
Form - 0040700013
Record 1998 - 1st:1 2nd:0 3rd:1 Ran:10
Pre1998 - 1st:1 2nd:1 3rd:0 Ran:3
Win Prizemoney £5,507 *Total Prizemoney* £8,374
Wins * 1998 *Oct Southw (STD) H 8f 55 63*
* 1997 Oct Newcas (G-F) 6f 86 <
1998 Turf 0-8: (5f, 6f, 7f 3, 8f, 9f 2) (g-s 2, gd 6) 1998 AW 1-2: (7f, 8f 1-1) (Fibr 1-2)
Above-average gelding, effective 6f, acts on gd, has worn blinkers. Turf high 77. AW high 63 (began Jly). **M Johnston [2-13] M Doyle.*

LOVE BLUES (USA) BHB 60f58a **RR 56f 58a** 4876[5]

2 b c Hansel (USA) 12.6f **(78)** - Jolie Bold (USA) (Bold Forbes (USA)) 8.9f **(59)**
Form - 6665
Record 1998 - 1st:0 2nd:0 3rd:0 Ran:4
1998 Turf 0-3: (7f 2, 9f) (gd 2, g-f) 1998 AW 0-1: (6f) (Fibr)
Fair colt. Turf high 56. **M Johnston [0-4] M Doyle.*

LOVEDAY **RR** 457[6]

3 br f Environment Friend 7.5f **(67)** - Always on a Sunday (Star Appeal) 9.6f **(65)**
Form - 6
Record 1998 - 1st:0 2nd:0 3rd:0 Ran:1
1998 AW 0-1: (9f) (Fibr)
Light-framed, currently very poor filly.
**S C Williams [0-1] Mrs D V C Whittingham.*

LOVE DIAMONDS (IRE) BHB 52f56a **RR 55f 56a** 4658[13]

2 b g Royal Academy (USA) 7.8f **(77)** - Baby Diamonds (Habitat) 9.4f **(70)**
Form - 5850
Record 1998 - 1st:0 2nd:0 3rd:0 Ran:4
1998 Turf 0-4: (6f 2, 7f, 8f) (gd 4)
Fair gelding. Turf high 55. **M Johnston [0-4] M Doyle.*

LOVE IS WELCOME (USA) **RR 57f** 1967[9]

4 b c Corporate Report (USA) - L'Emigress (CAN) (L'Emigrant (USA)) 10.5f **(62)**
Form - 00
Record 1998 - 1st:0 2nd:0 3rd:0 Ran:2
1998 Turf 0-2: (5f, 6f) (gd, g-f)
Strong, currently fair colt. Turf high 57. **M Johnston [0-2] M Doyle.*

LOVE KISS (IRE) BHB 82f **RR 82f** 1141[11]

3 b c Brief Truce (USA) 9.1f **(73)** - Pendulina (Prince Tenderfoot (USA)) 9f **(61)**
Form - 0
Record 1998 - 1st:0 2nd:0 3rd:0 Ran:1
Pre1998 - 1st:0 2nd:0 3rd:1 Ran:3
Win Prizemoney £0 *Total Prizemoney* £1,051
1998 Turf 0-1: (11f) (gd)
Workmanlike, decent colt. **M Johnston [0-4] M Doyle.*

LOVELY ISLAND (IRE) BHB 60f56a **RR 61f 56a** 5068[5]

2 b f Inchinor 8.9f **(64)** -Lovely Me (IRE) **(56f 57a)** (Vision (USA)) 9f **(64)**
Form - 5655
Record 1998 - 1st:0 2nd:0 3rd:0 Ran:4
1998 Turf 0-4: (5f 2, 6f 2) (gd, g-f 3)
Average filly. Turf high 59 (began Spt) - 6th of 14 getting 5lb from Ones Enough (25 Spt Folkestone 5f g-f RF 4471).
**R F JohnsonHoughton [0-4] Mrs J O'Halloran.*

LOVE ME DO (USA) BHB 62f60a **RR 67f 60a** 3237[9]

4 b g Minshaanshu Amad (USA) 11.3f **(53)** - I Assume (USA) (Young Emperor) 10.1f **(63)**

Form - 00

Record	**1998** -	1st:0	2nd:0	3rd:0	Ran:2
	Pre1998 -	1st:2	2nd:1	3rd:4	Ran:15

Win Prizemoney £6,264 *Total Prizemoney* £9,263

Wins	1997	Aug Redcar (FRM) H	14.1f	60	67	<
	1997	*Feb Southw (STD)*	*12f*		*55*	

1998 Turf 0-2: (12f, 14f) (frm 2)

Strong, above-average gelding, effective 11 to 17f, acts on gd to frm - acts on Fibr, likes left handed tracks, favours tight tracks, does well at Southwell. Turf high 45 (began Jly).

**Mrs Merrita Jones [0-2] Fabulous Four Partnership (from M Johnston [2-15] Aug 1997).*

LOVE OPERA BHB 49f **RR 46f** 5060[7]

3 ch f Pursuit of Love 9.5f **(69)** - Lets Fall In Love (USA) (Northern Baby (CAN)) 11.6f **(71)**

Form - 3487

Record	**1998** -	1st:0	2nd:0	3rd:1	Ran:4

Win Prizemoney £0 *Total Prizemoney* £757

1998 Turf 0-4: (5f 2, 6f, 8f) (sft, g-f 2, frm)

Lengthy, moderate filly. Turf high 59 (1st run) (began Aug) - 3rd of 9 to Bollin Ann (15 Aug Ripon 5f g-f RF 3657).

**J Berry [0-4] Mrs S Dalton.*

Strong, high-class filly, effective 7 to 9f, acts on gd to frm. Turf high 118 - 2nd of 10 getting 5lb from Decorated Hero (17 Oct Newmarket 7f gd RF 4849) - also 1st of 13 from Wren (8 Jly Newmarket RF 2637). She was disappointing in a maiden at the Craven Meeting on her reappearance, but bolted up in soft ground at Yarmouth next time. She ran very well to finish third in the Jersey, before stamping herself a high-class filly with a sparkling win in the Falmouth Stakes at Newmarket. She ran very poorly in soft ground at Deauville, but was a good third in a Group Two at Goodwood on a sounder surface, and only just lost out to Decorated Hero in the Challenge Stakes. Her last race came in the States when she finished a close fifth in a handicap on Breeders' Cup day.

**Sir Michael Stoute [2-8] Cheveley Park Stud (from D R Loder [0-1] Nov 1997).*

LOVER'S LEAP RR 73f 4139[2]

2 b g Pursuit of Love 9.5f **(69)** - Anna Karietta (Precocious) 8.6f **(62)**

Form - 02

Record	**1998** -	1st:0	2nd:1	3rd:0	Ran:2

Win Prizemoney £0 *Total Prizemoney* £1,020

1998 Turf 0-2: (6f, 7f) (g-f, frm)

Currently above-average gelding. Turf high 73 (began Jly) - 2nd of 15 to Culzean (8 Spt Leicester 7f g-f RF 4139).

**H Candy [0-2] The Earl Cadogan.*

Lovers Knot unravelled for a stylish win at Newmarket

LOVERS KNOT BHB 114f **RR 118f** 5161a[5]

3 b f Groom Dancer (USA) 9.5f **(75)** - Nemea (USA) (The Minstrel (CAN)) 10f **(72)**

Form - 01316325

Record	**1998** -	1st:2	2nd:1	3rd:2	Ran:8
	Pre1998 -	1st:0	2nd:1	3rd:0	Ran:1

Win Prizemoney £37,890 *Total Prizemoney* £74,745

Wins	* **1998**	Jly Newmar (G-F) G2	8f	110	<
	* **1998**	Jun Yarmou (SFT)	7f	86++	

1998 Turf 2-8: (7f 1-4, 8f 1-3, 9f) (sft, gd 3, g-f 1-2, frm 1-2)

LOVE VENTURE BHB 45f **RR 55f** 4402[8]

4 b f Pursuit of Love 9.5f **(69)** - Our Shirley (Shirley Heights) 10.3f **(74)**

Form - 08

Record	**1998** -	1st:0	2nd:0	3rd:0	Ran:2
	Pre1998 -	1st:0	2nd:1	3rd:1	Ran:8

Win Prizemoney £0 *Total Prizemoney* £2,297

1998 Turf 0-2: (8f, 10f) (g-f, frm)

Scopey, fair filly, effective 8f, acts on gd, likes left handed tracks, likes tight tracks. Turf high 40 (began Aug). Becoming disappointing. **Miss M E Rowland [0-7] GTanner&JRevell (from SWoods [0-8] Oct 1997).*

LOVEYOUMILLIONS (IRE) BHB 62f65a **RR 61f 65a** 2392[3]
6 b g Law Society(USA) 11.6f **(71)** -Warning Sound(Red Alert) 7.6f **(66)**
Form - 3
Record 1998 - 1st:0 2nd:0 3rd:1 Ran:1
Pre1998 - 1st:2 2nd:5 3rd:1 Ran:27
Win Prizemoney £73,266 *Total Prizemoney* £84,974
Wins 1994 Aug Currag (SFT) 6f 85+
1994 Jun Hamilt (G-F) 5f 77+
1998 Turf 0-1: (10f) (g-f)
Average gelding, has broken blood-vessels, has worn blinkers. Inconsistent. **M C Pipe [2-4] A G Fear (from N Tinkler [0-8] Apr 1997).*

LOVING CLAIM (USA) RR 112f 1918a[7]
3 b f Hansel (USA) 12.6f **(78)** - Ville D'Amore (USA) (Irish River (FR)) 8.6f **(78)**
Form - 527
1998 Turf 0-3: (8f, 10f, 11f) (sft, gd 2)
Group-class filly, has worn blinkers. Turf high 110 - 2nd of 9 to Zainta (17 May Longchamp 10f gd RF 1382a). Impressive when winning the Prix Marcel Boussac as a juvenile, she was lightly raced last season and could not handle soft ground in the Prix de Diane Hermes. **Mme C Head in FR [1-4] Maktoum Al Maktoum.*

LOVIN SPOONFUL (USA) BHB 66f **RR 71f** 4118[9]
3 ch f Dixieland Band (USA) 10.1f **(80)** - O My Darling (USA) (Mr Prospector (USA)) 8.8f **(78)**
Form - 03400
Record 1998 - 1st:0 2nd:0 3rd:1 Ran:5
Win Prizemoney £0 *Total Prizemoney* £802
1998 Turf 0-4: (6f 2, 8f 2) (g-f 2, frm 2) 1998 AW 0-1: (7f) (Fibr)
Scopey, above-average filly. Turf high 71 - 3rd of 12 to Cornflower Fields (29 May Bath 8f frm RF 1569).
**P F I Cole [0-5] Christopher Wright.*

LOXLEY'S GIRL (IRE) BHB 34f30a **RR 34f 30a** 36[9]
4 b f Lahib (USA) 8f **(69)** - Samnaun (USA) (Stop The Music (USA)) 9.2f **(71)**
Form - 0
Record 1998 - 1st:0 2nd:0 3rd:0 Ran:1
Pre1998 - 1st:0 2nd:0 3rd:1 Ran:8
Win Prizemoney £0 *Total Prizemoney* £542
1998 AW 0-1: (7f) (Equi)
Unfurnished, very moderate filly, effective 7 to 8f, acts on frm - acts on Fibr, has worn blinkers. Inconsistent.
**H Akbary [0-6] S R Hudson (from M W Easterby [0-3] Jun 1996).*

LOYAL TOAST (USA) BHB 75f **RR 78f** 3222[18]
3 b c Lyphard (USA) 10.6f **(75)** - Lisieux (USA) (Steady Growth (CAN)) 9.9f **(78)**
Form - 0051570
Record 1998 - 1st:1 2nd:0 3rd:0 Ran:7
Win Prizemoney £4,854 *Total Prizemoney* £4,854
Wins * **1998** Jun Goodwo (G-F) H 9.9f 73 78 <
1998 Turf 1-7: (7f, 8f 3, 9f, 10f 1-2) (sft, gd 2, frm 1-4)
Well made, above-average colt, effective 8 to 10f, best at 10f, acts on frm. Turf high 78 - 1st of 8 giving 3lb to Prince Batshoof (5 Jun Goodwood RF 1756). Looked a progressive sort when getting off the mark at Goodwood, and his running next time should be dismissed as he never saw daylight. Fair effort in a competitive race at Newmarket. **L M Cumani [1-7] Lord De La Warr.*

L S LOWRY (USA) BHB 65f **RR 78f** 5094[5]
2 b c Thorn Dance (USA) 8.2f **(77)** - Queluz (USA) (Saratoga Six (USA)) 7f **(73)**
Form - 015
Record 1998 - 1st:1 2nd:0 3rd:0 Ran:3
Win Prizemoney £6,027 *Total Prizemoney* £6,027
Wins * **1998** Oct Newmar (GD) S 7f 78 <
1998 Turf 1-3: (5f, 7f 1-1, 8f) (g-s, gd, frm 1-1)
Currently above-average colt. Turf high 78 (began Oct) - 1st of 28 from Cops (15 Oct Newmarket RF 4818). Beat a huge field in a valuable seller at Newmarket on his second start.
**P F I Cole [1-3] Richard Green (Fine Paintings).*

LUANSHYA BHB 73f **RR 70f** 4820[5]
2 b f First Trump - Blues Indigo (Music Boy) 6.8f **(57)**
Form - 3242535
Record 1998 - 1st:0 2nd:2 3rd:2 Ran:7
Win Prizemoney £0 *Total Prizemoney* £3,078
1998 Turf 0-7: (5f 5, 6f 2) (gd, g-f 3, frm 3)
Above-average filly, effective 5 to 6f, best at 5f, acts on gd to frm, best on g-f. Turf high 70 - 5th of 15 getting 16lb from Acicula (15 Oct Newmarket 6f frm RF 4820). **R M Whitaker [0-7] The PBT Group.*

LUCAYAN BEACH BHB 72f **RR 72f** 3928[6]
4 gr g Cyrano de Bergerac 7.3f **(58)** - Mrs Gray (Red Sunset) 8.2f **(63)**
Form - 136
Record 1998 - 1st:1 2nd:0 3rd:1 Ran:3
Pre1998 - 1st:0 2nd:1 3rd:0 Ran:6
Win Prizemoney £2,866 *Total Prizemoney* £4,803
Wins * **1998** Jly Kempto (G-F) C 6f 68 <
1998 Turf 1-3: (6f 1-3) (frm 1-3)
Workmanlike, above-average gelding, effective 6f, acts on frm. Turf high 72 (began Jly) - 3rd of 12 getting 4lb from Rushcutter Bay (31 Jly Newmarket 6f frm RF 3238).
**B Gubby [1-9] Brian Gubby Ltd.*

LUCAYAN INDIAN (IRE) BHB 106f **RR 111f** 2702[1]
3 ch c Indian Ridge 7.6f **(74)** - Eleanor Antoinette (IRE) (Double Schwartz) 7.9f **(55)**
Form - 231
Record 1998 - 1st:1 2nd:1 3rd:1 Ran:3
Pre1998 - 1st:2 2nd:0 3rd:0 Ran:3
Win Prizemoney £18,739 *Total Prizemoney* £29,709
Wins * **1998** Jly York (G-F) 7.9f 111 <
* 1997 Oct Newmar (G-S) 7f 91
* 1997 Oct Newcas (G-F) 6f 88
1998 Turf 1-3: (8f 1-3) (gd 2, frm 1-1)
Scopey, Group-class colt, effective 8f, acts on gd to frm. Turf high 111 - 1st of 4 getting 6lb from Bold Words (10 Jly York RF 2702). He was the medium of some hefty wagers in handicaps on his first two starts, but failed to deliver. He gave the impression that there was something left in the locker when winning a minor event at York in July, should train on into a smart four-year-old and will stay beyond a mile. **D R Loder [3-6] Lucayan Stud.*

LUCAYAN SPRING RR 87f 1608[2]
3 ch c Ela-Mana-Mou 12.7f **(72)** - Gorgeous Dancer (IRE) (Nordico (USA)) 6.5f **(62)**
Form - 52
Record 1998 - 1st:0 2nd:1 3rd:0 Ran:2
Win Prizemoney £0 *Total Prizemoney* £1,236
1998 Turf 0-2: (11f, 14f) (gd, g-f)
Strong, currently useful colt. Turf high 86 - 2nd of 3 to Laurentide (30 May Newmarket 14f g-f RF 1608). Promising efforts in maidens, but he did not look all that resolute when runner-up on his second start. **M Johnston [0-2] Lucayan Stud.*

LUCIDO (IRE) RR 82f 4946a[3]
2 b c Royal Academy (USA) 7.8f **(77)** - Lady Ambassador (General Assembly (USA)) 10f **(68)**
Form - 413
Record 1998 - 1st:1 2nd:0 3rd:1 Ran:3
Win Prizemoney £3,239 *Total Prizemoney* £17,056
Wins * **1998** Spt Salisb (HVY) 8f 82 <
1998 Turf 1-3: (7f, 8f 1-2) (hvy, gd 1-1, frm)
Currently decent colt. Turf high 82 (began Jly) - also 1st of 10 from Western Folly (30 Spt Salisbury RF 4584). **J L Dunlop [1-3].*

LUCKY ARCHER BHB 72f **RR 72f** 4319[5]
5 b g North Briton 8.2f **(53)** - Preobrajenska (Double Form) 7.3f **(58)**
Form - 111250025
Record 1998 - 1st:3 2nd:2 3rd:0 Ran:9
Pre1998 - 1st:0 2nd:2 3rd:3 Ran:17
Win Prizemoney £12,961 *Total Prizemoney* £20,243
Wins * **1998** Jun Carlis (G-S) H 8f 64 71 <
* **1998** May Yarmou (FRM) H 7f 55 67
* **1998** May Nottin (FRM) H 8.2f 55 59
1998 Turf 3-9: (7f 1-3, 8f 2-6) (gd 1-2, g-f 3, frm 2-4)
Above-average gelding, effective 7 to 8f, best at 8f, acts on gd to frm, best on frm, has worn blinkers, likes tight tracks, excels at Beverley. Turf high 72 - 2nd of 15 giving 7lb to Kass Alhawa (29 Aug Beverley 7f frm RF 3942) - also 1st of 18 getting 4lb from Colway Ritz (24 Jun Carlisle RF 2227). Comfortable winner of a weak race at Nottingham in May, he went on to complete a hat-

trick with victories at Yarmouth and Carlisle. The latter victory, in the historic Carlisle Bell, showed what a tough performer he is. Lost little in defeat next time, but the Handicapper then grabbed him.
**J M Bradley [3-12] The Parishioners (from C E Brittain [0-14] Oct 1996).*

LUCKY BEA BHB 42f **RR 45f** 4408[13]
5 b g Lochnager 6.9f **(50)** - Knocksharry (Palm Track) 9.8f **(50)**
Form - 00
Record 1998 - 1st:0 2nd:0 3rd:0 Ran:2
Pre1998 - 1st:1 2nd:3 3rd:5 Ran:28
Win Prizemoney £3,631 *Total Prizemoney* £8,297
Wins 1996 May Newcas (GD) H 8f 54 56 <
1998 Turf 0-2: (7f, 10f) (gd, g-f)
Moderate gelding, has worn blinkers. Turf high 28 (began Spt).
**G Holmes [0-2] Steve Ryan (from M W Easterby [2-34] Apr 1997).*

LUCKY BEGONIA (IRE) BHB 54f70a **RR 55f 70a** 5069[4]
5 br m Simply Great (FR) 11.9f **(61)** - Hostess (Be My Guest (USA)) 9.3f **(67)**
Form - 221515161004
Record 1998 - 1st:4 2nd:1 3rd:0 Ran:11
Pre1998 - 1st:0 2nd:4 3rd:0 Ran:12
Win Prizemoney £10,246 *Total Prizemoney* £14,656
Wins ** **1998** Aug Southw (STD) H 12f 65 68 <*
* **1998** Jun Mussel (SFT) 12f 50
** **1998** May Southw (STD) H 11f 55 60*
** **1998** Mar Southw (STD) H 8f 52 54*
1998 Turf 1-5: (12f 1-5) (gd 1-1, g-f, frm 3) 1998 AW 3-6: (8f 1-3, 11f 1-2, 12f 1-1) (Fibr 3-6)
Average filly, effective 11 to 12f, best at 12f, acts on frm - acts on Fibr, prefers tight tracks. Turf high 59 (1st run) - 5th of 8 giving 14lb to Phantom Waters (25 May Chepstow 12f frm RF 1445). AW high 68 - 1st of 10 giving 24lb to Miss Vita (14 Aug Southwell RF 3641) - also 1st of 16 giving 24lb to Makati (11 May Southwell RF 1152). She had finished runner-up more times than was desirable before March of 1998, but she has done very well since, winning three times on the Southwell Fibresand and once on turf at Musselburgh. She has won over a mile, but is much better over middle distances.
**A W Carroll [4-11] Serafino Agodino (from W J Musson [0-8] Nov 1997).*

LUCKY BY PHAR **RR** 3628[6]
3 b g Pharly (FR) 11.5f **(64)** - Lots of Luck (Neltino) 7.6f **(54)**
Form - 6
Record 1998 - 1st:0 2nd:0 3rd:0 Ran:1
1998 Turf 0-1: (12f) (g-f)
Workmanlike, currently very poor gelding, always wears blinkers - 6th of 6 to Petane (14 Aug Folkestone 12f g-f RF 3628).
**J Pearce [0-1] Phil Mackay.*

LUCKY COVE BHB 79f71a **RR 75f 71a** 4303[4]
2 gr c Lugana Beach 7f **(63)** - Port Na Blath (On Your Mark) 7.7f **(58)**
Form - 33024
Record 1998 - 1st:0 2nd:1 3rd:2 Ran:5
Win Prizemoney £0 *Total Prizemoney* £1,672
1998 Turf 0-2: (5f 2) (gd 2) 1998 AW 0-3: (5f 2, 6f) (Fibr 3)
Above-average colt. Turf high 75 (began Aug). AW high 69.
**B A McMahon [0-5] J R Smith.*

LUCKY DOUBLE BHB 66f **RR 72f** 4540[14]
3 b c Green Desert (USA) 7.8f **(78)** - Lady Bentley (Bellypha) 9.8f **(73)**
Form - 0346778010
Record 1998 - 1st:1 2nd:0 3rd:1 Ran:10
Pre1998 - 1st:1 2nd:0 3rd:0 Ran:3
Win Prizemoney £6,701 *Total Prizemoney* £7,536
Wins * **1998** Spt Leices (G-F) S 10f 61+
* 1997 Oct Salisb (GD) 7f 75 <
1998 Turf 1-10: (7f, 8f 3, 9f, 10f 1-5) (gd 3, frm 1-7)
Above-average colt, effective 7 to 10f, acts on gd to frm, best on frm. Turf high 76 - 4th of 16 getting 1lb from Circuiteer (22 May Pontefract 8f frm RF 1406). **R Hannon [2-13] Mohamed Suhail.*

LUCKY FEATHER (IRE) BHB 63f **RR 64f** 4873[12]
2 b f Lucky Guest - Hens Grove (Alias Smith (USA)) 9.8f **(58)**
Form - 005810
Record 1998 - 1st:1 2nd:0 3rd:0 Ran:6
Win Prizemoney £2,094 *Total Prizemoney* £2,094
Wins 1998 Oct Leices (G-S) S 10f 62+ <
1998 Turf 1-6: (7f 3, 8f 2, 10f 1-1) (gd 1-4, frm 2)
Average filly, effective 10f, acts on gd. Turf high 64 (began Jly) - also 1st of 18 from Medelai (12 Oct Leicester RF 4762).
**G Lewis [0-1] Geoff Lewis (from J L Dunlop [1-5] Oct 1998).*

LUCKY GITANO (IRE) BHB 80f **RR 81f** 5009[5]
2 b br c Lucky Guest - April Wind (Windjammer (USA)) 7f **(59)**
Form - 325
Record 1998 - 1st:0 2nd:1 3rd:1 Ran:3
Win Prizemoney £0 *Total Prizemoney* £1,165
1998 Turf 0-3: (8f 3) (sft, g-s, frm)
Currently decent colt. Turf high 81 (began Spt) - 2nd of 10 to Simply Noble (28 Spt Hamilton 8f g-s RF 4530).
**J L Dunlop [0-3] Anamoine Ltd.*

LUCKY LINDA (IRE) BHB 59f **RR 56f** 5138[7]
2 b f Bluebird (USA) 7.9f **(71)** - Spectacular Dawn (Spectacular Bid (USA)) 11.2f **(76)**
Form - 077
Record 1998 - 1st:0 2nd:0 3rd:0 Ran:3
1998 Turf 0-3: (6f, 7f 2) (sft, gd 2)
Currently fair filly. Turf high 56 (began Oct).
**J L Dunlop [0-3] Peter Winfield.*

LUCKY LOVER (IRE) BHB 65f **RR 73f** 3511[6]
3 b br c Ballad Rock 7.2f **(63)** -Petticoat Lane(Ela-Mana-Mou)10.1f **(70)**
Form - 846
Record 1998 - 1st:0 2nd:0 3rd:0 Ran:3
Win Prizemoney £0 *Total Prizemoney* £260
1998 Turf 0-3: (8f 3) (frm 2, hrd)
Scopey, currently above-average colt. Turf high 73 (began Jly).
**G B Balding [0-3] Ms Julia Doveton.*

LUCKY ME (IRE) BHB 47f50a **RR 51f 50a** 4955[5]
3 gr g Maledetto (IRE) - Silver Heart (Yankee Gold) 7.6f **(55)**
Form - 4000070435
Record 1998 - 1st:0 2nd:0 3rd:1 Ran:10
Win Prizemoney £0 *Total Prizemoney* £270
1998 Turf 0-8: (7f 5, 8f 2, 10f) (g-s, gd 4, g-f, frm 2) 1998 AW 0-2: (7f, 8f) (Equi, Fibr)
Workmanlike, fair gelding. Turf high 51. AW high 56.
**M H Tompkins [0-10] Michael Keogh.*

LUCKY MYST BHB 50f **RR 66f** 4883[11]
3 b g Mystiko (USA) 7.7f **(59)** -Lucky Omen(Queen's Hussar) 11.6f **(58)**
Form - 6500
Record 1998 - 1st:0 2nd:0 3rd:0 Ran:4
Pre1998 - 1st:0 2nd:0 3rd:1 Ran:1
Win Prizemoney £0 *Total Prizemoney* £490
1998 Turf 0-4: (6f, 8f, 10f 2) (g-s, gd, g-f 2)
Workmanlike, average gelding. Turf high 66 (began Aug).
**C E Brittain [0-5] R N Khan.*

LUCKY NEMO **RR 50f** 5039[16]
2 b c Sabrehill (USA) 8.5f **(64)** -Lucky Omen(Queen's Hussar)11.6f **(58)**
Form - 00
Record 1998 - 1st:0 2nd:0 3rd:0 Ran:2
1998 Turf 0-2: (6f, 8f) (g-s 2)
Currently fair colt. Turf high 50 (began Oct).
**C E Brittain [0-2] R N Khan.*

LUCKY RASCAL (IRE) **RR 66tf** 2742[16]
2 b c Indian Ridge 7.6f **(74)** - Chesnut Tree (USA) (Shadeed (USA)) 8.2f **(70)**
Form - 40
Record 1998 - 1st:0 2nd:0 3rd:0 Ran:2
Win Prizemoney £0 *Total Prizemoney* £214
1998 Turf 0-2: (6f 2) (g-f, frm)
Currently average colt. Turf high 66 (began Jly).
**B Hanbury [0-2] Abdullah Ali.*

LUCKY RED BHB 59f58a **RR 68f 58a** 4969[7]
2 b g Presidium 7.5f **(56)** - Judys Girl (IRE)(Simply Great (FR)) 8.2f **(65)**

Form - 2633537
Record 1998 - 1st:0 2nd:1 3rd:3 Ran:7
Win Prizemoney £0 *Total Prizemoney* £1,342
1998 Turf 0-6: (5f, 6f 2, 7f 3) (g-s 2, gd 2, g-f, frm) 1998 AW 0-1: (6f) (Fibr)
Average gelding, effective 6 to 7f, acts on g-s to g-f, often wears blinkers. Turf high 68 - 3rd of 20 giving 5lb to Enthaisingh (2 Oct Lingfield 6f g-s RF 4612).
**Pat Mitchell [0-1] Mrs G Dunlop (from K McAuliffe [0-6] Oct 1998).*

LUCKY UNO BHB 42f RR 30f 5139[16]

2 b c Rock City 8.8f **(62)** - Free Skip (Free State) 8.7f **(61)**
Form - 080
Record 1998 - 1st:0 2nd:0 3rd:0 Ran:3
1998 Turf 0-3: (6f, 8f 2) (sft, gd 2)
Currently very moderate colt. Turf high 30 (began Oct).
**C Smith [0-3] Lucky Racing.*

LUCREZIA (IRE) BHB 82f RR 79f 4824[10]

3 b f Machiavellian (USA) 9.8f **(83)** - Troyanna (Troy) 10.4f **(68)**
Form - 217810
Record 1998 - 1st:2 2nd:1 3rd:0 Ran:6
Win Prizemoney £10,698 *Total Prizemoney* £11,624
Wins * **1998** Oct Warwic (GD) H 12.5f 77 74 <
* **1998** Jun Chepst (G-S) 12.1f 73
1998 Turf 2-6: (10f 2, 12f 1-3, 13f 1-1) (gd 1-1, g-f 1-2, frm 3)
Workmanlike, above-average filly, effective 10 to 13f, acts on gd to frm, has worn blinkers. Turf high 79 - also 1st of 12 getting 9lb from Carlys Quest (4 Oct Warwick RF 4647).
**Sir Michael Stoute [2-6] Lord Weinstock.*

LUCY GLITTERS (USA) RR 48f 4087[16]

3 b f Cryptoclearance (USA) - Way of The World (USA) (Dance of Life (USA)) 7f **(66)**
Form - 00000
Record 1998 - 1st:0 2nd:0 3rd:0 Ran:5
Pre1998 - 1st:0 2nd:0 3rd:0 Ran:1
1998 Turf 0-5: (6f 3, 7f 2) (gd 3, g-f, frm)
Small, moderate filly. Turf high 48. **I A Balding [0-6] Paul Mellon.*

LUCY MARIELLA BHB 67f RR 71df 4881[5]

2 b f Mystiko (USA) 7.7f **(59)** - Deanta in Eirinn (Red Sunset) 8.2f **(63)**
Form - 37205
Record 1998 - 1st:0 2nd:1 3rd:1 Ran:5
Win Prizemoney £0 *Total Prizemoney* £1,240
1998 Turf 0-5: (5f 4, 6f) (g-s, gd 2, g-f, frm)
Above-average filly. Turf high 71. **J R Arnold [0-5] Terry Barwick.*

LUCY TUFTY BHB 33f28a RR 32f 28a 2065[7]

7 b m Vin St Benet 11.4f **(48)** - Manor Farm Toots (Royalty) 11.4f **(49)**
Form - 1677
Record 1998 - 1st:1 2nd:0 3rd:0 Ran:4
Pre1998 - 1st:1 2nd:0 3rd:1 Ran:14
Win Prizemoney £4,974 *Total Prizemoney* £5,448
Wins * **1998** Apr Ripon (SFT) SH 12.3f 33 44 <
* 1996 Nov Folkes (SFT) SH 12f 35 44 <
1998 Turf 1-4: (12f 1-3, 14f) (hvy, sft 1-1, gd, frm)
Very moderate mare, effective 12f, acts on sft. Turf high 44 (1st run) - 1st of 20 getting 24lb from Lancer (8 Apr Ripon RF 0609). Consistent. **J Pearce [4-47] G H Tufts.*

LUDERE (IRE) BHB 43f37a RR 46f 37a 3907[5]

3 ch g Desse Zenny (USA) 12f **(53)** - White Jasmin (Jalmood (USA)) 10.1f **(52)**
Form - 8534761254355
Record 1998 - 1st:1 2nd:1 3rd:2 Ran:12
Pre1998 - 1st:0 2nd:0 3rd:0 Ran:5
Win Prizemoney £2,372 *Total Prizemoney* £4,234
Wins 1998 May Mussel (GD) C 12f 40 <
1998 Turf 1-8: (12f 1-6, 14f, 16f) (gd 3, g-f 1-3, frm 2) 1998 AW 0-4: (8f 2, 11f, 12f) (Fibr 4)
Moderate gelding, effective 12f, acts on g-f, has worn blinkers, likes right handed tracks, favours tight tracks. Turf high 48 - 2nd of 12 getting 16lb from Hasta la Vista (18 May Musselburgh 12f g-f RF 1301) - also 1st of 5 getting 2lb from Ruby Bear (1 May Musselburgh RF 0954). AW high 38. Consistent. Won possibly one of the worst races ever run in Scotland, a Musselburgh claimer in May, but he could do no more than win.
**P Monteith [0-7] P Monteith (from J Hetherton [1-6] May 1998).*

LUGANA LADY RR 26f 3525[12]

2 b f Lugana Beach 7f **(63)** - Mrs Bacon (Balliol) 5f **(43)**
Form - 00
Record 1998 - 1st:0 2nd:0 3rd:0 Ran:2
1998 Turf 0-2: (5f, 6f) (g-f, frm)
Currently little account filly. Turf high 26 (began Jly).
**D HaydnJones [0-2] Stephen Owen.*

LUISIANA LADY BHB 37f RR 42f 3402[9]

3 b f Unfuwain (USA) 11.4f **(74)** - Ever Welcome (Be My Guest (USA)) 9.3f **(67)**
Form - 00000
Record 1998 - 1st:0 2nd:0 3rd:0 Ran:5
1998 Turf 0-5: (7f, 8f, 10f 3) (gd, g-f, frm 2, hrd)
Leggy, moderate filly. Turf high 42.
**B Hanbury [0-5] Mrs Holly Rincon.*

LUJAIN (USA) BHB 100f RR 120df 4851[6]

2 b c Seeking the Gold (USA) 7.4f **(80)** - Satin Flower (USA) (Shadeed (USA)) 8.2f **(70)**
Form - 1116
Record 1998 - 1st:3 2nd:0 3rd:0 Ran:4
Win Prizemoney £80,199 *Total Prizemoney* £82,249
Wins * **1998** Oct Newmar (gd) G1 6f 120++ <
* **1998** Spt York (GD) 6f 107++
* **1998** Jly Newmar (GD) 6f 90++
1998 Turf 3-4: (6f 3-3, 7f) (gd 1-2, g-f 1-1, frm 1-1)
Very high-class colt. Turf high 120 (began Jly) - 1st of 7 from Bertolini (1 Oct Newmarket RF 4593). Out of a mare who won the Jersey Stakes, he was an impressive winner of the Middle Park, albeit from some substandard opposition, having earlier impressed with fluent victories in a maiden and a novice event. He ran very disappointingly in the Dewhurst, and connections had no explanation for the poor show. He will join Godolphin for 1999, and if that last run is ignored, he looks a live candidate for the Guineas, although he may ultimately turn out to be a sprinter.
**D R Loder [3-4] Sheikh Mohammed.*

LUNAR LORD BHB 49f RR 46f 5145[8]

2 b c Elmaamul (USA) 8.1f **(70)** - Cache (Bustino) 10.4f **(64)**
Form - 708
Record 1998 - 1st:0 2nd:0 3rd:0 Ran:3
1998 Turf 0-3: (6f, 7f, 8f) (g-s, gd, g-f)
Currently moderate colt. Turf high 46 (began Oct).
**J S Moore [0-3] Alex Gorrie.*

LUNAR MIST BHB 68f RR 73df 2454[9]

5 b m Komaite (USA) 6.9f **(61)** - Sugar Token (Record Token) 6.3f **(53)**
Form - 70
Record 1998 - 1st:0 2nd:0 3rd:0 Ran:2
Pre1998 - 1st:6 2nd:1 3rd:3 Ran:18
Win Prizemoney £31,746 *Total Prizemoney* £35,197
Wins * 1995 Oct Newbur (G-S) H 6f 83 90 <
* 1995 Oct Newmar (G-F) H 6f 76 83
* 1995 Spt Newmar (GD) H 5f 62 74+
* 1995 Spt Haydoc (GD) H 6f 62 74
* 1995 Spt Mussel (GD) H 5f 62 66+
* 1995 May Haydoc (GD) S 5f 50
1998 Turf 0-2: (6f, 7f) (gd 2)
Above-average filly, effective 5 to 6f, best at 5f, acts on gd to g-f, best on gd. Turf high 48. **M Meade [6-20] Mrs P A Barratt.*

LUNAR MUSIC BHB 40f47a RR 42f 47a 4547[7]

4 b f Komaite (USA) 6.9f **(61)** -Lucky Candy (Lucky Wednesday) 8f **(50)**
Form - 0668001007
Record 1998 - 1st:1 2nd:0 3rd:0 Ran:10
Pre1998 - 1st:2 2nd:1 3rd:2 Ran:22
Win Prizemoney £8,103 *Total Prizemoney* £9,906
Wins * **1998** Aug Nottin (G-F) H 5.1f 34 42
1996 Aug Mussel (G-F) S 5f 80+ <
1996 Jly Lingfi (FRM) S 5f 65+
1998 Turf 1-7: (5f 1-4, 6f, 7f 2) (gd 1-3, g-f, frm 3) 1998 AW 0-3: (5f, 6f, 7f) (Fibr 3)
Scopey, moderate filly, effective 5f, - acts on AW, has worn blink-

ers. Turf high 42. AW high 45.
**S R Bowring [1-10] Paul Dixon (from Ronald Thompson [0-8] Jly 1997).*

7lb from Royal Result (14 Aug Catterick RF 3621).
**J Berry [3-10] S Aitken (from D Nicholls [3-13] Nov 1997).*

Lujain will relax in the Dubai sunshine this winter

LUNAR PROSPECTOR (IRE) BHB 73f **RR 77f** 4591[15]

2 ch f Second Set(IRE) 9.2f **(67)** -Eastern Aura(IRE)(Ahonoora)8.1f **(73)**
Form - 2363220

Record	**1998** -	1st:0	2nd:3	3rd:2	Ran:7

Win Prizemoney £0 *Total Prizemoney* £4,637
1998 Turf 0-7: (5f 7) (gd 4, g-f 3)
Above-average filly, effective 5f, acts on gd to g-f, best on g-f. Turf high 77 (1st run) - 2nd of 10 getting 5lb from Kastaway (4 May Doncaster 5f g-f RF 1005). A speedy sort, she has become frustrating.
**C A Dwyer [0-7] Bernard Hathaway.*

LUNCH PARTY BHB 60f **RR 64f** 4840[8]

6 b g Beveled (USA) 6.9f **(64)** - Crystal Sprite (Crystal Glitters (USA)) 11.3f **(79)**
Form - 3112614858

Record	**1998** -	1st:3	2nd:1	3rd:1	Ran:10
	Pre1998 -	1st:3	2nd:1	3rd:0	Ran:13

Win Prizemoney £18,898 *Total Prizemoney* £21,934

Wins								
	*** 1998**	Aug Catter	(G-F)	H	7f	60	63	<
	*** 1998**	May Catter	(G-S)	H	7f	52	57	
	*** 1998**	May Mussel	(G-F)	H	7.1f	47	49	
	1997	Nov Mussel	(G-S)	H	8f	40	49	
	1997	Spt Yarmou	(FRM)	H	7f	38	42	
	1996	May Thirsk	(G-F)	S	7f		57+	

1998 Turf 3-10: (7f 3-7, 8f 3) (sft, g-s, gd 1-3, g-f 1-3, frm 1-2)
Average gelding, effective 7 to 8f, best at 7f, acts on gd to frm, best on gd, likes right handed tracks, likes tight tracks, excels at Catterick, likes Musselburgh. Turf high 64 - 4th of 12 getting 8lb from Tiler (22 Aug Chester 8f gd RF 3801) - also 1st of 20 getting

LUNCHTIME GIRL BHB 40f40a **RR 35f 40a** 424[9]

3 ch f Cadeaux Genereux 7.9f **(76)** - Thewaari (USA) (Eskimo (USA))
Form - 00

Record	**1998** -	1st:0	2nd:0	3rd:0	Ran:2
	Pre1998 -	1st:0	2nd:0	3rd:0	Ran:4

1998 AW 0-2: (7f, 8f) (Fibr 2)
Lengthy, moderate filly. AW high 13.
**J D Bethell [0-6] Robert Gibbons.*

LUNE LASS **RR 60f** 2658[7]

2 br f Cyrano de Bergerac 7.3f **(58)** - Oubeck **(50f)** (Mummy's Game) 8.2f **(60)**
Form - 74617

Record	**1998** -	1st:1	2nd:0	3rd:0	Ran:5

Win Prizemoney £2,230 *Total Prizemoney* £2,230

Wins	*** 1998**	Jun Carlis	(G-S)	S	5f	60	<

1998 Turf 1-4: (5f 1-4) (gd 1-4) 1998 AW 0-1: (5f) (Fibr)
Average filly. Turf high 60 - 1st of 9 from Done And Dusted (25 Jun Carlisle RF 2261). (DEAD)
**E Weymes [1-5] Mrs A Birkett.*

LUSO BHB 118f **RR 119f** 4219a[7]

6 b h Salse (USA) 10.9f **(71)** - Lucayan Princess (High Line) 10.3f **(70)**
Form - 1745617

Record	**1998** -	1st:1	2nd:0	3rd:0	Ran:6
	Pre1998 -	1st:9	2nd:9	3rd:1	Ran:28

Win Prizemoney £1,179,885 *Total Prizemoney* £1,693,891

Wins						
	*** 1998**	Aug Gelsen	(GD)	G1	12f	119
	* 1997	Dec Sha Ti	(G-F)	G2	12f	119

* 1997	Jly	Dussel (GD)	G1	12f	121	
* 1997	May	Capann (G-F)	G2	12f	121	
* 1996	Dec	Sha Ti (G-F)	G2	12f	124	<
* 1996	Aug	Gelsen (GD)	G1	12f	118	
* 1996	May	Capann (G-F)	G2	8f	114+	
* 1996	Apr	Newmar (G-F)	G3	9f	117	
* 1995	May	Capann (G-F)	G1	12f	101	
* 1995	May	Cheste (G-F)	G3	12.3f	97	

1998 Turf 1-5: (12f 1-5) (sft, gd 1-3, g-f) 1998 AW 0-1: (10f) (Dirt)
High-class horse, effective 12f, acts on gd to frm, best on gd, prefers right handed tracks, and excels at Gelsenkirchen-Horst. Turf high 119 - 1st of 8 from Ungaro (9 Aug Gelsenkirchen-Horst RF 3616a). He has been globetrotting again, and gained another victory in a German Group One in August. He only made one appearance in this country in 1998, finishing down the field in the Coronation Cup. **C E Brittain [10-34] Saeed Manana.*

LUTINE BELL BHB 48f **RR 51f** 4666[8]
3 b g Fairy King (USA) 7.7f **(75)** - Bell Toll (High Line) 10.3f **(70)**
Form - 08
Record 1998 - 1st:0 2nd:0 3rd:0 Ran:2
Pre1998 - 1st:0 2nd:0 3rd:0 Ran:1
1998 Turf 0-2: (6f, 8f) (g-s, gd)
Leggy, currently fair gelding. Turf high 51 (began Spt).
**J E Banks [0-3] Giles Pritchard-Gordon.*

LUZ BAY (IRE) BHB 70f67a **RR 64f 67a** 4930[8]
2 b g Tenby 10.4f **(76)** - Cabcharge Princess (IRE) **(51f)** (Rambo Dancer (CAN))
Form - 58
Record 1998 - 1st:0 2nd:0 3rd:0 Ran:2
1998 Turf 0-2: (8f 2) (g-s, gd)
Currently average gelding. Turf high 64 (began Oct).
**R Charlton [0-2] S M De Zoete.*

LUZERN BHB 83f **RR 74f** 4846[5]
2 ch c Selkirk (USA) 7.9f **(76)** - Luana **(94f)** (Shaadi (USA))
Form - 735
Record 1998 - 1st:0 2nd:0 3rd:1 Ran:3
Win Prizemoney £0 *Total Prizemoney* £525
1998 Turf 0-3: (6f 2, 7f) (gd, g-f, frm)
Currently above-average colt. Turf high 74 (began Jly).
**C E Brittain [0-3] Saeed Manana.*

LV GIRL (IRE) BHB 58f **RR 65f** 4991[4]
2 ch f Mukaddamah (USA) 7.6f **(74)** - Penny Fan **(34f)** (Nomination) 7f **(60)**
Form - 7674
Record 1998 - 1st:0 2nd:0 3rd:0 Ran:4
Win Prizemoney £0 *Total Prizemoney* £505
1998 Turf 0-4: (5f 2, 7f 2) (sft, gd, g-f, frm)
Average filly. Turf high 65. **G B Balding [0-4] Mrs C A Richardson.*

LYCIAN (IRE) BHB 57f56a **RR 57f 56a** 4653[3]
3 b g Lycius (USA) 8.8f **(71)** - Perfect Time (IRE) (Dance of Life (USA)) 7f **(66)**
Form - 12153
Record 1998 - 1st:2 2nd:1 3rd:1 Ran:5
Pre1998 - 1st:0 2nd:0 3rd:0 Ran:4
Win Prizemoney £6,572 *Total Prizemoney* £7,817
Wins * **1998** Jly Bright (G-F) H 8f 52 57 <
* **1998** May Bath (G-F) H 8f 47 48
1998 Turf 2-4: (8f 2-4) (gd 1-1, g-f, frm 1-2) 1998 AW 0-1: (9f) (Fibr)
Well made, fair gelding, effective 8 to 9f, best at 8f, acts on gd to frm - acts on Fibr. Turf high 57 - 3rd of 15 getting 11lb from Drive Assured (5 Oct Brighton 8f g-f RF 4653) - also 1st of 12 getting 20lb from Soft Touch (23 Jly Brighton RF 3041). (1st run) - 2nd of 8 giving 1lb to Shipley Glen (17 Jun Wolverhampton 9f Fibr RF 2082).
**J A R Toller [2-5] A Ilsley (from Sir Mark Prescott [0-4] Oct 1997).*

LYRIST **RR 61f** 3736[13]
2 gr f Cozzene (USA) 10.1f **(87)** - La Llave (USA) (Risen Star (USA))
Form - 0
Record 1998 - 1st:0 2nd:0 3rd:0 Ran:1
1998 Turf 0-1: (7f) (frm)
Currently average filly. **C E Brittain [0-1] Saeed Manana.*

MA-ARIF (IRE) BHB 81f **RR 89f** 4761[5]
2 b f Alzao (USA) 9.8f **(73)** - Taqreem (IRE) **(75df)** (Nashwan (USA))
Form - 445
Record 1998 - 1st:0 2nd:0 3rd:0 Ran:3
Win Prizemoney £0 *Total Prizemoney* £612
1998 Turf 0-3: (7f 2, 8f) (gd, g-f 2)
Currently useful filly. Turf high 89 (began Spt) - 4th of 10 to Social Scene (16 Spt Sandown 8f g-f RF 4309).
**J H M Gosden [0-3] Hamdan Al Maktoum.*

MAAS (IRE) BHB 60f65a **RR 64f 65a** 4200[18]
3 br c Elbio 9f **(62)** - Payne's Grey (Godswalk (USA)) 7.3f **(58)**
Form - 400
Record 1998 - 1st:0 2nd:0 3rd:0 Ran:3
Pre1998 - 1st:0 2nd:0 3rd:0 Ran:1
1998 Turf 0-3: (5f 2, 6f) (gd, g-f, frm)
Average colt. Turf high 64 (began Jly).
**P J Makin [0-4] Brian Brackpool.*

MAAZOOM (IRE) BHB 43f **RR 45f** 4408[16]
3 b br g Be My Guest (USA) 10.2f **(66)** - Lancette (Double Jump) 9.4f **(58)**
Form - 50000
Record 1998 - 1st:0 2nd:0 3rd:0 Ran:5
Pre1998 - 1st:0 2nd:0 3rd:0 Ran:1
1998 Turf 0-5: (7f 2, 8f 2, 10f) (g-s, gd, g-f 2, frm)
Scopey, moderate gelding, has worn blinkers. Turf high 45.
**M E Sowersby [0-3] Newland Paint Partnership (from J H M Gosden [0-5] Jun 1998).*

MA BARNICLE (IRE) BHB 38f48a **RR 55f 48a** 2969[9]
5 ch m Al Hareb (USA) 9.4f **(53)** - Soltina (Sun Prince) 12.4f **(52)**
Form - 780
Record 1998 - 1st:0 2nd:0 3rd:0 Ran:3
Pre1998 - 1st:0 2nd:2 3rd:3 Ran:10
Win Prizemoney £0 *Total Prizemoney* £2,400
1998 Turf 0-1: (10f) (gd) 1998 AW 0-2: (8f, 15f) (Fibr 2)
Fair filly, effective 7f, acts on gd, has worn blinkers. AW high 32.
**P Eccles [0-10] The Ten Thousand To One Club (from D K Weld in IRE [0-10] Oct 1997).*

MACARI BHB 23f37a **RR 40f 37a** 4970[10]
4 gr g Arzanni - View Halloa (Al Sirat (USA))
Form - 00036080
Record 1998 - 1st:0 2nd:0 3rd:1 Ran:8
Pre1998 - 1st:0 2nd:0 3rd:1 Ran:10
Win Prizemoney £0 *Total Prizemoney* £643
1998 Turf 0-7: (8f, 10f 3, 11f 2, 12f) (g-s, g-f 3, frm 3) 1998 AW 0-1: (9f) (Fibr)
Workmanlike, moderate gelding, effective 10f, acts on frm. Turf high 40. **B P J Baugh [0-19] Iain Gillies.*

MACCA LUNA (IRE) BHB 72f **RR 62f** 1482[8]
3 b f Kahyasi 12.9f **(74)** -Medicosma (USA)(The Minstrel (CAN))10f **(72)**
Form - 8
Record 1998 - 1st:0 2nd:0 3rd:0 Ran:1
Pre1998 - 1st:1 2nd:0 3rd:0 Ran:2
Win Prizemoney £2,780 *Total Prizemoney* £2,780
Wins * 1997 Spt Hamilt (GD) 8.3f 62+ <
1998 Turf 0-1: (11f) (gd)
Scopey, currently average filly. **M H Tompkins [1-3] B McAllister.*

MACGILLYCUDDY (IRE) BHB 48f **RR 39f** 2890[10]
9 bb g Petorius 8f **(66)** - My Bonnie (Highland Melody) 6.3f **(55)**
Form - 000
Record 1998 - 1st:0 2nd:0 3rd:0 Ran:3
Pre1998 - 1st:0 2nd:1 3rd:1 Ran:16
Win Prizemoney £0 *Total Prizemoney* £1,288
1998 Turf 0-3: (5f, 6f 2) (frm 3)
Very moderate gelding, often wears blinkers. Turf high 38. Consistent.
**Mrs P N Dutfield [0-9] Mrs Nerys Dutfield (from Patrick Prendergast in IRE [0-10] Oct 1996).*

MACHIAVELLI BHB 74f **RR 65f** 5126[13]
4 b g Machiavellian (USA) 9.8f **(83)** - Forest Blossom (USA) (Green Forest (USA)) 9.9f **(68)**

Form - 000
Record 1998 - 1st:0 2nd:0 3rd:0 Ran:3
Pre1998 - 1st:1 2nd:0 3rd:1 Ran:6
Win Prizemoney £3,615 *Total Prizemoney* £5,118
Wins 1997 Jly Pontef (GD) 12f 87 <
1998 Turf 0-3: (10f, 12f 2) (g-s, g-f, frm)
Leggy, average gelding, effective 12f, acts on g-f to frm, has worn blinkers. Turf high 65. Consistent.
**G L Moore [2-7] B V & C J Pennick II (from H R A Cecil [1-6] Spt 1997).*

MACH ONE (FR) BHB 50f46a **RR 45f 46a** 1794[6]
3 b g Sanglamore (USA) 12.9f **(67)** - Douceur (USA) (Shadeed (USA)) 8.2f **(70)**
Form - 06
Record 1998 - 1st:0 2nd:0 3rd:0 Ran:2
Pre1998 - 1st:0 2nd:0 3rd:0 Ran:1
1998 Turf 0-1: (7f) (gd) 1998 AW 0-1: (7f) (Fibr)
Scopey, currently moderate gelding.
**Sir Mark Prescott [0-3] Roger Barby.*

MAC OATES BHB 39f44a **RR 37f 44a** 4653[12]
5 b g Bairn (USA) 9.4f **(55)** - Bit of a Lass (Wassl) 9.7f **(62)**
Form - 856000
Record 1998 - 1st:0 2nd:0 3rd:0 Ran:4
Pre1998 - 1st:1 2nd:1 3rd:0 Ran:14
Win Prizemoney £3,915 *Total Prizemoney* £4,788
Wins * 1997 Spt Goodwo (GD) CH 8f 44 51 <
1998 Turf 0-3: (6f, 8f 2) (sft, gd, g-f) 1998 AW 0-1: (8f) (Equi)
Moderate gelding, effective 7 to 8f, acts on frm - acts on Fibr, favours tight tracks. Turf high 37.
**P R Hedger [1-10] D N Larke (from D W P Arbuthnot [0-9] Spt 1996).*

MAC'S BACK (USA) BHB 35f52a **RR 41f 52a** 2922[10]
3 br g Momsfurrari (USA) - Peace Sister (USA) (Hold Your Peace (USA)) 9f **(72)**
Form - 333040770
Record 1998 - 1st:0 2nd:0 3rd:2 Ran:8
Pre1998 - 1st:0 2nd:0 3rd:1 Ran:2
Win Prizemoney £0 *Total Prizemoney* £1,042
1998 Turf 0-4: (8f, 10f, 12f, 14f) (gd 2, g-f, frm) 1998 AW 0-4: (8f 4) (Equi 3, Fibr)
Workmanlike, fair gelding, effective 8f, - acts on Equi, has worn blinkers, likes left handed tracks, likes tight tracks. Turf high 43. AW high 51. Inconsistent.
**Mrs L Stubbs [0-8] Joseph Smith (from W A O'Gorman [0-2] Dec 1997).*

MAC'S DELIGHT BHB 45a **RR 30f** 1270[16]
4 b g Machiavellian (USA) 9.8f **(83)** - Bashoosh (USA) (Danzig (USA)) 8.4f **(76)**
Form - 00
Record 1998 - 1st:0 2nd:0 3rd:0 Ran:2
Pre1998 - 1st:0 2nd:0 3rd:1 Ran:6
Win Prizemoney £0 *Total Prizemoney* £495
1998 Turf 0-1: (7f) (frm) 1998 AW 0-1: (7f) (Fibr)
Very moderate gelding, has worn blinkers.
**H Akbary [0-3] S R Hudson (from N M Babbage [0-3] May 1997).*

MAC'S DREAM (USA) BHB 50f **RR 54f** 2173[7]
3 b g Mister Frisky (USA) - Annie's Dream (USA) (Droll Role (USA))
Form - 7407
Record 1998 - 1st:0 2nd:0 3rd:0 Ran:4
1998 Turf 0-4: (7f 2, 8f 2) (gd 2, g-f 2)
Scopey, fair gelding. Turf high 54.
**J Noseda [0-4] Michael McDonnell.*

MAD ALEX BHB 36f24a **RR 44f 24a** 927[13]
5 b g Risk Me (FR) 8f **(53)**-Princess Mona(Prince Regent(FR)) 9.8f **(54)**
Form - 00
Record 1998 - 1st:0 2nd:0 3rd:0 Ran:2
Pre1998 - 1st:0 2nd:0 3rd:1 Ran:8
Win Prizemoney £0 *Total Prizemoney* £374
1998 Turf 0-2: (7f, 8f) (gd 2)
Moderate gelding, effective 8f, acts on gd. Turf high 35. Inconsistent. **M J Haynes [0-14] J P Saunders.*

MADAM ALISON BHB 74f **RR 71f** 4994[1]
2 b f Puissance 7.1f **(60)** - Copper Burn (Electric) 10.1f **(61)**
Form - 60841
Record 1998 - 1st:1 2nd:0 3rd:0 Ran:5
Win Prizemoney £2,658 *Total Prizemoney* £2,658
Wins * 1998 Oct Leices (HVY) 6f 71 <
1998 Turf 1-5: (5f 2, 6f 1-2, 7f) (sft 1-1, g-s, gd, g-f, frm)
Above-average filly. Turf high 71 (began Jly) - 1st of 9 from Mayville's Dancer (26 Oct Leicester RF 4994).
**R Hannon [1-5] William Kelly.*

MADAME CHINNERY BHB 55f70a **RR 40f 70a** 5125[7]
4 b f Weldnaas (USA) 8.4f **(55)** - Bel Esprit (Sagaro) 9.7f **(55)**
Form - 401247007
Record 1998 - 1st:1 2nd:1 3rd:0 Ran:9
Pre1998 - 1st:1 2nd:3 3rd:0 Ran:9
Win Prizemoney £6,734 *Total Prizemoney* £10,982
Wins 1998 Jun Haydoc (GD) C 11.9f 67
1996 Spt Yarmou (GD) H 7f 72 77 <
1998 Turf 1-7: (10f, 12f 1-4, 14f, 16f) (g-s, gd 1-3, g-f, frm 2) 1998 AW 0-2: (12f, 14f) (Fibr 2)
Lengthy, above-average filly, effective 11 to 14f, acts on frm - acts on Fibr, prefers tight tracks. Turf high 71. AW high 71 (1st run) - 2nd of 9 giving 1lb to Manileno (12 Jun Southwell 14f Fibr RF 1941).
**C Weedon [0-4] Atlantic Foods Ltd (from J M P Eustace [2-15] Jly 1998).*

MADAME CLAUDE (IRE) BHB 71f **RR 70f** 4751[18]
3 b f Paris House 5.9f **(64)** - Six Penny Express (Bay Express) 7.1f **(60)**
Form - 3744420
Record 1998 - 1st:0 2nd:1 3rd:1 Ran:7
Pre1998 - 1st:1 2nd:1 3rd:0 Ran:5
Win Prizemoney £3,882 *Total Prizemoney* £7,574
Wins * 1997 Spt Yarmou (FRM) 6f 78 <
1998 Turf 0-7: (6f, 7f 6) (gd 2, g-f, frm 3, hrd)
Leggy, above-average filly, effective 5 to 7f, acts on gd to frm, best on frm. Turf high 78 (1st run) - 3rd of 16 giving 19lb to Mountain Magic (16 May Newbury 7f frm RF 1262).
**J A R Toller [1-12] P C J Dalby.*

MADAME JIRY (USA) BHB 72f **RR 68f** 3374[6]
2 b f Rahy (USA) 9.1f **(80)** - Free Thinker (USA) (Shadeed (USA)) 8.2f **(70)**
Form - 476
Record 1998 - 1st:0 2nd:0 3rd:0 Ran:3
Win Prizemoney £0 *Total Prizemoney* £235
1998 Turf 0-3: (5f, 6f, 7f) (gd, frm 2)
Currently average filly. Turf high 68. Stayed on nicely on her debut but was put in her place subsequently.
**P F I Cole [0-3] Lord Lloyd-Webber.*

MADAME JONES (IRE) BHB 74f65a **RR 74f 65a** 4799[8]
3 ch f Lycius (USA) 8.8f **(71)** -Gold Braisim(IRE)(Jareer (USA)) 5.9f **(75)**
Form - 21137005456108
Record 1998 - 1st:3 2nd:1 3rd:1 Ran:14
Pre1998 - 1st:0 2nd:0 3rd:2 Ran:4
Win Prizemoney £12,033 *Total Prizemoney* £15,126
Wins * 1998 Spt Cheste (GD) 6.1f 68 <
1998 Jun Goodwo (GD) H 6f 68 68 <
1998 May Nottin (FRM) 6.1f 64
1998 Turf 3-13: (5f 2, 6f 3-7, 7f, 8f 3) (sft, g-s, gd 2-4, g-f 3, frm 1-4)
1998 AW 0-1: (7f) (Fibr)
Workmanlike, above-average filly, effective 6 to 8f, best at 6f, acts on gd to frm, likes tight tracks, excels at Goodwood, does well at Lingfield and Chester. Turf high 74 - 3rd of 11 giving 12lb to Zeppo (23 Jun Lingfield 6f g-f RF 2201) - also 1st of 11 getting 5lb from Swino (23 Spt Chester RF 4446). Gave both Mark Buckley and Andrew Murphy their first winners.
**A T Murphy [1-3] E H Jones (Paints) Ltd (from M A Buckley [2-11] Spt 1998).*

MADAME MAXI BHB 55f **RR 54f** 4927[8]
4 ch f Ron's Victory (USA) 9.2f **(52)** - New Pastures (Formidable (USA)) 9.2f **(63)**
Form - 2108
Record 1998 - 1st:1 2nd:1 3rd:0 Ran:4

Pre1998 - 1st:0 2nd:0 3rd:0 Ran:3
Win Prizemoney £2,706 *Total Prizemoney* £3,390
Wins * **1998** Spt Bath (G-S) H 8f 52 54 <
1998 Turf 1-4: (8f 1-2, 10f 2) (g-s, gd, g-f 1-1, frm)
Leggy, fair filly, effective 8f, acts on g-f to frm. Turf high 54 (began Spt) - 1st of 18 giving 3lb to Oare Kite (28 Spt Bath RF 4529).
**H S Howe [1-3] George Searle (from P R Hedger [0-4] Spt 1998).*

MADAM LUCY BHB 37f42a **RR 33f 42a** 2148[10]
4 ch f Efisio 7.7f **(69)** - Our Aisling (Blakeney) 10.5f **(64)**
Form - 700
Record 1998 - 1st:0 2nd:0 3rd:0 Ran:3
Pre1998 - 1st:1 2nd:1 3rd:2 Ran:16
Win Prizemoney £2,007 *Total Prizemoney* £3,270
Wins 1997 *Jly Wolver (STD) C 9.4f 50* <
1998 Turf 0-2: (11f 2) (g-f, frm) 1998 AW 0-1: (11f) (Fibr)
Workmanlike, moderate filly, effective 8 to 12f, - acts on Fibr, has worn blinkers, favours left handed tracks. Turf high 33.
**J L Spearing [0-13] Inthebing Ltd (from P Howling [0-1] Jly 1997).*

MADAM WAAJIB (IRE) BHB 55f **RR 56f** 4873[16]
2 ch f Waajib 8.9f **(67)** - Clogher Head (Sandford Lad) 7.8f **(54)**
Form - 0770
Record 1998 - 1st:0 2nd:0 3rd:0 Ran:4
1998 Turf 0-4: (6f 2, 7f, 8f) (gd, g-f, frm 2)
Fair filly, has worn blinkers. Turf high 54 (began Aug).
**B W Hills [0-4] Mrs J C Raper.*

MADAM ZANDO BHB 25f26a **RR 31f 26a** 215[8]
5 ch m Forzando 7.2f **(63)** - Madam Trilby (Grundy) 10.3f **(65)**
Form - 88
Record 1998 - 1st:0 2nd:0 3rd:0 Ran:2
Pre1998 - 1st:0 2nd:3 3rd:1 Ran:26
Win Prizemoney £0 *Total Prizemoney* £3,568
1998 AW 0-2: (7f 2) (Fibr 2)
Very moderate filly, has worn blinkers. AW high 20.
**J Balding [0-26] Mrs Gillian Jones (from J M P Eustace [0-2] Jly 1995).*

MADISON MIST BHB 57f **RR 64f** 414[11]
4 gr f Mystiko (USA) 7.7f **(59)** - Hi-Li (High Top) 10.2f **(67)**
Form - 0
Record 1998 - 1st:0 2nd:0 3rd:0 Ran:1
Pre1998 - 1st:0 2nd:0 3rd:0 Ran:5
Win Prizemoney £0 *Total Prizemoney* £559
1998 AW 0-1: (8f) (Fibr)
Scopey, average filly, effective 7f, acts on hrd. She has shown some ability, and looks to have a race in her.
**Mrs J R Ramsden [0-6] Mrs Alison Iles.*

MADJAMILA (IRE) BHB 80f **RR 85?f** 5043[3]
3 b f Doyoun 10.7f **(69)** -Madaniyya(USA) (Shahrastani (USA)) 8.8f **(72)**
Form - 53
Record 1998 - 1st:0 2nd:0 3rd:1 Ran:2
Pre1998 - 1st:1 2nd:0 3rd:0 Ran:1
Win Prizemoney £3,114 *Total Prizemoney* £3,803
Wins * 1997 Oct Lingfi (GD) 7f 84+ <
1998 Turf 0-2: (7f, 10f) (sft, gd)
Leggy, currently useful filly. Turf high 85 (began Spt).
**L M Cumani [1-3] H H Aga Khan.*

MADMAN'S MIRAGE (FR) BHB 55f65a **RR 53f 65a** 2562[4]
3 b g Green Desert (USA) 7.8f **(78)** - Layaali (USA) (Diesis) 9.3f **(69)**
Form - 1255067204
Record 1998 - 1st:1 2nd:2 3rd:0 Ran:10
Pre1998 - 1st:0 2nd:0 3rd:0 Ran:3
Win Prizemoney £2,085 *Total Prizemoney* £4,437
Wins 1998 *Feb Southw (STD) H 6f 60 78+* <
1998 Turf 0-6: (6f, 8f 3, 9f 2) (g-s, gd 3, g-f, frm) 1998 AW 1-4: (6f 1-3, 7f) (Equi, Fibr 1-3)
Scopey, above-average gelding, effective 6 to 7f, - acts on AW, prefers left handed tracks, likes tight tracks. Turf high 55. AW high 78 (1st run) - 1st of 15 getting 4lb from Ellenbrook (16 Feb Southwell RF 0295).
**V Thompson [0-2] Mouldshaugh Farms Ltd (from M Johnston [1-11] Jun 1998).*

MAD MILITANT (IRE) BHB 52f58a **RR 55f 58a** 4002[9]
9 b g Vision (USA) 10.4f **(57)** - Ullapool (Dominion) 8.5f **(63)**
Form - 3360
Record 1998 - 1st:0 2nd:0 3rd:2 Ran:4
Pre1998 - 1st:16 2nd:8 3rd:14 Ran:83
Win Prizemoney £63,273 *Total Prizemoney* £84,662
Wins * 1997 Jun Warwic (FRM) H 10.8f 55 60
* 1997 Mar Warwic (G-F) H 10.8f 52 55
1995 *Aug Southw (STD) C 8f 73*
1995 *Apr Wolver (STD) C 12f 67*
1995 *Feb Southw (STD) C 12f 58+*
1995 *Jan Wolver (STD) C 12f 66*
1994 May Cheste (G-F) H 12.3f 65 70
1994 *Feb Wolver (STD) H 12f 75 69*
1998 Turf 0-4: (10f, 11f 3) (gd, g-f, frm 2)
Average gelding, effective 10 to 12f, best at 12f, acts on gd to hrd - acts on Fibr, likes Warwick. Turf high 55 - 3rd of 13 getting 5lb from Flying Eagle (24 Jun Warwick 11f g-f RF 2255).
**A Streeter [2-23] K Nicholls (from A L Forbes [2-4] Aug 1995).*

MADMUN (IRE) BHB 75f **RR 76df** 4273[5]
4 ch g Cadeaux Genereux 7.9f **(76)** - Kates Cabin (Habitat) 9.4f **(70)**
Form - 03235
Record 1998 - 1st:0 2nd:1 3rd:2 Ran:5
Win Prizemoney £0 *Total Prizemoney* £2,280
1998 Turf 0-5: (6f 3, 7f, 8f) (gd 2, g-f, frm 2)
Rangy, above-average gelding, has worn blinkers. Turf high 76 - 2nd of 16 giving 5lb to Long Siege (31 Jly Salisbury 6f g-f RF 3247). **M P Tregoning [0-5] Hamdan Al Maktoum.*

MAEDALEY BHB 52f44a **RR 55f 44a** 335[9]
3 b f Charmer 9f **(59)** - Carousella (Rousillon (USA)) 8.2f **(74)**
Form - 80
Record 1998 - 1st:0 2nd:0 3rd:0 Ran:2
Pre1998 - 1st:0 2nd:1 3rd:2 Ran:8
Win Prizemoney £0 *Total Prizemoney* £1,357
1998 AW 0-2: (6f, 8f) (Fibr 2)
Scopey, fair filly, effective 6 to 7f, acts on g-f to frm.
**Ronald Thompson [0-3] Haggswood Partnerships (from P C Haslam [0-7] Spt 1997).*

MAESTEG RR 45f 4524[13]
2 b f Reprimand 8.2f **(63)** - Eluned May **(42df)** (Clantime)
Form - 00
Record 1998 - 1st:0 2nd:0 3rd:0 Ran:2
1998 Turf 0-2: (5f, 6f) (g-f, frm)
Currently moderate filly. Turf high 45 (began Spt).
**J W Hills [0-2] Derek D & Mrs Jean P Clee.*

MAFTUN (USA) BHB 45f51a **RR 48f 51a** 4875[7]
6 ch g Elmaamul (USA) 8.1f **(70)** - Allesheny (Be My Guest (USA)) 9.3f **(67)**
Form - 0506662067
Record 1998 - 1st:0 2nd:1 3rd:0 Ran:9
Pre1998 - 1st:2 2nd:5 3rd:3 Ran:22
Win Prizemoney £5,999 *Total Prizemoney* £13,580
Wins * 1997 *Feb Southw (STD) H 12f 54 62* <
* 1996 Jly Newcas (FRM) H 12.4f 52 57
1998 Turf 0-5: (14f, 16f 3, 17f) (gd 2, frm 3) 1998 AW 0-4: (11f, 12f 2, 14f) (Fibr 4)
Fair gelding, effective 11 to 12f, best at 12f, - acts on Fibr, favours left handed tracks, favours tight tracks. Turf high 48. AW high 55 - 7th of 9 to River Captain (19 Oct Southwell 12f Fibr RF 4875).
**G M Moore [2-29] Anmaf Partnership (from Major W R Hern [0-4] Spt 1995).*

MAGDA (IRE) BHB 91f **RR 83+f** 4853[14]
2 b f Turtle Island (IRE) - Pennine Drive (IRE) (Pennine Walk) 8.5f **(61)**
Form - 010
Record 1998 - 1st:1 2nd:0 3rd:0 Ran:3
Win Prizemoney £3,214 *Total Prizemoney* £3,214
Wins * **1998** Oct Nottin (SFT) 8.2f 83+ <
1998 Turf 1-3: (7f 2, 8f 1-1) (g-s 1-1, gd, frm)
Currently decent filly. Turf high 83 (began Aug) - 1st of 11 from Ramruma (6 Oct Nottingham RF 4665). **C E Brittain [1-3] B H Voak.*

MAGGICE BHB 43f35a **RR 50f 35a** 453[6]
3 b f Magic Ring (IRE) 6.5f **(64)** - Ice Chocolate (USA) (Icecapade (USA)) 11f **(62)**
Form - 0746506
Record 1998 - 1st:0 2nd:0 3rd:0 Ran:4
Pre1998 - 1st:0 2nd:0 3rd:0 Ran:9
1998 AW 0-4: (6f 3, 8f) (Fibr 4)
Light-framed, fair filly. AW high 44. **R Hollinshead [0-13] J A Forsyth.*

MAGHAARB RR 94f 2368[1]
2 ch f Machiavellian (USA) 9.8f **(83)** - Fida (IRE) (Persian Heights)
Form - 21
Record 1998 - 1st:1 2nd:1 3rd:0 Ran:2
Win Prizemoney £3,631 *Total Prizemoney* £4,721
Wins * **1998** Jun Goodwo (GD) 6f 94 <
1998 Turf 1-2: (6f 1-2) (gd 1-2)
Currently useful filly. Turf high 94 - 1st of 9 getting 5lb from Exeat (28 Jun Goodwood RF 2368). Runner-up on her Goodwood debut in June, she went on to win very easily at the same track later the same month but was not seen out again.
**M P Tregoning [1-2] Hamdan Al Maktoum.*

MAGICAL BABA (IRE) BHB 90f85a **RR 86f 85a** 429[5]
3 b c Magical Wonder (USA) 7.2f **(60)** - Mystery Treat (Plugged Nickle (USA)) 7.8f **(68)**
Form - 5
Record 1998 - 1st:0 2nd:0 3rd:0 Ran:1
Pre1998 - 1st:1 2nd:0 3rd:0 Ran:5
Win Prizemoney £4,795 *Total Prizemoney* £5,295
Wins 1997 May Currag (GD) 5f 71 <
1998 AW 0-1: (9f) (Fibr)
Useful colt, effective 6 to 9f, acts on g-f - acts on Fibr, has worn blinkers. (1st run) - 5th of 7 getting 18lb from Diamond Flame (14 Mar Wolverhampton 9f Fibr RF 0429).
**W J Haggas [0-1] Mrs Henrietta Charlet (from Patrick Prendergast in IRE [1-5] Jly 1997).*

MAGICAL COLOURS (IRE) BHB 60f **RR 60f** 784[7]
3 b f Rainbows For Life (CAN) 9.3f **(64)** - Immediate Impact (Caerleon (USA)) 8.6f **(71)**
Form - 57
Record 1998 - 1st:0 2nd:0 3rd:0 Ran:2
Pre1998 - 1st:0 2nd:0 3rd:0 Ran:2
1998 Turf 0-2: (7f, 10f) (sft, gd)
Light-framed, average filly. Turf high 60.
**J L Dunlop [0-4] Mrs A Pratt.*

MAGICAL DANCER (IRE) BHB 47f **RR 47f** 4574[3]
3 b f Magical Wonder (USA) 7.2f **(60)** - Diva Encore (Star Appeal) 9.6f **(65)**
Form - 7840328183
Record 1998 - 1st:1 2nd:1 3rd:2 Ran:10
Pre1998 - 1st:0 2nd:0 3rd:0 Ran:9
Win Prizemoney £2,763 *Total Prizemoney* £4,573
Wins * **1998** Aug Warwic (G-F) H 8f 43 45 <
1998 Turf 1-10: (5f, 6f, 8f 1-4, 9f, 10f 3) (g-s, gd 2, g-f 3, frm 1-4)
Leggy, moderate filly, likes left handed tracks, likes tight tracks. Turf high 47. Consistent. She's a half-sister to the useful sprinters Encore M'Lady and Don't Worry Me but lacks their zip.
**Mrs P N Dutfield [1-19] The Piccolo Boys.*

MAGIC COMBINATION (IRE) BHB 44f **RR 44f** 4938[7]
5 b g Scenic 10.6f **(66)** - Etage (Ile de Bourbon (USA)) 10.1f **(67)**
Form - 007
Record 1998 - 1st:0 2nd:0 3rd:0 Ran:3
Pre1998 - 1st:4 2nd:2 3rd:2 Ran:21
Win Prizemoney £11,867 *Total Prizemoney* £18,423
Wins * 1997 Jly Sandow (G-S) H 11.4f 69 72
1996 Aug Roscom (GD) H 12f 84 77+ <
1996 Jly Bellew (GD) H 14f 79 73
1996 Jun Leopar (GD) H 9f 75 65
1998 Turf 0-3: (14f 2, 16f) (gd 3)
Moderate gelding, effective 11 to 16f, acts on gd to g-f, best on gd, has worn blinkers, prefers right handed tracks. Turf high 44 (began Spt). Inconsistent.
**B J Curley [1-18] Mrs B J Curley (from K Prendergast in IRE [3-10] Nov 1996).*

MAGIC FALLS (IRE) BHB 37f **RR 54df** 2820[14]
3 b c River Falls 8.2f **(56)** - Simply Inch (Simply Great (FR)) 8.2f **(65)**
Form - 700
Record 1998 - 1st:0 2nd:0 3rd:0 Ran:3
Pre1998 - 1st:0 2nd:0 3rd:0 Ran:2
1998 Turf 0-3: (7f, 8f, 12f) (g-s, gd, g-f)
Scopey, fair colt. Turf high 8. **M J Polglase [0-5] K S Lee.*

MAGIC LIGHT (IRE) RR 60f 4756[8]
2 b c Dilum (USA) 7.1f **(56)** - Wynona (IRE) **(52f 41a)** (Cyrano de Bergerac) 6f **(68)**
Form - 0877608
Record 1998 - 1st:0 2nd:0 3rd:0 Ran:7
1998 Turf 0-7: (5f 3, 6f 2, 7f 2) (sft, gd, g-f, frm 4)
Average colt. Turf high 60 (began Jly).
**Sir Mark Prescott [0-7] Haydn Kelly.*

MAGIC MEMORIES BHB 64f **RR 74f** 5073[4]
2 b f Magic Ring (IRE) 6.5f **(64)** - Bay Runner (Bay Express) 7.1f **(60)**
Form - 82214844
Record 1998 - 1st:1 2nd:2 3rd:0 Ran:8
Win Prizemoney £2,290 *Total Prizemoney* £4,442
Wins * **1998** Aug Salisb (G-F) C 7f 73+ <
1998 Turf 1-8: (5f, 6f 3, 7f 1-2, 8f 2) (gd 2, g-f 1-2, frm 4)
Above-average filly, effective 5 to 7f, best at 7f, acts on gd to frm. Turf high 74 (began Jly) - 4th of 9 giving 3lb to Parisien Star (4 Spt Epsom 6f gd RF 4083) - also 1st of 11 getting 3lb from Shoot The Rapids (12 Aug Salisbury RF 3591).
**D R C Elsworth [1-8] Mrs Julie Lankshear.*

MAGIC MILL (IRE) BHB 73f72a **RR 72df 72a** 3520[2]
5 b h Simply Great (FR) 11.9f **(61)** - Rosy O'Leary (Majetta) 6.5f **(58)**
Form - 014450572
Record 1998 - 1st:1 2nd:1 3rd:0 Ran:8
Pre1998 - 1st:1 2nd:1 3rd:2 Ran:11
Win Prizemoney £7,543 *Total Prizemoney* £13,026
Wins 1998 Apr Newcas (SFT) H 7f 73 87? <
1995 Oct Redcar (FRM) 7f 82+
1998 Turf 1-8: (7f 1-3, 8f 4, 10f) (sft 1-1, g-s, gd 3, g-f 2, frm)
Above-average colt, effective 7 to 8f, acts on sft to g-s, has worn blinkers. Turf high 87 (1st run) - 1st of 11 getting 2lb from Over To You (13 Apr Newcastle RF 0663). Inconsistent.
**J S Goldie [0-3] A S Scott (from J L Eyre [1-14] Jun 1998).*

MAGIC MOMENT BHB 60f **RR 70f** 5012[14]
2 b f Magic Ring (IRE) 6.5f **(64)** - Epithet (Mill Reef (USA)) 10.5f **(78)**
Form - 0660
Record 1998 - 1st:0 2nd:0 3rd:0 Ran:4
1998 Turf 0-4: (5f, 6f 3) (g-s, gd, g-f, frm)
Above-average filly. Turf high 70 (began Aug).
**E Weymes [0-4] T A Scothern.*

MAGIC MONDAY (IRE) BHB 56f **RR 62f** 4276[11]
2 b f Petardia 8.2f **(58)** - Ultra (Stanford) 7.9f **(56)**
Form - 25080
Record 1998 - 1st:0 2nd:1 3rd:0 Ran:5
Win Prizemoney £0 *Total Prizemoney* £1,050
1998 Turf 0-5: (5f 3, 7f 2) (sft, gd 3, g-f)
Average filly. Turf high 62. **R Hannon [0-5] Bill Allan.*

MAGIC MORNING BHB 34f45a **RR 32f 45a** 3367[9]
3 ch g Magic Ring (IRE) 6.5f **(64)** - Incarnadine (Hot Spark) 7.6f **(62)**
Form - 6500000
Record 1998 - 1st:0 2nd:0 3rd:0 Ran:7
Pre1998 - 1st:0 2nd:0 3rd:0 Ran:2
1998 Turf 0-5: (6f 2, 7f 2, 10f) (gd 2, g-f 2, frm) 1998 AW 0-2: (6f, 7f) (Equi 2)
Moderate gelding. Turf high 32. AW high 49.
**W J Musson [0-9] Mrs Rita Brown.*

MAGIC OF ALOHA (IRE) BHB 63f **RR 75f** 4869[6]
3 ch f Diesis 9f **(80)** - Satz (USA) (The Minstrel (CAN)) 10f **(72)**
Form - 32556
Record 1998 - 1st:0 2nd:1 3rd:1 Ran:5
Pre1998 - 1st:0 2nd:0 3rd:0 Ran:1
Win Prizemoney £0 *Total Prizemoney* £2,124
1998 Turf 0-5: (7f, 10f 3, 12f) (gd 4, g-f)

Scopey, above-average filly. Turf high 75.
**B W Hills [0-6] J R Fleming.*

MAGIC PERFORMER RR 35f 4762[14]
2 b g Tragic Role (USA) 9.4f **(63)** - Hot Performer (Hotfoot) 10.5f **(59)**
Form - 70
Record 1998 - 1st:0 2nd:0 3rd:0 Ran:2
1998 Turf 0-2: (8f, 10f) (gd, g-f)
Currently very moderate gelding. Turf high 35 (began Spt).
**Miss J A Camacho [0-2] B W & J A Harland.*

MAGIC POWERS BHB 62f RR 57f 4765[3]
3 ch g Magical Wonder (USA) 7.2f **(60)** - Kissin' Cousin (Be Friendly) 9.3f **(53)**
Form - 003
Record 1998 - 1st:0 2nd:0 3rd:1 Ran:3
Pre1998 - 1st:0 2nd:0 3rd:0 Ran:3
Win Prizemoney £0 *Total Prizemoney* £633
1998 Turf 0-3: (7f 2, 8f) (gd, g-f, frm)
Leggy, fair gelding. Turf high 55. **G B Balding [0-6] The Wizards.*

MAGIC RAINBOW BHB 82f84a RR 85f 84a 4749[14]
3 b c Magic Ring (IRE) 6.5f **(64)** - Blues Indigo (Music Boy) 6.8f **(57)**
Form - 1041040060
Record 1998 - 1st:2 2nd:0 3rd:0 Ran:10
Pre1998 - 1st:1 2nd:0 3rd:0 Ran:3
Win Prizemoney £29,906 *Total Prizemoney* £31,518
Wins * **1998** May Newmar (G-F) H 6f 77 84 <
* **1998** *Mar Southw (STD) H 6f 76 80+*
* 1997 Jun Leices (GD) 5f 76
1998 Turf 1-9: (5f, 6f 1-8) (hvy, g-s, gd 2, g-f 1-3, frm 2) 1998 AW 1-1: (6f 1-1) (Fibr 1-1)
Leggy, useful colt, effective 5 to 6f, best at 6f, acts on gd to frm - acts on Fibr. Turf high 85 - 4th of 15 getting 7lb from Misbah (7 Jly Newmarket 6f frm RF 2582) - also 1st of 19 getting 12lb from Harmonic Way (30 May Newmarket RF 1611). (1st run) - 1st of 13 getting 3lb from Branston Berry (20 Mar Southwell RF 0452). A winner on the Southwell Fibresand in March, he later landed the valuable Coral Sprint at Newmarket. Seemed held by the Handicapper afterwards. **M Bell [3-13] P T Fenwick.*

MAGIC ROUNDABOUT (IRE) RR 2f 2081[7]
2 gr c Mac's Imp (USA) 5.6f **(54)** - Syndicate Wives (Godswalk (USA)) 7.3f **(58)**
Form - 007
Record 1998 - 1st:0 2nd:0 3rd:0 Ran:3
1998 Turf 0-1: (5f) (frm) 1998 AW 0-2: (5f 2) (Fibr 2)
Currently very poor colt, has worn blinkers. AW high 4.
**H S Howe [0-3] Mrs Maureen Shenkin.*

MAGIC SPRING (IRE) BHB 50f56a RR 62f 56a 4305[15]
3 ch f Persian Bold 10f **(69)** - Oasis (Valiyar) 8.5f **(73)**
Form - 666780
Record 1998 - 1st:0 2nd:0 3rd:0 Ran:6
Pre1998 - 1st:0 2nd:0 3rd:0 Ran:3
1998 Turf 0-5: (7f, 8f 3, 12f) (gd 2, g-f, frm 2) 1998 AW 0-1: (8f) (Fibr)
Light-framed, average filly. Turf high 62. Becoming disappointing.
**K McAuliffe [0-9] Fieldspring Racing.*

MAGIQUE ETOILE (IRE) BHB 50f RR 54f 5124[6]
2 b f Magical Wonder (USA) 7.2f **(60)** - Shes A Dancer (IRE) (Alzao (USA)) 7.1f **(68)**
Form - 07760406
Record 1998 - 1st:0 2nd:0 3rd:0 Ran:8
Win Prizemoney £0 *Total Prizemoney* £210
1998 Turf 0-8: (5f 2, 6f 2, 7f 3, 8f) (g-s 2, gd 2, g-f 2, frm 2)
Fair filly, has worn blinkers. Turf high 54.
**M P Muggeridge [0-8] Gallery Racing.*

MAGNI MOMENTI BHB 40f RR 51df 2312[11]
3 b f King's Signet (USA) 7f **(51)** - Halka (Daring March) 7.1f **(61)**
Form - 462560034280
Record 1998 - 1st:0 2nd:2 3rd:1 Ran:12
Pre1998 - 1st:0 2nd:0 3rd:0 Ran:1
Win Prizemoney £0 *Total Prizemoney* £2,238
1998 Turf 0-10: (6f 2, 7f 2, 8f, 10f 3, 12f 2) (sft 2, gd 3, g-f 4, frm) 1998 AW 0-2: (6f, 8f) (Fibr 2)

Workmanlike, fair filly, effective 6 to 10f, best at 10f, acts on sft to g-f. Turf high 59 (1st run) - 2nd of 13 getting 5lb from Cape Hope (2 Apr Leicester 6f sft RF 0544). AW high 31.
**J S Moore [0-12] Miss Susan Clarke (from R Hannon [0-1] Jun 1997).*

MAGNO (USA) BHB 100f RR 96f 4972[2]
2 b c El Gran Senor (USA) 8.9f **(85)** - Nice Noble (USA) (Vaguely Noble) 10.1f **(72)**
Form - 3312
Record 1998 - 1st:1 2nd:1 3rd:2 Ran:4
Win Prizemoney £7,122 *Total Prizemoney* £47,965
Wins * **1998** Oct York (GD) 7.9f 90 <
1998 Turf 1-4: (7f 2, 8f 1-2) (sft, gd 1-2, g-f)
Very useful colt. Turf high 96 (began Spt) - also 1st of 10 from Lightning Arrow (10 Oct York RF 4745). Tough and genuine, he was runner-up in the Racing Post Trophy on his final start, if no match for Commander Collins. This likeable sort lacks a turn of foot, and is likely to need middle-distances at three.
**P F I Cole [1-4] H R H Prince Fahd Salman.*

MAGPIES RR 374[10]
3 b g Puissance 7.1f **(60)** - Yankee Special (Bold Lad (IRE)) 8.4f **(68)**
Form - 50
Record 1998 - 1st:0 2nd:0 3rd:0 Ran:2
1998 AW 0-2: (6f, 7f) (Fibr 2)
Unfurnished, currently poor gelding. AW high 12.
**N Tinkler [0-2] The Toon Army Partnership.*

MAIDAAN RR 104+f 4542[1]
2 b c Midyan (USA) 9.9f **(64)**- Panache Arabelle **(66f)** (Nashwan (USA))
Form - 31
Record 1998 - 1st:1 2nd:0 3rd:1 Ran:2
Win Prizemoney £24,759 *Total Prizemoney* £25,303
Wins * **1998** Spt Newmar (GD) 7f 104+ <
1998 Turf 1-2: (6f, 7f 1-1) (g-f, frm 1-1)
Currently very useful colt. Turf high 104 (began Aug) - 1st of 26 from Houston Time (29 Spt Newmarket RF 4542). Beautifully bred, he was trained for the Tattersalls Houghton Sales Stakes by Mick Channon and did the job in fine style, lengthening his stride leaving the Dip and pulling away inside the final furlong. Out of a half-sister to Stagecraft, he should stay a mile and a quarter, and is a fascinating prospect for 1999, when he will race for Godolphin.
**M R Channon [1-2] Sheikh Ahmed Al Maktoum.*

MAIDEN'S BLUSH (USA) RR 67f 5072[7]
2 ch f Silver Hawk (USA) 11.2f **(85)** - Barmistress (USA) (Alydar (USA)) 9.1f **(76)**
Form - 7
Record 1998 - 1st:0 2nd:0 3rd:0 Ran:1
1998 Turf 0-1: (7f) (gd)
Currently average filly. **J H M Gosden [0-1] Sheikh Mohammed.*

MAID PLANS (IRE) BHB 51f RR 50f 4612[19]
2 br f Petardia 8.2f **(58)** - Ballerina Anna (IRE) (Dance of Life (USA)) 7f **(66)**
Form - 0860
Record 1998 - 1st:0 2nd:0 3rd:0 Ran:4
1998 Turf 0-4: (5f 3, 6f) (g-s, gd, frm 2)
Fair filly. Turf high 50.
**J Akehurst [0-4] The Plan Flow Leasing Partnership.*

MAID TO MEASURE RR 58f 3117[5]
2 b f Inchinor 8.9f **(64)** - Walking Saint (Godswalk (USA)) 7.3f **(58)**
Form - 3005
Record 1998 - 1st:0 2nd:0 3rd:1 Ran:4
Win Prizemoney £0 *Total Prizemoney* £738
1998 Turf 0-4: (6f 2, 7f 2) (g-s, gd, g-f, frm)
Fair filly. Turf high 58 (1st run) - 3rd of 14 to Claranna (26 Jun Newcastle 6f g-s RF 2310). **M Brittain [0-4] Mel Brittain.*

MAIELLA BHB 55f RR 60f 4393[12]
3 ch f Salse (USA) 10.9f **(71)** - Forelino (USA) (Trempolino (USA)) 12f **(71)**
Form - 8013305140
Record 1998 - 1st:2 2nd:0 3rd:2 Ran:10
Pre1998 - 1st:0 2nd:0 3rd:0 Ran:2
Win Prizemoney £4,849 *Total Prizemoney* £5,772

Wins * **1998** Aug Salisb (G-F) H 12f 56 60 <
* **1998** May Bright (FRM) SH 11.9f 52 59
1998 Turf 2-10: (10f 2, 11f, 12f 2-7) (g-s, g-f 1-2, frm 1-7)
Light-framed, average filly, effective 10 to 12f, best at 12f, acts on g-f to frm, best on g-f, likes tight tracks. Turf high 60 - 1st of 10 giving 1lb to Mighty Magic (12 Aug Salisbury RF 3592) - also 1st of 14 giving 7lb to Highbury Legend (28 May Brighton RF 1551).
**R Hannon [2-12] The Maiella Partnership.*

MAIL SHOT (IRE) BHB 40f34a **RR 50f 34a** 4861[15]
3 b g Maledetto (IRE) - Pallachine (FR) (Lichine (USA))
Form - 00423000
Record 1998 - 1st:0 2nd:1 3rd:1 Ran:8
Pre1998 - 1st:0 2nd:0 3rd:0 Ran:3
Win Prizemoney £0 *Total Prizemoney* £1,287
1998 Turf 0-7: (8f, 11f, 12f 2, 14f 2, 15f) (g-s, gd, g-f 2, frm 3) 1998 AW 0-1: (16f) (Equi)
Light-framed, fair gelding, effective 11 to 14f, acts on g-f to frm, likes tight tracks. Turf high 50 - 2nd of 15 getting 3lb from Pressurise (21 Jly Yarmouth 14f g-f RF 2981). Becoming disappointing. **S Dow [0-11] MacDonald Mailing.*

MAI TAI (IRE) BHB 54f **RR 56f** 4961[13]
3 b f Scenic 10.6f **(66)** - Oystons Propweekly (Swing Easy (USA)) 6.5f **(55)**
Form - 603447360000
Record 1998 - 1st:0 2nd:0 3rd:2 Ran:12
Pre1998 - 1st:0 2nd:0 3rd:1 Ran:2
Win Prizemoney £0 *Total Prizemoney* £1,663
1998 Turf 0-12: (5f, 6f 4, 7f 5, 8f 2) (g-s, gd 2, g-f 3, frm 6)
Workmanlike, fair filly, effective 6f, acts on g-f to frm, has worn blinkers. Turf high 59 - 3rd of 16 getting 20lb from Butrinto (27 May Newbury 6f g-f RF 1526). **Mrs P N Dutfield [0-14] One Over The Eight.*

MAITEAMIA BHB 60f67a **RR 64f 67a** 4921[17]
5 ch g Komaite (USA) 6.9f **(61)** - Mia Scintilla (Blazing Saddles (AUS)) 6.7f **(46)**
Form - 200225302065300
Record 1998 - 1st:0 2nd:4 3rd:2 Ran:15
Pre1998 - 1st:4 2nd:4 3rd:2 Ran:21
Win Prizemoney £11,736 *Total Prizemoney* £23,767
Wins * 1996 May Catter (GD) H 5f 63 61
* 1996 May Hamilt (HVY) H 5f 50 68
* 1996 *Apr Southw (STD) H 6f 61 73+* <
* 1996 *Mar Southw (STD) H 6f 50 51*
1998 Turf 0-13: (5f 7, 6f 3, 7f 3) (g-s 2, gd 4, g-f 4, frm 3) 1998 AW 0-2: (7f 2) (Fibr 2)
Above-average gelding, effective 5 to 7f, acts on gd to frm - acts on Fibr, mostly wears blinkers. Turf high 64. AW high 65 (began Jly) - 5th of 11 giving 15lb to Kosevo (25 Jly Southwell 7f Fibr RF 3128). Inconsistent. **S R Bowring [4-36] Mrs Zoe Grant.*

MAITREYA BHB 53f **RR 61f** 4644[11]
3 ch f Anshan 8.2f **(63)**- Princess Fair(Crowned Prince (USA))10.1f **(67)**
Form - 462080
Record 1998 - 1st:0 2nd:1 3rd:0 Ran:6
Win Prizemoney £0 *Total Prizemoney* £1,387
1998 Turf 0-6: (7f, 8f 4, 9f) (gd, g-f 3, frm 2)
Workmanlike, average filly, effective 7 to 8f, acts on frm. Turf high 61 (began Jly) - 2nd of 6 getting 5lb from Bering Gifts (14 Aug Warwick 8f frm RF 3645). **C N Allen [0-6] B Uniacke.*

MAJAARI BHB 97f **RR 95f** 4233[4]
3 b br c Marju (IRE) 9.2f **(76)** - Ahbab (IRE) (Ajdal (USA)) 9.2f **(89)**
Form - 364
Record 1998 - 1st:0 2nd:0 3rd:1 Ran:3
Pre1998 - 1st:1 2nd:1 3rd:0 Ran:3
Win Prizemoney £3,582 *Total Prizemoney* £6,717
Wins * 1997 Aug Ripon (G-F) 6f 81+ <
1998 Turf 0-3: (6f, 7f 2) (gd, g-f 2)
Workmanlike, very useful colt, effective 6f, acts on g-f. Turf high 95. **P T Walwyn [1-6] Hamdan Al Maktoum.*

MAJAL (IRE) BHB 30f44a **RR 37f 44a** 2566[12]
9 b g Caerleon (USA) 10.9f **(79)** - Park Special (Relkino) 8.9f **(65)**
Form - 440
Record 1998 - 1st:0 2nd:0 3rd:0 Ran:3
Pre1998 - 1st:2 2nd:6 3rd:5 Ran:48
Win Prizemoney £5,560 *Total Prizemoney* £15,959
Wins * 1995 *Feb Lingfi (STD) H 12f 52 54*
1998 Turf 0-3: (10f, 12f 2) (gd, g-f, frm)
Fair gelding, effective 9 to 12f, acts on gd to frm, has worn blinkers, favours tight tracks. Turf high 37.
**J S Wainwright [5-53] Mrs P Wake (from B Hanbury [1-16] Oct 1992).*

MAJALIS BHB 73f **RR 77f** 4751[23]
3 b br f Mujadil (USA) 7.7f **(70)** - Rose Barton (Pas de Seul) 9.1f **(67)**
Form - 022125350
Record 1998 - 1st:1 2nd:3 3rd:1 Ran:9
Pre1998 - 1st:0 2nd:0 3rd:1 Ran:3
Win Prizemoney £3,756 *Total Prizemoney* £9,247
Wins 1998 Jly Beverl (GD) 5f 74 <
1998 Turf 1-9: (5f 1-2, 6f 6, 7f) (gd 3, g-f 1-4, frm 2)
Workmanlike, above-average filly, effective 5 to 7f, acts on gd to frm, best on g-f. Turf high 77 - 2nd of 8 giving 3lb to Jocasta (17 Jly Newmarket 6f g-f RF 2883) - also 1st of 11 getting 5lb from Allmaites (4 Jly Beverley RF 2520).
**J L Eyre [0-1] Whitestonecliffe Racing Partnership (from R Guest [1-11] Spt 1998).*

MAJESTIC (IRE) BHB 70f64a **RR 78f 64a** 4987[2]
3 b g Belmez (USA) 11.4f **(65)** - Noble Lily (USA) (Vaguely Noble) 10.1f **(72)**
Form - 43434442
Record 1998 - 1st:0 2nd:1 3rd:2 Ran:8
Win Prizemoney £0 *Total Prizemoney* £3,242
1998 Turf 0-7: (9f, 10f, 12f 3, 14f, 16f) (sft, g-s, gd, g-f, frm 2, hrd) 1998 AW 0-1: (14f) (Fibr)
Workmanlike, above-average gelding, effective 12 to 14f, best at 12f, acts on sft to frm, has worn blinkers, favours tight tracks. Turf high 78 (began Jly) - 2nd of 11 getting 3lb from Silent Warning (25 Oct Leicester 12f sft RF 4987). **Ian Williams [0-8] Patrick Kelly.*

MAJESTIC HILLS BHB 76f **RR 66f** 1899[6]
3 b c Shirley Heights 12.1f **(76)** - Regent Miss (CAN) (Vice Regent (CAN)) 8.7f **(74)**
Form - 06
Record 1998 - 1st:0 2nd:0 3rd:0 Ran:2
Pre1998 - 1st:0 2nd:1 3rd:0 Ran:2
Win Prizemoney £0 *Total Prizemoney* £1,204
1998 Turf 0-2: (10f, 12f) (g-s, frm)
Scopey, average colt. Turf high 66. **J L Dunlop [0-4] Lady Harrison.*

MAJESTY (IRE) BHB 69f **RR 74df** 3482[9]
4 b g Sadler's Wells (USA) 11.3f **(87)** - Princesse Timide (USA) (Blushing Groom (FR)) 10.3f **(76)**
Form - 0
Record 1998 - 1st:0 2nd:0 3rd:0 Ran:1
Pre1998 - 1st:0 2nd:0 3rd:2 Ran:3
Win Prizemoney £0 *Total Prizemoney* £1,009
1998 Turf 0-1: (12f) (gd)
Leggy, above-average gelding.
**S Dow [0-3] The Sporting Divots (from P F I Cole [0-3] Spt 1997).*

MAJOR ATTRACTION RR 44f 3990[8]
3 gr g Major Jacko - My Friend Melody (Sizzling Melody)
Form - 88
Record 1998 - 1st:0 2nd:0 3rd:0 Ran:2
1998 Turf 0-2: (8f 2) (g-f, frm)
Leggy, currently moderate gelding. Turf high 44 (began Jly).
**M Mullineaux [0-2] Positive Partners.*

MAJOR CHANGE BHB 80f85a **RR 82f 85a** 4188[7]
6 gr g Sharrood (USA)11.1f **(67)**- May the Fourteenth(Thatching) 8f **(66)**
Form - 0847
Record 1998 - 1st:0 2nd:0 3rd:0 Ran:4
Pre1998 - 1st:3 2nd:3 3rd:6 Ran:28
Win Prizemoney £18,501 *Total Prizemoney* £42,880
Wins * 1997 Apr Epsom (GD) H 10.1f 86 92 <
1996 Jun Sandow (G-F) H 10f 87 91
1995 May Leices (G-F) 8f 76+
1998 Turf 0-3: (10f 3) (gd, g-f, frm) 1998 AW 0-1: (10f) (Equi)
Useful gelding, effective 10 to 12f, best at 10f, acts on gd to frm - acts on Fibr, best on gd, favours left handed tracks, likes tight

tracks. Turf high 82. Inconsistent. A little disappointing on the level 1998.
**Miss Gay Kelleway [4-22] A P Griffin (from R Hannon [2-16] Spt 1996).*

MAJOR GAMBLE BHB 46a **RR 47f** 4878^{15}
2 b g Cyrano de Bergerac 7.3f **(58)** - Nellie's Gamble **(36f 59a)** (Mummy's Game) 8.2f **(60)**
Form - 000007000
Record 1998 - 1st:0 2nd:0 3rd:0 Ran:9
1998 Turf 0-8: (5f 5, 6f, 7f 2) (g-s, gd 2, g-f 2, frm 3) 1998 AW 0-1: (7f) (Fibr)
Moderate gelding, has worn blinkers. Turf high 47.
**J J Quinn [0-9] C R Galloway.*

MAJOR'S LAW (IRE) BHB 52f63a **RR 57f 63a** 2398^{4}
9 b g Law Society (USA) 11.6f **(71)** - Maryinsky (USA) (Northern Dancer) 9.6f **(80)**
Form - 404
Record 1998 - 1st:0 2nd:0 3rd:0 Ran:3
Pre1998 - 1st:1 2nd:4 3rd:1 Ran:16
Win Prizemoney £2,924 *Total Prizemoney* £10,228
1998 Turf 0-3: (16f, 17f, 18f) (gd 2, g-f)
Fair gelding. Turf high 57. Becoming disappointing.
**R Simpson [3-8] Miss J Rumford (from C E Brittain [1-16] Oct 1992).*

MAKATI BHB 44f50a **RR 22f 50a** 4388^{2}
4 b g Efisio 7.7f **(69)** - Seleter (Hotfoot) 10.5f **(59)**
Form - 52741122
Record 1998 - 1st:2 2nd:3 3rd:0 Ran:8
Pre1998 - 1st:0 2nd:0 3rd:0 Ran:4
Win Prizemoney £4,329 *Total Prizemoney* £6,278
Wins * **1998** *Jly Wolver (STD) H 16.2f 30 41+ <*
* **1998** *Jly Southw (STD) H 14f 33 36+*
1998 Turf 0-2: (11f, 14f) (sft, gd) 1998 AW 2-6: (11f, 12f, 14f 1-2, 15f, 16f 1-1) (Fibr 2-6)
Strong, fair gelding, effective 12 to 16f, - acts on Fibr, prefers left handed tracks, prefers tight tracks. Turf high 15. AW high 50 - 2nd of 12 giving 3lb to Desert Spa (19 Spt Wolverhampton 12f Fibr RF 4388) - also 1st of 12 getting 8lb from Bella With A Zee (24 Jly Wolverhampton RF 3099). He showed much-improved form in modest Fibresand staying handicaps last season, winning two, and possibly catching a bit of a tartar in his hat-trick bid.
**Miss J A Camacho [2-8] Paul Wilson (from M J Camacho [0-4] Jly 1997).*

MAKE BELIEVE BHB 45f45a **RR 16f 45a** 2486^{9}
3 ch f Caerleon (USA) 10.9f **(79)** - Sleeping Beauty (Mill Reef (USA)) 10.5f **(78)**
Form - 50610576080
Record 1998 - 1st:1 2nd:0 3rd:0 Ran:10
Pre1998 - 1st:0 2nd:0 3rd:1 Ran:3
Win Prizemoney £3,548 *Total Prizemoney* £4,390
Wins * **1998** Apr Catter (GD) H 12f 58 64 <
1998 Turf 1-7: (10f 3, 12f 1-3, 15f) (sft, g-s, gd 1-2, g-f 2, frm) 1998 AW 0-3: (7f, 8f 2) (Equi, Fibr 2)
Unfurnished, moderate filly, effective 12f, acts on gd, has worn blinkers, likes left handed tracks, likes tight tracks. Turf high 64 (1st run) - 1st of 8 giving 10lb to Last Lap (1 Apr Catterick RF 0530). AW high 13. Becoming disappointing.
**M J Polglase [1-11] K S Lee (from R Charlton [0-2] Jun 1997).*

MAKEBELIEVE ISLAND (IRE) BHB 72f **RR 79f** 4845^{2}
2 b c Namaqualand (USA)- Zalamera **(44f 39a)** (Rambo Dancer (CAN))
Form - 445072
Record 1998 - 1st:0 2nd:1 3rd:0 Ran:6
Win Prizemoney £0 *Total Prizemoney* £2,628
1998 Turf 0-6: (6f 3, 8f 3) (gd, g-f, frm 3, hrd)
Above-average colt, effective 6 to 8f, best at 6f, acts on g-f to frm, best on frm, has worn blinkers. Turf high 79 - 4th of 8 to Muqtarib (5 Jun Goodwood 6f frm RF 1753). Fair form in maidens, and ran well in a nursery on his final start. **B W Hills [0-6] A D Shead.*

MAKEIT MUSIC BHB 35f **RR 38f** 4376^{18}
2 b g Komaite (USA) 6.9f **(61)** - Gandoorah (Record Token) 6.3f **(53)**
Form - 0000
Record 1998 - 1st:0 2nd:0 3rd:0 Ran:4
1998 Turf 0-4: (5f 2, 6f, 7f) (gd 2, g-f, frm)
Very moderate gelding. Turf high 38.
**Mrs A M Naughton [0-4] Raymond Miquel.*

MAKE READY BHB 39f55a **RR 43f 55a** 4334^{14}
4 b f Beveled (USA) 6.9f **(64)** - Prepare (IRE) (Millfontaine)
Form - 0766708280
Record 1998 - 1st:0 2nd:1 3rd:0 Ran:10
Pre1998 - 1st:2 2nd:1 3rd:2 Ran:16
Win Prizemoney £4,140 *Total Prizemoney* £6,613
Wins * 1996 *Spt Southw (STD) SH 5f 60 57 <*
* 1996 *Jly Southw (STD) S 5f 51*
1998 Turf 0-7: (5f 2, 6f 2, 7f 3) (gd, g-f 2, frm 4) 1998 AW 0-3: (5f, 6f 2) (Equi, Fibr 2)
Neat, moderate filly, effective 6f, acts on gd, has worn blinkers. Turf high 43 (began Jly). AW high 34. **J Neville [2-26] J Neville.*

MAKE WAY (USA) **RR 54f** 2554^{8}
2 b c Red Ransom (USA) 8.6f **(83)** - Way of The World (USA) (Dance of Life (USA)) 7f **(66)**
Form - 8
Record 1998 - 1st:0 2nd:0 3rd:0 Ran:1
1998 Turf 0-1: (6f) (g-f)
Currently fair colt. **I A Balding [0-1] Paul Mellon.*

MAKNAAS **RR 54f** 4699^{13}
2 ch c Wolfhound (USA) 7.3f **(71)** - White-Wash (Final Straw) 7.9f **(64)**
Form - 00
Record 1998 - 1st:0 2nd:0 3rd:0 Ran:2
1998 Turf 0-2: (6f, 7f) (gd 2)
Currently fair colt. Turf high 54 (began Spt).
**R W Armstrong [0-2] Hamdan Al Maktoum.*

MALAAH (IRE) **RR 66f** 2915^{8}
2 gr c Pips Pride 6.7f **(70)** - Lingdale Lass (Petong) 6.6f **(58)**
Form - 8
Record 1998 - 1st:0 2nd:0 3rd:0 Ran:1
1998 Turf 0-1: (6f) (frm)
Currently average colt. **R W Armstrong [0-1] Hamdan Al Maktoum.*

MALABI (USA) BHB 65f **RR 65f** 580^{8}
4 b c Danzig (USA) 8.1f **(88)** - Gmaasha (IRE) (Kris) 9.5f **(73)**
Form - 8
Record 1998 - 1st:0 2nd:0 3rd:0 Ran:1
Pre1998 - 1st:0 2nd:1 3rd:1 Ran:3
Win Prizemoney £0 *Total Prizemoney* £1,636
1998 Turf 0-1: (7f) (gd)
Strong, average colt. **J L Dunlop [0-4] Hamdan Al Maktoum.*

MALADERIE (IRE) BHB 73f **RR 70f** 5142^{7}
4 b g Thatching 7.8f **(69)** - Native Melody (Tudor Music) 6.8f **(59)**
Form - 5430226220361265140157
Record 1998 - 1st:3 2nd:5 3rd:2 Ran:22
Pre1998 - 1st:1 2nd:4 3rd:2 Ran:21
Win Prizemoney £19,537 *Total Prizemoney* £34,104
Wins **1998** Oct York (GD) H 5f 69 70
1998 Spt Haydoc (GD) H 5f 64 68
1998 Aug Windso (G-F) H 5f 58 60
1996 Jun Windso (G-F) 6f 76 <
1998 Turf 3-22: (5f 3-11, 6f 9, 7f 2) (sft, gd 1-10, g-f, frm 2-10)
Strong, above-average gelding, effective 5f, acts on gd to frm, best on gd, often wears blinkers (extremely effectively). Turf high 70 - 1st of 23 from Sue Me (7 Oct York RF 4701) - also 1st of 12 giving 1lb to Squire Corrie (5 Spt Haydock RF 4107). Consistent. In good form in 1998, ending a long losing run at Windsor in August. Sold for 19,000 guineas in October.
**M Dods [0-2] A G Watson (from M R Channon [4-41] Oct 1998).*

MALAYAN MOON BHB 45f **RR 49f** 4458^{14}
3 ch g Kris 10f **(75)**- Moon Carnival **(96f)** (Be My Guest (USA)) 9.3f **(67)**
Form - 0400840
Record 1998 - 1st:0 2nd:0 3rd:0 Ran:7
Win Prizemoney £0 *Total Prizemoney* £240
1998 Turf 0-7: (7f, 9f, 10f, 12f, 15f, 16f 2) (gd 3, g-f 2, frm 2)
Lengthy, moderate gelding. Turf high 62.
**Lady Herries [0-7] Angmering Park Stud.*

MALCHIK BHB 51f **RR 59f** 5094[15]

2 ch c Absalom 7.1f **(56)** - Very Good (Noalto) 5.7f **(49)**

Form - 0008703010070

Record 1998 - 1st:1 2nd:0 3rd:1 Ran:13

Win Prizemoney £2,080 *Total Prizemoney* £2,610

Wins * **1998** Spt Leices (G-S) SH 8f 52 59 <

1998 Turf 1-12: (5f 2, 6f 2, 7f 3, 8f 1-5) (gd 4, g-f 1-4, frm 4) 1998 AW 0-1: (6f) (Fibr)

Fair colt, effective 8f, acts on g-f, has worn blinkers. Turf high 59 - 1st of 20 getting 1lb from Miss Cody (8 Spt Leicester RF 4136). Inconsistent. **P Howling [1-13] I G Mirzoian.*

MALE-ANA-MOU (IRE) BHB 70f **RR 74f** 3595[6]

5 ch g Ela-Mana-Mou 12.7f **(72)** - Glasson Lady (GER) (Priamos (GER)) 11.1f **(61)**

Form - 247476

Record 1998 - 1st:0 2nd:1 3rd:0 Ran:6

Pre1998 - 1st:1 2nd:0 3rd:4 Ran:13

Win Prizemoney £4,240 *Total Prizemoney* £9,035

Wins * 1996 Jun Goodwo (G-F) 10f 79 <

1998 Turf 0-6: (12f 2, 13f, 14f 3) (gd, g-f 3, frm 2)

Above-average gelding, effective 12 to 16f, acts on gd, favours tight tracks. Turf high 82. Consistent.

**D R C Elsworth [1-19] Oh So Bright Syndicate.*

MALIBU MAN BHB 63f80a **RR 66f 80a** 3527[8]

6 ch g Ballacashtal (CAN) 7.9f **(51)** - National Time (USA) (Lord Avie (USA)) 5.3f **(61)**

Form - 046036008

Record 1998 - 1st:0 2nd:0 3rd:1 Ran:9

Pre1998 - 1st:6 2nd:5 3rd:6 Ran:41

Win Prizemoney £18,594 *Total Prizemoney* £28,002

Wins * 1997 Aug Bath (GD) H 5.1f 70 75

* 1997 *Jun Wolver (STD) H 5f 69 77* <

* 1997 Mar Folkes (GD) H 5f 65 74+

* 1996 Spt Chepst (G-F) H 5.1f 63 65

1995 *Jly Wolver (STD) H 5f 62 71+*

1995 *Jun Wolver (STD) H 6f 55 58*

1998 Turf 0-8: (5f 6, 6f 2) (sft, g-s, gd 2, g-f, frm 3) 1998 AW 0-1: (5f) (Fibr)

Above-average gelding, effective 5 to 6f, best at 5f, acts on g-s to frm - acts on Fibr, has worn blinkers, excels at Thirsk, does well at Wolverhampton. Turf high 73 - 4th of 7 to Daawe (17 Apr Thirsk 5f g-s RF 0738).

**E A Wheeler [4-32] Church Racing Partnership (from S Mellor [2-18] Apr 1996).*

MALLIA BHB 65f77a **RR 51f 77a** 4923[11]

5 b g Statoblest 6.4f **(63)** - Pronetta (USA) (Mr Prospector (USA)) 8.8f **(78)**

Form - 1101038000

Record 1998 - 1st:1 2nd:0 3rd:1 Ran:8

Pre1998 - 1st:4 2nd:4 3rd:0 Ran:22

Win Prizemoney £47,837 *Total Prizemoney* £54,955

Wins * **1998** Apr Ripon (SFT) H 6f 65 70

* 1997 *Dec Wolver (STD) H 6f 72 77*

* 1997 *Nov Southw (STD) H 6f 64 70+*

* 1996 Jun York (GD) H 6f 76 84 <

* 1995 May Hamilt (GD) 5f 78

1998 Turf 1-8: (5f, 6f 1-6, 7f) (sft 1-2, g-s 4, gd, g-f)

Above-average gelding, effective 6f, acts on sft to g-s - acts on Fibr, has worn blinkers (extremely effectively). Turf high 70 - 1st of 18 giving 2lb to Bee Health Boy (8 Apr Ripon RF 0610).

**T D Barron [5-30] H T Duddin.*

MALOZZA BHB 47f54a **RR 36f 54a** 531[16]

3 b f Michelozzo (USA) - Lis Na Mon (Gleason (USA))

Form - 00253380

Record 1998 - 1st:0 2nd:1 3rd:2 Ran:6

Pre1998 - 1st:2 2nd:0 3rd:2 Ran:10

Win Prizemoney £4,261 *Total Prizemoney* £5,871

Wins * 1997 *Spt Wolver (STD) S 6f 59* <

* 1997 *May Southw (STD) 5f 59* <

1998 Turf 0-1: (7f) (gd) 1998 AW 0-5: (6f 3, 8f 2) (Fibr 5)

Fair filly, effective 5 to 6f, best at 6f, - acts on Fibr, has worn blinkers. AW high 54. **P D Evans [2-16] D Maloney.*

MALTAYAR (IRE) RR 63f 1101[5]

3 ch c Be My Chief (USA) 10.2f **(62)** - Malwiya (USA) (Shahrastani (USA)) 8.8f **(72)**

Form - 5

Record 1998 - 1st:0 2nd:0 3rd:0 Ran:1

1998 Turf 0-1: (7f) (frm)

Scopey, currently average colt. **L M Cumani [0-1] H H Aga Khan.*

MAMBLE'S PENSION (IRE) BHB 36f36a **RR 47f 36a** 1926[7]

3 ch f Elmaamul (USA) 8.1f **(70)** - Chance All (FR) (Glenstal (USA)) 10.1f **(64)**

Form - 760407

Record 1998 - 1st:0 2nd:0 3rd:0 Ran:4

Pre1998 - 1st:0 2nd:0 3rd:0 Ran:3

1998 Turf 0-3: (6f 3) (sft 2, gd) 1998 AW 0-1: (9f) (Fibr)

Light-framed, moderate filly. Turf high 47.

**A Bailey [0-7] Sandybrow Stables Ltd.*

MAMMA'S BOY BHB 67f66a **RR 63f 66a** 5097[9]

3 b g Rock City 8.8f **(62)** - Henpot (IRE) (Alzao (USA)) 7.1f **(68)**

Form - 3842315726140

Record 1998 - 1st:2 2nd:2 3rd:2 Ran:13

Pre1998 - 1st:0 2nd:1 3rd:4 Ran:8

Win Prizemoney £7,340 *Total Prizemoney* £13,019

Wins * **1998** Spt Sandow (G-S) C 5f 63+

* **1998** Jun Doncas (GD) H 6f 69 72 <

1998 Turf 2-12: (5f 1-3, 6f 1-7, 7f 2) (sft, g-s, gd 2-9, frm) 1998 AW 0-1: (7f) (Fibr)

Strong, average gelding, effective 5 to 6f, best at 5f, acts on sft to frm, does well at Pontefract and Hamilton. Turf high 72 - 1st of 22 giving 9lb to Kings Arrow (27 Jun Doncaster RF 2331). Consistent.

**J Berry [2-21] G Tiribocchi.*

MAMMAS F-C (IRE) BHB 69f65a **RR 66f 65a** 4876[7]

2 ch f Case Law 6f **(64)** - Wasaif (IRE) (Lomond (USA)) 8.8f **(65)**

Form - 2272611628177

Record 1998 - 1st:3 2nd:4 3rd:0 Ran:13

Win Prizemoney £7,587 *Total Prizemoney* £10,389

Wins * **1998** Spt Haydoc (GD) C 6f 65

* **1998** Jun Mussel (G-F) C 5f 60+

* **1998** *Jun Southw (STD) 5f 66* <

1998 Turf 2-7: (5f 1-4, 6f 1-3) (g-s, gd 2, g-f 1-1, frm 1-3) 1998 AW 1-6: (5f 1-5, 6f) (Fibr 1-6)

Average filly, effective 5 to 6f, best at 5f, acts on g-f to frm - acts on Fibr. Turf high 66 - also 1st of 22 getting 17lb from Robber Red (4 Spt Haydock RF 4091). AW high 66 - 1st of 10 getting 5lb from Blue Star (12 Jun Southwell RF 1940). Consistent.

**J Berry [3-13] G Tiribocchi.*

MANCALA BHB 76f **RR 71f** 4499[6]

2 ch f Deploy 11.4f **(67)** - Alghabrah (Lomond (USA)) 8.8f **(65)**

Form - 036

Record 1998 - 1st:0 2nd:0 3rd:1 Ran:3

Win Prizemoney £0 *Total Prizemoney* £507

1998 Turf 0-3: (7f, 8f, 9f) (gd 2, frm)

Currently above-average filly. Turf high 71 (began Aug).

**P F I Cole [0-3] N C Kersey.*

MANCINI BHB 57f **RR** 4966[14]

5 b br g Nomination 7.3f **(57)** - Roman Blue (Charlottown) 10.9f **(57)**

Form - 0

Record 1998 - 1st:0 2nd:0 3rd:0 Ran:1

Pre1998 - 1st:1 2nd:1 3rd:0 Ran:9

Win Prizemoney £3,245 *Total Prizemoney* £4,719

Wins 1995 Aug Bright (FRM) 7f 84 <

1998 Turf 0-1: (10f) (sft)

Very poor gelding, has worn blinkers.

**J A B Old [0-1] Mrs Anne Yearley (from M Bell [1-9] Aug 1996).*

MANDEREZ (IRE) BHB 69f **RR 76f** 4577[4]

2 b c Up and At 'em - Tales of Eirann (Dara Monarch) 8.8f **(59)**

Form - 484

Record 1998 - 1st:0 2nd:0 3rd:0 Ran:3

1998 Turf 0-3: (5f 2, 7f) (gd 2, g-f)

Currently above-average colt. Turf high 76 (began Spt).

**J G FitzGerald [0-3] H R Atkinson & Co Ltd.*

MANDHAR (IRE) BHB 47f58a **RR 50f 58a** 4120[4]

3 b c Scenic 10.6f **(66)** - Clonross Lady (Red Alert) 7.6f **(66)**
Form - 20036624
Record 1998 - 1st:0 2nd:2 3rd:1 Ran:8
Pre1998 - 1st:0 2nd:0 3rd:0 Ran:2
Win Prizemoney £0 *Total Prizemoney* £2,087
1998 Turf 0-5: (7f, 8f, 9f, 10f, 12f) (gd 2, g-f, frm 2) 1998 AW 0-3: (8f, 9f, 12f) (Fibr 3)
Unfurnished, average colt, often wears blinkers. Turf high 50. AW high 64. **G Lewis [0-10] Abdulla Al Khalifa.*

MANDILAK (USA) BHB 103f **RR 105f** 4221a[4]

4 b c El Gran Senor (USA) 8.9f **(85)** - Madiriya (Diesis) 9.3f **(69)**
Form - 13804
Record 1998 - 1st:1 2nd:0 3rd:1 Ran:5
Pre1998 - 1st:1 2nd:2 3rd:0 Ran:6
Win Prizemoney £21,025 *Total Prizemoney* £35,646
Wins * **1998** May San Si (YLD) L 10f 105 <
* 1996 Oct Yarmou (GD) 8f 80
1998 Turf 1-5: (10f 1-3, 11f, 12f) (sft, g-s 1-1, gd 2, g-f)
Scopey, Pattern-class colt, effective 8 to 12f, acts on sft to g-f, best on g-f, excels at San Siro. Turf high 105 (1st run) - 1st of 6 from War Declaration (3 May San Siro RF 1094a). Consistent. He would probably have won a Group Two in Rome but for stumbling and hitting the rail a furlong from home. The passport will have to come out again if he is to land a similar prize. **L M Cumani [2-11].*

MANE FRAME BHB 59f **RR 78?f** 5119[3]

3 b c Unfuwain (USA) 11.4f **(74)** - Moviegoer (Pharly (FR)) 9.8f **(68)**
Form - 05430723
Record 1998 - 1st:0 2nd:1 3rd:2 Ran:8
Win Prizemoney £0 *Total Prizemoney* £2,668
1998 Turf 0-8: (10f 2, 12f 3, 14f, 16f, 17f) (sft, g-s, gd 3, g-f, frm 2)
Workmanlike, above-average colt, effective 12f, acts on sft, favours tight tracks. Turf high 78 - 2nd of 13 to Tom Paddington (27 Oct Bath 12f sft RF 5008). **H Morrison [0-8] A, J & M Arbib.*

MANFUL BHB 62f60a **RR 63f 60a** 5013[2]

6 b g Efisio 7.7f **(69)** - Mandrian (Mandamus) 12.6f **(56)**
Form - 00342133502
Record 1998 - 1st:1 2nd:2 3rd:3 Ran:10
Pre1998 - 1st:9 2nd:8 3rd:5 Ran:62
Win Prizemoney £37,015 *Total Prizemoney* £53,315
Wins * **1998** Aug Ayr (G-S) H 10f 60 62
* 1997 May Hamilt (SFT) H 11.1f 72 76
* 1997 Apr Hamilt (SFT) H 11.1f 68 73
1996 Dec Southw (SLW) H 11f 62 68
1996 Oct Lingfi (STD) H 12f 54 58
1996 Spt Hamilt (G-S) C 11.1f 69
1996 May Ayr (G-S) H 10.9f 62 67
1996 Mar Doncas (GD) H 10.3f 54 63
1994 Jly Newcas (G-F) 6f 79
1994 Jun Newcas (FRM) 6f 79
1998 Turf 1-10: (10f 1-3, 11f 5, 12f 2) (sft, g-s, gd 1-4, g-f, frm 3)
Average gelding, effective 11 to 12f, best at 11f, acts on g-s to gd, best on gd, often wears blinkers, likes right handed tracks, likes tight tracks. Turf high 66. Consistent.
**Miss L A Perratt [3-27] C D Barber-Lomax (from J Hetherton [2-35] Jan 1997).*

MANGUS (IRE) BHB 72f79a **RR 71f 79a** 3809[4]

4 b g Mac's Imp (USA) 5.6f **(54)** - Holly Bird (Runnett) 7f **(59)**
Form - 750010180684
Record 1998 - 1st:2 2nd:0 3rd:0 Ran:12
Pre1998 - 1st:1 2nd:3 3rd:1 Ran:13
Win Prizemoney £9,435 *Total Prizemoney* £14,455
Wins * ***1998*** *Jun Wolver (STD) H 5f 72 74* <
* **1998** May Lingfi (G-F) H 5f 67 72
* 1997 Apr Warwic (G-F) H 5f 70 72
1998 Turf 1-10: (5f 1-9, 6f) (g-s, gd 4, g-f 3, frm 1-2) 1998 AW 1-2: (5f 1-2) (Equi, Fibr 1-1)
Unfurnished, above-average gelding, effective 5f, acts on g-f to frm - acts on Fibr, likes left handed tracks. Turf high 72 - 1st of 13 giving 12lb to Facile Tigre (23 May Lingfield RF 1432). AW high 74 - 1st of 8 giving 10lb to Aljaz (17 Jun Wolverhampton RF 2080). Inconsistent. A fair sort in modest company over the minimum trip, he is suited by fast ground on Turf and can go on Fibresand too. **K O Cunningham-Brown [3-25] Danebury Racing Stables Ltd.*

MANIC MONDAY **RR** 4970[13]

3 b f Secret Appeal - Gilboa (Shirley Heights) 10.3f **(74)**
Form - 0
Record 1998 - 1st:0 2nd:0 3rd:0 Ran:1
1998 Turf 0-1: (10f) (g-s)
Unfurnished, currently very poor filly, has broken blood-vessels - 13th of 13 getting 10lb from Stone Ridge (24 Oct Doncaster 10f g-s RF 4970). **A Senior [0-1] Frank Youds.*

MANICURE (IRE) **RR 50f** 4668[12]

2 b f Lucky Guest - Mana (GER) (Windwurf (GER)) 12.7f **(72)**
Form - 0
Record 1998 - 1st:0 2nd:0 3rd:0 Ran:1
1998 Turf 0-1: (6f) (gd)
Currently fair filly. **E A L Dunlop [0-1] Anamoine Ltd.*

MANIKATO (USA) BHB 42f50a **RR 47f 50a** 4256[9]

4 b g Clever Trick (USA) 7.6f **(69)** - Pasampsi (USA) (Crow (FR)) 7.4f **(75)**
Form - 243344400
Record 1998 - 1st:0 2nd:0 3rd:2 Ran:8
Pre1998 - 1st:0 2nd:4 3rd:0 Ran:19
Win Prizemoney £0 *Total Prizemoney* £8,702
1998 Turf 0-2: (7f, 8f) (frm 2) 1998 AW 0-6: (7f, 8f 2, 10f 2, 12f) (Equi 4, Fibr 2)
Workmanlike, fair gelding, effective 7 to 8f, best at 8f, acts on gd - acts on Equi, has worn blinkers, favours tight tracks. Turf high 36. AW high 58.
**D J S Cosgrove [0-27] Edermine Bloodstock And Partners.*

MANILA MOON (USA) BHB 54f **RR 43f** 1561[5]

3 b c Manila (USA) 10f **(81)** - Sign Language (USA) (Silent Screen (USA)) 8.6f **(65)**
Form - 5
Record 1998 - 1st:0 2nd:0 3rd:0 Ran:1
Pre1998 - 1st:0 2nd:0 3rd:0 Ran:2
1998 Turf 0-1: (10f) (g-s)
Moderate colt. **J J O'Neill [0-3] Clayton Bigley Partnership Ltd.*

MANILENO BHB 70f77a **RR 65+f 77a** 1941[1]

4 ch g K-Battery 12.4f **(59)** - Andalucia (Rheingold) 10.4f **(62)**
Form - 11
Record 1998 - 1st:2 2nd:0 3rd:0 Ran:2
Pre1998 - 1st:3 2nd:0 3rd:3 Ran:9
Win Prizemoney £12,520 *Total Prizemoney* £13,868
Wins * ***1998*** *Jun Southw (STD) C 14f 73*
1998 *Jun Southw (STD) C 16f 74* <
1997 Jly Warwic (SFT) H 14.9f 57 65++
1997 Jun Lingfi (GD) H 11.5f 51 55+
1997 May Bright (FRM) SH 11.9f 45 48
1998 AW 2-2: (14f 1-1, 16f 1-1) (Fibr 2-2)
Unfurnished, above-average gelding, effective 14 to 17f, acts on gd to frm - acts on Fibr, has worn blinkers, prefers left handed tracks, favours tight tracks, excels at Southwell. AW high 74 (1st run) - 1st of 11 giving 1lb to Mister Aspecto (5 Jun Southwell RF 1764) - also 1st of 9 getting 1lb from Madame Chinnery (12 Jun Southwell RF 1941).
**Miss S J Wilton [1-1] John Pointon and Sons (from M C Pipe [8-14] Jun 1998).*

MANNEQUIN (IRE) BHB 68f **RR 75f** 4625[8]

3 b f In The Wings 11.2f **(77)** - Pretty Lady (High Top) 10.2f **(67)**
Form - 42522348
Record 1998 - 1st:0 2nd:3 3rd:1 Ran:8
Pre1998 - 1st:0 2nd:0 3rd:0 Ran:1
Win Prizemoney £0 *Total Prizemoney* £3,868
1998 Turf 0-8: (10f, 12f 4, 13f, 14f, 15f) (sft, gd, g-f 3, frm 3)
Neat, above-average filly, effective 12 to 15f, acts on gd to frm, has worn blinkers. Turf high 75 - 2nd of 7 giving 10lb to Aldwych Arrow (19 Jun Ayr 13f gd RF 2116).
**B W Hills [0-9] Mohammed Al Nabouda.*

MAN OF COURAGE **RR 79f** 2947[3]

3 b c Nashwan (USA) 10.3f **(79)**- Dafrah (USA)(Danzig (USA)) 8.4f **(76)**
Form - 63
Record 1998 - 1st:0 2nd:0 3rd:1 Ran:2
Win Prizemoney £0 *Total Prizemoney* £509

1998 Turf 0-2: (10f 2) (gd, frm)
Currently above-average colt. Turf high 79 (began Jly).
**E A L Dunlop [0-2] Maktoum Al Maktoum.*

MAN OF THE NIGHT BHB 65f **RR 69f** 4835[6]

2 b c Clantime 6.6f **(57)** - Forbidden Monkey (Gabitat) 5f **(44)**
Form - 186
Record 1998 - 1st:1 2nd:0 3rd:0 Ran:3
Win Prizemoney £2,556 *Total Prizemoney* £2,556
Wins * 1998 Aug Hamilt (SFT) S 5f 64+ <
1998 Turf 1-3: (5f 1-1, 6f, 7f) (g-s, gd 1-1, frm)
Currently average colt. Turf high 69 (began Aug) - also 1st of 8 from Red Amazon (12 Aug Hamilton RF 3577). Comfortable winner on his debut before finishing well held in the seller at the Ebor Meeting. **J J O'Neill [1-3] E A Brook.*

MANOLO (FR) BHB 65f70a **RR 57f 70a** 666[7]

5 b g Cricket Ball (USA) 7.9f **(75)** - Malouna (FR) (General Holme (USA)) 5.7f **(63)**
Form - 201177
Record 1998 - 1st:2 2nd:0 3rd:0 Ran:5
Pre1998 - 1st:2 2nd:4 3rd:1 Ran:22
Win Prizemoney £12,231 *Total Prizemoney* £18,296
Wins * 1998 *Feb Lingfi (SLW) H 5f 56 66* <
*** 1998** *Feb Lingfi (SLW) H 6f 58 65*
1997 Apr Pontef (G-F) H 5f 62 64
1996 Spt Beverl (G-F) 5f 62
1998 Turf 0-1: (5f) (sft) 1998 AW 2-4: (5f 1-1, 6f 1-3) (Equi 2-4)
Average gelding, effective 5 to 6f, best at 5f, acts on g-f to frm - acts on Equi, often wears blinkers, prefers left handed tracks, prefers tight tracks, excels at Pontefract, likes Lingfield. AW high 66 - 1st of 10 giving 9lb to La Doyenne (19 Feb Lingfield RF 0317) - also 1st of 9 getting 9lb from Ramsey Hope (10 Feb Lingfield RF 0263). Claimed to join David Loder after finishing runner-up on the Lingfield Equitrack in December, he won twice on the same track in February, the second time despite a slow start, but has not shown the same level of form since.
**D R Loder [2-5] Lucayan Stud (from J Berry [2-22] Dec 1997).*

MANORBIER BHB 80f **RR 81f** 4591[9]

2 ch g Shalford (IRE) 7.8f **(63)** - La Pirouette (USA) (Kennedy Road (CAN)) 10f **(66)**
Form - 61250
Record 1998 - 1st:1 2nd:1 3rd:0 Ran:5
Win Prizemoney £3,290 *Total Prizemoney* £4,275
Wins * 1998 Aug Chepst (G-F) 5.1f 79 <
1998 Turf 1-5: (5f 1-5) (gd 3, g-f, frm 1-1)
Decent gelding. Turf high 81 - 2nd of 6 giving 25lb to Tempramental (31 Aug Chepstow 5f gd RF 3979) - also 1st of 11 from Ecudamah (13 Aug Chepstow RF 3606). A real sprint type, he has run creditably in nurseries since winning his maiden.
**D W P Arbuthnot [1-5] Derrick Broomfield.*

MANSA MUSA (IRE) BHB 75f **RR 74f** 2752[7]

3 br c Hamas (IRE) 8f **(72)** - Marton Maid (Silly Season) 9.7f **(56)**
Form - 33252737
Record 1998 - 1st:0 2nd:2 3rd:3 Ran:8
Pre1998 - 1st:0 2nd:0 3rd:0 Ran:1
Win Prizemoney £0 *Total Prizemoney* £9,109
1998 Turf 0-8: (8f 3, 9f, 10f 3, 12f) (sft 2, gd 4, g-f, frm)
Unfurnished, above-average colt, effective 6 to 10f, best at 10f, acts on gd to frm, best on gd, prefers left handed tracks. Turf high 74 - 2nd of 11 getting 23lb from Dower House (5 Jun Epsom 10f gd RF 1750). Consistent. He has run some fine races in varied company, but has yet to get off the mark. He should be able to win a race if his sights were lowered a little.
**M R Channon [0-9] Surrey Laminators Ltd.*

MANTELLO BHB 50f **RR 59f** 4589[5]

3 ch c Mon Tresor 7.9f **(60)** - Laena (Roman Warrior) 5.6f **(57)**
Form - 00205005
Record 1998 - 1st:0 2nd:1 3rd:0 Ran:8
Pre1998 - 1st:0 2nd:0 3rd:0 Ran:3
Win Prizemoney £0 *Total Prizemoney* £752
1998 Turf 0-8: (6f, 7f, 8f 2, 10f 2, 13f, 14f) (gd 5, g-f, frm 2)
Fair colt, effective 7f, acts on gd, often wears blinkers (very effectively). Turf high 59 - 2nd of 20 getting 8lb from Gaily Mill (10 Jun Salisbury 7f gd RF 1883). A half-brother to Cape Merino, he ran his best race so far when tried in blinkers.
**Major D N Chappell [0-11] Super Sprinters.*

MANTLES PRIDE BHB 72f **RR 73?f** 5014[7]

3 b g Petong 7.6f **(58)** - State Romance (Free State) 8.7f **(61)**
Form - 33000707327
Record 1998 - 1st:0 2nd:1 3rd:3 Ran:11
Pre1998 - 1st:1 2nd:1 3rd:0 Ran:6
Win Prizemoney £3,322 *Total Prizemoney* £10,359
Wins 1997 Spt Folkes (FRM) H 5f 78 83 <
1998 Turf 0-11: (5f, 6f 8, 7f 2) (g-s 3, gd 3, g-f 5)
Neat, above-average gelding, effective 5f, acts on g-f, has worn blinkers. Turf high 84.
**P Calver [0-11] Kenneth MacPherson (from G Lewis [1-6] Oct 1997).*

MANTLES PRINCESS **RR 62f** 1012[9]

3 b f Rock City 8.8f **(62)** - Teslemi (USA) (Ogygian (USA))
Form - 0
Record 1998 - 1st:0 2nd:0 3rd:0 Ran:1
1998 Turf 0-1: (8f) (gd)
Scopey, currently average filly. **G Lewis [0-1] David Barker.*

MANTUSIS (IRE) BHB 89f **RR 90df** 4368[17]

3 ch c Pursuit of Love 9.5f **(69)** - Mana (GER) (Windwurf (GER)) 12.7f **(72)**
Form - 302000
Record 1998 - 1st:0 2nd:1 3rd:1 Ran:6
Pre1998 - 1st:1 2nd:1 3rd:0 Ran:2
Win Prizemoney £4,198 *Total Prizemoney* £9,036
Wins * 1997 Oct Leices (G-S) 8f 87 <
1998 Turf 0-6: (7f 3, 8f, 10f 2) (hvy, sft, g-s, g-f 3)
Scopey, useful colt, effective 7 to 8f, acts on g-s to gd. Turf high 90 - 2nd of 11 giving 4lb to Kayo (11 Jun Newbury 7f g-s RF 1900). Becoming disappointing. Appreciated the drop in trip from ten to seven furlongs when runner-up in heavy ground at Newbury, but faced some stiff tasks otherwise and showed little.
**P W Harris [1-8] The Romantics.*

MANUFAN BHB 62f **RR 73f** 4961[2]

3 b c Sabrehill (USA) 8.5f **(64)** - The Last Empress (IRE) (Last Tycoon) 8.5f **(62)**
Form - 04308022
Record 1998 - 1st:0 2nd:2 3rd:1 Ran:8
Pre1998 - 1st:0 2nd:0 3rd:0 Ran:1
Win Prizemoney £0 *Total Prizemoney* £4,130
1998 Turf 0-8: (7f, 8f, 10f, 12f 4, 14f) (gd 2, g-f, frm 5)
Lengthy, above-average colt, effective 12f, acts on gd. Turf high 74. Has joined Willie Muir.
**R F JohnsonHoughton [0-9] Anthony Pye-Jeary.*

MANZONI **RR 63f** 4889[8]

2 b c Warrshan (USA) 9.7f **(59)** - Arc Empress Jane (IRE) (Rainbow Quest (USA)) 10.4f **(75)**
Form - 8578
Record 1998 - 1st:0 2nd:0 3rd:0 Ran:4
1998 Turf 0-4: (6f 2, 7f, 8f) (gd 2, g-f 2)
Average colt. Turf high 58. **G Lewis [0-4] David Barker.*

MAPLE (IRE) BHB 92f **RR 89f** 4743[7]

2 ch c Soviet Lad (USA) 9.4f **(63)**-Little Red Rose (Precocious) 8.6f **(62)**
Form - 826242137
Record 1998 - 1st:1 2nd:3 3rd:1 Ran:9
Win Prizemoney £3,980 *Total Prizemoney* £8,534
Wins * 1998 Spt Newbur (GD) 6f 80 <
1998 Turf 1-9: (5f 4, 6f 1-3, 7f 2) (g-s, gd 3, g-f 1-3, frm 2)
Useful colt, effective 5 to 7f, best at 6f, acts on gd to frm. Turf high 89 - 3rd of 16 giving 12lb to Entwine (1 Oct Newmarket 5f gd RF 4591) - also 1st of 22 from Al Naba (19 Spt Newbury RF 4382). Put his experience to good use to land a fair Newbury maiden.
**D R C Elsworth [1-9] G Steinberg.*

MAPLE BAY (IRE) BHB 58f64a **RR 51f 64a** 573[9]

9 b g Bold Arrangement 8.7f **(57)** - Cannon Boy (USA) (Canonero (USA)) 7.8f **(71)**
Form - 50
Record 1998 - 1st:0 2nd:0 3rd:0 Ran:2
Pre1998 - 1st:11 2nd:7 3rd:7 Ran:70

Win Prizemoney £37,951 *Total Prizemoney* £49,871
Wins 1996 Spt Pontef (GD) H 8f 76 82 <
1996 Aug Nottin (G-S) H 8.2f 70 78
1996 Jly Mussel (GD) H 8.1f 68 71
1996 May Newcas (GD) H 8f 65 69
1996 Apr Nottin (GD) H 8.2f 62 72
1996 *Feb Wolver (STD) H 9.4f 80 80*
1996 *Jan Southw (STD) H 8f 59 74*
1996 *Jan Wolver (STD) S 8.5f 66*
1996 *Jan Wolver (STD) H 9.4f 59 63*
1994 *Jan Wolver (STD) H 7f 51 48*
1994 *Jan Wolver (STD) C 6f 48*
1998 Turf 0-1: (9f) (sft) 1998 AW 0-1: (8f) (Fibr)
Fair gelding, had worn blinkers. Consistent. (DEAD)
**B Ellison [1-18] Ferrograph Ltd (from A Bailey [9-41] Nov 1996).*

MARABELA (IRE) BHB 80f **RR 77df** 5141[7]
3 b f Shernazar 11.8f **(71)** - Mariyada (USA) (Diesis) 9.3f **(69)**
Form - 3167
Record 1998 - 1st:1 2nd:0 3rd:1 Ran:4
Win Prizemoney £3,132 *Total Prizemoney* £3,664
Wins * 1998 Jly Nottin (G-F) 8.2f 77 <
1998 Turf 1-4: (8f 1-2, 10f, 11f) (gd, g-f 1-2, frm)
Scopey, above-average filly. Turf high 77 (began Jly) - 1st of 11 from Miss Fara (24 Jly Nottingham RF 3083). Failed to progress after winning her maiden. **L M Cumani [1-4] H H Aga Khan.*

MARADI (IRE) BHB 41f71a **RR 46f 71a** 4486[2]
4 b g Marju (IRE) 9.2f **(76)** - Tigora (Ahonoora) 8.1f **(73)**
Form - 00042
Record 1998 - 1st:0 2nd:1 3rd:0 Ran:5
Pre1998 - 1st:1 2nd:1 3rd:5 Ran:18
Win Prizemoney £3,371 *Total Prizemoney* £9,548
Wins 1997 *Feb Southw (STD) 12f 53++* <
1998 Turf 0-5: (10f 4, 12f) (sft, g-s, gd, frm 2)
Well made, fair gelding, effective 10 to 13f, acts on gd to g-f, prefers left handed tracks, likes tight tracks. Turf high 46.
**B J Curley [0-10] Mrs B J Curley (from M Bell [1-10] Oct 1997).*

MARAHILL LAD BHB 35f **RR 47f** 4765[17]
3 b g Mazilier (USA) 8.5f **(56)** - Harmonious Sound (Auction Ring (USA)) 8.6f **(65)**
Form - 06700
Record 1998 - 1st:0 2nd:0 3rd:0 Ran:5
Pre1998 - 1st:0 2nd:0 3rd:0 Ran:4
1998 Turf 0-2: (7f, 10f) (g-s, gd) 1998 AW 0-3: (5f, 6f, 8f) (Fibr 3)
Workmanlike, moderate gelding. (began Spt). AW high 30.
**P Howling [0-10] Liam Sheridan.*

MARALINGA (IRE) BHB 96f98a **RR 99f 98a** 3802[7]
6 ch g Simply Great (FR) 11.9f **(61)** - Bellinzona (Northfields (USA)) 9f **(72)**
Form - 23647
Record 1998 - 1st:0 2nd:1 3rd:1 Ran:5
Pre1998 - 1st:4 2nd:3 3rd:3 Ran:26
Win Prizemoney £22,931 *Total Prizemoney* £54,376
Wins * 1997 Jun Cheste (G-F) 12.3f 85?
* 1996 Aug Windso (G-F) 10f 99 <
1995 *Apr Lingfi (STD) 10f 92*
1994 Jly Yarmou (GD) 7f 76
1998 Turf 0-5: (10f 2, 12f, 13f 2) (sft, gd 2, g-f, frm)
Very useful gelding, effective 10 to 12f, best at 10f, acts on gd to frm, prefers left handed tracks, prefers tight tracks. Turf high 99 (1st run) - 2nd of 5 getting 6lb from Salmon Ladder (10 May Bath 10f frm RF 1127). Inconsistent.
**Lady Herries [3-25] D K R & Mrs J B C Oliver (from M Bell [2-8] Jun 1995).*

MARATHON MAID BHB 55f **RR 64f** 4759[12]
4 gr f Kalaglow 11.2f **(67)** - El Rabab (USA) (Roberto (USA)) 10f **(76)**
Form - 8001650860
Record 1998 - 1st:1 2nd:0 3rd:0 Ran:10
Pre1998 - 1st:2 2nd:0 3rd:1 Ran:11
Win Prizemoney £12,101 *Total Prizemoney* £14,680
Wins * 1998 Jly Doncas (G-F) H 8f 60 64
* 1996 May Pontef (GD) 6f 84 <
* 1996 Apr Newcas (GD) 5f 67
1998 Turf 1-10: (8f 1-4, 10f 4, 12f 2) (sft, gd 3, g-f 2, frm 1-4)
Leggy, average filly, effective 8f, acts on frm, has worn blinkers, likes left handed tracks. Turf high 66 - also 1st of 9 getting 19lb from Royal Mark (15 Jly Doncaster RF 2819). She found winning form last season when dropped to a mile, though the form of that race is suspect.
**R A Fahey [3-21] John Stephenson & Sons (Nelson) Ltd.*

MARCH HARE BHB 52f **RR 56f** 4656[8]
3 b f Groom Dancer (USA) 9.5f **(75)** - Spring (Sadler's Wells (USA)) 10f **(76)**
Form - 034408
Record 1998 - 1st:0 2nd:0 3rd:1 Ran:6
Win Prizemoney £0 *Total Prizemoney* £451
1998 Turf 0-6: (8f, 9f, 10f, 12f 3) (gd 3, g-f, frm 2)
Small, fair filly, effective 12f, acts on g-f. Turf high 56.
**J L Dunlop [0-6] Lord Halifax.*

MARCHMAN BHB 44f **RR 53df** 3958[18]
13 b g Daring March 9f **(54)** - Saltation (Sallust) 8.4f **(63)**
Form - 080
Record 1998 - 1st:0 2nd:0 3rd:0 Ran:3
Pre1998 - 1st:3 2nd:5 3rd:3 Ran:25
Win Prizemoney £8,891 *Total Prizemoney* £14,169
Wins * 1996 May Nottin (G-F) SH 10f 45 53
1998 Turf 0-3: (10f, 12f, 13f) (g-f 2, frm)
Fair gelding. Turf high 39 (began Jly). **J S King [9-41] Mrs P M King.*

MARCH PARTY (FR) BHB 55f **RR 59f** 4136[11]
2 ch f Archway (IRE) 8.5f **(60)** - Social Gathering (IRE) (Dance of Life (USA)) 7f **(66)**
Form - 500801730
Record 1998 - 1st:1 2nd:0 3rd:1 Ran:9
Win Prizemoney £1,882 *Total Prizemoney* £2,262
Wins * 1998 *Jly Wolver (STD) S 7f 59* <
1998 Turf 0-7: (5f 2, 6f, 7f 3, 8f) (sft, g-s, g-f 2, frm 3) 1998 AW 1-2: (7f 1-2) (Fibr 1-2)
Fair filly, effective 7f, acts on g-f - acts on Fibr. Turf high 59 - 3rd of 11 getting 12lb from Cosmo Jack (22 Aug Sandown 7f g-f RF 3818). AW high 59 (1st run) (began Jly) - 1st of 11 from Brookhead Brandy (24 Jly Wolverhampton RF 3097).
**J G Portman [1-9] Madhatter Racing.*

MARCH STAR (IRE) BHB 105f **RR 110f** 4844[15]
4 b f Mac's Imp (USA) 5.6f **(54)** - Grade a Star (IRE) (Alzao (USA)) 7.1f **(68)**
Form - 08106100
Record 1998 - 1st:2 2nd:0 3rd:0 Ran:8
Pre1998 - 1st:2 2nd:1 3rd:2 Ran:8
Win Prizemoney £33,017 *Total Prizemoney* £36,759
Wins * 1998 Aug Leopar (G-F) G3 6f 110 <
*** 1998** Jun Yarmou (SFT) 6f 103
* 1997 Spt Yarmou (FRM) 6f 87
* 1996 May Newbur (SFT) 6f 68
1998 Turf 2-8: (6f 2-8) (g-s, gd 3, g-f 1-2, frm 1-2)
Workmanlike, Group-class filly, effective 6f, acts on g-f to frm. Turf high 110 - 1st of 8 giving 1lb to Bianconi (9 Aug Leopardstown RF 3557a) - also 1st of 4 giving 8lb to Thanksgiving (11 Jun Yarmouth RF 1905). Inconsistent. She ran the race of her life when winning a Group Three at Leopardstown in August, racing up with the pace and staying on doggedly. Well beaten afterwards, she will be hard pressed to score again at that level.
**J A R Toller [4-16] Mrs N O'Callaghan.*

MARCIANO **RR 11f** 4915[11]
2 b c Rock Hopper 10.6f **(54)** - Raintree Venture (Good Times (ITY)) 6.6f **(54)**
Form - 0
Record 1998 - 1st:0 2nd:0 3rd:0 Ran:1
1998 Turf 0-1: (6f) (g-s)
Currently poor colt. **C W Thornton [0-1] Guy Reed.*

MARCOMIR (USA) BHB 64a **RR 65+f 64a** 172[8]
5 b h Dayjur (USA) 6.8f **(79)** - Mariella (USA) (Roberto (USA)) 10f **(76)**
Form - 78
Record 1998 - 1st:0 2nd:0 3rd:0 Ran:2
Pre1998 - 1st:1 2nd:0 3rd:0 Ran:1
Win Prizemoney £4,260 *Total Prizemoney* £4,260

Wins 1995 Spt Hamilt (GD) 6f 71+ <
1998 AW 0-2: (6f, 7f) (Fibr 2)
Currently average colt. AW high 49.
**E J Alston [0-2] Mrs Carol McPhail (from M Johnston [1-1] Spt 1995).*

MARCO'S PAL BHB 57f RR 61+f 4410[9]

2 ch g Timeless Times (USA) 6.1f **(56)** - Parijoun (Manado) 9.6f **(63)**
Form - 7000
Record 1998 - 1st:0 2nd:0 3rd:0 Ran:4
1998 Turf 0-4: (5f, 6f, 7f 2) (gd, g-f, frm 2)
Average gelding. Turf high 61. **A P Jarvis [0-4] Ambrose Turnbull.*

MARCUS MAXIMUS (USA) BHB 109f RR 105f 4798[4]

3 ch c Woodman (USA) 9.7f **(77)** - Star Pastures (Northfields (USA)) 9f **(72)**
Form - 114
Record 1998 - 1st:2 2nd:0 3rd:0 Ran:3
Win Prizemoney £13,157 *Total Prizemoney* £13,529
Wins * **1998** Spt Doncas (GD) 10.3f 105 <
* **1998** Jly Yarmou (G-F) 11.5f 77
1998 Turf 2-3: (10f 1-1, 11f 1-1, 12f) (sft, g-f 2-2)
Workmanlike, currently Pattern-class colt. Turf high 105 (began Jly) - 1st of 5 from Dark Shell (11 Spt Doncaster RF 4223). He sprang a surprise when winning a decent minor event at Doncaster in September, and can be forgiven a disappointing effort on bad ground at Haydock the following month. Beautifully bred, he is open to improvement, but already weighted out of handicaps. **H R A Cecil [2-3] Wafic Said.*

MARDREW BHB 52f56a RR 53f 56a 2478[5]

4 b g Rambo Dancer (CAN) 8.4f **(59)** - Having Fun (Hard Fought) 8.8f **(62)**
Form - 456004505
Record 1998 - 1st:0 2nd:0 3rd:0 Ran:9
Pre1998 - 1st:1 2nd:3 3rd:5 Ran:19
Win Prizemoney £2,085 *Total Prizemoney* £8,340
Wins 1997 *Jan Southw (STD) S 8f 69* <
1998 Turf 0-6: (8f, 10f, 11f, 12f 3) (g-s, gd, g-f, frm, hrd 2) 1998 AW 0-3: (11f 3) (Fibr 3)
Neat, fair gelding, effective 8 to 12f, best at 8f, acts on gd to frm - acts on Fibr, best on gd, has worn blinkers, likes tight tracks, excels at Nottingham and Windsor. Turf high 58. AW high 58. Consistent.
**K G Wingrove [0-4] Terry Connors (from John Berry [0-10] Apr 1998).*

MAREMMA BHB 26f34a RR 37f 34a 3191[1]

4 b f Robellino (USA) 9.5f **(68)** - Maiden Way (Shareef Dancer (USA)) 9.9f **(73)**
Form - 0788534441
Record 1998 - 1st:1 2nd:0 3rd:1 Ran:10
Pre1998 - 1st:1 2nd:0 3rd:1 Ran:23
Win Prizemoney £5,071 *Total Prizemoney* £6,173
Wins * **1998** Jly Doncas (G-F) S 12f 37
* 1997 Jly Redcar (G-S) S 11f 46 <
1998 Turf 1-10: (11f 3, 12f 1-3, 14f 4) (sft, g-s, gd 5, g-f 1-3)
Neat, very moderate filly, effective 11 to 12f, acts on g-s to g-f, likes left handed tracks. Turf high 37. Consistent.
**Don Enrico Incisa [2-33] Don Enrico Incisa.*

MARENGO BHB 68a RR 65f 4121[12]

4 b g Never so Bold 7.1f **(62)** - Born to Dance (Dancing Brave (USA)) 8.4f **(76)**
Form - 11143500
Record 1998 - 1st:3 2nd:0 3rd:1 Ran:8
Pre1998 - 1st:0 2nd:2 3rd:2 Ran:14
Win Prizemoney £13,034 *Total Prizemoney* £18,678
Wins 1998 Apr Epsom (SFT) H 6f 62 65
1998 *Apr Wolver (STD) H 6f 57 66* <
1998 *Mar Southw (STD) H 6f 53 53*
1998 Turf 1-5: (6f 1-5) (sft 1-1, gd, g-f 2, frm) 1998 AW 2-3: (6f 2-3) (Fibr 2-3)
Unfurnished, average gelding, effective 6f, acts on sft to frm - acts on Fibr, best on frm, has worn blinkers, prefers left handed tracks, prefers tight tracks, and excels at Brighton. Turf high 66 - 4th of 13 getting 21lb from Bold Effort (17 May Kempton 6f frm RF 1281) - also 1st of 11 getting 13lb from Shamanic (22 Apr Epsom RF 0811). AW high 66 - 1st of 10 giving 10lb to Rude Awakening (4 Apr Wolverhampton RF 0570). A quirky customer, he took really well to Fibresand in 1998, winning narrowly at Southwell, and winning much more emphatically at Wolverhampton. He continued his good run back on turf with a smooth win at Epsom before losing his form. Now with Jack Berry, it would be no surprise to see him win a few more times for that yard, as likely as not back on Fibresand. **J Berry [0-2] J B Sharp (from J Akehurst [3-20] Jun 1998).*

MARGARETROSE ANNA BHB 33f37a RR 31f 37a 570[9]

6 b m Handsome Sailor 6.6f **(53)** - Be Bold (Bustino) 10.4f **(64)**
Form - 806440
Record 1998 - 1st:0 2nd:0 3rd:0 Ran:6
Pre1998 - 1st:0 2nd:1 3rd:1 Ran:22
Win Prizemoney £0 *Total Prizemoney* £1,441
1998 AW 0-6: (6f 6) (Fibr 6)
Moderate mare, effective 6f, - acts on Fibr, has worn blinkers. AW high 44.
**B P J Baugh [0-16] John Meredith (from P D Evans [0-1] May 1996).*

MARGARET'S DANCER BHB 62f43a RR 65f 43a 5147[12]

3 b g Rambo Dancer (CAN) 8.4f **(59)** - Cateryne (Ballymoss) 8.5f **(55)**
Form - 80313811020
Record 1998 - 1st:3 2nd:1 3rd:2 Ran:11
Pre1998 - 1st:0 2nd:0 3rd:0 Ran:8
Win Prizemoney £8,998 *Total Prizemoney* £11,002
Wins * **1998** Spt Beverl (G-F) H 8.5f 57 62 <
* **1998** Spt Thirsk (GD) S 8f 57
* **1998** Jun Pontef (SFT) S 8f 49
1998 Turf 3-10: (7f 2, 8f 3-8) (g-s 1-2, gd 4, g-f 1-1, frm 1-3) 1998 AW 0-1: (6f) (Fibr)
Unfurnished, average gelding, effective 8f, acts on g-s to frm, has worn blinkers, prefers left handed tracks, prefers tight tracks. Turf high 65 - 2nd of 10 getting 2lb from Brilliance (21 Oct Nottingham 8f g-s RF 4925) - also 1st of 16 getting 12lb from Master Caster (22 Spt Beverley RF 4407).
**J L Eyre [3-11] Gordon Batty (from C Smith [0-8] Spt 1997).*

MARGIN CALL (IRE) BHB 59f RR 74df 3975[12]

4 b f Tirol 8.1f **(64)** - Chive (St Chad) 6.7f **(67)**
Form - 040
Record 1998 - 1st:0 2nd:0 3rd:0 Ran:3
Pre1998 - 1st:0 2nd:0 3rd:0 Ran:3
Win Prizemoney £0 *Total Prizemoney* £367
1998 Turf 0-3: (8f, 9f, 11f) (g-s, gd, g-f)
Above-average filly, has broken blood-vessels, effective 9f, acts on gd. Turf high 74.
**K R Burke [0-1] Glenn Martin (from D T Hughes in IRE [0-5] Jun 1998).*

MARGONE (USA) BHB 60f RR 64f 3765[10]

3 b br f Dayjur (USA) 6.8f **(79)** - Whispered Secret (CAN) (Secretariat (USA)) 9f **(79)**
Form - 00272480
Record 1998 - 1st:0 2nd:2 3rd:0 Ran:8
Pre1998 - 1st:0 2nd:0 3rd:0 Ran:1
Win Prizemoney £0 *Total Prizemoney* £2,295
1998 Turf 0-8: (6f 2, 7f 3, 8f 3) (gd 3, frm 5)
Neat, average filly, effective 7 to 8f, acts on frm, often wears blinkers (extremely effectively). Turf high 64 - 2nd of 13 giving 17lb to Shocker (27 May Yarmouth 8f frm RF 1539). Consistent.
**G Wragg [0-9] Gestut Schlenderhan.*

MARIA ISABELLA (USA) RR 70+f 4935[1]

3 ch f Kris 10f **(75)** - Korveya (USA) (Riverman (USA)) 9.1f **(76)**
Form - 1
Record 1998 - 1st:1 2nd:0 3rd:0 Ran:1
Win Prizemoney £4,175 *Total Prizemoney* £4,175
Wins * **1998** Oct Nottin () 8.2f 70 <
1998 Turf 1-1: (8f 1-1) (gd 1-1)
Scopey, currently above-average filly. (1st run) - 1st of 15 getting 5lb from Tumbleweed Hero (22 Oct Nottingham RF 4935).
**L M Cumani [1-1] Gerald Leigh.*

MARIANA BHB 53a RR 46f 4919[2]

3 ch f Anshan 8.2f **(63)** - Maria Cappuccini (Siberian Express (USA)) 8.8f **(65)**
Form - 4247040072
Record 1998 - 1st:0 2nd:2 3rd:0 Ran:10
Pre1998 - 1st:0 2nd:0 3rd:1 Ran:6

Win Prizemoney £0 *Total Prizemoney* £1,907
1998 Turf 0-6: (6f, 7f, 8f 4) (g-s, g-f 2, frm 3) 1998 AW 0-4: (6f, 7f 2, 8f) (Equi 3, Fibr)
Leggy, fair filly, effective 5 to 7f, best at 7f, acts on frm - acts on Equi, has worn blinkers, likes tight tracks. Turf high 46 (began Jly). AW high 56. She has shown some placed form in modest company on turf and sand. **R M Whitaker [0-16] D Bass.*

MARIDPOUR (IRE) BHB 115f **RR 116f** 4719a^{7}

3 b c Shernazar 11.8f **(71)** - Maridana (USA) (Nijinsky (CAN)) 10.3f **(77)**
Form - 7211037

Record	**1998** -	1st:2	2nd:1	3rd:1	Ran:7

Win Prizemoney £39,177 *Total Prizemoney* £45,863

Wins	* **1998**	Jun	Ascot	(G-S)	G3	16.2f		105	<
	* **1998**	May	Hamilt	(GD)		12.1f		86+	

1998 Turf 2-7: (10f, 12f 1-2, 15f, 16f 1-3) (sft 2, gd 2-4, g-f)
Well made, high-class colt, effective 16f, acts on g-f. Turf high 116 - 3rd of 5 getting 14lb from Persian Punch (18 Aug York 16f g-f RF 3695). Unraced at two, he steadily progressed in each of his first four runs, beating a bunch of carthorses at Hamilton before putting up a brave performance to land the Queen's Vase. He ran very poorly in the Northumberland Plate, but that race may well have come too soon after Royal Ascot, and he lost out only narrowly to Persian Punch and Celeric in a York Group Three. He was very disappointing in the Prix de Lutece on his final start. Best with some give in the ground.
**Sir Michael Stoute [2-7] H H Aga Khan.*

Win Prizemoney £6,027 *Total Prizemoney* £6,960

Wins	* 1997	Oct	Newmar	(G-S)	S	7f		62	<

1998 Turf 0-7: (7f 2, 8f 5)(sft, g-s 3, gd, g-f, frm)1998 AW 0-1:(8f) (Equi)
Lengthy, fair filly, effective 7f, acts on gd, has worn blinkers. Turf high 60. **J R Arnold [1-16] J K Gale.*

MARIE LOUP (FR) BHB 89f **RR 89f** 4496^{6}

3 ch f Wolfhound (USA) 7.3f **(71)** - Marie de Fontenoy (FR) (Lightning (FR)) 7.9f **(74)**
Form - 212136

Record	**1998** -	1st:2	2nd:2	3rd:1	Ran:6
	Pre1998 -	1st:0	2nd:0	3rd:1	Ran:2

Win Prizemoney £7,080 *Total Prizemoney* £12,321

Wins	* **1998**	Jly	Chepst	(GD)	H	8.1f	79	89+	<
	* **1998**	Jun	Beverl	(G-S)		7.5f		57+	

1998 Turf 2-6: (7f 1-1, 8f 1-4, 9f) (gd 1-5, g-f 1-1)
Scopey, useful filly, effective 8 to 9f, best at 8f, acts on gd to g-f, best on gd. Turf high 89 - 1st of 8 giving 2lb to Only In Dreams (10 Jly Chepstow RF 2671). She showed ability before getting off the mark in a Beverley maiden in June, though she was not particularly impressive there. Fair effort in a handicap next time, though she looked short of a turn of foot, before strolling home at Chepstow. Looked on the upgrade at the Welsh track, but the Handicapper raised her 12lb. Fair effort at Goodwood nonetheless.
**L M Cumani [2-8] Robert Smith.*

Maridpour (right) came good at Royal Ascot

MARI-ELA (IRE) BHB 41f **RR 54f** 4990^{7}

3 ch f River Falls 8.2f **(56)** - Best Swinger (IRE) (Ela-Mana-Mou) 10.1f **(70)**
Form - 73740807

Record	**1998** -	1st:0	2nd:0	3rd:1	Ran:8
	Pre1998 -	1st:1	2nd:0	3rd:0	Ran:8

MARIGLIANO (USA) BHB 67f72a **RR 73+f 72a** 5079^{13}

5 b g Riverman (USA) 9.7f **(78)** - Mount Holyoke (Golden Fleece (USA)) 7.9f **(74)**
Form - 41317300240

Record	**1998** -	1st:2	2nd:1	3rd:2	Ran:11
	Pre1998 -	1st:1	2nd:0	3rd:3	Ran:5

Win Prizemoney £7,940 *Total Prizemoney* £12,098
Wins * **1998** *Jly Southw (STD) C 7f 69*
* **1998** Jun Mussel (SFT) C 7.1f 73+ <
1996 May Beverl (G-F) 7.5f 69+
1998 Turf 1-9: (6f, 7f 1-6, 8f 2) (sft, gd 1-2, g-f 2, frm 3, hrd) 1998 AW 1-2: (7f 1-2) (Fibr 1-2)
Above-average gelding, effective 7f, acts on gd to hrd - acts on Fibr, best on gd. Turf high 73 - 1st of 8 giving 6lb to Mamma's Boy (15 Jun Musselburgh RF 1992). AW high 69 (1st run) (began Jly) - 1st of 9 giving 4lb to Maiteamia (9 Jly Southwell RF 2653).
**K A Morgan [2-19] T R Pryke (from Sir Michael Stoute [1-4] Jun 1996).*

MARINO STREET BHB 36f33a RR 43f 33a 3908[10]
5 b m Totem (USA) 5f **(38)** - Demerger (Dominion) 8.5f **(63)**
Form - 4033053343028840
Record 1998 - 1st:0 2nd:1 3rd:5 Ran:16
Pre1998 - 1st:1 2nd:6 3rd:5 Ran:36
Win Prizemoney £2,571 *Total Prizemoney* £12,163
Wins * 1996 Jly Leices (G-F) 5f 48 <
1998 Turf 0-9: (5f 3, 6f 3, 7f 2, 8f) (g-f 3, frm 6) 1998 AW 0-7: (5f 3, 6f 3, 7f) (Equi, Fibr 6)
Moderate filly, effective 5f, acts on frm, mostly wears blinkers. Turf high 43 (began Jly). AW high 31. **P D Evans [1-52] Roy Penton.*

MARISA'S PET BHB 49f RR 48f 3901[8]
4 gr f Petong 7.6f **(58)** - Always on a Sunday (Star Appeal) 9.6f **(65)**
Form - 86040408
Record 1998 - 1st:0 2nd:0 3rd:0 Ran:7
Pre1998 - 1st:0 2nd:0 3rd:0 Ran:2
1998 Turf 0-7: (5f 2, 6f 2, 7f 3) (gd 3, g-f 2, frm 2)
Workmanlike, moderate filly. Turf high 55.
**T E Powell [0-8] Lawrence Pratt (from G Lewis [0-1] May 1997).*

MARISOL (IRE) BHB 35f RR 50f 3750[3]
5 b m Mujtahid (USA) 7.4f **(69)** - Stanerra's Star (Shadeed (USA)) 8.2f **(70)**
Form - 75523
Record 1998 - 1st:0 2nd:1 3rd:1 Ran:5
Win Prizemoney £0 *Total Prizemoney* £1,055
1998 Turf 0-5: (7f, 9f 2, 10f, 13f) (g-s 2, gd 2, frm)
Fair filly. Turf high 50 - 3rd of 8 giving 7lb to Amoroso (19 Aug Musselburgh 9f gd RF 3750). **P Monteith [0-7] Allan Melville.*

MARJORIE ROSE (IRE) BHB 52f56a RR 51f 56a 1075[10]
5 b m Magical Strike (USA) 5.5f **(61)** - Arrapata (Thatching) 8f **(66)**
Form - 60
Record 1998 - 1st:0 2nd:0 3rd:0 Ran:2
Pre1998 - 1st:3 2nd:3 3rd:2 Ran:28
Win Prizemoney £6,914 *Total Prizemoney* £10,976
Wins * 1996 *Dec Wolver (STD) C 6f 53*
* 1996 Spt Hamilt (GD) SH 5f 53 54 <
* 1996 *Jly Wolver (STD) H 5f 55 52*
1998 Turf 0-1: (6f) (hvy) 1998 AW 0-1: (5f) (Fibr)
Fair filly, effective 5f, - acts on Fibr, has worn blinkers, likes left handed tracks, likes tight tracks.
**A Bailey [3-30] Sandybrow Stables Ltd.*

MARKAN (USA) RR 89f 2909[1]
2 ch c Affirmed (USA) 10.3f **(75)** - Norma (USA) (Procida (USA))
Form - 01
Record 1998 - 1st:1 2nd:0 3rd:0 Ran:2
Win Prizemoney £7,924 *Total Prizemoney* £7,924
Wins * **1998** Jly Newbur (G-F) 7f 89 <
1998 Turf 1-2: (7f 1-2) (g-s, gd 1-1)
Currently useful colt. Turf high 89 - 1st of 8 giving 3lb to Gudlage (18 Jly Newbury RF 2909). Started favourite for the Chesham at Ascot, but failed to handle the soft ground. Left that run behind on a fast surface at Newbury and looks a useful recruit.
**P F I Cole [1-2] H R H Prince Fahd Salman.*

MARKAPEN (IRE) BHB 27f RR 14f 1065[13]
4 b f Classic Music (USA) 7.2f **(57)** - Dahsala (Top Ville) 11.7f **(68)**
Form - 870
Record 1998 - 1st:0 2nd:0 3rd:0 Ran:3
Pre1998 - 1st:0 2nd:0 3rd:0 Ran:1
Win Prizemoney £0 *Total Prizemoney* £238
1998 Turf 0-2: (12f, 16f) (g-s, gd) 1998 AW 0-1: (12f) (Fibr)
Poor filly. Turf high 14. **C N Allen [0-4] B Walker.*

MARK OF PROPHET (IRE) BHB 75f RR 75f 4841[1]
3 b g Scenic 10.6f **(66)** - Sure Flyer (IRE) (Sure Blade (USA)) 11.3f **(67)**
Form - 0021821
Record 1998 - 1st:2 2nd:2 3rd:0 Ran:7
Pre1998 - 1st:0 2nd:0 3rd:0 Ran:3
Win Prizemoney £10,505 *Total Prizemoney* £13,143
Wins * **1998** Oct Newmar (GD) H 14f 70 75 <
* **1998** Aug Leices (GD) 11.8f 72
1998 Turf 2-7: (7f, 10f, 12f 1-3, 14f 1-1, 15f) (sft, gd, g-f 1-2, frm 1-3)
Leggy, above-average gelding, effective 12 to 14f, best at 12f, acts on g-f to frm, best on g-f, prefers right handed tracks. Turf high 75 - 1st of 11 getting 20lb from Ivory Crown (16 Oct Newmarket RF 4841) - also 1st of 5 from Shohra Wa Jaah (5 Aug Leicester RF 3378). He showed much-improved form when stepped up to twelve furlongs, and got off the mark in a classified event at Leicester in August. He ended the season with a good victory over one mile six at Newmarket, and looks likely to make a decent stayer in 1999.
**J E Banks [2-10] P Cunningham.*

MARK TIME BHB 57f RR 58f 4936[8]
3 b c Pursuit of Love 9.5f **(69)**-Quiet Harbour(Mill Reef (USA))10.5f **(78)**
Form - 40004358
Record 1998 - 1st:0 2nd:0 3rd:1 Ran:8
Win Prizemoney £0 *Total Prizemoney* £595
1998 Turf 0-8: (7f 2, 8f 6) (g-s 3, gd 4, frm)
Scopey, fair colt, effective 7 to 8f, acts on g-s to gd. Turf high 58 - 4th of 17 getting 10lb from Great News (2 Oct Lingfield 7f g-s RF 4614). **M H Tompkins [0-8] J A Fuller.*

MARLENE RR 62f 787[3]
3 b f Komaite (USA) 6.9f **(61)** - Kaiserlinde (GER) (Frontal) 6.4f **(64)**
Form - 3
Record 1998 - 1st:0 2nd:0 3rd:1 Ran:1
Win Prizemoney £0 *Total Prizemoney* £385
1998 Turf 0-1: (10f) (g-s)
Light-framed, currently average filly. (1st run) - 3rd of 12 getting 5lb from Teroom (21 Apr Pontefract 10f g-s RF 0787).
**M R Channon [0-1] Sheet & Roll Convertors Ltd.*

MARMADUKE (IRE) RR 69f 5065[8]
2 ch c Perugino (USA) - Sympathy (Precocious) 8.6f **(62)**
Form - 18
Record 1998 - 1st:1 2nd:0 3rd:0 Ran:2
Win Prizemoney £8,596 *Total Prizemoney* £8,596
Wins * **1998** Oct San Si (SFT) 7.5f
1998 Turf 1-2: (8f 1-2) (sft 1-1, g-f)
Currently average colt. Turf high 69 (began Oct).
**L M Cumani [1-2] Anglia Bloodstock Syndicate 1997.*

MAROZIA (USA) BHB 65f75a RR 50f 75a 5069[10]
4 ch f Storm Bird (CAN) 8.5f **(82)** - Make Change (USA) (Roberto (USA)) 10f **(76)**
Form - 020710
Record 1998 - 1st:1 2nd:1 3rd:0 Ran:6
Pre1998 - 1st:0 2nd:1 3rd:1 Ran:3
Win Prizemoney £3,339 *Total Prizemoney* £6,219
Wins * **1998** *Oct Lingfi (STD) H 12f 65 75* <
1998 Turf 0-5: (8f, 10f 3, 12f) (g-s, g-f 3, frm) 1998 AW 1-1: (12f 1-1) (Equi 1-1)
Scopey, above-average filly, effective 8 to 12f, acts on g-f to frm - acts on Equi. Turf high 73 (began Spt) - 2nd of 9 giving 6lb to Vellum (25 Spt Folkestone 10f g-f RF 4477). (1st run) - 1st of 18 giving 3lb to Isabella Gonzaga (26 Oct Lingfield RF 5002). Inconsistent. **J H M Gosden [1-9] Sheikh Mohammed.*

MARSAD (IRE) BHB 83f RR 85f 1428[3]
4 ch c Fayruz 6.6f **(63)** - Broad Haven (IRE) (Be My Guest (USA)) 9.3f **(67)**
Form - 133
Record 1998 - 1st:1 2nd:0 3rd:2 Ran:3
Pre1998 - 1st:0 2nd:2 3rd:2 Ran:10
Win Prizemoney £3,842 *Total Prizemoney* £11,496
Wins * **1998** Apr Kempto (SFT) H 6f 69 79? <
1998 Turf 1-3: (6f 1-3) (sft 1-1, gd 2)
Scopey, useful colt, effective 6f, acts on sft to gd, best on gd. Turf

high 85 - 3rd of 13 giving 10lb to Supreme Angel (23 May Kempton 6f gd RF 1428) - also 1st of 24 getting 9lb from Johnny Staccato (13 Apr Kempton RF 0660). He beat a big field in soft ground on his reappearance. Good efforts since.
**J Akehurst [1-3] Canisbay Bloodstock Ltd (from R Akehurst [0-3] Jly 1997).*

MARSH MARIGOLD BHB 48f55a **RR 61f 55a** 4776[17]
4 br f Tina's Pet 7.4f **(56)** - Pulga (Blakeney) 10.5f **(64)**
Form - 080
Record 1998 - 1st:0 2nd:0 3rd:0 Ran:3
Pre1998 - 1st:2 2nd:3 3rd:3 Ran:24
Win Prizemoney £4,885 *Total Prizemoney* £9,218
Wins 1997 Jun Pontef (G-F) H 10f 57 65 <
1996 Oct Haydoc (SFT) SH 6f 60 61
1998 Turf 0-3: (10f 2, 11f) (sft, gd, frm)
Neat, average filly, effective 9 to 10f, acts on g-f, likes left handed tracks, favours tight tracks. Turf high 16. Becoming disappointing.
**G Fierro [0-5] G Fierro (from J Hetherton [1-11] Jly 1997).*

MARSH MELLOW RR 1216[20]
3 b g High Kicker (USA) 8.4f **(52)** -Snugfit Annie (Midyan (USA)) 6f **(60)**
Form - 0
Record 1998 - 1st:0 2nd:0 3rd:0 Ran:1
1998 Turf 0-1: (7f) (frm)
Light-framed, currently very poor gelding.
**R J Hodges [0-1] P E Axon.*

MARSKE MACHINE BHB 67f **RR 67f** 5147[13]
3 ch f Prince Daniel (USA) 11.4f **(46)** -Ciboure(Norwick (USA)) 7.2f **(56)**
Form - 070432216174410
Record 1998 - 1st:3 2nd:2 3rd:1 Ran:15
Pre1998 - 1st:2 2nd:1 3rd:1 Ran:14
Win Prizemoney £15,701 *Total Prizemoney* £20,979
Wins * **1998** Oct Newmar (G-S) H 9f 62 67 <
* **1998** Spt Newcas (GD) H 9f 58 64
* **1998** Aug Beverl (G-F) H 9.9f 55 61
* 1997 Aug Sandow (SFT) SH 7.1f 59 61
* 1997 Aug Leices (GD) SH 6f 55 56
1998Turf 3-15:(7f, 8f 6, 9f 2-4, 10f 1-3, 11f)(g-s 2, gd 4, g-f 2-5, frm 1-4)
Scopey, average filly, effective 7 to 10f, best at 9f, acts on gd to frm, often wears blinkers (extremely effectively), excels at Leicester. Turf high 67 - 1st of 22 getting 3lb from Elhabub (30 Oct Newmarket RF 5070) - also 1st of 18 getting 10lb from Knave's Ash (8 Spt Newcastle RF 4156). **N Tinkler [5-29] Marske Machine Co.*

MARTHA REILLY (IRE) BHB 53f **RR 52f** 4806[8]
2 ch f Rainbows For Life (CAN) 9.3f **(64)** - Debach Delight (Great Nephew) 9.9f **(64)**
Form - 800708
Record 1998 - 1st:0 2nd:0 3rd:0 Ran:6
1998 Turf 0-6: (6f 2, 7f 3, 8f) (gd 3, g-f, frm 2)
Fair filly. Turf high 52.
**Mrs Barbara Waring [0-6] McDonnell,H Shapter, Andrews.*

MARTINDALE (IRE) BHB 37f34a **RR 39df 34a** 4334[20]
5 b g Fairy King (USA) 7.7f **(75)**-Whist Awhile(Caerleon(USA)) 8.6f **(71)**
Form - 20701P000
Record 1998 - 1st:1 2nd:1 3rd:0 Ran:9
Pre1998 - 1st:0 2nd:0 3rd:0 Ran:7
Win Prizemoney £3,071 *Total Prizemoney* £3,701
Wins * **1998** Jly Ripon (G-F) H 6f 36 39 <
1998 Turf 1-5: (6f 1-5) (g-f 1-3, frm 2) 1998 AW 0-4: (5f 2, 6f, 7f) (Fibr 4)
Very moderate gelding, effective 5 to 6f, acts on g-f - acts on Fibr, often wears blinkers (very effectively). Turf high 39 - 1st of 20 getting 12lb from Bollin Ann (18 Jly Ripon RF 2939). AW high 43 (1st run) - 2nd of 10 giving 14lb to Stately Favour (6 Apr Southwell 5f Fibr RF 0572).
**R Bastiman [1-12] S R Johnson (from J Hanson [0-2] Jly 1997).*

MARTINE BHB 35f42a **RR 40f 42a** 5114[11]
4 ch f Clantime 6.6f **(57)** - Marcroft (Crofthall) 6.3f **(59)**
Form - 0007400
Record 1998 - 1st:0 2nd:0 3rd:0 Ran:6
Pre1998 - 1st:0 2nd:0 3rd:2 Ran:11
Win Prizemoney £0 *Total Prizemoney* £1,395
1998 Turf 0-6: (6f, 7f 4, 8f) (gd 2, g-f, frm 3)

Moderate filly, effective 7f, acts on frm, likes tight tracks. Turf high 40 - 4th of 14 getting 7lb from Desert Cat (14 Spt Musselburgh 7f frm RF 4255). Inconsistent. **A Bailey [0-17] Mrs M A Clayton.*

MARTON MOSS (SWE) BHB 91f **RR 91f** 5096[9]
3 b g Polish Patriot (USA) 7.8f **(70)** - Arrastra (Bustino) 10.4f **(64)**
Form - 452521520400630
Record 1998 - 1st:1 2nd:3 3rd:1 Ran:15
Pre1998 - 1st:2 2nd:0 3rd:0 Ran:7
Win Prizemoney £12,568 *Total Prizemoney* £33,440
Wins * **1998** Jun Ripon (SFT) H 6f 87 94 <
* 1997 Aug Ripon (G-F) 6f 78
* 1997 Jun Pontef (SFT) 5f 75+
1998 Turf 1-15: (5f, 6f 1-10, 7f 4) (sft 2, g-s 4, gd 1-7, g-f 2)
Leggy, useful gelding, effective 6 to 7f, best at 6f, acts on sft to g-f, best on gd, likes Ripon. Turf high 96 - 4th of 11 giving 10lb to Q Factor (21 Aug Chester 7f gd RF 3789) - also 1st of 10 giving 18lb to Pigeon (17 Jun Ripon RF 2074). Can act on varying ground and should win a race in 1999. **T D Easterby [3-22] T H Bennett.*

MARWEH RR 82df 1004[5]
3 b c Prince Sabo 6.6f **(64)** - Born to Dance (Dancing Brave (USA)) 8.4f **(76)**
Form - 25
Record 1998 - 1st:0 2nd:1 3rd:0 Ran:2
Win Prizemoney £0 *Total Prizemoney* £1,404
1998 Turf 0-2: (6f 2) (gd 2)
Scopey, currently decent colt. Turf high 82 (1st run) - 2nd of 16 to Caribbean Monarch (14 Apr Newmarket 6f gd RF 0683).
**A C Stewart [0-2] Hamdan Al Maktoum.*

MARX MISTRESS BHB 31f **RR 37f** 3850[5]
4 b f Batshoof 9.5f **(66)** - No Jazz (Jaazeiro (USA)) 9.2f **(54)**
Form - 75
Record 1998 - 1st:0 2nd:0 3rd:0 Ran:2
Pre1998 - 1st:0 2nd:0 3rd:0 Ran:1
1998 Turf 0-1: (10f) (frm) 1998 AW 0-1: (12f) (Fibr)
Workmanlike, very moderate filly, has worn blinkers. (1st run) - 5th of 12 giving 8lb to Moonlight Flit (25 Aug Pontefract 10f frm RF 3850). **P D Evans [0-1] John Pugh (from J G M O'Shea [0-5] Jly 1998).*

MARY CORNWALLIS BHB 82f78a **RR 86df 78a** 367[1]
4 ch f Primo Dominie 7.2f **(67)**-Infanta Real (Formidable (USA))9.2f **(63)**
Form - 040211
Record 1998 - 1st:2 2nd:1 3rd:0 Ran:3
Pre1998 - 1st:0 2nd:1 3rd:1 Ran:7
Win Prizemoney £6,807 *Total Prizemoney* £10,282
Wins * **1998** *Feb Lingfi (SLW) H 5f 73 74* <
* **1998** *Jan Lingfi (STD) H 5f 69 70*
1998 AW 2-3: (5f 2-2, 6f) (Equi 2-3)
Well made, useful filly, has worn blinkers. AW high 74. Inconsistent. Something of a talking horse before each of her first two races, she then became a disappointing and moody sort on turf and sand. Her new trainer eventually found the key to her, the minimum trip and blinkers, resulting in two fine front-running victories on the Lingfield Equitrack at the start of the year.
**R M H Cowell [2-6] Bottisham Heath Stud (from G Wragg [0-4] Spt 1997).*

MARY CULI BHB 42f **RR 46f** 5098[9]
4 gr f Liboi (USA) 11.5f **(56)** - Copper Trader (Faustus (USA)) 10f **(58)**
Form - 0863836100
Record 1998 - 1st:1 2nd:0 3rd:2 Ran:10
Pre1998 - 1st:0 2nd:0 3rd:1 Ran:9
Win Prizemoney £2,725 *Total Prizemoney* £4,131
Wins * **1998** Spt Sandow (GD) H 10f 41 46 <
1998 Turf 1-10: (10f 1-4, 11f 2, 12f 4) (sft, g-s, gd 1-4, g-f 4)
Workmanlike, moderate filly, effective 10 to 11f, best at 10f, acts on gd, has worn blinkers, likes left handed tracks. Turf high 49 - 3rd of 11 getting 14lb from Afon Alwen (13 Jun Lingfield 11f gd RF 1968) - also 1st of 19 getting 2lb from Famous (15 Spt Sandown RF 4270). Consistent. **H Candy [1-19] Mrs David Blackburn.*

MARY HANNAH RR 4676[14]
5 b m Lugana Beach 7f **(63)** - Bloomsbury Girl (Weepers Boy)
Form - 0
Record 1998 - 1st:0 2nd:0 3rd:0 Ran:1

1998 Turf 0-1: (6f) (g-f)
Currently poor filly. **A Senior [0-1] A Senior.*

MARY JANE BHB 47f58a RR 49f 58a 4469[10]

3 b f Tina's Pet 7.4f **(56)** - Fair Attempt (IRE) (Try My Best (USA)) 7.6f **(67)**
Form - 60414300706050
Record 1998 - 1st:1 2nd:0 3rd:1 Ran:13
Pre1998 - 1st:1 2nd:0 3rd:1 Ran:4
Win Prizemoney £4,683 *Total Prizemoney* £5,475
Wins * **1998** *Feb Wolver (STD) C 5f 54+*
* 1997 Oct Redcar (G-F) 5f 68 <
1998 Turf 0-6:(5f 6)(gd, g-f 2, frm 3)1998 AW1-7:(5f 1-7)(Equi, Fibr 1-6)
Workmanlike, average filly, effective 5f, acts on frm - acts on Fibr, has worn blinkers, likes left handed tracks, likes tight tracks. Turf high 49. AW high 61 - 4th of 7 giving 14lb to Dahlidya (18 Feb Wolverhampton 5f Fibr RF 0310). **J Berry [2-17] W R Milner.*

MARYLEBONE (IRE) RR 60f 4920[13]

4 ch g River Falls 8.2f **(56)** - Pasadena Lady (Captain James) 5f **(59)**
Form - 4624U306000640
Record 1998 - 1st:0 2nd:1 3rd:1 Ran:14
Pre1998 - 1st:0 2nd:4 3rd:0 Ran:11
Win Prizemoney £0 *Total Prizemoney* £6,040
1998 Turf 0-14: (6f 3, 7f 8, 8f 2, 9f) (g-s, gd 2, g-f 2, frm 9)
Scopey, average gelding, effective 5 to 7f, acts on gd to frm, best on frm, has worn blinkers, likes right handed tracks. Turf high 60 - 3rd of 11 giving 4lb to High Premium (4 Jly Carlisle 7f frm RF 2524).
**Martyn Wane [0-11] Mrs H Wane (from Mrs J R Ramsden [0-4] Jun 1998).*

MARY LOU (IRE) BHB 40f47a RR 43f 47a 784[6]

3 b f Tirol 8.1f **(64)** - Kilcsem Eile (IRE) (Commanche Run) 8.5f **(58)**
Form - 342547656
Record 1998 - 1st:0 2nd:1 3rd:0 Ran:7
Pre1998 - 1st:0 2nd:0 3rd:1 Ran:11
Win Prizemoney £0 *Total Prizemoney* £761
1998 Turf 0-3: (10f 2, 12f) (sft, g-s, gd) 1998 AW 0-4: (8f, 9f, 11f 2) (Fibr 4)
Leggy, fair filly, effective 8f, - acts on Fibr, has worn blinkers, likes left handed tracks, likes tight tracks. Turf high 43. AW high 55 (1st run) - 2nd of 11 to Sharway Lady (5 Jan Southwell 8f Fibr RF 0028).
**M R Channon [0-18] M A Ryan.*

MARYS PATH BHB 22f RR 24f 2922[6]

4 b f Rock Hopper 10.6f **(54)** - Jasmin Path (Warpath) 12.3f **(52)**
Form - 60766
Record 1998 - 1st:0 2nd:0 3rd:0 Ran:5
Pre1998 - 1st:0 2nd:0 3rd:0 Ran:5
1998 Turf 0-5: (12f 2, 14f 2, 16f) (gd, g-f 2, frm, hrd)
Unfurnished, little account filly. Turf high 24.
**S Gollings [0-10] R L Houlton.*

MARY STUART (IRE) RR 50f 4665[8]

2 b f Nashwan (USA) 10.3f **(79)**- Scots Lass (Shirley Heights) 10.3f **(74)**
Form - 8
Record 1998 - 1st:0 2nd:0 3rd:0 Ran:1
1998 Turf 0-1: (8f) (g-s)
Currently fair filly. **Sir Michael Stoute [0-1] Lord Weinstock.*

MARYTAVY BHB 62f65a RR 62f 65a 343[2]

4 b f Lycius (USA) 8.8f **(71)** - Rose Parade (Thatching) 8f **(66)**
Form - 2
Record 1998 - 1st:0 2nd:1 3rd:0 Ran:1
Pre1998 - 1st:1 2nd:2 3rd:0 Ran:7
Win Prizemoney £2,277 *Total Prizemoney* £4,482
Wins 1997 *Spt Southw (STD) H 11f 61 66* <
1998 AW 0-1: (12f) (Fibr)
Scopey, average filly. (1st run) - 2nd of 8 getting 2lb from Private Despatch (23 Feb Southwell 12f Fibr RF 0343). Inconsistent.
**P R Webber [0-4] Paul Webber (from Sir Mark Prescott [1-7] Spt 1997).*

MASAMADAS BHB 82f83a RR 83f 83a 4480[8]

3 ch c Elmaamul (USA) 8.1f **(70)** - Beau's Delight (USA) (Lypheor) 12f **(71)**
Form - 202126338
Record 1998 - 1st:1 2nd:2 3rd:2 Ran:8
Pre1998 - 1st:0 2nd:1 3rd:0 Ran:2
Win Prizemoney £3,629 *Total Prizemoney* £8,849
Wins * **1998** May Windso (G-F) H 11.6f 72 81+ <
1998 Turf 1-8: (7f, 10f, 11f 2, 12f 1-4) (g-s, gd 3, g-f, frm 1-3)
Scopey, decent colt, effective 10 to 12f, best at 12f, acts on g-s to frm, best on frm, prefers tight tracks. Turf high 83 - 3rd of 10 getting 2lb from Pairumani Star (28 Aug Goodwood 12f g-f RF 3921) - also 1st of 13 getting 3lb from High Tension (18 May Windsor RF 1314). Somewhat disappointing after a facile victory, he was sold for 31,000 guineas in October. **C F Wall [1-10] M Tilbrook.*

MASHAB BHB 67f RR 67f 4807[5]

3 b c Pursuit of Love 9.5f **(69)** - Kukri (Kris) 9.5f **(73)**
Form - 355
Record 1998 - 1st:0 2nd:0 3rd:1 Ran:3
Pre1998 - 1st:0 2nd:0 3rd:0 Ran:2
Win Prizemoney £0 *Total Prizemoney* £565
1998 Turf 0-3: (8f 3) (sft, gd, g-f)
Scopey, average colt. Turf high 67 - 5th of 17 giving 6lb to Brave Envoy (14 Oct Nottingham 8f gd RF 4807).
**N A Graham [0-5] Hamdan Al Maktoum.*

MASHA-IL (IRE) BHB 97f RR 95f 4367[20]

3 b c Danehill (USA) 9.1f **(79)** - Valley Lights (IRE) (Dance of Life (USA)) 7f **(66)**
Form - 402601710
Record 1998 - 1st:2 2nd:1 3rd:0 Ran:9
Pre1998 - 1st:1 2nd:0 3rd:1 Ran:3
Win Prizemoney £34,208 *Total Prizemoney* £37,169
Wins * **1998** Aug Goodwo (G-F) H 6f 92 95 <
* **1998** Jun Goodwo (GD) H 6f 85 89
* 1997 Nov Doncas (GD) 6f 79
1998 Turf 2-9: (6f 2-8, 7f) (hvy, sft, g-s, gd 1-3, g-f 1-2, frm)
Workmanlike, very useful colt, effective 6f, acts on gd to frm. Turf high 95 - 1st of 18 giving 5lb to Faraway Lass (29 Aug Goodwood RF 3947) - also 1st of 24 giving 1lb to Resist the Force (28 Jun Goodwood RF 2366). Running well prior to a clear cut win in the Stewards' Cup Trial at Goodwood, albeit from a plum draw. He ran quite well in the real thing when not quite so well drawn and confirmed himself a progressive sprinter with victory in another competitive Goodwood handicap in August. Should pay his way again in 1999. **J H M Gosden [3-12] Hamdan Al Maktoum.*

MASHKORAH (USA) BHB 30f35a RR 32f 35a 1807[8]

4 ch f Miswaki (USA) 8.1f **(81)** - Tom's Lassie (USA) (Tom Rolfe) 9.4f **(75)**
Form - 008
Record 1998 - 1st:0 2nd:0 3rd:0 Ran:3
Pre1998 - 1st:0 2nd:0 3rd:0 Ran:4
1998 Turf 0-2: (10f 2) (g-s, frm) 1998 AW 0-1: (7f) (Fibr)
Leggy, very moderate filly. Turf high 6.
**T Wall [0-3] Mrs E J Williams (from R Hannon [0-4] Jun 1997).*

MASONIC (IRE) BHB 60f RR 69f 5039[12]

2 ch c Grand Lodge (USA) - Winning Heart (Horage) 10.3f **(61)**
Form - 500
Record 1998 - 1st:0 2nd:0 3rd:0 Ran:3
1998 Turf 0-3: (8f 3) (g-s, gd, frm)
Currently average colt. Turf high 69 (began Spt).
**M H Tompkins [0-3] Mrs Beryl Lockey.*

MASSENET (IRE) BHB 79f RR 75f 3682[3]

3 b c Caerleon (USA) 10.9f **(79)** - Massawippi (Be My Native (USA)) 10.2f **(71)**
Form - 033
Record 1998 - 1st:0 2nd:0 3rd:2 Ran:3
Win Prizemoney £0 *Total Prizemoney* £1,049
1998 Turf 0-3: (10f, 11f, 12f) (gd, g-f, frm)
Well made, currently above-average colt. Turf high 75 - 3rd of 12 to Pegnitz (17 Aug Windsor 10f g-f RF 3682).
**J H M Gosden [0-3] Sheikh Mohammed.*

MASSYAR SEVENTEEN BHB 59f64a RR 66f 64a 5126[8]

4 b g Chilibang 7f **(55)** - Westminster Waltz (Dance In Time (CAN)) 8.9f **(59)**

1998 IN COLOUR

(Clockwise): **Kieren Fallon** - Champion Jockey for the 2nd consecutive year; **Sagamix** (Andre Fabre) with jockey Olivier Peslier and connections after winning the Prix de L'Arc de Triomphe at Longchamp in October; **Swain,** representing the all-conquering Godolphin team, is led in following his second King George VI and Queen Elizabeth Diamond Stakes victory at Ascot in July; Juddmonte International Stakes - one of the most thrilling finishes ever seen in a Group One race - (from right to left) **One So Wonderful** (Pat Eddery, L.Cumani) wins from **Faithful Son** (L Dettori, S.bin Suroor) and **Chester House** (K.Fallon, H.Cecil).

SAEED BIN SUROOR WRAPS UP THE SEASON

Champion trainer **Saeed bin Suroor** (bottom left) took the first and last Classics of the season, and plenty more races in between for the Godolphin operation; **Cape Verdi** and L. Dettori (top) winning the Sagitta 1000 Guineas in May; **Nedawi** and John Reid parade before winning the Pertemps St Leger (bottom right).

...BUT THE 2000 GUINEAS GOES TO IRELAND

Aidan O'Brien (top right) followed up the announcement that he would in future be concentrating on the Flat by taking the Sagitta 2000 Guineas with the brilliant, but now sadly retired, **King of Kings** (Michael Kinane); (top left) King of Kings comes home in front of Lend A Hand (M. Johnston, D. Holland) and Border Arrow (I. Balding, R. Cochrane).

EPSOM IN JUNE...

(Clockwise) **Shahtoush**, trainer Aidan O'Brien's first ever runner at Epsom, wins the Vodafone Oaks for owners Mrs D. Nagle and Mrs J. Magnier with Michael Kinane in the saddle; **Intikhab** (S. Suroor, L. Dettori) wins the Vodafone Diomed Stakes and would soon follow up with victory in the Queen Anne Stakes at Royal Ascot; **Silver Patriarch** (J. Dunlop, Pat Eddery) gained compensation for last year's Derby defeat when out-gunning Swain for victory in the Vodafone Coronation Cup.

... AND THE VODAFONE DERBY

High-Rise and Olivier Peslier (bottom) bring home a second Epsom Derby for trainer Luca Cumani in the third fastest time ever. He was sent out from the same box as Kahyasi, Cumani's first Derby winner 10 years ago; High-Rise, (top) carrying the colours of Sheikh Mohammed Obaid Al Maktoum, holds off City Honours (S. Suroor, J. Reid) to take the Blue Riband event.

IRISH DREAMS...

Dream Well (top) is first past the post in the Budweiser Irish Derby for trainer Pascal Bary and Cash Asmussen in the colours of the Niarchos Family and J. Bouchard. He was adding a second Classic to the Les Emirats Arabes Unis Prix du Jockey-Club already taken earlier in the year on home turf at Chantilly in May. **Tarascon** (bottom) gives 17 year old apprentice Jamie Spencer (bottom left) an historic victory in the Irish 1000 Guineas.

...AND ROYAL ASCOT MEMORIES

The emotion shows on the face of jockey Walter Swinburn as he is led in following his Coronation Stakes victory on **Exclusive** (top right), in a year when increasing weight problems forced an early close to his season. This was the first win for trainer **Sir Michael Stoute** (top left) since his knighthood for services to tourism in Barbados. **Kayf Tara** (S. Suroor, L. Dettori) (bottom) gets up to beat Double Trigger (D. Holland) in the Gold Cup. He would later in the year take the Irish St Leger, this time with John Reid in the saddle.

... IN BATTLE

Dr Fong (top), (H. Cecil, K. Fallon) wins the St James's Palace Stakes ahead of rival Desert Prince at Royal Ascot in June. The places are reversed (bottom) in the Queen Elizabeth II Stakes at Ascot in September. **Desert Prince** (D. Loder, O. Peslier), never out of the first three in his five European races this season, also took the Irish 2,000 Guineas and the Prix du Moulin de Longchamp for his connections.

A DIAMOND DOUBLE FOR SWAIN

Swain (top & bottom) becomes the first horse since Dahlia ('73/'74) to win the King George VI and Queen Elizabeth Diamond Stakes back to back. He is also the oldest winner of the race, beating Derby winner High-Rise (L. Cumani, O. Peslier) (right) and Royal Anthem (H. Cecil, K, Fallon) (centre). He followed up by taking the Irish Champion Stakes at Leopardstown in September for the Godolphin team of Saeed bin Suroor and Frankie Dettori.

1999? A HINT OF WHATS IN STORE...

Bint Allayl (M. Channon, L. Dettori) collects the Queen Mary Stakes at Royal Ascot (top) on the way to becoming one of the top-rated two-year-old fillies of the season, while (bottom left), **Wannabe Grand** and Pat Eddery provide trainer Jeremy Noseda (bottom right) with a first Group One success in his first season when winning the Shadwell Stud Cheveley Park Stakes at Newmarket in September.

AND FROM THE COLTS...

Commander Collins seen here winning at Newmarket in July (top left) finished his season with a convincing victory in the Racing Post Trophy at Doncaster in October for the new Manton team of jockey Jimmy Fortune, trainer Peter Chapple-Hyam, and owner Robert Sangster (bottom). **Auction House** put himself up for the title of top two-year-old with three wins, including the Champagne Stakes at Doncaster in September beating Commander Collins (middle), for the father-son team of Barry and Michael Hills.

A SURPRISE IN STORE...

Stravinsky,(top) in the colours of Michael Tabor and John Magnier, and produced by trainer Aidan O'Brien, arrived with a high reputation to win a York maiden stakes (top) in August under Michael Kinane. **Lujain**, for trainer David Loder and jockey Frankie Dettori, (bottom right) completed his hat-trick at Newmarket in the Middle Park Stakes but, like Stravinsky above, and **Enrique** (H. Cecil, K. Fallon) (inset) had his reputation upset by the surprise winner of the Dewhurst Stakes in October. (see over page)

... AT NEWMARKET IN OCTOBER

Mujahid, under Richard Hills, (top left) springs a surprise to some when taking the Dewhurst Stakes at 25/1 from Auction House, but not to his trainer John Dunlop (top right). **Alborada** (bottom left) is a popular Group One winner for the veteran jockey George Duffield and trainer Sir Mark Prescott (bottom right) in the Dubai Champion Stakes, beating Insatiable (O. Peslier)

SPRINTING THROUGH THE YEAR...

Elnadim (top) takes the July Cup ahead of Tamarisk (obscured) for trainer John Dunlop and jockey Richard Hills. **Tamarisk** and jockey Tim Sprake (bottom right) collect the Stanley Leisure Sprint Cup at Haydock in September to boost a difficult season for trainer Roger Charlton. The same owner-trainer-jockey team of Jeff Smith, Ian Balding and Frankie Dettori repeat Lochsong's 1993 Nunthorpe Stakes win with her half-sister **Lochangel** at York in August (bottom left)

... A REMINDER OF WHAT IT IS ALL ABOUT...

The prolific stayer **Double Trigger** was retired to stud after winning the Doncaster Cup for the third time in the colours of Ron Huggins. He is seen here, with jockey Darryll Holland aboard, being led in by trainer Mark Johnston for the last time (top left), with Frankie Dettori winning the race in 1996 (bottom right), and with Jason Weaver winning at Sandown in May 1995 (bottom left). His fourteen wins also included three Goodwood Cups and the 1995 Ascot Gold Cup.

RETIRING IN 1998

Lynda Ramsden (top right) anounced her retirement from training at the end of the year. She put the seal on her career when Bishops Court (top left) provided her with her first Group victory in France when taking the Prix du Petit Couvert in October (top right). **Lord Huntingdon** (bottom left), the Queen's trainer, also anounced his retirement this summer, and **Christy Roche**, winner of the 1984 Derby on Secreto, (bottom right) hung up his saddle in August to concentrate on training,

Form - 1305574723618

Record 1998 - 1st:1 2nd:1 3rd:1 Ran:10
Pre1998 - 1st:1 2nd:0 3rd:1 Ran:9

Win Prizemoney £5,582 *Total Prizemoney* £8,463

Wins * **1998** Oct Leices (HVY) H 8f 54 66 <
1997 *Nov Lingfi (STD) 10f 59*

1998 Turf 1-9: (8f 1-2, 10f 6, 11f) (sft 1-1, g-s, gd 2, g-f 2, frm 2, hrd)
1998 AW 0-1: (12f) (Equi)

Workmanlike, average gelding, effective 8 to 10f, best at 10f, acts on sft to hrd - acts on Equi, has worn blinkers. Turf high 66 - 1st of 11 getting 12lb from Bomb Alaska (26 Oct Leicester RF 4995). Generally ran well in '98, but does not always put it all in.

**P W D'Arcy [1-5] Exors of the late Derek Weeden (from H J Collingridge [1-14] Jly 1998).*

MASTER BEVELED BHB 72f65a **RR 72f 65a** 4698[6]

8 b g Beveled (USA) 6.9f **(64)** - Miss Anniversary (Tachypous) 8.6f **(55)**

Form - 46040603201006

Record 1998 - 1st:1 2nd:1 3rd:1 Ran:12
Pre1998 - 1st:10 2nd:7 3rd:8 Ran:81

Win Prizemoney £64,597 *Total Prizemoney* £85,631

Wins * **1998** Spt Ayr (g-s) H 10.9f 69 72
* 1996 Oct Warwic (FRM) 8f 67
* 1996 Oct Haydoc (SFT) 10.5f 74
* 1994 Oct Newmar (G-S) H 8f 80 85 <
* 1994 Oct York (G-S) H 8.9f 66 71
* 1994 Spt Haydoc (GD) 8.1f 64
* 1994 May Doncas (G-F) H 7f 60 58
* 1994 May Kempto (HVY) H 8f 54 63

1998 Turf 1-10: (8f 3, 9f, 10f 3, 11f 1-1, 12f 2) (sft, g-s, gd 1-3, g-f 3, frm 2) 1998 AW 0-2: (11f, 12f) (Equi, Fibr)

Above-average gelding, effective 8 to 12f, best at 10f, acts on gd to frm, best on gd, has worn blinkers, excels at Newbury, does well at York, likes Ayr. Turf high 74 (1st run) - 4th of 15 getting 5lb from Mowelga (4 May Doncaster 10f g-f RF 1008) - also 1st of 20 getting 1lb from River's Source (17 Spt Ayr RF 4321). AW high 5. Inconsistent. Has a useful turn of foot, and is effective both on the Flat and over hurdles, but does not find it easy to get his head in front.

**P D Evans [14-100] Mrs E J Williams (from A P Jones [0-9] Aug 1993).*

MASTER BOBBY BHB 28f32a **RR 27f 32a** 4573[14]

4 b g Touch of Grey 8.1f **(47)** -Young Lady(Young Generation) 7.7f **(63)**

Form - 000

Record 1998 - 1st:0 2nd:0 3rd:0 Ran:1
Pre1998 - 1st:0 2nd:0 3rd:0 Ran:7

1998 Turf 0-1: (12f) (g-f)

Workmanlike, little account gelding, has worn blinkers. Becoming disappointing.

**R M Flower [0-10] Richard Gurr (from R Boss [0-3] Mar 1997).*

MASTER CASTER (IRE) BHB 70f70a **RR 74f 70a** 4407[2]

3 b g Night Shift (USA) 8.1f **(73)** - Honourable Sheba (USA) (Roberto (USA)) 10f **(76)**

Form - 543136042628212

Record 1998 - 1st:2 2nd:4 3rd:2 Ran:15
Pre1998 - 1st:0 2nd:0 3rd:0 Ran:2

Win Prizemoney £6,618 *Total Prizemoney* £11,647

Wins * **1998** Spt Beverl (G-F) H 8.5f 63 68
1998 *Feb Lingfi (SLW) 10f 70* <

1998 Turf 1-10: (7f 4, 8f 1-4, 9f, 10f) (gd 5, g-f 2, frm 1-3) 1998 AW 1-5: (7f, 8f 2, 10f 1-2) (Equi 1-4, Fibr)

Unfurnished, above-average gelding, effective 7 to 10f, best at 8f, acts on gd to frm - acts on Equi, has worn blinkers, prefers right handed tracks, prefers tight tracks. Turf high 74 - 2nd of 16 giving 12lb to Margaret's Dancer (22 Spt Beverley 8f g-f RF 4407) - also 1st of 18 giving 2lb to Tipperary Sunset (16 Spt Beverley RF 4302). AW high 70 - 1st of 9 giving 5lb to Feel Free (26 Feb Lingfield RF 0366). Not one of the stable stars, and the steering is dodgy to boot. Now hurdling with Graham McCourt.

**Mrs J R Ramsden [1-10] Casting Partners A (from D R Loder [1-7] Feb 1998).*

MASTER HYDE (USA) BHB 44f54a **RR 42f 54a** 4958[12]

9 gr g Trempolino (USA) 11.9f **(77)** - Sandspur (USA) (Al Hattab (USA)) 9.3f **(74)**

Form - 670

Record 1998 - 1st:0 2nd:0 3rd:0 Ran:3
Pre1998 - 1st:5 2nd:6 3rd:5 Ran:47

Win Prizemoney £14,681 *Total Prizemoney* £22,691

Wins 1995 Jly Carlis (FRM) H 12f 55 62
1994 Aug Mussel (G-F) H 12.1f 49 52

1998 Turf 0-3: (15f, 16f 2) (g-f, frm 2)

Average gelding, has worn blinkers. Turf high 42 (began Aug). Inconsistent.

**J S Goldie [2-10] J S Goldie (from W Storey [5-25] Oct 1996).*

MASTER MAC (USA) BHB 73f **RR 72df** 2824[8]

3 br c Exbourne (USA) - Kentucky Blonde (USA) (General Assembly (USA)) 10f **(68)**

Form - 65508

Record 1998 - 1st:0 2nd:0 3rd:0 Ran:5
Pre1998 - 1st:2 2nd:1 3rd:0 Ran:8

Win Prizemoney £9,498 *Total Prizemoney* £12,533

Wins 1997 Jly Lingfi (G-F) H 6f 81 <
1997 Jun Goodwo (G-S) 7f 75

1998 Turf 0-5: (6f 4, 7f) (g-s, gd 2, g-f, frm)

Workmanlike, above-average colt, effective 6 to 7f, best at 7f, acts on gd to frm, best on gd. Turf high 72 - 5th of 7 giving 11lb to Madame Jones (12 Jun Goodwood 6f gd RF 1932). Inconsistent.

**J Akehurst [0-3] Normandy Developments (London) (from M A Jarvis [0-2] May 1998).*

MASTER MILLFIELD (IRE) BHB 57f68a **RR 58f 68a** 4748[17]

6 b g Prince Rupert(FR) 10.4f **(60)** -Calash(Indian King (USA)) 7.4f **(64)**

Form - 1150

Record 1998 - 1st:2 2nd:0 3rd:0 Ran:4
Pre1998 - 1st:6 2nd:5 3rd:9 Ran:51

Win Prizemoney £24,282 *Total Prizemoney* £35,661

Wins * **1998** Spt Goodwo (G-S) H 8f 49 58
* **1998** Spt Salisb (GD) H 8f 49 53
1997 Spt Folkes (FRM) H 6.9f 47 54
1995 Spt Bath (HRD) H 5.7f 65 65
1995 *Feb Lingfi (STD) H 7f 72 73* <
1994 *Dec Wolver (STD) H 7f 60 69*
1994 *Dec Wolver (STD) H 6f 60 71*
1994 *Dec Lingfi (STD) 7f 63*

1998 Turf 2-4: (8f 2-3, 9f) (gd 1-2, g-f 1-1, frm)

Average gelding, effective 7 to 8f, best at 8f, acts on gd to frm, has worn blinkers. Turf high 58 (began Spt) - 1st of 19 giving 11lb to Ardent (11 Spt Goodwood RF 4234) - also 1st of 17 getting 15lb from Sea Danzig (3 Spt Salisbury RF 4065). In fine form over hurdles in the summer, he won a Salisbury handicap in September on his first run on the Flat for eleven months, and followed up at Goodwood later in the month.

**R J Hodges [5-18] P Slade (from C J Hill [6-38] Oct 1997)*

MASTERPIECE BHB 53f **RR 56f** 1639[12]

4 br g Primo Dominie 7.2f **(67)** - Swift Return (Double Form) 7.3f **(58)**

Form - 00

Record 1998 - 1st:0 2nd:0 3rd:0 Ran:2
Pre1998 - 1st:0 2nd:1 3rd:0 Ran:7

Win Prizemoney £0 *Total Prizemoney* £627

1998 Turf 0-2: (6f 2) (g-f 2)

Scopey, fair gelding, effective 7f, acts on g-f. Turf high 36.

**R Hannon [0-9] Lady Tennant.*

MASTER REX BHB 52f **RR 51f** 5008[7]

3 ch g Interrex (CAN) 7.7f **(51)**-Whose Lady(USA)(Master Willie) 7f **(70)**

Form - 067

Record 1998 - 1st:0 2nd:0 3rd:0 Ran:3

1998 Turf 0-3: (12f 2, 14f) (sft, gd, frm)

Strong, currently fair gelding. Turf high 51 (began Spt).

**E A Wheeler [0-3] Miss Louise Challis.*

MASTERSTROKE BHB 48f55a **RR 24f 55a** 3094[9]

4 b g Timeless Times (USA) 6.1f **(56)** - Fauve (Dominion) 8.5f **(63)**

Form - 0

Record 1998 - 1st:0 2nd:0 3rd:0 Ran:1
Pre1998 - 1st:3 2nd:0 3rd:2 Ran:18

Win Prizemoney £8,018 *Total Prizemoney* £9,704

Wins 1997 *Jan Lingfi (STD) S 7f 68* <
1996 Jly Leices (G-F) H 6f 65
1996 Apr Bright (FRM) 5.3f 65

1998 AW 0-1: (8f) (Fibr)

Neat, little account gelding, effective 7f, - acts on Equi, has worn

blinkers, likes left handed tracks, likes tight tracks.
**A W Carroll [0-1] Simon Lewis (from B J Meehan [3-18] Spt 1997).*

MASTER TIROL (IRE) BHB 61f RR 59f — 4447[7]
2 ro c Tirol 8.1f **(64)** - Inisfail (Persian Bold) 9.3f **(66)**
Form - 6057
Record 1998 - 1st:0 2nd:0 3rd:0 Ran:4
1998 Turf 0-4: (5f, 6f 2, 7f) (gd 3, g-f)
Fair colt. Turf high 59. **R A Fahey [0-4] D A Read.*

MATOAKA BHB 52f58a RR 51f 58a — 5079[6]
4 b f Be My Chief (USA)10.2f **(62)**- Echoing (Formidable(USA))9.2f **(63)**
Form - 48007406425320046
Record 1998 - 1st:0 2nd:2 3rd:1 Ran:16
Pre1998 - 1st:1 2nd:2 3rd:0 Ran:10
Win Prizemoney £2,277 *Total Prizemoney* £7,397
Wins * 1997 Oct Bright (FRM) 8f 71 <
1998 Turf 0-15: (6f, 7f 11, 8f 3) (sft, g-s, gd 6, g-f 3, frm 4) 1998 AW 0-1: (7f) (Equi)
Neat, fair filly, effective 7 to 8f, best at 8f, acts on gd to frm, best on frm, likes left handed tracks. Turf high 56. Consistent.
**V Soane [1-21] The Stargazers (from R J R Williams [0-5] Jun 1997).*

MATTIMEO (IRE) BHB 82f70a RR 83f 70a — 1425[12]
5 b g Prince Rupert (FR) 10.4f **(60)**-Herila (FR)(Bold Lad(USA)) 10f **(65)**
Form - 0
Record 1998 - 1st:0 2nd:0 3rd:0 Ran:1
Pre1998 - 1st:3 2nd:3 3rd:1 Ran:17
Win Prizemoney £13,434 *Total Prizemoney* £18,810
Wins 1997 Aug Ascot (GD) H 10f 75 77 <
1997 Jun Newcas (GD) H 10.1f 70 75
1996 Aug Nottin (G-F) H 10f 70 71
1998 Turf 0-1: (10f) (gd)
Decent gelding, effective 10f, acts on gd to g-f, best on g-f.
**Lady Herries [0-1] Mrs Monica Keogh (from A P Jarvis [3-17] Nov 1997).*

MATTIOCCO (IRE) RR 96f — 4177a[18]
3 b f Last Tycoon 9.4f **(73)** - Purchasepaperchase (Young Generation) 7.7f **(63)**
Form - 46160
1998 Turf 1-5: (8f 1-4, 12f) (sft 1-2, gd 2, frm)
Very useful filly. Turf high 96 - also 1st of 10 from Baniyka (30 Jly Galway RF 3349a). **A P O'Brien in IRE [1-5] Michael Tabor.*

MAURANGI BHB 24f RR 25f — 2064[3]
7 b g Warning 8.1f **(77)** - Spin Dry (High Top) 10.2f **(67)**
Form - 043
Record 1998 - 1st:0 2nd:0 3rd:1 Ran:2
Pre1998 - 1st:2 2nd:1 3rd:2 Ran:33
Win Prizemoney £5,995 *Total Prizemoney* £9,727
Wins * 1994 Jly Beverl (G-F) H 8.5f 55 59 <
* 1994 Jun Ayr (G-S) H 8f 50 53
1998 Turf 0-2: (12f, 13f) (gd, hrd)
Little account gelding, has broken blood-vessels, effective 8 to 10f, best at 8f, acts on gd to frm, best on frm, has worn blinkers. Turf high 25. **B W Murray [3-38] M E Foxton.*

MAWARED (IRE) BHB 107f RR 99f — 3288[1]
5 ch h Nashwan (USA) 10.3f **(79)** - Harmless Albatross (Pas de Seul) 9.1f **(67)**
Form - 211
Record 1998 - 1st:2 2nd:1 3rd:0 Ran:3
Pre1998 - 1st:4 2nd:1 3rd:3 Ran:13
Win Prizemoney £49,012 *Total Prizemoney* £68,259
Wins * **1998** Aug Cheste (G-S) H 18.7f 99 99 <
* **1998** Jly Newbur (GD) H 16f 93 97
* 1997 Aug Newmar (GD) H 14.8f 77 86
* 1997 Aug Newbur (G-F) H 16f 77 83+
* 1997 Jly Sandow (G-F) H 14f 67 78
* 1997 Jly Sandow (G-F) H 14f 67 72
1998 Turf 2-3: (14f, 16f 1-1, 19f 1-1) (gd 1-1, g-f 1-2)
Very useful colt, effective 14 to 19f, best at 16f, acts on gd to g-f, best on g-f, likes right handed tracks, and does well at Newbury and Newmarket. Turf high 99 - 1st of 4 getting 1lb from Top Cees (2 Aug Chester RF 3288) - also 1st of 11 giving 3lb to Premier Night (12 Jly Newbury RF 2747). Improving. A most progressive stayer in 1997, he looked as good as ever when touched off on his return and proceeded to win his next two starts. Seemed to be improving with age, and it is a pity he was not seen out after early August. **J L Dunlop [6-16] Hamdan Al Maktoum.*

MAWINGO (IRE) BHB 73f RR 59f — 4822[18]
5 b h Taufan (USA) 8.3f **(65)** - Tappen Zee (Sandhurst Prince) 7.9f **(63)**
Form - 5000
Record 1998 - 1st:0 2nd:0 3rd:0 Ran:4
Pre1998 - 1st:3 2nd:2 3rd:2 Ran:15
Win Prizemoney £18,412 *Total Prizemoney* £25,405
Wins * 1996 Jun Newmar (G-F) H 8f 75 80 <
* 1996 Jun Newmar (G-F) H 8f 69 74
* 1996 May Warwic (FRM) H 7f 64 65
1998 Turf 0-4: (8f 3, 10f) (gd 2, frm 2)
Average colt, effective 7 to 8f, best at 8f, acts on g-s to frm, has worn blinkers. Turf high 59 (began Jly). Becoming disappointing.
**G Wragg [3-19] Mrs Claude Lilley.*

MAWSOOF BHB 94f RR 95f — 3289[1]
3 b c Alzao (USA) 9.8f **(73)** - Guilty Secret (IRE) (Kris) 9.5f **(73)**
Form - 22131
Record 1998 - 1st:2 2nd:2 3rd:1 Ran:5
Pre1998 - 1st:0 2nd:2 3rd:0 Ran:2
Win Prizemoney £11,269 *Total Prizemoney* £17,536
Wins * **1998** Aug Cheste (G-S) H 9.3f 89 95 <
* **1998** Jun Newcas (SFT) 8f 67
1998 Turf 2-5: (7f, 8f 1-2, 9f 1-1, 10f) (sft 1-1, gd 1-2, g-f, frm)
Very useful colt, effective 8 to 9f, acts on gd. Turf high 95 - 1st of 9 giving 23lb to Rebel County (2 Aug Chester RF 3289). Made all to win a competitive Chester handicap on his final start.
**Sir Michael Stoute [2-7] Abdulla Al Khalifa.*

MAXIME (IRE) BHB 63f RR 55f — 3254[17]
2 b f Mac's Imp (USA) 5.6f **(54)** - Ludovica (Bustino) 10.4f **(64)**
Form - 7630
Record 1998 - 1st:0 2nd:0 3rd:1 Ran:4
Win Prizemoney £0 *Total Prizemoney* £405
1998 Turf 0-4: (5f 3, 7f) (gd 4)
Fair filly. Turf high 55. **B J Meehan [0-4] Capt C M Ryan.*

MAYA COVE RR 55f — 3432[6]
2 b f Caerleon (USA) 10.9f **(79)** - Shining Water (Kalaglow) 9.8f **(67)**
Form - 6
Record 1998 - 1st:0 2nd:0 3rd:0 Ran:1
1998 Turf 0-1: (7f) (g-f)
Currently fair filly. **B W Hills [0-1] K Abdulla.*

MAYARO BAY BHB 83f RR 81f — 4820[2]
2 b f Robellino (USA) 9.5f **(68)** - Down the Valley (Kampala) 8.5f **(56)**
Form - 04312
Record 1998 - 1st:1 2nd:1 3rd:1 Ran:5
Win Prizemoney £3,046 *Total Prizemoney* £6,063
Wins * **1998** Oct Warwic (GD) 6f 76+ <
1998 Turf 1-5: (6f 1-5) (gd 2, g-f 1-1, frm 2)
Decent filly. Turf high 81 (began Jly) - 2nd of 15 getting 8lb from Acicula (15 Oct Newmarket 6f frm RF 4820) - also 1st of 10 getting 5lb from Ecudamah (4 Oct Warwick RF 4641).
**R Hannon [1-5] J R Shannon.*

MAYBE SPECIAL BHB 87f92a RR 79f 92a — 4546[1]
2 b g Then Again 7.4f **(52)** - With Love (Be My Guest (USA)) 9.3f **(67)**
Form - 222151
Record 1998 - 1st:2 2nd:3 3rd:0 Ran:6
Win Prizemoney £6,264 *Total Prizemoney* £9,564
Wins * **1998** *Spt Southw (STD) 8f 88* <
* **1998** Jly Redcar (G-F) H 7f 79
1998 Turf 1-4: (5f, 6f, 7f 1-1, 8f) (gd, frm, hrd 1-2) 1998 AW 1-2: (6f, 8f 1-1) (Fibr 1-2)
Useful gelding, effective 7 to 8f, acts on hrd - acts on Fibr. Turf high 79 - also 1st of 8 giving 11lb to Cashiki (25 Jly Redcar RF 3120). AW high 88 - 1st of 8 giving 4lb to Hyphen (29 Spt Southwell RF 4546). **P C Haslam [2-6] Les Buckley.*

MAYDORO BHB 50f45a RR 55f 45a — 2682[2]
5 b m Dominion Royale 7.8f **(63)** - Bamdoro (Cavo Doro) 10.6f **(57)**
Form - 10050182

Record 1998 - 1st:2 2nd:1 3rd:0 Ran:8
Pre1998 - 1st:0 2nd:0 3rd:0 Ran:9
Win Prizemoney £3,998 *Total Prizemoney* £4,848
Wins * **1998** Jun Newcas (SFT) S 5f 55 <
* ***1998*** *Jan Wolver (STD) C 6f 51*
1998 Turf 1-4: (5f 1-2, 6f 2) (g-s, gd 1-1, frm 2) 1998 AW 1-4: (6f 1-4) (Fibr 1-4)
Fair filly, effective 5 to 6f, best at 6f, acts on gd to frm - acts on Fibr. Turf high 55 - 1st of 9 from Souperficial (3 Jun Newcastle RF 1701). AW high 51 (1st run) - 1st of 13 getting 4lb from Hurgill Lady (14 Jan Wolverhampton RF 0086). Inconsistent. Popped up at double-carpet on the Wolverhampton Fibresand in January, but showed little until scoring over the minimum trip on soft ground in June. Ran better afterwards. **M Dods [2-17] M J K Dods.*

MAYFAIR BALLERINA BHB 49f54a **RR 63f 54a** 3108[3]

2 ch f King's Signet (USA) 7f **(51)** - Mayfair Cecilia (Brotherly (USA))
Form - 2074753
Record 1998 - 1st:0 2nd:1 3rd:1 Ran:7
Win Prizemoney £0 *Total Prizemoney* £1,122
1998 Turf 0-5: (5f 5) (g-s, g-f 2, frm 2) 1998 AW 0-2: (5f 2) (Equi, Fibr)
Average filly, effective 5f, acts on g-f - acts on Equi. Turf high 63 - 4th of 7 getting 4lb from Ruanbeg (25 May Leicester 5f g-f RF 1452). AW high 61 (1st run) - 2nd of 4 getting 5lb from Touch Up (3 Apr Lingfield 5f Equi RF 0553).
**W G M Turner [0-7] Mrs A F Horsington.*

MAY I SAY (IRE) BHB 74f **RR 76f** 4873[5]

2 b f Night Shift (USA) 8.1f **(73)** - Monoglow (Kalaglow) 9.8f **(67)**
Form - 73025
Record 1998 - 1st:0 2nd:1 3rd:1 Ran:5
Win Prizemoney £0 *Total Prizemoney* £1,472
1998 Turf 0-5: (7f 2, 8f 3) (gd, g-f, frm 3)
Above-average filly. Turf high 76 (began Jly) - 2nd of 7 giving 10lb to Sunset Lady (24 Spt Pontefract 8f frm RF 4466).
**P W Harris [0-5] Colairo, Coles & Harris.*

MAY KING MAYHEM BHB 44f41a **RR 42f 41a** 4656[1]

5 ch g Great Commotion (USA) 9.2f **(80)** - Queen Ranavalona (Sure Blade (USA)) 11.3f **(67)**
Form - 630F653063417031
Record 1998 - 1st:2 2nd:0 3rd:4 Ran:16
Pre1998 - 1st:1 2nd:1 3rd:2 Ran:22
Win Prizemoney £8,079 *Total Prizemoney* £11,230
Wins * **1998** Oct Pontef (GD) H 12f 37 42
* **1998** Aug Haydoc (GD) H 11.9f 31 34
* 1997 Jly Carlis (GD) H 12f 36 47 <
1998 Turf 2-15: (12f 2-8, 13f, 14f 4, 15f, 16f) (sft ^, g-s 2, gd 1-3, g-f 1-3, frm 4, hrd) 1998 AW 0-1: (14f) (Fibr)
Moderate gelding, effective 12 to 15f, best at 12f, acts on gd to frm, best on frm, has worn blinkers, likes tight tracks, excels at Carlisle and Pontefract. Turf high 42 - 1st of 15 from Cadmax (5 Oct Pontefract RF 4656).
**Mrs A L M King [3-36] S J Harrison (from W R Muir [0-2] Spt 1995).*

MAYLANE BHB 112f **RR 112f** 2085[7]

4 b g Mtoto 11.5f **(71)** - Possessive Dancer (Shareef Dancer (USA)) 9.9f **(73)**
Form - 87
Record 1998 - 1st:0 2nd:0 3rd:0 Ran:2
Pre1998 - 1st:4 2nd:2 3rd:0 Ran:10
Win Prizemoney £64,355 *Total Prizemoney* £71,375
Wins 1997 Spt Epsom (GD) G3 12f 112 <
1997 Jly Goodwo (G-F) H 12f 99 102
1997 Jun Goodwo (GD) 9f 93+
1996 Oct Lingfi (G-S) 7f 83+
1998 Turf 0-2: (12f, 20f) (g-s, g-f)
Light-framed, Group-class gelding, effective 12 to 20f, best at 12f, acts on g-s to g-f. Turf high 110 - 7th of 16 to Kayf Tara (18 Jun Ascot 20f g-s RF 2085). He has the ability to win almost any race, but believes that rules are only made to be broken. Very slow out of the gate when seventh in the Ascot Gold Cup, he seems to have been weeded out of the Godolphin operation and would probably have been better left with his original trainer, Alec Stewart.
**S bin Suroor [0-2] Godolphin.*

MAYO **RR 55f** 4779[19]

2 b c Nashwan (USA) 10.3f **(79)** - Nuryana (Nureyev (USA)) 8.7f **(78)**
Form - 60
Record 1998 - 1st:0 2nd:0 3rd:0 Ran:2
1998 Turf 0-2: (8f 2) (gd, frm)
Currently fair colt. Turf high 55 (began Spt).
**H R A Cecil [0-2] Burke's 5th Family Settlement.*

MAY QUEEN MEGAN BHB 52f38a **RR 54f 38a** 4698[13]

5 gr m Petorius 8f **(66)** - Siva (FR) (Bellypha) 9.8f **(73)**
Form - 0F1501003050
Record 1998 - 1st:2 2nd:0 3rd:1 Ran:12
Pre1998 - 1st:1 2nd:3 3rd:3 Ran:25
Win Prizemoney £10,023 *Total Prizemoney* £15,556
Wins * **1998** Jly Lingfi (G-F) H 9f 49 52 <
* **1998** Jun Nottin (GD) H 8.2f 38 48
* 1996 Jly Lingfi (G-F) H 6f 52 52 <
1998 Turf 2-11: (8f 1-6, 9f 1-1, 10f 4) (g-s, gd 1-2, g-f 3, frm 1-5) 1998 AW 0-1: (8f) (Fibr)
Fair filly, effective 8 to 10f, acts on gd to frm, best on frm, has worn blinkers, likes left handed tracks, likes tight tracks. Turf high 54 - also 1st of 13 giving 11lb to Little Miss Ribot (9 Jly Lingfield RF 2645). **Mrs A L M King [3-37] S J Harrison.*

MAYTONG BHB 54f54a **RR 63f 54a** 889[14]

3 gr f Petong 7.6f **(58)** - Bit O' May (Mummy's Pet) 7.7f **(60)**
Form - 80
Record 1998 - 1st:0 2nd:0 3rd:0 Ran:2
Pre1998 - 1st:0 2nd:0 3rd:0 Ran:3
1998 Turf 0-1: (6f) (gd) 1998 AW 0-1: (7f) (Fibr)
Scopey, average filly. **J Berry [0-5] & Mrs Peter Foden.*

MAYVILLE'S DANCER (IRE) BHB 70f **RR 67f** 4994[2]

2 ch f Up and At 'em - Cutlers Corner (Sharpen Up) 8.3f **(67)**
Form - 772
Record 1998 - 1st:0 2nd:1 3rd:0 Ran:3
Win Prizemoney £0 *Total Prizemoney* £738
1998 Turf 0-3: (6f 3) (sft, g-f 2)
Currently average filly. Turf high 67 (began Spt) - 2nd of 9 to Madam Alison (26 Oct Leicester 6f sft RF 4994).
**G A Butler [0-3] Jan Stenbeck.*

MAZBOON (USA) BHB 90f **RR 88f** 3496[6]

3 ch c Diesis 9f **(80)** - Secretaire (USA) (Secretariat (USA)) 9f **(79)**
Form - 46
Record 1998 - 1st:0 2nd:0 3rd:0 Ran:2
Pre1998 - 1st:2 2nd:0 3rd:0 Ran:2
Win Prizemoney £7,583 *Total Prizemoney* £8,126
Wins * 1997 Jly Yarmou (G-S) 7f 88
* 1997 Jun Newbur (G-F) 6f 93 <
1998 Turf 0-2: (8f, 10f) (gd, g-f)
Scopey, useful colt. Turf high 88.
**E A L Dunlop [2-4] Hamdan Al Maktoum.*

MAZEED (IRE) BHB 74f70a **RR 74f 70a** 3834[4]

5 ch g Lycius (USA) 8.8f **(71)** - Maraatib (IRE) (Green Desert (USA)) 8.6f **(78)**
Form - 01117311210234
Record 1998 - 1st:4 2nd:2 3rd:2 Ran:11
Pre1998 - 1st:4 2nd:1 3rd:1 Ran:16
Win Prizemoney £23,075 *Total Prizemoney* £30,048
Wins * **1998** Jly Beverl (GD) H 9.9f 71 73
* **1998** Jun Yarmou (G-F) H 10.1f 58 71
* **1998** May Yarmou (FRM) H 10.1f 58 68
* ***1998*** *Jan Lingfi (STD) 10f 69+*
* *1997 Dec Wolver (STD) H 9.4f 57 64+*
* *1997 Dec Wolver (STD) H 9.4f 43 56+*
1995 Aug Haydoc (G-F) 6f 84+ <
1995 Jun Newcas (FRM) 6f 81
1998 Turf 3-8: (10f 3-8) (g-f 1-3, frm 2-5) 1998 AW 1-3: (9f 2, 10f 1-1) (Equi 1-1, Fibr 2)
Above-average gelding, effective 9 to 10f, best at 10f, acts on g-f to frm - acts on AW, best on frm, often wears blinkers (extremely effectively), likes left handed tracks, likes tight tracks, and does well at Yarmouth and Beverley. Turf high 74 - 2nd of 9 giving 7lb to River's Source (5 Aug Pontefract 10f frm RF 3386) - also 1st of 8 giving 6lb to Lancer (4 Jly Beverley RF 2517). AW high 69 (1st run) - 1st of 7 giving 6lb to Awesome Power (1 Jan Lingfield RF 0003). Consistent. Was in fine form on the sand during the winter before the Handicapper took his measure, and carried on the good work

on Turf, winning three times in minor company. Has a turn of foot, and is usually produced late.
**P D Evans [6-19] Mrs L A Windsor (from H ThomsonJones [2-8] Aug 1996).*

MAZILLA BHB 38f41a **RR 47f 41a** 2924[5]
6 b m Mazilier (USA) 8.5f **(56)** - Mo Ceri (Kampala) 8.5f **(56)**
Form - 0326005
Record 1998 - 1st:0 2nd:1 3rd:1 Ran:7
Pre1998 - 1st:8 2nd:4 3rd:4 Ran:46
Win Prizemoney £20,386 *Total Prizemoney* £26,528

Wins	* 1996	Aug	Yarmou	(GD)	H	10.1f	52	59	
	* 1996	Jly	Nottin	(G-F)	H	10f	46	53+	
	* 1996	Jly	Warwic	(G-F)	SH	10.8f	40	52	
	* 1996	Jun	Nottin	(G-F)	SH	10f	37	42	
	* 1996	*Feb*	*Southw*	*(STD)*	*H*	*11f*	*47*	*51*	
	* 1996	*Feb*	*Southw*	*(STD)*	*SH*	*11f*	*42*	*45*	
	1995	*Jan*	*Wolver*	*(STD)*	*S*	*7f*		*60*	<
	1995	*Jan*	*Southw*	*(STD)*	*S*	*8f*		*51*	

1998 Turf 0-7: (8f, 9f, 10f 5) (gd 3, frm 4)
Moderate mare, effective 10 to 11f, acts on gd to frm, has worn blinkers. Turf high 47 - 2nd of 10 giving 11lb to Lady Rockstar (3 Jun Folkestone 10f gd RF 1692).
**A Streeter [6-43] M Rhodes (from A L Forbes [0-1] Jun 1995).*

MAZIRAH BHB 30f27a **RR 38df 27a** 4938[14]
7 b g Mazilier (USA) 8.5f **(56)** - Barbary Court (Grundy) 10.3f **(65)**
Form - 00
Record 1998 - 1st:0 2nd:0 3rd:0 Ran:2
Pre1998 - 1st:0 2nd:1 3rd:1 Ran:20
Win Prizemoney £0 *Total Prizemoney* £1,891
1998 Turf 0-1: (16f) (gd) 1998 AW 0-1: (12f) (Equi)
Very moderate gelding, has worn blinkers. Inconsistent.
**P Shakespeare [0-1] Michael Appleby (from R Curtis [0-11] Jan 1998).*

MAZZARELLO (IRE) BHB 18f36a **RR 15f 36a** 3647[12]
8 ch g Hatim (USA) 7.8f **(56)** - Royal Demon (Tarboosh (USA)) 10f **(55)**
Form - 0000
Record 1998 - 1st:0 2nd:0 3rd:0 Ran:4
Pre1998 - 1st:2 2nd:1 3rd:1 Ran:26
Win Prizemoney £7,817 *Total Prizemoney* £9,858

Wins	1995	Jun	Goodwo	(GD)	H	5f	39	38	<
	1995	May	Goodwo	(G-F)	H	5f	29	32	

1998 Turf 0-4: (5f 2, 10f, 12f) (g-f, frm 2, hrd)
Poor gelding, often wears blinkers. Turf high 15 (began Jly).
**R Ingram [0-6] D W Hoskyns (from R Curtis [2-23] Aug 1996).*

MAZZELMO BHB 61f61a **RR 62f 61a** 5118[15]
5 gr m Thethingaboutitis (USA) 16f **(44)** - Nattfari (Tyrnavos) 10.1f **(55)**
Form - 3517443413040
Record 1998 - 1st:2 2nd:0 3rd:3 Ran:13
Win Prizemoney £6,016 *Total Prizemoney* £8,847

Wins	* **1998**	Aug	Cheste	(GD)	H	15.9f	52	59	
	* **1998**	*Jun*	*Wolver*	*(STD)*	*C*	*16.2f*		*70*	<

1998 Turf 1-11: (14f, 16f 1-7, 17f 3) (sft, g-s, gd 1-3, g-f, frm 4, hrd)
1998 AW 1-2: (12f, 16f 1-1) (Fibr 1-2)
Above-average filly, effective 16f, acts on g-s to gd - acts on Fibr, favours tight tracks. Turf high 64 - 3rd of 11 giving 27lb to On The Mat (1 Spt Ripon 16f g-s RF 4015). AW high 70 - 1st of 8 giving 9lb to Monaco Gold (17 Jun Wolverhampton RF 2078).
**A Bailey [2-19] Miss E Oats.*

MBULWA BHB 48f55a **RR 50f 55a** 2021[10]
12 ch g Be My Guest (USA) 10.2f **(66)** - Bundu (FR) (Habitat) 9.4f **(70)**
Form - 050
Record 1998 - 1st:0 2nd:0 3rd:0 Ran:3
Pre1998 - 1st:7 2nd:9 3rd:6 Ran:61
Win Prizemoney £37,316 *Total Prizemoney* £52,217

Wins	* 1996	Jun	Epsom	(G-F)	H	8.5f	55	59
	* 1995	Oct	Redcar	(FRM)	H	8f	44	57
	1994	Spt	Thirsk	(G-F)	H	8f	49	50
	1994	May	Mussel	(FRM)	H	7.1f	40	40

1998 Turf 0-3: (7f 2, 9f) (gd, g-f 2)
Fair gelding, effective 8 to 9f, best at 8f, acts on g-f to frm, best on frm, has worn blinkers, likes right handed tracks, likes tight tracks. Turf high 42. Consistent.
**R A Fahey [2-27] Northumbria Leisure Ltd (from S E Kettlewell [5-37] Jly 1995).*

MCCALLUM'S TIME BHB 30f **RR 5f** 4671[28]
2 b f Timeless Times (USA) 6.1f **(56)** - Agnes Jane (Sweet Monday) 8.3f **(25)**
Form - 000
Record 1998 - 1st:0 2nd:0 3rd:0 Ran:3
1998 Turf 0-3: (5f, 7f 2) (g-f, frm 2)
Currently very poor filly. Turf high 5 (began Aug).
**N Bycroft [0-3] Stuart McCallum.*

MCFARLINE (IRE) BHB 68f **RR 67f** 3976[8]
2 b c Ela-Mana-Mou 12.7f **(72)**- Highland Ball (Bold Lad (IRE)) 8.4f **(68)**
Form - 068
Record 1998 - 1st:0 2nd:0 3rd:0 Ran:3
1998 Turf 0-3: (7f 2, 8f) (gd, g-f, frm)
Currently average colt. Turf high 67 (began Jly).
**J L Dunlop [0-3] Michael Watt.*

MCGILLYCUDDY REEKS (IRE)BHB70f74a **RR71f 74a** 5061[3]
7 b m Kefaah (USA) 11.2f **(64)** - Kilvarnet (Furry Glen) 8.9f **(63)**
Form - 85106404176606863
Record 1998 - 1st:2 2nd:0 3rd:1 Ran:17
Pre1998 - 1st:6 2nd:4 3rd:8 Ran:42
Win Prizemoney £32,175 *Total Prizemoney* £41,318

Wins	* **1998**	Aug	Thirsk	(GD)	H	12f	73	77	<
	* **1998**	Jun	Newcas	(SFT)	H	10.1f	70	73	
	* 1997	Oct	York	(GD)	H	10.4f	68	71	
	* 1997	Aug	Nottin	(G-F)	H	10f	53	65	
	* 1997	Jly	Beverl	(GD)	H	9.9f	46	59	
	* 1997	Jly	Beverl	(G-F)	H	9.9f	46	51	
	* 1997	Jly	Pontef	(GD)	H	8f	38	45	
	1994	Aug	Windso	(G-F)	S	10f		48	

1998 Turf 2-17: (8f 2, 9f, 10f 1-9, 11f, 12f 1-4) (sft, g-s 1-5, g-f 1-5, frm 5, hrd)
Above-average mare, effective 8 to 12f, best at 12f, acts on sft to frm, best on g-f, and excels at Newcastle. Turf high 77 - 1st of 8 getting 4lb from Crystal Falls (1 Aug Thirsk RF 3282) - also 1st of 9 from Desert Fighter (3 Jun Newcastle RF 1702).
**Don Enrico Incisa [7-36] Don Enrico Incisa (from N Tinkler [0-12] Nov 1996).*

MEADGATE'S DREAMER (IRE) BHB 28f **RR 34f** 3980[5]
3 br f Petardia 8.2f **(58)** - Avidal Park (Horage) 10.3f **(61)**
Form - 8505075
Record 1998 - 1st:0 2nd:0 3rd:0 Ran:7
Pre1998 - 1st:0 2nd:0 3rd:0 Ran:4
1998 Turf 0-7: (10f, 12f 5, 13f) (gd, g-f 3, frm 2, hrd)
Scopey, very moderate filly. Turf high 34.
**B Palling [0-11] Meadgate Homes Ltd.*

MEANS BUSINESS (IRE) BHB 65f75a **RR 58f 75a** 1758[10]
3 ch g Imp Society (USA) 7.1f **(63)** - Fantasise (FR) (General Assembly (USA)) 10f **(68)**
Form - 1124010
Record 1998 - 1st:3 2nd:1 3rd:0 Ran:7
Pre1998 - 1st:1 2nd:1 3rd:1 Ran:8
Win Prizemoney £8,762 *Total Prizemoney* £10,687

Wins	* **1998**	May	Ripon	(GD)	C	8f		58	
	* **1998**	*Feb*	*Lingfi*	*(SLW)*	*H*	*7f*	*65*	*75*	<
	* **1998**	*Jan*	*Southw*	*(STD)*	*S*	*7f*		*65*	
	1997	Jly	Lingfi	(G-F)	S	5f		62	

1998 Turf 1-3: (8f 1-3) (gd, g-f 1-1, frm) 1998 AW 2-4: (7f 2-3, 8f) (Equi 1-3, Fibr 1-1)
Leggy, above-average gelding, effective 7f, - acts on AW, best on Equi, has worn blinkers, likes left handed tracks, prefers tight tracks. Turf high 58. AW high 75 - 1st of 7 giving 24lb to Sharp Steel (5 Feb Lingfield RF 0225). Inconsistent. He likes to come very late. **J Hetherton [3-7] Keith West Partnership 1998 (from B J Meehan [1-8] Oct 1997).*

MEAUX (IRE) **RR 48f** 1897[10]
3 b c Fairy King (USA) 7.7f **(75)** - Mo Pheata (Petorius) 7.3f **(61)**
Form - 30
Record 1998 - 1st:0 2nd:0 3rd:1 Ran:2
Win Prizemoney £0 *Total Prizemoney* £879
1998 Turf 0-2: (7f, 8f) (sft, g-s)
Scopey, currently moderate colt. Turf high 62.
**C E Brittain [0-2] B H Voak.*

MECCA PRINCESS BHB 25f **RR** 4010[12]
3 ch f Weldnaas (USA) 8.4f **(55)** - Parfait Amour **(48f)** (Clantime)
Form - 00
Record 1998 - 1st:0 2nd:0 3rd:0 Ran:2
Pre1998 - 1st:0 2nd:0 3rd:0 Ran:1
1998 Turf 0-2: (8f 2) (g-s, g-f)
Currently very poor filly. (began Jly).
**R M Whitaker [0-3] Mecca Social Clubs.*

MECHILIE BHB 30f25a **RR 42f 25a** 3670[15]
4 b f Belmez (USA) 11.4f **(65)** - Tundra Goose (Habitat) 9.4f **(70)**
Form - 00
Record 1998 - 1st:0 2nd:0 3rd:0 Ran:2
Pre1998 - 1st:0 2nd:0 3rd:1 Ran:9
Win Prizemoney £0 *Total Prizemoney* £247
1998 Turf 0-2: (14f, 17f) (g-f, frm)
Strong, moderate filly, effective 14 to 16f, best at 14f, acts on g-f, has worn blinkers. Turf high 14 (began Jly). Inconsistent.
**J W Payne [0-11] Sir Simon Lycett Green.*

MEDAILLE MILITAIRE BHB 93f **RR 98df** 995[9]
6 gr h Highest Honor (FR) 10.9f **(72)** - Lovely Noor (USA) (Fappiano (USA)) 8.7f **(77)**
Form - 560
Record 1998 - 1st:0 2nd:0 3rd:0 Ran:3
Pre1998 - 1st:5 2nd:1 3rd:3 Ran:17
Win Prizemoney £57,019 *Total Prizemoney* £64,238
Wins 1996 Nov Doncas (SFT) L 12f 114 <
1996 Oct Yarmou (GD) 10.1f 90
1995 Aug York (G-F) H 10.4f 93 99+
1995 Jun Ascot (G-F) H 8f 84 92+
1995 Apr Newcas (G-F) 8f 54++
1998 Turf 0-3: (10f, 12f 2) (hvy, gd 2)
Very useful horse, effective 10f, acts on gd, has worn blinkers. Turf high 98. Inconsistent.
**M C Pipe [0-4] James Hartnett (from J L Dunlop [5-16] Aug 1997).*

MEDELAI BHB 58f **RR 69f** 5073[16]
2 b f Marju (IRE) 9.2f **(76)** - No Islands (Lomond (USA)) 8.8f **(65)**
Form - 06340210
Record 1998 - 1st:1 2nd:1 3rd:1 Ran:8
Win Prizemoney £2,197 *Total Prizemoney* £3,365
Wins * **1998** Oct Nottin (SFT) S 8.2f 69 <
1998 Turf 1-8: (6f, 7f 4, 8f 1-2, 10f) (gd 1-3, g-f 2, frm 3)
Average filly, effective 8f, acts on gd, likes tight tracks. Turf high 69 - 1st of 17 getting 5lb from Druridge Bay (22 Oct Nottingham RF 4934). Inconsistent.
**J D Bethell [1-8] Clarendon Thoroughbred Racing.*

MEDICINE BALL BHB 60f **RR 62df** 4150[6]
3 b f Rudimentary (USA) 8.2f **(66)** - Morica (Moorestyle) 6.9f **(64)**
Form - 046
Record 1998 - 1st:0 2nd:0 3rd:0 Ran:3
1998 Turf 0-3: (7f, 9f, 11f) (g-f 2, frm)
Scopey, currently average filly. Turf high 62 - 4th of 7 to Honeybird (25 Aug Lingfield 9f frm RF 3847).
**T R Watson [0-3] Newitt and Co Ltd.*

MEDINA MISS BHB 29f36a **RR 19f 36a** 3246[13]
3 b f Rudimentary (USA) 8.2f **(66)** - Podrida (Persepolis (FR)) 6.4f **(67)**
Form - 0800
Record 1998 - 1st:0 2nd:0 3rd:0 Ran:4
Pre1998 - 1st:0 2nd:2 3rd:1 Ran:8
Win Prizemoney £0 *Total Prizemoney* £1,353
1998 Turf 0-2: (6f, 12f) (g-f, frm) 1998 AW 0-2: (8f, 10f) (Equi 2)
Light-framed, moderate filly, effective 6f, acts on frm, has worn blinkers, likes left handed tracks, likes tight tracks. Turf high 9 (began Jly).
**M Madgwick [0-4] The I W Racing Club (from G M McCourt [0-2] Spt 1997).*

MEDLAND (IRE) BHB 36f34a **RR 30f 34a** 162[7]
8 ch g Imperial Frontier (USA) 7f **(65)** - Miami Dancer (Miami Springs) 9.9f **(59)**
Form - 8057
Record 1998 - 1st:0 2nd:0 3rd:0 Ran:2
Pre1998 - 1st:4 2nd:7 3rd:5 Ran:55
Win Prizemoney £10,405 *Total Prizemoney* £18,180
Wins 1995 *Jan Lingfi (STD) C 10f 50* <
1994 *Mar Lingfi (STD) H 8f 49 50* <
1994 *Mar Lingfi (STD) H 8f 43 46*
1998 AW 0-2: (6f, 8f) (Fibr 2)
Very moderate gelding, has worn blinkers. AW high 20.
**B J McMath [0-20] The Happy Go Lucky Partnership (from W G M Turner [1-4] Feb 1995).*

MEG BHB 61f **RR 61f** 4613[17]
2 b f Be My Chief (USA) 10.2f **(62)** - Megdale (IRE) **(41f)** (Waajib)
Form - 8830
Record 1998 - 1st:0 2nd:0 3rd:1 Ran:4
Win Prizemoney £0 *Total Prizemoney* £337
1998 Turf 0-4: (7f 4) (g-s, g-f, frm 2)
Average filly. Turf high 61 (began Jly) - 3rd of 11 getting 9lb from Archie Babe (5 Spt Thirsk 7f frm RF 4115).
**C F Wall [0-4] Sir Stanley and Lady Grinstead.*

MEGA (IRE) RR 64f 4189[9]
2 b f Petardia 8.2f **(58)** - Gobolino (Don) 7.7f **(64)**
Form - 0
Record 1998 - 1st:0 2nd:0 3rd:0 Ran:1
1998 Turf 0-1: (6f) (gd)
Currently average filly. **M H Tompkins [0-1] Mystic Meg Ltd.*

MEGA TID BHB 22f20a **RR 25f 20a** 1551[8]
6 b g Old Vic 12.8f **(72)** - Dunoof (Shirley Heights) 10.3f **(74)**
Form - 08
Record 1998 - 1st:0 2nd:0 3rd:0 Ran:1
Pre1998 - 1st:1 2nd:0 3rd:2 Ran:22
Win Prizemoney £3,741 *Total Prizemoney* £5,046
Wins 1995 *Feb Lingfi (STD) 10f 65* <
1998 Turf 0-1: (12f) (frm)
Little account gelding, has worn blinkers.
**J R Poulton [1-17] Come Racing Ltd (from B A Pearce [1-18] Jan 1997).*

MEG'S MEMORY (IRE) BHB 45f42a **RR 49f 42a** 4938[9]
5 b m Superlative 8.8f **(57)** - Meanz Beanz (High Top) 10.2f **(67)**
Form - 0460
Record 1998 - 1st:0 2nd:0 3rd:0 Ran:4
Pre1998 - 1st:1 2nd:2 3rd:2 Ran:17
Win Prizemoney £3,803 *Total Prizemoney* £6,561
Wins 1996 Apr Bath (GD) H 10.2f 55 59 <
1998 Turf 0-3: (16f 3) (gd 2, g-f) 1998 AW 0-1: (12f) (Fibr)
Moderate filly, effective 12 to 16f, acts on gd to g-f, has worn blinkers. Turf high 49 (1st run) (began Spt) - 4th of 18 giving 6lb to Old Red (14 Spt Nottingham 16f gd RF 4262).
**A Streeter [2-17] Centaur Racing Ltd (from John Berry [1-14] Aug 1996).*

MEGS PEARL RR 57f 2554[6]
2 gr f Petong 7.6f **(58)** - Heaven-Liegh-Grey (Grey Desire) 8.7f **(50)**
Form - 576
Record 1998 - 1st:0 2nd:0 3rd:0 Ran:3
1998 Turf 0-3: (6f 3) (g-s, g-f 2)
Currently fair filly. Turf high 57. **P D Evans [0-3] John Pugh.*

MEHMAAS BHB 80f **RR 83f** 4779[2]
2 b c Distant Relative 7f **(69)** - Guest List (Be My Guest (USA)) 9.3f **(67)**
Form - 8502
Record 1998 - 1st:0 2nd:1 3rd:0 Ran:4
Win Prizemoney £0 *Total Prizemoney* £1,216
1998 Turf 0-4: (6f, 7f 2, 8f) (gd 2, g-f, frm)
Decent colt, mostly wears blinkers. Turf high 83 (began Aug) - 2nd of 20 to Dollar Law (13 Oct Leicester 8f gd RF 4779).
**C J Benstead [0-4] Hamdan Al Maktoum.*

MEILLEUR (IRE) BHB 49f55a **RR 56f 55a** 5125[5]
4 b g Nordico (USA) 8.2f **(59)** - Lucy Limelight (Hot Spark) 7.6f **(62)**
Form - 243410675
Record 1998 - 1st:1 2nd:0 3rd:1 Ran:8
Pre1998 - 1st:0 2nd:1 3rd:1 Ran:8
Win Prizemoney £2,458 *Total Prizemoney* £3,996
Wins * **1998** Aug Hamilt (SFT) H 11.1f 51 52 <
1998 Turf 1-8: (10f 2, 11f 1-3, 12f 3) (g-s 2, gd 1-2, g-f 2, frm 2)

Scopey, fair gelding, effective 11 to 16f, acts on gd to frm - acts on Equi, has worn blinkers, likes right handed tracks, prefers tight tracks. Turf high 57 - 3rd of 10 getting 9lb from Admirals Secret (27 Jun Lingfield 11f frm RF 2336) - also 1st of 14 giving 23lb to Joli Fille (12 Aug Hamilton RF 3575).
**Lady Herries [1-16] The Cottage Racing Partnership.*

MELANJO (IRE) RR 14f 1276^{8}
2 b c River Falls 8.2f **(56)** - Chiltern Show **(18f 39a)** (Rambo Dancer (CAN))
Form - 8
Record 1998 - 1st:0 2nd:0 3rd:0 Ran:1
1998 Turf 0-1: (5f) (g-f)
Poor colt. (DEAD) **T D Easterby [0-1] C H Newton Jnr Ltd.*

MELBOURNEFIFTYSIX (IRE) BHB 26f RR 44f 4544^{9}
3 ch f Erins Isle 8.3f **(76)** - Flying Tribute (USA) (Fighting Fit (USA))
Form - 645000
Record 1998 - 1st:0 2nd:0 3rd:0 Ran:6
1998 Turf 0-4: (10f 2, 12f, 16f)(g-f 2, frm 2)1998 AW 0-2: (14f 2) (Fibr 2)
Unfurnished, moderate filly. Turf high 44. AW high 17 (began Aug).
**R Craggs [0-6] Ten For Sport Partnership.*

MELBOURNE PRINCESS BHB 38f31a RR 48f 31a 106^{4}
4 ch f Primo Dominie 7.2f **(67)** - Lurking (Formidable (USA)) 9.2f **(63)**
Form - 7054
Record 1998 - 1st:0 2nd:0 3rd:0 Ran:1
Pre1998 - 1st:0 2nd:2 3rd:2 Ran:21
Win Prizemoney £0 *Total Prizemoney* £2,491
1998 AW 0-1: (6f) (Equi)
Scopey, moderate filly, has worn blinkers.
**R M Whitaker [0-22] Country Lane Partnership.*

MELLORS (IRE) BHB 53f65a RR 52f 65a 4648^{4}
5 b h Common Grounds 8.1f **(66)** - Simply Beautiful (IRE) (Simply Great (FR)) 8.2f **(65)**
Form - 511312154
Record 1998 - 1st:4 2nd:1 3rd:1 Ran:9
Pre1998 - 1st:2 2nd:5 3rd:2 Ran:29
Win Prizemoney £15,236 *Total Prizemoney* £21,967

Wins								
* 1998	May	Bright	(FRM)	H	8f	46	52	
* 1998	Apr	Bright	(GD)	H	8f	41	50	
* 1998	*Feb*	*Lingfi*	*(SLW)*	*H*	*8f*	*51*	*68*	<
* 1998	*Feb*	*Lingfi*	*(SLW)*	*H*	*8f*	*51*	*56*	
* 1997	*Jan*	*Lingfi*	*(STD)*	*H*	*6f*	*57*	*60*	
1996	Jun	Catter	(GD)		6f		52	

1998 Turf 2-5: (8f 2-4, 9f) (gd 1-1, g-f, frm 1-3) 1998 AW 2-4: (7f, 8f 2-2, 9f) (Equi 2-3, Fibr)
Average colt, effective 6 to 8f, - acts on Equi, has worn blinkers, prefers left handed tracks, prefers tight tracks, and excels at Lingfield. Turf high 52. AW high 68 - 1st of 8 giving 3lb to Sea Spouse (26 Feb Lingfield RF 0363). In fine form in the first part of the season.
**M J Heaton-Ellis [5-26] Barbury Racing (from J A R Toller [1-14] Oct 1996).*

MELLOW MISS RR 63f 5063^{16}
2 b f Danehill (USA) 9.1f **(79)** - Like the Sun (USA) (Woodman (USA)) 9f **(74)**
Form - 70
Record 1998 - 1st:0 2nd:0 3rd:0 Ran:2
1998 Turf 0-2: (6f 2) (gd, g-f)
Currently average filly. Turf high 63 (began Spt).
**E A L Dunlop [0-2] Maktoum Al Maktoum.*

MELODIAN BHB 42f RR 41f 4677^{23}
3 b c Grey Desire 9.3f **(49)** - Mere Melody (Dunphy) 9.4f **(57)**
Form - 0801300
Record 1998 - 1st:1 2nd:0 3rd:1 Ran:7
Pre1998 - 1st:0 2nd:0 3rd:0 Ran:2
Win Prizemoney £2,431 *Total Prizemoney* £2,831

Wins								
* 1998	Jly	Newcas	(GD)	H	7f	38	41	<

1998 Turf 1-7: (6f 2, 7f 1-3, 8f 2) (gd 1-4, g-f 2, frm)
Leggy, moderate colt, effective 7f, acts on gd, often wears blinkers (very effectively). Turf high 41 - 1st of 20 getting 21lb from Jacobina (27 Jly Newcastle RF 3141). **M Brittain [1-9] Mel Brittain.*

MELODY ANNE BHB 19f RR 5114^{13}
9 ch m Clantime 6.6f **(57)** - Louisa Anne (Mummy's Pet) 7.7f **(60)**
Form - 000
Record 1998 - 1st:0 2nd:0 3rd:0 Ran:3
Pre1998 - 1st:0 2nd:0 3rd:0 Ran:9
1998 Turf 0-3: (5f 2, 8f) (sft, gd 2)
Very poor mare. (began Aug). **J S Haldane [0-12] J Kyle.*

MELODY BLUES BHB 47f52a RR 46f 52a 3934^{9}
2 b f Merdon Melody 6.8f **(56)** - Hsian (Shantung) 9.8f **(64)**
Form - 3350
Record 1998 - 1st:0 2nd:0 3rd:2 Ran:4
Win Prizemoney £0 *Total Prizemoney* £554
1998 Turf 0-2: (6f, 7f) (gd, frm) 1998 AW 0-2: (6f, 7f) (Fibr 2)
Fair filly. Turf high 46. AW high 56 (began Jly) - 5th of 11 to March Party (24 Jly Wolverhampton 7f Fibr RF 3097).
**M Dods [0-4] M J K Dods.*

MELODY LADY BHB 60f RR 66f 4612^{9}
2 ch f Dilum (USA) 7.1f **(56)** - Ansellady **(62f 60a)** (Absalom) 7.2f **(58)**
Form - 77530
Record 1998 - 1st:0 2nd:0 3rd:1 Ran:5
Win Prizemoney £0 *Total Prizemoney* £399
1998 Turf 0-5: (6f 4, 7f) (g-s, g-f 3, frm)
Average filly, has worn blinkers. Turf high 66 (began Aug) - 3rd of 16 giving 4lb to Helen's Stardust (25 Spt Folkestone 6f g-f RF 4473). **Mrs L Stubbs [0-5] Joseph Smith.*

MELODY QUEEN BHB 76f RR 73f 4845^{11}
2 b f Merdon Melody 6.8f **(56)**-Thabeh (Shareef Dancer(USA)) 9.9f **(73)**
Form - 7526122210
Record 1998 - 1st:2 2nd:4 3rd:0 Ran:10
Win Prizemoney £20,370 *Total Prizemoney* £25,025

Wins								
* 1998	Spt	Newmar	(GD)	H	7f	65	73	<
1998	Aug	Bright	(FRM)	S	7f		60	

1998 Turf 2-10: (6f 4, 7f 2-4, 8f 2) (gd 2, g-f 1-5, frm 1-3)
Above-average filly, effective 7f, acts on frm. Turf high 73 - 1st of 13 getting 12lb from Weaver of Words (29 Spt Newmarket RF 4538). Consistent. Effective in a modest grade, she won a valuable nursery at Newmarket off a low weight for her new connections, who bought her out of a seller.
**K R Burke [1-3] Nigel Shields (from Ronald Thompson [1-7] Aug 1998).*

MELS BABY (IRE) BHB 60f54a RR 45f 54a 5119^{9}
5 br g Contract Law (USA) 8.9f **(54)** - Launch The Raft (Home Guard (USA)) 9.3f **(66)**
Form - 40000
Record 1998 - 1st:0 2nd:0 3rd:0 Ran:5
Pre1998 - 1st:4 2nd:7 3rd:2 Ran:32
Win Prizemoney £20,523 *Total Prizemoney* £26,562

Wins								
* 1997	May	Beverl	(HVY)	H	9.9f	71	76	<
* 1996	Nov	Doncas	(SFT)	H	8f	61	68	
* 1996	Oct	Pontef	(GD)	H	8f	58	62	
* 1996	Spt	Redcar	(FRM)	H	8f	56	63	

1998 Turf 0-4: (10f, 11f, 12f 2) (gd 2, frm 2) 1998 AW 0-1: (12f) (Fibr)
Fair gelding, effective 8 to 10f, best at 10f, acts on g-s to gd, best on gd, has worn blinkers. Turf high 45 (began Spt).
**J L Eyre [4-37] John Roberts (Wakefield).*

MEMORISE (USA) BHB 107f RR 112f 3652^{3}
4 b c Lyphard (USA) 10.6f **(75)** - Shirley Valentine (Shirley Heights) 10.3f **(74)**
Form - 3513
Record 1998 - 1st:1 2nd:0 3rd:2 Ran:4
Pre1998 - 1st:2 2nd:2 3rd:0 Ran:9
Win Prizemoney £42,805 *Total Prizemoney* £66,924

Wins								
* 1998	Jun	Currag	(HVY)	G3	14f		112	<
* 1997	Jly	Newmar	(G-F)	H	10f	86	89	
* 1997	May	Newcas	(GD)		10.1f		82	

1998 Turf 1-4: (12f, 13f 2, 14f 1-1) (sft 1-1, gd, g-f 2)
Scopey, Group-class colt, effective 12 to 14f, acts on sft to frm, best on g-f, excels at Newmarket. Turf high 112 (1st run) - 3rd of 6 getting 5lb from Stretarez (7 May Chester 13f g-f RF 1071) - also 1st of 4 from Stage Affair (28 Jun Curragh RF 2435a). He does not always look an easy ride, and benefited from a typically robust Kieren Fallon effort when winning a Group Three at the Curragh in

June. He stayed a mile and three-quarters well that day and could develop into a Cup horse next term. **H R A Cecil [3-13] K Abdulla.*

MEMORY'S MUSIC BHB 32f43a RR 31f 43a 4931[2]

6 b g Dance of Life (USA) 9.3f **(69)** - Sheer Luck (Shergar) 10.4f **(66)**
Form - 63142
Record 1998 - 1st:1 2nd:1 3rd:1 Ran:4
Pre1998 - 1st:0 2nd:0 3rd:0 Ran:15
Win Prizemoney £1,864 *Total Prizemoney* £2,766
Wins * **1998** *Jan Lingfi (STD) SH 12f 34 39 <*
1998 Turf 0-1: (10f) (g-s) 1998 AW 1-3: (12f 1-3) (Equi 1-3)
Moderate gelding, effective 12f, - acts on Equi, has worn blinkers, favours left handed tracks. AW high 43 - 4th of 11 giving 2lb to Rajah (22 Jan Lingfield 12f Equi RF 0136) - also 1st of 11 getting 3lb from Krayyan Dawn (15 Jan Lingfield RF 0091).
**M Madgwick [2-21] Mrs J Phillips-Hill (from I A Balding [0-8] Spt 1995).*

MEMPARI (IRE) RR 102+f 4428a[3]

3 b f Fairy King (USA) 7.7f **(75)**- Sharaya (USA) (Youth (USA)) 9.8f **(64)**
Form - 6112673
1998 Turf 2-7: (5f 1-1, 7f 2, 8f 1-4) (sft, gd 2-5, frm)
Very useful filly, effective 5 to 8f, acts on gd to frm, best on gd. Turf high 102 (1st run) - 6th of 13 to Tarascon (24 May Curragh 8f gd RF 1513a) - also 1st of 8 getting 5lb from Rashay (22 Jly Naas RF 3178a). Inconsistent. She underlined her versatility by winning a five-furlong maiden and mile conditions event within seven days during July. Used as a pacemaker later in the season, she is not Group class yet. **A P O'Brien in IRE [2-12] Michael Tabor.*

MEMPHIS DANCER BHB 58f RR 67f 4816[2]

3 b f Shareef Dancer (USA) 10.1f **(67)** - Wollow Maid (Wollow) 8.2f **(61)**
Form - 206002
Record 1998 - 1st:0 2nd:2 3rd:0 Ran:6
Pre1998 - 1st:0 2nd:0 3rd:0 Ran:2
Win Prizemoney £0 *Total Prizemoney* £1,750
1998 Turf 0-6: (8f 2, 10f 2, 12f 2) (gd 2, g-f, frm 3)
Scopey, average filly, effective 8f, acts on frm. Turf high 67.
**J W Hills [0-8] Martin Boase.*

MENDELUCI (IRE) BHB 48f RR 16f 4416[16]

6 b g Nordico (USA) 8.2f **(59)** - Favourite Niece (Busted) 10.2f **(61)**
Form - 0
Record 1998 - 1st:0 2nd:0 3rd:0 Ran:1
Pre1998 - 1st:0 2nd:0 3rd:0 Ran:1
1998 Turf 0-1: (11f) (frm)
Poor gelding, always wears blinkers.
**J G M O'Shea [0-3] Robert Mullett (from J S Bolger in IRE [0-1] Spt 1996).*

MENDOZA BHB 46f46a RR 50f 46a 3593[7]

4 b g Rambo Dancer (CAN) 8.4f **(59)** - Red Poppy (IRE) (Coquelin (USA)) 8.4f **(58)**
Form - 0487330537
Record 1998 - 1st:0 2nd:0 3rd:3 Ran:9
Pre1998 - 1st:1 2nd:2 3rd:0 Ran:14
Win Prizemoney £3,290 *Total Prizemoney* £6,683
Wins 1997 *Jan Lingfi (STD) H 8f 55 53 <*
1998 Turf 0-6: (8f 3, 9f, 10f, 12f) (gd, g-f, frm 4) 1998 AW 0-3: (8f 3) (Equi 2, Fibr)
Workmanlike, fair gelding, effective 8 to 10f, best at 8f, acts on frm - acts on Equi, has worn blinkers, likes left handed tracks, favours tight tracks. Turf high 50. AW high 43.
**P Mitchell [0-6] Commsave Partnership (from D J G MurraySmith [1-17] Apr 1998).*

MENEER (USA) BHB 90f RR 84f 4204[10]

2 b or br c Silver Hawk (USA) 11.2f **(85)** - Mrs West (USA) (Gone West (USA)) 6.5f **(75)**
Form - 422130
Record 1998 - 1st:1 2nd:2 3rd:1 Ran:6
Win Prizemoney £3,590 *Total Prizemoney* £7,673
Wins * **1998** Jly Ayr (SFT) 7f 84 <
1998 Turf 1-6: (6f, 7f 1-4, 8f) (gd 1-2, g-f, frm 3)
Decent colt, effective 7f, acts on gd to frm. Turf high 84 - 2nd of 9 to Nimello (7 Jly Newmarket 7f frm RF 2578) - also 1st of 8 from Election Promise (20 Jly Ayr RF 2946). Got off the mark with a wide-margin win at Ayr, not before time, but was below par on fast ground after. **J H M Gosden [1-6] H E Sheikh Rashid Al Maktoum.*

MENSA BHB 95f RR 77f 3204[5]

2 ch c Rudimentary (USA) 8.2f **(66)** - Musianica (Music Boy) 6.8f **(57)**
Form - 53215
Record 1998 - 1st:1 2nd:1 3rd:1 Ran:5
Win Prizemoney £6,398 *Total Prizemoney* £7,854
Wins * **1998** Jly Sandow (GD) 7.1f 77 <
1998 Turf 1-5: (6f 3, 7f 1-2) (gd 1-3, g-f, frm)
Above-average colt, has worn blinkers. Turf high 77 - 3rd of 7 to Pistachio (11 Jun Yarmouth 6f g-f RF 1907) - also 1st of 4 getting 4lb from Gold Rush (3 Jly Sandown RF 2503). Has ability, but is a character too and no easy ride. Going to post early paid off when he won at Sandown in July, as he faced a stiff task in a Group Three at Glorious Goodwood next time.
**M H Tompkins [1-5] Mrs Beryl Lockey.*

MENTAL PRESSURE BHB 53f RR 49f 3123[8]

5 ch g Polar Falcon (USA) 9f **(74)** - Hysterical (High Top) 10.2f **(67)**
Form - 7778
Record 1998 - 1st:0 2nd:0 3rd:0 Ran:4
Pre1998 - 1st:0 2nd:4 3rd:3 Ran:9
Win Prizemoney £0 *Total Prizemoney* £11,429
1998 Turf 0-4: (12f, 14f 2, 16f) (gd, frm 2, hrd)
Moderate gelding. Turf high 49. Becoming disappointing.
**Mrs M Reveley [0-11] P D Savill (from M R Channon [0-2] Spt 1995).*

MERANIE GIRL (IRE) BHB 52f RR 68f 5042[11]

2 b f Mujadil (USA) 7.7f **(70)** - Christoph's Girl (Efisio)
Form - 0860580
Record 1998 - 1st:0 2nd:0 3rd:0 Ran:7
1998 Turf 0-7: (5f 5, 6f, 7f) (sft, gd, g-f 3, frm 2)
Average filly. Turf high 64. **J R Arnold [0-7] George Darling.*

MERANTI BHB 58f62a RR 66f 62a 4799[23]

5 b g Puissance 7.1f **(60)** - Sorrowful (Moorestyle) 6.9f **(64)**
Form - 00308161550000
Record 1998 - 1st:2 2nd:0 3rd:1 Ran:14
Pre1998 - 1st:3 2nd:2 3rd:0 Ran:30
Win Prizemoney £17,359 *Total Prizemoney* £21,262
Wins * **1998** Jly Thirsk (GD) H 6f 56 66 <
* **1998** Jly Salisb (FRM) H 6f 51 54
* 1997 Jly Salisb (G-F) H 6f 56 60
* 1997 Apr Thirsk (G-F) H 7f 43 55
* 1997 Apr Nottin (G-F) H 6.1f 43 57
1998 Turf 2-14: (6f 2-11, 7f 3) (sft, gd, g-f 1-7, frm 1-5)
Average gelding, effective 6f, acts on g-f to frm, best on g-f, excels at Salisbury and Thirsk. Turf high 66 - 1st of 16 getting 14lb from Benzoe (31 Jly Thirsk RF 3248). He took time to get his act together in '98, but managed victories at Salisbury and Thirsk when well drawn. **J M Bradley [5-29] John Wallis (from S Dow [0-8] Jly 1996).*

MERCHANT PRINCE RR 18f 4622[14]

2 b c Flying Tyke 7.2f **(42)** - Bellinote (FR) (Noir Et Or) 10f **(38)**
Form - 0
Record 1998 - 1st:0 2nd:0 3rd:0 Ran:1
1998 Turf 0-1: (5f) (g-f)
Currently poor colt. **A Smith [0-1] Park Racing Partnership.*

MERCH RHYD-Y-GRUG BHB 40f30a RR 38f 30a 120[7]

3 b f Sabrehill (USA) 8.5f **(64)** - Al Washl (USA) (The Minstrel (CAN)) 10f **(72)**
Form - 07
Record 1998 - 1st:0 2nd:0 3rd:0 Ran:1
Pre1998 - 1st:0 2nd:0 3rd:0 Ran:4
1998 AW 0-1: (8f) (Equi)
Leggy, very moderate filly. **D L Williams [0-5] Mouse Racing.*

MERCILESS BHB 93f RR 88df 1898[3]

3 gr f Last Tycoon 9.4f **(73)** - Galava (CAN) (Graustark) 10.1f **(70)**
Form - 83
Record 1998 - 1st:0 2nd:0 3rd:1 Ran:2
Pre1998 - 1st:1 2nd:0 3rd:0 Ran:1
Win Prizemoney £3,931 *Total Prizemoney* £5,671
Wins 1997 Oct Doncas (GD) 8f 88 <
1998 Turf 0-2: (10f 2) (g-s, gd)
Scopey, currently useful filly. Turf high 75. Won her only start at

two, but was well beaten in listed races last term.
**E A L Dunlop [0-1] Maktoum Al Maktoum (from S bin Suroor [1-2] May 1998).*

MERCILESS COP BHB 68f73a **RR 59f 73a** 773[11]
4 ch g Efisio 7.7f **(69)** - Naturally Bold (Bold Lad (IRE)) 8.4f **(68)**
Form - 0
Record 1998 - 1st:0 2nd:0 3rd:0 Ran:1
Pre1998 - 1st:4 2nd:0 3rd:3 Ran:21
Win Prizemoney £16,693 *Total Prizemoney* £19,577
Wins 1997 Jly Nottin (G-F) H 8.2f 63 69
1997 Jun Wolver (STD) H 9.4f 63 70
1997 Jun Goodwo (GD) C 8f 55
1996 Oct Lingfi (GD) H 7f 61 71 <
1998 Turf 0-1: (14f) (sft)
Above-average gelding, effective 8 to 9f, acts on frm - acts on Fibr, often wears blinkers (extremely effectively), prefers tight tracks.
**Mrs Merrita Jones [0-4] The Par Four (from B J Meehan [4-21] Aug 1997).*

MERCI MONSIEUR BHB 40f **RR 43f** 4383[10]
5 ch g Cadeaux Genereux 7.9f **(76)** - Night Encounter (Right Tack) 5.9f **(61)**
Form - 0
Record 1998 - 1st:0 2nd:0 3rd:0 Ran:1
Pre1998 - 1st:0 2nd:0 3rd:0 Ran:3
Win Prizemoney £0 *Total Prizemoney* £507
1998 AW 0-1: (8f) (Fibr)
Moderate gelding. Ex-French maiden. **J A B Old [0-4] S Emmet.*

MERCURY (IRE) BHB 25f41a **RR 30f 41a** 1621[11]
5 b g Contract Law (USA) 8.9f **(54)** - Monrovia (FR) (Dancers Image (USA)) 9.3f **(71)**
Form - 428U0264000
Record 1998 - 1st:0 2nd:1 3rd:0 Ran:7
Pre1998 - 1st:1 2nd:1 3rd:0 Ran:18
Win Prizemoney £2,717 *Total Prizemoney* £4,402
Wins 1996 *Jun Southw (STD) 8f 71+* <
1998 Turf 0-2: (8f, 10f) (g-f, frm) 1998 AW 0-5: (8f, 11f 2, 12f 2) (Fibr 5)
Moderate gelding, effective 10 to 12f, acts on frm - acts on Fibr, has worn blinkers, likes tight tracks. Turf high 15. AW high 46 - 2nd of 7 getting 4lb from State Approval (17 Mar Southwell 11f Fibr RF 0439).
**B P J Baugh [0-11] Nigel Taylor (from J A Glover [1-14] Aug 1997).*

MERE SLAD RR 45f 4144[9]
2 b f Beveled (USA) 6.9f **(64)** - Pallomere (Blue Cashmere) 6.4f **(54)**
Form - 0
Record 1998 - 1st:0 2nd:0 3rd:0 Ran:1
1998 Turf 0-1: (7f) (g-f)
Currently moderate filly. **A P Jones [0-1] The Lambourn Racing Club.*

MERIT (IRE) BHB 78f83a **RR 78f 83a** 648[13]
6 b h Rainbow Quest (USA) 11.2f **(81)** - Fur Hat (Habitat) 9.4f **(70)**
Form - 0
Record 1998 - 1st:0 2nd:0 3rd:0 Ran:1
Pre1998 - 1st:4 2nd:0 3rd:0 Ran:13
Win Prizemoney £52,398 *Total Prizemoney* £52,398
Wins * 1996 May Cheste (GD) H 18.7f 70 84 <
* 1995 Nov Doncas (G-F) H 16.5f 57 69+
* 1995 Nov Mussel (SFT) H 15.1f 57 72+
* 1995 *Oct Lingfi (STD) H 12f 58 72*
1998 Turf 0-1: (16f) (hvy)
Above-average horse, has worn blinkers.
**P F I Cole [4-14] H R H Prince Fahd Salman.*

MERLIN'S RING BHB 105f **RR 106f** 2908[8]
3 br c Magic Ring (IRE) 6.5f **(64)** - Dramatic Mood (Jalmood (USA)) 10.1f **(52)**
Form - 30278
Record 1998 - 1st:0 2nd:1 3rd:1 Ran:5
Pre1998 - 1st:4 2nd:1 3rd:1 Ran:7
Win Prizemoney £55,789 *Total Prizemoney* £70,357
Wins * 1997 Oct Saint-Cl (SFT) G3 6.5f 101 <
* 1997 Spt Maison (GD) L 6f 95
* 1997 Aug Goodwo (G-F) H 7f 85 95
* 1997 Jly York (GD) 6f 77+
1998 Turf 0-5: (6f, 7f 3, 8f) (sft, gd 3, g-f)
Unfurnished, Pattern-class colt, effective 7f, acts on sft to g-f, best on sft. Turf high 106 (1st run) - 3rd of 6 to Victory Note (18 Apr Newbury 7f sft RF 0742). A smart juvenile, he ran a fair race to finish third in the Greenham Stakes on his reappearance, but was mainly disappointing thereafter, and if he is to win again then it is most likely to be when the ground is very soft.
**I A Balding [4-12] Mrs Richard Plummer & Partners.*

MERLY NOTTY BHB 30f **RR 10f** 4671[29]
2 ch f Inchinor 8.9f **(64)** - Rambadale (Vaigly Great) 7f **(58)**
Form - 700
Record 1998 - 1st:0 2nd:0 3rd:0 Ran:3
1998 Turf 0-3: (5f 2, 7f) (gd 2, g-f)
Currently poor filly. Turf high 10. **J S Haldane [0-3] G J Johnston.*

MERRY MELODY RR 48f 4765[10]
3 b f Almoojid 7f **(36)** - Merry Marigold (Sonnen Gold) 6.6f **(47)**
Form - 580
Record 1998 - 1st:0 2nd:0 3rd:0 Ran:3
1998 Turf 0-3: (7f, 8f 2) (gd, g-f, frm)
Unfurnished, currently moderate filly. Turf high 48 (began Aug).
**R J Hodges [0-3] Mrs I E Penfold.*

MERRY PRINCE (IRE) BHB 62f **RR 65f** 4670[12]
3 b g Roi Danzig (USA) 10.5f **(62)**- Queen of the Brush(Averof)8.2f **(62)**
Form - 0055650
Record 1998 - 1st:0 2nd:0 3rd:0 Ran:7
1998 Turf 0-7: (7f, 8f 2, 10f 3, 11f) (g-s, gd 4, g-f 2)
Average gelding, effective 8f, acts on g-f. Turf high 65 - 5th of 11 to Roi de Danse (30 Spt Brighton 8f g-f RF 4571).
**M A Jarvis [0-7] D Fisher.*

MERRY WAKE RR 2342[5]
2 b c Keen 11.1f **(58)**- True Queen (USA) (Silver Hawk (USA)) 8.6f **(70)**
Form - 5
Record 1998 - 1st:0 2nd:0 3rd:0 Ran:1
1998 Turf 0-1: (6f) (g-s)
Very poor colt. (DEAD) **T J Etherington [0-1] David Abell.*

MERSEY BEAT BHB 83f **RR 80f** 1240[6]
4 ch c Rock Hopper 10.6f **(54)** - Handy Dancer (Green God) 9.6f **(68)**
Form - 86
Record 1998 - 1st:0 2nd:0 3rd:0 Ran:2
Pre1998 - 1st:1 2nd:1 3rd:1 Ran:5
Win Prizemoney £2,200 *Total Prizemoney* £6,080
Wins * 1996 *Nov Lingfi (STD) 10f 77+* <
1998 Turf 0-2: (12f 2) (sft, g-f)
Workmanlike, useful colt, effective 10f, acts on g-f - acts on Equi. Turf high 80. **G L Moore [1-10] Bryan Pennick.*

MESHTY (IRE) RR 86f 2075[3]
3 b g Lahib (USA) 8f **(69)** - Merry Devil (IRE) (Sadler's Wells (USA)) 10f **(76)**
Form - 3
Record 1998 - 1st:0 2nd:0 3rd:1 Ran:1
Win Prizemoney £0 *Total Prizemoney* £532
1998 Turf 0-1: (8f) (gd)
Workmanlike, currently useful gelding. (1st run) - 3rd of 9 to Alcazar (17 Jun Ripon 8f gd RF 2075).
**A C Stewart [0-1] Sheikh Ahmed Al Maktoum.*

MESOZOIC (USA) RR 75f 5015[2]
2 b c Barathea (IRE) - Wezzo (USA) (Bering) 7.4f **(61)**
Form - 2
Record 1998 - 1st:0 2nd:1 3rd:0 Ran:1
Win Prizemoney £0 *Total Prizemoney* £956
1998 Turf 0-1: (7f) (gd)
Currently above-average colt. (1st run) - 2nd of 5 giving 3lb to Come What May (27 Oct Redcar 7f gd RF 5015).
**D R Loder [0-1] Maktoum Al Maktoum.*

MESSENGER MISS (USA) RR 70f 4668[6]
2 b f Danehill (USA) 9.1f **(79)**-Foreign Courier (USA)(Sir Ivor) 10.2f **(70)**
Form - 6
Record 1998 - 1st:0 2nd:0 3rd:0 Ran:1
1998 Turf 0-1: (6f) (gd)

Currently above-average filly.
**Sir Michael Stoute [0-1] Maktoum Al Maktoum.*

METEORITE (IRE) RR 68f — 4779[12]

2 b c Bigstone (IRE)- Winning Appeal (FR)(Law Society (USA))9.9f **(70)**
Form - 0
Record 1998 - 1st:0 2nd:0 3rd:0 Ran:1
1998 Turf 0-1: (8f) (gd)
Currently average colt.
**R Hannon [0-1] W F Hawkings, M W Grant & T E Bucknall.*

METEOR STRIKE (USA) BHB 75f RR 71f — 1243[21]

4 ch g Lomond (USA) 9.9f **(74)** - Meteoric (High Line) 10.3f **(70)**
Form - 0
Record 1998 - 1st:0 2nd:0 3rd:0 Ran:1
Pre1998 - 1st:1 2nd:1 3rd:0 Ran:4
Win Prizemoney £3,101 *Total Prizemoney* £4,166
Wins * 1997 Jly Bath (GD) 10.2f 75 <
1998 Turf 0-1: (10f) (g-f)
Above-average gelding. **Mrs A J Perrett [1-6] S P Tindall.*

MEZZA LUNA RR 41f — 3377[14]

2 b f Distant Relative 7f **(69)** - Cox's Pippin (USA) (Cox's Ridge (USA)) 8f **(68)**
Form - 0
Record 1998 - 1st:0 2nd:0 3rd:0 Ran:1
1998 Turf 0-1: (6f) (frm)
Currently moderate filly. **B J McMath [0-1] The Nevis Partnership.*

MEZZORAMIO BHB 46f40a RR 51df 40a — 3469[9]

6 ch g Cadeaux Genereux 7.9f **(76)** - Hopeful Search (USA) (Vaguely Noble) 10.1f **(72)**
Form - 7343000
Record 1998 - 1st:0 2nd:0 3rd:2 Ran:7
Pre1998 - 1st:4 2nd:5 3rd:3 Ran:33
Win Prizemoney £13,217 *Total Prizemoney* £20,826
Wins * 1997 Jly Yarmou (G-F) H 7f 47 51 <
* 1996 Aug Newmar (G-F) H 8f 46 49
* 1996 Jly Leices (G-F) H 7f 40 45
* 1996 *Feb Southw (STD) H 8f 39 44*
1998 Turf 0-7: (6f 3, 7f 2, 8f 2) (gd 2, g-f, frm 2, hrd 2)
Fair gelding, effective 6 to 8f, best at 6f, acts on gd to hrd, best on frm, mostly wears blinkers (very effectively), likes Yarmouth. Turf high 54. Becoming disappointing.
**K A Morgan [4-39] T R Pryke (from Sir Mark Prescott [0-2] May 1995).*

MIAMI MOON BHB 35f45a RR 44f 45a — 2280[18]

4 ch f Keen 11.1f **(58)** - Two Moons (Bold Lad (IRE)) 8.4f **(68)**
Form - 33700
Record 1998 - 1st:0 2nd:0 3rd:0 Ran:3
Pre1998 - 1st:0 2nd:1 3rd:3 Ran:11
Win Prizemoney £0 *Total Prizemoney* £1,706
1998 Turf 0-2: (8f, 10f) (gd, frm) 1998 AW 0-1: (7f) (Fibr)
Moderate filly, effective 10 to 11f, acted on gd - acted on Equi. Turf high 44. (DEAD)
**G F JohnsonHoughton [0-7] M B Clemence (from C W Thornton [0-7] Jly 1997).*

MICE IDEAS (IRE) BHB 73f RR 76f — 4463[5]

2 ch g Fayruz 6.6f **(63)** - Tender Encounter (Prince Tenderfoot (USA)) 9f **(61)**
Form - 747425
Record 1998 - 1st:0 2nd:1 3rd:0 Ran:6
Win Prizemoney £0 *Total Prizemoney* £923
1998 Turf 0-6: (6f, 7f 3, 8f 2) (gd, g-f, frm 4)
Above-average gelding, effective 7f, acts on frm. Turf high 74 - 2nd of 11 giving 2lb to Edmo Heights (16 Spt Beverley 7f frm RF 4301).
**S Mellor [0-6] Silver Knight Exhibitions Ltd.*

MICHANDRA BOY RR — 517[11]

5 b g Skyliner 6.8f **(51)** - Magdalene (IRE) (Runnett) 7f **(59)**
Form - 0
Record 1998 - 1st:0 2nd:0 3rd:0 Ran:1
1998 Turf 0-1: (8f) (g-s)
Currently very poor gelding, always wears blinkers - 11th of 11 giving 5lb to Amenixa (31 Mar Nottingham 8f g-s RF 0517).
**Martyn Wane [0-3] Mrs Margaret Robson.*

MICHELEE BHB 62f63a RR 39f 63a — 269[5]

3 b f Merdon Melody 6.8f **(56)** - Hsian (Shantung) 9.8f **(64)**
Form - 5
Record 1998 - 1st:0 2nd:0 3rd:0 Ran:1
Pre1998 - 1st:2 2nd:0 3rd:1 Ran:4
Win Prizemoney £3,969 *Total Prizemoney* £4,305
Wins * *1997 Jun Wolver (STD) S 6f 65+*
* *1997 Jun Wolver (STD) S 6f 70+* <
1998 AW 0-1: (7f) (Fibr)
Leggy, above-average filly. **P D Evans [2-5] John Pugh.*

MICKY DEE RR 7f — 4395[16]

2 ch c Lion Cavern (USA) 7.5f **(74)** - Bellagio (Busted) 10.2f **(61)**
Form - 0
Record 1998 - 1st:0 2nd:0 3rd:0 Ran:1
1998 Turf 0-1: (8f) (frm)
Currently very poor colt. **A P Jarvis [0-1] Mrs Ann Jarvis.*

MID AIR RR 23f — 4818[23]

2 ch f Midyan (USA) 9.9f **(64)** - Alnasr Jewel (USA) (Al Nasr (FR)) 9.3f **(68)**
Form - 0
Record 1998 - 1st:0 2nd:0 3rd:0 Ran:1
1998 Turf 0-1: (7f) (frm)
Currently little account filly. **W J Musson [0-1] Mrs N A Ward.*

MIDDAY COWBOY (USA) BHB 18f RR 34df — 144[7]

5 b g Houston (USA) 7.7f **(65)** - Perfect Isn't Easy (USA) (Saratoga Six (USA)) 7f **(73)**
Form - 007
Record 1998 - 1st:0 2nd:0 3rd:0 Ran:3
Pre1998 - 1st:0 2nd:1 3rd:1 Ran:14
Win Prizemoney £0 *Total Prizemoney* £1,849
1998 AW 0-3: (8f, 11f, 12f) (Fibr 3)
Very moderate gelding, has worn blinkers.
**G Woodward [0-3] Wetherby Racing Bureau 29 (from M D Hammond [0-7] Jly 1997).*

MIDDLE EAST BHB 51f72a RR 52f 72a — 4811[4]

5 b g Beveled (USA) 6.9f **(64)** - Godara (Bustino) 10.4f **(64)**
Form - 100686075034
Record 1998 - 1st:0 2nd:0 3rd:1 Ran:11
Pre1998 - 1st:5 2nd:1 3rd:4 Ran:25
Win Prizemoney £14,476 *Total Prizemoney* £18,655
Wins * *1997 Nov Southw (STD) H 6f 65 67* <
* 1997 Oct Nottin (SFT) 6.1f 66
* 1997 Spt Nottin (G-F) 6.1f 60
* 1996 Jly Redcar (G-F) H 6f 71 66
* 1995 Jly Redcar (FRM) 5f 64+
1998 Turf 0-11: (5f 3, 6f 8) (g-s, gd 3, g-f 3, frm 4)
Average gelding, effective 6f, acts on gd to frm - acts on Fibr, often wears blinkers (very effectively). Turf high 57.
**T D Barron [5-36] Mrs J Hazell.*

MIDHISH TWO (IRE) BHB 83f RR 74df — 4357[12]

2 b c Midhish - Tudor Loom (Sallust) 8.4f **(63)**
Form - 4140
Record 1998 - 1st:1 2nd:0 3rd:0 Ran:4
Win Prizemoney £3,517 *Total Prizemoney* £4,060
Wins * **1998** Jun Newcas (SFT) 6f 71+ <
1998 Turf 1-4: (5f 2, 6f 1-1, 7f) (g-s 1-1, g-f 2, frm)
Above-average colt. Turf high 74 (1st run) - 4th of 9 getting 4lb from Cheyenne Gold (1 Jun Windsor 5f g-f RF 1637) - also 1st of 5 from Ice (27 Jun Newcastle RF 2342).
**Sir Michael Stoute [1-4] Saeed Suhail.*

MIDNIGHT COOKIE BHB 27f42a RR 21f 42a — 2764[10]

5 b g Midyan (USA) 9.9f **(64)** - Midnight's Reward (Night Shift (USA)) 7.2f **(69)**
Form - 5088660
Record 1998 - 1st:0 2nd:0 3rd:0 Ran:7
Pre1998 - 1st:0 2nd:1 3rd:0 Ran:17
Win Prizemoney £0 *Total Prizemoney* £621
1998 Turf 0-6: (5f 6) (g-s 2, gd, g-f, frm 2) 1998 AW 0-1: (5f) (Equi)
Little account gelding. Turf high 21.
**R J Hodges [0-11] Ms S A Joyner (from B A Pearce [0-13] Nov 1996).*

MIDNIGHT DISPLAY (IRE) BHB 76f **RR 77?f** 1676[3]
2 b f Midhish - Eimkar (Junius (USA)) 7.7f **(65)**
Form - 4363
Record 1998 - 1st:0 2nd:0 3rd:2 Ran:4
Win Prizemoney £0 *Total Prizemoney* £2,535
1998 Turf 0-4: (5f 3, 6f) (sft, gd 2, g-f)
Above-average filly, has worn blinkers. Turf high 77.
**C A Dwyer [0-4] Mrs J Lawthom.*

MIDNIGHT ESCAPE BHB 106f **RR 110df** 4203[8]
5 b g Aragon 7.7f **(58)** - Executive Lady (Night Shift (USA)) 7.2f **(69)**
Form - 610508
Record 1998 - 1st:1 2nd:0 3rd:0 Ran:6
Pre1998 - 1st:5 2nd:1 3rd:2 Ran:17
Win Prizemoney £61,847 *Total Prizemoney* £72,271

Wins								
* 1998	May	Kempto	(GD)	L	5f		110	<
* 1997	Spt	Leopar	(GD)	G3	5f		99+	
* 1996	Oct	Newmar	(GD)	H	5f	91	89	
* 1996	Jun	Ascot	(G-F)	H	5f	89	91	
* 1996	May	Windso	(GD)	H	5f	82	87	
* 1995	Jun	Lingfi	(G-F)		5f			

1998 Turf 1-6: (5f 1-6) (gd 4, frm 1-2)
Group-class gelding, effective 5f, acts on sft to frm. Turf high 110 - 1st of 9 giving 15lb to Cortachy Castle (30 May Kempton RF 1592). He won a Listed race at Kempton in May, but struggled when stepped into Group events. It is likely to be a similar story next term. **C F Wall [6-23] Mervyn Ayers.*

MIDNIGHT GUEST (IRE) RR 50f 1263[16]
3 b c Brief Truce (USA) 9.1f **(73)** - Rhoman Ruby (IRE) (Rhoman Rule (USA))
Form - 0
Record 1998 - 1st:0 2nd:0 3rd:0 Ran:1
1998 Turf 0-1: (10f) (frm)
Currently fair colt. **L M Cumani [0-1] I Helou.*

MIDNIGHT LINE (USA) BHB 115f **RR 113f** 3256[3]
3 ch f Kris S (USA) 9.3f **(76)** - Midnight Air (USA) (Green Dancer (USA)) 10.3f **(74)**
Form - 1233
Record 1998 - 1st:1 2nd:1 3rd:2 Ran:4
Pre1998 - 1st:3 2nd:0 3rd:0 Ran:5
Win Prizemoney £58,035 *Total Prizemoney* £106,585

Wins							
* 1998	May	Newmar	(GD)	L	10f	113+	<
* 1997	Spt	Doncas	(G-F)	G3	8f	105	
* 1997	Aug	Goodwo	(G-F)	G3	7f	103	
* 1997	Jly	Goodwo	(G-F)		7f	83+	

1998 Turf 1-4: (10f 1-3, 12f) (gd 1-4)
Scopey, Group-class filly, effective 7 to 10f, best at 10f, acts on gd to frm, best on gd, excels at Goodwood. Turf high 113 (1st run) - 1st of 11 giving 2lb to Leggera (3 May Newmarket RF 0992). This admirable filly developed into a leading Oaks fancy after running away with the Pretty Polly Stakes on her reappearance. She failed to stay when finishing third at Epsom, but ran her usual game race and should develop into a top-class broodmare.
**H R A Cecil [4-9] H R H Prince Fahd Salman.*

MIDNIGHT ORCHID (IRE) BHB 73f **RR 73f** 3957[12]
2 b f Petardia 8.2f **(58)** - Rosa Van Fleet (Sallust) 8.4f **(63)**
Form - 22165250
Record 1998 - 1st:1 2nd:3 3rd:0 Ran:8
Win Prizemoney £3,468 *Total Prizemoney* £7,605
Wins * **1998** Jun Hamilt (G-S) 6f 68 <
1998 Turf 1-7: (5f, 6f 1-6) (gd 2, g-f 1-4, frm) 1998 AW 0-1: (6f) (Fibr)
Above-average filly, effective 6f, acts on gd to g-f - acts on Fibr. Turf high 73 - 2nd of 14 getting 9lb from My Petal (28 Jly Goodwood 6f gd RF 3166) - also 1st of 7 getting 6lb from Cover Girl (24 Jun Hamilton RF 2244). (1st run) - 5th of 11 giving 14lb to Kilbowie Hill (24 Jly Wolverhampton 6f Fibr RF 3093). Despite her undoubted ability, she has shown a tendency to swish her tail under pressure and should be treated with some caution.
**J Berry [1-8] T Herbert-Jackson.*

MIDNIGHT STING BHB 38f **RR 40f** 4338[13]
3 gr f Inchinor 8.9f **(64)** - Halvoya (Bay Express) 7.1f **(60)**
Form - 00000
Record 1998 - 1st:0 2nd:0 3rd:0 Ran:5
Pre1998 - 1st:0 2nd:0 3rd:0 Ran:3
1998 Turf 0-5: (7f 2, 8f, 9f, 10f) (gd, frm 4)
Scopey, moderate filly, has worn blinkers. Turf high 40.
**J R Jenkins [0-5] The West's Awake Racing Partnership (from M A Jarvis [0-3] Oct 1997).*

MIDNIGHT TIMES BHB 46f26a **RR 32f 26a** 445[12]
4 b f Timeless Times (USA) 6.1f **(56)** - Midnight Lass (Today and Tomorrow)
Form - 408000
Record 1998 - 1st:0 2nd:0 3rd:0 Ran:3
Pre1998 - 1st:0 2nd:0 3rd:1 Ran:10
Win Prizemoney £0 *Total Prizemoney* £466
1998 AW 0-3: (5f 2, 6f) (Equi 3)
Very moderate filly, effective 5f, - acts on AW, has worn blinkers, favours left handed tracks, favours tight tracks. AW high 17.
**D C O'Brien [0-13] Mrs V O'Brien.*

MIDNIGHT WATCH (USA) BHB 68f **RR 76?f** 5126[19]
4 b g Capote (USA) 9.1f **(84)** - Midnight Air (USA) (Green Dancer (USA)) 10.3f **(74)**
Form - 0
Record 1998 - 1st:0 2nd:0 3rd:0 Ran:1
Pre1998 - 1st:0 2nd:1 3rd:1 Ran:5
Win Prizemoney £0 *Total Prizemoney* £2,520
1998 Turf 0-1: (10f) (g-s)
Light-framed, above-average gelding.
**P Winkworth [0-2] The Knowl Hill Billies (from H R A Cecil [0-5] Oct 1997).*

MIDRUSH (IRE) RR 27f 1628[12]
2 b f Polish Patriot (USA) 7.8f **(70)** - Midushi (USA) **(59df)** (Trapp Mountain (USA))
Form - 0600
Record 1998 - 1st:0 2nd:0 3rd:0 Ran:4
1998 Turf 0-4: (5f 2, 6f 2) (g-s, gd, g-f, frm)
Little account filly, has worn blinkers. Turf high 27.
**J S Wainwright [0-4] J H Pickard.*

MIDSUMMER NIGHT (IRE) BHB 55f **RR 55f** 3809[5]
3 b f Fairy King (USA) 7.7f **(75)** - Villota (Top Ville) 11.7f **(68)**
Form - 60575
Record 1998 - 1st:0 2nd:0 3rd:0 Ran:5
Pre1998 - 1st:0 2nd:1 3rd:1 Ran:5
Win Prizemoney £0 *Total Prizemoney* £1,912
1998 Turf 0-5: (5f 2, 6f 3) (gd 3, g-f, frm)
Leggy, fair filly, effective 5f, acts on g-f to frm, best on g-f. Turf high 55. **R Hannon [0-10] G Howard-Spink.*

MIDSUMMER ROMANCE (IRE) BHB 54f **RR 52df** 4995[9]
3 b f Fairy King (USA) 7.7f **(75)** - Jealous One (USA) (Raise A Native) 11.2f **(69)**
Form - 800040
Record 1998 - 1st:0 2nd:0 3rd:0 Ran:6
Pre1998 - 1st:0 2nd:0 3rd:0 Ran:1
1998 Turf 0-6: (8f 4, 10f 2) (sft, g-s, gd, g-f, frm 2)
Scopey, fair filly. Turf high 58. **B J Meehan [0-7] Theo Waddington.*

MIDYAN BLUE (IRE) BHB 40f65a **RR 42?f 65a** 5118[10]
8 ch g Midyan (USA) 9.9f **(64)** - Jarretiere (Star Appeal) 9.6f **(65)**
Form - 068070
Record 1998 - 1st:0 2nd:0 3rd:0 Ran:6
Pre1998 - 1st:4 2nd:8 3rd:6 Ran:58
Win Prizemoney £22,522 *Total Prizemoney* £71,615

Wins							
1995	Jly	Sandow	(G-F)	H	14f	72	79
1995	May	York	(GD)	H	13.9f	70	76

1998 Turf 0-6: (13f 2, 14f 2, 16f 2) (g-s 2, gd 4)
Fair gelding, effective 14f, acts on gd to frm, has worn blinkers, likes right handed tracks. Turf high 52. Becoming disappointing. He is on a very long losing run, and is a light of former days.
**I Semple [0-6] Stephen McCluskey (from J M P Eustace [4-58] Oct 1997).*

MIDYAN CALL BHB 99f **RR 96f** 1380a[4]
4 b c Midyan (USA) 9.9f **(64)** - Early Call (Kind of Hush) 10.1f **(62)**
Form - 564
Record 1998 - 1st:0 2nd:0 3rd:0 Ran:3

Pre1998 - 1st:1 2nd:2 3rd:0 Ran:7
Win Prizemoney £3,622 *Total Prizemoney* £9,680
Wins * 1997 Aug Newmar (G-F) 6f 82 <
1998 Turf 0-3: (6f, 7f, 8f) (sft, gd 2)
Well made, very useful colt, effective 6 to 8f, acts on gd to frm. Turf high 96 - 4th of 9 to Plumbird (17 May Capannelle 6f gd RF 1380a). **M Bell [1-10] Luciano Gaucci.*

MIDYAN QUEEN BHB 52f RR 57f 4547[6]

4 b f Midyan (USA) 9.9f **(64)** - Queen of Aragon (Aragon) 8.1f **(60)**
Form - 60006
Record 1998 - 1st:0 2nd:0 3rd:0 Ran:5
Pre1998 - 1st:1 2nd:0 3rd:2 Ran:11
Win Prizemoney £4,123 *Total Prizemoney* £5,482
Wins * 1997 Jly Warwic (G-F) H 7f 60 60 <
1998 Turf 0-4: (7f 2, 8f 2) (g-s, g-f 2, frm) 1998 AW 0-1: (7f) (Fibr)
Light-framed, fair filly, has broken blood-vessels, effective 7f, acts on g-f, likes left handed tracks, likes tight tracks. Turf high 57. Inconsistent. **R Hollinshead [1-16] Mrs Charles Lockhart.*

MIGHTY MAGIC BHB 53f RR 58f 4887[5]

3 b f Magic Ring (IRE) 6.5f **(64)** - Mighty Flash (Rolfe (USA)) 12.1f **(65)**
Form - 08002424305
Record 1998 - 1st:0 2nd:2 3rd:1 Ran:11
Pre1998 - 1st:0 2nd:0 3rd:1 Ran:6
Win Prizemoney £0 *Total Prizemoney* £3,428
1998 Turf 0-11: (7f, 8f 2, 9f, 10f 3, 12f 2, 14f, 16f)(g-s, gd 4, g-f 2, frm 4)
Scopey, fair filly, has worn blinkers. Turf high 58. Consistent.
**D R C Elsworth [0-11] R J Tory (from Mrs P N Dutfield [0-6] Spt 1997).*

MIGRATE (USA) BHB 73f RR 73f 3278[11]

3 ch f Storm Bird (CAN) 8.5f **(82)** - Home Leave (USA) (Alydar (USA)) 9.1f **(76)**
Form - 10
Record 1998 - 1st:1 2nd:0 3rd:0 Ran:2
Pre1998 - 1st:0 2nd:0 3rd:0 Ran:3
Win Prizemoney £3,080 *Total Prizemoney* £3,299
Wins * **1998** Jly Yarmou (G-F) H 8f 68 73 <
1998 Turf 1-2: (8f 1-2) (g-f 1-1, frm)
Scopey, above-average filly. Turf high 73 (1st run) (began Jly) - 1st of 12 giving 13lb to Daintree (15 Jly Yarmouth RF 2835). She looked a bit of a madam as a juvenile, but scored at Yarmouth on her belated return. Disappointed next time.
**J H M Gosden [1-5] Sheikh Mohammed.*

MIGWAR BHB 85f RR 95df 5078[25]

5 b g Unfuwain (USA) 11.4f **(74)**- Pick of the Pops (High Top) 10.2f **(67)**
Form - 60
Record 1998 - 1st:0 2nd:0 3rd:0 Ran:2
Pre1998 - 1st:2 2nd:2 3rd:0 Ran:8
Win Prizemoney £20,607 *Total Prizemoney* £22,925
Wins 1996 May Redcar (G-F) H 10f 89 95 <
1996 May Doncas (G-F) H 10.3f 83 85+
1998 Turf 0-2: (8f, 12f) (sft 2)
Very useful gelding. Turf high 26 (began Oct). Inconsistent. The winner of the 1996 Zetland Gold Cup, he has been lightly raced in recent seasons and has obviously had a problem.
**N P Littmoden [0-2] P Sandrovitch (from L M Cumani [2-8] Spt 1997).*

MIHNAH (IRE) BHB 86f RR 95f 4645[6]

3 br f Lahib (USA) 8f **(69)** - Nafhaat (USA) (Roberto (USA)) 10f **(76)**
Form - 216
Record 1998 - 1st:1 2nd:1 3rd:0 Ran:3
Pre1998 - 1st:1 2nd:1 3rd:0 Ran:4
Win Prizemoney £14,467 *Total Prizemoney* £18,440
Wins * **1998** Spt Goodwo (G-F) 8f 83
1997 Oct York (SFT) 6f 85+ <
1998 Turf 1-3: (7f, 8f 1-2) (gd, g-f, frm 1-1)
Tall, very useful filly, effective 6 to 7f, acts on g-s to gd. Turf high 95 (1st run) (began Spt) - 2nd of 7 getting 5lb from Hujoom (11 Spt Goodwood 7f gd RF 4233). Did not reappear until September, and landed a classified stakes at Goodwood on her second run. Looked a progressive sort, but disappointed on her final start.
**M P Tregoning [1-3] Hamdan Al Maktoum (from D Morley [1-4] Oct 1997).*

MIJAS BHB 50f59a RR 48f 59a 2688[7]

5 ch m Risk Me (FR) 8f **(53)** - Out of Harmony (Song) 7.2f **(61)**
Form - 0473047
Record 1998 - 1st:0 2nd:0 3rd:1 Ran:4
Pre1998 - 1st:2 2nd:1 3rd:0 Ran:25
Win Prizemoney £6,759 *Total Prizemoney* £9,118
Wins * 1996 *Dec Lingfi (STD) H 5f 59 65+*
* 1996 May Lingfi (G-F) 6f 74 <
1998 Turf 0-4: (5f 3, 6f) (frm 4)
Fair filly, effective 5f, - acted on Equi, had worn blinkers, liked left handed tracks, liked tight tracks. Turf high 48. (DEAD)
**L MontagueHall [2-29] The Mijas Partnership.*

MIKE'S DOUBLE (IRE) BHB 53f56a RR 54df 56a 4936[18]

4 br g Cyrano de Bergerac 7.3f **(58)** - Glass Minnow (IRE) (Alzao (USA)) 7.1f **(68)**
Form - 84324663531271848068000040
Record 1998 - 1st:2 2nd:2 3rd:2 Ran:23
Pre1998 - 1st:1 2nd:3 3rd:5 Ran:20
Win Prizemoney £12,665 *Total Prizemoney* £19,380
Wins * **1998** May Thirsk (GD) H 6f 57 61
* **1998** *Apr Wolver (STD) H 7f 55 62 <*
1997 *Jly Wolver (STD) 6f 62 <*
1998 Turf 1-13: (6f 1-6, 7f 4, 8f 3) (g-s 2, gd 1-4, g-f 5, frm, hrd) 1998 AW 1-10: (6f 5, 7f 1-4, 8f) (Fibr 1-10)
Light-framed, fair gelding, effective 6 to 7f, best at 7f, acts on gd - acts on AW, best on Fibr, often wears blinkers, likes left handed tracks, likes tight tracks, excels at Wolverhampton. Turf high 61 - 1st of 23 getting 11lb from Night Flight (15 May Thirsk RF 1254). AW high 65 - 2nd of 12 giving 4lb to Sis Garden (25 Apr Wolverhampton 7f Fibr RF 0875) - also 1st of 12 from Sis Garden (11 Apr Wolverhampton RF 0650).
**Mrs N Macauley [2-20] The Posse (from Miss Gay Kelleway [1-15] Feb 1998).*

MIKE SIMMONS BHB 45f40a RR 37f 40a 4773[7]

2 b g Ballacashtal (CAN) 7.9f **(51)**-Lady Crusty(Golden Dipper) 6.5f **(42)**
Form - 77
Record 1998 - 1st:0 2nd:0 3rd:0 Ran:2
1998 Turf 0-2: (7f 2) (gd 2)
Currently very moderate gelding. Turf high 37 (began Spt).
**L P Grassick [0-2] L P Grassick.*

MILAD (IRE) BHB 66f RR 73f 3899[11]

3 b c Green Desert (USA) 7.8f **(78)** - Arctic Winter (CAN) (Briartic (CAN)) 9.5f **(84)**
Form - 0U0030
Record 1998 - 1st:0 2nd:0 3rd:1 Ran:6
Pre1998 - 1st:0 2nd:0 3rd:0 Ran:3
Win Prizemoney £0 *Total Prizemoney* £708
1998 Turf 0-6: (6f, 8f 2, 9f, 10f 2) (g-s, gd 3, g-f, frm)
Above-average colt. Turf high 73. Inconsistent.
**K Bell [0-2] Mrs Joyce Wood (from K Prendergast in IRE [0-7] Jun 1998).*

MILADY LILLIE (IRE) RR 61f 2777[6]

2 b f Distinctly North (USA) 7.4f **(63)** - Millingdale Lillie (Tumble Wind (USA)) 7.5f **(57)**
Form - 876
Record 1998 - 1st:0 2nd:0 3rd:0 Ran:3
1998 Turf 0-3: (6f 3) (gd, frm 2)
Currently average filly. Turf high 61. **K T Ivory [0-3] K T Ivory.*

MILDON (IRE) RR 51f 2929[8]

2 ch c Dolphin Street (FR) - Lycia (Targowice (USA)) 11.4f **(70)**
Form - 8
Record 1998 - 1st:0 2nd:0 3rd:0 Ran:1
1998 Turf 0-1: (7f) (frm)
Currently fair colt. **E Weymes [0-1] Don Raper.*

MILE A MINUTE (IRE) BHB 34f RR 33f 2673[11]

7 b g Lomond (USA) 9.9f **(74)** - Pass The Secret (CAN) (King's Bishop (USA)) 7.1f **(74)**
Form - 20
Record 1998 - 1st:0 2nd:1 3rd:0 Ran:2
Pre1998 - 1st:0 2nd:0 3rd:0 Ran:1
Win Prizemoney £0 *Total Prizemoney* £864

1998 Turf 0-2: (12f, 13f) (g-f 2)
Very moderate gelding, always wears blinkers. Turf high 33 (began Jly).
**J Neville [0-2] George Moore (from Michael Flynn in IRE [1-4] Jly 1996).*

MILETRIAN CARES (IRE) RR 54f 3630[14]

2 b f Hamas (IRE) 8f **(72)** - Goodnight Girl (IRE) (Alzao (USA)) 7.1f **(68)**
Form - 050
Record 1998 - 1st:0 2nd:0 3rd:0 Ran:3
1998 Turf 0-3: (5f, 6f 2) (g-f 2, frm)
Currently fair filly. Turf high 54. **M R Channon [0-3] Miletrian Plc.*

MILETRIAN CITY BHB 29f RR 32f 2561[7]

5 gr g Petong 7.6f **(58)** - Blueit (FR) (Bold Lad (IRE)) 8.4f **(68)**
Form - 086457
Record 1998 - 1st:0 2nd:0 3rd:0 Ran:6
Pre1998 - 1st:1 2nd:4 3rd:1 Ran:32
Win Prizemoney £2,605 *Total Prizemoney* £6,339
Wins 1996 Aug Carlis (FRM) C 6.9f 59 <
1998 Turf 0-6: (7f, 8f 4, 9f) (g-s, gd 3, g-f, frm)
Very moderate gelding, effective 8f, acts on gd to frm, mostly wears blinkers. Turf high 34. Consistent.
**Miss L A Perratt [0-13] T P Finch (from J Berry [1-28] Jun 1997).*

MILETRIAN REFURB (IRE) BHB 51f30a RR 27f 30a 721[11]

5 b br g Anita's Prince 6f **(62)** - Lady of Man (So Blessed) 8.7f **(67)**
Form - 070
Record 1998 - 1st:0 2nd:0 3rd:0 Ran:2
Pre1998 - 1st:2 2nd:4 3rd:0 Ran:19
Win Prizemoney £4,517 *Total Prizemoney* £7,881
Wins * 1996 Mar Newcas (G-S) S 6f 62
* 1995 Spt Bright (GD) S 5.3f 65 <
1998 Turf 0-1: (5f) (g-s) 1998 AW 0-1: (7f) (Equi)
Little account gelding. **M R Channon [2-21] Miletrian Plc.*

MILINKY BHB 40f RR 38f 3831[11]

2 b f Batshoof 9.5f **(66)** - Attila the Honey (Connaught) 7.7f **(63)**
Form - 450880
Record 1998 - 1st:0 2nd:0 3rd:0 Ran:6
1998 Turf 0-4: (5f 3, 6f) (g-f 3, frm) 1998 AW 0-2: (5f, 6f) (Fibr 2)
Very moderate filly, has worn blinkers. Turf high 38 (began Jly). AW high 18. **D Shaw [0-6] Paul Murphy.*

MILKY WAY BHB 29a RR 26f 29a 30[8]

4 b f Statoblest 6.4f **(63)** - Evening Star (Red Sunset) 8.2f **(63)**
Form - 608
Record 1998 - 1st:0 2nd:0 3rd:0 Ran:1
Pre1998 - 1st:0 2nd:0 3rd:0 Ran:4
1998 AW 0-1: (8f) (Equi)
Workmanlike, little account filly.
**S P C Woods [0-3] Mrs C T Bletsoe (from A Hide [0-2] Nov 1997).*

MILL AFRIQUE BHB 67f RR 71f 4505[5]

2 b f Mtoto 11.5f **(71)** - Milinetta (Milford) 9f **(61)**
Form - 075
Record 1998 - 1st:0 2nd:0 3rd:0 Ran:3
1998 Turf 0-3: (5f, 8f 2) (gd 2, g-f)
Currently above-average filly. Turf high 71.
**C E Brittain [0-3] R Meredith.*

MILL BAY SAM RR 26f 2176[8]

7 b g Lighter 9.5f **(36)** - Emancipated (Mansingh (USA)) 7.4f **(55)**
Form - 8
Record 1998 - 1st:0 2nd:0 3rd:0 Ran:1
1998 Turf 0-1: (16f) (gd)
Little account gelding. **R Dickin [0-3] David John Robbins.*

MILLEMAY BHB 20f RR 7f 3580[10]

8 br m Respect 5.7f **(44)** - Ravenscraig (Impecunious)
Form - 00000
Record 1998 - 1st:0 2nd:0 3rd:0 Ran:5
Pre1998 - 1st:0 2nd:0 3rd:0 Ran:12
Win Prizemoney £0 *Total Prizemoney* £503
1998 Turf 0-5: (5f, 6f 2, 7f, 8f) (gd 2, g-f, frm 2)
Very poor mare. Turf high 12.
**J S Goldie [0-7] D St Clair (from P Monteith [0-14] Jun 1996).*

MILL END QUEST BHB 53f RR 55f 4921[10]

3 b f King's Signet (USA) 7f **(51)** - Milva (Jellaby) 6.4f **(58)**
Form - 304760
Record 1998 - 1st:0 2nd:0 3rd:1 Ran:6
Pre1998 - 1st:1 2nd:0 3rd:0 Ran:9
Win Prizemoney £2,916 *Total Prizemoney* £3,728
Wins * 1997 Jly Mussel (GD) 5f 66 <
1998 Turf 0-6: (5f 4, 6f 2) (g-s, gd 4, frm)
Neat, fair filly, effective 5f, acts on g-f. Turf high 55 (began Aug).
**M W Easterby [1-15] W T Allgood.*

MILL END VENTURE (IRE) BHB 50f RR 40f 3137[12]

2 b c Namaqualand (USA) - Risk All (Run The Gantlet (USA)) 12.1f **(59)**
Form - 000
Record 1998 - 1st:0 2nd:0 3rd:0 Ran:3
1998 Turf 0-3: (5f, 6f 2) (gd, frm 2)
Currently moderate colt. Turf high 40 (began Jly).
**M W Easterby [0-3] W T Allgood.*

MILLESIME (IRE) BHB 38f RR 40f 3681[8]

6 ch g Glow (USA) 10.2f **(61)** - Persian Myth (Persian Bold) 9.3f **(66)**
Form - 5066508
Record 1998 - 1st:0 2nd:0 3rd:0 Ran:7
Pre1998 - 1st:2 2nd:2 3rd:2 Ran:22
Win Prizemoney £6,285 *Total Prizemoney* £9,695
Wins 1995 Jly Bath (FRM) 5.1f 64
1995 Jly Chepst (G-F) 5.1f 66 <
1998 Turf 0-7: (5f 5, 6f 2) (g-s, gd 3, g-f, frm 2)
Moderate gelding, effective 6f, acts on gd, has worn blinkers. Turf high 42.
**Martyn Wane [0-12] Mrs P E Edmondson (from B Hanbury [2-17] Spt 1996).*

MILLING (IRE) BHB 81f RR 80f 4740[7]

3 b f In The Wings 11.2f **(77)** - Princess Pati (Top Ville) 11.7f **(68)**
Form - 52231687
Record 1998 - 1st:1 2nd:2 3rd:1 Ran:8
Pre1998 - 1st:0 2nd:0 3rd:0 Ran:1
Win Prizemoney £5,303 *Total Prizemoney* £7,917
Wins * **1998** Aug Hamilt (SFT) H 9.2f 77 80 <
1998 Turf 1-8: (8f, 9f 1-2, 10f 3, 12f 2) (g-s 3, gd 1-4, g-f)
Workmanlike, decent filly, effective 9 to 10f, acts on gd. Turf high 80 - 1st of 9 getting 2lb from Buzz (1 Aug Hamilton RF 3265). A half-sister to Pasternak, she had shown ability before getting off the mark in a Hamilton handicap, and looks well suited by give in the ground. **R Guest [1-9] C J Mills.*

MILLIONFORMERTHYR BHB 43f43a RR 59f 43a 5004[13]

2 b f Mon Tresor 7.9f **(60)** - Regal Salute (Dara Monarch) 8.8f **(59)**
Form - 632U37000
Record 1998 - 1st:0 2nd:1 3rd:2 Ran:9
Win Prizemoney £0 *Total Prizemoney* £1,127
1998 Turf 0-6: (5f 2, 6f, 7f 2, 8f) (sft, gd 2, g-f 2, frm) 1998 AW 0-3: (6f 3) (Fibr 3)
Fair filly, effective 6 to 7f, acts on gd - acts on Fibr, has worn blinkers. Turf high 59 - 3rd of 16 to Annie Apple (27 Aug Folkestone 7f gd RF 3897). AW high 55 (1st run) (began Jly) - 2nd of 8 getting 2lb from Lady Peppiatt (17 Jly Southwell 6f Fibr RF 2897). Becoming disappointing. **B Palling [0-9] Merthyr Motor Auctions.*

MILLISCENT BHB 53f RR 56f 4916[8]

2 b f Primo Dominie 7.2f **(67)** - Millaine (Formidable (USA)) 9.2f **(63)**
Form - 708
Record 1998 - 1st:0 2nd:0 3rd:0 Ran:3
1998 Turf 0-3: (6f 2, 7f) (g-s, frm 2)
Currently fair filly. Turf high 56 (began Aug).
**J Berry [0-3] T G & Mrs M E Holdcroft.*

MILLITRIX BHB 72f RR 77f 1791[9]

3 br f Doyoun 10.7f **(69)** - Galatrix (Be My Guest (USA)) 9.3f **(67)**
Form - 40
Record 1998 - 1st:0 2nd:0 3rd:0 Ran:2
Pre1998 - 1st:0 2nd:1 3rd:0 Ran:2
Win Prizemoney £0 *Total Prizemoney* £1,705
1998 Turf 0-2: (7f, 8f) (gd, hrd)
Unfurnished, above-average filly. Turf high 65.
**Sir Michael Stoute [0-4] Mrs G A E Smith.*

MILNE'S DREAM BHB 55f **RR 58f** 5004[3]
2 b f Reprimand 8.2f **(63)** - Milne's Way (The Noble Player (USA)) 6.5f **(67)**
Form - 7073
Record 1998 - 1st:0 2nd:0 3rd:1 Ran:4
Win Prizemoney £0 *Total Prizemoney* £278
1998 Turf 0-4: (5f 2, 6f 2) (sft, g-s, gd, g-f)
Fair filly. Turf high 58 (began Spt). **G Lewis [0-4] T P Milne.*

MILNGAVIE (IRE) BHB 30f33a **RR 37?f 33a** 308[6]
8 ch g Pharly (FR) 11.5f **(64)** - Wig And Gown (Mandamus) 12.6f **(56)**
Form - 0P66
Record 1998 - 1st:0 2nd:0 3rd:0 Ran:4
Pre1998 - 1st:10 2nd:16 3rd:15 Ran:82
Win Prizemoney £27,638 *Total Prizemoney* £49,941
Wins 1996 *Jly Wolver (STD) H* *16.2f 42 47*
1996 *Jan Lingfi (STD) H* *16f 29 39*
1995 Nov Folkes (G-F) CH 16.4f 26 37
1994 *Mar Wolver (STD) H* *14.8f 65 69* <
1994 *Feb Lingfi (STD) H* *16f 58 65+*
1994 *Jan Wolver (STD) H* *14.8f 48 55*
1994 *Jan Wolver (STD) H* *16f 48 53*
1998 AW 0-4: (12f, 13f, 15f, 16f) (Equi 3, Fibr)
Very moderate gelding, has worn blinkers. AW high 11. Becoming disappointing.
**B J McMath [0-4] Mrs Lisa Olley (from B Smart [1-4] Jly 1996).*

MILTON BHB 68f65a **RR 71f 65a** 418[6]
5 ch g Groom Dancer (USA) 9.5f **(75)** - Gold Flair (Tap On Wood) 10.3f **(65)**
Form - 56
Record 1998 - 1st:0 2nd:0 3rd:0 Ran:2
Pre1998 - 1st:0 2nd:1 3rd:1 Ran:3
Win Prizemoney £0 *Total Prizemoney* £1,723
1998 AW 0-2: (8f, 11f) (Fibr 2)
Above-average gelding. AW high 54.
**Mrs A Swinbank [0-2] Mrs Julie Martin (from P F I Cole [0-3] Jly 1996).*

MI'LUD BHB 52f **RR 48f** 1943[6]
3 ch g Dilum (USA) 7.1f **(56)** - Miellita (King Emperor (USA)) 9.4f **(58)**
Form - 056
Record 1998 - 1st:0 2nd:0 3rd:0 Ran:3
1998 Turf 0-2: (6f, 10f) (g-f, frm) 1998 AW 0-1: (8f) (Fibr)
Scopey, currently moderate gelding. Turf high 48.
**T J Etherington [0-3] J C Smith.*

MIMOSA BHB 48f52a **RR 49f 52a** 1788[3]
5 ch m Midyan (USA) 9.9f **(64)** - Figini (Glint of Gold) 9.3f **(66)**
Form - 4543
Record 1998 - 1st:0 2nd:0 3rd:1 Ran:4
Pre1998 - 1st:1 2nd:3 3rd:2 Ran:34
Win Prizemoney £2,735 *Total Prizemoney* £9,282
Wins 1996 Jun Salisb (G-F) H 8f 50 52 <
1998 Turf 0-4: (8f, 10f, 12f 2) (sft 2, frm, hrd)
Fair filly, effective 8 to 10f, best at 8f, acts on g-f to frm - acts on Equi, has worn blinkers. Turf high 51.
**M Pitman [0-8] Just Good Fun Club (from S Dow [1-29] Spt 1997).*

MINDANAO **RR 54f** 4812[7]
2 b f Most Welcome 8.6f **(66)** - Salala (Connaught) 7.7f **(63)**
Form - 7
Record 1998 - 1st:0 2nd:0 3rd:0 Ran:1
1998 Turf 0-1: (7f) (gd)
Currently fair filly. **Miss J A Camacho [0-1] Mrs S Camacho.*

MINDRACE BHB 48f **RR 49f** 3036[7]
5 b g Tina's Pet 7.4f **(56)** - High Velocity (Frimley Park) 6.5f **(67)**
Form - 08857
Record 1998 - 1st:0 2nd:0 3rd:0 Ran:5
Pre1998 - 1st:2 2nd:2 3rd:1 Ran:32
Win Prizemoney £10,087 *Total Prizemoney* £13,711
Wins * 1997 Jly Sandow (G-F) H 5f 59 61
* 1996 Jly Bath (FRM) H 5.1f 59 67 <
1998 Turf 0-5: (5f 4, 6f) (g-f, frm 4)
Moderate gelding, effective 5 to 6f, best at 5f, acts on gd to frm, best on frm, has worn blinkers. Turf high 49. Consistent.
**K T Ivory [2-37] D F Abbott.*

MINETTA **RR 75f** 4062[5]
3 ch f Mujtahid (USA) 7.4f **(69)** - Minwah (USA) (Diesis) 9.3f **(69)**
Form - 60042112355
Record 1998 - 1st:2 2nd:2 3rd:1 Ran:11
Pre1998 - 1st:1 2nd:0 3rd:1 Ran:6
Win Prizemoney £14,756 *Total Prizemoney* £19,311
Wins *** 1998** Jly Bath (GD) 8f 75 <
*** 1998** Jly Newmar (FRM) H 8f 68 74
* 1997 May Carlis (FRM) 5.9f 66
1998 Turf 2-11: (7f 2, 8f 2-7, 10f 2) (gd 1-4, g-f 4, frm 1-3)
Scopey, above-average filly, effective 7 to 8f, best at 8f, acts on gd to frm, has worn blinkers. Turf high 75 - 1st of 6 getting 9lb from Sovereigns Court (16 Jly Bath RF 2842) - also 1st of 10 getting 25lb from Plan-B (9 Jly Newmarket RF 2652). Consistent. She took time to find her form this season but did well in the summer, beating a decent field at Newmarket and following up with a narrow victory in a classified stakes at Bath. Has hung left on occasions.
**M Bell [3-17] Mrs G Rowland-Clark.*

MINI LODGE (IRE) BHB 92f **RR 87f** 4706[2]
2 ch c Grand Lodge (USA) - Mirea (USA) (The Minstrel (CAN)) 10f **(72)**
Form - 1722
Record 1998 - 1st:1 2nd:2 3rd:0 Ran:4
Win Prizemoney £3,208 *Total Prizemoney* £7,532
Wins *** 1998** Jly Newcas (G-F) 7f 78+ <
1998 Turf 1-4: (7f 1-3, 8f) (sft 2, gd 1-1, frm)
Useful colt. Turf high 87 (began Jly) - also 1st of 4 from Al Waffi (25 Jly Newcastle RF 3113).
**J G FitzGerald [1-4] Marquesa de Moratalla.*

MINIVET **RR 80f** 5062[2]
3 b g Midyan (USA) 9.9f **(64)** - Bronzewing (Beldale Flutter (USA)) 9.7f **(71)**
Form - 0232133622
Record 1998 - 1st:1 2nd:4 3rd:3 Ran:10
Pre1998 - 1st:0 2nd:0 3rd:1 Ran:1
Win Prizemoney £3,650 *Total Prizemoney* £12,820
Wins * **1998** Aug Redcar (G-F) 9f 44+ <
1998 Turf 1-10: (8f 2, 9f 1-3, 10f 3, 12f 2) (sft, gd 2, g-f 3, frm 1-4)
Neat, decent gelding, effective 8 to 12f, best at 10f, acts on gd to frm, best on gd, prefers left handed tracks, likes tight tracks. Turf high 80 - 2nd of 15 to Night City (8 Oct York 10f frm RF 4708). He had shown ability before landing an awful maiden at Redcar in August. He was 1/16 there but was not exactly impressive, and his subsequent efforts have suggested that he needs a greater test of stamina. **M Bell [1-11] Sir Thomas Pilkington.*

MINJARA BHB 48f **RR 45f** 4588[18]
3 b c Beveled (USA) 6.9f **(64)** - Honey Mill (Milford) 9f **(61)**
Form - 70000
Record 1998 - 1st:0 2nd:0 3rd:0 Ran:5
Pre1998 - 1st:0 2nd:0 3rd:0 Ran:2
1998 Turf 0-5: (7f 2, 8f, 10f, 14f) (gd 4, frm)
Workmanlike, moderate colt. Turf high 77.
**J G Smyth-Osbourne [0-2] Mrs V Youell (from A P Jones [0-5] May 1998).*

MINNESOTA BHB 73f **RR 91f** 4845[7]
2 b c Danehill (USA) 9.1f **(79)**- Santi Sana (Formidable (USA)) 9.2f **(63)**
Form - 321160087
Record 1998 - 1st:2 2nd:1 3rd:1 Ran:9
Win Prizemoney £7,605 *Total Prizemoney* £9,068
Wins *** 1998** Jly Newmar (G-F) H 7f 91 <
*** 1998** *Jun Southw (STD)* *7f* *78*
1998 Turf 1-8: (6f 4, 7f 1-1, 8f 3) (gd 2, g-f 2, frm 1-4) 1998 AW 1-1: (7f 1-1) (Fibr 1-1)
Useful colt, effective 7f, acts on frm, has worn blinkers. Turf high 91 - 1st of 7 giving 18lb to Tampa Lady (24 Jly Newmarket RF 3077). (1st run). He got off the mark with a battling victory on the Southwell Fibresand in June, and followed up with a fine victory under top weight in a Newmarket nursery, coming fast and late to snatch the race on the line. He seemed to lose his form after that but did not run badly in a Newmarket nursery on his final start.
**N A Callaghan [2-9] M Tabor & Mrs John Magnier.*

MINNISAM BHB 47f **RR 48f** 2974[5]
5 ch g Niniski (USA) 13.2f **(67)** - Wise Speculation (USA) (Mr

Prospector (USA)) 8.8f **(78)**
Form - 635
Record 1998 - 1st:0 2nd:0 3rd:1 Ran:3
Pre1998 - 1st:1 2nd:1 3rd:1 Ran:10
Win Prizemoney £2,381 *Total Prizemoney* £4,492
Wins 1996 Jly Folkes (FRM) H 12f 65 71 <
1998 Turf 0-3: (12f, 14f, 17f) (gd 2, g-f)
Moderate gelding, has worn blinkers. Turf high 48 (began Jly). Consistent.
**G A Ham [0-3] Mike Cornish (from J L Dunlop [1-10] Aug 1996).*

MINORITY RR 101f 4470b[3]
3 ch f Generous (IRE) 11.5f **(82)** - Minskip (USA) (The Minstrel (CAN)) 10f **(72)**
Form - 36243
1998 Turf 0-5: (11f 2, 12f, 13f, 14f) (sft 2, gd 2, g-f)
Very useful filly. Turf high 101. She was caught close home in a Group Three at Deauville in July but, that apart, failed to threaten in smart company. **P Bary in FR [0-5] K Abdulla.*

MINT CONDITION BHB 33f21a **RR 31f 21a** 97[11]
4 ch g Superlative 8.8f **(57)** - Penny Mint (Mummy's Game) 8.2f **(60)**
Form - 000
Record 1998 - 1st:0 2nd:0 3rd:0 Ran:2
Pre1998 - 1st:0 2nd:0 3rd:0 Ran:4
1998 AW 0-2: (6f, 8f) (Fibr 2)
Leggy, very moderate gelding.
**Don Enrico Incisa [0-3] Don Enrico Incisa (from Mrs L Stubbs [0-3] Spt 1996).*

MINTY RR 20f 5145[10]
2 b c Be My Chief (USA) 10.2f **(62)** - Mindomica (Dominion) 8.5f **(63)**
Form - 0
Record 1998 - 1st:0 2nd:0 3rd:0 Ran:1
1998 Turf 0-1: (8f) (gd)
Currently little account colt.
**C W Thornton [0-1] Ailsa Daniels & Guy Reed.*

MI PICASSO (IRE) BHB 45f **RR 40f** 4338[18]
3 ch g Be My Guest (USA) 10.2f **(66)** - Blue Infanta (Chief Singer) 8.9f **(66)**
Form - 7050
Record 1998 - 1st:0 2nd:0 3rd:0 Ran:4
Pre1998 - 1st:0 2nd:0 3rd:0 Ran:1
1998 Turf 0-4: (7f, 8f 2, 11f) (g-f 3, frm)
Moderate gelding. Turf high 40.
**M H Tompkins [0-4] Michael Keogh (from J S Bolger in IRE [0-1] Jly 1997).*

MIRACLE ISLAND BHB 74f75a **RR 74f 75a** 829[4]
3 b c Jupiter Island 10.4f **(57)** - Running Game (Run The Gantlet (USA)) 12.1f **(59)**
Form - 22144
Record 1998 - 1st:1 2nd:2 3rd:0 Ran:5
Win Prizemoney £3,468 *Total Prizemoney* £5,395
Wins * 1998 *Feb Wolver (STD) 9.4f 73* <
1998 Turf 0-1: (10f) (g-s) 1998 AW 1-4: (9f 1-2, 11f 2) (Fibr 1-4)
Neat, above-average colt, has worn blinkers. AW high 73 - 1st of 10 getting 16lb from Western Sonata (18 Feb Wolverhampton RF 0307). He won a maiden at Wolverhampton in February, but has looked to have a bit of temperament on more than one occasion. He is best left alone. **D R Loder [1-5] Mrs P T Fenwick.*

MIRACULOUS GUEST RR 69f 4389[7]
2 b f Be My Guest (USA) 10.2f **(66** - Mystery Ship (Decoy Boy) 6.7f **(56)**
Form - 67
Record 1998 - 1st:0 2nd:0 3rd:0 Ran:2
1998 Turf 0-2: (7f 2) (g-f, frm)
Currently average filly. Turf high 69 (began Spt).
**M Kettle [0-2] B H Simpson.*

MIRAGGIO RR 29f 5138[16]
2 b c Alhijaz 7.7f **(57)** - Doppio (Dublin Taxi) 6.4f **(55)**
Form - 0
Record 1998 - 1st:0 2nd:0 3rd:0 Ran:1
1998 Turf 0-1: (7f) (gd)
Currently very moderate colt.
**H Morrison [0-1] The Summerdown Partnership.*

MIRARIMA (IRE) RR 81f 4801[1]
3 ch f Shernazar 11.8f **(71)** - Mirana (IRE) (Ela-Mana-Mou) 10.1f **(70)**
Form - 71
Record 1998 - 1st:1 2nd:0 3rd:0 Ran:2
Win Prizemoney £3,680 *Total Prizemoney* £3,680
Wins * 1998 Oct Haydoc (SFT) 11.9f 81 <
1998 Turf 1-2: (8f, 12f 1-1) (sft 1-1, frm)
Leggy, currently decent filly. Turf high 81 (began Spt) - 1st of 10 getting 5lb from Bombastic (14 Oct Haydock RF 4801). Decisive winner of a back-end maiden. **L M Cumani [1-2] H H Aga Khan.*

MIRBECK (USA) RR 65f 4189[8]
2 ch f Gone West (USA) 7.8f **(82)** - Oakmead (IRE) (Lomond (USA)) 8.8f **(65)**
Form - 8
Record 1998 - 1st:0 2nd:0 3rd:0 Ran:1
1998 Turf 0-1: (6f) (gd)
Currently average filly.
**P W Chapple-Hyam [0-1] Mrs B V Sangster & B V Sangster.*

MIRY LEADER BHB 40f **RR 47f** 2566[3]
5 ch m Polar Falcon (USA) 9f **(74)** - Mrs Leader (USA) (Mr Leader (USA)) 9.8f **(66)**
Form - 703
Record 1998 - 1st:0 2nd:0 3rd:1 Ran:3
Win Prizemoney £0 *Total Prizemoney* £315
1998 Turf 0-3: (10f 3) (gd 2, g-f)
Moderate filly. Turf high 47. **Mrs J Cecil [0-6] Mrs M Slater.*

MISALLIANCE RR 73f 4759[7]
3 ch f Elmaamul (USA) 8.1f **(70)** - Cabaret Artiste (Shareef Dancer (USA)) 9.9f **(73)**
Form - 00568357
Record 1998 - 1st:0 2nd:0 3rd:1 Ran:8
Pre1998 - 1st:1 2nd:0 3rd:0 Ran:4
Win Prizemoney £2,239 *Total Prizemoney* £3,001
Wins * 1997 Oct Newcas (G-F) 7f 71+ <
1998 Turf 0-8: (8f 5, 9f, 10f, 11f) (g-s, gd 3, g-f, frm 3)
Scopey, above-average filly, effective 7 to 8f, acts on gd. Turf high 73 - 5th of 12 giving 1lb to Mustique Dream (8 Jun Nottingham 8f gd RF 1803). **C F Wall [1-12] The Lively Partners.*

MISBAH (USA) RR 98f 3946[6]
3 b c Gilded Time (USA) 7f **(76)** - For Dixie (USA) (Dixieland Band (USA)) 7f **(74)**
Form - 20106
Record 1998 - 1st:1 2nd:1 3rd:0 Ran:5
Pre1998 - 1st:1 2nd:1 3rd:0 Ran:3
Win Prizemoney £11,906 *Total Prizemoney* £16,702
Wins * 1998 Jly Newmar (G-F) H 6f 92 98 <
* 1997 Oct Yarmou (GD) 7f 91
1998 Turf 1-5: (6f 1-1, 7f 2, 8f 2) (gd, g-f 3, frm 1-1)
Scopey, very useful colt, effective 6 to 8f, best at 8f, acts on gd to frm. Turf high 98 (1st run) - 2nd of 4 getting 9lb from Sharp Play (16 May Thirsk 8f g-f RF 1275) - also 1st of 15 giving 9lb to Second Wind (7 Jly Newmarket RF 2582). He chased home Swiss Guineas winner Sharp Play at Thirsk on his reappearance, and was not beaten far in the Britannia. However, he was more impressive when brought back to six furlongs at Newmarket, but had the draw against him over seven at Ascot. Might need to drop a few pounds. **B Hanbury [2-8] Hamdan Al Maktoum.*

MISCONDUCT BHB 48f51a **RR 47+f 51a** 4589[4]
4 gr f Risk Me (FR) 8f **(53)** - Grey Cree (Creetown) 6.9f **(50)**
Form - 3235802151104
Record 1998 - 1st:3 2nd:1 3rd:0 Ran:10
Pre1998 - 1st:0 2nd:1 3rd:2 Ran:7
Win Prizemoney £7,640 *Total Prizemoney* £10,120
Wins * 1998 *Aug Lingfi (STD) H 10f 42 48+* <
*** 1998** Jly Bath (GD) H 10.2f 44 47+
*** 1998** Jun Salisb (G-F) H 9.9f 39 42
1998 Turf 2-6: (8f, 10f 2-4, 11f) (gd 2-4, g-f, frm) 1998 AW 1-4: (7f 2, 8f, 10f 1-1) (Equi 1-1, Fibr 3)
Lengthy, moderate filly, effective 7 to 10f, best at 10f, acts on gd - acts on Equi, likes left handed tracks, favours tight tracks, excels

at Lingfield. Turf high 47 - 1st of 15 from Mighty Magic (16 Jly Bath RF 2845) - also 1st of 18 getting 6lb from Polonaise Prince (25 Jun Salisbury RF 2280). AW high 48 - 1st of 11 giving 7lb to Sassy (1 Aug Lingfield RF 3272). Consistent. She looked only very modest until suddenly finding her form in the summer, winning twice on Turf and once on Equitrack. Ten furlongs looks to be her trip.

**G L Moore [3-17] Miss Samantha Sykes.*

MISKIN HEIGHTS (IRE) BHB 44f23a **RR 50f 23a** 4648^{12}

4 ch f Sharp Victor (USA) 10f **(56)** - Nurse Jo (USA) (J O Tobin (USA)) 9.4f **(67)**

Form - 687241130800

Record 1998 - 1st:2 2nd:1 3rd:1 Ran:10
Pre1998 - 1st:0 2nd:0 3rd:0 Ran:8

Win Prizemoney £6,166 *Total Prizemoney* £7,375

Wins * **1998** Jun Warwic (GD) H 8f 47 50 <
* **1998** May Bright (FRM) H 8f 41 49

1998 Turf 2-9: (8f 2-8, 10f) (g-s 1-1, gd 1-4, g-f 2, frm 2) 1998 AW 0-1: (9f) (Fibr)

Scopey, fair filly, effective 8 to 10f, best at 8f, acts on g-s to gd, best on gd, prefers left handed tracks. Turf high 50 - 1st of 16 from Up in Flames (3 Jun Warwick RF 1709) - also 1st of 13 getting 24lb from Out Line (22 May Brighton RF 1387).

**K R Burke [2-18] Brooknight Guarding Ltd.*

MISLEADING LADY **RR 62f** 2455^{5}

3 b f Warning 8.1f **(77)** - Much Too Risky (Bustino) 10.4f **(64)**

Form - 05

Record 1998 - 1st:0 2nd:0 3rd:0 Ran:2

1998 Turf 0-2: (8f, 11f) (g-f, frm)

Scopey, currently average filly. Turf high 62.

**Sir Michael Stoute [0-2] J M Greetham.*

MISLEMANI (IRE) BHB 40f29a **RR 41f 29a** 4234^{19}

8 b g Kris 10f **(75)** - Meis El-Reem (Auction Ring (USA)) 8.6f **(65)**

Form - 0735070

Record 1998 - 1st:0 2nd:0 3rd:1 Ran:5
Pre1998 - 1st:2 2nd:5 3rd:11 Ran:47

Win Prizemoney £8,009 *Total Prizemoney* £17,743

Wins * 1997 Jun Bath (GD) CH 8f 47 54
* 1995 Jly Epsom (GD) H 7f 51 59 <

1998 Turf 0-1: (8f) (gd) 1998 AW 0-4: (8f, 10f 2, 11f) (Equi 3, Fibr)

Moderate gelding, effective 8f, acts on gd. AW high 33.

**A G Newcombe [2-41] Mrs Pamela Cann (from Lady Herries [0-10] Spt 1994).*

MISMEWMEW BHB 42f44a **RR 39f 44a** 4865^{7}

3 b f Weldnaas (USA) 8.4f **(55)** - Joan's Gift (Doulab (USA)) 9.8f **(65)**

Form - 4400747

Record 1998 - 1st:0 2nd:0 3rd:0 Ran:7
Pre1998 - 1st:0 2nd:0 3rd:0 Ran:2

1998 Turf 0-4: (8f 3, 10f) (sft, g-f, frm 2) 1998 AW 0-3: (7f, 8f 2) (Equi 2, Fibr)

Unfurnished, moderate filly. Turf high 39. AW high 46.

**L A Dace [0-3] Eddie Davess (from C J Benstead [0-6] Jly 1998).*

MISPRINT BHB 54f **RR 61f** 4471^{10}

2 b f Minshaanshu Amad (USA) 11.3f **(53)** - Miss Copyforce (Aragon) 8.1f **(60)**

Form - 06550

Record 1998 - 1st:0 2nd:0 3rd:0 Ran:5

1998 Turf 0-5: (5f 3, 6f 2) (g-f 2, frm 3)

Average filly. Turf high 61 (began Jly).

**E A Wheeler [0-5] Benham Racing.*

MISS ALL ALONE BHB 48f50a **RR 50f 50a** 2654^{2}

3 ch f Crofthall 8.6f **(54)** - Uninvited (Be My Guest (USA)) 9.3f **(67)**

Form - 63252232

Record 1998 - 1st:0 2nd:4 3rd:2 Ran:8
Pre1998 - 1st:0 2nd:0 3rd:0 Ran:1

Win Prizemoney £0 *Total Prizemoney* £4,223

1998 Turf 0-5: (7f, 8f 4) (sft, g-s, gd 2, g-f)1998 AW 0-3:(7f, 8f 2)(Fibr 3)

Scopey, fair filly, effective 7 to 8f, best at 8f, acts on gd to g-f - acts on Fibr, has worn blinkers, prefers left handed tracks, prefers tight tracks. Turf high 50 - 3rd of 18 getting 23lb from Sunstreak (4 Jly Nottingham 8f g-f RF 2544). AW high 49 - 2nd of 15 getting 8lb from Hunt Hill (5 Jun Southwell 8f Fibr RF 1763). Consistent.

**J A Glover [0-9] Countrywide Classics Ltd.*

MISS AMANPURI BHB 93f **RR 90f** 4207^{9}

2 b f Alzao(USA) 9.8f **(73)**- Miss Rinjani **(88f)**(Shirley Heights)10.3f **(74)**

Form - 5410

Record 1998 - 1st:1 2nd:0 3rd:0 Ran:4

Win Prizemoney £4,110 *Total Prizemoney* £4,845

Wins * **1998** Aug Newmar (G-F) 7f 90 <

1998 Turf 1-4: (6f, 7f 1-2, 8f) (gd 2, frm 1-2)

Useful filly. Turf high 90 (began Jly) - 1st of 18 from Subito (28 Aug Newmarket RF 3926). Paid her Goodwood conqueror Bionic a compliment when beating a big field of maidens at Newmarket on her third start, but showed nothing in the May Hill on her final outing.

**G Wragg [1-4] J L C Pearce.*

MISS ARCH (IRE) BHB 49f **RR 59f** 4934^{17}

2 ch f Archway (IRE) 8.5f **(60)** - Zanskar (Godswalk (USA)) 7.3f **(58)**

Form - 0050

Record 1998 - 1st:0 2nd:0 3rd:0 Ran:4

1998 Turf 0-4: (6f, 7f, 8f, 9f) (gd, frm 3)

Fair filly. Turf high 59 (began Spt).

**Miss J F Craze [0-1] Robert Cook (from G R Oldroyd [0-3] Spt 1998).*

MISS BANANAS BHB 43f57a **RR 22f 57a** 4921^{20}

3 b f Risk Me (FR) 8f **(53)** - Astrid Gilberto (Runnett) 7f **(59)**

Form - 4324100000

Record 1998 - 1st:1 2nd:1 3rd:0 Ran:8
Pre1998 - 1st:0 2nd:1 3rd:1 Ran:6

Win Prizemoney £3,355 *Total Prizemoney* £5,023

Wins 1998 *Feb Lingfi (SLW) H 5f 58 63* <

1998 Turf 0-3:(5f 3) (g-s, gd, frm)1998 AW 1-5:(5f 1-5) (Equi 1-3, Fibr 2)

Neat, moderate filly, effective 5f, - acts on Equi, likes left handed tracks, likes tight tracks. Turf high 21 (began Aug). AW high 63 - 1st of 5 getting 25lb from Vista Alegre (21 Feb Lingfield RF 0332). Becoming disappointing. She had made the frame several times on sand, but did not get off the mark until taking a handicap over the minimum on the Lingfield Equitrack in February. She did not reproduce that effort after.

**C N Kellett [0-2] W Meah (from T T Bill [1-12] Aug 1998).*

MISS BUSSELL BHB 59f **RR 60f** 2544^{5}

3 ch f Sabrehill (USA) 8.5f **(64)** - Reel Foyle (USA) (Irish River (FR)) 8.6f **(78)**

Form - 4502155

Record 1998 - 1st:1 2nd:1 3rd:0 Ran:7
Pre1998 - 1st:0 2nd:0 3rd:0 Ran:1

Win Prizemoney £2,290 *Total Prizemoney* £3,168

Wins * **1998** Jun Hamilt (SFT) 8.3f 59 <

1998 Turf 1-6: (8f 1-5, 10f) (g-s, gd 1-1, g-f, frm 3) 1998 AW 0-1: (8f) (Equi)

Unfurnished, average filly, effective 8f, acts on gd to frm. Turf high 60 - 2nd of 14 giving 12lb to Lady Rockstar (5 Jun Haydock 8f frm RF 1758) - also 1st of 7 getting 3lb from Temper Lad (17 Jun Hamilton RF 2059). Consistent.

**B W Hills [1-8] W J Gredley.*

MISS CAMPANULA BHB 56f **RR 58f** 3831^{12}

2 b f Rudimentary (USA) 8.2f **(66)** - Miss Primula (Dominion) 8.5f **(63)**

Form - 57002530

Record 1998 - 1st:0 2nd:1 3rd:1 Ran:8

Win Prizemoney £0 *Total Prizemoney* £1,051

1998 Turf 0-7: (5f 5, 6f 2) (gd, g-f, frm 4, hrd) 1998 AW 0-1: (6f) (Fibr)

Fair filly, effective 5 to 6f, best at 5f, acts on gd to frm, best on frm. Turf high 58 - 2nd of 9 getting 3lb from Lightning Blaze (20 Jly Beverley 5f frm RF 2953). Inconsistent.

**M W Easterby [0-8] Mrs Jean Turpin.*

MISS CODY BHB 53f48a **RR 59f 48a** 4762^{7}

2 b f Noble Patriarch 12.2f **(43)** - Madam Cody (Hot Spark) 7.6f **(62)**

Form - 842562247

Record 1998 - 1st:0 2nd:3 3rd:0 Ran:9

Win Prizemoney £0 *Total Prizemoney* £2,177

1998 Turf 0-9: (7f 6, 8f 2, 10f) (gd, g-f 5, frm 3)

Fair filly, effective 7 to 8f, best at 8f, acts on g-f to frm, best on g-f, often wears blinkers (extremely effectively). Turf high 59 (began Jly) - 2nd of 20 giving 1lb to Malchik (8 Spt Leicester 8f g-f RF 4136).

**T D Easterby [0-9] M H Easterby.*

MISS DANGEROUS BHB 58f67a **RR 60f 67a** 4837[8]
3 b f Komaite (USA) 6.9f **(61)** - Khadine (Astec) 8.6f **(66)**
Form - 5128116481408
Record 1998 - 1st:4 2nd:1 3rd:0 Ran:13
Pre1998 - 1st:0 2nd:1 3rd:0 Ran:5
Win Prizemoney £10,828 *Total Prizemoney* £12,512
Wins * **1998** Jun Warwic (G-S) H 5f 57 60
* **1998** *Apr Wolver (STD) H 6f 55 67+* <
* **1998** Apr Folkes (SFT) C 5f 56
* **1998** *Jan Wolver (STD) S 5f 54*
1998 Turf 2-8: (5f 2-5, 6f 2, 7f) (sft 1-1, g-s 2, gd 4, frm 1-1) 1998 AW 2-5: (5f 1-3, 6f 1-2) (Fibr 2-5)
Unfurnished, average filly, effective 5 to 6f, acts on gd - acts on Fibr. Turf high 60. AW high 67 - 1st of 10 getting 24lb from Summer Deal (30 Apr Wolverhampton RF 0938). She was Mick Quinn's first winner as a trainer when winning a seller on the Wolverhampton Fibresand in January, and went on to win better events on Turf and back on Fibresand, before rather losing her form. Back to winning ways at Warwick in June, where the strong pace suited her.
**M Quinn [4-13] M Quinn (from M R Channon [0-5] Oct 1997).*

MISS DIVOT (IRE) BHB 65f **RR 42f** 1721[7]
3 b f Petardia 8.2f **(58)** - Kinosium (Relkino) 8.9f **(65)**
Form - 3807
Record 1998 - 1st:0 2nd:0 3rd:1 Ran:4
Win Prizemoney £0 *Total Prizemoney* £560
1998 Turf 0-4: (7f 4) (sft, gd 2, frm)
Light-framed, moderate filly. Turf high 73 (1st run) - 3rd of 7 to Oh Hebe (9 Apr Leicester 7f sft RF 0620).
**R Guest [0-4] Miss Jocelyn Booth.*

MISS DOODYBUSINESS RR 35f 2567[8]
2 b f Formidable (USA) 7.8f **(60)**- Miss Doody (Gorytus (USA)) 7.8f **(60)**
Form - 8
Record 1998 - 1st:0 2nd:0 3rd:0 Ran:1
1998 Turf 0-1: (5f) (gd)
Currently very moderate filly.
**C W Thornton [0-1] Racegoers Club Spigot Lodge Owners Group.*

MISS DRAGONFLY (IRE) BHB 77f **RR 78f** 4204[9]
2 b f Brief Truce (USA) 9.1f **(73)** - Winged Victory (IRE) **(89f)** (Dancing Brave (USA)) 8.4f **(76)**
Form - 1240
Record 1998 - 1st:1 2nd:1 3rd:0 Ran:4
Win Prizemoney £3,414 *Total Prizemoney* £4,789
Wins * **1998** Jly Leices (GD) 7f 71+ <
1998 Turf 1-4: (7f 1-3, 8f) (gd 2, g-f, frm 1-1)
Above-average filly. Turf high 78 (began Jly) - 4th of 12 getting 5lb from Tony Tie (22 Aug Chester 7f gd RF 3803) - also 1st of 20 getting 2lb from Goodwood Jazz (22 Jly Leicester RF 3027).
**B W Hills [1-4] Nigel Murray.*

MISSED DOMINO BHB 42f **RR 44f** 3121[6]
3 ch f Ron's Victory (USA) 9.2f **(52)** - Far Claim (USA) (Far North (CAN)) 9.7f **(75)**
Form - 06
Record 1998 - 1st:0 2nd:0 3rd:0 Ran:2
Pre1998 - 1st:0 2nd:0 3rd:0 Ran:3
1998 Turf 0-2: (10f, 11f) (g-f, hrd)
Light-framed, moderate filly. Turf high 29 (began Jly).
**Mrs A Swinbank [0-5] S Smith.*

MISSED THE CUT (IRE) BHB 69f66a **RR 72f 66a** 1262[2]
3 b f Classic Secret (USA) 8.8f **(56)** - Missish (Mummy's Pet) 7.7f **(60)**
Form - 412582
Record 1998 - 1st:1 2nd:2 3rd:0 Ran:6
Pre1998 - 1st:0 2nd:2 3rd:0 Ran:2
Win Prizemoney £2,712 *Total Prizemoney* £6,409
Wins * **1998** *Jan Lingfi (STD) 6f 69+* <
1998 Turf 0-2: (7f 2) (g-s, frm) 1998 AW 1-4: (5f, 6f 1-1, 7f 2) (Equi 1-4)
Light-framed, above-average filly, effective 5 to 7f, best at 5f, acts on g-s to frm - acts on Equi, best on frm. Turf high 71 - 2nd of 16 giving 12lb to Mountain Magic (16 May Newbury 7f frm RF 1262). AW high 70 - 2nd of 10 giving 8lb to Nautical Warning (20 Jan Lingfield 7f Equi RF 0119) - also 1st of 7 from Phantom Ring (17 Jan Lingfield RF 0107). **R Hannon [1-8] R Hannon.*

MISS ELIMINATOR BHB 51f50a **RR 47f 50a** 1964[7]
3 b f Komaite (USA) 6.9f **(61)** - Northern Line (Camden Town) 9.3f **(53)**
Form - 0707
Record 1998 - 1st:0 2nd:0 3rd:0 Ran:4
Pre1998 - 1st:1 2nd:0 3rd:1 Ran:6
Win Prizemoney £2,847 *Total Prizemoney* £3,264
Wins 1997 Jly Beverl (GD) 5f 62 <
1998 Turf 0-3: (6f 3) (gd 3) 1998 AW 0-1: (5f) (Fibr)
Lengthy, moderate filly, effective 5f, acts on frm, has worn blinkers (very effectively). Turf high 47.
**J L Harris [0-4] Mrs R Morley (from M W Easterby [1-6] Aug 1997).*

MISS EMM RR 36f 4387[9]
2 b f Sea Raven (IRE) - Chomolonga (High Top) 10.2f **(67)**
Form - 80
Record 1998 - 1st:0 2nd:0 3rd:0 Ran:2
1998 Turf 0-1: (7f) (frm) 1998 AW 0-1: (7f) (Fibr)
Currently very moderate filly. **J Wharton [0-2] Mrs Vera Craggs.*

MISS FARA (FR) BHB 78f **RR 75f** 4464[3]
3 ch f Galetto (FR) 11.7f **(86)** - Faracha (FR) (Kenmare (FR)) 6.5f **(72)**
Form - 2023
Record 1998 - 1st:0 2nd:2 3rd:1 Ran:4
Win Prizemoney £0 *Total Prizemoney* £2,720
1998 Turf 0-4: (8f 2, 10f 2) (gd, g-f 2, frm)
Above-average filly. Turf high 75 (began Jly) - 2nd of 17 getting 5lb from Gleaming Hill (8 Spt Leicester 10f g-f RF 4138).
**M C Pipe [0-4] Mrs Christine Painting.*

MISS FIT (IRE) BHB 88f **RR 85f** 4322[7]
2 b f Hamas (IRE) 8f **(72)** - Soucaro (Rusticaro (FR)) 8.2f **(65)**
Form - 11127
Record 1998 - 1st:3 2nd:1 3rd:0 Ran:5
Win Prizemoney £7,609 *Total Prizemoney* £9,255
Wins * **1998** Aug Redcar (G-F) 5f 85 <
* **1998** Jly Carlis (G-F) 5.9f 77+
* **1998** *Jun Southw (STD) 5f 70+*
1998 Turf 2-4: (5f 1-3, 6f 1-1) (g-s, gd, g-f 1-1, frm 1-1) 1998 AW 1-1: (5f 1-1) (Fibr 1-1)
Useful filly. Turf high 85 (began Jly) - 1st of 5 giving 4lb to Lunar Prospector (29 Aug Redcar RF 3964) - also 1st of 7 giving 7lb to Highly Fancied (4 Jly Carlisle RF 2523). (1st run). Very speedy, she showed progressive form to notch up a hat-trick. Not disgraced in a listed race at Ayr in September, she can make a useful sprinter at three. **Mrs G S Rees [3-5] Mrs G S Rees.*

MISS GILLY BHB 34f **RR 23f** 4765[8]
3 b f Thowra (FR) 11.2f **(47)** - Mey Madam (Song) 7.2f **(61)**
Form - 008
Record 1998 - 1st:0 2nd:0 3rd:0 Ran:3
1998 Turf 0-3: (7f, 8f, 12f) (gd, frm, hrd)
Currently little account filly. Turf high 23 (began Jly).
**R J R Williams [0-3] The Smine Partnership.*

MISS GRAPETTE (IRE) BHB 68f **RR 71f** 4518[5]
2 b f Brief Truce (USA) 9.1f **(73)** - Grapette (Nebbiolo) 8.1f **(75)**
Form - 332205
Record 1998 - 1st:0 2nd:2 3rd:2 Ran:6
Win Prizemoney £0 *Total Prizemoney* £3,233
1998 Turf 0-6: (5f 5, 6f) (g-s, gd, g-f 3, frm)
Above-average filly, effective 5 to 6f, best at 5f, acts on g-s to frm, best on g-f. Turf high 71 - 2nd of 7 to Ring of Love (11 Jly Chester 5f frm RF 2707). **J Berry [0-6] Mrs A E Robertson.*

MISS GREEN BHB 54f **RR 57f** 3901[11]
3 b f Greensmith - Miss Comedy (Comedy Star (USA)) 7.5f **(50)**
Form - 60500
Record 1998 - 1st:0 2nd:0 3rd:0 Ran:5
1998 Turf 0-5: (5f, 6f 2, 7f, 8f) (gd 2, g-f, frm 2)
Neat, fair filly. Turf high 57. **J W Hills [0-5] Miss J Wilkinson.*

MISS HILLSIDE BHB 60f59a **RR 57df 59a** 4201[10]
3 b f Reprimand 8.2f **(63)** - Miss Butterfield (Cure The Blues (USA)) 9.5f **(63)**
Form - 6300
Record 1998 - 1st:0 2nd:0 3rd:1 Ran:4
Win Prizemoney £0 *Total Prizemoney* £320

1998 Turf 0-3: (7f, 8f 2) (gd, g-f, frm) 1998 AW 0-1: (7f) (Equi)
Light-framed, fair filly. Turf high 61. **W Jarvis [0-4] Miss V R Jarvis.*

MISS HIT BHB 65f **RR 63f** 5142[11]
3 b f Efisio 7.7f **(69)** - Jennies' Gem (Sayf El Arab (USA)) 7.1f **(54)**
Form - 4523810
Record 1998 - 1st:1 2nd:1 3rd:1 Ran:7
Pre1998 - 1st:0 2nd:0 3rd:0 Ran:1
Win Prizemoney £5,088 *Total Prizemoney* £6,785
Wins * 1998 Oct Newmar () H 5f 60 63 <
1998 Turf 1-7: (5f 1-5, 6f 2) (gd 1-3, g-f, frm 3)
Scopey, average filly, effective 5f, acts on gd. Turf high 63 (began Jly) - also 1st of 24 getting 2lb from Sky Red (1 Oct Newmarket RF 4596).
**Miss Gay Kelleway [1-7] Brian Lovrey (from M R Channon [0-1] Apr 1997).*

MISSIDENT (IRE) RR 1f 544[11]
3 b f Dancing Dissident (USA) 6.8f **(65)** - My Miss Molly (IRE) (Entitled)
Form - 0
Record 1998 - 1st:0 2nd:0 3rd:0 Ran:1
1998 Turf 0-1: (6f) (sft)
Leggy, currently very poor filly.
**D J S Cosgrove [0-1] Edermine Bloodstock.*

MISSILE TOE (IRE) BHB 43f48a **RR 50f 48a** 4319[7]
5 b g Exactly Sharp (USA) 8.4f **(66)** - Debach Dust (Indian King (USA)) 7.4f **(64)**
Form - 000555307
Record 1998 - 1st:0 2nd:0 3rd:1 Ran:7
Pre1998 - 1st:1 2nd:5 3rd:2 Ran:27
Win Prizemoney £3,166 *Total Prizemoney* £10,228
Wins 1995 Jly Newcas (G-F) 6f 65 <
1998 Turf 0-7: (8f, 9f, 10f 5) (g-s, gd, g-f, frm 4)
Fair gelding, effective 10f, acts on g-f to frm, best on g-f, has worn blinkers, prefers left handed tracks, prefers tight tracks. Turf high 53 - 5th of 16 giving 1lb to Rear Window (8 May Nottingham 10f frm RF 1114). Inconsistent.
**D Morris [0-13] Stag and Huntsman (from J E Banks [1-21] Oct 1996).*

MISSING TED BHB 71f **RR 80f** 4732[13]
2 b f Formidable (USA) 7.8f **(60)** - Hat Hill (Roan Rocket) 7.8f **(57)**
Form - 63724531050
Record 1998 - 1st:1 2nd:1 3rd:2 Ran:11
Win Prizemoney £2,571 *Total Prizemoney* £5,192
Wins * 1998 Aug Bright (G-F) 6f 68 <
1998 Turf 1-11: (5f, 6f 1-4, 7f 6) (g-s, gd 3, g-f 3, frm 1-4)
Decent filly, effective 7f, acts on g-f to frm. Turf high 80 - 4th of 7 getting 10lb from Minnesota (24 Jly Newmarket 7f frm RF 3077). She had shown some ability in maiden and nursery company before getting off the mark in a Brighton maiden in August, but she made hard work of that and was beaten out of sight subsequently. **S Dow [1-11] Garvin-Jarvis.*

MISS KALAGLOW BHB 37f48a **RR 14f 48a** 3944[15]
4 b f Kalaglow 11.2f **(67)** - Dame du Moulin (Shiny Tenth) 9.2f **(56)**
Form - 000
Record 1998 - 1st:0 2nd:0 3rd:0 Ran:3
Pre1998 - 1st:0 2nd:1 3rd:0 Ran:5
Win Prizemoney £0 *Total Prizemoney* £739
1998 Turf 0-3: (8f, 10f, 12f) (g-s 2, frm)
Leggy, poor filly, effective 8f, acts on frm. Turf high 14. Becoming disappointing. **C F Wall [0-8] Mrs C A Wall.*

MISS LACROIX RR 34f 4394[13]
3 b f Picea 12.7f **(43)** - Smartie Lee (Dominion) 8.5f **(63)**
Form - U0
Record 1998 - 1st:0 2nd:0 3rd:0 Ran:2
1998 Turf 0-2: (11f, 12f) (gd, frm)
Tall, very moderate filly. Turf high 34.
**R Hollinshead [0-4] Mrs Norma Harris.*

MISS MAGNUM (IRE) RR 15f 1438[7]
3 b f Whitehall Bridge - Illiney Girl (Lochnager) 6f **(59)**
Form - 07
Record 1998 - 1st:0 2nd:0 3rd:0 Ran:2
1998 Turf 0-2: (10f, 11f) (frm 2)
Workmanlike, currently poor filly. Turf high 15.
**J Neville [0-2] Magnum Construction Ltd.*

MISS MAIN STREET (IRE) BHB 40f **RR 38f** 3085[10]
3 b f Shalford (IRE) 7.8f **(63)** - Bonvin (Taufan (USA)) 7f **(57)**
Form - 005000
Record 1998 - 1st:0 2nd:0 3rd:0 Ran:6
Pre1998 - 1st:1 2nd:0 3rd:0 Ran:7
Win Prizemoney £2,986 *Total Prizemoney* £3,225
Wins * 1997 Aug Newcas (G-F) H 7f 58 61 <
1998 Turf 0-6: (8f 6) (g-s, gd 3, frm 2)
Workmanlike, very moderate filly, effective 6 to 7f, best at 7f, acts on gd to frm, best on gd, has worn blinkers. Turf high 38. Inconsistent. **J J Quinn [1-13] The Main Street Partnership.*

MISS MONEY SPIDER (IRE) BHB 56f **RR 59f** 4614[5]
3 b f Statoblest 6.4f **(63)** - Dream of Jenny (Caerleon (USA)) 8.6f **(71)**
Form - 5703047135
Record 1998 - 1st:1 2nd:0 3rd:2 Ran:9
Pre1998 - 1st:0 2nd:0 3rd:0 Ran:2
Win Prizemoney £2,530 *Total Prizemoney* £3,616
Wins * 1998 Spt Yarmou (G-S) S 7f 55 <
1998 Turf 1-9: (5f 2, 6f 3, 7f 1-3, 8f) (g-s, gd 1-2, g-f 2, frm 4)
Neat, above-average filly, has worn blinkers. Turf high 59.
**N A Callaghan [1-9] Paul & Jenny Green (from R Hannon [0-2] Nov 1997).*

MISS MOUSE RR 2f 3331[7]
6 br m Arctic Lord 11.7f **(37)** - Gypsy's Barn Rat (Balliol) 5f **(43)**
Form - 7
Record 1998 - 1st:0 2nd:0 3rd:0 Ran:1
1998 Turf 0-1: (12f) (gd)
Very poor mare. **K C Comerford [0-5] Andrew Scott.*

MISS MUFFETT (IRE) BHB 45a **RR 49f** 3644[11]
3 b f Hero's Honor (USA) 9.2f **(76)** - Grain de Folie (FR) (Top Ville) 11.7f **(68)**
Form - 8770
Record 1998 - 1st:0 2nd:0 3rd:0 Ran:3
Pre1998 - 1st:0 2nd:0 3rd:0 Ran:7
Win Prizemoney £0 *Total Prizemoney* £251
1998 Turf 0-2: (7f, 8f) (frm 2) 1998 AW 0-1: (9f) (Fibr)
Unfurnished, moderate filly. Turf high 49 (began Jly). Inconsistent.
**L J Barratt [0-4] W O Morris (from P Mooney [0-7] Dec 1997).*

MISS MULTIPLY BHB 48f65a **RR 55f 65a** 4253[10]
2 b f Komaite (USA) 6.9f **(61)** - Miss Calculate (Mummy's Game) 8.2f **(60)**
Form - 472700
Record 1998 - 1st:0 2nd:1 3rd:0 Ran:6
Win Prizemoney £0 *Total Prizemoney* £814
1998 Turf 0-4: (5f 2, 6f 2) (gd 2, frm 2) 1998 AW 0-2: (5f, 6f) (Fibr 2)
Fair filly, effective 5f, - acts on Fibr. Turf high 55. AW high 59 (began Jly) - 2nd of 8 getting 1lb from Moocha Cha Man (20 Jly Wolverhampton 5f Fibr RF 2966). **Mrs G S Rees [0-6] Mike Keating.*

MISS PARADISO (IRE) BHB 42f **RR 35f** 4123[11]
3 b f Anita's Prince 6f **(62)** - Heavenly Blessed (Monseigneur (USA)) 7.7f **(63)**
Form - 5060
Record 1998 - 1st:0 2nd:0 3rd:0 Ran:4
1998 Turf 0-4: (7f, 8f 2, 9f) (sft, g-f, frm 2)
Unfurnished, very moderate filly. Turf high 60.
**B Palling [0-4] Rhiwbina Racing.*

MISS PENTON BHB 58f **RR 59f** 5006[11]
3 ch f Primo Dominie 7.2f **(67)** - On The House (FR) (Be My Guest (USA)) 9.3f **(67)**
Form - 450320
Record 1998 - 1st:0 2nd:1 3rd:1 Ran:6
Win Prizemoney £0 *Total Prizemoney* £1,786
1998 Turf 0-6: (6f 2, 7f, 8f 3) (sft, g-s, gd 2, frm 2)
Scopey, fair filly, effective 6 to 7f, best at 6f, acts on g-s to gd, best on gd. Turf high 59 (1st run) - 4th of 10 to Bolshaya (25 Jun Newcastle 6f gd RF 2273). **R Charlton [0-6] A E Oppenheimer.*

MISS PEREGRINE BHB 41f **RR 45f** 3379[7]
4 b f Polar Falcon (USA) 9f **(74)** - Good Thinking (USA) (Raja Baba (USA)) 10f **(64)**
Form - 048407
Record 1998 - 1st:0 2nd:0 3rd:0 Ran:6
Pre1998 - 1st:0 2nd:0 3rd:1 Ran:4
Win Prizemoney £0 *Total Prizemoney* £846
1998 Turf 0-5: (6f 2, 7f 2, 8f) (gd 2, g-f, frm 2) 1998 AW 0-1: (8f) (Fibr)
Moderate filly, effective 6 to 7f, acts on g-s to frm. Turf high 45. Inconsistent.
**N M Babbage [0-6] Alan Craddock (from R Guest [0-4] Jun 1997).*

MISS PIN UP BHB 59f63a **RR 63f 63a** 5069[6]
9 gr m Kalaglow 11.2f **(67)** - Allander Girl (Miralgo) 12.6f **(63)**
Form - 546245146
Record 1998 - 1st:1 2nd:1 3rd:0 Ran:9
Pre1998 - 1st:9 2nd:6 3rd:1 Ran:51
Win Prizemoney £33,438 *Total Prizemoney* £47,007
Wins * 1998 Aug Nottin (G-F) H 14.1f 59 63
1995 Jly Yarmou (G-F) H 11.5f 77 81 <
1994 Aug Ripon (G-F) H 12.3f 69 79
1998 Turf 1-8: (11f, 12f 4, 14f 1-2, 16f) (gd, g-f 1-5, frm 2) 1998 AW 0-1: (12f) (Equi)
Average mare, effective 11 to 16f, best at 14f, acts on gd to frm, best on g-f, has worn blinkers, favours tight tracks. Turf high 63 - 1st of 9 giving 3lb to Drift (29 Aug Nottingham RF 3963). Consistent.
**R McGhin [1-9] Ray McGhin (from W J Haggas [2-11] Aug 1995).*

MISS PUGH BHB 33f **RR 31f** 3582[12]
3 b f Puissance 7.1f **(60)** - Crymlyn (Welsh Pageant) 10f **(65)**
Form - 00700
Record 1998 - 1st:0 2nd:0 3rd:0 Ran:5
Pre1998 - 1st:0 2nd:0 3rd:0 Ran:2
1998 Turf 0-5: (6f 2, 7f 2, 9f) (gd 4, g-f)
Light-framed, very moderate filly. Turf high 31.
**Don Enrico Incisa [0-5] Don Enrico Incisa (from C W Fairhurst [0-2] Aug 1997).*

MISS RIMEX (IRE) BHB 78f **RR 81f** 4845[8]
2 b f Ezzoud (IRE) - Blue Guitar (Cure The Blues (USA)) 9.5f **(63)**
Form - 002310238
Record 1998 - 1st:1 2nd:2 3rd:2 Ran:9
Win Prizemoney £4,182 *Total Prizemoney* £7,660
Wins * 1998 Aug Kempto (G-F) H 6f 75 79 <
1998 Turf 1-9: (5f 2, 6f 1-3, 7f 2, 8f 2) (g-s, g-f 3, frm 1-5)
Decent filly, effective 6 to 8f, best at 8f, acts on g-f to frm, best on frm. Turf high 81 - also 1st of 7 getting 4lb from Casimir (5 Aug Kempton RF 3370). Consistent. Reasonable form in nurseries since winning one at Kempton.
**D R C Elsworth [1-9] Nightmare Partnership.*

MISS RIVIERA STAR BHB 57f **RR 69?f** 5098[15]
3 ch f Generous (IRE) 11.5f **(82)** - Miss Beaulieu (Northfields (USA)) 9f **(72)**
Form - 07300
Record 1998 - 1st:0 2nd:0 3rd:1 Ran:5
Win Prizemoney £0 *Total Prizemoney* £575
1998 Turf 0-5: (10f 5) (gd 2, g-f 3)
Workmanlike, average filly. Turf high 69 (began Aug).
**G Wragg [0-5] J L C Pearce.*

MISS ROBERTO (IRE) BHB 49f **RR 46f** 151[8]
5 ch m Don Roberto (USA) 15.6f **(39)** - Frau Ahuyentante (ARG) (Frari (ARG)) 11.6f **(74)**
Form - 8
Record 1998 - 1st:0 2nd:0 3rd:0 Ran:1
Pre1998 - 1st:1 2nd:0 3rd:0 Ran:6
Win Prizemoney £3,253 *Total Prizemoney* £3,253
Wins 1996 Jun Sligo (G-S) H 11f 55 46 <
1998 AW 0-1: (12f) (Equi)
Moderate filly, has worn blinkers.
**J G M O'Shea [2-6] M G Lilwall and Partners (2) (from M Brassil in IRE [2-4] Spt 1996).*

MISS SABRENA BHB 46f **RR 51f** 2179[13]
3 b f Sabrehill (USA) 8.5f **(64)** - Tebre (USA) (Sir Ivor) 10.2f **(70)**
Form - 0000
Record 1998 - 1st:0 2nd:0 3rd:0 Ran:4
1998 Turf 0-4: (7f, 10f 3) (gd, g-f 2, frm)
Neat, fair filly. Turf high 51. **S C Williams [0-4] Livingston Trading Ltd.*

MISS SALSA DANCER BHB 56f **RR 61f** 4917[2]
3 ch f Salse (USA) 10.9f **(71)**- Thakhayr (Sadler's Wells (USA)) 10f **(76)**
Form - 5413045404722
Record 1998 - 1st:1 2nd:2 3rd:1 Ran:13
Pre1998 - 1st:0 2nd:0 3rd:1 Ran:5
Win Prizemoney £7,720 *Total Prizemoney* £12,258
Wins * 1998 May Thirsk (G-F) H 8f 60 61 <
1998 Turf 1-13: (8f 1-5, 9f 2, 10f 4, 11f, 12f) (sft 2, g-s 3, gd 3, g-f 1-3, frm 2)
Neat, average filly, effective 6f, acts on g-f. Turf high 61. Consistent. **Denys Smith [1-18] Jim Blair.*

MISS SCOOTER BHB 47f48a **RR 37f 48a** 2019[15]
3 ch f Beveled (USA) 6.9f **(64)** - Donosa (Posse (USA)) 8.9f **(61)**
Form - 25840
Record 1998 - 1st:0 2nd:1 3rd:0 Ran:5
Pre1998 - 1st:0 2nd:1 3rd:0 Ran:4
Win Prizemoney £0 *Total Prizemoney* £1,117
1998 Turf 0-5: (5f 3, 6f, 7f) (sft 2, gd 2, frm)
Light-framed, very moderate filly, effective 5f, acts on sft. Turf high 48 (1st run) - 2nd of 7 getting 6lb from Miss Dangerous (7 Apr Folkestone 5f sft RF 0579). **A P Jones [0-9] A P Jones.*

MISS SERENGETI BHB 52f **RR 45f** 3518[10]
3 b f Tragic Role (USA) 9.4f **(63)** - Sea Siesta (Vaigly Great) 7f **(58)**
Form - 085500
Record 1998 - 1st:0 2nd:0 3rd:0 Ran:6
1998 Turf 0-6: (5f, 6f, 7f 4) (gd 3, g-f, frm, hrd)
Unfurnished, moderate filly. Turf high 45. **J Berry [0-6] Mark Pennell.*

MISS SHEMA (USA) RR 73f 4316[4]
2 b f Gulch (USA) 9.6f **(79)** - Fire and Shade (USA) (Shadeed (USA)) 8.2f **(70)**
Form - 4
Record 1998 - 1st:0 2nd:0 3rd:0 Ran:1
Win Prizemoney £0 *Total Prizemoney* £248
1998 Turf 0-1: (6f) (gd)
Currently above-average filly. **B Hanbury [0-1] Abdullah Ali.*

MISS SKYE (IRE) BHB 48f47a **RR 47f 47a** 1202[11]
3 b f Common Grounds 8.1f **(66)** - Swift Chorus (Music Boy) 6.8f **(57)**
Form - 3603245134400
Record 1998 - 1st:1 2nd:1 3rd:2 Ran:10
Pre1998 - 1st:0 2nd:0 3rd:1 Ran:9
Win Prizemoney £1,850 *Total Prizemoney* £3,276
Wins 1998 *Feb Lingfi (SLW) C 7f 50 <*
1998 Turf 0-1: (6f) (frm)1998 AW 1-9:(6f 2, 7f 1-4, 8f 3)(Equi 1-6, Fibr 3)
Leggy, fair filly. AW high 53.
**B A Pearce [0-5] Mrs Virginia Toft (from T J Naughton [1-14] Feb 1998).*

MISS TAKE (IRE) BHB 47f47a **RR 56f 47a** 4878[13]
2 ch f Red Sunset 9f **(57)** - Grave Error (Northern Treat (USA)) 6f **(50)**
Form - 7012573880080
Record 1998 - 1st:1 2nd:1 3rd:1 Ran:13
Win Prizemoney £1,725 *Total Prizemoney* £2,684
Wins * 1998 *Jun Wolver (STD) S 6f 63 <*
1998 Turf 0-7: (6f 2, 7f 5) (g-f 3, frm 3, hrd) 1998 AW 1-6: (5f 2, 6f 1-2, 7f 2) (Fibr 1-6)
Average filly, effective 6 to 7f, best at 7f, acts on g-f - acts on Fibr, mostly wears blinkers (very effectively), prefers left handed tracks, prefers tight tracks. Turf high 56 (began Jly) - 3rd of 10 getting 14lb from Dandy Dancer (22 Jly Catterick 7f g-f RF 3020). AW high 63 - 1st of 6 from Super Strides (20 Jun Wolverhampton RF 2165). Becoming disappointing.
**P D Evans [1-13] Crewe And Nantwich Racing Club.*

MISS TEHENTE (FR) RR 68f 4778[4]
3 gr f Tehente (FR) - Fairy Guile (FR) (Native Guile (USA))
Form - 4
Record 1998 - 1st:0 2nd:0 3rd:0 Ran:1
Win Prizemoney £0 *Total Prizemoney* £359

1998 Turf 0-1: (8f) (gd)
Strong, currently average filly. *R Simpson [0-1] Miss J Rumford.

MISS TRAXDATA BHB 46f **RR 40f** 4610[13]

2 gr f Absalom 7.1f **(56)** - Princess Sharpenup (Lochnager) 6f **(59)**
Form - 000
Record 1998 - 1st:0 2nd:0 3rd:0 Ran:3
1998 Turf 0-3: (5f 2, 6f) (g-s, frm, hrd)
Currently moderate filly. Turf high 40 (began Aug).
*M Bell [0-3] Traxdata.

MISS UNIVERSE (IRE) **RR 99f** 4974[3]

2 gr f Warning 8.1f **(77)** - Reine D'Beaute (Caerleon (USA)) 8.6f **(71)**
Form - 2313343
Record 1998 - 1st:1 2nd:1 3rd:4 Ran:7
Win Prizemoney £3,766 *Total Prizemoney* £20,989
Wins * **1998** Aug Windso (G-F) 6f 86 <
1998 Turf 1-7: (5f, 6f 1-4, 7f 2) (sft, gd 3, g-f, frm 1-2)
Very useful filly, effective 6f, acts on sft to frm. Turf high 99 - 4th of 9 to Wannabe Grand (29 Spt Newmarket 6f frm RF 4539). She stepped up on her previous form when only collared inside the last and beaten under two lengths in the Cheveley Park. She was subsequently beaten in heavy ground in a listed race, but should have no problem winning in that grade in 1999. Will need seven furlongs or a mile. *B W Hills [1-7] Mrs J M Corbett.

MISS VITA (USA) BHB 48f44a **RR 48f 44a** 4862[10]

4 b f Alleged (USA) 11.8f **(81)** - Torrid Tango (USA) (Green Dancer (USA)) 10.3f **(74)**
Form - 684221350
Record 1998 - 1st:1 2nd:2 3rd:1 Ran:9
Pre1998 - 1st:0 2nd:0 3rd:1 Ran:5
Win Prizemoney £1,955 *Total Prizemoney* £4,924
Wins * **1998** *Aug Wolver (STD) H 12f 43 48* <
1998 Turf 0-4: (12f 2, 13f, 16f) (g-f, frm 3) 1998 AW 1-5: (10f, 12f 1-4) (Equi, Fibr 1-4)
Neat, moderate filly, effective 10f, acts on g-f, likes tight tracks. Turf high 48. AW high 48. She was running pretty well on turf and sand prior to winning a very modest apprentice maiden handicap at Wolverhampton in August. *R J R Williams [1-14] Entente Cordiale.

MISS VIVIEN BHB 44f **RR 35f** 5120[12]

3 b f Puissance 7.1f **(60)** - Madam Bold (Never so Bold) 6.3f **(66)**
Form - 006406020000
Record 1998 - 1st:0 2nd:1 3rd:0 Ran:12
Pre1998 - 1st:1 2nd:0 3rd:0 Ran:5
Win Prizemoney £3,665 *Total Prizemoney* £4,971
Wins * 1997 Oct Pontef (G-F) H 6f 72 75 <
1998 Turf 0-12: (6f 3, 7f 8, 8f) (sft, g-s, gd 4, g-f 3, frm 3)
Scopey, very moderate filly, effective 6f, acts on g-f, likes left handed tracks, likes tight tracks. Turf high 63. Becoming disappointing. *Miss L A Perratt [1-17] T P Finch.

MISTER ASPECTO (IRE) BHB 52f74a **RR 57df 74a** 2001[13]

5 b g Caerleon (USA) 10.9f **(79)** - Gironde (USA) (Raise A Native) 11.2f **(69)**
Form - 11133230
Record 1998 - 1st:3 2nd:1 3rd:3 Ran:8
Pre1998 - 1st:7 2nd:6 3rd:7 Ran:39
Win Prizemoney £29,070 *Total Prizemoney* £40,531

Wins								
* **1998**	*Feb*	*Wolver*	*(STD)*	*C*	*14.8f*		*79*	<
* **1998**	*Jan*	*Wolver*	*(STD)*	*H*	*16.2f*	*78*	*79*	<
* **1998**	*Jan*	*Southw*	*(STD)*	*C*	*16f*		*73*	
* 1997	*Aug*	*Lingfi*	*(STD)*	*H*	*16f*	*69*	*75*	
* 1997	*Aug*	*Lingfi*	*(STD)*		*16f*		*67*	
* 1996	Aug	Hamilt	(G-F)	H	13f	68	71	
* 1996	Jly	Beverl	(G-F)	H	12f	63	69	
* 1996	*Apr*	*Southw*	*(STD)*	*H*	*11f*	*68*	*69*	
* 1996	*Mar*	*Lingfi*	*(STD)*	*H*	*10f*	*62*	*66*	
* 1996	*Feb*	*Lingfi*	*(STD)*		*12f*		*44*	

1998 Turf 0-1: (18f) (g-s) 1998 AW 3-7: (14f 2, 15f 1-1, 16f 2-4) (Equi, Fibr 3-6)
Above-average gelding, effective 12 to 16f, - acts on AW, best on Fibr, mostly wears blinkers (very effectively), prefers left handed tracks, and excels at Southwell and Wolverhampton. AW high 79 - 1st of 8 giving 8lb to Jaraab (18 Feb Wolverhampton RF 0308) - also 1st of 8 giving 12lb to Noufari (24 Jan Wolverhampton RF 0154). He is a very smart stayer on sand and boasts a fine strike rate on both All-Weather surfaces. A successful start to 1998 meant that he was rated too highly to qualify for almost all handicaps on sand, and claimers were his only option. Not seen after June. *M Johnston [10-47] Aspecto Clothing Co Ltd.

MISTER BENJAMIN (IRE) BHB 87f86a **RR 89f 86a** 5151[18]

3 b g Polish Patriot (USA) 7.8f **(70)** - Frau Ahuyentante (ARG) (Frari (ARG)) 11.6f **(74)**
Form - 1125120
Record 1998 - 1st:3 2nd:2 3rd:0 Ran:7
Pre1998 - 1st:1 2nd:0 3rd:0 Ran:3
Win Prizemoney £20,312 *Total Prizemoney* £38,614

Wins								
* **1998**	Aug	Ascot	(G-F)	H	10f	82	86	<
* **1998**	Jun	Haydoc	(GD)	H	10.5f	79	81	
* **1998**	Apr	Kempto	(HVY)	H	9f	75	78	
* 1997	*Spt*	*Southw*	*(STD)*		*7f*		*69+*	

1998 Turf 3-7:(9f 1-1, 10f 1-4, 11f 1-1, 12f)(hvy 1-1, gd, g-f 1-3, frm 1-2)
Scopey, useful gelding, effective 10 to 11f, best at 10f, acts on g-f to frm, best on g-f. Turf high 89 - 2nd of 19 getting 12lb from Brilliant Red (19 Spt Newbury 10f g-f RF 4379) - also 1st of 9 getting 14lb from Premier Generation (7 Aug Ascot RF 3426). Won nicely on heavy ground at Kempton on his reappearance, but has since shown that he acts well on a faster surface. Tends to race prominently and is an honest sort, but lacks a turn of foot.
*S P C Woods [4-10] Mrs Julie Choy.

MISTER JOLSON BHB 73f78a **RR 86f 78a** 4872[15]

9 br g Latest Model 5.4f **(48)** - Impromptu (My Swanee) 7.6f **(52)**
Form - 62184437425000
Record 1998 - 1st:1 2nd:2 3rd:1 Ran:14
Pre1998 - 1st:11 2nd:5 3rd:11 Ran:73
Win Prizemoney £50,558 *Total Prizemoney* £73,483

Wins								
* **1998**	May	Bath	(FRM)		5.1f		78	
* 1997	May	Kempto	(GD)	H	6f	74	76	
* 1996	Jun	Salisb	(G-F)	H	5f	75	78	
* 1996	Apr	Sandow	(GD)	H	5f	70	73	
* 1994	Oct	Newmar	(G-F)	H	5f	83	81	<
* 1994	Jly	Warwic	(G-F)	H	5f	79	78	
* 1994	May	Newbur	(SFT)	H	6f	73	74	
* 1994	Apr	Bath	(GD)	H	5.1f	66	69	

1998 Turf 1-14: (5f 1-10, 6f 4) (hvy, sft 2, g-s 2, gd 7, frm 1-2)
Useful gelding, effective 5 to 6f, best at 5f, acts on gd to frm, best on gd, has worn blinkers. Turf high 86 - 2nd of 7 getting 14lb from Cortachy Castle (22 Aug Sandown 5f gd RF 3820) - also 1st of 5 from At Large (18 May Bath RF 1296). Not easy to catch right, but hit form in the spring, and won well at Bath in May.
*R J Hodges [12-87] Bob Froome.

MISTER MAL (IRE) **RR 53f** 4575[8]

2 b c Scenic 10.6f **(66)** - Fashion Parade (Mount Hagen (FR)) 8.4f **(70)**
Form - 08
Record 1998 - 1st:0 2nd:0 3rd:0 Ran:2
1998 Turf 0-2: (6f, 7f) (g-f 2)
Currently fair colt. Turf high 53 (began Aug).
*J A Glover [0-2] Mrs Andrea Mallinson.

MISTER MUNNELLY (IRE) BHB 48f **RR 37f** 3691[9]

5 b g Imperial Frontier (USA) 7f **(65)** - Maid of The Ring (Stetchworth (USA))
Form - 26000
Record 1998 - 1st:0 2nd:1 3rd:0 Ran:5
Pre1998 - 1st:2 2nd:0 3rd:1 Ran:13
Win Prizemoney £7,192 *Total Prizemoney* £8,396

Wins								
1997	Jly	Killar	(G-S)	H	8.5f	55	68	<
1996	Jly	Leopar	(G-F)	H	7f	53	52	

1998 Turf 0-5: (7f, 8f 2, 10f 2) (g-f 3, frm 2)
Very moderate gelding, effective 8f, acts on g-s, likes left handed tracks. Turf high 57. Consistent.
J R Jenkins [0-5] Come Racing Ltd (from C Roche in IRE [1-6] Jly 1997).

MISTER NOW THEN **RR** 4155[P]

3 ch c Mister Mellon - Fidget (Workboy) 7.3f **(46)**
Form - P
Record 1998 - 1st:0 2nd:0 3rd:0 Ran:1
1998 Turf 0-1: (8f) (frm)
Very poor colt. (DEAD) *A Smith [0-1] A H Grant.

MISTER PQ BHB 54f **RR 64f** 4337^{16}
2 ch c Ardkinglass 5f **(64)** - Well Off (Welsh Pageant) 10f **(65)**
Form - 0500
Record 1998 - 1st:0 2nd:0 3rd:0 Ran:4
1998 Turf 0-4: (6f 2, 7f, 8f) (gd, g-f, frm 2)
Average colt. Turf high 64 (began Jly).
**J G Smyth-Osbourne [0-4] PQ International/Euromedia.*

MISTER RAIDER BHB 29f57a **RR 24f 57a** 5003^{5}
6 ch g Ballacashtal (CAN) 7.9f **(51)** - Martian Melody (Enchantment) 5.4f **(52)**
Form - 204367200605
Record 1998 - 1st:0 2nd:1 3rd:0 Ran:8
Pre1998 - 1st:4 2nd:3 3rd:3 Ran:45
Win Prizemoney £9,920 *Total Prizemoney* £13,924
Wins * 1997 Jun Leices (G-F) SH 6f 44 46
* *1996 Dec Lingfi (STD) H 5f 50 51* <
* *1996 Nov Lingfi (STD) H 5f 48 51* <
1996 Feb Lingfi (STD) 6f 48
1998 Turf 0-4: (5f, 6f 3) (gd, frm 3) 1998 AW 0-4: (5f 2, 6f, 7f) (Equi 4)
Average gelding, effective 5 to 7f, - acts on Equi, mostly wears blinkers (effectively), likes left handed tracks, likes tight tracks. Turf high 24. AW high 62 - 5th of 16 to Kafil (26 Oct Lingfield 7f Equi RF 5003). Inconsistent.
**E A Wheeler [3-32] Raiders Partnership (from S Mellor [1-21] Feb 1996).*

MISTER RAMBO BHB 86f **RR 91f** 4854^{5}
3 b g Rambo Dancer (CAN) 8.4f **(59)** - Ozra (Red Alert) 7.6f **(66)**
Form - 2550144505
Record 1998 - 1st:1 2nd:1 3rd:0 Ran:10
Pre1998 - 1st:1 2nd:0 3rd:0 Ran:1
Win Prizemoney £11,033 *Total Prizemoney* £13,969
Wins * **1998** Jun Frankf (GD) L 7.8f 91 <
* 1997 Oct Newbur (GD) 6f 87
1998 Turf 1-10: (7f 8, 8f 1-2) (gd 1-6, g-f 2, frm 2)
Well made, useful gelding, effective 6 to 8f, best at 8f, acts on gd. Turf high 91 - 1st of 10 from Chahrouzan (19 Jun Frankfurt RF 2282a). His victory came in a very weak German Listed event and he ran only respectably in handicaps.
**B J Meehan [2-11] Abbott Racing Ltd.*

MISTER TRICKY BHB 53f68a **RR 46f 68a** 2202^{4}
3 ch g Magic Ring (IRE) 6.5f **(64)** - Splintering (Sharpo) 7.7f **(59)**
Form - 6311004
Record 1998 - 1st:2 2nd:0 3rd:1 Ran:6
Pre1998 - 1st:0 2nd:0 3rd:0 Ran:2
Win Prizemoney £5,875 *Total Prizemoney* £6,382
Wins * **1998** *Apr Lingfi (STD) H 7f 53 62* <
* **1998** *Mar Lingfi (STD) H 8f 53 56*
1998 Turf 0-2: (6f, 8f) (g-f, frm) 1998 AW 2-4: (7f 1-1, 8f 1-3) (Equi 2-4)
Workmanlike, average gelding, effective 7 to 8f, - acts on Equi, prefers tight tracks. Turf high 41. AW high 62 - 1st of 10 getting 9lb from Best Quest (9 Apr Lingfield RF 0625) - also 1st of 7 giving 4lb to Roger Ross (30 Mar Lingfield RF 0508).
**P Mitchell [2-8] G P Triefus, D A Lucie-Smith & Others.*

MISTER WESTSOUND BHB 54f52a **RR 54f 52a** 5059^{3}
6 b g Cyrano de Bergerac 7.3f **(58)**-Captivate(Mansingh (USA))7.4f **(55)**
Form - 7035262050054153
Record 1998 - 1st:1 2nd:2 3rd:2 Ran:16
Pre1998 - 1st:5 2nd:8 3rd:7 Ran:55
Win Prizemoney £20,167 *Total Prizemoney* £38,473
Wins * **1998** Oct Ayr (HVY) H 6f 46 50
* 1997 Jun Ayr (GD) H 7f 36 49+
* 1997 Jun Hamilt (G-S) H 6f 37 49
* 1995 Aug Hamilt (FRM) H 6f 45 56
* 1995 Aug Ayr (G-F) H 6f 45 51
* 1994 Jly Mussel (G-F) C 5f 73
1998 Turf 1-16: (6f 1-15, 7f) (sft 1-3, gd 7, g-f 2, frm 4)
Fair gelding, effective 6 to 7f, best at 6f, acts on sft to frm, best on sft, mostly wears blinkers (effectively), and excels at Hamilton. Turf high 54 - 3rd of 19 giving 7lb to Bataleur (30 Oct Newcastle 6f sft RF 5059) - also 1st of 27 getting 5lb from Souperficial (13 Oct Ayr RF 4771). He is often hampered by his habit of conceding ground at the start. The heavy ground helped him score at Ayr in October.
**Miss L A Perratt [6-71] David Sutherland-Ian Hay.*

MISTLE SONG RR 70f 4505^{7}
2 b f Nashwan (USA) 10.3f **(79)** - Mistle Thrush (USA) **(86f)** (Storm Bird (CAN)) 10.3f **(74)**
Form - 7
Record 1998 - 1st:0 2nd:0 3rd:0 Ran:1
1998 Turf 0-1: (8f) (gd)
Currently above-average filly. **C E Brittain [0-1] Saeed Manana.*

MISTRAL LORD (IRE) BHB 39f28a **RR 43f 28a** 356^{8}
4 br g Fairy King (USA) 7.7f **(75)** -Walkyria (Lord Gayle (USA)) 8.8f **(62)**
Form - 78
Record 1998 - 1st:0 2nd:0 3rd:0 Ran:2
Pre1998 - 1st:0 2nd:0 3rd:0 Ran:3
1998 AW 0-2: (8f, 10f) (Equi 2)
Scopey, moderate gelding. AW high 24.
**M P Muggeridge [0-4] Zephyr Racing (from M Madgwick [0-3] Aug 1997).*

MISTY MOOR BHB 54f **RR 38f** 2373^{4}
3 b f Wolfhound (USA) 7.3f **(71)** - Corley Moor (Habitat) 9.4f **(70)**
Form - 6004
Record 1998 - 1st:0 2nd:0 3rd:0 Ran:4
Pre1998 - 1st:0 2nd:1 3rd:0 Ran:2
Win Prizemoney £0 *Total Prizemoney* £1,185
1998 Turf 0-4: (6f, 7f, 8f 2) (g-s, gd 2, frm)
Scopey, very moderate filly. Turf high 38.
**M Johnston [0-6] Greenland Park Ltd.*

MISTY POINT BHB 44f **RR 46f** 4886^{14}
4 ch f Sharpo 7.5f **(68)** - Clouded Vision (So Blessed) 8.7f **(67)**
Form - 740003680
Record 1998 - 1st:0 2nd:0 3rd:1 Ran:9
Pre1998 - 1st:0 2nd:1 3rd:1 Ran:8
Win Prizemoney £0 *Total Prizemoney* £2,040
1998 Turf 0-9: (5f, 6f 2, 7f 6) (g-s, gd 4, g-f 2, frm 2)
Scopey, moderate filly, effective 6 to 7f, acts on g-f, has worn blinkers. Turf high 55. **I A Balding [0-17] M E Wates.*

MISTY RAIN BHB 52f55a **RR 51f 55a** 186^{8}
4 br f Polar Falcon (USA) 9f **(74)** - Ballerine (USA) (Lyphard's Wish (FR)) 9f **(74)**
Form - 18
Record 1998 - 1st:1 2nd:0 3rd:0 Ran:2
Pre1998 - 1st:0 2nd:0 3rd:2 Ran:11
Win Prizemoney £1,735 *Total Prizemoney* £3,070
Wins * **1998** *Jan Southw (STD) H 12f 52 55* <
1998 AW 1-2: (12f 1-2) (Fibr 1-2)
Light-framed, fair filly, effective 10 to 12f, acts on gd - acts on Fibr, favours tight tracks. AW high 55 (1st run) - 1st of 10 giving 16lb to Toulston Lady (19 Jan Southwell RF 0118).
**J L Spearing [1-2] Last Chance Racing (from B W Hills [0-11] Oct 1997).*

MITCHAM (IRE) BHB 93f **RR 93f** 4735^{2}
2 br c Hamas (IRE) 8f **(72)** - Arab Scimetar (IRE) (Sure Blade (USA)) 11.3f **(67)**
Form - 412
Record 1998 - 1st:1 2nd:1 3rd:0 Ran:3
Win Prizemoney £2,859 *Total Prizemoney* £5,251
Wins * **1998** Spt Warwic (G-F) 6f 81 <
1998 Turf 1-3: (6f 1-3) (g-s, g-f, frm 1-1)
Currently useful colt. Turf high 93 (began Aug) - 2nd of 7 to Compton Arrow (9 Oct Ascot 6f g-s RF 4735). Got off the mark in a Warwick maiden on his second start and lost nothing in defeat in a decent event at Ascot next time. **T G Mills [1-3] T G Mills.*

MITCHIGAN (IRE) RR 87f 3313^{1}
2 b c Mujadil (USA) 7.7f **(70)** - Bomblet **(36df)** (Persian Bold) 9.3f **(66)**
Form - 11
Record 1998 - 1st:2 2nd:0 3rd:0 Ran:2
Win Prizemoney £8,001 *Total Prizemoney* £8,001
Wins * **1998** Aug Ripon (GD) 6f 87 <
1998 May Currag (G-F) 6f 86+
1998 Turf 2-2: (6f 2-2) (gd 2-2)
Currently useful colt. Turf high 87 - 1st of 6 giving 4lb to Abbajabba (3 Aug Ripon RF 3313) - also 1st of 16 from Moonis (24 May Curragh RF 1512a). A winner for Jim Bolger at the Curragh in

May, he is now with David Loder, and had to battle hard to win a novice event at Ripon in August.
**D R Loder [1-1] Prince Abdul Aziz Bin Saud (from J S Bolger in IRE [1-1] May 1998).*

MITHAK (USA) BHB 78f **RR 85f** 4369[4]
4 b g Silver Hawk (USA) 11.2f **(85)** - Kapalua Butterfly (USA) (Stage Door Johnny) 10.3f **(84)**
Form - 56854
Record 1998 - 1st:0 2nd:0 3rd:0 Ran:5
Pre1998 - 1st:1 2nd:2 3rd:3 Ran:10
Win Prizemoney £3,687 *Total Prizemoney* £16,337
Wins 1997 Mar Doncas (G-F) 10.3f 77+ <
1998 Turf 0-5: (13f, 14f, 16f 2, 19f) (sft 2, g-f, frm 2)
Workmanlike, useful gelding, effective 10 to 19f, best at 14f, acts on sft to frm, has worn blinkers. Turf high 87 (1st run) - 5th of 18 getting 7lb from Silence in Court (6 May Chester 19f g-f RF 1059). Consistent. He was one of a number to meet trouble in running in the Chester Cup, but shaped with promise nonetheless, and ran another good race in the Pitmen's Derby. Held subsequently.
**Mrs J R Ramsden [0-5] Platinum Syndicate Ltd (from B W Hills [1-10] Oct 1997).*

MITHALI BHB 93f **RR 95f** 973[13]
5 b h Unfuwain (USA) 11.4f **(74)** - Al Bahathri (USA) (Blushing Groom (FR)) 10.3f **(76)**
Form - 0
Record 1998 - 1st:0 2nd:0 3rd:0 Ran:1
Pre1998 - 1st:3 2nd:0 3rd:0 Ran:6
Win Prizemoney £14,242 *Total Prizemoney* £14,242
Wins * 1997 Oct Leices (G-F) 10f 95 <
* 1997 Spt Doncas (G-F) 10.3f 91
* 1997 Jun Nottin (SFT) 8.2f 79+
1998 Turf 0-1: (10f) (gd)
Very useful colt, effective 10f, acts on frm.
**B W Hills [3-7] Hamdan Al Maktoum.*

MITIE ACCESS (IRE) BHB 50f **RR 58f** 4318[13]
2 ch f Mujtahid (USA) 7.4f **(69)** - Simply Marilyn (IRE) (Simply Great (FR)) 8.2f **(65)**
Form - 030
Record 1998 - 1st:0 2nd:0 3rd:1 Ran:3
Win Prizemoney £0 *Total Prizemoney* £530
1998 Turf 0-3: (7f 3) (gd, frm 2)
Currently fair filly. Turf high 58 (began Jly) - 3rd of 3 getting 4lb from Sarraia (5 Aug Yarmouth 7f frm RF 3397).
**C A Dwyer [0-3] David Bowkett.*

MIXED CURRENCY (USA) RR 73f 5116[3]
2 b br c Silver Hawk (USA) 11.2f **(85)** - Copperhead (USA) (Hawaii) 9.4f **(66)**
Form - 3
Record 1998 - 1st:0 2nd:0 3rd:1 Ran:1
Win Prizemoney £0 *Total Prizemoney* £515
1998 Turf 0-1: (8f) (gd)
Currently above-average colt. (1st run) - 3rd of 9 to Raneen Nashwan (4 Nov Musselburgh 8f gd RF 5116).
**J H M Gosden [0-1] Sheikh Mohammed.*

MIXSTERTHETRIXSTER (USA) BHB 100f **RR 87f** 4870[3]
2 b c Alleged (USA) 11.8f **(81)** - Parliament House (USA) (General Assembly (USA)) 10f **(68)**
Form - 13143
Record 1998 - 1st:2 2nd:0 3rd:2 Ran:5
Win Prizemoney £8,410 *Total Prizemoney* £17,645
Wins * **1998** Spt Haydoc (GD) 8.1f 87 <
* **1998** Jun Newcas (GD) 7f 80+
1998 Turf 2-5: (7f 1-2, 8f 1-3) (gd 1-3, frm 1-2)
Useful colt. Turf high 87 - 3rd of 4 to Tayil (11 Jly York 7f frm RF 2735) - also 1st of 4 giving 5lb to Bienamado (5 Spt Haydock RF 4103). Beat an ordinary field in facile style on his debut and ran respectably in a conditions race next time. Dead-heated with a potentially useful sort on his third run, but well held in the Royal Lodge. Looks a stayer.
**T D Easterby [2-5] Burke's 5th Family Settlement.*

MIZHAR (USA) BHB 97f **RR 94f** 4634[1]
2 b br c Dayjur (USA) 6.8f **(79)** - Futuh (USA) (Diesis) 9.3f **(69)**
Form - 0411
Record 1998 - 1st:2 2nd:0 3rd:0 Ran:4
Win Prizemoney £9,310 *Total Prizemoney* £9,593
Wins * **1998** Oct Newmar () H 6f 91 94 <
* **1998** Spt Nottin (GD) 6.1f 82
1998 Turf 2-4: (6f 2-2, 7f 2) (gd 1-2, g-f 1-1, frm)
Useful colt. Turf high 94 (began Aug) - 1st of 8 giving 6lb to Acicula (3 Oct Newmarket RF 4634). A brother to Middle Park winner Hayil, he ended the season on a high with victories in a Nottingham maiden and a Newmarket nursery under top weight. He could be a nice little sprint handicapper next season.
**E A L Dunlop [2-4] Hamdan Al Maktoum.*

MIZ TAW BHB 55f **RR 58f** 3400[4]
2 b f Mizoram (USA) - Brown Taw (Whistlefield) 5f **(55)**
Form - 404
Record 1998 - 1st:0 2nd:0 3rd:0 Ran:3
1998 Turf 0-3: (5f 2, 6f) (g-f, frm 2)
Currently fair filly. Turf high 58. **J R Jenkins [0-3] Mrs Carol Davis.*

MODEST HOPE (USA) BHB 27f31a **RR 34f 31a** 4890[12]
11 b g Blushing Groom (FR) 10.2f **(80)** - Key Dancer (USA) (Nijinsky (CAN)) 10.3f **(77)**
Form - 30656838100
Record 1998 - 1st:1 2nd:0 3rd:2 Ran:11
Pre1998 - 1st:10 2nd:8 3rd:16 Ran:90
Win Prizemoney £29,709 *Total Prizemoney* £45,073
Wins * **1998** Aug Bright (FRM) SH 11.9f 26 34
1996 *Jan Southw (STD) H 11f 44 48*
1995 *Mar Southw (STD) H 11f 45 49*
1994 Spt Pontef (GD) H 12f 41 50
1994 Spt Yarmou (G-F) H 11.5f 42 45
1998 Turf 1-7: (11f, 12f 1-5, 14f) (sft, g-f 1-3, frm 2, hrd) 1998 AW 0-4: (11f 2, 12f 2) (Fibr 4)
Very moderate gelding, effective 12f, acts on g-f to frm, favours tight tracks. Turf high 34 - 1st of 13 getting 1lb from Country Thatch (12 Aug Brighton RF 3571). AW high 29.
**Mrs S Lamyman [1-13] J McManamon (from B Richmond [5-64] Spt 1996).*

MODESTY FORBIDS BHB 64f **RR 57f** 4643[13]
2 b f Formidable (USA) 7.8f **(60)** - Ming Blue (Primo Dominie) 6.2f **(80)**
Form - 5030
Record 1998 - 1st:0 2nd:0 3rd:1 Ran:4
Win Prizemoney £0 *Total Prizemoney* £292
1998 Turf 0-4: (6f, 7f 3) (g-f 2, frm 2)
Fair filly. Turf high 57 (began Jly) - 3rd of 12 to Bob's Princess (31 Aug Warwick 7f frm RF 4006). **P G Murphy [0-4] R D Willis.*

MOET (IRE) BHB 55f **RR 60f** 4811[14]
3 b f Mac's Imp (USA) 5.6f **(54)** - Comfrey Glen (Glenstal (USA)) 10.1f **(64)**
Form - 345150
Record 1998 - 1st:1 2nd:0 3rd:1 Ran:6
Pre1998 - 1st:0 2nd:0 3rd:0 Ran:1
Win Prizemoney £4,614 *Total Prizemoney* £5,384
Wins * **1998** Spt Thirsk (GD) 6f 60 <
1998 Turf 1-6: (6f 1-4, 7f, 8f) (gd 4, frm 1-2)
Scopey, average filly, effective 6f, acts on frm. Turf high 60 - 1st of 14 getting 5lb from Bahamian Pirate (5 Spt Thirsk RF 4113).
**J L Eyre [1-7] Mrs Kate Watson.*

MOGIN BHB 31f46a **RR 30f 46a** 3663[8]
5 ch m Komaite (USA) 6.9f **(61)** - Misdevious (USA) (Alleged (USA)) 10f **(76)**
Form - 361216726884008
Record 1998 - 1st:2 2nd:2 3rd:0 Ran:13
Pre1998 - 1st:1 2nd:1 3rd:2 Ran:21
Win Prizemoney £6,463 *Total Prizemoney* £9,895
Wins * **1998** *Jan Lingfi (STD) H 10f 42 46*
* **1998** *Jan Lingfi (STD) H 8f 38 41*
* 1996 Aug Bright (G-F) 7f 51 <
1998 Turf 0-6: (8f 2, 10f 3, 11f) (sft, g-s, gd, g-f 2, frm) 1998 AW 2-7: (8f 1-3, 10f 1-4) (Equi 2-7)
Moderate filly, effective 8 to 10f, best at 10f, - acts on Equi, favours

left handed tracks. Turf high 39. AW high 46 - 2nd of 12 giving 7lb to North Ardar (22 Jan Lingfield 10f Equi RF 0131) - also 1st of 8 giving 3lb to Don't Drop Bombs (29 Jan Lingfield RF 0183).
**T J Naughton [3-26] The Dream Partnership (from J Ffitch-Heyes [0-8] Apr 1996).*

MOGUL BHB 48f54a RR 39f 54a 2329[11]
4 b g Formidable (USA) 7.8f **(60)** - Madiyla (Darshaan) 9.9f **(84)**
Form - 0
Record 1998 - 1st:0 2nd:0 3rd:0 Ran:1
Pre1998 - 1st:0 2nd:2 3rd:0 Ran:9
Win Prizemoney £0 *Total Prizemoney* £1,666
1998 Turf 0-1: (12f) (gd)
Workmanlike, very moderate gelding, effective 10f, - acts on Equi, has worn blinkers, favours tight tracks.
**R J Baker [0-2] R J Baker (from N A Graham [0-9] Jly 1997).*

MOHAWK (IRE) RR 72f 1878[9]
3 b c Indian Ridge 7.6f **(74)**-Dazzling Fire(IRE)(Bluebird (USA))7.5f **(69)**
Form - 6140
Record 1998 - 1st:1 2nd:0 3rd:0 Ran:4
Pre1998 - 1st:0 2nd:0 3rd:2 Ran:6
Win Prizemoney £2,944 *Total Prizemoney* £4,657
Wins *** 1998** May Newcas (G-S) H 6f 66 72 <
1998 Turf 1-4: (6f 1-4) (g-s, gd 1-2, frm)
Workmanlike, above-average colt, effective 6f, acts on gd. Turf high 72 - 1st of 20 giving 1lb to Wait'n'see (4 May Newcastle RF 1021). Inconsistent. **J L Dunlop [1-10] John Darby.*

MOI CANARD BHB 34f42a RR 39f 42a 923[11]
5 ch h Bold Owl 9.7f **(47)** - Royal Scots Greys (Blazing Saddles (AUS)) 6.7f **(46)**
Form - 8500
Record 1998 - 1st:0 2nd:0 3rd:0 Ran:4
Pre1998 - 1st:6 2nd:7 3rd:2 Ran:38
Win Prizemoney £16,644 *Total Prizemoney* £24,252

Wins								
	1996	*Mar Lingfi*	*(STD)*	*H*	*7f*	*69*	*70*	*<*
	1996	*Feb Lingfi*	*(STD)*	*H*	*7f*	*62*	*68*	
	1995	*Nov Lingfi*	*(STD)*	*C*	*6f*		*66*	
	1995	Aug Hamilt	(FRM)	C	6f		66	
	1995	*May Wolver*	*(STD)*	*S*	*6f*		*66?*	
	1995	*May Southw*	*(STD)*	*S*	*5f*		*66*	

1998 Turf 0-1: (6f) (gd) 1998 AW 0-3: (6f, 7f 2) (Equi, Fibr 2)
Very moderate colt, effective 5f, acts on frm, has worn blinkers, likes left handed tracks. AW high 28.
**Pat Mitchell [0-4] Mrs Anna Sanders (from B A Pearce [2-25] Spt 1997).*

MOLA (IRE) BHB 67f RR 73df 2752[10]
3 b f Robellino (USA) 9.5f **(68)** - Epure (Bellypha) 9.8f **(73)**
Form - 450
Record 1998 - 1st:0 2nd:0 3rd:0 Ran:3
Win Prizemoney £0 *Total Prizemoney* £267
1998 Turf 0-3: (10f, 12f 2) (gd 2, g-f)
Scopey, currently above-average filly. Turf high 73.
**Mrs J Cecil [0-3] Greenbay Stables Ltd.*

MOLAKAI (USA) RR 82f 4778[2]
3 b f Nureyev (USA) 8.4f **(84)** -Yemanja (USA) (Alleged (USA)) 10f **(76)**
Form - 2
Record 1998 - 1st:0 2nd:1 3rd:0 Ran:1
Win Prizemoney £0 *Total Prizemoney* £1,819
1998 Turf 0-1: (8f) (gd)
Scopey, currently decent filly. **H R A Cecil [0-1] Niarchos Family.*

MOLE CREEK BHB 84f RR 83f 5043[2]
3 gr f Unfuwain (USA) 11.4f **(74)**- Nicholas Grey (Track Spare) 8.8f **(62)**
Form - 22522212
Record 1998 - 1st:1 2nd:6 3rd:0 Ran:8
Pre1998 - 1st:0 2nd:0 3rd:0 Ran:1
Win Prizemoney £3,501 *Total Prizemoney* £13,739
Wins *** 1998** Oct Warwic (GD) 10.8f 83 <
1998 Turf 1-8: (10f 5, 11f 1-1, 12f 2) (sft, gd, g-f 1-5, frm)
Leggy, decent filly, effective 10 to 12f, best at 10f, acts on sft to g-f. Turf high 83 - 1st of 4 from Red Leggings (4 Oct Warwick RF 4646). Consistent. Her victory was not coming out of turn.
**J R Fanshawe [1-9] Lord Vestey.*

MOLLY MACK BHB 45f RR 51f 3970[8]
2 b f Thowra (FR) 11.2f **(47)** - Gangawayhame (Lochnager) 6f **(59)**
Form - 0508
Record 1998 - 1st:0 2nd:0 3rd:0 Ran:4
1998 Turf 0-4: (6f 3, 7f) (g-f 2, frm 2)
Fair filly. Turf high 51 (began Jly). **A W Carroll [0-4] John Rutter.*

MOLLY MUSIC BHB 33f40a RR 33f 40a 4275[14]
4 b f Music Boy 6.5f **(56)** - Carlton Glory (Blakeney) 10.5f **(64)**
Form - 42557245705406040
Record 1998 - 1st:0 2nd:1 3rd:0 Ran:14
Pre1998 - 1st:1 2nd:3 3rd:5 Ran:22
Win Prizemoney £3,096 *Total Prizemoney* £8,049
Wins ** 1997 Jun Southw (STD) H 8f 55 65 <*
1998 Turf 0-5: (7f 2, 8f 2, 10f) (g-s 2, gd, frm 2) 1998 AW 0-9: (7f 2, 8f 7) (Fibr 9)
Neat, moderate filly, effective 7 to 8f, best at 7f, - acts on Fibr, has worn blinkers, likes left handed tracks, likes tight tracks. Turf high 33. AW high 46. **G G Margarson [1-36] William Hattersley.*

MOLLYTIME BHB 40f RR 36f 5093[10]
2 ch f Timeless Times (USA) 6.1f **(56)** - Merry Molly **(22f)** (Deploy)
Form - 000
Record 1998 - 1st:0 2nd:0 3rd:0 Ran:3
1998 Turf 0-3: (7f 3) (sft, gd, g-f)
Currently very moderate filly. Turf high 36 (began Oct).
**N Bycroft [0-3] G W H Burnett.*

MOMENTARILY (USA) BHB 56f RR 60f 3392[18]
3 b f Gilded Time (USA) 7f **(76)** - Saratoga Dame (USA) (Saratoga Six (USA)) 7f **(73)**
Form - 780
Record 1998 - 1st:0 2nd:0 3rd:0 Ran:3
Pre1998 - 1st:0 2nd:0 3rd:0 Ran:1
1998 Turf 0-3: (7f, 8f 2) (gd, g-f, frm)
Workmanlike, average filly. Turf high 60.
**E A L Dunlop [0-4] C Gordon-Watson.*

MONAASSIB BHB 110f RR 112f 3929[5]
7 ch g Cadeaux Genereux 7.9f **(76)** - Pluvial (Habat) 7.6f **(61)**
Form - 1460435
Record 1998 - 1st:1 2nd:0 3rd:1 Ran:7
Pre1998 - 1st:9 2nd:8 3rd:1 Ran:29
Win Prizemoney £108,121 *Total Prizemoney* £178,026

Wins							
	*** 1998**	Mar Doncas	(GD)	L	6f	114	<
	* 1997	Jly Deauvi	(GD)	G3	6f	113	
	* 1997	May Baden	(G-F)	G3	6f	107	
	* 1997	May Goodwo	(GD)		6f	110	
	* 1997	Apr Newmar	(GD)	L	6f	110	
	* 1997	Mar Kempto	(G-F)		6f	110	
	* 1996	Aug Yarmou	(G-F)		6f	100	
	* 1995	Oct Doncas	(G-F)		7f	100	
	1994	Jly Haydoc	(G-F)		6f	95	
	1994	May Salisb	(FRM)		6f	74	

1998 Turf 1-7: (6f 1-7) (gd 1-4, frm 3)
Group-class gelding, effective 6 to 7f, best at 6f, acts on gd to frm, best on gd, and excels at Deauville. Turf high 114 (1st run) - 1st of 9 from Cretan Gift (28 Mar Doncaster RF 0485). Consistent. A grand campaigner, he won a Listed event at Doncaster in March and went on to run some solid races, including when beaten just over five lengths in the July Cup.
**E A L Dunlop [8-31] Maktoum Al Maktoum (from A A Scott [2-5] Jly 1994).*

MONACO (IRE) BHB 42f RR 30f 1096[10]
4 b g Classic Music (USA) 7.2f **(57)** - Larosterna (Busted) 10.2f **(61)**
Form - 00
Record 1998 - 1st:0 2nd:0 3rd:0 Ran:2
Pre1998 - 1st:0 2nd:0 3rd:1 Ran:8
Win Prizemoney £0 *Total Prizemoney* £1,033
1998 Turf 0-2: (7f, 8f) (gd 2)
Scopey, very moderate gelding, effective 9 to 10f, acts on g-s to frm, likes tight tracks. Turf high 24.
**R Allan [0-9] Ian Flannigan (from L M Cumani [0-5] Aug 1997).*

MONACO GOLD (IRE) BHB 45f49a RR 45f 49a 2340[5]
6 b g Durgam (USA) 12.3f **(53)** - Monaco Ville (Rheingold) 10.4f **(62)**

Form - 13321525

Record 1998 - 1st:2 2nd:2 3rd:2 Ran:8
Pre1998 - 1st:4 2nd:1 3rd:0 Ran:16

Win Prizemoney £16,469 *Total Prizemoney* £19,019

Wins * **1998** *May Lingfi (STD) SH 16f 47 54*
* **1998** *Mar Southw (STD) C 14f 54*
1997 Jly Hamilt (SFT) C 11.1f 40
1997 Jun Hamilt (SFT) C 12.1f 63 <
1996 Aug Hamilt (G-F) H 13f 39 43
1996 Jun Ayr (G-F) H 13.1f 35 39

1998 Turf 0-2: (12f 2) (sft, g-s) 1998 AW 2-6: (13f, 14f 1-1, 16f 1-4) (Equi 1-3, Fibr 1-3)

Fair gelding, has broken blood-vessels, effective 12 to 16f, best at 16f, acts on gd - acts on AW, best on Fibr, has worn blinkers. Turf high 45. AW high 59 - 2nd of 8 getting 9lb from Mazzelmo (17 Jun Wolverhampton 16f Fibr RF 2078) - also 1st of 14 giving 8lb to Krayyan Dawn (23 May Lingfield RF 1430).

D J S Cosgrove [2-8] Winning Circle Racing Club Ltd (from Mrs M Reveley [4-13] Aug 1997).

MONARCHY (IRE) RR 57f 3443[14]

3 b f Common Grounds 8.1f **(66)** - Royal Rumpus (Prince Tenderfoot (USA)) 9f **(61)**

Form - 50

Record 1998 - 1st:0 2nd:0 3rd:0 Ran:2

1998 Turf 0-2: (7f, 8f) (g-f, frm)

Scopey, currently fair filly. Turf high 57 (began Jly).

J H M Gosden [0-2] Sheikh Mohammed.

MON BRUCE BHB 53f70a RR 55f 70a 3941[5]

4 ch g Beveled (USA) 6.9f **(64)** - Pendona (Blue Cashmere) 6.4f **(54)**

Form - 00703005

Record 1998 - 1st:0 2nd:0 3rd:1 Ran:8
Pre1998 - 1st:3 2nd:3 3rd:2 Ran:20

Win Prizemoney £7,531 *Total Prizemoney* £11,912

Wins * 1997 Spt Pontef (G-F) H 5f 57 60
1997 *Spt Southw (STD) C 5f 66* <
1997 *Apr Wolver (STD) 6f 53*

1998 Turf 0-8: (5f 8) (g-f 2, frm 6)

Unfurnished, average gelding, effective 5f, acts on gd to frm - acts on Fibr, likes left handed tracks, likes tight tracks. Turf high 55.

M Dods [1-13] N A Riddell (from W R Muir [2-15] Spt 1997).

MONCHANIA BHB 72f74a RR 3f 74a 1797[11]

3 ch f Mon Tresor 7.9f **(60)** - Sugar Owl (Bold Owl) 8.5f **(45)**

Form - 1600

Record 1998 - 1st:1 2nd:0 3rd:0 Ran:4

Win Prizemoney £3,647 *Total Prizemoney* £3,647

Wins * **1998** *Jan Wolver (STD) 8.5f 79+* <

1998 Turf 0-1: (8f) (g-s) 1998 AW 1-3: (8f 1-1, 9f 2) (Fibr 1-3)

Light-framed, above-average filly. AW high 79 (1st run) - 1st of 13 getting 20lb from Run Or Bust (7 Jan Wolverhampton RF 0037). Landed a touch when scoring on her racecourse bow at Wolverhampton in January. The opposition was not up to much, and she has been well and truly found out since.

J L Spearing [1-4] The Not So Risky Partnership.

MONDRAGON BHB 65f60a RR 67f 60a 5118[2]

8 b g Niniski (USA) 13.2f **(67)** - La Lutine (My Swallow) 9.2f **(71)**

Form - 5265345221312532

Record 1998 - 1st:2 2nd:5 3rd:3 Ran:15
Pre1998 - 1st:3 2nd:5 3rd:7 Ran:37

Win Prizemoney £15,953 *Total Prizemoney* £36,806

Wins * **1998** Aug Beverl (G-F) H 16.2f 59 62
* **1998** Jly Redcar (G-F) H 16f 55 57
* 1994 Jly Redcar (GD) H 16f 69 74 <

1998 Turf 2-12: (16f 2-10, 17f, 18f) (sft, g-s 2, gd 3, g-f 1-2, frm 1-3, hrd) 1998 AW 0-3: (16f 3) (Fibr 3)

Average gelding, effective 16f, acts on g-s to hrd - acts on Fibr, prefers right handed tracks, favours tight tracks, excels at Redcar and Beverley. Turf high 67 - 2nd of 16 getting 1lb from Silent Warning (4 Nov Musselburgh 16f gd RF 5118) - also 1st of 6 giving 9lb to Spa Lane (12 Aug Beverley RF 3564). AW high 60 (1st run) - 2nd of 11 getting 1lb from Whitley Grange Boy (9 Jan Southwell 16f Fibr RF 0054). Consistent. Well suited by fast ground and a strongly-run race.

Mrs M Reveley [6-53] D Young.

MONDSCHEIN BHB 93f RR 90f 5141[2]

3 b f Rainbow Quest (USA) 11.2f **(81)** - River Spey (Mill Reef (USA)) 10.5f **(78)**

Form - 143662

Record 1998 - 1st:1 2nd:1 3rd:1 Ran:6
Pre1998 - 1st:0 2nd:1 3rd:0 Ran:2

Win Prizemoney £4,240 *Total Prizemoney* £10,395

Wins * **1998** Apr Sandow (SFT) 10f 79 <

1998 Turf 1-6: (10f 1-4, 12f 2) (sft 1-2, g-s, gd, g-f, frm)

Light-framed, useful filly, effective 7 to 12f, best at 10f, acts on sft to frm, has worn blinkers. Turf high 91 - 3rd of 12 giving 8lb to Light Step (31 Aug Newcastle 10f frm RF 3992). Owned by Abba member Benny Andersson, she was the decisive winner of a soft-ground Sandown maiden on her reappearance, but met her Waterloo on faster ground at Goodwood next time. She did not win again, but proved a real Super Trouper by running well in a Newcastle listed handicap and a Doncaster conditions event on her final start. Soft ground looks the Name Of The Game.

J L Dunlop [1-8] Benny Andersson.

MONET BHB 70a RR 69f 4879[5]

3 b c Dynaformer (USA) 12f **(82)** - Ballerina Star (USA) (Forli (ARG)) 9.6f **(67)**

Form - 44220045

Record 1998 - 1st:0 2nd:2 3rd:0 Ran:8

Win Prizemoney £0 *Total Prizemoney* £2,591

1998 Turf 0-4: (10f, 12f 2, 14f) (gd 2, g-f, frm) 1998 AW 0-4: (9f 2, 12f, 14f) (Fibr 4)

Scopey, above-average colt, has broken blood-vessels, effective 9 to 12f, best at 12f, acts on frm - acts on Fibr, prefers left handed tracks. Turf high 80 - 4th of 6 getting 6lb from Casino Captive (25 May Chepstow 12f frm RF 1444). AW high 79 (1st run) (began Aug) - 2nd of 6 to Ionian Spring (7 Aug Wolverhampton 9f Fibr RF 3451). Inconsistent. *P W Chapple-Hyam [0-8] Mrs Jane Chapple-Hyam.*

MONGOL WARRIOR (USA) BHB 105f RR 113f 4348a[4]

5 b h Deputy Minister (CAN) 9.2f **(71)** - Surely Georgie's (USA) (Alleged (USA)) 10f **(76)**

Form - 15204

Record 1998 - 1st:0 2nd:1 3rd:0 Ran:4
Pre1998 - 1st:5 2nd:4 3rd:3 Ran:19

Win Prizemoney £147,294 *Total Prizemoney* £208,590

Wins * 1997 Dec Toulou (HVY) L 12f 113 <
* 1996 Nov La Zar (G-F) G3 12f 94
* 1996 Jun Frauen (GD) 12f 88
* 1996 May Munich (SFT) G3 11f 88
* 1996 Jan Cagnes (SFT) 8f 81

1998 Turf 0-4: (12f 2, 16f, 20f) (sft 2, g-s, gd)

Group-class colt, effective 11 to 16f, best at 12f, acts on hvy to gd, likes right handed tracks, excels at Cologne. Turf high 108 - 2nd of 7 giving 4lb to Solo Mio (16 May Baden-Baden 16f gd RF 1376a). He raced infrequently and never threatened in Group races.

Lord Huntingdon [5-23].

MONICA'S CHOICE (IRE) BHB 65f RR 68df 5060[5]

7 b g Shaadi (USA) 8.1f **(75)** - Tendermark (Prince Tenderfoot (USA)) 9f **(61)**

Form - 36145

Record 1998 - 1st:1 2nd:0 3rd:1 Ran:5
Pre1998 - 1st:0 2nd:0 3rd:1 Ran:3

Win Prizemoney £2,416 *Total Prizemoney* £3,146

Wins * **1998** May Carlis (G-S) C 6.9f 68 <

1998 Turf 1-5: (7f 1-3, 8f 2) (sft, gd 1-3, frm)

Average gelding. Turf high 68 - 1st of 11 giving 4lb to Dancing Lawyer (8 May Carlisle RF 1096).

Mrs M Reveley [2-11] Mrs E A Murray (from P Burke in IRE [0-7] Oct 1996).

MONIS (IRE) BHB 38f38a RR 41f 38a 4919[1]

7 ch g Waajib 8.9f **(67)** - Gratify (Grundy) 10.3f **(65)**

Form - 1

Record 1998 - 1st:1 2nd:0 3rd:0 Ran:1
Pre1998 - 1st:2 2nd:4 3rd:7 Ran:46

Win Prizemoney £7,974 *Total Prizemoney* £16,627

Wins * **1998** Oct Newcas (SFT) CH 8f 33 39
* 1997 Oct Newcas (G-F) CH 8f 30 37

1998 Turf 1-1: (8f 1-1) (g-s 1-1)

Moderate gelding, effective 8 to 12f, best at 8f, acts on g-s to frm,

has worn blinkers (extremely effectively). (1st run) - 1st of 20 getting 5lb from Mariana (21 Oct Newcastle RF 4919). Consistent.
**B Ellison [2-6] C E Sherry (from Ronald Thompson [0-8] Aug 1997).*

MONITOR BHB 91f **RR 91f** 4742[2]
4 ch g Machiavellian (USA) 9.8f **(83)** - Instant Desire (USA) (Northern Dancer) 9.6f **(80)**
Form - 0052182
Record 1998 - 1st:1 2nd:2 3rd:0 Ran:7
Pre1998 - 1st:1 2nd:1 3rd:2 Ran:5
Win Prizemoney £10,590 *Total Prizemoney* £19,550
Wins * **1998** Aug Yarmou (G-F) 10.1f 85+ <
* 1997 Aug Ripon (G-F) 10f 75t
1998 Turf 1-7: (9f, 10f 1-5, 12f) (sft, g-s, gd 2, g-f 1-1, frm 2)
Well made, useful gelding, effective 9 to 10f, best at 10f, acts on g-s to frm, best on gd. Turf high 91 - 2nd of 15 getting 7lb from Present Arms (10 Oct Ascot 10f g-s RF 4742) - also 1st of 4 giving 12lb to Shfoug (9 Aug Yarmouth RF 3497). He was runner-up in a couple of handicaps during the season, but his victory came in a four-runner Yarmouth conditions event.
**H R A Cecil [2-12] Buckram Oak Holdings.*

MONKSTON POINT (IRE) BHB 100f **RR 99+f** 4739[3]
2 b c Fayruz 6.6f **(63)** - Doon Belle (Ardoon) 7.3f **(53)**
Form - 13133413
Record 1998 - 1st:3 2nd:0 3rd:4 Ran:8
Win Prizemoney £16,493 *Total Prizemoney* £56,316
Wins * **1998** Spt Ayr (G-S) L 5f 99+ <
* **1998** Jun Bath (G-S) 5.1f 93
* **1998** Apr Bath (SFT) 5.1f 88
1998 Turf 3-8: (5f 3-7, 6f) (g-s 2-4, gd 1-4)
Very useful colt, effective 5f, acts on g-s to gd, best on gd. Turf high 99 - also 1st of 12 from Pips Magic (17 Spt Ayr RF 4322). Improving. Did his connections proud, winning three times including Ayr's Harry Rosebery Trophy. He also ran cracking races in defeat in most of the top two-year-old sprints. Very genuine, he was led out unsold at 60,000 gns at Newmarket in the autumn and is likely to stay with Arbuthnot.
**D W P Arbuthnot [3-8] Derrick Broomfield.*

MONO LADY (IRE) BHB 67f75a **RR 61df 75a** 5126[15]
5 b m Polish Patriot (USA) 7.8f **(70)** - Phylella (Persian Bold) 9.3f **(66)**
Form - 7262715700
Record 1998 - 1st:1 2nd:2 3rd:0 Ran:10
Pre1998 - 1st:5 2nd:3 3rd:3 Ran:26
Win Prizemoney £21,808 *Total Prizemoney* £28,990
Wins * **1998** Aug Leices (GD) H 11.8f 72 74 <
* 1997 Spt Bright (G-F) H 11.9f 60 68
* 1997 *May Lingfi (STD) H 10f 63 71*
* 1997 *Jan Southw (STD) H 8f 54 58*
* 1997 *Jan Wolver (SLW) H 9.4f 48 52*
* 1996 Oct Folkes (G-S) H 9.7f 51 57
1998 Turf 1-10: (10f 7, 11f, 12f 1-2) (sft, g-s 3, gd 3, g-f 2, frm 1-1)
Above-average filly, effective 10 to 12f, best at 10f, acts on gd to frm - acts on Equi, often wears blinkers (extremely effectively), likes left handed tracks. Turf high 74 - 1st of 7 giving 9lb to City Gambler (19 Aug Leicester RF 3743). Becoming disappointing.
**D HaydnJones [6-36] Monolithic Refractories Ltd.*

MONSAJEM (USA) BHB 96f **RR 89+f** 5043[1]
3 ch c Woodman (USA) 9.7f **(77)** - Fairy Dancer (USA) (Nijinsky (CAN)) 10.3f **(77)**
Form - 334611
Record 1998 - 1st:2 2nd:0 3rd:2 Ran:6
Pre1998 - 1st:1 2nd:0 3rd:0 Ran:5
Win Prizemoney £11,017 *Total Prizemoney* £18,880
Wins * **1998** Oct Yarmou (SFT) 10.1f 89+ <
* **1998** Oct Yarmou (G-S) H 10.1f 85 88
1997 Aug Chepst (GD) 8.1f 76
1998 Turf 2-6: (10f 2-4, 12f 2) (sft 1-1, gd, g-f 1-3, frm)
Scopey, useful colt, effective 10 to 12f, best at 10f, acts on sft to g-f, best on g-f. Turf high 89 (began Aug) - 1st of 6 giving 3lb to Mole Creek (28 Oct Yarmouth RF 5043) - also 1st of 13 giving 8lb to Fahs (20 Oct Yarmouth RF 4893). Improving. Two backend victories at Yarmouth stamp him as an improving sort.
**E A L Dunlop [2-6] Khalifa Sultan (from S bin Suroor [1-5] Oct 1997).*

MONTAGUE TIGG (IRE) BHB 68f **RR 76f** 4658[1]
2 b g Common Grounds 8.1f **(66)** - Astra (IRE) (Glenstal (USA)) 10.1f **(64)**
Form - 40023001
Record 1998 - 1st:1 2nd:1 3rd:1 Ran:8
Win Prizemoney £3,570 *Total Prizemoney* £5,288
Wins * **1998** Oct Pontef (GD) H 6f 63 64 <
1998 Turf 1-8: (6f 1-7, 7f) (gd 1-2, g-f, frm 5)
Above-average gelding, effective 6f, acts on frm. Turf high 76 (1st run) (began Jly) - 4th of 16 giving 7lb to Scoop (17 Jly Pontefract 6f frm RF 2884). **N Tinkler [1-8] Boz.*

MONTALCINO (IRE) RR 74f 4503[4]
2 b c Robellino (USA) 9.5f **(68)** - Only Gossip (USA) (Trempolino (USA)) 12f **(71)**
Form - 4
Record 1998 - 1st:0 2nd:0 3rd:0 Ran:1
Win Prizemoney £0 *Total Prizemoney* £273
1998 Turf 0-1: (7f) (frm)
Currently above-average colt.
**P W Chapple-Hyam [0-1] Dr Carlos Stelling.*

MONTE CALVO RR 66f 4664[5]
2 b f Shirley Heights 12.1f **(76)** - Slava (USA) (Diesis) 9.3f **(69)**
Form - 5
Record 1998 - 1st:0 2nd:0 3rd:0 Ran:1
1998 Turf 0-1: (8f) (g-s)
Currently average filly. **J L Dunlop [0-1] Capt J Macdonald-Buchanan.*

MONTE CAVO BHB 44f51a **RR 50f 51a** 4156[10]
7 b g Bustino 11f **(64)** - Dance Festival (Nureyev (USA)) 8.7f **(78)**
Form - 0000
Record 1998 - 1st:0 2nd:0 3rd:0 Ran:4
Pre1998 - 1st:3 2nd:4 3rd:5 Ran:34
Win Prizemoney £10,083 *Total Prizemoney* £16,621
Wins * 1997 Aug Newmar (GD) H 10f 52 58 <
* 1997 *Jun Southw (STD) H 8f 41 48*
* 1997 Jun Newmar (G-S) H 8f 30 45
1998 Turf 0-4: (9f, 10f 2, 11f) (g-s, g-f 2, frm)
Fair gelding, effective 8 to 10f, best at 10f, acts on gd to hrd, has worn blinkers, likes right handed tracks, excels at Newmarket. Turf high 31. Inconsistent.
**M Brittain [3-30] Mel Brittain (from C F Wall [0-3] Aug 1994).*

MONTECRISTO BHB 90f89a **RR 86f 89a** 4515[3]
5 br g Warning 8.1f **(77)** - Sutosky (Great Nephew) 9.9f **(64)**
Form - 131313441313
Record 1998 - 1st:4 2nd:0 3rd:4 Ran:10
Pre1998 - 1st:8 2nd:1 3rd:3 Ran:27
Win Prizemoney £41,125 *Total Prizemoney* £55,109
Wins * **1998** Spt Epsom (SFT) H 12f 83 86 <
* **1998** Jly Bright (GD) H 11.9f 77 82
* **1998** Mar Warwic (G-S) H 12.5f 73 77
* **1998** *Feb Wolver (STD) H 12f 72 71+*
* 1997 *Nov Wolver (STD) 12f 73+*
* 1997 Nov Nottin (GD) 14.1f 74
* 1997 *Oct Southw (STD) 12f 51*
* 1997 Spt Newbur (SFT) H 12f 66 70
* 1997 Aug Hamilt (G-F) H 11.1f 62 65
* 1996 Apr Beverl (G-F) C 9.9f 65
* 1996 *Feb Lingfi (STD) C 12f 54*
* 1996 *Feb Lingfi (STD) H 10f 60 70*
1998 Turf 3-8: (12f 2-5, 13f 1-1, 14f 2) (sft, g-s 1-1, gd 1-2, g-f 2, frm 1-2) 1998 AW 1-2: (12f 1-2) (Fibr 1-2)
Useful gelding, effective 12 to 14f, best at 12f, acts on sft to frm, best on gd, and excels at Epsom and Nottingham. Turf high 86 - 1st of 11 giving 19lb to Galapino (5 Spt Epsom RF 4100) - also 1st of 9 giving 16lb to Yet Again (1 Jly Brighton RF 2439). AW high 73. Consistent. Had a fine season, never out of the frame and ending the campaign with a staying-on third in a valuable Ascot handicap.
**R Guest [12-37] Rae Guest.*

MONTE LEMOS (IRE) BHB 87f **RR 91f** 4749[16]
3 b g Mukaddamah (USA)7.6f **(74)**- Crimbourne(Mummy's Pet)7.7f **(60)**
Form - 63000
Record 1998 - 1st:0 2nd:0 3rd:1 Ran:5
Pre1998 - 1st:3 2nd:0 3rd:2 Ran:6

Win Prizemoney £11,981 *Total Prizemoney* £14,292

Wins * 1997 Oct Newmar (G-F) H 6f 89 91 <
* 1997 Aug Sandow (GD) H 5f 84 85
* 1997 Jly Windso (G-F) 5f 80

1998 Turf 0-5: (5f 2, 6f 3) (gd 2, g-f, frm 2)

Useful gelding, effective 5 to 6f, best at 5f, acts on gd to frm, best on gd. Turf high 91. Becoming disappointing. Met with all sorts of trouble in running on his '98 reappearance, shaping promisingly in the circumstances, but did not really go on from there. Sold for 12,000 guineas in October to Italian interests.

**R Charlton [3-11] S M De Zoete.*

MONTE MAYOR RR 4f 2554[12]

2 b f Magic Ring (IRE) 6.5f **(64)** - Giblet Pie (Henbit (USA)) 9f **(61)**

Form - 0

Record 1998 - 1st:0 2nd:0 3rd:0 Ran:1

1998 Turf 0-1: (6f) (g-f)

Currently very poor filly. **D HaydnJones [0-1] Mrs E M HaydnJones.*

MONTENDRE BHB 65f RR 71f 4988[10]

11 b g Longleat (USA) 7.2f **(59)** - La Lutine (My Swallow) 9.2f **(71)**

Form - 18384231040

Record 1998 - 1st:2 2nd:1 3rd:2 Ran:11
Pre1998 - 1st:6 2nd:13 3rd:12 Ran:76

Win Prizemoney £58,803 *Total Prizemoney* £156,861

Wins * **1998** Aug Haydoc (GD) C 6f 66
* **1998** Apr Nottin (SFT) C 5.1f 62
1997 Spt Bath (GD) H 5.7f 75 78
1995 Mar Doncas (G-F) L 6f 102

1998 Turf 2-11: (5f 1-3, 6f 1-8) (sft 1-2, g-s, gd 1-4, g-f, frm 3)

Above-average gelding, effective 5 to 6f, best at 6f, acts on gd to frm, best on g-f, has worn blinkers. Turf high 72 - 3rd of 7 getting 18lb from Triple Hay (20 May Goodwood 6f g-f RF 1355). A marvellous veteran, he remains well capable of winning sprints in modest company.

**R J Hodges [2-21] David Mort (from M J Heaton-Ellis [1-5] Oct 1997).*

MONTFORT (USA) RR 106?f 964[10]

4 b g Manila (USA) 10f **(81)** - Sable Coated (Caerleon (USA)) 8.6f **(71)**

Form - 0

Record 1998 - 1st:0 2nd:0 3rd:0 Ran:1
Pre1998 - 1st:3 2nd:0 3rd:1 Ran:5

Win Prizemoney £15,844 *Total Prizemoney* £17,086

Wins * 1997 Jun Salisb (SFT) 14f 106+ <
* 1997 Jun York (G-S) 11.9f 92+
* 1997 May Bright (FRM) 11.9f 80

1998 Turf 0-1: (16f) (gd)

Scopey, Pattern-class gelding. **P F I Cole [3-6] Sir George Meyrick.*

MONTONE (IRE) BHB 35f47a RR 31f 47a 1709[12]

8 b g Pennine Walk 8.9f **(64)**-Aztec Princess(Indian King(USA))7.4f **(64)**

Form - 7000

Record 1998 - 1st:0 2nd:0 3rd:0 Ran:3
Pre1998 - 1st:11 2nd:14 3rd:7 Ran:84

Win Prizemoney £30,481 *Total Prizemoney* £45,294

Wins * 1997 *Feb Lingfi (STD) H 8f 60 66*
* 1996 *Nov Lingfi (STD) H 8f 58 60*
* 1996 Oct Newcas (G-F) H 8f 63 68 <
* 1996 Jun Folkes (FRM) H 9.7f 59 62
* 1996 *Jun Southw (STD) H 7f 48 61*
* 1996 Jun Warwic (FRM) H 8f 53 59
* 1996 May Warwic (GD) H 8f 48 55
1994 Aug Beverl (G-F) H 7.5f 57 59
1994 Jun Carlis (G-F) H 6.9f 50 53
1994 Apr Carlis (SFT) H 5.9f 42 46+

1998 Turf 0-3: (8f 3) (gd, frm 2)

Moderate gelding, effective 8 to 12f, best at 8f, - acts on AW, best on Equi, has worn blinkers, likes left handed tracks, favours tight tracks. Turf high 17.

**J R Jenkins [7-52] B Shirazi (from K R Burke [0-12] Aug 1995).*

MONTRAVE BHB 49f RR 54f 2116[4]

9 ch g Netherkelly - Streakella (Firestreak) 8.2f **(64)**

Form - 6724

Record 1998 - 1st:0 2nd:1 3rd:0 Ran:4
Pre1998 - 1st:0 2nd:0 3rd:0 Ran:1

Win Prizemoney £0 *Total Prizemoney* £624

1998 Turf 0-4: (11f, 12f, 13f 2) (g-s 2, gd 2)

Fair gelding. Turf high 54.

**J S Goldie [3-12] D St Clair (from P Monteith [0-1] Jly 1992).*

MONTY'S RETURN BHB 40f RR 37f 2928[20]

5 ch g Mon Tresor 7.9f **(60)** - Mrs Kogl (Ballad Rock) 7.8f **(63)**

Form - 4570

Record 1998 - 1st:0 2nd:0 3rd:0 Ran:4

Win Prizemoney £0 *Total Prizemoney* £242

1998 Turf 0-4: (7f, 8f, 12f 2) (gd, frm 3)

Very moderate gelding, always wears blinkers. Turf high 37.

**D Moffatt [0-4] The Sheroot Partnership.*

MONUMENT BHB 58f RR 63f 3980[2]

6 ch g Cadeaux Genereux 7.9f **(76)** - In Perpetuity (Great Nephew) 9.9f **(64)**

Form - 553182

Record 1998 - 1st:1 2nd:1 3rd:1 Ran:6
Pre1998 - 1st:4 2nd:0 3rd:2 Ran:20

Win Prizemoney £15,791 *Total Prizemoney* £18,769

Wins * **1998** Aug Kempto (G-F) H 12f 56 58
* 1997 Jly Nottin (G-F) 10f 65
* 1996 Jly Windso (G-F) H 10f 65 64
* 1996 Jun Salisb (G-F) C 8f 62
1995 Aug Kempto (G-F) 8f 79 <

1998 Turf 1-6: (10f, 11f, 12f 1-3, 14f) (gd, g-f, frm 1-4)

Average gelding, has broken blood-vessels, effective 10 to 12f, best at 10f, acts on gd to frm, prefers left handed tracks, excels at Kempton and Chepstow. Turf high 63 (1st run) - 5th of 8 getting 9lb from Carlys Quest (23 May Warwick 11f frm RF 1437) - also 1st of 7 giving 2lb to Mystagogue (5 Aug Kempton RF 3368). Consistent. **J S King [4-26] V Askew (from R Charlton [1-5] Spt 1995).*

MOOCHA CHA MAN BHB 66f70a RR 65f 70a 5144[14]

2 b c Sizzling Melody 6.3f **(49)** - Nilu (IRE) (Ballad Rock) 7.8f **(63)**

Form - 351060

Record 1998 - 1st:1 2nd:0 3rd:1 Ran:6

Win Prizemoney £2,234 *Total Prizemoney* £2,670

Wins * **1998** *Jly Wolver (STD) 5f 65* <

1998 Turf 0-4: (5f 4) (sft, gd 2, g-f) 1998 AW 1-2: (5f 1-1, 6f) (Fibr 1-2)

Average colt, effective 5f, - acts on Fibr. Turf high 65. AW high 65 (1st run) (began Jly) - 1st of 8 giving 1lb to Miss Multiply (20 Jly Wolverhampton RF 2966). **B A McMahon [1-6] Mrs J McMahon.*

MOON AT NIGHT BHB 57f RR 55f 4456[1]

3 gr g Pursuit of Love 9.5f **(69)** - La Nureyeva (USA) (Nureyev (USA)) 8.7f **(78)**

Form - 700001

Record 1998 - 1st:1 2nd:0 3rd:0 Ran:6

Win Prizemoney £4,011 *Total Prizemoney* £4,011

Wins * **1998** Spt Goodwo (G-F) CH 8f 50 55 <

1998 Turf 1-6: (6f, 7f 3, 8f 1-2) (gd, g-f, frm 1-4)

Workmanlike, fair gelding, effective 8f, acts on frm. Turf high 55 - 1st of 22 giving 2lb to Cherished (23 Spt Goodwood RF 4456).

**L G Cottrell [1-3] Mrs D Joly (from I A Balding [0-3] Jun 1998).*

MOON BLAST BHB 75f RR 66f 3331[3]

4 gr g Reprimand 8.2f **(63)** - Castle Moon (Kalamoun) 10.4f **(67)**

Form - 63

Record 1998 - 1st:0 2nd:0 3rd:1 Ran:2
Pre1998 - 1st:2 2nd:2 3rd:1 Ran:11

Win Prizemoney £6,882 *Total Prizemoney* £10,686

Wins * 1997 Jun Windso (G-F) 8.3f 86 <
* 1997 Apr Bright (FRM) 8f 71+

1998 Turf 0-2: (12f, 13f) (gd 2)

Scopey, average gelding, effective 8 to 12f, acts on gd to frm, has worn blinkers, favours tight tracks. Turf high 66 (began Jly). Consistent. A half-brother to Moon Madness and Sheriff's Star among others, he was beaten on his belated 1998 debut, and appeared only once more. **Lady Herries [2-14] Angmering Park Stud.*

MOON BUZZARD BHB 70f RR 69f 4070[8]

2 ch c Polar Falcon (USA) 9f **(74)** - Remany (Bellypha) 9.8f **(73)**

Form - 0134758

Record 1998 - 1st:1 2nd:0 3rd:1 Ran:7

Win Prizemoney £3,882 *Total Prizemoney* £5,300

Wins * **1998** May Folkes (G-F) 6f 69 <

1998 Turf 1-7: (5f, 6f 1-5, 8f) (g-s, gd 1-3, g-f, frm 2)

Average colt, effective 6f, acts on g-s to gd. Turf high 69 - also 1st of 9 from Jade Tiger (27 May Folkestone RF 1518).
**M Blanshard [1-7] G H S Bailey & N C D Hall.*

MOON COLONY BHB 79f **RR 79f** 4958[16]
5 b g Top Ville 11f **(71)** - Honeymooning (USA) (Blushing Groom (FR)) 10.3f **(76)**
Form - 2380116040
Record 1998 - 1st:2 2nd:1 3rd:1 Ran:10
Pre1998 - 1st:1 2nd:3 3rd:1 Ran:9
Win Prizemoney £13,837 *Total Prizemoney* £21,127
Wins * **1998** Jly Newmar (G-F) H 12f 76 79
* **1998** Jly Doncas (G-F) H 12f 73 74
* 1997 Oct Nottin (SFT) 14.1f 81 <
1998 Turf 2-10: (12f 2-5, 14f 2, 15f 2, 16f) (gd 4, g-f 2, frm 2-4)
Above-average gelding, effective 12 to 17f, best at 14f, acts on sft to frm, best on gd, likes right handed tracks, likes Doncaster. Turf high 79 - 1st of 11 giving 16lb to Ordained (31 Jly Newmarket RF 3237) - also 1st of 7 giving 17lb to Warning Reef (15 Jly Doncaster RF 2816). Inconsistent. Struck form this year when reverting to twelve furlongs from two miles, but disappointed lately. Usually makes the running. **Lady Herries [3-19] Mrs Berta Lazarus.*

MOON FAIRY BHB 53f58a **RR 18f 58a** 3647[19]
4 ch f Interrex (CAN) 7.7f **(51)** - Zamoon (Zambrano) 6.1f **(37)**
Form - 0000
Record 1998 - 1st:0 2nd:0 3rd:0 Ran:3
Pre1998 - 1st:1 2nd:2 3rd:0 Ran:5
Win Prizemoney £2,531 *Total Prizemoney* £4,277
Wins * 1997 Aug Nottin (G-F) 6.1f 57+ <
1998 Turf 0-3: (5f, 6f, 7f) (gd, frm, hrd)
Unfurnished, poor filly, effective 6 to 7f, acts on g-f to frm. Turf high 18. Becoming disappointing.
**J G Smyth-Osbourne [1-8] Edenwood Partnership.*

MOON GLOW (IRE) RR 76f 3813[4]
2 b g Fayruz 6.6f **(63)** - Jarmar Moon **(55f)** (Unfuwain (USA))
Form - 524
Record 1998 - 1st:0 2nd:1 3rd:0 Ran:3
Win Prizemoney £0 *Total Prizemoney* £1,410
1998 Turf 0-3: (6f, 7f 2) (g-f 2, frm)
Currently above-average gelding. Turf high 76 (began Jly).
**Miss S E Hall [0-3] C Platts.*

MOON GORGE BHB 72f **RR 77f** 4308[15]
3 b f Pursuit of Love 9.5f **(69)** - Highland Light (Home Guard (USA)) 9.3f **(66)**
Form - 1163533850
Record 1998 - 1st:2 2nd:0 3rd:3 Ran:10
Pre1998 - 1st:0 2nd:0 3rd:0 Ran:1
Win Prizemoney £10,455 *Total Prizemoney* £12,275
Wins * **1998** Mar Warwic (G-S) H 8f 71 78 <
* **1998** *Feb Southw (STD) 7f 63*
1998 Turf 1-9: (7f 6, 8f 1-3) (g-s 1-1, gd 4, g-f 3, frm) 1998 AW 1-1: (7f 1-1) (Fibr 1-1)
Workmanlike, above-average filly, effective 7 to 8f, best at 8f, acts on g-s to frm, prefers left handed tracks, prefers tight tracks, excels at Warwick. Turf high 79 - 3rd of 19 giving 1lb to Persiano (4 May Warwick 7f g-f RF 1028) - also 1st of 9 getting 4lb from Shaanxi Romance (28 Mar Warwick RF 0490). (1st run).
**W Jarvis [2-11] Lady Howard de Walden.*

MOONLIGHT (IRE) RR 47f 3766[7]
2 b f Night Shift (USA) 8.1f **(73)** - Local Custom (IRE) (Be My Native (USA)) 10.2f **(71)**
Form - 7
Record 1998 - 1st:0 2nd:0 3rd:0 Ran:1
1998 Turf 0-1: (6f) (frm)
Currently moderate filly.
**H R A Cecil [0-1] Dr Anne J F Gillespie & John Wilson.*

MOONLIGHT FLIT RR 43f 4920[10]
3 b f Presidium 7.5f **(56)** - Moonwalker (Night Shift (USA)) 7.2f **(69)**
Form - 0651060
Record 1998 - 1st:1 2nd:0 3rd:0 Ran:7
Pre1998 - 1st:1 2nd:0 3rd:0 Ran:5
Win Prizemoney £5,146 *Total Prizemoney* £5,146
Wins 1998 Aug Pontef (G-F) S 10f 43
1997 Spt Beverl (G-F) SH 7.5f 54 63 <
1998 Turf 1-7: (8f, 9f, 10f 1-4, 12f) (g-s, gd, g-f 3, frm 1-2)
Moderate filly, effective 7f, acts on frm, has worn blinkers, likes tight tracks. Turf high 43. Both of her wins to date have been in selling company and that looks her level.
**J L Eyre [0-3] Miss C King (from J G FitzGerald [2-9] Aug 1998).*

MOONLIGHT INVADER (IRE) BHB 41f **RR 43f** 4458[12]
4 br g Darshaan 11.9f **(81)** - Mashmoon (USA) (Habitat) 9.4f **(70)**
Form - 00
Record 1998 - 1st:0 2nd:0 3rd:0 Ran:2
Pre1998 - 1st:0 2nd:0 3rd:0 Ran:5
1998 Turf 0-2: (16f 2) (gd, frm)
Scopey, moderate gelding. Turf high 43 (began Spt).
**J G Portman [0-2] A S B Portman (from E A L Dunlop [0-5] Jly 1997).*

MOONLIGHT MONTY BHB 68f **RR 67f** 4663[14]
2 ch c Elmaamul (USA) 8.1f **(70)** - Lovers Light (Grundy) 10.3f **(65)**
Form - 8370
Record 1998 - 1st:0 2nd:0 3rd:1 Ran:4
Win Prizemoney £0 *Total Prizemoney* £496
1998 Turf 0-4: (7f 2, 8f, 10f) (g-s, gd, frm 2)
Average colt. Turf high 67 (began Jly).
**J L Dunlop [0-4] Credit Income Ltd.*

MOONLIGHT TRUCE (IRE) BHB 53f **RR 75f** 4375[10]
3 ro f Brief Truce (USA) 9.1f **(73)** - Moon Festival (Be My Guest (USA)) 9.3f **(67)**
Form - 330700
Record 1998 - 1st:0 2nd:0 3rd:2 Ran:6
Pre1998 - 1st:0 2nd:1 3rd:0 Ran:3
Win Prizemoney £0 *Total Prizemoney* £1,937
1998 Turf 0-6: (12f, 13f, 14f 2, 16f 2) (gd 2, g-f 3, frm)
Above-average filly, effective 9 to 14f, acts on sft to g-f. Turf high 75 (began Jly). Inconsistent.
**B J Curley [0-3] P Byrne (from C O'Brien in IRE [0-6] Jly 1998).*

MOONLIT WATER RR 62f 4309[9]
2 b f Rainbow Quest (USA) 11.2f **(81)** - Shimmer (FR) (Green Dancer (USA)) 10.3f **(74)**
Form - 00
Record 1998 - 1st:0 2nd:0 3rd:0 Ran:2
1998 Turf 0-2: (7f, 8f) (g-f, frm)
Currently average filly. Turf high 62 (began Aug).
**J L Dunlop [0-2] Aylesfield Farms Ltd.*

MOON MASQUERADE (IRE) BHB 60f **RR 72f** 4987[4]
3 b br f Darshaan 11.9f **(81)** - Moon Parade (Welsh Pageant) 10f **(65)**
Form - 4024
Record 1998 - 1st:0 2nd:1 3rd:0 Ran:4
Win Prizemoney £0 *Total Prizemoney* £1,678
1998 Turf 0-4: (10f, 12f 2, 14f) (sft, gd 2, frm)
Scopey, above-average filly, has worn blinkers. Turf high 72 (began Spt) - 2nd of 7 getting 5lb from Wave of Optimism (14 Oct Nottingham 14f gd RF 4809). **Sir Michael Stoute [0-4] P D Savill.*

MOON MISSION RR 10f 4415[11]
3 br f Interrex (CAN) 7.7f **(51)** - Zamoon (Zambrano) 6.1f **(37)**
Form - 0
Record 1998 - 1st:0 2nd:0 3rd:0 Ran:1
1998 Turf 0-1: (8f) (frm)
Light-framed, currently poor filly.
**J G Smyth-Osbourne [0-1] Edenwood Partnership.*

MOON QUEST RR 27f 4838[10]
3 ch c Rainbow Quest (USA) 11.2f **(81)** - Mrs Moonlight (Ajdal (USA)) 9.2f **(89)**
Form - 00
Record 1998 - 1st:0 2nd:0 3rd:0 Ran:2
1998 Turf 0-2: (10f, 12f) (g-s, frm)
Strong, currently little account colt. Turf high 27 (began Aug).
**K A Morgan [0-1] R G Marriott (from R Charlton [0-1] Aug 1998).*

MOONRAKING BHB 42f68a **RR 41f 68a** 5061[11]
5 gr g Rusticaro (FR) 11.3f **(45)** - Lunaire (Try My Best (USA)) 7.6f **(67)**
Form - 1222211500

Record 1998 - 1st:2 2nd:3 3rd:0 Ran:8
Pre1998 - 1st:2 2nd:3 3rd:4 Ran:16
Win Prizemoney £9,802 *Total Prizemoney* £16,914
Wins * **1998** *Mar Southw (STD) H 8f 58 68* <
* **1998** *Feb Southw (STD) H 11f 58 60*
* 1997 *Dec Southw (STD) H 11f 50 54*
* 1997 *Mar Southw (STD) H 12f 50 56*
1998 Turf 0-2: (10f 2) (sft, gd) 1998 AW 2-6: (8f 1-2, 11f 1-2, 12f 2) (Fibr 2-6)
Average gelding, effective 8 to 12f, best at 12f, - acts on Fibr, has worn blinkers (effectively), prefers left handed tracks, favours tight tracks, excels at Southwell. Turf high 27 (began Oct). AW high 68 - 1st of 8 from Swift (2 Mar Southwell RF 0385) - also 1st of 9 giving 18lb to Nakhal (23 Feb Southwell RF 0347).
**T J Etherington [4-24] Ian Bartlett.*

MOON RIVER (IRE) BHB 75f **RR 82df** 2918[10]
4 ch g Mujtahid (USA) 7.4f **(69)** - Moonsilk (Solinus) 9f **(71)**
Form - 0600
Record 1998 - 1st:0 2nd:0 3rd:0 Ran:4
Pre1998 - 1st:1 2nd:0 3rd:0 Ran:1
Win Prizemoney £2,885 *Total Prizemoney* £2,963
Wins * 1996 Nov Doncas (SFT) 8f 88+ <
1998 Turf 0-4: (10f 2, 14f, 15f) (g-s, gd, g-f, frm)
Decent gelding. Turf high 82. **J L Dunlop [1-5] Benny Andersson.*

MOON RIVER WONDER (IRE) **RR 64f** 4884[12]
2 b c Doyoun 10.7f **(69)** - Bayazida (Bustino) 10.4f **(64)**
Form - 80
Record 1998 - 1st:0 2nd:0 3rd:0 Ran:2
1998 Turf 0-2: (7f 2) (g-s, frm)
Currently average colt. Turf high 64 (began Spt).
**B W Hills [0-2] R A N Bonnycastle.*

MOONSHIFT BHB 27f40a **RR 43f 40a** 5038[9]
4 b g Cadeaux Genereux 7.9f **(76)** - Thewaari (USA) (Eskimo (USA))
Form - 704500
Record 1998 - 1st:0 2nd:0 3rd:0 Ran:5
Pre1998 - 1st:0 2nd:0 3rd:0 Ran:4
Win Prizemoney £0 *Total Prizemoney* £257
1998 Turf 0-5: (10f, 11f, 12f 2, 14f) (g-s 2, gd, g-f 2)
Scopey, moderate gelding, effective 10f, acts on g-f, has worn blinkers, likes left handed tracks, favours tight tracks. Turf high 43. Inconsistent.
**H J Collingridge [0-7] C V Lines (from Sir Michael Stoute [0-2] May 1997).*

MOON SHOT BHB 66f **RR 56+f** 5080[1]
2 gr c Pistolet Bleu (IRE) - La Luna (USA) (Lyphard (USA)) 9.9f **(72)**
Form - 08B1
Record 1998 - 1st:1 2nd:0 3rd:0 Ran:4
Win Prizemoney £2,490 *Total Prizemoney* £2,490
Wins * **1998** *Oct Wolver (STD) 6f 64+* <
1998 Turf 0-3: (6f 3) (g-f 2, frm) 1998 AW 1-1: (6f 1-1) (Fibr 1-1)
Average colt. Turf high 56 (began Spt). (1st run) - 1st of 13 giving 5lb to Trojan Girl (31 Oct Wolverhampton RF 5080). Unlucky to be brought down at Warwick when just about to launch a challenge, he made amends with a narrow victory at Wolverhampton next time on his Fibresand debut.
**Sir Mark Prescott [1-4] Eclipse Thoroughbreds.*

MOON SONG BHB 50f38a **RR 53f 38a** 256[7]
4 b f Presidium 7.5f **(56)** - Martian Melody (Enchantment) 5.4f **(52)**
Form - 53087
Record 1998 - 1st:0 2nd:0 3rd:1 Ran:4
Pre1998 - 1st:0 2nd:0 3rd:1 Ran:9
Win Prizemoney £0 *Total Prizemoney* £880
1998 AW 0-4: (6f 4) (Equi, Fibr 3)
Workmanlike, fair filly, often wears blinkers. AW high 45. Becoming disappointing. **A P Jarvis [0-13] Mrs D B Brazier.*

MOONSPELL BHB 53f **RR 63f** 41[9]
4 b f Batshoof 9.5f **(66)** - Shimmer (Bustino) 10.4f **(64)**
Form - 0
Record 1998 - 1st:0 2nd:0 3rd:0 Ran:1
Pre1998 - 1st:0 2nd:0 3rd:1 Ran:5
Win Prizemoney £0 *Total Prizemoney* £514
1998 AW 0-1: (12f) (Fibr)
Scopey, average filly, has worn blinkers.
**M J Wilkinson [0-4] The Diamond Seven Partnership (from R Charlton [0-5] May 1997).*

MOONSTONE (IRE) BHB 54f68a **RR 67f 68a** 4402[12]
3 b f Statoblest 6.4f **(63)** - Opening Day (Day Is Done) 6.3f **(67)**
Form - 400010500480
Record 1998 - 1st:1 2nd:0 3rd:0 Ran:12
Pre1998 - 1st:0 2nd:1 3rd:0 Ran:7
Win Prizemoney £3,557 *Total Prizemoney* £4,902
Wins * **1998** Jly Yarmou (GD) H 7f 63 67 <
1998 Turf 1-11: (7f 1-7, 8f 4) (gd 2, g-f 3, frm 1-6) 1998 AW 0-1: (9f) (Fibr)
Scopey, average filly, effective 6 to 7f, best at 6f, acts on gd to frm, has worn blinkers. Turf high 67 - 1st of 7 giving 7lb to Newala (1 Jly Yarmouth RF 2458). **A P Jarvis [1-19] Mrs D B Brazier.*

MOON STRIKE (FR) BHB 89f79a **RR 94f 79a** 4821[11]
8 b or br g Strike Gold (USA) 5.9f **(99)** - Lady Lamia (USA) (Secreto (USA)) 8.7f **(72)**
Form - 703850
Record 1998 - 1st:0 2nd:0 3rd:1 Ran:6
Pre1998 - 1st:8 2nd:4 3rd:3 Ran:32
Win Prizemoney £53,562 *Total Prizemoney* £64,787
Wins 1997 Aug Haydoc (G-F) H 5f 91 95 <
1997 Jun Newcas (GD) H 5f 83 94
1996 Aug Newmar (G-S) H 5f 74 79
1996 May Folkes (GD) C 6.9f 71+
1995 May Lingfi (FRM) H 7f 70 76
1995 *Jan Lingfi (STD) H 7f 77 79*
1998 Turf 0-6: (5f 6) (gd, g-f 4, frm)
Useful gelding, effective 5f, acts on gd to frm, best on gd, has worn blinkers. Turf high 94 - 3rd of 19 getting 3lb from Proud Native (8 Aug Haydock 5f gd RF 3464). A useful sprint handicapper, he ran a couple of good races last season, but was high enough in the handicap and did not manage to win.
**Mrs A E Johnson [0-6] A Foustok (from P Howling [1-5] Spt 1997).*

MOON TANGO (IRE) BHB 80f **RR 79f** 3956[11]
3 b f Last Tycoon 9.4f **(73)** - Dance It (USA) (Believe It (USA)) 9.4f **(70)**
Form - 01470
Record 1998 - 1st:1 2nd:0 3rd:0 Ran:5
Win Prizemoney £4,012 *Total Prizemoney* £4,537
Wins * **1998** Jun Lingfi (SFT) 6f 79 <
1998 Turf 1-5: (6f 1-3, 7f 2) (gd 1-3, g-f, frm)
Workmanlike, above-average filly. Turf high 79 - 1st of 12 from Uplifting (13 Jun Lingfield RF 1967). Unraced at two, she improved from her debut to score in soft ground at Lingfield. She took an age to get going there and looked suited by the seventh furlong next time, but has been rather out of form since.
**B W Hills [1-5] K Al-Said.*

MOORHALL LAD RR 3092[9]
6 b g Presidium 7.5f **(56)** - Forgiving (Jellaby) 6.4f **(58)**
Form - 00
Record 1998 - 1st:0 2nd:0 3rd:0 Ran:2
1998 AW 0-2: (8f 2) (Fibr 2)
Poor gelding. AW high 12. **A W Carroll [0-4] R S Brookhouse.*

MORATORIUM (USA) BHB 90f **RR 92f** 4467[8]
3 b c El Gran Senor (USA) 8.9f **(85)** -Substance (USA)(Diesis) 9.3f **(69)**
Form - 41308
Record 1998 - 1st:1 2nd:0 3rd:1 Ran:5
Pre1998 - 1st:0 2nd:0 3rd:0 Ran:1
Win Prizemoney £4,240 *Total Prizemoney* £7,482
Wins * **1998** May Ripon (G-F) 9f 84 <
1998 Turf 1-5: (9f 1-1, 10f 4) (gd, g-f, frm 1-3)
Scopey, useful colt, effective 9 to 10f, best at 10f, acts on gd to frm. Turf high 92 (1st run) - 4th of 10 to Casino Captive (5 May Chester 10f g-f RF 1041) - also 1st of 10 from Karasi (17 May Ripon RF 1290). Steadily improved to win a Ripon maiden on his second start of the season, and was only just beaten on his handicap debut at Epsom, but he disappointed in his final two outings.
**H R A Cecil [1-6] K Abdulla.*

MORE BILLS (IRE) BHB 21f28a **RR 17?f 28a** 2922P
6 b g Gallic League 6.3f **(58)** - Lady Portobello (Porto Bello) 8.9f **(43)**
Form - P
Record **1998** - 1st:0 2nd:0 3rd:0 Ran:1
Pre1998 - 1st:0 2nd:0 3rd:0 Ran:11
1998 Turf 0-1: (14f) (gd)
Poor gelding, has worn blinkers.
**B J Llewellyn [0-2] S Harrison (from J Neville [0-4] May 1997).*

MORGAN LE FAY BHB 65f **RR 65f** 4614[7]
3 b f Magic Ring (IRE) 6.5f **(64)** - Melody Park (Music Boy) 6.8f **(57)**
Form - 00302202037
Record **1998** - 1st:0 2nd:3 3rd:2 Ran:11
Win Prizemoney £0 *Total Prizemoney* £4,081
1998 Turf 0-11: (6f 2, 7f 7, 8f 2) (g-s 2, gd 3, g-f 3, frm 3)
Unfurnished, average filly, effective 6 to 7f, best at 7f, acts on g-s to frm, best on frm. Turf high 65 - 2nd of 16 giving 6lb to Jacobina (6 Aug Haydock 7f g-f RF 3410). **B J Meehan [0-11] Lord Portman.*

MORNING CHORUS BHB 64f **RR 71f** 4924[7]
2 b f Prince Sabo 6.6f **(64)** - Leave At Dawn (Slip Anchor) 9.8f **(73)**
Form - 627
Record **1998** - 1st:0 2nd:1 3rd:0 Ran:3
Win Prizemoney £0 *Total Prizemoney* £3,495
1998 Turf 0-3: (6f 3) (sft, g-f, frm)
Currently above-average filly. Turf high 71 (began Jly) - 2nd of 19 getting 5lb from Red Charger (19 Aug York 6f frm RF 3757). Dropped in grade to finish second in the seller at the Ebor Meeting. **M H Tompkins [0-3] Mark Tompkins Racing.*

MORNING GLORY **RR 62+f** 4575[7]
2 b f Polar Falcon (USA) 9f **(74)**- Round Midnight(Star Appeal) 9.6f **(65)**
Form - 77
Record **1998** - 1st:0 2nd:0 3rd:0 Ran:2
1998 Turf 0-2: (6f, 7f) (g-f, frm)
Currently average filly. Turf high 62 (began Spt).
**R A Fahey [0-2] Mrs A C Brown.*

MORNING MUSIC BHB 85f **RR 88f** 4389[1]
2 b f Green Desert (USA) 7.8f **(78)** - Blushing Storm (USA) (Blushing Groom (FR)) 10.3f **(76)**
Form - 2857231
Record **1998** - 1st:1 2nd:2 3rd:1 Ran:7
Win Prizemoney £3,030 *Total Prizemoney* £6,210
Wins * 1998 Spt Kempto (GD) 7f 88 <
1998 Turf 1-7: (5f, 6f 3, 7f 1-3) (gd, g-f 2, frm 1-4)
Useful filly, effective 5 to 7f, best at 7f, acts on frm. Turf high 88 - 1st of 16 from Dashiba (21 Spt Kempton RF 4389).
**R Hannon [1-7] Mohamed Suhail.*

MORNING STAR BHB 31f53a **RR 31f 53a** 3309[22]
4 b f Statoblest 6.4f **(63)** - Moushka (Song) 7.2f **(61)**
Form - 7040
Record **1998** - 1st:0 2nd:0 3rd:0 Ran:4
Pre1998 - 1st:1 2nd:0 3rd:0 Ran:8
Win Prizemoney £2,777 *Total Prizemoney* £2,777
Wins 1996 Oct Redcar (G-F) 5f 63+ <
1998 Turf 0-4: (5f 4) (gd 3, g-f)
Neat, very moderate filly. Turf high 31. Inconsistent.
**W McKeown [0-10] Mrs L E McKeown (from M Johnston [1-2] Oct 1996).*

MOROCCO (IRE) BHB 62f **RR 62f** 4962[15]
9 b g Cyrano de Bergerac 7.3f **(58)** - Lightning Laser (Monseigneur (USA)) 7.7f **(63)**
Form - 717440030
Record **1998** - 1st:1 2nd:0 3rd:1 Ran:9
Pre1998 - 1st:8 2nd:6 3rd:9 Ran:72
Win Prizemoney £31,748 *Total Prizemoney* £43,812
Wins * 1998 Jly Leices (GD) H 7f 58 58
* 1996 Spt Lingfi (FRM) H 7f 54 56
* 1996 May Salisb (G-F) H 7f 56 52
* 1995 Aug Carlis (HRD) 6.9f 65
* 1995 Jun Mussel (G-F) H 8.1f 55 57
* 1994 Aug Bath (G-F) S 8f 53
1998 Turf 1-9: (7f 1-5, 8f 4) (sft, gd 2, g-f 2, frm 1-4)
Average gelding, effective 7 to 8f, best at 7f, acts on gd to frm, best on frm, has worn blinkers. Turf high 62 (began Jly) - 4th of 11 giving 6lb to Prospector's Cove (18 Aug Brighton 8f frm RF 3691) - also 1st of 12 giving 3lb to Samara Song (16 Jly Leicester RF 2854).
**M R Channon [6-63] Mountgrange Stud (from R Charlton [3-18] Jun 1993).*

MORSELL **RR 58+f** 3970[2]
2 br f Dilum (USA) 7.1f **(56)** - Count On Me (No Mercy) 8f **(61)**
Form - 2
Record **1998** - 1st:0 2nd:1 3rd:0 Ran:1
Win Prizemoney £0 *Total Prizemoney* £730
1998 Turf 0-1: (6f) (frm)
Currently fair filly. (1st run) - 2nd of 12 to Clunie (29 Aug Windsor 6f frm RF 3970). **M J Heaton-Ellis [0-1] David Mort.*

MORTEENO BHB 53f **RR 57f** 4752[11]
2 b c Perpendicular - Petticoat Rule (Stanford) 7.9f **(56)**
Form - 000
Record **1998** - 1st:0 2nd:0 3rd:0 Ran:3
1998 Turf 0-3: (7f, 8f 2) (sft, g-s, gd)
Currently fair colt. Turf high 57 (began Spt).
**Miss L A Perratt [0-3] Four But Five.*

MORVINO BHB 60f **RR 63f** 4767[12]
2 b c Night Shift (USA) 8.1f **(73)** -Hard Task(Formidable (USA))9.2f **(63)**
Form - 508680
Record **1998** - 1st:0 2nd:0 3rd:0 Ran:6
1998 Turf 0-6: (6f, 7f 3, 8f 2) (sft, g-f 2, frm 3)
Average colt. Turf high 63.
**M A Jarvis [0-6] Thurloe Thoroughbreds III.*

MOSCOW MIST (IRE) BHB 72f65a **RR 71?f 65a** 4147[14]
7 b g Soviet Star (USA) 8.6f **(74)** -Ivory Dawn (USA) (Sir Ivor) 10.2f **(70)**
Form - 0P20
Record **1998** - 1st:0 2nd:1 3rd:0 Ran:3
Pre1998 - 1st:1 2nd:2 3rd:0 Ran:14
Win Prizemoney £48,250 *Total Prizemoney* £52,212
Wins 1996 Aug Goodwo (G-F) H 8f 70 85 <
1998 Turf 0-3: (7f 2, 8f) (g-f, frm, hrd)
Above-average gelding, effective 7 to 8f, acts on frm. Turf high 70 (began Aug) - 2nd of 17 giving 2lb to Myttons Mistake (19 Aug Kempton 7f frm RF 3739). Inconsistent. Sprang a 50/1 surprise in the 1996 Schweppes Golden Mile, but showed little subsequently until running a good race at Kempton in August. Never going next time.
**B Palling [0-8] Merthyr Motor Auctions (from Lady Herries [1-9] Spt 1996).*

MOSEY ALONG **RR 15f** 3924[7]
2 b f Petong 7.6f **(58)** - Mo's Star **(66f)** (Most Welcome)
Form - 7
Record **1998** - 1st:0 2nd:0 3rd:0 Ran:1
1998 Turf 0-1: (6f) (g-f)
Currently poor filly. **E L James [0-1] C James.*

MOSI-OA-TUNYA (IRE) **RR** 4772[17]
2 ch c River Falls 8.2f **(56)** - Heart to Heart (IRE) **(36f)** (Double Schwartz) 7.9f **(55)**
Form - 0
Record **1998** - 1st:0 2nd:0 3rd:0 Ran:1
1998 Turf 0-1: (7f) (gd)
Currently very poor colt. **K McAuliffe [0-1] The PBT Group.*

MOSQUERO (USA) **RR 77f** 4109[4]
2 b c Sky Classic (CAN) 10f **(83)** - Mosella (USA) (Lord At War (ARG))
Form - 54
Record **1998** - 1st:0 2nd:0 3rd:0 Ran:2
Win Prizemoney £0 *Total Prizemoney* £275
1998 Turf 0-2: (7f, 8f) (gd, frm)
Currently above-average colt. Turf high 77 (began Aug) - 4th of 8 to Moutahddee (5 Spt Thirsk 8f frm RF 4109).
**J H M Gosden [0-2] Sheikh Mohammed.*

MOST RESPECTFUL BHB 48f56a **RR 54f 56a** 4921[12]
5 ch g Respect 5.7f **(44)** - Active Movement (Music Boy) 6.8f **(57)**
Form - 507031410

Record 1998 - 1st:2 2nd:0 3rd:1 Ran:9
Pre1998 - 1st:0 2nd:0 3rd:0 Ran:5
Win Prizemoney £5,810 *Total Prizemoney* £6,425
Wins *** 1998** *Spt Southw (STD) H 6f 50 54* <
*** 1998** Aug Beverl (G-F) 5f 54 <
1998 Turf 1-8: (5f 1-2, 6f 5, 8f) (g-s, gd, g-f 2, frm 1-4) 1998 AW 1-1: (6f 1-1) (Fibr 1-1)
Fair gelding, effective 5 to 6f, acts on frm - acts on Fibr. Turf high 54 - 1st of 12 giving 7lb to Here And Now (29 Aug Beverley RF 3940). (1st run) - 1st of 16 from Baritone (29 Spt Southwell RF 4550).
**N Tinkler [2-9] R O Manners (from Denys Smith [0-7] May 1997).*

MOST WANTED (IRE) BHB 27f RR 26f 841[10]
5 ch m Priolo (USA) 10.9f **(71)** - Dewan's Niece (USA) (Dewan (USA)) 7.4f **(65)**
Form - 0
Record 1998 - 1st:0 2nd:0 3rd:0 Ran:1
Pre1998 - 1st:0 2nd:0 3rd:0 Ran:9
1998 Turf 0-1: (7f) (gd)
Little account filly. Inconsistent.
**W McKeown [1-10] Mrs L A Tinnion (from J J O'Neill [0-3] Spt 1996).*

MOTET BHB 85f RR 92f 4480[9]
4 b c Mtoto 11.5f **(71)** - Guest Artiste (Be My Guest (USA)) 9.3f **(67)**
Form - 082030
Record 1998 - 1st:0 2nd:1 3rd:1 Ran:6
Pre1998 - 1st:3 2nd:1 3rd:3 Ran:9
Win Prizemoney £14,042 *Total Prizemoney* £21,755
Wins * 1997 Spt Yarmou (FRM) H 18.2f 85 90 <
* 1997 Aug Newcas (GD) H 16.1f 82 84
* 1997 *Mar Lingfi (STD) 10f 66+*
1998 Turf 0-6: (12f 2, 14f, 15f, 16f 2) (gd 3, g-f 2, frm)
Scopey, useful colt, effective 12 to 18f, acts on gd to frm, best on g-f, has worn blinkers, prefers left handed tracks. Turf high 92 - 2nd of 4 getting 1lb from Top Cees (20 Jun Ayr 15f g-f RF 2145). A fair stayer in 1997, he only showed glimpses of form last term when runner-up to Top Cees at Ayr and third to Mowelga in a Newbury classified stakes. **G Wragg [3-15] A E Oppenheimer.*

MOTHER OF PEARL (IRE) RR 108f 4064[1]
2 b f Sadler's Wells (USA) 11.3f **(87)** - Sisania (High Top) 10.2f **(67)**
Form - 1
Record 1998 - 1st:1 2nd:0 3rd:0 Ran:1
Win Prizemoney £5,225 *Total Prizemoney* £5,225
Wins *** 1998** Spt Salisb (GD) 7f 77+ <
1998 Turf 1-1: (7f 1-1) (g-f 1-1)
Currently Pattern-class filly. (1st run) - 1st of 12 from Annapurna (3 Spt Salisbury RF 4064). Closely-related to Turtle Island, she can make her mark in much better company.
**P W Chapple-Hyam [1-1] Mrs J Magnier & R E Sangster.*

MOTHERS HELP BHB 58f RR 57f 4759[5]
3 b f Relief Pitcher 7.6f **(47)** - Laundry Maid (Forzando) 7.6f **(59)**
Form - 04035
Record 1998 - 1st:0 2nd:0 3rd:1 Ran:5
Pre1998 - 1st:0 2nd:0 3rd:0 Ran:1
Win Prizemoney £0 *Total Prizemoney* £628
1998 Turf 0-5: (8f 5) (gd 2, g-f 2, frm)
Leggy, fair filly, effective 8f, acts on gd to frm. Turf high 57 - 4th of 6 getting 5lb from Bering Gifts (14 Aug Warwick 8f frm RF 3645).
**H Candy [0-6] C J R Trotter.*

MOTTARET (IRE) BHB 49f RR 46f 3993[7]
2 ch f Forest Wind (USA) - Brazilian Princess (Absalom) 7.2f **(58)**
Form - 060077
Record 1998 - 1st:0 2nd:0 3rd:0 Ran:6
1998 Turf 0-6: (5f 2, 6f 2, 7f, 8f) (gd 2, g-f 3, frm)
Moderate filly. Turf high 46.
**B S Rothwell [0-6] The Action Racing Club Ltd.*

MOUCHE BHB 70f RR 70f 3965[7]
4 b br f Warning 8.1f **(77)** - Case for the Crown (USA) (Bates Motel (USA)) 6.5f **(77)**
Form - 800634820117
Record 1998 - 1st:2 2nd:1 3rd:1 Ran:12
Pre1998 - 1st:2 2nd:1 3rd:0 Ran:13
Win Prizemoney £11,610 *Total Prizemoney* £14,886
Wins *** 1998** Aug Leices (GD) H 8f 66 70 <
*** 1998** Jly Redcar (G-F) 7f 70 <
* 1997 Spt Nottin (G-F) H 6.1f 63 64
* 1997 Apr Nottin (G-F) 5.1f 67
1998 Turf 2-12: (6f 4, 7f 1-4, 8f 1-4) (g-s, gd 3, g-f 3, frm 1-4, hrd 1-1)
Lengthy, above-average filly, effective 5 to 8f, acts on gd to hrd, has worn blinkers, excels at Pontefract and Nottingham, likes Doncaster. Turf high 70 - 1st of 11 giving 16lb to Bestemor (5 Aug Leicester RF 3379) - also 1st of 11 giving 1lb to Peter's Imp (25 Jly Redcar RF 3119). Consistent. She always looked as though she would benefit from a longer trip, and duly scored over seven at Redcar and a mile at Leicester.
**Mrs J R Ramsden [4-25] Mrs Peter Hastings.*

MOULIN ROUGE BHB 76f RR 74f 2888[3]
3 b f Shareef Dancer (USA) 10.1f **(67)** - Pride of Paris (Troy) 10.4f **(68)**
Form - 3523
Record 1998 - 1st:0 2nd:1 3rd:2 Ran:4
Win Prizemoney £0 *Total Prizemoney* £2,167
1998 Turf 0-4: (10f 4) (g-f, frm 3)
Scopey, above-average filly. Turf high 74 - 3rd of 4 to Abi (17 Jly Pontefract 10f frm RF 2888). **E A L Dunlop [0-4] Paul Homewood.*

MOUNTAIN BIRD RR 48f 2884[10]
2 ch f Superlative 8.8f **(57)** - Northern Bird **(60+f)** (Interrex (CAN))
Form - 050
Record 1998 - 1st:0 2nd:0 3rd:0 Ran:3
1998 Turf 0-3: (5f 2, 6f) (gd 2, frm)
Currently moderate filly. Turf high 48 (began Jly).
**M Brittain [0-3] Northgate Silver.*

MOUNTAIN DREAM BHB 30f53a RR 38f 53a 3575[13]
5 b g Batshoof 9.5f **(66)** - Echoing (Formidable (USA)) 9.2f **(63)**
Form - 808500
Record 1998 - 1st:0 2nd:0 3rd:0 Ran:6
Pre1998 - 1st:0 2nd:0 3rd:1 Ran:7
Win Prizemoney £0 *Total Prizemoney* £382
1998 Turf 0-6: (7f, 8f 2, 9f 2, 11f) (gd 5, frm)
Very moderate gelding, has worn blinkers. Turf high 40. Inconsistent.
**R Allan [0-15] R Allan (from L M Cumani [0-3] Aug 1996).*

MOUNTAIN MAGIC BHB 49f RR 56f 4648[10]
3 b f Magic Ring (IRE) 6.5f **(64)** - Nevis (Connaught) 7.7f **(63)**
Form - 10050000
Record 1998 - 1st:1 2nd:0 3rd:0 Ran:8
Pre1998 - 1st:0 2nd:0 3rd:0 Ran:6
Win Prizemoney £4,042 *Total Prizemoney* £4,042
Wins *** 1998** May Newbur (G-F) H 7.3f 54 61 <
1998 Turf 1-8: (6f, 7f 1-4, 8f 3) (g-f 2, frm 1-5, hrd)
Workmanlike, fair filly, effective 7f, acts on frm. Turf high 61 (1st run) - 1st of 16 getting 12lb from Missed The Cut (16 May Newbury RF 1262). Becoming disappointing. Well below form since winning at Newbury on her reappearance.
**D J S ffrenchDavis [1-14] Hargood Ltd.*

MOUNTAIN SONG BHB 108f RR 111f 4755[1]
3 b c Tirol 8.1f **(64)** - Persian Song (Persian Bold) 9.3f **(66)**
Form - 26121
Record 1998 - 1st:2 2nd:2 3rd:0 Ran:5
Pre1998 - 1st:2 2nd:0 3rd:2 Ran:5
Win Prizemoney £22,136 *Total Prizemoney* £50,350
Wins *** 1998** Oct Ayr (G-S) 8f 84
*** 1998** Aug Windso (G-F) 10f 99 <
* 1997 Jun Salisb (SFT) 7f 94+
* 1997 Jun Thirsk (GD) 7f 71+
1998 Turf 2-5: (8f 1-1, 10f 1-4) (sft 1-1, gd, g-f 1-3)
Scopey, Group-class colt, effective 8 to 10f, best at 10f, acts on gd to g-f, best on g-f, excels at Windsor. Turf high 111 - 2nd of 9 getting 12lb from Annus Mirabilis (29 Aug Windsor 10f g-f RF 3973). Many trainers would have run up a blind alley with this seemingly hard-to-place colt, but Sir Mark Prescott managed to find a couple of decent minor heats. Game and genuine, he is just the sort to excel on the continent as a four-year-old.
**Sir Mark Prescott [4-10] Eclipse Thoroughbreds.*

MOUNT HOLLY (USA) BHB 73f74a **RR 80tf 74a** 3515[13]

4 b c Woodman (USA) 9.7f **(77)** -Mount Helena(Danzig (USA)) 8.4f **(76)**
Form - 3000613700
Record 1998 - 1st:1 2nd:0 3rd:2 Ran:10
Pre1998 - 1st:1 2nd:1 3rd:2 Ran:6
Win Prizemoney £12,510 *Total Prizemoney* £15,963
Wins * **1998** Jly Newmar (G-F) H 8f 70 77
1997 Oct Yarmou (GD) 8f 81 <
1998 Turf 1-9: (7f 3, 8f 1-4, 9f, 10f) (gd 2, g-f 4, frm 1-1, hrd 2) 1998 AW 0-1: (8f) (Equi)
Workmanlike, decent colt, effective 8f, acts on sft to frm, best on frm. Turf high 80 - also 1st of 20 getting 8lb from Wild Sky (7 Jly Newmarket RF 2579). Inconsistent. He was the shock winner of a competitive handicap at the Newmarket July Meeting, having shown little earlier in the season, including when acting as pace-maker. Fair efforts since, a mile looks to be his trip.
**K Mahdi [1-10] Hamad Al-Mutawa (from J H M Gosden [1-6] Nov 1997).*

MOUNT IRISH (USA) RR 80f 4989[1]

2 b c Irish River (FR) 9f **(77)** - Wajna (USA) (Nureyev (USA)) 8.7f **(78)**
Form - 1
Record 1998 - 1st:1 2nd:0 3rd:0 Ran:1
Win Prizemoney £3,704 *Total Prizemoney* £3,704
Wins * **1998** Oct Leices (SFT) 8f 80 <
1998 Turf 1-1: (8f 1-1) (sft 1-1)
Currently decent colt. (1st run) - 1st of 11 from Weet For Me (26 Oct Leicester RF 4989). Not over-impressive in his debut victory, but he should improve when tackling middle-distances.
**D R Loder [1-1] Sheikh Mohammed.*

MOUSEHOLE BHB 65f **RR 59f** 5007[8]

6 b g Statoblest 6.4f **(63)** - Alo Ez (Alzao (USA)) 7.1f **(68)**
Form - 00063321201750008
Record 1998 - 1st:2 2nd:2 3rd:2 Ran:17
Pre1998 - 1st:4 2nd:8 3rd:3 Ran:32
Win Prizemoney £17,506 *Total Prizemoney* £31,948
Wins * **1998** Aug Bath (FRM) 5.1f 77 <
* **1998** Jly Carlis (G-F) 5f 70
* 1997 Aug Bath (GD) 5.1f 72
* 1997 Jly Warwic (G-F) 5f 63
* 1996 Jun Windso (G-F) 5f 63
* 1995 Jun Thirsk (G-F) H 6f 63 65
1998 Turf 2-17: (5f 2-16, 6f) (sft 2, g-s, gd 4, g-f 3, frm 2-6, hrd)
Fair gelding, effective 5f, acts on gd to frm, best on frm, has worn blinkers, excels at Beverley and Bath. Turf high 77 - 1st of 12 giving 3lb to Bramble Bear (11 Aug Bath RF 3527) - also 1st of 4 giving 7lb to Break For Peace (17 Jly Carlisle RF 2870). Consistent. Quite a useful fast-ground sprinter on his day, he takes a few runs to find his form but was victorious twice last term. His wins in recent seasons have come in limited or classified stakes. Not the easiest of rides and requires strong handling.
**R Guest [6-49] Mrs Janet Linskey.*

MOUTAHDDEE (IRE) BHB 86f **RR 82f** 4109[1]

2 b c Alzao (USA) 9.8f **(73)** - Ah Ya Zein (Artaius (USA)) 9f **(69)**
Form - 801
Record 1998 - 1st:1 2nd:0 3rd:0 Ran:3
Win Prizemoney £4,055 *Total Prizemoney* £4,055
Wins * **1998** Spt Thirsk (GD) 8f 82 <
1998 Turf 1-3: (7f 2, 8f 1-1) (frm 1-3)
Currently decent colt. Turf high 82 (began Jly) - 1st of 8 from Just Name It (5 Spt Thirsk RF 4109).
**M P Tregoning [1-3] Sheikh Ahmed Al Maktoum.*

MOUTON (IRE) RR 74f 3890[2]

2 b f Dolphin Street (FR) - The Queen of Soul (Chief Singer) 8.9f **(66)**
Form - 02
Record 1998 - 1st:0 2nd:1 3rd:0 Ran:2
Win Prizemoney £0 *Total Prizemoney* £572
1998 Turf 0-2: (7f, 8f) (g-f, frm)
Currently above-average filly. Turf high 74 (began Aug) - 2nd of 9 getting 5lb from Colonel Mustard (26 Aug Lingfield 8f g-f RF 3890).
**J W Hills [0-2] Uplands Bloodstock.*

MOVING ARROW BHB 57f76a **RR 66f 76a** 4859[8]

7 ch g Indian Ridge 7.6f **(74)** - Another Move (Farm Walk) 11.6f **(55)**
Form - 8700702088
Record 1998 - 1st:0 2nd:1 3rd:0 Ran:10
Pre1998 - 1st:4 2nd:7 3rd:1 Ran:37
Win Prizemoney £26,848 *Total Prizemoney* £54,875
Wins * 1996 Jly Newmar (G-F) H 10f 92 98 <
* 1995 Oct York (GD) H 7.9f 90 94
* 1995 Aug Haydoc (G-F) H 8.1f 87 89
1998 Turf 0-10: (8f 8, 9f, 11f) (sft, gd 2, g-f 3, frm 4)
Average gelding, effective 8f, acts on g-f, has worn blinkers, likes left handed tracks. Turf high 77. **Miss S E Hall [4-47] G W Westgarth.*

MOVING PRINCESS BHB 62f **RR 69f** 4672[11]

3 b f Prince Sabo 6.6f **(64)** - Another Move (Farm Walk) 11.6f **(55)**
Form - 342642580
Record 1998 - 1st:0 2nd:2 3rd:1 Ran:9
Pre1998 - 1st:0 2nd:0 3rd:2 Ran:4
Win Prizemoney £0 *Total Prizemoney* £4,706
1998 Turf 0-9: (8f 5, 9f, 10f 3) (gd 3, g-f 4, frm 2)
Lengthy, average filly, effective 8 to 10f, best at 8f, acts on gd to frm, best on g-f, prefers left handed tracks, likes tight tracks. Turf high 69 - 2nd of 8 getting 6lb from Scene (12 Jly Haydock 8f g-f RF 2741). **Miss S E Hall [0-13] G W Westgarth.*

MOVING UP (IRE) BHB 30f31a **RR 28f 31a** 1039[12]

5 ch m Don't Forget Me 9.5f **(66)** - Our Pet (Mummy's Pet) 7.7f **(60)**
Form - 00
Record 1998 - 1st:0 2nd:0 3rd:0 Ran:2
Pre1998 - 1st:0 2nd:1 3rd:2 Ran:19
Win Prizemoney £0 *Total Prizemoney* £1,810
1998 Turf 0-2: (6f 2) (sft, gd)
Little account filly, has worn blinkers. Turf high 13. Inconsistent.
**T E Powell [0-8] W Powell (from G L Moore [0-13] Aug 1996).*

MOWBRAY (USA) BHB 105f **RR 106f** 5140[4]

3 b br c Opening Verse (USA) 11.8f **(70)** - Peppy Raja (USA) (Raja Baba (USA)) 10f **(64)**
Form - 442614
Record 1998 - 1st:1 2nd:1 3rd:0 Ran:6
Pre1998 - 1st:2 2nd:2 3rd:0 Ran:5
Win Prizemoney £13,396 *Total Prizemoney* £82,919
Wins * **1998** Oct Leices (HVY) 11.8f 100 <
* 1997 Aug Kempto (GD) 7f 97
* 1997 Aug Catter (G-F) 7f 77
1998 Turf 1-6: (10f, 12f 1-4, 15f) (sft 1-1, gd, g-f 4)
Strong, Pattern-class colt, effective 8 to 12f, best at 12f, acts on sft to g-f, best on g-f, prefers right handed tracks. Turf high 108 - 4th of 16 to Central Park (31 May Capannelle 12f g-f RF 1734a) - also 1st of 3 getting 4lb from Chist (26 Oct Leicester RF 4993). Consistent. He has not always looked the easiest of rides, and did not improve upon his juvenile form. He appeared not to stay 14 furlongs on his final start. **P F I Cole [3-11] Sir George Meyrick.*

MOWELGA BHB 96f **RR 99f** 4515[9]

4 ch c Most Welcome 8.6f **(66)** - Galactic Miss (Damister (USA)) 9f **(73)**
Form - 123110
Record 1998 - 1st:3 2nd:1 3rd:1 Ran:6
Pre1998 - 1st:1 2nd:0 3rd:1 Ran:3
Win Prizemoney £27,292 *Total Prizemoney* £34,522
Wins * **1998** Aug Newbur (GD) 12f 99 <
* **1998** Aug Pontef (G-F) H 12f 88 92
* **1998** May Doncas (G-F) H 10.3f 77 81
* 1997 Oct Newbur (GD) 10f 61
1998 Turf 3-6: (10f 1-3, 12f 2-3) (gd 2, g-f 2-3, frm 1-1)
Scopey, very useful colt, effective 12f, acts on g-f to frm, prefers left handed tracks. Turf high 99 - 1st of 6 giving 2lb to Aginor (15 Aug Newbury RF 3654) - also 1st of 9 giving 12lb to Domappel (5 Aug Pontefract RF 3390). A very useful middle-distance handicapper at his best, he was in fine form last season, winning handicaps at Doncaster and Pontefract, and a valuable classified event at Newbury. Best held up off a fast pace, and possibly still has some improvement in him. **Lady Herries [4-9] Hesmonds Stud.*

MOY (IRE) BHB 37f48a **RR 25f 48a** 5120[10]

3 ch f Beveled (USA) 6.9f **(64)** - Exceptional Beauty (Sallust) 8.4f **(63)**
Form - 030000206000
Record 1998 - 1st:0 2nd:1 3rd:1 Ran:12
Pre1998 - 1st:0 2nd:0 3rd:0 Ran:6
Win Prizemoney £0 *Total Prizemoney* £1,606

1998 Turf 0-10: (5f, 6f 5, 7f, 8f 3) (sft 2, g-s, gd 3, g-f 3, frm) 1998 AW 0-2: (6f, 8f) (Fibr 2)

Light-framed, very moderate filly, effective 7f, acts on g-f, has worn blinkers, likes tight tracks. Turf high 56. AW high 37.

**W M Brisbourne [0-6] Christopher Chell (from M Brittain [0-12] Jun 1998).*

MOZAMBIQUE (IRE) BHB 67f61a **RR 72f 61a** 4744[18]

4 b c Fayruz 6.6f **(63)** - Lightning Laser (Monseigneur (USA)) 7.7f **(63)**

Form - 14242010840

Record 1998 - 1st:1 2nd:1 3rd:0 Ran:8
Pre1998 - 1st:1 2nd:2 3rd:1 Ran:6

Win Prizemoney £18,620 *Total Prizemoney* £22,067

Wins * **1998** Mar Doncas (GD) H 8f 65 72 <
* 1997 *Nov Lingfi (STD) 7f 56*

1998 Turf 1-5: (7f, 8f 1-3, 10f) (hvy, g-s, gd 1-2, g-f) 1998 AW 0-3: (8f 3) (Equi, Fibr 2)

Scopey, above-average colt, effective 8f, acts on gd - acts on Equi, likes left handed tracks. Turf high 72 (1st run) - 1st of 24 getting 11lb from Wild Sky (27 Mar Doncaster RF 0479). AW high 63 - 2nd of 10 giving 8lb to Mellors (17 Feb Lingfield 8f Equi RF 0302). Inconsistent. **Mrs J Cecil [2-14] Mountgrange Stud.*

MR BERGERAC (IRE) BHB 77f73a **RR 83f 73a** 4749[11]

7 b g Cyrano de Bergerac 7.3f **(58)** -Makalu (Godswalk (USA)) 7.3f **(58)**

Form - 35338736000

Record 1998 - 1st:0 2nd:0 3rd:3 Ran:9
Pre1998 - 1st:8 2nd:9 3rd:7 Ran:64

Win Prizemoney £36,540 *Total Prizemoney* £71,364

Wins * 1997 Aug Newmar (G-F) H 6f 80 84
* 1997 May Leices (GD) H 6f 80 82
* 1996 Jly Newmar (GD) H 6f 79 83
* 1995 *Nov Wolver (STD) H 6f 85 86*
* 1995 Aug Sandow (G-F) H 5f 76 79
* 1995 Jly Sandow (G-F) H 5f 70 73

1998 Turf 0-9: (6f 8, 7f) (sft, g-s, gd 3, g-f 2, frm 2)

Decent gelding, effective 5 to 7f, best at 6f, acts on gd to frm, has worn blinkers, and excels at Leicester and Redcar. Turf high 83 (1st run) (began Jly) - 3rd of 10 giving 3lb to Cybertechnology (1 Jly Redcar 7f gd RF 2454). Consistent. **B Palling [8-73] P R John.*

MR BOMBASTIQUE (IRE) BHB 75f **RR 78f** 2954[5]

4 b g Classic Music (USA) 7.2f **(57)** - Duende (High Top) 10.2f **(67)**

Form - 7265

Record 1998 - 1st:0 2nd:1 3rd:0 Ran:4
Pre1998 - 1st:1 2nd:2 3rd:1 Ran:8

Win Prizemoney £2,882 *Total Prizemoney* £7,553

Wins 1996 Jly Chepst (G-F) 6.1f 71 <

1998 Turf 0-4: (10f 2, 11f 2) (gd 2, g-f, frm)

Scopey, above-average gelding, effective 10 to 11f, acts on sft to gd. Turf high 78 - 2nd of 6 giving 26lb to Tonnerre (17 Jun Ripon 10f gd RF 2073).

**Mrs J Brown [0-7] The Howarting's Partnership (from B W Hills [1-8] May 1997).*

MR BROWNING (USA) BHB 63f54a **RR 69df 54a** 4451[11]

7 br g Al Nasr (FR) 9.9f **(72)** - Crinoline (Blakeney) 10.5f **(64)**

Form - 36030160

Record 1998 - 1st:1 2nd:0 3rd:2 Ran:8
Pre1998 - 1st:3 2nd:4 3rd:1 Ran:32

Win Prizemoney £12,999 *Total Prizemoney* £21,337

Wins * **1998** Aug Bright (FRM) H 11.9f 60 69
1997 Jun Bright (FRM) H 11.9f 61 65
1995 Aug Goodwo (G-F) H 12f 68 73 <
1995 Jun Folkes (FRM) H 12f 61 68+

1998 Turf 1-8: (12f 1-6, 13f, 14f) (gd 2, g-f 1-5, frm)

Average gelding, effective 12 to 14f, best at 12f, acts on gd to frm, often wears blinkers (effectively), likes left handed tracks, favours tight tracks. Turf high 69 - 10th of 15 getting 10lb from Seignorial (28 Jly Goodwood 14f gd RF 3163) - also 1st of 8 giving 11lb to Castles Burning (12 Aug Brighton RF 3572). Inconsistent. He seems to need the ground bone hard, conditions under which he scored at Brighton in August. His only win in 1997 was at the same track under identical conditions.

**Miss Gay Kelleway [1-8] Mrs M E O'Shea (from R Akehurst [3-22] Spt 1997).*

MR CAHILL (USA) BHB 89f **RR 92f** 3955[12]

3 b c Cahill Road (USA) 8.5f **(82)** - Sympathetic Miss (USA) (Proudest Roman (USA)) 9f **(75)**

Form - 67180

Record 1998 - 1st:1 2nd:0 3rd:0 Ran:5
Pre1998 - 1st:1 2nd:0 3rd:0 Ran:2

Win Prizemoney £12,617 *Total Prizemoney* £12,702

Wins * **1998** Jly Ascot (G-F) H 10f 88 92 <
* 1997 Aug Yarmou (G-F) 7f 83+

1998 Turf 1-5: (7f, 10f 1-4) (gd 1-1, g-f, frm 3)

Scopey, useful colt, effective 7 to 10f, acts on gd to frm. Turf high 92 - 1st of 9 giving 4lb to Praetorian Gold (24 Jly Ascot RF 3064). Most of his efforts last season were poor, though he did win an Ascot handicap in July when fitted with a cross-noseband for the first time. **Sir Michael Stoute [2-7] Maktoum Al Maktoum.*

MR CASAUBON BHB 28f **RR 24?f** 2078[8]

7 ch g Kris 10f **(75)**- Lady Tippins(USA)(Star de Naskra (USA))9.7f **(65)**

Form - 8

Record 1998 - 1st:0 2nd:0 3rd:0 Ran:1
Pre1998 - 1st:0 2nd:0 3rd:0 Ran:3

1998 AW 0-1: (16f) (Fibr)

Little account gelding, mostly wears blinkers.

**K C Comerford [0-1] Foster, Danzebrink, Dodd (from P W Harris [0-3] Aug 1994).*

MR CHRISTIE BHB 36f **RR 33f** 880[11]

6 b g Doulab (USA) 7.4f **(61)** - Hi There (High Top) 10.2f **(67)**

Form - 0

Record 1998 - 1st:0 2nd:0 3rd:0 Ran:1
Pre1998 - 1st:0 2nd:0 3rd:2 Ran:15

Win Prizemoney £0 *Total Prizemoney* £1,629

1998 Turf 0-1: (22f) (g-s)

Very moderate gelding.

**Miss L C Siddall [3-46] David Mann Partnership.*

MR CUBE (IRE) BHB 36f44a **RR 41f 44a** 4275[4]

8 ch h Tate Gallery (USA) 8.2f **(63)** - Truly Thankful (CAN) (Graustark) 10.1f **(70)**

Form - 500867874

Record 1998 - 1st:0 2nd:0 3rd:0 Ran:9
Pre1998 - 1st:8 2nd:9 3rd:11 Ran:84

Win Prizemoney £24,905 *Total Prizemoney* £39,107

Wins * 1997 Jly Epsom (G-S) H 7f 49 59
* 1996 Spt Folkes (G-F) H 6.9f 50 54
* 1995 Jly Newcas (G-F) H 7f 55 61 <
* 1995 Jly Kempto (G-F) H 7f 53 58
* 1995 Jun Warwic (G-F) H 7f 49 58
* 1994 Jly Thirsk (FRM) H 8f 45 49

1998 Turf 0-9: (7f 4, 8f 5) (gd 5, g-f, frm 3)

Moderate horse, effective 7 to 8f, best at 7f, acts on gd to frm, best on frm, often wears blinkers. Turf high 48. Consistent.

**J M Bradley [6-77] R Miles (from P F I Cole [2-18] Nov 1993).*

MR FORTYWINKS (IRE) BHB 54f68a **RR 58f 68a** 5098[7]

4 ch g Fools Holme (USA) 10.3f **(64)** - Dream on (Absalom) 7.2f **(58)**

Form - 13213212000407

Record 1998 - 1st:2 2nd:3 3rd:1 Ran:12
Pre1998 - 1st:2 2nd:3 3rd:2 Ran:13

Win Prizemoney £9,159 *Total Prizemoney* £18,106

Wins * **1998** Apr Nottin (SFT) H 10f 53 58
* **1998** *Jan Southw (STD) H 11f 61 61+*
* 1997 *Nov Wolver (STD) H 12f 49 63* <
* 1997 Aug Hamilt (GD) S 9.2f 44

1998 Turf 1-9: (10f 1-3, 11f 2, 12f 4) (sft 1-2, g-s, gd 2, g-f, frm 3) 1998 AW 1-3: (11f 1-1, 12f 2) (Fibr 1-3)

Light-framed, average gelding, effective 10 to 12f, best at 12f, acts on sft to g-f - acts on AW, best on Fibr, likes right handed tracks, prefers tight tracks, excels at Wolverhampton and Hamilton. Turf high 62 - 2nd of 8 getting 4lb from Summerhill Special (1 May Musselburgh 12f g-f RF 0956) - also 1st of 16 getting 8lb from Zorba (20 Apr Nottingham RF 0775). AW high 67 (1st run) - 2nd of 10 getting 20lb from Swan Hunter (7 Jan Wolverhampton 12f Fibr RF 0041) - also 1st of 12 giving 11lb to Head Gardener (16 Jan Southwell RF 0099). Diana Jones gets on particularly well with him. **J L Eyre [4-25] Miss Nuala Cassidy.*

MR FROSTY BHB 60f60a **RR 56f 60a** 3605[5]
6 b g Absalom 7.1f **(56)** - Chadenshe (Taufan (USA)) 7f **(57)**
Form - 00002011858385
Record 1998 - 1st:2 2nd:1 3rd:1 Ran:12
Pre1998 - 1st:4 2nd:1 3rd:4 Ran:25
Win Prizemoney £16,564 *Total Prizemoney* £20,826
Wins * **1998** *Mar Wolver (STD) H 7f 60 67*
* **1998** *Mar Southw (STD) 7f 66*
* 1996 *Dec Wolver (STD) C 6f 77* <
* 1996 *Dec Wolver (STD) H 6f 60 62*
* 1996 *Dec Southw (SLW) H 6f 54 57*
* 1995 *Jan Lingfi (STD) 7f 56*
1998 Turf 0-2: (7f, 8f) (gd, frm) 1998 AW 2-10: (6f, 7f 2-7, 8f 2) (Equi 2, Fibr 2-8)
Fair gelding, effective 6 to 7f, best at 7f, acts on gd - acts on Fibr. Turf high 56. AW high 67 - 1st of 8 getting 6lb from Davis Rock (28 Mar Wolverhampton RF 0495) - also 1st of 9 from Domino Flyer (17 Mar Southwell RF 0434). Consistent. He does not seem to stay beyond seven furlongs, and is at his best when able to dominate.
**W Jarvis [6-38] D G Wright.*

MR FUND SWITCH BHB 28f35a **RR 2f 35a** 5070[22]
3 ch g Chilibang 7f **(55)** - Purple Fan (Dalsaan) 9.8f **(64)**
Form - 00026007000
Record 1998 - 1st:0 2nd:1 3rd:0 Ran:11
Pre1998 - 1st:0 2nd:0 3rd:0 Ran:10
Win Prizemoney £0 *Total Prizemoney* £730
1998 Turf 0-4: (6f, 8f 2, 9f) (g-s, gd, g-f 2) 1998 AW 0-7: (6f 2, 7f 2, 8f 3) (Fibr 7)
Neat, very moderate gelding, effective 8f, - acts on Fibr, has worn blinkers. Turf high 2. AW high 38 - 2nd of 9 getting 24lb from Killarney Jazz (23 Feb Southwell 8f Fibr RF 0341). Becoming disappointing.
**D Shaw [0-2] Justin Aaron (from S R Bowring [0-4] Aug 1998).*

MR GENEAOLOGY (USA) BHB 57f **RR 62f** 390[14]
8 b g Procida (USA) 9.6f **(72)** - Que Mona (USA) (Ribot) 15.4f **(65)**
Form - 0
Record 1998 - 1st:0 2nd:0 3rd:0 Ran:1
Pre1998 - 1st:4 2nd:3 3rd:3 Ran:17
Win Prizemoney £11,514 *Total Prizemoney* £15,281
Wins 1995 Aug Ripon (G-F) H 16f 55 62 <
1998 AW 0-1: (13f) (Equi)
Average gelding, mostly wears blinkers. Consistent.
**T P McGovern [0-6] Mrs Sally Rowe (from F Murphy [2-10] Aug 1995).*

MR HAMAD RR 49f 3682[11]
3 b c Rainbow Quest (USA) 11.2f **(81)** - Twafeaj (USA) (Topsider (USA)) 8.3f **(71)**
Form - 60
Record 1998 - 1st:0 2nd:0 3rd:0 Ran:2
1998 Turf 0-2: (8f, 10f) (gd, g-f)
Scopey, currently moderate colt. Turf high 49 (began Aug).
**B Hanbury [0-2] Abdullah Ali.*

MR LURPAK BHB 54f **RR 58f** 5013[3]
6 b g Minster Son 10.9f **(56)** - Ixia (I Say) 10f **(56)**
Form - 2523
Record 1998 - 1st:0 2nd:2 3rd:1 Ran:4
Win Prizemoney £0 *Total Prizemoney* £2,095
1998 Turf 0-4: (10f, 11f, 12f 2) (sft, gd 3)
Fair gelding. Turf high 58. **Mrs M Reveley [2-8] K G Reveley.*

MR MAJICA BHB 65f67a **RR 75f 67a** 3673[17]
4 b c Rudimentary (USA) 8.2f **(66)** - Pellinora (USA) (King Pellinore (USA)) 8.2f **(68)**
Form - 774572046140420
Record 1998 - 1st:1 2nd:2 3rd:0 Ran:13
Pre1998 - 1st:1 2nd:1 3rd:1 Ran:8
Win Prizemoney £6,271 *Total Prizemoney* £12,041
Wins 1998 Jun Salisb (G-F) C 8f 69
1997 Spt Yarmou (G-F) 6f 80 <
1998 Turf 1-12: (8f 1-12) (sft 2, g-s, gd 2, g-f, frm 1-5, hrd) 1998 AW 0-1: (7f) (Equi)
Workmanlike, above-average colt, effective 6 to 8f, best at 8f, acts on sft to frm, has worn blinkers, likes right handed tracks. Turf high 83 - 2nd of 10 getting 2lb from Therhea (24 Apr Sandown 8f sft RF 0847).
**A J McNae [0-1] A J McNae (from B J Meehan [2-20] Jly 1998).*

MR MIYAGI BHB 48f **RR 50f** 3518[11]
3 b g Full Extent (USA) 5.2f **(50)** - All the Girls (IRE) (Alzao (USA)) 7.1f **(68)**
Form - 8470
Record 1998 - 1st:0 2nd:0 3rd:0 Ran:4
Pre1998 - 1st:0 2nd:0 3rd:0 Ran:5
Win Prizemoney £0 *Total Prizemoney* £83
1998 Turf 0-3: (7f 2, 8f) (gd 2, frm) 1998 AW 0-1: (6f) (Fibr)
Small, fair gelding, often wears blinkers. Turf high 50.
**A Bailey [0-9] Sandybrow Stables Ltd.*

MR MONTAGUE (IRE) BHB 40f **RR 36f** 1114[12]
6 b g Pennine Walk 8.9f **(64)** - Ballyewry (Prince Tenderfoot (USA)) 9f **(61)**
Form - 00
Record 1998 - 1st:0 2nd:0 3rd:0 Ran:2
Pre1998 - 1st:0 2nd:0 3rd:0 Ran:5
1998 Turf 0-2: (10f 2) (gd, frm)
Very moderate gelding. Turf high 36.
**T W Donnelly [0-16] C I P Racing.*

MR MORIARTY (IRE) BHB 32f29a **RR 36f 29a** 2093[5]
7 ch g Tate Gallery (USA) 8.2f **(63)** - Bernica (FR) (Caro) 9.3f **(74)**
Form - 615
Record 1998 - 1st:1 2nd:0 3rd:0 Ran:3
Pre1998 - 1st:2 2nd:4 3rd:3 Ran:46
Win Prizemoney £11,736 *Total Prizemoney* £15,577
Wins * **1998** Jun Newmar (GD) H 12f 27 36
* 1996 *Feb Southw (STD) H 12f 36 41* <
* 1996 *Jan Southw (STD) H 12f 24 40*
1998 Turf 1-3: (12f 1-2, 16f) (g-s, gd, hrd 1-1)
Very moderate gelding, has worn blinkers (extremely effectively). Turf high 36 - 1st of 29 getting 16lb from Siberian Mystic (6 Jun Newmarket RF 1788).
**S R Bowring [10-52] D H Bowring (from A L Forbes [0-7] Jly 1994).*

MR NEVERMIND (IRE) BHB 42f58a **RR 41f 58a** 5003[13]
8 b g The Noble Player (USA) 7.7f **(58)** -Salacia (Seaepic(USA)) 9f **(56)**
Form - 77882300350
Record 1998 - 1st:0 2nd:1 3rd:2 Ran:11
Pre1998 - 1st:13 2nd:14 3rd:11 Ran:67
Win Prizemoney £42,414 *Total Prizemoney* £62,232
Wins * 1997 *Feb Wolver (STD) H 7f 85 85* <
* 1997 *Feb Lingfi (STD) H 7f 80 83*
* 1997 *Jan Lingfi (STD) H 8f 76 80*
* 1996 *Dec Lingfi (STD) C 8f 62+*
* 1996 *Nov Lingfi (STD) H 7f 73 74*
* 1996 Spt Bright (FRM) C 8f 67
* 1996 *Mar Lingfi (STD) C 7f 75*
* 1995 *Dec Lingfi (STD) C 8f 76*
* 1995 *Nov Lingfi (STD) 8f 67+*
* 1994 *Nov Lingfi (STD) H 7f 67 62*
1998 Turf 0-4: (7f, 8f 2, 10f) (gd, g-f 2, frm) 1998 AW 0-7: (7f, 8f 6) (Equi 6, Fibr)
Average gelding, effective 7 to 8f, best at 7f, - acts on AW, best on Equi, has worn blinkers, favours left handed tracks, favours tight tracks. Turf high 41 (began Jly). AW high 69.
**G L Moore [12-68] K Higson (from G Lewis [1-10] Spt 1992).*

MR OSCAR BHB 81f **RR 66?f** 2307[19]
6 b g Belfort (FR) 6.7f **(53)** - Moushka (Song) 7.2f **(61)**
Form - 0
Record 1998 - 1st:0 2nd:0 3rd:0 Ran:1
Pre1998 - 1st:2 2nd:0 3rd:0 Ran:10
Win Prizemoney £8,932 *Total Prizemoney* £8,932
Wins 1995 Spt Leices (GD) 5f 95+ <
1995 Aug Ripon (G-F) 5f 82+
1998 Turf 0-1: (5f) (gd)
Average gelding. Becoming disappointing.
**W McKeown [0-4] Mrs L E McKeown (from M Johnston [2-7] Jun 1996).*

MR PARADISE (IRE) BHB 62f71a **RR 62f 71a** 5014[4]
4 b g Salt Dome (USA) 6.5f **(59)** -Glowlamp (IRE)(Glow (USA))6.7f **(71)**

Form - 702253841524344
Record 1998 - 1st:1 2nd:2 3rd:2 Ran:12
Pre1998 - 1st:2 2nd:7 3rd:2 Ran:21
Win Prizemoney £8,394 *Total Prizemoney* £22,408
Wins *** 1998** *Jun Southw (STD) H 7f 63 67*
1997 Jun Lingfi (GD) 7f 73 <
1997 Jun Beverl (G-F) 8.5f 73 <
1998 Turf 0-6: (6f, 7f 5) (sft, g-s, gd 2, frm 2) 1998 AW 1-6: (7f 1-6) (Equi, Fibr 1-5)
Scopey, above-average gelding, effective 7 to 8f, best at 8f, acts on gd to frm - acts on Fibr, best on g-f, has worn blinkers, does well at Southwell. Turf high 61. AW high 71 - 2nd of 7 getting 8lb from First Maite (11 Jly Southwell 7f Fibr RF 2725) - also 1st of 13 giving 23lb to Sparkling Harry (5 Jun Southwell RF 1766). Consistent. **R M H Cowell [1-15] Paradise Partnership (from T J Naughton [2-18] Oct 1997).*

MR ROUGH BHB 44f31a **RR 48f 31a** 4456[9]

7 b g Fayruz 6.6f **(63)** - Rheinbloom (Rheingold) 10.4f **(62)**
Form - 78002107330
Record 1998 - 1st:1 2nd:1 3rd:2 Ran:10
Pre1998 - 1st:4 2nd:6 3rd:10 Ran:56
Win Prizemoney £15,954 *Total Prizemoney* £29,039
Wins *** 1998** Jly Bright (GD) S 8f 39
* 1997 Jun Yarmou (FRM) SH 8f 50 57
* 1995 Apr Bright (G-F) H 8f 58 64 <
* 1994 Spt Goodwo (G-F) CH 8f 51 51
1998 Turf 1-10: (8f 1-10) (g-s, gd 1-1, g-f, frm 6, hrd)
Moderate gelding, effective 8f, acts on frm, has worn blinkers. Turf high 48. **D Morris [5-67] D Morris.*

MRS MALAPROP BHB 65f **RR 69f** 4858[7]

3 b f Night Shift (USA) 8.1f **(73)** - Lightning Legacy (USA) (Super Concorde (USA)) 10.9f **(66)**
Form - 000272016200807
Record 1998 - 1st:1 2nd:3 3rd:0 Ran:15
Pre1998 - 1st:1 2nd:1 3rd:0 Ran:5
Win Prizemoney £5,750 *Total Prizemoney* £11,989
Wins *** 1998** Aug Salisb (G-F) H 6f 63 67
* 1997 Spt Catter (GD) 5f 82+ <
1998 Turf 1-15: (5f 7, 6f 1-8) (hvy, sft 2, g-s 2, gd 4, g-f 1-3, frm 3)
Scopey, average filly, effective 5f, acts on gd. Turf high 69. She regained winning form at Salisbury in August. Modest form afterwards, though she should have won at Epsom later the same month, but hung her chance away.
**M R Channon [2-20] Michael Foy.*

MRS MIDDLE BHB 41f **RR 46f** 4486[15]

3 b f Puissance 7.1f **(60)** - Ibadiyya (Tap On Wood) 10.3f **(65)**
Form - 00287088200
Record 1998 - 1st:0 2nd:2 3rd:0 Ran:11
Pre1998 - 1st:1 2nd:0 3rd:0 Ran:7
Win Prizemoney £3,122 *Total Prizemoney* £5,090
Wins 1997 Aug Warwic (G-S) H 6f 62 66 <
1998 Turf 0-11: (6f, 7f 2, 8f 5, 9f, 10f 2) (g-s, gd 6, g-f 2, frm 2)
Light-framed, moderate filly, effective 5 to 6f, acts on g-f to frm, prefers left handed tracks, likes tight tracks. Turf high 46.
**D W Chapman [0-6] Michael Hill (from N A Callaghan [1-12] Jly 1998).*

MR SOLITAIRE (IRE) BHB 60f **RR 66f** 4863[6]

2 ch c Bigstone (IRE)- Farewell Song (USA) (The Minstrel (CAN)) 10f **(72)**
Form - 535076
Record 1998 - 1st:0 2nd:0 3rd:1 Ran:6
Win Prizemoney £0 *Total Prizemoney* £440
1998 Turf 0-4: (6f 2, 7f, 8f) (gd, g-f 2, frm) 1998 AW 0-2: (6f, 7f) (Fibr 2)
Average colt, effective 6f, acts on gd, has worn blinkers. Turf high 66. AW high 64. **P F I Cole [0-6] Mrs Christopher Hanbury.*

MR SPEAKER (IRE) BHB 61f52a **RR 60f 52a** 4652[8]

5 ch g Statoblest 6.4f **(63)** - Casting Vote (USA) (Monteverdi) 6.5f **(61)**
Form - 7618
Record 1998 - 1st:1 2nd:0 3rd:0 Ran:4
Pre1998 - 1st:1 2nd:2 3rd:1 Ran:21
Win Prizemoney £6,238 *Total Prizemoney* £9,389
Wins *** 1998** Spt Beverl (G-F) H 7.5f 55 60 <
* 1996 Jly Chepst (G-F) H 6.1f 60 60 <
1998 Turf 1-3: (7f 1-3) (g-f 1-3) 1998 AW 0-1: (10f) (Equi)
Average gelding, effective 6 to 7f, best at 7f, acts on g-s to frm, best on g-f. Turf high 60 (began Spt) - also 1st of 17 getting 12lb from Kass Alhawa (22 Spt Beverley RF 4406).
**C F Wall [2-24] David Allan (from G C Bravery [0-2] Jan 1998).*

MR SPECULATOR BHB 45f51a **RR 14f 51a** 154[7]

5 ch g Kefaah (USA) 11.2f **(64)** - Humanity (Ahonoora) 8.1f **(73)**
Form - 7
Record 1998 - 1st:0 2nd:0 3rd:0 Ran:1
Pre1998 - 1st:3 2nd:1 3rd:4 Ran:22
Win Prizemoney £9,155 *Total Prizemoney* £11,032
Wins 1997 *Feb Wolver (STD) H 12f 51 52*
1996 *Dec Wolver (STD) H 12f 48 49*
1996 Jly Warwic (G-F) H 14.9f 56 60 <
1998 AW 0-1: (16f) (Fibr)
Fair gelding, effective 11 to 15f, best at 12f, - acts on Fibr, often wears blinkers (extremely effectively), prefers left handed tracks. Inconsistent.
**J L Spearing [0-2] North Kilworth Racing (from J E Banks [2-14] Oct 1997).*

MRS PICKLES BHB 34f36a **RR 36f 36a** 3629[2]

3 gr f Northern Park (USA) 10f **(57)** - Able Mabel (Absalom) 7.2f **(58)**
Form - 56880042
Record 1998 - 1st:0 2nd:1 3rd:0 Ran:8
Pre1998 - 1st:0 2nd:0 3rd:0 Ran:3
Win Prizemoney £0 *Total Prizemoney* £654
1998 Turf 0-6: (6f, 8f, 10f 2, 16f 2) (g-f 5, frm) 1998 AW 0-2: (9f, 12f) (Fibr 2)
Strong, very moderate filly, effective 9 to 16f, acts on g-f - acts on Fibr, likes tight tracks. Turf high 36 - 2nd of 6 getting 7lb from Lady Felix (14 Aug Folkestone 16f g-f RF 3629). AW high 34 (1st run) - 5th of 8 getting 12lb from Bint Nadia (7 Apr Wolverhampton 9f Fibr RF 0592). Consistent. **M D I Usher [0-11] Midweek Racing.*

MR SPONGE (USA) BHB 86a **RR 88f** 4360[20]

4 ch g Summer Squall (USA) 7f **(80)** - Dinner Surprise (USA) (Lyphard (USA)) 9.9f **(72)**
Form - 70
Record 1998 - 1st:0 2nd:0 3rd:0 Ran:2
Pre1998 - 1st:1 2nd:0 3rd:4 Ran:8
Win Prizemoney £3,691 *Total Prizemoney* £7,962
Wins * 1997 Jun Salisb (G-F) 7f 77 <
1998 Turf 0-2: (7f 2) (frm 2)
Scopey, useful gelding, effective 7 to 8f, best at 7f, acts on sft to frm. Turf high 79 (began Spt). **I A Balding [1-10] Paul Mellon.*

MRS SIDDONS (IRE) RR 84+f 4758[2]

2 ch f Royal Academy (USA) 7.8f **(77)** - White Water (FR) (Pharly (FR)) 9.8f **(68)**
Form - 2
Record 1998 - 1st:0 2nd:1 3rd:0 Ran:1
Win Prizemoney £0 *Total Prizemoney* £1,060
1998 Turf 0-1: (7f) (gd)
Currently decent filly. (1st run) - 2nd of 20 to Hawriyah (12 Oct Leicester 7f gd RF 4758). **G Wragg [0-1] Mrs R Philipps.*

MT SPECULATION (IRE) BHB 85f **RR 88f** 4752[2]

2 b c Common Grounds 8.1f **(66)** - Blue Alicia (Wolver Hollow) 8f **(56)**
Form - 272
Record 1998 - 1st:0 2nd:2 3rd:0 Ran:3
Win Prizemoney £0 *Total Prizemoney* £1,958
1998 Turf 0-3: (7f 3) (sft, gd, frm)
Currently useful colt. Turf high 88 (began Spt) - 2nd of 14 giving 5lb to Amarice (12 Oct Ayr 7f sft RF 4752).
**P W Chapple-Hyam [0-3] J Chapple-Hyam, A Peacock, Lady S Renouf.*

MUARA BAY BHB 48f54a **RR 52f 54a** 4962[3]

4 gr g Absalom 7.1f **(56)** - Inca Girl (Tribal Chief) 8.5f **(61)**
Form - 21240378082583
Record 1998 - 1st:1 2nd:2 3rd:2 Ran:13
Pre1998 - 1st:1 2nd:3 3rd:2 Ran:11
Win Prizemoney £5,179 *Total Prizemoney* £10,455
Wins *** 1998** *Jan Southw (STD) H 8f 46 52* <
* 1997 Aug Bright (G-F) H 8f 38 47
1998 Turf 0-9: (7f, 8f 8) (sft, g-s, gd 3, g-f 2, frm 2) 1998 AW 1-4: (7f, 8f

1-3) (Fibr 1-4)
Workmanlike, fair gelding, effective 7 to 10f, best at 8f, acts on gd to frm - acts on Fibr, has worn blinkers (effectively), prefers left handed tracks, likes tight tracks, and excels at Wolverhampton and Brighton. Turf high 52 - 2nd of 19 getting 2lb from Desert Valentine (11 Spt Goodwood 8f gd RF 4229). AW high 56 - 2nd of 13 getting 1lb from Green Bopper (28 Mar Wolverhampton 8f Fibr RF 0493) - also 1st of 9 getting 22lb from Benjamins Law (2 Jan Southwell RF 0009). **G Lewis [2-23] Khalifa Dasmal (from Miss Gay Kelleway [0-1] Nov 1996).*

MU-ARRIK BHB 31f20a **RR 28df 20a** 4485[23]

10 b or br h Aragon 7.7f **(58)** - Maravilla (Mandrake Major) 7.6f **(53)**
Form - 0605600
Record 1998 - 1st:0 2nd:0 3rd:0 Ran:4
Pre1998 - 1st:2 2nd:10 3rd:7 Ran:94
Win Prizemoney £5,396 *Total Prizemoney* £16,343
Wins * 1994 Spt Haydoc (GD) SH 6f 52 52 <
1998 Turf 0-1: (6f) (frm) 1998 AW 0-3: (6f 2, 7f) (Equi, Fibr 2)
Little account horse, effective 6f, acts on gd to frm, mostly wears blinkers. AW high 21.
**G R Oldroyd [1-56] Robert Cook (from B Beasley [0-5] Nov 1993).*

MUBRIK (IRE) BHB 101f **RR 103+f** 4494[4]

3 b c Lahib (USA) 8f **(69)** - Bequeath (USA) (Lyphard (USA)) 9.9f **(72)**
Form - 21124
Record 1998 - 1st:2 2nd:2 3rd:0 Ran:5
Pre1998 - 1st:0 2nd:0 3rd:1 Ran:2
Win Prizemoney £11,363 *Total Prizemoney* £24,459
Wins * **1998** Jly Sandow (GD) H 7.1f 93 96 <
* **1998** Jun Thirsk (SFT) 7f 83+
1998 Turf 2-5: (7f 2-4, 8f) (gd 2-4, frm)
Strong, very useful colt, effective 7 to 8f, best at 7f, acts on gd to frm, best on gd. Turf high 103 - 2nd of 10 giving 2lb to Florazi (18 Jly Newmarket 8f frm RF 2919) - also 1st of 14 giving 13lb to Fredora (3 Jly Sandown RF 2506). He did not run a bad race all season, and put up a super performance after a 10-week break when finishing fourth in the valuable Tote Festival Handicap at Ascot in September. He shaped as if he would stay beyond seven furlongs that day and, granted normal improvement, is just the sort to win a big handicap in 1999.
**J H M Gosden [2-7] Hamdan Al Maktoum.*

MUCH COMMENDED BHB 93f **RR 93f** 3216[8]

4 b f Most Welcome 8.6f **(66)** - Glowing With Pride (Ile de Bourbon (USA)) 10.1f **(67)**
Form - 3848
Record 1998 - 1st:0 2nd:0 3rd:1 Ran:4
Pre1998 - 1st:1 2nd:0 3rd:3 Ran:4
Win Prizemoney £3,987 *Total Prizemoney* £43,818
Wins * 1996 Spt Nottin (G-F) 6.1f 83+ <
1998 Turf 0-4: (7f, 8f 2, 9f) (gd 3, g-f)
Workmanlike, useful filly, effective 8f, acts on gd to g-f. Turf high 93 (1st run) - 3rd of 6 giving 12lb to Digitalize (21 May Goodwood 8f g-f RF 1364). In the frame in the German and Italian 1,000 Guineas at three, she was off the track for a year before reappearing last season but did not show a great deal. Not seen out after July. **G Wragg [1-8] A E Oppenheimer.*

MUCHEA BHB 112f **RR 116f** 4849[4]

4 ch c Shalford (IRE) 7.8f **(63)** - Bargouzine (Hotfoot) 10.5f **(59)**
Form - 1520158364
Record 1998 - 1st:2 2nd:1 3rd:1 Ran:10
Pre1998 - 1st:3 2nd:2 3rd:4 Ran:13
Win Prizemoney £93,195 *Total Prizemoney* £201,053
Wins * **1998** Jun Newmar (GD) G3 7f 115 <
* **1998** Apr Currag (HVY) G3 7f 111
* 1996 Aug Baden (GD) G2 6f 104
* 1996 Apr Newmar (G-F) 5f 84+
* 1996 Mar Catter (G-S) 5f 93
1998 Turf 2-10: (7f 2-4, 8f 6) (hvy 1-1, sft, gd 1-7, g-f)
Leggy, high-class colt, effective 7 to 8f, best at 7f, acts on hvy to gd, best on gd, excels at Newmarket. Turf high 116 - 3rd of 12 giving 3lb to Seeking The Pearl (9 Aug Deauville 7f gd RF 3614a) - also 1st of 10 from Ramooz (27 Jun Newmarket RF 2352). Consistent. He took a Curragh Group Three on his return, but then found it tough going for the rest of the season, usually taking on the best, and he only managed one more victory which came in another Group Three at Newmarket. He showed his best form with cut in the ground. **M R Channon [5-23] Andy Smith.*

MUCHO COLOR (IRE) **RR 69f** 2970[8]

2 ch c Pips Pride 6.7f **(70)** - Aubretia (USA) (Hatchet Man (USA)) 6.3f **(51)**
Form - 60508
Record 1998 - 1st:0 2nd:0 3rd:0 Ran:5
Win Prizemoney £0 *Total Prizemoney* £76
1998 Turf 0-5: (5f 3, 6f 2) (gd 3, frm 2)
Average colt, has worn blinkers. Turf high 69.
**B J Meehan [0-5] High Seas Leisure Ltd.*

MUDALAL (USA) BHB 85f **RR 86f** 2088[11]

3 b c Dixieland Band (USA) 10.1f **(80)** - Barakat (Bustino) 10.4f **(64)**
Form - 10
Record 1998 - 1st:1 2nd:0 3rd:0 Ran:2
Pre1998 - 1st:0 2nd:0 3rd:1 Ran:2
Win Prizemoney £4,110 *Total Prizemoney* £4,881
Wins * **1998** May Lingfi (GD) 10f 86 <
1998 Turf 1-2: (10f 1-1, 12f) (g-s, g-f 1-1)
Light-framed, useful colt. Turf high 86 (1st run) - 1st of 12 getting 15lb from Coulthard (9 May Lingfield RF 1121). Likely to prove suited by further than the ten furlongs over which he won his maiden.
**B W Hills [1-2] Hamdan Al Maktoum (from D Morley [0-2] Oct 1997).*

MUDEER BHB 108f **RR 110f** 5066[5]

3 b c Warning 8.1f **(77)** - Colorvista (Shirley Heights) 10.3f **(74)**
Form - 4025
Record 1998 - 1st:0 2nd:1 3rd:0 Ran:4
Pre1998 - 1st:2 2nd:1 3rd:0 Ran:3
Win Prizemoney £15,609 *Total Prizemoney* £58,963
Wins * 1997 Spt Ascot (G-F) 7f 98 <
* 1997 Spt Leices (G-F) 7f 87+
1998 Turf 0-4: (9f, 10f, 11f, 12f) (gd 2, g-f 2)
Well made, Group-class colt, effective 8 to 11f, acts on gd to g-f, best on gd. Turf high 110 (1st run) - 4th of 5 to Croco Rouge (10 May Longchamp 11f gd RF 1231a). He was touched off in the Group One Racing Post Trophy as a juvenile, but was still unable to score when dropped down to Listed company in October. Seemingly unable to stride out with any fluency, he may have a physical problem. **S bin Suroor [2-7] Godolphin.*

MUGELLO BHB 81f **RR 85f** 4508[20]

3 b f Emarati (USA) 6.6f **(63)** - Fleur de Foret (USA) (Green Forest (USA)) 9.9f **(68)**
Form - 00000
Record 1998 - 1st:0 2nd:0 3rd:0 Ran:5
Pre1998 - 1st:2 2nd:3 3rd:0 Ran:8
Win Prizemoney £6,457 *Total Prizemoney* £19,627
Wins * 1997 Jly Chepst (G-F) 5.1f 94 <
* 1997 Jun Warwic (G-F) 5f 77+
1998 Turf 0-4: (5f 2, 6f 2) (gd 2, g-f 2) 1998 AW 0-1: (5f) (Fibr)
Neat, useful filly, effective 5 to 6f, best at 5f, acts on gd to g-f, best on g-f. Turf high 85. Inconsistent. **A P Jarvis [2-13] Mrs Ann Jarvis.*

MUGHAMERR **RR 50f** 4956[10]

2 b br f Mr Prospector (USA) 8.6f **(88)** - Intrepidity **(116f)** (Sadler's Wells (USA)) 10f **(76)**
Form - 0
Record 1998 - 1st:0 2nd:0 3rd:0 Ran:1
1998 Turf 0-1: (8f) (frm)
Currently fair filly. **D R Loder [0-1] Sheikh Mohammed.*

MUHABA (USA) BHB 90f **RR 94f** 4993[3]

3 ch f Mr Prospector (USA) 8.6f **(88)** - Salsabil (Sadler's Wells (USA)) 10f **(76)**
Form - 453
Record 1998 - 1st:0 2nd:0 3rd:1 Ran:3
Pre1998 - 1st:1 2nd:0 3rd:0 Ran:3
Win Prizemoney £3,517 *Total Prizemoney* £8,129
Wins 1997 Spt Haydoc (GD) 8.1f 88+ <
1998 Turf 0-3: (10f 2, 12f) (sft, gd, frm)
Scopey, useful filly, effective 10f, acts on frm. Turf high 94 (began Spt) - 5th of 8 to Lady In Waiting (15 Oct Newmarket 10f frm RF 4819). She had been off the track for nearly a year before reap-

pearing in September, but did not show a great deal in two Listed races and a conditions event.
**J L Dunlop [0-3] Hamdan Al Maktoum (from S bin Suroor [1-3] Oct 1997).*

MUHANDIS BHB 52f50a **RR 55f 50a** 5125[3]

5 b h Persian Bold 10f **(69)** - Night At Sea (Night Shift (USA)) 7.2f **(69)**
Form - 08813

Record	**1998** -	1st:0	2nd:0	3rd:1	Ran:1
	Pre1998 -	1st:2	2nd:0	3rd:1	Ran:10

Win Prizemoney £5,640 *Total Prizemoney* £6,637

Wins * 1997 *Dec Lingfi (STD) H 10f 47 50*
1996 Jly Yarmou (FRM) 7f 77 <

1998 Turf 0-1: (12f) (g-s)
Fair colt, has worn blinkers, likes left handed tracks.
**G L Moore [1-7] A Moore (from J H M Gosden [1-4] Spt 1996).*

MUHIB (USA) BHB 103f **RR 103f** 4515[10]

3 b c Red Ransom (USA) 8.6f **(83)** - Sensorious (CAN) (Vice Regent (CAN)) 8.7f **(74)**
Form - 21710

Record	**1998** -	1st:2	2nd:1	3rd:0	Ran:5
	Pre1998 -	1st:0	2nd:0	3rd:1	Ran:2

Win Prizemoney £39,545 *Total Prizemoney* £41,452

Wins * **1998** Jly Goodwo (G-S) H 12f 96 103 <
* **1998** Jun Goodwo (G-F) 9f 85+

1998 Turf 2-5: (8f, 9f 1-1, 10f, 12f 1-2) (gd 1-2, g-f 1-1, frm 2)
Scopey, very useful colt, effective 12f, acts on gd. Turf high 103 - 1st of 15 giving 11lb to Rainbow High (29 Jly Goodwood RF 3206). His form chart resembles the Alps, the peak being an emphatic win in the Tote Gold Trophy Handicap at Glorious Goodwood. Immaturity might be at the root of his inconsistency, and he could well come back a totally different athlete next term. This colt has Group race potential. **Sir Michael Stoute [2-7] Hamdan Al Maktoum.*

MUHTADI (IRE) BHB 52f **RR 35f** 1788[17]

5 br g Marju (IRE) 9.2f **(76)** - Moon Parade (Welsh Pageant) 10f **(65)**
Form - 00

Record	**1998** -	1st:0	2nd:0	3rd:0	Ran:2
	Pre1998 -	1st:1	2nd:0	3rd:0	Ran:10

Win Prizemoney £3,137 *Total Prizemoney* £3,617

Wins 1996 Apr Ripon (GD) H 10f 70 71 <

1998 Turf 0-2: (8f, 12f) (frm, hrd)
Very moderate gelding, has worn blinkers. Turf high 35.
**D W Chapman [0-2] S B Clark (from Lady Herries [1-5] Jun 1997).*

MUHTAFEL BHB 93f **RR 92f** 4241[D]

4 b c Nashwan (USA) 10.3f **(79)** - The Perfect Life (IRE) (Try My Best (USA)) 7.6f **(67)**
Form - 6800005321213D

Record	**1998** -	1st:2	2nd:2	3rd:2	Ran:14
	Pre1998 -	1st:1	2nd:2	3rd:0	Ran:4

Win Prizemoney £13,052 *Total Prizemoney* £21,343

Wins * **1998** Aug Chepst (G-F) H 10.2f 81 86 <
1998 Jly Newmar (G-F) H 10f 72 77
1997 Jun Redcar (GD) 8f 81

1998 Turf 2-13: (8f 5, 10f 2-7, 12f) (hvy, g-s, gd 3, g-f 2, frm 2-5, hrd)
1998 AW 0-1: (12f) (Fibr)
Strong, useful colt, effective 8 to 10f, best at 10f, acts on frm, has worn blinkers. Turf high 92 - also 1st of 7 getting 8lb from Secret Spring (13 Aug Chepstow RF 3610). Improving. Formerly with John Dunlop, he started off the year with Mick Quinn and ended up with John Jenkins. He showed his best form in July and August, winning for both trainers, and was controversially disqualified after winning a valuable handicap at the St Leger meeting.
**J R Jenkins [1-4] Pertemps Group Ltd (from M Quinn [1-10] Jly 1998).*

MUHTATHIR BHB 120f **RR 121f** 4947a[9]

3 ch c Elmaamul (USA) 8.1f **(70)** -Majmu (USA) (Al Nasr (FR)) 9.3f **(68)**
Form - 3211170

Record	**1998** -	1st:3	2nd:1	3rd:1	Ran:7
	Pre1998 -	1st:2	2nd:1	3rd:0	Ran:5

Win Prizemoney £69,661 *Total Prizemoney* £126,482

Wins * **1998** Aug Goodwo (G-F) G2 8f 121 <
* **1998** Aug Newbur (G-F) G3 7.3f 118
* **1998** Jly Doncas (G-F) 8f 109+
* 1997 Jly Sandow (G-S) 7.1f 105+
* 1997 Jun Sandow (G-F) 7.1f 90

1998 Turf 3-7: (7f 1-2, 8f 2-4, 10f) (hvy, sft, gd 2, g-f 3-3)
Scopey, very high-class colt, effective 7 to 8f, best at 8f, acts on gd to g-f, best on g-f, does well at Sandown. Turf high 121 - 1st of 9 getting 9lb from Almushtarak (29 Aug Goodwood RF 3948) - also 1st of 9 getting 6lb from Danish Rhapsody (14 Aug Newbury RF 3633). Inconsistent. High-class as a juvenile, he was rather disappointing in the ten-furlong Thresher Classic Trial on his reappearance, seemingly not getting home in the very soft ground. Ran a lot better when runner-up in the French Guineas, and a facile victory at Doncaster set him up for an all-the-way win in the Hungerford Stakes. Followed up by making most in the Tripleprint Celebration Mile at Goodwood, but he was never able to dominate the QE II field in the same way and was well beaten. He failed to act on the heavy ground in the Prix de la Foret. He joins Godolphin in 1999, and has the potential to make a top miler.
**J H M Gosden [5-12].*

MUJADENE (IRE) BHB 99f **RR 87f** 4462[2]

2 br c Mujadil (USA) 7.7f **(70)** - Rossaldene (Mummy's Pet) 7.7f **(60)**
Form - 2217242

Record	**1998** -	1st:1	2nd:4	3rd:0	Ran:7

Win Prizemoney £2,916 *Total Prizemoney* £7,799

Wins * **1998** Jly Windso (G-F) 5f 80+ <

1998 Turf 1-7: (5f 1-4, 6f 3) (gd 2, g-f, frm 1-4)
Useful colt, effective 5 to 6f, best at 6f, acts on g-f to frm, best on frm. Turf high 87 - 2nd of 4 giving 3lb to Deadly Nightshade (24 Spt Goodwood 6f frm RF 4462) - also 1st of 11 giving 5lb to Corndavon (20 Jly Windsor RF 2959). Sold for 32,000 guineas at Tattersalls Autumn Horses-in-Training Sales. **B J Meehan [1-7] F D Allison.*

MUJAGEM (IRE) BHB 50f **RR 53f** 5094[13]

2 br f Mujadil (USA) 7.7f **(70)** - Lili Bengam (Welsh Saint) 7.6f **(64)**
Form - 5460000

Record	**1998** -	1st:0	2nd:0	3rd:0	Ran:7

Win Prizemoney £0 *Total Prizemoney* £257

1998 Turf 0-7: (5f 3, 6f 2, 8f 2) (gd 4, g-f 2, frm)
Fair filly. Turf high 62. **M W Easterby [0-7] C F Spence.*

MUJAHID (USA) BHB 100f **RR 116f** 4851[1]

2 b c Danzig (USA) 8.1f **(88)** -Elrafa Ah (USA) **(101f)** (Storm Cat (USA))
Form - 1151

Record	**1998** -	1st:3	2nd:0	3rd:0	Ran:4

Win Prizemoney £142,822 *Total Prizemoney* £145,012

Wins * **1998** Oct Newmar (GD) G1 7f 116 <
* **1998** Jly Salisb (G-F) 6f 95+
* **1998** Jly Newmar (G-F) 6f 98+

1998 Turf 3-4: (6f 2-3, 7f 1-1) (gd 1-1, g-f 1-1, frm 1-2)
High-class colt. Turf high 116 (began Jly) - 1st of 7 from Auction House (17 Oct Newmarket RF 4851). Showed a turn of foot to beat the highly regarded Belasco on his Newmarket debut. Faced a facile task next time before a somewhat disappointing run when upped in class in the Gimcrack, although he was later reported to have suffered sore shins after that race. However, he bounced back to cause a surprise by winning the Dewhurst. Some of his better-fancied rivals did not show their form, but you cannot make excuses for all of them and he was definitely the winner on merit. His dam never won beyond six furlongs, but he has already done so, and looks a credible Guineas candidate.
**J L Dunlop [3-4] Hamdan Al Maktoum.*

MUJA'S MAGIC (IRE) BHB 53f60a **RR 52f 60a** 5007[12]

3 b f Mujadil (USA) 7.7f **(70)** -Grave Error(Northern Treat (USA)) 6f **(50)**
Form - 23318235865146028530

Record	**1998** -	1st:1	2nd:2	3rd:2	Ran:16
	Pre1998 -	1st:1	2nd:1	3rd:3	Ran:16

Win Prizemoney £9,670 *Total Prizemoney* £14,307

Wins * **1998** Jun Bright (GD) H 6f 53 59 <
* 1997 *Dec Lingfi (STD) H 6f 54 58*

1998 Turf 1-12: (5f 2, 6f 1-8, 7f 2) (sft, gd 1-3, g-f 3, frm 5) 1998 AW 0-4: (5f, 6f, 7f 2) (Equi 3, Fibr)
Leggy, average filly, effective 6 to 7f, best at 7f, acts on gd to g-f - acts on Equi, often wears blinkers, likes left handed tracks, likes tight tracks, excels at Lingfield. Turf high 63 - 4th of 11 getting 1lb from Zeppo (23 Jun Lingfield 6f g-f RF 2201) - also 1st of 9 getting 15lb from Majalis (15 Jun Brighton RF 1989). AW high 61 - 3rd of 7 giving 8lb to Scotland Bay (10 Jan Lingfield 7f Equi RF 0062).
**K T Ivory [2-32] Mrs Valerie Hubbard.*

Muhtathir romps home in the Tripleprint Celebration Mile

MUJI BHB 50f52a **RR 57f 52a** 4317[17]

3 b f Safawan 6.6f **(60)** - Tame Duchess (Saritamer (USA)) 9.5f **(63)**

Form - 34150030

Record 1998 - 1st:1 2nd:0 3rd:2 Ran:8

Pre1998 - 1st:0 2nd:0 3rd:0 Ran:3

Win Prizemoney £2,402 *Total Prizemoney* £3,275

Wins * **1998** Jun Carlis (G-S) 5.9f 57 <

1998 Turf 1-6: (6f 1-2, 7f 2, 8f 2) (gd 2, g-f 1-2, frm 2) 1998 AW 0-2: (7f 2) (Fibr 2)

Unfurnished, fair filly, effective 6f, acts on g-f. Turf high 57 - 1st of 15 getting 3lb from Wishbone Alley (11 Jun Carlisle RF 1893). AW high 56. **A P Jarvis [1-11] Christopher Shankland.*

MUJKARI (IRE) BHB 41f **RR 47f** 4934[11]

2 ch c Mujtahid (USA) 7.4f **(69)** -Hot Curry (USA)(Sharpen Up) 8.3f **(67)**

Form - 076000

Record 1998 - 1st:0 2nd:0 3rd:0 Ran:6

1998 Turf 0-6: (5f 2, 7f 3, 8f) (g-s, gd 4, g-f)

Moderate colt, has worn blinkers. Turf high 47.

**R Hannon [0-6] Vernon Smith.*

MUJOVA (IRE) BHB 60f72a **RR 62f 72a** 4955[10]

4 b c Mujadil (USA) 7.7f **(70)** - Kirsova (Absalom) 7.2f **(58)**

Form - 78002540507060

Record 1998 - 1st:0 2nd:1 3rd:0 Ran:14

Pre1998 - 1st:2 2nd:2 3rd:4 Ran:25

Win Prizemoney £6,783 *Total Prizemoney* £13,966

Wins * 1997 Spt Sandow (G-F) 7.1f 79 <

* 1996 Jly Newcas (G-F) 6f 76

1998 Turf 0-13: (6f 3, 7f 7, 8f 3) (sft 2, gd 5, g-f, frm 5) 1998 AW 0-1: (8f) (Fibr)

Workmanlike, average colt, effective 7f, acts on g-f to frm, best on g-f. Turf high 75. **R Hollinshead [2-39] J D Graham.*

MUKARRAB (USA) BHB 49f42a **RR 46f 42a** 5059[5]

4 b br g Dayjur (USA) 6.8f **(79)** -Mahassin (NZ)(Biscay (AUS)) 6.5f **(51)**

Form - 0006830274402303231O8005

Record 1998 - 1st:1 2nd:3 3rd:4 Ran:22

Pre1998 - 1st:0 2nd:0 3rd:0 Ran:8

Win Prizemoney £3,317 *Total Prizemoney* £8,299

Wins * **1998** Spt Thirsk (GD) H 5f 47 56 <

1998 Turf 1-17: (5f 1-15, 6f 2) (sft, g-s 4, gd 4, g-f, frm 1-7) 1998 AW 0-5: (5f 2, 6f, 7f 2) (Fibr 5)

Moderate gelding, effective 5f, acts on frm, has worn blinkers. Turf high 56 - 1st of 24 getting 7lb from Ajnad (5 Spt Thirsk RF 4114). AW high 40.

**D W Chapman [1-24] Ian Armitage (from D K Weld in IRE [0-6] Jly 1997).*

MUKASOL RR 76f 5005[3]

2 b c Mukaddamah (USA) 7.6f **(74)** - So Long Boys (FR) (Beldale Flutter (USA)) 9.7f **(71)**

Form - 433

Record 1998 - 1st:0 2nd:0 3rd:2 Ran:3

Win Prizemoney £0 *Total Prizemoney* £3,478

1998 Turf 0-3: (8f 3) (sft, gd, g-f)

Currently above-average colt. Turf high 76 (began Spt).

**L M Cumani [0-3] Moro Viscomti.*

MUKHALIF (IRE) RR 102+f 4511[1]

2 ch c Caerleon (USA) 10.9f **(79)** - Potri Pe (ARG) (Potrillazo (ARG))

Form - 11

Record 1998 - 1st:2 2nd:0 3rd:0 Ran:2

Win Prizemoney £15,823 *Total Prizemoney* £15,823

Wins * **1998** Spt Ascot (SFT) 7f 102+ <

* **1998** Spt Leices (G-S) 7f 97+

1998 Turf 2-2: (7f 2-2) (gd 1-1, g-f 1-1)

Currently very useful colt. Turf high 102 (began Spt) - 1st of 9 giving 3lb to Zaajer (27 Spt Ascot RF 4511) - also 1st of 14 from Dollar Law (8 Spt Leicester RF 4142). 'If the Dewhurst had been run today and he had been running in it I would have expected him to win.' That was David Loder's telling comment after this highly promising colt ran out an easy winner from Zaajer at Ascot in September. Sent to winter in Dubai, he is very much a Classic candidate. By Caerleon and out of a mare who won a Grade One over a mile and a half in Argentina, he has the right make, shape, and pedigree for

Epsom. *D R Loder [2-2] Sheikh Mohammed.*

Currently very moderate colt. Turf high 33 (began Spt).
M Kettle [0-2] Greenacres.

Mukhalif looks an extremely exciting prospect for 1999

MUKHLLES (USA) BHB 43f48a **RR 45f 48a** 4529[8]
5 b h Diesis 9f **(80)** - Serenely (USA) (Alydar (USA)) 9.1f **(76)**
Form - 57008778

Record	**1998** -	1st:0	2nd:0	3rd:0	Ran:7
	Pre1998 -	1st:0	2nd:0	3rd:3	Ran:12

Win Prizemoney £0 *Total Prizemoney* £1,904
1998 Turf 0-6: (7f 2, 8f 4) (gd 2, g-f 2, frm 2) 1998 AW 0-1: (8f) (Fibr)
Moderate colt, effective 7 to 8f, best at 8f, acts on g-f to frm, best on frm, likes left handed tracks, likes tight tracks. Turf high 47. Consistent.
**Bob Jones [0-17] Mrs Daphne Downey (from Major W R Hern [0-2] Apr 1996).*

MULLAGH HILL LAD (IRE) BHB 52f45a **RR 59?f 45a** 4543[13]
5 b g Cyrano de Bergerac 7.3f **(58)** - Fantasise (FR) (General Assembly (USA)) 10f **(68)**
Form - 056267700

Record	**1998** -	1st:0	2nd:1	3rd:0	Ran:7
	Pre1998 -	1st:1	2nd:1	3rd:2	Ran:21

Win Prizemoney £2,085 *Total Prizemoney* £5,181
Wins 1995 *Nov Wolver (STD) S 5f 65* <
1998 AW 0-7: (5f, 6f 5, 7f) (Equi, Fibr 6)
Fair gelding, effective 5 to 6f, best at 6f, acts on gd - acts on Fibr, has worn blinkers. AW high 52 - 2nd of 11 giving 23lb to Kid Ory (16 Jan Southwell 6f Fibr RF 0097). Inconsistent.
**N P Littmoden [0-9] Nick Littmoden (from B A McMahon [1-19] Jly 1997).*

MULLAGHMORE (IRE) RR 33f 4697[21]
2 b c Petardia 8.2f **(58)** - Comfrey Glen (Glenstal (USA)) 10.1f **(64)**
Form - 00

Record	**1998** -	1st:0	2nd:0	3rd:0	Ran:2

1998 Turf 0-2: (8f 2) (gd, g-f)

MULLITOVER BHB 69f80a **RR 72f 80a** 5079[16]
8 ch g Interrex (CAN) 7.7f **(51)** - Atlantic Air (Air Trooper) 9.1f **(63)**
Form - 732046020

Record	**1998** -	1st:0	2nd:2	3rd:1	Ran:9
	Pre1998 -	1st:6	2nd:3	3rd:1	Ran:41

Win Prizemoney £26,862 *Total Prizemoney* £40,370

Wins								
* 1995	Oct	Newmar	(G-F)	H	7f	83	87	<
* 1995	Spt	Lingfi	(FRM)	H	7f	75	71	
* 1995	Aug	Kempto	(G-F)	H	7f	62	77	
* 1995	Aug	Windso	(G-F)	H	8.3f	62	71	
* 1994	*Nov*	*Southw*	*(STD)*	*H*	*7f*	*67*	*73*	

1998 Turf 0-9: (7f 7, 8f 2) (sft, gd 2, g-f 3, frm 2, hrd)
Above-average gelding, effective 7f, acts on gd. Turf high 72.
**M J Heaton-Ellis [6-50] Mrs D B Mulley.*

MULTICOLOURED (IRE) BHB 116f **RR 117?f** 3652[1]
5 b h Rainbow Quest (USA) 11.2f **(81)** - Greektown (Ela-Mana-Mou) 10.1f **(70)**
Form - 5321

Record	**1998** -	1st:1	2nd:1	3rd:1	Ran:4
	Pre1998 -	1st:1	2nd:4	3rd:0	Ran:6

Win Prizemoney £47,691 *Total Prizemoney* £75,681

Wins							
* **1998**	Aug	Newbur	(GD)	G2	13.3f	117?	<
* 1996	Oct	York	(GD)		10.4f	82+	

1998 Turf 1-4: (10f, 12f 2, 13f 1-1) (g-f 1-3, frm)
High-class colt, effective 10 to 13f, acts on gd to frm. Turf high 117 - 1st of 6 getting 6lb from Silver Patriarch (15 Aug Newbury RF 3652). Lightly raced, he ran too freely in his first two runs this term and was fitted with a net muzzle, but settled better when runner-up in the Princess of Wales's Stakes at Newmarket. Given a fine ride by Ryan, he made all the running to beat Silver Patriarch in the Geoffrey Freer, when he was able to enjoy an uncontested early

lead, but that was the last we saw of him.
**Sir Michael Stoute [2-10] Lord Weinstock.*

MULTI FRANCHISE BHB 36f35a **RR 39f 35a** 4143[6]
5 ch g Gabitat 8.5f **(44)** - Gabibti (IRE) (Dara Monarch) 8.8f **(59)**
Form - 16044463604448606
Record 1998 - 1st:0 2nd:0 3rd:1 Ran:13
Pre1998 - 1st:4 2nd:2 3rd:2 Ran:33
Win Prizemoney £10,045 *Total Prizemoney* £13,730
Wins * 1997 *Nov Lingfi (STD) H 10f 39 46*
1996 Aug Bright (FRM) C 8f 54
1996 *Feb Lingfi (STD) C 10f 57*
1995 *Jun Wolver (STD) S 7f 65* <
1998 Turf 0-5: (8f 3, 10f 2) (gd, g-f 2, frm 2) 1998 AW 0-8: (7f, 8f, 10f 6) (Equi 8)
Moderate gelding, effective 7 to 10f, acts on g-f to hrd - acts on Equi, has worn blinkers, likes right handed tracks, favours tight tracks, and excels at Windsor and Brighton. Turf high 41 - 4th of 14 getting 5lb from Mellors (28 May Brighton 8f frm RF 1550). AW high 44 - 3rd of 8 giving 6lb to Shanghai Lil (24 Feb Lingfield 10f Equi RF 0356). He won quite easily on the Lingfield Equitrack in November 1997, but has not added to that tally.
**R M Flower [1-29] The Equus Fugit Partnership (from B Gubby [3-19] Feb 1997).*

MUMKIN BHB 61f **RR 55f** 46[11]
4 b c Reprimand 8.2f **(63)** - Soon to Be (Hot Spark) 7.6f **(62)**
Form - 30
Record 1998 - 1st:0 2nd:0 3rd:0 Ran:1
Pre1998 - 1st:1 2nd:0 3rd:2 Ran:9
Win Prizemoney £3,306 *Total Prizemoney* £4,019
Wins 1996 Aug Windso (G-F) 6f 79 <
1998 AW 0-1: (7f) (Equi)
Workmanlike, fair colt, has worn blinkers.
**Mrs L Stubbs [0-5] R P Johns (from T ThomsonJones [1-5] Jly 1997).*

MUMMY NOSE BEST RR 39f 1026[7]
2 b f Cyrano de Bergerac 7.3f **(58)** - Wendy's Way **(44f 41a)** (Merdon Melody)
Form - 7
Record 1998 - 1st:0 2nd:0 3rd:0 Ran:1
1998 Turf 0-1: (5f) (g-f)
Currently very moderate filly. **V Soane [0-1] The Fillies Fanciers.*

MUNASIB (IRE) BHB 53f **RR 72f** 4677[6]
3 br g Treasure Kay 6.5f **(53)** - Pipe Opener (Prince Sabo) 7.2f **(62)**
Form - 03086
Record 1998 - 1st:0 2nd:0 3rd:1 Ran:5
Pre1998 - 1st:0 2nd:0 3rd:0 Ran:4
Win Prizemoney £0 *Total Prizemoney* £411
1998 Turf 0-5: (5f, 7f 3, 8f) (hvy, gd 2, g-f, frm)
Above-average gelding, effective 7f, acts on hvy. Turf high 72 - 3rd of 7 giving 5lb to Kenema (5 Aug Sligo 7f hvy RF 3544a). Becoming disappointing.
**S E Kettlewell [0-3] Cable Media Consultancy Ltd (from D Hanley in IRE [0-6] Aug 1998).*

MUNAZA (USA) BHB 62f **RR 70f** 4893[13]
3 b br c Trempolino (USA) 11.9f **(77)** - Known Feminist (USA) (Known Fact (USA)) 7.4f **(67)**
Form - 75400
Record 1998 - 1st:0 2nd:0 3rd:0 Ran:5
Win Prizemoney £0 *Total Prizemoney* £247
1998 Turf 0-5: (8f 2, 10f 3) (gd, g-f 2, frm 2)
Strong, above-average colt, has worn blinkers. Turf high 70 (began Jly). **R W Armstrong [0-5] Hamdan Al Maktoum.*

MUNDAHISH (IRE) BHB 78f **RR 75f** 4479[3]
2 b br c Marju (IRE) 9.2f **(76)** - Wakayi (Persian Bold) 9.3f **(66)**
Form - 6263
Record 1998 - 1st:0 2nd:1 3rd:1 Ran:4
Win Prizemoney £0 *Total Prizemoney* £1,547
1998 Turf 0-4: (6f 2, 7f, 8f) (g-f 2, frm 2)
Above-average colt. Turf high 75 (began Jly).
**P T Walwyn [0-4] Hamdan Al Maktoum.*

MUNDO RARO BHB 88f **RR 87f** 5078[21]
3 b c Zafonic (USA) 9f **(83)** - Star Spectacle (Spectacular Bid (USA)) 11.2f **(76)**
Form - 231020
Record 1998 - 1st:1 2nd:2 3rd:1 Ran:6
Win Prizemoney £3,566 *Total Prizemoney* £9,766
Wins * **1998** Aug Pontef (G-F) 8f 87 <
1998 Turf 1-6: (8f 1-4, 9f, 10f) (sft, gd, g-f 3, frm 1-1)
Lengthy, useful colt, effective 8f, acts on g-f to frm. Turf high 87 - 1st of 10 from Razor (16 Aug Pontefract RF 3675).
**J G FitzGerald [1-6] Marquesa de Moratalla.*

MUNEERA (USA) RR 61f 4394[7]
3 ch f Green Dancer (USA) 11.9f **(77)** - Hard Knocker (USA) (Raja Baba (USA)) 10f **(64)**
Form - 07
Record 1998 - 1st:0 2nd:0 3rd:0 Ran:2
1998 Turf 0-2: (12f 2) (frm 2)
Leggy, currently average filly. Turf high 61 (began Spt).
**M P Tregoning [0-2] Hamdan Al Maktoum.*

MUNGO DUFF (IRE) RR 62f 1937[13]
3 b c Priolo (USA) 10.9f **(71)** - Noble Dust (USA) (Dust Commander (USA)) 10.3f **(77)**
Form - 00
Record 1998 - 1st:0 2nd:0 3rd:0 Ran:2
1998 Turf 0-2: (10f 2) (gd 2)
Scopey, currently average colt. Turf high 62.
**P W Harris [0-2] J Jay & Mrs P W Harris.*

MUNGO PARK BHB 77f **RR 81f** 4872[3]
4 b g Selkirk (USA) 7.9f **(76)** - River Dove (USA) (Riverman (USA)) 9.1f **(76)**
Form - 241271510051440563
Record 1998 - 1st:4 2nd:2 3rd:1 Ran:18
Pre1998 - 1st:2 2nd:0 3rd:3 Ran:16
Win Prizemoney £23,175 *Total Prizemoney* £30,328
Wins * **1998** Jly Newcas (G-F) H 5f 77 80 <
* **1998** Jun Nottin (G-F) H 5.1f 75 76
* **1998** May Beverl (GD) H 5f 70 75
* **1998** Apr Newcas (SFT) H 5f 64 70
* 1997 Oct Newcas (G-F) H 5f 53 60
* 1997 May Carlis (FRM) 5f 51
1998 Turf 4-18: (5f 4-17, 6f) (sft 1-1, g-s 4, gd 1-8, g-f 1-2, frm 1-3)
Decent gelding, effective 5f, acts on gd to frm, has worn blinkers, excels at Newcastle. Turf high 81 - 4th of 12 giving 17lb to Maladerie (5 Spt Haydock 5f frm RF 4107) - also 1st of 10 getting 8lb from Lago Di Varano (25 Jly Newcastle RF 3114).
**Mrs J R Ramsden [6-34] Mrs H M Carr.*

MUNIF (USA) RR 54f 1589[9]
3 ch c Woodman (USA) 9.7f **(77)** - Garvin's Gal (USA) (Seattle Slew (USA)) 9.4f **(76)**
Form - 0
Record 1998 - 1st:0 2nd:0 3rd:0 Ran:1
1998 Turf 0-1: (7f) (gd)
Currently fair colt. **B Hanbury [0-1] Hamdan Al Maktoum.*

MUNJIZ (IRE) BHB 92f **RR 88f** 4706[3]
2 b br c Marju (IRE) 9.2f **(76)** - Absaar (USA) (Alleged (USA)) 10f **(76)**
Form - 4213
Record 1998 - 1st:1 2nd:1 3rd:1 Ran:4
Win Prizemoney £4,825 *Total Prizemoney* £10,691
Wins * **1998** Spt Goodwo (G-S) 6f 88 <
1998 Turf 1-4: (6f 1-3, 7f) (gd 1-1, g-f, frm 2)
Useful colt. Turf high 88 - 1st of 11 from Voracious (11 Spt Goodwood RF 4235). Not beaten far in a maiden on the July Course first time before chasing home Stravinsky at York. Boosted that form in a maiden at Goodwood, but failed to give his running latest. **B W Hills [1-4] Hamdan Al Maktoum.*

MUQTARB (IRE) RR 89f 3694[5]
2 ch c Cadeaux Genereux 7.9f **(76)** - Jasarah (IRE) (Green Desert (USA)) 8.6f **(78)**
Form - 15
Record 1998 - 1st:1 2nd:0 3rd:0 Ran:2
Win Prizemoney £6,775 *Total Prizemoney* £7,307
Wins * **1998** Jly Ascot (G-F) 6f 89+ <

1998 Turf 1-2: (6f 1-1, 7f) (g-f 1-2)
Currently useful colt. Turf high 89 (began Jly) - also 1st of 8 from Siege (25 Jly Ascot RF 3105). Beat a field of fellow debutants at Ascot with a bit to spare, but failed to settle in a listed race at York. Don't confuse him with Muqtarib, the Richmond Stakes winner in the same ownership.
**M P Tregoning [1-2] Hamdan Al Maktoum.*

MUQTARIB (USA) BHB 100f RR 100f 3217[1]

2 b c Gone West (USA) 7.8f **(82)** - Shicklah (USA) (The Minstrel (CAN)) 10f **(72)**
Form - 121
Record 1998 - 1st:2 2nd:1 3rd:0 Ran:3
Win Prizemoney £30,748 *Total Prizemoney* £32,152
Wins * 1998 Jly Goodwo (G-S) G2 6f 100 <
*** 1998** Jun Goodwo (GD) 6f 84+
1998 Turf 2-3: (6f 2-3) (gd 1-2, frm 1-1)
Currently very useful colt. Turf high 100 - 1st of 4 from Sarson (30 Jly Goodwood RF 3217). He was restricted to three outings over six furlongs at Goodwood, but showed enough when beating Sarson and Rosselli in the Richmond Stakes to suggest that he could develop into a leading sprinter next term. He has been held-up in all his races to date, and could prove even better on a stiff track. **J L Dunlop [2-3] Hamdan Al Maktoum.*

MURCHAN TYNE (IRE) BHB 61f RR 60f 4448[2]

5 ch m Good Thyne(USA) 11.8f **(60)** -Ardnamurchan(Ardross)10.6f **(68)**
Form - 21344272
Record 1998 - 1st:1 2nd:3 3rd:1 Ran:8
Pre1998 - 1st:0 2nd:0 3rd:0 Ran:5
Win Prizemoney £3,036 *Total Prizemoney* £9,206
Wins * 1998 Jun Leices (GD) H 11.8f 53 57 <
1998 Turf 1-8: (11f, 12f 1-3, 14f, 16f 3) (sft, gd 4, g-f, frm 1-2)
Average filly, effective 11 to 17f, best at 16f, acts on sft to frm, best on gd. Turf high 60 - 2nd of 12 getting 16lb from Sandbaggedagain (23 Spt Chester 16f gd RF 4448) - also 1st of 14 from Phantom Waters (1 Jun Leicester RF 1627). Consistent. She gained a gutsy success at Leicester in June, but has looked short of pace on other occasions and a step up to a marathon trip may be just what she needs. **E J Alston [2-16] Harrington-Worrall Racing.*

MURGHEM (IRE) BHB 100f RR 100f 4719a[3]

3 b c Common Grounds 8.1f **(66)** - Fabulous Pet (Somethingfabulous (USA)) 9.5f **(75)**
Form - 2582132223
Record 1998 - 1st:1 2nd:5 3rd:2 Ran:10
Win Prizemoney £3,566 *Total Prizemoney* £32,333
Wins * 1998 Jly Kempto (G-F) 12f 80 <
1998Turf 1-10:(8f 2, 10f 2, 12f 1-3, 14f, 15f, 16f)(sft, gd 2, g-f 5, frm 1-2)
Scopey, very useful colt, effective 12 to 16f, acts on sft to g-f, best on g-f, excels at York. Turf high 100 - 2nd of 11 getting 4lb from Churlish Charm (17 Spt Newbury 16f g-f RF 4331). This progressive colt was moved up in distance throughout the campaign, and was good enough to take his chance in a Group race by the autumn. A third place in the Prix du Lutece was the result of that adventure and, if he continues at this rate, there will be at least a Listed race in the bag by the end of 1999.
**B Hanbury [1-10] A Al Rostamani.*

MURMOON BHB 63f RR 71f 4807[4]

3 b c Danehill (USA) 9.1f **(79)** - Reflection (Mill Reef (USA)) 10.5f **(78)**
Form - 4037604824
Record 1998 - 1st:0 2nd:1 3rd:1 Ran:10
Pre1998 - 1st:0 2nd:0 3rd:1 Ran:3
Win Prizemoney £0 *Total Prizemoney* £2,933
1998 Turf 0-10: (6f, 8f 3, 9f 2, 10f 2, 11f, 12f) (g-s 2, gd 3, g-f 2, frm 3)
Scopey, above-average colt, effective 8 to 12f, acts on g-s to frm, best on frm, likes tight tracks. Turf high 71 - 2nd of 8 to Sconced (28 Spt Hamilton 9f g-s RF 4531). **B Hanbury [0-13] A Al-Rostamani.*

MURPHY'S GOLD (IRE) BHB 54f49a RR 53f 49a 4108[17]

7 ch g Salt Dome (USA) 6.5f **(59)** - Winter Harvest (Grundy) 10.3f **(65)**
Form - 463376618350
Record 1998 - 1st:1 2nd:0 3rd:3 Ran:12
Pre1998 - 1st:5 2nd:3 3rd:2 Ran:45
Win Prizemoney £24,421 *Total Prizemoney* £33,084
Wins * 1998 Jly Beverl (GD) H 8.5f 50 53
* 1997 Jun Beverl (G-F) H 8.5f 49 55 <
* 1995 Jly Beverl (G-F) H 8.5f 52 55 <
* 1995 Jun Beverl (G-F) H 7.5f 49 54
* 1994 Jly Ayr (G-F) H 8f 49 52
* 1994 Jun Carlis (G-F) H 6.9f 33 46
1998 Turf 1-12: (7f 5, 8f 1-7) (gd 3, g-f 1-5, frm 4)
Fair gelding, has broken blood-vessels, effective 7 to 8f, best at 8f, acts on gd to frm, best on g-f, has worn blinkers, likes right handed tracks, excels at Beverley. Turf high 53 - 5th of 15 getting 8lb from Kass Alhawa (29 Aug Beverley 7f frm RF 3942) - also 1st of 8 giving 5lb to Thatched (28 Jly Beverley RF 3158).
**R A Fahey [6-58] D A Read (from M H Easterby [0-1] Jun 1993).*

MURPHY'S LAW BHB 54f RR 67f 5041[8]

2 b g High Kicker (USA) 8.4f **(52)** - Mio Mementa (Streak) 10f **(58)**
Form - 008
Record 1998 - 1st:0 2nd:0 3rd:0 Ran:3
1998 Turf 0-3: (5f, 6f, 7f) (sft, gd, frm)
Currently average gelding. Turf high 67.
**M J Ryan [0-3] Norcroft Park Stud.*

MURRAY GREY BHB 50f RR 55df 1096[8]

4 gr f Be My Chief (USA) 10.2f **(62)** - Couleur de Rose (Kalaglow) 9.8f **(67)**
Form - 08
Record 1998 - 1st:0 2nd:0 3rd:0 Ran:2
Pre1998 - 1st:1 2nd:1 3rd:0 Ran:6
Win Prizemoney £2,827 *Total Prizemoney* £3,527
Wins * 1997 May Mussel (G-F) 8f 55 <
1998 Turf 0-2: (7f, 8f) (g-s, gd)
Scopey, fair filly. Turf high 22. **E Weymes [1-8] Mrs P M Weymes.*

MUSAFI (USA) BHB 90f99a RR 73f 99a 128[2]

4 b g Dayjur (USA) 6.8f **(79)** - Ra'a (USA) (Diesis) 9.3f **(69)**
Form - 12
Record 1998 - 1st:1 2nd:1 3rd:0 Ran:2
Pre1998 - 1st:0 2nd:0 3rd:1 Ran:1
Win Prizemoney £2,801 *Total Prizemoney* £4,433
Wins * 1998 *Jan Wolver (STD) 7f 86* <
1998 AW 1-2: (6f, 7f 1-1) (Fibr 1-2)
Scopey, currently very useful gelding. AW high 97 - 2nd of 7 giving 16lb to Wolfhunt (21 Jan Wolverhampton 6f Fibr RF 0128). He made his reappearance at Wolverhampton in January when winning a seven-furlong maiden in a canter, but was inexplicably dropped to six when turned over next time. He was not seen after that.
**K A Morgan [1-2] D & M Cased Hole (from Major W R Hern [0-1] May 1997).*

MUSALSAL (IRE) BHB 99f RR 99f 4239[11]

4 b c Sadler's Wells (USA) 11.3f **(87)** - Ozone Friendly (USA) (Green Forest (USA)) 9.9f **(68)**
Form - 2207420
Record 1998 - 1st:0 2nd:3 3rd:0 Ran:7
Pre1998 - 1st:2 2nd:0 3rd:2 Ran:8
Win Prizemoney £10,372 *Total Prizemoney* £36,751
Wins * 1997 Mar Doncas (G-F) 8f 104 <
* 1996 Oct Leices (GD) 8f 91+
1998 Turf 0-7: (8f 2, 10f 5) (gd 2, g-f 4, frm)
Scopey, very useful colt, effective 8 to 10f, best at 10f, acts on gd to g-f, best on gd, has worn blinkers. Turf high 109 (1st run) - 2nd of 11 to Insatiable (2 May Newmarket 10f gd RF 0977). Consistent. A particularly good-looking individual, he has been ridden from the front, but ran a good race when held up for a late burst at Newmarket in August. He is not easy to place.
**B W Hills [2-15] Maktoum Al Maktoum.*

MUSALSE BHB 59f59a RR 57+f 59a 4627[3]

3 b g Salse (USA) 10.9f **(71)** - Musical Sally (USA) (The Minstrel (CAN)) 10f **(72)**
Form - 007353512241113
Record 1998 - 1st:4 2nd:2 3rd:3 Ran:13
Pre1998 - 1st:0 2nd:0 3rd:0 Ran:3
Win Prizemoney £9,912 *Total Prizemoney* £12,380
Wins * 1998 Spt Warwic (G-F) H 16.1f 47 57+ <
*** 1998** Spt Catter (G-F) H 15.8f 47 54
*** 1998** *Aug Lingfi (STD) H 16f 42 51*
*** 1998** May Redcar (G-F) H 14.1f 35 41
1998 Turf 3-6: (10f, 14f 1-1, 16f 2-4) (gd, g-f 1-3, frm 2-2) 1998 AW 1-7:

(8f 2, 11f 2, 15f 2, 16f 1-1) (Equi 1-1, Fibr 6)
Workmanlike, fair gelding, effective 16f, acts on g-f to frm - acts on Equi, best on frm, has worn blinkers, favours left handed tracks, favours tight tracks. Turf high 57 - 1st of 9 getting 12lb from Rushen Raider (22 Spt Warwick RF 4417) - also 1st of 18 getting 8lb from Charter (19 Spt Catterick RF 4375). AW high 51 - 1st of 12 getting 16lb from Secrecy (26 Aug Lingfield RF 3888). Found his form in late summer and was just thwarted in his bid for a four-timer. **P C Haslam [4-16] Mrs C Barclay/Middleham Park Racing VIII.*

MUSHRAAF BHB 95f **RR 98df** 2548[13]
3 b br c Zafonic (USA) 9f **(83)** - Vice Vixen (CAN) (Vice Regent (CAN)) 8.7f **(74)**
Form - 140
Record 1998 - 1st:1 2nd:0 3rd:0 Ran:3
Pre1998 - 1st:1 2nd:0 3rd:0 Ran:3
Win Prizemoney £11,566 *Total Prizemoney* £13,816
Wins * **1998** Apr Nottin (G-S) 8.2f 98 <
* 1997 Aug Salisb (G-F) 6f 78
1998 Turf 1-3: (8f 1-2, 10f) (g-s 1-1, gd, g-f)
Scopey, very useful colt, effective 8f, acts on g-s. Turf high 98 (1st run) - 1st of 4 giving 2lb to Komistar (7 Apr Nottingham RF 0588). A Salisbury winner at two, he made a winning reappearance in a four-runner event at Nottingham in April, but was tailed off in the Dee Stakes and a Sandown handicap.
**J L Dunlop [2-6] Hamdan Al Maktoum.*

MUSICAL PET (IRE) BHB 23f **RR 25f** 4371[10]
3 ch f Petardia 8.2f **(58)** - Musical Gem (USA) (The Minstrel (CAN)) 10f **(72)**
Form - 0070
Record 1998 - 1st:0 2nd:0 3rd:0 Ran:4
Pre1998 - 1st:0 2nd:0 3rd:0 Ran:3
1998 Turf 0-4: (6f 2, 10f, 14f) (gd, g-f 2, frm)
Little account filly. Turf high 25. **J L Eyre [0-7] The Flowerpot Men.*

MUSICAL TONES (USA) RR 73+f 4956[2]
2 b f Diesis 9f **(80)** - Arsaan (USA) (Nureyev (USA)) 8.7f **(78)**
Form - 2
Record 1998 - 1st:0 2nd:1 3rd:0 Ran:1
Win Prizemoney £0 *Total Prizemoney* £1,230
1998 Turf 0-1: (8f) (frm)
Currently above-average filly. (1st run) - 2nd of 10 to Fatina (23 Oct Doncaster 8f frm RF 4956). **B W Hills [0-1] Maktoum Al Maktoum.*

MUSICAL TREAT (IRE) RR 94+f 3220[2]
2 ch f Royal Academy (USA) 7.8f **(77)** - Mountain Ash (Dominion) 8.5f **(63)**
Form - 2
Record 1998 - 1st:0 2nd:1 3rd:0 Ran:1
Win Prizemoney £0 *Total Prizemoney* £3,165
1998 Turf 0-1: (7f) (gd)
Currently useful filly. No match for Bionic on their respective debuts in a Goodwood maiden in July on what turned out to be her only start of the season. **P W Chapple-Hyam [0-1] R E Sangster.*

MUSICAL TWIST (USA) BHB 70f **RR 71f** 4482[6]
3 ch f Woodman (USA) 9.7f **(77)** - Musicale (USA) (The Minstrel (CAN)) 10f **(72)**
Form - 5363476
Record 1998 - 1st:0 2nd:0 3rd:2 Ran:7
Pre1998 - 1st:0 2nd:1 3rd:0 Ran:1
Win Prizemoney £0 *Total Prizemoney* £3,129
1998 Turf 0-7: (7f 4, 8f 2, 10f) (sft, g-f, frm 5)
Workmanlike, above-average filly, effective 6f, acts on g-f, has worn blinkers. Turf high 82. Consistent. Finished runner-up to a smart rival on her sole outing at two, but was something of a disappointment last season, being unable to take advantage of progressively easier company. Blinkers did not seem to work either, and she looks one to treat with caution.
**P W Chapple-Hyam [0-8] R E Sangster.*

MUSIC EXPRESS (IRE) BHB 44f42a **RR 44f 42a** 534[14]
4 b f Classic Music (USA) 7.2f **(57)** -Hetty Green Bay Express) 7.1f **(60)**
Form - 50
Record 1998 - 1st:0 2nd:0 3rd:0 Ran:2
Pre1998 - 1st:0 2nd:0 3rd:1 Ran:6
Win Prizemoney £0 *Total Prizemoney* £337
1998 Turf 0-1: (7f) (gd) 1998 AW 0-1: (12f) (Fibr)
Moderate filly, has worn blinkers. Becoming disappointing.
**J L Eyre [0-6] Watglea Racing (from A Harrison [0-2] Jly 1996).*

MUSICIAN RR 75f 4856[3]
2 b f Shirley Heights 12.1f **(76)** - Rose Alto (Adonijah) 10f **(61)**
Form - 43
Record 1998 - 1st:0 2nd:0 3rd:1 Ran:2
Win Prizemoney £0 *Total Prizemoney* £828
1998 Turf 0-2: (7f, 8f) (sft, gd)
Currently above-average filly. Turf high 75 (began Spt).
**J R Fanshawe [0-2] T & J Vestey.*

MUSTAFHEL BHB 78f **RR 66f** 5039[4]
2 b br c Wolfhound (USA) 7.3f **(71)** - Kadwah (USA) (Mr Prospector (USA)) 8.8f **(78)**
Form - 704
Record 1998 - 1st:0 2nd:0 3rd:0 Ran:3
Win Prizemoney £0 *Total Prizemoney* £262
1998 Turf 0-3: (7f, 8f 2) (g-s, gd, frm)
Currently average colt. Turf high 66 (began Spt).
**J H M Gosden [0-3] Hamdan Al Maktoum.*

MUSTANG BHB 42f52a **RR 49f 52a** 3815[10]
5 ch g Thatching 7.8f **(69)** - Lassoo (Caerleon (USA)) 8.6f **(71)**
Form - 217222272426670
Record 1998 - 1st:0 2nd:6 3rd:0 Ran:12
Pre1998 - 1st:2 2nd:2 3rd:0 Ran:19
Win Prizemoney £4,899 *Total Prizemoney* £11,993
Wins * 1997 *Nov Lingfi (STD) H 7f 33 45* <
* 1997 *Mar Wolver (STD) H 7f 27 32*
1998 Turf 0-6: (6f 3, 7f 2, 9f) (gd 3, g-f 2, frm) 1998 AW 0-6: (6f, 7f 4, 8f) (Equi 4, Fibr 2)
Fair gelding, effective 6 to 7f, best at 7f, acts on gd to g-f - acts on AW, best on Equi, often wears blinkers (extremely effectively), does well at Lingfield. Turf high 51 (1st run) - 2nd of 20 getting 1lb from Birchwood Sun (24 Apr Carlisle 6f gd RF 0845). AW high 56 - 2nd of 16 giving 2lb to Sure To Dream (18 May Southwell 6f Fibr RF 1310). Although he has found one too good more often than is desirable, there is no suggestion of lack of resolution.
**C W Thornton [2-31] Guy Reed.*

MUSTIQUE DREAM BHB 83f82a **RR 84f 82a** 4360[8]
3 b f Don't Forget Me 9.5f **(66)** - Jamaican Punch (IRE) (Shareef Dancer (USA)) 9.9f **(73)**
Form - 00112748
Record 1998 - 1st:2 2nd:1 3rd:0 Ran:8
Pre1998 - 1st:0 2nd:3 3rd:0 Ran:3
Win Prizemoney £8,545 *Total Prizemoney* £12,913
Wins * **1998** Jun Warwic (G-S) H 8f 79 82 <
* **1998** Jun Nottin (GD) H 8.2f 74 79
1998 Turf 2-7: (7f 2, 8f 2-4, 9f) (sft, gd 1-1, g-f 1-4, frm) 1998 AW 0-1: (8f) (Fibr)
Lengthy, decent filly, effective 6 to 8f, best at 8f, acts on gd to frm - acts on Fibr, best on g-f, likes tight tracks. Turf high 84 - 2nd of 7 giving 6lb to Hadith (4 Jly Beverley 8f g-f RF 2518) - also 1st of 10 giving 3lb to Indium (24 Jun Warwick RF 2256). Sold for 51,000 guineas at Tattersalls in October. **R Charlton [2-11] Wafic Said.*

MUSTN'T GRUMBLE (IRE) BHB 45f45a **RR 41f 45a** 3324[6]
8 b g Orchestra 7.5f **(44)** - Gentle Heiress (Prince Tenderfoot (USA)) 9f **(61)**
Form - 46106602056
Record 1998 - 1st:1 2nd:1 3rd:0 Ran:11
Pre1998 - 1st:6 2nd:9 3rd:6 Ran:52
Win Prizemoney £21,753 *Total Prizemoney* £32,119
Wins * **1998** *Mar Southw (STD) S 8f 47*
* 1996 Spt Leices (FRM) 8f 64 <
1994 *Nov Southw (STD) H 7f 66 62*
1994 Aug Redcar (G-F) H 7f 64 62
1994 Jun Hamilt (GD) H 6f 58 61
1994 *Mar Southw (STD) H 6f 57 57*
1998 Turf 0-4: (6f 2, 7f, 8f) (sft, gd, g-f 2) 1998 AW 1-7: (7f 3, 8f 1-4) (Fibr 1-7)
Fair gelding, has worn blinkers, favours left handed tracks, likes tight tracks. Turf high 41. AW high 59. **Miss S J Wilton [2-28] John Pointon and Sons (from D Nicholls [0-2] Mar 1996).*

MUTAAHAB (CAN) BHB 100f **RR 98f** 4512[1]
2 b c Dixieland Band (USA) 10.1f **(80)** - Serene Nobility (USA) (His Majesty (USA)) 10.9f **(82)**
Form - 145111
Record 1998 - 1st:4 2nd:0 3rd:0 Ran:6
Win Prizemoney £92,368 *Total Prizemoney* £95,393
Wins * **1998** Spt Ascot (SFT) G2 8f 98 <
* **1998** Spt Goodwo (G-S) L 8f 98 <
* **1998** Aug Redcar (G-F) 7f 69+
* **1998** May Yarmou (FRM) 6f 87+
1998 Turf 4-6: (6f 1-3, 7f 1-1, 8f 2-2) (gd 2-3, g-f 1-1, frm 1-2)
Very useful colt, effective 6 to 8f, best at 8f, acts on gd. Turf high 98 - 1st of 6 from Glamis (27 Spt Ascot RF 4512) - also 1st of 3 from Glamis (11 Spt Goodwood RF 4231). A good fourth in the Coventry, he was unsuited by the lack of pace in the July Stakes. Has then stepped up in trip to win his final three starts, culminating in a battling victory over old adversary Glamis in the Royal Lodge Stakes. Suited by a mile on soft ground, he is some way below the best of his generation but is an admirably genuine performer. **E A L Dunlop [4-6] Hamdan Al Maktoum.*

Mutaahab went into winter quarters on a hat-trick

MUTAAKKID (USA) BHB 81f **RR 78f** 5139[1]
2 b br c Dayjur (USA) 6.8f **(79)** - Arjuzah (IRE) **(108f)** (Ahonoora) 8.1f **(73)**
Form - 61
Record 1998 - 1st:1 2nd:0 3rd:0 Ran:2
Win Prizemoney £4,169 *Total Prizemoney* £4,169
Wins * **1998** Nov Doncas (SFT) 6f 78 <
1998 Turf 1-2: (6f 1-1, 7f) (sft, gd 1-1)
Currently above-average colt. Turf high 78 (began Oct) - 1st of 22 from Liberty Lines (6 Nov Doncaster RF 5139).
**J H M Gosden [1-2] Hamdan Al Maktoum.*

MUTABARI (USA) BHB 55f53a **RR 45f 53a** 5125[9]
4 ch c Seeking the Gold (USA) 7.4f **(80)** - Cagey Exuberance (USA) (Exuberant (USA)) 7.8f **(84)**
Form - 866000
Record 1998 - 1st:0 2nd:0 3rd:0 Ran:5
Pre1998 - 1st:0 2nd:0 3rd:2 Ran:11
Win Prizemoney £0 *Total Prizemoney* £1,416
1998 Turf 0-4: (7f 2, 8f, 12f) (hvy, sft, g-s, gd) 1998 AW 0-1: (7f) (Equi)
Leggy, moderate colt, effective 8 to 12f, acts on gd to g-f, likes tight tracks. Turf high 45.
**K Mahdi [0-11] Hamad Al-Mutawa (from D Morley [0-5] Apr 1997).*

MUTABASSIR (IRE) BHB 60f54a **RR 62f 54a** 4840[2]
4 ch g Soviet Star (USA) 8.6f **(74)** - Anghaam (USA) (Diesis) 9.3f **(69)**
Form - 28405351112
Record 1998 - 1st:3 2nd:2 3rd:1 Ran:11
Pre1998 - 1st:0 2nd:0 3rd:0 Ran:1
Win Prizemoney £9,348 *Total Prizemoney* £12,212
Wins * **1998** Spt Folkes (G-F) H 7f 53 57 <
* **1998** Spt Epsom (GD) H 7f 47 52
* **1998** Aug Bright (FRM) H 7f 40 50
1998 Turf 3-8: (7f 3-5, 8f, 9f, 10f) (g-s, gd 2-4, g-f 1-2, frm) 1998 AW 0-3: (10f 2, 12f) (Equi 3)
Strong, average gelding, effective 7f, acts on g-s to gd, best on gd, likes left handed tracks. Turf high 62 - 2nd of 13 getting 2lb from Peaceful Sarah (16 Oct Catterick 7f g-s RF 4840) - also 1st of 16 getting 7lb from Whatever's Right (25 Spt Folkestone RF 4475). AW high 48. Improving. He looked much improved when completing a hat-trick on turf during the autumn, and has looked a decent sort on sand too. Seven furlongs looks his trip, having been tried over much further at the start of the year.
**G L Moore [3-11] Danny Bloor (from A C Stewart [0-1] Aug 1997).*

MUTADARRA (IRE) BHB 64f64a **RR 68f 64a** 3472[D]
5 ch g Mujtahid (USA) 7.4f **(69)** - Silver Echo (Caerleon (USA)) 8.6f **(71)**
Form - 05022D
Record 1998 - 1st:0 2nd:2 3rd:0 Ran:6
Pre1998 - 1st:2 2nd:3 3rd:1 Ran:16
Win Prizemoney £8,660 *Total Prizemoney* £18,453
Wins * 1997 Jly Newmar (G-F) H 10f 62 69
1996 May Pontef (GD) 6f 80 <
1998 Turf 0-6: (8f, 10f 5) (gd, g-f 2, frm 2, hrd)
Average gelding, effective 10 to 12f, best at 10f, acts on gd to hrd, has worn blinkers, prefers right handed tracks, and excels at Newmarket. Turf high 68 - 2nd of 15 giving 9lb to Flag Fen (31 Jly Newmarket 10f frm RF 3241). A basically disappointing sort, with a tendency to pull and to hang to his left, he reserves his best for the Newmarket July Course.
**W J Musson [1-16] Mrs Rita Brown (from R W Armstrong [1-6] Jly 1996).*

MU-TADIL BHB 29f **RR 35f** 4588[7]
6 ch g Be My Chief (USA) 10.2f **(62)** - Inveraven (Alias Smith (USA)) 9.8f **(58)**
Form - 6S32637
Record 1998 - 1st:0 2nd:1 3rd:2 Ran:7
Pre1998 - 1st:0 2nd:0 3rd:0 Ran:5
Win Prizemoney £0 *Total Prizemoney* £1,552
1998 Turf 0-7: (14f 2, 17f 4, 18f) (gd 4, frm 3)
Very moderate gelding, effective 17 to 18f, best at 17f, acts on gd to frm, best on frm. Turf high 37 (1st run) - 6th of 15 getting 20lb from Witney-de-Bergerac (10 May Bath 17f frm RF 1133).
**R J Baker [0-29] Mrs V W Jones (from Major W R Hern [0-2] Spt 1995).*

MUTAFARIJ (USA) BHB 62f **RR 64f** 4667[6]
3 ch c Diesis 9f **(80)** - Madame Secretary (USA) (Secretariat (USA)) 9f **(79)**
Form - 566
Record 1998 - 1st:0 2nd:0 3rd:0 Ran:3
Pre1998 - 1st:0 2nd:0 3rd:0 Ran:2
1998 Turf 0-3: (10f, 12f, 16f) (g-s 2, g-f)
Strong, average colt. Turf high 64 (began Spt).
**E A L Dunlop [0-5] Hamdan Al Maktoum.*

MUTAFAWEQ (USA) RR 92f 4823[1]
2 b c Silver Hawk (USA) 11.2f **(85)** - The Caretaker (Caerleon (USA)) 8.6f **(71)**
Form - 21
Record 1998 - 1st:1 2nd:1 3rd:0 Ran:2

Win Prizemoney £7,632 *Total Prizemoney* £8,736
Wins * **1998** Oct Newmar (GD) 8f 92 <
1998 Turf 1-2: (8f 1-2) (frm 1-2)
Currently useful colt. Turf high 92 (began Spt) - 1st of 23 from Biennale (15 Oct Newmarket RF 4823). Needed his first run, but still showed promise to finish second, and went one better in a Newmarket maiden next time. **S bin Suroor [1-2] Godolphin.*

MUTAHADETH BHB 44f59a **RR 49f 59a** 4402[18]

4 ch g Rudimentary (USA) 8.2f **(66)** - Music in My Life (IRE) (Law Society (USA)) 9.9f **(70)**
Form - 41728360020500
Record **1998** - 1st:1 2nd:2 3rd:1 Ran:14
Pre1998 - 1st:1 2nd:2 3rd:3 Ran:18
Win Prizemoney £4,029 *Total Prizemoney* £8,970
Wins * **1998** *Jan Southw (STD) C 7f 68 <*
* 1997 *Feb Southw (STD) H 8f 58 60+*
1998 Turf 0-5: (7f 2, 8f 3) (gd 3, frm, hrd) 1998 AW 1-9: (7f 1-3, 8f 5, 9f) (Equi, Fibr 1-8)
Scopey, average gelding, effective 7 to 11f, best at 8f, - acts on AW, best on Fibr, often wears blinkers, likes left handed tracks, likes tight tracks, does well at Southwell. Turf high 49 (began Aug). AW high 68 - 1st of 10 giving 3lb to Robellion (5 Jan Southwell RF 0025). Inconsistent. He has been kept busy, but is at his most effective in modest company over seven furlongs to a mile at Southwell.
**D Shaw [2-28] K G Radford (from N A Graham [0-4] Spt 1996).*

MUTAMAKIN (USA) **RR 75+f** 4336[1]

2 b c Red Ransom (USA) 8.6f **(83)** - Won't She Tell (USA) (Banner Sport (USA)) 8.6f **(93)**
Form - 1
Record **1998** - 1st:1 2nd:0 3rd:0 Ran:1
Win Prizemoney £3,691 *Total Prizemoney* £3,691
Wins * **1998** Spt Yarmou (G-S) 8f 75+ <
1998 Turf 1-1: (8f 1-1) (frm 1-1)
Currently above-average colt. (1st run) - 1st of 13 from Mutafaweq (17 Spt Yarmouth RF 4336). Looks a staying type judged on his debut win. **B Hanbury [1-1] Hamdan Al Maktoum.*

MUTAMAM BHB 118f **RR 120f** 4852[4]

3 b c Darshaan 11.9f **(81)** - Petal Girl (Caerleon (USA)) 8.6f **(71)**
Form - 201114
Record **1998** - 1st:3 2nd:1 3rd:0 Ran:6
Pre1998 - 1st:2 2nd:0 3rd:1 Ran:3
Win Prizemoney £55,493 *Total Prizemoney* £96,277
Wins * **1998** Spt Goodwo (G-S) G3 9.9f 118+ <
* **1998** Aug Haydoc (GD) G3 10.5f 113+
* **1998** Jly Sandow (GD) 10f 116+
* 1997 Spt Cheste (GD) 7.6f 102++
* 1997 Aug Lingfi (G-S) 7.6f 86+
1998 Turf 3-6: (10f 2-4, 11f 1-1, 12f) (g-s 1-1, gd 1-2, g-f 1-3)
Workmanlike, very high-class colt, effective 8 to 11f, best at 10f, acts on g-s to g-f. Turf high 120 - 4th of 10 giving 3lb to Alborada (17 Oct Newmarket 10f gd RF 4852) - also 1st of 4 getting 4lb from Prince of Denial (12 Spt Goodwood RF 4245). He won his first two starts at two, and ran a fine third in the Racing Post Trophy when not getting the best of runs. He had pretensions to being a Derby candidate, but was a little disappointing when he was beaten in the Predominate, and as a 50/1 shot, ran no sort of race in the Derby. However, he bounced back to form when dropped in class, landing a Sandown conditions event and Group Threes at Haydock and Goodwood. He made all the running on the last two occasions, but was held up when raised in class in the Dubai Champion Stakes. He ran creditably nonetheless and, with some maturing to do over the winter, the top level may not prove beyond him in 1999. Has joined the Godolphin operation.
**A C Stewart [5-9] Hamdan Al Maktoum.*

MUTAMAYYAZ (USA) **RR 85+f** 3952[1]

2 b br c Nureyev (USA) 8.4f **(84)** -Ajfan (USA)(Woodman(USA)) 9f **(74)**
Form - 21
Record **1998** - 1st:1 2nd:1 3rd:0 Ran:2
Win Prizemoney £4,581 *Total Prizemoney* £5,699
Wins * **1998** Aug Newmar (G-F) 6f 85+ <
1998 Turf 1-2: (6f 1-2) (g-f, frm 1-1)
Currently useful colt. Turf high 85 (began Aug) - 1st of 11 from Swallow Flight (29 Aug Newmarket RF 3952). Out of a mare who was third in the 1000 Guineas, he was an unspectacular winner of a maiden on his second start. Failed to settle satisfactorily on his debut. Will stay beyond six furlongs.
**J H M Gosden [1-2] Hamdan Al Maktoum.*

MUTASAWWAR BHB 54f65a **RR 55f 65a** 5007[9]

4 ch g Clantime 6.6f **(57)** - Keen Melody (USA) (Sharpen Up) 8.3f **(67)**
Form - 251426608864 1000
Record **1998** - 1st:2 2nd:1 3rd:0 Ran:14
Pre1998 - 1st:0 2nd:2 3rd:0 Ran:10
Win Prizemoney £5,486 *Total Prizemoney* £8,452
Wins * **1998** Spt Chepst (G-S) H 5.1f 51 55
* **1998** *Jan Lingfi (STD) H 6f 60 61 <*
1998 Turf 1-9: (5f 1-4, 6f 5) (sft, gd 1-4, frm 4) 1998 AW 1-5: (6f 1-5) (Equi 1-5)
Scopey, average gelding, effective 5 to 7f, best at 6f, acts on gd - acts on AW, best on Equi, has worn blinkers, likes left handed tracks, likes tight tracks. Turf high 55. AW high 65 - 2nd of 14 giving 15lb to Sharp Imp (27 Jan Lingfield 6f Equi RF 0167) - also 1st of 8 giving 30lb to Wild Nettle (3 Jan Lingfield RF 0019).
**M S Saunders [2-19] M S Saunders (from E A L Dunlop [0-5] Jun 1997).*

MUTAWWAJ (IRE) BHB 107f **RR 110f** 4224[3]

3 b c Caerleon (USA) 10.9f **(79)** - Himmah (USA) (Habitat) 9.4f **(70)**
Form - 33513
Record **1998** - 1st:1 2nd:0 3rd:3 Ran:5
Pre1998 - 1st:1 2nd:1 3rd:2 Ran:4
Win Prizemoney £8,844 *Total Prizemoney* £62,279
Wins * **1998** Jly Newmar (G-F) 12f 110 <
* 1997 Spt Goodwo (GD) 8f 91
1998 Turf 1-5: (10f, 12f 1-4) (gd 2, g-f 2, frm 1-1)
Scopey, Group-class colt, effective 8 to 12f, best at 12f, acts on gd to frm, best on g-f, excels at Newmarket and Doncaster. Turf high 110 - 1st of 5 getting 20lb from Ismaros (17 Jly Newmarket RF 2879). Consistent. He kept hot company for most of the season and relished a drop in class when winning by seven lengths at Newmarket in July. Group races look just out of his reach at present. **S bin Suroor [2-9] Godolphin.*

MUTAZZ (USA) BHB 60f **RR 41f** 1133[13]

6 b g Woodman (USA) 9.7f **(77)** - Ghashtah (USA) (Nijinsky (CAN)) 10.3f **(77)**
Form - 0
Record **1998** - 1st:0 2nd:0 3rd:0 Ran:1
Pre1998 - 1st:0 2nd:2 3rd:1 Ran:8
Win Prizemoney £0 *Total Prizemoney* £2,875
1998 Turf 0-1: (17f) (frm)
Moderate gelding. Consistent.
**M P Tregoning [0-1] M P N Tregoning (from Major W R Hern [2-11] Apr 1996).*

MUYASSIR (IRE) BHB 67f70a **RR 73f 70a** 4996[1]

3 b c Brief Truce (USA) 9.1f **(73)** - Twine (Thatching) 8f **(66)**
Form - 273801
Record **1998** - 1st:1 2nd:1 3rd:1 Ran:6
Pre1998 - 1st:0 2nd:0 3rd:0 Ran:4
Win Prizemoney £3,157 *Total Prizemoney* £4,859
Wins * **1998** *Oct Lingfi (STD) H 10f 67 69 <*
1998 Turf 0-5: (8f 5) (gd, g-f 2, frm 2) 1998 AW 1-1: (10f 1-1) (Equi 1-1)
Scopey, above-average colt, effective 8 to 10f, best at 8f, acts on g-f to frm - acts on Equi. Turf high 73 - 3rd of 15 getting 5lb from Safey Ana (20 Aug Salisbury 8f g-f RF 3763). (1st run) - 1st of 14 giving 3lb to Bank On Him (26 Oct Lingfield RF 4996).
**P J Makin [1-6] William Otley (from C J Benstead [0-4] Oct 1997).*

MY ABBEY BHB 33f **RR 22f** 3742[14]

9 b m Hadeer 8.9f **(58)** - Rose Barton (Pas de Seul) 9.1f **(67)**
Form - 060
Record **1998** - 1st:0 2nd:0 3rd:0 Ran:3
Pre1998 - 1st:4 2nd:3 3rd:5 Ran:40
Win Prizemoney £14,229 *Total Prizemoney* £20,659
Wins 1995 May Thirsk (G-F) H 5f 55 53
1998 Turf 0-3: (5f 3) (frm 3)
Little account mare, has worn blinkers. Turf high 22 (began Jly).
**M Mullineaux [0-3] Abbey Racing (from A Bailey [0-2] Aug 1997).*

MY ALIBI (USA) RR 60f 4856[10]
2 b f Sheikh Albadou 9.2f **(75)** -Fellwaati (USA) (Alydar (USA)) 9.1f **(76)**
Form - 0
Record 1998 - 1st:0 2nd:0 3rd:0 Ran:1
1998 Turf 0-1: (7f) (sft)
Currently average filly. **E A L Dunlop [0-1] Maktoum Al Maktoum.*

MY BEST FRIEND RR 34f 1897[11]
3 b f Chilibang 7f **(55)** - My Diamond Ring (Sparkling Boy) 5f **(36)**
Form - 0
Record 1998 - 1st:0 2nd:0 3rd:0 Ran:1
1998 Turf 0-1: (7f) (g-s)
Unfurnished, currently very moderate filly. **W R Muir [0-1] F Hope.*

MY BEST VALENTINE BHB 117f85a **RR 119f 85a** 4726a[1]
8 b h Try My Best (USA) 7.8f **(68)** -Pas de Calais(Pas de Seul) 9.1f **(67)**
Form - 8245040251
Record 1998 - 1st:1 2nd:2 3rd:0 Ran:10
Pre1998 - 1st:8 2nd:9 3rd:6 Ran:61
Win Prizemoney £100,397 *Total Prizemoney* £176,304
Wins * **1998** Oct Longch (SFT) G1 5f 119 <
* 1997 Oct Newbur (GD) H 6f 103 111
* 1997 Oct Newmar (G-S) L 6f 104
* 1997 Jly Sandow (G-S) H 5f 95 102
1996 Apr Bright (FRM) H 7f 84 87
1994 Jun Epsom (G-F) H 7f 85 86
1998 Turf 1-10: (5f 1-6, 6f 4) (sft 1-1, g-s, gd 5, g-f, frm 2)
High-class horse, effective 5 to 6f, best at 6f, acts on sft to gd, best on sft, has worn blinkers, likes Newmarket. Turf high 119 - 1st of 14 from Averti (4 Oct Longchamp RF 4726a). Consistent. This veteran really seemed to thrive in 1997, winning three times including in Listed company, but he enjoyed his finest hour last term. He may well have needed his reappearance run, but then ran most creditably in high-class company, if appearing short of Group Class. That theory was blown when he provided a major shock by winning the Prix de l'Abbaye, and there was not the vestige of a fluke about it. That victory was thoroughly deserved, and he has now been retired to stud.
**V Soane [4-18] The Valentines (from J White [1-29] Jun 1997).*

MY BET BHB 48f53a **RR 47f 53a** 2451[2]
3 b f Noble Patriarch 12.2f **(43)** - Estefan (Taufan (USA)) 7f **(57)**
Form - 0U2
Record 1998 - 1st:0 2nd:1 3rd:0 Ran:3
Pre1998 - 1st:1 2nd:0 3rd:1 Ran:12
Win Prizemoney £2,277 *Total Prizemoney* £3,516
Wins * *1997 Apr Southw (STD) S 5f 55* <
1998 Turf 0-2: (10f 2) (gd 2) 1998 AW 0-1: (7f) (Fibr)
Light-framed, fair filly, effective 5f, acts on frm - acts on Fibr. Turf high 46. Had shown some ability on turf before scoring on sand at Southwell in April. Well held in varied company since.
**M W Easterby [1-15] W T Allgood.*

MY BOLD BOYO BHB 70f **RR 76f** 4744[15]
3 b g Never so Bold 7.1f **(62)** - My Rosie (Forzando) 7.6f **(59)**
Form - 43431500
Record 1998 - 1st:1 2nd:0 3rd:2 Ran:8
Win Prizemoney £2,070 *Total Prizemoney* £3,424
Wins * **1998** Aug Lingfi (GD) 7.6f 76 <
1998 Turf 1-8: (7f 4, 8f 1-3, 9f) (g-s, gd 4, g-f 1-1, frm 2)
Workmanlike, above-average gelding, effective 7 to 9f, acts on gd to frm. Turf high 76 - 1st of 10 from Seven (1 Aug Lingfield RF 3269). **D R C Elsworth [1-8] Mrs W Protheroe-Beynon.*

MYBOTYE BHB 61f56a **RR 60f 56a** 2454[4]
5 br g Rambo Dancer (CAN) 8.4f **(59)** -Sigh (Highland Melody) 6.3f **(55)**
Form - 44505634
Record 1998 - 1st:0 2nd:0 3rd:1 Ran:7
Pre1998 - 1st:4 2nd:1 3rd:4 Ran:25
Win Prizemoney £15,941 *Total Prizemoney* £20,795
Wins * 1997 Spt Chepst (GD) H 7.1f 58 64
1996 Jun Redcar (FRM) H 7f 76 77 <
1995 Aug Redcar (G-F) H 6f 64 65+
1995 Jun Pontef (GD) 5f 61+
1998 Turf 0-7: (7f 7) (g-s, gd 2, g-f 3, frm)
Average gelding, effective 7f, acts on sft to frm - acts on Fibr, best on gd, has worn blinkers, and excels at Thirsk. Turf high 60 - 3rd of 16 giving 12lb to Ochos Rios (16 Jun Thirsk 7f gd RF 2021). Consistent.
**R Bastiman [1-20] Anthony Moroney (from G R Oldroyd [3-12] Nov 1996).*

MY BROADSTAIRS JOY RR 65f 4530[6]
2 b g Terimon 8.7f **(58)** - Al Raja (Kings Lake (USA)) 10.8f **(67)**
Form - 086
Record 1998 - 1st:0 2nd:0 3rd:0 Ran:3
1998 Turf 0-3: (7f 2, 8f) (g-s, g-f, frm)
Currently average gelding. Turf high 65 (began Jly).
**J J O'Neill [0-3] Mrs Judy Hunt.*

MY BROTHER BHB 38f **RR 35f** 2511[15]
4 b g Lugana Beach 7f **(63)** - Lucky Love (Mummy's Pet) 7.7f **(60)**
Form - 00
Record 1998 - 1st:0 2nd:0 3rd:0 Ran:2
Pre1998 - 1st:0 2nd:0 3rd:0 Ran:1
1998 Turf 0-2: (8f 2) (g-f, frm)
Leggy, currently very moderate gelding. Turf high 31.
**S Earle [0-3] Robert & Cora Till.*

MY CAREER BHB 72f **RR 60f** 2076[7]
3 b c Caerleon (USA) 10.9f **(79)**-Lady Be Mine(USA)(Sir Ivor) 10.2f **(70)**
Form - 667
Record 1998 - 1st:0 2nd:0 3rd:0 Ran:3
1998 Turf 0-3: (8f, 10f, 12f) (gd, g-f, frm)
Light-framed, average colt. Turf high 60. (DEAD)
**E A L Dunlop [0-3] Dragon's Stud.*

MY DESPERADO (IRE) BHB 73f **RR 70f** 5141[5]
5 b m Un Desperado (FR) 9.3f **(42)** - Lady Kasbah (Lord Gayle (USA)) 8.8f **(62)**
Form - 6331046007701155
Record 1998 - 1st:3 2nd:0 3rd:2 Ran:16
Win Prizemoney £10,527 *Total Prizemoney* £11,786
Wins * **1998** Oct Redcar (SFT) 10f 65
* **1998** Oct Pontef (SFT) H 10f 66 69
* **1998** Jly Thirsk (GD) 8f 73 <
1998 Turf 3-16: (7f 2, 8f 1-5, 10f 2-8, 12f)(sft, g-s, gd 2-7, g-f 1-3, frm 4)
Above-average filly, effective 7 to 12f, acts on g-s to frm, likes left handed tracks. Turf high 73 (began Jly) - 1st of 12 giving 3lb to Minivet (31 Jly Thirsk RF 3251) - also 1st of 19 giving 24lb to Oxbane (19 Oct Pontefract RF 4869). Consistent.
**L R Lloyd-James [3-16] Mrs H Ratcliffe.*

MY DILEMMA BHB 49f **RR 36f** 4363[3]
2 b f Pursuit of Love 9.5f **(69)** - Butosky (Busted) 10.2f **(61)**
Form - 403
Record 1998 - 1st:0 2nd:0 3rd:1 Ran:3
Win Prizemoney £0 *Total Prizemoney* £833
1998 Turf 0-2: (7f, 8f) (sft, frm) 1998 AW 0-1: (7f) (Fibr)
Currently moderate filly. Turf high 36 (began Aug).
**K G Wingrove [0-3] Peter Scott.*

MY ELLIE RR 47?f 2440[9]
4 b f Picea 12.7f **(43)** - Loving You (Thatch (USA)) 9.8f **(62)**
Form - 60
Record 1998 - 1st:0 2nd:0 3rd:0 Ran:2
Win Prizemoney £0 *Total Prizemoney* £81
1998 Turf 0-2: (8f, 10f) (g-f, frm)
Currently moderate filly. Turf high 47.
**R Simpson [0-2] Miss J Rumford.*

MY EMILY BHB 66f **RR 62f** 3982[9]
2 b f King's Signet (USA) 7f **(51)** - Flying Wind **(33f 41a)** (Forzando) 7.6f **(59)**
Form - 32000
Record 1998 - 1st:0 2nd:1 3rd:1 Ran:5
Win Prizemoney £0 *Total Prizemoney* £1,346
1998 Turf 0-5: (5f, 6f, 7f 3) (gd 3, g-f, frm)
Average filly. Turf high 62 - 2nd of 13 getting 7lb from April Ace (27 Jun Bath 6f gd RF 2324). She showed ability in her first two starts but has disappointed since being tried beyond six.
**G L Moore [0-5] B V and C J Pennick.*

MY FLOOSIE BHB 43f **RR 55f** 4627[18]
3 b f Unfuwain (USA) 11.4f **(74)** - My Chiara (Ardross) 10.6f **(68)**
Form - 0300

Record	**1998** -	1st:0	2nd:0	3rd:1	Ran:4
	Pre1998 -	1st:0	2nd:0	3rd:0	Ran:1

Win Prizemoney £0 *Total Prizemoney* £512
1998 Turf 0-4: (11f, 12f 2, 16f) (gd 2, g-f 2)
Unfurnished, fair filly. Turf high 55. **P J Bevan [0-5] A Eaton.*

MY GODSON BHB 34f30a **RR 31f 30a** 3958[10]
8 br g Valiyar 9.6f **(54)** - Blessit (So Blessed) 8.7f **(67)**
Form - 70

Record	**1998** -	1st:0	2nd:0	3rd:0	Ran:2
	Pre1998 -	1st:5	2nd:5	3rd:4	Ran:65

Win Prizemoney £12,990 *Total Prizemoney* £18,606

Wins	1996	Aug	Catter	(G-F)	H	7f	51	57
	1996	Jly	Beverl	(G-F)	SH	7.5f	47	54
	1996	May	Newcas	(GD)	C	7f		49

1998 Turf 0-1: (10f) (g-f) 1998 AW 0-1: (7f) (Fibr)
Very moderate gelding, often wears blinkers.
**S R Bowring [0-2] Linkchallenge Ltd (from M Dods [0-7] Oct 1997).*

MY HANDSOME PRINCE BHB 27f27a **RR 31f 27a** 3677[11]
6 b g Handsome Sailor 6.6f **(53)** - My Serenade (USA) (Sensitive Prince (USA)) 9.1f **(60)**
Form - 07060

Record	**1998** -	1st:0	2nd:0	3rd:0	Ran:5
	Pre1998 -	1st:0	2nd:3	3rd:2	Ran:31

Win Prizemoney £0 *Total Prizemoney* £3,350
1998 Turf 0-4: (8f 2, 9f 2) (g-s, gd, g-f, frm) 1998 AW 0-1: (9f) (Fibr)
Very moderate gelding, effective 8f, acts on frm, has worn blinkers, likes right handed tracks. Turf high 31.
**P J Bevan [0-38] D B Holmes.*

MY HANDY MAN BHB 29f29a **RR 21f 29a** 531[15]
7 ch g Out of Hand - My Home (Homing) 7.8f **(59)**
Form - 07060

Record	**1998** -	1st:0	2nd:0	3rd:0	Ran:5
	Pre1998 -	1st:0	2nd:3	3rd:1	Ran:21

Win Prizemoney £0 *Total Prizemoney* £3,228
1998 Turf 0-1: (7f) (gd) 1998 AW 0-4: (8f 2, 11f, 12f) (Fibr 4)
Little account gelding, has worn blinkers. AW high 27.
**D W Barker [0-9] Mrs P A Barker (from R Allan [0-22] Apr 1996).*

MY HEARTS DESIRE BHB 49f **RR 45f** 2174[9]
3 b f Deploy 11.4f **(67)** - Blue Room (Gorytus (USA)) 7.8f **(60)**
Form - 000

Record	**1998** -	1st:0	2nd:0	3rd:0	Ran:3

1998 Turf 0-3: (8f, 10f 2) (gd 2, g-f)
Workmanlike, currently moderate filly. Turf high 45.
**D HaydnJones [0-3] G J Hicks.*

MY HERO (IRE) BHB 44f38a **RR 67?f 38a** 313[4]
4 b f Bluebird (USA) 7.9f **(71)** - Risacca (ITY) (Sir Gaylord) 10.6f **(64)**
Form - 404

Record	**1998** -	1st:0	2nd:0	3rd:0	Ran:2
	Pre1998 -	1st:0	2nd:0	3rd:0	Ran:5

Win Prizemoney £0 *Total Prizemoney* £248
1998 AW 0-2: (11f, 12f) (Equi, Fibr)
Scopey, average filly, has worn blinkers. AW high 19.
**T G Mills [0-9] Bill Brown and Peter Pepper Partnership.*

MY JESS BHB 38f **RR 34f** 1027[15]
4 b f Jester 8.5f **(43)** - Miss Levantine (Levanter)
Form - 0

Record	**1998** -	1st:0	2nd:0	3rd:0	Ran:1
	Pre1998 -	1st:0	2nd:0	3rd:0	Ran:3

1998 Turf 0-1: (6f) (g-f)
Scopey, very moderate filly. **S G Knight [0-4] Mrs P M Underhill.*

MYLANIA RR 50f 3952[10]
2 b f Midyan (USA) 9.9f **(64)** - Appelania (Star Appeal) 9.6f **(65)**
Form - 0

Record	**1998** -	1st:0	2nd:0	3rd:0	Ran:1

1998 Turf 0-1: (6f) (frm)
Currently fair filly. **M H Tompkins [0-1] J Ellis.*

MY LASS RR 72f 4928[2]
2 b f Elmaamul (USA) 8.1f **(70)** - Be My Lass (IRE) (Be My Guest (USA)) 9.3f **(67)**
Form - 42

Record	**1998** -	1st:0	2nd:1	3rd:0	Ran:2

Win Prizemoney £0 *Total Prizemoney* £1,026
1998 Turf 0-2: (7f 2) (g-s, gd)
Currently above-average filly. Turf high 72 (began Oct) - 2nd of 14 getting 5lb from Pagan King (22 Oct Brighton 7f g-s RF 4928).
**Sir Mark Prescott [0-2] Cheveley Park Stud.*

MY LEARNED FRIEND BHB 74f **RR 75f** 4932[P]
7 b or br g Broken Hearted 10.1f **(65)** - Circe (Main Reef) 9.6f **(57)**
Form - 222207212P

Record	**1998** -	1st:1	2nd:6	3rd:0	Ran:10
	Pre1998 -	1st:4	2nd:5	3rd:2	Ran:29

Win Prizemoney £20,211 *Total Prizemoney* £54,102

Wins	* 1998	Spt	Pontef	(G-F)		10f		75	
	1995	Aug	Newbur	(G-F)	H	12f	79	86	<
	1995	Jun	Goodwo	(G-F)	H	10f	75	80	
	1995	Jun	Haydoc	(GD)	H	10.5f	71	77	
	1994	Jun	Lingfi	(GF)		9f		57	

1998 Turf 1-10: (10f 1-3, 12f 7) (g-s 3, gd 3, g-f 2, frm 1-2)
Above-average gelding, effective 10 to 14f, acted on g-s to frm, best on g-f, had worn blinkers, liked right handed tracks, liked tight tracks. Turf high 75 - 1st of 9 from Burning Truth (24 Spt Pontefract RF 4470). Inconsistent. Ran his best race of 1997 when runner-up in the Old Newton Cup. Runner-up on his first four starts of 1998, he was best suited by big fields and a strong gallop. (DEAD)
**S P C Woods [1-10] Mrs J Roberts (from A Hide [4-29] Spt 1997).*

MY LEGAL EAGLE (IRE) BHB 49f50a **RR 48f 50a** 4775[14]
4 b g Law Society (USA) 11.6f **(71)** - Majestic Nurse (On Your Mark) 7.7f **(58)**
Form - 83004130

Record	**1998** -	1st:1	2nd:0	3rd:2	Ran:8
	Pre1998 -	1st:0	2nd:0	3rd:0	Ran:5

Win Prizemoney £2,550 *Total Prizemoney* £3,317

Wins	* 1998	Jly	Thirsk	(GD)	H	7f	45	47	<

1998 Turf 1-6: (7f 1-3, 8f 3) (gd 4, g-f 1-1, frm) 1998 AW 0-2: (8f, 9f) (Equi, Fibr)
Fair gelding, has worn blinkers, likes left handed tracks, likes tight tracks. Turf high 48. AW high 47.
**J W Hills [1-10] J W Hills (from M Cunningham in IRE [0-4] Oct 1996).*

MY LITTLE MAN BHB 53f **RR 62f** 5008[12]
3 b g Lugana Beach 7f **(63)** - Gay Ming (Gay Meadow)
Form - 8640

Record	**1998** -	1st:0	2nd:0	3rd:0	Ran:4

Win Prizemoney £0 *Total Prizemoney* £243
1998 Turf 0-4: (8f, 9f, 10f, 12f) (sft, g-s, g-f, frm)
Light-framed, average gelding. Turf high 62 (began Jly).
**B Smart [0-4] W Clifford.*

MY LOST LOVE BHB 58f53a **RR 58f 53a** 409[11]
3 b g Green Desert (USA) 7.8f **(78)** - Love of Silver (USA) (Arctic Tern (USA)) 8.9f **(69)**
Form - 0370

Record	**1998** -	1st:0	2nd:0	3rd:1	Ran:4
	Pre1998 -	1st:0	2nd:0	3rd:0	Ran:3

Win Prizemoney £0 *Total Prizemoney* £567
1998 AW 0-4: (5f, 6f 2, 7f) (Equi, Fibr 3)
Workmanlike, fair gelding, has worn blinkers. AW high 46.
**M Johnston [0-7] Ali Saeed.*

MY MAN FRIDAY BHB 57f **RR 55f** 4641[5]
2 b c Lugana Beach 7f **(63)** - My Ruby Ring **(61df 50a)** (Blushing Scribe (USA)) 6f **(45)**
Form - 005

Record	**1998** -	1st:0	2nd:0	3rd:0	Ran:3

1998 Turf 0-3: (5f, 6f, 7f) (g-f 2, frm)
Currently fair colt. Turf high 55. **W R Muir [0-3] Mrs Marion Wickham.*

MY MOTHER'S DREAM (IRE) BHB 47f48a **RR 57f 48a** 3979[5]
2 b f Fayruz 6.6f **(63)** - With Diamonds (Shirley Heights) 10.3f **(74)**
Form - 0037433065

Record 1998 - 1st:0 2nd:0 3rd:3 Ran:10
Win Prizemoney £0 *Total Prizemoney* £815
1998 Turf 0-6: (5f 3, 6f 3) (gd 2, g-f 2, frm 2) 1998 AW 0-4: (5f 2, 6f 2) (Fibr 4)
Fair filly, effective 5f, acts on g-f. Turf high 57 - 3rd of 10 getting 5lb from Cosmo Jack (6 Jly Bath 5f g-f RF 2555). AW high 43.
**M A Buckley [0-10] Dulverton Racing Partnership.*

MYNAH BIRD (IRE) BHB 70f RR 73f 4767[15]
2 b f Bluebird (USA) 7.9f **(71)** - Maribiya (FR) (Natroun (FR))
Form - 5530
Record 1998 - 1st:0 2nd:0 3rd:1 Ran:4
Win Prizemoney £0 *Total Prizemoney* £498
1998 Turf 0-4: (7f 2, 8f 2) (sft, frm 3)
Above-average filly. Turf high 73 (began Aug).
**Mrs J R Ramsden [0-4] J M Ranson.*

MYOSOTIS BHB 34f40a RR 19f 40a 4987[8]
4 ch g Don't Forget Me 9.5f **(66)** - Ella Mon Amour (Ela-Mana-Mou) 10.1f **(70)**
Form - 01650068
Record 1998 - 1st:1 2nd:0 3rd:0 Ran:7
Pre1998 - 1st:0 2nd:0 3rd:0 Ran:11
Win Prizemoney £2,295 *Total Prizemoney* £2,295
Wins * **1998** *Jan Lingfi (STD) H 12f 40 45 <*
1998 Turf 0-2: (12f 2) (sft, gd) 1998 AW 1-5: (10f, 12f 1-2, 13f, 16f) (Equi 1-5)
Workmanlike, moderate gelding, effective 12 to 16f, acts on gd - acts on Equi, often wears blinkers (effectively), favours tight tracks. Turf high 19. AW high 45 (1st run) - 1st of 17 getting 2lb from Don't Drop Bombs (17 Jan Lingfield RF 0105).
**P W Hiatt [1-14] Red Lion (Chipping Norton) Partnership (from P J Makin [0-10] Aug 1997).*

MY PETAL BHB 88f RR 85f 4185[8]
2 gr f Petong 7.6f **(58)** - Najariya (Northfields (USA)) 9f **(72)**
Form - 2118
Record 1998 - 1st:2 2nd:1 3rd:0 Ran:4
Win Prizemoney £11,039 *Total Prizemoney* £12,074
Wins * **1998** Jly Goodwo (GD) H 6f 85 <
* **1998** Jly Newbur (G-F) 5.2f 67
1998 Turf 2-4: (5f 1-1, 6f 1-3) (gd 1-2, g-f 1-2)
Useful filly. Turf high 85 (began Jly) - 1st of 14 giving 9lb to Midnight Orchid (28 Jly Goodwood RF 3166).
**R Hannon [2-4] Mrs P & P Jubert.*

MY PLEDGE (IRE) BHB 70f RR 71f 4092[6]
3 b c Waajib 8.9f **(67)** - Pollys Glow (IRE) (Glow (USA)) 6.7f **(71)**
Form - 47186
Record 1998 - 1st:1 2nd:0 3rd:0 Ran:5
Pre1998 - 1st:0 2nd:0 3rd:0 Ran:1
Win Prizemoney £3,668 *Total Prizemoney* £3,994
Wins * **1998** Jun Windso (SFT) H 10f 69 71 <
1998 Turf 1-5: (8f 2, 10f 1-2, 12f) (gd 1-2, g-f, frm 2)
Above-average colt, effective 10 to 12f, acts on gd to frm. Turf high 71 - 1st of 9 getting 11lb from Speaker's Chair (15 Jun Windsor RF 2006).
**C A Horgan [1-6] Mrs B Sumner.*

MY POPPET RR 43f 1211[9]
3 b f Midyan (USA) 9.9f **(64)** - Pretty Poppy (Song) 7.2f **(61)**
Form - 0
Record 1998 - 1st:0 2nd:0 3rd:0 Ran:1
1998 Turf 0-1: (10f) (frm)
Leggy, currently moderate filly. **S G Knight [0-1] Gordon Fox.*

MYRMIDON BHB 80f RR 73f 1106[10]
4 b g Midyan (USA) 9.9f **(64)** - Moorish Idol (Aragon) 8.1f **(60)**
Form - 040
Record 1998 - 1st:0 2nd:0 3rd:0 Ran:2
Pre1998 - 1st:1 2nd:3 3rd:0 Ran:13
Win Prizemoney £3,489 *Total Prizemoney* £10,816
Wins 1996 Nov Doncas (SFT) H 5f 80 98 <
1998 Turf 0-2: (6f, 8f) (sft, frm)
Above-average gelding, effective 5f, acts on sft to g-s, has worn blinkers. Turf high 67.
**Mrs L Stubbs [0-9] Michael Worth (from J L Dunlop [1-6] Nov 1996).*

MY SALTARELLO (IRE) BHB 38f RR 41f 937[6]
4 b g Salt Dome (USA) 6.5f **(59)** - Daidis (Welsh Pageant) 10f **(65)**
Form - 6
Record 1998 - 1st:0 2nd:0 3rd:0 Ran:1
Pre1998 - 1st:0 2nd:0 3rd:0 Ran:8
1998 AW 0-1: (6f) (Fibr)
Workmanlike, moderate gelding, has worn blinkers. Becoming disappointing. **A B Mulholland [0-9] R Wylie.*

MYSTAGOGUE BHB 58f70a RR 66f 70a 4838[3]
3 ch g Mystiko (USA) 7.7f **(59)** -Malibasta(Auction Ring (USA)) 8.6f **(65)**
Form - 212216235463
Record 1998 - 1st:1 2nd:3 3rd:2 Ran:10
Pre1998 - 1st:1 2nd:1 3rd:0 Ran:9
Win Prizemoney £5,247 *Total Prizemoney* £9,228
Wins * **1998** *Jan Lingfi (STD) H 10f 64 65+ <*
* *1997 Nov Lingfi (STD) 10f 54*
1998 Turf 0-6: (11f, 12f 3, 14f, 16f) (g-s, gd 3, g-f, frm) 1998 AW 1-4: (8f, 10f 1-3) (Equi 1-4)
Neat, above-average gelding, effective 8 to 14f, acts on gd to frm - acts on Equi, has worn blinkers, likes left handed tracks, prefers tight tracks, excels at Lingfield. Turf high 66 (began Aug) - 3rd of 13 getting 14lb from Paradise Navy (20 Aug Salisbury 14f gd RF 3762). AW high 72 (1st run) - 2nd of 11 giving 14lb to Impulsive Decision (1 Jan Lingfield 8f Equi RF 0001) - also 1st of 9 getting 6lb from Appyabo (27 Jan Lingfield RF 0169). He is an effective performer in modest company on Equitrack, including two victories over ten furlongs, but struggles against better opposition
**R Hannon [2-19] J S Threadwell.*

MYSTERIOUS ECOLOGY BHB 51f RR 64?f 4590[11]
3 gr f Mystiko (USA) 7.7f **(59)** -Ecologically Kind(Alleged (USA))10f **(76)**
Form - 7420
Record 1998 - 1st:0 2nd:1 3rd:0 Ran:4
Pre1998 - 1st:0 2nd:0 3rd:0 Ran:2
Win Prizemoney £0 *Total Prizemoney* £951
1998 Turf 0-4: (10f, 11f, 12f 2) (gd 2, g-f, frm)
Workmanlike, average filly, effective 11f, acts on gd. Turf high 58 (began Aug). Has joined Martin Pipe.
**B W Hills [0-5] W J Gredley (from C E Brittain [0-1] Jly 1997).*

MYSTERIUM BHB 39f41a RR 37f 41a 157[8]
4 gr c Mystiko (USA) 7.7f **(59)** - Way to Go (Troy) 10.4f **(68)**
Form - 048
Record 1998 - 1st:0 2nd:0 3rd:0 Ran:2
Pre1998 - 1st:1 2nd:1 3rd:1 Ran:9
Win Prizemoney £2,804 *Total Prizemoney* £3,633
Wins * *1997 Feb Wolver (STD) 7f 59 <*
1998 AW 0-2: (9f, 12f) (Fibr 2)
Light-framed, fair colt, effective 7f, - acts on Fibr, has worn blinkers, favours left handed tracks, favours tight tracks. AW high 36. Inconsistent. **N P Littmoden [1-11] Mrs G L Taylor.*

MYSTERY GUEST (IRE) BHB 59f RR 63f 4760[16]
3 b g Alzao (USA) 9.8f **(73)** -Lora's Guest(Be My Guest (USA)) 9.3f **(67)**
Form - 045240
Record 1998 - 1st:0 2nd:1 3rd:0 Ran:6
Pre1998 - 1st:0 2nd:1 3rd:0 Ran:4
Win Prizemoney £0 *Total Prizemoney* £2,551
1998 Turf 0-6: (8f, 9f, 10f 3, 11f) (g-s, gd 2, g-f, frm 2)
Scopey, average gelding, effective 10 to 11f, best at 10f, acts on gd to frm, likes left handed tracks, prefers tight tracks. Turf high 63 - 4th of 14 getting 12lb from Harmony Hall (4 Jly Nottingham 10f g-f RF 2545). Inconsistent. **Sir Mark Prescott [0-10] G Moore.*

MYSTERY MAN BHB 47f RR 27f 336[7]
3 gr g Mystiko (USA) 7.7f **(59)** - Baileys by Name (Nomination) 7f **(60)**
Form - 0257
Record 1998 - 1st:0 2nd:1 3rd:0 Ran:4
Pre1998 - 1st:0 2nd:0 3rd:0 Ran:2
Win Prizemoney £0 *Total Prizemoney* £488
1998 AW 0-4: (8f 4) (Fibr 4)
Workmanlike, fair gelding, effective 8f, - acts on Fibr. AW high 58 - 2nd of 9 getting 5lb from Emperor's Gold (12 Jan Southwell 8f Fibr RF 0076). **P C Haslam [0-6] N P Green.*

MYSTICAL BHB 56f68a **RR 33f 68a** 5059[11]
4 b f Mystiko (USA) 7.7f **(59)** - Midnight Imperial (Night Shift (USA)) 7.2f **(69)**
Form - 7121327142280050
Record 1998 - 1st:2 2nd:4 3rd:1 Ran:14
Pre1998 - 1st:3 2nd:3 3rd:1 Ran:16
Win Prizemoney £13,579 *Total Prizemoney* £20,635

Wins 1998 *Mar Lingfi (SLW) C 5f 73 <*
1998 *Jan Lingfi (STD) C 6f 61+*
1997 *Dec Lingfi (STD) C 6f 61*
1997 Aug Bright (G-F) H 6f 62 64
1997 Jun Mussel (G-S) SH 5f 51 58

1998 Turf 0-3: (5f, 6f 2) (sft, g-f, frm) 1998 AW 2-11: (5f 1-4, 6f 1-7) (Equi 2-11)
Leggy, above-average filly, effective 5 to 6f, best at 6f, - acts on Equi, mostly wears blinkers (extremely effectively), prefers left handed tracks, prefers tight tracks, excels at Lingfield. Turf high 33. AW high 75 - 2nd of 6 getting 7lb from Robo Magic (3 Apr Lingfield 6f Equi RF 0556) - also 1st of 9 giving 4lb to Palo Blanco (3 Mar Lingfield RF 0391).
**D Nicholls [0-1] Ian Blakey (from Mrs L Stubbs [5-29] Jly 1998).*

MYSTICAL RODGE BHB 41f49a **RR 40f 49a** 1475[24]
3 b g Mystiko (USA) 7.7f **(59)** - Deux Etoiles (Bay Express) 7.1f **(60)**
Form - 85330
Record 1998 - 1st:0 2nd:0 3rd:2 Ran:5
Pre1998 - 1st:0 2nd:0 3rd:0 Ran:2
Win Prizemoney £0 *Total Prizemoney* £500
1998 Turf 0-1: (6f) (g-f) 1998 AW 0-4: (5f 3, 6f) (Fibr 4)
Unfurnished, moderate gelding. AW high 49.
**M Dods [0-7] Doug Graham.*

MYSTICAL SONG BHB 39f **RR 36f** 2320[8]
3 ch f Mystiko (USA) 7.7f **(59)** - Jubilee Song (Song) 7.2f **(61)**
Form - 0088
Record 1998 - 1st:0 2nd:0 3rd:0 Ran:4
Pre1998 - 1st:0 2nd:0 3rd:0 Ran:1
1998 Turf 0-3: (5f 2, 6f) (gd 2, hrd) 1998 AW 0-1: (5f) (Fibr)
Neat, very moderate filly. Turf high 36. **R Guest [0-5] J Strange.*

MYSTIC FLIGHT (USA) RR 53f 1569[7]
3 b f Silver Hawk (USA) 11.2f **(85)** - Wand (IRE) (Reference Point) 6.8f **(70)**
Form - 7
Record 1998 - 1st:0 2nd:0 3rd:0 Ran:1
Pre1998 - 1st:0 2nd:0 3rd:0 Ran:1
1998 Turf 0-1: (8f) (frm)
Light-framed, currently fair filly. **R Charlton [0-2] Cliveden Stud.*

MYSTICISM BHB 61f **RR 65f** 1689[13]
3 ch f Mystiko (USA) 7.7f **(59)** - Abuzz (Absalom) 7.2f **(58)**
Form - 360
Record 1998 - 1st:0 2nd:0 3rd:1 Ran:3
Pre1998 - 1st:0 2nd:2 3rd:0 Ran:9
Win Prizemoney £0 *Total Prizemoney* £5,929
1998 Turf 0-2: (6f 2) (hvy, g-f) 1998 AW 0-1: (5f) (Equi)
Neat, average filly, effective 5f, acts on frm. Turf high 8. Far from disgraced when fifth in the Weatherbys Super Sprint at two, she has not run up to that form subsequently.
**C E Brittain [0-12] Mrs C E Brittain.*

MYSTIC LADY RR 9f 888[8]
2 gr f Mystiko (USA) 7.7f **(59)** -Eladale (IRE) (Ela-Mana-Mou) 10.1f **(70)**
Form - 38
Record 1998 - 1st:0 2nd:0 3rd:1 Ran:2
Win Prizemoney £0 *Total Prizemoney* £225
1998 Turf 0-1: (5f) (sft) 1998 AW 0-1: (5f) (Fibr)
Currently very poor filly. **S C Williams [0-2] Alasdair Simpson.*

MYSTIC LEGEND (IRE) BHB 27f20a **RR 37f 20a** 209[9]
6 gr g Standaan (FR) 5.4f **(46)** - Mandy Girl (Manado) 9.6f **(63)**
Form - 0
Record 1998 - 1st:0 2nd:0 3rd:0 Ran:1
Pre1998 - 1st:0 2nd:0 3rd:0 Ran:11
1998 AW 0-1: (10f) (Equi)
Very moderate gelding. Inconsistent.
**L Wells [0-2] Mrs Elizabeth Sinclair (from J J Sheehan [0-6] Nov 1996).*

MYSTIC QUEST (IRE) BHB 50f75a **RR 55f 75a** 4887[15]
4 b g Arcane (USA) 11.6f **(66)** - Tales of Wisdom (Rousillon (USA)) 8.2f **(74)**
Form - 30781500
Record 1998 - 1st:1 2nd:0 3rd:1 Ran:8
Pre1998 - 1st:2 2nd:3 3rd:2 Ran:16
Win Prizemoney £9,941 *Total Prizemoney* £14,220

Wins * 1998 Jly Folkes (G-F) H 12f 50 53
* 1997 *Oct Lingfi (STD) H 12f 70 77*
* 1996 *Spt Wolver (STD) 8.5f 83 <*

1998 Turf 1-7: (11f, 12f 1-4, 14f, 15f) (g-s 2, g-f, frm 1-4) 1998 AW 0-1: (12f) (Equi)
Scopey, above-average gelding, effective 12f, - acts on Equi, often wears blinkers, favours tight tracks. Turf high 55. (1st run) - 3rd of 5 to Quiet Arch (19 Mar Lingfield 12f Equi RF 0446). Inconsistent. His only win in 1998 was on fast ground at Folkestone, when the visor was left off.
**K McAuliffe [3-24] Delamere Cottage Racing Partners (1996).*

MYSTIC RIDGE BHB 45f **RR 50df** 5098[16]
4 ch g Mystiko (USA) 7.7f **(59)** - Vallauris (Faustus (USA)) 10f **(58)**
Form - 0000306328000
Record 1998 - 1st:0 2nd:1 3rd:2 Ran:13
Pre1998 - 1st:0 2nd:1 3rd:2 Ran:6
Win Prizemoney £0 *Total Prizemoney* £3,909
1998 Turf 0-13: (9f, 10f 3, 12f 7, 14f, 15f) (sft, g-s 3, gd 5, g-f 4)
Scopey, fair gelding, effective 10f, acts on frm, often wears blinkers. Turf high 55. Becoming disappointing.
**B J Curley [0-18] P Byrne (from D R C Elsworth [0-5] Jun 1997).*

MYSTIC RING (IRE) BHB 29f40a **RR 23f 40a** 3119[10]
8 b g Fairy King (USA) 7.7f **(75)** - Cheap And Sweet (USA) (Rising Market (USA))
Form - 700600
Record 1998 - 1st:0 2nd:0 3rd:0 Ran:6
Pre1998 - 1st:3 2nd:2 3rd:3 Ran:24
Win Prizemoney £8,220 *Total Prizemoney* £10,803

Wins 1997 May Fairyh (G-S) H 7f 63 67 <
1996 Spt Listow (GD) H 6f 59 57
1996 Spt Down R (FRM) H 7f 54 54

1998 Turf 0-5: (6f 2, 7f 2, 8f) (hvy, gd 2, frm, hrd) 1998 AW 0-1: (6f) (Fibr)
Little account gelding, effective 6 to 7f, acts on g-s to gd, has worn blinkers, likes right handed tracks. Turf high 23.
**J S Haldane [0-6] J S Haldane (from T Stack in IRE [3-24] Nov 1997).*

MYSTIC SPRING (IRE) RR 70f 5072[5]
2 gr f Royal Academy (USA) 7.8f **(77)** - Secret Sunday (USA) (Secreto (USA)) 8.7f **(72)**
Form - 05
Record 1998 - 1st:0 2nd:0 3rd:0 Ran:2
1998 Turf 0-2: (7f 2) (gd 2)
Currently above-average filly. Turf high 70 (began Oct).
**J Noseda [0-2] Fieldspring Racing.*

MYSTIQUE AIR (IRE) BHB 39f **RR 50f** 5098[11]
4 b f Mujadil (USA) 7.7f **(70)** -Romany Pageant(Welsh Pageant)10f **(65)**
Form - 0000006170
Record 1998 - 1st:1 2nd:0 3rd:0 Ran:10
Pre1998 - 1st:1 2nd:1 3rd:2 Ran:12
Win Prizemoney £4,943 *Total Prizemoney* £6,869

Wins * 1998 Oct Ayr (HVY) S 9.1f 50
* 1997 Jly Catter (G-F) 7f 58 <

1998 Turf 1-9: (7f 2, 8f 4, 9f 1-1, 10f 2) (sft 1-1, g-s 2, gd 3, g-f, frm 2)
1998 AW 0-1: (12f) (Fibr)
Neat, fair filly, effective 6 to 7f, best at 7f, acts on g-f to hrd, best on g-f, has worn blinkers, likes left handed tracks. Turf high 50.
**E Weymes [2-22] T A Scothern.*

MY TESS BHB 79f **RR 66f** 5146[5]
2 br f Lugana Beach 7f **(63)** - Barachois Princess (USA) (Barachois (CAN)) 8.3f **(63)**
Form - 635
Record 1998 - 1st:0 2nd:0 3rd:1 Ran:3
Win Prizemoney £0 *Total Prizemoney* £590
1998 Turf 0-3: (8f 3) (g-s, gd, frm)
Currently average filly. Turf high 66 (began Oct) - 3rd of 10 to

Fatina (23 Oct Doncaster 8f frm RF 4956).

**B A McMahon [0-3] J D Graham.*

MYTHICAL GIRL (USA) BHB 100f **RR 100f** 3772[6]

2 b f Gone West (USA) 7.8f **(82)** - Yousefia (USA) (Danzig (USA)) 8.4f **(76)**

Form - 116

Record	**1998 -**	1st:2	2nd:0	3rd:0	Ran:3

Win Prizemoney £29,596 *Total Prizemoney* £30,171

Wins						
*** 1998**	Jly	Ascot	(G-F)	G3	6f	100 <
*** 1998**	Jly	Newmar	(FRM)		6f	92+

1998 Turf 2-3: (6f 2-3) (g-f 1-1, frm 1-2)

Currently very useful filly. Turf high 100 (began Jly) - 1st of 6 from Gipsy Rose Lee (25 Jly Ascot RF 3101) - also 1st of 10 from Elhida (9 Jly Newmarket RF 2648). She seemed to have the world at her feet after winning the Group Three Princess Margaret Stakes at Ascot in July, but flattened out in the Lowther Stakes at York the following month. She did not appear to give her true running there - possibly due to some scrimmaging before the furlong pole - and is worth another chance. Her optimum trip is a moot point, but a mile might prove a step too far.

**D R Loder [2-3] Maktoum Al Maktoum.*

Form - 508370220631310700

Record					
1998 -	1st:2	2nd:2	3rd:3	Ran:16
Pre1998 -	1st:6	2nd:5	3rd:9	Ran:49

Win Prizemoney £28,983 *Total Prizemoney* £47,974

Wins							
*** 1998**	Aug	Kempto	(G-F)	H	7f	68	70
*** 1998**	Jly	Bath	(GD)	H	5.7f	64	67
1997	Oct	Leices	(GD)	CH	8f	62	78?
1997	Spt	Sandow	(G-F)	H	7.1f	59	64
1997	Aug	Beverl	(GD)	H	7.5f	57	60
1997	Jly	Cheste	(G-F)	H	7.6f	53	58
1995	Jly	Beverl	(G-F)		5f		85 <
1995	Jun	Ayr	(FRM)		7f		74+

1998 Turf 2-16: (6f 1-6, 7f 1-8, 8f, 9f) (sft 2, g-s 2, gd 1-6, g-f 2, frm 1-4)

Above-average gelding, effective 7 to 8f, acts on gd to frm, has worn blinkers. Turf high 70 - 1st of 17 getting 2lb from Moscow Mist (19 Aug Kempton RF 3739). Becoming disappointing. He won four times on Turf in a busy 1997. Kept on the go again this season, he has hit form back on Turf during the summer with wins at Bath and Kempton, and is quite a versatile sort considering he has won at distances ranging from an extended five furlongs to a mile. Probably best on a sound surface.

**R J Hodges [2-19] P Slade (from A Bailey [6-46] Oct 1997).*

Mythical Girl's Ascot win was real enough to her rivals

MYTTONS MISTAKE BHB 68f67a **RR 70f 67a** 4886[9]

5 b g Rambo Dancer (CAN) 8.4f **(59)** - Hi-Hunsley (Swing Easy (USA)) 6.5f **(55)**

MYTTON'S MOMENT (IRE) BHB 62f **RR 65f** 4767[13]

2 b g Waajib 8.9f **(67)** - Late Swallow (My Swallow) 9.2f **(71)**

Form - 8844040

Record 1998 - 1st:0 2nd:0 3rd:0 Ran:7
Win Prizemoney £0 *Total Prizemoney* £904
1998 Turf 0-7: (5f, 6f, 7f 2, 8f 3) (sft 2, gd, g-f 4)
Average gelding, has worn blinkers. Turf high 65.
**A Bailey [0-7] Gordon Mytton.*

MY TYSON (IRE) BHB 52f68a RR 52f 68a 2576[17]

3 b c Don't Forget Me 9.5f **(66)** - Shuckran Habibi (Thatching) 8f **(66)**
Form - 1780000
Record 1998 - 1st:0 2nd:0 3rd:0 Ran:6
Pre1998 - 1st:1 2nd:0 3rd:0 Ran:6
Win Prizemoney £2,916 *Total Prizemoney* £2,916
Wins ** 1997 Nov Lingfi (STD) 5f 66 <*
1998 Turf 0-5: (5f, 6f 2, 8f 2) (gd 2, g-f 3) 1998 AW 0-1: (6f) (Fibr)
Scopey, average colt, effective 5f, - acts on Equi. Turf high 52. Becoming disappointing. Was always prominent when winning a Lingfield maiden on Equitrack in November '97. Modest form since. **K Mahdi [1-12] Hamad Al-Mutawa.*

MYZOMELA (USA) BHB 70f RR 70f 4759[3]

3 b f Kris S (USA) 9.3f **(76)** - Myza (USA) (Danzig (USA)) 8.4f **(76)**
Form - 4187043
Record 1998 - 1st:1 2nd:0 3rd:1 Ran:7
Win Prizemoney £3,922 *Total Prizemoney* £4,996
Wins * **1998** May Windso (G-F) 8.3f 62++ <
1998 Turf 1-7: (7f, 8f 1-6) (gd 4, g-f 2, frm 1-1)
Workmanlike, above-average filly, effective 8f, acts on gd. Turf high 75. Unraced as a juvenile, she got off the mark in good style at Windsor but disappointed in handicaps.
**J H M Gosden [1-7] Sheikh Mohammed.*

NABHAAN (IRE) BHB 105f RR 105f 551a[4]

5 b h In The Wings 11.2f **(77)** - Miss Gris (USA) (Hail the Pirates (USA)) 11f **(78)**
Form - 14
1998 AW 1-2: (10f 1-2) (Dirt 1-2)
Pattern-class colt, effective 10 to 14f, best at 12f, acts on gd to g-f - acts on Dirt, has worn blinkers, excels at Haydock. AW high 109 (1st run) - 1st of 7 from Sunbeam Dance (5 Mar Nad Al Sheba RF 0448a). Consistent. A tricky ride, he won a decent prize in Dubai during March and has obviously adapted well to his new surroundings.
**E Charpy in UAE [1-2] Hamdan Al-Maktoum (from D Morley [3-22] Spt 1997).*

NABONASSAR RR 82+f 4774[2]

2 ch c Lion Cavern (USA) 7.5f **(74)** - Negligent (Ahonoora) 8.1f **(73)**
Form - 2
Record 1998 - 1st:0 2nd:1 3rd:0 Ran:1
Win Prizemoney £0 *Total Prizemoney* £988
1998 Turf 0-1: (7f) (gd)
Currently decent colt. (1st run) - 2nd of 18 to Little Rock (13 Oct Leicester 7f gd RF 4774). Son of a useful racemare, he was runner-up to a stablemate on his only run.
**Sir Michael Stoute [0-1] Sheikh Mohammed.*

NABURN LOCH BHB 30f RR 35f 316[8]

8 b m Lochnager 6.9f **(50)**-Balgownie (Prince Tenderfoot (USA)) 9f **(61)**
Form - 8
Record 1998 - 1st:0 2nd:0 3rd:0 Ran:1
Pre1998 - 1st:0 2nd:0 3rd:1 Ran:8
Win Prizemoney £0 *Total Prizemoney* £503
1998 AW 0-1: (6f) (Equi)
Very moderate mare.
**D M Hyde [0-5] J D Hankinson (from G P Kelly [0-8] Aug 1994).*

NADOUR AL BAHR (IRE) RR 114f 4219a[5]

3 b c Be My Guest (USA) 10.2f **(66)** - Nona (GER) (Cortez (GER)) 8.6f **(75)**
Form - 12235
1998 Turf 1-5: (10f 1-1, 12f 4) (hvy, sft, gd 1-2, g-f)
Group-class colt. Turf high 114 - 3rd of 8 getting 13lb from Luso (9 Aug Gelsenkirchen-horst 12f gd RF 3616a). Narrowly beaten on fast ground in the Italian Derby, and on a heavy surface in the German equivalent, he is a game but luckless individual.
**M Hofer in GER [1-5].*

NADWAH (USA) BHB 102f RR 103df 2700[6]

3 b f Shadeed (USA) 7.7f **(72)** - Tadwin (Never so Bold) 6.3f **(66)**
Form - 63526
Record 1998 - 1st:0 2nd:1 3rd:1 Ran:5
Pre1998 - 1st:2 2nd:0 3rd:2 Ran:5
Win Prizemoney £31,920 *Total Prizemoney* £47,000
Wins * 1997 Jun Ascot (G-F) G3 5f 97 <
* 1997 May Newbur (G-S) 5.2f 76+
1998 Turf 0-5: (6f 4, 7f) (sft, g-f 2, frm 2)
Scopey, very useful filly, effective 5 to 6f, acts on gd to g-f, has worn blinkers. Turf high 104. A Group-winning juvenile, she went backwards last season and did not seem to have trained on.
**P T Walwyn [2-10] Hamdan Al Maktoum.*

NAFITH RR 65f 4928[6]

2 ch c Elmaamul (USA) 8.1f **(70)** - Wanisa (USA) (Topsider (USA)) 8.3f **(71)**
Form - 66
Record 1998 - 1st:0 2nd:0 3rd:0 Ran:2
1998 Turf 0-2: (7f, 8f) (g-s, frm)
Currently average colt. Turf high 65 (began Spt).
**M P Tregoning [0-2] Hamdan Al Maktoum.*

NA HUIBHEACHU (IRE) BHB 30f31a RR 31f 31a 2984a[15]

7 ch g Nostrum (USA) - Royal Slip (Royal Match) 11.8f **(54)**
Form - 408000
Record 1998 - 1st:0 2nd:0 3rd:0 Ran:4
Pre1998 - 1st:0 2nd:3 3rd:0 Ran:13
Win Prizemoney £0 *Total Prizemoney* £2,108
1998 Turf 0-3: (8f 2, 14f) (g-s, gd, g-f) 1998 AW 0-1: (8f) (Equi)
Very moderate gelding, effective 9f, acts on frm, has worn blinkers, favours left handed tracks. Turf high 14. Becoming disappointing.
**P McCreery in IRE [0-3] Mrs Yona Caffrey (from J S Moore [0-5] Jan 1998).*

NAISSANT BHB 60f56a RR 61f 56a 4771[26]

5 b m Shaadi (USA) 8.1f **(75)** - Nophe (USA) (Super Concorde (USA)) 10.9f **(66)**
Form - 04002150010050
Record 1998 - 1st:2 2nd:1 3rd:0 Ran:14
Pre1998 - 1st:2 2nd:3 3rd:1 Ran:32
Win Prizemoney £17,081 *Total Prizemoney* £25,923
Wins * **1998** Aug Hamilt (SFT) H 6f 55 61
* **1998** Jun Hamilt (SFT) H 6f 51 53
1996 Aug Carlis (FRM) 6.9f 61
1996 Aug Ripon (G-S) H 6f 60 71 <
1998 Turf 2-14: (6f 2-13, 7f) (sft, g-s 3, gd 2-2, g-f 6, frm 2)
Average filly, effective 6f, acts on g-s to gd, best on gd. Turf high 61 - 1st of 9 getting 6lb from Mrs Malaprop (1 Aug Hamilton RF 3264) - also 1st of 10 giving 6lb to Mister Westsound (17 Jun Hamilton RF 2063).
**Martyn Wane [2-18] William Graham (from R M McKellar [2-19] May 1997).*

NAJJAR (USA) BHB 63f RR 66f 4807[9]

3 gr g El Prado (IRE) 8f **(74)** - With Strawberries (USA) (Maudlin (USA)) 8f **(74)**
Form - 450801100
Record 1998 - 1st:2 2nd:0 3rd:0 Ran:9
Pre1998 - 1st:0 2nd:0 3rd:1 Ran:3
Win Prizemoney £6,658 *Total Prizemoney* £7,145
Wins * **1998** Aug Leices (GD) H 8f 59 66 <
* **1998** Aug Newcas (GD) H 8f 57 58
1998 Turf 2-9: (7f 2, 8f 2-6, 10f) (sft, g-s, gd 4, g-f 1-1, frm 1-2)
Scopey, average gelding, effective 8f, acts on frm, has worn blinkers. Turf high 66 - 1st of 13 giving 4lb to Marske Machine (10 Aug Leicester RF 3500). Now running over hurdles.
**J G FitzGerald [2-9] John Smith's Ltd (from P T Walwyn [0-3] Spt 1997).*

NAJM AL BAHAR (FR) RR 54f 4135[8]

2 b f Caerleon (USA) 10.9f **(79)** - Noble Lily (USA) (Vaguely Noble) 10.1f **(72)**
Form - 8
Record 1998 - 1st:0 2nd:0 3rd:0 Ran:1
1998 Turf 0-1: (8f) (g-f)

Currently fair filly. **D R Loder [0-1] Sheikh Mohammed.*

NAKED OAT BHB 60f64a **RR 71f 64a** 589[13]

3 b g Imp Society (USA) 7.1f **(63)** - Bajina (Dancing Brave (USA)) 8.4f **(76)**

Form - 35432430

Record 1998 - 1st:0 2nd:1 3rd:2 Ran:5
Pre1998 - 1st:0 2nd:0 3rd:1 Ran:10

Win Prizemoney £0 *Total Prizemoney* £2,336

1998 Turf 0-1: (8f) (g-s) 1998 AW 0-4: (8f 2, 9f 2) (Fibr 4)

Above-average gelding, effective 8f, - acts on Fibr, has worn blinkers. AW high 60. He has had plenty of chances to get off the mark, especially on sand, but has become frustrating. He showed nothing when returning to turf. **B Smart [0-15] The Superioat Partnership.*

NAKHAL BHB 40f43a **RR 50f 43a** 3129[4]

5 b g Puissance 7.1f **(60)** - Rambadale (Vaigly Great) 7f **(58)**

Form - 772104804

Record 1998 - 1st:1 2nd:1 3rd:0 Ran:9
Pre1998 - 1st:0 2nd:4 3rd:2 Ran:19

Win Prizemoney £2,450 *Total Prizemoney* £8,527

Wins * 1998 *Mar Southw (STD) H 11f 41 45* <

1998 Turf 0-1: (10f) (g-f) 1998 AW 1-8: (11f 1-3, 12f 5) (Fibr 1-8)

Fair gelding, effective 10 to 12f, best at 10f, - acts on Equi, often wears blinkers, favours left handed tracks. AW high 48. He had plenty of chances to get off the mark, but had to wait until a poor maiden handicap on the Southwell Fibresand in March to achieve it. It was not much of a race, and he will struggle to find another one as bad. **D J G MurraySmith [1-28] Mrs Jill McNeill.*

NAMAS BHB 79f **RR 76f** 4758[7]

2 b f Alzao (USA) 9.8f **(73)** - Dafinah (USA) (Graustark) 10.1f **(70)**

Form - 357

Record 1998 - 1st:0 2nd:0 3rd:1 Ran:3

Win Prizemoney £0 *Total Prizemoney* £726

1998 Turf 0-3: (7f 3) (gd, frm 2)

Currently above-average filly. Turf high 76 (began Aug).
**Sir Michael Stoute [0-3] Mitaab Abdullah.*

NAMBUCCA **RR 66f** 271[7]

4 b f Shirley Heights 12.1f **(76)** - Cephira (FR) (Abdos) 10f **(77)**

Form - 7

Record 1998 - 1st:0 2nd:0 3rd:0 Ran:1
Pre1998 - 1st:0 2nd:1 3rd:0 Ran:1

Win Prizemoney £0 *Total Prizemoney* £1,100

1998 AW 0-1: (12f) (Equi)

Scopey, currently average filly. Ran a most promising race on her debut at Doncaster in March '97, but did not reappear until running poorly in a maiden on the Lingfield Equitrack in February. Her tongue was flapping out the side of her mouth in that race and she did not look at all happy. **Mrs J Cecil [0-2] Lord Howard de Walden.*

NAME OF OUR FATHER (USA) BHB 55f47a **RR 50?f 47a** 2015[26]

5 b g Northern Baby (CAN) 10.2f **(74)** - Ten Hail Marys (USA) (Halo (USA)) 10.6f **(75)**

Form - 0

Record 1998 - 1st:0 2nd:0 3rd:0 Ran:1
Pre1998 - 1st:0 2nd:1 3rd:0 Ran:9

Win Prizemoney £0 *Total Prizemoney* £1,581

1998 Turf 0-1: (20f) (gd)

Fair gelding. Becoming disappointing.
**P Bowen [7-27] T M Morris (from M J Fetherston-Godley [0-1] Apr 1996).*

NAMID **RR 90+f** 2802a[1]

2 b c Indian Ridge 7.6f **(74)**-Dawnsio (IRE)(Tate Gallery (USA))7.4f **(67)**

Form - 21

1998 Turf 1-2: (6f 1-2) (sft, gd 1-1)

Currently useful colt. Turf high 90 - 1st of 6 giving 3lb to Coralita (12 Jly Curragh RF 2802a). Made an encouraging debut when chasing home Camargo in the Railway Stakes, and was a clear-cut winner of the Anglesey Stakes on his only other appearance.
**J Oxx in IRE [1-2] Lady Clague.*

NANCY MALONEY (IRE) BHB 41f **RR 53f** 4574[7]

3 b f Persian Bold 10f **(69)** - Snoozy Time (Cavo Doro) 10.6f **(57)**

Form - 86065507

Record 1998 - 1st:0 2nd:0 3rd:0 Ran:8

1998 Turf 0-8: (8f 2, 9f 3, 10f 3) (sft, gd, g-f 2, frm 4)

Scopey, fair filly, effective 8 to 9f, acts on gd to frm, favours tight tracks. Turf high 55. Inconsistent.
**Miss Gay Kelleway [0-8] Brian Kennedy.*

NANOUSHKA (IRE) BHB 108f **RR 111?f** 4461[7]

3 b f Taufan (USA) 8.3f **(65)** - West Chazy (USA) (Gone West (USA)) 6.5f **(75)**

Form - 6101347

Record 1998 - 1st:2 2nd:0 3rd:1 Ran:7
Pre1998 - 1st:1 2nd:0 3rd:1 Ran:3

Win Prizemoney £31,018 *Total Prizemoney* £37,531

Wins * 1998 Jly York (G-F) L 6f 111? <
*** 1998** May Lingfi (GD) L 7f 100
* 1997 Aug Ascot (GD) 6f 89+

1998 Turf 2-7: (6f 1-3, 7f 1-3, 8f) (gd 3, g-f 1-1, frm 1-3)

Leggy, Group-class filly, effective 6f, acts on frm. Turf high 111 - 1st of 7 giving 4lb to Crazee Mental (10 Jly York RF 2700). Most impressive when making all at York in July, she can win Listed races but stumbles when stepped-up to Group events. Equally effective at six and seven furlongs, she did not seem to stay a mile at Royal Ascot. **R Hannon [3-10] Thurloe Thoroughbreds II.*

NANTON POINT (USA) BHB 82f **RR 84f** 4850[25]

6 b g Darshaan 11.9f **(81)** - Migiyas (Kings Lake (USA)) 10.8f **(67)**

Form - 10130110

Record 1998 - 1st:4 2nd:0 3rd:1 Ran:8
Pre1998 - 1st:4 2nd:3 3rd:0 Ran:23

Win Prizemoney £29,236 *Total Prizemoney* £47,935

Wins * 1998 Spt Bath (GD) H 17.2f 78 84 <
*** 1998** Aug Warwic (G-F) H 16.1f 76 77
*** 1998** Jly Beverl (GD) H 16.2f 69 73
*** 1998** Jun Haydoc (GD) H 16.2f 66 73
* 1995 Jly Redcar (FRM) H 16f 52 62
* 1995 Jly Redcar (FRM) H 14.1f 52 61+
* 1995 Jly Folkes (GD) H 15.4f 44 55+
* 1995 Jun Yarmou (FRM) H 14.1f 44 51

1998 Turf 4-8: (16f 3-5, 17f 1-1, 18f, 20f) (gd 2, g-f 2-4, frm 2-2)

Decent gelding, effective 14 to 20f, acts on g-f to frm, best on g-f, has worn blinkers, prefers left handed tracks, likes tight tracks, excels at Haydock. Turf high 84 - 1st of 12 giving 10lb to Paradise Navy (28 Spt Bath RF 4525) - also 1st of 8 giving 10lb to Treasure Chest (31 Aug Warwick RF 4003). Inconsistent. Had a good season, but ran a couple of unaccountably bad races.
**Lady Herries [8-28] The High Flying Partnership (from R Hannon [0-3] Spt 1994).*

NAPIER STAR BHB 33f57a **RR 41df 57a** 26[8]

5 b m Inca Chief (USA) 5.6f **(45)**-America Star (Norwick(USA)) 7.2f **(56)**

Form - 863078

Record 1998 - 1st:0 2nd:0 3rd:0 Ran:1
Pre1998 - 1st:4 2nd:8 3rd:8 Ran:50

Win Prizemoney £9,262 *Total Prizemoney* £18,928

Wins ** 1997 May Wolver (STD) H 5f 63 63* <
** 1996 Nov Wolver (STD) H 5f 60 61*
** 1996 Jly Wolver (STD) H 5f 51 51*
** 1996 Apr Southw (STD) 6f 57*

1998 AW 0-1: (6f) (Fibr)

Fair filly, effective 5 to 6f, best at 6f, - acts on Fibr, often wears blinkers (effectively), likes left handed tracks, likes tight tracks. Consistent. She runs regularly, though almost exclusively on sand these days. She has been most successful over the minimum trip at Wolverhampton, over which she has gained her last three victories. **Mrs N Macauley [4-51] P M Heaton.*

NAPOLEON'S RETURN BHB 38f40a **RR 39f 40a** 5114[2]

5 gr g Daring March 9f **(54)** - Miss Colenca (Petong) 6.6f **(58)**

Form - 64032

Record 1998 - 1st:0 2nd:1 3rd:1 Ran:5
Pre1998 - 1st:3 2nd:3 3rd:1 Ran:33

Win Prizemoney £9,121 *Total Prizemoney* £13,197

Wins * 1997 Jly Catter (G-F) H 7f 37 38
1996 Jun Ayr (G-F) H 8f 45 50
1995 Oct Redcar (FRM) C 7f 66 <

1998 Turf 0-5: (8f 4, 12f) (g-s 3, gd 2)

Very moderate gelding, effective 7 to 8f, best at 8f, acts on g-s to

gd, best on gd, has worn blinkers (extremely effectively). Turf high 39 (began Spt) - 3rd of 20 giving 5lb to Monis (21 Oct Newcastle 8f g-s RF 4919). Inconsistent.

**J L Eyre [1-16] J E Wilson (from A Harrison [1-11] Jly 1996).*

NAPOLEON'S SISTER (IRE) BHB 100f **RR 100f** 4186[6]

3 b f Alzao (USA) 9.8f **(73)** - Sheer Audacity (Troy) 10.4f **(68)**
Form - 515636
Record 1998 - 1st:1 2nd:0 3rd:1 Ran:6
Win Prizemoney £17,610 *Total Prizemoney* £19,759
Wins * 1998 May Goodwo (G-F) L 9.9f 96+ <
1998 Turf 1-6: (8f, 10f 1-1, 12f 2, 14f, 15f) (gd 3, g-f 1-2, frm)
Scopey, very useful filly, effective 10 to 14f, acts on g-f. Turf high 100 - 3rd of 3 getting 1lb from Ta-Lim (29 Aug Goodwood 14f g-f RF 3945) - also 1st of 8 from Putuna (20 May Goodwood RF 1356). She looked a genuine Oaks contender when coming from another parish to win the Lupe Stakes at Goodwood, but failed to fulfil that potential. She is open to improvement, but connections may decide her future lies at stud.

**D R C Elsworth [1-6] Mrs Anne Coughlan.*

NAPOLEON STAR (IRE) BHB 48f35a **RR 54f 35a** 4920[17]

7 ch g Mulhollande (USA) 6.6f **(68)** - Lady Portobello (Porto Bello) 8.9f **(43)**
Form - 00463860068625760700500
Record 1998 - 1st:0 2nd:1 3rd:1 Ran:20
Pre1998 - 1st:6 2nd:3 3rd:4 Ran:68
Win Prizemoney £16,057 *Total Prizemoney* £23,548
Wins 1997 Jun Catter (GD) H 6f 48 52
1997 Mar Warwic (G-F) H 5f 43 49
1997 Feb Southw (STD) SH 6f 43 43
1994 Jly Bath (FRM) 5.1f 72 <
1994 Jun Bright (FRM) 6f 57
1994 Jun Bath (FRM) C 5.1f 61
1998 Turf 0-16: (5f 3, 6f 8, 7f 2, 8f 3) (g-s, gd 7, g-f 2, frm 6) 1998 AW 0-4: (6f 2, 7f 2) (Fibr 4)
Fair gelding, effective 5 to 8f, best at 6f, acts on gd to frm, best on gd, often wears blinkers, likes left handed tracks. Turf high 54. AW high 29.

**Miss J F Craze [0-25] Miss J F Craze (from S R Bowring [3-20] Aug 1997).*

NARRABETH (IRE) **RR 114f** 3616a[4]

5 bl h Shaadi (USA) 8.1f **(75)** - Nocturna (IRE) (Diu Star)
Form - 0464
1998 Turf 0-4: (11f, 12f 3) (sft 2, gd 2)
Group-class colt, effective 10 to 12f, best at 12f, acts on sft to gd, best on gd. Turf high 109. Consistent. He is usually held-up and has been slowly away. There is nothing to suggest he will win a Group race next season.

**Uwe Stoltefuss in GER [0-7] Stall Silvretta (from H Jentzsch in GER [0-3] Jun 1997).*

NARROGIN (USA) BHB 62f74a **RR 60f 74a** 3436[7]

3 ch g Strike The Gold (USA) 8f **(79)** - Best Regalia (Sharpen Up) 8.3f **(67)**
Form - 22867
Record 1998 - 1st:0 2nd:2 3rd:0 Ran:5
Pre1998 - 1st:0 2nd:1 3rd:2 Ran:11
Win Prizemoney £0 *Total Prizemoney* £5,177
1998 Turf 0-3: (9f, 10f, 11f) (gd 2, g-f) 1998 AW 0-2: (10f 2) (Equi 2)
Workmanlike, above-average gelding, effective 8 to 10f, best at 8f, acts on gd to frm - acts on Equi, has worn blinkers. Turf high 60. AW high 72 (1st run) - 2nd of 6 to Netta Rufina (7 Feb Lingfield 10f Equi RF 0239). Now hurdling with Paul Webber.

**M R Channon [0-16] J G Rogers-Coltman.*

NASAAYEM (USA) BHB 84f **RR 80f** 4464[1]

3 b br f Gulch (USA) 9.6f **(79)** - Saffaanh (USA) (Shareef Dancer (USA)) 9.9f **(73)**
Form - 341
Record 1998 - 1st:1 2nd:0 3rd:1 Ran:3
Win Prizemoney £3,601 *Total Prizemoney* £4,568
Wins * 1998 Spt Goodwo (G-F) 9.9f 80 <
1998 Turf 1-3: (7f, 9f, 10f 1-1) (gd 1-3)
Workmanlike, currently decent filly. Turf high 80 - 1st of 6 from Mole Creek (24 Spt Goodwood RF 4464). A sister to Guineas winner Harayir, she was Godolphin's first runner of the year when third in a Newmarket maiden. One-paced next time, before securing that all-important victory.

**S bin Suroor [1-3] Godolphin.*

NASANICE (IRE) **RR 97f** 5109a[6]

3 b f Nashwan (USA) 10.3f **(79)** - Mathaayl (USA) (Shadeed (USA)) 8.2f **(70)**
Form - 221546
1998 Turf 1-6: (8f, 9f 1-1, 10f 3, 12f) (g-s 1-3, gd 2, g-f)
Very useful filly, effective 8 to 10f, acts on g-s to gd, has worn blinkers. Turf high 97 (began Jly) - 5th of 9 to Darina (3 Oct Curragh 10f g-s RF 4691a).

**D Hanley in IRE [1-6] Hamdan Al Maktoum.*

NASHEED (USA) BHB 88f **RR 91f** 4732[1]

2 b br f Riverman (USA) 9.7f **(78)** - Thawakib (IRE) (Sadler's Wells (USA)) 10f **(76)**
Form - 311
Record 1998 - 1st:2 2nd:0 3rd:1 Ran:3
Win Prizemoney £12,343 *Total Prizemoney* £13,195
Wins * 1998 Oct Ascot (SFT) H 7f 81 91 <
*** 1998** Aug Cheste (G-S) 7f 74
1998 Turf 2-3: (7f 2-3) (g-s 1-1, gd, g-f 1-1)
Currently useful filly. Turf high 91 (began Jly) - 1st of 15 getting 7lb from Parisien Star (9 Oct Ascot RF 4732). Showed definite promise when third on her Newbury debut. She went on to win a Chester maiden and gained a battling victory in an Ascot nursery, on both occasions with give in the ground.

**J L Dunlop [2-3] Hamdan Al Maktoum.*

NASKHI BHB 97f **RR 94f** 5052a[2]

3 b f Nashwan (USA) 10.3f **(79)** - Calpella (Ajdal (USA)) 9.2f **(89)**
Form - 50423111040732
Record 1998 - 1st:3 2nd:2 3rd:2 Ran:14
Pre1998 - 1st:1 2nd:0 3rd:1 Ran:5
Win Prizemoney £22,177 *Total Prizemoney* £29,799
Wins * 1998 Jly Beverl (G-F) H 9.9f 82 94 <
*** 1998** Jly Doncas (FRM) H 10.3f 82 93
*** 1998** Jun Newcas (SFT) H 10.1f 80 83
***** 1997 Spt Pontef (G-F) H 8f 77 79+
1998 Turf 3-14: (8f 3, 9f, 10f 3-8, 12f 2) (hvy, sft 1-1, g-s, gd 4, g-f 3, frm 2-4)
Scopey, useful filly, effective 8 to 10f, best at 10f, acts on hvy to frm, best on frm, excels at Newcastle. Turf high 94 - 1st of 6 giving 32lb to Thatched (20 Jly Beverley RF 2954) - also 1st of 8 getting 2lb from Zakuska (16 Jly Doncaster RF 2849). Consistent. She improved a lot after being stepped up to ten furlongs, completing a hat-trick at Newcastle, Doncaster and Beverley during the summer. Held by the handicapper since. **M Johnston [4-19].*

NASKRAMAR BHB 77f **RR 72f** 5043[4]

5 m Marju (IRE) 9.2f **(76)** - Blink Naskra(USA) (Naskra (USA)) 8.8f **(69)**
Form - 3874
Record 1998 - 1st:0 2nd:0 3rd:1 Ran:4
Pre1998 - 1st:0 2nd:0 3rd:0 Ran:1
Win Prizemoney £0 *Total Prizemoney* £1,174
1998 Turf 0-4: (8f 2, 10f, 12f) (sft, g-s, gd, frm)
Above-average filly. Turf high 72 (began Aug).

**A J McNae [0-4] The Iona Stud (from Trained in ITY [0-1] Apr 1996).*

NATALIE JAY BHB 78f **RR 73f** 4766[3]

2 b f Ballacashtal (CAN) 7.9f **(51)** - Falls of Lora (Scottish Rifle) 10f **(55)**
Form - 3633
Record 1998 - 1st:0 2nd:0 3rd:3 Ran:4
Win Prizemoney £0 *Total Prizemoney* £1,925
1998 Turf 0-4: (7f 2, 8f 2) (sft, gd, g-f 2)
Above-average filly. Turf high 73 (began Spt).

**M R Channon [0-4] Peter Jolliffe.*

NATALIE'S PET BHB 32f **RR 24f** 4275[18]

3 b f Merdon Melody 6.8f **(56)** - Tripolitaine (FR) (Nonoalco (USA)) 8.5f **(66)**
Form - 0500600
Record 1998 - 1st:0 2nd:0 3rd:0 Ran:7
Pre1998 - 1st:0 2nd:0 3rd:0 Ran:2
1998 Turf 0-7: (6f 2, 7f 2, 8f 3) (g-s, gd 2, g-f 2, frm 2)
Workmanlike, little account filly, effective 8f, acts on g-s, has worn blinkers. Turf high 50 - 5th of 13 getting 4lb from Miskin Heights

(22 May Brighton 8f g-s RF 1387).
**J C Poulton [0-4] Gerald West (from Lady Herries [0-2] Jly 1998).*

NATHAN'S BOY BHB 75f69a **RR 75f 69a** 5148[2]
2 gr c Tragic Role (USA) 9.4f **(63)** - Gold Belt (IRE) (Bellypha) 9.8f **(73)**
Form - 70303622
Record 1998 - 1st:0 2nd:2 3rd:2 Ran:8
Win Prizemoney £0 *Total Prizemoney* £3,756
1998 Turf 0-7: (6f 3, 7f 3, 8f) (gd, g-f 3, frm 3) 1998 AW 0-1: (8f) (Fibr)
Above-average colt, effective 6 to 8f, acts on gd to frm. Turf high 75 - 2nd of 22 giving 4lb to Rex Is Okay (7 Nov Doncaster 7f gd RF 5148). **R Hollinshead [0-8] Mrs J Hughes.*

NATHAN'S HERO (IRE) BHB 51f57a **RR 63f 57a** 4878[3]
2 ch c Forest Wind (USA) - Lapland Lights (USA) (Northern Prospect (USA)) 9.5f **(71)**
Form - 0077770353
Record 1998 - 1st:0 2nd:0 3rd:2 Ran:10
Win Prizemoney £0 *Total Prizemoney* £622
1998 Turf 0-7: (5f 3, 6f, 7f 3) (gd 3, g-f, frm 3) 1998 AW 0-3: (5f, 7f 2) (Fibr 3)
Average colt. Turf high 63. AW high 51 (began Jly).
**R Hollinshead [0-10] Mrs J Hughes.*

NATIONAL ACADEMY (GER) RR 93f 2666a[11]
3 b c Royal Academy (USA) 7.8f **(77)** - Narola (GER) (Nebos (GER)) 9f **(78)**
Form - 30
1998 Turf 0-2: (10f, 12f) (hvy, gd)
Useful colt. Turf high 93. **H Remmert in GER [0-4] Dr C Berglar*

NATIONAL ANTHEM RR 86f 4892[2]
2 b c Royal Academy (USA) 7.8f **(77)** - Heart's Harmony (Blushing Groom (FR)) 10.3f **(76)**
Form - 02
Record 1998 - 1st:0 2nd:1 3rd:0 Ran:2
Win Prizemoney £0 *Total Prizemoney* £1,058
1998 Turf 0-2: (7f 2) (gd 2)
Currently useful colt. Turf high 86 (began Oct) - 2nd of 5 to Asood (20 Oct Yarmouth 7f gd RF 4892).
**Sir Michael Stoute [0-2] Mrs Denis Haynes.*

NATIONAL WISH (USA) BHB 73f **RR 66f** 1711[5]
3 ch c Forty Niner (USA) 8.8f **(73)** - Regent's Walk (CAN) (Vice Regent (CAN)) 8.7f **(74)**
Form - 035
Record 1998 - 1st:0 2nd:0 3rd:1 Ran:3
Pre1998 - 1st:0 2nd:0 3rd:0 Ran:1
Win Prizemoney £0 *Total Prizemoney* £530
1998 Turf 0-3: (8f, 9f, 11f) (gd 2, g-f)
Scopey, average colt. Turf high 66 - 3rd of 6 to Porto Foricos (21 May Goodwood 9f g-f RF 1360).
**E A L Dunlop [0-4] Maktoum Al Maktoum.*

NATIVE JUSTICE (USA) RR 112f 4717a[4]
3 f Alleged (USA) 11.8f **(81)** - Fabulous Native (USA) (Le Fabuleux) 11.4f **(76)**
Form - 44
1998 Turf 0-2: (12f, 13f) (hvy, sft)
Currently Group-class filly. Turf high 112 (1st run) (began Spt) - 4th of 11 to Leggera (13 Spt Longchamp 12f hvy RF 4343a). She went from a Class E event in the provinces to finish fourth in the Group One Prix Vermeille at Longchamp. Given time, this filly could make her mark at the highest level.
**A Fabre in FR [0-2] K Abdulla.*

NATIVE QUEST RR 2322[7]
2 b c Alhijaz 7.7f **(57)** - Adana (FR) (Green Dancer (USA)) 10.3f **(74)**
Form - 07
Record 1998 - 1st:0 2nd:0 3rd:0 Ran:2
1998 AW 0-2: (6f, 7f) (Fibr 2)
Currently poor colt. AW high 13.
**N P Littmoden [0-2] Superfoods Plus.*

NATTIE BHB 31f39a **RR 43?f 39a** 404[12]
4 b g Almoojid 7f **(36)** - Defy Me (Bustino) 10.4f **(64)**
Form - 30
Record 1998 - 1st:0 2nd:0 3rd:1 Ran:2
Pre1998 - 1st:0 2nd:0 3rd:1 Ran:7
Win Prizemoney £0 *Total Prizemoney* £902
1998 AW 0-2: (7f, 12f) (Fibr 2)
Unfurnished, moderate gelding, has worn blinkers. AW high 15. Becoming disappointing.
**A Barrow [0-3] Duckhaven Stud (from C J Hill [0-1] Spt 1997).*

NATURAL EIGHT (IRE) BHB 63f **RR 62f** 4314[17]
4 b g In The Wings 11.2f **(77)** - Fenny Rough (Home Guard (USA)) 9.3f **(66)**
Form - 700
Record 1998 - 1st:0 2nd:0 3rd:0 Ran:3
Pre1998 - 1st:0 2nd:1 3rd:2 Ran:5
Win Prizemoney £0 *Total Prizemoney* £2,631
1998 Turf 0-3: (10f 3) (gd 3)
Neat, average gelding, effective 10f, acts on frm. Turf high 62. Becoming disappointing.
**R W Armstrong [0-4] Mrs Melody Siu (from B W Hills [0-4] May 1997).*

NATURAL KEY BHB 65f **RR 62f** 2756[8]
5 ch m Safawan 6.6f **(60)** - No Sharps Or Flats (USA) (Sharpen Up) 8.3f **(67)**
Form - 86018
Record 1998 - 1st:1 2nd:0 3rd:0 Ran:5
Pre1998 - 1st:7 2nd:4 3rd:3 Ran:32
Win Prizemoney £30,035 *Total Prizemoney* £37,201

Wins								
* **1998**	Jly	Hamilt	(FRM)	H	6f	60	62	
* 1997	Aug	Hamilt	(GD)	H	6f	65	66	
* 1996	Spt	Hamilt	(GD)	H	5f	65	68	
* 1996	Spt	Hamilt	(GD)	H	6f	60	61	
* 1996	Aug	Hamilt	(G-F)	H	6f	56	55	
* 1996	Jly	Hamilt	(G-F)	S	6f		49	
1995	Jly	Chepst	(G-F)	C	6.1f		64+	
1995	Jun	Ripon	(FRM)		5f		74	<

1998 Turf 1-5: (5f 3, 6f 1-2) (gd 3, frm 1-2)
Average filly, effective 5 to 7f, acts on g-f to frm, best on g-f, has worn blinkers. Turf high 62. A winner six times at Hamilton, the latest in July.
**D HaydnJones [6-34] Hugh O'Donnell (from Sir Mark Prescott [2-3] Jly 1995).*

NATURAL PEARL RR 54f 5063[12]
2 gr f Petong 7.6f **(58)** - Petriece (Mummy's Pet) 7.7f **(60)**
Form - 0
Record 1998 - 1st:0 2nd:0 3rd:0 Ran:1
1998 Turf 0-1: (6f) (g-f)
Currently fair filly. **C F Wall [0-1] Hintlesham Racing.*

NAUGHTY BLUE (USA) BHB 95f **RR 99f** 4617[12]
3 b c Danehill (USA) 9.1f **(79)** - Blue Note (FR) (Habitat) 9.4f **(70)**
Form - 0
Record 1998 - 1st:0 2nd:0 3rd:0 Ran:1
Pre1998 - 1st:1 2nd:0 3rd:0 Ran:3
Win Prizemoney £3,915 *Total Prizemoney* £5,525
Wins 1997 Spt Yarmou (FRM) 7f 85+ <
1998 Turf 0-1: (7f) (gd)
Rangy, very useful colt.
**J H M Gosden [0-1] Sheikh Mohammed (from S bin Suroor [1-3] Oct 1997).*

NAUGHTY CROWN (USA) RR 83f 5000[4]
2 b f Chief's Crown (USA) 10.2f **(75)** - Native Twine (Be My Native (USA)) 10.2f **(71)**
Form - 34
Record 1998 - 1st:0 2nd:0 3rd:1 Ran:2
Win Prizemoney £0 *Total Prizemoney* £689
1998 Turf 0-2: (7f, 8f) (sft, g-s)
Currently decent filly. Turf high 83 (1st run) (began Oct) - 3rd of 10 to Kristina (6 Oct Nottingham 8f g-s RF 4664).
**P F I Cole [0-2] G J Beck.*

NAUPLIE (BEL) BHB 10f **RR** 4955[16]
4 b f Commonwelsh - Charred (BEL) (Red Steps (USA))
Form - 000
Record 1998 - 1st:0 2nd:0 3rd:0 Ran:3
1998 Turf 0-3: (7f, 12f 2) (gd, g-f, frm)

Currently very poor filly. (began Oct). **J J Bridger [0-3] K J Walls.*

NAUTICAL STAR BHB 93f RR 94f 3984[1]

3 b c Slip Anchor 12.7f **(75)** - Comic Talent (Pharly (FR)) 9.8f **(68)**
Form - 140331
Record 1998 - 1st:2 2nd:0 3rd:2 Ran:6
Pre1998 - 1st:1 2nd:0 3rd:0 Ran:3
Win Prizemoney £20,257 *Total Prizemoney* £23,520
Wins * **1998** Aug Epsom (G-F) H 12f 89 94 <
* **1998** Apr Newmar (SFT) H 10f 83 91
* 1997 Aug Ayr (G-F) 7f 80+
1998 Turf 2-6: (10f 1-4, 12f 1-2) (g-s, gd 1-3, g-f 1-2)
Scopey, useful colt, effective 10 to 12f, best at 10f, acts on gd to g-f, best on gd, has worn blinkers. Turf high 94 - 1st of 11 giving 21lb to Opera Buff (31 Aug Epsom RF 3984) - also 1st of 11 getting 1lb from Noble Demand (16 Apr Newmarket RF 0708). Won a handicap on soft ground at Newmarket on his first start of the year, and landed the Moet & Chandon Silver Magnum on his last. He put in some fair efforts in decent handicap company in between. Game and genuine. **J W Hills [3-9] Michael Wauchope.*

NAUTICAL WARNING BHB 54f61a RR 57f 61a 4775[11]

3 b c Warning 8.1f **(77)** - Night At Sea (Night Shift (USA)) 7.2f **(69)**
Form - 150400
Record 1998 - 1st:1 2nd:0 3rd:0 Ran:6
Pre1998 - 1st:0 2nd:0 3rd:0 Ran:4
Win Prizemoney £2,274 *Total Prizemoney* £2,524
Wins * **1998** *Jan Lingfi (STD) H 7f 57 63* <
1998 Turf 0-4: (7f 3, 8f) (gd 2, g-f, frm) 1998 AW 1-2: (7f 1-2) (Equi 1-1, Fibr)
Strong, average colt, effective 7f, - acts on Equi. Turf high 57. AW high 63 (1st run) - 1st of 10 getting 8lb from Missed The Cut (20 Jan Lingfield RF 0119). He became the first winner trained by Jeremy Noseda when winning a modest apprentice handicap on the Lingfield Equitrack in January.
**J Noseda [1-6] B Schmidt-Bodner (from M H Tompkins [0-4] Nov 1997).*

NAUTIKER (GER) RR 106f 4214a[6]

7 h
Form - 6
1998 Turf 0-1: (6f) (gd)
Pattern-class horse. **P Remmert in GER [1-5].*

NAVAL GAMES BHB 51f46a RR 48f 46a 1114[7]

5 b g Slip Anchor 12.7f **(75)** - Plaything (High Top) 10.2f **(67)**
Form - 6500867
Record 1998 - 1st:0 2nd:0 3rd:0 Ran:3
Pre1998 - 1st:0 2nd:1 3rd:0 Ran:7
Win Prizemoney £0 *Total Prizemoney* £1,086
1998 Turf 0-3: (10f 2, 11f) (sft, g-f, frm)
Moderate gelding, effective 12f, acted on gd to g-f. Turf high 48. (DEAD) **J M Bradley [0-7] S G Martin (from M C Pipe [0-1] Oct 1997).*

NAVIASKY (IRE) BHB 66f RR 69f 4381[11]

3 b br g Scenic 10.6f **(66)** - Black Molly (IRE) (High Top) 10.2f **(67)**
Form - 007441332850
Record 1998 - 1st:1 2nd:1 3rd:2 Ran:12
Pre1998 - 1st:1 2nd:0 3rd:0 Ran:8
Win Prizemoney £6,352 *Total Prizemoney* £11,760
Wins 1998 Jun Carlis (G-S) H 8f 60 66
1997 Aug Thirsk (G-F) 5f 79+ <
1998 Turf 1-12: (7f 2, 8f 1-9, 10f) (g-s, gd 1-4, g-f 4, frm 3)
Strong, average gelding, effective 5f, acts on g-f. Turf high 69. Consistent.
**W R Muir [0-1] Perspicacious Punters Racing Club (from Mrs J R Ramsden [2-19] Aug 1998).*

NAYIB BHB 47f RR 40f 2270[13]

5 b g Bustino 11f **(64)** - Nicholas Grey (Track Spare) 8.8f **(62)**
Form - 40
Record 1998 - 1st:0 2nd:0 3rd:0 Ran:2
Pre1998 - 1st:0 2nd:1 3rd:0 Ran:3
Win Prizemoney £0 *Total Prizemoney* £1,124
1998 Turf 0-2: (13f, 16f) (g-s, gd)
Moderate gelding. Turf high 40.
**J I A Charlton [0-2] J I A Charlton (from D Morley [0-3] Jun 1996).*

NEBL BHB 73f RR 67f 4660[14]

3 ch f Persian Bold 10f **(69)** - Maraatib (IRE) (Green Desert (USA)) 8.6f **(78)**
Form - 00
Record 1998 - 1st:0 2nd:0 3rd:0 Ran:2
Pre1998 - 1st:1 2nd:0 3rd:1 Ran:3
Win Prizemoney £3,225 *Total Prizemoney* £3,694
Wins 1997 Spt Sandow (G-F) 8.1f 91 <
1998 Turf 0-2: (8f 2) (gd, g-f)
Workmanlike, average filly. Turf high 51 (began Spt).
**M P Tregoning [0-2] Hamdan Al Maktoum (from Major W R Hern [1-3] Oct 1997).*

NEBRANGUS (IRE) BHB 18f21a RR 14f 21a 3504[11]

6 ch g Nashamaa 8.1f **(58)** - Choral Park (Music Boy) 6.8f **(57)**
Form - 080
Record 1998 - 1st:0 2nd:0 3rd:0 Ran:3
Pre1998 - 1st:0 2nd:0 3rd:0 Ran:16
1998 Turf 0-3: (8f, 14f, 16f) (gd, frm 2)
Poor gelding, has worn blinkers. Turf high 14 (began Jly).
**N Bycroft [0-23] Bernard Rayner.*

NEBUCHADNEZZAR BHB 45f RR 32f 504[11]

3 gr g Absalom 7.1f **(56)** - Golden Decoy (Decoy Boy) 6.7f **(56)**
Form - 0
Record 1998 - 1st:0 2nd:0 3rd:0 Ran:1
Pre1998 - 1st:0 2nd:0 3rd:0 Ran:3
1998 Turf 0-1: (12f) (sft)
Workmanlike, very moderate gelding.
**J J O'Neill [0-4] Miss G Joughin.*

NEDAWI BHB 117f RR 117f 4240[1]

3 ch c Rainbow Quest (USA) 11.2f **(81)** - Wajd (USA) (Northern Dancer) 9.6f **(80)**
Form - 1311
Record 1998 - 1st:3 2nd:0 3rd:1 Ran:4
Win Prizemoney £221,990 *Total Prizemoney* £223,605
Wins * **1998** Spt Doncas (GD) G1 14.6f 117 <
* **1998** Jly Goodwo (GD) G3 12f 114
* **1998** Jun Goodwo (G-F) 12f 90+
1998 Turf 3-4: (12f 2-3, 15f 1-1) (gd 1-1, g-f 1-2, frm 1-1)
Scopey, high-class colt. Turf high 117 - 1st of 9 giving 3lb to High And Low (12 Spt Doncaster RF 4240) - also 1st of 6 from Rabah (28 Jly Goodwood RF 3162). Unraced at two, he turned a Goodwood maiden into a procession on his debut, and was a keeping-on third in a Haydock Listed race next time. He returned to winning form when dead-heating with Rabah in the Gordon Stakes, and gained his biggest moment when winning the St Leger, despite being hampered and running green. For a classic, it was a modest race, but he showed a bright turn of foot and looks sure to make his mark at the top level in 1999. **S bin Suroor [3-4] Godolphin.*

NEEDLE MATCH BHB 51f60a RR 54f 60a 4936[15]

5 ch g Royal Academy (USA) 7.8f **(77)** - Miss Tatting (USA) (Miswaki (USA)) 9f **(81)**
Form - 5000
Record 1998 - 1st:0 2nd:0 3rd:0 Ran:4
Pre1998 - 1st:3 2nd:2 3rd:4 Ran:27
Win Prizemoney £7,357 *Total Prizemoney* £10,894
Wins * 1997 Aug Carlis (FRM) 6.9f 66 <
* 1997 *Mar Southw (STD) H 6f 60 61*
* 1997 *Feb Wolver (STD) H 6f 53 56*
1998 Turf 0-1: (8f) (gd) 1998 AW 0-3: (7f, 8f 2) (Fibr 3)
Fair gelding, effective 6 to 8f, best at 7f, acts on g-f to frm - acts on Fibr, has worn blinkers, likes left handed tracks, prefers tight tracks, does well at Southwell. AW high 59 (1st run) - 5th of 12 giving 17lb to Pleasure Trick (12 Jan Southwell 7f Fibr RF 0070). Becoming disappointing.
**J J O'Neill [3-27] Clayton Bigley Partnership Ltd (from C F Wall [0-8] Spt 1996).*

NEED SOME SPACE BHB 19f RR 9f 3647[18]

3 br f Precocious 7.2f **(54)** - Time for Joy (Good Times (ITY)) 6.6f **(54)**
Form - 0700000
Record 1998 - 1st:0 2nd:0 3rd:0 Ran:7
1998 Turf 0-5: (5f 2, 6f 3) (sft, gd 2, frm, hrd) 1998 AW 0-2: (5f, 6f) (Equi, Fibr)

Workmanlike, very poor filly, has worn blinkers. Turf high 9.
**J M Bradley [0-7] Accomodation UK Ltd.*

NEEDWOOD LEGEND BHB 30f28a **RR 27f 28a** 3611[5]

5 b br g Rolfe (USA) 11.2f **(46)** - Enchanting Kate (Enchantment) 5.4f **(52)**
Form - 040055
Record 1998 - 1st:0 2nd:0 3rd:0 Ran:5
Pre1998 - 1st:0 2nd:0 3rd:0 Ran:6
1998 Turf 0-2: (12f 2) (frm 2) 1998 AW 0-3: (10f, 12f 2) (Equi, Fibr 2)
Little account gelding, has worn blinkers. Turf high 27 (began Jly). AW high 29. Inconsistent.
**A J Wilson [0-3] Mrs M J Wilson (from B C Morgan [0-8] Jan 1998).*

NEEDWOOD MERLIN BHB 61f **RR 57f** 4357[8]

2 b c Sizzling Melody 6.3f **(49)**-Enchanting Kate(Enchantment) 5.4f **(52)**
Form - 8858
Record 1998 - 1st:0 2nd:0 3rd:0 Ran:4
1998 Turf 0-3: (6f, 7f 2) (g-f, frm 2) 1998 AW 0-1: (6f) (Fibr)
Fair colt. Turf high 57 (began Aug).
**B C Morgan [0-4] Needwood Racing Ltd.*

NEEDWOOD MINSTREL BHB 59f **RR 66df** 4868[16]

2 b c Clantime 6.6f **(57)** - Azubah **(29a)** (Castle Keep) 8.3f **(57)**
Form - 0560
Record 1998 - 1st:0 2nd:0 3rd:0 Ran:4
1998 Turf 0-4: (5f, 6f 3) (gd, g-f, frm 2)
Average colt. Turf high 66 (began Spt).
**B C Morgan [0-4] Needwood Racing Ltd.*

NEEDWOOD MYSTIC BHB 53f **RR 66f** 4939[14]

3 b f Rolfe (USA) 11.2f **(46)** - Enchanting Kate (Enchantment) 5.4f **(52)**
Form - 574000
Record 1998 - 1st:0 2nd:0 3rd:0 Ran:6
Win Prizemoney £0 *Total Prizemoney* £260
1998 Turf 0-6: (8f, 10f 2, 11f 2, 12f) (sft, gd, g-f 2, frm 2)
Small, average filly, effective 8f, acts on frm. Turf high 66 (began Aug). **B C Morgan [0-6] Needwood Racing Ltd.*

NEEDWOOD NUTKIN BHB 34f32a **RR 44df 32a** 828[3]

5 b m Rolfe (USA) 11.2f **(46)** - Needwood Nut (Royben) 7.3f **(60)**
Form - 3
Record 1998 - 1st:0 2nd:0 3rd:1 Ran:1
Pre1998 - 1st:0 2nd:0 3rd:2 Ran:9
Win Prizemoney £0 *Total Prizemoney* £1,336
1998 Turf 0-1: (10f) (g-s)
Moderate filly, effective 10 to 12f, acts on g-s to frm. (1st run) - 3rd of 15 getting 19lb from Tycoon Tina (23 Apr Beverley 10f g-s RF 0828). **B C Morgan [0-16] Gromit Racing.*

NEEDWOOD SPIRIT BHB 60f55a **RR 64f 55a** 4839[1]

3 b c Rolfe (USA) 11.2f **(46)** - Needwood Nymph (Bold Owl) 8.5f **(45)**
Form - 4477365441
Record 1998 - 1st:1 2nd:0 3rd:1 Ran:10
Pre1998 - 1st:0 2nd:0 3rd:0 Ran:2
Win Prizemoney £2,845 *Total Prizemoney* £4,339
Wins * 1998 Oct Catter (SFT) 13.8f 61 <
1998 Turf 1-9: (8f, 10f 2, 11f, 12f 4, 14f 1-1) (g-s 1-5, gd, g-f, frm 2)
1998 AW 0-1: (15f) (Fibr)
Leggy, average colt, has worn blinkers, likes tight tracks. Turf high 71. Consistent. **B C Morgan [1-12] Needwood Racing Ltd.*

NEEDWOOD SPITFIRE BHB 45f **RR 42f** 4625[3]

3 b f Rolfe (USA) 11.2f **(46)** - Lime Brook (Rapid River) 5.7f **(51)**
Form - 00533
Record 1998 - 1st:0 2nd:0 3rd:2 Ran:5
Pre1998 - 1st:0 2nd:0 3rd:0 Ran:2
Win Prizemoney £0 *Total Prizemoney* £954
1998 Turf 0-4: (7f, 11f, 12f, 14f) (gd, g-f, frm 2) 1998 AW 0-1: (8f) (Fibr)
Light-framed, moderate filly, effective 12 to 14f, acts on g-f to frm. Turf high 42. **B C Morgan [0-7] Needwood Racing Ltd.*

NEIGES ETERNELLES (FR) **RR 98f** 4717a[7]

3 b f Exit To Nowhere (USA) 8.7f **(77)**-Nabita (FR) (Akarad (FR)) 9f **(76)**
Form - 37
1998 Turf 0-2: (13f 2) (sft, gd)
Currently very useful filly. Turf high 98 (began Aug).
**H-A Pantall in FR [0-2] Mrs M Pollard-Gill.*

NELLIE NORTH BHB 32f **RR 34f** 3844[11]

5 b m Northern State (USA) 12.6f **(45)** - Kimble Princess (Kala Shikari) 8.4f **(54)**
Form - 0003064734780
Record 1998 - 1st:0 2nd:0 3rd:2 Ran:13
Pre1998 - 1st:1 2nd:3 3rd:5 Ran:29
Win Prizemoney £3,647 *Total Prizemoney* £10,492
Wins 1995 Jly Windso (G-F) 5f 75 <
1998 Turf 0-13: (5f 7, 6f 6) (sft, g-f, frm 9, hrd 2)
Very moderate filly, effective 5 to 6f, acts on g-f to frm, often wears blinkers. Turf high 34. Consistent.
**A J Chamberlain [0-13] The Old Biddies (from G M McCourt [0-20] Spt 1997).*

NERO TIROL (IRE) **RR 80f** 2417a[18]

2 b br c Tirol 8.1f **(64)** - Saltoki (Ballad Rock) 7.8f **(63)**
Form - 450
Record 1998 - 1st:0 2nd:0 3rd:0 Ran:3
Win Prizemoney £0 *Total Prizemoney* £230
1998 Turf 0-3: (5f, 6f 2) (g-s, gd, g-f)
Currently decent colt, has worn blinkers. Turf high 80.
**A Kelleway [0-3] Osvaldo Pedroni & P A Kelleway.*

NERVOUS REX BHB 59f49a **RR 61f 49a** 4401[9]

4 b g Reprimand 8.2f **(63)** - Spinner (Blue Cashmere) 6.4f **(54)**
Form - 01010030
Record 1998 - 1st:2 2nd:0 3rd:1 Ran:8
Pre1998 - 1st:1 2nd:2 3rd:1 Ran:20
Win Prizemoney £8,305 *Total Prizemoney* £11,976
Wins * 1998 Jly Haydoc (G-S) H 7.1f 55 58 <
*** 1998** Jun Leices (GD) SH 6f 50 53
1997 Jun Carlis (FRM) S 5.9f 55
1998 Turf 2-8: (5f, 6f 1-4, 7f 1-3) (g-s, gd 2, frm 2-5)
Scopey, average gelding, effective 6 to 7f, best at 7f, acts on g-f to frm, best on frm, has worn blinkers, prefers right handed tracks, excels at Carlisle. Turf high 61 - 3rd of 13 to Salty Behaviour (13 Aug Chepstow 7f frm RF 3609) - also 1st of 14 giving 13lb to Gablesea (2 Jly Haydock RF 2468).
**D Nicholls [2-8] First Past The Post (from W R Muir [1-20] Oct 1997).*

NESSUN DORO BHB 61f55a **RR 65f 55a** 2166[8]

6 b g Hallgate 6.8f **(54)** - Bamdoro (Cavo Doro) 10.6f **(57)**
Form - 18
Record 1998 - 1st:1 2nd:0 3rd:0 Ran:2
Pre1998 - 1st:0 2nd:1 3rd:0 Ran:7
Win Prizemoney £2,433 *Total Prizemoney* £3,681
Wins * 1998 *Jan Southw (STD) 12f 56+* <
1998 AW 1-2: (12f 1-2) (Fibr 1-2)
Average gelding, has worn blinkers. AW high 56 (1st run) - 1st of 7 from Specialize (26 Jan Southwell RF 0159).
**S Mellor [4-24] Paul Porter & Partners.*

NETHERHALL BHB 39f **RR 40f** 4762[15]

2 ch c Rudimentary (USA) 8.2f **(66)** - Legal Precedent (Star Appeal) 9.6f **(65)**
Form - 00700
Record 1998 - 1st:0 2nd:0 3rd:0 Ran:5
1998 Turf 0-5: (5f, 6f 2, 7f, 10f) (gd 2, frm 3)
Moderate colt. Turf high 38. **M G Meagher [0-5] M R Johnson.*

NETTA RUFINA (IRE) BHB 75f79a **RR 74f 79a** 4154[10]

3 ch c Night Shift (USA) 8.1f **(73)** - Age of Elegance (Troy) 10.4f **(68)**
Form - 0412605512240
Record 1998 - 1st:2 2nd:3 3rd:0 Ran:13
Win Prizemoney £6,346 *Total Prizemoney* £10,318
Wins * 1998 Aug Ripon (GD) H 12.3f 65 70
*** 1998** *Feb Lingfi (SLW) 10f 74* <
1998 Turf 1-9: (10f, 12f 1-2, 13f 2, 14f 2, 16f 2) (g-s, gd 1-4, g-f 2, frm 2)
1998 AW 1-4: (8f 2, 9f, 10f 1-1) (Equi 1-2, Fibr 2)
Above-average colt, effective 9 to 16f, acts on gd to g-f - acts on AW, favours tight tracks, excels at Musselburgh. Turf high 74 - 2nd of 6 giving 7lb to Charity Crusader (19 Aug Musselburgh 16f gd RF 3748) - also 1st of 10 giving 2lb to Augustan (3 Aug Ripon RF 3310). AW high 78 - 2nd of 4 giving 4lb to Prince Ashleigh (25 Feb Wolverhampton 9f Fibr RF 0362) - also 1st of 6 from Narrogin (7

Feb Lingfield RF 0239). **M Johnston [2-13] Miss Belinda Lee.*

NEUWEST (USA) BHB 94f95a **RR 67f 95a** 4617[11]

6 b h Gone West (USA) 7.8f **(82)** - White Mischief (Dance In Time (CAN)) 8.9f **(59)**

Form - 00

Record	**1998** -	1st:0	2nd:0	3rd:0	Ran:2
	Pre1998 -	1st:6	2nd:6	3rd:2	Ran:27

Win Prizemoney £43,911 *Total Prizemoney* £54,954

Wins								
1997	Aug	Newmar	(G-F)	H	7f	92	97	<
1997	Jun	Newbur	(GD)	H	7f	85	92+	
1996	Aug	Lingfi	(G-F)		7f		85	
1996	Jun	Folkes	(FRM)	H	6.9f	78	83+	
1996	May	Lingfi	(G-F)	H	7f	73	76	
1995	Oct	Yarmou	(G-F)		8f		69	

1998 Turf 0-2: (7f 2) (g-s, gd)

Above-average horse, effective 7f, acts on frm. Turf high 67 (began Spt). Becoming disappointing.

**J Akehurst [0-2] Paul Green (from R Akehurst [2-5] Spt 1997).*

NEVER CAN TELL BHB 79f **RR 77f** 4703[13]

2 ch g Emarati (USA) 6.6f **(63)**-Farmer's Pet (Sharrood(USA))10.5f **(72)**

Form - 70420

Record	**1998** -	1st:0	2nd:1	3rd:0	Ran:5

Win Prizemoney £0 *Total Prizemoney* £1,897

1998 Turf 0-5: (6f 4, 7f) (sft, gd 2, g-f, hrd)

Above-average gelding. Turf high 77 - 2nd of 16 getting 2lb from Alastair Smellie (18 Spt Ayr 6f sft RF 4349). A pacey sort, he is up to winning a race or two. **J G FitzGerald [0-5] J Dick.*

NEVER THINK TWICE BHB 48f45a **RR 50f 45a** 1831[10]

5 b g Never so Bold 7.1f **(62)** - Hope and Glory (USA) (Well Decorated (USA)) 7.6f **(64)**

Form - 8748880

Record	**1998** -	1st:0	2nd:0	3rd:0	Ran:7
	Pre1998 -	1st:2	2nd:8	3rd:3	Ran:38

Win Prizemoney £6,141 *Total Prizemoney* £14,949

Wins								
1996	Aug	Folkes	(G-F)	H	6f	57	67	<
1996	Jly	Windso	(G-F)	H	6f	47	59	

1998 Turf 0-2: (6f, 7f) (gd, g-f) 1998 AW 0-5: (6f, 7f, 8f, 9f, 10f) (Equi 3, Fibr 2)

Fair gelding, effective 6 to 7f, acts on gd - acts on Equi, mostly wears blinkers. Turf high 50. AW high 51.

**P S McEntee [0-1] R J Lorenz (from P M McEntee [0-1] May 1998).*

NEW ABBEY **RR 72+f** 1001[1]

3 b f Sadler's Wells (USA) 11.3f **(87)** - Bahamian (Mill Reef (USA)) 10.5f **(78)**

Form - 1

Record	**1998** -	1st:1	2nd:0	3rd:0	Ran:1

Win Prizemoney £3,517 *Total Prizemoney* £3,517

Wins								
* **1998**	May	Salisb	(G-S)		12f		72	<

1998 Turf 1-1: (12f 1-1) (gd 1-1)

Well made, currently above-average filly. (1st run) - 1st of 11 getting 5lb from Churlish Charm (3 May Salisbury RF 1001). Beautifully bred, she was an odds-on shot when making a successful debut. Likely to improve with time, inexperience is her biggest enemy at this stage. **H R A Cecil [1-1] K Abdulla.*

NEWALA BHB 56f **RR 59f** 4961[12]

3 b f Royal Academy (USA) 7.8f **(77)** - African Dance (USA) (El Gran Senor (USA)) 9.6f **(76)**

Form - 620020

Record	**1998** -	1st:0	2nd:2	3rd:0	Ran:5
	Pre1998 -	1st:0	2nd:0	3rd:0	Ran:3

Win Prizemoney £0 *Total Prizemoney* £1,894

1998 Turf 0-5: (7f 3, 8f 2) (gd, frm 4)

Light-framed, fair filly, effective 7 to 8f, acts on frm. Turf high 59 (1st run) (began Jly) - 2nd of 7 getting 7lb from Moonstone (1 Jly Yarmouth 7f frm RF 2458). **W J Haggas [0-8] J D Ashenheim.*

NEWBRIDGE BOY BHB 44f51a **RR 50f 51a** 933[9]

5 b g Bustino 11f **(64)** - Martyrdom (USA) (Exceller (USA)) 12.5f **(74)**

Form - 30

Record	**1998** -	1st:0	2nd:0	3rd:0	Ran:1
	Pre1998 -	1st:1	2nd:2	3rd:1	Ran:16

Win Prizemoney £2,381 *Total Prizemoney* £4,584

Wins								
* 1996	*Jly*	*Wolver*	*(STD)*	*H*	*12f*	*52*	*57*	*<*

1998 Turf 0-1: (11f) (sft)

Fair gelding, effective 10f, acts on frm - acts on Equi. Inconsistent.

**M G Meagher [1-23] Alan Draper.*

NEW CAPRICORN (USA) BHB 49f **RR 48f** 5014[8]

8 ch g Green Forest (USA) 7.4f **(73)** - Size Six (USA) (Caerleon (USA)) 8.6f **(71)**

Form - 06058

Record	**1998** -	1st:0	2nd:0	3rd:0	Ran:5
	Pre1998 -	1st:5	2nd:3	3rd:4	Ran:28

Win Prizemoney £36,458 *Total Prizemoney* £51,074

Wins								
1994	May	Capann	(GD)	L	7f		97	<
1994	Apr	Bright	(GD)	H	7f	90	90	

1998 Turf 0-5: (6f, 7f 4) (sft 2, gd, g-f, hrd)

Moderate gelding, has worn blinkers. Turf high 48 (began Aug). Becoming disappointing.

**C Parker [0-8] & Mrs Raymond Anderson Green (from M A Jarvis [5-28] Jly 1995).*

NEWGATE NOBLESSE BHB 20f **RR 8?f** 4371[12]

3 b f Noble Patriarch 12.2f **(43)** - Mummys Colleen (Mummy's Pet) 7.7f **(60)**

Form - 00

Record	**1998** -	1st:0	2nd:0	3rd:0	Ran:2
	Pre1998 -	1st:0	2nd:0	3rd:0	Ran:3

1998 Turf 0-2: (10f, 14f) (g-f, frm)

Scopey, very poor filly. (began Aug) - 12th of 13 to Sweet Serenata (19 Spt Catterick 14f frm RF 4371).

**B W Murray [0-5] W P S Johnson.*

NEWHARGEN (IRE) BHB 33f **RR 34f** 2686[9]

3 b g Astronef 7.9f **(59)** - Brandywell (Skyliner) 7.3f **(53)**

Form - 00854680

Record	**1998** -	1st:0	2nd:0	3rd:0	Ran:8
	Pre1998 -	1st:0	2nd:1	3rd:0	Ran:9

Win Prizemoney £0 *Total Prizemoney* £835

1998 Turf 0-7: (5f 5, 6f 2) (g-s, gd 2, g-f, frm 3) 1998 AW 0-1: (5f) (Equi)

Light-framed, very moderate gelding, effective 6f, acts on frm, has worn blinkers. Turf high 34.

**M Quinn [0-8] Paul Green (Huyton) (from P D Evans [0-9] Aug 1997).*

NEWLANDS CORNER BHB 50f50a **RR 54f 50a** 5121[7]

5 b m Forzando 7.2f **(63)** - Nice Lady (Connaught) 7.7f **(63)**

Form - 377046000547

Record	**1998** -	1st:0	2nd:0	3rd:0	Ran:10
	Pre1998 -	1st:4	2nd:3	3rd:1	Ran:25

Win Prizemoney £11,461 *Total Prizemoney* £16,237

Wins								
* 1997	*Aug*	*Southw*	*(STD)*	*H*	*6f*	*54*	*58*	*<*
* 1996	Aug	Bright	(G-F)	H	6f	44	54	
* 1996	Aug	Salisb	(G-F)	CH	6f	44	47	
* 1996	Aug	Carlis	(FRM)	H	5.9f	39	40	

1998 Turf 0-8: (6f 8) (sft, g-s 3, gd, frm 3) 1998 AW 0-2: (6f, 7f) (Fibr 2)

Fair filly, effective 6 to 7f, best at 6f, acts on g-s to frm - acts on Fibr, mostly wears blinkers (very effectively), excels at Chepstow, does well at Leicester. Turf high 54 - 4th of 19 getting 26lb from Stand Tall (25 Oct Leicester 6f g-s RF 4988). AW high 33.

**J Akehurst [4-35] The Jolly Skolars.*

NEW MOON **RR 33f** 3996[8]

2 ch c Good Times (ITY) 8.7f **(53)**-Two Moons (Bold Lad(IRE)) 8.4f **(68)**

Form - 008

Record	**1998** -	1st:0	2nd:0	3rd:0	Ran:3

1998 Turf 0-3: (5f, 6f 2) (gd, g-f, frm)

Currently very moderate colt. Turf high 33 (began Jly).

**C W Thornton [0-3] Guy Reed.*

NEWTONS CORNER (IRE) BHB 37f **RR 33f** 90[8]

4 ch g Masterclass (USA) 5.9f **(63)** - Princess Galicia (Welsh Pageant) 10f **(65)**

Form - 8

Record	**1998** -	1st:0	2nd:0	3rd:0	Ran:1
	Pre1998 -	1st:0	2nd:0	3rd:0	Ran:3

1998 AW 0-1: (5f) (Fibr)

Workmanlike, very moderate gelding. **D Nicholls [0-4] Girls On Top.*

NEW YORKER (USA) BHB 57f60a **RR 60a** 4958[15]
3 ch c Gilded Time (USA) 7f **(76)** - Doris's Secret (USA) (Nikoli)
Form - 72260
Record 1998 - 1st:0 2nd:2 3rd:0 Ran:5
Win Prizemoney £0 *Total Prizemoney* £2,075
1998 Turf 0-1: (15f) (frm) 1998 AW 0-4: (10f, 12f 3) (Equi 3, Fibr)
Strong, average colt. AW high 64 - 2nd of 10 getting 21lb from Harik (12 Feb Lingfield 12f Equi RF 0271).
**Miss A Stokell [0-1] T J Ford (from P F I Cole [0-4] Mar 1998).*

NEXT ROUND (IRE) BHB 74f **RR 67f** 1219[6]
3 b f Common Grounds 8.1f **(66)** - Debbie's Next (USA) (Arctic Tern (USA)) 8.9f **(69)**
Form - 86
Record 1998 - 1st:0 2nd:0 3rd:0 Ran:2
Pre1998 - 1st:1 2nd:0 3rd:0 Ran:5
Win Prizemoney £3,694 *Total Prizemoney* £4,084
Wins * 1997 Jly Folkes (SFT) 6.9f 75 <
1998 Turf 0-2: (7f 2) (gd 2)
Light-framed, average filly, effective 7f, acts on gd. Turf high 67.
**M Bell [1-7] Deln Ltd.*

NGAERE PRINCESS BHB 30f **RR 29f** 3677[5]
3 br f Terimon 8.7f **(58)** - Zippy Zoe (Rousillon (USA)) 8.2f **(74)**
Form - 06580745
Record 1998 - 1st:0 2nd:0 3rd:0 Ran:8
Pre1998 - 1st:0 2nd:0 3rd:2 Ran:15
Win Prizemoney £0 *Total Prizemoney* £874
1998 Turf 0-8: (6f, 7f 2, 8f 2, 9f, 12f 2) (g-s 2, gd 4, g-f 2)
Unfurnished, little account filly, has worn blinkers. Turf high 40. Inconsistent. **W T Kemp [0-23] Drakemyre Racing.*

NIAGARO (GER) RR **101f** 4723a[5]
3
Form - 5
1998 Turf 0-1: (14f) (sft)
Currently very useful. (1st run) - 5th of 10 to Laveron (4 Oct Dortmund 14f sft RF 4723a). He was well beaten in a Group 2 at Dortmund in October and is not up to that class. **in GER [0-1].*

NICELY (IRE) BHB 79f **RR 73f** 5005[1]
2 gr f Bustino 11f **(64)** - Nichodoula (Doulab (USA)) 9.8f **(65)**
Form - 01
Record 1998 - 1st:1 2nd:0 3rd:0 Ran:2
Win Prizemoney £2,493 *Total Prizemoney* £2,493
Wins * **1998** Oct Bath (SFT) 8f 73 <
1998 Turf 1-2: (8f 1-2) (sft 1-1, g-f)
Currently above-average filly. Turf high 73 (began Oct) - 1st of 11 getting 5lb from Regal Philosopher (27 Oct Bath RF 5005).
**J W Hills [1-2] Mrs Claire Smith.*

NICE SPICE (IRE) BHB 40f **RR 41f** 4473[16]
2 b f Common Grounds 8.1f **(66)** - Your Village (IRE) (Be My Guest (USA)) 9.3f **(67)**
Form - 60700
Record 1998 - 1st:0 2nd:0 3rd:0 Ran:5
1998 Turf 0-5: (5f 2, 6f 2, 7f) (gd 2, g-f 2, frm)
Moderate filly. Turf high 41.
**G L Moore [0-1] A Moore (from R Hannon [0-4] Aug 1998).*

NICHOLAS MISTRESS BHB 61f55a **RR 62f 55a** 5117[2]
2 b f Beveled (USA) 6.9f **(64)** - Foreign Mistress (Darshaan) 9.9f **(84)**
Form - 253276452
Record 1998 - 1st:0 2nd:3 3rd:1 Ran:9
Win Prizemoney £0 *Total Prizemoney* £2,709
1998 Turf 0-9: (5f 7, 6f 2) (sft 2, gd, g-f 3, frm 3)
Average filly, effective 5f, acts on gd to frm, best on frm. Turf high 63 (1st run) (began Jly) - 2nd of 11 to Kilbowie Hill (16 Jly Leicester 5f frm RF 2853). **P D Evans [0-9] J E Abbey.*

NICHOL FIFTY BHB 71f **RR 76f** 4647[8]
4 b g Old Vic 12.8f **(72)**-Jawaher (IRE) (Dancing Brave (USA)) 8.4f **(76)**
Form - 8
Record 1998 - 1st:0 2nd:0 3rd:0 Ran:1
Pre1998 - 1st:2 2nd:1 3rd:1 Ran:10
Win Prizemoney £6,600 *Total Prizemoney* £9,002
Wins * 1997 Oct Leices (GD) 11.8f 73 <
* 1997 Jly Cheste (G-F) 12.3f 67
1998 Turf 0-1: (13f) (g-f)
Workmanlike, above-average gelding, effective 10 to 16f, acts on gd to frm, best on gd, favours tight tracks.
**M H Tompkins [3-14] Lloyd Bedack.*

NICKER BHB 24f31a **RR 31a** 4384[12]
4 b g Nicholas (USA) 6.1f **(63)** - Glimmer (Hot Spark) 7.6f **(62)**
Form - 70508000
Record 1998 - 1st:0 2nd:0 3rd:0 Ran:8
Pre1998 - 1st:0 2nd:1 3rd:1 Ran:7
Win Prizemoney £0 *Total Prizemoney* £1,399
1998 Turf 0-2:(10f, 16f) (frm 2)1998 AW 0-6: (8f, 9f 2, 12f 2, 15f)(Fibr 6)
Workmanlike, very poor gelding, effective 6 to 8f, acts on g-f to frm, has worn blinkers. AW high 35.
**M Waring [0-8] Dunstall Park Centre Ltd (from W Jarvis [0-7] Spt 1997).*

NICKLES BHB 72f **RR 77f** 4127[8]
3 b c Lugana Beach 7f **(63)** - Instinction (Never so Bold) 6.3f **(66)**
Form - 338
Record 1998 - 1st:0 2nd:0 3rd:2 Ran:3
Win Prizemoney £0 *Total Prizemoney* £1,073
1998 Turf 0-3: (5f 2, 6f) (g-s, g-f, frm)
Neat, currently above-average colt. Turf high 77 - 3rd of 10 giving 5lb to Jasmine (6 Jun Doncaster 5f g-f RF 1773).
**L G Cottrell [0-3] Ray Richards.*

NICOLA BELLA (IRE) RR **96f** 3719a[6]
3 b f Sadler's Wells (USA) 11.3f **(87)** - Valley Of Hope (USA) 00
Form - 22516P6
1998 Turf 1-7: (8f, 9f, 10f 1-4, 12f) (sft, gd 1-4, frm, hrd)
Very useful filly, effective 10f, acts on gd. Turf high 96 - also 1st of 9 getting 5lb from Battle On (10 Jly Gowran Park RF 2796a).
**J Oxx in IRE [1-7] Neil Jones.*

NICOLE PHARLY RR **107f** 1745[7]
4 b f Pharly (FR) 11.5f **(64)**-Debbie Harry (USA)(Alleged(USA)) 10f **(76)**
Form - 47
Record 1998 - 1st:0 2nd:0 3rd:0 Ran:2
Pre1998 - 1st:2 2nd:0 3rd:0 Ran:2
Win Prizemoney £191,118 *Total Prizemoney* £192,741
Wins 1997 May San Si (GD) G1 11f 97
1997 Apr Capann (GD) G2 8f 98 <
1998 Turf 0-2: (10f, 12f) (sft, gd)
Pattern-class filly. Turf high 107. She hates the stalls and became progressively temperamental as the season went on. One to leave alone.
**Sir Michael Stoute [0-2] M Nagashima (from A Verdesi in ITY [2-2] May 1997).*

NIFTY NORMAN BHB 57f **RR 47f** 4323[21]
4 b g Rock City 8.8f **(62)** - Nifty Fifty (IRE) (Runnett) 7f **(59)**
Form - 207807000
Record 1998 - 1st:0 2nd:1 3rd:0 Ran:9
Pre1998 - 1st:2 2nd:2 3rd:1 Ran:11
Win Prizemoney £8,943 *Total Prizemoney* £11,877
Wins * 1997 Jun Ayr (GD) H 5f 72 73
* 1997 May Beverl (HVY) 5f 82? <
1998 Turf 0-9: (5f 7, 6f 2) (sft 2, g-s 2, gd 3, g-f, frm)
Scopey, moderate gelding, effective 5 to 6f, best at 5f, acts on sft to gd. Turf high 73 (1st run) - 2nd of 12 giving 1lb to Arantxa (4 Apr Hamilton 6f sft RF 0560). Consistent. He ran well on heavy ground at Hamilton on his return, but does not seem to run two races alike and looks to have lost his way. **J Berry [2-20] Mrs Norma Peebles.*

NIGEL'S LAD (IRE) BHB 82f78a **RR 84f 78a** 4958[13]
6 b g Dominion Royale 7.8f **(63)**-Back To Earth (FR) (Vayrann) 9.7f **(74)**
Form - 1100
Record 1998 - 1st:2 2nd:0 3rd:0 Ran:4
Pre1998 - 1st:9 2nd:6 3rd:4 Ran:46
Win Prizemoney £44,994 *Total Prizemoney* £57,619
Wins * **1998** Jun Hamilt (SFT) H 13f 80 84
* **1998** May Ripon (GD) H 16f 75 76+
* 1997 Jun Pontef (G-F) H 17.1f 70 77+
* 1997 May Catter (G-F) H 15.8f 70 79
* 1997 May Ripon (G-F) H 16f 70 85

* 1995 Spt Newmar (GD) H 10f 79 87 <
* 1995 May Newcas (GD) H 8f 81 87 <
* 1995 May Hamilt (G-F) H 9.2f 70 75
* 1995 Apr Nottin (GD) 10f 72
* 1995 *Jan Lingfi (STD) H 10f 67 75*
* 1995 *Jan Lingfi (STD) H 10f 60 60*
1998 Turf 2-4: (13f 1-1, 14f, 15f, 16f 1-1) (g-s 1-1, gd, g-f 1-1, frm)
Decent gelding, effective 13 to 17f, best at 16f, acts on g-s to frm, likes right handed tracks, prefers tight tracks. Turf high 84 - 1st of 7 giving 32lb to Hill Farm Dancer (10 Jun Hamilton RF 1875) - also 1st of 10 giving 15lb to Astro Lines (27 May Ripon RF 1534). Inconsistent. Very smart on the Flat and over hurdles, he won his first two starts on the level, but ran below form on his last two after a three-month break. **P C Haslam [18-63] N C Dunnington.*

NIGHT AUCTION (IRE) BHB 49f52a **RR 60f 52a** 4811[17]
3 b f Night Shift (USA) 8.1f **(73)** - Maria Stuarda (Royal And Regal (USA)) 9.5f **(60)**
Form - 6501245000
Record 1998 - 1st:1 2nd:1 3rd:0 Ran:8
Pre1998 - 1st:0 2nd:0 3rd:0 Ran:7
Win Prizemoney £2,416 *Total Prizemoney* £3,381
Wins * **1998** Jly Redcar (G-S) C 6f 46 <
1998 Turf 1-8: (6f 1-7, 7f) (gd 1-3, g-f, frm 4)
Scopey, average filly, effective 6f, acts on frm. Turf high 60 - 2nd of 17 getting 9lb from Inchalong (20 Jly Windsor 6f frm RF 2963). Becoming disappointing. **B Palling [1-15] D Brennan.*

NIGHT CHORUS BHB 59f58a **RR 71f 58a** 4936[7]
4 b g Most Welcome 8.6f **(66)** - Choral Sundown (Night Shift (USA)) 7.2f **(69)**
Form - 7564133470007
Record 1998 - 1st:1 2nd:0 3rd:2 Ran:13
Pre1998 - 1st:1 2nd:2 3rd:1 Ran:14
Win Prizemoney £6,532 *Total Prizemoney* £12,943
Wins * **1998** Jun Mussel (SFT) H 8f 63 67
* 1997 Apr Nottin (GD) H 8.2f 67 73 <
1998 Turf 1-12: (7f, 8f 1-10, 9f) (g-s, gd 1-6, g-f, frm 4) 1998 AW 0-1: (9f) (Fibr)
Above-average gelding, effective 8 to 9f, best at 8f, acts on g-s to frm, best on gd, has worn blinkers, and excels at Hamilton. Turf high 71 - 3rd of 12 getting 8lb from Bollin Terry (25 Jly Newcastle 8f gd RF 3118) - also 1st of 6 giving 3lb to Broctune Gold (29 Jun Musselburgh RF 2374). **B S Rothwell [2-27] R M J MacNair.*

NIGHT CITY BHB 75f77a **RR 77f 77a** 5126[9]
7 b g Kris 10f **(75)** - Night Secret (Nijinsky (CAN)) 10.3f **(77)**
Form - 01331313617012211108110
Record 1998 - 1st:9 2nd:2 3rd:4 Ran:21
Pre1998 - 1st:4 2nd:3 3rd:0 Ran:25
Win Prizemoney £56,547 *Total Prizemoney* £66,914
Wins * **1998** Oct York (GD) C 10.4f 77
* **1998** Oct Bright (GD) C 11.9f 75
* **1998** Aug Lingfi (FRM) H 11.5f 70 77
* **1998** Aug Catter (GD) C 12f 66
* **1998** Jly Hamilt (FRM) C 12.1f 55
* **1998** May Thirsk (GD) C 12f 71
* **1998** Mar Hamilt (HVY) H 11.1f 65 75
* **1998** *Feb Lingfi (SLW) C 12f 75+*
* **1998** *Jan Lingfi (STD) C 12f 83+*
* 1997 *Dec Lingfi (STD) H 13f 70 73*
* 1997 *Nov Lingfi (STD) C 12f 68*
1996 May Newbur (SFT) H 9f 96 102 <
1995 Oct Chepst (SFT) 8.1f 84
1998 Turf 7-14: (10f 1-2, 11f 2-2, 12f 4-10) (sft 1-1, g-s 2, gd 2-3, g-f 2-5, frm 2-3) 1998 AW 2-7: (10f, 12f 2-5, 13f) (Equi 2-6, Fibr)
Decent gelding, effective 10 to 13f, best at 12f, acts on sft to frm - acts on Equi, has worn blinkers, excels at Lingfield, likes Hamilton. Turf high 77 - 1st of 15 from Minivet (8 Oct York RF 4708) - also 1st of 8 giving 13lb to Billaddie (26 Aug Lingfield RF 3894). AW high 83 - 1st of 4 giving 12lb to Chingachgook (20 Jan Lingfield RF 0121) - also 1st of 6 from Quiet Arch (19 Feb Lingfield RF 0313). He had been in the doldrums for quite a while, but won four times over middle-distances on the Lingfield Equitrack during the winter. Expertly placed to win nine times, he is a most effective sort when able to dominate, but has been known to sulk if crowded early on.
**K R Burke [11-31] Nigel Shields (from Lady Herries [2-16] May 1997).*

NIGHT DANCE BHB 56f60a **RR 57f 60a** 1614[10]
6 ch h Weldnaas (USA) 8.4f **(55)** - Shift Over (USA) (Night Shift (USA)) 7.2f **(69)**
Form - 080
Record 1998 - 1st:0 2nd:0 3rd:0 Ran:3
Pre1998 - 1st:5 2nd:2 3rd:1 Ran:25
Win Prizemoney £81,214 *Total Prizemoney* £86,066
Wins * 1997 Apr Beverl (G-F) 7.5f 78
1995 Oct Ascot (SFT) H 8f 90 97 <
1995 Spt Ascot (GD) H 7f 81 91
1995 Jly Sandow (GD) H 7.1f 76 79
1994 Jly Sandow (G-F) 7.1f 81+
1998 Turf 0-2: (8f 2) (g-f, frm) 1998 AW 0-1: (8f) (Fibr)
Fair horse, effective 7f, acts on frm. Turf high 52.
**K A Morgan [3-16] Racecourse Medical Officers Association (from G Lewis [4-19] Oct 1996).*

NIGHT DEVIL (GER) **RR 102?f** 4077a[3]
3 b c Nebos (GER) - Noble House (GER) (Siberian Express (USA)) 8.8f **(65)**
Form - 1003
1998 Turf 1-4: (8f 1-3, 12f) (hvy, sft 1-1, gd 2)
Very useful colt. Turf high 102 (1st run) - 1st of 9 from Adito (19 Apr Hoppegarten RF 0834a). He earned himself a crack at the German 2,000 Guineas when winning a Group Three in April, but flopped in the Classic and proved a disappointment.
**A Schutz in GER [1-4].*

NIGHT EXPRESS BHB 44f70a **RR 59df 70a** 3883[15]
4 ch g Night Shift (USA) 8.1f **(73)** -New Edition(Great Nephew) 9.9f **(64)**
Form - 0
Record 1998 - 1st:0 2nd:0 3rd:0 Ran:1
Pre1998 - 1st:0 2nd:1 3rd:3 Ran:13
Win Prizemoney £0 *Total Prizemoney* £3,108
1998 Turf 0-1: (7f) (gd)
Workmanlike, above-average gelding.
**Martin Todhunter [0-4] Barleylion Racing (from B Hanbury [0-13] Spt 1997).*

NIGHT FLIGHT BHB 80f **RR 80+f** 4799[18]
4 gr g Night Shift (USA) 8.1f **(73)** - Ancestry (Persepolis (FR)) 6.4f **(67)**
Form - 425160350030
Record 1998 - 1st:1 2nd:1 3rd:2 Ran:12
Pre1998 - 1st:1 2nd:2 3rd:3 Ran:14
Win Prizemoney £9,838 *Total Prizemoney* £19,034
Wins * **1998** Jun Newcas (GD) H 6f 71 80+
1997 Apr Pontef (GD) H 6f 72 82 <
1998 Turf 1-12: (5f 3, 6f 1-9) (sft 2, g-s, gd 1-5, g-f 2, frm 2)
Scopey, decent gelding, effective 5 to 6f, best at 6f, acts on gd to g-f, best on gd. Turf high 80 - 1st of 14 giving 17lb to Time To Tango (25 Jun Newcastle RF 2272).
**R A Fahey [1-12] C H Stevens (from J J O'Neill [1-14] Spt 1997).*

NIGHT FLYER BHB 73f **RR 77f** 4708[8]
3 b c Midyan (USA) 9.9f **(64)** - Scandalette (Niniski (USA)) 10.6f **(65)**
Form - 46207428
Record 1998 - 1st:0 2nd:2 3rd:0 Ran:8
Pre1998 - 1st:1 2nd:1 3rd:1 Ran:7
Win Prizemoney £8,325 *Total Prizemoney* £16,263
Wins * 1997 Aug Epsom (GD) H 7f 75 74 <
1998 Turf 0-8: (8f 7, 10f) (sft, gd, g-f 3, frm 3)
Unfurnished, above-average colt, effective 7 to 8f, best at 8f, acts on sft to frm, likes left handed tracks. Turf high 82 - 2nd of 5 to Khalas (28 May Ayr 8f g-f RF 1544). Consistent. Fourth in an Italian listed race on his 1998 debut, but has been exposed as ordinary in this country. **J W Hills [1-15] The Jampot Partnership.*

NIGHTGLADE (IRE) BHB 39f **RR 34f** 4301[11]
2 b c Night Shift (USA) 8.1f **(73)** - Woodland Garden (Godswalk (USA)) 7.3f **(58)**
Form - 000
Record 1998 - 1st:0 2nd:0 3rd:0 Ran:3
1998 Turf 0-3: (7f 2, 8f) (frm 3)
Currently very moderate colt. Turf high 33 (began Jly).
**M Brittain [0-3] Mel Brittain.*

NIGHTINGALE BHB 55f **RR 34f** 4584[7]
2 ro f Night Shift (USA) 8.1f **(73)** - Grey Angel (Kenmare (FR)) 6.5f **(72)**
Form - 007
Record 1998 - 1st:0 2nd:0 3rd:0 Ran:3
1998 Turf 0-3: (5f, 6f, 8f) (gd 2, frm)
Currently very moderate filly. Turf high 34.
**I A Balding [0-3] The Queen.*

NIGHTINGALE SONG BHB 46f65a **RR 46f 65a** 2559[19]
4 b f Tina's Pet 7.4f **(56)** - Songlines (Night Shift (USA)) 7.2f **(69)**
Form - 050
Record 1998 - 1st:0 2nd:0 3rd:0 Ran:3
Pre1998 - 1st:1 2nd:1 3rd:4 Ran:18
Win Prizemoney £2,332 *Total Prizemoney* £5,464
Wins * 1996 Jly Windso (GD) S 6f 63 <
1998 Turf 0-3: (5f 2, 6f) (g-f, frm 2)
Neat, average filly, effective 5 to 6f, best at 5f, acts on gd - acts on AW, prefers left handed tracks. Turf high 46.
**M Meade [1-21] Stephen Bayless.*

NIGHT LIFE (IRE) RR 60f 5144[10]
2 gr f Night Shift (USA) 8.1f **(73)** - Petula **(94f)** (Petong) 6.6f **(58)**
Form - 00010
Record 1998 - 1st:1 2nd:0 3rd:0 Ran:5
Win Prizemoney £3,054 *Total Prizemoney* £3,054
Wins * 1998 Oct Yarmou (SFT) H 5.2f 54 60 <
1998 Turf 1-5: (5f 1-4, 6f) (sft 1-1, g-s, gd 2, frm)
Average filly. Turf high 60 (began Spt) - 1st of 12 getting 9lb from Lively Lady (28 Oct Yarmouth RF 5042).
**M Bell [1-5] Mrs J M Corbett.*

NIGHT OF GLASS BHB 87f **RR 89f** 4985[8]
5 b g Mazilier (USA) 8.5f **(56)** - Donna Elvira (Chief Singer) 8.9f **(66)**
Form - 1111132033077831508
Record 1998 - 1st:6 2nd:1 3rd:4 Ran:19
Pre1998 - 1st:2 2nd:3 3rd:4 Ran:24
Win Prizemoney £34,549 *Total Prizemoney* £50,796

Wins	*** 1998**	Spt	Mussel	(GD)	H	7.1f	85	88	<
	*** 1998**	May	Beverl	(GD)	H	8.5f	84	87	
	*** 1998**	May	Thirsk	(GD)	H	7f	78	85	
	*** 1998**	Apr	Carlis	(G-S)	H	8f	68	79	
	*** 1998**	Apr	Thirsk	(G-S)	H	7f	68	74	
	*** 1998**	Apr	Catter	(GD)	H	7f	64	68	
	* 1997	Oct	Catter	(SFT)	H	7f	61	65	
	1996	Spt	Yarmou	(G-F)	H	8f	55	58	

1998 Turf 6-19:(7f 4-10, 8f 2-9)(sft, g-s 1-3, gd 3-5, g-f 1-3, frm 1-6, hrd)
Useful gelding, effective 7 to 8f, best at 7f, acts on sft to frm, best on frm, mostly wears blinkers (extremely effectively), likes left handed tracks, likes tight tracks, excels at Thirsk and Catterick. Turf high 89 - 3rd of 6 getting 7lb from Darnaway (16 May Newmarket 7f frm RF 1265) - also 1st of 13 giving 4lb to Smooth Sailing (27 Spt Musselburgh RF 4520). Consistent. He was in irresistible form at the start of the season, completing a nap hand of victories during April and May. The run came to an end in decent company at Newmarket, though he ran a fine race in defeat. Despite winning over a mile, his ideal conditions look to be seven furlongs on easy ground. The Handicapper has taken notice of his improvement, but he remains a credit to his trainer.
**J L Eyre [7-31] K Silvester and B Silvester (from D Morris [1-12] Nov 1996).*

NIGHT OWL BHB 65f **RR 67f** 4390[24]
3 b f Night Shift (USA) 8.1f **(73)**-Sarah Georgina(Persian Bold) 9.3f **(66)**
Form - 3550
Record 1998 - 1st:0 2nd:0 3rd:1 Ran:4
Pre1998 - 1st:0 2nd:0 3rd:1 Ran:4
Win Prizemoney £0 *Total Prizemoney* £1,074
1998 Turf 0-4: (6f 3, 7f) (gd, g-f, frm 2)
Neat, average filly, effective 6f, acts on g-f to frm. Turf high 67 (1st run) (began Jly) - 3rd of 6 to Kayoko (17 Jly Newmarket 6f frm RF 2880). **R Charlton [0-8] Mrs C F Van Straubenzee.*

NIGHT PLAYER (IRE) RR 103f 3783a[7]
4 b c Night Shift (USA) 8.1f **(73)** - Racquette (Ballymore) 7.3f **(64)**
Form - 7
1998 Turf 0-1: (8f) (gd)
Currently very useful colt, has worn blinkers. He is not a Group One horse and was wasting his time in the Prix Jacques le Marois.
**R Collet in FR [1-3] R C Strauss.*

NIGHT SHOT BHB 107f **RR 110f** 4492[7]
3 br g Night Shift (USA) 8.1f **(73)** - Optaria (Song) 7.2f **(61)**
Form - 152371661427
Record 1998 - 1st:3 2nd:2 3rd:1 Ran:12
Pre1998 - 1st:0 2nd:2 3rd:1 Ran:4
Win Prizemoney £33,879 *Total Prizemoney* £55,521

Wins	*** 1998**	Aug	York	(G-F)	H	5f	97	101+	<
	*** 1998**	Jun	Ascot	(G-S)	H	5f	90	95	
	*** 1998**	Mar	Warwic	(G-S)		5f		85	

1998 Turf 3-12: (5f 3-5, 6f 7) (g-s 1-2, gd 4, g-f 1-5, frm 1-1)
Neat, Group-class gelding, effective 5 to 6f, best at 5f, acts on gd to frm. Turf high 110 - 2nd of 12 getting 1lb from Cathedral (17 Spt Newbury 5f g-f RF 4330) - also 1st of 17 giving 12lb to The Limping Cat (19 Aug York RF 3758). A half-brother to Grey Shot. he made great strides after winning a maiden at Warwick in March, picking up valuable handicaps at Ascot and York and making the frame in a Listed contest. He should win at that level, but Group races are another matter. **I A Balding [3-16] J C Smith.*

NIGHT SPIRIT (IRE) BHB 56f **RR 45df** 4886[16]
3 b f Night Shift (USA) 8.1f **(73)** - Brentsville (USA) (Arctic Tern (USA)) 8.9f **(69)**
Form - 0100000
Record 1998 - 1st:1 2nd:0 3rd:0 Ran:7
Win Prizemoney £4,142 *Total Prizemoney* £4,142
Wins * 1998 May Folkes (G-F) 6f 82 <
1998 Turf 1-7: (6f 1-4, 7f 3) (g-s, gd 1-2, frm 4)
Workmanlike, moderate filly, effective 6f, acts on gd, has worn blinkers. Turf high 82 - 1st of 11 getting 5lb from East Winds (27 May Folkestone RF 1517). **C E Brittain [1-7] Eddy Grimstead Honda.*

NIGHT TIME BHB 45f37a **RR 45f 37a** 765[8]
6 b g Night Shift (USA) 8.1f **(73)** - Gathering Place (USA) (Hawaii) 9.4f **(66)**
Form - 58
Record 1998 - 1st:0 2nd:0 3rd:0 Ran:2
Pre1998 - 1st:0 2nd:1 3rd:3 Ran:20
Win Prizemoney £0 *Total Prizemoney* £3,191
1998 Turf 0-1: (12f) (g-s) 1998 AW 0-1: (8f) (Fibr)
Moderate gelding, has broken blood-vessels.
**H S Howe [0-2] Mrs Maureen Shenkin(from A G Hobbs [1-5] Jly 1997).*

NIGHT VIGIL (IRE) BHB 75f84a **RR 69f 84a** 2114[6]
3 b c Night Shift (USA) 8.1f **(73)** - Game Plan (Darshaan) 9.9f **(84)**
Form - 131056
Record 1998 - 1st:1 2nd:0 3rd:0 Ran:4
Pre1998 - 1st:1 2nd:0 3rd:1 Ran:6
Win Prizemoney £6,562 *Total Prizemoney* £7,133
Wins * 1998 *Feb Lingfi (SLW) H 10f 73 76* <
* 1997 *Nov Lingfi (STD) 8f 73*
1998 Turf 0-2: (9f, 10f) (gd 2) 1998 AW 1-2: (9f, 10f 1-1) (Equi 1-1, Fibr)
Strong, decent colt, effective 8 to 10f, - acts on AW, best on Equi, prefers left handed tracks, prefers tight tracks. Turf high 69. AW high 80 - 5th of 11 giving 1lb to Danzino (6 Jun Wolverhampton 9f Fibr RF 1797) - also 1st of 5 getting 1lb from Frankie Ferrari (14 Feb Lingfield RF 0291). **B W Hills [2-10] Saif Ali.*

NIGRASINE BHB 105f **RR 107f** 4971[3]
4 b c Mon Tresor 7.9f **(60)** - Early Gales (Precocious) 8.6f **(62)**
Form - 5301404520283
Record 1998 - 1st:1 2nd:2 3rd:2 Ran:13
Pre1998 - 1st:3 2nd:2 3rd:1 Ran:14
Win Prizemoney £26,113 *Total Prizemoney* £70,455

Wins	*** 1998**	Jun	Haydoc	(GD)	L	7.1f		107	<
	* 1997	Jly	Haydoc	(GD)	H	6f	99	103	
	* 1996	Jly	Pontef	(G-F)		6f		101	
	* 1996	Jun	Redcar	(G-F)		6f		73	

1998 Turf 1-13: (6f 7, 7f 1-4, 8f 2) (sft 2, g-s 2, gd 5, g-f, frm 1-3)
Workmanlike, Pattern-class colt, effective 6 to 8f, best at 6f, acts on gd to frm, best on frm, has worn blinkers, excels at Haydock, likes Doncaster. Turf high 107 - 1st of 7 from Jo Mell (6 Jun Haydock RF 1785). He finished fifth in the Lincoln and was still going strong in October. Tough and talented, he is equally effective at six and seven furlongs and has run well on all types of ground. **J L Eyre [4-27] Sunpak Potatoes.*

Night Shot carries the same colours as Lochangel to victory at York

NIKA NESGODA RR 69f 5071[6]
2 b f Suave Dancer (USA) 10.7f **(68)** - Highland Ceilidh (IRE) (Scottish Reel) 7f **(61)**
Form - 06
Record 1998 - 1st:0 2nd:0 3rd:0 Ran:2
1998 Turf 0-2: (7f, 8f) (gd 2)
Currently average filly. Turf high 69 (began Oct).
**J L Dunlop [0-2] Cyril Humphris.*

NIKI (IRE) BHB 85f **RR 77f** 2836[1]
3 b f Fairy King (USA) 7.7f **(75)** - Nicola Wynn (Nicholas Bill) 10.1f **(56)**
Form - 1
Record 1998 - 1st:1 2nd:0 3rd:0 Ran:1
Pre1998 - 1st:0 2nd:1 3rd:0 Ran:3
Win Prizemoney £3,655 *Total Prizemoney* £5,069
Wins * 1998 Jly Yarmou (G-F) 7f 74 <
1998 Turf 1-1: (7f 1-1) (g-f 1-1)
Above-average filly. (1st run) - 1st of 6 getting 5lb from Razor (15 Jly Yarmouth RF 2836). **J H M Gosden [1-4] George Strawbridge.*

NIKITA'S STAR (IRE) BHB 43f55a **RR 48f 55a** 2969[6]
5 ch g Soviet Lad (USA) 9.4f **(63)** - Sally Chase (Sallust) 8.4f **(63)**
Form - 2543463834356
Record 1998 - 1st:0 2nd:0 3rd:4 Ran:12
Pre1998 - 1st:5 2nd:5 3rd:1 Ran:34
Win Prizemoney £15,305 *Total Prizemoney* £23,328

Wins								
1996	*Nov*	*Wolver*	*(STD)*	*H*	*12f*	*73*	*75*	<
1996	Jly	Folkes	(G-F)	H	12f	60	64	
1996	*Jly*	*Southw*	*(STD)*	*C*	*11f*		*64*	
1996	*Mar*	*Wolver*	*(STD)*	*H*	*12f*	*66*	*69+*	
1996	*Feb*	*Wolver*	*(STD)*		*9.4f*		*55*	

1998 Turf 0-2: (13f, 14f) (gd, frm) 1998 AW 0-10: (12f 2, 14f 2, 15f 3, 16f 3) (Fibr 10)
Average gelding, effective 12 to 16f, - acts on Fibr, has worn blinkers, likes left handed tracks. Turf high 48. AW high 67 - 3rd of 11 getting 1lb from Manileno (5 Jun Southwell 16f Fibr RF 1764).
**M Brittain [0-7] D Parker (from D J G MurraySmith [5-39] Mar 1998).*

NIMELLO (USA) RR 87+f 2578[1]
2 b c Kingmambo (USA) 10.9f **(85)** - Zakota (IRE) (Polish Precedent (USA)) 10.2f **(60)**
Form - 1
Record 1998 - 1st:1 2nd:0 3rd:0 Ran:1
Win Prizemoney £5,299 *Total Prizemoney* £5,299
Wins * 1998 Jly Newmar (G-F) 7f 87+ <
1998 Turf 1-1: (7f 1-1) (frm 1-1)
Currently useful colt. (1st run) - 1st of 9 from Meneer (7 Jly Newmarket RF 2578). Looked in need of the race prior to making an impressive winning debut at the July Meeting, but was sidelined through injury for the rest of the campaign. Should progress to much better things. **P F I Cole [1-1] C Shiacolas.*

NIMINY-PIMINY (IRE) BHB 42f **RR 32f** 3882[12]
2 ch f Polish Patriot (USA) 7.8f **(70)** - Recherchee (Rainbow Quest (USA)) 10.4f **(75)**
Form - 700
Record 1998 - 1st:0 2nd:0 3rd:0 Ran:3
1998 Turf 0-3: (5f, 6f 2) (g-s, gd, hrd)
Currently very moderate filly. Turf high 32 (began Jly).
**M Johnston [0-3] P D Savill.*

NINIAN BELL BHB 31f **RR 35f** 4548[14]
2 ch g St Ninian - Ramas Silk (Amber Rama (USA)) 10.2f **(45)**
Form - 08000
Record 1998 - 1st:0 2nd:0 3rd:0 Ran:5
1998 Turf 0-4: (5f, 6f 2, 7f) (gd, frm 3) 1998 AW 0-1: (7f) (Fibr)
Very moderate gelding. Turf high 35. **Miss J F Craze [0-5] K Briggs.*

NIP IN SHARP RR 67f 4666[4]
5 b h Sharpo 7.5f **(68)**-Nip In The Air (USA) (Northern Dancer) 9.6f **(80)**
Form - 4
Record 1998 - 1st:0 2nd:0 3rd:0 Ran:1
Win Prizemoney £0 *Total Prizemoney* £275
1998 Turf 0-1: (8f) (g-s)
Currently average colt. **J L Eyre [0-1] P Ives.*

NIPPER RR 40f 1583[7]
2 b f Noble Patriarch 12.2f**(43)**-Gymcrak Lovebird(Taufan (USA))7f **(57)**
Form - 07
Record 1998 - 1st:0 2nd:0 3rd:0 Ran:2
1998 Turf 0-2: (5f, 6f) (gd, g-f)
Currently moderate filly. Turf high 40.
**T D Easterby [0-2] Mrs Jennifer Pallister.*

NISABA (IRE) BHB 53f69a **RR 59f 69a** 3692[7]
3 b f Belmez (USA) 11.4f **(65)** - Nibabu (FR) (Nishapour (FR)) 9.1f **(61)**
Form - 73111500207
Record 1998 - 1st:3 2nd:1 3rd:0 Ran:9
Pre1998 - 1st:0 2nd:0 3rd:1 Ran:6
Win Prizemoney £8,372 *Total Prizemoney* £9,819
Wins * **1998** *Jan Lingfi (STD) 10f 73*
* **1998** *Jan Lingfi (STD) H 10f 55 74 <*
* **1998** *Jan Lingfi (STD) 10f 58*
1998 Turf 0-5: (8f, 10f 3, 12f) (g-f 2, frm 3) 1998 AW 3-4: (10f 3-4) (Equi 3-4)
Lengthy, above-average filly, effective 10f, - acts on Equi, likes left handed tracks, likes tight tracks. Turf high 59 (began Jly). AW high 74 - 1st of 7 giving 3lb to Mystagogue (6 Jan Lingfield RF 0034) - also 1st of 4 getting 1lb from Dancing Rio (17 Jan Lingfield RF 0108). Inconsistent. She seems to have a liking for Equitrack, and landed a hat-trick of wins in modest company over ten furlongs on that surface at the beginning of '98. She was well beaten when meeting slightly better opposition afterwards, and has shown little on turf after a lengthy absence.
**J S Moore [3-11] Raymond Auld (from M Johnston [0-4] Oct 1997).*

NITE OWLER BHB 27f39a **RR 11f 39a** 4334[16]
4 b g Saddlers' Hall (IRE) 10.5f **(65)** - Lorne Lady (Local Suitor (USA)) 8.4f **(67)**
Form - 70610060
Record 1998 - 1st:1 2nd:0 3rd:0 Ran:8
Pre1998 - 1st:0 2nd:0 3rd:0 Ran:3
Win Prizemoney £2,637 *Total Prizemoney* £2,637
Wins * **1998** *Jun Southw (STD) H 6f 34 41 <*
1998 Turf 0-4: (5f 2, 6f 2) (gd, g-f, frm 2) 1998 AW 1-4: (5f, 6f 1-3) (Fibr 1-4)
Leggy, moderate gelding, effective 6f, - acts on Fibr, likes left handed tracks, likes tight tracks. Turf high 45. AW high 41 - 1st of 11 getting 9lb from Petraco (29 Jun Southwell RF 2386). Inconsistent.
**J Balding [1-8] Steer Arms Belton Racing Club (from J O'Reilly [0-2] Spt 1997).*

NITWITTY BHB 59f **RR 66f** 4799[21]
4 b g Nomination 7.3f **(57)** - Dawn Ditty (Song) 7.2f **(61)**
Form - 7300420000
Record 1998 - 1st:0 2nd:1 3rd:1 Ran:10
Pre1998 - 1st:0 2nd:0 3rd:0 Ran:1
Win Prizemoney £0 *Total Prizemoney* £1,235
1998 Turf 0-10: (5f 3, 6f 3, 7f 3, 8f) (sft, g-s, gd 2, g-f 3, frm 3)
Workmanlike, average gelding, effective 6 to 7f, acts on gd. Turf high 72 - 3rd of 8 giving 14lb to Stanott (7 Apr Folkestone 7f gd RF 0581).
**R J Hodges [0-10] Unity Farm Holiday Centre Ltd (from P D Cundell [0-1] Oct 1996).*

NKAPEN ROCKS (SPA) BHB 45f38a **RR 50f 38a** 4536[7]
5 b g Risk Me (FR) 8f **(53)** - Debutina Park (Averof) 8.2f **(62)**
Form - 81073507
Record 1998 - 1st:1 2nd:0 3rd:1 Ran:8
Pre1998 - 1st:0 2nd:3 3rd:2 Ran:23
Win Prizemoney £2,862 *Total Prizemoney* £7,234
Wins * **1998** May Mussel (G-S) H 8f 45 50 <
1998 Turf 1-8: (7f 2, 8f 1-6) (g-s 2, gd 1-3, g-f 3)
Fair gelding, effective 7 to 8f, best at 8f, acts on g-s to frm, best on gd, likes right handed tracks, likes tight tracks. Turf high 50 - 1st of 14 getting 10lb from Young Benson (30 May Musselburgh RF 1607). A disappointing type, he likes a bit of cut.
**Mrs G S Rees [1-8] Lady Lilford (from Capt J Wilson [0-23] Nov 1997).*

NOBALINO BHB 66f65a **RR 68f 65a** 3805[9]
4 ch c Sharpo 7.5f **(68)** - Zipperti Do (Precocious) 8.6f **(62)**
Form - 3412758253825470
Record 1998 - 1st:0 2nd:2 3rd:1 Ran:12
Pre1998 - 1st:1 2nd:4 3rd:1 Ran:10
Win Prizemoney £1,944 *Total Prizemoney* £9,519
Wins * 1997 *Dec Southw (STD) H 5f 59 67 <*
1998 Turf 0-7: (5f 7)(g-s, gd 3, g-f 3)1998 AW 0-5:(5f 4, 6f)(Equi, Fibr 4)
Workmanlike, average colt, effective 5f, acts on gd to frm - acts on AW, has worn blinkers (effectively). Turf high 72. AW high 64 - 2nd of 8 getting 8lb from Juwwi (9 Apr Lingfield 5f Equi RF 0624). Consistent. A genuine sort who usually runs his race, he deservedly scored over the minimum at Southwell in December '97. **Mrs N Macauley [1-22] Maurice Kirby.*

NOBBY BARNES BHB 43f32a **RR 52f 32a** 5060[3]
9 b g Nordance (USA) 7.4f **(69)**-Loving Doll (Godswalk (USA)) 7.3f **(58)**
Form - 6563872337067166463603 63
Record 1998 - 1st:1 2nd:1 3rd:6 Ran:24
Pre1998 - 1st:6 2nd:14 3rd:11 Ran:121
Win Prizemoney £23,137 *Total Prizemoney* £53,024
Wins * **1998** Jun Hamilt (SFT) H 9.2f 38 45
1994 Jun Lingfi (GF) H 9f 46 48
1998 Turf 1-18: (7f, 8f 7, 9f 1-9, 10f) (sft 3, g-s 3, gd 1-8, frm 4) 1998 AW 0-6: (7f, 8f 5) (Fibr 6)
Fair gelding, effective 8 to 9f, best at 9f, acts on sft to frm, best on gd, likes right handed tracks, does well at Hamilton. Turf high 52 - also 1st of 6 getting 32lb from High Premium (17 Jun Hamilton RF 2060). AW high 34. He recorded his first win since for four years at Hamilton but is pretty moderate these days and a bit of a thinker. Habitually slow to break, and best coming off a fast pace.
**Don Enrico Incisa [1-82] Don Enrico Incisa (from D A Wilson [6-51] Jly 1994).*

NOBBY BEACH BHB 37f **RR 25f** 2250[14]
4 ch g Sharpo 7.5f **(68)** - Sunshine Coast (Posse (USA)) 8.9f **(61)**
Form - 0
Record 1998 - 1st:0 2nd:0 3rd:0 Ran:1
Pre1998 - 1st:0 2nd:0 3rd:0 Ran:3
1998 Turf 0-1: (8f) (frm)
Workmanlike, little account gelding. **W R Muir [0-4] B Bull.*

NOBELIST RR 98f 1916a[3]
3 b c Bering 9.6f **(80)** - Noble Peregrine (Lomond)
Form - 3
1998 Turf 0-1: (8f) (sft)
Currently very useful colt. (1st run) - 3rd of 6 to Silic (7 Jun Chantilly 8f sft RF 1916a). **A Fabre in FR [0-1] Sheikh Mohammed.*

NOBLE CANONIRE BHB 22f22a **RR 28f 22a** 402[7]
6 b m Gunner B 11.2f **(45)** - Lucky Candy (Lucky Wednesday) 8f **(50)**
Form - 77
Record 1998 - 1st:0 2nd:0 3rd:0 Ran:2
Pre1998 - 1st:1 2nd:2 3rd:0 Ran:22
Win Prizemoney £2,296 *Total Prizemoney* £4,241
Wins 1996 *Feb Southw (STD) SH 11f 44 48 <*
1998 AW 0-2: (9f, 12f) (Fibr 2)
Little account mare, effective 8f, - acts on Fibr, has worn blinkers (very effectively), likes left handed tracks. AW high 1.
**D J Wintle [0-2] D J Wintle (from D Shaw [0-10] Jun 1997).*

NOBLE CHARGER (IRE) RR 42f 1018[12]
3 ch c Cadeaux Genereux 7.9f **(76)** - Shawgatny (USA) (Danzig Connection (USA)) 8f **(68)**
Form - 0
Record 1998 - 1st:0 2nd:0 3rd:0 Ran:1
1998 Turf 0-1: (8f) (gd)
Scopey, currently moderate colt.
**E A L Dunlop [0-1] Maktoum Al Maktoum.*

NOBLE CYRANO RR 71f 4138[9]
3 ch c Generous (IRE) 11.5f **(82)** - Miss Bergerac (Bold Lad (IRE)) 8.4f **(68)**
Form - 30
Record 1998 - 1st:0 2nd:0 3rd:1 Ran:2
Win Prizemoney £0 *Total Prizemoney* £520
1998 Turf 0-2: (8f, 10f) (g-f, frm)
Workmanlike, currently above-average colt. Turf high 71 (began Aug). **G Wragg [0-2] J L C Pearce.*

NOBLE DEMAND (USA) BHB 87f **RR 86f** 4966[11]

3 b g Red Ransom (USA) 8.6f **(83)** - Noble Nordic (USA) (Vaguely Noble) 10.1f **(72)**

Form - 2550

Record 1998 - 1st:0 2nd:1 3rd:0 Ran:4
Pre1998 - 1st:1 2nd:1 3rd:0 Ran:5

Win Prizemoney £8,480 *Total Prizemoney* £12,841

Wins 1997 Spt York (SFT) H 7.9f 72 83 <

1998 Turf 0-4: (10f 2, 12f 2) (sft, g-s, gd, g-f)

Workmanlike, useful gelding, effective 8 to 10f, best at 8f, acts on sft to gd, best on gd. Turf high 92 (1st run) - 2nd of 11 giving 1lb to Nautical Star (16 Apr Newmarket 10f gd RF 0708). Inconsistent. He failed by the minimum margin to make a winning reappearance in soft ground at Newmarket, but did not run up to that form in three subsequent starts. He has joined Toby Balding for a hurdling career.

**G B Balding [0-1] Mrs E A Haycock (from Mrs J R Ramsden [1-8] Jun 1998).*

NOBLE HERO BHB 44f46a **RR 51f 46a** 74[8]

4 b g Houston (USA) 7.7f **(65)** - Noble Devorcee (USA) (Vaguely Noble) 10.1f **(72)**

Form - 68

Record 1998 - 1st:0 2nd:0 3rd:0 Ran:1
Pre1998 - 1st:0 2nd:1 3rd:1 Ran:13

Win Prizemoney £0 *Total Prizemoney* £1,765

1998 AW 0-1: (12f) (Fibr)

Scopey, fair gelding, has worn blinkers.

**K A Morgan [0-2] D & M Cased Hole (from J J Sheehan [0-12] May 1997).*

NOBLE ONE RR 92++f 4622[1]

2 ch f Primo Dominie 7.2f **(67)** - Noble Destiny (Dancing Brave (USA)) 8.4f **(76)**

Form - 1

Record 1998 - 1st:1 2nd:0 3rd:0 Ran:1

Win Prizemoney £3,738 *Total Prizemoney* £3,738

Wins * **1998** Oct Catter (gd,) 5f 92++ <

1998 Turf 1-1: (5f 1-1) (g-f 1-1)

Currently useful filly. (1st run) - 1st of 15 getting 5lb from Waterford Spirit (3 Oct Catterick RF 4622). She won a Catterick maiden by a street on her debut in October, and though it was not a great race, she is one to bear in mind for next season.

**Sir Mark Prescott [1-1] Cheveley Park Stud.*

NOBLE PATRIOT BHB 43f **RR 47f** 2370[11]

3 b c Polish Patriot (USA) 7.8f **(70)** - Noble Form (Double Form) 7.3f **(58)**

Form - 00300

Record 1998 - 1st:0 2nd:0 3rd:1 Ran:5
Pre1998 - 1st:0 2nd:0 3rd:0 Ran:3

Win Prizemoney £0 *Total Prizemoney* £324

1998 Turf 0-5: (5f 2, 6f, 7f, 8f) (g-s, gd 3, g-f)

Scopey, fair colt, has worn blinkers. Turf high 47. Inconsistent.

**R Hollinshead [0-8] P D Savill.*

NOBLE PEARL (ITY) RR 95f 4950a[1]

2 b f Dashing Blade 7.9f **(80)** - Noble Girl (Be Friendly) 9.3f **(53)**

Form - 1

1998 Turf 1-1: (8f 1-1) (sft 1-1)

Currently very useful filly. (1st run) - 1st of 9 getting 3lb from Zindabad (18 Oct San Siro RF 4950a). Made all to win the Group One Grand Criterium under former crack apprentice Stephen Davies. **J Kujath in GER [1-1] Stall Haferkasten.*

NOBLE WATER (FR) BHB 33f **RR 24f** 4885[10]

3 b f Noblequest (FR) - Bulle d'Eau (FR)(Faraway Son (USA))10.3f **(55)**

Form - 000

Record 1998 - 1st:0 2nd:0 3rd:0 Ran:3

1998 Turf 0-3: (5f, 7f, 8f) (g-s, gd 2)

Currently little account filly. Turf high 24 (began Spt).

**J J Bridger [0-3] J J Bridger.*

NO CLICHES BHB 63f **RR 65f** 3603[6]

5 ch g Risk Me (FR) 8f **(53)**-Always on a Sunday(Star Appeal) 9.6f **(65)**

Form - 156863323346

Record 1998 - 1st:1 2nd:1 3rd:4 Ran:12
Pre1998 - 1st:1 2nd:5 3rd:0 Ran:24

Win Prizemoney £8,386 *Total Prizemoney* £19,207

Wins * **1998** Mar Doncas (GD) H 10.3f 60 66
1995 Spt Doncas (G-F) H 8f 72 79 <

1998 Turf 1-12: (9f, 10f 1-8, 12f 2, 14f) (g-s 2, gd 1-4, g-f 2, frm 4)

Average gelding, effective 8 to 12f, best at 10f, acts on gd to frm, best on frm, has worn blinkers, likes right handed tracks. Turf high 66 (1st run) - 1st of 17 giving 13lb to Dr Edgar (26 Mar Doncaster RF 0475). Consistent. Won an amateur riders' event at Doncaster on his reappearance despite looking in need of the run, but has been held since despite regularly reaching the frame.

**D Nicholls [1-23] J M G Promotions Ltd (from G Lewis [1-13] Oct 1996).*

NOCTURNE (IRE) BHB 55f55a **RR 61f 55a** 4875[2]

3 b f Tenby 10.4f **(76)** - Phylella (Persian Bold) 9.3f **(66)**

Form - 7454444522

Record 1998 - 1st:0 2nd:2 3rd:0 Ran:10
Pre1998 - 1st:0 2nd:0 3rd:0 Ran:1

Win Prizemoney £0 *Total Prizemoney* £2,028

1998 Turf 0-7: (8f 2, 9f, 10f 2, 12f, 16f) (g-f 5, frm 2) 1998 AW 0-3: (12f, 13f, 16f) (Equi 2, Fibr)

Unfurnished, average filly, effective 12 to 16f, best at 12f, acts on g-f - acts on AW, prefers left handed tracks, favours tight tracks. Turf high 61 - 4th of 10 getting 3lb from Grosvenor Spirit (31 Jly Thirsk 12f g-f RF 3250). AW high 60 (began Aug) - 2nd of 6 to Chocolate Box (2 Oct Lingfield 13f Equi RF 4615). Consistent.

**J W Hills [0-11] Highclere Thoroughbred Racing Ltd.*

NOEL (GER) RR 104f 4723a[4]

3

Form - 4

1998 Turf 0-1: (14f) (sft)

Currently very useful. (1st run) - 4th of 10 to Laveron (4 Oct Dortmund 14f sft RF 4723a). He will always struggle against strong foreign opposition judged on his fourth place at Dortmund in October. **in GER [0-1].*

NO EXTRAS (IRE) BHB 87f90a **RR 94f 90a** 4854[16]

8 b g Efisio 7.7f **(69)** - Parkland Rose (Sweet Candy (VEN)) 6.4f **(103)**

Form - 047314600720

Record 1998 - 1st:1 2nd:1 3rd:1 Ran:12
Pre1998 - 1st:8 2nd:11 3rd:9 Ran:68

Win Prizemoney £65,211 *Total Prizemoney* £130,194

Wins * **1998** Jun Newmar (GD) H 7f 87 92
* 1997 Jly Goodwo (G-F) H 8f 72 78
* 1997 Jun Goodwo (G-S) H 8f 62 67
* 1995 Aug Goodwo (G-F) H 6f 89 95 <
* 1994 Spt Baden (GD) 6f 88

1998 Turf 1-12: (6f, 7f 1-6, 8f 5) (sft, g-s, gd 4, g-f 1-3, frm 3)

Useful gelding, effective 6 to 8f, best at 8f, acts on gd to frm, has worn blinkers, likes tight tracks, excels at Goodwood. Turf high 94 - 6th of 22 getting 9lb from For Your Eyes Only (30 Jly Goodwood 8f gd RF 3219) - also 1st of 16 getting 5lb from Warningford (19 Jun Newmarket RF 2126). A versatile handicapper, he won a competitive handicap at Newmarket in June when very much racing on the favoured side of the track, and ran some good races to make the frame a couple of times at his beloved Goodwood.

**G L Moore [8-70] K Higson (from J Sutcliffe [1-10] Nov 1992).*

NO GROUSING (IRE) BHB 75f64a **RR 77f 64a** 158[8]

4 b g Robellino (USA) 9.5f **(68)**-Amenaide (Known Fact (USA)) 7.4f **(67)**

Form - 158

Record 1998 - 1st:0 2nd:0 3rd:0 Ran:2
Pre1998 - 1st:1 2nd:3 3rd:0 Ran:5

Win Prizemoney £2,294 *Total Prizemoney* £5,321

Wins * 1997 *Nov Wolver (STD) 7f 57* <

1998 AW 0-2: (8f, 11f) (Equi, Fibr)

Rangy, above-average gelding, effective 8f, acts on g-f to frm, prefers tight tracks. AW high 56.

**P C Haslam [1-7] The Glorious Twelfth Syndicate.*

NOIRIE BHB 42f **RR 45f** 2526[7]

4 br g Warning 8.1f **(77)**-Callipoli (USA)(Green Dancer (USA))10.3f **(74)**

Form - 014067

Record 1998 - 1st:1 2nd:0 3rd:0 Ran:6
Pre1998 - 1st:0 2nd:0 3rd:0 Ran:10

Win Prizemoney £2,237 *Total Prizemoney* £3,127

Wins *1998 Jun Pontef (HVY) H 10f 38 40 <
1998 Turf 1-6: (8f 3, 10f 1-2, 12f) (g-s 1-1, gd, g-f 2, frm 2)
Scopey, moderate gelding, has worn blinkers, likes tight tracks. Turf high 45. **M Brittain [1-16] Miss Debi Woods.*

NO MERCY RR 73f
5009[4]
2 ch c Faustus (USA) 9.1f **(54)** - Nashville Blues (IRE) **(74f)** (Try My Best (USA)) 7.6f **(67)**
Form - 744
Record 1998 - 1st:0 2nd:0 3rd:0 Ran:3
Win Prizemoney £0 *Total Prizemoney* £498
1998 Turf 0-3: (7f, 8f 2) (sft, g-f 2)
Currently above-average colt. Turf high 73 (began Jly).
**J W Hills [0-3] Freddy Bienstock.*

NOM FRANCAIS BHB 49f RR 50f
5072[15]
2 b f First Trump - Eastern Ember (Indian King (USA)) 7.4f **(64)**
Form - 680
Record 1998 - 1st:0 2nd:0 3rd:0 Ran:3
1998 Turf 0-3: (5f, 7f 2) (sft, g-s, gd)
Currently fair filly. Turf high 50. A half-sister to sprint handicapper Perryston View.
**R Guest [0-2] M Sakal (from Dr J D Scargill [0-1] Apr 1998).*

NOMINATOR LAD BHB 79f72a RR 79f 72a
5078[6]
4 b c Nomination 7.3f **(57)** - Ankara's Princess (USA) (Ankara (USA)) 8f **(71)**
Form - 061044521706
Record 1998 - 1st:2 2nd:1 3rd:0 Ran:12
Pre1998 - 1st:2 2nd:1 3rd:1 Ran:13
Win Prizemoney £30,469 *Total Prizemoney* £36,008
Wins *1998 Spt Ayr (G-S) H 8f 75 79 <
*1998 *Jun Wolver (STD) H 8.5f 70 70*
*1997 Spt Haydoc (GD) H 7.1f 67 71
*1997 Jly Nottin (G-F) 8.2f 72
1998 Turf 1-10: (7f 4, 8f 1-6) (sft 1-2, g-s, gd 5, g-f 2) 1998 AW 1-2: (8f 1-2) (Fibr 1-2)
Strong, above-average colt, effective 7 to 8f, best at 8f, acts on sft to frm - acts on Fibr, best on gd, prefers left handed tracks, prefers tight tracks, excels at Haydock. Turf high 79 - 1st of 20 giving 3lb to Jay-Owe-Two (19 Spt Ayr RF 4368). AW high 70 (1st run) - 1st of 5 getting 8lb from Sualtach (20 Jun Wolverhampton RF 2163). Won a modest handicap on the Fibresand in June, but was well beaten on grass next time. Returned to form on easy ground in the autumn, and scored under a forceful ride at the Ayr Western Meeting. **B A McMahon [4-25] J D Graham.*

NOMORE MR NICEGUY BHB 85f90a RR 94f 90a
4854[3]
4 b c Rambo Dancer (CAN) 8.4f **(59)** - Lariston Gale (Pas de Seul) 9.1f **(67)**
Form - 2065403124803000403
Record 1998 - 1st:1 2nd:2 3rd:3 Ran:19
Pre1998 - 1st:3 2nd:4 3rd:5 Ran:28
Win Prizemoney £22,724 *Total Prizemoney* £53,476
Wins *1998 Jun Cheste (GD) H 7f 79 90+ <
*1997 *Mar Wolver (STD) H 7f 84 88*
*1996 *Dec Wolver (STD) H 7f 78 84*
*1996 Jly Hamilt (GD) 5f 67
1998 Turf 1-18: (6f 6, 7f 1-10, 8f 2) (sft 2, g-s, gd 1-8, g-f 6, frm) 1998 AW 0-1: (8f) (Fibr)
Scopey, useful colt, effective 6 to 8f, best at 8f, acts on g-s to g-f - acts on Fibr, best on g-f, has worn blinkers, likes tight tracks, does well at Chester and likes Newmarket. Turf high 94 - 2nd of 11 getting 4lb from Superior Premium (24 Jun Chester 6f gd RF 2233) - also 1st of 14 giving 16lb to Myttons Mistake (3 Jun Chester RF 1682). (1st run) - 2nd of 13 giving 7lb to Fayik (14 Mar Wolverhampton 8f Fibr RF 0431). He managed just a solitary Chester victory from umpteen starts, but made the frame on five other occasions. He stands his racing well, and is a particularly effective performer on a tight left-handed track.
**E J Alston [4-47] Mrs Carol McPhail.*

NO NELLIE NO RR
4150[12]
4 ch f Formidable (USA)7.8f **(60)**-Now In Session(USA)(Diesis)9.3f **(69)**
Form - 0
Record 1998 - 1st:0 2nd:0 3rd:0 Ran:1
1998 Turf 0-1: (11f) (g-f)
Currently very poor filly. **L A Dace [0-1] Mrs V J Davey.*

NONIOS (IRE) BHB 43f RR 40f
4375[8]
7 b g Nashamaa 8.1f **(58)** - Bosquet (Queen's Hussar) 11.6f **(58)**
Form - 68
Record 1998 - 1st:0 2nd:0 3rd:0 Ran:2
Pre1998 - 1st:4 2nd:4 3rd:3 Ran:28
Win Prizemoney £14,309 *Total Prizemoney* £21,505
Wins 1994 Aug Bright (FRM) H 7f 78 80
1994 Jly Warwic (G-F) H 7f 73 73
1998 Turf 0-2: (12f, 16f) (frm 2)
Fair gelding, has worn blinkers. Turf high 40 (began Jly).
**G M Moore [2-33] Mrs Susan Moore (from B J Meehan [4-25] Oct 1994).*

NO NO NORA BHB 43f RR 58f
4545[16]
3 ch f Inchinor 8.9f **(64)** - Lucky Fingers (Hotfoot) 10.5f **(59)**
Form - 47680
Record 1998 - 1st:0 2nd:0 3rd:0 Ran:5
Win Prizemoney £0 *Total Prizemoney* £194
1998 Turf 0-4: (7f, 8f, 9f, 11f) (gd 2, g-f, frm) 1998 AW 0-1: (11f) (Fibr)
Leggy, fair filly, has worn blinkers. Turf high 58 (began Jly).
**S C Williams [0-5] Mrs A Stacey.*

NON VINTAGE (IRE) BHB 35f47a RR 34f 47a
1788[6]
7 ch g Shy Groom (USA) 8.2f **(59)** - Great Alexandra (Runnett) 7f **(59)**
Form - 06
Record 1998 - 1st:0 2nd:0 3rd:0 Ran:2
Pre1998 - 1st:2 2nd:5 3rd:7 Ran:44
Win Prizemoney £9,212 *Total Prizemoney* £21,408
Wins *1994 Aug Pontef (G-F) 18f 69
1998 Turf 0-2: (12f, 16f) (frm, hrd)
Fair gelding, has worn blinkers. Turf high 30.
**M C Chapman [5-78] Alan Mann (from M H Easterby [1-17] Aug 1994).*

NOPALEA BHB 60f58a RR 48f 58a
3527[9]
4 b f Warrshan (USA) 9.7f **(59)** - Nophe (USA) (Super Concorde (USA)) 10.9f **(66)**
Form - 000
Record 1998 - 1st:0 2nd:0 3rd:0 Ran:3
Pre1998 - 1st:1 2nd:3 3rd:6 Ran:16
Win Prizemoney £3,613 *Total Prizemoney* £10,094
Wins *1997 Jun Warwic (G-F) H 5f 66 66 <
1998 Turf 0-3: (5f 2, 6f) (gd, frm 2)
Workmanlike, moderate filly, effective 5f, acts on gd to frm, best on frm, likes left handed tracks. Turf high 45. Becoming disappointing.
**T J Naughton [1-13] T J Naughton (from C E Brittain [0-6] Oct 1996).*

NO PATTERN BHB 55f55a RR 62f 55a
4655[10]
6 ch g Rock City 8.8f **(62)** - Sunfleet (Red Sunset) 8.2f **(63)**
Form - 00
Record 1998 - 1st:0 2nd:0 3rd:0 Ran:2
Pre1998 - 1st:3 2nd:3 3rd:3 Ran:30
Win Prizemoney £9,189 *Total Prizemoney* £15,551
Wins *1995 Jly Lingfi (G-F) H 11.5f 73 75 <
*1995 *Jan Lingfi (STD) H 8f 74 72*
*1994 *Nov Lingfi (STD) 6f 69*
1998 Turf 0-1: (10f) (g-f) 1998 AW 0-1: (12f) (Equi)
Average gelding, has worn blinkers. Becoming disappointing.
**G L Moore [5-47] K Higson.*

NORCROFT JOY BHB 70f RR 70f
4763[5]
3 b f Rock Hopper 10.6f **(54)** - Greenhills Joy (Radetzky) 9.8f **(56)**
Form - 0212511105
Record 1998 - 1st:4 2nd:2 3rd:0 Ran:10
Pre1998 - 1st:0 2nd:0 3rd:0 Ran:3
Win Prizemoney £12,257 *Total Prizemoney* £14,013
Wins *1998 Spt Haydoc (GD) H 11.9f 61 70 <
*1998 Aug Beverl (G-F) H 12f 54 57
*1998 Aug Hamilt (SFT) H 12.1f 54 61
*1998 Jun Yarmou (SFT) H 14.1f 52 60
1998 Turf 4-10: (8f, 12f 3-7, 14f 1-2) (g-s 2-4, gd 3, g-f 1-2, frm 1-1)
Leggy, above-average filly, effective 12 to 14f, best at 12f, acts on g-s to frm, best on g-s, favours tight tracks. Turf high 70 - 1st of 19 getting 12lb from Creon (4 Spt Haydock RF 4092) - also 1st of 7 getting 16lb from Spartan Royale (17 Aug Hamilton RF 3676). Consistent. She performed much better after being stepped up in trip, winning four times in all. Her trainer Mick Ryan won eight

races during the season with another daughter of Rock Hopper, Lady Rockstar. **M J Ryan [4-13] Norcroft Park Stud.*

NORDIC BREEZE (IRE) BHB 65f70a RR 65f 70a 2719[9]

6 b or br g Nordico (USA) 8.2f **(59)** - Baby Clair (Gulf Pearl) 12f **(54)**
Form - 010
Record 1998 - 1st:1 2nd:0 3rd:0 Ran:3
Pre1998 - 1st:1 2nd:6 3rd:1 Ran:19
Win Prizemoney £6,063 *Total Prizemoney* £14,139
Wins * **1998** Jly Warwic (GD) H 12.5f 65 65 <
1995 Jun Ayr (G-F) H 7f 60 65 <
1998 Turf 1-3: (12f 2, 13f 1-1) (g-f 1-2, frm)
Average gelding, has worn blinkers (extremely effectively). Turf high 65 - 1st of 8 giving 29lb to Mile A Minute (3 Jly Warwick RF 2515). Inconsistent.
**M C Pipe [4-23] Malcolm Jones (from A Bailey [1-20] Aug 1996).*

NORDIC PIRJO BHB 50f RR 50f 585[17]

3 b f Nordico (USA) 8.2f **(59)** - Victoria Mill (Free State) 8.7f **(61)**
Form - 0
Record 1998 - 1st:0 2nd:0 3rd:0 Ran:1
Pre1998 - 1st:0 2nd:0 3rd:0 Ran:3
1998 Turf 0-1: (10f) (g-s)
Leggy, fair filly. **Mrs J R Ramsden [0-4] P J Carr.*

NORDINEX (IRE) BHB 40f47a RR 40f 47a 4229[9]

6 b g Nordico (USA) 8.2f **(59)** - Debbie's Next (USA) (Arctic Tern (USA)) 8.9f **(69)**
Form - 808400
Record 1998 - 1st:0 2nd:0 3rd:0 Ran:5
Pre1998 - 1st:4 2nd:0 3rd:5 Ran:30
Win Prizemoney £19,947 *Total Prizemoney* £24,095
Wins 1996 *Feb Lingfi (STD) H 8f 65 67*
1995 Jly Newmar (G-F) H 8f 75 78 <
1995 Jun Kempto (G-F) H 8f 70 75
1995 *Jan Lingfi (STD) H 8f 68 67*
1998 Turf 0-5: (8f 4, 11f) (gd 4, g-f)
Moderate gelding, has worn blinkers. Turf high 40. Consistent.
**P Hayward [0-7] A J Byrne (from D R C Elsworth [0-5] Nov 1997).*

NO RESERVE (USA) RR 68f 4779[9]

2 b f Gone West (USA) 7.8f **(82)** - Milly Ha Ha **(101f)** (Dancing Brave (USA)) 8.4f **(76)**
Form - 0
Record 1998 - 1st:0 2nd:0 3rd:0 Ran:1
1998 Turf 0-1: (8f) (gd)
Currently average filly. **H R A Cecil [0-1] Cliveden Stud.*

NORLING (IRE) BHB 30f39a RR 16f 39a 2721[15]

8 ch g Nashamaa 8.1f **(58)** - Now Then (Sandford Lad) 7.8f **(54)**
Form - 00
Record 1998 - 1st:0 2nd:0 3rd:0 Ran:2
Pre1998 - 1st:5 2nd:3 3rd:5 Ran:54
Win Prizemoney £12,211 *Total Prizemoney* £17,403
Wins * 1995 Aug Salisb (G-F) CH 6f 47 51
* 1994 Jly Folkes (G-F) 6f 44
1998 Turf 0-2: (6f 2) (gd, frm)
Moderate gelding, effective 6f, - acts on Equi, likes left handed tracks, likes tight tracks. Turf high 16. Becoming disappointing.
**K O Cunningham-Brown [2-39] S Pedersen (from N Tinkler [2-16] Oct 1993).*

NORMAN ARCHER (IRE) BHB 45f RR 41f 2254[F]

3 b c Archway (IRE) 8.5f **(60)** - Foxy Fairy (IRE) (Fairy King (USA)) 7.7f **(59)**
Form - 080F
Record 1998 - 1st:0 2nd:0 3rd:0 Ran:4
1998 Turf 0-4: (6f, 7f 3) (sft, gd, g-f, frm)
Workmanlike, moderate colt. Turf high 41. (DEAD)
**V Soane [0-4] Mrs M Watts And Miss R Hatley.*

NORMAN CONQUEST (USA) BHB 50f RR 57f 1615[7]

4 ch g Miswaki (USA) 8.1f **(81)** - Grand Luxe (CAN) (Sir Ivor) 10.2f **(70)**
Form - 7
Record 1998 - 1st:0 2nd:0 3rd:0 Ran:1
Pre1998 - 1st:0 2nd:0 3rd:0 Ran:9
Win Prizemoney £0 *Total Prizemoney* £219
1998 Turf 0-1: (13f) (g-f)
Scopey, fair gelding, effective 10f, acts on g-f, has worn blinkers.
**M D Hammond [0-5] B & K Associates (from I A Balding [0-9] Spt 1997).*

NORNAX LAD (USA) BHB 29f38a RR 30f 38a 87[7]

10 b g Northern Baby (CAN) 10.2f **(74)** - Naxos (USA) (Big Spruce (USA)) 11f **(71)**
Form - 7
Record 1998 - 1st:0 2nd:0 3rd:0 Ran:1
Pre1998 - 1st:4 2nd:1 3rd:2 Ran:22
Win Prizemoney £13,180 *Total Prizemoney* £15,014
Wins * 1997 Jun Hamilt (G-F) H 13f 52 49
* 1995 Aug Hamilt (FRM) 11.1f 60
* 1995 Aug Hamilt (FRM) H 13f 53 61
* 1994 *Feb Lingfi (STD) H 13f 65 68* <
1998 AW 0-1: (15f) (Fibr)
Moderate gelding, effective 13 to 17f, acts on gd to frm - acts on Equi, often wears blinkers (extremely effectively).
**M Meade [8-32] Ladyswood Racing Club.*

NORSKI LAD BHB 82f80a RR 81f 80a 4963[2]

3 b c Niniski (USA) 13.2f **(67)** - Lady Norcliffe (USA) (Norcliffe (CAN)) 14f **(72)**
Form - 12123112
Record 1998 - 1st:4 2nd:3 3rd:1 Ran:8
Pre1998 - 1st:0 2nd:0 3rd:0 Ran:4
Win Prizemoney £12,074 *Total Prizemoney* £15,933
Wins * **1998** Oct Pontef (G-S) H 17.1f 70 76 <
* **1998** Spt Newcas (GD) H 16.1f 70 75
* **1998** *Jun Southw (STD) H 12f 63 67*
* **1998** *Jun Wolver (STD) H 14.8f 55 62*
1998 Turf 2-4: (11f, 16f 1-2, 17f 1-1) (sft, gd 1-2, g-f 1-1) 1998 AW 2-4: (12f 1-1, 14f, 15f 1-2) (Fibr 2-4)
Scopey, decent colt, effective 15 to 17f, best at 16f, acts on sft to g-f - acts on Fibr, prefers left handed tracks, prefers tight tracks, excels at Wolverhampton. Turf high 81 - 2nd of 13 getting 15lb from Silver Wedge (23 Oct Newbury 16f sft RF 4963) - also 1st of 8 giving 8lb to Indigo Dawn (5 Oct Pontefract RF 4659). AW high 73 - 3rd of 9 getting 9lb from Philosophic (20 Jly Wolverhampton 15f Fibr RF 2969). A versatile, progressive performer, he made 62,000 guineas at Tattersalls Horses-in-Training Sale.
**Sir Mark Prescott [4-12] Hesmonds Stud.*

NORTH ARDAR BHB 53f47a RR 51?f 47a 340[6]

8 b g Ardar 9.5f **(63)** - Langwaite (Seaepic (USA)) 9f **(56)**
Form - 5514166
Record 1998 - 1st:2 2nd:0 3rd:0 Ran:6
Pre1998 - 1st:12 2nd:10 3rd:7 Ran:67
Win Prizemoney £39,222 *Total Prizemoney* £52,250
Wins * **1998** *Feb Lingfi (STD) H 12f 40 46*
* **1998** *Jan Lingfi (STD) H 10f 35 41*
1996 *Spt Southw (STD) H 8f 52 57*
1996 Aug Hamilt (G-F) S 8.3f 60
1996 Jly Ripon (GD) S 10f 57
1996 Jun Redcar (FRM) C 10f 60
1996 Jun Pontef (G-F) S 10f 53
1996 May Catter (GD) S 10.2f 60
1995 Jly Mussel (G-F) H 11.1f 53 58
1995 Jun Thirsk (G-F) H 12f 50 54
1994 Jun Pontef (G-F) S 10f 60
1998 AW 2-6: (9f, 10f 1-2, 12f 1-3) (Equi 2-4, Fibr 2)
Fair gelding, effective 10 to 12f, - acts on Equi, has worn blinkers. AW high 46 - 1st of 11 giving 2lb to Zorro (3 Feb Lingfield RF 0213) - also 1st of 12 getting 7lb from Mogin (22 Jan Lingfield RF 0131). Inconsistent. The old boy seemed to have been on the decline since the autumn of '96, but regained winning form in a handicap on the Lingfield Equitrack in January. He was given a poor ride when beaten in an amateur riders' event at the same track next time, but returned to winning ways with a last-gasp victory in a handicap there in February.
**N P Littmoden [2-7] Paul Stringer (from T Wall [0-8] Mar 1997).*

NORTHERN ACCORD BHB 45f RR 45f 4869[4]

4 b g Akarad (FR) 9.7f **(73)** - Sioux City (Simply Great (FR)) 8.2f **(65)**
Form - 014014
Record 1998 - 1st:2 2nd:0 3rd:0 Ran:6
Pre1998 - 1st:0 2nd:0 3rd:0 Ran:3

Win Prizemoney £5,222 *Total Prizemoney* £5,520
Wins *** 1998** Spt Beverl (G-F) H 9.9f 41 45 <
*** 1998** Aug Hamilt (SFT) H 8.3f 37 39
1998 Turf 2-6: (8f 1-1, 10f 1-2, 11f, 12f 2) (gd 1-5, g-f 1-1)
Lengthy, moderate gelding, effective 8 to 12f, best at 10f, acts on gd to g-f, best on gd, favours tight tracks. Turf high 45 (began Aug) - 4th of 19 getting 21lb from My Desperado (19 Oct Pontefract 10f gd RF 4869) - also 1st of 18 giving 5lb to Dr Woodstock (22 Spt Beverley RF 4408).
**Mrs J R Ramsden [2-10] Bernard Hathaway.*

NORTHERN BLESSING BHB 85f **RR 88f** 4111[4]
4 b f Waajib 8.9f **(67)** - Last Blessing (Final Straw) 7.9f **(64)**
Form - 005014
Record **1998** - 1st:1 2nd:0 3rd:0 Ran:6
Pre1998 - 1st:1 2nd:0 3rd:0 Ran:2
Win Prizemoney £7,679 *Total Prizemoney* £8,124
Wins *** 1998** Jly Lingfi (G-F) H 7.6f 77 84 <
* 1997 Spt Nottin (G-F) 8.2f 79
1998 Turf 1-5: (7f, 8f 1-4) (gd 2, frm 1-3) 1998 AW 0-1: (10f) (Equi)
Scopey, useful filly, effective 8f, acts on g-f to frm, best on frm. Turf high 86 - 4th of 18 giving 15lb to Queens Consul (5 Spt Thirsk 8f frm RF 4111) - also 1st of 5 giving 12lb to Carlton (25 Jly Lingfield RF 3109). **P W Harris [2-8] The Twelve Apostles.*

NORTHERN DRAKE (AUS) **RR 111f** 5133a[2]
4 br c Varick (USA) - Elizabeth Drake (Northfields (USA)) 9f **(72)**
Form - 2
1998 Turf 0-1: (10f) (gd)
Currently Group-class colt. (1st run) - 2nd of 11 giving 6lb to Champagne (31 Oct Flemington 10f gd RF 5133a).
**K Mann in AUS [0-1].*

NORTHERN JUDGE BHB 32f28a **RR 19f 28a** 336[10]
5 ch g Highest Honor (FR) 10.9f **(72)**-Nordica(Northfields (USA)) 9f **(72)**
Form - 680
Record **1998** - 1st:0 2nd:0 3rd:0 Ran:3
Pre1998 - 1st:1 2nd:2 3rd:0 Ran:21
Win Prizemoney £3,915 *Total Prizemoney* £6,388
Wins 1996 Aug Newmar (GD) C 7f 63 <
1998 AW 0-3: (6f, 8f, 9f) (Equi, Fibr 2)
Poor gelding, often wears blinkers. AW high 19.
**A P James [0-13] The Good Judgement Partnership (from B Hanbury [1-14] Oct 1996).*

NORTHERN LASS (IRE) BHB 48f **RR 43f** 4403[6]
3 br f Rainbows For Life (CAN) 9.3f **(64)** - Intrepid (Rousillon (USA)) 8.2f **(74)**
Form - 156686
Record **1998** - 1st:1 2nd:0 3rd:0 Ran:6
Pre1998 - 1st:0 2nd:0 3rd:0 Ran:3
Win Prizemoney £2,232 *Total Prizemoney* £2,232
Wins *** 1998** Apr Nottin (G-S) SH 10f 49 63 <
1998 Turf 1-6: (10f 1-3, 12f 2, 14f) (g-s 1-1, gd, g-f 2, frm 2)
Unfurnished, moderate filly, effective 10f, acts on g-s, has worn blinkers, likes tight tracks. Turf high 63 (1st run) - 1st of 17 getting 6lb from Little Cracker (7 Apr Nottingham RF 0585). Consistent.
**M H Tompkins [1-9] Mrs Brian Grice.*

NORTHERN MAESTRO BHB 28f **RR 28f** 1065[7]
4 ch g Rock Hopper 10.6f **(54)**-Thimbalina (Salmon Leap(USA))11f **(61)**
Form - 7
Record **1998** - 1st:0 2nd:0 3rd:0 Ran:1
Pre1998 - 1st:0 2nd:0 3rd:0 Ran:5
Win Prizemoney £0 *Total Prizemoney* £282
1998 Turf 0-1: (16f) (gd)
Workmanlike, little account gelding, effective 16f, acts on gd, has worn blinkers. (1st run) - 7th of 13 getting 7lb from Dally Boy (6 May Musselburgh 16f gd RF 1065). **Mrs M Reveley [1-15] A Sharratt.*

NORTHERN MOTTO BHB 56f51a **RR 60f 51a** 4355[7]
5 b g Mtoto 11.5f **(71)** - Soulful (FR) (Zino) 12.9f **(54)**
Form - 3001351417277
Record **1998** - 1st:3 2nd:1 3rd:2 Ran:13
Pre1998 - 1st:3 2nd:1 3rd:1 Ran:25
Win Prizemoney £25,993 *Total Prizemoney* £30,469
Wins *** 1998** Jly Cheste (G-F) H 15.9f 56 60 <
*** 1998** May Mussel (G-S) H 16f 55 58
*** 1998** Apr Mussel (G-S) H 16f 48 59
* 1997 Jun Doncas (G-F) H 12f 50 55
* 1997 *Feb Wolver (STD) H 12f 52 57*
* 1996 Nov Mussel (G-S) H 15.1f 47 54
1998 Turf 3-10: (15f, 16f 3-8, 17f) (sft, gd 2-6, frm 1-3) 1998 AW 0-3: (12f 2, 14f) (Fibr 3)
Average gelding, effective 12 to 20f, acts on gd to frm - acts on Fibr, prefers right handed tracks, excels at Ascot and Musselburgh. Turf high 60 - 2nd of 10 giving 28lb to Give An Inch (11 Aug Ayr 15f gd RF 3522) - also 1st of 9 getting 20lb from Domappel (11 Jly Chester RF 2705). AW high 47. Consistent.
**J S Goldie [6-32] Andrew Paterson (from W Storey [0-3] Oct 1996).*

NORTHERN SPRING (IRE) **RR 76f** 4524[2]
2 ch c Common Grounds 8.1f **(66)** - North Telstar (Sallust) 8.4f **(63)**
Form - 52
Record **1998** - 1st:0 2nd:1 3rd:0 Ran:2
Win Prizemoney £0 *Total Prizemoney* £1,055
1998 Turf 0-2: (6f 2) (g-f 2)
Currently above-average colt. Turf high 76 (began Spt) - 2nd of 14 giving 5lb to En Garde (28 Spt Bath 6f g-f RF 4524).
**M J Heaton-Ellis [0-2] Fieldspring Racing.*

NORTHERN SUN BHB 72f79a **RR 82df 79a** 5081[10]
4 b g Charmer 9f **(59)** - Princess Dancer (Alzao (USA)) 7.1f **(68)**
Form - 602860
Record **1998** - 1st:0 2nd:1 3rd:0 Ran:6
Pre1998 - 1st:3 2nd:0 3rd:2 Ran:13
Win Prizemoney £11,789 *Total Prizemoney* £14,592
Wins * 1997 Mar Kempto (GD) H 9f 79 85 <
* 1996 Aug Bright (FRM) H 7f 83 77
* 1996 Jly Bright (FRM) 7f 71
1998 Turf 0-4: (10f 3, 12f) (hvy, gd, g-f, frm) 1998 AW 0-2: (10f, 12f) (Equi, Fibr)
Workmanlike, decent gelding, effective 9 to 12f, acts on gd to frm, best on g-f, favours tight tracks. Turf high 82 - 2nd of 6 giving 3lb to Gift Token (8 May Nottingham 10f frm RF 1113). AW high 44. Inconsistent. **T G Mills [3-19] John Humphreys (Turf Accountants) Ltd.*

NORTHERN SVENGALI (IRE) BHB 82f **RR 82f** 4813[1]
2 b g Distinctly North (USA) 7.4f **(63)** - Trilby's Dream (IRE) (Mansooj)
Form - 027222220101
Record **1998** - 1st:2 2nd:6 3rd:0 Ran:12
Win Prizemoney £6,878 *Total Prizemoney* £13,389
Wins *** 1998** Oct Catter (G-S) H 5f 79 82 <
*** 1998** Spt Catter (G-F) 6f 80
1998 Turf 2-12: (5f 1-9, 6f 1-3) (gd 1-6, g-f 3, frm 1-3)
Decent gelding, effective 5 to 6f, best at 5f, acts on gd to frm, best on frm. Turf high 82 - 1st of 11 giving 12lb to Piggy Bank (15 Oct Catterick RF 4813) - also 1st of 12 from Diplomat (19 Spt Catterick RF 4370). **T D Barron [2-12] Timothy Cox.*

NORTHGATE (IRE) BHB 50f **RR 70f** 4575[11]
2 b c Thatching 7.8f **(69)** - Tender Time (Tender King) 6.8f **(54)**
Form - 0600
Record **1998** - 1st:0 2nd:0 3rd:0 Ran:4
1998 Turf 0-4: (6f 2, 7f 2) (g-f 2, frm 2)
Above-average colt. Turf high 70. **M Brittain [0-4] Mel Brittain.*

NORTH OF KALA (IRE) BHB 36f **RR 37f** 4474[6]
5 b g Distinctly North (USA) 7.4f **(63)** - Hi Kala (Kampala) 8.5f **(56)**
Form - 00006
Record **1998** - 1st:0 2nd:0 3rd:0 Ran:5
Pre1998 - 1st:0 2nd:0 3rd:0 Ran:1
1998 Turf 0-5: (12f, 13f 2, 15f, 16f) (hvy 2, g-s, gd, g-f)
Very moderate gelding. Turf high 37.
**G L Moore [0-1] B Lennard (from S J Treacy in IRE [0-15] Jun 1998).*

NORTH OFTHE BORDER BHB 80f **RR 81f** 991[P]
3 b c Primo Dominie 7.2f **(67)** - Valika (Valiyar) 8.5f **(73)**
Form - 2P
Record **1998** - 1st:0 2nd:1 3rd:0 Ran:2
Pre1998 - 1st:0 2nd:0 3rd:1 Ran:3
Win Prizemoney £0 *Total Prizemoney* £2,055
1998 Turf 0-2: (8f 2) (gd 2)
Workmanlike, decent colt. Turf high 76 (1st run) - 2nd of 14 getting

14lb from Strachin (24 Apr Carlisle 8f gd RF 0844).
**M Johnston [0-5] Robert Aird.*

NORTHWING RR 32f 4930[11]

2 b c Minshaanshu Amad (USA) 11.3f **(53)** - Kicking Bird (Bold Owl) 8.5f **(45)**
Form - 00
Record 1998 - 1st:0 2nd:0 3rd:0 Ran:2
1998 Turf 0-2: (6f, 8f) (g-s, frm)
Currently very moderate colt. Turf high 32 (began Jly).
**E A Wheeler [0-2] Mrs D Claessen-Brierton.*

NOSEY NATIVE BHB 49f41a RR 47f 41a 3768[5]

5 b g Cyrano de Bergerac 7.3f **(58)** - Native Flair (Be My Native (USA)) 10.2f **(71)**
Form - 3664563600515215
Record 1998 - 1st:2 2nd:1 3rd:1 Ran:13
Pre1998 - 1st:3 2nd:2 3rd:4 Ran:35
Win Prizemoney £16,287 *Total Prizemoney* £21,416

Wins
- * **1998** Aug Catter (G-F) H 12f 44 46
- * **1998** Jun Ripon (SFT) H 12.3f 40 41
- * 1997 Jun Ripon (GD) H 12.3f 61 58
- * 1996 Oct Haydoc (SFT) H 10.5f 51 71
- * 1995 Oct Yarmou (G-F) H 8f 74 82 <

1998 Turf 2-8: (10f 2, 11f 2, 12f 2-2, 14f, 17f) (sft, g-s 1-1, gd, g-f, frm 1-4) 1998 AW 0-5: (10f, 11f, 12f, 13f 2) (Equi 3, Fibr 2)
Moderate gelding, effective 11 to 14f, acts on g-f to frm, best on frm, has worn blinkers, prefers right handed tracks, excels at Ripon. Turf high 47. AW high 43. **J Pearce [5-48] Mrs Lydia Pearce.*

NO SHOES NO NEWS (IRE) BHB 30f RR 30f 2895[11]

3 br g Be My Native (USA) 11.2f **(62)** - Buffs Express (Bay Express) 7.1f **(60)**
Form - 080
Record 1998 - 1st:0 2nd:0 3rd:0 Ran:3
1998 Turf 0-3: (8f, 12f, 14f) (gd, g-f 2)
Lengthy, currently very moderate gelding. Turf high 30.
**M A Buckley [0-3] C C Buckley.*

NOSTALCHIA (FR) RR 96f 725a[3]

3 b f Genereux Genie - Assombrie (FR) (Hellios (USA))
Form - 33
1998 Turf 0-2: (7f 2) (hvy, sft)
Currently very useful filly. Turf high 96 - 3rd of 7 to Cortona (10 Apr Maisons-laffitte 7f hvy RF 0725a). **in FR [0-2].*

NOTAGAINTHEN BHB 58f RR 56f 5005[8]

2 b f Then Again 7.4f **(52)** - Fairy Ballerina (Fairy King (USA)) 7.7f **(59)**
Form - 548
Record 1998 - 1st:0 2nd:0 3rd:0 Ran:3
1998 Turf 0-3: (6f 2, 8f) (sft, gd, g-f)
Currently fair filly. Turf high 56 (began Jly).
**S G Knight [0-3] Mrs Ginny Withers.*

NOTATION (IRE) BHB 32f42a RR 34f 42a 4879[9]

4 b c Arazi (USA) 9.2f **(74)** - Grace Note (FR) (Top Ville) 11.7f **(68)**
Form - 818144322708463080
Record 1998 - 1st:0 2nd:2 3rd:2 Ran:14
Pre1998 - 1st:2 2nd:0 3rd:0 Ran:9
Win Prizemoney £4,238 *Total Prizemoney* £6,484

Wins
- * 1997 *Dec Southw (STD) H 14f 45 51* <
- * 1997 *Nov Southw (STD) H 14f 29 43*

1998 Turf 0-4: (16f 3, 18f) (g-s, gd 3) 1998 AW 0-10: (14f 4, 15f, 16f 5) (Fibr 10)
Fair colt, effective 14 to 16f, best at 16f, - acts on Fibr, has worn blinkers, prefers left handed tracks, favours tight tracks, excels at Southwell. Turf high 34. AW high 57 - 2nd of 12 giving 5lb to Glide Path (13 Feb Southwell 16f Fibr RF 0283).
**D W Chapman [2-23] J M Chapman.*

NOTEWORTHY RR 47f 4665[9]

2 br f Saddlers' Hall (IRE) 10.5f **(65)** - Rushing River (USA) (Irish River (FR)) 8.6f **(78)**
Form - 0
Record 1998 - 1st:0 2nd:0 3rd:0 Ran:1
1998 Turf 0-1: (8f) (g-s)
Currently moderate filly. **J Noseda [0-1] Wyck Hall Stud.*

NOT FORGOTTEN (USA) BHB 30f43a RR 49df 43a 3038[10]

4 b g St Jovite (USA) 11.8f **(75)** - Past Remembered (USA) (Solford (USA)) 13f **(71)**
Form - 000
Record 1998 - 1st:0 2nd:0 3rd:0 Ran:3
Pre1998 - 1st:0 2nd:0 3rd:0 Ran:13
Win Prizemoney £0 *Total Prizemoney* £979
1998 Turf 0-2: (12f, 22f) (g-s, gd) 1998 AW 0-1: (16f) (Equi)
Moderate gelding, often wears blinkers. Becoming disappointing.
**R P C Hoad [0-9] Jay Byrds Partnership (from P A Kelleway [0-13] Spt 1997).*

NOTLEY PARK BHB 69f RR 75f 3293[5]

3 ch f Wolfhound (USA) 7.3f **(71)** - Riviere Bleue (Riverman (USA)) 9.1f **(76)**
Form - 3245
Record 1998 - 1st:0 2nd:1 3rd:1 Ran:4
Win Prizemoney £0 *Total Prizemoney* £1,879
1998 Turf 0-4: (7f 3, 8f) (gd 2, g-f, frm)
Above-average filly. Turf high 75 - 2nd of 15 getting 5lb from Dushanbe (10 Jun Beverley 7f gd RF 1868).
**Miss L A Perratt [0-4] Mrs Seamus Burns.*

NOT OUT LAD BHB 24f RR 31df 3365[16]

4 b g Governor General 6.8f **(45)** - Sorcha (IRE) (Shernazar) 10.2f **(73)**
Form - 00
Record 1998 - 1st:0 2nd:0 3rd:0 Ran:2
Pre1998 - 1st:0 2nd:0 3rd:0 Ran:4
1998 Turf 0-2: (7f, 10f) (gd, g-f)
Strong, very moderate gelding. (began Jly).
**P Butler [0-6] Christopher Wilson.*

NOT QUITE GREY BHB 23f RR 21f 3599[10]

5 gr g Absalom 7.1f **(56)** - Strawberry Song (Final Straw) 7.9f **(64)**
Form - 00030
Record 1998 - 1st:0 2nd:0 3rd:1 Ran:5
Pre1998 - 1st:0 2nd:0 3rd:1 Ran:7
Win Prizemoney £0 *Total Prizemoney* £676
1998 Turf 0-5: (8f 2, 10f, 12f, 16f) (sft, gd, g-f, frm 2)
Little account gelding, has worn blinkers. Turf high 21.
**Miss J A Camacho [0-2] D D Davies (from T D McCarthy [0-6] May 1998).*

NOTTY RR 35f 1877[8]

3 ch f Nicholas Bill 9.8f **(56)** - Silver Empress (Octavo (USA)) 14.4f **(54)**
Form - 8
Record 1998 - 1st:0 2nd:0 3rd:0 Ran:1
1998 Turf 0-1: (12f) (g-s)
Leggy, currently very moderate filly.
**P Hayward [0-1] Mrs S A Coplestone.*

NOUFARI (FR) BHB 68f84a RR 75f 84a 5150[12]

7 b g Kahyasi 12.9f **(74)** - Noufiyla (Top Ville) 11.7f **(68)**
Form - 312110153205310200
Record 1998 - 1st:5 2nd:3 3rd:2 Ran:17
Pre1998 - 1st:6 2nd:8 3rd:12 Ran:51
Win Prizemoney £36,245 *Total Prizemoney* £68,049

Wins
- * **1998** Aug Newcas (GD) H 16.1f 64 67
- * **1998** *Apr Wolver (STD) H 14.8f 78 82* <
- * **1998** *Mar Wolver (STD) H 14.8f 74 77*
- * **1998** *Feb Southw (STD) H 16f 70 74*
- * **1998** *Jan Southw (STD) H 16f 60 66*
- * 1997 Jly Ayr (G-F) 13.1f 74
- * 1995 *Feb Wolver (STD) H 12f 80 79*
- * 1995 *Feb Wolver (STD) H 12f 72 78*
- * 1995 *Jan Wolver (STD) H 14f 61 69+*
- * 1994 *Dec Wolver (STD) H 12f 61 65*
- * 1994 *Dec Wolver (STD) H 12f 56 59*

1998 Turf 1-11: (15f, 16f 1-6, 17f, 18f 3) (g-s, gd 6, g-f 1-2, frm 2) 1998 AW 4-6: (15f 2-3, 16f 2-3) (Fibr 4-6)
Decent gelding, effective 13 to 18f, best at 15f, acts on gd to frm - acts on Fibr, favours left handed tracks, excels at Southwell and does well at Newcastle. Turf high 75 - 2nd of 5 getting 25lb from Sweetness Herself (31 Aug Newcastle 16f frm RF 3994). AW high 82 - 1st of 6 giving 14lb to Onefourseven (11 Apr Wolverhampton RF 0653) - also 1st of 9 getting 5lb from Jamaican Flight (14 Mar Wolverhampton RF 0432). Inconsistent. He went through a spell

where he just could not put his head in front where it matters, and looked to throw away winning chances on more than one occasion. However, he was in good form over long distances on Fibresand early in the year with a string of victories in staying events. He looked one to oppose on turf, but did win a race at Newcastle in August. **R Hollinshead [11-68] Ed Weetman.*

NOUKARI (IRE) BHB 53f53a **RR 68f 53a** 5081[2]

5 b g Darshaan 11.9f **(81)** - Noufiyla (Top Ville) 11.7f **(68)**
Form - 272
Record 1998 - 1st:0 2nd:2 3rd:0 Ran:3
Pre1998 - 1st:0 2nd:0 3rd:1 Ran:3
Win Prizemoney £0 *Total Prizemoney* £1,664
1998 Turf 0-2: (12f 2) (g-s, frm) 1998 AW 0-1: (12f) (Fibr)
Average gelding. Turf high 68.
**P D Evans [0-3] Mrs L A Windsor (from J Oxx in IRE [0-3] May 1997).*

NOUSHKEY **RR 83f** 5071[1]

2 b f Polish Precedent (USA) 9f **(73)** - Top of the League (High Top) 10.2f **(67)**
Form - 1
Record 1998 - 1st:1 2nd:0 3rd:0 Ran:1
Win Prizemoney £4,321 *Total Prizemoney* £4,321
Wins * **1998** Oct Newmar (SFT) 7f 83 <
1998 Turf 1-1: (7f 1-1) (gd 1-1)
Currently decent filly. (1st run) - 1st of 16 from Balladonia (31 Oct Newmarket RF 5071). A half-sister to San Sebastian, she looks a staying type. **M A Jarvis [1-1] Sheikh Ahmed Al Maktoum.*

NOUVEAU CHEVAL BHB 56f55a **RR 55f 55a** 3949[5]

3 b f Picea 12.7f **(43)** - Freeracer (Free State) 8.7f **(61)**
Form - 77135
Record 1998 - 1st:1 2nd:0 3rd:1 Ran:5
Win Prizemoney £2,469 *Total Prizemoney* £2,790
Wins 1998 May Leices (GD) C 8f 51 <
1998 Turf 1-3: (8f 1-2, 10f) (g-s, gd, g-f 1-1)1998AW 0-2: (7f, 9f) (Fibr 2)
Light-framed, fair filly. Turf high 55 - 5th of 22 getting 11lb from Galapino (29 Aug Goodwood 10f gd RF 3949) - also 1st of 12 giving 4lb to Mrs Middle (26 May Leicester RF 1469). AW high 47.
**M C Pipe [0-2] Knight Hawks Partnership (from J R Jenkins [1-3] May 1998).*

NOVELTY **RR 44f** 4010[8]

3 b f Primo Dominie 7.2f **(67)** - Nophe (USA) (Super Concorde (USA)) 10.9f **(66)**
Form - 78
Record 1998 - 1st:0 2nd:0 3rd:0 Ran:2
1998 Turf 0-2: (7f, 8f) (g-s, frm)
Unfurnished, currently moderate filly. Turf high 44 (began Jly).
**M Brittain [0-2] Mel Brittain.*

NO WARNING BHB 96f **RR 85f** 4746[5]

2 b c Warning 8.1f **(77)** - Norgabie (Northfields (USA)) 9f **(72)**
Form - 11175
Record 1998 - 1st:3 2nd:0 3rd:0 Ran:5
Win Prizemoney £12,121 *Total Prizemoney* £12,469
Wins * **1998** Jun Ripon (SFT) 6f 85+
* **1998** Jun Chepst (G-S) 6.1f 80+
* **1998** *May Wolver (STD) 6f 86++* <
1998 Turf 2-4: (6f 2-3, 7f) (g-s 1-1, gd 1-2, g-f) 1998 AW 1-1: (6f 1-1) (Fibr 1-1)
Useful colt. Turf high 85 - also 1st of 2 giving 8lb to Bon Ami (18 Jun Ripon RF 2090). (1st run) - 1st of 8 from Maybe Special (29 May Wolverhampton RF 1580). He won his first three starts, including one on the Wolverhampton Fibresand, but only held on by a whisker in a match at Ripon on his third outing, and finished stone last in the Solario. **Sir Mark Prescott [3-5] Hesmonds Stud.*

NOWELL HOUSE BHB 55f **RR 69f** 5094[10]

2 ch g Polar Falcon (USA) 9f **(74)** -Langtry Lady (Pas de Seul) 9.1f **(67)**
Form - 0330000
Record 1998 - 1st:0 2nd:0 3rd:2 Ran:7
Win Prizemoney £0 *Total Prizemoney* £1,066
1998 Turf 0-7: (5f 3, 6f, 7f, 8f 2) (gd 3, g-f 4)
Average gelding, effective 5f, acts on g-f. Turf high 69.
**M W Easterby [0-7] Bernard Bargh.*

NOWHERE TO EXIT BHB 91f **RR 83f** 4930[1]

2 b c Exit To Nowhere (USA) 8.7f **(77)** - Tromond **(92f)** (Lomond (USA)) 8.8f **(65)**
Form - 721
Record 1998 - 1st:1 2nd:1 3rd:0 Ran:3
Win Prizemoney £3,582 *Total Prizemoney* £4,558
Wins * **1998** Oct Bright (G-S) 8f 83 <
1998 Turf 1-3: (7f, 8f 1-2) (g-s 1-1, g-f, frm)
Currently decent colt. Turf high 83 (began Jly) - 1st of 11 from Blue (22 Oct Brighton RF 4930).
**J L Dunlop [1-3] Mrs Gary Pinchen.*

NOW IS THE HOUR BHB 46f **RR 55f** 4643[18]

2 ch g Timeless Times (USA) 6.1f **(56)** - Macs Maharanee **(71f 70a)** (Indian King (USA)) 7.4f **(64)**
Form - 804060
Record 1998 - 1st:0 2nd:0 3rd:0 Ran:6
Win Prizemoney £0 *Total Prizemoney* £232
1998 Turf 0-5: (5f 3, 6f, 7f) (gd, g-f 3, frm) 1998 AW 0-1: (5f) (Fibr)
Fair gelding. Turf high 55. **P S Felgate [0-6] John Martin.*

NOW LOOK HERE BHB 79f **RR 77f** 5139[4]

2 b c Reprimand 8.2f **(63)** - Where's Carol (Anfield) 8.5f **(59)**
Form - 634
Record 1998 - 1st:0 2nd:0 3rd:1 Ran:3
Win Prizemoney £0 *Total Prizemoney* £821
1998 Turf 0-3: (5f, 6f 2) (g-s, gd 2)
Currently above-average colt. Turf high 77 (began Oct) - 4th of 22 to Mutaakkid (6 Nov Doncaster 6f gd RF 5139).
**B A McMahon [0-3] S L Edwards.*

NOZOMI (IRE) BHB 72f **RR 69f** 4857[21]

2 b f Mujadil (USA) 7.7f **(70)** - Crimbourne (Mummy's Pet) 7.7f **(60)**
Form - 7610
Record 1998 - 1st:1 2nd:0 3rd:0 Ran:4
Win Prizemoney £2,532 *Total Prizemoney* £2,532
Wins * **1998** *Oct Wolver (sta) 6f 77* <
1998 Turf 0-3: (5f, 6f 2) (sft, gd, g-f) 1998 AW 1-1: (6f 1-1) (Fibr 1-1)
Above-average filly. Turf high 69. (1st run) - 1st of 11 getting 5lb from Bellamont Forest (3 Oct Wolverhampton RF 4637). Speedily-bred, she showed promise on turf before getting off the mark in a maiden on the Wolverhampton Fibresand in October.
**P J Makin [1-4] R P Marchant.*

NUANCE (IRE) **RR 68f** 4809[3]

3 ch f Rainbow Quest (USA) 11.2f **(81)** - Madame Dubois (Legend of France (USA)) 9.5f **(61)**
Form - 63
Record 1998 - 1st:0 2nd:0 3rd:1 Ran:2
Win Prizemoney £0 *Total Prizemoney* £580
1998 Turf 0-2: (12f, 14f) (gd, frm)
Workmanlike, currently average filly. Turf high 68 (began Spt) - 3rd of 7 getting 5lb from Wave of Optimism (14 Oct Nottingham 14f gd RF 4809). **H R A Cecil [0-2] Cliveden Stud.*

NUBILE BHB 43f31a **RR 46f 31a** 1638[10]

4 b f Pursuit of Love 9.5f **(69)** - Trojan Lady (USA) (Irish River (FR)) 8.6f **(78)**
Form - 05540
Record 1998 - 1st:0 2nd:0 3rd:0 Ran:4
Pre1998 - 1st:1 2nd:0 3rd:1 Ran:8
Win Prizemoney £2,146 *Total Prizemoney* £2,848
Wins 1997 Jly Windso (G-F) S 11.6f 46 <
1998 Turf 0-1: (12f) (g-f) 1998 AW 0-3: (16f 3) (Equi, Fibr 2)
Workmanlike, moderate filly, likes tight tracks. AW high 26.
**W J Musson [0-10] Windmill Racing (from B W Hills [1-5] Jly 1997).*

NUCLEAR DEBATE (USA) BHB 98f **RR 98f** 4516[4]

3 b g Geiger Counter (USA) 7.8f **(85)** - I'm An Issue (USA) (Cox's Ridge (USA)) 8f **(68)**
Form - 321510024
Record 1998 - 1st:2 2nd:2 3rd:1 Ran:9
Pre1998 - 1st:0 2nd:2 3rd:1 Ran:6
Win Prizemoney £20,985 *Total Prizemoney* £45,396
Wins * **1998** Jun Newcas (GD) H 5f 90 97 <
* **1998** May Thirsk (GD) 6f 88
1998 Turf 2-9: (5f 1-2, 6f 1-7) (g-s, gd 2-5, g-f 3)

Workmanlike, very useful gelding, effective 5 to 6f, best at 5f, acts on gd to g-f, best on gd. Turf high 98 - 4th of 9 getting 4lb from To the Roof (27 Spt Ascot 5f gd RF 4516) - also 1st of 19 giving 8lb to Gay Breeze (26 Jun Newcastle RF 2307). Consistent. A useful sprint handicapper, he landed the competitive Gosforth Park Cup at Newcastle when well drawn. He was not so well berthed in the Stewards' Cup, and that run can be pretty much ignored, and ran poorly at Ripon before putting in good runs when second in the Portland and at Ascot. With the retirement of Lynda Ramsden, he has joined John Hammond's yard in France.
**Mrs J R Ramsden [2-15] J R Chester.*

NUIT D'OR (IRE) BHB 69f58a **RR 66f 58a** 459[5]
3 ch g Night Shift (USA) 8.1f **(73)** - Sister Golden Hair (IRE) (Glint of Gold) 9.3f **(66)**
Form - 642105
Record 1998 - 1st:1 2nd:1 3rd:0 Ran:6
Pre1998 - 1st:0 2nd:0 3rd:0 Ran:4
Win Prizemoney £1,738 *Total Prizemoney* £2,461
Wins 1998 *Feb Wolver (STD) S 8.5f 62 <*
1998 AW 1-6: (6f, 7f, 8f 1-4) (Fibr 1-6)
Strong, average gelding, effective 8f, - acts on Fibr, has worn blinkers (extremely effectively). AW high 64 - 2nd of 8 getting 7lb from Pipe Music (23 Feb Southwell 8f Fibr RF 0342) - also 1st of 10 giving 5lb to Operatic (25 Feb Wolverhampton RF 0361). He seemed to improve when blinkered and stepped up to a mile on sand, and after being unluckily caught on the line at Southwell in February, made no mistake with an easy victory at Wolverhampton just two days later.
**N P Littmoden [0-2] Foley Steelstock (from M Johnston [1-8] Feb 1998).*

NUKUD (USA) BHB 17f26a **RR 43?f 26a** 4875[6]
6 b g Topsider (USA) 7.9f **(73)** - Summer Silence (USA) (Stop The Music (USA)) 9.2f **(71)**
Form - 0850506068006
Record 1998 - 1st:0 2nd:0 3rd:0 Ran:13
Pre1998 - 1st:0 2nd:1 3rd:1 Ran:16
Win Prizemoney £0 *Total Prizemoney* £851
1998 Turf 0-10: (7f, 8f 5, 9f, 12f 2, 14f) (gd 6, g-f 2, frm 2) 1998 AW 0-3: (8f, 11f, 12f) (Fibr 3)
Fair gelding, effective 12f, - acts on Fibr, often wears blinkers, likes left handed tracks. Turf high 43. AW high 55 (began Jly) - 6th of 9 to River Captain (19 Oct Southwell 12f Fibr RF 4875).
**Miss J F Craze [0-1] Robert Cook (from G R Oldroyd [0-30] Spt 1998).*

NULLI SECUNDUS RR 54f 5037[6]
2 b c Polar Falcon (USA) 9f **(74)** - Exclusive Virtue (USA) (Shadeed (USA)) 8.2f **(70)**
Form - 6
Record 1998 - 1st:0 2nd:0 3rd:0 Ran:1
1998 Turf 0-1: (7f) (g-s)
Currently fair colt. **J A R Toller [0-1] Duke of Devonshire.*

NUMERATOR RR 75+f 4860[3]
2 ch f Rudimentary (USA) 8.2f **(66)** - Half a Dozen (USA) (Saratoga Six (USA)) 7f **(73)**
Form - 3
Record 1998 - 1st:0 2nd:0 3rd:1 Ran:1
Win Prizemoney £0 *Total Prizemoney* £420
1998 Turf 0-1: (8f) (sft)
Currently above-average filly. (1st run) - 3rd of 9 getting 5lb from Bring Sweets (17 Oct Redcar 8f sft RF 4860).
**W J Haggas [0-1] Cheveley Park Stud.*

NUNTHORPE BHB 66f **RR 77f** 4660[15]
3 ch f Mystiko (USA) 7.7f**(59)**-Enchanting Melody(Chief Singer)8.9f **(66)**
Form - 0105760
Record 1998 - 1st:1 2nd:0 3rd:0 Ran:7
Pre1998 - 1st:0 2nd:1 3rd:0 Ran:3
Win Prizemoney £4,416 *Total Prizemoney* £5,678
Wins * 1998 May Beverl (G-F) H 8.5f 72 77 <
1998 Turf 1-7: (7f, 8f 1-6) (gd 2, g-f 4, hrd 1-1)
Leggy, above-average filly, effective 6 to 8f, acts on frm to hrd, prefers tight tracks. Turf high 77 - 1st of 14 giving 4lb to Pixielated (10 May Beverley RF 1134). **J A Glover [1-10] B H Farr.*

NUTCHAT BHB 62f **RR 73f** 4463[10]
2 ch c Beveled (USA) 6.9f **(64)** - Shapina (Sharp Edge) 10f **(56)**
Form - 60040
Record 1998 - 1st:0 2nd:0 3rd:0 Ran:5
Win Prizemoney £0 *Total Prizemoney* £208
1998 Turf 0-5: (5f, 6f, 7f 2, 8f) (gd 3, frm, hrd)
Above-average colt. Turf high 73. **A P Jones [0-5] J F O'Donovan.*

NUVELLINO BHB 73f **RR 71f** 4670[1]
3 b g Robellino (USA) 9.5f **(68)** - Furry Dance (USA) (Nureyev (USA)) 8.7f **(78)**
Form - 3551
Record 1998 - 1st:1 2nd:0 3rd:1 Ran:4
Pre1998 - 1st:0 2nd:0 3rd:0 Ran:1
Win Prizemoney £3,692 *Total Prizemoney* £4,202
Wins * 1998 Oct Nottin (SFT) H 10f 67 71 <
1998 Turf 1-4: (7f, 10f 1-1, 12f 2) (g-s 1-1, g-f, frm 2)
Leggy, above-average gelding. Turf high 71 (began Aug) - 1st of 16 giving 6lb to Wings Awarded (6 Oct Nottingham RF 4670).
**B R Millman [1-4] Richard Withers (from S G Knight [0-1] Aug 1997).*

OA BALDIXE (FR) RR 115f 4346a[3]
4 gr c Linamix (FR) 8.2f **(64)** - Bal d'Oa (FR) (Noir Et Or) 10f **(38)**
Form - 311373
1998 Turf 2-5: (12f 2-4, 13f) (hvy, sft 1-2, g-s 1-1, gd)
High-class colt, effective 12 to 13f, best at 12f, acts on hvy to gd. Turf high 115 - 3rd of 6 to Limnos (13 Spt Longchamp 12f hvy RF 4346a). Looked a fair sort in the spring when winning a Listed event and a Group Three at Longchamp, but was then found out in Group Two company. **P Bary in FR [2-7] F Prat.*

OAKBURY (IRE) BHB 35f70a **RR 44f 70a** 4262[7]
6 ch g Common Grounds 8.1f **(66)** - Doon Belle (Ardoon) 7.3f **(53)**
Form - 307
Record 1998 - 1st:0 2nd:0 3rd:1 Ran:3
Pre1998 - 1st:0 2nd:4 3rd:3 Ran:27
Win Prizemoney £0 *Total Prizemoney* £6,471
1998 Turf 0-3: (12f 2, 16f) (gd 3)
Moderate gelding, has worn blinkers. Turf high 44 (1st run) (began Aug) - 3rd of 8 getting 12lb from Ten Past Six (26 Aug Carlisle 12f gd RF 3885).
**Miss L C Siddall [2-47] Panther Racing Ltd (from R Hannon [0-14] Oct 1995).*

OAKEN WOOD (IRE) BHB 42f36a **RR 38f 36a** 388[10]
4 ch g Lycius (USA) 8.8f **(71)** - Little Red Rose (Precocious) 8.6f **(62)**
Form - 00
Record 1998 - 1st:0 2nd:0 3rd:0 Ran:2
Pre1998 - 1st:0 2nd:0 3rd:0 Ran:4
1998 AW 0-2: (6f, 8f) (Equi, Fibr)
Strong, very moderate gelding, has worn blinkers. AW high 17.
**N A Callaghan [0-7] Dean Graham Bostock.*

OAK VINTAGE (USA) BHB 65f62a **RR 72df 62a** 4996[5]
3 b f Seeking the Gold (USA) 7.4f **(80)** - Delicate Vine (USA) (Knights Choice (USA))
Form - 7545
Record 1998 - 1st:0 2nd:0 3rd:0 Ran:4
Win Prizemoney £0 *Total Prizemoney* £247
1998 Turf 0-3: (9f 2, 11f) (gd, frm 2) 1998 AW 0-1: (10f) (Equi)
Scopey, above-average filly. Turf high 72.
**J H M Gosden [0-4] Sheikh Mohammed.*

OARE KITE BHB 65f56a **RR 62f 56a** 4874[13]
3 b f Batshoof 9.5f **(66)** - Portvasco (Sharpo) 7.7f **(59)**
Form - 000850320210
Record 1998 - 1st:1 2nd:2 3rd:1 Ran:12
Pre1998 - 1st:0 2nd:0 3rd:1 Ran:3
Win Prizemoney £2,400 *Total Prizemoney* £4,653
Wins * 1998 Oct Leices (G-S) 7f 62 <
1998 Turf 1-11: (5f 2, 6f 4, 7f 1-3, 8f 2) (g-s, gd 1-3, g-f, frm 5, hrd)
1998 AW 0-1: (8f) (Fibr)
Scopey, average filly, effective 7f, acts on gd, often wears blinkers (effectively). Turf high 62 - 1st of 19 getting 5lb from I Wish You Love (12 Oct Leicester RF 4765).
**G L Moore [1-4] Joe Bates (Bloodstock) Ltd (from P T Walwyn [0-11] Aug 1998).*

OARE LINNET **RR 40f** 4758[15]
2 ch f Polish Precedent (USA) 9f **(73)** - Portvasco (Sharpo) 7.7f **(59)**
Form - 0
Record 1998 - 1st:0 2nd:0 3rd:0 Ran:1
1998 Turf 0-1: (7f) (gd)
Currently moderate filly. **P T Walwyn [0-1] Mrs Henry Keswick.*

OATH (IRE) BHB 91f **RR 77f** 4806[1]
2 b c Fairy King (USA) 7.7f **(75)** - Sheer Audacity (Troy) 10.4f **(68)**
Form - 531
Record 1998 - 1st:1 2nd:0 3rd:1 Ran:3
Win Prizemoney £3,752 *Total Prizemoney* £4,313
Wins * **1998** Oct Nottin (SFT) 8.2f 77 <
1998 Turf 1-3: (6f, 7f, 8f 1-1) (gd 1-2, frm)
Currently above-average colt. Turf high 77 - 1st of 8 from Chelsea Barracks (14 Oct Nottingham RF 4806).
**H R A Cecil [1-2] The Thoroughbred Corporation (from R Charlton [0-1] Jun 1998).*

OBAN BALL BHB 52f **RR 46f** 4261[18]
2 ch f Pursuit of Love 9.5f **(69)** - Highland Light (Home Guard (USA)) 9.3f **(66)**
Form - 0800
Record 1998 - 1st:0 2nd:0 3rd:0 Ran:4
1998 Turf 0-4: (5f, 6f 3) (gd, g-f, frm, hrd)
Moderate filly. Turf high 46. **R Hannon [0-4] Lady Howard de Walden.*

OBERON'S MISTRAL BHB 75f **RR 77f** 4332[12]
3 b f Fairy King (USA) 7.7f **(75)** - La Venta (USA) (Drone) 10.3f **(74)**
Form - 863140
Record 1998 - 1st:1 2nd:0 3rd:1 Ran:6
Pre1998 - 1st:0 2nd:1 3rd:1 Ran:3
Win Prizemoney £3,629 *Total Prizemoney* £6,320
Wins * **1998** Jly Windso (G-F) 8.3f 75 <
1998 Turf 1-6: (8f 1-4, 9f, 10f) (gd, g-f 2, frm 1-3)
Small, above-average filly, effective 7 to 8f, best at 8f, acts on g-f to frm, best on frm. Turf high 77 - also 1st of 11 from Search Party (27 Jly Windsor RF 3148). Consistent. Not one of the stable stars.
**H R A Cecil [1-9] Lord Lloyd-Webber.*

OCASA (GER) **RR 110f** 5053a[1]
3 b f Lagunas 10f **(110)** - Olaya (GER) (Acatenango (GER))
Form - 1
1998 Turf 1-1: (12f 1-1) (hvy 1-1)
Currently Group-class filly. (1st run) - 1st of 8 getting 12lb from Kenzo (25 Oct Dusseldorf RF 5053a).
**P Remmert in GER [1-1] H Lohndorf.*

OCEAN BREEZE BHB 25f **RR 33df** 3623[6]
4 ch g Most Welcome 8.6f **(66)** - Sea Power (Welsh Pageant) 10f **(65)**
Form - 05356
Record 1998 - 1st:0 2nd:0 3rd:1 Ran:5
Pre1998 - 1st:0 2nd:0 3rd:2 Ran:9
Win Prizemoney £0 *Total Prizemoney* £1,389
1998 Turf 0-5: (12f, 13f, 14f, 16f, 22f) (g-s, gd, g-f, frm 2)
Leggy, very moderate gelding, effective 13 to 17f, acts on frm, often wears blinkers, prefers right handed tracks. Turf high 33.
**J S Wainwright [0-15] Miss Nina Bridge.*

OCEAN DRIVE (IRE) BHB 69f **RR 80f** 5057[4]
2 b br c Dolphin Street (FR) - Blonde Goddess (IRE) (Godswalk (USA)) 7.3f **(58)**
Form - 364
Record 1998 - 1st:0 2nd:0 3rd:1 Ran:3
Win Prizemoney £0 *Total Prizemoney* £560
1998 Turf 0-3: (7f 2, 8f) (sft 2, gd)
Currently decent colt. Turf high 80 (began Spt).
**Miss L A Perratt [0-3] Sutherland Marett Hay.*

OCEAN LIGHT BHB 43f **RR 10f** 2677[6]
4 ch f Anshan 8.2f **(63)** - Waveguide (Double Form) 7.3f **(58)**
Form - 06
Record 1998 - 1st:0 2nd:0 3rd:0 Ran:2
Pre1998 - 1st:0 2nd:0 3rd:0 Ran:3
1998 Turf 0-2: (8f 2) (g-f, frm)
Light-framed, moderate filly, has worn blinkers. Turf high 10 (began Jly). **A Bailey [0-5] Nev Jones.*

OCEAN LINE (IRE) BHB 45f **RR 47f** 4052[12]
3 b g Kefaah (USA) 11.2f **(64)** - Tropic Sea (IRE) (Sure Blade (USA)) 11.3f **(67)**
Form - 880450
Record 1998 - 1st:0 2nd:0 3rd:0 Ran:6
Pre1998 - 1st:0 2nd:0 3rd:1 Ran:4
Win Prizemoney £0 *Total Prizemoney* £501
1998 Turf 0-5: (9f 3, 10f 2) (gd 2, g-f 2, frm) 1998 AW 0-1: (8f) (Equi)
Workmanlike, moderate gelding, effective 9 to 10f, acts on gd to g-f, prefers tight tracks. Turf high 47 - 5th of 12 getting 4lb from Water Force (29 Jly Epsom 9f g-f RF 3202).
**A P Jarvis [0-10] Christopher Shankland.*

OCEAN OF STORMS (IRE) **RR 106f** 4719a[2]
3 b c Arazi (USA) 9.2f **(74)** - Moon Cactus (Kris) 9.5f **(73)**
Form - 22
1998 Turf 0-2: (15f 2) (sft, gd)
Currently Pattern-class colt. Turf high 106 (1st run) (began Jly) - 2nd of 4 to Pozarica (25 Jly Maisons-laffitte 15f gd RF 3226a). He was a shade unlucky in a Group Two at Maisons-Laffitte in July, challenging along the rail when there was an easier option round the outside. He went on to hack-up in a Listed race and finish second in the Prix de Lutece. More will be heard of this progressive stayer, who has joined Godolphin.
**A Fabre in FR [0-2] Sheikh Mohammed Al Maktoum.*

OCEAN PARK BHB 57f75a **RR 60f 75a** 4932[5]
7 b g Dominion 8.9f **(65)** - Chiming Melody (Cure The Blues (USA)) 9.5f **(63)**
Form - 072015
Record 1998 - 1st:1 2nd:1 3rd:0 Ran:6
Pre1998 - 1st:5 2nd:4 3rd:2 Ran:30
Win Prizemoney £22,547 *Total Prizemoney* £28,299
Wins * **1998** Aug Warwic (G-F) S 10.8f 59
* 1996 Spt Folkes (G-F) 12f 66
* 1996 Apr Leices (GD) H 10f 65 66
* 1996 *Mar Lingfi (STD) H 10f 80 84* <
* 1996 *Feb Lingfi (STD) H 10f 76 77*
* 1996 *Jan Wolver (STD) 8.5f 75*
1998 Turf 1-6: (8f, 10f 3, 11f 1-1, 12f) (g-s, g-f, frm 1-4)
Decent gelding, effective 8 to 12f, best at 12f, acts on gd to hrd, has worn blinkers, excels at Folkestone. Turf high 60 - 7th of 13 giving 9lb to Smarter Charter (8 Jly Kempton 8f frm RF 2633) - also 1st of 17 giving 14lb to Brookhouse Lady (31 Aug Warwick RF 4002).
**Lady Herries [6-27] Lady Herries (from P J Makin [0-6] Oct 1994).*

OCEAN PRINCE (FR) **RR 52f** 4823[21]
2 b c Dolphin Street (FR) - Dumayla (Shernazar) 10.2f **(73)**
Form - 60
Record 1998 - 1st:0 2nd:0 3rd:0 Ran:2
1998 Turf 0-2: (8f 2) (gd, frm)
Currently fair colt. Turf high 52 (began Spt). **W R Muir [0-2] B Bull.*

OCEANS FRIENDLY (USA) **RR 74f** 4514[8]
2 br f Green Dancer (USA) 11.9f **(77)** - Sedra (Nebbiolo) 8.1f **(75)**
Form - 48
Record 1998 - 1st:0 2nd:0 3rd:0 Ran:2
Win Prizemoney £0 *Total Prizemoney* £240
1998 Turf 0-2: (8f 2) (gd, g-f)
Currently above-average filly. Turf high 74 (1st run) (began Spt) - 4th of 16 getting 5lb from Golden Snake (11 Spt Doncaster 8f g-f RF 4227). Shaped with promise on her debut in a Doncaster maiden. **B W Hills [0-2] W J Gredley.*

OCHOS RIOS (IRE) BHB 48f60a **RR 50f 60a** 4775[8]
7 br g Horage 11.4f **(58)** - Morgiana (Godswalk (USA)) 7.3f **(58)**
Form - 0011608
Record 1998 - 1st:2 2nd:0 3rd:0 Ran:7
Pre1998 - 1st:4 2nd:5 3rd:8 Ran:62
Win Prizemoney £27,019 *Total Prizemoney* £39,793
Wins * **1998** Jun Thirsk (SFT) H 7f 40 50
* **1998** Jun Beverl (GD) H 7.5f 40 43
* 1996 Spt York (GD) H 7f 56 59
* 1994 Spt Haydoc (G-S) H 7.1f 58 64
1998 Turf 2-7: (7f 2-7) (gd 2-4, g-f 2, frm)
Fair gelding, effective 7f, acts on gd to frm, best on gd, has worn

blinkers. Turf high 50. **B S Rothwell [6-69] J B Young.*

OCKER (IRE) BHB 80f70a RR 78f 70a 5142[1]

4 br g Astronef 7.9f **(59)** - Violet Somers (Will Somers) 5.9f **(59)**

Form - 0012002222081331000030001

Record 1998 - 1st:4 2nd:5 3rd:3 Ran:22
Pre1998 - 1st:0 2nd:2 3rd:0 Ran:15

Win Prizemoney £20,819 *Total Prizemoney* £33,354

Wins * **1998** Nov Doncas (SFT) H 5f 74 78 <
* **1998** Aug Newbur (GD) H 5.2f 74 77
* **1998** Jly Haydoc (G-F) H 5f 68 71
1998 Mar Nottin (G-S) H 6.1f 53 76

1998 Turf 4-22:(5f 3-10, 6f 1-11, 7f)(sft 3, g-s 1-4, gd 2-6, g-f 1-5, frm 4)

Scopey, above-average gelding, effective 5 to 6f, best at 5f, acts on sft to frm, best on gd, has worn blinkers, excels at Newcastle. Turf high 78 - 1st of 22 getting 6lb from Demolition Jo (6 Nov Doncaster RF 5142) - also 1st of 15 giving 12lb to River Tern (15 Aug Newbury RF 3656). By no means consistent, but an effective sprinter on his day. Suited by a fast-run five.

**Mrs N Macauley [3-18] J Teasdale (from M H Tompkins [1-19] Apr 1998).*

OCTAVIA HILL BHB 40f50a RR 22f 50a 2940[13]

5 ch m Prince Sabo 6.6f **(64)** - Clara Barton (Youth (USA)) 9.8f **(64)**

Form - 006000

Record 1998 - 1st:0 2nd:0 3rd:0 Ran:6
Pre1998 - 1st:1 2nd:1 3rd:2 Ran:11

Win Prizemoney £3,025 *Total Prizemoney* £5,069

Wins 1997 Spt Epsom (GD) H 7f 52 57 <

1998 Turf 0-6: (6f 2, 7f 2, 8f 2) (gd 3, g-f, frm 2)

Little account filly, effective 7f, acts on gd to frm, often wears blinkers. Turf high 22.

**J M Bradley [0-6] M G Ridley & Partners (from P W Harris [1-11] Spt 1997).*

ODDSANENDS BHB 78f81a RR 73?f 81a 3827[3]

2 b c Alhijaz 7.7f **(57)** - Jans Contessa (Rabdan) 5.9f **(53)**

Form - 54413

Record 1998 - 1st:1 2nd:0 3rd:1 Ran:5

Win Prizemoney £5,550 *Total Prizemoney* £9,030

Wins * **1998** Aug Ascot (G-F) H 7f 63 73? <

1998 Turf 1-3: (6f, 7f 1-2) (g-s, g-f 1-1, frm) 1998 AW 0-2: (6f 2) (Fibr 2)

Decent colt. Turf high 73. AW high 84 (began Jly) - 3rd of 13 to Blue Star (22 Aug Wolverhampton 6f Fibr RF 3827). He got off the mark by making all to land an Ascot nursery in August.

**C N Allen [1-5] J T B Racing.*

ODETTE BHB 70f RR 71f 3235[14]

3 b f Pursuit of Love 9.5f **(69)** - On Tiptoes (Shareef Dancer (USA)) 9.9f **(73)**

Form - 48110

Record 1998 - 1st:2 2nd:0 3rd:0 Ran:5
Pre1998 - 1st:0 2nd:2 3rd:2 Ran:4

Win Prizemoney £5,583 *Total Prizemoney* £9,149

Wins * **1998** Jly Warwic (G-F) 5f 71 <
* **1998** Jun Bath (G-S) 5.7f 65

1998 Turf 2-5: (5f 1-2, 6f 1-2, 7f) (gd 1-3, g-f, frm 1-1)

Workmanlike, above-average filly, effective 5 to 7f, best at 5f, acts on gd to frm, has worn blinkers. Turf high 71 - 1st of 5 giving 3lb to Mrs Malaprop (18 Jly Warwick RF 2945) - also 1st of 8 getting 10lb from Nitwitty (27 Jun Bath RF 2326).

**Sir Mark Prescott [2-9] J W Rowles.*

ODYSSEY BHB 71f RR 74f 4779[7]

2 b c Slip Anchor 12.7f **(75)** - Circe (Main Reef) 9.6f **(57)**

Form - 567

Record 1998 - 1st:0 2nd:0 3rd:0 Ran:3

1998 Turf 0-3: (7f, 8f 2) (gd 2, g-f)

Currently above-average colt. Turf high 74 (began Aug).

**P T Walwyn [0-3] A D G Oldrey.*

OFF HIRE BHB 46f RR 48f 5117[1]

2 b g Clantime 6.6f **(57)** - Lady Pennington (Blue Cashmere) 6.4f **(54)**

Form - 0001

Record 1998 - 1st:1 2nd:0 3rd:0 Ran:4

Win Prizemoney £2,745 *Total Prizemoney* £2,745

Wins * **1998** Nov Mussel (SFT) SH 5f 35 48 <

1998 Turf 1-4: (5f 1-2, 7f, 8f) (gd 1-1, frm 3)

Average gelding. Turf high 48 (began Aug) - 1st of 9 getting 22lb from Nicholas Mistress (4 Nov Musselburgh RF 5117).

**C Smith [1-4] John Martin-Hoyes.*

OFFICE HOURS BHB 30f40a RR 24f 40a 3385[5]

6 b g Danehill (USA) 9.1f **(79)**-Charmina (FR)(Nonoalco (USA))8.5f **(66)**

Form - 5

Record 1998 - 1st:0 2nd:0 3rd:0 Ran:1
Pre1998 - 1st:0 2nd:2 3rd:3 Ran:23

Win Prizemoney £0 *Total Prizemoney* £4,047

1998 Turf 0-1: (12f) (g-f)

Moderate gelding, has worn blinkers. Becoming disappointing.

**R Lee [0-1] Oakford Horse Transport (from W G M Turner [0-5] Apr 1997).*

OFF THE RAILS BHB 48f53a RR 55f 53a 1551[14]

4 b f Saddlers' Hall (IRE) 10.5f **(65)** - Sliprail (USA) (Our Native (USA)) 11.2f **(63)**

Form - 80

Record 1998 - 1st:0 2nd:0 3rd:0 Ran:2
Pre1998 - 1st:0 2nd:0 3rd:1 Ran:6

Win Prizemoney £0 *Total Prizemoney* £509

1998 Turf 0-1: (12f) (frm) 1998 AW 0-1: (10f) (Equi)

Scopey, fair filly.

**J G Portman [0-2] Mrs John Redvers (from H Candy [0-6] Spt 1997).*

OGGI BHB 80f RR 81f 4246[21]

7 gr g Efisio 7.7f **(69)** - Dolly Bevan (Another Realm) 6.6f **(55)**

Form - 600040

Record 1998 - 1st:0 2nd:0 3rd:0 Ran:6
Pre1998 - 1st:6 2nd:1 3rd:3 Ran:29

Win Prizemoney £27,667 *Total Prizemoney* £38,756

Wins * 1997 May Goodwo (G-S) H 6f 79 81 <
* 1997 Apr Leices (G-S) H 6f 72 78
* 1996 Oct Leices (G-F) H 6f 65 71
* 1996 Spt Haydoc (G-F) H 6f 59 65
* 1995 May Newbur (GD) H 6f 61 59

1998 Turf 0-6: (6f 6) (g-s, gd 2, g-f 2, frm)

Decent gelding, effective 6f, acts on gd to g-f, best on gd, has worn blinkers. Turf high 81. He seemed better than ever in '97, running well in some of the big sprint handicaps, but had a frustrating campaign in 1998. Probably retains his ability.

**P J Makin [5-32] Skyline Racing Ltd (from A G Foster [1-3] Apr 1994).*

OH FROBISHER (IRE) BHB 45f RR 49f 4623[8]

2 ch f Perugino (USA) - Poscimur (IRE) (Prince Rupert (FR))

Form - 7780408

Record 1998 - 1st:0 2nd:0 3rd:0 Ran:7

1998 Turf 0-7: (5f 3, 6f 3, 7f) (g-s, gd 2, g-f 2, frm 2)

Moderate filly, has worn blinkers. Turf high 49.

**C Parker [0-7] M C MacKenzie & Mrs S B MacKenzie.*

OH HEBE (IRE) BHB 71f RR 72f 2967[6]

3 b f Night Shift (USA) 8.1f **(73)** - Why so Silent (Mill Reef (USA)) 10.5f **(78)**

Form - 106556

Record 1998 - 1st:1 2nd:0 3rd:0 Ran:6
Pre1998 - 1st:0 2nd:0 3rd:1 Ran:2

Win Prizemoney £3,915 *Total Prizemoney* £4,852

Wins * **1998** Apr Leices (SFT) 7f 77 <

1998 Turf 1-5: (6f 2, 7f 1-1, 8f 2) (sft 1-1, gd 2, g-f, frm) 1998 AW 0-1: (6f) (Fibr)

Workmanlike, above-average filly, effective 7f, acts on sft. Turf high 77 (1st run) - 1st of 7 from Light Step (9 Apr Leicester RF 0620). Consistent. A half-sister to Poppy Carew and Calypso Grant, she won a maiden at Leicester in very testing ground on her reappearance. Though unplaced in some competitive handicaps since, she has been far from disgraced. Does not help her cause by pulling hard. **P W Harris [1-8] Mrs P W Harris.*

O' HIGGINS (IRE) BHB 44f RR 44f 4504[7]

3 b g Magical Wonder (USA) 7.2f **(60)** - Lightning Laser (Monseigneur (USA)) 7.7f **(63)**

Form - 000807

Record 1998 - 1st:0 2nd:0 3rd:0 Ran:6
Pre1998 - 1st:0 2nd:0 3rd:2 Ran:7

Win Prizemoney £0 *Total Prizemoney* £1,172
1998 Turf 0-6: (7f 2, 8f 4) (gd, g-f, frm 4)
Moderate gelding, effective 8f, acts on g-f, has worn blinkers. Turf high 44. Consistent.
**D Morris [0-6] T J Wells (from R Boss [0-7] Oct 1997).*

OH I SAY BHB 59f **RR 71f** 4863[12]
2 b f Primo Dominie 7.2f **(67)** - Isotonic (Absalom) 7.2f **(58)**
Form - 21616544080
Record 1998 - 1st:2 2nd:1 3rd:0 Ran:11
Win Prizemoney £8,028 *Total Prizemoney* £9,440
Wins * **1998** May Windso (G-F) 5f 71 <
* **1998** Apr Nottin (G-S) 5.1f 71 <
1998 Turf 2-9: (5f 2-7, 6f 2) (gd 1-2, g-f 2, frm 1-4, hrd) 1998 AW 0-2: (5f, 6f) (Equi, Fibr)
Decent filly, effective 5f, acts on gd to frm - acts on Equi. Turf high 71 (1st run) - 1st of 7 from First Musical (7 Apr Nottingham RF 0587) - also 1st of 7 giving 6lb to College Blue (18 May Windsor RF 1313). AW high 80 (1st run) - 2nd of 7 to Kastaway (30 Mar Lingfield 5f Equi RF 0505).
**M Bell [2-11] G L H Lederman & R A M Lederman.*

OH NO NOT HIM BHB 55f **RR 45f** 4803[5]
2 b c Reprimand 8.2f **(63)** - Lucky Mill **(23f)** (Midyan (USA)) 6f **(60)**
Form - 005
Record 1998 - 1st:0 2nd:0 3rd:0 Ran:3
1998 Turf 0-3: (7f 3) (sft, gd, g-f)
Currently moderate colt. Turf high 45 (began Spt).
**M A Jarvis [0-3] Little Stanneylands Stud.*

OH SO GRAND BHB 50f **RR 43f** 4665[11]
2 ch f Grand Lodge (USA) - Cutleaf (Kris) 9.5f **(73)**
Form - 060
Record 1998 - 1st:0 2nd:0 3rd:0 Ran:3
1998 Turf 0-3: (6f, 7f, 8f) (g-s, frm 2)
Currently moderate filly. Turf high 43 (began Jly).
**R M H Cowell [0-3] G W Byrne.*

OH SO HANDY BHB 28f29a **RR 34f 29a** 2110[10]
10 b g Nearly A Hand 10f **(36)** - Geordie Lass (Bleep-Bleep) 11f **(56)**
Form - 0
Record 1998 - 1st:0 2nd:0 3rd:0 Ran:1
Pre1998 - 1st:0 2nd:0 3rd:2 Ran:8
Win Prizemoney £0 *Total Prizemoney* £774
1998 Turf 0-1: (22f) (gd)
Very moderate gelding, often wears blinkers. Becoming disappointing. **R Curtis [6-52] Mrs R A Smith.*

OKAWANGO (SPA) RR 104f 4718a[7]
5 b h Don Roberto (USA) 15.6f **(39)** - Noche Gris (SPA) (Blue Skyer (SPA))
Form - 7
1998 Turf 0-1: (10f) (sft)
Currently very useful colt. He was never a factor behind Insatiable in the Prix Dollar. **M Delcher in SPA [1-2] Guijarro Zubiz.*

OKAY BABY (IRE) BHB 30f44a **RR 31f 44a** 3309[2]
6 b m Treasure Kay 6.5f **(53)** - Miss Tuko (Good Times (ITY)) 6.6f **(54)**
Form - 74062
Record 1998 - 1st:0 2nd:1 3rd:0 Ran:5
Pre1998 - 1st:1 2nd:4 3rd:1 Ran:25
Win Prizemoney £2,708 *Total Prizemoney* £7,096
Wins 1995 Jun Mussel (FRM) C 8.1f 45 <
1998 Turf 0-3: (5f, 6f, 7f) (sft, gd, g-f) 1998 AW 0-2: (6f 2) (Equi, Fibr)
Very moderate mare, effective 5 to 7f, best at 7f, acts on gd to frm, has worn blinkers. Turf high 31 - 2nd of 23 getting 22lb from Superbit (3 Aug Ripon 5f gd RF 3309). AW high 28.
**J M Bradley [0-19] J M Bradley (from M H Tompkins [1-12] Oct 1995).*

OK BABE BHB 60f70a **RR 56df 70a** 5128[11]
3 b f Bold Arrangement 8.7f **(57)** - Celtic Bird (Celtic Cone) 9.8f **(43)**
Form - 31542100000
Record 1998 - 1st:1 2nd:1 3rd:0 Ran:8
Pre1998 - 1st:1 2nd:0 3rd:1 Ran:5
Win Prizemoney £4,786 *Total Prizemoney* £6,144
Wins * **1998** *Feb Southw (STD) H 6f 65 73* <
* 1997 *Nov Wolver (STD) S 6f 67*
1998 Turf 0-4:(6f 3, 7f)(sft, g-s, gd, g-f)1998 AW1-4:(6f 1-3, 7f)(Fibr 1-4)
Light-framed, above-average filly, effective 6f, - acts on AW, best on Fibr, prefers left handed tracks, prefers tight tracks. Turf high 56 (began Spt). AW high 73 - 2nd of 14 giving 7lb to Fast Franc (23 Jan Southwell 6f Fibr RF 0139) - also 1st of 11 getting 10lb from Eminent (6 Feb Southwell RF 0235).
**J Akehurst [2-13] OK Partnership.*

O'KELLY (DEN) RR 23f 2484b[5]
3 b f Last Tycoon 9.4f **(73)** - Laser Show (IRE) (Wassl) 9.7f **(62)**
Form - 875
Record 1998 - 1st:0 2nd:0 3rd:0 Ran:3
Pre1998 - 1st:1 2nd:0 3rd:1 Ran:4
Win Prizemoney £3,522 *Total Prizemoney* £8,773
Wins * 1997 Aug Cheste (G-S) 7f 79 <
1998 Turf 0-3: (11f, 12f 2) (sft, g-s, g-f)
Light-framed, little account filly, effective 7f, acts on g-s. Turf high 23. **R Guest [1-7].*

OK JOHN (IRE) BHB 47f55a **RR 40f 55a** 2963[7]
3 b c Mac's Imp (USA) 5.6f **(54)** - Ching A Ling (Pampapaul) 10.9f **(63)**
Form - 0600007
Record 1998 - 1st:0 2nd:0 3rd:0 Ran:7
Pre1998 - 1st:0 2nd:2 3rd:2 Ran:6
Win Prizemoney £0 *Total Prizemoney* £1,993
1998 Turf 0-7: (5f 5, 6f 2) (g-s, gd 2, frm 4)
Workmanlike, average colt, effective 5f, acts on g-f to frm - acts on Fibr. Turf high 44. **J Akehurst [0-13] OK Partnership.*

OK MAITE BHB 56f **RR 30f** 3642[1]
2 ch f Komaite (USA) 6.9f **(61)** - Gleam of Gold (Crested Lark)
Form - 541
Record 1998 - 1st:1 2nd:0 3rd:0 Ran:3
Win Prizemoney £2,145 *Total Prizemoney* £2,145
Wins * **1998** *Aug Southw (STD) S 5f 66* <
1998 Turf 0-1: (5f) (gd) 1998 AW 1-2: (5f 1-2) (Fibr 1-2)
Currently average filly. AW high 66 (began Jly) - 1st of 16 from Risky Experience (14 Aug Southwell RF 3642).
**Miss J F Craze [1-3] Mrs Angela Wilson.*

OKRA BHB 55f50a **RR 49f 50a** 4547[11]
4 ch f Chilibang 7f **(55)** - Mollified (Lombard (GER)) 10.5f **(66)**
Form - 0
Record 1998 - 1st:0 2nd:0 3rd:0 Ran:1
Pre1998 - 1st:0 2nd:0 3rd:0 Ran:3
Win Prizemoney £0 *Total Prizemoney* £243
1998 AW 0-1: (7f) (Fibr)
Lengthy, moderate filly. **J D Bethell [0-4] Mrs G Fane.*

OLD GOLD N TAN BHB 20f24a **RR 11f 24a** 3385[4]
5 ch g Ballacashtal (CAN) 7.9f **(51)** - Raleigh Gazelle (Absalom) 7.2f **(58)**
Form - 5564
Record 1998 - 1st:0 2nd:0 3rd:0 Ran:4
Pre1998 - 1st:0 2nd:0 3rd:0 Ran:7
1998 Turf 0-2: (12f, 16f) (gd, g-f) 1998 AW 0-2: (8f, 12f) (Equi, Fibr)
Very moderate gelding, has worn blinkers. Turf high 11 (began Aug). AW high 32.
**A G Juckes [0-3] Stuart Hibbert (from J R Poulton [0-10] Feb 1998).*

OLD HUSH WING (IRE) BHB 43f35a **RR 44f 35a** 3099[5]
5 b g Tirol 8.1f **(64)** - Saneena (Kris) 9.5f **(73)**
Form - 40525
Record 1998 - 1st:0 2nd:1 3rd:0 Ran:4
Pre1998 - 1st:1 2nd:1 3rd:2 Ran:13
Win Prizemoney £2,780 *Total Prizemoney* £4,773
Wins * 1997 Jly Hamilt (G-F) H 13f 40 44 <
1998 Turf 0-1: (13f) (gd) 1998 AW 0-3: (16f 3) (Fibr 3)
Moderate gelding, effective 13 to 16f, best at 13f, acts on gd to frm - acts on Equi, has worn blinkers, favours tight tracks. (1st run) - 2nd of 5 giving 1lb to Urgent Reply (17 Jun Hamilton 13f gd RF 2064). AW high 33. **P C Haslam [3-24] Frank Hanson.*

OLD RED (IRE) BHB 47f65a **RR 48f 65a** 4262[1]
8 ch g Ela-Mana-Mou 12.7f **(72)** - Sea Port (Averof) 8.2f **(62)**
Form - 00532151
Record 1998 - 1st:2 2nd:1 3rd:1 Ran:8

Pre1998 - 1st:3 2nd:4 3rd:3 Ran:22
Win Prizemoney £58,733 *Total Prizemoney* £67,500
Wins * **1998** Spt Nottin (GD) H 16f 44 48
* **1998** Aug Nottin (G-F) H 16f 40 42
* 1995 Oct Newmar (G-F) H 18f 66 74 <
* 1994 Aug Redcar (G-F) H 14.1f 66 71
* 1994 *Mar Southw (STD) 11f 62*
1998 Turf 2-8: (14f 2, 16f 2-6) (gd 1-3, g-f 1-4, frm)
Average gelding, effective 14 to 16f, best at 16f, acts on gd to frm, best on g-f, favours left handed tracks, prefers tight tracks. Turf high 48 - 1st of 18 giving 2lb to Little Brave (14 Spt Nottingham RF 4262) - also 1st of 5 getting 12lb from Children's Choice (12 Aug Nottingham RF 3586). Won the 1995 Cesarewitch, but missed the following season and showed nothing in 1997. Gradually returned to form last term, although he is not as good as he was.
**Mrs M Reveley [5-25] A Flannigan (from P F I Cole [0-5] Spt 1993).*

OLD ROUVEL (USA) BHB 85f RR 91f 2110[5]
7 b g Riverman (USA) 9.7f **(78)** - Marie de Russy (FR) (Sassafras (FR)) 9.6f **(69)**
Form - 05
Record 1998 - 1st:0 2nd:0 3rd:0 Ran:2
Pre1998 - 1st:3 2nd:5 3rd:3 Ran:25
Win Prizemoney £13,803 *Total Prizemoney* £58,595
Wins * 1997 Spt Pontef (G-S) 18f 60+
* 1995 Oct Doncas (G-F) 16.5f 76+ <
* 1995 *Feb Lingfi (STD) 12f 61*
1998 Turf 0-2: (19f, 22f) (gd, g-f)
Useful gelding, effective 16 to 22f, acts on sft to gd, has worn blinkers. Turf high 91. Inconsistent. He is a useful stayer, but very hard to place on the Flat as his shortage of acceleration too often counts against him, and on occasions he has appeared to lack resolution. Only ran twice on the Flat in 1998.
**D J G MurraySmith [4-32] Mrs R D Cowell.*

OLD TRADITION (IRE) RR 69f 1904[2]
3 b br f Royal Academy (USA) 7.8f **(77)** - Desert Bride (USA) (Key to the Kingdom (USA)) 8.3f **(65)**
Form - 62
Record 1998 - 1st:0 2nd:1 3rd:0 Ran:2
Win Prizemoney £0 *Total Prizemoney* £1,070
1998 Turf 0-2: (7f 2) (gd, g-f)
Scopey, currently average filly. Turf high 69.
**E A L Dunlop [0-2] Maktoum Al Maktoum.*

OLIBERI BHB 57f RR 52f 2956[5]
2 b g First Trump - Rhiannon (Welsh Pageant) 10f **(65)**
Form - 455
Record 1998 - 1st:0 2nd:0 3rd:0 Ran:3
Win Prizemoney £0 *Total Prizemoney* £238
1998 Turf 0-3: (5f 2, 7f) (sft, gd, frm)
Currently fair gelding. Turf high 52. **J Berry [0-3] J K M Oliver.*

OLIVE THE TWIST (USA) BHB 92f RR 86+f 3069[7]
3 ch f Theatrical 11.5f **(78)** - Lady of the Light (USA) (The Minstrel (CAN)) 10f **(72)**
Form - 17
Record 1998 - 1st:1 2nd:0 3rd:0 Ran:2
Pre1998 - 1st:0 2nd:0 3rd:0 Ran:1
Win Prizemoney £4,854 *Total Prizemoney* £4,854
Wins * **1998** Jun Newmar (GD) 10f 85+ <
1998 Turf 1-2: (10f 1-2) (g-f 1-2)
Leggy, currently useful filly. Turf high 86 - also 1st of 15 getting 5lb from Generous Rosi (19 Jun Newmarket RF 2128). Lost her action and finished down the field in a Listed race, having looked well worth a try at that level. **J H M Gosden [1-3] Landon Knight.*

OLIVO (IRE) BHB 65f RR 68f 4525[10]
4 ch g Priolo (USA) 10.9f **(71)** - Honourable Sheba (USA) (Roberto (USA)) 10f **(76)**
Form - 441627470
Record 1998 - 1st:1 2nd:1 3rd:0 Ran:9
Pre1998 - 1st:1 2nd:1 3rd:3 Ran:11
Win Prizemoney £5,808 *Total Prizemoney* £12,405
Wins * **1998** Jly Salisb (FRM) 14.1f 67
* 1997 Jly Bright (FRM) H 8f 67 69 <
1998 Turf1-9:(8f, 12f, 13f, 14f 1-1, 15f, 16f 3, 17f)(g-s, gd, g-f 4, frm 1-3)
Scopey, average gelding, effective 8 to 16f, best at 8f, acts on g-s to frm, best on frm, excels at Brighton. Turf high 68 - 4th of 8 getting 8lb from Nanton Point (31 Aug Warwick 16f frm RF 4003) - also 1st of 6 from Durham (11 Jly Salisbury RF 2720). Consistent. He is no world beater, but won a small event over fourteen furlongs at Salisbury in July.
**C A Horgan [2-17] J L Harrison (from P F I Cole [0-3] Oct 1996).*

OLLIE'S CHUCKLE (IRE) BHB 55f61a RR 65f 61a 4670[14]
3 b g Mac's Imp (USA)5.6f **(54)**-Chenya (Beldale Flutter(USA)) 9.7f **(71)**
Form - 36026723800
Record 1998 - 1st:0 2nd:2 3rd:2 Ran:11
Pre1998 - 1st:0 2nd:0 3rd:0 Ran:2
Win Prizemoney £0 *Total Prizemoney* £2,800
1998 Turf 0-9: (6f, 7f 3, 8f, 9f, 10f 3) (g-s, gd 5, g-f, frm 2) 1998 AW 0-2: (6f 2) (Fibr 2)
Average gelding, effective 7f, acts on gd, likes left handed tracks, likes tight tracks. Turf high 80 - 2nd of 5 to Tankersley (30 May Catterick 7f gd RF 1587). AW high 51. Becoming disappointing.
**J J Quinn [0-11] & Mrs J S Pearson (from J A Glover [0-2] Aug 1997).*

OMAHA CITY (IRE) BHB 88f RR 100f 4508[15]
4 b g Night Shift (USA) 8.1f **(73)** - Be Discreet (Junius (USA)) 7.7f **(65)**
Form - 000437080
Record 1998 - 1st:0 2nd:0 3rd:1 Ran:9
Pre1998 - 1st:2 2nd:3 3rd:2 Ran:20
Win Prizemoney £13,900 *Total Prizemoney* £53,433
Wins * 1997 Aug Goodwo (G-F) H 7f 100 100 <
* 1996 Jun Cheste (G-F) 5.1f 73
1998 Turf 0-9: (6f 2, 7f 6, 8f) (g-s 2, gd 4, g-f 2, frm)
Strong, very useful gelding, effective 6 to 7f, best at 7f, acts on gd to frm, best on g-f, likes tight tracks. Turf high 100. Inconsistent. Ran good races in the Bunbury Cup and the Beeswing Stakes, but will continue to be hard to place. **B Gubby [2-29] Brian Gubby Ltd.*

OMAR'S ODYSSEY (IRE) BHB 29f RR 26f 3888[11]
3 ch g Sharifabad (IRE)-Tales Of Homer (Home Guard (USA)) 9.3f **(66)**
Form - 8648P000
Record 1998 - 1st:0 2nd:0 3rd:0 Ran:6
Pre1998 - 1st:0 2nd:0 3rd:0 Ran:4
Win Prizemoney £0 *Total Prizemoney* £245
1998 Turf 0-3: (9f, 11f, 12f)(g-f, frm 2)1998 AW 0-3: (10f 2, 16f) (Equi 3)
Scopey, moderate gelding, has worn blinkers. Turf high 26. AW high 45. Becoming disappointing. **P Mitchell [0-10] Richard Cohen.*

ON CALL BHB 98f RR 101f 4850[18]
3 gr f Alleged (USA) 11.8f **(81)** - Doctor Bid (USA) (Spectacular Bid (USA)) 11.2f **(76)**
Form - 1111113130
Record 1998 - 1st:7 2nd:0 3rd:2 Ran:10
Pre1998 - 1st:0 2nd:0 3rd:0 Ran:3
Win Prizemoney £30,942 *Total Prizemoney* £35,171
Wins * **1998** Aug Leopar (G-S) L 14f 101 <
* **1998** Aug Redcar (G-F) H 16f 76 83
* **1998** *Aug Lingfi (STD) 16f 68+*
* **1998** Jly Lingfi (G-F) H 16f 60 63
* **1998** Jly Bright (GD) 11.9f 67
* **1998** Jun Hamilt (G-S) H 12.1f 47 52
* **1998** Jun Yarmou (GD) H 14.1f 47 58+
1998 Turf 6-9: (12f 2-2, 14f 2-2, 15f, 16f 2-3, 18f) (gd 3-5, g-f 1-2, frm 2-2) 1998 AW 1-1: (16f 1-1) (Equi 1-1)
Scopey, very useful filly, effective 14 to 15f, acts on gd, prefers left handed tracks, likes tight tracks, excels at Lingfield. Turf high 101 - 1st of 6 getting 24lb from Ebadiyla (23 Aug Leopardstown RF 3880a). (1st run). This filly was one of 1998's success stories. She began the campaign by winning a Class E handicap off a mark of 48 at Yarmouth in June, and was notching up win number seven when beating Irish Oaks heroine Ebadiyla in a Listed contest at Leopardstown in August. If ever there was a living tribute to the skill of Sir Mark Prescott, it is this gutsy grey.
**Sir Mark Prescott [7-13] Mrs Chryss O'Reilly.*

ONCE MORE FOR LUCK (IRE) BHB75f70a RR 78f 70a 4970[4]
7 b g Petorius 8f **(66)** - Mrs Lucky (Royal Match) 11.8f **(54)**
Form - 72114314
Record 1998 - 1st:3 2nd:1 3rd:1 Ran:8
Pre1998 - 1st:5 2nd:7 3rd:6 Ran:39

Win Prizemoney £29,137 *Total Prizemoney* £46,968

Wins	* **1998**	Oct	Catter	(SFT)	C	12f		78	<
	* **1998**	Spt	Mussel	(GD)	H	12f	65	67	
	* **1998**	Spt	York	(GD)	H	10.4f	60	67	
	* 1997	Oct	Ayr	(SFT)	S	13.1f		53+	
	* 1996	Oct	Redcar	(G-F)	C	11f		67	
	* 1995	Oct	Catter	(G-F)	C	12f		61+	

1998 Turf 3-7: (10f 1-3, 12f 2-4) (g-s 1-2, gd, g-f 1-1, frm 1-3) 1998 AW 0-1: (12f) (Fibr)

Above-average gelding, effective 12f, acts on g-s to gd, likes tight tracks. Turf high 78 (began Aug) - 1st of 14 from Filial (16 Oct Catterick RF 4838).

**Mrs M Reveley [14-61] The Mary Reveley Racing Club (from M Johnston [0-8] Spt 1994).*

	Pre1998 -	1st:1	2nd:0	3rd:0	Ran:6

Win Prizemoney £3,663 *Total Prizemoney* £6,047

Wins * 1997 May Hamilt (SFT) 12.1f 75 <

1998 Turf 0-2: (14f, 16f) (frm 2)

Leggy, above-average gelding, effective 12 to 16f, acted on gd to frm, best on frm. Turf high 74 (began Jly) - 3rd of 10 getting 10lb from Premier Night (8 Jly Newmarket 16f frm RF 2640). Did not reappear for the season until July, but ran two good races in quick succession. (DEAD)

**M Johnston [1-8] G R Bailey Ltd (Baileys Horse Feeds).*

On Call made startling progress

ONE DINAR (FR) BHB 63f **RR 71f** 4776[14]

3 b c Generous (IRE) 11.5f **(82)** - Lypharitissima (FR) (Lightning (FR)) 7.9f **(74)**

Form - 005570

Record	**1998 -**	1st:0	2nd:0	3rd:0	Ran:6
	Pre1998 -	1st:0	2nd:0	3rd:0	Ran:2

1998 Turf 0-6: (7f, 8f, 9f, 10f 3) (gd 5, g-f)

Workmanlike, above-average colt, effective 10f, acts on gd, likes tight tracks. Turf high 71 - 5th of 13 giving 5lb to Royal Fontaine (15 Spt Sandown 10f gd RF 4265).

**K Mahdi [0-6] Greenfield Stud (from J H M Gosden [0-2] Spt 1997).*

ONE FINE MAN RR 3609[12]

5 gr g Savahra Sound 7.8f **(55)** - Chance to Dream (Petong) 6.6f **(58)**

Form - 0

Record 1998 - 1st:0 2nd:0 3rd:0 Ran:1

1998 Turf 0-1: (7f) (frm)

Formerly very poor gelding - 12th of 13 getting 5lb from Salty Behaviour (13 Aug Chepstow 7f frm RF 3609).

**H E Haynes [0-1] Mrs Theresa Walshe.*

ONE FOR BAILEYS BHB 75f **RR 74f** 2640[3]

4 b g Unfuwain (USA) 11.4f **(74)** - Three Stars (Star Appeal) 9.6f **(65)**

Form - 23

Record 1998 - 1st:0 2nd:1 3rd:1 Ran:2

ONEFORTHEDITCH (USA) BHB 64f70a **RR 62f 70a** 4760[1]

5 gr m With Approval (CAN) 8.7f **(80)** - Wee Dram (USA) (Nostrum (USA)) 9f **(84)**

Form - 24534711

Record	**1998 -**	1st:2	2nd:0	3rd:1	Ran:7
	Pre1998 -	1st:3	2nd:2	3rd:1	Ran:13

Win Prizemoney £15,943 *Total Prizemoney* £20,102

Wins	* **1998**	Oct	Leices	(G-S)		8f		62	
	* **1998**	Spt	Leices	(G-F)		8f		56	
	* 1997	Oct	Nottin	(G-F)		10f		61	
	* 1997	*Jan*	*Wolver*	*(STD)*	*H*	*9.4f*	*65*	*70*	<
	* 1997	*Jan*	*Wolver*	*(STD)*		*9.4f*		*69*	

1998 Turf 2-5: (8f 2-2, 10f 3) (g-s, gd 1-3, frm 1-1) 1998 AW 0-2: (9f, 12f) (Fibr 2)

Above-average filly, effective 8 to 9f, best at 9f, acts on gd - acts on Fibr, excels at Leicester and Wolverhampton. Turf high 62. AW high 68 (1st run) - 4th of 7 giving 3lb to Sualtach (14 Jan Wolverhampton 9f Fibr RF 0088). She took time to find her form this season, but did so when dropped back in trip, winning twice over a mile at Leicester in the autumn.

**J R Fanshawe [5-15] Onefortheditch Partnership (from J H M Gosden [0-6] Oct 1996).*

ONEFOURSEVEN BHB 66f64a **RR 70f 64a** 2334[4]

5 b g Jumbo Hirt (USA) 15.8f **(44)** - Dominance (Dominion) 8.5f **(63)**

Form - 22404

Record	**1998** -	1st:0	2nd:2	3rd:0	Ran:5
	Pre1998 -	1st:6	2nd:1	3rd:3	Ran:23

Win Prizemoney £22,177 *Total Prizemoney* £40,286

Wins	* 1997	*Spt*	*Wolver*	*(STD)*	*H*	*14.8f*	*57*	*64*
	* 1997	May	Thirsk	(GD)	H	16f	68	72 <
	* 1997	Mar	Doncas	(G-F)	H	18f	57	65
	* 1996	*Nov*	*Southw*	*(STD)*	*H*	*16f*	*52*	*58*
	* 1996	*Nov*	*Southw*	*(STD)*	*H*	*14f*	*45*	*46*
	* 1996	Spt	Catter	(G-F)	H	15.8f	36	47

1998 Turf 0-4: (14f, 15f, 16f, 18f) (g-s, gd 3) 1998 AW 0-1: (15f) (Fibr)

Above-average gelding, effective 16 to 20f, best at 16f, acts on sft to g-f, has worn blinkers. Turf high 70.

**J L Eyre [6-20] J Roundtree (from S R Bowring [0-8] Apr 1996).*

ONE LIFE TO LIVE (IRE) BHB 43f43a RR 43f 43a 883[10]

5 gr h Classic Music (USA) 7.2f **(57)** - Fine Flame (Le Prince) 5.8f **(49)**

Form - 40

Record	**1998** -	1st:0	2nd:0	3rd:0	Ran:2
	Pre1998 -	1st:0	2nd:1	3rd:0	Ran:13

Win Prizemoney £0 *Total Prizemoney* £1,759

1998 Turf 0-2: (10f, 11f) (sft, g-s)

Moderate colt, effective 9f, acts on g-f, has worn blinkers, likes tight tracks. Turf high 29. Becoming disappointing.

**D W Barker [0-2] R Fenwick-Gibson (from S E Kettlewell [0-5] Jly 1997).*

ONEMORETIME BHB 24f RR 13f 251[7]

4 b f Timeless Times (USA)6.1f **(56)**-Dear Glenda (Gold Song) 5.5f **(61)**

Form - 00867

Record	**1998** -	1st:0	2nd:0	3rd:0	Ran:4
	Pre1998 -	1st:0	2nd:0	3rd:0	Ran:9

Win Prizemoney £0 *Total Prizemoney* £215

1998 AW 0-4: (7f 3, 8f) (Fibr 4)

Unfurnished, very moderate filly. AW high 34.

**B W Murray [0-13] Mrs M Lingwood.*

ONE NIGHT STAND RR 41f 3191[2]

3 ch g Pursuit of Love 9.5f **(69)** - Relatively Easy (Relkino) 8.9f **(65)**

Form - 2

Record	**1998** -	1st:0	2nd:1	3rd:0	Ran:1

Win Prizemoney £0 *Total Prizemoney* £808

1998 Turf 0-1: (12f) (g-f)

Currently moderate gelding. (1st run) - 2nd of 5 getting 7lb from Maremma (29 Jly Doncaster 12f g-f RF 3191).

**Mrs J R Ramsden [0-1] Mrs D Ridley.*

ONEOFTHEOLDONES BHB 32f27a RR 38f 27a 111[11]

6 b g Deploy 11.4f **(67)** - Waveguide (Double Form) 7.3f **(58)**

Form - 0

Record	**1998** -	1st:0	2nd:0	3rd:0	Ran:1
	Pre1998 -	1st:1	2nd:0	3rd:3	Ran:22

Win Prizemoney £3,245 *Total Prizemoney* £5,047

Wins	1995	*Jun*	*Southw*	*(STD)*	*8f*	*60*	<

1998 AW 0-1: (8f) (Fibr)

Very moderate gelding, effective 7f, acted on frm. (DEAD)

**A Streeter [0-1] R Baker (from J Norton [0-19] Jly 1997).*

ONES ENOUGH BHB 84f RR 88f 5001[1]

2 b c Reprimand 8.2f **(63)** - Sea Fairy (Wollow) 8.2f **(61)**

Form - 3636511

Record	**1998** -	1st:2	2nd:0	3rd:2	Ran:7

Win Prizemoney £6,104 *Total Prizemoney* £7,079

Wins	* **1998**	Oct	Lingfi	(HVY)	5f	88	<
	* **1998**	Spt	Folkes	(G-F)	5f	70	

1998 Turf 2-7: (5f 2-4, 6f 2, 8f) (sft 1-1, gd, g-f 1-4, frm)

Useful colt, effective 5f, acts on sft, mostly wears blinkers. Turf high 88 - 1st of 9 giving 3lb to Ranaan (26 Oct Lingfield RF 5001).

**G L Moore [2-7] Heart Of The South Racing (3).*

ONE SHOT (IRE) BHB 36f27a RR 38f 27a 2069[13]

5 b g Fayruz 6.6f **(63)** - La Gravotte (FR) (Habitat) 9.4f **(70)**

Form - 0086060700

Record	**1998** -	1st:0	2nd:0	3rd:0	Ran:9
	Pre1998 -	1st:0	2nd:0	3rd:1	Ran:10

Win Prizemoney £0 *Total Prizemoney* £350

1998 Turf 0-5: (6f, 7f, 8f 2, 10f) (g-s, gd, g-f, frm 2) 1998 AW 0-4: (7f, 8f, 9f, 11f) (Fibr 4)

Very moderate gelding, often wears blinkers. Turf high 56. AW high 31. Inconsistent.

**W R Muir [0-19] R Haim.*

ONE SINGER BHB 62f90a RR 62f 90a 2019[17]

3 ch g Anshan 8.2f **(63)** - Moushka (Song) 7.2f **(61)**

Form - 3145008030

Record	**1998** -	1st:1	2nd:0	3rd:1	Ran:9
	Pre1998 -	1st:2	2nd:3	3rd:2	Ran:11

Win Prizemoney £7,578 *Total Prizemoney* £12,175

Wins	* **1998**	*Jan*	*Wolver*	*(STD)*	*H*	*7f*	*85*	*88+*
	1997	May	Redcar	(GD)		5f		92 <
	1997	*May*	*Wolver*	*(STD)*		*5f*		*78*

1998 Turf 0-7: (6f 2, 7f 2, 8f 2, 11f) (gd 6, frm) 1998 AW 1-2: (6f, 7f 1-1) (Fibr 1-2)

Light-framed, useful gelding, effective 5 to 7f, best at 7f, acts on frm - acts on Fibr, has worn blinkers, prefers left handed tracks, prefers tight tracks. Turf high 73. AW high 88 (1st run) - 1st of 5 giving 15lb to Impulsive Decision (10 Jan Wolverhampton RF 0067).

**N P Littmoden [1-10] Clayton Bigley Partnership Ltd (from M Johnston [2-10] Oct 1997).*

ONESINGER ONESONG RR 58f 2754[9]

2 b g Whittingham (IRE) -Classy Nancy (USA) (Cutlass (USA)) 8.5f **(76)**

Form - 660

Record	**1998** -	1st:0	2nd:0	3rd:0	Ran:3

1998 Turf 0-3: (6f 3) (gd, g-f, frm)

Currently fair gelding. Turf high 58.

**N Tinkler [0-3] Clayton Bigley Partnership Ltd.*

ONE SO WONDERFUL BHB 119f RR 118f 4852[5]

4 b f Nashwan (USA) 10.3f **(79)** - Someone Special (Habitat) 9.4f **(70)**

Form - 71145

Record	**1998** -	1st:2	2nd:0	3rd:0	Ran:5
	Pre1998 -	1st:3	2nd:0	3rd:0	Ran:3

Win Prizemoney £250,881 *Total Prizemoney* £263,481

Wins	* **1998**	Aug	York	(G-F)	G1	10.4f	118 <
	* **1998**	Jly	Chepst	(GD)	L	10.2f	103+
	* 1997	Oct	Newmar	(G-F)	G2	10f	116
	* 1997	Aug	Sandow	(SFT)	L	8.1f	104++
	* 1996	Spt	Kempto	(GD)		7f	92+

1998 Turf 2-5: (10f 2-5) (gd 3, g-f 2-2)

Scopey, high-class filly, effective 10f, acts on gd to frm, best on gd, does well at Newmarket. Turf high 118 - 4th of 8 getting 3lb from Swain (12 Spt Leopardstown 10f gd RF 4294a) - also 1st of 8 getting 3lb from Faithful Son (18 Aug York RF 3696). A member of a high-class family, this half-sister to Alnasr Alwasheek lost her unbeaten record first time out in the Brigadier Gerard Stakes, but bounced back with a fluent win in a Chepstow Listed race. She came out best in a three-way photo to the Juddmonte International, showing admirable battling qualities, although that was a relatively weak Group One. Fourth in the Irish Champion Stakes on unsuitably soft ground, she was hampered when unplaced in the Champion Stakes, which can probably be forgotten. She is a most likeable filly with a turn of foot and she has now been retired.

**L M Cumani [5-8] Helena Springfield Ltd.*

ONE TO GO (IRE) BHB 57f55a RR 53f 55a 4961[11]

3 b g Petorius 8f **(66)** - Caroline's Mark (On Your Mark) 7.7f **(58)**

Form - 404022320880210

Record	**1998** -	1st:1	2nd:4	3rd:1	Ran:15
	Pre1998 -	1st:0	2nd:1	3rd:0	Ran:6

Win Prizemoney £2,304 *Total Prizemoney* £6,491

Wins	* **1998**	Oct	Catter	(gd,)	6f	51	<

1998 Turf 1-12: (5f 2, 6f 1-3, 7f 5, 8f 2) (sft 2, gd 2, g-f 1-5, frm 3) 1998 AW 0-3: (6f 3) (Fibr 3)

Workmanlike, average gelding, effective 6f, - acts on Fibr, likes left handed tracks, likes tight tracks. Turf high 53. AW high 61 - 2nd of 9 to Press Ahead (10 Jly Wolverhampton 6f Fibr RF 2692).

**J Berry [1-21] David Hall.*

ONE WON ONE (USA) BHB 91f RR 106f 4907a[7]

4 b g Naevus (USA) 7.2f **(86)** - Havards Bay (ARG) 00

Form - 41102137

1998 Turf 3-8: (5f 1-2, 6f 2-6) (sft 2-4, g-s, gd 1-3)

Pattern-class gelding, effective 5 to 6f, best at 5f, acts on sft to gd, likes Curragh. Turf high 106 - 3rd of 10 giving 17lb to En Retard (3

Oct Curragh 5f g-s RF 4689a) - also 1st of 7 giving 23lb to Magic Annemarie (4 May Navan RF 1174a). He had a super season and must have given the Irish handicapper nightmares, moving from a rating of 78 to 104. This likeable gelding can win a Listed event.

**Ms J Morgan in IRE [5-17] Heavenly Syndicate.*

* 1997 May Cheste (SFT) 5.1f 84 <

1998 Turf 0-10: (6f 8, 7f 2) (sft, g-s 2, gd 4, g-f 2, frm)

Workmanlike, above-average colt, effective 5f, acts on g-s to frm. Turf high 79. Inconsistent.

**J Berry [2-13] John Milner & Stephen Milner.*

One So Wonderful (right) winning her first Group One at York

ONICE NERO RR 90f 4952a[1]

2 b c Primo Dominie 7.2f **(67)** - Nord's Lucy (IRE) (Nordico (USA)) 6.5f **(62)**

Form - 1

1998 Turf 1-1: (6f 1-1) (sft 1-1)

Currently useful colt. (1st run) - 1st of 9 from Tesiano (18 Oct San Siro RF 4952a). **B Grizzetti in ITY [1-1] B Grizzetti.*

ON LOCATION (IRE) BHB 68f **RR 65f** 4868[4]

2 b f Lear Fan (USA) 10.4f **(80)** - Marylou Whitney (USA) (Fappiano (USA)) 8.7f **(77)**

Form - 7554

Record 1998 - 1st:0 2nd:0 3rd:0 Ran:4

1998 Turf 0-4: (5f, 6f 2, 7f) (g-s, gd, g-f, frm)

Average filly. Turf high 65 (began Aug).

**M H Tompkins [0-4] Mrs M H Tompkins.*

ONLY FOR GOLD BHB 70f81a **RR 73f 81a** 5096[8]

3 b c Presidium 7.5f **(56)** - Calvanne Miss (Martinmas) 7.6f **(59)**

Form - 0000604008

Record 1998 - 1st:0 2nd:0 3rd:0 Ran:10

Pre1998 - 1st:2 2nd:0 3rd:0 Ran:3

Win Prizemoney £15,660 *Total Prizemoney* £17,940

Wins * 1997 Jun Beverl (G-F) 5f 84 <

ONLY IN DREAMS BHB 75f **RR 77f** 4198[8]

3 b f Polar Falcon (USA) 9f **(74)** - Dream Baby (Master Willie) 7f **(70)**

Form - 606208

Record 1998 - 1st:0 2nd:1 3rd:0 Ran:6

Pre1998 - 1st:1 2nd:0 3rd:1 Ran:3

Win Prizemoney £3,249 *Total Prizemoney* £5,006

Wins * 1997 Oct Leices (SFT) 7f 79 <

1998 Turf 0-6: (7f 2, 8f 2, 9f, 10f) (sft, gd 3, g-f 2)

Neat, above-average filly, effective 7f, acts on g-s. Turf high 77.

**B J Meehan [1-9] Mascalls Stud.*

ONLY JOSH (IRE) BHB 31f49a **RR 27f 49a** 1720[15]

4 gr g Waajib 8.9f **(67)** - Carlyle Suite (USA) (Icecapade (USA)) 11f **(62)**

Form - 00

Record 1998 - 1st:0 2nd:0 3rd:0 Ran:2

Pre1998 - 1st:0 2nd:0 3rd:1 Ran:8

Win Prizemoney £0 *Total Prizemoney* £782

1998 Turf 0-2: (7f, 8f) (g-f, frm)

Leggy, fair gelding, effective 8f, - acts on Fibr, has worn blinkers, likes left handed tracks, likes tight tracks. Turf high 7.

**J A Glover [0-2] Mrs Andrea Mallinson (from Mrs V A Aconley [0-1] Jun 1997).*

ON THE BLACK (IRE) BHB 40f **RR 34f** 4808[13]

2 br g Petardia 8.2f **(58)** - Salonniere (FR) (Bikala) 10.1f **(49)**

Form - 0000
Record 1998 - 1st:0 2nd:0 3rd:0 Ran:4
1998 Turf 0-4: (5f, 6f 2, 10f) (gd, g-f, frm 2)
Very moderate gelding, often wears blinkers. Turf high 34.
**M Kettle [0-4] Pillar To Post Racing.*

ON THE GREEN BHB 30f30a **RR 43f 30a** 3958[17]
5 br m Pharly (FR) 11.5f **(64)** - Regal Wonder (Stupendous) 8f **(49)**
Form - 0400
Record 1998 - 1st:0 2nd:0 3rd:0 Ran:3
Pre1998 - 1st:1 2nd:1 3rd:1 Ran:13
Win Prizemoney £2,346 *Total Prizemoney* £4,779
Wins 1997 Oct Newcas (G-F) CH 8f 36 43 <
1998 Turf 0-2: (10f, 11f) (g-f, frm) 1998 AW 0-1: (9f) (Fibr)
Moderate filly, effective 7 to 8f, best at 7f, acts on g-s to g-f, often wears blinkers (extremely effectively). (began Jly). Becoming disappointing.
**B Preece [0-9] H S & E M Yates (from A Hide [1-12] Oct 1997).*

ON THE MAT BHB 50f **RR 53f** 4871[4]
3 b g Reprimand 8.2f **(63)** - Secret Freedom (USA) (Secreto (USA)) 8.7f **(72)**
Form - 008501074
Record 1998 - 1st:1 2nd:0 3rd:0 Ran:9
Pre1998 - 1st:0 2nd:1 3rd:0 Ran:6
Win Prizemoney £3,003 *Total Prizemoney* £3,993
Wins * 1998 Spt Ripon (HVY) H 16f 48 53 <
1998 Turf 1-9: (8f 2, 9f, 12f, 14f, 16f 1-3, 18f) (g-s 1-1, gd, g-f 3, frm 4)
Fair gelding, effective 16f, acts on g-s, has worn blinkers, likes right handed tracks. Turf high 53. Inconsistent.
**J J O'Neill [2-16] Clayton Bigley Partnership Ltd.*

ON THE OFF CHANCE BHB 27f **RR 7f** 1890[14]
6 ch g French Gondolier (USA) - Off and on (Touching Wood (USA)) 8.2f **(55)**
Form - 8080
Record 1998 - 1st:0 2nd:0 3rd:0 Ran:4
Pre1998 - 1st:0 2nd:0 3rd:0 Ran:1
1998 Turf 0-3: (6f, 10f, 11f) (g-s 2, g-f) 1998 AW 0-1: (8f) (Fibr)
Very poor gelding, has worn blinkers. Turf high 7.
**R M McKellar [0-8] J G Hickie (from G Holmes [0-1] Spt 1995).*

ON THE RIDGE (IRE) BHB 102f **RR 98+f** 2679[2]
3 ch c Risk Me (FR) 8f **(53)** - Star Ridge (USA) (Storm Bird (CAN)) 10.3f **(74)**
Form - 3312
Record 1998 - 1st:1 2nd:1 3rd:2 Ran:4
Win Prizemoney £7,440 *Total Prizemoney* £12,129
Wins * 1998 Jun York (G-S) 7.9f 98+ <
1998 Turf 1-4: (8f 1-3, 10f) (g-s 1-1, g-f 2, frm)
Scopey, very useful colt. Turf high 98 - 2nd of 2 getting 12lb from Lord of Men (10 Jly Chester 10f frm RF 2679) - also 1st of 3 from The Gene Genie (13 Jun York RF 1984). Promising efforts in warm maidens, before winning a three-horse affair easily in soft ground. Well held by sole opponent Lord of Men when attempting ten furlongs for the first time. **H R A Cecil [1-4] Buckram Oak Holdings.*

ON TILL MORNING (IRE) BHB 69f **RR 68f** 4250[1]
2 ch f Never so Bold 7.1f **(62)** - Shamasiya (FR) (Vayrann) 9.7f **(74)**
Form - 32731
Record 1998 - 1st:1 2nd:1 3rd:2 Ran:5
Win Prizemoney £2,862 *Total Prizemoney* £4,954
Wins * 1998 Spt Mussel (GD) 5f 66 <
1998 Turf 1-5: (5f 1-3, 6f 2) (gd, g-f, frm 1-3)
Average filly. Turf high 68 (began Jly) - 2nd of 7 to Paleria (24 Jly Thirsk 6f frm RF 3089) - also 1st of 10 from Bayford Green (14 Spt Musselburgh RF 4250). **P Calver [1-5] D B Stanley.*

OO EE BE BHB 64f64a **RR 67f 64a** 5005[5]
2 b g Whittingham (IRE) - Miss Derby (USA) (Master Derby (USA)) 9.5f **(69)**
Form - 005306055
Record 1998 - 1st:0 2nd:0 3rd:1 Ran:9
Win Prizemoney £0 *Total Prizemoney* £345
1998 Turf 0-8: (5f, 6f 4, 7f 2, 8f) (sft, gd 2, g-f 2, frm 3) 1998 AW 0-1: (6f) (Fibr)
Average gelding, has worn blinkers. Turf high 67. Inconsistent.
**A T Murphy [0-2] West Down Racing Partnership (from M A Buckley [0-7] Aug 1998).*

OOH AH CANTONA BHB 52f **RR 45f** 5061[10]
7 b g Crofthall 8.6f **(54)** - Chablisse (Radetzky) 9.8f **(56)**
Form - 60
Record 1998 - 1st:0 2nd:0 3rd:0 Ran:2
Pre1998 - 1st:5 2nd:1 3rd:0 Ran:21
Win Prizemoney £15,707 *Total Prizemoney* £18,514
Wins 1995 Aug Redcar (FRM) H 10f 65 69
1995 Jly Beverl (G-F) H 9.9f 61 64
1995 Jun Newcas (FRM) H 10.1f 54 61
1998 Turf 0-2: (10f, 12f) (sft, g-f)
Moderate gelding. Turf high 45. Consistent.
**M D Hammond [0-6] Mrs Eve Sweetman (from J L Eyre [3-9] Spt 1995).*

OOZLEM (IRE) BHB 34f30a **RR 36f 30a** 15[4]
9 b g Burslem 9.4f **(56)** - Fingers (Lord Gayle (USA)) 8.8f **(62)**
Form - 8664
Record 1998 - 1st:0 2nd:0 3rd:0 Ran:1
Pre1998 - 1st:5 2nd:3 3rd:5 Ran:62
Win Prizemoney £13,772 *Total Prizemoney* £19,093
Wins 1996 *Feb Lingfi (STD) H 8f 39 48* <
1995 Aug Salisb (G-F) H 8f 34 43
1994 Aug Redcar (G-F) H 8f 37 38
1994 Aug Bright (FRM) H 8f 34 33
1994 Jun Newmar (GD) H 8f 34 34
1998 AW 0-1: (12f) (Equi)
Very moderate gelding, effective 10 to 12f, acts on g-f - acts on Equi, mostly wears blinkers.
**L MontagueHall [0-14] Brooknight Guarding Ltd (from J R Poulton [2-17] Aug 1996).*

OPAQUE BHB 75f **RR 79f** 5150[7]
6 b g Shirley Heights 12.1f **(76)** - Opale (Busted) 10.2f **(61)**
Form - 7124308607
Record 1998 - 1st:1 2nd:1 3rd:1 Ran:10
Pre1998 - 1st:2 2nd:4 3rd:1 Ran:17
Win Prizemoney £20,345 *Total Prizemoney* £36,862
Wins * 1998 May York (GD) H 13.9f 72 77 <
* 1997 Nov Doncas (SFT) H 16.5f 68 75
1996 May Newmar (GD) H 14f 66 71
1998 Turf 1-10: (14f 1-2, 15f, 16f 4, 17f, 18f 2) (sft, gd 1-6, g-f, frm 2)
Above-average gelding, effective 14 to 17f, best at 16f, acts on sft to frm, favours left handed tracks. Turf high 84 - 4th of 20 getting 3lb from Cyrian (27 Jun Newcastle 16f sft RF 2345) - also 1st of 12 getting 1lb from Totem Dancer (13 May York RF 1210). Consistent. He was running well in the summer, winning at York and running fine races at Haydock and in the Northumberland Plate. Goes best on a galloping track.
**W Storey [2-21] G J Keary (from L M Cumani [1-7] Jun 1996).*

OPEN ARMS BHB 75f **RR 80f** 4889[3]
2 ch c Most Welcome 8.6f **(66)** - Amber Fizz (USA) (Effervescing (USA)) 8.1f **(79)**
Form - 544273
Record 1998 - 1st:0 2nd:1 3rd:1 Ran:6
Win Prizemoney £0 *Total Prizemoney* £1,621
1998 Turf 0-6: (6f, 8f 4, 9f) (gd 2, g-f 2, frm 2)
Decent colt, effective 8f, acts on gd to frm. Turf high 80 - 4th of 10 giving 5lb to Canadian Approval (26 Aug Lingfield 8f g-f RF 3889).
**C E Brittain [0-6] Saeed Manana.*

OPENING NIGHT BHB 46a **RR 53f** 3829[11]
3 b g Theatrical Charmer 10.9f **(63)**-First Time Over (Derrylin) 8.8f **(54)**
Form - 080
Record 1998 - 1st:0 2nd:0 3rd:0 Ran:2
Pre1998 - 1st:0 2nd:0 3rd:0 Ran:3
1998 Turf 0-1: (8f) (frm) 1998 AW 0-1: (9f) (Fibr)
Light-framed, fair gelding. **R Simpson [0-5] Miss J Rumford.*

OPENING RANGE BHB 41f36a **RR 42f 36a** 3449[8]
7 b m Nordico (USA) 8.2f **(59)** - Waveguide (Double Form) 7.3f **(58)**
Form - 23068
Record 1998 - 1st:0 2nd:0 3rd:0 Ran:3
Pre1998 - 1st:2 2nd:2 3rd:1 Ran:17

Win Prizemoney £4,648 *Total Prizemoney* £6,565
Wins * 1997 Aug Windso (G-F) H 5f 35 42 <
* 1997 *Jly Wolver (STD) H 5f 35 34*
1998 Turf 0-1: (5f) (frm) 1998 AW 0-2: (5f 2) (Fibr 2)
Moderate mare, effective 5 to 6f, best at 6f, acts on gd to frm - acts on AW, best on frm, has worn blinkers. AW high 19 (began Jly).
**N E Berry [2-19] The Purple People Racing Partnership (from W J Musson [0-2] Jly 1994).*

OPEN SECRET (IRE) BHB 87f RR 87f 4405[1]

2 b br f Mac's Imp (USA) 5.6f **(54)**-Lady Montekin (Montekin) 11.1f **(55)**
Form - 22101
Record 1998 - 1st:2 2nd:2 3rd:0 Ran:5
Win Prizemoney £6,267 *Total Prizemoney* £32,677
Wins * **1998** Spt Beverl (G-F) 5f 87 <
* **1998** Aug Carlis (G-S) 5f 73+
1998 Turf 2-5: (5f 2-4, 6f) (gd 1-3, g-f 1-2)
Useful filly. Turf high 87 (began Jly) - 1st of 14 giving 9lb to Red Amazon (22 Spt Beverley RF 4405). Finished fast into second place in the Weatherbys Super Sprint, overcoming both inexperience and a moderate draw. She landed two small races later in the season, seeming suited by a stiff five furlongs. Should make a nice sprinter at three. **A C Stewart [2-5] Racing For Gold.*

OPERA BUFF (IRE) BHB 59f80a RR 62f 80a 4638[6]

7 br g Rousillon (USA) 10.4f **(69)** - Obertura (USA) (Roberto (USA)) 10f **(76)**
Form - 40200377464252666
Record 1998 - 1st:0 2nd:3 3rd:1 Ran:17
Pre1998 - 1st:9 2nd:2 3rd:8 Ran:42
Win Prizemoney £29,806 *Total Prizemoney* £42,506
Wins * 1997 Spt Folkes (FRM) 12f 72
* 1997 Aug Bright (G-F) H 11.9f 65 69
* 1997 May Bright (FRM) 11.9f 70
* 1997 *Jan Wolver (STD) H 12f 89 93* <
* 1995 *Nov Lingfi (STD) H 13f 63 78*
* 1995 *Nov Lingfi (STD) H 12f 50 67*
* 1995 *Nov Wolver (STD) H 12f 50 62+*
* 1995 Oct Nottin (G-F) 14.1f 70+
* 1995 Spt Salisb (G-S) CH 14f 50 58
1998 Turf 0-14: (11f 2, 12f 11, 16f) (gd 3, g-f 5, frm 6) 1998 AW 0-3: (10f, 12f 2) (Equi 2, Fibr)
Decent gelding, effective 12f, - acts on Fibr, has worn blinkers, likes tight tracks. Turf high 64. AW high 84 - 6th of 12 giving 7lb to Primary Colours (3 Oct Wolverhampton 12f Fibr RF 4638). Largely out of sorts in '98, like most of the yard.
**Miss Gay Kelleway [9-49] Dorchester Racing Club (from M C Pipe [0-6] Jly 1995).*

OPERA KING (USA) BHB 99f RR 98f 2088[16]

3 ch c Storm Bird (CAN) 8.5f **(82)** - Jewel In My Crown (CAN) (Secretariat (USA)) 9f **(79)**
Form - 10
Record 1998 - 1st:1 2nd:0 3rd:0 Ran:2
Pre1998 - 1st:1 2nd:1 3rd:0 Ran:2
Win Prizemoney £9,049 *Total Prizemoney* £10,463
Wins * **1998** May Lingfi (GD) 11.5f 98 <
* 1997 Jly Doncas (GD) 7f 85
1998 Turf 1-2: (11f 1-1, 12f) (g-s, g-f 1-1)
Well made, very useful colt. Turf high 98 (1st run) - 1st of 4 getting 3lb from Success And Glory (30 May Lingfield RF 1598). He battled on well to gain a narrow victory in a Lingfield conditions event on his return but finished down the field at Royal Ascot and was not seen again. **S bin Suroor [2-4] Godolphin.*

OPERA QUEEN (USA) RR 50f 2184[10]

3 b f Pleasant Colony (USA) 12.4f **(88)** - Cadeaux D'Amie (USA) (Lyphard (USA)) 9.9f **(72)**
Form - 0
Record 1998 - 1st:0 2nd:0 3rd:0 Ran:1
1998 Turf 0-1: (8f) (g-f)
Workmanlike, currently fair filly.
**E A L Dunlop [0-1] Gainsborough Stud.*

OPERATIC BHB 60f65a RR 66f 65a 4862[2]

3 b f Goofalik (USA) 15.4f **(66)** - Choir Mistress (Chief Singer) 8.9f **(66)**
Form - 42233363713338623232207301222
Record 1998 - 1st:2 2nd:9 3rd:10 Ran:29
Pre1998 - 1st:1 2nd:1 3rd:0 Ran:3
Win Prizemoney £6,691 *Total Prizemoney* £19,648
Wins * **1998** *Spt Wolver (STD) 14.8f 63* <
* **1998** May Yarmou (FRM) C 16f 57
1997 *Jly Wolver (STD) S 7f 54*
1998 Turf 1-16: (12f 3, 14f 7, 15f, 16f 1-4, 17f) (g-s 3, gd 4, g-f, frm 1-8)
1998 AW 1-13: (8f, 10f, 11f, 12f 5, 15f 1-4, 16f) (Equi 2, Fibr 1-11)
Workmanlike, average filly, effective 7 to 16f, acts on g-s to frm - acts on AW, mostly wears blinkers, favours left handed tracks, favours tight tracks, excels at Yarmouth, does well at Wolverhampton, likes Haydock and Nottingham. Turf high 66 - 3rd of 8 giving 4lb to Pressurise (24 Jly Nottingham 16f g-f RF 3084) - also 1st of 6 from Trakelor (27 May Yarmouth RF 1540). AW high 65 - 2nd of 12 giving 1lb to Isabella Gonzaga (17 Oct Wolverhampton 12f Fibr RF 4862) - also 1st of 12 from Kingdom Queen (19 Spt Wolverhampton RF 4384). Only small, she is as tough as they come and retained her form throughout an arduous season.
**P D Evans [2-29] Mrs Stephen Allen (from M Bell [1-3] Aug 1997).*

OPERETTA (FR) BHB 45f RR 41f 4815[10]

3 b f Lashkari 13.1f **(52)** - Lyric Opera (Sadler's Wells (USA)) 10f **(76)**
Form - 3700
Record 1998 - 1st:0 2nd:0 3rd:1 Ran:4
Win Prizemoney £0 *Total Prizemoney* £515
1998 Turf 0-4: (9f, 10f 2, 12f) (gd, g-f 2, frm)
Leggy, moderate filly. Turf high 55.
**Ian Williams [0-4] & Mrs John Poynton.*

OPOPMIL (IRE) BHB 65f RR 58f 500[5]

3 b f Pips Pride 6.7f **(70)** - Limpopo (Green Desert (USA)) 8.6f **(78)**
Form - 5
Record 1998 - 1st:0 2nd:0 3rd:0 Ran:1
Pre1998 - 1st:0 2nd:1 3rd:1 Ran:3
Win Prizemoney £0 *Total Prizemoney* £1,403
1998 Turf 0-1: (6f) (sft)
Workmanlike, fair filly. **T D Easterby [0-4] T H Bennett.*

OPPORTUNE (GER) BHB 48a RR 49f 1305[4]

3 br c Shirley Heights 12.1f **(76)** - On The Tiles (Thatch (USA)) 9.8f **(62)**
Form - 00314
Record 1998 - 1st:1 2nd:0 3rd:1 Ran:5
Pre1998 - 1st:0 2nd:0 3rd:0 Ran:7
Win Prizemoney £2,425 *Total Prizemoney* £2,740
Wins * **1998** May Beverl (GD) S 9.9f 49 <
1998 Turf 1-4: (8f, 10f 1-2, 12f) (g-s 3, frm 1-1) 1998 AW 0-1: (11f) (Fibr)
Scopey, moderate colt, effective 9f, acts on frm, likes tight tracks. Turf high 49.
**C A Smith [1-7] The Ox Hill Flyers (from D R C Elsworth [0-5] Spt 1997).*

OPTIMISTIC BHB 86f RR 89f 1597[9]

3 b f Reprimand 8.2f **(63)** - Arminda (Blakeney) 10.5f **(64)**
Form - 50
Record 1998 - 1st:0 2nd:0 3rd:0 Ran:2
Pre1998 - 1st:2 2nd:0 3rd:0 Ran:4
Win Prizemoney £15,049 *Total Prizemoney* £15,518
Wins * 1997 Aug York (GD) H 7f 73 81+ <
* 1997 Jly Yarmou (G-F) 7f 80+
1998 Turf 0-2: (10f 2) (gd, g-f)
Neat, useful filly, effective 7 to 10f, best at 7f, acts on gd to g-f, best on gd. Turf high 89 (1st run) - 5th of 11 getting 3lb from Bawsian (12 May York 10f gd RF 1165).
**M H Tompkins [2-6] Mystic Meg Ltd.*

OPTIMISTIC CHRIS BHB 58f RR 55f 2745[8]

3 b g Pharly (FR) 11.5f **(64)** -Gay Twenties (Lord Gayle (USA)) 8.8f **(62)**
Form - 788
Record 1998 - 1st:0 2nd:0 3rd:0 Ran:3
1998 Turf 0-3: (8f, 10f, 11f) (g-f 3)
Light-framed, currently fair gelding. Turf high 55.
**A Streeter [0-3] Optimistic Racing.*

OPTIONAL BHB 67f RR 77f 5068[10]

2 ch f Prince Sabo 6.6f **(64)** - My Polished Corner (IRE) (Tate Gallery

(USA)) 7.4f **(67)**
Form - 6264080
Record 1998 - 1st:0 2nd:1 3rd:0 Ran:7
Win Prizemoney £0 *Total Prizemoney* £1,301
1998 Turf 0-7: (5f 2, 6f 5) (g-s, gd, g-f 2, frm, hrd 2)
Above-average filly, effective 6f, acts on g-f, has worn blinkers. Turf high 77 - 2nd of 24 to Grey Princess (22 Jun Windsor 6f g-f RF 2182). **B J Meehan [0-7] Wyck Hall Stud.*

OPULENT BHB 64f **RR 67f** 2487^{7}

7 b g Robellino (USA) 9.5f **(68)** - One Half Silver (CAN) (Plugged Nickle (USA)) 7.8f **(68)**
Form - 00557
Record 1998 - 1st:0 2nd:0 3rd:0 Ran:5
Pre1998 - 1st:1 2nd:1 3rd:1 Ran:8
Win Prizemoney £5,466 *Total Prizemoney* £7,643
Wins * 1997 Jly Beverl (HVY) H 8.5f 71 74 <
1998 Turf 0-5: (8f 3, 10f 2) (g-s, gd 3, g-f)
Average gelding, effective 8 to 10f, acts on sft to gd. Turf high 67.
**Mrs M Reveley [1-10] Mrs Eileen Hawkey (from C A Dwyer [0-2] Oct 1996).*

ORANGE BUSH (IRE) BHB 57a **RR 56f 57a** 303^{3}

3 ch g Pips Pride 6.7f **(70)** - Kew Gift (Faraway Son (USA)) 10.3f **(55)**
Form - 401173
Record 1998 - 1st:2 2nd:0 3rd:1 Ran:4
Pre1998 - 1st:0 2nd:0 3rd:0 Ran:3
Win Prizemoney £3,546 *Total Prizemoney* £3,929
Wins 1998 *Feb Wolver (STD) S 6f 58 <*
1998 *Jan Lingfi (STD) 5f 58 <*
1998 AW 2-4: (5f 1-2, 6f 1-2) (Equi 1-2, Fibr 1-2)
Scopey, fair gelding, effective 5 to 6f, - acts on AW. AW high 58 (1st run) - 1st of 4 from Dande Times (10 Jan Lingfield RF 0060) - also 1st of 8 giving 5lb to Arcane Star (4 Feb Wolverhampton RF 0220). **B A Pearce [0-1] Richard Gray (from M Waring [0-1] Feb 1998).*

ORANGE PLACE (IRE) BHB 52f49a **RR 55f 49a** 4775^{13}

7 ch g Nordance (USA) 7.4f **(69)** - Little Red Hut (Habitat) 9.4f **(70)**
Form - 445080005660
Record 1998 - 1st:0 2nd:0 3rd:0 Ran:10
Pre1998 - 1st:5 2nd:3 3rd:4 Ran:38
Win Prizemoney £31,528 *Total Prizemoney* £39,089
Wins 1996 May Goodwo (SFT) H 7f 70 74
1994 Jun Epsom (GD) H 7f 88 89 <
1994 Apr Kempto (SFT) H 7f 85 85
1998 Turf 0-8: (6f, 7f 5, 8f 2) (sft, gd 5, frm 2) 1998 AW 0-2: (7f, 11f) (Fibr 2)
Fair gelding, effective 7 to 8f, best at 8f, acts on gd to frm, has worn blinkers. Turf high 62. AW high 45. Remains difficult to win with.
**B J Llewellyn [0-18] Lodge Cross Partnership (from T J Naughton [1-18] Jun 1997).*

ORBITAL STAR (IRE) BHB 67f **RR 64f** 5146^{4}

2 b c Contract Law (USA) 8.9f **(54)** - Sun Gift (Guillaume Tell (USA)) 13.2f **(54)**
Form - 004
Record 1998 - 1st:0 2nd:0 3rd:0 Ran:3
Win Prizemoney £0 *Total Prizemoney* £215
1998 Turf 0-3: (7f, 8f 2) (sft, gd 2)
Currently average colt. Turf high 64 (began Oct).
**P W Harris [0-3] Hornbuckle, Buckle, Daffey & Knight.*

ORDAINED BHB 61f45a **RR 61f 45a** 3237^{2}

5 b m Mtoto 11.5f **(71)** - In the Habit (USA) (Lyphard (USA)) 9.9f **(72)**
Form - 006282
Record 1998 - 1st:0 2nd:2 3rd:0 Ran:4
Pre1998 - 1st:3 2nd:5 3rd:5 Ran:34
Win Prizemoney £10,721 *Total Prizemoney* £22,404
Wins * 1997 Oct Newmar (G-F) H 12f 52 60
* 1996 Aug Redcar (FRM) H 11f 54 61 <
* 1996 Jun Redcar (G-F) H 10f 50 54
1998 Turf 0-3: (10f, 12f 2) (frm 3) 1998 AW 0-1: (12f) (Fibr)
Average filly, effective 10 to 12f, best at 12f, acts on g-f to frm, best on frm, prefers right handed tracks, excels at Newmarket, does well at Leicester. Turf high 61 (1st run) (began Jly) - 2nd of 11 giving 10lb to Indiana Princess (17 Jly Pontefract 12f frm RF 2885). Inconsistent.
**E J Alston [3-35] Peter Ebdon Racing (from T T Clement [0-3] Feb 1996).*

OREGON DREAM (IRE) BHB 51f **RR 35f** 4834^{10}

2 b f Seattle Dancer (USA) 10.1f **(74)** - Ibda (Mtoto)
Form - 830
Record 1998 - 1st:0 2nd:0 3rd:1 Ran:3
Win Prizemoney £0 *Total Prizemoney* £306
1998 Turf 0-2: (5f 2) (g-s, gd) 1998 AW 0-1: (6f) (Fibr)
Currently moderate filly. Turf high 35.
**M Bell [0-1] Desmond Fitzgerald (from M W Easterby [0-2] Jly 1998).*

ORFORD NESS (FR) **RR 116f** 3914a^{3}

4 b f Selkirk (USA) 7.9f **(76)** - Nesaah (USA) (Topsider (USA)) 8.3f **(71)**
Form - 353
1998 Turf 0-3: (8f 3) (sft, gd, g-f)
High-class filly. Turf high 116 (1st run) (began Jly) - 3rd of 9 getting 3lb from Fly To The Stars (12 Jly Deauville 8f g-f RF 2862a).
**P Bary in FR [1-4].*

ORIEL GIRL BHB 57f50a **RR 58f 50a** 5128^{4}

3 b f Beveled (USA) 6.9f **(64)** - St Helena (Monsanto (FR)) 6.5f **(59)**
Form - 5038570000014
Record 1998 - 1st:1 2nd:0 3rd:1 Ran:13
Pre1998 - 1st:3 2nd:3 3rd:2 Ran:16
Win Prizemoney £17,734 *Total Prizemoney* £21,276
Wins * **1998** Oct Yarmou (SFT) H 7f 49 58
1997 Aug Mussel (G-F) H 5f 66 71 <
1997 Jly Mussel (G-F) C 5f 65
1997 Jly Catter (SFT) S 5f 65
1998 Turf 1-7: (5f, 6f, 7f 1-3, 8f 2) (g-s 1-2, gd 3, g-f, frm) 1998 AW 0-6: (5f 5, 7f) (Equi 3, Fibr 3)
Unfurnished, fair filly, effective 5f, acts on gd to g-f, best on g-f, often wears blinkers (very effectively), excels at Musselburgh. Turf high 58. AW high 52.
**M J Ryan [1-6] M Byron (from G L Moore [0-7] Apr 1998).*

ORIEL STAR BHB 64f **RR 74f** 5144^{7}

2 b f Safawan 6.6f **(60)** - Silvers Era (Balidar) 7.9f **(63)**
Form - 30410338037
Record 1998 - 1st:1 2nd:0 3rd:4 Ran:11
Win Prizemoney £2,784 *Total Prizemoney* £4,890
Wins * **1998** Spt Ripon (SFT) 5f 74 <
1998 Turf 1-11: (5f 1-10, 6f) (sft, g-s, gd 1-6, g-f, frm 2)
Above-average filly, effective 5f, acts on gd to frm, mostly wears blinkers (very effectively). Turf high 74 - also 1st of 17 getting 7lb from Tread Softly (1 Spt Ripon RF 4009).
**P D Evans [1-11] Kendall White & Co Ltd.*

ORIENTAL EXPRESS (IRE) **RR 113f** 2104a^{2}

5 br h Green Desert (USA) 7.8f **(78)** - City Fortress (Troy) 10.4f **(68)**
Form - 212
1998 Turf 1-2: (8f, 10f 1-1) (hvy, g-f 1-1)
Currently Group-class colt. Turf high 113 - 2nd of 17 to Taiki Shuttle (14 Jun Fuchu 8f hvy RF 2104a) - also 1st of 11 getting 5lb from Vialli (19 Apr Sha Tin RF 0839a). He gained a narrow victory in the Queen Elizabeth II Cup at Sha Tin.
**I Allan in HK [1-3] Larry Yung.*

ORIENTAL FASHION (IRE) **RR 92+f** 4505^{1}

2 b f Marju (IRE) 9.2f **(76)** - Wijdan (USA) **(96f)** (Mr Prospector (USA)) 8.8f **(78)**
Form - 21
Record 1998 - 1st:1 2nd:1 3rd:0 Ran:2
Win Prizemoney £4,565 *Total Prizemoney* £5,670
Wins * **1998** Spt Nottin (G-F) 8.2f 92+ <
1998 Turf 1-2: (7f, 8f 1-1) (gd 1-1, frm)
Currently useful filly. Turf high 92 (began Aug) - 1st of 10 from Beryl (26 Spt Nottingham RF 4505). She showed promise on her Kempton debut, and went on to run away with a Nottingham maiden over a mile next time. She will stay middle distances next year.
**S bin Suroor [1-2] Godolphin.*

ORIENTAL PRIDE (IRE) **RR 45f** 5138^{11}

2 ch c Indian Ridge 7.6f **(74)** - Mercy Bien (IRE) (Be My Guest (USA)) 9.3f **(67)**
Form - 00

Record 1998 - 1st:0 2nd:0 3rd:0 Ran:2
1998 Turf 0-2: (7f 2) (g-s, gd)
Currently moderate colt. Turf high 45 (began Oct).
**E A L Dunlop [0-2] H R H Sultan Ahmad Shah.*

ORINOCO VENTURE (IRE) BHB 35f **RR 7f** 1301[11]

7 br g Doyoun 10.7f **(69)** - Push a Button (Bold Lad (IRE)) 8.4f **(68)**
Form - 00
Record 1998 - 1st:0 2nd:0 3rd:0 Ran:2
Pre1998 - 1st:0 2nd:0 3rd:2 Ran:9
Win Prizemoney £0 *Total Prizemoney* £1,232
1998 Turf 0-1: (12f) (g-f) 1998 AW 0-1: (11f) (Fibr)
Very poor gelding, has worn blinkers. Inconsistent.
**B P J Baugh [0-2] John Meredith (from S P C Woods [0-10] Spt 1994).*

ORIOLE BHB 53f50a **RR 50f 50a** 5014[9]

5 b g Mazilier (USA) 8.5f **(56)** - Odilese (Mummy's Pet) 7.7f **(60)**
Form - 050021008001450
Record 1998 - 1st:2 2nd:1 3rd:0 Ran:15
Pre1998 - 1st:4 2nd:3 3rd:4 Ran:40
Win Prizemoney £19,624 *Total Prizemoney* £26,621

Wins								
	* **1998**	Aug	Redcar	(G-F)	H	7f	47	49
	* **1998**	Jun	Carlis	(G-S)	H	6.9f	46	50
	* 1997	Aug	Redcar	(FRM)	H	7f	48	52
	* 1997	May	Redcar	(GD)	H	8f	33	39
	1996	Jly	Ayr	(G-S)	H	7f	46	49
	1995	Jly	Thirsk	(G-F)	H	6f		62 <

1998 Turf 2-14: (6f, 7f 2-9, 8f 4) (sft 2, gd 1-5, g-f 4, frm 1-3) 1998 AW 0-1: (8f) (Fibr)
Fair gelding, effective 7 to 8f, best at 8f, acts on gd to frm, best on g-f, has worn blinkers (very effectively), excels at Redcar. Turf high 50 - 1st of 14 getting 12lb from Step On Degas (24 Jun Carlisle RF 2226) - also 1st of 14 getting 20lb from Far Removed (9 Aug Redcar RF 3488). He runs regularly but wins in his turn, and seems to go well at Redcar.
**Don Enrico Incisa [4-28] Don Enrico Incisa (from N Tinkler [2-27] Oct 1996).*

ORLEANS (IRE) BHB 40f **RR 43f** 3575[5]

3 b g Scenic 10.6f **(66)** - Guest House (What A Guest) 7f **(62)**
Form - 80305
Record 1998 - 1st:0 2nd:0 3rd:1 Ran:5
Pre1998 - 1st:0 2nd:0 3rd:0 Ran:3
Win Prizemoney £0 *Total Prizemoney* £405
1998 Turf 0-5: (8f, 9f 2, 11f, 12f) (gd 4, g-f)
Workmanlike, moderate gelding, effective 11f, acts on gd. Turf high 43. Inconsistent. **T P Tate [0-8] C E Whiteley.*

ORMELIE (IRE) BHB 90f **RR 93f** 5155a[10]

3 b c Jade Hunter (USA) 10.4f **(72)**-Trolley Song (USA) (Caro) 9.3f **(74)**
Form - 5133150
Record 1998 - 1st:2 2nd:0 3rd:2 Ran:7
Win Prizemoney £8,857 *Total Prizemoney* £10,967

Wins								
	* **1998**	Aug	Newbur	(G-F)	H	13.3f	83	88 <
	* **1998**	May	Ayr	(GD)		10f		74

1998 Turf 2-7: (8f, 10f 1-1, 12f 3, 13f 1-1, 15f) (hvy, sft 2, g-s 1-1, g-f 1-2, frm)
Leggy, useful colt, effective 12 to 13f, acts on g-f. Turf high 93 - also 1st of 8 giving 9lb to Bathe In Light (14 Aug Newbury RF 3636). Scrambled home in an ordinary Ayr maiden, but showed better form in handicaps afterwards, including when displaying a turn of foot to win at Newbury. She did not figure when tried in Pattern company in France on her final two starts.
**P W Chapple-Hyam [2-7].*

ORNATE (IRE) BHB 44f **RR 64?f** 4775[20]

4 b g Arazi (USA) 9.2f **(74)** - Pretty Lady (High Top) 10.2f **(67)**
Form - 000
Record 1998 - 1st:0 2nd:0 3rd:0 Ran:3
Pre1998 - 1st:0 2nd:0 3rd:1 Ran:3
Win Prizemoney £0 *Total Prizemoney* £260
1998 Turf 0-3: (7f, 8f, 9f) (sft, gd, g-f)
Average gelding. Turf high 35 (began Spt).
**D Shaw [0-3] J C Fretwell (from J Oxx in IRE [0-3] May 1997).*

ORONTES (USA) BHB 42f54a **RR 44f 54a** 2325[10]

4 b g Lomond (USA) 9.9f **(74)** - Chateau Princess (USA) (Majestic Prince (USA)) 10f **(74)**
Form - 05880
Record 1998 - 1st:0 2nd:0 3rd:0 Ran:5
Pre1998 - 1st:1 2nd:0 3rd:1 Ran:9
Win Prizemoney £3,216 *Total Prizemoney* £4,326
Wins 1996 Aug Salisb (GD) 7f 79 <
1998 Turf 0-4: (8f 2, 12f, 17f) (gd, g-f, frm 2) 1998 AW 0-1: (8f) (Equi)
Scopey, moderate gelding, effective 8f, acts on gd, has worn blinkers, likes tight tracks. Turf high 48. Likely to need a mile plus.
**J S Moore [0-9] Oncebitten Syndicate (from R Hannon [1-9] Oct 1997).*

ORPEN (USA) RR 107f 3916a[1]

2 b c Lure (USA) - Bonita Francita (CAN)(Devil's Bag (USA)) 12.4f **(78)**
Form - 11
1998 Turf 2-2: (6f 2-2) (sft 1-1, gd 1-1)
Currently Pattern-class colt. Turf high 107 (began Aug) - 1st of 13 from Exeat (23 Aug Deauville RF 3916a). He looked outstandingly well before the Group One Prix Morny at Deauville in August, and put up a first-rate performance to win by a clear margin after being checked two furlongs out. A line through Zirconi suggests that he is not far behind the best of his generation, and he should hold his own in top-class company at up to a mile next season. He has avoided the hype surrounding his stablemate Stravinsky, but could yet prove the ace in Aidan O'Brien's pack.
**A P O'Brien in IRE [2-2] Mrs John Magnier.*

Orpen looks a super prospect for '99

ORSAY BHB 76f **RR 80f** 4893[6]

6 b g Royal Academy (USA) 7.8f **(77)** - Bellifontaine (FR) (Bellypha) 9.8f **(73)**
Form - 401076
Record 1998 - 1st:1 2nd:0 3rd:0 Ran:6
Pre1998 - 1st:2 2nd:2 3rd:3 Ran:14
Win Prizemoney £15,938 *Total Prizemoney* £23,929

Wins								
	* **1998**	Aug	Sandow	(G-F)	H	10f	76	80 <
	* 1997	Jun	Sandow	(G-F)	H	10f	76	79
	* 1995	Apr	Leices	(GD)		8f		69

1998 Turf 1-6: (8f, 10f 1-5) (gd, g-f 1-4, frm)
Decent gelding, effective 8 to 10f, best at 10f, acts on gd to frm, prefers right handed tracks, excels at Sandown and Newmarket.

Turf high 80 - 1st of 10 getting 6lb from Infatuation (22 Aug Sandown RF 3823). **W R Muir [3-21] D J Deer.*

ORSINO BHB 60f **RR 63f** 2185[9]
3 b g Theatrical Charmer 10.9f **(63)** - Sonoco (Song) 7.2f **(61)**
Form - 8050
Record 1998 - 1st:0 2nd:0 3rd:0 Ran:4
Pre1998 - 1st:0 2nd:0 3rd:0 Ran:3
1998 Turf 0-4: (8f, 10f, 14f 2) (g-s, g-f 2, frm)
Scopey, average gelding. Turf high 63.
**S Dow [0-7] Mrs Jackie Gittins.*

ORSUNO (GER) RR 98f 634a[3]
4
Form - 3
1998 Turf 0-1: (10f) (hvy)
Currently very useful. (1st run) - 3rd of 10 getting 7lb from Eden Rock (5 Apr Gelsenkirchen-horst 10f hvy RF 0634a).
**R Suerland in GER [0-1] Gestut Monchhof (from H Jentzsch in GER [0-1] May 1997).*

ORTOLAN BHB 77f66a **RR 83f 66a** 398[4]
5 gr h Prince Sabo 6.6f **(64)** - Kala Rosa (Kalaglow) 9.8f **(67)**
Form - 54
Record 1998 - 1st:0 2nd:0 3rd:0 Ran:2
Pre1998 - 1st:6 2nd:2 3rd:1 Ran:13
Win Prizemoney £23,411 *Total Prizemoney* £38,650
Wins 1996 Oct Pontef (GD) C 6f 83
1996 Aug Newmar (G-F) C 7f 62
1996 Aug Newmar (GD) C 7f 80
1996 Aug Salisb (G-F) C 6f 64
1996 May Goodwo (SFT) C 6f 76
1995 May Salisb (G-F) 5f 98+ <
1998 AW 0-2: (7f 2) (Fibr 2)
Decent colt. AW high 68.
**J L Eyre [0-2] Diamond Racing Ltd (from R Hannon [6-13] Oct 1996).*

OSCAR ROSE BHB 20f26a **RR 13f 26a** 2325[9]
5 b g Aragon 7.7f **(58)** - Mossy Rose (King of Spain) 7.8f **(52)**
Form - 300070
Record 1998 - 1st:0 2nd:0 3rd:1 Ran:6
Pre1998 - 1st:0 2nd:0 3rd:1 Ran:15
Win Prizemoney £0 *Total Prizemoney* £1,016
1998 Turf 0-4: (12f 2, 15f, 17f)(sft, gd 3) 1998 AW 0-2:(13f, 16f) (Equi 2)
Poor gelding, has worn blinkers. Turf high 13. AW high 19.
**M J Bolton [0-14] Mrs S P Elphick (from Lord Huntingdon [0-9] Aug 1996).*

OSUMI TYCOON (IRE) RR 122f 1378a[2]
7 b h Last Tycoon 9.4f **(73)** - Doff the Derby (USA) (Master Derby (USA)) 9.5f **(69)**
Form - 2
1998 Turf 0-1: (7f) (frm)
Currently very high-class horse. (1st run) - 2nd of 16 to Taiki Shuttle (16 May Fuchu 7f frm RF 1378a). **Y Take in JPN [0-1].*

OTAHUNA BHB 80f **RR 78f** 5138[2]
2 b c Selkirk (USA) 7.9f **(76)** - Stara (Star Appeal) 9.6f **(65)**
Form - 842
Record 1998 - 1st:0 2nd:1 3rd:0 Ran:3
Win Prizemoney £0 *Total Prizemoney* £1,257
1998 Turf 0-3: (7f 3) (sft, gd, frm)
Currently above-average colt. Turf high 78 (began Spt) - 2nd of 19 giving 5lb to Hesitation (6 Nov Doncaster 7f gd RF 5138).
**R Hollinshead [0-3] J D Graham.*

OTELLO BHB 72f **RR 85f** 4642[F]
2 b br c Tragic Role (USA) 9.4f **(63)** - Yankee Special (Bold Lad (IRE)) 8.4f **(68)**
Form - 0563F
Record 1998 - 1st:0 2nd:0 3rd:1 Ran:5
Win Prizemoney £0 *Total Prizemoney* £444
1998 Turf 0-5: (5f, 6f 4) (gd, g-f 2, frm 2)
Useful colt. Turf high 85 (began Jly) - 3rd of 14 giving 10lb to Diamond Geezer (15 Spt Sandown 5f gd RF 4264). (DEAD)
**D R C Elsworth [0-5] Mrs M E Slade.*

OTHER CLUB BHB 56f58a **RR 60f 58a** 4670[9]
4 ch g Kris 10f **(75)** - Tura (Northfields (USA)) 9f **(72)**
Form - 321810
Record 1998 - 1st:2 2nd:0 3rd:0 Ran:4
Pre1998 - 1st:0 2nd:1 3rd:1 Ran:4
Win Prizemoney £5,914 *Total Prizemoney* £7,469
Wins 1998 *Jun Wolver (STD) C 8.5f 61* <
1998 *Jan Wolver (STD) 8.5f 61* <
1998 Turf 0-1: (10f) (g-s) 1998 AW 2-3: (8f 2-3) (Fibr 2-3)
Scopey, average gelding, effective 8f, - acts on Fibr. AW high 61 (1st run) - 1st of 9 giving 5lb to Time of Night (21 Jan Wolverhampton RF 0125) - also 1st of 12 giving 15lb to Lady Eil (20 Jun Wolverhampton RF 2162).
**E A L Dunlop [0-1] Mrs E Peate (from J A R Toller [2-7] Jun 1998).*

OTTAVIO FARNESE BHB 38f47a **RR 37f 47a** 4094[8]
6 ch g Scottish Reel 8.6f **(58)**- Sense of Pride (Welsh Pageant) 10f **(65)**
Form - 008
Record 1998 - 1st:0 2nd:0 3rd:0 Ran:3
Pre1998 - 1st:1 2nd:1 3rd:0 Ran:9
Win Prizemoney £4,123 *Total Prizemoney* £5,359
Wins 1995 Oct Bright (GD) 10f 65 <
1998 Turf 0-3: (10f 2, 11f) (frm 3)
Very moderate gelding. Turf high 37 (began Jly). Inconsistent.
**G G Margarson [0-3] Anthony Hide (from A Hide [1-10] Nov 1996).*

OTTERINGTON GIRL BHB 45f **RR 42f** 4320[7]
2 b f Noble Patriarch 12.2f **(43)** - Bidweaya (USA) (Lear Fan (USA)) 8.5f **(73)**
Form - 00057
Record 1998 - 1st:0 2nd:0 3rd:0 Ran:5
1998 Turf 0-5: (5f 2, 6f, 7f, 8f) (sft, gd 2, g-f 2)
Moderate filly. Turf high 40. **Miss S E Hall [0-5] Mrs Joan Hodgson.*

OTTO RR 41f 4371[11]
3 b g Sure Blade (USA) 10.6f **(66)** - Nikatino (Bustino) 10.4f **(64)**
Form - 7500
Record 1998 - 1st:0 2nd:0 3rd:0 Ran:4
1998 Turf 0-4: (12f 2, 14f 2) (gd, g-f, frm 2)
Leggy, moderate gelding. Turf high 41 (began Jly).
**K McAuliffe [0-4] Mrs H Raw.*

OTTO E MEZZO BHB 69f **RR 75f** 4590[12]
6 bl g Persian Bold 10f **(69)** - Carolside (Music Maestro) 7.7f **(66)**
Form - 0
Record 1998 - 1st:0 2nd:0 3rd:0 Ran:1
Pre1998 - 1st:4 2nd:1 3rd:2 Ran:17
Win Prizemoney £30,597 *Total Prizemoney* £32,375
Wins 1994 Oct San Si (HVY) 7.5f 95
1994 Oct San Si (SFT) 7f
1994 Spt Maia (G-F) 8f 87+
1994 Jun San Si (G-F) 7f 83
1998 Turf 0-1: (12f) (gd)
Above-average gelding. Inconsistent.
**M J Polglase [1-15] M J Polglase (from J L Dunlop [4-7] Oct 1994).*

OUAISNE BHB 78f **RR 70f** 2449[10]
3 b g Warning 8.1f **(77)** - Noirmant (Dominion) 8.5f **(63)**
Form - 8000
Record 1998 - 1st:0 2nd:0 3rd:0 Ran:4
Pre1998 - 1st:1 2nd:0 3rd:0 Ran:4
Win Prizemoney £3,367 *Total Prizemoney* £5,836
Wins * 1997 Jun Redcar (GD) 5f 86+ <
1998 Turf 0-4: (5f 2, 6f, 8f) (gd 3, g-f)
Workmanlike, above-average gelding, has worn blinkers. Turf high 78. Inconsistent. Has completely lost his way and flopped in a claimer on his final run. **R Guest [1-8] MatthewsBreedingandRacing.*

OUDALMUTEENA (IRE) RR 67f 4888[3]
3 b c Lahib (USA) 8f **(69)** - Roxy Music (IRE) (Song) 7.2f **(61)**
Form - 03
Record 1998 - 1st:0 2nd:0 3rd:1 Ran:2
Win Prizemoney £0 *Total Prizemoney* £555
1998 Turf 0-2: (6f, 7f) (gd 2)
Strong, currently average colt. Turf high 67 (began Spt) - 3rd of 6 to Ally (20 Oct Yarmouth 7f gd RF 4888).
**A C Stewart [0-2] Hamdan Al Maktoum.*

OULTON BROAD BHB 57f **RR 55f** 4583[11]

2 b c Midyan (USA) 9.9f **(64)** - Lady Quachita (USA) (Sovereign Dancer (USA)) 11.2f **(68)**

Form - 800

Record	**1998 -**	1st:0	2nd:0	3rd:0	Ran:3

1998 Turf 0-3: (7f, 8f 2) (gd 2, g-f)

Currently fair colt. Turf high 55 (began Aug).

**J G Portman [0-3] A Masse-Stamberger.*

OUR ALBERT (IRE) BHB 33f **RR 35f** 4114[17]

5 b g Durgam (USA) 12.3f **(53)** - Power Girl (Tyrant (USA)) 6.6f **(59)**

Form - 80

Record	**1998 -**	1st:0	2nd:0	3rd:0	Ran:2
	Pre1998 -	1st:0	2nd:0	3rd:0	Ran:6

1998 Turf 0-2: (5f, 7f) (frm 2)

Very moderate gelding, has worn blinkers. Turf high 26 (began Jly).

**T W Donnelly [0-2] Mrs J A Beighton (from J A Glover [0-6] Oct 1996).*

OUR BANDBOX BHB 59f **RR 53f** 4146[8]

2 ch g Risk Me (FR) 8f **(53)** - Treble Top (USA) (Miswaki (USA)) 9f **(81)**

Form - 80078

Record	**1998 -**	1st:0	2nd:0	3rd:0	Ran:5

1998 Turf 0-5: (5f 2, 6f 3) (g-f 4, frm)

Fair gelding. Turf high 53. **S Mellor [0-5] The Bandbox Brigade.*

OUR DROWSY MAGGIE BHB 18f **RR 27f** 1944[10]

4 b f Puissance 7.1f **(60)** - Loadplan Lass (Nicholas Bill) 10.1f **(56)**

Form - 060

Record	**1998 -**	1st:0	2nd:0	3rd:0	Ran:3
	Pre1998 -	1st:0	2nd:0	3rd:0	Ran:3

1998 AW 0-3: (11f, 12f, 15f) (Fibr 3)

Leggy, little account filly.

**T Wall [0-2] Dennis Newton (from G Fierro [0-1] Jan 1998).*

OUR MAIN MAN BHB 32f60a **RR 28f 60a** 1157[5]

8 ch g Superlative 8.8f **(57)** - Ophrys (Nonoalco (USA)) 8.5f **(66)**

Form - 0562025

Record	**1998 -**	1st:0	2nd:2	3rd:0	Ran:5
	Pre1998 -	1st:3	2nd:2	3rd:3	Ran:29

Win Prizemoney £9,100 *Total Prizemoney* £13,320

Wins								
	* 1997	*Jun*	*Southw*	*(STD)*	*H*	*12f*	*50*	*57+*
	* 1995	Oct	Pontef	(FRM)	H	10f	49	56
	* 1995	Jly	Mussel	(FRM)		11.1f		58 <

1998 Turf 0-1: (16f) (gd) 1998 AW 0-4: (12f, 13f, 14f 2) (Equi, Fibr 3)

Average gelding, effective 12 to 14f, best at 12f, - acts on Fibr, has worn blinkers, favours left handed tracks, favours tight tracks. AW high 62 - 2nd of 12 giving 8lb to Monaco Gold (17 Mar Southwell 14f Fibr RF 0436). **R M Whitaker [4-49] R M Whitaker.*

OUR MATE MART **RR 50f** 4611[14]

2 ch g Keen 11.1f **(58)**-Princess Moodyshoe (Jalmood (USA))10.1f **(52)**

Form - 0

Record	**1998 -**	1st:0	2nd:0	3rd:0	Ran:1

1998 Turf 0-1: (6f) (g-s)

Currently fair gelding. **M Bell [0-1] Frank Farrant.*

OUR MOLLY MALONE BHB 50f **RR 24f** 4938[15]

3 ch f Deploy 11.4f **(67)** - Lady Clementine (He Loves Me) 7.9f **(55)**

Form - 30

Record	**1998 -**	1st:0	2nd:0	3rd:1	Ran:2
	Pre1998 -	1st:0	2nd:0	3rd:0	Ran:4

Win Prizemoney £0 *Total Prizemoney* £360

1998 Turf 0-1: (16f) (gd) 1998 AW 0-1: (13f) (Equi)

Unfurnished, fair filly.

**A C Stewart [0-2] The Foxons Fillies Partnership (from D Morley [0-4] Oct 1997).*

OUR PEOPLE BHB 57f48a **RR 58f 48a** 5119[8]

4 ch g Indian Ridge 7.6f **(74)** - Fair and Wise (High Line) 10.3f **(70)**

Form - 804370121503478

Record	**1998 -**	1st:2	2nd:1	3rd:2	Ran:15
	Pre1998 -	1st:1	2nd:0	3rd:2	Ran:10

Win Prizemoney £10,529 *Total Prizemoney* £15,265

Wins								
	* **1998**	Aug	Redcar	(G-F)	H	11f	56	60
	* **1998**	Jly	Carlis	(G-F)	H	8f	49	53
	* 1996	Oct	Leices	(G-F)		8f		84 <

1998 Turf 2-13: (7f 2, 8f 1-2, 10f 4, 11f 1-2, 12f 3) (sft 3, g-s 2, gd 2, g-f 1-2, frm 1-4) 1998 AW 0-2: (6f, 10f) (Equi, Fibr)

Rangy, fair gelding, has worn blinkers, likes tight tracks. Turf high 60. AW high 36. Consistent. **M Johnston [3-25] Dr Fuk To Chang.*

OUR RISK BHB 40f **RR 60f** 4403[12]

4 ch g Risk Me (FR) 8f **(53)** - Our Lucy (Porto Bello) 8.9f **(43)**

Form - 707600

Record	**1998 -**	1st:0	2nd:0	3rd:0	Ran:6
	Pre1998 -	1st:0	2nd:0	3rd:0	Ran:7

1998 Turf 0-6: (8f, 10f, 11f, 12f 2, 13f) (hvy, sft, g-s, gd, g-f 2)

Average gelding, effective 8f, acts on gd, has worn blinkers. Turf high 60 - 7th of 16 getting 2lb from Luminoso (2 Jly Bellewstown 8f gd RF 2603a). Inconsistent.

**B Ellison [0-2] Brian Ellison Racing Club (from P Mullins in IRE [1-16] Jly 1998).*

OUR SHADEE (USA) BHB 42f36a **RR 38f 36a** 244[7]

8 b g Shadeed (USA) 7.7f **(72)** - Nuppence (Reform) 8.9f **(62)**

Form - 060657

Record	**1998 -**	1st:0	2nd:0	3rd:0	Ran:5
	Pre1998 -	1st:8	2nd:11	3rd:16	Ran:108

Win Prizemoney £23,007 *Total Prizemoney* £41,621

Wins								
	* 1996	Aug	Lingfi	(G-F)	H	7.6f	49	52
	* 1996	*Apr*	*Lingfi*	*(STD)*	*H*	*6f*	*66*	*69* <
	* 1996	*Mar*	*Lingfi*	*(STD)*	*C*	*6f*		*69* <
	* 1996	*Feb*	*Lingfi*	*(STD)*	*H*	*6f*	*54*	*55*
	* 1995	*Feb*	*Lingfi*	*(STD)*	*H*	*6f*	*53*	*51*
	* 1995	*Feb*	*Lingfi*	*(STD)*		*6f*		*50*
	* 1994	Jun	Lingfi	(G-F)	SH	7f	43	45

1998 AW 0-5: (6f 2, 7f 2, 8f) (Equi 5)

Very moderate gelding, effective 8f, - acts on Equi, mostly wears blinkers. AW high 34. Consistent. Once very useful on Equitrack, he is on a very long losing run indeed. **K T Ivory [8-113] K T Ivory.*

OUR WAY BHB 49f53a **RR 53f 53a** 3504[2]

4 ch f Forzando 7.2f **(63)** - Hanglands (Bustino) 10.4f **(64)**

Form - 04055776254732

Record	**1998 -**	1st:0	2nd:2	3rd:1	Ran:14
	Pre1998 -	1st:1	2nd:2	3rd:0	Ran:11

Win Prizemoney £3,018 *Total Prizemoney* £8,275

Wins								
	1997	May	Yarmou	(G-F)	H	8f	68	72 <

1998 Turf 0-11: (8f 2, 10f 2, 12f 6, 16f) (sft, g-s, gd, g-f 2, frm 5, hrd)

1998 AW 0-3: (8f, 9f, 11f) (Fibr 3)

Scopey, fair filly, effective 8 to 9f, best at 8f, acts on gd to hrd, has worn blinkers. Turf high 59. AW high 55.

**M Brittain [0-14] Mel Brittain (from C E Brittain [1-11] Jly 1997).*

OUTCRY **RR 65+f** 5071[13]

2 b f Caerleon (USA) 10.9f **(79)** - In Full Cry (USA) (Seattle Slew (USA)) 9.4f **(76)**

Form - 80

Record	**1998 -**	1st:0	2nd:0	3rd:0	Ran:2

1998 Turf 0-2: (6f, 7f) (gd, g-f)

Currently average filly. Turf high 65 (began Oct).

**G Wragg [0-2] A E Oppenheimer.*

OUT LIKE MAGIC BHB 48f60a **RR 59df 60a** 4660[12]

3 ch f Magic Ring (IRE) 6.5f **(64)** - Thevetia (Mummy's Pet) 7.7f **(60)**

Form - 02750000

Record	**1998 -**	1st:0	2nd:0	3rd:0	Ran:5
	Pre1998 -	1st:1	2nd:6	3rd:0	Ran:15

Win Prizemoney £3,203 *Total Prizemoney* £12,632

Wins								
	* 1997	Apr	Ripon	(G-F)		5f		74 <

1998 Turf 0-5: (5f, 6f, 7f, 8f 2) (gd, g-f, frm 2, hrd)

Light-framed, fair filly, effective 5 to 7f, best at 6f, acts on gd to frm, has worn blinkers, likes Pontefract. Turf high 42 (began Jly).

**P D Evans [1-20] Mrs E A Dawson.*

OUT LINE BHB 79f **RR 81f** 4360[5]

6 gr m Beveled (USA) 6.9f **(64)** - Free Range (Birdbrook) 8.4f **(62)**

Form - 421301085

Record	**1998 -**	1st:2	2nd:1	3rd:1	Ran:9
	Pre1998 -	1st:2	2nd:2	3rd:2	Ran:19

Win Prizemoney £16,865 *Total Prizemoney* £22,134

Wins								
	* **1998**	Jly	Salisb	(G-F)	H	7f	78	81 <
	* **1998**	Jun	Goodwo	(GD)	H	6f	66	73

* 1997 Jly Lingfi (G-F) H 6f 61 64
* 1997 May Sandow (GD) H 7.1f 57 61
1998 Turf 2-9: (6f 1-3, 7f 1-5, 8f) (g-s, gd 1-3, g-f 1-4, frm)
Decent mare, effective 6 to 7f, best at 7f, acts on gd to g-f, best on g-f, likes tight tracks. Turf high 81 - 1st of 9 giving 16lb to Bold Tina (31 Jly Salisbury RF 3242) - also 1st of 15 giving 7lb to Maladerie (3 Jun Goodwood RF 1696). Consistent.
**M Madgwick [4-28] Miss D M Green.*

OUT OF SIGHT (IRE) BHB 75f **RR 77f** 1319[8]
4 ch c Salse (USA) 10.9f **(71)** - Starr Danias (USA) (Sensitive Prince (USA)) 9.1f **(60)**
Form - 468
Record 1998 - 1st:0 2nd:0 3rd:0 Ran:3
Pre1998 - 1st:1 2nd:0 3rd:0 Ran:10
Win Prizemoney £8,285 *Total Prizemoney* £10,928
Wins * 1997 May York (GD) H 7.9f 75 79 <
1998 Turf 0-3: (8f 3) (sft, gd, frm)
Scopey, above-average colt, effective 8f, acts on sft to gd. Turf high 77 (1st run) - 4th of 10 getting 3lb from Therhea (24 Apr Sandown 8f sft RF 0847). **B A McMahon [1-13] D J Allen.*

OUT ON A PROMISE (IRE) BHB 48f60a **RR 60?f 60a** 2684[4]
6 b g Night Shift (USA) 8.1f **(73)** - Lovers' Parlour (Beldale Flutter (USA)) 9.7f **(71)**
Form - 64
Record 1998 - 1st:0 2nd:0 3rd:0 Ran:2
Pre1998 - 1st:2 2nd:3 3rd:5 Ran:22
Win Prizemoney £7,590 *Total Prizemoney* £16,221
Wins 1995 Spt Doncas (G-F) 10.3f 87 <
1994 Nov Wolver (STD) 7f 68+
1998 Turf 0-2: (10f, 12f) (gd, frm)
Average gelding, has worn blinkers. Turf high 39.
**L Lungo [1-12] London & Clydeside Properties Ltd (from N J H Walker [1-10] Jan 1997).*

OUTPLACEMENT (USA) RR 21f 879[5]
3 b g Mountain Cat (USA) - Coolernearthelake (USA) (Hail the Pirates (USA)) 11f **(78)**
Form - 65
Record 1998 - 1st:0 2nd:0 3rd:0 Ran:2
1998 Turf 0-1: (12f) (g-s) 1998 AW 0-1: (11f) (Fibr)
Lengthy, currently little account gelding.
**C R Egerton [0-2] Miss Hilary Butler.*

OUTSET (IRE) BHB 74f **RR 75f** 5150[11]
8 ch g Persian Bold 10f **(69)** - It's Now Or Never (High Line) 10.3f **(70)**
Form - 150
Record 1998 - 1st:1 2nd:0 3rd:0 Ran:3
Pre1998 - 1st:2 2nd:1 3rd:0 Ran:8
Win Prizemoney £13,646 *Total Prizemoney* £14,714
Wins * **1998** Mar Newcas (G-S) H 16.1f 67 75 <
* 1997 Nov Mussel (G-S) H 16f 63 68
* 1997 Oct Redcar (G-F) H 14.1f 56 62
1998 Turf 1-3: (14f, 16f 1-1, 17f) (gd 1-3)
Above-average gelding. Turf high 75 - 5th of 12 giving 3lb to Opaque (13 May York 14f gd RF 1210) - also 1st of 15 giving 17lb to Arisaig (31 Mar Newcastle RF 0514).
**M D Hammond [8-30] Mark Kilner (from H Candy [0-2] Oct 1992).*

OUTSPOKEN RR 106f 4281a[5]
3 ch c Arazi (USA) 9.2f **(74)** - Oh So Sharp (Kris) 9.5f **(73)**
Form - 4221035
1998 Turf 1-7: (8f, 9f, 10f 1-4, 12f) (hvy, sft, gd 1-3, g-f 2)
Pattern-class colt, effective 8 to 10f, best at 10f, acts on sft to gd, best on gd, often wears blinkers. Turf high 106 - 2nd of 6 to Desert Fox (6 Jun Cork 10f gd RF 1858a) - also 1st of 2 giving 2lb to Hibernian Rhapsody (5 Jly Naas RF 2620a). He is bred to be a champion, but notched up just one win, and that in a two-runner affair. **J Oxx in IRE [2-8] Sheikh Mohammed.*

OVER KEEN BHB 52f **RR 59f** 4962[4]
4 b f Keen 11.1f **(58)** - Shift Over (USA) (Night Shift (USA)) 7.2f **(69)**
Form - 5674
Record 1998 - 1st:0 2nd:0 3rd:0 Ran:4
1998 Turf 0-4: (7f, 8f, 10f 2) (sft, g-f, frm 2)
Workmanlike, fair filly. Turf high 59 (began Jly).
**Miss Gay Kelleway [0-4] Miss J A Challen.*

OVER THE COUNTER (IRE) BHB 60a **RR 67f** 4866[9]
2 b f Persian Bold 10f **(69)** - Scotia Rose (Tap On Wood) 10.3f **(65)**
Form - 04145410600
Record 1998 - 1st:2 2nd:0 3rd:0 Ran:11
Win Prizemoney £4,578 *Total Prizemoney* £4,943
Wins * **1998** Aug Newcas (G-F) C 8f 67 <
* **1998** Jly Bright (GD) S 7f 59
1998 Turf 2-9: (6f, 7f 1-6, 8f 1-2) (gd, g-f 3, frm 2-5) 1998 AW 0-2: (7f, 8f) (Fibr 2)
Average filly, effective 7 to 8f, best at 7f, acts on frm - acts on Fibr, prefers left handed tracks. Turf high 67 - 1st of 8 giving 4lb to Miss Cody (31 Aug Newcastle RF 3993) - also 1st of 6 from Patsys Forem (1 Jly Brighton RF 2437). AW high 63 (1st run) (began Jly) - 4th of 11 giving 6lb to March Party (24 Jly Wolverhampton 7f Fibr RF 3097). **M R Channon [2-11] Over The Counter Partnership.*

OVER THE MARCH BHB 54f **RR 65f** 4779[14]
2 b f Deploy 11.4f **(67)** -Carn Maire (Northern Prospect (USA)) 9.5f **(71)**
Form - 060
Record 1998 - 1st:0 2nd:0 3rd:0 Ran:3
1998 Turf 0-3: (6f, 8f 2) (g-s, gd 2)
Currently average filly. Turf high 65 (began Spt).
**J E Banks [0-3] Giles Pritchard-Gordon.*

OVER THE MOON BHB 53f59a **RR 25f 59a** 4636[10]
4 ch f Beveled (USA) 6.9f **(64)** - Beyond the Moon (IRE) (Ballad Rock) 7.8f **(63)**
Form - 36558377161710
Record 1998 - 1st:3 2nd:0 3rd:2 Ran:14
Pre1998 - 1st:0 2nd:0 3rd:0 Ran:6
Win Prizemoney £6,588 *Total Prizemoney* £7,235
Wins 1998 *Spt Wolver (STD) C 7f 59*
1998 *Jly Wolver (STD) C 8.5f 56*
1998 *Jun Wolver (STD) C 7f 60* <
1998 Turf 0-1:(7f) (gd)1998 AW 3-13:(7f 2-5,8f 1-6, 9f 2)(Equi,Fibr 3-12)
Unfurnished, average filly, effective 7 to 8f, best at 7f, - acts on Fibr, has worn blinkers, likes left handed tracks, likes tight tracks. AW high 60 - 1st of 7 getting 12lb from Elite Hope (6 Jun Wolverhampton RF 1795) - also 1st of 12 getting 11lb from Abtaal (5 Spt Wolverhampton RF 4117). Inconsistent. She took her time in getting off the mark, but has found her level in modest company on Fibresand, winning two claimers and an apprentice event at Wolverhampton in 1998.
**Miss S J Wilton [0-1] John Pointon and Sons (from N P Littmoden [3-13] Spt 1998).*

OVER THE TOP (IRE) BHB 45f **RR 45f** 5145[13]
2 b g Up and At 'em - Latin Mass (Music Boy) 6.8f **(57)**
Form - 0080
Record 1998 - 1st:0 2nd:0 3rd:0 Ran:4
1998 Turf 0-4: (6f, 7f 2, 8f) (sft, gd 2, g-f)
Moderate gelding. Turf high 45 (began Spt).
**H Candy [0-4] Simon Broke and Partners.*

OVER TO YOU (USA) BHB 70f **RR 76f** 2073[5]
4 ch c Rubiano (USA) 7.1f **(87)** - Overnight (USA) (Mr Leader (USA)) 9.8f **(66)**
Form - 820305
Record 1998 - 1st:0 2nd:1 3rd:1 Ran:6
Pre1998 - 1st:1 2nd:0 3rd:2 Ran:9
Win Prizemoney £5,280 *Total Prizemoney* £9,309
Wins 1996 Oct Nottin (GD) 8.2f 83 <
1998 Turf 0-6: (7f 2, 8f, 10f 3) (sft, g-s, gd 3, frm)
Light-framed, above-average colt, effective 8 to 10f, best at 10f, acts on gd to frm, best on frm, has worn blinkers. Turf high 76 - 3rd of 19 getting 13lb from Party Romance (17 May Ripon 10f frm RF 1287). Inconsistent.
**T D Barron [0-6] Dave Scott (from E A L Dunlop [1-9] Spt 1997).*

OVERTURE (IRE) BHB 76f **RR 75f** 2711[8]
3 gr c Fairy King (USA) 7.7f **(75)** - Everything Nice (Sovereign Path) 9.3f **(55)**
Form - 60058
Record 1998 - 1st:0 2nd:0 3rd:0 Ran:5
Pre1998 - 1st:1 2nd:1 3rd:1 Ran:4

Win Prizemoney £3,160 *Total Prizemoney* £4,581
Wins * 1997 Jun Sandow (G-F) 5f 81+ <
1998 Turf 0-5: (6f 2, 7f 2, 8f) (gd 2, g-f, frm 2)
Neat, above-average colt, effective 5f, acts on g-f to frm. Turf high 75. **R Hannon [1-9] J A Lazzari.*

OXALAGU (GER) RR 118f 4718a[5]

6 gr h Lagunas 10f **(110)** - Oxalis (GER) (Ashmore (FR)) 8.5f **(65)**
Form - 252315
1998 Turf 1-5: (10f 1-3, 11f 2) (sft 3, gd 1-2)
High-class horse, effective 10 to 11f, best at 10f, acts on hvy to gd, best on sft. Turf high 118 - 5th of 10 giving 5lb to Insatiable (3 Oct Longchamp 10f sft RF 4718a) - also 1st of 9 from Kalatos (20 Spt Frankfurt RF 4470h). Consistent. A top-class German middle-distance performer, he did not have the same success last term that he enjoyed in 1997. He did manage to win a Group Two at Frankfurt in September, but was well held behind Insatiable in the Prix Dollar.
**A Schutz in GER [1-5] Gestut Rietberg (from B Schutz in GER [6-14] Nov 1997).*

OXBANE BHB 48f38a RR 50f 38a 5098[2]

4 b f Soviet Star (USA) 8.6f **(74)** - Oxslip (Owen Dudley) 8.3f **(61)**
Form - 0400600845202
Record 1998 - 1st:0 2nd:2 3rd:0 Ran:10
Pre1998 - 1st:0 2nd:1 3rd:1 Ran:16
Win Prizemoney £0 *Total Prizemoney* £3,764
1998 Turf 0-9: (6f, 7f 3, 8f, 10f 3, 12f) (gd 4, g-f 2, frm 2, hrd) 1998 AW 0-1: (6f) (Equi)
Scopey, fair filly, effective 6 to 10f, acts on gd to frm, has worn blinkers. Turf high 50 (began Jly) - 2nd of 17 getting 11lb from Bold Amusement (2 Nov Redcar 10f gd RF 5098).
**Mrs S Lamyman [0-9] John Purcell (from C A Dwyer [0-10] Jan 1998).*

PABELLA BLUEBIRD (IRE) BHB 27f RR 26f 3749[12]

3 b f Mac's Imp (USA) 5.6f **(54)** - Blue Diana (IRE) (Bluebird (USA)) 7.5f **(69)**
Form - 0080060000
Record 1998 - 1st:0 2nd:0 3rd:0 Ran:10
Pre1998 - 1st:0 2nd:0 3rd:0 Ran:4
1998 Turf 0-10: (5f 9, 6f) (g-s, gd 6, g-f, frm 2)
Light-framed, little account filly, often wears blinkers. Turf high 26.
**G R Oldroyd [0-14] C Raine.*

PACAERA (GER) RR 57f 4823[16]

2 b f Caerleon (USA) 10.9f **(79)** - Pamplona (GER) (Surumu (GER)) 10f **(83)**
Form - 0
Record 1998 - 1st:0 2nd:0 3rd:0 Ran:1
1998 Turf 0-1: (8f) (frm)
Currently fair filly. **J L Dunlop [0-1] Mrs H Focke.*

PACIFIC ALLIANCE (IRE) RR 64f 4412[10]

2 b c Fayruz 6.6f **(63)** - La Gravotte (FR) (Habitat) 9.4f **(70)**
Form - 50
Record 1998 - 1st:0 2nd:0 3rd:0 Ran:2
1998 Turf 0-2: (6f 2) (frm 2)
Currently average colt. Turf high 64 (began Aug).
**R W Armstrong [0-2] Horst Geicke.*

PACIFYC (IRE) BHB 53f RR 61f 4839[9]

3 b c Brief Truce (USA) 9.1f **(73)** - Ocean Blue (IRE) (Bluebird (USA)) 7.5f **(69)**
Form - 03000000
Record 1998 - 1st:0 2nd:0 3rd:1 Ran:8
Win Prizemoney £0 *Total Prizemoney* £447
1998 Turf 0-8: (8f 2, 10f 2, 12f 2, 14f 2) (g-s, gd, g-f 3, frm 3)
Neat, average colt, effective 8f, acts on gd. Turf high 76 - 3rd of 10 to Cyber World (23 May Kempton 8f gd RF 1429). Inconsistent.
**W R Muir [0-8] Terry Benson.*

PACKITIN RR 1890[15]

5 b g Rich Charlie 5.9f **(50)** - Sound Type (Upper Case (USA)) 8.2f **(55)**
Form - 0
Record 1998 - 1st:0 2nd:0 3rd:0 Ran:1
Pre1998 - 1st:0 2nd:0 3rd:0 Ran:1
1998 Turf 0-1: (6f) (g-f)
Currently very poor gelding.
**F Watson [0-2] M D Hetherington (Packaging) Ltd.*

PADAUK BHB 50f47a RR 59f 47a 4887[13]

4 b c Warrshan (USA) 9.7f **(59)** - Free on Board (Free State) 8.7f **(61)**
Form - 404320258550
Record 1998 - 1st:0 2nd:2 3rd:1 Ran:10
Pre1998 - 1st:0 2nd:1 3rd:4 Ran:15
Win Prizemoney £0 *Total Prizemoney* £6,264
1998 Turf 0-10: (12f 2, 13f, 14f 5, 15f, 16f) (g-s 2, gd 2, g-f 4, frm 2)
Average colt, effective 11 to 16f, acts on g-s to frm - acts on Equi, best on frm, has worn blinkers, favours tight tracks, and excels at Lingfield and Kempton. Turf high 59 - 2nd of 4 giving 19lb to Tarashaan (10 Jun Kempton 14f g-s RF 1880). A brother to dual-purpose winner Courbaril, he has managed a string of placed efforts in small staying events, but is one-paced and has not been able to get his head in front.
**M J Haynes [0-25] Butler, Bob Pettis, Haynes.*

PADDOCK INSPECTION (IRE)BHB56f63aRR58f 63a 4671[20]

2 ch g Archway (IRE) 8.5f **(60)** - Lauretta Blue (IRE) (Bluebird (USA)) 7.5f **(69)**
Form - 0370
Record 1998 - 1st:0 2nd:0 3rd:1 Ran:4
Win Prizemoney £0 *Total Prizemoney* £263
1998 Turf 0-3: (5f, 7f 2) (gd, g-f, frm) 1998 AW 0-1: (5f) (Fibr)
Average gelding, often wears blinkers. Turf high 58 (began Spt).
**G Lewis [0-4] Brooke Rankin.*

PADDY MCGOON (USA) BHB 69f RR 69f 2391[5]

3 ch g Irish River (FR) 9f **(77)** - Flame McGoon (USA) (Staff Writer (USA)) 10f **(54)**
Form - 5535
Record 1998 - 1st:0 2nd:0 3rd:1 Ran:4
Pre1998 - 1st:0 2nd:0 3rd:0 Ran:2
Win Prizemoney £0 *Total Prizemoney* £840
1998 Turf 0-4: (10f, 12f 3) (gd 2, g-f, frm)
Scopey, average gelding, effective 10 to 12f, acts on gd to g-f. Turf high 69 - 3rd of 8 giving 2lb to Praetorian Gold (12 Jun Goodwood 10f gd RF 1929). **D R C Elsworth [0-6] J C Smith.*

PADDY'S RICE BHB 47f RR 54f 4049[9]

7 ch g Hadeer 8.9f **(58)** - Requiem (Song) 7.2f **(61)**
Form - 00107500
Record 1998 - 1st:1 2nd:0 3rd:0 Ran:8
Pre1998 - 1st:4 2nd:3 3rd:3 Ran:37
Win Prizemoney £16,402 *Total Prizemoney* £20,826

Wins	* 1998	Jun	Bath	(G-S)	CH	8f	49	54	
	* 1997	May	Bright	(FRM)	H	8f	53	52	
	1996	Jun	Warwic	(FRM)		7f		60	<
	1995	May	Lingfi	(FRM)	H	6f	49	49	
	1994	Jly	Windso	(G-F)	SH	6f	48	43	

1998 Turf 1-8: (7f 3, 8f 1-5) (gd 1-4, g-f, frm 3)
Fair gelding, effective 8f, acts on gd to frm, has worn blinkers, likes left handed tracks, likes tight tracks. Turf high 54 - 1st of 18 giving 7lb to Warring (27 Jun Bath RF 2328).
**M Blanshard [2-16] Mrs R G Wellman (from M McCormack [1-7] Aug 1996).*

PADHAMS GREEN BHB 72f RR 64f 4650[4]

2 b c Aragon 7.7f **(58)** - Double Dutch (Nicholas Bill) 10.1f **(56)**
Form - 474
Record 1998 - 1st:0 2nd:0 3rd:0 Ran:3
Win Prizemoney £0 *Total Prizemoney* £444
1998 Turf 0-3: (5f 2, 6f) (g-f 2, frm)
Currently average colt. Turf high 64 (began Jly).
**M H Tompkins [0-3] D J Anderson.*

PAGAN RR 48f 3460[4]

3 b c Last Tycoon 9.4f **(73)** - Temple Row (Ardross) 10.6f **(68)**
Form - 44
Record 1998 - 1st:0 2nd:0 3rd:0 Ran:2
Win Prizemoney £0 *Total Prizemoney* £607
1998 Turf 0-2: (11f, 12f) (g-f 2)
Lengthy, currently moderate colt. Turf high 48 (began Jly).
**L M Cumani [0-2] Lord Hartington.*

PAGAN KING (IRE) BHB 88f **RR 78f** 4928[1]

2 b c Unblest - Starinka (Risen Star (USA))
Form - 041

Record	**1998 -**	1st:1	2nd:0	3rd:0	Ran:3

Win Prizemoney £2,941 *Total Prizemoney* £3,198

Wins	* **1998**	Oct	Bright	(G-S)		7f	78	<

1998 Turf 1-3: (6f 2, 7f 1-1) (g-s 1-1, g-f, frm)

Currently above-average colt. Turf high 78 (began Jly) - 1st of 14 giving 5lb to My Lass (22 Oct Brighton RF 4928).
**J A R Toller [1-3] The Gap Partnership.*

PAGEBOY BHB 45f65a **RR 40f 65a** 3621[16]

9 b g Tina's Pet 7.4f **(56)** - Edwin's Princess (Owen Dudley) 8.3f **(61)**
Form - 157570000

Record	**1998 -**	1st:1	2nd:0	3rd:0	Ran:9
	Pre1998 -	1st:10	2nd:12	3rd:6	Ran:87

Win Prizemoney £35,667 *Total Prizemoney* £58,117

Wins	* **1998**	*Jan*	*Lingfi*	*(STD)*	*H*	*6f*	*70*	*75*	<
	* 1997	*Jan*	*Lingfi*	*(STD)*	*H*	*6f*	*73*	*75*	<
	* 1996	*Spt*	*Wolver*	*(STD)*	*H*	*6f*	*67*	*65*	
	* 1996	Aug	Hamilt	(G-F)	H	6f	58	66+	
	* 1996	*Jan*	*Lingfi*	*(STD)*	*H*	*6f*	*61*	*63*	
	* 1995	*Jan*	*Lingfi*	*(STD)*	*H*	*6f*	*62*	*63+*	
	* 1994	May	Hamilt	(FRM)	H	6f	60	73+	
	* 1994	May	Hamilt	(GD)	H	6f	53	64+	
	* 1994	May	Thirsk	(FRM)	H	6f	53	57	

1998 Turf 0-5: (6f 4, 7f) (gd, g-f, frm 3) 1998 AW 1-4: (6f 1-4) (Equi 1-2, Fibr 2)

Above-average gelding, effective 6f, - acts on Equi, has worn blinkers (very effectively), likes left handed tracks, likes tight tracks. Turf high 40. AW high 75 (1st run) - 1st of 11 giving 5lb to Half Tone (1 Jan Lingfield RF 0004). Becoming disappointing. The time to catch him is within the first week of the year on the Lingfield Equitrack. The rest of the year is spent getting his handicap mark down. **P C Haslam [11-96] Lord Scarsdale.*

PAGE'S KING **RR 104f** 4829a[2]

3 b c Konigsstuhl (GER) 9f **(115)** - Page Bleue (GER) (Sadler's Wells (USA)) 10f **(76)**
Form - 262

1998 Turf 0-3: (9f, 11f, 12f) (hvy 3)

Currently very useful colt. Turf high 104 - 2nd of 11 getting 6lb from Tres Heureux (11 Oct Dusseldorf 9f hvy RF 4829a). He finished a well beaten sixth in the German Derby and is no better than that performance suggests. **A Lowe in GER [0-3] Stall Muhlgut*

PAGODA TREE (USA) BHB 74f **RR 76f** 3485[5]

3 b f Nureyev (USA) 8.4f **(84)** - Desert Holly (Vain (AUS)) 7.1f **(76)**
Form - 15

Record	**1998 -**	1st:1	2nd:0	3rd:0	Ran:2

Win Prizemoney £3,517 *Total Prizemoney* £3,517

Wins	* **1998**	Jly	Chepst	(GD)		7.1f	76	<

1998 Turf 1-2: (7f 1-2) (gd 1-2)

Scopey, currently above-average filly. Turf high 76 (1st run) (began Jly) - 1st of 9 from Hebony (4 Jly Chepstow RF 2529).
**P W Chapple-Hyam [1-2] R E Sangster.*

PAINT IT BLACK BHB 52f47a **RR 43f 47a** 109[6]

5 ch g Double Schwartz 7f **(60)**-Tableaux(FR) (Welsh Pageant) 10f **(65)**
Form - 083166

Record	**1998 -**	1st:1	2nd:0	3rd:1	Ran:5
	Pre1998 -	1st:2	2nd:1	3rd:1	Ran:28

Win Prizemoney £8,539 *Total Prizemoney* £11,063

Wins	* **1998**	*Jan*	*Lingfi*	*(STD)*	*S*	*7f*		*47*	
	* 1997	Apr	Thirsk	(G-F)	H	8f	50	54+	
	1995	Spt	Epsom	(GD)		7f		76	<

1998 AW 1-5: (7f 1-2, 8f 3) (Equi 1-4, Fibr)

Moderate gelding, effective 6 to 8f, best at 8f, acts on g-f to frm - acts on AW, has worn blinkers, prefers left handed tracks, favours tight tracks. AW high 49 - 3rd of 9 giving 14lb to Square Mile Miss (6 Jan Lingfield 8f Equi RF 0030) - also 1st of 14 from Rocky Waters (8 Jan Lingfield RF 0046).
**D Nicholls [2-19] M A Scaife (from R Hannon [1-14] Oct 1996).*

PAIRUMANI STAR (IRE) BHB 90f **RR 90f** 4841[3]

3 ch c Caerleon (USA) 10.9f **(79)** - Dawn Star (High Line) 10.3f **(70)**
Form - 221316123

Record	**1998 -**	1st:3	2nd:3	3rd:2	Ran:9
	Pre1998 -	1st:0	2nd:0	3rd:0	Ran:3

Win Prizemoney £14,608 *Total Prizemoney* £24,540

Wins	* **1998**	Aug	Goodwo	(G-F)	H	12f	85	87	<
	* **1998**	Jly	Salisb	(GD)	H	12f	80	86	
	* **1998**	Jun	Haydoc	(GD)	H	14f	78	80	

1998 Turf 3-9: (12f 2-3, 13f, 14f 1-4, 15f) (g-s, gd 2, g-f 1-4, frm 2-2)

Workmanlike, useful colt, effective 12 to 14f, acts on gd to frm, best on g-f, has worn blinkers, prefers right handed tracks, does well at Goodwood. Turf high 90 - 3rd of 11 giving 20lb to Mark of Prophet (16 Oct Newmarket 14f g-f RF 4841) - also 1st of 10 giving 18lb to Billaddie (28 Aug Goodwood RF 3921). Consistent. Quite a useful young handicapper, he won three times during the season and looks equally at home at trips between twelve and fourteen furlongs, but never made it look easy. He certainly knows how to battle. **J L Dunlop [3-12] Windflower Overseas Holdings Inc.*

PALACEGATE GOLD (IRE) BHB 38f29a **RR 43f 29a** 4311[4]

9 b g Sarab 9.2f **(60)** - Habilite (Habitat) 9.4f **(70)**
Form - 0004

Record	**1998 -**	1st:0	2nd:0	3rd:0	Ran:4
	Pre1998 -	1st:5	2nd:3	3rd:11	Ran:62

Win Prizemoney £13,266 *Total Prizemoney* £21,777

Wins	1994	Apr	Folkes	(HVY)	5f	51	

1998 Turf 0-4: (5f, 6f, 7f 2) (gd 2, g-f, frm)

Moderate gelding, has worn blinkers. Turf high 43 (began Jly).
**J E Long [0-4] J King (from R J Hodges [3-53] Apr 1996).*

PALACEGATE JACK (IRE) BHB 51f63a **RR 53f 63a** 4450[9]

7 gr g Neshad (USA) 5.5f **(59)** -Pasadena Lady (Captain James) 5f **(59)**
Form - 10255240516502873250

Record	**1998 -**	1st:1	2nd:4	3rd:1	Ran:18
	Pre1998 -	1st:13	2nd:6	3rd:9	Ran:58

Win Prizemoney £127,214 *Total Prizemoney* £143,790

Wins	* **1998**	May	Catter	(SFT)	C	5f		56
	* 1997	*Nov*	*Lingfi*	*(STD)*	*H*	*5f*	*68*	*72*
	* 1997	*Spt*	*Southw*	*(STD)*	*C*	*5f*		*67*
	* 1997	Jly	Mussel	(G-F)	H	5f	65	67
	* 1997	Jun	Hamilt	(G-S)	S	5f		55
	* 1997	Jun	Newcas	(FRM)	S	5f		49
	1996	Nov	Redcar	(G-F)		5f		75
	* 1996	*Spt*	*Southw*	*(STD)*	*C*	*5f*		*75*
	* 1995	Jun	Catter	(GD)	C	5f		84
	* 1994	Oct	Haydoc	(SFT)		5f		76

1998 Turf 1-11: (5f 1-11) (gd 1-8, g-f, frm 2) 1998 AW 0-7: (5f 6, 6f) (Equi 3, Fibr 4)

Above-average gelding, effective 5f, acts on g-f - acts on AW, best on Equi, often wears blinkers (very effectively), and excels at Lingfield. Turf high 56. AW high 71 (1st run) - 2nd of 6 giving 4lb to Anokato (8 Jan Lingfield 5f Equi RF 0047). He is still an effective performer in modest grade either on turf or sand, though his best days are probably behind him. Give him the minimum trip and an uncontested early lead and he will give you a run for your money.
**J Berry [13-66] William Burns (from C A Dwyer [1-10] Apr 1997).*

PALACEGATE JO (IRE) BHB 29f29a **RR 14f 29a** 4862[9]

7 b m Drumalis 8.8f **(73)** - Welsh Rhyme (Welsh Term) 9.9f **(71)**
Form - 263138000

Record	**1998 -**	1st:1	2nd:1	3rd:2	Ran:9
	Pre1998 -	1st:11	2nd:10	3rd:3	Ran:66

Win Prizemoney £35,231 *Total Prizemoney* £46,977

Wins	* **1998**	*Feb*	*Wolver*	*(STD)*	*H*	*12f*	*24*	*37*
	* 1995	*Jly*	*Wolver*	*(STD)*	*H*	*12f*	*50*	*53*
	1995	*May*	*Southw*	*(STD)*	*C*	*12f*		*65*
	1995	*Feb*	*Southw*	*(STD)*	*H*	*12f*	*57*	*63+*
	1995	*Jan*	*Southw*	*(STD)*	*H*	*11f*	*57*	*57*
	1994	*May*	*Wolver*	*(STD)*	*C*	*8.5f*		*49++*
	1994	*May*	*Wolver*	*(STD)*	*C*	*9.4f*		*60+*
	1994	*Feb*	*Wolver*	*(STD)*	*C*	*6f*		*48*
	1994	*Feb*	*Southw*	*(STD)*	*H*	*6f*	*61*	*56*

1998 AW 1-9: (8f 3, 12f 1-6) (Fibr 1-9)

Very moderate mare, has broken blood-vessels, effective 12f, - acts on Fibr, has worn blinkers. AW high 37 - 1st of 6 getting 32lb from State Approval (21 Feb Wolverhampton RF 0340). Becoming disappointing. She pops up on Fibresand from time to time, and duly landed a modest handicap at Wolverhampton in February.
**D W Chapman [2-32] David Chapman (from R Hollinshead [3-19] May 1995).*

PALACEGATE TOUCH BHB 57f75a **RR 64f 75a** 4799[10]
8 gr g Petong 7.6f **(58)**-Dancing Chimes (London Bells (CAN)) 5.8f **(53)**
Form - 12301423506155441110370
Record 1998 - 1st:5 2nd:1 3rd:3 Ran:21
Pre1998 - 1st:20 2nd:9 3rd:7 Ran:83
Win Prizemoney £82,869 *Total Prizemoney* £104,151

Wins								
* **1998**	Jly	Catter	(GD)	C	6f		58	
* **1998**	Jly	Catter	(FRM)	S	6f		55	
* **1998**	Jly	Hamilt	(FRM)	S	6f		60	
* **1998**	Jun	Warwic	(GD)	C	6f		64	
* **1998**	*Jan*	*Lingfi*	*(STD)*	*C*	*6f*		*72*	
* 1997	*Nov*	*Lingfi*	*(STD)*	*H*	*7f*	*72*	*76*	
* 1997	Aug	Haydoc	(G-F)	C	6f		72	
* 1997	Jly	Hamilt	(G-S)	H	6f	77	78	
* 1997	May	Catter	(G-F)	C	5f		64	
* 1997	May	Doncas	(GD)	C	5f		75	
* 1996	Oct	Catter	(GD)	H	5f	74	78	
* 1996	Spt	Sandow	(G-F)	C	5f		75	
* 1996	Aug	Catter	(G-F)	C	5f		65	
* 1996	Jly	Warwic	(FRM)		5f		72	
* 1996	*Jly*	*Lingfi*	*(STD)*	*C*	*5f*		*66*	
* 1996	Apr	Carlis	(G-S)	C	6.9f		65	
* 1995	Apr	Ripon	(G-S)	H	6f	86	90	<
* 1994	Apr	Ripon	(GD)	H	6f	88	84	

1998 Turf 4-14: (5f 5, 6f 4-9) (sft 3, gd 1-4, g-f 1-3, frm 2-4) 1998 AW 1-7: (6f 1-4, 7f 3) (Equi 1-5, Fibr 2)
Above-average gelding, effective 5 to 7f, best at 6f, acts on gd to frm - acts on AW, best on g-f, mostly wears blinkers (effectively), likes left handed tracks, likes tight tracks, excels at Southwell, likes Catterick and Lingfield and Hamilton. Turf high 64. AW high 76 - 3rd of 10 giving 10lb to Depreciate (9 Mar Southwell 6f Fibr RF 0413) - also 1st of 4 giving 10lb to Ultra Beet (29 Jan Lingfield RF 0178). He is a prolific winner on both turf and Equitrack and is well capable of adding to his tally in the right grade.
**J Berry [25-104] A B Parr.*

PALACE GREEN (IRE) BHB 65f65a **RR 67f 65a** 4863[2]
2 ch f Rudimentary (USA) 8.2f **(66)** - Show Home (Music Boy) 6.8f **(57)**
Form - 2861143732423652
Record 1998 - 1st:2 2nd:4 3rd:3 Ran:16
Win Prizemoney £3,712 *Total Prizemoney* £8,729
Wins 1998 *May Southw (STD) S 6f 60* <
1998 *May Southw (STD) S 5f 60* <
1998 Turf 0-10: (5f 7, 6f 3) (hvy, g-s 2, gd 2, g-f 3, frm 2) 1998 AW 2-6: (5f 1-2, 6f 1-4) (Fibr 2-6)
Above-average filly, effective 5 to 6f, best at 5f, acts on g-f to frm - acts on Fibr, excels at Southwell. Turf high 67 - 3rd of 9 giving 9lb to Hadeqa (9 Aug Redcar 6f frm RF 3486). AW high 70 - 2nd of 7 getting 6lb from Jackie's Baby (11 Jly Southwell 5f Fibr RF 2723). Something of a character, she is often taken to post early.
**D W Chapman [0-11] J M Chapman (from M R Channon [2-5] May 1998).*

PALAEMON BHB 50f **RR 54f** 2895[4]
4 b g Slip Anchor 12.7f **(75)** - Palace Street (USA) (Secreto (USA)) 8.7f **(72)**
Form - 434
Record 1998 - 1st:0 2nd:0 3rd:1 Ran:3
Pre1998 - 1st:0 2nd:1 3rd:4 Ran:13
Win Prizemoney £0 *Total Prizemoney* £3,971
1998 Turf 0-3: (14f, 17f, 18f) (g-s, gd 2)
Workmanlike, fair gelding, effective 11 to 18f, best at 16f, acts on g-s to frm, has worn blinkers, likes tight tracks. Turf high 54. Consistent. He tries hard, but is very one-paced and keeps finding one or two too good. **G B Balding [0-20] Miss B Swire.*

PALAIS (IRE) BHB 72f **RR 74f** 2447[4]
3 b c Darshaan 11.9f **(81)** - Dance Festival (Nureyev (USA)) 8.7f **(78)**
Form - 45664
Record 1998 - 1st:0 2nd:0 3rd:0 Ran:5
Win Prizemoney £0 *Total Prizemoney* £495
1998 Turf 0-5: (8f 2, 10f, 11f, 12f) (gd 2, frm 3)
Tall, above-average colt, has worn blinkers. Turf high 74.
**Sir Michael Stoute [0-5] Sheikh Mohammed.*

PALAMON (USA) BHB 68f **RR 72f** 2553[10]
5 ch h Sanglamore (USA) 12.9f **(67)** - Gantlette (Run The Gantlet (USA)) 12.1f **(59)**
Form - 0
Record 1998 - 1st:0 2nd:0 3rd:0 Ran:1
Pre1998 - 1st:1 2nd:2 3rd:1 Ran:11
Win Prizemoney £2,880 *Total Prizemoney* £5,949
Wins 1996 Jly Leices (G-F) 10f 78 <
1998 Turf 0-1: (11f) (gd)
Above-average colt, effective 12f, acted on g-s to frm, had worn blinkers, preferred tight tracks. Inconsistent. (DEAD)
**P Eccles [3-10] Orchard Press (from J White [0-9] May 1997).*

PALAWAN RR 54f 5139[10]
2 br c Polar Falcon (USA) 9f **(74)** - Krameria (Kris) 9.5f **(73)**
Form - 00
Record 1998 - 1st:0 2nd:0 3rd:0 Ran:2
1998 Turf 0-2: (6f 2) (sft, gd)
Currently fair colt. Turf high 54 (began Oct).
**I A Balding [0-2] Robert Hitchins.*

PALDOUNA (IRE) RR 97f 4470a[3]
3 gr f Kaldoun (FR) 9.9f **(84)** - Palavera (Bikala) 10.1f **(49)**
Form - 3
1998 Turf 0-1: (8f) (sft)
Currently very useful filly. (1st run) - 3rd of 11 to Astorg (4 Aug Deauville 8f sft RF 4470a). **A Fabre in FR [0-1] J-L Lagardere.*

PALERIA (USA) BHB 75f **RR 71f** 3461[5]
2 ch f Zilzal (USA) 8.5f **(79)** - Placer Queen (Habitat) 9.4f **(70)**
Form - 015
Record 1998 - 1st:1 2nd:0 3rd:0 Ran:3
Win Prizemoney £3,647 *Total Prizemoney* £3,647
Wins * 1998 Jly Thirsk (FRM) 6f 71 <
1998 Turf 1-3: (6f 1-3) (gd, frm 1-2)
Currently above-average filly. Turf high 71 (began Jly) - 1st of 7 from On Till Morning (24 Jly Thirsk RF 3089).
**P W Harris [1-3] Resplendent Racing Ltd.*

PALETTE (IRE) RR 90f 4296a[5]
6 b m Scenic 10.6f **(66)** - Spun Gold (Thatch (USA)) 9.8f **(62)**
Form - 7825
1998 Turf 0-4: (14f, 16f 2, 17f) (gd 3, hrd)
Useful mare. Turf high 90 - 2nd of 5 getting 5lb from Moscow Express (27 Aug Tralee 17f gd RF 4027a).
**W P Mullins in IRE [5-30] Mayden Syndicate.*

PALIO SKY BHB 105f **RR 113f** 4632[7]
4 b c Niniski (USA) 13.2f **(67)**-Live Ammo (Home Guard (USA))9.3f **(66)**
Form - 0251677
Record 1998 - 1st:1 2nd:1 3rd:0 Ran:7
Pre1998 - 1st:4 2nd:2 3rd:1 Ran:9
Win Prizemoney £46,055 *Total Prizemoney* £96,319

Wins							
* **1998**	Jly	Chanti	(GD)	L	15f	113	<
* 1997	Spt	Chanti	(SFT)	L	15f	113+	
* 1997	Apr	Epsom	(GD)		12f	96	
* 1997	Mar	Kempto	(GD)		10f	91	
* 1996	Spt	Haydoc	(GD)		8.1f	88	

1998 Turf 1-7: (12f 2, 13f, 15f 1-2, 16f 2) (sft 2, gd 1-2, g-f 3)
Workmanlike, Group-class colt, effective 13 to 15f, best at 15f, acts on sft to g-f, excels at Chantilly. Turf high 113 - 2nd of 6 getting 5lb from Stretarez (7 May Chester 13f g-f RF 1071) - also 1st of 5 giving 3lb to Asolo (6 Jly Chantilly RF 2859a). He finished runner-up in the Ormonde Stakes, and though that may have been another event that was less competitive than usual, it was a fair performance. He lost his way after winning a Listed event at Chantilly, but was ridden from the front there and may need things all his own way. **J L Dunlop [5-16] J E Nash.*

PALISANDER (IRE) BHB 43f56a **RR 50f 56a** 1449[13]
4 ch g Conquering Hero (USA) 10.6f **(50)** - Classic Choice (Patch) 11.5f **(51)**
Form - 1888315080
Record 1998 - 1st:1 2nd:0 3rd:1 Ran:8
Pre1998 - 1st:1 2nd:0 3rd:0 Ran:11
Win Prizemoney £5,417 *Total Prizemoney* £5,884
Wins 1998 *Feb Lingfi (SLW) H 13f 55 60* <
1997 *Nov Lingfi (STD) H 10f 55 60* <
1998 Turf 0-2: (10f 2) (gd, g-f) 1998 AW 1-6: (10f 3, 12f, 13f 1-1, 16f) (Equi 1-6)

Scopey, average gelding, effective 10 to 13f, best at 10f, - acts on Equi, has worn blinkers (extremely effectively), favours left handed tracks, likes tight tracks. Turf high 31. AW high 60 - 1st of 13 giving 12lb to Aquavita (12 Feb Lingfield RF 0270).

**Mrs A E Johnson [0-1] A Foustok (from P Howling [0-2] Apr 1998).*

PALLIUM (IRE) BHB 38f59a RR 44f 59a 4130^{6}

10 b g Try My Best (USA) 7.8f **(68)** - Jungle Gardenia (Nonoalco (USA)) 8.5f **(66)**

Form - 000520347674076

Record	**1998** -	1st:0	2nd:1	3rd:1	Ran:15
	Pre1998 -	1st:7	2nd:13	3rd:12	Ran:111

Win Prizemoney £21,855 *Total Prizemoney* £46,469

Wins	Year	Month	Course	Going	Type	Dist		
	* 1997	Jly	Hamilt	(G-F)	H	5f	45	47
	1995	Jly	Ripon	(G-F)	SH	5f	55	56
	1995	Jly	Mussel	(G-F)	H	5f	52	53

1998 Turf 0-15: (5f 13, 6f 2) (sft, g-s, gd 8, g-f 3, frm 2)

Moderate gelding, effective 5 to 6f, best at 5f, acts on gd to frm, best on gd, has worn blinkers (very effectively), and likes Hamilton. Turf high 51 - 2nd of 11 giving 8lb to Kolby (18 May Musselburgh 5f gd RF 1299).

**D A Nolan [1-33] Mrs J McFadyen-Murray (from Mrs A M Naughton [2-31] Spt 1996).*

PALMETTO BAY (IRE) BHB 63f RR 60?f 4883^{13}

3 b c Royal Academy (USA) 7.8f **(77)** - Surmise (USA) (Alleged (USA)) 10f **(76)**

Form - 0

Record	**1998** -	1st:0	2nd:0	3rd:0	Ran:1
	Pre1998 -	1st:0	2nd:0	3rd:2	Ran:4

Win Prizemoney £0 *Total Prizemoney* £1,249

1998 Turf 0-1: (10f) (g-s)

Scopey, average colt. Modest form in a fair maiden and a conditions event.

**J R Poulton [0-1] F Willson (from Sir Michael Stoute [0-4] Oct 1997).*

PALO BLANCO BHB 58f59a RR 66f 59a 4260^{6}

7 b m Precocious 7.2f **(54)** - Linpac Mapleleaf (Dominion) 8.5f **(63)**

Form - 3662744463555286

Record	**1998** -	1st:0	2nd:2	3rd:1	Ran:15
	Pre1998 -	1st:4	2nd:6	3rd:6	Ran:37

Win Prizemoney £13,494 *Total Prizemoney* £29,998

Wins	Year	Month	Course	Going	Type	Dist		
	1997	Spt	Sandow	(G-F)	C	5f		58
	1996	May	Ayr	(GD)	H	6f	71	73 <
	1994	Aug	Thirsk	(GD)	H	5f	70	67
	1994	May	Doncas	(G-F)		5f		61+

1998 Turf 0-9: (5f 3, 6f 3, 7f 3) (gd 2, g-f 2, frm 5) 1998 AW 0-6: (5f 2, 6f 3, 7f) (Equi 4, Fibr 2)

Average mare, effective 5 to 7f, best at 5f, acts on gd to g-f - acts on Equi, best on gd, likes tight tracks. Turf high 66 (began Jly). AW high 69 - 2nd of 9 getting 4lb from Mystical (3 Mar Lingfield 5f Equi RF 0391).

**M J Ryan [0-9] A S Reid (from G L Moore [1-19] Apr 1998).*

PAL OF MINE BHB 80f RR 84f 4095^{1}

2 b c Zafonic (USA) 9f **(83)**-Dana Springs(IRE) **(93df)**(Aragon) 8.1f **(60)**

Form - 721

Record	**1998** -	1st:1	2nd:1	3rd:0	Ran:3

Win Prizemoney £3,420 *Total Prizemoney* £5,108

Wins	Year	Month	Course	Going	Type	Dist		
	* **1998**	Spt	Epsom	(SFT)		6f		84 <

1998 Turf 1-3: (5f, 6f 1-2) (gd 1-1, frm 2)

Currently decent colt. Turf high 84 (began Jly) - 1st of 8 giving 5lb to Lady Melbourne (5 Spt Epsom RF 4095). He seems to inheerited some of his dam's toughness and will appreciate a longer trip.

**R Hannon [1-3] G Howard-Spink.*

PALVIC LADY BHB 59f RR 54f 4509^{8}

2 b f Cotation (FR) - Palvic Grey (Kampala) 8.5f **(56)**

Form - 008

Record	**1998** -	1st:0	2nd:0	3rd:0	Ran:3

1998 Turf 0-3: (6f, 7f 2) (gd, g-f 2)

Currently fair filly. Turf high 54 (began Jly).

**C Smith [0-3] Alan Pickard.*

PANAMA HOUSE BHB 71f RR 73f 4957^{1}

3 ch g Rudimentary (USA)8.2f **(66)**-Lustrous(Golden Act(USA))8.8f **(67)**

Form - 67003071

Record	**1998** -	1st:1	2nd:0	3rd:1	Ran:8
	Pre1998 -	1st:2	2nd:4	3rd:0	Ran:8

Win Prizemoney £11,151 *Total Prizemoney* £15,772

Wins	Year	Month	Course	Going	Type	Dist		
	* **1998**	Oct	Doncas	(SFT)	H	10.3f	69	73
	* 1997	Oct	Doncas	(GD)	H	8f	73	81 <
	* 1997	Aug	Thirsk	(G-F)		7f		70+

1998 Turf 1-8: (7f, 8f 5, 9f, 10f 1-1) (g-s, gd 3, g-f 3, frm 1-1)

Scopey, above-average gelding, effective 6 to 10f, best at 6f, acts on g-f to frm, best on frm, likes left handed tracks. Turf high 73 - 3rd of 16 giving 11lb to Margaret's Dancer (22 Spt Beverley 8f g-f RF 4407) - also 1st of 7 getting 5lb from First Master (23 Oct Doncaster RF 4957). Inconsistent. **T D Easterby [3-16] P England.*

PANDJOJOE (IRE) BHB 56f RR 65f 4479^{5}

2 b c Archway (IRE) 8.5f **(60)** - Vital Princess (Prince Sabo) 7.2f **(62)**

Form - 85605

Record	**1998** -	1st:0	2nd:0	3rd:0	Ran:5

1998 Turf 0-5: (5f 3, 6f 2) (sft, gd, g-f 2, frm)

Average colt. Turf high 65. **R A Fahey [0-5] J Dixon.*

PAN GALACTIC (USA) RR 111f $4712a^{2}$

3 b f Lear Fan (USA) 10.4f **(80)** - Scierpan (USA)(Sharpen Up) 8.3f **(67)**

Form - 222

1998 Turf 0-3: (8f 3) (sft 3)

Currently Group-class filly. Turf high 111 (began Aug) - 2nd of 11 getting 3lb from Soeur Ti (22 Aug Deauville 8f sft RF 3914a). She was narrowly beaten in three Listed races and deserves a change of luck. **M Zilber in FR [0-3] K Abdulla.*

PANOORAS LORD (IRE) BHB 20f28a RR 15?f 28a 3944^{17}

4 b g Topanoora 8.3f **(67)** - Ladyship (Windjammer (USA)) 7f **(59)**

Form - 70

Record	**1998** -	1st:0	2nd:0	3rd:0	Ran:2
	Pre1998 -	1st:0	2nd:0	3rd:0	Ran:2

1998 Turf 0-1: (10f) (frm) 1998 AW 0-1: (12f) (Fibr)

Poor gelding. **J S Wainwright [0-8] G R Brett.*

PANSY BHB 69f RR 74f 3377^{8}

2 br f Lugana Beach 7f **(63)** - Smah (Mtoto)

Form - 548

Record	**1998** -	1st:0	2nd:0	3rd:0	Ran:3

Win Prizemoney £0 *Total Prizemoney* £201

1998 Turf 0-3: (5f, 6f 2) (frm 3)

Currently above-average filly. Turf high 74 (began Jly).

**J M P Eustace [0-3] Racing Post Syndicate.*

PANTAR (IRE) BHB 100f RR 100f 4631^{3}

3 b c Shirley Heights 12.1f **(76)** - Spring Daffodil (Pharly (FR)) 9.8f **(68)**

Form - 8342130503

Record	**1998** -	1st:1	2nd:1	3rd:3	Ran:10
	Pre1998 -	1st:0	2nd:0	3rd:0	Ran:2

Win Prizemoney £14,980 *Total Prizemoney* £37,884

Wins	Year	Month	Course	Going	Type	Dist		
	* **1998**	Jun	Goodwo	(GD)	H	8f	90	96 <

1998 Turf 1-10: (8f 1-8, 9f, 10f) (gd 1-7, g-f 2, frm)

Very useful colt, effective 8 to 9f, best at 8f, acts on gd to g-f, best on gd. Turf high 100 - 3rd of 35 giving 7lb to Lear Spear (3 Oct Newmarket 9f g-f RF 4631) - also 1st of 20 giving 1lb to Sweet Wilhelmina (28 Jun Goodwood RF 2365). A good sort, he ran up a string of placed efforts before winning a valuable handicap at Goodwood in June. Excuse notes were written for some below par performances after that success, and he proved them to be valid when finishing third in the Cambridgeshire on his final outing. He is never going to be shown much respite from the handicapper, but is open to some improvement and could develop into a leading contender for the Royal Hunt Cup.

**I A Balding [1-12] Robert Hitchins.*

PANTHER (IRE) BHB 36f37a RR 34f 37a 3908^{8}

8 ch g Primo Dominie 7.2f **(67)** - High Profile (High Top) 10.2f **(67)**

Form - 067780708

Record	**1998** -	1st:0	2nd:0	3rd:0	Ran:8
	Pre1998 -	1st:7	2nd:8	3rd:14	Ran:86

Win Prizemoney £24,288 *Total Prizemoney* £38,151

Wins	Year	Month	Course	Going	Type	Dist		
	1996	Aug	Cheste	(G-S)	H	5.1f	68	69 <
	1996	Jun	Warwic	(FRM)	C	6f		57
	1996	May	Redcar	(G-F)	C	6f		63
	1996	Apr	Catter	(GD)		6f		57

1995 Apr Hamilt (SFT) H 6f 53 53
1995 Jan Wolver (STD) 6f 50
1994 Apr Pontef (GD) S 6f 47
1998 Turf 0-7:(5f 3, 7f 3, 8f)(g-s, gd 3, g-f 2, frm)1998AW 0-1: (7f) (Fibr)
Very moderate gelding, effective 6f, acts on g-f, has worn blinkers. Turf high 44. Consistent.
**J L Eyre[0-8]TrebleChancePartnership(from PD Evans[1-20]Nov1997).*

PANZEER BHB 78f **RR 73f** 4767[10]

2 ch c Arazi (USA) 9.2f **(74)** - Pushy (Sharpen Up) 8.3f **(67)**
Form - 334010
Record 1998 - 1st:1 2nd:0 3rd:2 Ran:6
Win Prizemoney £3,442 *Total Prizemoney* £4,752
Wins * 1998 Spt Yarmou (G-S) H 8f 70 73 <
1998 Turf 1-6: (6f 3, 7f, 8f 1-2) (sft, gd 2, g-f, frm 1-2)
Above-average colt, effective 6 to 8f, acts on gd to frm. Turf high 73 - 1st of 20 from Open Arms (17 Spt Yarmouth RF 4337).
**L M Cumani [1-6] Umm Qarn Racing.*

PAPER FLIGHT BHB 57f **RR 65f** 3849[15]

2 gr f Petong 7.6f **(58)** - Tissue Paper (Touch Paper) 6.8f **(57)**
Form - 6400
Record 1998 - 1st:0 2nd:0 3rd:0 Ran:4
Win Prizemoney £0 *Total Prizemoney* £198
1998 Turf 0-4: (5f, 6f 2, 7f) (gd 2, g-f, frm)
Average filly, has worn blinkers. Turf high 65.
**P D Evans [0-4] Mrs E A Dawson.*

PAPER TIGER (USA) RR 53f 2305[6]

3 b g Quest for Fame 12.8f **(75)** - Absara's Dancer (USA) (Bombay Duck (USA)) 12.1f **(72)**
Form - 6
Record 1998 - 1st:0 2nd:0 3rd:0 Ran:1
1998 Turf 0-1: (10f) (gd)
Leggy, currently fair gelding. **R Charlton [0-1] Lord De La Warr.*

PAPILLON SAUVAGE RR 44f 4935[9]

3 b f Theatrical Charmer 10.9f **(63)**-Gotcher (Jalmood (USA)) 10.1f **(52)**
Form - 0
Record 1998 - 1st:0 2nd:0 3rd:0 Ran:1
1998 Turf 0-1: (8f) (gd)
Lengthy, currently moderate filly. **W R Muir [0-1] Paul Bourdon.*

PAPITA (IRE) BHB 58f50a **RR 60df 50a** 287[7]

4 b f Law Society (USA) 11.6f **(71)** - Fantasise (FR) (General Assembly (USA)) 10f **(68)**
Form - 07
Record 1998 - 1st:0 2nd:0 3rd:0 Ran:1
Pre1998 - 1st:1 2nd:0 3rd:1 Ran:15
Win Prizemoney £7,132 *Total Prizemoney* £7,816
Wins 1996 Jly Goodwo (G-F) 6f 88 <
1998 AW 0-1: (8f) (Equi)
Workmanlike, average filly, has worn blinkers. Becoming disappointing.
**N M Lampard [0-4] Roses Wood Racing (from S Dow [1-14] Jly 1997).*

PAPUA RR 89f 1780[12]

4 ch g Green Dancer (USA) 11.9f **(77)** - Fairy Tern (Mill Reef (USA)) 10.5f **(78)**
Form - 20
Record 1998 - 1st:0 2nd:1 3rd:0 Ran:2
Pre1998 - 1st:3 2nd:2 3rd:2 Ran:15
Win Prizemoney £32,409 *Total Prizemoney* £51,849
Wins * 1996 Oct Newmar (GD) 7f 93
* 1996 Aug Doncas (G-F) 7f 95 <
* 1996 Jly Lingfi (G-F) 7f 84
1998 Turf 0-2: (12f 2) (g-f 2)
Scopey, useful gelding, effective 10 to 12f, acts on gd to g-f, has worn blinkers, prefers tight tracks. Turf high 89. Inconsistent. Fair effort on his return to the Flat, having been hurdling, but well beaten afterwards. **I A Balding [4-20] Robert Hitchins.*

PARADE GROUND (USA) RR 122f 4953a[3]

3 b c Kingmambo (USA) 10.9f **(85)** - Battle Creek Girl (USA) (His Majesty (USA)) 10.9f **(82)**
Form - 3
1998 Turf 0-1: (12f) (frm)
Currently very high-class colt. (1st run) - 3rd of 8 to Royal Anthem (18 Oct Woodbine 12f frm RF 4953a). This American-trained colt ran a good third to Royal Anthem and Chief Bearhart in the Canadian International. That form makes him an interesting prospect for 1999. **N Drysdale in USA [0-1] W S Farish & S Hilbert.*

PARADISE LANE RR 52f 1440[4]

2 ch g Alnasr Alwasheek 9.4f **(62)** - La Belle Vie (Indian King (USA)) 7.4f **(64)**
Form - 4
Record 1998 - 1st:0 2nd:0 3rd:0 Ran:1
1998 Turf 0-1: (5f) (frm)
Currently fair gelding. **B R Millman [0-1] Robin Lawson.*

PARADISE NAVY BHB 67f52a **RR 71f 52a** 4861[4]

9 b g Slip Anchor 12.7f **(75)** - Ivory Waltz (USA) (Sir Ivor) 10.2f **(70)**
Form - 564331327418000274
Record 1998 - 1st:2 2nd:2 3rd:3 Ran:17
Pre1998 - 1st:7 2nd:6 3rd:10 Ran:62
Win Prizemoney £30,083 *Total Prizemoney* £53,524
Wins * 1998 Aug Salisb (G-F) H 14.1f 67 71
*** 1998** May Nottin (FRM) H 16f 63 65
* 1997 Oct Yarmou (FRM) C 14.1f 56
* 1997 Aug Yarmou (G-F) H 14.1f 70 74 <
* 1997 Jly Doncas (GD) H 16.5f 64 66
* 1997 Apr Folkes (G-F) H 15.4f 65 71
* *1996 Aug Lingfi (STD) H 16f 65 66*
* 1996 Jly Bath (FRM) H 17.2f 64 69+
1994 Mar Doncas (GD) H 18f 60 62+
1998 Turf 2-16: (12f, 14f 1-5, 15f 3, 16f 1-4, 17f 3) (sft 2, g-s 2, gd 1-3, g-f 5, frm 1-4) 1998 AW 0-1: (12f) (Fibr)
Above-average gelding, effective 14 to 17f, acts on sft to frm - acts on Fibr, best on g-f, often wears blinkers (very effectively), likes left handed tracks, likes tight tracks, excels at Yarmouth and Bath and does well at Warwick. Turf high 71 - 2nd of 8 getting 1lb from Bowcliffe Court (17 Jly Newbury 16f g-f RF 2875) - also 1st of 13 giving 7lb to Last Laugh (20 Aug Salisbury RF 3762). Kept on the go, he pays his way in minor company. He is a very difficult ride who needs to be left to do it his way, but when he is likely to show his best is very difficult to predict.
**C R Egerton [8-75] Elite Racing Club (from M C Pipe [2-7] Apr 1994).*

PARADISE SOUL (USA) BHB 78f **RR 80f** 4841[7]

3 b f Dynaformer (USA) 12f **(82)** - River Valley (FR) (Riverman (USA)) 9.1f **(76)**
Form - 417517
Record 1998 - 1st:2 2nd:0 3rd:0 Ran:6
Pre1998 - 1st:0 2nd:0 3rd:2 Ran:3
Win Prizemoney £10,592 *Total Prizemoney* £12,042
Wins * 1998 Oct Nottin (SFT) H 16f 75 80 <
*** 1998** Aug Yarmou (G-F) H 14.1f 75 78
1998 Turf 2-6: (11f, 14f 1-4, 16f 1-1) (g-s 1-1, g-f, frm 1-4)
Neat, decent filly, effective 9 to 16f, acts on g-s to frm, prefers left handed tracks, prefers tight tracks, excels at Redcar and Yarmouth. Turf high 80 - 1st of 9 giving 13lb to Golden Hawk (6 Oct Nottingham RF 4667) - also 1st of 5 giving 15lb to Operatic (5 Aug Yarmouth RF 3393). Consistent. Looks an out-and-out stayer in the making.
**C E Brittain [2-6] Mohammed Jaber (from D R Loder [0-3] Oct 1997).*

PARAISO BOY (IRE) BHB 49f **RR 47f** 4009[14]

2 ch g Forest Wind (USA) - Tinnycross (Sallust) 8.4f **(63)**
Form - 500
Record 1998 - 1st:0 2nd:0 3rd:0 Ran:3
1998 Turf 0-3: (5f 2, 6f) (gd 2, frm)
Currently moderate gelding. Turf high 47.
**B S Rothwell [0-3] Mrs Greta Sparks.*

PARDAN BHB 35f31a **RR 47f 31a** 4588[8]

4 b g Pharly (FR) 11.5f **(64)** - Silent Pool (Relkino) 8.9f **(65)**
Form - 5834345208
Record 1998 - 1st:0 2nd:1 3rd:2 Ran:10
Pre1998 - 1st:0 2nd:0 3rd:1 Ran:9
Win Prizemoney £0 *Total Prizemoney* £1,650
1998 Turf 0-7: (14f 3, 16f 3, 17f) (gd 5, g-f, frm) 1998 AW 0-3: (6f, 7f, 13f) (Equi, Fibr 2)
Workmanlike, moderate gelding, has worn blinkers. Turf high 47. AW high 35. **B Palling [0-22] A F Syndicate.*

PARISIAN BLUE (IRE) RR 38f 1580[7]
2 gr c Paris House 5.9f **(64)** - Thatched Roof (IRE) **(49a)** (Thatching) 8f **(66)**
Form - 07
Record 1998 - 1st:0 2nd:0 3rd:0 Ran:2
1998 Turf 0-1: (5f) (g-f) 1998 AW 0-1: (6f) (Fibr)
Currently very moderate colt. **N P Littmoden [0-2] T Clarke.*

PARISIAN LADY (IRE) BHB 80f **RR 92f** 4496[14]
3 b f Paris House 5.9f **(64)** - Mia Gigi (Hard Fought) 8.8f **(62)**
Form - 43084000
Record 1998 - 1st:0 2nd:0 3rd:1 Ran:8
Pre1998 - 1st:2 2nd:1 3rd:0 Ran:5
Win Prizemoney £5,449 *Total Prizemoney* £14,583
Wins * 1997 Jly Salisb (G-F) 6f 93+ <
* 1997 Jun Salisb (G-F) 6f 80
1998 Turf 0-8: (6f 3, 7f 4, 8f) (sft, gd 3, g-f 3, hrd)
Leggy, useful filly, effective 6 to 7f, acts on g-f to frm. Turf high 92 - 3rd of 9 getting 5lb from Volontiers (6 Jun Epsom 7f g-f RF 1779). Becoming disappointing. She ran her best race of the season when third in an Epsom Listed event in June, but faced stiff tasks throughout the campaign and was not up to it.
**A G Newcombe [2-13] Advanced Marketing Services Ltd.*

PARISIENNE HILL BHB 40f **RR 55f** 4934[12]
2 b f Lapierre - Snarry Hill (Vitiges (FR)) 8.2f **(59)**
Form - 700
Record 1998 - 1st:0 2nd:0 3rd:0 Ran:3
1998 Turf 0-3: (6f, 7f, 8f) (gd, g-f, frm)
Currently fair filly. Turf high 55 (began Spt).
**R A Fahey [0-3] Roy Robinson.*

PARISIEN STAR (IRE) BHB 94f **RR 98f** 5065[4]
2 ch g Paris House 5.9f **(64)** - Auction Maid (IRE) (Auction Ring (USA)) 8.6f **(65)**
Form - 00031124
Record 1998 - 1st:2 2nd:1 3rd:1 Ran:8
Win Prizemoney £9,155 *Total Prizemoney* £12,746
Wins * **1998** Spt Newbur (gd) H 7.3f 80 82 <
* **1998** Spt Epsom (GD) H 6f 74 76
1998 Turf 2-8: (5f 2, 6f 1-3, 7f 1-2, 8f) (g-s, gd 1-1, g-f 3, frm 1-3)
Very useful gelding, effective 7f, acts on g-s. Turf high 98 - 2nd of 15 giving 7lb to Nasheed (9 Oct Ascot 7f g-s RF 4732). Inconsistent. Following a gelding operation, he showed improved form to win a brace of nurseries in September. Stayed the mile well on his final start. **G Lewis [2-8] E & B Productions (Theatre) Ltd.*

PARIS SPORT (FR) RR 100f 4233[3]
3 gr c Highest Honor (FR) 10.9f **(72)** - Plessaya (USA) (Nureyev (USA)) 8.7f **(78)**
Form - 43
Record 1998 - 1st:0 2nd:0 3rd:1 Ran:2
Win Prizemoney £0 *Total Prizemoney* £1,544
1998 Turf 0-2: (7f, 8f) (gd, frm)
Unfurnished, currently very useful colt. Turf high 100 (began Aug) - 3rd of 7 to Hujoom (11 Spt Goodwood 7f gd RF 4233). An ex-German colt, he ran well at Goodwood in September and will have greater scope when he is qualified for handicaps.
**E A L Dunlop [0-2] Jaber Abdullah.*

PARK ROYAL BHB 39f **RR 33f** 4939[7]
3 b g Secret Appeal - Mohibbah (USA) (Conquistador Cielo (USA)) 8.8f **(69)**
Form - 570707
Record 1998 - 1st:0 2nd:0 3rd:0 Ran:6
1998 Turf 0-5: (7f 2, 8f, 10f 2) (gd 4, g-f) 1998 AW 0-1: (8f) (Equi)
Leggy, very moderate gelding. Turf high 59.
**P Butler [0-6] Alan Wood.*

PARLEZ MOI D'AMOUR (IRE) BHB 43f **RR 43f** 3907[3]
3 gr f Precocious 7.2f **(54)** - Normanby Lass (Bustino) 10.4f **(64)**
Form - 383
Record 1998 - 1st:0 2nd:0 3rd:2 Ran:3
Pre1998 - 1st:0 2nd:0 3rd:0 Ran:2
Win Prizemoney £0 *Total Prizemoney* £694
1998 Turf 0-2: (11f, 12f) (gd, g-f) 1998 AW 0-1: (7f) (Fibr)
Scopey, moderate filly. Turf high 43 (1st run) (began Aug) - 8th of 14 getting 12lb from Meilleur (12 Aug Hamilton 11f gd RF 3575).
**C W Thornton [0-5] Guy Reed.*

PARONOMASIA BHB 20f20a **RR 26f 20a** 4375[16]
6 b g Precocious 7.2f **(54)** - The Crying Game (Manor Farm Boy)
Form - 0850500000400
Record 1998 - 1st:0 2nd:0 3rd:0 Ran:11
Pre1998 - 1st:0 2nd:3 3rd:1 Ran:31
Win Prizemoney £0 *Total Prizemoney* £2,597
1998 Turf 0-6: (10f, 11f, 12f 2, 16f, 17f) (gd 2, frm 3, hrd) 1998 AW 0-5: (10f 2, 11f, 12f, 16f) (Equi 4, Fibr)
Little account gelding, effective 10f, - acts on Equi, has worn blinkers. Turf high 26. AW high 17.
**J L Harris [0-33] Paddy Barrett (from M Bell [0-9] Feb 1996).*

PARTICULAR FRIEND BHB 70f **RR 75f** 4662[4]
3 ch f Cadeaux Genereux 7.9f **(76)** - Pamela Peach (Habitat) 9.4f **(70)**
Form - 44
Record 1998 - 1st:0 2nd:0 3rd:0 Ran:2
Pre1998 - 1st:0 2nd:1 3rd:0 Ran:2
Win Prizemoney £0 *Total Prizemoney* £2,102
1998 Turf 0-2: (8f 2) (gd, g-f)
Above-average filly. Turf high 58 (began Spt).
**E A L Dunlop [0-4] Maktoum Al Maktoum.*

PARTING ECHO BHB 67f60a **RR 67f 60a** 4865[3]
3 ch g Aragon 7.7f **(58)** - Annabrianna (Night Shift (USA)) 7.2f **(69)**
Form - 544473
Record 1998 - 1st:0 2nd:0 3rd:1 Ran:6
Win Prizemoney £0 *Total Prizemoney* £861
1998 Turf 0-5: (7f 3, 8f 2) (gd, g-f 4) 1998 AW 0-1: (7f) (Fibr)
Neat, average gelding. Turf high 67.
**J A R Toller [0-6] Forum Trustees Ltd A/C Rannerdale.*

PARTNER'S HERO (USA) RR 115 5164a[8]
4 b c Storm Cat (USA) 7f **(86)**
Form - 8
1998 AW 0-1: (6f) (Dirt)
Currently high-class colt. **D W Lukas in USA [0-1] Horton Stables.*

PARTY ROMANCE (USA) BHB 78f **RR 86f** 4314[11]
4 gr c Black Tie Affair 10.5f **(64)** - Tia Juanita (USA) (My Gallant (USA)) 9f **(71)**
Form - 416558460
Record 1998 - 1st:1 2nd:0 3rd:0 Ran:9
Pre1998 - 1st:2 2nd:2 3rd:1 Ran:14
Win Prizemoney £12,292 *Total Prizemoney* £21,332
Wins * **1998** May Ripon (G-F) H 10f 85 90 <
* 1997 Jly Newcas (GD) H 10.1f 84 89
* 1997 May Ayr (G-F) 10f 85
1998 Turf 1-9: (8f, 10f 1-8) (gd, g-f 6, frm 1-2)
Scopey, useful colt, effective 10f, acts on gd to frm, best on frm, has worn blinkers, likes left handed tracks, likes tight tracks. Turf high 90 - 1st of 19 giving 9lb to Sky Dome (17 May Ripon RF 1287). He scored a game victory at Ripon in May, but was held in handicap company afterwards. **B Hanbury [3-23] Abdullah Ali.*

PAS DE MEMOIRES (IRE) BHB 72f85a **RR 72f 85a** 4854[13]
3 b c Don't Forget Me 9.5f **(66)** - Bally Pourri (IRE) (Law Society (USA)) 9.9f **(70)**
Form - 11663430
Record 1998 - 1st:0 2nd:0 3rd:2 Ran:6
Pre1998 - 1st:2 2nd:1 3rd:0 Ran:6
Win Prizemoney £5,686 *Total Prizemoney* £10,010
Wins 1997 *Nov Wolver (STD) H 7f 70 91+* <
1997 *Nov Southw (STD) H 7f 65 88+*
1998 Turf 0-6: (6f, 7f 2, 8f 2, 10f) (gd 4, g-f, frm)
Decent colt, effective 7f, - acts on Fibr, likes left handed tracks, prefers tight tracks. Turf high 72.
**K R Burke [0-5] Nigel Shields (from M P Bielby [0-1] Jun 1998).*

PAS DE PROBLEME (IRE) RR 69f 5148[8]
2 ch c Ela-Mana-Mou 12.7f **(72)** - Torriglia (USA) (Nijinsky (CAN)) 10.3f **(77)**
Form - 2658
Record 1998 - 1st:0 2nd:1 3rd:0 Ran:4
Win Prizemoney £0 *Total Prizemoney* £1,692

1998 Turf 0-4: (6f 3, 7f) (gd 2, frm 2)
Average colt. Turf high 69 (1st run) - 2nd of 7 getting 7lb from Champagne Rider (23 May Kempton 6f gd RF 1424).
**M Blanshard [0-4] Capt Francis Burne.*

PAS DE REPONSE (USA) RR 120f 3614a^{8}

4 b f Danzig (USA) 8.1f **(88)** - Soundings (USA) (Mr Prospector (USA)) 8.8f **(78)**
Form - 2258
1998 Turf 0-4: (5f, 6f, 7f 2) (gd 3, frm)
Very high-class filly, effective 5 to 7f, acts on gd to frm, best on gd, has worn blinkers. Turf high 120 - 2nd of 6 giving 1lb to Hidden Meadow (26 May Longchamp 7f gd RF 1728a). Twice second in France in May, finding five furlongs too short and seven too far, she ran a fine fifth in the July Cup from an unfavourable draw. She disappointed at Deauville next time and was retired to stud soon afterwards. **Mme C Head in FR [4-12] Wertheimer Brothers.*

PASHA RR 32f 3026^{8}

2 b f Ardkinglass 5f **(64)** - Infanta Maria (King of Spain) 7.8f **(52)**
Form - 624078
Record 1998 - 1st:0 2nd:1 3rd:0 Ran:6
Win Prizemoney £0 *Total Prizemoney* £672
1998 Turf 0-3: (5f 3) (gd 2, frm) 1998 AW 0-3: (5f 3) (Fibr 3)
Average filly, has worn blinkers. Turf high 31. AW high 63.
**N Tinkler [0-6] T & M Partnership.*

PASOLINI RR 108f 4721a^{2}

7 b h Cagliostro - Passeggiata (USA) (Elocutionist (USA)) 8f **(77)**
Form - 2
1998 Turf 0-1: (15f) (hvy)
Pattern-class horse. (1st run) - 2nd of 8 giving 10lb to Generosity (3 Oct San Siro 15f hvy RF 4721a). He is a grand old campaigner, but could not concede age and weight to Generosity at San Siro in October.
**W Kujath in GER [1-3] (from J Kujath in GER [0-1] Aug 1995).*

PASSAGE CREEPING (IRE) BHB 48f50a RR 42f 50a 1642^{9}

5 b m Persian Bold 10f **(69)** - Tiptoe (Dance In Time (CAN)) 8.9f **(59)**
Form - 0
Record 1998 - 1st:0 2nd:0 3rd:0 Ran:1
Pre1998 - 1st:0 2nd:6 3rd:3 Ran:19
Win Prizemoney £0 *Total Prizemoney* £7,566
1998 Turf 0-1: (12f) (g-f)
Fair filly, effective 8 to 10f, acts on g-f to frm, has worn blinkers. Becoming disappointing.
**L A Dace [0-2] Mike D'Arcy Quinn (from S Dow [0-11] Oct 1997).*

PASSIONATE PURSUIT BHB 79f RR 76f 2636^{13}

3 b f Pursuit of Love 9.5f **(69)** - Flambera (FR) (Akarad (FR)) 9f **(76)**
Form - 04510
Record 1998 - 1st:1 2nd:0 3rd:0 Ran:5
Win Prizemoney £3,720 *Total Prizemoney* £3,970
Wins * 1998 Jun Lingfi (G-F) 10f 76 <
1998 Turf 1-5: (10f 1-4, 12f) (gd, g-f 1-2, frm 2)
Scopey, above-average filly. Turf high 76 - 1st of 10 from Hever Golf Passion (23 Jun Lingfield RF 2199).
**S Dow [1-5] Mrs A M Upsdell.*

PASSION FOR LIFE BHB 80f RR 80f 2366^{24}

5 br g Charmer 9f **(59)** - Party Game (Red Alert) 7.6f **(66)**
Form - 0060
Record 1998 - 1st:0 2nd:0 3rd:0 Ran:4
Pre1998 - 1st:5 2nd:2 3rd:2 Ran:21
Win Prizemoney £58,234 *Total Prizemoney* £67,032
Wins 1996 Jun Baden (GD) G3 6f 112
1996 Apr Newmar (G-F) L 6f 115+ <
1996 Apr Kempto (GD) H 6f 86 103+
1995 Apr Warwic (G-F) 5f 74+t
1995 Apr Haydoc (GD) 5f 86+t
1998 Turf 0-4: (5f, 6f 3) (gd 3, frm)
Decent gelding, has worn blinkers. Turf high 80.
**W Jarvis [0-4] Canisbay Bloodstock Ltd (from G Lewis [5-21] Spt 1997).*

PASS THE REST (IRE) BHB 77f87a RR 79f 87a 4232^{10}

3 b c Shalford (IRE) 7.8f **(63)** - Brown Foam (Horage) 10.3f **(61)**
Form - 2710120
Record 1998 - 1st:2 2nd:2 3rd:0 Ran:7
Pre1998 - 1st:0 2nd:1 3rd:1 Ran:3
Win Prizemoney £9,556 *Total Prizemoney* £13,441
Wins * 1998 *Aug Wolver (STD) H 8.5f 79 85* <
*** 1998** Jun Ripon (SFT) H 8f 76 79
1998 Turf 1-5: (7f 2, 8f 1-2, 9f) (sft, g-s 1-1, gd 2, g-f) 1998 AW 1-2: (8f 1-2) (Fibr 1-2)
Scopey, useful colt, effective 7 to 8f, best at 8f, acts on g-s - acts on Fibr. Turf high 79 - 1st of 8 giving 13lb to Hit The Spot (18 Jun Ripon RF 2092). AW high 85 (began Aug) - 2nd of 16 giving 12lb to Goldfame (14 Aug Southwell 8f Fibr RF 3640) - also 1st of 7 giving 5lb to Hit The Spot (7 Aug Wolverhampton RF 3452). In the frame in maidens, and appreciated the step up to a mile when scoring at Ripon on his handicap debut. He looks a real soft-ground type on turf, so he had little trouble with the Wolverhampton Fibresand when taking a handicap on that surface in August.
**J Noseda [2-7] J Roundtree (from J L Eyre [0-3] Nov 1997).*

PASTERNAK BHB 103f RR 103f 4843^{6}

5 b h Soviet Star (USA) 8.6f **(74)** - Princess Pati (Top Ville) 11.7f **(68)**
Form - 22006
Record 1998 - 1st:0 2nd:2 3rd:0 Ran:5
Pre1998 - 1st:4 2nd:1 3rd:2 Ran:11
Win Prizemoney £124,028 *Total Prizemoney* £158,092
Wins * 1997 Oct Newmar (G-F) H 9f 91 100+ <
* 1997 Jly York (GD) H 10.4f 85 89++
* 1996 Oct York (GD) H 10.4f 75 85
* 1996 Spt Bath (G-S) 10.2f 79
1998 Turf 0-5: (8f, 9f 3, 10f) (gd, g-f 3, frm)
Very useful colt, effective 9 to 10f, best at 9f, acts on g-f to frm, best on frm. Turf high 103 (1st run) (began Jly) - 2nd of 20 giving 21lb to Porto Foricos (11 Jly York 10f frm RF 2738). He may well have won the Magnet Cup on his reappearance had Porto Foricos not stolen first run, and pulled too hard for his own good when touched off at Leopardstown a week later. Very disappointing at Glorious Goodwood, he came back to something like his best in the autumn, but is too high in the handicap at present. If anyone can find an opening for this popular gelding it is Sir Mark Prescott, but that may mean clocking up some air miles.
**Sir Mark Prescott [4-16] Graham Rock.*

PATHAZE BHB 25f35a RR 25f 35a 3765^{6}

5 b m Totem (USA) 5f **(38)** - Stilvella (Camden Town) 9.3f **(53)**
Form - 006000800006
Record 1998 - 1st:0 2nd:0 3rd:0 Ran:11
Pre1998 - 1st:1 2nd:6 3rd:6 Ran:34
Win Prizemoney £2,676 *Total Prizemoney* £11,912
Wins * 1995 Jun Ayr (FRM) 5f 58 <
1998 Turf 0-10:(5f 5,6f 3,7f 2)(g-s,gd 3, g-f,frm5)1998AW 0-1: (7f) (Fibr)
Little account filly, effective 5 to 6f, acts on gd to frm, has worn blinkers. Turf high 26. **N Bycroft [1-45] J A Swinburne.*

PATINA BHB 31f37a RR 33f 37a 4014^{6}

4 ch f Rudimentary (USA) 8.2f **(66)** -Appledorn (Doulab (USA)) 9.8f **(65)**
Form - 67307621740288886
Record 1998 - 1st:1 2nd:2 3rd:0 Ran:14
Pre1998 - 1st:0 2nd:1 3rd:5 Ran:18
Win Prizemoney £2,095 *Total Prizemoney* £6,954
Wins * 1998 *Feb Southw (STD) H 8f 35 39* <
1998 Turf 0-5: (7f 2, 8f 3) (g-s, gd 2, frm 2) 1998 AW 1-9: (6f, 7f 3, 8f 1-4, 12f) (Fibr 1-9)
Light-framed, very moderate filly, effective 7 to 8f, best at 7f, acts on gd - acts on Fibr, has worn blinkers, likes left handed tracks, and does well at Wolverhampton. Turf high 33. AW high 39.
**R Hollinshead [1-32] R Hollinshead.*

PATONY (IRE) BHB 62f58a RR 57f 58a 3097^{7}

2 ch f Pips Pride 6.7f **(70)** - Panalpina (Petorius) 7.3f **(61)**
Form - 255137
Record 1998 - 1st:1 2nd:1 3rd:1 Ran:6
Win Prizemoney £1,917 *Total Prizemoney* £2,735
Wins * 1998 Jun Yarmou (SFT) S 7f 57 <
1998 Turf 1-5: (5f 3, 6f, 7f 1-1) (gd 3, g-f 1-1, hrd) 1998 AW 0-1: (7f) (Fibr)
Fair filly, effective 7f, acts on g-f. Turf high 57 - 1st of 10 getting 5lb from La Tavernetta (11 Jun Yarmouth RF 1903).
**D J S Cosgrove [1-6] Winning Circle Racing Club Ltd.*

PATRINIA BHB 48f **RR 45f** 4880[11]
2 ch f Superlative 8.8f **(57)** - Dame du Moulin (Shiny Tenth) 9.2f **(56)**
Form - 000
Record 1998 - 1st:0 2nd:0 3rd:0 Ran:3
1998 Turf 0-3: (6f, 7f, 8f) (g-s, g-f, frm)
Currently moderate filly. Turf high 45 (began Aug).
**M J Ryan [0-3] P E Axon.*

PATRIOT BHB 100f **RR 98f** 4974[6]
2 b c Whittingham (IRE) - Gibaltarik (IRE)**(63f)** (Jareer (USA)) 5.9f **(75)**
Form - 2152336
Record 1998 - 1st:1 2nd:2 3rd:2 Ran:7
Win Prizemoney £2,950 *Total Prizemoney* £40,396
Wins * 1998 May Warwic (G-F) 5f 73 <
1998 Turf 1-7: (5f 1-3, 6f 4) (sft, g-s 2, gd 2, frm 1-2)
Very useful colt, effective 6f, acts on gd. Turf high 98 - 3rd of 22 giving 5lb to Boomerang Blade (9 Spt Doncaster 6f gd RF 4185). A fairly useful sprinting juvenile, he seemed unsuited by heavy ground on his final two starts. **B Smart [1-7] W Clifford.*

PATRITA PARK BHB 32f43a **RR 33+f 43a** 4050[1]
4 br f Flying Tyke 7.2f **(42)** - Bellinote (FR) (Noir Et Or) 10f **(38)**
Form - 36576751
Record 1998 - 1st:1 2nd:0 3rd:1 Ran:8
Pre1998 - 1st:0 2nd:0 3rd:0 Ran:10
Win Prizemoney £2,473 *Total Prizemoney* £2,830
Wins * 1998 Spt Bright (FRM) H 10f 26 33+ <
1998 Turf 1-8: (7f, 8f 2, 10f 1-4, 12f) (gd, g-f 2, frm 1-5)
Unfurnished, very moderate filly, effective 10f, acts on g-f to frm, likes tight tracks. Turf high 33 - 1st of 16 from Top Shelf (2 Spt Brighton RF 4050).
**W G M Turner [1-10] Park Racing Partnership (from W W Haigh [0-8] Aug 1997).*

PATRON SAINT **RR 79f** 4732[9]
2 b c Primo Dominie 7.2f **(67)**-Tender Loving Care(Final Straw)7.9f **(64)**
Form - 53234630
Record 1998 - 1st:0 2nd:1 3rd:3 Ran:8
Win Prizemoney £0 *Total Prizemoney* £3,770
1998 Turf 0-8: (6f 3, 7f 3, 8f 2) (g-s, gd 2, g-f 3, frm 2)
Above-average colt, effective 6 to 8f, acts on g-f to frm, best on frm, has worn blinkers. Turf high 79 - 3rd of 11 giving 11lb to Hoh No (24 Spt Goodwood 8f frm RF 4463). Consistent. Sold for 20,000 guineas in October. **R Hannon [0-8] The Royal Ascot Racing Club.*

PATSY CULSYTH BHB 50f **RR 50f** 4153[11]
3 b f Tragic Role (USA) 9.4f **(63)**-Regal Salute (Dara Monarch) 8.8f **(59)**
Form - 0064010
Record 1998 - 1st:1 2nd:0 3rd:0 Ran:7
Pre1998 - 1st:1 2nd:4 3rd:1 Ran:12
Win Prizemoney £4,963 *Total Prizemoney* £8,959
Wins * 1998 Aug Ayr (G-S) SH 7f 45 50
1997 Aug Beverl (G-S) C 5f 62 <
1998 Turf1-6:(5f 2, 6f 3,7f 1-1)(gd 1-2, g-f, frm 3)1998AW 0-1: (7f) (Fibr)
Light-framed, fair filly, effective 5f, acts on gd to g-f, best on gd, often wears blinkers (effectively). Turf high 50 (began Jly).
**N Tinkler [1-10] Don Enrico Incisa (from Mrs L Stubbs [1-2] Aug 1997).*

PATSY GRIMES BHB 76f80a **RR 80f 80a** 4397[18]
8 b m Beveled (USA) 6.9f **(64)** - lue Angel (Lord Gayle (USA)) 8.8f **(62)**
Form - 544780444500
Record 1998 - 1st:0 2nd:0 3rd:0 Ran:12
Pre1998 - 1st:10 2nd:10 3rd:9 Ran:69
Win Prizemoney £37,650 *Total Prizemoney* £63,932
Wins * 1997 Spt Haydoc (GD) H 5f 87 88
* 1996 Aug Newbur (GD) H 6f 88 91 <
* 1996 Jly Yarmou (G-F) H 7f 76 84
* 1996 May Chepst (G-S) H 6.1f 67 73
* 1996 May Salisb (G-F) H 6f 64 65
1995 Jun Windso (GD) 6f 61
1994 Spt Salisb (GD) H 5f 65 63
1998 Turf 0-12: (5f 3, 6f 4, 7f 5) (hvy, g-s, gd 4, g-f 5, frm)
Decent mare, effective 5f, acts on sft to g-f, has worn blinkers. Turf high 89. **J S Moore [5-45] J K Grimes (from L J Holt [2-14] Spt 1995).*

PATSYS FOREM BHB 52f **RR 55f** 4473[10]
2 b f Then Again 7.4f **(52)** - Sheesha (USA) (Shadeed (USA)) 8.2f **(70)**
Form - 7244430
Record 1998 - 1st:0 2nd:1 3rd:1 Ran:7
Win Prizemoney £0 *Total Prizemoney* £864
1998 Turf 0-7: (6f 4, 7f 3) (gd 2, g-f 2, frm 3)
Fair filly, effective 6 to 7f, acts on frm. Turf high 55 - 3rd of 12 to Clunie (29 Aug Windsor 6f frm RF 3970).
**M Blanshard [0-7] H C Promotions Ltd.*

PATSY STONE BHB 65f **RR 64f** 5148[11]
2 b f Jester 8.5f **(43)** - Third Dam **(47f 45a)** (Slip Anchor) 9.8f **(73)**
Form - 020304320
Record 1998 - 1st:0 2nd:2 3rd:2 Ran:9
Win Prizemoney £0 *Total Prizemoney* £2,424
1998 Turf 0-9: (5f, 6f 5, 7f 3) (g-s, gd 2, g-f 2, frm 4)
Average filly, effective 6 to 7f, best at 6f, acts on g-s to frm. Turf high 64 - 3rd of 8 giving 2lb to Beverley Monkey (26 Aug Lingfield 6f g-f RF 3891). Consistent. **M Kettle [0-9] I Fraser.*

PAT THE FIDDLER (IRE) **RR 54f** 1095[2]
2 b c Night Shift (USA) 8.1f **(73)** - Lucky Song (USA) (Seattle Song (USA)) 9f **(77)**
Form - 2
Record 1998 - 1st:0 2nd:1 3rd:0 Ran:1
Win Prizemoney £0 *Total Prizemoney* £944
1998 Turf 0-1: (5f) (gd)
Currently fair colt. **M W Easterby [0-1] Burke's 5th Family Settlement.*

PAULA'S JOY BHB 80f **RR 84f** 2234[8]
2 b f Danehill (USA) 9.1f **(79)**-Pernilla(IRE)(Tate Gallery(USA)) 7.4f **(67)**
Form - 31738
Record 1998 - 1st:1 2nd:0 3rd:2 Ran:5
Win Prizemoney £3,470 *Total Prizemoney* £5,372
Wins * 1998 May Thirsk (G-F) 5f 84 <
1998 Turf 1-5: (5f 1-4, 6f) (gd 2, g-f 1-3)
Decent filly. Turf high 84 - 1st of 8 getting 6lb from Rose's Treasure (16 May Thirsk RF 1276). **M R Channon [1-5] John Breslin.*

PAULINES STAR BHB 30f **RR 29f** 5004[17]
2 b br f Superlative 8.8f **(57)** - Champion Girl (Blazing Saddles (AUS)) 6.7f **(46)**
Form - 000
Record 1998 - 1st:0 2nd:0 3rd:0 Ran:3
1998 Turf 0-3: (6f 2, 8f) (sft, gd 2)
Currently little account filly. Turf high 29 (began Oct).
**E A Wheeler [0-3] G W Witheford.*

PAVILLON PANAMA (FR) **RR 97f** 278a[3]
4 ch c Common Grounds 8.1f **(66)** - Corolina (USA) (Nashua) 10.3f **(67)**
Form - 3
1998 Turf 0-1: (11f) (gd)
Currently very useful colt. (1st run) - 3rd of 20 giving 4lb to Fier Danseur (8 Feb Cagnes-Sur-Mer 11f gd RF 0278a).
**R Collet in FR [0-1].*

PAWSIBLE (IRE) **RR 57f** 4082[8]
2 b f Mujadil (USA) 7.7f **(70)** - Kentucky Wildcat (Be My Guest (USA)) 9.3f **(67)**
Form - 08
Record 1998 - 1st:0 2nd:0 3rd:0 Ran:2
1998 Turf 0-2: (5f, 7f) (gd, hrd)
Currently fair filly. Turf high 57 (began Aug).
**D W P Arbuthnot [0-2] The Pawsible Partnership.*

PAY HOMAGE BHB 56f **RR 59f** 4506[8]
10 ch g Primo Dominie 7.2f **(67)** - Embraceable Slew (USA) (Seattle Slew (USA)) 9.4f **(76)**
Form - 01867638308
Record 1998 - 1st:1 2nd:0 3rd:2 Ran:11
Pre1998 - 1st:10 2nd:11 3rd:10 Ran:91
Win Prizemoney £94,677 *Total Prizemoney* £127,263
Wins * 1998 May Warwic (GD) H 10.8f 64 67
* 1997 Jly Bath (FRM) 11.7f 69
* 1995 May Goodwo (G-F) H 9f 81 83
* 1994 Mar Doncas (GD) L 8f 100
1998 Turf 1-11: (10f 2, 11f 1-2, 12f 6, 14f) (sft, gd 3, g-f 1-4, frm 3)
Fair gelding, effective 11 to 13f, best at 12f, acts on g-f to frm, best on frm, has worn blinkers, likes left handed tracks, favours tight

tracks, excels at Warwick, does well at Bath. Turf high 67 - 1st of 18 giving 14lb to Atlantic Mist (4 May Warwick RF 1032). Consistent. **I A Balding [11-105] Miss A V Hill.*

PAYLANDER BHB 40f RR 27f 4047[8]

2 ch c Karinga Bay - Bichette **(43f 47a)** (Lidhame) 9.2f **(50)**
Form - 008
Record 1998 - 1st:0 2nd:0 3rd:0 Ran:3
1998 Turf 0-3: (7f 3) (gd 2, frm)
Currently little account colt. Turf high 27 (began Jly).
**G L Moore [0-3] B V and C J Pennick.*

PAY ME BACK (IRE) RR 107f 1729a[2]

8 ch h Master Willie 9.2f **(67)** - Princess Reema (USA) (Affirmed (USA)) 9.3f **(79)**
Form - 2
1998 Turf 0-1: (12f) (g-f)
Pattern-class horse. (1st run) - 2nd of 8 to War Declaration (30 May Capannelle 12f g-f RF 1729a). He is a tough old character and earned some useful place money in valuable Italian Group races. He seems to stay middle-distances in his dotage.
**G Verricelli in ITY [0-6] (from ITY [2-2] Aug 1994).*

PAY ON RED (USA) BHB 78f RR 81f 4619[13]

3 br c Red Ransom (USA) 8.6f **(83)** - Mo Jo Kate (USA) (Mr Leader (USA)) 9.8f **(66)**
Form - 37120100
Record 1998 - 1st:2 2nd:1 3rd:1 Ran:8
Pre1998 - 1st:0 2nd:0 3rd:2 Ran:5
Win Prizemoney £6,937 *Total Prizemoney* £11,718
Wins * 1998 Spt Epsom (SFT) H 8.5f 75 81 <
*** 1998** Aug Epsom (G-F) 7f 80
1998 Turf 2-8: (7f 1-2, 8f, 9f 1-3, 10f 2) (sft, gd 2-5, g-f 2)
Well made, decent colt, effective 7 to 9f, acts on gd, prefers tight tracks. Turf high 81 - 1st of 15 getting 1lb from Transylvania (5 Spt Epsom RF 4101) - also 1st of 7 from Doraid (9 Aug Epsom RF 3484). Has progressed steadily in 1998, winning twice at Epsom. Goes well with some cut in the ground. **P F I Cole [2-13] Terry Neill.*

PAY THE PIED PIPER (USA) RR 58f 5138[10]

2 b c Red Ransom (USA) 8.6f **(83)** -Fife (IRE) (Lomond (USA)) 8.8f **(65)**
Form - 00
Record 1998 - 1st:0 2nd:0 3rd:0 Ran:2
1998 Turf 0-2: (7f 2) (gd, frm)
Currently fair colt. Turf high 58 (began Oct).
**E A L Dunlop [0-2] Maktoum Al Maktoum.*

PC'S EUROCRUISER (IRE) BHB 49f47a RR 50f 47a 5080[7]

2 b g Fayruz 6.6f **(63)** - Kuwait Night (Morston (FR)) 9.4f **(55)**
Form - 88087
Record 1998 - 1st:0 2nd:0 3rd:0 Ran:5
1998 Turf 0-2: (5f 2) (g-f, frm) 1998 AW 0-3: (5f, 6f 2) (Fibr 3)
Fair gelding. Turf high 50 (began Jly). AW high 43.
**N P Littmoden [0-5] PC Racing Partners.*

PEACEFUL RR 76f 3937[8]

2 br f Primo Dominie 7.2f **(67)**-Ideal Home(Home Guard (USA))9.3f **(66)**
Form - 2128
Record 1998 - 1st:1 2nd:2 3rd:0 Ran:4
Win Prizemoney £2,723 *Total Prizemoney* £4,518
Wins * 1998 Jly Carlis (G-F) 5f 67+ <
1998 Turf 1-4: (5f 1-2, 6f 2) (gd, g-f, frm 1-2)
Above-average filly. Turf high 76 (began Jly) - also 1st of 5 getting 6lb from Gold Spice (17 Jly Carlisle RF 2865).
**T D Easterby [1-4] C H Stevens.*

PEACEFUL SARAH BHB 72f RR 73f 5147[6]

3 b f Sharpo 7.5f **(68)** - Red Gloves (Red God) 8.5f **(65)**
Form - 56023148136
Record 1998 - 1st:2 2nd:1 3rd:2 Ran:11
Pre1998 - 1st:0 2nd:0 3rd:0 Ran:3
Win Prizemoney £6,857 *Total Prizemoney* £8,999
Wins * 1998 Oct Catter (SFT) H 7f 63 73
*** 1998** Aug Epsom (G-F) 7f 74? <
1998 Turf 2-11: (7f 2-6, 8f 2, 10f 3) (g-s 1-2, gd 7, g-f 1-1, frm)
Leggy, above-average filly, effective 7f, acts on g-s to g-f, likes left handed tracks, likes tight tracks. Turf high 74 - 1st of 4 getting 5lb from Grangeville (31 Aug Epsom RF 3988) - also 1st of 13 giving 2lb to Mutabassir (16 Oct Catterick RF 4840). Inconsistent.
**R Ingram [2-6] Byna Sheils and Peter Mooney (from B Hanbury [0-5] Jly 1998).*

PEACE OF MIND RR 81f 4395[1]

2 ch c Nashwan (USA) 10.3f **(79)** - De Stael (USA) (Nijinsky (CAN)) 10.3f **(77)**
Form - 31
Record 1998 - 1st:1 2nd:0 3rd:1 Ran:2
Win Prizemoney £3,468 *Total Prizemoney* £4,340
Wins * 1998 Spt Kempto (GD) 8f 81 <
1998 Turf 1-2: (7f, 8f 1-1) (frm 1-2)
Currently decent colt. Turf high 81 (began Jly) - 1st of 17 from Lightning Arrow (21 Spt Kempton RF 4395). From an excellent middle-distance family, he should pay to follow at three.
**R Charlton [1-2] K Abdulla.*

PEACE PACT RR 4915[12]

2 b f Brief Truce (USA) 9.1f **(73)** - Royal Mazi **(25f)** (Kings Lake (USA)) 10.8f **(67)**
Form - 0
Record 1998 - 1st:0 2nd:0 3rd:0 Ran:1
1998 Turf 0-1: (6f) (g-s)
Currently very poor filly. **G P Kelly [0-1] A M McArdle.*

PEAJAY (USA) RR 63f 4823[13]

2 b c Dehere (USA) - Petroleuse (Habitat) 9.4f **(70)**
Form - 0
Record 1998 - 1st:0 2nd:0 3rd:0 Ran:1
1998 Turf 0-1: (8f) (frm)
Currently average colt.
**M A Jarvis [0-1] Burke's 5th Family Settlement.*

PEAK PATH (IRE) BHB 112f RR 112f 3697[4]

3 b c Polish Precedent (USA) 9f **(73)** - Road To The Top (Shirley Heights) 10.3f **(74)**
Form - 144
Record 1998 - 1st:1 2nd:0 3rd:0 Ran:3
Pre1998 - 1st:0 2nd:0 3rd:1 Ran:1
Win Prizemoney £3,111 *Total Prizemoney* £8,013
Wins * 1998 Apr Bath (SFT) 10.2f 92 <
1998 Turf 1-3: (10f 1-2, 12f) (g-s 1-1, g-f, frm)
Scopey, Group-class colt. Turf high 112 - 4th of 6 to Sea Wave (18 Aug York 12f g-f RF 3697). A half-brother to, amongst others, Craven Stakes winner Painter's Row, he has been very lightly raced. Fourth in the Great Voltigeur at York, keeping on well after being outpaced, he promises to stay two miles as a four-year-old and has more improvement in him.
**Sir Michael Stoute [1-4] Lord Weinstock.*

PEAK PERFORMANCE RR 50f 4779[16]

2 b c Shirley Heights 12.1f **(76)** - Sharp Castan (Sharpen Up) 8.3f **(67)**
Form - 0
Record 1998 - 1st:0 2nd:0 3rd:0 Ran:1
1998 Turf 0-1: (8f) (gd)
Currently fair colt. **I A Balding [0-1] J C Smith.*

PEARL ANNIVERSARY (IRE) BHB 37f37a RR 23f 37a 4120[6]

5 ch g Priolo (USA) 10.9f **(71)** - Tony Award (USA) (Kirtling) 10.9f **(54)**
Form - 0245306
Record 1998 - 1st:0 2nd:0 3rd:1 Ran:4
Pre1998 - 1st:2 2nd:4 3rd:1 Ran:17
Win Prizemoney £4,451 *Total Prizemoney* £7,360
Wins 1996 *May Wolver (STD) S 12f 63* <
1996 *May Wolver (STD) S 12f 51*
1998 Turf 0-1: (12f) (frm) 1998 AW 0-3: (12f 2, 15f) (Fibr 3)
Very moderate gelding, effective 15f, - acts on Fibr, has worn blinkers, likes left handed tracks. AW high 38.
**Miss S J Wilton [0-9] John Pointon and Sons (from M Johnston [2-13] Spt 1996).*

PEARL BARLEY (IRE) RR 49f 4629[11]

2 ch f Polish Precedent (USA) 9f **(73)** - Pearl Kite (USA) **(101df)** (Silver Hawk (USA)) 8.6f **(70)**
Form - 0

Record 1998 - 1st:0 2nd:0 3rd:0 Ran:1
1998 Turf 0-1: (6f) (g-f)
Currently moderate filly. **C E Brittain [0-1] Saeed Manana.*

PEARL DAWN (IRE) BHB 45f32a **RR 52f 32a** 3039[10]

8 b m Jareer (USA) 10.2f **(54)** - Spy Girl (Tanfirion) 7f **(61)**
Form - 0

Record	**1998 -**	1st:0	2nd:0	3rd:0	Ran:1
	Pre1998 -	1st:3	2nd:3	3rd:6	Ran:45

Win Prizemoney £8,037 *Total Prizemoney* £13,649

Wins	1996	Jly	Bright	(FRM) S	8f	47	
	1995	Aug	Bath	(HRD) C	5.1f	66	<
	1995	Aug	Bath	(HRD) C	5.7f	62	

1998 Turf 0-1: (7f) (gd)
Fair mare, effective 5 to 7f, best at 7f, acts on g-f to frm, best on frm. **P C Clarke [0-16] Mrs E Keep (from G L Moore [1-21] Oct 1996).*

PEARLY QUEEN BHB 42f50a **RR 31f 50a** 2337[5]

3 ch f Superlative 8.8f **(57)** - Miss Kimmy (Tower Walk) 10f **(62)**
Form - 5433332346037005

Record	**1998 -**	1st:0	2nd:1	3rd:5	Ran:13
	Pre1998 -	1st:0	2nd:0	3rd:1	Ran:4

Win Prizemoney £0 *Total Prizemoney* £2,752
1998 Turf 0-3:(7f 3)(gd 3)1998 AW0-10:(5f, 6f 3, 7f 5, 8f)(Equi 6, Fibr 4)
Neat, fair filly, effective 6 to 7f, best at 7f, - acts on AW, best on Fibr, favours left handed tracks, favours tight tracks. Turf high 31. AW high 57 - 2nd of 5 to Hevergolf Princess (12 Feb Lingfield 7f Equi RF 0274). She has made the frame regularly in modest company on sand, but has not had a lot of luck, and always seems to find a way to get herself beat. **G C Bravery [0-17] R Allder.*

PEARTREE HOUSE (IRE) BHB 90f **RR 92f** 5078[24]

4 b c Simply Majestic (USA) 7.8f **(72)** - Fashion Front (Habitat) 9.4f **(70)**
Form - 00140

Record	**1998 -**	1st:1	2nd:0	3rd:0	Ran:5
	Pre1998 -	1st:3	2nd:1	3rd:1	Ran:13

Win Prizemoney £16,910 *Total Prizemoney* £27,286

Wins	* **1998**	May	Lingfi	(GD)	7.6f	92	
	* 1997	May	Doncas	(G-S)	8f	97	<
	1996	Aug	Catter	(G-F)	7f	89	
	1996	Jun	Ayr	(G-F)	6f	60+	

1998 Turf 1-5: (8f 1-5) (sft 2, gd, g-f, frm 1-1)
Useful colt, effective 8f, acts on gd to frm, best on gd. Turf high 92 - 1st of 10 giving 11lb to King Slayer (8 May Lingfield RF 1106). Inconsistent. He started off the season running in top handicap company, though his victory at Lingfield in May was in a limited stakes, and he was off the track for five months before finishing down the field at Newmarket in October.
**W R Muir [2-13] Fayzad Thoroughbred Ltd (from B W Hills [2-5] Spt 1996).*

PEBBLE MOON BHB 63f **RR 67f** 4643[9]

2 gr c Efisio 7.7f **(69)** - Jazz (Sharrood (USA)) 10.5f **(72)**
Form - 74700
Record 1998 - 1st:0 2nd:0 3rd:0 Ran:5
Win Prizemoney £0 *Total Prizemoney* £413
1998 Turf 0-5: (6f, 7f 4) (gd, g-f 2, frm 2)
Average colt, has worn blinkers. Turf high 67.
**M A Jarvis [0-5] Mrs Christine Stevenson.*

PECULIARITY BHB 92f **RR 90+f** 4697[1]

2 b c Perpendicular - Pretty Pollyanna (General Assembly (USA)) 10f **(68)**
Form - 031
Record 1998 - 1st:1 2nd:0 3rd:1 Ran:3
Win Prizemoney £7,434 *Total Prizemoney* £7,946
Wins * **1998** Oct York (GD) 7.9f 90+ <
1998 Turf 1-3: (8f 1-3) (g-f 1-2, frm)
Currently useful colt. Turf high 90 (began Spt) - 1st of 25 from Regal Philosopher (7 Oct York RF 4697). He seems to be going the right way judged by his runaway win in a median auction event at York on his final start. **B Smart [1-3] The Family Partnership.*

PEDRO (IRE) BHB 90f **RR 88f** 3935[1]

3 b c Brief Truce (USA) 9.1f **(73)** - Mrs Fisher (IRE) (Salmon Leap (USA)) 11f **(61)**
Form - 1

Record	**1998 -**	1st:1	2nd:0	3rd:0	Ran:1
	Pre1998 -	1st:1	2nd:0	3rd:0	Ran:3

Win Prizemoney £10,260 *Total Prizemoney* £10,260

Wins	* **1998**	Aug	Thirsk	(G-F)	8f	88	<
	* 1997	*Spt*	*Wolver*	*(STD)*	*8.5f*	*76+*	

1998 Turf 1-1: (8f 1-1) (frm 1-1)
Strong, useful colt. (1st run) - 1st of 8 getting 10lb from Virtual Reality (28 Aug Thirsk RF 3935). **Sir Mark Prescott [2-4] G D Waters.*

PEGASUS BAY BHB 43f52a **RR 46f 52a** 4313[7]

7 b g Tina's Pet 7.4f **(56)** - Mossberry Fair (Mossberry) 7.4f **(51)**
Form - 64237

Record	**1998 -**	1st:0	2nd:1	3rd:1	Ran:5
	Pre1998 -	1st:2	2nd:2	3rd:1	Ran:7

Win Prizemoney £5,019 *Total Prizemoney* £7,480

Wins	*1997*	*Oct*	*Lingfi*	*(STD)*	*7f*	*64*	<
	1997	Spt	Yarmou	(FRM) S	10.1f	56+	

1998 Turf 0-3: (10f 2, 12f) (gd, g-f, frm) 1998 AW 0-2: (8f 2) (Equi 2)
Average gelding, effective 7 to 10f, best at 10f, acts on gd to frm - acts on Equi, prefers left handed tracks, favours tight tracks. Turf high 46 (began Aug). AW high 62.
**D E Cantillon [1-13] Don Cantillon (from Mrs A E Johnson [2-7] Nov 1997).*

PEGNITZ (USA) BHB 100f **RR 105?f** 3682[1]

3 b c Lear Fan (USA) 10.4f **(80)** - Likely Split (USA) (Little Current (USA)) 9.6f **(75)**
Form - 403021

Record	**1998 -**	1st:1	2nd:1	3rd:1	Ran:6
	Pre1998 -	1st:0	2nd:1	3rd:0	Ran:2

Win Prizemoney £3,668 *Total Prizemoney* £17,401
Wins * **1998** Aug Windso () 10f 80 <
1998 Turf 1-6: (8f, 9f 2, 10f 1-2, 12f) (gd 3, g-f 1-3)
Scopey, Pattern-class colt, effective 10f, acts on g-f. Turf high 105 - 3rd of 6 to Rabah (19 May Goodwood 10f g-f RF 1325). After spending his early career running in Group and Listed races, he finally came good when struggling home in a maiden at Windsor. He is not as good as his connections believe.
**C E Brittain [1-8] B H Voak.*

PEKAN HEIGHTS (USA) BHB 75f **RR 75+f** 4541[8]

2 b c Green Dancer (USA) 11.9f **(77)** - Battle Drum (USA) (Alydar (USA)) 9.1f **(76)**
Form - 358
Record 1998 - 1st:0 2nd:0 3rd:1 Ran:3
Win Prizemoney £0 *Total Prizemoney* £514
1998 Turf 0-3: (7f, 8f 2) (g-f 2, frm)
Currently above-average colt. Turf high 75 (1st run) (began Jly) - 3rd of 5 to Pilot's Harbour (28 Jly Beverley 7f g-f RF 3156).
**E A L Dunlop [0-3] H R H Sultan Ahmad Shah.*

PEKAY BHB 73f70a **RR 78f 70a** 1982[2]

5 b g Puissance 7.1f **(60)** - K-Sera (Lord Gayle (USA)) 8.8f **(62)**
Form - 12

Record	**1998 -**	1st:1	2nd:1	3rd:0	Ran:2
	Pre1998 -	1st:2	2nd:4	3rd:5	Ran:19

Win Prizemoney £10,637 *Total Prizemoney* £22,870

Wins	* **1998**	Jun	Salisb	(G-S) H	12f	70	70	<
	1997	Oct	Ayr	(SFT) H	10.9f	64	69	
	1997	Jun	Hamilt	(G-F) H	9.2f	60	64	

1998 Turf 1-2: (12f 1-2) (g-s, gd 1-1)
Above-average gelding, effective 11 to 12f, best at 12f, acts on g-s to gd, best on gd, has worn blinkers, likes left handed tracks. Turf high 78 - 2nd of 13 getting 7lb from Whitechapel (13 Jun York 12f g-s RF 1982) - also 1st of 14 giving 23lb to Herbshan Dancer (9 Jun Salisbury RF 1833). Won an amateurs' race at Salisbury in June and ran well under a penalty in a similar event next time. Suited by cut in the ground.
**M C Pipe [3-8] Moran, Nelson & Newman (from M Johnston [2-15] Oct 1997).*

PELAGOS (FR) BHB 81f **RR 84f** 3199[5]

3 gr c Exit To Nowhere (USA) 8.7f **(77)** - Southern Maid (USA) (Northern Dancer) 9.6f **(80)**
Form - 185305

Record	**1998 -**	1st:1	2nd:0	3rd:1	Ran:6
	Pre1998 -	1st:0	2nd:0	3rd:0	Ran:2

Win Prizemoney £3,030 *Total Prizemoney* £3,938

Wins * **1998** Apr Bright (GD) 8f 77+ <
1998 Turf 1-6: (8f 1-2, 10f 2, 11f, 12f) (g-s 1-1, g-f 3, frm 2)
Workmanlike, decent colt, effective 8 to 11f, acts on g-s to frm. Turf high 84 - 3rd of 6 giving 7lb to Mister Benjamin (6 Jun Haydock 11f frm RF 1782) - also 1st of 8 from Krisamba (20 Apr Brighton RF 0769). Consistent. **R Charlton [1-8] Niarchos Family.*

PENALTY MISS BHB 43f **RR 34f** 5004[8]

2 gr f Midyan (USA) 9.9f **(64)**-Between the Sticks (Pharly (FR)) 9.8f **(68)**
Form - 008
Record 1998 - 1st:0 2nd:0 3rd:0 Ran:3
1998 Turf 0-3: (6f 2, 7f) (sft, gd, frm)
Currently very moderate filly. Turf high 34 (began Spt).
**A G Newcombe [0-3] Bain, Beard, Harley, Meredith.*

PENANG PEARL (FR) BHB 67f **RR 62f** 4663[11]

2 b f Bering 9.6f **(80)** - Guapa (Shareef Dancer (USA)) 9.9f **(73)**
Form - 55520
Record 1998 - 1st:0 2nd:1 3rd:0 Ran:5
Win Prizemoney £0 *Total Prizemoney* £1,020
1998 Turf 0-5: (6f, 7f 2, 8f, 10f) (g-s, gd 2, g-f 2)
Average filly. Turf high 62 - 2nd of 8 to Stolen Tear (7 Spt Hamilton 8f gd RF 4131). **M Quinn [0-5] Mrs A K H Ooi.*

PENDANT BHB 78f **RR 76f** 4236[8]

3 b c Warning 8.1f **(77)**-Emerald (USA) (El Gran Senor (USA)) 9.6f **(76)**
Form - 318
Record 1998 - 1st:1 2nd:0 3rd:1 Ran:3
Win Prizemoney £3,501 *Total Prizemoney* £4,033
Wins * **1998** Aug Yarmou (G-F) 11.5f 72 <
1998 Turf 1-3: (11f 1-1, 12f 2) (gd, g-f 1-1, frm)
Currently above-average colt. Turf high 76 (1st run) (began Jly) - 3rd of 8 to Brigade Charge (7 Jly Pontefract 12f frm RF 2589) - also 1st of 4 from Aliabad (9 Aug Yarmouth RF 3495).
**H R A Cecil [1-3] K Abdulla.*

PEN FRIEND RR 54f 2521[2]

4 b g Robellino (USA) 9.5f **(68)** - Nibbs Point (IRE) (Sure Blade (USA)) 11.3f **(67)**
Form - 2
Record 1998 - 1st:0 2nd:1 3rd:0 Ran:1
Pre1998 - 1st:2 2nd:1 3rd:1 Ran:9
Win Prizemoney £5,941 *Total Prizemoney* £8,684
Wins * 1997 Aug Thirsk (G-F) H 16f 47 53 <
* 1997 Jly Beverl (G-F) H 16.2f 43 48
1998 Turf 0-1: (16f) (g-f)
Lengthy, fair gelding, effective 16f, acts on g-f to frm, best on g-f, likes tight tracks, excels at Beverley. (1st run) - 2nd of 7 getting 15lb from Nanton Point (4 Jly Beverley 16f g-f RF 2521). Improving.
**W J Haggas [2-10] B Haggas.*

PENMAR BHB 55f50a **RR 56f 50a** 5114[1]

6 b g Reprimand 8.2f **(63)** - Latakia (Morston (FR)) 9.4f **(55)**
Form - 371
Record 1998 - 1st:1 2nd:0 3rd:1 Ran:3
Pre1998 - 1st:1 2nd:3 3rd:3 Ran:20
Win Prizemoney £6,196 *Total Prizemoney* £10,599
Wins * **1998** Nov Mussel (SFT) H 8f 49 56
1996 *May Wolver (STD) H 9.4f 56 60* <
1998 Turf 1-3: (8f 1-3) (gd 1-1, g-f, frm)
Average gelding, has worn blinkers (very effectively). Turf high 56 (began Jly) - 1st of 13 giving 11lb to Napoleon's Return (4 Nov Musselburgh RF 5114).
**M A Peill [1-3] J F Wright (from T J Etherington [1-16] Oct 1996).*

PENMAYNE BHB 95f **RR 89f** 4853[8]

2 ch f Inchinor 8.9f **(64)** - Salanka (IRE) **(65df 56a)** (Persian Heights)
Form - 072413438
Record 1998 - 1st:1 2nd:1 3rd:2 Ran:9
Win Prizemoney £3,517 *Total Prizemoney* £9,814
Wins * **1998** Jly Sandow (GD) 7.1f 78 <
1998 Turf 1-9: (5f 2, 6f 2, 7f 1-5) (gd 2, g-f 1-3, frm 4)
Useful filly, effective 7f, acts on frm. Turf high 89. Benefited from the step up to seven furlongs when scoring at Sandown, but has not really improved on that. **D R C Elsworth [1-9] Mrs M E Slade.*

PENNILESS (IRE) BHB 48f47a **RR 53f 47a** 3938[9]

3 b f Common Grounds 8.1f **(66)** - Tizzy (Formidable (USA)) 9.2f **(63)**
Form - 8835758581520080
Record 1998 - 1st:1 2nd:1 3rd:1 Ran:14
Pre1998 - 1st:2 2nd:0 3rd:1 Ran:11
Win Prizemoney £8,561 *Total Prizemoney* £10,538
Wins * **1998** Jun Catter (G-S) H 5f 47 52
* 1997 Jun Beverl (SFT) C 5f 73 <
* 1997 Apr Thirsk (G-F) 5f 68
1998 Turf 1-10: (5f 1-5, 6f 4, 7f) (sft, gd 1-3, g-f, frm 4, hrd) 1998 AW 0-4: (6f 4) (Fibr 4)
Leggy, fair filly, effective 5f, acts on gd to frm. Turf high 53. AW high 50. Becoming disappointing.
**N Tinkler [3-25] The Penniless Partnership.*

PENNY APPEAL RR 772[8]

4 ch f Clantime 6.6f **(57)** - Petroc Concert (Tina's Pet) 6.8f **(59)**
Form - 08
Record 1998 - 1st:0 2nd:0 3rd:0 Ran:2
1998 Turf 0-1: (5f) (sft) 1998 AW 0-1: (8f) (Equi)
Strong, formerly very poor filly. **J W Mullins [0-4] Seamus Mullins.*

PENNY MOOR BHB 78f **RR 80f** 4377[11]

2 b f Polish Precedent (USA) 9f **(73)** - Corley Moor (Habitat) 9.4f **(70)**
Form - 425100
Record 1998 - 1st:1 2nd:1 3rd:0 Ran:6
Win Prizemoney £3,341 *Total Prizemoney* £4,489
Wins * **1998** Aug Beverl (G-F) H 5f 76 80 <
1998 Turf 1-6: (5f 1-4, 6f 2) (sft, gd 1-3, g-f, frm)
Decent filly, effective 5f, acts on gd. Turf high 80 - 1st of 6 giving 18lb to Wind In Winnipeg (12 Aug Beverley RF 3563). She showed some ability in her first three starts, and put up a dour performance to win an ordinary-looking Beverley nursery.
**M Johnston [1-6] Greenland Park Ltd.*

PENNYS FROM HEAVEN RR 74f 3430[4]

4 gr g Generous (IRE) 11.5f **(82)** - Heavenly Cause (USA) (Grey Dawn II) 11.1f **(72)**
Form - 034
Record 1998 - 1st:0 2nd:0 3rd:1 Ran:3
Pre1998 - 1st:1 2nd:1 3rd:3 Ran:13
Win Prizemoney £3,670 *Total Prizemoney* £8,683
Wins 1997 Aug Bath (GD) H 11.7f 75 77 <
1998 Turf 0-3: (12f 3) (gd, g-f, frm)
Scopey, above-average gelding, effective 12f, acts on gd to frm, best on gd, has worn blinkers, does well at Goodwood. Turf high 74 - 3rd of 6 giving 1lb to Colleville (22 Jly Leicester 12f frm RF 3028). **L M Cumani [0-3] SKSC Racing(from HCandy [1-13] Oct 1997).*

PENNY'S MILL (IRE) RR 44f 3443[11]

3 ch f Belmez (USA) 11.4f **(65)** - Repique (USA) (Sharpen Up) 8.3f **(67)**
Form - 0
Record 1998 - 1st:0 2nd:0 3rd:0 Ran:1
1998 Turf 0-1: (8f) (frm)
Workmanlike, currently moderate filly.
**D R C Elsworth [0-1] Miss R Wakeford.*

PENNY WHISTLE BHB 36f **RR 37f** 2931[10]

3 b f Clantime 6.6f **(57)** - Penny Hasset **(64f)** (Lochnager) 6f **(59)**
Form - 0403660
Record 1998 - 1st:0 2nd:0 3rd:1 Ran:7
Pre1998 - 1st:0 2nd:0 3rd:0 Ran:3
Win Prizemoney £0 *Total Prizemoney* £492
1998 Turf 0-7: (5f 5, 6f 2) (g-s, gd 5, frm)
Small, very moderate filly. Turf high 37.
**T D Easterby [0-10] Simon Bhullar.*

PENROSE (IRE) BHB 62f **RR 70df** 4886[8]

3 ch f Wolfhound (USA) 7.3f **(71)** - Mill Path (Mill Reef (USA)) 10.5f **(78)**
Form - 55238
Record 1998 - 1st:0 2nd:1 3rd:1 Ran:5
Pre1998 - 1st:0 2nd:0 3rd:0 Ran:1
Win Prizemoney £0 *Total Prizemoney* £1,628
1998 Turf 0-5: (6f 2, 7f, 8f 2) (g-s, g-f 2, frm 2)
Unfurnished, above-average filly, effective 7f, acts on frm. Turf high 70 (began Aug) - 2nd of 10 to Dhirina (25 Spt Haydock 7f frm RF 4482). **B W Hills [0-6] Madhad Ali.*

PENSION FUND BHB 78f **RR 82f** 5151[4]
4 b g Emperor Fountain 10f **(82)** - Navarino Bay (Averof) 8.2f **(62)**
Form - 88231704
Record 1998 - 1st:1 2nd:1 3rd:1 Ran:8
Pre1998 - 1st:3 2nd:4 3rd:1 Ran:19
Win Prizemoney £25,864 *Total Prizemoney* £40,604
Wins * **1998** Spt Ripon (HVY) H 10f 77 82 <
* 1997 Aug Beverl (G-S) H 9.9f 69 70
* 1996 Aug York (GD) H 7f 75 72
* 1996 Jly Redcar (G-F) 5f 63
1998 Turf 1-8: (10f 1-5, 12f 3) (g-s 1-1, gd 2, g-f 2, frm 3)
Rangy, decent gelding, effective 10 to 12f, best at 12f, acts on g-s to frm, has worn blinkers, likes right handed tracks. Turf high 82 - 1st of 7 giving 2lb to Aim High (1 Spt Ripon RF 4012). Retains his ability and was a good third at York in August, a track where he has a useful record, before scoring in heavy ground at Ripon. Disappointing afterwards. **M W Easterby [4-27] Stephen Curtis.*

PENTAGON LAD BHB 55f **RR 57f** 5137[13]
2 ch c Secret Appeal - Gilboa (Shirley Heights) 10.3f **(74)**
Form - 700
Record 1998 - 1st:0 2nd:0 3rd:0 Ran:3
1998 Turf 0-3: (6f, 7f, 8f) (gd, g-f, frm)
Currently fair colt. Turf high 57 (began Spt).
**J L Eyre [0-3] Creskeld Racing.*

PENYBONT RR 82f 5000[3]
2 b f Unfuwain (USA) 11.4f **(74)** - Morgannwg (IRE) (Simply Great (FR)) 8.2f **(65)**
Form - 083
Record 1998 - 1st:0 2nd:0 3rd:1 Ran:3
Win Prizemoney £0 *Total Prizemoney* £515
1998 Turf 0-3: (6f, 7f 2) (sft, gd, g-f)
Currently decent filly. Turf high 82 (began Oct) - 3rd of 10 to Balisada (26 Oct Lingfield 7f sft RF 5000).
**M Bell [0-3] K J Mercer & Mrs S Mercer.*

PEPPERDINE (IRE) BHB 81f **RR 83f** 4643[1]
2 b c Indian Ridge 7.6f **(74)** - Rahwah (Northern Baby (CAN)) 11.6f **(71)**

Form - 225061
Record 1998 - 1st:1 2nd:2 3rd:0 Ran:6
Win Prizemoney £3,550 *Total Prizemoney* £5,625
Wins * **1998** Oct Warwic (GD) H 7f 78 83 <
1998 Turf 1-6: (6f 3, 7f 1-3) (gd 2, g-f 1-3, frm)
Decent colt, effective 6 to 7f, best at 6f, acts on gd to g-f, best on g-f, has worn blinkers. Turf high 83 (began Jly) - 1st of 20 giving 3lb to Sari (4 Oct Warwick RF 4643). **W Jarvis [1-6] P D Savill.*

PEPPERS (IRE) BHB 53f51a **RR 58f 51a** 4126[7]
5 b m Bluebird (USA) 7.9f **(71)** - Pepilin (Coquelin (USA)) 8.4f **(58)**
Form - 5722353737
Record 1998 - 1st:0 2nd:2 3rd:3 Ran:10
Pre1998 - 1st:0 2nd:3 3rd:3 Ran:17
Win Prizemoney £0 *Total Prizemoney* £8,665
1998 Turf 0-8: (8f, 9f, 10f 4, 12f, 13f) (g-s 2, gd, g-f, frm 4) 1998 AW 0-2: (10f 2) (Equi 2)
Fair filly, effective 10 to 12f, best at 10f, acts on gd to frm, best on gd, has worn blinkers, prefers left handed tracks, favours tight tracks. Turf high 59. AW high 53. Consistent.
**K R Burke [0-24] M Nelmes-Crocker (from L M Cumani [0-3] Oct 1995).*

PEPPIATT BHB 75f **RR 74f** 5096[5]
4 ch g Efisio 7.7f **(69)** - Fleur du Val (Valiyar) 8.5f **(73)**
Form - 008474333321705
Record 1998 - 1st:1 2nd:1 3rd:4 Ran:15
Pre1998 - 1st:2 2nd:1 3rd:0 Ran:3
Win Prizemoney £22,522 *Total Prizemoney* £29,737
Wins **1998** Spt Goodwo (SFT) H 6f 71 77
1997 Jly Lingfi (G-F) H 7f 80 79 <
1997 Apr Folkes (G-F) 6f 75
1998 Turf 1-15: (6f 1-8, 7f 5, 8f 2) (sft, g-s 1-2, gd 4, g-f 5, frm 2, hrd)
Workmanlike, above-average gelding, effective 6 to 7f, best at 6f, acts on g-s to frm, has worn blinkers, excels at Lingfield. Turf high 77 - 1st of 21 giving 5lb to Carlton (12 Spt Goodwood RF 4246). Consistent. Found his form gradually, culminating in winning a competitive handicap over six at Goodwood in September.
**N Bycroft [0-1] J A Swinburne (from D Nicholls [1-14] Oct 1998).*

PERADVENTURE (IRE) BHB 84f **RR 83f** 4855[8]
3 b c Persian Bold 10f **(69)** - Missed Opportunity (IRE) (Exhibitioner) 8.7f **(61)**
Form - 0324555138
Record 1998 - 1st:1 2nd:1 3rd:2 Ran:10
Win Prizemoney £6,290 *Total Prizemoney* £9,428
Wins * **1998** Spt York (GD) 10.4f 79 <
1998 Turf 1-10: (8f 2, 9f, 10f 1-2, 11f, 12f 3, 13f) (sft, g-s 2, gd, g-f 3, frm 1-3)
Workmanlike, decent colt, effective 10 to 13f, acts on g-s to frm, prefers left handed tracks. Turf high 83 - 5th of 17 getting 14lb from Double Classic (18 Jun Ascot 12f g-s RF 2088) - also 1st of 6 giving 5lb to Royal Fontaine (2 Spt York RF 4057). Consistent. Had had plenty of chances prior to making all in a maiden at York in September. **R Hannon [1-10] Hippodrome Racing.*

PERCHANCER (IRE) BHB 57f **RR 57df** 4658[16]
2 ch g Perugino (USA) - Irish Hope (Nishapour (FR)) 9.1f **(61)**
Form - 803860
Record 1998 - 1st:0 2nd:0 3rd:1 Ran:6
Win Prizemoney £0 *Total Prizemoney* £492
1998 Turf 0-6: (6f 6) (gd 2, g-f 3, frm)
Fair gelding. Turf high 57. **P C Haslam [0-6] N P Green.*

PERCY BHB 40f50a **RR 41f 50a** 4708[14]
3 ch g Precocious 7.2f **(54)** - Manna Green (Bustino) 10.4f **(64)**
Form - 7500000
Record 1998 - 1st:0 2nd:0 3rd:0 Ran:7
Pre1998 - 1st:0 2nd:1 3rd:1 Ran:7
Win Prizemoney £0 *Total Prizemoney* £844
1998 Turf 0-4:(8f, 9f, 10f, 12f)(g-f, frm 3) 1998 AW 0-3: (7f, 8f 2) (Fibr 3)
Small, fair gelding, effective 8f, - acts on Fibr, has worn blinkers, likes left handed tracks, likes tight tracks. Turf high 33 (began Jly). AW high 54 (1st run) - 7th of 12 getting 2lb from Sharp Monkey (2 Feb Southwell 8f Fibr RF 0206). Inconsistent.
**J Hetherton [0-9] Mrs O K Steele (from J F Bottomley [0-5] Aug 1997).*

PERCY-P BHB 72f **RR 76f** 2628[9]
3 ch c Superpower 6.6f **(58)** - Song's Best (Never so Bold) 6.3f **(66)**
Form - 310
Record 1998 - 1st:1 2nd:0 3rd:1 Ran:3
Pre1998 - 1st:0 2nd:0 3rd:1 Ran:2
Win Prizemoney £2,276 *Total Prizemoney* £3,207
Wins * **1998** May Bath (G-F) C 5.1f 76 <
1998 Turf 1-3: (5f 1-1, 6f 2) (gd, frm 1-2)
Workmanlike, above-average colt. Turf high 76 - 1st of 9 from Emperor Naheem (29 May Bath RF 1568) (DEAD)
**W R Muir [1-5] Perspicacious Punters Racing Club.*

PERECAPA (IRE) BHB 35f33a **RR 42f 33a** 3850[3]
3 b f Archway (IRE) 8.5f **(60)** - Cupid Miss (Anita's Prince)
Form - 05403333
Record 1998 - 1st:0 2nd:0 3rd:4 Ran:8
Pre1998 - 1st:0 2nd:0 3rd:0 Ran:2
Win Prizemoney £0 *Total Prizemoney* £1,127
1998 Turf 0-7: (8f, 10f 2, 11f 2, 12f 2) (g-s, g-f 2, frm 2, hrd 2) 1998 AW 0-1: (9f) (Fibr)
Light-framed, moderate filly, effective 10 to 12f, acts on g-f to frm, favours tight tracks. Turf high 45. Inconsistent.
**B Palling [0-10] Davies And Williams Partnership.*

PERFECT PAL (IRE) BHB 57f **RR 60f** 4202[9]
7 ch g Mulhollande (USA) 6.6f **(68)** - Gone (Whistling Wind) 10f **(55)**
Form - 00830
Record 1998 - 1st:0 2nd:0 3rd:1 Ran:5
Pre1998 - 1st:0 2nd:1 3rd:0 Ran:6
Win Prizemoney £0 *Total Prizemoney* £1,497
1998 Turf 0-5: (6f, 7f 2, 8f, 10f) (g-s, gd, g-f, frm 2)
Average gelding, effective 7f, acts on frm. Turf high 60.
**M J Weeden [0-9] Peter Bolton (from Miss Gay Kelleway [2-12] Aug 1997).*

PERFECT PARADIGM (IRE) BHB 100f **RR 102f** 4515[14]
4 b c Alzao (USA) 9.8f **(73)** - Brilleaux (Manado) 9.6f **(63)**

Form - 767172330
Record 1998 - 1st:1 2nd:1 3rd:2 Ran:9
Pre1998 - 1st:2 2nd:2 3rd:0 Ran:6
Win Prizemoney £46,172 *Total Prizemoney* £55,946
Wins * **1998** Jly Haydoc (G-F) H 11.9f 94 98
* 1997 May Cheste (SFT) H 12.3f 88 101+ <
* 1997 Mar Newcas (G-F) 12.4f 82+
1998 Turf 1-9: (12f 1-5, 13f, 14f 3) (sft, g-s, gd 3, g-f 1-3, frm)
Workmanlike, very useful colt, effective 12 to 14f, acts on g-s to g-f, best on gd, has worn blinkers (extremely effectively), likes left handed tracks, prefers tight tracks, excels at Chester. Turf high 102 - 2nd of 5 giving 6lb to Sadian (8 Aug Ascot 12f g-f RF 3455) - also 1st of 8 giving 8lb to Bay of Islands (4 Jly Haydock RF 2537). Inconsistent. He ran appallingly on his first three starts and the Stewards quite rightly demanded an explanation when he roared back to form at Haydock in July. John Gosden informed them that the horse had choked on his previous start and was improved by the application of a first time visor, as well as a shorter trip on faster ground. A model of consistency on his next four starts, he flopped in the mud at Ascot in September and must be avoided if encountering such a surface next term.
**J H M Gosden [3-15] Sheikh Mohammed.*

PERFECT PEACH BHB 75f **RR 77f** 3758[7]
3 b f Lycius (USA) 8.8f **(71)** - Perfect Timing (Comedy Star (USA)) 7.5f **(50)**
Form - 4637
Record 1998 - 1st:0 2nd:0 3rd:1 Ran:4
Pre1998 - 1st:2 2nd:1 3rd:0 Ran:5
Win Prizemoney £7,954 *Total Prizemoney* £9,911
Wins 1997 Aug Beverl (G-S) H 5f 75 78 <
1997 Aug Thirsk (GD) 5f 78 <
1998 Turf 0-4: (5f 4) (g-f 2, frm 2)
Workmanlike, above-average filly, effective 5f, acts on gd to frm, best on gd. Turf high 75. Consistent.
**C W Fairhurst [0-2] Mrs Ann Morris (from D W Chapman [0-2] Jun 1998).*

PERFECT POPPY BHB 57f47a **RR 58f 47a** 2392[4]
4 b f Shareef Dancer (USA) 10.1f **(67)** - Benazir (High Top) 10.2f **(67)**
Form - 05B5814
Record 1998 - 1st:1 2nd:0 3rd:0 Ran:7
Pre1998 - 1st:0 2nd:0 3rd:2 Ran:11
Win Prizemoney £1,725 *Total Prizemoney* £2,986
Wins * **1998** Jun Lingfi (G-F) H 10f 37 45+ <
1998 Turf 1-7: (8f 3, 10f 1-3, 11f) (sft, g-s, gd 3, g-f 1-2)
Light-framed, fair filly, effective 7 to 8f, acts on gd to frm. Turf high 58. Inconsistent. Not the most trustworthy of fillies, she managed to win an apprentice handicap at Lingfield in June, though she has not shown much otherwise.
**S Dow [1-10] Mrs I P Blance (from J R Fanshawe [0-8] Jun 1997).*

PERFECT SCOUNDREL (IRE) **RR 98f** 4562a[5]
3 b c Mujadil (USA) 7.7f **(70)** - Park Lady (Tap On Wood) 10.3f **(65)**
Form - 35
1998 Turf 0-2: (9f, 10f) (g-s 2)
Currently very useful colt. Turf high 98 (1st run) (began Jly) - 3rd of 11 to Fairy Ridge (9 Jly Tipperary 9f g-s RF 2791a).
**G A Cusack in IRE [0-2] John McKay.*

PERFECT VINTAGE **RR 106f** 4076a[1]
8 b h Shirley Heights 12.1f **(76)** - Fair Salinia (Petingo) 11f **(72)**
Form - 1
1998 Turf 1-1: (8f 1-1) (gd 1-1)
Pattern-class horse. (1st run) - 1st of 6 giving 8lb to Sand Falcon (29 Aug Deauville RF 4076a). A smashing horse who retains his enthusiasm despite clutching a bus pass, he came with a storming finish to win the Group Three Prix Quincey at Deauville in August.
**Mme P Barbe in FR [1-3] Np Bloodstock Ltd.*

PERICLES BHB 70f77a **RR 71f 77a** 4308[5]
4 b g Primo Dominie 7.2f **(67)** - Egalite (FR) (Luthier) 9.8f **(71)**
Form - 8603013608525
Record 1998 - 1st:1 2nd:1 3rd:2 Ran:13
Pre1998 - 1st:4 2nd:4 3rd:2 Ran:22
Win Prizemoney £17,104 *Total Prizemoney* £24,932
Wins * **1998** Jun Folkes (GD) 7f 71
1997 *Oct Wolver (STD) C* *7f* *85* <
1997 *Jun Wolver (STD) H* *7f* *80 80*
1997 Jun Leices (GD) H 7f 70 74
1996 *Spt Wolver (STD)* *6f* *77+*
1998 Turf 1-11: (7f 1-9, 8f 2) (g-s, gd 1-3, g-f 3, frm 4) 1998 AW 0-2: (7f, 8f) (Equi, Fibr)
Scopey, above-average gelding, effective 7 to 8f, best at 7f, acts on g-f - acts on Fibr, has worn blinkers. Turf high 71. AW high 62. His victory came in a weak amateurs' race, but he has run well in better company since.
**Miss Gay Kelleway [1-16] Miss Gay Kelleway (from M Johnston [4-20] Oct 1997).*

PERIDOT **RR 79f** 4310[11]
3 b f Green Desert (USA) 7.8f **(78)** - Alinova (USA) (Alleged (USA)) 10f **(76)**
Form - 241570
Record 1998 - 1st:1 2nd:1 3rd:0 Ran:6
Pre1998 - 1st:0 2nd:0 3rd:0 Ran:1
Win Prizemoney £3,629 *Total Prizemoney* £4,923
Wins * **1998** Jly Windso (GD) 10f 79 <
1998 Turf 1-6: (8f, 10f 1-2, 11f 2, 12f) (gd 3, g-f 1-3)
Workmanlike, above-average filly, effective 10 to 11f, acts on gd to g-f, has worn blinkers. Turf high 79 - 1st of 7 getting 5lb from Aim High (13 Jly Windsor RF 2769).
**J H M Gosden [1-7] Sheikh Mohammed.*

PERIGEUX (IRE) BHB 85f92a **RR 79f 92a** 4349[15]
2 b c Perugino (USA) - Rock On (IRE) (Ballad Rock) 7.8f **(63)**
Form - 2511100
Record 1998 - 1st:3 2nd:1 3rd:0 Ran:7
Win Prizemoney £11,853 *Total Prizemoney* £12,695
Wins * **1998** *Jly Wolver (STD)* *6f* *86* <
* **1998** Jly Ayr (GD) H 6f 79
* **1998** *Jly Southw (STD)* *6f* *79*
1998 Turf 1-5: (6f 1-5) (sft, gd 1-3, g-f) 1998 AW 2-2: (6f 2-2) (Fibr 2-2)
Useful colt, effective 6f, acts on gd - acts on Fibr. Turf high 79 - 1st of 6 giving 18lb to Vosburgh (18 Jly Ayr RF 2904). AW high 86 (began Jly) - 1st of 4 giving 1lb to Spirit Willing (24 Jly Wolverhampton RF 3096) - also 1st of 14 from Hyphen (9 Jly Southwell RF 2657). A winner on the Southwell and Wolverhampton Fibresand tracks, he landed an Ayr nursery in between. He was involved in a most unfortunate incident when mistakenly running instead of the three-year-old filly Royal Dream in a Hamilton handicap in August, getting upset in the stalls and finishing tailed off. Hopefully the experience will not ruin him.
**J Berry [3-7] Mrs Valerie Hubbard.*

PERISTRODIUM BHB 22f **RR 10f** 1807[9]
3 b c Presidium 7.5f **(56)** - Countess of Honour (USA) (Troy) 10.4f **(68)**
Form - 000
Record 1998 - 1st:0 2nd:0 3rd:0 Ran:3
1998 Turf 0-3: (8f, 10f 2) (sft, g-s, frm)
Lengthy, currently poor colt. Turf high 10.
**R Bastiman [0-3] J F Wright.*

PERLA DI SASSO (GER) **RR 60f** 4477[5]
3 br f Caerleon (USA) 10.9f **(79)** - Pebbles (Sharpen Up) 8.3f **(67)**
Form - 55
Record 1998 - 1st:0 2nd:0 3rd:0 Ran:2
1998 Turf 0-2: (9f, 10f) (gd, g-f)
Unfurnished, currently average filly. Turf high 60 (began Spt).
**C E Brittain [0-2] Sheikh Mohammed.*

PERPETUAL LIGHT BHB 37f58a **RR 37f 58a** 1741[9]
5 b m Petoski 10.4f **(56)** - Butosky (Busted) 10.2f **(61)**
Form - 303477640
Record 1998 - 1st:0 2nd:0 3rd:1 Ran:8
Pre1998 - 1st:3 2nd:0 3rd:1 Ran:17
Win Prizemoney £7,863 *Total Prizemoney* £9,097
Wins * 1997 *Oct Wolver (STD) H* *9.4f* *55 63*
* 1996 *Jun Southw (STD) H* *8f* *62 68* <
* 1996 *Apr Southw (STD)* *8f* *59*
1998 Turf 0-3: (9f, 10f, 12f) (gd 2, frm) 1998 AW 0-5: (8f, 9f 2, 10f, 11f) (Equi, Fibr 4)
Average filly, effective 9f, - acts on Fibr, has worn blinkers, favours left handed tracks, favours tight tracks. Turf high 37. AW high 64 - 3rd of 8 getting 13lb from Tough Leader (4 Feb Wolverhampton 9f Fibr RF 0221).

J J Quinn [4-32] The Four Point Partnership.

PERPETUAL TIARA RR 24f 4155[10]

3 b f Green Desert (USA) 7.8f **(78)** - Joud (Dancing Brave (USA)) 8.4f **(76)**

Form - 0

Record 1998 - 1st:0 2nd:0 3rd:0 Ran:1

1998 Turf 0-1: (8f) (frm)

Neat, currently little account filly. *J D Bethell [0-1] Robert Gibbons.*

PERRYSTON VIEW BHB 89f **RR 92f** 4367[11]

6 b h Primo Dominie 7.2f **(67)** - Eastern Ember (Indian King (USA)) 7.4f **(64)**

Form - 605100

Record 1998 - 1st:1 2nd:0 3rd:0 Ran:6
Pre1998 - 1st:8 2nd:1 3rd:3 Ran:28

Win Prizemoney £92,251 *Total Prizemoney* £101,881

Wins * **1998** Aug Ripon (GD) H 6f 86 92 <
* 1997 Spt Ayr (GD) H 6f 81 92 <
* 1997 May Newmar (GD) H 6f 78 80
* 1995 Jly Newmar (G-F) H 6f 86 81
* 1995 Jun Newmar (GD) H 6f 81 82
* 1995 Apr Catter (GD) H 5f 67 76+
* 1995 Apr Newcas (G-F) H 5f 67 72+
* 1994 Nov Doncas (SFT) H 5f 64 74
* 1994 Spt Redcar (GD) H 6f 60 60

1998 Turf 1-6: (5f, 6f 1-5) (sft, gd 1-4, g-f)

Useful horse, effective 5 to 6f, best at 6f, acts on gd, mostly wears blinkers (effectively). Turf high 92 - 1st of 9 from Lago Di Varano (3 Aug Ripon RF 3312). He returned to form at Ripon in August, but that was by far his best performance of the season. Suited by good ground and likes to race prominently.

P Calver [9-34] Mrs Janis MacPherson.

PERSEPHONE BHB 20f17a **RR 25f 17a** 4375[11]

5 ch m Lycius (USA) 8.8f **(71)** - Elarrih (USA) (Sharpen Up) 8.3f **(67)**

Form - 0

Record 1998 - 1st:0 2nd:0 3rd:0 Ran:1
Pre1998 - 1st:0 2nd:1 3rd:0 Ran:20

Win Prizemoney £0 *Total Prizemoney* £1,115

1998 Turf 0-1: (16f) (frm)

Little account filly, often wears blinkers.

C N Allen [0-2] Roger Langley (from J L Harris [0-10] Spt 1997).

PERSEVERE BHB 40f44a **RR 41f 44a** 4927[R]

4 b f Pursuit of Love 9.5f **(69)**-Seastream (USA)(Alleged (USA))10f **(76)**

Form - 480606R

Record 1998 - 1st:0 2nd:0 3rd:0 Ran:7
Pre1998 - 1st:0 2nd:0 3rd:1 Ran:5

Win Prizemoney £0 *Total Prizemoney* £1,033

1998 Turf 0-4: (8f 2, 10f 2) (g-s, gd, g-f 2) 1998 AW 0-3: (7f, 8f 2) (Equi 2, Fibr)

Lengthy, moderate filly, effective 6f, acts on gd, has worn blinkers, likes left handed tracks. Turf high 41. AW high 44.

Graeme Roe [0-2] Graeme Roe (from Lord Huntingdon [0-10] May 1998).

PERSIAN FANTASIA BHB 56f **RR 55f** 2590[13]

3 b f Alzao (USA) 9.8f **(73)** - Persian Fantasy (Persian Bold) 9.3f **(66)**

Form - 700

Record 1998 - 1st:0 2nd:0 3rd:0 Ran:3
Pre1998 - 1st:0 2nd:0 3rd:0 Ran:1

1998 Turf 0-3: (8f, 10f 2) (g-s, frm 2)

Neat, fair filly. Turf high 55.

J L Dunlop [0-4] Windflower Overseas Holdings Inc.

PERSIAN FAYRE BHB 80f **RR 86+f** 4581[3]

6 b g Persian Heights 10.5f **(61)** - Dominion Fayre (Dominion) 8.5f **(63)**

Form - 77415520703

Record 1998 - 1st:1 2nd:1 3rd:1 Ran:11
Pre1998 - 1st:5 2nd:7 3rd:3 Ran:40

Win Prizemoney £36,008 *Total Prizemoney* £55,811

Wins * **1998** Jun Haydoc (GD) 7.1f 86+ <
* 1996 Nov Newmar (GD) H 7f 79 83
* 1996 Oct York (GD) H 7f 75 78
* 1996 Aug Newcas (GD) H 7f 67 77
* 1995 May Ayr (G-F) 8f 73
* 1994 May Ayr (GF) 5f 61

1998 Turf 1-11: (7f 1-11) (sft 2, g-s, gd 3, g-f 2, frm 1-2, hrd)

Useful gelding, effective 7 to 8f, best at 7f, acts on gd to frm, best on frm, prefers left handed tracks, prefers tight tracks, excels at Haydock and Ayr. Turf high 86 - 1st of 7 getting 6lb from Refuse To Lose (5 Jun Haydock RF 1762). Consistent. A front-running seven-furlong specialist, he wins only rarely but usually runs an honest race. *J Berry [6-51] Murray Grubb.*

PERSIAN FORTUNE BHB 44f49a **RR 41f 49a** 4401[10]

3 b f Forzando 7.2f **(63)** - Persian Air (Persian Bold) 9.3f **(66)**

Form - 037606080

Record 1998 - 1st:0 2nd:0 3rd:1 Ran:9
Pre1998 - 1st:1 2nd:2 3rd:2 Ran:10

Win Prizemoney £2,277 *Total Prizemoney* £4,940

Wins * 1997 *May Southw (STD) S 5f 57* <

1998 Turf 0-7: (5f 2, 6f 3, 7f, 8f) (g-s, gd, g-f, frm 4) 1998 AW 0-2: (6f, 7f) (Fibr 2)

Light-framed, fair filly, effective 5 to 7f, acts on gd to frm - acts on Fibr. Turf high 53 - 6th of 9 getting 13lb from I Cried For You (22 May Brighton 5f frm RF 1388). AW high 36.

W G M Turner [1-19] J G Charlton.

PERSIANLUX RR 97f 4715a[2]

2 b c Persian Bold 10f **(69)** - Luxurioux (Lyphard (USA)) 9.9f **(72)**

Form - 2

1998 Turf 0-1: (9f) (sft)

Currently very useful colt. (1st run) - 2nd of 5 to Bienamado (3 Oct Longchamp 9f sft RF 4715a). No match for Bienamado in a Longchamp Group Three, he should make a useful three-year-old.

A Fabre in FR [0-1] J-L Lagardere.

PERSIANO BHB 98f **RR 99+f** 1413[1]

3 ch c Efisio 7.7f **(69)** - Persiandale (Persian Bold) 9.3f **(66)**

Form - 4111

Record 1998 - 1st:3 2nd:0 3rd:0 Ran:4
Pre1998 - 1st:0 2nd:0 3rd:0 Ran:4

Win Prizemoney £16,823 *Total Prizemoney* £18,004

Wins * **1998** May Doncas (GD) H 7f 90 99+ <
* **1998** May Salisb (FRM) H 7f 75 89+
* **1998** May Warwic (GD) H 7f 75 83

1998 Turf 3-4: (6f, 7f 3-3) (hvy, g-f 2-2, frm 1-1)

Lengthy, very useful colt, effective 7f, acts on g-f to frm. Turf high 99 - 1st of 8 getting 8lb from Night of Glass (23 May Doncaster RF 1413). Improving. He had shown ability in his early races, but found his form when stepped up to seven furlongs, winning three times in the style of a rapidly-improving colt. Not seen after May.

J R Fanshawe [3-8] Miss A Church.

PERSIAN PUNCH (IRE) BHB 118f **RR 120f** 5153a[3]

5 ch g Persian Heights 10.5f **(61)** - Rum Cay (USA) (Our Native (USA)) 11.2f **(63)**

Form - 131613

Record 1998 - 1st:3 2nd:0 3rd:2 Ran:6
Pre1998 - 1st:5 2nd:2 3rd:4 Ran:15

Win Prizemoney £133,185 *Total Prizemoney* £288,008

Wins * **1998** Aug York (G-F) G3 15.9f 115
* **1998** May Sandow (GD) G3 16.4f 119
* **1998** May Newmar (G-S) G3 16f 120 <
* 1997 May Sandow (G-F) G3 16.4f 115
* 1997 May Newbur (SFT) L 13.3f 116
* 1996 Jly Newmar (GD) L 14.8f 106
* 1996 Jun Salisb (GD) 14f 90
* 1996 May Windso (G-F) 10f 79+

1998 Turf 3-6: (14f, 16f 3-4, 20f) (g-s, gd 1-3, g-f 2-2)

Very high-class gelding, effective 13 to 20f, acts on g-s to frm, best on gd, excels at Sandown and York. Turf high 120 - 3rd of 24 giving 11lb to Jezabeel (3 Nov Flemington 16f gd RF 5153a) - also 1st of 10 giving 3lb to Busy Flight (1 May Newmarket RF 0964). Consistent. He developed into a smart stayer in 1997, and made a winning reappearance in 1998 in the Sagaro Stakes, before taking the Henry II for the second time. For the second successive year he did not figure in the Ascot Gold Cup, and the evidence seems to suggest that he does not stay much beyond two miles, but he is a very effective performer at that trip as he showed when a battling winner of York's Lonsdale Stakes. He was sent to Australia for his final run, in the Melbourne Cup and, despite an interrupted preparation due to ringworm, put up a terrific performance to take third place giving the first two 11lb. He is likely to stay in training

with a return to Australia as the target.
*D R C Elsworth [8-21] J C Smith.

Form - 7840371072
Record 1998 - 1st:1 2nd:1 3rd:1 Ran:10

Persian Punch ran a terrific race in the Melbourne Cup

PERSIAN SABRE BHB 58f **RR 56f** 4194[13]
3 b f Sabrehill (USA) 8.5f **(64)** - Wassl's Sister (Troy) 10.4f **(68)**
Form - 5002410
Record 1998 - 1st:1 2nd:1 3rd:0 Ran:7
Pre1998 - 1st:0 2nd:0 3rd:0 Ran:5
Win Prizemoney £2,070 *Total Prizemoney* £2,802
Wins * **1998** Aug Lingfi (G-F) H 10f 54 56 <
1998 Turf 1-7: (8f 3, 9f, 10f 1-2, 12f) (sft, gd, g-f 2, frm 1-3)
Unfurnished, fair filly, effective 10f, acts on frm, likes tight tracks. Turf high 56 - 1st of 15 getting 3lb from Harlequin Walk (25 Aug Lingfield RF 3848). *V Soane [1-12] Persian War Racing.*

PERSIAN WATERS (IRE) BHB 70f **RR 68f** 4873[1]
2 b c Persian Bold 10f **(69)** - Emerald Waters (Kings Lake (USA)) 10.8f **(67)**
Form - 47041
Record 1998 - 1st:1 2nd:0 3rd:0 Ran:5
Win Prizemoney £3,692 *Total Prizemoney* £3,938
Wins * **1998** Oct Pontef (SFT) H 8f 64 68 <
1998 Turf 1-5: (7f 3, 8f 1-1, 10f) (g-s, gd 1-1, g-f 2, frm)
Average colt. Turf high 68 (began Jly) - 1st of 20 getting 4lb from Evasive Step (19 Oct Pontefract RF 4873).
Mrs J R Ramsden [1-5] Paul Green.

PERTEMPS CRAIC RR 4989[11]
2 b g Gildoran 11.6f **(58)** - Pertemps Partner **(41f 52a)** (Bairn (USA)) 7.7f **(59)**
Form - 0
Record 1998 - 1st:0 2nd:0 3rd:0 Ran:1
1998 Turf 0-1: (8f) (sft)
Currently very poor gelding - 11th of 11 to Mount Irish (26 Oct Leicester 8f sft RF 4989). *A G Newcombe [0-1] Pertemps Group Ltd.*

PERTEMPS MISSION BHB 42f **RR 45f** 4458[2]
4 b g Safawan 6.6f **(60)** - Heresheis (Free State) 8.7f **(61)**
Pre1998 - 1st:0 2nd:0 3rd:0 Ran:6
Win Prizemoney £2,994 *Total Prizemoney* £4,736
Wins * **1998** Aug Catter (G-F) H 15.8f 35 38+ <
1998 Turf 1-10: (14f 2, 15f 2, 16f 1-5, 17f) (sft, g-s 2, gd 2, g-f, frm 1-4)
Rangy, moderate gelding, effective 16f, acts on gd to frm, best on frm, has worn blinkers (very effectively), likes tight tracks. Turf high 45 - 2nd of 16 getting 7lb from Danegold (24 Spt Goodwood 16f frm RF 4458) - also 1st of 7 getting 1lb from Es Go (14 Aug Catterick RF 3623). He showed signs of ability at two, but then became very disappointing before managing to find a particularly poor Catterick maiden in August. He will be fortunate to find another race quite as bad. *J Pearce [1-16] Michael Whatley.*

PERTINO BHB 59f **RR 61f** 4503[9]
2 b g Terimon 8.7f **(58)** - Persian Fountain (IRE) (Persian Heights)
Form - 050
Record 1998 - 1st:0 2nd:0 3rd:0 Ran:3
1998 Turf 0-3: (6f, 7f, 8f) (frm 3)
Currently average gelding. Turf high 61 (began Aug).
J M Jefferson [0-3] Mrs P Butler, Pryke, Willis & Fouracres.

PERUGINO BAY (IRE) BHB 100f **RR 103f** 4974[2]
2 b c Perugino (USA) - Dublah (USA)(Private Account (USA)) 8.5f **(74)**
Form - 2151430332
Record 1998 - 1st:2 2nd:2 3rd:3 Ran:10
Win Prizemoney £10,203 *Total Prizemoney* £33,075
Wins * **1998** Jly York (FRM) H 5f 103 <
* **1998** Apr Ripon (SFT) 5f 85
1998 Turf 2-10: (5f 2-8, 6f 2) (sft 1-3, gd 3, g-f 2, frm 1-2)
Very useful colt, effective 5 to 6f, best at 6f, acts on sft to frm, best on sft. Turf high 103 - 1st of 7 giving 15lb to Northern Svengali (11 Jly York RF 2740). A credit to Bryan McMahon, this tough juvenile began his campaign at Doncaster in March and finished it back there in a Listed race during November. Beaten just a neck by Two Clubs that day, he goes on any ground or track and never lies

down without a fight. **B A McMahon [2-10] J C Fretwell.*

PERUSING (IRE) BHB 99f **RR 98f** 4964[5]

2 b c Perugino (USA) - Sweet Reprieve (Shirley Heights) 10.3f **(74)**
Form - 45115
Record 1998 - 1st:2 2nd:0 3rd:0 Ran:5
Win Prizemoney £10,974 *Total Prizemoney* £11,454
Wins * **1998** Oct York (GD) 7f 98+ <
* **1998** Spt Beverl (G-F) 7.5f 83+
1998 Turf 2-5: (6f, 7f 2-4) (sft, gd, frm 2-3)
Very useful colt. Turf high 98 (began Aug) - 1st of 3 getting 3lb from Mini Lodge (8 Oct York RF 4706). Showed promise in hot maidens before getting off the mark. Failed to handle a step up in class in testing ground on his final start.
**L M Cumani [2-5] Mrs V Shelton.*

PESCARA (IRE) **RR 99f** 3916a[5]

2 b f Common Grounds 8.1f **(66)** - Mackla (Caerleon (USA)) 8.6f **(71)**
Form - 35
1998 Turf 0-2: (6f 2) (sft, frm)
Currently very useful filly. Turf high 99 (1st run) (began Jly) - 3rd of 10 to Wannabe Grand (7 Jly Newmarket 6f frm RF 2580). Won on her second start at Maisons-Laffitte before finishing third in the Cherry Hinton and fifth in the Prix Morny.
**Mme C Head in FR [0-2] G A Oldham.*

PESHTIGO (USA) **RR 82f** 4541[5]

2 b c Kris S (USA) 9.3f **(76)** - Fume (USA) (Secretariat (USA)) 9f **(79)**
Form - 55
Record 1998 - 1st:0 2nd:0 3rd:0 Ran:2
1998 Turf 0-2: (7f, 8f) (g-f, frm)
Currently decent colt. Turf high 82 (began Spt).
**B W Hills [0-2] Maktoum Al Maktoum.*

PETAK (IRE) BHB 40f **RR 37f** 4878[9]

2 b f Petardia 8.2f **(58)** - Wicken Wonder (IRE) **(56f)** (Distant Relative)
Form - 7000
Record 1998 - 1st:0 2nd:0 3rd:0 Ran:4
1998 Turf 0-3: (5f, 6f, 7f) (gd, g-f, frm) 1998 AW 0-1: (7f) (Fibr)
Very moderate filly. Turf high 37.
**D J S ffrenchDavis [0-4] Miss Henrietta Senn.*

PETANE (IRE) BHB 39f **RR 58f** 5002[14]

3 b g Petardia 8.2f **(58)** - Senane (Vitiges (FR)) 8.2f **(59)**
Form - 0040501030
Record 1998 - 1st:1 2nd:0 3rd:1 Ran:10
Pre1998 - 1st:0 2nd:0 3rd:0 Ran:4
Win Prizemoney £1,725 *Total Prizemoney* £2,256
Wins 1998 Aug Folkes (G-F) S 12f 47 <
1998 Turf 1-9: (10f 4, 12f 1-4, 14f) (gd 2, g-f 1-6, frm) 1998 AW 0-1: (12f) (Equi)
Neat, fair gelding, effective 10f, acts on g-f, often wears blinkers (very effectively). Turf high 60 - 4th of 11 getting 3lb from Konker (27 May Newbury 10f g-f RF 1528).
**L A Dace [0-1] A Rahman (from J R Arnold [1-13] Oct 1998).*

PETARA (IRE) BHB 43f **RR 52f** 4919[12]

3 ch c Petardia 8.2f **(58)** - Romangoddess (IRE) (Rhoman Rule (USA))
Form - 470554260500
Record 1998 - 1st:0 2nd:1 3rd:0 Ran:12
Pre1998 - 1st:1 2nd:0 3rd:3 Ran:12
Win Prizemoney £3,564 *Total Prizemoney* £6,639
Wins * 1997 Spt Catter (G-F) H 7f 60 65 <
1998 Turf 0-12: (7f 2, 8f 7, 9f, 10f, 12f) (g-s, gd 2, g-f 4, frm 5)
Workmanlike, fair colt, effective 6 to 7f, acts on g-f, mostly wears blinkers (effectively), likes left handed tracks, likes tight tracks. Turf high 52. His victory in a Catterick nursery has been his only success in a busy career to date. **J S Wainwright [1-24] J H Pickard.*

PETARGA BHB 77f **RR 76f** 4596[3]

3 b f Petong 7.6f **(58)** - One Half Silver (CAN) (Plugged Nickle (USA)) 7.8f **(68)**
Form - 30643
Record 1998 - 1st:0 2nd:0 3rd:2 Ran:5
Pre1998 - 1st:1 2nd:1 3rd:0 Ran:5
Win Prizemoney £2,917 *Total Prizemoney* £6,064
Wins * 1997 Jun Bath (G-F) 5.1f 72 <
1998 Turf 0-5: (5f 2, 6f 3) (gd, g-f 2, frm 2)
Neat, above-average filly, effective 5 to 6f, best at 5f, acts on g-f to frm, best on g-f. Turf high 81 (1st run) - 3rd of 13 giving 8lb to Double Brandy (16 May Newbury 6f frm RF 1261).
**J A R Toller [1-10] Mrs R W Gore-Andrews.*

PETER PERFECT BHB 45f46a **RR 57df 46a** 4775[15]

4 gr g Chilibang 7f **(55)** - Misdevious (USA) (Alleged (USA)) 10f **(76)**
Form - 00
Record 1998 - 1st:0 2nd:0 3rd:0 Ran:2
Pre1998 - 1st:0 2nd:3 3rd:1 Ran:12
Win Prizemoney £0 *Total Prizemoney* £3,186
1998 Turf 0-1: (7f) (gd) 1998 AW 0-1: (6f) (Fibr)
Scopey, fair gelding, effective 7f, acts on frm, often wears blinkers (effectively), likes tight tracks. Becoming disappointing.
**Mrs S Lamyman [0-2] P Lamyman (from R Curtis [0-2] Spt 1997).*

PETER QUINCE BHB 60f **RR 29f** 4704[22]

8 b h Kris 10f **(75)** - Our Reverie (USA) (J O Tobin (USA)) 9.4f **(67)**
Form - 0
Record 1998 - 1st:0 2nd:0 3rd:0 Ran:1
Pre1998 - 1st:3 2nd:2 3rd:2 Ran:12
Win Prizemoney £20,302 *Total Prizemoney* £27,624
Wins 1994 Jun Beverl (G-F) 12f 108+ <
1994 Apr Pontef (SFT) 10f 105
1998 Turf 0-1: (12f) (frm)
Little account horse. Becoming disappointing.
**M Brittain [0-3] Mel Brittain (from H R A Cecil [3-10] Jun 1994).*

PETER'S IMP (IRE) BHB 68f64a **RR 75f 64a** 4636[9]

3 b g Imp Society (USA) 7.1f **(63)** - Catherine Clare (Sallust) 8.4f **(63)**
Form - 008312060
Record 1998 - 1st:1 2nd:1 3rd:1 Ran:9
Pre1998 - 1st:1 2nd:0 3rd:3 Ran:7
Win Prizemoney £7,067 *Total Prizemoney* £9,559
Wins * **1998** Jly Haydoc (G-F) 7.1f 68
* 1997 Aug Newcas (G-F) H 6f 77 81 <
1998 Turf 1-8: (6f 2, 7f 1-5, 8f) (g-s, gd 2, g-f 1-2, frm 2, hrd) 1998 AW 0-1: (7f) (Fibr)
Scopey, above-average gelding, effective 6 to 7f, best at 6f, acts on gd to hrd, has worn blinkers (extremely effectively). Turf high 75 - 3rd of 10 giving 1lb to Ray of Sunshine (1 Jly Redcar 6f gd RF 2450). **J Berry [2-16] & Mrs Peter Foden.*

PET EXPRESS BHB 58f56a **RR 60f 56a** 284[P]

4 b g Petoski 10.4f **(56)** - Hush it Up (Tina's Pet) 6.8f **(59)**
Form - 065P
Record 1998 - 1st:0 2nd:0 3rd:0 Ran:3
Pre1998 - 1st:3 2nd:2 3rd:1 Ran:14
Win Prizemoney £8,282 *Total Prizemoney* £10,647
Wins * *1997 Jan Southw (STD) H 6f 52 56+* <
* *1997 Jan Southw (STD) H 6f 44 48*
* *1997 Jan Southw (STD) H 7f 30 38*
1998 AW 0-3: (6f 2, 8f) (Fibr 3)
Workmanlike, average gelding, has broken blood-vessels, effective 6 to 7f, best at 7f, acts on gd to g-f - acts on Fibr. AW high 47. Inconsistent. **P C Haslam [3-17] Pet Express (W&R) Ltd.*

PET EXPRESS FLYER (IRE) BHB 90f **RR 92f** 4960[8]

2 b c Mukaddamah (USA) 7.6f **(74)** - Take The Option (USA) (Bold Bidder) 8.8f **(67)**
Form - 3121310838
Record 1998 - 1st:3 2nd:1 3rd:3 Ran:10
Win Prizemoney £8,509 *Total Prizemoney* £11,233
Wins * **1998** Jly Ayr (GD) H 7f 92 <
* **1998** Jun Mussel (G-F) 7.1f 72+
* **1998** Jun Hamilt (GD) 6f 78
1998 Turf 3-10: (5f, 6f 1-3, 7f 2-4, 8f 2) (g-s 2, gd 1-2, g-f 1-3, frm 1-3)
Useful colt, effective 7 to 8f, acts on gd to g-f. Turf high 92 - 3rd of 20 getting 1lb from Fair Flight (16 Oct Newmarket 8f g-f RF 4845) - also 1st of 7 giving 23lb to Dispol Safa (13 Jly Ayr RF 2755). A tough and genuine juvenile, he was very consistent in his first six starts, including winning three small races in Scotland. He did not run quite as well afterwards, except for when finishing a fine third in a valuable Newmarket nursery in October.
**P C Haslam [3-10] Pet Express (W&R) Ltd.*

PETITE DANSEUSE BHB 47f44a **RR 50f 44a** 4775[6]
4 b f Aragon 7.7f **(58)** - Let Her Dance (USA) (Sovereign Dancer (USA)) 11.2f **(68)**
Form - 5550764037734703204 56
Record 1998 - 1st:0 2nd:1 3rd:3 Ran:19
Pre1998 - 1st:4 2nd:5 3rd:4 Ran:29
Win Prizemoney £13,515 *Total Prizemoney* £25,503
Wins 1997 Spt Leices (G-F) C 6f 61
1997 Aug Leices (GD) C 7f 59+
1996 May Windso (GD) 5f 75 <
1996 May Bath (G-F) 5.1f 72
1998 Turf 0-13: (5f 2, 6f 7, 7f 4) (g-s 2, gd 5, g-f 2, frm 4) 1998 AW 0-6: (6f 5, 7f) (Equi, Fibr 5)
Neat, fair filly, effective 6f, acts on frm - acts on Equi, has worn blinkers. Turf high 58. AW high 48. Consistent.
**D W Chapman [0-22] T S Redman (from C A Dwyer [2-14] Spt 1997).*

PETITE LADY BHB 40f **RR 44f** 453[11]
3 b f Noble Patriarch 12.2f **(43)** - Rough Guess (IRE) (Believe It (USA)) 9.4f **(70)**
Form - 0
Record 1998 - 1st:0 2nd:0 3rd:0 Ran:1
Pre1998 - 1st:0 2nd:0 3rd:0 Ran:2
Win Prizemoney £0 *Total Prizemoney* £199
1998 AW 0-1: (6f) (Fibr)
Light-framed, currently moderate filly. **P D Evans [0-3] R F F Mason.*

PETITE SABO RR 22f 476[10]
2 b f Prince Sabo 6.6f **(64)** - La Reine de France (Queen's Hussar) 11.6f **(58)**
Form - 0
Record 1998 - 1st:0 2nd:0 3rd:0 Ran:1
1998 Turf 0-1: (5f) (gd)
Currently little account filly. **M Brittain [0-1] Northgate Silver.*

PETIT PALAIS (IRE) RR 44f 4327[21]
2 gr c Paris House 5.9f **(64)**-Renzola(Dragonara Palace(USA)) 6.1f **(55)**
Form - 0
Record 1998 - 1st:0 2nd:0 3rd:0 Ran:1
1998 Turf 0-1: (7f) (g-f)
Currently moderate colt. **B J Meehan [0-1] Ted Voute.*

PETIT VERSAILLES (FR) RR 104f 836a[3]
3 gr c Gairloch - Chakini (FR) (Dom Pasquini (FR))
Form - 33
1998 Turf 0-2: (10f, 11f) (hvy, gd)
Currently very useful colt. Turf high 104 - 3rd of 5 to Croco Rouge (19 Apr Longchamp 11f hvy RF 0836a). He seems a little one-paced, but is honest and ran well behind Croco Rouge at Longchamp in April. **Jean-Marc Capitte in FR [0-2] J de Cock.*

PETOSKIN BHB 40f54a **RR 47f 54a** 4879[8]
6 b g Petoski 10.4f **(56)** - Farcical (Pharly (FR)) 9.8f **(68)**
Form - 483174030043088
Record 1998 - 1st:1 2nd:0 3rd:3 Ran:13
Pre1998 - 1st:9 2nd:2 3rd:4 Ran:38
Win Prizemoney £24,562 *Total Prizemoney* £31,864
Wins * 1998 *Jan Wolver (STD) H 14.8f 62 66*
* 1997 Jly Bath (G-F) S 11.7f 52
* 1997 *Jun Wolver (STD) C 16.2f 63*
* 1997 *May Lingfi (STD) C 16f 68* <
* 1997 Apr Bright (FRM) C 11.9f 55
* 1997 *Feb Wolver (STD) C 14.8f 68* <
* 1996 *Dec Wolver (STD) S 14.8f 66*
* 1996 *Nov Wolver (STD) C 14.8f 67*
* 1996 Oct Yarmou (G-F) SH 11.5f 50 58
1994 Apr Kempto (G-S) 5f 66
1998 Turf 0-4: (12f 2, 14f, 16f) (g-f, frm 3) 1998 AW 1-9: (14f, 15f 1-3, 16f 5) (Equi, Fibr 1-8)
Average gelding, effective 15 to 16f, best at 16f, - acts on AW, best on Equi, has worn blinkers, likes left handed tracks, favours tight tracks, and excels at Lingfield. Turf high 47 (began Jly). AW high 66 - 1st of 10 getting 3lb from Premier Dance (14 Jan Wolverhampton RF 0087). Normally a real force in modest staying events on sand, he has run very poorly since winning at Wolverhampton in January, and should be avoided until showing some of his old sparkle.
**J Pearce [9-42] Mrs Jean Routledge (from R Hannon [1-9] Oct 1994).*

PETRACO (IRE) BHB 43f42a **RR 46f 42a** 4093[10]
10 b g Petorius 8f **(66)** - Merrie Moira (Bold Lad (IRE)) 8.4f **(68)**
Form - 0354285100020
Record 1998 - 1st:1 2nd:2 3rd:1 Ran:13
Pre1998 - 1st:8 2nd:6 3rd:10 Ran:104
Win Prizemoney £29,738 *Total Prizemoney* £44,136
Wins * 1998 Jly Salisb (GD) CH 6f 42 45
* 1996 Spt Haydoc (GD) SH 6f 56 60
* 1995 Aug Pontef (G-F) H 5f 59 63
* 1995 Jun Leices (GD) SH 6f 55 62
1998 Turf 1-11: (5f 4, 6f 1-6, 7f) (gd, g-f 4, frm 1-6) 1998 AW 0-2: (6f 2) (Fibr 2)
Moderate gelding, effective 5 to 6f, acts on gd to frm, has worn blinkers. Turf high 46. AW high 43.
**N A Smith [6-83] Mrs Penny Day (from L J Codd [3-35] May 1993).*

PETRA NOVA BHB 55f **RR 58f** 4937[12]
2 ch f First Trump - Spinner (Blue Cashmere) 6.4f **(54)**
Form - 2000
Record 1998 - 1st:0 2nd:1 3rd:0 Ran:4
Win Prizemoney £0 *Total Prizemoney* £1,493
1998 Turf 0-4: (5f 3, 6f) (gd 3, g-f)
Fair filly. Turf high 51. **R M Whitaker [0-4] Mrs Margaret Schofield.*

PETREIO RR 5131a[3]
2 ch c Salse (USA) 10.9f **(71)** - Pear Drop (Bustino) 10.4f **(64)**
Form - 3
Record 1998 - 1st:0 2nd:0 3rd:1 Ran:1
Win Prizemoney £0 *Total Prizemoney* £1,650
1998 Turf 0-1: (9f) (sft)
Currently very poor colt. **Miss Gay Kelleway [0-1].*

PETROVNA (IRE) RR 76f 4538[13]
2 ch f Petardia 8.2f **(58)** - Efficient Funding (IRE) (Entitled)
Form - 51520
Record 1998 - 1st:1 2nd:1 3rd:0 Ran:5
Win Prizemoney £3,290 *Total Prizemoney* £4,370
Wins * 1998 Aug Windso (G-F) 5f 76 <
1998 Turf 1-5: (5f 1-2, 6f 2, 7f) (gd, frm 3, hrd 1-1)
Above-average filly. Turf high 76 (began Aug) - 1st of 13 getting 7lb from Dangerous Dancer (17 Aug Windsor RF 3686). She looked good when winning a maiden auction event at Windsor on her second start, but has been well beaten otherwise.
**P L Gilligan [1-5] Dr Susan Barnes.*

PETRUS (IRE) BHB 78f **RR 84f** 4891[6]
2 b c Perugino (USA) - Love With Honey (USA) (Full Pocket (USA)) 14.1f **(61)**
Form - 6886
Record 1998 - 1st:0 2nd:0 3rd:0 Ran:4
Win Prizemoney £0 *Total Prizemoney* £253
1998 Turf 0-4: (6f 2, 7f 2) (gd, g-f, frm 2)
Decent colt. Turf high 84 (began Aug). **C E Brittain [0-4] C E Brittain.*

PETTY FRANCE (IRE) RR 71f 3664[2]
2 b br f Petardia 8.2f **(58)** - Business Centre (IRE) (Digamist (USA))
Form - 2
Record 1998 - 1st:0 2nd:1 3rd:0 Ran:1
Win Prizemoney £0 *Total Prizemoney* £1,002
1998 Turf 0-1: (6f) (frm)
Currently above-average filly. (1st run) - 2nd of 7 to Precocious Miss (16 Aug Lingfield 6f frm RF 3664).
**J A R Toller [0-1] Racing Options.*

PETUCHINO (IRE) BHB 64f **RR 63f** 4813[6]
2 b f Petardia 8.2f **(58)** - Cappuchino (IRE) **(59a)** (Roi Danzig (USA))
Form - 033786
Record 1998 - 1st:0 2nd:0 3rd:2 Ran:6
Win Prizemoney £0 *Total Prizemoney* £836
1998 Turf 0-6: (5f 5, 6f) (g-s 2, gd 2, g-f, frm)
Average filly. Turf high 63. Not beaten far in most of her races, she was sold for 5,000 gns at Tattersalls in October, reportedly to a German buyer. **R F JohnsonHoughton [0-6] Woodway Racing.*

PETUNTSE BHB 46f **RR 48+f** 1720[1]
4 b g Phountzi (USA) 9.6f **(60)** - Alipampa (IRE) (Glenstal (USA)) 10.1f **(64)**
Form - 4621
Record 1998 - 1st:1 2nd:1 3rd:0 Ran:4
Pre1998 - 1st:0 2nd:0 3rd:1 Ran:5
Win Prizemoney £2,250 *Total Prizemoney* £3,265
Wins * **1998** Jun Yarmou (G-F) SH 8f 38 48+ <
1998 Turf 1-3: (7f, 8f 1-1, 10f) (gd, frm 1-2) 1998 AW 0-1: (8f) (Fibr)
Lengthy, moderate gelding, effective 8 to 10f, acts on frm, has worn blinkers. Turf high 48 - also 1st of 19 getting 22lb from Severity (4 Jun Yarmouth RF 1720). Consistent.
**J Pearce [1-4] T H Rossiter (from J G Smyth-Osbourne [0-5] Oct 1997).*

PETURA (IRE) BHB 64f **RR 73f** 4151[4]
2 br g Petardia 8.2f **(58)** - Roman Heights (IRE) (Head for Heights) 9.6f **(55)**
Form - 4044
Record 1998 - 1st:0 2nd:0 3rd:0 Ran:4
Win Prizemoney £0 *Total Prizemoney* £598
1998 Turf 0-4: (6f 2, 7f, 8f) (g-f 2, frm 2)
Above-average gelding. Turf high 73.
**J S Wainwright [0-4] J H Pickard.*

PHANTOM RING BHB 58f60a **RR 56f 60a** 4757[4]
3 ch f Magic Ring (IRE) 6.5f **(64)** - Follow the Stars (Sparkler) 8.4f **(55)**
Form - 252222000104
Record 1998 - 1st:1 2nd:3 3rd:0 Ran:9
Pre1998 - 1st:0 2nd:2 3rd:0 Ran:7
Win Prizemoney £3,692 *Total Prizemoney* £8,641
Wins * **1998** Spt Beverl (G-F) 5f 56 <
1998 Turf 1-4:(5f 1-4)(sft, gd 1-3)1998 AW 0-5: (5f 4, 6f) (Equi 2, Fibr 3)
Average filly, effective 5f, - acts on Fibr. Turf high 56 (began Spt). AW high 65 - 2nd of 7 giving 14lb to Dahlidya (18 Feb Wolverhampton 5f Fibr RF 0310). Inconsistent.
**A Bailey [1-16] Ray Bailey.*

PHANTOM THREEONINE BHB 38f **RR 48f** 3995[8]
2 ch f Hatim (USA) 7.8f **(56)** - Glenrock Dancer (IRE) **(32f)** (Glenstal (USA)) 10.1f **(64)**
Form - 0846P768
Record 1998 - 1st:0 2nd:0 3rd:0 Ran:8
1998 Turf 0-8: (5f 3, 6f 4, 7f) (g-s 2, gd 3, g-f 2, hrd)
Moderate filly, has worn blinkers. Turf high 48.
**W T Kemp [0-8] A J Thurgood.*

PHANTOM WATERS BHB 73f **RR 76f** 4194[14]
3 b f Pharly (FR) 11.5f **(64)** - Idle Waters (Mill Reef (USA)) 10.5f **(78)**
Form - 441221680
Record 1998 - 1st:2 2nd:2 3rd:0 Ran:9
Pre1998 - 1st:0 2nd:0 3rd:0 Ran:6
Win Prizemoney £10,260 *Total Prizemoney* £12,962
Wins * **1998** Jly Bright (GD) H 11.9f 74 76 <
* **1998** May Chepst (G-F) H 12.1f 63 68
1998 Turf 2-9: (10f, 12f 2-7, 14f) (gd 1-4, g-f, frm 1-4)
Workmanlike, above-average filly, effective 12f, acts on gd to frm, prefers tight tracks. Turf high 76 - 1st of 7 getting 9lb from Danesman (13 Jly Brighton RF 2763) - also 1st of 8 getting 19lb from Venetian Scene (25 May Chepstow RF 1445). Consistent early in the season, including wins over twelve furlongs at Chepstow and Brighton, her subsequent modest efforts can probably be put down to either softer ground or a longer trip.
**R F JohnsonHoughton [2-15] R Crutchley.*

PHARAOH'S JOY BHB 54f58a **RR 57f 58a** 3208[17]
5 b m Robellino (USA) 9.5f **(68)** - Joyce's Best (Tolomeo) 5.6f **(60)**
Form - 001053253450
Record 1998 - 1st:1 2nd:1 3rd:2 Ran:10
Pre1998 - 1st:3 2nd:1 3rd:5 Ran:27
Win Prizemoney £11,865 *Total Prizemoney* £17,108
Wins * **1998** *May Southw (STD) H 5f 49 56*
1996 Aug Yarmou (G-F) H 5.2f 58 60
1996 Jun Carlis (FRM) H 5f 51 58
1995 Jly Nottin (G-F) 6.1f 67 <
1998 Turf 0-3:(5f, 6f 2)(gd, frm 2)1998 AW1-7:(5f 1-3, 6f 3, 7f) (Fibr 1-7)
Average filly, effective 5 to 6f, best at 5f, acts on frm - acts on Fibr, has worn blinkers. Turf high 57 - 5th of 11 getting 12lb from Positive Air (29 Jun Pontefract 6f frm RF 2377). AW high 61 - 2nd of 12 getting 1lb from Desert Invader (20 Jun Wolverhampton 6f Fibr RF 2161) - also 1st of 12 giving 10lb to Super Geil (7 May Southwell RF 1086).
**A G Newcombe [1-15] M Patel (from J W Payne [3-22] Aug 1997).*

PHARATTA (IRE) RR 111f 3421a[4]
3 b f Fairy King (USA) 7.7f **(75)** - Sharata (IRE) (Darshaan) 9.9f **(84)**
Form - 1414
1998 Turf 2-4: (8f 1-3, 12f 1-1) (sft 1-1, gd 1-3)
Group-class filly. Turf high 111 - 1st of 10 from Soeur Ti (31 May Chantilly RF 1735a). She had only just recovered from an abscess on her foot when finishing fourth in the Poule d'Essai des Pouliches (French 1,000 Guineas), and made no mistake when winning a Group Three at Chantilly later in May. This useful filly is definitely worth trying beyond a mile.
**C Laffon-Parias in FR [2-4] D Hinojosa.*

PHAR CLOSER BHB 23f **RR 29?f** 629[9]
5 br m Phardante (FR) 12.8f **(46)** - Forever Together (Hawaiian Return (USA))
Form - 0
Record 1998 - 1st:0 2nd:0 3rd:0 Ran:1
Pre1998 - 1st:0 2nd:1 3rd:3 Ran:12
Win Prizemoney £0 *Total Prizemoney* £2,010
1998 Turf 0-1: (16f) (gd)
Little account filly, has worn blinkers. **W T Kemp [0-16] W T Kemp.*

PHAREEKH RR 78tf 4058[7]
2 b c Caerleon (USA) 10.9f **(79)** - Sephala (USA) (Mr Prospector (USA)) 8.8f **(78)**
Form - 47
Record 1998 - 1st:0 2nd:0 3rd:0 Ran:2
Win Prizemoney £0 *Total Prizemoney* £652
1998 Turf 0-2: (7f 2) (g-f, frm)
Currently above-average colt. Turf high 78 (1st run) (began Aug) - 4th of 5 giving 5lb to Valentine Girl (14 Aug Newbury 7f g-f RF 3631). Started odds-on for a listed race on his debut but finished only fourth of five, and found little under pressure on his second run. A half-brother to the useful stayer Brier Creek, she might do better in time. **D R Loder [0-2] Sheikh Mohammed.*

PHARLY DANCER BHB 38f54a **RR 37f 54a** 1739[3]
9 b g Pharly (FR) 11.5f **(64)** - Martin-Lavell Mail (Dominion) 8.5f **(63)**
Form - 1340420553
Record 1998 - 1st:0 2nd:1 3rd:1 Ran:7
Pre1998 - 1st:12 2nd:9 3rd:8 Ran:49
Win Prizemoney £33,752 *Total Prizemoney* £44,934
Wins 1997 *Nov Southw (STD) H 14f 52 57*
1996 *Dec Southw (SLW) C 14f 68*
1996 *Nov Wolver (STD) C 12f 67*
1996 Jly Haydoc (GD) C 11.9f 57
1996 Jly Catter (G-F) C 12f 63
1996 *Jun Southw (STD) C 14f 65*
1995 Apr Catter (GD) H 12f 56 62
1995 *Mar Southw (STD) H 12f 79 77*
1995 *Jan Southw (STD) H 12f 67 78* <
1995 *Jan Southw (STD) H 12f 67 70*
1994 *Nov Southw (STD) C 14f 65+*
1998 Turf 0-3: (12f, 13f, 14f) (sft, g-s, gd) 1998 AW 0-4: (14f 2, 16f 2) (Fibr 4)
Fair gelding, effective 12 to 16f, best at 14f, - acts on Fibr, has worn blinkers, favours left handed tracks. Turf high 37. AW high 57 - 2nd of 7 getting 12lb from Jaraab (9 Mar Southwell 14f Fibr RF 0412). Fourteen-furlong Southwell claimers look to be his cup of tea these days.
**J Hetherton [0-7] A Marucci (from W W Haigh [12-49] Dec 1997).*

PHASE EIGHT GIRL BHB 37f **RR 36f** 4671[27]
2 b f Warrshan (USA) 9.7f **(59)** - Bugsy's Sister (Aragon) 8.1f **(60)**
Form - 0060
Record 1998 - 1st:0 2nd:0 3rd:0 Ran:4
1998 Turf 0-4: (5f 2, 6f, 7f) (gd 2, g-f, frm)
Very moderate filly. Turf high 36 (began Aug).
**J Hetherton [0-4] Peter Urquhart.*

PHAYUHA KIRI LOVE RR 23f 2009[21]
3 b c Pursuit of Love 9.5f **(69)** - My Moody Girl (IRE) (Alzao (USA)) 7.1f **(68)**
Form - 40
Record 1998 - 1st:0 2nd:0 3rd:0 Ran:2
Win Prizemoney £0 *Total Prizemoney* £251
1998 Turf 0-2: (10f 2) (gd, frm)
Strong, currently little account colt. Turf high 23.
**A G Newcombe [0-2] Roger Johns.*

PHEBUS (FR) RR 96f 1914a[3]
3 b c Last Tycoon 9.4f **(73)** - Consolation (Troy) 10.4f **(68)**
Form - 3
1998 Turf 0-1: (13f) (sft)
Currently very useful colt. (1st run) - 3rd of 6 to Epistolaire (6 Jun Maisons-laffitte 13f sft RF 1914a). **P Bary in FR [0-1] J-L Bouchard.*

PHILATELIC LADY (IRE) RR 75f 4389[6]
2 ch f Pips Pride 6.7f **(70)** - Gold Stamp (Golden Act (USA)) 8.8f **(67)**
Form - 06
Record 1998 - 1st:0 2nd:0 3rd:0 Ran:2
1998 Turf 0-2: (6f, 7f) (gd, frm)
Currently above-average filly. Turf high 75 (began Spt).
**M J Haynes [0-2] Bob Pettis, Gordon F Haynes.*

PHILGEM BHB 17f19a **RR 17f 19a** 4838[12]
5 b m Precocious 7.2f **(54)** - Andalucia (Rheingold) 10.4f **(62)**
Form - 7880
Record 1998 - 1st:0 2nd:0 3rd:0 Ran:4
Pre1998 - 1st:1 2nd:0 3rd:2 Ran:24
Win Prizemoney £2,458 *Total Prizemoney* £3,684
Wins 1997 May Hamilt (SFT) SH 11.1f 27 28 <
1998 Turf 0-4: (9f, 11f, 12f, 16f) (g-s, gd 2, g-f)
Poor filly, effective 11 to 12f, acts on gd to g-f, has worn blinkers, likes right handed tracks. Turf high 17 (began Aug).
**T A K Cuthbert [0-4] T A K Cuthbert (from C W Fairhurst [1-20] Spt 1997).*

PHILISTAR BHB 77f71a **RR 81f 71a** 4822[10]
5 ch h Bairn (USA) 9.4f **(55)** - Philgwyn (Milford) 9f **(61)**
Form - 3713144D106P0743200
Record 1998 - 1st:3 2nd:1 3rd:3 Ran:19
Pre1998 - 1st:5 2nd:3 3rd:3 Ran:30
Win Prizemoney £57,053 *Total Prizemoney* £72,059
Wins * **1998** Jun Epsom (GD) H 8.5f 75 81 <
* **1998** *Apr Lingfi (STD) H 7f 67 71*
* **1998** *Feb Lingfi (SLW) 7f 70*
* 1997 Jun Bright (FRM) 10f 70
* 1997 Jun Hamilt (GD) H 8.3f 60 70
* 1997 Jun Epsom (GD) H 8.5f 65 77
* 1997 Jun Newcas (FRM) 9f 61
1996 *Jly Lingfi (STD) H 10f 60 65*
1998 Turf 1-13: (8f 4, 9f 1-7, 10f 2) (g-s, gd 1-7, g-f, frm 4) 1998 AW 2-6: (7f 2-3, 8f 2, 9f) (Equi 2-5, Fibr)
Decent colt, effective 7 to 10f, best at 9f, acts on gd to frm - acts on Equi, best on g-f, has worn blinkers, likes left handed tracks, likes tight tracks, excels at Epsom and does well at Goodwood. Turf high 81 - 1st of 14 getting 5lb from Secret Spring (5 Jun Epsom RF 1748). AW high 71. Consistent. Shrewdly placed to rattle off a quick four-timer in June '97, he was in good form on the Lingfield Equitrack after new year, including winning twice over seven furlongs. He maintained his good form back on turf, winning a valuable handicap at Epsom in game fashion. Held since, although was runing well at the end of the season.
**K R Burke [7-32] Nigel Shields (from J M P Eustace [1-17] May 1997).*

PHILMIST BHB 42f42a **RR 57f 42a** 4754[7]
6 b m Hard Fought 8.9f **(51)** - Andalucia (Rheingold) 10.4f **(62)**
Form - 53615007
Record 1998 - 1st:1 2nd:0 3rd:1 Ran:7
Pre1998 - 1st:5 2nd:6 3rd:4 Ran:44
Win Prizemoney £16,514 *Total Prizemoney* £25,257
Wins * **1998** Aug Hamilt (SFT) S 12.1f 47+
* 1997 Spt Ayr (G-S) H 10.9f 45 50 <
* 1997 Aug Hamilt (GD) H 11.1f 40 48
* 1997 Jly Hamilt (G-S) H 11.1f 40 40
1996 *May Southw (STD) H 11f 48 50* <
1995 *Jly Southw (STD) H 12f 48 49*
1998 Turf 1-7: (10f, 11f 2, 12f 1-2, 13f 2) (sft, gd 1-6)
Fair mare, effective 11 to 15f, best at 15f, acts on g-s to frm - acts on Fibr, mostly wears blinkers (very effectively), and excels at Wolverhampton. Turf high 57. Becoming disappointing.
**Miss L A Perratt [4-21] C D Barber-Lomax (from J Hetherton [0-9] Feb 1997).*

PHILOSOPHIC BHB 49f72a **RR 51f 72a** 4887[9]
4 b g Be My Chief (USA) 10.2f **(62)** - Metaphysique (FR) (Law Society (USA)) 9.9f **(70)**
Form - 3111864312010120
Record 1998 - 1st:6 2nd:2 3rd:2 Ran:16
Pre1998 - 1st:0 2nd:2 3rd:1 Ran:9
Win Prizemoney £16,612 *Total Prizemoney* £21,417
Wins * **1998** Spt Folkes (G-F) H 15.4f 46 48
* **1998** *Aug Lingfi (STD) H 16f 69 73* <
* **1998** *Jly Wolver (STD) H 14.8f 66 69*
* **1998** *Mar Lingfi (SLW) H 16f 53 65*
* **1998** *Feb Lingfi (SLW) H 16f 53 59+*
* **1998** *Jan Lingfi (STD) H 13f 48 49*
1998 Turf 1-8: (12f 2, 14f, 15f 1-2, 16f 2, 17f) (g-s, gd 3, g-f 1-2, frm 2)
1998 AW 5-8: (12f, 13f 1-1, 15f 1-1, 16f 3-5) (Equi 4-6, Fibr 1-2)
Above-average gelding, effective 12 to 16f, - acts on AW, best on Fibr, prefers left handed tracks, excels at Wolverhampton and Lingfield. Turf high 51. AW high 74 - 2nd of 12 getting 5lb from Primary Colours (3 Oct Wolverhampton 12f Fibr RF 4638) - also 1st of 14 giving 29lb to Sheltered Cove (22 Aug Lingfield RF 3811). Inconsistent. Not many stay was well as him on the artificial surfaces.
**Mrs L C Jewell [6-16] Gallagher Equine Ltd (from Sir Mark Prescott [0-9] Oct 1997).*

PHILSUN RR 35f 4325[7]
2 ch f Ardkinglass 5f **(64)** - Andalucia (Rheingold) 10.4f **(62)**
Form - 7
Record 1998 - 1st:0 2nd:0 3rd:0 Ran:1
1998 Turf 0-1: (7f) (gd)
Very moderate filly. (DEAD) **J Hetherton [0-1] C D Barber-Lomax.*

PHOENIX PRINCESS BHB 47f50a **RR 54f 50a** 5127[4]
4 b f Nomination 7.3f **(57)** - Princess Poquito (Hard Fought) 8.8f **(62)**
Form - 107400820404
Record 1998 - 1st:0 2nd:1 3rd:0 Ran:9
Pre1998 - 1st:2 2nd:1 3rd:3 Ran:13
Win Prizemoney £4,571 *Total Prizemoney* £7,504
Wins 1997 *Nov Southw (STD) H 6f 55 58* <
1997 *Jly Southw (STD) H 8f 49 50*
1998 Turf 0-5: (6f 3, 7f 2) (g-s 2, gd 2, frm) 1998 AW 0-4: (6f, 7f 2, 8f) (Fibr 4)
Scopey, fair filly, effective 6 to 8f, best at 6f, acts on g-s to gd - acts on Fibr, has worn blinkers (effectively). Turf high 57 - 2nd of 8 getting 3lb from Shifting Time (13 Jun Leicester 6f gd RF 1964). AW high 31.
**Miss Gay Kelleway [0-9] F L Ho (from B A McMahon [2-13] Nov 1997).*

PHONETIC BHB 66f **RR 70df** 1751[17]
5 b g Shavian 7.7f **(67)** - So True (So Blessed) 8.7f **(67)**
Form - 400
Record 1998 - 1st:0 2nd:0 3rd:0 Ran:3
Pre1998 - 1st:1 2nd:0 3rd:1 Ran:13
Win Prizemoney £7,782 *Total Prizemoney* £9,050
Wins * 1997 May Newbur (SFT) H 8f 71 77 <
1998 Turf 0-3: (9f, 10f 2) (sft, gd, frm)
Above-average gelding, effective 8 to 10f, acts on sft to gd. Turf high 70 (1st run) - 4th of 16 giving 16lb to Mr Fortywinks (20 Apr Nottingham 10f sft RF 0775). Inconsistent.
**G B Balding [1-16] Miss B Swire.*

PHUKET PARK BHB 48f48a **RR 54f 48a** 4473[8]
2 gr f Petong 7.6f **(58)** - Peace In The Park (IRE) (Ahonoora) 8.1f **(73)**
Form - 4458
Record 1998 - 1st:0 2nd:0 3rd:0 Ran:4
1998 Turf 0-3: (6f 3) (g-f 3) 1998 AW 0-1: (7f) (Fibr)
Fair filly, has worn blinkers. Turf high 54 (began Aug).
**Sir Mark Prescott [0-4] J R Newton.*

PHYLOZZO BHB 40f **RR 41f** 4612[14]
2 ch f Michelozzo (USA) - Phyllida Fox (Healaugh Fox) 10f **(46)**
Form - 50
Record 1998 - 1st:0 2nd:0 3rd:0 Ran:2
1998 Turf 0-2: (5f, 6f) (g-s, frm)
Currently moderate filly. Turf high 41 (began Spt).
**P D Evans [0-2] Mrs C W Middleton.*

PIAF BHB 65f **RR 64df** 4189[13]
2 b f Pursuit of Love 9.5f **(69)** - Pippas Song (Reference Point) 6.8f **(70)**

Form - 080
Record 1998 - 1st:0 2nd:0 3rd:0 Ran:3
1998 Turf 0-3: (6f 3) (gd, g-f, frm)
Currently average filly. Turf high 64 (began Aug).
**B W Hills [0-3] S P Tindall.*

PIANIST (IRE) BHB 54f **RR 51f** 2259[8]
3 ch g Balla Cove - Hit For Six (Tap On Wood) 10.3f **(65)**
Form - 658
Record 1998 - 1st:0 2nd:0 3rd:0 Ran:3
Pre1998 - 1st:0 2nd:2 3rd:0 Ran:7
Win Prizemoney £0 *Total Prizemoney* £1,414
1998 Turf 0-3: (10f, 14f, 15f) (g-s, g-f, frm)
Fair gelding, effective 7 to 10f, acts on gd to g-f, has worn blinkers, likes tight tracks. Turf high 51. Consistent.
**Miss K M George [0-2] Exterior Profiles Ltd (from D L Williams [0-1] Jun 1998).*

PICASSO'S HERITAGE BHB 63f **RR 74f** 4230[8]
2 gr c Greensmith - Jane Herring (Nishapour (FR)) 9.1f **(61)**
Form - 8658
Record 1998 - 1st:0 2nd:0 3rd:0 Ran:4
1998 Turf 0-4: (5f 2, 6f, 7f) (g-s, gd, g-f, frm)
Above-average colt. Turf high 74. **M C Pipe [0-4] P M Cain.*

PICCADILLY BHB 35f **RR 34f** 5038[8]
3 ch f Belmez (USA) 11.4f **(65)** - Polly's Pear (USA) (Sassafras (FR)) 9.6f **(69)**
Form - 3306500608
Record 1998 - 1st:0 2nd:0 3rd:2 Ran:10
Pre1998 - 1st:0 2nd:0 3rd:0 Ran:3
Win Prizemoney £0 *Total Prizemoney* £1,227
1998 Turf 0-10: (10f 2, 12f 3, 14f 3, 16f, 18f) (g-s, gd 4, g-f, frm 4)
Workmanlike, very moderate filly, effective 12f, acts on gd, has worn blinkers, likes left handed tracks. Turf high 65 (1st run) - 3rd of 12 giving 7lb to Kilnamartyra Girl (4 May Newcastle 12f gd RF 1025). Consistent. **T J Etherington [0-13] W R Green.*

PICCOLO CATIVO BHB 57f49a **RR 55f 49a** 5142[8]
3 b f Komaite (USA) 6.9f **(61)** - Malcesine (IRE) **(38f 31a)** (Auction Ring (USA)) 8.6f **(65)**
Form - 5000140612042700648
Record 1998 - 1st:2 2nd:2 3rd:0 Ran:17
Pre1998 - 1st:1 2nd:0 3rd:0 Ran:4
Win Prizemoney £9,835 *Total Prizemoney* £11,683
Wins * **1998** Jun Carlis (G-S) H 5f 60 64
* **1998** May Hamilt (GD) H 5f 54 55
1997 *May Southw (STD) 5f 68 <*
1998 Turf 2-14: (5f 2-8, 6f 6) (sft 2, g-s, gd 2-8, g-f, frm 2) 1998 AW 0-3: (5f, 7f 2) (Fibr 3)
Strong, fair filly, effective 5 to 6f, best at 5f, acts on gd - acts on Fibr. Turf high 64 - 1st of 14 getting 5lb from D'Marti (25 Jun Carlisle RF 2264). AW high 26. Consistent.
**Mrs G S Rees [2-16] J W Gittins (from Capt J Wilson [1-5] Jan 1998).*

PICHON BARON (USA) BHB 56f **RR 16f** 5095[9]
3 ch g Zilzal (USA) 8.5f **(79)** - Flora Lady (USA) (Track Barron (USA))
Form - 000
Record 1998 - 1st:0 2nd:0 3rd:0 Ran:3
Pre1998 - 1st:0 2nd:0 3rd:0 Ran:3
Win Prizemoney £0 *Total Prizemoney* £403
1998 Turf 0-3: (8f 2, 11f) (gd 3)
Leggy, poor gelding. Turf high 16 (began Oct). Won two claimers when trained in France, but has been pitched in too high in this country. **M J Ryan [0-3] A S Reid (from B J Meehan [0-3] Oct 1997).*

PICKENS (USA) BHB 60f62a **RR 51f 62a** 440[6]
6 b g Theatrical 11.5f **(78)** - Alchi (USA) (Alleged (USA)) 10f **(76)**
Form - 453221112146
Record 1998 - 1st:4 2nd:3 3rd:0 Ran:9
Pre1998 - 1st:2 2nd:0 3rd:1 Ran:16
Win Prizemoney £13,249 *Total Prizemoney* £15,565
Wins * **1998** *Feb Southw (STD) H 12f 54 66+ <*
* **1998** *Feb Southw (STD) S 11f 52*
* **1998** *Jan Southw (STD) S 11f 53*
* **1998** *Jan Southw (STD) S 12f 55+*
* 1997 Oct Redcar (G-F) C 11f 41
1996 Jly Beverl (G-F) S 12f 52
1998 AW 4-9: (11f 2-4, 12f 2-5) (Fibr 4-9)
Average gelding, effective 11 to 14f, - acts on Fibr, has worn blinkers, favours left handed tracks, favours tight tracks, excels at Southwell. AW high 66 - 1st of 10 getting 3lb from Blooming Amazing (27 Feb Southwell RF 0375). Consistent. He really hit form with a string of victories over middle distances on the Southwell Fibresand at the start of '98, starting off in selling company, and eventually proving successful in much better grade, though he looked to be going off the boil at the end of March.
**Don Enrico Incisa [5-18] Don Enrico Incisa (from N Tinkler [2-16] Nov 1996).*

PICK OF AFFECTION **RR 52f** 5137[8]
2 gr c Salse (USA) 10.9f **(71)** - High Matinee (Shirley Heights) 10.3f **(74)**
Form - 08
Record 1998 - 1st:0 2nd:0 3rd:0 Ran:2
1998 Turf 0-2: (7f, 8f) (g-s, gd)
Currently fair colt. Turf high 52 (began Oct).
**E A L Dunlop [0-2] H R H Sultan Ahmad Shah.*

PICTURE PUZZLE **RR 36f** 5138[12]
2 b f Royal Academy (USA) 7.8f **(77)** - Cloudslea (USA) (Chief's Crown (USA)) 9.8f **(72)**
Form - 0
Record 1998 - 1st:0 2nd:0 3rd:0 Ran:1
1998 Turf 0-1: (7f) (gd)
Currently very moderate filly. **W J Haggas [0-1] M H Wilson.*

PICULA BIERE (IRE) BHB 31f **RR 39f** 3025[7]
3 ch g Balla Cove - Loreo (IRE) (Lord Chancellor (USA))
Form - 6507
Record 1998 - 1st:0 2nd:0 3rd:0 Ran:4
1998 Turf 0-4: (7f, 8f 2, 11f) (gd, g-f 2, frm)
Leggy, very moderate gelding, has worn blinkers. Turf high 39.
**N M Babbage [0-4] St James Racing Club Cheltenham.*

PIERPOINT (IRE) BHB 70f **RR 73f** 4323[10]
3 ch g Archway (IRE) 8.5f **(60)** - Lavinia (Habitat) 9.4f **(70)**
Form - 02720285700
Record 1998 - 1st:0 2nd:3 3rd:0 Ran:11
Pre1998 - 1st:2 2nd:2 3rd:2 Ran:8
Win Prizemoney £6,083 *Total Prizemoney* £13,480
Wins 1997 Jly Hamilt (G-F) H 5f 78 <
1997 Jun Hamilt (G-F) C 5f 69+
1998 Turf 0-11: (5f, 6f 5, 7f 4, 8f) (sft, g-s 2, gd 5, g-f 2, frm)
Scopey, above-average gelding, effective 5 to 8f, best at 5f, acts on gd to frm, best on frm, has worn blinkers, excels at Hamilton. Turf high 75.
**D Nicholls [0-7] John Wilman (from R A Fahey [2-12] Jun 1998).*

PIERRE AUGUSTE (FR) **RR 101f** 2283a[3]
4 b c Saumarez 15.1f **(87)** - Antartica (FR) (Arctic Tern (USA)) 8.9f **(69)**
Form - 3
1998 Turf 0-1: (12f) (sft)
Currently very useful colt. (1st run) - 3rd of 9 getting 3lb from Go Boldly (20 Jun Lyon Parilly 12f sft RF 2283a). He ran creditably in a Listed race at Lyon Parilly during June, but is unlikely to make startling progress. **in FR [0-1].*

PIETRA BHB 43f **RR 56f** 5073[14]
2 b f Puissance 7.1f **(60)** - Femme Formidable (Formidable (USA)) 9.2f **(63)**
Form - 60000
Record 1998 - 1st:0 2nd:0 3rd:0 Ran:5

1998 Turf 0-5: (6f 3, 7f, 8f) (gd 2, g-f, frm 2)
Fair filly. Turf high 56 (began Jly). **P Howling [0-5] P Gwilliam.*

PIGEON BHB 78f **RR 79f** 4872[5]

3 b f Casteddu 7.4f **(54)** - Wigeon (Divine Gift) 6.6f **(57)**
Form - 0702112523770730145

Record	**1998 -**	1st:3	2nd:3	3rd:2	Ran:19
	Pre1998 -	1st:1	2nd:1	3rd:1	Ran:4

Win Prizemoney £12,181 *Total Prizemoney* £19,342

Wins								
	*** 1998**	Spt	Cheste	(GD)	H	5.1f	74	78 <
	*** 1998**	Jun	Catter	(G-S)	H	6f	58	71
	*** 1998**	May	Catter	(SFT)	H	6f	58	71
	* 1997	May	Catter	(G-F)	S	6f		63

1998 Turf 3-18: (5f 1-7, 6f 2-11) (sft, g-s, gd 3-8, g-f 5, frm 3) 1998 AW 0-1: (6f) (Fibr)
Leggy, above-average filly, effective 5 to 6f, best at 5f, acts on gd to frm, best on g-f, likes left handed tracks, likes tight tracks, and does well at Catterick. Turf high 79 - also 1st of 13 getting 11lb from Classy Cleo (23 Spt Chester RF 4450). Speedy front-running sprint handicapper. **D W Barker [4-23] D W Barker.*

PIGGY BANK BHB 72f **RR 68f** 5144[2]

2 b f Emarati (USA) 6.6f **(63)** - Granny's Bank (Music Boy) 6.8f **(57)**
Form - 560470564122

Record	**1998 -**	1st:1	2nd:2	3rd:0	Ran:12

Win Prizemoney £3,517 *Total Prizemoney* £6,363

Wins								
	*** 1998**	Oct	Haydoc	(SFT)	H	5f	60	66 <

1998 Turf 1-12: (5f 1-8, 6f 3, 8f) (sft 1-2, g-s, gd 6, g-f, frm 2)
Average filly, effective 5 to 6f, best at 5f, acts on sft to gd, best on gd. Turf high 68 - 2nd of 20 getting 13lb from Danielle's Lad (6 Nov Doncaster 5f gd RF 5144) - also 1st of 18 getting 13lb from Ecudamah (14 Oct Haydock RF 4796).
**M W Easterby [1-12] Stephen Curtis.*

PILOT'S HARBOUR BHB 85f **RR 85f** 4204[11]

2 b c Distant Relative 7f **(69)** - Lillemor 00
Form - 352110

Record	**1998 -**	1st:2	2nd:1	3rd:1	Ran:6

Win Prizemoney £9,359 *Total Prizemoney* £11,096

Wins								
	*** 1998**	Aug	Newmar	(G-F)	H	8f	83	85 <
	*** 1998**	Jly	Beverl	(GD)		7.5f		80

1998 Turf 2-6: (6f 2, 7f 1-2, 8f 1-2) (gd 2, g-f 1-2, frm 1-2)
Useful colt, effective 6 to 8f, best at 7f, acts on g-f to frm, best on g-f. Turf high 85 - 1st of 12 giving 10lb to Godley (28 Aug Newmarket RF 3932) - also 1st of 5 from Riverblue (28 Jly Beverley RF 3156). Progressing well, and finished in good style to land a Newmarket nursery in August, staying the mile well. However, he disappointed in a similar race at Doncaster.
**J L Dunlop [2-6] M Berger.*

PINCHINCHA (FR) BHB 75f76a **RR 78f 76a** 4314[7]

4 b g Priolo (USA) 10.9f **(71)** - Western Heights (Shirley Heights) 10.3f **(74)**
Form - 64487

Record	**1998 -**	1st:0	2nd:0	3rd:0	Ran:5
	Pre1998 -	1st:4	2nd:3	3rd:2	Ran:17

Win Prizemoney £13,611 *Total Prizemoney* £23,386

Wins								
	* 1997	Jun	Pontef	(G-F)	H	10f	75	78 <
	* 1997	May	Doncas	(G-S)		10.3f		71
	* 1997	Apr	Folkes	(G-F)	H	9.7f	65	67
	* 1996	*Nov*	*Southw*	*(STD)*	*S*	*8f*		*72*

1998 Turf 0-5: (10f 4, 11f) (gd, g-f 2, frm 2)
Workmanlike, above-average gelding, effective 10f, acts on gd to frm, excels at Pontefract, does well at Doncaster. Turf high 78 (began Jly) - 4th of 7 giving 22lb to Riccarton (29 Jly Doncaster 10f g-f RF 3195). **D Morris [4-22] T J Wells.*

PINE RIDGE LAD (IRE) BHB 60f58a **RR 62f 58a** 1630[10]

8 gr g Taufan (USA) 8.3f **(65)** - Rosserk (Roan Rocket) 7.8f **(57)**
Form - 373183624202180

Record	**1998 -**	1st:2	2nd:3	3rd:2	Ran:13
	Pre1998 -	1st:14	2nd:12	3rd:10	Ran:89

Win Prizemoney £46,235 *Total Prizemoney* £65,583

Wins								
	*** 1998**	May	Redcar	(GD)	H	8f	57	62
	*** 1998**	*Jan*	*Southw*	*(STD)*	*S*	*7f*		*59+*
	* 1997	Spt	Hamilt	(GD)	H	8.3f	50	54
	* 1996	Jly	Cheste	(G-F)	H	7.6f	57	65
	* 1996	Mar	Beverl	(GD)	H	7.5f	54	63
	* 1996	*Feb*	*Wolver*	*(STD)*	*H*	*7f*	*79*	*79* <
	* 1996	*Feb*	*Southw*	*(STD)*	*H*	*8f*	*71*	*78*
	* 1995	*Nov*	*Southw*	*(STD)*	*C*	*8f*		*61*
	* 1995	Jun	Carlis	(FRM)	H	6.9f	53	56
	* 1995	*Feb*	*Southw*	*(STD)*	*C*	*7f*		*66*
	* 1995	*Jan*	*Southw*	*(STD)*	*C*	*6f*		*58*

1998 Turf 1-5: (6f, 8f 1-3, 9f) (g-s, gd 1-2, g-f 2) 1998 AW 1-8: (7f 1-2, 8f 6) (Fibr 1-8)
Average gelding, has broken blood-vessels, effective 7 to 8f, acts on gd - acts on Fibr, has worn blinkers. Turf high 62 - 1st of 14 getting 11lb from Alpine Hideaway (11 May Redcar RF 1148). AW high 66.
**J L Eyre [11-59] Whitestonecliffe Racing Partnership (from B Beasley [1-26] Oct 1994).*

PINKARAL **RR 90f** 5157a[1]

2 b c Akarad (FR) 9.7f **(73)** -Pinaflore (FR) (Formidable (USA)) 9.2f **(63)**
Form - 1
1998 Turf 1-1: (8f 1-1) (g-s 1-1)
Currently useful colt. (1st run) - 1st of 4 from Wicked Clutch (7 Nov Saint-Cloud RF 5157a). Easy winner of a backend Group Three.
**A Fabre in FR [1-1] J-L Lagardere.*

PINK CORAL (IRE) **RR 103f** 5019a[1]

2 b fSadler's Wells(USA)11.3f**(87)**-Coral Fury(Mill Reef(USA))10.5f **(78)**
Form - 302441
1998 Turf 1-6: (7f 2, 8f 1-4) (hvy 1-1, sft, gd 4)
Very useful filly, effective 8f, acts on hvy to sft. Turf high 103 (began Aug) - 1st of 17 from Twizzle (21 Oct Navan RF 5019a). She was beaten in a maiden after contesting the Group One Moyglare Stud Stakes, but proved that she is indeed a smart filly when finishing fourth in the Prix Marcel Boussac. An easy win at Navan in October will have come as a welcome relief, and she should go on to land a decent prize in 1999. By Sadler's Wells and out of a Mill Reef mare, she will stay all day. **A P O'Brien in IRE [1-6] Mrs T Hyde.*

PINK TICKET BHB 50f47a **RR 52f 47a** 405[6]

3 b f Emarati (USA) 6.6f **(63)** - Foreign Mistress (Darshaan) 9.9f **(84)**
Form - 076

Record	**1998 -**	1st:0	2nd:0	3rd:0	Ran:2
	Pre1998 -	1st:1	2nd:1	3rd:4	Ran:12

Win Prizemoney £1,725 *Total Prizemoney* £3,429

Wins								
	* 1997	*Oct*	*Wolver*	*(STD)*	*S*	*8.5f*		*62* <

1998 AW 0-2: (8f 2) (Fibr 2)
Light-framed, fair filly, effective 8f, - acts on Fibr, likes left handed tracks, likes tight tracks. AW high 29. Becoming disappointing. She is no great shakes, but has some form in All-Weather sellers including a win at Wolverhampton in October. A mile on Fibresand looks her optimum trip. **P D Evans [1-14] John Pugh.*

PINMIX (FR) **RR 109f** 1230a[7]

3 gr c Linamix (FR) 8.2f **(64)**-Pinaflore (FR)(Formidable (USA)) 9.2f **(63)**
Form - 37
1998 Turf 0-2: (8f 2) (hvy, gd)
Currently Pattern-class colt. Turf high 107 (1st run) - 3rd of 7 to With The Flow (19 Apr Longchamp 8f hvy RF 0837a). He did not improve on his Group Three win as a juvenile. **A Fabre in FR [1-3].*

PINMOOR HILL **RR 45f** 4227[14]

2 b c Saddlers' Hall (IRE) 10.5f **(65)** - Pennine Pink (IRE) **(75f 60a)** (Pennine Walk) 8.5f **(61)**
Form - 70

Record	**1998 -**	1st:0	2nd:0	3rd:0	Ran:2

1998 Turf 0-2: (7f, 8f) (g-f, hrd)
Currently moderate colt. Turf high 45 (began Aug).
**Mrs J R Ramsden [0-2] J E Swiers.*

PINNACLE **RR 71+f** 2710[2]

2 b f Shirley Heights 12.1f **(76)** - Manhattan Sunset (USA) **(62f)** (El Gran Senor (USA)) 9.6f **(76)**
Form - 2

Record	**1998 -**	1st:0	2nd:1	3rd:0	Ran:1

Win Prizemoney £0 *Total Prizemoney* £1,150
1998 Turf 0-1: (7f) (frm)
Currently above-average filly. (1st run) - 2nd of 6 getting 7lb from Diablo Dancer (11 Jly Lingfield 7f frm RF 2710).
**W J Haggas [0-1] Mrs Barbara Bassett.*

PINSHARP (IRE) BHB 25f **RR 33f** 4271^{10}
3 b c Sharp Victor (USA) 10f **(56)** - Binnissima (USA) (Tilt Up (USA)) 9.8f **(55)**
Form - 06807700
Record 1998 - 1st:0 2nd:0 3rd:0 Ran:8
Pre1998 - 1st:0 2nd:0 3rd:0 Ran:3
1998 Turf 0-8: (5f, 6f, 7f 3, 8f, 11f, 12f) (gd 3, g-f 2, frm 2, hrd)
Scopey, very moderate colt, often wears blinkers. Turf high 61.
**P Howling [0-11] K Weston.*

PINUP BHB 44f44a **RR 54f 44a** 518^{13}
3 gr f Risk Me (FR) 8f **(53)** - Princess Tara (Prince Sabo) 7.2f **(62)**
Form - 00061350
Record 1998 - 1st:1 2nd:0 3rd:1 Ran:5
Pre1998 - 1st:0 2nd:0 3rd:0 Ran:8
Win Prizemoney £2,179 *Total Prizemoney* £2,558
Wins ** **1998** Jan Lingfi (STD) H 6f 38 44 <*
1998 Turf 0-1: (6f) (g-s) 1998 AW 1-4: (6f 1-2, 7f 2) (Equi 1-4)
Neat, fair filly, effective 6f, acts on frm - acts on Equi. AW high 44. She had shown precious little until showing improved form on the Lingfield Equitrack at the start of '98, including a victory in a poor handicap. She has not shown much on turf.
**C A Dwyer [1-8] Wessex House Racing (from G Lewis [0-5] Oct 1997).*

PIPA BHB 73f **RR 74f** 4983^{5}
2 b f Suave Dancer (USA) 10.7f **(68)** - Pipitina (Bustino) 10.4f **(64)**
Form - 825
Record 1998 - 1st:0 2nd:1 3rd:0 Ran:3
Win Prizemoney £0 *Total Prizemoney* £1,120
1998 Turf 0-3: (7f, 8f 2) (g-s, gd, frm)
Currently above-average filly. Turf high 74 (began Spt) - 2nd of 10 getting 5lb from Kattegat (14 Oct Nottingham 8f gd RF 4805).
**J L Dunlop [0-3] Sir Eric Parker.*

PIPADOR (IRE) BHB 63f **RR 56f** 4642^{5}
2 ch c Pips Pride 6.7f **(70)** - Dorado Llave (USA) (Well Decorated (USA)) 7.6f **(64)**
Form - 005
Record 1998 - 1st:0 2nd:0 3rd:0 Ran:3
1998 Turf 0-3: (5f 2, 6f) (gd, g-f, frm)
Currently fair colt. Turf high 56 (began Spt).
**R Hannon [0-3] Noodles Racing.*

PIPALONG (IRE) BHB 100f **RR 100f** 4857^{1}
2 b f Pips Pride 6.7f **(70)** - Limpopo (Green Desert (USA)) 8.6f **(78)**
Form - 112241
Record 1998 - 1st:3 2nd:2 3rd:0 Ran:6
Win Prizemoney £90,867 *Total Prizemoney* £111,327
Wins * **1998** Oct Redcar (HVY) 6f 100 <
* **1998** May York (GD) 5f 95
* **1998** Apr Ripon (SFT) 5f 99+
1998 Turf 3-6: (5f 2-3, 6f 1-2, 7f) (sft 1-1, g-s 1-1, gd 1-2, g-f, frm)
Very useful filly, effective 5 to 7f, best at 6f, acts on sft to frm. Turf high 100 - 1st of 22 getting 5lb from Pistachio (17 Oct Redcar RF 4857) - also 1st of 13 from College Music (16 Apr Ripon RF 0716). The only filly to lower Bint Allayl's colours last season, she proved a real money-spinner for Tim Easterby, winning three times and making the frame in two Group races. Thrown in at the weights when battling home on heavy ground in the valuable Comcast Teesside Two-Year-Old Trophy on her final start, she did not appear to stay seven furlongs at Newmarket in October and looks a sprinter pure and simple. Whatever happens in 1999, she does not owe her connections a shilling. **T D Easterby [3-6] T H Bennett.*

PIPED ABOARD (IRE) BHB 83f **RR 85f** 4188^{6}
3 b g Pips Pride 6.7f **(70)** - Last Gunboat (Dominion) 8.5f **(63)**
Form - 1222246
Record 1998 - 1st:1 2nd:4 3rd:0 Ran:7
Pre1998 - 1st:0 2nd:0 3rd:0 Ran:3
Win Prizemoney £2,337 *Total Prizemoney* £7,756
Wins 1998 Apr Thirsk (G-S) 7f 71 <
1998 Turf 1-7: (7f 1-1, 8f 4, 10f 2) (g-s 1-1, gd 5, g-f)
Scopey, useful gelding, effective 8 to 10f, best at 8f, acts on gd to g-f, best on gd, has worn blinkers. Turf high 85 - 4th of 8 getting 8lb from Brave Reward (21 Aug Chester 10f gd RF 3792). Consistent. Created a favourable impression when winning at Thirsk over what looked an inadequate trip, and has run some sound races since, although regularly coming up against one too good. A winning hurdler in October.
**M C Pipe [0-2] & Mrs M Jones (from J L Dunlop [1-8] Jly 1998).*

PIPE MUSIC (IRE) BHB 60f65a **RR 62f 65a** 2813^{4}
3 b g Mujadil (USA) 7.7f **(70)** - Sunset Cafe (IRE)(Red Sunset) 8.2f **(63)**
Form - 55140075324
Record 1998 - 1st:1 2nd:1 3rd:1 Ran:10
Pre1998 - 1st:0 2nd:0 3rd:0 Ran:3
Win Prizemoney £1,735 *Total Prizemoney* £3,908
Wins ** **1998** Feb Southw (STD) H 8f 60 71 <*
1998 Turf 0-8: (8f, 10f 3, 11f 2, 12f 2) (g-s, gd 3, g-f, frm 3) 1998 AW 1-2: (7f, 8f 1-1) (Equi, Fibr 1-1)
Scopey, average gelding, effective 8 to 12f, acts on gd - acts on Fibr, has worn blinkers, likes left handed tracks. Turf high 71 (1st run) - 4th of 15 getting 12lb from Bawsian (26 Mar Doncaster 10f gd RF 0471). AW high 71 - 1st of 8 giving 7lb to Nuit d'Or (23 Feb Southwell RF 0342). **P C Haslam [1-13] Lord Scarsdale.*

PIPERI (IRE) RR 109f $4726a^{9}$
4 b c Machiavellian (USA) 9.8f **(83)** - Gwydion (USA) (Raise A Cup (USA)) 7.6f **(74)**
Form - 32030
1998 Turf 0-5: (5f 5) (sft, gd 4)
Pattern-class colt, effective 5f, acts on gd, has worn blinkers. Turf high 109 - 2nd of 8 giving 11lb to Sainte Marine (30 May Chantilly 5f gd RF 1731a). He is useful, but not a match for the top sprinters.
**J E Pease in FR [0-7] Niarchos Family.*

PIPIJI (IRE) BHB 33f **RR 34f** 4939^{10}
3 gr f Pips Pride 6.7f **(70)** - Blue Alicia (Wolver Hollow) 8f **(56)**
Form - 804000
Record 1998 - 1st:0 2nd:0 3rd:0 Ran:6
Win Prizemoney £0 *Total Prizemoney* £248
1998 Turf 0-4:(8f, 10f, 11f, 12f)(gd 3, g-f) 1998AW 0-2:(12f, 15f) (Fibr 2)
Very moderate filly. Turf high 34. AW high 3.
**Mrs G S Rees [0-6] Brooke Rankin.*

PIPPAS PRIDE (IRE) BHB 41f **RR 37f** 5006^{6}
3 ch g Pips Pride 6.7f **(70)** - Al Shany (Burslem) 8.8f **(53)**
Form - 006
Record 1998 - 1st:0 2nd:0 3rd:0 Ran:3
Pre1998 - 1st:0 2nd:0 3rd:0 Ran:3
1998 Turf 0-3: (7f, 8f 2) (sft 2, g-f)
Scopey, very moderate gelding. Turf high 37 (began Oct).
**M J Fetherston-Godley [0-6] Mrs Anthony Vickers.*

PIP'S ADDITION (IRE) BHB 49f62a **RR 39f 62a** 4919^{18}
3 ch f Pips Pride 6.7f **(70)** - Mint Addition (Tate Gallery (USA)) 7.4f **(67)**
Form - 3211236800
Record 1998 - 1st:1 2nd:1 3rd:1 Ran:7
Pre1998 - 1st:1 2nd:1 3rd:2 Ran:6
Win Prizemoney £4,293 *Total Prizemoney* £6,872
Wins ** **1998** Jan Southw (STD) H 7f 60 68 <*
** 1997 Dec Southw (STD) S 7f 59*
1998 Turf 0-3: (7f 2, 8f) (g-s, gd, g-f) 1998 AW 1-4: (7f 1-4) (Fibr 1-4)
Scopey, moderate filly, effective 6 to 7f, best at 7f, - acts on Fibr, prefers left handed tracks, prefers tight tracks. Turf high 39 (began Aug). AW high 68 (1st run) - 1st of 13 giving 1lb to I'm Tef (2 Jan Southwell RF 0011). Becoming disappointing.
**J A Glover [2-13] Miss A C Radford.*

PIP'S BRAVE RR 57f 2350^{6}
2 b c Be My Chief (USA) 10.2f **(62)** - Pipistrelle (Shareef Dancer (USA)) 9.9f **(73)**
Form - 6
Record 1998 - 1st:0 2nd:0 3rd:0 Ran:1
1998 Turf 0-1: (7f) (g-f)
Currently fair colt. **M J Polglase [0-1] M J Polglase.*

PIPSISEWA (IRE) RR 51f 3653^{19}
2 ch f Pips Pride 6.7f **(70)** - Algonquin Park (High Line) 10.3f **(70)**
Form - 80
Record 1998 - 1st:0 2nd:0 3rd:0 Ran:2
1998 Turf 0-2: (5f, 7f) (gd 2)
Currently fair filly. Turf high 59.
**D R C Elsworth [0-2] Michael Jackson Bloodstock Ltd.*

Pipalong (left) beating Bint Allayl at York

PIPS MAGIC (IRE) BHB 94f **RR 86f** 5074[9]
2 b c Pips Pride 6.7f **(70)** - Kentucky Starlet (USA) (Cox's Ridge (USA)) 8f **(68)**
Form - 0371100502440
Record 1998 - 1st:2 2nd:1 3rd:1 Ran:13
Win Prizemoney £7,312 *Total Prizemoney* £12,889
Wins * **1998** May Ayr (G-F) 5f 84 <
* **1998** May Ripon (G-F) 6f 66
1998 Turf 2-13: (5f 1-7, 6f 1-6) (sft 2, g-s 4, gd 4, g-f 1-1, frm 1-2)
Useful colt, effective 5f, acts on g-f. Turf high 86 - also 1st of 6 giving 4lb to Henry Hall (28 May Ayr RF 1542). Consistent. He showed gradually improving form, ultimately winning small events at Ripon and Ayr, but has been found wanting in a couple of hot events. **J S Goldie [2-13] Frank Brady.*

PIPS SONG (IRE) BHB 70f79a **RR 74f 79a** 3471[13]
3 ch g Pips Pride 6.7f **(70)** - Friendly Song (Song) 7.2f **(61)**
Form - 1046430
Record 1998 - 1st:1 2nd:0 3rd:1 Ran:7
Pre1998 - 1st:0 2nd:0 3rd:0 Ran:1
Win Prizemoney £2,322 *Total Prizemoney* £5,132
Wins * **1998** *Apr Wolver (STD) 6f 63* <
1998 Turf 0-6:(5f, 6f 4, 7f)(gd, g-f 4, hrd)1998 AW 1-1: (6f 1-1) (Fibr 1-1)
Leggy, above-average gelding. Turf high 74. (1st run). Consistent. He got off the mark in a maiden on the Wolverhampton Fibresand in April, a race which may well have been above average for its type. Ran a cracker in a warm Newmarket handicap in May, but has not really progressed from that. Has looked a tricky ride at times.
**Dr J D Scargill [1-7] P J Edwards (from I A Balding [0-1] Jly 1997).*

PIRONGIA BHB 29f **RR 18f** 2559[16]
4 b f Wing Park - Gangawayhame (Lochnager) 6f **(59)**
Form - 000
Record 1998 - 1st:0 2nd:0 3rd:0 Ran:3
Pre1998 - 1st:0 2nd:0 3rd:0 Ran:5
1998 Turf 0-3: (5f, 6f 2) (gd, g-f, frm)
Neat, poor filly. Turf high 18.
**B R Millman [0-3] Orby Racing (from P Howling [0-5] Jun 1997).*

PIRRO (IRE) RR 101f 2420a[1]
3 ch g Persian Bold 10f **(69)** - Kindness Itself
Form - 21
1998 Turf 1-2: (8f 1-2) (g-s 1-1, gd)
Currently very useful gelding. Turf high 101 - 1st of 7 from Dual Star (26 Jun Curragh RF 2420a). He justified short-priced favouritism at Galway in June, but was not seen out again. He would have been an interesting runner in classy handicaps, and could have a future over hurdles. **J Oxx in IRE [1-2] Lady Clague.*

PISCES LAD BHB 78f **RR 82f** 2855[6]
2 b c Cyrano de Bergerac 7.3f **(58)** - Tarnside Rosal **(56f)** (Mummy's Game) 8.2f **(60)**
Form - 425236
Record 1998 - 1st:0 2nd:2 3rd:1 Ran:6
Win Prizemoney £0 *Total Prizemoney* £2,735
1998 Turf 0-6: (5f 5, 6f) (gd 2, g-f, frm 3)
Decent colt. Turf high 82. **S Dow [0-6] J Falvey & G Williamson.*

PISTACHIO BHB 100f **RR 104f** 4857[2]
2 gr c Unblest - Cashew **(77f)** (Sharrood (USA)) 10.5f **(72)**
Form - 113422

Record 1998 - 1st:2 2nd:2 3rd:1 Ran:6
Win Prizemoney £5,580 *Total Prizemoney* £39,931
Wins * **1998** Jun Ripon (SFT) 5f 89+ <
* **1998** Jun Yarmou (SFT) 6f 82+
1998 Turf 2-6: (5f 1-1, 6f 1-4, 7f) (sft, gd 1-2, g-f 1-1, frm 2)
Very useful colt, effective 6f, acts on sft to gd. Turf high 104 - 2nd of 22 giving 5lb to Pipalong (17 Oct Redcar 6f sft RF 4857). He won his first two starts in good style, but failed to stay seven furlongs at Salisbury in July. He went on to run a couple of smashing races in the autumn, notably when touched off by Pipalong at Redcar. He should win a Listed race over sprint distances in 1999, and will probably be at his most effective on easy ground.
**J R Fanshawe [2-6] Lord Vestey.*

PISTOL (IRE) BHB 65f RR 66f 2556[2]
8 ch g Glenstal (USA) 10f **(59)** - First Wind (Windjammer (USA)) 7f **(59)**
Form - 0542
Record 1998 - 1st:0 2nd:1 3rd:0 Ran:4
Pre1998 - 1st:6 2nd:6 3rd:5 Ran:51
Win Prizemoney £18,700 *Total Prizemoney* £32,745
Wins * 1996 Aug Bath (GD) H 11.7f 73 75 <
* 1996 Jly Bath (FRM) 11.7f 73
* 1996 Jly Folkes (G-F) 9.7f 67
* 1996 Jly Folkes (FRM) H 9.7f 59 64
* 1995 May Folkes (G-F) H 9.7f 59 58
* 1994 Aug Folkes (GD) H 9.7f 59 64
1998 Turf 0-4: (10f 3, 12f) (gd, g-f 2, frm)
Average gelding, effective 10 to 12f, best at 10f, acts on gd to g-f, best on g-f, has worn blinkers, prefers tight tracks. Turf high 66 - 2nd of 12 getting 7lb from Diminutive (6 Jly Bath 10f g-f RF 2556). Consistent. **C Horgan[6-48] Mrs B Sumner(fromP Cole[0-8]Dec1992).*

PISUM SATIVUM BHB 27f30a RR 30a 450[7]
4 ch f Ron's Victory (USA) 9.2f **(52)** - Trojan Desert (Troy) 10.4f **(68)**
Form - 47
Record 1998 - 1st:0 2nd:0 3rd:0 Ran:2
Pre1998 - 1st:0 2nd:0 3rd:0 Ran:2
Win Prizemoney £0 *Total Prizemoney* £282
1998 AW 0-2: (7f, 12f) (Fibr 2)
Strong, very poor filly. AW high 9. **J L Harris [0-4] Paddy Barrett.*

PIXIELATED (IRE) BHB 77f RR 76f 2872[4]
3 b f Fairy King (USA) 7.7f **(75)** - Last Embrace (IRE) (Shernazar) 10.2f **(73)**
Form - 22214
Record 1998 - 1st:1 2nd:3 3rd:0 Ran:5
Pre1998 - 1st:0 2nd:0 3rd:0 Ran:3
Win Prizemoney £3,468 *Total Prizemoney* £7,002
Wins * **1998** Jly Chepst (GD) H 10.2f 72 76 <
1998 Turf 1-5: (8f, 10f 1-4) (g-s, gd 1-1, g-f, frm, hrd)
Unfurnished, above-average filly, effective 8 to 10f, best at 10f, acts on g-s to hrd. Turf high 76 - 1st of 7 getting 8lb from Happy Go Lucky (4 Jly Chepstow RF 2530). Consistent. She caught the eye on both of her first two starts as a juvenile, and ran well on her three-year-old bow. Fluent winner of a fillies' handicap at Chepstow in July, but well held off a 5lb higher mark.
**D R Loder [1-8] E J Loder.*

PIZZICATO BHB 55f59a RR 55f 59a 2686[8]
4 b f Statoblest 6.4f **(63)** - Musianica (Music Boy) 6.8f **(57)**
Form - 7230348
Record 1998 - 1st:0 2nd:1 3rd:2 Ran:7
Pre1998 - 1st:2 2nd:0 3rd:0 Ran:5
Win Prizemoney £4,554 *Total Prizemoney* £6,038
Wins * 1997 Jly Bright (FRM) 5.3f 59 <
* 1997 *Jun Wolver (STD) 5f 52*
1998 Turf 0-3: (5f 2, 6f) (gd, frm 2) 1998 AW 0-4: (5f 4) (Equi, Fibr 3)
Scopey, fair filly, effective 5f, acts on g-f - acts on Fibr, prefers left handed tracks. Turf high 55. AW high 57 - 2nd of 8 giving 19lb to Sunset Harbour (25 Apr Wolverhampton 5f Fibr RF 0877).
**R J R Williams [2-12] Richard Morris Jr.*

PLAISIR D'AMOUR (IRE) BHB 80f RR 79f 2838[4]
4 b f Danehill (USA) 9.1f **(79)**-Mira Adonde (USA)(Sharpen Up)8.3f **(67)**
Form - 5027074
Record 1998 - 1st:0 2nd:1 3rd:0 Ran:7
Pre1998 - 1st:4 2nd:3 3rd:1 Ran:15
Win Prizemoney £27,611 *Total Prizemoney* £43,474
Wins * 1997 Aug York (GD) H 6f 85 90 <
* 1997 Jly Epsom (SFT) H 6f 80 82
* 1997 Apr Leices (FRM) H 7f 74 82
* 1997 Mar Leices (G-F) H 7f 74 81+
1998 Turf 0-7: (6f 4, 7f 3) (sft, g-s, gd 2, g-f 2, frm)
Scopey, above-average filly, effective 6 to 7f, best at 6f, acts on gd to frm, best on frm, has worn blinkers, and excels at Leicester. Turf high 93 - 2nd of 6 getting 4lb from Darnaway (16 May Newmarket 7f frm RF 1265). She ran well to finish runner up in a Newmarket rated stakes on her third start of the season, but was well held otherwise and proved difficult to place.
**N A Callaghan [4-22] M Tabor & Mrs John Magnier.*

PLAN-B BHB 98f RR 99+f 2652[2]
3 b c Polish Precedent (USA) 9f **(73)** - Draft Board (Rainbow Quest (USA)) 10.4f **(75)**
Form - 6312
Record 1998 - 1st:1 2nd:1 3rd:1 Ran:4
Pre1998 - 1st:0 2nd:1 3rd:0 Ran:2
Win Prizemoney £29,700 *Total Prizemoney* £36,072
Wins * **1998** Jun Ascot (G-S) H 8f 88 97 <
1998 Turf 1-4: (7f, 8f 1-3) (gd 1-2, g-f, frm)
Scopey, very useful colt, effective 8f, acts on gd to frm. Turf high 99 - 2nd of 10 giving 25lb to Minetta (9 Jly Newmarket 8f frm RF 2652) - also 1st of 31 giving 2lb to Pantar (16 Jun Ascot RF 2014). Put an unlucky run at Chester behind him to take the ultra-competitive Britannia Handicap at Royal Ascot. Suited by being held up in a strongly-run race, the slow pace was against him next time at Newmarket and he failed to peg back Minetta. Did not reappear.
**J H M Gosden [1-6] Sheikh Mohammed.*

PLAN FOR PROFIT (IRE) BHB 72f84a RR 77f 84a 4970[2]
4 b g Polish Patriot (USA) 7.8f **(70)** - Wild Sable (IRE) (Kris) 9.5f **(73)**
Form - 1142232605168002
Record 1998 - 1st:2 2nd:4 3rd:1 Ran:15
Pre1998 - 1st:3 2nd:4 3rd:2 Ran:27
Win Prizemoney £17,916 *Total Prizemoney* £30,917
Wins * **1998** Spt York (GD) C 8.9f 70
* **1998** *Jan Southw (STD) C 8f 83* <
* 1997 *Nov Lingfi (STD) H 8f 75 79*
* 1997 May Sandow (GD) H 7.1f 75 76
* 1996 Jly Hamilt (G-F) H 5f 63
1998 Turf 1-8: (8f 3, 9f 1-3, 10f 2) (sft, g-s, gd 2, g-f, frm 1-3) 1998 AW 1-7: (7f, 8f 1-5, 9f) (Equi 3, Fibr 1-4)
Scopey, useful gelding, effective 7 to 9f, best at 8f, acts on gd to frm - acts on AW, best on Equi, prefers tight tracks, excels at Ripon and Lingfield. Turf high 77 (began Jly). AW high 88 - 2nd of 6 giving 3lb to Ursa Major (7 Feb Lingfield 8f Equi RF 0243) - also 1st of 9 giving 4lb to Rambo Waltzer (2 Jan Southwell RF 0010). A rather in-and-out character, he came back to form with two good victories over a mile on sand at the beginning of '98, and has since run with credit against some of the best sand performers around. Able on turf too, a winner of a York claimer in September.
**M Johnston [5-42] Professional Racing Partnership.*

PLAN MAISON RR 94f 833a[4]
3 f
Form - 4
1998 Turf 0-1: (8f) (sft)
Currently useful filly. **G Ligas in ITY [0-1].*

PLAYACTING (USA) RR 102f 4428a[5]
3 b c Forty Niner (USA) 8.8f **(73)** - Mystery Play (IRE) (Sadler's Wells (USA)) 10f **(76)**
Form - 215643345
1998 Turf 1-9: (7f, 8f 1-5, 9f, 10f 2) (hvy, sft 1-2, gd 5, g-f)
Very useful colt, effective 8 to 10f, best at 8f, acts on hvy to g-f, best on gd, has worn blinkers, and does well at Leopardstown. Turf high 102 - 3rd of 7 getting 2lb from Lil's Boy (28 Aug Tralee 8f gd RF 4034a) - also 1st of 13 giving 5lb to Blushing Melody (2 May Curragh RF 1051a). Consistent. He faced some stiff tasks after winning his maiden and, significantly, seemed to run his best races in handicaps. **J Oxx in IRE [1-9] Sheikh Mohammed.*

PLAYGROUP BHB 66f RR 64f 1262[15]
3 ch f Rudimentary (USA) 8.2f **(66)** - Miss Paige (AUS) (Luskin Star (AUS)) 6.3f **(71)**
Form - 680

Record 1998 - 1st:0 2nd:0 3rd:0 Ran:3
Pre1998 - 1st:0 2nd:0 3rd:0 Ran:1
1998 Turf 0-3: (7f 3) (sft, gd, frm)
Scopey, average filly. Turf high 64.
**Mrs J Cecil [0-4] Lord Howard de Walden.*

2 b c First Trump - Alo Ez (Alzao (USA)) 7.1f **(68)**
Form - 08
Record 1998 - 1st:0 2nd:0 3rd:0 Ran:2
1998 Turf 0-2: (6f, 7f) (g-f, frm)
Currently fair colt. Turf high 57 (began Aug).
**Miss J A Camacho [0-2] Shangri-La Racing Club.*

Plan-B winning the Britannia Handicap at Ascot

PLEADING RR 70f 2344[6]
5 b g Never so Bold 7.1f **(62)** - Ask Mama (Mummy's Pet) 7.7f **(60)**
Form - 001006
Record 1998 - 1st:1 2nd:0 3rd:0 Ran:6
Pre1998 - 1st:2 2nd:1 3rd:0 Ran:14
Win Prizemoney £14,775 *Total Prizemoney* £25,776
Wins * **1998** Apr Pontef (G-S) H 6f 65 70
1996 May Leices (G-S) H 6f 80 91+ <
1996 May Salisb (GD) 6f 77
1998 Turf 1-6: (6f 1-6) (sft, g-s 1-3, gd, frm)
Above-average gelding, effective 6f, acts on gd. Turf high 70.
**W J Musson [1-7] Lloyd Bennett (from H Candy [2-13] Oct 1997).*

PLEASANT DREAMS BHB 56f **RR 56f** 4660[10]
3 ch f Sabrehill (USA) 8.5f **(64)** - Tafila (Adonijah) 10f **(61)**
Form - 50452188100
Record 1998 - 1st:2 2nd:1 3rd:0 Ran:11
Pre1998 - 1st:0 2nd:0 3rd:0 Ran:3
Win Prizemoney £5,252 *Total Prizemoney* £6,000
Wins * **1998** Spt Ripon (HVY) C 8f 56 <
* **1998** Jly Carlis (G-F) H 9.3f 48 55
1998 Turf 2-11: (8f 1-3, 9f 1-4, 10f 4)(sft, g-s 1-2, gd 1-4, g-f 2, frm, hrd)
Leggy, fair filly, effective 8 to 9f, best at 8f, acts on g-s to frm, prefers right handed tracks. Turf high 56 - also 1st of 11 getting 7lb from Flower O'Cannie (1 Spt Ripon RF 4014).
**Denys Smith [2-14] Jim Blair.*

PLEASANT MOUNT RR 57f 4298[8]

PLEASE RR 64f 1041[9]
3 b f Kris 10f **(75)** - Tanz (IRE) (Sadler's Wells (USA)) 10f **(76)**
Form - 00
Record 1998 - 1st:0 2nd:0 3rd:0 Ran:2
1998 Turf 0-2: (8f, 10f) (sft, g-f)
Scopey, currently average filly. Turf high 64.
**B W Hills [0-2] Mrs Jane Bailey.*

PLEASING PROSPECT (USA) RR 62f 4396[6]
2 b f Mr Prospector (USA) 8.6f **(88)** - Promising Girl (USA) (Youth (USA)) 9.8f **(64)**
Form - 6
Record 1998 - 1st:0 2nd:0 3rd:0 Ran:1
1998 Turf 0-1: (7f) (frm)
Currently average filly. **J H M Gosden [0-1] Sheikh Mohammed.*

PLEASURE BHB 57f55a **RR 54f 55a** 4961[1]
3 ch f Most Welcome 8.6f **(66)** - Peak Squaw (USA) (Icecapade (USA)) 11f **(62)**
Form - 38001
Record 1998 - 1st:1 2nd:0 3rd:1 Ran:5
Pre1998 - 1st:0 2nd:0 3rd:0 Ran:1
Win Prizemoney £3,113 *Total Prizemoney* £3,408
Wins * **1998** Oct Doncas (SFT) H 7f 51 54 <
1998 Turf 1-5: (5f 2, 6f 2, 7f 1-1) (g-s, gd, frm 1-2, hrd)
Fair filly, effective 7f, acts on frm. Turf high 54 - 1st of 22 getting 9lb from Manufan (23 Oct Doncaster RF 4961).
**A Smith [1-5] The Rufus Partnership (from R W Armstrong [0-1] Nov 1997).*

PLEASURELAND (IRE) BHB 54f49a **RR 65df 49a** 1690[9]
5 ch g Don't Forget Me 9.5f **(66)** - Elminya (IRE) (Sure Blade (USA)) 11.3f **(67)**
Form - 840
Record **1998** - 1st:0 2nd:0 3rd:0 Ran:3
Pre1998 - 1st:0 2nd:0 3rd:2 Ran:12
Win Prizemoney £0 *Total Prizemoney* £1,035
1998 Turf 0-2: (14f, 16f) (gd 2) 1998 AW 0-1: (16f) (Equi)
Average gelding, effective 20f, acts on g-f, has worn blinkers. Turf high 55.
**R Curtis [2-19] Mrs Sylvia McGarvie (from P J Makin [0-9] Spt 1996).*

PLEASURE TIME BHB 70f65a **RR 70f 65a** 4837[7]
5 ch g Clantime 6.6f **(57)** - First Experience (Le Johnstan) 7.4f **(55)**
Form - 122871007
Record **1998** - 1st:2 2nd:2 3rd:0 Ran:9
Pre1998 - 1st:3 2nd:3 3rd:5 Ran:31
Win Prizemoney £16,316 *Total Prizemoney* £25,798

Wins							
* **1998**	Aug	Thirsk	(G-F)	H	5f	65	70
* **1998**	May	Nottin	(G-F)	H	5.1f	60	66
* 1997	May	Nottin	(GD)	H	5.1f	58	63
* 1995	Aug	Haydoc	(G-F)	H	5f	65	67
* 1995	May	Redcar	(FRM)		5f		71 <

1998 Turf 2-9: (5f 2-9) (g-s 2, gd 3, g-f, frm 2-3)
Above-average gelding, effective 5f, acts on g-s to frm, best on frm, often wears blinkers (very effectively). Turf high 70 - 1st of 15 giving 14lb to Sunset Harbour (28 Aug Thirsk RF 3938) - also 1st of 17 giving 17lb to Soaked (15 May Nottingham RF 1246).
**C Smith [5-40] A E Needham.*

PLEASURE TRICK (USA) BHB 39f58a **RR 39f 58a** 5120[5]
7 br g Clever Trick (USA) 7.6f **(69)** - Pleasure Garden (USA) (Foolish Pleasure (USA)) 8.9f **(72)**
Form - 01323816380065
Record **1998** - 1st:2 2nd:1 3rd:3 Ran:13
Pre1998 - 1st:7 2nd:3 3rd:2 Ran:54
Win Prizemoney £29,818 *Total Prizemoney* £35,832

Wins							
* **1998**	*Feb*	*Southw*	*(STD)*	*H*	*7f*	*55*	*58*
* **1998**	*Jan*	*Southw*	*(STD)*	*H*	*7f*	*49*	*50*
* 1997	Jly	Pontef	(G-F)	H	8f	41	47
* 1997	*Feb*	*Southw*	*(STD)*	*H*	*8f*	*49*	*56*
* 1997	*Jan*	*Southw*	*(STD)*	*H*	*7f*	*42*	*46*
* 1996	*Nov*	*Southw*	*(STD)*	*H*	*7f*	*34*	*43*
1995	Jly	Pontef	(G-F)	C	8f		64 <
1994	Aug	Catter	(GD)	H	7f	62	57
1994	Jun	Catter	(FRM)	H	7f	57	57+

1998 Turf 0-5: (8f 5)(gd 2, g-f, frm 2)1998 AW 2-8:(7f 2-3, 8f 5)(Fibr 2-8)
Fair gelding, effective 7 to 8f, best at 7f, - acts on Fibr, has worn blinkers, likes left handed tracks, favours tight tracks, excels at Southwell. Turf high 39 (began Jly). AW high 58 - 3rd of 12 giving 8lb to Up in Flames (30 Jan Southwell 8f Fibr RF 0190) - also 1st of 9 getting 11lb from Davis Rock (27 Feb Southwell RF 0373). He is rather difficult to predict, but when in the mood he has the ability to snatch races from a seemingly impossible position. Seven furlongs or a mile at Southwell seem to suit him best.
**Don Enrico Incisa [6-46] Don Enrico Incisa (from N Tinkler [1-12] Spt 1995).*

PLEIN GAZ (FR) BHB 36f44a **RR 36f 44a** 2390[7]
5 ch g Lesotho (USA) 6f **(53)**-Gazzara (USA) (Irish River (FR)) 8.6f **(78)**
Form - 07387814483060057
Record **1998** - 1st:1 2nd:0 3rd:2 Ran:16
Pre1998 - 1st:0 2nd:1 3rd:0 Ran:4
Win Prizemoney £1,830 *Total Prizemoney* £3,710

Wins							
* **1998**	*Feb*	*Lingfi*	*(SLW)*	*S*	*6f*		*46 <*

1998 Turf 0-5: (5f, 6f 3, 7f) (sft, gd 2, g-f, frm) 1998 AW 1-11: (5f 5, 6f 1-4, 7f 2) (Equi 1-10, Fibr)
Average gelding, effective 5f, - acts on Equi, likes left handed tracks, favours tight tracks. Turf high 36. AW high 65 - 3rd of 6 getting 2lb from Anokato (8 Jan Lingfield 5f Equi RF 0047).
**J J Bridger [1-17] Exors of the late M R Pascall (from Andre Hermans in BEL [0-3] Jan 1996).*

PLENTY OF SUNSHINE BHB 26f **RR 5f** 3885[8]
5 ch m Pharly (FR) 11.5f **(64)** - Zipperti Do (Precocious) 8.6f **(62)**
Form - 8008
Record **1998** - 1st:0 2nd:0 3rd:0 Ran:4
Pre1998 - 1st:0 2nd:0 3rd:0 Ran:2
1998 Turf 0-3: (8f 2, 12f) (gd 2, hrd) 1998 AW 0-1: (8f) (Fibr)
Little account filly. Turf high 5.
**Mrs N Macauley [0-4] Maurice Kirby (from I Campbell [0-2] Feb 1997).*

PLISSETSKAIA (FR) **RR 90+f** 3612a[1]
2 br f Caerleon (USA) 10.9f **(79)** - Soviet Squaw (USA) (Nureyev (USA)) 8.7f **(78)**
Form - 1
1998 Turf 1-1: (7f 1-1) (gd 1-1)
Currently useful filly. (1st run) - 1st of 10 getting 4lb from Stella Berine (4 Aug Deauville RF 3612a).
**C Laffon-Parias in FR [1-1] Wertheimer Brothers.*

PLUMBIRD **RR 101f** 1380a[1]
4 b c Statoblest 6.4f **(63)** - Plum Bold (Be My Guest (USA)) 9.3f **(67)**
Form - 1
1998 Turf 1-1: (6f 1-1) (gd 1-1)
Currently very useful colt. (1st run) - 1st of 9 giving 9lb to Blu Carillon (17 May Capannelle RF 1380a). He is a threat in Group Three company, but would struggle if asked to climb any higher.
**A Calchetti in ITY [1-2] San Paolo Agri Stud.*

PLUM FIRST BHB 56f43a **RR 64f 43a** 4751[16]
8 b g Nomination 7.3f **(57)** - Plum Bold (Be My Guest (USA)) 9.3f **(67)**
Form - 4743030087070
Record **1998** - 1st:0 2nd:0 3rd:2 Ran:11
Pre1998 - 1st:5 2nd:11 3rd:11 Ran:96
Win Prizemoney £18,673 *Total Prizemoney* £42,795

Wins							
1995	May	Warwic	(FRM)		6f		58
1995	Apr	Pontef	(GD)		5f		56
1994	Jun	Redcar	(FRM)	H	6f	53	53

1998 Turf 0-11: (5f 7, 6f 3, 7f) (gd 3, g-f, frm 7)
Average gelding, effective 5f, acts on gd, often wears blinkers. Turf high 64 (began Jly) - 3rd of 5 to Fairy Prince (28 Jly Beverley 5f gd RF 3160).
**J S Wainwright [0-6] J B Slatcher (from L R Lloyd-James [2-35] Aug 1998).*

PLURALIST (IRE) BHB 79f **RR 76f** 3655[8]
2 b c Mujadil (USA) 7.7f **(70)** - Encore Une Fois (IRE) **(75f)** (Shirley Heights) 10.3f **(74)**
Form - 5228
Record **1998** - 1st:0 2nd:2 3rd:0 Ran:4
Win Prizemoney £0 *Total Prizemoney* £3,025
1998 Turf 0-4: (6f 2, 7f 2) (g-f 3, frm)
Above-average colt. Turf high 76 - 2nd of 11 giving 5lb to Lady Muck (29 Jly Epsom 7f g-f RF 3198). Looks a surefire future winner, probably over seven furlongs.
**W Jarvis [0-4] The Pluralist Partnership.*

PLUS A SONG BHB 50f **RR 55f** 3621[18]
3 b c Energy Plus - Barkston Singer (Runnett) 7f **(59)**
Form - 0085060
Record **1998** - 1st:0 2nd:0 3rd:0 Ran:7
1998 Turf 0-7: (5f 2, 6f 3, 7f 2) (gd 4, frm 2, hrd)
Unfurnished, fair colt, effective 5f, acts on gd. Turf high 55 - 5th of 9 giving 9lb to Penniless (5 Jun Catterick 5f gd RF 1742).
**J L Eyre [0-7] T H Morris.*

POCO (IRE) BHB 52f54a **RR 60f 54a** 3499[5]
2 b f Distinctly North (USA) 7.4f **(63)** - Lady Roberta (USA) (Roberto (USA)) 10f **(76)**
Form - 4717075
Record **1998** - 1st:1 2nd:0 3rd:0 Ran:7
Win Prizemoney £2,390 *Total Prizemoney* £2,615

Wins							
* **1998**	May	Beverl	(GD)	S	5f		60 <

1998 Turf 1-5: (5f 1-2, 6f 2, 7f) (sft, gd, frm 1-3) 1998 AW 0-2: (5f, 6f) (Fibr 2)
Average filly, effective 5f, acts on frm. Turf high 60 - 1st of 10 from Sweet As A Nut (19 May Beverley RF 1317). AW high 37.
**M R Channon [1-7] Tim Corby.*

POCONO KNIGHT BHB 25f **RR** 3067[12]
8 gr g Petong 7.6f **(58)** - Avahra (Sahib) 12.1f **(52)**
Form - 0
Record **1998** - 1st:0 2nd:0 3rd:0 Ran:1
Pre1998 - 1st:0 2nd:0 3rd:0 Ran:6

1998 Turf 0-1: (12f) (g-f)
Very poor gelding, has worn blinkers.
**K McAuliffe [0-1] Miss B Small (from M Madgwick [0-6] Jly 1993).*

PODDINGTON BHB 80f RR 76f 2881[8]

7 b g Crofthall 8.6f **(54)** - Bold Gift (Persian Bold) 9.3f **(66)**
Form - 058
Record 1998 - 1st:0 2nd:0 3rd:0 Ran:3
Pre1998 - 1st:1 2nd:0 3rd:1 Ran:4
Win Prizemoney £3,893 *Total Prizemoney* £5,129
Wins 1996 Jly Lingfi (G-F) 9f 76 <
1998 Turf 0-3: (10f 3) (sft, frm 2)
Above-average gelding. Turf high 76. (DEAD)
**J Akehurst [0-3] Miss Vivian Pratt (from R Akehurst [1-4] Jun 1997).*

PODIUM BHB 59f RR 56f 4808[4]

2 b g Presidium 7.5f **(56)** - Sally Tadpole (Jester)
Form - 004
Record 1998 - 1st:0 2nd:0 3rd:0 Ran:3
1998 Turf 0-3: (8f 2, 10f) (gd, g-f, frm)
Currently fair gelding. Turf high 56 (began Spt).
**P W Harris [0-3] The Saboteurs.*

POETRY IN MOTION (IRE) BHB 64f RR 69df 4596[20]

3 gr f Ballad Rock 7.2f **(63)** - Nasseem (FR) (Zeddaan) 9f **(76)**
Form - 20000
Record 1998 - 1st:0 2nd:1 3rd:0 Ran:5
Pre1998 - 1st:0 2nd:0 3rd:0 Ran:3
Win Prizemoney £0 *Total Prizemoney* £1,070
1998 Turf 0-5: (5f 4, 6f) (g-s, gd 2, g-f, frm)
Scopey, average filly, effective 5f, acts on g-s. Turf high 69 (1st run) (began Jly) - 2nd of 13 giving 2lb to D'Marti (3 Jly Sandown 5f g-s RF 2508). **E J Alston [0-8] Peter Ebdon Racing.*

POETS PRIDE BHB 47f39a RR 62f 39a 5144[20]

2 br f Cyrano de Bergerac 7.3f **(58)** - Pattis Pet (Mummy's Pet) 7.7f **(60)**
Form - 00468600
Record 1998 - 1st:0 2nd:0 3rd:0 Ran:8
Win Prizemoney £0 *Total Prizemoney* £192
1998 Turf 0-7:(5f 3, 6f 3, 7f)(sft, gd 2,g-f 2,frm 2)1998 AW 0-1:(5f) (Fibr)
Average filly, has worn blinkers. Turf high 62 (began Aug).
**K A Ryan [0-8] Two Jays Partnership.*

POETTO BHB 48f59a RR 49f 59a 4486[10]

3 ch g Casteddu 7.4f **(54)** - Steamy Windows (Dominion) 8.5f **(63)**
Form - 65752344005570
Record 1998 - 1st:0 2nd:1 3rd:1 Ran:12
Pre1998 - 1st:0 2nd:2 3rd:1 Ran:10
Win Prizemoney £0 *Total Prizemoney* £4,261
1998 Turf 0-6: (6f 2, 7f 2, 8f, 10f) (g-s, gd 3, frm 2) 1998 AW 0-6: (6f 2, 7f 3, 8f) (Fibr 6)
Leggy, average gelding, effective 6f, acts on gd, has worn blinkers. Turf high 49. AW high 64. He has made the frame regularly on turf and sand, but cannot get his head in front and is proving expensive to follow.
**Mrs J Brown [0-4] H R Hewitt (from J Hetherton [0-10] Jun 1998).*

POINT OF DISPUTE BHB 82f RR 82df 2074[10]

3 b g Cyrano de Bergerac 7.3f **(58)**-Opuntia (Rousillon (USA)) 8.2f **(74)**
Form - 0180
Record 1998 - 1st:1 2nd:0 3rd:0 Ran:4
Win Prizemoney £3,143 *Total Prizemoney* £3,143
Wins * **1998** May Salisb (G-S) 6f 82 <
1998 Turf 1-4: (6f 1-3, 7f) (gd 1-3, g-f)
Well made, decent gelding. Turf high 82 - 1st of 18 giving 5lb to Uplifting (3 May Salisbury RF 0998).
**P J Makin [1-4] Mrs B J Carrington.*

POKEIT BHB 56f50a RR 60f 50a 4929[13]

2 b g Cyrano de Bergerac 7.3f **(58)** - Entourage (Posse (USA)) 8.9f **(61)**
Form - 44030040
Record 1998 - 1st:0 2nd:0 3rd:1 Ran:8
Win Prizemoney £0 *Total Prizemoney* £647
1998 Turf 0-6: (5f 2, 6f 3, 7f) (g-s, gd, g-f 3, frm) 1998 AW 0-2: (5f, 6f) (Fibr 2)
Average gelding, effective 5f, acts on g-f, has worn blinkers, likes left handed tracks, likes tight tracks. Turf high 63. AW high 44 (began Jly). **G L Moore [0-8] Joe Bates (Bloodstock) Ltd.*

POKER-B (IRE) RR 102f 3870a[6]

4 ch c Shalford (IRE) 7.8f **(63)** - Far From Home (Habitat) 9.4f **(70)**
Form - 4536576
1998 Turf 0-7: (5f, 6f 5, 7f) (sft 3, gd 2, g-f, frm)
Very useful colt, effective 6 to 7f, best at 7f, acts on sft to g-f, best on sft, has worn blinkers, likes left handed tracks. Turf high 102 - 3rd of 5 to Tumbleweed Ridge (10 Jun Leopardstown 7f sft RF 2036a). He won a Listed race as a three-year-old, but has been highly tried, and mostly outclassed, since then. Sold for 45,000 guineas in October to race in Bahrain.
**D Gillespie in IRE [3-22] Patrick Headon.*

POKER SCHOOL (IRE) BHB 44f58a RR 40f 58a 1818[13]

4 b g Night Shift (USA) 8.1f **(73)** - Mosaique Bleue (Shirley Heights) 10.3f **(74)**
Form - 83300000
Record 1998 - 1st:0 2nd:0 3rd:2 Ran:8
Pre1998 - 1st:1 2nd:2 3rd:1 Ran:9
Win Prizemoney £2,740 *Total Prizemoney* £5,658
Wins 1997 May Dundal (GD) 9f 75 <
1998 Turf 0-5: (8f, 10f, 12f 3) (gd 2, g-f 2, frm) 1998 AW 0-3: (10f 2, 12f) (Equi 2, Fibr)
Average gelding, effective 8 to 9f, best at 8f, acts on g-s to gd, best on g-s, has worn blinkers, prefers left handed tracks. Turf high 42. AW high 64. Inconsistent.
**N A Callaghan [0-14] D Westley (from C O'Brien in IRE [1-5] May 1997).*

POKUSSION (IRE) RR 24f 2089[7]

3 b f Polski Boy (USA) - Tambourine Girl (USA) (The Minstrel (CAN)) 10f **(72)**
Form - 7
Record 1998 - 1st:0 2nd:0 3rd:0 Ran:1
1998 Turf 0-1: (10f) (g-s)
Light-framed, currently little account filly.
**M Brittain [0-1] Mel Brittain.*

POLAIRE (IRE) RR 95f 4690a[3]

2 b f Polish Patriot (USA) 7.8f **(70)** - Headrest (Habitat) 9.4f **(70)**
Form - 614363
1998 Turf 1-6: (6f 2, 7f 1-4) (sft, g-s, gd 1-2, g-f, frm)
Very useful filly, effective 6 to 7f, acts on gd to frm. Turf high 95 - also 1st of 11 getting 5lb from Beauty Go Leor (10 Jly Gowran Park RF 2794a). Won her maiden, and then ran useful races in high-class company afterwards. **K Prendergast in IRE [1-6] M J Halligan.*

POLAR CHAMP BHB 73f77a RR 75f 77a 4893[4]

5 b g Polar Falcon (USA) 9f **(74)** - Ceramic (USA) (Raja Baba (USA)) 10f **(64)**
Form - 30503212215D644
Record 1998 - 1st:2 2nd:3 3rd:2 Ran:15
Pre1998 - 1st:3 2nd:4 3rd:2 Ran:19
Win Prizemoney £21,828 *Total Prizemoney* £31,756
Wins * **1998** Jly Ripon (G-F) H 10f 73 75
* **1998** Jun Ripon (SFT) 10f 73
* 1997 *Oct Wolver (STD) H 12f 75 79*
* 1997 May Doncas (G-S) H 10.3f 74 84 <
* 1996 Spt Leices (FRM) 10f 66
1998 Turf 2-14: (10f 2-9, 11f, 12f 4) (sft 2, g-s 1-2, gd 2, g-f 1-4, frm 3, hrd) 1998 AW 0-1: (12f) (Equi)
Decent gelding, effective 10 to 12f, best at 10f, acts on g-s to hrd - acts on Fibr, often wears blinkers, excels at Ripon and Yarmouth. Turf high 75 - 2nd of 8 giving 24lb to Elba Magic (2 Jly Yarmouth 10f hrd RF 2478) - also 1st of 6 giving 19lb to Foxes Tail (18 Jly Ripon RF 2936). A bit of a character and a hard ride, he is now with Nick Gaselee. **S P C Woods [5-34] P K L Chu.*

POLAR ECLIPSE BHB 50f76a RR 50f 76a 3839[9]

5 ch g Polar Falcon (USA) 9f **(74)** - Princess Zepoli (Persepolis (FR)) 6.4f **(67)**
Form - 458030
Record 1998 - 1st:0 2nd:0 3rd:1 Ran:6
Pre1998 - 1st:1 2nd:1 3rd:1 Ran:15
Win Prizemoney £4,320 *Total Prizemoney* £8,931
Wins 1995 Oct Haydoc (G-S) 7.1f 89+ <

1998 Turf 0-6: (6f 2, 7f 3, 8f) (g-s 2, gd, g-f, frm 2)
Fair gelding, has worn blinkers. Turf high 55. Consistent.
**B J Meehan [0-9] J R Good (from M Johnston [1-12] May 1997).*

POLAR FAIR RR 69f 2629[8]

2 ch f Polar Falcon (USA) 9f **(74)** - Fair Country (Town And Country) 8.1f **(68)**
Form - 08
Record 1998 - 1st:0 2nd:0 3rd:0 Ran:2
1998 Turf 0-2: (6f 2) (g-f, frm)
Currently average filly. Turf high 69.
**J Noseda [0-2] Sir Gordon Brunton.*

POLAR ICE RR 83f 4967[5]

2 b c Polar Falcon (USA) 9f **(74)** - Sweet Slew (USA) (Seattle Slew (USA)) 9.4f **(76)**
Form - 25
Record 1998 - 1st:0 2nd:1 3rd:0 Ran:2
Win Prizemoney £0 *Total Prizemoney* £1,020
1998 Turf 0-2: (6f 2) (sft, g-f)
Currently decent colt. Turf high 83 (1st run) (began Spt) - 2nd of 14 to Sir Jack (30 Spt Newcastle 6f g-f RF 4579).
**Sir Mark Prescott [0-2] Cheveley Park Stud.*

POLAR MIST BHB 65f64a RR 44f 64a 4864[6]

3 b g Polar Falcon (USA) 9f **(74)** - Post Mistress (IRE) **(71f)** (Cyrano de Bergerac) 6f **(68)**
Form - 231586
Record 1998 - 1st:1 2nd:0 3rd:1 Ran:5
Pre1998 - 1st:0 2nd:1 3rd:0 Ran:1
Win Prizemoney £3,452 *Total Prizemoney* £4,941
Wins 1998 *Jan Wolver (STD) 6f 73 <*
1998 Turf 0-1: (6f) (frm) 1998 AW 1-4: (5f, 6f 1-3) (Fibr 1-4)
Neat, average gelding, effective 6f, - acts on Fibr. AW high 73 - 1st of 7 from Sara Moon Classic (28 Jan Wolverhampton RF 0171). He had a simple task in a Wolverhampton maiden in January and made no mistake. His shrewd trainer no doubt will find a race or two more for him.
**Mrs N Macauley [0-1] Stephen Roots (from Sir Mark Prescott [1-5] Spt 1998).*

POLAR PEAK BHB 44f RR 59f 5073[13]

2 ch f Polar Falcon (USA) 9f **(74)** - Hilly (Town Crier) 10.2f **(55)**
Form - 0760
Record 1998 - 1st:0 2nd:0 3rd:0 Ran:4
1998 Turf 0-4: (7f, 8f, 10f 2) (gd 3, g-f)
Fair filly, has worn blinkers. Turf high 59 (began Spt).
**G G Margarson [0-4] D P Martin.*

POLAR PRINCE (IRE) BHB 116f RR 117f 4329[6]

5 b h Distinctly North (USA) 7.4f **(63)** - Staff Approved (Teenoso (USA)) 9.9f **(72)**
Form - 414576
Record 1998 - 1st:1 2nd:0 3rd:0 Ran:6
Pre1998 - 1st:6 2nd:4 3rd:3 Ran:22
Win Prizemoney £154,421 *Total Prizemoney* £195,253
Wins * **1998** May Capann (GD) G1 10f 118 <
* 1997 Jun Epsom (GD) G3 8.5f 112
* 1997 May Capann (G-F) L 7f 101
* 1996 Spt Goodwo (G-F) 7f 105
* 1996 Aug Newmar (G-F) H 7f 96 103
* 1996 Jun Epsom (G-F) H 7f 90 93
* 1995 Spt Haydoc (GD) 7.1f 76+
1998 Turf 1-6: (8f, 10f 1-4, 11f) (sft 2, gd 1-2, g-f 2)
High-class colt, effective 8 to 11f, acts on gd to g-f, best on gd, likes right handed tracks, excels at Capannelle. Turf high 118 - 1st of 7 from Annus Mirabilis (17 May Capannelle RF 1381a). An admirable performer with a potent turn of foot, he found the soft ground against him on his seasonal debut, but won a weak Group One in Rome next time when stepped up to ten furlongs. He ran some decent races afterwards, but was held in the highest class in this country. **M A Jarvis [7-28] Mrs Christine Stevenson.*

POLAR PROSPECT BHB 60f RR 60f 1074[3]

5 b g Polar Falcon (USA) 9f **(74)** - Littlemisstrouble (USA) (My Gallant (USA)) 9f **(71)**
Form - 3
Record 1998 - 1st:0 2nd:0 3rd:1 Ran:1
Pre1998 - 1st:2 2nd:2 3rd:1 Ran:15
Win Prizemoney £6,881 *Total Prizemoney* £14,403
Wins 1997 Oct Redcar (G-F) H 9f 56 60
1996 Jun Beverl (G-F) 7.5f 66 <
1998 Turf 0-1: (12f) (g-f)
Average gelding, effective 8 to 12f, acts on g-f to frm, best on g-f. (1st run) - 3rd of 11 getting 10lb from Domappel (7 May Chester 12f g-f RF 1074).
**P J Hobbs [3-8] & Mrs Don Last and Bill Yates (from B Hanbury [2-15] Oct 1997).*

POLAR REFRAIN BHB 32f25a RR 29f 25a 2266[2]

5 ch m Polar Falcon (USA) 9f **(74)**-Cut No Ice (Great Nephew) 9.9f **(64)**
Form - 12
Record 1998 - 1st:1 2nd:1 3rd:0 Ran:2
Pre1998 - 1st:0 2nd:1 3rd:3 Ran:19
Win Prizemoney £2,010 *Total Prizemoney* £5,039
Wins * **1998** Jun Redcar (G-S) H 8f 25 29 <
1998 Turf 1-2: (7f, 8f 1-1) (gd 1-2)
Very moderate filly, effective 7 to 8f, acts on gd, has worn blinkers. Turf high 29 - 2nd of 13 to Priory Gardens (25 Jun Carlisle 7f gd RF 2266) - also 1st of 8 getting 7lb from Ikis Girl (20 Jun Redcar RF 2160). **J L Eyre [1-2] Billy Parker (from J Norton [0-5] Jun 1997).*

POLES APART (IRE) BHB 95f RR 98f 4237[5]

2 b c Distinctly North (USA) 7.4f **(63)** -Slightly Latin (Ahonoora) 8.1f **(73)**
Form - 3145
Record 1998 - 1st:1 2nd:0 3rd:1 Ran:4
Win Prizemoney £2,905 *Total Prizemoney* £12,327
Wins * **1998** Aug Folkes (G-F) 6f 84+ <
1998 Turf 1-4: (6f 1-4) (gd, g-f 1-2, frm)
Very useful colt. Turf high 98 (began Jly) - 4th of 27 giving 5lb to Amazing Dream (29 Aug Curragh 6f gd RF 4039a). Not beaten far in a valuable sales race at the Curragh, but failed to confirm the form on his final start.
**M H Tompkins [1-4] Flint Fairyhouse Partnership.*

POLISH LEGION BHB 54f RR 56f 4669[16]

5 b g Polish Precedent (USA) 9f **(73)** - Crystal Bright (Bold Lad (IRE)) 8.4f **(68)**
Form - 70000
Record 1998 - 1st:0 2nd:0 3rd:0 Ran:5
Pre1998 - 1st:1 2nd:0 3rd:0 Ran:1
Win Prizemoney £3,850 *Total Prizemoney* £3,850
Wins 1995 Apr Newbur (G-F) 5.2f 86+t <
1998 Turf 0-5: (6f 4, 8f) (g-s, gd, g-f 2, frm)
Fair gelding. Turf high 56.
**J Akehurst [0-5] R J P J Partnership (from J H M Gosden [1-1] Apr 1995).*

POLISH PILOT (IRE) BHB 52f67a RR 65f 67a 4574[17]

3 b c Polish Patriot (USA) 7.8f **(70)** -Va Toujours (Alzao (USA))7.1f **(68)**
Form - 76850000
Record 1998 - 1st:0 2nd:0 3rd:0 Ran:7
Pre1998 - 1st:0 2nd:0 3rd:1 Ran:4
Win Prizemoney £0 *Total Prizemoney* £429
1998 Turf 0-7: (8f, 9f, 10f 4, 13f) (gd, g-f, frm 5)
Workmanlike, average colt, effective 9f, acts on frm, has worn blinkers, likes tight tracks. Turf high 65. Becoming disappointing.
**W R Muir [0-11] Mrs Barbara Jean Martin.*

POLISH SPIRIT BHB 60f RR 69f 4799[20]

3 b g Emarati (USA) 6.6f **(63)**-Gentle Star (Comedy Star(USA))7.5f **(50)**
Form - 7010050
Record 1998 - 1st:1 2nd:0 3rd:0 Ran:7
Win Prizemoney £3,687 *Total Prizemoney* £3,687
Wins * **1998** Jly Warwic (G-F) 7f 69 <
1998 Turf 1-7: (6f, 7f 1-4, 8f 2) (sft, g-f 2, frm 1-4)
Unfurnished, average gelding, effective 7f, acts on frm. Turf high 69 - 1st of 7 from Great News (11 Jly Warwick RF 2731).
**B R Millman [1-7] Mrs Izabel Palmer.*

POLIZIANO (USA) RR 72+f 1895[2]

2 ch c Storm Bird (CAN) 8.5f **(82)** - Polemic (USA) (Roberto (USA)) 10f **(76)**
Form - 2

Record 1998 - 1st:0 2nd:1 3rd:0 Ran:1
Win Prizemoney £0 *Total Prizemoney* £1,144
1998 Turf 0-1: (6f) (g-s)
Currently above-average colt. Promising debut in yielding ground at Newbury. **H R A Cecil [0-1] K Abdulla.*

POLKA RR 6f 3383[6]

3 b c Slip Anchor 12.7f **(75)** - Peace Dance (Bikala) 10.1f **(49)**
Form - 6
Record 1998 - 1st:0 2nd:0 3rd:0 Ran:1
1998 Turf 0-1: (9f) (g-f)
Currently very poor colt. **C W Thornton [0-1] Guy Reed.*

POLLYDUU BHB 30a RR 30a 73[5]

3 ch f Casteddu 7.4f **(54)** - Polly Packer (Reform) 8.9f **(62)**
Form - 0065
Record 1998 - 1st:0 2nd:0 3rd:0 Ran:1
Pre1998 - 1st:0 2nd:0 3rd:0 Ran:3
1998 AW 0-1: (6f) (Fibr)
Poor filly, has worn blinkers. **N P Littmoden [0-4] David Hall.*

POLLY GOLIGHTLY BHB 67f50a RR 68f 50a 5142[9]

5 ch m Weldnaas (USA) 8.4f **(55)** - Polly's Teahouse (Shack (USA)) 5.8f **(53)**
Form - 04471172304570700
Record 1998 - 1st:2 2nd:1 3rd:1 Ran:17
Pre1998 - 1st:5 2nd:3 3rd:6 Ran:42
Win Prizemoney £29,667 *Total Prizemoney* £43,239
Wins * 1998 Jun York (G-S) H 5f 56 73
*** 1998** Jun Cheste (GD) H 5.1f 56 76?
* 1997 Oct Catter (SFT) H 5f 54 60
* 1997 Jun Goodwo (G-F) H 5f 59 64
* 1997 May Lingfi (G-F) H 5f 54 57
1995 Nov Doncas (G-F) H 5f 77 80 <
1995 May Bath (GD) 5.1f 60
1998 Turf 2-17: (5f 2-17) (sft, g-s 1-2, gd 1-8, frm 6)
Average filly, effective 5f, acts on g-s to frm, mostly wears blinkers (effectively), excels at York. Turf high 76 - 2nd of 8 getting 21lb from Blessingindisguise (10 Jly York 5f frm RF 2698) - also 1st of 7 giving 5lb to Napoleon Star (3 Jun Chester RF 1686). Consistent. A speedy mare, she runs from the front and was in fine form in June, winning at Chester and York. She is most effective over an easy five. **M Blanshard [5-50] David Sykes (from B Smart [2-9] Nov 1995).*

POLLY MILLS BHB 74f72a RR 78?f 72a 5068[6]

2 b f Lugana Beach 7f **(63)** - Danseuse Davis (FR) **(46f 42a)** (Glow (USA)) 6.7f **(71)**
Form - 71243504408046
Record 1998 - 1st:1 2nd:1 3rd:1 Ran:14
Win Prizemoney £2,304 *Total Prizemoney* £4,554
Wins * 1998 Jun Windso (SFT) S 5f 66 <
1998 Turf 1-13: (5f 1-10, 6f 3) (g-s, gd 1-4, g-f 5, frm 3) 1998 AW 0-1: (5f) (Fibr)
Above-average filly, effective 5f, acts on gd to g-f, has worn blinkers. Turf high 78 - 4th of 6 getting 4lb from Angie Baby (26 Aug Lingfield 5f g-f RF 3893). She showed the right sort of attitude to land a Windsor seller on her second start, handling the soft ground well, and has faced some impossible tasks since. She did not seem to stay when tried beyond the minimum.
**P D Evans [1-14] Mrs H Raw.*

POLLYTEKNICK BHB 27f31a RR 10f 31a 1768[6]

3 gr f Terimon 8.7f **(58)** - Flute Royale (Horage) 10.3f **(61)**
Form - 06
Record 1998 - 1st:0 2nd:0 3rd:0 Ran:2
Pre1998 - 1st:0 2nd:0 3rd:0 Ran:3
1998 Turf 0-1: (7f) (gd) 1998 AW 0-1: (5f) (Fibr)
Light-framed, little account filly.
**J L Eyre [0-2] The Polly Partnership (from N P Littmoden [0-3] Jly 1997).*

POLONAISE PRINCE (USA) BHB 50f45a RR 53f 45a 4065[P]

5 b g Alleged (USA) 11.8f **(81)** - La Polonaise (USA) (Danzig (USA)) 8.4f **(76)**
Form - 2731P
Record 1998 - 1st:1 2nd:1 3rd:1 Ran:5
Pre1998 - 1st:0 2nd:0 3rd:0 Ran:5
Win Prizemoney £2,472 *Total Prizemoney* £3,658
Wins * 1998 Aug Bath (FRM) H 8f 46 53 <
1998 Turf 1-5: (8f 1-3, 10f 2) (gd, g-f, frm 1-3)
Fair gelding, effective 8 to 10f, acted on gd to frm, had worn blinkers, favoured tight tracks. Turf high 53 - 1st of 18 getting 4lb from Bestemor (11 Aug Bath RF 3524). (DEAD)
**P J Makin [1-5] Four Seasons Racing Ltd (from V Soane [0-4] Oct 1997).*

POLO VENTURE BHB 63f68a RR 71f 68a 3275[7]

3 ch g Polar Falcon (USA) 9f **(74)** - Ceramic (USA) (Raja Baba (USA)) 10f **(64)**
Form - 3321557
Record 1998 - 1st:1 2nd:1 3rd:2 Ran:7
Pre1998 - 1st:0 2nd:0 3rd:2 Ran:5
Win Prizemoney £2,898 *Total Prizemoney* £5,983
Wins * 1998 *May Lingfi (STD) 10f 69 <*
1998 Turf 0-3: (10f, 12f 2) (sft, frm 2) 1998 AW 1-4: (9f, 10f 1-1, 12f 2) (Equi 1-2, Fibr 2)
Leggy, above-average gelding, effective 8 to 12f, acts on gd to frm - acts on Equi, likes left handed tracks. Turf high 71. AW high 71 - 2nd of 9 getting 3lb from Blueprint (13 May Lingfield 12f Equi RF 1204) - also 1st of 8 getting 20lb from Ki Chi Saga (23 May Lingfield RF 1435). Consistent. **S P C Woods [1-12] Dr Frank Chao.*

POLRUAN BHB 78f RR 77f 5148[7]

2 ch c Elmaamul (USA) 8.1f **(70)** - Trelissick (Electric) 10.1f **(61)**
Form - 2402517
Record 1998 - 1st:1 2nd:2 3rd:0 Ran:7
Win Prizemoney £3,030 *Total Prizemoney* £5,261
Wins * 1998 Oct Warwic (GD) 6f 74+ <
1998 Turf 1-7: (5f, 6f 1-3, 7f 3) (gd 5, g-f 1-1, frm)
Above-average colt, effective 6 to 7f, best at 6f, acts on gd to g-f, best on gd. Turf high 77 - 2nd of 11 giving 5lb to Schnitzel (11 Spt Goodwood 7f gd RF 4230) - also 1st of 10 from Bartholomew (4 Oct Warwick RF 4642). **B R Millman [1-7] Michael WingfieldDigby.*

POLSKA MODELLE (FR) BHB 82f RR 82f 3852[6]

3 ch c Polish Precedent (USA) 9f **(73)** - Model Village (Habitat) 9.4f **(70)**
Form - 0250156
Record 1998 - 1st:1 2nd:1 3rd:0 Ran:7
Pre1998 - 1st:0 2nd:0 3rd:0 Ran:1
Win Prizemoney £6,076 *Total Prizemoney* £7,228
Wins * 1998 Jly Nottin (G-F) H 8.2f 80 82 <
1998 Turf 1-7: (8f 1-6, 10f) (gd 1-5, g-f, frm)
Scopey, decent colt, effective 8f, acts on gd, prefers left handed tracks, prefers tight tracks. Turf high 82 - 1st of 6 giving 15lb to Silken Dalliance (18 Jly Nottingham RF 2925). He has shown some ability in varied company but has also looked short of pace.
**J H M Gosden [1-8] Sheikh Mohammed.*

POLY BLUE (IRE) BHB 69f RR 83f 5079[24]

3 ch f Thatching 7.8f **(69)** - Mazarine Blue (USA) (Chief's Crown (USA)) 9.8f **(72)**
Form - 2684304500
Record 1998 - 1st:0 2nd:1 3rd:1 Ran:10
Pre1998 - 1st:1 2nd:0 3rd:0 Ran:4
Win Prizemoney £3,902 *Total Prizemoney* £7,997
Wins * 1997 Spt Newbur (G-S) 6f 80 <
1998 Turf 0-10: (6f, 7f 9) (sft, g-s 2, gd 4, frm 3)
Unfurnished, decent filly, effective 6 to 7f, best at 7f, acts on gd to frm, best on frm, has worn blinkers. Turf high 84.
**Miss Gay Kelleway [1-14] Sheet & Roll Convertors Ltd.*

POLYPHONY (USA) BHB 54f RR 54f 1879[10]

4 b c Cox's Ridge (USA) 9.4f **(72)** - Populi (USA) (Star Envoy (USA)) 9.6f **(78)**
Form - 760
Record 1998 - 1st:0 2nd:0 3rd:0 Ran:3
Pre1998 - 1st:1 2nd:1 3rd:1 Ran:4
Win Prizemoney £3,363 *Total Prizemoney* £5,191
Wins 1997 Apr Carlis (GD) 12f 70 <
1998 Turf 0-3: (12f, 14f, 15f) (sft, g-s, frm)
Light-framed, average colt, effective 12 to 14f, acts on gd, has worn blinkers. Turf high 54.
**D C O'Brien [0-4] Michael Gearon (from R Charlton [1-4] Jun 1997).*

POLY RULER (IRE) BHB 50f **RR 65f** 4762[5]
2 b c Dancing Dissident (USA) 6.8f **(65)** - Love Me Tight (Tyrant (USA)) 6.6f **(59)**
Form - 0705
Record 1998 - 1st:0 2nd:0 3rd:0 Ran:4
1998 Turf 0-4: (7f, 8f 2, 10f) (gd 4)
Average colt. Turf high 65 (began Aug).
**M R Channon [0-4] Sheet & Roll Convertors Ltd.*

PORCELLINO (IRE) BHB 44f60a **RR 51f 60a** 4885[6]
3 b g Last Tycoon 9.4f **(73)** - Supportive (IRE) (Nashamaa) 7.1f **(66)**
Form - 02500300306
Record 1998 - 1st:0 2nd:1 3rd:2 Ran:11
Pre1998 - 1st:0 2nd:0 3rd:0 Ran:4
Win Prizemoney £0 *Total Prizemoney* £1,272
1998 Turf 0-9: (7f 7, 8f, 9f) (sft, g-s 2, gd 4, g-f, frm) 1998 AW 0-2: (8f, 9f) (Fibr 2)

Porto Foricos winning at York

POOL MUSIC BHB 91f **RR 90f** 2582[8]
3 ch c Forzando 7.2f **(63)** - Sunfleet (Red Sunset) 8.2f **(63)**
Form - 85308
Record 1998 - 1st:0 2nd:0 3rd:1 Ran:5
Pre1998 - 1st:2 2nd:0 3rd:2 Ran:7
Win Prizemoney £12,667 *Total Prizemoney* £24,115
Wins * 1997 May Sandow (G-F) L 5f 94+ <
* 1997 May Salisb (G-F) 5f 85+
1998 Turf 0-5: (6f 3, 7f 2) (sft, g-s, gd, frm 2)
Scopey, useful colt, effective 5 to 6f, acts on gd to g-f. Turf high 90. He paid for his success as a two-year-old by starting the season too high in the handicap. He was well held in Listed events early on, and even when his handicap mark dropped it made little difference. **R Hannon [2-12] Mrs Caroline Parker.*

POPPY TOO (IRE) BHB 40f **RR 45f** 2173[13]
3 br f Petardia 8.2f **(58)** - My Natalie (Rheingold) 10.4f **(62)**
Form - 60070
Record 1998 - 1st:0 2nd:0 3rd:0 Ran:5
1998 Turf 0-5: (8f, 10f 3, 12f) (sft, gd 3, frm)
Unfurnished, moderate filly, has worn blinkers. Turf high 45.
**M R Channon [0-5] T S M Cunningham.*

Fair gelding, has worn blinkers. Turf high 57. AW high 44.
**K R Burke [0-11] The Ginge Racing Partnership (from D K Weld in IRE [0-4] Aug 1997).*

PORLOCK LADY BHB 37f **RR 31f** 4004[12]
3 b f King's Signet (USA) 7f **(51)** - Miramede (Norwick (USA)) 7.2f **(56)**
Form - 600
Record 1998 - 1st:0 2nd:0 3rd:0 Ran:3
1998 Turf 0-3: (5f 2, 6f) (gd, g-f, frm)
Light-framed, currently very moderate filly. Turf high 31 (began Jly). **R J Hodges [0-3] John Davey Beverton.*

PORTENT **RR 27f** 1836[14]
3 ch f Most Welcome 8.6f **(66)** - Foreseen (Reform) 8.9f **(62)**
Form - 00
Record 1998 - 1st:0 2nd:0 3rd:0 Ran:2
1998 Turf 0-2: (8f 2) (gd 2)
Neat, currently little account filly, often wears blinkers. Turf high 27. **Lady Herries [0-2] Hesmonds Stud.*

PORTHILLY BUOY BHB 43f40a **RR 52f 40a** 1291[13]
3 ch g Keen 11.1f **(58)** - Hissma (Midyan (USA)) 6f **(60)**
Form - 7570

Record 1998 - 1st:0 2nd:0 3rd:0 Ran:3
Pre1998 - 1st:0 2nd:0 3rd:0 Ran:4
1998 Turf 0-1: (8f) (frm) 1998 AW 0-2: (8f 2) (Equi 2)
Workmanlike, fair gelding. AW high 31.
**M J Haynes [0-7] Porthilly Partners.*

PORTITE SOPHIE BHB 39f27a **RR 41f 27a** 4549[6]
7 b m Doulab (USA) 7.4f **(61)**-Impropriety (Law Society (USA)) 9.9f **(70)**
Form - 58028451736
Record 1998 - 1st:1 2nd:1 3rd:1 Ran:11
Pre1998 - 1st:2 2nd:9 3rd:4 Ran:53
Win Prizemoney £7,018 *Total Prizemoney* £17,385
Wins * **1998** Spt Hamilt (SFT) S 9.2f 41
* 1997 *Jly Southw (STD) C 11f 45* <
* 1996 *Jly Wolver (STD) H 8.5f 29 32*
1998 Turf 1-6: (9f 1-1, 10f 2, 11f 2, 12f) (g-s, gd 1-3, g-f 2) 1998 AW 0-5: (8f, 9f, 11f, 12f 2) (Fibr 5)
Moderate mare, effective 8 to 12f, acts on gd to frm - acts on Fibr, has worn blinkers, likes right handed tracks, favours tight tracks, and likes Beverley. Turf high 41 - 1st of 11 giving 6lb to Priolette (7 Spt Hamilton RF 4133). AW high 16.
**M Brittain [3-64] Ms Maureen Hanlon.*

PORT MEADOW (IRE) **RR 62f** 5146[6]
2 b c Common Grounds 8.1f **(66)** - Kharimata (IRE) (Kahyasi)
Form - 06
Record 1998 - 1st:0 2nd:0 3rd:0 Ran:2
1998 Turf 0-2: (8f 2) (gd, g-f)
Currently average colt. Turf high 62 (began Oct).
**R Charlton [0-2] Lady Vestey.*

PORTO FORICOS (USA) BHB 100f **RR 102f** 5136a[7]
3 b c Mr Prospector (USA) 8.6f **(88)** - Gallanta (FR) (Nureyev (USA)) 8.7f **(78)**
Form - 331107407
Record 1998 - 1st:2 2nd:0 3rd:2 Ran:9
Pre1998 - 1st:0 2nd:0 3rd:0 Ran:2
Win Prizemoney £74,470 *Total Prizemoney* £76,795
Wins * **1998** Jly York (FRM) H 10.4f 90 94 <
* **1998** May Goodwo (G-F) 9f 74
1998 Turf 2-9: (7f, 8f 3, 9f 1-3, 10f 1-2) (gd 2, g-f 1-4, frm 1-3)
Scopey, very useful colt, effective 8 to 10f, acts on g-f to frm. Turf high 102 - also 1st of 20 getting 21lb from Pasternak (11 Jly York RF 2738). Henry Cecil is usually very patient with his horses, but this colt was an exception. Rushed into the Group One Sussex Stakes (he was supplemented at a cost of £18,000) after winning the John Smith's Cup off a mark of 90, he lost his way and ended the season looking thoroughly dejected. He is set to continue his career in California. **H R A Cecil [2-11].*

PORTOLANO (FR) BHB 25f27a **RR 17f 27a** 175[7]
7 b g Reference Point 12f **(66)** - Kottna (USA) (Lyphard (USA)) 9.9f **(72)**
Form - 7
Record 1998 - 1st:0 2nd:0 3rd:0 Ran:1
Pre1998 - 1st:0 2nd:1 3rd:2 Ran:16
Win Prizemoney £0 *Total Prizemoney* £1,674
1998 AW 0-1: (15f) (Fibr)
Poor gelding, has worn blinkers.
**B P J Baugh [0-4] T A Peake (from W Clay [0-6] Aug 1995).*

PORTUGUESE LIL BHB 34f **RR 49f** 4409[10]
5 ch m Master Willie 9.2f **(67)** - Sabonis (USA) (The Minstrel (CAN)) 10f **(72)**
Form - 006500800
Record 1998 - 1st:0 2nd:0 3rd:0 Ran:9
Pre1998 - 1st:0 2nd:0 3rd:1 Ran:10
Win Prizemoney £0 *Total Prizemoney* £582
1998 Turf 0-9: (8f 2, 10f 5, 12f 2) (gd, g-f 4, frm 3, hrd)
Moderate filly, effective 10f, acts on g-f, has worn blinkers, likes right handed tracks, favours tight tracks. Turf high 49 - 5th of 8 getting 19lb from Mazeed (4 Jly Beverley 10f g-f RF 2517). Inconsistent.
**M E Sowersby [0-9] Mrs G W Bloom (from J L Eyre [0-1] Jun 1997).*

POSATIVE BHB 41f29a **RR 43f 29a** 4529[7]
4 ch f Charmer 9f **(59)** - Suprette (Superlative) 7.2f **(56)**
Form - 757
Record 1998 - 1st:0 2nd:0 3rd:0 Ran:3
Pre1998 - 1st:0 2nd:0 3rd:0 Ran:1
1998 Turf 0-1: (8f) (g-f) 1998 AW 0-2: (6f, 7f) (Equi 2)
Scopey, moderate filly. **M Salaman [0-4] M J Lewin.*

POSEIDON BHB 99f **RR 106f** 3634[7]
4 b c Polar Falcon (USA) 9f **(74)** - Nastassia (FR) (Noble Decree (USA)) 10.2f **(76)**
Form - 1565357
Record 1998 - 1st:1 2nd:0 3rd:1 Ran:7
Pre1998 - 1st:2 2nd:2 3rd:0 Ran:10
Win Prizemoney £22,200 *Total Prizemoney* £41,238
Wins * **1998** Mar Doncas (GD) 12f 109 <
* 1997 Jun Doncas (G-F) 10.3f 104
* 1996 Spt San Si (GD) 6f
1998 Turf 1-7: (10f 2, 11f, 12f 1-4) (gd 1-5, g-f 2)
Pattern-class colt, effective 10 to 12f, best at 12f, acts on g-s to frm, best on gd. Turf high 109 (1st run) - 1st of 8 giving 2lb to Sacho (28 Mar Doncaster RF 0487). Consistent. He was fortunate to be awarded a race at Doncaster in March and regressed as the season went on.
**M R Channon [3-17] Allevamento La Nuova Sbarra SRL.*

POSIDONAS BHB 119f **RR 122f** 4951a[2]
6 b h Slip Anchor 12.7f **(75)** -Tamassos(Dance In Time (CAN)) 8.9f **(59)**
Form - 2161302
Record 1998 - 1st:2 2nd:1 3rd:1 Ran:6
Pre1998 - 1st:6 2nd:3 3rd:4 Ran:19
Win Prizemoney £274,583 *Total Prizemoney* £509,602
Wins * **1998** Jun Ascot (G-S) G2 12f 122
* **1998** Apr Newbur (HVY) G3 12f 115
* 1997 Spt Newbur (G-F) L 11f 113
* 1996 Jly Newmar (GD) G2 12f 123 <
* 1995 Spt San Si (SFT) G1 12f 108
* 1995 Spt Goodwo (GD) 12f 105
* 1995 Apr Newbur (GD) 11f 93
* 1994 Spt Goodwo (GD) 8f 69t
1998 Turf 2-6: (11f, 12f 2-5) (sft 1-3, gd 1-2, g-f)
Very high-class horse, effective 11 to 12f, best at 12f, acts on sft to frm, has worn blinkers, excels at Newbury. Turf high 122 - 1st of 7 from Germano (19 Jun Ascot RF 2106) - also 1st of 12 from Sacho (18 Apr Newbury RF 0741). Consistent. Ninth in the 1997 Arc, he began the season with a battling victory in the John Porter Stakes, handling the heavy ground well, but was well beaten in the Coronation Cup before taking the Hardwicke at Ascot. Beaten at Newbury after a break, he ran below expectations in the Arc this term. He came back from that to give Silver Patriarch a battle in the valuable Gran Premio del Jockey-Club in Milan. He races with his head high, but his gameness cannot be questioned.
**P F I Cole [8-25].*

POSIE CHAIN BHB 22f22a **RR 18f 22a** 1578[6]
5 b m Rakaposhi King 9.3f **(55)** - Call Me Daisy (Callernish) 12.6f **(58)**
Form - 255006
Record 1998 - 1st:0 2nd:1 3rd:0 Ran:6
Win Prizemoney £0 *Total Prizemoney* £585
1998 Turf 0-1: (7f) (gd) 1998 AW 0-5: (9f, 11f, 12f 2, 16f) (Equi, Fibr 4)
Moderate filly, effective 11f, - acts on Fibr. AW high 40 (1st run) - 2nd of 10 to Cruz Santa (5 Jan Southwell 11f Fibr RF 0024).
**N P Littmoden [0-6] Mrs P M Daniel.*

POSITIVE AIR BHB 72f **RR 82f** 4751[19]
3 b f Puissance 7.1f **(60)** - Breezy Day (Day Is Done) 6.3f **(67)**
Form - 00371660700
Record 1998 - 1st:1 2nd:0 3rd:1 Ran:11
Pre1998 - 1st:0 2nd:3 3rd:1 Ran:10
Win Prizemoney £7,304 *Total Prizemoney* £11,747
Wins * **1998** Jun Pontef (GD) H 6f 75 78 <
1998 Turf 1-11: (6f 1-8, 7f 3) (gd 6, g-f, frm 1-4)
Scopey, decent filly, effective 6f, acts on gd to frm, best on gd, has worn blinkers. Turf high 82 - also 1st of 11 giving 2lb to Angel Hill (29 Jun Pontefract RF 2377). Inconsistent.
**B A McMahon [1-21] R Thornhill.*

POSTLIP GOLD **RR** 3317[18]
3 b f Derrylin 12.7f **(38)** - Wilhemina Crusty (Jester)
Form - 00

Record 1998 - 1st:0 2nd:0 3rd:0 Ran:2
1998 Turf 0-2: (10f 2) (g-f, frm)
Workmanlike, currently very poor filly. (began Jly).
**L P Grassick [0-2] Alan Waller And Mrs Pat Beck.*

the easy winner Intikhab in the Queen Anne before finding ten furlongs too far in the Eclipse. Reverting to a mile, his last run was a disappointing effort in the Sussex, and he still fails to inspire punters with confidence. **L M Cumani [2-11] Gary Tanaka.*

Posidonas put up a brave performance to win the Hardwicke

POTEEN (USA) RR 113f 3205[6]
4 b c Irish River (FR) 9f(**77**)-Chaleur (CAN)(Rouge Sang (USA))7f (**118**)
Form - 2356

Record	**1998 -**	1st:0	2nd:1	3rd:1	Ran:4
	Pre1998 -	1st:2	2nd:2	3rd:1	Ran:7

Win Prizemoney £7,851 *Total Prizemoney* £113,606

Wins	* 1997 Apr	Newmar (GD)	7f	99	<
	* 1996 Oct	Haydoc (SFT)	7.1f	92+	

1998 Turf 0-4: (8f 3, 10f) (gd 3, frm)
Scopey, Group-class colt, effective 7 to 8f, best at 8f, acts on gd to frm, has worn blinkers. Turf high 120 (1st run) - 2nd of 10 to Cape Cross (16 May Newbury 8f frm RF 1260). Consistent. He always runs in the highest class, but since winning on his reappearance in 1997, has been an 'almost' horse. Once again his best performance of the season was on his reappearance, going down by just a neck in a weak-looking renewal of the Lockinge. He ran third to

POWER FLAME (GER) RR 116f 4599a[1]
5 ch g Dashing Blade 7.9f (**80**)-Pikante (GER) (Surumu (GER)) 10f (**83**)
Form - 111
1998 Turf 3-3: (8f 3-3) (sft 2-2, gd 1-1)
High-class gelding. Turf high 116 (began Aug) - 1st of 9 giving 8lb to Tannenkonig (26 Spt Cologne RF 4599a) - also 1st of 7 giving 19lb to Equity Princess (1 Spt Baden-Baden RF 4212a). A useful German miler who has gained a string of Group Two and Group Three victories in his home country over the last couple of seasons. Difficult to know how good he is until he takes on decent company outside Germany.
**A Wohler in GER [5-5] Renstall Darboven.*

POWER GAME BHB 30f49a **RR 53f 49a** 4536[12]
5 b g Puissance 7.1f (**60**) - Play the Game (Mummy's Game) 8.2f (**60**)
Form - 50000

Record 1998 - 1st:0 2nd:0 3rd:0 Ran:5
Pre1998 - 1st:6 2nd:3 3rd:9 Ran:35
Win Prizemoney £16,798 *Total Prizemoney* £25,967
Wins 1997 May Mussel (G-F) H 8f 51 59
1997 May Mussel (G-S) S 8f 54
1996 Oct Leices (GD) C 8f 66 <
1996 Spt Hamilt (GD) C 8.3f 64
1996 Spt Thirsk (G-F) S 8f 59
1996 Aug Haydoc (G-F) S 8.1f 58
1998 Turf 0-5: (8f 4, 9f) (g-s 2, gd, g-f, frm)
Fair gelding, effective 8f, acts on gd to g-f, often wears blinkers, likes right handed tracks. Turf high 53. Becoming disappointing.
**D A Nolan [0-5] Mrs J McFadyen-Murray (from J Berry [6-35] Jly 1997).*

POWER GLOW RR 43f 3581[13]

2 gr c Puissance 7.1f **(60)** - Kala Rosa (Kalaglow) 9.8f **(67)**
Form - 000
Record 1998 - 1st:0 2nd:0 3rd:0 Ran:3
1998 Turf 0-3: (5f, 6f 2) (gd 2, g-f)
Currently moderate colt. Turf high 43 (began Jly).
**J M Bradley [0-3] B Paling.*

POWERGOLD (IRE) BHB 72f RR 70f 3961[12]

2 ch g Second Set (IRE) 9.2f **(67)** - Madaraya (USA) (Shahrastani (USA)) 8.8f **(72)**
Form - 0420
Record 1998 - 1st:0 2nd:1 3rd:0 Ran:4
Win Prizemoney £0 *Total Prizemoney* £1,345
1998 Turf 0-4: (6f 3, 7f) (g-f 2, frm 2)
Above-average gelding. Turf high 70 (began Jly).
**W A O'Gorman [0-4] N S Yong.*

POW WOW BHB 36f50a RR 31df 50a 2468[12]

4 b c Efisio 7.7f **(69)** - Mill Hill (USA) (Riva Ridge (USA)) 8.2f **(68)**
Form - 572751000
Record 1998 - 1st:1 2nd:1 3rd:0 Ran:9
Pre1998 - 1st:0 2nd:0 3rd:0 Ran:5
Win Prizemoney £2,295 *Total Prizemoney* £3,105
Wins * **1998** *Mar Wolver (STD) H 7f 45 53 <*
1998 Turf 0-2: (6f, 7f) (gd, frm) 1998 AW 1-7: (7f 1-7) (Fibr 1-7)
Unfurnished, fair colt, effective 7f, - acts on Fibr, favours left handed tracks, favours tight tracks. AW high 55 - 2nd of 11 to Zalotto (23 Jan Southwell 7f Fibr RF 0142) - also 1st of 12 giving 1lb to Hever Golf Passion (7 Mar Wolverhampton RF 0404). Inconsistent.
**E J Alston [1-9] Valley Paddocks Racing Ltd (from P Eccles [0-2] Spt 1997).*

POZARICA RR 106f 3226a[1]

3 b c Rainbow Quest (USA) 11.2f **(81)** - Anna Matrushka (Mill Reef (USA)) 10.5f **(78)**
Form - 11
1998 Turf 2-2: (15f 2-2) (gd 2-2)
Currently Pattern-class colt. Turf high 106 (began Jly) - 1st of 4 from Ocean of Storms (25 Jly Maisons-laffitte RF 3226a) - also 1st of 5 from Blushing Risk (1 Jly Chantilly RF 2662a). He almost earned a crack at the St Leger after winning two Group races in the summer. In the event connections kept their powder dry; they have a super prospect for the top long-distance prizes next term.
**N Clement in FR [2-2] Sheikh Mohammed Al Maktoum.*

PRAEDITUS BHB 60f60a RR 58f 60a 3067[6]

4 b g Cadeaux Genereux 7.9f **(76)** - Round Midnight (Star Appeal) 9.6f **(65)**
Form - 036
Record 1998 - 1st:0 2nd:0 3rd:1 Ran:3
Pre1998 - 1st:1 2nd:0 3rd:1 Ran:11
Win Prizemoney £3,190 *Total Prizemoney* £4,369
Wins 1997 May Lingfi (GD) 7f 76 <
1998 Turf 0-2: (10f, 12f) (g-f, frm) 1998 AW 0-1: (8f) (Fibr)
Scopey, fair gelding, effective 7f, acts on frm, has worn blinkers. Turf high 56 (began Jly).
**M C Pipe [0-3] B A Kilpatrick (from R Hannon [1-11] Oct 1997).*

PRAETORIAN GOLD BHB 82f RR 87f 4763[11]

3 ch c Presidium 7.5f **(56)** - Chinese Princess (Sunny Way) 9f **(53)**
Form - 03112040
Record 1998 - 1st:2 2nd:1 3rd:1 Ran:8
Pre1998 - 1st:1 2nd:0 3rd:1 Ran:7
Win Prizemoney £12,497 *Total Prizemoney* £17,412
Wins * **1998** Jun Chepst (G-S) H 10.2f 76 80 <
* **1998** Jun Goodwo (GD) H 9.9f 68 75
* 1997 Spt Nottin (GD) 6.1f 66
1998 Turf 2-8: (9f, 10f 2-6, 12f) (gd 2-5, g-f, frm 2)
Useful colt, effective 10f, acts on gd, likes right handed tracks. Turf high 87 - 2nd of 9 getting 4lb from Mr Cahill (24 Jly Ascot 10f gd RF 3064) - also 1st of 8 giving 1lb to Alcayde (30 Jun Chepstow RF 2397). He has improved tremendously during the summer, winning most impressively over ten furlongs at Goodwood and Chepstow. Well beaten latterly, however.
**R Hannon [3-15] The Gold Buster Syndicate (2).*

PRAIRIE FALCON (IRE) BHB 84f RR 85f 4973[9]

4 b c Alzao (USA) 9.8f **(73)** - Sea Harrier (Grundy) 10.3f **(65)**
Form - 87231180
Record 1998 - 1st:2 2nd:1 3rd:1 Ran:8
Pre1998 - 1st:1 2nd:1 3rd:1 Ran:9
Win Prizemoney £10,092 *Total Prizemoney* £13,212
Wins * **1998** Spt Goodwo (G-F) H 12f 81 85 <
* **1998** Spt Haydoc (GD) H 10.5f 80 80
* 1997 May Chepst (GD) 12.1f 80
1998 Turf 2-8: (10f, 11f 1-1, 12f 1-6) (sft, g-s, gd, g-f, frm 2-4)
Scopey, useful colt, effective 11 to 12f, best at 12f, acts on gd to frm, prefers tight tracks. Turf high 85 (began Jly) - 1st of 12 giving 20lb to Billaddie (23 Spt Goodwood RF 4451) - also 1st of 10 giving 16lb to Shaffishayes (4 Spt Haydock RF 4094). Regularly ridden by Charles Hills. **B W Hills [3-17] Mrs B W Hills.*

PRAIRIE MINSTREL (USA) BHB 41f RR 51f 4417[7]

4 b g Regal Intention (CAN) - Prairie Sky (USA) (Gone West (USA)) 6.5f **(75)**
Form - 57
Record 1998 - 1st:0 2nd:0 3rd:0 Ran:2
Pre1998 - 1st:0 2nd:0 3rd:0 Ran:8
Win Prizemoney £0 *Total Prizemoney* £249
1998 Turf 0-2: (12f, 16f) (g-f, frm)
Workmanlike, fair gelding, has worn blinkers. Turf high 41. Consistent. **R Dickin [2-23] Martin Brook.*

PRAIRIE WOLF RR 56f 4997[6]

2 ch c Wolfhound (USA) 7.3f **(71)** - Bay Queen **(75f)** (Damister (USA)) 9f **(73)**
Form - 06
Record 1998 - 1st:0 2nd:0 3rd:0 Ran:2
1998 Turf 0-2: (7f, 8f) (sft, frm)
Currently fair colt. Turf high 56 (began Oct).
**M Bell [0-2] B J Warren.*

PRAISE BE (FR) BHB 24a RR 24a 375[7]

8 b g Baillamont (USA) 9.7f **(80)** - Louange (Green Dancer (USA)) 10.3f **(74)**
Form - 00707
Record 1998 - 1st:0 2nd:0 3rd:0 Ran:3
Pre1998 - 1st:0 2nd:0 3rd:0 Ran:2
1998 AW 0-3: (8f, 11f, 12f) (Fibr 3)
Formerly very poor gelding, has worn blinkers.
**D W Chapman [0-5] David Chapman.*

PRE CATELAN BHB 52f53a RR 44f 53a 1985[6]

3 ch f Polar Falcon (USA) 9f **(74)** - Anneli Rose (Superlative) 7.2f **(56)**
Form - 486
Record 1998 - 1st:0 2nd:0 3rd:0 Ran:3
Pre1998 - 1st:0 2nd:0 3rd:0 Ran:3
Win Prizemoney £0 *Total Prizemoney* £202
1998 Turf 0-2: (6f, 7f) (gd 2) 1998 AW 0-1: (6f) (Fibr)
Workmanlike, fair filly, effective 6f, - acts on Fibr. Turf high 44. (1st run) - 4th of 14 getting 13lb from Kayo (27 Apr Southwell 6f Fibr RF 0887). **M Bell [0-6] M B Hawtin.*

PRECIOUS CHOICE (USA) RR 90f 3561a[5]

3 ch f Jade Hunter (USA) 10.4f **(72)** - Brorita (USA) (Caro) 9.3f **(74)**
Form - 35
1998 Turf 0-2: (7f, 8f) (g-s, gd)
Currently useful filly. Turf high 90 (1st run) - 3rd of 7 getting 5lb

from Pirro (26 Jun Curragh 8f g-s RF 2420a).
**C O'Brien in IRE [0-2] Mrs P Myerscough.*

PRECIOUS PRINCESS BHB 56a RR 56a 467[4]

3 br f Precocious 7.2f **(54)** - Magyar Princess (Beldale Flutter (USA)) 9.7f **(71)**
Form - 52574
Record 1998 - 1st:0 2nd:0 3rd:0 Ran:2
Pre1998 - 1st:0 2nd:1 3rd:0 Ran:3
Win Prizemoney £0 *Total Prizemoney* £644
1998 AW 0-2: (5f, 6f) (Fibr 2)
Leggy, average filly. AW high 46. **R Guest [0-5] Mrs Lesley Mills.*

PRECIOUS YEARS RR 51f 4666[13]

3 ch g Dilum (USA) 7.1f **(56)** - Tantot (Charlottown) 10.9f **(57)**
Form - 00
Record 1998 - 1st:0 2nd:0 3rd:0 Ran:2
1998 Turf 0-2: (7f, 8f) (g-s, g-f)
Workmanlike, currently fair gelding. Turf high 51 (began Aug).
**R Simpson [0-2] Miss Kate Waddington.*

PRECISELY (IRE) BHB 51f52a RR 44f 52a 4543[15]

3 b g Petorius 8f **(66)** - Indigent (IRE) (Superlative) 7.2f **(56)**
Form - 0815700
Record 1998 - 1st:1 2nd:0 3rd:0 Ran:5
Pre1998 - 1st:0 2nd:0 3rd:0 Ran:4
Win Prizemoney £1,830 *Total Prizemoney* £1,830
Wins * **1998** *Mar Wolver (STD) SH 5f 45 53* <
1998 Turf 0-1: (5f) (gd) 1998 AW 1-4: (5f 1-3, 6f) (Fibr 1-4)
Fair gelding, has broken blood-vessels, effective 5f, - acts on Fibr, often wears blinkers (very effectively). AW high 53 (1st run) - 1st of 10 getting 5lb from Indian Splendour (4 Mar Wolverhampton RF 0401). Inconsistent. **J Wharton [1-9] Mrs S M Moore.*

PRECISION RR 17f 2295[10]

3 b c Kris 10f **(75)** - Sweetly (FR) (Lyphard (USA)) 9.9f **(72)**
Form - 0
Record 1998 - 1st:0 2nd:0 3rd:0 Ran:1
1998 Turf 0-1: (6f) (g-f)
Workmanlike, currently poor colt.
**R Charlton [0-1] Highclere Thoroughbred Racing Ltd.*

PRECISION FINISH BHB 61f RR 63f 2254[3]

3 ch f Safawan 6.6f **(60)** - Tricky Tracey (Formidable (USA)) 9.2f **(63)**
Form - 0063
Record 1998 - 1st:0 2nd:0 3rd:1 Ran:4
Pre1998 - 1st:0 2nd:0 3rd:0 Ran:1
Win Prizemoney £0 *Total Prizemoney* £326
1998 Turf 0-4: (6f, 7f, 8f 2) (g-s, g-f 2, frm)
Scopey, average filly. Turf high 63 - 3rd of 11 to Pride of My Heart (24 Jun Salisbury 7f frm RF 2254).
**J Cullinan [0-5] Alan Spargo Ltd Toolmakers.*

PRECOCIOUS MISS (USA) RR 85+f 3664[1]

2 b f Diesis 9f **(80)** - Kissogram Girl (USA) (Danzig (USA)) 8.4f **(76)**
Form - 21
Record 1998 - 1st:1 2nd:1 3rd:0 Ran:2
Win Prizemoney £3,310 *Total Prizemoney* £4,448
Wins * **1998** Aug Lingfi (G-F) 6f 71 <
1998 Turf 1-2: (6f 1-2) (frm 1-2)
Currently useful filly. Turf high 85 (1st run) (began Aug) - 2nd of 18 to Miss Universe (3 Aug Windsor 6f frm RF 3318). She ran a most promising race on her debut, but made hard work of landing the odds next time. She needs to calm down a bit.
**Sir Michael Stoute [1-2] Maktoum Al Maktoum.*

PREDAPPIO BHB 124f RR 126f 4346a[6]

5 b h Polish Precedent (USA) 9f **(73)** - Khalafiya (Darshaan) 9.9f **(84)**
Form - 06
Record 1998 - 1st:0 2nd:0 3rd:0 Ran:2
Pre1998 - 1st:4 2nd:2 3rd:2 Ran:10
Win Prizemoney £114,295 *Total Prizemoney* £175,493
Wins * 1997 Jun Ascot (GD) G2 12f 125 <
1996 Oct Currag (SFT) G2 11f 111
1996 Spt Galway (G-F) L 12f 109+
1996 Jly Gowran (GD) 8f 89
1998 Turf 0-1: (12f) (hvy) 1998 AW 0-1: (10f) (Dirt)
Top-class colt, effective 10 to 12f, best at 12f, acts on gd to frm, best on gd, has worn blinkers. Showed top-class form in 1997, but was restricted to just two runs last season, well beaten in the Dubai World Cup and the Prix Foy.
**S bin Suroor [1-6] Godolphin (from S bin Suroor in UAE [0-1] Mar 1998).*

PRELUDE TO FAME (USA) BHB 40f RR 47?f 985[7]

5 b g Affirmed (USA) 10.3f **(75)** - Dance Call (USA) (Nijinsky (CAN)) 10.3f **(77)**
Form - 87
Record 1998 - 1st:0 2nd:0 3rd:0 Ran:2
Pre1998 - 1st:0 2nd:0 3rd:0 Ran:3
1998 Turf 0-2: (13f, 16f) (g-s, gd)
Moderate gelding, has worn blinkers. Turf high 25.
**Miss Kate Milligan [1-8] Jumbo Racing Club (from T Stack in IRE [0-3] May 1996).*

PREMIER BARON BHB 74f70a RR 74f 70a 4854[15]

3 b c Primo Dominie 7.2f **(67)** - Anna Karietta (Precocious) 8.6f **(62)**
Form - 634264030
Record 1998 - 1st:0 2nd:1 3rd:2 Ran:9
Win Prizemoney £0 *Total Prizemoney* £2,884
1998 Turf 0-6: (6f 3, 7f 3) (g-s, gd 3, g-f 2) 1998 AW 0-3: (6f 2, 8f) (Equi, Fibr 2)
Leggy, above-average colt, effective 6 to 7f, best at 7f, acts on g-s to g-f. Turf high 79 (1st run) - 4th of 16 to Caribbean Monarch (14 Apr Newmarket 6f gd RF 0683). AW high 47.
**T T Clement [0-9] Miss T J Fitzgerald.*

PREMIER BAY BHB 92f RR 94f 4742[10]

4 b c Primo Dominie 7.2f **(67)** - Lydia Maria (Dancing Brave (USA)) 8.4f **(76)**
Form - 0
Record 1998 - 1st:0 2nd:0 3rd:0 Ran:1
Pre1998 - 1st:2 2nd:2 3rd:2 Ran:13
Win Prizemoney £14,736 *Total Prizemoney* £24,959
Wins 1997 Jun York (G-S) H 10.4f 95 97 <
1996 May Newbur (SFT) 6f 87+
1998 Turf 0-1: (10f) (g-s)
Workmanlike, useful colt, effective 8 to 10f, best at 10f, acts on gd to frm, best on gd, has worn blinkers, prefers left handed tracks.
**P J Hobbs [1-6] E M Thornton (from P W Harris [2-13] Oct 1997).*

PREMIER DANCE BHB 40f48a RR 47f 48a 4384[6]

11 ch g Bairn (USA) 9.4f **(55)** - Gigiolina (King Emperor (USA)) 9.4f **(58)**

Form - 037244736466
Record 1998 - 1st:0 2nd:1 3rd:1 Ran:10
Pre1998 - 1st:12 2nd:17 3rd:20 Ran:114
Win Prizemoney £32,750 *Total Prizemoney* £55,964
Wins * *1997 May Wolver (STD) H 12f 66 68*
* *1997 Mar Wolver (STD) H 14.8f 60 62*
* *1996 May Wolver (STD) H 12f 68 74* <
* *1996 Feb Wolver (STD) H 12f 65 64*
* *1996 Jan Southw (STD) H 12f 62 61*
* *1995 Dec Wolver (STD) H 12f 56 61*
* *1995 Jan Wolver (STD) H 14f 55 58+*
* *1994 Jly Wolver (STD) H 12f 52 53*
* *1994 Feb Wolver (STD) H 12f 44 49+*
1998 Turf 0-1: (11f) (gd) 1998 AW 0-9: (12f 2, 14f 2, 15f 4, 16f) (Equi, Fibr 8)
Average gelding, effective 12 to 16f, best at 12f, - acts on Fibr, has worn blinkers, favours left handed tracks, excels at Wolverhampton. AW high 67 - 2nd of 10 giving 3lb to Petoskin (14 Jan Wolverhampton 15f Fibr RF 0087). He is not getting any younger, but seems to retain some ability. **D HaydnJones [12-124] J S Fox and Sons.*

PREMIERE DIVISION BHB 52f RR 48df 4658[11]

2 b f Be My Chief (USA) 10.2f **(62)** - One Half Silver (CAN) (Plugged Nickle (USA)) 7.8f **(68)**
Form - 7800
Record 1998 - 1st:0 2nd:0 3rd:0 Ran:4
1998 Turf 0-4: (6f 4) (g-s, gd 3)
Moderate filly. Turf high 48 (began Jly).
**Miss L A Perratt [0-4] Lostford Manor Stud.*

Premier Night hit top form at Newmarket

PREMIER GENERATION (IRE) BHB 90f72a **RR 91f 72a** 4631[4]

5 b g Cadeaux Genereux 7.9f **(76)** - Bristle (Thatch (USA)) 9.8f **(62)**

Form - 36022412416127054

Record	**1998 -**	1st:3	2nd:4	3rd:0	Ran:16
	Pre1998 -	1st:1	2nd:3	3rd:2	Ran:19

Win Prizemoney £22,927 *Total Prizemoney* £41,186

Wins							
* **1998**	Jly	Sandow (G-F)	H	10f	83	87	<
* **1998**	Jun	Nottin (GD)	H	10f	80	83	
* **1998**	May	Newbur (GD)	H	10f	73	77	
* 1997	May	Newbur (SFT)	H	10f	63	70	

1998 Turf 3-14: (9f 2, 10f 3-10, 11f, 12f) (sft 2, g-s, gd 1-3, g-f 1-6, frm 1-2) 1998 AW 0-2: (8f, 12f) (Fibr 2)

Useful gelding, effective 9 to 10f, best at 10f, acts on gd to frm, best on g-f, excels at Newbury. Turf high 91 - 4th of 35 giving 3lb to Lear Spear (3 Oct Newmarket 9f g-f RF 4631) - also 1st of 13 giving 5lb to Shalad'or (23 Jly Sandown RF 3046). AW high 48. Consistent. After running fairly well over hurdles last winter, he performed consistently well in a very busy Flat campaign, including winning three times over ten furlongs. He has now joined Nicky Henderson, where he has already won impressively over hurdles. **D W P Arbuthnot [4-39] Mrs W A Oram.*

PREMIER JET RR 14f 3247[15]

3 br f Dilum (USA) 7.1f **(56)** - Lady Shikari (Kala Shikari) 8.4f **(54)**

Form - 0

Record	**1998 -**	1st:0	2nd:0	3rd:0	Ran:1
	Pre1998 -	1st:0	2nd:0	3rd:0	Ran:1

1998 Turf 0-1: (6f) (g-f)

Workmanlike, currently poor filly. **M Madgwick [0-2] T G N Burrage.*

PREMIER LEAGUE (IRE) BHB 49f37a **RR 52f 37a** 4731[11]

8 gr g Don't Forget Me 9.5f **(66)** - Kilmara (USA) (Caro) 9.3f **(74)**

Form - 0063011700

Record	**1998 -**	1st:2	2nd:0	3rd:1	Ran:10
	Pre1998 -	1st:2	2nd:2	3rd:1	Ran:26

Win Prizemoney £13,262 *Total Prizemoney* £16,156

Wins						
* **1998**	Aug	Windso (G-F)	H	11.6f	48	52
* **1998**	Jly	Windso (G-F)	SH	11.6f	43	48

1998 Turf 2-9: (10f, 12f 2-7, 14f) (sft, g-s 2, gd, g-f 2, frm 2-3) 1998 AW 0-1: (12f) (Equi)

Fair gelding, effective 12f, acts on g-f to frm, best on frm, likes tight tracks. Turf high 52 - 1st of 11 getting 12lb from Koraloona (3 Aug Windsor RF 3315) - also 1st of 20 getting 6lb from Sharpest (20 Jly Windsor RF 2958). He won twice at Windsor, but is a second division performer nowadays.

**K O Cunningham-Brown [2-10] The Harkander Partnership (from J E Long [0-19] Apr 1997).*

PREMIER NIGHT BHB 95f **RR 93f** 2747[2]

5 b m Old Vic 12.8f **(72)** - Warm Welcome (General Assembly (USA)) 10f **(68)**

Form - 41412

Record	**1998 -**	1st:2	2nd:1	3rd:0	Ran:5
	Pre1998 -	1st:2	2nd:2	3rd:1	Ran:14

Win Prizemoney £22,006 *Total Prizemoney* £31,694

Wins							
* **1998**	Jly	Newmar (G-F)	H	16.1f	85	89	<
* **1998**	May	Kempto (G-F)	H	16f	80	84	
* 1997	May	Newbur (G-F)	H	13.3f	76	78	
* 1997	Apr	Folkes (FRM)		12f		70	

1998 Turf 2-5: (12f, 14f, 16f 2-3) (gd 1-3, g-f, frm 1-1)

Useful filly, effective 16f, acts on gd to frm, best on gd, likes right

handed tracks. Turf high 93 - 2nd of 11 getting 3lb from Mawared (12 Jly Newbury 16f gd RF 2747) - also 1st of 10 getting 5lb from Jaseur (8 Jly Newmarket RF 2640). A decent staying handicapper, she won two such events at Kempton and Newmarket. She was covered by Shaamit in the spring and was retired in July.
**S Dow [4-19] D G Churston.*

PREMIUM PRINCESS BHB 61f56a RR 64f 56a 4961[17]
3 b f Distant Relative 7f **(69)** - Solemn Occasion (USA) (Secreto (USA)) 8.7f **(72)**
Form - 748434020

Record		1st	2nd	3rd	Ran
	1998 -	1st:0	2nd:1	3rd:1	Ran:9
	Pre1998 -	1st:0	2nd:3	3rd:1	Ran:8

Win Prizemoney £0 *Total Prizemoney* £4,901
1998 Turf 0-9: (6f, 7f 7, 8f) (gd 3, g-f, frm 5)
Lengthy, average filly, effective 5 to 7f, best at 6f, acts on gd to frm, best on frm, excels at Nottingham and Redcar. Turf high 64 - 4th of 14 giving 11lb to Oriole (9 Aug Redcar 7f frm RF 3488).
**J J Quinn [0-17] Premium Bloodstock Plc.*

PREMIUM PURSUIT BHB 61f RR 66f 4485[19]
3 b g Pursuit of Love 9.5f **(69)** - Music in My Life (IRE) (Law Society (USA)) 9.9f **(70)**
Form - 05866000

Record		1st	2nd	3rd	Ran
	1998 -	1st:0	2nd:0	3rd:0	Ran:8
	Pre1998 -	1st:1	2nd:2	3rd:1	Ran:8

Win Prizemoney £3,304 *Total Prizemoney* £6,305
Wins * 1997 Jun Doncas (GD) 6f 81 <
1998 Turf 0-8: (6f 3, 7f 3, 8f 2) (gd 4, g-f 2, frm 2)
Average gelding, effective 5 to 8f, best at 6f, acts on gd to g-f, best on gd, has worn blinkers. Turf high 76 - 5th of 13 giving 7lb to Bodfari Pride (5 May Chester 8f g-f RF 1044).
**R A Fahey [1-16] J C Parsons.*

PREMIUM QUEST BHB 53f53a RR 51f 53a 2901[10]
3 b g Forzando 7.2f **(63)** - Sabonis (USA) (The Minstrel (CAN)) 10f **(72)**
Form - 08763820

Record		1st	2nd	3rd	Ran
	1998 -	1st:0	2nd:1	3rd:1	Ran:8
	Pre1998 -	1st:1	2nd:0	3rd:1	Ran:5

Win Prizemoney £3,925 *Total Prizemoney* £6,115
Wins * 1997 Oct Pontef (G-S) H 8f 66 70 <
1998 Turf 0-6: (8f 2, 9f, 10f, 11f, 12f) (g-s 2, gd 2, g-f, frm) 1998 AW 0-2: (11f, 12f) (Fibr 2)
Workmanlike, fair gelding, effective 7 to 8f, acts on gd, has worn blinkers. Turf high 51. AW high 54 (began Jly).
**R A Fahey [1-13] J C Parsons.*

PREMIUM RATE (USA) BHB 85f RR 83f 2014[20]
3 ch c Phone Trick (USA) 7f **(62)** - Excitable Gal (USA) (Secretariat (USA)) 9f **(79)**
Form - 3010

Record		1st	2nd	3rd	Ran
	1998 -	1st:1	2nd:0	3rd:1	Ran:4
	Pre1998 -	1st:0	2nd:0	3rd:1	Ran:1

Win Prizemoney £3,392 *Total Prizemoney* £4,586
Wins * **1998** May Redcar (G-F) 7f 83 <
1998 Turf 1-4: (6f, 7f 1-1, 8f 2) (gd 3, g-f 1-1)
Scopey, decent colt. Turf high 83 - 1st of 4 getting 11lb from Sugarfoot (26 May Redcar RF 1476). A well-named colt, he shaped very well in decent maidens before winning at Redcar. Down the field at Royal Ascot.
**E A L Dunlop [1-5] Bernard Gover Bloodstock Trading Ltd.*

PRENDS CA (IRE) BHB 89f RR 83f 2700[5]
5 b m Reprimand 8.2f **(63)**-Cri de Coeur (USA)(Lyphard (USA))9.9f **(72)**
Form - 665

Record		1st	2nd	3rd	Ran
	1998 -	1st:0	2nd:0	3rd:0	Ran:3
	Pre1998 -	1st:5	2nd:2	3rd:2	Ran:26

Win Prizemoney £44,806 *Total Prizemoney* £55,733

Wins	Year	Month	Course	Going		Dist			
*	1997	Spt	Haydoc	(GD)	H	6f	81	88	
	1996	Oct	Newmar	(G-F)	H	6f	86	93	<
	1996	May	Cheste	(GD)	H	7.6f	88	89	
	1995	Oct	Ascot	(SFT)	H	7f	82	86	
	1995	Jun	Goodwo	(G-F)		6f		63+	

1998 Turf 0-3: (6f 3) (sft, g-f, frm)
Decent filly, effective 6f, acts on gd to g-f, best on gd, has worn blinkers. Turf high 80. Consistent. Proved tricky to place in '98, as she seems just below listed class.
**W R Muir [1-15] B Bull (from R Hannon [4-14] Oct 1996).*

PREPOSITION BHB 40f RR 35f 3996[16]
2 b g Then Again 7.4f **(52)** - Little Emmeline **(39df)** (Emarati (USA))
Form - 4800

Record		1st	2nd	3rd	Ran
	1998 -	1st:0	2nd:0	3rd:0	Ran:4

Win Prizemoney £0 *Total Prizemoney* £267
1998 Turf 0-4: (5f 2, 6f 2) (g-s, gd 2, g-f)
Very moderate gelding. Turf high 35.
**M A Peill [0-2] Ms V B Foster (from Mrs J R Ramsden [0-2] May 1998).*

PRESELI MAGIC BHB 62f RR 59f 4400[16]
2 gr f Puissance 7.1f **(60)** - Swallow Bay (Penmarric (USA))
Form - 63660

Record		1st	2nd	3rd	Ran
	1998 -	1st:0	2nd:0	3rd:1	Ran:5

Win Prizemoney £0 *Total Prizemoney* £270
1998 Turf 0-5: (5f 3, 6f 2) (gd 2, g-f, frm, hrd)
Fair filly. Turf high 59. **D HaydnJones [0-5] The Preseli Partnership.*

PRESENT ARMS (USA) BHB 97f RR 103f 5151[19]
5 b h Affirmed (USA) 10.3f **(75)** - Au Printemps (USA) (Dancing Champ (USA)) 8.8f **(80)**
Form - 72467510

Record		1st	2nd	3rd	Ran
	1998 -	1st:1	2nd:1	3rd:0	Ran:8
	Pre1998 -	1st:5	2nd:2	3rd:2	Ran:15

Win Prizemoney £49,219 *Total Prizemoney* £58,957

Wins	Year	Month	Course	Going		Dist			
*	**1998**	Oct	Ascot	(SFT)	H	10f	98	103	<
*	1997	Jly	Ascot	(SFT)	H	10f	94	100	
*	1997	Jun	Doncas	(G-S)	H	10.3f	88	92	
*	1996	Oct	Leices	(G-F)	H	11.8f	81	83	
*	1996	Aug	Windso	(G-F)	H	11.6f	75	80	
*	1996	Jly	Newcas	(FRM)		10.1f		74	

1998 Turf 1-8: (10f 1-5, 12f 3) (hvy, sft, g-s 1-1, gd 4, g-f)
Very useful colt, effective 10f, acts on sft to gd, best on gd, has worn blinkers (effectively), likes right handed tracks, excels at Ascot. Turf high 103 - 1st of 15 giving 7lb to Monitor (10 Oct Ascot RF 4742). He is not particularly consistent, but goes well when fresh and came back from a three month sabbatical to win at Ascot in October. He needs to drop in the weights before scoring again. **P F I Cole [6-23] H R H Prince Fahd Salman.*

PRESENT CHANCE BHB 76f60a RR 80f 60a 4750[21]
4 ch c Cadeaux Genereux 7.9f **(76)** - Chance All (FR) (Glenstal (USA)) 10.1f **(64)**
Form - 24343315070

Record		1st	2nd	3rd	Ran
	1998 -	1st:1	2nd:1	3rd:3	Ran:11
	Pre1998 -	1st:0	2nd:3	3rd:3	Ran:14

Win Prizemoney £7,002 *Total Prizemoney* £18,280
Wins * **1998** Jly Goodwo (G-S) 6f 80 <
1998 Turf 1-10: (5f 3, 6f 1-6, 7f) (g-s 2, gd 1-3, g-f, frm 4) 1998 AW 0-1: (5f) (Fibr)
Scopey, decent colt, effective 5 to 7f, best at 6f, acts on g-s to frm. Turf high 85 (1st run) - 2nd of 15 giving 12lb to Night Shot (28 Mar Warwick 5f g-s RF 0492) - also 1st of 9 getting 6lb from Delta Soleil (31 Jly Goodwood RF 3234). **B A McMahon [1-25] Brian Pennington.*

PRESENT GENERATION BHB 76f RR 83f 4923[7]
5 ch g Cadeaux Genereux 7.9f **(76)** - Penny Mint (Mummy's Game) 8.2f **(60)**
Form - 1085077

Record		1st	2nd	3rd	Ran
	1998 -	1st:1	2nd:0	3rd:0	Ran:7
	Pre1998 -	1st:1	2nd:6	3rd:0	Ran:14

Win Prizemoney £6,953 *Total Prizemoney* £13,943

Wins	Year	Month	Course	Going		Dist			
*	**1998**	Jly	Bright	(GD)	H	8f	77	83	<
*	1997	Aug	Epsom	(GD)		7f		77	

1998 Turf 1-7: (6f, 7f 2, 8f 1-3, 9f) (sft, gd 1-5, g-f)
Decent gelding, has broken blood-vessels, effective 6 to 8f, acts on gd to g-f, best on gd, likes tight tracks. Turf high 83 (1st run) (began Jly) - 1st of 10 giving 7lb to Barbason (14 Jly Brighton RF 2780). Suited by a sharp downhill track. **R Guest [2-21] S Lury.*

PRESENTIMENT BHB 34f31a RR 39f 31a 4955[17]
4 b g Puissance 7.1f **(60)** - Octavia (Sallust) 8.4f **(63)**
Form - 844854764050

Record		1st	2nd	3rd	Ran
	1998 -	1st:0	2nd:0	3rd:0	Ran:10
	Pre1998 -	1st:0	2nd:1	3rd:1	Ran:17

Win Prizemoney £0 *Total Prizemoney* £1,654
1998 Turf 0-7: (5f 3, 6f 2, 7f, 8f) (sft, g-s, gd 2, g-f, frm 2) 1998 AW 0-3: (6f, 7f 2) (Fibr 3)

Light-framed, very moderate gelding, effective 8f, acts on g-s, has worn blinkers, likes left handed tracks. Turf high 46. AW high 31.
**S R Bowring [0-13] Anchor Racing (from Martyn Wane [0-7] Aug 1997).*

PRESENT LAUGHTER RR 86+f 4880[2]

2 b c Cadeaux Genereux 7.9f **(76)** - Ever Genial (Brigadier Gerard) 9.3f **(58)**
Form - 2
Record 1998 - 1st:0 2nd:1 3rd:0 Ran:1
Win Prizemoney £0 *Total Prizemoney* £967
1998 Turf 0-1: (7f) (g-s)
Currently useful colt. (1st run) - 2nd of 13 giving 12lb to Saint Ella (20 Oct Folkestone 7f g-s RF 4880). **P F I Cole [0-1] Lord Portman.*

PRESENT 'N CORRECT BHB 43f33a RR 42f 33a 4921[3]

5 ch g Cadeaux Genereux 7.9f **(76)** - Emerald Eagle (Sandy Creek) 8.9f **(59)**
Form - 5065423
Record 1998 - 1st:0 2nd:1 3rd:1 Ran:7
Pre1998 - 1st:1 2nd:0 3rd:1 Ran:13
Win Prizemoney £3,142 *Total Prizemoney* £4,741
Wins 1996 Spt Thirsk (G-F) H 5f 45 45 <
1998 Turf 0-7: (5f 5, 6f 2) (g-s, gd, g-f, frm 3, hrd)
Moderate gelding, effective 5 to 6f, best at 6f, acts on g-s to frm. Turf high 42 (began Aug) - 2nd of 19 getting 9lb from Loganlea (17 Spt Yarmouth 6f frm RF 4339).
**J M Bradley [0-7] M B Clemence (from C B B Booth [1-13] Jly 1997).*

PRESENT SITUATION BHB 52f62a RR 60f 62a 4655[3]

7 ch g Cadeaux Genereux 7.9f **(76)** - Storm Warning (Tumble Wind (USA)) 7.5f **(57)**
Form - 6838053
Record 1998 - 1st:0 2nd:0 3rd:2 Ran:7
Pre1998 - 1st:9 2nd:6 3rd:5 Ran:40
Win Prizemoney £33,277 *Total Prizemoney* £46,967
Wins * 1997 Aug Epsom (G-S) H 8.5f 59 69
* 1997 *Feb Lingfi (STD) H 8f 67 70*
* 1996 Oct Leices (G-F) 8f 71+ <
* 1996 Jun Goodwo (G-F) H 7f 55 63
* 1996 *Jan Lingfi (STD) 7f 69*
* 1995 *Feb Lingfi (STD) H 7f 65 68*
* 1994 *Nov Lingfi (STD) H 8f 62 64*
* 1994 *Spt Southw (STD) H 8f 54 59*
* 1994 *Spt Wolver (STD) H 8.5f 50 50*
1998 Turf 0-6: (8f, 9f 2, 10f 3) (gd 4, g-f 2) 1998 AW 0-1: (8f) (Equi)
Above-average gelding, effective 8 to 9f, acts on gd - acts on Equi, likes left handed tracks, likes tight tracks. Turf high 60.
**Lord Huntingdon [9-47] Chris van Hoorn.*

PRESS AGAIN BHB 37f26a RR 39f 26a 2854[12]

6 ch m Then Again 7.4f **(52)** - Silver Empress (Octavo (USA)) 14.4f **(54)**
Form - 0030
Record 1998 - 1st:0 2nd:0 3rd:1 Ran:4
Pre1998 - 1st:0 2nd:0 3rd:0 Ran:11
Win Prizemoney £0 *Total Prizemoney* £452
1998 Turf 0-4: (7f, 8f 2, 12f) (gd, g-f 2, frm)
Very moderate mare, effective 7 to 8f, acts on g-f. Turf high 39 - 3rd of 18 getting 10lb from Final Settlement (29 Jun Windsor 8f g-f RF 2387). **P Hayward [0-17] J Sawyer.*

PRESS AHEAD BHB 48f60a RR 46f 60a 2692[1]

3 b c Precocious 7.2f **(54)** - By Line (High Line) 10.3f **(70)**
Form - 582071
Record 1998 - 1st:1 2nd:1 3rd:0 Ran:6
Pre1998 - 1st:0 2nd:0 3rd:0 Ran:4
Win Prizemoney £2,322 *Total Prizemoney* £3,138
Wins * **1998** *Jly Wolver (STD) 6f 65* <
1998 Turf 0-3: (5f 2, 8f) (sft, g-f, frm) 1998 AW 1-3: (5f, 6f 1-2) (Fibr 1-3)
Workmanlike, average colt, effective 5 to 6f, - acts on Fibr. Turf high 46. AW high 65 - 1st of 9 from One To Go (10 Jly Wolverhampton RF 2692). Inconsistent.
**B A McMahon [1-10] R L Bedding.*

PRESS TIMES (USA) RR 47f 1810[6]

2 b c Press Card (USA) - Doubling Time (USA) (Timeless Moment (USA)) 6f **(72)**
Form - 6
Record 1998 - 1st:0 2nd:0 3rd:0 Ran:1
1998 Turf 0-1: (6f) (g-s)
Currently moderate colt. **T D Easterby [0-1] Times of Wigan.*

PRESSURISE BHB 63f RR 64+f 3084[1]

3 ch g Sanglamore (USA) 12.9f **(67)** - Employ Force (USA) (Alleged (USA)) 10f **(76)**
Form - 11
Record 1998 - 1st:2 2nd:0 3rd:0 Ran:2
Pre1998 - 1st:0 2nd:0 3rd:0 Ran:3
Win Prizemoney £5,794 *Total Prizemoney* £5,794
Wins * **1998** Jly Nottin (G-F) H 16f 51 64 <
* **1998** Jly Yarmou (G-F) H 14.1f 51 59+
1998 Turf 2-2: (14f 1-1, 16f 1-1) (g-f 2-2)
Scopey, average gelding. Turf high 64 (began Jly) - 1st of 8 giving 16lb to Musalse (24 Jly Nottingham RF 3084) - also 1st of 15 giving 3lb to Mail Shot (21 Jly Yarmouth RF 2981). Followed the classic Prescott pattern of having three runs over inadequate trips at two, before finding his feet when tackling a suitable trip. A big individual, he can progress to much better things.
**Sir Mark Prescott [2-5] Charles Walker & Jonathon Carroll.*

PRETTY ASH RR 4926[7]

3 ch f Superlative 8.8f **(57)** - Petty Cash (Midyan (USA)) 6f **(60)**
Form - 7
Record 1998 - 1st:0 2nd:0 3rd:0 Ran:1
1998 Turf 0-1: (10f) (g-s)
Workmanlike, currently very poor filly.
**A T Murphy [0-1] Cee-Jay-Dee.*

PRETTY OBVIOUS BHB 57f RR 59f 4767[2]

2 ch f Pursuit of Love 9.5f **(69)** - Settlement (USA) (Irish River (FR)) 8.6f **(78)**
Form - 4672
Record 1998 - 1st:0 2nd:1 3rd:0 Ran:4
Win Prizemoney £0 *Total Prizemoney* £1,128
1998 Turf 0-4: (6f 3, 8f) (sft, g-s, g-f, frm)
Fair filly. Turf high 59 - 2nd of 16 getting 12lb from Sunset Lady (13 Oct Ayr 8f sft RF 4767). **R A Fahey [0-4] H Hurst.*

PRETTY WOMAN (IRE) RR 72f 4983[4]

2 b f Alzao (USA) 9.8f **(73)** - Simply Gorgeous (Hello Gorgeous (USA)) 9.7f **(63)**
Form - 44
Record 1998 - 1st:0 2nd:0 3rd:0 Ran:2
Win Prizemoney £0 *Total Prizemoney* £472
1998 Turf 0-2: (8f 2) (g-s 2)
Currently above-average filly. Turf high 72 (began Oct).
**P F I Cole [0-2] Faisal Salman.*

PREVALENCE BHB 87f RR 89f 1981[16]

3 ch c Cadeaux Genereux 7.9f **(76)** - Tabdea (USA) (Topsider (USA)) 8.3f **(71)**
Form - 0110
Record 1998 - 1st:2 2nd:0 3rd:0 Ran:4
Pre1998 - 1st:0 2nd:1 3rd:0 Ran:2
Win Prizemoney £6,775 *Total Prizemoney* £8,105
Wins * **1998** May Kempto (GD) H 7f 79 89 <
* **1998** May Kempto (G-F) 7f 63
1998 Turf 2-4: (6f, 7f 2-2, 8f) (g-s, gd 1-2, g-f 1-1)
Useful colt, effective 7f, acts on gd to g-f, has worn blinkers. Turf high 89 - 1st of 17 giving 7lb to Smooth Sailing (30 May Kempton RF 1591). Was well supported and showed encouragement in two maidens in Ireland in 1997, and looked useful in two victories for Noseda at three. Never going when favourite in a valuable handicap at York.
**J Noseda [2-4] Mrs J M Ryan (from J S Bolger in IRE [0-2] Spt 1997).*

PRICE OF PASSION BHB 84f RR 81f 4857[19]

2 b f Dolphin Street (FR) - Food of Love (Music Boy) 6.8f **(57)**
Form - 870623010
Record 1998 - 1st:1 2nd:1 3rd:1 Ran:9
Win Prizemoney £3,781 *Total Prizemoney* £5,321
Wins * **1998** Spt Folkes (G-F) H 5f 77 81 <
1998 Turf 1-9: (5f 1-6, 6f 3) (sft, gd 2, g-f 1-2, frm 4)
Decent filly, effective 5f, acts on g-f to frm. Turf high 81 - 1st of 9

getting 6lb from Grey Princess (25 Spt Folkestone RF 4472). Finally came good in a nursery. **D W P Arbuthnot [1-9] Noel Cronin.*

PRIDDY FAIR BHB 38f51a **RR 21f 51a** 186[9]
5 b m North Briton 8.2f **(53)** - Rainbow Ring (Rainbow Quest (USA)) 10.4f **(75)**
Form - 0
Record 1998 - 1st:0 2nd:0 3rd:0 Ran:1
Pre1998 - 1st:0 2nd:0 3rd:0 Ran:7
Win Prizemoney £0 *Total Prizemoney* £220
1998 AW 0-1: (12f) (Fibr)
Little account filly.
**D W Barker [1-10] The Ebor Partnership (from R Boss [0-6] Oct 1995).*

PRIDDY GREEN BHB 47f40a **RR 49f 40a** 2654[15]
3 b f Formidable (USA)7.8f **(60)** - No Can Tell(USA)(Clev Er Tell (USA))
Form - 080
Record 1998 - 1st:0 2nd:0 3rd:0 Ran:3
Pre1998 - 1st:0 2nd:0 3rd:0 Ran:2
1998 AW 0-3: (8f 2, 11f) (Fibr 3)
Neat, moderate filly, has worn blinkers. AW high 20.
**J Hetherton [0-3] Miss S Dent (from H Candy [0-2] Oct 1997).*

PRIDE OF BRIXTON BHB 48f63a **RR 60f 63a** 4837[12]
5 b g Dominion 8.9f **(65)** - Caviar Blini (What A Guest) 7f **(62)**
Form - 0017450105000
Record 1998 - 1st:2 2nd:0 3rd:0 Ran:11
Pre1998 - 1st:1 2nd:3 3rd:2 Ran:20
Win Prizemoney £11,665 *Total Prizemoney* £15,905
Wins 1998 *Aug Wolver (STD) S 5f 65*
1998 May Carlis (G-S) 5f 64
1996 May Cheste (GD) H 5.1f 78 81 <
1998 Turf 1-8: (5f 1-7, 6f) (g-s, gd 1-4, g-f, frm 2) 1998 AW 1-3: (5f 1-1, 6f 2) (Fibr 1-3)
Average gelding, effective 5 to 6f, best at 5f, acts on gd - acts on Fibr. Turf high 64 (1st run) - 1st of 10 giving 9lb to Charlies Bride (8 May Carlisle RF 1099). AW high 65 (1st run) (began Aug) - 1st of 8 giving 5lb to Tinker's Surprise (7 Aug Wolverhampton RF 3453). Becoming disappointing.
**P D Evans [0-5] Treble Chance Partnership (from C W Thornton [2-14] Aug 1998).*

PRIDE OF BRYN BHB 42f **RR 44f** 3141[11]
3 br f Efisio 7.7f **(69)** - Alpine Sunset (Auction Ring (USA)) 8.6f **(65)**
Form - 220804400
Record 1998 - 1st:0 2nd:2 3rd:0 Ran:9
Pre1998 - 1st:0 2nd:1 3rd:0 Ran:7
Win Prizemoney £0 *Total Prizemoney* £3,199
1998 Turf 0-9: (7f 2, 8f 7) (gd 5, g-f 3, frm)
Moderate filly, effective 6 to 8f, best at 8f, acts on gd to frm, likes right handed tracks. Turf high 53 (1st run) - 2nd of 14 getting 7lb from Saintes (9 Apr Musselburgh 8f gd RF 0632).
**Denys Smith [0-16] Jim Blair.*

PRIDE OF DINGLE (IRE) RR 5056a[3]
2 b c Dolphin Street (FR)
Form - 13
Record 1998 - 1st:1 2nd:0 3rd:1 Ran:2
Win Prizemoney £6,876 *Total Prizemoney* £11,002
Wins * **1998** Spt San Si (HVY) 12f
1998 Turf 1-2: (9f, 12f 1-1) (hvy 1-2)
Currently very poor colt. (began Spt) - 3rd of 7 to Light Burner (25 Oct San Siro 9f hvy RF 5056a) - also 1st of 7 from Steel Lancer (27 Spt San Siro RF 4606a). **M Bell [1-2].*

PRIDE OF KASHMIR BHB 41f **RR 42?f** 1833[9]
5 gr g Petong 7.6f **(58)** - Proper Madam (Mummy's Pet) 7.7f **(60)**
Form - 0
Record 1998 - 1st:0 2nd:0 3rd:0 Ran:1
Pre1998 - 1st:0 2nd:1 3rd:2 Ran:18
Win Prizemoney £0 *Total Prizemoney* £2,287
1998 Turf 0-1: (12f) (gd)
Moderate gelding, has worn blinkers. Consistent. Sprint-bred, he is always likely to need an easy track.
**P J Hobbs [4-12] Frank & Cicely Berry (from P W Harris [0-18] Oct 1996).*

PRIDE OF LONDUBH (IRE) BHB 57f **RR 44f** 4878[16]
2 b f Pips Pride 6.7f **(70)** - Londubh (Tumble Wind (USA)) 7.5f **(57)**
Form - 4374020
Record 1998 - 1st:0 2nd:1 3rd:1 Ran:7
Win Prizemoney £0 *Total Prizemoney* £923
1998 Turf 0-3: (5f, 6f 2) (gd 3) 1998 AW 0-4: (5f 2, 7f, 8f) (Fibr 4)
Average filly, effective 8f, - acts on Fibr. Turf high 54. AW high 65 - 2nd of 13 to Blue Glass (17 Oct Wolverhampton 8f Fibr RF 4866).
**M R Channon [0-3] & Mrs Gary Pinchen (from M Quinn [0-4] Jun 1998).*

PRIDE OF MY HEART BHB 59f **RR 69f** 4571[6]
3 b f Lion Cavern (USA) 7.5f **(74)** - Hearten (Hittite Glory) 8.7f **(50)**
Form - 0501430746
Record 1998 - 1st:1 2nd:0 3rd:1 Ran:10
Pre1998 - 1st:0 2nd:0 3rd:0 Ran:3
Win Prizemoney £2,402 *Total Prizemoney* £3,721
Wins * **1998** Jun Salisb (G-F) 7f 69 <
1998 Turf 1-10: (7f 1-1, 8f 5, 9f, 10f 3) (g-s, gd, g-f 5, frm 1-3)
Leggy, average filly. Turf high 69. **I A Balding [1-13] Nigel Harris.*

PRIDE OF PENDLE BHB 64f **RR 72f** 4848[24]
9 ro m Grey Desire 9.3f **(49)** - Pendle's Secret (Le Johnstan) 7.4f **(55)**
Form - 05385373000777187000
Record 1998 - 1st:1 2nd:0 3rd:3 Ran:20
Pre1998 - 1st:15 2nd:11 3rd:8 Ran:108
Win Prizemoney £106,115 *Total Prizemoney* £142,025
Wins * **1998** Spt York (GD) H 7.9f 65 68
* 1997 Aug Newcas (GD) 9f 77
* 1997 Jun Doncas (G-S) H 8f 67 71
1996 Spt Ayr (G-F) H 8f 66 74
1995 Aug Cheste (G-F) H 7.6f 74 79 <
1995 Jun York (G-F) H 8.9f 69 73
1995 May Thirsk (G-F) H 8f 66 70
1994 Aug Redcar (G-F) H 8f 66 68
1994 Jly York (GD) H 7.9f 63 66
1998 Turf 1-20: (7f 3, 8f 1-14, 9f 3) (hvy, g-s 2, gd 7, g-f 4, frm 1-6)
Above-average mare, effective 7 to 9f, best at 8f, acts on gd to frm, best on gd, likes left handed tracks, does well at Doncaster, likes York. Turf high 72 - also 1st of 24 giving 6lb to Suez Tornado (2 Spt York RF 4056). A most tough and genuine mare, she only managed one win in a busy '98, but owes nothing to anyone. She requires luck in running, and is suited by a strongly-run race and a big field.
**Martyn Wane [3-38] Mrs Linda Miller (from D Nicholls [6-51] Oct 1996).*

PRIDEWAY (IRE) BHB 68f **RR 72f** 4447[6]
2 b f Pips Pride 6.7f **(70)** - Up The Gates (Captain James) 5f **(59)**
Form - 75362406
Record 1998 - 1st:0 2nd:1 3rd:1 Ran:8
Win Prizemoney £0 *Total Prizemoney* £2,520
1998 Turf 0-8: (5f, 6f 2, 7f 5) (gd 4, g-f 3, frm)
Above-average filly, effective 7f, acts on gd, has worn blinkers. Turf high 72 - 2nd of 12 getting 19lb from Tony Tie (22 Aug Chester 7f gd RF 3803). **A Bailey [0-8] Nev Jones.*

PRIENA (IRE) BHB 90f **RR 90f** 1364[5]
4 ch f Priolo (USA) 10.9f **(71)** - Isabena (Star Appeal) 9.6f **(65)**
Form - 85
Record 1998 - 1st:0 2nd:0 3rd:0 Ran:2
Pre1998 - 1st:1 2nd:3 3rd:1 Ran:9
Win Prizemoney £3,377 *Total Prizemoney* £20,410
Wins 1996 Spt Redcar (FRM) 7f 78+ <
1998 Turf 0-2: (8f, 9f) (gd, g-f)
Lengthy, useful filly, effective 8 to 10f, best at 8f, acts on gd to g-f, best on g-f, has worn blinkers (effectively). Turf high 90. Consistent. Well beaten in two Listed events in May and did not reappear. **W Jarvis [0-2] Cuadra Africa (from DR Loder [1-9]Oct 1997).*

PRIMA FACIE RR 60f 1415[5]
3 b f Primo Dominie 7.2f **(67)** - Soluce (Junius (USA)) 7.7f **(65)**
Form - 05
Record 1998 - 1st:0 2nd:0 3rd:0 Ran:2
Pre1998 - 1st:0 2nd:0 3rd:0 Ran:1
1998 Turf 0-2: (5f 2) (g-f, hrd)
Scopey, currently average filly. Turf high 54.
**J R Fanshawe[0-2]Cheveley Park Stud(from DR Loder[0-1] Nov 1997).*

PRIMARY COLOURS BHB 63f86a **RR 61f 86a** 4939[4]
3 b f Saddlers' Hall (IRE) 10.5f **(65)**-Go For Red(IRE)(Thatching) 8f **(66)**
Form - 1224710114
Record 1998 - 1st:3 2nd:0 3rd:0 Ran:7
Pre1998 - 1st:1 2nd:2 3rd:1 Ran:5
Win Prizemoney £13,329 *Total Prizemoney* £15,872
Wins * **1998** Oct Haydoc (SFT) H 10.5f 58 61
* **1998** *Oct Wolver (sta) H 12f 83 87* <
* **1998** *Aug Wolver (STD) H 9.4f 75 83*
1997 *Nov Southw (STD) S 8f 77*
1998 Turf 1-4: (9f, 10f 2, 11f 1-1) (sft 1-1, gd 2, hrd) 1998 AW 2-3: (8f, 9f 1-1, 12f 1-1) (Fibr 2-3)
Workmanlike, useful filly, effective 7 to 12f, - acts on AW, best on Fibr, prefers left handed tracks, prefers tight tracks, excels at Southwell, does well at Wolverhampton. Turf high 61 (began Aug). AW high 87 - 1st of 12 giving 5lb to Philosophic (3 Oct Wolverhampton RF 4638) - also 1st of 13 from Amico (22 Aug Wolverhampton RF 3826). Inconsistent. She won a seller at Southwell as a two-year-old, but rather lost her way at the start of this year before bouncing back with a victory at Wolverhampton in August. She followed up with a hard-fought victory at the same track in October when stepped up to twelve furlongs, and scored back on turf at Haydock.
**J Pearce [3-9] Saracen Racing (from W J Haggas [1-3] Nov 1997).*

PRIMATICCIO (IRE) BHB 52f58a **RR 50+f 58a** 4627[5]
3 b g Priolo (USA) 10.9f **(71)** - Martinova (Martinmas) 7.6f **(59)**
Form - 058621615
Record 1998 - 1st:2 2nd:1 3rd:0 Ran:9
Pre1998 - 1st:0 2nd:0 3rd:0 Ran:1
Win Prizemoney £4,850 *Total Prizemoney* £5,730
Wins * **1998** *Spt Southw (STD) H 14f 48 50+* <
* **1998** Jly Folkes (G-F) H 15.4f 42 50
1998 Turf 1-6: (7f, 12f, 13f, 15f 1-2, 16f) (gd 2, g-f, frm 1-3) 1998 AW 1-3: (7f, 9f, 14f 1-1) (Fibr 1-3)
Fair gelding, effective 12 to 16f, acts on g-f to frm - acts on Fibr, has worn blinkers (extremely effectively), prefers tight tracks. Turf high 50 - 1st of 5 getting 18lb from Operatic (27 Jly Folkestone RF 3134). AW high 50 - 1st of 11 getting 12lb from Dangerus Precedent (29 Spt Southwell RF 4544). Went for 20,000 guineas at Tattersalls Horses-in-Training sale.
**Sir Mark Prescott [2-10] Cyril Humphris.*

PRIMAVERA BHB 60f **RR 68f** 1706[7]
3 b f Anshan 8.2f **(63)** - Fair Maid of Kent (USA) (Diesis) 9.3f **(69)**
Form - 007
Record 1998 - 1st:0 2nd:0 3rd:0 Ran:3
Pre1998 - 1st:0 2nd:1 3rd:0 Ran:3
Win Prizemoney £0 *Total Prizemoney* £1,021
1998 Turf 0-3: (6f, 7f 2) (gd 2, g-f)
Unfurnished, average filly, effective 7f, acts on g-f. Turf high 40.
**M J Haynes [0-6] G Steinberg.*

PRIMA VERDE BHB 78f **RR 78+f** 2354[4]
5 b m Leading Counsel (USA) 7.7f **(78)** - Bold Green (FR) (Green Dancer (USA)) 10.3f **(74)**
Form - 4
Record 1998 - 1st:0 2nd:0 3rd:0 Ran:1
Pre1998 - 1st:2 2nd:0 3rd:1 Ran:4
Win Prizemoney £9,475 *Total Prizemoney* £10,373
Wins * 1997 Jun Newmar (SFT) H 8f 75 78 <
* 1997 Jun Beverl (SFT) 7.5f 62+
1998 Turf 0-1: (8f) (gd)
Above-average filly. (1st run) - 4th of 9 giving 13lb to Sweet Pea (27 Jun Newmarket 8f gd RF 2354).
**L M Cumani [2-5] The Lawster Partnership.*

PRIME HAND BHB 80f **RR 81f** 4626[3]
3 ch f Primo Dominie 7.2f **(67)** - Rechanit (IRE) (Local Suitor (USA)) 8.4f **(67)**
Form - 2513
Record 1998 - 1st:1 2nd:1 3rd:1 Ran:4
Pre1998 - 1st:0 2nd:1 3rd:0 Ran:1
Win Prizemoney £4,240 *Total Prizemoney* £6,659
Wins * **1998** Spt Nottin (G-F) 6.1f 81 <
1998 Turf 1-4: (6f 1-4) (g-s, gd 1-2, g-f)
Workmanlike, decent filly. Turf high 81 - 3rd of 8 to Clef of Silver (3 Oct Catterick 6f g-f RF 4626) - also 1st of 13 from Sprite (26 Spt Nottingham RF 4510). **W J Haggas [1-5] Mrs M M Haggas.*

PRIME OFFER RR 38f 4937[13]
2 b c Primo Dominie 7.2f **(67)**-Single Bid (Auction Ring (USA)) 8.6f **(65)**
Form - 0
Record 1998 - 1st:0 2nd:0 3rd:0 Ran:1
1998 Turf 0-1: (5f) (gd)
Currently very moderate colt. **K A Morgan [0-1] D & M Cased Hole.*

PRIME PARTNER BHB 33f40a **RR 30f 40a** 3901[12]
5 b g Formidable (USA) 7.8f **(60** -Baileys by Name (Nomination) 7f **(60)**
Form - 040
Record 1998 - 1st:0 2nd:0 3rd:0 Ran:3
Pre1998 - 1st:1 2nd:1 3rd:4 Ran:27
Win Prizemoney £2,873 *Total Prizemoney* £5,997
Wins 1997 Jun Ripon (GD) SH 8f 33 37 <
1998 Turf 0-2: (6f, 7f) (g-f, hrd) 1998 AW 0-1: (11f) (Fibr)
Very moderate gelding, effective 7 to 8f, best at 8f, acts on sft to frm, best on frm, has worn blinkers. Turf high 27 (began Aug).
**Pat Mitchell [0-2] D Cruickshank (from Ronald Thompson [0-1] Feb 1998).*

PRIMERO (IRE) BHB 38f45a **RR 45a** 521[14]
4 b g Lycius (USA) 8.8f **(71)** - Pipitina (Bustino) 10.4f **(64)**
Form - 700
Record 1998 - 1st:0 2nd:0 3rd:0 Ran:1
Pre1998 - 1st:0 2nd:0 3rd:0 Ran:4
Win Prizemoney £0 *Total Prizemoney* £142
1998 Turf 0-1: (14f) (g-s)
Scopey, moderate gelding, has worn blinkers.
**A Barrow [0-8] Alan Harrington.*

PRIME SURPRISE BHB 50f **RR 60f** 4934[6]
2 b f Primo Dominie 7.2f **(67)** - My Surprise (Welsh Pageant) 10f **(65)**
Form - 006
Record 1998 - 1st:0 2nd:0 3rd:0 Ran:3
1998 Turf 0-3: (6f, 7f, 8f) (gd 2, g-f)
Currently average filly. Turf high 60 (began Spt).
**C A Dwyer [0-3] T Calver.*

PRIME TIME GIRL RR 57f 791[8]
3 b f Primo Dominie 7.2f **(67)** - Timely Raise (USA) (Raise A Man (USA)) 7.8f **(78)**
Form - 8
Record 1998 - 1st:0 2nd:0 3rd:0 Ran:1
Pre1998 - 1st:0 2nd:0 3rd:0 Ran:1
1998 Turf 0-1: (6f) (g-s)
Unfurnished, currently fair filly. **I A Balding [0-2] J C Smith.*

PRIMEVAL BHB 63f **RR 63f** 621[2]
4 b g Primo Dominie 7.2f **(67)** - Class Adorns (Sadler's Wells (USA)) 10f **(76)**
Form - 2
Record 1998 - 1st:0 2nd:1 3rd:0 Ran:1
Pre1998 - 1st:0 2nd:0 3rd:1 Ran:2
Win Prizemoney £0 *Total Prizemoney* £1,665
1998 AW 0-1: (10f) (Equi)
Strong, currently average gelding. (1st run) - 2nd of 9 giving 5lb to Raspberry Sauce (9 Apr Lingfield 10f Equi RF 0621).
**P W Harris [0-3] Mrs G A Godfrey.*

PRIMO LARA BHB 95f91a **RR 94f 91a** 5096[11]
6 ch h Primo Dominie 7.2f **(67)** - Clara Barton (Youth (USA)) 9.8f **(64)**
Form - 320010
Record 1998 - 1st:1 2nd:1 3rd:0 Ran:5
Pre1998 - 1st:4 2nd:2 3rd:6 Ran:25
Win Prizemoney £43,326 *Total Prizemoney* £56,977
Wins * **1998** Oct York (GD) H 6f 90 94 <
* 1997 Nov Redcar (GD) H 6f 84 87
* 1996 Spt Haydoc (G-F) H 7.1f 82 87
* 1996 Apr Thirsk (G-F) H 7f 65 82+
* 1996 Apr Beverl (G-F) H 7.5f 65 70+
1998 Turf 1-5: (6f 1-3, 7f 2) (gd 1-3, frm 2)
Useful horse, effective 6 to 7f, best at 6f, acts on gd to frm - acts on Fibr, best on frm. Turf high 94 (began Jly) - 1st of 23 giving 11lb to Prince Dome (10 Oct York RF 4749). He has become rather inconsistent, but did manage to win a very valuable sprint handi-

cap at York in August. He races prominently and looks best over six furlongs.
**P W Harris [5-29] Resplendent Racing Ltd (from P W Harris [0-1] May 1995).*

PRINCE ASHLEIGH BHB 75f79a **RR 77f 79a** 719[7]

3 b g Anshan 8.2f **(63)** - Fen Princess (IRE) (Trojan Fen) 8.1f **(62)**
Form - 523117
Record 1998 - 1st:2 2nd:1 3rd:1 Ran:5
Pre1998 - 1st:0 2nd:2 3rd:0 Ran:7
Win Prizemoney £7,770 *Total Prizemoney* £11,438
Wins * **1998** *Feb Wolver (STD) H 9.4f 76 77* <
* **1998** *Jan Wolver (STD) 9.4f 72*
1998 Turf 0-1: (12f) (g-s) 1998 AW 2-4: (7f, 8f, 9f 2-2) (Fibr 2-4)
Scopey, above-average gelding, effective 7 to 9f, acts on g-s to gd - acts on Fibr, prefers left handed tracks, prefers tight tracks, excels at Wolverhampton. AW high 77 - 1st of 4 getting 4lb from Netta Rufina (25 Feb Wolverhampton RF 0362) - also 1st of 11 from Miracle Island (24 Jan Wolverhampton RF 0152).
**P C Haslam [2-12] S A B Dinsmore.*

PRINCE BABAR BHB 96f **RR 101f** 5078[2]

7 b g Fairy King (USA) 7.7f **(75)** - Bell Toll (High Line) 10.3f **(70)**
Form - 0577012
Record 1998 - 1st:1 2nd:1 3rd:0 Ran:7
Pre1998 - 1st:3 2nd:6 3rd:4 Ran:21
Win Prizemoney £196,333 *Total Prizemoney* £269,025
Wins * **1998** Oct Newmar (GD) H 7f 85 92 <
* 1996 Oct Ascot (GD) 8f 83
1998 Turf 1-7: (7f 1-2, 8f 2, 9f, 10f 2) (sft, gd 1-3, g-f 2, frm)
Very useful gelding, effective 7 to 8f, best at 8f, acts on sft to gd, best on gd, has worn blinkers. Turf high 101 - 2nd of 26 giving 8lb to Raheen (31 Oct Newmarket 8f sft RF 5078). Ran in all the top handicaps last season, usually running well, and gained due reward by beating a big field at Newmarket in October. He ran another game race on his final start over a mile on soft ground. He will be knocking on the door in all the big handicaps again in 1999.
**J E Banks [2-20] Giles Pritchard-Gordon (from G A Pritchard-Gordon [2-8] Jun 1994).*

PRINCE BATSHOOF BHB 70f **RR 75f** 3436[3]

3 b g Batshoof 9.5f **(66)** - Sipsi Fach (Prince Sabo) 7.2f **(62)**
Form - 2202433
Record 1998 - 1st:0 2nd:3 3rd:2 Ran:7
Pre1998 - 1st:0 2nd:0 3rd:1 Ran:3
Win Prizemoney £0 *Total Prizemoney* £6,973
1998 Turf 0-7: (8f, 9f 2, 10f 3, 11f) (g-s, gd 3, g-f 2, frm)
Above-average gelding, effective 7 to 11f, acts on g-s to frm, prefers right handed tracks, prefers tight tracks. Turf high 75 - 2nd of 8 getting 3lb from Loyal Toast (5 Jun Goodwood 10f frm RF 1756). Consistent. **M Bell [0-10] Frank Farrant.*

PRINCE CONFEY (IRE) BHB 35f23a **RR 8f 23a** 8[10]

4 b c Tirol 8.1f **(64)** - Filet Mignon (USA) (Topsider (USA)) 8.3f **(71)**
Form - 000
Record 1998 - 1st:0 2nd:0 3rd:0 Ran:1
Pre1998 - 1st:0 2nd:0 3rd:0 Ran:11
1998 AW 0-1: (8f) (Fibr)
Poor colt, has worn blinkers.
**D J Wintle [0-4] D J Wintle (from G P Creaner in IRE [0-9] Oct 1997).*

PRINCE CONSORT **RR 75f** 4473[2]

2 b c Clantime 6.6f **(57)** - Miss Petella (Dunphy) 9.4f **(57)**
Form - 245072
Record 1998 - 1st:0 2nd:2 3rd:0 Ran:6
Win Prizemoney £0 *Total Prizemoney* £1,724
1998 Turf 0-6: (5f 2, 6f 3, 8f) (gd, g-f 3, frm 2)
Above-average colt, effective 5 to 6f, acts on g-f to frm, has worn blinkers. Turf high 75 (began Jly) - 2nd of 16 giving 11lb to Helen's Stardust (25 Spt Folkestone 6f g-f RF 4473).
**Mrs J R Ramsden [0-6] P D Savill.*

PRINCE DANZIG (IRE) BHB 47f65a **RR 50f 65a** 1642[8]

7 ch g Roi Danzig (USA) 10.5f **(62)** - Veldt (High Top) 10.2f **(67)**
Form - 50068
Record 1998 - 1st:0 2nd:0 3rd:0 Ran:3
Pre1998 - 1st:9 2nd:10 3rd:9 Ran:68
Win Prizemoney £29,018 *Total Prizemoney* £48,339
Wins * 1996 *Dec Wolver (STD) H 12f 79 83* <
* 1996 May Bright (FRM) H 11.9f 63 64
* 1996 *Feb Lingfi (STD) H 12f 77 76*
* 1995 Jly Bright (FRM) H 11.9f 54 60
* 1995 *Mar Lingfi (STD) H 12f 77 78*
* 1995 *Jan Lingfi (STD) C 12f 59+*
* 1994 Aug Bright (G-F) H 10f 52 59
* 1994 *Mar Lingfi (STD) H 10f 75 73*
1998 Turf 0-2: (12f 2) (gd, g-f) 1998 AW 0-1: (12f) (Equi)
Average gelding, effective 10f, - acts on Equi, has worn blinkers, likes left handed tracks, favours tight tracks. Turf high 47.
**D J G MurraySmith [9-71] A H Ulrick.*

PRINCE DE BERRY BHB 38f **RR 36f** 118[5]

7 ch g Ballacashtal (CAN) 7.9f **(51)** - Hoonah (FR) (Luthier) 9.8f **(71)**
Form - 5
Record 1998 - 1st:0 2nd:0 3rd:0 Ran:1
Pre1998 - 1st:0 2nd:0 3rd:2 Ran:13
Win Prizemoney £0 *Total Prizemoney* £1,018
1998 AW 0-1: (12f) (Fibr)
Very moderate gelding, has worn blinkers.
**G A Ham [0-6] N G Ahier (from B J Meehan [0-5] Aug 1996).*

PRINCE DOME (IRE) BHB 80f **RR 82f** 4918[16]

4 ch g Salt Dome (USA) 6.5f **(59)** - Blazing Glory (IRE) (Glow (USA)) 6.7f **(71)**
Form - 000608611747300020
Record 1998 - 1st:2 2nd:1 3rd:1 Ran:18
Pre1998 - 1st:3 2nd:1 3rd:2 Ran:13
Win Prizemoney £39,511 *Total Prizemoney* £55,875
Wins * **1998** Jly York (FRM) H 6f 79 82
* **1998** Jly Haydoc (G-S) H 6f 74 75
* 1997 Jun Ascot (SFT) H 5f 80 87 <
* 1997 Jun Newcas (FRM) H 6f 74 81
* 1997 Apr Beverl (G-F) 5f 70
1998 Turf 2-18: (5f 7, 6f 2-11) (g-s 4, gd 8, g-f 4, frm 2-2)
Unfurnished, decent gelding, effective 5 to 6f, best at 5f, acts on gd to frm, best on gd, excels at York. Turf high 82 - 1st of 17 getting 9lb from Venture Capitalist (11 Jly York RF 2739). Took time to recapture his form, but a promising run at Newcastle in June heralded a win in a competitive handicap at Haydock. Followed up at York over six, and has continued to run well. Gets six, but that trip stretches his stamina. **Martyn Wane [5-31] G W Jones.*

PRINCELY DREAM (IRE) BHB 85f **RR 87f** 4349[4]

2 br c Night Shift (USA) 8.1f **(73)** - Princess of Zurich (IRE) (Law Society (USA)) 9.9f **(70)**
Form - 22014
Record 1998 - 1st:1 2nd:2 3rd:0 Ran:5
Win Prizemoney £5,576 *Total Prizemoney* £8,176
Wins * **1998** Aug Pontef (G-F) 5f 82 <
1998 Turf 1-5: (5f 1-2, 6f 3) (sft, g-s 2, g-f, frm 1-1)
Useful colt. Turf high 87 - 2nd of 9 to Focus (13 Jun York 6f g-s RF 1979) - also 1st of 11 from Pal of Mine (16 Aug Pontefract RF 3669). Stepped up on his debut with a game win at York, just getting the better of a sustained duel with Focus although subsequently disqualified. He ran poorly in the Goffs Challenge at the Curragh, but regained winning form over the minimum at Pontefract in August.
**R A Fahey [1-5] I Bray.*

PRINCELY HEIR (IRE) **RR 110f** 4205[2]

3 b c Fairy King (USA) 7.7f **(75)** - Meis El-Reem (Auction Ring (USA)) 8.6f **(65)**
Form - 4483352
Record 1998 - 1st:0 2nd:1 3rd:2 Ran:7
Pre1998 - 1st:3 2nd:0 3rd:1 Ran:4
Win Prizemoney £92,430 *Total Prizemoney* £115,698
Wins * 1997 Aug Leopar (G-S) G1 6f 104 <
* 1997 Jly Beverl (HVY) 5f 101+
* 1997 May Ripon (G-F) 5f 76+
1998 Turf 0-7: (6f, 7f, 8f 5) (g-s, gd 4, g-f, frm)
Lengthy, Group-class colt, effective 5 to 8f, best at 8f, acts on sft to frm, best on gd, has worn blinkers, excels at Doncaster. Turf high 110 - 3rd of 8 getting 9lb from Green Card (15 Jly Doncaster 8f frm RF 2818). Consistent. He found life tough under a Group One penalty incurred as a result of his win in the Heinz 57 Phoenix Stakes in 1997. He is capable of winning a minor Group race on

soft ground. **M Johnston [3-11] Maktoum Al Maktoum.*

PRINCE NICHOLAS BHB 50f **RR 50f** 3575[11]
3 ch g Midyan (USA) 9.9f **(64)** - Its My Turn (Palm Track) 9.8f **(50)**
Form - 22050
Record 1998 - 1st:0 2nd:2 3rd:0 Ran:5
Pre1998 - 1st:0 2nd:0 3rd:0 Ran:4
Win Prizemoney £0 *Total Prizemoney* £1,510
1998 Turf 0-5: (8f, 9f, 10f 2, 11f) (sft 3, gd 2)
Fair gelding, effective 8 to 10f, acts on sft, prefers tight tracks. Turf high 50. Inconsistent. **K W Hogg [0-9] Auldyn Stud Ltd.*

PRINCE OF ARAGON BHB 59f **RR 65df** 4796[17]
2 b g Aragon 7.7f **(58)** - Queens Welcome (Northfields (USA)) 9f **(72)**
Form - 07700
Record 1998 - 1st:0 2nd:0 3rd:0 Ran:5
1998 Turf 0-5: (5f 3, 6f 2) (sft, gd, g-f, frm 2)
Average gelding. Turf high 65. **K T Ivory [0-5] K T Ivory.*

PRINCE OF DENIAL BHB 102f99a **RR 98f 99a** 5149[2]
4 b c Soviet Star (USA) 8.6f **(74)** - Gleaming Water (Kalaglow) 9.8f **(67)**
Form - 64315000362452
Record 1998 - 1st:1 2nd:2 3rd:2 Ran:13
Pre1998 - 1st:3 2nd:1 3rd:1 Ran:12
Win Prizemoney £42,309 *Total Prizemoney* £65,555
Wins * **1998** May York (GD) H 10.4f 95 97 <
* 1997 Oct Newbur (G-S) H 9f 89 94
* 1997 Spt Newbur (G-S) H 8f 83 89
* 1997 May Kempto (GD) H 9f 76 78
1998 Turf 1-13: (10f 1-8, 11f 2, 12f 3) (hvy, sft 2, g-s, gd 1-5, g-f 3, frm)
Leggy, very useful colt, effective 10 to 11f, best at 10f, acts on g-s to gd, best on gd, likes right handed tracks, likes tight tracks, excels at Newbury. Turf high 109 - 2nd of 4 giving 4lb to Mutamam (12 Spt Goodwood 10f g-s RF 4245). Consistent. He ran above himself when finishing second to Mutamam in a Group Three at Goodwood in September and was sold for 80,000 guineas in October to race in Germany. **D W P Arbuthnot [4-25] J S Gutkin.*

PRINCE OF INDIA BHB 85f80a **RR 90f 80a** 399[6]
6 b g Night Shift (USA) 8.1f **(73)** - Indian Queen (Electric) 10.1f **(61)**
Form - 36
Record 1998 - 1st:0 2nd:0 3rd:1 Ran:2
Pre1998 - 1st:2 2nd:1 3rd:2 Ran:19
Win Prizemoney £18,314 *Total Prizemoney* £30,738
Wins * 1994 Aug Bordea (GD) L 6f 95
* 1994 Jly Goodwo (GF) 6f 88+
1998 AW 0-2: (7f, 8f) (Equi, Fibr)
Useful gelding. AW high 70.
**Lord Huntingdon [2-21] Sir Gordon Brunton.*

PRINCE OF MY HEART BHB 90f **RR 96df** 4631[29]
5 ch h Prince Daniel (USA) 11.4f **(46)** - Blue Room (Gorytus (USA)) 7.8f **(60)**
Form - 40883400
Record 1998 - 1st:0 2nd:0 3rd:1 Ran:8
Pre1998 - 1st:3 2nd:1 3rd:4 Ran:22
Win Prizemoney £18,589 *Total Prizemoney* £46,544
Wins 1997 May Newbur (SFT) H 9f 100 108? <
1996 Apr Catter (GD) 12f 87++
1995 Oct York (GD) 7.9f 85
1998 Turf 0-8: (8f 5, 9f, 10f 2) (hvy, gd 4, g-f 3)
Very useful colt, effective 9 to 10f, acts on gd to g-f, has worn blinkers. Turf high 96. Ran his best race for quite a while when third in the Royal Hunt Cup and put in another good performance at Glorious Goodwood, but remains hard to win with.
**D HaydnJones [0-8] G J Hicks (from B W Hills [3-22] Aug 1997).*

PRINCE OF SALSA BHB 40f46a **RR 37f 46a** 3689[8]
3 b g Emarati (USA) 6.6f **(63)** - Salinas (Bay Express) 7.1f **(60)**
Form - 670008
Record 1998 - 1st:0 2nd:0 3rd:0 Ran:6
Pre1998 - 1st:0 2nd:0 3rd:0 Ran:1
1998 Turf 0-4:(6f 2, 10f, 12f) (gd, frm 3) 1998 AW 0-2: (6f 2) (Equi, Fibr)
Unfurnished, moderate gelding, has worn blinkers. Turf high 37. AW high 47. **K McAuliffe [0-7] The PBT Group.*

PRINCE OF SPADES BHB 35f **RR 25f** 2255[P]
6 ch g Shavian 7.7f **(67)** - Diamond Princess (Horage) 10.3f **(61)**
Form - 0P
Record 1998 - 1st:0 2nd:0 3rd:0 Ran:2
Pre1998 - 1st:2 2nd:0 3rd:0 Ran:11
Win Prizemoney £6,903 *Total Prizemoney* £6,903
Wins 1995 Jly Bright (FRM) H 10f 59 64 <
1995 Jly Ripon (G-F) S 10f 63
1998 Turf 0-2: (11f 2) (gd, g-f)
Little account gelding. Becoming disappointing.
**M Quinn[0-2] M & K Sports & Promotions(from F Jordan[0-5]Jly 1996).*

PRINCE OXLEY BHB 46f40a **RR 44f 40a** 3202[10]
3 ch g King's Signet (USA) 7f **(51)** - Precious Air (IRE) (Precocious) 8.6f **(62)**
Form - 43460780
Record 1998 - 1st:0 2nd:0 3rd:1 Ran:7
Pre1998 - 1st:0 2nd:0 3rd:0 Ran:4
Win Prizemoney £0 *Total Prizemoney* £735
1998 Turf 0-1: (9f) (g-f) 1998 AW 0-6: (7f 3, 8f 2, 10f) (Equi 6)
Scopey, moderate gelding, effective 8f, - acts on Equi, has worn blinkers, likes left handed tracks, likes tight tracks. AW high 46.
**G L Moore [0-11] Bryan Pennick.*

PRINCE POWHATAN (FR) RR 92f 5154a[1]
2 ch c Hero's Honor (USA) 9.2f **(76)** - Wish For Diamonds (USA) (Lyphard's Wish (FR)) 9f **(74)**
Form - 1
1998 Turf 1-1: (8f 1-1) (hvy 1-1)
Currently useful colt. (1st run) - 1st of 6 giving 3lb to Mumtaz (2 Nov Nantes RF 5154a). **H-A Pantall in FR [1-1] J Poiroux.*

PRINCE PROSPECT BHB 82f **RR 86f** 4796[15]
2 b c Lycius (USA) 8.8f **(71)**-Princess Dechtra (IRE) (Bellypha) 9.8f **(73)**
Form - 422330
Record 1998 - 1st:0 2nd:2 3rd:2 Ran:6
Win Prizemoney £0 *Total Prizemoney* £3,299
1998 Turf 0-6: (5f, 6f 5) (sft, gd, g-f 2, frm 2)
Useful colt, effective 6f, acts on frm, has worn blinkers. Turf high 86 - 3rd of 7 giving 18lb to Retaliator (16 Jly Leicester 6f frm RF 2855). **J Noseda [0-6] Harvey Rosenblatt & Norman Mandell.*

PRINCE SLAYER RR 75f 5138[5]
2 b c Batshoof 9.5f **(66)** - Top Sovereign (High Top) 10.2f **(67)**
Form - 5
Record 1998 - 1st:0 2nd:0 3rd:0 Ran:1
1998 Turf 0-1: (7f) (gd)
Currently above-average colt. **B Smart [0-1] A Khaleq.*

PRINCESS BELFORT BHB 20f20a **RR 20f 20a** 1581[7]
5 b m Belfort (FR) 6.7f **(53)** - Domino Rose (Dominion) 8.5f **(63)**
Form - 07
Record 1998 - 1st:0 2nd:0 3rd:0 Ran:2
Pre1998 - 1st:0 2nd:0 3rd:0 Ran:3
1998 AW 0-2: (12f 2) (Fibr 2)
Little account filly.
**W Clay [0-3] Barry Leavy (from G Barnett [0-1] Jly 1997).*

PRINCESS DANIELLE BHB 53f **RR 60f** 4776[6]
6 b m Prince Daniel (USA) 11.4f **(46)** - Bells of St Martin (Martinmas) 7.6f **(59)**
Form - 506466436
Record 1998 - 1st:0 2nd:0 3rd:1 Ran:9
Pre1998 - 1st:4 2nd:3 3rd:9 Ran:33
Win Prizemoney £14,534 *Total Prizemoney* £24,040
Wins * 1997 Jun Windso (G-F) H 10f 61 67 <
* 1997 May Leices (G-F) H 10f 59 64
1995 Spt Salisb (G-S) H 10f 54 55
1995 Jun Nottin (G-F) H 8.2f 52 54
1998 Turf 0-9: (10f 9) (sft, gd 5, g-f, frm 2)
Average mare, effective 10 to 12f, best at 10f, acts on gd to frm, best on g-f, prefers tight tracks, excels at Windsor. Turf high 60 - 4th of 7 to Pixielated (4 Jly Chepstow 10f gd RF 2530). Consistent.
**W R Muir [2-28] Mrs Marion Wickham (from C C Elsey [2-9] Apr 1996).*

PRINCESS EILEEN BHB 52f **RR 45f** 2300[15]
4 b f Lord Bud 8.2f **(52)** - Too Familiar (Oats) 8.9f **(46)**

Form - 0800
Record 1998 - 1st:0 2nd:0 3rd:0 Ran:4
1998 Turf 0-4: (7f 2, 8f, 10f) (gd, g-f, frm 2)
Moderate filly. Turf high 45. **D C O'Brien [0-4] Mrs J Scudder.*

PRINCESSE ZELDA (FR) RR 3829[9]
4 b f Defensive Play (USA) - Brisk Waters (USA) (Saratoga Six (USA)) 7f **(73)**
Form - 0
Record 1998 - 1st:0 2nd:0 3rd:0 Ran:1
1998 AW 0-1: (9f) (Fibr)
Currently poor filly. **D J G MurraySmith [0-1] D MurraySmith.*

PRINCESS FOLEY (IRE) BHB 62f58a RR 63f 58a 4812[8]
2 ch f Forest Wind (USA) - Taniokey (Grundy) 10.3f **(65)**
Form - 563438
Record 1998 - 1st:0 2nd:0 3rd:2 Ran:6
Win Prizemoney £0 *Total Prizemoney* £724
1998 Turf 0-6: (5f 3, 6f 2, 7f) (gd 2, g-f 2, frm 2)
Average filly, effective 5f, acts on g-f. Turf high 63 - 3rd of 14 getting 5lb from Ones Enough (25 Spt Folkestone 5f g-f RF 4471).
**W G M Turner [0-5] Foley Steelstock (from D HaydnJones [0-1] May 1998).*

PRINCESS LATIFA RR 63f 1410[4]
2 b f Wolfhound (USA) 7.3f **(71)** - Moorish Idol (Aragon) 8.1f **(60)**
Form - 74
Record 1998 - 1st:0 2nd:0 3rd:0 Ran:2
Win Prizemoney £0 *Total Prizemoney* £227
1998 Turf 0-2: (6f 2) (g-f, frm)
Currently average filly. Turf high 63. **B J Meehan [0-2] J A Lazzari.*

PRINCESS LONDIS BHB 47f RR 48df 4962[19]
3 ch f Interrex (CAN) 7.7f **(51)** - Princess Lucianne (Stanford) 7.9f **(56)**
Form - 0000
Record 1998 - 1st:0 2nd:0 3rd:0 Ran:4
Pre1998 - 1st:0 2nd:0 3rd:0 Ran:3
Win Prizemoney £0 *Total Prizemoney* £398
1998 Turf 0-4: (6f 2, 7f 2) (sft, gd, frm 2)
Neat, moderate filly, has worn blinkers. Turf high 48.
**N E Berry [0-1] C Richards (from P Shakespeare [0-3] Jun 1998).*

PRINCESS MO BHB 56f RR 62f 5001[6]
2 b f Prince Sabo 6.6f **(64)** - Morica (Moorestyle) 6.9f **(64)**
Form - 506
Record 1998 - 1st:0 2nd:0 3rd:0 Ran:3
1998 Turf 0-3: (5f 3) (sft, g-s, gd)
Currently average filly. Turf high 62 (began Oct).
**Pat Mitchell [0-3] Had A Mad Mo-Ment Partnership.*

PRINCESS NATALIE BHB 64f RR 66f 4596[12]
3 b f Rudimentary (USA) 8.2f **(66)** - X-Data (On Your Mark) 7.7f **(58)**
Form - 37160
Record 1998 - 1st:1 2nd:0 3rd:1 Ran:5
Pre1998 - 1st:1 2nd:0 3rd:0 Ran:7
Win Prizemoney £7,765 *Total Prizemoney* £8,215
Wins * 1998 Aug Leices (GD) H 5f 61 66
1997 Jun Doncas (G-S) 5f 79+ <
1998 Turf 1-5: (5f 1-4, 6f) (gd 2, g-f 2, frm 1-1)
Scopey, average filly, effective 5f, acts on g-s. Turf high 66. Brought back to the minimum, she beat a big field in a Leicester handicap in August.
**M A Jarvis [1-3] Burke's 5th Family Settlement (from M W Easterby [0-7] Jun 1998).*

PRINCESS OF HEARTS BHB 39f43a RR 44f 43a 3884[17]
4 b f Prince Sabo 6.6f **(64)** - Constant Delight (Never so Bold) 6.3f **(66)**
Form - 5678700
Record 1998 - 1st:0 2nd:0 3rd:0 Ran:7
Pre1998 - 1st:2 2nd:3 3rd:3 Ran:21
Win Prizemoney £4,054 *Total Prizemoney* £9,513
Wins 1997 Apr Nottin (G-F) S 8.2f 59 <
1996 Aug Folkes (G-F) S 6.9f 58
1998 Turf 0-3: (8f 2, 10f) (gd, g-f 2) 1998 AW 0-4: (8f 2, 10f, 12f) (Equi 3, Fibr)
Scopey, moderate filly, effective 8 to 10f, best at 8f, acts on gd to frm, often wears blinkers (very effectively). Turf high 42 (began Jly). AW high 45. Inconsistent. She has become very disappointing and there has to be a big question about her resolution.
**M J Ryan [0-3] A S Reid (from G L Moore [0-4] Feb 1998).*

PRINCESS OLIVIA BHB 31f45a RR 27f 45a 4275[13]
3 b f Prince Sabo 6.6f **(64)** - Les Amis (Alzao (USA)) 7.1f **(68)**
Form - 08000000
Record 1998 - 1st:0 2nd:0 3rd:0 Ran:8
Pre1998 - 1st:0 2nd:0 3rd:0 Ran:2
Win Prizemoney £0 *Total Prizemoney* £228
1998 Turf 0-6: (5f, 6f, 7f 4) (gd 5, frm) 1998 AW 0-2: (8f, 11f) (Fibr 2)
Neat, little account filly. Turf high 27. AW high 2.
**M J Ryan [0-10] Mrs W L Sole.*

PRINCESS SCEPTRE BHB 56f RR 53f 2948[8]
3 ch f Cadeaux Genereux 7.9f **(76)** - Sans Blague (USA) (The Minstrel (CAN)) 10f **(72)**
Form - 0568
Record 1998 - 1st:0 2nd:0 3rd:0 Ran:4
1998 Turf 0-4: (7f, 8f, 10f, 11f) (gd 4)
Light-framed, fair filly. Turf high 60. **B W Hills [0-4] Sceptre Racing.*

PRINCESS TOPAZ BHB 74f RR 78f 4497[16]
4 b f Midyan (USA) 9.9f **(64)** - Diamond Princess (Horage) 10.3f **(61)**
Form - 4016000
Record 1998 - 1st:1 2nd:0 3rd:0 Ran:7
Pre1998 - 1st:2 2nd:3 3rd:3 Ran:16
Win Prizemoney £11,834 *Total Prizemoney* £24,098
Wins * 1998 Jly Newmar (GD) H 14.8f 75 78 <
* 1997 Aug Sandow (G-F) H 14f 68 72
* 1997 Aug Newmar (GD) H 12f 61 65
1998 Turf 1-6: (14f, 15f 1-2, 16f 3) (sft, gd 2, frm 1-3) 1998 AW 0-1: (12f) (Equi)
Light-framed, above-average filly, effective 14 to 16f, best at 16f, acts on gd to frm, best on gd, prefers right handed tracks. Turf high 78 - 1st of 10 getting 1lb from Domappel (18 Jly Newmarket RF 2918). Inconsistent. Twice a winner last season, she had not shown much for a while before bouncing back with a victory at Newmarket in July. She seems to like it there, and needs fast ground. **C A Cyzer [3-23] Stephen Crown.*

PRINCE ZANDO BHB 42f RR 43f 5128[3]
4 b g Forzando 7.2f **(63)** - Paradise Forum (Prince Sabo) 7.2f **(62)**
Form - 000800256073
Record 1998 - 1st:0 2nd:1 3rd:1 Ran:12
Pre1998 - 1st:0 2nd:0 3rd:2 Ran:5
Win Prizemoney £0 *Total Prizemoney* £2,041
1998 Turf 0-12: (5f 2, 6f 2, 7f 5, 8f 2, 10f) (g-s, gd 3, g-f 4, frm 4)
Unfurnished, moderate gelding, has worn blinkers. Turf high 50.
**C A Horgan [0-17] Mrs B Sumner.*

PRINCIPAL BOY (IRE) BHB 41f38a RR 40f 38a 1083[11]
5 br g Cyrano de Bergerac 7.3f **(58)** - Shenley Lass (Prince Tenderfoot (USA)) 9f **(61)**
Form - 66125740
Record 1998 - 1st:1 2nd:1 3rd:0 Ran:6
Pre1998 - 1st:4 2nd:4 3rd:2 Ran:36
Win Prizemoney £14,319 *Total Prizemoney* £20,979
Wins * *1998 Jan Southw (STD) H 8f 37 40*
1997 Jun Hamilt (G-S) H 9.2f 44 47
1997 May Hamilt (SFT) H 8.3f 35 45
1996 May Southw (STD) H 7f 52 52 <
1996 Feb Southw (STD) H 7f 42 45
1998 Turf 0-1: (8f) (sft) 1998 AW 1-5: (7f, 8f 1-4) (Fibr 1-5)
Moderate gelding, effective 8 to 9f, best at 9f, acts on gd to frm, best on g-f, has worn blinkers, prefers right handed tracks, excels at Hamilton. AW high 40 (1st run). Twice a winner at Hamilton in '97, he has shown some ability on Fibresand too, though the apprentice handicap he won at Southwell in January was very modest.
**J A Glover [1-7] Chris Moreno (from T J Etherington [4-41] Nov 1997).*

PRINCIPAL DANCER BHB 54f RR 65f 4873[18]
2 b f Shareef Dancer (USA) 10.1f **(67)** - Little Beaut **(67df 60a)** (Prince Sabo) 7.2f **(62)**
Form - 403000
Record 1998 - 1st:0 2nd:0 3rd:1 Ran:6

Win Prizemoney £0 *Total Prizemoney* £751
1998 Turf 0-6: (5f 3, 6f 2, 8f) (g-s, gd 2, g-f 2, frm)
Average filly. Turf high 65. **J A Glover [0-6] M O'Horan.*

PRINCIPALITY (IRE) BHB 96f **RR 92f** 4857[8]

2 b c College Chapel - Desert Palace (Green Desert (USA)) 8.6f **(78)**
Form - 2122420368
Record 1998 - 1st:1 2nd:4 3rd:1 Ran:10
Win Prizemoney £2,996 *Total Prizemoney* £15,029
Wins * 1998 Apr Newcas (SFT) 5f 75 <
1998 Turf 1-10: (5f 1-4, 6f 6) (sft 1-2, gd 6, g-f, frm)
Useful colt, effective 5 to 6f, best at 6f, acts on gd to frm, best on gd, has worn blinkers. Turf high 92. Consistent. He had quite a busy juvenile season, winning at Newcastle and finishing runner-up four times in his first six starts. His form deteriorated as the better two-year-olds appeared in the second half of the season and he was sold in the autumn, apparently to race abroad.
**J Berry [1-10] Mrs John Magnier.*

PRINCIPLED BHB 26f **RR 30f** 1478[15]

3 b c Prince Sabo 6.6f **(64)** - Payvashooz (Ballacashtal (CAN)) 5.3f **(50)**
Form - 08000
Record 1998 - 1st:0 2nd:0 3rd:0 Ran:5
1998 Turf 0-5: (7f, 8f, 10f, 12f, 14f) (sft, g-s, gd, g-f, frm)
Unfurnished, very moderate colt, mostly wears blinkers. Turf high 36. **M Brittain [0-5] M J Paver.*

PRIOLETTE (IRE) BHB 40f **RR 46f** 4133[2]

3 b f Priolo (USA) 10.9f **(71)** - Celestial Path (Godswalk (USA)) 7.3f **(58)**

Form - 0634602
Record 1998 - 1st:0 2nd:1 3rd:1 Ran:7
Pre1998 - 1st:0 2nd:0 3rd:0 Ran:5
Win Prizemoney £0 *Total Prizemoney* £2,555
1998 Turf 0-7: (8f 3, 9f 2, 10f 2) (g-s 2, gd 2, g-f, frm 2)
Workmanlike, moderate filly. Turf high 46.
**J G FitzGerald [0-12] J Dick.*

PRIORS MOOR BHB 56f57a **RR 53f 57a** 4338[1]

3 br g Petong 7.6f **(58)** - Jaziyah (IRE) (Lead on Time (USA)) 8f **(65)**
Form - 4001
Record 1998 - 1st:1 2nd:0 3rd:0 Ran:3
Pre1998 - 1st:0 2nd:0 3rd:0 Ran:5
Win Prizemoney £2,994 *Total Prizemoney* £3,186
Wins * 1998 Spt Yarmou (G-S) H 8f 48 53 <
1998 Turf 1-3: (8f 1-1, 9f, 11f) (gd, g-f, frm 1-1)
Scopey, fair gelding, effective 8f, acts on frm, has worn blinkers. Turf high 53 - 1st of 20 getting 8lb from Newala (17 Spt Yarmouth RF 4338). **R W Armstrong [1-8] Mrs L Alexander.*

PRIORY GARDENS (IRE) BHB 38f **RR 36f** 4339[15]

4 b g Broken Hearted 10.1f **(65)** - Rosy O'Leary (Majetta) 6.5f **(58)**
Form - 80411080
Record 1998 - 1st:2 2nd:0 3rd:0 Ran:8
Pre1998 - 1st:1 2nd:0 3rd:0 Ran:11
Win Prizemoney £9,023 *Total Prizemoney* £9,243
Wins * 1998 Jun Carlis (G-S) H 6.9f 30 34
*** 1998** Jun Goodwo (GD) H 6f 30 36
* 1997 Jun Thirsk (GD) H 6f 40 47 <
1998 Turf 2-8: (6f 1-4, 7f 1-4) (sft, gd 1-2, g-f 1-2, frm 3)
Leggy, very moderate gelding, effective 6f, acts on frm. Turf high 36. **J M Bradley [3-19] Gwilym Fry.*

PRIVATE AUDIENCE (USA) BHB 48f55a **RR 46?f 55a** 469[20]

5 b h Private Account (USA) 10.1f **(80)** - Monroe (USA) (Sir Ivor) 10.2f **(70)**
Form - 4605040
Record 1998 - 1st:0 2nd:0 3rd:0 Ran:3
Pre1998 - 1st:0 2nd:0 3rd:0 Ran:6
Win Prizemoney £0 *Total Prizemoney* £231
1998 Turf 0-1: (12f) (gd) 1998 AW 0-2: (12f 2) (Equi, Fibr)
Fair colt, effective 12f, - acts on Equi, has worn blinkers, likes tight tracks. AW high 55. Inconsistent.
**W R Muir [0-9] John Davies (from H R A Cecil [0-2] May 1996).*

PRIVATE DESPATCH (USA) BHB 50f55a **RR 9f 55a** 3811[14]

8 ch h Private Account (USA) 10.1f **(80)** - Soft Dawn (USA) (Grey Dawn II) 11.1f **(72)**
Form - 122102000
Record 1998 - 1st:2 2nd:3 3rd:0 Ran:9
Pre1998 - 1st:0 2nd:1 3rd:0 Ran:1
Win Prizemoney £4,797 *Total Prizemoney* £6,900
Wins * 1998 *Feb Southw (STD) C 12f 68 <*
1998 *Jan Lingfi (STD) C 10f 60+*
1998 Turf 0-1: (12f) (gd) 1998 AW 2-8: (10f 1-3, 11f, 12f 1-2, 16f 2) (Equi 1-4, Fibr 1-4)
Average horse, effective 10 to 12f, best at 12f, - acts on AW, best on Fibr, favours tight tracks. AW high 68 - 1st of 8 giving 2lb to Marytavy (23 Feb Southwell RF 0343) - also 1st of 7 from Awesome Power (24 Jan Lingfield RF 0148). Becoming disappointing.
**M Quinn [1-7] Frank Adams & & Mrs Gary Pinchen (from J Martens in BEL [1-2] Feb 1998).*

PRIVATE FIXTURE (IRE) BHB 50f63a **RR 50f 63a** 100[2]

7 ch g The Noble Player (USA) 7.7f **(58)** - Pennyala (Skyliner) 7.3f **(53)**
Form - 362
Record 1998 - 1st:0 2nd:1 3rd:0 Ran:1
Pre1998 - 1st:4 2nd:4 3rd:5 Ran:38
Win Prizemoney £9,989 *Total Prizemoney* £15,771
Wins * 1997 *Jly Southw (STD) S 12f 72*
* 1997 *Jun Southw (STD) C 11f 67*
1998 AW 0-1: (16f) (Fibr)
Above-average gelding, effective 11 to 16f, - acts on Fibr, has worn blinkers, favours left handed tracks. (1st run) - 2nd of 9 getting 2lb from Mister Aspecto (16 Jan Southwell 16f Fibr RF 0100).
**D Marks [2-29] John Jackson (from W Jarvis [2-10] Jun 1994).*

PRIVATE PERCIVAL BHB 29f33a **RR 23f 33a** 2336[6]

5 b g Arrasas (USA) 14.4f **(37)** - Romacina (Roman Warrior) 5.6f **(57)**
Form - 06
Record 1998 - 1st:0 2nd:0 3rd:0 Ran:2
Pre1998 - 1st:0 2nd:0 3rd:0 Ran:6
1998 Turf 0-2: (11f, 12f) (frm, hrd)
Little account gelding. Turf high 23. **J R Poulton [0-9] Mrs J Druce.*

PRIVATE SEAL BHB 43f59a **RR 39f 59a** 4571[10]

3 b g King's Signet (USA) 7f **(51)** - Slender (Aragon) 8.1f **(60)**
Form - 33200550
Record 1998 - 1st:0 2nd:0 3rd:0 Ran:5
Pre1998 - 1st:1 2nd:2 3rd:3 Ran:10
Win Prizemoney £1,984 *Total Prizemoney* £4,322
Wins 1997 Oct Bright (FRM) S 5.3f 69 <
1998 Turf 0-5: (7f 2, 8f 2, 10f) (gd, g-f 2, frm 2)
Leggy, average gelding, effective 5 to 7f, acts on g-f to frm - acts on Equi, prefers left handed tracks, prefers tight tracks. Turf high 39. **J C Poulton [0-3] Gerald West (from G L Moore [1-12] Jly 1998).*

PRIWINGS (IRE) **RR 94f** 4722a[2]

3 b c In The Wings 11.2f **(77)** - Primisca (Double Form) 7.3f **(58)**
Form - 2
1998 Turf 0-1: (9f) (hvy)
Currently useful colt. (1st run) - 2nd of 12 to Green Tea (3 Oct San Siro 9f hvy RF 4722a). **I Tellini in ITY [1-2].*

PRIX DE CLERMONT (IRE) BHB 32f38a **RR 35f 38a** 5002[9]

4 b g Petorius 8f **(66)** - Sandra's Choice (Sandy Creek) 8.9f **(59)**
Form - 6416738370700
Record 1998 - 1st:0 2nd:0 3rd:2 Ran:9
Pre1998 - 1st:1 2nd:0 3rd:0 Ran:9
Win Prizemoney £2,453 *Total Prizemoney* £3,071
Wins 1997 *Dec Wolver (STD) H 12f 45 49 <*
1998 Turf 0-2: (12f 2) (frm 2) 1998 AW 0-7: (12f 6, 16f) (Equi 3, Fibr 4)
Leggy, moderate gelding, effective 10 to 12f, - acts on AW, has worn blinkers, likes left handed tracks, favours tight tracks. Turf high 35 (began Jly). AW high 48.
**G L Moore [0-5] R Kiernan (from G Lewis [1-14] Mar 1998).*

PRIX STAR BHB 75f **RR 66f** 5096[17]

3 ch g Superpower 6.6f **(58)** - Celestine **(40f 44a)** (Skyliner) 7.3f **(53)**
Form - 330000
Record 1998 - 1st:0 2nd:0 3rd:2 Ran:6
Pre1998 - 1st:1 2nd:3 3rd:0 Ran:7
Win Prizemoney £3,225 *Total Prizemoney* £12,901
Wins * 1997 Jly Hamilt (G-S) 5f 76 <

1998 Turf 0-6: (6f 6) (g-s 2, gd 2, g-f 2)
Workmanlike, average gelding, effective 5 to 6f, best at 5f, acts on g-s to g-f, best on g-f, often wears blinkers. Turf high 81 - 3rd of 22 getting 14lb from Friar Tuck (13 Jun York 6f g-s RF 1981). Consistent. **C W Fairhurst [1-13] M J Grace.*

PRIZEFIGHTER BHB 62f63a **RR 64f 63a** 2540^{5}

7 b g Rambo Dancer (CAN)8.4f **(59)** - Jaisalmer (Castle Keep) 8.3f **(57)**
Form - 625

Record		1st	2nd	3rd	Ran
	1998 -	1st:0	2nd:1	3rd:0	Ran:3
	Pre1998 -	1st:9	2nd:3	3rd:1	Ran:36

Win Prizemoney £29,151 *Total Prizemoney* £34,307

Wins							
1996	Aug Carlis	(FRM)	H	8f	62	64	
1996	*Feb Southw*	*(STD)*	*H*	*8f*	*66*	*62*	
1995	*Dec Lingfi*	*(STD)*	*H*	*8f*	*62*	*66*	
1995	Aug Sandow	(G-F)	H	8.1f	60	64	
1994	Jly Newmar	(GD)	H	8f	74	74	<
1994	Jly Sandow	(G-F)	H	8.1f	69	68	
1994	Jun Haydoc	(GD)	H	8.1f	64	69	
1994	May Mussel	(FRM)	H	8.1f	60	61	

1998 Turf 0-2: (10f, 11f) (gd, g-f) 1998 AW 0-1: (12f) (Fibr)
Average gelding, had worn blinkers. Turf high 64 (1st run) - 2nd of 5 giving 4lb to Ellopassoff (12 Jun Chepstow 10f gd RF 1924). (DEAD) **B J Llewellyn [1-11] J Milton (from J L Eyre [7-19] Mar 1997).*

PROCEDURE (USA) **RR 78f** 4997^{3}

2 b br c Strolling Along (USA) - Bold Courtesan (USA) (Bold Bidder) 8.8f **(67)**
Form - 63
Record 1998 - 1st:0 2nd:0 3rd:1 Ran:2
Win Prizemoney £0 *Total Prizemoney* £500
1998 Turf 0-2: (7f 2) (sft, gd)
Currently above-average colt. Turf high 78 (began Oct) - 3rd of 10 to Bound For Pleasure (26 Oct Lingfield 7f sft RF 4997).
**Sir Michael Stoute [0-2] Highclere Thoroughbred Racing Ltd.*

PRODIGAL SON (IRE) BHB 51f53a **RR 60f 53a** 4865^{2}

3 b g Waajib 8.9f **(67)** - Nouveau Lady (IRE) (Taufan (USA)) 7f **(57)**
Form - 040453202
Record 1998 - 1st:0 2nd:2 3rd:1 Ran:9
Pre1998 - 1st:0 2nd:0 3rd:0 Ran:4
Win Prizemoney £0 *Total Prizemoney* £2,500
1998 Turf 0-8: (8f 3, 9f, 10f 2, 14f, 15f) (gd, g-f 5, frm 2) 1998 AW 0-1: (7f) (Fibr)
Workmanlike, average gelding, effective 8 to 9f, acts on g-f to frm, has worn blinkers, likes left handed tracks, likes tight tracks. Turf high 60. **R J R Williams [0-13] Richard Morris Jr.*

PROFESSION BHB 28f20a **RR 60?f 20a** 63^{6}

7 b g Shareef Dancer (USA) 10.1f **(67)** - Mrs Warren (USA) (Hail To Reason) 10.1f **(82)**
Form - 0876
Record 1998 - 1st:0 2nd:0 3rd:0 Ran:1
Pre1998 - 1st:0 2nd:0 3rd:0 Ran:10
Win Prizemoney £0 *Total Prizemoney* £209
1998 AW 0-1: (16f) (Equi)
Average gelding. Becoming disappointing.
**G P Enright [0-8] Frederick Gray (from C E Brittain [0-3] Jly 1994).*

PROFILER (USA) BHB 82f **RR 82f** 4392^{5}

3 b c Capote (USA) 9.1f **(84)** - Magnificent Star (USA) (Silver Hawk (USA)) 8.6f **(70)**
Form - 27215
Record 1998 - 1st:1 2nd:2 3rd:0 Ran:5
Win Prizemoney £3,615 *Total Prizemoney* £5,865
Wins * **1998** Aug Ripon (G-F) 12.3f 80 <
1998 Turf 1-5: (10f 2, 12f 1-3) (gd 1-2, frm 3)
Workmanlike, decent colt. Turf high 82 (1st run) - 2nd of 17 to Forest Ending (19 May Beverley 10f frm RF 1321) - also 1st of 9 from Eurolink Apache (31 Aug Ripon RF 4000).
**H R A Cecil [1-5] Buckram Oak Holdings.*

PROFIT MAKER (USA) BHB 60f **RR 60df** 3750^{8}

3 b g Hansel (USA) 12.6f **(78)** - Bineyah (IRE) (Sadler's Wells (USA)) 10f **(76)**
Form - 5858
Record 1998 - 1st:0 2nd:0 3rd:0 Ran:4
1998 Turf 0-4: (8f 2, 9f 2) (sft, gd 2, g-f)
Tall, average gelding. Turf high 60.
**W McKeown [0-2] Elsa Crankshaw & G Allan (from M Johnston [0-2] Jly 1998).*

PROKOFIEV (USA) **RR 68+f** 5037^{3}

2 br c Nureyev (USA) 8.4f **(84)**-Aviara (USA)(Cox's Ridge (USA))8f **(68)**
Form - 3
Record 1998 - 1st:0 2nd:0 3rd:1 Ran:1
Win Prizemoney £0 *Total Prizemoney* £451
1998 Turf 0-1: (7f) (g-s)
Currently average colt. Found less than had looked likely when let down on his debut.
**Sir Michael Stoute [0-1] M Tabor & Mrs John Magnier.*

PROLIX BHB 114f **RR 112f** 4223^{3}

3 ch c Kris 10f **(75)** - Ajuga (USA) (The Minstrel (CAN)) 10f **(72)**
Form - 2115533
Record 1998 - 1st:2 2nd:1 3rd:2 Ran:7
Pre1998 - 1st:0 2nd:3 3rd:0 Ran:3
Win Prizemoney £36,714 *Total Prizemoney* £91,950

Wins						
* **1998**	May Cheste	(G-F)	L	10.3f	110+	<
* **1998**	Apr Thirsk	(G-S)		8f	107	

1998 Turf 2-7: (8f 1-2, 10f 1-3, 12f 2) (g-s 1-1, gd 3, g-f 1-3)
Scopey, Group-class colt, effective 8 to 12f, best at 10f, acts on g-s to g-f, best on g-f. Turf high 112 - 3rd of 6 to Sea Wave (18 Aug York 12f g-f RF 3697) - also 1st of 4 from Scorned (7 May Chester RF 1070). Consistent. He is a hot colt and went off at a suicidal pace when finishing fifth in the Prix du Jockey-Club (French Derby). He ran creditably in all his subsequent starts, but is not really a Group One performer. **B W Hills [2-10] K Abdulla.*

PROPELLANT BHB 40f50a **RR 29f 50a** 3623^{7}

4 b g Formidable (USA) 7.8f **(60)** - Kirsheda (Busted) 10.2f **(61)**
Form - 7
Record 1998 - 1st:0 2nd:0 3rd:0 Ran:1
Pre1998 - 1st:0 2nd:0 3rd:0 Ran:7
1998 Turf 0-1: (16f) (frm)
Leggy, little account gelding. Inconsistent.
**D W Barker [0-1] David Metcalfe (from C W Thornton [0-7] Jun 1997).*

PROPER BLUE (USA) BHB 97f **RR 104f** 4843^{12}

5 b h Proper Reality (USA) 10f **(106)** - Blinking (USA) (Tom Rolfe) 9.4f **(75)**
Form - 2783400
Record 1998 - 1st:0 2nd:1 3rd:1 Ran:7
Pre1998 - 1st:3 2nd:2 3rd:5 Ran:15
Win Prizemoney £26,767 *Total Prizemoney* £46,306

Wins							
* 1996	Nov Newmar	(GD)	L	10f		106	<
* 1996	Oct Ascot	(GD)	H	10f	90	95	
* 1995	Aug Bright	(FRM)	H	7f	84	92	

1998 Turf 0-7: (9f, 10f 4, 12f 2) (g-s, gd, g-f 4, frm)
Very useful colt, effective 9 to 12f, best at 10f, acts on gd to frm, best on g-f, likes right handed tracks, does well at Goodwood, likes Newmarket. Turf high 104 (1st run) - 2nd of 6 getting 3lb from Redbridge (6 Jun Doncaster 10f g-f RF 1771). He has bags of ability, but is almost impossible to place and seemed to have had enough when disappointing in the autumn. Connections let him go for 58,000 guineas at the Tattersalls Autumn Horses In Training Sales. **T G Mills [3-22] M J Legg.*

PROPHITS PRIDE (IRE) BHB 50f **RR 54f** 2372^{2}

6 ch g Carmelite House (USA) 8.2f **(52)**-Asinara (Julio Mariner)7.2f **(57)**
Form - 142
Record 1998 - 1st:1 2nd:1 3rd:0 Ran:3
Pre1998 - 1st:0 2nd:0 3rd:0 Ran:2
Win Prizemoney £2,248 *Total Prizemoney* £3,215
Wins * **1998** May Ayr (G-F) C 10f 50 <
1998 Turf 1-3: (10f 1-1, 12f 2) (gd, g-f 1-2)
Fair gelding. Turf high 54 - 2nd of 3 giving 5lb to Lucky Begonia (29 Jun Musselburgh 12f gd RF 2372) - also 1st of 9 giving 17lb to Eager Hero (28 May Ayr RF 1546).
**P Monteith [1-12] Mrs Maud Monteith.*

PROSPECTOR'S COVE BHB 61f50a **RR 62f 50a** 4936^{5}

5 b g Dowsing (USA) 7f **(61)** - Pearl Cove (Town And Country) 8.1f **(68)**
Form - 5300540140735

Record 1998 - 1st:1 2nd:0 3rd:2 Ran:13
Pre1998 - 1st:2 2nd:0 3rd:2 Ran:14
Win Prizemoney £10,173 *Total Prizemoney* £12,673
Wins * **1998** Aug Bright (FRM) H 8f 56 62
* 1996 Apr Kempto (GD) 10f 86 <
* 1995 Nov Mussel (SFT) 7.1f 83+
1998 Turf 1-11: (8f 1-8, 12f 3) (sft, gd 4, g-f 4, frm 1-2) 1998 AW 0-2: (13f, 16f) (Equi, Fibr)
Average gelding, has worn blinkers. Turf high 62. AW high 46. Consistent. **J Pearce [3-30] Saracen Racing.*

Wins * **1998** May Lingfi (GD) 7f 69 <
1998 Turf 1-4: (7f 1-2, 8f, 9f) (gd 2, frm 1-2)
Light-framed, decent filly. Turf high 80 - 2nd of 11 giving 13lb to Roger Ross (11 Jly Salisbury 8f frm RF 2718). She showed promise on her sole start at two, and made a winning reappearance in a Lingfield maiden. She faced stiff tasks in her next two starts, but ran better at Salisbury. A mile looks to be the limit of her stamina. **Lord Huntingdon [1-5] Mrs S Y Thomas.*

Prolix, an easy winner at Chester

PROSPECTORS QUEEN BHB 64f **RR 69f** 4756[7]
2 b f Robellino (USA) 9.5f **(68)** - Pronetta (USA) (Mr Prospector (USA)) 8.8f **(78)**
Form - 56367
Record 1998 - 1st:0 2nd:0 3rd:1 Ran:5
Win Prizemoney £0 *Total Prizemoney* £536
1998 Turf 0-5: (6f 3, 7f 2) (sft, g-f, frm 3)
Average filly. Turf high 69 (began Jly) - 3rd of 12 getting 5lb from Northern Svengali (19 Spt Catterick 6f frm RF 4370). **Miss S E Hall [0-5] Mrs James McAllister.*

PROSPECTRESS (USA) BHB 80f **RR 80f** 2718[2]
3 ch f Mining (USA) 7.8f **(78)** - Seductive Smile (USA) (Silver Hawk (USA)) 8.6f **(70)**
Form - 1072
Record 1998 - 1st:1 2nd:1 3rd:0 Ran:4
Pre1998 - 1st:0 2nd:0 3rd:1 Ran:1
Win Prizemoney £3,460 *Total Prizemoney* £5,708

PROSPERITY (IRE) **RR 74f** 3018[4]
2 b g Catrail (USA) - Bequeath (USA) (Lyphard (USA)) 9.9f **(72)**
Form - 434
Record 1998 - 1st:0 2nd:0 3rd:1 Ran:3
Win Prizemoney £0 *Total Prizemoney* £1,036
1998 Turf 0-3: (6f 3) (g-s, g-f 2)
Currently above-average gelding. Turf high 74. **T D Easterby [0-3] Reg Griffin and Jim McGrath.*

PROSPEROUS (IRE) **RR 81f** 4856[2]
2 ch f Generous (IRE) 11.5f **(82)** - Amwag (USA) (El Gran Senor (USA)) 9.6f **(76)**
Form - 2
Record 1998 - 1st:0 2nd:1 3rd:0 Ran:1
Win Prizemoney £0 *Total Prizemoney* £1,076
1998 Turf 0-1: (7f) (sft)
Currently decent filly. (1st run) - 2nd of 16 to Capistrano Day (17 Oct Redcar 7f sft RF 4856). **B W Hills [0-1] R A Scarborough.*

PROTARAS BAY BHB 46f37a **RR 51f 37a** 5114[7]
4 b c Superpower 6.6f **(58)** - Vivid Impression (Cure The Blues (USA)) 9.5f **(63)**
Form - 423525625017
Record 1998 - 1st:1 2nd:2 3rd:1 Ran:10
Pre1998 - 1st:0 2nd:2 3rd:1 Ran:10
Win Prizemoney £1,668 *Total Prizemoney* £5,815
Wins * **1998** Oct Newcas (SFT) CH 8f 43 51 <
1998 Turf 1-8: (8f 1-2, 9f, 10f 3, 11f, 12f) (g-s 1-1, gd 3, g-f, frm 3) 1998 AW 0-2: (9f, 11f) (Fibr 2)
Neat, fair colt, effective 8 to 10f, best at 10f, acts on g-s to frm, has worn blinkers (extremely effectively). Turf high 51 - 1st of 17 getting 5lb from Top Floor (21 Oct Newcastle RF 4920). AW high 36.
**P L Gilligan [1-17] The Cavotoro Partnership (from T T Clement [0-3] Jly 1996).*

PROTOCOL (IRE) BHB 72f83a **RR 74f 83a** 5147[15]
4 ch g Taufan (USA) 8.3f **(65)** - Ukraine's Affair (USA) (The Minstrel (CAN)) 10f **(72)**
Form - 5365731146070600
Record 1998 - 1st:2 2nd:0 3rd:2 Ran:16
Pre1998 - 1st:1 2nd:3 3rd:0 Ran:12
Win Prizemoney £9,934 *Total Prizemoney* £14,897
Wins * **1998** Apr Leices (SFT) H 10f 79 83 <
* **1998** Mar Doncas (GD) H 12f 73 78
1997 May Sandow (G-F) H 11.4f 73 74
1998 Turf 2-10: (8f, 10f 1-4, 11f, 12f 1-3, 16f) (sft 1-2, g-s, gd 1-3, g-f 2, frm, hrd) 1998 AW 0-6: (7f, 9f, 11f, 12f, 16f 2) (Fibr 6)
Leggy, decent gelding, effective 9 to 12f, best at 10f, acts on sft to hrd - acts on Fibr, likes right handed tracks. Turf high 87 - also 1st of 12 giving 11lb to Premier Generation (9 Apr Leicester RF 0618). AW high 80 - 3rd of 7 getting 4lb from Diamond Flame (14 Mar Wolverhampton 9f Fibr RF 0429).
**Mrs S Lamyman [2-17] P Lamyman (from J W Hills [1-12] Oct 1997).*

PROTON BHB 56f64a **RR 50?f 64a** 3199[9]
8 b g Sure Blade (USA) 10.6f **(66)** - Banket (Glint of Gold) 9.3f **(66)**
Form - 0
Record 1998 - 1st:0 2nd:0 3rd:0 Ran:1
Pre1998 - 1st:3 2nd:4 3rd:4 Ran:34
Win Prizemoney £16,788 *Total Prizemoney* £32,282
Wins 1995 Aug Epsom (G-F) H 12f 76 83 <
1994 Spt Lingfi (G-S) 11.5f 54
1994 Aug Lingfi (GD) H 11.5f 55 64
1998 Turf 0-1: (12f) (g-f)
Fair gelding, has worn blinkers.
**J Akehurst [0-1] Persian War Racing (from R Akehurst [3-22] Oct 1996).*

PROUD BRIGADIER (IRE) BHB 35f **RR 39f** 4201[3]
10 b g Auction Ring (USA) 8.4f **(62)** - Naughty One Gerard (Brigadier Gerard) 9.3f **(58)**
Form - 000073
Record 1998 - 1st:0 2nd:0 3rd:1 Ran:6
Pre1998 - 1st:4 2nd:5 3rd:6 Ran:62
Win Prizemoney £11,564 *Total Prizemoney* £18,415
Wins 1994 Jly Leices (G-F) 7f 63
1998 Turf 0-6: (8f 2, 9f, 10f, 11f, 12f) (gd, g-f, frm 4)
Very moderate gelding. Turf high 39.
**M R Bosley [0-15] S J Edwards (from P Burgoyne [0-6] Oct 1996).*

PROUD MONK BHB 35f41a **RR 51f 41a** 4931[16]
5 gr g Aragon 7.7f **(58)** - Silent Sister (Kind of Hush) 10.1f **(62)**
Form - 0507000740600350400
Record 1998 - 1st:0 2nd:0 3rd:1 Ran:18
Pre1998 - 1st:1 2nd:2 3rd:5 Ran:26
Win Prizemoney £4,146 *Total Prizemoney* £14,762
Wins 1995 Oct Newbur (G-S) H 7.3f 72 82 <
1998 Turf 0-15: (7f, 8f 5, 9f, 10f 5, 11f, 12f 2) (sft, g-s 3, gd 3, g-f 2, frm 6) 1998 AW 0-3: (8f 2, 10f) (Equi, Fibr 2)
Fair gelding, effective 10 to 11f, acts on frm, has worn blinkers, likes left handed tracks, likes tight tracks. Turf high 51 - 3rd of 9 getting 25lb from River's Source (5 Aug Pontefract 10f frm RF 3386). AW high 45. He is on a long losing run now, and even a big drop in the handicap does not seem to have made much difference.
**M R Bosley [0-21] S J Edwards (from G L Moore [1-25] Oct 1997).*

PROUD NATIVE (IRE) BHB 106f **RR 112f** 4330[6]
4 b g Imp Society (USA) 7.1f **(63)** - Karamana (Habitat) 9.4f **(70)**
Form - 107807010156
Record 1998 - 1st:3 2nd:0 3rd:0 Ran:12
Pre1998 - 1st:5 2nd:1 3rd:0 Ran:15
Win Prizemoney £127,386 *Total Prizemoney* £143,408
Wins * **1998** Aug Nottin (G-F) 5.1f 112 <
* **1998** Aug Haydoc (GD) H 5f 98 103
* **1998** Mar Doncas (GD) H 5f 100 105
1997 Aug Yarmou (G-F) 6f 101
1996 Oct Redcar (G-F) 6f 103
1996 Jun Epsom (GD) L 6f 105
1996 May York (G-F) 6f 84
1996 Apr Ripon (GD) 5f 78
1998 Turf 3-12: (5f 3-7, 6f 5) (gd 2-9, g-f 1-3)
Group-class gelding, effective 5f, acts on gd to g-f, best on gd. Turf high 112 - 1st of 6 from Almaty (29 Aug Nottingham RF 3962) - also 1st of 18 giving 21lb to Lord High Admiral (26 Mar Doncaster RF 0472). David Nicholl's has seen a healthy return on the 40,000 guineas this fellow cost at Newmarket in 1997. The winner of valuable handicaps at Doncaster and Haydock, he is capable of landing a Listed event as a five-year-old.
**D Nicholls [3-12] P D Savill (from A P Jarvis [5-15] Spt 1997).*

PROUD PICTURE (IRE) BHB 58f **RR 61f** 4145[12]
2 b g Pips Pride 6.7f **(70)** - Mint Addition (Tate Gallery (USA)) 7.4f **(67)**
Form - 0080
Record 1998 - 1st:0 2nd:0 3rd:0 Ran:4
1998 Turf 0-4: (5f, 6f 2, 7f) (g-f, frm 3)
Average gelding. Turf high 61.
**J G Smyth-Osbourne [0-4] The G N I Partnership.*

PTARMIGAN RIDGE **RR 87?f** 4836[1]
2 b c Sea Raven (IRE) - Panayr (Faraway Times (USA)) 7.4f **(52)**
Form - 1
Record 1998 - 1st:1 2nd:0 3rd:0 Ran:1
Win Prizemoney £3,626 *Total Prizemoney* £3,626
Wins * **1998** Oct Catter (SFT) 5f 87? <
1998 Turf 1-1: (5f 1-1) (g-s 1-1)
Currently useful colt. (1st run) - 1st of 5 from Waterford Spirit (16 Oct Catterick RF 4836). **Miss L A Perratt [1-1] Miss Heather Galbraith.*

PUBLIC PURSE (USA) **RR 119f** 4219a[3]
4 b c Private Account (USA) 10.1f **(80)** - Prodigious (FR) (Pharly (FR)) 9.8f **(68)**
Form - 113
1998 Turf 2-3: (10f 1-1, 12f, 13f 1-1) (sft 2-3)
Scopey, high-class colt. Turf high 119 - 3rd of 8 giving 11lb to Tiger Hill (6 Spt Baden-Baden 12f sft RF 4219a) - also 1st of 11 from Farasan (18 Jun Longchamp RF 2281a). Won a Group Two and a Group Three in France in the summer, but was only third to Tiger Hill in the Grosser Preis Von Baden after that.
**A Fabre in FR [2-4].*

PUBLIC WAY (IRE) BHB 30f **RR 35f** 609[7]
8 b g Common Grounds 8.1f **(66)** - Kilpeacon (Florescence) 6.2f **(54)**
Form - 47
Record 1998 - 1st:0 2nd:0 3rd:0 Ran:2
Pre1998 - 1st:3 2nd:1 3rd:5 Ran:40
Win Prizemoney £9,304 *Total Prizemoney* £12,655
Wins * 1994 Apr Hamilt (G-S) H 9.2f 48 50
1998 Turf 0-2: (9f, 12f) (sft 2)
Very moderate gelding. Turf high 35 (1st run) - 4th of 9 getting 5lb from Zorba (30 Mar Hamilton 9f sft RF 0501). Inconsistent.
**N Chamberlain [3-48] N Chamberlain (from M H Easterby [0-2] May 1992).*

PUBLISHER (USA) **RR 93f** 3684[3]
3 b c Kris S (USA) 9.3f **(76)** - Andover Way (USA) (His Majesty (USA)) 10.9f **(82)**
Form - 3
Record 1998 - 1st:0 2nd:0 3rd:1 Ran:1
Pre1998 - 1st:1 2nd:0 3rd:0 Ran:1
Win Prizemoney £4,173 *Total Prizemoney* £5,063
Wins * 1997 Oct Yarmou (FRM) 8f 82++ <
1998 Turf 0-1: (10f) (g-f)
Strong, currently useful colt. (1st run) - 3rd of 5 to Mountain Song

(17 Aug Windsor 10f g-f RF 3684). A big colt built like a tank, he won his only start at two, and his third place in a Windsor conditions event in August was his only start at three. He obviously has his problems. **J R Fanshawe [1-2] Joseph Allen.*

PUIWEE BHB 40f **RR 47f** 4919[20]

3 b f Puissance 7.1f **(60)** - Glow Again (The Brianstan) 5.9f **(55)**

Form - 00836302000

Record 1998 - 1st:0 2nd:1 3rd:2 Ran:11
Pre1998 - 1st:0 2nd:0 3rd:0 Ran:1

Win Prizemoney £0 *Total Prizemoney* £1,535

1998 Turf 0-10: (6f, 7f 4, 8f 5) (sft, g-s, gd 4, g-f 3, frm) 1998 AW 0-1: (8f) (Fibr)

Moderate filly, effective 7 to 8f, acts on gd to frm. Turf high 47 - 2nd of 16 giving 2lb to Dancing Em (24 Jly Thirsk 8f frm RF 3085).

**P T Dalton [0-12] J R Hall.*

PULAU TIOMAN BHB 88f **RR 87f** 4709[5]

2 b c Robellino (USA) 9.5f **(68)** - Ella Mon Amour (Ela-Mana-Mou) 10.1f **(70)**

Form - 3415

Record 1998 - 1st:1 2nd:0 3rd:1 Ran:4

Win Prizemoney £3,886 *Total Prizemoney* £5,027

Wins * **1998** Aug Nottin (G-F) 8.2f 82 <

1998 Turf 1-4: (7f 2, 8f 1-2) (gd 2, g-f 1-1, frm)

Useful colt. Turf high 87 (began Jly) - 4th of 11 to Enrique (31 Jly Goodwood 7f gd RF 3233) - also 1st of 8 from Western Folly (29 Aug Nottingham RF 3959).

**M A Jarvis [1-4] H R H Sultan Ahmad Shah.*

PUNISHMENT BHB 97f **RR 98f** 5151[15]

7 b h Midyan (USA) 9.9f **(64)** - In the Shade (Bustino) 10.4f **(64)**

Form - 2025027810

Record 1998 - 1st:1 2nd:3 3rd:0 Ran:10
Pre1998 - 1st:0 2nd:1 3rd:0 Ran:11

Win Prizemoney £7,746 *Total Prizemoney* £66,990

Wins * **1998** Oct Leices (SFT) H 10f 94 98 <

1998 Turf 1-10: (8f 2, 10f 1-3, 12f 4, 14f) (sft 1-2, g-s, gd 6, frm)

Very useful horse, effective 8 to 14f, best at 10f, acts on sft to frm, best on sft. Turf high 98 - 1st of 7 giving 1lb to Weet-A-Minute (25 Oct Leicester RF 4986). He has kept useful company for much of his career and has been difficult to place. A fine second for French-based trainer John Hammond in the ten-furlong Hong Kong Trophy this year, he has been stepped up in trip since without proving he stays. Second in a weak Group Three at Epsom in September, and landed a small race at Leicester, produced late as he needs to be.

**K O Cunningham-Brown [1-7] A J Richards (from J E Hammond in FR [0-3] Jly 1998).*

PUNKAH (USA) BHB 52f67a **RR 56f 67a** 3197[5]

5 b g Lear Fan (USA) 10.4f **(80)** - Gentle Persuasion(Bustino) 10.4f **(64)**

Form - 005

Record 1998 - 1st:0 2nd:0 3rd:0 Ran:3
Pre1998 - 1st:3 2nd:0 3rd:1 Ran:15

Win Prizemoney £11,267 *Total Prizemoney* £12,844

Wins * 1997 *Feb Lingfi (STD) H 10f 74 76* <
1996 Jun Windso (G-F) H 10f 72 71
1996 *Feb Lingfi (STD) 10f 47*

1998 Turf 0-2: (10f 2) (g-f 2) 1998 AW 0-1: (10f) (Equi)

Fair gelding, effective 8 to 10f, - acts on AW, likes left handed tracks, likes tight tracks. Turf high 48.

**G M McCourt [5-21] McCourt Fine Meats Ltd & D J Rushen (from Lord Huntingdon [2-6] Jun 1996).*

PURE COINCIDENCE BHB 83f **RR 80f** 4975[4]

3 b c Lugana Beach 7f **(63)** - Esilam (Frimley Park) 6.5f **(67)**

Form - 0070034

Record 1998 - 1st:0 2nd:0 3rd:1 Ran:7
Pre1998 - 1st:2 2nd:2 3rd:1 Ran:8

Win Prizemoney £5,199 *Total Prizemoney* £38,615

Wins * 1997 Aug Redcar (FRM) 5f 75+
* 1997 *Jun Southw (STD) 5f 77+* <

1998 Turf 0-6: (5f 4, 6f, 7f) (sft, g-s, gd 3, frm) 1998 AW 0-1: (5f) (Fibr)

Scopey, decent colt, effective 5f, acts on g-f. Turf high 80. Sold for 22, 000 guineas in October to join Willie Musson.

**G Lewis [2-15] Mrs Andry Muinos.*

PURE GOLD BHB 82f **RR 79f** 4360[19]

3 b f Dilum (USA) 7.1f **(56)** - Gold Runner (Runnett) 7f **(59)**

Form - 14200

Record 1998 - 1st:1 2nd:1 3rd:0 Ran:5

Win Prizemoney £3,647 *Total Prizemoney* £6,274

Wins * **1998** Jun Sandow (SFT) 7.1f 72 <

1998 Turf 1-5: (7f 1-3, 8f, 9f) (g-s 1-1, gd, g-f, frm 2)

Scopey, above-average filly. Turf high 79 - 2nd of 4 getting 4lb from Tadwiga (1 Jly Kempton 8f gd RF 2444) - also 1st of 11 getting 5lb from Razor (13 Jun Sandown RF 1977).

**H Candy [1-5] H R H Prince Fahd Salman.*

PURE NOBILITY (IRE) BHB 80f **RR 82f** 4958[10]

3 br c Darshaan 11.9f **(81)**-Ma Pavlova (USA) (Irish River (FR))8.6f **(78)**

Form - 44440

Record 1998 - 1st:0 2nd:0 3rd:0 Ran:5
Pre1998 - 1st:1 2nd:0 3rd:1 Ran:3

Win Prizemoney £3,436 *Total Prizemoney* £6,229

Wins * 1997 Spt Cheste (GD) 7f 85 <

1998 Turf 0-5: (11f, 12f 2, 13f, 15f) (gd 2, g-f, frm 2)

Workmanlike, decent colt, effective 7 to 13f, best at 7f, acts on gd to frm, best on gd, has worn blinkers. Turf high 82 - 4th of 14 getting 12lb from Tessajoe (19 Spt Catterick 12f frm RF 4372).

**B W Hills [1-8] Bassam Freiha.*

PURNADAS ROAD (IRE) BHB 54f **RR 44f** 1887[10]

3 ch f Petardia 8.2f **(58)** - Choral Park (Music Boy) 6.8f **(57)**

Form - 050

Record 1998 - 1st:0 2nd:0 3rd:0 Ran:3

1998 Turf 0-3: (6f, 7f 2) (gd 2, g-f)

Workmanlike, currently moderate filly. Turf high 44.

**J A R Toller [0-3] R A C Toller.*

PURPLE DAWN (IRE) BHB 52f **RR 69f** 5073[5]

2 b f Tirol 8.1f **(64)** - Tuesday Morning (Sadler's Wells (USA)) 10f **(76)**

Form - 000270055

Record 1998 - 1st:0 2nd:1 3rd:0 Ran:9

Win Prizemoney £0 *Total Prizemoney* £760

1998 Turf 0-9: (6f, 7f 5, 8f 2, 10f) (g-s, gd 4, g-f, frm 3)

Average filly, effective 7f, acts on gd. Turf high 69 - 2nd of 8 getting 9lb from Spy (19 Aug Musselburgh 7f gd RF 3746).

**J S Moore [0-9] Mrs Angela Speyer.*

PURPLE FLING BHB 57f62a **RR 59f 62a** 4669[9]

7 ch g Music Boy 6.5f **(56)** - Divine Fling (Imperial Fling (USA)) 7.1f **(58)**

Form - 885505000

Record 1998 - 1st:0 2nd:0 3rd:0 Ran:9
Pre1998 - 1st:8 2nd:5 3rd:3 Ran:41

Win Prizemoney £27,504 *Total Prizemoney* £37,508

Wins 1997 Jly Redcar (G-S) 7f 76 <
1997 Jun Salisb (G-F) H 6f 68 70
1996 Oct Folkes (G-S) 6f 68
1995 Jly Carlis (FRM) 6.9f 76 <
1995 Jly Doncas (FRM) 6f 71
1995 *Jun Southw (STD) 6f 67*
1994 Jly Carlis (FRM) 5.9f 73

1998 Turf 0-8: (5f 3, 6f 4, 7f) (gd 2, g-f 3, frm 3) 1998 AW 0-1: (6f) (Fibr)

Fair gelding, effective 6 to 7f, best at 6f, acts on gd to hrd, best on gd. Turf high 64.

**A J McNae [0-8] The Sun Punters Club (from D W Chapman [1-6] Mar 1998).*

PURPLE LACE RR 1462[10]

6 b m Salse (USA) 10.9f **(71)** - Purple Prose (Rainbow Quest (USA)) 10.4f **(75)**

Form - 0

Record 1998 - 1st:0 2nd:0 3rd:0 Ran:1

1998 Turf 0-1: (16f) (g-f)

Formerly very poor mare - 10th of 11 getting 6lb from Persian Punch (25 May Sandown 16f g-f RF 1462).

**H S Howe [0-5] Kevin Daniel Crabb.*

PURSUANT BHB 35f **RR 48f** 3934[13]

2 b c Puissance 7.1f **(60)** - Payvashooz (Ballacashtal (CAN)) 5.3f **(50)**

Form - 000

Record 1998 - 1st:0 2nd:0 3rd:0 Ran:3

1998 Turf 0-3: (5f, 7f 2) (frm 3)

Currently moderate colt. Turf high 48 (began Jly).
**M Brittain [0-3] M J Paver.*

PURSUIT OF GOLD BHB 77f **RR 81f** 4397[12]
3 ch c Pursuit of Love 9.5f **(69)** - Tenderetta (Tender King) 6.8f **(54)**
Form - 810
Record 1998 - 1st:1 2nd:0 3rd:0 Ran:3
Win Prizemoney £3,631 *Total Prizemoney* £3,631
Wins * 1998 Spt Bath (GD) 5.7f 81 <
1998 Turf 1-3: (5f, 6f 1-1, 8f) (frm 1-3)
Scopey, currently decent colt. Turf high 81 (began Jly) - 1st of 16 from Loch Laird (7 Spt Bath RF 4127). **A Kelleway [1-3] Classic Gold.*

PURSUIT VENTURE BHB 56f56a **RR 68f 56a** 4759[18]
3 b f Pursuit of Love 9.5f **(69)** - Our Shirley (Shirley Heights) 10.3f **(74)**
Form - 245367330
Record 1998 - 1st:0 2nd:1 3rd:3 Ran:9
Pre1998 - 1st:0 2nd:1 3rd:1 Ran:2
Win Prizemoney £0 *Total Prizemoney* £4,122
1998 Turf 0-7: (7f, 8f 4, 10f, 11f) (sft, gd 2, g-f, frm 3) 1998 AW 0-2: (8f 2) (Fibr 2)
Leggy, average filly, effective 7 to 8f, acts on sft to gd, has worn blinkers. Turf high 76 (1st run) - 2nd of 8 getting 5lb from Ethereal (13 Apr Newcastle 8f sft RF 0665). AW high 55 (began Spt). She has run pretty well in maiden company, but is still looking for that first win. **S P C Woods [0-11] Dr Frank Chao.*

PURSUIVANT BHB 59f **RR 80df** 4263[8]
4 b g Pursuit of Love 9.5f **(69)** - Collapse (Busted) 10.2f **(61)**
Form - 6638
Record 1998 - 1st:0 2nd:0 3rd:1 Ran:4
Pre1998 - 1st:0 2nd:2 3rd:2 Ran:5
Win Prizemoney £0 *Total Prizemoney* £2,586
1998 Turf 0-4: (7f 2, 9f, 10f) (g-s 2, gd 2)
Decent gelding, effective 7 to 8f, acts on gd to g-f, has worn blinkers. Turf high 67.
**M D Hammond [0-1] Andy Peake (from N Meade in IRE [0-8] Aug 1998).*

PURSUMI **RR 36f** 3089[6]
2 b f Pursuit of Love 9.5f **(69)** - Alacrity **(58df)** (Alzao (USA)) 7.1f **(68)**
Form - 06
Record 1998 - 1st:0 2nd:0 3rd:0 Ran:2
1998 Turf 0-2: (6f 2) (gd, frm)
Currently very moderate filly. Turf high 36.
**R M Whitaker [0-2] G F Pemberton.*

PUSEY STREET GIRL BHB 65f **RR 50f** 660[23]
5 ch m Gildoran 11.6f **(58)** - Pusey Street (Native Bazaar) 6.9f **(62)**
Form - 00
Record 1998 - 1st:0 2nd:0 3rd:0 Ran:2
Pre1998 - 1st:1 2nd:0 3rd:1 Ran:7
Win Prizemoney £3,947 *Total Prizemoney* £5,017
Wins 1996 May Warwic (GD) 7f 68 <
1998 Turf 0-2: (6f, 7f) (sft, g-s)
Fair filly. Turf high 17.
**M R Bosley [0-5] Marks (Banbury) (from J R Bosley [1-4] Jun 1996).*

PUSSY GALORE BHB 68f **RR 74df** 4935[8]
3 b f Pursuit of Love 9.5f **(69)** - Zinzi (Song) 7.2f **(61)**
Form - 508
Record 1998 - 1st:0 2nd:0 3rd:0 Ran:3
1998 Turf 0-3: (7f, 8f 2) (gd 2, g-f)
Workmanlike, currently above-average filly. Turf high 74.
**D R C Elsworth [0-3] Raymond Tooth.*

PUTERI WENTWORTH BHB 79f **RR 81f** 4850[4]
4 b f Sadler's Wells (USA) 11.3f **(87)** - Sweeping (Indian King (USA)) 7.4f **(64)**
Form - 7141044
Record 1998 - 1st:2 2nd:0 3rd:0 Ran:7
Pre1998 - 1st:1 2nd:0 3rd:0 Ran:6
Win Prizemoney £21,324 *Total Prizemoney* £27,585
Wins * 1998 Jly Goodwo (GD) H 20f 72 74 <
*** 1998** Jun Doncas (GD) H 14.6f 68 72
* 1997 Nov Mussel (G-S) H 12f 60 68
1998 Turf 2-7: (14f, 15f 1-2, 16f 2, 18f, 20f 1-1) (gd 2-4, g-f, frm 2)
Scopey, decent filly, effective 15 to 20f, acts on gd to frm, best on gd, likes right handed tracks. Turf high 81 - also 1st of 11 getting 4lb from Etterby Park (29 Jly Goodwood RF 3203). A progressive stayer, she landed the Goodwood Handicap but never got into it next time. Creditable efforts last two starts and she can win more races, although she may not want the ground too fast.
**Miss Gay Kelleway [3-13] H R H Sultan Ahmad Shah.*

PUTUNA BHB 95f **RR 96f** 4742[6]
3 b f Generous (IRE) 11.5f **(82)**-Ivoronica (Targowice (USA)) 11.4f **(70)**
Form - 162175306
Record 1998 - 1st:2 2nd:1 3rd:1 Ran:9
Pre1998 - 1st:0 2nd:0 3rd:2 Ran:2
Win Prizemoney £15,645 *Total Prizemoney* £27,440
Wins * 1998 Jun Newbur (SFT) L 10f 93+ <
*** 1998** Apr Epsom (SFT) 8.5f 83
1998 Turf 2-9: (9f 1-1, 10f 1-6, 11f, 12f) (sft 1-1, g-s 1-3, gd, g-f 3, frm)
Very useful filly, effective 10 to 11f, best at 10f, acts on g-s to g-f, best on g-f, prefers left handed tracks. Turf high 96 - also 1st of 4 from Zante (11 Jun Newbury RF 1898). Consistent. Made a winning reappearance in an Epsom maiden despite looking unsuited by the track. She has mostly done well in Listed company since, and easily won a four-runner event of that type in heavy ground at Newbury in June, but was unable to make much impact when tried in Group company. **I A Balding [2-11] Robert Hitchins.*

PUZZLEMENT BHB 72f78a **RR 73f 78a** 4776[8]
4 gr g Mystiko (USA) 7.7f **(59)** - Abuzz (Absalom) 7.2f **(58)**
Form - 1130008665113028
Record 1998 - 1st:2 2nd:1 3rd:1 Ran:13
Pre1998 - 1st:4 2nd:1 3rd:1 Ran:19
Win Prizemoney £26,027 *Total Prizemoney* £36,482
Wins * 1998 Aug Beverl (G-F) H 9.9f 63 71+
*** 1998** Aug Beverl (G-F) H 9.9f 59 61
** 1997 Nov Lingfi (STD) H 8f 70 73* <
** 1997 Nov Lingfi (STD) H 8f 63 66*
** 1997 Feb Wolver (STD) H 9.4f 52 60*
** 1997 Feb Lingfi (STD) H 8f 57 59*
1998 Turf 2-11: (8f, 10f 2-9, 11f) (g-s 2, gd 3, g-f 1-4, frm 1-2) 1998 AW 0-2: (8f, 10f) (Equi 2)
Scopey, useful gelding, favours tight tracks, excels at Beverley, does well at Lingfield. Turf high 73. AW high 64.
**C E Brittain [6-32] Mrs C E Brittain.*

PYTHIOS (IRE) **RR 32tf** 3259[8]
2 b c Danehill (USA) 9.1f **(79)** - Pithara (GR) (Never so Bold) 6.3f **(66)**
Form - 8
Record 1998 - 1st:0 2nd:0 3rd:0 Ran:1
1998 Turf 0-1: (6f) (gd)
Currently very moderate colt. **H R A Cecil [0-1] Mrs H G Cambanis.*

QANDIL (USA) **RR 53f** 4595[21]
2 ch c Riverman (USA) 9.7f **(78)** - Confirmed Affair (USA) (Affirmed (USA)) 9.3f **(79)**
Form - 0
Record 1998 - 1st:0 2nd:0 3rd:0 Ran:1
1998 Turf 0-1: (7f) (gd)
Currently fair colt. **M P Tregoning [0-1] Hamdan Al Maktoum.*

Q FACTOR BHB 82f72a **RR 88f 72a** 4360[17]
6 br m Tragic Role (USA) 9.4f **(63)** - Dominiana (Dominion) 8.5f **(63)**
Form - 071060
Record 1998 - 1st:1 2nd:0 3rd:0 Ran:6
Pre1998 - 1st:7 2nd:3 3rd:10 Ran:48
Win Prizemoney £35,559 *Total Prizemoney* £48,179
Wins * 1998 Aug Cheste (GD) H 7f 80 88 <
* 1997 Aug Salisb (G-F) H 7f 78 84
* 1997 Jun Folkes (SFT) H 6.9f 73 80+
* 1996 Oct Haydoc (SFT) H 7.1f 75 79
* 1996 Aug Windso (G-F) H 8.3f 70 71
* 1996 Jly Windso (G-F) H 8.3f 64 71
* 1996 Jun Nottin (G-F) H 8.2f 62 60
* 1994 Nov Doncas (HVY) 6f 63
1998 Turf 1-6: (7f 1-3, 8f 3) (gd 1-2, g-f 2, frm 2)
Useful mare, effective 7 to 8f, best at 7f, acts on sft to frm, has worn blinkers, likes tight tracks, excels at Chester. Turf high 88 (began Aug) - 1st of 11 from Jeffrey Anotherred (21 Aug Chester RF 3789). Slow to strike form in '98, she was able to dominate

when making all at Chester in August. Held since.
**D HaydnJones [8-54] H G Collis.*

QHAZEENAH BHB 100f RR 103f 4364[7]

2 b f Marju (IRE) 9.2f **(76)** - Nafhaat (USA) (Roberto (USA)) 10f **(76)**
Form - 35117
Record 1998 - 1st:2 2nd:0 3rd:1 Ran:5
Win Prizemoney £24,302 *Total Prizemoney* £25,126
Wins * **1998** Spt Doncas (GD) H 6.5f 93 103 <
* **1998** Aug Folkes (G-F) 6.9f 82
1998 Turf 2-5: (6f 2, 7f 2-3) (sft, gd 2-3, frm)
Very useful filly. Turf high 103 (began Jly) - 1st of 15 getting 3lb from Blue Melody (9 Spt Doncaster RF 4183). She caught the eye in no uncertain terms on her debut, and looked the part when winning a valuable nursery at Doncaster in September. Sent off favourite for a Listed race at Ayr on the strength of that performance, she was soon off the bridle and outpaced, but had a valid excuse as she came home lame. She has plenty of scope and can pick up a decent prize. **J L Dunlop [2-5] Hamdan Al Maktoum.*

QILIN (IRE) BHB 88f RR 97f 4821[13]

3 b f Second Set (IRE) 9.2f **(67)** - Usance (GER) (Kronenkranich (GER)) 6f **(97)**
Form - 0201300500
Record 1998 - 1st:1 2nd:1 3rd:1 Ran:10
Pre1998 - 1st:1 2nd:0 3rd:0 Ran:3
Win Prizemoney £10,304 *Total Prizemoney* £14,872
Wins * **1998** Jun Newmar (GD) 6f 97 <
* 1997 Oct Newmar (G-F) 6f 91
1998 Turf 1-10: (5f, 6f 1-7, 7f, 8f) (sft, gd 3, g-f 1-3, frm 3)
Scopey, very useful filly, effective 6f, acts on g-f to frm. Turf high 97 - 1st of 5 giving 4lb to Nadwah (26 Jun Newmarket RF 2317). Well beaten in Pattern company last season, but much more successful in small-field conditions races, including winning such an event at Newmarket in June. Held in competitive sprint handicaps.
**M H Tompkins [2-13] Ian Lochhead.*

QISMAT RR 30f 37[5]

3 b f Selkirk (USA) 7.9f **(76)** - Plaything (High Top) 10.2f **(67)**
Form - 25
Record 1998 - 1st:0 2nd:0 3rd:0 Ran:1
Pre1998 - 1st:0 2nd:1 3rd:0 Ran:2
Win Prizemoney £0 *Total Prizemoney* £747
1998 AW 0-1: (8f) (Fibr)
Light-framed, currently average filly. **H Akbary [0-3] S R Hudson.*

QUADROON (USA) RR 43f 3769[4]

4 b g Shadeed (USA) 7.7f **(72)** - Only Yours (Aragon) 8.1f **(60)**
Form - 84
Record 1998 - 1st:0 2nd:0 3rd:0 Ran:2
Win Prizemoney £0 *Total Prizemoney* £247
1998 Turf 0-2: (8f, 10f) (frm, hrd)
Scopey, currently moderate gelding. Turf high 43 (began Aug).
**C A Cyzer [0-2] Gerald Leigh.*

QUARME LADY RR 4387[R]

2 ch f Interrex (CAN) 7.7f **(51)** - Miss Examiner (Absalom) 7.2f **(58)**
Form - 0R
Record 1998 - 1st:0 2nd:0 3rd:0 Ran:2
1998 Turf 0-1: (7f) (gd) 1998 AW 0-1: (7f) (Fibr)
Currently very poor filly. **W G M Turner [0-2] R B Cody-Boutcher.*

QUARTERSTAFF BHB 49f43a RR 54f 43a 1944[7]

4 b g Charmer 9f **(59)** - Quaranta (Hotfoot) 10.5f **(59)**
Form - 587
Record 1998 - 1st:0 2nd:0 3rd:0 Ran:3
Pre1998 - 1st:0 2nd:0 3rd:1 Ran:6
Win Prizemoney £0 *Total Prizemoney* £366
1998 Turf 0-1: (7f) (gd) 1998 AW 0-2: (11f 2) (Fibr 2)
Lengthy, fair gelding, effective 10f, acts on frm, has worn blinkers, favours tight tracks. AW high 29.
**Mrs A Swinbank [0-3] S Smith (from C F Wall [0-6] Spt 1997).*

QUE BELLE (USA) RR 119f 1375a[5]

4 b f Seattle Dancer (USA) 10.1f **(74)** - Qui Bid (GER) (Spectacular Bid (USA)) 11.2f **(76)**
Form - 25
1998 Turf 0-2: (11f, 12f) (sft, gd)
High-class filly, effective 11 to 12f, best at 12f, acts on sft to gd, best on gd. Turf high 119 (1st run) - 2nd of 4 getting 3lb from Astarabad (26 Apr Longchamp 11f sft RF 0950a). A very high-class German filly, she ran well when runner-up in the Prix Ganay on her reappearance, but not so well in a Group Two next time.
**H Remmert in GER [2-6].*

QUEDEX BHB 61f RR 71f 5124[4]

2 b c Deploy 11.4f **(67)** - Alwal (Pharly (FR)) 9.8f **(68)**
Form - 484004
Record 1998 - 1st:0 2nd:0 3rd:0 Ran:6
Win Prizemoney £0 *Total Prizemoney* £240
1998 Turf 0-6: (5f, 6f, 7f 2, 8f 2) (g-s, gd, g-f 2, frm 2)
Above-average colt. Turf high 71. **E L James [0-6] E James.*

QUEEN OF SCOTLAND (IRE) BHB 50f RR 62f 4885[5]

3 b f Mujadil (USA) 7.7f **(70)** - Hitopah (Bustino) 10.4f **(64)**
Form - 61063643005
Record 1998 - 1st:1 2nd:0 3rd:2 Ran:11
Win Prizemoney £3,826 *Total Prizemoney* £4,724
Wins * **1998** Apr Kempto (SFT) 7f 82 <
1998 Turf 1-11: (5f, 7f 1-6, 8f 3, 9f) (hvy 1-1, g-s 3, gd 4, g-f 3)
Unfurnished, average filly, effective 7f, acts on hvy. Turf high 82 - 1st of 12 getting 19lb from Bushwhacker (13 Apr Kempton RF 0656). **M R Channon [1-11] Noel Wabe.*

QUEEN OF SHANNON (IRE) BHB 51f35a RR 58f 35a 4201[4]

10 b m Nordico (USA) 8.2f **(59)** - Raj Kumari (Vitiges (FR)) 8.2f **(59)**
Form - 04412404
Record 1998 - 1st:1 2nd:1 3rd:0 Ran:7
Pre1998 - 1st:4 2nd:5 3rd:3 Ran:48
Win Prizemoney £19,875 *Total Prizemoney* £27,929
Wins * **1998** Jun Ripon (SFT) SH 8f 48 54
* 1997 Jly Warwic (SFT) SH 8f 49 61
* 1996 Aug Windso (G-F) SH 8.3f 44 52+
1998 Turf 1-7: (8f 1-5, 9f 2) (g-s, gd 1-3, g-f 3)
Fair mare, effective 7 to 8f, best at 8f, acts on gd to g-f, best on gd, has worn blinkers, likes left handed tracks. Turf high 58 - 2nd of 20 giving 19lb to Holloway Melody (3 Jly Warwick 8f g-f RF 2510) - also 1st of 20 giving 25lb to Conic Hill (17 Jun Ripon RF 2071). She is not getting any younger but still has ability, especially when racing over a mile on soft ground. Goes well for an apprentice.
**A W Carroll [3-27] J Wigmore Racing Partnership (from B J Meehan [0-5] Jan 1995).*

QUEEN OF SILK (IRE) RR 96f 4795a[13]

3 b f Brief Truce (USA) 9.1f **(73)** - Danzig Lass (USA) 00
Form - 6200
1998 Turf 0-4: (7f, 8f, 9f, 10f) (sft, g-s, gd, frm)
Very useful filly, effective 7 to 9f, acts on gd to frm, has worn blinkers. Turf high 96 - 2nd of 4 to Susun Kelapa (10 Aug Cork 9f frm RF 3703a). **D K Weld in IRE [1-7] Mrs P McAllister.*

QUEEN OF THE KEYS RR 41f 4542[26]

2 b f Royal Academy (USA) 7.8f **(77)** - Piano Belle (USA) (Fappiano (USA)) 8.7f **(77)**
Form - 80
Record 1998 - 1st:0 2nd:0 3rd:0 Ran:2
1998 Turf 0-2: (6f, 7f) (gd, frm)
Currently moderate filly. Turf high 41. **S Dow [0-2] Mrs A M Upsdell.*

QUEEN OF TIDES (IRE) BHB 47f RR 17f 4922[9]

3 b f Soviet Star (USA) 8.6f **(74)** - Tidesong (Top Ville) 11.7f **(68)**
Form - 00
Record 1998 - 1st:0 2nd:0 3rd:0 Ran:2
Pre1998 - 1st:0 2nd:0 3rd:0 Ran:2
1998 Turf 0-2: (12f, 14f) (g-s, g-f)
Scopey, poor filly. Turf high 17 (began Oct).
**S Dow [0-2] S Dow (from Sir Michael Stoute [0-2] Spt 1997).*

QUEEN OMAH (IRE) BHB 70f RR 68f 5000[9]

2 b f Dolphin Street (FR) - Quilting (Mummy's Pet) 7.7f **(60)**
Form - 440
Record 1998 - 1st:0 2nd:0 3rd:0 Ran:3
Win Prizemoney £0 *Total Prizemoney* £534
1998 Turf 0-3: (6f, 7f 2) (sft, g-s, g-f)

Currently average filly. Turf high 68 (began Spt).
**R Hannon [0-3] Buddy Hackett.*

QUEEN SARABI (IRE) RR 59f 4566a[9]

3 b f Mujtahid (USA) 7.4f **(69)** - Sharp Slipper (Sharpo) 7.7f **(59)**
Form - 123400000
1998 Turf 1-9: (5f 1-3, 6f 5, 7f) (hvy 1-1, sft 2, g-s, gd 4, hrd)
Fair filly, effective 6f, acts on sft to gd, has worn blinkers. Turf high 92 - 2nd of 8 getting 2lb from Record Entry (13 Apr Cork 6f sft RF 0793a). Becoming disappointing.
**E Lynam in IRE [1-11] Paul Redmond.*

QUEENS CONSUL (IRE) BHB 72f65a RR 74f 65a 4748[18]

8 gr m Kalaglow 11.2f **(67)** -Queens Connection (Bay Express) 7.1f **(60)**
Form - 0007086231040

Record	**1998** -	1st:1	2nd:1	3rd:1	Ran:13
	Pre1998 -	1st:10	2nd:13	3rd:8	Ran:83

Win Prizemoney £50,668 *Total Prizemoney* £82,908

Wins								
	* **1998**	Spt Thirsk	(GD)	H	8f	70	74	
	* 1997	Aug Cheste	(SFT)	H	7.6f	79	84	<
	* 1997	Aug Haydoc	(G-F)	H	8.1f	74	80	
	* 1997	Jly Beverl	(GD)	H	8.5f	69	75	
	* 1996	Aug Thirsk	(FRM)		8f		82	
	* 1996	Jun Catter	(GD)	H	7f	78	81	
	* 1995	Jun Thirsk	(G-F)	H	8f	75	77	
	* 1994	Aug Nottin	(G-F)	H	8.2f	67	73+	
	* 1994	Aug Nottin	(G-F)	H	8.2f	54	69	
	* 1994	Jly Beverl	(G-F)	H	8.5f	54	58	
	* 1994	*Jan Southw*	*(STD)*		*8f*		*47*	

1998 Turf 1-13: (7f, 8f 1-11, 9f) (gd 6, g-f 3, frm 1-4)
Above-average mare, effective 8f, acts on sft to frm, likes left handed tracks, likes tight tracks. Turf high 79. Consistent.
**B S Rothwell [12-102] Miss Heather Davison.*

QUEENS DAGGER (USA) BHB 80f RR 66df 4985[20]

3 b f Rahy (USA) 9.1f **(80)** - Katies First (USA) (Kris) 9.5f **(73)**
Form - 45100

Record	**1998** -	1st:1	2nd:0	3rd:0	Ran:5

Win Prizemoney £6,706 *Total Prizemoney* £6,969

Wins							
	* **1998**	Spt York	(GD)	7.9f		66+	<

1998 Turf 1-5: (7f 2, 8f 1-3) (g-s, gd 3, g-f 1-1)
Scopey, average filly. Turf high 71 - also 1st of 8 getting 5lb from Cellini (3 Spt York RF 4071).
**J H M Gosden [1-5] Sheikh Mohammed.*

QUEEN'S HAT BHB 60f57a RR 64f 57a 2896[6]

3 b f Cadeaux Genereux 7.9f **(76)** - Greenlet (IRE) (Green Desert (USA)) 8.6f **(78)**
Form - 0346

Record	**1998** -	1st:0	2nd:0	3rd:1	Ran:4
	Pre1998 -	1st:0	2nd:0	3rd:0	Ran:1

Win Prizemoney £0 *Total Prizemoney* £520
1998 Turf 0-3: (6f, 7f, 9f) (gd 3) 1998 AW 0-1: (8f) (Fibr)
Well made, average filly. Turf high 64 - 3rd of 10 to Bolshaya (25 Jun Newcastle 6f gd RF 2273). **B Hanbury [0-5] Abdullah Ali.*

QUEEN'S INSIGNIA (USA) BHB 49f RR 52f 4234[9]

5 b m Gold Crest (USA) 7.5f **(77)**-Years (USA)(Secretariat(USA))9f **(79)**
Form - 223700

Record	**1998** -	1st:0	2nd:2	3rd:1	Ran:6
	Pre1998 -	1st:3	2nd:2	3rd:1	Ran:19

Win Prizemoney £9,957 *Total Prizemoney* £15,502

Wins								
	1997	Jun Windso	(G-S)	H	8.3f	53	58	
	1995	Spt Goodwo	(GD)	H	8f	61	67	<
	1995	Jun Windso	(GD)	S	6f		59+	

1998 Turf 0-6: (8f 5, 9f) (sft, g-s 2, gd 2, frm)
Fair filly, effective 8f, acts on sft to hrd, has worn blinkers. Turf high 57 (1st run) - 2nd of 13 getting 21lb from Topatori (2 Apr Leicester 8f sft RF 0542). Consistent.
**D W P Arbuthnot [0-6] W H Ponsonby (from P F I Cole [3-19] Oct 1997).*

QUEENSLAND STAR (IRE) BHB 100f RR 94f 4857[16]

2 b c College Chapel - Zenga (Try My Best (USA)) 7.6f **(67)**
Form - 1140026020

Record	**1998** -	1st:2	2nd:2	3rd:0	Ran:10

Win Prizemoney £11,613 *Total Prizemoney* £17,144

Wins						
* **1998**	May Cheste	(GD)	5.1f		94+	<
* **1998**	Apr Newmar	(SFT)	5f		88+	

1998 Turf 2-10: (5f 2-6, 6f 3, 7f) (sft, g-s 2, gd 1-4, g-f 1-2, frm)
Useful colt, effective 5f, acts on gd to g-f, best on g-f. Turf high 94 - 1st of 7 giving 8lb to Golden Silca (5 May Chester RF 1040) - also 1st of 5 from Bodfari Muka (16 Apr Newmarket RF 0713). He knew his job when winning at Newmarket on his debut, giving the Manchester United boss Alex Ferguson his first winner with his first runner as an owner, and followed up in style from a good draw at Chester. He was then found out in better company for the rest of the season though he did run quite well to finish runner-up on two occasions at Ascot. **J Berry [2-10] The Right Angle Club.*

QUEEN'S PAGEANT BHB 73f84a RR 73f 84a 5147[11]

4 ch f Risk Me (FR) 8f **(53)** - Mistral's Dancer (Shareef Dancer (USA)) 9.9f **(73)**
Form - 53280005100

Record	**1998** -	1st:1	2nd:1	3rd:0	Ran:9
	Pre1998 -	1st:1	2nd:0	3rd:2	Ran:9

Win Prizemoney £15,182 *Total Prizemoney* £18,847

Wins								
	* **1998**	Oct York	(GD)	H	7f	70	73	<
	* 1996	Oct Haydoc	(SFT)		5f		68	

1998 Turf 1-7: (6f, 7f 1-3, 8f 3) (sft 2, gd 1-3, g-f, frm) 1998 AW 0-2: (8f, 9f) (Fibr 2)
Leggy, decent filly, has worn blinkers, likes left handed tracks. Turf high 73. AW high 80. She was running pretty well on Fibresand at the start of the year, but had shown little on turf until winning a handicap at York in October.
**J L Spearing [2-18] Mrs Robert Heathcote.*

QUEENS STROLLER (IRE) BHB 33f36a RR 31f 36a 4050[10]

7 b m Pennine Walk 8.9f **(64)** - Mount Isa (Miami Springs) 9.9f **(59)**
Form - 204470050

Record	**1998** -	1st:0	2nd:0	3rd:0	Ran:7
	Pre1998 -	1st:6	2nd:9	3rd:4	Ran:57

Win Prizemoney £19,951 *Total Prizemoney* £30,018

Wins								
	* 1997	*May Southw*	*(STD)*	*H*	*8f*	*30*	*38*	
	1995	Mar Folkes	(GD)	H	9.7f	56	57	
	1995	*Mar Wolver*	*(STD)*	*H*	*9.4f*	*66*	*66*	<
	1994	*Feb Southw*	*(STD)*	*H*	*7f*	*65*	*59*	

1998 Turf 0-4: (8f 2, 10f 2) (frm 4) 1998 AW 0-3: (8f, 10f 2) (Equi 3)
Very moderate mare, effective 8 to 10f, acts on g-f - acts on Fibr, has worn blinkers, likes left handed tracks, likes tight tracks. Turf high 31 (began Aug). AW high 35.
**R E Peacock [1-21] R E Peacock (from T Wall [0-7] Jun 1996).*

QUEEN TITANIA (IRE) BHB 63f RR 59f 4318[8]

2 b f Elbio 9f **(62)** - Astania (GER) (Arratos (FR)) 12.2f **(60)**
Form - 608

Record	**1998** -	1st:0	2nd:0	3rd:0	Ran:3

1998 Turf 0-3: (6f, 7f, 8f) (gd, g-f, frm)
Currently fair filly. Turf high 59 (began Aug).
**A J McNae [0-3] The Iona Stud.*

QUEEN ZENOBIA RR 80f 4411[6]

2 b f Danehill (USA) 9.1f **(79)** - Persia (IRE) (Persian Bold) 9.3f **(66)**
Form - 66

Record	**1998** -	1st:0	2nd:0	3rd:0	Ran:2

1998 Turf 0-2: (6f, 7f) (frm 2)
Currently decent filly. Turf high 80 (began Aug) - 6th of 17 to Kalidasa (22 Spt Warwick 7f frm RF 4411).
**J H M Gosden [0-2] Mrs Madelyn Jason.*

QUEL SENOR (FR) RR 109f 4470e[1]

3 g
Form - 341
1998 Turf 1-3: (10f 1-3) (sft 1-2, gd)
Pattern-class gelding. Turf high 109 (began Jly) - 1st of 4 from Barbola (19 Spt Longchamp RF 4470e). He deserved his Group Three win at Longchamp in September and, being a gelding, should be around for some time yet. **F Doumen in FR [1-4] Martin.*

QUESTAN BHB 51f46a RR 56f 46a 4648[11]

6 b g Rainbow Quest (USA) 11.2f **(81)** - Vallee Dansante (USA) (Lyphard (USA)) 9.9f **(72)**
Form - 65412855070

Record 1998 - 1st:1 2nd:1 3rd:0 Ran:11
Win Prizemoney £3,011 *Total Prizemoney* £4,151
Wins * **1998** May Bath (FRM) H 8f 51 57 <
1998 Turf 1-7: (7f 2, 8f 1-5) (gd 3, g-f 2, frm 1-2) 1998 AW 0-4: (8f, 10f, 12f, 14f) (Equi 2, Fibr 2)
Fair gelding, effective 7 to 8f, best at 8f, acts on gd to frm, favours tight tracks. Turf high 57 (1st run) - 1st of 18 giving 5lb to Mellors (18 May Bath RF 1292). AW high 49. Becoming disappointing.
**B Smart [1-11] B Smart.*

QUESTUARY (IRE) RR 48f — 4336[8]

2 b f Rainbow Quest (USA) 11.2f **(81)**-Pelf (USA)(Al Nasr (FR))9.3f **(68)**
Form - 08
Record 1998 - 1st:0 2nd:0 3rd:0 Ran:2
1998 Turf 0-2: (7f, 8f) (g-f, frm)
Currently moderate filly. Turf high 48 (began Spt).
**M P Tregoning [0-2] Sheikh Mohammed.*

QUEZON CITY BHB 45f56a RR 50f 56a — 4549[5]

4 ch c Keen 11.1f **(58)** - Calachuchi (Martinmas) 7.6f **(59)**
Form - 805
Record 1998 - 1st:0 2nd:0 3rd:0 Ran:3
Pre1998 - 1st:1 2nd:1 3rd:1 Ran:8
Win Prizemoney £2,416 *Total Prizemoney* £4,556
Wins 1997 Jun Hamilt (G-F) 12.1f 61 <
1998 Turf 0-1: (12f) (frm) 1998 AW 0-2: (11f, 12f) (Fibr 2)
Unfurnished, fair colt, effective 11 to 12f, acts on g-f to frm. AW high 31 (began Spt). Becoming disappointing.
**Miss J A Camacho [0-3] Middleham Park Racing XI (from M J Camacho [1-8] Jly 1997).*

QUIBBLING BHB 31f36a RR 42f 36a — 3328[3]

4 b f Salse (USA) 10.9f **(71)** - Great Exception (Grundy) 10.3f **(65)**
Form - 504443
Record 1998 - 1st:0 2nd:0 3rd:1 Ran:6
Pre1998 - 1st:0 2nd:1 3rd:1 Ran:9
Win Prizemoney £0 *Total Prizemoney* £1,964
1998 Turf 0-4: (12f 2, 13f, 16f) (gd, g-f 2, frm) 1998 AW 0-2: (11f, 12f) (Fibr 2)
Leggy, moderate filly, effective 7f, acts on gd, has worn blinkers. Turf high 42. AW high 36. Consistent.
**K C Comerford [0-6] S J V Construction (from H Candy [0-9] Oct 1997).*

QUICKSTEP RR 75f — 4327[18]

2 ch f Salse (USA) 10.9f **(71)** - Short And Sharp (Sharpen Up) 8.3f **(67)**
Form - 630
Record 1998 - 1st:0 2nd:0 3rd:1 Ran:3
Win Prizemoney £0 *Total Prizemoney* £770
1998 Turf 0-3: (7f 3) (g-f 2, frm)
Currently above-average filly. Turf high 75 (began Aug) - 3rd of 12 to Mother of Pearl (3 Spt Salisbury 7f g-f RF 4064).
**R Hannon [0-3] Lady Tennant.*

QUIET ARCH (IRE) BHB 60f73a RR 63f 73a — 4654[6]

5 b g Archway (IRE) 8.5f **(60)** - My Natalie (Rheingold) 10.4f **(62)**
Form - 7222213103416
Record 1998 - 1st:3 2nd:4 3rd:2 Ran:12
Pre1998 - 1st:3 2nd:4 3rd:5 Ran:27
Win Prizemoney £17,023 *Total Prizemoney* £30,132
Wins * **1998** Jun Bright (FRM) C 10f 63
* **1998** *Mar Lingfi (STD) 12f 73*
* **1998** *Feb Lingfi (SLW) H 12f 70 75* <
* 1997 *Jan Lingfi (STD) H 10f 57 67*
* 1997 *Jan Lingfi (STD) 10f 51*
1996 *Jun Lingfi (STD) 8f 69*
1998 Turf 1-4: (10f 1-1, 12f 3) (gd, g-f 1-3) 1998 AW 2-8: (10f, 12f 2-6, 13f) (Equi 2-8)
Above-average gelding, effective 10 to 12f, best at 12f, acts on g-f - acts on Equi, has worn blinkers, likes left handed tracks, likes Lingfield. Turf high 63. AW high 75 - 1st of 4 giving 8lb to Harik (24 Feb Lingfield RF 0349) - also 1st of 5 getting 2lb from Amadour (19 Mar Lingfield RF 0446). His victories over the past couple of seasons have all come on Equitrack, though he has ability on turf. He probably does not win as often as he should, and needs to come late off a strong pace.
**W R Muir [5-27] John Davies (from C A Cyzer [1-13] Oct 1996).*

QUIET ASSURANCE (USA) BHB 96f RR 102f — 4494[25]

3 ch c St Jovite (USA) 11.8f **(75)** - Silent Turn (USA) (Silent Cal (USA)) 14.5f **(91)**
Form - 52480
Record 1998 - 1st:0 2nd:1 3rd:0 Ran:5
Pre1998 - 1st:1 2nd:2 3rd:1 Ran:5
Win Prizemoney £7,573 *Total Prizemoney* £21,042
Wins * 1997 Oct Newmar (GD) 7f 96+ <
1998 Turf 0-5: (7f 4, 8f) (g-s, gd 2, g-f, frm)
Scopey, very useful colt, effective 7 to 8f, best at 7f, acts on gd to g-f, best on gd. Turf high 102 - 2nd of 6 giving 3lb to Lone Piper (3 May Newmarket 7f gd RF 0990). He seemed certain to win races after chasing Lone Piper home at Newmarket in May, but was lightly raced and disappointing thereafter. Life will not be much easier in 1999. **E A L Dunlop [1-10] Maktoum Al Maktoum.*

QUIET MILLFIT (USA) RR 66f — 5138[14]

2 b c Quiet American (USA) 7.9f **(60)** - Millfit (USA) (Blushing Groom (FR)) 10.3f **(76)**
Form - 00
Record 1998 - 1st:0 2nd:0 3rd:0 Ran:2
1998 Turf 0-2: (6f, 7f) (gd, g-f)
Currently average colt. Turf high 66 (began Oct).
**B Hanbury [0-2] Hilal Salem.*

QUIET VENTURE BHB 81f RR 78f — 4617[9]

4 b g Rainbow Quest (USA) 11.2f **(81)** - Jameelaty (USA) (Nureyev (USA)) 8.7f **(78)**
Form - 0001110
Record 1998 - 1st:3 2nd:0 3rd:0 Ran:7
Pre1998 - 1st:0 2nd:0 3rd:1 Ran:4
Win Prizemoney £12,198 *Total Prizemoney* £13,007
Wins * **1998** Aug Newcas (GD) H 7f 76 78 <
* **1998** Aug Mussel (G-F) 7.1f 74
* **1998** Aug Redcar (G-F) 8f 65
1998 Turf 3-6: (7f 2-3, 8f 1-2, 9f) (gd 1-4, frm 1-1, hrd 1-1) 1998 AW 0-1: (12f) (Fibr)
Scopey, useful gelding, effective 7 to 10f, best at 7f, acts on gd to hrd. Turf high 78 - 1st of 11 from Tiler (31 Aug Newcastle RF 3989) - also 1st of 8 from Pericles (19 Aug Musselburgh RF 3751). Inconsistent. He had shown little for quite a while, but bounced back to form with all-the-way wins at Redcar, Musselburgh and Newcastle in August. Those tactics seem to suit him.
**I Semple [3-7] Gee Kay Gee Gees (from E A L Dunlop [0-4] Oct 1997).*

QUIGLEYS POINT (IRE) RR 7f — 5139[20]

2 b c Royal Academy (USA) 7.8f **(77)** - Remind Me (USA) (Riverman (USA)) 9.1f **(76)**
Form - 0
Record 1998 - 1st:0 2nd:0 3rd:0 Ran:1
1998 Turf 0-1: (6f) (gd)
Currently very poor colt. **B W Hills [0-1] John Grant.*

QUILT BHB 62f RR 61f — 5005[9]

2 b f Terimon 8.7f **(58)** - Quaranta (Hotfoot) 10.5f **(59)**
Form - 820
Record 1998 - 1st:0 2nd:1 3rd:0 Ran:3
Win Prizemoney £0 *Total Prizemoney* £702
1998 Turf 0-2: (8f, 10f) (sft, gd) 1998 AW 0-1: (8f) (Fibr)
Currently average filly. Turf high 61 (1st run) (began Oct) - 2nd of 13 getting 5lb from Whistling Jack (14 Oct Nottingham 10f gd RF 4808). **Sir Mark Prescott [0-3] Lord Fairhaven.*

QUINSTARS (IRE) RR 99+f — 4439a[3]

3 b g Thatching 7.8f **(69)** - Legal Steps
Form - 222153
1998 Turf 1-6: (5f 1-3, 6f, 7f 2) (sft, g-s, gd 1-4)
Very useful gelding, effective 5 to 7f, acts on sft to gd, best on gd, often wears blinkers. Turf high 99 (began Jly) - 1st of 10 giving 5lb to Benefits Galore (29 Aug Curragh RF 4036a).
**J Oxx in IRE [1-6] Benny Kwong.*

QUINTUS (USA) BHB 83f RR 87f — 4457[1]

3 ch c Sky Classic (CAN) 10f **(83)** - Superbe Dawn (USA) (Grey Dawn II) 11.1f **(72)**
Form - 2354261821
Record 1998 - 1st:2 2nd:3 3rd:1 Ran:10

Pre1998 - 1st:0 2nd:1 3rd:0 Ran:3
Win Prizemoney £7,796 *Total Prizemoney* £14,129
Wins * **1998** Spt Goodwo (G-F) H 9.9f 79 81 <
* **1998** Aug Windso (G-F) 10f 70
1998 Turf 2-10: (10f 2-9, 12f) (g-s, gd 1-5, g-f 3, frm 1-1)
Scopey, useful colt, effective 7 to 10f, best at 10f, acts on gd to g-f, best on g-f, has worn blinkers, excels at Doncaster. Turf high 89 - 3rd of 11 getting 1lb from Nautical Star (16 Apr Newmarket 10f gd RF 0708) - also 1st of 20 getting 1lb from Borani (23 Spt Goodwood RF 4457). Does not always produce much off the bridle. **P F I Cole [2-13] Sir George Meyrick.*

QUITE HAPPY (IRE) BHB 71f **RR 67f** 2316[7]

3 b f Statoblest 6.4f **(63)** - Four-Legged Friend (Aragon) 8.1f **(60)**
Form - 031737
Record 1998 - 1st:1 2nd:0 3rd:2 Ran:6
Pre1998 - 1st:0 2nd:1 3rd:0 Ran:2
Win Prizemoney £2,950 *Total Prizemoney* £4,603
Wins * **1998** May Folkes (G-F) H 5f 68 76? <
1998 Turf 1-6: (5f 1-5, 6f) (gd 1-2, g-f 3, frm)
Scopey, average filly, effective 5f, acts on gd. Turf high 76 - 1st of 11 giving 8lb to Runs in the Family (27 May Folkestone RF 1519).
**Dr J D Scargill [1-8] M Sakal.*

QUIZ MASTER BHB 46f39a **RR 68f 39a** 4877[9]

3 ch g Superpower 6.6f **(58)** - Ask Away (Midyan (USA)) 6f **(60)**
Form - 0265778000
Record 1998 - 1st:0 2nd:1 3rd:0 Ran:10
Pre1998 - 1st:0 2nd:3 3rd:3 Ran:13
Win Prizemoney £0 *Total Prizemoney* £5,524
1998 Turf 0-9: (5f, 6f 6, 7f 2) (gd 5, g-f 2, frm 2) 1998 AW 0-1: (6f) (Fibr)
Scopey, average gelding, effective 5f, acts on g-s to gd, often wears blinkers. Turf high 68. **E Weymes [0-23] Mrs R L Heaton.*

QUIZ SHOW BHB 81f **RR 86f** 5152[8]

3 b f Primo Dominie 7.2f **(67)**-Aryaf (CAN) (Vice Regent(CAN)) 8.7f **(74)**
Form - 425108037528
Record 1998 - 1st:1 2nd:2 3rd:1 Ran:12
Pre1998 - 1st:0 2nd:0 3rd:0 Ran:5
Win Prizemoney £3,727 *Total Prizemoney* £7,876
Wins * **1998** Jun Newbur (SFT) 7f 73 <
1998 Turf 1-12: (6f 4, 7f 1-7, 8f) (sft, g-s 1-1, gd 4, g-f 2, frm 3, hrd)
Scopey, useful filly, effective 7f, acts on gd to g-f. Turf high 86. A half-sister to Mind Games, she finally got off the mark when winning a soft-ground maiden at Newbury. Running well in handicap company at the back-end. **R Hannon [1-17] Lostford Manor Stud.*

QUWS **RR 112f** 4430a[7]

4 b c Robellino (USA) 9.5f **(68)** - Fleeting Rainbow (Rainbow Quest (USA)) 10.4f **(75)**
Form - 231537
1998 Turf 1-6: (8f, 10f 1-4, 14f) (sft, gd 1-4, hrd)
Group-class colt, effective 8 to 10f, best at 10f, acts on sft to hrd, likes right handed tracks, excels at Curragh. Turf high 117 (1st run) - 2nd of 9 giving 28lb to Tarry Flynn (29 Mar Curragh 8f sft RF 0526a) - also 1st of 6 giving 18lb to Takarian (5 Jun Curragh RF 1853a). Consistent. A consistent colt in Ireland, he won a Group Three at the Curragh in June, but was held in higher grade in Britain and Ireland afterwards.
**K Prendergast in IRE [6-16] Hamdan Al Maktoum.*

RAAHAT ALGHARB (USA) **RR 36f** 4983[13]

2 b f Gone West (USA) 7.8f **(82)**-Mount Helena (Danzig(USA)) 8.4f **(76)**
Form - 00
Record 1998 - 1st:0 2nd:0 3rd:0 Ran:2
1998 Turf 0-2: (7f, 8f) (g-s, gd)
Currently very moderate filly. Turf high 36 (began Oct).
**M A Jarvis [0-2] Sheikh Ahmed Al Maktoum.*

RAAQI **RR 77f** 4359[5]

2 b c Nashwan (USA) 10.3f **(79)** - Mehthaaf (USA) **(122f)** (Nureyev (USA)) 8.7f **(78)**
Form - 55
Record 1998 - 1st:0 2nd:0 3rd:0 Ran:2
Win Prizemoney £0 *Total Prizemoney* £321
1998 Turf 0-2: (7f, 8f) (gd, g-f)
Currently above-average colt. Turf high 77 (began Jly).
**J L Dunlop [0-2] Hamdan Al Maktoum.*

RAASED BHB 40f44a **RR 38f 44a** 5098[13]

6 b g Unfuwain (USA) 11.4f **(74)** - Sajjaya (USA) (Blushing Groom (FR)) 10.3f **(76)**
Form - 4180273020
Record 1998 - 1st:1 2nd:2 3rd:1 Ran:10
Pre1998 - 1st:1 2nd:1 3rd:2 Ran:14
Win Prizemoney £4,951 *Total Prizemoney* £9,824
Wins * **1998** *Feb Southw (STD) H 8f 36 43*
1995 Apr Bright (GD) 10f 71 <
1998 Turf 0-7: (8f 5, 9f, 10f) (g-s, gd 2, g-f, frm 3) 1998 AW 1-3: (8f 1-3) (Fibr 1-3)
Moderate gelding, effective 8f, acts on g-s to frm - acts on Fibr, has worn blinkers, favours tight tracks, excels at Southwell. Turf high 38 (began Jly) - 7th of 14 getting 15lb from Swinging The Blues (24 Jly Nottingham 8f g-f RF 3082). AW high 43 - 1st of 10 getting 18lb from Batsman (13 Feb Southwell RF 0286). He has had wind problems in the past, and wore a tongue-strap when winning on the Southwell Fibresand in February.
**F Watson [1-19] Linkchallenge Ltd (from J L Dunlop [1-5] Jun 1995).*

RAAZI BHB 45f **RR 43f** 3305[7]

3 ch f My Generation 6.5f **(68)** - Botvyle Flame (IRE) (Reprimand)
Form - 003057
Record 1998 - 1st:0 2nd:0 3rd:1 Ran:6
Pre1998 - 1st:0 2nd:0 3rd:0 Ran:3
Win Prizemoney £0 *Total Prizemoney* £539
1998 Turf 0-6: (6f 4, 7f 2) (gd 4, g-f 2)
Light-framed, moderate filly, effective 6 to 7f, acts on gd to g-f. Turf high 43 - 5th of 16 getting 7lb from My Legal Eagle (31 Jly Thirsk 7f g-f RF 3253).
**R A Fahey [0-6] A R Nemazee (from R M Stronge [0-3] Jun 1997).*

RABAH BHB 115f **RR 114f** 4491[2]

3 b c Nashwan (USA) 10.3f **(79)** - The Perfect Life (IRE) (Try My Best (USA)) 7.6f **(67)**
Form - 611122
Record 1998 - 1st:3 2nd:2 3rd:0 Ran:6
Pre1998 - 1st:2 2nd:2 3rd:1 Ran:6
Win Prizemoney £63,065 *Total Prizemoney* £106,919
Wins * **1998** Jly Goodwo (GD) G3 12f 114 <
* **1998** Jly Haydoc (G-F) L 11.9f 114 <
* **1998** May Goodwo (G-F) L 9.9f 106
* 1997 Oct Newmar (G-F) 8f 94
* 1997 Aug Redcar (FRM) 7f 78
1998 Turf 3-6: (10f 1-2, 12f 2-4) (gd 1-3, g-f 2-3)
Workmanlike, Group-class colt, effective 10 to 12f, best at 12f, acts on gd to g-f, best on gd, excels at Goodwood. Turf high 114 - 2nd of 9 giving 3lb to Capri (26 Spt Ascot 12f gd RF 4491) - also 1st of 6 from Nedawi (28 Jly Goodwood RF 3162). Improving. Quarried rather than foaled, this ultra tough front-runner figured in some titanic finishes, notably when dead-heating with Nedawi in the Gordon Stakes at Glorious Goodwood. He looked better than ever when chasing Capri home at Ascot on his final start and can never be left out of the calculations on fast ground.
**J L Dunlop [5-12] Hamdan Al Maktoum.*

RABEA (USA) BHB 53f **RR 61f** 4917[18]

3 b f Devil's Bag (USA) 9.3f **(73)** - Racing Blue (Reference Point) 6.8f **(70)**
Form - 6328830
Record 1998 - 1st:0 2nd:1 3rd:2 Ran:7
Pre1998 - 1st:0 2nd:0 3rd:0 Ran:2
Win Prizemoney £0 *Total Prizemoney* £1,521
1998 Turf 0-7: (10f, 12f 2, 15f, 16f 3) (g-s, gd 2, g-f 2, frm 2)
Average filly, effective 15 to 16f, acts on g-f to frm, likes tight tracks. Turf high 61 - 2nd of 11 giving 5lb to Albrighton (20 Jly Beverley 16f frm RF 2952). **J L Dunlop [0-9] Mrs H Focke.*

RABI (IRE) BHB 113f **RR 117f** 2949[2]

3 b c Alzao (USA) 9.8f **(73)** - Sharakawa (IRE) (Darshaan) 9.9f **(84)**
Form - 272
Record 1998 - 1st:0 2nd:2 3rd:0 Ran:3
Pre1998 - 1st:2 2nd:0 3rd:0 Ran:2
Win Prizemoney £9,556 *Total Prizemoney* £18,482
Wins 1997 Spt Leices (G-F) 7f 96+ <
1997 Aug Newmar (G-F) 7f 91+

1998 Turf 0-3: (7f 2, 10f) (gd 2, g-f)

Well made, high-class colt. Turf high 117 (1st run) - 2nd of 4 giving 5lb to Diktat (26 May Leicester 7f g-f RF 1470). Joined the Godolphin operation after an unbeaten juvenile campaign, but did not scale the heights this term that once seemed likely. Runner-up to Diktat first time out, he was well beaten at Newmarket before finishing second to Winter Romance in the Scottish Classic. That was the last we saw of him.

**S bin Suroor [0-3] Godolphin (from E A L Dunlop [2-2] Spt 1997).*

RACHAELS NORTH (IRE) BHB 83f **RR 93f** 4631[28]

3 gr c Night Shift (USA) 8.1f **(73)**-Anne de Beaujeu (Ahonoora) 8.1f **(73)**

Form - 63110070

Record 1998 - 1st:2 2nd:0 3rd:1 Ran:8
Pre1998 - 1st:0 2nd:0 3rd:0 Ran:1

Win Prizemoney £12,384 *Total Prizemoney* £12,996

Wins * 1998 Jun Ascot (G-S) 8f 93 <
*** 1998** May Nottin (FRM) H 8.2f 78 82

1998 Turf 2-8: (7f 2, 8f 2-4, 9f, 10f) (gd 2, g-f 1-4, frm 1-2)

Scopey, useful colt, effective 8f, acts on g-f. Turf high 93 - 1st of 6 giving 3lb to The Sandfly (20 Jun Ascot RF 2139). He gradually improved before winning consecutive races at Nottingham and Ascot, but then ran poorly in each of his four subsequent starts.

**R W Armstrong [2-9] P J Vela.*

RACING HAWK (USA) BHB 34f40a **RR 40?f 40a** 3670[5]

6 ch g Silver Hawk (USA) 11.2f **(85)** - Lorn Lady (Lorenzaccio) 10f **(64)**

Form - 5

Record 1998 - 1st:0 2nd:0 3rd:0 Ran:1
Pre1998 - 1st:1 2nd:1 3rd:2 Ran:19

Win Prizemoney £3,857 *Total Prizemoney* £5,746

Wins 1996 Jly Nottin (FRM) H 10f 48 50 <

1998 Turf 0-1: (17f) (frm)

Moderate gelding, has broken blood-vessels, effective 10 to 17f, acts on g-f to frm, has worn blinkers, favours left handed tracks. (1st run) - 5th of 17 getting 4lb from Batoutoftheblue (16 Aug Pontefract 17f frm RF 3670).

**P Bowen [4-19] G Morris (from M S Saunders [1-17] Jun 1997).*

RACING TELEGRAPH BHB 37f27a **RR 34f 27a** 10[6]

8 b g Claude Monet (USA) 7.2f **(54)** - Near Enough (English Prince) 10.1f **(61)**

Form - 6

Record 1998 - 1st:0 2nd:0 3rd:0 Ran:1
Pre1998 - 1st:1 2nd:1 3rd:6 Ran:43

Win Prizemoney £3,106 *Total Prizemoney* £7,500

1998 AW 0-1: (8f) (Fibr)

Very moderate gelding, has worn blinkers. Inconsistent.

**C N Allen [0-16] Newmarket Connections Ltd (from J W Payne [0-7] Feb 1996).*

RADAR (IRE) BHB 79f **RR 81f** 5078[11]

3 b c Petardia 8.2f **(58)** - Soignee (Night Shift (USA)) 7.2f **(69)**

Form - 471655520

Record 1998 - 1st:1 2nd:1 3rd:0 Ran:9
Pre1998 - 1st:1 2nd:1 3rd:0 Ran:5

Win Prizemoney £10,527 *Total Prizemoney* £14,331

Wins * 1998 Jun Sandow (SFT) H 9f 77 81 <
* 1997 Oct Nottin (GD) H 8.2f 66 79+

1998 Turf 1-9: (8f 5, 9f 1-3, 10f) (hvy, sft, g-s 1-1, gd 4, g-f 2)

Scopey, decent colt, effective 8 to 9f, best at 8f, acts on g-s to gd, best on gd, prefers tight tracks. Turf high 81 - 1st of 10 getting 3lb from Silver Strand (13 Jun Sandown RF 1974). Consistent. He won over nine furlongs in testing ground at Sandown in June, but did not seem to quite stay ten furlongs when tried over it. Worth another chance at that trip. **M A Jarvis [2-14] John Sims.*

RADAR O'REILLY BHB 50f45a **RR 50f 45a** 4120[9]

4 b g Almoojid 7f **(36)** - Travel Bye (Miller's Mate) 7f **(63)**

Form - 000348060

Record 1998 - 1st:0 2nd:0 3rd:1 Ran:9
Pre1998 - 1st:1 2nd:1 3rd:2 Ran:6

Win Prizemoney £3,372 *Total Prizemoney* £5,011

Wins * 1997 Jly Bright (FRM) 7f 68+ <

1998 Turf 0-6: (7f 3, 8f 3) (g-s, gd 2, g-f, frm 2) 1998 AW 0-3: (7f, 8f, 12f) (Fibr 3)

Leggy, fair gelding, effective 7 to 9f, acts on g-s to g-f, likes left handed tracks, likes tight tracks. Turf high 50. AW high 45 (began Jly). Becoming disappointing.

**R J R Williams [1-15] Harry Ormesher.*

RADA'S DAUGHTER **RR 66f** 4665[5]

2 br f Robellino (USA) 9.5f **(68)** - Drama School (Young Generation) 7.7f **(63)**

Form - 45

Record 1998 - 1st:0 2nd:0 3rd:0 Ran:2

Win Prizemoney £0 *Total Prizemoney* £208

1998 Turf 0-2: (7f, 8f) (g-s, frm)

Currently average filly. Turf high 66 (began Spt).

**I A Balding [0-2] Mrs Richard Plummer.*

RAED BHB 69f78a **RR 67f 78a** 3157[2]

5 b h Nashwan (USA) 10.3f **(79)** - Awayed (USA) (Sir Ivor) 10.2f **(70)**

Form - 2111272222

Record 1998 - 1st:2 2nd:5 3rd:0 Ran:8
Pre1998 - 1st:1 2nd:3 3rd:1 Ran:19

Win Prizemoney £8,564 *Total Prizemoney* £21,030

Wins * 1998 *Feb Southw (STD) H 11f 62 72* <
*** 1998** *Feb Southw (STD) H 11f 62 65*
* 1997 *Dec Southw (STD) H 11f 57 62*

1998 Turf 0-4: (9f 2, 10f 2) (gd, g-f, frm 2) 1998 AW 2-4: (9f, 11f 2-2, 12f) (Fibr 2-4)

Above-average colt, effective 7 to 12f, acts on g-f to hrd - acts on Fibr, likes left handed tracks, likes tight tracks, excels at Southwell. Turf high 67 - 2nd of 10 giving 13lb to Iron Mountain (28 Jly Beverley 10f g-f RF 3157). AW high 76 - 2nd of 6 getting 12lb from Cashmere Lady (23 Mar Southwell 12f Fibr RF 0466) - also 1st of 6 giving 10lb to Moonraking (16 Feb Southwell RF 0297). Consistent. It took him a long time to get off the mark, but he looked an improved horse when tried on the Southwell Fibresand, completing a hat-trick over middle-distances. He does not find much off the bridle, but George Duffield is the right man to keep him up to his work. Continued to run well on turf.

**Mrs A Swinbank [3-18] David Young (from P T Walwyn [0-9] Oct 1996).*

RAELEEN **RR 21f** 4984[11]

2 b f Jupiter Island 10.4f **(57)** - Ballintava (Better By Far)

Form - 0

Record 1998 - 1st:0 2nd:0 3rd:0 Ran:1

1998 Turf 0-1: (7f) (g-s)

Currently little account filly. **G M McCourt [0-1] D A N Ross.*

RAFFAELLO (IRE) BHB 92f **RR 93f** 3228a[3]

3 b c Fairy King (USA) 7.7f **(75)** - Silver Dollar (Shirley Heights) 10.3f **(74)**

Form - 1220303

Record 1998 - 1st:1 2nd:2 3rd:2 Ran:7
Pre1998 - 1st:0 2nd:0 3rd:0 Ran:1

Win Prizemoney £3,550 *Total Prizemoney* £17,093

Wins * 1998 Apr Kempto (SFT) 11.1f 77+ <

1998 Turf 1-7: (8f 3, 10f 3, 11f 1-1) (hvy 1-1, gd 4, g-f, frm)

Useful colt, effective 8 to 10f, acts on gd to g-f. Turf high 93 - 3rd of 6 to Rachaels North (20 Jun Ascot 8f g-f RF 2139). Easy winner of a soft-ground maiden on his reappearance, he did not win again but ran with credit to make the frame in two handicaps, a classified stakes and an Italian Listed event. **M R Channon [1-8].*

RAFFLES ROOSTER BHB 75f74a **RR 80f 74a** 101[2]

6 ch g Galetto (FR) 11.7f **(86)** - Singapore Girl (FR) (Lyphard (USA)) 9.9f **(72)**

Form - 2

Record 1998 - 1st:0 2nd:1 3rd:0 Ran:1
Pre1998 - 1st:4 2nd:5 3rd:3 Ran:20

Win Prizemoney £21,179 *Total Prizemoney* £38,992

Wins * 1997 Jun York (G-S) H 11.9f 66 74 <
* 1997 *Apr Wolver (STD) H 12f 63 73+*
* 1997 *Jan Southw (STD) H 11f 56 60*
* 1997 *Jan Southw (STD) H 12f 56 60*

1998 AW 0-1: (12f) (Fibr)

Decent gelding, effective 12 to 19f, best at 12f, acts on hvy to g-f - acts on Fibr, best on gd, prefers tight tracks, excels at Chester, does well at Southwell. (1st run) - 2nd of 6 to China Castle (16 Jan Southwell 12f Fibr RF 0101). Consistent.

**A G Newcombe [4-26] Mark Leatham.*

RAFTERS MUSIC (IRE) BHB 55f **RR 61f** 4644[8]
3 b g Thatching 7.8f **(69)** - Princess Dixieland (USA) (Dixieland Band (USA)) 7f **(74)**
Form - 008
Record 1998 - 1st:0 2nd:0 3rd:0 Ran:3
1998 Turf 0-3: (7f, 8f 2) (g-f 3)
Workmanlike, currently average gelding. Turf high 61 (began Spt).
**Mrs A J Perrett [0-3] C Duncan.*

RAFTING (IRE) BHB 76f **RR 80f** 3771[10]
3 b f Darshaan 11.9f **(81)** - White Water (FR) (Pharly (FR)) 9.8f **(68)**
Form - 214430
Record 1998 - 1st:1 2nd:1 3rd:1 Ran:6
Win Prizemoney £3,548 *Total Prizemoney* £6,093
Wins * **1998** May Thirsk (G-F) 12f 57+ <
1998 Turf 1-6: (11f, 12f 1-3, 14f 2) (g-s, gd 2, g-f 1-1, frm 2)
Rangy, decent filly, effective 11 to 14f, best at 14f, acts on g-s to frm, has worn blinkers. Turf high 80 - 4th of 11 getting 8lb from Generosity (1 Aug Goodwood 14f gd RF 3258).
**M Johnston [1-6] Alan Lillingston.*

RAGAMUFFIN ROMEO BHB 40f41a **RR 41a** 567[7]
9 b g Niniski (USA) 13.2f **(67)** - Interviewme (USA) (Olden Times) 11.4f **(67)**
Form - 8554357
Record 1998 - 1st:0 2nd:0 3rd:1 Ran:5
Pre1998 - 1st:0 2nd:1 3rd:1 Ran:10
Win Prizemoney £0 *Total Prizemoney* £1,531
1998 AW 0-5: (14f, 16f 4) (Fibr 5)
Fair gelding, has worn blinkers. AW high 51.
**H J Collingridge [1-12] Mrs D Sawyer (from N C Wright [0-6] Jly 1993).*

RAGTIME COWGIRL BHB 20f33a **RR 8f 33a** 3677[12]
5 ch m Aragon 7.7f **(58)** - Echo Chamber (Music Boy) 6.8f **(57)**
Form - 0767800
Record 1998 - 1st:0 2nd:0 3rd:0 Ran:7
Pre1998 - 1st:3 2nd:0 3rd:7 Ran:25
Win Prizemoney £7,784 *Total Prizemoney* £10,392
Wins * 1997 Jun Hamilt (SFT) H 5f 30 23
1996 Aug Mussel (G-F) C 11.1f 37 <
1996 Jly Pontef (G-F) SH 12f 35 37 <
1998 Turf 0-7: (5f, 6f, 7f, 9f 3, 11f) (sft, g-s 2, gd 4)
Very moderate filly, effective 5f, acts on gd. Turf high 8.
**D A Nolan [1-21] Mrs J McFadyen-Murray (from C W Thornton [2-11] Aug 1996).*

RAHAYEB BHB 82f **RR 75f** 4135[2]
2 b f Arazi (USA) 9.2f **(74)** - Bashayer (USA) (Mr Prospector (USA)) 8.8f **(78)**
Form - 352
Record 1998 - 1st:0 2nd:1 3rd:1 Ran:3
Win Prizemoney £0 *Total Prizemoney* £1,730
1998 Turf 0-3: (7f 2, 8f) (g-f, frm 2)
Currently above-average filly. Turf high 75 (began Jly) - 2nd of 13 to Ashbourne Pat (8 Spt Leicester 8f g-f RF 4135).
**J L Dunlop [0-3] Hamdan Al Maktoum.*

RAHCAK (IRE) RR 78f 4983[3]
2 b f Generous (IRE) 11.5f **(82)** - Homage (Ajdal (USA)) 9.2f **(89)**
Form - 3
Record 1998 - 1st:0 2nd:0 3rd:1 Ran:1
Win Prizemoney £0 *Total Prizemoney* £557
1998 Turf 0-1: (8f) (g-s)
Currently above-average filly. **D R Loder [0-1] Sheikh Mohammed.*

RAHEEN (USA) BHB 89f87a **RR 93f 87a** 5078[1]
5 b h Danzig (USA) 8.1f **(88)** - Belle de Jour (USA) (Speak John) 10.7f **(72)**
Form - 3045060871
Record 1998 - 1st:1 2nd:0 3rd:1 Ran:10
Pre1998 - 1st:1 2nd:1 3rd:2 Ran:10
Win Prizemoney £26,368 *Total Prizemoney* £35,074
Wins * **1998** Oct Newmar (SFT) H 8f 82 93 <
1996 Dec Wolver (STD) 8.5f 81+
1998 Turf 1-10: (7f, 8f 1-6, 9f 2, 10f) (sft 1-1, g-s, gd 3, g-f 3, frm 2)
Useful colt, effective 7 to 9f, best at 8f, acts on sft to frm, has worn blinkers, likes left handed tracks. Turf high 93 - 1st of 26 getting 8lb from Prince Babar (31 Oct Newmarket RF 5078). Creditable efforts in some competitive handicaps, but he looked held until landing the Ladbroke Autumn Handicap on his final start.
**R A Fahey [1-10] Basheer Kielany (from W G M Turner [1-6] Jly 1997).*

RAHIKA ROSE RR 98f 4442a[5]
3 b f Unfuwain (USA) 11.4f **(74)** - Rahik (Wassl) 9.7f **(62)**
Form - 12015105
1998 Turf 3-8: (7f 2-4, 8f 1-3, 9f) (g-s 1-1, gd 1-5, frm 1-1, hrd)
Very useful filly, effective 7f, acts on frm. Turf high 98 - 1st of 2 getting 2lb from Key Provider (20 Aug Tipperary RF 3868a).
**C Collins in IRE [3-12] John Costello.*

RAINALD (USA) BHB 110f **RR 109f** 4470g[7]
3 b c Danzig (USA) 8.1f **(88)** - Ristna (Kris) 9.5f **(73)**
Form - 51137
Record 1998 - 1st:2 2nd:0 3rd:1 Ran:5
Win Prizemoney £10,087 *Total Prizemoney* £11,208
Wins * **1998** Jly Newbur (G-F) 7.3f 106+ <
* **1998** Jly Haydoc (G-S) 7.1f 85
1998 Turf 2-5: (7f 2-4, 8f) (sft, gd, g-f 1-2, frm 1-1)
Tall, Pattern-class colt. Turf high 109 - 3rd of 4 giving 13lb to Baltic State (2 Aug Newcastle 7f g-f RF 3296) - also 1st of 9 from King Slayer (17 Jly Newbury RF 2874). He has ability and temperament. Impressive when beating a useful field at Newbury in July, he looked in a foul mood when disappointing at Newcastle and Longchamp later in the campaign and is not one to trust implicitly.
**J H M Gosden [2-5] George Strawbridge.*

RAINBOW AMETHYST (IRE) RR 94f 4178a[7]
2 b f Brief Truce (USA) 9.1f **(73)** - Khatiynza
Form - 36513337
1998 Turf 1-8: (5f 2, 6f 1-4, 7f 2) (sft, g-s 1-2, gd 3, g-f, frm)
Useful filly, effective 6 to 7f, acts on g-s to gd. Turf high 94 - 3rd of 27 to Amazing Dream (29 Aug Curragh 6f gd RF 4039a). She had a busy season, and ran well in several good races. However, her only win was in a Navan maiden.
**A P O'Brien in IRE [1-8] Miss Katherine Magnier.*

RAINBOW FRONTIER (IRE) BHB 86f **RR 86f** 2345[2]
4 b g Law Society (USA) 11.6f **(71)** - Tatchers Mate (Thatching) 8f **(66)**
Form - 22
Record 1998 - 1st:0 2nd:2 3rd:0 Ran:2
Pre1998 - 1st:3 2nd:3 3rd:3 Ran:15
Win Prizemoney £10,617 *Total Prizemoney* £49,351
Wins 1997 Jly Killar (G-S) H 14f 79 75+
1997 Jun Currag (G-S) H 11f 75 79 <
1997 May Wexfor (GD) 13f 79 <
1998 Turf 0-2: (16f, 20f) (sft, gd)
Useful gelding, effective 11 to 20f, best at 16f, acts on sft to gd, best on sft, likes Curragh. Turf high 86 - 2nd of 20 getting 3lb from Cyrian (27 Jun Newcastle 16f sft RF 2345). Consistent. A useful hurdler too, he was a good second in the Ascot Stakes and the Northumberland Plate in June.
**M C Pipe [1-5] Clive Smith (from A P O'Brien in IRE [6-18] Oct 1997).*

RAINBOW HIGH BHB 93f **RR 96f** 4824[4]
3 b c Rainbow Quest (USA) 11.2f **(81)** - Imaginary (IRE) (Dancing Brave (USA)) 8.4f **(76)**
Form - 125524
Record 1998 - 1st:1 2nd:2 3rd:0 Ran:6
Pre1998 - 1st:0 2nd:0 3rd:0 Ran:3
Win Prizemoney £3,517 *Total Prizemoney* £20,045
Wins * **1998** Jun Ripon (SFT) 12.3f 76 <
1998 Turf 1-6: (12f 1-5, 14f) (gd 1-2, g-f 2, frm 2)
Scopey, very useful colt, effective 12 to 14f, best at 12f, acts on gd to frm, best on frm, and excels at York. Turf high 96 - 4th of 13 giving 5lb to Rainbow Ways (15 Oct Newmarket 12f frm RF 4824). Showed promise as a juvenile, and went some way to fulfilling that by winning a Ripon maiden on his return. A good second in the Tote Gold Trophy at Goodwood, he ran two respectable races at York on ground a shade fast for him and ended the campaign with an excellent effort at Newmarket. **B W Hills [1-9] K Abdulla.*

RAINBOW RAIN (USA) BHB 57f68a **RR 57f 68a** 4652[15]
4 b g Capote (USA) 9.1f **(84)** - Grana (USA) (Miswaki (USA)) 9f **(81)**
Form - 0088006000032561000

Record 1998 - 1st:1 2nd:1 3rd:1 Ran:18
Pre1998 - 1st:1 2nd:1 3rd:1 Ran:13
Win Prizemoney £10,725 *Total Prizemoney* £15,441
Wins * **1998** *Aug Lingfi (STD) H 7f 59 69*
1997 Jun Carlis (FRM) H 8f 73 75 <
1998 Turf 0-17: (6f 3, 7f 6, 8f 5, 10f 2, 13f) (sft 2, gd 6, g-f 6, frm 3)
1998 AW 1-1: (7f 1-1) (Equi 1-1)
Workmanlike, average gelding, effective 6 to 8f, acts on g-f to frm - acts on Equi, likes tight tracks. Turf high 57. (1st run) - 1st of 16 getting 6lb from Best Quest (26 Aug Lingfield RF 3895).
**S Dow [1-20] P McCarthy (from M Johnston [1-11] Jly 1997).*

RAINBOW RAVER (IRE) BHB 56f RR 66?f 5094[11]
2 ch f Rainbows For Life (CAN) 9.3f **(64)** - Foolish Passion (USA) (Secretariat (USA)) 9f **(79)**
Form - 5085680
Record 1998 - 1st:0 2nd:0 3rd:0 Ran:7
Win Prizemoney £0 *Total Prizemoney* £138
1998 Turf 0-7: (5f 2, 6f, 7f, 8f 3) (gd 4, g-f, frm 2)
Average filly. Turf high 66. **C Smith [0-7] A E Needham.*

RAINBOW ROMEO (IRE) BHB 61f55a RR 62f 55a 4876[10]
2 br c Rainbows For Life (CAN) 9.3f **(64)** - Splendid Chance (Random Shot) 11.4f **(52)**
Form - 500570
Record 1998 - 1st:0 2nd:0 3rd:0 Ran:6
1998 Turf 0-5: (6f 3, 7f 2) (g-s, gd, g-f, frm 2) 1998 AW 0-1: (6f) (Fibr)
Average colt. Turf high 62. **P T Walwyn [0-6] Eric Perry.*

RAINBOW WAYS BHB 92f RR 93f 4824[1]
3 b c Rainbow Quest (USA) 11.2f **(81)** - Siwaayib (Green Desert (USA)) 8.6f **(78)**
Form - 342111
Record 1998 - 1st:3 2nd:1 3rd:1 Ran:6
Pre1998 - 1st:0 2nd:1 3rd:0 Ran:2
Win Prizemoney £20,681 *Total Prizemoney* £24,619
Wins * **1998** Oct Newmar (GD) H 12f 88 93 <
* **1998** Spt Haydoc (G-F) H 11.9f 81 84
* **1998** Aug Newmar (G-F) 12f 74
1998 Turf 3-6: (10f, 12f 3-5) (gd, frm 2-4, hrd 1-1)
Light-framed, useful colt, effective 7 to 12f, best at 12f, acts on frm, has worn blinkers. Turf high 93 - 1st of 13 getting 19lb from Rokeby Bowl (15 Oct Newmarket RF 4824) - also 1st of 11 getting 5lb from Slipper (25 Spt Haydock RF 4480). Although making the frame in varied company, it was not until he was fitted with blinkers that he struck winning form, and completed a hat-trick with the headgear in progressively better company.
**B W Hills [3-8] Maktoum Al Maktoum.*

RAINDEER QUEST BHB 47f35a RR 51f 35a 475[13]
6 ch m Hadeer 8.9f **(58)** - Rainbow Ring (Rainbow Quest (USA)) 10.4f **(75)**
Form - 03460
Record 1998 - 1st:0 2nd:0 3rd:1 Ran:4
Pre1998 - 1st:4 2nd:3 3rd:3 Ran:33
Win Prizemoney £11,175 *Total Prizemoney* £15,397
Wins * 1997 Aug Carlis (FRM) H 8f 43 48
* 1996 *Dec Southw (SLW) H 11f 31 41+*
* 1996 Apr Pontef (GD) SH 8f 40 42
1994 May Hamilt (GD) 5f 56
1998 Turf 0-1: (10f) (gd) 1998 AW 0-3: (11f, 12f 2) (Fibr 3)
Fair mare, effective 8 to 11f, best at 10f, acts on gd to frm - acts on Fibr, excels at Redcar. AW high 37. Inconsistent.
**J L Eyre [3-32] Whitestonecliffe Racing Partnership (from C Smith [1-7] Spt 1995).*

RAINMAKER BHB 57f53a RR 54f 53a 1727a[3]
3 b c Last Tycoon 9.4f **(73)** - Starr Danias (USA) (Sensitive Prince (USA)) 9.1f **(60)**
Form - 7073
Record 1998 - 1st:0 2nd:0 3rd:1 Ran:3
Pre1998 - 1st:0 2nd:0 3rd:0 Ran:4
Win Prizemoney £0 *Total Prizemoney* £314
1998 AW 0-3: (8f 2, 10f) (Equi, Fibr, Dirt)
Scopey, fair colt. AW high 53.
**J Huber in SWE [0-1] (from M A Jarvis [0-6] Jan 1998).*

RAIN RAIN GO AWAY (USA) RR 86f 5041[3]
2 ch c Miswaki (USA) 8.1f **(81)** - Stormagain (USA) 00
Form - 3
Record 1998 - 1st:0 2nd:0 3rd:1 Ran:1
Win Prizemoney £0 *Total Prizemoney* £446
1998 Turf 0-1: (7f) (sft)
Currently useful colt. **E A L Dunlop [0-1] Maktoum Al Maktoum.*

RAINSTORM RR 61f 4666[5]
3 b c Rainbow Quest (USA) 11.2f **(81)** - Katsina (USA) (Cox's Ridge (USA)) 8f **(68)**
Form - 605
Record 1998 - 1st:0 2nd:0 3rd:0 Ran:3
1998 Turf 0-3: (8f, 10f 2) (g-s, gd, frm)
Lengthy, currently average colt. Turf high 61 (began Spt).
**J H M Gosden [0-3] K Abdulla.*

RAINWATCH BHB 98f RR 109?f 4515[15]
4 b c Rainbow Quest (USA) 11.2f **(81)** - Third Watch (Slip Anchor) 9.8f **(73)**
Form - 00
Record 1998 - 1st:0 2nd:0 3rd:0 Ran:2
Pre1998 - 1st:3 2nd:1 3rd:0 Ran:9
Win Prizemoney £13,991 *Total Prizemoney* £15,857
Wins 1997 Oct Haydoc (SFT) 11.9f 109? <
1997 Jun Salisb (G-S) H 12f 90 97
1997 Jun Newbur (GD) H 12f 81 89
1998 Turf 0-2: (12f 2) (sft, gd)
Workmanlike, Pattern-class colt, effective 12 to 13f, acts on g-s to gd, likes left handed tracks. Turf high 14. Inconsistent.
**M C Pipe [2-7] Mrs Alison Farrant (from J L Dunlop [3-9] Oct 1997).*

RAISE A GRAND (IRE) BHB 100f RR 106f 4851[5]
2 ch c Grand Lodge (USA) - Atyaaf (USA) (Irish River (FR)) 8.6f **(78)**
Form - 311215
Record 1998 - 1st:3 2nd:1 3rd:1 Ran:6
Win Prizemoney £23,548 *Total Prizemoney* £37,742
Wins * **1998** Aug Sandow (G-F) G3 7.1f 99 <
* **1998** Jly Yarmou (GD) 7f 89+
* **1998** Jun Nottin (GD) 6.1f 79
1998 Turf 3-6: (6f 1-2, 7f 2-4) (gd 1-3, g-f 1-1, frm, hrd 1-1)
Pattern-class colt, effective 7f, acts on g-f. Turf high 106 - also 1st of 7 from Compton Admiral (21 Aug Sandown RF 3796). He is Pip Payne's most expensive purchase at 190,000 guineas and developed into a classy juvenile. Second to Aljabr at Goodwood, he produced a sustained burst to win the Group Three Solario Stakes at Sandown and was by no means disgraced in the Dewhurst. A mile on fast ground would appear his ideal. He will win another Group race or two if kept away from the very best, and is probably an ideal type for the Italian or German 2000 Guineas.
**J W Payne [3-6] Nagy Azar.*

RAISE A KING BHB 95f RR 96f 2548[11]
3 b g Ardkinglass 5f **(64)** - Bias (Royal Prerogative) 7f **(98)**
Form - 5740
Record 1998 - 1st:0 2nd:0 3rd:0 Ran:4
Pre1998 - 1st:2 2nd:1 3rd:1 Ran:4
Win Prizemoney £7,702 *Total Prizemoney* £10,935
Wins * 1997 Spt Yarmou (FRM) 6f 94+ <
* 1997 Aug Sandow (GD) 5f 89+
1998 Turf 0-4: (7f 2, 8f 2) (gd 4)
Leggy, very useful gelding, effective 5 to 8f, best at 6f, acts on gd to frm, best on frm. Turf high 96 - 4th of 6 to Speedfit Too (23 May Kempton 8f gd RF 1426). Consistent. Made a solid reappearance at Newmarket, keeping on well, and ran a good race stepped up to a mile in listed company on his third start.
**J W Payne [2-8] Marwan Tabsh.*

RAISE A PRINCE (FR) BHB 100f95a RR 92f 95a 5149[4]
5 b g Machiavellian (USA) 9.8f **(83)** - Enfant D'Amour (USA) (Lyphard (USA)) 9.9f **(72)**
Form - 141245401134
Record 1998 - 1st:3 2nd:1 3rd:1 Ran:10
Pre1998 - 1st:3 2nd:2 3rd:1 Ran:15
Win Prizemoney £71,242 *Total Prizemoney* £84,701
Wins * **1998** Spt Ascot (SFT) H 12f 90 92 <
* **1998** Spt Ayr (G-S) H 13.1f 89 92 <

* **1998** Apr Newmar (SFT) H 12f 79 89
* 1997 *Nov Lingfi (STD) 12f 82*
* 1997 Oct Newbur (G-S) C 12f 81+
1997 Jly Nottin (SFT) H 10f 69 69

1998 Turf 3-10: (12f 2-7, 13f 1-1, 14f 2) (sft 2-3, g-s, gd 1-3, g-f 3)

Useful gelding, effective 12 to 14f, acts on sft to g-f - acts on Equi, has worn blinkers, likes tight tracks. Turf high 92 - 4th of 7 giving 1lb to Henry Island (20 May Goodwood 14f g-f RF 1357) - also 1st of 16 getting 7lb from Yavana's Pace (27 Spt Ascot RF 4515). Very much suited by soft ground, conditions under which he won three times during the season, the last of which was the Sunday Special Handicap at the Ascot Festival. His trainer reports the gelding has problems with his feet and requires time between his races.

**S P C Woods [5-13] George Tong (from J W Hills [1-9] Jly 1997).*

1998 Turf 0-4: (12f 4) (sft, g-f 2, frm) 1998 AW 1-4: (12f 1-2, 13f, 15f) (Equi 1-2, Fibr 2)

Moderate gelding, effective 12 to 15f, - acts on AW, prefers left handed tracks. Turf high 33. AW high 46 - 1st of 11 giving 3lb to Shanghai Lil (22 Jan Lingfield RF 0136).

**C W Thornton [2-16] Guy Reed.*

RAJAIYMA (IRE) BHB 95f **RR 98f** 5140[2]

3 b f Kahyasi 12.9f **(74)** - Rajaura (IRE) (Storm Bird (CAN)) 10.3f **(74)**

Form - 122

Record 1998 - 1st:1 2nd:2 3rd:0 Ran:3

Win Prizemoney £3,517 *Total Prizemoney* £6,089

Wins * 1998 Jly Kempto (G-S) 10f 76 <

1998 Turf 1-3: (10f 1-2, 15f) (gd 1-3)

Raise a Grand was worth every penny

RAIVUE BHB 80f **RR 79f** 4392[6]

4 ch g Beveled (USA) 6.9f **(64)** - Halka (Daring March) 7.1f **(61)**

Form - 7166

Record 1998 - 1st:1 2nd:0 3rd:0 Ran:4
Pre1998 - 1st:1 2nd:1 3rd:1 Ran:7

Win Prizemoney £7,977 *Total Prizemoney* £9,560

Wins * 1998 Aug Ripon (G-F) H 12.3f 76 79 <
* 1997 Jun Ripon (GD) 10f 71

1998 Turf 1-4: (12f 1-4) (g-f 1-3, frm)

Above-average gelding, effective 10 to 12f, best at 10f, acts on g-f to frm, best on frm. Turf high 79 (began Aug) - 1st of 8 giving 12lb to Warning Reef (22 Aug Ripon RF 3814). Sold for 34,000 gns to join Tim Easterby. **E Weymes [2-11] Mrs A Birkett.*

RAJAH BHB 32f44a **RR 33f 44a** 3161[5]

5 b br g Be My Chief (USA) 10.2f **(62)** - Pretty Thing (Star Appeal) 9.6f **(65)**

Form - 861408055

Record 1998 - 1st:1 2nd:0 3rd:0 Ran:8
Pre1998 - 1st:1 2nd:0 3rd:1 Ran:8

Win Prizemoney £4,407 *Total Prizemoney* £5,030

Wins * 1998 *Jan Lingfi (STD) 12f 46* <
* 1996 *Mar Wolver (STD) H 8.5f 45 46* <

Workmanlike, currently very useful filly. Turf high 98 (began Jly) - 2nd of 4 getting 9lb from Craigsteel (6 Nov Doncaster 15f gd RF 5140). Unraced at two, she won nicely at Kempton on her debut and only went down narrowly at Doncaster next time. No match for Craigsteel on her final start at the backend, she uses her tail like a propeller but seems genuine enough.

**L M Cumani [1-3] H H Aga Khan.*

RAJATI (USA) BHB 58f55a **RR 58f 55a** 1152[5]

3 b g Chief's Crown (USA) 10.2f **(75)** - Charming Life (NZ) (Sir Tristram) 10.7f **(76)**

Form - 54515

Record 1998 - 1st:1 2nd:0 3rd:0 Ran:5
Pre1998 - 1st:0 2nd:0 3rd:0 Ran:1

Win Prizemoney £0 *Total Prizemoney* £235

Wins * 1998 May Newmar (GD) 8f 58 <

1998 Turf 1-4: (8f 1-2, 10f 2) (sft 2, gd 1-2) 1998 AW 0-1: (11f) (Fibr)

Well made, fair gelding, effective 8f, acts on gd, has worn blinkers. Turf high 58 - also 1st of 2 giving 5lb to High Demand (3 May Newmarket RF 0997). A half-brother to Kingfisher Mill, he is beginning to look a rather disappointing sort. His win came in the Newmarket Challenge Whip, so technically he remains a maiden.

**Mrs J Cecil [1-6] Lord Howard de Walden.*

RAJJAAF RR 99f
4296a[8]

3 ch c Unfuwain (USA) 11.4f **(74)** - Forest Lair (Habitat) 9.4f **(70)**
Form - 4112308
1998 Turf 2-7: (9f, 12f 2-5, 14f) (hvy 2, g-s 1-1, gd 2, g-f, hrd 1-1)
Very useful colt, effective 12f, acts on gd to hrd, has worn blinkers. Turf high 99 - 3rd of 14 giving 2lb to Dragon Triumph (14 Jly Down Royal 12f g-f RF 2992a) - also 1st of 5 from Dragon Triumph (3 May Gowran Park RF 1056a).
**D K Weld in IRE [2-7] Hamdan Al Maktoum.*

RAJMATA (IRE) BHB 62f RR 70f
5042[9]

2 b f Prince Sabo 6.6f **(64)** - Heart of India (IRE) (Try My Best (USA)) 7.6f **(67)**
Form - 56500
Record 1998 - 1st:0 2nd:0 3rd:0 Ran:5
1998 Turf 0-5: (5f 5) (sft 2, gd, frm 2)
Above-average filly. Turf high 70.
**Sir Mark Prescott [0-5] Mrs C R Philipson.*

RAJWHAN (USA) RR 74f
4327[4]

2 br c Lear Fan (USA) 10.4f **(80)** - Samra(USA) (Solford (USA)) 13f **(71)**
Form - 04
Record 1998 - 1st:0 2nd:0 3rd:0 Ran:2
Win Prizemoney £0 *Total Prizemoney* £821
1998 Turf 0-2: (6f, 7f) (g-f, frm)
Currently above-average colt. Turf high 74 (began Aug).
**C E Brittain [0-2] Mohammed Jaber.*

RAKEEB (USA) BHB 87f RR 94f
4537[11]

3 ch c Irish River (FR) 9f **(77)** - Ice House (Northfields (USA)) 9f **(72)**
Form - 033110
Record 1998 - 1st:2 2nd:0 3rd:2 Ran:6
Win Prizemoney £7,083 *Total Prizemoney* £8,188

Wins								
* 1998	Aug	Haydoc	(G-S)	H	11.9f	85	91	
* 1998	Jly	Ayr	(SFT)		10f		94	<

1998 Turf 2-6: (8f, 10f 1-2, 11f, 12f 1-2) (gd 1-4, g-f 1-1, frm)
Useful colt, effective 10 to 12f, acts on gd to g-f. Turf high 94 - 1st of 5 giving 5lb to Magic of Aloha (20 Jly Ayr RF 2947) - also 1st of 6 giving 1lb to Indimaaj (6 Aug Haydock RF 3411). He seemed to really come to himself when faced with a test of stamina, winning nicely at Ayr and Haydock, and goes particularly well on soft ground. Tailed off on his final start, however, and was sold for 10,500 gns in October. **A C Stewart [2-6] Hamdan Al Maktoum.*

RAKIS (IRE) BHB 67f85a RR 78f 85a
4936[17]

8 b or br g Alzao (USA) 9.8f **(73)** - Bristle (Thatch (USA)) 9.8f **(62)**
Form - 7024540030
Record 1998 - 1st:0 2nd:1 3rd:1 Ran:10
Pre1998 - 1st:9 2nd:4 3rd:5 Ran:47
Win Prizemoney £40,817 *Total Prizemoney* £55,485

Wins								
* 1997	*Feb*	*Wolver*	*(STD)*	*H*	*7f*	*87*	*87*	<
* 1996	Spt	Sandow	(G-F)	H	7.1f	75	77	
* 1996	Jun	Sandow	(G-F)	H	7.1f	72	79	
1996	*Feb*	*Lingfi*	*(STD)*	*H*	*7f*	*82*	*85*	
1996	*Jan*	*Lingfi*	*(STD)*	*H*	*7f*	*72*	*79*	
1996	*Jan*	*Lingfi*	*(STD)*	*H*	*7f*	*72*	*77*	
1996	*Jan*	*Lingfi*	*(STD)*	*H*	*7f*	*64*	*58*	
1995	*Dec*	*Wolver*	*(STD)*	*H*	*7f*	*57*	*65*	

1998 Turf 0-9: (7f 5, 8f 4) (gd 4, g-f 4, frm) 1998 AW 0-1: (7f) (Fibr)
Useful gelding, effective 7 to 8f, best at 7f, acts on gd to frm - acts on Fibr, best on frm, has worn blinkers, likes left handed tracks, and does well at Lingfield. Turf high 78 - 2nd of 15 getting 10lb from Sharp Rebuff (12 Jun Sandown 7f gd RF 1936). A seven-furlong specialist, but despite numerous efforts has not won since February 1997.
**Mrs L Stubbs [3-37] P G Shorrock (from M Brittain [5-8] Feb 1996).*

RAMBLERS COURT (IRE) RR 92f
4432a[22]

3 br g Distinctly North (USA) 7.4f **(63)** - Flash The Gold (Ahonoora) 8.1f **(73)**
Form - 50578760
1998 Turf 0-8: (7f 3, 8f 2, 9f 2, 10f) (sft, g-s, gd 6)
Useful gelding. Turf high 92. **T A Regan in IRE [0-8] P J Barrett.*

RAMBLING BEAR BHB 106f RR 109f
4330[10]

5 ch h Sharrood (USA) 11.1f **(67)** - Supreme Rose (Frimley Park) 6.5f **(67)**
Form - 16607825860
Record 1998 - 1st:1 2nd:1 3rd:0 Ran:11
Pre1998 - 1st:5 2nd:3 3rd:4 Ran:25
Win Prizemoney £68,985 *Total Prizemoney* £89,408

Wins							
* 1998	May	Goodwo	(G-F)		6f	109	
* 1996	Jly	Goodwo	(G-F)	G3	5f	107	
* 1996	Jun	Lingfi	(G-F)	L	6f	114	<
* 1996	May	Newbur	(G-F)		6f	108	
* 1995	Spt	Kempto	(GD)	L	6f	92	
* 1995	Jly	Windso	(G-F)		5f	91	

1998 Turf 1-11: (5f 5, 6f 1-6) (g-s, gd 5, g-f 1-4, frm)
Pattern-class colt, effective 5 to 7f, best at 6f, acts on gd to frm, best on g-f. Turf high 109 (1st run) - 1st of 7 from To the Roof (19 May Goodwood RF 1328). He ran his best race for some time when finishing fifth in the Nunthorpe Stakes at York. He needs fast ground and is unlikely to be good enough to win another Group race next season. **M Blanshard [6-36] Mrs Michael Hill.*

RAMBLING ROSE RR 110f
4717a[6]

3 ch f Cadeaux Genereux 7.9f **(76)** - Blush Rambler (IRE) (Blushing Groom (FR)) 10.3f **(76)**
Form - 232316
Record 1998 - 1st:1 2nd:2 3rd:2 Ran:6
Pre1998 - 1st:1 2nd:2 3rd:1 Ran:4
Win Prizemoney £22,536 *Total Prizemoney* £63,690

Wins							
* 1998	Aug	York	(FRM)	L	11.9f	104	<
* 1997	Spt	Nottin	(G-F)		8.2f	83	

1998 Turf 1-6: (11f, 12f 1-3, 13f, 14f) (sft, g-s, gd, g-f 2, frm 1-1)
Scopey, Group-class filly, effective 12f, acts on g-s to frm. Turf high 110 - 3rd of 9 to Bahr (18 Jun Ascot 12f g-s RF 2083) - also 1st of 8 getting 6lb from Bristol Channel (20 Aug York RF 3776). This thoroughly likeable filly ran a string of good races in the summer, culminating in a victory in the Galtres Stakes at York. She was not at her best when unplaced at Longchamp in October and was immediately retired to stud.
**Sir Michael Stoute [2-10] Sir Evelyn De Rothschild.*

RAMBOLD BHB 51f60a RR 39f 60a
5121[8]

7 b m Rambo Dancer (CAN) 8.4f **(59)** - Boldie (Bold Lad (IRE)) 8.4f **(68)**
Form - 0100140008
Record 1998 - 1st:2 2nd:0 3rd:0 Ran:10
Pre1998 - 1st:5 2nd:4 3rd:4 Ran:46
Win Prizemoney £25,076 *Total Prizemoney* £31,351

Wins							
* 1998	Jly	Bright	(G-F)		6f		58
* 1998	May	Chepst	(G-F)	H	6.1f	47	51
* 1996	Aug	Yarmou	(GD)	H	6f	60	65
* 1996	Jun	Hamilt	(GD)		6f		48
1994	Jun	Lingfi	(GF)	H	6f	66	65

1998 Turf 2-10: (6f 2-10) (g-s, gd 1-2, frm 1-7)
Fair mare, effective 6f, acts on gd to frm. Turf high 61 - also 1st of 9 from Rainbow Rain (23 Jly Brighton RF 3042).
**N E Berry [4-35] Ron Collins (from T M Jones [3-21] Jan 1995).*

RAMBO TANGO BHB 34f30a RR 38f 30a
756[9]

4 b g Rambo Dancer (CAN) 8.4f **(59)** - Jumra (Thatch (USA)) 9.8f **(62)**
Form - 0
Record 1998 - 1st:0 2nd:0 3rd:0 Ran:1
Pre1998 - 1st:0 2nd:0 3rd:0 Ran:6
1998 AW 0-1: (16f) (Fibr)
Light-framed, very moderate gelding.
**B R Cambidge [1-13] A S Blackham.*

RAMBO WALTZER BHB 63f86a RR 59f 86a
4804[5]

6 b g Rambo Dancer (CAN) 8.4f **(59)** - Vindictive Lady (USA) (Foolish Pleasure (USA)) 8.9f **(72)**
Form - 5232126321000535
Record 1998 - 1st:2 2nd:4 3rd:3 Ran:15
Pre1998 - 1st:12 2nd:6 3rd:4 Ran:52
Win Prizemoney £55,881 *Total Prizemoney* £70,319

Wins								
* 1998	*Apr*	*Southw*	*(STD)*	*H*	*8f*	*81*	*87*	<
* 1998	*Jan*	*Wolver*	*(STD)*	*H*	*9.4f*	*76*	*78*	
* 1997	Apr	Hamilt	(G-S)	H	8.3f	65	71	
* 1997	*Mar*	*Wolver*	*(STD)*	*H*	*8.5f*	*78*	*78*	
* 1997	*Feb*	*Southw*	*(STD)*	*H*	*8f*	*70*	*76*	
* 1997	*Jan*	*Southw*	*(STD)*	*C*	*7f*		*70+*	

* 1997	*Jan*	*Southw*	*(STD)*	*C*	*8f*		*81+*
* 1996	Apr	Ripon	(GD)	H	8f	61	68
* 1996	Apr	Thirsk	(G-F)	H	8f	55	64
* 1996	Apr	Hamilt	(G-S)	H	8.3f	55	58
* 1996	*Jan*	*Wolver*	*(STD)*	*C*	*7f*		*78*
* 1996	*Jan*	*Southw*	*(STD)*	*C*	*8f*		*75+*
1994	*Jly*	*Southw*	*(STD)*		*6f*		*75*
1994	*Jly*	*Southw*	*(STD)*		*7f*		*61*

1998 Turf 0-6: (7f 2, 8f, 9f 2, 10f) (sft 2, gd 2, g-f, frm) 1998 AW 2-9: (7f 2, 8f 1-4, 9f 1-3) (Fibr 2-9)

Useful gelding, effective 8 to 9f, best at 8f, - acts on Fibr, has worn blinkers, favours tight tracks, and excels at Wolverhampton. Turf high 72. AW high 87 - 1st of 11 giving 23lb to Danzino (6 Apr Southwell RF 0573) - also 1st of 5 giving 3lb to Roderick Hudson (28 Jan Wolverhampton RF 0176). He is a consistent performer, and though most of his wins in recent seasons have been on Fibresand, a surface on which he is particularly effective, he remains perfectly capable of winning on turf. A turning track suits him best, and he seems to need at least a mile now.

**D Nicholls [12-52] W G Swiers (from S G Norton [2-15] Nov 1995).*

best on gd, has worn blinkers, and does well at Curragh. Turf high 115 - 2nd of 10 to Muchea (27 Jun Newmarket 7f gd RF 2352) - also 1st of 9 giving 14lb to Gulf Shaadi (13 May York RF 1208). Consistent. He is a very useful sort in Listed or Group races between seven furlongs and a mile. Often successfully campaigned abroad, one of his two victories in a busy season came at the Curragh. Best when held up for a late run off a strong gallop, he is admirably consistent.

**B Hanbury [8-37] Hilal Salem.*

RAMRUMA (USA) RR 91f 4665^{2}

2 ch f Diesis 9f **(80)** - Princess of Man (Green God) 9.6f **(68)**

Form - 32

Record 1998 - 1st:0 2nd:1 3rd:1 Ran:2

Win Prizemoney £0 *Total Prizemoney* £1,478

1998 Turf 0-2: (8f 2) (g-s, g-f)

Currently useful filly. Turf high 91 (1st run) (began Spt) - 3rd of 10 to Social Scene (16 Spt Sandown 8f g-f RF 4309). In the frame in fair maiden company, looking a stayer.

**H R A Cecil [0-2] H R H Prince Fahd Salman.*

Rambling Rose gained an overdue first success at York

RAMOOZ (USA) BHB 112f RR 109f 5152^{4}

5 b h Rambo Dancer (CAN) 8.4f **(59)** - My Shafy (Rousillon (USA)) 8.2f **(74)**

Form - 214243831734

Record 1998 - 1st:2 2nd:2 3rd:3 Ran:12
Pre1998 - 1st:6 2nd:7 3rd:2 Ran:25

Win Prizemoney £110,822 *Total Prizemoney* £204,790

Wins									
* **1998**	Spt	Currag	(SFT)	G3	7f		109+	
* **1998**	May	York	(GD)	LH	7.9f	110	112	
* 1997	Jly	Currag	(GD)	G3	8f		115	<
* 1997	Jun	Newmar	(SFT)	G3	7f		108	
* 1996	Jun	Epsom	(GD)		7f		98	
* 1996	Apr	Thirsk	(G-F)		8f		94	
* 1995	Spt	Newbur	(G-S)	H	7.3f	88	100	
* 1995	Aug	York	(G-F)	H	7.9f	80	79	

1998 Turf 2-12: (6f, 7f 1-5, 8f 1-4, 9f 2) (sft, g-s, gd 2-7, g-f 3)

Pattern-class colt, effective 7 to 8f, best at 8f, acts on gd to g-f,

RAMSEY HOPE BHB 40f46a RR 41f 46a 4867^{10}

5 b h Timeless Times (USA) 6.1f **(56)** - Marfen (Lochnager) 6f **(59)**

Form - 16832454268540056005 80

Record 1998 - 1st:0 2nd:1 3rd:0 Ran:17
Pre1998 - 1st:7 2nd:7 3rd:4 Ran:58

Win Prizemoney £20,137 *Total Prizemoney* £32,112

Wins								
* 1997	*Nov*	*Southw*	*(STD)*	*C*	*6f*		*64*	
* 1997	Jun	Carlis	(FRM)	H	5f	59	59	
* 1997	*Feb*	*Lingfi*	*(STD)*	*H*	*5f*	*73*	*74*	
* 1996	*Nov*	*Lingfi*	*(STD)*	*H*	*5f*	*65*	*69*	
* 1996	*Oct*	*Wolver*	*(STD)*	*H*	*5f*	*58*	*60*	
* 1995	Aug	Ripon	(G-F)		6f		84	<
* 1995	Jun	Hamilt	(FRM)		6f		84	<

1998 Turf 0-4: (5f, 6f 3) (g-f 2, frm 2) 1998 AW 0-13: (5f 5, 6f 6, 7f, 8f) (Equi 4, Fibr 9)

Moderate colt, effective 5 to 6f, best at 5f, - acts on AW, best on

Fibr, often wears blinkers (effectively), likes left handed tracks, likes tight tracks, and likes Lingfield. Turf high 41. AW high 62.
**C W Fairhurst [7-75] C D Barber-Lomax.*

RANAAN (IRE) RR 72f 5139[6]
2 ch c Brief Truce (USA) 9.1f **(73)** - Ma Minti (Mummy's Pet) 7.7f **(60)**
Form - 26
Record 1998 - 1st:0 2nd:1 3rd:0 Ran:2
Win Prizemoney £0 *Total Prizemoney* £975
1998 Turf 0-2: (5f, 6f) (sft, gd)
Currently above-average colt. Turf high 72 (began Oct) - 6th of 22 to Mutaakkid (6 Nov Doncaster 6f gd RF 5139).
**M R Channon [0-2] Ahmed Al Shafar.*

RANDOM KINDNESS BHB 70f92a **RR 75f 92a** 4850[27]
5 b g Alzao (USA) 9.8f **(73)** - Lady Tippins (USA) (Star de Naskra (USA)) 9.7f **(65)**
Form - 16812312284880
Record 1998 - 1st:2 2nd:3 3rd:1 Ran:13
Pre1998 - 1st:4 2nd:5 3rd:2 Ran:18
Win Prizemoney £20,458 *Total Prizemoney* £30,637
Wins * **1998** May Bright (FRM) 11.9f 70
* **1998** *Apr Lingfi (STD) 12f 84* <
* 1997 *Nov Wolver (STD) H 12f 77 82*
* 1997 Oct Lingfi (FRM) 11.5f 62
* 1997 *Apr Wolver (STD) H 14.8f 66 77*
* 1997 *Mar Wolver (STD) 16.2f 77*
1998 Turf 1-11: (12f 1-7, 13f, 14f, 16f, 18f) (g-s, gd 4, g-f 3, frm 1-3)
1998 AW 1-2: (12f 1-1, 16f) (Equi 1-1, Fibr)
Useful gelding, effective 12 to 16f, best at 12f, acts on g-f - acts on AW, best on Fibr, prefers left handed tracks, prefers tight tracks, and excels at Wolverhampton. Turf high 75 - 2nd of 9 getting 6lb from Flying Eagle (29 Jly Epsom 12f g-f RF 3199). AW high 84 - 1st of 5 giving 2lb to Opera Buff (9 Apr Lingfield RF 0623). He looks very useful on Fibresand, but over the past couple of seasons he has shown that he is perfectly capable of winning races on Equitrack and on turf too. Effective from twelve to sixteen furlongs, he is versatile as well as game and genuine.
**R Ingram [6-26] 949 Racing (from P W Harris [0-5] Jly 1996).*

RANDSOM'S HANDSOME (USA) RR 73f 3985[6]
3 br g Red Ransom (USA) 8.6f **(83)** - Best of My Love (USA) (Best Turn (USA)) 10.2f **(78)**
Form - 6
Record 1998 - 1st:0 2nd:0 3rd:0 Ran:1
Win Prizemoney £0 *Total Prizemoney* £87
1998 Turf 0-1: (10f) (g-f)
Scopey, currently above-average gelding.
**E A L Dunlop [0-1] Jaber Abdullah.*

RANEEN NASHWAN BHB 82f **RR 77f** 5116[1]
2 b c Nashwan (USA) 10.3f **(79)** - Raneen Alwatar (Sadler's Wells (USA)) 10f **(76)**
Form - 6541
Record 1998 - 1st:1 2nd:0 3rd:0 Ran:4
Win Prizemoney £3,512 *Total Prizemoney* £3,765
Wins * **1998** Nov Mussel (SFT) 8f 77 <
1998 Turf 1-4: (7f, 8f 1-3) (g-s, gd 1-3)
Above-average colt. Turf high 77 (began Spt) - 1st of 9 from Tier Worker (4 Nov Musselburgh RF 5116).
**M R Channon [1-4] Sheikh Ahmed Al Maktoum.*

RANGATIRA (IRE) BHB 60f **RR 61f** 4531[5]
3 ch g Royal Academy (USA) 7.8f **(77)** - Chief's Quest (USA) (Chief's Crown (USA)) 9.8f **(72)**
Form - 435
Record 1998 - 1st:0 2nd:0 3rd:1 Ran:3
Win Prizemoney £0 *Total Prizemoney* £882
1998 Turf 0-3: (8f 2, 9f) (sft, g-s, gd)
Currently average gelding. Turf high 61.
**M Johnston [0-3] J W Robb.*

RANGER SLOANE BHB 41f30a **RR 43f 30a** 1247[4]
6 ch g Gunner B 11.2f **(45)** - Lucky Amy (Lucky Wednesday) 8f **(50)**
Form - 004
Record 1998 - 1st:0 2nd:0 3rd:0 Ran:2
Pre1998 - 1st:1 2nd:2 3rd:0 Ran:15
Win Prizemoney £3,096 *Total Prizemoney* £4,923
Wins * 1997 Spt Catter (GD) H 15.8f 38 43 <
1998 Turf 0-2: (16f 2) (frm 2)
Moderate gelding, effective 16 to 17f, best at 16f, acts on gd to frm, has worn blinkers. Turf high 39 - 4th of 8 getting 20lb from Paradise Navy (15 May Nottingham 16f frm RF 1247). Inconsistent.
**G Fierro [4-31] G Fierro.*

RAPID MOVER BHB 27f **RR 28f** 2680[12]
11 ch g Final Straw 10f **(52)** - Larive (Blakeney) 10.5f **(64)**
Form - 0800
Record 1998 - 1st:0 2nd:0 3rd:0 Ran:4
Pre1998 - 1st:1 2nd:1 3rd:4 Ran:55
Win Prizemoney £1,646 *Total Prizemoney* £4,363
1998 Turf 0-4: (6f 3, 11f) (hvy, sft, g-f, frm)
Little account gelding, effective 6f, acts on g-f, mostly wears blinkers. Turf high 28.
**D A Nolan [3-83] Mrs J McFadyen-Murray (from T Craig [1-15] Jly 1993).*

RAPID RELIANCE BHB 40f52a **RR 49f 52a** 4275[16]
3 b f Emarati (USA) 6.6f **(63)** - Chiquitita (Reliance II) 9.9f **(58)**
Form - 884074700
Record 1998 - 1st:0 2nd:0 3rd:0 Ran:7
Pre1998 - 1st:1 2nd:0 3rd:0 Ran:8
Win Prizemoney £2,882 *Total Prizemoney* £3,087
Wins 1997 Spt Sandow (GD) C 5f 68 <
1998 Turf 0-7: (5f, 6f, 7f 2, 10f 2, 12f) (sft, gd 3, g-f 2, frm)
Neat, fair filly, effective 5f, acts on gd, has worn blinkers. Turf high 49. Inconsistent.
**K R Burke [0-1] Brooknight Guarding Ltd (from R Ingram [0-10] Jly 1998).*

RAPIER BHB 83f **RR 88df** 4132[5]
4 b g Sharpo 7.5f **(68)** - Sahara Breeze (Ela-Mana-Mou) 10.1f **(70)**
Form - 031005
Record 1998 - 1st:1 2nd:0 3rd:1 Ran:6
Pre1998 - 1st:1 2nd:2 3rd:3 Ran:11
Win Prizemoney £18,918 *Total Prizemoney* £29,314
Wins * **1998** Jun York (G-S) H 8.9f 82 88 <
1996 Spt Bright (FRM) 8f 77
1998 Turf 1-6: (8f 3, 9f 1-1, 10f 2) (g-s 1-1, gd 2, g-f, frm 2)
Workmanlike, useful gelding, effective 8 to 9f, best at 8f, acts on g-s to frm. Turf high 88 - 1st of 17 giving 17lb to Dispol Diamond (13 Jun York RF 1980). Inconsistent. After a promising run at Haydock, he won well at York in June. Yet to prove he stays ten furlongs.
**M D Hammond [1-6] Mrs A Kane (from R Hannon [1-11] Oct 1997).*

RAQQASA BHB 71f **RR 72f** 5095[4]
3 b f Groom Dancer (USA) 9.5f **(75)** - Khandjar (Kris) 9.5f **(73)**
Form - 236224
Record 1998 - 1st:0 2nd:3 3rd:1 Ran:6
Win Prizemoney £0 *Total Prizemoney* £4,873
1998 Turf 0-6: (10f 2, 11f 2, 12f 2) (gd 3, g-f 2, frm)
Leggy, above-average filly, effective 10 to 12f, best at 10f, acts on gd to frm, best on g-f. Turf high 72 - 2nd of 5 getting 5lb from Kimberley (7 Oct York 10f g-f RF 4702).
**H R A Cecil [0-6] Lord Howard de Walden.*

RA RA RASPUTIN BHB 54f82a **RR 54f 82a** 5006[2]
3 b c Petong 7.6f **(58)** - Ra Ra Girl (Shack (USA)) 5.8f **(53)**
Form - 005304800402
Record 1998 - 1st:0 2nd:1 3rd:1 Ran:12
Pre1998 - 1st:1 2nd:0 3rd:0 Ran:7
Win Prizemoney £18,555 *Total Prizemoney* £20,621
Wins * 1997 *Aug Wolver (STD) 6f 82* <
1998 Turf 0-12: (5f, 6f, 7f 4, 8f 6) (sft, gd 6, g-f 3, frm 2)
Scopey, decent colt, effective 6f, - acts on Fibr, likes left handed tracks, likes tight tracks. Turf high 56. Inconsistent. Scored a 50/1 shock win in the Weatherbys Dash at Wolverhampton in '97 and obviously likes Fibresand. A tight left-handed track suits, as he has run some of his best races on turf at Chester.
**B A McMahon [1-19] D J Allen.*

RARE ROCK (USA) RR 5164a[9]
5 b h Danzig Connection (USA) 8.2f **(75)**

Form - 0
1998 AW 0-1: (6f) (Dirt)
Currently Group-class colt, always wears blinkers.
**T Pletcher in USA [0-1] Betty Massey & J Pletcher.*

RARE TALENT BHB 58f **RR 65f** 4540[15]

4 b c Mtoto 11.5f **(71)** - Bold As Love (Lomond (USA)) 8.8f **(65)**
Form - 301413848700
Record **1998** - 1st:2 2nd:0 3rd:2 Ran:12
Pre1998 - 1st:2 2nd:1 3rd:1 Ran:14
Win Prizemoney £12,970 *Total Prizemoney* £16,201
Wins * **1998** Jly Cheste (G-F) H 10.3f 60 63
* **1998** Jun Doncas (GD) H 10.3f 55 59
1997 Spt Leices (G-F) S 10f 60
1997 Aug Ripon (G-F) SH 10f 60 65 <
1998 Turf 2-12: (8f 2, 10f 2-10) (gd, g-f 1-4, frm 1-6, hrd)
Workmanlike, average colt, effective 10 to 12f, best at 12f, acts on gd to hrd, best on gd, likes right handed tracks, likes tight tracks. Turf high 65 - 3rd of 5 giving 17lb to Kingdom Queen (20 Jly Beverley 10f frm RF 2957) - also 1st of 10 getting 3lb from No Cliches (11 Jly Chester RF 2709). A fair handicapper on his day, his best form has been over ten furlongs on good or faster ground.
**S Gollings [2-15] John King, Bill Hobs King (from M R Channon [2-11] Spt 1997).*

RASHAY (IRE) RR 98+ 4442a[16]

3 ch c Archway (IRE) 8.5f **(60)** - Brierley Lodge (Lorenzaccio) 10f **(64)**
Form - 7521800
1998 Turf 1-7: (5f, 6f, 7f 1-4, 8f) (sft 1-1, gd 5, hrd)
Pattern-class colt, effective 5 to 7f, acts on sft to gd. Turf high 106 - 2nd of 8 giving 5lb to Mempari (22 Jly Naas 5f gd RF 3178a) - also 1st of 8 from Quinstars (28 Jly Galway RF 3340a). He struggled after winning a run-of-the-mill maiden at Galway.
**N Meade in IRE [1-7] P R Charles.*

RASIN CHARGE BHB 29a **RR 25df 29a** 163[11]

7 b g Governor General 6.8f **(45)** - Airlanka (Corvaro (USA)) 9f **(53)**
Form - 0
Record **1998** - 1st:0 2nd:0 3rd:0 Ran:1
Pre1998 - 1st:0 2nd:0 3rd:0 Ran:2
1998 AW 0-1: (6f) (Fibr)
Little account gelding, has worn blinkers.
**R Craggs [0-4] Ray Craggs.*

RASPBERRY SAUCE BHB 59f57a **RR 62f 57a** 3272[4]

4 b f Niniski (USA) 13.2f **(67)** - Sobranie (High Top) 10.2f **(67)**
Form - 7423621147364
Record **1998** - 1st:2 2nd:2 3rd:2 Ran:11
Pre1998 - 1st:0 2nd:0 3rd:0 Ran:3
Win Prizemoney £7,205 *Total Prizemoney* £9,981
Wins * **1998** Apr Bath (SFT) H 11.7f 58 62 <
* **1998** *Apr Lingfi (STD) 10f 54*
1998 Turf 1-3: (10f, 12f 1-2) (g-s 1-1, gd, g-f) 1998 AW 1-8: (8f, 10f 1-5, 12f, 13f) (Equi 1-8)
Workmanlike, average filly, effective 10 to 12f, best at 12f, acts on g-s to g-f - acts on Equi. Turf high 62 (1st run) - 1st of 10 giving 7lb to Limelight (28 Apr Bath RF 0896). AW high 54 - 1st of 9 getting 5lb from Primeval (9 Apr Lingfield RF 0621). She was beginning to look a rather frustrating sort until putting previous experience of the surface to good effect to land a maiden on the Lingfield Equitrack in April. She followed up in a handicap on turf at Bath, but a rise in the handicap has found her out since.
**C A Cyzer [2-14] R M Cyzer.*

RAS SHAIKH (USA) BHB 91f **RR 83f** 4067[3]

2 b f Sheikh Albadou 9.2f **(75)** - Aneesati (Kris) 9.5f **(73)**
Form - 313
Record **1998** - 1st:1 2nd:0 3rd:2 Ran:3
Win Prizemoney £2,994 *Total Prizemoney* £4,992
Wins * **1998** Aug Leices (GD) 6f 83 <
1998 Turf 1-3: (6f 1-3) (gd, g-f, frm 1-1)
Currently decent filly. Turf high 83 (began Jly) - 1st of 21 getting 5lb from Alhasad (5 Aug Leicester RF 3377). Showed promise on her debut, and went on to score in clear-cut fashion at Leicester next time. There looks to be plenty of improvement in her.
**B W Hills [1-3] Salem Bel Obaida.*

RATATUIA RR 88f 4930[3]

2 b f Zafonic (USA) 9f **(83)**-Refilee (IRE) (Sadler's Wells (USA)) 10f **(76)**
Form - 823
Record **1998** - 1st:0 2nd:1 3rd:1 Ran:3
Win Prizemoney £0 *Total Prizemoney* £1,488
1998 Turf 0-3: (8f 3) (g-s 2, gd)
Currently useful filly. Turf high 88 (began Spt) - 2nd of 10 to Kristina (6 Oct Nottingham 8f g-s RF 4664).
**L M Cumani [0-3] Scuderia Rencati Srl.*

RAVENWOOD LADY RR 62f 4761[9]

2 ch f Unfuwain (USA) 11.4f **(74)** - Sylvatica (Thatching) 8f **(66)**
Form - 0
Record **1998** - 1st:0 2nd:0 3rd:0 Ran:1
1998 Turf 0-1: (7f) (gd)
Currently average filly. **S C Williams [0-1] W J de Ruiter.*

RAVIER (ITY) RR 111f 3059a[1]

7 gr h Highest Honor (FR) 10.9f **(72)** - Revarola (ITY) (Marracci)
Form - 71
1998 Turf 1-2: (8f 1-2) (sft, g-f 1-1)
Group-class horse. Turf high 95.
**E Borromeo in ITY [2-6] Razza Dormello-Olgiata (from ITY [1-5] Jun 1998).*

RAYIK BHB 78f **RR 81f** 4138[5]

3 br g Marju (IRE) 9.2f **(76)** - Matila (IRE) (Persian Bold) 9.3f **(66)**
Form - 45
Record **1998** - 1st:0 2nd:0 3rd:0 Ran:2
Pre1998 - 1st:0 2nd:0 3rd:0 Ran:1
Win Prizemoney £0 *Total Prizemoney* £309
1998 Turf 0-2: (8f, 10f) (g-f, frm)
Workmanlike, currently decent gelding. Turf high 78 (1st run) (began Aug) - 4th of 9 to Cool Vibes (29 Aug Newmarket 8f frm RF 3954). Lightly raced, he will be one to keep an eye on when competing in handicaps. **R W Armstrong [0-3] Hamdan Al Maktoum.*

RAY OF LIGHT (IRE) RR 91f 4781a[1]

2 b c Rainbows For Life (CAN) 9.3f **(64)** - Topmost 00
Form - 33065411
1998 Turf 2-8: (6f 3, 7f 2-3, 8f 2) (g-s 1-2, gd 1-5, g-f)
Useful colt, effective 7f, acts on g-s to gd, has worn blinkers. Turf high 91 - 1st of 16 giving 25lb to Mrs Evans (7 Oct Fairyhouse RF 4781a) - also 1st of 15 giving 5lb to Tribal (19 Spt Down Royal RF 4434a). He had shown reasonable form in maidens at the top Irish tracks before getting off the mark at Down Royal. Put up a better performance when following up in a Fairyhouse nursery.
**M Halford in IRE [2-8] Mrs M Halford.*

RAY OF SUNSHINE (IRE) BHB 86f **RR 88f** 4365[19]

3 ch g Rainbows For Life (CAN) 9.3f **(64)** - Maura's Guest (IRE) (Be My Guest (USA)) 9.3f **(67)**
Form - 0611140
Record **1998** - 1st:3 2nd:0 3rd:0 Ran:7
Pre1998 - 1st:1 2nd:1 3rd:0 Ran:5
Win Prizemoney £15,215 *Total Prizemoney* £16,587
Wins * **1998** Jly Pontef (G-F) H 6f 74 84 <
* **1998** Jly Redcar (G-S) H 6f 75 82
* **1998** Jun Thirsk (SFT) H 6f 70 71
* 1997 Oct Catter (SFT) H 7f 70 73
1998 Turf 3-7: (6f 3-5, 7f, 8f) (sft, gd 2-3, g-f, frm 1-2)
Scopey, useful gelding, effective 6f, acts on gd to frm, best on frm. Turf high 88 - 4th of 9 giving 12lb to Sea-Deer (24 Jly Newmarket 6f frm RF 3076) - also 1st of 15 giving 21lb to Time To Tango (7 Jly Pontefract RF 2588). Inconsistent. He has looked to have two very different ways of running in the past, but was in fine form in the summer, completing a quickfire hat-trick. Appreciates soft ground.
**Mrs J R Ramsden [4-12] Charlton Bloodstock Ltd.*

RAYWARE BOY (IRE) BHB 48f **RR 48f** 5012[9]

2 b c Scenic 10.6f **(66)** - Amata (USA) (Nodouble (USA)) 8.8f **(68)**
Form - 7000
Record **1998** - 1st:0 2nd:0 3rd:0 Ran:4
1998 Turf 0-2: (6f 2) (gd, g-f) 1998 AW 0-2: (6f, 7f) (Fibr 2)
Moderate colt, has worn blinkers. Turf high 48 (began Aug). AW high 41 (began Aug). **D Shaw [0-4] Rayton Racing.*

RAYWARE LAD (IRE) RR 44f 3126[9]
2 b g Paris House 5.9f **(64)** - Track Twenty Nine (IRE) (Standaan (FR)) 7f **(55)**
Form - 0700
Record 1998 - 1st:0 2nd:0 3rd:0 Ran:4
1998 Turf 0-3: (5f 2, 6f) (gd, g-f, frm) 1998 AW 0-1: (6f) (Fibr)
Moderate gelding, has worn blinkers. Turf high 44.
**D Shaw [0-4] Rayton Racing.*

RAZIK (CAN) RR 105f 4177a[10]
3 b c Dayjur (USA) 6.8f **(79)** - Sirona (CAN) (Irish Stronghold (USA))
Form - 123230
1998 Turf 1-6: (8f 1-5, 9f) (sft, gd 1-4, g-f)
Strong, Pattern-class colt, effective 8 to 9f, acts on gd to g-f, has worn blinkers. Turf high 106 - 2nd of 4 to Desert Fox (21 May Tipperary 9f g-f RF 1496a). He faced some stiff tasks after winning on his reappearance, but was not disgraced under a big weight in the Irish Cambridgeshire. He may well stay beyond nine furlongs.
**D K Weld in IRE [1-6] Hamdan Al Maktoum.*

RAZOR BHB 84f **RR 84f** 4483[3]
3 b c Warning 8.1f **(77)** - Smarten Up (Sharpen Up) 8.3f **(67)**
Form - 32022413
Record 1998 - 1st:1 2nd:3 3rd:2 Ran:8
Pre1998 - 1st:0 2nd:0 3rd:0 Ran:1
Win Prizemoney £3,517 *Total Prizemoney* £8,132
Wins * **1998** Spt Newcas (GD) 8f 67 <
1998 Turf 1-8: (6f, 7f 4, 8f 1-3) (g-s, gd, g-f, frm 1-5)
Decent colt, effective 7 to 8f, best at 8f, acts on g-s to frm, best on frm. Turf high 84 - 3rd of 11 giving 10lb to Sualtach (25 Spt Haydock 8f frm RF 4483). A half-brother to top-class sprinter Cadeaux Genereux and useful stayer Brightner, he was sold for 75,000 gns in the autumn to race abroad.
**S C Williams [1-9] Ivyclose.*

REACTION BALL RR 53f 3646[9]
2 b f Simply Great (FR) 11.9f **(61)**-Empty Purse(Pennine Walk) 8.5f **(61)**
Form - 0
Record 1998 - 1st:0 2nd:0 3rd:0 Ran:1
1998 Turf 0-1: (7f) (frm)
Currently fair filly. **T R Watson [0-1] Newitt and Co Ltd.*

REACTIVE (IRE) BHB 61f70a **RR 70f 70a** 4863[1]
2 ch c Nucleon (USA) - Wind In The Willow (Tumble Wind (USA)) 7.5f **(57)**
Form - 6060301
Record 1998 - 1st:1 2nd:0 3rd:1 Ran:7
Win Prizemoney £2,784 *Total Prizemoney* £3,061
Wins * **1998** *Oct Wolver (STD) C 6f 69 <*
1998 Turf 0-5: (5f, 6f, 7f 3) (gd, g-f 3, frm) 1998 AW 1-2: (6f 1-1, 7f) (Fibr 1-2)
Above-average colt, effective 6f, - acts on Fibr. Turf high 70 (began Jly). AW high 69 (began Spt) - 1st of 13 giving 5lb to Palace Green (17 Oct Wolverhampton RF 4863). He did not show much on turf but improved significantly when tried on Fibresand, winning a Wolverhampton claimer in game style from a field that included previous winners on the surface.
**N P Littmoden [1-7] Clayton Bigley Partnership Ltd.*

READING RHONDA (USA) RR 58f 2330[5]
2 b f Eastern Echo (USA) 8f **(61)** - Higher Learning (USA) (Fappiano (USA)) 8.7f **(77)**
Form - 5
Record 1998 - 1st:0 2nd:0 3rd:0 Ran:1
1998 Turf 0-1: (7f) (gd)
Currently fair filly. **I A Balding [0-1] Paul Mellon.*

READY FONTAINE BHB 37f **RR 9f** 5006[17]
3 b g Dilum (USA) 7.1f **(56)** - Prepare (IRE) (Millfontaine)
Form - 25332000
Record 1998 - 1st:0 2nd:2 3rd:2 Ran:8
Pre1998 - 1st:0 2nd:0 3rd:0 Ran:3
Win Prizemoney £0 *Total Prizemoney* £2,494
1998 Turf 0-8: (6f 5, 7f 2, 8f) (sft, gd 4, g-f, frm 2)
Strong, very poor gelding, effective 6f, acts on gd to frm, best on gd. Turf high 45 - 3rd of 18 getting 24lb from Ray of Sunshine (16 Jun Thirsk 6f gd RF 2019). Becoming disappointing. He showed ability in modest handicap company last season, but remains a maiden. **J Neville [0-11] T A Wadsworth.*

READY TEDDY (IRE) BHB 28f **RR 25f** 1604[9]
5 b m Fayruz 6.6f **(63)** - Racey Naskra (USA) (Star de Naskra (USA)) 9.7f **(65)**
Form - 0
Record 1998 - 1st:0 2nd:0 3rd:0 Ran:1
Pre1998 - 1st:0 2nd:2 3rd:3 Ran:18
Win Prizemoney £0 *Total Prizemoney* £2,839
1998 Turf 0-1: (5f) (gd)
Little account filly, effective 5f, acts on g-f, has worn blinkers. Inconsistent. **Miss L A Perratt [0-19] David White (Bothwell).*

REAL MADRID BHB 32f36a **RR 28f 36a** 136[8]
7 b g Dreams to Reality (USA) 8f **(46)** - Spanish Princess (King of Spain) 7.8f **(52)**
Form - 8
Record 1998 - 1st:0 2nd:0 3rd:0 Ran:1
Pre1998 - 1st:3 2nd:2 3rd:1 Ran:33
Win Prizemoney £5,304 *Total Prizemoney* £7,203
Wins * 1996 *Jan Lingfi (STD) H 10f 39 42 <*
* 1995 Nov Groene (HVY) H 9.3f
* 1994 *Dec Sterre (STD) 8f 41*
1998 AW 0-1: (12f) (Equi)
Very moderate gelding, often wears blinkers.
**G P Enright [4-40] Chris Wall.*

REALMS OF GOLD (USA) RR 51f 4668[11]
2 ch f Gulch (USA) 9.6f **(79)** - Royal Pageant (USA) (Majestic Light (USA)) 10.6f **(75)**
Form - 00
Record 1998 - 1st:0 2nd:0 3rd:0 Ran:2
1998 Turf 0-2: (6f 2) (gd, g-f)
Currently fair filly. Turf high 51 (began Spt).
**I A Balding [0-2] Paul Mellon.*

REAL QUIET (USA) RR 123f 1913a[2]
3 b c Quiet American (USA) 7.9f **(60)** - Really Blue (USA) (Believe It (USA)) 9.4f **(70)**
Form - 112
1998 Turf 1-1: (10f 1-1) (frm 1-1) 1998 AW 1-2: (10f 1-1, 12f) (Dirt 1-2)
Currently top-class colt. (1st run) - 1st of 15 from Victory Gallop (2 May Churchill Downs RF 1090a). AW high 126 (1st run) - 1st of 10 from Victory Gallop (16 May Pimlico RF 1377a). Took the Kentucky Derby and the Preakness Stakes, but his Triple Crown bid was narrowly foiled by Victory Gallop in the Belmont. His career was ended by injury shortly afterwards.
**B Baffert in USA [2-3] Mike Pegram.*

REAL TING BHB 35f **RR 8f** 4612[20]
2 br g Forzando 7.2f **(63)** - St Helena (Monsanto (FR)) 6.5f **(59)**
Form - 000
Record 1998 - 1st:0 2nd:0 3rd:0 Ran:3
1998 Turf 0-2: (6f 2) (g-s, frm) 1998 AW 0-1: (5f) (Fibr)
Currently little account gelding. Turf high 8 (began Aug).
**P D Evans [0-1] P D Evans (from P C Haslam [0-2] Aug 1998).*

REAMZAFONIC RR 4800[9]
2 b f Grand Lodge (USA) -Eye Witness (IRE)(Don't Forget Me) 8.3f **(74)**
Form - 0
Record 1998 - 1st:0 2nd:0 3rd:0 Ran:1
1998 Turf 0-1: (7f) (sft)
Currently very poor filly - 9th of 9 to Credit-A-Plenty (14 Oct Haydock 7f sft RF 4800). **E J Alston [0-1] Miss F Fenley.*

REAP REWARDS BHB 67f **RR 76df** 3836[9]
3 gr c Barrys Gamble 7f **(50)** - Bo' Babbity (Strong Gale) 5.6f **(66)**
Form - 400
Record 1998 - 1st:0 2nd:0 3rd:0 Ran:3
Pre1998 - 1st:1 2nd:0 3rd:1 Ran:3
Win Prizemoney £2,934 *Total Prizemoney* £5,212
Wins * 1997 May Ayr (G-F) 6f 72 <
1998 Turf 0-3: (7f, 8f 2) (gd, g-f 2)
Lengthy, above-average colt, effective 5 to 6f, acts on gd to frm. Turf high 51. **J G FitzGerald [1-6] Marquesa de Moratalla.*

REAR WINDOW BHB 58f60a **RR 59f 60a** 2962^{16}
4 b g Night Shift (USA) 8.1f **(73)** - Last Clear Chance (USA) (Alleged (USA)) 10f **(76)**
Form - 12212600
Record 1998 - 1st:2 2nd:3 3rd:0 Ran:8
Pre1998 - 1st:0 2nd:0 3rd:1 Ran:5
Win Prizemoney £5,404 *Total Prizemoney* £8,499
Wins * **1998** May Nottin (G-F) H 10f 54 60
* **1998** *Mar Southw (STD) H 12f 53 61* <
1998 Turf 1-7: (10f 1-4, 12f 2, 16f) (sft 2, g-f 2, frm 1-3) 1998 AW 1-1: (12f 1-1) (Fibr 1-1)
Scopey, average gelding, effective 10 to 16f, best at 10f, acts on sft to frm - acts on AW, best on frm, has worn blinkers, prefers left handed tracks, prefers tight tracks. Turf high 60 - 1st of 16 giving 1lb to Mister Munnelly (8 May Nottingham RF 1114). (1st run) - 1st of 14 giving 13lb to Kierans Bridge (20 Mar Southwell RF 0455).
**G M McCourt [2-8] Dawn Build Ltd (from Lord Huntingdon [0-5] Oct 1997).*

REBECCA JAY BHB 55f **RR 69f** 5080^{5}
2 b f Rambo Dancer (CAN) 8.4f **(59)**-Having Fun(Hard Fought) 8.8f **(62)**
Form - 00505
Record 1998 - 1st:0 2nd:0 3rd:0 Ran:5
1998 Turf 0-4: (5f, 6f, 7f 2) (sft, gd 2, frm) 1998 AW 0-1: (6f) (Fibr)
Average filly. Turf high 69. **M G Meagher [0-5] B Collier.*

REBEL COUNTY (IRE) BHB 60f75a **RR 59f 75a** 5120^{4}
5 b m Maelstrom Lake 8.8f **(53)** - Haven Bridge (Connaught) 7.7f **(63)**
Form - 000007212514000004
Record 1998 - 1st:2 2nd:2 3rd:0 Ran:18
Pre1998 - 1st:7 2nd:6 3rd:3 Ran:42
Win Prizemoney £43,971 *Total Prizemoney* £58,726
Wins * **1998** Aug Epsom (G-F) H 8.5f 61 65
* **1998** Jly Bath (GD) H 8f 54 58
* 1996 Oct Haydoc (SFT) H 8.1f 84 88 <
* 1996 Spt Ayr (G-F) H 10f 80 80
* 1996 Aug Epsom (GD) H 8.5f 69 75
1996 Jun Cheste (G-F) C 10.3f 53+
1996 May Leices (G-S) C 8f 60
1996 May Newmar (GD) C 8f 57
1995 Spt Lingfi (G-F) 6f 76
1998 Turf 2-18: (8f 1-11, 9f 1-4, 10f, 12f 2) (sft, gd 2-9, g-f 3, frm 4, hrd)
Average filly, effective 8 to 10f, acts on gd, has worn blinkers, likes left handed tracks, likes tight tracks. Turf high 65 - also 1st of 12 getting 3lb from Hyde Park (9 Aug Epsom RF 3481). She will pay her way again when dropped a few pounds. An effective sort on left-handed tracks with a bit of cut in the ground.
**A Bailey [5-45] Showtime Ice Cream Concessionaire (from M C Pipe [1-3] Jun 1996).*

REBEL TIGER (IRE) BHB 58f **RR 64f** 3619^{2}
2 b c Desse Zenny (USA) 12f **(53)** - Rebel's Lyric (USA) (Mutineer (USA))
Form - 05442
Record 1998 - 1st:0 2nd:1 3rd:0 Ran:5
Win Prizemoney £0 *Total Prizemoney* £1,007
1998 Turf 0-5: (6f, 7f 4) (gd 2, g-f, frm 2)
Average colt, has worn blinkers. Turf high 64 - 2nd of 13 to Lashkari Gold (14 Aug Catterick 7f frm RF 3619).
**B S Rothwell [0-5] Jim Browne.*

REBUFF RR 95f $4470I^{2}$
3 ch f Kris 10f **(75)** - Throw Away Line (USA) (Assert) 10.6f **(85)**
Form - 2
1998 Turf 0-1: (10f) (gd)
Currently very useful filly. (1st run) - 2nd of 4 giving 5lb to Snow Polina (20 Spt Toulouse 10f gd RF 4470I).
**H-A Pantall in FR [0-1] Sheikh Mohammed Al Maktoum.*

RECOGNITION BHB 65f58a **RR 60f 58a** 4117^{10}
3 b c Rock City 8.8f **(62)** - Star Face (African Sky) 7.9f **(63)**
Form - 6415P350
Record 1998 - 1st:1 2nd:0 3rd:1 Ran:8
Pre1998 - 1st:0 2nd:1 3rd:1 Ran:5
Win Prizemoney £1,838 *Total Prizemoney* £3,327
Wins 1998 *Jan Lingfi (STD) S 7f 66* <
1998 Turf 0-2: (6f, 8f) (g-s, gd) 1998 AW 1-6: (5f, 7f 1-4, 9f) (Equi 1-2, Fibr 4)
Scopey, average colt, effective 6 to 7f, acts on g-f - acts on Equi, has worn blinkers. Turf high 45. AW high 66 - 1st of 8 from Figawin (13 Jan Lingfield RF 0080).
**R A Fahey [0-4] Tommy Staunton (from Miss Gay Kelleway [0-1] Mar 1998).*

RECORD LOVER (IRE) BHB 22f25a **RR 44f 25a** 283^{12}
8 b g Alzao (USA) 9.8f **(73)** - Spun Gold (Thatch (USA)) 9.8f **(62)**
Form - 0250
Record 1998 - 1st:0 2nd:1 3rd:0 Ran:4
Pre1998 - 1st:3 2nd:3 3rd:6 Ran:45
Win Prizemoney £8,350 *Total Prizemoney* £15,059
Wins * 1996 *Feb Southw (STD) H 16f 36 39*
1998 AW 0-4: (12f 2, 16f 2) (Fibr 4)
Moderate gelding. AW high 24. Inconsistent.
**M C Chapman [1-63] Tony Satchell (from Lord Huntingdon [2-8] Aug 1993).*

RECORD TIME RR 64f 2707^{6}
2 ch f Clantime 6.6f **(57)** - On the Record (Record Token) 6.3f **(53)**
Form - 76
Record 1998 - 1st:0 2nd:0 3rd:0 Ran:2
1998 Turf 0-2: (5f 2) (frm 2)
Currently average filly. Turf high 64. **E J Alston [0-2] Peter Onslow.*

RED AMAZON BHB 74f **RR 77?f** 4756^{11}
2 b g Magic Ring (IRE) 6.5f **(64)** - Lindfield Belle (IRE) (Fairy King (USA)) 7.7f **(59)**
Form - 02700326210
Record 1998 - 1st:1 2nd:3 3rd:1 Ran:11
Win Prizemoney £8,952 *Total Prizemoney* £11,497
Wins * **1998** Spt Hamilt (SFT) H 6f 59 77? <
1998 Turf 1-11: (5f 5, 6f 1-6) (sft, g-s 1-3, gd 3, g-f 3, frm)
Above-average gelding, effective 5 to 6f, acts on g-s to g-f. Turf high 77 - 1st of 13 from Wind In Winnipeg (28 Spt Hamilton RF 4533). **J Berry [1-11] The Red Shirt Brigade Ltd.*

RED APOLLO RR 50f 5139^{13}
2 gr c Petong 7.6f **(58)** - Scarlet Veil (Tyrnavos) 10.1f **(55)**
Form - 00
Record 1998 - 1st:0 2nd:0 3rd:0 Ran:2
1998 Turf 0-2: (6f 2) (g-s, gd)
Currently above-average colt. Turf high 50 (began Oct).
**A C Stewart [0-2] S J Hammond.*

RED BORDEAUX BHB 60f **RR 71f** 4816^{1}
3 b c Alzao (USA) 9.8f **(73)** - Marie de Flandre (FR) (Crystal Palace (FR)) 12.5f **(76)**
Form - 57730541
Record 1998 - 1st:1 2nd:0 3rd:1 Ran:8
Win Prizemoney £2,290 *Total Prizemoney* £3,065
Wins * **1998** Oct Catter (G-S) 12f 64 <
1998 Turf 1-8: (7f 2, 10f 2, 12f 1-2, 15f, 16f) (gd 1-5, g-f, frm 2)
Above-average colt, effective 7f, acts on gd. Turf high 81 (1st run) - 5th of 13 to Chattan (27 Mar Doncaster 7f gd RF 0481).
**B W Hills [1-8] Wafic Said.*

REDBRIDGE (USA) BHB 105f **RR 115+f** 4366^{3}
4 b c Alleged (USA) 11.8f **(81)** - Red Slippers (USA) (Nureyev (USA)) 8.7f **(78)**
Form - 1411453
Record 1998 - 1st:3 2nd:0 3rd:1 Ran:7
Pre1998 - 1st:0 2nd:0 3rd:1 Ran:1
Win Prizemoney £20,393 *Total Prizemoney* £26,394
Wins * **1998** Jun Leices (SFT) L 11.8f 102
* **1998** Jun Doncas (GD) 10.3f 115+ <
* **1998** *Apr Wolver (STD) 12f 99+*
1998 Turf 2-6: (10f 1-2, 11f, 12f 1-2, 13f) (sft, gd 1-1, g-f 1-4) 1998 AW 1-1: (12f 1-1) (Fibr 1-1)
Scopey, high-class colt, effective 10 to 13f, acts on g-f. Turf high 115 - 1st of 6 giving 3lb to Proper Blue (6 Jun Doncaster RF 1771). (1st run). A son of Sun Chariot winner Red Slippers, he won a maiden on the Wolverhampton Fibresand in a canter having been off the track for a year, but possibly found the ground too fast when asked a big question in the Ormonde Stakes. Picked up victories in a minor event at Doncaster and a Leicester Listed event

before proving rather disappointing.
**J H M Gosden [3-8] Sheikh Mohammed.*

RED BROOK LAD BHB 32f **RR 36f** 1468[10]

3 ch g Nomadic Way (USA) - Silently Yours (USA) (Silent Screen (USA)) 8.6f **(65)**
Form - 00
Record 1998 - 1st:0 2nd:0 3rd:0 Ran:2
Pre1998 - 1st:0 2nd:0 3rd:0 Ran:2
1998 Turf 0-2: (10f, 12f) (gd, g-f)
Workmanlike, very moderate gelding. Turf high 8.
**S Dow [0-4] Dr B H Seal.*

RED CAFE (IRE) BHB 58f **RR 62f** 3581[3]

2 ch f Perugino (USA) - Test Case (Busted) 10.2f **(61)**
Form - 4073
Record 1998 - 1st:0 2nd:0 3rd:1 Ran:4
Win Prizemoney £0 *Total Prizemoney* £533
1998 Turf 0-3: (6f 3) (gd 2, frm) 1998 AW 0-1: (6f) (Fibr)
Average filly. Turf high 62 - 3rd of 14 to Bodfari Anna (12 Aug Nottingham 6f gd RF 3581). **P D Evans [0-4] Men Behaving Badly.*

Decent gelding, effective 6 to 7f, acts on frm. Turf high 82 - 1st of 5 from Thank Heavens (15 Jly Catterick RF 2808) - also 1st of 19 giving 5lb to Morning Chorus (19 Aug York RF 3757). His three wins included the valuable seller at York. Has joined David Nicholls.
**D Nicholls [0-2] Geoff Carr (from J Berry [3-8] Aug 1998).*

RED DECEMBER (IRE) **RR 53f** 4576[5]

2 b c Soviet Lad (USA) 9.4f **(63)** - Late Date (Goldhill) 8.5f **(55)**
Form - 05
Record 1998 - 1st:0 2nd:0 3rd:0 Ran:2
1998 Turf 0-2: (8f 2) (g-f, frm)
Currently fair colt. Turf high 53 (began Spt).
**A P Jarvis [0-2] Ambrose Turnbull.*

RED DELIRIUM BHB 95f **RR 93f** 4587[4]

2 b c Robellino (USA) 9.5f **(68)** - Made of Pearl (USA) (Nureyev (USA)) 8.7f **(78)**
Form - 61776285024
Record 1998 - 1st:1 2nd:2 3rd:0 Ran:11
Win Prizemoney £4,581 *Total Prizemoney* £7,142
Wins * 1998 May Goodwo (G-F) 6f 88+ <

Red Charger looked better than plating class at York

RED CHARGER (IRE) BHB 71f **RR 82f** 4519[6]

2 ch g Up and At 'em - Smashing Pet (Mummy's Pet) 7.7f **(60)**
Form - 3154135106
Record 1998 - 1st:3 2nd:0 3rd:2 Ran:10
Win Prizemoney £16,155 *Total Prizemoney* £17,130

Wins	**1998**	Aug York	(G-F)	S	6f	79
	1998	Jly Catter	(FRM)		7f	82 <
	1998	May Redcar	(GD)		5f	67

1998 Turf 3-9: (5f 1-3, 6f 1-2, 7f 1-4) (g-s, gd 1-2, g-f 2, frm 2-3, hrd)
1998 AW 0-1: (6f) (Fibr)
1998 Turf 1-11: (5f 2, 6f 1-5, 7f 3, 8f) (gd 5, g-f 1-2, frm 3, hrd)
Useful colt, effective 6 to 7f, best at 7f, acts on g-f to frm, best on g-f. Turf high 93 - also 1st of 10 from Rhapsodist (20 May Goodwood RF 1359). A useful juvenile, just found wanting at Group level, he failed to get the run of the race on his nursery debut at York, and his form was a little in-and-out afterwards.
**R Hannon [1-11] Terry Neill.*

REDEPLOY BHB 64f **RR 69f** 4779[18]

2 b c Deploy 11.4f **(67)** - Baino Clinic (USA) (Sovereign Dancer (USA))

11.2f **(68)**
Form - 660
Record 1998 - 1st:0 2nd:0 3rd:0 Ran:3
1998 Turf 0-3: (8f 2, 10f) (gd, g-f, frm)
Currently average colt. Turf high 69 (began Spt).
**B R Millman [0-3] Take Six.*

RED FREESIA RR 53f
2567[6]
2 ch f Timeless Times (USA) 6.1f **(56)** - Miss Drummond (The Brianstan) 5.9f **(55)**
Form - 7066
Record 1998 - 1st:0 2nd:0 3rd:0 Ran:4
1998 Turf 0-4: (5f 4) (gd 4)
Fair filly. Turf high 49. **Denys Smith [0-4] Vic Roper.*

RED LAD (IRE) RR 50f
3927[18]
2 ch g Mujtahid (USA) 7.4f **(69)** - Gustavia (IRE) **(79df 83a)** (Red Sunset) 8.2f **(63)**
Form - 0
Record 1998 - 1st:0 2nd:0 3rd:0 Ran:1
1998 Turf 0-1: (7f) (frm)
Currently fair gelding. **R W Armstrong [0-1] Mrs Robert Armstrong.*

RED LEGGINGS BHB 74f RR 74f
5069[11]
3 b f Shareef Dancer (USA) 10.1f **(67)** - Anchorage (IRE) (Slip Anchor) 9.8f **(73)**
Form - 334420
Record 1998 - 1st:0 2nd:1 3rd:2 Ran:6
Pre1998 - 1st:1 2nd:0 3rd:0 Ran:3
Win Prizemoney £3,848 *Total Prizemoney* £7,354
Wins * 1997 Oct Warwic (G-F) 7f 76 <
1998 Turf 0-6: (10f 3, 11f 2, 12f) (gd 2, g-f 3, frm)
Neat, above-average filly, effective 7 to 11f, best at 10f, acts on gd to frm, likes left handed tracks, prefers tight tracks. Turf high 76 - 3rd of 6 getting 5lb from River Beat (28 Jun Goodwood 10f gd RF 2364). Consistent. **J W Hills [1-9] Mrs Claire Smith.*

RED LION BHB 90f RR 90f
4969[6]
2 ch g Lion Cavern (USA) 7.5f **(74)** -Fleur Rouge (Pharly (FR)) 9.8f **(68)**
Form - 141736
Record 1998 - 1st:2 2nd:0 3rd:1 Ran:6
Win Prizemoney £6,038 *Total Prizemoney* £7,362
Wins * 1998 Jun Windso (GD) 5f 83
* 1998 May Redcar (G-F) 5f 89 <
1998 Turf 2-6: (5f 2-2, 6f 3, 7f) (g-s, gd 1-3, frm 1-2)
Useful gelding, effective 5 to 6f, best at 5f, acts on gd to frm, best on gd. Turf high 90 - 3rd of 16 giving 13lb to Achilles Star (7 Oct York 6f gd RF 4703) - also 1st of 9 giving 5lb to Rose's Treasure (25 May Redcar RF 1455). Showed himself to be highly-strung and quirky in his early races. That did not stop him winning two of his first three, but he found things harder under top weight in nurseries later on. He should stay further as a three-year-old and, if he matures mentally, has the ability to win more races.
**J W Payne [2-6] Lhendup Dorji.*

RED MAY (IRE) RR 59f
3032[9]
2 b br f Persian Bold 10f **(69)** - Stay That Way (Be My Guest (USA)) 9.3f **(67)**
Form - 50
Record 1998 - 1st:0 2nd:0 3rd:0 Ran:2
Win Prizemoney £0 *Total Prizemoney* £157
1998 Turf 0-2: (6f, 7f) (frm 2)
Currently fair filly. Turf high 59. **R Hannon [0-2] Terry Neill.*

REDONES (USA) RR 79+f
3995[2]
2 b c Seeking the Gold (USA) 7.4f **(80)** - Red Slippers (USA) (Nureyev (USA)) 8.7f **(78)**
Form - 2
Record 1998 - 1st:0 2nd:1 3rd:0 Ran:1
Win Prizemoney £0 *Total Prizemoney* £1,135
1998 Turf 0-1: (7f) (hrd)
Currently above-average colt. (1st run) - 2nd of 9 to Iscan (31 Aug Newcastle 7f hrd RF 3995). Has joined Godolphin for 1999.
**L M Cumani [0-1] Sheikh Mohammed.*

REDOUBLE BHB 71f RR 84f
5148[19]
2 b c First Trump - Sunflower Seed (Mummy's Pet) 7.7f **(60)**
Form - 63662030
Record 1998 - 1st:0 2nd:1 3rd:2 Ran:8
Win Prizemoney £0 *Total Prizemoney* £1,593
1998 Turf 0-8: (5f, 6f 2, 7f 4, 8f) (g-s, gd 4, g-f 2, frm)
Decent colt, effective 7 to 8f, acts on g-f to frm. Turf high 84 - 2nd of 10 giving 5lb to Canadian Approval (26 Aug Lingfield 8f g-f RF 3889). **R Hannon [0-8] J P Kenny.*

REDOUBTABLE (USA) BHB 73f77a RR 75df 77a
5014[11]
7 b h Grey Dawn II 6.8f **(76)** - Seattle Rockette (USA) (Seattle Slew (USA)) 9.4f **(76)**
Form - 71143700310510706062000
Record 1998 - 1st:3 2nd:1 3rd:2 Ran:21
Pre1998 - 1st:3 2nd:2 3rd:2 Ran:16
Win Prizemoney £37,679 *Total Prizemoney* £75,397
Wins * 1998 Jun Newcas (SFT) H 7f 72 77
* 1998 May Ayr (G-F) H 7f 68 69
* 1998 *Jan Lingfi (STD) H 7f 67 73+*
* 1997 *Dec Wolver (STD) H 6f 60 65+*
1998 Turf 2-17: (5f, 6f 7, 7f 2-7, 8f 2) (sft 2, g-s 1-3, gd 3, g-f 1-6, frm 3)
1998 AW 1-4: (5f, 6f, 7f 1-2) (Equi 1-2, Fibr 2)
Decent horse, effective 6 to 7f, best at 7f, acts on g-s to frm - acts on Equi, has worn blinkers, likes left handed tracks, likes tight tracks, excels at Lingfield. Turf high 77 - 1st of 9 getting 11lb from Kayo (27 Jun Newcastle RF 2343). AW high 80 - 3rd of 16 giving 3lb to Fayik (17 Jan Lingfield 7f Equi RF 0110) - also 1st of 8 getting 17lb from Banzhaf (3 Jan Lingfield RF 0022). Becoming disappointing. He was picked up cheaply by present connections and rewarded them with two impressive victories on sand around new year. He does not seem to have any problem with either All-Weather surface, as he continued to run well against decent opposition. Generally running well on turf since, appreciating the soft ground when winning at Newcastle in June.
**D W Chapman [4-25] David Chapman (from R Hannon [2-12] Aug 1994).*

RED PEPPER (IRE) BHB 50f50a RR 44f 50a
3806[11]
3 br g Chilibang 7f **(55)** - Magic Flame (Sayf El Arab (USA)) 7.1f **(54)**
Form - 872252150020000
Record 1998 - 1st:1 2nd:3 3rd:0 Ran:12
Pre1998 - 1st:0 2nd:1 3rd:1 Ran:12
Win Prizemoney £2,200 *Total Prizemoney* £5,104
Wins * 1998 *Feb Lingfi (SLW) 6f 61* <
1998 Turf 0-4: (5f, 6f, 7f, 8f) (gd 2, frm 2) 1998 AW 1-8: (5f, 6f 1-4, 7f 2, 8f) (Equi 1-6, Fibr 2)
Workmanlike, average gelding, effective 5f, acts on g-f. Turf high 44. AW high 61. Becoming disappointing.
**P Howling [1-24] Rosefield UK Ltd.*

RED PHANTOM (IRE) BHB 60f45a RR 18f 45a
175[6]
6 ch g Kefaah (USA) 11.2f **(64)** - Highland Culture (Lomond (USA)) 8.8f **(65)**
Form - 236
Record 1998 - 1st:0 2nd:0 3rd:1 Ran:2
Pre1998 - 1st:3 2nd:1 3rd:5 Ran:17
Win Prizemoney £7,022 *Total Prizemoney* £9,442
Wins * 1997 *Aug Wolver (STD) S 9.4f 52*
* 1995 *Aug Wolver (STD) C 9.4f 69* <
* 1995 *Jly Southw (STD) C 12f 65*
1998 AW 0-2: (12f, 15f) (Fibr 2)
Fair gelding, effective 9 to 12f, - acts on Fibr, has worn blinkers. AW high 48. **S Mellor [3-24] Silver Knight Exhibitions Ltd.*

RED PRAIRIE (USA) BHB 100f RR 102f
4739[6]
2 b c El Prado (IRE) 8f **(74)** - Kates Delimma (USA) (Tank's Prospect (USA))
Form - 01183136
Record 1998 - 1st:3 2nd:0 3rd:2 Ran:8
Win Prizemoney £22,489 *Total Prizemoney* £33,261
Wins * 1998 Aug York (G-F) L 5f 93 <
* 1998 May Pontef (G-F) 6f 82
* 1998 May Hamilt (G-S) 5f 78
1998 Turf 3-8: (5f 2-5, 6f 1-3) (g-s 1-2, gd 2, g-f 2, frm 2-2)
Very useful colt, effective 5 to 6f, best at 5f, acts on g-f to frm, best on g-f. Turf high 102 - 3rd of 13 to Sheer Viking (12 Spt Doncaster 5f g-f RF 4242) - also 1st of 7 from Trinity (19 Aug York RF 3756). He is very tough and stood up well to a busy season. The best of his wins came in a Listed event at York in August, but he per-

formed equally well when placed in the Group Two Flying Childers Stakes at Doncaster the following month. He may not improve much as a three-year-old, but has already done his job.
**M Bell [3-8] Terry Neill.*

RED RABBIT BHB 75f55a **RR 77f 55a** 3638[13]

3 b f Suave Dancer (USA) 10.7f **(68)** - Turban (Glint of Gold) 9.3f **(66)**
Form - 536550

Record	**1998 -**	1st:0	2nd:0	3rd:1	Ran:6
	Pre1998 -	1st:0	2nd:2	3rd:0	Ran:3

Win Prizemoney £0 *Total Prizemoney* £2,459
1998 Turf 0-1: (10f) (gd) 1998 AW 0-5:(7f, 8f 2, 10f, 14f) (Equi 2, Fibr 3)
Unfurnished, above-average filly, effective 7f, acts on gd. AW high 51. Becoming disappointing. **B W Hills [0-9] S P Tindall.*

RED RAJA BHB 55f52a **RR 63?f 52a** 3403[9]

5 b g Persian Heights 10.5f **(61)** - Jenny Splendid (John Splendid) 8.1f **(62)**
Form - 0

Record	**1998 -**	1st:0	2nd:0	3rd:0	Ran:1
	Pre1998 -	1st:0	2nd:1	3rd:0	Ran:10

Win Prizemoney £0 *Total Prizemoney* £627
1998 Turf 0-1: (12f) (frm)
Average gelding. Inconsistent. **P Mitchell [3-21] J R Ali.*

RED RAMONA BHB 90f **RR 91f** 5151[5]

3 b c Rudimentary (USA) 8.2f **(66)**-Apply (Kings Lake (USA)) 10.8f **(67)**
Form - 2156045

Record	**1998 -**	1st:1	2nd:1	3rd:0	Ran:7

Win Prizemoney £2,406 *Total Prizemoney* £4,273

Wins	**1998**	Jun	Folkes	(GD)		12f	75	<

1998 Turf 1-7: (10f, 12f 1-5, 13f) (g-s 2, gd 1-2, g-f 2, frm)
Strong, useful colt, effective 12f, acts on g-s to g-f. Turf high 99 - 5th of 6 to Dark Moondancer (20 Jun Ascot 12f g-f RF 2137). A keen sort, he was the comfortable winner of a Folkestone maiden and has shown mixed form in better company since. Just lacks a turn of foot, and might not stay thirteen furlongs. Changed hands for 50,000 gns at Newmarket autumn sales, and ran well for his new connections in the November Handicap.
**J Akehurst [0-1] A D Spence (from R Charlton [1-6] Oct 1998).*

RED RISK BHB 25f41a **RR 29f 41a** 4990[11]

3 ch g Risk Me (FR) 8f **(53)** - Red Sails (Town And Country) 8.1f **(68)**
Form - 76367860800

Record	**1998 -**	1st:0	2nd:0	3rd:1	Ran:9
	Pre1998 -	1st:0	2nd:0	3rd:0	Ran:6

Win Prizemoney £0 *Total Prizemoney* £414
1998 Turf 0-6: (8f 2, 10f 4) (sft, g-s, gd, frm 3) 1998 AW 0-3: (7f 2, 8f) (Fibr 3)
Light-framed, very moderate gelding. Turf high 29. AW high 35.
**P W Harris [0-15] The Red Connection.*

RED ROSES (IRE) RR 5159a[7]

2 f
Form - 7

Record	**1998 -**	1st:0	2nd:0	3rd:0	Ran:1

1998 Turf 0-1: (8f) (hvy)
Currently very poor filly - 7th of 9 to Jordy (7 Nov San Siro 8f hvy RF 5159a). **L M Cumani [0-1].*

RED SEA RR 105f 5162a[12]

2 b c Barathea (IRE) - Up Anchor (IRE) (Slip Anchor) 9.8f **(73)**
Form - U11720

Record	**1998 -**	1st:2	2nd:1	3rd:0	Ran:6

Win Prizemoney £38,175 *Total Prizemoney* £78,579

Wins	*** 1998**	Jun	Ascot	(G-S)	G3	6f	105	<
	*** 1998**	May	York	(GD)		6f	93+	

1998 Turf 2-5: (5f, 6f 2-3, 8f) (sft, g-s, gd 2-3) 1998 AW 0-1: (9f) (Dirt)
Pattern-class colt, effective 6 to 8f, acts on g-s to gd, often wears blinkers. Turf high 105 - 1st of 17 from Be The Chief (16 Jun Ascot RF 2013). After an inauspicious debut - he unseated Richard Quinn - this colt developed into a smart juvenile. Blinkers helped him concentrate when winning the Coventry Stakes at Royal Ascot and they remained part of his armoury. There is no doubting his bravery, however, as was shown by a battling second place on atrocious ground in the Grand Criterium at Longchamp in October. Disappointing in the Breeders' Cup Juvenile, where he lost the race due breaking out of the stalls and never really fired. If he matures mentally, he should win a Group race at around a mile in 1999. **P F I Cole [2-6] H R H Prince Fahd Salman.*

RED SHIFT (IRE) BHB 67f **RR 72f** 4127[5]

3 b g Night Shift (USA) 8.1f **(73)** - Histoire Douce (USA) (Chief's Crown (USA)) 9.8f **(72)**
Form - 55

Record	**1998 -**	1st:0	2nd:0	3rd:0	Ran:2
	Pre1998 -	1st:0	2nd:0	3rd:0	Ran:1

1998 Turf 0-2: (6f 2) (frm 2)
Strong, currently above-average gelding. Turf high 72 (began Aug).
**D R C Elsworth [0-2] Mrs R F Lowe (from R Hannon [0-1] Oct 1997).*

RED SPECTRUM (IRE) BHB 60f **RR 58f** 4814[8]

2 ch g Rainbows For Life(CAN) 9.3f **(64)**-Theda(Mummy's Pet) 7.7f **(60)**
Form - 788

Record	**1998 -**	1st:0	2nd:0	3rd:0	Ran:3

1998 Turf 0-3: (5f, 6f, 8f) (g-s, gd, frm)
Currently fair gelding, has worn blinkers. Turf high 58 (began Spt).
**J Berry [0-3] The Red Shirt Brigade Ltd.*

REDSPET BHB 20f25a **RR 24f 25a** 234[8]

4 ch f Tina's Pet 7.4f **(56)** - Manabel (Manado) 9.6f **(63)**
Form - 088

Record	**1998 -**	1st:0	2nd:0	3rd:0	Ran:2
	Pre1998 -	1st:0	2nd:0	3rd:0	Ran:11

1998 AW 0-2: (5f, 8f) (Fibr 2)
Little account filly, has worn blinkers.
**S R Bowring [0-13] A H Ripley.*

REDSWAN BHB 74f68a **RR 76f 68a** 2916[2]

3 ch g Risk Me (FR) 8f **(53)** - Bocas Rose (Jalmood (USA)) 10.1f **(52)**
Form - 5312

Record	**1998 -**	1st:1	2nd:1	3rd:1	Ran:4
	Pre1998 -	1st:0	2nd:0	3rd:0	Ran:2

Win Prizemoney £4,045 *Total Prizemoney* £5,837

Wins	*** 1998**	Jun	Newmar	(GD)	C	8f	67+	<

1998 Turf 1-3: (7f, 8f 1-2) (g-f 1-1, frm 2) 1998 AW 0-1: (8f) (Fibr)
Leggy, above-average gelding, effective 7 to 8f, acts on g-f to frm. Turf high 76 - 2nd of 11 getting 6lb from Huntswood (18 Jly Newmarket 7f frm RF 2916) - also 1st of 12 giving 13lb to Shalyah (27 Jun Newmarket RF 2349). Facile winner of a Newmarket claimer, at a time the yard was just returning to form. Can hold his own in better company. **S C Williams [1-6] P Geoghan.*

RED SYMPHONY BHB 70f **RR 72f** 4813[8]

2 b f Merdon Melody 6.8f **(56)** - Woodland Steps (Bold Owl) 8.5f **(45)**
Form - 412134618

Record	**1998 -**	1st:3	2nd:1	3rd:1	Ran:9

Win Prizemoney £7,144 *Total Prizemoney* £8,497

Wins	*** 1998**	Spt	Mussel	(GD)	H	5f	60	72	<
	1998	May	Mussel	(G-S)	S	5f		55	
	1998	*Apr*	*Wolver*	*(STD)*	*S*	*5f*		*48+*	

1998 Turf 2-7: (5f 2-7) (gd 1-5, frm 1-2) 1998 AW 1-2: (5f 1-2) (Fibr 1-2)
Above-average filly, effective 5f, acts on frm. Turf high 72 - 1st of 17 getting 9lb from Charlie Girl (14 Spt Musselburgh RF 4253). AW high 48. **I Semple [1-4] W Edward (from J Berry [2-5] Jun 1998).*

RED TIARA (USA) RR 64+f 5071[7]

2 b br f Mr Prospector (USA) 8.6f **(88)** - Heart of Joy (USA) (Lypheor) 12f **(71)**
Form - 7

Record	**1998 -**	1st:0	2nd:0	3rd:0	Ran:1

1998 Turf 0-1: (7f) (gd)
Currently average filly. **Sir Michael Stoute [0-1] Cheveley Park Stud.*

RED TIME BHB 40f26a **RR 44f 26a** 114[10]

5 br g Timeless Times(USA) 6.1f **(56)**-Crimson Dawn(Manado) 9.6f **(63)**
Form - 00

Record	**1998 -**	1st:0	2nd:0	3rd:0	Ran:1
	Pre1998 -	1st:0	2nd:0	3rd:2	Ran:19

Win Prizemoney £0 *Total Prizemoney* £905
1998 AW 0-1: (7f) (Fibr)
Moderate gelding, has worn blinkers.
**M S Saunders [0-25] M S Saunders.*

Red Sea at Royal Ascot

RED TULLE (USA) BHB 66f **RR 66df** 3990[5]
3 b f A P Indy (USA) - Namaqua (USA) (Storm Bird (CAN)) 10.3f **(74)**
Form - 355
Record 1998 - 1st:0 2nd:0 3rd:1 Ran:3
Win Prizemoney £0 *Total Prizemoney* £532
1998 Turf 0-3: (8f 2, 10f) (gd, frm 2)
Workmanlike, currently average filly, has worn blinkers. Turf high 66 (began Jly). **Sir Michael Stoute [0-3] Cheveley Park Stud.*

RED VENUS (IRE) BHB 65f58a **RR 62?f 58a** 4834[3]
2 ch f Perugino (USA) - Reflection Time (IRE) (Fayruz)
Form - 7030663
Record 1998 - 1st:0 2nd:0 3rd:2 Ran:7
Win Prizemoney £0 *Total Prizemoney* £898
1998 Turf 0-4: (5f 4) (g-s, gd 3) 1998 AW 0-3: (5f 3) (Fibr 3)
Average filly, mostly wears blinkers. Turf high 62. AW high 60. **J Berry [0-7] The Red Shirt Brigade Ltd.*

REEFA'S MILL (IRE) BHB 39f **RR 40f** 2534[4]
6 b g Astronef 7.9f **(59)** - Pharly's Myth (Pharly (FR)) 9.8f **(68)**
Form - 4
Record 1998 - 1st:0 2nd:0 3rd:0 Ran:1
Pre1998 - 1st:0 2nd:3 3rd:2 Ran:15
Win Prizemoney £0 *Total Prizemoney* £5,671
1998 Turf 0-1: (18f) (gd)
Moderate gelding, has worn blinkers. Becoming disappointing. **B J Llewellyn [1-3] David Lewis (from J Neville [0-9] Aug 1996).*

REFERENDUM (IRE) BHB 95f **RR 97f** 4675[5]
4 b c Common Grounds 8.1f **(66)** - Final Decision (Tap On Wood) 10.3f **(65)**
Form - 0205
Record 1998 - 1st:0 2nd:1 3rd:0 Ran:4
Pre1998 - 1st:1 2nd:3 3rd:1 Ran:8
Win Prizemoney £4,513 *Total Prizemoney* £63,559
Wins * 1996 Aug Goodwo (GD) 6f 94 <
1998 Turf 0-4: (5f, 6f 2, 7f) (sft, g-f 3)
Scopey, very useful colt. Turf high 97 (began Aug). High-class at two, he had a curtailed campaign in '97 and finished down the field on his return from a long absence at York in August. Was proving hard to place, but if anyone can find the key it is David Nicholls, whose yard he joined following 39,000 gns sale in the autumn. **G Lewis [1-12] Highclere Thoroughbred Racing Ltd.*

REFINED (IRE) BHB 91f **RR 93df** 4315[6]
3 b f Statoblest 6.4f **(63)** - Annsfield Lady (Red Sunset) 8.2f **(63)**
Form - 06
Record 1998 - 1st:0 2nd:0 3rd:0 Ran:2
Pre1998 - 1st:2 2nd:0 3rd:0 Ran:3
Win Prizemoney £6,808 *Total Prizemoney* £6,871
Wins * 1997 Oct Catter (SFT) H 5f 85 93+ <
* 1997 Spt Kempto (GD) 5f 76+
1998 Turf 0-2: (5f, 6f) (gd, frm)
Scopey, useful filly. Turf high 69 (began Aug). A half-sister to Pipe Major, she won twice at two but did not appear in '98 until finishing down the field off topweight in a competitive handicap at the Ebor meting. **L M Cumani [2-5] Sheikh Mohammed.*

REFUSE TO LOSE BHB 92f98a **RR 95f 98a** 3219[11]
4 ch c Emarati (USA) 6.6f **(63)** - Petrol (Troy) 10.4f **(68)**
Form - 1422142180
Record 1998 - 1st:3 2nd:3 3rd:0 Ran:10
Pre1998 - 1st:1 2nd:2 3rd:0 Ran:8
Win Prizemoney £76,869 *Total Prizemoney* £99,437
Wins * **1998** Jun Ascot (G-S) H 8f 83 95
* **1998** *May Lingfi (STD) H 8f 90 98* <

* 1998 *Feb Lingfi (SLW) H 8f 76 89*
* 1996 Oct Leices (GD) 6f 73+

1998 Turf 1-6: (7f, 8f 1-4, 10f) (gd 1-3, g-f, frm 2) 1998 AW 2-4: (8f 2-3, 10f) (Equi 2-3, Fibr)

Scopey, very useful colt, effective 7 to 10f, best at 8f, acts on gd to frm - acts on AW, best on Equi, prefers left handed tracks, prefers tight tracks, excels at Lingfield. Turf high 95 - 1st of 32 getting 28lb from Fly To The Stars (17 Jun Ascot RF 2056). AW high 98 - 1st of 11 giving 21lb to Danzino (13 May Lingfield RF 1203) - also 1st of 10 getting 9lb from Plan For Profit (28 Feb Lingfield RF 0380). Consistent. Made a big impression on his Lingfield Equitrack debut in February of this year, winning twice and finishing runner-up in the Winter Derby. He translated that good form on to turf, culminating in an all-the-way win in the Royal Hunt Cup, but found the extended ten furlongs stretching his stamina at York. Fair effort at Goodwood on his final start.

**J M P Eustace [4-18] J C Smith.*

REGAL ACADEMY (IRE) BHB 46f RR 51f 4572[6]

4 b f Royal Academy (USA) 7.8f **(77)** - Polistatic (Free State) 8.7f **(61)**

Form - 507F56

Record	**1998** -	1st:0	2nd:0	3rd:0	Ran:6
	Pre1998 -	1st:0	2nd:0	3rd:0	Ran:1

1998 Turf 0-6: (8f, 9f, 10f 2, 11f, 12f) (gd, g-f 2, frm 3)

Unfurnished, fair filly. Turf high 51. **C A Horgan [0-7] Mrs B Sumner.*

REGAL ARROW BHB 35f RR 44f 1216[14]

3 br g Superlative 8.8f **(57)** - A Little Hot (Petong) 6.6f **(58)**

Form - 000

Record	**1998** -	1st:0	2nd:0	3rd:0	Ran:3
	Pre1998 -	1st:0	2nd:0	3rd:0	Ran:2

1998 Turf 0-3: (7f 2, 10f) (gd 2, frm)

Scopey, moderate gelding, has worn blinkers. Turf high 13.

**P Shakespeare [0-3] Regal (Witney) Ltd (from A G Foster [0-2] Nov 1997).*

REGAL BRIDGET BHB 65f RR 64f 4527[4]

3 ch f Gildoran 11.6f **(58)** - Bridge Street Lady (Decoy Boy) 6.7f **(56)**

Form - 523074

Record	**1998** -	1st:0	2nd:1	3rd:1	Ran:6

Win Prizemoney £0 *Total Prizemoney* £1,906

1998 Turf 0-6: (10f 4, 12f 2) (g-f 3, frm 3)

Unfurnished, average filly, effective 10 to 12f, best at 10f, acts on g-f to frm, best on frm. Turf high 64 (began Jly) - 3rd of 9 to Cuff (12 Aug Sandown 10f frm RF 3598).

**D R C Elsworth [0-6] M A Wilkins & J Wilkins.*

REGAL EXIT (FR) RR 71f 4745[3]

2 ch c Exit To Nowhere (USA) 8.7f **(77)** - Regalante (Gairloch) 7f **(63)**

Form - 53

Record	**1998** -	1st:0	2nd:0	3rd:1	Ran:2

Win Prizemoney £0 *Total Prizemoney* £1,028

1998 Turf 0-2: (7f, 8f) (gd, frm)

Currently above-average colt. Turf high 71 (began Spt).

**M R Channon [0-2] Brian Buckley.*

REGAL FAN (IRE) BHB 72f RR 61f 3827[10]

2 br f Taufan (USA) 8.3f **(65)**-Regal Rhapsody (Owen Dudley) 8.3f **(61)**

Form - 10

Record	**1998** -	1st:1	2nd:0	3rd:0	Ran:2

Win Prizemoney £2,490 *Total Prizemoney* £2,490

Wins 1998 Jly Warwic (G-F) 7f 61 <

1998 Turf 1-1: (7f 1-1) (frm 1-1) 1998 AW 0-1: (6f) (Fibr)

Currently average filly. (1st run) - 1st of 15 from Lady Muck (11 Jly Warwick RF 2732).

**D T Thom [0-1] T Mustafa (from C Drew [1-1] Jly 1998).*

REGALO BHB 62f RR 58f 1315[11]

3 b c Nalchik (USA) 12.6f **(44)** - Stardrop (Starch Reduced) 11.5f **(52)**

Form - 00

Record	**1998** -	1st:0	2nd:0	3rd:0	Ran:2
	Pre1998 -	1st:0	2nd:0	3rd:1	Ran:8

Win Prizemoney £0 *Total Prizemoney* £826

1998 Turf 0-2: (5f, 8f) (gd, frm)

Workmanlike, fair colt, effective 5f, acts on gd. Turf high 46.

**D M Hyde [0-10] The Spanish Connection.*

REGAL PATRIARCH (IRE) BHB 70f RR 67f 1320[4]

3 br c Marju (IRE) 9.2f **(76)**-Early Rising (USA)(Grey Dawn II) 11.1f **(72)**

Form - 74

Record	**1998** -	1st:0	2nd:0	3rd:0	Ran:2
	Pre1998 -	1st:0	2nd:0	3rd:0	Ran:3

1998 Turf 0-2: (10f, 12f) (sft, frm)

Workmanlike, average colt. Turf high 67.

**J L Dunlop [0-5] Peter Winfield.*

REGAL PHILOSOPHER BHB 83f RR 78+f 5005[2]

2 b c Faustus (USA) 9.1f **(54)** - Princess Lucy (Local Suitor (USA)) 8.4f **(67)**

Form - 3022

Record	**1998** -	1st:0	2nd:2	3rd:1	Ran:4

Win Prizemoney £0 *Total Prizemoney* £3,910

1998 Turf 0-4: (7f 2, 8f 2) (sft, g-f 2, frm)

Above-average colt. Turf high 78 (began Spt) - 2nd of 11 giving 5lb to Nicely (27 Oct Bath 8f sft RF 5005).

**J W Hills [0-4] Trajan Partners.*

REGAL REVOLUTION BHB 90f RR 90f 3661[19]

3 br f Hamas (IRE) 8f **(72)** - True Queen (USA) (Silver Hawk (USA)) 8.6f **(70)**

Form - 06740

Record	**1998** -	1st:0	2nd:0	3rd:0	Ran:5
	Pre1998 -	1st:5	2nd:1	3rd:0	Ran:7

Win Prizemoney £34,054 *Total Prizemoney* £37,543

Wins	* 1997 Spt Ayr	(G-S) L	6f		97 <
	* 1997 Spt Salisb	(G-S)	6f		82
	* 1997 Aug Windso	(G-F) H	6f	78	82
	* 1997 Jly Ayr	(G-F) H	6f		79
	* 1997 Jly Folkes	(GD)	6f		59+

1998 Turf 0-5: (6f 3, 7f, 8f) (sft, gd, g-f 2, frm)

Workmanlike, useful filly, effective 6 to 7f, acts on gd, has worn blinkers, excels at Ayr. Turf high 90. A wonderful bargain at just 2,500 guineas, she won five times at two including a Listed race at Ayr. She was not up to Pattern company as a three-year-old, and returned to handicaps later on. She did not look to have trained on, but owes connections nothing.

**P T Walwyn [5-12] S W E J Slack.*

REGAL SONG (IRE) BHB 62f RR 59f 5144[3]

2 b c Anita's Prince 6f **(62)** - Song Beam (Song) 7.2f **(61)**

Form - 057633

Record	**1998** -	1st:0	2nd:0	3rd:2	Ran:6

Win Prizemoney £0 *Total Prizemoney* £961

1998 Turf 0-6: (5f 2, 6f 3, 8f) (sft, gd 2, g-f 3)

Fair colt, effective 6f, acts on gd, has worn blinkers. Turf high 59 (began Jly) - 3rd of 14 giving 11lb to Vale of Leven (27 Oct Redcar 6f gd RF 5012). **T J Etherington [0-6] J C Smith.*

REGAL SPLENDOUR (CAN) BHB 60a RR 14f 4458[16]

5 ch g Vice Regent (CAN) 7.3f **(70)** - Seattle Princess (USA) (Seattle Slew (USA)) 9.4f **(76)**

Form - 00707000000

Record	**1998** -	1st:0	2nd:0	3rd:0	Ran:10
	Pre1998 -	1st:1	2nd:2	3rd:0	Ran:11

Win Prizemoney £2,427 *Total Prizemoney* £4,387

Wins 1997 *Feb Lingfi (STD) H 8f 60 62* <

1998 Turf 0-9: (8f 2, 9f 2, 10f 3, 12f, 16f) (g-s, gd, g-f, frm 6) 1998 AW 0-1: (10f) (Equi)

Little account gelding, effective 8f, - acts on Equi, likes left handed tracks. Turf high 14.

**J J Bridger [0-11] Miss Sarah Jones (from R J O'Sullivan [1-7] May 1997).*

REGENCY TIMES (USA) BHB 53f RR 68f 4255[3]

3 b g Vice Regent (CAN) 7.3f **(70)** - High Noon Ridge (USA) (Raja Baba (USA)) 10f **(64)**

Form - 4444500753

Record	**1998** -	1st:0	2nd:0	3rd:1	Ran:10

Win Prizemoney £0 *Total Prizemoney* £1,352

1998 Turf 0-10: (5f, 6f, 7f 7, 8f) (gd 3, g-f 2, frm 5)

Average gelding, has worn blinkers. Turf high 68.

**T D Easterby [0-10] Times of Wigan.*

REGENT RR 41f 4968[11]
3 ch g Zafonic (USA) 9f **(83)** - Queen Midas (Glint of Gold) 9.3f **(66)**
Form - 00
Record 1998 - 1st:0 2nd:0 3rd:0 Ran:2
1998 Turf 0-2: (8f, 10f) (sft, g-f)
Workmanlike, currently moderate gelding. Turf high 41 (began Oct). **C P Morlock [0-2] P J Morgan.*

REGGIE BUCK (USA) BHB 48f53a **RR 39f 53a** 1114[16]
4 b br g Alleged (USA) 11.8f **(81)** - Hello Memphis (USA) (Super Concorde (USA)) 10.9f **(66)**
Form - 30600
Record 1998 - 1st:0 2nd:0 3rd:1 Ran:5
Pre1998 - 1st:0 2nd:1 3rd:1 Ran:3
Win Prizemoney £0 *Total Prizemoney* £2,521
1998 Turf 0-2: (10f, 14f) (g-s, frm) 1998 AW 0-3: (8f, 11f, 16f) (Equi 2, Fibr)
Neat, fair gelding, effective 8f, acts on gd, has worn blinkers. Turf high 29. AW high 55.
**J L Harris [0-3] L Pipe (from R J O'Sullivan [0-6] Mar 1998).*

REGGIE BYRNE RR 4641[10]
2 b c Mon Tresor 7.9f **(60)** - Failand (Kala Shikari) 8.4f **(54)**
Form - 0
Record 1998 - 1st:0 2nd:0 3rd:0 Ran:1
1998 Turf 0-1: (6f) (g-f)
Currently very poor colt. **R Dickin [0-1] Mrs Tessa Byrne.*

REGIUS RR 12f 2477[17]
4 b g Ron's Victory (USA) 9.2f **(52)** - Shirlstar Investor (Some Hand) 9f **(50)**
Form - 00
Record 1998 - 1st:0 2nd:0 3rd:0 Ran:2
1998 Turf 0-2: (8f 2) (gd, hrd)
Currently poor gelding. Turf high 12.
**Mrs S Lamyman [0-2] John Purcell.*

REHAAB BHB 47f58a **RR 44f 58a** 3513[P]
5 b m Mtoto 11.5f **(71)** - Top Treat (USA) (Topsider (USA)) 8.3f **(71)**
Form - 183245231207880P
Record 1998 - 1st:1 2nd:2 3rd:1 Ran:11
Pre1998 - 1st:2 2nd:5 3rd:1 Ran:25
Win Prizemoney £8,675 *Total Prizemoney* £15,654
Wins * 1998 *Feb Lingfi (SLW) H 12f 55 62 <*
* 1997 *Nov Lingfi (STD) 10f 52*
1996 Jly Nottin (G-F) 10f 61
1998 Turf 0-3: (9f, 11f, 12f) (gd, frm, hrd) 1998 AW 1-8: (10f 4, 12f 1-4) (Equi 1-8)
Average filly, effective 10 to 13f, best at 12f, - acts on Equi, often wears blinkers (very effectively), likes left handed tracks, favours tight tracks, excels at Lingfield. Turf high 44 (began Jly). AW high 63 - 2nd of 7 giving 30lb to Little Miss Ribot (19 Feb Lingfield 10f Equi RF 0314) - also 1st of 6 giving 22lb to Raspberry Sauce (14 Feb Lingfield RF 0293). Inconsistent.
**Miss B Sanders [2-19] Mrs J M Laycock (from D Morris [0-13] Aug 1997).*

REIMEI BHB 49f **RR 50f** 1833[13]
9 b g Top Ville 11f **(71)** - Brilliant Reay (Ribero) 9.3f **(56)**
Form - 0
Record 1998 - 1st:0 2nd:0 3rd:0 Ran:1
Pre1998 - 1st:3 2nd:1 3rd:2 Ran:18
Win Prizemoney £14,277 *Total Prizemoney* £16,838
Wins 1996 Jun Newmar (G-F) H 12f 65 67 <
1994 Jly Sandow (G-F) H 11.4f 63 65
1994 May Leices (GD) H 11.8f 58 62
1998 Turf 0-1: (12f) (gd)
Fair gelding, has worn blinkers.
**K C Comerford [0-5] Dr A Kimber (from R Akehurst [3-16] Apr 1997).*

REINE CERISE BHB 62f **RR 70f** 4987[6]
3 b f Shareef Dancer (USA) 10.1f **(67)** - Sakura Queen (IRE) (Woodman (USA)) 9f **(74)**
Form - 77621747006
Record 1998 - 1st:1 2nd:1 3rd:0 Ran:11
Win Prizemoney £3,488 *Total Prizemoney* £4,677
Wins * 1998 Jun Beverl (GD) H 12f 69 70 <
1998 Turf 1-11: (7f, 8f, 10f 3, 11f, 12f 1-5) (sft 2, g-s, gd 1-3, g-f 4, frm)
Neat, above-average filly, effective 10 to 12f, acts on gd to g-f, has worn blinkers, favours tight tracks. Turf high 70 - 1st of 5 getting 13lb from Winsome George (10 Jun Beverley RF 1867). Becoming disappointing. **S P C Woods [1-11] Ian Deane.*

REINHARDT (IRE) BHB 33f26a **RR 34tf 26a** 3748[5]
5 b g Bluebird (USA) 7.9f **(71)** - Rhein Bridge (Rheingold) 10.4f **(62)**
Form - 605
Record 1998 - 1st:0 2nd:0 3rd:0 Ran:3
Pre1998 - 1st:1 2nd:2 3rd:5 Ran:26
Win Prizemoney £2,232 *Total Prizemoney* £9,451
Wins 1997 Jun Beverl (G-F) H 5f 40 44 <
1998 Turf 0-2: (12f, 16f) (gd 2) 1998 AW 0-1: (11f) (Fibr)
Very moderate gelding, effective 5 to 7f, acts on frm, has worn blinkers. Turf high 34.
**L R Lloyd-James [0-9] Nelson Unit Ltd (from D Nicholls [1-11] Spt 1997).*

REJECTED BHB 66f **RR 63f** 1712[6]
3 b c Puissance 7.1f **(60)** - Dalby Dancer (Bustiki) 8.7f **(78)**
Form - 0056
Record 1998 - 1st:0 2nd:0 3rd:0 Ran:4
Pre1998 - 1st:1 2nd:0 3rd:1 Ran:7
Win Prizemoney £3,420 *Total Prizemoney* £4,221
Wins * 1997 Jun Haydoc (G-F) 5f 86+ <
1998 Turf 0-4: (5f, 6f, 7f 2) (gd 2, frm 2)
Scopey, average colt, effective 5 to 6f, acts on g-f. Turf high 63. Inconsistent. **R Hannon [1-11] T G Holdcroft.*

RELATE BACK (IRE) BHB 78f **RR 74f** 4959[5]
2 ch c College Chapel - Kip's Sister (Cawston's Clown) 8f **(60)**
Form - 755
Record 1998 - 1st:0 2nd:0 3rd:0 Ran:3
1998 Turf 0-3: (6f, 7f 2) (g-f, frm, hrd)
Currently above-average colt. Turf high 74 (began Aug).
**B W Hills [0-3] J Hanson.*

RELATIVE SHADE BHB 86f **RR 74f** 5156a[7]
2 b f Distant Relative 7f **(69)** - In the Shade (Bustino) 10.4f **(64)**
Form - 81157
Record 1998 - 1st:2 2nd:0 3rd:0 Ran:5
Win Prizemoney £9,699 *Total Prizemoney* £9,699
Wins * 1998 Aug Epsom (G-F) H 7f 72 74 <
*** 1998** Aug Lingfi (G-F) 6f 68
1998 Turf 2-5: (6f 1-3, 7f 1-1, 8f) (sft, gd, g-f 2-2, frm)
Above-average filly. Turf high 74 (began Aug) - 7th of 12 getting 3lb from Magiustrina (3 Nov Capannelle 8f gd RF 5156a) - also 1st of 13 giving 1lb to Schnitzel (31 Aug Epsom RF 3982). Her wins at Lingfield and Epsom were narrow, but she showed real battling qualities and seems to get seven well enough. Never figured in two runs in Italy. **Lord Huntingdon [2-5].*

RELIABLY WON BHB 60f **RR 73df** 4862[12]
3 b f Sabrehill (USA) 8.5f **(64)** - Way to Go (Troy) 10.4f **(68)**
Form - 0828060
Record 1998 - 1st:0 2nd:1 3rd:0 Ran:7
Win Prizemoney £0 *Total Prizemoney* £1,246
1998 Turf 0-6: (8f, 10f 5) (sft, gd 2, g-f 3) 1998 AW 0-1: (12f) (Fibr)
Scopey, above-average filly, effective 10f, acts on gd, likes tight tracks. Turf high 73 - 2nd of 21 getting 18lb from Coulthard (15 Jun Windsor 10f gd RF 2009).
**D Marks [0-4] C R Buttery (from B W Hills [0-3] Jun 1998).*

REMARKABLE STYLE (USA) RR 98f 3536a[6]
3 b f Danzig (USA) 8.1f **(88)** - Ophidian (USA)
Form - 4026
1998 Turf 0-4: (5f, 6f 3) (sft 2, gd, g-f)
Very useful filly, effective 6f, acts on g-s, has worn blinkers. Turf high 98. Inconsistent. **J S Bolger in IRE [2-8] Henryk de Kwiatkowski.*

RENAISSANCE LADY (IRE) RR 56f 4110[10]
2 ch f Imp Society (USA) 7.1f **(63)** - Easter Morning (FR) (Nice Havrais (USA))
Form - 00
Record 1998 - 1st:0 2nd:0 3rd:0 Ran:2
1998 Turf 0-2: (7f 2) (frm 2)

Currently fair filly. Turf high 56 (began Aug).
**T R Watson [0-2] Alan Wright.*

RENGE (IRE) RR 93+f
5109a[7]

4 ch f Generous (IRE) 11.5f **(82)** - Lyphard's Lady (USA)
Form - 7622517
1998 Turf 1-7: (9f, 10f 1-5, 12f) (g-s, gd 1-5, g-f)
Useful filly, effective 9 to 12f, best at 10f, acts on g-s to g-f, best on gd, prefers right handed tracks, and likes Curragh. Turf high 93 - 1st of 11 giving 5lb to Darina (17 Spt Gowran Park RF 4426a). Consistent. **J Oxx in IRE [3-14] Takahiro Wada.*

RENNYHOLME BHB 36f34a RR 35f 34a
3479[5]

7 ch g Rich Charlie 5.9f **(50)** - Jacqui Joy (Music Boy) 6.8f **(57)**
Form - 448507045

Record	**1998 -**	1st:0	2nd:0	3rd:0	Ran:6
	Pre1998 -	1st:1	2nd:3	3rd:3	Ran:46

Win Prizemoney £2,070 *Total Prizemoney* £7,150
Wins 1996 *Mar Wolver (STD) S 5f 58 <*
1998 Turf 0-3: (5f, 6f 2) (g-s, g-f, frm) 1998 AW 0-3: (5f 2, 6f) (Fibr 3)
Very moderate gelding, effective 5f, acts on gd to hrd, often wears blinkers. Turf high 35. AW high 35. He has won only once in his long career, which just about says it all.
**K A Ryan [0-2] The Gloria Darley Racing Partnership (from A B Mulholland [0-14] Apr 1998).*

RENOWN BHB 66f67a RR 68f 67a
3950[3]

6 b g Soviet Star (USA) 8.6f **(74)** - Starlet (Teenoso (USA)) 9.9f **(72)**
Form - 0013

Record	**1998 -**	1st:1	2nd:0	3rd:1	Ran:4
	Pre1998 -	1st:4	2nd:3	3rd:1	Ran:18

Win Prizemoney £16,667 *Total Prizemoney* £21,307

Wins								
	* **1998**	Aug	Salisb	(G-F)	H	9.9f	62	68
	* 1996	Jun	Bright	(FRM)	H	11.9f	64	69
	* 1996	*Mar*	*Lingfi*	*(STD)*	*H*	*10f*	*67*	*73 <*
	* 1995	*Dec*	*Lingfi*	*(STD)*	*H*	*10f*	*65*	*65*
	* 1995	*Feb*	*Lingfi*	*(STD)*		*7f*		*51*

1998 Turf 1-3: (9f, 10f 1-1, 12f) (gd 1-2, g-f) 1998 AW 0-1: (10f) (Equi)
Above-average gelding, effective 9 to 12f, best at 10f, acts on gd to frm - acts on Equi, favours tight tracks. Turf high 68 (began Jly) - 1st of 11 giving 10lb to Silver Groom (12 Aug Salisbury RF 3588). He has apparently suffered from many niggling problems in recent seasons, but bounced back to form with a victory over ten furlongs at Salisbury in August.
**Lord Huntingdon [5-22] D H Caslon Partners.*

RENZO (IRE) BHB 83f RR 83f
5150[1]

5 b g Alzao (USA) 9.8f **(73)** - Watership (USA) (Foolish Pleasure (USA)) 8.9f **(72)**
Form - 5082501

Record	**1998 -**	1st:1	2nd:1	3rd:0	Ran:7
	Pre1998 -	1st:2	2nd:3	3rd:3	Ran:13

Win Prizemoney £14,996 *Total Prizemoney* £24,003

Wins								
	* **1998**	Nov	Doncas	(SFT)	H	16.5f	78	83
	1997	Spt	Kempto	(GD)	H	14.4f	79	86 <
	1996	Nov	Redcar	(G-F)	H	11f	77	83

1998 Turf 1-7: (14f 3, 15f, 16f, 17f 1-1, 18f) (gd 1-5, frm 2)
Decent gelding, effective 12 to 17f, acts on gd to frm, best on gd, has worn blinkers, excels at Kempton, likes Sandown. Turf high 83 - 1st of 14 giving 17lb to Bridie's Pride (7 Nov Doncaster RF 5150). He possesses the ability to win a decent race but carries his head awkwardly and may not be one to trust entirely. Made a good start for his new trainer when taking a Doncaster handicap.
**J L Harris [1-1] Cleartherm Ltd (from Mrs A J Perrett [1-13] Oct 1998).*

REPERTORY BHB 106f RR 108f
5054a[3]

5 b g Anshan 8.2f **(63)** - Susie's Baby (Balidar) 7.9f **(63)**
Form - 2722101423

Record	**1998 -**	1st:2	2nd:4	3rd:1	Ran:10
	Pre1998 -	1st:2	2nd:3	3rd:1	Ran:19

Win Prizemoney £59,375 *Total Prizemoney* £97,696

Wins								
	* **1998**	Aug	Epsom	(G-F)	H	5f	98	106
	* **1998**	Jly	Currag	(G-S)	LH	5f		107 <
	* 1997	Apr	Newbur	(G-F)	H	5.2f	88	88
	1995	May	Salisb	(GD)		5f		85+

1998 Turf 2-10: (5f 2-9, 6f) (hvy, gd 1-3, g-f 1-5, frm)
Pattern-class gelding, effective 5f, acts on hvy to g-f, excels at Newbury. Turf high 108 - 3rd of 7 to Bishops Court (25 Oct Longchamp 5f hvy RF 5054a) - also 1st of 11 getting 3lb from Carhue Lass (12 Jly Curragh RF 2804a). He is an absolute flying machine and very hard to catch when on song. Just 0.42 seconds outside the rather dubious five furlong world record when winning at Epsom in August, he could spring a surprise in a Group race next season.
**M S Saunders [3-21] M S Saunders (from M R Channon [1-8] Oct 1996).*

REPOSE (IRE) BHB 30f RR 33df
4920[15]

3 gr f Posen (USA) 8.6f **(59)**-Dream Trader (Auction Ring (USA)) 8.6f **(65)**
Form - 005070

Record	**1998 -**	1st:0	2nd:0	3rd:0	Ran:6
	Pre1998 -	1st:0	2nd:0	3rd:0	Ran:2

1998 Turf 0-6: (6f, 7f, 8f 2, 11f, 14f) (g-s 2, gd, frm 2, hrd)
Neat, very moderate filly. Turf high 33.
**G R Oldroyd [0-8] Ms Janet McLeod.*

REPTON BHB 55f52a RR 64f 52a
5016[3]

3 ch g Rock City 8.8f **(62)** - Hasty Key (USA) (Key To The Mint (USA)) 9.4f **(75)**
Form - 010063

Record	**1998 -**	1st:1	2nd:0	3rd:1	Ran:6
	Pre1998 -	1st:0	2nd:0	3rd:0	Ran:3

Win Prizemoney £3,162 *Total Prizemoney* £3,458
Wins * **1998** Jly Redcar (G-S) H 10f 50 58+ <
1998 Turf 1-5: (7f, 8f, 9f, 10f 1-2) (gd 1-4, frm) 1998 AW 0-1: (12f) (Fibr)
Leggy, average gelding, effective 10f, acts on gd, prefers left handed tracks, likes tight tracks. Turf high 64 - 3rd of 4 getting 4lb from My Desperado (27 Oct Redcar 10f gd RF 5016) - also 1st of 6 giving 2lb to My Bet (1 Jly Redcar RF 2451).
**Mrs A Swinbank [1-9] Mrs Julie Martin.*

REPUBLIC (IRE) BHB 68f RR 70f
4651[4]

2 b c Anita's Prince 6f **(62)** - Sweet Finale (Sallust) 8.4f **(63)**
Form - 455304

Record	**1998 -**	1st:0	2nd:0	3rd:1	Ran:6

Win Prizemoney £0 *Total Prizemoney* £684
1998 Turf 0-6: (5f 5, 6f) (gd 2, g-f 2, frm 2)
Above-average colt, effective 5 to 6f, best at 5f, acts on gd to frm, best on frm. Turf high 70 - 3rd of 6 giving 16lb to Tempramental (31 Aug Chepstow 5f gd RF 3979). **R Hannon [0-6] Michael Pescod.*

REQUESTOR BHB 82f RR 83f
1219[15]

3 br c Distinctly North (USA) 7.4f **(63)** - Bebe Altesse (GER) (Alpenkonig (GER)) 10.8f **(76)**
Form - 70

Record	**1998 -**	1st:0	2nd:0	3rd:0	Ran:2
	Pre1998 -	1st:0	2nd:3	3rd:2	Ran:6

Win Prizemoney £0 *Total Prizemoney* £4,568
1998 Turf 0-2: (7f, 8f) (gd, g-f)
Decent colt, effective 6f, acts on g-f to frm. Turf high 74.
**J G FitzGerald [0-8] Marquesa de Moratalla.*

RERAISE (USA) RR
5164a[1]

3 b g Danzatore (CAN) 9f **(59)**-Get Us To Paris (USA) (Policeman (FR))
Form - 1
1998 AW 1-1: (6f 1-1) (Dirt 1-1)
Currently top-class gelding. (1st run) - 1st of 14 from Grand Slam (7 Nov Churchill Downs RF 5164a). Brilliant American speed merchant, beaten just once prior to his all-the-way victory in the Breeders' Cup Sprint.
**C Dollase in USA [1-1] B Fey & M Han & C Dollase.*

RESALAH BHB 83f RR 80f
4673[1]

2 ch f Zafonic (USA) 9f **(83)** -Ghzaalh(USA) (Northern Dancer) 9.6f **(80)**
Form - 31

Record	**1998 -**	1st:1	2nd:0	3rd:1	Ran:2

Win Prizemoney £3,330 *Total Prizemoney* £3,846
Wins * **1998** Oct Redcar (g-s) 6f 78 <
1998 Turf 1-2: (6f 1-2) (g-f 1-1, frm)
Currently decent filly. Turf high 80 (1st run) (began Spt) - 3rd of 10 to Truly Bewitched (25 Spt Redcar 6f frm RF 4489) - also 1st of 10 from Fayruzah (6 Oct Redcar RF 4673).
**M P Tregoning [1-2] Hamdan Al Maktoum.*

Repertory scores an easy victory at the Curragh

RESEMBLANCE RR 271[10]
4 b f State Diplomacy (USA) - Pretty Pollyanna (General Assembly (USA)) 10f **(68)**
Form - 0
Record 1998 - 1st:0 2nd:0 3rd:0 Ran:1
1998 AW 0-1: (12f) (Equi)
Currently very poor filly - 10th of 10 getting 5lb from Harik (12 Feb Lingfield 12f Equi RF 0271). *°B Smart [0-1] Mrs V R Smart.*

RESIDUAL VALUE (USA) RR 72+f 4595[9]
2 b c Lear Fan (USA) 10.4f **(80)** - Riverlyph (USA) (Lyphard (USA)) 9.9f **(72)**
Form - 0
Record 1998 - 1st:0 2nd:0 3rd:0 Ran:1
1998 Turf 0-1: (7f) (gd)
Currently above-average colt.
°Sir Michael Stoute [0-1] The Thoroughbred Corporation.

RESIST THE FORCE (USA) BHB 83f65a **RR 85f 65a** 3947[12]
8 br g Shadeed (USA) 7.7f **(72)** - Countess Tully (Hotfoot) 10.5f **(59)**
Form - 351273140
Record 1998 - 1st:2 2nd:1 3rd:1 Ran:7
Pre1998 - 1st:3 2nd:3 3rd:2 Ran:20
Win Prizemoney £17,783 *Total Prizemoney* £29,111
Wins • **1998** Aug Epsom (G-F) 7f 85 <
• **1998** Jun Folkes (GD) H 6f 66 74+
• 1997 Jly Bright (FRM) H 6f 55 68
• 1997 Jly Bright (FRM) 6f 64
• 1997 *May Lingfi (STD) H 8f 55 60*
1998 Turf 2-7: (5f, 6f 1-4, 7f 1-1, 8f) (gd 1-3, g-f 1-3, frm)
Useful gelding, effective 6 to 8f, acts on gd to frm, best on gd, likes left handed tracks, and excels at Brighton. Turf high 85 - 1st of 6 getting 3lb from Salty Jack (9 Aug Epsom RF 3485). Impressive winner at Folkestone first time, he has run well since and was very impressive at Epsom when stepped up to seven.
°C A Cyzer [5-27] Mrs Barbara Hogan.

RESPOND BHB 62f73a **RR 74f 73a** 4883[7]
3 b f Reprimand 8.2f **(63)** - Kina (USA) (Bering) 7.4f **(61)**
Form - 147016855647
Record 1998 - 1st:1 2nd:0 3rd:0 Ran:11
Pre1998 - 1st:1 2nd:0 3rd:2 Ran:8
Win Prizemoney £5,113 *Total Prizemoney* £6,448
Wins • **1998** Jun Salisb (G-F) H 8f 67 74
• 1997 *Dec Lingfi (STD) H 8f 68 78* <
1998 Turf 1-11: (8f 1-5, 9f 3, 10f 3) (g-s, gd 4, g-f 4, frm 1-2)
Leggy, above-average filly, effective 8 to 9f, best at 8f, acts on gd to frm - acts on Equi. Turf high 74 - 1st of 14 giving 9lb to Lauren's Lad (25 Jun Salisbury RF 2279).
°G L Moore [2-19] B V and C J Pennick.

RESTIGNE (FR) BHB 48f **RR 56f** 4671[14]
2 b c Polytain (FR) - Dissidence (IRE) (Dancing Dissident (USA))
Form - 0650

Record 1998 - 1st:0 2nd:0 3rd:0 Ran:4
1998 Turf 0-3: (7f 3) (g-f 3) 1998 AW 0-1: (8f) (Fibr)
Fair colt. Turf high 56 (began Jly). **J W Hills [0-4] Salisbury Farms.*

RESURRECTION (IRE) BHB 39f **RR 20f** 2331[19]

3 b f Midyan (USA) 9.9f **(64)** - Tolstoya (Northfields (USA)) 9f **(72)**
Form - 000
Record 1998 - 1st:0 2nd:0 3rd:0 Ran:3
Pre1998 - 1st:0 2nd:0 3rd:0 Ran:4
1998 Turf 0-3: (6f, 8f, 10f) (gd 2, frm)
Light-framed, little account filly.
**M C Chapman [0-3] Mrs N Gidleywright (from R Hannon [0-4] Oct 1997).*

RETALIATOR BHB 72f **RR 80f** 4820[10]

2 b f Rudimentary (USA) 8.2f **(66)**-Redgrave Design (Nebbiolo)8.1f **(75)**
Form - 63315430
Record 1998 - 1st:1 2nd:0 3rd:3 Ran:8
Win Prizemoney £3,752 *Total Prizemoney* £6,736
Wins * 1998 Jly Leices (GD) H 6f 70 <
1998 Turf 1-7: (5f 2, 6f 1-3, 7f 2) (gd 2, g-f 2, frm 1-3) 1998 AW 0-1: (5f) (Fibr)
Decent filly, effective 6 to 7f, acts on frm. Turf high 80 - 5th of 7 getting 10lb from Minnesota (24 Jly Newmarket 7f frm RF 3077).
**M Bell [1-8] Peter Ward.*

RETENDER (USA) BHB 33f37a **RR 21f 37a** 3135[15]

9 br g Storm Bird (CAN) 8.5f **(82)** - Dandy Bury (FR) (Exbury) 9f **(73)**
Form - 0000
Record 1998 - 1st:0 2nd:0 3rd:0 Ran:3
Pre1998 - 1st:3 2nd:3 3rd:7 Ran:35
Win Prizemoney £13,146 *Total Prizemoney* £23,830
Wins 1994 Jun Newcas (FRM) H 12.4f 63 66
1994 Apr Newcas (GD) H 12.4f 57 66
1998 Turf 0-2: (12f, 14f) (gd, frm) 1998 AW 0-1: (12f) (Equi)
Moderate gelding, has broken blood-vessels. Turf high 21 (began Jly). Becoming disappointing.
**J Pearce [0-9] Jeff Pearce (from Mrs J R Ramsden [2-22] Apr 1995).*

RET FREM (IRE) BHB 49f **RR 53df** 5013[5]

5 b g Posen (USA) 8.6f **(59)** - New Light (Reform) 8.9f **(62)**
Form - 505
Record 1998 - 1st:0 2nd:0 3rd:0 Ran:3
Pre1998 - 1st:2 2nd:1 3rd:1 Ran:11
Win Prizemoney £9,260 *Total Prizemoney* £11,252
Wins 1996 Jly Doncas (G-F) H 8f 65 70 <
1996 Jun Windso (G-F) H 8.3f 58 62
1998 Turf 0-3: (8f, 9f, 11f) (sft, gd, g-f)
Fair gelding. Turf high 53 (began Spt). Inconsistent.
**C Parker [1-11] & Mrs Raymond Anderson Green (from M A Jarvis [2-9] Jly 1996).*

RETURN OF AMIN BHB 97f84a **RR 99f 84a** 4707[6]

4 ch c Salse (USA) 10.9f **(71)** - Ghassanah (Pas de Seul) 9.1f **(67)**
Form - 60616220026
Record 1998 - 1st:1 2nd:3 3rd:0 Ran:11
Pre1998 - 1st:3 2nd:4 3rd:2 Ran:19
Win Prizemoney £49,114 *Total Prizemoney* £78,860
Wins * 1998 Jun Pontef (SFT) H 6f 85 89 <
* 1997 Jun York (G-S) H 6f 66 78
* 1996 *Nov Southw (STD) H 7f 70 82*
* 1996 Nov Folkes (SFT) H 6.9f 61 68
1998 Turf 1-10: (6f 1-7, 7f 3) (sft 2, g-s 1-2, gd 4, g-f, frm) 1998 AW 0-1: (7f) (Fibr)
Scopey, very useful colt, effective 6 to 7f, best at 6f, acts on g-s to frm, best on gd, does well at York. Turf high 99 - 2nd of 12 giving 9lb to Salty Jack (2 Oct Newmarket 7f gd RF 4617). He appreciated the cut in the ground to win the William Hill Trophy at York in '97 and has run some more good races over six furlongs with soft conditions, including when sixth in the Wokingham. Capable of recapturing winning ways when encountering cut in the ground, but might need the Handicapper to relent a little.
**J D Bethell [4-30] Sheikh Amin Dahlawi.*

RETURN OF THE MAC BHB 41a **RR 41a** 306[10]

6 b g Machiavellian (USA) 9.8f **(83)** - Home Truth (Known Fact (USA)) 7.4f **(67)**
Form - 1570
Record 1998 - 1st:1 2nd:0 3rd:0 Ran:4
Win Prizemoney £2,137 *Total Prizemoney* £2,137
Wins * 1998 *Jan Lingfi (STD) C 12f 47 <*
1998 AW 1-4: (10f, 12f 1-2, 13f) (Equi 1-4)
Moderate gelding, has worn blinkers. AW high 47 (1st run) - 1st of 8 getting 18lb from Filial (3 Jan Lingfield RF 0015). Showed nothing in bumpers, but caused a real shock when scoring at 33/1 on his first outing on Equitrack in January, flooring the odds-on Filial in the process. The form looked suspect at the time however, an impression confirmed by his subsequent efforts.
**M R Bosley [1-6] Mrs R Brackenbury.*

RETURN TO BRIGHTON BHB 34f27a **RR 40f 27a** 3958[7]

6 b m Then Again 7.4f **(52)** - Regency Brighton (Royal Palace) 9f **(56)**
Form - 027
Record 1998 - 1st:0 2nd:1 3rd:0 Ran:3
Pre1998 - 1st:1 2nd:1 3rd:1 Ran:20
Win Prizemoney £2,837 *Total Prizemoney* £4,821
Wins * 1996 Jun Ripon (G-F) SH 8f 45 47 <
1998 Turf 0-3: (8f, 10f 2) (g-f 2, frm)
Moderate mare, effective 8 to 10f, acts on g-f, likes tight tracks. Turf high 40 - 2nd of 18 getting 5lb from Rival Bid (25 May Leicester 10f g-f RF 1449).
**J M Bradley [1-23] Alan Purvis (from P C Clarke [0-3] May 1995).*

REUNION (IRE) BHB 100f **RR 100f** 3458[24]

4 br f Be My Guest (USA) 10.2f **(66)** - Phylella (Persian Bold) 9.3f **(66)**
Form - 27050
Record 1998 - 1st:0 2nd:1 3rd:0 Ran:5
Pre1998 - 1st:2 2nd:0 3rd:1 Ran:4
Win Prizemoney £22,442 *Total Prizemoney* £25,430
Wins * 1997 Apr Newmar (GD) G3 7f 113 <
* 1996 May Redcar (G-F) 6f 69+
1998 Turf 0-5: (7f 3, 8f 2) (gd, g-f 3, frm)
Workmanlike, very useful filly, effective 7f, acts on gd. Turf high 100. She was sidelined for a year after finishing unplaced in the 1997 1,000 Guineas, and never threatened to regain the lost momentum as a four-year-old. Her future lies at stud.
**J W Hills [2-9] Highclere Thoroughbred Racing Ltd.*

REVENGE IS SWEET BHB 42f **RR 48f** 4304[16]

3 b c Absalom 7.1f **(56)** - Welsh Secret (Welsh Captain) 5f **(60)**
Form - 07080
Record 1998 - 1st:0 2nd:0 3rd:0 Ran:5
Pre1998 - 1st:0 2nd:0 3rd:0 Ran:2
1998 Turf 0-4: (5f 3, 6f) (g-s, gd 2, frm) 1998 AW 0-1: (5f) (Fibr)
Moderate colt. Turf high 48. **B A McMahon [0-7] Ian Guise.*

REVOLUTION BHB 55f **RR 60f** 4402[19]

4 b c Suave Dancer (USA) 10.7f **(68)** - Sunny Flower (FR) (Dom Racine (FR)) 9.2f **(62)**
Form - 54440
Record 1998 - 1st:0 2nd:0 3rd:0 Ran:5
Win Prizemoney £0 *Total Prizemoney* £501
1998 Turf 0-4: (8f 3, 12f) (sft, g-s, gd, frm) 1998 AW 0-1: (12f) (Fibr)
Average colt. Turf high 60. **R J R Williams [0-5] Entente Cordiale.*

REWARDIA (IRE) BHB 38f63a **RR 47f 63a** 3573[4]

3 b f Petardia 8.2f **(58)** - Riwaya (IRE) (Nishapour (FR)) 9.1f **(61)**
Form - 58247554
Record 1998 - 1st:0 2nd:1 3rd:0 Ran:8
Pre1998 - 1st:0 2nd:0 3rd:2 Ran:6
Win Prizemoney £0 *Total Prizemoney* £2,080
1998 Turf 0-8: (6f, 7f 2, 8f 3, 10f 2) (gd 4, g-f 3, frm)
Light-framed, moderate filly, effective 7f, acts on gd to g-f, has worn blinkers, likes left handed tracks, likes tight tracks. Turf high 59. **P D Evans [0-14] Treble Chance Partnership.*

REX IS OKAY BHB 76f **RR 77f** 5148[1]

2 ch c Mazilier (USA) 8.5f **(56)** - Cocked Hat Girl (Ballacashtal (CAN)) 5.3f **(50)**
Form - 03553311
Record 1998 - 1st:2 2nd:0 3rd:3 Ran:8
Win Prizemoney £12,037 *Total Prizemoney* £13,333
Wins * 1998 Nov Doncas (SFT) H 7f 66 77 <
*** 1998** Oct Leices (HVY) H 7f 59 65

1998 Turf 2-8: (5f, 6f 3, 7f 2-3, 8f) (sft 1-1, g-s, gd 1-6)
Above-average colt, effective 7f, acts on gd. Turf high 77 - 1st of 22 getting 4lb from Nathan's Boy (7 Nov Doncaster RF 5148). Improving. **S R Bowring [2-8] The Belfitt Family.*

REX MUNDI BHB 60f60a **RR 61f 60a** 13[1]

6 b g Gunner B 11.2f **(45)** - Rose Standish (Gulf Pearl) 12f **(54)**
Form - 78311

Record	**1998 -**	1st:1	2nd:0	3rd:0	Ran:1
	Pre1998 -	1st:4	2nd:3	3rd:6	Ran:27

Win Prizemoney £15,472 *Total Prizemoney* £22,995

Wins								
	*** 1998**	*Jan Southw*	*(STD)*	*S*	*11f*		*61*	
	* 1997	*Dec Wolver*	*(STD)*	*S*	*12f*		*56*	
	* 1997	*Oct Wolver*	*(STD)*		*12f*		*66*	<
	* 1997	Jly Cheste	(G-F)	H	15.9f	61	66	<
	* 1996	Spt Ayr	(G-F)	H	10.9f	56	60	

1998 AW 1-1: (11f 1-1) (Fibr 1-1)
Average gelding, effective 11 to 16f, best at 12f, acted on sft to frm - acted on Fibr, had worn blinkers, excelled at Wolverhampton. (1st run) - 1st of 12 from Pickens (2 Jan Southwell RF 0013). Consistent. Showed good form at middle-distances on Fibresand, winning a limited stakes at Wolverhampton in October, and sellers at Wolverhampton and Southwell around new year. (DEAD)
**P D Evans [5-27] J W Littler (from W M Brisbourne [0-1] Aug 1994).*

1998 Turf 1-1: (8f 1-1) (gd 1-1)
Currently useful colt. (1st run) - 1st of 13 from Adnaan (14 Spt Nottingham RF 4257). Came to his Nottingham debut with a big reputation, and justified it with a comfortable win. He is a half-brother to Darazari and Kilimanjaro, from a fine middle-distance family, and is one to follow at three.
**D R Loder [1-1] Maktoum Al Maktoum.*

RHAPSODIST (USA) BHB 100f **RR 95f** 4597a[3]

2 b c Affirmed (USA) 10.3f **(75)** - Secret Rhapsody (USA) (Secreto (USA)) 8.7f **(72)**
Form - 21273

Record	**1998 -**	1st:1	2nd:2	3rd:1	Ran:5

Win Prizemoney £23,875 *Total Prizemoney* £32,796

Wins	*** 1998**	Jun Ascot	(SFT)	L	7f	87	<

1998 Turf 1-5: (6f, 7f 1-3, 8f) (g-s 1-1, gd 2, g-f, frm)
Very useful colt. Turf high 95 - 3rd of 6 to Slickly (22 Spt Chantilly 8f gd RF 4597a) - also 1st of 10 from Compton Admiral (18 Jun Ascot RF 2087). Improved from his debut to land the Chesham at Royal Ascot over an extra furlong, although he may have been a fortunate winner. It was no disgrace at all failing to concede 7lb to newcomer Commander Collins next time but he ran inexplicably poorly at Goodwood. Fair effort at Chantilly on his final start, but looks exposed. **J H M Gosden [1-5] Sheikh Mohammed Al Maktoum.*

Rhapsodist battled on for a game victory at Royal Ascot

REYNOLDS (IRE) **RR 56f** 4959[12]

2 b c Royal Academy (USA) 7.8f **(77)** - In Perpetuity (Great Nephew) 9.9f **(64)**
Form - 0

Record	**1998 -**	1st:0	2nd:0	3rd:0	Ran:1

1998 Turf 0-1: (7f) (frm)
Currently fair colt. **R Charlton [0-1] Lady Rothschild.*

RHAGAAS **RR 94+f** 4257[1]

2 b c Sadler's Wells (USA) 11.3f **(87)** - Darara (Top Ville) 11.7f **(68)**
Form - 1

Record	**1998 -**	1st:1	2nd:0	3rd:0	Ran:1

Win Prizemoney £3,900 *Total Prizemoney* £3,900

Wins	*** 1998**	Spt Nottin	(GD)	8.2f	94+	<

RHAPSODY IN BLUE (IRE) BHB 40f **RR 28f** 3271[13]

3 b g Magical Strike (USA) 5.5f **(61)** - Palace Blue (IRE) (Dara Monarch) 8.8f **(59)**
Form - 000

Record	**1998 -**	1st:0	2nd:0	3rd:0	Ran:3
	Pre1998 -	1st:0	2nd:0	3rd:0	Ran:3

1998 Turf 0-3: (8f, 11f, 12f) (g-f 2, frm)
Leggy, little account gelding. Turf high 28.
**Andrew Turnell [0-6] The Eternal Optimists.*

RHEINBOLD BHB 57f **RR 66f** 4640[5]

4 br g Never so Bold 7.1f **(62)** - Rheinbloom (Rheingold) 10.4f **(62)**
Form - 0567633065

Record	**1998 -**	1st:0	2nd:0	3rd:2	Ran:10

Pre1998 - 1st:1 2nd:2 3rd:0 Ran:7
Win Prizemoney £2,617 *Total Prizemoney* £5,986
Wins * 1997 May Mussel (G-S) 12f 64+ <
1998 Turf 0-9: (7f, 8f, 9f, 10f 2, 12f 4) (g-s, gd, g-f 6, frm) 1998 AW 0-1: (9f) (Fibr)
Lengthy, average gelding, effective 10 to 12f, best at 10f, acts on gd to frm, favours tight tracks. Turf high 75 - 5th of 10 giving 9lb to Break the Rules (5 May Chester 10f g-f RF 1043). Consistent. Has joined Mark Johnston. **T J Etherington [1-17] E Oliver.*

RHEIN HILL (IRE) BHB 54f **RR 61f** 4887[14]

3 b c Danehill (USA) 9.1f **(79)** - Rhein Bridge (Rheingold) 10.4f **(62)**
Form - 4708040
Record 1998 - 1st:0 2nd:0 3rd:0 Ran:7
Pre1998 - 1st:0 2nd:0 3rd:0 Ran:2
Win Prizemoney £0 *Total Prizemoney* £452
1998 Turf 0-7: (7f, 8f, 10f, 12f 4) (g-s, gd, g-f 2, frm 3)
Scopey, average colt. Turf high 63.
**P W Harris [0-9] The Danehill Connection.*

RHEIN LADY BHB 40f **RR 40f** 2627[5]

4 b f Gildoran 11.6f **(58)** - Houston Belle (Milford) 9f **(61)**
Form - 78775
Record 1998 - 1st:0 2nd:0 3rd:0 Ran:5
Pre1998 - 1st:0 2nd:0 3rd:0 Ran:1
Win Prizemoney £0 *Total Prizemoney* £271
1998 Turf 0-5: (7f, 8f, 11f, 12f, 14f) (g-s, gd 2, g-f, frm)
Workmanlike, moderate filly. Turf high 40.
**R Rowe [0-6] The Cinder Syndicate.*

RHINEFIELD BEAUTY (IRE) BHB 31f **RR 13f** 4771[20]

3 ch f Shalford (IRE) 7.8f **(63)**-Humble Mission (Shack (USA)) 5.8f **(53)**
Form - 00000
Record 1998 - 1st:0 2nd:0 3rd:0 Ran:5
Pre1998 - 1st:0 2nd:0 3rd:0 Ran:7
Win Prizemoney £0 *Total Prizemoney* £400
1998 Turf 0-5: (5f 3, 6f, 8f) (sft, g-s, gd 2, frm)
Poor filly. Turf high 13 (began Aug). Becoming disappointing.
**J S Goldie [0-12] Frank Brady.*

RHINE VALLEY (USA) **RR 100f** 4907a[4]

3 b f Danzig (USA) 8.1f **(88)** - Lake Valley (USA) (Mr Prospector (USA)) 8.8f **(78)**
Form - 211124
1998 Turf 3-6: (5f 2-3, 6f 1-3) (sft, gd 1-3, g-f 1-1, frm 1-1)
Very useful filly, effective 5 to 6f, best at 5f, acts on gd to frm, best on gd, has worn blinkers. Turf high 100 - 4th of 9 getting 13lb from Burden Of Proof (17 Oct Curragh 6f gd RF 4907a) - also 1st of 4 getting 12lb from Best Before Dawn (20 Aug Tipperary RF 3863a). Notched up a hat-trick of victories in the Summer, and ran two game races although in defeat at the end of the season. Fast ground is needed for her to show her best, and a decent sprint could be within her grasp. **J Oxx in IRE [3-6] Sheikh Mohammed.*

RIBBLE ASSEMBLY BHB 49f **RR 57f** 4408[7]

3 ch g Presidium 7.5f **(56)** - Spring Sparkle (Lord Gayle (USA)) 8.8f **(62)**

Form - 120857000037
Record 1998 - 1st:1 2nd:1 3rd:1 Ran:12
Pre1998 - 1st:0 2nd:2 3rd:0 Ran:5
Win Prizemoney £3,035 *Total Prizemoney* £6,167
Wins 1998 May Carlis (G-S) H 8f 52 60 <
1998 Turf 1-12: (7f, 8f 1-6, 9f 2, 10f 2, 12f) (gd 1-5, g-f 3, frm 4)
Workmanlike, fair gelding, effective 6 to 8f, best at 8f, acts on gd to frm, best on gd, has worn blinkers. Turf high 61 - 2nd of 7 getting 20lb from Rachaels North (15 May Nottingham 8f frm RF 1249) - also 1st of 18 giving 2lb to Technician (8 May Carlisle RF 1098).
**K A Ryan [0-9] Swan At Whalley Partnership (from R A Fahey [1-8] May 1998).*

RIBBLE PRINCESS BHB 68f **RR 65f** 3086[7]

3 b f Selkirk (USA) 7.9f **(76)** - Ricochet Romance (USA) (Shadeed (USA)) 8.2f **(70)**
Form - 437
Record 1998 - 1st:0 2nd:0 3rd:1 Ran:3
Win Prizemoney £0 *Total Prizemoney* £761
1998 Turf 0-3: (7f, 8f 2) (gd, frm 2)
Leggy, currently average filly. Turf high 65.
**K A Ryan [0-3] Swan At Whalley Partnership.*

RIBBLESDALE BHB 72f **RR 78f** 4883[5]

3 b f Northern Park (USA) 10f **(57)** - Tarib (Habitat) 9.4f **(70)**
Form - 13552675
Record 1998 - 1st:1 2nd:1 3rd:1 Ran:8
Pre1998 - 1st:0 2nd:0 3rd:0 Ran:3
Win Prizemoney £3,340 *Total Prizemoney* £6,583
Wins * **1998** Apr Nottin (SFT) 10f 78+ <
1998 Turf 1-8: (8f 2, 9f, 10f 1-4, 12f) (sft 1-1, g-s, gd 2, g-f 2, frm 2)
Scopey, above-average filly, effective 9 to 10f, best at 10f, acts on sft to gd, best on gd, often wears blinkers, prefers tight tracks. Turf high 78 - 2nd of 20 giving 4lb to Tallulah Belle (30 Jly Goodwood 9f gd RF 3222) - also 1st of 7 from Robin Lane (20 Apr Nottingham RF 0776). She showed little at two, but made a winning reappearance in a modest event at Nottingham in April despite running green. She has since been found out in handicap company, looking a bit one-paced, but was a little unlucky not to score at Glorious Goodwood. A hard ride.
**J L Dunlop [1-11] Cooper (Susan Abbott Racing).*

RIBERAC BHB 95f **RR 90f** 4364[6]

2 b f Efisio 7.7f **(69)** - Ciboure (Norwick (USA)) 7.2f **(56)**
Form - 01356
Record 1998 - 1st:1 2nd:0 3rd:1 Ran:5
Win Prizemoney £3,241 *Total Prizemoney* £5,174
Wins * **1998** Jly Windso (G-F) 5f 74+ <
1998 Turf 1-5: (5f 1-3, 6f 2) (sft, g-s, gd, frm 1-2)
Useful filly. Turf high 90 (began Jly) - 3rd of 7 to Amazing Dream (15 Aug Newbury 5f gd RF 3651). After landing her maiden, she ran a good third in a listed race before competing twice in three days in listed company at the Ayr Western meeting. Has given trouble at the stalls. **W J Haggas [1-5] & Mrs G Middlebrook.*

RICCARTON BHB 60f **RR 61f** 4869[11]

5 b g Nomination 7.3f **(57)** - Legendary Dancer (Shareef Dancer (USA)) 9.9f **(73)**
Form - 101431480
Record 1998 - 1st:3 2nd:0 3rd:1 Ran:9
Pre1998 - 1st:1 2nd:2 3rd:5 Ran:17
Win Prizemoney £12,681 *Total Prizemoney* £18,631
Wins * **1998** Jly Doncas (G-F) H 10.3f 60 61 <
* **1998** Jun Hamilt (GD) H 9.2f 56 57
* **1998** Apr Redcar (SFT) H 11f 52 55+
* 1997 Aug Beverl (GD) H 9.9f 46 52
1998 Turf 3-9: (9f 1-2, 10f 1-4, 11f 1-3) (sft 1-1, gd 3, g-f 2-3, frm 2)
Average gelding, effective 9 to 11f, best at 10f, acts on sft to frm, has worn blinkers, excels at Doncaster and Hamilton. Turf high 61 - 1st of 7 getting 13lb from Tankersley (29 Jly Doncaster RF 3195) - also 1st of 6 giving 3lb to Jona Holley (1 Jun Hamilton RF 1617). Consistent. He had a good season by winning three times in handicap company. Has hung left on occasions.
**P Calver [4-26] Kenneth MacPherson.*

RICH CHOICE BHB 54f **RR 66f** 4304[15]

3 gr f Presidium 7.5f **(56)** - Gratclo (Belfort (FR)) 6.8f **(63)**
Form - 354600
Record 1998 - 1st:0 2nd:0 3rd:1 Ran:6
Pre1998 - 1st:0 2nd:1 3rd:1 Ran:5
Win Prizemoney £0 *Total Prizemoney* £2,579
1998 Turf 0-6: (5f 2, 6f 3, 7f) (gd 3, g-f 2, frm)
Scopey, average filly, effective 6f, acts on frm, has worn blinkers. Turf high 66. Becoming disappointing. A half-sister to the yard's July Stakes winner Rich Ground, she has ability but has failed to settle and hung on occasions. **J D Bethell [0-11] Mrs J E Vickers.*

RICH DOMINION BHB 54f **RR 66f** 5012[8]

2 ch c First Trump - Tiszta Sharok (Song) 7.2f **(61)**
Form - 70507808
Record 1998 - 1st:0 2nd:0 3rd:0 Ran:8
1998 Turf 0-8: (5f 5, 6f 3) (gd 4, g-f, frm 3)
Average colt, has worn blinkers. Turf high 66.
**J D Bethell [0-8] Mrs J E Vickers.*

RICH GLOW BHB 31f45a **RR 33f 45a** 4485[21]

7 b g Rich Charlie 5.9f **(50)** - Mayglow (Sparkling Boy) 5f **(36)**

Form - 06666660000000
Record 1998 - 1st:0 2nd:0 3rd:0 Ran:14
Pre1998 - 1st:6 2nd:8 3rd:4 Ran:78
Win Prizemoney £20,529 *Total Prizemoney* £36,611
Wins * 1997 May Ayr (SFT) H 5f 46 49
* 1996 Aug Pontef (G-F) H 5f 60 58 <
* 1996 Jly Ayr (G-S) H 5f 53 54
* 1995 Jun Ayr (FRM) H 5f 54 55
* 1995 Jun Ayr (G-F) H 5f 50 47
* 1995 May Ayr (G-F) H 5f 47 47
1998 Turf 0-13: (5f 9, 6f 3, 7f) (gd 4, g-f 3, frm 6) 1998 AW 0-1: (6f) (Fibr)
Very moderate gelding, effective 5f, acts on sft to frm, best on gd, has worn blinkers. Turf high 40. **N Bycroft [6-92] M J Bateson.*

RICH IN LOVE (IRE) BHB 85f RR 92f 4819[7]
4 b f Alzao (USA) 9.8f **(73)** - Chief's Quest (USA) (Chief's Crown (USA)) 9.8f **(72)**
Form - 27200781122687
Record 1998 - 1st:2 2nd:4 3rd:0 Ran:14
Pre1998 - 1st:2 2nd:2 3rd:0 Ran:17
Win Prizemoney £23,236 *Total Prizemoney* £35,811
Wins * **1998** Aug Yarmou (G-F) H 7f 72 78 <
* **1998** Jly Ascot (G-F) H 7f 65 71
* 1997 Aug Yarmou (G-F) H 7f 69 75
* 1996 Jun Ripon (G-F) 6f 73
1998 Turf 2-14: (6f 2, 7f 2-8, 8f 2, 10f 2) (gd 5, g-f 2-6, frm 3)
Leggy, useful filly, effective 7f, acts on gd to g-f, has worn blinkers. Turf high 92 - 6th of 14 giving 1lb to Ashraakat (10 Spt Doncaster 7f gd RF 4208). Largely disappointing last season until picking up a valuable ladies' handicap at Ascot. Quickly followed up at Yarmouth and would probably have completed the hat-trick at the same track had it not been for a slipping saddle. Has continued to run very well, and seven furlongs on fast ground look to be her ideal conditions. **C A Cyzer [4-31] R M Cyzer.*

RICHMOND HILL BHB 73f RR 71f 1813[5]
3 b c Sabrehill (USA) 8.5f **(64)** - Mrs Warren (USA) (Hail To Reason) 10.1f **(82)**
Form - 225
Record 1998 - 1st:0 2nd:2 3rd:0 Ran:3
Pre1998 - 1st:0 2nd:0 3rd:0 Ran:1
Win Prizemoney £0 *Total Prizemoney* £1,831
1998 Turf 0-3: (10f, 11f, 12f) (g-s, gd 2)
Workmanlike, above-average colt. Turf high 71 (1st run) - 2nd of 12 to Teroom (21 Apr Pontefract 10f g-s RF 0787).
**B W Hills [0-4] Saif Ali.*

RICH PLAIN (IRE) BHB 39f RR 32f 4530[10]
2 b g Roi Danzig (USA) 10.5f **(62)** - Winter Tern (USA) (Arctic Tern (USA)) 8.9f **(69)**
Form - 000
Record 1998 - 1st:0 2nd:0 3rd:0 Ran:3
1998 Turf 0-3: (6f 2, 8f) (g-s, g-f 2)
Currently very moderate gelding. Turf high 32.
**C F Wall [0-3] The Boardroom Syndicate.*

RICHTER SCALE (USA) RR 110a 5164a[12]
4 b c Habitony
Form - 0
1998 AW 0-1: (6f) (Dirt)
Currently Group-class colt.
**Mary Jo Lohmeier in USA [0-1] Nancy & Richard Kaster & Nathan Fox (from P Byrne in USA [0-1] Nov 1997).*

RIDAIYMA (IRE) BHB 101f RR 100f 3754[6]
4 b f Kahyasi 12.9f **(74)** - Riyda (Be My Guest (USA)) 9.3f **(67)**
Form - 2436
Record 1998 - 1st:0 2nd:1 3rd:1 Ran:4
Pre1998 - 1st:3 2nd:0 3rd:1 Ran:6
Win Prizemoney £56,220 *Total Prizemoney* £75,340
Wins * 1997 Spt Ascot (G-F) H 12f 92 97 <
* 1997 Aug Kempto (GD) H 12f 85 92
* 1997 Jun Chepst (G-F) 12.1f 80
1998 Turf 0-4: (12f 2, 14f 2) (gd, g-f, frm 2)
Scopey, very useful filly, effective 12 to 14f, best at 12f, acts on gd to frm, excels at York. Turf high 100 - 6th of 21 giving 10lb to Tuning (19 Aug York 14f frm RF 3754). Consistent. She was collared close home in a Group Two at San Siro in June and ran three super races in valuable handicaps afterwards. She appeared to be struck into when finishing a brave sixth in the Tote Ebor, and was not seen out again. **L M Cumani [3-10] H H Aga Khan.*

RIDDLE RR 44f 1571[12]
2 ch f Superlative 8.8f **(57)** - Griddle Cake (IRE) **(65df)** (Be My Guest (USA)) 9.3f **(67)**
Form - 500
Record 1998 - 1st:0 2nd:0 3rd:0 Ran:3
1998 Turf 0-3: (5f 2, 6f) (gd 3)
Currently moderate filly. Turf high 44. **P D Evans [0-3] R F F Mason.*

RIDGEWAY (IRE) BHB 107f RR 110f 1042[4]
3 b c Indian Ridge 7.6f **(74)** - Regal Promise (Pitskelly) 8.5f **(53)**
Form - 124
Record 1998 - 1st:1 2nd:1 3rd:0 Ran:3
Pre1998 - 1st:0 2nd:0 3rd:0 Ran:2
Win Prizemoney £4,337 *Total Prizemoney* £10,288
Wins * **1998** Apr Nottin (G-S) 8.2f 90 <
1998 Turf 1-3: (8f 1-2, 12f) (g-s 1-2, g-f)
Well made, Group-class colt. Turf high 110 - 2nd of 6 giving 3lb to Prolix (18 Apr Thirsk 8f g-s RF 0752). He looked a horse with a future when running Prolix to a head at Thirsk in April, but was given a pacemaker's role to Gulland at Chester and was not seen again. We have not seen the best of this attractive colt.
**G Wragg [1-5] Mollers Racing.*

RIDWAN (GER) RR 113f 3424a[4]
5
Form - 4
1998 Turf 0-1: (10f) (sft)
Currently Group-class. (1st run) - 4th of 7 giving 15lb to Elle Danzig (2 Aug Munich 10f sft RF 3424a). Fourth in a Group 1 during August, he is a useful gelding.
**Frau J Mayer in GER [0-1] Frau A Seitz.*

RIFIFI BHB 76f75a RR 80f 75a 4854[14]
5 ch g Aragon 7.7f **(58)** - Bundled Up (USA) (Sharpen Up) 8.3f **(67)**
Form - 07800066114370
Record 1998 - 1st:2 2nd:0 3rd:1 Ran:14
Pre1998 - 1st:5 2nd:0 3rd:1 Ran:21
Win Prizemoney £39,644 *Total Prizemoney* £43,152
Wins * **1998** Aug Sandow (G-F) H 5f 69 72
* **1998** Aug Newbur (G-F) H 6f 71 72
* 1997 Aug Goodwo (G-F) H 6f 71 80 <
* 1997 Aug Newmar (GD) H 6f 64 71
* 1997 Jun Windso (G-F) H 6f 58 61
* *1997 Feb Lingfi (STD) H 5f 60 66*
* *1997 Feb Lingfi (STD) 5f 66*
1998 Turf 2-14: (5f 1-1, 6f 1-12, 7f) (sft, g-s, gd 1-5, g-f 1-4, frm 3)
Decent gelding, likes Lingfield. Turf high 80. Consistent. Kept very busy, he won twice during August, just as he had done in 1997. Six furlongs on fast ground seem to suit him, and he is also very effective over the minimum trip on Equitrack.
**R Ingram [7-33] Brooknight Guarding Ltd (from J L Dunlop [0-2] Oct 1995).*

RIGADOON (IRE) BHB 61f RR 55f 3566[8]
2 b g Be My Chief (USA) 10.2f **(62)** - Loucoum (FR) (Iron Duke (FR)) 8.8f **(60)**
Form - 008
Record 1998 - 1st:0 2nd:0 3rd:0 Ran:3
1998 Turf 0-3: (5f, 6f, 7f) (gd, g-f, frm)
Currently fair gelding. Turf high 55 (began Jly).
**M W Easterby [0-3] Mybank Racing.*

RIGGING RR 50f 3604[11]
2 b f Warning 8.1f **(77)** - Pilot (Kris) 9.5f **(73)**
Form - 0
Record 1998 - 1st:0 2nd:0 3rd:0 Ran:1
1998 Turf 0-1: (5f) (gd)
Currently fair filly. **B W Hills [0-1] R D Hollingsworth.*

RIGHT JOB (IRE) RR 90f 5028a[6]
3 ch c Sharp Victor (USA) 10f **(56)** - Mlle Le Fabuleux (USA)
Form - 11152180586

1998 Turf 3-10:(7f, 8f 1-4, 9f 2-4, 11f)(hvy 1-2, sft1-4, g-s, gd 2, frm 1-1)
Tall, useful colt, effective 8 to 9f, best at 9f, acts on hvy to frm. Turf high 100 - 1st of 5 getting 2lb from Sense Of Honour (12 Apr Cork RF 0694a) - also 1st of 6 getting 2lb from Key Provider (1 Jun Leopardstown RF 1841a). He improved throughout his juvenile campaign, and kept up the good work in the first half of 1998. However, the handicapper got a grip of him in the summer and he is still trying to break free. **P J Flynn in IRE [4-15] Patrick McGinn.*

RIGHT WING (IRE) BHB 100f RR 100f 4700[6]

4 b c In The Wings 11.2f **(77)** - Nekhbet (Artaius (USA)) 9f **(69)**
Form - 3480316
Record 1998 - 1st:1 2nd:0 3rd:2 Ran:7
Pre1998 - 1st:2 2nd:0 3rd:3 Ran:8
Win Prizemoney £26,333 *Total Prizemoney* £45,656
Wins * **1998** Spt Doncas (GD) H 8f 97 100 <
1997 Oct Ayr (SFT) 8f 88+
1997 Jun Ascot (SFT) 8f 89
1998 Turf 1-7: (7f, 8f 1-6) (sft, gd 4, g-f 1-2)
Scopey, very useful colt, effective 8f, acts on sft to frm, has worn blinkers, excels at Doncaster. Turf high 100 - 1st of 12 giving 7lb to Silk St John (12 Spt Doncaster RF 4239). He is not easy to win with and was making his debut in a visor when landing a valuable handicap at Doncaster in September. He enjoys easy ground and has enough ability to pick up a Listed race.
**J L Dunlop [1-7] The Earl Cadogan (from Major W R Hern [2-8] Oct 1997).*

RIGOLETTO BHB 54f RR 58f 4935[12]

3 ch c Machiavellian (USA)9.8f **(83)**-Sally Brown (Posse(USA))8.9f **(61)**
Form - 600
Record 1998 - 1st:0 2nd:0 3rd:0 Ran:3
1998 Turf 0-3: (7f, 8f 2) (gd, frm 2)
Strong, currently fair colt. Turf high 58 (began Jly).
**C W Thornton [0-3] Guy Reed.*

RIMBA (USA) RR 75f 3429[4]

2 b f Dayjur (USA) 6.8f **(79)** - Ristna (Kris) 9.5f **(73)**
Form - 64
Record 1998 - 1st:0 2nd:0 3rd:0 Ran:2
Win Prizemoney £0 *Total Prizemoney* £378
1998 Turf 0-2: (6f 2) (gd, g-f)
Currently above-average filly. Turf high 75 (began Jly) - 4th of 6 to Itlak (7 Aug Ascot 6f g-f RF 3429). Out of a Sun Chariot winner, she ran a better race on her second start.
**J H M Gosden [0-2] George Strawbridge.*

RIMMAS (IRE) RR 35f 3735[16]

2 b c River Falls 8.2f **(56)** - Abbessingh (Mansingh (USA)) 7.4f **(55)**
Form - 00
Record 1998 - 1st:0 2nd:0 3rd:0 Ran:2
1998 Turf 0-2: (6f 2) (g-f, frm)
Currently very moderate colt. Turf high 35 (began Aug).
**B J Meehan [0-2] The Chantilly Partnership.*

RING CHEQUER'S RR 20f 2457[13]

3 ch g Magic Ring (IRE) 6.5f **(64)** - Sharp Silk (Sharpo) 7.7f **(59)**
Form - 0
Record 1998 - 1st:0 2nd:0 3rd:0 Ran:1
1998 Turf 0-1: (7f) (frm)
Light-framed, currently little account gelding.
**T T Clement [0-1] The Chequers.*

RING DANCER BHB 92f RR 89f 5074[8]

3 b c Polar Falcon (USA) 9f **(74)** - Ring Cycle (Auction Ring (USA)) 8.6f **(65)**
Form - 288438
Record 1998 - 1st:0 2nd:1 3rd:1 Ran:6
Pre1998 - 1st:1 2nd:1 3rd:0 Ran:2
Win Prizemoney £3,223 *Total Prizemoney* £7,727
Wins * 1997 Aug Ripon (GD) 6f 93+ <
1998 Turf 0-6: (5f, 6f 4, 7f) (g-s, gd, g-f 2, frm 2)
Lengthy, useful colt, effective 6 to 7f, best at 6f, acts on gd to frm, best on gd. Turf high 95 (1st run) - 2nd of 7 giving 9lb to Zelah (13 May Lingfield 7f frm RF 1201). Consistent. In the frame in sprint handicaps, his stable was out of form for much of the season and he can do quite a bit better. **P J Makin [1-8] Mrs Tricia Mitchell.*

RINGLEADER BHB 48f RR 46f 4408[18]

3 b g Magic Ring (IRE) 6.5f **(64)** - Kinlet Vision (IRE) (Vision (USA)) 9f **(64)**
Form - 0008P0
Record 1998 - 1st:0 2nd:0 3rd:0 Ran:6
Pre1998 - 1st:1 2nd:0 3rd:1 Ran:9
Win Prizemoney £4,110 *Total Prizemoney* £5,179
Wins 1997 Nov Newmar (G-F) S 8f 70 <
1998 Turf 0-6: (7f, 8f 3, 10f 2) (sft, g-f, frm 4)
Light-framed, fair gelding, has broken blood-vessels, effective 7 to 8f, best at 8f, acts on gd to frm, often wears blinkers. Turf high 46. Inconsistent. **N Tinkler [0-6] Axom (from P F I Cole [1-9] Nov 1997).*

RING OF LOVE BHB 74f RR 76f 3624[7]

2 b f Magic Ring (IRE) 6.5f **(64)** - Fine Honey (USA) (Drone) 10.3f **(74)**
Form - 521037
Record 1998 - 1st:1 2nd:1 3rd:1 Ran:6
Win Prizemoney £4,250 *Total Prizemoney* £5,795
Wins * **1998** Jly Cheste (G-F) 5.1f 76 <
1998 Turf 1-6: (5f 1-6) (hvy, g-s, gd, g-f 2, frm 1-1)
Above-average filly, effective 5f, acts on g-f to frm. Turf high 76 - 1st of 7 from Miss Grapette (11 Jly Chester RF 2707).
**M Bell [1-6] K Ratcliffe.*

RINGSIDE JACK BHB 80f RR 83f 4398[4]

2 b c Batshoof 9.5f **(66)** - Celestine **(40f 44a)** (Skyliner) 7.3f **(53)**
Form - 0013204
Record 1998 - 1st:1 2nd:1 3rd:1 Ran:7
Win Prizemoney £3,302 *Total Prizemoney* £5,051
Wins * **1998** Jun Redcar (G-S) 5f 70 <
1998 Turf 1-7: (5f 1-2, 6f 2, 7f 2, 8f) (gd 1-4, g-f, frm 2)
Decent colt, effective 7f, acts on frm. Turf high 83 - 2nd of 10 giving 15lb to Tous Les Jours (13 Aug Beverley 7f frm RF 3601).
**C W Fairhurst [1-7] M J G Partnership.*

RING THE CHIEF BHB 37f35a RR 40f 35a 7[3]

6 b g Chief Singer 8.6f **(62)** - Lomond Ring (Lomond (USA)) 8.8f **(65)**
Form - 03
Record 1998 - 1st:0 2nd:0 3rd:1 Ran:1
Pre1998 - 1st:3 2nd:3 3rd:7 Ran:38
Win Prizemoney £6,283 *Total Prizemoney* £11,683
Wins * 1997 Aug Salisb (G-S) H 7f 34 42 <
* *1997 Jun Southw (STD) SH 7f 33 39*
* *1997 Feb Southw (STD) H 7f 30 34*
1998 AW 0-1: (8f) (Fibr)
Moderate gelding, effective 6 to 10f, best at 10f, acts on gd to hrd - acts on Fibr, best on frm, and excels at Windsor.
**M D I Usher [3-29] G A Summers (from R Akehurst [0-7] Aug 1995).*

RING THE RAFTERS BHB 42f RR 51f 4662[7]

3 b f Batshoof 9.5f **(66)** - Soprano (Kris) 9.5f **(73)**
Form - 77
Record 1998 - 1st:0 2nd:0 3rd:0 Ran:2
Pre1998 - 1st:0 2nd:0 3rd:0 Ran:1
1998 Turf 0-2: (7f, 8f) (gd, frm)
Workmanlike, currently fair filly. Turf high 35 (began Spt).
**B P J Baugh [0-2] Mrs Joan Chrimes (from I A Balding [0-1] Apr 1997).*

RING TRUE RR 53f 4934[15]

2 b f Robellino (USA) 9.5f **(68)** - Dahlawise (IRE) (Caerleon (USA)) 8.6f **(71)**
Form - 05600
Record 1998 - 1st:0 2nd:0 3rd:0 Ran:5
1998 Turf 0-5: (6f 3, 7f, 8f) (g-s, gd 2, g-f, frm)
Fair filly. Turf high 53. **J D Bethell [0-5] The Gordon Partnership.*

RINUS MAGIC BHB 25f25a RR 31f 25a 932[6]

5 ch g Timeless Times (USA) 6.1f **(56)** - Callace (Royal Palace) 9f **(56)**
Form - 7006
Record 1998 - 1st:0 2nd:0 3rd:0 Ran:4
Pre1998 - 1st:0 2nd:0 3rd:0 Ran:5
1998 Turf 0-2: (7f 2) (sft, gd) 1998 AW 0-2: (8f, 11f) (Fibr 2)
Very moderate gelding, has worn blinkers. Turf high 31. AW high 8. **E J Alston [0-9] A M Proos.*

RIO (IRE) BHB 58f51a RR 69f 51a 1459[F]

3 b g Superpower 6.6f **(58)** - Apocalypse (Auction Ring (USA)) 8.6f **(65)**

Form - F
Record 1998 - 1st:0 2nd:0 3rd:0 Ran:1
Pre1998 - 1st:0 2nd:0 3rd:1 Ran:6
Win Prizemoney £0 *Total Prizemoney* £428
1998 Turf 0-1: (6f) (gd)
Lengthy, average gelding, effective 5f, acted on frm. (DEAD)
**P T Dalton [0-1] Mrs Julie Martin (from J Berry [0-6] Oct 1997).*

RIOJA BHB 69f **RR 77df** 4106[14]
3 ch g Anshan 8.2f **(63)** - Executive Flare (Executive Man) 6f **(77)**
Form - 10000
Record 1998 - 1st:1 2nd:0 3rd:0 Ran:5
Pre1998 - 1st:0 2nd:1 3rd:1 Ran:5
Win Prizemoney £8,220 *Total Prizemoney* £9,616
Wins * **1998** Apr Newmar (SFT) H 6f 70 77 <
1998 Turf 1-5: (6f 1-3, 7f 2) (g-s, gd 1-1, g-f, frm 2)
Workmanlike, above-average gelding, effective 6 to 7f, acts on gd to frm. Turf high 77 (1st run) - 1st of 15 getting 14lb from Epsom Cyclone (16 Apr Newmarket RF 0711). He showed ability at two, and made the perfect start to his three-year-old season with a gutsy victory in very soft ground at Newmarket. Most disappointing since. **T P Tate [1-10] Mrs Sylvia Clegg.*

RIPSNORTER (IRE) BHB 30f29a **RR 34f 29a** 4995[7]
9 ch g Rousillon (USA) 10.4f **(69)** - Formulate (Reform) 8.9f **(62)**
Form - 061360700087
Record 1998 - 1st:1 2nd:0 3rd:1 Ran:12
Pre1998 - 1st:3 2nd:5 3rd:2 Ran:43
Win Prizemoney £9,433 *Total Prizemoney* £15,091
Wins * **1998** *Feb Lingfi (SLW) SH 8f 26 36*
1994 Apr Ripon (G-S) H 8f 50 54
1998 Turf 0-3: (8f 2, 9f) (sft, gd, frm) 1998 AW 1-9: (8f 1-7, 9f, 10f) (Equi 1-4, Fibr 5)
Moderate gelding, effective 8f, - acts on Equi, likes left handed tracks. Turf high 34. AW high 43 - also 1st of 10 from Sarum (21 Feb Lingfield RF 0328).
**P D Purdy [1-12] P D Purdy (from K Bishop [0-8] Aug 1996).*

RISCATTO (USA) BHB 42f45a **RR 41f 45a** 4931[3]
4 b g Red Ransom (USA) 8.6f **(83)** - Ultima Cena (USA) (Leonardo da Vinci (FR)) 10f **(55)**
Form - 3
Record 1998 - 1st:0 2nd:0 3rd:1 Ran:1
Pre1998 - 1st:1 2nd:1 3rd:1 Ran:12
Win Prizemoney £1,984 *Total Prizemoney* £3,202
Wins * 1997 Apr Nottin (G-F) SH 10f 48 46 <
1998 Turf 0-1: (10f) (g-s)
Scopey, fair gelding, effective 8 to 10f, acts on g-f - acts on Fibr, has worn blinkers, prefers left handed tracks.
**W R Muir [1-14] F Hope.*

RISE ABOVE (IRE) BHB 31f **RR 39f** 1551[11]
4 b f Simply Great (FR) 11.9f **(61)** - La Tanque (USA) (Last Raise (USA)) 7f **(51)**
Form - 000
Record 1998 - 1st:0 2nd:0 3rd:0 Ran:3
Pre1998 - 1st:0 2nd:0 3rd:0 Ran:1
1998 Turf 0-3: (8f, 10f, 12f) (gd, frm 2)
Scopey, very moderate filly. Turf high 14.
**R Simpson [0-3] G Piper (from T Hind [0-1] Jun 1997).*

RISE 'N SHINE BHB 40f53a **RR 28f 53a** 3584[9]
4 ch f Night Shift (USA) 8.1f **(73)** - Clunk Click (Star Appeal) 9.6f **(65)**
Form - 321323600
Record 1998 - 1st:1 2nd:2 3rd:3 Ran:9
Pre1998 - 1st:0 2nd:3 3rd:2 Ran:15
Win Prizemoney £2,221 *Total Prizemoney* £8,874
Wins * **1998** *Feb Lingfi (SLW) H 5f 42 51* <
1998 Turf 0-1: (5f) (gd) 1998 AW 1-8: (5f 1-5, 6f 3) (Equi 1-7, Fibr)
Strong, fair filly, effective 5 to 6f, best at 5f, - acts on Equi, has worn blinkers, prefers left handed tracks, prefers tight tracks. AW high 55 - 3rd of 8 getting 21lb from Krystal Max (19 Mar Lingfield 5f Equi RF 0444) - also 1st of 10 getting 15lb from Just Dissident (12 Feb Lingfield RF 0272). A half-sister to Crazy Paving, she has been placed many times on turf and sand, but had to wait until her eighteenth race before getting off the mark on the Lingfield Equitrack in February. She has not shown much since however.
**C A Cyzer [1-24] R M Cyzer.*

RISIAT (IRE) RR 108f 4833a[8]
4 b c Waajib 8.9f **(67)** - Ratafia (Rousillon (USA)) 8.2f **(74)**
Form - 738
1998 Turf 0-2: (8f 2) (sft, g-s)
Pattern-class colt, effective 8 to 10f, best at 8f, acts on sft to gd. Turf high 107 (1st run) - 3rd of 11 to Waky Nao (7 Jun San Siro 8f sft RF 1920a). He ran too badly to be true at San Siro in October and is a useful performer on his day. **E Borromeo in ITY [1-7].*

RISING CHORUS (USA) RR 61f 4488[1]
3 b f Gone West (USA) 7.8f **(82)** - Devon Diva (USA) (The Minstrel (CAN)) 10f **(72)**
Form - 1
Record 1998 - 1st:1 2nd:0 3rd:0 Ran:1
Win Prizemoney £3,730 *Total Prizemoney* £3,730
Wins * **1998** Spt Redcar (G-F) 7f 61 <
1998 Turf 1-1: (7f 1-1) (frm 1-1)
Currently average filly. (1st run) - 1st of 14 from Aoife (25 Spt Redcar RF 4488). **J H M Gosden [1-1] K Abdulla.*

RISING MANE BHB 40f **RR 43f** 4249[10]
3 b c Reprimand 8.2f **(63)** - Petastra (Petoski) 5.7f **(62)**
Form - 00
Record 1998 - 1st:0 2nd:0 3rd:0 Ran:2
Pre1998 - 1st:0 2nd:0 3rd:0 Ran:1
1998 Turf 0-2: (8f, 10f) (g-s, frm)
Workmanlike, currently moderate colt. Turf high 26 (began Aug).
**Miss Gay Kelleway [0-2] D R Windebank (from D R C Elsworth [0-1] Oct 1997).*

RISING OF THE MOON (IRE) BHB 87f **RR 83f** 3229[13]
3 gr f Warning 8.1f **(77)**-Dazzlingly Radiant(Try My Best(USA)) 7.6f **(67)**
Form - 50
Record 1998 - 1st:0 2nd:0 3rd:0 Ran:2
Pre1998 - 1st:2 2nd:0 3rd:0 Ran:3
Win Prizemoney £6,634 *Total Prizemoney* £6,854
Wins 1997 Apr Warwic (G-F) 5f 82 <
1997 Mar Doncas (G-F) 5f 81
1998 Turf 0-2: (7f 2) (gd, frm)
Scopey, decent filly. Turf high 80 (began Jly).
**E A L Dunlop [0-2] Miss L Regis (from R Hannon [2-3] Jly 1997).*

RISING SPRAY BHB 68f **RR 70f** 4476[2]
7 ch g Waajib 8.9f **(67)** - Rose Bouquet (General Assembly (USA)) 10f **(68)**
Form - 456302
Record 1998 - 1st:0 2nd:1 3rd:1 Ran:6
Pre1998 - 1st:4 2nd:3 3rd:6 Ran:35
Win Prizemoney £14,201 *Total Prizemoney* £22,499
Wins * 1997 May Salisb (G-F) H 14f 67 71 <
* 1997 Apr Folkes (G-F) H 12f 62 66
* 1996 Aug Folkes (G-F) H 12f 44 53+
* 1996 Aug Folkes (G-F) H 12f 44 52
1998 Turf 0-6: (11f, 12f 3, 14f 2) (gd 2, g-f 2, frm 2)
Above-average gelding, effective 11 to 14f, best at 12f, acts on gd to frm, best on frm, has worn blinkers, likes right handed tracks, likes tight tracks, and excels at Salisbury. Turf high 70 - 2nd of 8 giving 3lb to Happy Go Lucky (25 Spt Folkestone 12f g-f RF 4476). Consistent.
**C A Horgan [4-33] Exors of the late J T Heritage (from P W Harris [0-8] Spt 1994).*

RISK MATERIAL (IRE) RR 114+f 4910a[6]
3 b c Danehill (USA) 9.1f **(79)** - Spear Dance (Gay Fandango (USA)) 8.5f **(59)**
Form - 211378416
1998 Turf 3-9: (9f 1-1, 10f 2-5, 11f, 12f 2) (sft 2, gd 3-5, g-f, hrd)
Group-class colt, effective 8 to 10f, best at 10f, acts on sft to gd, best on gd. Turf high 114 - also 1st of 6 giving 8lb to Dabaya (24 May Curragh RF 1515a). He is tough and consistent, but that is not enough against Group One opposition. Firmly put in his place in the Irish Derby and King George, he is a Listed or Group Three colt and does not stay a mile and a half.
**A P O'Brien in IRE [7-13] Castleblake Racing Syndicate.*

RISK ONE FARTHING RR 29f 1798[6]
2 ch f Risk Me (FR) 8f **(53)** - Farinara (Dragonara Palace (USA)) 6.1f

(55)
Form - 576
Record 1998 - 1st:0 2nd:0 3rd:0 Ran:3
1998 Turf 0-1: (5f) (frm) 1998 AW 0-2: (5f 2) (Fibr 2)
Currently little account filly. AW high 35.
**J Berry [0-3] Brooke Rankin.*

Form - 87333
Record 1998 - 1st:0 2nd:0 3rd:3 Ran:5
Pre1998 - 1st:1 2nd:0 3rd:0 Ran:2
Win Prizemoney £3,347 *Total Prizemoney* £4,561
Wins * 1997 Jun Pontef (GD) 6f 66 <
1998 Turf 0-4: (10f, 12f, 14f 2) (sft, frm 3) 1998 AW 0-1: (15f) (Fibr)

Risk Material had a busy season but lost none of his enthusiasm

RISKY EXPERIENCE BHB 53f55a **RR 70f 55a** 4349[12]
2 ch f Risk Me (FR) 8f **(53)** - First Experience (Le Johnstan) 7.4f **(55)**
Form - 6037685280
Record 1998 - 1st:0 2nd:1 3rd:1 Ran:10
Win Prizemoney £0 *Total Prizemoney* £1,098
1998 Turf 0-8: (5f 5, 6f 3) (sft, g-s, gd 3, g-f, frm 2) 1998 AW 0-2: (5f, 6f) (Fibr 2)
Above-average filly, effective 5f, - acts on Fibr, has worn blinkers. Turf high 70. AW high 66 (began Jly) - 2nd of 16 to Ok Maite (14 Aug Southwell 5f Fibr RF 3642). **P D Evans [0-10] D E Simpson.*

RISKY FLIGHT BHB 25f28a **RR 31f 28a** 4114[21]
4 ch g Risk Me (FR) 8f **(53)** - Stairway to Heaven (IRE) (Godswalk (USA)) 7.3f **(58)**
Form - 0
Record 1998 - 1st:0 2nd:0 3rd:0 Ran:1
Pre1998 - 1st:0 2nd:0 3rd:0 Ran:11
1998 Turf 0-1: (5f) (frm)
Light-framed, very moderate gelding, has worn blinkers.
**A Smith [0-15] Mrs Sheila Oakes.*

RISKY GIRL BHB 50f50a **RR 54f 50a** 3454[3]
3 ro f Risk Me (FR) 8f **(53)** - Jove's Voodoo (USA) (Northern Jove (CAN)) 9.7f **(66)**
Leggy, fair filly, effective 6f, acts on gd, has worn blinkers, likes tight tracks. Turf high 54. Won over hurdles in November.
**M J Heaton-Ellis [1-7] F J Sainsbury.*

RISKY LOVER BHB 36f30a **RR 25tf 30a** 873[8]
5 b m Risk Me (FR) 8f **(53)** - Dawn Love (He Loves Me) 7.9f **(55)**
Form - 08
Record 1998 - 1st:0 2nd:0 3rd:0 Ran:1
Pre1998 - 1st:0 2nd:0 3rd:0 Ran:5
1998 AW 0-1: (8f) (Fibr)
Little account filly, has worn blinkers.
**T T Bill [0-5] Bill Cahill (from D Shaw [0-4] Apr 1997).*

RISKY MONEY BHB 44f **RR 46f** 4765[7]
3 b c Risk Me (FR) 8f **(53)** - Where's the Money (Lochnager) 6f **(59)**
Form - 0007
Record 1998 - 1st:0 2nd:0 3rd:0 Ran:4
1998 Turf 0-3: (7f 2, 8f) (gd 2, g-f) 1998 AW 0-1: (6f) (Fibr)
Workmanlike, moderate colt. Turf high 46.
**V Soane [0-4] The Risky Investors-Four Seasons Racing.*

RISKY VALENTINE BHB 59f59a **RR 72f 59a** 5144[12]
2 ch f Risk Me (FR)8f **(53)**-Mandrake Madam(Mandrake Major)7.6f **(53)**
Form - 31382052357320

Record 1998 - 1st:1 2nd:3 3rd:4 Ran:14
Win Prizemoney £2,343 *Total Prizemoney* £5,486
Wins * **1998** *Apr Wolver (STD) 5f 55* <
1998 Turf 0-8: (5f 5, 6f 3) (sft 2, g-s 2, gd 3, frm) 1998 AW 1-6: (5f 1-1, 6f 3, 7f 2) (Fibr 1-6)
Above-average filly, effective 5 to 6f, acts on g-s. Turf high 72 - 3rd of 8 giving 4lb to Dispol Clan (28 Apr Nottingham 5f g-s RF 0900). AW high 61. **J L Spearing [1-14] T A Pearson.*

RISKY WAY BHB 60f62a **RR 67f 62a** 4376[9]

2 b g Risk Me (FR) 8f **(53)** - Hot Sunday Sport (Star Appeal) 9.6f **(65)**
Form - 656213030
Record 1998 - 1st:1 2nd:1 3rd:2 Ran:9
Win Prizemoney £2,024 *Total Prizemoney* £3,493
Wins * **1998** Jly Catter (GD) S 7f 67 <
1998 Turf 1-7: (5f, 6f 2, 7f 1-4) (gd 2, g-f 1-2, frm 3) 1998 AW 0-2: (5f, 7f) (Fibr 2)
Average gelding, effective 7f, acts on g-f - acts on Fibr. Turf high 67 - 1st of 14 from Lashkari Gold (22 Jly Catterick RF 3019). AW high 68 - 3rd of 9 giving 6lb to Cable Media Boy (7 Aug Wolverhampton 7f Fibr RF 3450).
**B S Rothwell [1-9] J M G Promotions Ltd.*

RISKY WHISKY BHB 53f60a **RR 43f 60a** 4757[9]

3 b g Risk Me (FR) 8f **(53)**-Desert Gem (Green Desert (USA)) 8.6f **(78)**
Form - 054321132000
Record 1998 - 1st:2 2nd:2 3rd:2 Ran:10
Pre1998 - 1st:4 2nd:1 3rd:0 Ran:14
Win Prizemoney £13,780 *Total Prizemoney* £16,356
Wins * **1998** *Mar Wolver (STD) S 6f 73*
* **1998** *Feb Wolver (STD) S 6f 54*
* 1997 *Nov Lingfi (STD) H 5f 63 64*
* 1997 Jun Carlis (GD) S 5f 70
* 1997 *Jun Wolver (STD) S 5f 64*
* 1997 Mar Haydoc (SFT) 5f 76 <
1998 Turf 0-4:(5f 4) (sft, g-s, gd, g-f)1998 AW 2-6:(5f 3, 6f 2-3)(Fibr 2-6)
Light-framed, average gelding, effective 5 to 6f, best at 5f, acts on sft to hrd - acts on Fibr, mostly wears blinkers, likes left handed tracks, likes tight tracks, likes Wolverhampton. Turf high 64. AW high 73 - 1st of 11 giving 11lb to Stravsea (14 Mar Wolverhampton RF 0428). **J Berry [6-24] W J Kelly.*

RISQUE LADY BHB 104f **RR 100f** 4496[1]

3 ch f Kenmare (FR) 9.6f **(76)** - Christine Daae (Sadler's Wells (USA)) 10f **(76)**
Form - 305033231
Record 1998 - 1st:1 2nd:1 3rd:4 Ran:9
Pre1998 - 1st:2 2nd:0 3rd:0 Ran:4
Win Prizemoney £26,600 *Total Prizemoney* £38,484
Wins * **1998** Spt Ascot (GD) LH 8f 97 100 <
* 1997 Spt Haydoc (GD) 5f 96
* 1997 Aug Windso (G-F) 5f 83+
1998 Turf 1-9: (7f 6, 8f 1-3) (gd 1-6, g-f 2, hrd)
Neat, very useful filly, effective 5 to 8f, acts on gd to g-f, best on gd, excels at Doncaster. Turf high 100 - 1st of 17 giving 10lb to Confidante (26 Spt Ascot RF 4496). She ran a series of fine races in the autumn and thoroughly deserved a Listed success at Ascot in September. A tendency to pull hard makes her an uncomfortable ride, but she is willing and does not flinch under pressure.
**P W Harris [3-13] Godwin Hollis Lawren Rice.*

RISSAGA RR 759[P]

4 ch f Meqdaam (USA) - Crosby Place (Crooner) 9.9f **(49)**
Form - P
Record 1998 - 1st:0 2nd:0 3rd:0 Ran:1
Pre1998 - 1st:0 2nd:0 3rd:0 Ran:1
1998 AW 0-1: (12f) (Fibr)
Poor filly. (DEAD)
**T Wall [0-1] D Bunn (from C W Fairhurst [0-1] Nov 1996).*

RITA'S ROCK APE BHB 58f **RR 57f** 4649[3]

3 b f Mon Tresor 7.9f **(60)** - Failand (Kala Shikari) 8.4f **(54)**
Form - 38060323
Record 1998 - 1st:0 2nd:1 3rd:3 Ran:8
Pre1998 - 1st:0 2nd:2 3rd:0 Ran:5
Win Prizemoney £0 *Total Prizemoney* £4,898
1998 Turf 0-8: (5f 8) (g-s, gd, g-f 2, frm 3, hrd)
Neat, fair filly, has broken blood-vessels, effective 5f, acts on gd. Turf high 58. Consistent. She has bags of pace, but is something of a short-runner. **R Brotherton [0-13] Mrs Janet Pearce.*

RITUAL RR 71f 3031[6]

3 ch g Selkirk (USA) 7.9f **(76)** - Pure Formality (Forzando) 7.6f **(59)**
Form - 4306
Record 1998 - 1st:0 2nd:0 3rd:1 Ran:4
Pre1998 - 1st:0 2nd:0 3rd:0 Ran:1
Win Prizemoney £0 *Total Prizemoney* £820
1998 Turf 0-4: (7f 2, 8f 2) (g-s, g-f 2, frm)
Light-framed, above-average gelding. Turf high 71 (1st run) - 4th of 13 to Jalaab (4 May Doncaster 7f g-f RF 1010).
**H Candy [0-5] The Hon Mrs M A Marten.*

RITUAL RUN BHB 57f **RR 56f** 3588[11]

3 b c Rudimentary (USA) 8.2f **(66)** - Roussalka (Habitat) 9.4f **(70)**
Form - 06800
Record 1998 - 1st:0 2nd:0 3rd:0 Ran:5
1998 Turf 0-5: (7f 3, 8f, 10f) (g-s, gd 3, g-f)
Well made, fair colt. Turf high 56. **R Hannon [0-5] Mohamed Suhail.*

RIVAL BID (USA) BHB 36f28a **RR 46f 28a** 3958[8]

10 b g Cannonade (USA) 9.9f **(79)** - Love Triangle (USA) (Nodouble (USA)) 8.8f **(68)**
Form - 0761608608
Record 1998 - 1st:1 2nd:0 3rd:0 Ran:10
Pre1998 - 1st:9 2nd:10 3rd:10 Ran:77
Win Prizemoney £33,591 *Total Prizemoney* £49,418
Wins * **1998** May Leices (GD) SH 10f 37 45
* 1996 Oct Leices (G-F) H 10f 63 67
* 1996 Jun Warwic (FRM) H 10.8f 64 70
* 1996 *Jan Lingfi (STD) 10f 61*
* 1995 Oct Leices (FRM) H 10f 62 68
* 1995 Oct Warwic (G-S) CH 10.8f 57 66
1994 Aug York (G-F) C 8.9f 70
1998 Turf 1-5: (10f 1-4, 12f) (gd 2, g-f 1-2, frm) 1998 AW 0-5: (8f, 9f, 11f, 12f 2) (Fibr 5)
Moderate gelding, effective 10f, acts on g-f, has worn blinkers. Turf high 46 - also 1st of 18 giving 5lb to Return To Brighton (25 May Leicester RF 1449). AW high 40. Inconsistent. He is a character and rarely gets away on level terms, but he can finish well. However, he wins only infrequently these days.
**Mrs N Macauley [6-52] Mrs N Macauley (from M A Jarvis [4-42] Aug 1995).*

RIVENDELL RR 4135[13]

2 b f Saddlers' Hall (IRE) 10.5f **(65)** - Fairy Kingdom (Prince Sabo) 7.2f **(62)**
Form - 0
Record 1998 - 1st:0 2nd:0 3rd:0 Ran:1
1998 Turf 0-1: (8f) (g-f)
Currently very poor filly. **Mrs N Macauley [0-1] Maurice Kirby.*

RIVER BAY (USA) RR 114+f 5167a[11]

5 ch h Irish River (FR) 9f **(77)** - Buckeye Gal (USA) (Good Counsel (USA)) 6.9f **(69)**
Form - 0
1998 Turf 0-1: (12f) (frm)
Group-class colt, has worn blinkers.
**R Frankel in USA [0-1] Ecurie Chalhoub (from J E Hammond in FR [2-4] Apr 1997).*

RIVER BEAT (IRE) BHB 85f **RR 88f** 4986[7]

3 b g River Falls 8.2f **(56)** - Aughamore Beauty (IRE) (Dara Monarch) 8.8f **(59)**
Form - 3711110807
Record 1998 - 1st:4 2nd:0 3rd:1 Ran:10
Pre1998 - 1st:0 2nd:0 3rd:0 Ran:3
Win Prizemoney £15,749 *Total Prizemoney* £16,187
Wins * **1998** Jun Goodwo (GD) H 9.9f 87 88 <
* **1998** Jun Ayr (GD) H 9.1f 71 85
* **1998** Jun Carlis (G-S) H 9.3f 64 76
* **1998** Jun Windso (G-F) H 8.3f 64 71
1998 Turf 4-10:(8f 1-1, 9f 2-3,10f 1-5,12f)(sft, g-s, gd 3-5, g-f 1-1, frm 2)
Workmanlike, useful gelding, effective 9 to 10f, acts on gd, likes right handed tracks. Turf high 88 - 1st of 6 giving 4lb to Sick As A Parrot (28 Jun Goodwood RF 2364) - also 1st of 6 getting 3lb from

Naskhi (19 Jun Ayr RF 2114). This progressive gelding rattled up a four-timer before the run came to an end at the July Meeting. In the Handicapper's grip later. Sold for 18,000 gns in October.
**M H Tompkins [4-13] Grangewood Sales & Marketing.*

RIVERBIRD (IRE) RR 64f 5064[5]
2 b f Mujadil (USA) 7.7f **(70)** - Ruby River (Red God) 8.5f **(65)**
Form - 85
Record 1998 - 1st:0 2nd:0 3rd:0 Ran:2
1998 Turf 0-2: (5f, 6f) (g-f 2)
Currently average filly. Turf high 64 (began Spt).
**Major D N Chappell [0-2] R C C Villers.*

RIVERBLUE (IRE) BHB 89f **RR 91+f** 3937[1]
2 b c Bluebird (USA) 7.9f **(71)** - La Riveraine (USA) **(81f)** (Riverman (USA)) 9.1f **(76)**
Form - 342151
Record 1998 - 1st:2 2nd:1 3rd:1 Ran:6
Win Prizemoney £7,707 *Total Prizemoney* £9,711
Wins * **1998** Aug Thirsk (G-F) H 6f 80 91+ <
* **1998** Aug Catter (GD) 7f 76
1998 Turf 2-6: (5f, 6f 1-2, 7f 1-3) (gd 1-1, g-f 2, frm 1-3)
Useful colt, effective 6f, acts on frm. Turf high 91 - 1st of 11 giving 15lb to The Nurse (28 Aug Thirsk RF 3937). Progressed well, and should have further improvement in him.
**Mrs J R Ramsden [2-6] Mrs Joan Egan.*

RIVER BOY (IRE) BHB 53f **RR 44f** 4337[18]
2 b g River Falls 8.2f **(56)** - Natty Gann (IRE) (Mister Majestic)
Form - 0460
Record 1998 - 1st:0 2nd:0 3rd:0 Ran:4
1998 Turf 0-3: (7f 2, 8f) (g-f, frm 2) 1998 AW 0-1: (7f) (Fibr)
Moderate gelding. Turf high 44 (began Jly).
**P Shakespeare [0-4] Mrs M Shakespeare.*

RIVER CAPTAIN (USA) BHB 54f60a **RR 48f 60a** 4875[1]
5 ch g Riverman (USA) 9.7f **(78)** - Katsura (USA) (Northern Dancer) 9.6f **(80)**
Form - 71530201
Record 1998 - 1st:2 2nd:1 3rd:1 Ran:8
Pre1998 - 1st:1 2nd:0 3rd:0 Ran:5
Win Prizemoney £7,786 *Total Prizemoney* £9,265
Wins * **1998** *Oct Southw (STD) 12f 61*
* **1998** *Mar Southw (STD) H 12f 54 57*
* 1997 *Mar Southw (STD) 11f 62* <
1998 Turf 0-1: (12f) (gd) 1998 AW 2-7: (11f, 12f 2-5, 14f) (Fibr 2-7)
Average gelding, effective 11 to 12f, best at 12f, - acts on Fibr. AW high 61 - 1st of 9 giving 10lb to Nocturne (19 Oct Southwell RF 4875) - also 1st of 10 getting 2lb from Komreyev Dancer (9 Mar Southwell RF 0417). Inconsistent. He has apparently suffered from a back problem, but came back to win his second race at Southwell in March on his second run back after an eight-month break, and added another right at the end of the season. He obviously likes it there.
**D J G MurraySmith [3-12] The Joiners Arms Racing Club Quarndon (from J H M Gosden [0-1] Apr 1996).*

RIVER COURT RR 68f 3252[13]
2 b g River Falls 8.2f **(56)** - Point of Law (Law Society (USA)) 9.9f **(70)**
Form - 06850
Record 1998 - 1st:0 2nd:0 3rd:0 Ran:5
1998 Turf 0-5: (6f, 7f 4) (gd, g-f 3, frm)
Average gelding, has worn blinkers. Turf high 68.
**E A L Dunlop [0-5] The Serendipity Partnership.*

RIVERDANCE (IRE) RR 70f 4937[17]
2 ch c College Chapel - Valmarana (USA) (Danzig Connection (USA)) 8f **(68)**
Form - 50640
Record 1998 - 1st:0 2nd:0 3rd:0 Ran:5
Win Prizemoney £0 *Total Prizemoney* £258
1998 Turf 0-5: (5f 4, 6f) (g-s, gd 2, g-f 2)
Above-average colt, has worn blinkers. Turf high 70.
**K McAuliffe [0-5] Gallagher Equine Ltd.*

RIVER ENSIGN BHB 40f40a **RR 41f 40a** 5128[5]
5 br m River God (USA) 6f **(37)** - Ensigns Kit (Saucy Kit) 6f **(43)**
Form - 33541533420551082446587305
Record 1998 - 1st:2 2nd:2 3rd:3 Ran:22
Pre1998 - 1st:1 2nd:0 3rd:3 Ran:14
Win Prizemoney £10,096 *Total Prizemoney* £14,147
Wins * **1998** Apr Nottin (SFT) H 6.1f 39 44 <
* **1998** *Jan Southw (STD) H 6f 35 36*
* 1997 Aug Thirsk (GD) H 6f 35 41
1998 Turf 1-10: (6f 1-9, 8f) (sft 2, g-s 1-2, gd 2, g-f 2, frm 2) 1998 AW 1-12: (5f 2, 6f 1-7, 7f 2, 8f) (Fibr 1-12)
Moderate filly, effective 6 to 8f, best at 6f, acts on sft to g-f - acts on Fibr, does well at Southwell. Turf high 44 (1st run) - 1st of 20 getting 11lb from Grace (28 Apr Nottingham RF 0899). AW high 40 - 2nd of 7 getting 25lb from Antonias Melody (20 Feb Southwell 6f Fibr RF 0327) - also 1st of 10 getting 28lb from La Petite Fusee (5 Jan Southwell RF 0026). Consistent.
**W M Brisbourne [3-36] Crispandave Racing Associates.*

RIVER FLARE (USA) RR 92f 4724a[3]
3 ch f Riverman (USA) 9.7f **(78)** - Proflare (USA) (Mr Prospector (USA)) 8.8f **(78)**
Form - 3
1998 Turf 0-1: (10f) (sft)
Currently useful filly. (1st run) - 3rd of 11 giving 4lb to Moteck (4 Oct Longchamp 10f sft RF 4724a).
**Mme C Head in FR [0-2] K Abdulla.*

RIVER FRONTIER (IRE) BHB 36f31a **RR 40f 31a** 4544[6]
3 b f Imperial Frontier (USA) 7f **(65)** - River Low (IRE) (Lafontaine (USA)) 8.7f **(62)**
Form - 30845424345356516
Record 1998 - 1st:1 2nd:1 3rd:2 Ran:15
Pre1998 - 1st:0 2nd:0 3rd:1 Ran:9
Win Prizemoney £2,425 *Total Prizemoney* £4,056
Wins * **1998** Aug Ripon (G-F) SH 10f 30 40 <
1998 Turf 1-5: (8f 2, 10f 1-2, 16f) (g-s, gd, g-f 1-2, frm) 1998 AW 0-10: (7f 3, 8f 3, 10f, 12f, 14f, 15f) (Equi 5, Fibr 5)
Neat, moderate filly, effective 8 to 10f, best at 10f, acts on g-f - acts on AW, likes tight tracks. Turf high 40 - 1st of 13 getting 3lb from Fairy Three (22 Aug Ripon RF 3812). AW high 44 - 4th of 10 getting 21lb from Dancing Rio (10 Feb Lingfield 10f Equi RF 0259).
**M D I Usher [1-24] Sporting Partners.*

RIVER JUNCTION (IRE) BHB 31f60a **RR 34f 60a** 2971[11]
7 b g Cyrano de Bergerac 7.3f **(58)** -Lovestream(Sandy Creek) 8.9f **(59)**
Form - 05450
Record 1998 - 1st:0 2nd:0 3rd:0 Ran:5
Pre1998 - 1st:3 2nd:3 3rd:0 Ran:13
Win Prizemoney £8,843 *Total Prizemoney* £11,887
Wins 1994 *Aug Wolver (STD) H 9.4f 59 62* <
1994 *Aug Wolver (STD) H 9.4f 53 54*
1994 *Jly Wolver (STD) H 8.5f 46 54*
1998 Turf 0-5: (10f 2, 12f 2, 14f) (sft, gd 2, g-f, frm)
Average gelding. Turf high 34.
**B Smart [0-5] The Dyball Partnership (from P C Haslam [3-13] Aug 1994).*

RIVER NORTH (IRE) BHB 100f **RR 110df** 2283a[8]
8 ch g Lomond (USA) 9.9f **(74)** - Petillante (USA) (Riverman (USA)) 9.1f **(76)**
Form - 48
Record 1998 - 1st:0 2nd:0 3rd:0 Ran:2
Pre1998 - 1st:7 2nd:6 3rd:5 Ran:26
Win Prizemoney £160,333 *Total Prizemoney* £220,565
Wins * 1997 Jly Vichy (SFT) L 14f 104
* 1994 Aug Gelsen (GD) G1 12f 116 <
* 1994 Jun Newmar (GS) L 12f 113
1998 Turf 0-2: (10f, 12f) (sft, g-f)
Group-class gelding, effective 14 to 16f, acts on sft to gd. Turf high 101. He underwent major surgery on a sinus problem in 1996 and is a shadow of his former self.
**Lady Herries [7-29] Lady Herries (from Sir Michael Stoute [0-1] Oct 1992).*

RIVER SAINT (USA) RR 73f 4316[5]
2 ch f Irish River (FR) 9f **(77)**-Imagining (USA)(Northfields (USA))9f **(72)**
Form - 5
Record 1998 - 1st:0 2nd:0 3rd:0 Ran:1
1998 Turf 0-1: (6f) (gd)

Currently above-average filly.
**Sir Michael Stoute [0-1] Cheveley Park Stud.*

RIVERSDALE (IRE) RR 62f 4868[6]
2 b c Elbio 9f **(62)** - Embustera (Sparkler) 8.4f **(55)**
Form - 76
Record 1998 - 1st:0 2nd:0 3rd:0 Ran:2
1998 Turf 0-2: (6f, 7f) (gd, frm)
Currently average colt. Turf high 62 (began Spt).
**J G FitzGerald [0-2] J G FitzGerald.*

RIVERSDALE FLYER RR 5f 4779[20]
2 br c Prince des Coeurs (USA) - Pink N' Perky (Tickled Pink) 6.5f **(59)**
Form - 70
Record 1998 - 1st:0 2nd:0 3rd:0 Ran:2
1998 Turf 0-2: (6f, 8f) (gd, g-f)
Currently very poor colt. Turf high 5 (began Oct).
**E A Wheeler [0-2] Afondale Racing.*

RIVERS MAGIC BHB 30f30a RR 39f 30a 1520[10]
5 b g Dominion 8.9f **(65)** - Rivers Maid (Rarity) 10.1f **(60)**
Form - 0604480000
Record 1998 - 1st:0 2nd:0 3rd:0 Ran:9
Pre1998 - 1st:1 2nd:0 3rd:0 Ran:10
Win Prizemoney £4,008 *Total Prizemoney* £4,008
Wins 1996 Jly Haydoc (G-S) 7.1f 82 <
1998 Turf 0-3: (6f 2, 7f) (sft, gd 2) 1998 AW 0-6: (7f, 8f 4, 12f) (Equi 6)
Moderate gelding, has worn blinkers. Turf high 20. AW high 47.
**J J Bridger [0-16] J F Walls (from Major D N Chappell [1-4] Oct 1996).*

RIVERSMEET RR 41f 1596[7]
4 b g Soviet Star (USA) 8.6f **(74)** - Zepha (Great Nephew) 9.9f **(64)**
Form - 7
Record 1998 - 1st:0 2nd:0 3rd:0 Ran:1
1998 Turf 0-1: (10f) (g-f)
Leggy, currently moderate gelding. (DEAD)
**L G Cottrell [0-3] H C Seymour.*

RIVERS RAINBOW BHB 33f RR 23f 3848[15]
3 b f Primo Dominie 7.2f **(67)** - Rivers Maid (Rarity) 10.1f **(60)**
Form - 0000
Record 1998 - 1st:0 2nd:0 3rd:0 Ran:4
1998 Turf 0-4: (7f, 8f, 10f 2) (gd, g-f, frm 2)
Scopey, little account filly. Turf high 23.
**Major D N Chappell [0-4] Rex Mead.*

RIVER'S SOURCE (USA) BHB 70f RR 72f 4966[4]
4 b g Irish River (FR) 9f**(77)**-Singing (USA)(The Minstrel (CAN))10f **(72)**
Form - 50264512204
Record 1998 - 1st:1 2nd:3 3rd:0 Ran:11
Pre1998 - 1st:1 2nd:2 3rd:1 Ran:8
Win Prizemoney £8,939 *Total Prizemoney* £15,275
Wins * **1998** Aug Pontef (G-F) H 10f 68 68
* 1997 Apr Newmar (G-F) H 10f 82 78 <
1998 Turf 1-11: (8f, 9f, 10f 1-7, 11f, 12f) (sft 2, g-s, gd 2, g-f 4, frm 1-2)
Scopey, above-average gelding, effective 9 to 11f, best at 10f, acts on sft to frm, best on g-f, has worn blinkers, likes tight tracks. Turf high 76 (1st run) - 5th of 15 getting 7lb from Kewarra (22 Apr Epsom 10f sft RF 0814). Consistent. **B W Hills [2-19] Mrs B W Hills.*

RIVER'S SPARKLE (IRE) BHB 43f RR 29f 4007[8]
2 b f River Falls 8.2f **(56)** - El Zaana (Priamos (GER)) 11.1f **(61)**
Form - 0068
Record 1998 - 1st:0 2nd:0 3rd:0 Ran:4
1998 Turf 0-4: (6f, 7f 3) (g-f 2, frm 2)
Little account filly. Turf high 29.
**G B Balding [0-4] Mrs K L Perrin & Mrs P D Gulliver.*

RIVER TERN BHB 61f63a RR 62f 63a 4502[6]
5 b g Puissance 7.1f **(60)** - Millaine (Formidable (USA)) 9.2f **(63)**
Form - 8370542306
Record 1998 - 1st:0 2nd:1 3rd:2 Ran:10
Pre1998 - 1st:4 2nd:2 3rd:4 Ran:26
Win Prizemoney £12,811 *Total Prizemoney* £20,603
Wins * 1997 Aug Catter (G-F) C 5f 62
* 1997 Jly Warwic (G-F) H 5f 63 64
* 1997 May Redcar (GD) C 6f 65 <
1996 Spt Thirsk (G-F) 6f 59
1998 Turf 0-10: (5f 10) (gd 3, g-f 4, frm 3)
Average gelding, effective 5 to 6f, best at 5f, acts on gd to frm, best on frm, has worn blinkers. Turf high 64. Inconsistent. Ran a number of good races without reward in 1998.
**J M Bradley [3-24] Martyn James (from J Berry [1-12] Oct 1996).*

RIVER TIMES (USA) BHB 89f RR 77f 4089[1]
2 b c Runaway Groom (CAN) 8.1f **(69)** - Miss Riverton (USA) (Fred Astaire (USA))
Form - 5341
Record 1998 - 1st:1 2nd:0 3rd:1 Ran:4
Win Prizemoney £2,899 *Total Prizemoney* £4,364
Wins * **1998** Spt Haydoc (GD) 8.1f 77 <
1998 Turf 1-4: (5f, 6f, 7f, 8f 1-1) (g-f 2, frm 1-2)
Above-average colt. Turf high 77 (began Jly) - 1st of 17 from Canta Ke Brave (4 Spt Haydock RF 4089).
**T D Easterby [1-4] Times of Wigan.*

RIYADIAN BHB 110f RR 114f 1484[4]
6 ch h Polish Precedent (USA) 9f **(73)** - Knight's Baroness (Rainbow Quest (USA)) 10.4f **(75)**
Form - 354
Record 1998 - 1st:0 2nd:0 3rd:1 Ran:3
Pre1998 - 1st:5 2nd:2 3rd:2 Ran:10
Win Prizemoney £83,000 *Total Prizemoney* £193,595
Wins * 1997 Jun Hamilt (GD) 9.2f 106+
* 1996 May Newmar (G-F) G2 12f 116 <
* 1995 Spt Ascot (GD) G3 12f 116 <
* 1995 Spt Doncas (G-S) 10.3f 110+
* 1995 Apr Kempto (GD) 10f 84
1998 Turf 0-3: (10f 2, 13f) (sft, gd, g-f)
Group-class horse. Turf high 114 (1st run) - 3rd of 5 to Germano (25 Apr Sandown 10f sft RF 0869). Consistent. A very useful performer who has been lightly-raced in recent seasons due to injury, there is still some mileage left in him, though has never fulfilled the promise of his victory in the Jockey Club Stakes in 1996. His best chance of further Pattern race victories probably lies abroad.
**P F I Cole [5-13] H R H Prince Fahd Salman.*

RM AGAIN RR 32f 3374[9]
2 b c Primo Dominie 7.2f **(67)** - La Cabrilla (Carwhite) 7.2f **(61)**
Form - 00
Record 1998 - 1st:0 2nd:0 3rd:0 Ran:2
1998 Turf 0-2: (5f 2) (frm 2)
Currently very moderate colt. Turf high 27 (began Jly).
**R Guest [0-2] RM Partnership Architectural Consultants.*

ROBANNA BHB 48f RR 53f 4922[2]
3 b f Robellino (USA) 9.5f **(68)** - Pounelta (Tachypous) 8.6f **(55)**
Form - 0000470042
Record 1998 - 1st:0 2nd:1 3rd:0 Ran:10
Pre1998 - 1st:0 2nd:0 3rd:0 Ran:3
Win Prizemoney £0 *Total Prizemoney* £783
1998 Turf 0-10: (6f, 7f, 8f 2, 10f 3, 11f, 14f 2) (g-s 2, gd 2, g-f 2, frm 4)
Light-framed, fair filly. Turf high 53.
**J Akehurst [0-10] Peter Valentine (from R Akehurst [0-3] Oct 1997).*

ROBBER RED BHB 76f RR 83f 4634[5]
2 b c Mon Tresor 7.9f **(60)** - Starisk **(33f)** (Risk Me (FR)) 5.9f **(53)**
Form - 542022512025
Record 1998 - 1st:1 2nd:5 3rd:0 Ran:12
Win Prizemoney £1,972 *Total Prizemoney* £6,848
Wins * **1998** Aug Lingfi (FRM) C 6f 78 <
1998 Turf 1-12: (5f 6, 6f 1-5, 7f) (gd 5, g-f 1-3, frm 4)
Decent colt, effective 5 to 6f, best at 5f, acts on gd to frm, has worn blinkers. Turf high 83 - 2nd of 14 giving 5lb to Diamond Geezer (15 Spt Sandown 5f gd RF 4264) - also 1st of 5 giving 8lb to Itsallhappening (26 Aug Lingfield RF 3892). Quite a useful juvenile sprinter, but faced some stiff tasks and has only a solitary fast-ground Lingfield victory to show for his pains so far.
**B J Meehan [1-12] David Allen.*

ROBBIES DREAM (IRE) BHB 69f RR 71f 4845[19]
2 ch c Balla Cove - Royal Golden (IRE) (Digamist (USA))
Form - 0060
Record 1998 - 1st:0 2nd:0 3rd:0 Ran:4

1998 Turf 0-4: (6f 2, 7f, 8f) (g-s, g-f 2, frm)
Above-average colt. Turf high 71. **D Morris [0-4] James Brown.*

ROBBO BHB 59f70a **RR 61f 70a** 4850[16]

4 b g Robellino (USA) 9.5f **(68)** - Basha (USA) (Chief's Crown (USA)) 9.8f **(72)**
Form - 2330
Record 1998 - 1st:0 2nd:0 3rd:2 Ran:3
Pre1998 - 1st:3 2nd:2 3rd:2 Ran:14
Win Prizemoney £6,039 *Total Prizemoney* £10,015
Wins 1997 *Oct Wolver (STD) H 14.8f 60 70 <*
1997 *Spt Wolver (STD) 14.8f 63+*
1997 *Aug Southw (STD) H 14f 54 61*
1998 Turf 0-3: (16f, 17f, 18f) (gd 3)
Light-framed, above-average gelding, effective 14 to 16f, best at 15f, acts on g-s - acts on Fibr, often wears blinkers (extremely effectively), prefers left handed tracks, favours tight tracks. Turf high 60 (began Spt). Consistent.
**Mrs M Reveley [2-7] The Scarth Racing Partnership (from C W Thornton [3-14] Nov 1997).*

ROBEENA BHB 60f48a **RR 48f 48a** 5059[19]

3 b f Robellino (USA) 9.5f**(68)**-Raheena (USA)(Lyphard (USA))9.9f **(72)**
Form - 060
Record 1998 - 1st:0 2nd:0 3rd:0 Ran:3
Pre1998 - 1st:0 2nd:0 3rd:2 Ran:6
Win Prizemoney £0 *Total Prizemoney* £1,155
1998 Turf 0-1: (6f) (sft) 1998 AW 0-2: (7f, 10f) (Equi, Fibr)
Neat, moderate filly, effective 6f, acts on gd. AW high 31. Becoming disappointing.
**J L Eyre [0-1] Village Green Racing (from C N Allen [0-8] Jan 1998).*

ROBELLION BHB 60f67a **RR 66f 67a** 3605[8]

7 b g Robellino (USA) 9.5f **(68)** - Tickled Trout (Red Alert) 7.6f **(66)**
Form - 4622213151520638
Record 1998 - 1st:3 2nd:3 3rd:2 Ran:13
Pre1998 - 1st:7 2nd:9 3rd:9 Ran:75
Win Prizemoney £30,111 *Total Prizemoney* £50,677
Wins * **1998** *Mar Southw (STD) H 7f 62 67*
* **1998** *Feb Lingfi (SLW) 8f 62*
1998 *Jan Lingfi (STD) C 8f 62*
1997 Oct Salisb (GD) H 6f 47 53
1996 Aug Newmar (GD) H 6f 61 69
1996 Jly Chepst (G-F) H 5.1f 61 63
1996 *Feb Lingfi (STD) H 10f 63 62*
1996 *Jan Lingfi (STD) H 8f 58 55*
1995 Jly Chepst (G-F) H 5.1f 68 69
1998 Turf 0-5: (6f 2, 7f 2, 8f) (hvy, g-f, frm 2, hrd) 1998 AW 3-8: (7f 1-3, 8f 2-5) (Equi 2-5, Fibr 1-3)
Average gelding, effective 6 to 10f, best at 8f, acts on hvy - acts on AW, best on Equi, often wears blinkers (extremely effectively), prefers left handed tracks, prefers tight tracks, excels at Lingfield. Turf high 66. AW high 67 - 1st of 10 giving 12lb to Time of Night (2 Mar Southwell RF 0386) - also 1st of 9 getting 6lb from Anonym (22 Jan Lingfield RF 0133).
**Mrs L Stubbs [2-10] The Forty Ninth Partnership (from D W P Arbuthnot [8-78] Jan 1998).*

ROBELLITA BHB 48f **RR 43f** 2329[10]

4 b g Robellino (USA) 9.5f **(68)** - Miellita (King Emperor (USA)) 9.4f **(58)**
Form - 000
Record 1998 - 1st:0 2nd:0 3rd:0 Ran:3
1998 Turf 0-3: (10f 2, 12f) (gd 3)
Strong, moderate gelding. Turf high 43.
**C P Morlock [0-6] Angels Racing Syndicate.*

ROBERGERIE (IRE) BHB 54f **RR 54f** 4548[4]

2 b c Robellino (USA) 9.5f **(68)** - Daisy Grey (Nordance (USA)) 7.5f **(52)**
Form - 078704
Record 1998 - 1st:0 2nd:0 3rd:0 Ran:6
1998 Turf 0-5: (7f 4, 8f) (gd, g-f 2, frm 2) 1998 AW 0-1: (7f) (Fibr)
Fair colt, often wears blinkers. Turf high 54.
**M R Channon [0-6] R M Brehaut.*

ROBERT ELLIS **RR 31f** 5001[9]

2 ch c Anshan 8.2f **(63)** - Susie's Baby (Balidar) 7.9f **(63)**
Form - 00
Record 1998 - 1st:0 2nd:0 3rd:0 Ran:2
1998 Turf 0-2: (5f, 6f) (sft, g-f)
Currently very moderate colt. Turf high 31 (began Oct).
**J Cullinan [0-2] W H Joyce.*

ROBERTICO **RR 110f** 3785a[3]

3 b c Robellino (USA) 9.5f **(68)** - Dance On The Stage (Dancing Brave (USA)) 8.4f **(76)**
Form - 313
1998 Turf 1-3: (11f, 12f 1-2) (hvy 1-2, gd)
Currently Group-class colt. Turf high 110 - 1st of 19 from Nadour Al Bahr (5 Jly Hamburg RF 2666a). Described as a 'cart-horse' by his trainer, he ran out a courageous winner of the German Derby, where the ground was heavy. Outpaced on a faster surface later in the season, he may need a stern test of stamina.
**A Schutz in GER [1-3] Gestut Hof Vesterberg.*

ROBIN GOODFELLOW **RR 86f** 4985[14]

3 b c Fairy King (USA) 7.7f **(75)** - La Tuerta (Hot Spark) 7.6f **(62)**
Form - 2105080
Record 1998 - 1st:1 2nd:1 3rd:0 Ran:7
Pre1998 - 1st:1 2nd:0 3rd:0 Ran:3
Win Prizemoney £10,890 *Total Prizemoney* £12,690
Wins * **1998** May Salisb (G-S) H 6f 81 86 <
* 1997 Oct Catter (SFT) 6f 83
1998 Turf 1-7: (5f, 6f 1-4, 7f 2) (hvy, g-s 2, gd 1-3, g-f)
Scopey, useful colt, effective 6f, acts on g-s to gd, best on g-s. Turf high 86 - 1st of 9 getting 4lb from Eleventh Duke (3 May Salisbury RF 1002). Inconsistent. **P T Walwyn [2-10] Michael Gough.*

ROBIN LANE BHB 92f **RR 88f** 4973[1]

3 b f Tenby 10.4f **(76)** - Hiawatha's Song (USA) (Chief's Crown (USA)) 9.8f **(72)**
Form - 42012114040711
Record 1998 - 1st:5 2nd:2 3rd:0 Ran:14
Pre1998 - 1st:0 2nd:0 3rd:0 Ran:5
Win Prizemoney £33,528 *Total Prizemoney* £41,084
Wins * **1998** Oct Doncas (HVY) H 12f 85 88 <
* **1998** Oct Ascot (SFT) H 12f 81 85
* **1998** Jly Hamilt (FRM) H 9.2f 72 79
* **1998** Jun Hamilt (G-S) H 9.2f 70 74
* **1998** May Redcar (G-F) 10f 71
1998 Turf 5-14: (8f, 9f 2-2, 10f 1-8, 12f 2-3) (sft 1-4, g-s 1-1, gd 1-5, g-f 1-2, frm 1-2)
Scopey, useful filly, effective 9 to 12f, best at 12f, acts on sft to frm, likes right handed tracks, excels at Hamilton. Turf high 88 - 1st of 12 getting 1lb from Carlys Quest (24 Oct Doncaster RF 4973) - also 1st of 11 getting 11lb from Elhayq (9 Oct Ascot RF 4734). She improved a great deal this season, winning five times including competitive handicaps at Ascot and Doncaster in October when stepped up in trip. Tough and genuine.
**M Johnston [5-14] & Mrs G Middlebrook (from I A Balding [0-5] Oct 1997).*

ROBO MAGIC (USA) BHB 41f82a **RR 43f 82a** 2857[14]

6 b g Tejano (USA) 6.5f **(64)** - Bubble Magic (USA) (Clever Trick (USA)) 6.6f **(77)**
Form - 25881528215400
Record 1998 - 1st:2 2nd:2 3rd:0 Ran:11
Pre1998 - 1st:8 2nd:5 3rd:5 Ran:57
Win Prizemoney £34,465 *Total Prizemoney* £44,368
Wins * **1998** *Apr Lingfi (STD) H 6f 78 83*
* **1998** *Feb Lingfi (STD) H 6f 71 73*
* 1997 *May Wolver (STD) H 5f 78 85 <*
* 1997 *Jan Lingfi (STD) C 6f 66*
* 1996 *Feb Lingfi (STD) H 6f 70 74*
* 1996 *Feb Lingfi (STD) H 6f 70 69*
* 1995 *Dec Lingfi (STD) H 6f 67 66*
* 1995 Aug Lingfi (G-F) H 6f 54 49
1995 *Feb Lingfi (STD) S 6f 67*
1994 *Nov Lingfi (STD) H 6f 62 67*
1998 Turf 0-3: (5f, 6f, 7f) (g-f, frm 2) 1998 AW 2-8: (5f 2, 6f 2-5, 8f) (Equi 2-7, Fibr)
Decent gelding, effective 5 to 7f, best at 5f, - acts on AW, best on Equi, has worn blinkers, prefers left handed tracks, prefers tight tracks, does well at Lingfield. Turf high 43. AW high 83 - 1st of 6 giving 7lb to Mystical (3 Apr Lingfield RF 0556). Becoming disappointing. He bounced back to win a couple of times over six fur-

longs on the Lingfield Equitrack early in the year, his optimum conditions, but is very difficult to predict these days.
**L MontagueHall [8-54] A D Green and Partners (from A Moore [2-6] Feb 1995).*

ROBORANT BHB 79f **RR 80f** 4957[3]
3 b g Robellino (USA) 9.5f **(68)** - Sunny Davis (USA) (Alydar (USA)) 9.1f **(76)**
Form - 03100P13
Record 1998 - 1st:2 2nd:0 3rd:2 Ran:8
Pre1998 - 1st:0 2nd:0 3rd:1 Ran:5
Win Prizemoney £9,047 *Total Prizemoney* £10,771
Wins * **1998** Oct Bright (GD) H 10f 76 79 <
* **1998** Jun Beverl (GD) H 9.9f 74 76
1998 Turf 2-8: (8f, 9f, 10f 2-6) (gd 2, g-f 1-3, frm 1-3)
Unfurnished, decent gelding, effective 8 to 10f, best at 10f, acts on g-f to frm, best on frm, has worn blinkers, likes tight tracks. Turf high 80 - 3rd of 7 giving 10lb to Panama House (23 Oct Doncaster 10f frm RF 4957) - also 1st of 10 getting 1lb from My Learned Friend (5 Oct Brighton RF 4655). Inconsistent. Has joined John Akehurst. **J L Dunlop [2-13] Lord Wakeham.*

ROBSART (IRE) BHB 84f **RR 84f** 4501[4]
3 b f Robellino (USA) 9.5f **(68)** - Sharp Girl (FR) (Sharpman) 11.3f **(66)**
Form - 10174
Record 1998 - 1st:2 2nd:0 3rd:0 Ran:5
Pre1998 - 1st:0 2nd:1 3rd:0 Ran:2
Win Prizemoney £9,952 *Total Prizemoney* £11,938
Wins * **1998** Jly Lingfi (G-F) 10f 84 <
* **1998** Apr Folkes (SFT) 7f 73
1998 Turf 2-5: (7f 1-1, 8f, 10f 1-2, 11f) (gd 1-3, frm 1-2)
Neat, decent filly, effective 10f, acts on frm. Turf high 84 - 1st of 5 getting 1lb from Just In Time (9 Jly Lingfield RF 2644). Bred to stay further than the seven furlongs over which she made a winning reappearance, she was stepped up to ten furlongs when winning a modest classified stakes at Lingfield in July. Held in a Listed race.
**J R Fanshawe [2-7] Lord Vestey.*

ROCA MURADA (IRE) BHB 52f **RR 55f** 2972[5]
9 br g Cyrano de Bergerac 7.3f **(58)** - Keppols (Furry Glen) 8.9f **(63)**
Form - 6505
Record 1998 - 1st:0 2nd:0 3rd:0 Ran:4
Pre1998 - 1st:5 2nd:4 3rd:3 Ran:29
Win Prizemoney £16,209 *Total Prizemoney* £21,864
1998 Turf 0-4: (7f 3, 8f) (gd 3, g-f)
Fair gelding, has worn blinkers. Turf high 55.
**L G Cottrell [0-4] Mrs Angela Tincknell (from P J Hobbs [0-1] Oct 1994).*

ROCHEA BHB 28f31a **RR 15f 31a** 2654[4]
4 br f Rock City 8.8f **(62)** - Pervenche (Latest Model) 6f **(62)**
Form - 004554260804
Record 1998 - 1st:0 2nd:1 3rd:0 Ran:12
Pre1998 - 1st:0 2nd:2 3rd:5 Ran:22
Win Prizemoney £0 *Total Prizemoney* £4,241
1998 Turf 0-2: (5f, 10f) (gd, frm) 1998 AW 0-10: (6f 3, 7f 6, 8f) (Fibr 10)
Moderate filly, effective 7 to 10f, best at 8f, acts on gd to g-f - acts on Fibr, best on g-f, has worn blinkers, and excels at Leicester. Turf high 15. AW high 44 - 4th of 11 getting 5lb from Zalotto (23 Jan Southwell 7f Fibr RF 0142). Becoming disappointing.
**K R Burke [0-3] Nigel Shields (from Mrs N Macauley [0-26] May 1998).*

ROCKCRACKER (IRE) BHB 51f46a **RR 51f 46a** 1553[8]
6 ch g Ballad Rock 7.2f **(63)** - Forest Blaze (USA) (Green Forest (USA)) 9.9f **(68)**
Form - 8568
Record 1998 - 1st:0 2nd:0 3rd:0 Ran:3
Pre1998 - 1st:4 2nd:2 3rd:3 Ran:42
Win Prizemoney £13,020 *Total Prizemoney* £16,948
Wins * 1997 Jun Folkes (G-F) H 6f 48 51
* 1996 Jly Warwic (G-F) H 6f 60 62 <
* 1996 May Warwic (FRM) 6f 54
1994 Jly Bath (FRM) 5.7f 57
1998 Turf 0-2: (6f 2) (frm 2) 1998 AW 0-1: (8f) (Equi)
Fair gelding, effective 6f, acts on gd to frm, best on frm, often wears blinkers (effectively). Turf high 51 (1st run) - 6th of 17 getting 1lb from Step On Degas (22 May Brighton 6f frm RF 1389).
**G G Margarson [3-34] P E Axon (from R Charlton [1-11] Oct 1995).*

ROCKETTE BHB 40f47a **RR 30f 47a** 2965[9]
3 ch f Rock Hopper 10.6f **(54)** - Primulette (Mummy's Pet) 7.7f **(60)**
Form - 10457700000
Record 1998 - 1st:1 2nd:0 3rd:0 Ran:11
Pre1998 - 1st:0 2nd:0 3rd:0 Ran:5
Win Prizemoney £1,880 *Total Prizemoney* £1,880
Wins 1998 *Jan Lingfi (STD) S 8f 52* <
1998 Turf 0-3: (8f, 10f, 11f) (frm 3) 1998 AW 1-8: (6f, 8f 1-5, 11f 2) (Equi 1-2, Fibr 6)
Fair filly, effective 8f, - acts on Equi, has worn blinkers (effectively). Turf high 17. AW high 53 - also 1st of 9 from Easy Virtue (20 Jan Lingfield RF 0120).
**S G Knight [0-2] Miss K Di Marte (from R J Baker [0-1] Jun 1998).*

ROCK FALCON (IRE) BHB 102f **RR 102f** 4971[4]
5 ch g Polar Falcon (USA) 9f **(74)** - Rockfest (USA) (Stage Door Johnny) 10.3f **(84)**
Form - 010201414
Record 1998 - 1st:3 2nd:1 3rd:0 Ran:9
Pre1998 - 1st:3 2nd:0 3rd:0 Ran:7
Win Prizemoney £37,892 *Total Prizemoney* £41,250
Wins * **1998** Spt Bath (G-S) 8f 97+
* **1998** Aug Goodwo (G-F) H 7f 97 101 <
* **1998** May Kempto (G-F) H 8f 85 93
* 1997 Oct Ascot (HVY) H 8f 80 91
* 1997 Spt Chepst (GD) S 8.1f 67+
* 1997 May Lingfi (GD) 7f 80
1998 Turf 3-9: (7f 1-5, 8f 2-4) (sft 2, g-s, gd, g-f 3-3, frm 2)
Very useful gelding, effective 7 to 8f, best at 7f, acts on g-f to frm, best on g-f, mostly wears blinkers (effectively), likes tight tracks. Turf high 102 - also 1st of 12 getting 3lb from Swiss Law (29 Aug Goodwood RF 3946). He has temperament and ability in equal measure, but was on his best behaviour when making all to win at Kempton, Goodwood and Bath. It is only fitting that this equine joker is owned by the comedian Enn Reitel.
**Lady Herries [6-16] E Reitel.*

ROCK FROM THE SUN BHB 40f38a **RR 51f 38a** 2900[12]
3 b f Rock City 8.8f **(62)** - Amathus Glory (Mummy's Pet) 7.7f **(60)**
Form - 40
Record 1998 - 1st:0 2nd:0 3rd:0 Ran:2
Pre1998 - 1st:1 2nd:0 3rd:2 Ran:10
Win Prizemoney £1,984 *Total Prizemoney* £2,594
Wins * 1997 *Jun Wolver (STD) S 7f 56* <
1998 AW 0-2: (7f, 9f) (Fibr 2)
Leggy, fair filly, effective 7f, - acts on Fibr, often wears blinkers, likes left handed tracks, likes tight tracks. AW high 10 (began Jly).
**W G M Turner [1-12] O J Stokes.*

ROCK ISLAND LINE (IRE) BHB 58f53a **RR 56f 53a** 3637[3]
4 b g New Express 6.8f **(54)** - Gail's Crystal (Crofter (USA)) 8.4f **(56)**
Form - 01513354834423
Record 1998 - 1st:2 2nd:1 3rd:4 Ran:14
Pre1998 - 1st:2 2nd:2 3rd:2 Ran:10
Win Prizemoney £8,873 *Total Prizemoney* £13,083
Wins * **1998** *Feb Southw (STD) C 8f 52*
* **1998** *Jan Southw (STD) C 7f 58*
* 1997 May Newcas (GD) C 7f 62 <
* 1997 Apr Hamilt (SFT) S 8.3f 53
1998 Turf 0-3: (7f 2, 8f) (sft, gd, frm) 1998 AW 2-11: (7f 1-8, 8f 1-3) (Fibr 2-11)
Workmanlike, average gelding, effective 7 to 8f, best at 7f, acts on g-f - acts on Fibr, and excels at Newcastle. Turf high 56. AW high 62 - 2nd of 14 giving 6lb to Kosevo (17 Jly Southwell 7f Fibr RF 2900). **J Berry [4-24] J Berry.*

ROCKLANDS LANE RR 59f 5001[8]
2 b c Puissance 7.1f **(60)** - Dancing Daughter (Dance In Time (CAN)) 8.9f **(59)**
Form - 48
Record 1998 - 1st:0 2nd:0 3rd:0 Ran:2
Win Prizemoney £0 *Total Prizemoney* £272
1998 Turf 0-2: (5f 2) (sft, g-s)
Currently fair colt. Turf high 59 (began Oct).
**R F JohnsonHoughton [0-2] Lord Leverhulme.*

ROCK RIVER BHB 48f **RR 47f** 1881[12]
4 ch f Rock Hopper 10.6f **(54)** - Emmer Green (Music Boy) 6.8f **(57)**
Form - 700
Record 1998 - 1st:0 2nd:0 3rd:0 Ran:3
Pre1998 - 1st:0 2nd:0 3rd:0 Ran:1
1998 Turf 0-3: (7f, 8f, 10f) (g-s, frm 2)
Workmanlike, moderate filly. Turf high 47.
**D C O'Brien [0-4] Mrs R M Blake.*

ROCK SCENE (IRE) BHB 44f55a **RR 49f 55a** 4072[8]
6 b g Scenic 10.6f **(66)** - Rockeater (Roan Rocket) 7.8f **(57)**
Form - 6081008
Record 1998 - 1st:1 2nd:0 3rd:0 Ran:7
Pre1998 - 1st:0 2nd:0 3rd:0 Ran:4
Win Prizemoney £3,036 *Total Prizemoney* £3,036
Wins * **1998** Jly Warwic (GD) H 10.8f 42 49 <
1998 Turf 1-7: (8f 3, 10f, 11f 1-1, 12f 2) (gd, g-f 1-5, frm)
Average gelding, favours tight tracks. Turf high 49.
**A Streeter [1-8] Mrs J Hughes (from R Hollinshead [0-3] Aug 1995).*

ROCKSWAIN (IRE) BHB 67a **RR 24f 67a** 428[5]
3 ch g Ballad Rock 7.2f **(63)** - Uninvited Guest (Be My Guest (USA)) 9.3f **(67)**
Form - 14323315
Record 1998 - 1st:1 2nd:1 3rd:3 Ran:7
Pre1998 - 1st:1 2nd:0 3rd:0 Ran:2
Win Prizemoney £4,597 *Total Prizemoney* £6,680
Wins * **1998** *Mar Wolver (STD) H 6f 59 67* <
* 1997 *Nov Wolver (STD) S 5f 65*
1998 AW 1-7: (5f 2, 6f 1-5) (Equi 2, Fibr 1-5)
Average gelding, effective 5 to 6f, best at 5f, - acts on Fibr, favours left handed tracks, favours tight tracks. AW high 67 - 1st of 13 getting 9lb from Russian Romeo (7 Mar Wolverhampton RF 0409).
**P C Haslam [2-9] Martin Wickens.*

ROCK THE BARNEY (IRE) BHB 31f35a **RR 20f 35a** 2958[12]
9 b h Coquelin (USA) 9.7f **(55)** - Lady Loire (Wolverlife) 9.3f **(54)**
Form - 0000
Record 1998 - 1st:0 2nd:0 3rd:0 Ran:4
Pre1998 - 1st:5 2nd:6 3rd:5 Ran:55
Win Prizemoney £15,963 *Total Prizemoney* £24,881
Wins 1997 Spt Sandow (G-F) H 10f 40 49
* 1995 Jun Kempto (G-F) H 12f 52 59 <
* 1995 Jun Sandow (G-F) H 11.4f 48 53
* 1994 May Leices (GD) H 10f 42 49
1998 Turf 0-4: (10f, 12f 2, 14f) (gd 2, g-f, frm)
Very moderate horse, effective 10 to 12f, best at 10f, acts on gd to hrd, best on gd, has worn blinkers, prefers right handed tracks, favours tight tracks. Turf high 20. Inconsistent.
**P Burgoyne [4-46] Mrs Satu Marks (from M D I Usher [1-12] Oct 1997).*

ROCK TO THE TOP (IRE) BHB 35f57a **RR 33f 57a** 3895[14]
4 b c Rudimentary (USA) 8.2f **(66)** - Well Bought (IRE) (Auction Ring (USA)) 8.6f **(65)**
Form - 0000800
Record 1998 - 1st:0 2nd:0 3rd:0 Ran:7
Pre1998 - 1st:0 2nd:1 3rd:1 Ran:7
Win Prizemoney £0 *Total Prizemoney* £1,258
1998 Turf 0-6: (5f, 6f, 7f 2, 8f, 12f) (gd 3, g-f 2, frm) 1998 AW 0-1: (7f) (Equi)
Scopey, average colt, effective 6f, - acts on Equi, likes tight tracks. Turf high 33. Inconsistent.
**J J Sheehan [0-14] Mrs Christina Dowling.*

ROCKYS REVENGE BHB 51f **RR 63f** 4934[7]
2 b g Deploy 11.4f **(67)** - Unique Treasure (Young Generation) 7.7f **(63)**
Form - 507
Record 1998 - 1st:0 2nd:0 3rd:0 Ran:3
1998 Turf 0-2: (7f, 8f) (gd, frm) 1998 AW 0-1: (6f) (Fibr)
Currently average gelding. Turf high 63 (began Oct).
**W J Musson [0-3] Mike Hawkett.*

ROCKY STALLONE RR 1253[19]
3 b c Rock City 8.8f **(62)** - City Link Pet (Tina's Pet) 6.8f **(59)**
Form - 0
Record 1998 - 1st:0 2nd:0 3rd:0 Ran:1
1998 Turf 0-1: (6f) (gd)
Light-framed, currently very poor colt - 19th of 19 to Nuclear Debate (15 May Thirsk 6f gd RF 1253). **W McKeown [0-1] C H Dyne.*

ROCKY WATERS (USA) BHB 27f48a **RR 34f 48a** 4804[17]
9 b or br g Rocky Marriage (USA) 6.6f **(93)** - Running Melody (Rheingold) 10.4f **(62)**
Form - 62243135000
Record 1998 - 1st:1 2nd:1 3rd:2 Ran:9
Pre1998 - 1st:5 2nd:10 3rd:5 Ran:65
Win Prizemoney £23,166 *Total Prizemoney* £38,057
Wins 1998 *Mar Lingfi (STD) C 6f 58*
1994 *Nov Lingfi (STD) H 6f 78 76*
1998 Turf 0-3: (7f, 8f 2) (gd 3) 1998 AW 1-6: (6f 1-2, 7f 2, 8f 2) (Equi 1-4, Fibr 2)
Fair gelding, effective 6f, - acts on AW, has worn blinkers (effectively), likes left handed tracks, favours tight tracks. AW high 58 - 1st of 14 getting 6lb from Mister Raider (19 Mar Lingfield RF 0445). Becoming disappointing. He ended a long losing run when winning a claimer on the Lingfield Equitrack in March, and seems most suited by that surface.
**Mrs L Stubbs [0-5] Doug Kirk and Darren Kirk (from M D I Usher [1-14] Mar 1998).*

RODERICK HUDSON BHB 68f75a **RR 33f 75a** 3986[12]
6 b g Elmaamul (USA) 8.1f **(70)** - Moviegoer (Pharly (FR)) 9.8f **(68)**
Form - 200
Record 1998 - 1st:0 2nd:1 3rd:0 Ran:3
Pre1998 - 1st:1 2nd:2 3rd:0 Ran:10
Win Prizemoney £3,100 *Total Prizemoney* £6,453
Wins 1995 Jun Newbur (G-F) 7f 77+ <
1998 Turf 0-1: (9f) (g-f) 1998 AW 0-2: (8f, 9f) (Equi, Fibr)
Above-average gelding. AW high 75 (1st run) - 2nd of 5 getting 3lb from Rambo Waltzer (28 Jan Wolverhampton 9f Fibr RF 0176). Lightly-raced on the Flat in recent seasons.
**J R Poulton [0-1] G G Grayson (from J A R Toller [2-16] May 1998).*

ROEMOOR GIRL (IRE) BHB 53f50a **RR 67f 50a** 4834[13]
2 b br f Turtle Island (IRE) - Ozone (Auction Ring (USA)) 8.6f **(65)**
Form - 5750600
Record 1998 - 1st:0 2nd:0 3rd:0 Ran:7
1998 Turf 0-7: (5f 4, 6f 3) (g-s, gd, frm 4, hrd)
Average filly. Turf high 67. **R Hannon [0-7] Jimm Racing.*

ROFFEY SPINNEY (IRE) BHB 60f57a **RR 67f 57a** 5003[10]
4 ch g Masterclass (USA) 5.9f **(63)** - Crossed Line (Thatching) 8f **(66)**
Form - 033080770120356010
Record 1998 - 1st:2 2nd:1 3rd:3 Ran:18
Pre1998 - 1st:2 2nd:0 3rd:4 Ran:12
Win Prizemoney £10,098 *Total Prizemoney* £13,783
Wins 1998 Oct Leices (G-S) SH 7f 54 67
1998 Jly Folkes (GD) C 7f 50
1997 *Feb Lingfi (STD) H 5f 66 69* <
1997 *Feb Lingfi (STD) 6f 63*
1998 Turf 2-12: (6f 5, 7f 2-5, 8f 2) (g-s, gd 2-7, g-f, frm 3) 1998 AW 0-6: (6f 2, 7f 3, 8f) (Equi 6)
Unfurnished, average gelding, effective 5 to 8f, acts on gd - acts on Equi, and excels at Folkestone. Turf high 67 - 1st of 20 giving 6lb to Tayovullin (13 Oct Leicester RF 4775). AW high 69 - 3rd of 9 giving 10lb to Robellion (22 Jan Lingfield 8f Equi RF 0133).
**J Cullinan [0-1] Alan Spargo Ltd Toolmakers (from R Hannon [4-29] Oct 1998).*

ROGER ROSS BHB 75f63a **RR 75f 63a** 4848[15]
3 b c Touch of Grey 8.1f **(47)** - Foggy Dew (Smoggy) 8f **(50)**
Form - 83776211812833010
Record 1998 - 1st:4 2nd:2 3rd:3 Ran:16
Pre1998 - 1st:0 2nd:0 3rd:0 Ran:1
Win Prizemoney £21,863 *Total Prizemoney* £25,227
Wins * **1998** Oct Ascot (SFT) H 8f 71 75 <
* **1998** Jly Salisb (FRM) H 8f 62 69
* **1998** Jun Sandow (G-S) H 8.1f 52 64
* **1998** Jun Salisb (G-S) H 8f 52 65
1998 Turf 4-11: (8f 4-9, 9f 2) (g-s 1-1, gd 2-5, g-f 3, frm 1-2) 1998 AW 0-5: (7f, 8f 4) (Equi 5)
Small, above-average colt, effective 8f, acts on g-s to frm, excels at Salisbury and Sandown. Turf high 75 - 1st of 20 getting 15lb from Therhea (10 Oct Ascot RF 4744) - also 1st of 11 getting 13lb from Prospectress (11 Jly Salisbury RF 2718). AW high 52. He has

had a busy season but has improved through it, winning four times on ground ranging from soft to firm. A mile is his trip.
**R M Flower [4-17] H Lawrence.*

ROI DE DANSE BHB 71f **RR 71f** 4962[8]

3 ch c Komaite (USA) 6.9f **(61)** - Princess Lucy (Local Suitor (USA)) 8.4f **(67)**
Form - 00058128

Record					
1998 -	1st:1	2nd:1	3rd:0	Ran:8	
Pre1998 -	1st:1	2nd:0	3rd:0	Ran:6	

Win Prizemoney £5,411 *Total Prizemoney* £8,927

Wins						
* **1998**	Spt	Bright	(GD)	8f	71	
* 1997	Aug	Kempto	(GD)	6f	72	<

1998 Turf 1-8: (7f 4, 8f 1-3, 9f) (sft, g-s, gd 3, g-f 1-2, frm)
Scopey, above-average colt, effective 6 to 9f, acts on gd to frm, best on g-f. Turf high 71 - 1st of 11 getting 3lb from Acid Test (30 Spt Brighton RF 4571). **J W Hills [2-14] A N Miller.*

ROI GIRONDE (IRE) **RR 101f** 4214a[9]

3 b c Fairy King (USA) 7.7f **(75)** - Girouette (USA) (Nodouble (USA)) 8.8f **(68)**
Form - 3700
1998 Turf 0-4: (6f, 7f 2, 8f) (hvy, gd 3)
Very useful colt, effective 6 to 7f, best at 7f, acts on sft. Turf high 100. Becoming disappointing. He won a Group 2 in 1997, but never looked like improving on that last term. Connections seemed to be in the dark as to his favoured trip and tactics. Will continue his career in the States. **Mme C Head in FR [1-8].*

ROISIN SPLENDOUR (IRE) BHB 64f **RR 77f** 4633[25]

3 ch f Inchinor 8.9f **(64)** - Oriental Splendour (Runnett) 7f **(59)**
Form - 4324100080

Record				
1998 -	1st:1	2nd:1	3rd:1	Ran:10
Pre1998 -	1st:0	2nd:0	3rd:1	Ran:2

Win Prizemoney £2,762 *Total Prizemoney* £5,638

Wins						
* **1998**	Jly	Bright	(GD)	7f	77	<

1998 Turf 1-10: (6f 2, 7f 1-8) (g-s, gd 1-4, g-f 4, frm)
Workmanlike, above-average filly, effective 7f, acts on gd to g-f, best on gd. Turf high 77 - 1st of 5 getting 5lb from Splendid Isolation (14 Jly Brighton RF 2779). A consistent sort, her win at Brighton in July was the result of an enterprising ride by her rider.
**S Dow [1-12] Brighthelm Racing.*

RO-JO **RR** 2511[16]

4 b g Roviris - Joan Addison (Jolly Good) 10.7f **(73)**
Form - 0

Record				
1998 -	1st:0	2nd:0	3rd:0	Ran:1

1998 Turf 0-1: (8f) (g-f)
Neat, formerly very poor gelding.
**A J Chamberlain [0-4] Mrs A G Sims.*

ROKEBY BOWL BHB 102f **RR 105f** 4824[2]

6 b g Salse (USA) 10.9f **(71)** - Rose Bowl (USA) (Habitat) 9.4f **(70)**
Form - 52211282

Record				
1998 -	1st:2	2nd:4	3rd:0	Ran:8
Pre1998 -	1st:4	2nd:5	3rd:3	Ran:25

Win Prizemoney £60,288 *Total Prizemoney* £106,937

Wins								
* **1998**	Aug	York	(FRM)	H	11.9f	93	96	<
* **1998**	Aug	Epsom	(G-F)	H	12f	90	93	
* 1997	Aug	Newbur	(G-F)		12f		96	<
* 1997	Jly	Sandow	(G-F)		11.4f		91	
* 1995	Jun	Sandow	(GD)	H	9f	84	83	
* 1995	Jun	Pontef	(GD)	H	10f	76	83	

1998 Turf 2-8: (10f 2, 12f 2-6) (g-s, gd 1-3, g-f, frm 1-3)
Pattern-class gelding, effective 12f, acts on g-f to frm, best on frm, prefers left handed tracks. Turf high 105 - 2nd of 13 giving 19lb to Rainbow Ways (15 Oct Newmarket 12f frm RF 4824) - also 1st of 14 giving 11lb to Jaazim (20 Aug York RF 3771). Improving. His wins are like buses, arriving infrequently but in pairs. A fast ground specialist, he should continue to give his connections some fun in the better middle-distance handicaps.
**I A Balding [6-33] Paul Mellon.*

ROLE MODEL **RR** 2467[8]

2 b f Tragic Role (USA) 9.4f **(63)** - Emerald Gulf (IRE) (Wassl) 9.7f **(62)**
Form - 8

Record				
1998 -	1st:0	2nd:0	3rd:0	Ran:1

1998 Turf 0-1: (6f) (frm)
Currently very poor filly. **R M Whitaker [0-1] The PBT Group.*

ROLI ABI (FR) **RR 105f** 1737a[13]

3 b c Bering 9.6f **(80)** - All Found (FR) (Alleged (USA)) 10f **(76)**
Form - 240
1998 Turf 0-3: (11f 2, 12f) (hvy, sft, gd)
Currently Pattern-class colt. Turf high 105 (1st run) - 2nd of 6 to Special Quest (13 Apr Longchamp 11f hvy RF 0830a). He had a tough race for an inexperienced horse on his reappearance and seemed to be feeling that for the remainder of the campaign.
**F Belmont in FR [0-3].*

ROLLER **RR 70f** 3664[3]

2 b c Bluebird (USA) 7.9f **(71)** - Tight Spin (High Top) 10.2f **(67)**
Form - 43

Record				
1998 -	1st:0	2nd:0	3rd:1	Ran:2

Win Prizemoney £0 *Total Prizemoney* £759
1998 Turf 0-2: (6f 2) (frm 2)
Currently above-average colt. Turf high 70 (began Aug) - 3rd of 7 giving 5lb to Precocious Miss (16 Aug Lingfield 6f frm RF 3664).
**H Candy [0-2] H R H Prince Fahd Salman.*

ROLLING HIGH (IRE) **RR** 236[6]

3 ch c Roi Danzig (USA) 10.5f **(62)** - Sally Chase (Sallust) 8.4f **(63)**
Form - 6

Record				
1998 -	1st:0	2nd:0	3rd:0	Ran:1
Pre1998 -	1st:0	2nd:0	3rd:0	Ran:1

1998 AW 0-1: (11f) (Fibr)
Lengthy, currently very poor colt.
**D J G MurraySmith [0-2] D Twomey.*

Rokeby Bowl loves to hear his feet rattle

ROLLING PATCH (IRE) BHB 46f43a **RR 44f 43a** 5098[14]

4 b f Tirol 8.1f **(64)** - Shprinza (Vitiges (FR)) 8.2f **(59)**
Form - 750080

Record 1998 - 1st:0 2nd:0 3rd:0 Ran:6
1998 Turf 0-5: (6f, 10f 3, 12f) (sft, gd, g-f 3) 1998 AW 0-1: (8f) (Fibr)
Moderate filly. Turf high 56.
**E J Alston [0-5] Only Fools Have Horses (from B King in IRE [0-2] May 1998).*

ROLLING RIO BHB 60f64a RR 60f 64a 4013[11]

2 b g Chaddleworth (IRE) - Broughton's Gold (IRE) **(18f)** (Trojan Fen) 8.1f **(62)**
Form - 00460
Record 1998 - 1st:0 2nd:0 3rd:0 Ran:5
Win Prizemoney £0 *Total Prizemoney* £191
1998 Turf 0-4: (5f 2, 6f 2) (sft, gd, g-f, frm) 1998 AW 0-1: (7f) (Fibr)
Average gelding. Turf high 60.
**P C Haslam [0-5] Rio Stainless Engineering Ltd.*

ROLO TOMASI (IRE) RR 102f 4686a[2]

2 b c Mujtahid (USA) 7.4f **(69)** - Elegant Bloom (Be My Guest (USA)) 9.3f **(67)**
Form - 1152
1998 Turf 2-4: (5f 1-1, 6f 1-2, 7f) (sft 1-2, g-s 1-2)
Very useful colt. Turf high 102 - 2nd of 7 giving 5lb to Immovable Option (3 Oct Curragh 6f g-s RF 4686a) - also 1st of 20 from Alabama Jacks (26 Jun Curragh RF 2417a). He looked a tremendous raw talent when winning his first two starts, but disappointed on both his outings in the autumn. However, there were excuses for those performances - he was hampered in the Prix de la Salamandre and left with too much to do in a Listed event at the Curragh - so all is not lost. This colt has a heap of ability and should win a Group race. **E Lynam in IRE [2-4] Gerard Purcell.*

ROMA BHB 53f RR 62f 4802[5]

3 b f Second Set (IRE) 9.2f **(67)** - Villasanta (Corvaro (USA)) 9f **(53)**
Form - 0835
Record 1998 - 1st:0 2nd:0 3rd:1 Ran:4
Win Prizemoney £0 *Total Prizemoney* £512
1998 Turf 0-3: (8f, 9f, 11f) (sft, g-s, frm) 1998 AW 0-1: (7f) (Fibr)
Rangy, average filly. Turf high 62 (began Spt) - 3rd of 8 getting 5lb from Sconced (28 Spt Hamilton 9f g-s RF 4531).
**C W Thornton [0-4] Guy Reed.*

ROMALITO BHB 40f32a RR 42f 32a 202[8]

8 b g Robellino (USA) 9.5f **(68)** - Princess Zita (Manado) 9.6f **(63)**
Form - 08
Record 1998 - 1st:0 2nd:0 3rd:0 Ran:1
Pre1998 - 1st:1 2nd:6 3rd:5 Ran:51
Win Prizemoney £2,070 *Total Prizemoney* £11,077
Wins * 1995 Jly Nottin (FRM) SH 14.1f 41 48 <
1998 AW 0-1: (16f) (Fibr)
Moderate gelding, effective 15 to 17f, best at 16f, acts on gd to frm, best on g-f, has worn blinkers, favours tight tracks. Inconsistent.
**M Blanshard [1-71] M Blanshard.*

ROMANOV (IRE) BHB 116f RR 117f 3103[5]

4 b c Nureyev (USA) 8.4f **(84)** - Morning Devotion (USA) (Affirmed (USA)) 9.3f **(79)**
Form - 125
Record 1998 - 1st:1 2nd:1 3rd:0 Ran:3
Pre1998 - 1st:3 2nd:1 3rd:4 Ran:8
Win Prizemoney £66,311 *Total Prizemoney* £309,056

Wins							
* **1998**	May	Newmar	(G-S)	G2	12f	117	<
* 1997	Aug	Haydoc	(G-F)	G3	10.5f	109	
* 1997	Apr	Sandow	(G-F)		8.1f	98	
* 1997	Mar	Haydoc	(SFT)		7.1f	80	

1998 Turf 1-3: (12f 1-3) (gd 1-2, g-f)
Well made, high-class colt, effective 10 to 12f, best at 12f, acts on gd to frm, best on gd, prefers left handed tracks, does well at Saint-Cloud and Haydock. Turf high 117 - 2nd of 9 to Fragrant Mix (28 Jun Saint-cloud 12f gd RF 2483a) - also 1st of 8 getting 5lb from Silver Patriarch (1 May Newmarket RF 0961). Consistent. Unraced at two, he developed into a high-class colt last year, and beat Silver Patriarch in the Jockey Club Stakes on his reappearance. He again finished ahead of that rival when runner-up in the Grand Prix de Saint-Cloud. Never really in the hunt in the King George, he was retired to stud in Kentucky afterwards.
**P W Chapple-Hyam [4-11] Sangster, Kraft Pays Collins.*

ROMAN REEL (USA) BHB 58f61a RR 59f 61a 4050[11]

7 ch g Sword Dance 9.4f **(67)** - Our Mimi (USA) (Believe It (USA)) 9.4f **(70)**
Form - 186120230610
Record 1998 - 1st:3 2nd:2 3rd:1 Ran:12
Pre1998 - 1st:8 2nd:6 3rd:9 Ran:61
Win Prizemoney £26,660 *Total Prizemoney* £37,025

Wins								
* **1998**	Aug	Bright	(FRM)	H	10f	55	59	
* **1998**	*Mar*	*Lingfi*	*(STD)*	*H*	*8f*	*56*	*63*	
* **1998**	*Jan*	*Lingfi*	*(STD)*	*H*	*10f*	*53*	*65*	
* 1997	Spt	Bright	(G-F)	H	10f	47	52	
* 1997	Jun	Bright	(FRM)	C	10f	-	55	
* 1997	*Mar*	*Lingfi*	*(STD)*	*H*	*8f*	*54*	*58*	
* 1996	Jun	Bright	(FRM)	C	10f		70	<
* 1996	May	Bright	(FRM)	S	10f		61	
* 1995	Jly	Chepst	(G-F)	H	8.1f	62	69	
* 1995	*Feb*	*Lingfi*	*(STD)*	*H*	*10f*	*57*	*57*	
* 1994	Aug	Bright	(FRM)		10f		62	

1998 Turf 1-7: (8f 2, 9f, 10f 1-4) (gd, g-f, frm 1-4, hrd) 1998 AW 2-5: (7f, 8f 1-2, 10f 1-2) (Equi 2-4, Fibr)
Average gelding, effective 8 to 10f, best at 10f, acts on g-f to frm - acts on Equi. Turf high 59 - 1st of 12 from Guesstimation (18 Aug Brighton RF 3693). AW high 65 (1st run) - 1st of 9 getting 6lb from Bon Guest (29 Jan Lingfield RF 0182) - also 1st of 12 getting 3lb from Anchor Venture (19 Mar Lingfield RF 0441). Pays his way at a low level, and goes particularly well on the Lingfield Equitrack and at Brighton. He is not very consistent, but is a good ride for an inexperienced pilot. **G L Moore [11-73] Mrs J Moore.*

ROMANTIC SECRET BHB 30f RR 25f 3092[10]

3 ch f Executive Man 8.9f **(52)**-Tria Romantica(Another Realm) 6.6f **(55)**
Form - 0
Record 1998 - 1st:0 2nd:0 3rd:0 Ran:1
Pre1998 - 1st:0 2nd:0 3rd:0 Ran:2
1998 AW 0-1: (8f) (Fibr)
Light-framed, currently little account filly.
**A G Juckes [0-1] Mrs K C Price (from R T Juckes [0-2] Jly 1997).*

ROMERO BHB 65f RR 65f 4752[7]

2 b c Robellino (USA) 9.5f **(68)** - Casamurrae (Be My Guest (USA)) 9.3f **(67)**
Form - 037
Record 1998 - 1st:0 2nd:0 3rd:1 Ran:3
Win Prizemoney £0 *Total Prizemoney* £497
1998 Turf 0-3: (6f, 7f, 8f) (sft, gd, g-f)
Currently average colt. Turf high 65 (began Aug).
**C W Thornton [0-3] Guy Reed.*

RONDA RR 90f 2663a[3]

2 b f Bluebird (USA) 7.9f **(71)** - Memory's Gold (USA) **(61f)** (Java Gold (USA))
Form - 3
1998 Turf 0-1: (5f) (gd)
Currently useful filly. **C Laffon-Parias in FR [0-1] D Hinojosa.*

RONDAN (ITY) RR 99f 5135a[1]

3 b c Danehill (USA) 9.1f **(79)**-Rontry (ITY)(Try My Best(USA)) 7.6f **(67)**
Form - 31
1998 Turf 1-2: (15f 1-2) (hvy, g-s 1-1)
Currently very useful colt. Turf high 99 (began Oct) - 1st of 7 getting 3lb from Generosity (31 Oct Tesio RF 5135a).
**V Caruso in ITY [1-2] Incolinx.*

RONQUISTA D'OR BHB 49f47a RR 52f 47a 4879[7]

4 b c Ron's Victory (USA) 9.2f **(52)** - Gild the Lily (Ile de Bourbon (USA)) 10.1f **(67)**
Form - 6140705142007
Record 1998 - 1st:2 2nd:1 3rd:0 Ran:12
Pre1998 - 1st:0 2nd:2 3rd:1 Ran:11
Win Prizemoney £4,539 *Total Prizemoney* £7,364

Wins								
* **1998**	Jly	Warwic	(G-F)	SH	12.5f	43	52	
* **1998**	*Jan*	*Southw*	*(STD)*	*H*	*12f*	*46*	*56+*	<

1998 Turf 1-6: (12f 2, 13f 1-1, 14f 3) (gd 3, g-f, frm 1-2) 1998 AW 1-6: (11f, 12f 1-2, 13f, 14f, 16f) (Equi, Fibr 1-5)
Strong, fair colt, effective 12 to 14f, acts on g-f to hrd - acts on AW, often wears blinkers (very effectively), likes left handed tracks, favours tight tracks. Turf high 52 - 2nd of 8 giving 1lb to Zibeth (13

Aug Chepstow 12f frm RF 3611) - also 1st of 12 getting 15lb from Java Shrine (18 Jly Warwick RF 2944). AW high 56 (1st run) - 1st of 15 getting 11lb from Dalwhinnie (2 Jan Southwell RF 0014). Becoming disappointing. **G A Ham [2-23] D M Drury.*

RON'S PET BHB 68f RR 72f 4962^{5}

3 ch g Ron's Victory (USA) 9.2f **(52)** - Penny Mint (Mummy's Game) 8.2f **(60)**

Form - 08005585

Record 1998 - 1st:0 2nd:0 3rd:0 Ran:8
Pre1998 - 1st:1 2nd:4 3rd:1 Ran:8

Win Prizemoney £2,992 *Total Prizemoney* £9,489

Wins * 1997 Aug Bright (GD) 7f 79 <

1998 Turf 0-8: (7f 2, 8f 4, 10f 2) (sft, gd 2, g-f, frm 4)

Scopey, above-average gelding, effective 5 to 8f, acts on g-s to frm, best on g-f. Turf high 75. **R Hannon [1-16] George Teo.*

RON'S ROUND BHB 57f55a RR 59f 55a 4141^{2}

4 ch g Ron's Victory (USA) 9.2f **(52)**-Magical Spirit (Top Ville) 11.7f **(68)**

Form - 3755323111422

Record 1998 - 1st:3 2nd:3 3rd:3 Ran:13
Pre1998 - 1st:0 2nd:2 3rd:1 Ran:10

Win Prizemoney £7,736 *Total Prizemoney* £13,423

Wins * **1998** *Jly Wolver (STD) H 9.4f 35 46+*
* **1998** *Jly Southw (STD) H 11f 35 49+*
1998 Jun Nottin (G-S) SH 10f 48 56 <

1998 Turf 1-8: (8f, 10f 1-7) (gd 1-2, g-f 3, frm 3) 1998 AW 2-5: (9f 1-1, 10f, 11f 1-2, 12f) (Equi 2, Fibr 2-3)

Workmanlike, fair gelding, effective 8 to 10f, best at 10f, acts on gd to frm, best on frm, excels at Leicester, does well at Nottingham. Turf high 59 - 2nd of 15 getting 4lb from Cherokee Flight (31 Aug Chepstow 10f frm RF 3981) - also 1st of 18 giving 14lb to Acquittal (17 Jun Nottingham RF 2069). AW high 49. Consistent. Sold to join the Martin Pipe team after wining a seller at Nottingham in June, he gave his new connections plenty of fun. Not a straightforward ride, he will now been seen out over hurdles.

**M C Pipe [2-5] David Manning Associates (from C A Dwyer [1-16] Jun 1998).*

ROOKIE RR 47f 4146^{12}

2 b g Magic Ring (IRE) 6.5f **(64)** - Shot At Love (IRE) **(83f)** (Last Tycoon) 8.5f **(62)**

Form - 0

Record 1998 - 1st:0 2nd:0 3rd:0 Ran:1

1998 Turf 0-1: (6f) (g-f)

Currently moderate gelding. **C A Cyzer [0-1] R M Cyzer.*

ROOSTER BHB 69f RR 68f 4155^{7}

3 b g Roi Danzig (USA) 10.5f **(62)** - Jussoli (Don) 7.7f **(64)**

Form - 467

Record 1998 - 1st:0 2nd:0 3rd:0 Ran:3

Win Prizemoney £0 *Total Prizemoney* £253

1998 Turf 0-3: (8f, 11f, 12f) (gd, g-f, frm)

Workmanlike, average gelding. Turf high 68 (began Jly).
**Miss S E Hall [0-3] C Platts.*

ROSA CANINA RR 62f 5005^{10}

2 b f Bustino 11f **(64)** - Moon Spin (Night Shift (USA)) 7.2f **(69)**

Form - 00

Record 1998 - 1st:0 2nd:0 3rd:0 Ran:2

1998 Turf 0-2: (8f 2) (sft, gd)

Currently average filly. Turf high 62 (began Oct).
**J L Dunlop [0-2] J L Dunlop.*

ROSA ROYALE BHB 46f43a RR 48f 43a 4815^{8}

4 b f Arazi (USA) 9.2f **(74)** - Gussy Marlowe (Final Straw) 7.9f **(64)**

Form - 0328384788

Record 1998 - 1st:0 2nd:1 3rd:2 Ran:10
Pre1998 - 1st:0 2nd:0 3rd:0 Ran:4

Win Prizemoney £0 *Total Prizemoney* £1,958

1998 Turf 0-9: (8f 3, 9f 3, 12f 2, 16f) (g-s 2, gd 5, frm 2) 1998 AW 0-1: (12f) (Fibr)

Lengthy, moderate filly, effective 8 to 12f, acts on gd. Turf high 52 - 3rd of 15 giving 4lb to Genuine John (15 May Hamilton 8f gd RF 1234). Inconsistent.
**W Storey [0-10] Mrs V A Ward (from Mrs J Cecil [0-4] Spt 1997).*

ROSE BAY RR 65f 4758^{11}

2 b f Shareef Dancer (USA) 10.1f **(67)** - Cormorant Bay (Don't Forget Me) 8.3f **(74)**

Form - 0

Record 1998 - 1st:0 2nd:0 3rd:0 Ran:1

1998 Turf 0-1: (7f) (gd)

Currently average filly. **C E Brittain [0-1] Saeed Manana.*

ROSE CROIX (USA) BHB 69f RR 69f 5041^{7}

2 b f Chief's Crown (USA) 10.2f **(75)** - La Papagena (Habitat) 9.4f **(70)**

Form - 747

Record 1998 - 1st:0 2nd:0 3rd:0 Ran:3

Win Prizemoney £0 *Total Prizemoney* £235

1998 Turf 0-3: (6f, 7f 2) (sft, gd 2)

Currently average filly. Turf high 69 (began Spt).
**W Jarvis [0-3] Lord Howard de Walden.*

ROSE FLYER (IRE) BHB 25f RR 13f 294^{9}

8 b m Nordico (USA) 8.2f **(59)** - String of Straw (Thatching) 8f **(66)**

Form - 0

Record 1998 - 1st:0 2nd:0 3rd:0 Ran:1
Pre1998 - 1st:3 2nd:5 3rd:5 Ran:38

Win Prizemoney £5,961 *Total Prizemoney* £11,855

1998 AW 0-1: (8f) (Fibr)

Poor mare. Becoming disappointing.
**M C Chapman [3-39] A M Packaging Ltd.*

ROSE HILL BHB 75f RR 74f 4845^{10}

2 b f Sabrehill (USA) 8.5f **(64)** - Petite Rosanna (Ile de Bourbon (USA)) 10.1f **(67)**

Form - 160

Record 1998 - 1st:1 2nd:0 3rd:0 Ran:3

Win Prizemoney £2,203 *Total Prizemoney* £2,285

Wins * **1998** Aug Warwic (G-F) 7f 68+ <

1998 Turf 1-3: (7f 1-1, 8f 2) (gd, g-f, frm 1-1)

Currently above-average filly. Turf high 74 (began Aug) - 6th of 7 getting 5lb from Bathwick (15 Spt Sandown 8f gd RF 4266) - also 1st of 11 from Emma-Lyne (31 Aug Warwick RF 4007).
**T G Mills [1-3] Chancery Bourse Inv Stud).*

ROSE OF MOONCOIN (IRE) BHB 100f RR 98f 3101^{5}

2 b f Brief Truce (USA) 9.1f **(73)** - Sharp Deposit (Sharpo) 7.7f **(59)**

Form - 145

Record 1998 - 1st:1 2nd:0 3rd:0 Ran:3

Win Prizemoney £4,308 *Total Prizemoney* £5,958

Wins * **1998** Jun Newmar (GD) 6f 79 <

1998 Turf 1-3: (6f 1-3) (g-f, frm, hrd 1-1)

Currently very useful filly. Turf high 98 - 4th of 10 to Wannabe Grand (7 Jly Newmarket 6f frm RF 2580). Won a warm maiden on her debut on the Newmarket July Course before finishing fourth over course and distance in the Cherry Hinton. Fifth in the Princess Margaret at Ascot, a seventh furlong might suit.
**J E Banks [1-3] P Cunningham.*

ROSE OF SHUAIB (IRE) BHB 57f RR 59f 4263^{10}

3 ch f Caerleon (USA) 10.9f **(79)** - Almuhtarama (IRE) (Rainbow Quest (USA)) 10.4f **(75)**

Form - 3000

Record 1998 - 1st:0 2nd:0 3rd:1 Ran:4

Win Prizemoney £0 *Total Prizemoney* £578

1998 Turf 0-4: (8f, 10f 3) (gd 2, frm 2)

Scopey, fair filly. Turf high 59 (1st run) - 3rd of 18 to Myzomela (18 May Windsor 8f frm RF 1316).
**L M Cumani [0-4] Sheikh Ahmed Al Maktoum.*

ROSE PETAL (USA) RR 100f $3880a^{3}$

3 ch f Majestic Light (USA) 9.5f **(78)** - Gdansk Victory (USA)

Form - 1111123

1998 Turf 5-7: (9f 1-1, 10f 4-5, 14f) (g-s 1-1, gd 2-4, g-f 2-2)

Very useful filly, effective 10 to 14f, best at 10f, acts on gd to g-f, best on gd, and likes Leopardstown. Turf high 100 - 2nd of 7 giving 8lb to Draft Of Vintage (9 Aug Leopardstown 10f gd RF 3559a) - also 1st of 7 giving 5lb to Balizac (2 Aug Cork RF 3358a). She must have given the handicapper nightmares, winning five races off the bounce despite rising 25lb in the ratings. Placed in a Listed event on her final start, she is a credit to her trainer and will be hard to keep out of the winners' enclosure in 1999.

**J S Bolger in IRE [5-8] Henryk de Kwiatkowski.*

ROSES FROM RIDEY (IRE) RR 78f 4812^{9}
2 b f Petorius 8f **(66)** - Minnie Habit (Habitat) 9.4f **(70)**
Form - 60
Record 1998 - 1st:0 2nd:0 3rd:0 Ran:2
1998 Turf 0-2: (6f, 7f) (gd, g-f)
Currently above-average filly. Turf high 78 (1st run) (began Oct) - 6th of 14 to Georgette (3 Oct Newmarket 6f g-f RF 4629).
**B W Hills [0-2] Mrs Drusilla Thomas.*

ROSE'S TREASURE (IRE) BHB 71f **RR 72f** 4243^{13}
2 b f Treasure Kay 6.5f **(53)**-Euro Miss(IRE)(Double Schwartz) 7.9f **(55)**
Form - 122254550
Record 1998 - 1st:1 2nd:3 3rd:0 Ran:9
Win Prizemoney £4,305 *Total Prizemoney* £7,788
Wins * 1998 Mar Doncas (GD) 5f 76 <
1998 Turf 1-9: (5f 1-7, 6f 2) (g-s, gd 1-2, g-f 4, frm 2)
Above-average filly, effective 5f, acts on g-s to g-f, often wears blinkers. Turf high 84 - 2nd of 9 getting 5lb from Red Lion (25 May Redcar 5f gd RF 1455) - also 1st of 22 getting 10lb from Perugino Bay (28 Mar Doncaster RF 0482). Consistent. She showed the right sort of attitude to win a maiden auction event at Doncaster on her debut, and has run some respectable races since.
**B S Rothwell [1-9] Jack Kee.*

ROSEUM RR 39f 4994^{8}
2 b f Lahib (USA) 8f **(69)** - Rose Barton (Pas de Seul) 9.1f **(67)**
Form - 8
Record 1998 - 1st:0 2nd:0 3rd:0 Ran:1
1998 Turf 0-1: (6f) (sft)
Currently very moderate filly. **R Guest [0-1] Mrs B Mills.*

ROSEWOOD LADY (IRE) BHB 46f45a **RR 51f 45a** 3329^{19}
3 b f Maledetto (IRE) - Thrill Seeker (IRE) (Treasure Kay)
Form - 3000
Record 1998 - 1st:0 2nd:0 3rd:1 Ran:4
Pre1998 - 1st:1 2nd:3 3rd:0 Ran:9
Win Prizemoney £2,738 *Total Prizemoney* £5,787
Wins * 1997 Aug Windso (GD) S 6f 59 <
1998 Turf 0-4: (7f, 8f 3) (gd 3, g-f)
Light-framed, fair filly, effective 5 to 8f, best at 6f, acts on gd to g-f - acts on Fibr, best on gd, has worn blinkers. Turf high 51 (1st run) - 3rd of 17 getting 2lb from Swoosh (22 Jun Nottingham 8f gd RF 2173). **K R Burke [1-13] Maurice Charge.*

ROSIE JAQUES BHB 49f48a **RR 45f 48a** 3641^{6}
3 b f Doyoun 10.7f **(69)** - Premier Princess (Hard Fought) 8.8f **(62)**
Form - 8054176
Record 1998 - 1st:1 2nd:0 3rd:0 Ran:7
Win Prizemoney £1,773 *Total Prizemoney* £1,773
Wins * 1998 *Jly Wolver (STD) C 9.4f 38* <
1998 Turf 0-3:(10f, 12f 2)(gd, frm 2)1998 AW 1-4: (9f 1-3, 12f) (Fibr 1-4)
Workmanlike, moderate filly, effective 9f, - acts on Fibr. Turf high 45. AW high 38 - 1st of 7 getting 5lb from Amber Regent (10 Jly Wolverhampton RF 2693). **N P Littmoden [1-7] La Piette Partnership.*

ROSMADEC (FR) RR 92f $1091a^{7}$
3
Form - 7
1998 Turf 0-1: (11f) (sft)
Currently useful. **E Lellouche in FR [0-1].*

ROSSEL (USA) BHB 60f **RR 62f** 4769^{2}
5 b g Blushing John (USA) 8.9f **(75)** - Northern Aspen (USA) (Northern Dancer) 9.6f **(80)**
Form - 133022
Record 1998 - 1st:1 2nd:2 3rd:2 Ran:6
Pre1998 - 1st:1 2nd:0 3rd:2 Ran:14
Win Prizemoney £9,268 *Total Prizemoney* £15,407
Wins * 1998 Apr Hamilt (HVY) H 13f 57 62
1996 Jly Mussel (GD) C 12.1f 63 <
1998 Turf 1-6: (11f, 12f 2, 13f 1-2, 16f) (sft 1-2, g-s, gd 3)
Average gelding, effective 12 to 13f, best at 13f, acts on sft to g-s, best on g-s, has worn blinkers, prefers right handed tracks. Turf high 62 - 2nd of 17 getting 1lb from Voila Premiere (28 Spt Hamilton 12f g-s RF 4532) - also 1st of 7 getting 11lb from Ledgendry Line (4 Apr Hamilton RF 0562). He looks best suited by a trip short of two miles on the Flat.
**P Monteith [6-31] Allan Melville (from Sir Michael Stoute [1-6] Jly 1996).*

ROSSELLI (USA) BHB 100f **RR 102df** 3755^{7}
2 b c Puissance 7.1f **(60)** - Miss Rossi (Artaius (USA)) 9f **(69)**
Form - 11137
Record 1998 - 1st:3 2nd:0 3rd:1 Ran:5
Win Prizemoney £42,917 *Total Prizemoney* £47,292
Wins * 1998 Jun Ascot (SFT) G3 5f 102 <
*** 1998** Jun Beverl (G-S) 5f 94
*** 1998** May Newcas (G-F) 5f 78+
1998 Turf 3-5: (5f 3-3, 6f 2) (g-s 1-1, gd 1-2, frm 1-2)
Very useful colt. Turf high 102 - 1st of 15 from Sheer Viking (18 Jun Ascot RF 2084) - also 1st of 3 from Principality (3 Jun Beverley RF 1678). He looked the pick of the early-season juveniles when winning the Group Three Norfolk Stakes at Royal Ascot, but was put in his place later in the summer. Jack Berry believes he is the spitting image of Mind Games, and it will be interesting to see if he develops as well as that admirable sprinter.
**J Berry [3-5] T G Holdcroft.*

ROTOSTAR BHB 50f **RR 64f** 3904^{8}
2 ch f Aragon 7.7f **(58)** - Davinia (Gold Form) 5.6f **(55)**
Form - 066448
Record 1998 - 1st:0 2nd:0 3rd:0 Ran:6
1998 Turf 0-5: (5f, 6f 3, 7f) (g-f 2, frm 3) 1998 AW 0-1: (5f) (Fibr)
Average filly, effective 6f, acts on frm. Turf high 64.
**P D Evans [0-6] Treble Chance Partnership.*

ROUGE BHB 54f59a **RR 21f 59a** 873^{3}
3 gr f Rudimentary (USA) 8.2f **(66)**-Couleur de Rose(Kalaglow)9.8f **(67)**
Form - 403
Record 1998 - 1st:0 2nd:0 3rd:1 Ran:3
Win Prizemoney £0 *Total Prizemoney* £475
1998 Turf 0-1: (8f) (g-s) 1998 AW 0-2: (7f, 8f) (Fibr 2)
Currently fair filly. AW high 55 - 3rd of 13 giving 1lb to Landrfun (25 Apr Wolverhampton 8f Fibr RF 0873).
**J P Leigh [0-3] J M Greetham.*

ROUGE ETOILE RR 80f 4882^{1}
2 b f Most Welcome 8.6f **(66)** - Choral Sundown (Night Shift (USA)) 7.2f **(69)**
Form - 31
Record 1998 - 1st:1 2nd:0 3rd:1 Ran:2
Win Prizemoney £2,763 *Total Prizemoney* £3,458
Wins * 1998 Oct Folkes (G-S) 6f 80 <
1998 Turf 1-2: (6f 1-2) (g-s 1-2)
Currently decent filly. Turf high 80 (began Oct) - 1st of 16 getting 5lb from Tayif (20 Oct Folkestone RF 4882).
**A J McNae [1-2] Astaire & Partners (Holdings) Ltd.*

ROUND ROBIN (IRE) BHB 58f49a **RR 68df 49a** 4970^{9}
4 ch g Royal Academy (USA) 7.8f **(77)**-Flying Fantasy(Habitat) 9.4f **(70)**
Form - 0400
Record 1998 - 1st:0 2nd:0 3rd:0 Ran:3
Pre1998 - 1st:0 2nd:1 3rd:1 Ran:6
Win Prizemoney £0 *Total Prizemoney* £2,064
1998 Turf 0-1: (10f) (g-s) 1998 AW 0-2: (8f, 12f) (Fibr 2)
Scopey, average gelding, effective 7f, acts on sft, often wears blinkers, likes left handed tracks, favours tight tracks. AW high 44. Inconsistent. His Ayr second in August '97 flatters him.
**Mrs A E Johnson [0-3] The Daisy Chain Partnership (from C W Thornton [0-8] Feb 1998).*

ROUTE SIXTY SIX (IRE) BHB 77f **RR 72f** 4929^{1}
2 b f Brief Truce (USA) 9.1f **(73)** - Lyphards Goddess (IRE) (Lyphard's Special (USA)) 10.3f **(72)**
Form - 827661
Record 1998 - 1st:1 2nd:1 3rd:0 Ran:6
Win Prizemoney £3,053 *Total Prizemoney* £4,005
Wins * 1998 Oct Bright (G-S) H 7f 72 72 <
1998 Turf 1-6: (6f, 7f 1-5) (g-s 1-1, gd, g-f, frm 3)
Above-average filly, effective 7f, acts on g-s to frm. Turf high 72 (began Jly) - 1st of 17 giving 8lb to Glastonbury (22 Oct Brighton RF 4929). **G L Moore [1-6] J B R Leisure Ltd.*

Rosselli - the next Mind Games?

ROVERETTO RR 23f 2157[8]
3 b c Robellino (USA) 9.5f **(68)** - Spring Flyer (IRE) **(56f 64a)** (Waajib)
Form - 8
Record 1998 - 1st:0 2nd:0 3rd:0 Ran:1
1998 Turf 0-1: (8f) (gd)
Lengthy, currently little account colt.
**Mrs M Reveley [0-1] Codan Trust Company Ltd.*

ROWLANDSONS CHARM (IRE) BHB 40f47a **RR 38f 47a** 2958[17]
5 b m Fayruz 6.6f **(63)** - Magic Gold (Sallust) 8.4f **(63)**
Form - 60128820

Record					
1998 -	1st:1	2nd:2	3rd:0	Ran:6	
Pre1998 -	1st:3	2nd:5	3rd:4	Ran:26	

Win Prizemoney £9,928 *Total Prizemoney* £17,602

Wins						
*** 1998**	*Feb Lingfi*	*(SLW) SH*	*13f*	*40*	*40*	
1996	*Mar Lingfi*	*(STD) C*	*8f*		*46*	
1996	*Jan Lingfi*	*(STD) S*	*8f*		*64*	<
1996	*Jan Lingfi*	*(STD) C*	*8f*		*58*	

1998 Turf 0-2:(8f, 12f) (gd, frm) 1998 AW 1-4: (13f 1-2, 16f 2) (Equi 1-4)
Moderate filly, effective 13 to 16f, - acts on Equi, mostly wears blinkers (effectively), prefers left handed tracks. Turf high 38. AW high 47 - 2nd of 11 giving 17lb to Coastguards Hero (27 Jun Lingfield 13f Equi RF 2340). Inconsistent.
**Miss B Sanders [1-12] J M Quinn (from A Moore [0-1] May 1996).*

ROWLANDSONS STUD (IRE) BHB 38f46a **RR 25f 46a** 3806[10]
5 b br g Distinctly North (USA) 7.4f **(63)** - Be My Million (Taufan (USA)) 7f **(57)**
Form - 34301700

Record				
1998 -	1st:1	2nd:0	3rd:1	Ran:7
Pre1998 -	1st:1	2nd:2	3rd:6	Ran:27

Win Prizemoney £4,320 *Total Prizemoney* £8,619

Wins						
*** 1998**	*Jun Lingfi*	*(STD) SH*	*7f*	*46*	*50*	
1996	*Mar Lingfi*	*(STD) H*	*6f*	*55*	*61*	<

1998 Turf 0-1:(7f)(frm) 1998 AW 1-6:(5f, 6f 3, 7f 1-1, 8f)(Equi 1-2,Fibr 4)
Very moderate gelding, effective 5 to 7f, best at 5f, acts on frm - acts on Equi, has worn blinkers, favours left handed tracks, likes tight tracks. AW high 50 - 1st of 15 giving 8lb to Kosevo (13 Jun Lingfield RF 1965). Consistent.
**K C Comerford [1-14] S Comerford (from P Burgoyne [0-6] Nov 1996).*

ROY BHB 53a **RR 60tf** 3638[10]
3 ch g Keen 11.1f **(58)** - Billante (USA) (Graustark) 10.1f **(70)**
Form - 3050

Record				
1998 -	1st:0	2nd:0	3rd:1	Ran:4
Pre1998 -	1st:0	2nd:0	3rd:0	Ran:1

Win Prizemoney £0 *Total Prizemoney* £588
1998 Turf 0-3: (12f, 14f, 17f) (gd, g-f 2) 1998 AW 0-1: (14f) (Fibr)
Scopey, average gelding, has worn blinkers. Turf high 60.
**H Morrison [0-5] The D T M Partnership.*

ROYAL ACCLAIM BHB 27f32a **RR 47f 32a** 9[6]
13 ch g Tender King 8.1f **(54)** - Glimmer (Hot Spark) 7.6f **(62)**
Form - 6

Record				
1998 -	1st:0	2nd:0	3rd:0	Ran:1
Pre1998 -	1st:5	2nd:9	3rd:6	Ran:85

Win Prizemoney £14,756 *Total Prizemoney* £24,682

Wins					
1997	*Jan Southw*	*(STD) H*	*11f*	*32*	*36*

1998 AW 0-1: (8f) (Fibr)
Moderate gelding, mostly wears blinkers.
**B Preece [0-1] M Ephgrave (from K R Burke [0-9] Oct 1997).*

ROYAL AFFINITY (IRE) RR 95f 4695a[6]
4 ch c Royal Academy (USA) 7.8f **(77)** - Tuyenu

Form - 73056
1998 Turf 0-5: (5f, 6f, 7f 2, 8f) (hvy 2, gd 3)
Very useful colt, effective 5 to 6f, best at 6f, acts on g-s to frm, has worn blinkers. Turf high 95 - 3rd of 11 giving 15lb to Coconut Creek (3 Aug Leopardstown 6f gd RF 3536a). Becoming disappointing. **A P O'Brien in IRE [1-12] Ronald Arculli.*

ROYAL ALIBI RR 72f 2455[4]
4 b c Royal Academy (USA) 7.8f **(77)** - Excellent Alibi (USA) (Exceller (USA)) 12.5f **(74)**
Form - 4
Record 1998 - 1st:0 2nd:0 3rd:0 Ran:1
Win Prizemoney £0 *Total Prizemoney* £240
1998 Turf 0-1: (11f) (frm)
Light-framed, currently above-average colt.
**H R A Cecil [0-1] Lordship Stud.*

ROYAL AMARETTO (IRE) BHB 106f RR 105f 2912[5]
4 b c Fairy King (USA) 7.7f **(75)** - Melbourne Miss (Chaparral (FR)) 13.7f **(90)**
Form - 8835
Record 1998 - 1st:0 2nd:0 3rd:1 Ran:4
Pre1998 - 1st:2 2nd:1 3rd:2 Ran:8
Win Prizemoney £11,799 *Total Prizemoney* £23,783
Wins * 1997 Apr Newbur (G-F) 10f 110+ <
* 1996 Spt Chepst (G-F) 7.1f 86
1998 Turf 0-4: (10f 3, 12f) (sft, gd 3)
Scopey, Pattern-class colt, effective 10f, acts on gd. Turf high 105. He moves like a dream and is often ridden from the front. However, while those tactics make use of his stride, they proved singularly unsuccessful last season. There is a good race lurking within this under-achieving colt.
**B J Meehan [2-12] The Harlequin Partnership.*

ROYAL ANTHEM (USA) BHB 125f RR 125f 5167a[7]
3 b c Theatrical 11.5f **(78)** - In Neon (USA) (Ack Ack (USA)) 12.7f **(82)**
Form - 111317
Record 1998 - 1st:4 2nd:0 3rd:1 Ran:6
Win Prizemoney £359,412 *Total Prizemoney* £422,412
Wins * **1998** Oct Woodbi (FRM) 12f 125 <
* **1998** Jun Ascot (G-S) G2 12f 115
* **1998** Jun Newmar (GD) L 10f 109
* **1998** May Newbur (G-F) 10f 92
1998 Turf 4-6: (10f 2-2, 12f 2-4) (gd 1-1, g-f, frm 2-3, hrd 1-1)
Well made, top-class colt, effective 12f, acts on gd to frm. Turf high 125 - 1st of 8 getting 7lb from Chief Bearhart (18 Oct Woodbine RF 4953a). Unraced at two, he won his first three starts last year, including the Group Two King Edward VII Stakes at Royal Ascot, before running a fine third for one so inexperienced in the King George. Given a three-month break, he came back with a fine win in the Canadian International at Woodbine before running poorly in the Breeders' Cup Turf. Cecil expressed regrets about letting such a long-striding colt take his chance on the loose turf and tight corners at Churchill Downs, especially after the horse suffered an injury scare in the build-up to the race. It is to be hoped that this talented individual returns in good order in 1999. **H R A Cecil [4-6] The Thoroughbred Corporation.*

ROYAL ARROW (IRE) RR 7f 4968[12]
3 b f Royal Academy (USA) 7.8f **(77)** - Fighting Run (Runnett) 7f **(59)**
Form - 00
Record 1998 - 1st:0 2nd:0 3rd:0 Ran:2
1998 Turf 0-2: (7f, 10f) (sft, gd)
Scopey, currently very poor filly. Turf high 7.
**I A Balding [0-2] R P B Michaelson & Wafic Said.*

ROYAL BLUE BHB 42f RR 43f 4383[8]
3 ch g Ron's Victory (USA) 9.2f **(52)** - Angels Are Blue (Stanford) 7.9f **(56)**
Form - 004808
Record 1998 - 1st:0 2nd:0 3rd:0 Ran:6
Pre1998 - 1st:0 2nd:0 3rd:0 Ran:3
Win Prizemoney £0 *Total Prizemoney* £251
1998 Turf 0-5: (5f, 6f 4) (g-s, gd 2, g-f, frm) 1998 AW 0-1: (8f) (Fibr)
Leggy, moderate gelding. Turf high 43.
**M D I Usher [0-9] The Ridgeway Partnership.*

ROYAL CARLTON (IRE) BHB 36f53a RR 44f 53a 4927[9]
6 b g Mulhollande (USA) 6.6f **(68)** - Saintly Angel (So Blessed) 8.7f **(67)**
Form - 0007000768040
Record 1998 - 1st:0 2nd:0 3rd:0 Ran:10
Pre1998 - 1st:3 2nd:1 3rd:1 Ran:19
Win Prizemoney £8,661 *Total Prizemoney* £10,682
Wins 1997 *Jan Lingfi (STD) H 8f 65 68*
1997 *Jan Lingfi (STD) H 7f 60 70* <
1996 *Dec Lingfi (STD) 8f 59*
1998 Turf 0-8: (8f 4, 9f 2, 10f 2) (g-s 2, gd 3, g-f 2, frm) 1998 AW 0-2: (8f, 10f) (Equi 2)
Moderate gelding, effective 7 to 8f, best at 8f, - acts on Equi, favours left handed tracks. Turf high 44. AW high 30.
**K C Comerford [0-1] Ian Hutchins (from G L Moore [3-21] Jly 1998).*

ROYAL CASCADE (IRE) BHB 44f60a RR 42f 60a 4635[11]
4 b g River Falls 8.2f **(56)** - Relative Stranger (Cragador) 6f **(67)**
Form - 67514116082570
Record 1998 - 1st:3 2nd:1 3rd:0 Ran:12
Pre1998 - 1st:1 2nd:1 3rd:0 Ran:10
Win Prizemoney £8,390 *Total Prizemoney* £9,994
Wins * **1998** *Mar Wolver (STD) C 6f 65*
* **1998** *Feb Southw (STD) C 6f 69* <
* **1998** *Jan Southw (STD) S 6f 53*
* 1997 *Feb Wolver (STD) S 6f 51*
1998 Turf 0-4: (5f, 6f 3) (g-s, gd, g-f, frm) 1998 AW 3-8: (6f 3-7, 7f) (Fibr 3-8)
Unfurnished, average gelding, effective 6f, - acts on Fibr, has worn blinkers (extremely effectively), prefers left handed tracks, prefers tight tracks. Turf high 42. AW high 69 - 1st of 5 getting 6lb from Palacegate Touch (20 Feb Southwell RF 0323) - also 1st of 10 getting 1lb from Elite Hope (28 Mar Wolverhampton RF 0494). Inconsistent. **B A McMahon [4-22] R L Bedding.*

ROYAL CASTLE (IRE) BHB 77f RR 79f 4958[11]
4 b c Caerleon (USA) 10.9f**(79)**-Sun Princess(English Prince)10.1f **(61)**
Form - 420
Record 1998 - 1st:0 2nd:1 3rd:0 Ran:3
Pre1998 - 1st:2 2nd:0 3rd:1 Ran:8
Win Prizemoney £7,252 *Total Prizemoney* £10,751
Wins 1997 Oct Redcar (G-F) H 14.1f 74 80 <
1997 Jun Pontef (G-F) H 12f 70 73
1998 Turf 0-3: (12f, 14f, 15f) (frm 3)
Scopey, above-average colt, effective 12 to 14f, best at 14f, acts on gd to frm, best on frm, prefers tight tracks, excels at Redcar. Turf high 79 (began Spt) - 2nd of 7 getting 13lb from Aginor (25 Spt Redcar 14f frm RF 4487).
**M P Tregoning [0-3] Lord Weinstock (from Major W R Hern [2-8] Oct 1997).*

ROYAL CEILIDH (IRE) BHB 60f55a RR 68f 55a 151[6]
5 b m Prince Rupert (FR) 10.4f **(60)**-Isa (Dance In Time (CAN))8.9f **(59)**
Form - 746
Record 1998 - 1st:0 2nd:0 3rd:0 Ran:3
Pre1998 - 1st:3 2nd:2 3rd:4 Ran:28
Win Prizemoney £15,887 *Total Prizemoney* £23,859
Wins 1996 May Thirsk (G-F) H 8f 69 71
1995 Oct Catter (G-F) H 7f 67 73
1995 May Newcas (GD) 5f 84+ <
1998 AW 0-3: (10f, 12f 2) (Equi 3)
Average filly, effective 8 to 10f, acts on g-f, has worn blinkers, likes left handed tracks. AW high 54. Inconsistent.
**D L Williams [0-5] G C Farr (from Denys Smith [3-28] Oct 1997).*

ROYAL CIRCUS BHB 29f28a RR 28f 28a 3939[4]
9 b g Kris 10f **(75)** - Circus Ring (High Top) 10.2f **(67)**
Form - 0033850304
Record 1998 - 1st:0 2nd:0 3rd:3 Ran:8
Pre1998 - 1st:7 2nd:6 3rd:2 Ran:50
Win Prizemoney £19,286 *Total Prizemoney* £27,832
Wins 1997 Jly Bath (GD) SH 13.1f 37 43
1996 *Jan Lingfi (STD) H 12f 39 44* <
1995 *Feb Lingfi (STD) H 13f 35 35*
1995 *Jan Lingfi (STD) H 13f 33 37*
1994 Aug Hamilt (FRM) H 12.1f 39 38
1994 Jun Catter (GD) H 11.5f 38 40
1994 May Hamilt (FRM) H 12.1f 38 40

1998 Turf 0-2: (12f, 13f) (frm 2) 1998 AW 0-6: (12f, 13f 3, 16f 2) (Equi 6)
Very moderate gelding, effective 13 to 15f, best at 13f, acts on g-f to frm - acts on Equi, has worn blinkers, favours left handed tracks. Turf high 28 (began Jly). AW high 37 (1st run) - 3rd of 8 giving 3lb to Coastguards Hero (8 Jan Lingfield 13f Equi RF 0051).
**P W Hiatt [7-54] P W Hiatt (from Ian Williams [1-4] Aug 1997).*

ROYAL CROWN (IRE) BHB 78f RR 81df 4335[5]

4 b g Sadler's Wells (USA) 11.3f **(87)** - Rose of Jericho (USA) (Alleged (USA)) 10f **(76)**
Form - 7685

Record	**1998 -**	1st:0	2nd:0	3rd:0	Ran:4
	Pre1998 -	1st:0	2nd:3	3rd:1	Ran:7

Royal Anthem should be on song next term

ROYAL CITIZEN (IRE) BHB 44f55a RR 46f 55a 2930[4]

9 b g Caerleon (USA) 10.9f **(79)** - Taking Steps (Gay Fandango (USA)) 8.5f **(59)**
Form - 7024

Record	**1998 -**	1st:0	2nd:1	3rd:0	Ran:4
	Pre1998 -	1st:3	2nd:7	3rd:2	Ran:30

Win Prizemoney £7,356 *Total Prizemoney* £16,514

Wins						
1995	*Feb Wolver*	*(STD)*	*C*	*14f*		*53*
1995	*Feb Wolver*	*(STD)*	*C*	*14f*		*61*
1994	*Jan Southw*	*(STD)*	*H*	*12f*	*55*	*62* <

1998 Turf 0-3: (14f, 16f 2) (gd 2, frm) 1998 AW 0-1: (14f) (Fibr)
Fair gelding, effective 15f, - acts on Fibr, has worn blinkers (extremely effectively), likes tight tracks. Turf high 46.
**J Hetherton [0-6] Qualitair Holdings Ltd (from J F Bottomley [6-44] Apr 1997).*

Win Prizemoney £0 *Total Prizemoney* £5,835
1998 Turf 0-4: (13f, 16f, 18f, 20f) (gd 2, g-f, frm)
Well made, decent gelding, effective 12 to 16f, acts on gd to frm, best on gd, prefers left handed tracks, likes tight tracks. Turf high 81. **C E Brittain [0-4] Michael Watt (from P W Chapple-Hyam [0-7] Oct 1997).*

ROYAL DOLPHIN (IRE) RR 5137[19]

2 b c Dolphin Street (FR)-Diamond Lake (Kings Lake (USA)) 10.8f **(67)**
Form - 0

Record	**1998 -**	1st:0	2nd:0	3rd:0	Ran:1

1998 Turf 0-1: (7f) (gd)
Currently very poor colt. **B A McMahon [0-1] R L Bedding.*

ROYAL DOME (IRE) BHB 70f75a **RR 66f 75a** 4872[7]

6 b g Salt Dome (USA) 6.5f **(59)** - Brook's Dilemma (Known Fact (USA)) 7.4f **(67)**

Form - 060343250510107

Record					
1998 -	1st:2	2nd:1	3rd:2	Ran:15
Pre1998 -	1st:7	2nd:8	3rd:2	Ran:44

Win Prizemoney £44,615 *Total Prizemoney* £57,785

Wins							
* **1998**	Spt	Newcas	(GD)	H	5f	66	66
* **1998**	Aug	Carlis	(G-S)	H	5f	61	65
* 1997	Jly	Beverl	(GD)		5f		76 <
* 1997	Jun	Pontef	(GD)		5f		61
* 1996	Aug	Haydoc	(G-F)	H	5f	70	73
* 1996	Jly	Beverl	(G-F)		5f		68
* 1995	Oct	York	(GD)	H	5f	67	70
* 1995	Spt	Pontef	(GD)	H	5f	64	64
* 1995	Aug	Nottin	(G-F)	H	5.1f	54	60+

1998 Turf 2-15: (5f 2-15) (gd 1-6, g-f 1-5, frm 4)

Average gelding, effective 5 to 6f, best at 5f, acts on gd to frm, has worn blinkers. Turf high 66.

**Martyn Wane [9-58] Darren & Annaley Yates (from M W Easterby [0-1] Jun 1994).*

ROYAL DREAM BHB 71f68a **RR 79f 68a** 4872[14]

3 b f Ardkinglass 5f **(64)** - Faraway Grey (Absalom) 7.2f **(58)**

Form - 4044134340350

Record				
1998 -	1st:1	2nd:0	3rd:3	Ran:13
Pre1998 -	1st:2	2nd:0	3rd:1	Ran:7

Win Prizemoney £9,980 *Total Prizemoney* £14,408

Wins							
* **1998**	Jun	Beverl	(GD)	H	5f	69	75 <
* 1997	Jun	Ripon	(GD)		6f		73
* 1997	May	Beverl	(G-S)	S	5f		71

1998 Turf 1-10: (5f 1-4, 6f 6) (gd 1-5, g-f 3, frm 2) 1998 AW 0-3: (6f 3) (Fibr 3)

Unfurnished, above-average filly, effective 5 to 6f, best at 6f, acts on gd to frm, best on g-f, excels at Ripon and Beverley. Turf high 79 - 4th of 11 giving 2lb to Positive Air (29 Jun Pontefract 6f frm RF 2377) - also 1st of 18 giving 16lb to Hiltons Executive (10 Jun Beverley RF 1864). AW high 61. **J Berry [3-20] Mrs B A Matthews.*

ROYALE FINALE (IRE) BHB 49f49a **RR 45f 49a** 2477[U]

4 ch g Royal Academy (USA) 7.8f **(77)** - Final Farewell (USA) (Proud Truth (USA))

Form - 68000U

Record				
1998 -	1st:0	2nd:0	3rd:0	Ran:6
Pre1998 -	1st:0	2nd:0	3rd:1	Ran:3

Win Prizemoney £0 *Total Prizemoney* £587

1998 Turf 0-4: (6f, 8f 2, 11f) (gd, g-f 2, hrd) 1998 AW 0-2: (5f, 7f) (Equi, Fibr)

Scopey, moderate gelding, often wears blinkers. Turf high 45. AW high 31. Becoming disappointing.

**R F Marvin [0-8] Underwoods Racing (from H R A Cecil [0-3] May 1997).*

ROYAL FONTAINE (IRE) BHB 78f **RR 84f** 4265[1]

3 b f Royal Academy (USA) 7.8f **(77)** - Bellifontaine (FR) (Bellypha) 9.8f **(73)**

Form - 2221

Record				
1998 -	1st:1	2nd:3	3rd:0	Ran:4

Win Prizemoney £3,696 *Total Prizemoney* £7,954

Wins						
* **1998**	Spt	Sandow	(GD)	10f		72 <

1998 Turf 1-4: (8f, 10f 1-3) (gd 1-2, g-f, frm)

Workmanlike, decent filly. Turf high 82 (began Aug) - 2nd of 13 to De Mille (21 Aug Sandown 10f g-f RF 3794). Unraced at two, she ran a most promising race on her Sandown debut, only going down narrowly. Found one too good on her next two runs, doing little wrong, before making all at Sandown. **J W Hills [1-4] D J Deer.*

ROYAL FUSILIER (IRE) BHB 61f **RR 73f** 4658[17]

2 b c Case Law 6f **(64)**-Tropical Rain (Rainbow Quest (USA)) 10.4f **(75)**

Form - 02000

Record				
1998 -	1st:0	2nd:1	3rd:0	Ran:5

Win Prizemoney £0 *Total Prizemoney* £831

1998 Turf 0-5: (6f, 7f 3, 8f) (sft, gd, g-f 2, frm)

Above-average colt. Turf high 73 (began Jly) - 2nd of 8 to Gypsy (27 Jly Yarmouth 7f g-f RF 3152). **M Bell [0-5] W H Ponsonby.*

ROYAL HOUSE (FR) RR 96f 2807a[5]

3 b f Royal Academy (USA) 7.8f **(77)** - Reine Caroline (FR)

Form - 15

1998 Turf 1-2: (8f 1-2) (sft 1-1, gd)

Very useful filly. Turf high 96 (1st run) - 1st of 7 getting 12lb from Free To Speak (27 Jun Curragh RF 2427a).

**J Oxx in IRE [2-4] Mrs Arlene O'Neill.*

ROYAL INTRUSION BHB 24f **RR 3f** 1926[15]

5 ch g Roman Warrior - Image of War (Warpath) 12.3f **(52)**

Form - 0

Record				
1998 -	1st:0	2nd:0	3rd:0	Ran:1
Pre1998 -	1st:0	2nd:0	3rd:0	Ran:5

1998 Turf 0-1: (6f) (gd)

Very poor gelding. **R J Hodges [0-6] D H Smith.*

ROYAL LEGEND BHB 61f55a **RR 63f 55a** 4655[5]

6 b g Fairy King (USA) 7.7f **(75)** - Legend of Arabia (Great Nephew) 9.9f **(64)**

Form - 34031158365

Record				
1998 -	1st:2	2nd:0	3rd:2	Ran:10
Pre1998 -	1st:1	2nd:1	3rd:4	Ran:12

Win Prizemoney £11,014 *Total Prizemoney* £14,881

Wins							
* **1998**	Jun	Goodwo	(G-F)	H	9.9f	51	60 <
* **1998**	Jun	Lingfi	(G-S)	H	10f	51	54
1997	*May*	*Southw*	*(STD)*	*C*	*11f*		*51*

1998 Turf 2-10: (8f, 10f 2-8, 12f) (gd 2-4, g-f 2, frm 4)

Average gelding, effective 10f, acts on gd to frm, best on gd, has worn blinkers, prefers tight tracks. Turf high 63 - 3rd of 19 giving 21lb to Mary Culi (15 Spt Sandown 10f gd RF 4270) - also 1st of 13 getting 10lb from Diminutive (19 Jun Goodwood RF 2119).

**R M Flower [2-11] Jan Rieck (from J Pearce [1-10] Jun 1997).*

ROYAL MARK (IRE) BHB 80f **RR 84f** 4854[11]

5 b g Fairy King (USA) 7.7f **(75)** - Take Your Mark (USA) (Round Table) 9.5f **(81)**

Form - 00044218000

Record				
1998 -	1st:1	2nd:1	3rd:0	Ran:11
Pre1998 -	1st:3	2nd:2	3rd:2	Ran:18

Win Prizemoney £19,439 *Total Prizemoney* £31,459

Wins							
* **1998**	Jly	Newcas	(GD)	H	7f	81	84
1997	Aug	Newcas	(GD)	H	7f	82	86 <
1995	Aug	Newmar	(G-F)	H	7f	78	85+
1995	Jly	Ayr	(GD)		7f		84

1998 Turf 1-11: (6f 3, 7f 1-7, 8f) (sft, gd 1-6, g-f 2, frm, hrd)

Decent gelding, effective 7 to 8f, best at 7f, acts on g-s to frm, has worn blinkers, likes left handed tracks. Turf high 84 - 1st of 14 giving 20lb to Thwaab (27 Jly Newcastle RF 3140). Consistent. Took time to find his form in 1998, but scored at Newcastle in July and has a useful turn of foot when things go his way.

**T D Easterby [1-11] Burke's 5th Family Settlement (from T D Barron [1-6] Aug 1997).*

ROYAL MIDYAN RR 89f 4177a[2]

5 b g Midyan (USA) 9.9f **(64)** - Royal Agreement (USA) (Vaguely Noble) 10.1f **(72)**

Form - 26145472

1998 Turf 1-8: (8f 2, 9f, 10f 1-4, 11f) (hvy, sft, gd 1-5, g-f)

Useful gelding, effective 8 to 10f, acts on hvy to gd, best on gd. Turf high 92 - 1st of 10 giving 8lb to Crystal Wind (23 May Curragh RF 1505a). Consistent. **J F Bailey Jun in IRE [2-21] J F Bailey Jun.*

ROYAL MOUNT RR 72+f 1979[5]

2 ch c Cadeaux Genereux 7.9f **(76)** - Hawait Al Barr (Green Desert (USA)) 8.6f **(78)**

Form - 5

Record				
1998 -	1st:0	2nd:0	3rd:0	Ran:1

1998 Turf 0-1: (6f) (g-s)

Currently above-average colt. Shaped quite well on her debut.

**M Johnston [0-1] Maktoum Al Maktoum.*

ROYAL ORIGINE (IRE) BHB 90f **RR 80f** 4462[4]

2 b c Royal Academy (USA) 7.8f **(77)** - Belle Origine (USA) (Exclusive Native (USA)) 9.1f **(81)**

Form - 334

Record				
1998 -	1st:0	2nd:0	3rd:2	Ran:3

Win Prizemoney £0 *Total Prizemoney* £1,915

1998 Turf 0-3: (5f, 6f 2) (g-f 2, frm)
Currently decent colt. Turf high 80 - 3rd of 10 to Red Delirium (20 May Goodwood 6f g-f RF 1359).
**M R Channon [0-3] & Mrs Gary Pinchen.*

ROYAL PARADE (IRE) BHB 40f **RR 33f** 3281[19]
3 b g Pips Pride 6.7f **(70)** - Route Royale (Roi Soleil) 8.7f **(57)**
Form - 0080000
Record 1998 - 1st:0 2nd:0 3rd:0 Ran:7
1998 Turf 0-7: (6f 2, 7f 2, 8f 3) (gd, g-f 3, frm 3)
Strong, very moderate gelding, has worn blinkers. Turf high 44.
**J M Bradley [0-7] Craftbook Ltd.*

ROYAL PATRON RR 59f 5072[8]
2 ch f Royal Academy (USA) 7.8f **(77)**-Indian Queen(Electric) 10.1f **(61)**
Form - 8
Record 1998 - 1st:0 2nd:0 3rd:0 Ran:1
1998 Turf 0-1: (7f) (gd)
Currently fair filly. **J L Dunlop [0-1] Sir Gordon Brunton.*

ROYAL PLAYBOY BHB 58f **RR 48f** 3843[9]
2 ch c Clantime 6.6f **(57)** - First Play **(45df)** (Primo Dominie) 6.2f **(80)**
Form - 070
Record 1998 - 1st:0 2nd:0 3rd:0 Ran:3
1998 Turf 0-3: (5f 2, 6f) (gd, frm 2)
Currently moderate colt, has worn blinkers. Turf high 48 (began Jly). **G Lewis [0-3] Lhendup Dorji.*

ROYAL PREVIEW (IRE) BHB 55f **RR 48f** 2182[12]
2 b f Prince Sabo 6.6f **(64)** - Visible Form (Formidable (USA)) 9.2f **(63)**
Form - 050
Record 1998 - 1st:0 2nd:0 3rd:0 Ran:3
1998 Turf 0-3: (5f, 6f 2) (g-f 2, frm)
Currently moderate filly. Turf high 48. **M Bell [0-3] Sir Peter Davis.*

ROYAL PRINCESS RR 49f 4579[14]
2 b f Rock City 8.8f **(62)** - Royal Girl **(55f)** (Kafu) 6f **(47)**
Form - 50
Record 1998 - 1st:0 2nd:0 3rd:0 Ran:2
1998 Turf 0-2: (5f, 6f) (g-f, frm)
Currently moderate filly. Turf high 49 (began Spt).
**Miss S E Hall [0-2] Mrs T Hall.*

ROYAL REBEL RR 87f 4440a[4]
2 b c Robellino (USA) 9.5f **(68)** - Greenvera (USA) (Riverman (USA)) 9.1f **(76)**
Form - 474
Record 1998 - 1st:0 2nd:0 3rd:0 Ran:3
Win Prizemoney £0 *Total Prizemoney* £7,282
1998 Turf 0-3: (7f 2, 8f) (gd, g-f, frm)
Currently useful colt. Turf high 87 (began Jly). A promising fourth in a listed race on his debut, keeping on well at the end, he failed to progress from that next time, running green. Fourth in an Irish Group One, a maiden success will be a formallity.
**M Johnston [0-3] P D Savill.*

ROYAL REPRIMAND (IRE) BHB 54f **RR 42f** 3487[2]
3 b g Reprimand 8.2f **(63)**-Lake Ormond (Kings Lake (USA)) 10.8f **(67)**
Form - 602
Record 1998 - 1st:0 2nd:1 3rd:0 Ran:3
Win Prizemoney £0 *Total Prizemoney* £1,025
1998 Turf 0-3: (8f, 9f 2) (g-f 2, frm)
Tall, currently moderate gelding. Turf high 42 (began Jly) - 2nd of 3 to Minivet (9 Aug Redcar 9f frm RF 3487).
**R E Barr [0-3] J C Garbutt.*

ROYAL RESULT (USA) BHB 82f **RR 80f** 4520[9]
5 b br g Gone West (USA) 7.8f **(82)**-Norette (Northfields (USA)) 9f **(72)**
Form - 07037436281410
Record 1998 - 1st:2 2nd:1 3rd:2 Ran:14
Pre1998 - 1st:2 2nd:1 3rd:1 Ran:17
Win Prizemoney £34,047 *Total Prizemoney* £39,451
Wins * **1998** Spt Ayr (G-S) H 6f 76 80 <
* **1998** Spt York (GD) H 7f 70 75
1997 Oct Newmar (G-F) H 7f 65 72
1996 Aug Thirsk (G-F) 8f 56
1998 Turf 2-14: (6f 1-1, 7f 1-7, 8f 6) (sft 1-1, gd 4, g-f 1-2, frm 7)
Decent gelding, effective 6 to 7f, best at 7f, acts on sft to frm, has worn blinkers. Turf high 80 - 1st of 29 getting 3lb from Grey Kingdom (19 Spt Ayr RF 4365) - also 1st of 24 giving 10lb to Gymcrak Flyer (3 Spt York RF 4066). Steadily returned to a fair mark last term, winning over seven at York and putting up a fine performance to win the Ayr Silver Cup. He has a potent turn of foot.
**D Nicholls [2-7] Burke's 5th Family Settlement (from M W Easterby [1-12] Jly 1998).*

ROYAL ROULETTE BHB 45f53a **RR 51f 53a** 4887[8]
4 ch f Risk Me (FR) 8f **(53)** - Princess Lily (Blakeney) 10.5f **(64)**
Form - 10468
Record 1998 - 1st:0 2nd:0 3rd:0 Ran:2
Pre1998 - 1st:2 2nd:2 3rd:4 Ran:18
Win Prizemoney £5,071 *Total Prizemoney* £7,665
Wins * 1997 *Nov Lingfi (STD) H 12f 59 60 <*
1997 *Jan Southw (STD) S 8f 58*
1998 Turf 0-1: (12f) (g-s) 1998 AW 0-1: (12f) (Equi)
Workmanlike, fair filly, effective 8 to 12f, best at 12f, - acts on AW, best on Fibr, often wears blinkers, prefers left handed tracks. She is an effective sort in modest handicaps on sand. Twelve furlongs is the very limit of her stamina.
**Miss B Sanders [1-5] Mrs P J Sheen (from S P C Woods [1-15] Oct 1997).*

ROYAL SHOW (IRE) RR 65f 4926[3]
3 b f Sadler's Wells (USA) 11.3f **(87)** - Regal Beauty (USA) (Princely Native (USA)) 8.6f **(81)**
Form - 3
Record 1998 - 1st:0 2nd:0 3rd:1 Ran:1
Win Prizemoney £0 *Total Prizemoney* £555
1998 Turf 0-1: (10f) (g-s)
Light-framed, currently average filly. (1st run) - 3rd of 7 getting 5lb from Father Krismas (21 Oct Nottingham 10f g-s RF 4926).
**H R A Cecil [0-1] Michael Poland.*

ROYAL SHYNESS BHB 100f **RR 96f** 1779[7]
3 b f Royal Academy (USA) 7.8f **(77)** - Miss Demure (Shy Groom (USA)) 10f **(66)**
Form - 747
Record 1998 - 1st:0 2nd:0 3rd:0 Ran:3
Pre1998 - 1st:1 2nd:1 3rd:2 Ran:4
Win Prizemoney £3,550 *Total Prizemoney* £19,079
Wins * 1997 Spt Kempto (GD) 6f 96 <
1998 Turf 0-3: (6f, 7f 2) (gd, g-f, frm)
Neat, very useful filly, effective 6f, acts on frm. Turf high 94. Third in the Cheveley Park at two, she failed to run up to that form in a light season at three. **G Lewis [1-7] R D Hubbard.*

ROYAL SIGNET BHB 55f **RR 66f** 4477[6]
3 ch f King's Signet (USA) 7f **(51)** - Ladiz (Persian Bold) 9.3f **(66)**
Form - 68606
Record 1998 - 1st:0 2nd:0 3rd:0 Ran:5
1998 Turf 0-5: (7f, 8f, 10f 3) (gd 2, g-f 2, frm)
Scopey, average filly. Turf high 66 (began Jly).
**M J Weeden [0-5] Peter Bolton.*

ROYAL SUZUKA (IRE) RR 109f 2104a[4]
5 h Royal Academy (USA) 7.8f **(77)** - Godzilla (Gyr (USA)) 9.5f **(65)**
Form - 4
1998 Turf 0-1: (8f) (hvy)
Currently Pattern-class colt. **M Hashida in JPN [0-1] K Nagai.*

ROYAL TARRAGON BHB 47f **RR 60f** 5004[12]
2 b f Aragon 7.7f **(58)** - Lady Philippa (IRE) (Taufan (USA)) 7f **(57)**
Form - 000P470
Record 1998 - 1st:0 2nd:0 3rd:0 Ran:7
1998 Turf 0-7: (5f 2, 6f 4, 7f) (sft, gd, g-f 3, frm 2)
Average filly, often wears blinkers. Turf high 60.
**J R Arnold [0-7] Brooke Rankin, Green & Else.*

ROYAL VELVET BHB 55f **RR 50f** 67[5]
3 b f Perpendicular - Stellaris (Star Appeal) 9.6f **(65)**
Form - 5
Record 1998 - 1st:0 2nd:0 3rd:0 Ran:1
Pre1998 - 1st:0 2nd:0 3rd:0 Ran:3

1998 AW 0-1: (7f) (Fibr)
Leggy, fair filly. **C W Fairhurst [0-4] Brearley and McLain Partnership.*

ROYAL WAVE (IRE) RR 72f 4142[5]

2 b br c Polish Precedent (USA) 9f **(73)** - Mashmoon (USA) (Habitat) 9.4f **(70)**
Form - 5
Record 1998 - 1st:0 2nd:0 3rd:0 Ran:1
1998 Turf 0-1: (7f) (g-f)
Currently above-average colt. **Sir Michael Stoute [0-1] Saeed Suhail.*

ROY BOY BHB 52f50a RR 49f 50a 3806[9]

6 b g Emarati (USA) 6.6f **(63)** - Starky's Pet (Mummy's Pet) 7.7f **(60)**
Form - 0000
Record 1998 - 1st:0 2nd:0 3rd:0 Ran:4
Pre1998 - 1st:0 2nd:1 3rd:2 Ran:13
Win Prizemoney £0 *Total Prizemoney* £2,246
1998 Turf 0-3: (6f, 7f 2) (gd, frm 2) 1998 AW 0-1: (8f) (Equi)
Moderate gelding, has worn blinkers. Turf high 49 (began Jly).
**C A Horgan [0-6] Bill Brown (from Mrs M Reveley [0-15] Jun 1996).*

ROYRACE BHB 30f25a RR 39f 25a 4448[11]

6 b g Wace (USA) - Royal Tycoon (Tycoon II) 8.7f **(47)**
Form - 0
Record 1998 - 1st:0 2nd:0 3rd:0 Ran:1
Pre1998 - 1st:0 2nd:0 3rd:0 Ran:12
1998 Turf 0-1: (16f) (gd)
Very moderate gelding, has worn blinkers. Becoming disappointing. **W M Brisbourne [0-21] Andrew Evans.*

RUACANA FALLS (USA) BHB 95f RR 86f 4853[9]

2 b f Storm Bird (CAN) 8.5f **(82)** - Obeah (Cure The Blues (USA)) 9.5f **(63)**
Form - 410
Record 1998 - 1st:1 2nd:0 3rd:0 Ran:3
Win Prizemoney £3,745 *Total Prizemoney* £4,093
Wins * **1998** Spt Haydoc (G-F) 8.1f 82 <
1998 Turf 1-3: (7f 2, 8f 1-1) (gd 2, frm 1-1)
Currently useful filly. Turf high 86 (began Spt) - also 1st of 7 from Tudor Hall (26 Spt Haydock RF 4499).
**P W Chapple-Hyam [1-3] R E Sangster.*

RUANBEG (IRE) BHB 56f RR 71f 4136[13]

2 ch f Up and At 'em - Riverwave (USA) (Riverman (USA)) 9.1f **(76)**
Form - 1760R0
Record 1998 - 1st:1 2nd:0 3rd:0 Ran:6
Win Prizemoney £2,259 *Total Prizemoney* £2,259
Wins * **1998** May Leices (GD) C 5f 71 <
1998 Turf 1-6: (5f 1-1, 6f 3, 7f, 8f) (g-f 1-5, frm)
Above-average filly, effective 5f, acts on g-f, has worn blinkers. Turf high 71 (1st run) - 1st of 7 getting 1lb from Shirley Not (25 May Leicester RF 1452). **C A Dwyer [1-6] Ms B Murphy.*

RUBAMMA BHB 55f65a RR 67f 65a 4321[20]

3 b c Kris 10f **(75)** - Idle Gossip (USA) (Lyphard (USA)) 9.9f **(72)**
Form - 33066754700
Record 1998 - 1st:0 2nd:0 3rd:0 Ran:8
Pre1998 - 1st:0 2nd:0 3rd:3 Ran:7
Win Prizemoney £0 *Total Prizemoney* £1,964
1998 Turf 0-8: (7f, 8f, 9f, 10f 3, 11f, 12f) (hvy, g-s, gd 3, g-f, frm 2)
Neat, average colt, effective 7f, acts on g-s, likes left handed tracks. Turf high 68. Inconsistent.
**P T Walwyn [0-17] Mrs P T Walwyn.*

RUBY AFFAIR (IRE) BHB 59f RR 55f 4759[10]

3 b br f Night Shift (USA) 8.1f **(73)** - Tiavanita (USA) (J O Tobin (USA)) 9.4f **(67)**
Form - 2750
Record 1998 - 1st:0 2nd:1 3rd:0 Ran:4
Win Prizemoney £0 *Total Prizemoney* £930
1998 Turf 0-4: (7f 2, 8f 2) (gd, g-f 2, frm)
Unfurnished, fair filly. Turf high 55 (1st run) - 2nd of 9 getting 5lb from Prevalence (17 May Kempton 7f g-f RF 1284).
**J R Fanshawe [0-4] Peter and Noreen Hodgson.*

RUBY ANGEL BHB 35f32a RR 16f 32a 1601[8]

5 ch m Superlative 8.8f **(57)** - Queen Angel (Anfield) 8.5f **(59)**
Form - 08
Record 1998 - 1st:0 2nd:0 3rd:0 Ran:2
Pre1998 - 1st:0 2nd:0 3rd:1 Ran:5
Win Prizemoney £0 *Total Prizemoney* £278
1998 Turf 0-2: (7f, 8f) (sft, g-f)
Moderate filly. Turf high 16.
**Miss B Sanders [0-3] Mrs J M Laycock (from H Candy [0-4] Jan 1997).*

RUBY BEAR BHB 35f32a RR 40f 32a 4753[6]

3 gr f Thethingaboutitis (USA) 16f **(44)** - Hitravelscene (Mansingh (USA)) 7.4f **(55)**
Form - 28220832336
Record 1998 - 1st:0 2nd:4 3rd:3 Ran:11
Pre1998 - 1st:0 2nd:0 3rd:0 Ran:3
Win Prizemoney £0 *Total Prizemoney* £4,593
1998 Turf 0-9: (8f, 10f, 11f, 12f 2, 13f, 14f 3) (sft 2, g-s, gd 2, g-f 3, frm)
1998 AW 0-2: (9f, 15f) (Fibr 2)
Leggy, moderate filly, effective 8 to 14f, acts on sft to g-f, has worn blinkers. Turf high 51 - 2nd of 6 getting 5lb from Cut Diamond (18 May Musselburgh 14f g-f RF 1300). AW high 21.
**W M Brisbourne [0-14] D J Kirkland.*

RUDCROFT BHB 35f RR 20f 3993[8]

2 ch g Presidium 7.5f **(56)** - Stilvella (Camden Town) 9.3f **(53)**
Form - 000008
Record 1998 - 1st:0 2nd:0 3rd:0 Ran:6
1998 Turf 0-4: (5f 3, 8f) (gd, g-f, frm 2) 1998 AW 0-2: (5f 2) (Fibr 2)
Little account gelding, has worn blinkers. Turf high 20.
**N Bycroft [0-6] J A Swinburne.*

RUDE AWAKENING BHB 45f50a RR 51f 50a 3671[18]

4 b g Rudimentary (USA) 8.2f **(66)** - Final Call (Town Crier) 10.2f **(55)**
Form - 0130326545368520700
Record 1998 - 1st:1 2nd:2 3rd:3 Ran:19
Pre1998 - 1st:1 2nd:2 3rd:0 Ran:17
Win Prizemoney £7,367 *Total Prizemoney* £14,424
Wins * **1998** *Feb Southw (STD) H 6f 44 49*
1996 Apr Pontef (G-F) 5f 94 <
1998 Turf 0-8: (5f 6, 6f 2) (gd 2, frm 6) 1998 AW 1-11: (5f 3, 6f 1-7, 7f) (Fibr 1-11)
Scopey, fair gelding, effective 8f, acts on frm, has worn blinkers, likes tight tracks. Turf high 52. AW high 53.
**C W Fairhurst [1-30] William Hill (from G Lewis [1-6] Oct 1996).*

RUDE SHOCK BHB 41f RR 41f 2376[P]

3 gr g Rudimentary (USA) 8.2f **(66)** - Frighten The Life (Kings Lake (USA)) 10.8f **(67)**
Form - 060P
Record 1998 - 1st:0 2nd:0 3rd:0 Ran:4
Pre1998 - 1st:0 2nd:0 3rd:0 Ran:4
1998 Turf 0-4: (8f 2, 10f, 12f) (gd, frm 2, hrd)
Neat, moderate gelding. Turf high 41. (DEAD)
**M H Tompkins [0-8] M H Tompkins.*

RUDI KNIGHT BHB 74f RR 73f 4763[R]

3 ch g Rudimentary (USA) 8.2f **(66)** - Fleeting Affair (Hotfoot) 10.5f **(59)**
Form - 0001134R
Record 1998 - 1st:2 2nd:0 3rd:1 Ran:8
Win Prizemoney £5,250 *Total Prizemoney* £7,399
Wins * **1998** Aug Salisb (G-F) H 12f 67 70 <
* **1998** Jly Bath (GD) 11.7f 64
1998 Turf 2-8: (10f 3, 12f 2-3, 13f 2) (gd 1-3, g-f 3, frm 1-2)
Scopey, above-average gelding, effective 12 to 13f, best at 12f, acts on gd to frm. Turf high 73 - 3rd of 8 getting 13lb from Ormelie (14 Aug Newbury 13f g-f RF 3636) - also 1st of 8 giving 15lb to Chocolate Box (7 Aug Salisbury RF 3444).
**M J Fetherston-Godley [2-8] Derek D & Mrs Jean P Clee.*

RUDI SECRET RR 63f 3602[8]

2 ch c Rudimentary (USA) 8.2f **(66)**-Twilight Secret(Vaigly Great)7f **(58)**
Form - 0558
Record 1998 - 1st:0 2nd:0 3rd:0 Ran:4
1998 Turf 0-4: (5f, 7f 3) (gd, frm 3)
Average colt. Turf high 63. (DEAD) **T D Easterby [0-4] C J Murphy.*

RUDI'S GIRL RR 17f 3741[14]

2 b f Rudimentary (USA) 8.2f **(66)**-Charlton Athletic (Bustino) 10.4f **(64)**

Form - 050
Record 1998 - 1st:0 2nd:0 3rd:0 Ran:3
1998 Turf 0-2: (6f 2) (gd, frm) 1998 AW 0-1: (5f) (Fibr)
Currently moderate filly. Turf high 17.
**W R Muir [0-3] William Adams-Tom Gleason.*

RUDI'S PET (IRE) BHB 73f **RR 73f** 5142^{17}

4 ch c Don't Forget Me 9.5f **(66)** - Pink Fondant (Northfields (USA)) 9f **(72)**
Form - 00560000000000
Record 1998 - 1st:0 2nd:0 3rd:0 Ran:14
Pre1998 - 1st:4 2nd:1 3rd:2 Ran:21
Win Prizemoney £21,949 *Total Prizemoney* £29,919

Wins								
1997	Oct	Doncas	(GD)	H	5f	88	97	
1997	Aug	Sandow	(SFT)	H	5f	80	88	
1996	Aug	Sandow	(GD)	H	5f	92	99	<
1996	Jly	Windso	(GD)		5f		74	

1998 Turf 0-14: (5f 4, 6f 7, 7f 2, 8f) (sft 2, gd 8, g-f 3, frm)
Workmanlike, above-average colt, effective 5f, acts on gd, often wears blinkers (effectively). Turf high 87. Disappointed all year, but is gradually coming down in the weights.
**Mrs J R Ramsden [0-14] Jonathan Ramsden (from R Hannon [4-21] Oct 1997).*

RUMINATE (IRE) BHB 64f **RR 60+f** 4960^{4}

2 b c Night Shift (USA) 8.1f **(73)** - Top Knot (High Top) 10.2f **(67)**
Form - 05674
Record 1998 - 1st:0 2nd:0 3rd:0 Ran:5
Win Prizemoney £0 *Total Prizemoney* £265
1998 Turf 0-5: (6f 3, 7f, 8f) (gd 2, frm 3)
Average colt. Turf high 60 (began Spt).
**Mrs J R Ramsden [0-5] Paul Green.*

RUM LAD BHB 60f68a **RR 66f 68a** 4988^{12}

4 gr g Efisio 7.7f **(69)** - She's Smart (Absalom) 7.2f **(58)**
Form - 00307336245100
Record 1998 - 1st:1 2nd:1 3rd:3 Ran:14
Pre1998 - 1st:3 2nd:1 3rd:1 Ran:21
Win Prizemoney £11,037 *Total Prizemoney* £18,005

Wins									
*	**1998**	*Oct*	*Wolver*	*(sta)*	*H*	*6f*	*64*	*66*	
*	1997	Jly	Catter	(SFT)	H	6f	55	69	<
*	1997	Jun	Carlis	(GD)	H	5f	56	61	
*	1997	May	Catter	(G-F)		6f		53	

1998 Turf 0-13: (5f 5, 6f 7, 7f) (sft, g-s 4, gd 3, g-f 3, frm 2) 1998 AW 1-1: (6f 1-1) (Fibr 1-1)
Strong, average gelding, effective 5 to 7f, best at 6f, acts on sft to hrd - acts on Fibr, prefers left handed tracks, likes tight tracks, excels at Carlisle and Catterick. Turf high 66 - 2nd of 16 giving 1lb to Royal Dome (26 Aug Carlisle 5f gd RF 3886). (1st run) - 1st of 13 giving 2lb to Cool Prospect (3 Oct Wolverhampton RF 4635). A come-from-behind sprint handicapper who won three times in the summer of '97, he was possibly unlucky not to have won a race in 1998 before making a successful Fibresand debut at Wolverhampton in October. **J J Quinn [4-35] B Shaw.*

RUM POINTER (IRE) BHB 64f **RR 67f** 5094^{12}

2 b c Turtle Island (IRE) - Osmunda (Mill Reef (USA)) 10.5f **(78)**
Form - 45670
Record 1998 - 1st:0 2nd:0 3rd:0 Ran:5
Win Prizemoney £0 *Total Prizemoney* £292
1998 Turf 0-5: (7f 3, 8f, 10f) (g-s, gd, g-f 2, frm)
Average colt, has worn blinkers. Turf high 67.
**T D Easterby [0-5] Burke's 5th Family Settlement.*

RUNADRUM BHB 28f **RR 25f** 4350^{15}

3 b g Prince Daniel (USA) 11.4f **(46)** - Runabay (Run The Gantlet (USA)) 12.1f **(59)**
Form - 0000
Record 1998 - 1st:0 2nd:0 3rd:0 Ran:4
Pre1998 - 1st:0 2nd:0 3rd:0 Ran:2
1998 Turf 0-4: (8f, 9f, 12f 2) (sft, g-f 2, frm)
Light-framed, little account gelding, has worn blinkers. Turf high 25 (began Jly).
**J Hetherton [0-4] Mrs Helen Godfrey (from W W Haigh [0-2] Nov 1997).*

RUNAROUND BHB 29f **RR 29f** 3396^{9}

3 b f Northern Park (USA) 10f **(57)** - Party Game (Red Alert) 7.6f **(66)**
Form - 007000
Record 1998 - 1st:0 2nd:0 3rd:0 Ran:6
Pre1998 - 1st:0 2nd:0 3rd:0 Ran:3
1998 Turf 0-6: (7f, 8f 2, 10f, 11f, 14f) (g-s, gd, g-f 2, frm 2)
Strong, little account filly. Turf high 29. Inconsistent.
**N A Callaghan [0-6] Mrs G R Smith (from S Dow [0-3] Aug 1997).*

RUNAWAY BAY **RR 55f** 4612^{12}

2 gr c Lugana Beach 7f **(63)** - Absaloui (Absalom) 7.2f **(58)**
Form - 8840
Record 1998 - 1st:0 2nd:0 3rd:0 Ran:4
1998 Turf 0-4: (5f 3, 6f) (g-s, gd, g-f, frm)
Fair colt. Turf high 55 (began Aug). **Mrs L Stubbs [0-4] Ian Blakey.*

RUN FOR RUSS (IRE) BHB 40f **RR 1f** 954^{5}

3 br f Mujtahid (USA) 7.4f **(69)** - Gold Maid (FR) (Green Dancer (USA)) 10.3f **(74)**
Form - 475
Record 1998 - 1st:0 2nd:0 3rd:0 Ran:3
Win Prizemoney £0 *Total Prizemoney* £238
1998 Turf 0-2: (10f, 12f) (g-s, g-f) 1998 AW 0-1: (10f) (Equi)
Leggy, currently moderate filly. Turf high 1.
**S C Williams [0-3] D Jordan.*

RUNIC SYMBOL BHB 26f28a **RR 31f 28a** 2841^{7}

7 b g Warning 8.1f **(77)** - Pagan Deity (Brigadier Gerard) 9.3f **(58)**
Form - 778087
Record 1998 - 1st:0 2nd:0 3rd:0 Ran:4
Pre1998 - 1st:1 2nd:4 3rd:8 Ran:51
Win Prizemoney £3,288 *Total Prizemoney* £11,264
Wins * 1996 Jun Nottin (G-F) H 10f 36 42 <
1998 Turf 0-4: (8f, 10f 2, 12f) (gd 2, g-f 2)
Very moderate gelding, effective 11f, acts on gd, has worn blinkers. Turf high 31. Consistent. **M Blanshard [1-61] D Sloan.*

RUNNING BEAR BHB 25f **RR 21tf** 2939^{8}

4 ch g Sylvan Express 9.6f **(45)** - Royal Girl **(55f)** (Kafu) 6f **(47)**
Form - 8
Record 1998 - 1st:0 2nd:0 3rd:0 Ran:1
Pre1998 - 1st:0 2nd:0 3rd:0 Ran:3
Win Prizemoney £0 *Total Prizemoney* £201
1998 Turf 0-1: (6f) (g-f)
Workmanlike, little account gelding. **Miss S E Hall [0-4] C Platts.*

RUNNING GREEN BHB 53f56a **RR 57df 56a** 932^{7}

7 b g Green Desert (USA) 7.8f **(78)** - Smeralda (GER) (Dschingis Khan) 11.3f **(75)**
Form - 7
Record 1998 - 1st:0 2nd:0 3rd:0 Ran:1
Pre1998 - 1st:2 2nd:2 3rd:2 Ran:19
Win Prizemoney £4,422 *Total Prizemoney* £6,849

Wins									
*	1997	Jun	Ayr	(GD)	SH	8f	58	62	<
*	*1996*	*Dec*	*Southw*	*(SLW)*	*H*	*8f*	*48*	*59*	

1998 Turf 0-1: (7f) (sft)
Fair gelding, effective 8f, acts on gd to frm, often wears blinkers (very effectively), prefers right handed tracks, prefers tight tracks, excels at Musselburgh, likes Ayr.
**D Moffatt [2-20] Die-Hard Racing Club (from T Dyer [0-5] Apr 1995).*

RUNNING STAG (USA) BHB 115f119a **RR 115f 119a** $5168a^{7}$

4 b c Cozzene (USA) 10.1f **(87)** - Fruhlingstag (FR) (Orsini) 10f **(71)**
Form - 22156031347
Record 1998 - 1st:2 2nd:0 3rd:2 Ran:9
Pre1998 - 1st:1 2nd:5 3rd:0 Ran:11
Win Prizemoney £60,557 *Total Prizemoney* £161,972

Wins								
*	**1998**	Aug	Deauvi	(SFT)	G3	10f	115	<
*	**1998**	*Mar*	*Lingfi*	*(STD)*		*10f*	*104+*	
*	1997	*Feb*	*Lingfi*	*(STD)*		*10f*	*59++*	

1998 Turf 1-5: (10f 1-3, 12f 2) (hvy, sft 2, gd 1-1, g-f) 1998 AW 1-4: (9f, 10f 1-3) (Equi 1-1, Dirt 3)
Workmanlike, high-class colt, effective 10f, acts on gd, likes left handed tracks, likes tight tracks. Turf high 115 - 1st of 11 from Garuda (16 Aug Deauville RF 3782a). AW high 119. A fine winner of the Winter Derby on Lingfield's Equitrack in March, he looked held on turf until finally managing to win a Group Three at Deauville in

August. He was then sent on an adventurous mission to the United States, starting off with a most creditable third of five in the Woodward at Belmont Park. He was quite a well-beaten fourth in atrocious conditions in the Jockey Club Gold Cup at the same track, but was far from disgraced, though only seventh, in the Breeders' Cup Classic. **P Mitchell [3-20] Richard Cohen.*

RUN OR BUST (IRE) BHB 65a **RR 48f 65a** 95[5]

5 b m Commanche Run 10.3f **(63)** - Busteds Fancy (Busted) 10.2f **(61)**
Form - 25
Record 1998 - 1st:0 2nd:1 3rd:0 Ran:2
Pre1998 - 1st:0 2nd:0 3rd:0 Ran:1
Win Prizemoney £0 *Total Prizemoney* £1,105
1998 AW 0-2: (8f, 10f) (Equi, Fibr)
Currently fair filly. AW high 57. **R Ingram [0-3] Roger Ingram.*

RUNS IN THE FAMILY BHB 53f33a **RR 65f 33a** 4649[14]

6 b m Distant Relative 7f **(69)** - Stoneydale (Tickled Pink) 6.5f **(59)**
Form - 808730275401202000
Record 1998 - 1st:1 2nd:3 3rd:1 Ran:18
Pre1998 - 1st:3 2nd:5 3rd:5 Ran:41
Win Prizemoney £12,651 *Total Prizemoney* £25,327
Wins * **1998** Jly Bright (GD) 5.3f 47
* 1997 Jun Warwic (GD) H 5f 57 60
* 1997 May Lingfi (GD) H 5f 46 53
1994 Oct Warwic (SFT) 6f 64
1998 Turf 1-16: (5f 1-14, 6f 2) (g-s 2, gd 1-5, g-f 5, frm 4) 1998 AW 0-2: (5f 2) (Fibr 2)
Average mare, effective 5 to 6f, best at 5f, acts on gd to g-f, best on gd, mostly wears blinkers (effectively), likes Chepstow. Turf high 65 - 2nd of 13 getting 1lb from Songsheet (24 Jly Chepstow 5f g-f RF 3071). AW high 4. A speedy front-runner, she wins in her turn.
**G M McCourt [3-41] Christopher Shankland (from P G Murphy [1-18] Oct 1995).*

RUSHCUTTER BAY BHB 81f **RR 81f** 4508[4]

5 br g Mon Tresor 7.9f **(60)** - Llwy Bren (Lidhame) 9.2f **(50)**
Form - 0157044
Record 1998 - 1st:1 2nd:0 3rd:0 Ran:7
Pre1998 - 1st:2 2nd:1 3rd:2 Ran:22
Win Prizemoney £14,565 *Total Prizemoney* £22,928
Wins * **1998** Jly Newmar (G-F) H 6f 77 81
1996 Jun Nottin (G-F) H 5.1f 79 83 <
1995 Jly Windso (GD) 5f 63
1998 Turf 1-7: (5f 3, 6f 1-4) (gd 2, g-f 2, frm 1-3)
Decent gelding, effective 5 to 6f, best at 5f, acts on gd to frm, best on frm, has worn blinkers, excels at Nottingham and Ascot. Turf high 81 (began Jly) - 1st of 12 giving 12lb to Stylish Ways (31 Jly Newmarket RF 3238). Returned to form at Newmarket in July and has run well since.
**P L Gilligan [1-11] Treasure Seekers Partnership (from T T Clement [2-18] Jly 1997).*

RUSHED (IRE) **RR 46f** 712[13]

3 b g Fairy King (USA) 7.7f **(75)** - Exotic Bride (USA) (Blushing Groom (FR)) 10.3f **(76)**
Form - 0
Record 1998 - 1st:0 2nd:0 3rd:0 Ran:1
1998 Turf 0-1: (7f) (gd)
Neat, currently moderate gelding.
**Sir Michael Stoute [0-1] Sir Evelyn De Rothschild.*

RUSHEN RAIDER BHB 50f **RR 56f** 4417[2]

6 br g Reprimand 8.2f **(63)** - Travel Storm (Lord Gayle (USA)) 8.8f **(62)**
Form - 4654042
Record 1998 - 1st:0 2nd:1 3rd:0 Ran:7
Pre1998 - 1st:6 2nd:0 3rd:0 Ran:24
Win Prizemoney £18,620 *Total Prizemoney* £20,838
Wins * 1996 Aug Beverl (GD) H 16.2f 63 73 <
* 1996 Aug Catter (G-F) C 12f 65
* 1996 Jly Doncas (G-F) S 12f 66
* 1996 Jly Leices (G-F) C 11.8f 66
* 1995 Aug Redcar (FRM) C 10f 65
* 1995 May Thirsk (G-F) S 7f 45+
1998 Turf 0-7: (14f 2, 16f 4, 17f) (gd 2, g-f, frm 4)
Fair gelding, has broken blood-vessels, effective 14 to 16f, best at 16f, acts on gd to frm, best on frm, prefers left handed tracks, favours tight tracks. Turf high 56 (1st run) - 4th of 10 getting 5lb from The Butterwick Kid (25 May Redcar 14f gd RF 1460).
**K W Hogg [7-38] Mrs Thelma White.*

RUSH ME NOT (IRE) BHB 45f **RR 32f** 385[8]

5 b g Treasure Kay 6.5f **(53)** - Elegant Act (USA) (Shecky Greene (USA)) 8f **(50)**
Form - 8
Record 1998 - 1st:0 2nd:0 3rd:0 Ran:1
Pre1998 - 1st:0 2nd:0 3rd:0 Ran:3
1998 AW 0-1: (8f) (Fibr)
Very moderate gelding.
**J P Leigh [0-1] Mrs C D Buckland (from M P Bielby [0-3] Jun 1997).*

RUSH OFF BHB 57f **RR 62f** 2396[11]

3 b g Robellino (USA) 9.5f **(68)** - Arusha (IRE) (Dance of Life (USA)) 7f **(66)**
Form - 00
Record 1998 - 1st:0 2nd:0 3rd:0 Ran:2
Pre1998 - 1st:0 2nd:0 3rd:0 Ran:1
1998 Turf 0-2: (10f 2) (gd, g-f)
Scopey, currently average gelding. Turf high 48.
**R Hannon [0-2] Raymond Tooth (from R Akehurst [0-1] Oct 1997).*

RUSK BHB 70f **RR 75?f** 4747[15]

5 b g Pharly (FR) 11.5f **(64)** - Springwell (Miami Springs) 9.9f **(59)**
Form - 010
Record 1998 - 1st:1 2nd:0 3rd:0 Ran:3
Pre1998 - 1st:1 2nd:2 3rd:1 Ran:13
Win Prizemoney £12,764 *Total Prizemoney* £17,415
Wins * **1998** Spt Beverl (G-F) S 12f 48
1997 Jly Ascot (GD) H 16.2f 75 75 <
1998 Turf 1-3: (12f 1-1, 14f, 18f) (gd 2, g-f 1-1)
Above-average gelding, effective 12 to 16f, acts on g-s to g-f. Turf high 48. Inconsistent. Improved for the step up to two miles when winning under top weight at Ascot in July.
**T D Easterby [1-7] Mrs Jean Connew (from J Pearce [1-13] Oct 1997).*

RUSSIAN ABOUT (IRE) BHB 52f46a **RR 64f 46a** 941[12]

3 b f Polish Patriot (USA) 7.8f **(70)** - Molly Carter (IRE) (Dr Carter (USA))
Form - 80
Record 1998 - 1st:0 2nd:0 3rd:0 Ran:2
Pre1998 - 1st:0 2nd:1 3rd:0 Ran:7
Win Prizemoney £0 *Total Prizemoney* £547
1998 AW 0-2: (7f, 9f) (Fibr 2)
Leggy, average filly, effective 6f, acts on gd. AW high 39.
**D T Thom [0-2] Mrs Alison Thom (from M R Channon [0-7] Spt 1997).*

RUSSIAN ASPECT BHB 46f **RR 49f** 5118[11]

4 br g Al Nasr (FR) 9.9f **(72)** - Bourbon Topsy (Ile de Bourbon (USA)) 10.1f **(67)**
Form - 0240
Record 1998 - 1st:0 2nd:1 3rd:0 Ran:4
Pre1998 - 1st:0 2nd:0 3rd:0 Ran:4
Win Prizemoney £0 *Total Prizemoney* £1,192
1998 Turf 0-4: (10f, 12f 2, 16f) (sft, g-s, gd 2)
Leggy, moderate gelding, effective 12f, acts on gd, has worn blinkers. Turf high 49 - 2nd of 14 getting 1lb from Sing And Dance (15 Oct Catterick 12f gd RF 4815). Inconsistent.
**M W Easterby [0-14] A G Black.*

RUSSIAN DELIGHT (IRE) BHB 45f **RR 53f** 4653[13]

3 b f Soviet Lad (USA) 9.4f **(63)**-Geraldville (Lord Gayle (USA))8.8f **(62)**
Form - 600
Record 1998 - 1st:0 2nd:0 3rd:0 Ran:3
Pre1998 - 1st:0 2nd:0 3rd:0 Ran:2
1998 Turf 0-3: (8f 3) (g-f, frm 2)
Workmanlike, fair filly. Turf high 53 (began Aug).
**J S Moore [0-3] Kennet Valley Thorou I (from R Hannon [0-2] Oct 1997).*

RUSSIAN HOPE (IRE) **RR 107f** 4719a[1]

3 ch c Rock Hopper 10.6f **(54)** - Dievotchka (GER) (Dancing Brave (USA)) 8.4f **(76)**
Form - 31
1998 Turf 1-2: (11f, 15f 1-1) (sft 1-1, gd)

Currently Pattern-class colt. Turf high 107 (began Aug) - 1st of 8 from Ocean of Storms (3 Oct Longchamp RF 4719a). He was due to come under the hammer at the Goffs Arc Sale, but promptly ran away with the Group Three Prix de Lutece and was removed from the catalogue. He stays in training and is likely to be trained for the Cup races. **H-A Pantall in FR [1-2] Baron Edouard de Rothschild.*

RUSSIAN MUSIC BHB 88f100a **RR 86f 100a** 3458^{18}

5 b g Forzando 7.2f **(63)** - Sunfleet (Red Sunset) 8.2f **(63)**
Form - 42437000
Record 1998 - 1st:0 2nd:1 3rd:1 Ran:7
Pre1998 - 1st:3 2nd:6 3rd:8 Ran:27
Win Prizemoney £21,772 *Total Prizemoney* £72,645
Wins * 1997 Spt Doncas (G-F) H 8f 100 105
* 1997 Mar Warwic (G-F) 7f 108 <
* 1996 May Lingfi (G-F) 7f 70
1998 Turf 0-7: (7f, 8f 4, 10f 2) (hvy, gd 3, g-f 2, frm)
Useful gelding, effective 7 to 10f, best at 8f, acts on gd to frm, best on gd, has worn blinkers, likes left handed tracks. Turf high 101 (1st run) - 2nd of 8 to Hornbeam (26 Mar Doncaster 8f gd RF 0473). Connections gave him a couple of spins over 10 furlongs, but he is better at a mile. Disappointing in the second half of the campaign, he will be well handicapped next term and could pop up at a decent price.
**Miss Gay Kelleway [3-32] The Seventh Heaven Partnership (from P C Haslam [0-2] Aug 1995).*

RUSSIAN PARTY (IRE) BHB 78f **RR 72f** 1929^{6}

3 ch c Lycius (USA) 8.8f **(71)** - Sherkova (USA) (State Dinner (USA)) 9.4f **(74)**
Form - 16
Record 1998 - 1st:1 2nd:0 3rd:0 Ran:2
Pre1998 - 1st:0 2nd:0 3rd:1 Ran:2
Win Prizemoney £3,030 *Total Prizemoney* £3,516
Wins * **1998** Apr Bright (GD) 8f 64+ <
1998 Turf 1-2: (8f 1-1, 10f) (g-s 1-1, gd)
Above-average colt. Turf high 72.
**A C Stewart [1-4] Sheikh Ahmed Al Maktoum.*

RUSSIAN RELATION (IRE) RR 54f 4529^{18}

4 ch g Soviet Star(USA) 8.6f **(74)**-Anjaab (USA) (Alydar (USA))9.1f **(76)**
Form - 6084000
Record 1998 - 1st:0 2nd:0 3rd:0 Ran:7
Pre1998 - 1st:0 2nd:3 3rd:0 Ran:5
Win Prizemoney £0 *Total Prizemoney* £2,858
1998 Turf 0-7: (6f, 7f 2, 8f 2, 10f 2) (sft, gd, g-f 5)
Fair gelding, effective 7 to 8f, acts on g-s to gd, often wears blinkers (extremely effectively). Turf high 54.
**Mrs P N Dutfield [0-7] Mrs Jan Fuller (from J S Bolger in IRE [0-5] Oct 1997).*

RUSSIAN REVIVAL (USA) BHB 114f **RR 115f** 4849^{5}

5 ch h Nureyev (USA) 8.4f **(84)** - Memories (USA) (Hail the Pirates (USA)) 11f **(78)**
Form - 2340125
Record 1998 - 1st:1 2nd:1 3rd:1 Ran:6
Pre1998 - 1st:4 2nd:4 3rd:2 Ran:16
Win Prizemoney £89,648 *Total Prizemoney* £262,376
Wins * **1998** Spt Newbur (GD) L 7.3f 115
* 1997 Spt Newbur (G-F) L 7f 117 <
1996 Oct Newmar (GD) L 6f 114
1996 Spt Yarmou (G-F) 6f 110?
1995 May Newbur (G-F) 6f 97+
1998 Turf 1-6: (6f 2, 7f 1-4) (gd 4, g-f 1-1, frm)
High-class colt, effective 6 to 7f, best at 7f, acts on gd to frm, best on gd, excels at Newbury. Turf high 117 (1st run) - 3rd of 6 to Hidden Meadow (26 May Longchamp 7f gd RF 1728a) - also 1st of 11 from Kahal (17 Spt Newbury RF 4328). Consistent. A useful performer at six and seven furlongs, he is not quite up to Group class, though he did make the frame at that level in the Prix du Palais-Royal and the Diadem. His only victory came in the same Newbury Listed event that he won the previous year.
**J H M Gosden [2-10] Maktoum Al Maktoum (from S bin Suroor [2-9] May 1997).*

RUSSIAN RIVER RR 58^{6}

6 b g Sulaafah (USA) 8.6f **(44)** - Ninotchka (Niniski (USA)) 10.6f **(65)**
Form - 6
Record 1998 - 1st:0 2nd:0 3rd:0 Ran:1
1998 AW 0-1: (13f) (Equi)
Very poor gelding. **J J Bridger [0-5] Mrs R M MacLean.*

RUSSIAN ROMEO (IRE) BHB 63f60a **RR 72df 60a** 4469^{18}

3 b c Soviet Lad (USA) 9.4f **(63)**-Aotearoa (IRE)(Flash of Steel)7.2f **(53)**
Form - 82472001R0000
Record 1998 - 1st:1 2nd:1 3rd:0 Ran:11
Pre1998 - 1st:2 2nd:1 3rd:0 Ran:15
Win Prizemoney £8,176 *Total Prizemoney* £10,078
Wins * **1998** Jun Cheste (GD) C 6.1f 72
* 1997 *Oct Wolver (STD) C 6f 74* <
* 1997 Aug Leices (GD) S 6f 74 <
1998 Turf 1-5: (5f 3, 6f 1-2) (g-s, gd 1-1, g-f, frm 2) 1998 AW 0-6: (5f 2, 6f 4) (Fibr 6)
Light-framed, above-average colt, effective 6f, acts on gd to g-f - acts on Fibr, often wears blinkers (very effectively). Turf high 72 - 1st of 12 giving 6lb to Pierpoint (3 Jun Chester RF 1685). AW high 73 - 2nd of 13 giving 9lb to Rockswain (7 Mar Wolverhampton 6f Fibr RF 0409). Inconsistent. Has a suspect temperament, and is best when able to dominate. **B A McMahon [3-26] R L Bedding.*

RUSSIAN ROSE (IRE) BHB 78f **RR 79f** 1280^{2}

5 b m Soviet Lad (USA) 9.4f **(63)** - Thornbeam (Beldale Flutter (USA)) 9.7f **(71)**
Form - 2
Record 1998 - 1st:0 2nd:1 3rd:0 Ran:1
Pre1998 - 1st:2 2nd:2 3rd:0 Ran:10
Win Prizemoney £6,511 *Total Prizemoney* £10,751
Wins * 1997 Jun Bath (G-F) H 17.2f 65 70 <
1996 Jun Ripon (G-F) 10f 62
1998 Turf 0-1: (14f) (g-f)
Above-average filly, effective 13 to 17f, acts on gd to frm, best on g-f. (1st run) - 2nd of 8 getting 1lb from Life of Riley (17 May Kempton 14f g-f RF 1280). Improving.
**J A R Toller [1-7] Ash Partnership (from A Hide [1-4] Aug 1996).*

RUSSIAN RULER (IRE) BHB 74f79a **RR 75f 79a** 4112^{13}

4 b g Bering 9.6f **(80)** - Whitecairn (Sure Blade (USA)) 11.3f **(67)**
Form - 1051650
Record 1998 - 1st:2 2nd:0 3rd:0 Ran:7
Pre1998 - 1st:0 2nd:1 3rd:1 Ran:6
Win Prizemoney £6,775 *Total Prizemoney* £8,812
Wins * **1998** Jly Yarmou (G-F) H 11.5f 70 75 <
* **1998** *Mar Southw (STD) 12f 75* <
1998 Turf 1-5: (10f, 11f 1-1, 12f 3) (gd, g-f 1-2, frm 2) 1998 AW 1-2: (12f 1-2) (Fibr 1-2)
Neat, above-average gelding, effective 10 to 12f, acts on g-f to frm - acts on Fibr, prefers tight tracks. Turf high 75 - 1st of 11 giving 10lb to Miss Pin Up (15 Jly Yarmouth RF 2839). AW high 75 (1st run) - 1st of 6 from Andaman (9 Mar Southwell RF 0411). Inconsistent. **A P Jarvis [2-13] A L R Morton.*

RUSSIAN VELVET (IRE) BHB 43f **RR 33f** 4834^{11}

2 br f Soviet Lad (USA) 9.4f **(63)** - Ballylesson Girl (IRE) (Nashamaa) 7.1f **(66)**
Form - 00
Record 1998 - 1st:0 2nd:0 3rd:0 Ran:2
1998 Turf 0-2: (5f, 6f) (g-s 2)
Currently moderate filly. Turf high 33 (began Oct).
**M Quinn [0-2] Glendale Partnership Ltd.*

RUSTIC (IRE) BHB 100f **RR 95f** 3101^{3}

2 b f Grand Lodge (USA) - Style Of Life (USA) (The Minstrel (CAN)) 10f **(72)**
Form - 613
Record 1998 - 1st:1 2nd:0 3rd:1 Ran:3
Win Prizemoney £3,647 *Total Prizemoney* £8,047
Wins * **1998** Jly Haydoc (G-F) 6f 80+ <
1998 Turf 1-3: (6f 1-3) (g-f 1-3)
Currently very useful filly. Turf high 95 - 3rd of 6 to Mythical Girl (25 Jly Ascot 6f g-f RF 3101). Lost her chance at the start on her debut but was an impressive winner on her second run at Haydock. Not disgraced upped to Group Three company at Ascot, but did not reappear. **R Charlton [1-3] K Abdulla.*

RUTH'S GAMBLE BHB 33f33a **RR 1f 33a** 4476[8]
10 b g Kabour 6.1f **(36)** - Hilly's Daughter (Hillandale) 8f **(60)**
Form - 56358

Record	**1998** -	1st:0	2nd:0	3rd:1	Ran:5
	Pre1998 -	1st:3	2nd:1	3rd:4	Ran:27

Win Prizemoney £8,554 *Total Prizemoney* £12,275
1998 Turf 0-1: (12f) (g-f) 1998 AW 0-4: (10f, 11f 2, 16f) (Equi 2, Fibr 2)
Very moderate gelding, has worn blinkers. AW high 31. Inconsistent.
**Mrs L C Jewell [5-49] Mrs A Emanuel (from D W Chapman [3-25] Oct 1992).*

RUTHS GEM (IRE) BHB 25f **RR** 423[10]
3 ch f Imperial Frontier (USA) 7f **(65)** - Hossvend (Malinowski (USA)) 10f **(56)**
Form - 660

Record	**1998** -	1st:0	2nd:0	3rd:0	Ran:3
	Pre1998 -	1st:0	2nd:0	3rd:0	Ran:3

1998 AW 0-3: (6f 2, 8f) (Equi, Fibr 2)
Light-framed, very poor filly, has worn blinkers. AW high 6.
**D T Thom [0-5] Mrs R Nash (from B A Pearce [0-1] May 1997).*

RUTLAND CHANTRY (USA) BHB 72f69a **RR 72f 69a** 4698[7]
4 b g Dixieland Band (USA) 10.1f **(80)** - Christchurch (FR) (So Blessed) 8.7f **(67)**
Form - 1607

Record	**1998** -	1st:1	2nd:0	3rd:0	Ran:4
	Pre1998 -	1st:1	2nd:2	3rd:0	Ran:5

Win Prizemoney £10,592 *Total Prizemoney* £12,893

Wins								
* **1998**	Apr	Newbur	(HVY)	H	10f	66	72	<
* 1997	Oct	Pontef	(G-S)	H	10f	60	66	

1998 Turf 1-4: (10f 1-3, 12f) (sft 1-1, g-f 3)
Workmanlike, above-average gelding, effective 10f, acts on sft to g-f, prefers left handed tracks. Turf high 72 - 7th of 15 getting 2lb from Abuhail (7 Oct York 10f g-f RF 4698) - also 1st of 18 getting 5lb from Premier Generation (18 Apr Newbury RF 0740). He put up a decent front running performance in a competitive heavy-ground handicap at Newbury on his reappearance, and is obviously suited by ten furlongs with cut. **Lord Huntingdon [2-9] The Queen.*

RUZEN (IRE) BHB 83f **RR 79f** 3464[16]
3 b g Fayruz 6.6f **(63)** - Stifen (Burslem) 8.8f **(53)**
Form - 61106070

Record	**1998** -	1st:2	2nd:0	3rd:0	Ran:8
	Pre1998 -	1st:1	2nd:1	3rd:1	Ran:4

Win Prizemoney £12,209 *Total Prizemoney* £14,778

Wins								
* **1998**	May	Leices	(GD)		6f		89	<
* **1998**	May	Windso	(G-F)	H	6f	78	88	
* 1997	Apr	Leices	(G-S)		5f		84	

1998 Turf 2-8: (5f 4, 6f 2-4) (g-s 2, gd 3, g-f 1-2, frm 1-1)
Workmanlike, above-average gelding, effective 5 to 6f, best at 6f, acts on gd to frm, best on g-f, has worn blinkers. Turf high 89 - 1st of 4 giving 1lb to Qilin (26 May Leicester RF 1472) - also 1st of 23 giving 18lb to Zeppo (11 May Windsor RF 1160).
**B Palling [3-12] Five To Follow.*

RYEFIELD BHB 70f **RR 72f** 5147[22]
3 b c Petong 7.6f **(58)** - Octavia (Sallust) 8.4f **(63)**
Form - 43201800400

Record	**1998** -	1st:1	2nd:1	3rd:1	Ran:11
	Pre1998 -	1st:0	2nd:2	3rd:0	Ran:2

Win Prizemoney £3,517 *Total Prizemoney* £7,939

Wins								
* **1998**	Jly	Carlis	(G-F)		6.9f		76	<

1998 Turf 1-11: (6f 4, 7f 1-3, 8f 4) (sft 2, g-s, gd 4, g-f, frm 1-3)
Rangy, above-average colt, effective 6 to 7f, best at 6f, acts on gd to frm, best on gd. Turf high 84 - 2nd of 8 getting 14lb from Astrac (29 May Ayr 6f gd RF 1560) - also 1st of 8 giving 5lb to Come Up Smiling (17 Jly Carlisle RF 2868).
**Miss L A Perratt [1-13] Mrs Elaine Aird.*

RYEFIELD STAR BHB 43f55a **RR 40f 55a** 4002[14]
3 b g Marju (IRE) 9.2f **(76)** - Awayed (USA) (Sir Ivor) 10.2f **(70)**
Form - 40730640

Record	**1998** -	1st:0	2nd:0	3rd:1	Ran:7
	Pre1998 -	1st:0	2nd:0	3rd:0	Ran:3

Win Prizemoney £0 *Total Prizemoney* £615
1998 Turf 0-5: (7f, 8f, 9f, 10f, 11f) (g-s, g-f 2, frm, hrd) 1998 AW 0-2: (6f, 8f) (Fibr 2)
Strong, average gelding, often wears blinkers. Turf high 41. AW high 53. Inconsistent.
**D McCain [0-2] D McCain (from J Berry [0-9] Jun 1998).*

RYMER'S RASCAL BHB 62f55a **RR 61f 55a** 5014[1]
6 b g Rymer 7.1f **(58)** - City Sound (On Your Mark) 7.7f **(58)**
Form - 0554025330035701

Record	**1998** -	1st:1	2nd:1	3rd:3	Ran:16
	Pre1998 -	1st:4	2nd:3	3rd:5	Ran:38

Win Prizemoney £27,350 *Total Prizemoney* £36,751

Wins								
* **1998**	Oct	Redcar	(SFT)	H	7f	59	61	
* 1997	Spt	York	(SFT)	H	7f	60	64	<
* 1997	Aug	Catter	(G-F)	H	7f	56	61	
* 1997	Jly	Beverl	(G-F)	H	7.5f	54	60	
* 1994	Oct	Pontef	(G-S)		6f		59	

1998 Turf 1-16: (7f 1-12, 8f 4) (g-s, gd 1-6, g-f 5, frm 4)
Average gelding, effective 7 to 8f, best at 7f, acts on sft to frm, and excels at Musselburgh and Redcar. Turf high 61 - 2nd of 10 getting 20lb from Cybertechnology (1 Jly Redcar 7f gd RF 2454) - also 1st of 11 getting 19lb from Saint Express (27 Oct Redcar RF 5014).
**E J Alston [5-50] Brian Chambers (from P C Haslam [0-4] Jun 1994).*

SAAFEND ROCK BHB 97f **RR 90f** 4739[7]
2 b br c Dilum (USA) 7.1f **(56)** - Sharp Silk (Sharpo) 7.7f **(59)**
Form - 441141327

Record	**1998** -	1st:3	2nd:1	3rd:1	Ran:9

Win Prizemoney £24,874 *Total Prizemoney* £29,569

Wins								
* **1998**	Aug	Newmar	(G-F)	H	6f		90	<
* **1998**	Jly	Lingfi	(G-F)	H	6f		84	
* **1998**	Jun	Lingfi	(G-F)		5f		80	

1998 Turf 3-9: (5f 1-4, 6f 2-5) (g-s, gd 2, g-f 1-2, frm 2-4)
Useful colt, effective 5 to 6f, best at 6f, acts on g-f to frm, best on frm. Turf high 90 - 1st of 7 giving 4lb to Tamara (1 Aug Newmarket RF 3277) - also 1st of 7 giving 16lb to Missing Ted (11 Jly Lingfield RF 2713). Won twice at Lingfield, and a valuable Newmarket nursery, and was twice in the frame in listed company. A pacey sort, he is usually taken to post early. Sold for 40,000 guineas in October.
**R Hannon [3-9] J B R Leisure Ltd.*

SAAFEYA (IRE) BHB 109f **RR 114f** 4948a[2]
4 b f Sadler's Wells (USA) 11.3f **(87)** - Safa (Shirley Heights) 10.3f **(74)**
Form - 711142

Record	**1998** -	1st:3	2nd:1	3rd:0	Ran:6
	Pre1998 -	1st:3	2nd:1	3rd:3	Ran:8

Win Prizemoney £82,327 *Total Prizemoney* £106,082

Wins								
* **1998**	Spt	Yarmou	(G-S)	L	10.1f		114	<
* **1998**	Aug	Deauvi	(SFT)	L	10f		101	
* **1998**	Aug	Newmar	(FRM)		10f		97	
* 1997	Oct	Newmar	(G-F)	L	10f		101+	
* 1997	Spt	Haydoc	(GD)	H	10.5f	84	91	
* 1997	Aug	Pontef	(G-F)		8f		70++	

1998 Turf 3-6: (9f, 10f 3-4, 12f) (hvy, sft 1-1, gd 1-2, g-f, frm 1-1)
Workmanlike, Group-class filly, effective 10 to 12f, acts on hvy to gd. Turf high 114 - 1st of 6 giving 11lb to Innuendo (15 Spt Yarmouth RF 4272). She was in rare form during the late summer, winning three conditions races, none by more than half a length. As that suggests, she is not a lady to argue with, an attitude that bodes well for her future at stud. Best on fast ground.
**J H M Gosden [6-14] Sheikh Ahmed Al Maktoum.*

SAATCHMO BHB 44f **RR 20f** 2719[13]
6 b g Forzando 7.2f **(63)** - Into the Fire (Dominion) 8.5f **(63)**
Form - 0

Record	**1998** -	1st:0	2nd:0	3rd:0	Ran:1
	Pre1998 -	1st:0	2nd:0	3rd:1	Ran:6

Win Prizemoney £0 *Total Prizemoney* £293
1998 Turf 0-1: (12f) (frm)
Very moderate gelding.
**J L Spearing [0-11] J Spearing (from J M P Eustace [0-1] Aug 1994).*

SABADILLA (USA) BHB 112f **RR 111f** 3231[1]
4 b c Sadler's Wells (USA) 11.3f **(87)** - Jasmina (USA) (Forli (ARG)) 9.6f **(67)**
Form - 2251

Record	**1998** -	1st:1	2nd:2	3rd:0	Ran:4
	Pre1998 -	1st:2	2nd:1	3rd:0	Ran:5

Win Prizemoney £60,527 *Total Prizemoney* £81,042

Wins * 1998 Jly Goodwo (G-S) LH 12f 110 111 <
* 1997 Nov Doncas (SFT) H 12f 80 94+
* 1997 Oct Haydoc (HVY) 11.9f 83
1998 Turf 1-4: (12f 1-4) (gd 1-2, g-f, frm)
Scopey, Group-class colt, effective 12f, acts on gd to frm, best on gd. Turf high 111 - 1st of 9 giving 14lb to Yavana's Pace (31 Jly Goodwood RF 3231). Improving. His has been a career of constant progress, culminating in a Listed win at Glorious Goodwood. His absence in the second half of the season is a worry, but this horse will win more races if all is well.
**J H M Gosden [3-9] Sheikh Mohammed.*

SABHAAN BHB 81f **RR 83f** 4360[6]
3 b c Green Desert (USA) 7.8f **(78)** - Al Theraab (USA) (Roberto (USA)) 10f **(76)**
Form - 382166
Record 1998 - 1st:1 2nd:1 3rd:1 Ran:6
Pre1998 - 1st:0 2nd:1 3rd:2 Ran:3
Win Prizemoney £3,468 *Total Prizemoney* £7,822
Wins * 1998 Jun Bright (FRM) 7f 83 <
1998 Turf 1-6: (6f, 7f 1-4, 8f) (g-s, gd, g-f 1-2, frm 2)
Scopey, decent colt, effective 6 to 7f, best at 7f, acts on g-f. Turf high 88 - 2nd of 11 to Lonesome Dude (17 May Kempton 7f g-f RF 1283) - also 1st of 7 from Grand Slam (2 Jun Brighton RF 1644). He always looked to have ability but it took him a long time to get off the mark. He finally managed to do so at Brighton in May in what looked a very modest event, though it should have boosted his confidence.
**M P Tregoning [1-6] Hamdan Al Maktoum (from Major W R Hern [0-3] Spt 1997).*

SABLE CLOAK BHB 20f **RR** 326[6]
3 b f Prince Sabo 6.6f **(64)**-Edge of Darkness **(52f)**(Vaigly Great) 7f **(58)**
Form - 06
Record 1998 - 1st:0 2nd:0 3rd:0 Ran:2
Pre1998 - 1st:0 2nd:0 3rd:0 Ran:1
1998 AW 0-2: (5f, 7f) (Fibr 2)
Tall, currently very poor filly - 6th of 6 getting 5lb from Heathyards Sheik (20 Feb Southwell 7f Fibr RF 0326).
**J L Harris [0-3] David Abell.*

SABO'S JOY BHB 48f **RR 43f** 3153[10]
3 b f Prince Sabo 6.6f **(64)** - Port Na Blath (On Your Mark) 7.7f **(58)**
Form - 500
Record 1998 - 1st:0 2nd:0 3rd:0 Ran:3
Pre1998 - 1st:0 2nd:0 3rd:0 Ran:1
1998 Turf 0-1: (7f) (g-f) 1998 AW 0-2: (6f 2) (Fibr 2)
Lengthy, moderate filly. AW high 48.
**C N Allen [0-4] Conrad's Angels.*

SABO SONIC BHB 39f **RR 49f** 3331[8]
3 b f Syrtos 8.1f **(57)** - Sabo Song **(28f)** (Prince Sabo) 7.2f **(62)**
Form - 006008
Record 1998 - 1st:0 2nd:0 3rd:0 Ran:6
1998 Turf 0-6: (7f, 8f 3, 9f, 12f) (gd 4, g-f, frm)
Neat, moderate filly. Turf high 49.
**Martyn Wane [0-6] James Kennerley.*

SABOT BHB 76f85a **RR 68f 85a** 1545[8]
5 b h Polar Falcon (USA) 9f **(74)** - Power Take Off (Aragon) 8.1f **(60)**
Form - 0008
Record 1998 - 1st:0 2nd:0 3rd:0 Ran:4
Pre1998 - 1st:1 2nd:6 3rd:0 Ran:13
Win Prizemoney £3,821 *Total Prizemoney* £15,396
Wins 1996 Jun Thirsk (FRM) 7f 65 <
1998 Turf 0-4: (6f 3, 7f) (sft, gd 2, g-f)
Useful colt, effective 7 to 8f, best at 8f, acts on gd - acts on Fibr. Turf high 68. Becoming disappointing.
**C W Thornton [0-9] Guy Reed (from B W Hills [1-8] Spt 1996).*

SABOTIERE (IRE) RR 81f 4583[1]
2 b f Unfuwain (USA) 11.4f **(74)** - Vaigly Star (Star Appeal) 9.6f **(65)**
Form - 1
Record 1998 - 1st:1 2nd:0 3rd:0 Ran:1
Win Prizemoney £2,107 *Total Prizemoney* £2,107
Wins * 1998 Spt Salisb (HVY) 8f 81 <
1998 Turf 1-1: (8f 1-1) (gd 1-1)
Currently decent filly. (1st run) - 1st of 13 getting 5lb from Deal Fair (30 Spt Salisbury RF 4583).
**D R Loder [1-1] Maktoum Al Maktoum.*

SABRE BUTT BHB 44f **RR 46f** 3883[10]
3 gr g Sabrehill (USA) 8.5f **(64)** - Butsova (Formidable (USA)) 9.2f **(63)**
Form - 456880
Record 1998 - 1st:0 2nd:0 3rd:0 Ran:6
Pre1998 - 1st:0 2nd:0 3rd:0 Ran:3
1998 Turf 0-6: (7f, 8f 2, 10f, 11f 2) (gd 3, g-f, frm 2)
Workmanlike, moderate gelding, often wears blinkers. Turf high 46. **M H Tompkins [0-9] Mark Tompkins Elite.*

SABRE DANCER RR 24f 3579[9]
4 b g Rambo Dancer (CAN) 8.4f **(59)** - My Candy (Lorenzaccio) 10f **(64)**
Form - 660
Record 1998 - 1st:0 2nd:0 3rd:0 Ran:3
Pre1998 - 1st:0 2nd:1 3rd:1 Ran:5
Win Prizemoney £0 *Total Prizemoney* £1,432
1998 Turf 0-3: (9f, 12f, 16f) (gd, g-f, frm)
Little account gelding, effective 10f, acts on gd. Turf high 24. Becoming disappointing.
**R Allan [0-8] R Allan (from T Stack in IRE [0-4] May 1997).*

SABRE GIRL BHB 29f **RR 30f** 4004[13]
3 b f Sabrehill (USA) 8.5f **(64)** - Yasmeen Valley (USA) (Danzig Connection (USA)) 8f **(68)**
Form - 07070
Record 1998 - 1st:0 2nd:0 3rd:0 Ran:5
Pre1998 - 1st:0 2nd:0 3rd:0 Ran:4
1998 Turf 0-4: (5f, 6f, 7f, 8f) (gd, g-f 2, frm) 1998 AW 0-1: (7f) (Fibr)
Neat, very moderate filly, has worn blinkers. Turf high 30. Becoming disappointing.
**K T Ivory [0-5] Taker Bloodstock (from R Hannon [0-4] Spt 1997).*

SABU BHB 48f **RR 24f** 2809[8]
6 gr g Jumbo Hirt (USA) 15.8f **(44)** - Shankhouse Girl (General Ironside)
Form - 8
Record 1998 - 1st:0 2nd:0 3rd:0 Ran:1
Pre1998 - 1st:0 2nd:0 3rd:0 Ran:5
1998 Turf 0-1: (12f) (frm)
Little account gelding. (DEAD)
**R A Fahey [0-1] Mrs R C Carr (from J I A Charlton [0-8] Jly 1997).*

SACHO (IRE) BHB 113f **RR 115f** 1462[6]
5 b h Sadler's Wells (USA) 11.3f **(87)** - Oh So Sharp (Kris) 9.5f **(73)**
Form - 2246
Record 1998 - 1st:0 2nd:2 3rd:0 Ran:4
Pre1998 - 1st:1 2nd:2 3rd:0 Ran:4
Win Prizemoney £4,091 *Total Prizemoney* £22,881
Wins 1997 Spt Leices (G-F) 10f 86 <
1998 Turf 0-4: (12f 2, 14f, 16f) (sft, gd 2, g-f)
High-class colt, effective 12 to 14f, acts on sft to gd. Turf high 115 - 2nd of 12 to Posidonas (18 Apr Newbury 12f sft RF 0741). He changed stables before the start of the season, and ran very well for his new connections in decent company during the spring without quite managing to win. Best over twelve furlongs, he goes well when there is give in the ground.
**J L Harris [0-4] J H Henderson (from J H M Gosden [1-4] Spt 1997).*

SACHSENKING (IRE) RR 100f 4714a[3]
5 b h High Estate 10.5f **(66)** - Salviostra (Cagliostro (GER))
Form - 3
1998 Turf 0-1: (10f) (sft)
Currently very useful colt, always wears blinkers. He was well beaten in a Group Three during October and is too old to progress significantly. **E Groschel in GER [0-1] Henriette Troger.*

SACRED LOCH (USA) BHB 36f **RR 42?f** 3191[4]
5 ch g Lomond (USA) 9.9f **(74)** - Cypria Sacra (USA) (Sharpen Up) 8.3f **(67)**
Form - 034
Record 1998 - 1st:0 2nd:0 3rd:1 Ran:3
Pre1998 - 1st:0 2nd:0 3rd:0 Ran:2
Win Prizemoney £0 *Total Prizemoney* £480
1998 Turf 0-3: (10f, 11f, 12f) (gd, g-f 2)

Moderate gelding. Turf high 42 (began Jly).
**M Dods [0-3] M J K Dods (from G Harwood [0-2] Oct 1996).*

SADA BHB 66f67a **RR 64f 67a** 2678[10]
3 b br f Mujtahid (USA) 7.4f **(69)** - Peace Girl (Dominion) 8.5f **(63)**
Form - 3000070
Record 1998 - 1st:0 2nd:0 3rd:0 Ran:5
Pre1998 - 1st:0 2nd:0 3rd:4 Ran:10
Win Prizemoney £0 *Total Prizemoney* £2,666
1998 Turf 0-4: (5f, 6f, 7f 2) (g-f, frm 2, hrd) 1998 AW 0-1: (6f) (Fibr)
Unfurnished, above-average filly, effective 5 to 6f, best at 5f, acts on gd to frm - acts on Equi, has worn blinkers, likes left handed tracks. Turf high 64.
**C A Dwyer [0-7] Times of Wigan (from Major W R Hern [0-8] Oct 1997).*

SADDLERS' GLORY BHB 62f **RR 56f** 4499[7]
2 b f Saddlers' Hall (IRE) 10.5f **(65)** - Hope and Glory (USA) (Well Decorated (USA)) 7.6f **(64)**
Form - 007
Record 1998 - 1st:0 2nd:0 3rd:0 Ran:3
1998 Turf 0-3: (7f, 8f 2) (g-f, frm 2)
Currently fair filly. Turf high 56 (began Spt).
**C W Fairhurst [0-3] Tony Sweetman.*

SADDLER'S PROSPECT RR 66f 5077[7]
2 b c Saddlers' Hall (IRE) 10.5f **(65)** - Blonde Prospect (USA) (Mr Prospector (USA)) 8.8f **(78)**
Form - 07
Record 1998 - 1st:0 2nd:0 3rd:0 Ran:2
1998 Turf 0-2: (7f, 10f) (g-s, frm)
Currently average colt. Turf high 66 (began Spt).
**P S McEntee [0-2] R B Collier.*

SADDLERS' ROE (IRE) BHB 69f **RR 66f** 2089[4]
3 b g Saddlers' Hall (IRE) 10.5f **(65)** - Ladyfish (Pampapaul) 10.9f **(63)**
Form - 84
Record 1998 - 1st:0 2nd:0 3rd:0 Ran:2
Pre1998 - 1st:0 2nd:0 3rd:1 Ran:4
Win Prizemoney £0 *Total Prizemoney* £636
1998 Turf 0-2: (10f 2) (g-s, frm)
Workmanlike, average gelding, effective 6f, acts on g-f. Turf high 66. Now with David Nicholson. **B W Hills [0-6] Ford Farm Racing.*

SADEEBAH BHB 45f **RR 51f** 3750[4]
3 b g Prince Sabo 6.6f **(64)**-Adeebah (USA)(Damascus (USA)) 8.9f **(71)**
Form - 00267044
Record 1998 - 1st:0 2nd:1 3rd:0 Ran:8
Pre1998 - 1st:0 2nd:0 3rd:0 Ran:3
Win Prizemoney £0 *Total Prizemoney* £625
1998 Turf 0-8: (7f 3, 8f 4, 9f) (gd 5, g-f 2, frm)
Unfurnished, fair gelding, effective 8 to 9f, best at 8f, acts on gd to frm, best on gd, has worn blinkers, prefers tight tracks. Turf high 51 - 4th of 8 giving 3lb to Amoroso (19 Aug Musselburgh 9f gd RF 3750).
**Martin Todhunter [0-1] G C G Racing Partnership (from M Johnston [0-10] Jly 1998).*

SADIAN BHB 111f **RR 115f** 4240[4]
3 b c Shirley Heights 12.1f **(76)** - Rafha (Kris) 9.5f **(73)**
Form - 1270114
Record 1998 - 1st:3 2nd:1 3rd:0 Ran:7
Pre1998 - 1st:1 2nd:0 3rd:0 Ran:1
Win Prizemoney £20,220 *Total Prizemoney* £47,320

Wins	* **1998**	Spt	Salisb	(GD)	14.1f	109	<
	* **1998**	Aug	Ascot	(G-F)	12f	109	<
	1998	Apr	Bath	(SFT)	10.2f	99	
	1997	Aug	Lingfi	(G-S)	7.6f	83+	

1998 Turf 3-7: (10f 1-1, 11f, 12f 1-3, 14f 1-1, 15f) (sft, g-s 1-1, gd 1-1, g-f 1-4)
Scopey, high-class colt, effective 11 to 15f, acts on gd to g-f, best on g-f, excels at Lingfield. Turf high 115 - 2nd of 6 to High-Rise (9 May Lingfield 11f g-f RF 1125) - also 1st of 3 giving 4lb to Secret Archive (3 Spt Salisbury RF 4063). Trained by Henry Cecil when winning a small event at Bath on his reappearance, he just lost out in a battle royal with High-Rise in the Lingfield Derby Trial, but finished much further behind that horse in the Blue Riband. He finished lame in the Irish version, and moved to John Dunlop's yard, for whom he made a winning debut in an Ascot conditions event. Scrambled home at Salisbury and was supplemented for the St Leger, but in the event he could only manage to finish a one-paced fourth.
**J L Dunlop [2-3] Prince A A Faisal (from H R A Cecil [2-5] Jun 1998).*

SADLER'S BLAZE (IRE) BHB 59f **RR 62f** 3963[9]
4 b g Alzao (USA) 9.8f **(73)** - Christine Daae (Sadler's Wells (USA)) 10f **(76)**
Form - 41231560
Record 1998 - 1st:2 2nd:1 3rd:1 Ran:8
Pre1998 - 1st:0 2nd:0 3rd:1 Ran:6
Win Prizemoney £6,655 *Total Prizemoney* £8,997

Wins	* **1998**	Jun	Nottin	(GD)	H	14.1f	57	62	<
	* **1998**	Apr	Nottin	(SFT)	H	14.1f	50	54	

1998 Turf 2-8: (12f, 14f 2-6, 16f) (sft, g-s 1-1, gd 1-4, g-f, frm)
Average gelding, effective 14 to 16f, best at 14f, acts on g-s to frm, best on gd, often wears blinkers (extremely effectively), prefers left handed tracks, excels at Nottingham. Turf high 62 - 1st of 18 giving 12lb to Spa Lane (8 Jun Nottingham RF 1804) - also 1st of 16 getting 7lb from Slipstream (28 Apr Nottingham RF 0904).
**P W Harris [2-14] Newly United.*

SAD MAD BAD (USA) BHB 56f48a **RR 58f 48a** 4871[2]
4 b g Sunny's Halo (CAN) 8f **(80)** - Quite Attractive (USA) (Well Decorated (USA)) 7.6f **(64)**
Form - 742
Record 1998 - 1st:0 2nd:1 3rd:0 Ran:3
Pre1998 - 1st:1 2nd:2 3rd:2 Ran:14
Win Prizemoney £3,173 *Total Prizemoney* £7,472
Wins 1996 Aug Lingfi (G-S) 7.6f 80 <
1998 Turf 0-3: (13f, 16f, 18f) (gd 2, g-f)
Well made, fair gelding, effective 15f, acts on g-s. Turf high 58. Disappointing on the level and looked a difficult ride at times, but won over fences in November.
**Mrs M Reveley [3-14] P D Savill (from M Johnston [1-8] Jun 1997).*

SAFABEE BHB 42f39a **RR 47df 39a** 4338[15]
3 ch f Safawan 6.6f **(60)** - Bewails (IRE) (Caerleon (USA)) 8.6f **(71)**
Form - 0
Record 1998 - 1st:0 2nd:0 3rd:0 Ran:1
Pre1998 - 1st:0 2nd:0 3rd:0 Ran:6
1998 Turf 0-1: (8f) (frm)
Unfurnished, moderate filly.
**J Cullinan [0-3] Alan Walder (from M J Haynes [0-4] Spt 1997).*

SAFE SHARP JO (IRE) BHB 56f **RR 61df** 4672[12]
3 ch g Case Law 6f**(64)**-Kentucky Wildcat(Be My Guest (USA))9.3f **(67)**
Form - 084000
Record 1998 - 1st:0 2nd:0 3rd:0 Ran:6
Win Prizemoney £0 *Total Prizemoney* £204
1998 Turf 0-6: (6f, 8f 3, 9f 2) (gd, g-f 3, frm 2)
Workmanlike, average gelding. Turf high 61 (began Jly).
**M A Jarvis [0-6] Mrs Greta Sarfaty Marchant.*

SAFETY IN NUMBERS BHB 94f **RR 110?f** 2110[7]
8 b g Slip Anchor 12.7f **(75)** - Winter Queen (Welsh Pageant) 10f **(65)**
Form - 7
Record 1998 - 1st:0 2nd:0 3rd:0 Ran:1
Pre1998 - 1st:7 2nd:5 3rd:2 Ran:22
Win Prizemoney £82,226 *Total Prizemoney* £92,943

Wins	* 1994	Spt	Longch	(GD)	G3	15.5f		116?	<
	* 1994	Apr	Ascot	(G-S)	G3	16.2f		105	
	* 1994	Apr	Newbur	(G-S)	H	16f	88	95+	

1998 Turf 0-1: (22f) (gd)
Group-class gelding. A high-class stayer back in 1994 until injury intervened, and was having his first run since October of that year when well beaten in the Queen Alexandra.
**Lady Herries [7-15] A L Merry (from Mrs J R Ramsden [0-8] Jun 1993).*

SAFEY ANA (USA) BHB 72f **RR 75f** 4391[15]
7 b g Dixieland Band (USA) 10.1f **(80)** - Whatsoraire (USA) (Mr Prospector (USA)) 8.8f **(78)**
Form - 2033406100
Record 1998 - 1st:1 2nd:1 3rd:2 Ran:10
Pre1998 - 1st:6 2nd:2 3rd:3 Ran:39

Win Prizemoney £25,929 *Total Prizemoney* £34,628

Wins * **1998** Aug Salisb (G-F) H 8f 70 75 <
* 1997 Spt Lingfi (GD) H 7f 66 71
* 1997 Jly Lingfi (G-F) H 7.6f 64 69
* 1997 May Yarmou (G-F) H 7f 61 67
* 1997 Apr Bright (FRM) H 8f 59 65
* 1995 Jly Newbur (GD) H 7f 70 71
* 1995 May Redcar (FRM) 7f 69

1998 Turf 1-10: (7f 5, 8f 1-5) (g-f 1-4, frm 6)

Above-average gelding, effective 7 to 8f, best at 8f, acts on g-f to hrd, best on g-f, has worn blinkers, excels at Lingfield, likes Yarmouth. Turf high 75 - 1st of 15 giving 12lb to Bomb Alaska (20 Aug Salisbury RF 3763). A winner four times last term, he ran well in 1998 but did not get off the mark until landing a Salisbury handicap in August. **B Hanbury [7-49] The Optimists Racing Partnership.*

SAFFLEUR BHB 22f RR 4624[11]

3 b f Safawan 6.6f **(60)** - Hinari Hi Fi (Song) 7.2f **(61)**

Form - 00000

Record 1998 - 1st:0 2nd:0 3rd:0 Ran:5

1998 Turf 0-4: (6f, 7f, 8f 2) (gd, g-f 2, hrd) 1998 AW 0-1: (8f) (Fibr)

Lengthy, formerly very poor filly. (began Jly).

**K A Morgan [0-5] D & M Cased Hole.*

SAFFRON BHB 70a RR 75f 4376[1]

2 ch f Alhijaz 7.7f **(57)** - Silver Lodge (Homing) 7.8f **(59)**

Form - 32272551

Record 1998 - 1st:1 2nd:3 3rd:1 Ran:8

Win Prizemoney £3,246 *Total Prizemoney* £7,227

Wins * **1998** Spt Catter (G-F) H 7f 70 74 <

1998 Turf 1-7: (5f 2, 6f 3, 7f 1-2) (gd 3, g-f 2, frm 1-2) 1998 AW 0-1: (6f) (Fibr)

Above-average filly, effective 6 to 7f, best at 6f, acts on g-f to frm - acts on Fibr. Turf high 75 - 2nd of 15 to Courtesan (6 Jun Doncaster 6f g-f RF 1769) - also 1st of 18 giving 6lb to Zechariah (19 Spt Catterick RF 4376). (1st run) - 5th of 13 getting 5lb from Blue Star (22 Aug Wolverhampton 6f Fibr RF 3827).

**J A Glover [1-8] Ernest Bennett.*

SAFFRON ROSE BHB 62f RR 74f 4759[19]

4 b f Polar Falcon (USA) 9f **(74)** - Tweedling (USA) (Sir Ivor) 10.2f **(70)**

Form - 3452004700

Record 1998 - 1st:0 2nd:1 3rd:1 Ran:10
Pre1998 - 1st:2 2nd:0 3rd:0 Ran:13

Win Prizemoney £6,660 *Total Prizemoney* £9,320

Wins * 1997 Jly Nottin (SFT) H 8.2f 70 73 <
* 1997 Jun Nottin (GD) H 8.2f 63 70

1998 Turf 0-10: (8f 9, 10f) (g-s 2, gd 3, g-f, frm 4)

Unfurnished, above-average filly, effective 8 to 10f, best at 8f, acts on g-s to frm, best on g-s, prefers left handed tracks, prefers tight tracks, excels at Nottingham. Turf high 74 - 2nd of 12 getting 3lb from Star Invader (10 Jun Kempton 8f g-s RF 1881). Inconsistent. Won twice over the Nottingham mile in 1997 before the run came to an end over course and distance on ground too fast for her. Running well this year until a poor effort at Nottingham in June.

**M Blanshard [2-23] The Lower Bowden II Syndicate.*

SAFFRON WALDON (FR) RR 94f 5108a[2]

2 b c Sadler's Wells (USA) 11.3f **(87)** - Or Vision (USA) (Irish River (FR)) 8.6f **(78)**

Form - 2

1998 Turf 0-1: (7f) (gd)

Currently useful colt. (1st run) - 2nd of 6 giving 3lb to Athlumney Lady (26 Oct Leopardstown 7f gd RF 5108a). A Sadler's Wells half-brother to Dolphin Street, and a 1.2m guinea yearling, he ran green but showed plenty of promise on his sole outing in a Group Three, and will certainly come on for the outing. He can develop into a possible classic outsider. **A P O'Brien in IRE [0-1] Mrs John Magnier.*

SAFI BHB 70f67a RR 69f 67a 3095[9]

3 b g Generous (IRE) 11.5f **(82)** - Jasarah (IRE) (Green Desert (USA)) 8.6f **(78)**

Form - 4350

Record 1998 - 1st:0 2nd:0 3rd:1 Ran:4

Win Prizemoney £0 *Total Prizemoney* £812

1998 Turf 0-3: (6f, 7f 2) (gd, frm 2) 1998 AW 0-1: (9f) (Fibr)

Workmanlike, average gelding. Turf high 69.

**D McCain [0-4] Clayton Bigley Partnership Ltd.*

SAFIO BHB 84f70a RR 83f 70a 2650[19]

5 ch g Efisio 7.7f **(69)** - Marcroft (Crofthall) 6.3f **(59)**

Form - 8631310

Record 1998 - 1st:2 2nd:0 3rd:2 Ran:7
Pre1998 - 1st:5 2nd:1 3rd:3 Ran:28

Win Prizemoney £37,495 *Total Prizemoney* £47,131

Wins * **1998** Jly Haydoc (GD) H 7.1f 80 83 <
* **1998** Jun Goodwo (G-F) H 7f 77 79
* 1997 Spt Doncas (G-F) H 7f 75 78
* 1997 Aug Newcas (GD) H 7f 70 74
* 1997 Aug Ayr (G-F) H 6f 65 66
* 1997 Jly Newcas (GD) H 7f 61 65
1995 Apr Thirsk (GD) 5f 67t

1998 Turf 2-7: (6f, 7f 2-6) (sft, gd, g-f 2, frm 2-3)

Decent gelding, effective 7 to 8f, best at 7f, acts on gd to frm, best on frm, likes tight tracks, excels at Ayr, does well at Newmarket and Newcastle. Turf high 83 - 1st of 7 getting 14lb from Rock Falcon (3 Jly Haydock RF 2499) - also 1st of 12 getting 3lb from Final Tango (5 Jun Goodwood RF 1754). He completed a sparkling four-timer between July and September 1997, before the Handicapper got stuck in, and has recorded two more victories this year. A fast-run seven furlongs on a sound surface look to be his optimum conditions.

**A Bailey [6-22] Mrs M A Clayton (from C Smith [1-13] Aug 1996).*

SAGAMIX (FR) RR 127f 4727a[1]

3 br c Linamix (FR) 8.2f **(64)** - Saganeca (USA) (Sagace (FR)) 8f **(124)**

Form - 11

1998 Turf 2-2: (12f 2-2) (hvy 1-1, sft 1-1)

Currently top-class colt. Turf high 127 (began Spt) - 1st of 14 giving 3lb to Leggera (4 Oct Longchamp RF 4727a) - also 1st of 6 from Croco Rouge (13 Spt Longchamp RF 4345a). Beat Dream Well on heavy ground in the spring and, following a mid-term break, returned to take the scalps of both Croco Rouge and Dream Well in the Prix Niel. Confirmed himself a top-notch colt with victory in the Arc, catching Leggera well inside the final furlong but winning a shade comfortably in the end. All four of his runs have been over twelve furlongs with cut in the ground, and he would not want to tackle any shorter. **A Fabre in FR [2-2] J-L Lagardere.*

SAGEBRUSH ROLLER BHB 45f47a RR 49f 47a 627[14]

10 br g Sharpo 7.5f **(68)** - Sunita (Owen Dudley) 8.3f **(61)**

Form - 00

Record 1998 - 1st:0 2nd:0 3rd:0 Ran:2
Pre1998 - 1st:6 2nd:13 3rd:8 Ran:79

Win Prizemoney £24,992 *Total Prizemoney* £53,692

Wins 1994 Spt Newcas (GD) C 7f 68
1994 Mar Doncas (GF) H 6f 80 84 <

1998 Turf 0-1: (8f) (gd) 1998 AW 0-1: (7f) (Fibr)

Moderate gelding, effective 10f, acts on gd, has worn blinkers, likes left handed tracks. Once a useful handicapper for Bill Watts, he is now with Jonjo O'Neill but he seems to have gone completely sour, and his retirement cannot be too far away.

**J J O'Neill [0-7] A K Collins (from J W Watts [6-79] Spt 1997).*

SAGUARO BHB 54f RR 44f 2331[18]

4 b g Green Desert (USA) 7.8f **(78)** - Badawi (USA) (Diesis) 9.3f **(69)**

Form - 7000

Record 1998 - 1st:0 2nd:0 3rd:0 Ran:4
Pre1998 - 1st:0 2nd:1 3rd:0 Ran:1

Win Prizemoney £0 *Total Prizemoney* £744

1998 Turf 0-4: (6f, 7f, 8f, 9f) (sft, g-s, gd, g-f)

Lengthy, moderate gelding, has worn blinkers. Turf high 44. Finished runner-up on his belated racecourse bow at Leicester in October, though it was a pretty poor race, and he showed little in 1998. **J H M Gosden [0-5] Sheikh Marwan Al Maktoum.*

SAHARA BHB 80f RR 84f 4332[6]

3 b f Green Desert (USA) 7.8f **(78)** - Marie D'Argonne (FR) (Jefferson) 7.9f **(89)**

Form - 05211666

Record 1998 - 1st:2 2nd:1 3rd:0 Ran:8
Pre1998 - 1st:0 2nd:1 3rd:0 Ran:3

Win Prizemoney £7,714 *Total Prizemoney* £10,311

Wins * **1998** Jly Ayr (GD) 10f 84 <
* **1998** Jly Bright (GD) 8f 80

1998 Turf 2-8: (7f, 8f 1-3, 10f 1-3, 12f) (gd 1-3, g-f, frm 1-4)

Light-framed, decent filly, effective 8 to 10f, best at 8f, acts on gd

to frm, best on frm, has worn blinkers, prefers left handed tracks. Turf high 84 - 1st of 4 giving 3lb to Silver Strand (18 Jly Ayr RF 2905) - also 1st of 13 from Lea Grande (1 Jly Brighton RF 2440). Consistent. A half-sister to the top-class Polar Falcon, she has secured her paddocks value with two wins in modest company.
**P F I Cole [2-11] Lord Lloyd-Webber.*

SAHHAR BHB 38f51a **RR 51?f 51a** 2566[8]
5 ch h Sayf El Arab (USA) 8.2f **(57)** - Native Magic (Be My Native (USA)) 10.2f **(71)**
Form - 08
Record 1998 - 1st:0 2nd:0 3rd:0 Ran:2
Pre1998 - 1st:0 2nd:1 3rd:1 Ran:8
Win Prizemoney £0 *Total Prizemoney* £1,209
1998 Turf 0-2: (10f 2) (gd, g-f)
Fair colt. Turf high 26. Inconsistent.
**P J Bevan [0-6] Mrs P J Bevan (from R W Armstrong [0-8] Spt 1996).*

SAIFAN BHB 70f65a **RR 76f 65a** 4848[11]
9 ch g Beveled (USA) 6.9f **(64)** - Superfrost (Tickled Pink) 6.5f **(59)**
Form - 700372000
Record 1998 - 1st:0 2nd:1 3rd:1 Ran:8
Pre1998 - 1st:10 2nd:4 3rd:9 Ran:67
Win Prizemoney £86,551 *Total Prizemoney* £108,185

Wins								
* 1997	Aug	Redcar	(G-F)	H	8f	83	87	
* 1996	Nov	Newmar	(GD)	H	8f	83	88	<
* 1996	Jly	Yarmou	(FRM)	H	8f	77	82	
* 1996	Jun	Newmar	(G-F)	H	8f	72	77	
* 1995	Aug	Leices	(GD)	H	7f	72	78	
* 1995	Jly	Yarmou	(G-F)	H	8f	66	73	

1998 Turf 0-8: (8f 8) (sft, gd 3, g-f, frm 2, hrd)
Above-average gelding, has broken blood-vessels, effective 7 to 8f, best at 8f, acts on gd to frm, best on gd, mostly wears blinkers. Turf high 76. He is not getting any younger, and apart from winning at Redcar last season, he has faced some very stiff tasks in competitive events. He ran his best race for a while when third in a Yarmouth claimer in July, and was only just touched off in a Redcar handicap the following month, but he is finding it hard to win. **D Morris [10-68] D Morris (from J C Fox [0-7] Nov 1991).*

SAILEP (FR) RR 27f 1953[8]
6 ch g Holst (USA) - Sweet Cashmere (FR) (Kashmir II) 11.7f **(48)**
Form - 8
Record 1998 - 1st:0 2nd:0 3rd:0 Ran:1
1998 Turf 0-1: (10f) (gd)
Little account gelding. **R J Hodges [1-18] P Slade.*

SAILING SHOES (IRE) BHB 100f **RR 102f** 4857[20]
2 b c Lahib (USA) 8f **(69)** - Born To Glamour (Ajdal (USA)) 9.2f **(89)**
Form - 414250
Record 1998 - 1st:1 2nd:1 3rd:0 Ran:6
Win Prizemoney £3,434 *Total Prizemoney* £34,882
Wins * 1998 Jun Cheste (GD) 5.1f 85+ <
1998 Turf 1-6: (5f 1-2, 6f 4) (sft, g-s, gd 1-3, frm)
Very useful colt, effective 6f, acts on frm. Turf high 102. He ran out of his skin when adopting forcing tactics in the Gimcrack Stakes at York in August, only being collared inside the final furlong by Josr Algarhoud. Below that form on his two remaining starts, he should make a useful sprinter, but needs to progress to trouble the best. **R Hannon [1-6] Hippodrome Racing.*

SAIL-ON BUN BHB 57f **RR 62f** 4983[9]
2 gr f Beveled (USA) 6.9f **(64)** - Sea Farer Lake (Gairloch) 7f **(63)**
Form - 000
Record 1998 - 1st:0 2nd:0 3rd:0 Ran:3
1998 Turf 0-3: (7f 2, 8f) (g-s, frm 2)
Currently average filly. Turf high 62 (began Spt).
**K McAuliffe [0-3] Mrs S D Fidler.*

SAIL ON SALLY RR 61f 5122[5]
2 ch f Clantime 6.6f **(57)** - Croft Sally (Crofthall) 6.3f **(59)**
Form - 85
Record 1998 - 1st:0 2nd:0 3rd:0 Ran:2
1998 Turf 0-2: (6f, 7f) (sft, g-s)
Currently average filly. Turf high 61 (began Oct).
**J Akehurst [0-2] Miss Vivian Pratt.*

SAILOR JACK (USA) RR 82f 5041[4]
2 b c Green Dancer (USA) 11.9f **(77)** - Chateaubrook (USA) (Alleged (USA)) 10f **(76)**
Form - 84
Record 1998 - 1st:0 2nd:0 3rd:0 Ran:2
Win Prizemoney £0 *Total Prizemoney* £200
1998 Turf 0-2: (6f, 7f) (sft, g-f)
Currently decent colt. Turf high 82 (began Oct).
**C E Brittain [0-2] R A Pledger.*

SAILORMAITE BHB 57f73a **RR 37?f 73a** 519[R]
7 ch g Komaite (USA) 6.9f **(61)** - Marina Plata (Julio Mariner) 7.2f **(57)**
Form - 4R
Record 1998 - 1st:0 2nd:0 3rd:0 Ran:1
Pre1998 - 1st:9 2nd:5 3rd:3 Ran:48
Win Prizemoney £34,932 *Total Prizemoney* £48,764

Wins								
* 1996	May	Haydoc	(G-S)	H	5f	78	81	
* 1995	*Jun*	*Wolver*	*(STD)*	*H*	*6f*	*82*	*84*	<
* 1995	Jun	Haydoc	(G-S)	H	6f	72	73	
* 1994	Oct	Leices	(GD)	H	6f	66	66	
* 1994	Spt	Beverl	(GD)	H	8.5f	60	62+	
* 1994	*Aug*	*Southw*	*(STD)*	*H*	*8f*	*70*	*76*	
* 1994	*Aug*	*Southw*	*(STD)*	*H*	*7f*	*70*	*71*	
* 1994	*Jly*	*Southw*	*(STD)*	*H*	*6f*	*61*	*61*	
* 1994	*Jun*	*Southw*	*(STD)*		*6f*		*59*	

1998 Turf 0-1: (6f) (g-s)
Average gelding, has worn blinkers. Inconsistent. He has been reluctant to race on occasions and is not one to rely on.
**S R Bowring [9-48] S R Bowring (from Miss J F Craze [0-3] Aug 1997).*

SAINT ALBERT BHB 66f **RR 67+f** 3768[2]
3 ch g Keen 11.1f **(58)** - Thimbalina (Salmon Leap (USA)) 11f **(61)**
Form - 72321212
Record 1998 - 1st:2 2nd:4 3rd:1 Ran:8
Pre1998 - 1st:0 2nd:0 3rd:0 Ran:4
Win Prizemoney £4,822 *Total Prizemoney* £8,224

Wins								
* **1998**	Jly	Doncas	(G-F)	H	16.5f	61	67	<
* **1998**	Jly	Salisb	(FRM)	H	12f	55	59	

1998 Turf 2-8: (7f, 11f 2, 12f 1-3, 14f, 17f 1-1) (g-s, g-f 1-2, frm 1-5)
Scopey, average gelding, effective 12 to 17f, acts on g-f to frm, best on g-f, has worn blinkers. Turf high 67 - 1st of 11 giving 1lb to Nosey Native (30 Jly Doncaster RF 3210) - also 1st of 15 getting 30lb from Flying Eagle (11 Jly Salisbury RF 2719).
**P T Walwyn [2-12] Mrs D C Samworth.*

SAINT ELLA (IRE) BHB 76f **RR 75f** 4880[1]
2 b f High Estate 10.5f **(66)** - Paul's Lass (IRE) (Al Hareb (USA))
Form - 51
Record 1998 - 1st:1 2nd:0 3rd:0 Ran:2
Win Prizemoney £3,246 *Total Prizemoney* £3,246
Wins * 1998 Oct Folkes (G-S) 7f 75 <
1998 Turf 1-2: (6f, 7f 1-1) (g-s 1-1, g-f)
Currently above-average filly. Turf high 75 (began Spt) - 1st of 13 getting 12lb from Present Laughter (20 Oct Folkestone RF 4880).
**Lord Huntingdon [1-2] Coriolan Partnership.*

SAINTE MARINE (IRE) RR 112f 4726a[3]
3 b f Kenmare (FR) 9.6f **(76)** - Pont-Aven (Try My Best (USA)) 7.6f **(67)**
Form - 11523
1998 Turf 2-5: (5f 2-5) (sft, gd 2-3, frm)
Group-class filly, effective 5f, acts on sft to frm. Turf high 112 - 1st of 8 getting 11lb from Piperi (30 May Chantilly RF 1731a) - also 1st of 6 getting 11lb from Pas De Reponse (10 May Longchamp RF 1228a). One of France's leading sprinters, although that is not a strong division, she might have found the ground on the soft side when fifth in the King's Stand, but it was a good effort nonetheless. Showed lightning speed in the Nunthorpe, but was picked off inside the last by Lochangel. It was a similar story in the Abbaye, again on soft. **R Collet in FR [3-8] R C Strauss.*

SAINTES BHB 58f **RR 60f** 4672[13]
3 b g Be My Chief (USA) 10.2f **(62)** - Latakia (Morston (FR)) 9.4f **(55)**
Form - 41022500
Record 1998 - 1st:1 2nd:2 3rd:0 Ran:8
Pre1998 - 1st:0 2nd:0 3rd:0 Ran:4
Win Prizemoney £3,096 *Total Prizemoney* £6,218
Wins * 1998 Apr Mussel (G-S) H 8f 57 61 <

1998 Turf 1-8: (5f, 7f, 8f 1-3, 9f 2, 11f) (g-s, gd 1-5, g-f, frm)
Workmanlike, average gelding, effective 8 to 9f, best at 8f, acts on g-s to frm. Turf high 61 - 1st of 14 giving 7lb to Pride of Bryn (9 Apr Musselburgh RF 0632). Inconsistent. Got off the mark with a hard-fought victory in a maiden handicap at Musselburgh in April. Ran a couple of solid races at Newcastle after.
**W McKeown [1-12] Mrs L E McKeown.*

SAINT EXPRESS BHB 80f **RR 80f** 5096[4]

8 ch g Clantime 6.6f **(57)** - Redgrave Design (Nebbiolo) 8.1f **(75)**
Form - 8727815300024
Record 1998 - 1st:1 2nd:2 3rd:1 Ran:13
Pre1998 - 1st:6 2nd:9 3rd:9 Ran:60
Win Prizemoney £32,831 *Total Prizemoney* £87,395
Wins * **1998** Aug Redcar (G-F) H 8f 80 83
* 1997 Oct Redcar (G-F) H 7f 80 83
* 1995 Jun York (G-F) H 5f 94 100 <
1994 Jun York (G-F) H 5f 84 86
1998 Turf 1-13: (6f 4, 7f 7, 8f 1-2) (gd 10, frm 1-3)
Decent gelding, effective 6 to 8f, best at 7f, acts on gd to frm, best on frm, has worn blinkers, excels at Redcar. Turf high 83 - 1st of 13 giving 6lb to Saifan (8 Aug Redcar RF 3476). Once a useful sprint handicapper, he seems to have developed a bit of stamina in his old age, winning over seven furlongs at Redcar on his final start of '97, and over a mile at the same track in August of this year. He needs the ground fast.
**Mrs M Reveley [3-46] D S Hall (from N Tinkler [0-1] Jun 1994).*

SAINT GEORGE (IRE) BHB 60f **RR 56f** 4307[10]

2 b c Unblest - Jumana (Windjammer (USA)) 7f **(59)**
Form - 0060
Record 1998 - 1st:0 2nd:0 3rd:0 Ran:4
1998 Turf 0-4: (5f, 6f 3) (gd 2, g-f, frm)
Fair colt. Turf high 56 (began Jly).
**G B Balding [0-4] Russell Publishing Ltd.*

SAINTLY THOUGHTS (USA) BHB 58f54a **RR 71f 54a** 4731[14]

3 b br c St Jovite (USA) 11.8f **(75)** - Free Thinker (USA) (Shadeed (USA)) 8.2f **(70)**
Form - 704525362000
Record 1998 - 1st:0 2nd:2 3rd:1 Ran:12
Win Prizemoney £0 *Total Prizemoney* £2,674
1998 Turf 0-11: (10f, 12f 4, 13f, 14f, 16f 2, 17f 2) (g-s 2, gd, g-f 5, frm 3)
1998 AW 0-1: (12f) (Equi)
Well made, above-average colt, effective 13 to 17f, acts on g-f to frm, best on g-f, has worn blinkers, prefers left handed tracks. Turf high 71 - 2nd of 7 to The Blues Academy (6 Jly Bath 17f g-f RF 2558). Becoming disappointing. **G Lewis [0-12] Khalifa Dasmal.*

SAKHA BHB 100f **RR 102+f** 3461[1]

2 ch f Wolfhound (USA) 7.3f **(71)** - Harmless Albatross (Pas de Seul) 9.1f **(67)**
Form - 311
Record 1998 - 1st:2 2nd:0 3rd:1 Ran:3
Win Prizemoney £7,483 *Total Prizemoney* £8,319
Wins * **1998** Aug Haydoc (GD) 6f 102+ <
* **1998** Jly Kempto (G-F) 6f 84
1998 Turf 2-3: (6f 2-3) (gd 1-1, g-f, frm 1-1)
Currently very useful filly. Turf high 102 - 1st of 6 getting 2lb from Blue Melody (8 Aug Haydock RF 3461). She improved on each of her three starts, putting up a smart display when running away with a conditions event at Haydock in August. She would have been an interesting runner in Group company judged on that effort, but went on the missing list. Hopefully she will be able to make up for lost time in 1999. **J L Dunlop [2-3] Hamdan Al Maktoum.*

SAKHAROV BHB 33f42a **RR 46df 42a** 4931[5]

9 b g Bay Express 7.1f **(53)**-Supreme Kingdom (Take A Reef) 7.5f **(59)**
Form - 747611403406405
Record 1998 - 1st:2 2nd:0 3rd:1 Ran:14
Pre1998 - 1st:7 2nd:5 3rd:3 Ran:43
Win Prizemoney £25,449 *Total Prizemoney* £32,120
Wins 1998 *Apr Wolver (STD) H 9.4f 45 47*
1998 *Apr Lingfi (STD) H 10f 35 43*
1996 May Redcar (G-F) S 7f 62 <
1994 Aug Folkes (GD) H 6.9f 53 55
1994 Jun Carlis (G-F) H 5.9f 51 49
1998 Turf 0-3: (10f 2, 11f) (g-s, gd, g-f) 1998 AW 2-11: (7f, 8f 3, 9f 1-4, 10f 1-1, 11f 2) (Equi 1-2, Fibr 1-9)
Fair gelding, effective 9 to 11f, best at 9f, - acts on AW, best on Fibr, has worn blinkers, favours left handed tracks. Turf high 46. AW high 52 - 3rd of 8 getting 6lb from Ten Past Six (18 May Southwell 11f Fibr RF 1307) - also 1st of 11 getting 4lb from Warning Reef (11 Apr Wolverhampton RF 0655). He ended a long losing run when winning over ten furlongs on the Lingfield Equitrack in April, looking to be suited by the longer trip, and followed up with a narrow victory on the Wolverhampton Fibresand later the same month.
**J Neville [0-4] Mrs B J Harkins (from B Palling [0-7] Jun 1998).*

SALAMAH BHB 86f **RR 86f** 2447[1]

4 b g Sadler's Wells (USA) 11.3f **(87)** - Ala Mahlik (Ahonoora) 8.1f **(73)**
Form - 0521
Record 1998 - 1st:1 2nd:1 3rd:0 Ran:4
Pre1998 - 1st:1 2nd:1 3rd:0 Ran:4
Win Prizemoney £6,928 *Total Prizemoney* £9,972
Wins * **1998** Jly Kempto (G-S) H 12f 81 86
* 1997 May Lingfi (SFT) 10f 87 <
1998 Turf 1-4: (11f, 12f 1-3) (sft, gd 1-2, g-f)
Well made, useful gelding, effective 10 to 12f, best at 12f, acts on g-s to g-f. Turf high 86 - 1st of 8 giving 10lb to Bryony Brind (1 Jly Kempton RF 2447). Relatively lightly-raced, he beat the useful Bryony Brind in June but has not been seen since.
**R Charlton [2-8] K Abdulla.*

SALAMAN (FR) BHB 65f **RR 57f** 2015[27]

6 b g Saumarez 15.1f **(87)** - Merry Sharp (Sharpen Up) 8.3f **(67)**
Form - 30
Record 1998 - 1st:0 2nd:0 3rd:1 Ran:2
Pre1998 - 1st:4 2nd:0 3rd:4 Ran:18
Win Prizemoney £21,144 *Total Prizemoney* £25,420
Wins 1995 Aug Pontef (G-F) 18f 56+
1995 Jly Cheste (GD) H 18.7f 78 85+ <
1995 Jly Beverl (G-F) H 16.2f 72 77+
1995 Jun Warwic (FRM) H 14.9f 67 73+
1998 Turf 0-2: (14f, 20f) (g-s, gd)
Fair gelding, has worn blinkers. Turf high 57. Inconsistent.
**D C O'Brien [1-10] Mrs V O'Brien (from J L Dunlop [4-18] Spt 1996).*

SALBUS BHB 35f38a **RR 34f 38a** 4549[1]

8 b g Salse (USA) 10.9f **(71)** - Busca (USA) (Mr Prospector (USA)) 8.8f **(78)**
Form - 7071
Record 1998 - 1st:1 2nd:0 3rd:0 Ran:4
Pre1998 - 1st:2 2nd:3 3rd:1 Ran:24
Win Prizemoney £11,081 *Total Prizemoney* £13,902
Wins * **1998** *Spt Southw (STD) C 11f 41*
1995 Jan Wolver (STD) C 12f 60 <
1998 Turf 0-2: (11f 2) (g-f, frm) 1998 AW 1-2: (9f, 11f 1-1) (Fibr 1-2)
Moderate gelding, has worn blinkers (very effectively). Turf high 34. AW high 41 (began Jly).
**G L Moore [1-4] Graham Parker (from F J Yardley [1-6] Mar 1995).*

SALEELA (USA) BHB 80f **RR 78+f** 3648[1]

3 b f Nureyev (USA) 8.4f **(84)** - Allegretta (Lombard (GER)) 10.5f **(66)**
Form - 481
Record 1998 - 1st:1 2nd:0 3rd:0 Ran:3
Pre1998 - 1st:0 2nd:0 3rd:0 Ran:1
Win Prizemoney £3,882 *Total Prizemoney* £4,151
Wins * **1998** Aug Warwic (G-F) H 12.5f 74 78 <
1998 Turf 1-3: (8f, 10f, 13f 1-1) (gd, frm 1-2)
Light-framed, above-average filly. Turf high 78 - 1st of 4 giving 20lb to Hastate (14 Aug Warwick RF 3648). A half-sister to Arc winner Urban Sea, she looked in need of plenty of time on her debut but showed a hint of ability. Won a Warwick handicap at the third time of asking. **J L Dunlop [1-4] Hamdan Al Maktoum.*

SALESTRIA BHB 81f **RR 76f** 3943[3]

2 b f Salse (USA) 10.9f **(71)**-Lydia Maria(Dancing Brave (USA))8.4f **(76)**
Form - 6323
Record 1998 - 1st:0 2nd:1 3rd:2 Ran:4
Win Prizemoney £0 *Total Prizemoney* £2,265
1998 Turf 0-4: (7f 4) (gd 2, g-f, frm)
Above-average filly. Turf high 76 (began Jly) - 3rd of 7 to Green Snake (29 Aug Beverley 7f frm RF 3943).
**P W Harris [0-4] Mrs P W Harris.*

SALFORD EXPRESS (IRE) RR 93f 4542[7]
2 ch c Be My Guest (USA) 10.2f **(66)** - Summer Fashion (Moorestyle) 6.9f **(64)**
Form - 27
Record 1998 - 1st:0 2nd:1 3rd:0 Ran:2
Win Prizemoney £0 *Total Prizemoney* £1,675
1998 Turf 0-2: (7f 2) (gd, frm)
Currently useful colt. Turf high 93 (began Spt). Not beaten far into seventh in the Tattersalls Houghton Sales Stakes, he looks sure to pay his way when tackling a mile or further.
**D R C Elsworth [0-2] A J Thompson.*

SALFORD FLYER BHB 66f **RR 72f** 4889[2]
2 b c Pharly (FR) 11.5f **(64)**-Edge of Darkness**(52f)**(Vaigly Great)7f **(58)**
Form - 840402
Record 1998 - 1st:0 2nd:1 3rd:0 Ran:6
Win Prizemoney £0 *Total Prizemoney* £883
1998 Turf 0-5: (6f, 7f, 8f 3) (gd, g-f 3, frm) 1998 AW 0-1: (7f) (Fibr)
Above-average colt, effective 7 to 8f, acts on gd to g-f. Turf high 72 (began Jly) - 4th of 8 giving 3lb to Gypsy (27 Jly Yarmouth 7f g-f RF 3152). **G Wragg [0-6] A J Thompson.*

SALFORD LAD BHB 24f35a **RR 33f 35a** 4275[11]
4 b c Don't Forget Me 9.5f **(66)** - Adjusting (IRE) (Busted) 10.2f **(61)**
Form - 000780
Record 1998 - 1st:0 2nd:0 3rd:0 Ran:6
Pre1998 - 1st:0 2nd:0 3rd:0 Ran:3
1998 Turf 0-4: (7f, 8f 2, 11f) (gd, g-f, frm 2) 1998 AW 0-2: (7f, 8f) (Equi, Fibr)
Scopey, very moderate colt. Turf high 25 (began Jly).
**J Pearce [0-4] Jeff Pearce (from G Wragg [0-5] May 1998).*

SALIGO (IRE) BHB 80f **RR 79f** 4748[1]
3 b f Elbio 9f **(62)** - Doppio Filo (Vision (USA)) 9f **(64)**
Form - 42211061
Record 1998 - 1st:3 2nd:2 3rd:0 Ran:8
Pre1998 - 1st:0 2nd:0 3rd:1 Ran:6
Win Prizemoney £26,926 *Total Prizemoney* £29,186
Wins * **1998** Oct York (GD) H 8.9f 76 79 <
* **1998** Jun Leices (GD) H 10f 73 77
* **1998** May Salisb (FRM) H 8f 67 73
1998 Turf 3-8: (6f, 7f 2, 8f 1-1, 9f 1-1, 10f 1-2, 12f) (g-s 2, gd 1-3, g-f, frm 2-2)
Unfurnished, above-average filly, effective 7 to 10f, acts on gd to frm, best on frm, has worn blinkers. Turf high 79 - 1st of 26 giving 4lb to Super Monarch (10 Oct York RF 4748) - also 1st of 17 giving 2lb to Clarity (1 Jun Leicester RF 1624). She took her time getting off the mark, but has won handicaps at Salisbury, Leicester and York, looking better as she has gone up in trip.
**H Morrison [3-14] The Beach Club.*

SALLYANDAR RR 37f 4671[30]
2 b f Milieu - Megan's Move (Move Off) 15f **(41)**
Form - 00
Record 1998 - 1st:0 2nd:0 3rd:0 Ran:2
1998 Turf 0-2: (6f, 7f) (g-f, frm)
Currently very moderate filly. Turf high 37 (began Spt).
**W Storey [0-2] H S Hutchinson.*

SALLY GREEN (IRE) BHB 65f73a **RR 68f 73a** 4582[9]
4 b f Common Grounds 8.1f **(66)** - Redwood Hut (Habitat) 9.4f **(70)**
Form - 006627640
Record 1998 - 1st:0 2nd:1 3rd:0 Ran:9
Pre1998 - 1st:2 2nd:1 3rd:2 Ran:12
Win Prizemoney £5,948 *Total Prizemoney* £9,119
Wins * 1997 Jly Sandow (G-S) H 5f 68 68 <
* 1996 *Nov Southw (STD) 6f 66*
1998 Turf 0-9: (5f 6, 6f 3) (hvy, gd 2, g-f 4, frm 2)
Average filly, effective 5 to 6f, best at 5f, acts on gd to frm. Turf high 68 - 2nd of 12 getting 1lb from Ivory Dawn (10 Jly Lingfield 6f frm RF 2688). **C F Wall [2-21] K V Stenborg.*

SALLY'S DANCER RR 791[R]
3 b f Shareef Dancer (USA) 10.1f **(67)** - Spica (USA) (Diesis) 9.3f **(69)**
Form - 07R
Record 1998 - 1st:0 2nd:0 3rd:0 Ran:3
1998 Turf 0-1: (6f) (g-s) 1998 AW 0-2: (6f, 8f) (Fibr 2)
Light-framed, currently little account filly, often wears blinkers. AW high 20. **B A McMahon [0-3] Mrs Sally Fields.*

SALMON LADDER (USA) BHB 94f **RR 96f** 5151[14]
6 b h Bering 9.6f **(80)** - Ballerina Princess (USA) (Mr Prospector (USA)) 8.8f **(78)**
Form - 113582070
Record 1998 - 1st:2 2nd:1 3rd:1 Ran:9
Pre1998 - 1st:6 2nd:5 3rd:1 Ran:20
Win Prizemoney £101,554 *Total Prizemoney* £154,423
Wins * **1998** May Bath (GD) 10.2f 106
* **1998** May Hamilt (G-S) 9.2f 79+
* 1997 Aug Windso (G-F) 10f 106
* 1996 Oct Newbur (SFT) G3 12f 115 <
* 1996 Aug Goodwo (G-F) LH 12f 108 113
* 1996 Jun Ascot (G-F) H 10f 102 107
* 1996 Jun Hamilt (GD) 9.2f 88+
* 1994 Oct York (G-S) 7.9f 94+
1998 Turf 2-9:(9f 1-1, 10f 1-1, 11f, 12f 6)(sft, g-s 1-1,gd 3,g-f 2, frm 1-2)
Very useful horse, effective 10 to 12f, acts on gd to frm, best on gd, has worn blinkers, likes tight tracks. Turf high 106 - also 1st of 5 giving 6lb to Maralinga (10 May Bath RF 1127). He seems to have been around forever and finally started to give best to Old Father Time in 1998. **P F I Cole [8-29] M Arbib.*

SALORY RR 55f 5064[9]
2 b c Salse (USA) 10.9f **(71)** - Mory Kante (USA) (Icecapade (USA)) 11f **(62)**
Form - 00
Record 1998 - 1st:0 2nd:0 3rd:0 Ran:2
1998 Turf 0-2: (6f, 7f) (g-f, frm)
Currently fair colt. Turf high 55 (began Oct).
**R T Phillips [0-2] Sanford Racing.*

SALSEE LAD BHB 33f45a **RR 37f 45a** 5118[13]
4 b g Salse (USA) 10.9f **(71)** - Jamarj (Tymavos) 10.1f **(55)**
Form - 4724670700
Record 1998 - 1st:0 2nd:1 3rd:0 Ran:10
Pre1998 - 1st:0 2nd:0 3rd:1 Ran:8
Win Prizemoney £0 *Total Prizemoney* £1,364
1998 Turf 0-10: (12f 2, 13f 4, 14f 2, 16f 2) (g-s 2, gd 3, g-f, frm 4)
Fair gelding, effective 13 to 14f, best at 13f, acts on gd to frm, best on frm, has worn blinkers, prefers right handed tracks, favours tight tracks. Turf high 54 - 2nd of 8 giving 2lb to Silankka (3 Jly Hamilton 13f frm RF 2496).
**I Semple [0-11] Rycon Ltd (from J R Fanshawe [0-8] Oct 1997).*

SALSETTE BHB 64f **RR 72f** 3765[9]
3 b f Salse (USA) 10.9f **(71)** - Amber Fizz (USA) (Effervescing (USA)) 8.1f **(79)**
Form - 803030
Record 1998 - 1st:0 2nd:0 3rd:2 Ran:6
Pre1998 - 1st:0 2nd:0 3rd:1 Ran:4
Win Prizemoney £0 *Total Prizemoney* £1,742
1998 Turf 0-6: (5f, 6f 3, 7f, 8f) (gd 2, g-f, frm 2, hrd)
Scopey, above-average filly, effective 5f, acts on g-f, has worn blinkers. Turf high 72 - 3rd of 7 giving 3lb to Facile Tigre (2 Jun Brighton 5f g-f RF 1645). **C E Brittain [0-10] Saeed Manana.*

SALSIAN BHB 30f40a **RR 42f 40a** 2340[10]
5 b m Salse (USA) 10.9f **(71)** - Phylae (Habitat) 9.4f **(70)**
Form - 0
Record 1998 - 1st:0 2nd:0 3rd:0 Ran:1
Pre1998 - 1st:0 2nd:0 3rd:0 Ran:8
1998 AW 0-1: (13f) (Equi)
Moderate filly, has worn blinkers.
**P Winkworth [0-4] N A Dunger (from S C Williams [0-8] Jly 1996).*

SALSIFY RR 61f 5065[11]
2 b c Salse (USA) 10.9f **(71)** - Amaranthus (Shirley Heights) 10.3f **(74)**
Form - 0
Record 1998 - 1st:0 2nd:0 3rd:0 Ran:1
1998 Turf 0-1: (8f) (g-f)
Currently average colt.
**R Charlton [0-1] Highclere Thoroughbred Racing Ltd.*

SALSKA BHB 69f45a **RR 71f 45a** 4054[6]
7 b m Salse (USA) 10.9f **(71)** - Anzeige (GER) (Soderini) 13.5f **(68)**
Form - 112256

Record	**1998** -	1st:2	2nd:2	3rd:0	Ran:6
	Pre1998 -	1st:5	2nd:4	3rd:3	Ran:43

Win Prizemoney £23,381 *Total Prizemoney* £32,514

Wins							
* **1998**	Jun	Newcas	(GD)	H	16.1f	60	66 <
* **1998**	Jun	Nottin	(GD)	H	14.1f	60	66 <
* 1997	Jly	Redcar	(G-F)	H	16f	58	61
* 1997	Jun	Nottin	(G-F)	H	14.1f	56	61
* 1996	Jly	Redcar	(G-F)	H	14.1f	46	57+
* 1996	Jly	Warwic	(G-F)	H	14.9f	46	54+
* 1995	Spt	Haydoc	(GD)	H	14f	43	50

1998 Turf 2-6: (14f 1-2, 16f 1-4) (gd 2-2, frm 3, hrd)
Above-average mare, effective 14 to 16f, best at 16f, acts on gd to hrd, best on frm, has worn blinkers, prefers left handed tracks, likes tight tracks, excels at Redcar and Nottingham. Turf high 71 - 2nd of 9 giving 1lb to Hullbank (25 Jly Redcar 16f hrd RF 3123) - also 1st of 12 giving 17lb to Siberian Mystic (17 Jun Nottingham RF 2065). Consistent. A tough mare, she won staying handicaps at Nottingham and Newcastle on her first two starts of the season, but has struggled from higher marks. Her victories this term have shown that she handles yielding ground well.
**A Streeter [7-31] P L Clinton (from A L Forbes [0-4] Aug 1995).*

SALTY BEHAVIOUR (IRE) BHB 67f65a **RR 71f 65a** 4636[7]
4 ch c Salt Dome (USA) 6.5f**(59)**-Good Behaviour(Artaius (USA))9f **(69)**
Form - 71742517147

Record	**1998** -	1st:2	2nd:1	3rd:0	Ran:9
	Pre1998 -	1st:4	2nd:1	3rd:1	Ran:11

Win Prizemoney £18,505 *Total Prizemoney* £21,783

Wins						
* **1998**	Aug	Chepst	(G-F)	S	7.1f	68
* **1998**	Jly	Epsom	(G-F)	C	6f	70
* 1997	*Dec*	*Lingfi*	*(STD)*	*C*	*8f*	*70*
* 1997	Aug	Salisb	(G-F)	C	6f	70
* 1996	Nov	Folkes	(SFT)		5f	76 <
* 1996	Jly	Salisb	(G-F)		6f	76 <

1998 Turf 2-7: (5f, 6f 1-5, 7f 1-1) (gd 2, g-f 1-2, frm 1-3) 1998 AW 0-2: (7f, 8f) (Equi, Fibr)
Leggy, above-average colt, effective 6 to 8f, best at 6f, acts on gd to frm - acts on Equi, best on g-f, likes tight tracks. Turf high 71 - 2nd of 14 giving 14lb to Double March (15 Jun Windsor 6f gd RF 2007) - also 1st of 7 getting 8lb from Shamanic (29 Jly Epsom RF 3201). AW high 38. A winner on both turf and Equitrack, he is probably best over six furlongs despite his victory over a mile on sand. **R Hannon [6-20] J R Shannon.*

SALTY JACK (IRE) BHB 89f74a **RR 90f 74a** 4985[18]
4 b c Salt Dome (USA) 6.5f **(59)** - Play The Queen (IRE) (King of Clubs) 7.1f **(57)**
Form - 41203136482123110

Record	**1998** -	1st:4	2nd:2	3rd:3	Ran:14
	Pre1998 -	1st:2	2nd:1	3rd:4	Ran:12

Win Prizemoney £30,358 *Total Prizemoney* £39,694

Wins							
* **1998**	Oct	Newmar	(GD)	H	7f	85	90 <
* **1998**	Spt	Doncas	(GD)	H	7f	81	84
* **1998**	Jly	Epsom	(G-F)	H	7f	75	78
* **1998**	Apr	Folkes	(SFT)		6.9f		74
* 1997	*Dec*	*Lingfi*	*(STD)*	*H*	*7f*	*65*	*69*
1996	Aug	Salisb	(GD)		6f		75

1998 Turf 4-11: (7f 4-11) (sft 1-1, g-s, gd 2-6, g-f 1-2, frm) 1998 AW 0-3: (7f 2, 8f) (Equi 3)
Strong, useful colt, effective 7f, acts on gd. Turf high 90 - 1st of 12 getting 9lb from Return of Amin (2 Oct Newmarket RF 4617) - also 1st of 20 giving 7lb to Sheer Face (10 Spt Doncaster RF 4209). AW high 74. Developed through the year into a useful handicapper, suited by hold-up tactics in a fast-run race. Ray Cochrane timed his run to perfection at Doncaster, coming from virtually last place a furlong out to get up on the line for an astonishing victory. Has a great turn of foot, and is sure to win more races.
**V Soane [5-20] Salts Of The Earth (from S Dow [1-6] Spt 1996).*

SALZBURG (IRE) RR 24f 5064[16]
2 b g Salse (USA) 10.9f **(71)** - Sally Rose (Sallust) 8.4f **(63)**
Form - 0

Record	**1998** -	1st:0	2nd:0	3rd:0	Ran:1

1998 Turf 0-1: (6f) (g-f)
Currently little account gelding. **B J Meehan [0-1] B J Meehan.*

SAMANID (IRE) BHB 70f **RR 50f** 1772[7]
6 b g Shardari 12.1f **(59)** - Samarzana (USA) (Blushing Groom (FR)) 10.3f **(76)**
Form - 7

Record	**1998** -	1st:0	2nd:0	3rd:0	Ran:1
	Pre1998 -	1st:0	2nd:0	3rd:0	Ran:3

1998 Turf 0-1: (12f) (g-f)
Fair gelding, has worn blinkers.
**Miss L C Siddall [2-20] Mrs Theresa O'Toole (from P Burke in IRE [1-8] Jly 1996).*

SAMARAKAND RR 5f 2274[18]
2 b g Then Again 7.4f **(52)** - Whitchurch Silk (IRE) (Runnett) 7f **(59)**
Form - 00

Record	**1998** -	1st:0	2nd:0	3rd:0	Ran:2

1998 Turf 0-2: (7f 2) (gd, frm)
Currently very poor gelding. Turf high 5.
**G B Balding [0-2] Baldings (Training) Ltd.*

SAMARA SONG BHB 63f57a **RR 64f 57a** 4633[10]
5 ch g Savahra Sound 7.8f **(55)** - Hosting (Thatching) 8f **(66)**
Form - 684522163040

Record	**1998** -	1st:1	2nd:2	3rd:1	Ran:12
	Pre1998 -	1st:1	2nd:6	3rd:3	Ran:24

Win Prizemoney £10,953 *Total Prizemoney* £22,026

Wins							
* **1998**	Aug	Sandow	(GD)	H	7.1f	59	63 <
* 1997	Spt	Leices	(G-F)	H	7f	53	54

1998 Turf 1-12: (7f 1-10, 8f 2) (gd 1-3, g-f 5, frm 4)
Average gelding, effective 7 to 8f, best at 7f, acts on gd to frm, best on gd, has worn blinkers, likes left handed tracks, excels at Leicester and Chepstow and Bath. Turf high 64 - 4th of 18 getting 3lb from The Green Grey (21 Spt Kempton 8f frm RF 4391) - also 1st of 5 getting 19lb from Huntswood (2 Aug Sandown RF 3300). Consistent. He was in good form in 1997, but had become expensive to follow before his victory at Leicester, where the seven furlongs proved just right. It was the same story in 1998, several good efforts but not winning until Sandown in August.
**Ian Williams [2-23] Turton Builders (from W G M Turner [0-10] Oct 1996).*

SAMATA ONE (IRE) BHB 58f **RR 62f** 4048[11]
3 b c River Falls 8.2f **(56)** - Abadila (IRE) (Shernazar) 10.2f **(73)**
Form - 525280

Record	**1998** -	1st:0	2nd:2	3rd:0	Ran:6
	Pre1998 -	1st:0	2nd:0	3rd:0	Ran:2

Win Prizemoney £0 *Total Prizemoney* £2,170
1998 Turf 0-6: (7f 3, 8f 2, 9f) (gd 3, g-f, frm 2)
Light-framed, average colt, effective 7 to 8f, acts on gd to g-f, has worn blinkers. Turf high 62 - 2nd of 18 getting 12lb from Sunstreak (4 Jly Nottingham 8f g-f RF 2544). **W J Haggas [0-8] S Hassiakos.*

SAMBAKONIG (GER) RR 106f 4829a[3]
5 h
Form - 286423
1998 Turf 0-6: (9f, 10f 3, 11f 2) (hvy 2, sft 2, gd 2)
Pattern-class colt, effective 9 to 11f, best at 10f, acts on hvy to gd, best on sft, does well at Baden-Baden and Frankfurt. Turf high 106 - 2nd of 9 giving 11lb to Elle Danzig (3 Oct Hoppegarten 10f sft RF 4714a). Consistent. He was banging his head against a brick wall in Group Two and Three events. A drop in class is required.
**H Horwart in GER [0-9] A von Mulert.*

SAMMAL (IRE) BHB 72f **RR 76f** 4591[13]
2 b g Petardia 8.2f **(58)** - Prime Site (IRE) (Burslem) 8.8f **(53)**
Form - 3127700

Record	**1998** -	1st:1	2nd:1	3rd:1	Ran:7

Win Prizemoney £3,195 *Total Prizemoney* £4,743

Wins						
* **1998**	Apr	Carlis	(G-S)	5f		74 <

1998 Turf 1-7: (5f 1-5, 6f 2) (gd 1-4, frm 3)
Above-average gelding, effective 5f, acts on gd to frm. Turf high 76 - 2nd of 4 giving 6lb to Rosselli (21 May Newcastle 5f frm RF 1366) - also 1st of 18 giving 5lb to First Musical (24 Apr Carlisle RF 0840). Ran well on his Doncaster debut, and improved on that to win a Carlisle maiden next time. Despite the large field, it was not a particularly competitive race, and he had little to spare at the end. Runner-up to Rosselli on his third run, but well held since.
**J A Glover [1-7] Mrs Andrea Mallinson.*

SAMMY'S SHUFFLE BHB 47f37a **RR 47f 37a** 5070[6]
3 b c Touch of Grey 8.1f **(47)** - Cabinet Shuffle (Thatching) 8f **(66)**
Form - 0888676745124016
Record 1998 - 1st:2 2nd:1 3rd:0 Ran:13
Pre1998 - 1st:0 2nd:0 3rd:0 Ran:3
Win Prizemoney £5,150 *Total Prizemoney* £5,946
Wins * **1998** Spt Bright (GD) H 10f 43 47 <
* **1998** Jly Bright (G-F) H 10f 30 35
1998 Turf 2-8: (9f, 10f 2-6, 12f) (gd 1-3, g-f 1-4, frm) 1998 AW 0-5: (7f, 8f 2, 10f 2) (Equi 5)
Neat, moderate colt, effective 10f, acts on g-f to frm, best on g-f, mostly wears blinkers (extremely effectively), favours left handed tracks, favours tight tracks. Turf high 47 - 1st of 20 getting 17lb from Simlet (30 Spt Brighton RF 4574). AW high 36. Consistent.
**R M Flower [2-16] Mrs G M Temmerman.*

SAM PEEB BHB 30f32a **RR 38f 32a** 904[12]
4 b g Keen 11.1f **(58)** - Lutine Royal (Formidable (USA)) 9.2f **(63)**
Form - 00040
Record 1998 - 1st:0 2nd:0 3rd:0 Ran:5
Pre1998 - 1st:1 2nd:0 3rd:2 Ran:9
Win Prizemoney £2,277 *Total Prizemoney* £3,175
Wins * 1997 *May Southw (STD) H 12f 36 42* <
1998 Turf 0-2: (12f, 14f) (sft, g-s) 1998 AW 0-3: (11f, 12f 2) (Fibr 3)
Leggy, very moderate gelding, effective 12f, - acts on Fibr, has worn blinkers, likes left handed tracks. Turf high 32. AW high 13. Inconsistent. **R A Fahey [1-14] Mrs M A Brown.*

SAMPOWER LADY BHB 53f60a **RR 34f 60a** 1532[10]
3 ch f Rock City 8.8f **(62)** - Travel On (Tachypous) 8.6f **(55)**
Form - 0
Record 1998 - 1st:0 2nd:0 3rd:0 Ran:1
Pre1998 - 1st:0 2nd:0 3rd:0 Ran:5
Win Prizemoney £0 *Total Prizemoney* £656
1998 Turf 0-1: (6f) (g-f)
Workmanlike, fair filly. **W J Musson [0-6] Sampower Racing Club.*

SAMPOWER STAR BHB 90f82a **RR 83f 82a** 4743[4]
2 b c Cyrano de Bergerac 7.3f **(58)** - Green Supreme (Primo Dominie) 6.2f **(80)**
Form - 281135044
Record 1998 - 1st:2 2nd:1 3rd:1 Ran:9
Win Prizemoney £5,498 *Total Prizemoney* £7,778
Wins * **1998** Jly Salisb (GD) 7f 82 <
* **1998** Jly Folkes (G-F) 6f 71+
1998 Turf 2-8: (5f 2, 6f 1-2, 7f 1-3, 8f) (g-s, gd 3, g-f 1-2, frm 1-2) 1998 AW 0-1: (6f) (Fibr)
Decent colt, effective 7 to 8f, acts on gd to frm. Turf high 83 - also 1st of 7 getting 2lb from Bathwick (17 Jly Salisbury RF 2891). He won small races at Folkestone and Salisbury, but was been rather highly tried after. **R Simpson [2-9] Sampower Racing Club.*

SAMRAAN (USA) BHB 110f **RR 111f** 4632[3]
5 br h Green Dancer (USA) 11.9f **(77)** - Sedra (Nebbiolo) 8.1f **(75)**
Form - 32853
Record 1998 - 1st:0 2nd:1 3rd:2 Ran:5
Pre1998 - 1st:5 2nd:2 3rd:2 Ran:20
Win Prizemoney £67,258 *Total Prizemoney* £137,090
Wins * 1997 Oct San Si (G-F) L 15f 111+ <
* 1996 Spt Salisb (FRM) 14f 110
* 1996 Jun Ascot (G-F) H 12f 94 99
* 1996 May Newbur (GD) H 12f 90 95
* 1996 Apr Kempto (GD) 10f 85+
1998 Turf 0-5: (16f 5) (gd 2, g-f 3)
Group-class colt, effective 12 to 16f, best at 16f, acts on gd to frm, best on gd, excels at Newmarket and York. Turf high 116 - 2nd of 11 getting 3lb from Persian Punch (25 May Sandown 16f g-f RF 1462). Consistent. Ran good races on his first two starts of 1998, making the frame behind Persian Punch each time, but missed the Gold Cup due to the soft ground. He was well beaten at both Goodwood and York, but ran a little better when third in the Jockey Club Cup. He looks to need a trip in excess of two miles now. **J L Dunlop [5-25] K M Al-Mudhaf.*

SAMSON'S LILLY BHB 64f **RR 78f** 4697[13]
2 b g Lugana Beach 7f **(63)** -Rosy Diamond (Jalmood (USA)) 10.1f **(52)**
Form - 2730300
Record 1998 - 1st:0 2nd:1 3rd:2 Ran:7
Win Prizemoney £0 *Total Prizemoney* £1,764
1998 Turf 0-7: (6f 2, 7f 2, 8f 3) (g-s, gd 2, g-f, frm 2, hrd)
Above-average gelding, effective 7 to 8f, acts on frm. Turf high 78 (1st run) (began Jly) - 2nd of 8 to Sicnee (18 Jly Redcar 7f frm RF 2929). **J J O'Neill [0-7] Clayton Bigley Partnership Ltd.*

SAMSPET BHB 20f30a **RR 28f 30a** 2561[11]
4 ch g Pharly (FR) 11.5f **(64)** - Almond Blossom (Grundy) 10.3f **(65)**
Form - 76000
Record 1998 - 1st:0 2nd:0 3rd:0 Ran:5
Pre1998 - 1st:0 2nd:2 3rd:0 Ran:17
Win Prizemoney £0 *Total Prizemoney* £1,542
1998 Turf 0-5: (7f, 8f 3, 10f) (hvy, g-s, gd, g-f, frm)
Very moderate gelding, effective 7 to 8f, acts on sft to gd, has worn blinkers, likes right handed tracks, favours tight tracks. Turf high 28. **R A Fahey [0-22] Peter Tingey.*

SAMUT (IRE) BHB 92f **RR 93f** 4628[9]
2 b f Danehill (USA) 9.1f **(79)** - Simaat (USA) (Mr Prospector (USA)) 8.8f **(78)**
Form - 510
Record 1998 - 1st:1 2nd:0 3rd:0 Ran:3
Win Prizemoney £3,829 *Total Prizemoney* £3,829
Wins * **1998** Spt Beverl (G-F) 7.5f 89+ <
1998 Turf 1-3: (7f 1-3) (g-f, frm 1-2)
Currently useful filly. Turf high 93 (began Aug) - also 1st of 15 from Auspicious (16 Spt Beverley RF 4299). Showed a bright turn of foot to win at Beverley but failed to handle a step up in class.
**J H M Gosden [1-3] Hamdan Al Maktoum.*

SAMWAR BHB 67f71a **RR 70f 71a** 5040[13]
6 b g Warning 8.1f **(77)** - Samaza (USA) (Arctic Tern (USA)) 8.9f **(69)**
Form - 04047730658030
Record 1998 - 1st:0 2nd:0 3rd:2 Ran:14
Pre1998 - 1st:2 2nd:3 3rd:0 Ran:23
Win Prizemoney £22,745 *Total Prizemoney* £37,816
Wins 1996 Aug Ripon (GD) H 6f 78 89 <
1995 *Dec Lingfi (STD) 7f 70+*
1998 Turf 0-11: (5f 3, 6f 7, 7f) (sft, g-s, gd 2, g-f 3, frm 4) 1998 AW 0-3: (6f 2, 7f) (Fibr 3)
Above-average gelding, effective 5 to 6f, best at 6f, acts on sft to frm, best on frm, has worn blinkers (effectively). Turf high 71 - 4th of 18 giving 4lb to Divine Miss-P (10 May Bath 5f frm RF 1132). AW high 67.
**Mrs N Macauley [0-6] G Wiltshire (from Miss Gay Kelleway [2-20] Jly 1998).*

SANDBAGGEDAGAIN BHB 77f **RR 76f** 4448[1]
4 b g Prince Daniel (USA) 11.4f **(46)** - Paircullis (Tower Walk) 10f **(62)**
Form - 0083321131
Record 1998 - 1st:3 2nd:1 3rd:3 Ran:10
Pre1998 - 1st:1 2nd:2 3rd:5 Ran:15
Win Prizemoney £26,393 *Total Prizemoney* £41,059
Wins * **1998** Spt Cheste (GD) H 15.9f 74 76 <
* **1998** Jly Ascot (G-F) H 16.2f 64 68
* **1998** Jly Catter (GD) H 15.8f 62 63
* 1997 Jun York (G-S) 11.9f 76+
1998 Turf 3-10: (7f 3, 10f, 12f 2, 16f 3-4) (g-s, gd 2-4, g-f, frm 1-4)
Leggy, above-average gelding, effective 8 to 16f, best at 16f, acts on g-s to frm, has worn blinkers, likes left handed tracks, likes tight tracks. Turf high 76 - 1st of 12 giving 16lb to Murchan Tyne (23 Spt Chester RF 4448) - also 1st of 15 getting 4lb from Olivo (24 Jly Ascot RF 3062). Improving. He gradually ran into form this year, eventually scoring in a small Catterick handicap, and has improved for the step up in distance. Stays well, and can win decent handicaps in 1999.
**M W Easterby [4-27] Mrs Christopher Hanbury.*

SANDBLASTER BHB 40f32a **RR 46f 32a** 1035[14]
5 ch m Most Welcome 8.6f **(66)** - Honeychurch (USA) (Bering) 7.4f **(61)**
Form - 86U0
Record 1998 - 1st:0 2nd:0 3rd:0 Ran:4
Pre1998 - 1st:1 2nd:2 3rd:2 Ran:22
Win Prizemoney £2,802 *Total Prizemoney* £6,073
Wins 1997 Jun Mussel (G-S) H 8f 39 46 <
1998 Turf 0-1: (10f) (gd) 1998 AW 0-3: (6f, 8f 2) (Equi, Fibr 2)
Moderate filly, effective 8f, acts on gd, has worn blinkers.

AW high 15.
**W G M Turner [0-4] R B Cody-Boutcher (from J L Eyre [1-8] Aug 1997).*

SAND CAY (USA) BHB 45f **RR 40f** 4573[6]
4 ch g Geiger Counter (USA) 7.8f **(85)** - Lily Lily Rose (USA) (Lypheor) 12f **(71)**
Form - 060006
Record 1998 - 1st:0 2nd:0 3rd:0 Ran:6
Pre1998 - 1st:0 2nd:1 3rd:0 Ran:9
Win Prizemoney £0 *Total Prizemoney* £991
1998 Turf 0-6: (8f, 10f, 12f 3, 16f) (g-s, gd, g-f 2, frm 2)
Workmanlike, moderate gelding, effective 8 to 12f, acts on frm to hrd. Turf high 54 - 6th of 15 giving 1lb to Veronica Franco (14 May Salisbury 12f frm RF 1218).
**R J O'Sullivan [0-8] B S Chatwal And Partners (from R Hannon [0-9] Spt 1997).*

SANDERLING (IRE) BHB 65f **RR 72df** 4884[5]
2 b f Exit To Nowhere (USA) 8.7f **(77)** - Tartique Twist (USA) (Arctic Tern (USA)) 8.9f **(69)**
Form - 675
Record 1998 - 1st:0 2nd:0 3rd:0 Ran:3
1998 Turf 0-3: (7f 2, 8f) (g-s, gd, frm)
Currently above-average filly. Turf high 72 (1st run) (began Aug) - 6th of 21 getting 5lb from Forest Shadow (15 Aug Newbury 7f gd RF 3653). **J L Dunlop [0-3] Sir Thomas Pilkington.*

SAND FALCON RR 106f 4076a[2]
3 ch g Polar Falcon (USA) 9f **(74)** - Sand Grouse (USA) (Arctic Tern (USA)) 8.9f **(69)**
Form - 12
1998 Turf 1-2: (8f 1-2) (gd 1-2)
Currently Pattern-class gelding. Turf high 106 (1st run) (began Aug) - 1st of 7 from Florazi (11 Aug Deauville RF 3778a). He was out-sprinted in a tactically run Group Three at Deauville in August. By Polar Falcon, he could come into his own on soft ground.
**P Bary in FR [1-2] K Abdulla.*

SAND HAWK BHB 49f **RR 50f** 5006[12]
3 ch g Polar Falcon (USA) 9f **(74)** - Ghassanah (Pas de Seul) 9.1f **(67)**
Form - 00300320
Record 1998 - 1st:0 2nd:1 3rd:2 Ran:8
Win Prizemoney £0 *Total Prizemoney* £1,758
1998 Turf 0-7: (5f, 6f 3, 7f, 8f 2) (sft 2, gd, g-f 2, frm 2) 1998 AW 0-1: (6f) (Fibr)
Leggy, fair gelding, effective 7f, acts on g-f, has worn blinkers. Turf high 50 - 2nd of 29 getting 18lb from Hebony (6 Oct Redcar 7f g-f RF 4677). Inconsistent. **D Shaw [0-8] J C Fretwell.*

SANDIA POINT (IRE) BHB 54f **RR 48f** 1816[19]
3 b g Sharpo 7.5f **(68)** - Andbell (Trojan Fen) 8.1f **(62)**
Form - 000
Record 1998 - 1st:0 2nd:0 3rd:0 Ran:3
1998 Turf 0-3: (7f 2, 10f) (g-s, gd, frm)
Workmanlike, currently moderate gelding. Turf high 48.
**J A Glover [0-3] Ernest Bennett.*

SANDICLIFFE (USA) BHB 53f50a **RR 56f 50a** 3763[5]
5 b m Imp Society (USA) 7.1f **(63)** - Sad Song (USA) (Roberto (USA)) 10f **(76)**
Form - 6635
Record 1998 - 1st:0 2nd:0 3rd:1 Ran:4
Pre1998 - 1st:2 2nd:0 3rd:0 Ran:14
Win Prizemoney £6,226 *Total Prizemoney* £7,107
Wins * 1997 Aug Newmar (G-F) H 8f 50 60 <
1997 May Folkes (G-F) C 6.9f 52
1998 Turf 0-4: (8f 4) (gd, g-f 2, hrd)
Fair filly, effective 7 to 8f, best at 8f, acts on gd to hrd, best on frm, and excels at Yarmouth. Turf high 56 - 6th of 12 getting 2lb from Migrate (15 Jly Yarmouth 8f g-f RF 2835). Consistent.
**J A R Toller [1-8] Ash Partnership (from B W Hills [1-10] May 1997).*

SANDMOOR TARTAN BHB 56f **RR 54f** 4677[10]
3 b g Komaite (USA) 6.9f **(61)** - Sky Fighter (Hard Fought) 8.8f **(62)**
Form - 670073536610
Record 1998 - 1st:1 2nd:0 3rd:2 Ran:12
Pre1998 - 1st:1 2nd:0 3rd:1 Ran:9
Win Prizemoney £5,808 *Total Prizemoney* £7,425
Wins * **1998** Spt Nottin (G-F) SH 8.2f 51 54
* 1997 Aug Cheste (G-F) H 6.1f 56 55 <
1998 Turf 1-12: (5f, 6f 2, 7f 2, 8f 1-5, 9f, 10f) (gd 1-5, g-f 3, frm 3, hrd)
Workmanlike, fair gelding, effective 5 to 8f, acts on g-s to frm, prefers left handed tracks, prefers tight tracks. Turf high 54 - 1st of 17 giving 5lb to Final Claim (26 Spt Nottingham RF 4504). Consistent. **T D Easterby [2-21] Sandmoor Textiles Co Ltd.*

SANDOVA (IRE) RR 66f 4856[7]
2 b f Green Desert (USA) 7.8f **(78)** - Alinova (USA) (Alleged (USA)) 10f **(76)**
Form - 7
Record 1998 - 1st:0 2nd:0 3rd:0 Ran:1
1998 Turf 0-1: (7f) (sft)
Currently average filly. **Sir Michael Stoute [0-1] Sheikh Mohammed.*

SANDPOINT RR 3143[16]
2 b f Lugana Beach 7f **(63)** - Instinction (Never so Bold) 6.3f **(66)**
Form - 0
Record 1998 - 1st:0 2nd:0 3rd:0 Ran:1
1998 Turf 0-1: (6f) (frm)
Currently very poor filly. **L G Cottrell [0-1] L G Cottrell.*

SANDSIDE BHB 63f56a **RR 63f 56a** 3453[4]
3 b g Mazaad 8.5f **(53)** - Deverells Walk (IRE) (Godswalk (USA)) 7.3f **(58)**
Form - 07460104
Record 1998 - 1st:1 2nd:0 3rd:0 Ran:8
Pre1998 - 1st:3 2nd:2 3rd:1 Ran:12
Win Prizemoney £9,974 *Total Prizemoney* £12,798
Wins * **1998** Jly Redcar (G-F) SH 5f 58 63
* 1997 Aug Hamilt (GD) C 5f 85 <
* 1997 May Redcar (G-F) 5f 70
* 1997 May Mussel (G-S) 5f 70
1998 Turf 1-6: (5f 1-4, 6f 2) (gd 3, g-f 2, frm 1-1) 1998 AW 0-2: (5f, 6f) (Fibr 2)
Average gelding, effective 5f, acts on g-f, has worn blinkers. Turf high 63. AW high 48 (began Jly). **J Berry [4-20] J K Brown.*

SANDSPIDER RR 1f 4510[F]
3 ch f Clantime 6.6f **(57)** - Forbidden Monkey (Gabitat) 5f **(44)**
Form - 0F
Record 1998 - 1st:0 2nd:0 3rd:0 Ran:2
1998 Turf 0-2: (5f, 6f) (gd, frm)
Small, currently very poor filly. Turf high 1 (began Aug).
**L R Lloyd-James [0-2] J Morris.*

SANDVILLE LAD RR 58[5]
6 gr g Librate 10.4f **(37)** - Inglifield (Whistlefield) 5f **(55)**
Form - 85
Record 1998 - 1st:0 2nd:0 3rd:0 Ran:2
1998 AW 0-2: (10f, 13f) (Equi 2)
Little account gelding. AW high 29. **B Palling [0-2] Mrs D Thomas.*

SANDY SADDLER BHB 43f60a **RR 56f 60a** 4931[17]
4 ch g Most Welcome 8.6f **(66)** - Beryl's Jewel (Siliconn) 8.4f **(55)**
Form - 005760000
Record 1998 - 1st:0 2nd:0 3rd:0 Ran:8
Pre1998 - 1st:0 2nd:0 3rd:0 Ran:4
Win Prizemoney £0 *Total Prizemoney* £236
1998 Turf 0-8: (7f 3, 8f 2, 10f 3) (g-s, gd 2, g-f 2, frm 3)
Unfurnished, fair gelding, has worn blinkers. Turf high 65. Becoming disappointing.
**P Mitchell [0-4] J A Redmond (from S Dow [0-8] Jun 1998).*

SANDY SHORE BHB 65f57a **RR 62f 57a** 2655[6]
3 b f Lugana Beach 7f **(63)** - City Link Lass (Double Jump) 9.4f **(58)**
Form - 876
Record 1998 - 1st:0 2nd:0 3rd:0 Ran:3
Pre1998 - 1st:0 2nd:2 3rd:1 Ran:7
Win Prizemoney £0 *Total Prizemoney* £2,394
1998 Turf 0-2: (6f, 8f) (gd, g-f) 1998 AW 0-1: (7f) (Fibr)
Light-framed, average filly, effective 5 to 6f, acts on gd to frm. Turf high 28. Becoming disappointing.
**J Hetherton [0-3] J Rose (from J Wharton [0-7] Spt 1997).*

SAN GLAMORE MELODY (FR) BHB 40f45a **RR 46f 45a** 4572[8]

4 b g Sanglamore (USA) 12.9f **(67)** - Lypharitissima (FR) (Lightning (FR)) 7.9f **(74)**

Form - 00607243237508

Record 1998 - 1st:0 2nd:2 3rd:2 Ran:14
Pre1998 - 1st:0 2nd:1 3rd:1 Ran:6

Win Prizemoney £0 *Total Prizemoney* £4,416

1998 Turf 0-13: (8f 3, 10f 4, 11f, 12f 3, 13f, 14f) (g-s, gd, g-f 8, frm 3)
1998 AW 0-1: (9f) (Fibr)

Moderate gelding, effective 9 to 12f, best at 10f, acts on g-f to frm - acts on Fibr, best on g-f, has worn blinkers, favours tight tracks. Turf high 46 - 2nd of 11 getting 14lb from Chief Cashier (29 Jly Epsom 10f g-f RF 3197). (1st run) - 3rd of 13 giving 4lb to Ron's Round (20 Jly Wolverhampton 9f Fibr RF 2964). Consistent.

**R Ingram [0-15] 949 Racing (from J H M Gosden [0-5] Jly 1997).*

SANGRIA RR 20f 1968[11]

4 b f Aragon 7.7f **(58)** - Singora (Blue Cashmere) 6.4f **(54)**

Form - 0000

Record 1998 - 1st:0 2nd:0 3rd:0 Ran:4

1998 Turf 0-4: (6f, 8f 2, 11f) (gd 2, frm 2)

Light-framed, little account filly. Turf high 20.

**Mark Campion [0-4] Mrs P A Roberts.*

SANIWOOD (IRE) BHB 23f **RR 14f** 1430[8]

5 b m Law Society (USA) 11.6f **(71)** - Art Duo (Artaius (USA)) 9f **(69)**

Form - 6708

Record 1998 - 1st:0 2nd:0 3rd:0 Ran:4

1998 Turf 0-1: (10f) (gd) 1998 AW 0-3: (10f 2, 16f) (Equi 3)

Little account filly. AW high 20. **J J Bridger [0-9] M R Pascall.*

SANKATY LIGHT (USA) RR 60f 4761[10]

2 b f Summer Squall (USA) 7f **(80)** - Brave And True (USA) (Fappiano (USA)) 8.7f **(77)**

Form - 00

Record 1998 - 1st:0 2nd:0 3rd:0 Ran:2

1998 Turf 0-2: (6f, 7f) (gd, g-f)

Currently average filly. Turf high 60 (began Spt).

**I A Balding [0-2] Paul Mellon.*

San Sebastian annihilated the opposition at Ascot

SAN SEBASTIAN RR 105f 4850[20]

4 ch g Niniski (USA) 13.2f **(67)**-Top of the League (High Top) 10.2f **(67)**

Form - 2221130

1998 Turf 2-6: (14f 1-2, 16f, 18f, 20f 1-2) (sft, g-s, gd 2-4)

Pattern-class gelding, effective 14 to 20f, acts on sft to gd, best on gd, often wears blinkers (effectively), prefers right handed tracks, excels at Wexford. Turf high 105 - 3rd of 9 to Invermark (3 Oct Longchamp 20f sft RF 4716a) - also 1st of 8 giving 8lb to Broken Rites (30 May Gowran Park RF 1666a). A poor run in the Cesarewitch apart, he had a fine season, winning the Ascot Handicap at the Royal Meeting and finishing third in the Group One Prix du Cadran. The greater the test of stamina the better his chance. **M J Grassick in IRE [6-16] Mrs Michael Watt & R Sanz.*

SANS EGALE (FR) BHB 45f **RR 47f** 4393[13]

4 ch f Lashkari 13.1f **(52)** - Lady Gerardina (Levmoss) 11.4f **(66)**

Form - 0860

Record 1998 - 1st:0 2nd:0 3rd:0 Ran:4

1998 Turf 0-4: (8f 2, 10f, 11f) (frm 4)

Light-framed, moderate filly. Turf high 47.

**Lady Herries [0-4] Without Equal Partnership.*

SANSKRIT RR 49f 2766[14]

2 ch f Sabrehill (USA) 8.5f **(64)** - Alipura (Anfield) 8.5f **(59)**

Form - 00

Record 1998 - 1st:0 2nd:0 3rd:0 Ran:2

1998 Turf 0-2: (6f 2) (g-f, frm)

Currently moderate filly. Turf high 49.

**J L Dunlop [0-2] Francis Martin III.*

SANS RIVALE BHB 48f47a **RR 52f 47a** 4661[10]

3 ch f Elmaamul (USA) 8.1f **(70)**-Strawberry Song(Final Straw) 7.9f **(64)**

Form - 076128800

Record 1998 - 1st:1 2nd:1 3rd:0 Ran:9
Pre1998 - 1st:1 2nd:1 3rd:1 Ran:6

Win Prizemoney £4,818 *Total Prizemoney* £6,537

Wins * 1998 Apr Catter (GD) 5f 60
1997 Aug Mussel (GD) S 5f 71 <

1998 Turf 1-6: (5f 1-3, 6f 3) (gd 1-2, frm 4) 1998 AW 0-3: (5f, 6f, 7f) (Fibr 3)

Neat, fair filly, effective 5 to 6f, acts on gd to frm. Turf high 60 (1st run). AW high 43.

**J L Eyre [1-10] David Mann (from B J Meehan [1-5] Aug 1997).*

SANTA COURT BHB 56f **RR 60f** 1888[6]

3 b g Be My Native (USA)11.2f **(62)**-Christmas Show (Petorius)7.3f **(61)**

Form - 7506

Record 1998 - 1st:0 2nd:0 3rd:0 Ran:4
Pre1998 - 1st:0 2nd:1 3rd:0 Ran:5

Win Prizemoney £0 *Total Prizemoney* £1,135

1998 Turf 0-4: (8f 3, 10f) (g-s 2, gd, g-f)

Neat, average gelding, effective 6f, acts on g-f. Turf high 60.

**R Dickin [0-9] Derek & Cheryl Holder.*

SANTA FAYE (IRE) BHB 67f78a **RR 61f 78a** 3840[5]

3 b f Fayruz 6.6f **(63)** - Florissa (FR) (Persepolis (FR)) 6.4f **(67)**

Form - 5008015

Record 1998 - 1st:1 2nd:0 3rd:0 Ran:6
Pre1998 - 1st:2 2nd:0 3rd:1 Ran:6

Win Prizemoney £8,362 *Total Prizemoney* £8,812

Wins * 1998 Aug Leices (GD) C 7f 61
* 1997 *Oct Southw (STD) H 6f 76 74* <
* 1997 Aug Chepst (G-F) 5.1f 74 <

1998 Turf 1-5: (6f, 7f 1-4) (gd, frm 1-4) 1998 AW 0-1: (6f) (Fibr)

Workmanlike, above-average filly, effective 5 to 7f, acted on frm - acted on Fibr, had worn blinkers. Turf high 71. (DEAD)

**B Palling [3-12] Mrs R M Williams.*

SANTANDRE BHB 75f **RR 75f** 4991[7]

2 ch c Democratic (USA) - Smartie Lee (Dominion) 8.5f **(63)**

Form - 44414682367

Record 1998 - 1st:1 2nd:1 3rd:1 Ran:11

Win Prizemoney £3,647 *Total Prizemoney* £5,995

Wins * 1998 Jly Thirsk (GD) H 5f 75+ <

1998 Turf 1-10: (5f 1-2, 6f 6, 7f 2) (sft, g-s, gd 2, g-f 1-3, frm 3) 1998 AW 0-1: (6f) (Fibr)

Above-average colt, effective 5 to 7f, acts on g-s to frm. Turf high 75 - 2nd of 13 giving 9lb to Clunie (25 Spt Haydock 6f frm RF 4479) - also 1st of 8 giving 2lb to Luanshya (31 Jly Thirsk RF 3249). Consistent. **R Hollinshead [1-11] Geoff Lloyd.*

SANTARENE (IRE) BHB 41f52a **RR 43f 52a** 4890^{7}
3 b f Scenic 10.6f **(66)** - Rising Spirits (Cure The Blues (USA)) 9.5f **(63)**
Form - 5780247
Record 1998 - 1st:0 2nd:1 3rd:0 Ran:7
Pre1998 - 1st:0 2nd:0 3rd:0 Ran:2
Win Prizemoney £0 *Total Prizemoney* £636
1998 Turf 0-6:(8f 2, 10f 3, 11f)(g-f 3, frm 2, hrd)1998 AW 0-1:(11f) (Fibr)
Leggy, moderate filly. Turf high 43. **P Howling [0-9] R N Khan.*

SANTILLANA (USA) BHB 110f **RR 112f** $2293a^{2}$
5 ch h El Gran Senor (USA) 8.9f **(85)** - Galway (FR) (Irish River (FR)) 8.6f **(78)**
Form - 44712
Record 1998 - 1st:1 2nd:1 3rd:0 Ran:4
Pre1998 - 1st:4 2nd:0 3rd:1 Ran:6
Win Prizemoney £64,401 *Total Prizemoney* £152,510
Wins * **1998** May Newbur (GD) 10f 105
* 1997 Oct Newmar (G-S) 10f 103
* 1996 Apr Sandow (GD) G3 10f 112 <
* 1996 Apr Ripon (GD) 9f 95+
* 1995 Nov Mussel (SFT) 8.1f 82+
1998 Turf 1-4: (9f, 10f 1-2, 12f) (sft, gd, g-f 1-2)
Group-class colt, effective 10 to 12f, best at 10f, acts on gd to g-f, best on g-f. Turf high 112 - 2nd of 10 to Ungaro (21 Jun San Siro 12f g-f RF 2293a) - also 1st of 7 getting 7lb from Taufan's Melody (27 May Newbury RF 1527). Consistent. He goes well when fresh and seemed to enjoy waiting tactics when winning at Newbury in May. Now proven over a mile and a half when runner-up in an Italian Group One, he could continue to do well on the continent.
**J H M Gosden [5-10].*

SANTISSIMA (IRE) RR 43f 4148^{7}
2 ch f Grand Lodge (USA) - Ship's Twine (IRE) **(48df)** (Slip Anchor) 9.8f **(73)**
Form - 07
Record 1998 - 1st:0 2nd:0 3rd:0 Ran:2
1998 Turf 0-2: (6f, 7f) (g-f 2)
Currently moderate filly, often wears blinkers. Turf high 43 (began Aug). **B J Meehan [0-2] M O'Leary.*

SANTONE (IRE) BHB 72f **RR 72f** 1323^{5}
3 b c Fairy King (USA) 7.7f **(75)** - Olivia Jane (IRE) (Ela-Mana-Mou) 10.1f **(70)**
Form - 855
Record 1998 - 1st:0 2nd:0 3rd:0 Ran:3
Pre1998 - 1st:0 2nd:0 3rd:0 Ran:3
Win Prizemoney £0 *Total Prizemoney* £225
1998 Turf 0-3: (8f 2, 10f) (gd, g-f 2)
Neat, above-average colt. Turf high 72.
**R Hannon [0-6] Stonethorn Stud Farms Ltd.*

SANTOVITO (IRE) RR 92f $5106a^{2}$
2 bb c Project Manager 7.2f **(47)** - Nordic Pageant (IRE) (Nordico (USA)) 6.5f **(62)**
Form - 8532
1998 Turf 0-4: (6f 2, 7f 2) (g-s, gd 3)
Useful colt. Turf high 92 (began Spt).
**J S Bolger in IRE [0-4] D H W Dobson.*

SAPERLIPOUPETTE (FR) RR 104f $4600a^{3}$
6 gr m Highest Honor (FR) 10.9f **(72)** - Emmanuelle (FR) (Margouillat (FR)) 10.2f **(76)**
Form - 13
1998 Turf 1-2: (10f, 11f 1-1) (hvy, gd 1-1)
Currently very useful mare. Turf high 104 (1st run) - 1st of 11 giving 13lb to Intuition (27 Jun Hamburg RF 2481a). She is a game old mare and battled on well to win a Group 3 at Hamburg in June.
**J BertranDeBalanda in FR [1-2] Mme F Teboul.*

SAPHIRE BHB 95f **RR 89f** 4364^{9}
2 ch f College Chapel - Emerald Eagle (Sandy Creek) 8.9f **(59)**
Form - 2871132550
Record 1998 - 1st:2 2nd:2 3rd:1 Ran:10
Win Prizemoney £8,667 *Total Prizemoney* £16,285
Wins * **1998** Jun York (G-S) 6f 73 <
* **1998** Jun Newcas (SFT) 5f 73 <
1998 Turf 2-10: (5f 1-8, 6f 1-2) (sft 2, g-s 1-2, gd 1-5, g-f)
Useful filly, effective 5f, acts on g-s. Turf high 89 - 2nd of 6 getting 5lb from Sarson (3 Jly Sandown 5f g-s RF 2504). Deservedly got off the mark at the fourth time of asking, and followed up at York, relishing the soft ground. Ran another good race when third in useful company at Ascot and was just collared in a listed race at Sandown. **C B B Booth [2-10] Mrs Marian Rogers.*

SAPPHIRE RING BHB 98f **RR 93f** 2271^{3}
3 b f Marju (IRE) 9.2f **(76)** - Mazarine Blue (Bellypha) 9.8f **(73)**
Form - 523
Record 1998 - 1st:0 2nd:1 3rd:1 Ran:3
Pre1998 - 1st:2 2nd:2 3rd:0 Ran:5
Win Prizemoney £8,682 *Total Prizemoney* £27,898
Wins * 1997 Jun York (G-S) 6f 93+ <
* 1997 May Leices (GD) 6f 77+
1998 Turf 0-3: (6f, 7f, 8f) (gd 2, frm)
Light-framed, useful filly, effective 6 to 8f, best at 7f, acts on gd to frm, excels at Leicester. Turf high 93 - 3rd of 7 getting 10lb from Hunters of Brora (25 Jun Newcastle 8f gd RF 2271). Paid her way in useful company at two, and was in the frame in conditions races last term, meeting trouble in running on her third start.
**R Charlton [2-8] The Thoroughbred Corporation.*

SAPPHIRE SON (IRE) BHB 34f29a **RR 33f 29a** 5002^{16}
6 ch g Maelstrom Lake 8.8f **(53)** - Gluhwein (Ballymoss) 8.5f **(55)**
Form - 780080
Record 1998 - 1st:0 2nd:0 3rd:0 Ran:6
Pre1998 - 1st:3 2nd:8 3rd:4 Ran:43
Win Prizemoney £8,604 *Total Prizemoney* £16,480
Wins * 1997 Aug Lingfi (G-F) H 11.5f 46 48
1994 Spt Bright (GD) C 7f 58
1994 Aug Lingfi (GD) S 6f 58
1998 Turf 0-5: (10f, 12f 4) (gd, g-f 2, frm, hrd) 1998 AW 0-1: (12f) (Equi)
Very moderate gelding, effective 11 to 12f, best at 12f, acts on frm, has worn blinkers. Turf high 33 (began Jly).
**P C Clarke [1-31] D Cobb (from D Morris [0-7] Aug 1996).*

SARAH STOKES (IRE) BHB 73f **RR 73f** 1611^{15}
3 b f Brief Truce (USA) 9.1f **(73)** - Almaaseh (IRE) (Dancing Brave (USA)) 8.4f **(76)**
Form - 10
Record 1998 - 1st:1 2nd:0 3rd:0 Ran:2
Pre1998 - 1st:0 2nd:2 3rd:0 Ran:4
Win Prizemoney £3,452 *Total Prizemoney* £6,306
Wins * **1998** Apr Pontef (G-S) 6f 66 <
1998 Turf 1-2: (6f 1-2) (g-s 1-1, g-f)
Light-framed, above-average filly, effective 5 to 6f, best at 5f, acts on g-s to frm. Turf high 66 (1st run) - 1st of 9 from Blueberry Parkes (21 Apr Pontefract RF 0791). This half-sister to the useful Almaty got off the mark in a Pontefract maiden in April.
**R Guest [1-6] Matthews Breeding and Racing.*

SARALEA (FR) RR 99f $1382a^{8}$
3 b f Sillery (USA) - Solidarite (USA) (Far North (CAN)) 9.7f **(75)**
Form - 238
1998 Turf 0-3: (8f, 10f, 12f) (sft, g-s, gd)
Very useful filly, effective 12f, acts on sft. Turf high 90 - 3rd of 6 to Zainta (26 Apr Cologne 12f sft RF 0949a). **D Smaga in FR [1-6].*

SARA MOON CLASSIC (IRE) BHB 51f57a **RR 49f 57a** 5003^{15}
3 b g Fayruz 6.6f **(63)** - Irish Affaire (IRE) (Fairy King (USA)) 7.7f **(59)**
Form - 3233660050000
Record 1998 - 1st:0 2nd:1 3rd:2 Ran:12
Pre1998 - 1st:0 2nd:0 3rd:1 Ran:6
Win Prizemoney £0 *Total Prizemoney* £2,860
1998 Turf 0-7: (6f 4, 8f 3) (sft, g-s, gd 3, g-f, frm) 1998 AW 0-5: (6f 2, 7f 3) (Equi 2, Fibr 3)
Unfurnished, average gelding, effective 6f, - acts on Fibr, often wears blinkers (effectively), likes left handed tracks, likes tight tracks. Turf high 73. AW high 69 (1st run) - 2nd of 7 to Polar Mist (28 Jan Wolverhampton 6f Fibr RF 0171).
**K McAuliffe [0-18] Highgrove Developments Ltd.*

SARASI BHB 57f30a **RR 55f 30a** 339^{6}
6 ch g Midyan (USA) 9.9f **(64)** - Early Call (Kind of Hush) 10.1f **(62)**
Form - 64056

Record 1998 - 1st:0 2nd:0 3rd:0 Ran:4
Pre1998 - 1st:5 2nd:3 3rd:2 Ran:25
Win Prizemoney £15,623 *Total Prizemoney* £20,892
Wins 1997 *Feb Southw (STD) C 8f 56*
1997 *Jan Southw (STD) S 11f 43*
1996 *Feb Southw (STD) H 8f 63 68*
1995 *Dec Wolver (STD) S 9.4f 68*
1995 *Jan Lingfi (STD) H 7f 63 71* <
1998 AW 0-4: (8f, 9f, 11f 2) (Fibr 4)
Fair gelding, effective 8f, - acts on Fibr, has worn blinkers. AW high 26. Becoming disappointing.
**Miss J A Camacho [0-4] Axom (from M J Camacho [4-18] Dec 1997).*

SARASOTA STORM BHB 41f **RR 46f** 2974[9]

6 b g Petoski 10.4f **(56)** - Challanging (Mill Reef (USA)) 10.5f **(78)**
Form - 50
Record 1998 - 1st:0 2nd:0 3rd:0 Ran:2
Pre1998 - 1st:4 2nd:0 3rd:1 Ran:23
Win Prizemoney £11,214 *Total Prizemoney* £12,958
Wins 1996 Spt Mussel (G-F) H 15.1f 50 58
1996 Jly Mussel (G-F) H 15.1f 48 53
1996 Jun Mussel (G-F) H 15.1f 46 50
1995 Mar Mussel (G-S) 11.1f 67 <
1998 Turf 0-2: (17f 2) (gd, frm)
Moderate gelding, has worn blinkers. Turf high 46. Consistent.
**R G Frost [0-7] Mrs G A Robarts (from M Bell [4-23] Spt 1997).*

SARATOGA RED (USA) BHB 47f63a **RR 47f 63a** 3677[1]

4 ch c Saratoga Six (USA) 8.7f **(74)** - Wajibird (USA) (Storm Bird (CAN)) 10.3f **(74)**
Form - 380506001
Record 1998 - 1st:1 2nd:0 3rd:0 Ran:7
Pre1998 - 1st:1 2nd:2 3rd:4 Ran:16
Win Prizemoney £6,295 *Total Prizemoney* £9,738
Wins * 1998 Aug Hamilt (SFT) SH 9.2f 44 44
1997 *Nov Lingfi (STD) 7f 65* <
1998 Turf 1-7: (6f, 7f 3, 8f 2, 9f 1-1) (g-s 1-1, gd, g-f, frm 3, hrd)
Workmanlike, average colt, effective 7 to 8f, best at 8f, acts on gd to g-f - acts on AW, often wears blinkers (effectively), likes tight tracks. Turf high 51. Previous experience of sand probably won him the day at Lingfield in November 1997, but he did not show much on turf until landing a seller on soft ground at Hamilton in August.
**M J Ryan [1-2] Mrs A M Byrne (from W A O'Gorman [1-21] Jly 1998).*

SARATOGA SAGA (USA) BHB 27f **RR 36f** 4938[12]

3 b g Lyphard (USA) 10.6f **(75)** - Rob Roy's Breeze (CAN) (Carteret)
Form - 00700
Record 1998 - 1st:0 2nd:0 3rd:0 Ran:5
1998 Turf 0-4: (8f 2, 10f, 16f) (gd 2, g-f, frm) 1998 AW 0-1: (11f) (Fibr)
Neat, very moderate gelding, has worn blinkers. Turf high 36.
**P S McEntee [0-4] Racing Thoroughbreds Plc (from M A Jarvis [0-4] Jly 1998).*

SARATOGA SPRINGS (CAN) **RR 119f** 2432a[6]

3 ch c El Gran Senor (USA) 8.9f **(85)** - Population (General Assembly (USA)) 10f **(68)**
Form - 1406
1998 Turf 1-4: (10f 1-1, 12f 3) (sft, gd 1-2, g-f)
High-class colt, effective 7 to 12f, acts on gd, has worn blinkers, excels at York. Turf high 119 (1st run) - 1st of 6 from City Honours (13 May York RF 1207). A top two-year-old, he made a fine start to 1998, coming fast and late to beat a good field in the Dante, but looked a bit short of toe when fourth in the Prix du Jockey Club. With his two stable-companions, he had a rushed journey over to Epsom on Derby day, and that, together with the race being only six days after his run in France, probably contributed to a moderate performance. He did not really do any better when sixth in the Irish version and that was the last that was seen of him. He will join Godolphin for 1999. **A P O'Brien in IRE [5-11] Michael Tabor.*

SARAYAN (IRE) **RR 106f** 4433a[4]

3 b c Lahib (USA) 8f **(69)** - Yaqatha 00
Form - 41722324
1998 Turf 1-8: (10f 1-1, 11f, 12f 4, 14f 2) (g-s 1-1, gd 5, g-f, hrd)
Pattern-class colt, effective 10 to 12f, acts on g-s to gd. Turf high 106 - 1st of 7 from Mardani (26 Jun Curragh RF 2415a). He is no world-beater, but tries hard and has a decent handicap in him.
**K Prendergast in IRE [1-10] Hamdan Al Maktoum.*

SARENARA (IRE) **RR 91f** 4207[4]

2 b f Darshaan 11.9f **(81)** - Saraposa (IRE) (Ahonoora) 8.1f **(73)**
Form - 14
1998 Turf 1-2: (8f 1-2) (gd 1-2)
Currently useful filly. Turf high 91 (began Aug) - 4th of 10 to Calando (10 Spt Doncaster 8f gd RF 4207). Looked a stayer when fourth to Calando in the May Hill at Doncaster.
**J Oxx in IRE [1-2] H H Aga Khan.*

SARI BHB 78f **RR 81f** 4812[1]

2 b f Faustus (USA) 9.1f **(54)** - Fire Lily **(48df)** (Unfuwain (USA))
Form - 304221
Record 1998 - 1st:1 2nd:2 3rd:1 Ran:6
Win Prizemoney £2,960 *Total Prizemoney* £5,574
Wins * 1998 Oct Catter (G-S) 7f 80 <
1998 Turf 1-6: (6f 4, 7f 1-2) (gd 1-1, g-f 2, frm 3)
Decent filly, effective 6 to 7f, best at 7f, acts on gd to frm. Turf high 81 (1st run) (began Jly) - 3rd of 20 to Alegria (13 Jly Windsor 6f frm RF 2766) - also 1st of 9 from Awwaliya (15 Oct Catterick RF 4812). **P F I Cole [1-6] R A Instone.*

SARIGOR (IRE) **RR 102+f** 3720a[1]

3 ch c Polar Falcon (USA) 9f **(74)** - Saraposa (IRE)(Ahonoora) 8.1f **(73)**
Form - 22101
1998 Turf 2-5: (5f 1-2, 6f 1-2, 7f) (sft, gd 1-2, g-f, hrd 1-1)
Very useful colt, often wears blinkers. Turf high 102 - 1st of 6 giving 5lb to Zilina (1 Jly Bellewstown RF 2597a). He put up an improved effort when winning a handicap at The Curragh in August. Still lightly raced, he should pay his way in 1999.
**J Oxx in IRE [2-5] H H Aga Khan.*

SARRAIA BHB 77f **RR 75f** 4538[8]

2 b f Formidable (USA) 7.8f **(60)** - Lili Cup (FR) (Fabulous Dancer (USA)) 9.4f **(70)**
Form - 71168
Record 1998 - 1st:2 2nd:0 3rd:0 Ran:5
Win Prizemoney £6,605 *Total Prizemoney* £6,605
Wins * 1998 Aug Yarmou (G-F) 7f 70 <
*** 1998** Jly Lingfi (G-F) 7f 69
1998 Turf 2-5: (6f, 7f 2-3, 8f) (frm 2-3, hrd 2)
Above-average filly. Turf high 75 - also 1st of 3 getting 1lb from Powergold (5 Aug Yarmouth RF 3397).
**J L Dunlop [2-5] Kuwait Racing Syndicate.*

SARSON BHB 100f **RR 95f** 3217[2]

2 b c Efisio 7.7f **(69)** - Sarcita (Primo Dominie) 6.2f **(80)**
Form - 22212
Record 1998 - 1st:1 2nd:4 3rd:0 Ran:5
Win Prizemoney £10,308 *Total Prizemoney* £28,898
Wins * 1998 Jly Sandow (G-S) L 5f 95 <
1998 Turf 1-5: (5f 1-4, 6f) (g-s 1-1, gd 3, frm)
Very useful colt. Turf high 95 - 2nd of 4 to Muqtarib (30 Jly Goodwood 6f gd RF 3217) - also 1st of 6 giving 5lb to Saphire (3 Jly Sandown RF 2504). Out of a mare who won the Portland and the Ayr Gold Cup, he found one too good for him on each of his first three starts, but it was no disgrace going down to Flanders in the Windsor Castle. Needed every yard of the five when getting up to win a Sandown listed race in July, and proved suited by the step up to six when second of four in the Richmond Stakes. Should win more races at three. **R Hannon [1-5] Raymond Tooth.*

SARTEANO BHB 32f **RR 13f** 3082[14]

4 ch f Anshan 8.2f **(63)** - Daisy Girl (Main Reef) 9.6f **(57)**
Form - 000
Record 1998 - 1st:0 2nd:0 3rd:0 Ran:3
Pre1998 - 1st:0 2nd:0 3rd:1 Ran:2
Win Prizemoney £0 *Total Prizemoney* £524
1998 Turf 0-3: (8f, 10f 2) (g-f, frm 2)
Leggy, poor filly. (began Jly).
**T W Donnelly [0-3] S Taberner (from J Mackie [0-2] Aug 1996).*

SARTORIAL (IRE) **RR 82f** 5063[4]

2 b c Elbio 9f **(62)** - Madam Slaney (Prince Tenderfoot (USA)) 9f **(61)**
Form - 4
Record 1998 - 1st:0 2nd:0 3rd:0 Ran:1

Win Prizemoney £0 *Total Prizemoney* £237
1998 Turf 0-1: (6f) (g-f)
Currently decent colt. **P J Makin [0-1] Mrs Greta Sarfaty Marchant.*

SARUM BHB 23f25a **RR 14f 25a** 4609[11]
12 b g Tina's Pet 7.4f **(56)** - Contessa (HUN) (Peleid) 7.6f **(37)**
Form - 6027000070000
Record 1998 - 1st:0 2nd:1 3rd:0 Ran:13
Pre1998 - 1st:8 2nd:9 3rd:13 Ran:96
Win Prizemoney £19,785 *Total Prizemoney* £34,778
Wins 1996 *Mar Lingfi (STD) H 8f 50 49*
1994 *Feb Lingfi (STD) H 7f 56 55*
1994 *Jan Lingfi (STD) H 8f 50 49*
1998 Turf 0-5: (7f, 8f, 9f, 10f, 12f) (gd, g-f, frm 3) 1998 AW 0-8: (7f 2, 8f 3, 10f, 12f, 13f) (Equi 5, Fibr 3)
Very moderate gelding, effective 8f, - acts on Equi. Turf high 14. AW high 35. Once a useful performer on sand at Lingfield, his best days are well and truly behind him.
**J E Long [0-30] Terry Waters (from C P Wildman [8-79] May 1996).*

SASEEDO (USA) BHB 54f57a **RR 47f 57a** 3571[10]
8 ch g Afleet (CAN) 6.2f **(83)** - Barbara's Moment (USA) (Super Moment (USA)) 6.2f **(92)**
Form - 86566400
Record 1998 - 1st:0 2nd:0 3rd:0 Ran:8
Pre1998 - 1st:7 2nd:2 3rd:6 Ran:52
Win Prizemoney £58,949 *Total Prizemoney* £69,356
Wins 1996 Jly Haydoc (GD) H 7.1f 86 90
1996 Jly Pontef (G-F) H 6f 86 90
1996 May Newmar (GD) H 7f 86 91 <
1995 Oct Yarmou (FRM) 6f 75
1995 May Newmar (GD) H 6f 84 88
1998 Turf 0-4: (8f, 10f, 11f, 12f) (g-s, g-f 2, frm) 1998 AW 0-4: (8f 2, 11f, 12f) (Equi, Fibr 3)
Average gelding, has worn blinkers. Turf high 47. AW high 65. Inconsistent. Once a useful sprinter for Bill O'Gorman, his best days are behind him, and he is being tried over all sorts of distances nowadays.
**L A Dace [0-2] Mike D'Arcy Quinn (from Mrs A E Johnson [0-2] Jun 1998).*

SASSY (IRE) BHB 39f44a **RR 51f 44a** 4996[14]
3 b f Imp Society (USA) 7.1f **(63)** - Merrie Moment (IRE) (Taufan (USA)) 7f **(57)**
Form - 44875035253100
Record 1998 - 1st:1 2nd:1 3rd:2 Ran:14
Pre1998 - 1st:1 2nd:1 3rd:0 Ran:9
Win Prizemoney £4,370 *Total Prizemoney* £6,683
Wins 1998 *Spt Southw (STD) C 11f 45*
1997 Jly Windso (G-F) S 6f 65 <
1998 Turf 0-6: (8f 2, 10f 3, 11f) (g-s, gd, g-f 4) 1998 AW 1-8: (8f 2, 9f, 10f 2, 11f 1-1, 12f 2) (Equi 2, Fibr 1-6)
Workmanlike, fair filly, effective 6 to 7f, best at 6f, acts on g-f to frm, best on frm. Turf high 51. AW high 54. Appreciated the drop in class when the landing a Windsor seller in workmanlike style in July '97. Her form tailed off rather after that, though she has shown a little ability on sand, winning a Southwell claimer, and changing stables afterwards.
**B J McMath [0-2] Robert Clark (from A P Jarvis [2-21] Spt 1998).*

SASSY LADY (IRE) RR 20f 1539[12]
3 b f Brief Truce (USA) 9.1f **(73)**-Taken By Force(Persian Bold)9.3f **(66)**
Form - 0700
Record 1998 - 1st:0 2nd:0 3rd:0 Ran:4
Pre1998 - 1st:0 2nd:0 3rd:0 Ran:3
Win Prizemoney £0 *Total Prizemoney* £232
1998 Turf 0-4: (6f, 7f 2, 8f) (sft, g-s, frm 2)
Unfurnished, little account filly, has worn blinkers. Turf high 20.
**C A Dwyer [0-7] G Middlemiss.*

SASURU BHB 110f **RR 109f** 4852[10]
5 b h Most Welcome 8.6f **(66)** - Sassalya (Sassafras (FR)) 9.6f **(69)**
Form - 5330
Record 1998 - 1st:0 2nd:0 3rd:2 Ran:4
Pre1998 - 1st:5 2nd:3 3rd:1 Ran:11
Win Prizemoney £127,769 *Total Prizemoney* £145,504
Wins * 1997 May Longch (SFT) G1 9.3f 118
* 1997 Apr Sandow (G-S) G3 10f 119+ <
* 1996 Aug Deauvi (GD) G2 10f 109
* 1996 Jun York (GD) H 10.4f 100 104+
* 1996 May Newcas (GD) 10.1f 94
1998 Turf 0-4: (10f 3, 12f) (g-s, gd 3)
Pattern-class colt, effective 9 to 10f, acts on sft to gd, has worn blinkers, prefers right handed tracks. Turf high 109 (began Aug). Consistent. Any horse who cracks his pelvis twice can be counted as unlucky, and fortune has certainly not favoured this fellow. Connections have done well to get him back on the racecourse, and, apart from running quite well at Ascot in September when third to Capri, he was a shadow of his former self in 1998.
**G Wragg [5-15] A E Oppenheimer.*

SATIN CAR (FR) RR 107f 4728a[6]
3 Cardoun (FR) - Miss Satin (Satingo) 8.9f **(69)**
Form - 6
1998 Turf 0-1: (8f) (sft)
Currently Pattern-class. He could not match strides with Fly To The Stars at Longchamp in October.
**R Collet in FR [0-1] Antoine Segura.*

SATIN SLIPPER (IRE) BHB 70f **RR 71f** 3688[7]
2 ch f Petardia 8.2f **(58)** - Lomond Heights (IRE) (Lomond (USA)) 8.8f **(65)**
Form - 881437
Record 1998 - 1st:1 2nd:0 3rd:1 Ran:6
Win Prizemoney £2,529 *Total Prizemoney* £3,238
Wins * **1998** Jly Bright (GD) 5.3f 71 <
1998 Turf 1-6: (5f 1-5, 6f) (gd 1-2, g-f 2, frm 2)
Above-average filly, effective 5f, acts on gd. Turf high 71 - 1st of 4 from Bayonet (13 Jly Brighton RF 2759).
**K T Ivory [1-6] Mrs G E Maloney.*

SATIS (IRE) BHB 43f52a **RR 41f 52a** 2370[12]
3 b f Last Tycoon 9.4f **(73)** - Nazwa (Tarboosh (USA)) 10f **(55)**
Form - 0600
Record 1998 - 1st:0 2nd:0 3rd:0 Ran:3
Pre1998 - 1st:0 2nd:2 3rd:0 Ran:8
Win Prizemoney £0 *Total Prizemoney* £1,571
1998 Turf 0-3: (5f 2, 6f) (gd, g-f 2)
Leggy, moderate filly, effective 5 to 6f, acts on gd - acts on Fibr. Turf high 41. Inconsistent.
**M R Channon [0-11] Barry Walters Catering.*

SATISFY RR 2900[14]
3 b g Alhijaz 7.7f **(57)** - Snake Song (Mansingh (USA)) 7.4f **(55)**
Form - 0
Record 1998 - 1st:0 2nd:0 3rd:0 Ran:1
1998 AW 0-1: (7f) (Fibr)
Strong, currently very poor gelding - 14th of 14 getting 7lb from Kosevo (17 Jly Southwell 7f Fibr RF 2900).
**R M H Cowell [0-1] Bylon Farmers.*

SATRIA (IRE) RR 26f 5137[17]
2 b c Shareef Dancer (USA) 10.1f **(67)** - Inderaputeri **(68f 60a)** (Bold Fort)
Form - 0
Record 1998 - 1st:0 2nd:0 3rd:0 Ran:1
1998 Turf 0-1: (7f) (gd)
Currently little account colt.
**Miss Gay Kelleway [0-1] H R H Sultan Ahmad Shah.*

SATWA BOULEVARD BHB 41f **RR 40f** 5006[10]
3 ch f Sabrehill (USA) 8.5f **(64)** - Winnie Reckless (Local Suitor (USA)) 8.4f **(67)**
Form - 80060
Record 1998 - 1st:0 2nd:0 3rd:0 Ran:5
1998 Turf 0-5: (7f 2, 8f 2, 10f) (sft, g-s, g-f 2, frm)
Unfurnished, fair filly. Turf high 49 (began Spt).
**M R Channon [0-5] A Merza.*

SAUCY DANCER RR 308[7]
5 ch m Chilibang 7f **(55)** - Silent Dancer (Quiet Fling (USA)) 11.8f **(36)**
Form - 637
Record 1998 - 1st:0 2nd:0 3rd:1 Ran:3
Win Prizemoney £0 *Total Prizemoney* £502
1998 AW 0-3: (12f 2, 15f) (Equi, Fibr 2)

Little account filly. AW high 29. **G A Ham [0-3] Miss S J Burgin.*

SAUDI BHB 58f **RR 53f** 1926[14]

3 b c Green Desert (USA) 7.8f **(78)** - Emaline (FR) (Empery (USA)) 11.2f **(69)**
Form - 0700
Record 1998 - 1st:0 2nd:0 3rd:0 Ran:4
Pre1998 - 1st:0 2nd:0 3rd:0 Ran:3
1998 Turf 0-4: (5f, 6f, 7f 2) (gd 2, g-f, frm)
Scopey, fair colt, often wears blinkers. Turf high 53.
**P F I Cole [0-7] H R H Prince Fahd Salman.*

SAUGERTIES (USA) RR 110f 4603a[6]

4 ch c Trempolino (USA) 11.9f **(77)** - Stalwart Moment (USA) (Stalwart (USA)) 9.9f **(78)**
Form - 70756
1998 Turf 0-5: (11f 2, 12f 3) (sft 3, gd 2)
Group-class colt, effective 12f, acts on sft to gd, favours right handed tracks. Turf high 110 - 5th of 7 to Ungaro (26 Jly Dusseldorf 12f gd RF 3227a). He won a Group race as a three-year-old, but struggled throughout 1998.
**P Schiergen in GER [0-5] Baron G Von Ullmann (from H Jentzsch in GER [1-3] Oct 1997).*

SAUSALITO BAY BHB 90f **RR 97f** 4380[7]

4 b c Salse (USA) 10.9f **(71)** - Cantico (Green Dancer (USA)) 10.3f **(74)**
Form - 44007057
Record 1998 - 1st:0 2nd:0 3rd:0 Ran:8
Pre1998 - 1st:3 2nd:1 3rd:1 Ran:10
Win Prizemoney £37,643 *Total Prizemoney* £47,052
Wins * 1997 Spt Doncas (G-F) H 14.6f 92 100 <
* 1997 Aug York (GD) H 13.9f 85 92
* 1996 Oct Chepst (SFT) 8.1f 82
1998 Turf 0-8: (12f, 13f 2, 14f 2, 15f, 16f 2) (sft 2, gd 2, g-f, frm 3)
Scopey, very useful colt, effective 13 to 16f, acts on sft to frm, has worn blinkers, excels at Longchamp and Doncaster. Turf high 102 (1st run) - 4th of 5 to Tajoun (26 Apr Longchamp 16f sft RF 0951a). Consistent. He went backwards in 1998, and is now extremely well handicapped. He will win races if connections can rekindle the fire. **I A Balding [3-18] J C Smith.*

SAVILE ROW BHB 76f **RR 77f** 2938[2]

3 b g Elmaamul (USA) 8.1f **(70)** - Ural Dancer (Corvaro (USA)) 9f **(53)**
Form - 232
Record 1998 - 1st:0 2nd:2 3rd:1 Ran:3
Win Prizemoney £0 *Total Prizemoney* £2,010
1998 Turf 0-3: (7f, 8f, 9f) (gd, g-f 2)
Scopey, currently above-average gelding. Turf high 77 - 2nd of 8 giving 5lb to Buzzy Bomb (18 Jly Ripon 9f g-f RF 2938).
**J R Arnold [0-3] Lady Whent.*

SAVMO ONE BHB 36f **RR 30f** 4657[7]

2 b f Distinctly North (USA) 7.4f **(63)** - Dear Heart (Blakeney) 10.5f **(64)**
Form - 007
Record 1998 - 1st:0 2nd:0 3rd:0 Ran:3
1998 Turf 0-3: (5f, 7f, 10f) (gd 2, hrd)
Currently very moderate filly. Turf high 30.
**C Smith [0-3] M F R S Racing Partnership.*

SAVOIR FAIRE (IRE) BHB 58f **RR 57f** 4673[10]

2 b f College Chapel - Arctic Splendour (USA) (Arctic Tern (USA)) 8.9f **(69)**
Form - 000
Record 1998 - 1st:0 2nd:0 3rd:0 Ran:3
1998 Turf 0-3: (6f 2, 7f) (gd, g-f 2)
Currently fair filly. Turf high 57 (began Jly).
**M A Buckley [0-3] Mrs D J Buckley.*

SAVOURY BHB 53f **RR 42f** 2762[8]

3 b f Salse (USA) 10.9f **(71)** - Metaphysique (FR) (Law Society (USA)) 9.9f **(70)**
Form - 7608
Record 1998 - 1st:0 2nd:0 3rd:0 Ran:4
Pre1998 - 1st:0 2nd:0 3rd:0 Ran:3
Win Prizemoney £0 *Total Prizemoney* £219
1998 Turf 0-4: (8f, 10f 3) (g-s, gd 2, frm)
Workmanlike, moderate filly, has worn blinkers. Turf high 60.
**J L Dunlop [0-7] A Burrell.*

SAXON VICTORY (USA) BHB 39f43a **RR 39f 43a** 3396[3]

3 b g Nicholas (USA) 6.1f **(63)** - Saxon Shore (USA) (Halo (USA)) 10.6f **(75)**
Form - 6502063
Record 1998 - 1st:0 2nd:1 3rd:1 Ran:7
Pre1998 - 1st:0 2nd:0 3rd:1 Ran:4
Win Prizemoney £0 *Total Prizemoney* £1,599
1998 Turf 0-5: (8f, 9f, 10f 2, 12f) (g-s, gd, g-f 2, frm) 1998 AW 0-2: (9f 2) (Fibr 2)
Leggy, moderate gelding, has worn blinkers. Turf high 39. AW high 41. **W J Haggas [0-11] Mrs L Wallis.*

SAXOPHONE (USA) RR 99f 4561a[6]

3 b f Quest for Fame 12.8f **(75)** - Miss Jazz (USA)
Form - 242416
1998 Turf 1-6: (10f 1-4, 11f, 12f) (sft 1-2, g-s, gd 3)
Very useful filly, effective 10f, acts on g-s, has worn blinkers. Turf high 99 - 4th of 7 getting 5lb from Sarayan (26 Jun Curragh 10f g-s RF 2415a). **J S Bolger in IRE [1-6] Mrs J S Bolger.*

SAYARSHAN (FR) RR 113f 1737a[8]

3 b c Darshaan 11.9f **(81)** - Sayyara (Kris) 9.5f **(73)**
Form - 18
1998 Turf 1-2: (11f 1-1, 12f) (sft 1-1, gd)
Currently Group-class colt. Turf high 113 (1st run) - 1st of 7 from Sestino (3 May Chantilly RF 1091a). He could never get to grips with his stable-mates Dream Well and Croco Rouge in the Prix du Jockey Club (French Derby), but is a useful colt in his own right.
**P Bary in FR [1-2].*

SAYTARRA (USA) RR 90+f 4340a[1]

2 b f Seeking the Gold (USA) 7.4f **(80)** - Snow Bride (USA) (Blushing Groom (FR)) 10.3f **(76)**
Form - 11
Record 1998 - 1st:2 2nd:0 3rd:0 Ran:2
Win Prizemoney £25,918 *Total Prizemoney* £25,918
Wins * **1998** Spt Chanti (SFT) G3 8f 90+ <
* **1998** Jly Sandow (G-F) 7.1f 74+
1998 Turf 2-2: (7f 1-1, 8f 1-1) (sft 1-1, frm 1-1)
Currently useful filly. Turf high 90 (began Jly) - 1st of 8 from Juvenia (9 Spt Chantilly RF 4340a). A half-sister to Lammtarra, out of a high-class racemare, she made all to beat subsequent Marcel Boussac winner Juvenia in a Group Three at Chantilly. Should take high rank at three. **D R Loder [2-2] Saeed Maktoum Al Maktoum.*

SCARLET BHB 54f50a **RR 65f 50a** 5094[18]

2 ch f Bluebird (USA) 7.9f **(71)** - Taza **(40f)** (Persian Bold) 9.3f **(66)**
Form - 6060
Record 1998 - 1st:0 2nd:0 3rd:0 Ran:4
1998 Turf 0-4: (6f, 7f 2, 8f) (g-s, gd 2, frm)
Average filly. Turf high 65 (began Aug).
**C W Thornton [0-4] Guy Reed.*

SCARLET CRESCENT BHB 53f57a **RR 56f 57a** 4759[9]

4 b f Midyan (USA) 9.9f **(64)** - Scarlet Veil (Tyrnavos) 10.1f **(55)**
Form - 60
Record 1998 - 1st:0 2nd:0 3rd:0 Ran:2
Pre1998 - 1st:2 2nd:0 3rd:4 Ran:13
Win Prizemoney £6,589 *Total Prizemoney* £8,907
Wins 1997 Jun Nottin (G-F) H 8.2f 70 70 <
1996 Aug Warwic (GD) 7f 67
1998 Turf 0-2: (8f, 10f) (gd 2)
Light-framed, fair filly, has broken blood-vessels, effective 8f, acts on g-f to frm, has worn blinkers, prefers left handed tracks, likes tight tracks. Turf high 56 (began Spt). Consistent.
**M D I Usher [0-5] Midweek Racing (from P T Walwyn [2-13] Oct 1997).*

SCARLET RAIDER (USA) RR 82f 4495[4]

2 b f Red Ransom (USA) 8.6f **(83)** - Dariela (USA) (Manila (USA)) 9.3f **(71)**
Form - 14
Record 1998 - 1st:1 2nd:0 3rd:0 Ran:2
Win Prizemoney £6,810 *Total Prizemoney* £7,795
Wins * **1998** Spt York (GD) 7f 78 <
1998 Turf 1-2: (7f 1-2) (gd, frm 1-1)

Currently decent filly. Turf high 82 (began Spt) - also 1st of 11 from Weaver of Words (2 Spt York RF 4058). Got up close home to win on her debut, looking as if she will be suited by a mile.
**P F I Cole [1-2] M Arbib.*

SCARLET SCEPTRE (USA) RR 59f 4956[6]

2 b f Red Ransom (USA) 8.6f **(83)** - Wand (IRE) (Reference Point) 6.8f **(70)**
Form - 6
Record 1998 - 1st:0 2nd:0 3rd:0 Ran:1
1998 Turf 0-1: (8f) (frm)
Currently above-average filly. **R Charlton [0-1] Mrs M Bryce-Smith.*

SCARLETT'S BOY RR 62a 4637[U]

2 b g Emarati (USA) 6.6f **(63)** - Katie Scarlett (Lochnager) 6f **(59)**
Form - 2U
Record 1998 - 1st:0 2nd:1 3rd:0 Ran:2
Win Prizemoney £0 *Total Prizemoney* £1,097
1998 AW 0-2: (6f, 7f) (Fibr 2)
Currently average gelding. AW high 62 (began Aug).
**N P Littmoden [0-2] John Pugh.*

SCARROTS BHB 64f56a RR 42f 56a 2954[6]

4 b c Mazilier (USA) 8.5f **(56)** - Bath (Runnett) 7f **(59)**
Form - 6
Record 1998 - 1st:0 2nd:0 3rd:0 Ran:1
Pre1998 - 1st:3 2nd:1 3rd:1 Ran:17
Win Prizemoney £8,693 *Total Prizemoney* £10,963

Wins								
1997	Jun	Carlis	(FRM)	H	12f	64	69	<
1997	May	Leices	(G-F)	H	11.8f	59	63	
1996	Spt	Beverl	(G-F)	SH	7.5f	59	64	

1998 Turf 0-1: (10f) (frm)
Moderate colt, effective 11 to 12f, best at 12f, acts on gd to frm, best on frm, has worn blinkers, likes right handed tracks. Inconsistent.
**S Gollings [0-2] R A Redmile (from S C Williams [3-17] Oct 1997).*

SCATHEBURY BHB 48f53a RR 54f 53a 5127[6]

5 b g Aragon 7.7f **(58)** - Lady Bequick (Sharpen Up) 8.3f **(67)**
Form - 334152044762860016
Record 1998 - 1st:2 2nd:2 3rd:2 Ran:18
Pre1998 - 1st:5 2nd:9 3rd:4 Ran:44
Win Prizemoney £19,870 *Total Prizemoney* £33,619

Wins								
* **1998**	Oct	Newcas	(SFT)	S	8f		54	
* **1998**	Apr	Catter	(GD)	S	7f		64+	
* 1997	Oct	Leices	(G-S)	SH	7f	47	54	
* 1997	May	Windso	(SFT)	C	8.3f		64	
* 1997	Apr	Mussel	(G-F)	SH	8f	55	60	
* 1996	Aug	Mussel	(G-F)	H	7.1f	55	58	
1995	*Jly*	*Wolver*	*(STD)*		*6f*		*71*	<

1998 Turf 2-14: (7f 1-6, 8f 1-8) (sft 1-3, g-s 3, gd 1-2, g-f 2, frm 3, hrd)
1998 AW 0-4: (7f 3, 8f) (Fibr 4)
Fair gelding, effective 6 to 8f, acts on sft to frm, best on gd, has worn blinkers. Turf high 64 (1st run) - 1st of 19 giving 18lb to Snappy Times (1 Apr Catterick RF 0531). AW high 58.
**K R Burke [6-50] Christopher Neal (from S P C Woods [1-14] May 1996).*

SCATTERGUN BHB 93f RR 93f 4742[7]

4 ch c Rainbow Quest (USA) 11.2f **(81)** - Cattermole (USA) (Roberto (USA)) 10f **(76)**
Form - 14037
Record 1998 - 1st:1 2nd:0 3rd:1 Ran:5
Pre1998 - 1st:0 2nd:1 3rd:0 Ran:1
Win Prizemoney £3,782 *Total Prizemoney* £7,904

Wins								
* **1998**	May	Thirsk	(GD)		12f		83	<

1998 Turf 1-5: (10f 2, 12f 1-3) (g-s, gd 1-3, g-f)
Scopey, useful colt, effective 10 to 12f, acts on gd to g-f. Turf high 93 - 3rd of 20 giving 9lb to Himself (12 Spt Doncaster 10f g-f RF 4241). Unraced at two, he made a promising debut at three but was then off the track for a year. Won a Thirsk maiden gamely on his reappearance, but has faced some very stiff tasks since and has been found wanting. **J H M Gosden [1-6] K Abdulla.*

SCENE (IRE) BHB 72f RR 77f 4936[2]

3 b f Scenic 10.6f **(66)** - Avebury Ring (Auction Ring (USA)) 8.6f **(65)**
Form - 70101308P3842
Record 1998 - 1st:2 2nd:1 3rd:2 Ran:13
Pre1998 - 1st:1 2nd:0 3rd:2 Ran:10
Win Prizemoney £11,994 *Total Prizemoney* £20,233

Wins								
* **1998**	Jly	Haydoc	(G-F)	H	8.1f	72	77	<
* **1998**	Jun	Thirsk	(SFT)	H	8f	68	76	
1997	Nov	Doncas	(G-S)	H	7f	63	70	

1998 Turf 2-13: (7f 2, 8f 2-7, 9f, 10f 2, 11f) (gd 1-7, g-f 1-3, frm 3)
Light-framed, above-average filly, effective 7 to 9f, best at 8f, acts on sft to g-f, best on gd, likes left handed tracks, likes tight tracks. Turf high 77 - 1st of 8 giving 6lb to Moving Princess (12 Jly Haydock RF 2741) - also 1st of 11 getting 11lb from Marie Loup (16 Jun Thirsk RF 2022). She made a successful debut for her new trainer in a soft-ground Thirsk handicap in June but was well beaten under a penalty, reportedly in season. Bounced back to score at Haydock, proving she handles fast ground, but held afterwards.
**J A Glover [2-11] Paul Dixon (from M Meade [1-12] Apr 1998).*

SCENIC BEAUTY (IRE) BHB 67f RR 66f 4148[4]

2 b f Scenic 10.6f **(66)** - East River (FR) (Arctic Tern (USA)) 8.9f **(69)**
Form - 534
Record 1998 - 1st:0 2nd:0 3rd:1 Ran:3
Win Prizemoney £0 *Total Prizemoney* £566
1998 Turf 0-3: (6f, 7f 2) (g-f, frm 2)
Currently average filly. Turf high 66 (began Aug).
**R Hannon [0-3] Major A M Everett.*

SCENIC LADY (IRE) RR 24f 4583[13]

2 b f Scenic 10.6f **(66)** - Tu Tu Maori (IRE)(Kings Lake (USA))10.8f **(67)**
Form - 00
Record 1998 - 1st:0 2nd:0 3rd:0 Ran:2
1998 Turf 0-2: (7f, 8f) (gd, g-f)
Currently little account filly. Turf high 24 (began Spt).
**J J Sheehan [0-2] Mrs Christina Dowling.*

SCENICRIS (IRE) BHB 46f28a RR 47f 28a 300[5]

5 b m Scenic 10.6f **(66)** - Princesse Smile (Balidar) 7.9f **(63)**
Form - 50685
Record 1998 - 1st:0 2nd:0 3rd:0 Ran:5
Pre1998 - 1st:1 2nd:6 3rd:9 Ran:45
Win Prizemoney £3,626 *Total Prizemoney* £14,517

Wins								
* 1996	Oct	Nottin	(SFT)	H	8.2f	60	65	<

1998 AW 0-5: (8f 4, 11f) (Fibr 5)
Moderate filly, effective 8f, acts on g-f. AW high 29. Becoming disappointing. **R Hollinshead [1-50] Mrs Christine Johnson.*

SCENT OF SUCCESS (USA) RR 80f 4381[13]

3 b f Quiet American (USA) 7.9f **(60)** - Mousquet (USA) (Shadeed (USA)) 8.2f **(70)**
Form - 000633110
Record 1998 - 1st:2 2nd:0 3rd:2 Ran:9
Pre1998 - 1st:1 2nd:1 3rd:1 Ran:4
Win Prizemoney £10,475 *Total Prizemoney* £13,672

Wins								
* **1998**	Aug	Windso	(G-F)	H	8.3f	70	80	
* **1998**	Aug	Beverl	(G-F)	H	7.5f	70	78	
* 1997	Spt	Beverl	(G-F)		7.5f		81	<

1998 Turf 2-9: (7f 1-4, 8f 1-4, 9f) (g-s, gd 2, g-f 2-6)
Tall, decent filly, effective 7 to 8f, best at 7f, acts on g-f to frm, best on frm, often wears blinkers, prefers tight tracks. Turf high 80 - 1st of 12 giving 14lb to Daintree (29 Aug Windsor RF 3975) - also 1st of 9 giving 7lb to Master Caster (24 Aug Beverley RF 3836).
**Sir Michael Stoute [3-13] Saeed Suhail.*

SCHARNHORST BHB 51f62a RR 18f 62a 3576[17]

6 b g Tacheron 6.8f **(79)** - Stardyn (Star Appeal) 9.6f **(65)**
Form - 00
Record 1998 - 1st:0 2nd:0 3rd:0 Ran:2
Pre1998 - 1st:5 2nd:1 3rd:1 Ran:30
Win Prizemoney £19,379 *Total Prizemoney* £21,334

Wins								
1996	May	Kempto	(G-S)	H	6f	73	79	<
1996	Apr	Folkes	(FRM)		6.9f		74	
1996	Mar	Leices	(SFT)	H	7f	66	70	
1995	May	Sandow	(GD)	H	7.1f	63	64	
1995	May	Salisb	(G-F)	H	7f	57	45	

1998 Turf 0-2: (5f, 6f) (gd, frm)
Moderate gelding, has worn blinkers. Turf high 18 (began Jly). Becoming disappointing.
**A R Dicken [0-6] M G Mackenzie (from S Dow [5-26] Spt 1996).*

SCHNITZEL (IRE) BHB 79f75a **RR 76f 75a** 4538[4]
2 b f Tirol 8.1f **(64)** - Good Reference (IRE) (Reference Point) 6.8f **(70)**
Form - 517214
Record 1998 - 1st:2 2nd:1 3rd:0 Ran:6
Win Prizemoney £6,042 *Total Prizemoney* £9,472
Wins * **1998** Spt Goodwo (G-S) H 7f 71 73 <
* **1998** *Jly Southw (STD)* *7f* *71*
1998 Turf 1-5: (7f 1-5)(gd 1-1, g-f 3, frm)1998 AW 1-1: (7f 1-1)(Fibr 1-1)
Above-average filly, effective 7f, acts on gd to g-f - acts on Fibr. Turf high 76 (began Jly) - also 1st of 11 getting 5lb from Polruan (11 Spt Goodwood RF 4230). (1st run) - 1st of 6 from Juanita (25 Jly Southwell RF 3127). **M Bell [2-6] Mrs G Rowland-Clark.*

SCHNOZZLE (IRE) BHB 48f **RR 51f** 2152[10]
7 b g Cyrano de Bergerac 7.3f **(58)** - Sun Gift (Guillaume Tell (USA)) 13.2f **(54)**
Form - 830
Record 1998 - 1st:0 2nd:0 3rd:1 Ran:3
Pre1998 - 1st:1 2nd:2 3rd:5 Ran:15
Win Prizemoney £3,039 *Total Prizemoney* £9,504
Wins * 1997 Jun Warwic (GD) H 12.5f 44 52 <
1998 Turf 0-3: (9f, 10f, 11f) (gd, frm 2)
Fair gelding, effective 13 to 15f, acts on gd to g-f. Turf high 51.
**K S Bridgwater [1-12] Willsford Racing Incorporated (from M J Fetherston-Godley [0-12] Oct 1994).*

SCINTILATING SOUND BHB 32f **RR 32f** 4990[9]
3 ch f Savahra Sound 7.8f **(55)** - Mia Scintilla (Blazing Saddles (AUS)) 6.7f **(46)**
Form - 038000
Record 1998 - 1st:0 2nd:0 3rd:1 Ran:6
Win Prizemoney £0 *Total Prizemoney* £500
1998 Turf 0-6: (5f 4, 8f 2) (sft, g-s, gd, g-f, frm 2)
Unfurnished, very moderate filly, has worn blinkers. Turf high 32 (began Jly). **S R Bowring [0-6] Mrs Zoe Grant.*

SCISSOR RIDGE BHB 53f70a **RR 56f 70a** 4962[7]
6 ch g Indian Ridge 7.6f **(74)** - Golden Scissors (Kalaglow) 9.8f **(67)**
Form - 32436434645721200807007
Record 1998 - 1st:1 2nd:2 3rd:2 Ran:20
Pre1998 - 1st:6 2nd:12 3rd:5 Ran:73
Win Prizemoney £23,004 *Total Prizemoney* £44,616
Wins * **1998** Jly Folkes (GD) H 6f 50 56
* 1996 *Dec Lingfi (STD) H 5f 60 65* <
* 1996 *Nov Lingfi (STD) H 6f 60 65* <
* 1996 Spt Goodwo (G-F) H 5f 58 60
* 1996 Jun Goodwo (G-F) H 6f 43 52
* 1995 *Dec Lingfi (STD) H 7f 46 47*
1994 *Jly Wolver (STD) S 7f 62+*
1998 Turf 1-13: (5f 2, 6f 1-9, 7f 2) (sft, g-s, gd 4, g-f 3, frm 1-4) 1998 AW 0-7: (6f 3, 7f 4) (Equi 7)
Above-average gelding, effective 5 to 7f, - acts on Equi, has worn blinkers, prefers left handed tracks, prefers tight tracks, excels at Lingfield. Turf high 56. AW high 70. Ran well in July, breaking a long losing run at Folkestone and finding only Double Oscar too good in a big field at Goodwood, but has gone off the boil again since.
**J J Bridger [6-85] Donald Smith (from M R Channon [1-8] Aug 1994).*

SCOLD BHB 32f **RR 18f** 2361[10]
3 gr f Reprimand 8.2f **(63)** - Hopea (USA) (Drone) 10.3f **(74)**
Form - 000
Record 1998 - 1st:0 2nd:0 3rd:0 Ran:3
1998 Turf 0-3: (7f, 8f, 12f) (gd, g-f, frm)
Unfurnished, currently poor filly. Turf high 18.
**J S Wainwright [0-3] A M McArdle.*

SCOLDING BHB 45f **RR 50f** 4919[7]
3 b f Reprimand 8.2f **(63)** - Tinkerbird (Music Boy) 6.8f **(57)**
Form - 070410767
Record 1998 - 1st:1 2nd:0 3rd:0 Ran:9
Pre1998 - 1st:0 2nd:0 3rd:0 Ran:5
Win Prizemoney £2,910 *Total Prizemoney* £2,910
Wins * **1998** Aug Pontef (G-F) H 8f 44 48 <
1998 Turf 1-9: (6f, 8f 1-7, 10f) (g-s, gd 3, g-f 2, frm 1-3)
Lengthy, fair filly, effective 8f, acts on g-s to frm, prefers left handed tracks, likes tight tracks. Turf high 50 - also 1st of 19 getting 5lb from Starliner (5 Aug Pontefract RF 3392). She showed nothing in her first eight starts, but after a much more encouraging effort at Nottingham, got off the mark in a Pontefract handicap in August. She can probably get a bit better yet.
**G Woodward [1-9] Michael Worth (from K A Morgan [0-5] Aug 1997).*

SCONCED (USA) BHB 73f **RR 73f** 4763[4]
3 ch c Affirmed (USA) 10.3f **(75)** - Quaff (USA) (Raise A Cup (USA)) 7.6f **(74)**
Form - 314
Record 1998 - 1st:1 2nd:0 3rd:1 Ran:3
Pre1998 - 1st:0 2nd:0 3rd:0 Ran:3
Win Prizemoney £3,468 *Total Prizemoney* £4,806
Wins * **1998** Spt Hamilt (SFT) 9.2f 73 <
1998 Turf 1-3: (9f 1-1, 10f, 12f) (g-s 1-1, gd 2)
Well made, above-average colt, effective 9 to 10f, acts on g-s to gd. Turf high 73 (began Spt) - 1st of 8 from Murmoon (28 Spt Hamilton RF 4531). **G Wragg [1-6] Mrs H H Morriss.*

SCOOP (IRE) RR 76df 5094[6]
2 b f Scenic 10.6f **(66)** - Big Story (Cadeaux Genereux)
Form - 31304306
Record 1998 - 1st:1 2nd:0 3rd:3 Ran:8
Win Prizemoney £3,386 *Total Prizemoney* £5,053
Wins 1998 Jly Pontef (G-F) 6f 76 <
1998 Turf 1-8: (6f 1-2, 7f 2, 8f 4) (gd 2, g-f 2, frm 1-4)
Above-average filly, effective 6f, acts on frm, has worn blinkers. Turf high 76 - 1st of 16 getting 7lb from Robber Red (17 Jly Pontefract RF 2884).
**S E Kettlewell [0-2] J Tennant (from Mrs J R Ramsden [1-6] Spt 1998).*

SCORCHED AIR BHB 34f26a **RR 32f 26a** 2772[12]
8 b m Elegant Air 9.6f **(64)** - Misfire (Gunner B) 11.2f **(58)**
Form - 400040
Record 1998 - 1st:0 2nd:0 3rd:0 Ran:6
Pre1998 - 1st:2 2nd:3 3rd:6 Ran:21
Win Prizemoney £6,511 *Total Prizemoney* £13,679
1998 Turf 0-2: (14f, 16f) (gd, frm) 1998 AW 0-4: (11f, 14f 2, 16f) (Fibr 4)
Very moderate mare. Turf high 32. AW high 27. Inconsistent.
**Mrs S Lamyman [1-11] P Lamyman (from J G M O'Shea [0-5] Spt 1995).*

SCORNED (GER) BHB 111f **RR 116f** 4491[7]
3 b c Selkirk (USA) 7.9f **(76)** -Spurned (USA)(Robellino (USA)) 7.6f **(80)**
Form - 112234217
Record 1998 - 1st:3 2nd:3 3rd:1 Ran:9
Pre1998 - 1st:1 2nd:0 3rd:0 Ran:2
Win Prizemoney £45,041 *Total Prizemoney* £96,349
Wins * **1998** Spt Newbur (GD) L 11f 116 <
* **1998** Apr Kempto (HVY) 10f 106+
* **1998** Mar Doncas (GD) 8f 106+
* 1997 Nov Doncas (GD) 7f 88
1998 Turf 3-9: (8f 1-1, 10f 1-3, 11f 1-2, 12f 3) (hvy 1-1, g-s, gd 1-4, g-f 1-3)
Scopey, high-class colt, effective 8 to 12f, acts on hvy to g-f, excels at Doncaster. Turf high 116 - 1st of 7 getting 7lb from Taipan (17 Spt Newbury RF 4329). Consistent. Started off the new season in fine style with impressive victories at Doncaster and Kempton. He kept making the frame in Group and Listed company at home and abroad afterwards, but did not gain another victory until landing a valuable Listed event at Newbury in September. His disappointing final effort may have come too soon after that.
**I A Balding [4-11] George Strawbridge.*

SCORPION ORCHID (IRE) RR 70f 1121[7]
3 gr f Caerleon (USA) 10.9f **(79)** - Negligence (Roan Rocket) 7.8f **(57)**
Form - 7
Record 1998 - 1st:0 2nd:0 3rd:0 Ran:1
1998 Turf 0-1: (10f) (g-f)
Workmanlike, currently above-average filly. From a useful family, she was easy to back before a rather disappointing debut.
**H R A Cecil [0-1] Mrs John Magnier & M Tabor.*

SCORPIUS BHB 30f **RR 40df** 501[8]
8 b h Soviet Star (USA) 8.6f **(74)** - Sally Brown (Posse (USA)) 8.9f **(61)**
Form - 8
Record 1998 - 1st:0 2nd:0 3rd:0 Ran:1

Pre1998 - 1st:1 2nd:0 3rd:0 Ran:16
Win Prizemoney £3,465 *Total Prizemoney* £3,719
1998 Turf 0-1: (9f) (sft)
Moderate horse, has worn blinkers. Becoming disappointing.
**T T Clement [0-10] Mrs C Clement (from C N Williams [0-4] Spt 1995).*

Win Prizemoney £19,591 *Total Prizemoney* £25,629
Wins * 1996 Apr Folkes (G-F) H 9.7f 56 58
1998 Turf 0-2: (10f 2) (sft, g-f)
Fair gelding. Turf high 51. Consistent.
**P R Webber [6-28] William Kelly (from R Hannon [5-33] Jun 1995).*

Scorned laughed in the face of the opposition

SCOTCH TIME BHB 34f **RR 28f** 4374[11]
3 ch g Timeless Times (USA) 6.1f **(56)** - Scotch Imp (Imperial Fling (USA)) 7.1f **(58)**
Form - 0000000
Record 1998 - 1st:0 2nd:0 3rd:0 Ran:7
Pre1998 - 1st:0 2nd:0 3rd:0 Ran:4
1998 Turf 0-7: (6f 4, 7f 3) (gd 3, frm 4)
Strong, little account gelding, has worn blinkers. Turf high 41.
**R A Fahey [0-11] James Ritchie.*

SCOTLAND BAY BHB 56f62a **RR 60f 62a** 5127[11]
3 b f Then Again 7.4f **(52)** - Down the Valley (Kampala) 8.5f **(56)**
Form - 441423346010
Record 1998 - 1st:2 2nd:1 3rd:2 Ran:10
Pre1998 - 1st:0 2nd:0 3rd:0 Ran:3
Win Prizemoney £4,260 *Total Prizemoney* £5,818
Wins 1998 Oct Folkes (G-S) S 7f 60 <
1998 *Jan Lingfi (STD) H 7f 54 59*
1998 Turf 1-7: (6f, 7f 1-6) (sft, g-s 1-2, gd 3, frm) 1998 AW 1-3: (6f, 7f 1-2) (Equi 1-3)
Workmanlike, average filly, effective 7f, acts on g-s - acts on Equi, likes left handed tracks. Turf high 60 - 1st of 16 from Hoh Navigator (20 Oct Folkestone RF 4885). AW high 66 - 2nd of 9 getting 18lb from Philistar (21 Feb Lingfield 7f Equi RF 0334) - also 1st of 7 giving 3lb to Hevergolf Princess (10 Jan Lingfield RF 0062).
**P Butler [0-1] Christopher Wilson (from R Hannon [2-12] Oct 1998).*

SCOTTISH BAMBI BHB 54f **RR 56f** 1471[4]
10 ch g Scottish Reel 8.6f **(58)** - Bambolona (Bustino) 10.4f **(64)**
Form - 54
Record 1998 - 1st:0 2nd:0 3rd:0 Ran:2
Pre1998 - 1st:6 2nd:5 3rd:2 Ran:38

SCOTTISH HERO BHB 38f **RR 24f** 1449[14]
5 b g North Briton 8.2f **(53)** - Tartan Pimpernel (Blakeney) 10.5f **(64)**
Form - 00
Record 1998 - 1st:0 2nd:0 3rd:0 Ran:2
Pre1998 - 1st:0 2nd:0 3rd:0 Ran:7
Win Prizemoney £0 *Total Prizemoney* £232
1998 Turf 0-2: (8f, 10f) (gd, g-f)
Little account gelding, has worn blinkers. Turf high 23. Becoming disappointing.
**Lady Herries [0-5] Mrs Linda McCalla (from J R Fanshawe [0-4] Aug 1996).*

SCRAGGYS DREAM (IRE) RR 40f 4930[10]
2 ch c Shalford (IRE) 7.8f **(63)** - Massive Powder (Caerleon (USA)) 8.6f **(71)**
Form - 0
Record 1998 - 1st:0 2nd:0 3rd:0 Ran:1
1998 Turf 0-1: (8f) (g-s)
Currently moderate colt. **P Mitchell [0-1] Mrs Sue O'Keeffe.*

SCROOGE (IRE) BHB 49f **RR 49f** 5041[9]
2 b c Tirol 8.1f **(64)** - Gay Appeal (Star Appeal) 9.6f **(65)**
Form - 000
Record 1998 - 1st:0 2nd:0 3rd:0 Ran:3
1998 Turf 0-3: (7f 3) (sft, gd 2)
Currently moderate colt. Turf high 49 (began Spt).
**M H Tompkins [0-3] Richard Flatt.*

SCURRILOUS BHB 58f **RR 25f** 594[5]
3 ch f Sharpo 7.5f **(68)** - Tea and Scandals (USA) (Key to the Kingdom (USA)) 8.3f **(65)**
Form - 25

Record 1998 - 1st:0 2nd:1 3rd:0 Ran:2
Pre1998 - 1st:0 2nd:0 3rd:0 Ran:2
Win Prizemoney £0 *Total Prizemoney* £1,075
1998 AW 0-2: (6f 2) (Fibr 2)
Light-framed, fair filly. AW high 54 (1st run) - 2nd of 14 getting 5lb from Erro Codigo (23 Feb Southwell 6f Fibr RF 0345).
**M Bell [0-4] The Hon Peter Stanley.*

SEA ALMOND (USA) RR 60f 1596[2]

3 b f Nureyev (USA) 8.4f **(84)** - Dear Dorothy (USA) (Riverman (USA)) 9.1f **(76)**
Form - 2
Record 1998 - 1st:0 2nd:1 3rd:0 Ran:1
Win Prizemoney £0 *Total Prizemoney* £1,080
1998 Turf 0-1: (10f) (g-f)
Leggy, currently average filly, always wears blinkers.
**H R A Cecil [0-1] M Tabor & Mrs John Magnier.*

SEA-BELLE (IRE) BHB 73f RR 79f 4276[10]

2 ch f Mukaddamah (USA) 7.6f **(74)** - Blue Bell Lady (Dunphy) 9.4f **(57)**
Form - 4340
Record 1998 - 1st:0 2nd:0 3rd:1 Ran:4
Win Prizemoney £0 *Total Prizemoney* £1,092
1998 Turf 0-4: (6f 2, 7f 2) (gd, g-f 2, frm)
Above-average filly. Turf high 79 (1st run) (began Jly) - 4th of 20 to Alegria (13 Jly Windsor 6f frm RF 2766).
**A P Jarvis [0-4] Christopher Shankland.*

SEA CRYSTAL RR 26f 5139[15]

2 ch f Arazi (USA) 9.2f **(74)** - Crystal Land (Kris) 9.5f **(73)**
Form - 0
Record 1998 - 1st:0 2nd:0 3rd:0 Ran:1
1998 Turf 0-1: (6f) (gd)
Currently little account filly. **M Johnston [0-1] Maktoum Al Maktoum.*

SEA DANZIG BHB 61f72a RR 65f 72a 4776[16]

5 ch g Roi Danzig (USA) 10.5f **(62)** - Tosara (Main Reef) 9.6f **(57)**
Form - 430411245016410532000
Record 1998 - 1st:4 2nd:2 3rd:1 Ran:18
Pre1998 - 1st:3 2nd:5 3rd:4 Ran:45
Win Prizemoney £21,450 *Total Prizemoney* £34,548

Wins								
* **1998**	Jly	Folkes	(G-F)		9.7f		63	
* **1998**	Jun	Goodwo	(G-F)	H	9f	52	61	
* **1998**	*Jan*	*Lingfi*	*(STD)*	*H*	*10f*	*68*	*73*	<
* **1998**	*Jan*	*Lingfi*	*(STD)*	*H*	*10f*	*68*	*73*	<
* 1997	*Nov*	*Lingfi*	*(STD)*	*H*	*10f*	*67*	*69*	
* 1997	*Jan*	*Lingfi*	*(STD)*	*H*	*7f*	*63*	*58*	
* 1996	Oct	Lingfi	(GD)	H	7f	62	66	

1998 Turf 2-12: (8f 3, 9f 1-3, 10f 1-5, 12f) (gd 4, g-f 2, frm 2-5, hrd)
1998 AW 2-6: (10f 2-5, 12f) (Equi 2-6)
Above-average gelding, effective 7 to 10f, best at 10f, acts on g-f to frm - acts on Equi, likes left handed tracks, likes Lingfield. Turf high 65 - 2nd of 17 giving 15lb to Master Millfield (3 Spt Salisbury 8f g-f RF 4065). AW high 73 - 1st of 8 getting 3lb from Classic Find (20 Jan Lingfield RF 0122) - also 1st of 5 from Quiet Arch (13 Jan Lingfield RF 0078). He has looked better on Equitrack than on turf in the past, but won twice on Turf in 1998, having previously won his share on sand during the winter. Suited by eight to ten furlongs, he is difficult to catch when able to dominate, but it is a different story if he is taken on.
**J J Bridger [7-52] P Cook (from P Howling [0-11] Jly 1996).*

SEA-DEER BHB 66f80a RR 69f 80a 5040[5]

9 ch g Hadeer 8.9f **(58)** - Hi-Tech Girl (Homeboy) 6.6f **(55)**
Form - 2006464337104300805
Record 1998 - 1st:1 2nd:0 3rd:3 Ran:17
Pre1998 - 1st:13 2nd:11 3rd:9 Ran:70
Win Prizemoney £58,535 *Total Prizemoney* £88,293

Wins								
* **1998**	Jly	Newmar	(G-F)	H	6f	69	73	
* 1997	Jun	Yarmou	(GD)		6f		87	
* 1996	*Aug*	*Wolver*	*(STD)*	*H*	*6f*	*74*	*77*	
* 1996	Jly	Newmar	(GD)		5f		96	<
* 1996	Jun	Yarmou	(FRM)	H	6f	73	71	
* 1996	Jun	Yarmou	(FRM)	H	6f	67	72	
1996	May	Catter	(GD)	C	5f		49	
1996	May	Newcas	(GD)	S	5f		60	
1994	Jly	Goodwo	(GF)	H	5f	79	78	
1994	Jly	Newmar	(G-F)	H	5f	73	75	
1994	Jun	Nottin	(G-F)	H	5.1f	65	65+	
1994	May	Windso	(SFT)		6f		64	

1998 Turf 1-17: (5f, 6f 1-13, 7f 3) (sft, g-s, gd 4, g-f 5, frm 1-5, hrd)
Above-average gelding, effective 5 to 6f, best at 6f, acts on gd to frm, likes Newmarket. Turf high 74.
**C A Dwyer [6-45] M M Foulger (from D W Chapman [2-12] May 1996).*

SEA FIG BHB 44f58a RR 50f 58a 3749[6]

3 gr f Robellino (USA) 9.5f **(68)** - Aimee Jane (USA) (Our Native (USA)) 11.2f **(63)**
Form - 628700270207886
Record 1998 - 1st:0 2nd:3 3rd:0 Ran:15
Pre1998 - 1st:0 2nd:0 3rd:0 Ran:1
Win Prizemoney £0 *Total Prizemoney* £2,663
1998 Turf 0-11: (5f, 6f 5, 7f 4, 8f) (g-s, gd 6, g-f 3, frm) 1998 AW 0-4: (6f 2, 8f 2) (Fibr 4)
Average filly, has broken blood-vessels, effective 6f, - acts on Fibr, has worn blinkers, likes left handed tracks, likes tight tracks. Turf high 50. AW high 67 - 2nd of 8 getting 5lb from Euro Venture (14 Jan Wolverhampton 6f Fibr RF 0085). Ran well at Carlisle in June when dropped back to six and fitted with blinkers for the first time.
**T D Barron [0-16] J Baggott.*

SEA FREEDOM BHB 68f RR 69f 5150[4]

7 b h Slip Anchor 12.7f **(75)** - Rostova (Blakeney) 10.5f **(64)**
Form - 4336318004
Record 1998 - 1st:1 2nd:0 3rd:3 Ran:10
Pre1998 - 1st:3 2nd:8 3rd:5 Ran:39
Win Prizemoney £39,525 *Total Prizemoney* £64,511

Wins								
* **1998**	Jun	Chepst	(G-S)	H	18f	67	71	<
* 1997	Jun	Ascot	(GD)	H	20f	65	71	<
* 1997	Apr	Nottin	(GD)	H	14.1f	63	71	<
* 1997	Apr	Hamilt	(G-S)	H	13f	58	66	

1998 Turf 1-10: (14f, 16f 5, 17f, 18f 1-2, 20f) (hvy, sft, gd 1-8)
Average horse, effective 12 to 20f, acts on sft to frm, best on gd, often wears blinkers (extremely effectively), likes tight tracks, and excels at Salisbury. Turf high 71 - 1st of 7 giving 14lb to Bridie's Pride (30 Jun Chepstow RF 2398). A good third in the Ascot Stakes, a race he had won in '97, he showed real grit and determination to score at Chepstow. Well beaten after, he stays particularly well, but is not an easy ride. **G B Balding [4-53] Miss B Swire.*

SEA GOD BHB 18f32a RR 31f 32a 3768[8]

7 ch g Rainbow Quest (USA) 11.2f **(81)** - Sea Pageant (Welsh Pageant) 10f **(65)**
Form - P6800008
Record 1998 - 1st:0 2nd:0 3rd:0 Ran:7
Pre1998 - 1st:1 2nd:3 3rd:2 Ran:28
Win Prizemoney £3,077 *Total Prizemoney* £6,122

Wins								
* 1996	*Feb*	*Southw*	*(STD)*	*H*	*11f*	*44*	*48*	<

1998 Turf 0-4: (12f 3, 14f) (sft, gd, frm, hrd) 1998 AW 0-3: (11f, 12f, 14f) (Fibr 3)
Very moderate gelding, effective 11 to 12f, best at 12f, - acts on Fibr, favours left handed tracks, favours tight tracks. Turf high 31. AW high 26.
**M C Chapman [1-50] McCann Ltd (from B W Hills [0-3] May 1994).*

SEALED BY FATE (IRE) BHB 50f51a RR 56f 51a 4304[12]

3 b g Mac's Imp (USA) 5.6f **(54)** - Fairy Don (Don) 7.7f **(64)**
Form - 04363000824360
Record 1998 - 1st:0 2nd:1 3rd:3 Ran:13
Pre1998 - 1st:0 2nd:0 3rd:0 Ran:7
Win Prizemoney £0 *Total Prizemoney* £1,832
1998 Turf 0-9: (5f 6, 6f 3) (g-s, gd 3, g-f 2, frm 2, hrd) 1998 AW 0-4: (6f 2, 7f 2) (Fibr 4)
Strong, fair gelding, effective 5f, acts on frm, often wears blinkers. Turf high 56 - 2nd of 14 giving 13lb to Distant King (23 Jun Beverley 5f frm RF 2196). AW high 53.
**J S Wainwright [0-20] B Selective Partnership.*

SEA MAGIC (IRE) RR 76f 3834[9]

3 b br f Distinctly North (USA) 7.4f **(63)** - Danger Ahead (Mill Reef (USA)) 10.5f **(78)**
Form - 00680
Record 1998 - 1st:0 2nd:0 3rd:0 Ran:5
Pre1998 - 1st:1 2nd:1 3rd:2 Ran:7
Win Prizemoney £3,473 *Total Prizemoney* £7,072

Wins								
* 1997	May	Haydoc	(G-S)		5f		76	<

1998 Turf 0-5: (7f 2, 8f 2, 10f) (sft, gd, g-f 3)
Lengthy, above-average filly, effective 5 to 7f, best at 7f, acts on gd to frm. Turf high 76. **B W Hills [1-12] Ray Richards.*

SEA MARK RR 83f
4846[2]

2 br c Warning 8.1f **(77)** - Mettlesome (Lomond (USA)) 8.8f **(65)**
Form - 02

Record	**1998 -**	1st:0	2nd:1	3rd:0	Ran:2

Win Prizemoney £0 *Total Prizemoney* £1,820
1998 Turf 0-2: (6f 2) (g-f 2)
Currently decent colt. Turf high 83 (began Spt) - 2nd of 19 to Al Naba (16 Oct Newmarket 6f g-f RF 4846). **B W Hills [0-2] K Abdulla.*

SEA MINSTREL BHB 55f RR 62f
4400[7]

2 b f Sea Raven (IRE) - Give Us a Treat (Cree Song)
Form - 5773407

Record	**1998 -**	1st:0	2nd:0	3rd:1	Ran:7

Win Prizemoney £0 *Total Prizemoney* £756
1998 Turf 0-7: (5f 3, 6f 3, 8f) (gd 2, g-f 2, frm 3)
Average filly. Turf high 62. **M E Sowersby [0-7] Paul Clifton.*

SEANCHAI (IRE) BHB 32f36a RR 36a
1945[14]

5 b g Treasure Kay 6.5f **(53)** - Blue Infanta (Chief Singer) 8.9f **(66)**
Form - 10000

Record	**1998 -**	1st:1	2nd:0	3rd:0	Ran:5
	Pre1998 -	1st:0	2nd:0	3rd:0	Ran:7

Win Prizemoney £1,388 *Total Prizemoney* £1,388
Wins * **1998** *Jan Wolver (STD) H 6f 22 42 <*
1998 AW 1-5: (6f 1-4, 7f) (Fibr 1-5)
Moderate gelding, effective 6f, - acts on Fibr, likes left handed tracks, likes tight tracks. AW high 42 (1st run) - 1st of 10 getting 31lb from Elite Hope (7 Jan Wolverhampton RF 0043). A very moderate performer these days, he was fortunate to be awarded an amateur riders' event in the Stewards' room at Wolverhampton in January. **P S Felgate [1-12] A E Blee.*

SEA PENNANT BHB 51a RR
164[7]

4 br f Adbass (USA) 12.2f **(45)** - Doubtfire (Jalmood (USA)) 10.1f **(52)**
Form - 02677

Record	**1998 -**	1st:0	2nd:0	3rd:0	Ran:2
	Pre1998 -	1st:0	2nd:1	3rd:0	Ran:3

Sea Wave stormed home at York

Win Prizemoney £0 *Total Prizemoney* £461
1998 AW 0-2: (11f 2) (Fibr 2)
Tall, moderate filly. AW high 43. **Mrs H L Walton [0-5] R Thompson.*

SEA PICTURE (IRE) RR 79+f 5072[2]

2 b f Royal Academy (USA) 7.8f **(77)** - Grecian Sea (FR) (Homeric) 9.8f **(67)**
Form - 2
Record 1998 - 1st:0 2nd:1 3rd:0 Ran:1
Win Prizemoney £0 *Total Prizemoney* £1,288
1998 Turf 0-1: (7f) (gd)
Currently above-average filly. (1st run) - 2nd of 16 to Eden (31 Oct Newmarket 7f gd RF 5072). **Sir Michael Stoute [0-1] Lord Weinstock.*

SEARCH PARTY RR 74f 3148[2]

3 b f Rainbow Quest (USA) 11.2f **(81)** - Quest (USA) (The Minstrel (CAN)) 10f **(72)**
Form - 822
Record 1998 - 1st:0 2nd:2 3rd:0 Ran:3
Win Prizemoney £0 *Total Prizemoney* £2,161
1998 Turf 0-3: (8f, 10f 2) (gd, frm, hrd)
Lengthy, currently above-average filly. Turf high 74 - 2nd of 8 to Rajaiyma (1 Jly Kempton 10f gd RF 2443).
**L M Cumani [0-3] Mohammed Bin Hendi.*

SEASON OF HOPE RR 46f 2977[9]

2 ch f Komaite (USA) 6.9f **(61)** - Honour and Glory (Hotfoot) 10.5f **(59)**
Form - 500
Record 1998 - 1st:0 2nd:0 3rd:0 Ran:3
1998 Turf 0-3: (6f, 7f 2) (g-f, frm, hrd)
Currently moderate filly. Turf high 42 (began Jly).
**D J S Cosgrove [0-3] Mrs Christine Willmott.*

SEA SPOUSE BHB 35f67a RR 39f 67a 4229[11]

7 ch g Jalmood (USA) 11.1f **(59)** - Bambolona (Bustino) 10.4f **(64)**
Form - 440214370561120300
Record 1998 - 1st:3 2nd:2 3rd:2 Ran:16
Pre1998 - 1st:6 2nd:3 3rd:6 Ran:46
Win Prizemoney £23,378 *Total Prizemoney* £32,267

Wins								
*	**1998**	*Jun Lingfi*	*(STD)*		*8f*		*74*	<
*	**1998**	*Jun Lingfi*	*(STD)*		*8f*		*63*	
*	**1998**	*Mar Southw*	*(STD)*	*H*	*8f*	*58*	*61*	
*	1997	*Jan Southw*	*(STD)*	*H*	*8f*	*61*	*66*	
*	1997	*Jan Southw*	*(STD)*	*H*	*8f*	*61*	*66*	
*	1996	*Jun Southw*	*(STD)*	*H*	*7f*	*57*	*64*	
*	1996	Mar Folkes	(G-S)	H	6.9f	41	45	
*	1996	*Feb Southw*	*(STD)*	*H*	*8f*	*48*	*59*	
*	1995	*Apr Southw*	*(STD)*	*S*	*12f*		*61*	

1998 Turf 0-5: (7f, 8f 2, 10f, 12f) (gd 2, g-f 3) 1998 AW 3-11: (8f 3-10, 9f) (Equi 2-3, Fibr 1-8)
Above-average gelding, effective 8f, - acts on AW, best on Fibr, likes left handed tracks, favours tight tracks, and excels at Lingfield. Turf high 39. AW high 74 - 1st of 8 giving 4lb to Bapsford (23 Jun Lingfield RF 2202). Inconsistent.
**M Blanshard [9-62] Seven Seas Racing.*

SEATTLE RIBBON (USA) BHB 64f RR 71f 4477[4]

3 ch f Seattle Dancer (USA) 10.1f **(74)** - Golden Rhyme (Dom Racine (FR)) 9.2f **(62)**
Form - 0353624
Record 1998 - 1st:0 2nd:1 3rd:2 Ran:7
Win Prizemoney £0 *Total Prizemoney* £1,830
1998 Turf 0-7: (7f, 8f, 9f, 10f 4) (gd 3, g-f 2, frm 2)
Workmanlike, above-average filly, effective 9f, acts on frm. Turf high 71. Sister to ill-fated Racing Post Trophy winner Seattle Rhyme. Fair placed form in maiden company.
**D R C Elsworth [0-7] J C Smith.*

SEA WAVE (IRE) BHB 120f RR 122f 4727a[9]

3 b c Sadler's Wells (USA) 11.3f **(87)** -Three Tails (Blakeney) 10.5f **(64)**
Form - 2111U0
Record 1998 - 1st:3 2nd:1 3rd:0 Ran:6
Pre1998 - 1st:0 2nd:0 3rd:0 Ran:1
Win Prizemoney £65,617 *Total Prizemoney* £67,746

Wins							
*	**1998**	Aug York	(G-F)	G2	11.9f	119+	<
*	**1998**	Jun Leices	(SFT)		11.8f	109+	
*	**1998**	May Lingfi	(GD)		10f	84	

1998 Turf 3-6: (10f 1-1, 12f 2-5) (hvy, sft, gd 1-2, g-f 2-2)
Workmanlike, very high-class colt, effective 12f, acts on sft to g-f. Turf high 122 - 9th of 14 to Sagamix (4 Oct Longchamp 12f sft RF 4727a) - also 1st of 6 from Rabah (18 Aug York RF 3697). Very much an improving sort, he won a couple of small events at Lingfield and Leicester in effortless style, and had no trouble tackling a steep rise in class when an impressive winner of the Great Voltigeur. Broke the track record on the fast ground at York and looked to have a fine chance in the St Leger, but was re-routed to the Prix Niel. Unfortunately connections learnt little about the colt's Arc prospects as he veered sharply left leaving the stalls and decanted Frankie Dettori. He ran reasonably well in the race itself and, with a winter in the sun to help him mature, can make up into a leading middle distance colt in 1999. However, like his half-brother Three Cheers he has shown signs of waywardness, and he needs to overcome this if he is to reach the top.
**S bin Suroor [3-7] Godolphin.*

SEA YA MAITE BHB 42f69a RR 46f 69a 4874[4]

4 b g Komaite (USA) 6.9f **(61)** - Marina Plata (Julio Mariner) 7.2f **(57)**
Form - 03010330004
Record 1998 - 1st:1 2nd:0 3rd:3 Ran:11
Pre1998 - 1st:2 2nd:1 3rd:3 Ran:14
Win Prizemoney £6,950 *Total Prizemoney* £11,078

Wins								
*	**1998**	*May Southw*	*(STD)*	*H*	*8f*	*63*	*67*	<
*	1997	*Oct Wolver*	*(STD)*	*H*	*8.5f*	*58*	*65*	
*	1997	*Jly Southw*	*(STD)*	*H*	*6f*	*52*	*56*	

1998 Turf 0-6: (6f, 7f, 9f, 10f 2, 12f) (gd 2, g-f 3, frm) 1998 AW 1-5: (7f, 8f 1-4) (Fibr 1-5)
Leggy, average gelding, effective 8f, - acts on Fibr, has worn blinkers, likes left handed tracks, likes tight tracks. Turf high 46. AW high 68 - 3rd of 16 giving 2lb to Goldfame (14 Aug Southwell 8f Fibr RF 3640) - also 1st of 16 giving 4lb to Kailey Goddess (18 May Southwell RF 1304). Inconsistent. **S R Bowring [3-25] S R Bowring.*

SECOND EMPIRE (IRE) RR 123f 5165a[6]

3 b c Fairy King (USA) 7.7f **(75)**-Welsh Love (Ela-Mana-Mou) 10.1f **(70)**
Form - 381336
1998 Turf 1-6: (8f 1-5, 12f) (sft, gd 2, g-f, frm, hrd 1-1)
Very high-class colt, effective 8f, acts on sft to hrd. Turf high 123 - 1st of 7 giving 3lb to Centre Stalls (15 Aug Curragh RF 3721a). Consistent. One of a string of Classic prospects in the care of Aidan O'Brien, he had physical problems at the start of 1998, and enjoyed a rather patchy season. A controversial third in the Irish Guineas, he then had a nightmare journey over for the Epsom Derby and did not show at all in the race itself. He came back to win a Group Two at the Curragh in August, but again rather disappointed when only third in the Moulin, and was never nearer when filling the same position in the QE II. Nevertheless, he took his chance in the Breeders' Cup Mile, and was certainly not disgraced in finishing sixth. There is stamina on his dam's side, and ten furlongs should not be beyond him next term.
**A P O'Brien in IRE [4-9] M Tabor.*

SECOND NATURE (IRE) BHB 75f RR 74f 4997[4]

2 b c Second Set (IRE) 9.2f **(67)** - Tittlemouse (Castle Keep) 8.3f **(57)**
Form - 054
Record 1998 - 1st:0 2nd:0 3rd:0 Ran:3
Win Prizemoney £0 *Total Prizemoney* £225
1998 Turf 0-3: (7f 3) (sft 2, g-f)
Currently above-average colt. Turf high 74 (began Spt) - 4th of 10 to Bound For Pleasure (26 Oct Lingfield 7f sft RF 4997).
**J L Dunlop [0-3] Hesmonds Stud.*

SECONDS AWAY BHB 32f22a RR 36f 22a 4535[11]

7 b g Hard Fought 8.9f **(51)** - Keep Mum (Mummy's Pet) 7.7f **(60)**
Form - 05133800
Record 1998 - 1st:1 2nd:0 3rd:2 Ran:8
Pre1998 - 1st:1 2nd:4 3rd:6 Ran:46
Win Prizemoney £4,964 *Total Prizemoney* £12,104

Wins								
*	**1998**	Jun Ayr	(GD)	SH	8f	31	36	<
*	1997	Jly Mussel	(G-F)	H	8f	30	35	

1998 Turf 1-8: (8f 1-6, 9f, 10f) (g-s, gd 1-4, frm 3)
Very moderate gelding, effective 5 to 10f, best at 9f, acts on gd to frm, best on gd, has worn blinkers, and does well at Hamilton and Ayr. Turf high 36 - 1st of 10 getting 27lb from Coscoroba (19 Jun Ayr RF 2111). Consistent. Has a very poor wins to runs ratio.

**J S Goldie [2-57] J S Goldie (from A Harrison [0-9] Apr 1995).*

SECOND SECRET RR 3850[12]
3 b f Second Set (IRE) 9.2f **(67)** - Miss Bali Beach (Nonoalco (USA)) 8.5f **(66)**
Form - 00
Record 1998 - 1st:0 2nd:0 3rd:0 Ran:2
1998 Turf 0-2: (8f, 10f) (g-s, frm)
Tall, currently very poor filly. **M Brittain [0-2] Mel Brittain.*

Win Prizemoney £4,213 *Total Prizemoney* £7,792
Wins * 1997 Apr Newmar (G-F) 5f 79 <
1998 Turf 0-8: (5f, 6f 3, 7f 3, 8f) (g-s, gd 3, frm 4)
Scopey, useful colt, effective 5 to 6f, acts on g-f to frm. Turf high 86 - 2nd of 15 getting 9lb from Misbah (7 Jly Newmarket 6f frm RF 2582). A half-brother to Kerrera and Rock City, both high-class performers, he ran his best race so far this year when runner-up at the July Meeting, having been dropped back to six furlongs.
**P F I Cole [1-9] David Simpson.*

Second Empire, a good miler, but his future could lie over 10 furlongs

SECOND SUN BHB 44f41a **RR 53f 41a** 4127[15]
3 ch g Clantime 6.6f **(57)** - Sun Follower (Relkino) 8.9f **(65)**
Form - 744080030
Record 1998 - 1st:0 2nd:0 3rd:1 Ran:9
Pre1998 - 1st:0 2nd:0 3rd:0 Ran:5
Win Prizemoney £0 *Total Prizemoney* £800
1998 Turf 0-6: (6f 6) (gd 2, g-f 2, frm 2) 1998 AW 0-3: (5f, 6f 2) (Equi 3)
Light-framed, fair gelding, has worn blinkers. Turf high 53. AW high 44. **J J Bridger [0-14] Mrs J M Stamp.*

SECOND TERM (IRE) BHB 36f **RR 40f** 4535[15]
3 b f Second Set (IRE) 9.2f **(67)** - Trinida (Jaazeiro (USA)) 9.2f **(54)**
Form - 0428800
Record 1998 - 1st:0 2nd:1 3rd:0 Ran:7
Pre1998 - 1st:0 2nd:0 3rd:0 Ran:3
Win Prizemoney £0 *Total Prizemoney* £1,285
1998 Turf 0-7: (8f 3, 10f 2, 12f, 13f) (g-s, gd 2, g-f 3, frm)
Leggy, moderate filly. Turf high 40. Inconsistent.
**W Storey [0-10] Black Type Racing.*

SECOND WIND BHB 76f **RR 86f** 4988[11]
3 ch c Kris 10f **(75)** - Rimosa's Pet (Petingo) 11f **(72)**
Form - 55278600
Record 1998 - 1st:0 2nd:1 3rd:0 Ran:8
Pre1998 - 1st:1 2nd:0 3rd:0 Ran:1

SECRECY BHB 50f53a **RR 55f 53a** 4092[18]
3 b c Polish Precedent (USA) 9f **(73)** - Blonde Prospect (USA) (Mr Prospector (USA)) 8.8f **(78)**
Form - 84820
Record 1998 - 1st:0 2nd:1 3rd:0 Ran:4
Pre1998 - 1st:0 2nd:0 3rd:0 Ran:3
Win Prizemoney £0 *Total Prizemoney* £654
1998 Turf 0-3: (12f 3) (gd, g-f, frm) 1998 AW 0-1: (16f) (Equi)
Well made, fair colt, effective 16f, - acts on Equi, has worn blinkers. Turf high 51. (1st run) - 2nd of 12 giving 16lb to Musalse (26 Aug Lingfield 16f Equi RF 3888).
**P F I Cole [0-7] H R H Prince Fahd Salman.*

SECRET ALWAYS (FR) RR 90f 184a[1]
5 b h Always Fair (USA) 14f **(61)** - Secret Feeling (FR) (Riverman (USA)) 9.1f **(76)**
Form - 1
1998 Turf 1-1: (7f 1-1) (sft 1-1)
Currently useful colt. (1st run) - 1st of 16 giving 3lb to Yosna (21 Jan Cagnes-Sur-Mer RF 0184a). **Mme A Rossio in FR [1-1] P Dreux.*

SECRET ARCHIVE BHB 104f **RR 105f** 4481[2]
3 b c Salse (USA) 10.9f **(71)** - Lycia (USA) (Lyphard (USA)) 9.9f **(72)**
Form - 1450122
Record 1998 - 1st:2 2nd:2 3rd:0 Ran:7

Pre1998 - 1st:1 2nd:0 3rd:1 Ran:2
Win Prizemoney £16,142 *Total Prizemoney* £21,468
Wins * **1998** Aug Newbur (G-F) H 11f 100 105 <
* **1998** May Salisb (FRM) 12f 104
* 1997 Aug Kempto (GD) 7f 79
1998 Turf 2-7: (11f 1-1, 12f 1-4, 14f 2) (gd 2, g-f 1-3, frm 1-2)
Scopey, Pattern-class colt, effective 11 to 14f, best at 14f, acts on gd to frm, does well at Haydock and Salisbury. Turf high 105 - 1st of 7 from The Editor (14 Aug Newbury RF 3634) - also 1st of 4 from Kahtan (14 May Salisbury RF 1214). Made all to win a small four-runner event on fast ground at Salisbury on his reappearance, seeming to get the twelve furlongs well enough, but has been found out in rather better company since. Very game winner at Newbury in August. He is not quite Group class and unless he improves, races might be hard to come by next season.
**R Hannon [3-9] Mohamed Suhail.*

SECRET BALLOT (IRE) BHB 72f RR 77df 3472[8]

4 b c Taufan (USA) 8.3f **(65)** - Ballet Society (FR) (Sadler's Wells (USA)) 10f **(76)**
Form - 080384272808
Record 1998 - 1st:0 2nd:2 3rd:1 Ran:12
Pre1998 - 1st:3 2nd:2 3rd:2 Ran:15
Win Prizemoney £9,636 *Total Prizemoney* £18,216
Wins * 1997 Oct Leices (SFT) H 11.8f 61 71 <
* 1997 Oct Nottin (SFT) H 10f 62 64
* 1997 Jly Nottin (SFT) 10f 62+
1998 Turf 0-12: (8f, 10f 7, 12f 4) (sft 3, g-s, gd 5, g-f 2, hrd)
Workmanlike, above-average colt, effective 8 to 12f, acts on sft to g-f, best on gd, likes left handed tracks, likes tight tracks, excels at Sandown, likes Nottingham. Turf high 78 - 3rd of 10 getting 3lb from Therhea (24 Apr Sandown 8f sft RF 0847). Becoming disappointing. Ran quite well in the first half of the year without managing to get his head in front.
**K Mahdi [3-24] Waleed Al-Mutawa (from R Hannon [0-3] Oct 1996).*

SECRET BOURNE (USA) BHB 50f RR 52f 4356[13]

3 b f Exbourne (USA) - Secret Angel (Halo (USA)) 10.6f **(75)**
Form - 00
Record 1998 - 1st:0 2nd:0 3rd:0 Ran:2
Pre1998 - 1st:0 2nd:0 3rd:0 Ran:1
1998 Turf 0-2: (7f, 8f) (gd, g-f)
Workmanlike, currently fair filly. Turf high 45.
**B W Hills [0-3] K Abdulla.*

SECRET DELL (IRE) BHB 61f RR 74f 5093[7]

2 b c Doyoun 10.7f **(69)** - Summer Silence (USA) (Stop The Music (USA)) 9.2f **(71)**
Form - 867
Record 1998 - 1st:0 2nd:0 3rd:0 Ran:3
1998 Turf 0-3: (7f 2, 8f) (g-s, gd 2)
Currently above-average colt. Turf high 74 (began Oct).
**E A L Dunlop [0-3] Ahmed Ali.*

SECRETERN (FR) RR 98f 830a[4]

3 c
Form - 4
1998 Turf 0-1: (11f) (hvy)
Currently very useful colt. (1st run) - 4th of 6 to Special Quest (13 Apr Longchamp 11f hvy RF 0830a). **E Lellouche in FR [0-1].*

SECRET HARMONY BHB 43f RR 48f 3846[15]

3 gr f Mystiko (USA) 7.7f **(59)** - Mimram Melody (Music Boy) 6.8f **(57)**
Form - 7860
Record 1998 - 1st:0 2nd:0 3rd:0 Ran:4
1998 Turf 0-2: (8f 2) (g-f, frm) 1998 AW 0-2: (8f 2) (Equi 2)
Light-framed, moderate filly. Turf high 48 (began Jly). AW high 13.
**V Soane [0-4] The Mystics-Four Seasons Racing.*

SECRET HAVEN BHB 50f RR 57f 2187[3]

2 b f Lugana Beach 7f **(63)** -Embroglio (USA)(Empery (USA)) 11.2f **(69)**
Form - 5453
Record 1998 - 1st:0 2nd:0 3rd:1 Ran:4
Win Prizemoney £0 *Total Prizemoney* £250
1998 Turf 0-4: (5f 3, 6f) (gd 3, g-f)
Fair filly. Turf high 57. **B J Meehan [0-4] David Powell.*

SECRET SAVER (USA) BHB 107f RR 103++f 2269[1]

3 ch c Green Dancer (USA) 11.9f **(77)** - Vachti (FR) (Crystal Palace (FR)) 12.5f **(76)**
Form - 0121
Record 1998 - 1st:2 2nd:1 3rd:0 Ran:4
Win Prizemoney £15,623 *Total Prizemoney* £16,686
Wins * **1998** Jun Newcas (GD) H 12.4f 94 103++ <
* **1998** May Hamilt (G-S) 11.1f 83+
1998 Turf 2-4: (8f, 10f, 11f 1-1, 12f 1-1) (sft, g-s 1-1, gd 1-1, frm)
Well made, very useful colt. Turf high 103 - 1st of 7 giving 8lb to Corniche (25 Jun Newcastle RF 2269). He was developing into a smart colt when going AWOL in the middle of the season. A mile and a half looks to be his trip and he may need to get his toe in. There is a big handicap waiting for this fellow.
**Sir Michael Stoute [2-4] Saeed Suhail.*

SECRET'S OUT BHB 90f RR 78f 4576[2]

2 b c Polish Precedent (USA) 9f **(73)** - Secret Obsession (USA) (Secretariat (USA)) 9f **(79)**
Form - 2222
Record 1998 - 1st:0 2nd:4 3rd:0 Ran:4
Win Prizemoney £0 *Total Prizemoney* £5,182
1998 Turf 0-4: (7f 2, 8f 2) (gd, g-f, frm 2)
Above-average colt. Turf high 77 (began Jly) - 2nd of 7 to Ebinzayd (30 Spt Newcastle 8f g-f RF 4576). Although runner-up on each of his four starts, his attitude is not in question.
**Sir Michael Stoute [0-4] Sir Evelyn De Rothschild.*

SECRET SPRING (FR) BHB 88f90a RR 89f 90a 4631[15]

6 b g Dowsing (USA) 7f **(61)** - Nordica (Northfields (USA)) 9f **(72)**
Form - 562251620
Record 1998 - 1st:1 2nd:3 3rd:0 Ran:8
Pre1998 - 1st:3 2nd:3 3rd:3 Ran:17
Win Prizemoney £16,796 *Total Prizemoney* £32,089
Wins * **1998** Jly Kempto (G-F) H 10f 82 87 <
* 1997 Oct Bright (G-F) 8f 81
* 1996 *Feb Lingfi (STD) H 8f 82 83*
* 1996 *Feb Lingfi (STD) 8f 81*
1998 Turf 1-8: (8f 2, 9f 2, 10f 1-4) (gd 4, g-f, frm 1-3)
Useful gelding, effective 8 to 10f, best at 10f, acts on gd to frm, best on frm, likes tight tracks. Turf high 89 - 2nd of 7 giving 8lb to Muhtafel (13 Aug Chepstow 10f frm RF 3610) - also 1st of 13 giving 23lb to Mutadarra (8 Jly Kempton RF 2631). Consistent.
**P R Hedger [6-28] M K George (from R Charlton [0-6] Oct 1995).*

SECRET STYLE RR 83?f 3972[4]

3 b c Shirley Heights 12.1f **(76)** - Rosie Potts (Shareef Dancer (USA)) 9.9f **(73)**
Form - 44
Record 1998 - 1st:0 2nd:0 3rd:0 Ran:2
Win Prizemoney £0 *Total Prizemoney* £856
1998 Turf 0-2: (12f 2) (g-f 2)
Scopey, currently decent colt. Turf high 83 (began Aug) - 4th of 4 getting 10lb from Ferny Hill (29 Aug Windsor 12f g-f RF 3972).
**E A L Dunlop [0-2] Jaber Abdullah.*

SECRET TANGO BHB 33f RR 34f 295[15]

3 ch f Interrex (CAN) 7.7f **(51)** - Seymour Ann (Krayyan) 8.5f **(49)**
Form - 0
Record 1998 - 1st:0 2nd:0 3rd:0 Ran:1
Pre1998 - 1st:0 2nd:0 3rd:0 Ran:4
1998 AW 0-1: (6f) (Fibr)
Leggy, very moderate filly. **A P Jones [0-5] A P Jones.*

SECRET TREASURE BHB 64f RR 60f 4761[11]

2 b f Dilum (USA) 7.1f **(56)** - Surprise Surprise (Robellino (USA)) 7.6f **(80)**
Form - 070
Record 1998 - 1st:0 2nd:0 3rd:0 Ran:3
1998 Turf 0-3: (6f 2, 7f) (gd 2, frm)
Currently average filly. Turf high 60 (began Aug).
**H Candy [0-3] Amanda Dixon and Partners.*

SEDRAH (USA) RR 76f 3926[6]

2 ch f Dixieland Band (USA) 10.1f **(80)** - Madame Secretary (USA) (Secretariat (USA)) 9f **(79)**
Form - 56

Record 1998 - 1st:0 2nd:0 3rd:0 Ran:2
1998 Turf 0-2: (7f 2) (frm 2)
Currently above-average filly. Turf high 76 (began Jly). A half-sister to French 1000 Guineas winner Ta Rib, she has shown ability in maidens but is not getting home as yet.
**E A L Dunlop [0-2] Hamdan Al Maktoum.*

SEDVICTA BHB 30f **RR 16f** 514[11]
6 b g Primitive Rising (USA) 8.1f **(48)** - Annes Gift (Ballymoss) 8.5f **(55)**
Form - 0
Record 1998 - 1st:0 2nd:0 3rd:0 Ran:1
Pre1998 - 1st:0 2nd:1 3rd:0 Ran:10
Win Prizemoney £0 *Total Prizemoney* £840
1998 Turf 0-1: (16f) (gd)
Poor gelding. (DEAD)
**Mrs M Reveley [3-22] The Mary Reveley Racing Club.*

SEEFINN RR 92f 4691a[7]
3 b f Night Shift (USA) 8.1f **(73)** - Adjusting (IRE) (Busted) 10.2f **(61)**
Form - 13647
1998 Turf 1-5: (8f, 9f 1-3, 10f) (g-s, gd 1-3, frm)
Useful filly, effective 8 to 10f, best at 9f, acts on g-s to frm. Turf high 92 (began Aug) - 7th of 9 to Darina (3 Oct Curragh 10f g-s RF 4691a) - also 1st of 12 getting 5lb from Shah Of Persia (2 Aug Cork RF 3360a). **D Hanley in IRE [1-7] McLoughlin Family Syndicate.*

SEEKING THE PEARL (USA) RR 118f 4217a[5]
4 b f Seeking the Gold (USA) 7.4f **(80)** - Page Proof (USA) (Seattle Slew (USA)) 9.4f **(76)**
Form - 15
1998 Turf 1-2: (7f 1-1, 8f) (sft, gd 1-1)
Currently high-class filly. Turf high 118 (1st run) (began Aug) - 1st of 12 getting 3lb from Jim And Tonic (9 Aug Deauville RF 3614a). She won the Prix Maurice de Gheest and made history in the process by becoming the first ever Japanese-trained horse to win a Group One race in Europe. She seemed to find the extra furlong and a half of the Moulin beyond her the following month.
**H Mori in JPN [1-2].*

SEFTON BLAKE BHB 47f42a **RR 54f 42a** 1407[13]
4 b g Roscoe Blake 7.4f **(51)** - Rainbow Lady (Jaazeiro (USA)) 9.2f **(54)**
Form - 570
Record 1998 - 1st:0 2nd:0 3rd:0 Ran:1
Pre1998 - 1st:0 2nd:0 3rd:0 Ran:8
1998 Turf 0-1: (12f) (frm)
Workmanlike, fair gelding, has worn blinkers. Becoming disappointing. **M G Meagher [0-14] Sefton Surfacing Co Ltd.*

SEGALA (IRE) BHB 56f58a **RR 61f 58a** 2147[5]
7 b g Petorius 8f **(66)** - Cerosia (Pitskelly) 8.5f **(53)**
Form - 5375245
Record 1998 - 1st:0 2nd:1 3rd:1 Ran:7
Pre1998 - 1st:3 2nd:1 3rd:1 Ran:14
Win Prizemoney £11,998 *Total Prizemoney* £16,975
Wins 1994 Oct Redcar (GD) H 8f 72 77
1994 Aug Hamilt (FRM) H 8.3f 69 71
1998 Turf 0-6: (8f 2, 9f, 11f, 12f 2) (sft, g-s 2, gd 2, g-f) 1998 AW 0-1: (8f) (Fibr)
Average gelding, effective 8 to 12f, acts on sft to g-s, has worn blinkers, prefers tight tracks. Turf high 64 (1st run) - 3rd of 11 to Filial (8 Apr Ripon 12f sft RF 0612).
**J J O'Neill [2-21] F S Williams & Geoff Salters (from Sir Mark Prescott [3-10] Spt 1995).*

SEGAVIEW (IRE) BHB 66f **RR 66?f** 4337[6]
2 b c Scenic 10.6f **(66)** - Little Sega (FR) (Bellypha) 9.8f **(73)**
Form - 0046
Record 1998 - 1st:0 2nd:0 3rd:0 Ran:4
1998 Turf 0-4: (7f 3, 8f) (gd, frm 3)
Average colt. Turf high 66. **Mrs P Sly [0-4] Thorney Racing Club.*

SEIGNORIAL (USA) BHB 98f **RR 101f** 4719a[6]
3 b c Kingmambo (USA) 10.9f **(85)** - Suavite (USA) (Alleged (USA)) 10f **(76)**
Form - 157186
Record 1998 - 1st:2 2nd:0 3rd:0 Ran:6
Win Prizemoney £38,970 *Total Prizemoney* £38,970
Wins * **1998** Jly Goodwo (GD) H 14f 95 99 <
* **1998** Apr Beverl (SFT) 12f 81
1998 Turf 2-6: (12f 1-3, 13f, 14f 1-1, 15f) (sft, g-s 1-1, gd 1-2, g-f 2)
Rangy, very useful colt, effective 14f, acts on gd. Turf high 101 - also 1st of 15 getting 22lb from Street General (28 Jly Goodwood RF 3163). He is not within a country mile of his half-brother Suave Dancer, but showed himself above average when winning a valuable handicap at Glorious Goodwood. Out of his depth in Group and Listed races afterwards, he will not be particularly easy to place. **P W Chapple-Hyam [2-6] John Gunther.*

SELBERRY BHB 75f64a **RR 81f 64a** 282[2]
4 b g Selkirk (USA) 7.9f **(76)** - Choke Cherry (Connaught) 7.7f **(63)**
Form - 062
Record 1998 - 1st:0 2nd:1 3rd:0 Ran:2
Pre1998 - 1st:1 2nd:2 3rd:0 Ran:7
Win Prizemoney £4,940 *Total Prizemoney* £7,894
Wins * 1997 *Jan Wolver (STD) H 8.5f 77 78 <*
1998 AW 0-2: (12f 2) (Equi, Fibr)
Rangy, decent gelding, effective 8 to 10f, acts on gd - acts on Fibr, has worn blinkers. AW high 62.
**P C Haslam [1-11] Middleham Park Racing VI.*

SELECT CHOICE (IRE) BHB 63f **RR 49f** 3129[P]
4 b g Waajib 8.9f **(67)** - Stella Ann (Ahonoora) 8.1f **(73)**
Form - 00P
Record 1998 - 1st:0 2nd:0 3rd:0 Ran:3
Pre1998 - 1st:0 2nd:2 3rd:2 Ran:11
Win Prizemoney £0 *Total Prizemoney* £3,386
1998 Turf 0-2: (6f, 8f) (gd, frm) 1998 AW 0-1: (12f) (Fibr)
Workmanlike, moderate gelding. Turf high 18. Becoming disappointing. (DEAD) **A P Jarvis [0-14] Mrs Ann Jarvis.*

SELECT STAR (IRE) BHB 27f50a **RR 21f 50a** 1764[8]
4 b g Arcane (USA) 11.6f **(66)** - Chevrefeuille (Ile de Bourbon (USA)) 10.1f **(67)**
Form - 508
Record 1998 - 1st:0 2nd:0 3rd:0 Ran:3
Pre1998 - 1st:0 2nd:2 3rd:3 Ran:16
Win Prizemoney £0 *Total Prizemoney* £3,738
1998 Turf 0-1: (12f) (frm) 1998 AW 0-2: (10f, 16f) (Equi, Fibr)
Strong, little account gelding, effective 10 to 12f, acts on gd to g-f, best on g-f, has worn blinkers, favours left handed tracks. AW high 6. Becoming disappointing. He runs as many bad races as good ones and has not always looked to have the right attitude.
**G M McCourt [0-6] R Argles (from A P Jarvis [0-16] Oct 1997).*

SELFISH BHB 85f **RR 91?f** 1107[1]
4 ch f Bluebird (USA) 7.9f **(71)** - Sariza (Posse (USA)) 8.9f **(61)**
Form - 1
Record 1998 - 1st:1 2nd:0 3rd:0 Ran:1
Pre1998 - 1st:0 2nd:2 3rd:2 Ran:5
Win Prizemoney £3,460 *Total Prizemoney* £7,001
Wins * **1998** May Lingfi (GD) 7f 67+ <
1998 Turf 1-1: (7f 1-1) (frm 1-1)
Scopey, useful filly, effective 8f, acts on gd. (1st run). She bolted up in a Lingfield maiden on her reappearance and may have a future as a handicapper. **H R A Cecil [1-6] L Marinopoulos.*

SELHURSTPARK FLYER (IRE) BHB 103f **RR 105f** 4367[15]
7 b g Northiam (USA) 6f **(69)** - Wisdom to Know (Bay Express) 7.1f **(60)**
Form - 84611060
Record 1998 - 1st:2 2nd:0 3rd:0 Ran:8
Pre1998 - 1st:8 2nd:5 3rd:6 Ran:46
Win Prizemoney £173,835 *Total Prizemoney* £203,623
Wins * **1998** Jun Ascot (G-S) H 6f 92 105 <
* **1998** Jun Epsom (GD) H 6f 92 105 <
* 1997 Jun Ascot (G-S) H 6f 94 105 <
* 1996 Spt Epsom (G-F) 6f 94+
* 1996 Jun Epsom (GD) H 6f 79 86
* 1996 May Carlis (G-F) H 5.9f 70 75
1998 Turf 2-8: (6f 2-8) (sft 2, gd 1-4, g-f 1-1, frm)
Pattern-class gelding, effective 6f, acts on gd to g-f, best on gd, has worn blinkers, likes left handed tracks, likes tight tracks. Turf high 105 - 1st of 29 giving 8lb to Dancethenightaway (19 Jun Ascot RF 2107) - also 1st of 16 giving 20lb to White Emir (6 Jun Epsom RF 1781). He became the first horse in 65 years to win successive runnings of the Wokingham Handicap and is a grand old stick. He

will win again when the Handicapper relents.
**J Berry [10-54] Chris & Antonia Deuters.*

Win Prizemoney £13,918 *Total Prizemoney* £14,336
Wins * 1997 Spt Ayr (G-S) H 17.5f 47 49 <

Selhurstpark Flyer (noseband) does the Wokingham double

SELIANA RR 43f 5138[9]
2 b f Unfuwain (USA) 11.4f **(74)** - Anafi (Slip Anchor) 9.8f **(73)**
Form - 0
Record 1998 - 1st:0 2nd:0 3rd:0 Ran:1
1998 Turf 0-1: (7f) (gd)
Currently moderate filly. **G Wragg [0-1] L Marinopoulos.*

SELKIRK ROSE (IRE) BHB 63f **RR 72f** 4757[5]
3 b f Pips Pride 6.7f **(70)** - Red Note (Rusticaro (FR)) 8.2f **(65)**
Form - 474604005
Record 1998 - 1st:0 2nd:0 3rd:0 Ran:9
Pre1998 - 1st:1 2nd:1 3rd:0 Ran:6
Win Prizemoney £2,892 *Total Prizemoney* £5,335
Wins * 1997 Aug Carlis (G-F) 5f 75+ <
1998 Turf 0-9: (5f, 7f 6, 8f 2) (sft 2, gd 2, g-f 5)
Scopey, above-average filly, effective 5 to 8f, acts on g-f to frm, best on g-f, has worn blinkers, likes left handed tracks, likes tight tracks. Turf high 76 (1st run) - 4th of 5 getting 3lb from Khalas (28 May Ayr 8f g-f RF 1544). Inconsistent.
**Miss L A Perratt [1-15] Jim McLaren.*

SELLETTE (IRE) BHB 69f **RR 68f** 4995[6]
4 ch f Selkirk (USA) 7.9f **(76)** - Near the End (Shirley Heights) 10.3f **(74)**
Form - 007536
Record 1998 - 1st:0 2nd:0 3rd:1 Ran:6
Pre1998 - 1st:1 2nd:3 3rd:3 Ran:11
Win Prizemoney £3,642 *Total Prizemoney* £10,231
Wins * 1997 Jun Windso (SFT) 8.3f 73 <
1998 Turf 0-6: (8f 4, 10f, 11f) (sft, gd 3, g-f, frm)
Scopey, average filly, effective 8 to 11f, best at 11f, acts on gd to g-f, best on g-f, likes left handed tracks. Turf high 68 (began Aug).
**D HaydnJones [1-17] Mrs Judy Mihalop.*

SELMESTON (IRE) BHB 30f37a **RR 33f 37a** 4871[8]
6 b g Double Schwartz 7f **(60)** - Baracuda (FR) (Zeddaan) 9f **(76)**
Form - 70708
Record 1998 - 1st:0 2nd:0 3rd:0 Ran:4
Pre1998 - 1st:4 2nd:0 3rd:1 Ran:19
* 1997 Aug Beverl (G-S) SH 16.2f 40 48
* 1997 Jun Bath (GD) SH 17.2f 40 42
1996 *Mar Southw (STD) H 16f 35 46*
1998 Turf 0-4: (16f 2, 17f, 18f) (sft, gd 2, g-f)
Very moderate gelding, effective 16 to 17f, best at 17f, acts on gd, prefers tight tracks. Turf high 33. Inconsistent. Seems suited by having plenty of time between his races.
**S C Williams [3-11] Chris Wright (from P S Felgate [1-11] May 1996).*

SEMI CIRCLE BHB 52f **RR 61f** 4817[5]
3 b f Noble Patriarch 12.2f **(43)** - True Ring (High Top) 10.2f **(67)**
Form - 481211374645
Record 1998 - 1st:3 2nd:1 3rd:1 Ran:12
Pre1998 - 1st:1 2nd:0 3rd:0 Ran:5
Win Prizemoney £12,300 *Total Prizemoney* £14,450
Wins * **1998** Jly Ripon (GD) H 12.3f 52 61 <
* **1998** Jly Redcar (G-S) H 14.1f 52 56
* **1998** Jun Beverl (G-S) H 12f 49 54
* 1997 Jly Catter (G-F) S 7f 60
1998 Turf 3-12: (11f, 12f 2-7, 14f 1-2, 16f 2) (g-s, gd 3-5, g-f 3, frm 3)
Scopey, average filly, effective 7 to 14f, acts on g-s to frm, best on gd, often wears blinkers (extremely effectively), favours tight tracks, excels at Ripon and Redcar and Beverley. Turf high 61 - 1st of 6 getting 3lb from Pipe Music (6 Jly Ripon RF 2568) - also 1st of 6 getting 11lb from Royal Citizen (1 Jly Redcar RF 2452). Consistent. **T D Easterby [4-17] C H Stevens.*

SENA DESERT BHB 90f **RR 71f** 4514[6]
2 b f Green Desert (USA) 7.8f **(78)** - Sueboog (IRE)(Darshaan) 9.9f **(84)**
Form - 036
Record 1998 - 1st:0 2nd:0 3rd:1 Ran:3
Win Prizemoney £0 *Total Prizemoney* £565
1998 Turf 0-3: (7f, 8f 2) (gd, g-f, frm)
Currently above-average filly. Turf high 71 (began Aug). A daughter of a Fred Darling Stakes winner, she needed the run on her debut but kept on well for third next time.
**C E Brittain [0-3] Mohamed Obaida.*

SENOR HURST BHB 47f **RR 49f** 3329[13]
3 b g Young Senor (USA) 8f **(43)** - Broadhurst (Workboy) 7.3f **(46)**
Form - 28180
Record **1998** - 1st:1 2nd:1 3rd:0 Ran:5
Pre1998 - 1st:0 2nd:0 3rd:0 Ran:1
Win Prizemoney £2,700 *Total Prizemoney* £3,336
Wins *** 1998** Jly Yarmou (GD) C 8f 49 <
1998 Turf 1-5: (7f 2, 8f 1-1, 10f, 11f) (gd 2, frm 2, hrd 1-1)
Scopey, moderate gelding, effective 8 to 11f, acts on frm to hrd. Turf high 49 - 1st of 20 getting 6lb from Mr Rough (2 Jly Yarmouth RF 2477). **Mrs P Sly [1-6] Mrs P M Sly.*

SENSE OF HONOUR (USA) RR 91f 2037a[1]
4 ch f Be My Guest (USA) 10.2f **(66)** - Well Supported (USA) 00
Form - 5022551
1998 Turf 1-6: (8f 2, 9f 1-3, 10f) (hvy 2, sft 3, g-s 1-1)
Useful filly, effective 8 to 10f, best at 9f, acts on hvy to gd, mostly wears blinkers (extremely effectively). Turf high 91 - 1st of 7 from Renge (10 Jun Leopardstown RF 2037a).
**D K Weld in IRE [2-13] Mrs C L Weld.*

SENSE OF PRIORITY BHB 44f51a **RR 40f 51a** 346[7]
9 ch g Primo Dominie 7.2f **(67)**-Sense of Pride (Welsh Pageant)10f **(65)**
Form - 85577
Record **1998** - 1st:0 2nd:0 3rd:0 Ran:5
Pre1998 - 1st:20 2nd:9 3rd:10 Ran:81
Win Prizemoney £50,696 *Total Prizemoney* £61,836
Wins * 1997 *Feb Wolver (STD) C* *7f* *52*
* 1997 *Feb Southw (STD) S* *6f* *59*
* 1997 *Jan Southw (STD) C* *6f* *70*
* 1997 *Jan Southw (STD) S* *6f* *58*
* 1997 *Jan Southw (STD) S* *7f* *70*
* 1996 Jun Carlis (FRM) S 5.9f 66
* 1996 *Feb Southw (STD) S* *6f* *66*
* 1996 *Feb Southw (STD) C* *6f* *68*
* 1996 *Jan Wolver (STD) C* *6f* *65*
* 1995 *Jly Wolver (STD) C* *6f* *61*
* 1995 Jly Catter (G-F) S 6f 52
1998 AW 0-5: (5f, 6f 3, 7f) (Fibr 5)
Moderate gelding, effective 6 to 7f, - acts on Fibr, has worn blinkers, likes left handed tracks, likes tight tracks. AW high 46. Showed a tendency to hang left in some of his races in 1998. If that can be sorted out, then he is in the right yard to squeeze another victory or two out of him.
**D Nicholls [11-46] M A Scaife (from M H Easterby [9-40] May 1995).*

SENSORY BHB 104f **RR 106f** 4971[1]
3 b c Selkirk (USA) 7.9f **(76)** - Illusory (Kings Lake (USA)) 10.8f **(67)**
Form - 2536551
Record **1998** - 1st:1 2nd:1 3rd:1 Ran:7
Pre1998 - 1st:1 2nd:1 3rd:0 Ran:3
Win Prizemoney £13,186 *Total Prizemoney* £27,567
Wins *** 1998** Oct Doncas (HVY) 7f 106 <
* 1997 Spt Leices (G-F) 7f 87+
1998 Turf 1-7: (7f 1-2, 8f, 9f, 10f 3) (sft 1-1, gd 2, g-f 3, hrd)
Scopey, Pattern-class colt, effective 7 to 10f, best at 7f, acts on sft to g-f, best on gd. Turf high 106 - 1st of 7 giving 5lb to Dazilyn Lady (24 Oct Doncaster RF 4971). Consistent. He was ridden in all sorts of ways over a variety of trips before finally getting his act together on appalling ground at Doncaster in November. That timely return to form was enough to see him sold for 205,000 guineas at that Tattersalls Autumn Horses In Training Sales, and he will continue his career in Saudi Arabia.
**B W Hills [2-10] K Abdulla.*

SENTRY DUTY RR 45f 3406[11]
3 b g Nashwan (USA) 10.3f **(79)** - Third Watch (Slip Anchor) 9.8f **(73)**
Form - 0
Record **1998** - 1st:0 2nd:0 3rd:0 Ran:1
1998 Turf 0-1: (11f) (g-f)
Light-framed, currently moderate gelding.
**W J Haggas [0-1] B Haggas.*

SENURE (USA) BHB 86f **RR 87f** 4772[1]
2 b c Nureyev (USA) 8.4f **(84)** - Diese (USA) (Diesis) 9.3f **(69)**
Form - 701
Record **1998** - 1st:1 2nd:0 3rd:0 Ran:3
Win Prizemoney £3,327 *Total Prizemoney* £3,327
Wins *** 1998** Oct Leices (G-S) 7f 87 <
1998 Turf 1-3: (6f, 7f 1-2) (gd 1-1, g-f, frm)
Currently useful colt. Turf high 87 (began Aug) - 1st of 17 from Ya-Ain (13 Oct Leicester RF 4772). Out of a half-sister to Xaar, he caught the eye under sympathetic handling on his debut, and scored at the third attempt on easier ground.
**R Charlton [1-3] K Abdulla.*

SEPTEMBER HARVEST (USA) BHB 75f **RR 81f** 4929[3]
2 ch c Mujtahid (USA) 7.4f **(69)** - Shawgatny (USA) (Danzig Connection (USA)) 8f **(68)**
Form - 005035703
Record **1998** - 1st:0 2nd:0 3rd:2 Ran:9
Win Prizemoney £0 *Total Prizemoney* £909
1998 Turf 0-9: (5f, 7f 6, 8f 2) (g-s, gd, g-f 2, frm 5)
Decent colt, effective 7 to 8f, best at 7f, acts on g-f to frm, best on frm, has worn blinkers. Turf high 79 - 5th of 12 getting 3lb from Pilot's Harbour (28 Aug Newmarket 8f frm RF 3932).
**B J Meehan [0-9] J S Dunningham.*

SERAPE BHB 32f30a **RR 39f 30a** 4920[16]
5 b m Primo Dominie 7.2f **(67)** - Absaloute Service (Absalom) 7.2f **(58)**
Form - 80237200500
Record **1998** - 1st:0 2nd:2 3rd:1 Ran:11
Pre1998 - 1st:0 2nd:2 3rd:0 Ran:14
Win Prizemoney £0 *Total Prizemoney* £3,642
1998 Turf 0-10: (6f 4, 7f 3, 8f 2, 9f) (sft, g-s, gd, g-f 5, frm 2) 1998 AW 0-1: (7f) (Fibr)
Very moderate filly, effective 7f, acts on g-f, likes left handed tracks. Turf high 39. Inconsistent.
**M A Peill [0-16] Ms V B Foster (from Mrs L Stubbs [0-10] Jly 1997).*

SERDAAL BHB 66f **RR 70f** 1712[4]
3 b c Warning 8.1f **(77)** - Negeen (USA) (Danzig (USA)) 8.4f **(76)**
Form - 0074
Record **1998** - 1st:0 2nd:0 3rd:0 Ran:4
1998 Turf 0-4: (7f 2, 8f, 9f) (gd 3, frm)
Workmanlike, above-average colt, has worn blinkers. Turf high 70.
**A C Stewart [0-4] Sheikh Ahmed Al Maktoum.*

SERENA (IRE) RR 98f 5019a[4]
2 ch f Rainbow Quest (USA) 11.2f **(81)** - Green Lucia (Green Dancer (USA)) 10.3f **(74)**
Form - 44
1998 Turf 0-2: (8f 2) (hvy, gd)
Currently very useful filly. Turf high 98 (began Aug) - 4th of 17 to Pink Coral (21 Oct Navan 8f hvy RF 5019a).
**C Collins in IRE [0-2] Gerald Jennings.*

SERENDIPITY (FR) BHB 59f55a **RR 63f 55a** 5081[5]
5 b g Mtoto11.5f **(71)** -Bint Damascus (USA)(Damascus (USA))8.9f **(71)**
Form - 33832105
Record **1998** - 1st:1 2nd:1 3rd:3 Ran:8
Pre1998 - 1st:1 2nd:0 3rd:4 Ran:22
Win Prizemoney £5,571 *Total Prizemoney* £12,297
Wins *** 1998** Aug Chepst (G-F) C 12.1f 63
1996 May Beverl (G-F) 9.9f 75 <
1998 Turf 1-7: (10f 3, 11f 2, 12f 1-2) (gd 2, g-f 3, frm 1-2) 1998 AW 0-1: (12f) (Fibr)
Average gelding, effective 8 to 12f, acts on gd to frm, best on gd, has worn blinkers, likes left handed tracks, prefers tight tracks, excels at Salisbury. Turf high 63 - 1st of 11 getting 2lb from Monument (31 Aug Chepstow RF 3980). He looks one-paced on the Flat these days.
**M C Pipe [2-12] M J Horton (from B R Millman [0-10] Oct 1997).*

SEREN HILL BHB 74f **RR 76f** 5094[1]
2 ch f Sabrehill (USA) 8.5f **(64)** - Seren Quest **(81f)** (Rainbow Quest (USA)) 10.4f **(75)**
Form - 6641
Record **1998** - 1st:1 2nd:0 3rd:0 Ran:4
Win Prizemoney £3,330 *Total Prizemoney* £3,558
Wins *** 1998** Nov Redcar (G-S) H 8f 69 76 <
1998 Turf 1-4: (7f 3, 8f 1-1) (gd 1-2, frm 2)
Above-average filly. Turf high 76 - 1st of 22 giving 16lb to Top Fit (2 Nov Redcar RF 5094).

G A Butler [1-1] The Fairy Story Partnership (from J W Hills [0-3] Aug 1998).

SEREN TEG BHB 68f **RR 70f** 4668[7]
2 ch f Timeless Times (USA) 6.1f **(56)** - Hill of Fare (Brigadier Gerard) 9.3f **(58)**
Form - 535657
Record 1998 - 1st:0 2nd:0 3rd:1 Ran:6
Win Prizemoney £0 *Total Prizemoney* £485
1998 Turf 0-6: (5f 2, 6f 4) (gd 2, g-f, frm 2, hrd)
Above-average filly, effective 5 to 6f, best at 6f, acts on g-f to hrd. Turf high 70 (began Aug) - 5th of 20 getting 7lb from Central Coast (29 Aug Nottingham 6f g-f RF 3961).
B Palling [0-6] K & D Computers Ltd.

SERGEANT IMP (IRE) BHB 47f41a **RR 51f 41a** 4996[9]
3 b g Mac's Imp (USA) 5.6f **(54)** - Genzyme Gene (Riboboy (USA)) 14f **(54)**
Form - 0610070550760
Record 1998 - 1st:1 2nd:0 3rd:0 Ran:13
Pre1998 - 1st:0 2nd:0 3rd:0 Ran:9
Win Prizemoney £2,550 *Total Prizemoney* £2,550
Wins * **1998** Apr Bright (GD) 6f 48 <
1998 Turf 1-11: (6f 1-5, 7f 2, 8f, 9f, 10f 2) (g-s 1-1, gd 6, g-f 3, frm) 1998 AW 0-2: (7f, 10f) (Equi 2)
Strong, fair gelding, has worn blinkers (effectively), likes left handed tracks. Turf high 51. AW high 38. *P Mitchell [1-22] W R Mann.*

SERGEANT YORK BHB 91f **RR 95f** 4533[3]
2 b c Be My Chief (USA) 10.2f **(62)** - Metaphysique (FR) (Law Society (USA)) 9.9f **(70)**
Form - 1038243
Record 1998 - 1st:1 2nd:1 3rd:2 Ran:7
Win Prizemoney £3,436 *Total Prizemoney* £6,671
Wins * **1998** May Hamilt (SFT) 5f 69 <
1998 Turf 1-7: (5f 1-2, 6f 4, 7f) (hvy 1-1, g-s, gd 2, g-f 2, hrd)
Very useful colt, effective 6f, acts on g-s. Turf high 95 - 3rd of 13 giving 25lb to Red Amazon (28 Spt Hamilton 6f g-s RF 4533). A fairly useful juvenile, he was not entirely disgraced in hot company at Royal Ascot and Newbury. Can win races at three at a more realistic level. *C Smith [1-7] A E Needham.*

SERIOUS ACCOUNT (USA) BHB 38f35a **RR 48df 35a**190[10]
5 b h Danzig (USA) 8.1f **(88)** - Topicount (USA) (Private Account (USA)) 8.5f **(74)**
Form - 0
Record 1998 - 1st:0 2nd:0 3rd:0 Ran:1
Pre1998 - 1st:0 2nd:0 3rd:1 Ran:4
Win Prizemoney £0 *Total Prizemoney* £507
1998 AW 0-1: (8f) (Fibr)
Moderate colt.
J L Eyre [0-4] Ms Heidi McKenna (from H R A Cecil [0-1] May 1996).

SERIOUS TRUST BHB 51f59a **RR 59f 59a** 3034[10]
5 b g Alzao (USA) 9.8f **(73)** - Mill Line (Mill Reef (USA)) 10.5f **(78)**
Form - 00640
Record 1998 - 1st:0 2nd:0 3rd:0 Ran:5
Pre1998 - 1st:2 2nd:1 3rd:2 Ran:19
Win Prizemoney £6,784 *Total Prizemoney* £8,834
Wins * 1997 Aug Salisb (G-F) H 14f 47 53
1996 May Salisb (G-F) H 12f 52 55 <
1998 Turf 0-4: (12f, 14f 2, 15f) (sft, gd, frm 2) 1998 AW 0-1: (16f) (Fibr)
Fair gelding, effective 12 to 14f, best at 14f, acts on g-f to frm, best on frm, likes right handed tracks. Turf high 59. Inconsistent.
Mrs L C Jewell [1-14] Peter Allen (from Sir Mark Prescott [1-10] Aug 1996).

SERPENTINE **RR 92f** 4410[1]
2 ch c Grand Lodge (USA) -Lake Pleasant (IRE) (Elegant Air) 13.2f **(61)**
Form - 331
Record 1998 - 1st:1 2nd:0 3rd:2 Ran:3
Win Prizemoney £4,050 *Total Prizemoney* £5,069
Wins * **1998** Spt Warwic (G-F) 7f 92 <
1998 Turf 1-3: (6f 2, 7f 1-1) (g-f, frm 1-2)
Currently useful colt. Turf high 92 (began Jly) - 1st of 14 from Gauntlet (22 Spt Warwick RF 4410). Appreciated the step up to seven to win his maiden. Lacks a bit of size.

J R Fanshawe [1-3] Lord Vestey.

SERRATE BHB 36f **RR 38f** 1246[15]
4 ch f Sharpo 7.5f **(68)** - Baino Clinic (USA) (Sovereign Dancer (USA)) 11.2f **(68)**
Form - 706050
Record 1998 - 1st:0 2nd:0 3rd:0 Ran:6
1998 Turf 0-3: (5f, 6f, 8f) (sft, g-s, frm) 1998 AW 0-3: (5f, 8f 2) (Fibr 3)
Very moderate filly, often wears blinkers. Turf high 38. AW high 31.
D Shaw [0-6] Mrs J Wilson.

SESTINO (FR) **RR 112f** 4948a[5]
3 b c Shirley Heights 12.1f **(76)** - Stellina (IRE) (Caerleon (USA)) 8.6f **(71)**
Form - 2335
1998 Turf 0-4: (10f, 11f, 12f 2) (hvy, sft 2, gd)
Group-class colt. Turf high 112 (1st run) - 2nd of 7 to Sayarshan (3 May Chantilly 11f sft RF 1091a). It was a surprise to see him dropped back in trip after finishing third in the Prix du Jockey-Club (French Derby). By Shirley Heights and out of a Caerleon mare, he will still beyond middle-distances.
Mme C Head in FR [0-4].

SET AND MATCH (IRE) **RR 47f** 4999[5]
2 ch c Second Set (IRE) 9.2f **(67)** - Kate Labelle (Teenoso (USA)) 9.9f **(72)**
Form - 5
Record 1998 - 1st:0 2nd:0 3rd:0 Ran:1
1998 Turf 0-1: (7f) (sft)
Currently moderate colt. *Miss Gay Kelleway [0-1] A P Griffin.*

SET TRAIL (IRE) BHB 54f **RR 53f** 4917[16]
3 b f Second Set (IRE) 9.2f **(67)** - Trail (Thatch (USA)) 9.8f **(62)**
Form - 68000
Record 1998 - 1st:0 2nd:0 3rd:0 Ran:5
Pre1998 - 1st:1 2nd:1 3rd:0 Ran:4
Win Prizemoney £3,376 *Total Prizemoney* £4,904
Wins * 1997 Oct Ayr (SFT) 7f 71 <
1998 Turf 0-5: (7f, 8f 2, 10f 2) (sft, g-s 2, gd, frm)
Scopey, fair filly, effective 7f, acts on sft to gd, prefers left handed tracks. Turf high 53. Inconsistent. *J Hanson [1-9] J Hanson.*

SEVEN BHB 64f **RR 69f** 4614[6]
3 ch g Weldnaas (USA) 8.4f **(55)** - Polly's Teahouse (Shack (USA)) 5.8f **(53)**
Form - 8865256
Record 1998 - 1st:0 2nd:1 3rd:0 Ran:7
Pre1998 - 1st:0 2nd:0 3rd:0 Ran:3
Win Prizemoney £0 *Total Prizemoney* £570
1998 Turf 0-7: (6f 2, 7f 3, 8f, 9f) (g-s, gd 2, g-f 2, frm 2)
Workmanlike, average gelding, effective 8f, acts on g-f, often wears blinkers (effectively). Turf high 69 - 2nd of 10 to My Bold Boyo (1 Aug Lingfield 8f g-f RF 3269). *B Smart [0-10] The Smart Set.*

SEVEN CROWNS (USA) BHB 27f **RR 50?f** 4545[12]
5 b g Chief's Crown (USA) 10.2f **(75)** - Ivory Dance (USA) (Sir Ivor) 10.2f **(70)**
Form - 000
Record 1998 - 1st:0 2nd:0 3rd:0 Ran:3
Pre1998 - 1st:0 2nd:0 3rd:2 Ran:12
Win Prizemoney £0 *Total Prizemoney* £1,679
1998 Turf 0-1: (14f) (gd) 1998 AW 0-2: (11f, 14f) (Fibr 2)
Fair gelding, has worn blinkers. (began Aug). Becoming disappointing.
R C Spicer [0-3] Mrs J A Nichols (from R Hannon [0-11] Spt 1996).

SEVEN SPRINGS (IRE) **RR 62?f** 4924[2]
2 b c Unblest - Zaydeen (Sassafras (FR)) 9.6f **(69)**
Form - 02
Record 1998 - 1st:0 2nd:1 3rd:0 Ran:2
Win Prizemoney £0 *Total Prizemoney* £708
1998 Turf 0-2: (6f, 7f) (sft, hrd)
Currently above-average colt. Turf high 62 (began Aug).
R Hollinshead [0-2] R Hollinshead.

SEVEN STARS **RR 62f** 4818[10]
2 b g Rudimentary (USA) 8.2f **(66)** - Carlton Glory (Blakeney) 10.5f **(64)**

Form - 000
Record 1998 - 1st:0 2nd:0 3rd:0 Ran:3
1998 Turf 0-3: (5f, 6f, 7f) (g-f, frm 2)
Currently average gelding. Turf high 62.
**M H Tompkins [0-3] Magnificent Seven.*

SEVENTEENS LUCKY BHB 76f65a **RR 78f 65a** 3826[9]
6 gr g Touch of Grey 8.1f **(47)** - Westminster Waltz (Dance In Time (CAN)) 8.9f **(59)**
Form - 0
Record 1998 - 1st:0 2nd:0 3rd:0 Ran:1
Pre1998 - 1st:3 2nd:5 3rd:4 Ran:31
Win Prizemoney £21,754 *Total Prizemoney* £31,136
Wins 1996 Spt York (GD) H 7.9f 75 78 <
1996 Jun Kempto (G-F) H 8f 68 72
1995 Oct York (GD) H 8.9f 67 71
1998 AW 0-1: (9f) (Fibr)
Above-average gelding, has broken blood-vessels, has worn blinkers. This tough handicapper has recorded two of his three career wins at York.
**M C Pipe [0-3] D M Cameron (from Bob Jones [3-31] Oct 1996).*

SEVERITY BHB 45f **RR 66f** 3830[9]
4 b c Reprimand 8.2f **(63)** - Neenah (Bold Lad (IRE)) 8.4f **(68)**
Form - 230200040
Record 1998 - 1st:0 2nd:2 3rd:1 Ran:9
Pre1998 - 1st:0 2nd:0 3rd:2 Ran:3
Win Prizemoney £0 *Total Prizemoney* £3,103
1998 Turf 0-6: (7f 2, 8f 3, 12f) (sft, g-f 2, frm 2, hrd) 1998 AW 0-3: (8f, 10f, 12f) (Equi 2, Fibr)
Workmanlike, above-average colt, effective 8f, acts on frm - acts on Equi. Turf high 66 - 2nd of 19 giving 22lb to Petuntse (4 Jun Yarmouth 8f frm RF 1720). AW high 75 (1st run) - 2nd of 7 giving 19lb to Call The Boss (21 Feb Lingfield 8f Equi RF 0333).
**B J McMath [0-5] Robert Clark (from W J Haggas [0-7] Jun 1998).*

SEWARDS FOLLY RR 58f 1278[4]
2 b f Rudimentary (USA) 8.2f **(66)** - Anchorage (IRE) (Slip Anchor) 9.8f **(73)**
Form - 4
Record 1998 - 1st:0 2nd:0 3rd:0 Ran:1
Win Prizemoney £0 *Total Prizemoney* £258
1998 Turf 0-1: (6f) (frm)
Currently fair filly. (1st run) - 4th of 12 to Dark Albatross (17 May Kempton 6f frm RF 1278). **J A R Toller [0-1] G M Cobey.*

SEYAASI (IRE) BHB 85f **RR 70+f** 3990[1]
3 ch c Indian Ridge 7.6f **(74)** - Good Policy (IRE) (Thatching) 8f **(66)**
Form - 51
Record 1998 - 1st:1 2nd:0 3rd:0 Ran:2
Win Prizemoney £4,221 *Total Prizemoney* £4,221
Wins * 1998 Aug Newcas (G-F) 8f 70+ <
1998 Turf 1-2: (7f, 8f 1-1) (g-f, frm 1-1)
Scopey, currently above-average colt. Turf high 70 (began Aug) - 1st of 8 giving 5lb to Stylish Storm (31 Aug Newcastle RF 3990).
**J H M Gosden [1-2] Sheikh Ahmed Al Maktoum.*

SHAANXI ROMANCE (IRE) BHB 77f **RR 81f** 4893[11]
3 b g Darshaan 11.9f **(81)** - Easy Romance (USA) (Northern Jove (CAN)) 9.7f **(66)**
Form - 120
Record 1998 - 1st:1 2nd:1 3rd:0 Ran:3
Pre1998 - 1st:0 2nd:0 3rd:1 Ran:2
Win Prizemoney £3,273 *Total Prizemoney* £5,883
Wins 1998 *Mar Wolver (STD) 8.5f 67 <*
1998 Turf 0-2: (8f, 10f) (g-s, g-f) 1998 AW 1-1: (8f 1-1) (Fibr 1-1)
Scopey, decent gelding. Turf high 81 (1st run) - 2nd of 9 giving 4lb to Moon Gorge (28 Mar Warwick 8f g-s RF 0490). (1st run). He showed a little bit of ability on turf at two, but got off the mark in a maiden on the Wolverhampton Fibresand in March with a smoothly-gained success.
**J Noseda [0-1] K Y Lim (from M Bell [1-4] Mar 1998).*

SHABAASH (IRE) BHB 60f **RR 70f** 4570[3]
2 b c Mujadil (USA) 7.7f **(70)** - Folly Vision (IRE) (Vision (USA)) 9f **(64)**
Form - 407184553
Record 1998 - 1st:1 2nd:0 3rd:1 Ran:9
Win Prizemoney £2,976 *Total Prizemoney* £3,763
Wins * 1998 Jly Folkes (G-F) H 5f 70 <
1998 Turf 1-9: (5f 1-7, 6f 2) (g-s, gd 3, g-f 1-3, frm 2)
Above-average colt, effective 5f, acts on g-f. Turf high 70 - 1st of 6 getting 8lb from Lightning Blaze (8 Jly Folkestone RF 2621).
**G Lewis [1-9] B S Chatwal.*

SHADES OF LOVE BHB 50f65a **RR 52f 65a** 4402[7]
4 b c Pursuit of Love 9.5f **(69)** - Shadiliya (Red Alert) 7.6f **(66)**
Form - 351700047
Record 1998 - 1st:1 2nd:0 3rd:0 Ran:8
Pre1998 - 1st:0 2nd:1 3rd:1 Ran:8
Win Prizemoney £3,501 *Total Prizemoney* £4,781
Wins * 1998 *Mar Southw (STD) H 7f 57 64 <*
1998 Turf 0-4: (7f 2, 8f 2) (gd 2, g-f, frm) 1998 AW 1-4: (7f 1-2, 8f 2) (Equi, Fibr 1-3)
Workmanlike, average colt, effective 6 to 7f, best at 7f, acts on frm - acts on Fibr, prefers left handed tracks, prefers tight tracks. Turf high 52. AW high 64 - 1st of 10 giving 9lb to Hever Golf Passion (20 Mar Southwell RF 0450). **V Soane [1-16] The Pursuers.*

SHADIRWAN (IRE) BHB 50f **RR 56f** 4588[13]
7 b h Kahyasi 12.9f **(74)** - Shademah (Thatch (USA)) 9.8f **(62)**
Form - 5470080
Record 1998 - 1st:0 2nd:0 3rd:0 Ran:7
Pre1998 - 1st:2 2nd:3 3rd:0 Ran:21
Win Prizemoney £10,708 *Total Prizemoney* £20,134
Wins 1996 Mar Doncas (G-S) H 18f 70 83 <
1995 May Thirsk (G-F) H 16f 72 77+
1998 Turf 0-7: (14f, 15f, 16f 2, 20f 2, 22f) (sft, g-s, gd 5)
Fair horse, effective 17 to 20f, acts on g-f to frm, has worn blinkers, likes tight tracks. Turf high 62. Becoming disappointing. Has joined Chris Popham.
**Mrs A J Perrett [0-7] Clive Batt (from R Akehurst [2-24] Nov 1997).*

Shadoof (right) battled on to just hold Future Perfect

SHADOOF BHB 87f **RR 88f** 4631[23]
4 b c Green Desert (USA) 7.8f **(78)** - Bermuda Classic (Double Form) 7.3f **(58)**
Form - 511028200
Record 1998 - 1st:2 2nd:2 3rd:0 Ran:9
Pre1998 - 1st:1 2nd:0 3rd:3 Ran:9
Win Prizemoney £49,187 *Total Prizemoney* £58,388
Wins * 1998 Jun Epsom (GD) H 10.1f 84 88 <
*** 1998** May Redcar (G-F) H 10f 77 85

* 1997 Jun Haydoc (G-F) H 10.5f 75 78

1998 Turf 2-9: (9f, 10f 2-8) (gd 1-4, g-f 1-4, frm)

Workmanlike, useful colt, effective 10 to 11f, best at 10f, acts on gd to g-f, best on g-f, prefers tight tracks, excels at Epsom. Turf high 88 - 11th of 20 giving 1lb to Yavana's Pace (3 Jly Sandown 10f gd RF 2505) - also 1st of 14 getting 15lb from Future Perfect (6 Jun Epsom RF 1777). Consistent. A winner once in quite a busy three-year-old campaign, he was in fine form earlier this season, winning two very valuable handicaps at Redcar and Epsom. Respectable efforts since. **W R Muir [3-18] Mrs H Levy.*

SHADOW CREEK (IRE) BHB 85f **RR 86f** 4494[9]

3 b c Fairy King (USA) 7.7f **(75)** - Daniela Samuel (USA) (No Robbery) 8.7f **(80)**

Form - 31620

Record	**1998 -**	1st:1	2nd:1	3rd:1	Ran:5

Win Prizemoney £3,754 *Total Prizemoney* £6,594

Wins	* **1998**	Jly	Thirsk	(FRM)		7f		86	<

1998 Turf 1-5: (7f 1-5) (gd, g-f, frm 1-3)

Scopey, useful colt. Turf high 86 (began Jly) - 1st of 9 from Wajori (24 Jly Thirsk RF 3086). **R W Armstrong [1-5] P J Vela.*

SHADOW DANCE (FR) **RR 103f** 3612b[2]

3 ch c Galetto (FR) 11.7f **(86)** - Swim Dance (USA) (Riverman (USA)) 9.1f **(76)**

Form - 2

1998 Turf 0-1: (13f) (gd)

Currently very useful colt. (1st run) - 2nd of 3 giving 1lb to Dark Moondancer (6 Aug Deauville 13f gd RF 3612b). He was outpaced by Dark Moondancer at Deauville in August and looks a stayer. ** in FR [0-1].*

SHADOW JURY BHB 44f43a **RR 51f 43a** 1310[5]

8 ch g Doulab (USA) 7.4f **(61)** - Texita (Young Generation) 7.7f **(63)**

Form - 35667605

Record	**1998 -**	1st:0	2nd:0	3rd:0	Ran:6
	Pre1998 -	1st:17	2nd:14	3rd:18	Ran:129

Win Prizemoney £59,035 *Total Prizemoney* £84,942

Wins	* 1997	May	Mussel	(G-F)	H	5f	60	60
	* 1997	May	Warwic	(FRM)		6f		63
	* 1996	Jly	Newmar	(GD)	H	5f	60	61
	* 1996	*Jan*	*Wolver*	*(STD)*	*H*	*5f*	*72*	*70*
	* 1995	*Jly*	*Southw*	*(STD)*	*H*	*5f*	*58*	*69*
	* 1995	Jly	Ayr	(GD)	H	5f	68	72
	* 1995	Jly	Haydoc	(G-F)	H	5f	64	65
	* 1995	Jun	Hamilt	(FRM)	H	5f	58	62
	* 1995	May	Redcar	(FRM)	H	5f	54	53
	* 1995	*Feb*	*Southw*	*(STD)*	*H*	*6f*	*53*	*52*

1998 Turf 0-1: (6f) (sft) 1998 AW 0-5: (5f 4, 6f) (Fibr 5)

Fair gelding, effective 5 to 6f, best at 5f, acts on gd to g-f - acts on Fibr, mostly wears blinkers. AW high 45.

**D W Chapman [13-120] Mrs Jeanne Chapman (from C Tinkler [0-1] Spt 1992).*

SHADY DEAL **RR 70f** 4735[7]

2 b c No Big Deal - Taskalady (Touching Wood (USA)) 8.2f **(55)**

Form - 077

Record	**1998 -**	1st:0	2nd:0	3rd:0	Ran:3

1998 Turf 0-3: (6f 3) (g-s, frm 2)

Currently above-average colt. Turf high 70 (began Jly) - 7th of 13 getting 3lb from Kangaroo Island (22 Spt Warwick 6f frm RF 4413). **M D I Usher [0-3] The Sundial Partnership.*

SHAFFISHAYES BHB 67f65a **RR 73f 65a** 4754[2]

6 ch g Clantime 6.6f **(57)** - Mischievous Miss (Niniski (USA)) 10.6f **(65)**

Form - 510405532102

Record	**1998 -**	1st:2	2nd:2	3rd:1	Ran:12
	Pre1998 -	1st:4	2nd:5	3rd:4	Ran:22

Win Prizemoney £21,948 *Total Prizemoney* £34,017

Wins	* **1998**	Spt	Nottin	(GD)		10f		73	<
	* **1998**	Apr	Thirsk	(G-S)		12f		73	<
	* 1997	Jun	Newmar	(SFT)	H	12f	68	70	
	* 1997	May	Newcas	(GD)	H	12.4f	65	69	
	* 1996	Apr	Pontef	(G-F)		8f		66	
	* 1995	Apr	Mussel	(GD)		7.1f		45	

1998 Turf 2-12:(10f 1-5, 11f 2,12f 1-5)(sft 2, g-s 1-3, gd1-2, g-f 2, frm 3)

Above-average gelding, effective 10 to 13f, acts on sft to frm, best on g-s, prefers left handed tracks, excels at Doncaster and Ayr. Turf high 73 - 1st of 6 from My Learned Friend (18 Apr Thirsk RF 0748) - also 1st of 16 giving 8lb to Wings Awarded (14 Spt Nottingham RF 4263). **Mrs M Reveley [6-34] P Davidson-Brown.*

SHAFT OF LIGHT BHB 92f83a **RR 92f 83a** 2660a[6]

6 gr g Sharrood (USA) 11.1f **(67)** -Reflection (Mill Reef (USA))10.5f **(78)**

Form - 6446

Record	**1998 -**	1st:0	2nd:0	3rd:0	Ran:4
	Pre1998 -	1st:5	2nd:4	3rd:5	Ran:17

Win Prizemoney £34,678 *Total Prizemoney* £59,367

Wins	* 1997	Aug	Epsom	(G-S)	H	12f	87	97	<
	* 1997	Aug	Cheste	(G-F)	H	18.7f	83	86	
	* 1995	Jly	Salisb	(G-F)	H	12f	70	77+	
	* 1995	*Mar*	*Lingfi*	*(STD)*	*H*	*10f*	*65*	*63*	
	* 1995	*Feb*	*Southw*	*(STD)*		*11f*		*60+*	

1998 Turf 0-4: (12f 3, 16f) (hvy, gd 2, g-f)

Useful gelding, effective 12 to 16f, acts on gd to frm, best on gd, often wears blinkers, prefers left handed tracks. Turf high 91 - 4th of 15 giving 3lb to Hajr (6 Jun Epsom 12f g-f RF 1780). Seemed to need the run on his seasonal debut in '98, but ran very well at both Epsom and Royal Ascot in June.

**Lord Huntingdon [5-21] Queen Elizabeth.*

SHAHER (USA) **RR 48f** 3406[7]

3 ch c Shadeed (USA) 7.7f **(72)** -Desirable (Lord Gayle (USA)) 8.8f **(62)**

Form - 07

Record	**1998 -**	1st:0	2nd:0	3rd:0	Ran:2

1998 Turf 0-2: (8f, 11f) (g-f, frm)

Scopey, currently moderate colt. Turf high 48 (began Jly).

**J L Dunlop [0-2] Hamdan Al Maktoum.*

SHAHIK (USA) BHB 60f51a **RR 58f 51a** 1751[4]

8 b g Spectacular Bid (USA) 10.8f **(63)** - Sham Street (USA) (Sham (USA)) 9.5f **(68)**

Form - 080004

Record	**1998 -**	1st:0	2nd:0	3rd:0	Ran:4
	Pre1998 -	1st:2	2nd:4	3rd:2	Ran:24

Win Prizemoney £6,782 *Total Prizemoney* £9,395

Wins	1996	*Nov*	*Wolver*	*(STD)*	*H*	*9.4f*	*60*	*65*	
	1996	Oct	Salisb	(G-S)	H	10f	61	68	<

1998 Turf 0-2: (8f, 9f) (frm 2) 1998 AW 0-2: (8f 2) (Equi, Fibr)

Fair gelding, effective 10f, acts on frm, has worn blinkers. Turf high 58. AW high 41.

**K C Comerford [0-7] Dr A Kimber (from D HaydnJones [2-14] Aug 1997).*

SHAHRANI BHB 33f **RR 36df** 4871[7]

6 b g Lear Fan (USA) 10.4f **(80)** - Windmill Princess (Gorytus (USA)) 7.8f **(60)**

Form - 6207

Record	**1998 -**	1st:0	2nd:1	3rd:0	Ran:4
	Pre1998 -	1st:0	2nd:0	3rd:0	Ran:9

Win Prizemoney £0 *Total Prizemoney* £831

1998 Turf 0-4: (14f, 16f 2, 18f) (gd, g-f 2, frm)

Very moderate gelding. Turf high 36 (began Jly) - 2nd of 8 getting 14lb from Danegold (27 Jly Yarmouth 16f g-f RF 3149).

**M C Chapman [0-5] Mrs E C Rosbottom (from M C Pipe [2-8] Jly 1996).*

SHAHRUR (USA) BHB 66f **RR 67f** 5150[6]

5 b br g Riverman (USA) 9.7f **(78)** - Give Thanks (Relko) 9.9f **(59)**

Form - 3806

Record	**1998 -**	1st:0	2nd:0	3rd:1	Ran:4
	Pre1998 -	1st:1	2nd:1	3rd:0	Ran:5

Win Prizemoney £1,712 *Total Prizemoney* £3,565

Wins	1997	May	Down R	(Y-S)	14f	77	<

1998 Turf 0-4: (16f 2, 17f, 18f) (g-s, gd 3)

Average gelding, effective 14 to 16f, acts on g-s to gd, prefers right handed tracks. Turf high 72 (1st run) - 3rd of 11 getting 10lb from Premier Night (23 May Kempton 16f gd RF 1427). Consistent. Ex-Irish, he enjoyed a good season over hurdles and ran well back on the Flat in May. Well held since on the level.

**G L Moore [4-12] Mrs Elizabeth Kiernan (from D K Weld in IRE [1-5] Jun 1997).*

SHAHTOUSH (IRE) **RR 117f** 4294a[8]

3 b f Alzao (USA) 9.8f **(73)** - Formulate (Reform) 8.9f **(62)**

Form - 120158
1998 Turf 2-6: (8f 1-3, 10f, 12f 1-2) (hvy 1-1, gd 1-4, frm)
High-class filly, effective 12f, acts on gd. Turf high 117 - 1st of 8 from Bahr (5 Jun Epsom RF 1747). A winner in heavy ground at the Curragh on her return, she chased home Cape Verdi at a respectable distance in the 1000 Guineas, but ran no sort of race on much faster ground in the Irish version. Stepped up to twelve furlongs and back on an easier surface, she showed a useful turn of foot to go past and then outbattle Bahr to land the Epsom Oaks, but her subsequent form, and indeed that of the rest of the field, must cast a doubt on the quality of the race. Has been retired.
**A P O'Brien in IRE [3-11] Mrs David Nagle.*

SHAJI (IRE) BHB 65f **RR 62f** 4086[4]
3 ch c Mukaddamah (USA) 7.6f **(74)** - Alkariyh (USA) (Alydar (USA)) 9.1f **(76)**
Form - 35864

Record	**1998 -**	1st:0	2nd:0	3rd:1	Ran:5
	Pre1998 -	1st:0	2nd:0	3rd:0	Ran:1

Win Prizemoney £0 *Total Prizemoney* £995
1998 Turf 0-5: (6f, 7f 2, 8f, 9f) (gd, g-f, frm 3)
Scopey, average colt, effective 6 to 7f, acts on gd to frm. Turf high 69 (1st run) - 3rd of 11 giving 5lb to Prospectress (8 May Lingfield 7f frm RF 1101). **C J Benstead [0-6] Hamdan Al Maktoum.*

SHAKA RR 113f 1554a[4]
4 b c Exit To Nowhere (USA) 8.7f **(77)** - Serafica (FR) (No Pass No Sale) 11.9f **(85)**
Form - 54
1998 Turf 0-2: (8f, 9f) (g-s, gd)
Group-class colt, effective 10 to 11f, acts on gd. Turf high 113.
**J-C Rouget in FR [2-7].*

SHAKEN UP BHB 52f **RR 61f** 450[10]
4 b g Kendor (FR) 12.2f **(66)** - Oshawa (Alzao (USA)) 7.1f **(68)**
Form - 0

Record	**1998 -**	1st:0	2nd:0	3rd:0	Ran:1
	Pre1998 -	1st:0	2nd:0	3rd:0	Ran:4

1998 AW 0-1: (7f) (Fibr)
Strong, average gelding.
**Mrs D Haine [0-6] Mrs Solna ThomsonJones.*

SHAKIRA (IRE) RR 22f 4998[9]
2 b f Lycius (USA) 8.8f **(71)** - Shakanda (IRE) (Shernazar) 10.2f **(73)**
Form - 0

Record	**1998 -**	1st:0	2nd:0	3rd:0	Ran:1

1998 Turf 0-1: (7f) (sft)
Currently little account filly. **I A Balding [0-1] Mrs P Reditt.*

SHAKIYR (FR) BHB 38f64a **RR 44f 64a** 2866[7]
7 gr g Lashkari 13.1f **(52)** - Shakamiyn (Nishapour (FR)) 9.1f **(61)**
Form - 862120773657

Record	**1998 -**	1st:1	2nd:1	3rd:1	Ran:9
	Pre1998 -	1st:5	2nd:5	3rd:5	Ran:41

Win Prizemoney £18,775 *Total Prizemoney* £29,716

Wins	*** 1998**	*Jan*	*Wolver*	*(STD)*	*H*	*16.2f*	*60*	*63*	
	* 1997	*Jan*	*Wolver*	*(STD)*	*S*	*14.8f*		*59*	
	* 1996	*Jan*	*Wolver*	*(STD)*	*H*	*16.2f*	*65*	*70*	<
	* 1995	*Apr*	*Wolver*	*(STD)*	*H*	*12f*	*61*	*66*	
	* 1995	*Feb*	*Wolver*	*(STD)*	*H*	*12f*	*55*	*57*	
	* 1995	*Jan*	*Southw*	*(STD)*		*11f*		*48*	

1998 Turf 0-8: (14f 2, 15f, 16f 3, 18f, 22f) (g-s, gd 4, frm 3) 1998 AW 1-1: (16f 1-1) (Fibr 1-1)
Average gelding, effective 14 to 16f, - acts on Fibr, has worn blinkers, likes left handed tracks, favours tight tracks. Turf high 49. (1st run) - 1st of 6 getting 2lb from Indigo Dawn (10 Jan Wolverhampton RF 0069). He does all his winning on Fibresand, though he has shown the odd bit of form on turf this season. Not entirely consistent. **R Hollinshead [6-50] L & R Roadlines.*

SHALAAL (USA) BHB 70f57a **RR 78?f 57a** 102[8]
4 b g Sheikh Albadou 9.2f **(75)** - One Fine Day (USA) (Quadratic (USA)) 7f **(75)**
Form - 0848

Record	**1998 -**	1st:0	2nd:0	3rd:0	Ran:2
	Pre1998 -	1st:1	2nd:0	3rd:0	Ran:10

Win Prizemoney £2,679 *Total Prizemoney* £2,924

Wins	***** 1997	Oct	Leices	(SFT)		7f		78	<

1998 AW 0-2: (8f, 11f) (Fibr 2)
Scopey, above-average gelding, effective 7f, acts on g-s. AW high 56.
**M C Chapman [1-8] Eric Knowles (from E A L Dunlop [0-4] Apr 1997).*

SHALABELLA (IRE) BHB 42f **RR 17f** 1387[10]
3 br f Shalford (IRE) 7.8f **(63)** - Perfect Swinger (Shernazar) 10.2f **(73)**
Form - 00

Record	**1998 -**	1st:0	2nd:0	3rd:0	Ran:2
	Pre1998 -	1st:0	2nd:0	3rd:1	Ran:4

Win Prizemoney £0 *Total Prizemoney* £259
1998 Turf 0-2: (6f, 8f) (sft, g-s)
Workmanlike, poor filly, effective 7f, acts on g-f.
**J W Mullins [0-2] Mrs Jeni Fisher (from M R Channon [0-4] Spt 1997).*

SHALAD'OR BHB 90f **RR 92f** 4496[17]
3 b f Golden Heights 7.1f **(50)** - Shalati (FR) (High Line) 10.3f **(70)**
Form - 43112620

Record	**1998 -**	1st:2	2nd:2	3rd:1	Ran:8
	Pre1998 -	1st:1	2nd:2	3rd:0	Ran:6

Win Prizemoney £12,500 *Total Prizemoney* £23,471

Wins	*** 1998**	Jly	Windso	(GD)	H	8.3f	83	91+	<
	*** 1998**	Jun	Bath	(G-S)	H	8f	79	83	
	* 1997	Jly	Leices	(GD)		7f		61	

1998 Turf 2-8: (7f, 8f 2-5, 10f 2) (g-s, gd 1-3, g-f 1-3, frm)
Light-framed, useful filly, effective 8 to 10f, best at 8f, acts on gd to frm, best on g-f, prefers tight tracks. Turf high 92 - 2nd of 13 getting 5lb from Premier Generation (23 Jly Sandown 10f frm RF 3046) - also 1st of 10 giving 4lb to Sweet Pea (13 Jly Windsor RF 2768). She ran very well in a competitive handicap at Epsom on her second start of '98, and went on to win nicely at Bath and Windsor over a mile. Suited by making the running, she finds ten furlongs just stretching her stamina. **B R Millman [3-14] G Palmer.*

SHALAMA (IRE) BHB 89f **RR 85f** 1793[2]
3 b f Kahyasi 12.9f **(74)** - Shademah (Thatch (USA)) 9.8f **(62)**
Form - 222

Record	**1998 -**	1st:0	2nd:3	3rd:0	Ran:3

Win Prizemoney £0 *Total Prizemoney* £3,357
1998 Turf 0-3: (9f, 10f 2) (gd, frm, hrd)
Scopey, currently useful filly. Turf high 85 - 2nd of 11 to Silver Rhapsody (6 Jun Newmarket 10f hrd RF 1793). This half-sister to Shahrastani looks a sure-fire maiden winner, and connections will be looking to get some black type into her record.
**Sir Michael Stoute [0-3] H H Aga Khan.*

SHALARI (IRE) BHB 47f **RR 55f** 5094[8]
2 b f Shalford (IRE) 7.8f **(63)** - Hinari Disk Deck (Indian King (USA)) 7.4f **(64)**
Form - 50765008

Record	**1998 -**	1st:0	2nd:0	3rd:0	Ran:8

1998 Turf 0-7: (5f 4, 6f, 7f, 8f) (g-s, gd 3, g-f, frm 2) 1998 AW 0-1: (7f) (Fibr)
Fair filly. Turf high 61. **J L Eyre [0-8] Wetherby Racing Bureau 33.*

SHALATEENO BHB 71f **RR 80f** 4963[11]
5 b m Teenoso (USA) 10.5f **(62)** - Shalati (FR) (High Line) 10.3f **(70)**
Form - 73261P0630

Record	**1998 -**	1st:1	2nd:1	3rd:2	Ran:10
	Pre1998 -	1st:2	2nd:5	3rd:3	Ran:21

Win Prizemoney £9,993 *Total Prizemoney* £23,729

Wins	*** 1998**	Jun	Salisb	(G-S)	H	12f	72	80	<
	* 1997	Jun	Salisb	(G-F)	H	12f	64	62	
	* 1996	Aug	Chepst	(GD)	H	10.2f	56	63	

1998 Turf 1-10:(10f 2, 12f 1-2, 13f 3,14f,16f 2)(sft 2, gd 1-3, g-f 2, frm 3)
Decent filly, has broken blood-vessels, effective 10 to 16f, acts on gd to frm, best on gd, excels at Salisbury. Turf high 80 - 1st of 9 giving 10lb to Milling (10 Jun Salisbury RF 1886). A front-runner, she took advantage of a lenient mark to score at Salisbury. Handled the softish ground well there.
**B R Millman [3-23] G Palmer (from M R Channon [0-8] Jly 1996).*

SHALIMAR GARDEN (IRE) BHB 85f **RR 81f** 4769[3]
3 b f Caerleon (USA) 10.9f **(79)** - Producer (USA) (Nashua) 10.3f **(67)**
Form - 4423

Record	**1998 -**	1st:0	2nd:1	3rd:1	Ran:4

Win Prizemoney £0 *Total Prizemoney* £2,750
1998 Turf 0-4: (10f 2, 12f, 13f) (sft, frm 2, hrd)
Decent filly. Turf high 81 - 2nd of 10 to Careful Timing (24 Jly Newmarket 12f frm RF 3078). **L M Cumani [0-4] Mrs John Magnier.*

SHALSTAYHOLY (IRE) BHB 60f58a **RR 40f 58a** 4121[13]
4 ch f Shalford (IRE) 7.8f **(63)** - Saintly Guest (What A Guest) 7f **(62)**
Form - 0008700
Record 1998 - 1st:0 2nd:0 3rd:0 Ran:7
Pre1998 - 1st:3 2nd:3 3rd:2 Ran:17
Win Prizemoney £10,477 *Total Prizemoney* £18,496
Wins * 1997 Jly Sandow (G-F) H 5f 66 70 <
* 1997 Jun Newmar (GD) H 6f 60 65
* 1997 *Feb Lingfi (STD) 7f 57*
1998 Turf 0-4: (5f 2, 6f, 7f) (gd, g-f 3) 1998 AW 0-3: (6f 3) (Equi 2, Fibr)
Strong, moderate filly, effective 5f, acts on gd to g-f, has worn blinkers. Turf high 40 (began Jly). AW high 47.
**G L Moore [3-24] J B R Leisure Ltd.*

SHALYAH (IRE) BHB 46f **RR 48f** 4550[10]
3 ch f Shalford (IRE) 7.8f **(63)** - Baheejah (Northfields (USA)) 9f **(72)**
Form - 040288320
Record 1998 - 1st:0 2nd:2 3rd:1 Ran:9
Pre1998 - 1st:0 2nd:1 3rd:1 Ran:7
Win Prizemoney £0 *Total Prizemoney* £4,563
1998 Turf 0-7: (7f, 8f 5, 10f) (gd 2, g-f 2, frm 3) 1998 AW 0-2: (6f, 8f) (Fibr 2)
Workmanlike, moderate filly, effective 5 to 7f, acts on g-f to frm. Turf high 51. AW high 46 (began Spt).
**N P Littmoden [0-2] Ciaran McClintock (from Mrs V C Ward [0-1] Aug 1998).*

SHAMANIC BHB 68f **RR 77f** 4390[21]
6 b g Fairy King (USA) 7.7f **(75)** - Annie Albright (USA) (Verbatim (USA)) 8.5f **(64)**
Form - 2464200
Record 1998 - 1st:0 2nd:2 3rd:0 Ran:7
Pre1998 - 1st:3 2nd:5 3rd:1 Ran:31
Win Prizemoney £15,479 *Total Prizemoney* £38,734
Wins 1995 May Salisb (G-F) 6f 96 <
1994 May Cheste (G-F) 5.1f 82+
1994 Apr Windso (GD) 5f 94+
1998 Turf 0-7: (6f 7) (sft, g-f 4, frm 2)
Above-average gelding, effective 6 to 7f, best at 6f, acts on sft to frm, has worn blinkers. Turf high 77. Despite often making the frame in handicaps over six to seven furlongs, he has not managed to win a race since May 1995.
**S P C Woods [0-14] I Goldsmith (from R Hannon [3-24] Spt 1996).*

SHAMAWAN (IRE) RR 87f 4968[1]
3 b c Kris 10f **(75)** - Shamawna (IRE) (Darshaan) 9.9f **(84)**
Form - 51
Record 1998 - 1st:1 2nd:0 3rd:0 Ran:2
Win Prizemoney £3,782 *Total Prizemoney* £3,782
Wins * **1998** Oct Newbur (HVY) 10f 77 <
1998 Turf 1-2: (10f 1-2) (sft 1-1, gd)
Well made, currently useful colt. Turf high 87. Sold for 100,000 guineas at Tattersalls in October, and has joined Frank Berry.
**L M Cumani [1-2] H H Aga Khan.*

SHAMBLES BHB 33f29a **RR 41f 29a** 5038[4]
3 ch f Elmaamul (USA) 8.1f **(70)** - Rambadale (Vaigly Great) 7f **(58)**
Form - 00087332734544
Record 1998 - 1st:0 2nd:1 3rd:3 Ran:14
Pre1998 - 1st:0 2nd:0 3rd:0 Ran:2
Win Prizemoney £0 *Total Prizemoney* £1,573
1998 Turf 0-12: (7f, 8f, 10f, 11f 3, 12f 5, 14f) (g-s, gd 3, g-f 4, frm 3, hrd)
1998 AW 0-2: (7f, 16f) (Equi, Fibr)
Light-framed, moderate filly, effective 11 to 14f, acts on g-s to hrd, prefers tight tracks, excels at Beverley and Windsor, likes Yarmouth. Turf high 45 - 3rd of 12 getting 10lb from Coalminersdaughter (15 Spt Yarmouth 11f gd RF 4271). AW high 25. Consistent. **G G Margarson [0-16] The Shambles Partnership.*

SHAMEL BHB 69f **RR 76df** 4805[6]
2 b c Unfuwain (USA) 11.4f **(74)** - Narjis (USA) (Blushing Groom (FR)) 10.3f **(76)**
Form - 206
Record 1998 - 1st:0 2nd:1 3rd:0 Ran:3
Win Prizemoney £0 *Total Prizemoney* £1,100
1998 Turf 0-3: (7f, 8f 2) (gd 2, frm)
Currently above-average colt. Turf high 76 (1st run) (began Jly) - 2nd of 9 giving 5lb to Shoogle (11 Jly Salisbury 7f frm RF 2716).
**J L Dunlop [0-3] Hamdan Al Maktoum.*

SHAMOKIN BHB 28f28a **RR 18f 28a** 3490[7]
6 b g Green Desert (USA) 7.8f **(78)** - Shajan (Kris) 9.5f **(73)**
Form - 038007
Record 1998 - 1st:0 2nd:0 3rd:1 Ran:6
Pre1998 - 1st:0 2nd:0 3rd:1 Ran:14
Win Prizemoney £0 *Total Prizemoney* £603
1998 Turf 0-2: (8f 2) (frm 2) 1998 AW 0-4: (8f 4) (Fibr 4)
Very moderate gelding, has worn blinkers. Turf high 7. AW high 30. Inconsistent. **F Watson [0-20] F Watson.*

SHAMPOOED (IRE) BHB 59f **RR 72f** 4195[8]
4 b f Law Society (USA) 11.6f **(71)** - White Caps (Shirley Heights) 10.3f **(74)**
Form - 055128
Record 1998 - 1st:1 2nd:1 3rd:0 Ran:6
Pre1998 - 1st:1 2nd:0 3rd:1 Ran:7
Win Prizemoney £5,308 *Total Prizemoney* £6,695
Wins 1998 Jun Thurle (GD) 16f 72 <
1997 Jun Tralee (FRM) H 11f 60 63
1998 Turf 1-6: (11f, 12f, 14f, 16f 1-2, 17f) (hvy, sft, gd 1-3, frm)
Above-average filly, effective 11 to 17f, acts on sft to frm, has worn blinkers. Turf high 72 - 1st of 9 from In Generosity (20 Jun Thurles RF 2220a).
**R Dickin [0-2] Warwick Members Racing Club (from J G Murphy in IRE [2-7] Jun 1998).*

SHAMWARI SONG BHB 58f70a **RR 58f 70a** 5147[10]
3 b g Sizzling Melody 6.3f **(49)** - Spark Out (Sparkler) 8.4f **(55)**
Form - 61123400000
Record 1998 - 1st:2 2nd:1 3rd:1 Ran:11
Pre1998 - 1st:1 2nd:0 3rd:0 Ran:7
Win Prizemoney £7,984 *Total Prizemoney* £10,392
Wins 1998 May Newcas (G-F) H 8f 67 72 <
1998 May Beverl (G-F) C 7.5f 57
1997 Oct Newcas (G-F) 7f 63
1998 Turf 2-10: (7f 1-4, 8f 1-6) (sft, g-s 2, gd 3, g-f, frm 1-2, hrd 1-1)
1998 AW 0-1: (7f) (Equi)
Scopey, average gelding, effective 8f, acts on g-f to frm. Turf high 78 - 3rd of 11 to Guaranteed (19 Jun Newmarket 8f g-f RF 2127) - also 1st of 20 giving 5lb to Saintes (21 May Newcastle RF 1368).
**N A Callaghan [0-5] Gallagher Equine Ltd (from Mrs L C Jewell [0-1] Jun 1998).*

SHANAZ BHB 32f **RR 32f** 4201[12]
3 b f Then Again 7.4f **(52)** - Trecauldah (Treboro (USA))
Form - 058000
Record 1998 - 1st:0 2nd:0 3rd:0 Ran:6
1998 Turf 0-6: (7f, 8f 2, 10f 3) (g-s, gd 2, frm 3)
Unfurnished, very moderate filly. Turf high 53.
**D Burchell [0-6] The Valleys Partners.*

SHANGHAI LADY RR 61f 5071[8]
2 b f Sabrehill (USA) 8.5f **(64)** - Session (Reform) 8.9f **(62)**
Form - 8
Record 1998 - 1st:0 2nd:0 3rd:0 Ran:1
1998 Turf 0-1: (7f) (gd)
Currently average filly. **J H M Gosden [0-1] Pacific Hawk (HK) Ltd.*

SHANGHAI LIL BHB 28f47a **RR 31f 47a** 4362[5]
6 b m Petong 7.6f **(58)** - Toccata (USA) (Mr Leader (USA)) 9.8f **(66)**
Form - 5542311045105
Record 1998 - 1st:3 2nd:1 3rd:1 Ran:11
Pre1998 - 1st:3 2nd:3 3rd:2 Ran:33
Win Prizemoney £14,214 *Total Prizemoney* £18,287
Wins * **1998** *Jun Wolver (STD) H 12f 44 46*
* **1998** *Mar Wolver (STD) C 12f 47*
* **1998** *Feb Lingfi (SLW) 10f 41*
* **1997** *Jan Lingfi (STD) H 8f 46 51* <
* **1996** *Dec Lingfi (STD) H 8f 40 45*

*1995 *Apr Wolver (STD) H 6f 40 42*
1998 Turf 0-1: (12f) (frm) 1998 AW 3-10: (10f 1-2, 11f 2, 12f 2-6) (Equi 1-5, Fibr 2-5)
Moderate mare, effective 8 to 12f, best at 8f, - acts on AW, best on Equi, has worn blinkers, favours left handed tracks, favours tight tracks, does well at Wolverhampton, likes Lingfield. AW high 47.
**M J Fetherston-Godley [6-44] M J Fetherston-Godley.*

SHANILLO BHB 75f **RR 75f** 1219[12]
3 gr g Anshan 8.2f **(63)** - Sea Fret (Habat) 7.6f **(61)**
Form - 410
Record 1998 - 1st:1 2nd:0 3rd:0 Ran:3
Pre1998 - 1st:0 2nd:0 3rd:0 Ran:1
Win Prizemoney £3,209 *Total Prizemoney* £3,209
Wins * 1998 Apr Folkes (SFT) 6f 75 <
1998 Turf 1-3: (6f 1-2, 7f) (sft 1-1, gd 2)
Above-average gelding. Turf high 75 - 1st of 11 from Faute de Mieux (21 Apr Folkestone RF 0780).
**M R Channon [1-4] The Piccolo Boys.*

SHANNON'S DREAM RR 11f 4967[14]
2 b f Anshan 8.2f **(63)** - Jenny's Call (Petong) 6.6f **(58)**
Form - 00
Record 1998 - 1st:0 2nd:0 3rd:0 Ran:2
1998 Turf 0-2: (6f 2) (sft, g-f)
Currently poor filly. Turf high 11 (began Spt).
**G M McCourt [0-1] Mrs B Taylor (from B J Meehan [0-1] Spt 1998).*

SHAN'T RR 1897[16]
3 ch c Shalford (IRE) 7.8f **(63)** - Silent Girl (Krayyan) 8.5f **(49)**
Form - 0
Record 1998 - 1st:0 2nd:0 3rd:0 Ran:1
1998 Turf 0-1: (7f) (g-s)
Scopey, currently very poor colt - 16th of 16 giving 5lb to Quiz Show (11 Jun Newbury 7f g-s RF 1897).
**P T Walwyn [0-1] Mrs P T Walwyn.*

SHANTHI BHB 32f39a **RR 24f 39a** 2926[8]
3 b f Reprimand 8.2f **(63)** - Scarlett Holly (Red Sunset) 8.2f **(63)**
Form - 7808
Record 1998 - 1st:0 2nd:0 3rd:0 Ran:4
Pre1998 - 1st:0 2nd:1 3rd:4 Ran:8
Win Prizemoney £0 *Total Prizemoney* £2,386
1998 Turf 0-4: (7f, 8f 2, 11f) (gd 3, frm)
Light-framed, little account filly, effective 5 to 7f, acts on gd to frm, has worn blinkers. Turf high 24.
**B J Llewellyn [0-4] B J Llewellyn (from P J Makin [0-8] Oct 1997).*

SHANTUNG (IRE) RR 54f 4624[5]
3 ch f Anshan 8.2f **(63)** - Bamian (USA) (Topsider (USA)) 8.3f **(71)**
Form - 806005
Record 1998 - 1st:0 2nd:0 3rd:0 Ran:6
Pre1998 - 1st:0 2nd:0 3rd:0 Ran:3
Win Prizemoney £0 *Total Prizemoney* £198
1998 Turf 0-6: (6f, 7f 4, 10f) (gd 3, g-f 2, frm)
Neat, fair filly, has worn blinkers. Turf high 54.
**K McAuliffe [0-9] K & B Wetherell, Mrs Burke, C Krosinsky.*

SHANUKE (IRE) BHB 25f48a **RR 30f 48a** 4654[8]
6 b m Contract Law (USA) 8.9f **(54)** - Auntie Ponny (Last Fandango) 7.8f **(61)**
Form - 70010008
Record 1998 - 1st:1 2nd:0 3rd:0 Ran:8
Pre1998 - 1st:0 2nd:0 3rd:0 Ran:9
Win Prizemoney £2,040 *Total Prizemoney* £2,453
Wins * 1998 Jly Bright (G-F) SH 11.9f 30 30 <
1998 Turf 1-8: (7f, 8f, 10f, 11f, 12f 1-2, 14f 2) (gd 1-4, g-f 2, frm 2)
Very moderate mare, effective 12f, acts on gd, likes tight tracks. Turf high 30 - 1st of 11 giving 4lb to Coastguards Hero (23 Jly Brighton RF 3038).
**S Woodman [1-9] R Howitt (from J S Moore [0-9] Jun 1995).*

SHAPE SHIFTER (IRE) RR 78f 1786[8]
3 ch c Night Shift (USA) 8.1f **(73)** - Zabeta (Diesis) 9.3f **(69)**
Form - 248
Record 1998 - 1st:0 2nd:1 3rd:0 Ran:3
Pre1998 - 1st:0 2nd:0 3rd:0 Ran:1
Win Prizemoney £0 *Total Prizemoney* £1,472
1998 Turf 0-3: (8f 3) (sft, frm 2)
Neat, above-average colt. Turf high 78 - 4th of 12 giving 5lb to Bryony Brind (8 May Nottingham 8f frm RF 1111). (DEAD)
**R Hannon [0-4] G Howard-Spink.*

SHARAF (IRE) BHB 49f53a **RR 53f 53a** 4871[6]
5 b g Sadler's Wells (USA) 11.3f **(87)** - Marie de Flandre (FR) (Crystal Palace (FR)) 12.5f **(76)**
Form - 543521324276
Record 1998 - 1st:1 2nd:3 3rd:2 Ran:12
Pre1998 - 1st:1 2nd:2 3rd:1 Ran:18
Win Prizemoney £6,918 *Total Prizemoney* £15,728
Wins * 1998 Jly Bath (GD) H 17.2f 47 51
1996 Apr Folkes (G-F) 12f 80+ <
1998 Turf 1-12: (14f 2, 16f 4, 17f 1-5, 18f) (sft, gd 1-5, g-f 4, frm 2)
Fair gelding, effective 14 to 17f, best at 17f, acts on gd to frm, has worn blinkers, favours tight tracks, excels at Sandown and Bath. Turf high 53 - 2nd of 12 getting 4lb from Fast Forward Fred (21 Aug Sandown 16f g-f RF 3797) - also 1st of 12 from Fast Forward Fred (21 Jly Bath RF 2974). Consistent.
**W R Muir [1-24] D J Deer (from J L Dunlop [1-7] Jly 1996).*

SHARAZAN (IRE) BHB 75f **RR 71f** 2551[12]
5 b g Akarad (FR) 9.7f **(73)** - Sharaniya (USA) (Alleged (USA)) 10f **(76)**
Form - 00
Record 1998 - 1st:0 2nd:0 3rd:0 Ran:2
Pre1998 - 1st:2 2nd:3 3rd:1 Ran:9
Win Prizemoney £10,960 *Total Prizemoney* £16,568
Wins 1997 Jly Currag (GD) H 16f 94 109 <
1996 May Leopar (GD) 12f 70
1998 Turf 0-2: (16f, 19f) (gd, g-f)
Above-average gelding, effective 16f, acts on gd, has worn blinkers, prefers right handed tracks. Turf high 71. Consistent.
**O O'Neill [0-4] Frank Clarke (from J Oxx in IRE [2-9] Aug 1997).*

SHARBADARID (IRE) BHB 62f62a **RR 73df 62a** 1280[7]
4 b g Night Shift (USA) 8.1f **(73)** - Sharenara (USA) (Vaguely Noble) 10.1f **(72)**
Form - 214707
Record 1998 - 1st:1 2nd:1 3rd:0 Ran:6
Pre1998 - 1st:0 2nd:1 3rd:2 Ran:6
Win Prizemoney £3,403 *Total Prizemoney* £6,750
Wins * 1998 *Feb Lingfi (SLW) 12f 70+* <
1998 Turf 0-2: (10f, 14f) (sft, g-f) 1998 AW 1-4:(10f 2,12f 1-2) (Equi 1-4)
Scopey, above-average gelding, effective 10 to 12f, acts on gd - acts on Equi, has worn blinkers, likes tight tracks. Turf high 49. AW high 70 - 1st of 6 giving 21lb to New Yorker (5 Feb Lingfield RF 0227). Inconsistent. Showed ability on turf without breaking his duck, but after joining Simon Dow, won a maiden on the Lingfield Equitrack with the utmost ease in February. He has disappointed since, however.
**S Dow [1-8] Mrs Anne Devine (from L M Cumani [0-6] Spt 1997).*

SHARDELOW RR 71f 1836[4]
3 b f Belmez (USA) 11.4f **(65)** - Sliprail (USA) (Our Native (USA)) 11.2f **(63)**
Form - 4
Record 1998 - 1st:0 2nd:0 3rd:0 Ran:1
Win Prizemoney £0 *Total Prizemoney* £268
1998 Turf 0-1: (8f) (gd)
Workmanlike, currently above-average filly.
**H Candy [0-1] Major M G Wyatt.*

SHARE DELIGHT (IRE) BHB 51f75a **RR 52f 75a** 4456[11]
4 b g Common Grounds 8.1f **(66)** - Dorado Llave (USA) (Well Decorated (USA)) 7.6f **(64)**
Form - 000800
Record 1998 - 1st:0 2nd:0 3rd:0 Ran:6
Pre1998 - 1st:1 2nd:1 3rd:0 Ran:11
Win Prizemoney £4,110 *Total Prizemoney* £5,115
Wins 1997 Mar Doncas (G-F) H 7f 70 79 <
1998 Turf 0-6: (6f, 7f 3, 8f, 10f) (g-s, gd 2, g-f, frm 2)
Scopey, fair gelding, effective 7 to 8f, acts on gd. Turf high 52. Inconsistent.
**D Nicholls [0-6] Miss V H Owen (from B W Hills [1-11] Aug 1997).*

SHARERA (IRE) BHB 84f **RR 83f** 4973[12]
3 b f Kahyasi 12.9f **(74)** - Sharenara (USA) (Vaguely Noble) 10.1f **(72)**
Form - 142620
Record 1998 - 1st:1 2nd:2 3rd:0 Ran:6
Pre1998 - 1st:0 2nd:0 3rd:0 Ran:1
Win Prizemoney £3,077 *Total Prizemoney* £7,346
Wins * **1998** May Salisb (G-F) 9.9f 76+ <
1998 Turf 1-6: (10f 1-4, 12f 2) (sft, gd 3, frm 1-2)
Neat, decent filly, effective 10f, acts on gd to frm. Turf high 83 - 2nd of 8 getting 8lb from Souffle (2 Aug Sandown 10f gd RF 3298) - also 1st of 9 from Lucrezia (14 May Salisbury RF 1217).
**L M Cumani [1-7] H H Aga Khan.*

SHARH RR 66f 3369[12]
2 ch c Elmaamul (USA) 8.1f **(70)** - Depeche (FR) (Kings Lake (USA)) 10.8f **(67)**
Form - 0
Record 1998 - 1st:0 2nd:0 3rd:0 Ran:1
1998 Turf 0-1: (7f) (frm)
Currently average colt. **Mrs J Cecil [0-1] Hamdan Al Maktoum.*

SHARK (IRE) BHB 39f **RR 39f** 4134[6]
5 b g Tirol 8.1f **(64)** - Gay Appeal (Star Appeal) 9.6f **(65)**
Form - 056
Record 1998 - 1st:0 2nd:0 3rd:0 Ran:3
Pre1998 - 1st:1 2nd:0 3rd:2 Ran:7
Win Prizemoney £3,886 *Total Prizemoney* £4,575
Wins * 1997 Spt Yarmou (FRM) H 8f 42 49 <
1998 Turf 0-3: (8f, 12f 2) (gd, g-f, frm)
Very moderate gelding, effective 8f, acts on frm. Turf high 39 (began Jly).
**K A Morgan [1-15] M J Harmer (from H ThomsonJones [0-1] May 1996).*

SHAROURA RR 61f 4006[2]
2 ch f Inchinor 8.9f **(64)** - Kinkajoo (Precocious) 8.6f **(62)**
Form - 2
Record 1998 - 1st:0 2nd:1 3rd:0 Ran:1
Win Prizemoney £0 *Total Prizemoney* £614
1998 Turf 0-1: (7f) (frm)
Currently average filly. (1st run) - 2nd of 12 to Bob's Princess (31 Aug Warwick 7f frm RF 4006). **K Mahdi [0-1] Solaiman Alsaiary.*

SHARP CATCH (IRE) RR 99f 5027a[1]
3 b f Common Grounds 8.1f **(66)** - Dear Lorraine (FR) (Nonoalco (USA)) 8.5f **(66)**
Form - 0475561
1998 Turf 1-7: (5f 2, 6f 3, 8f 1-2) (hvy 1-1, sft, gd 3, frm 2)
Strong, very useful filly, effective 5f, acts on g-s to frm, has worn blinkers. Turf high 99. Well beaten in the Irish 1000 Guineas on her reappearance, she reverted to sprinting and took a minor event on her final start. **A P O'Brien in IRE [2-8] Mrs H M Keaveney.*

SHARP COMMAND BHB 46f41a **RR 46f 41a** 567[4]
5 ch g Sharpo 7.5f **(68)** - Bluish (USA) (Alleged (USA)) 10f **(76)**
Form - 4
Record 1998 - 1st:0 2nd:0 3rd:0 Ran:1
Pre1998 - 1st:1 2nd:1 3rd:0 Ran:16
Win Prizemoney £2,085 *Total Prizemoney* £2,703
Wins * 1996 *Nov Wolver (STD) H 14.8f 48 48* <
1998 AW 0-1: (16f) (Fibr)
Moderate gelding, has worn blinkers. Inconsistent.
**P Eccles [4-26] A P Holland (from R W Armstrong [0-5] Jun 1996).*

SHARP CRACKER (IRE) BHB 78f **RR 80f** 4933[1]
3 b f Hamas (IRE) 8f **(72)** - Ascensiontide (Ela-Mana-Mou) 10.1f **(70)**
Form - 82461
Record 1998 - 1st:1 2nd:1 3rd:0 Ran:5
Pre1998 - 1st:1 2nd:3 3rd:3 Ran:10
Win Prizemoney £5,733 *Total Prizemoney* £11,638
Wins * **1998** Oct Bright (G-S) 8f 80 <
* 1997 Oct Pontef (G-S) 6f 74
1998 Turf 1-5: (7f, 8f 1-2, 10f 2) (sft 2, g-s 1-1, frm 2)
Scopey, decent filly, effective 6 to 10f, best at 8f, acts on g-s to frm, best on frm, prefers left handed tracks, prefers tight tracks, excels at Pontefract. Turf high 80 - 1st of 9 getting 6lb from Further Outlook (22 Oct Brighton RF 4933). **M Johnston [2-15] Mrs I Bird.*

SHARP DEED (IRE) BHB 46f30a **RR 48f 30a** 270[11]
4 ch g Sharp Victor (USA) 10f **(56)** - Fabulous Deed (USA) (Shadeed (USA)) 8.2f **(70)**
Form - 670
Record 1998 - 1st:0 2nd:0 3rd:0 Ran:3
Pre1998 - 1st:0 2nd:1 3rd:0 Ran:11
Win Prizemoney £0 *Total Prizemoney* £933
1998 AW 0-3: (10f, 13f, 16f) (Equi 3)
Workmanlike, moderate gelding, effective 8 to 10f, acts on gd to frm, has worn blinkers, favours tight tracks. AW high 42.
**M Madgwick [0-4] W V Roker (from P J Makin [0-11] Nov 1997).*

SHARP DOMINO RR 96f 4214a[7]
3 ch c Sharpo 7.5f **(68)** - Prompting (Primo Dominie) 6.2f **(80)**
Form - 7
1998 Turf 0-1: (6f) (gd)
Currently very useful colt. **R Suerland in GER [0-2].*

SHARP EDGE BOY BHB 65f **RR 72f** 4591[16]
2 gr c Mystiko (USA) 7.7f **(59)** - Leap Castle (Never so Bold) 6.3f **(66)**
Form - 0805630
Record 1998 - 1st:0 2nd:0 3rd:1 Ran:7
Win Prizemoney £0 *Total Prizemoney* £545
1998 Turf 0-7: (5f 5, 6f, 7f) (sft, gd 3, g-f 2, frm)
Above-average colt. Turf high 72.
**E J Alston [0-7] N Gilbert & A Shandley.*

SHARP ENDING (IRE) BHB 58f **RR 50f** 4395[14]
2 b c Keen 11.1f **(58)** - Last Finale (USA) (Stop The Music (USA)) 9.2f **(71)**
Form - 0800
Record 1998 - 1st:0 2nd:0 3rd:0 Ran:4
1998 Turf 0-4: (7f 3, 8f) (frm 4)
Fair colt. Turf high 50. **A P Jarvis [0-4] Ambrose Turnbull.*

SHARPEST BHB 45f **RR 52f** 4887[4]
4 ch g Sharpo 7.5f **(68)** - Anna Karietta (Precocious) 8.6f **(62)**
Form - 007022004
Record 1998 - 1st:0 2nd:2 3rd:0 Ran:9
Pre1998 - 1st:0 2nd:0 3rd:0 Ran:3
Win Prizemoney £0 *Total Prizemoney* £1,271
1998 Turf 0-8: (8f, 10f 3, 12f 3, 14f) (g-s, gd 3, g-f 2, frm 2) 1998 AW 0-1: (9f) (Fibr)
Light-framed, fair gelding. Turf high 52. Inconsistent.
**J S Moore [0-9] Terry Pasquale (from J L Dunlop [0-3] Oct 1996).*

SHARP FELLOW BHB 39f50a **RR 47f 50a** 4504[5]
3 ch g Keen 11.1f **(58)** - Clarandal (Young Generation) 7.7f **(63)**
Form - 00076085
Record 1998 - 1st:0 2nd:0 3rd:0 Ran:7
Pre1998 - 1st:0 2nd:0 3rd:0 Ran:3
1998 Turf 0-7: (6f 2, 7f, 8f 4) (g-s, gd 4, frm 2)
Leggy, fair gelding, has worn blinkers. Turf high 47.
**I A Balding [0-10] Park House Partnership.*

SHARP GAYLE BHB 48f **RR 48f** 4130[P]
3 b f Sharpo 7.5f **(68)** - Storm Gayle(IRE)(Sadler's Wells (USA))10f **(76)**
Form - 067030P
Record 1998 - 1st:0 2nd:0 3rd:1 Ran:7
Win Prizemoney £0 *Total Prizemoney* £338
1998 Turf 0-7: (5f 3, 6f 2, 7f, 8f) (gd 7)
Moderate filly, effective 5f, acts on gd. Turf high 51.
**I Semple [0-7] David McKenzie.*

SHARP HAT BHB 77f **RR 86f** 4060[8]
4 ch c Shavian 7.7f **(67)** - Madam Trilby (Grundy) 10.3f **(65)**
Form - 0086300008
Record 1998 - 1st:0 2nd:0 3rd:1 Ran:10
Pre1998 - 1st:3 2nd:3 3rd:1 Ran:17
Win Prizemoney £13,908 *Total Prizemoney* £31,942
Wins * 1997 May Newbur (SFT) H 6f 85 90 <
* 1996 Spt Doncas (G-F) H 6f 78 83
* 1996 Aug Warwic (GD) H 6f 70 67
1998 Turf 0-10: (5f 2, 6f 7, 8f) (gd 6, g-f 4)
Scopey, useful colt, effective 6 to 7f, best at 6f, acts on g-s to frm, has worn blinkers. Turf high 86. Not at his best in '98, and will need the Handicapper to relent. **R Hannon [3-27] J C Smith.*

SHARP HINT BHB 50f **RR 52f** 4921^{19}
3 ch f Sharpo 7.5f **(68)** - May Hinton (Main Reef) 9.6f **(57)**
Form - 8400750
Record 1998 - 1st:0 2nd:0 3rd:0 Ran:7
1998 Turf 0-7: (5f 5, 6f, 7f) (sft, g-s, gd 2, g-f, frm 2)
Workmanlike, fair filly. Turf high 59.
**D Nicholls [0-3] V Greaves (from J L Dunlop [0-4] Jun 1998).*

SHARP IMP BHB 53f49a **RR 56f 49a** 4475^{8}
8 b g Sharpo 7.5f **(68)** - Implore (Ile de Bourbon (USA)) 10.1f **(67)**
Form - 43048146507388032648
Record 1998 - 1st:1 2nd:1 3rd:2 Ran:17
Pre1998 - 1st:8 2nd:17 3rd:9 Ran:82
Win Prizemoney £23,615 *Total Prizemoney* £44,974

Wins							
* **1998**	*Jan Lingfi*	*(STD)*	*H*	*6f*	*49*	*50*	
* 1997	Aug Folkes	(G-F)		6f		63	<
* 1997	*Jan Lingfi*	*(STD)*	*H*	*6f*	*59*	*62*	
* 1996	Aug Bright	(RFM)		7f		60	
* 1996	Jun Bright	(FRM)	H	6f	48	51	
* 1996	*Jan Lingfi*	*(STD)*	*H*	*6f*	*50*	*54*	
* 1995	Aug Folkes	(FRM)		6f		50	
* 1995	Jly Bright	(FRM)	H	6f	33	38	
* 1994	Jun Yarmou	(G-F)	H	7f	35	33	

1998 Turf 0-11: (6f 5, 7f 6) (gd 4, g-f 5, frm 2) 1998 AW 1-6: (6f 1-4, 7f 2) (Equi 1-6)
Fair gelding, effective 6 to 7f, best at 6f, acts on g-f to frm - acts on Equi, best on frm, mostly wears blinkers (effectively), likes left handed tracks, and excels at Brighton. Turf high 64 - 3rd of 9 giving 13lb to Academy (28 May Brighton 7f frm RF 1549). AW high 50. Effective around Lingfield's Equitrack and at Brighton, he needs to be brought late. Basically difficult to win with.
**R M Flower [9-92] Mrs G M Temmerman (from J Sutcliffe [0-7] Jun 1993).*

SHARP LABEL BHB 35f **RR 29f** 76^{7}
3 ch f Sharpo 7.5f **(68)** -Labelon Lady (Touching Wood (USA)) 8.2f **(55)**
Form - 07
Record 1998 - 1st:0 2nd:0 3rd:0 Ran:1
Pre1998 - 1st:0 2nd:0 3rd:0 Ran:3
1998 AW 0-1: (8f) (Fibr)
Unfurnished, little account filly, has worn blinkers.
**J L Harris [0-4] P T Bell.*

SHARP LOVE BHB 60f **RR 54f** 3143^{9}
2 b f Pursuit of Love 9.5f **(69)** - Sweet Decision (IRE) **(64f 66a)** (Common Grounds)
Form - 7600
Record 1998 - 1st:0 2nd:0 3rd:0 Ran:4
1998 Turf 0-4: (5f, 6f 2, 7f) (frm 4)
Fair filly. Turf high 54. **M J Ryan [0-4] A J Hollis.*

SHARP MATT RR 104f $3416a^{2}$
7 ch h Sharpo 7.5f **(68)** - Matoa (USA)
Form - 2
1998 Turf 0-1: (7f) (sft)
Currently very useful horse. (1st run) - 2nd of 13 giving 8lb to Shawdon (30 Jly Ovrevoll 7f sft RF 3416a). He is a tough old horse and almost caught Shawdon in a Listed event during July. Like most of his sire's stock, he acts on easy ground.
**M Kahn in SWE [1-2] Stall Kebo.*

SHARP MONKEY BHB 42f50a **RR 10f 50a** 4123^{18}
3 b g Man Among Men (IRE) 8f **(47)** - Sharp Thistle (Sharpo) 7.7f **(59)**
Form - 522834116225803030U0
Record 1998 - 1st:2 2nd:2 3rd:3 Ran:16
Pre1998 - 1st:0 2nd:2 3rd:0 Ran:8
Win Prizemoney £4,171 *Total Prizemoney* £7,120

Wins							
* **1998**	*Feb Southw*	*(STD)*	*SH*	*8f*	*54*	*63*	<
* **1998**	*Jan Southw*	*(STD)*	*C*	*8f*		*63*	<

1998 Turf 0-4: (7f, 8f 3) (g-s, gd, frm 2) 1998 AW 2-12: (7f 3, 8f 2-6, 9f 2, 11f) (Fibr 2-12)
Leggy, moderate gelding, effective 7 to 9f, best at 8f, - acts on Fibr, mostly wears blinkers (extremely effectively), favours left handed tracks, favours tight tracks, and excels at Southwell. Turf high 10. AW high 65 - 2nd of 9 getting 2lb from Killarney Jazz (2 Mar Southwell 8f Fibr RF 0384) - also 1st of 12 giving 1lb to Sharway Lady (26 Jan Southwell RF 0160). Becoming disappointing.
**Mrs N Macauley [2-24] J Teasdale.*

SHARP MOVE BHB 30f21a **RR 45f 21a** 4^{10}
6 ch m Night Shift (USA) 8.1f **(73)** - Judeah (Great Nephew) 9.9f **(64)**
Form - 00
Record 1998 - 1st:0 2nd:0 3rd:0 Ran:1
Pre1998 - 1st:0 2nd:0 3rd:0 Ran:10
1998 AW 0-1: (6f) (Equi)
Moderate mare.
**B A Pearce [0-3] S B Components (from Mrs J Cecil [0-5] Nov 1996).*

SHARP PEARL BHB 70f66a **RR 66df 66a** 5127^{12}
5 ch g Sharpo 7.5f **(68)** - Silent Pearl (USA) (Silent Screen (USA)) 8.6f **(65)**
Form - 030000
Record 1998 - 1st:0 2nd:0 3rd:1 Ran:6
Pre1998 - 1st:3 2nd:3 3rd:3 Ran:30
Win Prizemoney £9,944 *Total Prizemoney* £17,691

Wins							
1997	Aug Newmar	(G-F)	H	5f	77	79	<
1997	Apr Bright	(FRM)	H	5.3f	70	75	
1996	Jun Bright	(FRM)	H	5.3f	70	75	

1998 Turf 0-6: (5f 3, 6f, 7f 2) (g-s 2, gd 2, g-f, frm)
Average gelding, effective 5 to 6f, best at 5f, acts on gd to frm, best on gd, often wears blinkers (very effectively), likes Brighton. Turf high 80 (began Jly) - 3rd of 9 giving 7lb to Batchworth Belle (5 Spt Epsom 5f gd RF 4097).
**D J S Cosgrove [0-3] Dennis Yardy (from P R Webber [1-11] Spt 1998).*

SHARP PET BHB 31f **RR** 4401^{18}
3 b f Petong 7.6f **(58)** - Harmony Park (Music Boy) 6.8f **(57)**
Form - 0
Record 1998 - 1st:0 2nd:0 3rd:0 Ran:1
Pre1998 - 1st:0 2nd:0 3rd:0 Ran:3
1998 Turf 0-1: (6f) (frm)
Unfurnished, very poor filly, has worn blinkers.
**D McCain [0-4] A Spruce.*

SHARP PLAY BHB 105f **RR 109f** 3774^{3}
3 b c Robellino (USA) 9.5f **(68)** - Child's Play (USA) (Sharpen Up) 8.3f **(67)**
Form - 141163
Record 1998 - 1st:3 2nd:0 3rd:1 Ran:6
Pre1998 - 1st:1 2nd:1 3rd:0 Ran:4
Win Prizemoney £27,839 *Total Prizemoney* £38,814

Wins						
* **1998**	May Thirsk	(G-F)	8f		109	<
* **1998**	May Dielsd	(G-S)	8f		85	
* **1998**	Apr Ripon	(SFT)	9f		93	
.* 1997	Jly York	(GD)	7f		80+	

1998 Turf 3-6: (8f 2-4, 9f 1-1, 12f) (sft 1-1, g-s 1-2, g-f 1-2, frm)
Scopey, Pattern-class colt, effective 7 to 8f, best at 8f, acts on gd to frm, best on g-f, excels at York. Turf high 109 - 1st of 4 giving 9lb to Misbah (16 May Thirsk RF 1275). He was well placed to win three minor events and failed to stay a mile and a half in the Swiss Derby. A mile on fast ground could prove his optimum.
**M Johnston [4-10] Mrs I Bird.*

SHARP REBUFF BHB 89f85a **RR 90f 85a** 4804^{2}
7 b h Reprimand 8.2f **(63)** - Kukri (Kris) 9.5f **(73)**
Form - 40142
Record 1998 - 1st:1 2nd:1 3rd:0 Ran:5
Pre1998 - 1st:4 2nd:4 3rd:4 Ran:25
Win Prizemoney £21,511 *Total Prizemoney* £35,341

Wins							
* **1998**	Jun Sandow	(G-S)	H	7.1f	85	90	<
* 1997	Jun Warwic	(GD)	H	8f	79	83	
* 1996	Jly Kempto	(GD)	H	8f	74	81	
* 1995	Jun Warwic	(GD)	H	8f	69	73	
* 1994	Jly Ayr	(GD)	H	7f	59	64	

1998 Turf 1-5: (7f 1-2, 8f 3) (gd 1-4, frm)
Useful horse, effective 7 to 8f, best at 7f, acts on gd to frm, best on gd. Turf high 90 - 1st of 15 giving 10lb to Rakis (12 Jun Sandown RF 1936). Ran a fine fourth in the Lincoln on his reappearance but returned lame next time. Suited by the stiff seven when scoring at Sandown. **P J Makin [5-30] D M Ahier.*

SHARP RHYTHM (IRE) BHB 48f **RR 37f** 5012^{4}
2 b f Mujadil (USA) 7.7f **(70)** - Welsh Note (USA) (Sharpen Up) 8.3f **(67)**

Form - 8054
Record 1998 - 1st:0 2nd:0 3rd:0 Ran:4
1998 Turf 0-4: (5f 3, 6f) (hvy, g-s, gd 2)
Very moderate filly. Turf high 37. **M Johnston [0-4] Mrs I Bird.*

SHARP SARAH BHB 45f **RR 60df** 4321[16]

3 ch f Sabrehill (USA) 8.5f **(64)**-Sarah's Love (Caerleon (USA))8.6f **(71)**
Form - 0732000
Record 1998 - 1st:0 2nd:1 3rd:1 Ran:7
Win Prizemoney £0 *Total Prizemoney* £1,417
1998 Turf 0-7: (10f 3, 11f 2, 13f, 16f) (gd 3, g-f 3, frm)
Light-framed, average filly. Turf high 60.
**D Nicholls [0-3] J O'Connor (from B W Hills [0-4] Jun 1998).*

SHARP SHOOTER (IRE) BHB 43f **RR 48f** 3155[10]

3 b g Sabrehill (USA) 8.5f **(64)** - Kermesse (IRE) (Reference Point) 6.8f **(70)**
Form - 03250
Record 1998 - 1st:0 2nd:1 3rd:1 Ran:5
Pre1998 - 1st:0 2nd:0 3rd:0 Ran:5
Win Prizemoney £0 *Total Prizemoney* £1,024
1998 Turf 0-5: (8f, 10f, 12f 2, 13f) (gd, g-f 2, frm 2)
Scopey, moderate gelding, effective 10 to 12f, acts on g-f to frm, likes tight tracks. Turf high 48 - 3rd of 9 getting 10lb from Prophits Pride (28 May Ayr 10f g-f RF 1546).
**S E Kettlewell [0-4] Alan Thompson (from Mrs J R Ramsden [0-6] May 1998).*

SHARP SHUFFLE (IRE) BHB 62f70a **RR 71+f 70a** 4955[2]

5 ch g Exactly Sharp (USA) 8.4f **(66)** - Style (Homing) 7.8f **(59)**
Form - 55502372113802
Record 1998 - 1st:2 2nd:3 3rd:2 Ran:13
Pre1998 - 1st:3 2nd:6 3rd:5 Ran:28
Win Prizemoney £20,233 *Total Prizemoney* £37,279
Wins * **1998** Aug Newmar (G-F) C 7f 71+
* **1998** Jly Newmar (G-F) S 8f 61
* 1997 Jun Goodwo (G-F) H 8f 75 78+ <
* 1997 Apr Bright (FRM) 8f 74
* 1996 Spt Kempto (GD) H 7f 68 74
1998 Turf 2-13: (7f 1-3, 8f 1-9, 10f) (g-s 2, gd 4, g-f, frm 1-5, hrd 1-1)
Above-average gelding, effective 8 to 9f, best at 8f, acts on gd to frm, likes right handed tracks, excels at Goodwood, does well at Newmarket. Turf high 71. Had to drop into a seller to get off the mark for the year, but followed up in a claimer. Usually held up, he has a turn of foot and is suited by a strongly-run race.
**R Hannon [5-41] Mrs H F Prendergast.*

SHARP SPICE **RR 63f** 4882[5]

2 b f Lugana Beach 7f **(63)** - Ewar Empress (IRE) **(11f 35a)** (Persian Bold) 9.3f **(66)**
Form - 85
Record 1998 - 1st:0 2nd:0 3rd:0 Ran:2
1998 Turf 0-2: (6f 2) (g-s, gd)
Currently average filly. Turf high 63 (began Spt).
**Lord Huntingdon [0-2] The Nags Head Racing Syndicate.*

SHARP STEEL BHB 55f **RR 45f** 493[5]

3 ch g Beveled (USA) 6.9f **(64)** - Shift Over (USA) (Night Shift (USA)) 7.2f **(69)**
Form - 2515
Record 1998 - 1st:1 2nd:1 3rd:0 Ran:4
Pre1998 - 1st:0 2nd:0 3rd:0 Ran:3
Win Prizemoney £1,922 *Total Prizemoney* £2,699
Wins 1998 *Mar Southw (STD) S 7f 61* <
1998 AW 1-4: (7f 1-3, 8f) (Equi 2, Fibr 1-2)
Leggy, average gelding, effective 7f, - acts on Fibr. AW high 61 - 1st of 15 giving 5lb to Stately Favour (20 Mar Southwell RF 0454).
**Miss S J Wilton [0-1] John Pointon and Sons (from G L Moore [1-6] Mar 1998).*

SHARP STOCK BHB 60f **RR 56f** 3208[18]

5 b g Tina's Pet 7.4f **(56)** - Mrewa (Runnymede) 9.3f **(50)**
Form - 0816180
Record 1998 - 1st:2 2nd:0 3rd:0 Ran:7
Pre1998 - 1st:0 2nd:1 3rd:1 Ran:15
Win Prizemoney £10,780 *Total Prizemoney* £12,631
Wins * **1998** Jun Salisb (G-S) H 5f 50 56 <
* **1998** May Goodwo (G-F) H 5f 44 46
1998 Turf 2-7: (5f 2-6, 6f) (g-s 2, gd 1-4, g-f 1-1)
Fair gelding, effective 5f, acts on gd to frm, best on gd, has worn blinkers. Turf high 56 - 1st of 13 getting 5lb from Kram (10 Jun Salisbury RF 1885).
**R J Hodges [2-18] Mrs M Fairbairn (from B J Meehan [0-4] May 1996).*

SHART (IRE) BHB 80f **RR 85f** 4113[6]

3 b c Last Tycoon 9.4f **(73)** - Simaat (USA) (Mr Prospector (USA)) 8.8f **(78)**
Form - 26
Record 1998 - 1st:0 2nd:1 3rd:0 Ran:2
Pre1998 - 1st:0 2nd:1 3rd:2 Ran:3
Win Prizemoney £0 *Total Prizemoney* £3,811
1998 Turf 0-2: (6f, 7f) (g-f, frm)
Well made, useful colt, has worn blinkers. Turf high 79 (began Aug). He has shown ability in maidens.
**J H M Gosden [0-5] Hamdan Al Maktoum.*

SHARWAY LADY BHB 48f51a **RR 44f 51a** 842[9]

3 b f Shareef Dancer (USA) 10.1f **(67)** - Eladale (IRE) (Ela-Mana-Mou) 10.1f **(70)**
Form - 000162870660
Record 1998 - 1st:1 2nd:1 3rd:0 Ran:9
Pre1998 - 1st:0 2nd:0 3rd:0 Ran:3
Win Prizemoney £1,738 *Total Prizemoney* £2,421
Wins * **1998** *Jan Southw (STD) S 8f 60* <
1998 Turf 0-2:(9f, 10f)(sft, gd) 1998 AW1-7:(8f 1-3, 9f 2, 12f 2)(Fibr 1-7)
Average filly, effective 8f, - acts on Fibr, mostly wears blinkers (very effectively), favours left handed tracks, favours tight tracks. Turf high 44. AW high 60 - 2nd of 12 getting 1lb from Sharp Monkey (26 Jan Southwell 8f Fibr RF 0160) - also 1st of 11 from Mary Lou (5 Jan Southwell RF 0028).
**B A McMahon [1-12] Sharway Contracts.*

SHASKA BHB 88f **RR 89f** 5066[6]

4 ch f Kris 10f **(75)** - Dance Machine (Green Dancer (USA)) 10.3f **(74)**
Form - 303106
Record 1998 - 1st:1 2nd:0 3rd:2 Ran:6
Pre1998 - 1st:1 2nd:1 3rd:0 Ran:3
Win Prizemoney £7,988 *Total Prizemoney* £14,565
Wins * **1998** Spt Doncas (GD) 10.3f 89 <
* 1997 Aug Sandow (G-S) 10f 72
1998 Turf 1-6: (10f 1-5, 13f) (gd 1-4, g-f 2)
Workmanlike, useful filly, effective 10f, acts on gd, has worn blinkers. Turf high 89 - 1st of 10 giving 5lb to Rajaiyma (9 Spt Doncaster RF 4188). Closely-related to the top-class Halling, she ran a very eye-catching third on her reappearance but never got into it in a hotly-contested handicap next time. Failed to stay when stepped up three furlongs plus to a mile and five at Newbury but landed a decent minor event over shorter over shorter.
**J H M Gosden [2-9] Sheikh Mohammed.*

SHAVELING **RR 73f** 2184[4]

3 ch c Sharpo 7.5f **(68)** - Sancta (So Blessed) 8.7f **(67)**
Form - 4
Record 1998 - 1st:0 2nd:0 3rd:0 Ran:1
Pre1998 - 1st:0 2nd:0 3rd:0 Ran:1
Win Prizemoney £0 *Total Prizemoney* £272
1998 Turf 0-1: (8f) (g-f)
Scopey, currently above-average colt. Closely related to the useful Carmelite House, he shaped with promise on his return, but was not seen again. **Mrs J Cecil [0-2] Lord Howard de Walden.*

SHAWDON BHB 99f **RR 102f** 3416a[1]

3 b c Inchinor 8.9f **(64)** - Play With Me (IRE) (Alzao (USA)) 7.1f **(68)**
Form - 1
1998 Turf 1-1: (7f 1-1) (sft 1-1)
Neat, very useful colt, effective 5 to 7f, acts on sft to frm, excels at Yarmouth. (1st run) - 1st of 13 getting 8lb from Sharp Matt (30 Jly Ovrevoll RF 3416a). Formerly trained by Sir Mark Prescott, he has done well in Scandinavia, winning a Listed race during July.
**M Kahn in SWE [1-1] Stall Lambada & Stall Gransaeter (from Sir Mark Prescott [4-10] Oct 1997).*

SHAYA BHB 104f **RR 109f** 3634[5]

4 ch c Nashwan (USA) 10.3f **(79)** - Gharam (USA) (Green Dancer

(USA)) 10.3f **(74)**
Form - 5
Record 1998 - 1st:0 2nd:0 3rd:0 Ran:1
Pre1998 - 1st:1 2nd:4 3rd:0 Ran:7
Win Prizemoney £3,533 *Total Prizemoney* £12,518
Wins 1997 Aug Sandow (GD) 10f 76 <
1998 Turf 0-1: (11f) (g-f)
Lengthy, Pattern-class colt, effective 12f, acts on frm. A creditable seventh in the Leger in '97, he was well held on his belated come-back.
**M P Tregoning [0-1] Hamdan Al Maktoum (from Major W R Hern [1-7] Oct 1997).*

SHAYLAN (IRE) RR 72f 4803[2]
2 br c Primo Dominie 7.2f **(67)** - Shayraz (Darshaan) 9.9f **(84)**
Form - 2
Record 1998 - 1st:0 2nd:1 3rd:0 Ran:1
Win Prizemoney £0 *Total Prizemoney* £935
1998 Turf 0-1: (7f) (sft)
Currently above-average colt.
**Sir Michael Stoute [0-1] H H Aga Khan.*

SHE BAT RR 104f 4833a[5]
4 f
Form - 5
1998 Turf 0-1: (8f) (g-s)
Currently very useful filly. **V Caruso in ITY [1-3].*

SHECANDO (IRE) BHB 30f **RR 35f** 2820[12]
3 ch f Second Set (IRE) 9.2f **(67)** - Carado (Manado) 9.6f **(63)**
Form - 0050
Record 1998 - 1st:0 2nd:0 3rd:0 Ran:4
Pre1998 - 1st:0 2nd:0 3rd:0 Ran:5
1998 Turf 0-4: (7f, 8f, 10f, 12f) (gd, g-f, frm 2)
Leggy, very moderate filly, has worn blinkers. Turf high 35.
**E L James [0-4] Nicholas Cowan (from C James [0-5] Spt 1997).*

Pre1998 - 1st:0 2nd:0 3rd:0 Ran:7
Win Prizemoney £0 *Total Prizemoney* £778
1998 AW 0-5: (8f, 11f 2, 12f 2) (Fibr 5)
Average filly. AW high 36.
**J Parkes [0-6] J Parkes (from N Meade in IRE [0-6] Oct 1997).*

SHEER DANZIG (IRE) BHB 111f **RR 110f** 5153a[12]
6 b h Roi Danzig (USA) 10.5f **(62)** - Sheer Audacity (Troy) 10.4f **(68)**
Form - 07120
Record 1998 - 1st:1 2nd:1 3rd:0 Ran:5
Pre1998 - 1st:5 2nd:4 3rd:4 Ran:25
Win Prizemoney £90,373 *Total Prizemoney* £152,442

Wins									
	*** 1998**	Jly	York	(FRM)	LH	13.9f	103	106	<
	* 1997	Mar	Doncas	(G-F)		12f		102+	
	* 1996	Jly	Sandow	(G-F)	H	10f	85	94	
	* 1995	Oct	York	(GD)	H	10.4f	80	87	
	* 1995	Jly	Newmar	(GD)	H	8f	71	76	
	* 1995	*Mar*	*Southw*	*(STD)*		*8f*		*67*	

1998 Turf 1-5: (10f 2, 14f 1-2, 16f) (gd 3, frm 1-2)
Group-class horse, effective 10 to 14f, best at 14f, acts on gd to frm, best on frm, likes left handed tracks. Turf high 110 - 2nd of 21 giving 16lb to Tuning (19 Aug York 14f frm RF 3754) - also 1st of 8 giving 7lb to Dream of Nurmi (11 Jly York RF 2737). Lightly raced in 1998, he won a Listed race at York in July and went back there to finish second under a welter-weight in the Tote Ebor. That was a career best effort and he was immediately put to one side and trained for the Foster's Melbourne Cup. Unfortunately the trip 'down under' proved something of a disappointment as, according to his Australian rider, he felt jarred up in the last 300 metres before weakening into twelfth place. All being well, this old soldier will be back in winning form next term. **R W Armstrong [6-30].*

SHEER FACE BHB 72f70a **RR 76f 70a** 4822[25]
4 b c Midyan (USA) 9.9f **(64)** - Rock Face (Ballad Rock) 7.8f **(63)**
Form - 00105072000
Record 1998 - 1st:1 2nd:1 3rd:0 Ran:11

Sheer Danzig winning at York

SHEEFIN (IRE) BHB 41f34a **RR 66f 34a** 419[4]
4 b f Danehill (USA) 9.1f **(79)** - Starlust (Sallust) 8.4f **(63)**
Form - 043544
Record 1998 - 1st:0 2nd:0 3rd:1 Ran:5

Pre1998 - 1st:2 2nd:3 3rd:3 Ran:19
Win Prizemoney £14,636 *Total Prizemoney* £25,641

Wins									
	*** 1998**	Jun	Goodwo	(G-F)	H	8f	69	74	
	* 1996	Spt	Bath	(G-F)	H	8f	86	90	<

* 1996 Aug Bright (FRM) 7f 81+
1998 Turf 1-10: (7f, 8f 1-8, 9f) (gd 5, g-f 1-2, frm 2, hrd) 1998 AW 0-1: (9f) (Fibr)
Strong, above-average colt, effective 7 to 10f, best at 8f, acts on g-s to frm, has worn blinkers, likes left handed tracks, excels at Doncaster. Turf high 76 - 2nd of 20 getting 7lb from Salty Jack (10 Spt Doncaster 7f gd RF 4209). Becoming disappointing. Recorded his first victory since September 1996 when scoring at Goodwood in June. Held subsequently, but was just touched off at Doncaster in September. **W R Muir [3-30] A J de V Patrick.*

SHEER HARMONY (USA) RR 54f 4059[9]
2 b br f Woodman (USA) 9.7f **(77)** - Memories Of Pam (USA) (Graustark) 10.1f **(70)**
Form - 0
Record 1998 - 1st:0 2nd:0 3rd:0 Ran:1
1998 Turf 0-1: (7f) (g-f)
Currently fair filly. **Sir Michael Stoute [0-1] Lordship Stud.*

SHEER NATIVE BHB 76f RR 78f 4389[5]
2 b f In The Wings 11.2f **(77)** - Native Magic (Be My Native (USA)) 10.2f **(71)**
Form - 7005
Record 1998 - 1st:0 2nd:0 3rd:0 Ran:4
1998 Turf 0-4: (7f 4) (gd 2, frm 2)
Above-average filly. Turf high 78. **B W Hills [0-4] R J Arculli.*

SHEER VIKING (IRE) BHB 100f RR 105f 4593[7]
2 b c Danehill (USA) 9.1f **(79)** - Schlefalora (Mas Media)
Form - 1324617
Record 1998 - 1st:2 2nd:1 3rd:1 Ran:7
Win Prizemoney £34,133 *Total Prizemoney* £49,036
Wins * **1998** Spt Doncas (GD) G2 5f 105 <
* **1998** May Newmar (G-S) 5f 90+
1998 Turf 2-7: (5f 2-3, 6f 4) (g-s, gd 1-3, g-f 1-1, frm 2)
Pattern-class colt, effective 5f, acts on g-f. Turf high 105 - 1st of 13 from Borromini (12 Spt Doncaster RF 4242). He kept the best company after a winning debut, and gained just reward for some solid efforts when winning the Group Two Flying Childers Stakes. Possibly over the top when a hard-pulling last of seven in the Middle Park Stakes on his final start, he may be best over the minimum trip and is just the sort to run well in the Palace House Stakes at Newmarket next spring. **B W Hills [2-7] R J Arculli.*

SHEER WARNING (IRE) BHB 53f RR 60df 4875[9]
4 b g Warning 8.1f **(77)** - Native Magic (Be My Native (USA)) 10.2f **(71)**
Form - 7880
Record 1998 - 1st:0 2nd:0 3rd:0 Ran:4
1998 Turf 0-3: (7f, 8f 2) (frm 3) 1998 AW 0-1: (12f) (Fibr)
Average gelding. Turf high 60. **R W Armstrong [0-4] R J Arculli.*

SHEILA-B RR 57f 492[10]
3 ch f Formidable (USA) 7.8f **(60)** - Good Woman (Good Times (ITY)) 6.6f **(54)**
Form - 0
Record 1998 - 1st:0 2nd:0 3rd:0 Ran:1
Pre1998 - 1st:0 2nd:0 3rd:0 Ran:1
1998 Turf 0-1: (5f) (g-s)
Currently fair filly.
**B R Millman [0-1] D L C Hodges (from P J Makin [0-1] Oct 1997).*

SHELLEY BHB 35f RR 13f 4967[15]
2 b c Nomination 7.3f **(57)** - Kimble Princess (Kala Shikari) 8.4f **(54)**
Form - 000
Record 1998 - 1st:0 2nd:0 3rd:0 Ran:3
1998 Turf 0-3: (6f 3) (sft, g-f, frm)
Currently poor colt. Turf high 13 (began Aug).
**G M McCourt [0-3] Mrs Dulcie Newman.*

SHELTERED COVE (IRE) BHB 34f39a RR 34f 39a 5002[4]
7 ch g Bold Arrangement 8.7f **(57)** - Racing Home (FR) (Dom Racine (FR)) 9.2f **(62)**
Form - 57667214
Record 1998 - 1st:1 2nd:1 3rd:0 Ran:8
Pre1998 - 1st:2 2nd:4 3rd:1 Ran:22
Win Prizemoney £8,021 *Total Prizemoney* £13,668
Wins * **1998** Spt Salisb (HVY) CH 14.1f 30 34
* *1995 Feb Lingfi (STD) H 16f 50 55 <*
* 1994 Aug Bath (G-F) H 17.2f 51 49
1998 Turf 1-4: (12f, 14f 1-2, 17f) (gd 1-2, frm, hrd) 1998 AW 0-4: (12f, 16f 3) (Equi 3, Fibr)
Moderate gelding, effective 16f, - acts on Equi, has worn blinkers. Turf high 34. AW high 45 (1st run) - 5th of 14 getting 2lb from Monaco Gold (23 May Lingfield 16f Equi RF 1430).
**K O Cunningham-Brown [3-24] A J Richards (from C E Brittain [0-8] Jun 1994).*

SHELTERING SKY (IRE) BHB 98f RR 100f 4844[10]
4 b c Selkirk (USA) 7.9f **(76)** - Shimmering Sea (Slip Anchor) 9.8f **(73)**
Form - 512500
Record 1998 - 1st:1 2nd:1 3rd:0 Ran:6
Pre1998 - 1st:1 2nd:1 3rd:1 Ran:5
Win Prizemoney £29,665 *Total Prizemoney* £38,862
Wins * **1998** May Newmar (G-S) H 6f 86 90 <
* 1997 Jly Haydoc (G-S) 7.1f 84
1998 Turf 1-6: (6f 1-4, 7f 2) (sft, gd 1-3, g-f, frm)
Scopey, very useful colt, effective 6f, acts on gd. Turf high 100 - 5th of 29 getting 1lb from Selhurstpark Flyer (19 Jun Ascot 6f gd RF 2107). He produced a scintillating performance to win a handicap at Newmarket in May and, with any sort of luck in running, would have followed up at York later that month. Disappointed after but he is talented and capable of winning a Listed contest.
**J L Dunlop [2-11] Victor Behrens (Susa Racing).*

SHENCK RR 90f 1733a[2]
3 b f Zafonic (USA) 9f **(83)** -Buckwig (USA) (Buckfinder (USA)) 8.1f **(71)**
Form - 2
1998 Turf 0-1: (6f) (g-f)
Currently useful filly. (1st run) - 2nd of 9 to Chiquita Linda (31 May Capannelle 6f g-f RF 1733a). **B Grizzetti in ITY [0-1].*

SHERATON GIRL BHB 33f28a RR 16f 28a 1154[16]
4 b f Mon Tresor 7.9f **(60)** - Sara Sprint (Formidable (USA)) 9.2f **(63)**
Form - 7000
Record 1998 - 1st:0 2nd:0 3rd:0 Ran:4
Pre1998 - 1st:1 2nd:0 3rd:1 Ran:16
Win Prizemoney £2,277 *Total Prizemoney* £2,630
Wins * 1997 *Apr Southw (STD) H 7f 38 42 <*
1998 AW 0-4: (6f, 7f, 8f 2) (Equi, Fibr 3)
Scopey, poor filly, effective 7f, - acts on Fibr, has worn blinkers, likes left handed tracks, favours tight tracks. AW high 7.
**N P Littmoden [1-11] Happy Times Ahead Partnership (from M Johnston [0-9] Spt 1996).*

SHERBET FIZZ (IRE) RR 30f 3150[5]
2 b f Petardia 8.2f **(58)** - Skiddaw (USA) (Grey Dawn II) 11.1f **(72)**
Form - 05
Record 1998 - 1st:0 2nd:0 3rd:0 Ran:2
1998 Turf 0-2: (6f, 7f) (g-f, frm)
Currently very moderate filly. Turf high 30 (began Jly).
**N Tinkler [0-2] Elite Racing Club.*

SHERGANZAR BHB 75f RR 75f 2553[4]
3 b g Shernazar 11.8f **(71)** - Victory Kingdom (CAN) (Viceregal (CAN)) 6.8f **(64)**
Form - 5762254
Record 1998 - 1st:0 2nd:2 3rd:0 Ran:7
Pre1998 - 1st:0 2nd:0 3rd:1 Ran:5
Win Prizemoney £0 *Total Prizemoney* £2,732
1998 Turf 0-7: (8f, 9f, 11f 2, 12f 3) (g-s, gd 4, g-f, frm)
Scopey, above-average gelding, effective 8 to 12f, acts on g-s to g-f, best on gd, excels at Sandown. Turf high 76 - 6th of 8 getting 4lb from Generosity (26 May Sandown 11f gd RF 1482). Consistent. Has shown plenty of ability in fair maiden and handicap company and should win a race or two, possibly over ten furlongs, although he has become rather frustrating. Now hurdling with oliver Sherwood.
**R Hannon [0-7] Antony Sofroniou (from M Salaman [0-5] Nov 1997).*

SHERIFF BHB 55f75a RR 51f 75a 2729[4]
7 b g Midyan (USA) 9.9f **(64)** - Daisy Warwick (USA) (Ribot) 15.4f **(65)**
Form - 1114
Record 1998 - 1st:3 2nd:0 3rd:0 Ran:4
Pre1998 - 1st:2 2nd:3 3rd:3 Ran:23

Win Prizemoney £13,508 *Total Prizemoney* £18,535
Wins ** **1998** Feb Lingfi (SLW) H 16f 70 76 <*
** **1998** Feb Lingfi (SLW) H 16f 60 75+*
** **1998** Jan Lingfi (STD) H 16f 53 59*
** 1996 Feb Lingfi (STD) H 16f 52 56+*
1998 Turf 0-1: (15f) (frm) 1998 AW 3-3: (16f 3-3) (Equi 3-3)
Above-average gelding, effective 16f, - acts on Equi, has worn blinkers. AW high 76 - 1st of 6 giving 15lb to Coleridge (21 Feb Lingfield RF 0329) - also 1st of 8 giving 11lb to Broughtons Formula (10 Feb Lingfield RF 0262). He was in brilliant form on the Lingfield Equitrack at the start of '98, completing a hat-trick over two miles. There is no reason why the sequence should have ended. **J W Hills [10-46] Terry Milson.*

SHE'S A CRACKER BHB 49f32a **RR 53f 32a** 24P
4 b f Deploy 11.4f **(67)** - Red Secret (IRE) (Valiyar) 8.5f **(73)**
Form - 06P
Record 1998 - 1st:0 2nd:0 3rd:0 Ran:1
Pre1998 - 1st:0 2nd:0 3rd:0 Ran:6
Win Prizemoney £0 *Total Prizemoney* £170
1998 AW 0-1: (11f) (Fibr)
Fair filly, has worn blinkers.
**Mrs N Macauley [0-6] Maurice Kirby (from C A Dwyer [0-1] Spt 1996).*

SHE'S A GEM BHB 46f62a **RR 45f 62a** 4385[8]
3 b f Robellino (USA) 9.5f **(68)** -Rose Gem (IRE) (Taufan (USA)) 7f **(57)**
Form - 5311613607304768
Record 1998 - 1st:3 2nd:0 3rd:2 Ran:14
Pre1998 - 1st:0 2nd:0 3rd:1 Ran:3
Win Prizemoney £6,788 *Total Prizemoney* £8,146
Wins ** **1998** Mar Southw (STD) H 7f 64 68 <*
** **1998** Jan Wolver (STD) H 7f 58 63*
** **1998** Jan Southw (STD) S 7f 52*
1998 Turf 0-5: (5f, 6f 2, 7f 2) (gd 4, frm) 1998 AW 3-9: (6f 2, 7f 3-7) (Equi, Fibr 3-8)
Light-framed, average filly, effective 7f, - acts on Fibr, prefers left handed tracks, prefers tight tracks. Turf high 45. AW high 68 - 3rd of 6 getting 13lb from Darwell's Folly (21 Mar Wolverhampton 7f Fibr RF 0459) - also 1st of 9 giving 7lb to Kustom Kit Kate (11 Mar Southwell RF 0424). **Mrs N Macauley [3-17] Maurice Kirby.*

SHE-WOLFF (IRE) BHB 97f **RR 84f** 2389[2]
2 b f Pips Pride 6.7f **(70)** - Royal Wolff(Prince Tenderfoot (USA)) 9f **(61)**
Form - 152
Record 1998 - 1st:1 2nd:1 3rd:0 Ran:3
Win Prizemoney £3,273 *Total Prizemoney* £4,969
Wins * **1998** May Bath (G-F) 5.7f 80+ <
1998 Turf 1-3: (5f, 6f 1-2) (gd, frm 1-2)
Currently decent filly. Turf high 84 - 2nd of 8 to Gipsy Rose Lee (29 Jun Windsor 6f frm RF 2389) - also 1st of 14 from Little Gem (29 May Bath RF 1566). Considering she had previously won a Bath maiden over a slightly longer trip on her debut, she ran a blinder to finish fifth in the Queen Mary, and was beaten by a very useful sort next time. She looks sure to win more races.
**P J Makin [1-3] P E Cooper.*

SHFOUG (USA) BHB 102f **RR 104f** 5066[1]
3 b f Sheikh Albadou 9.2f **(75)** - Pure Misk (Rainbow Quest (USA)) 10.4f **(75)**
Form - 4334241121
Record 1998 - 1st:3 2nd:2 3rd:2 Ran:10
Pre1998 - 1st:1 2nd:0 3rd:1 Ran:2
Win Prizemoney £30,662 *Total Prizemoney* £42,953
Wins * **1998** Oct Newmar (G-S) L 10f 104 <
* **1998** Oct Newmar (GD) H 10f 81 96+
* **1998** Spt Haydoc (G-F) H 10.5f 81 82+
* 1997 Oct Catter (SFT) 7f 77
1998 Turf 3-10:(7f 2, 8f, 9f, 10f 2-4,11f 1-1, 12f)(gd 1-3, g-f 1-4, frm 1-3)
Scopey, very useful filly, effective 10f, acts on gd to frm. Turf high 104 - 1st of 6 getting 10lb from Silence Reigns (30 Oct Newmarket RF 5066) - also 1st of 14 giving 3lb to Sharera (2 Oct Newmarket RF 4619). Ran some good races in 1998, and finished the season off with a game win in a Listed race at Newmarket in October. Now the key has been found to her, further success should come her way. **B W Hills [4-12] Hilal Salem.*

SHIELD-DIAGNOSTIC (IRE) **RR 59f** 1286[8]
2 b c Distinctly North (USA) 7.4f **(63)** - Steel Tap (IRE) (Flash of Steel) 7.2f **(53)**
Form - 708
Record 1998 - 1st:0 2nd:0 3rd:0 Ran:3
1998 Turf 0-3: (5f 2, 6f) (g-s, frm 2)
Fair colt. Turf high 59. (DEAD) **J M Bradley [0-3] Steve Evans.*

SHIFTALONG (IRE) BHB 35f **RR 35f** 3475[14]
2 b f Then Again 7.4f **(52)** - Reshift (Night Shift (USA)) 7.2f **(69)**
Form - 08000
Record 1998 - 1st:0 2nd:0 3rd:0 Ran:5
1998 Turf 0-5: (5f 2, 6f 2, 7f) (gd 3, g-f, frm)
Very moderate filly. Turf high 35. **M Brittain [0-5] Northgate Lodgers.*

SHIFTING BHB 47f50a **RR 29f 50a** 4760[15]
3 ch f Night Shift (USA) 8.1f **(73)** - Preening (Persian Bold) 9.3f **(66)**
Form - 036000
Record 1998 - 1st:0 2nd:0 3rd:1 Ran:5
Pre1998 - 1st:0 2nd:0 3rd:1 Ran:4
Win Prizemoney £0 *Total Prizemoney* £1,022
1998 Turf 0-3: (8f 2, 12f) (gd 2, g-f) 1998 AW 0-2: (8f, 11f) (Fibr 2)
Scopey, fair filly. Turf high 29 (began Aug). AW high 51. Becoming disappointing. **C W Thornton [0-9] Guy Reed and Mrs Ailsa Daniels.*

SHIFTING TIME BHB 57f43a **RR 60f 43a** 3200[4]
4 b f Night Shift (USA) 8.1f **(73)** - Timely Raise (USA) (Raise A Man (USA)) 7.8f **(78)**
Form - 841554
Record 1998 - 1st:1 2nd:0 3rd:0 Ran:6
Pre1998 - 1st:0 2nd:1 3rd:0 Ran:8
Win Prizemoney £3,288 *Total Prizemoney* £5,682
Wins * **1998** Jun Leices (SFT) H 6f 51 60 <
1998 Turf 1-3: (6f 1-2, 7f) (gd 1-1, g-f, frm) 1998 AW 0-3: (5f, 6f, 7f) (Fibr 3)
Scopey, average filly, effective 6 to 7f, acts on gd to g-f. Turf high 60 (1st run) - 1st of 8 giving 3lb to Phoenix Princess (13 Jun Leicester RF 1964). AW high 44.
**Lord Huntingdon [1-6] Tim Corby (from I A Balding [0-8] Jly 1997).*

SHII-TAKE BHB 92f **RR 94df** 3610P
4 b c Deploy 11.4f **(67)** - Super Sally (Superlative) 7.2f **(56)**
Form - 400P
Record 1998 - 1st:0 2nd:0 3rd:0 Ran:4
Pre1998 - 1st:1 2nd:2 3rd:2 Ran:8
Win Prizemoney £3,127 *Total Prizemoney* £11,886
Wins 1996 Spt Epsom (G-F) 7f 92+ <
1998 Turf 0-4: (10f 2, 12f 2) (gd, g-f 2, frm)
Scopey, useful colt, effective 8 to 10f, acted on gd to g-f. Turf high 94. He was far from disgraced in very useful company in '97. Not seen out again until fourth in a Listed race in May for his new trainer, but pulled up lame on his final start. (DEAD)
**Mrs A J Perrett [0-4] Clive Batt (from R Akehurst [1-8] Jun 1997).*

SHIKARI'S SON BHB 73f **RR 76?f** 1428[10]
11 br g Kala Shikari 6f **(48)** - Have Form (Haveroid) 6f **(48)**
Form - 0
Record 1998 - 1st:0 2nd:0 3rd:0 Ran:1
Pre1998 - 1st:12 2nd:9 3rd:3 Ran:73
Win Prizemoney £88,444 *Total Prizemoney* £107,053
Wins 1995 Jly Goodwo (G-F) H 6f 88 97 <
1995 Apr Bright (GD) C 6f 67
1994 Aug Bright (G-F) H 5.3f 84 82
1994 Jun Epsom (G-F) H 6f 79 73
1994 Jun Bright (FRM) H 8f 76 76
1998 Turf 0-1: (6f) (gd)
Above-average gelding. Consistent. He is without a win since the 1995 Stewards' Cup, and was off the track for almost two years. His best chance of further victories could be at Brighton, where he has won nine times.
**J Cullinan [0-10] Alan Spargo Ltd Toolmakers (from J White [10-55] Spt 1995).*

SHILLING (IRE) BHB 57f52a **RR 60df 52a** 781[9]
4 b f Bob Back (USA) 11.5f **(71)** - Quiche (Formidable (USA)) 9.2f **(63)**
Form - 30
Record 1998 - 1st:0 2nd:0 3rd:1 Ran:2
Pre1998 - 1st:0 2nd:1 3rd:1 Ran:7
Win Prizemoney £0 *Total Prizemoney* £1,969
1998 Turf 0-2: (14f, 15f) (sft, g-s)

Workmanlike, average filly, effective 12 to 14f, best at 12f, acts on g-s to frm, likes left handed tracks. Turf high 60 (1st run) - 3rd of 14 giving 1lb to Alpine Panther (31 Mar Nottingham 14f g-s RF 0521). Consistent.
**Miss H C Knight [0-6] MillionMind Partnership (7) (from A C Stewart [0-7] Oct 1997).*

SHIMAAL BHB 95f RR 91f 4724a[11]

3 b f Sadler's Wells (USA) 11.3f **(87)** - Grace Note (FR) (Top Ville) 11.7f **(68)**
Form - 4210
Record 1998 - 1st:1 2nd:1 3rd:0 Ran:4
Pre1998 - 1st:0 2nd:1 3rd:0 Ran:2
Win Prizemoney £3,727 *Total Prizemoney* £7,080
Wins * 1998 Jly Windso (GD) 8.3f 79+ <
1998 Turf 1-4: (8f 1-1, 10f, 11f, 12f) (sft, gd, g-f 1-2)
Leggy, useful filly, effective 7 to 12f, acts on gd to frm. Turf high 91 (1st run) - 4th of 6 to Bristol Channel (9 May Lingfield 11f g-f RF 1124). Closely related to King George winner Belmez, she got the all-important win under her belt but was not up to listed class.
**S bin Suroor [1-6] Godolphin.*

SHINDIUM BHB 40f RR 35f 1521[11]

3 b f Presidium 7.5f **(56)**-Shining Wood(Touching Wood (USA))8.2f **(55)**
Form - 00
Record 1998 - 1st:0 2nd:0 3rd:0 Ran:2
Pre1998 - 1st:0 2nd:0 3rd:0 Ran:2
1998 Turf 0-2: (6f, 7f) (g-s, gd)
Scopey, very moderate filly, has worn blinkers. Turf high 3.
**C A Dwyer [0-4] Mrs Shelley Dwyer.*

SHINEROLLA BHB 72f83a RR 72f 83a 4241[2]

6 b g Thatching 7.8f **(69)** - Primrolla (Relko) 9.9f **(59)**
Form - 702
Record 1998 - 1st:0 2nd:1 3rd:0 Ran:3
Pre1998 - 1st:3 2nd:5 3rd:3 Ran:26
Win Prizemoney £12,841 *Total Prizemoney* £39,904
Wins 1995 Oct Pontef (G-F) H 8f 75 79 <
1995 May Pontef (GD) H 8f 66 65+
1995 May Pontef (FRM) 8f 63
1998 Turf 0-3: (7f, 8f, 10f) (g-f, frm, hrd)
Decent gelding, effective 8f, acts on frm - acts on Fibr, has worn blinkers. Turf high 71 (began Aug). Ran well in competitive handicaps at Doncaster and Newmarket in the autumn.
**C Parker [1-18] & Mrs Raymond Anderson Green (from Mrs J R Ramsden [3-16] Oct 1995).*

SHINING CLOUD BHB 44f RR 48f 5069[7]

5 ch m Indian Ridge 7.6f **(74)**-Hardiheroine (Sandhurst Prince) 7.9f **(63)**
Form - 7020248007
Record 1998 - 1st:0 2nd:2 3rd:0 Ran:10
Pre1998 - 1st:1 2nd:1 3rd:3 Ran:13
Win Prizemoney £3,594 *Total Prizemoney* £8,300
Wins * 1996 Spt Nottin (G-F) 6.1f 65 <
1998 Turf 0-10: (5f, 6f, 7f, 8f 5, 9f, 12f) (gd 2, g-f 5, frm 3)
Moderate filly, effective 6 to 8f, acts on g-f, has worn blinkers. Turf high 55 - 2nd of 16 getting 1lb from Sis Garden (1 Aug Lingfield 8f g-f RF 3267).
**M Bell [1-19] Mrs Anne Yearley (from L G Cottrell [0-4] Aug 1996).*

SHINING DANCER BHB 55f53a RR 55f 53a 4737[8]

6 b m Rainbow Quest (USA) 11.2f **(81)** - Strike Home (Be My Guest (USA)) 9.3f **(67)**
Form - 68085503128
Record 1998 - 1st:1 2nd:1 3rd:1 Ran:11
Pre1998 - 1st:2 2nd:1 3rd:5 Ran:26
Win Prizemoney £13,080 *Total Prizemoney* £19,441
Wins * 1998 Spt Sandow (GD) H 14f 47 51
* 1997 May Kempto (GD) H 16f 60 64 <
* 1996 Jun Windso (G-F) H 10f 55 60
1998 Turf 1-11: (12f, 14f 1-4, 15f 2, 16f 4) (g-s, gd 4, g-f 1-5, frm)
Fair mare, effective 14 to 20f, best at 20f, acts on gd to g-f, best on g-f, prefers right handed tracks, and excels at Kempton. Turf high 55. She showed a good turn of foot for a stayer when scoring at Kempton in 1997, but has become rather disappointing since then. Tends to pull.
**S Dow [3-35] The Lalemaha Partnership (from Sir Michael Stoute [0-3] Jly 1995).*

SHINING DESERT (IRE) BHB 83f RR 86df 4067[6]

2 b f Green Desert (USA) 7.8f **(78)** - Riyoom (USA) (Vaguely Noble) 10.1f **(72)**
Form - 10356
Record 1998 - 1st:1 2nd:0 3rd:1 Ran:5
Win Prizemoney £3,533 *Total Prizemoney* £4,310
Wins 1998 Jun Haydoc (GD) 5f 85++ <
1998 Turf 1-5: (5f 1-2, 6f 3) (gd 3, g-f, frm 1-1)
Useful filly. Turf high 86 - also 1st of 11 getting 5lb from Sarson (6 Jun Haydock RF 1783). Made all at Haydock first time but was outpaced in the Windsor Castle on her second start. Below par subsequently.
**J Berry [0-3] Microtrain Ltd (from M Johnston [1-2] Jun 1998).*

SHINING EXAMPLE BHB 66f69a RR 63f 69a 2227[18]

6 ch g Hadeer 8.9f **(58)** - Kick the Habit (Habitat) 9.4f **(70)**
Form - 030
Record 1998 - 1st:0 2nd:0 3rd:1 Ran:3
Pre1998 - 1st:3 2nd:4 3rd:1 Ran:23
Win Prizemoney £12,226 *Total Prizemoney* £17,498
Wins 1997 Jun Goodwo (GD) H 9f 66 69
1996 May Windso (G-F) 10f 77 <
1995 Oct Newmar (G-F) H 9f 67 77 <
1998 Turf 0-3: (8f 2, 12f) (gd 2, frm)
Average gelding, effective 9 to 10f, best at 9f, acts on gd to frm, prefers right handed tracks, prefers tight tracks. Turf high 63.
**J J O'Neill [0-8] Mrs L R Joughin (from P J Makin [3-23] Oct 1997).*

SHIPLEY GLEN BHB 55f59a RR 54+f 59a 2546[4]

3 b c Green Desert (USA) 7.8f **(78)** - Lady Shipley (Shirley Heights) 10.3f **(74)**
Form - 214
Record 1998 - 1st:1 2nd:1 3rd:0 Ran:3
Pre1998 - 1st:0 2nd:0 3rd:0 Ran:3
Win Prizemoney £2,427 *Total Prizemoney* £3,315
Wins * 1998 *Jun Wolver (STD) H 9.4f 51 57+* <
1998 Turf 0-2: (9f, 10f) (gd, g-f) 1998 AW 1-1: (9f 1-1) (Fibr 1-1)
Fair colt, effective 9f, acts on gd - acts on Fibr. Turf high 54. (1st run) - 1st of 8 getting 1lb from Lycian (17 Jun Wolverhampton RF 2082). Showed nothing at two, but improved last season, looking suited by longer trips. He looks the sort who will get better with age and even longer trips. **Sir Mark Prescott [1-6] Mrs L Burnet.*

SHIRA-A BHB 30f34a RR 56f 34a 2457[14]

3 b g Soviet Star (USA) 8.6f **(74)** - Hamama (USA) (Majestic Light (USA)) 10.6f **(75)**
Form - 666000
Record 1998 - 1st:0 2nd:0 3rd:0 Ran:6
Pre1998 - 1st:0 2nd:0 3rd:0 Ran:1
1998 Turf 0-2: (6f, 7f) (g-s, frm) 1998 AW 0-4: (6f, 7f, 8f, 10f) (Equi 2, Fibr 2)
Fair gelding, often wears blinkers. Turf high 10. AW high 21.
**M J Polglase [0-6] K S Lee (from K Prendergast in IRE [0-1] Oct 1997).*

SHIRAZAN (IRE) BHB 45a RR 35f 45a 13[12]

4 b g Doyoun 10.7f **(69)** - Sharaniya (USA) (Alleged (USA)) 10f **(76)**
Form - 0
Record 1998 - 1st:0 2nd:0 3rd:0 Ran:1
Pre1998 - 1st:0 2nd:0 3rd:0 Ran:2
1998 AW 0-1: (11f) (Fibr)
Scopey, currently very moderate gelding.
**J A Glover [0-1] J A Glover (from L M Cumani [0-2] Jun 1997).*

SHIRLEY NOT BHB 75f RR 76f 4152[2]

2 gr g Paris House 5.9f **(64)** - Hollia (Touch Boy) 5f **(66)**
Form - 1225172
Record 1998 - 1st:2 2nd:3 3rd:0 Ran:7
Win Prizemoney £5,390 *Total Prizemoney* £7,814
Wins * 1998 Aug Cheste (G-S) H 5.1f 73 <
1998 *Apr Southw (STD) S 5f 51*
1998 Turf 1-6: (5f 1-6) (g-f 1-3, frm 3) 1998 AW 1-1: (5f 1-1) (Fibr 1-1)
Above-average gelding, effective 5f, acts on g-f to frm, best on g-f. Turf high 76 - 2nd of 6 giving 2lb to Cartmel Park (8 Spt Newcastle 5f frm RF 4152) - also 1st of 7 getting 7lb from Aa-Youknownothing (2 Aug Chester RF 3290). (1st run). He was a pacey juvenile, and

has the scope to do well at three.
**S Gollings [1-4] Whinham Brown Kenwor Stelling (from J Berry [1-3] May 1998).*

SHIRTY BHB 38f **RR 27f** 1247[8]
4 b g Shirley Heights 12.1f **(76)** - Sassy Lassy (IRE) (Taufan (USA)) 7f **(57)**
Form - 878
Record 1998 - 1st:0 2nd:0 3rd:0 Ran:3
Pre1998 - 1st:0 2nd:0 3rd:0 Ran:1
1998 Turf 0-2: (12f, 16f) (sft, frm) 1998 AW 0-1: (12f) (Fibr)
Lengthy, little account gelding. Turf high 2.
**T T Bill [0-3] Willwewontwe Club (from D Morley [0-1] Aug 1997).*

SHIVA (JPN) RR 89f 1593[1]
3 ch f Hector Protector (USA) 9f **(89)**-Lingerie(Shirley Heights)10.3f **(74)**
Form - 1
Record 1998 - 1st:1 2nd:0 3rd:0 Ran:1
Win Prizemoney £3,680 *Total Prizemoney* £3,680
Wins * **1998** May Kempto (GD) 9f 89 <
1998 Turf 1-1: (9f 1-1) (gd 1-1)
Well made, currently useful filly. (1st run) - 1st of 14 from Shalama (30 May Kempton RF 1593). A comfortable winner of a maiden, she was not seen again. **H R A Cecil [1-1] Niarchos Family.*

SHMOOSE (IRE) BHB 105f **RR 101f** 4844[3]
3 b f Caerleon (USA) 10.9f **(79)** - Kerrera (Diesis) 9.3f **(69)**
Form - 33
Record 1998 - 1st:0 2nd:0 3rd:2 Ran:2
Pre1998 - 1st:1 2nd:0 3rd:0 Ran:2
Win Prizemoney £4,276 *Total Prizemoney* £10,889
Wins * 1997 Aug Newbur (G-F) 6f 89+ <
1998 Turf 0-2: (6f 2) (gd, g-f)
Well made, very useful filly. Turf high 101 (began Spt) - 3rd of 16 getting 5lb from Bold Edge (16 Oct Newmarket 6f g-f RF 4844). Extremely lightly-raced, she has shown enough to suggest that there is a Listed or Group contest in the locker. It would be interesting to see her ridden with restraint. **S bin Suroor [1-4] Godolphin.*

SHOCKER (IRE) BHB 67f **RR 70df** 3906[6]
3 b f Sabrehill (USA) 8.5f **(64)** - Fenjaan (Trojan Fen) 8.1f **(62)**
Form - 66111356
Record 1998 - 1st:3 2nd:0 3rd:1 Ran:7
Pre1998 - 1st:0 2nd:0 3rd:0 Ran:3
Win Prizemoney £8,788 *Total Prizemoney* £9,196
Wins * **1998** Jly Ripon (GD) H 8f 62 70+ <
* **1998** Jun Mussel (G-F) H 8f 55 57+
* **1998** May Yarmou (FRM) H 8f 48 51
1998 Turf 3-7: (7f 2, 8f 3-5) (gd 1-2, g-f 2, frm 2-3)
Unfurnished, above-average filly, effective 7 to 8f, best at 8f, acts on gd to g-f, best on g-f. Turf high 70 - 1st of 15 giving 1lb to Swinging The Blues (6 Jly Ripon RF 2570). Her effort at Southwell in November caught the attention of the stewards, and resulted in a thirty-day ban for the horse. Helped by the application of a tongue-strap when notching a hat-trick, she was later held by the Handicapper. **W J Haggas [3-10] Ali K Al Jafleh.*

SHOGUN (IRE) BHB 82f **RR 85?f** 3816[4]
3 b c Zafonic (USA) 9f **(83)** - Sheriyna (FR) (Darshaan) 9.9f **(84)**
Form - 4224
Record 1998 - 1st:0 2nd:2 3rd:0 Ran:4
Win Prizemoney £0 *Total Prizemoney* £2,977
1998 Turf 0-4: (8f 3, 10f) (g-f 2, frm 2)
Scopey, useful colt. Turf high 85 - 2nd of 9 giving 5lb to La Rochelle (5 Aug Pontefract 8f frm RF 3387).
**J H M Gosden [0-4] George Strawbridge.*

SHOHRA WA JAAH BHB 63f **RR 69f** 3770[2]
3 b g Mtoto 11.5f **(71)** - Pipina (USA) (Sir Gaylord) 10.6f **(64)**
Form - 433522
Record 1998 - 1st:0 2nd:2 3rd:2 Ran:6
Pre1998 - 1st:0 2nd:0 3rd:0 Ran:2
Win Prizemoney £0 *Total Prizemoney* £2,630
1998 Turf 0-6: (10f, 12f 2, 14f 2, 17f) (g-f 3, frm 3)
Light-framed, average gelding, effective 10 to 17f, acts on g-f to frm, best on g-f, favours tight tracks. Turf high 69 - 2nd of 5 to Mark of Prophet (5 Aug Leicester 12f frm RF 3378). Consistent.

**M A Jarvis [0-8] Sheikh Ahmed Al Maktoum.*

SHONA (USA) RR 54f 2645[11]
4 ch f Lyphard (USA) 10.6f **(75)** - Klarifi (Habitat) 9.4f **(70)**
Form - 54050
Record 1998 - 1st:0 2nd:0 3rd:0 Ran:5
Win Prizemoney £0 *Total Prizemoney* £209
1998 Turf 0-5: (8f 2, 9f, 10f 2) (g-s, gd 2, frm 2)
Fair filly. Turf high 61. **R Hannon [0-5] Stonethorn Stud Farms Ltd.*

SHONTAINE BHB 55f65a **RR 54f 65a** 4936[16]
5 b g Pharly (FR) 11.5f **(64)**-Hinari Televideo (Caerleon (USA)) 8.6f **(71)**
Form - 33545212150
Record 1998 - 1st:2 2nd:2 3rd:0 Ran:7
Pre1998 - 1st:8 2nd:4 3rd:9 Ran:58
Win Prizemoney £27,552 *Total Prizemoney* £37,122
Wins * **1998** *Feb Southw (STD) H 8f 60 63*
* **1998** *Jan Southw (STD) H 8f 51 56*
* 1997 Spt Hamilt (GD) H 8.3f 55 59
* 1997 Aug Thirsk (G-F) SH 8f 51 57
* 1997 May Carlis (FRM) H 6.9f 50 56
* 1997 *Mar Lingfi (STD) C 6f 52*
* 1996 *Nov Southw (STD) H 7f 60 67*
* 1996 Jly Catter (GD) SH 7f 60 64
* 1995 Jly Newcas (G-F) 6f 78 <
* 1995 Jly Doncas (GD) 6f 74
1998 Turf 0-1: (8f) (gd) 1998 AW 2-6: (8f 2-6) (Equi, Fibr 2-5)
Average gelding, effective 7 to 8f, best at 8f, acts on g-f to frm - acts on Fibr, likes right handed tracks, likes tight tracks. AW high 63 - also 1st of 11 getting 10lb from First Maite (9 Feb Southwell RF 0254). **M Johnston [10-65] Paul Dean.*

SHOOGLE (USA) BHB 80f **RR 77f** 4892[5]
2 ch f A P Indy (USA) - Dokki (USA) (Northern Dancer) 9.6f **(80)**
Form - 165
Record 1998 - 1st:1 2nd:0 3rd:0 Ran:3
Win Prizemoney £3,642 *Total Prizemoney* £3,642
Wins * **1998** Jly Salisb (FRM) 7f 72+ <
1998 Turf 1-3: (7f 1-3) (gd, frm 1-2)
Currently above-average filly. Turf high 77 (began Jly) - also 1st of 9 getting 5lb from Shamel (11 Jly Salisbury RF 2716).
**J H M Gosden [1-3] K Abdulla.*

SHOOTING LIGHT (IRE) BHB 73f **RR 78f** 4850[7]
5 b g Shernazar 11.8f **(71)** - Church Light (Caerleon (USA)) 8.6f **(71)**
Form - 07
Record 1998 - 1st:0 2nd:0 3rd:0 Ran:2
Pre1998 - 1st:2 2nd:1 3rd:2 Ran:9
Win Prizemoney £6,043 *Total Prizemoney* £8,684
Wins * 1997 Aug Sandow (SFT) H 14f 72 77 <
1996 May Hamilt (SFT) 12.1f 66
1998 Turf 0-2: (16f, 18f) (gd, g-f)
Above-average gelding, has worn blinkers. Turf high 78 (began Spt). **P G Murphy [3-15] J M Brown (from M A Jarvis [1-5] Jun 1996).*

SHOOT THE RAPIDS (IRE) RR 69f 4243[19]
2 b g River Falls 8.2f **(56)** - Petit Nom (IRE) (Nomination) 7f **(60)**
Form - 53200
Record 1998 - 1st:0 2nd:1 3rd:1 Ran:5
Win Prizemoney £0 *Total Prizemoney* £910
1998 Turf 0-5: (6f 3, 7f 2) (gd, g-f 3, frm)
Average gelding. Turf high 69 (began Jly).
**R Hannon [0-5] D Boocock.*

SHOP WINDOW BHB 58f **RR 63+f** 4873[13]
2 b f Noble Patriarch 12.2f **(43)** - Warning Bell (Bustino) 10.4f **(64)**
Form - 3600
Record 1998 - 1st:0 2nd:0 3rd:1 Ran:4
Win Prizemoney £0 *Total Prizemoney* £340
1998 Turf 0-4: (6f, 7f 2, 8f) (gd, frm 3)
Average filly. Turf high 63 (1st run) (began Aug) - 3rd of 18 to The Nurse (8 Aug Redcar 6f frm RF 3475). **T D Easterby [0-4] A Arton.*

SHORT ROMANCE (IRE) BHB 58f **RR 60f** 4393[7]
3 b f Brief Truce (USA) 9.1f **(73)** - Lady's Turn (Rymer) 12f **(61)**
Form - 8504177
Record 1998 - 1st:1 2nd:0 3rd:0 Ran:7

Pre1998 - 1st:0 2nd:0 3rd:2 Ran:5
Win Prizemoney £3,494 *Total Prizemoney* £5,134
Wins * **1998** Aug Folkes (G-F) H 12f 58 60 <
1998 Turf 1-7: (8f, 10f 3, 11f, 12f 1-2) (gd 2, g-f 1-2, frm 3)
Average filly, effective 8 to 12f, best at 8f, acts on g-f to frm, best on g-f, prefers right handed tracks, excels at Folkestone. Turf high 60 - 1st of 16 from Snow Partridge (27 Aug Folkestone RF 3900). Consistent. **J W Hills [1-12] Abbott Racing Partners.*

SHOTLEY MARIE (IRE) BHB 33f RR 31f 3392[12]
3 b f Scenic 10.6f **(66)** - Hana Marie (Formidable (USA)) 9.2f **(63)**
Form - 0600
Record 1998 - 1st:0 2nd:0 3rd:0 Ran:4
Pre1998 - 1st:0 2nd:0 3rd:0 Ran:3
1998 Turf 0-4: (8f 2, 9f, 11f) (g-f 2, frm 2)
Light-framed, very moderate filly, has worn blinkers. Turf high 31.
**N Bycroft [0-7] J A Swinburne.*

SHOT SILK BHB 65f RR 64f 4299[10]
2 ch f Kris 10f **(75)** - Flaming Rose (USA) (Upper Nile (USA)) 8.5f **(75)**
Form - 060
Record 1998 - 1st:0 2nd:0 3rd:0 Ran:3
1998 Turf 0-3: (6f, 7f 2) (frm 2, hrd)
Currently average filly. Turf high 64 (began Aug).
**Mrs J R Ramsden [0-3] Mrs J D Trotter.*

SHOUK BHB 90f RR 94f 4819[4]
4 b f Shirley Heights 12.1f **(76)** - Souk (IRE) (Ahonoora) 8.1f **(73)**
Form - 4524
Record 1998 - 1st:0 2nd:1 3rd:0 Ran:4
Pre1998 - 1st:1 2nd:1 3rd:0 Ran:4
Win Prizemoney £3,452 *Total Prizemoney* £8,307
Wins * 1997 May Haydoc (SFT) 10.5f 77+ <
1998 Turf 0-4: (10f, 12f 3) (g-f, frm 3)
Scopey, useful filly, effective 10f, acts on frm. Turf high 94 - 4th of 8 giving 5lb to Lady In Waiting (15 Oct Newmarket 10f frm RF 4819). Improving. **L M Cumani [1-8] Fittocks Stud.*

SHOWBOAT BHB 86f RR 91f 4854[12]
4 b c Warning 8.1f **(77)** - Boathouse (Habitat) 9.4f **(70)**
Form - 330640060
Record 1998 - 1st:0 2nd:0 3rd:2 Ran:9
Pre1998 - 1st:2 2nd:0 3rd:1 Ran:6
Win Prizemoney £8,489 *Total Prizemoney* £20,590
Wins * 1997 Aug Salisb (G-F) 8f 93 <
* 1996 Oct Leices (G-F) 7f 93+
1998 Turf 0-9: (7f 7, 8f 2) (sft, gd 5, g-f 2, frm)
Scopey, useful colt, effective 7 to 8f, best at 8f, acts on sft to frm, excels at Newmarket. Turf high 97 - 3rd of 9 getting 14lb from Ramooz (13 May York 8f gd RF 1208). Took a Salisbury conditions event in August '97, and ran a couple of good races in decent company last season, including a blinder in the Tote International Handicap when drawn on the wrong side of the track. Can land a nice seven-furlong prize. **B W Hills [2-15] R D Hollingsworth.*

SHOW FAITH (IRE) BHB 58f55a RR 59f 55a 2392[8]
8 ch g Exhibitioner 8.4f **(56)** - Keep the Faith (Furry Glen) 8.9f **(63)**
Form - 88
Record 1998 - 1st:0 2nd:0 3rd:0 Ran:2
Pre1998 - 1st:4 2nd:2 3rd:6 Ran:42
Win Prizemoney £35,902 *Total Prizemoney* £60,405
Wins * 1997 Aug Goodwo (G-F) H 9f 54 59
* 1995 Jly Newbur (GD) H 8f 81 84
1998 Turf 0-2: (10f, 11f) (gd, g-f)
Fair gelding, has worn blinkers. Turf high 49.
**R Hannon [4-50] I A N Wight.*

SHOW ME THE MONEY (IRE) RR 108f 4739[1]
2 b f Mujadil (USA) 7.7f **(70)**-Snappy Dresser (Nishapour (FR)) 9.1f **(61)**
Form - 1433111
1998 Turf 4-7: (5f 3-4, 6f 1-3) (hvy 1-1, g-s 1-2, gd 2-3, frm)
Pattern-class filly, effective 5f, acts on g-s. Turf high 108 - 1st of 12 from Deadly Nightshade (10 Oct Ascot RF 4739). She came good in the second half of the season, beating Deadly Nightshade in a strong renewal of the Group Three Cornwallis Stakes at Ascot. Suited by the soft ground there, she is a sprinter plain and simple, and will surely win another Group race when there is some give underfoot. **N Meade in IRE [4-7] L Queally.*

SHREDDER (GER) RR 99f 4470h[6]
5
Form - 6
1998 Turf 0-1: (10f) (gd)
Currently very useful. **in GER [0-1].*

SHTURM (RUS) RR 97f 4605a[3]
5 ch h Raut (RUS) - Askanija (RUS)
Form - 1313
1998 Turf 2-4: (9f 1-1, 12f 2, 15f 1-1) (sft, gd 2-3)
Very useful colt, effective 9 to 15f, acts on gd. Turf high 97 - 3rd of 9 getting 5lb from Trait De Genie (27 Spt Dielsdorf 12f gd RF 4605a). Consistent. **M Weiss in SWI [2-10].*

SHUDDER BHB 94f RR 95f 2838[6]
3 b c Distant Relative 7f **(69)** - Oublier L'Ennui (FR) (Bellman (FR)) 8.4f **(77)**
Form - 6
Record 1998 - 1st:0 2nd:0 3rd:0 Ran:1
Pre1998 - 1st:1 2nd:1 3rd:2 Ran:4
Win Prizemoney £3,590 *Total Prizemoney* £25,906
Wins * 1997 Aug Goodwo (G-F) 6f 85+ <
1998 Turf 0-1: (7f) (g-f)
Workmanlike, very useful colt. **W J Haggas [1-5] Ali K Al Jafleh.*

SHUHRAH (USA) BHB 102f RR 98f 1364[2]
3 b br f Danzig (USA) 8.1f **(88)** - Sajjaya (USA) (Blushing Groom (FR)) 10.3f **(76)**
Form - 32
Record 1998 - 1st:0 2nd:1 3rd:1 Ran:2
Pre1998 - 1st:1 2nd:0 3rd:1 Ran:3
Win Prizemoney £7,035 *Total Prizemoney* £14,436
Wins * 1997 Jly Ascot (GD) 6f 90+ <
1998 Turf 0-2: (7f, 8f) (g-f 2)
Scopey, very useful filly. Turf high 97 (1st run) - 3rd of 9 to Nanoushka (9 May Lingfield 7f g-f RF 1126). Fair efforts in Listed company. **S bin Suroor [1-5] Godolphin.*

SHUTTLECOCK BHB 24f31a RR 31f 31a 4549[10]
7 ch g Pharly (FR) 11.5f **(64)**-Upper Sister (Upper Case(USA)) 8.2f **(55)**
Form - 4547034682340
Record 1998 - 1st:0 2nd:1 3rd:2 Ran:11
Pre1998 - 1st:4 2nd:6 3rd:7 Ran:64
Win Prizemoney £10,088 *Total Prizemoney* £18,974
Wins *1995 Jan Southw (STD) C 8f 69* <
1995 Jan Southw (STD) C 8f 53
1994 Jun Wolver (STD) H 8.5f 58 56
1998 Turf 0-3: (11f 2, 12f) (hvy, gd, g-f) 1998 AW 0-8: (11f 2, 12f 3, 13f, 14f 2) (Equi, Fibr 7)
Very moderate gelding, effective 12f, - acts on Fibr, has worn blinkers, favours left handed tracks. Turf high 31. AW high 33. He is without a win on the Flat since 1995, and despite one or two fair efforts, he looks one to leave alone.
**D W Chapman [0-18] David Chapman (from Mrs N Macauley [2-35] Feb 1997).*

SIBERIAN MYSTIC BHB 43f RR 45f 3067[8]
5 gr m Siberian Express (USA) 9f **(58)** - Mystic Crystal (IRE) (Caerleon (USA)) 8.6f **(71)**
Form - 32258
Record 1998 - 1st:0 2nd:2 3rd:1 Ran:5
Pre1998 - 1st:2 2nd:1 3rd:0 Ran:12
Win Prizemoney £5,239 *Total Prizemoney* £8,848
Wins * 1997 Oct Pontef (G-F) H 12f 35 43 <
* 1996 Aug Beverl (G-F) H 9.9f 30 36
1998 Turf 0-5: (12f 4, 14f) (gd, g-f 2, frm, hrd)
Moderate filly, effective 12 to 14f, best at 12f, acts on gd to hrd, likes tight tracks. Turf high 45 - 2nd of 12 getting 17lb from Salska (17 Jun Nottingham 14f gd RF 2065). A winning hurdler, she pays her way on the level too. Often the subject of market support.
**P G Murphy [6-30] Glenferry And Partners.*

SIBLING RIVAL (USA) RR 114f 4079a[2]
4 b c Quest for Fame 12.8f **(75)** - Perfect Sister (USA) (Perrault)
Form - 22

1998 Turf 0-2: (12f, 13f) (sft, gd)
Currently Group-class colt. Turf high 114 - 2nd of 8 giving 11lb to Epistolaire (30 Aug Deauville 13f gd RF 4079a). He suffered the indignity of being narrowly beaten by stable-mates in Group races at Deauville and Chantilly. This game colt deserves to land a decent prize. **A Fabre in FR [0-2] Sheikh Mohammed.*

SICK AS A PARROT BHB 83f **RR 84f** 4631[21]
3 ch c Casteddu 7.4f **(54)** - Sianiski (Niniski (USA)) 10.6f **(65)**
Form - 012661600
Record 1998 - 1st:2 2nd:1 3rd:0 Ran:9
Pre1998 - 1st:3 2nd:2 3rd:1 Ran:7
Win Prizemoney £21,025 *Total Prizemoney* £26,919
Wins * **1998** Aug Redcar (G-F) H 11f 84 84
* **1998** May Beverl (GD) H 8.5f 80 85 <
* 1997 Oct Yarmou (GD) H 8f 75 79
* 1997 Spt Yarmou (FRM) H 8f 70 72
* 1997 Jun Yarmou (FRM) S 7f 58
1998 Turf 2-9: (8f 1-2, 9f 2, 10f 4, 11f 1-1) (gd 5, g-f 2, frm 2-2)
Unfurnished, decent colt, effective 8 to 11f, acts on gd to frm, best on frm, has worn blinkers, prefers tight tracks, excels at Yarmouth, does well at Goodwood. Turf high 85 - 1st of 8 getting 5lb from Sualtach (19 May Beverley RF 1319) - also 1st of 5 giving 4lb to Allgrit (9 Aug Redcar RF 3489). He won over eleven furlongs at Redcar in August, but that race was slowly run, and he has yet to convince that he really stays beyond ten furlongs.
**C A Dwyer [5-16] First Class Mobile.*

SICNEE (USA) BHB 100f **RR 104f** 4964[2]
2 gr c Rubiano (USA) 7.1f **(87)** - Lets Be Personal (CAN) (Grey Dawn II) 11.1f **(72)**
Form - 1212
Record 1998 - 1st:2 2nd:2 3rd:0 Ran:4
Win Prizemoney £17,819 *Total Prizemoney* £26,564
Wins * **1998** Aug Deauvi (GD) L 7f 91+ <
* **1998** Jly Redcar (G-F) 7f 84+
1998 Turf 2-4: (7f 2-4) (sft, gd 1-2, frm 1-1)
Very useful colt. Turf high 104 (began Jly) - 2nd of 6 to Brancaster (23 Oct Newbury 7f sft RF 4964). A striking, near-white individual, he won easily on his Redcar debut, but did not seem to get home at Sandown next time after looking home and hosed. Redeemed his reputation with a comfortable listed win at Deauville, and ended the campaign with a brave display against the useful Brancaster in the Horris Hill at Newbury, only just losing out in a tight finish. He looks a very useful prospect in the making.
**D R Loder [2-4] Maktoum Al Maktoum.*

SIDE BAR BHB 24f20a **RR 16f 20a** 2340[6]
8 b g Mummy's Game 9.2f **(56)** - Joli's Girl (Mansingh (USA)) 7.4f **(55)**
Form - 786
Record 1998 - 1st:0 2nd:0 3rd:0 Ran:3
Pre1998 - 1st:2 2nd:1 3rd:3 Ran:25
Win Prizemoney £4,473 *Total Prizemoney* £6,446
Wins 1995 *Feb Lingfi (STD) SH 13f 28 34*
1998 AW 0-3: (12f, 13f 2) (Equi 3)
Poor gelding, often wears blinkers. AW high 13.
**K C Comerford [0-6] Exell, Bailey And Penwright (from P Mooney [0-4] May 1997).*

SIDE BY SIDE (GER) **RR 57f** 3589[8]
5 b m Conquering Hero (USA) 10.6f **(50)** - Sarpanitu (Simply Great (FR)) 8.2f **(65)**
Form - 8
Record 1998 - 1st:0 2nd:0 3rd:0 Ran:1
1998 Turf 0-1: (10f) (gd)
Currently fair filly. **Mrs A E Johnson [0-1] Mrs S N J Embiricos.*

SIDNEY THE KIDNEY BHB 26f26a **RR 30f 26a** 5081[7]
4 b f Mystiko (USA) 7.7f **(59)** - Martin-Lavell Mail (Dominion) 8.5f **(63)**
Form - 04353554734307
Record 1998 - 1st:0 2nd:0 3rd:3 Ran:11
Pre1998 - 1st:0 2nd:1 3rd:2 Ran:11
Win Prizemoney £0 *Total Prizemoney* £2,337
1998 Turf 0-2: (10f, 11f) (g-s, g-f) 1998 AW 0-9: (11f 3, 12f 6) (Fibr 9)
Neat, moderate filly, effective 10f, acts on g-f. Turf high 27 (began Oct). AW high 40. **M J Ryan [0-22] Norcroft Park Stud.*

SIEGE (IRE) BHB 100f **RR 96f** 4542[5]
2 br c Indian Ridge 7.6f **(74)** - Above Water (IRE) (Reference Point) 6.8f **(70)**
Form - 2335
Record 1998 - 1st:0 2nd:1 3rd:2 Ran:4
Win Prizemoney £0 *Total Prizemoney* £5,770
1998 Turf 0-4: (6f 3, 7f) (g-f, frm 3)
Very useful colt. Turf high 96 (began Jly) - 5th of 26 to Maidaan (29 Spt Newmarket 7f frm RF 4542). Runner-up on his debut, he failed to settle and was a shade disappointing behind Stravinsky at York next time. Looked to need seven furlongs, and ran well at that trip in a valuable sales race at Newmarket.
**Sir Michael Stoute [0-4] The Royal Ascot Racing Club.*

SIENA (GER) BHB 47f **RR 34f** 4574[14]
3 ch f Platini (GER) - Smeralda (GER) (Nebos (GER)) 9f **(78)**
Form - 080
Record 1998 - 1st:0 2nd:0 3rd:0 Ran:3
Pre1998 - 1st:1 2nd:0 3rd:0 Ran:5
Win Prizemoney £3,385 *Total Prizemoney* £3,385
Wins 1997 Spt Goodwo (G-F) S 9f 61 <
1998 Turf 0-3: (8f, 10f, 12f) (gd, g-f 2)
Leggy, very moderate filly, effective 9f, acts on frm, has worn blinkers. Turf high 34.
**Miss K M George [0-6] Exterior Profiles Ltd (from M R Channon [1-5] Oct 1997).*

SIFAT BHB 72f **RR 76f** 4925[3]
3 b f Marju (IRE) 9.2f **(76)** - Reine Maid (USA) (Mr Prospector (USA)) 8.8f **(78)**
Form - 4635513
Record 1998 - 1st:1 2nd:0 3rd:2 Ran:7
Win Prizemoney £3,647 *Total Prizemoney* £5,066
Wins * **1998** Oct Pontef (G-S) 8f 76 <
1998 Turf 1-7: (8f 1-5, 10f 2) (g-s, gd 1-3, g-f, frm 2)
Scopey, above-average filly, effective 8f, acts on g-s to gd, best on gd, has worn blinkers, prefers tight tracks. Turf high 76 (began Jly) - 1st of 8 from Forest Call (5 Oct Pontefract RF 4662).
**M P Tregoning [1-7] Hamdan Al Maktoum.*

SIFWA BHB 35f32a **RR 35f 32a** 1567[7]
4 ch f Safawan 6.6f **(60)** - Wigeon (Divine Gift) 6.6f **(57)**
Form - 0557
Record 1998 - 1st:0 2nd:0 3rd:0 Ran:2
Pre1998 - 1st:0 2nd:1 3rd:0 Ran:6
Win Prizemoney £0 *Total Prizemoney* £813
1998 Turf 0-1: (17f) (frm) 1998 AW 0-1: (12f) (Equi)
Light-framed, very moderate filly. **D C O'Brien [0-14] A Runacre.*

SIGER WATER BHB 25f **RR** 4108[18]
5 ch m Rakaposhi King 9.3f **(55)** - Kates Fling (USA) (Quiet Fling (USA)) 11.8f **(36)**
Form - 40
Record 1998 - 1st:0 2nd:0 3rd:0 Ran:2
Pre1998 - 1st:0 2nd:0 3rd:0 Ran:1
Win Prizemoney £0 *Total Prizemoney* £288
1998 Turf 0-2: (8f, 12f) (gd, frm)
Formerly very poor filly. (began Aug) - 18th of 18 getting 6lb from Margaret's Dancer (5 Spt Thirsk 8f frm RF 4108).
**W M Brisbourne [0-2] P Evans (from R F Fisher [0-1] Apr 1995).*

SIGGIEWI BHB 25f **RR 39f** 4051[10]
4 ro f Mystiko (USA) 7.7f **(59)** - Shadiyama (Nishapour (FR)) 9.1f **(61)**
Form - 00
Record 1998 - 1st:0 2nd:0 3rd:0 Ran:2
Pre1998 - 1st:0 2nd:0 3rd:0 Ran:2
1998 Turf 0-1: (12f) (frm) 1998 AW 0-1: (12f) (Fibr)
Scopey, very moderate filly. **N M Babbage [0-4] N M Babbage.*

SIGNED AND SEALED (USA) BHB 52f57a **RR 51f 57a** 3454[11]
4 b g Rahy (USA) 9.1f **(80)**-Heaven's Mine (USA) (Graustark) 10.1f **(70)**
Form - 02134842611040
Record 1998 - 1st:2 2nd:1 3rd:0 Ran:10
Pre1998 - 1st:1 2nd:1 3rd:1 Ran:10
Win Prizemoney £7,532 *Total Prizemoney* £9,023
Wins * **1998** *Apr Wolver (STD) H 16.2f 54 58* <

* **1998** *Apr Wolver (STD) H 16.2f 45 52*
* 1997 *Dec Lingfi (G-S) 16f 56*
1998 AW 2-10: (14f, 15f, 16f 2-8) (Equi 5, Fibr 2-5)
Scopey, fair gelding, effective 16f, - acts on AW, best on Fibr, often wears blinkers (extremely effectively), likes left handed tracks, favours tight tracks. AW high 58 - 1st of 13 giving 9lb to Aquavita (18 Apr Wolverhampton RF 0756) - also 1st of 11 getting 10lb from Imad (4 Apr Wolverhampton RF 0567). He showed some good form when put over the extended two miles on the Wolverhampton Fibresand, winning twice in April in determined style.
**C A Cyzer [3-20] R M Cyzer.*

SIGNORINA CATTIVA (USA) RR 99+f 4983[1]

2 b f El Gran Senor (USA) 8.9f **(85)** - Assez Cuite (USA) (Graustark) 10.1f **(70)**
Form - 71
Record 1998 - 1st:1 2nd:0 3rd:0 Ran:2
Win Prizemoney £3,761 *Total Prizemoney* £3,761
Wins * 1998 Oct Leices (SFT) 8f 99+ <
1998 Turf 1-2: (7f, 8f 1-1) (g-s 1-1, gd)
Currently very useful filly. Turf high 99 (began Oct) - 1st of 14 from Genesis (25 Oct Leicester RF 4983). Bolted up by ten lengths on her second start. A half-sister to high-class stayer El Cuite, she will be suited by middle-distances at three.
**J L Dunlop [1-2] Mrs Maria Mai Goransson.*

SIGNS AND WONDERS BHB 65f66a RR 69f 66a 3821[4]

4 b f Danehill (USA) 9.1f **(79)** - Front Line Romance (Caerleon (USA)) 8.6f **(71)**
Form - 105520684
Record 1998 - 1st:1 2nd:1 3rd:0 Ran:9
Pre1998 - 1st:0 2nd:4 3rd:2 Ran:16
Win Prizemoney £3,460 *Total Prizemoney* £10,216
Wins * 1998 *Mar Lingfi (STD) H 10f 62 66* <
1998 Turf 0-6: (6f 2, 8f 2, 9f, 10f) (gd 3, g-f, frm 2) 1998 AW 1-3: (8f, 10f 1-2) (Equi 1-3)
Unfurnished, average filly, effective 6 to 10f, best at 8f, acts on g-f to frm - acts on Equi, best on frm, likes left handed tracks, excels at Lingfield. Turf high 69. AW high 66 (1st run) - 1st of 7 giving 17lb to Mogin (30 Mar Lingfield RF 0506).
**C A Cyzer [1-25] R M Cyzer.*

SIHAFI (USA) BHB 75f80a RR 71f 80a 5142[15]

5 ch g Elmaamul (USA) 8.1f **(70)** - Kit's Double (USA) (Spring Double) 6.8f **(76)**
Form - 0517880312111141263527801 10
Record 1998 - 1st:9 2nd:3 3rd:2 Ran:26
Pre1998 - 1st:2 2nd:4 3rd:0 Ran:25
Win Prizemoney £41,320 *Total Prizemoney* £50,251
Wins * 1998 *Oct Wolver (STD) H 6f 75 77* <
* **1998** Spt Haydoc (G-F) H 5f 70 71
* **1998** Jly Sandow (G-F) H 5f 60 70+
* **1998** Jly Salisb (GD) H 5f 56 64
* **1998** Jly Lingfi (G-F) H 5f 46 53+
* **1998** Jly Folkes (G-F) H 5f 46 51+
* **1998** Jly Bath (GD) H 5.1f 46 61
* **1998** Jun Windso (GD) H 6f 41 54+
* **1998** *Jan Lingfi (STD) H 6f 61 64*
1997 *Feb Lingfi (STD) H 6f 56 57*
1996 *Dec Lingfi (STD) H 6f 50 51*
1998 Turf 7-21: (5f 6-15, 6f 1-5, 7f) (g-s 2, gd 5, g-f 2-5, frm 5-9) 1998 AW 2-5: (6f 2-5) (Equi 1-4, Fibr 1-1)
Above-average gelding, has broken blood-vessels, effective 5 to 6f, best at 5f, acts on frm - acts on Fibr, excels at Windsor, likes Lingfield. Turf high 71 - 1st of 18 giving 3lb to Unshaken (26 Spt Haydock RF 4502) - also 1st of 12 getting 23lb from Storyteller (22 Jly Sandown RF 3036). AW high 77 - 1st of 13 getting 9lb from Italian Symphony (17 Oct Wolverhampton RF 4864). He had a brilliant 1998, and equalled the twentieth-century record of nine handicap wins in a season when scoring on the Wolverhampton Fibresand in October. The fact that he has achieved this feat by winning races on turf, Equitrack and Fibresand pays testament to his versatility. He is yet another example of his trainer's skills.
**D Nicholls [9-27] John Gilbertson (from J M Carr [2-17] Aug 1997).*

SILANKKA BHB 53f48a RR 53f 48a 3454[7]

4 b f Slip Anchor 12.7f **(75)** - Mary Sunley (Known Fact (USA)) 7.4f **(67)**
Form - 53556127137
Record 1998 - 1st:2 2nd:1 3rd:2 Ran:11
Pre1998 - 1st:0 2nd:0 3rd:0 Ran:2
Win Prizemoney £4,608 *Total Prizemoney* £5,816
Wins * 1998 *Jly Southw (STD) H 12f 45 51*
* **1998** Jly Hamilt (FRM) H 13f 50 53 <
1998 Turf 1-3: (10f, 12f, 13f 1-1) (gd, g-f, frm 1-1) 1998 AW 1-8: (10f 3, 11f, 12f 1-3, 15f) (Equi 4, Fibr 1-4)
Unfurnished, fair filly, effective 10 to 13f, acts on frm. Turf high 53. AW high 51. She managed to win on turf and on Fibresand during the summer, but both races were pretty moderate.
**M R Channon [2-13] Simon Legg and Partners.*

SILCA BLANKA (IRE) BHB 80f RR 88f 4494[16]

6 b h Law Society (USA) 11.6f **(71)** - Reality (Known Fact (USA)) 7.4f **(67)**
Form - 033700410200
Record 1998 - 1st:1 2nd:1 3rd:2 Ran:12
Pre1998 - 1st:3 2nd:1 3rd:0 Ran:20
Win Prizemoney £34,617 *Total Prizemoney* £56,365
Wins * 1998 Jly Warwic (G-F) 7f 86
1995 Jun Epsom (FRM) 7f 98
1994 Jun Epsom (GD) L 6f 100+ <
1994 Apr Newmar (SFT) 5f 69
1998 Turf 1-12: (7f 1-5, 8f 6, 9f) (sft, gd 4, g-f 4, frm 1-3)
Useful horse, effective 7 to 8f, best at 8f, acts on sft to frm, best on frm. Turf high 88 - 2nd of 12 giving 6lb to Vicimar (16 Aug San Sebastian 8f sft RF 3786a) - also 1st of 5 giving 1lb to La Modiste (18 Jly Warwick RF 2943). Now back in training in this country after a spell at stud, he showed some fair form last season, but has been highly tried on other occasions.
**A G Newcombe [1-12] Duckhaven Stud (from M R Channon [3-20] Aug 1996).*

SILCA KEY SERVICE BHB 100f RR 102?f 4712a[3]

3 b f Bering 9.6f **(80)** - Aquaglow (Caerleon (USA)) 8.6f **(71)**
Form - 157083
Record 1998 - 1st:1 2nd:0 3rd:1 Ran:6
Pre1998 - 1st:0 2nd:0 3rd:0 Ran:2
Win Prizemoney £3,980 *Total Prizemoney* £7,616
Wins 1998 Apr Newbur (HVY) 8f 79 <
1998 Turf 1-6: (8f 1-5, 12f) (sft 1-3, g-s, gd 2)
Unfurnished, very useful filly, effective 8f, acts on gd. Turf high 102. She was highly tried and mostly outclassed after winning a maiden at Newbury in the spring. She has been sold and will continue her career in America.
**C F Wall [0-2] David Hutson (from M R Channon [1-6] Jun 1998).*

SILENCE IN COURT (IRE) BHB 112f RR 113f 2085[4]

7 b g Law Society (USA) 11.6f **(71)** - Fair Flutter (Beldale Flutter (USA)) 9.7f **(71)**
Form - 14
Record 1998 - 1st:1 2nd:0 3rd:0 Ran:2
Pre1998 - 1st:5 2nd:2 3rd:2 Ran:16
Win Prizemoney £69,375 *Total Prizemoney* £87,936
Wins * 1998 May Cheste (GD) H 18.7f 88 94 <
1994 Spt Newcas (GD) H 16.1f 86 91+
1994 Aug Newmar (GD) H 14.8f 76 81
1994 Jly Goodwo (FRM) H 14f 74 78
1994 May Nottin (GD) H 14.1f 69 71
1994 Apr Ripon (G-S) H 12.3f 65 71
1998 Turf 1-2: (19f 1-1, 20f) (g-s, g-f 1-1)
Group-class gelding. Turf high 113 - 4th of 16 giving 2lb to Kayf Tara (18 Jun Ascot 20f g-s RF 2085). A very useful stayer in '95, he was having his first run for two and a half years when an excellent second at Doncaster in October 1997, and it was a fine feat of training to produce him ready to win the Chester Cup first time out in 1998. He ran a blinder to finish fourth in the Ascot Gold Cup, despite proving very awkward in the preliminaries, and it was therefore a tragedy for connections when he died of colic in June. (DEAD)
**A Bailey [1-3] Peter Freeman (from B A McMahon [5-15] May 1995).*

SILENCE REIGNS BHB 105f RR 108f 5066[2]

4 b g Saddlers' Hall (IRE) 10.5f **(65)** - Rensaler (USA) (Stop The Music (USA)) 9.2f **(71)**
Form - 4144262
Record 1998 - 1st:1 2nd:2 3rd:0 Ran:7
Pre1998 - 1st:1 2nd:2 3rd:0 Ran:4

Win Prizemoney £9,267 *Total Prizemoney* £28,721
Wins * **1998** Jun Doncas (GD) 10.3f 109 <
* 1997 Jun Pontef (SFT) 10f 73++
1998 Turf 1-7: (9f, 10f 1-3, 11f 3) (sft, gd 2, g-f 1-4)
Workmanlike, Pattern-class gelding, effective 9 to 12f, best at 10f, acts on gd to g-f, best on g-f. Turf high 109 - 1st of 7 giving 15lb to Mountain Song (28 Jun Doncaster RF 2357). He reeled in the free-running Great Dane at Doncaster in June, but could not catch that colt when they met again at York in September. He does not look an obvious improver. **Sir Michael Stoute [2-11] Cheveley Park Stud.*

SILENTLY BHB 78f **RR 75f** 5150[10]
6 b g Slip Anchor 12.7f **(75)** - Land of Ivory (USA) (The Minstrel (CAN)) 10f **(72)**
Form - 832830131351060
Record 1998 - 1st:3 2nd:1 3rd:4 Ran:15
Pre1998 - 1st:3 2nd:8 3rd:3 Ran:31
Win Prizemoney £23,389 *Total Prizemoney* £45,389
Wins * **1998** Spt Mussel (GD) H 16f 78 85 <
* **1998** Aug Mussel (GD) H 14f 72 76
1998 Aug Redcar (G-F) C 14.1f 63
1995 Jly Bath (HRD) H 10.2f 72 83+
1995 Jly Pontef (G-F) H 10f 72 76
1995 Apr Ripon (G-S) H 10f 70 70+
1998 Turf 3-15: (12f, 13f 2, 14f 2-5, 15f 3, 16f 1-3, 17f) (sft, gd 4, g-f 2-6, frm 1-4)
Above-average gelding, effective 12 to 16f, best at 14f, acts on gd to frm, best on g-f, has worn blinkers, likes right handed tracks, prefers tight tracks, excels at Musselburgh, does well at Sandown. Turf high 85 - 1st of 8 from Forgie (27 Spt Musselburgh RF 4521) - also 1st of 12 giving 29lb to General Glow (27 Aug Musselburgh RF 3905). Consistent. An able fast-ground stayer, he changed stables after winning a Redcar claimer in August, and has won two handicaps at Musselburgh for his new yard since then.
**K A Ryan [2-8] The Gloria Darley Racing Partnership (from J S King [1-11] Aug 1998).*

SILENT PRIDE (IRE) BHB 30f36a **RR 26f 36a** 3365[15]
3 ch f Pips Pride 6.7f **(70)** - Suppression (Kind of Hush) 10.1f **(62)**
Form - 445700060
Record 1998 - 1st:0 2nd:0 3rd:0 Ran:9
Pre1998 - 1st:0 2nd:2 3rd:1 Ran:15
Win Prizemoney £0 *Total Prizemoney* £2,588
1998 Turf 0-8: (7f, 8f, 10f 4, 11f, 12f) (gd 2, g-f 3, frm 3) 1998 AW 0-1: (7f) (Fibr)
Light-framed, moderate filly, effective 6f, acts on g-f. Turf high 41.
**M D I Usher [0-24] Miss D G Kerr.*

SILENT SOUND (IRE) BHB 62f **RR 71f** 4873[11]
2 b c Be My Guest (USA) 10.2f **(66)** - Whist Awhile (Caerleon (USA)) 8.6f **(71)**
Form - 5560
Record 1998 - 1st:0 2nd:0 3rd:0 Ran:4
1998 Turf 0-4: (7f 2, 8f 2) (gd, g-f, frm 2)
Above-average colt. Turf high 71.
**P Calver [0-4] Mrs Janis MacPherson.*

SILENT VALLEY BHB 48a **RR 50f** 1025[5]
4 b f Forzando 7.2f **(63)** - Tremmin (Horage) 10.3f **(61)**
Form - 75
Record 1998 - 1st:0 2nd:0 3rd:0 Ran:2
Pre1998 - 1st:1 2nd:2 3rd:3 Ran:23
Win Prizemoney £2,940 *Total Prizemoney* £5,431
Wins * 1997 Jly Nottin (G-F) 10f 56 <
1998 Turf 0-1: (12f) (gd) 1998 AW 0-1: (9f) (Fibr)
Scopey, fair filly, effective 8 to 10f, best at 8f, acts on gd to frm, best on gd, often wears blinkers (extremely effectively), likes left handed tracks, likes tight tracks.
**Miss L C Siddall [3-24] Mrs S E Cooper (from D Nicholls [0-4] Jan 1997).*

SILENT VOTE BHB 10f **RR 7f** 4955[18]
3 b f Nomination 7.3f **(57)** - Whispering Sea (Bustino) 10.4f **(64)**
Form - 000
Record 1998 - 1st:0 2nd:0 3rd:0 Ran:3
1998 Turf 0-3: (6f, 7f, 8f) (frm 3)
Small, currently very poor filly, has worn blinkers. Turf high 7 (began Spt). **S R Bowring [0-3] G M Sheppard.*

SILENT WARNING BHB 82f86a **RR 83+f 86a** 5118[1]
3 b c Ela-Mana-Mou 12.7f **(72)** - Buzzbomb (Bustino) 10.4f **(64)**
Form - 404111
Record 1998 - 1st:3 2nd:0 3rd:0 Ran:6
Pre1998 - 1st:0 2nd:0 3rd:0 Ran:2
Win Prizemoney £13,489 *Total Prizemoney* £14,110
Wins * **1998** Nov Mussel (SFT) H 16f 73 79+
* **1998** Oct Leices (SFT) 11.8f 83 <
* **1998** *Oct Southw (STD) H 14f 69 75*
1998 Turf 2-5: (7f, 9f, 10f, 12f 1-1, 16f 1-1) (sft 1-1, gd 1-2, frm, hrd)
1998 AW 1-1: (14f 1-1) (Fibr 1-1)
Workmanlike, useful colt, effective 12 to 16f, acts on sft to gd - acts on Fibr, prefers tight tracks. Turf high 83 (began Jly) - 1st of 11 giving 3lb to Majestic (25 Oct Leicester RF 4987) - also 1st of 16 giving 1lb to Mondragon (4 Nov Musselburgh RF 5118). (1st run) - 1st of 9 giving 17lb to Yaverland (19 Oct Southwell RF 4879).
**Sir Mark Prescott [3-8] Eclipse Thoroughbreds.*

SILENT WELLS BHB 21f35a **RR 20f 35a** 1475[26]
4 b f Saddlers' Hall (IRE) 10.5f **(65)** - Silent Plea (Star Appeal) 9.6f **(65)**
Form - 000
Record 1998 - 1st:0 2nd:0 3rd:0 Ran:3
Pre1998 - 1st:0 2nd:0 3rd:0 Ran:5
1998 Turf 0-3: (6f, 7f, 8f) (g-s, gd, g-f)
Light-framed, little account filly. Turf high 9.
**J J Quinn [0-7] Phillip Kneafsey (from L R Lloyd-James [0-1] May 1997).*

SILESIA (IRE) BHB 73f **RR 79df** 3106[10]
4 b c Sadler's Wells (USA) 11.3f **(87)** - Ghariba (Final Straw) 7.9f **(64)**
Form - 556640
Record 1998 - 1st:0 2nd:0 3rd:0 Ran:6
Win Prizemoney £0 *Total Prizemoney* £747
1998 Turf 0-6: (8f, 10f 4, 12f) (gd 3, g-f 3)
Above-average colt. Turf high 95. **R Simpson [0-6] G Piper.*

SILIC (FR) RR 114f 4728a[4]
3 c
Form - 214
1998 Turf 1-3: (7f, 8f 1-2) (hvy, sft 1-2)
Group-class colt. Turf high 114. He was shaping into a high-class miler before meeting with a training set-back in the summer. Bearing that in mind, he shaped encouragingly to finish fourth in the Prix du Rond Point on his comeback and is the sort to do well as a four-year-old. **P Bary in FR [1-4] Ecurie Stella Maris.*

SILK COTTAGE BHB 47f50a **RR 46f 50a** 5059[8]
6 b g Superpower 6.6f **(58)** - Flute Royale (Horage) 10.3f **(61)**
Form - 406374280352703640006 28
Record 1998 - 1st:0 2nd:3 3rd:3 Ran:20
Pre1998 - 1st:2 2nd:10 3rd:5 Ran:57
Win Prizemoney £5,052 *Total Prizemoney* £20,564
Wins 1997 *Mar Wolver (STD) S 5f 48*
1996 Jly Mussel (GD) H 5f 54 57 <
1998 Turf 0-15: (5f 14, 6f) (sft 2, g-s 2, gd 3, g-f 3, frm 5) 1998 AW 0-5: (5f, 6f 3, 7f) (Fibr 5)
Moderate gelding, effective 5 to 6f, best at 6f, acts on gd - acts on Fibr, has worn blinkers. Turf high 52 - 4th of 23 getting 3lb from Superbit (3 Aug Ripon 5f gd RF 3309). AW high 46. Consistent. He has made the frame regularly on Fibresand, but is on a long losing run stretching back to March '97.
**R Bastiman [0-19] Mrs W Walmsley (from R M Whitaker [2-58] Jan 1998).*

SILKEN RR 69f 4846[6]
2 b f Danehill (USA) 9.1f **(79)** - Our Reverie (USA) (J O Tobin (USA)) 9.4f **(67)**
Form - 66
Record 1998 - 1st:0 2nd:0 3rd:0 Ran:2
1998 Turf 0-2: (6f, 7f) (g-f 2)
Currently average filly. Turf high 69 (began Spt).
**Mrs A J Perrett [0-2] K J Buchanan.*

SILKEN DALLIANCE BHB 84f79a **RR 83f 79a** 4848[1]
3 b f Rambo Dancer (CAN) 8.4f **(59)** - A Sharp (Sharpo) 7.7f **(59)**
Form - 215271011
Record 1998 - 1st:4 2nd:2 3rd:0 Ran:9

	Pre1998 -	1st:0	2nd:1	3rd:0	Ran:3		

Win Prizemoney £72,437 *Total Prizemoney* £75,683

Wins	* **1998**	Oct	Newmar (GD)	H	8f	79	83	<
	* **1998**	Spt	Ascot (SFT)	H	8f	74	76	
	* **1998**	Spt	Kempto (SFT)	H	8f	67	74+	
	* **1998**	*Mar*	*Southw (STD)*		*6f*		*56*	

1998 Turf 3-7: (8f 3-6, 9f) (gd 3-6, g-f) 1998 AW 1-2: (6f 1-2) (Fibr 1-2)

Lengthy, decent filly, effective 6 to 8f, best at 8f, acts on gd - acts on Fibr. Turf high 83 - 1st of 30 giving 8lb to Giko (17 Oct Newmarket RF 4848) - also 1st of 24 getting 22lb from Silk St John (27 Spt Ascot RF 4513). AW high 65. She ran well on her first two starts on sand, and duly got off the mark at Southwell in March. Being stepped up to a mile on turf finally paid dividends in soft ground at Kempton in September, but she was given a less than satisfactory ride at Newbury in the Rothmans Semi-Final next time. Won the Mail On Sunday and Rothmans Finals on her next two outings and is improving.

**Lord Huntingdon [4-12] The C H F Partnership.*

Wins	* **1998**	Aug	Windso (G-F)	H	8.3f	86	90	<
	* **1998**	Jly	Newbur (GD)	H	8f	82	87	
	* **1998**	Jun	Windso (GD)		8.3f		83	
	* **1998**	May	Chepst (G-F)		8.1f		83	
	* 1997	Aug	Newmar (GD)	H	8f	74	78	

1998 Turf 4-15: (7f, 8f 4-13, 9f) (sft, gd 1-5, g-f 2-6, frm 1-3) 1998 AW 0-2: (11f 2) (Fibr 2)

Scopey, useful gelding, effective 8f, acts on gd to frm, best on g-f, excels at Windsor. Turf high 93 - 2nd of 12 getting 7lb from Right Wing (12 Spt Doncaster 8f g-f RF 4239) - also 1st of 10 giving 2lb to Shalad'or (29 Aug Windsor RF 3974). AW high 64. Consistent. A game sort, he was in fine form for most of the campaign, his four victories including a competitive handicap at Newbury. He was also disqualified after winning at Haydock, and ran a cracker when runner-up to Silken Dalliance in a valuable handicap at Ascot in September. A model of consistency, he is usually held up, and is suited by a strongly-run race. **M J Ryan [5-32] C R S Partners.*

Silken Dalliance put up a smooth performance at Newmarket

SILK PRINCESS BHB 63f **RR 64f** 4968[6]

3 gr f Touch of Grey 8.1f **(47)**-Young Lady (Young Generation) 7.7f **(63)**

Form - 006

Record 1998 - 1st:0 2nd:0 3rd:0 Ran:3

1998 Turf 0-3: (7f, 10f 2) (sft, gd, g-f)

Workmanlike, currently average filly. Turf high 64 (began Spt).

**R M Flower [0-3] Richard Gurr.*

SILK ST JOHN BHB 95f81a **RR 93f 81a** 5078[5]

4 b g Damister (USA) 9.1f **(66)** - Silk St James (Pas de Seul) 9.1f **(67)**

Form - 38647D1213167712205

Record	**1998** -	1st:4	2nd:3	3rd:1	Ran:17
	Pre1998 -	1st:1	2nd:3	3rd:3	Ran:15

Win Prizemoney £23,878 *Total Prizemoney* £46,433

SILK WING BHB 40f **RR 43f** 4264[13]

2 b f Wing Park - Little Park (Cragador) 6f **(67)**

Form - 060

Record 1998 - 1st:0 2nd:0 3rd:0 Ran:3

1998 Turf 0-3: (5f 2, 6f) (gd, g-f, frm)

Currently moderate filly. Turf high 43 (began Jly).

**T T Clement [0-3] J Burns.*

SILLY MID-ON **RR 48f** 978[4]

4 b f Midyan (USA) 9.9f **(64)** -Height of Folly (Shirley Heights) 10.3f **(74)**

Form - 4

Record 1998 - 1st:0 2nd:0 3rd:0 Ran:1

Win Prizemoney £0 *Total Prizemoney* £254

1998 Turf 0-1: (12f) (gd)

Lengthy, currently moderate filly.
**Lady Herries [0-1] Lady Sarah Clutton.*

SILVERADO (IRE) BHB 82f **RR 88?f** 4086[1]
3 gr g Indian Ridge 7.6f **(74)** - Tajarib (IRE) (Last Tycoon) 8.5f **(62)**
Form - 231
Record 1998 - 1st:1 2nd:1 3rd:1 Ran:3
Pre1998 - 1st:0 2nd:0 3rd:2 Ran:3
Win Prizemoney £3,355 *Total Prizemoney* £5,870
Wins * 1998 Spt Epsom (GD) 8.5f 70 <
1998 Turf 1-3: (8f 2, 9f 1-1) (gd 1-2, frm)
Useful gelding, effective 8f, acts on gd to frm, has worn blinkers. Turf high 88 (1st run) - 2nd of 11 giving 5lb to Absoluta (16 May Cork 8f gd RF 1347a).
**R Hannon [1-2] The Irish Connection (from D K Weld in IRE [0-4] May 1998).*

SILVER APPLE (IRE) RR 82f 2703[2]
2 gr c Danehill (USA) 9.1f **(79)** - Moon Festival (Be My Guest (USA)) 9.3f **(67)**
Form - 2
Record 1998 - 1st:0 2nd:1 3rd:0 Ran:1
Win Prizemoney £0 *Total Prizemoney* £1,824
1998 Turf 0-1: (7f) (frm)
Currently decent colt. **P F I Cole [0-1] Anthony Speelman.*

SILVER BLADE RR 59f 4991[9]
2 gr f Mystiko (USA) 7.7f **(59)** - Blade of Grass (Kris) 9.5f **(73)**
Form - 00760
Record 1998 - 1st:0 2nd:0 3rd:0 Ran:5
1998 Turf 0-5: (6f 2, 7f 2, 8f) (sft, gd, g-f 3)
Fair filly. Turf high 59.
**A T Murphy [0-1] D M Beresford (from M A Buckley [0-1] Aug 1998).*

SILVERBULLETDAY (USA) RR 5163a[1]
2 b f Silver Deputy (CAN) - Rokeby Rose (USA) 0**0**
Form - 1
1998 AW 1-1: (9f 1-1) (Dirt 1-1)
Currently Group-class filly. (1st run) - 1st of 11 from Excellent Meeting (7 Nov Churchill Downs RF 5163a). Showed a fine turn of speed to justify favouritism in the Breeders' Cup Juvenile Fillies.
**B Baffert in USA [1-1] Mike Pegram.*

SILVER CASTOR (IRE) BHB 59f **RR 65f** 4861[9]
3 b f Indian Ridge 7.6f **(74)** - Bayazida (Bustino) 10.4f **(64)**
Form - 4800
Record 1998 - 1st:0 2nd:0 3rd:0 Ran:4
Win Prizemoney £0 *Total Prizemoney* £255
1998 Turf 0-4: (12f 3, 14f) (g-s, gd, frm 2)
Lengthy, average filly. Turf high 65 (began Aug).
**P W Harris [0-4] John Hamshaw.*

SILVER CHARM (USA) RR 118f 5168a[2]
4 ro c Silver Buck (USA) - Bonnie's Poker (USA) (Poker (USA))
Form - 12
1998 AW 1-2: (10f 1-2) (Dirt 1-2)
Top-class colt. AW high 128 - 2nd of 10 to Awesome Again (7 Nov Churchill Downs 10f Dirt RF 5168a) - also 1st of 9 from Swain (28 Mar Nad Al Sheba RF 0552a). A streetfighter of a racehorse, he edged out Swain in the Dubai World Cup and was only caught close home by Awesome Again in the Breeders' Cup Classic.
**B Baffert in USA [3-5] B & R Lewis.*

SILVERDALE COUNT BHB 35f **RR** 1739[10]
6 b g Nomination 7.3f **(57)** - Its My Turn (Palm Track) 9.8f **(50)**
Form - 0
Record 1998 - 1st:0 2nd:0 3rd:0 Ran:1
Pre1998 - 1st:1 2nd:0 3rd:0 Ran:8
Win Prizemoney £2,675 *Total Prizemoney* £2,675
Wins * 1995 Aug Ayr (FRM) S 13.1f 51 <
1998 Turf 0-1: (14f) (gd)
Very poor gelding. **K W Hogg [1-9] Anthony White.*

SILVER FUN (FR) RR 109f 1383a[6]
4 b f Saumarez 15.1f **(87)** - Riviere d'Argent (FR) (Nijinsky (CAN)) 10.3f **(77)**
Form - 6
1998 Turf 0-1: (16f) (gd)
Pattern-class filly. (1st run) - 6th of 6 to Tajoun (17 May Longchamp 16f gd RF 1383a). She has bled in her races and did not improve on her three-year-old form. **Mme C Head in FR [1-5].*

SILVER GROOM (IRE) BHB 52f **RR 61f** 4270[7]
8 gr g Shy Groom (USA) 8.2f **(59)** - Rustic Lawn (Rusticaro (FR)) 8.2f **(65)**
Form - 80708207
Record 1998 - 1st:0 2nd:1 3rd:0 Ran:8
Pre1998 - 1st:3 2nd:7 3rd:3 Ran:45
Win Prizemoney £40,798 *Total Prizemoney* £69,389
Wins 1995 Jly Goodwo (FRM) H 10f 65 73+ <
1998 Turf 0-8: (10f 6, 11f, 12f) (gd 4, g-f 3, frm)
Average gelding, effective 10f, acts on g-f to frm, has worn blinkers, prefers right handed tracks. Turf high 68. Has been a useful handicapper in his day under both codes, but is hard to win with nowadays.
**M R Channon [0-10] The Silver Darling Partnership (from R Akehurst [4-36] Spt 1997).*

SILVER GYRE (IRE) BHB 71f **RR 69f** 4956[9]
2 b f Silver Hawk (USA) 11.2f **(85)** - Kraemer (USA) (Lyphard (USA)) 9.9f **(72)**
Form - 400
Record 1998 - 1st:0 2nd:0 3rd:0 Ran:3
Win Prizemoney £0 *Total Prizemoney* £246
1998 Turf 0-3: (7f 2, 8f) (frm 3)
Currently average filly. Turf high 69 (began Aug).
**Mrs J R Ramsden [0-3] Mrs Joan Egan.*

SILVER HARROW BHB 45f26a **RR 49f 26a** 4456[12]
5 ch g Belmez (USA) 11.4f **(65)** - Dancing Diana (Raga Navarro (ITY)) 8f **(64)**
Form - 807474450
Record 1998 - 1st:0 2nd:0 3rd:0 Ran:8
Pre1998 - 1st:1 2nd:6 3rd:6 Ran:32
Win Prizemoney £3,015 *Total Prizemoney* £12,065
Wins * 1996 Oct Leices (G-F) SH 7f 53 59 <
1998 Turf 0-6: (6f, 8f 5) (g-f 4, frm 2) 1998 AW 0-2: (8f 2) (Fibr 2)
Moderate gelding, effective 7 to 8f, best at 8f, acts on gd to frm, has worn blinkers, likes left handed tracks. Turf high 49. AW high 30.
**A G Newcombe [1-33] M Patel (from Sir Mark Prescott [0-7] Oct 1995).*

SILVER HOPE (IRE) BHB 34f41a **RR 29f 41a** 4120[10]
3 ch c Silver Kite (USA) 10.2f **(51)** - Cloven Dancer (USA) (Hurok (USA)) 7.7f **(60)**
Form - 648710000
Record 1998 - 1st:1 2nd:0 3rd:0 Ran:9
Pre1998 - 1st:0 2nd:0 3rd:0 Ran:5
Win Prizemoney £2,406 *Total Prizemoney* £2,406
Wins * 1998 *Apr Wolver (STD) H 12f 41 45* <
1998 Turf 0-3: (12f 3) (g-s 2, g-f) 1998 AW 1-6: (8f, 11f, 12f 1-2, 15f, 16f) (Fibr 1-6)
Moderate colt, effective 12f, - acts on Fibr, has worn blinkers (very effectively), likes left handed tracks. Turf high 24. AW high 45 - also 1st of 6 getting 13lb from Vincent (30 Apr Wolverhampton RF 0942). Inconsistent. **R Hollinshead [1-14] John Smallman.*

SILVERING (FR) BHB 82f82a **RR 83f 82a** 4586[7]
6 b h Polish Precedent (USA) 9f **(73)** - Silvermine (FR) (Bellypha) 9.8f **(73)**
Form - 457721707
Record 1998 - 1st:1 2nd:1 3rd:0 Ran:9
Pre1998 - 1st:0 2nd:0 3rd:1 Ran:3
Win Prizemoney £5,865 *Total Prizemoney* £16,299
Wins * 1998 Jun Ayr (G-F) H 7f 82 83 <
1998 Turf 1-7: (6f 2, 7f 1-1, 8f 4) (sft, gd 2, g-f 1-3, frm) 1998 AW 0-2: (7f, 8f) (Equi, Fibr)
Decent horse, effective 6 to 8f, acts on g-f. Turf high 83 - 1st of 7 giving 17lb to Smokey From Caplaw (20 Jun Ayr RF 2143). AW high 69. Sold for 15,000 guineas at Tattersalls in October.
**M Meade [1-6] David Caddy (from R M H Cowell [0-3] Mar 1998).*

SILVER JOY BHB 36f33a **RR 21f 33a** 3094[7]

3 b f Silver Kite (USA) 10.2f **(51)** - Oh My Joy (Grundy) 10.3f **(65)**

Form - 06670067

Record	**1998** -	1st:0	2nd:0	3rd:0	Ran:7
	Pre1998 -	1st:0	2nd:0	3rd:0	Ran:3

1998 Turf 0-4: (6f, 7f 2, 8f) (gd 2, g-f, frm) 1998 AW 0-3: (7f, 8f, 12f) (Equi 2, Fibr)

Unfurnished, little account filly, has worn blinkers. Turf high 43. AW high 27. **K McAuliffe [0-10] Gallagher Equine Ltd.*

SILVER KRISTAL BHB 76f **RR 77f** 4147[9]

4 gr f Kris 10f **(75)** - Reine D'Beaute (Caerleon (USA)) 8.6f **(71)**

Form - 86170

Record	**1998** -	1st:1	2nd:0	3rd:0	Ran:5
	Pre1998 -	1st:0	2nd:2	3rd:1	Ran:7

Win Prizemoney £3,980 *Total Prizemoney* £7,350

Wins	* **1998**	Jly	Yarmou	(G-F)	H	7f	73	77	<

1998 Turf 1-5: (6f, 7f 1-2, 8f 2) (g-s, g-f 1-3, frm)

Scopey, above-average filly, effective 7 to 8f, best at 7f, acts on gd to g-f, best on g-f. Turf high 77 - 1st of 13 giving 30lb to Dina Line (21 Jly Yarmouth RF 2978). Though running quite well, she did not break her duck until landing a modest Yarmouth handicap in July.
**R W Armstrong [1-5] Sir Eric Parker (from R Akehurst [0-7] Oct 1997).*

SILVER LINING BHB 47f **RR 49f** 4456[20]

4 b g Beveled (USA) 6.9f **(64)** - Seymour Ann (Krayyan) 8.5f **(49)**

Form - 0050043770

Record	**1998** -	1st:0	2nd:0	3rd:1	Ran:10
	Pre1998 -	1st:3	2nd:0	3rd:1	Ran:12

Win Prizemoney £8,892 *Total Prizemoney* £10,101

Wins	* 1997	Jly	Leices	(GD)	H	7f	60	64	
	* 1997	Jun	Salisb	(G-F)	H	7f	58	63	
	* 1996	Jly	Leices	(G-F)	S	5f		70+	<

1998 Turf 0-10: (7f 6, 8f 4) (gd, g-f 3, frm 6)

Leggy, moderate gelding, effective 5 to 7f, best at 7f, acts on gd to frm, best on frm. Turf high 51.
**A P Jones [3-22] The Lambourn Racing Club.*

SILVER MIST BHB 54f **RR 53f** 4668[10]

2 b f Lugana Beach 7f **(63)** - Highland Bonnie (Dreams to Reality (USA)) 6.4f **(73)**

Form - 8040

Record	**1998** -	1st:0	2nd:0	3rd:0	Ran:4

Win Prizemoney £0 *Total Prizemoney* £392

1998 Turf 0-4: (5f 2, 6f 2) (gd, g-f, frm 2)

Fair filly. Turf high 53 (began Jly).
**B A McMahon [0-4] Dr Neil Dorward.*

SILVER MOON BHB 36a **RR 18f** 24[9]

4 gr f Environment Friend 7.5f **(67)** - High and Bright (Shirley Heights) 10.3f **(74)**

Form - 0

Record	**1998** -	1st:0	2nd:0	3rd:0	Ran:1
	Pre1998 -	1st:0	2nd:0	3rd:0	Ran:7

1998 AW 0-1: (11f) (Fibr)

Little account filly. Becoming disappointing.
**B A McMahon [0-8] Michael Sturgess.*

SILVER PATRIARCH (IRE) BHB 126f **RR 122f** 4951a[1]

4 gr c Saddlers' Hall (IRE) 10.5f **(65)** - Early Rising (USA) (Grey Dawn II) 11.1f **(72)**

Form - 2146221

Record	**1998** -	1st:2	2nd:3	3rd:0	Ran:7
	Pre1998 -	1st:4	2nd:2	3rd:1	Ran:10

Win Prizemoney £428,522 *Total Prizemoney* £750,657

Wins	* **1998**	Oct	San Si	(SFT)	G1	12f	122	<
	* **1998**	Jun	Epsom	(GD)	G1	12f	122	<
	* 1997	Spt	Doncas	(G-F)	G1	14.6f	121	
	* 1997	May	Lingfi	(SFT)	G3	11.5f	102+	
	* 1996	Nov	Newmar	(GD)	L	10f	105	
	* 1996	Oct	Pontef	(GD)		10f	82+	

1998 Turf 2-7: (12f 2-5, 13f, 14f) (sft 1-1, gd 1-4, g-f 2)

Scopey, very high-class colt, effective 10 to 15f, best at 12f, acts on sft to g-f, prefers left handed tracks, likes Epsom. Turf high 122 - 1st of 6 from Posidonas (18 Oct San Siro RF 4951a) - also 1st of 7

Silver Patriarch (left) laid his Epsom ghost to rest.

from Swain (5 Jun Epsom RF 1745). Consistent. The winner of the St Leger and runner-up in the Derby in 1997, he ran very creditably on his reappearance when second to Romanov in the Jockey Club Stakes. He went one better with a fine win in the Coronation Cup, despite again not handling the downhill run into the straight. He was not suited by the slow pace in the Grand Prix de Saint-Cloud next time, then ran poorly in the King George. His inability to do anything quickly once again proved his undoing when he was beaten by Multicoloured in the Geoffrey Freer, before being out-stayed by Kayf Tara in the Irish St Leger. He finished the season in style when beating compatriot Posidonas in the valuable Gran Premio del Jockey-Club in Milan. He needs a strongly-run race to be at his most effective, and connections are likely to step him up in distance in 1999 with the Ascot Gold Cup as the target.

**J L Dunlop [6-17] Peter Winfield.*

SILVER PREY (USA) BHB 65f **RR 61f** 5040[10]

5 b g Silver Hawk (USA) 11.2f **(85)** - Truly My Style (USA) (Mount Hagen (FR)) 8.4f **(70)**

Form - 50077000

Record 1998 - 1st:0 2nd:0 3rd:0 Ran:8
Pre1998 - 1st:1 2nd:0 3rd:2 Ran:4

Win Prizemoney £4,952 *Total Prizemoney* £7,170

Wins 1995 Aug Newbur (G-F) 7f 80 <

1998 Turf 0-8: (7f 2, 8f 5, 9f) (g-s, gd 4, frm 3)

Average gelding. Turf high 80. Inconsistent.

**M J Bolton [0-8] A R M Galbraith (from E A L Dunlop [1-4] Oct 1996).*

Win Prizemoney £35,414 *Total Prizemoney* £40,099

Wins * **1998** Oct Ascot (SFT) G3 12f 110 <
* **1998** Jun Newmar (GD) 10f 85

1998 Turf 2-4: (10f 1-1, 12f 1-3) (g-s 1-2, g-f, hrd 1-1)

Lengthy, Group-class filly. Turf high 110 - 1st of 7 getting 10lb from Delilah (10 Oct Ascot RF 4740). Her stable was out of sorts when she ran poorly in the re-scheduled St Simon Stakes at Newmarket in October. Better judged on a decisive win in the Princess Royal Stakes, she is a resolute galloper and should do well if kept in training. **H R A Cecil [2-5] Lordship Stud.*

SILVER ROBIN (USA) RR 80+f 5137[2]

2 b br c Silver Hawk (USA) 11.2f **(85)** - Wedge Musical (What A Guest) 7f **(62)**

Form - 2

Record 1998 - 1st:0 2nd:1 3rd:0 Ran:1

Win Prizemoney £0 *Total Prizemoney* £1,040

1998 Turf 0-1: (7f) (gd)

Currently decent colt. (1st run) - 2nd of 20 to Ettrick (6 Nov Doncaster 7f gd RF 5137).

**L M Cumani [0-1] W V M W & Mrs E S Robins.*

SILVER SABRE (USA) RR 77df 1269[5]

3 b c Silver Hawk (USA) 11.2f **(85)** - Explosive Tobin (USA) (Explodent (USA)) 9.4f **(87)**

Form - 35

Silver Rhapsody on song at Ascot

SILVER RHAPSODY (USA) BHB 109f **RR 110f** 5075[5]

3 b f Silver Hawk (USA) 11.2f **(85)** - Sister Chrys (USA) (Fit To Fight (USA)) 9.7f **(45)**

Form - 1315

Record 1998 - 1st:2 2nd:0 3rd:1 Ran:4
Pre1998 - 1st:0 2nd:1 3rd:0 Ran:1

Record 1998 - 1st:0 2nd:0 3rd:1 Ran:2

Win Prizemoney £0 *Total Prizemoney* £537

1998 Turf 0-2: (10f, 12f) (gd, frm)

Workmanlike, currently above-average colt. Turf high 77 (1st run) - 3rd of 9 to Al-Fateh (4 May Newcastle 10f gd RF 1024).

**E A L Dunlop [0-2] Maktoum Al Maktoum.*

SILVER SANDS BHB 41f **RR 20f** 584[14]
4 gr f Chilibang 7f **(55)** - Sayida-Shahira (Record Run) 8f **(42)**
Form - 00
Record 1998 - 1st:0 2nd:0 3rd:0 Ran:2
Pre1998 - 1st:0 2nd:0 3rd:0 Ran:3
1998 Turf 0-2: (7f, 10f) (sft, g-s)
Workmanlike, little account filly. Turf high 20.
**T P McGovern [0-8] The Best Of Luck Partnership.*

SILVER SEA (USA) RR 47f 4529[14]
3 gr ro f Java Gold (USA) 9.3f **(67)** - Gray And Red (USA) (Wolf Power (SAF))
Form - 0000
Record 1998 - 1st:0 2nd:0 3rd:0 Ran:4
Pre1998 - 1st:0 2nd:0 3rd:0 Ran:1
1998 Turf 0-4: (6f, 7f, 8f 2) (g-f 3, frm)
Workmanlike, moderate filly. Turf high 47 (began Jly).
**I A Balding [0-5] Paul Mellon.*

SILVER SECRET BHB 48f **RR 49f** 5040[9]
4 ro g Absalom 7.1f **(56)** - Secret Dance (Sadler's Wells (USA)) 10f **(76)**
Form - 640040
Record 1998 - 1st:0 2nd:0 3rd:0 Ran:6
Pre1998 - 1st:1 2nd:0 3rd:1 Ran:11
Win Prizemoney £2,277 *Total Prizemoney* £3,614
Wins 1997 Aug Folkes (G-F) 6f 60 <
1998 Turf 0-6: (7f 3, 8f, 10f 2) (sft, g-s, g-f, frm 3)
Workmanlike, moderate gelding, effective 6 to 8f, acts on g-f, has worn blinkers. Turf high 57 (began Jly).
**S Gollings [0-6] R Attwood (from M J Heaton-Ellis [1-11] Spt 1997).*

SILVERSMITH (FR) RR 67f 4128[18]
3 b c Always Fair (USA) 14f **(61)** - Phargette (FR) (Lyphard (USA)) 9.9f **(72)**
Form - 605000
Record 1998 - 1st:0 2nd:0 3rd:0 Ran:6
Pre1998 - 1st:0 2nd:2 3rd:0 Ran:3
Win Prizemoney £0 *Total Prizemoney* £2,120
1998 Turf 0-6: (6f, 7f 3, 8f 2) (gd 2, g-f, frm 3)
Workmanlike, average colt. Turf high 67 (began Jly). Becoming disappointing. **S Dow [0-9] D G Churston.*

SILVER SNAKE (IRE) RR 48f 4842[5]
2 b c Salse (USA) 10.9f **(71)** - Ibtisamm (USA) (Caucasus (USA)) 8.2f **(74)**
Form - 5
Record 1998 - 1st:0 2nd:0 3rd:0 Ran:1
Win Prizemoney £0 *Total Prizemoney* £170
1998 Turf 0-1: (7f) (g-f)
Currently moderate colt. **C E Brittain [0-1] Mohamed Obaida.*

SILVER SPIDER RR 36f 2195[7]
3 gr g Terimon 8.7f **(58)** - Quetta's Girl (Orchestra) 9.7f **(52)**
Form - 07
Record 1998 - 1st:0 2nd:0 3rd:0 Ran:2
1998 Turf 0-2: (8f, 10f) (frm 2)
Scopey, currently very moderate gelding. Turf high 36.
**Mrs S Lamyman [0-2] P Lamyman.*

SILVER STAR (FR) RR 103f 4725a[5]
2 b f Zafonic (USA) 9f **(83)** - Monroe (USA) (Sir Ivor) 10.2f **(70)**
Form - 5
1998 Turf 0-1: (8f) (sft)
Currently very useful filly. (1st run) - 5th of 11 to Juvenia (4 Oct Longchamp 8f sft RF 4725a). A sister to Xaar, she made a promising debut at Chantilly in September, and was only beaten a length when finishing fifth in the Group One Prix Marcel Boussac the following month. She has a bright future and should stay beyond a mile. **A Fabre in FR [0-1] K Abdulla.*

SILVER STRAND (IRE) BHB 73f **RR 80f** 4933[8]
3 b f Waajib 8.9f **(67)** - Jendeal (Troy) 10.4f **(68)**
Form - 62423308
Record 1998 - 1st:0 2nd:2 3rd:2 Ran:8
Pre1998 - 1st:1 2nd:1 3rd:0 Ran:3
Win Prizemoney £3,486 *Total Prizemoney* £9,717
Wins * 1997 Jly Nottin (SFT) 6.1f 71 <
1998 Turf 0-8: (7f, 8f 2, 9f 2, 10f 2, 12f) (sft, g-s 2, gd 3, g-f 2)
Well made, decent filly, effective 6 to 10f, acts on g-s to g-f. Turf high 80 - 2nd of 10 giving 3lb to Radar (13 Jun Sandown 9f g-s RF 1974). **B W Hills [1-11] Miss Susan McIntyre.*

SILVER SUN BHB 68f **RR 72f** 4644[6]
3 gr f Green Desert (USA) 7.8f **(78)**-Catch The Sun (Kalaglow) 9.8f **(67)**
Form - 738420256
Record 1998 - 1st:0 2nd:2 3rd:1 Ran:9
Pre1998 - 1st:0 2nd:0 3rd:0 Ran:1
Win Prizemoney £0 *Total Prizemoney* £3,083
1998 Turf 0-9: (7f, 8f 4, 10f 4) (g-s, gd 3, g-f 3, frm 2)
Light-framed, above-average filly, effective 8 to 10f, best at 10f, acts on g-f to frm, best on frm. Turf high 72.
**D R C Elsworth [0-10] C J Harper.*

SILVER SYMPHONY RR 35f 1291[6]
3 gr f Kylian (USA) 8.1f **(66)** - Brave Maiden (Three Legs) 11.1f **(54)**
Form - 6
Record 1998 - 1st:0 2nd:0 3rd:0 Ran:1
1998 Turf 0-1: (8f) (frm)
Scopey, currently very moderate filly. **B R Millman [0-1] G Palmer.*

SILVERTOWN BHB 49f **RR 44f** 5095[8]
3 b c Danehill (USA) 9.1f **(79)** - Docklands (USA) (Theatrical)
Form - 3054260008
Record 1998 - 1st:0 2nd:1 3rd:1 Ran:10
Pre1998 - 1st:0 2nd:1 3rd:0 Ran:2
Win Prizemoney £0 *Total Prizemoney* £2,971
1998 Turf 0-10: (7f, 8f, 9f, 10f 2, 11f, 12f 4) (g-s, gd 5, g-f 2, frm 2)
Scopey, moderate colt, effective 7f, acts on frm, likes tight tracks. Turf high 68. Consistent. Looks to have his share of temperament.
**B J Curley [0-7] Mrs B J Curley (from J H M Gosden [0-5] Jun 1998).*

SILVER WEDDING BHB 53f **RR 54f** 4477[8]
3 gr f Warning 8.1f **(77)** - Best Girl Friend (Sharrood (USA)) 10.5f **(72)**
Form - 7788
Record 1998 - 1st:0 2nd:0 3rd:0 Ran:4
1998 Turf 0-4: (8f 2, 10f 2) (g-s, g-f, frm, hrd)
Workmanlike, fair filly. Turf high 54 (began Jly).
**Lady Herries [0-4] Mrs Denis Haynes.*

SILVER WEDGE (USA) BHB 90f **RR 102?f** 4963[1]
7 ch g Silver Hawk (USA) 11.2f **(85)** - Wedge Musical (What A Guest) 7f **(62)**
Form - 1
Record 1998 - 1st:1 2nd:0 3rd:0 Ran:1
Pre1998 - 1st:3 2nd:3 3rd:2 Ran:14
Win Prizemoney £53,424 *Total Prizemoney* £63,098
Wins * **1998** Oct Newbur (HVY) H 16f 85 87
1994 Jun Ascot (G-F) G3 16.2f 100 <
1994 May Newbur (G-F) H 12f 85 88
1998 Turf 1-1: (16f 1-1) (sft 1-1)
Very useful gelding, has worn blinkers (very effectively). (1st run). One of the top staying hurdlers a few seasons back, he caused a big surprise when overcoming an absence of two and a half years to win on the Flat at Newbury.
**N J Henderson [1-1] W V M W & Mrs E S Robins (from Lord Huntingdon [0-2] Spt 1995).*

SILVERY BHB 36f **RR 42f** 3900[16]
4 gr f Petong 7.6f **(58)** - Petit Peu (IRE) (Kings Lake (USA)) 10.8f **(67)**
Form - 0008080
Record 1998 - 1st:0 2nd:0 3rd:0 Ran:7
Pre1998 - 1st:1 2nd:1 3rd:0 Ran:7
Win Prizemoney £3,850 *Total Prizemoney* £4,709
Wins 1997 Spt Goodwo (GD) 10f 66 <
1998 Turf 0-7: (10f 4, 12f 3) (sft 2, gd, g-f 4)
Light-framed, moderate filly, effective 10f, acts on gd, likes right handed tracks. Turf high 46. Inconsistent.
**S Woodman [0-7] The Hallmark Partnership (from J A R Toller [1-7] Oct 1997).*

SIMLET BHB 60f70a **RR 72f 70a** 4708[7]
3 b g Forzando 7.2f **(63)** - Besito (Wassl) 9.7f **(62)**
Form - 13233775527
Record 1998 - 1st:1 2nd:2 3rd:3 Ran:11

Pre1998 - 1st:0 2nd:2 3rd:0 Ran:5
Win Prizemoney £2,169 *Total Prizemoney* £7,702
Wins * **1998** *Feb Lingfi (SLW) 8f 57+* <
1998 Turf 0-9: (8f 2, 9f, 10f 4, 11f, 12f) (g-s, gd, g-f 3, frm 4) 1998 AW 1-2: (8f 1-1, 9f) (Equi 1-1, Fibr)
Small, above-average gelding, effective 7 to 9f, best at 9f, acts on g-s to frm - acts on Fibr, often wears blinkers, excels at Lingfield. Turf high 75 (1st run) - 2nd of 20 giving 7lb to Dancing Lawyer (4 May Warwick 8f g-f RF 1031). AW high 74 - 3rd of 4 to Prince Ashleigh (25 Feb Wolverhampton 9f Fibr RF 0362). Has joined David Nicholls. **W Jarvis [1-16] Mrs Doris Allen.*

SIMPLE IDEALS (USA) BHB 38f **RR 67f** 4890[5]
4 bb g Woodman (USA) 9.7f **(77)** - Comfort and Style (Be My Guest (USA)) 9.3f **(67)**
Form - 507700785
Record 1998 - 1st:0 2nd:0 3rd:0 Ran:9
Pre1998 - 1st:0 2nd:0 3rd:2 Ran:6
Win Prizemoney £0 *Total Prizemoney* £813
1998 Turf 0-9: (10f, 11f 3, 12f 4, 14f) (hvy, sft, g-s, g-f 2, frm 4)
Average gelding, effective 10f, acts on g-s, has worn blinkers. Turf high 67. Becoming disappointing.
**N Tinkler [0-5] J Parks (from M Torrens in IRE [0-9] Aug 1998).*

SIMPLY GIFTED BHB 79f **RR 84f** 3407[6]
3 b g Simply Great (FR) 11.9f **(61)** - Souveniers (Relko) 9.9f **(59)**
Form - 2376
Record 1998 - 1st:0 2nd:1 3rd:1 Ran:4
Pre1998 - 1st:1 2nd:0 3rd:2 Ran:4
Win Prizemoney £2,869 *Total Prizemoney* £10,796
Wins * 1997 Jly Newcas (GD) 7f 60 <
1998 Turf 0-4: (10f 2, 11f, 12f) (g-s, gd, g-f, frm)
Leggy, decent gelding, effective 8 to 10f, acts on sft to g-s. Turf high 84 (1st run) - 2nd of 6 getting 17lb from Evening World (13 Jun York 10f g-s RF 1983). Progressive at two, he ran a good race at York on his return, but his response off the bit was rather disappointing next time. Has switched successfully to hurdles.
**T D Easterby [1-8] Steve Hammond.*

SIMPLY MAGICAL BHB 58f **RR 53f** 5000[5]
2 b f Magic Ring (IRE) 6.5f **(64)** - Naulakha **(55f)** (Bustino) 10.4f **(64)**
Form - 055
Record 1998 - 1st:0 2nd:0 3rd:0 Ran:3
1998 Turf 0-3: (7f 2, 8f) (sft, gd 2)
Currently fair filly. Turf high 53 (began Spt).
**P Mitchell [0-3] The Chint Racing Club.*

SIMPLY NOBLE BHB 81f **RR 81f** 4530[1]
2 b c Noble Patriarch 12.2f **(43)** - Simply Candy (IRE) (Simply Great (FR)) 8.2f **(65)**
Form - 771
Record 1998 - 1st:1 2nd:0 3rd:0 Ran:3
Win Prizemoney £2,738 *Total Prizemoney* £2,738
Wins * **1998** Spt Hamilt (SFT) 8.3f 81 <
1998 Turf 1-3: (6f, 8f 1-2) (g-s 1-1, g-f 2)
Currently decent colt. Turf high 81 (began Jly) - 1st of 10 from Lucky Gitano (28 Spt Hamilton RF 4530).
**K McAuliffe [1-3] MCKPS Equine Ltd.*

SIMPLY SPECIAL (IRE) RR 31f 4664[9]
2 ch f Petit Loup (USA) - Triste Oeil (USA) (Raise A Cup (USA)) 7.6f **(74)**
Form - 0
Record 1998 - 1st:0 2nd:0 3rd:0 Ran:1
1998 Turf 0-1: (8f) (g-s)
Currently very moderate filly. **B Hanbury [0-1] Abdullah Ali.*

SIMPLY SUPER BHB 54f65a **RR 70f 65a** 4760[18]
3 ch f Superlative 8.8f **(57)** - Real Princess (Aragon) 8.1f **(60)**
Form - 0032040070
Record 1998 - 1st:0 2nd:1 3rd:1 Ran:10
Pre1998 - 1st:1 2nd:0 3rd:0 Ran:2
Win Prizemoney £2,484 *Total Prizemoney* £4,765
Wins * 1997 Aug Bright (G-F) 6f 63 <
1998 Turf 0-9:(7f, 8f 5, 9f 2, 10f)(gd 4, g-f 4,frm)1998 AW 0-1:(7f) (Equi)
Scopey, above-average filly, effective 6 to 8f, acts on gd to g-f, often wears blinkers. Turf high 70 - 3rd of 7 to London Be Good (29 Jly Doncaster 8f g-f RF 3194). Inconsistent.
**C E Brittain [1-12] C E Brittain.*

SIMPSON'S DOMAIN (IRE) BHB 50f40a **RR 59f 40a** 5073[3]
2 b f Woods of Windsor (USA) - Admiralella **(62f)** (Dominion) 8.5f **(63)**
Form - 63545567063
Record 1998 - 1st:0 2nd:0 3rd:2 Ran:11
Win Prizemoney £0 *Total Prizemoney* £1,050
1998 Turf 0-9: (5f 3, 6f 3, 7f 2, 8f) (g-s, gd 5, frm 3) 1998 AW 0-2: (7f 2) (Fibr 2)
Fair filly, has worn blinkers. Turf high 58. AW high 48 (began Jly).
**J S Moore [0-11] Mrs P M Ratcliffe.*

SINCH BHB 50f43a **RR 43f 43a** 139[8]
3 ch f Inchinor 8.9f **(64)** - Swinging Gold (Swing Easy (USA)) 6.5f **(55)**
Form - 88
Record 1998 - 1st:0 2nd:0 3rd:0 Ran:2
Pre1998 - 1st:0 2nd:0 3rd:0 Ran:2
Win Prizemoney £0 *Total Prizemoney* £227
1998 AW 0-2: (6f, 7f) (Fibr 2)
Leggy, moderate filly. AW high 31. **T D Barron [0-4] Geoffrey Martin.*

SING AND DANCE BHB 48f **RR 50f** 5119[5]
5 b m Rambo Dancer (CAN) 8.4f **(59)** - Musical Princess (Cavo Doro) 10.6f **(57)**
Form - 48343121644015
Record 1998 - 1st:3 2nd:1 3rd:2 Ran:14
Pre1998 - 1st:1 2nd:2 3rd:3 Ran:25
Win Prizemoney £13,555 *Total Prizemoney* £20,001
Wins * **1998** Oct Catter (G-S) H 12f 47 50 <
* **1998** Jly Newcas (GD) H 12.4f 44 46
* **1998** Jun Mussel (G-F) H 12f 39 42
* 1997 Aug Redcar (G-F) H 10f 38 44
1998 Turf 3-14: (9f, 10f 2, 11f 2, 12f 3-9) (g-s, gd 2-6, g-f 3, frm 1-4)
Fair filly, effective 10 to 12f, best at 12f, acts on g-s to frm, best on gd, has worn blinkers, excels at Musselburgh and Newcastle, does well at Redcar. Turf high 50 - 1st of 14 giving 1lb to Russian Aspect (15 Oct Catterick RF 4815) - also 1st of 7 getting 15lb from Vanadium Ore (27 Jly Newcastle RF 3142). Consistent.
**E Weymes [4-39] Mrs N Napier.*

SINGER SARGENT (USA) BHB 75f **RR 76f** 3148[5]
3 ch c Kingmambo (USA) 10.9f **(85)** - Puppet Dance (USA) (Northern Dancer) 9.6f **(80)**
Form - 0725
Record 1998 - 1st:0 2nd:1 3rd:0 Ran:4
Win Prizemoney £0 *Total Prizemoney* £1,140
1998 Turf 0-4: (8f 4) (sft, gd, frm 2)
Well made, above-average colt. Turf high 76 - 2nd of 9 to Cadette (16 Jly Doncaster 8f frm RF 2850). Will not live up to his pedigree - he's out of a half-sister to Sadler's Wells - or to the 880,000gns price tag which made him the top lot at the 1996 Highflyer Sale.
**Sir Michael Stoute [0-4] Tabor Mrs Magnier & Niarchos Family.*

SING FOR ME (IRE) BHB 37f44a **RR 43f 44a** 4550[5]
3 b br f Songlines (FR) 5f **(68)** - Running For You (FR) (Pampabird) 7.5f **(73)**
Form - 468831460258036075
Record 1998 - 1st:1 2nd:1 3rd:2 Ran:15
Pre1998 - 1st:0 2nd:0 3rd:1 Ran:12
Win Prizemoney £1,738 *Total Prizemoney* £3,226
Wins * **1998** *Feb Wolver (STD) S 5f 53* <
1998 Turf 0-8: (5f 2, 6f 5, 8f) (g-s, gd 2, g-f, frm 4) 1998 AW 1-7: (5f 1-2, 6f 4, 8f) (Fibr 1-7)
Moderate filly, effective 6f, acts on gd, has worn blinkers. Turf high 48. AW high 53. Consistent. **R Hollinshead [1-27] J Doxey.*

SING FOR ROSIE BHB 53f **RR 55f** 5123[8]
2 br f Petong 7.6f **(58)** - Turbo Rose (Taufan (USA)) 7f **(57)**
Form - 0708
Record 1998 - 1st:0 2nd:0 3rd:0 Ran:4
1998 Turf 0-4: (6f 3, 7f) (g-s, g-f, frm 2)
Fair filly. Turf high 55 (began Aug).
**P J Makin [0-4] Four Seasons Racing Ltd.*

SINGFORYOURSUPPER BHB 34f **RR 14df** 4339[19]
4 ch f Superlative 8.8f **(57)** - Suzannah's Song (Song) 7.2f **(61)**

Form - 000
Record 1998 - 1st:0 2nd:0 3rd:0 Ran:3
Pre1998 - 1st:1 2nd:1 3rd:0 Ran:15
Win Prizemoney £3,420 *Total Prizemoney* £5,142
Wins * 1996 Aug Sandow (G-F) SH 5f 50 50 <
1998 Turf 0-3: (5f 2, 6f) (g-f, frm 2)
Scopey, very moderate filly, effective 5f, acts on gd. (began Aug). Becoming disappointing. *G G Margarson [1-18] Mrs S M Martin.*

SINGLE EMPIRE (IRE) BHB 112f **RR 116f** 3917a[8]
4 ch c Kris 10f **(75)** - Captive Island (Northfields (USA)) 9f **(72)**
Form - 668
Record 1998 - 1st:0 2nd:0 3rd:0 Ran:3
Pre1998 - 1st:3 2nd:0 3rd:0 Ran:5
Win Prizemoney £250,195 *Total Prizemoney* £250,767
Wins * 1997 May Capann (G-F) G1 12f 101 <
* 1997 May Newmar (GD) 12f 89
* 1997 Mar Kempto (G-F) 11.1f 83
1998 Turf 0-3: (12f, 13f, 15f) (sft, g-f, frm)
Scopey, high-class colt, effective 12f, acts on frm. Turf high 116 (1st run) (began Jly) - 6th of 7 giving 18lb to Fruits of Love (7 Jly Newmarket 12f frm RF 2581). Winner of the 1997 Derby Italiano, he showed very little in three outings in 1998.
P W Chapple-Hyam [3-8] A K Collins.

SINGLE SHOT (USA) BHB 83f **RR 82f** 5115[1]
2 b c Hermitage (USA) 8.6f **(84)** - Bourbon Miss (USA) (Smile (USA))
Form - 032221
Record 1998 - 1st:1 2nd:3 3rd:1 Ran:6
Win Prizemoney £3,148 *Total Prizemoney* £7,045
Wins * **1998** Nov Mussel (SFT) 7.1f 72 <
1998 Turf 1-6: (6f 2, 7f 1-3, 8f) (sft, gd 1-1, g-f 2, frm 2)
Decent colt, effective 6 to 8f, acts on sft to frm. Turf high 82 (began Jly) - 2nd of 9 to Bring Sweets (17 Oct Redcar 8f sft RF 4860).
L M Cumani [1-6] Donald Kahn.

SING WITH THE BAND BHB 42f65a **RR 46f 65a** 72[8]
7 b m Chief Singer 8.6f **(62)** - Ra Ra Girl (Shack (USA)) 5.8f **(53)**
Form - 8
Record 1998 - 1st:0 2nd:0 3rd:0 Ran:1
Pre1998 - 1st:3 2nd:9 3rd:5 Ran:51
Win Prizemoney £8,244 *Total Prizemoney* £24,329
Wins 1996 Jun Warwic (FRM) H 5f 58 64+
1995 Jun Southw (STD) H 5f 63 65 <
1995 May Southw (STD) H 5f 60 60
1998 AW 0-1: (7f) (Fibr)
Average mare, effective 5f, - acts on Fibr, has worn blinkers, likes left handed tracks, likes tight tracks.
R Hollinshead [0-1] The Three R's (from B A McMahon [3-51] Spt 1997).

SINON (IRE) BHB 101f **RR 102f** 2647[4]
3 ch c Ela-Mana-Mou 12.7f **(72)**-Come In(Be My Guest (USA)) 9.3f **(67)**
Form - 144
Record 1998 - 1st:1 2nd:0 3rd:0 Ran:3
Pre1998 - 1st:1 2nd:0 3rd:0 Ran:2
Win Prizemoney £13,134 *Total Prizemoney* £17,004
Wins * **1998** May York (GD) 13.9f 96 <
* 1997 Spt Redcar (FRM) 9f 85+
1998 Turf 1-3: (14f 1-1, 15f, 16f) (gd 1-2, frm)
Scopey, very useful colt. Turf high 102 - 4th of 8 to Maridpour (17 Jun Ascot 16f gd RF 2057) - also 1st of 5 from Elhayq (12 May York RF 1169). He did not look happy on fast ground at Newmarket in July and is an out-and-out stayer. *M Johnston [2-5] Ridings Racing.*

SIOUX BHB 55f62a **RR 63f 62a** 4875[3]
4 ch f Kris 10f **(75)** - Lassoo (Caerleon (USA)) 8.6f **(71)**
Form - 503
Record 1998 - 1st:0 2nd:0 3rd:1 Ran:3
Pre1998 - 1st:0 2nd:0 3rd:1 Ran:7
Win Prizemoney £0 *Total Prizemoney* £920
1998 Turf 0-2: (12f 2) (g-s, frm) 1998 AW 0-1: (12f) (Fibr)
Leggy, average filly. Turf high 61 (began Spt).
C W Thornton [0-10] Guy Reed.

SIOUXANNA BHB 30f **RR 29f** 3119[9]
3 b f Totem (USA) 5f **(38)** - Adder Howe (Amboise)
Form - 07600
Record 1998 - 1st:0 2nd:0 3rd:0 Ran:5
1998 Turf 0-5: (7f, 8f 2, 10f, 12f) (g-s 2, g-f, frm, hrd)
Little account filly. Turf high 29.
J R Turner [0-5] Mrs Susan Johnson.

SIPOWITZ BHB 60f59a **RR 64f 59a** 874[3]
4 b g Warrshan (USA) 9.7f **(59)**-Springs Welcome (Blakeney) 10.5f **(64)**
Form - 03
Record 1998 - 1st:0 2nd:0 3rd:1 Ran:1
Pre1998 - 1st:5 2nd:1 3rd:1 Ran:15
Win Prizemoney £14,226 *Total Prizemoney* £16,543
Wins * 1997 Oct Pontef (G-S) H 18f 56 64 <
* 1997 Oct Pontef (G-F) H 17.1f 53 57
* *1997 Aug Lingfi (G-S) H 16f 46 50*
* 1997 Jly Lingfi (G-F) H 16f 44 52
* *1997 Jun Wolver (STD) H 14.8f 44 41*
1998 AW 0-1: (15f) (Fibr)
Leggy, average gelding, effective 15 to 18f, acts on gd to g-f - acts on Fibr, prefers left handed tracks, and excels at Pontefract and Wolverhampton. (1st run) - 3rd of 6 getting 21lb from Star Rage (25 Apr Wolverhampton 15f Fibr RF 0874). *C A Cyzer [5-16] R M Cyzer.*

SIR ECHO (FR) BHB 75f **RR 75f** 5138[6]
2 b c Saumarez 15.1f **(87)** - Echoes (FR) (Niniski (USA)) 10.6f **(65)**
Form - 0646
Record 1998 - 1st:0 2nd:0 3rd:0 Ran:4
Win Prizemoney £0 *Total Prizemoney* £248
1998 Turf 0-4: (7f 2, 8f 2) (sft, gd 2, frm)
Above-average colt. Turf high 75 (began Jly).
H Candy [0-4] P A Deal.

SIREN SONG (IRE) **RR 60f** 1127[4]
7 b g Warning 8.1f **(77)** - Nazwa (Tarboosh (USA)) 10f **(55)**
Form - 4
Record 1998 - 1st:0 2nd:0 3rd:0 Ran:1
Win Prizemoney £0 *Total Prizemoney* £490
1998 Turf 0-1: (10f) (frm)
Average gelding. *C E Brittain [0-1] Michael Watt.*

SIRINNDI (IRE) **RR 94f** 4898a[5]
4 b g Shahrastani (USA) 11.5f **(69)** - Sinntara 00
Form - 65
1998 Turf 0-2: (14f 2) (sft, g-s)
Useful gelding, effective 16f, acts on gd, prefers right handed tracks. Turf high 94.
C Roche in IRE [0-5] Mrs Joan Brosnan (from J Oxx in IRE [2-7] Oct 1997).

SIR JACK BHB 87f **RR 88f** 4857[22]
2 b c Distant Relative 7f **(69)** - Frasquita (Song) 7.2f **(61)**
Form - 210
Record 1998 - 1st:1 2nd:1 3rd:0 Ran:3
Win Prizemoney £3,371 *Total Prizemoney* £4,356
Wins * **1998** Spt Newcas (GD) 6f 88 <
1998 Turf 1-3: (6f 1-3) (sft, gd, g-f 1-1)
Currently useful colt, has worn blinkers. Turf high 88 (began Spt) - 1st of 14 from Polar Ice (30 Spt Newcastle RF 4579). His win came in an ordinary maiden. *D R Loder [1-3] Lucayan Stud.*

SIR JOEY (USA) BHB 62f80a **RR 64f 80a** 4128[14]
9 ch g Honest Pleasure (USA) 5.6f **(91)** - Sougoli (Realm) 8.1f **(65)**
Form - 70046600500
Record 1998 - 1st:0 2nd:0 3rd:0 Ran:10
Pre1998 - 1st:7 2nd:8 3rd:14 Ran:75
Win Prizemoney £31,159 *Total Prizemoney* £83,605
Wins * 1996 Jun Salisb (GD) H 6f 81 82
* 1995 Jly Chepst (G-F) H 5.1f 84 83
* 1994 Jly York (G-F) H 6f 84 86 <
1998 Turf 0-10: (5f 2, 6f 8) (hvy, gd 3, g-f 2, frm 4)
Decent gelding, effective 6 to 7f, best at 6f, acts on gd to hrd - acts on Fibr. Turf high 76 - 4th of 13 giving 3lb to Supreme Angel (23 May Kempton 6f gd RF 1428). This grand old campaigner is not as good as he was. A strongly-run race suits him best, but he is on a long losing run and gets little change out of the Handicapper.
P G Murphy [6-80] Mrs A G Sims (from R J Holder [1-5] Oct 1992).

SIR PERSE BHB 64f **RR 65f** 5122[6]
2 b c Precocious 7.2f **(54)** - Anne's Bank (IRE) (Burslem) 8.8f **(53)**
Form - 006
Record 1998 - 1st:0 2nd:0 3rd:0 Ran:3
1998 Turf 0-3: (6f 3) (g-s, g-f 2)
Currently average colt. Turf high 62 (began Oct).
**G L Moore [0-3] Mrs L B Jones.*

SIR SANDROVITCH (IRE) **RR 62f** 4088[6]
2 b g Polish Patriot (USA) 7.8f **(70)** - Old Downie (Be My Guest (USA)) 9.3f **(67)**
Form - 6
Record 1998 - 1st:0 2nd:0 3rd:0 Ran:1
1998 Turf 0-1: (5f) (frm)
Currently average gelding.
**R A Fahey [0-1] Sandrovitch Partnership A.*

SIR TALBOT BHB 86f **RR 89?f** 4824[11]
4 b g Ardross 12.4f **(67)** - Bermuda Lily (Dunbeath (USA)) 7.8f **(70)**
Form - 0
Record 1998 - 1st:0 2nd:0 3rd:0 Ran:1
Pre1998 - 1st:2 2nd:1 3rd:0 Ran:8
Win Prizemoney £8,383 *Total Prizemoney* £10,753
Wins 1997 Jly Windso (G-F) H 10f 85 89 <
1997 Mar Leices (G-F) 8f 79
1998 Turf 0-1: (12f) (frm)
Scopey, useful gelding, effective 8 to 10f, acts on g-f to frm, best on frm. **J A B Old [1-3] W E Sturt (from R Hannon [2-8] Aug 1997).*

SIR TASKER BHB 41f39a **RR 48f 39a** 388[6]
10 b h Lidhame 6.7f **(54)** - Susie's Baby (Balidar) 7.9f **(63)**
Form - 0006466
Record 1998 - 1st:0 2nd:0 3rd:0 Ran:5
Pre1998 - 1st:16 2nd:14 3rd:12 Ran:151
Win Prizemoney £56,760 *Total Prizemoney* £74,336
Wins * 1997 *Feb Lingfi (STD) 6f 42*
* 1995 Aug Newmar (GD) H 6f 54 56
* 1995 *Mar Lingfi (STD) H 6f 75 75* <
* 1995 *Mar Lingfi (STD) C 6f 74*
* 1995 *Feb Lingfi (STD) H 6f 67 63*
* 1995 *Jan Wolver (STD) C 5f 62*
* 1994 Apr Thirsk (GD) H 5f 54 57
1998 AW 0-5: (6f 5) (Fibr 5)
Moderate horse, effective 5 to 6f, best at 6f, acts on g-f - acts on AW, has worn blinkers, likes left handed tracks, likes tight tracks. AW high 44. **J L Harris [16-147] J L Harris (from M Bell [0-6] Jly 1991).*

SI SENORITA BHB 32f **RR 43f** 3305[16]
3 b f Young Senor (USA) 8f **(43)** - Raunchy Rita (Brigadier Gerard) 9.3f **(58)**
Form - 05000
Record 1998 - 1st:0 2nd:0 3rd:0 Ran:5
Pre1998 - 1st:0 2nd:0 3rd:0 Ran:1
1998 Turf 0-5: (5f 2, 6f, 7f, 8f) (gd 4, frm)
Leggy, moderate filly. Turf high 23. **B Mactaggart [0-6] Eden Racing.*

SIS GARDEN BHB 57f70a **RR 58f 70a** 4636[5]
5 b m Damister (USA) 9.1f **(66)** - Miss Nanna (Vayrann) 9.7f **(74)**
Form - 8210447131705
Record 1998 - 1st:3 2nd:1 3rd:1 Ran:13
Pre1998 - 1st:5 2nd:5 3rd:4 Ran:35
Win Prizemoney £18,940 *Total Prizemoney* £26,368
Wins * **1998** Aug Lingfi (GD) H 7.6f 53 58
* **1998** *Jly Wolver (STD) 7f 69* <
* **1998** *Apr Wolver (STD) H 7f 57 64*
* 1997 Aug Chepst (G-F) H 8.1f 54 60
* 1997 May Bright (FRM) H 8f 47 50
* 1996 *Nov Wolver (STD) 7f 61*
1996 *Spt Wolver (STD) C 7f 58*
1996 Aug Ayr (GD) SH 7f 43 48
1998 Turf 1-8: (7f 2, 8f 1-6) (gd, g-f 1-4, frm 2, hrd) 1998 AW 2-5: (7f 2-5) (Fibr 2-5)
Average filly, effective 7 to 8f, best at 7f, acts on g-f to frm - acts on Fibr, has worn blinkers, does well at Wolverhampton. Turf high 58. AW high 69 - 1st of 10 giving 11lb to Hit The Spot (10 Jly Wolverhampton RF 2695) - also 1st of 12 getting 4lb from Mike's Double (25 Apr Wolverhampton RF 0875). Her best efforts are normally when going around a sharp left-hand bend, either on sand or turf, and she is particularly effective over seven furlongs on the Wolverhampton Fibresand. She can win on a straight track, as she showed by winning a Chepstow ladies' race over the straight mile in 1997, and an apprentice event over the extended seven at Lingfield.
**J Cullinan [6-32] Alan Spargo Ltd Toolmakers (from T D Easterby [2-13] Spt 1996).*

SISTER KIT (IRE) BHB 34f49a **RR 40f 49a** 4777[10]
5 b m Glacial Storm (USA)-Good Holidays (Good Times (ITY)) 6.6f **(54)**
Form - 000
Record 1998 - 1st:0 2nd:0 3rd:0 Ran:3
Pre1998 - 1st:0 2nd:0 3rd:1 Ran:8
Win Prizemoney £0 *Total Prizemoney* £311
1998 Turf 0-3: (12f 2, 14f) (g-s, gd, frm)
Moderate filly. Turf high 40.
**B J Llewellyn [0-2] Caleb Davies (from B Palling [0-9] Mar 1998).*

SISTER PATRICE (IRE) BHB 48f **RR 54f** 4569[9]
2 b f Petorius 8f **(66)** - Top Nurse (High Top) 10.2f **(67)**
Form - 07866000
Record 1998 - 1st:0 2nd:0 3rd:0 Ran:8
1998 Turf 0-8: (5f 6, 6f 2) (gd 2, g-f, frm 5)
Fair filly, has worn blinkers. Turf high 54.
**Mrs P N Dutfield [0-8] In For The Crack.*

SIX FOR LUCK BHB 24f **RR 19f** 3908[11]
6 b g Handsome Sailor 6.6f **(53)** -Fire Sprite (Mummy's Game) 8.2f **(60)**
Form - 76080
Record 1998 - 1st:0 2nd:0 3rd:0 Ran:5
Pre1998 - 1st:1 2nd:2 3rd:2 Ran:34
Win Prizemoney £2,348 *Total Prizemoney* £5,242
Wins 1994 May Mussel (G-F) 5f 58+
1998 Turf 0-5: (5f 5) (gd 3, g-f, frm)
Poor gelding, has worn blinkers. Turf high 19.
**D A Nolan [0-33] Mrs J McFadyen-Murray (from J Berry [1-6] Jun 1995).*

SIZZLING BHB 49f50a **RR 51df 50a** 3739[9]
6 b g Sizzling Melody 6.3f **(49)** - Oriental Splendour (Runnett) 7f **(59)**
Form - 265317500
Record 1998 - 1st:1 2nd:0 3rd:1 Ran:6
Pre1998 - 1st:3 2nd:2 3rd:2 Ran:29
Win Prizemoney £12,626 *Total Prizemoney* £16,450
Wins * **1998** May Bright (FRM) H 6f 48 53
* 1997 Apr Bright (FRM) C 6f 56
* 1995 Oct Leices (FRM) H 6f 59 63 <
* 1995 May Bath (G-F) 5.1f 61
1998 Turf 1-5: (6f 1-3, 7f 2) (gd, g-f, frm 1-3) 1998 AW 0-1: (6f) (Equi)
Fair gelding, effective 6 to 7f, best at 6f, acts on gd to frm - acts on Equi, best on frm, has worn blinkers, prefers left handed tracks, prefers tight tracks. Turf high 53 (1st run) - 1st of 11 getting 11lb from Maladerie (28 May Brighton RF 1553). (1st run) - 3rd of 11 getting 19lb from Pageboy (1 Jan Lingfield 6f Equi RF 0004).
**R Hannon [4-35] P & Mrs P Jubert.*

SKELTON COUNTESS (IRE) BHB 30f31a **RR 27f 31a** 5120[9]
5 ch m Imperial Frontier (USA) 7f **(65)** - Running Brook (Run The Gantlet (USA)) 12.1f **(59)**
Form - 00000
Record 1998 - 1st:0 2nd:0 3rd:0 Ran:5
Pre1998 - 1st:0 2nd:0 3rd:2 Ran:17
Win Prizemoney £0 *Total Prizemoney* £1,187
1998 Turf 0-4: (5f 2, 7f, 8f) (gd, g-f 2, frm) 1998 AW 0-1: (6f) (Fibr)
Little account filly. Turf high 27 (began Jly). Inconsistent.
**R E Barr [0-4] P B Burnell (from R Hollinshead [0-18] Jan 1998).*

SKELTON SOVEREIGN (IRE) BHB 46f60a **RR 51f 60a** 68[R]
4 b c Contract Law (USA) 8.9f **(54)**-Mrs Lucky (Royal Match) 11.8f **(54)**
Form - 30R
Record 1998 - 1st:0 2nd:0 3rd:0 Ran:1
Pre1998 - 1st:2 2nd:4 3rd:7 Ran:36
Win Prizemoney £4,537 *Total Prizemoney* £11,353
Wins * 1997 *May Wolver (STD) S 12f 57*
* 1996 Oct Leices (G-F) S 10f 63 <
1998 AW 0-1: (12f) (Fibr)

Light-framed, average colt, effective 11 to 14f, best at 12f, acts on gd to frm - acts on Fibr, has worn blinkers, prefers left handed tracks, favours tight tracks, does well at Wolverhampton.
**R Hollinshead [2-37] G Bailey.*

SKERRAY BHB 68f RR 64f 4859[6]

3 b f Soviet Star (USA) 8.6f **(74)** - Reuval (Sharpen Up) 8.3f **(67)**
Form - 3736
Record 1998 - 1st:0 2nd:0 3rd:2 Ran:4
Win Prizemoney £0 *Total Prizemoney* £1,164
1998 Turf 0-4: (7f, 8f 3) (sft, gd, frm 2)
Scopey, average filly. Turf high 65 (1st run) (began Aug) - 3rd of 7 getting 5lb from Lear Spear (2 Aug Sandown 8f gd RF 3302).
**J R Fanshawe [0-4] Dr Catherine Wills.*

SKI JUMP (IRE) BHB 66f RR 60f 4261[19]

2 ch f Mukaddamah (USA) 7.6f **(74)**-Ski Slope (Niniski (USA))10.6f **(65)**
Form - 8600110
Record 1998 - 1st:2 2nd:0 3rd:0 Ran:7
Win Prizemoney £5,044 *Total Prizemoney* £5,044
Wins * **1998** Aug Ripon (G-F) S 6f 60 <
* **1998** Aug Hamilt (SFT) C 6f 56
1998 Turf 2-7: (6f 2-5, 7f 2) (g-s 1-1, gd 1-3, g-f 2, frm)
Average filly, effective 6f, acts on g-s to gd, has worn blinkers. Turf high 60 - 1st of 17 from Melody Queen (31 Aug Ripon RF 3996) - also 1st of 9 getting 21lb from Smokin (17 Aug Hamilton RF 3678). **M Dods [2-7] M J K Dods.*

SKI LODGE (IRE) BHB 83f RR 82f 4761[1]

2 br f Persian Bold 10f **(69)** - Place of Honour (Be My Guest (USA)) 9.3f **(67)**
Form - 571
Record 1998 - 1st:1 2nd:0 3rd:0 Ran:3
Win Prizemoney £3,509 *Total Prizemoney* £3,509
Wins * **1998** Oct Leices (G-S) 7f 82 <
1998 Turf 1-3: (6f, 7f 1-2) (gd 1-2, frm)
Currently decent filly. Turf high 82 (began Spt) - 1st of 18 from Balladonia (12 Oct Leicester RF 4761).
**C E Brittain [1-3] Mrs Sean Collins.*

SKIP AWAY (USA) RR 115f 5168a[6]

5 gr h Skip Trial (USA) 9f **(128)** - Ingot Way (USA) (Diplomat Way) 7.5f **(74)**
Form - 136
1998 AW 1-3: (9f 1-1, 10f 2) (Dirt 1-3)
Top-class colt, has worn blinkers. AW high 128 (1st run) (began Spt) - 1st of 3 from Gentlemen (19 Spt Belmont Park RF 4470d). One of America's highest career earners, he took his unbeaten run to nine before a defeat behind Wagon Limit in the Jockey Club Gold Cup. Sustained an injury there and was below his best in the Breeders' Cup Classic. He has been retired to stud in Kentucky at a fee of $50,000. **H Hine in USA [2-6] Mrs Carolyn Hine.*

SKIP CHURCH (IRE) BHB 66f RR 66f 4634[4]

2 ch f College Chapel - Be Nimble (Wattlefield) 5.8f **(71)**
Form - 0654
Record 1998 - 1st:0 2nd:0 3rd:0 Ran:4
Win Prizemoney £0 *Total Prizemoney* £388
1998 Turf 0-4: (5f 3, 6f) (gd, g-f, frm, hrd)
Average filly. Turf high 66 (began Aug).
**Lord Huntingdon [0-4] Lord Huntingdon.*

SKY DOME (IRE) BHB 70f RR 73f 5079[10]

5 ch g Bluebird (USA) 7.9f **(71)** -God Speed Her (Pas de Seul) 9.1f **(67)**
Form - 2607004400
Record 1998 - 1st:0 2nd:1 3rd:0 Ran:10
Pre1998 - 1st:4 2nd:0 3rd:0 Ran:17
Win Prizemoney £29,047 *Total Prizemoney* £33,803
Wins * 1996 Aug Goodwo (GD) H 8f 84 89 <
* 1996 Aug Newmar (GD) H 8f 78 86
* 1996 Apr Newmar (G-F) H 7f 75 80
* 1995 Apr Carlis (GD) 5f 74t
1998 Turf 0-10: (7f 2, 8f 5, 10f 3) (sft 2, g-s 2, gd 3, g-f, frm 2)
Above-average gelding, effective 10f, acts on frm. Turf high 81 (1st run) - 2nd of 19 getting 9lb from Party Romance (17 May Ripon 10f frm RF 1287). Inconsistent. A tough and genuine performer at his best, he ran well first time out but has been held since, though he ran a couple of fair races in big-field handicaps in the autumn.
**M H Tompkins [4-27] Miss D J Merson.*

SKYERS A KITE BHB 50f RR 47f 4817[3]

3 b f Deploy 11.4f **(67)** - Milady Jade (IRE) (Drumalis) 12f **(54)**
Form - 0032102513
Record 1998 - 1st:2 2nd:2 3rd:2 Ran:9
Pre1998 - 1st:0 2nd:0 3rd:0 Ran:2
Win Prizemoney £6,741 *Total Prizemoney* £8,723
Wins * **1998** Oct Catter (gd,) H 12f 42 45 <
* **1998** Jly Beverl (GD) SH 12f 40 45 <
1998 Turf 2-9: (8f, 10f, 11f, 12f 2-5, 16f) (gd 2, g-f 2-3, frm 3, hrd)
Unfurnished, moderate filly, effective 11 to 12f, best at 12f, acts on g-f to hrd, best on g-f, likes left handed tracks. Turf high 47 (began Jly) - also 1st of 13 from Suggest (3 Oct Catterick RF 4625). Consistent. **Ronald Thompson [2-11] Ronald Thompson.*

SKYERS FLYER (IRE) BHB 46f65a RR 67f 65a 4771[11]

4 b br f Magical Wonder (USA) 7.2f **(60)** - Siwana (IRE) (Dom Racine (FR)) 9.2f **(62)**
Form - 3250300460007760
Record 1998 - 1st:0 2nd:1 3rd:2 Ran:16
Pre1998 - 1st:4 2nd:4 3rd:5 Ran:25
Win Prizemoney £10,345 *Total Prizemoney* £20,687
Wins 1997 Aug Newcas (G-F) S 6f 48
1997 Apr Nottin (GD) S 6.1f 68
1996 Aug Bright (FRM) H 5.3f 85 72 <
1996 May Beverl (G-F) S 5f 47
1998 Turf 0-16: (5f, 6f 7, 7f 8) (sft, gd 8, g-f 2, frm 5)
Unfurnished, average filly, effective 6 to 8f, best at 6f, acts on gd to frm, best on gd, likes right handed tracks, likes tight tracks. Turf high 67. Mixed efforts in '98. She reportedly has problems with her joints and prefers good ground.
**Martyn Wane [0-16] Mrs Linda Miller (from Ronald Thompson [4-25] Aug 1997).*

SKYERS TRYER BHB 39f43a RR 41f 43a 3609[6]

4 b f Lugana Beach 7f **(63)** - Saltina (Bustino) 10.4f **(64)**
Form - 0004836
Record 1998 - 1st:0 2nd:0 3rd:1 Ran:6
Pre1998 - 1st:1 2nd:0 3rd:0 Ran:10
Win Prizemoney £2,697 *Total Prizemoney* £3,111
Wins 1996 Spt Mussel (G-F) 5f 70 <
1998 Turf 0-6: (5f, 6f 3, 7f, 8f) (gd, g-f 2, frm 3)
Light-framed, moderate filly. Turf high 41.
**B P J Baugh [0-6] M J Lyons (from Ronald Thompson [1-10] Dec 1997).*

SKYLIGHT BHB 38f RR 31f 1302[12]

5 ch g Domynsky 7.8f **(58)** - Indian Flower (Mansingh (USA)) 7.4f **(55)**
Form - 0
Record 1998 - 1st:0 2nd:0 3rd:0 Ran:1
Pre1998 - 1st:0 2nd:0 3rd:0 Ran:3
1998 Turf 0-1: (7f) (g-f)
Very moderate gelding. **Miss Kate Milligan [0-6] Mrs J M L Milligan.*

SKYMISTRESS BHB 43f45a RR 43f 45a 4863[9]

2 ch f Emarati (USA) 6.6f **(63)** - Divissima (Music Boy) 6.8f **(57)**
Form - 0783474400
Record 1998 - 1st:0 2nd:0 3rd:1 Ran:10
Win Prizemoney £0 *Total Prizemoney* £260
1998 Turf 0-6: (5f 2, 6f 3, 7f) (g-s, gd 2, g-f, frm 2) 1998 AW 0-4: (5f 2, 6f 2) (Fibr 4)
Fair filly, has worn blinkers. Turf high 43. AW high 56 (began Jly).
**M Dods [0-10] K Chapman.*

SKY MOUNTAIN (IRE) BHB 47f47a RR 44f 47a 3085[11]

3 b g Danehill (USA) 9.1f **(79)** - Molvina (ITY) (Final Straw) 7.9f **(64)**
Form - 40733762485644550
Record 1998 - 1st:0 2nd:1 3rd:2 Ran:17
Pre1998 - 1st:0 2nd:0 3rd:1 Ran:4
Win Prizemoney £0 *Total Prizemoney* £1,899
1998 Turf 0-8: (6f 5, 8f 3) (sft, g-s 3, gd 2, g-f, frm) 1998 AW 0-9: (6f 2, 7f 3, 8f 3, 11f) (Fibr 9)
Workmanlike, fair gelding, effective 6 to 8f, acts on g-s - acts on Fibr, has worn blinkers. Turf high 61 (1st run) - 2nd of 20 giving 2lb to Kustom Kit Kate (31 Mar Nottingham 6f g-s RF 0518). AW high

56 - 3rd of 9 getting 3lb from Killarney Jazz (23 Feb Southwell 8f Fibr RF 0341). Placed in modest company on turf and sand, his best trip remains a mystery.

**S R Bowring [0-17] Roland Wheatley (from G Lewis [0-4] Jly 1997).*

SKY OF HOPE (FR) BHB 77f RR 71f 4959[7]

2 b c Zieten (USA) - Rain Or Shine (FR) (Nonoalco (USA)) 8.5f **(66)**

Form - 007

Record 1998 - 1st:0 2nd:0 3rd:0 Ran:3

1998 Turf 0-3: (6f, 7f 2) (gd, g-f, frm)

Currently above-average colt. Turf high 71 (began Spt).

**R Hannon [0-3] Lucayan Stud.*

SKY RED BHB 66f65a RR 65f 65a 4701[22]

3 gr f Night Shift (USA) 8.1f **(73)** - Noble Haven (Indian King (USA)) 7.4f **(64)**

Form - 3601550113720

Record 1998 - 1st:3 2nd:1 3rd:2 Ran:13
Pre1998 - 1st:0 2nd:0 3rd:0 Ran:3

Win Prizemoney £7,578 *Total Prizemoney* £10,554

Wins * **1998** Aug Windso (G-F) H 5f 60 64 <
* **1998** Aug Yarmou (G-F) H 5.2f 61 64 <
* **1998** Jun Mussel (G-F) 5f 49

1998 Turf 3-12: (5f 3-11, 6f) (g-s, gd 4, g-f 1-2, frm 1-4, hrd 1-1) 1998 AW 0-1: (6f) (Fibr)

Neat, average filly, effective 5f, acts on gd to hrd. Turf high 65 - 2nd of 24 giving 2lb to Miss Hit (1 Oct Newmarket 5f gd RF 4596) - also 1st of 5 giving 19lb to Marino Street (5 Aug Yarmouth RF 3398). Her first win at Musselburgh came in a particularly dire event, but she has done well since, gaining back to back wins at Yarmouth and an apprentice event at Windsor. Suited by fast ground and the minimum trip. **M Bell [3-16] Terry Neill.*

SKY ROCKET BHB 92f RR 86f 3255[6]

3 ch c Storm Cat (USA) 7f **(86)** - Oriental Mystique (Kris) 9.5f **(73)**

Form - 606

Record 1998 - 1st:0 2nd:0 3rd:0 Ran:3
Pre1998 - 1st:1 2nd:1 3rd:0 Ran:2

Win Prizemoney £4,550 *Total Prizemoney* £6,623

Wins * 1997 Oct Nottin (G-F) 6.1f 75++ <

1998 Turf 0-3: (7f 2, 8f) (gd 2, frm)

Scopey, useful colt. Turf high 86.

**Sir Michael Stoute [1-5] Saeed Suhail.*

SKY STORM RR 59f 4934[14]

2 ch g Lycius (USA) 8.8f **(71)** - Beijing (USA) (Northjet) 10.3f **(74)**

Form - 00

Record 1998 - 1st:0 2nd:0 3rd:0 Ran:2

1998 Turf 0-2: (7f, 8f) (gd 2)

Currently fair gelding. Turf high 59 (began Oct).

**B J Meehan [0-2] Mrs Sylvia Mead.*

SLAPY DAM BHB 33f50a RR 22f 50a 4890[11]

6 b g Deploy 11.4f **(67)** - Key to the River (USA) (Irish River (FR)) 8.6f **(78)**

Form - 0

Record 1998 - 1st:0 2nd:0 3rd:0 Ran:1
Pre1998 - 1st:3 2nd:1 3rd:1 Ran:31

Win Prizemoney £11,270 *Total Prizemoney* £13,410

Wins 1995 Oct Leices (GD) H 11.8f 57 60 <
1995 Spt Folkes (SFT) H 12f 48 59
1995 Apr Mussel (GD) H 11.1f 48 53

1998 Turf 0-1: (11f) (g-f)

Fair gelding, effective 12f, acts on gd to frm, has worn blinkers.

**C A Smith [0-7] The Ox Hill Flyers (from J Mackie [2-19] Spt 1996).*

SLASHER JACK (IRE) BHB 60f54a RR 59f 54a 2497[1]

7 b g Alzao (USA) 9.8f **(73)** - Sherkraine (Shergar) 10.4f **(66)**

Form - 02044501

Record 1998 - 1st:1 2nd:1 3rd:0 Ran:8
Pre1998 - 1st:5 2nd:2 3rd:2 Ran:27

Win Prizemoney £24,031 *Total Prizemoney* £39,563

Wins * **1998** Jly Haydoc (GD) C 11.9f 59
1995 May Haydoc (G-F) H 11.9f 78 87 <
1994 Jly York (GD) H 11.9f 80 86+
1994 Jun Pontef (FRM) H 12f 72 73
1994 Apr Mussel (GD) H 11.1f 70 65

1998 Turf 1-7: (12f 1-6, 14f) (sft 2, g-s, gd 2, frm 1-2) 1998 AW 0-1: (16f) (Fibr)

Fair gelding, effective 12f, acts on sft to frm, has worn blinkers, likes tight tracks. Turf high 68 (1st run) - 2nd of 11 giving 3lb to Filial (8 Apr Ripon 12f sft RF 0612) - also 1st of 6 getting 14lb from Night City (3 Jly Haydock RF 2497).

**R A Fahey [1-13] T C Chiang (from D Nicholls [0-3] Apr 1997).*

SLEAVE SILK (IRE) BHB 36f RR 43f 4970[8]

3 b f Unfuwain (USA) 11.4f **(74)** - Shanira (Shirley Heights) 10.3f **(74)**

Form - 708

Record 1998 - 1st:0 2nd:0 3rd:0 Ran:3

1998 Turf 0-3: (8f, 9f, 10f) (g-s 3)

Workmanlike, currently moderate filly. Turf high 43 (began Spt).

**W J Musson [0-3] Broughton Bloodstock.*

SLEEPLESS BHB 84f RR 78f 4985[11]

4 b f Night Shift (USA) 8.1f **(73)** - Late Evening (USA) (Riverman (USA)) 9.1f **(76)**

Form - 1765510

Record 1998 - 1st:2 2nd:0 3rd:0 Ran:7
Pre1998 - 1st:1 2nd:1 3rd:2 Ran:9

Win Prizemoney £14,771 *Total Prizemoney* £19,345

Wins * **1998** Spt Newcas (GD) 7f 76
* **1998** Apr Leices (SFT) H 7f 84 94+ <
* 1997 May Newbur (SFT) H 7.3f 78 90

1998 Turf 2-7: (7f 2-6, 8f) (sft 1-1, g-s 2, gd, g-f 1-2, frm)

Scopey, above-average filly, effective 7 to 8f, best at 7f, acts on sft to gd. Turf high 94 (1st run) - 1st of 20 giving 10lb to Boater (2 Apr Leicester RF 0548). Consistent.

**N A Graham [3-16] Mrs Audrey Scotney.*

SLEEPY BABY BHB 40f RR 45f 4624[7]

3 b c Paris House 5.9f **(64)** - Pertinent (Persepolis (FR)) 6.4f **(67)**

Form - 256500007

Record 1998 - 1st:0 2nd:1 3rd:0 Ran:9

Win Prizemoney £0 *Total Prizemoney* £628

1998 Turf 0-9: (5f 2, 6f 4, 7f 3) (g-s, gd 3, g-f 2, frm 3)

Unfurnished, moderate colt, has broken blood-vessels, has worn blinkers. Turf high 74.

**W T Kemp [0-6] A J Thurgood (from I Semple [0-4] Jly 1998).*

SLEEPYTIME (IRE) BHB 120f RR 119df 696[7]

4 b f Royal Academy (USA) 7.8f **(77)** - Alidiva (Chief Singer) 8.9f **(66)**

Form - 7

Record 1998 - 1st:0 2nd:0 3rd:0 Ran:1
Pre1998 - 1st:2 2nd:0 3rd:2 Ran:5

Win Prizemoney £108,540 *Total Prizemoney* £148,444

Wins * 1997 May Newmar (GD) G1 8f 119 <
* 1996 Spt Sandow (G-F) 7.1f 79++

1998 Turf 0-1: (9f) (sft)

High-class filly. The 1997 1000 Guineas heroine, she was found out by the lack of pace on her only subsequent appearance in the Coronation Stakes. Looked sure to appreciate the nine furlongs of the Earl of Sefton on her reappearance, but she trailed in last on the soft ground, reportedly slightly lame, and was retired to stud.

**H R A Cecil [2-6] Greenbay Stables Ltd.*

SLICKLY (FR) RR 99f 4597a[1]

2 gr c Linamix (FR) 8.2f **(64)** - Slipstream Queen (FR) (Conquistador Cielo (USA)) 8.8f **(69)**

Form - 1

1998 Turf 1-1: (8f 1-1) (gd 1-1)

Currently very useful colt. (1st run) - 1st of 6 from Irish Prize (22 Spt Chantilly RF 4597a). Game winner of the Prix la Rochette.

**A Fabre in FR [1-1] J-L Lagardere.*

SLIEU WHALLIAN BHB 48f RR 46f 151[7]

4 b f In The Wings 11.2f **(77)** - Ladyfish (Pampapaul) 10.9f **(63)**

Form - 77

Record 1998 - 1st:0 2nd:0 3rd:0 Ran:2
Pre1998 - 1st:0 2nd:0 3rd:0 Ran:4

1998 AW 0-2: (12f 2) (Equi 2)

Scopey, moderate filly. AW high 36.

**R Hannon [0-6] Barouche Stud Ltd.*

SLIEVENAMON BHB 38f42a **RR 21f 42a** 172^{12}
5 br g Warning 8.1f **(77)** - Twice A Fool (USA) (Foolish Pleasure (USA)) 8.9f **(72)**
Form - 83050
Record 1998 - 1st:0 2nd:0 3rd:0 Ran:2
Pre1998 - 1st:2 2nd:0 3rd:1 Ran:13
Win Prizemoney £5,523 *Total Prizemoney* £6,051
Wins 1996 *Dec Southw (SLW) H 8f 44 52* <
1996 *Nov Wolver (STD) H 9.4f 41 46*
1998 AW 0-2: (7f, 12f) (Fibr 2)
Moderate gelding, effective 7f, - acts on Equi, has worn blinkers (very effectively), favours left handed tracks, favours tight tracks. Inconsistent.
**R Simpson [0-5] Miss J Rumford (from J E Banks [2-10] Spt 1997).*

SLIGHTLY DUSTY RR 42f 1271^{7}
2 b f Deploy 11.4f **(67)** - Dusty's Darling (Doyoun) 9f **(69)**
Form - 7
Record 1998 - 1st:0 2nd:0 3rd:0 Ran:1
1998 Turf 0-1: (5f) (g-f)
Currently moderate filly. **P D Evans [0-1] Kendall White & Co Ltd.*

SLIGHTLY OLIVER (IRE) BHB 54f34a **RR 44?f 34a** 106^{R}
4 b g Silver Kite (USA) 10.2f **(51)** - Red Note (Rusticaro (FR)) 8.2f **(65)**
Form - 080RR
Record 1998 - 1st:0 2nd:0 3rd:0 Ran:4
Pre1998 - 1st:0 2nd:1 3rd:1 Ran:6
Win Prizemoney £0 *Total Prizemoney* £883
1998 AW 0-4: (6f 3, 12f) (Equi 2, Fibr 2)
Workmanlike, moderate gelding, mostly wears blinkers.
**D L Williams [0-5] P F Moore (from Mrs N Macauley [0-1] Nov 1996).*

SLIGHTLY SPECIAL (IRE) BHB 25f21a **RR 24f 21a** 2981^{9}
6 ch g Digamist (USA) 8.8f **(56)** - Tunguska (Busted) 10.2f **(61)**
Form - 84700
Record 1998 - 1st:0 2nd:0 3rd:0 Ran:5
Pre1998 - 1st:0 2nd:0 3rd:0 Ran:3
1998 Turf 0-4: (12f, 14f 2, 17f) (gd 3, g-f) 1998 AW 0-1: (16f) (Fibr)
Very moderate gelding. Turf high 24. Inconsistent.
**D T Thom [1-16] Mrs R Nash.*

SLIM PRIOR BHB 54f55a **RR 54f 55a** 1082^{4}
3 gr g Norton Challenger 10f **(41)** -Hopeful Katie (Full of Hope) 8.5f **(64)**
Form - 1464335384
Record 1998 - 1st:0 2nd:0 3rd:3 Ran:8
Pre1998 - 1st:1 2nd:0 3rd:0 Ran:8
Win Prizemoney £1,998 *Total Prizemoney* £3,019
Wins 1997 *Nov Lingfi (STD) S 7f 57* <
1998 Turf 0-2: (6f, 8f) (sft, g-s) 1998 AW 0-6: (7f 4, 8f 2) (Equi 3, Fibr 3)
Leggy, average gelding, effective 7f, - acts on AW, has worn blinkers, likes left handed tracks, likes tight tracks. Turf high 54. AW high 63 - 3rd of 6 giving 6lb to Heathyards Sheik (20 Feb Southwell 7f Fibr RF 0326).
**J L Harris [0-2] Peter Castle (from K R Burke [1-14] Mar 1998).*

SLIMS LADY BHB 59f **RR 64f** 5124^{3}
2 b f Theatrical Charmer 10.9f **(63)** - Lady Antoinette (Pharly (FR)) 9.8f **(68)**
Form - 86333
Record 1998 - 1st:0 2nd:0 3rd:3 Ran:5
Win Prizemoney £0 *Total Prizemoney* £1,169
1998 Turf 0-5: (6f 2, 7f 2, 8f) (g-s, gd, g-f 2, frm)
Average filly. Turf high 64. **K R Burke [0-5] Stuart Prior.*

SLIPPER BHB 89f **RR 86f** 4480^{2}
3 b f Suave Dancer (USA) 10.7f **(68)** - Horseshoe Reef (Mill Reef (USA)) 10.5f **(78)**
Form - 5172
Record 1998 - 1st:1 2nd:1 3rd:0 Ran:4
Pre1998 - 1st:0 2nd:0 3rd:0 Ran:2
Win Prizemoney £3,525 *Total Prizemoney* £5,805
Wins * 1998 Jun Lingfi (G-F) H 11.5f 79 79 <
1998 Turf 1-4: (10f, 11f 1-1, 12f, 14f) (g-f 1-2, frm, hrd)
Neat, useful filly, effective 11 to 14f, acts on g-f to frm, best on g-f. Turf high 86 - 2nd of 11 giving 5lb to Rainbow Ways (25 Spt Haydock 12f frm RF 4480) - also 1st of 7 giving 7lb to In The Sun (23 Jun Lingfield RF 2203). Always seemed likely to find her niche in middle-distance handicaps, and won such an event at Lingfield in June despite not handling the track too well. Did not get the run of the race next time and is capable of further improvement.
**L M Cumani [1-6] Lord Halifax.*

SLIPSTREAM RR 59f 2729^{7}
4 b g Slip Anchor 12.7f **(75)** - Butosky (Busted) 10.2f **(61)**
Form - 862041037
Record 1998 - 1st:1 2nd:1 3rd:1 Ran:9
Pre1998 - 1st:0 2nd:0 3rd:0 Ran:2
Win Prizemoney £2,234 *Total Prizemoney* £3,923
Wins * 1998 May Ayr (GD) 13.1f 60+ <
1998 Turf 1-8: (12f, 13f 1-1, 14f 3, 15f, 16f, 20f) (sft, g-s 1-2, gd 4, frm)
1998 AW 0-1: (9f) (Fibr)
Neat, fair gelding, likes tight tracks. Turf high 60.
**R Guest [1-11] Matthews Breeding and Racing.*

SLIP STREAM (USA) RR 88++f 4984^{1}
2 ch c Irish River (FR) 9f **(77)** - Sous Entendu (USA) (Shadeed (USA)) 8.2f **(70)**
Form - 1
Record 1998 - 1st:1 2nd:0 3rd:0 Ran:1
Win Prizemoney £3,631 *Total Prizemoney* £3,631
Wins * 1998 Oct Leices (SFT) 7f 88++ <
1998 Turf 1-1: (7f 1-1) (g-s 1-1)
Currently useful colt. (1st run) - 1st of 12 from Zanay (25 Oct Leicester RF 4984). **D R Loder [1-1] Maktoum Al Maktoum.*

SLIP THE NET (IRE) BHB 67f **RR 70f** 4871^{5}
4 b g Slip Anchor 12.7f **(75)** - Circus Ring (High Top) 10.2f **(67)**
Form - 457745
Record 1998 - 1st:0 2nd:0 3rd:0 Ran:6
Pre1998 - 1st:0 2nd:1 3rd:0 Ran:2
Win Prizemoney £0 *Total Prizemoney* £2,573
1998 Turf 0-6: (12f 2, 14f 2, 15f, 18f) (sft, g-s, gd 3, g-f)
Scopey, above-average gelding, has worn blinkers. Turf high 71. Ran fairly well in two outings as a two-year-old, but missed the whole of 1997. No real promise since his return.
**P F I Cole [0-8] J S Gutkin.*

SLIP VENTURE BHB 60f65a **RR 63f 65a** 4927^{1}
3 b c Slip Anchor 12.7f **(75)** - Sherkraine (Shergar) 10.4f **(66)**
Form - 100676531
Record 1998 - 1st:2 2nd:0 3rd:1 Ran:9
Pre1998 - 1st:0 2nd:0 3rd:0 Ran:3
Win Prizemoney £5,700 *Total Prizemoney* £6,096
Wins * 1998 Oct Nottin (SFT) 10f 63
*** 1998** *Apr Lingfi (STD) 10f 70+* <
1998 Turf 1-8: (8f, 10f 1-5, 16f 2) (g-s 1-2, gd 2, g-f 3, frm) 1998 AW 1-1: (10f 1-1) (Equi 1-1)
Unfurnished, above-average colt, effective 8 to 10f, best at 10f, acts on g-s to gd - acts on Equi, has worn blinkers, prefers left handed tracks, prefers tight tracks. Turf high 63 - 1st of 16 getting 7lb from Amico (21 Oct Nottingham RF 4927). (1st run) - 1st of 4 from Browning (3 Apr Lingfield RF 0555). Showed little on turf in 1997, but made a winning reappearance in a four-runner maiden on the Lingfield Equitrack in April. Looks to be improving.
**S P C Woods [2-12] Dr Frank Chao.*

SLMAAT BHB 60f40a **RR 56df 40a** 375^{10}
7 ch m Sharpo 7.5f **(68)** - Wasslaweyeh (USA) (Damascus (USA)) 8.9f **(71)**
Form - 0
Record 1998 - 1st:0 2nd:0 3rd:0 Ran:1
Pre1998 - 1st:5 2nd:2 3rd:1 Ran:27
Win Prizemoney £18,015 *Total Prizemoney* £21,391
Wins 1995 *Jan Southw (STD) H 11f 64 63+*
1994 *Nov Wolver (STD) 12f 61*
1994 Oct Haydoc (SFT) H 10.5f 63 67 <
1994 *Mar Wolver (STD) 7f 64*
1998 AW 0-1: (12f) (Fibr)
Fair mare, has worn blinkers.
**B R Cambidge [0-1] G A Farndon (from R D E Woodhouse [0-2] Mar 1996).*

SLUMBERING (IRE) BHB 92f **RR 95f** 5148^{5}
2 b c Thatching 7.8f **(69)** - Bedspread (USA) (Seattle Dancer (USA))

Form - 74155
Record 1998 - 1st:1 2nd:0 3rd:0 Ran:5
Win Prizemoney £6,914 *Total Prizemoney* £7,368
Wins * **1998** Oct York (GD) 6f 84 <
1998 Turf 1-5: (6f 1-3, 7f 2) (g-s, gd 1-2, g-f 2)
Very useful colt. Turf high 95 (began Spt).
**B J Meehan [1-5] Mrs Christine Painting.*

SMALL RISK BHB 42f **RR 1f** 4402[20]
4 b f Risk Me (FR) 8f **(53)** - Small Double (IRE) (Double Schwartz) 7.9f **(55)**
Form - 0
Record 1998 - 1st:0 2nd:0 3rd:0 Ran:1
Pre1998 - 1st:0 2nd:1 3rd:1 Ran:5
Win Prizemoney £0 *Total Prizemoney* £1,085
1998 Turf 0-1: (8f) (frm)
Poor filly, has worn blinkers.
**J W Hills [0-1] Miss Elizabeth Herbert (from T T Clement [0-2] Jun 1997).*

SMART (IRE) RR 396[8]
3 b f Last Tycoon 9.4f **(73)** - Belle Origine (USA) (Exclusive Native (USA)) 9.1f **(81)**
Form - 058
Record 1998 - 1st:0 2nd:0 3rd:0 Ran:3
1998 AW 0-3: (7f 2, 8f) (Fibr 3)
Currently very moderate filly. AW high 31.
**Sir Mark Prescott [0-3] A S Reid.*

SMART BOY (IRE) BHB 61f73a **RR 59f 73a** 4932[2]
4 ch c Polish Patriot (USA) 7.8f **(70)** - Bouffant (High Top) 10.2f **(67)**
Form - 66152440702
Record 1998 - 1st:1 2nd:2 3rd:0 Ran:10
Pre1998 - 1st:3 2nd:0 3rd:1 Ran:9
Win Prizemoney £11,974 *Total Prizemoney* £14,799
Wins * **1998** *Feb Wolver (STD) H 12f 70 77* <
* 1997 *May Lingfi (STD) 10f 69*
* 1997 *May Lingfi (STD) 10f 69*
* 1996 May Lingfi (G-F) 5f 60t
1998 Turf 0-6: (12f 3, 14f 3) (g-s 3, gd 3) 1998 AW 1-4: (10f, 12f 1-3) (Equi, Fibr 1-3)
Neat, above-average colt, effective 10 to 14f, best at 12f, acts on g-s - acts on AW, best on Fibr, has worn blinkers, prefers left handed tracks, prefers tight tracks, excels at Wolverhampton, likes Lingfield. Turf high 71 (1st run) - 2nd of 14 giving 6lb to Alpine Panther (31 Mar Nottingham 14f g-s RF 0521). AW high 77 - 1st of 8 giving 32lb to Drama King (18 Feb Wolverhampton RF 0312). He won an apprentice handicap on the Wolverhampton Fibresand in February when he was able to dominate. He was found out in better company afterwards, and has not seemed to quite get home over fourteen furlongs on Turf.
**P F I Cole [4-19] H R H Sultan Ahmad Shah.*

SMART DOMINION BHB 40f **RR 31f** 4666[15]
4 b c Sharpo 7.5f **(68)** - Anodyne (Dominion) 8.5f **(63)**
Form - 0
Record 1998 - 1st:0 2nd:0 3rd:0 Ran:1
Pre1998 - 1st:0 2nd:0 3rd:0 Ran:2
1998 Turf 0-1: (8f) (g-s)
Scopey, currently very moderate colt. Has shown little so far.
**Mrs A E Johnson [0-1] George Ward (from Lord Huntingdon [0-2] May 1997).*

SMARTER CHARTER BHB 57f46a **RR 65f 46a** 4962[6]
5 br g Master Willie 9.2f **(67)** - Irene's Charter (Persian Bold) 9.3f **(66)**
Form - 02110006
Record 1998 - 1st:2 2nd:1 3rd:0 Ran:7
Pre1998 - 1st:2 2nd:3 3rd:3 Ran:26
Win Prizemoney £15,518 *Total Prizemoney* £22,682
Wins * **1998** Jly Beverl (G-F) H 7.5f 60 65
* **1998** Jly Kempto (G-F) H 8f 56 57
1996 Jly Beverl (G-F) H 8.5f 70 75 <
1996 May Beverl (G-F) H 7.5f 58 61
1998 Turf 2-7: (7f 1-2, 8f 1-5) (sft, g-f 2, frm 2-4)
Average gelding, effective 7 to 8f, acts on gd to frm, prefers right handed tracks, prefers tight tracks. Turf high 65. In good heart in July before losing his way.
**Mrs L Stubbs [2-19] A P Griffin (from Mrs J R Ramsden [2-14] Aug 1996).*

SMART GUEST BHB 29f36a **RR 35f 36a** 5173a[12]
6 ch g Be My Guest (USA) 10.2f **(66)** - Konbola (Superlative) 7.2f **(56)**
Form - 8383087087000
Record 1998 - 1st:0 2nd:0 3rd:2 Ran:13
Pre1998 - 1st:4 2nd:1 3rd:2 Ran:27
Win Prizemoney £24,225 *Total Prizemoney* £28,420
Wins 1996 Apr Pontef (GD) S 6f 62
1995 May Newmar (GD) C 8f 81+
1994 Aug Currag (SFT) G3 6.3f 92+
1994 Jly Yarmou (GD) 6f 78
1998 Turf 0-11: (6f 2, 7f 6, 8f 2, 10f) (sft 2, gd 6, g-f, frm 2) 1998 AW 0-2: (7f 2) (Fibr 2)
Very moderate gelding, effective 7f, acts on gd to g-f, best on gd, has worn blinkers. Turf high 53 - 3rd of 11 getting 3lb from Birchwood Sun (4 May Newcastle 7f gd RF 1022). AW high 26.
**M M Treacy in IRE [0-2] Barrow Vale Syndicate (from J Parkes [0-9] Jly 1998).*

SMART KID (IRE) BHB 68f75a **RR 67f 75a** 4822[11]
4 b g Lahib (USA) 8f **(69)** -Diamond Lake (Kings Lake (USA)) 10.8f **(67)**
Form - 0880
Record 1998 - 1st:0 2nd:0 3rd:0 Ran:4
Pre1998 - 1st:1 2nd:0 3rd:0 Ran:4
Win Prizemoney £3,143 *Total Prizemoney* £3,143
Wins 1997 May Salisb (G-F) 6f 70 <
1998 Turf 0-4: (8f 3, 10f) (gd, g-f, frm 2)
Scopey, average gelding, effective 6f, acts on g-f. Turf high 67. Consistent.
**Miss Gay Kelleway [0-4] H R H Sultan Ahmad Shah (from P F I Cole [1-4] Oct 1997).*

SMARTLY TAX (USA) RR 102f 1231a[5]
3 c
Form - 65
1998 Turf 0-2: (11f 2) (hvy, gd)
Currently very useful colt. Turf high 102. He has been used as a pacemaker for Special Quest. **Mme C Head in FR [0-2].*

SMART PRINCE BHB 53f **RR 36f** 3392[19]
3 b g Prince Sabo 6.6f **(64)** - She's Smart (Absalom) 7.2f **(58)**
Form - 0000
Record 1998 - 1st:0 2nd:0 3rd:0 Ran:4
Pre1998 - 1st:0 2nd:0 3rd:0 Ran:5
1998 Turf 0-4: (6f 3, 8f) (g-s, gd, frm 2)
Neat, very moderate gelding. Turf high 36. Inconsistent.
**J J Quinn [0-9] B Shaw.*

SMART SAVANNAH BHB 98f **RR 88+f** 4542[13]
2 b c Primo Dominie 7.2f **(67)** - High Savannah (Rousillon (USA)) 8.2f **(74)**
Form - 310
Record 1998 - 1st:1 2nd:0 3rd:1 Ran:3
Win Prizemoney £3,533 *Total Prizemoney* £4,389
Wins * **1998** Spt Sandow (GD) 7.1f 88+ <
1998 Turf 1-3: (7f 1-3) (g-f 1-1, frm 2)
Currently useful colt. Turf high 88 (began Aug) - 1st of 4 getting 6lb from Diggit (16 Spt Sandown RF 4306).
**R Charlton [1-3] George Ward.*

SMART SNIP RR 2f 3097[8]
2 ch f Weldnaas (USA) 8.4f **(55)** - Scottish Lady (Dunbeath (USA)) 7.8f **(70)**
Form - 88
Record 1998 - 1st:0 2nd:0 3rd:0 Ran:2
1998 Turf 0-1: (6f) (gd) 1998 AW 0-1: (7f) (Fibr)
Currently poor filly. **B Smart [0-2] B Smart.*

SMART SPIRIT (IRE) BHB 45f **RR 49f** 3944[10]
4 b f Persian Bold 10f **(69)** - Sharp Ego (USA) (Sharpen Up) 8.3f **(67)**
Form - 608270
Record 1998 - 1st:0 2nd:1 3rd:0 Ran:6
Pre1998 - 1st:0 2nd:1 3rd:2 Ran:12
Win Prizemoney £0 *Total Prizemoney* £3,553
1998 Turf 0-6: (8f 2, 9f, 10f, 11f, 12f) (sft 2, gd 2, g-f, frm)

Rangy, moderate filly, effective 8f, acts on g-f. Turf high 49. Inconsistent. **Mrs M Reveley [2-21] Mrs Stephanie Smith.*

SMART SQUALL (USA) BHB 102f **RR 107f** 4723a[2]
3 b c Summer Squall (USA) 7f **(80)** - Greek Wedding (USA) (Blushing Groom (FR)) 10.3f **(76)**
Form - 104232
Record 1998 - 1st:0 2nd:2 3rd:1 Ran:5
Pre1998 - 1st:3 2nd:0 3rd:0 Ran:5
Win Prizemoney £26,668 *Total Prizemoney* £59,555
Wins * 1997 Dec Toulou (HVY) L 8f 99 <
* 1997 Oct Ascot (HVY) H 7f 83 95+
* 1997 Spt Chepst (GD) 7.1f 81
1998 Turf 0-5: (10f 2, 12f 2, 14f) (sft 2, g-s, gd, g-f)
Small, Pattern-class colt, effective 8 to 14f, acts on hvy to g-f. Turf high 107 - 2nd of 10 to Laveron (4 Oct Dortmund 14f sft RF 4723a). Consistent. He clocked up more air miles than Alan Whicker and gained the reputation of a game, but luckless, colt.
**Lord Huntingdon [3-10].*

SMITTENBY (IRE) BHB 100f **RR 105f** 4628[1]
2 b f Tenby 10.4f **(76)** - Moira My Girl (Henbit (USA)) 9f **(61)**
Form - 245003121
Record 1998 - 1st:2 2nd:2 3rd:1 Ran:9
Win Prizemoney £13,487 *Total Prizemoney* £19,799
Wins * **1998** Oct Newmar (gd) L 7f 105 <
* **1998** Aug Windso (G-F) H 6f 77 83
1998 Turf 2-9: (5f 5, 6f 1-2, 7f 1-2) (gd 3, g-f 1-4, frm, hrd 1-1)
Pattern-class filly, effective 7f, acts on g-f. Turf high 105 - 1st of 10 from Fragrant Oasis (3 Oct Newmarket RF 4628). Fifth of seven in a Class E race at Lingfield in May, this filly came on in leaps and bounds in the second half of the season, beating some blue-blooded rivals to win a Listed race at Newmarket in October. There was absolutely no fluke about that success and she will improve again when tackling a mile. She has been sold to America.
**Mrs P N Dutfield [2-9] W A Harrison-Allan.*

SMOKED PEARL RR 19f 3019[12]
2 gr f Petong 7.6f **(58)** - Spun Gold (Thatch (USA)) 9.8f **(62)**
Form - 070
Record 1998 - 1st:0 2nd:0 3rd:0 Ran:3
1998 Turf 0-3: (5f 2, 7f) (gd 2, g-f)
Currently poor filly. Turf high 19.
**M W Easterby [0-3] K Hodgson & Mrs J Hodgson.*

SMOKEY FROM CAPLAW BHB 70f **RR 69f** 3140[13]
4 b g Sizzling Melody 6.3f **(49)** - Mary From Dunlow (Nicholas Bill) 10.1f **(56)**
Form - 0608322010
Record 1998 - 1st:1 2nd:2 3rd:1 Ran:10
Pre1998 - 1st:4 2nd:1 3rd:0 Ran:19
Win Prizemoney £16,780 *Total Prizemoney* £21,570
Wins * **1998** Jly Carlis (G-F) H 6.9f 67 69
* 1997 Oct Redcar (G-F) H 7f 65 67
* 1997 May Thirsk (GD) H 6f 62 70 <
* 1997 May Newcas (GD) H 6f 62 64
* 1996 May Hamilt (G-F) C 6f 66
1998 Turf 1-10: (6f 3, 7f 1-5, 8f 2) (sft, g-s, gd 4, g-f 2, frm 1-2)
Scopey, average gelding, effective 6 to 8f, acts on gd to frm, best on frm, excels at Redcar. Turf high 69 - 1st of 13 giving 31lb to Komlucky (17 Jly Carlisle RF 2869). **J J O'Neill [5-29] G P Bernacchi.*

SMOKIN (IRE) BHB 62f56a **RR 69f 56a** 4878[8]
2 b g Magic Ring (IRE) 6.5f **(64)** - Casbah Girl (Native Bazaar) 6.9f **(62)**
Form - 34347021068
Record 1998 - 1st:1 2nd:1 3rd:2 Ran:11
Win Prizemoney £2,722 *Total Prizemoney* £4,603
Wins * **1998** Aug Thirsk (G-F) S 7f 66 <
1998 Turf 1-10: (5f 5, 6f 3, 7f 1-2) (g-s 5, g-f, frm 1-3, hrd) 1998 AW 0-1: (7f) (Fibr)
Average gelding, effective 5 to 7f, acts on g-s to frm, has worn blinkers. Turf high 71 - 4th of 8 giving 5lb to Dispol Clan (28 Apr Nottingham 5f g-s RF 0900) - also 1st of 14 from Bodfari Signet (28 Aug Thirsk RF 3934). Inconsistent. **J Berry [1-11] H B Hughes.*

SMOOTH PRINCESS (IRE) BHB 43f57a **RR 43f 57a** 4874[5]
3 gr f Roi Danzig (USA) 10.5f **(62)**-Sashi Woo (Rusticaro (FR)) 8.2f **(65)**
Form - 2087005025
Record 1998 - 1st:0 2nd:1 3rd:0 Ran:8
Pre1998 - 1st:1 2nd:1 3rd:0 Ran:7
Win Prizemoney £1,984 *Total Prizemoney* £3,777
Wins * *1997 Oct Southw (STD) S 7f 78+* <
1998 Turf 0-5: (6f, 7f, 8f 3) (gd 2, g-f, frm 2) 1998 AW 0-3: (7f 2, 8f) (Fibr 3)
Scopey, fair filly, effective 7f, - acts on Fibr, likes left handed tracks, likes tight tracks. Turf high 43. AW high 51. Inconsistent.
**J G FitzGerald [1-15] J G FitzGerald.*

SMOOTH SAILING BHB 88f78a **RR 90f 78a** 4985[2]
3 gr g Beveled (USA) 6.9f **(64)** - Sea Farer Lake (Gairloch) 7f **(63)**
Form - 707760521304R022
Record 1998 - 1st:1 2nd:3 3rd:1 Ran:15
Pre1998 - 1st:1 2nd:2 3rd:1 Ran:11
Win Prizemoney £7,778 *Total Prizemoney* £20,549
Wins * **1998** Jun Leices (SFT) H 7f 78 80 <
* 1997 Apr Sandow (GD) 5f 78
1998 Turf 1-15: (6f 3, 7f 1-11, 8f) (sft, g-s 2, gd 1-5, g-f 4, frm 3)
Leggy, useful gelding, effective 7 to 8f, best at 7f, acts on g-s to frm, has worn blinkers, prefers right handed tracks, does well at Leicester. Turf high 90 - 2nd of 20 getting 2lb from Young Precedent (25 Oct Leicester 7f g-s RF 4985). A fair juvenile, he lost his way when upped in class. He showed better form last season when put over seven furlongs, winning a small handicap at Leicester, and finishing runner-up on three occasions. Seems to go well with some give these days. **K McAuliffe [2-26] A R Parrish.*

SMUGGLER'S POINT (USA) BHB 51f47a **RR 50?f 47a** 63[5]
8 b g Lyphard (USA) 10.6f **(75)** - Smuggly (USA) (Caro) 9.3f **(74)**
Form - 5
Record 1998 - 1st:0 2nd:0 3rd:0 Ran:1
Pre1998 - 1st:1 2nd:0 3rd:0 Ran:13
Win Prizemoney £3,231 *Total Prizemoney* £3,579
1998 AW 0-1: (16f) (Equi)
Fair gelding, has worn blinkers. Becoming disappointing.
**J J Bridger [2-30] Mrs V R Hoare (from J H M Gosden [1-4] Jly 1993).*

SNAP CRACKER BHB 78f **RR 78f** 4533[10]
2 b f Inchinor 8.9f **(64)** - Valkyrie (Bold Lad (IRE)) 8.4f **(68)**
Form - 163115246300
Record 1998 - 1st:3 2nd:1 3rd:2 Ran:12
Win Prizemoney £9,397 *Total Prizemoney* £12,900
Wins * **1998** Jun Cheste (G-S) 5.1f 78 <
* **1998** Jun Leices (SFT) 5f 64+
* **1998** Apr Sandow (HVY) 5f 65
1998 Turf 3-12: (5f 3-11, 6f) (hvy 1-1, g-s 2, gd 2-6, g-f 2, frm)
Above-average filly, effective 5f, acts on gd. Turf high 78 - 1st of 9 getting 1lb from Bon Ami (24 Jun Chester RF 2234). Consistent. A winner of three races in modest company so far, she is well suited by plenty of give in the ground. **M Quinn [3-12] J Miller.*

SNAPPY TIMES BHB 40f54a **RR 49f 54a** 4661[13]
3 ch g Timeless Times (USA) 6.1f **(56)** - Hill of Fare (Brigadier Gerard) 9.3f **(58)**
Form - 005043280054200
Record 1998 - 1st:0 2nd:2 3rd:1 Ran:15
Pre1998 - 1st:1 2nd:1 3rd:3 Ran:12
Win Prizemoney £1,984 *Total Prizemoney* £4,982
Wins * *1997 Oct Wolver (STD) S 6f 57* <
1998 Turf 0-9: (5f 2, 6f 2, 7f 4, 8f) (gd 6, frm 3) 1998 AW 0-6: (6f 4, 7f, 8f) (Fibr 6)
Fair gelding, effective 5 to 7f, acts on gd to g-f - acts on Fibr, best on g-f, often wears blinkers. Turf high 54 (1st run) - 2nd of 19 getting 18lb from Scathebury (1 Apr Catterick 7f gd RF 0531). AW high 58. **M Dods [1-27] J A Wynn-Williams.*

SNOW AND ICE BHB 70f75a **RR 23f 75a** 1028[19]
3 b f Chilibang 7f **(55)** - Nisha (Nishapour (FR)) 9.1f **(61)**
Form - 160
Record 1998 - 1st:1 2nd:0 3rd:0 Ran:3
Win Prizemoney £3,517 *Total Prizemoney* £3,517
Wins * **1998** *Jan Lingfi (STD) 8f 69+* <
1998 Turf 0-1: (7f) (g-f) 1998 AW 1-2: (8f 1-2) (Equi 1-2)
Unfurnished, average filly. AW high 69 (1st run) - 1st of 10 getting 5lb from Appyabo (8 Jan Lingfield RF 0048). (DEAD)
**H Candy [1-3] Girsonfield Ltd.*

SNOWBALLS BHB 33f **RR 41f** 3518[12]

3 gr g Chilibang 7f **(55)** - Golden Panda (Music Boy) 6.8f **(57)**

Form - 407035700

Record 1998 - 1st:0 2nd:0 3rd:1 Ran:9
Pre1998 - 1st:0 2nd:0 3rd:1 Ran:3

Win Prizemoney £0 *Total Prizemoney* £712

1998 Turf 0-9: (5f, 6f, 7f 5, 8f, 10f) (gd 5, g-f 4)

Strong, moderate gelding, often wears blinkers. Turf high 66. Inconsistent. **Miss L A Perratt [0-12] Cree Lodge Racing Club.*

SNOWBERRY RR 13f 4860[9]

2 b f Alhijaz 7.7f **(57)** - Dear Person (Rainbow Quest (USA)) 10.4f **(75)**

Form - 0

Record 1998 - 1st:0 2nd:0 3rd:0 Ran:1

1998 Turf 0-1: (8f) (sft)

Currently poor filly. **Miss S E Hall [0-1] Miss S E Hall.*

SNOW PARTRIDGE (USA) BHB 55f **RR 61f** 4704[18]

4 ch c Arctic Tern (USA) 12.2f **(71)** - Lady Sharp (FR) (Sharpman) 11.3f **(66)**

Form - 084037622010

Record 1998 - 1st:1 2nd:2 3rd:1 Ran:12
Pre1998 - 1st:0 2nd:2 3rd:3 Ran:8

Win Prizemoney £3,011 *Total Prizemoney* £11,349

Wins * 1998 Spt Bright (GD) H 11.9f 48 50 <

1998 Turf 1-12: (10f 4, 11f, 12f 1-5, 13f, 14f) (gd 4, g-f 1-3, frm 4, hrd)

Scopey, average colt, effective 10 to 14f, acts on g-f to frm, best on g-f, has worn blinkers, favours tight tracks. Turf high 61.
**P F I Cole [1-20] M Arbib.*

SNOW POLINA (USA) RR 101f 4470I[1]

3 ch f Trempolino (USA) 11.9f **(77)** - Snow House (IRE) (Vacarme (USA)) 8.5f **(68)**

Form - 1

1998 Turf 1-1: (10f 1-1) (gd 1-1)

Currently very useful filly. (1st run) - 1st of 4 getting 5lb from Rebuff (20 Spt Toulouse RF 4470I).
**J-C Rouget in FR [1-1] Ecurie La Clauzade.*

SNOWY MANTLE BHB 40f **RR 37f** 1630[2]

5 b m Siberian Express (USA) 9f **(58)** - Mollified (Lombard (GER)) 10.5f **(66)**

Form - 02

Record 1998 - 1st:0 2nd:1 3rd:0 Ran:2
Pre1998 - 1st:1 2nd:1 3rd:3 Ran:14

Win Prizemoney £3,772 *Total Prizemoney* £7,996

Wins * 1997 Jly Nottin (G-F) H 8.2f 37 48+ <

1998 Turf 0-2: (8f 2) (g-f, hrd)

Very moderate filly, effective 8 to 10f, best at 10f, acts on g-f to frm, best on frm, likes right handed tracks. Turf high 37. Inconsistent. **J D Bethell [1-16] Mrs G Fane.*

SOAKED BHB 62f70a **RR 63f 70a** 4864[10]

5 b g Dowsing (USA) 7f **(61)**-Water Well (Sadler's Wells (USA)) 10f **(76)**

Form - 5245173041211110010400

Record 1998 - 1st:7 2nd:2 3rd:1 Ran:21
Pre1998 - 1st:0 2nd:1 3rd:1 Ran:18

Win Prizemoney £20,566 *Total Prizemoney* £24,306

Wins * 1998 Spt Pontef (G-F) H 5f 56 63
*** 1998** *Jun Southw (STD) H 5f 50 67* <
*** 1998** *Jun Southw (STD) H 5f 48 63+*
*** 1998** Jun Hamilt (GD) H 6f 46 56
*** 1998** May Mussel (G-S) H 5f 46 57
*** 1998** May Mussel (GD) H 5f 35 44
*** 1998** *Mar Southw (STD) SH 6f 41 49*

1998 Turf 4-11: (5f 3-9, 6f 1-2) (g-s 2, gd 1-3, g-f 2-3, frm 1-3) 1998 AW 3-10: (5f 2-4, 6f 1-5, 7f) (Fibr 3-10)

Average gelding, effective 5 to 6f, best at 5f, acts on gd to frm - acts on Fibr, often wears blinkers, and excels at Musselburgh. Turf high 63 - 1st of 18 getting 14lb from Bilko (24 Spt Pontefract RF 4469). AW high 67 - 1st of 8 giving 9lb to Press Ahead (12 Jun Southwell RF 1942) - also 1st of 16 getting 8lb from Aljaz (5 Jun Southwell RF 1768). Inconsistent. He used to be a bit of a short runner who did not seem to get home, especially when running beyond the minimum, but he did not have that problem last season, winning five times from six starts during May and June. He has won races on turf and Fibresand, and though winning over six, is still best suited by a fast five. He is very quickly away from the stalls and likes to do it from the front.
**D W Chapman [7-34] David Chapman (from J R Fanshawe [0-5] Jly 1996).*

SOAKING BHB 45f49a **RR 51f 49a** 4143[9]

8 b g Dowsing (USA) 7f **(61)** - Moaning Low (Burglar) 7.2f **(49)**

Form - 00754085410

Record 1998 - 1st:1 2nd:0 3rd:0 Ran:9
Pre1998 - 1st:9 2nd:7 3rd:3 Ran:62

Win Prizemoney £29,788 *Total Prizemoney* £38,352

Wins * 1998 *Aug Lingfi (STD) SH 8f 39 51*
* 1997 *Jan Lingfi (STD) C 8f 64*
* 1996 *Dec Lingfi (STD) H 8f 66 74*
* 1996 Jly Kempto (GD) H 7f 47 51
* 1996 *Jan Lingfi (STD) H 7f 63 66*
1995 Jly Chepst (G-F) S 7.1f 62
1994 *Nov Lingfi (STD) C 7f 56*
1994 Aug Bright (FRM) C 7f 53

1998 Turf 0-2: (7f, 8f) (gd, frm) 1998 AW 1-7: (7f, 8f 1-5, 10f) (Equi 1-6, Fibr)

Fair gelding, effective 8f, - acts on Equi, has worn blinkers, likes left handed tracks, likes tight tracks. Turf high 51 (began Jly). AW high 52. Inconsistent. **P Burgoyne [5-29] Image Office Supplies Ltd (from M D I Usher [0-12] Feb 1998).*

SOAP STONE BHB 29f **RR 29f** 3431[15]

3 b f Gunner B 11.2f **(45)** - Tzarina (USA) (Gallant Romeo (USA)) 8.4f **(64)**

Form - 000

Record 1998 - 1st:0 2nd:0 3rd:0 Ran:1
Pre1998 - 1st:0 2nd:0 3rd:0 Ran:3

1998 Turf 0-1: (12f) (g-f)

Light-framed, little account filly. **A Bailey [0-4] G V Gann.*

SOCIALIZER (USA) RR 51f 4937[5]

2 b c Glitterman (USA) - Speckofsun (USA) (Sunny North (USA))

Form - 5

Record 1998 - 1st:0 2nd:0 3rd:0 Ran:1

1998 Turf 0-1: (5f) (gd)

Currently average colt. **W Jarvis [0-1] H J W Steckmest And Partners.*

SOCIAL ROUND (FR) BHB 63f **RR 20f** 4765[9]

3 ch c Cadeaux Genereux 7.9f **(76)** - Dome Lawel (USA) (Blushing Groom (FR)) 10.3f **(76)**

Form - 80

Record 1998 - 1st:0 2nd:0 3rd:0 Ran:2

1998 Turf 0-2: (7f, 8f) (gd 2)

Rangy, currently fair colt. Turf high 59.
**T E Powell [0-1] W Powell (from E A L Dunlop [0-1] Apr 1998).*

SOCIAL SCENE (IRE) RR 99f 4725a[10]

2 ch f Grand Lodge (USA) - Ardmelody (Law Society (USA)) 9.9f **(70)**

Form - 210

Record 1998 - 1st:1 2nd:1 3rd:0 Ran:3

Win Prizemoney £3,517 *Total Prizemoney* £4,737

Wins * 1998 Spt Sandow (GD) 8.1f 94 <

1998 Turf 1-3: (7f, 8f 1-2) (sft, gd, g-f 1-1)

Currently very useful filly. Turf high 99 (began Aug) - 10th of 11 to Juvenia (4 Oct Longchamp 8f sft RF 4725a) - also 1st of 10 from Kristina (16 Spt Sandown RF 4309). Put her debut experience to good use to win an ordinary Sandown maiden. Took her chance in the Prix Marcel Boussac, finishing last after making the running but not beaten far. **P W Chapple-Hyam [1-3] R E Sangster.*

SOCIETY GIRL BHB 60f53a **RR 61f 53a** 151[9]

5 b m Shavian 7.7f **(67)** - Sirene Bleu Marine (USA) (Secreto (USA)) 8.7f **(72)**

Form - 0

Record 1998 - 1st:0 2nd:0 3rd:0 Ran:1
Pre1998 - 1st:6 2nd:3 3rd:3 Ran:23

Win Prizemoney £20,009 *Total Prizemoney* £24,779

Wins 1996 Spt Thirsk (G-F) H 8f 58 61
1996 Aug Hamilt (G-F) C 8.3f 60
1996 Jly Ayr (G-S) C 10f 60
1996 May Ripon (GD) C 8f 60
1995 Jly Newmar (G-F) S 7f 74+ <

1995 Jun Thirsk (G-F) S 6f 67
1998 AW 0-1: (12f) (Equi)
Average filly. She has been well beaten on her runs so far.
**J G M O'Shea [0-8] The Cross Racing Club (from C W Thornton [6-23] Spt 1996).*

SOCIETY KING (IRE) RR 63f 4540[25]

3 b c Fairy King (USA) 7.7f **(75)**-Volga (USA)(Riverman(USA)) 9.1f **(76)**
Form - 3000
Record 1998 - 1st:0 2nd:0 3rd:1 Ran:4
Pre1998 - 1st:0 2nd:0 3rd:0 Ran:1
Win Prizemoney £0 *Total Prizemoney* £450
1998 Turf 0-4: (7f 2, 8f, 10f) (gd 3, frm)
Workmanlike, average colt. Turf high 63. **J E Banks [0-5] R Sabey.*

SOCIETY SNOOP (IRE) BHB 99f RR 95f 4204[14]

2 b c Warning 8.1f **(77)** - Aljood (Kris) 9.5f **(73)**
Form - 12220
Record 1998 - 1st:1 2nd:3 3rd:0 Ran:5
Win Prizemoney £3,338 *Total Prizemoney* £7,067
Wins * 1998 Jun Hamilt (SFT) 6f 75+ <
1998 Turf 1-5: (6f 1-2, 7f 2, 8f) (gd 1-3, g-f, hrd)
Very useful colt. Turf high 95 - 2nd of 7 giving 25lb to Oddsanends (8 Aug Ascot 7f g-f RF 3459). Overcame greenness to score at Hamilton on his debut, and finished runner-up in his next three starts, the third of which was under top weight in an Ascot nursery. Raced alone and beaten quickly on his final start.
**M Johnston [1-5] Maktoum Al Maktoum.*

SODA POP (IRE) BHB 25f RR 20f 2958[11]

4 b g River Falls 8.2f **(56)** - Riviere Salee (FR) (Luthier) 9.8f **(71)**
Form - 050780
Record 1998 - 1st:0 2nd:0 3rd:0 Ran:6
Pre1998 - 1st:1 2nd:2 3rd:0 Ran:12
Win Prizemoney £1,984 *Total Prizemoney* £3,666
Wins 1997 Jly Bright (FRM) SH 11.9f 60 65 <
1998 Turf 0-4: (11f, 12f 3) (gd, g-f, frm 2) 1998 AW 0-2: (12f, 13f) (Equi, Fibr)
Scopey, little account gelding, effective 10 to 12f, best at 12f, acts on g-f to frm, best on g-f, has worn blinkers, favours tight tracks. Turf high 20. AW high 27.
**G L Moore [0-10] C F Sparrowhawk (from C E Brittain [1-8] Jly 1997).*

SODEN (IRE) BHB 47f64a RR 49f 64a 4862[11]

4 b f Mujadil (USA) 7.7f **(70)** - Elminya (IRE) (Sure Blade (USA)) 11.3f **(67)**
Form - 003018080
Record 1998 - 1st:1 2nd:0 3rd:0 Ran:6
Pre1998 - 1st:2 2nd:0 3rd:4 Ran:18
Win Prizemoney £8,303 *Total Prizemoney* £9,975
Wins * 1998 *Jun Wolver (STD) H 12f 63 68*
* 1997 *Aug Lingfi (STD) H 10f 65 68*
* 1996 Aug Redcar (G-F) 7f 69 <
1998 Turf 0-3: (9f, 11f 2) (gd, frm 2) 1998 AW 1-3: (12f 1-3) (Fibr 1-3)
Strong, average filly, effective 10 to 13f, best at 10f, acts on frm - acts on AW, has worn blinkers, prefers left handed tracks. Turf high 43. AW high 68 (1st run) - 1st of 9 giving 30lb to By Jay (17 Jun Wolverhampton RF 2077). Inconsistent.
**T G Mills [3-24] Albert Soden Ltd.*

SOEUR TI (FR) RR 115f 4947a[5]

3 b f Kaldoun (FR) 9.9f **(84)** - Habigael (FR) (Habitat) 9.4f **(70)**
Form - 726155
1998 Turf 1-6: (7f, 8f 1-4, 9f) (hvy, sft 1-2, gd 3)
High-class filly, effective 8f, acts on sft to gd. Turf high 115 - 1st of 11 giving 3lb to Pan Galactic (22 Aug Deauville RF 3914a).
**G Collet in FR [0-1] (from R Collet in FR [2-7] Oct 1998).*

SOFT TOUCH (IRE) BHB 69f RR 74f 4802[8]

3 b f Petorius 8f **(66)** - Fingers (Lord Gayle (USA)) 8.8f **(62)**
Form - 4133272348
Record 1998 - 1st:1 2nd:2 3rd:3 Ran:10
Pre1998 - 1st:0 2nd:3 3rd:1 Ran:7
Win Prizemoney £2,333 *Total Prizemoney* £29,209
Wins * 1998 May Bright (FRM) 8f 65+ <
1998 Turf 1-10: (8f 1-5, 10f 3, 11f 2) (sft, g-s, gd 3, g-f 2, frm 1-3)
Leggy, above-average filly, effective 5 to 10f, best at 8f, acts on gd to g-f, best on gd, has worn blinkers, likes left handed tracks, excels at Brighton. Turf high 74 - 2nd of 12 giving 20lb to Lycian (23 Jly Brighton 8f gd RF 3041). She has lived up to her name somewhat, filling the frame regularly but only having managed victory in a very poor Brighton maiden so far.
**Miss Gay Kelleway [1-17] Mind The Gap Partnership.*

SOFYAAN (USA) BHB 78f RR 81f 520[6]

5 b g Silver Hawk (USA) 11.2f **(85)** - Tanwi (Vision (USA)) 9f **(64)**
Form - 6
Record 1998 - 1st:0 2nd:0 3rd:0 Ran:1
Pre1998 - 1st:1 2nd:2 3rd:1 Ran:11
Win Prizemoney £2,740 *Total Prizemoney* £5,688
Wins 1996 May Dundal (G-S) 9f 83 <
1998 Turf 0-1: (10f) (g-s)
Decent gelding, effective 10 to 12f, best at 12f, acts on gd to frm.
**Lady Herries [2-12] E Reitel (from K Prendergast in IRE [1-5] Jun 1996).*

SO KEEN BHB 33f28a RR 31f 28a 2369[4]

5 ch g Keen 11.1f **(58)** - Diana's Bow (Great Nephew) 9.9f **(64)**
Form - 4
Record 1998 - 1st:0 2nd:0 3rd:0 Ran:1
Pre1998 - 1st:0 2nd:0 3rd:0 Ran:12
1998 Turf 0-1: (16f) (gd)
Very moderate gelding. **A Bailey [0-19] Ray Bailey.*

SOLAR STORM BHB 95f RR 95f 484[22]

4 ch c Polar Falcon (USA) 9f **(74)** - Sister Sophie (USA) (Effervescing (USA)) 8.1f **(79)**
Form - 0
Record 1998 - 1st:0 2nd:0 3rd:0 Ran:1
Pre1998 - 1st:3 2nd:0 3rd:0 Ran:5
Win Prizemoney £36,433 *Total Prizemoney* £36,736
Wins * 1997 Oct York (G-S) H 7.9f 89 95 <
* 1997 Spt Ayr (GD) H 8f 85 89
* 1997 Spt York (SFT) 7.9f 82
1998 Turf 0-1: (8f) (gd)
Unfurnished, very useful colt, effective 8f, acts on g-s to gd. In good form at the end of '97, winning at York twice, and at Ayr, he started favourite for the Lincoln on his reappearance, but in the event only beat one home. It transpired that he had gone lame, and is unlikely to race again. **M Bell [3-6] Lordship Stud.*

SOLDIER (USA) RR 4765[18]

3 b g Sheikh Albadou 9.2f **(75)** - His Ginger (USA) (Fred Astaire (USA))
Form - 00
Record 1998 - 1st:0 2nd:0 3rd:0 Ran:2
1998 Turf 0-2: (7f, 8f) (g-s, gd)
Strong, currently very poor gelding, often wears blinkers. (began Oct). **R F Marvin [0-2] William Verry Partnership.*

SOLDIER COVE (USA) BHB 46f49a RR 50f 49a 42[3]

8 ch g Manila (USA) 10f **(81)** - Secret Form (Formidable (USA)) 9.2f **(63)**
Form - 483
Record 1998 - 1st:0 2nd:0 3rd:1 Ran:1
Pre1998 - 1st:4 2nd:2 3rd:0 Ran:22
Win Prizemoney £9,076 *Total Prizemoney* £10,966
Wins 1997 Mar Mussel (SFT) SH 8f 42 50
1997 *Mar Southw (STD) C 8f 55*
1997 *Mar Wolver (STD) S 9.4f 56* <
1997 *Feb Lingfi (STD) SH 8f 46 50*
1998 AW 0-1: (9f) (Fibr)
Fair gelding, effective 8 to 9f, best at 9f, acts on gd - acts on AW, best on Fibr. (1st run) - 3rd of 8 to Ethbaat (7 Jan Wolverhampton 9f Fibr RF 0042). In fine form on the All-Weather during the winter, completing a hat-trick in modest company.
**D Burchell [0-6] Mrs Ruth Burchell (from M Meade [4-21] Aug 1997).*

SOLDIER'S SONG BHB 50f RR 51df 542[9]

5 b m Infantry 10f **(54)** - Top Soprano (High Top) 10.2f **(67)**
Form - 0
Record 1998 - 1st:0 2nd:0 3rd:0 Ran:1
Pre1998 - 1st:0 2nd:0 3rd:0 Ran:3
1998 Turf 0-1: (8f) (sft)
Fair filly. **R J Hodges [0-6] Mrs P R Stocker.*

SOLE SINGER (GER) RR 74f 4999^{4}
2 b c Slip Anchor 12.7f **(75)** - Singer on the Roof (Chief Singer) 8.9f **(66)**
Form - 84
Record 1998 - 1st:0 2nd:0 3rd:0 Ran:2
Win Prizemoney £0 *Total Prizemoney* £222
1998 Turf 0-2: (7f 2) (sft, gd)
Currently above-average colt. Turf high 74 (began Oct).
**I A Balding [0-2] J C Smith.*

SOLLY'S PAL RR 51f 1408^{9}
3 gr g Petong 7.6f **(58)** - Petriece (Mummy's Pet) 7.7f **(60)**
Form - 00
Record 1998 - 1st:0 2nd:0 3rd:0 Ran:2
1998 Turf 0-2: (6f 2) (gd, frm)
Scopey, currently fair gelding. Turf high 51.
**I A Balding [0-2] Mrs Paul Levinson.*

SOLO MIO (IRE) BHB 100f **RR 110f** $4218a^{2}$
4 b c Sadler's Wells (USA) 11.3f **(87)** - Marie de Flandre (FR) (Crystal Palace (FR)) 12.5f **(76)**
Form - 3312
1998 Turf 1-4: (16f 1-4) (sft 3, gd 1-1)
Well made, Group-class colt, effective 12 to 16f, best at 16f, acts on sft to gd, best on sft, prefers right handed tracks, excels at Longchamp and Newmarket. Turf high 110 - 2nd of 5 giving 4lb to Tiraaz (6 Spt Longchamp 16f sft RF 4218a) - also 1st of 7 getting 4lb from Mongol Warrior (16 May Baden-Baden RF 1376a). Improving. He justified his 120,000 guinea purchase out of Barry Hills' yard when winning a Group Three at Baden-Baden. Still on the upgrade, he could develop into a candidate for major staying honours next season. **J E Hammond in FR [1-4] Platinum Syndicate Ltd.*

SOLO SONG BHB 30f **RR 17f** 5114^{12}
3 ch f Executive Man 8.9f **(52)** - Aosta (Shack (USA)) 5.8f **(53)**
Form - 007000
Record 1998 - 1st:0 2nd:0 3rd:0 Ran:6
Pre1998 - 1st:0 2nd:0 3rd:0 Ran:3
1998 Turf 0-6: (5f 3, 7f 2, 8f) (sft, gd 3, g-f, frm)
Leggy, poor filly. Turf high 21 (began Jly).
**A R Dicken [0-5] The Low Flyers (Thoroughbreds) Ltd (Monteith [0-1] Jly 1998).*

SOLO SPIRIT BHB 50f **RR 64df** 4550^{12}
3 b f Northern Park (USA) 10f **(57)** - Brown Taw (Whistlefield) 5f **(55)**
Form - 000770000
Record 1998 - 1st:0 2nd:0 3rd:0 Ran:9
Pre1998 - 1st:1 2nd:0 3rd:0 Ran:5
Win Prizemoney £3,938 *Total Prizemoney* £4,438
Wins * 1997 Oct Leices (GD) 6f 81 <
1998 Turf 0-8: (5f 2, 6f 5, 7f) (hvy, gd 2, g-f, frm 4) 1998 AW 0-1: (6f) (Fibr)
Unfurnished, average filly, effective 6f, acts on gd, has worn blinkers. Turf high 64. Becoming disappointing.
**J R Jenkins [1-14] Mrs I Hampson.*

SOMAYDA (IRE) BHB 89f **RR 90f** 4986^{3}
3 b c Last Tycoon 9.4f **(73)** - Flame of Tara (Artaius (USA)) 9f **(69)**
Form - 1513
Record 1998 - 1st:2 2nd:0 3rd:1 Ran:4
Pre1998 - 1st:0 2nd:0 3rd:0 Ran:2
Win Prizemoney £17,365 *Total Prizemoney* £18,786
Wins * 1998 Spt Goodwo (G-S) H 9f 83 89+ <
*** 1998** Jun Redcar (G-S) 8f 65+
1998 Turf 2-4: (8f 1-2, 9f 1-1, 10f) (sft, gd 2-3)
Scopey, useful colt, effective 8 to 10f, acts on sft to gd, best on gd. Turf high 90 - 3rd of 7 getting 10lb from Punishment (25 Oct Leicester 10f sft RF 4986) - also 1st of 14 getting 13lb from Lonesome Dude (11 Spt Goodwood RF 4232). A brother to Marju and half-brother to Salsabil, he cost 550,000 gns as a yearling but showed only fair form in a couple of maidens at two. He made a winning reappearance at Redcar in June, despite showing a very moderate action both before and during the race, and although winning a valuable handicap at Goodwood in September, has not turned out as good as his breeding would have suggested.
**J L Dunlop [2-6] Hamdan Al Maktoum.*

SOME MIGHT SAY BHB 72f72a **RR 71f 72a** 1112^{2}
3 b c Be My Chief (USA) 10.2f **(62)** - Willowbed (Wollow) 8.2f **(61)**
Form - 22312
Record 1998 - 1st:1 2nd:3 3rd:1 Ran:5
Win Prizemoney £3,355 *Total Prizemoney* £6,675
Wins * 1998 *Mar Lingfi (SLW) 10f 76* <
1998 Turf 0-1: (14f) (frm) 1998 AW 1-4: (8f, 9f, 10f 1-2) (Equi 1-3, Fibr)
Workmanlike, above-average colt. (1st run) - 2nd of 12 giving 4lb to St Enodoc (8 May Nottingham 14f frm RF 1112). AW high 76 - 1st of 6 from Highbury Legend (3 Mar Lingfield RF 0392). Placed in All-Weather maidens at the start of '98, he did not seem to be progressing, but managed to find a pretty desperate affair on the Lingfield Equitrack in March in which to get off the mark. He won by a very wide margin, but will be fortunate to find another race quite as bad. **M Johnston [1-5] Stable Investments Ltd.*

SOMERTON BOY (IRE) BHB 64f73a **RR 67f 73a** 4970^{7}
8 b h Thatching 7.8f **(69)** - Bonnie Bess (Ardoon) 7.3f **(53)**
Form - 007133307
Record 1998 - 1st:1 2nd:0 3rd:3 Ran:9
Pre1998 - 1st:5 2nd:3 3rd:5 Ran:35
Win Prizemoney £22,509 *Total Prizemoney* £39,193
Wins * 1998 Jly Ayr (GD) H 9.1f 62 65+
* 1997 May Ayr (G-F) H 8f 64 73 <
* 1996 Jun Ayr (G-F) H 7f 68 72
* 1995 Jly Ayr (GD) H 7f 71 73 <
* 1995 May Newcas (GD) H 8f 67 69
* 1994 May Ayr (FRM) H 7f 69 66
1998 Turf 1-9: (7f, 8f 3, 9f 1-3, 10f 2) (sft, g-s 2, gd 1-3, g-f, frm 2)
Average horse, effective 7 to 9f, best at 8f, acts on gd to g-f, best on gd, likes left handed tracks, likes tight tracks, excels at Ayr, does well at Doncaster. Turf high 67 - 3rd of 9 getting 12lb from Abajany (11 Aug Ayr 8f gd RF 3520) - also 1st of 10 giving 8lb to Rebel County (18 Jly Ayr RF 2907). Reserves his best for Ayr, and won quite nicely there in July, tackling nine furlongs for the first time. Usually held up, and can finish strongly.
**P Calver [6-44] Mrs Janis MacPherson.*

SOMEWEEKEND (IRE) RR 34f 2555^{10}
2 b f Balla Cove - Penultimate Cress (IRE) (My Generation)
Form - 850
Record 1998 - 1st:0 2nd:0 3rd:0 Ran:3
1998 Turf 0-3: (5f 2, 6f) (gd, g-f 2)
Currently very moderate filly. Turf high 34.
**J S Moore [0-3] D P Johnson.*

SOMMERSBY (IRE) BHB 40f37a **RR 29f 37a** 575^{11}
7 b g Vision (USA) 10.4f **(57)** - Echoing (Formidable (USA)) 9.2f **(63)**
Form - 0
Record 1998 - 1st:0 2nd:0 3rd:0 Ran:1
Pre1998 - 1st:2 2nd:2 3rd:3 Ran:28
Win Prizemoney £6,049 *Total Prizemoney* £9,028
Wins * 1995 *Spt Wolver (STD) H 12f 58 67* <
1995 *May Wolver (STD) H 12f 56 64+*
1998 AW 0-1: (12f) (Fibr)
Little account gelding, has worn blinkers. He is not the horse he once was.
**Mrs N Macauley [1-30] Andy Peake (from A C Stewart [1-8] May 1995).*

SOMOSIERRA (IRE) BHB 60a **RR 53f** 4955^{3}
3 b g Paris House 5.9f **(64)** - Island Heather (IRE) (Salmon Leap (USA)) 11f **(61)**
Form - 7160833473
Record 1998 - 1st:1 2nd:0 3rd:3 Ran:10
Pre1998 - 1st:0 2nd:0 3rd:0 Ran:6
Win Prizemoney £2,318 *Total Prizemoney* £3,955
Wins * 1998 May Catter (G-S) 6f 70 <
1998 Turf 1-8: (5f 3, 6f 1-4, 7f) (gd 1-4, g-f 2, frm 2) 1998 AW 0-2: (6f 2) (Fibr 2)
Scopey, fair gelding, effective 6f, acts on gd, has worn blinkers, likes left handed tracks. Turf high 70 - 1st of 10 from Barren Lands (30 May Catterick RF 1584). AW high 58 (began Jly). Consistent.
**J Berry [1-16] Chris & Antonia Deuters.*

SONEVA (IRE) BHB 43f **RR 37f** 4662^{6}
3 b f Alzao (USA) 9.8f **(73)** - Rathvindon (Realm) 8.1f **(65)**

Form - 70706
Record 1998 - 1st:0 2nd:0 3rd:0 Ran:5
1998 Turf 0-5: (8f 2, 10f 3) (gd 2, g-f, frm 2)
Workmanlike, very moderate filly. Turf high 37.
**M A Buckley [0-5] C C Buckley.*

SONGINO (IRE) BHB 43f **RR 40f** 5094[19]
2 ch g Perugino (USA) - Sonbere (Electric) 10.1f **(61)**
Form - 0080
Record 1998 - 1st:0 2nd:0 3rd:0 Ran:4
1998 Turf 0-4: (5f, 6f, 7f, 8f) (gd 2, g-f 2)
Moderate gelding, has worn blinkers. Turf high 40 (began Jly).
**E J Alston [0-4] Jacksons Timber.*

SONG 'N DANCE MAN BHB 77f **RR 69f** 4845[17]
2 b c Prince Sabo 6.6f **(64)** - Born to Dance (Dancing Brave (USA)) 8.4f **(76)**
Form - 7550
Record 1998 - 1st:0 2nd:0 3rd:0 Ran:4
1998 Turf 0-4: (6f 2, 7f, 8f) (gd, g-f 2, frm)
Average colt. Turf high 68.
**J Noseda [0-4] Schmidt-Bodner & The late Mrs Tillman.*

SONG OF PARADISE (GER) **RR 98f** 1227a[9]
3 c
Form - 0
1998 Turf 0-1: (8f) (gd)
Currently very useful colt. **H Steinmetz in GER [0-1].*

SONG OF SKYE BHB 65f **RR 74f** 3666[8]
4 b f Warning 8.1f **(77)** - Song of Hope (Chief Singer) 8.9f **(66)**
Form - 763700808

Record	**1998 -**	1st:0	2nd:0	3rd:1	Ran:9
	Pre1998 -	1st:1	2nd:2	3rd:1	Ran:13

Win Prizemoney £3,493 *Total Prizemoney* £9,391
Wins * 1996 Jly Newbur (G-F) 5.2f 69 <
1998 Turf 0-9: (7f 2, 8f 6, 9f) (sft 2, gd 2, g-f 2, frm 2, hrd)
Leggy, above-average filly, effective 7 to 9f, best at 7f, acts on gd to frm, best on gd, has worn blinkers, likes right handed tracks, likes tight tracks, does well at Sandown. Turf high 76 - 3rd of 10 giving 2lb to Confidante (25 May Sandown 7f g-f RF 1461).
**T J Naughton [1-22] E J Fenaroli.*

SONGSHEET BHB 67f55a **RR 71f 55a** 3527[3]
5 b m Dominion 8.9f **(65)** - Songstead (Song) 7.2f **(61)**

Form - 4206563017503

Record	**1998 -**	1st:1	2nd:1	3rd:2	Ran:12
	Pre1998 -	1st:4	2nd:7	3rd:2	Ran:35

Win Prizemoney £13,483 *Total Prizemoney* £23,810

Wins	* **1998**	Jly	Chepst	(GD)	H	5.1f	64	71	
	* 1997	Jly	Yarmou	(G-S)		5.2f		72	<
	* 1997	Jun	Windso	(G-F)		5f		65	
	* 1997	May	Folkes	(G-F)	H	5f	62	66	
	1996	Apr	Bath	(GD)	S	5.1f		62+	

1998 Turf 1-9:(5f 1-9)(gd 2, g-f 1-6, frm)1998AW 0-3:(6f 3)(Equi 2, Fibr)
Above-average filly, effective 5f, acts on gd to g-f, best on g-f, excels at Chepstow and Folkestone. Turf high 71 - 1st of 13 giving 1lb to Runs in the Family (24 Jly Chepstow RF 3071). AW high 52. She had a good first half of last season around the minor tracks, and was a ready winner at Chepstow in July. Mixed form since. Suited by a fast-run race.
**M S Saunders [4-34] Mrs J Turner (from M Meade [0-9] Oct 1996).*

Song of Freedom was well tuned up for Ascot

SONG OF FREEDOM BHB 98f **RR 100f** 3752[10]
4 ch c Arazi (USA) 9.2f **(74)** - Glorious Song (CAN) (Halo (USA)) 10.6f **(75)**
Form - 284150

Record	**1998 -**	1st:1	2nd:1	3rd:0	Ran:6
	Pre1998 -	1st:2	2nd:1	3rd:0	Ran:8

Win Prizemoney £22,021 *Total Prizemoney* £30,831

Wins	* **1998**	Jly	Ascot	(G-F)	H	10f	95	100	<
	* 1997	Aug	Newbur	(G-F)	H	10f	86	86+	
	* 1997	Jly	Pontef	(GD)		10f		82	

1998 Turf 1-6: (10f 1-6) (gd, g-f 1-3, frm 2)
Strong, very useful colt, effective 10f, acts on gd to frm. Turf high 100 - 1st of 10 giving 3lb to Yavana's Pace (25 Jly Ascot RF 3100). A half-brother to Singspiel, he loves fast ground and had everything in his favour when winning a valuable handicap at Ascot in July. He is a summer horse.
**J H M Gosden [3-14] Sheikh Mohammed.*

SONIC SAPPHIRE RR 71f 4779[4]
2 b f Royal Academy (USA) 7.8f **(77)** - Sit Alkul (USA) (Mr Prospector (USA)) 8.8f **(78)**
Form - 4
Record 1998 - 1st:0 2nd:0 3rd:0 Ran:1
Win Prizemoney £0 *Total Prizemoney* £274
1998 Turf 0-1: (8f) (gd)
Currently above-average filly.
**E A L Dunlop [0-1] Maktoum Al Maktoum.*

SON OF ARAGON RR 2319[9]
4 b g Aragon 7.7f **(58)** - Golden Swallow (NZ) (Star Way)
Form - 0
Record 1998 - 1st:0 2nd:0 3rd:0 Ran:1
1998 AW 0-1: (12f) (Fibr)
Rangy, formerly very poor gelding.
**C W Thornton [0-6] W G Thornton.*

SON OF SKELTON BHB 47f **RR 50f** 4839[10]
3 ch g Minster Son 10.9f **(56)** - Skelton (Derrylin) 8.8f **(54)**
Form - 0050
Record 1998 - 1st:0 2nd:0 3rd:0 Ran:4
Pre1998 - 1st:0 2nd:1 3rd:0 Ran:2
Win Prizemoney £0 *Total Prizemoney* £804
1998 Turf 0-4: (8f 2, 11f, 14f) (g-s, gd 3)
Scopey, fair gelding, effective 7f, acts on g-s. Turf high 50.
**J S Haldane [0-4] Mrs Hugh Fraser (from J Wharton [0-2] Jly 1997).*

SON OF SNURGE (FR) BHB 74f **RR 76f** 5116[5]
2 b c Snurge - Swift Spring (FR) (Bluebird (USA)) 7.5f **(69)**
Form - 265
Record 1998 - 1st:0 2nd:1 3rd:0 Ran:3
Win Prizemoney £0 *Total Prizemoney* £1,037
1998 Turf 0-3: (8f, 10f 2) (gd 2, g-f)
Currently above-average colt. Turf high 76 (1st run) (began Spt) - 2nd of 11 to Bergamo (28 Spt Bath 10f g-f RF 4526).
**P F I Cole [0-3] M Arbib.*

SOOJAMA (IRE) BHB 57f49a **RR 55?f 49a** 3243[R]
8 b g Mansooj 10.6f **(53)** - Pyjama Game (Cavo Doro) 10.6f **(57)**
Form - RR
Record 1998 - 1st:0 2nd:0 3rd:0 Ran:2
Pre1998 - 1st:6 2nd:8 3rd:4 Ran:46
Win Prizemoney £21,014 *Total Prizemoney* £30,283

Wins	* 1997	May	Newmar	(GD)	H	14f	52	60	<
	* 1997	*Feb*	*Lingfi*	*(STD)*	*H*	*16f*	*41*	*53*	
	* 1997	*Feb*	*Lingfi*	*(STD)*	*H*	*12f*	*41*	*44*	
	* 1996	Jun	Newmar	(G-F)	H	12f	42	51	
	* 1995	Jun	Folkes	(GD)	H	16.4f	36	41	
	* 1995	Apr	Folkes	(G-F)	H	15.4f	35	38	

1998 Turf 0-2: (14f 2) (gd, frm)
Fair gelding, effective 14 to 16f, best at 15f, acts on gd to g-f - acts on Equi, best on gd, often wears blinkers (very effectively). Becoming disappointing. He has been most reluctant to take part in his recent races and is one to be very wary of.
**R M Flower [6-33] M G Rogers (from R Voorspuy [0-17] May 1994).*

SOOTY TERN BHB 43f36a **RR 60f 36a** 3839[4]
11 br h Wassl 9.8f **(62)** - High Tern (High Line) 10.3f **(70)**
Form - 0600037086604
Record 1998 - 1st:0 2nd:0 3rd:1 Ran:13
Pre1998 - 1st:19 2nd:18 3rd:9 Ran:115
Win Prizemoney £67,565 *Total Prizemoney* £93,320

Wins	* 1997	Jly	Bright	(FRM)	H	8f	67	75	<
	* 1997	Jly	Epsom	(G-S)	H	8.5f	67	68	
	* 1997	Jun	Bright	(FRM)	H	8f	64	68	
	* 1996	Aug	Hamilt	(G-F)	H	8.3f	62	74	
	* 1996	*May*	*Lingfi*	*(STD)*	*H*	*8f*	*47*	*48*	
	* 1995	Jly	Hamilt	(FRM)	H	8.3f	67	72	
	* 1995	Jun	Bright	(G-F)	H	8f	63	67	
	* 1995	Jun	Kempto	(GD)	H	8f	63	67	
	* 1994	Jly	Thirsk	(FRM)	H	8f	64	68	
	* 1994	Jun	Chepst	(G-F)	H	8.1f	61	62	
	* 1994	May	Hamilt	(SFT)	H	8.3f	57	58	

1998 Turf 0-9: (8f 6, 10f 3) (gd 2, g-f 3, frm 4) 1998 AW 0-4: (8f 3, 9f) (Equi, Fibr 3)
Average horse, effective 8 to 9f, best at 8f, acts on gd to frm. Turf high 60. AW high 34. A marvellous veteran, he was out of form for most of this year. As a half-brother to High-Rise, there should be a place at stud for him.
**J M Bradley [19-128] J M Bradley (from J W Watts [1-4] Jun 1990).*

SOPRAFFINO (USA) RR 108f 3781a[3]
3 ch c Nureyev (USA) 8.4f **(84)** - Sierra Roberta (FR) (Don Roberto (USA))
Form - 3
1998 Turf 0-1: (10f) (gd)
Currently Pattern-class colt. (1st run) - 3rd of 6 to Kabool (15 Aug Deauville 10f gd RF 3781a). He was not far behind Xaar in a Group 2 at Deauville and can win in a slightly lower grade.
**E Lellouche in FR [0-1] H Yokoyama.*

SOPRAN LONDA (IRE) RR 105f 1558a[8]
3 b f Danehill (USA) 9.1f **(79)** - Longobarda (FR) (Crystal Palace (FR)) 12.5f **(76)**
Form - 18
1998 Turf 1-2: (8f 1-1, 11f) (hvy, sft 1-1)
Pattern-class filly. Turf high 105 (1st run) - 1st of 16 from Deep Sea (19 Apr Capannelle RF 0833a). She ran out a convincing winning of the Premio Regina Elena (Italian 1,000 Guineas), but pulled hard and did not give herself any chance of staying in the Oaks d'Italia.
**L Camici in ITY [2-4].*

SORISKY BHB 34f34a **RR 42f 34a** 2841[11]
6 ch g Risk Me (FR) 8f **(53)** - Minabella (Dance In Time (CAN)) 8.9f **(59)**
Form - 040
Record 1998 - 1st:0 2nd:0 3rd:0 Ran:3
Pre1998 - 1st:1 2nd:0 3rd:0 Ran:18
Win Prizemoney £2,505 *Total Prizemoney* £2,505

Wins	* 1996	*Jan*	*Lingfi*	*(STD)*	*SH*	*13f*	*38*	*43*	<

1998 Turf 0-2: (12f 2) (gd, g-f) 1998 AW 0-1: (16f) (Equi)
Moderate gelding, had worn blinkers. Turf high 42. Inconsistent. (DEAD) **B Gubby [1-25] Brian Gubby Ltd.*

SORRIDAR BHB 67f72a **RR 73df 72a** 2156[5]
3 b f Puissance 7.1f **(60)** - Sorrowful (Moorestyle) 6.9f **(64)**
Form - 134114405
Record 1998 - 1st:3 2nd:0 3rd:1 Ran:9
Pre1998 - 1st:0 2nd:0 3rd:0 Ran:4
Win Prizemoney £6,361 *Total Prizemoney* £7,432

Wins	* **1998**	Mar	Hamilt	(HVY)	H	6f	67	73	<
	* **1998**	*Mar*	*Southw*	*(STD)*	*H*	*7f*	*62*	*73*	<
	* **1998**	*Feb*	*Wolver*	*(STD)*	*S*	*6f*		*60*	

1998 Turf 1-4: (6f 1-3, 7f) (sft 1-1, g-s, gd 2) 1998 AW 2-5: (6f 1-4, 7f 1-1) (Fibr 2-5)
Leggy, above-average filly, effective 6 to 7f, acts on sft - acts on Fibr, likes left handed tracks, likes tight tracks. Turf high 73 (1st run) - 1st of 8 giving 3lb to Barrelbio (30 Mar Hamilton RF 0500). AW high 73 - 1st of 9 giving 9lb to Bank On Him (11 Mar Southwell RF 0425). Becoming disappointing. **J L Eyre [3-13] K Birkinshaw.*

SOSSUS VLEI BHB 97f **RR 87f** 5065[2]
2 b c Inchinor 8.9f **(64)** - Sassalya (Sassafras (FR)) 9.6f **(69)**
Form - 0102
Record 1998 - 1st:1 2nd:1 3rd:0 Ran:4
Win Prizemoney £4,272 *Total Prizemoney* £6,369

Wins	* **1998**	Aug	Newmar	(G-F)		7f		87	<

1998 Turf 1-4: (7f 1-3, 8f) (g-f, frm 1-3)
Useful colt. Turf high 87 (began Jly) - 2nd of 13 giving 2lb to Lightning Arrow (30 Oct Newmarket 8f g-f RF 5065) - also 1st of 20 from Desaru (28 Aug Newmarket RF 3927). Showed little on his debut, but the yard was bang out of form then and he left that form behind on his second run. A half-brother to the stable's Sasuru, he lost little in defeat on his last two starts, and looks an interesting long-term prospect. **G Wragg [1-4] A E Oppenheimer.*

SOSTENUTO BHB 20f **RR 1f** 2099[13]
5 b m Northern State (USA) 12.6f **(45)** - Pride of Ayr (Recoil)
Form - 0
Record 1998 - 1st:0 2nd:0 3rd:0 Ran:1
Pre1998 - 1st:0 2nd:0 3rd:0 Ran:3
1998 AW 0-1: (8f) (Fibr)
Very poor filly. (DEAD) **R Hollinshead [0-4] Mrs B E Woodward.*

SOTONIAN (HOL) BHB 49f45a **RR 48f 45a** 4334[9]
5 br g Statoblest 6.4f **(63)** - Visage (Vision (USA)) 9f **(64)**
Form - 500833612330
Record 1998 - 1st:1 2nd:1 3rd:4 Ran:12
Pre1998 - 1st:2 2nd:1 3rd:3 Ran:26
Win Prizemoney £8,457 *Total Prizemoney* £13,893
Wins * **1998** *Aug Wolver (STD) H 5f 36 46* <
* 1997 *Jan Wolver (STD) H 5f 30 44*
* 1997 *Jan Wolver (STD) H 5f 30 44*
1998 Turf 0-6: (5f 5, 6f)(gd, frm 4, hrd)1998AW1-6: (5f 1-5, 6f) (Fibr 1-6)
Moderate gelding, effective 5f, acts on gd to hrd - acts on Fibr, has worn blinkers, likes left handed tracks, and excels at Warwick. Turf high 48 - 3rd of 11 getting 32lb from Westcourt Magic (22 Aug Chester 5f gd RF 3805). AW high 46 - 1st of 13 getting 20lb from Sue Me (7 Aug Wolverhampton RF 3449). Consistent.
**P S Felgate [3-35] Tim Dean (from Mrs L Stubbs [0-3] Jly 1996).*

SOTTVUS (IRE) BHB 90f **RR 90f** 4943a[1]
3 b c Royal Academy (USA) 7.8f **(77)** - Lorne Lady (Local Suitor (USA)) 8.4f **(67)**
Form - 343331
Record 1998 - 1st:1 2nd:0 3rd:4 Ran:6
Pre1998 - 1st:1 2nd:0 3rd:0 Ran:1
Win Prizemoney £16,518 *Total Prizemoney* £22,513
Wins * **1998** Oct San Si (SFT) 8f 90 <
* 1997 Spt San Si (GD) 7f
1998 Turf 1-6: (7f 2, 8f 1-3, 10f) (sft 1-1, gd, g-f 2, frm, hrd)
Useful colt, effective 8f, acts on sft to g-f. Turf high 90 - 1st of 6 getting 4lb from Lake Storm (17 Oct San Siro RF 4943a).
**L M Cumani [2-7] Scuderia Rencati.*

SOUFFLE BHB 97f **RR 100f** 5067[2]
3 b f Zafonic (USA) 9f **(83)** - One Way Street (Habitat) 9.4f **(70)**
Form - 311442
Record 1998 - 1st:2 2nd:1 3rd:1 Ran:6
Win Prizemoney £9,330 *Total Prizemoney* £16,543
Wins * **1998** Aug Sandow (GD) H 10f 90 94+ <
* **1998** Jly Haydoc (G-F) 10.5f 69+
1998 Turf 2-6: (10f 1-2, 11f 1-1, 12f, 15f, 16f) (gd 1-2, g-f 1-2, frm, hrd)
Tall, very useful filly, effective 10 to 16f, acts on gd to frm. Turf high 100 - 2nd of 6 giving 5lb to Etterby Park (30 Oct Newmarket 16f g-f RF 5067) - also 1st of 8 giving 8lb to Sharera (2 Aug Sandown RF 3298). She is a game filly and ran well in the face of some stiff tasks after winning at Haydock and Sandown. Well bred and placed in Listed company, she will make a valuable broodmare. **H R A Cecil [2-6] H R H Prince Fahd Salman.*

SOUND APPEAL BHB 53f **RR 57f** 4458[6]
4 b f Robellino (USA) 9.5f **(68)** - Son Et Lumiere (Rainbow Quest (USA)) 10.4f **(75)**
Form - 6
Record 1998 - 1st:0 2nd:0 3rd:0 Ran:1
Pre1998 - 1st:0 2nd:0 3rd:0 Ran:10
Win Prizemoney £0 *Total Prizemoney* £210
1998 Turf 0-1: (16f) (frm)
Leggy, fair filly, effective 8 to 10f, acts on gd to hrd, often wears blinkers (extremely effectively). Has shown very little on the level, but is a lot better over hurdles.
**G M McCourt [0-1] R W and J R Fidler (from A G Foster [0-10] Spt 1997).*

SOUND'S ACE BHB 68f **RR 67f** 5144[6]
2 ch f Savahra Sound 7.8f **(55)** - Ace Girl (Stanford) 7.9f **(56)**
Form - 751316
Record 1998 - 1st:2 2nd:0 3rd:1 Ran:6
Win Prizemoney £6,583 *Total Prizemoney* £7,200
Wins * **1998** Oct Newmar (G-S) H 5f 64 67 <
* **1998** Aug Beverl (G-F) S 5f 64
1998 Turf 2-6: (5f 2-5, 6f) (g-s, gd 2, g-f 2-2, frm)
Average filly, effective 5f, acts on gd to g-f, best on g-f, has worn blinkers. Turf high 67 - 1st of 10 getting 14lb from Elegant Lady (30 Oct Newmarket RF 5068) - also 1st of 16 from Bank On Mee (24 Aug Beverley RF 3831). **D Shaw [2-6] Paul Dixon.*

SOUNDS COOL BHB 47f52a **RR 47f 52a** 4490[12]
2 b c Savahra Sound 7.8f **(55)** -Lucky Candy(Lucky Wednesday) 8f **(50)**
Form - 7000
Record 1998 - 1st:0 2nd:0 3rd:0 Ran:4
1998 Turf 0-4: (5f 2, 6f 2) (gd 3, frm)
Fair colt. Turf high 47. **S R Bowring [0-4] Paul Dixon.*

SOUNDS LUCKY BHB 52f **RR 54f** 3642[7]
2 b c Savahra Sound 7.8f **(55)** - Sweet And Lucky (Lucky Wednesday) 8f **(50)**
Form - 567
Record 1998 - 1st:0 2nd:0 3rd:0 Ran:3
1998 Turf 0-1: (5f) (g-f) 1998 AW 0-2: (5f, 6f) (Fibr 2)
Currently fair colt. AW high 59 (began Jly).
**N P Littmoden [0-3] Paul Dixon.*

SOUNDS SOLO BHB 62f **RR** 4878[1]
2 b c Savahra Sound 7.8f **(55)** - Sola Mia (Tolomeo) 5.6f **(60)**
Form - 21
Record 1998 - 1st:1 2nd:1 3rd:0 Ran:2
Win Prizemoney £2,094 *Total Prizemoney* £2,734
Wins * **1998** *Oct Southw (STD) S 7f 56* <
1998 AW 1-2: (7f 1-2) (Fibr 1-2)
Currently average colt, always wears blinkers. AW high 64 (1st run) (began Spt) - 2nd of 15 to Hannibal Lad (29 Spt Southwell 7f Fibr RF 4548) - also 1st of 16 from Vale of Leven (19 Oct Southwell RF 4878). Has only one eye, but that has not stopped him from showing some ability on Fibresand. Runner-up in a Southwell seller on his debut, he made virtually all in a similar event next time.
**S R Bowring [1-2] Paul Dixon.*

SOUNDS SWEET BHB 46f40a **RR 50f 40a** 4863[13]
2 ch f Savahra Sound 7.8f **(55)** - Be My Sweet (Galivanter) 7.8f **(56)**
Form - 0556400
Record 1998 - 1st:0 2nd:0 3rd:0 Ran:7
1998 Turf 0-6: (5f 2, 6f, 7f 3) (gd 2, frm 4) 1998 AW 0-1: (6f) (Fibr)
Fair filly. Turf high 50. **J J O'Neill [0-7] Paul Dixon.*

SOUND THE TRUMPET (IRE) BHB 44f43a **RR 35f 43a** 536[8]
6 b g Fayruz 6.6f **(63)** - Red Note (Rusticaro (FR)) 8.2f **(65)**
Form - 1508
Record 1998 - 1st:1 2nd:0 3rd:0 Ran:4
Pre1998 - 1st:1 2nd:5 3rd:3 Ran:37
Win Prizemoney £5,805 *Total Prizemoney* £13,483
Wins * **1998** *Jan Lingfi (STD) H 5f 30 50*
1994 Mar Newcas (GD) 5f 64
1998 Turf 0-1: (5f) (gd) 1998 AW 1-3: (5f 1-3) (Equi 1-3)
Fair gelding, effective 5 to 7f, acts on gd to g-f - acts on Equi, best on g-f, has worn blinkers. AW high 50 (1st run) - 1st of 9 getting 24lb from Friendly Brave (13 Jan Lingfield RF 0081). He ended a very long losing run when winning a handicap on the Lingfield Equitrack in January. He won very easily, but his previous and subsequent performances do not inspire confidence that he can repeat the feat.
**R C Spicer [1-28] Mrs J A Nichols (from A Streeter [0-4] Oct 1995).*

SOUPERFICIAL BHB 52f40a **RR 52f 40a** 5059[7]
7 gr g Petong 7.6f **(58)** - Duck Soup (Decoy Boy) 6.7f **(56)**
Form - 0821178653027
Record 1998 - 1st:2 2nd:2 3rd:1 Ran:11
Pre1998 - 1st:8 2nd:5 3rd:3 Ran:66
Win Prizemoney £29,835 *Total Prizemoney* £39,193
Wins * **1998** Jun Hamilt (SFT) S 5f 56
* **1998** Jun Carlis (G-S) C 5.9f 56
1997 Jly Hamilt (SFT) 6f 46
1996 Spt Leices (FRM) H 5f 50 52
1996 Aug Nottin (G-F) H 5.1f 46 47
1995 Jly Pontef (G-F) H 6f 57 62
1995 May Wolver (STD) H 7f 56 63 <
1995 Apr Wolver (STD) H 6f 52 55
1995 Mar Southw (STD) H 6f 43 45
1994 Jly Pontef (G-F) H 5f 44 41
1998 Turf 2-11: (5f 1-3, 6f 1-7, 7f) (sft 2, gd 1-3, g-f 1-2, frm 4)
Fair gelding, effective 5 to 6f, best at 6f, acts on sft to frm, mostly wears blinkers (effectively), excels at Hamilton. Turf high 56 - 1st of 15 from Naissant (11 Jun Carlisle RF 1890) - also 1st of 8 from Henry the Hawk (17 Jun Hamilton RF 2062). Consistent. Running well in '98, successful in claiming and selling company in June.
**Don Enrico Incisa [2-13] Mrs Christine Cawley (from N Tinkler [1-17] Oct 1997).*

SOUTHBOUND TRAIN BHB 55f **RR 67f** 5004[6]
2 ch g Superlative 8.8f **(57)** - Louisianalightning (Music Boy) 6.8f **(57)**
Form - 8806
Record 1998 - 1st:0 2nd:0 3rd:0 Ran:4
1998 Turf 0-4: (6f 2, 7f 2) (sft, g-s, frm 2)
Average gelding. Turf high 67 (began Spt).
**G B Balding [0-4] Baldings (Training) Ltd.*

SOUTH CHINA SEA BHB 35f **RR 43f** 3396[12]
4 b f Robellino (USA) 9.5f **(68)** - Danzig Harbour (USA) (Private Account (USA)) 8.5f **(74)**
Form - 4400
Record 1998 - 1st:0 2nd:0 3rd:0 Ran:4
Pre1998 - 1st:0 2nd:0 3rd:0 Ran:4
Win Prizemoney £0 *Total Prizemoney* £353
1998 Turf 0-4: (7f 2, 8f 2) (sft, gd 2, frm)
Workmanlike, moderate filly. Turf high 43.
**J L Harris [0-4] J L Harris (from P F I Cole [0-4] Spt 1997).*

SOUTHDOWN CYRANO (IRE) BHB 46f **RR 41f** 4200[20]
3 b g Cyrano de Bergerac 7.3f **(58)** - Value Voucher (IRE) (Kings Lake (USA)) 10.8f **(67)**
Form - 0
Record 1998 - 1st:0 2nd:0 3rd:0 Ran:1
Pre1998 - 1st:0 2nd:0 3rd:0 Ran:3
1998 Turf 0-1: (5f) (gd)
Unfurnished, moderate gelding. **P Butler [0-4] P Butler.*

SOUTHERN-BE-GEORGE **RR 43f** 2589[8]
3 b g Be My Chief (USA) 10.2f **(62)** - Southern Sky (Comedy Star (USA)) 7.5f **(50)**
Form - 8
Record 1998 - 1st:0 2nd:0 3rd:0 Ran:1
Pre1998 - 1st:0 2nd:0 3rd:0 Ran:1
1998 Turf 0-1: (12f) (frm)
Strong, moderate gelding. **W G M Turner [0-2] A Wilkinson.*

SOUTHERN DOMINION BHB 58f56a **RR 61f 56a** 4921[18]
6 ch g Dominion 8.9f **(65)** - Southern Sky (Comedy Star (USA)) 7.5f **(50)**
Form - 37780406156510000
Record 1998 - 1st:2 2nd:0 3rd:0 Ran:15
Pre1998 - 1st:5 2nd:8 3rd:8 Ran:65
Win Prizemoney £22,932 *Total Prizemoney* £35,435
Wins * **1998** Aug Mussel (GD) H 5f 52 61 <
* **1998** Jly Mussel (GD) H 5f 48 51
* 1997 Nov Doncas (GD) H 5f 51 56
* 1997 Oct Ayr (SFT) H 5f 45 54
* 1997 May Mussel (G-F) H 5f 40 40
1995 Nov Lingfi (STD) H 6f 52 50
1995 May Bath (GD) S 5.1f 57
1998 Turf 2-14: (5f 2-14) (sft, g-s 3, gd 4, g-f 1-3, frm 1-2, hrd) 1998 AW 0-1: (5f) (Fibr)
Average gelding, effective 5 to 6f, best at 5f, acts on g-s to frm - acts on Fibr, often wears blinkers, excels at Doncaster, does well at Musselburgh. Turf high 61 - 1st of 17 from William's Well (27 Aug Musselburgh RF 3908). Usually blazes from the stalls and it is just a question of whether he can hold on. Best suited by an easy five, he can act on sand as well.
**Miss J F Craze [5-38] Mrs Angela Wilson (from C N Allen [0-8] Oct 1996).*

SOUTHERN DUNES **RR** 1144[12]
2 b c Ardkinglass 5f **(64)** - Leprechaun Lady (Royal Blend) 11.9f **(58)**
Form - 0
Record 1998 - 1st:0 2nd:0 3rd:0 Ran:1
1998 Turf 0-1: (6f) (gd)
Currently very poor colt, always wears blinkers - 12th of 12 to Strike A Blow (10 May Haydock 6f gd RF 1144).
**N Tinkler [0-1] Speedlith Group.*

SOUTHERN HARMONY (IRE) **RR 39f** 3903[8]
2 b f Mujadil (USA) 7.7f **(70)** - Fleur-de-Luce (Tumble Wind (USA)) 7.5f **(57)**
Form - 8
Record 1998 - 1st:0 2nd:0 3rd:0 Ran:1
1998 Turf 0-1: (5f) (g-f)
Currently moderate filly.
**Miss L A Perratt [0-1] The Happy Monday Club.*

SOUTHERN JAKE **RR** 1934[7]
2 b c Dilum (USA) 7.1f **(56)** - Southern Sky (Comedy Star (USA)) 7.5f **(50)**
Form - 7
Record 1998 - 1st:0 2nd:0 3rd:0 Ran:1
1998 Turf 0-1: (7f) (gd)
Currently very poor colt. **W G M Turner [0-1] A Wilkinson.*

SOUTHERN MEMORIES (IRE) BHB 37f27a **RR 37f 27a** 386[5]
8 b g Don't Forget Me 9.5f **(66)** - Our Pet (Mummy's Pet) 7.7f **(60)**
Form - 0555
Record 1998 - 1st:0 2nd:0 3rd:0 Ran:3
Pre1998 - 1st:3 2nd:1 3rd:1 Ran:29
Win Prizemoney £9,764 *Total Prizemoney* £12,481
Wins * 1995 Aug Goodwo (G-F) H 8f 50 54
1998 AW 0-3: (7f 3) (Fibr 3)
Very moderate gelding, has worn blinkers. AW high 26.
**W J Musson [1-13] Broughton Thermal Insulation (from R Hannon [2-19] May 1994).*

SOUTHERN RIDGE BHB 40f47a **RR 38f 47a** 3067[4]
7 b g Indian Ridge 7.6f **(74)** - Southern Sky (Comedy Star (USA)) 7.5f **(50)**
Form - 4
Record 1998 - 1st:0 2nd:0 3rd:0 Ran:1
Pre1998 - 1st:1 2nd:0 3rd:0 Ran:15
Win Prizemoney £4,500 *Total Prizemoney* £4,500
1998 Turf 0-1: (12f) (g-f)
Very moderate gelding.
**R G Frost [1-10] N J Holdsworth (from R J Baker [0-2] Feb 1996).*

SOVEREIGN BHB 34f **RR 35f** 2534[6]
4 b f Interrex (CAN) 7.7f **(51)** - Shiny Penny (Glint of Gold) 9.3f **(66)**
Form - 46
Record 1998 - 1st:0 2nd:0 3rd:0 Ran:2
Pre1998 - 1st:0 2nd:0 3rd:0 Ran:4
1998 Turf 0-2: (12f, 18f) (g-s, gd)
Workmanlike, very moderate filly. Turf high 35.
**M P Muggeridge [0-16] The Gaelic Five.*

SOVEREIGN ABBEY (IRE) BHB 70f68a **RR 72f 68a** 4998[3]
2 b f Royal Academy (USA) 7.8f **(77)** - Elabella (Ela-Mana-Mou) 10.1f **(70)**
Form - 03
Record 1998 - 1st:0 2nd:0 3rd:1 Ran:2
Win Prizemoney £0 *Total Prizemoney* £520
1998 Turf 0-2: (7f 2) (sft, g-s)
Currently above-average filly. Turf high 72 (began Oct) - 3rd of 10 to City of Gold (26 Oct Lingfield 7f sft RF 4998).
**Sir Mark Prescott [0-2] G S Shropshire.*

SOVEREIGN CREST (IRE) BHB 45f **RR 45f** 4458[9]
5 gr g Priolo (USA) 10.9f **(71)** - Abergwrle (Absalom) 7.2f **(58)**
Form - 43718830
Record 1998 - 1st:1 2nd:0 3rd:2 Ran:8
Pre1998 - 1st:1 2nd:0 3rd:2 Ran:14
Win Prizemoney £6,253 *Total Prizemoney* £8,157
Wins * **1998** Jly Lingfi (G-F) H 14f 42 43
* 1997 Jly Bright (FRM) H 11.9f 45 47 <
1998 Turf 1-8: (11f, 12f 4, 14f 1-2, 16f) (gd, g-f 2, frm 1-5)
Moderate gelding, effective 10 to 14f, best at 12f, acts on g-f to frm, best on frm, has worn blinkers, prefers left handed tracks, and excels at Lingfield. Turf high 45 - 3rd of 8 getting 5lb from Flying Bold (16 Aug Lingfield 11f frm RF 3663) - also 1st of 7 getting 28lb from Random Kindness (9 Jly Lingfield RF 2646). Consistent. Had run some good races prior to landing a handicap in July when tried in a visor. Often slowly away. **C A Horgan [2-22] Mrs B Sumner.*

SOVEREIGNS COURT BHB 74f **RR 76f** 3102[9]
5 ch g Statoblest 6.4f **(63)** - Clare Celeste (Coquelin (USA)) 8.4f **(58)**
Form - 531720
Record 1998 - 1st:1 2nd:1 3rd:1 Ran:6
Pre1998 - 1st:2 2nd:1 3rd:1 Ran:16
Win Prizemoney £9,885 *Total Prizemoney* £13,753

Wins * **1998** Jun Newbur (HVY) H 10f 74 74 <
* 1997 Nov Nottin (GD) H 10f 65 73
* 1997 Oct Nottin (SFT) H 8.2f 56 71

1998 Turf 1-6: (8f 2, 10f 1-4) (g-s 1-1, gd 3, g-f, frm)

Above-average gelding, effective 8 to 10f, best at 10f, acts on g-s to gd, best on gd, has worn blinkers, prefers left handed tracks, likes tight tracks. Turf high 76 - 2nd of 6 giving 9lb to Minetta (16 Jly Bath 8f gd RF 2842) - also 1st of 9 getting 3lb from River's Source (11 Jun Newbury RF 1901). Consistent.

**L G Cottrell [3-15] E Gadsden (from Major D N Chappell [0-7] Oct 1996).*

SOVIET ARTIC (FR) RR 83f
2275[3]

4 ch f Bering 9.6f **(80)** - Soviet Squaw (USA) (Nureyev (USA)) 8.7f **(78)**

Form - 63

Record 1998 - 1st:0 2nd:0 3rd:1 Ran:2

Win Prizemoney £0 *Total Prizemoney* £1,000

1998 Turf 0-2: (9f, 14f) (gd 2)

Currently decent filly, often wears blinkers. Turf high 83. Ex-French, a winner on soft ground at Clairefontaine in October '97, she showed mulish tendencies on both runs in this country.

**P W Chapple-Hyam [0-2] R E Sangster.*

SOVIET BUREAU (IRE) BHB 110f RR 112f
4945a[6]

3 ch c Soviet Lad (USA) 9.4f **(63)** - Redwood Hut (Habitat) 9.4f **(70)**

Form - 40413156

Record 1998 - 1st:2 2nd:0 3rd:1 Ran:8
Pre1998 - 1st:1 2nd:0 3rd:0 Ran:1

Win Prizemoney £22,000 *Total Prizemoney* £28,086

Wins * **1998** Aug Salisb (G-F) 8f 112 <
* **1998** Jun Goodwo (GD) 8f 105
* 1997 Aug Salisb (G-F) 7f 92+

1998 Turf 2-8: (7f, 8f 2-5, 9f, 10f) (sft, gd 1-4, g-f 1-3)

Scopey, Group-class colt, effective 8f, acts on gd to g-f. Turf high 112 - also 1st of 3 giving 11lb to Zaya (20 Aug Salisbury RF 3761). Described by Gay Kelleway as 'the best horse I have ever trained', he proved a shade disappointing when push came to shove. He ran his last race for the Kelleway yard when unplaced in the Grade Two Jamaica Handicap at Belmont Park in October and is to be trained in America. **Miss Gay Kelleway [3-9].*

SOVIET GIRL (IRE) BHB 59f RR 58f
1897[9]

3 b f Soviet Star (USA) 8.6f **(74)** - Crystal City (Kris) 9.5f **(73)**

Form - 070

Record 1998 - 1st:0 2nd:0 3rd:0 Ran:3

1998 Turf 0-3: (7f 3) (g-s, gd, g-f)

Unfurnished, currently fair filly. Turf high 58.

**B J Meehan [0-3] F C T Wilson.*

SOVIET LADY (IRE) BHB 30f RR 34f
4938[16]

4 b f Soviet Lad (USA) 9.4f **(63)**-La Vosgienne (Ashmore (FR)) 8.5f **(65)**

Form - 005470300

Record 1998 - 1st:0 2nd:0 3rd:1 Ran:9
Pre1998 - 1st:1 2nd:0 3rd:4 Ran:16

Win Prizemoney £2,845 *Total Prizemoney* £4,324

Wins 1996 Aug Thirsk (FRM) S 7f 59 <

1998 Turf 0-7: (6f, 7f 2, 8f 3, 16f) (g-s, gd 4, g-f, frm) 1998 AW 0-2: (6f, 8f) (Equi, Fibr)

Light-framed, very moderate filly, effective 7 to 8f, acts on gd to frm, has worn blinkers, favours tight tracks. Turf high 46 - 4th of 18 giving 12lb to Jato Dancer (18 May Windsor 8f frm RF 1311). AW high 12.

**R Ingram [0-1] Gerry Boyer (from B A Pearce [0-8] Jly 1998).*

SO WILLING BHB 64f63a RR 69f 63a
4253[13]

2 gr g Keen 11.1f **(58)** - Sweet Whisper **(14f 46a)** (Petong) 6.6f **(58)**

Form - 3648640

Record 1998 - 1st:0 2nd:0 3rd:1 Ran:7

Win Prizemoney £0 *Total Prizemoney* £565

1998 Turf 0-6: (5f 5, 6f) (gd 2, g-f 2, frm 2) 1998 AW 0-1: (6f) (Fibr)

Average gelding, effective 5 to 6f, best at 5f, acts on gd to g-f - acts on Fibr. Turf high 69 - 4th of 14 to Light Fingered (11 Jun Carlisle 5f g-f RF 1889). (1st run) - 6th of 11 giving 9lb to Kilbowie Hill (24 Jly Wolverhampton 6f Fibr RF 3093).

**M Dods [0-7] A G Watson.*

SPACE BABE BHB 54f RR 61f
4643[17]

2 br f Cosmonaut - Concorde Lady (Hotfoot) 10.5f **(59)**

Form - 6770

Record 1998 - 1st:0 2nd:0 3rd:0 Ran:4

1998 Turf 0-4: (5f, 7f 3) (gd, g-f 2, frm)

Average filly. Turf high 61 (began Jly). **R Hannon [0-4] Lady Davis.*

SPACE RACE BHB 77f77a RR 80f 77a
1105[10]

4 b g Rock Hopper 10.6f **(54)**-Melanoura (Imperial Fling(USA)) 7.1f **(58)**

Form - 200

Record 1998 - 1st:0 2nd:1 3rd:0 Ran:3
Pre1998 - 1st:1 2nd:1 3rd:0 Ran:6

Win Prizemoney £2,556 *Total Prizemoney* £4,947

Wins * 1997 May Bath (GD) 8f 70 <

1998 AW 0-3: (8f 2, 9f) (Equi, Fibr 2)

Scopey, decent gelding, effective 8 to 10f, best at 8f, acts on gd to frm - acts on Fibr, prefers tight tracks. AW high 80 (1st run) - 2nd of 6 giving 4lb to Sualtach (4 Apr Wolverhampton 8f Fibr RF 0568). He ran an encouraging race on his reappearance on the Wolverhampton Fibresand in April, but has run poorly since.

**C A Cyzer [1-9] R M Cyzer.*

SPA LANE BHB 51f42a RR 54f 42a
4958[7]

5 ch g Presidium 7.5f **(56)** - Sleekit (Blakeney) 10.5f **(64)**

Form - 132462227357

Record 1998 - 1st:1 2nd:4 3rd:2 Ran:12
Pre1998 - 1st:2 2nd:2 3rd:1 Ran:20

Win Prizemoney £8,858 *Total Prizemoney* £17,512

Wins * **1998** May Beverl (GD) H 16.2f 35 40
1996 Aug Nottin (G-S) 14.1f 58 <
1996 Jun Nottin (G-F) 10f 54

1998 Turf 1-12:(14f, 15f, 16f 1-6, 17f 2, 18f 2)(g-s 2, gd 2, g-f 3, frm 1-5)

Fair gelding, effective 12 to 18f, acts on g-s to frm, best on frm, likes tight tracks, excels at Beverley. Turf high 54 - 3rd of 5 getting 26lb from Etterby Park (17 Spt Yarmouth 18f frm RF 4335).

**Mrs S Lamyman [1-12] Sotby Farming Company Ltd (from M P Bielby [0-11] Oct 1997).*

SPANISH EYES BHB 65a RR 59f
4572[3]

3 b f Belmez (USA) 11.4f **(65)** - Night Transaction (Tina's Pet) 6.8f **(59)**

Form - 403233

Record 1998 - 1st:0 2nd:1 3rd:3 Ran:6
Pre1998 - 1st:0 2nd:0 3rd:0 Ran:1

Win Prizemoney £0 *Total Prizemoney* £2,803

1998 Turf 0-5: (8f 2, 10f 3) (gd, g-f 2, frm 2) 1998 AW 0-1: (8f) (Fibr)

Neat, fair filly, effective 8f, acts on g-f to frm, prefers tight tracks. Turf high 67 (1st run) - 4th of 12 to Cornflower Fields (29 May Bath 8f frm RF 1569). **J A R Toller [0-7] Alan Gibson.*

SPANISH FERN (USA) BHB 92f RR 92+f
4208[12]

3 b br f El Gran Senor (USA) 8.9f **(85)** - Chain Fern (USA) (Blushing Groom (FR)) 10.3f **(76)**

Form - 2110

Record 1998 - 1st:2 2nd:1 3rd:0 Ran:4
Pre1998 - 1st:0 2nd:0 3rd:1 Ran:1

Win Prizemoney £11,767 *Total Prizemoney* £13,272

Wins * **1998** Aug Newmar (G-F) H 7f 84 92+ <
* **1998** Jun Haydoc (GD) 7.1f 81

1998 Turf 2-4: (7f 2-3, 8f) (gd 1-3, frm 1-1)

Well made, useful filly, mostly wears blinkers. Turf high 92 - 1st of 17 from Blakeset (29 Aug Newmarket RF 3956). Just touched off on her three-year-old bow, she got off the mark with a clear cut victory in a Haydock maiden next time. Off the track for almost three months before bolting up in a Newmarket handicap, but was very disappointing at the Leger meeting. Capable of much better.

**R Charlton [2-5] K Abdulla.*

SPANISH KNOT (USA) BHB 65f52a RR 71f 52a
300[7]

4 b f El Gran Senor (USA) 8.9f **(85)** - Ingenuity (Clever Trick (USA)) 6.6f **(77)**

Form - 47

Record 1998 - 1st:0 2nd:0 3rd:0 Ran:2
Pre1998 - 1st:0 2nd:2 3rd:0 Ran:5

Win Prizemoney £0 *Total Prizemoney* £2,492

1998 AW 0-2: (7f, 8f) (Equi, Fibr)

Light-framed, above-average filly. AW high 20.

**Lord Huntingdon [0-7] The Queen.*

SPANISH LADY (IRE) RR 39f 5137[9]
2 b f Bering 9.6f **(80)** - Belle Arrivee (Bustino) 10.4f **(64)**
Form - 0
Record 1998 - 1st:0 2nd:0 3rd:0 Ran:1
1998 Turf 0-1: (7f) (gd)
Currently very moderate filly.
**J L Dunlop [0-1] Windflower Overseas Holdings Inc.*

SPANISH STRIPPER (USA) BHB 30f25a **RR 43?f 25a** 98[8]
7 b g El Gran Senor (USA) 8.9f **(85)** - Gourmet Dinner (USA) (Raise A Cup (USA)) 7.6f **(74)**
Form - 778
Record 1998 - 1st:0 2nd:0 3rd:0 Ran:3
Pre1998 - 1st:1 2nd:3 3rd:4 Ran:57
Win Prizemoney £3,113 *Total Prizemoney* £7,877
Wins * 1995 May Redcar (FRM) H 6f 53 63 <
1998 AW 0-3: (6f, 7f, 8f) (Fibr 3)
Moderate gelding, effective 10f, acts on frm, has worn blinkers. AW high 31. Inconsistent. Occasionally flatters to deceive, but often gives trouble before the start. Definitely not one to trust.
**M C Chapman [1-61] Tony Satchell (from J A R Toller [0-2] Spt 1994).*

SPANISH VERDICT BHB 27f **RR 35f** 5013[4]
11 b g King of Spain 7.3f **(55)** - Counsel's Verdict (Firestreak) 8.2f **(64)**
Form - 0000000004
Record 1998 - 1st:0 2nd:0 3rd:0 Ran:10
Pre1998 - 1st:13 2nd:15 3rd:14 Ran:132
Win Prizemoney £50,106 *Total Prizemoney* £76,729
Wins * 1996 Jun Thirsk (FRM) H 8f 59 61
* 1995 Aug Ripon (GD) H 8f 69 73
* 1995 Jly Carlis (FRM) H 8f 67 74 <
* 1994 Jly Mussel (G-F) H 8.1f 68 73
* 1994 Apr Thirsk (FRM) H 8f 64 64
1998 Turf 0-10: (8f 6, 9f, 11f 3) (g-s, gd 3, g-f 4, frm 2)
Very moderate gelding, effective 8f, acts on g-f to frm, best on frm, has worn blinkers. Turf high 36.
**Denys Smith [13-137] Cox & Allen (Kendal) Ltd (from Miss S E Hall [1-10] Oct 1990).*

SPARE SET (IRE) BHB 45f **RR 45f** 4656[15]
3 b f Second Set (IRE) 9.2f **(67)** - Troja (Troy) 10.4f **(68)**
Form - 6000
Record 1998 - 1st:0 2nd:0 3rd:0 Ran:4
1998 Turf 0-4: (8f, 10f 2, 12f) (gd, g-f 2, frm)
Leggy, moderate filly. Turf high 45 (began Aug).
**M G Meagher [0-4] Trevor Hemmings.*

SPARKLING DIAMOND RR 44f 3970[9]
2 b f Tina's Pet 7.4f **(56)** - Kate Kimberley (Sparkler) 8.4f **(55)**
Form - 00
Record 1998 - 1st:0 2nd:0 3rd:0 Ran:2
1998 Turf 0-2: (6f, 7f) (frm 2)
Currently moderate filly. Turf high 44 (began Jly).
**S C Williams [0-2] Bainey Racing Partnership.*

SPARKLING HARRY BHB 37f60a **RR 39f 60a** 4917[15]
4 ch g Tina's Pet 7.4f **(56)** - Sparkling Hock (Hot Spark) 7.6f **(62)**
Form - 6702804031010
Record 1998 - 1st:2 2nd:1 3rd:1 Ran:13
Pre1998 - 1st:0 2nd:0 3rd:1 Ran:18
Win Prizemoney £6,339 *Total Prizemoney* £7,767
Wins * **1998** *Oct Wolver (sta) H 9.4f 56 61* <
* **1998** *Spt Wolver (STD) H 8.5f 46 53*
1998 Turf 0-7: (6f, 7f 2, 8f 3, 10f) (g-s 3, gd 2, g-f, frm) 1998 AW 2-6: (7f 2, 8f 1-3, 9f 1-1) (Fibr 2-6)
Neat, average gelding, effective 6 to 9f, acts on frm - acts on Fibr, has worn blinkers. Turf high 50. AW high 61 - 1st of 13 getting 4lb from Windy Gulch (3 Oct Wolverhampton RF 4640) - also 1st of 13 giving 2lb to Shalyah (19 Spt Wolverhampton RF 4383). Inconsistent. Shows better form on sand than on turf. He got off the mark at the twenty-eighth attempt in a maiden handicap at Wolverhampton in September, and won over a slightly longer trip at the same track the following month.
**Miss L C Siddall [2-31] Lynn Siddall Racing.*

SPARKY BHB 66f **RR 68f** 1677[7]
4 b g Warrshan (USA) 9.7f **(59)** - Pebble Creek (IRE) (Reference Point) 6.8f **(70)**
Form - 5457
Record 1998 - 1st:0 2nd:0 3rd:0 Ran:4
Pre1998 - 1st:3 2nd:4 3rd:3 Ran:22
Win Prizemoney £7,966 *Total Prizemoney* £14,359
Wins * 1997 *Jun Southw (STD) H 8f 57 60+*
* 1996 Aug Beverl (FRM) H 7.5f 54 65 <
* 1996 Aug Bright (FRM) S 6f 65 <
1998 Turf 0-3: (8f 2, 10f) (gd, g-f, frm) 1998 AW 0-1: (9f) (Fibr)
Workmanlike, above-average gelding, effective 8 to 12f, best at 8f, acts on g-f to frm - acts on Fibr, mostly wears blinkers (extremely effectively), prefers right handed tracks, favours tight tracks. Turf high 67 (1st run) - 4th of 19 getting 19lb from Party Romance (17 May Ripon 10f frm RF 1287). Consistent.
**M W Easterby [3-30] Abbots Salford Carav Park.*

SPARTAN HEARTBEAT BHB 70f66a **RR 76f 66a** 759[2]
5 b g Shareef Dancer (USA) 10.1f **(67)**-Helen's Dream (Troy) 10.4f **(68)**
Form - 02
Record 1998 - 1st:0 2nd:1 3rd:0 Ran:2
Pre1998 - 1st:0 2nd:2 3rd:3 Ran:13
Win Prizemoney £0 *Total Prizemoney* £6,454
1998 Turf 0-1: (18f) (gd) 1998 AW 0-1: (12f) (Fibr)
Above-average gelding, has worn blinkers. He has spurned what looked to be easy winning opportunities on more than one occasion, but he had been set some impossible tasks prior to that. He seems to have gone sour, and though he ran quite well in a maiden on the Wolverhampton Fibresand in April, he cannot be trusted to replicate it. However, he was in good form over hurdles in the summer.
**J G M O'Shea [0-2] K W Bell (from C E Brittain [0-13] Nov 1997).*

SPARTAN ROYALE BHB 56f **RR 58f** 4355[6]
4 b g Shareef Dancer (USA) 10.1f **(67)** - Cormorant Creek (Gorytus (USA)) 7.8f **(60)**
Form - 372106
Record 1998 - 1st:1 2nd:1 3rd:1 Ran:6
Pre1998 - 1st:0 2nd:1 3rd:0 Ran:5
Win Prizemoney £2,346 *Total Prizemoney* £5,325
Wins * **1998** Aug Carlis (G-S) H 17.2f 55 58 <
1998 Turf 1-6: (11f, 12f 3, 17f 1-2) (sft, g-s, gd 1-4)
Scopey, fair gelding, effective 10f, acts on gd, likes right handed tracks. Turf high 58 (began Aug). Inconsistent.
**P Monteith [1-6] P Monteith (from C E Brittain [0-5] Oct 1997).*

SPAT RR 3933[16]
2 b f Casteddu 7.4f **(54)** - Amoureuse (IRE) (Petorius) 7.3f **(61)**
Form - 70
Record 1998 - 1st:0 2nd:0 3rd:0 Ran:2
1998 Turf 0-2: (5f, 6f) (frm 2)
Currently very poor filly. (began Jly).
**T H Caldwell [0-2] R S G Jones.*

SPEAKER'S CHAIR BHB 80f **RR 82f** 2644[3]
3 b c Shirley Heights 12.1f **(76)** - Lead Note (USA) (Nijinsky (CAN)) 10.3f **(77)**
Form - 3723
Record 1998 - 1st:0 2nd:1 3rd:2 Ran:4
Pre1998 - 1st:0 2nd:1 3rd:1 Ran:3
Win Prizemoney £0 *Total Prizemoney* £4,256
1998 Turf 0-4: (10f 2, 12f 2) (g-s, gd, g-f, frm)
Scopey, decent colt, effective 7 to 10f, best at 10f, acted on gd to frm. Turf high 82 - 2nd of 9 giving 11lb to My Pledge (15 Jun Windsor 10f gd RF 2006). He managed to make the frame in maiden and handicap company without quite managing to get his head in front. (DEAD) **R Charlton [0-7] K Abdulla.*

SPECIALIZE BHB 31f34a **RR 38df 34a** 264[8]
6 b g Faustus (USA) 9.1f **(54)** - Scholastika (GER) (Alpenkonig (GER)) 10.8f **(76)**
Form - 248
Record 1998 - 1st:0 2nd:1 3rd:0 Ran:3
Pre1998 - 1st:0 2nd:0 3rd:0 Ran:9
Win Prizemoney £0 *Total Prizemoney* £683
1998 AW 0-3: (12f 3) (Fibr 3)
Fair gelding, has worn blinkers. AW high 55 (1st run) - 2nd of 7 to Nessun Doro (26 Jan Southwell 12f Fibr RF 0159). Inconsistent.
**K R Burke [0-16] Mrs Diane Smith.*

SPECIAL-K BHB 35f37a **RR 42f 37a** 4010[11]
6 br m Treasure Kay 6.5f **(53)** - Lissi Gori (FR) (Bolkonski) 7.6f **(64)**
Form - 4830850800

Record	**1998 -**	1st:0	2nd:0	3rd:1	Ran:10
	Pre1998 -	1st:6	2nd:4	3rd:4	Ran:38

Win Prizemoney £17,392 *Total Prizemoney* £25,084

Wins								
1997	Jly	Ripon	(G-F)	S	8f		50	
1997	Jly	Beverl	(HVY)	SH	7.5f	44	49	
1995	Aug	Ripon	(G-F)	C	8f		68	<
1995	Jly	Beverl	(GD)	C	7.5f		68	<
1995	Jly	Redcar	(FRM)	C	7f		61	
1994	Jun	Doncas	(G-F)	S	6f		61	

1998 Turf 0-9: (5f, 7f 3, 8f 5) (g-s, gd 4, g-f 2, frm 2) 1998 AW 0-1: (7f) (Fibr)
Moderate mare, effective 7 to 8f, best at 8f, acts on sft to frm, best on frm, has worn blinkers. Turf high 51. Becoming disappointing.
**J R Turner [0-10] G Falshaw (from E Weymes [6-38] Oct 1997).*

SPECIAL PERSON (IRE) BHB 56f58a **RR 52f 58a** 3272[10]
3 ch f Ballad Rock 7.2f **(63)** - Hada Rani (Jaazeiro (USA)) 9.2f **(54)**
Form - 2401020

Record	**1998 -**	1st:1	2nd:1	3rd:0	Ran:6
	Pre1998 -	1st:0	2nd:1	3rd:0	Ran:1

Win Prizemoney £3,183 *Total Prizemoney* £4,793

Wins								
* **1998**	*Jun*	*Lingfi*	*(STD)*	*H*	*8f*	*55*	*60*	<

1998 Turf 0-3: (7f 2, 9f) (gd, frm 2) 1998 AW 1-3: (8f 1-2, 10f) (Equi 1-3)
Leggy, average filly, effective 8f, - acts on Equi. Turf high 52. AW high 60 (1st run) - 1st of 11 from Bank On Him (20 Jun Lingfield RF 2153). She has shown her best form to date on Equitrack, including winning a maiden handicap at Lingfield in June, but ran poorly when tried over ten furlongs.
**P Mitchell [1-7] Matthews Breeding and Racing.*

SPECIAL QUEST (FR) RR 113f 3781a[5]
3 c
Form - 13445
1998 Turf 1-5: (10f 3, 11f 1-2) (hvy 1-1, sft, gd 3)
Group-class colt, effective 10 to 11f, best at 10f, acts on hvy to gd, best on gd, often wears blinkers. Turf high 113 - 3rd of 5 to Croco Rouge (10 May Longchamp 11f gd RF 1231a) - also 1st of 6 from Roli Abi (13 Apr Longchamp RF 0830a). A very nervous individual, he sports special tight blinkers, but is game enough. He was involved in some fierce battles in the spring, including when just failing to stay an extended mile and a quarter at Longchamp in May. Possibly unlucky in a blanket finish behind Dr Fong at Maisons-Laffitte in July, he will appreciate his winter break and should do well in 10-furlong Group races next term.
**Mme C Head in FR [2-7] Wertheimer Brothers.*

SPECIAL ROLE BHB 44f39a **RR 43f 39a** 4866[12]
2 b f Tragic Role (USA) 9.4f **(63)** - Simmie's Special **(67a)** (Precocious) 8.6f **(62)**
Form - 6500

Record	**1998 -**	1st:0	2nd:0	3rd:0	Ran:4

1998 Turf 0-1: (5f) (g-f) 1998 AW 0-3: (5f, 6f, 8f) (Fibr 3)
Moderate filly. AW high 36 (began Jly). **P D Evans [0-4] J E Abbey.*

SPECIAL STAR RR 104f 4221a[2]
4 ch c Soviet Star (USA) 8.6f **(74)** - Sharpina (Sharpen Up) 8.3f **(67)**
Form - 62
1998 Turf 0-2: (10f, 11f) (sft, gd)
Very useful colt. Turf high 104 - 2nd of 5 getting 4lb from War Declaration (6 Spt San Siro 11f sft RF 4221a). He ran his best race for some time when narrowly beaten in a Group Three at San Siro in September.
**A Tortorella in ITY [0-2] (from P Guarsegnati in ITY [0-1] May 1997).*

SPECIAL TREAT BHB 92f **RR 92f** 1267[7]
3 b f Wolfhound (USA) 7.3f **(71)** - Just a Treat (IRE) (Glenstal (USA)) 10.1f **(64)**
Form - 587

Record	**1998 -**	1st:0	2nd:0	3rd:0	Ran:3
	Pre1998 -	1st:2	2nd:1	3rd:0	Ran:5

Win Prizemoney £10,065 *Total Prizemoney* £13,707

Wins								
1997	Oct	York	(GD)	H	6f	82	82	<
1997	Spt	Redcar	(FRM)		6f		82	<

1998 Turf 0-3: (7f 2, 8f) (hvy, g-f, frm)
Neat, useful filly, effective 6f, acts on gd to frm, best on gd, often wears blinkers (extremely effectively). Turf high 83. No promise in listed events.
**G Wragg [0-3] Cheveley Park Stud (from D R Loder [2-5] Oct 1997).*

SPECKLED GEM BHB 43f **RR 46f** 5004[15]
2 b f Precocious 7.2f **(54)** - My Diamond Ring (Sparkling Boy) 5f **(36)**
Form - 585500

Record	**1998 -**	1st:0	2nd:0	3rd:0	Ran:6

1998 Turf 0-3: (5f, 6f 2) (sft, gd 2) 1998 AW 0-3: (5f 2, 8f) (Fibr 3)
Moderate filly, has worn blinkers. Turf high 46. AW high 41.
**P D Evans [0-6] James Fenlon.*

SPECULATIVE BHB 27f **RR 27f** 2071[18]
4 b c Suave Dancer (USA) 10.7f **(68)** - Gull Nook (Mill Reef (USA)) 10.5f **(78)**
Form - 0060

Record	**1998 -**	1st:0	2nd:0	3rd:0	Ran:4
	Pre1998 -	1st:0	2nd:0	3rd:0	Ran:3

1998 Turf 0-4: (8f, 11f, 12f, 14f) (gd 4)
Workmanlike, little account colt, has worn blinkers. Turf high 27.
**W Storey [0-10] Tony Stafford.*

SPEEDFIT TOO (IRE) BHB 108f **RR 107f** 3633[4]
3 b c Scenic 10.6f **(66)** - Safka (USA) (Irish River (FR)) 8.6f **(78)**
Form - 581644

Record	**1998 -**	1st:1	2nd:0	3rd:0	Ran:6
	Pre1998 -	1st:2	2nd:1	3rd:2	Ran:7

Win Prizemoney £31,608 *Total Prizemoney* £46,121

Wins								
* **1998**	May	Kempto	(G-F)	L	8f		99+	<
* 1997	Aug	Newmar	(G-F)	H	6f	97	97	
* 1997	Aug	Windso	(GD)		6f		94	

1998 Turf 1-6: (7f 2, 8f 1-4) (sft, gd 1-4, g-f)
Workmanlike, Pattern-class colt, effective 8f, acts on gd, likes right handed tracks. Turf high 109. Consistent. He was not beaten far in the 2000 Guineas and deserved his Listed win at Kempton. The apple of his trainer's eye, he is a useful horse in that grade provided the ground rides fast. **G G Margarson [3-13] John Guest.*

SPEED ON BHB 81f **RR 91f** 4988[15]
5 b g Sharpo 7.5f **(68)** - Pretty Poppy (Song) 7.2f **(61)**
Form - 100006050

Record	**1998 -**	1st:1	2nd:0	3rd:0	Ran:9
	Pre1998 -	1st:1	2nd:2	3rd:3	Ran:12

Win Prizemoney £10,220 *Total Prizemoney* £17,152

Wins								
* **1998**	Apr	Bath	(SFT)		5.1f		97	<
* 1996	May	Beverl	(G-F)		5f		83	

1998 Turf 1-9: (5f 1-6, 6f 3) (g-s 1-3, gd 4, g-f, frm)
Useful gelding, effective 5f, acts on g-s to g-f, has worn blinkers. Turf high 97 (1st run) - 1st of 8 giving 5lb to Lochangel (28 Apr Bath RF 0892). He is a pacey sort well capable of winning sprint handicaps, as he showed when scoring at Bath in decisive fashion on his reappearance, but things have not gone his way since.
**H Candy [2-21] P A Deal.*

SPEEDY CLASSIC (USA) BHB 60f87a **RR 58f 87a** 4475[15]
9 br g Storm Cat (USA) 7f **(86)** - Shadows Lengthen (Star Appeal) 9.6f **(65)**
Form - 52105300010

Record	**1998 -**	1st:2	2nd:0	3rd:1	Ran:9
	Pre1998 -	1st:12	2nd:9	3rd:8	Ran:74

Win Prizemoney £45,110 *Total Prizemoney* £60,073

Wins								
* **1998**	Aug	Chepst	(G-F)	H	6.1f	55	58	
* **1998**	*Jan*	*Lingfi*	*(STD)*	*H*	*7f*	*84*	*86*	<
* 1997	Oct	Yarmou	(FRM)	H	7f	53	60	
* 1997	*Mar*	*Lingfi*	*(STD)*	*H*	*6f*	*80*	*79*	
* 1996	*Dec*	*Lingfi*	*(STD)*	*H*	*7f*	*72*	*80*	
* 1996	Spt	Chepst	(G-F)	H	7.1f	54	57	
* 1996	*Aug*	*Lingfi*	*(STD)*	*H*	*7f*	*63*	*74*	
* 1996	*Feb*	*Lingfi*	*(STD)*	*C*	*7f*		*67*	
* 1994	*Dec*	*Lingfi*	*(STD)*	*H*	*6f*	*56*	*62*	
* 1994	*Nov*	*Lingfi*	*(STD)*	*H*	*5f*	*49*	*58+*	
* 1994	Jly	Chepst	(G-F)	H	5.1f	56	58	
* 1994	Jun	Windso	(G-F)	H	6f	48	50	
* 1994	*Jan*	*Southw*	*(STD)*	*H*	*6f*	*46*	*46*	

1998 Turf 1-5: (6f 1-1, 7f 4) (gd 2, frm 1-3) 1998 AW 1-4: (6f, 7f 1-2, 8f) (Equi 1-4)
Useful gelding, effective 6 to 7f, best at 6f, - acts on Equi, has worn

blinkers, likes left handed tracks, likes tight tracks, excels at Lingfield. Turf high 58. AW high 86 (1st run) - 1st of 8 giving 16lb to Barbason (3 Jan Lingfield RF 0021). Inconsistent. Better on sand than on turf these days, though he did beat a big field in a Yarmouth handicap in October 1997. He has to be able to lead early in order to show his best. Seven furlongs looks to be his best trip.
**M J Heaton-Ellis [14-75] South Wales Shower S Faucets (from B W Hills [0-3] Oct 1992).*

SPEEDY JAMES (IRE) BHB 100f RR 97df 4242^{10}

2 ch c Fayruz 6.6f **(63)** - Haraabah (USA) (Topsider (USA)) 8.3f **(71)**
Form - 1128300
Record 1998 - 1st:2 2nd:1 3rd:1 Ran:7
Win Prizemoney £8,156 *Total Prizemoney* £15,272
Wins * **1998** Apr Newmar (SFT) 5f 98++ <
* **1998** Mar Newcas (G-S) 5f 84++
1998 Turf 2-7: (5f 2-7) (g-s, gd 2-4, g-f, frm)
Very useful colt, effective 5f, acts on gd, has worn blinkers. Turf high 98 - also 1st of 5 giving 9lb to Strike A Blow (16 Apr Newmarket RF 0715). He won in scintillating style at Newcastle and Newmarket before put in his place by the filly Bint Allayl at Sandown. He was rather disappointing when unplaced in the Norfolk, although it later transpired that he had spread a plate, and has had his limitations exposed since. Last in the Nunthorpe against older horses. **J Berry [2-7] Lucayan Stud.*

SPELUNAR (FR) RR 106f 943a^{1}

4 gr c Hard Leaf (FR) - Spelunca (FR) (Kaldoun (FR)) 10.3f **(68)**
Form - 1
1998 Turf 1-1: (6f 1-1) (g-s 1-1)
Currently Pattern-class colt. (1st run) - 1st of 5 giving 12lb to Zelding (20 Apr Chantilly RF 0943a). He won a competitive Listed event at Chantilly in April, but did not mount a challenge for the top sprint prizes. **M Bouland in FR [1-1] Mme M Tartrou.*

SPENCER'S REVENGE BHB 37f52a RR 39f 52a 1970^{7}

9 ch g Bay Express 7.1f **(53)** - Armour of Light (Hot Spark) 7.6f **(62)**
Form - 807
Record 1998 - 1st:0 2nd:0 3rd:0 Ran:3
Pre1998 - 1st:13 2nd:10 3rd:8 Ran:53
Win Prizemoney £39,002 *Total Prizemoney* £51,019
Wins * 1997 *Feb Lingfi (STD) C 10f 58*
1996 *Apr Southw (STD) C 8f 68*
1996 *Jan Southw (STD) C 8f 64*
1995 *Dec Lingfi (STD) C 8f 75*
1995 Oct Yarmou (FRM) H 7f 67 70
1995 *Spt Wolver (STD) C 7f 74*
1995 May Salisb (GD) H 7f 63 68
1995 *Feb Wolver (STD) C 7f 67*
1995 *Jan Lingfi (STD) 7f 66+*
1995 *Jan Lingfi (STD) S 7f 57+*
1998 Turf 0-2: (8f, 9f) (frm 2) 1998 AW 0-1: (8f) (Equi)
Fair gelding, effective 7 to 10f, best at 8f, - acts on Equi, has worn blinkers, prefers left handed tracks, favours tight tracks. Turf high 39. Becoming disappointing.
**P Butler [1-11] Mrs Janet Coleman (from N Tinkler [1-11] Jan 1997).*

SPENDER BHB 68f84a RR 67f 84a 5007^{15}

9 b or br g Last Tycoon 9.4f **(73)** - Lady Hester (Native Prince) 5.5f **(50)**
Form - 06000030
Record 1998 - 1st:0 2nd:0 3rd:1 Ran:8
Pre1998 - 1st:15 2nd:7 3rd:9 Ran:66
Win Prizemoney £54,146 *Total Prizemoney* £67,740
Wins * 1997 Spt Yarmou (G-F) H 5.2f 77 82
* 1997 Jun Bath (G-F) H 5.7f 76 79
* 1997 Apr Bright (FRM) H 6f 74 77
* 1996 *Mar Lingfi (STD) H 5f 82 87* <
* 1995 Aug Bath (HRD) H 5.1f 71 72
* 1995 *Mar Lingfi (STD) H 5f 76 76*
* 1995 *Jan Lingfi (STD) H 5f 73 73*
* 1994 Apr Thirsk (FRM) H 5f 58 58
* 1994 Apr Bright (GD) H 5.3f 53 55
* 1994 *Mar Lingfi (STD) H 6f 66 63*
* 1994 *Feb Lingfi (STD) 6f 54+*
* 1994 *Feb Lingfi (STD) H 6f 55 58*
1998 Turf 0-8: (5f 7, 6f) (sft 2, g-s, gd 2, g-f 2, frm)
Useful gelding, effective 5 to 6f, best at 5f, acts on g-f to frm - acts on Equi, likes left handed tracks. Turf high 67. This game and genuine sprinter wins in his turn, but has been lightly raced in '98.
**P W Harris [15-74] The Entrepreneurs.*

SPENDTHEPROC-EDE'S BHB 65f RR 64f 3591^{5}

2 b f Dilum (USA) 7.1f **(56)** - Karonga (Main Reef) 9.6f **(57)**
Form - 552585
Record 1998 - 1st:0 2nd:1 3rd:0 Ran:6
Win Prizemoney £0 *Total Prizemoney* £1,040
1998 Turf 0-6: (5f 2, 6f, 7f 3) (gd 3, g-f, frm 2)
Average filly, effective 6f, acts on frm. Turf high 60 - 2nd of 7 to Unicamp (22 May Nottingham 6f frm RF 1400).
**W G M Turner [0-6] Ede's (UK) Ltd.*

SPICE BOY BHB 33f RR 33f 3657^{8}

3 ch g Imp Society (USA) 7.1f **(63)** - Lewista (Mandrake Major) 7.6f **(53)**
Form - 00008
Record 1998 - 1st:0 2nd:0 3rd:0 Ran:5
1998 Turf 0-5: (5f 2, 6f, 7f, 8f) (g-s, gd, g-f, frm, hrd)
Leggy, very moderate gelding, has worn blinkers. Turf high 33.
**R M Whitaker [0-5] A Bunch Of Fives.*

SPICE GIRL BHB 33f39a RR 38f 39a 1478^{6}

3 ch f Alhijaz 7.7f **(57)** - Imagery (Vision (USA)) 9f **(64)**
Form - 576
Record 1998 - 1st:0 2nd:0 3rd:0 Ran:3
Pre1998 - 1st:0 2nd:0 3rd:0 Ran:3
1998 Turf 0-1: (14f) (g-f) 1998 AW 0-2: (9f, 12f) (Fibr 2)
Light-framed, very moderate filly, often wears blinkers. AW high 36. **P D Evans [0-6] Treble Chance Partnership.*

SPICETRESS BHB 35f30a RR 56f 30a 157^{9}

4 gr f Chilibang 7f **(55)** - Foreign Mistress (Darshaan) 9.9f **(84)**
Form - 00
Record 1998 - 1st:0 2nd:0 3rd:0 Ran:1
Pre1998 - 1st:0 2nd:0 3rd:0 Ran:5
1998 AW 0-1: (9f) (Fibr)
Leggy, fair filly, has worn blinkers.
**Ian Williams [0-2] M F C A Ltd (from J L Spearing [0-4] Spt 1997).*

SPICK AND SPAN BHB 51a RR 52f 4458^{4}

4 b g Anshan 8.2f **(63)** - Pretty Thing (Star Appeal) 9.6f **(65)**
Form - 2834
Record 1998 - 1st:0 2nd:0 3rd:1 Ran:2
Pre1998 - 1st:0 2nd:1 3rd:1 Ran:8
Win Prizemoney £0 *Total Prizemoney* £1,943
1998 Turf 0-1: (16f) (frm) 1998 AW 0-1: (12f) (Fibr)
Leggy, fair gelding, effective 12 to 16f, best at 12f, acts on gd to frm - acts on Fibr, likes tight tracks. (1st run) - 4th of 16 getting 1lb from Danegold (24 Spt Goodwood 16f frm RF 4458). (1st run) - 3rd of 11 giving 5lb to Grovefair Lad (9 Mar Southwell 12f Fibr RF 0416). Consistent.
**P R Hedger [0-6] Essandess Partners (from C W Thornton [0-8] Nov 1997).*

SPINDRIFT (IRE) BHB 104f RR 102f 2252^{1}

3 b c Mukaddamah (USA) 7.6f **(74)** - Win For Me (Bonne Noel) 10.7f **(71)**
Form - 211
Record 1998 - 1st:2 2nd:1 3rd:0 Ran:3
Win Prizemoney £9,384 *Total Prizemoney* £11,050
Wins * **1998** Jun Salisb (G-F) 7f 102 <
* **1998** May Newmar (G-F) 8f 96
1998 Turf 2-3: (7f 1-1, 8f 1-2) (gd, g-f 1-1, frm 1-1)
Well made, currently very useful colt. Turf high 102 - 1st of 8 giving 9lb to Doomna (24 Jun Salisbury RF 2252) - also 1st of 12 from Lear Spear (30 May Newmarket RF 1613). He did well to beat Lear Spear in May, and coped with a drop back to seven furlongs when following up at Salisbury in June. Withdrawn after banging his head at Glorious Goodwood, he remains unexposed and very much one to follow. **L M Cumani [2-3] M J Dawson.*

SPINNER TOY RR 12f 2642^{10}

3 ch g Seven Hearts - Priory Bay (Petong) 6.6f **(58)**
Form - 0
Record 1998 - 1st:0 2nd:0 3rd:0 Ran:1
1998 Turf 0-1: (8f) (frm)

Light-framed, currently poor gelding.
**J C Fox [0-1] Miss Sarah-Jane Durman.*

SPIRAL DREAM (USA) RR 55f 3044[U]

3 b f El Gran Senor (USA) 8.9f **(85)** - Amalise (Valiyar) 8.5f **(73)**
Form - 40U
Record 1998 - 1st:0 2nd:0 3rd:0 Ran:3
Win Prizemoney £0 *Total Prizemoney* £274
1998 Turf 0-3: (8f 3) (frm 3)
Leggy, currently fair filly. Turf high 55 (1st run) - 4th of 18 to Myzomela (18 May Windsor 8f frm RF 1316).
**P W Chapple-Hyam [0-3] R E Sangster.*

SPIRAL FLYER (IRE) BHB 33f25a RR 35f 25a 4938[1]

5 b br m Contract Law (USA) 8.9f **(54)** - Souveniers (Relko) 9.9f **(59)**
Form - 87081
Record 1998 - 1st:1 2nd:0 3rd:0 Ran:5
Pre1998 - 1st:0 2nd:1 3rd:1 Ran:17
Win Prizemoney £3,057 *Total Prizemoney* £4,128
Wins * 1998 Oct Nottin () H 16f 20 35 <
1998 Turf 1-4: (12f 2, 16f 1-1, 17f) (gd 1-1, g-f, frm, hrd) 1998 AW 0-1: (11f) (Fibr)
Very moderate filly, effective 16 to 17f, best at 17f, acts on gd to frm, best on gd, has worn blinkers, prefers left handed tracks, prefers tight tracks. Turf high 35 - 1st of 17 getting 4lb from Dutch Dyane (22 Oct Nottingham RF 4938).
**M D I Usher [2-35] G A Summers.*

SPIRIT LADY BHB 35f RR 12tf 3944[18]

4 b f Salse (USA) 10.9f **(71)** - Wanda (Taufan (USA)) 7f **(57)**
Form - 00
Record 1998 - 1st:0 2nd:0 3rd:0 Ran:2
Pre1998 - 1st:0 2nd:0 3rd:0 Ran:4
Win Prizemoney £0 *Total Prizemoney* £245
1998 Turf 0-2: (8f, 10f) (gd, frm)
Leggy, poor filly. (began Aug).
**D Nicholls [0-2] E J Mangan (from J S King [0-4] Spt 1997).*

SPIRITO BHB 40f RR 51f 3084[6]

3 b g Mystiko (USA) 7.7f **(59)** - Classic Beam (Cut Above) 14.1f **(56)**
Form - 0006
Record 1998 - 1st:0 2nd:0 3rd:0 Ran:4
Pre1998 - 1st:0 2nd:0 3rd:0 Ran:1
1998 Turf 0-4: (10f 2, 12f, 16f) (g-f 3, frm)
Fair gelding, has worn blinkers. Turf high 51.
**Lord Huntingdon [0-5] The W I Syndicate.*

SPIRIT OF LOVE (USA) BHB 108f99a RR 112+f 99a 4850[1]

3 ch c Trempolino (USA) 11.9f **(77)** - Dream Mary (USA) (Marfa (USA)) 14.9f **(73)**
Form - 01323114131
Record 1998 - 1st:5 2nd:1 3rd:3 Ran:10
Pre1998 - 1st:0 2nd:0 3rd:0 Ran:2
Win Prizemoney £104,805 *Total Prizemoney* £108,110
Wins * 1998 Oct Newmar (GD) H 18f 91 112+ <

Spirit of Love and Olivier Peslier win the Cesarewitch

* **1998** Spt Doncas (GD) H 14.6f 91 99
* **1998** Aug Ascot (G-F) H 16.2f 83 90
* **1998** May Doncas (G-F) H 14.6f 77 81
* **1998** *Jan Southw (STD) 11f 70*

1998 Turf 4-6: (14f 2, 15f 2-2, 16f 1-1, 18f 1-1) (gd 2-2, g-f 2-2, frm 2)
1998 AW 1-4: (10f, 11f 1-2, 12f) (Equi, Fibr 1-3)

Scopey, Group-class colt, effective 18f, acts on gd. Turf high 112 - 1st of 29 giving 3lb to Etterby Park (17 Oct Newmarket RF 4850). AW high 77. Improving. Whether he is the second coming of Double Trigger remains to be seen, but there is no quibbling with his runaway win in the Cesarewitch. Granted normal progress from three to four, he will make life uncomfortable for the established stayers in the Cup races. It is worth noting that he goes very well when fresh and has improved for every step up in trip.
**M Johnston [5-12] A W Robinson.*

SPIRITO LIBRO (USA) BHB 77f RR 73?f 973[14]

5 b m Lear Fan (USA) 10.4f **(80)** - Teeming Shore (USA) (L'Emigrant (USA)) 10.5f **(62)**
Form - 0
Record 1998 - 1st:0 2nd:0 3rd:0 Ran:1
Pre1998 - 1st:4 2nd:2 3rd:3 Ran:18
Win Prizemoney £37,773 *Total Prizemoney* £68,425
Wins 1996 Jun Epsom (GD) H 10.1f 73 78 <
1996 May Newmar (G-F) H 8f 58 73
1995 Spt Folkes (G-F) C 6f 65
1995 Aug Mussel (G-F) S 5f 58+
1998 Turf 0-1: (10f) (gd)
Above-average filly.
**Martyn Wane [0-1] J R Bamforth (from D J S Cosgrove [0-2] Jun 1997).*

SPIRIT WILLING (IRE) BHB 100f RR 97f 4974[7]

2 b f Fairy King (USA) 7.7f **(75)** - Pro Patria (Petingo) 11f **(72)**
Form - 31527
Record 1998 - 1st:1 2nd:1 3rd:1 Ran:5
Win Prizemoney £5,654 *Total Prizemoney* £9,220
Wins * **1998** Jun Ascot (G-S) 6f 95+ <
1998 Turf 1-4: (6f 1-4) (sft, g-f 1-1, frm, hrd) 1998 AW 0-1: (6f) (Fibr)
Very useful filly. Turf high 97 - 5th of 10 to Wannabe Grand (7 Jly Newmarket 6f frm RF 2580) - also 1st of 10 from Penmayne (20 Jun Ascot RF 2140). Easy winner at Ascot on her second start before finishing fifth in the Cherry Hinton. The fast ground was against her there, but she ran poorly on her final two starts, on Wolverhampton's Fibresand and on heavy. One to reserve judgement on, she might need seven furlongs. **D R Loder [1-5] E J Loder.*

SPITZBERGEN BHB 83f RR 82f 5124[1]

2 ch c Polar Falcon (USA) 9f **(74)** - Soba (Most Secret) 7.1f **(58)**
Form - 811
Record 1998 - 1st:2 2nd:0 3rd:0 Ran:3
Win Prizemoney £6,637 *Total Prizemoney* £6,637
Wins * **1998** Nov Bright (SFT) H 8f 77 82 <
* **1998** Oct Folkes (G-S) 7f 82 <
1998 Turf 2-3: (6f, 7f 1-1, 8f 1-1) (g-s 2-2, gd)
Currently decent colt. Turf high 82 (began Oct) - 1st of 9 from West Escape (5 Nov Brighton RF 5124) - also 1st of 13 giving 7lb to Cinnamon Lady (20 Oct Folkestone RF 4884). Improved with each run, he got off the mark with a last-gasp victory in a Folkestone maiden, and followed up with a battling success in a Brighton nursery. Should be suited by middle distances next season. **M Johnston [2-3] Brian Yeardley Continental Ltd.*

SPLASHED BHB 34f47a RR 36f 47a 3524[10]

4 gr f Absalom 7.1f **(56)** - Riverain (Bustino) 10.4f **(64)**
Form - 470050
Record 1998 - 1st:0 2nd:0 3rd:0 Ran:6
Pre1998 - 1st:0 2nd:0 3rd:2 Ran:9
Win Prizemoney £0 *Total Prizemoney* £1,984
1998 Turf 0-3: (6f, 7f, 8f) (gd, frm 2) 1998 AW 0-3: (7f, 8f, 10f) (Equi, Fibr 2)
Scopey, very moderate filly. Turf high 32. AW high 50. Consistent. (DEAD)
**Paddy Farrell [0-6] Mrs Roz Virasinghe (from T D Barron [0-9] May 1997).*

SPLENDIDA IDEA (IRE) RR 96f 4600a[6]

3 f
Form - 66
1998 Turf 0-2: (10f, 11f) (hvy 2)
Currently very useful filly. Turf high 96. Sixth in the Italian Oaks.
**F Camici in ITY [0-2].*

SPLENDID ISOLATION (USA) BHB 85f RR 93f 4621[4]

3 b br c Hermitage (USA) 8.6f **(84)** - Hord (USA) (Private Account (USA)) 8.5f **(74)**
Form - 220220174
Record 1998 - 1st:1 2nd:4 3rd:0 Ran:9
Pre1998 - 1st:0 2nd:0 3rd:1 Ran:2
Win Prizemoney £3,501 *Total Prizemoney* £8,239
Wins * **1998** Aug Salisb (G-F) 7f 93+ <
1998 Turf 1-9: (7f 1-3, 8f 5, 10f) (gd 5, g-f 1-3, frm)
Scopey, useful colt, effective 6 to 8f, best at 8f, acts on gd to g-f, best on g-f. Turf high 93 - 1st of 11 from Shart (20 Aug Salisbury RF 3764). He got off the mark at Yarmouth in August, but should have done so earlier having finished runner-up four times in his first five starts of the year. A mile looks to be the very limit of his stamina, and he will continue his career in the States, having been sold for 75,000 guineas.
**L M Cumani [1-11] Lord De La Warr & Mrs T Von Halle.*

SPLIT THE ACES (IRE) BHB 60f RR 43f 2394[7]

2 gr c Balla Cove - Hazy Lady (Habitat) 9.4f **(70)**
Form - 487
Record 1998 - 1st:0 2nd:0 3rd:0 Ran:3
Win Prizemoney £0 *Total Prizemoney* £242
1998 Turf 0-3: (5f 2, 6f) (hvy, g-s, gd)
Currently moderate colt. Turf high 43. **R Hannon [0-3] A F Merritt.*

SPONDULICKS (IRE) BHB 50f42a RR 45f 42a 283[10]

4 b g Silver Kite (USA) 10.2f **(51)** - Greek Music (Tachypous) 8.6f **(55)**
Form - 00
Record 1998 - 1st:0 2nd:0 3rd:0 Ran:2
Pre1998 - 1st:0 2nd:4 3rd:3 Ran:22
Win Prizemoney £0 *Total Prizemoney* £4,722
1998 AW 0-2: (12f, 16f) (Fibr 2)
Scopey, fair gelding, effective 9 to 14f, acts on g-s to frm - acts on Fibr, has worn blinkers. AW high 12.
**B P J Baugh [0-12] Mrs Joan Chrimes (from R Hannon [0-12] Spt 1996).*

SPONTANEITY (IRE) BHB 71f70a RR 78f 70a 4960[6]

2 ch f Shalford (IRE) 7.8f **(63)** - Mariyda (IRE) (Vayrann) 9.7f **(74)**
Form - 531056
Record 1998 - 1st:1 2nd:0 3rd:1 Ran:6
Win Prizemoney £3,805 *Total Prizemoney* £4,204
Wins * **1998** Aug Thirsk (G-F) 7f 78 <
1998 Turf 1-5: (6f 3, 7f 1-1, 8f) (gd 2, frm 1-2, hrd) 1998 AW 0-1: (8f) (Fibr)
Above-average filly, effective 6 to 7f, acts on frm to hrd. Turf high 78 (began Jly) - 1st of 16 getting 7lb from Moon Glow (10 Aug Thirsk RF 3507). **P D Evans [1-6] Colin Booth.*

SPOONFUL OF SUGAR RR 78f 5146[2]

2 b f Sabrehill (USA) 8.5f **(64)** - Pacific Gull (USA) (Storm Bird (CAN)) 10.3f **(74)**
Form - 62
Record 1998 - 1st:0 2nd:1 3rd:0 Ran:2
Win Prizemoney £0 *Total Prizemoney* £1,010
1998 Turf 0-2: (7f, 8f) (gd 2)
Currently above-average filly. Turf high 78 (began Oct) - 2nd of 13 getting 5lb from Chelsea Barracks (7 Nov Doncaster 8f gd RF 5146). **B W Hills [0-2] H R H Prince Fahd Salman.*

SPORTING LAD (USA) BHB 99f RR 89f 4964[4]

2 b c Danzig (USA) 8.1f **(88)** - Lydara (USA) (Alydar (USA)) 9.1f **(76)**
Form - 52214
Record 1998 - 1st:1 2nd:2 3rd:0 Ran:5
Win Prizemoney £3,626 *Total Prizemoney* £9,149
Wins * **1998** Aug Cheste (GD) 7f 89 <
1998 Turf 1-5: (6f, 7f 1-4) (sft, gd 1-3, g-f)
Useful colt. Turf high 89 - 1st of 7 from King Adam (21 Aug Chester RF 3791). **P F I Cole [1-5] M Arbib.*

SPORTS ROAD (IRE) BHB 76f **RR 85f** 5042[5]
2 b c Common Grounds 8.1f **(66)** - Sports Post Lady (IRE) (M Double M (USA)) 14.1f **(52)**
Form - 6222405
Record 1998 - 1st:0 2nd:3 3rd:0 Ran:7
Win Prizemoney £0 *Total Prizemoney* £3,453
1998 Turf 0-7: (5f 2, 6f 5) (sft, gd, g-f 3, frm 2)
Useful colt, effective 5 to 6f, best at 6f, acts on g-f to frm, best on frm. Turf high 85 - 2nd of 20 to Compton Arrow (6 Aug Haydock 6f g-f RF 3409). **R Hannon [0-7] Noodles Racing.*

SPORTY SPICE (IRE) BHB 29f **RR 44f** 5070[10]
3 b f Indian Ridge 7.6f **(74)** - Intrinsic (Troy) 10.4f **(68)**
Form - 00854000
Record 1998 - 1st:0 2nd:0 3rd:0 Ran:8
Pre1998 - 1st:0 2nd:0 3rd:0 Ran:3
1998 Turf 0-7: (8f, 9f, 10f, 11f 3, 14f) (gd 3, g-f 3, frm) 1998 AW 0-1: (12f) (Fibr)
Light-framed, moderate filly, has worn blinkers. Turf high 44.
**J L Harris [0-9] Dr C W Ashpole (from Mrs J R Ramsden [0-2] Jun 1998).*

SPOTTED EAGLE BHB 51f41a **RR 52f 41a** 3953[4]
5 ch g Risk Me (FR) 8f **(53)** - Egnoussa (Swing Easy (USA)) 6.5f **(55)**
Form - 08722604
Record 1998 - 1st:0 2nd:2 3rd:0 Ran:8
Pre1998 - 1st:2 2nd:0 3rd:1 Ran:16
Win Prizemoney £5,608 *Total Prizemoney* £8,169
Wins 1997 Jly Catter (G-F) S 6f 46
1996 Apr Folkes (FRM) 6f 72 <
1998 Turf 0-6: (5f 3, 6f 3) (gd, g-f 2, frm 3) 1998 AW 0-2: (5f 2) (Fibr 2)
Fair gelding, likes left handed tracks, likes tight tracks. Turf high 52 (began Jly). AW high 28. Inconsistent.
**D Nicholls [0-11] W G Swiers (from Martyn Wane [1-6] Jly 1997).*

SPREE ROSE BHB 41f44a **RR 22f 44a** 2765[8]
3 ch f Dancing Spree (USA) 8f **(59)** - Pinkie Rose (FR) (Kenmare (FR)) 6.5f **(72)**
Form - 0550008
Record 1998 - 1st:0 2nd:0 3rd:0 Ran:5
Pre1998 - 1st:0 2nd:1 3rd:0 Ran:5
Win Prizemoney £0 *Total Prizemoney* £1,153
1998 Turf 0-3: (7f, 10f, 12f) (g-f 2, frm) 1998 AW 0-2: (8f 2) (Equi 2)
Leggy, moderate filly, effective 7f, acts on g-f, likes tight tracks. Turf high 22. AW high 6. **K O Cunningham-Brown [0-10] D Bass.*

SPREE VISION BHB 88f **RR 82f** 5057[1]
2 b c Suave Dancer (USA) 10.7f **(68)** - Regent's Folly (IRE) (Touching Wood (USA)) 8.2f **(55)**
Form - 041
Record 1998 - 1st:1 2nd:0 3rd:0 Ran:3
Win Prizemoney £2,717 *Total Prizemoney* £2,934
Wins * 1998 Oct Newcas (SFT) 8f 82 <
1998 Turf 1-3: (7f, 8f 1-2) (sft 1-1, gd 2)
Currently decent colt. Turf high 82 (began Spt) - 1st of 6 giving 4lb to Tonic (30 Oct Newcastle RF 5057).
**S C Williams [1-3] S Demanuele.*

SPRING ANCHOR (FR) BHB 82f **RR 83f** 4500[2]
3 b c Slip Anchor 12.7f **(75)** -Swift Spring (FR)(Bluebird (USA)) 7.5f **(69)**
Form - 22233212
Record 1998 - 1st:1 2nd:5 3rd:2 Ran:8
Win Prizemoney £2,490 *Total Prizemoney* £10,342
Wins * 1998 Spt Lingfi (G-S) 11.5f 74 <
1998 Turf 1-7: (10f, 11f 1-1, 12f 2, 14f 3) (sft, gd 4, g-f 1-1, frm) 1998 AW 0-1: (12f) (Fibr)
Rangy, decent colt, effective 12 to 14f, best at 14f, acts on gd, favours tight tracks. Turf high 88. It took him an age to get off the mark, despite regularly making the frame in maidens, but he managed it under a positive ride at Lingfield in September.
**P F I Cole [1-8] M Arbib.*

SPRING BEACON BHB 43f48a **RR 43f 48a** 4123[13]
3 ch f Pharly (FR) 11.5f **(64)** - Vernair (USA) (Super Concorde (USA)) 10.9f **(66)**
Form - 5002270440
Record 1998 - 1st:0 2nd:2 3rd:0 Ran:10
Win Prizemoney £0 *Total Prizemoney* £1,123
1998 Turf 0-4: (6f, 7f 2, 8f) (sft, gd 2, frm) 1998 AW 0-6: (7f, 8f 3, 9f, 11f) (Fibr 6)
Lengthy, moderate filly, effective 7 to 8f, acts on gd - acts on Fibr, likes left handed tracks, likes tight tracks. Turf high 43 - 4th of 13 getting 2lb from Patsy Culsyth (11 Aug Ayr 7f gd RF 3518). AW high 49 - 2nd of 8 getting 15lb from Killarney Jazz (7 May Southwell 8f Fibr RF 1082). Inconsistent.
**C N Allen [0-10] Newmarket Connections Ltd.*

SPRINGER BHB 57f **RR 54f** 5080[10]
2 b g Cyrano de Bergerac 7.3f **(58)** - Spring Collection (Tina's Pet) 6.8f **(59)**
Form - 000
Record 1998 - 1st:0 2nd:0 3rd:0 Ran:3
1998 Turf 0-2: (6f, 7f) (sft, g-f) 1998 AW 0-1: (6f) (Fibr)
Currently fair gelding. Turf high 54 (began Spt).
**J L Eyre [0-3] Watglea Racing.*

SPRING FEVER BHB 74f **RR 84f** 4645[5]
3 b c Indian Ridge 7.6f **(74)** - Tender Moment (IRE) (Caerleon (USA)) 8.6f **(71)**
Form - 44417005
Record 1998 - 1st:1 2nd:0 3rd:0 Ran:8
Pre1998 - 1st:0 2nd:0 3rd:0 Ran:3
Win Prizemoney £3,722 *Total Prizemoney* £6,017
Wins * 1998 Jly Ayr (GD) 8f 82 <
1998 Turf 1-8: (8f 1-3, 9f, 10f 4) (sft, gd 1-4, g-f 2, frm)
Workmanlike, decent colt, effective 8 to 10f, acts on gd, has worn blinkers, prefers left handed tracks. Turf high 84 - 4th of 11 getting 13lb from Dower House (5 Jun Epsom 10f gd RF 1750) - also 1st of 3 giving 5lb to Blow Me A Kiss (18 Jly Ayr RF 2906).
**B W Hills [1-11] Ray Richards.*

SPRING HAVEN (USA) RR 99f 4896a[13]
3 br f Lear Fan (USA) 10.4f **(80)** - Native Twine (Be My Native (USA)) 10.2f **(71)**
Form - 305055830
1998 Turf 0-9: (8f, 11f, 12f 6, 16f) (hvy, sft 2, g-s 2, gd 2, g-f 2)
Very useful filly, effective 12f, acts on gd, likes right handed tracks. Turf high 99 - 5th of 8 to Star Begonia (5 Jun Curragh 12f gd RF 1856a). **A P O'Brien in IRE [0-9] Paul Shanahan.*

SPRING LOADED BHB 28f37a **RR 37a** 3579[10]
7 b g Last Tycoon 9.4f **(73)** - Time For Romance (Cure The Blues (USA)) 9.5f **(63)**
Form - 50
Record 1998 - 1st:0 2nd:0 3rd:0 Ran:2
Pre1998 - 1st:4 2nd:3 3rd:5 Ran:28
Win Prizemoney £11,377 *Total Prizemoney* £15,663
Wins 1994 Jly Ayr (G-F) C 13.1f 56
1994 Jly Ripon (G-F) S 10f 43
1994 Apr Hamilt (SFT) C 8.3f 57
1998 Turf 0-2: (9f, 12f) (gd, frm)
Little account gelding, has worn blinkers. (began Jly). Becoming disappointing.
**D A Nolan [0-3] F Jestin (from J G M O'Shea [0-9] Feb 1995).*

SPRING MARATHON (USA) BHB 50f **RR 54f** 880[3]
8 b g Topsider (USA) 7.9f **(73)** - April Run (Run The Gantlet (USA)) 12.1f **(59)**
Form - 3
Record 1998 - 1st:0 2nd:0 3rd:1 Ran:1
Pre1998 - 1st:0 2nd:2 3rd:0 Ran:7
Win Prizemoney £0 *Total Prizemoney* £2,968
1998 Turf 0-1: (22f) (g-s)
Fair gelding. Becoming disappointing.
**Mrs P N Dutfield [4-27] Mrs Nerys Dutfield (from D R C Elsworth [0-3] Oct 1993).*

SPRING PURSUIT RR 85f 2257[7]
2 b c Rudimentary (USA) 8.2f **(66)** - Pursuit of Truth (USA) (Irish River (FR)) 8.6f **(78)**
Form - 7107
Record 1998 - 1st:1 2nd:0 3rd:0 Ran:4
Win Prizemoney £3,330 *Total Prizemoney* £3,330
Wins * 1998 Jun Warwic (GD) 6f 85 <

1998 Turf 1-4: (6f 1-2, 7f 2) (g-s, gd 1-1, g-f, frm)
Useful colt, has worn blinkers. Turf high 85 - 1st of 8 getting 1lb from Al Fahda (3 Jun Warwick RF 1705).
**R Charlton [1-4] Fieldspring Racing.*

SPRINGS BHB 50f **RR 55f** 4808[6]
2 b f Anshan 8.2f **(63)** - College Supreme (Mansingh (USA)) 7.4f **(55)**
Form - 06006
Record 1998 - 1st:0 2nd:0 3rd:0 Ran:5
1998 Turf 0-5: (6f, 7f 3, 10f) (gd, g-f 2, frm 2)
Fair filly. Turf high 48 (began Jly).
**J L Spearing [0-5] Abbots Salford Carav Park.*

SPRINGS NOBLEQUEST BHB 65f **RR 65f** 4013[12]
2 b f Noble Patriarch 12.2f **(43)** - Primum Tempus **(42df)** (Primo Dominie) 6.2f **(80)**
Form - 313880
Record 1998 - 1st:1 2nd:0 3rd:2 Ran:6
Win Prizemoney £3,113 *Total Prizemoney* £4,040
Wins * **1998** May Carlis (G-S) 5f 65 <
1998 Turf 1-6: (5f 1-3, 6f 3) (g-s, gd 1-3, frm 2)
Average filly, effective 5f, acts on gd. Turf high 65 - also 1st of 9 getting 5lb from Pat The Fiddler (8 May Carlisle RF 1095).
**T D Easterby [1-6] Springs Equestrian Ltd.*

SPRING TO ACTION BHB 75f **RR 50f** 2573[6]
8 b g Shareef Dancer (USA) 10.1f **(67)** - Light Duty (Queen's Hussar) 11.6f **(58)**
Form - 6
Record 1998 - 1st:0 2nd:0 3rd:0 Ran:1
Pre1998 - 1st:2 2nd:2 3rd:0 Ran:8
Win Prizemoney £13,249 *Total Prizemoney* £15,269
1998 Turf 0-1: (12f) (g-f)
Fair gelding. Consistent. **I A Balding [2-9] David Watson.*

SPRITE BHB 60f **RR 70f** 4652[13]
3 b f Fairy King (USA) 7.7f **(75)** - Cubby Hole (Town And Country) 8.1f **(68)**
Form - 383544020
Record 1998 - 1st:0 2nd:1 3rd:2 Ran:9
Win Prizemoney £0 *Total Prizemoney* £2,709
1998 Turf 0-9: (6f, 7f 5, 8f 2, 9f) (gd 3, g-f 6)
Neat, above-average filly, effective 7 to 9f, best at 7f, acts on gd to g-f, best on g-f, has worn blinkers. Turf high 70 - 3rd of 9 to Pagoda Tree (4 Jly Chepstow 7f gd RF 2529). Inconsistent.
**R Hannon [0-9] Lord Carnarvon.*

SPUNKIE BHB 87f **RR 92f** 4850[3]
5 ch g Jupiter Island 10.4f **(57)** - Super Sol (Rolfe (USA)) 12.1f **(65)**
Form - 15613
Record 1998 - 1st:2 2nd:0 3rd:1 Ran:5
Win Prizemoney £18,239 *Total Prizemoney* £28,845
Wins * **1998** Spt Ascot (GD) H 16.2f 76 76 <
* **1998** Jly Salisb (GD) 14.1f 73
1998 Turf 2-5: (12f 2, 14f 1-1, 16f 1-1, 18f) (gd 2-3, g-f 2)
Useful gelding. Turf high 92 (began Jly). He was fit from hurdling when winning a Salisbury maiden in July, and after facing a couple of very tough tasks, came late to land a valuable handicap at Ascot in September. Third in the Cesarewitch, never threatening to win, he is a tough individual who clearly stays very well.
**R F JohnsonHoughton [3-9] Jim Short.*

SPUN SILK (IRE) **RR 53f** 4299[15]
2 ch f Brief Truce (USA) 9.1f **(73)** - Silk Route (USA) **(55f)** (Shahrastani (USA)) 8.8f **(72)**
Form - 0
Record 1998 - 1st:0 2nd:0 3rd:0 Ran:1
1998 Turf 0-1: (7f) (frm)
Currently fair filly. **N Tinkler [0-1] Richard Green (Fine Paintings).*

SPY (IRE) BHB 80f **RR 87f** 3746[1]
2 b c Mac's Imp (USA) 5.6f **(54)** - Mystery Bid (Auction Ring (USA)) 8.6f **(65)**
Form - 04251
Record 1998 - 1st:1 2nd:1 3rd:0 Ran:5
Win Prizemoney £2,560 *Total Prizemoney* £3,480
Wins * **1998** Aug Mussel (G-F) 7.1f 84 <
1998 Turf 1-5: (5f, 6f 3, 7f 1-1) (g-s, gd 1-4)
Useful colt. Turf high 87 - 2nd of 14 to Hyphen (5 Aug Newcastle 6f gd RF 3380) - also 1st of 8 giving 9lb to Purple Dawn (19 Aug Musselburgh RF 3746). He got off the mark in good style at Musselburgh in August. It was not a great race, but he seemed to appreciate the seventh furlong and faster ground there, and should be able to win again. **C W Thornton [1-5] Guy Reed.*

SQUABBLE BHB 59f **RR 59f** 3375[5]
3 b f Reprimand 8.2f **(63)** - Hability (Habitat) 9.4f **(70)**
Form - 405
Record 1998 - 1st:0 2nd:0 3rd:0 Ran:3
Pre1998 - 1st:0 2nd:0 3rd:0 Ran:1
Win Prizemoney £0 *Total Prizemoney* £297
1998 Turf 0-3: (8f 2, 10f) (gd, frm 2)
Lengthy, fair filly. Turf high 59.
**R F JohnsonHoughton [0-4] T D Holland-Martin.*

SQUARE DANCER **RR 70+f** 4709[8]
2 b c Then Again 7.4f **(52)** - Cubist (IRE) (Tate Gallery (USA)) 7.4f **(67)**
Form - 54778
Record 1998 - 1st:0 2nd:0 3rd:0 Ran:5
Win Prizemoney £0 *Total Prizemoney* £303
1998 Turf 0-5: (6f 3, 8f 2) (gd, g-f 2, frm 2)
Above-average colt. Turf high 70 (began Aug).
**Mrs J R Ramsden [0-5] Bernard Hathaway.*

SQUARE DEAL (FR) BHB 48f52a **RR 25f 52a** 104[11]
7 b g Sharpo 7.5f **(68)** - River Dove (USA) (Riverman (USA)) 9.1f **(76)**
Form - 0
Record 1998 - 1st:0 2nd:0 3rd:0 Ran:1
Pre1998 - 1st:2 2nd:3 3rd:0 Ran:19
Win Prizemoney £4,926 *Total Prizemoney* £7,442
Wins * 1997 *Mar Southw (STD) C 8f 51* <
* 1996 *Jan Southw (STD) 7f 51* <
1998 AW 0-1: (8f) (Fibr)
Fair gelding, effective 8f, - acts on Fibr, has worn blinkers, prefers left handed tracks. Becoming disappointing.
**S R Bowring [2-21] Padraig Flanagan.*

SQUARE MILE MISS (IRE) BHB 40f43a **RR 19f 43a** 3242[8]
5 b m Last Tycoon 9.4f **(73)** - Call Me Miss (Hello Gorgeous (USA)) 9.7f **(63)**
Form - 62116538
Record 1998 - 1st:2 2nd:0 3rd:1 Ran:6
Pre1998 - 1st:0 2nd:2 3rd:1 Ran:18
Win Prizemoney £5,111 *Total Prizemoney* £7,750
Wins * **1998** *Jan Lingfi (STD) H 7f 35 43* <
* **1998** *Jan Lingfi (STD) H 8f 35 39*
1998 Turf 0-1: (7f) (g-f) 1998 AW 2-5: (7f 1-1, 8f 1-4) (Equi 2-5)
Moderate filly, effective 7 to 9f, best at 8f, acts on g-f to frm - acts on Equi, prefers left handed tracks, prefers tight tracks. AW high 43 - 1st of 11 getting 5lb from Castle Ashby Jack (15 Jan Lingfield RF 0096) - also 1st of 9 getting 18lb from Be Warned (6 Jan Lingfield RF 0030).
**N E Berry [2-8] P Rawson (from P Howling [0-16] Aug 1997).*

SQUIRE CORRIE BHB 62f70a **RR 66f 70a** 4701[10]
6 b g Distant Relative 7f **(69)** - Fast Car (FR) (Carwhite) 7.2f **(61)**
Form - 7880507788002253800
Record 1998 - 1st:0 2nd:2 3rd:1 Ran:19
Pre1998 - 1st:10 2nd:8 3rd:9 Ran:65
Win Prizemoney £44,197 *Total Prizemoney* £68,182
Wins * 1997 Jun Ayr (GD) H 5f 71 82
* 1997 Jun York (G-S) H 5f 71 84 <
* 1997 Jun Hamilt (GD) H 5f 71 76
* 1997 May Thirsk (GD) H 5f 69 70
* 1997 *Feb Lingfi (STD) H 6f 68 69*
* 1997 *Feb Wolver (STD) H 5f 58 63*
1996 Spt Salisb (FRM) H 5f 57 63
1996 Aug Sandow (GD) H 5f 57 60
1996 Jly Sandow (G-F) H 5f 55 57
1995 Spt Newmar (GD) H 5f 59 64
1998 Turf 0-16: (5f 13, 6f 2, 7f) (g-s 5, gd 4, g-f, frm 6) 1998 AW 0-3: (5f 3) (Equi, Fibr 2)
Above-average gelding, effective 5f, acts on gd to g-f, best on gd, has worn blinkers. Turf high 76. AW high 70. Becoming disappointing. Very speedy, he enjoyed a highly successful '97. Took

time to fire in '98, but he recaptured his form at the end of August.
**D W Chapman [6-50] FirstAssist (from G Harwood [3-19] Oct 1996).*

SQUIRE'S OCCASION (CAN)BHB 35f53a **RR 24f 53a** 1454[13]
5 b g Black Tie Affair 10.5f **(64)** -Tayana (USA) (Wajima (USA)) 10f **(68)**
Form - 7034000
Record 1998 - 1st:0 2nd:0 3rd:1 Ran:6
Pre1998 - 1st:1 2nd:0 3rd:2 Ran:14
Win Prizemoney £2,484 *Total Prizemoney* £3,339
Wins 1997 *Jan Lingfi (STD) H 12f 60 64 <*
1998 Turf 0-2: (12f 2) (gd, g-f) 1998 AW 0-4: (11f, 12f 2, 13f) (Equi 2, Fibr 2)
Fair gelding, effective 11 to 12f, best at 12f, - acts on AW, best on Equi, has worn blinkers, prefers left handed tracks. AW high 57 - 3rd of 12 getting 2lb from The Butterwick Kid (19 Jan Southwell 11f Fibr RF 0116). Becoming disappointing.
**R Curtis [1-17] Chelgate Public Relations Ltd (from R Akehurst [2-10] Feb 1997).*

STACCATO RR 29f 4113[11]
3 b g Forzando 7.2f **(63)** - Fast Car (FR) (Carwhite) 7.2f **(61)**
Form - 0
Record 1998 - 1st:0 2nd:0 3rd:0 Ran:1
1998 Turf 0-1: (6f) (frm)
Currently little account gelding. **C W Thornton [0-1] Guy Reed.*

STAGE AFFAIR (USA) RR 111+f 4281a[4]
4 bb g Theatrical 11.5f **(78)** - Wooing 00
Form - 112424
1998 Turf 2-6: (10f 1-2, 12f 1-3, 14f) (hvy, sft 1-2, g-s 1-1, gd 2)
Group-class gelding, effective 10 to 14f, best at 10f, acts on sft to gd, excels at Curragh. Turf high 111 (1st run) - 1st of 6 giving 9lb to Blue Saddle (18 Apr Listowel RF 0801a) - also 1st of 6 from Fort Morgan (2 May Curragh RF 1049a). Consistent. He did not progress after winning two races in the spring and had been gelded before finishing a poor fourth on heavy ground at Galway in September. The unkindest cut of all may be the prelude to a career over hurdles, and he would have a bright future at that game.
**D K Weld in IRE [5-10] Michael Smurfit.*

STAGE WHISPER BHB 74f75a **RR 67f 75a** 1782[6]
3 b c Alzao (USA) 9.8f **(73)** - Starlet (Teenoso (USA)) 9.9f **(72)**
Form - 16
Record 1998 - 1st:0 2nd:0 3rd:0 Ran:1
Pre1998 - 1st:1 2nd:0 3rd:0 Ran:2
Win Prizemoney £2,659 *Total Prizemoney* £2,984
Wins * 1997 *Dec Wolver (STD) 8.5f 67 <*
1998 Turf 0-1: (11f) (frm)
Workmanlike, currently average colt.
**Lord Huntingdon [1-3] The Queen.*

STALWART LEGION (IRE) BHB 31f **RR 45f** 3812[8]
3 b f Distinctly North (USA) 7.4f **(63)** - La Posada (Procida (USA))
Form - 0088
Record 1998 - 1st:0 2nd:0 3rd:0 Ran:4
Pre1998 - 1st:0 2nd:0 3rd:0 Ran:4
1998 Turf 0-4: (10f 2, 11f, 16f) (g-f 4)
Workmanlike, moderate filly. Turf high 45.
**J W Hills [0-8] Royal British Legion Racing Club.*

STAND ASIDE RR 55f 5093[6]
2 b c In The Wings 11.2f **(77)** - Honourable Sheba (USA) (Roberto (USA)) 10f **(76)**
Form - 6
Record 1998 - 1st:0 2nd:0 3rd:0 Ran:1
1998 Turf 0-1: (7f) (gd)
Currently fair colt. **Lady Herries [0-1] Chris Hardy.*

STAND TALL BHB 82f80a **RR 84f 80a** 5096[16]
6 b g Unfuwain (USA) 11.4f **(74)** - Antilla (Averof) 8.2f **(62)**
Form - 42032000010
Record 1998 - 1st:1 2nd:2 3rd:1 Ran:11
Pre1998 - 1st:9 2nd:6 3rd:4 Ran:35
Win Prizemoney £38,840 *Total Prizemoney* £58,499
Wins * **1998** Oct Leices (SFT) H 6f 78 84 <
* 1997 Spt Nottin (GD) H 6.1f 74 78
* 1997 Spt Pontef (G-S) H 6f 68 71
* 1997 Aug Folkes (G-F) H 6f 61 66
* 1997 May Bright (FRM) 7f 61
1996 Jly Hamilt (GD) H 6f 56 60
1996 *Mar Lingfi (STD) H 6f 69 76*
1996 *Feb Southw (STD) H 6f 59 64*
1996 *Jan Southw (STD) H 6f 55 54*
1995 *Nov Lingfi (STD) H 6f 46 50*
1998 Turf 1-11: (6f 1-10, 7f) (sft 2, g-s 1-1, gd 4, g-f 4)
Decent gelding, effective 6f, acts on sft, prefers left handed tracks. Turf high 97 - 2nd of 13 giving 4lb to Hever Golf Rose (2 Jun Taby 6f sft RF 1911a). He had a very rewarding season in 1997 and held his form well, but was rather high in the weights as a result. His best run of last term was when second in a listed race in Sweden, and he did win a Leicester handicap at the back-end. His final run can be disregarded.
**Lady Herries [5-22] Chris Hardy (from C W Thornton [5-24] Spt 1996).*

STANLEY WIGFIELD (USA) RR 57f 4503[8]
2 b c Woodman (USA) 9.7f **(77)** - Las Meninas (IRE) **(110f)** (Glenstal (USA)) 10.1f **(64)**
Form - 08
Record 1998 - 1st:0 2nd:0 3rd:0 Ran:2
1998 Turf 0-2: (7f, 8f) (gd, frm)
Currently fair colt. Turf high 57 (began Spt).
**E A L Dunlop [0-2] Burke's 5th Family Settlement.*

STANOTT (IRE) BHB 104f **RR 95f** 3228a[2]
3 b c Mukaddamah (USA) 7.6f **(74)** - Seme de Lys (USA) (Slew O' Gold (USA)) 8f **(75)**
Form - 14142
Record 1998 - 1st:2 2nd:1 3rd:0 Ran:5
Pre1998 - 1st:0 2nd:0 3rd:0 Ran:1
Win Prizemoney £20,358 *Total Prizemoney* £28,583
Wins * **1998** May Capann (G-F) L 8f 93 <
* **1998** Apr Folkes (SFT) 7f 78
1998 Turf 2-5: (7f 1-2, 8f 1-2, 10f) (gd 1-2, g-f 1-2, frm)
Very useful colt, effective 8f, acts on gd to g-f. Turf high 95 - 2nd of 12 giving 4lb to Adieu (26 Jly San Siro 8f gd RF 3228a) - also 1st of 6 getting 6lb from Teishebaini (31 May Capannelle RF 1732a). Won in listed company in Italy, but would not be good enough in that grade in this country. **L M Cumani [2-6].*

STAR BEGONIA RR 110f 4430a[5]
3 b f Sadler's Wells (USA) 11.3f **(87)** - Alexandrie (USA) (Val de L'Orne (FR)) 12f **(75)**
Form - 322125
1998 Turf 1-6: (10f 3, 12f 1-2, 14f) (hvy, sft, g-s, gd 1-3)
Group-class filly, effective 10 to 12f, best at 12f, acts on g-s to gd, best on gd. Turf high 110 - 2nd of 9 to Bahr (18 Jun Ascot 12f g-s RF 2083) - also 1st of 8 getting 5lb from Mardani (5 Jun Curragh RF 1856a). Inconsistent. A sister to Poliglote and a half-sister to King Alex, she was given a cagey ride when finishing second to Bahr in the Ribblesdale Stakes at Royal Ascot, letting the winner go and then securing second spot to gain that all important black-type. Outclassed in the Irish St Leger, her future probably lies at stud. **A P O'Brien in IRE [1-8] Michael Tabor.*

STARBOARD TACK (FR) RR 70f 5071[5]
2 b f Saddlers' Hall (IRE) 10.5f **(65)** - North Wind (IRE) (Lomond (USA)) 8.8f **(65)**
Form - 5
Record 1998 - 1st:0 2nd:0 3rd:0 Ran:1
1998 Turf 0-1: (7f) (gd)
Currently above-average filly.
**B W Hills [0-1] H R H Princess Michael of Kent.*

STARBOROUGH BHB 114f **RR 115f** 3948[7]
4 ch c Soviet Star (USA) 8.6f **(74)** - Flamenco Wave (USA) (Desert Wine (USA)) 9.7f **(80)**
Form - 647
Record 1998 - 1st:0 2nd:0 3rd:0 Ran:3
Pre1998 - 1st:4 2nd:1 3rd:1 Ran:9
Win Prizemoney £194,245 *Total Prizemoney* £269,802
Wins 1997 Jun Ascot (GD) G1 8f 118 <
1997 Jun Chanti (GD) G1 9f 105
1997 Apr Thirsk (G-F) 8f 102
1996 Aug Thirsk (FRM) 6f 76++
1998 Turf 0-3: (8f 2, 10f) (gd, g-f 2)

Scopey, high-class colt, effective 8f, acts on gd to g-f, best on g-f. Turf high 115 - 4th of 10 to Among Men (29 Jly Goodwood 8f gd RF 3205). Consistent. A high-class miler at three for David Loder, after which he was moved to Godolphin. However, he did not enjoy a similar level of success.
**S bin Suroor [0-2] Godolphin (from S bin Suroor in UAE [0-1] Apr 1998).*

STAR CRYSTAL (IRE) BHB 90f **RR 98df** 3163[14]
3 b f Brief Truce (USA) 9.1f **(73)** - Crystal Spray (Beldale Flutter (USA)) 9.7f **(71)**
Form - 51170
Record **1998** - 1st:2 2nd:0 3rd:0 Ran:5
Pre1998 - 1st:0 2nd:1 3rd:0 Ran:1
Win Prizemoney £8,904 *Total Prizemoney* £10,152
Wins * **1998** Jun Salisb (G-S) 14.1f 98+ <
* **1998** May Haydoc (GD) 11.9f 92
1998 Turf 2-5: (11f, 12f 1-1, 14f 1-2, 16f) (gd 2-5)
Light-framed, very useful filly, effective 12 to 14f, acts on gd. Turf high 98 - 1st of 3 getting 5lb from Last Christmas (10 Jun Salisbury RF 1884) - also 1st of 5 from Shimaal (22 May Haydock RF 1395). From a useful middle-distance family, she looked a progressive stayer with wins at Haydock and Salisbury. Tailed off when upped in class in the Queen's Vase, and well beaten in her first handicap. **H R A Cecil [2-6] Michael Poland.*

STAR FANTASY (USA) **RR 68f** 3682[5]
3 ch g Sky Classic (CAN) 10f **(83)** - Wanda's Dream (USA) (Miswaki (USA)) 9f **(81)**
Form - 5
Record **1998** - 1st:0 2nd:0 3rd:0 Ran:1
1998 Turf 0-1: (10f) (g-f)
Scopey, currently average gelding. **P F I Cole [0-1] M Arbib.*

STAR INVADER BHB 80f **RR 78f** 2365[F]
4 b c Nashwan (USA) 10.3f **(79)** - Sahara Star (Green Desert (USA)) 8.6f **(78)**
Form - 181F
Record **1998** - 1st:2 2nd:0 3rd:0 Ran:4
Pre1998 - 1st:0 2nd:0 3rd:1 Ran:3
Win Prizemoney £12,667 *Total Prizemoney* £13,360
Wins * **1998** Jun Kempto (HVY) H 8f 73 78+ <
* **1998** May Cheste (G-F) H 7.6f 69 71
1998 Turf 2-4: (7f, 8f 2-3) (g-s 1-1, gd 2, g-f 1-1)
Scopey, above-average colt, effective 8f, acted on g-s to g-f. Turf high 78 - 1st of 12 giving 3lb to Saffron Rose (10 Jun Kempton RF 1881) - also 1st of 18 giving 6lb to Twin Creeks (7 May Chester RF 1069). Won at Chester on his handicap debut by courtesy of the stewards. (DEAD) **Sir Michael Stoute [2-7] Maktoum Al Maktoum.*

STARLINER (IRE) BHB 45f **RR 52f** 4504[16]
3 ch f Statoblest 6.4f **(63)** - Dancing Line (High Line) 10.3f **(70)**
Form - 6870275060
Record **1998** - 1st:0 2nd:1 3rd:0 Ran:10
Pre1998 - 1st:0 2nd:0 3rd:1 Ran:6
Win Prizemoney £0 *Total Prizemoney* £1,284
1998 Turf 0-10: (6f 3, 7f, 8f 5, 10f) (gd 4, g-f 2, frm 4)
Leggy, fair filly, has worn blinkers. Turf high 52.
**M Brittain [0-16] Northgate Lodge Partnerships.*

STAR MANAGER (USA) BHB 68f **RR 71f** 3483[6]
8 b g Lyphard (USA) 10.6f **(75)** - Angel Clare (FR) (Mill Reef (USA)) 10.5f **(78)**
Form - 506176
Record **1998** - 1st:1 2nd:0 3rd:0 Ran:6
Pre1998 - 1st:5 2nd:1 3rd:5 Ran:40
Win Prizemoney £44,761 *Total Prizemoney* £74,962
Wins * **1998** Jun Epsom (GD) C 8.5f 71
* 1996 Apr Sandow (GD) H 8.1f 78 89 <
* 1995 Apr Newbur (GD) H 8f 78 82
* 1994 Jun Haydoc (GD) H 8.1f 78 77
1998 Turf 1-6: (8f 2, 9f 1-2, 10f, 11f) (sft, gd 3, g-f 1-1, frm)
Above-average gelding, effective 8 to 12f, best at 10f, acts on gd to frm, best on gd, likes left handed tracks, likes tight tracks, excels at Epsom. Turf high 78. Consistent. A useful handicapper who goes well when fresh, he was dropped into claiming company for a comfortable victory at Epsom in June. **P F I Cole [6-51] M Arbib.*

STAR OF GROSVENOR (IRE) BHB 72f **RR 72f** 1262[14]
3 b f Last Tycoon 9.4f **(73)** - Castilian Queen (USA) (Diesis) 9.3f **(69)**
Form - 0
Record **1998** - 1st:0 2nd:0 3rd:0 Ran:1
Pre1998 - 1st:1 2nd:0 3rd:0 Ran:4
Win Prizemoney £3,643 *Total Prizemoney* £3,643
Wins * 1997 Aug Folkes (G-F) 6.9f 77 <
1998 Turf 0-1: (7f) (frm)
Neat, above-average filly, has worn blinkers.
**P W Chapple-Hyam [1-5] R E Sangster.*

STAR OF QATAR BHB 55f **RR 40f** 4650[8]
2 ch c Cigar 6.3f **(43)** - Bella Brown (Bairn (USA)) 7.7f **(59)**
Form - 008
Record **1998** - 1st:0 2nd:0 3rd:0 Ran:3
1998 Turf 0-3: (6f 2, 7f) (gd, g-f 2)
Currently moderate colt. Turf high 40 (began Aug).
**R J Hodges [0-3] A J Al Mudaikhi.*

STAR OF RING (IRE) BHB 45f **RR 51f** 4456[8]
5 b g Taufan (USA) 8.3f **(65)** - Karine (Habitat) 9.4f **(70)**
Form - 523008
Record **1998** - 1st:0 2nd:1 3rd:1 Ran:6
Pre1998 - 1st:1 2nd:0 3rd:0 Ran:9
Win Prizemoney £2,722 *Total Prizemoney* £3,756
Wins 1997 Apr Thirsk (G-F) 7f 61+ <
1998 Turf 0-5: (7f 4, 8f) (g-f 3, frm 2) 1998 AW 0-1: (7f) (Fibr)
Fair gelding, effective 7f, acts on g-f, likes left handed tracks, likes tight tracks. Turf high 51.
**Miss Gay Kelleway [0-6] N Parker (from M J Heaton-Ellis [1-9] Oct 1997).*

STAR OF THE COURSE (USA) BHB 75f **RR 75f** 4802[2]
3 b f Theatrical 11.5f **(78)** - Water Course (USA) (Irish River (FR)) 8.6f **(78)**
Form - 051112
Record **1998** - 1st:3 2nd:1 3rd:0 Ran:6
Pre1998 - 1st:0 2nd:0 3rd:0 Ran:2
Win Prizemoney £9,652 *Total Prizemoney* £11,085
Wins * **1998** Spt Bright (FRM) H 11.9f 66 73+ <
* **1998** Aug Bright (FRM) H 11.9f 58 62+
* **1998** Aug Folkes (G-F) H 12f 54 59
1998 Turf 3-6: (7f, 11f, 12f 3-4) (sft, gd, g-f, frm 3-3)
Light-framed, above-average filly, effective 11 to 12f, acts on sft to frm, favours tight tracks. Turf high 75 - 2nd of 12 giving 17lb to Primary Colours (14 Oct Haydock 11f sft RF 4802) - also 1st of 10 getting 2lb from Clarity (2 Spt Brighton RF 4051). Improving. She did not show much in her first two starts, but hit form with a quick-fire hat-trick on fast ground. **P F I Cole [3-8] M Arbib.*

STAR OF THE ROAD BHB 34f **RR 1f** 1403[P]
4 b c Risk Me (FR) 8f **(53)** - Astrid Gilberto (Runnett) 7f **(59)**
Form - 0P
Record **1998** - 1st:0 2nd:0 3rd:0 Ran:2
Pre1998 - 1st:0 2nd:0 3rd:1 Ran:10
Win Prizemoney £0 *Total Prizemoney* £422
1998 Turf 0-2: (6f, 8f) (g-s, frm)
Lengthy, very poor colt, effective 6f, acts on frm. Becoming disappointing.
**L R Lloyd-James [0-2] David Dyer (from J M Carr [0-10] Spt 1997).*

STAR PRECISION BHB 87f **RR 81f** 5141[4]
4 ch f Shavian 7.7f **(67)** - Accuracy (Gunner B) 11.2f **(58)**
Form - 33205844
Record **1998** - 1st:0 2nd:1 3rd:2 Ran:8
Pre1998 - 1st:4 2nd:0 3rd:0 Ran:11
Win Prizemoney £16,382 *Total Prizemoney* £27,166
Wins * 1997 Oct Leices (G-S) 8f 94 <
* 1997 May Chepst (GD) H 12.1f 72 92++
* 1997 May Bath (G-S) H 13.1f 72 82+
* 1997 Apr Nottin (GD) H 10f 64 71
1998 Turf 0-8: (8f, 9f, 10f 4, 12f 2) (hvy, g-s, gd 5, g-f)
Unfurnished, decent filly, effective 8 to 12f, acts on gd, prefers left handed tracks, prefers tight tracks. Turf high 98 - 2nd of 7 to Arriving (13 May York 10f gd RF 1206). Becoming disappointing. She showed progressive form in '97, winning four times and finishing fourth in a Group Three, but did not run up to that form last

season after finishing in the frame in listed races early in the year.
**G B Balding [4-19] Miss B Swire.*

STAR RAGE (IRE) BHB 74f80a **RR 77f 80a** 2551[5]

8 b g Horage 11.4f **(58)** - Star Bound (Crowned Prince (USA))10.1f **(67)**
Form - 5106225

Record		1st	2nd	3rd	Ran
1998 -		1st:1	2nd:2	3rd:0	Ran:7
Pre1998 -		1st:13	2nd:12	3rd:8	Ran:62

Win Prizemoney £57,174 *Total Prizemoney* £83,567

Wins								
* **1998**	*Apr*	*Wolver*	*(STD)*	*H*	*14.8f*	*78*	*80*	
* 1997	Aug	Redcar	(FRM)	H	16f	75	77	
* 1995	Aug	Newcas	(GD)	H	16.1f	77	84	<
* 1995	Aug	Beverl	(G-F)	H	16.2f	70	80	
* 1995	Aug	Newcas	(FRM)	H	16.1f	70	79	
* 1994	Aug	Beverl	(G-F)	H	16.2f	71	75	
* 1994	Jly	Beverl	(G-F)	H	16.2f	64	70	
* 1994	Jly	Mussel	(GD)	H	15.1f	64	66	
* 1994	Jun	Warwic	(FRM)	H	16.1f	61	66	
* 1994	Jun	Doncas	(G-F)	H	16.5f	51	56	
* 1994	*May*	*Wolver*	*(STD)*	*H*	*12f*	*56*	*58*	
* 1994	*May*	*Southw*	*(STD)*	*H*	*11f*	*41*	*53*	
* 1994	May	Beverl	(G-F)	H	12f	39	49	
* 1994	May	Mussel	(G-F)	CH	12.1f	39	43	

1998 Turf 0-5: (14f, 16f 3, 17f) (gd 3, g-f, frm) 1998 AW 1-2: (15f 1-2) (Fibr 1-2)

Decent gelding, effective 12 to 17f, best at 16f, acts on gd to frm - acts on AW, best on gd, likes tight tracks, excels at Wolverhampton. Turf high 77 - 2nd of 9 giving 15lb to Witney-de-Bergerac (13 Jun Bath 17f gd RF 1955). AW high 80 - 1st of 6 getting 1lb from Jaraab (25 Apr Wolverhampton RF 0874). Consistent. After a spell hurdling during the winter, this tough stayer gained a gritty victory on the Wolverhampton Fibresand in April.
**M Johnston [16-68] David Abell (from J L Harris [5-21] Apr 1997).*

STARRY NIGHT **RR 78+f** 4803[1]

2 b f Sheikh Albadou 9.2f **(75)** - My Ballerina (USA) (Sir Ivor) 10.2f **(70)**
Form - 1

Record	1st	2nd	3rd	Ran
1998 -	1st:1	2nd:0	3rd:0	Ran:1

Win Prizemoney £3,095 *Total Prizemoney* £3,095

Wins							
* **1998**	Oct	Haydoc	(SFT)		7.1f	78+	<

1998 Turf 1-1: (7f 1-1) (sft 1-1)

Currently above-average filly. (1st run) - 1st of 7 getting 5lb from Shaylan (14 Oct Haydock RF 4803).
**J L Dunlop [1-1] H R H Prince Fahd Salman.*

STAR TALENT (USA) BHB 76f72a **RR 76f 72a** 3168[4]

7 b g Local Talent (USA) 7.5f **(72)** - Sedra (Nebbiolo) 8.1f **(75)**
Form - 08730404

Record	1st	2nd	3rd	Ran
1998 -	1st:0	2nd:0	3rd:1	Ran:8
Pre1998 -	1st:7	2nd:6	3rd:5	Ran:42

Win Prizemoney £31,659 *Total Prizemoney* £57,272

Wins								
* 1997	Apr	Sandow	(G-F)	H	8.1f	82	89	
1997	Apr	Warwic	(G-F)	C	8f		75+	
1996	Apr	Bright	(FRM)		7f		82	
1996	*Jan*	*Lingfi*	*(STD)*	*S*	*7f*		*69*	
1995	Apr	Warwic	(GD)		7f		108	<

1998 Turf 0-8: (7f 2, 8f 5, 9f) (sft, g-s, gd 2, g-f 2, frm 2)

Above-average gelding, effective 8 to 9f, best at 8f, acted on gd to frm, had worn blinkers, preferred right handed tracks, excelled at Sandown. Turf high 78. He required the ground on the fast side and a strongly-run race, but though he had ability, his style of racing meant that he regularly met trouble in running. (DEAD)
**I A Balding [1-17] R P B Michaelson & D F Allport (from Miss Gay Kelleway [3-22] Apr 1997).*

STARTOO **RR 64f** 4650[3]

2 ch f King's Signet (USA) 7f **(51)** - Shall We Run (Hotfoot) 10.5f **(59)**
Form - 03

Record	1st	2nd	3rd	Ran
1998 -	1st:0	2nd:0	3rd:1	Ran:2

Win Prizemoney £0 *Total Prizemoney* £495
1998 Turf 0-2: (5f, 6f) (gd, g-f)

Currently average filly. Turf high 64 (began Spt) - 3rd of 9 getting 5lb from Learned Friend (5 Oct Brighton 6f g-f RF 4650).
**R F JohnsonHoughton [0-2] R C Naylor.*

STARTRECK BHB 65f **RR 71df** 5098[10]

3 b f Night Shift (USA) 8.1f **(73)** - Shirley Superstar (Shirley Heights) 10.3f **(74)**
Form - 06300

Record	1st	2nd	3rd	Ran
1998 -	1st:0	2nd:0	3rd:1	Ran:5

Win Prizemoney £0 *Total Prizemoney* £530
1998 Turf 0-5: (8f, 10f 4) (gd 2, g-f, frm, hrd)

Strong, above-average filly. Turf high 71 - 3rd of 10 to Passionate Pursuit (23 Jun Lingfield 10f g-f RF 2199).
**P J Makin [0-5] Helena Springfield Ltd.*

STAR TURN (IRE) BHB 49f49a **RR 45f 49a** 3830[11]

4 ch g Night Shift (USA) 8.1f **(73)**-Ringtail (Auction Ring (USA))8.6f **(65)**
Form - 452500

Record	1st	2nd	3rd	Ran
1998 -	1st:0	2nd:1	3rd:0	Ran:6
Pre1998 -	1st:0	2nd:2	3rd:2	Ran:12

Win Prizemoney £0 *Total Prizemoney* £4,024
1998 Turf 0-2: (7f, 8f) (g-f, frm) 1998 AW 0-4: (7f, 8f 2, 12f)(Equi, Fibr 3)

Scopey, average gelding, effective 7 to 8f, best at 7f, acts on g-s to g-f - acts on Equi, excels at Lingfield and Nottingham. Turf high 45 (began Jly). AW high 60 - 2nd of 9 to Without Friends (14 Feb Lingfield 8f Equi RF 0290). Becoming disappointing.
**B J Llewellyn [0-3] K & D Computers Ltd (from M Bell [0-15] Feb 1998).*

STARVINE BHB 40f45a **RR 58f 45a** 4490[13]

2 b f Superlative 8.8f **(57)** - Girl Next Door **(35df 36a)** (Local Suitor (USA)) 8.4f **(67)**
Form - 776638700

Record	1st	2nd	3rd	Ran
1998 -	1st:0	2nd:0	3rd:1	Ran:9

Win Prizemoney £0 *Total Prizemoney* £252
1998 Turf 0-4: (5f 4) (sft, frm 3) 1998 AW 0-5: (5f 5) (Fibr 5)

Fair filly. Turf high 58. AW high 58. Becoming disappointing.
**R C Spicer [0-9] M G Vines.*

STAR WITNESS (IRE) BHB 48f27a **RR 21f 27a** 417[10]

6 b g Contract Law (USA) 8.9f **(54)** - Star Heading (Upper Case (USA)) 8.2f **(55)**
Form - 055540

Record	1st	2nd	3rd	Ran
1998 -	1st:0	2nd:0	3rd:0	Ran:4
Pre1998 -	1st:1	2nd:3	3rd:1	Ran:16

Win Prizemoney £2,566 *Total Prizemoney* £7,335

Wins					
1994	Jun	Doncas	(G-F)	7f	73

1998 AW 0-4: (12f 2, 13f, 16f) (Equi 2, Fibr 2)

Very moderate gelding, has worn blinkers. AW high 30.
**A G Newcombe [0-8] Alan Cocker (from J S Moore [0-2] Jan 1995).*

STATAJACK (IRE) BHB 58f65a **RR 60f 65a** 4887[10]

10 b g King of Clubs 9.3f **(61)** - Statira (Skymaster) 8.7f **(71)**
Form - 3170810460210

Record	1st	2nd	3rd	Ran
1998 -	1st:3	2nd:1	3rd:0	Ran:12
Pre1998 -	1st:11	2nd:9	3rd:12	Ran:64

Win Prizemoney £57,158 *Total Prizemoney* £77,568

Wins								
* **1998**	Oct	Leices	(G-S)	C	11.8f		55	
* **1998**	May	Kempto	(GD)	H	12f	62	65	
* **1998**	Apr	Folkes	(SFT)	H	9.7f	60	65	
* 1997	Nov	Nottin	(GD)	S	10f		58	
* 1997	Spt	Folkes	(GD)	S	12f		61	
* 1996	Jun	Goodwo	(G-F)	H	10f	75	81	<
* 1996	Jun	Goodwo	(G-F)	C	12f		65	
* 1994	Jly	Ascot	(G-F)	H	12f	79	76	
* 1994	Jly	Newmar	(G-F)	H	10f	76	81	<
* 1994	May	Kempto	(SFT)	H	10f	71	75	

1998 Turf 3-12: (10f 1-2, 11f, 12f 2-8, 13f) (sft 1-1, g-s 2, gd 2-3, g-f 4, frm 2)

Average gelding, effective 10 to 12f, best at 12f, acts on sft to frm - acts on Equi, mostly wears blinkers (very effectively), likes left handed tracks, favours tight tracks, excels at Lingfield, does well at Folkestone and Kempton. Turf high 65 (1st run) - 1st of 15 giving 12lb to Rear Window (7 Apr Folkestone RF 0584) - also 1st of 8 getting 12lb from Secret Ballot (30 May Kempton RF 1594). A real character, he will continue to win races when in the mood, but is an exasperating sort and a very tricky ride. Goes well for Richard Quinn. **D R C Elsworth [16-105] The Nutschalling Partnership.*

STATE APPROVAL BHB 58f69a **RR 61f 69a** 1944[2]

5 b g Pharly (FR) 11.5f **(64)** - Tabeeba (Diesis) 9.3f **(69)**
Form - 071142151112

Record	1st	2nd	3rd	Ran
1998 -	1st:6	2nd:2	3rd:0	Ran:10
Pre1998 -	1st:4	2nd:5	3rd:3	Ran:31

Win Prizemoney £21,120 *Total Prizemoney* £27,516

Wins						
* **1998**	*May*	*Wolver*	*(STD)*	*S*	*12f*	*66+*

* 1998 *Apr Southw (STD) C 12f 64*
* 1998 *Apr Southw (STD) S 12f 66*
* 1998 *Mar Southw (STD) S 11f 55*
* 1998 *Jan Wolver (STD) S 12f 57+*
1998 *Jan Wolver (STD) S 12f 57+*
1997 *Jun Wolver (STD) H 12f 62 74* <
1997 *Mar Wolver (STD) H 12f 57 62*
1996 *Aug Wolver (STD) H 12f 56 68+*
1996 Aug Kempto (G-F) H 12f 58 61+
1998 AW 6-10: (11f 1-3, 12f 5-7) (Fibr 6-10)
Average gelding, effective 12f, - acts on Fibr, favours left handed tracks, and excels at Wolverhampton. AW high 66 - 1st of 11 from Private Despatch (6 Apr Southwell RF 0575) - also 1st of 8 from Avanti Blue (29 May Wolverhampton RF 1581). Consistent. He is at his most effective when able to dominate in modest company over middle-distances on Fibresand, though he struggles outside of plating company.
**Miss S J Wilton [5-9] John Pointon and Sons (from P Eccles [3-14] Jan 1998).*

STATE FAIR BHB 74f73a RR 85f 73a 4963[10]
4 b c Shirley Heights 12.1f **(76)** - Lobinda (Shareef Dancer (USA)) 9.9f **(73)**
Form - 54077005207060
Record 1998 - 1st:0 2nd:1 3rd:0 Ran:14
Pre1998 - 1st:2 2nd:2 3rd:2 Ran:14
Win Prizemoney £13,827 *Total Prizemoney* £32,270
Wins * 1996 Aug Newbur (GD) L 7f 88
* 1996 Aug Cheste (G-F) 7f 98+ <
1998 Turf 0-13: (12f 4, 14f 2, 15f, 16f 4, 19f, 20f) (sft 3, g-s, gd 3, g-f 4, frm 2) 1998 AW 0-1: (10f) (Equi)
Workmanlike, useful colt, effective 12 to 15f, acts on gd to frm, has worn blinkers. Turf high 89. An able but disappointing sort, he is high in the handicap and proving very hard to place, but he ran a better race when second at Ascot in July. Has joined Gerald Ham.
**B W Hills [2-27] Ray Richards (from J L Dunlop [0-1] May 1997).*

STATELY FAVOUR BHB 50f47a RR 51f 47a 1685[9]
3 ch f Statoblest 6.4f **(63)** - Dixie Favor (USA) (Dixieland Band (USA)) 7f **(74)**
Form - 4321500
Record 1998 - 1st:1 2nd:1 3rd:1 Ran:6
Pre1998 - 1st:0 2nd:0 3rd:0 Ran:5
Win Prizemoney £2,280 *Total Prizemoney* £3,310
Wins * 1998 *Apr Southw (STD) C 5f 44* <
1998 Turf 0-1: (6f) (gd) 1998 AW 1-5: (5f 1-1, 6f 3, 7f) (Fibr 1-5)
Workmanlike, fair filly. AW high 51.
**Miss J A Camacho [1-6] Elite Racing Club (from M J Camacho [0-5] Nov 1997).*

STATELY PRINCESS BHB 62f60a RR 60f 60a 5121[4]
3 b f Robellino (USA) 9.5f **(68)** - Affair of State (IRE) (Tate Gallery (USA)) 7.4f **(67)**
Form - 5006683251634
Record 1998 - 1st:1 2nd:1 3rd:2 Ran:13
Pre1998 - 1st:1 2nd:0 3rd:1 Ran:5
Win Prizemoney £6,298 *Total Prizemoney* £9,079
Wins * 1998 Spt Leices (G-F) C 6f 58
* 1997 Mar Newcas (G-F) 5f 71 <
1998 Turf 1-13: (5f 3, 6f 1-8, 7f 2) (sft, g-s 2, gd 3, g-f 3, frm 1-4)
Workmanlike, average filly, effective 5f, acts on gd, has worn blinkers. Turf high 63. Consistent. Generally running well in handicaps, and was dropped in grade to win a claimer at Leicester.
**M R Channon [2-18] Stephen Crown.*

STATE OF CAUTION BHB 69f99a RR 71f 99a 4988[3]
5 b g Reprimand 8.2f **(63)** - Hithermoor Lass (Red Alert) 7.6f **(66)**
Form - 2266305070004223
Record 1998 - 1st:0 2nd:3 3rd:2 Ran:15
Pre1998 - 1st:5 2nd:2 3rd:4 Ran:20
Win Prizemoney £23,054 *Total Prizemoney* £35,604
Wins * 1997 *Nov Wolver (STD) H 7f 95 96* <
* 1997 *Oct Wolver (STD) H 6f 88 90*
* 1997 *Spt Wolver (STD) H 6f 82 84*
* 1997 *Mar Southw (STD) H 7f 77 80*
* 1997 *Jan Southw (STD) 7f 71+*
1998 Turf 0-13: (5f 4, 6f 6, 7f 3) (sft 3, g-s 3, gd 5, g-f 2) 1998 AW 0-2: (5f, 6f) (Fibr 2)
Very useful gelding, effective 5 to 7f, best at 7f, - acts on Fibr, mostly wears blinkers (very effectively), prefers left handed tracks, prefers tight tracks, excels at Southwell and Wolverhampton. Turf high 80. AW high 102 (1st run) - 2nd of 12 giving 2lb to Cretan Gift (14 Mar Wolverhampton 5f Fibr RF 0430). He had a long and tiring season, but was most consistent and deserved more than a string of placed efforts. Much better on the All-Weather, he is one to watch during the winter, although winning opportunities may be limited due to his high rating. Has joined Karl Burke.
**D Shaw [5-27] J C Fretwell (from J L Dunlop [0-8] Oct 1996).*

STATE WIND (IRE) BHB 59f RR 54f 4637[7]
2 ch g Forest Wind (USA) - Kowalski (IRE)(Cyrano de Bergerac) 6f **(68)**
Form - 077
Record 1998 - 1st:0 2nd:0 3rd:0 Ran:3
1998 Turf 0-1: (6f) (frm) 1998 AW 0-2: (6f, 7f) (Fibr 2)
Currently fair gelding. AW high 59 (began Aug).
**N P Littmoden [0-3] The Denton Partnership.*

STATISTICIAN BHB 50f46a RR 59f 46a 441[3]
6 b g Statoblest 6.4f **(63)** - Sharp Lady (Sharpen Up) 8.3f **(67)**
Form - 514333
Record 1998 - 1st:1 2nd:0 3rd:3 Ran:6
Pre1998 - 1st:1 2nd:6 3rd:3 Ran:26
Win Prizemoney £5,380 *Total Prizemoney* £12,399
Wins * **1998** *Jan Lingfi (STD) 6f 45*
* 1995 Jly Catter (G-F) H 6f 66 70 <
1998 AW 1-6: (6f 1-2, 7f 3, 8f) (Equi 1-5, Fibr)
Fair gelding, effective 6 to 8f, best at 8f, - acts on Equi, often wears blinkers (very effectively), favours left handed tracks, favours tight tracks. AW high 49 - 3rd of 12 getting 9lb from Roman Reel (19 Mar Lingfield 8f Equi RF 0441). **John Berry [2-32] Richard Sims.*

STATOYORK BHB 57f46a RR 57f 46a 4469[11]
5 b g Statoblest 6.4f **(63)** - Ultimate Dream (Kafu) 6f **(47)**
Form - 00086633486302256620165630
Record 1998 - 1st:1 2nd:3 3rd:4 Ran:23
Pre1998 - 1st:1 2nd:1 3rd:0 Ran:18
Win Prizemoney £8,190 *Total Prizemoney* £13,049
Wins * **1998** Aug Pontef (G-F) H 5f 52 57 <
1996 Jun Ayr (G-F) 7f 48+
1998 Turf 1-17: (5f 1-11, 6f 6) (g-s, gd 4, g-f 2, frm 1-10) 1998 AW 0-6: (5f 4, 6f 2) (Equi, Fibr 5)
Fair gelding, effective 5 to 7f, best at 7f, acts on g-f to frm, best on frm, has worn blinkers. Turf high 57 - 3rd of 20 getting 21lb from Dil (21 Spt Leicester 5f frm RF 4397) - also 1st of 18 getting 8lb from Jackerin (16 Aug Pontefract RF 3671). AW high 41. Consistent. Despite the odd good effort on turf and sand, his victory at Pontefract in August was his first since June 1996. He appears to travel well through his races but finds little off the bridle, and needs to be held up for a late run.
**D Shaw [1-27] Starburst Racing (from B W Hills [1-14] Jly 1997).*

STAVANGER (IRE) BHB 53f60a RR 59f 60a 3937[9]
2 b c Distinctly North (USA) 7.4f **(63)** - Card Queen (Lord Gayle (USA)) 8.8f **(62)**
Form - 30600
Record 1998 - 1st:0 2nd:0 3rd:1 Ran:5
Win Prizemoney £0 *Total Prizemoney* £426
1998 Turf 0-4: (5f 2, 6f 2) (gd 2, g-f, frm) 1998 AW 0-1: (5f) (Equi)
Average colt. Turf high 59. (1st run) - 3rd of 4 to Touch Up (3 Apr Lingfield 5f Equi RF 0553). **J Berry [0-5] Chris & Antonia Deuters.*

ST CLAIR RIDGE (IRE) RR 90+f 4037a[1]
2 ch f Indian Ridge 7.6f **(74)** - St Clair Star (Sallust) 8.4f **(63)**
Form - 32211
1998 Turf 2-5: (6f, 7f 2-3, 8f) (sft, gd 1-3, frm 1-1)
Useful filly. Turf high 90 (began Jly) - 1st of 9 getting 3lb from Mus-If (29 Aug Curragh RF 4037a) - also 1st of 13 from Desert Magic (20 Aug Tipperary RF 3867a). Beaten a neck by Sunspangled in a Galway maiden in July, she showed progressive form afterwards, and had subsequent National Stakes winner Mus-If behind when landing the Futurity Stakes at the Curragh.
**J S Bolger in IRE [2-5] Terence Molony.*

STEADY READY GO (IRE) BHB 70f RR 61f 2138[11]
6 b g Night Shift (USA) 8.1f **(73)** - Smeralda (GER) (Dschingis Khan)

11.3f **(75)**
Form - 00
Record 1998 - 1st:0 2nd:0 3rd:0 Ran:2
Pre1998 - 1st:2 2nd:1 3rd:0 Ran:5
Win Prizemoney £11,042 *Total Prizemoney* £16,689
Wins 1995 Jun San Si (SFT) 10f 99 <
1994 Nov San Si (HVY) 7.5f
1998 Turf 0-2: (10f 2) (gd, g-f)
Average gelding. Turf high 61.
**J R Poulton [0-3] V R V Partnership (from L M Cumani [2-4] Jun 1995).*

STEAMROLLER STANLY BHB 70f97a **RR 77df 97a** 3822^{8}

5 b g Shirley Heights 12.1f **(76)** - Miss Demure (Shy Groom (USA)) 10f **(66)**
Form - 1158038
Record 1998 - 1st:2 2nd:0 3rd:1 Ran:7
Pre1998 - 1st:4 2nd:1 3rd:3 Ran:16
Win Prizemoney £23,130 *Total Prizemoney* £31,394
Wins * **1998** *Feb Lingfi (SLW) 10f 93* <
* **1998** *Feb Lingfi (SLW) 10f 91*
* 1997 *Feb Lingfi (STD) 10f 90*
* 1997 *Jan Lingfi (STD) H 12f 80 90*
* 1996 *Nov Lingfi (STD) 12f 84*
* 1996 Jun Newbur (G-F) H 13.3f 65 69
1998 Turf 0-4: (10f, 14f 2, 15f) (gd 2, g-f 2) 1998 AW 2-3: (10f 2-3) (Equi 2-3)
Useful gelding, effective 10 to 12f, best at 10f, - acts on Equi, has worn blinkers, prefers left handed tracks, prefers tight tracks. Turf high 77. AW high 93 - 1st of 6 from White Plains (28 Feb Lingfield RF 0378) - also 1st of 6 from White Plains (10 Feb Lingfield RF 0260). Inconsistent. Although a winner on turf, he is a much better horse over middle-distances on the Lingfield Equitrack, and boasts a tremendous record on that track. He came back from a four-month break to run out the easy winner of a ten-furlong conditions event on his favourite surface in February, and beat a very talented field there next time. The race did not really go his way in the Winter Derby at Lingfield, as he is a much better performer when able to stay close to the pace, something he was unable to do in that race. Opportunities for him on sand remain very limited. Has joined Karl Burke. **C A Cyzer [6-23] R M Cyzer.*

STELLA BERINE (FR) **RR 98f** $4825a^{1}$

2 ch f Bering 9.6f **(80)** - Beaujolaise (FR) (Thatching) 8f **(66)**
Form - 22221
1998 Turf 1-5: (5f, 7f 1-4) (sft 1-1, gd 3, g-f)
Very useful filly. Turf high 98 (began Jly) - 1st of 7 getting 3lb from Zirconi (7 Oct Saint-Cloud RF 4825a). Genuine French filly, winner of the Prix Eclipse at Saint-Cloud.
**P Bary in FR [1-5] Ecurie Stella Maris.*

ST ENODOC (FR) **RR 83f** 2670^{3}

3 ch g Sanglamore (USA) 12.9f **(67)** - Exemina (USA) (Slip Anchor) 9.8f **(73)**
Form - 133
Record 1998 - 1st:1 2nd:0 3rd:2 Ran:3
Pre1998 - 1st:0 2nd:0 3rd:0 Ran:3
Win Prizemoney £3,100 *Total Prizemoney* £4,975
Wins * **1998** May Nottin (G-F) H 14.1f 66 74+ <
1998 Turf 1-3: (14f 1-1, 16f 2) (g-f 2, frm 1-1)
Decent gelding, effective 14 to 16f, best at 16f, acts on g-f to frm, best on g-f. Turf high 83 - 3rd of 14 giving 9lb to Bridie's Pride (20 Jun Ascot 16f g-f RF 2141) - also 1st of 12 getting 4lb from Some Might Say (8 May Nottingham RF 1112). A likeable half-brother to St Mawes. **J L Dunlop [1-6] Exors of the late Rt Hon Lord Swaythling.*

STEPHANGEORGE BHB 28f **RR 18f** 3812^{10}

3 b g La Grange Music - Telegraph Callgirl (Northern Tempest (USA))
Form - 00000
Record 1998 - 1st:0 2nd:0 3rd:0 Ran:5
Pre1998 - 1st:0 2nd:0 3rd:0 Ran:5
1998 Turf 0-5: (6f 2, 8f 2, 10f) (g-f 3, frm 2)
Light-framed, poor gelding, has worn blinkers. Turf high 18.
**M Brittain [0-10] Cliff Woof.*

STEPHENSONS ROCKET BHB 38f34a **RR 36f 34a** 1607^{7}

7 ch g Music Boy 6.5f **(56)** - Martian Princess (Cure The Blues (USA)) 9.5f **(63)**
Form - 67067
Record 1998 - 1st:0 2nd:0 3rd:0 Ran:5
Pre1998 - 1st:5 2nd:4 3rd:4 Ran:47
Win Prizemoney £19,070 *Total Prizemoney* £25,821
Wins 1994 Aug Thirsk (FRM) H 5f 77 71 <
1994 Jly Newcas (G-F) 5f 69
1994 Jun Ayr (G-S) H 5f 76 71 <
1994 Apr Catter (GD) H 5f 72 71 <
1998 Turf 0-4: (6f 3, 8f) (sft, g-s, gd 2) 1998 AW 0-1: (6f) (Fibr)
Very moderate gelding, effective 6f, acts on gd to frm, has worn blinkers (effectively). Turf high 36. Consistent.
**R A Fahey [0-19] John Stephenson & Sons (Nelson) Ltd (from D Nicholls [0-11] Nov 1996).*

STEP ON DEGAS BHB 56f60a **RR 60f 60a** 4652^{7}

5 b m Superpower 6.6f **(58)** - Vivid Impression (Cure The Blues (USA)) 9.5f **(63)**
Form - 001625886777
Record 1998 - 1st:1 2nd:1 3rd:0 Ran:11
Pre1998 - 1st:3 2nd:5 3rd:2 Ran:26
Win Prizemoney £9,998 *Total Prizemoney* £16,702
Wins * **1998** May Bright (FRM) H 6f 54 58
1997 Aug Bright (G-F) 7f 54
1997 *Jan Lingfi (STD) H 7f 63 63*
1996 Jun Warwic (FRM) H 5f 63 64 <
1998 Turf 1-10: (6f 1-2, 7f 6, 8f 2) (gd 2, g-f 4, frm 1-4) 1998 AW 0-1: (8f) (Equi)
Average filly, effective 6 to 8f, best at 7f, acts on gd to frm - acts on Equi, has worn blinkers, likes left handed tracks, prefers tight tracks, and does well at Brighton. Turf high 60 - 2nd of 14 giving 12lb to Oriole (24 Jun Carlisle 7f gd RF 2226) - also 1st of 17 getting 6lb from Anokato (22 May Brighton RF 1389). Consistent. A well-named mare, she is not easy to catch right but won at Brighton in May, getting up in the last stride of the six-furlong trip.
**Mrs A L M King [1-11] Mrs Pennie Muir (from M J Fetherston-Godley [3-22] Nov 1997).*

STEPSTONE **RR 61f** 4059^{5}

2 b f Slip Anchor 12.7f **(75)** - Stedham (Jaazeiro (USA)) 9.2f **(54)**
Form - 5
Record 1998 - 1st:0 2nd:0 3rd:0 Ran:1
1998 Turf 0-1: (7f) (g-f)
Currently average filly. **H Candy [0-1] Major M G Wyatt.*

STERNSINGER (USA) **RR 66f** 685^{9}

3 b c Seeking the Gold (USA) 7.4f **(80)** - Song Maker (IRE) (Sadler's Wells (USA)) 10f **(76)**
Form - 0
Record 1998 - 1st:0 2nd:0 3rd:0 Ran:1
Pre1998 - 1st:0 2nd:0 3rd:0 Ran:1
1998 Turf 0-1: (10f) (gd)
Scopey, currently average colt.
**H R A Cecil [0-2] Gestut Schlenderhan.*

STERO HEIGHTS (IRE) BHB 74f **RR 74f** 4801^{5}

3 b c Shirley Heights 12.1f **(76)** - Trystero (Shareef Dancer (USA)) 9.9f **(73)**
Form - 735
Record 1998 - 1st:0 2nd:0 3rd:1 Ran:3
Win Prizemoney £0 *Total Prizemoney* £520
1998 Turf 0-3: (10f, 11f, 12f) (sft, gd, frm)
Scopey, currently above-average colt. Turf high 74 (began Spt) - 3rd of 7 giving 5lb to Andalish (25 Spt Haydock 11f frm RF 4478). He has joined David Cosgrove.
**E A L Dunlop [0-3] Gainsborough Stud.*

STEVE'S HOT BHB 41f **RR 44f** 4136^{4}

2 gr g Terimon 8.7f **(58)** - Flammable (IRE) (Prince Rupert (FR))
Form - 0004
Record 1998 - 1st:0 2nd:0 3rd:0 Ran:4
1998 Turf 0-4: (6f, 7f 2, 8f) (gd, g-f, frm 2)
Moderate gelding. Turf high 44 - 4th of 20 getting 9lb from Malchik (8 Spt Leicester 8f g-f RF 4136). **M A Jarvis [0-4] Mrs B Sadowska.*

STEWARD (FR) **RR 115f** $3415a^{1}$

5 b h Saumarez 15.1f **(87)** - 00
Form - 101
1998 Turf 2-3: (10f 1-1, 11f 1-1, 12f) (g-s 1-1, gd 1-2)

High-class colt, effective 10 to 12f, acts on g-s to gd, best on gd. Turf high 115 (1st run) - 1st of 9 from Ferrari (24 May Baden-Baden RF 1556a) - also 1st of 7 giving 6lb to Foggy Day (29 Jly Vichy RF 3415a). He managed to win a Group Two in Germany and a Group Three in the French provinces this year.
**D Sepulchre in FR [4-7] G Coude.*

ST HELENSFIELD BHB 96f **RR 87f** 812[4]
3 ch c Kris 10f **(75)** - On Credit (FR) (No Pass No Sale) 11.9f **(85)**
Form - 4
Record **1998** - 1st:0 2nd:0 3rd:0 Ran:1
Pre1998 - 1st:1 2nd:1 3rd:1 Ran:3
Win Prizemoney £3,291 *Total Prizemoney* £7,154
Wins * 1997 Spt Bath (G-F) 10.2f 86+ <
1998 Turf 0-1: (12f) (sft)
Leggy, useful colt. Won over ten furlongs on his Bath debut in September '97, and ran with credit in fair company afterwards. However, he was beaten a long way on his reappearance at Epsom. **M Johnston [1-4] Paul Dean.*

ST HILARY RR 3083[11]
3 b f Formidable (USA) 7.8f **(60)**-Positive Attitude(Red Sunset) 8.2f **(63)**
Form - 00
Record **1998** - 1st:0 2nd:0 3rd:0 Ran:2
1998 Turf 0-2: (8f 2) (g-f 2)
Workmanlike, currently very poor filly - 11th of 11 to Marabela (24 Jly Nottingham 8f g-f RF 3083). **J E Banks [0-2] K J Mercer.*

STILL WATERS BHB 69a **RR 71f** 3828[13]
3 b g Rainbow Quest (USA) 11.2f **(81)** - Krill (Kris) 9.5f **(73)**
Form - 0200
Record **1998** - 1st:0 2nd:1 3rd:0 Ran:4
Pre1998 - 1st:0 2nd:0 3rd:0 Ran:1
Win Prizemoney £0 *Total Prizemoney* £990
1998 Turf 0-3: (8f 2, 10f) (g-s, g-f, frm) 1998 AW 0-1: (8f) (Fibr)
Workmanlike, above-average gelding. Turf high 71 - 2nd of 10 to Captain's Log (4 May Warwick 8f g-f RF 1030).
**K Bell [0-1] Mrs Joyce Wood (from R Charlton [0-4] Jun 1998).*

STINGRAY (IRE) BHB 70f **RR 76f** 4500[5]
3 b g Darshaan 11.9f **(81)** - Sovereign Dona (Sovereign Path) 9.3f **(55)**
Form - 135
Record **1998** - 1st:1 2nd:0 3rd:1 Ran:3
Pre1998 - 1st:0 2nd:0 3rd:0 Ran:2
Win Prizemoney £3,730 *Total Prizemoney* £4,686
Wins * **1998** Apr Nottin (G-S) 14.1f 76 <
1998 Turf 1-3: (14f 1-2, 16f) (g-s 1-1, g-f, frm)
Leggy, above-average gelding. Turf high 76 (1st run) - 1st of 3 getting 20lb from Highly Prized (7 Apr Nottingham RF 0590).
**M Johnston [1-5] M J Pilkington.*

STINGRAY CITY (USA) BHB 25f **RR 16f** 3618[6]
9 b g Raft (USA) 10.7f **(77)** - Out of This World (High Top) 10.2f **(67)**
Form - 6
Record **1998** - 1st:0 2nd:0 3rd:0 Ran:1
Pre1998 - 1st:1 2nd:10 3rd:2 Ran:23
Win Prizemoney £2,403 *Total Prizemoney* £11,235
1998 Turf 0-1: (12f) (frm)
Poor gelding, has worn blinkers. Becoming disappointing.
**R M McKellar [0-5] Mrs Linda Mckellar (from L Lungo [2-8] Oct 1994).*

ST LAWRENCE (CAN) BHB 72f **RR 72f** 3572[4]
4 gr g With Approval (CAN) 8.7f **(80)** - Mingan Isle (USA) (Lord Avie (USA)) 5.3f **(61)**
Form - 0034
Record **1998** - 1st:0 2nd:0 3rd:1 Ran:4
Pre1998 - 1st:0 2nd:3 3rd:0 Ran:5
Win Prizemoney £0 *Total Prizemoney* £3,979
1998 Turf 0-4: (10f 2, 12f 2) (sft, g-f 3)
Unfurnished, above-average gelding, effective 10f, acts on g-f, has worn blinkers. Turf high 72 - 3rd of 7 giving 12lb to Riccarton (29 Jly Doncaster 10f g-f RF 3195). **C E Brittain [0-9] Saeed Manana.*

STOCK CITY BHB 49f **RR 66f** 4818[15]
2 b c Rock City 8.8f **(62)** - Cousin Jenny (Midyan (USA)) 6f **(60)**
Form - 73686670
Record **1998** - 1st:0 2nd:0 3rd:1 Ran:8
Win Prizemoney £0 *Total Prizemoney* £447
1998 Turf 0-8: (5f 4, 6f 3, 7f) (gd 5, g-f, frm 2)
Average colt, has worn blinkers. Turf high 66.
**V Soane [0-8] Breeze In/Breeze Out Club.*

STOCK HILL DANCER BHB 34f31a **RR 38f 31a** 5128[15]
4 ch f Interrex (CAN) 7.7f **(51)** - Stocktina (Tina's Pet) 6.8f **(59)**
Form - 08823045602000
Record **1998** - 1st:0 2nd:2 3rd:1 Ran:14
Pre1998 - 1st:0 2nd:0 3rd:1 Ran:11
Win Prizemoney £0 *Total Prizemoney* £2,196
1998 Turf 0-12: (5f 7, 6f 4, 7f) (sft, g-s 4, gd 2, frm 5) 1998 AW 0-2: (5f, 6f) (Equi, Fibr)
Unfurnished, very moderate filly, effective 6f, acts on frm, has worn blinkers. Turf high 38. AW high 12. Becoming disappointing.
**R J Hodges [0-2] Wayne Sweeting (from K R Burke [0-15] Aug 1998).*

STOLEN MUSIC (IRE) BHB 38f **RR 41f** 5118[7]
5 b m Taufan (USA) 8.3f **(65)** - Causa Sua(Try My Best (USA)) 7.6f **(67)**
Form - 003047474611517
Record **1998** - 1st:3 2nd:0 3rd:1 Ran:15
Pre1998 - 1st:0 2nd:0 3rd:0 Ran:14
Win Prizemoney £7,643 *Total Prizemoney* £8,216
Wins * **1998** Oct Redcar (HVY) H 14.1f 33 36 <
* **1998** Spt Beverl (G-F) H 9.9f 29 33
* **1998** Aug Beverl (G-F) H 9.9f 25 30
1998 Turf 3-15: (7f 2, 8f, 10f 2-6, 11f 2, 12f 2, 14f 1-1, 16f) (g-s 1-2, gd 6, g-f 1-3, frm 1-4)
Moderate filly, effective 12 to 14f, acts on g-s to gd, has worn blinkers, favours tight tracks. Turf high 41 - 5th of 14 getting 7lb from Sing And Dance (15 Oct Catterick 12f gd RF 4815) - also 1st of 15 getting 32lb from Galapino (17 Oct Redcar RF 4861). Took a long time to get off the mark, but did her small yard proud last term. Stays well and needs to be brought late.
**R E Barr [3-27] P Cartmell (from Major D N Chappell [0-3] Spt 1996).*

STOLEN TEAR (FR) BHB 85f **RR 75f** 4466[7]
2 ch f Cadeaux Genereux 7.9f **(76)** - Durrah (USA) (Nijinsky (CAN)) 10.3f **(77)**
Form - 317
Record **1998** - 1st:1 2nd:0 3rd:1 Ran:3
Win Prizemoney £3,371 *Total Prizemoney* £3,859
Wins * **1998** Spt Hamilt (SFT) 8.3f 70+ <
1998 Turf 1-3: (7f, 8f 1-2) (gd 1-1, frm 2)
Currently above-average filly. Turf high 75 (began Aug) - also 1st of 8 from Penang Pearl (7 Spt Hamilton RF 4131).
**M Johnston [1-3] Maktoum Al Maktoum.*

STONE BECK BHB 65f **RR 69f** 4324[3]
3 b f Lapierre - Dovey (Welsh Pageant) 10f **(65)**
Form - 4403043
Record **1998** - 1st:0 2nd:0 3rd:2 Ran:7
Pre1998 - 1st:0 2nd:0 3rd:0 Ran:3
Win Prizemoney £0 *Total Prizemoney* £2,505
1998 Turf 0-7: (8f, 10f, 12f 4, 15f) (g-s, gd 2, frm 3, hrd)
Workmanlike, average filly, effective 8 to 15f, best at 8f, acts on g-s to hrd, best on gd, has worn blinkers. Turf high 69 - 3rd of 7 getting 10lb from Yanabi (17 Spt Ayr 15f gd RF 4324). Consistent.
**J M Jefferson [0-10] & Mrs J M Davenport.*

STONED IMACULATE (IRE) BHB 68f **RR 69f** 2640[6]
4 ch f Durgam (USA) 12.3f **(53)** - Rose Deer (Whistling Deer) 16.4f **(48)**
Form - 6
Record **1998** - 1st:0 2nd:0 3rd:0 Ran:1
Pre1998 - 1st:3 2nd:0 3rd:1 Ran:6
Win Prizemoney £8,490 *Total Prizemoney* £9,016
Wins * 1997 Spt Nottin (G-F) H 16f 56 69 <
* 1997 Spt Nottin (G-F) H 16f 56 64
* 1997 Aug Carlis (FRM) H 17.2f 49 56+
1998 Turf 0-1: (16f) (frm)
Scopey, average filly, effective 16f, acts on g-f. Completed a late-season hat-trick in '97 after being stepped up in trip, and also won over hurdles. Ran in snatches on her belated '98 bow.
**F Murphy [5-13] M Rowsell.*

STONEHAM GIRL BHB 25f **RR 28f** 2809[7]
6 b m Nomination 7.3f **(57)** -Persian Tapestry (Tap On Wood) 10.3f **(65)**

Form - 7
Record 1998 - 1st:0 2nd:0 3rd:0 Ran:1
Pre1998 - 1st:0 2nd:1 3rd:0 Ran:10
Win Prizemoney £0 *Total Prizemoney* £612
1998 Turf 0-1: (12f) (frm)
Little account mare.
**F Murphy [0-1] Richard Wheeler (from P Butler [0-10] Oct 1995).*

STONE OF DESTINY BHB 75f **RR 85f** 4661[1]
3 ch c Ballad Rock 7.2f **(63)** - Shamasiya (FR) (Vayrann) 9.7f **(74)**
Form - 4870001
Record 1998 - 1st:1 2nd:0 3rd:0 Ran:7
Pre1998 - 1st:1 2nd:2 3rd:0 Ran:7
Win Prizemoney £6,035 *Total Prizemoney* £10,811
Wins * **1998** Oct Pontef (G-S) C 6f 85
* 1997 Oct Folkes (GD) 6.9f 91 <
1998 Turf 1-7: (6f 1-1, 7f 5, 8f) (gd 1-3, g-f, frm 3)
Scopey, useful colt, effective 6 to 7f, best at 7f, acts on gd to frm, has worn blinkers. Turf high 89 - also 1st of 16 giving 7lb to Detroit City (5 Oct Pontefract RF 4661). **B J Meehan [2-14] P Heath.*

STONE RIDGE (IRE) BHB 75f **RR 78f** 4970[1]
6 b g Indian Ridge 7.6f **(74)** - Cut in Stone (USA) (Assert) 10.6f **(85)**
Form - 00172550068061
Record 1998 - 1st:2 2nd:1 3rd:0 Ran:14
Pre1998 - 1st:3 2nd:1 3rd:1 Ran:25
Win Prizemoney £87,273 *Total Prizemoney* £91,348
Wins * **1998** Oct Doncas (HVY) C 10.3f 77
* **1998** May Windso (G-F) 10f 78
* 1996 Mar Doncas (SFT) H 8f 87 97 <
* 1995 Oct Newmar (G-F) H 8f 82 89
* 1995 Apr Bright (G-F) 8f 80
1998 Turf 2-14: (8f 2, 10f 2-11, 12f) (hvy, g-s 1-1, gd 4, g-f 5, frm 1-3)
Above-average gelding, effective 10f, acts on g-s to frm, has worn blinkers. Turf high 78 - 1st of 10 from Brandon Jack (11 May Windsor RF 1161) - also 1st of 13 getting 2lb from Plan For Profit (24 Oct Doncaster RF 4970). **R Hannon [5-40] Mrs Chris Harrington.*

STONEY LANE RR 50f 1322[7]
3 b g Petoski 10.4f **(56)** - Everingham Park (Record Token) 6.3f **(53)**
Form - 7
Record 1998 - 1st:0 2nd:0 3rd:0 Ran:1
1998 Turf 0-1: (7f) (frm)
Currently fair gelding. **T D Easterby [0-1] A D Bottomley.*

STOP OUT BHB 95f **RR 83f** 3239[5]
3 b f Rudimentary (USA) 8.2f **(66)** - Breakaway (Song) 7.2f **(61)**
Form - 5
Record 1998 - 1st:0 2nd:0 3rd:0 Ran:1
Pre1998 - 1st:1 2nd:1 3rd:0 Ran:4
Win Prizemoney £3,208 *Total Prizemoney* £6,828
Wins * 1997 Jun Sandow (G-F) 5f 79 <
1998 Turf 0-1: (6f) (frm)
Scopey, decent filly.
**H Morrison [1-5] Sheran Macdonald-Buchanan & Partners.*

STOPPES BROW BHB 69f70a **RR 68f 70a** 5147[24]
6 b g Primo Dominie 7.2f **(67)** - So Bold (Never so Bold) 6.3f **(66)**
Form - 234042620251675236826 80
Record 1998 - 1st:1 2nd:5 3rd:1 Ran:21
Pre1998 - 1st:7 2nd:6 3rd:7 Ran:46
Win Prizemoney £31,743 *Total Prizemoney* £55,092
Wins * **1998** May Goodwo (G-F) H 8f 67 72
* 1996 May Newbur (SFT) H 6f 70 71
* 1995 Aug Goodwo (G-F) H 7f 62 66
* 1995 *Feb Lingfi (STD) H 6f 84 81* <
* 1995 *Jan Lingfi (STD) H 6f 74 77*
* 1995 *Jan Lingfi (STD) H 5f 74 71*
* 1994 *Nov Lingfi (STD) H 5f 68 76*
* 1994 *Nov Lingfi (STD) H 5f 58 68*
1998 Turf 1-15: (7f 7, 8f 1-6, 9f, 10f) (sft 2, gd 6, g-f 1-5, frm 2) 1998 AW 0-6: (7f 6) (Equi 5, Fibr)
Above-average gelding, effective 7 to 8f, best at 7f, acts on gd to frm - acts on Fibr, mostly wears blinkers, likes right handed tracks. Turf high 72 - 1st of 16 giving 6lb to Zurs (20 May Goodwood RF 1358). AW high 77. Consistent. Ended a long losing run at Goodwood in May but has been readily beatable since off higher marks. **G L Moore [8-67] C J Pennick.*

STOPWATCH (IRE) RR 91f 4297a[6]
3 b c Lead on Time (USA) 7.5f **(69)** - Rose Bonbon (FR) 00
Form - 71055246
1998 Turf 1-8: (8f 1-4, 9f 2, 10f 2) (hvy, sft 2, g-s 1-1, gd 3, frm)
Useful colt, effective 8f, acts on g-s to gd, has worn blinkers. Turf high 91 - also 1st of 11 giving 5lb to Azarina (13 Apr Cork RF 0795a). **T Stack in IRE [1-10] R E Sangster.*

STORM CAT BHB 76a **RR 70f** 4234[10]
3 ch g Interrex (CAN) 7.7f **(51)** - Albion Polka (Dance In Time (CAN)) 8.9f **(59)**
Form - 0420500
Record 1998 - 1st:0 2nd:1 3rd:0 Ran:7
Win Prizemoney £0 *Total Prizemoney* £1,004
1998 Turf 0-6:(8f 2, 9f 2, 10f, 12f)(gd 4, g-f, frm)1998 AW 0-1: (9f) (Fibr)
Above-average gelding, effective 9f, acts on frm, often wears blinkers, likes tight tracks. Turf high 70 - 2nd of 10 to Jamorin Dancer (27 Jun Lingfield 9f frm RF 2341). **K McAuliffe [0-7] A Ezen.*

STORM COMMAND BHB 54f **RR 56f** 1486[15]
4 b g Gildoran 11.6f **(58)** - Summer Sky (Skyliner) 7.3f **(53)**
Form - 80
Record 1998 - 1st:0 2nd:0 3rd:0 Ran:2
Pre1998 - 1st:0 2nd:0 3rd:0 Ran:1
1998 Turf 0-2: (8f, 10f) (gd, g-f)
Leggy, currently fair gelding. Turf high 56.
**D W P Arbuthnot [0-3] Henry Ponsonby & Partners (2).*

STORM CRY (USA) BHB 79f **RR 81f** 3229[16]
3 b c Hermitage (USA) 8.6f **(84)** - Doonesbury Lady (USA) (Doonesbury (USA)) 7.7f **(99)**
Form - 1530
Record 1998 - 1st:1 2nd:0 3rd:1 Ran:4
Pre1998 - 1st:0 2nd:1 3rd:0 Ran:2
Win Prizemoney £2,444 *Total Prizemoney* £4,580
Wins * **1998** May Bath (FRM) 8f 64+ <
1998 Turf 1-4: (7f, 8f 1-2, 9f) (g-s, gd, frm 1-2)
Light-framed, decent colt, effective 7 to 8f, acts on gd to frm. Turf high 81 - 3rd of 10 giving 10lb to Minetta (9 Jly Newmarket 8f frm RF 2652). He made a winning reappearance in a modest Bath maiden, but got totally bogged down in the soft ground at Sandown next time. Unsuited by a slowly-run race at Newmarket in July, but was a little disappointing nonetheless.
**Major D N Chappell [1-6] Rathmore Racing.*

STORM FROMTHE EAST BHB 79f **RR 84f** 1697[1]
3 b g Formidable (USA) 7.8f **(60)** - Callas Star (Chief Singer) 8.9f **(66)**
Form - 571
Record 1998 - 1st:1 2nd:0 3rd:0 Ran:3
Pre1998 - 1st:0 2nd:3 3rd:0 Ran:6
Win Prizemoney £3,720 *Total Prizemoney* £7,248
Wins * **1998** Jun Goodwo (GD) 7f 81 <
1998 Turf 1-3: (6f 2, 7f 1-1) (gd 1-3)
Scopey, decent gelding, effective 5 to 7f, best at 6f, acts on gd to frm, best on gd. Turf high 81 - 1st of 8 giving 5lb to Hebony (3 Jun Goodwood RF 1697). Consistent. **R Hannon [1-9] N Hayes.*

STORMIN (IRE) RR 54f 3027[18]
2 b c Perugino (USA) - Unalaska (IRE) (High Estate)
Form - 00
Record 1998 - 1st:0 2nd:0 3rd:0 Ran:2
1998 Turf 0-2: (6f, 7f) (frm 2)
Currently fair colt, always wears blinkers. Turf high 54 (began Jly).
**Mrs J R Ramsden [0-2] Mrs Joan Egan.*

STORMLESS BHB 66f **RR 69f** 1562[4]
7 b g Silly Prices 6.8f **(51)** - Phyl's Pet (Aberdeen) 9.4f **(55)**
Form - 2614
Record 1998 - 1st:1 2nd:1 3rd:0 Ran:4
Pre1998 - 1st:3 2nd:3 3rd:3 Ran:21
Win Prizemoney £14,585 *Total Prizemoney* £20,598
Wins * **1998** May Hamilt (SFT) H 8.3f 58 69 <
1997 May Hamilt (SFT) H 8.3f 53 59
1996 Aug Ayr (G-F) H 10f 48 54
1996 Jun Ayr (G-F) H 10f 43 47
1998 Turf 1-4: (8f 1-3, 10f) (hvy 1-1, sft, g-s, gd)
Average gelding, effective 8 to 10f, best at 10f, acts on hvy to gd.

Turf high 69 - 1st of 13 getting 4lb from Zorba (7 May Hamilton RF 1079). **J S Goldie [1-10] D St Clair (from P Monteith [3-17] May 1997).*

STORM TROOPER (USA) BHB 111f RR 118f 4953a[4]

5 b h Diesis 9f **(80)** - Stormette (USA) (Assert) 10.6f **(85)**
Form - 4
1998 Turf 0-1: (12f) (frm)
High-class colt. (1st run) - 4th of 8 giving 7lb to Royal Anthem (18 Oct Woodbine 12f frm RF 4953a).
**N Drysdale in USA [0-1] (from H R A Cecil [2-11] Spt 1996).*

STORM WEAVE (IRE) RR 68f 4505[8]

2 ch f Polar Falcon (USA) 9f **(74)** - Kaliala (FR) (Pharly (FR)) 9.8f **(68)**
Form - 68
Record 1998 - 1st:0 2nd:0 3rd:0 Ran:2
1998 Turf 0-2: (6f, 8f) (gd 2)
Currently average filly. Turf high 68 (began Aug).
**Mrs A Swinbank [0-2] Mrs Dee Shotton.*

STORMY SKYE (IRE) BHB 95f RR 84?f 4972[5]

2 b c Bluebird (USA) 7.9f **(71)** - Canna (Caerleon (USA)) 8.6f **(71)**
Form - 5835
Record 1998 - 1st:0 2nd:0 3rd:1 Ran:4
Win Prizemoney £0 *Total Prizemoney* £1,872
1998 Turf 0-4: (7f 2, 8f 2) (sft, g-s, gd, frm)
Decent colt. Turf high 84 (began Jly). Ran in hot company in testing ground on his last two starts, finishing third in a listed race and fifth in the Racing Post Trophy. Will win races at a lower level.
**A J McNae [0-4] The Iona Stud.*

STORYTELLER (IRE) BHB 85f RR 89f 4323[2]

4 b g Thatching 7.8f **(69)** - Please Believe Me (Try My Best (USA)) 7.6f **(67)**
Form - 622214111212572
Record 1998 - 1st:5 2nd:6 3rd:0 Ran:15
Pre1998 - 1st:1 2nd:0 3rd:1 Ran:11
Win Prizemoney £21,362 *Total Prizemoney* £30,977

Wins								
* **1998**	Jly	Pontef	(G-F)	H	5f	77	84	<
* **1998**	Jly	Beverl	(GD)	H	5f	65	76	
* **1998**	Jly	Haydoc	(GD)	H	5f	65	67	
* **1998**	Jun	Ayr	(GD)	H	5f	58	62	
* **1998**	Jun	Carlis	(G-S)	H	5f	58	61	
1997	Jly	Doncas	(GD)	H	5f	50	54	

1998 Turf 5-15: (5f 5-13, 6f 2) (g-s 2, gd 1-6, g-f 3-4, frm 1-3)
Workmanlike, useful gelding, effective 5f, acts on frm, mostly wears blinkers (extremely effectively). Turf high 89 - 2nd of 12 giving 23lb to Sihafi (22 Jly Sandown 5f frm RF 3036) - also 1st of 8 giving 28lb to Rude Awakening (17 Jly Pontefract RF 2886). Consistent. He was in terrific form in the summer, winning a string of races at five furlongs. Comes from behind and finishes strongly.
**M Dods [5-15] Mrs Karen Pratt (from Mrs J R Ramsden [1-10] Oct 1997).*

STOWAWAY BHB 119f RR 117f 550a[1]

4 b c Slip Anchor 12.7f **(75)** - On Credit (FR) (No Pass No Sale) 11.9f **(85)**
Form - 1
1998 Turf 1-1: (12f 1-1) (g-f 1-1)
Strong, high-class colt. (1st run) - 1st of 13 getting 2lb from For Valour (28 Mar Nad Al Sheba RF 0550a). He won a valuable event at Nad Al Sheba in March, but that turned out to be his only start of the season as he reportedly suffered a setback in June.
**S bin Suroor in UAE [1-1] Godolphin (from S bin Suroor [2-4] Oct 1997).*

STRACHIN BHB 84f RR 93?f 4944a[3]

4 b c Salse (USA) 10.9f **(71)** - Collage (Ela-Mana-Mou) 10.1f **(70)**
Form - 213
Record 1998 - 1st:1 2nd:1 3rd:1 Ran:3
Pre1998 - 1st:0 2nd:1 3rd:0 Ran:2
Win Prizemoney £3,566 *Total Prizemoney* £11,820
Wins * **1998** Apr Carlis (G-S) 8f 80 <
1998 Turf 1-3: (8f 1-2, 12f) (sft 2, gd 1-1)
Useful colt. Turf high 83. **L M Cumani [1-5].*

STRATEGIC RR 92f 3554a[1]

2 b c Caerleon (USA) 10.9f **(79)** - Game Plan (Darshaan) 9.9f **(84)**
Form - 41
1998 Turf 1-2: (7f, 8f 1-1) (sft, gd 1-1)
Currently useful colt. Turf high 92 - 1st of 11 giving 5lb to St Clair Ridge (9 Aug Leopardstown RF 3554a). Son of an Oaks runner-up, he showed a useful level of form in Irish maidens.
**J Oxx in IRE [1-2] Sheikh Mohammed.*

STRATEGIC AIR BHB 50f RR 48f 1478[16]

3 ch g Anshan 8.2f **(63)** - Kimbolton Katie (Aragon) 8.1f **(60)**
Form - 080
Record 1998 - 1st:0 2nd:0 3rd:0 Ran:3
Pre1998 - 1st:0 2nd:0 3rd:0 Ran:3
1998 Turf 0-3: (9f, 10f, 14f) (gd, g-f, frm)
Moderate gelding. Turf high 29. **E Weymes [0-6] T A Scothern.*

STRATEGIC CHOICE (USA) BHB 110f RR 113df 5149[5]

7 b h Alleged (USA) 11.8f **(81)** - Danlu (USA) (Danzig (USA)) 8.4f **(76)**
Form - 24365
Record 1998 - 1st:0 2nd:1 3rd:1 Ran:5
Pre1998 - 1st:6 2nd:4 3rd:4 Ran:24
Win Prizemoney £338,403 *Total Prizemoney* £827,925

Wins								
* 1997	Spt	Velief	(FRM)		12f	113+		
* 1996	Aug	Deauvi	(GD)	G2	12.5f	118		
* 1996	Jun	San Si	(GD)	G1	12f	116		
* 1995	Spt	Currag	(GD)	G1	14f	119		<
* 1995	Apr	Newbur	(GD)	G3	12f	113		
* 1994	May	Newbur	(G-F)		10f	70		

1998 Turf 0-5: (12f 2, 13f 2, 14f) (gd 4, g-f)
Group-class horse, effective 12 to 14f, acts on gd to frm, best on gd, has worn blinkers, likes right handed tracks. Turf high 113 (1st run) - 2nd of 6 to Busy Flight (14 May York 14f gd RF 1221). Consistent. His sculptured physique never fails to impress and, even at seven, he remains capable of high-class form, even if he has toured Europe more times than Jill Dando. Whether there is another Group race to be won is another matter.
**P F I Cole [6-29] M Arbib.*

STRAT'S LEGACY BHB 32f26a RR 37f 26a 31[6]

11 b g Chukaroo 13.7f **(73)** - State Romance (Free State) 8.7f **(61)**
Form - 676
Record 1998 - 1st:0 2nd:0 3rd:0 Ran:1
Pre1998 - 1st:10 2nd:9 3rd:4 Ran:80
Win Prizemoney £27,291 *Total Prizemoney* £37,253

Wins							
* 1995	Jly	Chepst	(G-F)	H	12.1f	43	50
* 1994	Jly	Chepst	(FRM)	H	12.1f	40	46

1998 AW 0-1: (13f) (Equi)
Very moderate gelding, effective 14f, acts on g-f, has worn blinkers, likes tight tracks. **D W P Arbuthnot [10-81] Jack Blumenow.*

STRAT'S QUEST BHB 51f48a RR 40f 48a 5128[9]

4 b f Nicholas (USA) 6.1f **(63)** - Eagle's Quest (Legal Eagle) 7.3f **(54)**
Form - 0736005700
Record 1998 - 1st:0 2nd:0 3rd:1 Ran:10
Pre1998 - 1st:2 2nd:0 3rd:0 Ran:17
Win Prizemoney £7,064 *Total Prizemoney* £8,428

Wins								
* 1997	May	Windso	(SFT)	H	6f	64	58	
* 1996	Oct	Chepst	(SFT)	H	6.1f	64	64	<

1998 Turf 0-10: (5f 3, 6f 6, 7f) (hvy, sft 2, g-s 2, gd 4, frm)
Light-framed, moderate filly, effective 5 to 6f, acts on hvy to gd. Turf high 61 - 3rd of 13 getting 29lb from The Gay Fox (24 Apr Sandown 5f hvy RF 0852). Consistent. Clearly likes soft ground, and won a twenty-five runner handicap on that surface at Windsor in '97. Generally well beaten since.
**D W P Arbuthnot [2-27] Jack Blumenow.*

STRAVINSKY (USA) RR 111f 4851[3]

2 b c Nureyev (USA) 8.4f **(84)** - Fire the Groom (USA) (Blushing Groom (FR)) 10.3f **(76)**
Form - 1D3
1998 Turf 1-3: (6f 1-1, 7f 2) (sft, gd, frm 1-1)
Currently Group-class colt. Turf high 111 (began Aug) - 3rd of 7 to Mujahid (17 Oct Newmarket 7f gd RF 4851) - also 1st of 6 from Munjiz (20 Aug York RF 3775). Quoted as low as 4-1 for the 2000 Guineas after a winning debut at York, his reputation had taken two sharp knocks by the end of the campaign. Beaten on merit by

Aljabr in the Prix de la Salamandre at Longchamp in September, he failed to quicken significantly when third behind Mujahid and Auction House in the Dewhurst Stakes at Newmarket in mid October. Connections have blamed soft and tacky ground for his defeats and, being essentially a speed horse, he may indeed require a firm surface. Aidan O'Brien has stated that the 2000 Guineas remains the aim, and his unstinting faith in this handsome colt makes him dangerous to dismiss.

**A P O'Brien in IRE [1-3] M Tabor & Mrs John Magnier.*

worn blinkers. Turf high 98 - 5th of 6 giving 5lb to Darnaway (16 May Newmarket 7f frm RF 1265). He failed to recapture his best form last term.

**Lady Herries [2-15] E Reitel (from J H M Gosden [2-4] Jly 1996).*

STREAKER BHB 26f RR 32f 4150[7]

3 gr f Petong 7.6f **(58)** - Northern Dynasty (Breeders Dream) 10.8f **(47)**

Form - 00007

Record 1998 - 1st:0 2nd:0 3rd:0 Ran:5

Stravinsky hits the right note at York

STRAVSEA BHB 43f50a RR 49f 50a 4504[13]

3 b f Handsome Sailor 6.6f **(53)**-La Stravaganza (Slip Anchor) 9.8f **(73)**

Form - 22522373000

Record				
1998 -	1st:0	2nd:4	3rd:2	Ran:11
Pre1998 -	1st:0	2nd:1	3rd:0	Ran:5

Win Prizemoney £0 *Total Prizemoney* £3,642

1998 Turf 0-3: (6f 2, 8f) (gd, frm 2) 1998 AW 0-8: (5f, 6f 3, 7f 4) (Fibr 8)

Scopey, fair filly, effective 6 to 7f, best at 6f, acts on gd - acts on Fibr. Turf high 49. AW high 61 - 2nd of 11 getting 11lb from Risky Whisky (14 Mar Wolverhampton 6f Fibr RF 0428). Becoming disappointing. She has finished runner-up in moderate company on turf and sand, and a seller is within her grasp.

**B P J Baugh [0-16] E Bennion.*

STRAZO (IRE) BHB 90f RR 91f 4467[11]

5 b g Alzao (USA) 9.8f **(73)** - Ministra (USA) (Deputy Minister (CAN)) 7.4f **(80)**

Form - 5500400

Record				
1998 -	1st:0	2nd:0	3rd:0	Ran:7
Pre1998 -	1st:4	2nd:2	3rd:0	Ran:12

Win Prizemoney £19,724 *Total Prizemoney* £28,371

Wins					
* 1997	Nov	Nottin (GD)	8.2f	100	<
* 1997	Oct	Newmar (G-F)	8f	94	
1996	Jun	Salisb (G-F)	7f	84	
1996	May	Chepst (G-S)	8.1f	82+	

1998 Turf 0-7: (7f, 8f 5, 10f) (gd 3, g-f 2, frm 2)

Useful gelding, effective 7 to 9f, acts on gd to frm, best on gd, has

1998 Turf 0-5: (8f 3, 10f, 11f) (g-f 2, frm 2, hrd)

Workmanlike, very moderate filly, has worn blinkers. Turf high 32.

**E A Wheeler [0-5] M F Kentish.*

STREAK FREE (IRE) BHB 65f RR 66f 4115[9]

2 b f Distinctly North (USA) 7.4f **(63)** - Camden Rye (Camden Town) 9.3f **(53)**

Form - 0460

Record 1998 - 1st:0 2nd:0 3rd:0 Ran:4

Win Prizemoney £0 *Total Prizemoney* £272

1998 Turf 0-3: (6f 2, 7f) (gd, g-f, frm) 1998 AW 0-1: (6f) (Fibr)

Average filly. Turf high 66 (began Aug).

**G C Bravery [0-4] M J Timms & Son Ltd.*

STREET GENERAL BHB 105f RR 107f 3754[F]

4 b c Generous (IRE) 11.5f **(82)** - Hotel Street (USA) (Alleged (USA)) 10f **(76)**

Form - 2232F

Record				
1998 -	1st:0	2nd:3	3rd:1	Ran:5
Pre1998 -	1st:1	2nd:1	3rd:1	Ran:3

Win Prizemoney £4,464 *Total Prizemoney* £25,792

Wins * 1997 Apr Newmar (GD) 12f 82 <

1998 Turf 0-5: (12f 2, 14f 3) (gd 3, frm 2)

Scopey, Pattern-class colt, effective 12 to 14f, best at 14f, acts on gd to frm, best on gd. Turf high 107 - 2nd of 15 giving 22lb to Seignorial (28 Jly Goodwood 14f gd RF 3163). He fell when still going well in the Tote Ebor, breaking three of Willie Ryan's ribs

but apparently returning without serious injury himself. Do not be put off by a pounding action that is better suited to kneading dough than galloping on fast ground - this game horse seems effective on any going. **H R A Cecil [1-8] Luciano Gaucci.*

STREET WALKER (IRE) RR 15f 5072[16]

2 b f Dolphin Street (FR) - Foolish Dame (USA) (Foolish Pleasure (USA)) 8.9f **(72)**
Form - 0
Record 1998 - 1st:0 2nd:0 3rd:0 Ran:1
1998 Turf 0-1: (7f) (gd)
Currently poor filly. **C F Wall [0-1] The Boardroom Syndicate.*

STRENGTH OF VISION BHB 28f30a RR 31f 30a 2545[12]

4 b g Unfuwain (USA) 11.4f **(74)** - Tootsiepop (USA) (Robellino (USA)) 7.6f **(80)**
Form - 00
Record 1998 - 1st:0 2nd:0 3rd:0 Ran:2
Pre1998 - 1st:0 2nd:1 3rd:0 Ran:5
Win Prizemoney £0 *Total Prizemoney* £1,050
1998 Turf 0-2: (10f, 12f) (g-f, frm)
Very moderate gelding. Turf high 15.
**C R Egerton [0-8] Austin Allison.*

best on g-s. Turf high 118 (1st run) - 1st of 6 giving 5lb to Palio Sky (7 May Chester RF 1071). Formerly trained in France, he moved to Venetia Williams' yard with the intention of going jumping, but showed that he still has what it takes on the Flat by winning the Ormonde Stakes in fine style. He did not figure in the Ascot Gold Cup, but connections still have a problem as to what to do with him from now on.
**Miss Venetia Williams [1-2] The Winning Line (Sport & Leisure) Ltd (from D Sepulchre in FR [4-6] Oct 1997).*

STRIDING KING BHB 69f60a RR 67f 60a 1926[5]

3 ch g King's Signet (USA) 7f **(51)** - Stride Home (Absalom) 7.2f **(58)**
Form - 2235
Record 1998 - 1st:0 2nd:2 3rd:1 Ran:4
Pre1998 - 1st:0 2nd:0 3rd:2 Ran:4
Win Prizemoney £0 *Total Prizemoney* £3,162
1998 Turf 0-1: (6f) (gd) 1998 AW 0-3: (6f, 7f 2) (Equi 2, Fibr)
Scopey, average gelding. AW high 51.
**M R Channon [0-8] Peter Taplin.*

STRIKE A BLOW (USA) BHB 100f RR 90f 4720a[1]

2 b c Red Ransom (USA) 8.6f **(83)** - Lilian Bayliss (IRE) (Sadler's Wells (USA)) 10f **(76)**

Stretarez (left) stretched the rest at Chester

STRETAREZ (FR) RR 118f 2085[10]

5 b h Saumarez 15.1f **(87)** -Street Opera (Sadler's Wells(USA)) 10f **(76)**
Form - 10
Record 1998 - 1st:1 2nd:0 3rd:0 Ran:2
Pre1998 - 1st:4 2nd:0 3rd:0 Ran:6
Win Prizemoney £139,659 *Total Prizemoney* £139,659

Wins								
	*1998	May	Cheste	(G-F)	G3	13.4f	118	
	1997	May	Longch	(SFT)	G2	15.5f	111	
	1997	Apr	Longch	(SFT)	G3	15.5f	114	
	1996	Nov	Nantes	(SFT)	L	12f	120	<
	1996	Oct	Deauvi	(G-S)	L	12.5f	101	

1998 Turf 1-2: (13f 1-1, 20f) (g-s, g-f 1-1)
High-class colt, effective 13 to 16f, best at 16f, acts on g-s to g-f,

Form - 2135111
Record 1998 - 1st:4 2nd:1 3rd:1 Ran:7
Win Prizemoney £55,171 *Total Prizemoney* £59,826

Wins								
	*1998	Oct	San Si	(HVY)	L	8f	90	<
	*1998	Jly	Maia	(G-S)	L	7.5f	83+	
	*1998	Jly	San Si	(G-F)	L	7.5f	83+	
	*1998	May	Haydoc	(GD)		6f	70+	

1998 Turf 4-7:(5f, 6f 1-2, 7f, 8f 3-3)(hvy 1-1, g-s1-1, gd 1-3, g-f 1-1, frm)
Useful colt, effective 8f, acts on hvy to g-f. Turf high 90 - 1st of 5 giving 2lb to Alabama Jacks (3 Oct San Siro RF 4720a) - also 1st of 6 from Canaima (19 Jly San Siro RF 3058a). Got off the mark in a Haydock maiden in May, but looked unsuited by the track at Epsom next time, despite staying on. Not disgraced in a Listed

race over seven furlongs at the July Meeting, he rattled up a hat-trick in Italy on various types of ground after that. The form of those victories is difficult to evaluate. **P F I Cole [4-7] J S Gutkin.*

STRIKE HARD (IRE) RR 111f 2804a[7]

3 b f Green Desert (USA) 7.8f **(78)** - Chinese Justice (USA) (Diesis) 9.3f **(69)**

Form - 11287

1998 Turf 2-5: (5f 2, 6f 2-3) (sft, gd 2-3, frm)

Group-class filly, effective 5f, acts on frm. Turf high 111 - 2nd of 7 getting 3lb from Lidanna (1 Jun Leopardstown 5f frm RF 1839a). Inconsistent. Presumably a 'good thing' when winning a handicap from a rating of 94 in May, she picked-up the Group Three Greenland Stakes later that month. That, however, was the end of the line.

**J Oxx in IRE [3-8] Sheikh Mohammed.*

STRILLO BHB 50f RR 57df 1304[16]

4 b g Safawan 6.6f **(60)** - Silvers Era (Balidar) 7.9f **(63)**

Form - 00

Record					
1998 -	1st:0	2nd:0	3rd:0	Ran:2
Pre1998 -	1st:0	2nd:0	3rd:0	Ran:2

1998 Turf 0-1: (8f) (g-s) 1998 AW 0-1: (8f) (Fibr)

Workmanlike, fair gelding. **N M Babbage [0-4] A M Tombs.*

STRINGERS (IRE) BHB 48f RR 48f 1713[9]

3 ch c Shalford (IRE) 7.8f **(63)** - Rebecca's Girl (IRE) (Nashamaa) 7.1f **(66)**

Form - 700

Record 1998 - 1st:0 2nd:0 3rd:0 Ran:3

1998 Turf 0-3: (7f, 10f 2) (g-s, gd 2)

Rangy, currently moderate colt. Turf high 48.

**S E Kettlewell [0-3] J S Calvert.*

STRIP SEARCH BHB 55f RR 62f 4463[8]

2 b f Bluebird (USA) 7.9f **(71)** - Swift Pursuit (Posse (USA)) 8.9f **(61)**

Form - 6808

Record 1998 - 1st:0 2nd:0 3rd:0 Ran:4

1998 Turf 0-4: (6f 3, 8f) (gd, frm 3)

Average filly. Turf high 62 (began Jly).

**J G Smyth-Osbourne [0-4] J G Smyth-Osbourne.*

STRONG CHOICE (IRE) BHB 50f46a RR 65f 46a 270[13]

6 br m Strong Gale - Innocent Choice (Deep Run) 18f **(46)**

Form - 30

Record					
1998 -	1st:0	2nd:0	3rd:1	Ran:2
Pre1998 -	1st:1	2nd:0	3rd:2	Ran:7

Win Prizemoney £2,740 *Total Prizemoney* £3,718

Wins 1997 Aug Tramor (GD) 14f 65 <

1998 AW 0-2: (12f, 13f) (Equi 2)

Average mare, effective 14 to 16f, acts on gd. AW high 35. Becoming disappointing.

**J W Mullins [0-4] Mrs Sandra McCarthy (from P Mullins in IRE [2-13] Spt 1997).*

STUDLEY PARK BHB 70f RR 64f 4053[1]

2 b f Northern Park (USA) 10f **(57)** - B A Poundstretcher (Laser Light) 9f **(68)**

Form - 301

Record 1998 - 1st:1 2nd:0 3rd:1 Ran:3

Win Prizemoney £7,226 *Total Prizemoney* £7,742

Wins * **1998** Spt York (GD) 7.9f 64 <

1998 Turf 1-3: (6f, 7f, 8f 1-1) (g-f, frm 1-2)

Currently average filly. Turf high 64 (began Jly) - 1st of 16 from Brenda Dee (2 Spt York RF 4053). Ran well on her debut, but was reportedly in season next time. Got up on the line to win an ordinary maiden auction at York on her third start.

**P Calver [1-3] The Ripon Ringers.*

STUFFED BHB 79f RR 76f 4872[6]

6 ch g Clantime 6.6f **(57)** - Puff Pastry (Reform) 8.9f **(62)**

Form - 25210006

Record					
1998 -	1st:1	2nd:2	3rd:0	Ran:8
Pre1998 -	1st:4	2nd:6	3rd:0	Ran:26

Win Prizemoney £36,470 *Total Prizemoney* £49,183

Wins								
* **1998**	May	York	(GD)	H	5f	80	83	<
* 1996	Oct	Newcas	(G-F)	H	5f	72	80	
* 1996	Oct	Pontef	(GD)	H	5f	72	74	
* 1996	Apr	Thirsk	(G-F)	H	5f	60	63	
* 1994	Jun	Thirsk	(FRM)	S	6f		58+	

1998 Turf 1-8: (5f 1-7, 6f) (hvy, g-s 2, gd 1-5)

Above-average gelding, effective 5f, acts on gd, has worn blinkers. Turf high 83 - 1st of 16 getting 20lb from Brave Edge (13 May York RF 1205). **M W Easterby [5-34] Early Morning Breakfast Syndicate.*

STURGEON (IRE) BHB 66f RR 69f 4132[6]

4 ch g Caerleon (USA) 10.9f **(79)** - Ridge The Times (USA) (Riva Ridge (USA)) 8.2f **(68)**

Form - 374466

Record					
1998 -	1st:0	2nd:0	3rd:1	Ran:6
Pre1998 -	1st:0	2nd:2	3rd:1	Ran:6

Win Prizemoney £0 *Total Prizemoney* £4,147

1998 Turf 0-6: (8f 2, 9f, 10f 2, 11f) (gd 2, g-f 4)

Strong, average gelding, effective 8f, acts on gd, favours tight tracks. Turf high 69. Consistent.

**K A Morgan [0-6] J Cleeve (from P F I Cole [0-6] Aug 1997).*

STUTTON GAL (IRE) BHB 38f42a RR 50f 42a 4818[25]

2 b f Up and At 'em - Sashi Woo (Rusticaro (FR)) 8.2f **(65)**

Form - 44000

Record 1998 - 1st:0 2nd:0 3rd:0 Ran:5

1998 Turf 0-4: (6f, 7f 2, 8f) (gd, g-f 2, frm) 1998 AW 0-1: (5f) (Fibr)

Fair filly. Turf high 50 (began Jly). **J Wharton [0-5] T A Hughes.*

STYLE DANCER (IRE) BHB 68f RR 73f 4520[6]

4 b g Dancing Dissident (USA) 6.8f **(65)** - Showing Style (Pas de Seul) 9.1f **(67)**

Form - 001675506

Record					
1998 -	1st:1	2nd:0	3rd:0	Ran:9
Pre1998 -	1st:1	2nd:3	3rd:6	Ran:22

Win Prizemoney £10,742 *Total Prizemoney* £19,176

Wins								
* **1998**	Jly	York	(FRM)	H	7f	70	73	<
* 1996	Oct	Redcar	(G-F)	H	6f	70	72	

1998 Turf 1-9: (6f 2, 7f 1-5, 8f 2) (gd 4, g-f 2, frm 1-2, hrd)

Leggy, above-average gelding, effective 6 to 7f, best at 6f, acts on gd to frm, best on gd, has worn blinkers (effectively), prefers left handed tracks, likes tight tracks, excels at Ripon. Turf high 73 - 1st of 10 getting 8lb from Saint Express (11 Jly York RF 2736).

**R M Whitaker [2-31] Mrs C A Hodgetts.*

STYLISH FLIGHT (USA) RR 48f 1937[15]

3 b g Alleged (USA) 11.8f **(81)** - Willa Joe (IRE) (El Gran Senor (USA)) 9.6f **(76)**

Form - 0

Record 1998 - 1st:0 2nd:0 3rd:0 Ran:1

1998 Turf 0-1: (10f) (gd)

Scopey, currently moderate gelding.

**E A L Dunlop [0-1] Maktoum Al Maktoum.*

STYLISH STORM (USA) BHB 70f RR 57f 4527[8]

3 b f Storm Bird (CAN) 8.5f **(82)**-Purify (USA) (Fappiano(USA)) 8.7f **(77)**

Form - 428

Record					
1998 -	1st:0	2nd:1	3rd:0	Ran:3
Pre1998 -	1st:0	2nd:0	3rd:0	Ran:1

Win Prizemoney £0 *Total Prizemoney* £1,654

1998 Turf 0-3: (7f, 8f, 10f) (g-f 2, frm)

Scopey, fair filly. Turf high 57 (began Aug) - 2nd of 8 getting 5lb from Seyaasi (31 Aug Newcastle 8f frm RF 3990).

**B W Hills [0-4] Newbyth Stud.*

STYLISH WAYS (IRE) BHB 77f RR 76f 5096[6]

6 b g Thatching 7.8f **(69)** - Style Of Life (USA) (The Minstrel (CAN)) 10f **(72)**

Form - 332237210156

Record					
1998 -	1st:2	2nd:3	3rd:3	Ran:12
Pre1998 -	1st:2	2nd:0	3rd:4	Ran:22

Win Prizemoney £20,706 *Total Prizemoney* £41,195

Wins								
* **1998**	Oct	Haydoc	(SFT)	H	6f	71	76	
* **1998**	Aug	Newmar	(G-F)	H	6f	67	69	
1995	May	Leices	(G-F)		6f		93	<
1994	Spt	Nottin	(SFT)		6.1f		89++	

1998 Turf 2-12: (6f 2-12) (hvy, sft 1-1, g-s 2, gd 2, g-f, frm 1-5)

Above-average gelding, effective 6f, acts on sft to frm. Turf high 76 - 1st of 23 giving 7lb to Juwwi (14 Oct Haydock RF 4799) - also 1st

Deservedly broke a lengthy losing run when scoring at Newmarket in August.
**J Pearce [2-18] Ian Hall (from Miss S E Hall [0-8] Nov 1996).*

SUALTACH (IRE) BHB 73f78a **RR 76f 78a** 4970[12]

5 b h Marju (IRE) 9.2f **(76)**-Astra Adastra (Mount Hagen (FR)) 8.4f **(70)**
Form - 521736156106285220241400010
Record 1998 - 1st:5 2nd:5 3rd:1 Ran:25
Pre1998 - 1st:4 2nd:4 3rd:2 Ran:34
Win Prizemoney £32,372 *Total Prizemoney* £48,896
Wins * **1998** Spt Haydoc (G-F) H 8.1f 70 72
* **1998** *Jly Wolver (STD) C 8.5f 76*
* **1998** *Apr Wolver (STD) H 8.5f 73 78*
* **1998** *Feb Wolver (STD) H 8.5f 72 71*
* **1998** *Jan Wolver (STD) H 9.4f 69 71*
* 1997 Oct Redcar (G-F) H 8f 69 74
* 1996 *May Wolver (STD) H 7f 70 81*
* 1996 Mar Doncas (SFT) H 7f 75 83
* 1995 Jun Nottin (G-F) 6.1f 87+ <
1998 Turf 1-13: (7f, 8f 1-9, 10f 3) (g-s, gd 4, g-f 5, frm 1-3) 1998 AW 4-12: (7f, 8f 3-6, 9f 1-5) (Fibr 4-12)
Above-average colt, effective 7 to 10f, best at 8f, acts on gd to frm - acts on Fibr, has worn blinkers, likes tight tracks, and excels at Haydock. Turf high 77 - 2nd of 8 giving 5lb to Sick As A Parrot (19 May Beverley 8f frm RF 1319) - also 1st of 11 getting 6lb from Bergen (25 Spt Haydock RF 4483). AW high 78 - 1st of 6 getting 4lb from Space Race (4 Apr Wolverhampton RF 0568) - also 1st of 10 giving 8lb to Yeoman Oliver (24 Jly Wolverhampton RF 3092). Inconsistent, and difficult to predict.
**R Hollinshead [9-59] Noel Sweeney.*

SUAVE FRANKIE BHB 55f **RR 57f** 5064[13]

2 ch c Suave Dancer (USA) 10.7f **(68)** - Francia **(58f)** (Legend of France (USA)) 9.5f **(61)**
Form - 000
Record 1998 - 1st:0 2nd:0 3rd:0 Ran:3
1998 Turf 0-3: (6f, 7f 2) (gd, g-f 2)
Currently fair colt. Turf high 57 (began Spt).
**S C Williams [0-3] Bruce Wyatt.*

SUBAROO SAM BHB 28a **RR 28a** 304[5]

4 gr g Arzanni - Nuns Little One (Celtic Cone) 9.8f **(43)**
Form - 075
Record 1998 - 1st:0 2nd:0 3rd:0 Ran:2
Pre1998 - 1st:0 2nd:0 3rd:0 Ran:1
1998 AW 0-2: (9f, 10f) (Equi, Fibr)
Very poor gelding. AW high 7. **J M Bradley [0-3] D A Jones.*

SUBEEN BHB 100f **RR 99f** 4539[3]

2 b f Caerleon (USA) 10.9f **(79)** - Khamsin (USA) (Mr Prospector (USA)) 8.8f **(78)**
Form - 313
Record 1998 - 1st:1 2nd:0 3rd:2 Ran:3
Win Prizemoney £3,781 *Total Prizemoney* £21,145
Wins * **1998** Spt Yarmou (G-S) 6f 87+ <
1998 Turf 1-3: (6f 1-3) (gd 1-1, frm 2)
Currently very useful filly. Turf high 99 (began Aug) - 3rd of 9 to Wannabe Grand (29 Spt Newmarket 6f frm RF 4539). Easy winner of a maiden before finishing third to Wannabe Grand in the Group One Cheveley Park Stakes. A pacey filly, she has more improvement in her, and will probably stay a mile.
**D R Loder [1-3] Maktoum Al Maktoum.*

SUBITO BHB 100f **RR 94f** 4853[13]

2 b f Darshaan 11.9f **(81)** - Rapid Repeat (IRE) (Exactly Sharp (USA))
Form - 2510
Record 1998 - 1st:1 2nd:1 3rd:0 Ran:4
Win Prizemoney £12,486 *Total Prizemoney* £13,716
Wins * **1998** Spt Ascot (GD) 7f 94 <
1998 Turf 1-4: (7f 1-3, 8f) (gd 1-3, frm)
Useful filly. Turf high 94 (began Aug) - 1st of 8 getting 3lb from Intimaa (26 Spt Ascot RF 4495). Ran a cracker on her debut, and was far from disgraced in the May Hill. She got off the mark with a clear-cut victory in the Blue Seal at Ascot but was most disappointing next time. She should have little difficulty staying a mile plus at three. **L M Cumani [1-4] Lord Hartington.*

SUBTLE INFLUENCE (IRE) BHB 88f **RR 87f** 2640[4]

4 b c Sadler's Wells (USA) 11.3f **(87)** - Campestral (USA) (Alleged (USA)) 10f **(76)**
Form - 0440534
Record 1998 - 1st:0 2nd:0 3rd:1 Ran:7
Win Prizemoney £0 *Total Prizemoney* £4,353
1998 Turf 0-7: (10f, 12f 3, 16f 3) (sft, gd 4, g-f, frm)
Useful colt, effective 16f, acts on sft to frm, has worn blinkers. Turf high 87 - 3rd of 12 giving 1lb to Life of Riley (4 Jly Sandown 16f gd RF 2551). He has faced some very difficult tasks this season and has taken time to find his form, but ran a couple of good races in July. **N A Callaghan [0-7] M Tabor.*

SUCCESS AND GLORY (IRE) BHB 100f **RR 101f** 1963[3]

3 b c Alzao (USA) 9.8f **(73)** - More Fizz (Morston (FR)) 9.4f **(55)**
Form - 123
Record 1998 - 1st:1 2nd:1 3rd:1 Ran:3
Pre1998 - 1st:1 2nd:1 3rd:1 Ran:4
Win Prizemoney £8,969 *Total Prizemoney* £14,025
Wins * **1998** May Bath (FRM) 10.2f 95 <
* 1997 Spt Newmar (G-F) 8f 93
1998 Turf 1-3: (10f 1-1, 11f, 12f) (gd, g-f, frm 1-1)
Neat, very useful colt, effective 8 to 11f, acts on g-f to frm, best on g-f. Turf high 101 - 2nd of 4 giving 3lb to Opera King (30 May Lingfield 11f g-f RF 1598) - also 1st of 4 from Secret Saver (18 May Bath RF 1293). He lacks pace and is best when able to dominate. He is surely worth a try beyond middle-distances.
**H R A Cecil [2-7] The Thoroughbred Corporation.*

SUCH BOLDNESS BHB 56f **RR 58f** 5098[3]

4 b c Persian Bold 10f **(69)** - Bone China (IRE) (Sadler's Wells (USA)) 10f **(76)**
Form - 3373443
Record 1998 - 1st:0 2nd:0 3rd:4 Ran:7
Pre1998 - 1st:0 2nd:1 3rd:0 Ran:3
Win Prizemoney £0 *Total Prizemoney* £2,818
1998 Turf 0-7: (10f, 12f 2, 14f 3, 17f) (gd 3, g-f, frm 3)
Workmanlike, fair colt, effective 12f, acts on gd, likes tight tracks. Turf high 63. Consistent.
**Miss Gay Kelleway [0-7] Mrs M E O'Shea (from R Akehurst [0-3] Jly 1997).*

SUDDEN SPIN BHB 31f65a **RR 33f 65a** 514[13]

8 b g Doulab (USA) 7.4f **(61)** - Lightning Legacy (USA) (Super Concorde (USA)) 10.9f **(66)**
Form - 0
Record 1998 - 1st:0 2nd:0 3rd:0 Ran:1
Pre1998 - 1st:6 2nd:1 3rd:6 Ran:42
Win Prizemoney £18,061 *Total Prizemoney* £22,143
Wins * 1997 *Jan Southw (STD) H 16f 61 67* <
* 1996 Apr Beverl (G-F) H 16.2f 42 50
1995 *Spt Wolver (STD) H 9.4f 58 64*
1995 *Jun Southw (STD) C 11f 64*
1995 *Jan Southw (STD) H 11f 40 44+*
1998 Turf 0-1: (16f) (gd)
Average gelding, effective 16f, - acts on Fibr, has worn blinkers (extremely effectively), likes left handed tracks, likes tight tracks. Becoming disappointing.
**J Norton [2-20] Billy Parker (from S G Norton [5-15] Nov 1995).*

SUDDEN SQUALL (USA) BHB 79f **RR 76f** 4960[3]

2 ch c Gulch (USA) 9.6f **(79)** - Sudden Storm Bird (USA) (Storm Bird (CAN)) 10.3f **(74)**
Form - 66513
Record 1998 - 1st:1 2nd:0 3rd:1 Ran:5
Win Prizemoney £3,494 *Total Prizemoney* £4,074
Wins * **1998** Oct Lingfi (SFT) H 7f 71 76 <
1998 Turf 1-5: (7f 1-3, 8f, 9f) (g-s 1-1, gd 2, g-f, frm)
Above-average colt. Turf high 76 (began Jly) - 3rd of 11 giving 7lb to Crackle (23 Oct Doncaster 8f frm RF 4960) - also 1st of 18 giving 10lb to Patsy Stone (2 Oct Lingfield RF 4613). Ridden differently when winning a maiden, having shown a wayward streak in his earlier races. **J H M Gosden [1-5] Sheikh Mohammed.*

SUDEST (IRE) BHB 64f **RR 66f** 4958[9]

4 b g Taufan (USA) 8.3f **(65)** - Frill (Henbit (USA)) 9f **(61)**
Form - 0884200

Record 1998 - 1st:0 2nd:1 3rd:0 Ran:7
Pre1998 - 1st:3 2nd:1 3rd:1 Ran:14
Win Prizemoney £9,648 *Total Prizemoney* £13,633
Wins * 1997 Jun Bath (G-F) 11.7f 73 <
* 1997 May Bath (G-F) H 17.2f 64 69
* 1997 May Warwic (FRM) H 12.5f 59 64
1998 Turf 0-7: (12f, 14f, 15f 2, 16f 3) (hvy, sft, g-s, gd, g-f 2, frm)
Workmanlike, average gelding, effective 12 to 17f, acts on gd to frm, best on frm, prefers left handed tracks, excels at Bath. Turf high 66 - 2nd of 9 getting 4lb from Puteri Wentworth (27 Jun Doncaster 15f gd RF 2334). Inconsistent.
**I A Balding [3-21] Robert Hitchins.*

SUEDORO BHB 38f **RR 34f** 4771[15]

8 b m Hard Fought 8.9f **(51)** - Bamdoro (Cavo Doro) 10.6f **(57)**
Form - 00000
Record 1998 - 1st:0 2nd:0 3rd:0 Ran:5
Pre1998 - 1st:4 2nd:0 3rd:4 Ran:39
Win Prizemoney £12,979 *Total Prizemoney* £15,585
Wins * 1997 Spt Hamilt (G-S) H 5f 40 45
1995 Aug Hamilt (FRM) H 6f 45 46 <
1995 Jly Hamilt (FRM) H 6f 40 42
1995 Jun Hamilt (FRM) H 6f 41 45
1998 Turf 0-5: (5f 3, 6f 2) (sft, g-s, gd, g-f, frm)
Very moderate mare, effective 5 to 6f, best at 6f, acts on gd to frm, does well at Hamilton. Turf high 34 (began Aug).
**J S Goldie [1-22] Tough Construction Ltd (from R M McKellar [3-16] Jly 1996).*

SUELLAJOY BHB 49f51a **RR 44f 51a** 4869[8]

3 ch f Weldnaas (USA) 8.4f **(55)** - Jeethgaya (USA) (Critique (USA))
Form - 030408
Record 1998 - 1st:0 2nd:0 3rd:1 Ran:6
Pre1998 - 1st:0 2nd:0 3rd:1 Ran:3
Win Prizemoney £0 *Total Prizemoney* £1,278
1998 Turf 0-5: (10f 2, 12f 2, 13f) (sft, g-s, gd 2, g-f) 1998 AW 0-1: (8f) (Fibr)
Workmanlike, moderate filly, effective 8f, acts on gd, has worn blinkers. Turf high 49. **B Smart [0-9] K H Burks.*

SUE ME (IRE) BHB 73f63a **RR 70f 63a** 4771[14]

6 b or br g Contract Law (USA) 8.9f **(54)** - Pink Fondant (Northfields (USA)) 9f **(72)**
Form - 4311004015664102577O120
Record 1998 - 1st:5 2nd:2 3rd:1 Ran:23
Pre1998 - 1st:1 2nd:4 3rd:4 Ran:37
Win Prizemoney £20,333 *Total Prizemoney* £30,912
Wins * **1998** *Spt Southw (STD) H 6f 56 58*
* **1998** Jly Doncas (G-F) H 5f 62 68
* **1998** Apr Pontef (G-S) H 5f 59 62
* **1998** *Feb Southw (STD) H 6f 43 49*
* **1998** *Jan Southw (STD) H 6f 44 45*
1994 Oct York (SFT) H 6f 65 75
1998 Turf 2-15: (5f 2-9, 6f 6) (sft 2, g-s 1-5, gd 3, g-f, frm 1-4) 1998 AW 3-8: (5f 2, 6f 3-5, 7f) (Fibr 3-8)
Above-average gelding, effective 5f, acts on g-s to frm, best on frm, has worn blinkers, likes left handed tracks, likes tight tracks, excels at Southwell. Turf high 70 - 2nd of 23 to Maladerie (7 Oct York 5f gd RF 4701) - also 1st of 15 giving 7lb to Ajnad (15 Jly Doncaster RF 2814). AW high 58.
**D Nicholls [5-30] T G Meynell (from W R Muir [1-30] Jan 1997).*

SUEZ TORNADO (IRE) BHB 59f64a **RR 59f 64a** 5114[4]

5 ch g Mujtahid (USA) 7.4f **(69)** - So Stylish (Great Nephew) 9.9f **(64)**
Form - 5454340207044
Record 1998 - 1st:0 2nd:1 3rd:1 Ran:13
Pre1998 - 1st:2 2nd:0 3rd:2 Ran:26
Win Prizemoney £7,242 *Total Prizemoney* £14,602
Wins * 1997 Jun Newmar (G-S) H 8f 61 63
1996 Jly Killar (GD) 8.5f 68 <
1998 Turf 0-9: (8f 9) (gd 5, g-f 2, frm 2)1998 AW 0-4: (8f 2, 9f 2) (Fibr 4)
Average gelding, effective 7 to 8f, acts on gd to frm, often wears blinkers. Turf high 62 (began Jly). AW high 64. Ex-Irish, he had been out of sorts in '98 until putting in a decent run at York in September. Needs at least a stiff seven and acts on softish ground.
**E J Alston [1-32] Papermates Racing (from D K Weld in IRE [1-7] Aug 1996).*

SUGA HAWK (IRE) BHB 62f55a **RR 65f 55a** 1578[10]

6 b g Pennine Walk 8.9f **(64)** - Ishtar Abu (St Chad) 6.7f **(67)**
Form - 623650
Record 1998 - 1st:0 2nd:1 3rd:1 Ran:6
Pre1998 - 1st:2 2nd:1 3rd:5 Ran:22
Win Prizemoney £6,203 *Total Prizemoney* £11,597
Wins 1997 Aug Ripon (G-F) H 12.3f 58 65 <
1997 Mar Wolver (STD) H 9.4f 54 60
1998 AW 0-6: (9f, 11f, 12f 3, 15f) (Fibr 6)
Average gelding, effective 9 to 12f, best at 12f, acts on gd to frm - acts on Fibr, best on frm, has worn blinkers. AW high 57 - 2nd of 7 getting 12lb from Montecristo (11 Feb Wolverhampton 12f Fibr RF 0267). Inconsistent.
**J G M O'Shea [0-1] Graham Brown (from E J Alston [2-22] Mar 1998).*

SUGAR CUBE TREAT BHB 59f **RR 65f** 4447[10]

2 b f Lugana Beach 7f **(63)** - Fair Eleanor (Saritamer (USA)) 9.5f **(63)**
Form - 8445300
Record 1998 - 1st:0 2nd:0 3rd:1 Ran:7
Win Prizemoney £0 *Total Prizemoney* £981
1998 Turf 0-7: (5f 4, 7f 2, 8f) (g-s, gd 3, g-f, frm 2)
Average filly, effective 7f, acts on gd. Turf high 65 - 3rd of 12 getting 19lb from Tony Tie (22 Aug Chester 7f gd RF 3803).
**M Mullineaux [0-7] Abbey Racing.*

SUGAR DANCE BHB 47f **RR 46f** 4506[14]

3 b c Salse (USA) 10.9f **(71)** - Springtime Sugar (USA) (Halo (USA)) 10.6f **(75)**
Form - 06000
Record 1998 - 1st:0 2nd:0 3rd:0 Ran:5
1998 Turf 0-5: (10f, 12f 3, 14f) (gd 3, frm 2)
Workmanlike, moderate colt, has worn blinkers. Turf high 46.
**M J Heaton-Ellis [0-5] John Manser.*

SUGARFOOT BHB 104f **RR 104f** 4700[1]

4 ch c Thatching 7.8f **(69)** - Norpella (Northfields (USA)) 9f **(72)**
Form - 0024215121
Record 1998 - 1st:3 2nd:3 3rd:0 Ran:10
Pre1998 - 1st:1 2nd:1 3rd:1 Ran:6
Win Prizemoney £55,834 *Total Prizemoney* £85,261
Wins * **1998** Oct York (GD) H 7.9f 99 104 <
* **1998** Aug York (FRM) H 7.9f 92 97
* **1998** Jly Ascot (G-F) H 8f 87 92
* 1996 Jly Ayr (G-F) 6f 82+
1998 Turf 3-10: (7f 3, 8f 3-5, 10f 2) (gd 5, g-f 2-4, frm 1-1)
Scopey, very useful colt, effective 7 to 8f, best at 8f, acts on gd to frm. Turf high 104 - 1st of 7 giving 13lb to China Red (7 Oct York RF 4700) - also 1st of 14 from Generous Rosi (20 Aug York RF 3774). Improving. He did connections proud, winning three valuable handicaps and invariably grabbing a share of the prize money. Game and progressive, he is well worth a chance in Listed company. **N Tinkler [4-16] Mrs D Wright.*

SUGAR PLUM BHB 50f47a **RR 40f 47a** 314[7]

4 br f Primo Dominie 7.2f **(67)** - Ile de Danse (Ile de Bourbon (USA)) 10.1f **(67)**
Form - 7
Record 1998 - 1st:0 2nd:0 3rd:0 Ran:1
Pre1998 - 1st:0 2nd:0 3rd:0 Ran:4
1998 AW 0-1: (10f) (Equi)
Workmanlike, moderate filly.
**W G M Turner [0-1] Major R P Thorman (from R Hannon [0-4] May 1997).*

SUGGEST BHB 47f **RR 50f** 5062[5]

3 b g Midyan (USA) 9.9f **(64)**-Awham (USA) (Lear Fan (USA)) 8.5f **(73)**
Form - 80080365006235
Record 1998 - 1st:0 2nd:1 3rd:2 Ran:14
Pre1998 - 1st:2 2nd:0 3rd:0 Ran:7
Win Prizemoney £6,630 *Total Prizemoney* £9,138
Wins * 1997 Aug Newmar (G-F) S 7f 70 <
* 1997 Aug Thirsk (GD) C 7f 70 <
1998 Turf 0-14: (7f, 8f 3, 9f, 10f, 11f, 12f 6, 16f) (sft, gd 5, g-f 4, frm 3, hrd)
Fair gelding, effective 7f, acts on g-f to frm, has worn blinkers. Turf high 50. **W Storey [2-18] Mrs M Tindale (from M Meade [0-1] Jly 1997).*

Sugarfoot (nearside) tasted success three times last season

SUHAIL (IRE) RR 52f 3833[9]
2 b c Wolfhound (USA) 7.3f **(71)** - Sharayif (IRE) (Green Desert (USA)) 8.6f **(78)**
Form - 00
Record 1998 - 1st:0 2nd:0 3rd:0 Ran:2
1998 Turf 0-2: (7f, 8f) (g-f 2)
Currently fair colt. Turf high 52 (began Jly).
**B Hanbury [0-2] Hamdan Al Maktoum.*

SUITE FACTORS BHB 68f47a **RR 69f 47a** 5127[10]
4 b g Timeless Times (USA) 6.1f **(56)** - Uptown Girl (Caruso) 5.8f **(63)**
Form - 20413136180
Record 1998 - 1st:3 2nd:1 3rd:2 Ran:11
Pre1998 - 1st:1 2nd:7 3rd:5 Ran:34
Win Prizemoney £11,343 *Total Prizemoney* £22,904

Wins								
* **1998**	Spt	Yarmou	(G-S)	H	7f	63	69	
* **1998**	Aug	Folkes	(G-F)	H	6f	46	62	
* **1998**	Jly	Folkes	(G-F)	H	7f	46	60	
1996	Aug	Nottin	(G-F)	C	5.1f		71	<

1998 Turf 3-10: (5f, 6f 1-3, 7f 2-6) (g-s, gd 2-2, g-f 4, frm 1-3) 1998 AW 0-1: (6f) (Fibr)
Light-framed, average gelding, effective 5 to 7f, best at 6f, acts on gd to frm, has worn blinkers. Turf high 69 - 1st of 18 getting 3lb from Marigliano (16 Spt Yarmouth RF 4317) - also 1st of 13 getting 16lb from Bandbox (6 Aug Folkestone RF 3401). Made all for his three victories.
**K R Burke [3-39] Nigel Shields (from J A Glover [1-6] Aug 1996).*

SUJUD (IRE) BHB 33f45a **RR 29f 45a** 2772[7]
6 b br m Shaadi (USA) 8.1f **(75)** - Sit Elnaas (USA) (Sir Ivor) 10.2f **(70)**
Form - 07
Record 1998 - 1st:0 2nd:0 3rd:0 Ran:2
Pre1998 - 1st:0 2nd:1 3rd:1 Ran:10
Win Prizemoney £0 *Total Prizemoney* £1,775
1998 Turf 0-2: (16f 2) (frm 2)
Very moderate mare. Turf high 29. Becoming disappointing.
**M A Peill [0-2] D J Lever (from M D Hammond [2-4] Mar 1997).*

SUKOON (IRE) RR 69?f 3427[8]
3 b f Shareef Dancer (USA) 10.1f **(67)** - Mist of the Marsh (USA) (Seattle Slew (USA)) 9.4f **(76)**
Form - 8
Record 1998 - 1st:0 2nd:0 3rd:0 Ran:1
1998 Turf 0-1: (8f) (g-f)
Scopey, currently average filly. Ex-German filly, out of her depth on her British debut. **E A L Dunlop [0-1] Jaber Abdullah.*

SULALAT RR 71f 1792[5]
2 br f Hamas (IRE) 8f **(72)** - Enaya (Caerleon (USA)) 8.6f **(71)**
Form - 5
Record 1998 - 1st:0 2nd:0 3rd:0 Ran:1
1998 Turf 0-1: (6f) (hrd)
Currently above-average filly.
**R W Armstrong [0-1] Hamdan Al Maktoum.*

SULAWESI (IRE) BHB 48f **RR 60f** 3315[9]
5 b m In The Wings 11.2f **(77)** - Royal Loft (Homing) 7.8f **(59)**
Form - 0
Record 1998 - 1st:0 2nd:0 3rd:0 Ran:1
Pre1998 - 1st:0 2nd:0 3rd:0 Ran:3
1998 Turf 0-1: (12f) (frm)
Average filly. Lightly-raced in recent seasons, she won a handicap hurdle very easily at Kempton in October and should win again.
**N A Twiston-Davies [2-7] Jack Joseph (from W Jarvis [0-3] Oct 1996).*

SULEYMAN BHB 64f68a **RR 70df 68a** 5003[3]
3 b c Alhijaz 7.7f **(57)** - Aonia (Mummy's Pet) 7.7f **(60)**
Form - 83030813
Record 1998 - 1st:1 2nd:0 3rd:3 Ran:8
Win Prizemoney £2,406 *Total Prizemoney* £3,599
Wins * **1998** *Oct Southw (STD) 6f 73 <*
1998 Turf 0-5: (8f 4, 10f) (g-f 3, frm 2) 1998 AW 1-3: (6f 1-1, 7f, 9f) (Equi, Fibr 1-2)
Unfurnished, above-average colt, effective 6 to 7f, - acts on AW, often wears blinkers (extremely effectively), favours tight tracks.

Turf high 70. AW high 73 (began Aug) - 1st of 13 from Ellway Prince (19 Oct Southwell RF 4877). He has shown his best form on sand, and was quite impressive when winning a Southwell maiden in October. He can probably win more races on that surface for his new handler, David Nicholls.

**R Charlton [1-8] Lady Annabel Goldsmith.*

SULTANA BHB 82f **RR 80f** 3209[9]

3 b f Unfuwain (USA) 11.4f **(74)** - Lambay (Lorenzaccio) 10f **(64)**

Form - 1450

Record 1998 - 1st:1 2nd:0 3rd:0 Ran:4

Win Prizemoney £5,127 *Total Prizemoney* £6,193

Wins * **1998** Apr Newmar (SFT) 7f 77 <

1998 Turf 1-4: (7f 1-1, 8f, 9f, 10f) (sft 1-1, gd, g-f 2)

Scopey, decent filly. Turf high 80 - also 1st of 15 from Aloha Dancer (15 Apr Newmarket RF 0699). From a decent family, she sprang a 50/1 surprise in a maiden at the Craven Meeting. She has not gone on from that though she has faced some stiff tasks.

**J G Smyth-Osbourne [1-4] Lady Rothschild.*

SULU (IRE) RR 62f 2274[4]

2 b c Elbio 9f **(62)** - Foxy Fairy (IRE) (Fairy King (USA)) 7.7f **(59)**

Form - 4

Record 1998 - 1st:0 2nd:0 3rd:0 Ran:1

1998 Turf 0-1: (7f) (frm)

Currently average colt. (1st run) - 4th of 18 to Kingston Venture (25 Jun Salisbury 7f frm RF 2274). **I A Balding [0-1] Robert Hitchins.*

SUMBAWA (IRE) BHB 38f41a **RR 57f 41a** 4574[16]

3 ch f Magic Ring (IRE) 6.5f **(64)** - Tittlemouse (Castle Keep) 8.3f **(57)**

Form - 0547440050

Record 1998 - 1st:0 2nd:0 3rd:0 Ran:10

Pre1998 - 1st:0 2nd:0 3rd:0 Ran:3

Win Prizemoney £0 *Total Prizemoney* £212

1998 Turf 0-9: (8f 4, 10f 3, 11f, 12f) (g-s, gd, g-f 3, frm 4) 1998 AW 0-1: (8f) (Fibr)

Leggy, fair filly, has worn blinkers. Turf high 57.

**D HaydnJones [0-13] J K Ruggles & Mrs A R Ruggles.*

SUMITAS (GER) RR 98++f 4946a[1]

2 br c Lomitas - Subia (GER) (Konigsstuhl (GER)) 11.2f **(76)**

Form - 1

1998 Turf 1-1: (8f 1-1) (hvy 1-1)

Currently very useful colt. (1st run) - 1st of 11 from Kaldono (18 Oct Cologne RF 4946a). Very promising German colt, one to keep a close eye on. **P Schiergen in GER [1-1] Baron G Von Ullmann.*

SUMMER BOUNTY BHB 78f **RR 69f** 4568[5]

2 b c Lugana Beach 7f **(63)** - Tender Moment (IRE) (Caerleon (USA)) 8.6f **(71)**

Form - 035

Record 1998 - 1st:0 2nd:0 3rd:1 Ran:3

Win Prizemoney £0 *Total Prizemoney* £820

1998 Turf 0-3: (7f 3) (gd, g-f, frm)

Currently average colt. Turf high 69 (began Aug).

**B W Hills [0-3] Ray Richards.*

SUMMER BREEZE RR 100f 5051a[3]

2 br f Rainbow Quest (USA) 11.2f **(81)** - Suntrap (USA) (Roberto (USA)) 10f **(76)**

Form - 3

1998 Turf 0-1: (8f) (hvy)

Currently very useful filly. (1st run) - 3rd of 6 to Comillas (20 Oct Deauville 8f hvy RF 5051a). **A Fabre in FR [0-1] K Abdullah.*

SUMMER DAY BLUES (IRE) BHB 47f **RR 32f** 2258[11]

3 b f Petorius 8f **(66)** - Atmospheric Blues (IRE) (Double Schwartz) 7.9f **(55)**

Form - 0000

Record 1998 - 1st:0 2nd:0 3rd:0 Ran:4

Pre1998 - 1st:0 2nd:0 3rd:0 Ran:4

1998 Turf 0-4: (5f 2, 6f 2) (g-s, gd, frm 2)

Workmanlike, very moderate filly, has worn blinkers. Turf high 32. Consistent.

**C F Wall [0-4] David Crichton-Watt (from C Murray [0-4] Jly 1997).*

SUMMER DEAL (USA) BHB 79f81a **RR 77df 81a** 2529[5]

3 b f Summer Squall (USA) 7f **(80)** - Dariela (USA) (Manila (USA)) 9.3f **(71)**

Form - 32245

Record 1998 - 1st:0 2nd:2 3rd:0 Ran:4

Pre1998 - 1st:0 2nd:3 3rd:4 Ran:9

Win Prizemoney £0 *Total Prizemoney* £8,897

1998 Turf 0-3: (7f 3) (gd, g-f, frm) 1998 AW 0-1: (6f) (Fibr)

Unfurnished, decent filly, effective 5 to 8f, best at 7f, acts on gd to frm, best on frm, has worn blinkers. Turf high 77 (1st run) - 2nd of 12 to Aloha Dancer (23 May Warwick 7f frm RF 1439). She has reached the frame a number of times, but is a disappointing sort.

**P F I Cole [0-13] M Arbib.*

SUMMERHILL SPECIAL (IRE) BHB 58f **RR 58f** 5119[12]

7 b m Roi Danzig (USA) 10.5f **(62)** -Special Thanks (Kampala) 8.5f **(56)**

Form - 64120202465020500

Record 1998 - 1st:1 2nd:4 3rd:0 Ran:17

Pre1998 - 1st:4 2nd:3 3rd:0 Ran:30

Win Prizemoney £13,560 *Total Prizemoney* £21,454

Wins * **1998** May Mussel (GD) H 12f 63 68

* 1997 Aug Catter (G-F) H 12f 65 71 <

* 1997 May Ayr (G-F) 13.1f 60

* 1997 Apr Ripon (G-F) H 12.3f 55 59

1996 Oct Folkes (G-S) H 12f 45 55

1998 Turf 1-17: (10f, 12f 1-16) (sft, g-s 3, gd 6, g-f 1-2, frm 5)

Fair mare, effective 11 to 12f, best at 12f, acts on sft to frm, best on g-f, has worn blinkers, likes right handed tracks, likes tight tracks, and excels at Ripon. Turf high 69 - 2nd of 10 giving 28lb to Nosey Native (18 Jun Ripon 12f g-s RF 2093) - also 1st of 8 giving 4lb to Mr Fortywinks (1 May Musselburgh RF 0956). A truly-run twelve furlongs on fast ground suits her best.

**D W Barker [4-37] Alba Racing Syndicate (from Mrs P N Dutfield [2-24] Oct 1996).*

SUMMER MIST (USA) RR 75f 3954[3]

3 b f Miswaki (USA) 8.1f **(81)** - Miss Summer (Luthier) 9.8f **(71)**

Form - 3

Record 1998 - 1st:0 2nd:0 3rd:1 Ran:1

Win Prizemoney £0 *Total Prizemoney* £678

1998 Turf 0-1: (8f) (frm)

Well made, currently above-average filly. (1st run) - 3rd of 9 getting 5lb from Cool Vibes (29 Aug Newmarket 8f frm RF 3954).

**R Charlton [0-1] K Abdulla.*

SUMMER QUEEN BHB 63f55a **RR 65f 55a** 5003[12]

4 b f Robellino (USA) 9.5f **(68)** - Carolside (Music Maestro) 7.7f **(66)**

Form - 626530357740

Record 1998 - 1st:0 2nd:1 3rd:2 Ran:12

Pre1998 - 1st:1 2nd:0 3rd:2 Ran:11

Win Prizemoney £6,408 *Total Prizemoney* £9,052

Wins * 1997 Apr Newmar (GD) H 7f 72 79 <

1998 Turf 0-10: (6f 2, 7f 8) (sft, gd 3, g-f 4, frm 2) 1998 AW 0-2: (7f 2) (Equi, Fibr)

Unfurnished, average filly, effective 7f, acts on gd to frm, has worn blinkers. Turf high 68. AW high 43 (began Jly).

**S P C Woods [1-23] Arashan Ali.*

SUMMERSEAT BHB 60f64a **RR 42f 64a** 12[4]

3 b f Thatching 7.8f **(69)** - Sudden Hope (FR) (Darshaan) 9.9f **(84)**

Form - 0114

Record 1998 - 1st:0 2nd:0 3rd:0 Ran:1

Pre1998 - 1st:3 2nd:0 3rd:1 Ran:8

Win Prizemoney £6,508 *Total Prizemoney* £7,198

Wins * 1997 *Dec Southw (STD) H 5f 62 68* <

* 1997 *Nov Wolver (STD) S 7f 63*

1997 *May Wolver (STD) S 5f 56*

1998 AW 0-1: (6f) (Fibr)

Leggy, average filly, effective 5 to 7f, - acts on Fibr, has worn blinkers.

**G Holmes [2-5] Miss J Salt (from C W Fairhurst [1-4] Spt 1997).*

SUMMER SPELL (USA) BHB 95f **RR 100f** 1780[8]

5 b br g Alleged (USA) 11.8f **(81)** - Summertime Lady (USA) (No Robbery) 8.7f **(80)**

Form - 8

Record 1998 - 1st:0 2nd:0 3rd:0 Ran:1

Pre1998 - 1st:1 2nd:1 3rd:1 Ran:5
Win Prizemoney £3,785 *Total Prizemoney* £8,237
Wins 1996 Mar Doncas (G-S) 10.3f 92 <
1998 Turf 0-1: (12f) (g-f)
Very useful gelding. (DEAD)
**N J Henderson [2-10] W V M W & Mrs E S Robins (from R Charlton [1-5] Oct 1996).*

SUMMER SPLENDOUR (USA) RR 78f 4505[3]

2 ch f Summer Squall (USA) 7f **(80)** - Sin Lucha (USA) (Northfields (USA)) 9f **(72)**
Form - 23
Record 1998 - 1st:0 2nd:1 3rd:1 Ran:2
Win Prizemoney £0 *Total Prizemoney* £1,635
1998 Turf 0-2: (8f 2) (gd 2)
Currently above-average filly. Turf high 78 (1st run) (began Aug) - 2nd of 7 to El Nafis (31 Aug Chepstow 8f gd RF 3977).
**B W Hills [0-2] K Abdulla.*

SUMMER THYME BHB 40f RR 33f 828[11]

4 b f Henbit (USA) 10.2f **(46)** - Hasty Sarah (Gone Native)
Form - 0
Record 1998 - 1st:0 2nd:0 3rd:0 Ran:1
Pre1998 - 1st:0 2nd:0 3rd:1 Ran:3
Win Prizemoney £0 *Total Prizemoney* £507
1998 Turf 0-1: (10f) (g-s)
Light-framed, very moderate filly. **J Berry [0-4] Mrs Brigitte Pollard.*

SUMMERVILLE WOOD BHB 51f37a RR 49f 37a 133[7]

4 b g Nomination 7.3f **(57)** - Four Love (Pas de Seul) 9.1f **(67)**
Form - 007
Record 1998 - 1st:0 2nd:0 3rd:0 Ran:1
Pre1998 - 1st:2 2nd:0 3rd:4 Ran:22
Win Prizemoney £4,186 *Total Prizemoney* £6,110
Wins * 1997 Apr Folkes (G-F) H 6f 58 64 <
* 1996 Aug Nottin (G-F) S 6.1f 58
1998 AW 0-1: (8f) (Equi)
Workmanlike, moderate gelding, effective 6f, acts on gd, often wears blinkers. **P Mooney [2-23] Likely Lads Partnership.*

SUMO AGAIN (IRE) BHB 38f RR 30f 4762[17]

2 ch g Then Again 7.4f **(52)** - Foresta Verde (USA) **(24f 42a)** (Green Forest (USA)) 9.9f **(68)**
Form - 8000
Record 1998 - 1st:0 2nd:0 3rd:0 Ran:4
1998 Turf 0-3: (8f, 10f 2) (gd, g-f 2) 1998 AW 0-1: (7f) (Fibr)
Very moderate gelding, has worn blinkers. Turf high 30 (began Spt). **M Quinn [0-4] M Quinn.*

SUN ALERT (USA) BHB 34f31a RR 33f 31a 3504[4]

4 b f Alysheba (USA) 12.1f **(78)**-Sunerta (USA) (Roberto (USA))10f **(76)**
Form - 77330084
Record 1998 - 1st:0 2nd:0 3rd:2 Ran:8
Pre1998 - 1st:1 2nd:0 3rd:3 Ran:15
Win Prizemoney £3,826 *Total Prizemoney* £7,341
Wins * 1997 Jun Yarmou (GD) 14.1f 70 <
1998 Turf 0-6: (12f 2, 15f, 16f, 17f, 22f) (sft, g-s, gd 2, frm, hrd) 1998 AW 0-2: (12f, 16f) (Equi 2)
Leggy, very moderate filly, effective 12 to 14f, acts on g-f, has worn blinkers. Turf high 44. AW high 29.
**M J Polglase [4-32] K S Lee.*

SUNBEAM DANCE (USA) BHB 95f RR 108?f 551a[5]

4 b c Gone West (USA) 7.8f **(82)** - Encorelle (FR) (Arctic Tern (USA)) 8.9f **(69)**
Form - 25
1998 AW 0-2: (10f 2) (Dirt 2)
Well made, Pattern-class colt, effective 10 to 11f, acts on gd - acts on Dirt, has worn blinkers. AW high 108 (1st run) - 2nd of 7 to Nabhaan (5 Mar Nad Al Sheba 10f Dirt RF 0448a). Inconsistent. A half-brother to crack German miler Royal Abjar, he was out of his depth behind Annus Mirabilis in the Dubai Duty Free Trophy in March and falls some way short of the top class.
**W D Mather in UAE [0-2] Sheikh Rashid bin Maktoum Al Maktoum (from S bin Suroor [1-8] Oct 1997).*

SUNDAE GIRL (USA) BHB 74f RR 69f 3991[13]

2 b f Green Dancer (USA) 11.9f **(77)** - Charmie Carmie (USA) (Lyphard (USA)) 9.9f **(72)**
Form - 5170
Record 1998 - 1st:1 2nd:0 3rd:0 Ran:4
Win Prizemoney £3,445 *Total Prizemoney* £3,602
Wins * 1998 Jun Folkes (GD) 6f 67 <
1998 Turf 1-4: (5f, 6f 1-2, 8f) (g-f 1-2, frm, hrd)
Average filly. Turf high 69 - also 1st of 9 from Cappella (3 Jun Folkestone RF 1688). **P F I Cole [1-4] Christopher Wright.*

SUN DANCER BHB 30f RR 29f 2692[9]

3 b g Sizzling Melody 6.3f **(49)** - Petite Melusine (IRE) (Fairy King (USA)) 7.7f **(59)**
Form - 00070
Record 1998 - 1st:0 2nd:0 3rd:0 Ran:5
Pre1998 - 1st:0 2nd:0 3rd:0 Ran:1
1998 Turf 0-2: (8f, 12f) (sft, gd) 1998 AW 0-3: (5f, 6f, 9f) (Fibr 3)
Little account gelding. Turf high 29. AW high 17.
**N A Smith [0-6] Edwin Smith.*

SUN DANCING (IRE) BHB 69f74a RR 63f 74a 3264[8]

3 ch f Magical Wonder (USA) 7.2f **(60)** - Lockwood Girl (Prince Tenderfoot (USA)) 9f **(61)**
Form - 1208
Record 1998 - 1st:0 2nd:0 3rd:0 Ran:2
Pre1998 - 1st:1 2nd:1 3rd:0 Ran:3
Win Prizemoney £2,294 *Total Prizemoney* £3,131
Wins 1997 *Nov Southw (STD) 5f 66* <
1998 Turf 0-2: (6f, 7f) (gd 2)
Workmanlike, decent filly. Turf high 63 (began Jly).
**P Monteith [0-2] Allan Melville (from J Berry [1-3] Nov 1997).*

SUNDAY MAIL TOO (IRE) BHB 26f RR 22f 3908[3]

6 b m Fayruz 6.6f **(63)** - Slick Chick (Shiny Tenth) 9.2f **(56)**
Form - 45500383
Record 1998 - 1st:0 2nd:0 3rd:2 Ran:8
Pre1998 - 1st:3 2nd:3 3rd:2 Ran:56
Win Prizemoney £9,224 *Total Prizemoney* £13,563
Wins * 1996 Jly Ayr (G-F) SH 5f 44 43
* 1996 Jun Hamilt (GD) H 6f 31 40
1994 Apr Hamilt (G-S) 5f 47
1998 Turf 0-8: (5f 8) (sft, gd 4, g-f 2, frm)
Little account mare, effective 5f, acts on g-f, has worn blinkers. Turf high 23.
**Miss L A Perratt [2-63] T P Finch (from J Berry [1-6] Oct 1994).*

SUNDAY NIGHT (GER) RR 56f 3473[5]

3 b f Bakharoff (USA) - Santina (GER) (Gimont (GER))
Form - 5
Record 1998 - 1st:0 2nd:0 3rd:0 Ran:1
1998 Turf 0-1: (6f) (hrd)
Currently fair filly. **E A L Dunlop [0-1] Jaber Abdullah.*

SUNLEY SEEKER BHB 77f82a RR 81f 82a 1930[1]

3 b f Elmaamul (USA) 8.1f **(70)** - Sunley Sinner (Try My Best (USA)) 7.6f **(67)**
Form - 001
Record 1998 - 1st:1 2nd:0 3rd:0 Ran:3
Pre1998 - 1st:2 2nd:0 3rd:0 Ran:4
Win Prizemoney £11,977 *Total Prizemoney* £11,977
Wins * 1998 Jun Goodwo (GD) C 8f 71
* 1997 Spt Newbur (G-S) H 7.3f 75 81 <
* 1997 *Jly Southw (STD) 7f 81* <
1998 Turf 1-3: (7f, 8f 1-2) (sft, gd 1-2)
Neat, decent filly, effective 7 to 8f, best at 7f, acts on gd - acts on Fibr. Turf high 71. **M R Channon [3-7] Mrs J M Jeyes.*

SUNLEY SENSE BHB 99f RR 94f 4739[5]

2 b c Komaite (USA) 6.9f **(61)**-Brown Velvet (Mansingh (USA)) 7.4f **(55)**
Form - 52552321125
Record 1998 - 1st:2 2nd:4 3rd:1 Ran:11
Win Prizemoney £8,758 *Total Prizemoney* £15,837
Wins * 1998 Spt Newbur (GD) H 5.2f 76 94 <
*** 1998** Spt Sandow (G-S) H 5f 76 80
1998 Turf 2-11: (5f 2-11) (g-s, gd 1-4, g-f 1-3, frm 3)
Useful colt, effective 5f, acts on gd to g-f. Turf high 94 - also 1st of

13 giving 6lb to Corndavon (19 Spt Newbury RF 4377). Improving. Although placed in maidens, he had looked a little bit of a short runner, but he came good with two nursery wins in quick succession in September. Ended the season with a good fifth in the Cornwallis Stakes, showing plenty of dash.
**M R Channon [2-11] John Sunley.*

SUN LION (IRE) BHB 47f **RR 46f** 5070[16]

3 b g Shalford (IRE) 7.8f **(63)** - Susie Sunshine (IRE) (Waajib)
Form - 00000020
Record 1998 - 1st:0 2nd:1 3rd:0 Ran:8
Pre1998 - 1st:0 2nd:1 3rd:0 Ran:6
Win Prizemoney £0 *Total Prizemoney* £1,783
1998 Turf 0-8: (8f 4, 9f 2, 10f 2) (hvy, g-s, gd 2, g-f, frm 3)
Moderate gelding, has worn blinkers. Turf high 46.
**Mrs P N Dutfield [0-8] Simon Dutfield (from C O'Brien in IRE [0-6] Oct 1997).*

SUN MARK (IRE) BHB 60f **RR 61f** 609[20]

7 ch g Red Sunset 9f **(57)** - Vivungi (USA) (Exbury) 9f **(73)**
Form - 0
Record 1998 - 1st:0 2nd:0 3rd:0 Ran:1
Pre1998 - 1st:3 2nd:1 3rd:2 Ran:11
Win Prizemoney £7,562 *Total Prizemoney* £9,353
Wins 1997 Aug Hamilt (GD) S 12.1f 49
1997 Jly Ripon (GD) S 10f 55
1997 May Hamilt (SFT) 12.1f 61 <
1998 Turf 0-1: (12f) (sft)
Average gelding, effective 9 to 12f, best at 12f, acts on gd to frm, best on gd, has worn blinkers, excels at Hamilton.
**Miss J F Craze [0-1] W Cooper (from Mrs A Swinbank [3-9] Aug 1997).*

SUNNY CHIEF BHB 47f **RR 31f** 2532[15]

2 ch c Be My Chief (USA) 10.2f **(62)** - Sunny Davis (USA) (Alydar (USA)) 9.1f **(76)**
Form - 600
Record 1998 - 1st:0 2nd:0 3rd:0 Ran:3
1998 Turf 0-3: (6f 3) (gd 2, g-f)
Currently very moderate colt. Turf high 31.
**Sir Mark Prescott [0-3] Hesmonds Stud.*

SUNNY FACT (USA) **RR 72f** 3735[5]

2 ch c Known Fact (USA) 8.3f **(72)** - Sunerta (USA) (Roberto (USA)) 10f **(76)**
Form - 25
Record 1998 - 1st:0 2nd:1 3rd:0 Ran:2
Win Prizemoney £0 *Total Prizemoney* £1,742
1998 Turf 0-2: (6f 2) (g-f, frm)
Currently above-average colt. Turf high 72 (began Jly).
**R Charlton [0-2] K Abdulla.*

SUNNY ISLE BHB 83f **RR 83+f** 4966[3]

4 b f Cadeaux Genereux 7.9f **(76)** - Highsplasher (USA) (Bucksplasher (USA)) 10.3f **(75)**
Form - 83103
Record 1998 - 1st:1 2nd:0 3rd:2 Ran:5
Pre1998 - 1st:1 2nd:0 3rd:2 Ran:3
Win Prizemoney £10,841 *Total Prizemoney* £13,354
Wins * **1998** Spt Ayr (G-S) H 10f 75 83+ <
* 1997 Spt Haydoc (GD) 10.5f 63
1998 Turf 1-5: (8f 2, 10f 1-3) (sft 1-3, g-f 2)
Light-framed, decent filly, effective 8 to 11f, best at 10f, acts on sft to g-f, best on sft. Turf high 83 - 1st of 14 giving 11lb to Flower O'Cannie (18 Spt Ayr RF 4351). **C F Wall [2-8] S Fustok.*

SUN O'TIROL (IRE) BHB 40f32a **RR 37f 32a** 442[11]

4 b g Tirol 8.1f **(64)** - Nous (Le Johnstan) 7.4f **(55)**
Form - 70
Record 1998 - 1st:0 2nd:0 3rd:0 Ran:2
Pre1998 - 1st:1 2nd:0 3rd:0 Ran:16
Win Prizemoney £2,381 *Total Prizemoney* £3,330
Wins 1996 Jly Folkes (G-F) 6.9f 68 <
1998 AW 0-2: (8f 2) (Equi 2)
Scopey, very moderate gelding, effective 8f, acts on frm, has worn blinkers, likes tight tracks. AW high 17.
**J R Arnold [0-10] Mrs Annette Barwick (from M R Channon [1-8] Spt 1996).*

SUN OVER SANTIAGO (IRE) RR 3996[17]

2 ch f Dolphin Street (FR) - Deydarika (IRE) (Kahyasi)
Form - 00
Record 1998 - 1st:0 2nd:0 3rd:0 Ran:2
1998 Turf 0-2: (6f, 7f) (gd, g-f)
Currently very poor filly. (began Jly).
**H Alexander [0-2] Rosaly Racing.*

SUNRISE FLAG (JPN) RR 125f 2287a[1]

4 br c Real Shadai (JPN) - Heian Dame (JPN) (Tosho Boy (JPN))
Form - 1
1998 Turf 1-1: (10f 1-1) (hvy 1-1)
Currently top-class colt. (1st run) - 1st of 14 from Air Groove (21 Jun Hanshin RF 2287a). Winner of a hugely valuable race in Japan in June. **I Yasuda in JPN [1-1].*

SUNSET FOREST RR 8f 2149[8]

2 ch f Forest Wind (USA) - Superetta (Superlative) 7.2f **(56)**
Form - 68
Record 1998 - 1st:0 2nd:0 3rd:0 Ran:2
1998 Turf 0-2: (5f, 6f) (gd, frm)
Currently very poor filly. Turf high 8. **M R Channon [0-2] Noel Wabe.*

Sunshine Street ran the race of his life at Epsom

SUNSET HARBOUR (IRE) BHB 51f44a **RR 52f 44a** 3938[2]

5 br m Prince Sabo 6.6f **(64)** - City Link Pet (Tina's Pet) 6.8f **(59)**

Form - 026560101381632

Record 1998 - 1st:3 2nd:1 3rd:2 Ran:12
Pre1998 - 1st:2 2nd:3 3rd:7 Ran:35

Win Prizemoney £13,630 *Total Prizemoney* £21,869

Wins * **1998** Aug Catter (GD) H 5f 47 50 <
* **1998** May Newcas (G-F) H 5f 42 44
* **1998** *Apr Wolver (STD) H 5f 37 40*
* 1997 Jun Beverl (G-S) H 5f 40 41
* 1996 Jly Redcar (FRM) SH 5f 44 45

1998 Turf 2-8: (5f 2-7, 6f) (gd 1-4, frm 1-4) 1998 AW 1-4: (5f 1-3, 6f) (Fibr 1-4)

Fair filly, effective 5 to 6f, best at 5f, acts on gd to frm, best on frm, has worn blinkers. Turf high 52 - 3rd of 12 giving 16lb to L A Touch (20 Aug Yarmouth 6f frm RF 3765) - also 1st of 17 getting 17lb from Lady Sheriff (4 Aug Catterick RF 3332). AW high 40.

**S E Kettlewell [5-29] J Tennant (from T J Naughton [0-10] Jly 1996).*

SUNSET LADY (IRE) BHB 73f **RR 74f** 4767[1]

2 b br f Red Sunset 9f **(57)** - Lady of Man (So Blessed) 8.7f **(67)**

Form - 01455121

Record 1998 - 1st:3 2nd:1 3rd:0 Ran:8

Win Prizemoney £9,690 *Total Prizemoney* £10,840

Wins * **1998** Oct Ayr (SFT) H 8f 65 74 <
* **1998** Spt Pontef (G-F) H 8f 61 66
* **1998** Jun Thirsk (GD) S 6f 66

1998 Turf 3-8: (5f, 6f 1-2, 7f 2, 8f 2-2, 10f) (sft 1-1, g-s, gd 2, g-f 1-2, frm 1-2)

Above-average filly, effective 6 to 10f, best at 8f, acts on sft to frm. Turf high 74 - 1st of 16 giving 12lb to Pretty Obvious (13 Oct Ayr RF 4767) - also 1st of 7 getting 10lb from May I Say (24 Spt Pontefract RF 4466).

**P C Haslam [3-8] The Jack Of All Trades Partnership.*

Sunspangled (right) gained revenge over Edabiya

SUNSHINE STREET (USA) RR 121f 5167a[5]

3 b c Sunshine Forever (USA) 13.2f **(76)** - Meadow Spirit (USA) (Chief's Crown (USA)) 9.8f **(72)**

Form - 222401235

1998 Turf 1-9: (10f 4, 12f 1-4, 15f) (hvy, sft 2, gd 1-2, g-f 2, frm, hrd)

Very high-class colt, effective 12 to 15f, best at 12f, acts on gd to frm, best on g-f, prefers left handed tracks. Turf high 121 - 5th of 13 getting 4lb from Buck's Boy (7 Nov Churchill Downs 12f frm RF 5167a). He ran the race of his life to lead the Derby field until the last furlong, finally finishing a fine fourth. His proximity to the principals can be viewed negatively, but he showed that was no fluke, taking a listed race before finishing third in the St Leger, where he seemed to stay well enough. He then took his chance in the Breeders' Cup Turf and, despite being a complete outsider, proved to be the best of the European raiders, running a similar race to his Epsom Derby run. His future may lay on the other side of the Atlantic but, if he races in Europe in 1999, he will surely win the big prize he deserves. **N Meade in IRE [1-11] P Garvey.*

SUNSPANGLED (IRE) RR 99f 4514[1]

2 ch f Caerleon (USA) 10.9f **(79)** - Filia Ardross (Ardross) 10.6f **(68)**

Form - 1251

1998 Turf 2-4: (7f 1-3, 8f 1-1) (sft 1-1, gd 1-3)

Very useful filly. Turf high 99 (began Jly) - 1st of 8 from Calando (27 Spt Ascot RF 4514) - also 1st of 11 from St Clair Ridge (28 Jly Galway RF 3337a). A half-sister to the ill-fated French Ballerina, she won her maiden at Galway, and then twice finished behind Edabiya, including when fifth in the Moyglare Stud Stakes. She was not helped by racing into a string headwind at the Curragh, and reversed the form in the Group One Fillies' Mile at Ascot. She battled well there, is likely to stay a mile and a half next season, and will no doubt have more battles with her old rival in 1999.

**A P O'Brien in IRE [2-4] M Tabor & Mrs John Magnier.*

SUNSTREAK BHB 98f **RR 102+f** 4222[2]

3 ch c Primo Dominie 7.2f **(67)** - Florentynna Bay (Aragon) 8.1f **(60)**

Form - 401112

Record 1998 - 1st:3 2nd:1 3rd:0 Ran:6
Pre1998 - 1st:0 2nd:0 3rd:0 Ran:2

Win Prizemoney £14,587 *Total Prizemoney* £16,327

Wins * **1998** Aug Sandow (G-F) H 8.1f 80 102+ <
* **1998** Aug Newmar (G-F) H 8f 74 82

* **1998** Jly Nottin (G-F) H 8.2f 69 75
1998 Turf 3-6: (7f 2, 8f 3-4) (g-f 2-4, frm 1-2)
Leggy, very useful colt, effective 8f, acts on g-f. Turf high 102 - 1st of 11 giving 6lb to Pay On Red (21 Aug Sandown RF 3795). Inconsistent. He blew a decent handicap mark when winning by 10 lengths at Sandown in August, and had to be stepped into conditions races. Second after pulling fiercely at Doncaster in September, he should improve over the winter and develop into a Listed class performer. **C F Wall [3-8] Ray Rice.*

SUPACALIFRAGILISTK BHB 34f45a **RR 45f 45a** 4877[10]
3 b f Sabrehill (USA) 8.5f **(64)** - Lucky Thing (Green Desert (USA)) 8.6f **(78)**
Form - 708000080064680
Record 1998 - 1st:0 2nd:0 3rd:0 Ran:15
Pre1998 - 1st:0 2nd:1 3rd:0 Ran:6
Win Prizemoney £0 *Total Prizemoney* £1,614
1998 Turf 0-12: (5f 2, 6f 4, 7f 3, 8f 2, 10f) (gd 8, g-f 2, frm 2) 1998 AW 0-3: (6f, 7f 2) (Fibr 3)
Neat, moderate filly, effective 7f, acts on g-f, has worn blinkers, likes left handed tracks, likes tight tracks. Turf high 45.
**J Balding [0-15] Josef Fusenich & Whitegate Travel (from B W Hills [0-3] Nov 1997).*

SUPERAPPAROS BHB 35f39a **RR 2f 39a** 70[8]
4 b g Superpower 6.6f **(58)** - Ayodessa (Lochnager) 6f **(59)**
Form - 7448
Record 1998 - 1st:0 2nd:0 3rd:0 Ran:2
Pre1998 - 1st:0 2nd:0 3rd:1 Ran:11
Win Prizemoney £0 *Total Prizemoney* £446
1998 AW 0-2: (7f, 8f) (Fibr 2)
Workmanlike, very moderate gelding, effective 7f, - acts on Fibr, has worn blinkers, likes left handed tracks, likes tight tracks. AW high 35. **S R Bowring [0-13] S R Bowring.*

SUPERBIT BHB 56f50a **RR 57f 50a** 5007[4]
6 b g Superpower 6.6f **(58)** - On A Bit (Mummy's Pet) 7.7f **(60)**
Form - 03004610005024
Record 1998 - 1st:1 2nd:1 3rd:1 Ran:14
Pre1998 - 1st:4 2nd:2 3rd:10 Ran:50
Win Prizemoney £12,848 *Total Prizemoney* £21,725
Wins * **1998** Aug Ripon (GD) SH 5f 50 54
* 1997 Jun Nottin (SFT) H 6.1f 60 64 <
* 1996 Oct Nottin (GD) 5.1f 60
* 1996 Spt Haydoc (GD) SH 6f 49 53
* 1995 Jun Bath (GD) C 5.1f 58
1998 Turf 1-14: (5f 1-9, 6f 5) (sft, gd 1-6, frm 7)
Fair gelding, effective 5 to 6f, best at 6f, acts on gd, has worn blinkers. Turf high 57 - 2nd of 20 to Agent Mulder (14 Oct Nottingham 6f gd RF 4811). He has a poor wins to runs ratio, and needed to be dropped into selling company in order to score at Ripon in August.
**B A McMahon [5-60] Neville Smith (from J G FitzGerald [0-4] Spt 1994).*

SUPERBOB **RR 69f** 3438[6]
2 b c Superlative 8.8f **(57)** - Beebob (Norwick (USA)) 7.2f **(56)**
Form - 006
Record 1998 - 1st:0 2nd:0 3rd:0 Ran:3
1998 Turf 0-3: (6f, 7f 2) (g-f, frm 2)
Currently average colt. Turf high 69 (began Jly).
**R J R Williams [0-3] Beebob.*

SUPERCAL BHB 95f **RR 100f** 4733[5]
4 gr f Environment Friend 7.5f **(67)** - Sorayah (Persian Bold) 9.3f **(66)**
Form - 62460678333745
Record 1998 - 1st:0 2nd:1 3rd:3 Ran:14
Pre1998 - 1st:4 2nd:2 3rd:2 Ran:17
Win Prizemoney £25,898 *Total Prizemoney* £73,707
Wins * 1997 May Lingfi (GD) L 7f 98 <
* 1997 Mar Kempto (GD) H 6f 89 88
* 1996 Jun Epsom (G-F) 6f 91
* 1996 May Folkes (GD) 6f 83
1998 Turf 0-14: (7f 3, 8f 8, 9f 3) (sft 2, g-s, gd 4, g-f 5, frm 2)
Scopey, very useful filly, effective 7 to 9f, best at 8f, acts on gd to g-f, best on gd, likes right handed tracks, excels at Curragh and Lingfield. Turf high 100 - 4th of 9 giving 16lb to Nanoushka (9 May Lingfield 7f g-f RF 1126). She is always a danger in Listed races, but has not won since the spring of 1997.
**D R C Elsworth [4-31] The Caledonian Racing Society.*

SUPERCHIEF BHB 49f **RR 51f** 4093[24]
3 b g Precocious 7.2f **(54)** - Rome Express (Siberian Express (USA)) 8.8f **(65)**
Form - 6008060
Record 1998 - 1st:0 2nd:0 3rd:0 Ran:7
Pre1998 - 1st:0 2nd:0 3rd:0 Ran:1
1998 Turf 0-7: (5f 2, 6f 2, 7f, 9f, 10f) (gd 2, g-f 3, frm 2)
Scopey, fair gelding, has worn blinkers. Turf high 51. Inconsistent.
**J E Banks [0-7] Sir Freddie Laker (from Miss B Sanders [0-1] Spt 1997).*

SUPER DOLLAR (IRE) BHB 68f **RR 68f** 4997[7]
2 ch c Great Commotion (USA) 9.2f **(80)** - L'Americaine (USA) (Verbatim (USA)) 8.5f **(64)**
Form - 357
Record 1998 - 1st:0 2nd:0 3rd:1 Ran:3
Win Prizemoney £0 *Total Prizemoney* £445
1998 Turf 0-3: (6f, 7f 2) (sft, gd, g-f)
Currently average colt. Turf high 68 (began Oct).
**P F I Cole [0-3] P S Partnership.*

SUPER FORUM BHB 60f70a **RR 70f 70a** 4960[10]
2 b c Superpower 6.6f **(58)** - Moushka (Song) 7.2f **(61)**
Form - 25472000
Record 1998 - 1st:0 2nd:2 3rd:0 Ran:8
Win Prizemoney £0 *Total Prizemoney* £1,884
1998 Turf 0-7: (5f 2, 6f 2, 8f 3) (g-s, gd, g-f, frm 4) 1998 AW 0-1: (5f) (Fibr)
Above-average colt, effective 5 to 8f, best at 5f, acts on gd to frm - acts on Fibr. Turf high 70 - 2nd of 6 getting 9lb from Baisse d'Argent (14 Spt Musselburgh 8f frm RF 4251). (1st run) - 4th of 10 giving 5lb to Mammas F-C (12 Jun Southwell 5f Fibr RF 1940). Becoming disappointing. **M Johnston [0-8] Mrs Jacqueline Conroy.*

SUPERFRILLS BHB 49f46a **RR 47f 46a** 4921[1]
5 b m Superpower 6.6f **(58)** - Pod's Daughter (IRE) (Tender King) 6.8f **(54)**
Form - 7000213001401
Record 1998 - 1st:3 2nd:1 3rd:1 Ran:13
Pre1998 - 1st:0 2nd:1 3rd:3 Ran:24
Win Prizemoney £7,899 *Total Prizemoney* £12,470
Wins * **1998** Oct Newcas (SFT) H 5f 45 47 <
* **1998** Aug Hamilt (SFT) H 5f 39 47 <
* **1998** Jun Hamilt (G-S) H 5f 33 40
1998 Turf 3-11: (5f 3-11) (g-s 2-2, gd 1-5, g-f 2, frm 2) 1998 AW 0-2: (5f 2) (Fibr 2)
Moderate filly, effective 5f, acts on g-s to g-f, best on g-s. Turf high 47 - 1st of 17 getting 2lb from Dubai Nurse (17 Aug Hamilton RF 3681) - also 1st of 20 getting 1lb from Silk Cottage (21 Oct Newcastle RF 4921). AW high 26. Consistent.
**Miss L C Siddall [3-37] Podso Racing.*

SUPER GEIL BHB 51f51a **RR 50f 51a** 2563[8]
3 b f Superlative 8.8f **(57)** - Mild Deception (IRE) (Glow (USA)) 6.7f **(71)**
Form - 236467260418
Record 1998 - 1st:1 2nd:1 3rd:0 Ran:9
Pre1998 - 1st:1 2nd:1 3rd:2 Ran:10
Win Prizemoney £4,707 *Total Prizemoney* £6,835
Wins * **1998** Jun Mussel (SFT) SH 5f 45 50
* 1997 *Spt Southw (STD) SH 5f 48 57* <
1998 Turf 1-5: (5f 1-5) (sft, gd 1-3, frm) 1998 AW 0-4: (5f 4) (Equi, Fibr 3)
Unfurnished, fair filly, effective 5f, acts on gd - acts on Fibr, has worn blinkers (effectively). Turf high 50 - 1st of 12 getting 5lb from Three Tenners (29 Jun Musselburgh RF 2370). AW high 47.
**C A Dwyer [2-19] E R Kettenacker.*

SUPER-GEM BHB 40f **RR 47f** 5070[14]
3 ch g Superpower 6.6f **(58)** - Ela-Yianni-Mou (Anfield) 8.5f **(59)**
Form - 0000
Record 1998 - 1st:0 2nd:0 3rd:0 Ran:4
1998 Turf 0-4: (9f, 10f 2, 11f) (gd, g-f 3)
Leggy, moderate gelding, has worn blinkers. Turf high 47 (began Aug). **D J S Cosgrove [0-4] Mrs J R Bamforth.*

SUPER IMPOSE BHB 34a **RR** 401^{10}
3 ch g Superpower 6.6f **(58)** - Sharp Lady (Sharpen Up) 8.3f **(67)**
Form - 87600
Record 1998 - 1st:0 2nd:0 3rd:0 Ran:4
Pre1998 - 1st:0 2nd:0 3rd:0 Ran:1
1998 AW 0-4: (5f, 6f, 7f, 8f) (Equi, Fibr 3)
Workmanlike, very moderate gelding, always wears blinkers. AW high 32. **John Berry [0-5] Mrs V Bampton.*

SUPERIOR FORCE BHB 42f57a **RR 33f 57a** 4609^{12}
5 ch g Superlative 8.8f **(57)** - Gleeful (Sayf El Arab (USA)) 7.1f **(54)**
Form - 65030
Record 1998 - 1st:0 2nd:0 3rd:1 Ran:5
Pre1998 - 1st:2 2nd:1 3rd:2 Ran:25
Win Prizemoney £9,390 *Total Prizemoney* £12,147
Wins * 1996 Spt Sandow (G-F) H 8.1f 58 60
* 1996 Jun Lingfi (STD) H 8f 59 63 <
1998 Turf 0-3: (10f, 11f, 14f) (frm 3) 1998 AW 0-2: (10f, 12f) (Equi 2)
Average gelding, effective 8 to 10f, - acts on Equi, has worn blinkers, likes left handed tracks. Turf high 33. AW high 63 (1st run) (began Spt) - 3rd of 13 getting 3lb from Java Shrine (8 Spt Lingfield 10f Equi RF 4143). **Miss B Sanders [2-30] Copyforce Ltd.*

SUPERIOR PREMIUM BHB 106f **RR 107f** 4367^{18}
4 br c Forzando 7.2f **(63)** - Devils Dirge (Song) 7.2f **(61)**
Form - 7287311150
Record 1998 - 1st:3 2nd:1 3rd:1 Ran:10
Pre1998 - 1st:3 2nd:3 3rd:1 Ran:15
Win Prizemoney £85,220 *Total Prizemoney* £114,519
Wins * **1998** Aug Goodwo (GD) H 6f 99 105 <
* **1998** Jly Haydoc (GD) 6f 95
* **1998** Jun Cheste (G-S) H 6.1f 94 98
* 1997 Mar Haydoc (SFT) L 5f 100
* 1996 Oct Haydoc (SFT) 5f 90
* 1996 Apr Nottin (G-S) 5.1f 79
1998 Turf 3-10: (6f 3-10) (sft, gd 2-6, g-f 1-2, frm)
Scopey, Pattern-class colt, effective 5 to 6f, best at 6f, acts on sft to gd, best on gd, excels at Haydock. Turf high 107 - also 1st of 29 giving 18lb to Ansellman (1 Aug Goodwood RF 3257). A shade unfortunate with the draw when a close third in the Wokingham Handicap at Royal Ascot, he gained recompense by winning his next three starts, including the Stewards' Cup. Fifth in the Group One Stanley Leisure Sprint Cup at Haydock in September, he loves soft ground and can win a Pattern race when conditions are in his favour. **R A Fahey [6-25] J C Parsons.*

SUPERLAO (BEL) BHB 43f33a **RR 54f 33a** 408^{6}
6 b m Bacalao (USA) 5f **(27)** - Princess of Import (Import) 6.6f **(68)**
Form - 056655646
Record 1998 - 1st:0 2nd:0 3rd:0 Ran:7
Pre1998 - 1st:1 2nd:1 3rd:7 Ran:43
Win Prizemoney £3,096 *Total Prizemoney* £7,492
Wins * 1997 Jun Lingfi (SFT) H 5f 38 41 <
1998 AW 0-7: (5f 2, 6f 5) (Equi 6, Fibr)
Fair mare, has worn blinkers. AW high 32.
**J J Bridger [1-44] J J Bridger (from Andre Hermans in BEL [0-6] Jan 1996).*

SUPERMATCH RR 37f 3321^{10}
2 ch f Superlative 8.8f **(57)** - Matching Lines (Thatching) 8f **(66)**
Form - 0
Record 1998 - 1st:0 2nd:0 3rd:0 Ran:1
1998 Turf 0-1: (5f) (g-f)
Currently very moderate filly. **M R Channon [0-1] Mrs Jean Keegan.*

SUPERMICK BHB 37f42a **RR 43f 42a** 4654^{12}
7 ch g Faustus (USA) 9.1f **(54)** - Lardana (Burglar) 7.2f **(49)**
Form - 0
Record 1998 - 1st:0 2nd:0 3rd:0 Ran:1
Pre1998 - 1st:2 2nd:4 3rd:2 Ran:21
Win Prizemoney £7,093 *Total Prizemoney* £11,282
Wins 1996 Jly Epsom (GD) H 12f 33 38 <
1996 Jly Nottin (G-F) SH 14.1f 30 32
1998 Turf 0-1: (12f) (g-f)
Moderate gelding, effective 11 to 12f, best at 12f, acts on g-f to frm, best on g-f, has worn blinkers. Inconsistent.
**M C Pipe [4-14] P Clarke (from W R Muir [4-33] Spt 1997).*

SUPERMODEL BHB 50f55a **RR 55f 55a** 412^{7}
6 ch m Unfuwain (USA) 11.4f **(74)** - Well Off (Welsh Pageant) 10f **(65)**
Form - 7
Record 1998 - 1st:0 2nd:0 3rd:0 Ran:1
Pre1998 - 1st:0 2nd:1 3rd:1 Ran:4
Win Prizemoney £0 *Total Prizemoney* £1,286
1998 AW 0-1: (14f) (Fibr)
Fair mare, has worn blinkers.
**Mrs N Macauley [1-12] Miss S Rudge (from M Johnston [0-1] Jan 1996).*

SUPER MONARCH BHB 77f72a **RR 78f 72a** 5078^{17}
4 ch g Cadeaux Genereux 7.9f **(76)** - Miss Fancy That (USA) (The Minstrel (CAN)) 10f **(72)**
Form - 4005018002000627210
Record 1998 - 1st:2 2nd:3 3rd:0 Ran:18
Pre1998 - 1st:0 2nd:1 3rd:0 Ran:5
Win Prizemoney £11,117 *Total Prizemoney* £20,208
Wins * **1998** Oct Newmar (GD) H 8f 68 78 <
1998 *Feb Lingfi (SLW) 7f 56*
1998 Turf 1-15: (6f, 7f 3, 8f 1-8, 9f, 10f, 11f) (sft 4, g-s, gd 4, g-f 3, frm 1-3) 1998 AW 1-3: (7f 1-1, 8f, 10f) (Equi 1-3)
Scopey, above-average gelding, effective 7 to 9f, best at 7f, acts on g-s to frm, likes left handed tracks, likes tight tracks. Turf high 78 - 1st of 28 giving 11lb to Manufan (15 Oct Newmarket RF 4822). AW high 56. He has changed stables a few times during his career, and has looked a tricky customer on occasions, but was in fine form in the autumn, including beating a big field in a handicap at Newmarket in October.
**K R Burke [1-7] Chelgate Public Relations Ltd (from S Dow [1-12] Jly 1998).*

SUPER PARK BHB 21f31a **RR 27f 31a** 3280^{16}
6 b g Superpower 6.6f **(58)** - Everingham Park (Record Token) 6.3f **(53)**
Form - 60636500
Record 1998 - 1st:0 2nd:0 3rd:1 Ran:8
Pre1998 - 1st:1 2nd:0 3rd:2 Ran:30
Win Prizemoney £3,453 *Total Prizemoney* £12,185
Wins 1994 Oct Newcas (G-S) 6f 74
1998 Turf 0-6: (6f, 7f 4, 8f) (gd 2, g-f 2, frm 2) 1998 AW 0-2: (7f, 8f) (Equi, Fibr)
Little account gelding, effective 7f, acts on g-f, has worn blinkers. Turf high 27. AW high 21.
**J Pearce [0-26] Jeff Pearce (from M H Easterby [1-12] Oct 1995).*

SUPERPRIDE BHB 56f **RR 55f** 2147^{2}
6 b g Superpower 6.6f **(58)**-Lindrake's Pride (Mandrake Major) 7.6f **(53)**
Form - 132
Record 1998 - 1st:1 2nd:1 3rd:1 Ran:3
Pre1998 - 1st:2 2nd:5 3rd:4 Ran:33
Win Prizemoney £8,550 *Total Prizemoney* £18,298
Wins * **1998** May Carlis (G-S) H 9.3f 52 55
* 1996 Aug Ayr (G-F) H 7f 55 64 <
1994 Jun Ayr (G-S) 6f 54
1998 Turf 1-3: (9f 1-2, 11f) (gd 1-1, g-f 2)
Fair gelding, effective 7 to 11f, acts on sft to frm, has worn blinkers, prefers right handed tracks, and excels at Carlisle. Turf high 55 (1st run) - 1st of 16 giving 13lb to Protaras Bay (8 May Carlisle RF 1097). Consistent. A keen type who often makes the pace, he can hang in the early stages and does not look entirely trustworthy. Winning hurdler.
**Mrs M Reveley [5-34] Mrs Muriel Ward (from T D Barron [1-6] Jun 1995).*

SUPER SNIP BHB 57f **RR 57f** 1584^{7}
3 ch g Superpower 6.6f **(58)** - Marcroft (Crofthall) 6.3f **(59)**
Form - 507
Record 1998 - 1st:0 2nd:0 3rd:0 Ran:3
Pre1998 - 1st:0 2nd:0 3rd:0 Ran:2
1998 Turf 0-3: (5f, 6f 2) (g-s, gd 2)
Scopey, fair gelding. Turf high 57. Half-brother to Safio.
**A Bailey [0-5] Mrs M A Clayton.*

SUPERSONIC RR 23f 5137^{16}
2 b f Shirley Heights 12.1f **(76)** - Bright Landing (Sun Prince) 12.4f **(52)**
Form - 0
Record 1998 - 1st:0 2nd:0 3rd:0 Ran:1

1998 Turf 0-1: (7f) (gd)
Currently little account filly.*R F JohnsonHoughton [0-1] J W Rowles.*

SUPER SONIC SONIA (IRE) RR 94f 3351a7
3 b f Tirol 8.1f **(64)** - Lunulae (Tumble Wind (USA)) 7.5f **(57)**
Form - 4587
1998 Turf 0-3: (8f, 10f, 12f) (hvy 2, gd)
Useful filly, effective 8f, acts on gd. Turf high 90. Inconsistent.
**M Brassil in IRE [0-3] P Sheridan (from A P O'Brien in IRE [1-5] Nov 1997).*

SUPER STRIDES BHB 38f52a RR 46f 52a 5117[4]
2 b f Superpower 6.6f **(58)** - Go Tally-Ho (Gorytus (USA)) 7.8f **(60)**
Form - 407222U40504
Record 1998 - 1st:0 2nd:3 3rd:0 Ran:12
Win Prizemoney £0 *Total Prizemoney* £1,733
1998 Turf 0-5: (5f 2, 6f 3) (gd 4, frm) 1998 AW 0-7: (5f 4, 6f 3) (Fibr 7)
Fair filly, effective 6f, - acts on Fibr. Turf high 46. AW high 56 - 2nd of 6 to Miss Take (20 Jun Wolverhampton 6f Fibr RF 2165). Inconsistent. **C W Fairhurst [0-12] William Hill.*

SUPERTOP BHB 57f RR 58f 2866[5]
10 b or br g High Top 11f **(60)** - Myth (Troy) 10.4f **(68)**
Form - 5215

Record	**1998** -	1st:1	2nd:1	3rd:0	Ran:4
	Pre1998 -	1st:6	2nd:4	3rd:4	Ran:36

Win Prizemoney £21,783 *Total Prizemoney* £28,828

Wins	* **1998**	Jly	Carlis	(G-F)	H	12f	55	56	
	* 1997	Apr	Ayr	(GD)	H	10f	50	54	
	1994	Jun	Yarmou	(G-F)	H	10.1f	58	64	<

1998 Turf 1-4: (12f 1-1, 14f 2, 16f) (gd 2, frm 1-2)
Fair gelding. Turf high 58 - 2nd of 15 getting 5lb from Salska (25 Jun Newcastle 16f gd RF 2270) - also 1st of 8 giving 5lb to Back Row (4 Jly Carlisle RF 2526). Consistent.
**L Lungo [11-30] Mrs Barbara Lungo (from P W Harris [5-32] Oct 1994).*

SUPER ZOE RR 47f 4671[10]
2 b f Bustino 11f **(64)** - Chain Dance (Shareef Dancer (USA)) 9.9f **(73)**
Form - 00
Record 1998 - 1st:0 2nd:0 3rd:0 Ran:2
1998 Turf 0-2: (7f 2) (gd, g-f)
Currently moderate filly. Turf high 47 (began Spt).
**W Jarvis [0-2] J M Greetham.*

SUPLIZI (IRE) BHB 96f RR 102?f 1279[2]
7 b h Alzao (USA) 9.8f **(73)** - Sphinx (GER) (Alpenkonig (GER)) 10.8f **(76)**
Form - 362

Record	**1998** -	1st:0	2nd:1	3rd:1	Ran:3
	Pre1998 -	1st:3	2nd:3	3rd:1	Ran:11

Win Prizemoney £28,324 *Total Prizemoney* £53,022

Wins	1996	Apr	Ripon	(GD)		12.3f		100	
	1994	May	Capann	(FRM)	L	10f		103	<

1998 Turf 0-3: (8f, 10f, 12f) (hvy, gd, g-f)
Very useful horse. Turf high 102. He returned to form in 1998, but still found winning difficult. The ability is there, but races are hard to find. **B J Llewellyn [0-3] T G Price (from P Bowen [0-2] Nov 1997).*

SUPPLY AND DEMAND BHB 97f RR 99f 4986[5]
4 b g Belmez (USA) 11.4f **(65)** - Sipsi Fach (Prince Sabo) 7.2f **(62)**
Form - 0310205

Record	**1998** -	1st:1	2nd:1	3rd:1	Ran:7
	Pre1998 -	1st:2	2nd:4	3rd:0	Ran:12

Win Prizemoney £45,455 *Total Prizemoney* £70,116

Wins	* **1998**	Jly	Goodwo	(GD)	H	9.9f	94	99	<
	* 1997	May	Lingfi	(SFT)	H	9f	90	93	
	* 1997	Apr	Epsom	(GD)		8.5f		75	

1998 Turf 1-7: (9f, 10f 1-5, 12f) (sft, gd 1-2, g-f 3, frm)
Workmanlike, very useful gelding, effective 8 to 10f, best at 10f, acts on sft to g-f, best on gd, has worn blinkers, prefers tight tracks, excels at Goodwood and Epsom. Turf high 99 - 1st of 17 giving 2lb to Yavana's Pace (28 Jly Goodwood RF 3165). Inconsistent. Landed a gamble in the valuable Chesterfield Cup at Goodwood in first-time blinkers but was most disappointing at York. Bounced back with a good effort in an Epsom conditions event and put in a decent run from a modest draw in the Cambridgeshire. **G L Moore [5-23] Action.*

SUPREME ANGEL BHB 83f RR 57f 4965[11]
3 b f Beveled (USA) 6.9f **(64)** - Blue Angel (Lord Gayle (USA)) 8.8f **(62)**
Form - 30100700

Record	**1998** -	1st:1	2nd:0	3rd:1	Ran:8
	Pre1998 -	1st:2	2nd:2	3rd:0	Ran:7

Win Prizemoney £14,370 *Total Prizemoney* £17,369

Wins	* **1998**	May	Kempto	(GD)	H	6f	82	84	<
	* 1997	Oct	Haydoc	(HVY)	H	5f	75	81	
	* 1997	Apr	Newbur	(G-F)		5.2f		69	

1998 Turf 1-8: (5f, 6f 1-7) (sft, gd 1-3, g-f 4)
Unfurnished, fair filly, effective 5 to 6f, acts on g-s to gd. Turf high 84 - 1st of 13 getting 10lb from Distinctive Dream (23 May Kempton RF 1428). Becoming disappointing. She put up a fair effort in a Kempton conditions event on her return, if well beaten by the winner, and won a handicap there on her third start. She has faced some very stiff tasks since.
**M P Muggeridge [3-15] Least Moved Partners.*

SUPREME SOUND BHB 100f RR 100f 4631[33]
4 b c Superlative 8.8f **(57)** - Sing Softly (Luthier) 9.8f **(71)**
Form - 40101217411300

Record	**1998** -	1st:5	2nd:1	3rd:1	Ran:14
	Pre1998 -	1st:3	2nd:1	3rd:2	Ran:13

Win Prizemoney £65,827 *Total Prizemoney* £73,394

Wins	* **1998**	Aug	York	(G-F)	H	10.4f	96	100	<
	* **1998**	Aug	Yarmou	(G-F)	H	10.1f	90	94	
	* **1998**	Jly	Newbur	(G-F)	H	9f	85	91	
	* **1998**	May	Folkes	(G-F)	H	9.7f	76	80	
	* **1998**	May	Beverl	(G-F)	H	9.9f	72	75	
	* 1997	Spt	Yarmou	(FRM)	H	10.1f	68	73	
	* 1997	Aug	Lingfi	(G-F)	H	10f	61	67	
	* 1996	Oct	Nottin	(GD)		10f		67+	

1998 Turf 5-14: (9f 1-2, 10f 4-10, 11f, 12f) (sft 2, gd 2-4, g-f 1-6, frm 1-1, hrd 1-1)
Scopey, very useful colt, effective 9 to 10f, best at 10f, acts on gd to frm, best on g-f, prefers left handed tracks, likes tight tracks, excels at Newbury and Yarmouth. Turf high 100 - 1st of 12 giving 6lb to Give Me A Ring (19 Aug York RF 3752) - also 1st of 6 giving 1lb to Shadoof (9 Aug Yarmouth RF 3496). He is a ten-furlong, fast ground specialist and enjoyed a smashing season. However, the handicapper needs to relent before he wins again.
**P W Harris [8-27] Mrs P W Harris.*

SUPREME THOUGHT BHB 50f39a RR 54f 39a 5121[13]
6 b m Emarati (USA) 6.6f **(63)** - Who's That Girl (Skyliner) 7.3f **(53)**
Form - 7788004040

Record	**1998** -	1st:0	2nd:0	3rd:0	Ran:10
	Pre1998 -	1st:1	2nd:2	3rd:0	Ran:14

Win Prizemoney £3,226 *Total Prizemoney* £5,041

Wins	1997	Aug	Salisb	(G-S)	H	6f	55	58	<

1998 Turf 0-5: (6f 3, 7f 2) (sft, g-s, gd, g-f, frm) 1998 AW 0-5: (6f, 7f 3, 8f) (Equi 2, Fibr 3)
Fair mare, effective 6f, acts on gd. Turf high 54. AW high 39. Inconsistent.
**Mrs A E Johnson [0-2] S R Hudson (from T J Naughton [0-7] Jun 1998).*

SURE QUEST BHB 60f RR 61f 4393[4]
3 b f Sure Blade (USA) 10.6f **(66)** -Eagle's Quest (Legal Eagle)7.3f **(54)**
Form - 5733164

Record	**1998** -	1st:1	2nd:0	3rd:2	Ran:7
	Pre1998 -	1st:0	2nd:0	3rd:0	Ran:2

Win Prizemoney £3,158 *Total Prizemoney* £4,507

Wins	* **1998**	Aug	Folkes	(G-F)	H	9.7f	57	61	<

1998 Turf 1-7: (8f, 10f 1-5, 11f) (gd 2, g-f, frm 1-4)
Light-framed, average filly, effective 10 to 11f, best at 10f, acts on gd to frm, best on frm, prefers tight tracks. Turf high 61 - 1st of 12 getting 1lb from Mystery Guest (6 Aug Folkestone RF 3404). Consistent. **D W P Arbuthnot [1-9] Miss P E Decker.*

SURE TO DREAM (IRE) BHB 40f53a RR 43f 53a 5121[11]
5 b m Common Grounds 8.1f **(66)**-Hard to Stop (Hard Fought) 8.8f **(62)**
Form - 154231240

Record	**1998** -	1st:1	2nd:2	3rd:1	Ran:6
	Pre1998 -	1st:1	2nd:0	3rd:0	Ran:7

Win Prizemoney £4,364 *Total Prizemoney* £6,265

Wins	* **1998**	*May*	*Southw*	*(STD)*	*H*	*6f*	*49*	*54*	<
	* 1997	*Nov*	*Lingfi*	*(STD)*		*6f*		*41*	

1998 Turf 0-3: (5f, 6f 2) (g-s, gd, frm) 1998 AW 1-3: (6f 1-3) (Equi 2, Fibr 1-1)
Fair filly, effective 6f, - acts on AW, best on Equi, prefers left handed tracks, prefers tight tracks. Turf high 43 (began Spt). AW high 54 - 1st of 16 getting 2lb from Mustang (18 May Southwell RF 1310). **R T Phillips [2-13] Dozen Dreamers Partnership.*

SURHAAN (IRE) RR 67f 4584[4]
2 ch c Rainbow Quest (USA)11.2f **(81)**-Kartajana(Shernazar) 10.2f **(73)**
Form - 4
Record 1998 - 1st:0 2nd:0 3rd:0 Ran:1
Win Prizemoney £0 *Total Prizemoney* £221
1998 Turf 0-1: (8f) (gd)
Currently average colt. **D R Loder [0-1] Sheikh Mohammed.*

SURPRESA CARA BHB 54f **RR 49f** 1883[15]
3 ch f Risk Me (FR) 8f **(53)** - Yukosan (Absalom) 7.2f **(58)**
Form - 00
Record 1998 - 1st:0 2nd:0 3rd:0 Ran:2
Pre1998 - 1st:0 2nd:0 3rd:0 Ran:3
1998 Turf 0-2: (6f, 7f) (gd 2)
Scopey, moderate filly. Turf high 48. **G Lewis [0-5] Ms E A Whelton.*

SURPRISED BHB 65f **RR 62f** 2736[9]
3 b g Superpower 6.6f **(58)** - Indigo (Primo Dominie) 6.2f **(80)**
Form - 0860
Record 1998 - 1st:0 2nd:0 3rd:0 Ran:4
Pre1998 - 1st:0 2nd:1 3rd:0 Ran:3
Win Prizemoney £0 *Total Prizemoney* £1,348
1998 Turf 0-4: (6f 3, 7f) (gd 3, frm)
Average gelding. Turf high 62. A sprint-bred half-brother to the owner's Surprise Mission and Bishops Court, he is improving gradually and will no doubt be placed to advantage.
**Mrs J R Ramsden [0-7] D R Brotherton.*

SURPRISE ENCOUNTER RR 88f 4542[10]
2 ch c Cadeaux Genereux 7.9f **(76)** - Scandalette (Niniski (USA)) 10.6f **(65)**
Form - 00
Record 1998 - 1st:0 2nd:0 3rd:0 Ran:2
1998 Turf 0-2: (7f 2) (g-f, frm)
Currently useful colt. Turf high 88 (began Spt).
**E A L Dunlop [0-2] Ahmed Ali.*

SURPRISE PRESENT (IRE) BHB 58f **RR 53f** 2328[12]
3 ch c Indian Ridge 7.6f **(74)** - Lady Redford (Bold Lad (IRE)) 8.4f **(68)**
Form - 00080
Record 1998 - 1st:0 2nd:0 3rd:0 Ran:5
Pre1998 - 1st:0 2nd:0 3rd:0 Ran:2
1998 Turf 0-5: (5f, 6f, 7f, 8f 2) (gd 4, frm)
Well made, fair colt. Turf high 65. **R Hannon [0-7] Mohamed Suhail.*

SURPRISE WISH (USA) RR 63f 4998[7]
2 gr f El Prado (IRE) 8f **(74)** - Cozier (USA) (Copelan (USA))
Form - 7
Record 1998 - 1st:0 2nd:0 3rd:0 Ran:1
1998 Turf 0-1: (7f) (sft)
Currently average filly.
**Sir Michael Stoute [0-1] The Thoroughbred Corporation.*

SURVEYOR BHB 97f **RR 98f** 4508[5]
3 ch c Lycius (USA) 8.8f **(71)** - Atacama (Green Desert (USA)) 8.6f **(78)**
Form - 73005
Record 1998 - 1st:0 2nd:0 3rd:1 Ran:5
Pre1998 - 1st:2 2nd:1 3rd:0 Ran:4
Win Prizemoney £7,211 *Total Prizemoney* £11,848
Wins * 1997 Spt Kempto (GD) H 6f 90 93 <
* 1997 Aug Lingfi (G-F) 6f 83+
1998 Turf 0-5: (6f 5) (gd 3, g-f 2)
Scopey, very useful colt, effective 6f, acts on sft to frm, best on gd, excels at Lingfield. Turf high 98 - 3rd of 15 getting 7lb from Brave Edge (12 Jly Newbury 6f gd RF 2749). A useful juvenile, he put up a fair effort on his return in a competitive handicap, but did not have much luck afterwards. He endured a terrible passage at Newbury, and had no chance from his draw in the Stewards' Cup. He never quite lived up to expectations, but he was high in the handicap and, if he comes down a few pounds, may be a better proposition in 1999. **J L Dunlop [2-9] The Earl Cadogan.*

SURVIVAL VENTURE BHB 56f **RR 66f** 4889[11]
2 b c Unfuwain (USA) 11.4f **(74)** - Sherkraine (Shergar) 10.4f **(66)**
Form - 0800
Record 1998 - 1st:0 2nd:0 3rd:0 Ran:4
1998 Turf 0-4: (7f, 8f 3) (gd 2, frm 2)
Average colt. Turf high 66 (began Aug). Out of a useful daughter of Shergar, he has shown little in maidens.
**S P C Woods [0-4] Dr Frank Chao.*

SUSANNE RR 49f 5005[6]
2 b f Batshoof 9.5f **(66)** - Clarandal (Young Generation) 7.7f **(63)**
Form - 86
Record 1998 - 1st:0 2nd:0 3rd:0 Ran:2
1998 Turf 0-2: (7f, 8f) (sft, g-f)
Currently moderate filly. Turf high 49 (began Spt).
**Lord Huntingdon [0-2] S Hastings-Bass.*

SUSAN'S DOWRY BHB 74f **RR 76?f** 2523[4]
2 b f Efisio 7.7f **(69)** - Adjusting (IRE) (Busted) 10.2f **(61)**
Form - 64164
Record 1998 - 1st:1 2nd:0 3rd:0 Ran:5
Win Prizemoney £3,615 *Total Prizemoney* £3,807
Wins * **1998** Jun Pontef (SFT) 6f 76+ <
1998 Turf 1-5: (5f 2, 6f 1-2, 7f) (g-s, gd 1-2, g-f, frm)
Above-average filly. Turf high 76 - 1st of 10 from Saffron (15 Jun Pontefract RF 1998). **T D Easterby [1-5] Mrs Claire Hollowood.*

SUSUN KELAPA (USA) RR 96f 3722a[6]
3 ch f St Jovite (USA) 11.8f **(75)** - Tiramisu (USA) (Roberto (USA)) 10f **(76)**
Form - 832716
1998 Turf 1-6: (8f, 9f 1-2, 10f, 11f, 12f) (sft, gd 2, g-f, frm 1-1, hrd)
Very useful filly, effective 7 to 10f, acts on sft to frm, best on g-f, has worn blinkers. Turf high 96 - 1st of 4 from Queen Of Silk (10 Aug Cork RF 3703a). She won a Dundalk maiden on her debut at two, but was highly tried after and did not look up to it. She managed to win a small race at Cork when dropped in class.
**A P O'Brien in IRE [2-10] Michael Tabor.*

SUSY WELLS (IRE) BHB 44f **RR 52f** 4919[5]
3 b f Masad (IRE) - My Best Susy (IRE) (Try My Best (USA)) 7.6f **(67)**
Form - 53826065
Record 1998 - 1st:0 2nd:1 3rd:1 Ran:8
Win Prizemoney £0 *Total Prizemoney* £1,048
1998 Turf 0-8: (7f 2, 8f 4, 10f 2) (g-s 2, gd, g-f 3, frm 2)
Workmanlike, fair filly, effective 7 to 8f, best at 8f, acts on g-s to frm, has worn blinkers. Turf high 52 - 2nd of 10 getting 5lb from Times O'War (6 Aug Haydock 8f g-f RF 3408).
**J Parkes [0-8] C W Moore.*

SUTTON BANK RR 57f 5093[11]
2 b c Clantime 6.6f **(57)** - Saja (USA) (Ferdinand (USA))
Form - 000
Record 1998 - 1st:0 2nd:0 3rd:0 Ran:3
1998 Turf 0-3: (6f 2, 7f) (gd 2, frm)
Currently fair colt. Turf high 57 (began Spt).
**J L Eyre [0-3] F M Smithson.*

SWAFFHAM RR 52+f 499[4]
2 ch c Whittingham (IRE) - Nellie O'Dowd (USA) (Diesis) 9.3f **(69)**
Form - 04
Record 1998 - 1st:0 2nd:0 3rd:0 Ran:2
Win Prizemoney £0 *Total Prizemoney* £192
1998 Turf 0-2: (5f 2) (sft, gd)
Currently fair colt. Turf high 52. **M W Easterby [0-2] P D Savill.*

SWAGGER RR 33+f 4915[7]
2 ch c Generous (IRE) 11.5f **(82)** - Widows Walk (Habitat) 9.4f **(70)**
Form - 7
Record 1998 - 1st:0 2nd:0 3rd:0 Ran:1
1998 Turf 0-1: (6f) (g-s)
Currently very moderate colt. **Sir Mark Prescott [0-1] G Moore.*

SWAIN (IRE) BHB 129f **RR 129+f** 5168a[3]

6 b h Nashwan (USA) 10.3f **(79)** - Love Smitten (CAN) (Key To The Mint (USA)) 9.4f **(75)**

Form - 223113

Record				
1998 -	1st:2	2nd:2	3rd:2	Ran:6
Pre1998 -	1st:6	2nd:2	3rd:4	Ran:14

Win Prizemoney £1,003,539 *Total Prizemoney* £2,313,300

Wins							
* **1998**	Spt	Leopar	(SFT)	G1	10f	124+	
* **1998**	Jly	Ascot	(G-F)	G1	12f	127	
* 1997	Jly	Ascot	(SFT)	G1	12f	129	<
1996	Spt	Longch	(GD)	G3	12f	115+	
1996	Jun	Epsom	(GD)	G1	12f	118+	
1995	Aug	Deauvi	(GD)	G2	12.5f	112	
1995	Aug	Deauvi	(GD)	L	12.5f	104	
1995	Jun	Saint-C	(GD)	G3	14f	103	

1998 Turf 2-4: (10f 1-1, 12f 1-3) (gd 1-3, g-f 1-1) 1998 AW 0-2: (10f 2) (Dirt 2)

Top-class horse, effective 10 to 12f, best at 12f, acts on gd to frm - acts on Dirt, likes Ascot. Turf high 127 - 1st of 8 giving 12lb to High-Rise (25 Jly Ascot RF 3103) - also 1st of 8 giving 10lb to Alborada (12 Spt Leopardstown RF 4294a). AW high 128 (1st run) - 2nd of 9 to Silver Charm (28 Mar Nad Al Sheba 10f Dirt RF 0552a). Consistent. One of the very best middle-distance performers in recent seasons both for Andre Fabre and Godolphin, he ran a blinder to go down by inches in the Dubai World Cup on his reappearance, but was a little disappointing in both the Coronation Cup and Hardwicke Stakes. However, he then returned to his very best, completing a memorable double in the King George, and gaining his first win over ten furlongs when beating a top-class field in the Irish Champion Stakes. It is a shame his swansong on the racecourse, when he finished third in the Breeders' Cup Classic, will be remembered for Dettori's controversial ride, which might even have cost this hard-as-nails battler the victory.

**S bin Suroor [3-10] Godolphin.*

Swain going to post for the King George

SWALLOW FLIGHT (IRE) BHB 99f **RR 84f** 4870[2]
2 b c Bluebird (USA) 7.9f **(71)** - Mirage (Red Sunset) 8.2f **(63)**
Form - 7232
Record 1998 - 1st:0 2nd:2 3rd:1 Ran:4
Win Prizemoney £0 *Total Prizemoney* £7,301
1998 Turf 0-4: (6f 2, 7f, 8f) (gd 2, g-f, frm)
Decent colt. Turf high 84 (began Jly) - 2nd of 7 giving 2lb to Three Green Leaves (19 Oct Pontefract 8f gd RF 4870). Ran an improved race on his second start and should make the grade. Looks the type to make a three-year-old. **G Wragg [0-4] Mollers Racing.*

SWALLOW WARRIOR (IRE) BHB 31f35a **RR 17f 35a** 2403[7]
3 b g Warrshan (USA) 9.7f **(59)** - Pica (Diesis) 9.3f **(69)**
Form - 680007
Record 1998 - 1st:0 2nd:0 3rd:0 Ran:4
Pre1998 - 1st:0 2nd:0 3rd:0 Ran:3
1998 Turf 0-3: (11f, 14f, 17f) (gd 2, g-f) 1998 AW 0-1: (15f) (Fibr)
Strong, moderate gelding, has worn blinkers. Turf high 17.
**T J Etherington [0-7] Foreneish Racing.*

SWAMPY (IRE) BHB 71f **RR 77f** 4196[6]
2 b c Second Set (IRE) 9.2f **(67)** - Mystery Lady (USA) (Vaguely Noble) 10.1f **(72)**
Form - 006
Record 1998 - 1st:0 2nd:0 3rd:0 Ran:3
1998 Turf 0-3: (5f, 7f 2) (gd 3)
Currently above-average colt. Turf high 77 (began Jly).
**K McAuliffe [0-3] Gallagher Equine Ltd.*

SWAN AT WHALLEY BHB 52f49a **RR 49f 49a** 3805[11]
6 b g Statoblest 6.4f **(63)** - My Precious Daisy (Sharpo) 7.7f **(59)**
Form - 0000002820060
Record 1998 - 1st:0 2nd:2 3rd:0 Ran:12
Pre1998 - 1st:4 2nd:4 3rd:3 Ran:36
Win Prizemoney £15,517 *Total Prizemoney* £25,586

Wins	1997	Spt	Cheste	(GD)	H	5.1f	63	64	
	1997	Jun	Doncas	(G-S)	H	5f	63	70	<
	1996	Jly	Mussel	(GD)	H	5f	60	67	
	1994	Jly	Cheste	(G-F)		5.1f		63	

1998 Turf 0-10:(5f 10)(g-s 2, gd 3, g-f, frm 4)1998 AW 0-2: (5f 2)(Fibr 2)
Moderate gelding, has broken blood-vessels, effective 5f, acts on gd to frm, best on gd, has worn blinkers. Turf high 63 - 2nd of 14 getting 20lb from First Maite (17 May Ripon 5f frm RF 1288). AW high 19.
**K A Ryan [0-6] Mrs C M Barlow (from R A Fahey [2-17] May 1998).*

SWANDALE FLYER BHB 25f22a **RR 31f 22a** 2496[8]
6 ch g Weldnaas (USA) 8.4f **(55)** - Misfire (Gunner B) 11.2f **(58)**
Form - 7000388
Record 1998 - 1st:0 2nd:0 3rd:1 Ran:7
Pre1998 - 1st:0 2nd:1 3rd:0 Ran:23
Win Prizemoney £0 *Total Prizemoney* £1,613
1998 Turf 0-5: (12f, 13f 3, 16f) (sft, gd 2, g-f, frm) 1998 AW 0-2: (11f, 12f) (Fibr 2)
Very moderate gelding, effective 12 to 13f, acts on gd - acts on Fibr, likes left handed tracks, favours tight tracks. Turf high 31 - 3rd of 7 getting 18lb from Aldwych Arrow (19 Jun Ayr 13f gd RF 2116). AW high 34. Inconsistent. **N Bycroft [1-37] Andrew Carruthers.*

SWAN HUNTER BHB 67f84a **RR 69f 84a** 4747[12]
5 b h Sharrood (USA) 11.1f **(67)** - Cache (Bustino) 10.4f **(64)**
Form - 11165400
Record 1998 - 1st:1 2nd:0 3rd:0 Ran:6
Pre1998 - 1st:5 2nd:3 3rd:0 Ran:18
Win Prizemoney £15,926 *Total Prizemoney* £19,956

Wins	* **1998**	*Jan*	*Wolver*	*(STD)*	*H*	*12f*	*77*	*84*	<
	* 1997	*Dec*	*Wolver*	*(STD)*	*H*	*12f*	*68*	*74+*	
	* 1997	*Nov*	*Wolver*	*(STD)*	*H*	*14.8f*	*62*	*67*	
	* 1997	Oct	Catter	(SFT)	C	12f		57+	
	* 1997	Oct	Leices	(G-S)	C	11.8f		62	
	* 1996	Apr	Mussel	(GD)		11.1f		63	

1998 Turf 0-3: (12f, 14f, 17f) (gd 2, g-f) 1998 AW 1-3: (9f, 12f 1-2) (Fibr 1-3)
Useful colt, effective 12f, - acts on Fibr, prefers tight tracks. Turf high 69 (began Spt). AW high 84 (1st run) - 1st of 10 giving 20lb to Mr Fortywinks (7 Jan Wolverhampton RF 0041). He was in fine form in the autumn of '97, winning his last two starts on turf, and continued the improvement during the winter with a sparkling hat-trick on the Wolverhampton Fibresand. Unfortunately, he finished unsound when tailed-off at the same track in February, and has been unable to regain his form since.
**D J S Cosgrove [6-24] Derrick Yarwood.*

SWAN ISLAND BHB 46f63a **RR 64f 63a** 4874[9]
4 ch f Hubbly Bubbly (USA) 9.5f **(43)** - Green's Cassatt (USA) (Apalachee (USA)) 9.4f **(71)**
Form - 67353218840600
Record 1998 - 1st:1 2nd:1 3rd:2 Ran:14
Pre1998 - 1st:0 2nd:2 3rd:1 Ran:12
Win Prizemoney £2,220 *Total Prizemoney* £7,301

Wins	* **1998**	*Jly*	*Southw*	*(STD)*	*8f*	*63*	<

1998 Turf 0-9: (8f 5, 9f, 10f 2, 11f) (g-s, gd 3, g-f 2, frm 3) 1998 AW 1-5: (8f 1-5) (Fibr 1-5)
Scopey, average filly, effective 6 to 8f, acts on frm - acts on Fibr, has worn blinkers, likes left handed tracks, favours tight tracks. Turf high 64 - 2nd of 6 giving 9lb to Akarita (10 Jly Chester 8f frm RF 2677). AW high 65 - also 1st of 8 from Chinaberry (17 Jly Southwell RF 2896).
**W M Brisbourne [1-17] K K Baron (from B Palling [0-9] May 1997).*

SWAN LAKE (IRE) BHB 46f **RR 43f** 3453[5]
4 b f Waajib 8.9f **(67)** - Atlanta Royale (Prince Tenderfoot (USA)) 9f **(61)**
Form - 008735
Record 1998 - 1st:0 2nd:0 3rd:1 Ran:6
Pre1998 - 1st:0 2nd:0 3rd:1 Ran:7
Win Prizemoney £0 *Total Prizemoney* £909
1998 Turf 0-5: (6f 5) (g-f, frm 3, hrd) 1998 AW 0-1: (5f) (Fibr)
Moderate filly, effective 5f, acts on gd, has worn blinkers. Turf high 43.
**B J Meehan [0-6] J F O'Malley (from D K Weld in IRE [0-7] Aug 1997).*

SWANMORE LADY (IRE) BHB 50f59a **RR 38f 59a** 2576[16]
3 b f Forzando 7.2f **(63)** - Steffi (Precocious) 8.6f **(62)**
Form - 5000
Record 1998 - 1st:0 2nd:0 3rd:0 Ran:3
Pre1998 - 1st:1 2nd:2 3rd:2 Ran:12
Win Prizemoney £3,561 *Total Prizemoney* £6,032

Wins	* 1997	Spt	Leices	(G-F)	H	6f	53	58	<

1998 Turf 0-3: (6f 3) (g-f 3)
Workmanlike, average filly, effective 5 to 6f, best at 5f, acts on frm - acts on Equi. Turf high 28. Becoming disappointing.
**S C Williams [1-15] A G Axton.*

SWAYBUS BHB 40f35a **RR 52f 35a** 206[10]
3 ch f Pursuit of Love 9.5f **(69)** - Gong (Bustino) 10.4f **(64)**
Form - 70
Record 1998 - 1st:0 2nd:0 3rd:0 Ran:2
Pre1998 - 1st:0 2nd:0 3rd:0 Ran:3
Win Prizemoney £0 *Total Prizemoney* £263
1998 AW 0-2: (7f, 8f) (Fibr 2)
Strong, fair filly. AW high 18.
**M Johnston [0-5] Mrs Jacqueline Conroy.*

SWEET APOLLO BHB 46f **RR 48f** 4818[26]
2 b f Common Grounds 8.1f **(66)** - Moon Watch (Night Shift (USA)) 7.2f **(69)**
Form - 400
Record 1998 - 1st:0 2nd:0 3rd:0 Ran:3
Win Prizemoney £0 *Total Prizemoney* £222
1998 Turf 0-3: (5f 2, 7f) (gd, frm 2)
Currently moderate filly. Turf high 48.
**C A Dwyer [0-3] The Newmarket Stablemates Partnership.*

SWEET AS A NUT (IRE) BHB 76f **RR 83f** 4533[11]
2 ch f Pips Pride 6.7f **(70)** - My First Paige (IRE) **(41f 48a)** (Runnett) 7f **(59)**
Form - 402011310550
Record 1998 - 1st:3 2nd:1 3rd:1 Ran:12
Win Prizemoney £8,213 *Total Prizemoney* £9,334

Wins	* **1998**	Jly	Doncas	(FRM)	H	5f	83	<
	* **1998**	Jun	Hamilt	(SFT)	C	5f	75	
	* **1998**	Jun	Beverl	(GD)	C	5f	58	

1998 Turf 3-11: (5f 3-7, 6f 4) (g-s, gd 2-6, g-f, frm 1-3) 1998 AW 0-1: (5f) (Fibr)

Decent filly, effective 5 to 6f, best at 5f, acts on gd to frm, best on frm. Turf high 83 - 1st of 6 giving 3lb to Northern Svengali (16 Jly Doncaster RF 2847) - also 1st of 6 giving 16lb to Dispol Clan (17 Jun Hamilton RF 2061). **C A Dwyer [3-12] Wessex House Racing.*

SWEET BETTSIE BHB 40f **RR 31f** 5128^{16}

4 b f Presidium 7.5f **(56)**-Sweet and Sure (Known Fact (USA)) 7.4f **(67)**
Form - 5005000
Record 1998 - 1st:0 2nd:0 3rd:0 Ran:7
Pre1998 - 1st:0 2nd:0 3rd:0 Ran:4
1998 Turf 0-7: (6f 5, 7f, 8f) (sft, g-s 2, gd, g-f 3)
Workmanlike, very moderate filly, has worn blinkers. Turf high 43. Inconsistent.
**K R Burke [0-7] The Five Legged Partnership (from A G Foster [0-4] May 1997).*

SWEET CHARITY (IRE) BHB 74f **RR 67f** 4370^{4}

2 ch f Bigstone (IRE) - Tolstoya (Northfields (USA)) 9f **(72)**
Form - 432334
Record 1998 - 1st:0 2nd:1 3rd:3 Ran:6
Win Prizemoney £0 *Total Prizemoney* £3,408
1998 Turf 0-6: (5f 2, 6f 4) (gd, g-f, frm 4)
Average filly, effective 5 to 6f, acts on frm. Turf high 67.
**M A Jarvis [0-6] Mrs Christine Stevenson.*

SWEET CISEAUX (IRE) BHB 31f40a **RR 20f 40a** 1788^{26}

5 b g Be My Guest (USA) 10.2f **(66)** - Wild Abandon (USA) (Graustark) 10.1f **(70)**
Form - 0
Record 1998 - 1st:0 2nd:0 3rd:0 Ran:1
Pre1998 - 1st:1 2nd:0 3rd:0 Ran:14
Win Prizemoney £2,397 *Total Prizemoney* £2,397
Wins 1996 Jun Tipper (FRM) H 7f 50 53 <
1998 Turf 0-1: (12f) (hrd)
Little account gelding, effective 11f, acts on frm, has worn blinkers, likes left handed tracks, favours tight tracks.
**P Bowen [2-10] The Bear (Neath) Racing Club (from B J Llewellyn [0-4] Jly 1997).*

SWEET COMPLIANCE BHB 69f **RR 77f** 4276^{8}

2 ch f Safawan 6.6f **(60)** - Sianiski (Niniski (USA)) 10.6f **(65)**
Form - 02368818
Record 1998 - 1st:1 2nd:1 3rd:1 Ran:8
Win Prizemoney £3,287 *Total Prizemoney* £4,482
Wins * 1998 Spt Lingfi (G-S) H 7f 59 77 <
1998 Turf 1-6: (5f, 6f 2, 7f 1-3) (gd 2, g-f 1-3, frm) 1998 AW 0-2: (5f 2) (Fibr 2)
Above-average filly, effective 7f, acts on g-f, has worn blinkers. Turf high 77 - 1st of 17 getting 9lb from Ghita (8 Spt Lingfield RF 4145). AW high 66. Became her trainer's first ever winner when scoring at Lingfield in September, though her victory owed much to her getting over to the vastly-favoured stands'-side rail.
**P Shakespeare [1-8] Mike Hyde.*

SWEET DREAMS RR 75f 5061^{9}

3 b f Selkirk (USA) 7.9f **(76)** - Ahohoney (Ahonoora) 8.1f **(73)**
Form - 1525630
Record 1998 - 1st:1 2nd:1 3rd:1 Ran:7
Pre1998 - 1st:0 2nd:0 3rd:0 Ran:3
Win Prizemoney £3,553 *Total Prizemoney* £5,513
Wins * 1998 Apr Nottin (SFT) H 8.2f 70 82+ <
1998 Turf 1-7: (8f 1-5, 10f 2) (sft 2, g-s 1-1, gd 3, frm)
Above-average filly, effective 8f, acts on g-s to gd. Turf high 82 (1st run) - 1st of 18 giving 12lb to Fawning (28 Apr Nottingham RF 0902). **J L Dunlop [1-10] Miss K Rausing.*

SWEET GLOW (FR) BHB 57f **RR 60f** 4963^{12}

11 b g Crystal Glitters (USA) 8f **(89)** - Very Sweet (Bellypha) 9.8f **(73)**
Form - 160
Record 1998 - 1st:1 2nd:0 3rd:0 Ran:3
Pre1998 - 1st:1 2nd:0 3rd:1 Ran:12
Win Prizemoney £28,051 *Total Prizemoney* £28,051
Wins * 1998 Jun Bath (G-S) SH 17.2f 52 60++
* 1994 Jun Ascot (G-F) H 20f 71 78+ <
1998 Turf 1-3: (16f 2, 17f 1-1) (sft, gd 1-2)
Average gelding. Turf high 60 (1st run). **M C Pipe [13-60] M C Pipe.*

SWEET MAGIC BHB 54f52a **RR 55f 52a** 1933^{10}

7 ch g Sweet Monday 8.3f **(43)** - Charm Bird (Daring March) 7.1f **(61)**
Form - 0500
Record 1998 - 1st:0 2nd:0 3rd:0 Ran:4
Pre1998 - 1st:3 2nd:3 3rd:2 Ran:27
Win Prizemoney £13,801 *Total Prizemoney* £25,671
Wins * 1997 Aug Sandow (G-S) H 5f 59 63
1995 Jly Newmar (GD) H 5f 81 81 <
1994 Jly Sandow (GD) H 5f 64 66
1998 Turf 0-4: (5f 4) (gd 3, frm)
Fair gelding, effective 5f, acts on g-s to g-f, has worn blinkers. Turf high 55. Inconsistent.
**P Howling [1-20] C Hammond (from L J Holt [2-11] Aug 1995).*

SWEET MATE BHB 47f40a **RR 42f 40a** 464^{7}

6 ch g Komaite (USA) 6.9f **(61)** - Be My Sweet (Galivanter) 7.8f **(56)**
Form - 67707
Record 1998 - 1st:0 2nd:0 3rd:0 Ran:5
Pre1998 - 1st:4 2nd:3 3rd:4 Ran:42
Win Prizemoney £8,828 *Total Prizemoney* £13,582
Wins * 1997 *May Southw (STD) H 6f 45 49*
* 1997 May Nottin (GD) H 6.1f 44 41
* 1996 *Feb Southw (STD) H 7f 55 57* <
* 1995 *May Southw (STD) H 6f 42 41*
1998 AW 0-5: (6f 2, 7f 2, 8f) (Fibr 5)
Moderate gelding, effective 5 to 6f, best at 6f, acts on g-s to gd - acts on Fibr, mostly wears blinkers (effectively). AW high 35.
**S R Bowring [4-39] S R Bowring (from M Meade [0-4] Jan 1997).*

SWEET MEADOW RR 3328^{7}

4 b g Sylvan Express 9.6f **(45)** - River Bark (Rapid River) 5.7f **(51)**
Form - 77
Record 1998 - 1st:0 2nd:0 3rd:0 Ran:2
1998 Turf 0-2: (11f, 16f) (gd 2)
Workmanlike, currently very poor gelding. (began Jly) - 7th of 7 giving 20lb to Last Lap (4 Aug Catterick 16f gd RF 3328).
**Mrs A M Naughton [0-3] D H Montgomerie.*

SWEETNESS HERSELF BHB 105f **RR 101f** 5140^{2}

5 ch m Unfuwain (USA) 11.4f **(74)** - No Sugar Baby (FR) (Crystal Glitters (USA)) 11.3f **(79)**
Form - 1445332813312
Record 1998 - 1st:2 2nd:2 3rd:4 Ran:12
Pre1998 - 1st:8 2nd:2 3rd:4 Ran:22
Win Prizemoney £71,777 *Total Prizemoney* £136,762
Wins * 1998 Oct Currag (SFT) H 16f 101+
*** 1998** Aug Newcas (GD) H 16.1f 93 101
* 1997 Dec Maison (HVY) L 15f 105 <
* 1997 Nov Doncas (GD) 14.6f 101
* 1997 Mar Haydoc (SFT) 16.2f 95?
* 1996 Nov Doncas (SFT) H 16.5f 76 83
* 1996 Oct Nottin (SFT) H 14.1f 66 78
* 1996 Oct Chepst (SFT) H 12.1f 66 73
* 1996 Oct Haydoc (SFT) H 14f 62 66
* 1996 Aug Leices (GD) 11.8f 65
1998 Turf 2-11: (14f 2, 15f 2, 16f 2-7) (hvy, sft 2, g-s 1-2, gd 2, g-f, frm 1-3) 1998 AW 0-1: (12f) (Fibr)
Very useful filly, effective 13 to 16f, acts on hvy to frm, likes left handed tracks, excels at Newcastle and Newbury and Maisons-laffitte and Haydock, likes Doncaster. Turf high 101 - 1st of 15 giving 8lb to Quinze (3 Oct Curragh RF 4688a) - also 1st of 5 giving 25lb to Noufari (31 Aug Newcastle RF 3994). Consistent. A tremendous servant to Mick Ryan's stable, she capped another excellent campaign by becoming the first British-trained horse to win the Irish Cesarewitch. Soft ground plus an extreme test of stamina are her requirements and she rarely comes off second best in a head-to-head. **M J Ryan [10-34] Mrs M J Lavell.*

SWEET NOTE (IRE) BHB 31f **RR 29f** 1874^{7}

4 ch f La Grange Music - Screenable (USA) (Silent Screen (USA)) 8.6f **(65)**
Form - 370307
Record 1998 - 1st:0 2nd:0 3rd:2 Ran:6
Pre1998 - 1st:0 2nd:0 3rd:1 Ran:13
Win Prizemoney £0 *Total Prizemoney* £1,545
1998 Turf 0-6: (8f 3, 9f 2, 11f) (hvy, sft 2, g-s 2, gd)
Neat, little account filly, effective 9f, acts on g-s. Turf high 33. Inconsistent. **Miss L A Perratt [0-19] T P Finch.*

SWEET PATOOPIE BHB 46f59a **RR 47f 59a** 3154[4]
4 b f Indian Ridge 7.6f **(74)** - Patriotic (Hotfoot) 10.5f **(59)**
Form - 206324
Record 1998 - 1st:0 2nd:2 3rd:1 Ran:6
Pre1998 - 1st:0 2nd:0 3rd:0 Ran:2
Win Prizemoney £0 *Total Prizemoney* £2,470
1998 Turf 0-4:(8f 2, 10f 2)(g-s, g-f 2, hrd)1998 AW 0-2: (6f, 10f) (Equi 2)
Workmanlike, fair filly, effective 6 to 10f, - acts on Equi, has worn blinkers, favours left handed tracks. Turf high 47. AW high 59 - 2nd of 12 giving 5lb to Hawksbill Henry (10 Jly Lingfield 10f Equi RF 2691). **B Hanbury [0-8] Mrs B Newton.*

SWEET PEA BHB 79f **RR 80f** 3209[12]
3 b f Persian Bold 10f **(69)** - Silk Petal (Petorius) 7.3f **(61)**
Form - 021120
Record 1998 - 1st:2 2nd:2 3rd:0 Ran:6
Win Prizemoney £8,359 *Total Prizemoney* £11,517
Wins * **1998** Jun Newmar (GD) H 8f 75 80 <
* **1998** May Bath (G-F) 8f 74
1998 Turf 2-6: (7f, 8f 2-4, 9f) (gd 1-3, g-f, frm 1-2)
Scopey, decent filly, effective 8f, acts on gd to frm. Turf high 80 - 1st of 9 giving 11lb to Minetta (27 Jun Newmarket RF 2354) - also 1st of 12 from Cornflower Fields (29 May Bath RF 1569). Steadily improving with each run, she managed to force a dead-heat at Bath on her third start, and was a game winner at Newmarket next time. Disappointing at Glorious Goodwood latest.
**J L Dunlop [2-6] Nicholas Jones.*

SWEET REWARD BHB 66f **RR 67f** 5147[8]
3 ch c Beveled (USA) 6.9f **(64)** - Sweet Revival (Claude Monet (USA))
Form - 386335008
Record 1998 - 1st:0 2nd:0 3rd:3 Ran:9
Pre1998 - 1st:1 2nd:0 3rd:1 Ran:4
Win Prizemoney £3,392 *Total Prizemoney* £6,850
Wins * 1997 Jun Leices (GD) 6f 72 <
1998 Turf 0-9: (7f, 8f 6, 10f 2) (g-s 2, gd 7)
Leggy, average colt, effective 6 to 8f, best at 8f, acts on g-s to gd, best on g-s, likes tight tracks. Turf high 80 (1st run) - 3rd of 13 getting 2lb from Fizzed (23 Apr Beverley 7f g-s RF 0826). Consistent.
**J G Smyth-Osbourne [1-13] Mrs V Youell.*

SWEET SENORITA BHB 27f **RR 38f** 4150[11]
3 b f Young Senor (USA) 8f **(43)**-Sweet N' Twenty (High Top) 10.2f **(67)**
Form - 0660
Record 1998 - 1st:0 2nd:0 3rd:0 Ran:4
Pre1998 - 1st:0 2nd:0 3rd:0 Ran:3
1998 Turf 0-4: (7f, 10f, 11f, 16f) (g-f 3, frm)
Leggy, very moderate filly. Turf high 38 (began Aug).
**M Madgwick [0-7] W E Baird.*

SWEET SERANADE (IRE) BHB 21f **RR** 4403[13]
5 b m Ballad Rock 7.2f **(63)** - Little Honey (Prince Bee) 12f **(46)**
Form - 0
Record 1998 - 1st:0 2nd:0 3rd:0 Ran:1
Pre1998 - 1st:0 2nd:0 3rd:0 Ran:2
1998 Turf 0-1: (12f) (g-f)
Very poor filly.
**J P Leigh [0-1] Mrs D Dukes (from N P Littmoden [0-2] Apr 1996).*

SWEET SERENATA BHB 39f **RR 48f** 4371[1]
3 gr f Keen 11.1f **(58)** - Serenata (Larrinaga) 13.8f **(53)**
Form - 477040751
Record 1998 - 1st:1 2nd:0 3rd:0 Ran:9
Win Prizemoney £2,010 *Total Prizemoney* £2,010
Wins * **1998** Spt Catter (G-F) S 13.8f 43 <
1998 Turf 1-8: (7f, 10f 2, 12f, 14f 1-2, 16f 2) (gd 2, g-f 3, frm 1-3) 1998 AW 0-1: (9f) (Fibr)
Lengthy, moderate filly, effective 14f, acts on frm, favours tight tracks. Turf high 49 - also 1st of 13 getting 6lb from Last Lap (19 Spt Catterick RF 4371). **S C Williams [1-9] Rib And Co.*

SWEET SHE AIN'T RR 18f 3669[11]
2 b f King's Signet (USA) 7f **(51)** - Just Run (IRE) (Runnett) 7f **(59)**
Form - 0
Record 1998 - 1st:0 2nd:0 3rd:0 Ran:1
1998 Turf 0-1: (5f) (frm)
Currently poor filly. **D Nicholls [0-1] R J H Ltd.*

SWEET SORROW (IRE) BHB 78f **RR 78f** 4802[3]
3 b f Lahib (USA) 8f **(69)** - So Long Boys (FR) (Beldale Flutter (USA)) 9.7f **(71)**
Form - 33333
Record 1998 - 1st:0 2nd:0 3rd:5 Ran:5
Pre1998 - 1st:0 2nd:0 3rd:0 Ran:2
Win Prizemoney £0 *Total Prizemoney* £4,613
1998 Turf 0-5: (8f 2, 10f 2, 11f) (sft, gd, g-f 3)
Leggy, above-average filly, effective 8 to 11f, acts on sft to g-f. Turf high 78 - 3rd of 12 giving 20lb to Primary Colours (14 Oct Haydock 11f sft RF 4802). **C F Wall [0-7] Mrs Yoshiko Allan.*

SWEET SUMMERTIME (IRE) RR 95f 4719a[4]
3 g Second Set (IRE) 9.2f **(67)** - Taeesha (Mill Reef (USA)) 10.5f **(78)**
Form - 4
1998 Turf 0-1: (15f) (sft)
Currently very useful gelding. **R Collet in FR [0-1] R C Strauss.*

SWEET SUPPOSIN (IRE) BHB 52f57a **RR 30f 57a** 395[5]
7 b h Posen (USA) 8.6f **(59)** - Go Honey Go (General Assembly (USA)) 10f **(68)**
Form - 524343505
Record 1998 - 1st:0 2nd:0 3rd:2 Ran:6
Pre1998 - 1st:13 2nd:6 3rd:8 Ran:54
Win Prizemoney £36,579 *Total Prizemoney* £46,729
Wins * 1997 *Mar Lingfi (STD) H 10f 62 64*
* 1997 *Feb Lingfi (STD) H 10f 60 62*
* 1996 *May Wolver (STD) C 9.4f 65*
* 1996 *Mar Lingfi (STD) C 12f 77*
* 1996 *Feb Lingfi (STD) C 10f 77*
* 1996 *Feb Lingfi (STD) C 10f 77*
* 1995 *Nov Wolver (STD) C 9.4f 59*
* 1995 *Aug Wolver (STD) C 7f 81* <
1995 *Jly Wolver (STD) C 7f 74+*
1995 *Jun Wolver (STD) C 8.5f 78*
1995 *Feb Lingfi (STD) C 7f 68*
1995 *Feb Lingfi (STD) C 7f 68*
1994 *Dec Lingfi (STD) H 8f 61 64+*
1998 AW 0-6: (8f, 10f 2, 11f 2, 12f) (Equi 3, Fibr 3)
Fair horse, effective 8 to 11f, best at 8f, - acts on AW, best on Equi, mostly wears blinkers (effectively), favours left handed tracks, favours tight tracks, does well at Lingfield. AW high 59 - 4th of 12 to The Butterwick Kid (19 Jan Southwell 11f Fibr RF 0116). He generally holds his form well, but is without a win since March '97. Frankie Dettori has a very good record on him.
**C A Dwyer [8-40] G Middlemiss (from John Berry [0-5] Oct 1996).*

SWEET TRENTINO (IRE) BHB 34f42a **RR 32f 42a** 3605[12]
7 b g High Estate 10.5f **(66)** - Sweet Adelaide (USA) (The Minstrel (CAN)) 10f **(72)**
Form - 00080
Record 1998 - 1st:0 2nd:0 3rd:0 Ran:5
Pre1998 - 1st:2 2nd:4 3rd:0 Ran:23
Win Prizemoney £7,355 *Total Prizemoney* £12,073
Wins 1994 Jun Newmar (GD) C 8f 69 <
1994 Jun Goodwo (GF) C 8f 58
1998 Turf 0-5: (8f 2, 10f, 11f, 12f) (sft, g-f, frm 2, hrd)
Moderate gelding, has worn blinkers. Turf high 32.
**M Tate [1-22] R C Smith (from C A Smith [0-5] Mar 1995).*

SWEET WILHELMINA BHB 77f76a **RR 82f 76a** 4848[28]
5 b m Indian Ridge 7.6f **(74)** - Henpot (IRE) (Alzao (USA)) 7.1f **(68)**
Form - 2821208600
Record 1998 - 1st:1 2nd:3 3rd:0 Ran:10
Pre1998 - 1st:5 2nd:3 3rd:1 Ran:17
Win Prizemoney £21,257 *Total Prizemoney* £46,197
Wins * **1998** Jun Goodwo (G-F) H 7f 74 76
* 1997 May Leices (GD) H 8f 60 68
* 1997 *Feb Lingfi (STD) 7f 66+*
* 1997 *Feb Lingfi (STD) 8f 61+*
* 1995 *Nov Lingfi (STD) H 8f 67 78+* <
* 1995 *Nov Wolver (STD) 7f 73*
1998 Turf 1-9: (7f 1-3, 8f 5, 9f) (sft 2, g-s, gd 3, g-f 1-3) 1998 AW 0-1: (8f) (Equi)
Decent filly, effective 7 to 8f, best at 8f, acts on g-s to g-f - acts on Equi, likes left handed tracks, prefers tight tracks, excels at Lingfield, does well at Goodwood. Turf high 82 - 2nd of 20 getting 1lb from Pantar (28 Jun Goodwood 8f gd RF 2365) - also 1st of 12

giving 9lb to Roisin Splendour (19 Jun Goodwood RF 2121). (1st run) - 2nd of 12 getting 2lb from Zimiri (8 May Lingfield 8f Equi RF 1105). Inconsistent. **Lord Huntingdon [6-27] Chris van Hoorn.*

SWELL BETTY (IRE) BHB 69f **RR 70f** 4538[7]
2 b f Distinctly North (USA) 7.4f **(63)** - Cambridge Lodge (Tower Walk) 10f **(62)**
Form - 65637
Record 1998 - 1st:0 2nd:0 3rd:1 Ran:5
Win Prizemoney £0 *Total Prizemoney* £510
1998 Turf 0-5: (5f 2, 6f, 7f 2) (gd, g-f 2, frm 2)
Above-average filly. Turf high 70. **R Hannon [0-5] Lady G Parker.*

SWIFT BHB 57f63a **RR 63df 63a** 4760[8]
4 ch g Sharpo 7.5f **(68)**-Three Terns (USA)(Arctic Tern (USA)) 8.9f **(69)**
Form - 430206663020504205004408
Record 1998 - 1st:0 2nd:3 3rd:2 Ran:24
Pre1998 - 1st:4 2nd:2 3rd:3 Ran:27
Win Prizemoney £12,464 *Total Prizemoney* £24,010
Wins * 1997 Jun Redcar (GD) H 7f 62 66 <
* 1997 May Ripon (G-F) H 6f 57 63
* 1997 *Mar Wolver (STD) 8.5f 61*
* 1996 Oct Catter (GD) 5f 61
1998 Turf 0-19: (7f 6, 8f 12, 10f) (sft, g-s 2, gd 6, g-f 6, frm 4) 1998 AW 0-5: (7f, 8f 4) (Equi 2, Fibr 3)
Workmanlike, average gelding, effective 6 to 8f, best at 8f, acts on gd to frm - acts on AW, excels at Wolverhampton. Turf high 66 - 3rd of 18 giving 21lb to Wings Awarded (11 May Windsor 8f frm RF 1158). AW high 64 - 3rd of 9 getting 16lb from Weetman's Weigh (18 Feb Wolverhampton 7f Fibr RF 0309).
**M J Polglase [4-51] Gen Sir Geoffrey Howlett.*

SWIFT TIME BHB 44f **RR 24f** 2258[16]
3 b f Timeless Times (USA)6.1f **(56)**-Bustling Around(Bustino)10.4f **(64)**
Form - 00
Record 1998 - 1st:0 2nd:0 3rd:0 Ran:2
Pre1998 - 1st:0 2nd:1 3rd:0 Ran:7
Win Prizemoney £0 *Total Prizemoney* £774
1998 Turf 0-2: (5f 2) (g-f, frm)
Small, little account filly, effective 5f, acts on gd. Turf high 6.
**M R Bosley [0-9] Marks (Banbury).*

SWIFTWAY BHB 48f **RR 49f** 3748[U]
4 ch g Anshan 8.2f **(63)** - Solemn Occasion (USA) (Secreto (USA)) 8.7f **(72)**
Form - 60514U
Record 1998 - 1st:1 2nd:0 3rd:0 Ran:6
Pre1998 - 1st:0 2nd:1 3rd:3 Ran:12
Win Prizemoney £3,036 *Total Prizemoney* £5,995
Wins * **1998** Jly Beverl (G-F) H 16.2f 44 49 <
1998 Turf 1-6: (14f, 16f 1-5) (gd 2, g-f 2, frm 1-2)
Workmanlike, moderate gelding, effective 12 to 16f, best at 16f, acts on gd to frm, best on frm, prefers right handed tracks, prefers tight tracks. Turf high 49. **K W Hogg [1-18] Anthony White.*

SWING ALONG BHB 85f **RR 86f** 1354[7]
3 ch f Alhijaz 7.7f **(57)** - So it Goes (Free State) 8.7f **(61)**
Form - 27
Record 1998 - 1st:0 2nd:1 3rd:0 Ran:2
Pre1998 - 1st:0 2nd:1 3rd:0 Ran:1
Win Prizemoney £0 *Total Prizemoney* £3,402
1998 Turf 0-2: (7f 2) (gd, g-f)
Strong, currently useful filly. Turf high 86 (1st run) - 2nd of 15 to Jinsiyah (1 May Newmarket 7f gd RF 0965).
**C F Wall [0-3] W G Bovill.*

SWING BALL RR 51f 1291[9]
3 b f Always Fair (USA) 14f **(61)** - Lady Anchor (Slip Anchor) 9.8f **(73)**
Form - 00
Record 1998 - 1st:0 2nd:0 3rd:0 Ran:2
1998 Turf 0-2: (8f 2) (g-s, frm)
Lengthy, currently fair filly. Turf high 51.
**T R Watson [0-2] Newitt and Co Ltd.*

SWINGING THE BLUES (IRE) BHB 66f **RR 66f** 4936[11]
4 b g Bluebird (USA) 7.9f **(71)** - Winsong Melody (Music Maestro) 7.7f **(66)**
Form - 302133210
Record 1998 - 1st:2 2nd:2 3rd:3 Ran:9
Pre1998 - 1st:0 2nd:0 3rd:0 Ran:7
Win Prizemoney £6,581 *Total Prizemoney* £10,504
Wins * **1998** Oct Redcar (g-s) H 9f 62 66 <
1998 Jly Nottin (G-F) H 8.2f 53 56
1998 Turf 2-9: (8f 1-8, 9f 1-1) (gd 4, g-f 2-4, frm)
Scopey, average gelding, effective 8 to 9f, best at 8f, acts on gd to g-f, best on g-f, has worn blinkers. Turf high 66 - 1st of 15 giving 5lb to Amoroso (6 Oct Redcar RF 4672).
**C A Dwyer [1-3] The Fairy Story Partnership (from J W Hills [1-6] Spt 1998).*

SWING JOB BHB 67f **RR 67f** 4650[6]
2 b f Ezzoud (IRE) - Leave Her Be (USA) (Known Fact (USA)) 7.4f **(67)**
Form - 566
Record 1998 - 1st:0 2nd:0 3rd:0 Ran:3
1998 Turf 0-3: (6f, 7f 2) (gd, g-f 2)
Currently average filly. Turf high 67 (began Aug).
**T G Mills [0-3] Shipman Racing.*

SWINGTIME BHB 31f **RR 20f** 3980[11]
3 ch f Beveled (USA) 6.9f **(64)** - Superfina (USA) (Fluorescent Light (USA))
Form - 0000
Record 1998 - 1st:0 2nd:0 3rd:0 Ran:4
Pre1998 - 1st:0 2nd:0 3rd:0 Ran:2
1998 Turf 0-4: (8f 3, 12f) (g-f, frm 3)
Strong, little account filly. Turf high 20 (began Jly).
**G F H Charles-Jones [0-4] J M Cook (from A G Foster [0-2] Oct 1997).*

SWING WEST (USA) BHB 58f61a **RR 48f 61a** 2514[7]
4 b c Gone West (USA) 7.8f **(82)** -Danlu (USA) (Danzig (USA)) 8.4f **(76)**
Form - 107
Record 1998 - 1st:1 2nd:0 3rd:0 Ran:3
Pre1998 - 1st:0 2nd:1 3rd:1 Ran:7
Win Prizemoney £2,450 *Total Prizemoney* £3,543
Wins * **1998** *Feb Southw (STD) H 16f 54 55* <
1998 Turf 0-2: (15f, 16f) (hvy, g-f) 1998 AW 1-1: (16f 1-1) (Fibr 1-1)
Scopey, fair colt, effective 11 to 16f, best at 11f, acts on gd to frm - acts on Fibr, prefers tight tracks. Turf high 48. (1st run) - 1st of 9 getting 11lb from Chabrol (2 Feb Southwell RF 0202).
**P Eccles [2-11] Noel Glynn (from P F I Cole [0-7] Aug 1997).*

SWINO BHB 74f70a **RR 81f 70a** 4799[19]
4 b g Forzando 7.2f **(63)** - St Helena (Monsanto (FR)) 6.5f **(59)**
Form - 0852167145470002800
Record 1998 - 1st:2 2nd:2 3rd:0 Ran:17
Pre1998 - 1st:2 2nd:7 3rd:2 Ran:30
Win Prizemoney £26,276 *Total Prizemoney* £39,780
Wins * **1998** May Haydoc (GD) H 6f 80 84
* **1998** Apr Thirsk (G-S) H 5f 72 84
* 1997 Oct Redcar (G-F) 5f 66
* 1996 Aug Carlis (FRM) 5f 85 <
1998 Turf 2-17: (5f 1-7, 6f 1-9, 7f) (sft 3, g-s 1-3, gd 1-8, g-f 3)
Light-framed, decent gelding, effective 5 to 6f, best at 5f, acts on g-s to gd, best on g-s, often wears blinkers. Turf high 84 - 1st of 12 giving 1lb to First Maite (10 May Haydock RF 1143) - also 1st of 20 getting 12lb from Ziggy's Dancer (18 Apr Thirsk RF 0750). Inconsistent. Mixed form in 1998, although he displayed a great turn of foot when winning at Thirsk in April and is clearly useful on his day. **P D Evans [4-47] Swinnerton Transport Ltd.*

SWISS LAW BHB 102f **RR 102f** 4494[11]
4 b c Machiavellian (USA) 9.8f **(83)** - Seductress (Known Fact (USA)) 7.4f **(67)**
Form - 3420
Record 1998 - 1st:0 2nd:1 3rd:1 Ran:4
Pre1998 - 1st:1 2nd:4 3rd:0 Ran:8
Win Prizemoney £5,040 *Total Prizemoney* £26,171
Wins 1997 May Newmar (GD) 7f 96 <
1998 Turf 0-4: (7f 3, 8f) (gd 2, g-f, frm)
Scopey, very useful colt, effective 7 to 8f, best at 7f, acts on gd to g-f, best on g-f. Turf high 102 - 2nd of 12 giving 3lb to Rock Falcon (29 Aug Goodwood 7f g-f RF 3946). Consistent. John Gosden was not happy with his attitude after a narrow defeat at Goodwood, declaring that the horse had 'chucked it'. He is probably right and this frustrating character is best left alone.

J H M Gosden [0-7] Maktoum Al Maktoum (from S bin Suroor [1-3] Jun 1997).

SWISSMATIC BHB 57f53a **RR 65f 53a** 4671[13]
2 gr f Petong 7.6f **(58)** - Last Blessing (Final Straw) 7.9f **(64)**
Form - 8640
Record 1998 - 1st:0 2nd:0 3rd:0 Ran:4
1998 Turf 0-3: (5f, 6f, 7f) (gd, g-f, frm) 1998 AW 0-1: (7f) (Fibr)
Average filly. Turf high 65 (began Jly).
P C Haslam [0-4] Mrs E Chung.

SWISS TONI BHB 62f **RR 67f** 4671[5]
2 gr g Petong 7.6f **(58)** - Dash Cascade (Absalom) 7.2f **(58)**
Form - 8275025
Record 1998 - 1st:0 2nd:2 3rd:0 Ran:7
Win Prizemoney £0 *Total Prizemoney* £1,345
1998 Turf 0-7: (5f 2, 6f, 7f 4) (gd 2, g-f, frm 4)
Average gelding, effective 7f, acts on frm. Turf high 67 - 2nd of 10 giving 2lb to Catch Me (23 Jun Beverley 7f frm RF 2197). Won a claimer on the All-Weather in November and has gone to race in Sweden. *D Nicholls [0-7] Trilby Racing.*

SWISS VALLEY LAD RR 271[8]
4 b g Meqdaam (USA) - Jokers High (USA) (Vaguely Noble) 10.1f **(72)**
Form - 8
Record 1998 - 1st:0 2nd:0 3rd:0 Ran:1
1998 AW 0-1: (12f) (Equi)
Currently very poor gelding - 8th of 10 to Harik (12 Feb Lingfield 12f Equi RF 0271). *N M Babbage [0-1] Miss S S Pigot.*

SWOOSH BHB 55f51a **RR 57f 51a** 5070[11]
3 gr g Absalom 7.1f **(56)** - Valldemosa (Music Boy) 6.8f **(57)**
Form - 08005617644400
Record 1998 - 1st:1 2nd:0 3rd:0 Ran:14
Pre1998 - 1st:0 2nd:1 3rd:1 Ran:5
Win Prizemoney £2,250 *Total Prizemoney* £3,719
Wins * **1998** Jun Nottin (GD) SH 8.2f 54 56 <
1998 Turf 1-11: (6f 3, 8f 1-3, 9f 2, 10f 3) (g-s 2, gd 1-2, g-f 5, frm 2)
1998 AW 0-3: (6f, 7f, 8f) (Fibr 3)
Workmanlike, fair gelding, effective 6f, acts on gd to g-f, has worn blinkers. Turf high 57. AW high 51.
J A Glover [1-14] Sports Mania (from B J Meehan [0-5] Jun 1997).

SWORD OF DAMOCLES (USA) BHB 66f **RR 62f** 4889[9]
2 ch c Sword Dance 9.4f **(67)** - Exceptional Jan (USA) (Give Me Strength (USA))
Form - 0840
Record 1998 - 1st:0 2nd:0 3rd:0 Ran:4
Win Prizemoney £0 *Total Prizemoney* £253
1998 Turf 0-4: (7f 2, 8f 2) (gd, g-f, frm 2)
Average colt, has worn blinkers. Turf high 62 (began Aug).
J H M Gosden [0-4] Ms Rachel Hood.

SWYNFORD CHARMER BHB 25f29a **RR 38f 29a** 267[7]
4 ch g Charmer 9f **(59)** - Qualitairess (Kampala) 8.5f **(56)**
Form - 067
Record 1998 - 1st:0 2nd:0 3rd:0 Ran:2
Pre1998 - 1st:0 2nd:0 3rd:0 Ran:7
1998 AW 0-2: (8f, 12f) (Fibr 2)
Very moderate gelding, has worn blinkers. AW high 16.
J Hetherton [0-5] Qualitair Holdings Ltd (from J F Bottomley [0-5] Aug 1997).

SWYNFORD DREAM BHB 57f60a **RR 57f 60a** 4582[16]
5 b g Statoblest 6.4f **(63)** - Qualitair Dream (Dreams to Reality (USA)) 6.4f **(73)**
Form - 7080000642001680
Record 1998 - 1st:1 2nd:1 3rd:0 Ran:15
Pre1998 - 1st:4 2nd:3 3rd:2 Ran:31
Win Prizemoney £23,320 *Total Prizemoney* £34,570
Wins * **1998** Jly Catter (GD) H 5f 55 57
1996 Oct Newmar (G-F) H 5f 79 82
1995 Oct Catter (G-F) H 5f 77 84+ <
1995 Spt Redcar (GD) H 5f 65 73+
1995 Spt Ayr (GD) S 5f 67
1998 Turf 1-13: (5f 1-13) (g-s 2, gd 3, g-f 1-5, frm 3) 1998 AW 0-2: (5f 2) (Fibr 2)
Fair gelding, has worn blinkers. Turf high 57. AW high 19.
J Hetherton [1-20] Qualitair Holdings Ltd (from J F Bottomley [4-26] Aug 1997).

SWYNFORD LORD BHB 57f **RR 69f** 5094[14]
2 b g Formidable (USA) 7.8f **(60)**-Princess Lieven(Royal Palace) 9f **(56)**
Form - 0050
Record 1998 - 1st:0 2nd:0 3rd:0 Ran:4
1998 Turf 0-4: (6f, 7f, 8f 2) (gd, g-f, frm 2)
Average gelding. Turf high 69 (began Aug).
J Hetherton [0-4] Qualitair Holdings Ltd.

SWYNFORD PLEASURE BHB 61f **RR 66f** 5148[14]
2 b f Reprimand 8.2f **(63)** - Pleasuring (Good Times (ITY)) 6.6f **(54)**
Form - 42200
Record 1998 - 1st:0 2nd:2 3rd:0 Ran:5
Win Prizemoney £0 *Total Prizemoney* £1,391
1998 Turf 0-5: (6f, 7f 2, 8f 2) (sft, gd, g-f 2, frm)
Average filly, has worn blinkers. Turf high 66 - 2nd of 7 getting 12lb from Three Green Leaves (8 Spt Newcastle 8f frm RF 4151).
J Hetherton [0-5] Qualitair Holdings Ltd.

SWYNFORD WELCOME BHB 72f **RR 76f** 4820[11]
2 b f Most Welcome 8.6f **(66)** - Qualitair Dream (Dreams to Reality (USA)) 6.4f **(73)**
Form - 24213700
Record 1998 - 1st:1 2nd:2 3rd:1 Ran:8
Win Prizemoney £2,973 *Total Prizemoney* £7,497
Wins * **1998** Jly Redcar (G-F) 6f 76 <
1998 Turf 1-8: (5f 4, 6f 1-4) (gd, g-f, frm 5, hrd 1-1)
Above-average filly, effective 5 to 6f, best at 6f, acts on g-f to hrd. Turf high 76 - 1st of 7 from Bollin Rita (25 Jly Redcar RF 3122).
J Hetherton [1-8] Qualitair Holdings Ltd.

SYCAMORE LODGE (IRE) BHB 53f48a **RR 53f 48a** 4775[5]
7 ch g Thatching 7.8f **(69)** - Bell Tower (Lyphard's Wish (FR)) 9f **(74)**
Form - 00575235235
Record 1998 - 1st:0 2nd:2 3rd:2 Ran:10
Pre1998 - 1st:1 2nd:6 3rd:4 Ran:25
Win Prizemoney £3,470 *Total Prizemoney* £15,404
Wins 1996 Jun Doncas (G-F) H 6f 67 67 <
1998 Turf 0-9: (5f, 6f 5, 7f 3) (gd 4, frm 5) 1998 AW 0-1: (7f) (Fibr)
Fair gelding, effective 6 to 7f, best at 6f, acts on gd to frm, best on frm, has worn blinkers. Turf high 53 - 3rd of 19 giving 4lb to Loganlea (17 Spt Yarmouth 6f frm RF 4339). Improving.
D Nicholls [0-10] Hollow Legs Syndicate (from M A Peill [0-7] Nov 1997).

SYDNEY SAFEHANDS BHB 81f **RR 81f** 4836[4]
2 b c Presidium 7.5f **(56)** - Like Amber (Aragon) 8.1f **(60)**
Form - 13040364
Record 1998 - 1st:1 2nd:0 3rd:2 Ran:8
Win Prizemoney £2,070 *Total Prizemoney* £3,513
Wins * **1998** *Apr Wolver (STD) 5f 76+* <
1998 Turf 0-5: (5f 5) (g-s 2, gd, g-f 2) 1998 AW 1-3: (5f 1-1, 6f 2) (Fibr 1-3)
Useful colt, effective 5 to 6f, acts on gd - acts on Fibr. Turf high 81 - 3rd of 12 giving 6lb to Sunley Sense (15 Spt Sandown 5f gd RF 4269). AW high 89 - 4th of 11 giving 25lb to Kilbowie Hill (24 Jly Wolverhampton 6f Fibr RF 3093). Inconsistent. He won a Wolverhampton Fibresand maiden nicely on his debut, but has faced some stiff tasks since then. *N P Littmoden [1-8] S R Leoni.*

SYDNEYTWOTHOUSAND (IRE) BHB 46f **RR 52f** 4887[3]
4 b g Ela-Mana-Mou 12.7f **(72)** - Fleuretta (USA) (The Minstrel (CAN)) 10f **(72)**
Form - 585003
Record 1998 - 1st:0 2nd:0 3rd:1 Ran:6
Pre1998 - 1st:0 2nd:0 3rd:0 Ran:1
Win Prizemoney £0 *Total Prizemoney* £270
1998 Turf 0-6: (8f 2, 9f, 12f 2, 14f) (sft 2, g-s 3, gd)
Fair gelding, often wears blinkers. Turf high 58.
R Rowe [0-2] Michael Watt (from D K Weld in IRE [0-5] May 1998).

SYLPHIDE BHB 20f **RR** 454[14]
3 b f Ballet Royal (USA) - Shafayif (Ela-Mana-Mou) 10.1f **(70)**
Form - 700

Record 1998 - 1st:0 2nd:0 3rd:0 Ran:3
Pre1998 - 1st:0 2nd:0 3rd:0 Ran:1
1998 AW 0-3: (7f 2, 10f) (Equi 2, Fibr)
Light-framed, formerly very poor filly.
**M P Muggeridge [0-3] H J Manners (from A J Chamberlain [0-1] Aug 1997).*

SYLVA LEGEND (USA) RR 71f 1744[6]

2 b c Lear Fan (USA) 10.4f **(80)** - Likeashot (CAN) (Gunshot (USA))
Form - 06
Record 1998 - 1st:0 2nd:0 3rd:0 Ran:2
1998 Turf 0-2: (6f 2) (gd, frm)
Currently above-average colt. Turf high 71.
**C E Brittain [0-2] Eddy Grimstead Honda.*

SYLVAN DANCER (IRE) BHB 35f31a RR 42f 31a 4114[13]

4 b br f Dancing Dissident (USA) 6.8f **(65)** - Unspoiled (Tina's Pet) 6.8f **(59)**
Form - 40060407407744232304030
Record 1998 - 1st:0 2nd:2 3rd:3 Ran:20
Pre1998 - 1st:0 2nd:1 3rd:2 Ran:13
Win Prizemoney £0 *Total Prizemoney* £5,187
1998 Turf 0-13: (5f 10, 6f 3) (gd 4, g-f, frm 7, hrd) 1998 AW 0-7: (5f 2, 6f 4, 7f) (Equi 4, Fibr 3)
Light-framed, moderate filly, effective 5 to 6f, acts on gd to frm, has worn blinkers. Turf high 45. AW high 37.
**G C Bravery [0-22] J J May (from C F Wall [0-11] Oct 1997).*

SYLVAN JUBILACION BHB 27f RR 11f 3811[9]

4 b g Sylvan Express 9.6f **(45)** - This Sensation (Balidar) 7.9f **(63)**
Form - 600
Record 1998 - 1st:0 2nd:0 3rd:0 Ran:3
Pre1998 - 1st:0 2nd:0 3rd:0 Ran:5
1998 Turf 0-1: (12f) (g-f) 1998 AW 0-2: (10f, 16f) (Equi 2)
Little account gelding. AW high 26 (began Jly).
**P Mitchell [0-8] Mrs S Teal.*

SYLVAN PRINCESS BHB 64f67a RR 69f 67a 962[23]

5 b m Sylvan Express 9.6f **(45)** - Ela-Yianni-Mou (Anfield) 8.5f **(59)**
Form - 0
Record 1998 - 1st:0 2nd:0 3rd:0 Ran:1
Pre1998 - 1st:6 2nd:2 3rd:2 Ran:26
Win Prizemoney £18,415 *Total Prizemoney* £23,553
Wins 1997 Apr Leices (FRM) H 8f 67 69 <
1996 Aug Yarmou (G-F) 8f 66
1996 Aug Bright (FRM) 8f 55
1996 Aug Salisb (G-F) H 8f 48 58
1996 Jly Newcas (G-F) H 7f 48 54
1996 Jly Sandow (G-F) H 7.1f 45 50
1998 Turf 0-1: (10f) (gd)
Average filly, effective 8f, acts on gd to frm, best on g-f, has worn blinkers. Becoming disappointing.
**Martyn Wane [0-1] J R Bamforth (from D J S Cosgrove [1-9] Jly 1997).*

SYLVAN SABRE (IRE) BHB 40f43a RR 38f 43a 1945[16]

9 b g Flash of Steel 9.7f **(64)** - Flute (FR) (Luthier) 9.8f **(71)**
Form - 0
Record 1998 - 1st:0 2nd:0 3rd:0 Ran:1
Pre1998 - 1st:5 2nd:3 3rd:4 Ran:42
Win Prizemoney £18,689 *Total Prizemoney* £24,684
1998 AW 0-1: (7f) (Fibr)
Very moderate gelding, has worn blinkers. Becoming disappointing. **D Shaw [1-11] J C Fretwell (from K A Morgan [4-18] Aug 1996).*

SYLVA PARADISE (IRE) BHB 81f RR 83f 4741[9]

5 b g Dancing Dissident (USA) 6.8f **(65)** - Brentsville (USA) (Arctic Tern (USA)) 8.9f **(69)**
Form - 00334803440
Record 1998 - 1st:0 2nd:0 3rd:3 Ran:11
Pre1998 - 1st:2 2nd:4 3rd:2 Ran:25
Win Prizemoney £10,460 *Total Prizemoney* £42,688
Wins * 1996 Jly Yarmou (FRM) H 6f 84 93 <
* 1995 Spt Folkes (SFT) 6f 77
1998 Turf 0-11: (5f 8, 6f 3) (g-s, gd 7, g-f, frm 2)
Decent gelding, effective 5 to 6f, acts on gd, has worn blinkers. Turf high 83. Consistent. **C E Brittain [2-36] Eddy Grimstead Honda.*

SYMONDS INN BHB 94f RR 102f 3994[5]

4 ch c In The Wings 11.2f **(77)** - Shining Eyes (USA) (Mr Prospector (USA)) 8.8f **(78)**
Form - 452065
Record 1998 - 1st:0 2nd:1 3rd:0 Ran:6
Pre1998 - 1st:1 2nd:1 3rd:2 Ran:5
Win Prizemoney £9,681 *Total Prizemoney* £21,385
Wins * 1997 May York (GD) 10.4f 92 <
1998 Turf 0-6: (12f 2, 14f 2, 16f 2) (sft 2, gd, g-f, frm 2)
Very useful colt, effective 12f, acts on g-f, has worn blinkers. Turf high 103. He has been most disappointing on the Flat since finishing seventh in the 1997 Derby, but has made a successful start to his career as a hurdler. **J G FitzGerald [1-11] Marquesa de Moratalla.*

SYRAH RR 19f 5073[12]

2 b f Minshaanshu Amad (USA) 11.3f **(53)** - La Domaine (Dominion) 8.5f **(63)**
Form - 0
Record 1998 - 1st:0 2nd:0 3rd:0 Ran:1
1998 Turf 0-1: (8f) (gd)
Currently average filly. **G Lewis [0-1] White Bear Ltd.*

TABAREEH (IRE) RR 79+f 5039[2]

2 b c Marju (IRE) 9.2f **(76)** - Rosia Bay (High Top) 10.2f **(67)**
Form - 2
Record 1998 - 1st:0 2nd:1 3rd:0 Ran:1
Win Prizemoney £0 *Total Prizemoney* £1,186
1998 Turf 0-1: (8f) (g-s)
Currently above-average colt. A half-brother to Roseate Tern and Ibn Bey, from the family of Teleprompter, he was slammed by Dubai Millennium on his debut but still looks an intriguing middle-distance prospect. **M P Tregoning [0-1] Hamdan Al Maktoum.*

TABASCO (IRE) BHB 65f RR 65f 2690[5]

3 b f Salse (USA) 10.9f **(71)** - El Taranda (Ela-Mana-Mou) 10.1f **(70)**
Form - 75
Record 1998 - 1st:0 2nd:0 3rd:0 Ran:2
Pre1998 - 1st:0 2nd:0 3rd:0 Ran:2
1998 Turf 0-2: (8f, 11f) (g-s, frm)
Average filly. Turf high 64. **M R Channon [0-4] Martin Myers.*

TABERNACLE RR 42tf 2396[7]

3 ch c Selkirk (USA) 7.9f **(76)** -Tabyan (USA) (Topsider (USA)) 8.3f **(71)**
Form - 07
Record 1998 - 1st:0 2nd:0 3rd:0 Ran:2
1998 Turf 0-2: (10f 2) (gd, g-f)
Lengthy, currently moderate colt. Turf high 42.
**R Charlton [0-2] Martin Myers.*

TABORITE (USA) BHB 27f RR 8f 4917[20]

4 gr g Gulch (USA) 9.6f **(79)** - Ziska (USA) (Danzig (USA)) 8.4f **(76)**
Form - 0
Record 1998 - 1st:0 2nd:0 3rd:0 Ran:1
Pre1998 - 1st:0 2nd:0 3rd:0 Ran:3
1998 Turf 0-1: (10f) (g-s)
Tall, very poor gelding.
**G Woodward [0-1] Wetherby Racing Bureau 32 (from E J Alston [0-3] Oct 1997).*

TACHYCARDIA BHB 32f40a RR 20f 40a 5128[12]

6 ch m Weldnaas (USA) 8.4f **(55)** - Gold Ducat (Young Generation) 7.7f **(63)**
Form - 54000
Record 1998 - 1st:0 2nd:0 3rd:0 Ran:3
Pre1998 - 1st:5 2nd:3 3rd:6 Ran:53
Win Prizemoney £13,159 *Total Prizemoney* £19,666
Wins 1997 *Jan Lingfi (STD) H 6f 34 41*
1997 *Jan Lingfi (STD) H 6f 34 38*
1995 Jun Bright (G-F) H 5.3f 42 53
1994 *Oct Wolver (STD) SH 8.5f 51 56*
1994 Jly Windso (G-F) S 6f 54
1998 Turf 0-3: (5f, 6f, 8f) (g-s, gd 2)
Moderate mare, effective 6 to 7f, best at 6f, acts on g-f - acts on Equi, likes tight tracks. Turf high 20.
**N E Berry [0-1] Lancing Racing Syndicate (from F P Murtagh [0-4] Jun 1998).*

TACT BHB 35f **RR 36f** 3502[10]
3 b f Deploy 11.4f **(67)** - Yes (Blakeney) 10.5f **(64)**
Form - 680
Record 1998 - 1st:0 2nd:0 3rd:0 Ran:3
1998 Turf 0-3: (7f 2, 8f) (g-f, frm 2)
Neat, currently very moderate filly. Turf high 36.
**D T Thom [0-3] Exors of the late W F Coleman.*

TACTFUL REMARK (USA) BHB 77f **RR 77f** 5039[7]
2 ch c Lord At War (ARG) 6.6f **(67)** - Right Word (USA) (Verbatim (USA)) 8.5f **(64)**
Form - 877
Record 1998 - 1st:0 2nd:0 3rd:0 Ran:3
1998 Turf 0-3: (8f 3) (g-s, g-f, frm)
Currently above-average colt. Turf high 77 (began Aug).
**J H M Gosden [0-3] Sheikh Mohammed.*

TACTICAL CAT (USA) RR 5162a[8]
2 gr c Storm Cat (USA) 7f **(86)** - Terre Haute (USA) 00
Form - 8
1998 AW 0-1: (9f) (Dirt)
Currently useful colt. **D W Lukas in USA [0-1] Overbrook Farm et al.*

Pre1998 - 1st:7 2nd:6 3rd:4 Ran:42
Win Prizemoney £81,222 *Total Prizemoney* £110,649

Wins									
	* **1998**	Aug	Fairyh	(G-F)	L	6f		102	
	* **1998**	May	Haydoc	(G-S)	H	5f	97	105	<
	* 1997	Spt	Nottin	(GD)		5.1f		95	
	* 1997	Aug	Ripon	(G-F)	H	6f	95	101	
	* 1997	Jly	Newmar	(GD)	H	5f	92	93	
	* 1996	Oct	Ascot	(GD)	H	5f	91	95	
	* 1996	Oct	Haydoc	(SFT)		5f		93	
	* 1995	Oct	Lingfi	(GD)		5f		95+	
	1995	May	Carlis	(FRM)		5f		62	

1998 Turf 2-10: (5f 1-6, 6f 1-4) (sft, gd 1-5, g-f 1-4)
Pattern-class gelding, effective 5 to 6f, best at 5f, acts on gd to frm, best on g-f, excels at Ripon. Turf high 105 - also 1st of 9 giving 17lb to Ansellman (23 May Haydock RF 1416). Better than ever as a five-year-old, he bullied his rivals when making all to land a Listed event at Fairyhouse. A stiff six furlongs tests his stamina to the limit and his best performances have come when the emphasis is on pure speed.
**M Johnston [8-45] (from M R Channon [1-7] Jly 1995).*

TADWIGA BHB 102f **RR 100f** 4733[8]
3 b f Fairy King (USA) 7.7f **(75)** - Euromill (Shirley Heights) 10.3f **(74)**

Tadwiga relishes give underfoot

TADEO BHB 104f **RR 105f** 4347a[6]
5 ch g Primo Dominie 7.2f **(67)** - Royal Passion (Ahonoora) 8.1f **(73)**
Form - 4130808136
Record 1998 - 1st:2 2nd:0 3rd:2 Ran:10

Form - 113518
Record 1998 - 1st:3 2nd:0 3rd:1 Ran:6
Pre1998 - 1st:1 2nd:3 3rd:1 Ran:6
Win Prizemoney £96,198 *Total Prizemoney* £109,684

Wins * **1998** Spt Currag (SFT) G3 8f 100 <
* **1998** Jly Kempto (G-S) 8f 87
* **1998** Apr Kempto (HVY) L 8f 98
* 1997 Jun Currag (G-S) 6.3f 83+

1998 Turf 3-6: (8f 3-5, 10f) (hvy 1-1, g-s, gd 2-2, g-f 2)

Neat, very useful filly, effective 6 to 8f, best at 8f, acts on hvy to frm, best on gd, excels at Curragh and Kempton. Turf high 100 - 1st of 7 from Darina (6 Spt Curragh RF 4179a) - also 1st of 8 from Dazilyn Lady (11 Apr Kempton RF 0646). She had a mid-season break after being found lame before the Italian 1000 Guineas, but came back better than ever in the autumn, winning a Group Three at the Curragh in September. Soft ground suits her admirably.

**R Hannon [4-12] Stonethorn Stud Farms Ltd.*

TAEL OF SILVER BHB 41f25a RR 48f 25a 4920[7]

6 b m Today and Tomorrow 6.2f **(45)** - Schula (Kala Shikari) 8.4f **(54)**

Form - 007

Record 1998 - 1st:0 2nd:0 3rd:0 Ran:2
Pre1998 - 1st:3 2nd:5 3rd:3 Ran:42

Win Prizemoney £10,050 *Total Prizemoney* £17,935

Wins * 1996 Jun Doncas (G-F) H 7f 59 66 <
1995 Jun Warwic (FRM) H 5f 62 65+
1995 Apr Nottin (GD) S 6.1f 58

1998 Turf 0-1: (8f) (g-s) 1998 AW 0-1: (7f) (Equi)

Moderate mare, effective 7 to 8f, best at 8f, acts on gd to frm, has worn blinkers, prefers left handed tracks, prefers tight tracks. Inconsistent.

**A Bailey [1-23] Peter Freeman (from K R Burke [2-21] May 1996).*

TAFFS WELL BHB 60f RR 60f 5059[2]

5 b g Dowsing (USA) 7f **(61)** - Zahiah (So Blessed) 8.7f **(67)**

Form - 0525606007002

Record 1998 - 1st:0 2nd:2 3rd:0 Ran:13
Pre1998 - 1st:0 2nd:2 3rd:1 Ran:6

Win Prizemoney £0 *Total Prizemoney* £5,816

1998 Turf 0-13: (6f 3, 7f, 8f 7, 9f 2) (sft 2, g-s 2, gd 3, g-f 4, frm 2)

Average gelding, effective 7 to 8f, best at 7f, acts on g-s to frm, likes tight tracks. Turf high 77 - 2nd of 15 giving 14lb to Dispol Diamond (21 Apr Pontefract 8f g-s RF 0789).

**Mrs J R Ramsden [0-13] Jonathan Ramsden (from R Akehurst [0-6] Oct 1997).*

TAIKI SHUTTLE (USA) RR 123f 3783a[1]

4 ch c Devil's Bag (USA) 9.3f **(73)** - Welsh Muffin (Caerleon (USA)) 8.6f **(71)**

Form - 111

1998 Turf 3-3: (7f 1-1, 8f 2-2) (hvy 1-1, gd 1-1, frm 1-1)

Currently very high-class colt. Turf high 123 (1st run) - 1st of 16 from Osumi Tycoon (16 May Fuchu RF 1378a) - also 1st of 8 from Among Men (16 Aug Deauville RF 3783a). Won the two big spring prizes in Japan, looking better on the soft ground on the second occasion. He then came to Europe, and put an international field in its place in the Prix Jacques le Marois. A very smart winner of ten of his 11 races, he is likely to be popular at stud in his homeland and, with his American pedigree, may well attract overseas breeders as well.

**K Fujisawa in JPN [3-3] Taiki Farm Co Ltd.*

TAILWIND BHB 49f50a RR 47f 50a 4811[15]

4 ch g Clantime 6.6f **(57)** - Casbar Lady (Native Bazaar) 6.9f **(62)**

Form - 740760070300

Record 1998 - 1st:0 2nd:0 3rd:1 Ran:9
Pre1998 - 1st:1 2nd:1 3rd:3 Ran:17

Win Prizemoney £3,561 *Total Prizemoney* £6,997

Wins * 1997 May Redcar (G-F) 6f 65 <

1998 Turf 0-7: (5f 2, 6f 5) (gd, g-f, frm 5) 1998 AW 0-2: (7f, 8f) (Equi 2)

Leggy, moderate gelding, effective 6 to 8f, acts on g-f - acts on Equi. Turf high 47 (began Jly). AW high 37. **W R Muir [1-26] R Haim.*

TAIPAN (IRE) BHB 121f RR 120f 4603a[1]

6 b h Last Tycoon 9.4f **(73)** - Alidiva (Chief Singer) 8.9f **(66)**

Form - 1336621

Record 1998 - 1st:1 2nd:1 3rd:2 Ran:6
Pre1998 - 1st:7 2nd:2 3rd:3 Ran:17

Win Prizemoney £526,910 *Total Prizemoney* £674,869

Wins * **1998** Spt Cologn (SFT) G1 12f 120
* 1997 Nov Capann (HVY) G1 10f 121 <
* 1997 Spt Cologn (GD) G1 12f 120
* 1997 Aug Deauvi (SFT) G2 12.5f 114
* 1996 Jun Lyon P (GD) L 12f 106
* 1996 May Goodwo (G-S) H 12f 98 105
* 1996 Apr Haydoc (GD) H 11.9f 90 96
* 1994 Nov Doncas (SFT) 7f 82

1998 Turf 1-6: (10f 3, 11f 2, 12f 1-1) (sft 1-2, g-s, gd 2, g-f)

Very high-class horse, effective 10 to 13f, best at 10f, acts on hvy to frm, does well at San Siro and Cologne and Longchamp. Turf high 120 - 1st of 9 from Garuda (27 Spt Cologne RF 4603a). Consistent. A half-brother to Ali-Royal and Sleepytime, he ran well without winning in top company in the first half of 1998. He came back from a break to be just touched off in the Arc trial at Newbury, then hit winning form when avoiding the top performers. He took the Europa-Preis at Cologne before following up in the Premio Roma. He retires to stud in Ireland with earnings of three-quarters of a million pounds, and should prove a popular stallion at a reasonable fee. **J L Dunlop [8-23] Lord Swaythling.*

TAISCE (IRE) RR 99f 5026a[3]

2 b f Treasure Kay 6.5f **(53)** - Mothers Blessing (Wolver Hollow) 8f **(56)**

Form - 5542333

1998 Turf 0-7: (6f 2, 7f 2, 8f 3) (hvy 2, sft 2, g-s, gd, g-f)

Very useful filly, effective 8f, acts on hvy, has worn blinkers. Turf high 99 (began Jly) - 3rd of 17 to Pink Coral (21 Oct Navan 8f hvy RF 5019a). Placed in the last four of her seven runs when stepped up in trip, she looks capable of winning races and definitely prefers it on the soft side.

**J S Bolger in IRE [0-7] Mrs Patricia O'Rourke.*

TAISPEAIN (IRE) RR 97f 3189a[11]

3 b f Petorius 8f **(66)** - Nordic Pride (Horage) 10.3f **(61)**

Form - 060

1998 Turf 0-3: (5f, 7f 2) (sft, g-s, g-f)

Very useful filly, effective 6f, acts on g-s, often wears blinkers (effectively). Turf high 97. **J S Bolger in IRE [1-9] Michael Smurfit.*

TAI TAI RR 26f 4389[15]

2 b f Mujtahid (USA) 7.4f **(69)** - Duwon (IRE) **(53df)** (Polish Precedent (USA)) 10.2f **(60)**

Form - 0

Record 1998 - 1st:0 2nd:0 3rd:0 Ran:1

1998 Turf 0-1: (7f) (frm)

Currently little account filly. **M Blanshard [0-1] James Watkins.*

TAI TAM WARRIOR RR 76df 2852[7]

3 ch c Risk Me (FR) 8f **(53)** - Sunday Sport Gem (Lomond (USA)) 8.8f **(65)**

Form - 27

Record 1998 - 1st:0 2nd:1 3rd:0 Ran:2

Win Prizemoney £0 *Total Prizemoney* £898

1998 Turf 0-2: (10f, 11f) (gd, frm)

Tall, currently above-average colt. Turf high 76 (1st run) - 2nd of 7 to Tory Boy (8 Jun Warwick 11f gd RF 1813).

**H J Collingridge [0-2] P A Skerrett.*

TAJAR (USA) BHB 48f46a RR 52f 46a 4409[12]

6 b g Slew O' Gold (USA) 10.2f **(73)** - Mashaarif (USA) (Mr Prospector (USA)) 8.8f **(78)**

Form - 60381881300

Record 1998 - 1st:2 2nd:0 3rd:2 Ran:10
Pre1998 - 1st:1 2nd:2 3rd:3 Ran:22

Win Prizemoney £8,313 *Total Prizemoney* £12,915

Wins * **1998** Aug Warwic (G-F) 10.8f 52 <
* **1998** Jly Pontef (G-F) H 10f 40 45
* 1997 Jly Chepst (G-F) H 12.1f 30 35

1998 Turf 2-10: (10f 1-4, 11f 1-2, 12f 4) (g-f 4, frm 2-6)

Fair gelding, effective 10 to 11f, best at 10f, acts on frm, has worn blinkers, likes left handed tracks, likes tight tracks. Turf high 52 - 1st of 10 giving 2lb to Snow Partridge (14 Aug Warwick RF 3649) - also 1st of 15 getting 5lb from Tapatch (7 Jly Pontefract RF 2585). Returned from three months off to spring a surprise in an amateurs' handicap, having been beaten in sellers previously. Fair efforts after, although he has not always looked keen.

**T Keddy [3-22] The Veg Chef Partnership (from M Dods [0-5] Apr 1997).*

TAJASUR (IRE) BHB 100f RR 100f 990[3]

3 ch c Imperial Frontier (USA) 7f **(65)** - Safiya (USA) (Riverman (USA))

9.1f **(76)**
Form - 23
Record 1998 - 1st:0 2nd:1 3rd:1 Ran:2
Pre1998 - 1st:1 2nd:0 3rd:0 Ran:1
Win Prizemoney £3,485 *Total Prizemoney* £6,199
Wins * 1997 Jun Doncas (G-S) 6f 79+ <
1998 Turf 0-2: (6f, 7f) (sft, gd)
Well made, currently very useful colt. Turf high 100 - 3rd of 6 giving 3lb to Lone Piper (3 May Newmarket 7f gd RF 0990). He looked an unlucky loser on his reappearance, but flashed his tail when narrowly beaten at Newmarket in May and may not be the toughest individual. That said, John Dunlop bought him back for 13,000 guineas at the Tattersalls Autumn Horses In Training Sales.
**J L Dunlop [1-3] Hamdan Al Maktoum.*

TAJAWALL (USA) RR 104f
3423a[1]

6 b h Dixieland Band (USA) 10.1f **(80)** - Conjinx
Form - 1
1998 Turf 1-1: (7f 1-1) (sft 1-1)
Very useful horse. (1st run) - 1st of 9 getting 5lb from Indian Point (2 Aug Munich RF 3423a). He is tough, and put up a fair performance when winning a Listed event at Munich in August. He may be best at distances short of a mile.
**D Richardson in GER [1-3] K U Zeimer (from A Wohler in GER [0-1] May 1995).*

TAJAWUZ BHB 78f RR 78f
4111[13]

3 ch f Kris 10f **(75)** - Na-Ayim (IRE) (Shirley Heights) 10.3f **(74)**
Form - 100
Record 1998 - 1st:1 2nd:0 3rd:0 Ran:3
Pre1998 - 1st:0 2nd:0 3rd:0 Ran:2
Win Prizemoney £3,850 *Total Prizemoney* £4,382
Wins 1998 May Lingfi (G-F) 10f 78 <
1998 Turf 1-3: (8f, 9f, 10f 1-1) (gd, frm 1-2)
Above-average filly. Turf high 78 (1st run) - 1st of 11 from Ivory Crown (23 May Lingfield RF 1433).
**M P Tregoning [0-1] Hamdan Al Maktoum (from S bin Suroor [1-4] Jly 1998).*

TAJINE (IRE) BHB 38f44a RR 45f 44a
4869[19]

3 ch g Indian Ridge 7.6f **(74)** - Simply Marilyn (IRE) (Simply Great (FR)) 8.2f **(65)**
Form - 587000500
Record 1998 - 1st:0 2nd:0 3rd:0 Ran:9
1998Turf 0-8:(8f 3, 9f, 10f 4)(sft, gd 2, g-f 4, frm)1998 AW 0-1:(8f) (Fibr)
Scopey, moderate gelding, has worn blinkers. Turf high 66.
**P W Harris [0-9] Mrs Godfrey,Mrs Horgan and Mrs Harris.*

TAJ MAHAL (IRE) BHB 34f40a RR 38f 40a
3580[12]

3 b g High Estate 10.5f **(66)** - Verthumna (Indian King (USA)) 7.4f **(64)**
Form - 0760000
Record 1998 - 1st:0 2nd:0 3rd:0 Ran:5
Pre1998 - 1st:0 2nd:0 3rd:0 Ran:3
1998 Turf 0-2: (6f, 8f) (gd 2) 1998 AW 0-3: (7f, 8f, 11f) (Equi, Fibr 2)
Very moderate gelding. (began Aug). AW high 32. Becoming disappointing. **C W Thornton [0-8] Guy Reed.*

TAJMIL (IRE) BHB 54f48a RR 63f 48a
5040[6]

3 ch f Wolfhound (USA) 7.3f **(71)** - Nouvelle Star (AUS) (Luskin Star (AUS)) 6.3f **(71)**
Form - 084058286
Record 1998 - 1st:0 2nd:1 3rd:0 Ran:9
Pre1998 - 1st:0 2nd:0 3rd:1 Ran:5
Win Prizemoney £0 *Total Prizemoney* £1,755
1998 Turf 0-9: (6f, 7f 7, 8f) (g-s, gd 3, g-f, frm 3, hrd)
Neat, average filly, effective 6 to 7f, best at 7f, acts on g-s to frm, has worn blinkers. Turf high 63 - 5th of 9 getting 3lb from Acid Test (20 Jun Lingfield 7f frm RF 2151).
**D Morris [0-9] Bloomsbury Stud (from Major W R Hern [0-5] Oct 1997).*

TAJOUN (FR) RR 114f
3917a[3]

4 b g General Holme (USA) 5.7f **(58)** - Taeesha (Mill Reef (USA)) 10.5f **(78)**
Form - 21113
1998 Turf 3-4: (15f, 16f 3-3) (sft 2-3, gd 1-1)
Group-class gelding. Turf high 114 - 3rd of 8 giving 2lb to Arctic Owl (23 Aug Deauville 15f sft RF 3917a) - also 1st of 6 from Lucky Dream (17 May Longchamp RF 1383a). He put up his very best performance on testing ground in the Group Two Prix de Barbeville at Longchamp in April. Put in his place by Arctic Owl at Deauville in August, he is a smart stayer but may struggle against the best long-distance horses from England who, on the whole, appear superior to their French counterparts.
**A deRoyerDupre in FR [3-5] H H Aga Khan.*

TAKARIAN (IRE) RR 116+f
3188a[1]

3 b c Doyoun 10.7f **(69)** - Takarouna (USA) (Green Dancer (USA)) 10.3f **(74)**
Form - 3251
1998 Turf 1-4: (10f 1-3, 12f) (sft, gd 2, g-f 1-1)
High-class colt, effective 10f, acts on gd to g-f. Turf high 116 - also 1st of 4 from Make No Mistake (25 Jly Curragh RF 3188a). He made the frame in a couple of Irish Group Threes early in the season, and did not run badly in the Irish Derby. He earned his black type when winning the Meld Stakes at the Curragh, but was not seen again. **J Oxx in IRE [2-7] H H Aga Khan.*

TAKARIYA (IRE) RR 90f
2803a[1]

2 b f Arazi (USA) 9.2f **(74)** - Takarouna (USA) (Green Dancer (USA)) 10.3f **(74)**
Form - 1
1998 Turf 1-1: (6f 1-1) (gd 1-1)
Currently useful filly. (1st run) - 1st of 11 from Antinnaz (12 Jly Curragh RF 2803a). **J Oxx in IRE [1-1] H H Aga Khan.*

TAKE A RISK BHB 44f RR 30f
4093[17]

3 ch f Risk Me (FR) 8f **(53)** -Hinari Televideo (Caerleon (USA)) 8.6f **(71)**
Form - 00000
Record 1998 - 1st:0 2nd:0 3rd:0 Ran:5
Pre1998 - 1st:1 2nd:0 3rd:0 Ran:5
Win Prizemoney £2,937 *Total Prizemoney* £3,187
Wins 1997 Spt Mussel (G-F) 5f 61 <
1998 Turf 0-5: (6f 5) (sft, gd, g-f, frm 2)
Workmanlike, very moderate filly, effective 5f, acts on g-f. Turf high 36.
**A G Newcombe [0-5] P McMahon (from M Johnston [1-5] Oct 1997).*

TAKE A TURN BHB 74f76a RR 75f 76a
4457[5]

3 br g Forzando 7.2f **(63)** - Honeychurch (USA) (Bering) 7.4f **(61)**
Form - 372560614535
Record 1998 - 1st:1 2nd:1 3rd:2 Ran:12
Pre1998 - 1st:1 2nd:2 3rd:1 Ran:11
Win Prizemoney £8,732 *Total Prizemoney* £13,804
Wins * **1998** Jly Salisb (G-F) H 8f 69 75
1997 Aug Cheste (SFT) H 7f 77 79 <
1998 Turf 1-9: (7f, 8f 1-3, 9f 3, 10f 2) (hvy, g-s, gd 5, g-f 1-2) 1998 AW 0-3: (7f, 8f 2) (Equi 2, Fibr)
Unfurnished, above-average gelding, effective 5 to 10f, best at 7f, acts on hvy to frm - acts on Equi, often wears blinkers (effectively), prefers tight tracks, excels at Chester. Turf high 75 - 1st of 18 from Roger Ross (31 Jly Salisbury RF 3245). AW high 76 (1st run) - 3rd of 5 getting 2lb from Blue Shadow (19 Feb Lingfield 7f Equi RF 0318).
**Miss Gay Kelleway [1-6] Sheet & Roll Convertors Ltd (from M R Channon [1-17] May 1998).*

TAKE NOTICE BHB 27f36a RR 23f 36a
4768[12]

5 b g Warning 8.1f **(77)** - Metair (Laser Light) 9f **(68)**
Form - 00048603060000
Record 1998 - 1st:0 2nd:0 3rd:1 Ran:14
Pre1998 - 1st:0 2nd:0 3rd:1 Ran:12
Win Prizemoney £0 *Total Prizemoney* £1,237
1998 Turf 0-9: (5f 3, 6f 3, 7f, 9f 2) (sft 3, gd 2, g-f 2, frm 2) 1998 AW 0-5: (5f 2, 6f, 8f 2) (Fibr 5)
Moderate gelding, effective 5f, - acts on Fibr, has worn blinkers. Turf high 31. AW high 49 - 4th of 10 giving 23lb to Stately Favour (6 Apr Southwell 5f Fibr RF 0572).
**Martyn Wane [0-18] J P Slattery (from R M McKellar [0-7] May 1997).*

TAKER CHANCE BHB 66f61a RR 70f 61a
4876[11]

2 b g Puissance 7.1f **(60)** - Flower Princess (Slip Anchor) 9.8f **(73)**
Form - 3060
Record 1998 - 1st:0 2nd:0 3rd:1 Ran:4
Win Prizemoney £0 *Total Prizemoney* £520

1998 Turf 0-3: (6f 2, 7f) (g-f 2, frm) 1998 AW 0-1: (6f) (Fibr)
Above-average gelding. Turf high 70 (1st run) (began Jly) - 3rd of 8 giving 3lb to Cover Girl (15 Jly Yarmouth 6f g-f RF 2834).
**W J Haggas [0-4] Taker Bloodstock.*

TAKHLID (USA) BHB 67f63a **RR 59f 63a** 5017[8]

7 b h Nureyev (USA) 8.4f **(84)** - Savonnerie (USA) (Irish River (FR)) 8.6f **(78)**
Form - 034748D36214143836300008

Record	**1998 -**	1st:2	2nd:1	3rd:4	Ran:21
	Pre1998 -	1st:5	2nd:2	3rd:5	Ran:33

Win Prizemoney £28,623 *Total Prizemoney* £38,131

Wins								
	*** 1998**	Jun	Hamilt	(SFT)	H	8.3f	61	72+
	*** 1998**	Jun	Thirsk	(GD)	H	8f	57	62
	* 1997	*Spt*	*Wolver*	*(STD)*	*H*	*6f*	*68*	*73*
	* 1997	*Apr*	*Southw*	*(STD)*	*H*	*8f*	*63*	*69*
	* 1997	*Mar*	*Wolver*	*(STD)*	*H*	*6f*	*61*	*59*
	1995	Spt	Epsom	(G-S)	H	8.5f	79	84 <
	1995	Aug	Bright	(FRM)	H	7f	77	79

1998 Turf 2-13: (6f, 7f 2, 8f 2-10) (g-s 1-1, gd 4, g-f 1-3, frm 5) 1998 AW 0-8: (6f 3, 7f 2, 8f 3) (Equi 2, Fibr 6)
Average horse, effective 6 to 9f, best at 7f, acts on g-s to frm - acts on Fibr, best on frm, and likes Hamilton and Wolverhampton. Turf high 76 - 3rd of 14 giving 27lb to Oriole (9 Aug Redcar 7f frm RF 3488) - also 1st of 4 giving 9lb to Segala (10 Jun Hamilton RF 1873). AW high 66. Consistent. He has shown ability on the Wolverhampton Fibresand, but his two victories in '98 came on turf at Thirsk and Hamilton. He did not show much after August.
**D W Chapman [5-47] Miss N F Thesiger (from H ThomsonJones [2-7] Spt 1995).*

TALAH **RR 94f** 5063[2]

2 b f Danehill (USA) 9.1f **(79)** - Kerrera (Diesis) 9.3f **(69)**
Form - 2

Record	**1998 -**	1st:0	2nd:1	3rd:0	Ran:1

Win Prizemoney £0 *Total Prizemoney* £1,100
1998 Turf 0-1: (6f) (g-f)
Currently useful filly. (1st run) - 2nd of 16 to Flavian (30 Oct Newmarket 6f g-f RF 5063). A half-brother to the speedy Shmoose, out of a 1000 Guineas runner-up, she was a promising second on her sole run at two and ought to make the grade.
**D R Loder [0-1] Sheikh Mohammed.*

TALARIA (IRE) **RR 75f** 2109[6]

2 ch f Petardia 8.2f **(58)** - Million At Dawn (IRE) (Fayruz)
Form - 46

Record	**1998 -**	1st:0	2nd:0	3rd:0	Ran:2

Win Prizemoney £0 *Total Prizemoney* £600
1998 Turf 0-2: (5f 2) (gd, frm)
Currently above-average filly. Turf high 75. Sure to find a sprint maiden. **G Wragg [0-2] Mrs Claude Lilley.*

TALAVERA BHB 54f **RR 43f** 5060[6]

3 gr g Paris House 5.9f **(64)** - Gem of Gold (Jellaby) 6.4f **(58)**
Form - 10588006

Record	**1998 -**	1st:1	2nd:0	3rd:0	Ran:8

Win Prizemoney £3,663 *Total Prizemoney* £3,663
Wins *** 1998** May Beverl (G-F) 5f 67 <
1998 Turf 1-8: (5f 1-4, 6f, 7f, 8f 2) (sft, gd 2, g-f 2, frm 2, hrd 1-1)
Tall, moderate gelding, effective 5f, acts on hrd, has worn blinkers. Turf high 67 (1st run) - 1st of 16 from Faute de Mieux (10 May Beverley RF 1137). Becoming disappointing. Sprint-bred, he won a Beverley maiden on his belated racecourse debut, but has shown little since. **J Berry [1-8] Chris & Antonia Deuters.*

TALEBAN BHB 89f **RR 75?f** 2818[8]

3 b c Alleged (USA) 11.8f **(81)** - Triode (USA) (Sharpen Up) 8.3f **(67)**
Form - 1578

Record	**1998 -**	1st:0	2nd:0	3rd:0	Ran:3
	Pre1998 -	1st:1	2nd:0	3rd:0	Ran:1

Win Prizemoney £11,571 *Total Prizemoney* £11,571
Wins * 1997 Nov San Si (HVY) 8f 93 <
1998 Turf 0-3: (8f, 10f 2) (g-f, frm, hrd)
Above-average colt. Turf high 75. Has joined Charlie Mann.
**L M Cumani [1-4] Fittocks Stud.*

TALES OF BOUNTY (IRE) BHB 65f **RR 69f** 5008[3]

3 b g Ela-Mana-Mou 12.7f **(72)** - Tales of Wisdom (Rousillon (USA)) 8.2f **(74)**
Form - 6083043

Record	**1998 -**	1st:0	2nd:0	3rd:2	Ran:7
	Pre1998 -	1st:0	2nd:0	3rd:0	Ran:1

Win Prizemoney £0 *Total Prizemoney* £1,262
1998 Turf 0-7: (10f 2, 12f 5) (sft, g-s 2, frm 4)
Scopey, average gelding, effective 12f, acts on frm. Turf high 72.
**D R C Elsworth [0-8] Mrs Michael Meredith.*

TALIB (USA) BHB 56f **RR 58f** 2239[8]

4 b g Silver Hawk (USA) 11.2f **(85)** - Dance For Lucy (USA) (Dance Bid (USA)) 11.6f **(71)**
Form - 27178

Record	**1998 -**	1st:1	2nd:1	3rd:0	Ran:5
	Pre1998 -	1st:0	2nd:0	3rd:0	Ran:5

Win Prizemoney £2,388 *Total Prizemoney* £3,476
Wins 1998 Jun Windso (GD) C 11.6f 58 <
1998 Turf 1-5: (11f 2, 12f 1-3) (gd, g-f 1-2, frm 2)
Light-framed, fair gelding, effective 12f, acts on gd. Turf high 64 (1st run) - 2nd of 12 giving 20lb to Kilnamartyra Girl (4 May Newcastle 12f gd RF 1025).
**P Mitchell [0-2] Mrs Barbara Gerber & Richard J Cohen (from Mrs J Cecil [1-3] Jun 1998).*

Ta-Lim, an improving stayer for next year

TA-LIM BHB 110f **RR 112f** 4240[5]

3 b c Ela-Mana-Mou 12.7f **(72)** - Alkaffeyeh (IRE) (Sadler's Wells (USA)) 10f **(76)**
Form - 316415

Record	**1998 -**	1st:2	2nd:0	3rd:1	Ran:6

Win Prizemoney £17,475 *Total Prizemoney* £19,615

Wins						
*** 1998**	Aug	Goodwo (G-F)	L	14f	105	<
*** 1998**	Jun	Goodwo (GD)		12f	88	

1998 Turf 2-6: (10f, 12f 1-2, 14f 1-2, 15f) (gd 1-1, g-f 1-4, frm)
Lengthy, Group-class colt, effective 14 to 15f, acts on g-f. Turf high 112 - 5th of 9 to Nedawi (12 Spt Doncaster 15f g-f RF 4240) -

also 1st of 3 from Generous Terms (29 Aug Goodwood RF 3945). He quickly put a poor performance at Sandown behind him and was quite impressive when winning the Listed March Stakes at Goodwood in August. That bought him a ticket for the St Leger and, in finishing five lengths fifth behind Nedawi, he ran his best race to date. He should make up into an imposing four-year-old and may develop into a Group-class stayer.

**Sir Michael Stoute [2-6] Hamdan Al Maktoum.*

TALK BACK (IRE) BHB 57f **RR 55f** 1268[1]

6 br g Bob Back (USA) 11.5f **(71)** - Summit Talk (Head for Heights) 9.6f **(55)**

Form - 1

Record **1998** - 1st:1 2nd:0 3rd:0 Ran:1
Pre1998 - 1st:0 2nd:0 3rd:0 Ran:4

Win Prizemoney £4,662 *Total Prizemoney* £4,662

Wins * **1998** May Newmar (G-F) H 8f 48 55 <

1998 Turf 1-1: (8f 1-1) (frm 1-1)

Fair gelding. (1st run) - 1st of 28 getting 5lb from Grooms Gold (16 May Newmarket RF 1268).

**Lady Herries [1-1] V McCalla (from G Lewis [0-3] Jly 1997).*

TALLULAH BELLE BHB 68f76a **RR 68f 76a** 3950[8]

5 b m Crowning Honors (CAN) 9.9f **(36)** - Fine a Leau (USA) (Youth (USA)) 9.8f **(64)**

Form - 2013637421418

Record **1998** - 1st:3 2nd:2 3rd:2 Ran:13
Pre1998 - 1st:5 2nd:4 3rd:7 Ran:43

Win Prizemoney £28,344 *Total Prizemoney* £40,360

Wins * **1998** Aug Yarmou (FRM) 10.1f 68
* **1998** Jly Goodwo (G-S) H 9f 61 65
* **1998** *May Lingfi (STD) H 10f 69 71* <
* 1997 Oct Redcar (G-F) 10f 68
* 1997 Spt Kempto (G-F) H 11.1f 56 65
* 1997 Apr Beverl (G-F) H 9.9f 57 56
* 1997 *Feb Lingfi (STD) H 10f 57 66*
* 1997 *Jan Wolver (STD) 9.4f 56*

1998 Turf 2-10: (9f 1-2, 10f 1-7, 12f) (gd 1-4, g-f 2, frm 1-4) 1998 AW 1-3: (9f 2, 10f 1-1) (Equi 1-1, Fibr 2)

Above-average filly, effective 9 to 11f, best at 10f, acts on gd to frm - acts on AW, best on Fibr, has worn blinkers, favours tight tracks, and excels at Beverley and Lingfield. Turf high 68 - 1st of 6 giving 9lb to Shohra Wa Jaah (20 Aug Yarmouth RF 3770) - also 1st of 20 getting 4lb from Ribblesdale (30 Jly Goodwood RF 3222). AW high 73 - 3rd of 11 giving 5lb to Danzino (6 Jun Wolverhampton 9f Fibr RF 1797) - also 1st of 8 giving 16lb to Peppers (8 May Lingfield RF 1102). She managed to win five times on both sand and turf in 1997. Not as prolific in 1998, she won on Equitrack before teaming up with Peslier to win a handicap at Glorious Goodwood, and also took a small race at Yarmouth in good style.

**N P Littmoden [8-59] Trojan Racing.*

TAL-Y-LLYN (IRE) BHB 36f44a **RR 17f 44a** 4962[16]

4 ch g Common Grounds 8.1f **(66)** - Welsh Fantasy (Welsh Pageant) 10f **(65)**

Form - 00000000

Record **1998** - 1st:0 2nd:0 3rd:0 Ran:8
Pre1998 - 1st:1 2nd:1 3rd:0 Ran:10

Win Prizemoney £3,533 *Total Prizemoney* £4,840

Wins 1997 May Newbur (SFT) 7.3f 79 <

1998 Turf 0-5: (6f, 7f 3, 8f)(sft, g-f, frm 3)1998 AW 0-3:(6f, 7f, 8f)(Fibr 3)

Workmanlike, very moderate gelding, effective 7f, acts on gd, has worn blinkers, likes left handed tracks. Turf high 32. AW high 33.

**N E Berry [0-8] B Beale (from B W Hills [1-10] Oct 1997).*

TAMARA BHB 89f **RR 86f** 4538[12]

2 b f Marju (IRE) 9.2f **(76)** - Ivory Palm (USA) (Sir Ivor) 10.2f **(70)**

Form - 010280

Record **1998** - 1st:1 2nd:1 3rd:0 Ran:6

Win Prizemoney £2,346 *Total Prizemoney* £7,546

Wins * **1998** May Catter (SFT) 5f 68 <

1998 Turf 1-6: (5f 1-3, 6f, 7f 2) (gd 1-3, g-f, frm 2)

Useful filly, effective 6f, acts on frm. Turf high 86 - 2nd of 7 getting 4lb from Saafend Rock (1 Aug Newmarket 6f frm RF 3277). She was suited by the soft ground when landing a Catterick maiden, but was outclassed in the Queen Mary before going down narrowly on her nursery debut. **J D Bethell [1-6] Mrs John Wilson.*

TAMARISK (IRE) **RR 122f** 4105[1]

3 b c Green Desert (USA) 7.8f **(78)** - Sine Labe (USA) (Vaguely Noble) 10.1f **(72)**

Form - 01210

Record **1998** - 1st:2 2nd:1 3rd:0 Ran:5
Pre1998 - 1st:3 2nd:1 3rd:0 Ran:4

Win Prizemoney £115,662 *Total Prizemoney* £191,028

Wins * **1998** Spt Haydoc (GD) G1 6f 122 <
* **1998** May Lingfi (GD) L 6f 112+
* 1997 Spt Newmar (G-F) 7f 106+
* 1997 Spt Kempto (GD) 7f 103+
* 1997 Aug Goodwo (G-F) 6f 86+

1998 Turf 2-4: (6f 2-3, 8f) (gd, g-f 1-1, frm 1-2) AW: (0-1) (fst 0-1)

Scopey, very high-class colt, effective 6f, acts on g-f to frm, best on frm. Turf high 122 - 1st of 13 getting 2lb from Bolshoi (5 Spt Haydock RF 4105). Improving. He ran poorly in the Guineas on his return, but he probably did not stay and his stable was out of form. It was a very different story when he was dropped back to six furlongs in a Listed event at Lingfield, where he won quite nicely. He followed up by chasing home Elnadim in the July Cup, and then took the Stanley Leisure Sprint Cup in dominant fashion. He went to America afterwards, but was excluded from the Breeders' Cup Sprint after a poor effort at Keeneland in his prep race, and has now been retired to Coolmore Stud.

**D W Lukas [0-1] Highclere Thoroughbred Racing Ltd (fromR Charlton [5-8] Sept 1998).*

TAMBARANN (IRE) BHB 82f **RR 79f** 3833[3]

2 b c Ezzoud (IRE) - Tamarzana (IRE) (Lear Fan (USA)) 8.5f **(73)**

Form - 5343

Record **1998** - 1st:0 2nd:0 3rd:2 Ran:4

Win Prizemoney £0 *Total Prizemoney* £1,202

1998 Turf 0-4: (6f 2, 7f, 8f) (gd, g-f 3)

Above-average colt, has worn blinkers. Turf high 78 (began Jly) - 3rd of 9 to Inducement (24 Aug Beverley 8f g-f RF 3833).

**Sir Michael Stoute [0-4] H H Aga Khan.*

TAMERIN BAY BHB 37f **RR 19f** 4339[18]

3 b g Lugana Beach 7f **(63)** - Quenlyn (Welsh Pageant) 10f **(65)**

Form - 000000

Record **1998** - 1st:0 2nd:0 3rd:0 Ran:6
Pre1998 - 1st:1 2nd:1 3rd:0 Ran:6

Win Prizemoney £2,682 *Total Prizemoney* £3,972

Wins 1997 Jun Pontef (G-F) 5f 69 <

1998 Turf 0-6: (5f 3, 6f, 7f, 8f) (gd 2, frm 4)

Scopey, poor gelding, effective 5 to 6f, acts on g-f, often wears blinkers. Turf high 19. Becoming disappointing.

**M Brittain [0-6] P Asquith (from R Boss [1-6] Aug 1997).*

TAMGEED (USA) **RR 54f** 5000[6]

2 ch f Woodman (USA) 9.7f **(77)** - Toujours Elle (USA) (Lyphard (USA)) 9.9f **(72)**

Form - 06

Record **1998** - 1st:0 2nd:0 3rd:0 Ran:2

1998 Turf 0-2: (6f, 7f) (sft, g-f)

Currently fair filly. Turf high 54 (began Oct).

**J L Dunlop [0-2] Hamdan Al Maktoum.*

TAMING (IRE) **RR 79f** 4257[3]

2 ch c Lycius (USA) 8.8f **(71)** - Black Fighter (USA) (Secretariat (USA)) 9f **(79)**

Form - 53

Record **1998** - 1st:0 2nd:0 3rd:1 Ran:2

Win Prizemoney £0 *Total Prizemoney* £561

1998 Turf 0-2: (7f, 8f) (gd, frm)

Currently above-average colt. Turf high 79 (began Jly).

**H R A Cecil [0-2] Buckram Oak Holdings.*

TAMMAM (IRE) BHB 87f **RR 79f** 3369[3]

2 b c Priolo (USA) 10.9f **(71)** - Bristle (Thatch (USA)) 9.8f **(62)**

Form - 2333

Record **1998** - 1st:0 2nd:1 3rd:3 Ran:4

Win Prizemoney £0 *Total Prizemoney* £2,546

1998 Turf 0-4: (6f 2, 7f 2) (gd, g-f, frm 2)

Above-average colt. Turf high 79. Placed in maidens on his first three runs, and looks sure to find a race. His trainer John Benstead has retired. **C J Benstead [0-4] Hamdan Al Maktoum.*

TAMPA LADY (IRE) BHB 66f **RR 72f** 3932[11]
2 ch f Up and At 'em- Fantasise (FR)(General Assembly(USA)) 10f **(68)**
Form - 2450110220
Record 1998 - 1st:2 2nd:3 3rd:0 Ran:10
Win Prizemoney £7,579 *Total Prizemoney* £10,809
Wins * **1998** Jly Newmar (G-F) S 7f 72 <
* **1998** Jun Hamilt (G-S) S 6f 61
1998 Turf 2-10: (5f 2, 6f 1-2, 7f 1-5, 8f) (sft, gd 1-3, g-f 2, frm 1-4)
Above-average filly, effective 7f, acts on gd to frm, best on frm. Turf high 72 - 1st of 12 getting 5lb from Ace of Trumps (8 Jly Newmarket RF 2638). Looked a decent plater when winning at the July Meeting, and has shown mixed form in nurseries since. Not an easy ride. **M Johnston [2-10] R Fabrizius.*

TAMURE (IRE) BHB 115f **RR 116f** 4079a[8]
6 b h Sadler's Wells (USA) 11.3f **(87)** -Three Tails (Blakeney) 10.5f **(64)**
Form - 318
Record 1998 - 1st:1 2nd:0 3rd:1 Ran:3
Pre1998 - 1st:4 2nd:3 3rd:1 Ran:14
Win Prizemoney £55,071 *Total Prizemoney* £354,099
Wins * **1998** Jun Newmar (GD) L 12f 116 <
1995 Spt Longch (SFT) G3 10f 112
1995 May York (GD) 10.4f 105
1995 May Newmar (GD) 12f 90
1995 Apr Newbur (G-F) 11f 94+
1998 Turf 1-3: (12f 1-2, 13f) (gd 2, g-f 1-1)
High-class horse, effective 10 to 13f, best at 12f, acts on sft to g-f, best on g-f, prefers right handed tracks. Turf high 116 - 1st of 7 getting 3lb from Taufan's Melody (27 Jun Newmarket RF 2351). Runner-up in the 1995 Derby, he has been rather disappointing since, but regained winning form in a Listed race at Newmarket in June, making all despite veering sharply to the left in the closing stages. He was not seen after disappointing at Deauville next time.
**L M Cumani [1-3] Scuderia Rencati Srl (from J H M Gosden [4-14] Nov 1997).*

TANAASA (IRE) BHB 105f **RR 92f** 4454[4]
4 b c Sadler's Wells (USA) 11.3f **(87)** - Mesmerize (Mill Reef (USA)) 10.5f **(78)**
Form - 4
Record 1998 - 1st:0 2nd:0 3rd:0 Ran:1
Pre1998 - 1st:1 2nd:1 3rd:1 Ran:3
Win Prizemoney £3,572 *Total Prizemoney* £16,857
Wins * 1997 Apr Leices (G-S) 10f 83+ <
1998 Turf 0-1: (10f) (gd)
Scopey, useful colt. Runner-up to Silver Patriarch in the Lingfield Derby Trial on his last start of 1997, he finished last in useful company on his only run. **Sir Michael Stoute [1-4] Maktoum Al Maktoum.*

TANCRED ARMS BHB 60f **RR 70f** 5012[6]
2 b f Clantime 6.6f **(57)** - Mischievous Miss (Niniski (USA)) 10.6f **(65)**
Form - 6002660226
Record 1998 - 1st:0 2nd:3 3rd:0 Ran:10
Win Prizemoney £0 *Total Prizemoney* £2,873
1998 Turf 0-10: (5f 5, 6f 5) (sft, gd 5, g-f 2, frm 2)
Above-average filly, effective 5f, acts on gd. Turf high 70 - 2nd of 8 getting 11lb from Pistachio (17 Jun Ripon 5f gd RF 2072).
**D W Barker [0-10] D W Barker.*

TANCRED MISCHIEF BHB 37f **RR 39f** 5118[12]
7 b m Northern State (USA) 12.6f **(45)** - Mischievous Miss (Niniski (USA)) 10.6f **(65)**
Form - 68050568410
Record 1998 - 1st:1 2nd:0 3rd:0 Ran:11
Pre1998 - 1st:2 2nd:1 3rd:2 Ran:20
Win Prizemoney £9,825 *Total Prizemoney* £12,193
Wins * **1998** Oct Pontef (SFT) H 18f 27 39 <
* 1997 Jun Pontef (GD) H 18f 30 39 <
* 1997 Apr Mussel (G-F) H 16f 28 30
1998 Turf 1-11: (14f 3, 16f 5, 17f, 18f 1-1, 22f) (g-s, gd 1-7, g-f, frm 2)
Very moderate mare, effective 16 to 18f, best at 18f, acts on sft to gd, best on gd, has worn blinkers, likes right handed tracks, does well at Musselburgh, likes Pontefract. Turf high 39 - 1st of 9 getting 21lb from Sad Mad Bad (19 Oct Pontefract RF 4871).
**D W Barker [3-23] D W Barker (from W L Barker [1-18] Jun 1996).*

TANCRED TIMES BHB 58f53a **RR 62f 53a** 4757[12]
3 ch f Clantime 6.6f **(57)** - Mischievous Miss (Niniski (USA)) 10.6f **(65)**
Form - 00434751250830
Record 1998 - 1st:1 2nd:1 3rd:2 Ran:14
Pre1998 - 1st:2 2nd:0 3rd:1 Ran:7
Win Prizemoney £9,209 *Total Prizemoney* £11,962
Wins * **1998** Aug Carlis (G-S) H 5.9f 56 62
* 1997 Jly Catter (G-F) H 7f 68 <
* 1997 Jun Thirsk (GD) S 6f 64
1998 Turf 1-14: (5f 4, 6f 1-8, 7f, 10f) (sft 2, gd 1-5, g-f, frm 5, hrd)
Light-framed, average filly, effective 5 to 7f, acts on gd to frm, best on frm, excels at Thirsk, does well at Catterick. Turf high 62 - 2nd of 11 giving 2lb to Wishbone Alley (10 Aug Thirsk 5f frm RF 3506) - also 1st of 19 giving 14lb to Guest Envoy (3 Aug Carlisle RF 3305).
**D W Barker [3-21] Tom Carrick.*

TANGAZI (USA) RR 109f 4945a[2]
3 b c Jade Hunter (USA) 10.4f **(72)** - Miss Leonora (USA) (Theatrical)
Form - 2
1998 Turf 0-1: (9f) (gd)
Currently Pattern-class colt. (1st run) - 2nd of 10 getting 1lb from Vergennes (18 Oct Belmont Park 9f gd RF 4945a).
**W Mott in USA [0-1].*

TANGERINE FLYER BHB 60f75a **RR 51f 75a** 3809[8]
3 ch g Presidium 7.5f **(56)** - Factuelle (Known Fact (USA)) 7.4f **(67)**
Form - 1113305578
Record 1998 - 1st:2 2nd:0 3rd:2 Ran:9
Pre1998 - 1st:1 2nd:2 3rd:0 Ran:7
Win Prizemoney £8,451 *Total Prizemoney* £11,071
Wins 1998 *Jan Lingfi (STD) C 5f 80+* <
1998 *Jan Lingfi (STD) H 5f 73 80+* <
1997 *Dec Lingfi (STD) 5f 72*
1998 Turf 0-4: (5f 3, 6f) (g-f 2, frm 2) 1998 AW 2-5: (5f 2-5) (Equi 2-4, Fibr)
Unfurnished, fair gelding, effective 5f, - acts on Equi, prefers left handed tracks, prefers tight tracks. Turf high 51. AW high 80 (1st run) - 1st of 6 giving 23lb to Dande Times (3 Jan Lingfield RF 0016) - also 1st of 3 giving 10lb to Dande Times (24 Jan Lingfield RF 0146). Becoming disappointing. He hit form with a hat-trick over the minimum on the Lingfield Equitrack during the winter. He looks a speedy and progressive sort, but less effective on Turf.
**P D Evans [0-4] M W Lawrence (from J Berry [3-12] May 1998).*

TANGO (IRE) BHB 82f **RR 90f** 4617[10]
3 b c Dancing Dissident (USA) 6.8f **(65)** - Tunguska (Busted) 10.2f **(61)**
Form - 5812700
Record 1998 - 1st:1 2nd:1 3rd:0 Ran:7
Win Prizemoney £3,875 *Total Prizemoney* £5,473
Wins * **1998** May Pontef (G-F) 6f 90 <
1998 Turf 1-6: (6f 1-5, 7f) (gd 3, g-f, frm 1-2) 1998 AW 0-1: (8f) (Equi)
Leggy, useful colt, effective 6f, acts on g-f to frm. Turf high 90 - 2nd of 8 to Caribbean Monarch (1 Jun Windsor 6f g-f RF 1636) - also 1st of 17 from Zihaam (22 May Pontefract RF 1408). Has found it tough since winning a maiden in good style. Has joined Kim Bailey. **R Hannon [1-7] Noodles Racing.*

TANGO KING BHB 46f **RR 61f** 3099[12]
4 b g Suave Dancer (USA) 10.7f **(68)** - Be My Queen (Be My Guest (USA)) 9.3f **(67)**
Form - 0040
Record 1998 - 1st:0 2nd:0 3rd:0 Ran:4
Pre1998 - 1st:1 2nd:1 3rd:0 Ran:8
Win Prizemoney £3,252 *Total Prizemoney* £4,425
Wins 1997 May Nottin (GD) H 14.1f 69 70 <
1998 Turf 0-3: (12f, 14f, 16f) (gd 2, frm) 1998 AW 0-1: (16f) (Fibr)
Leggy, average gelding, effective 11 to 14f, best at 14f, acts on g-s to frm, best on frm, likes left handed tracks. Turf high 61. Becoming disappointing.
**J G Portman [0-4] A S B Portman (from J L Dunlop [1-8] Aug 1997).*

TANGO QUEEN RR 33f 3408[7]
3 b f Rambo Dancer (CAN) 8.4f **(59)** - Formidable Task (Formidable (USA)) 9.2f **(63)**
Form - 07
Record 1998 - 1st:0 2nd:0 3rd:0 Ran:2
1998 Turf 0-2: (8f 2) (g-f 2)

Currently very moderate filly. Turf high 33 (began Jly).
**Miss S E Hall [0-2] C Platts.*

TANIMBAR (IRE) BHB 48f **RR 50f** 3690[4]
3 b g Persian Bold 10f **(69)** -Try My Rosie (Try My Best (USA)) 7.6f **(67)**
Form - 77054
Record 1998 - 1st:0 2nd:0 3rd:0 Ran:5
Pre1998 - 1st:0 2nd:0 3rd:0 Ran:2
1998 Turf 0-5: (6f, 7f 2, 8f 2) (gd 2, g-f 2, frm)
Workmanlike, fair gelding, effective 8f, acts on frm, has worn blinkers. Turf high 50 - 4th of 14 giving 3lb to Lady Yavanna (18 Aug Brighton 8f frm RF 3690).
**D HaydnJones [0-7] J K Ruggles & Mrs A R Ruggles.*

TANKERSLEY BHB 78f **RR 84f** 4226[12]
3 ch c Timeless Times (USA) 6.1f **(56)** -Busted Love (Busted) 10.2f **(61)**
Form - 2106200
Record 1998 - 1st:1 2nd:2 3rd:0 Ran:7
Pre1998 - 1st:0 2nd:0 3rd:0 Ran:1
Win Prizemoney £2,889 *Total Prizemoney* £5,203
Wins * 1998 May Catter (G-S) 7f 81 <
1998 Turf 1-7: (7f 1-2, 8f, 10f 2, 12f 2) (gd 1-3, g-f 2, frm 2)
Scopey, decent colt, effective 7 to 10f, best at 7f, acts on gd to g-f, best on gd, prefers left handed tracks. Turf high 90 (1st run) - 2nd of 11 giving 5lb to Confidante (2 May Thirsk 7f gd RF 0980) - also 1st of 5 from Ollie's Chuckle (30 May Catterick RF 1587). Struggled when faced with a simple task in a maiden, and has shown modest form since. A tough sort.
**P W D'Arcy [1-7] Walt Sylvester (from A Hide [0-1] Nov 1997).*

TANNENKONIG (GER) RR 111f 5132a[2]
3 b c Fairy King (USA) 7.7f **(75)** - Tannenalm (IRE) (Luciano) 11.2f **(65)**
Form - 3342262
1998 Turf 0-7: (7f, 8f 5, 10f) (sft 3, g-s 2, gd 2)
Group-class colt, effective 7 to 10f, best at 8f, acts on sft to gd, best on sft, does well at Cologne. Turf high 111 - 2nd of 9 getting 8lb from Power Flame (26 Spt Cologne 8f sft RF 4599a). He looked out of his depth when sent to Italy for a Group One in October.
**W Kujath in GER [0-6] M Grau et al.*

TANSHAN BHB 65f **RR 75f** 3846[7]
3 ch c Anshan 8.2f **(63)** - Nafla (FR) (Arctic Tern (USA)) 8.9f **(69)**
Form - 4347
Record 1998 - 1st:0 2nd:0 3rd:1 Ran:4
Win Prizemoney £0 *Total Prizemoney* £641
1998 Turf 0-4: (8f 2, 9f, 11f) (gd 2, frm 2)
Scopey, above-average colt. Turf high 75 (1st run) - 4th of 10 to Cyber World (23 May Kempton 8f gd RF 1429).
**A C Stewart [0-4] M Hawkes.*

TANTISPER RR 37f 5057[5]
2 ch c Anshan 8.2f **(63)** - Fine Asset (Hot Spark) 7.6f **(62)**
Form - 5
Record 1998 - 1st:0 2nd:0 3rd:0 Ran:1
1998 Turf 0-1: (8f) (sft)
Currently very moderate colt. **Mrs A Swinbank [0-1] Brooke Rankin.*

TANUSIUS BHB 85f **RR 86f** 4870[5]
2 b c Warning 8.1f **(77)** - Tanz (IRE) (Sadler's Wells (USA)) 10f **(76)**
Form - 235
Record 1998 - 1st:0 2nd:1 3rd:1 Ran:3
Win Prizemoney £0 *Total Prizemoney* £1,948
1998 Turf 0-3: (7f 2, 8f) (gd 2, g-f)
Currently useful colt. Turf high 86 (1st run) (began Spt) - 2nd of 7 to J R Stevenson (23 Spt Chester 7f gd RF 4445).
**C E Brittain [0-3] Abdullah Saeed Bul Hab.*

TAOISTE BHB 80f **RR 85f** 3104[12]
5 ch h Kris 10f **(75)** - Tenue de Soiree (USA) (Lyphard (USA)) 9.9f **(72)**
Form - 042200
Record 1998 - 1st:0 2nd:2 3rd:0 Ran:6
Pre1998 - 1st:0 2nd:0 3rd:1 Ran:8
Win Prizemoney £0 *Total Prizemoney* £5,332
1998 Turf 0-6: (5f 3, 6f 2, 7f) (g-s, gd, g-f 2, frm 2)
Useful colt, effective 5 to 6f, best at 6f, acts on g-s to g-f, has worn blinkers. Turf high 85 - 2nd of 4 giving 7lb to Cortachy Castle (13 Jun Sandown 5f g-s RF 1975). Inconsistent. An ex-French performer who has won at up to a mile in France but seems better over shorter, he has plenty of ability but is rather difficult to place.
**R W Armstrong [0-14] Po Shing Woo.*

TAPATCH (IRE) BHB 48f55a **RR 50f 55a** 4072[6]
10 b g Thatching 7.8f **(69)** - Knees Up (USA) (Dancing Champ (USA)) 8.8f **(80)**
Form - 31256
Record 1998 - 1st:1 2nd:1 3rd:1 Ran:5
Pre1998 - 1st:1 2nd:2 3rd:4 Ran:22
Win Prizemoney £5,330 *Total Prizemoney* £13,708
Wins * 1998 Jun Pontef (GD) H 10f 45 49 <
1998 Turf 1-5: (8f 2, 10f 1-3) (g-s, g-f, frm 1-3)
Average gelding, has worn blinkers. Turf high 50. A consistent sort on the Flat and over fences, his Pontefract win in June was his first on the level for eight years.
**M W Easterby [5-28] Miss V Foster (from J S Wainwright [0-1] Feb 1995).*

TAP ON TOOTSIE BHB 43f37a **RR 46f 37a** 2659[10]
6 b m Faustus (USA) 9.1f **(54)** - My Tootsie (Tap On Wood) 10.3f **(65)**
Form - 510
Record 1998 - 1st:1 2nd:0 3rd:0 Ran:3
Pre1998 - 1st:0 2nd:0 3rd:1 Ran:10
Win Prizemoney £2,430 *Total Prizemoney* £2,980
Wins * 1998 Jun Carlis (G-S) H 17.2f 36 46 <
1998 Turf 1-2: (16f, 17f 1-1) (gd 1-2) 1998 AW 0-1: (14f) (Fibr)
Moderate mare. Turf high 46 - 1st of 15 giving 8lb to Last Lap (24 Jun Carlisle RF 2229). Inconsistent.
**T Wall [2-14] R Cowper (from I Campbell [0-6] Dec 1995).*

TAP TO MUSIC (USA) RR 5166a[5]
3 f Pleasant Tap (USA) - Nuryette (USA) (Nureyev (USA))
Form - 5
1998 AW 0-1: (9f) (Dirt)
Currently very useful filly, always wears blinkers.
**J Orseno in USA [0-1] Stronach Stables.*

TARA (IRE) BHB 41f **RR 46f** 4264[11]
2 br f Petardia 8.2f **(58)** - Genzyme Gene (Riboboy (USA)) 14f **(54)**
Form - 6000400
Record 1998 - 1st:0 2nd:0 3rd:0 Ran:7
Win Prizemoney £0 *Total Prizemoney* £243
1998 Turf 0-4: (5f, 6f 2, 8f) (gd, g-f 3) 1998 AW 0-3: (5f 2, 7f) (Fibr 3)
Moderate filly, has worn blinkers. Turf high 46. AW high 13.
**K T Ivory [0-7] K T Ivory.*

TARADIYA (IRE) RR 82f 3220[6]
2 b f Danehill (USA) 9.1f **(79)** - Tarakana (USA) (Shahrastani (USA)) 8.8f **(72)**
Form - 66
Record 1998 - 1st:0 2nd:0 3rd:0 Ran:2
1998 Turf 0-2: (6f, 7f) (gd, frm)
Currently decent filly. Turf high 82 (began Jly).
**L M Cumani [0-2] H H Aga Khan.*

TARAKAN (IRE) RR 87f 701[4]
3 b c Doyoun 10.7f **(69)** - Tarakana (USA)(Shahrastani (USA)) 8.8f **(72)**
Form - 4
Record 1998 - 1st:0 2nd:0 3rd:0 Ran:1
Win Prizemoney £0 *Total Prizemoney* £378
1998 Turf 0-1: (8f) (sft)
Currently useful colt. (1st run) - 4th of 19 giving 5lb to The Sandfly (15 Apr Newmarket 8f sft RF 0701). Promising debut effort, and he should stay ten furlongs. *L M Cumani [0-1] H H Aga Khan.*

TARASCO (FR) BHB 75f **RR 74f** 4845[16]
2 b g Deploy 11.4f **(67)** -Moucha (FR)(Fabulous Dancer(USA)) 9.4f **(70)**
Form - 00010
Record 1998 - 1st:1 2nd:0 3rd:0 Ran:5
Win Prizemoney £5,998 *Total Prizemoney* £5,998
Wins * 1998 Spt Ayr (G-S) H 8f 63 74+ <
1998 Turf 1-5: (6f 3, 8f 1-2) (sft 1-1, g-f 2, frm 2)
Above-average gelding. Turf high 74 (began Aug) - 1st of 11 getting 18lb from Ice (18 Spt Ayr RF 4352). Showed little in six-furlong maidens, but a tongue tie and step up to a mile did the trick in a nursery. **Mrs J R Ramsden [1-5] Mrs D Ridley.*

TARASCON (IRE) **RR 109f** 4294a[5]

3 b f Tirol 8.1f **(64)** - Breyani (Commanche Run) 8.5f **(58)**

Form - 01675

1998 Turf 1-5: (8f 1-3, 10f, 12f) (gd 1-5)

Pattern-class filly, effective 7 to 8f, acts on gd. Turf high 109 - 1st of 13 from Kitza (24 May Curragh RF 1513a). She got herself into a rare stew in the stalls before the 1000 Guineas at Newmarket, and showed her performance there to be all wrong when winning the Irish equivalent under a fine ride from young Jamie Spencer. A non-stayer when tried beyond a mile later in the season, she will not be remembered as an outstanding Classic winner, but was a smart filly nonetheless. **T Stack in IRE [3-9] Mrs Jane Rowlinson.*

TARASHAAN BHB 91f **RR 87f** 4850[5]

3 b g Darshaan 11.9f **(81)** - Tarasova (USA) (Green Forest (USA)) 9.9f **(68)**

Form - 61115145

Record 1998 - 1st:4 2nd:0 3rd:0 Ran:8
Pre1998 - 1st:1 2nd:0 3rd:0 Ran:5

Win Prizemoney £17,645 *Total Prizemoney* £18,075

Wins								
* **1998**	Spt	Newcas	(GD)	H	16.1f	80	87	<
* **1998**	Jly	Chepst	(GD)	H	16.2f	80	83	
* **1998**	Jly	Haydoc	(G-S)	H	14f	75	79+	
* **1998**	Jun	Kempto	(HVY)		14.4f		66+	
* 1997	Spt	Nottin	(G-F)	H	10f	71	74	

1998 Turf 4-8: (10f, 12f, 14f 2-2, 15f, 16f 2-2, 18f) (g-s 1-1, gd 2, g-f 1-3, frm 2-2)

Scopey, useful gelding, effective 14 to 16f, best at 16f, acts on g-f to frm, best on frm, prefers left handed tracks, prefers tight tracks. Turf high 87 - 1st of 10 giving 25lb to Give An Inch (8 Spt Newcastle RF 4154) - also 1st of 3 giving 13lb to Cut Diamond (24 Jly Chepstow RF 3072). He returned to form by landing a hat-trick in small staying events during the summer, but he only beat a total of eight runners in the process, and when stepped down in trip against some quite useful rivals was well and truly found out. A patron of Noel Meade's yard paid 74,000 gns for him in October.
**Sir Mark Prescott [5-13] E B Rimmer.*

TARAWAN BHB 86f **RR 80f** 4959[2]

2 ch c Nashwan (USA) 10.3f **(79)** - Soluce (Junius (USA)) 7.7f **(65)**

Form - 702

Record 1998 - 1st:0 2nd:1 3rd:0 Ran:3

Win Prizemoney £0 *Total Prizemoney* £1,410

1998 Turf 0-3: (7f 3) (frm 3)

Currently decent colt. Turf high 80. **I A Balding [0-3] Robert Hitchins.*

TAR BABY **RR 30f** 4765[13]

3 b f Handsome Sailor 6.6f **(53)** - Queen of Aragon (Aragon) 8.1f **(60)**

Form - 00

Record 1998 - 1st:0 2nd:0 3rd:0 Ran:2

1998 Turf 0-2: (7f 2) (gd, frm)

Scopey, currently very moderate filly. Turf high 30 (began Spt).
**R Hollinshead [0-2] Mrs Charles Lockhart.*

TARHELM (IRE) **RR 107f** 1094a[3]

6 br h Helm Reef - Tarabella (Dance In Time (CAN)) 8.9f **(59)**

Form - 3

1998 Turf 0-1: (10f) (g-s)

Pattern-class horse. Consistent.
**G Colleo in ITY [2-8] (from ITY [2-3] Oct 1994).*

TARRADALE BHB 43f **RR 43f** 5017[2]

4 br g Interrex (CAN) 7.7f **(51)** - Encore L'Amour (USA) (Monteverdi) 6.5f **(61)**

Form - 04126582

Record 1998 - 1st:1 2nd:2 3rd:0 Ran:8
Pre1998 - 1st:0 2nd:0 3rd:0 Ran:10

Win Prizemoney £2,983 *Total Prizemoney* £4,925

Wins * **1998** Jun Hamilt (G-S) H 8.3f 32 35 <

1998 Turf 1-8: (8f 1-4, 9f 2, 10f, 12f) (g-s, gd 4, g-f 1-1, frm 2)

Strong, moderate gelding, likes right handed tracks, likes tight tracks. Turf high 43. **C B B Booth [1-20] Ashley Carr Racing.*

TARRY BHB 57f56a **RR 58f 56a** 93[11]

5 b m Salse (USA) 10.9f **(71)** - Waitingformargaret (Kris) 9.5f **(73)**

Form - 250

Record 1998 - 1st:0 2nd:0 3rd:0 Ran:2
Pre1998 - 1st:3 2nd:3 3rd:1 Ran:18

Win Prizemoney £8,831 *Total Prizemoney* £12,486

Wins								
* 1997	Oct	Salisb	(GD)	CH	14f	46	54	
1997	Aug	Chepst	(GD)	C	12.1f		50	
1995	Aug	Newmar	(G-F)	S	7f		60	<

1998 AW 0-2: (13f, 16f) (Equi 2)

Fair filly, has broken blood-vessels, effective 12 to 14f, acts on gd to frm - acts on Equi, has worn blinkers. AW high 38.
**Miss Gay Kelleway [1-7] The Pieces Of Eight Partnership (from A Streeter [2-8] Aug 1997).*

TARRY FLYNN (IRE) **RR 93f** 915a[2]

4 br g Kenmare (FR) 9.6f **(76)** - Danzig Lass (USA) 00

Form - 122

1998 Turf 1-3: (7f, 8f 1-1, 9f) (hvy, sft 1-2)

Useful gelding, effective 7 to 9f, acts on hvy to sft, best on sft, has worn blinkers. Turf high 93 - 2nd of 7 giving 13lb to Blue Stocking (26 Apr Cork 9f hvy RF 0915a) - also 1st of 9 getting 28lb from Quws (29 Mar Curragh RF 0526a). Inconsistent.
**D K Weld in IRE [2-8] Mrs C L Weld.*

TARSKI BHB 60f **RR 77f** 4744[11]

4 ch g Polish Precedent (USA) 9f **(73)** - Illusory (Kings Lake (USA)) 10.8f **(67)**

Form - 7600070

Record 1998 - 1st:0 2nd:0 3rd:0 Ran:7
Pre1998 - 1st:1 2nd:1 3rd:0 Ran:4

Win Prizemoney £4,240 *Total Prizemoney* £6,349

Wins 1996 Jly Sandow (G-F) 7.1f 92+ <

1998 Turf 0-7: (8f 4, 9f, 10f, 12f) (g-s, gd 3, frm 3)

Scopey, above-average gelding, effective 8f, acts on g-f, has worn blinkers. Turf high 77.
**L G Cottrell [0-7] E Gadsden (from H R A Cecil [1-4] Spt 1997).*

TART (FR) BHB 55a **RR 46f** 364[5]

5 br m Warning 8.1f **(77)** - Sharp Girl (FR) (Sharpman) 11.3f **(66)**

Form - 045

Record 1998 - 1st:0 2nd:0 3rd:0 Ran:3
Pre1998 - 1st:2 2nd:3 3rd:5 Ran:23

Win Prizemoney £5,876 *Total Prizemoney* £12,262

Wins								
1997	Spt	Redcar	(FRM)	SH	10f	42	46	
1996	Spt	Yarmou	(GD)	C	11.5f		68	<

1998 AW 0-3: (8f, 12f 2) (Equi, Fibr 2)

Moderate filly, effective 12f, acts on g-f - acts on Fibr, has worn blinkers, likes tight tracks. AW high 47.
**D Nicholls [0-6] M A Scaife (from J Pearce [1-13] Spt 1997).*

TARTAN LASS BHB 67f **RR 66f** 4260[12]

3 b f Selkirk (USA) 7.9f **(76)** - Gwiffina (Welsh Saint) 7.6f **(64)**

Form - 350

Record 1998 - 1st:0 2nd:0 3rd:0 Ran:2
Pre1998 - 1st:0 2nd:0 3rd:1 Ran:3

Win Prizemoney £0 *Total Prizemoney* £322

1998 Turf 0-2: (6f, 7f) (gd 2)

Scopey, average filly. Turf high 66.
**R Guest [0-5] Matthews Breeding and Racing.*

TARXIEN BHB 84f **RR 88f** 4769[4]

4 b g Kendor (FR) 12.2f **(66)** -Tanz (IRE)(Sadler's Wells (USA)) 10f **(76)**

Form - 33114105084

Record 1998 - 1st:3 2nd:0 3rd:2 Ran:11
Pre1998 - 1st:2 2nd:3 3rd:1 Ran:11

Win Prizemoney £17,547 *Total Prizemoney* £25,063

Wins								
* **1998**	Jun	Goodwo	(G-F)	H	14f	85	88	<
* **1998**	May	Newbur	(GD)	H	13.3f	73	86	
* **1998**	May	Haydoc	(G-S)	H	14f	73	77+	
* 1997	Spt	Pontef	(G-S)		12f		68	
* 1997	Aug	Haydoc	(G-F)	H	11.9f	62	68	

1998 Turf 3-11: (12f 4, 13f 1-2, 14f 2-5)(sft, g-s 2, gd 2-5, g-f 1-1, frm 2)

Scopey, useful gelding, effective 13 to 14f, acts on gd to g-f, likes left handed tracks. Turf high 88 - 1st of 10 giving 2lb to Life of Riley (26 Jun Goodwood RF 2302) - also 1st of 6 giving 2lb to Dead Aim (27 May Newbury RF 1525). In good form earlier in the year, winning three times, but looked held by the Handicapper later. **K R Burke [5-22] The Ginge Racing Partnership.*

TASHKENT BHB 35f **RR 6f** 3797^{11}
6 b g Thowra (FR) 11.2f **(47)** - Royal Bat (Crowned Prince (USA)) 10.1f **(67)**
Form - 0000
Record 1998 - 1st:0 2nd:0 3rd:0 Ran:4
Pre1998 - 1st:0 2nd:0 3rd:0 Ran:4
1998 Turf 0-4: (6f, 7f, 8f, 16f) (gd, g-f 2, frm)
Very poor gelding, has worn blinkers. Turf high 6. Becoming disappointing.
**R Simpson [0-7] Miss J Rumford (from Miss K M George [0-3] Jly 1996).*

TASIK CHINI (USA) BHB 57f **RR 61f** 4003^{8}
4 b br g St Jovite (USA) 11.8f **(75)** - Ten Hail Marys (USA) (Halo (USA)) 10.6f **(75)**
Form - 3108
Record 1998 - 1st:1 2nd:0 3rd:1 Ran:4
Pre1998 - 1st:1 2nd:0 3rd:1 Ran:13
Win Prizemoney £5,767 *Total Prizemoney* £6,873
Wins * **1998** May Bath (G-F) H 17.2f 56 61
* 1997 Mar Folkes (G-F) H 12f 70 72 <
1998 Turf 1-4: (16f 2, 17f 1-2) (gd, frm 1-3)
Scopey, average gelding, effective 12 to 13f, acts on g-f to frm, has worn blinkers, favours tight tracks. Turf high 61. His form indicates he is best fresh, but he is not one to place too much trust in.
**P F I Cole [2-17] H R H Sultan Ahmad Shah.*

TASK FORCE BHB 66f **RR 67f** 4319^{10}
3 b g Soviet Star (USA) 8.6f **(74)** - Devon Defender (Home Guard (USA)) 9.3f **(66)**
Form - 835100
Record 1998 - 1st:1 2nd:0 3rd:1 Ran:6
Win Prizemoney £2,637 *Total Prizemoney* £3,159
Wins * **1998** Aug Leices (GD) C 8f 63 <
1998 Turf 1-6: (8f 1-5, 9f) (sft, gd 3, frm 1-2)
Neat, average gelding. Turf high 77. The drop into claiming company paid dividends at Leicester in August.
**S P C Woods [1-6] Robert Russell.*

TASKONE RR 13f 1998^{8}
2 ch f Be My Chief (USA) 10.2f **(62)** - Good as Gold (IRE) (Glint of Gold) 9.3f **(66)**
Form - 8
Record 1998 - 1st:0 2nd:0 3rd:0 Ran:1
1998 Turf 0-1: (6f) (gd)
Currently poor filly. **R A Fahey [0-1] Task Training Ltd.*

TASSILI (IRE) BHB 54a **RR 39f** 2965^{10}
5 b g Old Vic 12.8f **(72)** - Topsy (Habitat) 9.4f **(70)**
Form - 00
Record 1998 - 1st:0 2nd:0 3rd:0 Ran:2
Pre1998 - 1st:0 2nd:0 3rd:0 Ran:5
Win Prizemoney £0 *Total Prizemoney* £229
1998 Turf 0-1: (10f) (gd) 1998 AW 0-1: (8f) (Fibr)
Very moderate gelding, has worn blinkers.
**J G Portman [0-4] Madhatter Racing (from Lady Herries [0-4] Jly 1997).*

TASSO DANCER RR 48f 4967^{8}
2 gr f Dilum (USA) 7.1f **(56)** -Dancing Diana(Raga Navarro (ITY))8f **(64)**
Form - 8
Record 1998 - 1st:0 2nd:0 3rd:0 Ran:1
1998 Turf 0-1: (6f) (sft)
Currently moderate filly. **B J Meehan [0-1] Mrs J Tredwell.*

TASTE OF SUCCESS BHB 65f **RR 65f** 3607^{4}
3 b c Thatching 7.8f **(69)** - Tastiera (USA) (Diesis) 9.3f **(69)**
Form - 4
Record 1998 - 1st:0 2nd:0 3rd:0 Ran:1
Pre1998 - 1st:0 2nd:0 3rd:0 Ran:2
Win Prizemoney £0 *Total Prizemoney* £483
1998 Turf 0-1: (7f) (frm)
Strong, currently average colt. **P W Harris [0-3] First Taste.*

TATTINGER BHB 88f **RR 94f** 4498^{8}
3 b f Prince Sabo 6.6f **(64)** - Tight (Lochnager) 6f **(59)**
Form - 21020438
Record 1998 - 1st:1 2nd:2 3rd:1 Ran:8
Pre1998 - 1st:0 2nd:0 3rd:1 Ran:2
Win Prizemoney £3,756 *Total Prizemoney* £8,708
Wins * **1998** May Redcar (G-F) 6f 66 <
1998 Turf 1-8: (6f 1-7, 7f) (gd 1-2, g-f 2, frm 4)
Workmanlike, useful filly, effective 6f, acts on gd. Turf high 94 - 3rd of 7 getting 7lb from Kumait (16 Spt Yarmouth 6f gd RF 4315). Simple task in a modest Redcar maiden before found wanting in decent handicap company. **J R Fanshawe [1-10] Mrs E Fanshawe.*

TATTLING RR 83f 4856^{5}
2 b f Warning 8.1f **(77)** - Tatouma (USA) (The Minstrel (CAN)) 10f **(72)**
Form - 25
Record 1998 - 1st:0 2nd:1 3rd:0 Ran:2
Win Prizemoney £0 *Total Prizemoney* £1,288
1998 Turf 0-2: (7f 2) (sft, frm)
Currently decent filly. Turf high 83 (1st run) (began Spt) - 2nd of 17 to Kalidasa (22 Spt Warwick 7f frm RF 4411).
**B W Hills [0-2] K Abdulla.*

TAUFAN BOY BHB 64f70a **RR 66f 70a** 4747^{2}
5 b g Taufan (USA) 8.3f **(65)** - Lydia Maria (Dancing Brave (USA)) 8.4f **(76)**
Form - 54142
Record 1998 - 1st:1 2nd:1 3rd:0 Ran:5
Pre1998 - 1st:1 2nd:2 3rd:5 Ran:22
Win Prizemoney £7,123 *Total Prizemoney* £17,259
Wins * **1998** May Haydoc (G-S) H 14f 58 63
1995 *Spt Southw (STD) 7f 80* <
1998 Turf 1-5: (12f, 14f 1-4) (sft, g-s, gd 1-2, frm)
Above-average gelding, effective 14f, acts on gd to frm, best on frm, has worn blinkers. Turf high 66 - 2nd of 17 getting 8lb from Foundry Lane (10 Oct York 14f gd RF 4747).
**G B Balding [1-9] Supreme Team (from P W Harris [1-22] Oct 1997).*

TAUFAN'S MELODY BHB 117f **RR 119f** 5153a^{4}
7 b g Taufan (USA) 8.3f **(65)** - Glorious Fate (Northfields (USA)) 9f **(72)**
Form - 1D225114
Record 1998 - 1st:2 2nd:2 3rd:0 Ran:6
Pre1998 - 1st:8 2nd:10 3rd:2 Ran:28
Win Prizemoney £474,231 *Total Prizemoney* £598,477
Wins * **1998** Oct Caulfi (GD) G1 12f 114 <
* **1998** Spt Baden (GD) L 16f 103
* 1997 Nov Lyon P (HVY) L 12f 111
* 1997 Nov Doncas (SFT) L 12f 114 <
* 1997 May Lingfi (G-F) 11.5f 103+
* 1996 Jun Lingfi (G-F) 11.5f 110
* 1995 Nov Nantes (G-S) L 12f 104
* 1995 Oct Lyon P (GD) L 12f 108
* 1995 Spt Ascot (G-S) H 12f 100 109
* 1994 Jun Goodwo (FRM) 9f 73+
1998 Turf 2-6: (10f, 12f 1-3, 16f 1-2) (sft, gd 2-3, g-f 2)
High-class gelding, effective 10 to 16f, best at 12f, acts on hvy to g-f, best on gd, likes left handed tracks, excels at Newbury. Turf high 119 - 4th of 24 giving 10lb to Jezabeel (3 Nov Flemington 16f gd RF 5153a) - also 1st of 17 giving 11lb to Lisa's Game (17 Oct Caulfield RF 4941a). Seemingly exposed as Listed class in Europe, this wonderfully tough gelding ran the race of his life to beat the Aussies in their own back yard and land the Foster's Caulfield Cup as an unconsidered 66-1 shot. He caused havoc when drifting left-handed under Ray Cochrane, who was later handed a one-month ban and £7,800 fine. He went on to run a super race to finish fourth in the Melbourne Cup after being ridden from the rear, which was in stark contrast to his trainer's instructions. He seems to act on any track or ground. **Lady Herries [10-34] All At Sea Partnership.*

TAUREAN BHB 38f **RR 24f** 376^{5}
3 b c Dilum (USA) 7.1f **(56)** - Herora (IRE) **(66f)** (Heraldiste (USA))
Form - 685
Record 1998 - 1st:0 2nd:0 3rd:0 Ran:3
Pre1998 - 1st:0 2nd:0 3rd:0 Ran:3
1998 AW 0-3: (6f, 8f 2) (Equi 2, Fibr)
Small, moderate colt. AW high 47.
**N A Graham [0-6] Mrs Lesley Graham.*

TAURUS BAY (IRE) RR 18f 3019^{13}
2 b g River Falls 8.2f **(56)** - Farriers Slipper (Prince Tenderfoot (USA)) 9f **(61)**

Form - 0060
Record 1998 - 1st:0 2nd:0 3rd:0 Ran:4
1998 Turf 0-4: (5f 3, 7f) (g-f 3, frm)
Poor gelding. Turf high 18.
**Ronald Thompson [0-4] Mrs Janet McCabe.*

TAVERNER SOCIETY (IRE) BHB 92f RR 102f 4734[10]

3 b c Imp Society(USA) 7.1f **(63)** -Straw Boater(Thatch (USA)) 9.8f **(62)**
Form - 43625500
Record 1998 - 1st:0 2nd:1 3rd:1 Ran:8
Pre1998 - 1st:1 2nd:1 3rd:0 Ran:4
Win Prizemoney £3,387 *Total Prizemoney* £10,563
Wins * 1997 Spt Kempto (G-F) 8f 81 <
1998 Turf 0-8: (10f 4, 12f 4) (sft, g-s, gd, g-f 4, frm)
Very useful colt, effective 10f, acts on gd to g-f. Turf high 102 (1st run) - 4th of 6 getting 3lb from Dr Fong (1 May Newmarket 10f gd RF 0960). Becoming disappointing. He proved difficult to place after running a super race on his reappearance. Connections cut their losses at the back-end, selling him for 15,000 guineas at the Tattersalls Autumn Horses In Training Sales.
**R W Armstrong [1-12] Pink & Blue Ribbon Racing Syndicate.*

TAWAFEK (USA) BHB 60f63a RR 59f 63a 3790[6]

5 br g Silver Hawk (USA) 11.2f **(85)** - Tippy Tippy Toe (USA) (Nureyev (USA)) 8.7f **(78)**
Form - 66
Record 1998 - 1st:0 2nd:0 3rd:0 Ran:2
Pre1998 - 1st:2 2nd:1 3rd:4 Ran:19
Win Prizemoney £6,133 *Total Prizemoney* £9,594
Wins 1997 Jly Salisb (G-F) 14f 68 <
1997 Jan Lingfi (STD) 10f 56
1998 Turf 0-2: (14f, 16f) (gd 2)
Average gelding, effective 14 to 15f, best at 14f, acts on gd to frm, best on frm. Turf high 59 (began Aug).
**J Mackie [0-2] A J Winterton (from S Dow [2-14] Oct 1997).*

TAWWAG (IRE) RR 78f 2578[5]

2 b c Shirley Heights 12.1f **(76)** - Albertville (USA) (Polish Precedent (USA)) 10.2f **(60)**
Form - 5
Record 1998 - 1st:0 2nd:0 3rd:0 Ran:1
1998 Turf 0-1: (7f) (frm)
Currently above-average colt. Bred to require middle distances, he shaped quite well on his debut over seven.
**M A Jarvis [0-1] Sheikh Ahmed Al Maktoum.*

TAYIF RR 77+f 4882[2]

2 gr c Taufan (USA) 8.3f **(65)** - Rich Lass (Broxted) 6.7f **(65)**
Form - 2
Record 1998 - 1st:0 2nd:1 3rd:0 Ran:1
Win Prizemoney £0 *Total Prizemoney* £768
1998 Turf 0-1: (6f) (g-s)
Currently above-average colt. (1st run) - 2nd of 16 giving 5lb to Rouge Etoile (20 Oct Folkestone 6f g-s RF 4882).
**J W Payne [0-1] G Jabre.*

TAYIL (IRE) BHB 100f RR 97f 4542[4]

2 b c Caerleon (USA) 10.9f **(79)** - Desert Bluebell (Kalaglow) 9.8f **(67)**
Form - 11664
Record 1998 - 1st:2 2nd:0 3rd:0 Ran:5
Win Prizemoney £11,294 *Total Prizemoney* £13,200
Wins * **1998** Jly York (FRM) 7f 89 <
* **1998** Jun Newmar (GD) 7f 77
1998 Turf 2-5: (7f 2-5) (gd, g-f 1-2, frm 1-2)
Very useful colt. Turf high 97 - 4th of 26 to Maidaan (29 Spt Newmarket 7f frm RF 4542) - also 1st of 4 from Distant Moon (11 Jly York RF 2735). Narrow winner of a maiden on the July Course and maintained his unbeaten record at York. However, he found Group races too much for him on his next two starts, and only returned to something like his form when dropped in class.
**J L Dunlop [2-5] Hamdan Al Maktoum.*

TAYLOR'S PRIDE BHB 39f40a RR 40f 40a 4817[10]

3 b f Nordico (USA) 8.2f **(59)** - Jendor (Condorcet (FR)) 12.3f **(62)**
Form - 25080
Record 1998 - 1st:0 2nd:1 3rd:0 Ran:5
Pre1998 - 1st:0 2nd:0 3rd:0 Ran:3
Win Prizemoney £0 *Total Prizemoney* £485
1998 Turf 0-1: (16f) (gd) 1998 AW 0-4: (11f 3, 12f) (Fibr 4)
Tall, fair filly. AW high 50. Becoming disappointing.
**C W Fairhurst [0-3] H Taylor & Sons (from T D Barron [0-5] Mar 1998).*

TAYOVULLIN (IRE) BHB 50f52a RR 60f 52a 5127[2]

4 ch f Shalford (IRE) 7.8f **(63)** - Fifth Quarter (Cure The Blues (USA)) 9.5f **(63)**
Form - 700000150205202
Record 1998 - 1st:1 2nd:3 3rd:0 Ran:15
Pre1998 - 1st:1 2nd:1 3rd:1 Ran:11
Win Prizemoney £5,957 *Total Prizemoney* £9,815
Wins * **1998** Jun Newmar (GD) H 7f 44 48
* *1997 Apr Southw (STD) H 7f 56 63* <
1998 Turf 1-12: (7f 1-9, 8f 2, 12f) (sft 2, g-s, gd 1-4, g-f 4, frm) 1998 AW 0-3: (7f, 8f 2) (Equi 2, Fibr)
Workmanlike, average filly, effective 7 to 8f, best at 7f, acts on g-s to frm - acts on Fibr, has worn blinkers, and excels at Brighton. Turf high 60 - 2nd of 20 getting 6lb from Roffey Spinney (13 Oct Leicester 7f gd RF 4775). AW high 53.
**H Morrison [2-24] H Morrison (from R Charlton [0-2] Spt 1996).*

TAYSEER (USA) BHB 85f RR 100f 5078[23]

4 ch g Sheikh Albadou 9.2f **(75)** - Millfit (USA) (Blushing Groom (FR)) 10.3f **(76)**
Form - 50
Record 1998 - 1st:0 2nd:0 3rd:0 Ran:2
Pre1998 - 1st:2 2nd:0 3rd:1 Ran:7
Win Prizemoney £24,054 *Total Prizemoney* £27,489
Wins 1997 May York (GD) H 7f 89 95 <
1996 Nov Redcar (G-F) 7f 95 <
1998 Turf 0-2: (7f, 8f) (sft, g-f)
Scopey, very useful gelding, effective 7f, acts on gd to g-f, best on gd. Turf high 91 (1st run) - 5th of 5 to Crumpton Hill (17 May Kempton 7f g-f RF 1282). He has been very lightly raced since being injured after finishing fourth in the 1997 Bunbury Cup, and was sold for just 16,000 gns at Newmarket in October of that year.
**W R Muir [0-2] Mrs H Levy (from E A L Dunlop [2-7] Jly 1997).*

TAZKIYA BHB 40f RR 41f 3949[11]

3 ch f King's Signet (USA) 7f **(51)** - Irene's Charter (Persian Bold) 9.3f **(66)**
Form - 6380070
Record 1998 - 1st:0 2nd:0 3rd:1 Ran:7
Pre1998 - 1st:0 2nd:0 3rd:0 Ran:1
Win Prizemoney £0 *Total Prizemoney* £345
1998 Turf 0-7: (7f 5, 10f 2) (gd 5, g-f, frm)
Scopey, moderate filly. Turf high 46. **C J Benstead [0-8] D Turner.*

TAZ MANIA BHB 49f RR 54f 4490[9]

2 b g Savahra Sound 7.8f **(55)** - Sugar Token (Record Token) 6.3f **(53)**
Form - 0560
Record 1998 - 1st:0 2nd:0 3rd:0 Ran:4
1998 Turf 0-4: (5f 3, 6f) (gd 2, frm 2)
Fair gelding. Turf high 54.
**S R Bowring [0-1] Mrs P A Barratt (from M Meade [0-3] Jun 1998).*

TEACHER (IRE) BHB 32f RR 1605[10]

8 b g Caerleon (USA) 10.9f **(79)** - Clunk Click (Star Appeal) 9.6f **(65)**
Form - 0
Record 1998 - 1st:0 2nd:0 3rd:0 Ran:1
Pre1998 - 1st:0 2nd:0 3rd:1 Ran:15
Win Prizemoney £0 *Total Prizemoney* £1,635
1998 Turf 0-1: (16f) (gd)
Very poor gelding, has worn blinkers.
**R Allan [0-6] R Allan (from J D Bethell [0-10] Oct 1994).*

TEA DANCER BHB 45f RR 41f 2393[5]

3 b f Thowra (FR) 11.2f **(47)** - Miss Lawsuit (Neltino) 7.6f **(54)**
Form - 47884605
Record 1998 - 1st:0 2nd:0 3rd:0 Ran:8
Win Prizemoney £0 *Total Prizemoney* £196
1998 Turf 0-7: (8f 2, 10f 4, 11f)(gd 3, g-f, frm 3) 1998 AW 0-1: (9f) (Fibr)
Workmanlike, moderate filly, had worn blinkers. Turf high 55. (DEAD) **B J Meehan [0-8] Vintage Services Ltd.*

TEAM OF THREE RR 25f 5138^{17}

2 b g Jumbo Hirt (USA) 15.8f **(44)** - Dominance (Dominion) 8.5f **(63)**

Form - 0

Record 1998 - 1st:0 2nd:0 3rd:0 Ran:1

1998 Turf 0-1: (7f) (gd)

Currently little account gelding. **D Shaw [0-1] J Roundtree.*

TEAPOT ROW (IRE) BHB 106f **RR 110f** 4843^{5}

3 b c Generous (IRE) 11.5f **(82)** - Secrage (USA) (Secreto (USA)) 8.7f **(72)**

Form - 62285

Record 1998 - 1st:0 2nd:2 3rd:0 Ran:5
Pre1998 - 1st:3 2nd:0 3rd:0 Ran:4

Win Prizemoney £82,737 *Total Prizemoney* £94,260

Wins * 1997 Spt Ascot (G-F) G2 8f 107 <
* 1997 Spt Doncas (G-F) 7f 102
* 1997 Aug Newmar (GD) 6f 93+

1998 Turf 0-5: (8f 2, 9f, 10f, 11f) (gd 2, g-f 2, frm)

Group-class colt, effective 7 to 11f, acts on gd to frm, excels at Doncaster and Newmarket. Turf high 110 - 2nd of 8 getting 9lb from Green Card (15 Jly Doncaster 8f frm RF 2818). Consistent. A mighty atom as a two-year-old, he did not grow much over the winter and was usually dwarfed by his opponents. He promises to stay a mile and a quarter, but is unlikely to improve and looks listed class on recent evidence. **J A R Toller [3-9] Duke of Devonshire.*

TEARAWAY BHB 73f **RR 74f** 1023^{3}

3 gr c Efisio 7.7f **(69)** - Hoosie (Niniski (USA)) 10.6f **(65)**

Form - 043

Record 1998 - 1st:0 2nd:0 3rd:1 Ran:3
Pre1998 - 1st:0 2nd:1 3rd:3 Ran:6

Win Prizemoney £0 *Total Prizemoney* £4,898

1998 Turf 0-3: (8f 2, 11f) (sft, g-s, gd)

Leggy, above-average colt, effective 8f, acted on g-s to gd, best on g-s, liked tight tracks. Turf high 73 - 4th of 11 getting 7lb from Ambiguous (16 Apr Ripon 8f g-s RF 0718). (DEAD)

**J J O'Neill [0-3] Out The Box Racing (from J W Watts [0-6] Oct 1997).*

TEAR WHITE (IRE) BHB 64f65a **RR 61f 65a** 4649^{1}

4 b g Mac's Imp (USA) 5.6f **(54)** - Exemplary (Sovereign Lord) 6.5f **(76)**

Form - 328664401

Record 1998 - 1st:1 2nd:0 3rd:0 Ran:6
Pre1998 - 1st:3 2nd:4 3rd:4 Ran:31

Win Prizemoney £16,551 *Total Prizemoney* £24,480

Wins * **1998** Oct Bright (GD) H 5.3f 60 61
* 1997 Aug Goodwo (G-F) H 5f 67 69 <
* 1997 Jun Bright (FRM) H 5.3f 62 62
* 1996 Jly Ripon (G-F) 5f 52

1998 Turf 1-5: (5f 1-5) (g-f 1-4, frm) 1998 AW 0-1: (5f) (Fibr)

Workmanlike, average gelding, effective 5 to 6f, best at 5f, acts on gd to frm - acts on Equi, has worn blinkers, likes left handed tracks, likes tight tracks, does well at Lingfield and Brighton. Turf high 61 - also 1st of 16 giving 7lb to Ivory's Grab Hire (5 Oct Brighton RF 4649). He used to be a very tricky ride, but was transformed in 1997 by a gelding operation and the discarding of the headgear he used to wear. Possesses plenty of toe and is suited by downhill tracks on turf. **T G Mills [4-37] A W Lawson & Co Ltd.*

TEBYAAN (USA) RR 79f 3429^{2}

2 b f Silver Hawk (USA) 11.2f **(85)** - Umniyatee (Green Desert (USA)) 8.6f **(78)**

Form - 2

Record 1998 - 1st:0 2nd:1 3rd:0 Ran:1

Win Prizemoney £0 *Total Prizemoney* £1,632

1998 Turf 0-1: (6f) (g-f)

Currently above-average filly. (1st run) - 2nd of 6 to Itlak (7 Aug Ascot 6f g-f RF 3429). A half-sister to Meshhed, out of a useful racemare, she should have no trouble winning a maiden.

**B Hanbury [0-1] Hamdan Al Maktoum.*

TECHNICIAN (IRE) BHB 62f52a **RR 69df 52a** 4848^{13}

3 ch g Archway (IRE) 8.5f **(60)** - How It Works (Commanche Run) 8.5f **(58)**

Form - 5203242084225335200

Record 1998 - 1st:0 2nd:6 3rd:3 Ran:18
Pre1998 - 1st:0 2nd:0 3rd:0 Ran:4

Win Prizemoney £0 *Total Prizemoney* £6,496

1998 Turf 0-14: (7f 7, 8f 6, 9f) (gd 8, g-f 5, frm) 1998 AW 0-4: (7f, 8f 3) (Equi, Fibr 3)

Scopey, average gelding, effective 7 to 8f, best at 7f, acts on g-f to frm, best on g-f, often wears blinkers (very effectively), likes right handed tracks. Turf high 69 - 2nd of 14 giving 16lb to Donna's Double (14 Spt Musselburgh 7f frm RF 4256). AW high 54.

**E J Alston [0-14] The Bibby Halliday Partnership (from M A Jarvis [0-8] Feb 1998).*

TEDBURROW BHB 110f **RR 111f** 4844^{2}

6 b g Dowsing (USA) 7f **(61)** - Gwiffina (Welsh Saint) 7.6f **(64)**

Form - 3158016122

Record 1998 - 1st:3 2nd:2 3rd:1 Ran:10
Pre1998 - 1st:10 2nd:2 3rd:2 Ran:38

Win Prizemoney £123,184 *Total Prizemoney* £156,830

Wins * **1998** Spt Leopar (SFT) G3 5f 110+ <
* **1998** Jly Cheste (G-F) L 5.1f 110
* **1998** Apr Newmar (G-S) L 6f 110
* 1997 Spt Ascot (G-F) H 5f 105 108
* 1997 Jly Cheste (G-F) 5.1f 100
* 1997 Jun York (G-S) H 6f 95 98
* 1997 May Haydoc (G-S) H 5f 88 94
1996 Jly Newmar (G-F) H 5f 88 91
1995 Jly Doncas (FRM) H 6f 72 82
1995 Jly Sandow (G-F) H 5f 72 75+
1995 Jly Sandow (GD) H 5f 64 67
1995 Jun Ayr (FRM) H 5f 61 56
1994 Jun Mussel (FRM) C 5f 63

1998 Turf 3-10: (5f 2-6, 6f 1-4) (sft, gd 2-7, g-f, frm 1-1)

Group-class gelding, effective 5 to 6f, best at 5f, acts on sft to frm, excels at Chester, does well at Newmarket. Turf high 111 - 2nd of 16 giving 5lb to Bold Edge (16 Oct Newmarket 6f g-f RF 4844) - also 1st of 7 giving 4lb to Rhine Valley (12 Spt Leopardstown RF 4293a). Consistent. He has improved throughout his career and, after some close scrapes, won his first Group race at Leopardstown in September. He acts on any ground and is a credit to Eric Alston, who certainly knows how to keep older horses on top of their game. It should be business as usual in races like the Abernant Stakes at Newmarket next spring.

**E J Alston [7-20] Philip Davies (from Mrs A M Naughton [5-25] Oct 1996).*

TEEJAY'N'AITCH (IRE) BHB 25f **RR 19f** 2116^{6}

6 b g Maelstrom Lake 8.8f **(53)** - Middle Verde (USA) (Sham (USA)) 9.5f **(68)**

Form - 86

Record 1998 - 1st:0 2nd:0 3rd:0 Ran:2
Pre1998 - 1st:0 2nd:1 3rd:4 Ran:28

Win Prizemoney £0 *Total Prizemoney* £3,484

1998 Turf 0-2: (13f 2) (g-s, gd)

Poor gelding, effective 12f, acts on gd, has worn blinkers. Turf high 19.

**J S Goldie [6-65] Mrs Alice Goldie (from R Ingram [0-3] Jly 1994).*

TEEN IDOL (IRE) RR 33f 3363^{9}

2 ch f Red Sunset 9f **(57)** - Truly Flattering (Hard Fought) 8.8f **(62)**

Form - 8000

Record 1998 - 1st:0 2nd:0 3rd:0 Ran:4

1998 Turf 0-4: (5f, 7f 3) (gd, g-f 3)

Very moderate filly. Turf high 33. **J J Bridger [0-4] Miss Sarah Jones.*

TEEPLOY GIRL BHB 41a **RR 41a** 407^{8}

3 b f Deploy 11.4f **(67)** - Intoxication (Great Nephew) 9.9f **(64)**

Form - 30088

Record 1998 - 1st:0 2nd:0 3rd:0 Ran:3
Pre1998 - 1st:0 2nd:0 3rd:1 Ran:2

Win Prizemoney £0 *Total Prizemoney* £273

1998 AW 0-3: (6f, 8f, 12f) (Fibr 3)

Leggy, very poor filly, has worn blinkers.

**N P Littmoden [0-5] Evergreen Partnership.*

TEGYRA (IRE) RR 77f 4499^{3}

2 ch f Trempolino (USA) 11.9f **(77)** - Tegwen (USA) **(81df)** (Nijinsky (CAN)) 10.3f **(77)**

Form - 03

Record 1998 - 1st:0 2nd:0 3rd:1 Ran:2

Win Prizemoney £0 *Total Prizemoney* £555

1998 Turf 0-2: (7f, 8f) (frm 2)

Currently above-average filly. Turf high 77 (began Aug) - 3rd of 7 to Ruacana Falls (26 Spt Haydock 8f frm RF 4499).
**M A Jarvis [0-2] Abdullah Saeed Bul Hab.*

Form - 304
Record 1998 - 1st:0 2nd:0 3rd:1 Ran:3
Win Prizemoney £0 *Total Prizemoney* £771

Tedburrow ran his rivals into the ground at Leopardstown

TEISHEBAINI (IRE) RR **96f** 1732a2
3 ch c Hamas (IRE) 8f **(72)** - Tea House (Sassafras (FR)) 9.6f **(69)**
Form - 2
1998 Turf 0-1: (8f) (g-f)
Currently very useful colt. (1st run) - 2nd of 6 giving 6lb to Stanott (31 May Capannelle 8f g-f RF 1732a).
**A Calchetti in ITY [0-1] (from A Colchetti in ITY [0-1] Spt 1997).*

TELLION BHB 60f59a **RR 66df 59a** 229816
4 b g Mystiko (USA) 7.7f **(59)** - Salchow (Niniski (USA)) 10.6f **(65)**
Form - 6360
Record 1998 - 1st:0 2nd:0 3rd:1 Ran:4
Pre1998 - 1st:0 2nd:0 3rd:1 Ran:7
Win Prizemoney £0 *Total Prizemoney* £1,562
1998 Turf 0-4: (12f 4) (sft, gd 2, g-f)
Light-framed, average gelding, effective 10 to 12f, best at 12f, acts on gd to g-f, best on gd, favours tight tracks. Turf high 66 - 3rd of 15 giving 28lb to Cohiba (5 May Brighton 12f gd RF 1037). Consistent.
**J R Jenkins [0-4] Come Racing Ltd (from Major W R Hern [0-7] Oct 1997).*

TELL THEM ALL BHB 74f **RR 74f** 44684
2 ch c Kris 10f **(75)** - Just Cause (Law Society (USA)) 9.9f **(70)**
1998 Turf 0-3: (7f, 8f 2) (g-f, frm 2)
Currently above-average colt. Turf high 74 (began Jly).
**M Johnston [0-3] Maktoum Al Maktoum.*

TELMAR BHB 45f **RR 48f** 24399
4 b g Picea 12.7f **(43)** - Freeracer (Free State) 8.7f **(61)**
Form - 0730
Record 1998 - 1st:0 2nd:0 3rd:1 Ran:4
Win Prizemoney £0 *Total Prizemoney* £354
1998 Turf 0-3: (12f 3) (gd, frm 2) 1998 AW 0-1: (12f) (Fibr)
Neat, moderate gelding. Turf high 48.
**J Cullinan [0-7] Dodson & Partners.*

TEMERAIRE (USA) BHB 88f **RR 93f** 48548
3 b g Dayjur (USA) 6.8f **(79)** - Key Dancer (USA) (Nijinsky (CAN)) 10.3f **(77)**
Form - 21108
Record 1998 - 1st:2 2nd:1 3rd:0 Ran:5
Pre1998 - 1st:0 2nd:0 3rd:0 Ran:1
Win Prizemoney £10,693 *Total Prizemoney* £11,823
Wins * 1998 Jly Lingfi (G-F) 7.6f 93 <
*** 1998** Jun Windso (G-F) 8.3f 84+
1998 Turf 2-5: (7f 2, 8f 2-3) (gd 3, g-f 1-1, frm 1-1)
Well made, useful gelding, effective 7 to 8f, best at 8f, acts on gd

to frm. Turf high 93 - 1st of 5 from King Slayer (10 Jly Lingfield RF 2689) - also 1st of 17 from Henry Heald (22 Jun Windsor RF 2184). Went down fighting on his debut at Kempton and was an easy winner next time. Scraped home at Lingfield but was down the field against hardened handicappers at Goodwood and Newmarket.
**Mrs A J Perrett [2-6] K Abdulla.*

TEME VALLEY RR 70f 2454[10]
4 br g Polish Precedent (USA) 9f **(73)** - Sudeley (Dancing Brave (USA)) 8.4f **(76)**
Form - 60
Record 1998 - 1st:0 2nd:0 3rd:0 Ran:2
Pre1998 - 1st:0 2nd:2 3rd:1 Ran:3
Win Prizemoney £0 *Total Prizemoney* £2,757
1998 Turf 0-2: (7f, 10f) (gd 2)
Scopey, above-average gelding. Turf high 59.
**Mrs A Swinbank [0-2] Eddie Shotton (from R Charlton [0-3] Spt 1997).*

TEMPERATE RR 4197[9]
2 ch g Librate 10.4f **(37)** - Miss Moody (Jalmood (USA)) 10.1f **(52)**
Form - 00
Record 1998 - 1st:0 2nd:0 3rd:0 Ran:2
1998 Turf 0-2: (6f, 7f) (gd 2)
Currently very poor gelding, often wears blinkers. (began Aug).
**J M Bradley [0-2] Miss Diane Hill.*

TEMPERING BHB 37f29a **RR 20f 29a** 436[9]
12 b g Kris 10f **(75)** - Mixed Applause (USA) (Nijinsky (CAN)) 10.3f **(77)**
Form - 08004580
Record 1998 - 1st:0 2nd:0 3rd:0 Ran:6
Pre1998 - 1st:22 2nd:13 3rd:11 Ran:111
Win Prizemoney £54,206 *Total Prizemoney* £69,503
Wins * 1996 *Mar Southw (STD) H 12f 53 58*
* 1996 *Feb Southw (STD) H 11f 50 49*
* 1995 *Jan Southw (STD) H 11f 54 58*
* 1994 *Feb Southw (STD) C 11f 59*
* 1994 *Jan Southw (STD) C 12f 61*
1998 AW 0-6: (11f 2, 12f 3, 14f) (Fibr 6)
Little account gelding, has worn blinkers. AW high 26. This Southwell-specialist made a surprise return to action in November 1997 after a 16-month absence, but he has not shown much and it is hard to see him adding to his impressive score at his time of life.
**D W Chapman [22-120] David Chapman (from W Jarvis [0-3] Aug 1990).*

TEMPER LAD (USA) BHB 63f **RR 62f** 2245[2]
3 b c Riverman(USA) 9.7f **(78)** -Dokki (USA)(Northern Dancer) 9.6f **(80)**
Form - 0722
Record 1998 - 1st:0 2nd:2 3rd:0 Ran:4
Pre1998 - 1st:0 2nd:0 3rd:0 Ran:1
Win Prizemoney £0 *Total Prizemoney* £1,544
1998 Turf 0-4: (7f, 8f 3) (gd 2, g-f 2)
Scopey, average colt, has worn blinkers. Turf high 62 - 2nd of 14 giving 18lb to Tarradale (24 Jun Hamilton 8f g-f RF 2245).
**J H M Gosden [0-5] K Abdulla.*

TEMPRAMENTAL (IRE) BHB 58f **RR 61f** 4651[5]
2 ch f Midhish - Musical Horn (Music Boy) 6.8f **(57)**
Form - 74503566105
Record 1998 - 1st:1 2nd:0 3rd:1 Ran:11
Win Prizemoney £3,257 *Total Prizemoney* £3,988
Wins * 1998 Aug Chepst (G-F) H 5.1f 54 60 <
1998 Turf 1-11: (5f 1-6, 6f 4, 7f) (hvy, gd 1-5, g-f 3, frm 2)
Average filly, effective 5f, acts on gd, often wears blinkers (very effectively). Turf high 61 - also 1st of 6 getting 25lb from Manorbier (31 Aug Chepstow RF 3979). Consistent.
**D HaydnJones [1-11] Hugh O'Donnell.*

TEMPTING PROSPECT BHB 95f **RR 97f** 1206[3]
4 b f Shirley Heights 12.1f **(76)** - Trying for Gold (USA) (Northern Baby (CAN)) 11.6f **(71)**
Form - 3
Record 1998 - 1st:0 2nd:0 3rd:1 Ran:1
Pre1998 - 1st:1 2nd:1 3rd:1 Ran:6
Win Prizemoney £4,793 *Total Prizemoney* £16,442
Wins * 1996 Oct Newbur (SFT) 8f 90 <
1998 Turf 0-1: (10f) (gd)
Leggy, very useful filly. (1st run) - 3rd of 7 to Arriving (13 May York 10f gd RF 1206). Some promise on her 1998 return, but she was not seen again.
**Lord Huntingdon [1-7] The Queen.*

TEMPTRESS BHB 53f45a **RR 53f 45a** 1074[5]
5 br m Kalaglow 11.2f **(67)** - Circe (Main Reef) 9.6f **(57)**
Form - 0360055
Record 1998 - 1st:0 2nd:0 3rd:0 Ran:3
Pre1998 - 1st:2 2nd:1 3rd:6 Ran:28
Win Prizemoney £6,696 *Total Prizemoney* £14,029
Wins 1996 Jun Newbur (G-F) H 12f 60 62 <
1996 May Ayr (SFT) 10f 50
1998 Turf 0-3: (12f 3) (sft 2, g-f)
Fair filly, effective 12f, acts on gd to g-f, has worn blinkers. Turf high 53.
**J L Harris [0-12] Paddy Barrett (from John Harris [0-6] Oct 1997).*

TEMPUS FUGIT BHB 60f **RR 63f** 4799[13]
3 ch f Timeless Times (USA) 6.1f **(56)** - Kabella (Kabour)
Form - 000
Record 1998 - 1st:0 2nd:0 3rd:0 Ran:3
Pre1998 - 1st:1 2nd:2 3rd:1 Ran:7
Win Prizemoney £3,148 *Total Prizemoney* £5,523
Wins * 1997 Jun Nottin (GD) 5.1f 77 <
1998 Turf 0-3: (5f 2, 6f) (sft, gd, frm)
Scopey, average filly, effective 5f, acts on gd to g-f, best on g-f. Turf high 45 (began Spt). Becoming disappointing.
**B R Millman [1-10] The Keepers.*

TEN BOB (IRE) RR 91+f 1693[P]
3 br c Bob Back (USA) 11.5f **(71)** - Tiempo (King of Spain) 7.8f **(52)**
Form - 2P
Record 1998 - 1st:0 2nd:0 3rd:0 Ran:1
Pre1998 - 1st:1 2nd:1 3rd:0 Ran:3
Win Prizemoney £3,629 *Total Prizemoney* £12,608
Wins * 1997 Nov Mussel (G-S) 8f 91+ <
1998 Turf 0-1: (10f) (gd)
Workmanlike, useful colt. (DEAD)
**M H Tompkins [1-4] Mrs M H Tompkins.*

TENBY HEIGHTS (IRE) BHB 54f **RR 67f** 4657[8]
2 b c Tenby 10.4f **(76)** - Alpine Spring (Head for Heights) 9.6f **(55)**
Form - 405008
Record 1998 - 1st:0 2nd:0 3rd:0 Ran:6
Win Prizemoney £0 *Total Prizemoney* £483
1998 Turf 0-6: (6f 3, 7f, 8f, 10f) (gd 2, g-f 3, frm)
Average colt. Turf high 67 (began Jly).
**R Hollinshead [0-6] J D Graham.*

TEN KINGDOMS (USA) RR 65f 3927[14]
2 b c Mr Prospector (USA) 8.6f **(88)** - Chinese Empress (USA) (Nijinsky (CAN)) 10.3f **(77)**
Form - 80
Record 1998 - 1st:0 2nd:0 3rd:0 Ran:2
1998 Turf 0-2: (7f 2) (frm 2)
Currently average colt. Turf high 65 (began Jly).
**J H M Gosden [0-2] Sheikh Mohammed.*

TENNESSEE (SWI) RR 104f 2286a[3]
3 b c Homme de Loi (IRE) - Tocaima (SWI) (Nebos (GER)) 9f **(78)**
Form - 3
1998 Turf 0-1: (12f) (g-f)
Currently very useful colt - 3rd of 11 to Copeland (21 Jun Frauenfeld 12f g-f RF 2286a). He looked one paced in the Swiss Derby.
**R Stadelmann in SWI [0-2].*

TENOR BELL (IRE) RR 59f 5143[5]
2 b c Tenby 10.4f **(76)** - Top Bloom (Thatch (USA)) 9.8f **(62)**
Form - 05
Record 1998 - 1st:0 2nd:0 3rd:0 Ran:2
1998 Turf 0-2: (8f 2) (gd, g-f)
Currently fair colt. Turf high 59 (began Oct).
**L M Cumani [0-2] Mrs E H Vestey.*

TEN PAST SIX BHB 54f60a **RR 57f 60a** 4409[13]
6 ch g Kris 10f **(75)** - Tashinsky (USA) (Nijinsky (CAN)) 10.3f **(77)**

Form - 5010012221050
Record 1998 - 1st:3 2nd:3 3rd:0 Ran:13
Pre1998 - 1st:2 2nd:4 3rd:0 Ran:20
Win Prizemoney £13,139 *Total Prizemoney* £24,983
Wins * **1998** Aug Carlis (G-S) C 12f 57
* **1998** Jun Hamilt (G-S) C 11.1f 56
* **1998** *May Southw (STD) C 11f 64*
* 1997 Apr Ripon (GD) S 10f 59
1995 May Haydoc (G-F) 7.1f 76 <
1998 Turf 2-11: (8f, 9f 2, 10f, 11f 1-1, 12f 1-6) (g-s 2, gd 2-5, g-f, frm 3)
1998 AW 1-2: (11f 1-1, 16f) (Fibr 1-2)
Average gelding, effective 9 to 12f, acts on gd to frm - acts on Fibr, best on gd, has worn blinkers (very effectively), favours tight tracks. Turf high 57 - 1st of 8 giving 14lb to Cromer Pier (26 Aug Carlisle RF 3885) - also 1st of 7 giving 8lb to Durgams First (30 Jun Hamilton RF 2403). AW high 64 (1st run) - 1st of 8 giving 8lb to Errant (18 May Southwell RF 1307).
**Martyn Wane [4-32] James S Kennerley and Miss Jenny Hall (from B W Hills [1-6] Spt 1995).*

TENSILE (IRE) BHB 83f **RR 86f** 4841^{8}
3 b c Tenby 10.4f **(76)** - Bonnie Isle (Pitcairn) 9.5f **(60)**
Form - 157258
Record 1998 - 1st:1 2nd:1 3rd:0 Ran:6
Pre1998 - 1st:0 2nd:1 3rd:0 Ran:5
Win Prizemoney £3,938 *Total Prizemoney* £7,619
Wins * **1998** Apr Beverl (SFT) H 9.9f 77 87 <
1998 Turf 1-6: (10f 1-1, 11f, 12f 2, 14f 2) (g-s 1-2, gd 2, g-f 2)
Well made, useful colt, effective 10 to 14f, acts on g-s to g-f. Turf high 87 (1st run) - 1st of 13 giving 7lb to Masamadas (23 Apr Beverley RF 0829). Made a winning reappearance in a soft-ground Beverley handicap, having been stepped up in trip. He has run pretty well in some decent handicaps since and looks as if he really needs two miles now. **L M Cumani [1-11] Mrs V Shelton.*

TEOFILIO (IRE) BHB 70f **RR 65f** 5079^{26}
4 ch c Night Shift (USA) 8.1f **(73)** - Rivoltade (USA) (Sir Ivor) 10.2f **(70)**
Form - 00600
Record 1998 - 1st:0 2nd:0 3rd:0 Ran:5
Pre1998 - 1st:1 2nd:2 3rd:1 Ran:6
Win Prizemoney £3,860 *Total Prizemoney* £10,509
Wins 1997 Apr Beverl (G-F) 8.5f 74 <
1998 Turf 0-5: (5f, 6f, 7f, 8f, 9f) (sft 2, gd 2, frm)
Strong, average colt, effective 8f, acts on g-f. Turf high 65 (began Aug). **A J McNae [0-5] The Iona Stud (from D R Loder [1-6] Jun 1997).*

TEQUILA BHB 80f **RR 82f** 3899^{2}
3 b c Mystiko (USA) 7.7f **(59)** - Black Ivor (USA) (Sir Ivor) 10.2f **(70)**
Form - 4316602
Record 1998 - 1st:1 2nd:1 3rd:1 Ran:7
Win Prizemoney £3,817 *Total Prizemoney* £6,536
Wins * **1998** Jun Goodwo (G-F) 8f 78 <
1998 Turf 1-7: (8f 1-4, 9f, 10f 2) (hvy, g-s, gd, g-f 2, frm 1-2)
Decent colt, effective 8 to 10f, best at 8f, acts on g-f to frm, best on frm. Turf high 82 - 2nd of 12 giving 1lb to Bering Gifts (27 Aug Folkestone 10f g-f RF 3899) - also 1st of 12 from Grand Slam (5 Jun Goodwood RF 1755). **L M Cumani [1-7] Paul Silver.*

TERDAD (USA) BHB 64f **RR 61f** 3936^{10}
5 ch g Lomond (USA) 9.9f **(74)** - Istiska (FR) (Irish River (FR)) 8.6f **(78)**
Form - 610
Record 1998 - 1st:1 2nd:0 3rd:0 Ran:3
Pre1998 - 1st:1 2nd:3 3rd:2 Ran:15
Win Prizemoney £5,948 *Total Prizemoney* £9,670
Wins * **1998** Aug Thirsk (G-F) H 16f 60 61
1997 Jun Mussel (G-S) 7.1f 64 <
1998 Turf 1-3: (12f, 16f 1-2) (frm 1-3)
Average gelding, effective 7 to 16f, best at 8f, acts on gd to frm - acts on Fibr, best on gd, has worn blinkers, does well at Thirsk. Turf high 61 (began Jly) - 1st of 11 giving 12lb to Our Way (10 Aug Thirsk RF 3504). He was known as a miler on the Flat, but had a successful season over hurdles in 1997/98, and stepping up to two miles on the level paid dividends at Thirsk in August. He seemed to stay well enough and can probably win more staying races.
**Mrs M Reveley [4-10] Les De La Haye (from T D Barron [1-11] Jly 1997).*

TERESHKOVA'S JOY RR 51f 3642^{10}
2 b f Cosmonaut - Joyful Escapade (Precocious) 8.6f **(62)**
Form - 76650
Record 1998 - 1st:0 2nd:0 3rd:0 Ran:5
1998 Turf 0-3: (5f 2, 6f) (frm 3) 1998 AW 0-2: (5f 2) (Fibr 2)
Fair filly, has worn blinkers. Turf high 51. AW high 45.
**K G Wingrove [0-5] Ms Clare Sharp.*

TEREYNA BHB 49f **RR 52df** 4312^{14}
3 gr f Terimon 8.7f **(58)** - Lareyna (Welsh Pageant) 10f **(65)**
Form - 8045240
Record 1998 - 1st:0 2nd:1 3rd:0 Ran:7
Pre1998 - 1st:0 2nd:0 3rd:0 Ran:1
Win Prizemoney £0 *Total Prizemoney* £1,084
1998 Turf 0-7: (10f, 11f, 12f, 14f 3, 15f) (gd, g-f 4, frm 2)
Light-framed, fair filly, effective 15f, acts on frm, favours tight tracks. Turf high 55. **R F JohnsonHoughton [0-8] Mrs P Robeson.*

TEROOM BHB 78f **RR 80f** 3483^{2}
3 br c Mtoto 11.5f **(71)** - Ballad Opera (Sadler's Wells (USA)) 10f **(76)**
Form - 13332
Record 1998 - 1st:1 2nd:1 3rd:3 Ran:5
Pre1998 - 1st:0 2nd:0 3rd:0 Ran:1
Win Prizemoney £2,788 *Total Prizemoney* £7,594
Wins * **1998** Apr Pontef (G-S) 10f 73 <
1998 Turf 1-5: (10f 1-2, 11f 2, 12f) (g-s 1-1, gd 2, g-f, frm)
Light-framed, decent colt, effective 10 to 12f, acts on g-s to frm. Turf high 80 - 2nd of 8 giving 10lb to Hardy Dancer (9 Aug Epsom 10f gd RF 3483) - also 1st of 12 from Richmond Hill (21 Apr Pontefract RF 0787). Got off the mark in a ten-furlong Pontefract maiden in April, but has looked a bit one paced since despite making the frame, and has not looked the most straightforward of rides. **A C Stewart [1-6] Sheikh Ahmed Al Maktoum.*

TERTIUM (IRE) BHB 81f72a **RR 88f 72a** 4854^{29}
6 b g Nordico (USA) 8.2f **(59)** - Nouniya (Vayrann) 9.7f **(74)**
Form - 0435170U083027107000
Record 1998 - 1st:2 2nd:1 3rd:2 Ran:20
Pre1998 - 1st:2 2nd:7 3rd:2 Ran:38
Win Prizemoney £59,236 *Total Prizemoney* £114,922
Wins * **1998** Aug Newmar (G-F) H 7f 79 88 <
* **1998** May Kempto (GD) H 8f 71 79
1996 May Beverl (G-F) H 8.5f 77 83
1995 May Kempto (G-F) 8f 82+
1998 Turf 2-18: (7f 1-5, 8f 1-11, 9f 2) (g-s 3, gd 1-8, g-f 4, frm 2, hrd 1-1) 1998 AW 0-2: (8f 2) (Fibr 2)
Useful gelding, effective 7 to 10f, best at 8f, acts on gd to hrd, likes right handed tracks, likes Ascot. Turf high 88 - 1st of 15 getting 6lb from Consort (8 Aug Newmarket RF 3471) - also 1st of 20 getting 20lb from Labeq (4 May Kempton RF 1014). AW high 69. He was kept very busy last term, landing the Jubilee at Kempton in May and a valuable handicap at Newmarket in August. Has a turn of foot. He has had wind problems and is often tongue-tied.
**N P Littmoden [2-20] M Barton (from Martyn Wane [1-32] Oct 1997).*

TERTULLIAN (USA) RR 112f $5132a^{1}$
3 ch c Miswaki (USA) 8.1f **(81)** - Turbaine (USA) (Trempolino (USA)) 12f **(71)**
Form - 21
1998 Turf 1-2: (7f 1-1, 9f) (sft 1-1, gd)
Currently Group-class colt. Turf high 112 - 1st of 9 from Tannenkonig (30 Oct San Siro RF 5132a). He finished second in a weak Group Three at Frankfurt in September.
**P Schiergen in GER [1-2] Gestut Schlenderhan.*

TESS BHB 75f **RR 72f** 4595^{20}
2 b f Emarati (USA) 6.6f **(63)** - Everdene (Bustino) 10.4f **(64)**
Form - 580
Record 1998 - 1st:0 2nd:0 3rd:0 Ran:3
1998 Turf 0-3: (5f, 7f 2) (gd, g-f 2)
Currently above-average filly. Turf high 72 (began Jly).
**B W Hills [0-3] S P Tindall.*

TESSAJOE BHB 88f **RR 88f** 4372^{1}
6 ch g Clantime 6.6f **(57)** - Busted Love (Busted) 10.2f **(61)**
Form - 083851
Record 1998 - 1st:1 2nd:0 3rd:1 Ran:6

Pre1998 - 1st:10 2nd:2 3rd:2 Ran:32
Win Prizemoney £46,506 *Total Prizemoney* £54,214

Wins									
*	1998	Spt	Catter	(G-F)	H	12f	85	88	<
	1997	Spt	Catter	(G-F)	H	12f	85	88	<
	1997	Jly	Ripon	(G-F)	H	12.3f	78	80	
	1997	Jun	Thirsk	(GD)	H	12f	75	79	
	1997	Jun	Thirsk	(FRM)	H	12f	73	77	
	1996	Spt	Catter	(G-F)	H	12f	71	73	
	1996	Apr	Thirsk	(G-F)		12f		75	
	1995	Jly	Ripon	(G-F)	H	12.3f	69	72	
	1995	Jly	Ayr	(GD)	H	10.9f	64	70	
	1995	Jly	Catter	(G-F)	H	12f	58	61	
	1995	Apr	Ripon	(G-F)	H	12.3f	54	57	

1998 Turf 1-6: (12f 1-5, 14f) (g-s, gd, g-f, frm 1-3)
Useful gelding, effective 12f, acts on g-f to frm, best on frm, prefers tight tracks, excels at Thirsk and Ripon, does well at Catterick. Turf high 88 - 1st of 14 giving 18lb to Summerhill Special (19 Spt Catterick RF 4372).
**Miss J A Camacho [1-6] Riley Partnership (from M J Camacho [10-32] Oct 1997).*

TESSARA RR 18f — 2273[9]

3 ch f Kasakov - Sum Music (Music Boy) 6.8f **(57)**
Form - 0
Record 1998 - 1st:0 2nd:0 3rd:0 Ran:1
1998 Turf 0-1: (6f) (gd)
Lengthy, currently poor filly.
**C W Thornton [0-1] Elephant & Castle Partnership-Wakefield.*

TEST THE WATER (IRE) BHB 72f RR 74df — 5147[4]

4 ch c Maelstrom Lake 8.8f **(53)** - Baliana (CAN) (Riverman (USA)) 9.1f **(76)**
Form - 8600301204
Record 1998 - 1st:1 2nd:1 3rd:1 Ran:10
Pre1998 - 1st:1 2nd:3 3rd:2 Ran:12
Win Prizemoney £11,620 *Total Prizemoney* £18,836

Wins									
*	1998	Jly	Sandow	(G-F)	C	8.1f		74	
*	1996	Oct	Ascot	(GD)	H	7f	85	90	<

1998 Turf 1-10: (7f, 8f 1-5, 9f 4) (sft 2, gd 4, g-f 2, frm 1-2)
Scopey, above-average colt, effective 8f, acts on sft to frm, has worn blinkers, likes tight tracks. Turf high 77 - 6th of 15 getting 6lb from Yabint El Sultan (18 Apr Newbury 8f sft RF 0743) - also 1st of 9 getting 2lb from Hugwity (22 Jly Sandown RF 3031). Has plenty of ability, but is by no means consistent.
**R Hannon [2-22] Peter Crane.*

TETHKAR RR 76f — 4499[4]

2 b f Machiavellian (USA) 9.8f **(83)** - Munnaya (USA) **(99f)** (Nijinsky (CAN)) 10.3f **(77)**
Form - 74
Record 1998 - 1st:0 2nd:0 3rd:0 Ran:2
Win Prizemoney £0 *Total Prizemoney* £265
1998 Turf 0-2: (7f, 8f) (frm 2)
Currently above-average filly. Turf high 76 (began Aug) - 4th of 7 to Ruacana Falls (26 Spt Haydock 8f frm RF 4499). Things did not go her way on her debut and she found a mile too far second time, but more will be heard of this attractively-bred filly.
**D R Loder [0-2] Maktoum Al Maktoum.*

TEZAAB BHB 40f49a RR 46f 49a — 2328[17]

4 gr g Petong 7.6f **(58)** -Very Nice (FR)(Green Dancer (USA)) 10.3f **(74)**
Form - 0
Record 1998 - 1st:0 2nd:0 3rd:0 Ran:1
Pre1998 - 1st:0 2nd:0 3rd:3 Ran:11
Win Prizemoney £0 *Total Prizemoney* £1,120
1998 Turf 0-1: (8f) (gd)
Lengthy, moderate gelding, effective 8 to 10f, best at 8f, acts on g-f to frm, best on g-f. Inconsistent.
**R J Baker [0-1] N F Coleman (from B Hanbury [0-11] Spt 1997).*

THAAYER BHB 60f RR 61f — 5059[12]

3 b g Wolfhound (USA) 7.3f **(71)** - Hamaya (USA) (Mr Prospector (USA)) 8.8f **(78)**
Form - 0670
Record 1998 - 1st:0 2nd:0 3rd:0 Ran:4
1998 Turf 0-4: (6f 2, 7f 2) (sft, gd, g-f 2)
Scopey, average gelding. Turf high 68.
**K Bell [0-3] Mrs Joyce Wood (from M P Tregoning [0-1] Apr 1998).*

THALEROS BHB 38f35a RR 27df 35a — 2147[13]

8 b g Green Desert (USA) 7.8f **(78)** - Graecia Magna (USA) (Private Account (USA)) 8.5f **(74)**
Form - 000
Record 1998 - 1st:0 2nd:0 3rd:0 Ran:1
Pre1998 - 1st:3 2nd:4 3rd:8 Ran:42
Win Prizemoney £10,946 *Total Prizemoney* £20,263

Wins								
1995	Aug	Ripon	(G-F)	H	10f	57	59	
1995	Jly	Catter	(G-F)	C	12f		52+	
1995	*Jan*	*Southw*	*(STD)*		*12f*		*70*	<

1998 Turf 0-1: (11f) (g-f)
Little account gelding, has worn blinkers. Inconsistent.
**J S Wainwright [0-7] M Gleason (from G M Moore [3-33] Jun 1996).*

THAMES DANCER (USA) RR 70f — 4541[14]

2 ch c Green Dancer (USA) 11.9f **(77)** - Hata (FR) (Kaldoun (FR)) 10.3f **(68)**
Form - 60
Record 1998 - 1st:0 2nd:0 3rd:0 Ran:2
1998 Turf 0-2: (7f, 8f) (g-f, frm)
Currently above-average colt. Turf high 70 (began Spt).
**K McAuliffe [0-2] J S Dunningham.*

THANK HEAVENS BHB 97f RR 95f — 4618[4]

2 b c Theatrical Charmer 10.9f **(63)** - Harmonia (Glint of Gold) 9.3f **(66)**
Form - 021324314
Record 1998 - 1st:2 2nd:2 3rd:2 Ran:9
Win Prizemoney £7,760 *Total Prizemoney* £14,023

Wins								
*	**1998**	Spt	Ayr	(G-S)	7f		86	<
*	**1998**	Jun	Thirsk	(SFT)	7f		71+	

1998 Turf 2-9: (5f, 6f, 7f 2-5, 8f 2) (sft 1-1, gd 1-5, g-f 2, frm)
Very useful colt, effective 7f, acts on sft. Turf high 95 - also 1st of 5 getting 4lb from Mini Lodge (18 Spt Ayr RF 4353). Improving. Steadily improving, he won a Thirsk median auction maiden event in a canter on his third start, seeming to appreciate the seventh furlong. Has continued to acquit himself well, and scored again at Ayr in September. Loves soft ground.
**M R Channon [2-9] Miss Bridget Coyle.*

THANKSGIVING (IRE) BHB 88f RR 96f — 4620[5]

3 ch f Indian Ridge 7.6f **(74)** -Thank One's Stars (Alzao (USA)) 7.1f **(68)**
Form - 332035
Record 1998 - 1st:0 2nd:1 3rd:3 Ran:6
Pre1998 - 1st:1 2nd:0 3rd:3 Ran:5
Win Prizemoney £4,577 *Total Prizemoney* £14,990

Wins								
*	1997	Spt	Folkes	(GD)	5f		89	<

1998 Turf 0-6: (5f, 6f 4, 7f) (gd 2, g-f 4)
Workmanlike, very useful filly, effective 5 to 6f, acts on gd to g-f. Turf high 96. Inconsistent. Placed in Listed company at two, she again made the frame several times in 1998 without winning, proving difficult to place as she was too high in the handicap, and yet not really Pattern class. **Major D N Chappell [1-11] Mrs G C Maxwell.*

THANKS KEITH BHB 37f46a RR 53f 46a — 4938[5]

3 ch g Risk Me (FR) 8f **(53)** - Nannie Annie (Persian Bold) 9.3f **(66)**
Form - 004525402665
Record 1998 - 1st:0 2nd:2 3rd:0 Ran:12
Pre1998 - 1st:0 2nd:0 3rd:1 Ran:4
Win Prizemoney £0 *Total Prizemoney* £2,233
1998 Turf 0-11: (8f, 9f, 11f, 12f 2, 14f, 16f 3, 17f 2) (gd 10, frm) 1998 AW 0-1: (14f) (Fibr)
Leggy, fair gelding, often wears blinkers. Turf high 54.
**J J O'Neill [0-17] Clayton Bigley Partnership Ltd.*

THATCHED (IRE) BHB 46f RR 48f — 4056[15]

8 b g Thatching 7.8f **(69)** - Shadia (USA) (Naskra (USA)) 8.8f **(69)**
Form - 01605022080
Record 1998 - 1st:1 2nd:2 3rd:0 Ran:11
Pre1998 - 1st:9 2nd:4 3rd:9 Ran:76
Win Prizemoney £35,452 *Total Prizemoney* £50,797

Wins									
*	1998	May	Redcar	(G-F)	H	9f	41	44	
*	1997	Apr	Carlis	(GD)	H	8f	51	56	
*	1996	Oct	Redcar	(G-F)	H	8f	48	52	
*	1996	Spt	Beverl	(G-F)	H	8.5f	47	43	
*	1996	Jly	Beverl	(G-F)	H	7.5f	43	46	
*	1995	Aug	Carlis	(HRD)	H	8f	50	64+	<
*	1995	Jly	Mussel	(G-F)	H	8.1f	44	51	

* 1995 Apr Newcas (G-F) H 8f 42 44
* 1994 Jly Redcar (G-F) H 8f 40 47
* 1994 Jun Mussel (G-F) H 8.1f 36 38

1998 Turf 1-11: (7f, 8f 6, 9f 1-2, 10f 2) (gd 3, g-f 1-3, frm 5)

Moderate gelding, effective 7 to 10f, best at 8f, acts on gd to frm, best on frm, has worn blinkers, likes right handed tracks, prefers tight tracks, and excels at Carlisle. Turf high 48 - 2nd of 8 getting 5lb from Murphy's Gold (28 Jly Beverley 8f g-f RF 3158). He has won his fair share of fast-ground handicaps at around a mile, including one at Redcar in May.

**R E Barr [10-84] C W Marwood (from C F Wall [0-9] Spt 1993).*

THATCHMASTER (IRE) BHB 69f RR 71f 4731^{7}

7 b g Thatching 7.8f **(69)** - Key Maneuver (USA) (Key To Content (USA)) 8f **(54)**

Form - 5071515237

Record 1998 - 1st:2 2nd:1 3rd:1 Ran:10
Pre1998 - 1st:3 2nd:3 3rd:2 Ran:25

Win Prizemoney £19,069 *Total Prizemoney* £25,405

Wins * **1998** Jly Windso (G-F) H 11.6f 63 67 <
* **1998** Jun Windso (GD) H 11.6f 60 62
* 1997 Aug Goodwo (G-F) CH 10f 59 67 <
* 1996 Aug Goodwo (G-F) CH 10f 52 58
* 1996 Jly Sandow (G-F) SH 8.1f 46 51

1998 Turf 2-10: (10f 4, 12f 2-5, 13f) (g-s, gd 3, g-f 1-4, frm 1-2)

Above-average gelding, effective 10 to 12f, best at 10f, acts on gd to frm, has worn blinkers, likes tight tracks, excels at Windsor and Goodwood. Turf high 71 - 2nd of 22 giving 8lb to Galapino (29 Aug Goodwood 10f gd RF 3949) - also 1st of 13 giving 22lb to Zibeth (27 Jly Windsor RF 3147). **C A Horgan [5-35] Mrs B Sumner.*

THAT MAN AGAIN BHB 72f72a RR 77?f 72a 4311^{11}

6 ch g Prince Sabo 6.6f **(64)** - Milne's Way (The Noble Player (USA)) 6.5f **(67)**

Form - 605330801470140

Record 1998 - 1st:2 2nd:0 3rd:2 Ran:12
Pre1998 - 1st:5 2nd:4 3rd:4 Ran:45

Win Prizemoney £35,697 *Total Prizemoney* £52,008

Wins * **1998** Aug Lingfi (G-F) C 5f 65
* **1998** Jun Folkes (G-F) H 5f 71 77?
1995 Aug Haydoc (G-F) H 5f 94 96 <
1995 Jly Bath (FRM) H 5.1f 90 92
1995 Jly Sandow (GD) H 5f 83 88
1994 Oct Catter (G-F) H 5f 76 84+
1994 Aug Bright (FRM) H 5.3f 65 69

1998 Turf 2-10: (5f 2-6, 6f 4) (g-s, gd 2, g-f 2-6, frm) 1998 AW 0-2: (5f 2) (Equi, Fibr)

Above-average gelding, effective 5f, acts on gd to frm, best on gd, often wears blinkers (extremely effectively). Turf high 77 - 1st of 8 giving 1lb to Bramble Bear (26 Jun Folkestone RF 2297). AW high 73. Still an effective sprint handicapper at the minor tracks, he seems at his best over the minimum on fast ground.

**S C Williams [2-26] J T Duffy & R E Duffy (from G Lewis [5-31] Spt 1996).*

THATOLDBLACKMAGIC (IRE) BHB 43f RR 45f 4486^{16}

3 b f Contract Law (USA) 8.9f **(54)** - Spinelle (Great Nephew) 9.9f **(64)**

Form - 3800

Record 1998 - 1st:0 2nd:0 3rd:1 Ran:4

Win Prizemoney £0 *Total Prizemoney* £302

1998 Turf 0-4: (5f, 7f 2, 10f) (frm 4)

Moderate filly. Turf high 45 (began Jly).

**W Storey [0-4] Tony Stafford.*

THATS LIFE BHB 72f RR 74f 3999^{9}

3 b c Mukaddamah (USA) 7.6f **(74)** - Run Faster (IRE) (Commanche Run) 8.5f **(58)**

Form - 458100

Record 1998 - 1st:1 2nd:0 3rd:0 Ran:6

Win Prizemoney £2,768 *Total Prizemoney* £2,979

Wins * **1998** Jly Folkes (G-F) 6f 74 <

1998 Turf 1-6: (6f 1-3, 7f 2, 8f) (gd 3, g-f 1-2, frm)

Leggy, above-average colt, effective 6f, acts on g-f. Turf high 77 - also 1st of 4 giving 5lb to Glowing (8 Jly Folkestone RF 2623). Looks the type to make a nice handicapper.

**T G Mills [1-6] T G Mills.*

THATS LOGIC (IRE) RR 92f $4567a^{7}$

4 b g Cyrano de Bergerac 7.3f **(58)** - Allberry (Alzao (USA)) 7.1f **(68)**

Form - 1742257

1998 Turf 0-6: (7f, 8f 5) (sft 3, gd 3)

Useful gelding, effective 7 to 8f, best at 8f, acts on hvy to gd, has worn blinkers, excels at Cork, likes Leopardstown. Turf high 92 - 2nd of 8 giving 9lb to Canzona (16 May Cork 8f gd RF 1345a).

**D Hassett in IRE [4-22] D M Murphy.*

THE ACCOUNTANT BHB 54f RR 59f 3810^{12}

3 ch g Suave Dancer (USA) 10.7f **(68)** - Fairy Tern (Mill Reef (USA)) 10.5f **(78)**

Form - 03000

Record 1998 - 1st:0 2nd:0 3rd:1 Ran:5

Win Prizemoney £0 *Total Prizemoney* £525

1998 Turf 0-5: (7f, 8f 3, 10f) (sft, g-f, frm 3)

Neat, fair gelding. Turf high 59. **Mrs J Cecil [0-5] Mrs M Slater.*

THE ANGEL GABRIEL RR 4531^{8}

3 ch c My Generation 6.5f **(68)** - Minsk **(30df)** (Kabour)

Form - 8

Record 1998 - 1st:0 2nd:0 3rd:0 Ran:1

1998 Turf 0-1: (9f) (g-s)

Currently very poor colt - 8th of 8 to Sconced (28 Spt Hamilton 9f g-s RF 4531). **D A Nolan [0-1] Mrs J McFadyen-Murray.*

THE ARTFUL DODGER BHB 56f52a RR 63f 52a 4116^{12}

3 b g Alhijaz 7.7f **(57)** - Madam Millie (Milford) 9f **(61)**

Form - 4650430

Record 1998 - 1st:0 2nd:0 3rd:1 Ran:7
Pre1998 - 1st:0 2nd:0 3rd:0 Ran:2

Win Prizemoney £0 *Total Prizemoney* £643

1998 Turf 0-6: (7f 2, 8f 2, 9f, 10f) (gd 2, g-f 3, frm) 1998 AW 0-1: (8f) (Fibr)

Workmanlike, average gelding, effective 9f, acts on g-f. Turf high 63. Inconsistent. **R J R Williams [0-9] Equinimity.*

THEATRE MAGIC BHB 29f55a RR 19f 55a 4543^{2}

5 b g Sayf El Arab(USA) 8.2f **(57)** -Miss Orient (Damister (USA)) 9f **(73)**

Form - 6510228476370052

Record 1998 - 1st:1 2nd:3 3rd:1 Ran:14
Pre1998 - 1st:3 2nd:4 3rd:5 Ran:37

Win Prizemoney £9,455 *Total Prizemoney* £18,939

Wins * **1998** *Jan Southw (STD) C 7f 63+*
* *1997 May Wolver (STD) H 7f 64 68 <*
* *1997 Apr Wolver (STD) H 7f 57 66*
1995 Nov Southw (STD) H 7f 55

1998 Turf 0-1: (6f) (g-f) 1998 AW 1-13: (5f, 6f 4, 7f 1-8) (Equi, Fibr 1-12)

Fair gelding, effective 6 to 7f, best at 7f, - acts on Fibr, has worn blinkers, likes left handed tracks, likes tight tracks. AW high 67 - also 1st of 11 getting 10lb from Yeoman Oliver (5 Jan Southwell RF 0023). He takes a keen hold, but is a useful sort in modest grade on sand. He started off 1998 in good style and was unlucky not to win more than just the one race at Southwell. Modest form after that but hinted at a return to form in the autumn. Seven furlongs looks his best trip.

**D Shaw [3-27] Green Diamond Racing (from S R Bowring [1-19] Dec 1996).*

THEATRE OF DREAMS BHB 55f RR 60f 2321^{P}

3 b f Tragic Role (USA) 9.4f **(63)** - Impala Lass (Kampala) 8.5f **(56)**

Form - 000240P

Record 1998 - 1st:0 2nd:1 3rd:0 Ran:7
Pre1998 - 1st:1 2nd:1 3rd:1 Ran:4

Win Prizemoney £2,565 *Total Prizemoney* £4,648

Wins 1997 May Mussel (G-F) C 5f 71 <

1998 Turf 0-5: (6f, 7f, 8f 3) (hvy, gd 2, g-f, frm) 1998 AW 0-2: (5f, 7f) (Fibr 2)

Leggy, average filly, effective 5f, acted on gd to g-f, best on g-f, had worn blinkers. Turf high 60. AW high 51. A half-sister to three winners, notably Oops Pettie, she got off the mark in a poor claimer at Musselburgh in May 1997. However, he was not seen out again until March 1998, and her best effort was second in a Windsor claimer, form she could not repeat. (DEAD)

**K R Burke [0-7] Nigel Shields (from P D Evans [1-4] May 1997).*

THEATREWORLD (IRE) RR 98f 3754[U]

6 b g Sadler's Wells (USA) 11.3f **(87)** - Chamonis (USA) (Affirmed (USA)) 9.3f **(79)**

Form - 4336331U

1998 Turf 1-8: (12f 1-3, 14f 3, 16f, 22f) (hvy 1-1, sft 2, g-s 2, gd 2, frm)

Very useful gelding, effective 12 to 16f, best at 12f, acts on sft to gd, likes right handed tracks, does well at Curragh and Galway. Turf high 98. Though better known as a hurdler these days, he is no mean performer on the Flat either, as he proved with three victories on the level in 1997. Won at Galway in 1998 before being brought down in the Ebor, sustaining a minor injury.

**A P O'Brien in IRE [13-42] Mrs John Magnier (from Sir Michael Stoute [0-1] Spt 1994).*

THE BARNSLEY BELLE (IRE) BHB 37f43a **RR 38f 43a** 4874[15]

5 b m Distinctly North (USA) 7.4f **(63)** - La Tanque (USA) (Last Raise (USA)) 7f **(51)**

Form - 34754370000

Record	**1998 -**	1st:0	2nd:0	3rd:1	Ran:9
	Pre1998 -	1st:2	2nd:5	3rd:3	Ran:30

Win Prizemoney £4,934 *Total Prizemoney* £10,545

Wins	1997	*Apr Southw (STD)*	*7f*	*63*	<
	1996	*Nov Southw (STD) H*	*7f*	*47*	*49*

1998 Turf 0-2: (8f 2) (sft, gd) 1998 AW 0-7: (7f 4, 8f 3) (Fibr 7)

Very moderate filly, effective 7f, - acts on Fibr. Turf high 31. AW high 51. **G Woodward [0-1] K Meynell (from J L Eyre [2-32] May 1998).*

THE BAT BHB 60f **RR 61f** 4072[20]

5 b h Chauve Souris - Jamra (Upper Case (USA)) 8.2f **(55)**

Form - 5370

Record	**1998 -**	1st:0	2nd:0	3rd:1	Ran:4

Win Prizemoney £0 *Total Prizemoney* £505

1998 Turf 0-4: (10f 2, 11f, 12f) (g-f 2, frm 2)

Average colt. Turf high 61 (began Jly). **A P Jarvis [0-7] Mrs P Stroud.*

THE BLUES ACADEMY (IRE) BHB 65f **RR 71f** 4659[8]

3 b g Royal Academy (USA) 7.8f **(77)** - She's the Tops (Shernazar) 10.2f **(73)**

Form - 002413008

Record	**1998 -**	1st:1	2nd:1	3rd:1	Ran:9
	Pre1998 -	1st:0	2nd:0	3rd:0	Ran:3

Win Prizemoney £3,533 *Total Prizemoney* £6,522

Wins	*** 1998**	Jly Bath (GD) H	17.2f	67	71 <

1998 Turf 1-9: (10f, 11f, 15f 2, 16f 2, 17f 1-2, 20f)(g-s, gd 5, g-f 1-2, frm)

Workmanlike, above-average gelding, effective 15 to 17f, acts on gd to frm, has worn blinkers. Turf high 71 - 3rd of 15 getting 10lb from Sandbaggedagain (24 Jly Ascot 16f gd RF 3062) - also 1st of 7 from Saintly Thoughts (6 Jly Bath RF 2558). Becoming disappointing. His form has improved as he has been stepped right up in trip, and stamina definitely won him the day at Bath in July. It was only a moderate maiden handicap, but he ran well in better company next time.

**M A Buckley [1-9] C C Buckley (from M Johnston [0-3] Oct 1997).*

THE BOMBER LISTON (IRE) RR 89f 4794a[4]

2 b c Perugino (USA) - Berenice (ITY) 00

Form - 511524

1998 Turf 2-6: (5f, 6f 1-3, 7f 1-2) (hvy 1-1, sft, g-s, gd 2, hrd 1-1)

Useful colt, effective 6 to 7f, best at 7f, acts on hvy to hrd. Turf high 90 - 1st of 15 giving 3lb to Cobourg Lodge (15 Aug Curragh RF 3716a) - also 1st of 11 giving 8lb to Legend Falls (5 Aug Sligo RF 3545a). **J S Bolger in IRE [2-6] Sporting Quest Racing Club.*

THE BOOZING BRIEF (USA) BHB 44f47a **RR 40f 47a** 629[13]

5 b g Turkoman (USA)- Evening Silk (USA)(Damascus (USA)) 8.9f **(71)**

Form - 0

Record	**1998 -**	1st:0	2nd:0	3rd:0	Ran:1
	Pre1998 -	1st:0	2nd:2	3rd:0	Ran:12

Win Prizemoney £0 *Total Prizemoney* £3,008

1998 Turf 0-1: (16f) (gd)

Moderate gelding, has worn blinkers. Becoming disappointing.

**C Parker [0-8] & Mrs Raymond Anderson Green (from M A Jarvis [0-10] Spt 1996).*

THE BOWER (IRE) RR 94f 5028a[8]

9 br g Don't Forget Me 9.5f **(66)** - Nyama (USA) (Pretense (USA)) 6.3f **(88)**

Form - 53568

1998 Turf 0-5: (6f, 8f 2, 9f 2) (hvy, sft 2, gd, frm)

Useful gelding, effective 8f, acts on sft to gd, mostly wears blinkers (effectively). Turf high 94. Inconsistent.

**C Collins in IRE [2-24] Mrs C Collins.*

THE BUTTERWICK KID BHB 70f66a **RR 70f 66a** 2015[10]

5 ch g Interrex (CAN) 7.7f **(51)** - Ville Air (Town Crier) 10.2f **(55)**

Form - 1333130

Record	**1998 -**	1st:2	2nd:0	3rd:4	Ran:7
	Pre1998 -	1st:5	2nd:3	3rd:1	Ran:23

Win Prizemoney £25,874 *Total Prizemoney* £32,535

Wins	*** 1998**	May Redcar (G-F) H	14.1f	62	66+
	*** 1998**	*Jan Southw (STD) H*	*11f*	*59*	*60*
	* 1997	May Mussel (G-S) H	12f	54	57+
	* 1997	May Cheste (HVY) H	12.3f	52	59
	* 1997	Apr Nottin (G-F) H	14.1f	45	49
	* 1996	Spt Hamilt (GD) H	12.1f	44	45
	* 1995	Jly Beverl (GD) C	5f		69 <

1998 Turf 1-6: (11f, 12f, 13f 2, 14f 1-1, 20f) (sft 2, gd 1-3, g-f) 1998 AW 1-1: (11f 1-1) (Fibr 1-1)

Above-average gelding, effective 11 to 14f, acts on sft to g-f - acts on Fibr, has worn blinkers, likes left handed tracks, favours tight tracks, excels at Hamilton. Turf high 70 - 3rd of 7 getting 2lb from Carburton (1 Jun Thirsk 12f g-f RF 1629) - also 1st of 10 giving 13lb to Highfield Fizz (25 May Redcar RF 1460). (1st run). Consistent. Lost his way in the latter part of the 1997 season, but regained winning form on the Southwell Fibresand in January, having previously shown good form over hurdles. He continued to run with credit back on turf, and was an unlucky-in-running tenth at Royal Ascot over two and a half miles.

**R A Fahey [8-35] Robert Chambers & Mrs M W Kenyon.*

THE CANNIE ROVER BHB 51f50a **RR 46f 50a** 1547[3]

3 ch c Beveled (USA) 6.9f **(64)** - Sister Rosarii (USA) (Properantes (USA)) 8.3f **(51)**

Form - 63

Record	**1998 -**	1st:0	2nd:0	3rd:1	Ran:2
	Pre1998 -	1st:0	2nd:0	3rd:0	Ran:8

Win Prizemoney £0 *Total Prizemoney* £324

1998 Turf 0-1: (9f) (g-f) 1998 AW 0-1: (8f) (Fibr)

Unfurnished, moderate colt. Inconsistent.

**M W Easterby [0-10] Mrs E Rhind.*

THECOMEBACKKING BHB 54f47a **RR 55f 47a** 259[9]

3 ch c Mystiko (USA) 7.7f **(59)** - Nitouche (Scottish Reel) 7f **(61)**

Form - 300

Record	**1998 -**	1st:0	2nd:0	3rd:1	Ran:3
	Pre1998 -	1st:0	2nd:0	3rd:0	Ran:7

Win Prizemoney £0 *Total Prizemoney* £585

1998 AW 0-3: (8f, 9f, 10f) (Equi, Fibr 2)

Workmanlike, fair colt, effective 9f, - acts on Fibr, likes tight tracks. AW high 54 (1st run) - 3rd of 10 getting 10lb from Accystan (10 Jan Wolverhampton 9f Fibr RF 0065).

**B P J Baugh [0-2] Mrs J Gill (from S C Williams [0-8] Jan 1998).*

THE COTTONWOOL KID BHB 28f34a **RR 23?f 34a** 2922[12]

6 b g Blakeney 11.9f **(53)** - Relatively Smart (Great Nephew) 9.9f **(64)**

Form - 0

Record	**1998 -**	1st:0	2nd:0	3rd:0	Ran:1
	Pre1998 -	1st:0	2nd:0	3rd:2	Ran:10

Win Prizemoney £0 *Total Prizemoney* £629

1998 Turf 0-1: (14f) (gd)

Very moderate gelding. Becoming disappointing.

**Miss L C Siddall [0-1] Mrs S E Cooper (from T Kersey [0-2] Spt 1996).*

THE DEALER BHB 53f **RR 61f** 4837[6]

3 b c No Big Deal - Not Alone (Pas de Seul) 9.1f **(67)**

Form - 76046

Record	**1998 -**	1st:0	2nd:0	3rd:0	Ran:5

1998 Turf 0-5: (5f 2, 6f 2, 7f) (g-s, gd, g-f, frm 2)

Leggy, average colt. Turf high 61 (began Jly).

**J A R Toller [0-5] & Mrs Daniel Day-Robinson.*

THE DIRK BHB 35f **RR 37f** 5124[9]

2 b c Petong 7.6f **(58)** - Nahawand (High Top) 10.2f **(67)**

Form - 07000
Record 1998 - 1st:0 2nd:0 3rd:0 Ran:5
1998 Turf 0-5: (5f, 6f 2, 7f, 8f) (sft, g-s, gd, g-f, frm)
Very moderate colt. Turf high 37. **J C Fox [0-5] John Homer Racing.*

THE DONK (IRE) BHB 52f45a RR 62f 45a 4934[16]

2 b g Case Law 6f **(64)** - Peep of Day (USA) (Lypheor) 12f **(71)**
Form - 33033200
Record 1998 - 1st:0 2nd:1 3rd:4 Ran:8
Win Prizemoney £0 *Total Prizemoney* £1,696
1998 Turf 0-4:(5f, 6f, 7f, 8f)(g-s 2, gd 2) 1998 AW 0-4:(5f 2, 6f 2)(Fibr 4)
Average gelding, effective 5 to 7f, acts on gd - acts on Fibr, has worn blinkers. Turf high 62 - 2nd of 10 giving 5lb to Fizzy Whizzy (20 Jun Redcar 7f gd RF 2154). AW high 59. Inconsistent. A less-than-flattering name, but he would seem to have a small amount of ability. He lost a Redcar seller in the stewards' room, but should be able to find a similar event. **B S Rothwell [0-8] Mrs Greta Sparks.*

THE DOWNTOWN FOX BHB 77f RR 82f 4988[9]

3 br c Primo Dominie 7.2f **(67)** -Sara Sprint(Formidable (USA)) 9.2f **(63)**
Form - 21768550000
Record 1998 - 1st:1 2nd:1 3rd:0 Ran:11
Pre1998 - 1st:0 2nd:1 3rd:2 Ran:5
Win Prizemoney £8,285 *Total Prizemoney* £13,558
Wins * **1998** Apr Leices (SFT) H 7f 82 88 <
1998 Turf 1-11: (6f 4, 7f 1-6, 8f) (sft 1-1, g-s 3, gd 3, g-f 4)
Unfurnished, decent colt, effective 6 to 7f, best at 6f, acts on sft to gd, has worn blinkers. Turf high 88 - 1st of 11 getting 3lb from Goodwood Cavalier (9 Apr Leicester RF 0619). Went down narrowly at Doncaster on his reappearance before scoring at Leicester. Below form since apart from a good effort at York in June in his favoured soft ground. **B A McMahon [1-16] G Whitaker.*

THE DRUMMER (IRE) RR 52f 1298[12]

2 b c River Falls 8.2f **(56)** - Tribal Rhythm (IRE) (Double Schwartz) 7.9f **(55)**
Form - 550
Record 1998 - 1st:0 2nd:0 3rd:0 Ran:3
1998 Turf 0-3: (5f 3) (sft, g-s, gd)
Currently fair colt. Turf high 52.
**Miss L A Perratt [0-3] C D Barber-Lomax.*

THE EDITOR BHB 104f RR 106f 3634[2]

3 b c Alzao(USA) 9.8f **(73)** -Litani River (USA)(Irish River (FR)) 8.6f **(78)**
Form - 512572
Record 1998 - 1st:1 2nd:2 3rd:0 Ran:6
Win Prizemoney £3,834 *Total Prizemoney* £7,740
Wins * **1998** May Thirsk (GD) 8f 87 <
1998 Turf 1-6: (8f 1-4, 10f, 11f) (sft, gd 1-3, g-f, frm)
Scopey, Pattern-class colt, effective 8 to 11f, best at 8f, acts on gd to frm. Turf high 106 - 2nd of 7 to Secret Archive (14 Aug Newbury 11f g-f RF 3634). He won a run-of-the-mill maiden at Thirsk and trod water before being stepped-up to middle-distances. Like most of Alzao's stock, he is worth a try in soft ground, although it has been reported he is likely to continue his career in the United States. **H R A Cecil [1-6] The Thoroughbred Corporation.*

THE EXETER MAN (USA) RR 5164a[13]

6 b g Capote (USA) 9.1f **(84)** - Nakiska Wind (USA) (Lyphard (USA))
Form - 0
1998 AW 0-1: (6f) (Dirt)
Currently Pattern-class gelding.
**R Frankel in USA [0-1] Super Horse Inc.*

THE EXHIBITION FOX RR 51f 4745[8]

2 b c Be My Chief(USA) 10.2f **(62)** -Swift Return(Double Form) 7.3f **(58)**
Form - 8
Record 1998 - 1st:0 2nd:0 3rd:0 Ran:1
1998 Turf 0-1: (8f) (gd)
Currently fair colt. **B A McMahon [0-1] G Whitaker.*

THE FARAWAY TREE BHB 94f RR 100f 4186[9]

4 b f Suave Dancer (USA) 10.7f **(68)** - Sassalya (Sassafras (FR)) 9.6f **(69)**
Form - 352450
Record 1998 - 1st:0 2nd:1 3rd:1 Ran:6
Pre1998 - 1st:2 2nd:2 3rd:1 Ran:8
Win Prizemoney £9,401 *Total Prizemoney* £28,264
Wins * 1997 Spt Haydoc (GD) 14f 102 <
* 1996 Spt Yarmou (G-F) 6f 80+
1998 Turf 0-6: (12f 2, 13f, 14f 2, 15f) (sft, gd 2, frm 3)
Workmanlike, very useful filly, effective 10 to 15f, acts on gd to frm, has worn blinkers, likes left handed tracks. Turf high 100 - 2nd of 4 giving 14lb to Generous Terms (25 Jun Salisbury 14f gd RF 2275). Like most of Geoff Wragg's horses, she was below par in 1998. She might be worth a spin in handicap company off her current mark. **G Wragg [2-14] A E Oppenheimer.*

THE FED BHB 32f29a RR 30f 29a 90[6]

8 ch g Clantime 6.6f **(57)** - Hyde Princess (Touch Paper) 6.8f **(57)**
Form - 046
Record 1998 - 1st:0 2nd:0 3rd:0 Ran:1
Pre1998 - 1st:4 2nd:4 3rd:10 Ran:58
Win Prizemoney £12,904 *Total Prizemoney* £21,293
Wins 1994 Spt Nottin (GS) H 5.1f 55 55
1994 Aug Mussel (G-F) H 5f 52 50
1994 Aug Nottin (G-F) H 5.1f 46 46
1998 AW 0-1: (5f) (Fibr)
Very moderate gelding, has worn blinkers. Consistent.
**J L Eyre [0-5] Nicholas Wright (from J A Pickering [0-7] Jun 1996).*

THE FLY BHB 105f RR 107f 4616[5]

4 gr c Pharly (FR) 11.5f **(64)** - Nelly Do Da (Derring-Do) 11.1f **(64)**
Form - 33375245
Record 1998 - 1st:0 2nd:1 3rd:3 Ran:8
Pre1998 - 1st:3 2nd:0 3rd:2 Ran:9
Win Prizemoney £46,512 *Total Prizemoney* £96,536
Wins * 1997 May York (GD) H 10.4f 93 102+ <
* 1996 Aug Newcas (GD) H 8f 85 94+
* 1996 Aug Ayr (GD) 7f 82
1998 Turf 0-8: (12f 7, 13f) (sft, gd 4, g-f 3)
Pattern-class colt, effective 12 to 15f, best at 12f, acts on sft to frm, likes left handed tracks, does well at Doncaster and Newmarket. Turf high 115 - 3rd of 12 getting 1lb from Posidonas (18 Apr Newbury 12f sft RF 0741). Consistent. Ran in three Classics in 1997, his best performance probably being his third in the St Leger, and should have won comfortably at Doncaster on his reappearance this season, but was disqualified after causing havoc. He has made the frame in Pattern company since then, but has also spurned easier opportunities, and it looks as if he has forgotten how to win, something he has not achieved since landing a York handicap on his 1997 reappearance.
**B W Hills [3-17] Mrs J M Corbett.*

THE FLYING PIG (IRE) RR 97f 5175a[11]

2 b g Case Law 6f **(64)** - Miss Quotation 00
Form - 072120500
1998 Turf 1-9: (5f 1-1, 6f 5, 7f, 8f 2) (sft, g-s 3, gd 1-5)
Very useful gelding, effective 5 to 6f, acts on gd, has worn blinkers. Turf high 97 - 5th of 27 giving 5lb to Amazing Dream (29 Aug Curragh 6f gd RF 4039a). Inconsistent. Had shown reasonable form, but was a 33/1 outsider when a close fifth in the valuable Tattersalls Breeders' Stakes.
**Patrick Prendergast in IRE [1-9] Ms Maura Horan.*

THE FRISKY FARMER BHB 41f36a RR 38f 36a 5121[15]

5 b g Emarati (USA) 6.6f **(63)** -Farceuse (Comedy Star (USA)) 7.5f **(50)**
Form - 66283506040
Record 1998 - 1st:0 2nd:1 3rd:1 Ran:11
Pre1998 - 1st:3 2nd:6 3rd:4 Ran:37
Win Prizemoney £7,083 *Total Prizemoney* £16,241
Wins * 1997 Aug Bright (G-F) S 6f 58
* 1996 Mar Leices (SFT) S 6f 67 <
* 1995 Apr Beverl (G-F) S 5f 62+t
1998 Turf 0-7: (5f, 6f 6) (g-s 2, gd 2, frm 3) 1998 AW 0-4: (6f 4) (Equi 3, Fibr)
Very moderate gelding, effective 6 to 7f, best at 6f, acts on gd to frm - acts on Equi, has worn blinkers, likes left handed tracks, likes tight tracks. Turf high 50 - 3rd of 11 giving 2lb to Halmanerror (30 Apr Brighton 6f gd RF 0923). AW high 39.
**W G M Turner [3-48] G J Bush.*

THE FUGATIVE BHB 73f64a RR 72f 64a 5097[6]

5 b m Nicholas (USA) 6.1f **(63)** - Miss Runaway (Runnett) 7f **(59)**
Form - 013324101650266

Record 1998 - 1st:3 2nd:2 3rd:2 Ran:15
Pre1998 - 1st:3 2nd:2 3rd:0 Ran:19
Win Prizemoney £19,222 *Total Prizemoney* £25,183
Wins * **1998** Jun Epsom (GD) H 6f 70 72
* **1998** May Lingfi (GD) H 6f 65 68
* **1998** Apr Folkes (SFT) 5f 73 <
* 1997 Jly Folkes (GD) H 5f 61 66
* 1997 Jun Folkes (SFT) H 5f 50 60
* 1997 Jun Epsom (G-S) H 6f 50 56
1998 Turf 3-15: (5f 1-7, 6f 2-5, 7f 3) (sft 1-2, gd 8, g-f 2-4, frm)
Above-average filly, effective 5 to 7f, acts on sft to frm, best on g-f, does well at Epsom and Lingfield and Folkestone. Turf high 73 - 1st of 4 getting 6lb from Ocker (7 Apr Folkestone RF 0578) - also 1st of 9 giving 7lb to Cauda Equina (24 Jun Epsom RF 2242). Likes to race prominently and is difficult to catch when on song. Goes well on a fast track. **P Mitchell [6-34] J A Redmond.*

THE GAMBOLLER (USA) BHB 68f **RR 69f** 4883[10]
3 b c Irish Tower (USA) 7.3f **(69)** - Lady Limbo (USA) (Dance Spell (USA)) 9.6f **(75)**
Form - 4271U800
Record 1998 - 1st:1 2nd:1 3rd:0 Ran:8
Win Prizemoney £2,427 *Total Prizemoney* £3,306
Wins * **1998** Jly Leices (GD) 10f 69 <
1998 Turf 1-8: (8f 2, 10f 1-5, 12f) (g-s, gd 3, g-f, frm 1-3)
Scopey, average colt, likes tight tracks. Turf high 84.
**Mrs A J Perrett [1-8] Simon Karmel.*

THE GAY FOX BHB 84f **RR 88f** 4975[5]
4 b gr c Never so Bold 7.1f **(62)** - School Concert (Music Boy) 6.8f **(57)**
Form - 37103866500008725
Record 1998 - 1st:1 2nd:1 3rd:2 Ran:17
Pre1998 - 1st:3 2nd:3 3rd:1 Ran:21
Win Prizemoney £20,451 *Total Prizemoney* £36,758
Wins * **1998** Apr Sandow (HVY) H 5f 87 90 <
* 1997 Jly Cheste (G-F) H 5.1f 81 83
* 1997 Jun Newmar (SFT) H 5f 74 76
* 1997 May Warwic (FRM) H 7f 73 70
1998 Turf 1-17: (5f 1-11, 6f 6) (hvy 1-1, sft 3, g-s 2, gd 7, g-f 2, frm 2)
Workmanlike, useful colt, effective 5f, acts on hvy to g-f, prefers left handed tracks, excels at Chester, does well at Newmarket. Turf high 94 - 3rd of 8 giving 6lb to Westcourt Magic (7 May Chester 5f g-f RF 1072) - also 1st of 13 giving 12lb to Mister Jolson (24 Apr Sandown RF 0852). Ran a fine race on his Doncaster reappearance, and took advantage of his good draw in order to score on heavy ground at Sandown. Has seemed held by the Handicapper since, although he is now back on a winning mark.
**B A McMahon [4-38] G Whitaker.*

THE GENE GENIE BHB 79f **RR 76df** 5008[6]
3 b g Syrtos 8.1f **(57)** - Sally Maxwell (Roscoe Blake) 11f **(66)**
Form - 62256
Record 1998 - 1st:0 2nd:2 3rd:0 Ran:5
Pre1998 - 1st:0 2nd:2 3rd:0 Ran:4
Win Prizemoney £0 *Total Prizemoney* £7,103
1998 Turf 0-5: (8f 3, 11f, 12f) (sft, g-s, gd, g-f, frm)
Workmanlike, above-average gelding, effective 7 to 10f, acts on g-f, has worn blinkers. Turf high 81. Looks one with his own ideas about the game, although he has the ability to win races.
**M J Heaton-Ellis [0-9] Fieldspring Racing.*

THE GLOW-WORM (IRE) BHB 110f **RR 111df** 5075[3]
3 b c Doyoun 10.7f **(69)** - Shakanda (IRE) (Shernazar) 10.2f **(73)**
Form - 126583
Record 1998 - 1st:1 2nd:1 3rd:1 Ran:6
Pre1998 - 1st:2 2nd:0 3rd:2 Ran:5
Win Prizemoney £19,560 *Total Prizemoney* £50,958
Wins * **1998** Apr Epsom (SFT) 12f 99+ <
* 1997 Oct Newmar (G-S) H 8f 89 96
* 1997 Jun Newmar (SFT) 7f 73
1998 Turf 1-6: (12f 1-5, 15f) (sft 1-1, g-s, g-f 4)
Scopey, Group-class colt, effective 12f, acts on g-f. Turf high 113. Unkindly nicknamed The Slow-Worm, he had a tough race when short-headed by Gulland in the Chester Vase and did not progress. Sixth in the Derby and eighth of nine in the St Leger, he does not look Group One material and would benefit from a confidence booster in the minor leagues.
**B W Hills [3-11] Mrs J M Corbett.*

THE GRADUATE BHB 52f **RR 52f** 4760[17]
4 ch g Indian Ridge 7.6f **(74)** - Queen's Eyot (Grundy) 10.3f **(65)**
Form - 7600
Record 1998 - 1st:0 2nd:0 3rd:0 Ran:4
Win Prizemoney £0 *Total Prizemoney* £85
1998 Turf 0-4: (8f 3, 10f) (gd 4)
Fair gelding. Turf high 64. **J A R Toller [0-4] Miss L Robertson.*

THE GREEN GREY BHB 69f52a **RR 70f 52a** 4653[5]
4 gr g Environment Friend 7.5f **(67)** - Pea Green (Try My Best (USA)) 7.6f **(67)**
Form - 6807112115
Record 1998 - 1st:4 2nd:1 3rd:0 Ran:8
Pre1998 - 1st:1 2nd:1 3rd:0 Ran:13
Win Prizemoney £17,243 *Total Prizemoney* £18,722
Wins * **1998** Spt Kempto (GD) H 8f 67 70 <
1998 Spt Bright (FRM) C 8f 68
1998 Aug Bath (FRM) S 8f 61
1998 Aug Yarmou (G-F) SH 8f 43 49
1997 Spt Bath (G-F) H 8f 42 51
1998 Turf 4-8: (8f 4-7, 10f) (gd, g-f 2, frm 4-5)
Scopey, above-average gelding, effective 8f, acts on frm, has worn blinkers. Turf high 70 - 1st of 18 from Super Monarch (21 Spt Kempton RF 4391) - also 1st of 13 giving 2lb to Burning (2 Spt Brighton RF 4049). He is only a plater, but an effective one on fast ground, conditions under which he gained back-to-back selling wins at Yarmouth and Bath, and later at Brighton and Kempton.
**Derrick Morris [1-2] J Daniels (from W R Muir [4-20] Spt 1998).*

THE GROOM IS RED (USA) RR 5162a[6]
2 b c Runaway Groom (CAN) 8.1f **(69)** - Sheenasgold (USA) **00**
Form - 6
1998 AW 0-1: (9f) (Dirt)
Currently very useful colt. **N Zito in USA [0-1] Celtic Pride Stable.*

THE GYPSY TIPPLER BHB 53f **RR 53f** 5121[9]
3 ch f Romany Rye - Eidolon (Rousillon (USA)) 8.2f **(74)**
Form - 506003850
Record 1998 - 1st:0 2nd:0 3rd:1 Ran:9
Win Prizemoney £0 *Total Prizemoney* £610
1998 Turf 0-9: (6f 6, 7f 2, 8f) (g-s 2, gd 3, g-f 2, frm 2)
Light-framed, fair filly. Turf high 63 (began Jly). Inconsistent.
**B Palling [0-9] Lindsay Hiscock.*

THE HAKA BHB 59f **RR 64f** 4889[13]
2 ch c Sabrehill(USA) 8.5f **(64)** -Exotic Forest **68df)**(Dominion) 8.5f **(63)**
Form - 76535F060
Record 1998 - 1st:0 2nd:0 3rd:1 Ran:9
Win Prizemoney £0 *Total Prizemoney* £532
1998 Turf 0-8: (5f, 6f 3, 7f 2, 8f, 10f) (g-s, gd 2, g-f 4, frm) 1998 AW 0-1: (7f) (Fibr)
Average colt, effective 6f, acts on frm, has worn blinkers. Turf high 64. Inconsistent. **G C Bravery [0-9] The TT Partnership.*

THE HAULIER RR 81f 5012[2]
2 ch c Ardkinglass 5f **(64)** - Ask Away (Midyan (USA)) 6f **(60)**
Form - 5365517502
Record 1998 - 1st:1 2nd:1 3rd:1 Ran:10
Win Prizemoney £2,827 *Total Prizemoney* £4,078
Wins * **1998** Aug Newcas (GD) H 7f 74 79 <
1998 Turf 1-10: (5f 2, 6f 2, 7f 1-4, 8f 2) (sft 2, gd 1-3, g-f 2, frm 2, hrd)
Decent colt, effective 6 to 7f, best at 6f, acts on gd to frm, best on gd. Turf high 79 - 1st of 9 giving 6lb to Tampa Lady (5 Aug Newcastle RF 3381).
**T D Easterby [1-10] T E F Freight (Scarborough) Ltd.*

THE HONORABLE LADY BHB 43f **RR 38f** 2278[6]
3 b f Mystiko(USA) 7.7f **(59)** -Mrs Thatcher(Law Society(USA)) 9.9f **(70)**
Form - 778546
Record 1998 - 1st:0 2nd:0 3rd:0 Ran:6
Pre1998 - 1st:1 2nd:1 3rd:2 Ran:10
Win Prizemoney £2,406 *Total Prizemoney* £3,824
Wins * 1997 Jly Yarmou (G-F) S 7f 67 <
1998 Turf 0-5: (6f, 7f 3, 9f) (gd 3, frm 2) 1998 AW 0-1: (9f) (Fibr)
Neat, moderate filly, effective 7f, acts on frm, has worn blinkers. Turf high 38. Consistent.
**M R Channon [1-16] Henry Ponsonby & Partners (1).*

THE IMPOSTER (IRE) BHB 50f52a **RR 56df 52a** 3094[6]
3 ch g Imp Society (USA) 7.1f **(63)** - Phoenix Dancer (IRE) (Gorytus (USA)) 7.8f **(60)**
Form - 5763056
Record 1998 - 1st:0 2nd:0 3rd:1 Ran:7
Pre1998 - 1st:0 2nd:0 3rd:1 Ran:3
Win Prizemoney £0 *Total Prizemoney* £601
1998 Turf 0-1: (7f) (gd) 1998 AW 0-6: (7f, 8f 4, 9f) (Fibr 6)
Workmanlike, fair gelding, effective 6 to 7f, acts on frm - acts on Fibr. AW high 53 - 5th of 14 getting 7lb from Kosevo (17 Jly Southwell 7f Fibr RF 2900). **D J G MurraySmith [0-10] D MurraySmith.*

THE INSTITUTE BOY BHB 50f49a **RR 47f 49a** 367[5]
8 b g Fairy King (USA) 7.7f **(75)** - To Oneiro (Absalom) 7.2f **(58)**
Form - 7005
Record 1998 - 1st:0 2nd:0 3rd:0 Ran:4
Pre1998 - 1st:5 2nd:11 3rd:10 Ran:76
Win Prizemoney £14,495 *Total Prizemoney* £28,260
Wins 1996 Jly Catter (G-F) H 5f 42 47
1996 *Mar Lingfi (STD) H 6f 60 64*
1996 *Feb Lingfi (STD) H 5f 52 57*
1998 AW 0-4: (5f 3, 6f) (Equi 4)
Moderate gelding, effective 5 to 6f, - acts on Equi, has worn blinkers. AW high 44. Becoming disappointing. A fair sprinter over the years on turf and sand, he was off the track for eleven months after February 1997, showing little since his return.
**K R Burke [2-25] Mrs J Addleshaw (from Miss J F Craze [3-43] Feb 1997).*

THEKRYAATI (IRE) RR 62f 996[16]
3 ch c Indian Ridge 7.6f **(74)** -Lamu Lady(IRE)(Lomond(USA)) 8.8f **(65)**
Form - 0
Record 1998 - 1st:0 2nd:0 3rd:0 Ran:1
1998 Turf 0-1: (8f) (gd)
Workmanlike, currently average colt. **B Hanbury [0-1] Saif Ali.*

THE LAD BHB 35f36a **RR 37f 36a** 2065[9]
9 b g Bold Owl 9.7f **(47)** - Solbella (Starch Reduced) 11.5f **(52)**
Form - 00
Record 1998 - 1st:0 2nd:0 3rd:0 Ran:2
Pre1998 - 1st:3 2nd:0 3rd:0 Ran:9
Win Prizemoney £8,147 *Total Prizemoney* £8,358
Wins 1996 Jly Chepst (G-F) H 12.1f 44 52 <
1996 Apr Folkes (FRM) H 15.4f 36 48
1996 *Feb Lingfi (STD) H 16f 27 32*
1998 Turf 0-2: (12f, 14f) (gd, g-f)
Very moderate gelding. Turf high 24. Consistent.
**Mrs L Stubbs [0-2] Treberth Partnership (from L MontagueHall [3-9] Spt 1996).*

THE LAMBTON WORM BHB 44f **RR 45f** 3024[10]
4 b g Superpower 6.6f **(58)** - Springwell (Miami Springs) 9.9f **(59)**
Form - 6000050
Record 1998 - 1st:0 2nd:0 3rd:0 Ran:7
Pre1998 - 1st:1 2nd:3 3rd:1 Ran:16
Win Prizemoney £3,493 *Total Prizemoney* £8,761
Wins * 1996 Jly Ayr (GD) 6f 77 <
1998 Turf 0-7: (6f, 7f 4, 8f 2) (hvy, gd 2, g-f 3, frm)
Moderate gelding, has worn blinkers. Turf high 45.
**Denys Smith [1-23] Lord Durham.*

THELANDY BHB 36f **RR 44?f** 4816[6]
3 b g Noble Patriarch 12.2f **(43)** - Choir (High Top) 10.2f **(67)**
Form - 6006
Record 1998 - 1st:0 2nd:0 3rd:0 Ran:4
1998 Turf 0-3: (7f, 8f, 12f) (gd, g-f, frm) 1998 AW 0-1: (8f) (Fibr)
Scopey, moderate gelding. Turf high 44.
**R Craggs [0-2] A Skelton (from J L Eyre [0-2] Jun 1998).*

THE LAST WORD BHB 40f **RR 32f** 5004[9]
2 b c Cosmonaut - Jolizal (Good Times (ITY)) 6.6f **(54)**
Form - 00
Record 1998 - 1st:0 2nd:0 3rd:0 Ran:2
1998 Turf 0-2: (6f 2) (sft, g-s)
Currently very moderate colt. Turf high 32 (began Oct).
**R Hollinshead [0-2] Mrs Patricia Lunn.*

THE LIMPING CAT (IRE) BHB 87f **RR 85f** 4821[8]
3 b c Emarati (USA) 6.6f **(63)** - Little Madam (Habat) 7.6f **(61)**
Form - 60502068
Record 1998 - 1st:0 2nd:1 3rd:0 Ran:8
Pre1998 - 1st:1 2nd:0 3rd:1 Ran:3
Win Prizemoney £3,588 *Total Prizemoney* £10,383
Wins * 1997 Jly Nottin (G-F) 5.1f 84 <
1998 Turf 0-8: (5f 7, 6f) (gd, g-f 2, frm 5)
Workmanlike, useful colt, effective 5f, acts on frm. Turf high 85 - 8th of 18 getting 14lb from Almaty (15 Oct Newmarket 5f frm RF 4821). He looked held by the Handicapper last season until running a good second at York in August.
**B C Morgan [1-11] G Whitaker.*

THELONIUS (IRE) BHB 72f **RR 75f** 4748[24]
3 ch c Statoblest 6.4f **(63)** - Little Sega (FR) (Bellypha) 9.8f **(73)**
Form - 348U52310
Record 1998 - 1st:1 2nd:1 3rd:2 Ran:9
Pre1998 - 1st:0 2nd:1 3rd:0 Ran:5
Win Prizemoney £3,858 *Total Prizemoney* £6,372
Wins * **1998** Oct Warwic (GD) 8f 75 <
1998 Turf 1-9: (6f, 7f 5, 8f 1-2, 9f) (g-s, gd 3, g-f 1-4, frm)
Neat, above-average colt, effective 7 to 8f, best at 8f, acts on g-f to frm, best on g-f, prefers left handed tracks, prefers tight tracks. Turf high 75 - 1st of 18 from Kennet (4 Oct Warwick RF 4644).
**J G Smyth-Osbourne [1-14] Mrs E T Smyth-Osbourne & Partners.*

THE MAGISTRATE (IRE) BHB 53f **RR 49f** 4475[14]
3 br c Case Law 6f **(64)** - Bel Ria (Gay Fandango (USA)) 8.5f **(59)**
Form - 0570000
Record 1998 - 1st:0 2nd:0 3rd:0 Ran:7
Pre1998 - 1st:0 2nd:0 3rd:0 Ran:4
Win Prizemoney £0 *Total Prizemoney* £197
1998 Turf 0-7: (6f, 7f 3, 8f 3) (gd 3, g-f 2, frm 2)
Moderate colt. Turf high 59. Becoming disappointing.
**M Blanshard [0-11] J A Oliver.*

THE MANX TOUCH (IRE) BHB 53f **RR 53f** 4509[11]
2 gr f Petardia 8.2f **(58)** - Chapter And Verse (Dancers Image (USA)) 9.3f **(71)**
Form - 800
Record 1998 - 1st:0 2nd:0 3rd:0 Ran:3
1998 Turf 0-3: (6f 2, 7f) (gd, frm 2)
Currently fair filly. Turf high 53 (began Aug).
**J J Quinn [0-3] Mrs S Quinn.*

THEME TUNE BHB 58f **RR 67f** 5079[22]
3 b f Dilum (USA) 7.1f **(56)** - Souadah (USA) (General Holme (USA)) 5.7f **(63)**
Form - 0
Record 1998 - 1st:0 2nd:0 3rd:0 Ran:1
Pre1998 - 1st:0 2nd:1 3rd:0 Ran:3
Win Prizemoney £0 *Total Prizemoney* £869
1998 Turf 0-1: (7f) (sft)
Light-framed, average filly. **Dr J D Scargill [0-4] G W Cossey.*

THE MUNRO'S BHB 58f57a **RR 59f 57a** 3140[9]
4 b c Safawan 6.6f **(60)** - Some Cherry (Some Hand) 9f **(50)**
Form - 28108040
Record 1998 - 1st:1 2nd:1 3rd:0 Ran:8
Pre1998 - 1st:0 2nd:0 3rd:0 Ran:3
Win Prizemoney £2,486 *Total Prizemoney* £3,391
Wins * **1998** May Ayr (GD) H 8f 51 66 <
1998 Turf 1-7: (7f 2, 8f 1-2, 9f 3) (sft, g-s 1-2, gd 3, frm) 1998 AW 0-1: (7f) (Fibr)
Unfurnished, fair colt, effective 8f, acted on g-s, liked left handed tracks, liked tight tracks. Turf high 66 - 1st of 11 from Rosa Royale (29 May Ayr RF 1564). Comfortable winner at Ayr in May, but beaten on both sand debut and when upped in class on turf afterwards. (DEAD) **J S Goldie [1-11] Aberdeenshire Racing Club.*

THE NEGOTIATOR BHB 55f **RR 56?f** 2887[P]
4 ch g Nebos (GER) - Baie des Anges (Pas de Seul) 9.1f **(67)**
Form - P
Record 1998 - 1st:0 2nd:0 3rd:0 Ran:1
Pre1998 - 1st:0 2nd:1 3rd:0 Ran:8
Win Prizemoney £0 *Total Prizemoney* £1,321

1998 Turf 0-1: (8f) (frm)
Leggy, fair gelding, effective 7f, acts on g-f.
**M J Heaton-Ellis [0-13] F J Sainsbury.*

THE NOBLEMAN (USA) RR 40f 4823[22]

2 b c Quiet American (USA) 7.9f **(60)** - Furajet (USA) (The Minstrel (CAN)) 10f **(72)**
Form - 0
Record 1998 - 1st:0 2nd:0 3rd:0 Ran:1
1998 Turf 0-1: (8f) (frm)
Currently moderate colt.
**Sir Michael Stoute [0-1] Maktoum Al Maktoum.*

THE NURSE (IRE) BHB 67f RR 69f 4703[8]

2 b f Mujadil (USA) 7.7f **(70)** -Nurse Jo (USA)(J O Tobin(USA)) 9.4f **(67)**
Form - 46142308
Record 1998 - 1st:1 2nd:1 3rd:1 Ran:8
Win Prizemoney £2,500 *Total Prizemoney* £5,200
Wins * 1998 Aug Redcar (G-F) S 6f 64 <
1998 Turf 1-7: (5f 2, 6f 1-5) (g-s, gd 3, frm 1-3) 1998 AW 0-1: (5f) (Fibr)
Average filly, effective 6f, acts on gd to frm, best on frm. Turf high 69 - 2nd of 11 getting 15lb from Riverblue (28 Aug Thirsk 6f frm RF 3937) - also 1st of 18 from Bodfari Anna (8 Aug Redcar RF 3475).
**K A Ryan [1-6] Clayton Bigley Partnership Ltd (from R J R Williams [0-2] Jun 1998).*

THE PEDALER ROCHE (IRE) BHB 44f RR 39f 1943[8]

3 b g Project Manager 7.2f **(47)** -Southern Song (Persian Bold) 9.3f **(66)**
Form - 0658
Record 1998 - 1st:0 2nd:0 3rd:0 Ran:4
1998 Turf 0-3: (7f 2, 9f) (hvy, sft, gd) 1998 AW 0-1: (8f) (Fibr)
Very moderate gelding. Turf high 39.
**R Craggs [0-4] Ten For Sport Partnership.*

THE PRESIDENT BHB 63f RR 69f 4252[14]

3 b c Yaheeb (USA) - When The Saints (Bay Express) 7.1f **(60)**
Form - 64650
Record 1998 - 1st:0 2nd:0 3rd:0 Ran:5
Win Prizemoney £0 *Total Prizemoney* £247
1998 Turf 0-5: (10f, 11f, 12f 3) (g-s, gd, g-f, frm 2)
Strong, average colt. Turf high 69 - 4th of 10 to Rainbow High (17 Jun Ripon 12f gd RF 2076). **J L Eyre [0-5] North Racing Partnership.*

THE PUZZLER (IRE) BHB 80f RR 81f 4749[17]

7 b or br g Sharpo 7.5f **(68)** - Enigma (Ahonoora) 8.1f **(73)**
Form - 64306000000
Record 1998 - 1st:0 2nd:0 3rd:1 Ran:11
Pre1998 - 1st:3 2nd:2 3rd:3 Ran:21
Win Prizemoney £26,301 *Total Prizemoney* £36,504
Wins * 1997 Oct Newmar (G-S) H 5f 98 99
* 1996 Oct Newbur (SFT) H 6f 100 106 <
1998 Turf 0-11: (5f 3, 6f 8) (gd 10, g-f)
Decent gelding, effective 5 to 6f, acts on gd, has worn blinkers. Turf high 99. He ran moderately in 1998 apart from when third at York in the spring. Best on soft ground.
**B W Hills [2-25] Lady Richard Wellesley (from M Kauntze in IRE [0-3] Jun 1995).*

THE QUARE FELLOW (IRE) RR 65f 4395[5]

2 ch c Elmaamul (USA) 8.1f **(70)** - Bizarre Lady (Dalsaan) 9.8f **(64)**
Form - 5
Record 1998 - 1st:0 2nd:0 3rd:0 Ran:1
1998 Turf 0-1: (8f) (frm)
Currently average colt. **J H M Gosden [0-1] David Simpson.*

THE RAIN LADY BHB 65f RR 59f 4088[5]

2 b f Lugana Beach 7f **(63)** - Rain Splash **(18f)** (Petong) 6.6f **(58)**
Form - 075
Record 1998 - 1st:0 2nd:0 3rd:0 Ran:3
1998 Turf 0-3: (5f 3) (gd 2, frm)
Currently fair filly. Turf high 59. **R Hollinshead [0-3] John Smallman.*

THE REAL MCCOY BHB 35a RR 41f 4409[14]

4 b g Deploy 11.4f **(67)** - Mukhayyalah (Dancing Brave (USA)) 8.4f **(76)**
Form - 150
Record 1998 - 1st:1 2nd:0 3rd:0 Ran:3
Pre1998 - 1st:0 2nd:0 3rd:0 Ran:4
Win Prizemoney £1,735 *Total Prizemoney* £1,735
Wins * 1998 *Jan Southw (STD) H 12f 35 43* <
1998 Turf 0-2: (10f 2) (gd, g-f) 1998 AW 1-1: (12f 1-1) (Fibr 1-1)
Scopey, moderate gelding. Turf high 41. (1st run) - 1st of 14 giving 6lb to Record Lover (30 Jan Southwell RF 0186).
**Mrs J R Ramsden [1-6] M R Charlton (from Ian Williams [0-1] Jly 1997).*

THERE BE DEMONS (USA) BHB 90f RR 77f 3066[4]

3 b c Devil's Bag (USA) 9.3f **(73)** - Krisalya (Kris) 9.5f **(73)**
Form - 44
Record 1998 - 1st:0 2nd:0 3rd:0 Ran:2
Pre1998 - 1st:0 2nd:0 3rd:0 Ran:1
Win Prizemoney £0 *Total Prizemoney* £801
1998 Turf 0-2: (7f, 10f) (gd 2)
Scopey, currently above-average colt. Turf high 77.
**G Wragg [0-3] A E Oppenheimer.*

THERHEA (IRE) BHB 85f RR 88f 4744[2]

5 b g Pennine Walk 8.9f **(64)** - Arab Art (Artaius (USA)) 9f **(69)**
Form - 431023505532
Record 1998 - 1st:1 2nd:2 3rd:3 Ran:12
Pre1998 - 1st:3 2nd:5 3rd:2 Ran:29
Win Prizemoney £22,679 *Total Prizemoney* £51,219
Wins * 1998 Apr Sandow (SFT) 8.1f 86 <
* 1997 Spt York (SFT) H 7.9f 76 81
* 1997 Jun Nottin (GD) H 8.2f 62 65
* 1996 Apr Newbur (G-S) H 8f 77 81+
1998 Turf 1-12: (7f, 8f 1-10, 9f) (sft 1-3, g-s, gd 6, g-f, frm)
Useful gelding, effective 8 to 9f, best at 8f, acts on sft to frm, best on gd, has worn blinkers, likes left handed tracks, does well at Goodwood and likes Newbury. Turf high 88 - 3rd of 13 getting 11lb from For Your Eyes Only (4 Jly Sandown 8f gd RF 2548) - also 1st of 10 giving 2lb to Mr Majica (24 Apr Sandown RF 0847). Consistent. He ran consistently well for most of the season, including a game victory at Sandown in April and good efforts in some hot handicaps. A mile in soft ground suits him admirably.
**B R Millman [4-41] Ray Gudge, Colin Lew Calvert.*

THERMOPYLAE RR 75f 4998[2]

2 b f Tenby 10.4f **(76)** - Tamassos (Dance In Time (CAN)) 8.9f **(59)**
Form - 42
Record 1998 - 1st:0 2nd:1 3rd:0 Ran:2
Win Prizemoney £0 *Total Prizemoney* £1,295
1998 Turf 0-2: (7f, 8f) (sft, g-s)
Currently above-average filly. Turf high 75 (began Oct) - 2nd of 10 to City of Gold (26 Oct Lingfield 7f sft RF 4998).
**P F I Cole [0-2] Athos Christodoulou.*

THE ROBE BHB 43f35a RR 44f 35a 4588[2]

3 b f Robellino (USA) 9.5f **(68)** -Outward's Gal (Ashmore (FR)) 8.5f **(65)**
Form - 6440063632
Record 1998 - 1st:0 2nd:1 3rd:2 Ran:7
Pre1998 - 1st:0 2nd:0 3rd:0 Ran:5
Win Prizemoney £0 *Total Prizemoney* £1,673
1998 Turf 0-6: (11f, 12f 2, 14f, 16f 2) (gd, g-f 2, frm 3) 1998 AW 0-1: (16f) (Equi)
Scopey, moderate filly, effective 7 to 8f, acts on g-f - acts on Equi. Turf high 44 (began Jly).
**A W Carroll [0-7] Gordon Day (from B J Meehan [0-5] Dec 1997).*

THE SANDFLY (USA) BHB 84f RR 90f 2139[2]

3 b f Sheikh Albadou 9.2f **(75)** - Sweet Simone (FR) (Green Dancer (USA)) 10.3f **(74)**
Form - 172
Record 1998 - 1st:1 2nd:1 3rd:0 Ran:3
Win Prizemoney £5,754 *Total Prizemoney* £8,777
Wins * 1998 Apr Newmar (SFT) 8f 89 <
1998 Turf 1-3: (8f 1-2, 12f) (sft 1-1, gd, g-f)
Workmanlike, currently useful filly. Turf high 90 - 2nd of 6 getting 3lb from Rachaels North (20 Jun Ascot 8f g-f RF 2139) - also 1st of 19 getting 5lb from Alyriva (15 Apr Newmarket RF 0701). Won the Wood Ditton with a bit to spare in soft ground, but seemed not to stay twelve furlongs next time. Just touched off on her third start back at a mile. **B W Hills [1-3] Mrs J M Corbett.*

THESEUS (IRE) RR 71f 4959[6]
2 b c Danehill (USA) 9.1f **(79)** - Graecia Magna (USA) (Private Account (USA)) 8.5f **(74)**
Form - 066
Record 1998 - 1st:0 2nd:0 3rd:0 Ran:3
1998 Turf 0-3: (7f 2, 8f) (gd, frm 2)
Currently above-average colt. Turf high 71 (began Aug).
**Sir Michael Stoute [0-3] Athos Christodoulou.*

THE SHADOW RR 77f 4884[3]
2 br c Polar Falcon (USA) 9f **(74)** - Shadiliya (Red Alert) 7.6f **(66)**
Form - 03
Record 1998 - 1st:0 2nd:0 3rd:1 Ran:2
Win Prizemoney £0 *Total Prizemoney* £456
1998 Turf 0-2: (7f, 8f) (g-s, gd)
Currently above-average colt. Turf high 77 (began Spt) - 3rd of 13 getting 2lb from Spitzbergen (20 Oct Folkestone 7f g-s RF 4884).
**D W P Arbuthnot [0-2] Mrs B J Lee.*

THE SILK THIEF RR 4990[12]
3 b g Thowra (FR) 11.2f **(47)** - Fine N Fancy (Netherkelly) 5.6f **(46)**
Form - 00
Record 1998 - 1st:0 2nd:0 3rd:0 Ran:2
1998 Turf 0-2: (7f, 8f) (sft, gd)
Workmanlike, currently very poor gelding. (began Oct).
**J R Jenkins [0-2] Mrs M A Bateley.*

THE STAGER (IRE) BHB 49f56a **RR 41f 56a** 4874[7]
6 b g Danehill (USA) 9.1f **(79)** - Wedgewood Blue (USA) (Sir Ivor) 10.2f **(70)**
Form - 56087
Record 1998 - 1st:0 2nd:0 3rd:0 Ran:5
Pre1998 - 1st:2 2nd:2 3rd:1 Ran:20
Win Prizemoney £7,779 *Total Prizemoney* £11,995
Wins * 1996 May Newmar (GD) 7f 75 <
* 1995 Apr Beverl (G-F) H 7.5f 65 67
1998 Turf 0-1: (7f) (frm) 1998 AW 0-4: (7f, 8f 3) (Equi 2, Fibr 2)
Fair gelding, has worn blinkers. AW high 51. Consistent.
**J R Jenkins [2-29] Julian Duncan.*

THE SWALLOW BHB 33f **RR** 492[15]
3 b g Runnett 6.7f **(56)** - Minshaar (Jalmood (USA)) 10.1f **(52)**
Form - 000
Record 1998 - 1st:0 2nd:0 3rd:0 Ran:3
1998 Turf 0-1: (5f) (g-s) 1998 AW 0-2: (5f, 7f) (Fibr 2)
Neat, currently very poor gelding. **K S Bridgwater [0-3] Aubrey Ellis.*

THE TAYSIDE FARMER RR 28f 4671[24]
2 ch c Bay Tern (USA) - Polly Potter (Pollerton)
Form - 00
Record 1998 - 1st:0 2nd:0 3rd:0 Ran:2
1998 Turf 0-2: (7f, 8f) (gd, g-f)
Currently little account colt. Turf high 28 (began Spt).
**D Moffatt [0-2] Tayside Farming.*

THE THRUSTER BHB 67f **RR 67f** 4475[10]
3 b g Elmaamul (USA) 8.1f **(70)** -Moon Spin(Night Shift (USA)) 7.2f **(69)**
Form - 7210
Record 1998 - 1st:1 2nd:1 3rd:0 Ran:4
Pre1998 - 1st:0 2nd:1 3rd:0 Ran:4
Win Prizemoney £3,546 *Total Prizemoney* £5,382
Wins * 1998 Aug Lingfi (G-F) H 7.6f 60 67 <
1998 Turf 1-4: (7f 2, 8f 1-2) (gd, g-f 2, frm 1-1)
Scopey, average gelding, effective 7 to 8f, best at 8f, acts on g-f to frm, best on frm, often wears blinkers (extremely effectively). Turf high 67 (began Jly) - 1st of 16 getting 5lb from Caversfield (25 Aug Lingfield RF 3846).
**M P Tregoning [1-4] J R Wallis (from Major W R Hern [0-4] Spt 1997).*

THE VALE (IRE) BHB 28f **RR 27f** 4403[10]
6 b g Satco (FR) 14.2f **(57)** - Lady Kasbah (Lord Gayle (USA)) 8.8f **(62)**
Form - 7500
Record 1998 - 1st:0 2nd:0 3rd:0 Ran:4
Pre1998 - 1st:0 2nd:0 3rd:0 Ran:4
Win Prizemoney £0 *Total Prizemoney* £244
1998 Turf 0-4: (11f 2, 12f, 13f) (sft 2, g-s, g-f)
Little account gelding, has worn blinkers. Turf high 27.
**L R Lloyd-James [0-1] Willie Smith (from R M McKellar [0-14] May 1998).*

THE WAD BHB 53f55a **RR 58f 55a** 536[7]
5 b g Emarati (USA) 6.6f **(63)** -Fair Melys (FR)(Welsh Pageant) 10f **(65)**
Form - 7
Record 1998 - 1st:0 2nd:0 3rd:0 Ran:1
Pre1998 - 1st:3 2nd:4 3rd:4 Ran:37
Win Prizemoney £8,554 *Total Prizemoney* £14,296
Wins 1997 Jly Catter (G-F) C 6f 58
1996 Jly Ripon (GD) H 6f 66 67 <
1996 Apr Nottin (G-F) S 6.1f 53
1998 Turf 0-1: (5f) (gd)
Fair gelding, effective 5 to 6f, best at 5f, acts on gd to g-f, best on g-f, has worn blinkers.
**John Berry [0-1] Miss J V May (from D Nicholls [3-32] Spt 1997).*

THE WHISTLING TEAL RR 63f 5137[6]
2 b c Rudimentary (USA) 8.2f **(66)** - Lonely Shore (Blakeney) 10.5f **(64)**
Form - 66
Record 1998 - 1st:0 2nd:0 3rd:0 Ran:2
1998 Turf 0-2: (7f 2) (g-s, gd)
Currently average colt. Turf high 63 (began Oct).
**J G Smyth-Osbourne [0-2] Mrs F A Veasey.*

THE WILD WIDOW BHB 64f **RR 70f** 4670[10]
4 gr f Saddlers' Hall (IRE) 10.5f **(65)** - No Cards (No Mercy) 8f **(61)**
Form - 3425600
Record 1998 - 1st:0 2nd:1 3rd:1 Ran:7
Pre1998 - 1st:0 2nd:1 3rd:0 Ran:1
Win Prizemoney £0 *Total Prizemoney* £3,474
1998 Turf 0-7: (8f 2, 10f 4, 12f) (sft, g-s 2, gd, g-f 2, frm)
Workmanlike, above-average filly, effective 8 to 10f, best at 10f, acts on g-s to frm. Turf high 70 - 2nd of 12 getting 14lb from Brandon Jack (8 Jun Windsor 10f g-f RF 1820).
**J M P Eustace [0-8] Mrs A Johnstone.*

THE WOODCOCK BHB 64f **RR 74f** 4955[12]
3 b g Handsome Sailor 6.6f **(53)** - Game Germaine (Mummy's Game) 8.2f **(60)**
Form - 604816000
Record 1998 - 1st:1 2nd:0 3rd:0 Ran:9
Pre1998 - 1st:0 2nd:0 3rd:0 Ran:1
Win Prizemoney £2,616 *Total Prizemoney* £2,616
Wins * 1998 Aug Nottin (G-F) 6.1f 74 <
1998 Turf 1-9: (5f, 6f 1-6, 7f 2) (g-s, gd 1-4, g-f 2, frm 2)
Leggy, above-average gelding, effective 6f, acts on gd to frm. Turf high 79 - 4th of 15 giving 5lb to Coronet (8 May Nottingham 6f frm RF 1109) - also 1st of 13 giving 5lb to Glowing (12 Aug Nottingham RF 3582). Becoming disappointing.
**J Hanson [1-9] Mrs J R Woodhouse (from B W Hills [0-1] Oct 1997).*

THE WYANDOTTE INN BHB 51f58a **RR 42df 58a** 4635[8]
4 ch g Ballacashtal (CAN) 7.9f **(51)** - Carolynchristensen (Sweet Revenge) 7.2f **(54)**
Form - 688730645308
Record 1998 - 1st:0 2nd:0 3rd:2 Ran:12
Pre1998 - 1st:3 2nd:9 3rd:3 Ran:27
Win Prizemoney £10,857 *Total Prizemoney* £22,436
Wins 1997 *Feb Lingfi (STD) H 7f 77 79* <
1997 *Jan Wolver (STD) H 6f 72 73*
1996 *Dec Lingfi (STD) 6f 70*
1998 Turf 0-2: (6f 2) (g-s, frm) 1998 AW 0-10: (6f 3, 7f 5, 8f, 9f) (Equi 5, Fibr 5)
Fair gelding, effective 6 to 7f, best at 7f, acts on frm - acts on AW, has worn blinkers, favours tight tracks. Turf high 7. AW high 59.
**R J Hodges [0-9] Mrs Anna Sanders (from K R Burke [0-3] Feb 1998).*

THICKET BHB 93f **RR 93f** 3232[9]
2 ch f Wolfhound (USA) 7.3f **(71)** - Sharpthorne (USA) (Sharpen Up) 8.3f **(67)**
Form - 510
Record 1998 - 1st:1 2nd:0 3rd:0 Ran:3
Win Prizemoney £3,176 *Total Prizemoney* £3,176
Wins * 1998 Jly Bath (GD) 5.1f 93+ <
1998 Turf 1-3: (5f 1-2, 6f) (gd 1-2, g-f)
Currently useful filly. Turf high 93 (began Jly) - 1st of 9 getting

11lb from Red Delirium (21 Jly Bath RF 2970). A good winner at Bath before disappointing in the Molecomb Stakes on a softer surface. **R Charlton [1-3] K Abdulla.*

THIEF OF HEARTS (IRE) RR 104f
1737a[9]

3 c In The Wings 11.2f **(77)** - Love Smitten (CAN) (Key To The Mint (USA)) 9.4f **(75)**
Form - 50
1998 Turf 0-2: (11f, 12f) (sft, gd)
Currently very useful colt. Turf high 104. He is a half-brother to Swain but, unlike that horse, did not progress from two to three. Very disappointing in the French Derby, he has a large question mark against his name. **A Fabre in FR [1-3] Sheikh Mohammed.*

THIHN (IRE) RR 61f
4935[7]

3 ch g Machiavellian (USA) 9.8f **(83)** - Hasana (USA) (Private Account (USA)) 8.5f **(74)**
Form - 07
Record 1998 - 1st:0 2nd:0 3rd:0 Ran:2
1998 Turf 0-2: (8f 2) (gd, g-f)
Workmanlike, currently average gelding. Turf high 61 (began Oct). **N E Berry [0-2] Messrs P Cowan, S Daniels & B Beale.*

THINK AGAIN (IRE) BHB 35f RR 42df
629[12]

4 b g Long Pond - Either Or (Boreen (FR))
Form - 0
Record 1998 - 1st:0 2nd:0 3rd:0 Ran:1
Pre1998 - 1st:0 2nd:0 3rd:0 Ran:5
1998 Turf 0-1: (16f) (gd)
Leggy, moderate gelding. **R Craggs [0-7] Ray Craggs.*

THIRD COUSIN (IRE) BHB 67f73a RR 71f 73a
4957[4]

3 b c Distant Relative 7f **(69)** - Queen Caroline (USA) (Chief's Crown (USA)) 9.8f **(72)**
Form - 006486467234
Record 1998 - 1st:0 2nd:1 3rd:1 Ran:12
Pre1998 - 1st:1 2nd:0 3rd:1 Ran:4
Win Prizemoney £2,277 *Total Prizemoney* £5,666
Wins * 1997 Oct Folkes (GD) 5f 82 <
1998 Turf 0-10: (7f 4, 8f 5, 10f) (sft, gd 5, g-f, frm 3) 1998 AW 0-2: (6f, 9f) (Fibr 2)
Lengthy, above-average colt, effective 5 to 6f, acts on gd - acts on Fibr. Turf high 72. AW high 67. Ran a useful race over a mile at the July Meeting, but generally disappointed. **M J Heaton-Ellis [1-16] P G Lowe.*

THIRD PARTY BHB 52f40a RR 51f 40a
443[8]

4 gr f Terimon 8.7f **(58)** - Party Game (Red Alert) 7.6f **(66)**
Form - 008
Record 1998 - 1st:0 2nd:0 3rd:0 Ran:3
Pre1998 - 1st:1 2nd:0 3rd:2 Ran:13
Win Prizemoney £2,862 *Total Prizemoney* £4,791
Wins * 1997 Jun Bright (FRM) 6f 66 <
1998 AW 0-3: (6f, 7f 2) (Equi 2, Fibr)
Unfurnished, fair filly, effective 6f, acts on frm, likes left handed tracks, likes tight tracks. AW high 37. **S Dow [1-16] Mrs G R Smith.*

THISONESFORALICE BHB 28f31a RR 22f 31a
2369[6]

10 b g Lochnager 6.9f **(50)** - Bamdoro (Cavo Doro) 10.6f **(57)**
Form - 6876
Record 1998 - 1st:0 2nd:0 3rd:0 Ran:4
Pre1998 - 1st:2 2nd:6 3rd:4 Ran:42
Win Prizemoney £5,147 *Total Prizemoney* £12,774
Wins 1994 Jly Mussel (G-F) H 8.1f 35 38 <
1998 Turf 0-4: (12f 2, 14f, 16f) (gd 3, frm)
Little account gelding, effective 11 to 15f, acts on g-f to frm, best on g-f, has worn blinkers, favours tight tracks. Turf high 22. Becoming disappointing.
**J S Goldie [0-26] Mrs Alice Goldie (from A Harrison [2-33] May 1995).*

THISTLE PARK BHB 72f RR 73f
1254[20]

3 ch g Selkirk (USA) 7.9f **(76)** - Kimberley Park (Try My Best (USA)) 7.6f **(67)**
Form - 0
Record 1998 - 1st:0 2nd:0 3rd:0 Ran:1
Pre1998 - 1st:0 2nd:0 3rd:2 Ran:3
Win Prizemoney £0 *Total Prizemoney* £1,065
1998 Turf 0-1: (6f) (gd)
Leggy, above-average gelding. **T D Barron [0-4] Mrs J Hazell.*

THOMAS HENRY (IRE) BHB 72f RR 72f
4732[15]

2 br c Petardia 8.2f **(58)** - Hitopah (Bustino) 10.4f **(64)**
Form - 074840
Record 1998 - 1st:0 2nd:0 3rd:0 Ran:6
Win Prizemoney £0 *Total Prizemoney* £367
1998 Turf 0-6: (6f, 7f 4, 8f) (g-s, gd 2, g-f, frm 2)
Above-average colt, has worn blinkers. Turf high 72 (began Jly). **J S Moore [0-6] Ernie Houghton.*

THOMAS JO (USA) RR
1913a[3]

3 gr c Strong Performance (USA) - Advanette (USA) (Iron Constitution (USA))
Form - 3
1998 AW 0-1: (12f) (Dirt)
Currently very high-class colt. (1st run) - 3rd of 11 to Victory Gallop (6 Jun Belmont Park 12f Dirt RF 1913a). He finished a close third in a desperate finish to the Belmont Stakes. **J Jerkens in USA [0-1] Earle I Mack & Team Valor.*

THOMAS O'MALLEY BHB 45f RR 49f
3571[7]

3 ch g Wing Park - Martini Time (Ardoon) 7.3f **(53)**
Form - 0007
Record 1998 - 1st:0 2nd:0 3rd:0 Ran:4
Pre1998 - 1st:0 2nd:0 3rd:0 Ran:4
1998 Turf 0-4: (8f 3, 12f) (gd, g-f 3)
Lengthy, moderate gelding. Turf high 49. Becoming disappointing. **R J O'Sullivan [0-8] C A Washbourn.*

THORNABY GIRL (IRE) BHB 68f RR 61f
1271[3]

2 b f Fayruz 6.6f **(63)** - Anita's Love (IRE) (Anita's Prince)
Form - 13
Record 1998 - 1st:1 2nd:0 3rd:1 Ran:2
Win Prizemoney £2,784 *Total Prizemoney* £3,152
Wins * 1998 May Mussel (GD) C 5f 61 <
1998 Turf 1-2: (5f 1-2) (gd 1-1, g-f)
Currently average filly. Turf high 61 - also 1st of 6 giving 6lb to Red Symphony (6 May Musselburgh RF 1063). **T D Barron [1-2] Dave Scott.*

THORNBY PARK BHB 85f RR 86f
5150[8]

4 b f Unfuwain (USA) 11.4f **(74)** - Wantage Park (Pas de Seul) 9.1f **(67)**
Form - 1875318
Record 1998 - 1st:2 2nd:0 3rd:1 Ran:7
Pre1998 - 1st:1 2nd:2 3rd:0 Ran:11
Win Prizemoney £17,550 *Total Prizemoney* £23,045
Wins * 1998 Oct Doncas (SFT) H 14.6f 82 86 <
*** 1998** May Salisb (G-S) H 14.1f 80 86 <
* 1997 Jun Goodwo (G-S) H 14f 78 86+
1998 Turf 2-7: (14f 1-3, 15f 1-1, 16f 2, 17f) (g-s, gd 1-4, frm 1-2)
Workmanlike, useful filly, effective 12 to 16f, best at 14f, acts on g-s to frm, best on gd, has worn blinkers, prefers tight tracks, does well at Goodwood. Turf high 86 - 1st of 16 giving 18lb to Burundi (23 Oct Doncaster RF 4958) - also 1st of 6 giving 4lb to Moon Colony (3 May Salisbury RF 1003). Consistent. **J L Dunlop [3-18] Appleby Lodge Stud.*

THORNEYHOLME BOY BHB 42f RR 46f
3996[15]

2 gr g Terimon 8.7f **(58)** - Real Silver (Silly Season) 9.7f **(56)**
Form - 060
Record 1998 - 1st:0 2nd:0 3rd:0 Ran:3
1998 Turf 0-3: (5f, 6f 2) (gd 3)
Currently moderate gelding. Turf high 46 (began Aug). **K A Ryan [0-3] Mrs Candice Reilly.*

THORNTOUN BELLE (IRE) BHB 49f RR 15f
2246[10]

3 b f Rainbows For Life (CAN) 9.3f **(64)** - Manzala (USA) (Irish River (FR)) 8.6f **(78)**
Form - 003000
Record 1998 - 1st:0 2nd:0 3rd:1 Ran:6
Pre1998 - 1st:0 2nd:0 3rd:0 Ran:1
Win Prizemoney £0 *Total Prizemoney* £421
1998 Turf 0-6: (6f, 8f 2, 9f 2, 11f) (g-s, gd 2, g-f 2, frm)
Unfurnished, poor filly, effective 8f, acts on frm. Turf high 49 - 3rd of 20 getting 16lb from Shamwari Song (21 May Newcastle 8f frm

RF 1368). **J S Goldie [0-7] W M Johnstone.*

THORNTOUN GOLD (IRE) BHB 50f **RR 55f** 4767[7]

2 ch f Lycius (USA) 8.8f **(71)** -Gold Braisim(IRE)(Jareer (USA)) 5.9f **(75)**
Form - 547477
Record 1998 - 1st:0 2nd:0 3rd:0 Ran:6
Win Prizemoney £0 *Total Prizemoney* £210
1998 Turf 0-6: (6f 2, 7f 2, 8f 2) (sft, gd 2, g-f 3)
Fair filly, effective 8f, acts on gd. Turf high 55 - 4th of 16 to Family Tree (17 Spt Ayr 8f gd RF 4320).
**J S Goldie [0-3] W M Johnstone (from M Johnston [0-3] Jly 1998).*

THORNTOUN HOUSE (IRE) BHB 25f30a **RR 29f 30a** 4254[11]

5 b g Durgam (USA) 12.3f **(53)** - Commanche Song (Commanche Run) 8.5f **(58)**
Form - 0
Record 1998 - 1st:0 2nd:0 3rd:0 Ran:1
Pre1998 - 1st:0 2nd:0 3rd:0 Ran:4
1998 Turf 0-1: (16f) (frm)
Little account gelding, has worn blinkers.
**J S Goldie [0-8] W M Johnstone.*

THOUGHTFUL KATE BHB 40f46a **RR 47f 46a** 2691[3]

4 b f Rock Hopper 10.6f **(54)** - Beloved Visitor (USA) (Miswaki (USA)) 9f **(81)**
Form - 44025003
Record 1998 - 1st:0 2nd:1 3rd:1 Ran:8
Pre1998 - 1st:0 2nd:0 3rd:0 Ran:4
Win Prizemoney £0 *Total Prizemoney* £1,333
1998 Turf 0-2:(10f 2)(gd, frm) 1998 AW 0-6:(8f, 9f, 10f 4)(Equi 4, Fibr 2)
Moderate filly, effective 9f, acts on gd, has worn blinkers. Turf high 28. AW high 42.
**B Palling [0-8] David L'Estrange (from J G Burns in IRE [0-4] Oct 1997).*

THRASHING BHB 70f **RR 65f** 4008[5]

3 b c Kahyasi 12.9f **(74)** - White-Wash (Final Straw) 7.9f **(64)**
Form - 34005
Record 1998 - 1st:0 2nd:0 3rd:1 Ran:5
Pre1998 - 1st:0 2nd:0 3rd:0 Ran:1
Win Prizemoney £0 *Total Prizemoney* £1,566
1998 Turf 0-5: (8f, 12f 2, 14f 2) (gd 3, g-f, frm)
Average colt, often wears blinkers. Turf high 76. He faced some impossible tasks in his early starts, but has yet to really show much. **C E Brittain [0-6] Saeed Manana.*

THREADNEEDLE (USA) BHB 62f80a **RR 55f 80a** 4704[19]

5 b g Danzig Connection (USA) 8.2f **(75)** - Sleeping Beauty (Mill Reef (USA)) 10.5f **(78)**
Form - 45117820000060
Record 1998 - 1st:2 2nd:1 3rd:0 Ran:13
Pre1998 - 1st:1 2nd:0 3rd:0 Ran:4
Win Prizemoney £9,839 *Total Prizemoney* £11,632
Wins **1998** *Feb Lingfi (SLW) C 10f 78+*
1998 *Feb Lingfi (STD) C 10f 81* <
1996 Spt Newbur (G-F) 8f 75
1998 Turf 0-5: (8f 3, 9f, 12f) (gd 2, g-f 2, frm) 1998 AW 2-8: (8f 2, 9f, 10f 2-4, 12f) (Equi 2-4, Fibr 4)
Decent gelding, effective 10f, - acts on Equi, has worn blinkers, likes left handed tracks, likes tight tracks. Turf high 55. AW high 83 - 2nd of 9 giving 17lb to Digpast (19 Mar Lingfield 10f Equi RF 0447) - also 1st of 9 giving 14lb to Private Despatch (3 Feb Lingfield RF 0209). Appreciated the drop into claiming company when twice winning easily on the Lingfield Equitrack in February. He has struggled since in handicaps, though he was unfortunate to meet Digpast on a going day at the same track in March. Has changed hands, and has shown very little on turf.
**K R Burke [0-10] Nigel Shields (from Lord Huntingdon [3-7] Feb 1998).*

THREAT RR 97?f 3658[3]

2 br c Zafonic (USA) 9f **(83)** - Prophecy (IRE) **(99f)** (Warning)
Form - 13
Record 1998 - 1st:1 2nd:0 3rd:1 Ran:2
Win Prizemoney £6,872 *Total Prizemoney* £7,705
Wins * 1998 Jly Goodwo (G-S) 6f 97+ <
1998 Turf 1-2: (6f 1-2) (gd 1-1, g-f)
Currently very useful colt. Turf high 97 (1st run) (began Jly) - 1st of 5 from Belasco (29 Jly Goodwood RF 3207). He won a very controversial maiden at Glorious Goodwood, missing the break badly, but given a second bite of the cherry when the field was recalled after three furlongs. Showed a smart turn of foot in the re-run, but the form should be taken with a pinch of salt, and he was beaten fair and square at Ripon. **J H M Gosden [1-2] K Abdulla.*

THREE ANGELS (IRE) RR 79f 4751[3]

3 b g Houmayoun (FR) 7.1f **(79)** -Mullaghroe (Tarboosh (USA)) 10f **(55)**
Form - 80115323463
Record 1998 - 1st:2 2nd:1 3rd:3 Ran:11
Pre1998 - 1st:0 2nd:1 3rd:1 Ran:3
Win Prizemoney £5,648 *Total Prizemoney* £11,754
Wins * 1998 Jun Haydoc (GD) H 7.1f 61 75 <
*** 1998** May Folkes (G-F) 7f 70
1998 Turf 2-11: (6f, 7f 2-8, 9f, 12f) (gd 2-7, frm 4)
Scopey, above-average gelding, effective 6 to 7f, best at 7f, acts on gd to frm, best on gd, has worn blinkers, excels at Sandown. Turf high 79 - 6th of 11 giving 3lb to Easter Ogil (15 Spt Sandown 7f gd RF 4267) - also 1st of 16 giving 12lb to Bollin Ethos (4 Jun Haydock RF 1712). Consistent. Got off the mark in a Folkestone maiden in May, and followed up in a Haydock handicap. He was unable to complete the hat-trick on faster ground and in a better race, but has continued to perform with credit.
**M H Tompkins [2-14] Bernard Bloom.*

THREE ARCH BRIDGE BHB 76f69a **RR 77f 69a** 254[6]

6 ch m Sayf El Arab (USA) 8.2f **(57)** -Alanood (Northfields(USA)) 9f **(72)**
Form - 0F2856
Record 1998 - 1st:0 2nd:1 3rd:0 Ran:4
Pre1998 - 1st:13 2nd:10 3rd:8 Ran:69
Win Prizemoney £45,647 *Total Prizemoney* £63,217
Wins * 1997 May Ripon (G-F) H 8f 70 77 <
* 1997 May Beverl (SFT) H 8.5f 65 73
* 1997 Mar Newcas (G-F) H 7f 64 66
* 1997 *Feb Southw (STD) H 8f 66 69*
* 1997 *Jan Southw (STD) H 8f 60 66*
* 1996 Jun Carlis (FRM) H 8f 57 69
* 1996 Jun Beverl (G-F) H 7.5f 57 68
* 1996 Jun Hamilt (GD) H 9.2f 57 65
* 1995 Spt Beverl (GD) H 8.5f 58 65
* 1995 Jly Hamilt (FRM) H 9.2f 55 61
* 1995 Jly Hamilt (FRM) 8.3f 57
* 1995 *Apr Southw (STD) H 7f 54 59+*
* 1994 May Hamilt (FRM) 6f 50
1998 AW 0-4: (7f, 8f, 9f 2) (Fibr 4)
Above-average mare, effective 8 to 9f, best at 8f, acts on g-s to frm - acts on Fibr, mostly wears blinkers (effectively), and excels at Wolverhampton. AW high 71 - 5th of 8 getting 5lb from Tough Leader (4 Feb Wolverhampton 9f Fibr RF 0221). She gained five victories in the first half of 1997, but did not show show the same level of form last season when returning after a six-month break.
**M Johnston [13-73] R N Pennell.*

THREE CHEERS (IRE) RR 117f 5055a[5]

4 b br g Slip Anchor 12.7f **(75)** - Three Tails (Blakeney) 10.5f **(64)**
Form - 8434455
Record 1998 - 1st:0 2nd:0 3rd:1 Ran:7
Pre1998 - 1st:3 2nd:1 3rd:1 Ran:6
Win Prizemoney £38,818 *Total Prizemoney* £79,828
Wins * 1997 Oct Longch (GD) G3 15f 110 <
* 1997 Jly Newmar (G-F) L 14.8f 97
* 1997 May Newmar (G-F) 14f 78
1998 Turf 0-7: (16f 4, 18f, 20f 2) (hvy, sft, g-s, gd 3, g-f)
Scopey, high-class gelding, effective 15 to 20f, best at 16f, acts on g-s to g-f, mostly wears blinkers (effectively), likes Newmarket. Turf high 117 - 3rd of 16 to Kayf Tara (18 Jun Ascot 20f g-s RF 2085). He looked a progressive young stayer in 1997, but did not manage a victory last term. His best effort was when a close third in the Ascot Gold Cup, and though he finished well behind Double Trigger at Goodwood, he ran a bit of a moody race and showed similar tendencies in his subsequent starts.
**J H M Gosden [3-13] Sheikh Mohammed Al Maktoum.*

THREE FOR A POUND BHB 63f60a **RR 63f 60a** 5098[12]

4 b g Risk Me (FR) 8f **(53)** - Lompoa (Lomond (USA)) 8.8f **(65)**
Form - 4177672085020
Record 1998 - 1st:1 2nd:2 3rd:0 Ran:13

Pre1998 - 1st:2 2nd:0 3rd:1 Ran:12
Win Prizemoney £10,547 *Total Prizemoney* £13,340
Wins **1998** Apr Thirsk (G-S) H 8f 63 68
1997 Jly Catter (SFT) H 7f 63 66
1997 Mar Catter (GD) 6f 74 <
1998 Turf 1-13: (7f 2, 8f 1-6, 9f 2, 10f 3) (g-s 1-2, gd 6, g-f 2, frm 3)
Workmanlike, average gelding, effective 6 to 8f, acts on sft to frm, has worn blinkers, likes right handed tracks, likes tight tracks. Turf high 68 - 1st of 18 giving 6lb to Finisterre (17 Apr Thirsk RF 0734).
·Don Enrico Incisa [0-4] Mrs Christine Cawley (from J A Glover [3-21] Spt 1998).

THREE GREEN LEAVES (IRE) BHB 99f **RR 84+f** 5077[4]
2 ch f Environment Friend 7.5f **(67)** - Kick the Habit (Habitat) 9.4f **(70)**
Form - 8U321311114
Record **1998** - 1st:5 2nd:1 3rd:2 Ran:11
Win Prizemoney £40,207 *Total Prizemoney* £42,902
Wins **· 1998** Oct Pontef (SFT) L 8f 84 <
· 1998 Oct Cork (G-S) 7f 84+
· 1998 Spt Newcas (GD) 8f 84+
· 1998 Jly Beverl (G-F) 7.5f 77
· 1998 Jun Beverl (GD) 7.5f 77
1998 Turf 5-11: (5f 2, 6f 2, 7f 3-4, 8f 2-2, 10f) (sft, g-s, gd 2-4, frm 3-4, hrd)
Decent filly, effective 7 to 10f, acts on g-s to frm, best on gd. Turf high 84 - 4th of 7 getting 3lb from Adnaan (31 Oct Newmarket 10f g-s RF 5077) - also 1st of 7 getting 2lb from Swallow Flight (19 Oct Pontefract RF 4870). Improving. She has not looked back since being stepped up to seven furlongs plus, winning five times, the last of which was quite a valuable event at Cork in October when she won very easily. May have been over the top when a little disappointing in the Zetland Stakes at the end of the season.
·M Johnston [5-11] R N Pennell.

THREE LEADERS (IRE) BHB 51f **RR 42f** 4622[13]
2 ch g Up and At 'em - Wolviston (Wolverlife) 9.3f **(54)**
Form - 080
Record **1998** - 1st:0 2nd:0 3rd:0 Ran:3
1998 Turf 0-3: (5f 2, 6f) (gd, g-f, frm)
Currently moderate gelding. Turf high 42. *·D Nicholls [0-3] R J H Ltd.*

THREEPLAY (IRE) BHB 43f38a **RR 57f 38a** 408[10]
4 b c Mac's Imp (USA) 5.6f **(54)** - Houwara (IRE) (Darshaan) 9.9f **(84)**
Form - 750
Record **1998** - 1st:0 2nd:0 3rd:0 Ran:2
Pre1998 - 1st:0 2nd:2 3rd:2 Ran:16
Win Prizemoney £0 *Total Prizemoney* £2,574
1998 AW 0-2: (5f, 6f) (Equi, Fibr)
Neat, fair colt, effective 5f, - acts on Fibr, has worn blinkers. AW high 26. Becoming disappointing.
·J Akehurst [0-18] The For Fore Four Partnership.

THREE RING (USA) RR 5163a[3]
2 ch f Notebook (USA) - My Nichole (USA) 00
Form - 3
1998 AW 0-1: (9f) (Dirt)
Currently Pattern-class filly. (1st run) - 3rd of 11 to Silverbulletday (7 Nov Churchill Downs 9f Dirt RF 5163a). Ran a fine race when third to Silverbulletday in the Breeders' Cup Juvenile Fillies.
·E Plesa Jr in USA [0-1] Schwartz, Hauman & Dahlman.

THREE STAR RATED (IRE) BHB 76f **RR 81f** 1703[8]
3 b f Pips Pride 6.7f **(70)** - Preponderance (IRE) (Cyrano de Bergerac) 6f **(68)**
Form - 78
Record **1998** - 1st:0 2nd:0 3rd:0 Ran:2
Pre1998 - 1st:1 2nd:1 3rd:0 Ran:4
Win Prizemoney £3,015 *Total Prizemoney* £3,891
Wins 1997 Spt Mussel (G-F) H 5f 70 81+ <
1998 Turf 0-2: (5f, 6f) (gd, g-f)
Workmanlike, decent filly, effective 5f, acts on g-f to frm. Turf high 69. *·G Holmes [0-2] Miss J Salt (from T D Barron [1-3] Spt 1997).*

THREE TENNERS BHB 47f47a **RR 52f 47a** 4401[11]
3 b f Distinctly North (USA) 7.4f **(63)** - Hollia (Touch Boy) 5f **(66)**
Form - 70208000
Record **1998** - 1st:0 2nd:1 3rd:0 Ran:8
Pre1998 - 1st:1 2nd:0 3rd:0 Ran:8
Win Prizemoney £2,542 *Total Prizemoney* £3,652
Wins 1997 Jly Haydoc (G-S) S 6f 68 <
1998 Turf 0-7: (5f 2, 6f 2, 7f, 8f, 10f) (gd 2, g-f 3, frm 2) 1998 AW 0-1: (7f) (Fibr)
Scopey, fair filly, effective 6f, acts on gd, often wears blinkers. Turf high 52. *·D Nicholls [0-7] N J Wilson (from J Berry [1-9] May 1998).*

THRIFTY BHB 65f **RR 67f** 4411[10]
2 b f Night Shift (USA) 8.1f **(73)** - Gena Ivor (USA) (Sir Ivor) 10.2f **(70)**
Form - 000
Record **1998** - 1st:0 2nd:0 3rd:0 Ran:3
1998 Turf 0-3: (6f, 7f, 8f) (gd, g-f, frm)
Currently average filly. Turf high 67 (began Spt).
·M J Ryan [0-3] A J Hollis.

THROUGH THE RYE RR 85f 5065[5]
2 ch c Sabrehill (USA) 8.5f **(64)** - Baharlilys (Green Dancer (USA)) 10.3f **(74)**
Form - 45
Record **1998** - 1st:0 2nd:0 3rd:0 Ran:2
Win Prizemoney £0 *Total Prizemoney* £1,156
1998 Turf 0-2: (7f, 8f) (gd, g-f)
Currently useful colt. Turf high 85 (began Spt).
·B W Hills [0-2] W J Gredley.

THRUST BHB 87f **RR 89f** 4196[2]
2 br c Prince Sabo 6.6f **(64)** - La Piaf (FR) (Fabulous Dancer (USA)) 9.4f **(70)**
Form - 272
Record **1998** - 1st:0 2nd:2 3rd:0 Ran:3
Win Prizemoney £0 *Total Prizemoney* £2,598
1998 Turf 0-2: (6f, 7f) (gd, g-f) 1998 AW 0-1: (6f) (Fibr)
Currently useful colt. Turf high 89 (began Aug) - 2nd of 11 to Beat All (10 Spt Chepstow 7f gd RF 4196). *·W R Muir [0-3] Mrs H Levy.*

THUNDER CAVE (IRE) RR 91f 4791a[5]
2 ch g Perugino (USA) - Perfect Chance (Petorius) 7.3f **(61)**
Form - 53355
1998 Turf 0-5: (6f 3, 7f, 8f) (g-s 3, gd, hrd)
Useful gelding, has worn blinkers. Turf high 91 - 3rd of 15 giving 3lb to The Bomber Liston (15 Aug Curragh 6f hrd RF 3716a).
·D K Weld in IRE [0-5] Mrs D K Weld.

THUNDER DRAGON (IRE) BHB 100f **RR 99f** 4225[8]
2 b c Zieten (USA) - Kiriyaki (USA) (Secretariat (USA)) 9f **(79)**
Form - 21038
Record **1998** - 1st:1 2nd:1 3rd:1 Ran:5
Win Prizemoney £4,466 *Total Prizemoney* £18,849
Wins **· 1998** May Windso (G-F) 5f 85+ <
1998 Turf 1-5: (5f 1-2, 6f 2, 7f) (gd 2, g-f, frm 1-2)
Very useful colt. Turf high 99 - 3rd of 8 to Josr Algarhoud (19 Aug York 6f frm RF 3755). He looked a useful early two-year-old but was disappointing in the Coventry. Off the track until finishing a good third in the Gimcrack, keeping on really well after being outpaced early, he then finished a disappointing last in the Champagne Stakes. He will continue his career in the States, having made 70,000 gns at Tattersalls in October.
·R Hannon [1-5] Lucayan Stud.

THUNDERING PAPOOSE BHB 34f **RR 27f** 2185[8]
3 b f Be My Chief (USA) 10.2f **(62)** - Thunder Bug (USA) (Secreto (USA)) 8.7f **(72)**
Form - 08
Record **1998** - 1st:0 2nd:0 3rd:0 Ran:2
Pre1998 - 1st:0 2nd:0 3rd:0 Ran:3
1998 Turf 0-2: (12f, 14f) (g-f, frm)
Little account filly. Turf high 15.
·N A Graham [0-2] C N & Mrs J C Wright (from A P James [0-3] Spt 1997).

THUNDER SKY BHB 100f **RR 85f** 4542[12]
2 b c Zafonic (USA) 9f **(83)** - Overcast (IRE) (Caerleon (USA)) 8.6f **(71)**
Form - 5540
Record **1998** - 1st:0 2nd:0 3rd:0 Ran:4
Win Prizemoney £0 *Total Prizemoney* £4,453

1998 Turf 0-4: (7f 4) (g-f 2, frm 2)
Useful colt. Turf high 85 (began Aug). Showed promise on his first start, and had little chance in the Solario on his second. He can win a race if not too highly tried. **C E Brittain [0-4] Ali Saeed.*

THWAAB BHB 58f53a **RR 63f 53a** 4751[14]
6 b g Dominion 8.9f **(65)** - Velvet Habit (Habitat) 9.4f **(70)**
Form - 0781270040
Record 1998 - 1st:1 2nd:1 3rd:0 Ran:10
Pre1998 - 1st:3 2nd:4 3rd:5 Ran:36
Win Prizemoney £14,210 *Total Prizemoney* £27,374
Wins * 1998 Jly Doncas (FRM) H 7f 56 58
* 1996 Aug Redcar (G-F) H 6f 59 61 <
* 1996 Jly Ayr (G-F) H 6f 52 56
* 1996 Jun Ayr (G-F) H 6f 45 50
1998 Turf 1-10: (6f 4, 7f 1-5, 8f) (gd 5, g-f 2, frm 1-3)
Average gelding, effective 6 to 8f, best at 6f, acts on gd to frm, best on frm, often wears blinkers, excels at Redcar. Turf high 63 - 2nd of 14 getting 20lb from Royal Mark (27 Jly Newcastle 7f gd RF 3140) - also 1st of 17 getting 3lb from Maiteamia (16 Jly Doncaster RF 2851). **F Watson [4-46] F Watson.*

THWING BHB 43f **RR 24f** 2520[7]
3 b f Presidium 7.5f **(56)** - Swinging Baby (Swing Easy (USA)) 6.5f **(55)**
Form - 07
Record 1998 - 1st:0 2nd:0 3rd:0 Ran:2
Pre1998 - 1st:0 2nd:0 3rd:0 Ran:1
1998 Turf 0-2: (5f, 7f) (gd, g-f)
Tall, currently moderate filly. Turf high 24.
**M W Easterby [0-3] R H Mason.*

TIBBI BLUES BHB 24f **RR 23f** 3579[7]
11 b m Cure The Blues (USA) 7.1f **(38)** - Tiberly (FR) (Lyphard (USA)) 9.9f **(72)**
Form - 6607
Record 1998 - 1st:0 2nd:0 3rd:0 Ran:4
Pre1998 - 1st:0 2nd:2 3rd:2 Ran:10
Win Prizemoney £0 *Total Prizemoney* £2,040
1998 Turf 0-4: (8f, 9f, 11f 2) (gd 4)
Little account mare, effective 7f, acts on sft, favours tight tracks. Turf high 23.
**J S Goldie [0-9] Miss Barbara Spittal (from W Storey [0-4] Aug 1996).*

TIBBIE SHIELS BHB 52f **RR 44f** 4623[7]
2 b f Deploy 11.4f **(67)** - Bajina (Dancing Brave (USA)) 8.4f **(76)**
Form - 6847
Record 1998 - 1st:0 2nd:0 3rd:0 Ran:4
Win Prizemoney £0 *Total Prizemoney* £206
1998 Turf 0-4: (7f 4) (gd, g-f, frm 2)
Moderate filly. Turf high 44 (began Jly).
**Mrs J R Ramsden [0-4] Ronald Thorburn.*

TIBETAN BHB 70f **RR 70f** 1210[4]
6 b g Reference Point 12f **(66)** -Winter Queen (Welsh Pageant) 10f **(65)**
Form - 4
Record 1998 - 1st:0 2nd:0 3rd:0 Ran:1
Pre1998 - 1st:0 2nd:2 3rd:0 Ran:5
Win Prizemoney £0 *Total Prizemoney* £3,555
1998 Turf 0-1: (14f) (gd)
Above-average gelding. **Lady Herries [3-20] Mrs Wendy Brown.*

TICKA TICKA TIMING BHB 30f32a **RR 15f 32a** 597[7]
5 b g Timeless Times (USA) 6.1f **(56)** - Belltina (Belfort (FR)) 6.8f **(63)**
Form - 064557
Record 1998 - 1st:0 2nd:0 3rd:0 Ran:4
Pre1998 - 1st:1 2nd:0 3rd:2 Ran:21
Win Prizemoney £2,489 *Total Prizemoney* £3,224
Wins * 1995 *Jly Southw (STD) S 6f 69?* <
1998 AW 0-4: (5f, 6f 3) (Fibr 4)
Very moderate gelding, effective 5f, - acts on Fibr, has worn blinkers, likes left handed tracks, likes tight tracks. AW high 38. Inconsistent. **B W Murray [1-25] Mrs M Lingwood.*

TICKLISH RR 69f 4835[8]
2 b f Cadeaux Genereux 7.9f **(76)** - Exit Laughing (Shaab)
Form - 36331518
Record 1998 - 1st:2 2nd:0 3rd:3 Ran:8
Win Prizemoney £6,774 *Total Prizemoney* £7,969
Wins * 1998 Spt Bright (GD) H 6f 66 69 <
*** 1998** Spt Ripon (HVY) H 6f 61 67
1998 Turf 2-8: (5f, 6f 2-5, 7f 2) (sft, g-s, gd 1-3, g-f 1-1, frm, hrd)
Average filly, effective 6f, acts on gd to g-f. Turf high 69 - 1st of 13 getting 10lb from Achilles Star (30 Spt Brighton RF 4570) - also 1st of 16 giving 1lb to Bodfari Anna (1 Spt Ripon RF 4013).
**W J Haggas [2-8] J W Bogie.*

TICK N PICK BHB 65f60a **RR 65f 60a** 4928[5]
2 br f Reprimand 8.2f **(63)** - My Preference (Reference Point) 6.8f **(70)**
Form - 005
Record 1998 - 1st:0 2nd:0 3rd:0 Ran:3
1998 Turf 0-3: (7f 2, 8f) (g-s, g-f, frm)
Currently average filly. Turf high 65 (began Spt).
**E A L Dunlop [0-3] A Burrell & P Burrell.*

TICKNTIMA BHB 48f **RR 53f** 1630[13]
4 ch g Precocious 7.2f **(54)** - Stolon Time (Good Times (ITY)) 6.6f **(54)**
Form - 600
Record 1998 - 1st:0 2nd:0 3rd:0 Ran:3
Pre1998 - 1st:0 2nd:0 3rd:1 Ran:6
Win Prizemoney £0 *Total Prizemoney* £682
1998 Turf 0-3: (8f 3) (gd 2, g-f)
Scopey, fair gelding. Turf high 53. Inconsistent.
**M D Hammond [0-12] Andy Peake.*

TIE BREAK (IRE) BHB 50f62a **RR 55f 62a** 3907[1]
3 ch g Second Set (IRE) 9.2f **(67)** - Karayasha (Posse (USA)) 8.9f **(61)**
Form - 30500311
Record 1998 - 1st:2 2nd:0 3rd:1 Ran:7
Pre1998 - 1st:0 2nd:0 3rd:1 Ran:2
Win Prizemoney £5,151 *Total Prizemoney* £5,774
Wins * 1998 Aug Mussel (GD) C 12f 52
*** 1998** Aug Leices (GD) C 10f 55 <
1998 Turf 2-7: (6f, 8f 2, 10f 1-3, 12f 1-1) (g-s, gd, g-f 1-1, frm 1-4)
Well made, average gelding, effective 5f, - acts on Fibr, often wears blinkers (extremely effectively). Turf high 55. He found his form when stepped up to middle distances, winning claimers at Leicester and Musselburgh, but does not look the most resolute of sorts. **W J Haggas [2-9] M H Wilson.*

TIEBREAKER (IRE) BHB 68f60a **RR 72f 60a** 3832[4]
3 b g Second Set (IRE) 9.2f **(67)** - Millionetta (IRE) (Danehill (USA)) 10f **(72)**
Form - 0878134
Record 1998 - 1st:1 2nd:0 3rd:1 Ran:7
Win Prizemoney £2,532 *Total Prizemoney* £2,952
Wins * 1998 Jly Nottin (G-F) 10f 68 <
1998 Turf 1-6: (8f 3, 10f 1-2, 12f) (g-s, gd 1-3, g-f, frm) 1998 AW 0-1: (8f) (Equi)
Strong, above-average gelding, effective 10 to 12f, best at 10f, acts on gd to frm. Turf high 68 - 4th of 12 giving 14lb to Norcroft Joy (24 Aug Beverley 12f g-f RF 3832) - also 1st of 7 from Ollie's Chuckle (18 Jly Nottingham RF 2927).
**N A Graham [1-7] The Tiebreakers.*

TIERGARTEN (IRE) RR 53f 4983[10]
2 b f Brief Truce (USA) 9.1f **(73)** - Lady In The Park (IRE) (Last Tycoon) 8.5f **(62)**
Form - 0
Record 1998 - 1st:0 2nd:0 3rd:0 Ran:1
1998 Turf 0-1: (8f) (g-s)
Currently fair filly. **A C Stewart [0-1] Mrs M E Domvile.*

TIERRA DEL FUEGO BHB 30f **RR 14f** 4927[14]
4 b f Chilibang 7f **(55)** - Dolly Bevan (Another Realm) 6.6f **(55)**
Form - 700
Record 1998 - 1st:0 2nd:0 3rd:0 Ran:2
Pre1998 - 1st:0 2nd:0 3rd:0 Ran:2
1998 Turf 0-2: (7f, 10f) (g-s, g-f)
Workmanlike, little account filly. Turf high 14 (began Spt).
**H J Collingridge [0-4] H J Collingridge.*

TIER WORKER BHB 80f **RR 76f** 5116[2]
2 b c Tenby 10.4f **(76)** - On the Tide **(67f)** (Slip Anchor) 9.8f **(73)**
Form - 732

Record 1998 - 1st:0 2nd:1 3rd:1 Ran:3
Win Prizemoney £0 *Total Prizemoney* £1,572
1998 Turf 0-3: (6f, 8f 2) (g-s, gd 2)
Currently above-average colt. Turf high 76 (began Oct) - 2nd of 9 to Raneen Nashwan (4 Nov Musselburgh 8f gd RF 5116).
**T D Easterby [0-3] Burke's 5th Family Settlement.*

TIE THE KNOT (AUS) RR 118f 4941a[3]

4 ch g Nassipour (USA) - Whisked (AUS) (Whiskey Road)
Form - 30
1998 Turf 0-1: (12f) (gd)
Currently high-class gelding. (1st run) - 3rd of 17 giving 4lb to Taufan's Melody (17 Oct Caulfield 12f gd RF 4941a).
**G Walter in AUS [0-1].*

TIGER GRASS (IRE) BHB 85f RR 80f 4842[4]

2 gr c Ezzoud (IRE) - Rustic Lawn (Rusticaro (FR)) 8.2f **(65)**
Form - 724
Record 1998 - 1st:0 2nd:1 3rd:0 Ran:3
Win Prizemoney £0 *Total Prizemoney* £1,520
1998 Turf 0-3: (7f 2, 8f) (g-f 2, frm)
Currently decent colt. Turf high 80 (began Spt). Runner-up in an ordinary maiden on his second start, he shapes as if needing a mile.
**W R Muir [0-3] M J Caddy.*

TIGER HILL (IRE) RR 126f 4727a[3]

3 b c Danehill (USA) 9.1f **(79)** - The Filly (GER) (Apiani (GER))
Form - 110213
1998 Turf 3-6: (8f 1-2, 10f 1-1, 12f 1-3) (hvy, sft 1-2, g-s 1-1, gd 1-2)
Top-class colt, effective 12f, acts on sft. Turf high 126 - 3rd of 14 to Sagamix (4 Oct Longchamp 12f sft RF 4727a) - also 1st of 8 getting 11lb from Caitano (6 Spt Baden-Baden RF 4219a). A very useful German performer, he won the local version of the 2000 Guineas in the spring and beat Caitano in the Grosser Preis von Baden in September. Surpassed himself with a fine third in the Arc, and remains in training at four.
**P Schiergen in GER [3-6] Baron G Von Ullmann.*

TIGER LAKE BHB 67f RR 68f 4100[5]

5 ch g Nashwan (USA) 10.3f **(79)** - Tiger Flower (Sadler's Wells (USA)) 10f **(76)**
Form - 8355
Record 1998 - 1st:0 2nd:0 3rd:1 Ran:4
Pre1998 - 1st:1 2nd:0 3rd:0 Ran:4
Win Prizemoney £4,092 *Total Prizemoney* £5,132
Wins 1996 Jun Goodwo (G-F) 12f 73 <
1998 Turf 0-4: (12f 3, 14f) (gd, g-f 3)
Average gelding. Turf high 68 (began Jly) - 3rd of 8 giving 11lb to Warning Reef (7 Aug Ascot 12f g-f RF 3430).
**S Dow [0-7] Brian Solomon and Miss Jo-Ann Wood (from S bin Suroor [1-3] Jun 1996).*

TIGER SHARK (USA) RR 72f 5015[4]

2 b c Chief's Crown (USA) 10.2f **(75)** - Life At the Top (Habitat) 9.4f **(70)**
Form - 64
Record 1998 - 1st:0 2nd:0 3rd:0 Ran:2
Win Prizemoney £0 *Total Prizemoney* £349
1998 Turf 0-2: (7f 2) (g-s, gd)
Currently above-average colt. Turf high 72 (began Oct) - 4th of 5 giving 3lb to Come What May (27 Oct Redcar 7f gd RF 5015).
**Lord Huntingdon [0-2] Henryk De Kwiatkowski.*

TIGER TALK BHB 81f RR 73f 5145[2]

2 ch c Sabrehill (USA) 8.5f **(64)** - Tebre (USA) (Sir Ivor) 10.2f **(70)**
Form - 00022
Record 1998 - 1st:0 2nd:2 3rd:0 Ran:5
Win Prizemoney £0 *Total Prizemoney* £1,714
1998 Turf 0-5: (7f 2, 8f 3) (sft, gd 2, g-f, frm)
Above-average colt. Turf high 73 (began Spt) - 2nd of 13 to Escort (7 Nov Doncaster 8f gd RF 5145).
**B W Hills [0-5] H R H Prince Fahd Salman.*

TIGGY SILVANO BHB 20f30a RR 26f 30a 4922[5]

3 b f Tigani - Infanta Maria (King of Spain) 7.8f **(52)**
Form - 05440000005
Record 1998 - 1st:0 2nd:0 3rd:0 Ran:10
Pre1998 - 1st:0 2nd:0 3rd:0 Ran:2
1998 Turf 0-6: (9f, 10f 3, 12f, 14f) (g-s 4, gd, frm) 1998 AW 0-4: (8f 2, 10f, 14f) (Equi 2, Fibr 2)
Lengthy, very moderate filly, has worn blinkers. Turf high 26. AW high 38. Inconsistent.
**M Quinn [0-11] M Quinn (from M R Channon [0-1] Jly 1997).*

TIGHTROPE BHB 68f67a RR 66f 67a 4776[15]

3 b c Alzao (USA) 9.8f **(73)** - Circus Act (Shirley Heights) 10.3f **(74)**
Form - 500
Record 1998 - 1st:0 2nd:0 3rd:0 Ran:3
Pre1998 - 1st:1 2nd:1 3rd:0 Ran:7
Win Prizemoney £3,956 *Total Prizemoney* £5,372
Wins * 1997 Oct Leices (G-F) H 8f 70 79+ <
1998 Turf 0-3: (8f, 9f, 10f) (gd 2, frm)
Workmanlike, average colt, effective 6 to 8f, acts on g-f to frm. Turf high 56.
**Sir Mark Prescott [1-10] W E Sturt.*

TIGI BHB 36f RR 36f 3749[11]

3 ch f Tigani - Molly Brazen (Risk Me (FR)) 5.9f **(53)**
Form - 400
Record 1998 - 1st:0 2nd:0 3rd:0 Ran:3
Pre1998 - 1st:0 2nd:0 3rd:0 Ran:4
1998 Turf 0-3: (5f 2, 6f) (gd 2, frm)
Leggy, very moderate filly. Turf high 36 (began Jly).
**Mrs M Reveley [0-7] Geoff Pickering.*

TIGRELLO BHB 80f RR 87f 1014[19]

4 ch c Efisio 7.7f **(69)** - Prejudice (Young Generation) 7.7f **(63)**
Form - 0
Record 1998 - 1st:0 2nd:0 3rd:0 Ran:1
Pre1998 - 1st:1 2nd:2 3rd:0 Ran:10
Win Prizemoney £3,349 *Total Prizemoney* £7,845
Wins * 1997 May Warwic (FRM) 8f 85 <
1998 Turf 0-1: (8f) (gd)
Strong, useful colt, effective 8f, acts on gd to frm.
**G Lewis [1-11] A M Al-Midani.*

TIGULLIO (IRE) BHB 71f RR 74f 4763[7]

3 b c Rainbows For Life (CAN) 9.3f **(64)** - L'Americaine (USA) (Verbatim (USA)) 8.5f **(64)**
Form - 82311207
Record 1998 - 1st:2 2nd:2 3rd:1 Ran:8
Pre1998 - 1st:0 2nd:0 3rd:0 Ran:2
Win Prizemoney £5,851 *Total Prizemoney* £8,029
Wins * **1998** Jly Lingfi (G-F) H 11.5f 62 67 <
* **1998** Jun Windso (G-F) H 11.6f 56 61
1998 Turf 2-8: (8f, 10f, 11f 1-3, 12f 1-3) (gd 4, g-f 1-1, frm 1-3)
Light-framed, above-average colt, effective 11f, acts on frm, prefers tight tracks. Turf high 74 - 2nd of 5 giving 10lb to Final Settlement (25 Jly Lingfield 11f frm RF 3111) - also 1st of 9 getting 3lb from Forest Fire (10 Jly Lingfield RF 2690). Ran a couple of good races before getting off the mark in a weakly-contested handicap at Windsor, and followed up at Lingfield the following month. Sold for 28,000 gns at Tattersalls in October.
**C F Wall [2-10] Ettore Landi.*

TIHEROS GLENN BHB 59f RR 51?f 5148[21]

2 ch c Toxotis - Warthill Girl (Anfield) 8.5f **(59)**
Form - 0740
Record 1998 - 1st:0 2nd:0 3rd:0 Ran:4
Win Prizemoney £0 *Total Prizemoney* £344
1998 Turf 0-4: (6f, 7f 2, 8f) (sft, gd, g-f 2)
Fair colt. Turf high 51 (began Jly). **D McCain [0-4] Mrs H F Mahr.*

TIJUANA RR 37f 3117[11]

2 ch f Gabitat 8.5f **(44)** - Gabibti (IRE) (Dara Monarch) 8.8f **(59)**
Form - 00
Record 1998 - 1st:0 2nd:0 3rd:0 Ran:2
1998 Turf 0-2: (5f, 6f) (gd, g-f)
Currently very moderate filly. Turf high 37 (began Jly).
**B Gubby [0-2] Brian Gubby Ltd.*

TIKOPIA BHB 59f56a RR 70f 56a 4810[5]

4 b g Saddlers' Hall (IRE) 10.5f **(65)** - Shesadelight (Shirley Heights) 10.3f **(74)**
Form - 30600475
Record 1998 - 1st:0 2nd:0 3rd:1 Ran:8

Pre1998 - 1st:1 2nd:2 3rd:2 Ran:8
Win Prizemoney £4,011 *Total Prizemoney* £8,228
Wins 1997 Spt Bath (GD) 11.7f 72 <
1998 Turf 0-7: (12f 3, 13f 2, 14f, 16f) (g-s, gd 3, g-f 2, frm) 1998 AW 0-1: (12f) (Equi)
Scopey, above-average gelding, effective 10 to 13f, best at 12f, acts on g-s to g-f, has worn blinkers, favours tight tracks, excels at Goodwood. Turf high 77 (1st run) - 3rd of 8 giving 4lb to Montecristo (28 Mar Warwick 13f g-s RF 0489).
**Mrs A J Perrett [0-7] The Tikopians (from I A Balding [1-11] Mar 1998).*

TIKOTINO BHB 57f RR 58f 4991[6]

2 ch f Mystiko (USA) 7.7f **(59)** - Tino-Ella (Bustino) 10.4f **(64)**
Form - 0876
Record 1998 - 1st:0 2nd:0 3rd:0 Ran:4
1998 Turf 0-4: (6f 3, 7f) (sft, g-f 2, frm)
Fair filly. Turf high 58 (began Aug). **J A Glover [0-4] Ted Revill.*

TILAAL (USA) BHB 43f RR 43f 3580[5]

6 ch g Gulch (USA) 9.6f **(79)** -Eye Drop (USA)(Irish River (FR))8.6f **(78)**
Form - 544457435
Record 1998 - 1st:0 2nd:0 3rd:1 Ran:9
Pre1998 - 1st:0 2nd:0 3rd:4 Ran:12
Win Prizemoney £0 *Total Prizemoney* £3,453
1998 Turf 0-9: (7f 2, 8f 5, 10f, 11f) (gd 3, g-f 2, frm 4)
Moderate gelding, effective 7 to 11f, acts on g-f to frm, best on frm, has worn blinkers, prefers left handed tracks, prefers tight tracks. Turf high 46 - 4th of 15 getting 7lb from Lucky Archer (22 May Nottingham 8f frm RF 1402). Consistent.
**M D Hammond [0-20] M D Hammond (from E A L Dunlop [0-7] Spt 1995).*

TILBURG BHB 35f40a RR 38f 40a 2656[8]

3 b f High Kicker (USA) 8.4f **(52)** -Touch My Heart(Steel Heart) 8.3f **(58)**
Form - 05425657058
Record 1998 - 1st:0 2nd:1 3rd:0 Ran:10
Pre1998 - 1st:0 2nd:0 3rd:0 Ran:9
Win Prizemoney £0 *Total Prizemoney* £488
1998 AW 0-10: (5f 4, 6f 4, 7f, 8f) (Fibr 10)
Leggy, moderate filly, effective 5f, - acts on Fibr. AW high 48.
**Mrs N Macauley [0-19] J Teasdale.*

TILER (IRE) BHB 76f80a RR 75f 80a 5096[3]

6 br g Ballad Rock 7.2f **(63)** - Fair Siobahn (Petingo) 11f **(72)**
Form - 03266807341205803
Record 1998 - 1st:1 2nd:2 3rd:3 Ran:17
Pre1998 - 1st:5 2nd:8 3rd:6 Ran:55
Win Prizemoney £40,773 *Total Prizemoney* £77,829
Wins *** 1998** Aug Cheste (G-S) H 7.6f 73 74
* 1997 Jly Ayr (G-F) H 6f 74 75
* 1996 Jly Thirsk (FRM) H 6f 78 83
* 1995 Aug York (G-F) H 6f 78 84 <
* 1994 Aug Ayr (G-S) 7f 76
* 1994 Jly Leices (G-F) 7f 69
1998 Turf 1-17: (6f 10, 7f 5, 8f 1-2) (sft, g-s, gd 1-8, g-f 3, frm 3, hrd)
Above-average gelding, effective 5 to 8f, best at 6f, acts on gd to hrd, has worn blinkers, excels at Ripon and Redcar. Turf high 80 - 3rd of 12 getting 2lb from Swino (10 May Haydock 6f gd RF 1143) - also 1st of 12 getting 1lb from Nominator Lad (22 Aug Chester RF 3801). Consistent. A front-running, fast-ground sprinter, he has messed about at the start on occasions, and lost several lengths in the process, which means he has not won as many times as he should have. Mixed form in 1998, winning at Chester in August.
**M Johnston [6-72] Mrs C Robinson.*

TILIA RR 55f 4570[12]

2 b f Primo Dominie 7.2f **(67)** -Bermuda Lily (Dunbeath (USA)) 7.8f **(70)**
Form - 0780
Record 1998 - 1st:0 2nd:0 3rd:0 Ran:4
1998 Turf 0-4: (5f, 6f 3) (g-f, frm 3)
Fair filly. Turf high 55 (began Jly).
**R Hannon [0-4] Mrs W H GibsonFleming.*

TIMAHS RR 93+f 4972[4]

2 b c Mtoto 11.5f **(71)** - Shomoose (Habitat) 9.4f **(70)**
Form - 14
Record 1998 - 1st:1 2nd:0 3rd:0 Ran:2
Win Prizemoney £5,708 *Total Prizemoney* £13,683
Wins * 1998 Spt Newmar (GD) 8f 93+ <
1998 Turf 1-2: (8f 1-2) (sft, frm 1-1)
Currently useful colt. Turf high 93 (1st run) (began Spt) - 1st of 19 from Biennale (29 Spt Newmarket RF 4541). A full brother to Shaamit, he was supplemented for the Racing Post Trophy, but appeared not to handle the testing ground and was a well-beaten fourth. Worth another chance to confirm the promise of his maiden win at Newmarket. **D R Loder [1-2] Sheikh Ahmed Al Maktoum.*

TIMBERHILL BHB 53f RR 54f 4808[5]

2 b g Aragon 7.7f **(58)** - Hability (Habitat) 9.4f **(70)**
Form - 0005
Record 1998 - 1st:0 2nd:0 3rd:0 Ran:4
1998 Turf 0-4: (5f, 6f, 8f, 10f) (gd 4)
Fair gelding. Turf high 54.
**M R Channon [0-4] Timberhill Racing Partnership.*

TIMBERVATI (USA) BHB 86f RR 81f 3209[14]

3 br f Woodman (USA) 9.7f **(77)** - Never Scheme (USA) (Never Bend) 13.1f **(70)**
Form - 170
Record 1998 - 1st:1 2nd:0 3rd:0 Ran:3
Pre1998 - 1st:0 2nd:1 3rd:0 Ran:1
Win Prizemoney £3,850 *Total Prizemoney* £4,795
Wins * 1998 Jun Yarmou (G-F) 7f 81+ <
1998 Turf 1-3: (7f 1-2, 9f) (gd, frm 1-2)
Light-framed, decent filly. Turf high 81 (1st run) - 1st of 8 from Foxie Lady (4 Jun Yarmouth RF 1721). Well held since winning her maiden, and looks harshly treated. **H R A Cecil [1-4] P D Savill.*

TIME AND AGAIN RR 54f 4873[17]

2 ch f Timeless Times (USA) 6.1f **(56)** -Busted Love (Busted) 10.2f **(61)**
Form - 0300
Record 1998 - 1st:0 2nd:0 3rd:1 Ran:4
Win Prizemoney £0 *Total Prizemoney* £461
1998 Turf 0-4: (5f, 6f 2, 8f) (g-s, gd 2, g-f)
Fair filly. Turf high 54 (began Jly). **Mrs G S Rees [0-4] A Rhodes.*

TIME CAN TELL BHB 52f60a RR 55f 60a 2192[4]

4 ch g Sylvan Express 9.6f **(45)** - Stellaris (Star Appeal) 9.6f **(65)**
Form - 54213243634
Record 1998 - 1st:1 2nd:2 3rd:3 Ran:10
Pre1998 - 1st:1 2nd:3 3rd:4 Ran:26
Win Prizemoney £4,809 *Total Prizemoney* £13,944
Wins 1998 *Jan Lingfi (STD) C 13f 69* <
1996 Oct Nottin (GD) S 8.2f 62
1998 Turf 0-1: (12f) (frm) 1998 AW 1-9: (10f, 12f 2, 13f 1-1, 16f 5) (Equi 1-5, Fibr 4)
Tall, average gelding, effective 8 to 16f, acts on g-f to frm - acts on AW, best on g-f, has worn blinkers, likes left handed tracks, likes tight tracks. AW high 69 - 1st of 5 giving 1lb to English Invader (13 Jan Lingfield RF 0079). His victory in a claimer on the Lingfield Equitrack in January ended a 22-race losing run. He often makes the frame but usually finds one or two to beat him, and may not be one to place too much faith in.
**R T Juckes [0-8] A C W Price (from J W Payne [1-3] Jan 1998).*

TIME FOR ACTION (IRE) BHB 70f RR 81f 4828a[12]

6 b g Alzao (USA) 9.8f **(73)** - Beyond Words (Ballad Rock) 7.8f **(63)**
Form - 00
Record 1998 - 1st:0 2nd:0 3rd:0 Ran:2
Pre1998 - 1st:3 2nd:1 3rd:3 Ran:26
Win Prizemoney £16,650 *Total Prizemoney* £23,341
Wins 1997 Oct Doncas (GD) C 10.3f 81
1996 Aug Pontef (G-F) H 12f 78 85 <
1994 Spt Hamilt (GD) 8.3f 82
1998 Turf 0-2: (15f, 17f) (gd, g-f)
Decent gelding, effective 10 to 12f, best at 10f, acts on gd to g-f - acts on Dirt. Turf high 23 (began Spt). Inconsistent.
**C J Mann [1-7] (from M H Tompkins [3-26] Oct 1997).*

TIME FOR LAGER BHB 43f41a RR 43f 41a 1081[4]

3 gr f Timeless Times (USA) 6.1f **(56)** -Laura Lager (Warpath)12.3f **(52)**
Form - 08434
Record 1998 - 1st:0 2nd:0 3rd:1 Ran:5
Win Prizemoney £0 *Total Prizemoney* £327

1998 Turf 0-2: (8f, 10f) (g-s 2) 1998 AW 0-3: (6f, 7f, 12f) (Fibr 3)
Leggy, moderate filly. Turf high 43. AW high 34.
**J Wharton [0-5] Mrs Vera Craggs.*

TIME IN MOTION BHB 33f35a **RR 51f 35a** 5117[7]
2 ch f Timeless Times (USA) 6.1f **(56)** - Times Zando **(13f 47a)** (Forzando) 7.6f **(59)**
Form - 000008807
Record 1998 - 1st:0 2nd:0 3rd:0 Ran:9
1998 Turf 0-5: (5f 5) (gd 3, g-f, frm) 1998 AW 0-4: (5f, 6f, 7f, 8f) (Fibr 4)
Fair filly. Turf high 51. AW high 38.
**Mrs G S Rees [0-9] Miss Judith Bond.*

TIMEKEEPER (USA) BHB 90f **RR 99f** 4707[11]
3 b br c Exbourne (USA) - Falabella (Steel Heart) 8.3f **(58)**
Form - 14040460

Record					
1998 -	1st:1	2nd:0	3rd:0	Ran:8
Pre1998 -	1st:3	2nd:2	3rd:2	Ran:9

Win Prizemoney £66,580 *Total Prizemoney* £87,810

Wins							
* **1998**	Apr	San Ro	(SFT)	L	7.5f	84	<
* 1997	Aug	Bettol	(GD)	L	7.5f	82	
* 1997	Jly	San Si	(GD)	L	7.5f	82	
* 1997	Apr	Carlis	(GD)		5f	82	

1998 Turf 1-8: (7f 2, 8f 1-5, 10f) (hvy 2, sft 1-1, gd 4, frm)
Scopey, very useful colt, effective 8f, acts on gd, prefers right handed tracks. Turf high 99 - 4th of 11 giving 21lb to French Connection (23 May Haydock 8f gd RF 1418). He enjoyed success in listed company in Italy early in the season, and appears infrequently in this country. Not easy to place, ten furlongs looks his trip. **M Bell [4-17] C M Watt.*

TIMELEE BHB 83f **RR 78f** 4405[9]
2 ch f Clantime 6.6f **(57)** - Lyndseylee (Swing Easy (USA)) 6.5f **(55)**
Form - 10
Record 1998 - 1st:1 2nd:0 3rd:0 Ran:2
Win Prizemoney £4,391 *Total Prizemoney* £4,391
Wins * **1998** Aug Thirsk (G-F) 6f 78 <
1998 Turf 1-2: (5f, 6f 1-1) (g-f, frm 1-1)
Currently above-average filly. Turf high 78 (1st run) (began Aug) - 1st of 16 from Dahshah (28 Aug Thirsk RF 3933).
**A Bailey [1-2] The Dark Horse Confederacy.*

TIME LIMIT (IRE) RR 105+f 4426a[8]
3 b f Alzao (USA) 9.8f **(73)** - Assya (Double Form) 7.3f **(58)**
Form - 10758
1998 Turf 1-5: (8f 1-4, 10f) (sft 1-1, gd 4)
Pattern-class filly. Turf high 105 (1st run) - 1st of 9 from Forget About It (11 May Killarney RF 1331a). She went from a maiden race to the Irish 1000 Guineas in one jump and never got back on an even keel. **T Stack in IRE [1-5] R E Sangster.*

TIME LOSS BHB 80f **RR 82f** 4647[9]
3 ch c Kenmare (FR) 9.6f **(76)** - Not Before Time (IRE) (Polish Precedent (USA)) 10.2f **(60)**
Form - 68100
Record 1998 - 1st:1 2nd:0 3rd:0 Ran:5
Win Prizemoney £3,566 *Total Prizemoney* £3,566
Wins * **1998** Jun Chepst (G-S) 10.2f 82 <
1998 Turf 1-5: (8f 2, 10f 1-2, 13f) (gd 1-3, g-f 2)
Scopey, decent colt. Turf high 82 - 1st of 12 from King Tango (30 Jun Chepstow RF 2396). A grandson of Time Charter, he looked to be suited by the longer trip when scoring over ten furlongs at Chepstow on his third start. Disappointed in handicap company.
**H Candy [1-5] R Barnett.*

TIME MILL RR 26f 4142[13]
2 b c Shirley Heights 12.1f **(76)** - Not Before Time (IRE) (Polish Precedent (USA)) 10.2f **(60)**
Form - 0
Record 1998 - 1st:0 2nd:0 3rd:0 Ran:1
1998 Turf 0-1: (7f) (g-f)
Currently little account colt. A half-brother to Time Loss, he is likely to come into his own as a three-year-old.
**J W Hills [0-1] George Tong.*

TIME OF NIGHT (USA) BHB 47f58a **RR 45f 58a** 4547[12]
5 gr ro m Night Shift (USA) 8.1f **(73)** - Tihama (USA) (Sassafras (FR)) 9.6f **(69)**
Form - 4202121164340

Record					
1998 -	1st:3	2nd:3	3rd:1	Ran:12
Pre1998 -	1st:0	2nd:2	3rd:4	Ran:23

Win Prizemoney £6,898 *Total Prizemoney* £14,741

Wins								
* **1998**	*Apr*	*Southw*	*(STD)*		*7f*		*60*	<
* **1998**	*Mar*	*Southw*	*(STD)*		*7f*		*60*	<
* **1998**	*Feb*	*Wolver*	*(STD)*	*H*	*7f*	*46*	*53*	

1998 Turf 0-4: (7f 2, 8f 2) (hvy, g-s, gd, frm) 1998 AW 3-8: (7f 3-5, 8f 3) (Fibr 3-8)
Average filly, effective 7 to 8f, best at 7f, acts on gd - acts on Fibr, has worn blinkers, likes left handed tracks, likes tight tracks. Turf high 45. AW high 60 - 1st of 13 getting 1lb from U-No-Harry (6 Apr Southwell RF 0574) - also 1st of 9 getting 1lb from C-Harry (17 Mar Southwell RF 0438). She had plenty of chances to break her maiden, but it took her a long time to do it, eventually getting off the mark in a modest maiden handicap on the Wolverhampton Fibresand in February. She has gained two further victories in limited stakes at Southwell since, but has needed Fallon to be at his strongest in order to achieve them.
**J L Eyre [3-15] J L Eyre (from R Guest [0-20] Jun 1997).*

TIME ON MY HANDS RR 56f 5115[5]
2 b g Most Welcome 8.6f **(66)** - Zareeta (Free State) 8.7f **(61)**
Form - 005
Record 1998 - 1st:0 2nd:0 3rd:0 Ran:3
1998 Turf 0-3: (6f 2, 7f) (gd 2, g-f)
Currently fair gelding. Turf high 56 (began Spt).
**C W Thornton [0-3] Guy Reed.*

TIME OUT BHB 39f **RR 37f** 4865[5]
3 ch f Timeless Times (USA) 6.1f **(56)** -Tangalooma (Hotfoot) 10.5f **(59)**
Form - 50005
Record 1998 - 1st:0 2nd:0 3rd:0 Ran:5
1998 Turf 0-3: (6f, 7f, 8f) (g-s, g-f, frm) 1998 AW 0-2: (7f 2) (Fibr 2)
Very moderate filly. Turf high 37 (began Spt). AW high 37 (began Aug). **G M Moore [0-5] Mrs D N B Pearson.*

TIME PROJECT (IRE) BHB 55f **RR 65f** 896[10]
4 b f Project Manager 7.2f **(47)** - Bright Era (Artaius (USA)) 9f **(69)**
Form - 0

Record					
1998 -	1st:0	2nd:0	3rd:0	Ran:1
Pre1998 -	1st:1	2nd:0	3rd:2	Ran:9

Win Prizemoney £8,220 *Total Prizemoney* £9,028
Wins 1997 Jly Down R (G-F) H 10f 58 65 <
1998 Turf 0-1: (12f) (g-s)
Average filly, effective 8 to 10f, best at 10f, acts on sft to frm, has worn blinkers. Inconsistent.
**C R Barwell [0-5] Lady Maria Coventry (from J S Bolger in IRE [1-9] Jly 1997).*

TIMES O'WAR (USA) BHB 63f **RR 67f** 4961[19]
3 ch g Lord At War (ARG) 6.6f **(67)** - Sun Bird (USA) (Arctic Tern (USA)) 8.9f **(69)**
Form - 604451700
Record 1998 - 1st:1 2nd:0 3rd:0 Ran:9
Win Prizemoney £2,290 *Total Prizemoney* £2,788
Wins * **1998** Aug Haydoc (G-S) S 8.1f 64+ <
1998 Turf 1-9: (7f 3, 8f 1-5, 10f) (sft, gd 3, g-f 1-2, frm 3)
Unfurnished, average gelding, effective 8f, acts on g-f to frm. Turf high 67 - also 1st of 10 giving 5lb to Susy Wells (6 Aug Haydock RF 3408). **T D Easterby [1-9] Times of Wigan.*

TIME TEMPTRESS BHB 60f **RR 62f** 5094[4]
2 b f Timeless Times (USA) 6.1f **(56)** - Tangalooma (Hotfoot) 10.5f **(59)**
Form - 85744724
Record 1998 - 1st:0 2nd:1 3rd:0 Ran:8
Win Prizemoney £0 *Total Prizemoney* £748
1998 Turf 0-7:(5f 3, 6f, 7f 2, 8f) (gd 4, g-f, frm 2) 1998 AW 0-1:(5f) (Fibr)
Average filly, effective 7 to 8f, acts on gd to g-f. Turf high 62 (began Jly) - 4th of 22 getting 10lb from Seren Hill (2 Nov Redcar 8f gd RF 5094). **G M Moore [0-8] Middleham Racing Bureau/G Heap.*

TIME TO FLY BHB 50f80a **RR 36f 80a** 1579[10]
5 b g Timeless Times (USA) 6.1f **(56)** - Dauntless Flight (Golden Mallard) 5.7f **(38)**
Form - 5211122400

Record	1998 -	1st:3	2nd:2	3rd:0	Ran:8
	Pre1998 -	1st:2	2nd:3	3rd:3	Ran:26

Win Prizemoney £11,146 *Total Prizemoney* £17,944

Wins									
	* 1998	Jan	Lingfi	(STD)	H	6f	68	72	<
	* 1998	Jan	Wolver	(STD)	H	5f	52	70	
	* 1998	Jan	Wolver	(STD)	H	6f	52	61	
	* 1997	Jun	Southw	(STD)	H	6f	42	46	
	* 1997	Apr	Wolver	(STD)	H	5f	32	43	

1998 Turf 0-1:(5f) (g-s) 1998 AW 3-7:(5f 1-3, 6f 2-4) (Equi 1-1, Fibr 2-6)

Useful gelding, effective 5 to 6f, - acts on Fibr, often wears blinkers (extremely effectively), prefers left handed tracks, prefers tight tracks, excels at Wolverhampton. AW high 85 - 2nd of 8 to Double-O (25 Feb Wolverhampton 5f Fibr RF 0360). Started off 1998 in particularly fine form with victories over five and six furlongs on both Fibresand and Equitrack. He is very difficult to catch if able to dominate, but struggles a bit if taken on.

**B W Murray [5-34] B Murray.*

TIME TO HUNT BHB 45f **RR 41f** 4677[28]

3 gr c Timeless Times (USA) 6.1f **(56)** - Hunting Gold (Sonnen Gold) 6.6f **(47)**

Form - 800

Record	1998 -	1st:0	2nd:0	3rd:0	Ran:3
	Pre1998 -	1st:0	2nd:0	3rd:0	Ran:2

1998 Turf 0-3: (6f, 7f 2) (sft, g-f 2)

Moderate colt. Turf high 33. **B W Murray [0-5] Miss N A Harrod.*

TIME TO TANGO BHB 58f **RR 61f** 4864[7]

5 b m Timeless Times (USA) 6.1f **(56)** -Tangalooma (Hotfoot) 10.5f **(59)**

Form - 062023200417087

Record	1998 -	1st:1	2nd:3	3rd:1	Ran:15
	Pre1998 -	1st:2	2nd:1	3rd:2	Ran:14

Win Prizemoney £8,952 *Total Prizemoney* £16,119

Wins									
	* 1998	Spt	Nottin	(GD)	H	6.1f	56	61	
	* 1996	Jly	Carlis	(FRM)	H	5f	65	68	<
	* 1996	Jun	Mussel	(G-F)		5f		49	

1998 Turf 1-14: (5f 3, 6f 1-11) (sft, gd 1-4, g-f 2, frm 7) 1998 AW 0-1: (6f) (Fibr)

Average filly, effective 6f, acts on gd to frm. Turf high 61 - 1st of 20 getting 1lb from Broadway Melody (14 Spt Nottingham RF 4260).

**G M Moore [3-29] Mrs D N B Pearson.*

TIME TO WYN BHB 61f **RR 64f** 4873[9]

2 b c Timeless Times (USA) 6.1f **(56)** -Wyn-Bank (Green God) 9.6f **(68)**

Form - 8676130

Record	1998 -	1st:1	2nd:0	3rd:1	Ran:7

Win Prizemoney £2,530 *Total Prizemoney* £3,055

Wins									
	* 1998	Spt	Beverl	(G-F)	SH	7.5f	52	57	<

1998 Turf 1-6:(6f, 7f 1-4, 8f)(gd 3, g-f 2, frm 1-1) 1998 AW 0-1:(7f) (Fibr)

Average colt, effective 7f, acts on g-f to frm, prefers tight tracks. Turf high 64 - 3rd of 20 getting 19lb from Pepperdine (4 Oct Warwick 7f g-f RF 4643) - also 1st of 17 getting 6lb from Swiss Toni (16 Spt Beverley RF 4300). **J G FitzGerald [1-7] Michael Ng.*

TIME ZONE **RR 87f** 5077[3]

2 b c Shirley Heights 12.1f **(76)** - Forthwith **(94f)** (Midyan (USA)) 6f **(60)**

Form - 23

Record	1998 -	1st:0	2nd:1	3rd:1	Ran:2

Win Prizemoney £0 *Total Prizemoney* £3,489

1998 Turf 0-2: (10f 2) (g-s, gd)

Currently useful colt. Turf high 87 (began Oct) - 3rd of 7 getting 3lb from Adnaan (31 Oct Newmarket 10f g-s RF 5077).

**C E Brittain [0-2] Wyck Hall Stud.*

TINA HEIGHTS **RR 71+f** 2832[1]

3 b f Shirley Heights 12.1f **(76)** - Catina (Nureyev (USA)) 8.7f **(78)**

Form - 1

Record	1998 -	1st:1	2nd:0	3rd:0	Ran:1

Win Prizemoney £3,533 *Total Prizemoney* £3,533

Wins								
	* 1998	Jly	Sandow	(GD)	10f		71	<

1998 Turf 1-1: (10f 1-1) (g-f 1-1)

Scopey, currently above-average filly. (1st run) - 1st of 8 from Key Academy (15 Jly Sandown RF 2832). Recovered from a tardy start to win a Sandown maiden on her sole run.

**J R Fanshawe [1-1] Mrs James McAllister.*

TINA'S ROYALE BHB 70f **RR 74f** 4796[3]

2 b f Prince Sabo 6.6f **(64)** - Aventina (Averof) 8.2f **(62)**

Form - 05633

Record	1998 -	1st:0	2nd:0	3rd:2	Ran:5

Win Prizemoney £0 *Total Prizemoney* £1,080

1998 Turf 0-5: (5f 4, 6f) (sft, g-s, gd, g-f, frm)

Above-average filly. Turf high 74 - 3rd of 13 to Inkberry (2 Oct Lingfield 5f g-s RF 4610).

**H Candy [0-5] Wickfield Stud and Hartshill Stud.*

TINA'S TUNE RR 3885[7]

3 b f Turbo Speed - Tina's Song (Tina's Pet) 6.8f **(59)**

Form - 7

Record	1998 -	1st:0	2nd:0	3rd:0	Ran:1

1998 Turf 0-1: (12f) (gd)

Small, currently very poor filly.

**B Mactaggart [0-1] Miss Shelley Johnstone.*

TINDAYA BHB 33f27a **RR 31f 27a** 2727[7]

3 b g Polar Falcon (USA) 9f **(74)** - Flitcham (Elegant Air) 13.2f **(61)**

Form - 8467

Record	1998 -	1st:0	2nd:0	3rd:0	Ran:4
	Pre1998 -	1st:0	2nd:0	3rd:0	Ran:4

Win Prizemoney £0 *Total Prizemoney* £236

1998 Turf 0-2: (12f, 13f) (gd, frm) 1998 AW 0-2: (9f, 12f) (Fibr 2)

Light-framed, very moderate gelding. Turf high 31. Inconsistent.

**P D Evans [0-8] J R Bostock.*

TIN DRUM (IRE) **RR 39f** 4058[11]

2 b c Roi Danzig (USA) 10.5f **(62)** - Triumphant (Track Spare) 8.8f **(62)**

Form - 00

Record	1998 -	1st:0	2nd:0	3rd:0	Ran:2

1998 Turf 0-2: (7f 2) (frm 2)

Currently very moderate colt. Turf high 39 (began Aug).

**R Hannon [0-2] Michael Pescod.*

TINKER AMELIA BHB 46a **RR 101f 46a** 5169a[3]

6 b m Damister (USA) 9.1f **(66)** - Miss Primula (Dominion) 8.5f **(63)**

Form - 3838040005223

1998 Turf 0-13: (5f 8, 6f 5) (hvy 2, sft 2, g-s 2, gd 6, g-f)

Very useful mare, effective 5 to 6f, best at 6f, acts on sft to gd, best on sft, has worn blinkers. Turf high 101 - 2nd of 9 getting 12lb from Burden Of Proof (17 Oct Curragh 6f gd RF 4907a).

**J G McDonnell in IRE [4-38] J G McDonnell (from W R Muir [0-5] Mar 1995).*

TINKER OSMASTON BHB 58f **RR 60f** 4128[12]

7 br m Dunbeath (USA) 9.9f **(53)** - Miss Primula (Dominion) 8.5f **(63)**

Form - 000323377560

Record	1998 -	1st:0	2nd:1	3rd:3	Ran:12
	Pre1998 -	1st:5	2nd:6	3rd:3	Ran:54

Win Prizemoney £15,617 *Total Prizemoney* £29,044

Wins								
	* 1997	Jun	Windso	(G-S)	H	6f	58	64
	1995	Oct	Chepst	(G-S)	H	5.1f	65	70
	1995	May	Bath	(G-F)	H	5.7f	60	62

1998 Turf 0-12: (5f 3, 6f 9) (sft, g-s, gd 2, g-f 3, frm 5)

Average mare, effective 5 to 6f, best at 6f, acts on g-s to frm, has worn blinkers, and excels at Windsor. Turf high 60 - 3rd of 19 giving 7lb to Carlton (22 Jun Windsor 6f g-f RF 2180). Consistent. She often makes the frame in modest sprint handicaps, but does not win very often. She is probably better suited by six furlongs than five these days, and appreciates a bit of cut in the ground.

**R J Hodges [1-22] John Luff (from M S Saunders [2-27] May 1997).*

TINKER'S SURPRISE (IRE) BHB 40f46a **RR 44f 46a** 4543[9]

4 b g Cyrano de Bergerac 7.3f **(58)** - Lils Fairy (Fairy King (USA)) 7.7f **(59)**

Form - 60478508220

Record	1998 -	1st:0	2nd:2	3rd:0	Ran:11
	Pre1998 -	1st:1	2nd:3	3rd:3	Ran:22

Win Prizemoney £3,460 *Total Prizemoney* £8,652

Wins								
1996	Jun	Goodwo	(G-F)	S	5f		69	<

1998 Turf 0-7: (5f 7) (g-s, gd 3, g-f 2, frm) 1998 AW 0-4: (5f 2, 6f 2) (Fibr 4)

Unfurnished, fair gelding, effective 5f, acts on g-f - acts on Fibr, has worn blinkers. Turf high 44 - 4th of 12 getting 21lb from Broadstairs Beauty (1 Jun Thirsk 5f g-f RF 1633). AW high 52

(began Jly) - 2nd of 8 getting 5lb from Pride of Brixton (7 Aug Wolverhampton 5f Fibr RF 3453).
**J Balding [0-22] Classic Racing (from B J Meehan [1-11] Spt 1996).*

TINKLERS FOLLY BHB 43f35a RR 46f 35a 3571[9]

6 ch g Bairn (USA) 9.4f **(55)** -Lucky Straw(Tumble Wind (USA))7.5f **(57)**
Form - 8060540

Record	**1998** -	1st:0	2nd:0	3rd:0	Ran:7
	Pre1998 -	1st:5	2nd:3	3rd:4	Ran:39

Win Prizemoney £14,754 *Total Prizemoney* £20,402

Wins	1996	Aug	Newcas	(G-F)	H	7f	63	61	<
	1996	Jun	Carlis	(FRM)	H	6.9f	50	60	
	1996	Jun	Mussel	(FRM)	H	8.1f	50	56	
	1996	Apr	Mussel	(GD)	H	7.1f	46	52	
	1995	Jly	Mussel	(FRM)	H	8.1f	41	52	

1998 Turf 0-5: (7f, 8f, 10f 2, 12f) (gd, g-f 3, frm) 1998 AW 0-2: (7f 2) (Equi, Fibr)
Moderate gelding, effective 8f, acts on g-f, has worn blinkers. Turf high 46. AW high 23. He looks to be very much on the decline.
**G G Margarson [0-7] William Hattersley (from R M Whitaker [0-11] Oct 1997).*

TIPPERARY SUNSET (IRE) BHB 62f RR 64f 5147[3]

4 gr g Red Sunset 9f **(57)** - Chapter And Verse (Dancers Image (USA)) 9.3f **(71)**
Form - 0850417250333

Record	**1998** -	1st:1	2nd:1	3rd:3	Ran:13
	Pre1998 -	1st:4	2nd:1	3rd:2	Ran:12

Win Prizemoney £17,554 *Total Prizemoney* £22,504

Wins	* **1998**	Aug	Hamilt	(SFT)	H	8.3f	54	55	
	* 1997	Nov	Doncas	(G-S)	H	8f	56	64	<
	* 1997	Oct	Newmar	(G-F)	H	9f	54	58	
	* 1997	Aug	Ripon	(G-F)	H	10f	41	48	
	* 1997	Aug	Pontef	(G-F)	H	8f	35	44	

1998 Turf 1-13: (7f 2, 8f 1-7, 9f 2, 10f 2) (sft, g-s 1-4, gd 4, g-f, frm 2, hrd)
Scopey, average gelding, effective 7 to 10f, best at 8f, acts on sft to frm, excels at Doncaster and does well at Pontefract. Turf high 64 - 3rd of 16 giving 7lb to Slip Venture (21 Oct Nottingham 10f g-s RF 4927) - also 1st of 13 getting 4lb from Amico (17 Aug Hamilton RF 3679). Consistent. **J J Quinn [5-25] Harold Bray.*

TIPSY RR 39f 4318[12]

2 ch f Kris 10f **(75)** - Heady (Rousillon (USA)) 8.2f **(74)**
Form - 0

Record	**1998** -	1st:0	2nd:0	3rd:0	Ran:1

1998 Turf 0-1: (7f) (gd)
Currently very moderate filly. **W J Haggas [0-1] Cheveley Park Stud.*

TIPSY CREEK (USA) BHB 112f RR 114f 4492[6]

4 b c Dayjur (USA) 6.8f **(79)** - Copper Creek (Habitat) 9.4f **(70)**
Form - 71084116

Record	**1998** -	1st:3	2nd:0	3rd:0	Ran:8
	Pre1998 -	1st:2	2nd:1	3rd:1	Ran:7

Win Prizemoney £49,708 *Total Prizemoney* £55,557

Wins	* **1998**	Aug	Newmar	(G-F)	L	6f	114	<
	* **1998**	Aug	Yarmou	(G-F)		6f	109	
	* **1998**	Jun	Haydoc	(GD)		6f	96	
	* 1996	Jun	Ascot	(G-F)	G3	5f	112	
	* 1996	May	Salisb	(G-F)		5f	81+	

1998 Turf 3-8: (5f 3, 6f 3-5) (sft, gd 1-4, g-f 1-1, frm 1-2)
Scopey, Group-class colt, effective 5 to 6f, best at 6f, acts on g-f to frm, best on g-f. Turf high 114 - 1st of 7 giving 3lb to Bold Edge (28 Aug Newmarket RF 3929) - also 1st of 6 from Rambling Bear (9 Aug Yarmouth RF 3493). Built like a brick out-house, he rediscovered his form in 1998, winning three times, including a Listed event at Newmarket. Six furlongs and an uncontested lead suit him ideally. **B Hanbury [5-15] Hamdan Al Maktoum.*

TIP THE BALANCE (IRE) RR 51f 1628[10]

2 b f Ballad Rock 7.2f **(63)** - Daidis (Welsh Pageant) 10f **(65)**
Form - 50

Record	**1998** -	1st:0	2nd:0	3rd:0	Ran:2

1998 Turf 0-2: (5f, 6f) (gd, g-f)
Currently fair filly. Turf high 51. **J Parkes [0-2] Mrs E Comer.*

TIRAAZ (USA) RR 112f 5055a[1]

4 b c Lear Fan (USA) 10.4f **(80)** - Tarikhana (Mouktar)
Form - 121
1998 Turf 2-3: (16f 2-2, 20f) (hvy 1-1, sft 1-2)
Currently Group-class colt. Turf high 112 (began Spt) - 1st of 7 giving 12lb to Erudite (25 Oct Longchamp RF 5055a) - also 1st of 5 getting 4lb from Solo Mio (6 Spt Longchamp RF 4218a). He was nailed close home by Invermark in the Group One Prix du Cadran, having beaten that colt in the Prix Gladiateur. Two miles may be his optimum distance. **A deRoyerDupre in FR [2-3] H H Aga Khan.*

TISSIFER RR 85f 4909a[5]

2 b c Polish Precedent (USA) 9f **(73)** - Ingozi **(74f)** (Warning)
Form - 115

Record	**1998** -	1st:2	2nd:0	3rd:0	Ran:3

Win Prizemoney £7,910 *Total Prizemoney* £7,910

Wins	* **1998**	Spt	Kempto	(SFT)	7f	82	<
	* **1998**	Aug	Epsom	(G-F)	6f	81+	

1998 Turf 2-3: (6f 1-1, 7f 1-1, 8f) (gd 1-2, g-f 1-1)
Currently useful colt. Turf high 85 (began Aug) - 5th of 9 to Festival Hall (17 Oct Curragh 8f gd RF 4909a) - also 1st of 7 giving 5lb to Salford Express (9 Spt Kempton RF 4192). Earned a crack at an Irish Group Three, but was exposed for lack of pace.
**M Johnston [2-3] Burke's 5th Family S'ment.*

TITAN BHB 65f RR 62f 2782[13]

3 b c Lion Cavern (USA) 7.5f **(74)** - Sutosky (Great Nephew) 9.9f **(64)**
Form - 003070

Record	**1998** -	1st:0	2nd:0	3rd:1	Ran:6
	Pre1998 -	1st:1	2nd:2	3rd:0	Ran:6

Win Prizemoney £4,110 *Total Prizemoney* £7,615

Wins	* 1997	Spt	Goodwo	(GD)	H	7f	74	76	<

1998 Turf 0-6: (6f, 7f 4, 8f) (hvy, sft, gd, g-f 3)
Scopey, average colt, effective 7f, acts on gd to frm, prefers right handed tracks, prefers tight tracks. Turf high 70 - 3rd of 10 getting 13lb from Adjutant (19 May Goodwood 7f g-f RF 1324). Inconsistent. **S Dow [1-12] J & S Kelly.*

TITANIC (IRE) RR 90f 3650[3]

3 b c Nashwan (USA) 10.3f **(79)** - White Star Line (USA) (Northern Dancer) 9.6f **(80)**
Form - 5303

Record	**1998** -	1st:0	2nd:0	3rd:2	Ran:4
	Pre1998 -	1st:2	2nd:0	3rd:1	Ran:5

Win Prizemoney £8,070 *Total Prizemoney* £15,605

Wins	* 1997	Jly	Yarmou	(G-F)	5.2f	90+	
	* 1997	Jly	Doncas	(GD)	5f	93+	<

1998 Turf 0-4: (5f, 6f 2, 7f) (g-s, g-f 2, frm)
Scopey, useful colt, effective 5f, acts on g-f. Turf high 90. Inconsistent. Failed to progress at three, but had more than once looked like he needed a longer trip, and he ran with promise on his final start over an extended seven.
**J H M Gosden [2-9] Sheikh Mohammed.*

TITANIUM DANCER (IRE) BHB 44f RR 32f 2760[6]

3 ch g Common Grounds 8.1f **(66)** - Grayfoot (Grundy) 10.3f **(65)**
Form - 007006

Record	**1998** -	1st:0	2nd:0	3rd:0	Ran:6

1998 Turf 0-6: (6f 2, 7f 2, 8f 2) (sft, gd 5)
Workmanlike, very moderate gelding. Turf high 58. (DEAD)
**B J Meehan [0-6] Ms A M Cone-Farran.*

TITTA RUFFO BHB 60f RR 76f 4002[7]

4 b g Reprimand 8.2f **(63)** - Hithermoor Lass (Red Alert) 7.6f **(66)**
Form - 07376771007

Record	**1998** -	1st:1	2nd:0	3rd:1	Ran:11
	Pre1998 -	1st:1	2nd:2	3rd:2	Ran:9

Win Prizemoney £5,865 *Total Prizemoney* £11,224

Wins	* **1998**	Aug	Windso	(G-F)	S	11.6f		51	
	* 1997	Jun	Goodwo	(GD)	H	10f	80	84	<

1998 Turf 1-11: (10f 7, 11f 2, 12f 1-2) (gd 3, g-f 5, frm 2, hrd 1-1)
Workmanlike, above-average gelding, effective 7 to 11f, acts on gd to frm, best on frm, has worn blinkers, excels at Sandown, likes Windsor. Turf high 76 - 7th of 13 getting 6lb from Premier Generation (23 Jly Sandown 10f frm RF 3046). He had become a very disappointing sort, and had to be dropped into selling grade in order to gain his first victory of the season. He won easily

enough, but the amount paid in order to keep him afterwards was somewhat surprising. **B J Meehan [2-20] Mario Lanfranchi.*

TIYE BHB 55f **RR 61df** 3585[6]
3 b f Salse (USA) 10.9f **(71)** - Kiya (USA) (Dominion) 8.5f **(63)**
Form - 562386
Record 1998 - 1st:0 2nd:1 3rd:1 Ran:6
Pre1998 - 1st:0 2nd:0 3rd:0 Ran:2
Win Prizemoney £0 *Total Prizemoney* £1,491
1998 Turf 0-5: (8f, 10f, 12f, 14f, 16f) (g-f 3, frm 2) 1998 AW 0-1: (10f) (Equi)
Unfurnished, average filly, effective 10 to 16f, acts on g-f to frm, has worn blinkers. Turf high 61 - 2nd of 11 getting 5lb from Konker (27 May Newbury 10f g-f RF 1528). Inconsistent.
**D L Williams [0-3] P F Moore (from R Hannon [0-5] May 1998).*

TOBLERSONG BHB 67f **RR 74f** 4990[5]
3 b c Tirol 8.1f **(64)** - Winsong Melody (Music Maestro) 7.7f **(66)**
Form - 600055
Record 1998 - 1st:0 2nd:0 3rd:0 Ran:6
Pre1998 - 1st:2 2nd:1 3rd:0 Ran:5
Win Prizemoney £7,805 *Total Prizemoney* £9,890
Wins 1997 Oct Yarmou (GD) 6f 93 <
1997 Jly Epsom (SFT) 6f 77+
1998 Turf 0-6: (6f 2, 7f 3, 8f) (sft, gd 3, g-f, frm)
Scopey, above-average colt, effective 6f, acts on gd to frm, has worn blinkers. Turf high 84. Becoming disappointing. Twice a winner for Reg Akehurst at two, he did not show any real form in 1998.
**C A Dwyer [0-2] The Fairy Story Partnership (from J W Hills [0-4] Aug 1998).*

TOBRUK (IRE) RR 84f 4595[2]
2 b c Red Ransom (USA) 8.6f **(83)** - Memories (USA) (Hail the Pirates (USA)) 11f **(78)**
Form - 2
Record 1998 - 1st:0 2nd:1 3rd:0 Ran:1
Win Prizemoney £0 *Total Prizemoney* £2,466
1998 Turf 0-1: (7f) (gd)
Currently decent colt. (1st run) - 2nd of 27 to Easaar (1 Oct Newmarket 7f gd RF 4595). A half-brother to Russian Revival, he found only a Godolphin hotpot too good in a huge field on his debut. **P W Chapple-Hyam [0-1] R E Sangster & A K Collins.*

TOFFOLUX BHB 30f **RR 33f** 3637[10]
3 b f Sharpo 7.5f **(68)** - Coca (Levmoss) 11.4f **(66)**
Form - 7060
Record 1998 - 1st:0 2nd:0 3rd:0 Ran:4
Pre1998 - 1st:0 2nd:0 3rd:0 Ran:2
1998 Turf 0-3: (7f, 8f 2) (g-f 2, hrd) 1998 AW 0-1: (7f) (Fibr)
Leggy, very moderate filly, often wears blinkers. Turf high 33.
**P W D'Arcy [0-4] G C Neate (from H J Collingridge [0-2] Oct 1997).*

TOI TOI (IRE) BHB 66f70a **RR 65f 70a** 4195[1]
4 b f In The Wings 11.2f **(77)** - Walliser (Niniski (USA)) 10.6f **(65)**
Form - 415471
Record 1998 - 1st:1 2nd:0 3rd:0 Ran:3
Pre1998 - 1st:1 2nd:2 3rd:2 Ran:15
Win Prizemoney £5,046 *Total Prizemoney* £9,170
Wins * **1998** Spt Kempto (G-S) H 14.4f 60 65
* 1997 *Nov Southw (STD) H 14f 65 70* <
1998 Turf 1-3: (12f, 14f 1-1, 16f) (gd 1-1, g-f, frm)
Workmanlike, above-average filly, effective 10 to 16f, best at 12f, acts on g-s to g-f - acts on Fibr, best on g-f, has worn blinkers. Turf high 65 (began Aug). Out of a sister to that good stayer Assessor, she has shown improved form since being stepped up to middle-distances. **D W P Arbuthnot [2-18] Noel Cronin.*

TOKAY BHB 45f **RR 47f** 3134[5]
3 b f Kylian (USA) 8.1f **(66)** - Tokyo (Mtoto)
Form - 374355
Record 1998 - 1st:0 2nd:0 3rd:2 Ran:6
Pre1998 - 1st:0 2nd:0 3rd:0 Ran:1
Win Prizemoney £0 *Total Prizemoney* £745
1998 Turf 0-6: (8f, 10f, 12f, 13f, 14f, 15f) (g-s, gd 2, g-f 2, frm)
Moderate filly, has worn blinkers. Turf high 61.
**P F I Cole [0-7] Mrs Jenny Willment.*

TOM BHB 34f42a **RR 48f 42a** 4401[13]
3 gr g Petong 7.6f **(58)** - Wanton (Kris) 9.5f **(73)**
Form - 50025056300000
Record 1998 - 1st:0 2nd:1 3rd:1 Ran:14
Pre1998 - 1st:0 2nd:0 3rd:1 Ran:6
Win Prizemoney £0 *Total Prizemoney* £1,261
1998 Turf 0-12: (6f 5, 7f 4, 8f 2, 9f) (sft, gd 7, frm 4) 1998 AW 0-2: (6f, 7f) (Fibr 2)
Workmanlike, fair gelding, effective 7f, - acts on Fibr, often wears blinkers. Turf high 48. AW high 56 - 3rd of 14 getting 7lb from Kosevo (17 Jly Southwell 7f Fibr RF 2900). He is very modest, and the closest he has come to winning has been in claiming company.
**C W Fairhurst [0-1] C D Barber-Lomax (from J Hetherton [0-15] Aug 1998).*

TOMAL BHB 34f30a **RR 33f 30a** 3900[12]
6 b g King Among Kings 7.4f **(49)** - Jacinda (Thatching) 8f **(66)**
Form - 770
Record 1998 - 1st:0 2nd:0 3rd:0 Ran:3
Pre1998 - 1st:1 2nd:3 3rd:3 Ran:35
Win Prizemoney £2,643 *Total Prizemoney* £7,628
Wins * 1994 Jly Redcar (G-F) 5f 62
1998 Turf 0-3: (8f 2, 12f) (gd, g-f 2)
Very moderate gelding, has worn blinkers. Turf high 45. Consistent. **R Ingram [1-46] The Emerald Gang.*

TOMASEAN RR 82+f 4735[4]
2 b c Forzando 7.2f **(63)** - Bunny Gee **(54f)** (Last Tycoon) 8.5f **(62)**
Form - 24
Record 1998 - 1st:0 2nd:1 3rd:0 Ran:2
Win Prizemoney £0 *Total Prizemoney* £1,726
1998 Turf 0-2: (6f 2) (g-s, frm)
Currently decent colt. Turf high 82 (1st run) (began Spt) - 2nd of 13 giving 5lb to Dominant Dancer (24 Spt Pontefract 6f frm RF 4465). **J Noseda [0-2] John Breslin.*

TOMASZEWSKI (FR) BHB 68f **RR 64f** 4249[9]
3 b c Polish Precedent(USA) 9f **(73)** -Circus Plume(High Top) 10.2f **(67)**
Form - 650
Record 1998 - 1st:0 2nd:0 3rd:0 Ran:3
1998 Turf 0-3: (10f 3) (g-s, g-f, frm)
Scopey, currently average colt. Turf high 64 (began Aug). A cleverly-named son of an Oaks winner, he showed promise on his belated debut but ran poorly on his second start.
**P W Harris [0-3] Mrs P W Harris.*

TOMBA BHB 116f **RR 118f** 4947a[1]
4 ch c Efisio 7.7f **(69)**- Indian Love Song (Be My Guest (USA)) 9.3f **(67)**
Form - 44103411
Record 1998 - 1st:3 2nd:0 3rd:1 Ran:8
Pre1998 - 1st:8 2nd:3 3rd:3 Ran:19
Win Prizemoney £218,168 *Total Prizemoney* £288,857

Wins								
* **1998**	Oct	Longch	(HVY)	G1	7f		118	<
* **1998**	Oct	Munich	(SFT)	G3	6.5f		115	
* **1998**	Jun	Ascot	(SFT)	G2	6f		117	
* 1997	Aug	Hoppeg	(GD)	G3	6.5f		111	
* 1997	Jun	Newcas	(HVY)	L	6f		115	
* 1997	May	Haydoc	(G-S)	LH	6f	109	109	
* 1997	May	Newbur	(G-S)		6f		107	
* 1997	May	Haydoc	(SFT)		6f		98	
* 1996	Nov	Evry	(HLD)	L	6f		104	
* 1996	Oct	Salisb	(G-S)		6f		106	
* 1996	Aug	Epsom	(GD)		6f		80	

1998 Turf 3-8: (6f 1-5, 7f 2-3) (hvy 1-1, sft 1-1, g-s 1-2, gd 2, g-f, frm)
Scopey, high-class colt, effective 6 to 7f, best at 6f, acts on hvy to frm, excels at Haydock. Turf high 118 - 1st of 9 giving 2lb to Charge D'Affaires (18 Oct Longchamp RF 4947a) - also 1st of 12 from Dyhim Diamond (18 Jun Ascot RF 2086). Ran creditably on most starts during the season, but it was only when conditions became testing that we saw the very best of him. Victories in the Cork And Orrery and a German Group Three were very creditable, but his finest hour came when victorious in the Prix de la Foret, his first Group One win. **B J Meehan [11-27] J R Good.*

TOM DOUGAL BHB 85f **RR 86f** 4854[19]
3 b c Ron's Victory (USA) 9.2f **(52)** - Fabulous Rina (FR) (Fabulous

Dancer (USA)) 9.4f **(70)**
Form - 371130800
Record 1998 - 1st:2 2nd:0 3rd:2 Ran:9
Pre1998 - 1st:0 2nd:1 3rd:0 Ran:7
Win Prizemoney £24,045 *Total Prizemoney* £30,263
Wins * **1998** May York (GD) H 7.9f 83 90+ <
* **1998** May Newmar (GD) H 8f 75 86
1998 Turf 2-9: (7f 2, 8f 2-7) (g-s, gd 2-7, g-f)
Leggy, useful colt, effective 8f, acts on gd, likes left handed tracks. Turf high 93 - 3rd of 11 giving 13lb to French Connection (23 May Haydock 8f gd RF 1418) - also 1st of 16 giving 6lb to Carambo (14 May York RF 1223). Beat a huge field at 33/1 at Newmarket, although there appeared no fluke about it. He confirmed that opinion when following up at York and when just touched off at Haydock. Finished well down a massive field at Royal Ascot, however, and was off the track nearly three months.
**C Smith [2-16] Mrs N Stewart.*

TOMISUE'S DELIGHT (USA) RR 5166a[4]
4 ch f A P Indy (USA) - Prospectors Delite (USA)(Mr Prospector (USA))
Form - 4
1998 AW 0-1: (9f) (Dirt)
Currently very useful filly. Ran on well in the closing stages, but was unable to reach the principals in the Breeders' Cup Distaff. ** N Howard in USA [0-1] S Hilbert.*

TOM MORGAN BHB 40f RR 42f 1409[19]
7 b g Faustus(USA) 9.1f **(54)** -Pirate Maid(Auction Ring(USA)) 8.6f **(65)**
Form - 650
Record 1998 - 1st:0 2nd:0 3rd:0 Ran:3
Pre1998 - 1st:5 2nd:2 3rd:2 Ran:26
Win Prizemoney £14,316 *Total Prizemoney* £18,747
Wins * 1994 Aug Newmar (GD) H 7f 77 78 <
* 1994 Jly Lingfi (GD) 7.6f 76
* 1994 Jun Redcar (G-F) 6f 68
* 1994 Apr Newmar (G-F) 8f 54+
1998 Turf 0-3: (6f, 7f, 8f) (sft, gd, g-f)
Moderate gelding, had worn blinkers. Turf high 42. (DEAD)
**P T Walwyn [5-29] Michael White.*

TOMMY CARSON RR 74f 4968[3]
3 b g Last Tycoon 9.4f **(73)** - Ivory Palm (USA) (Sir Ivor) 10.2f **(70)**
Form - 83
Record 1998 - 1st:0 2nd:0 3rd:1 Ran:2
Win Prizemoney £0 *Total Prizemoney* £548
1998 Turf 0-2: (10f 2) (sft, gd)
Scopey, currently above-average gelding. Turf high 74 (began Spt) - 3rd of 12 to Shamawan (23 Oct Newbury 10f sft RF 4968).
**D R C Elsworth [0-2] DGH Partnership.*

TOMMY'S TROUBLES RR 1565[6]
3 b g Nalchik (USA) 12.6f **(44)** -Secret Ingredient(Most Secret) 7.1f **(58)**
Form - 6
Record 1998 - 1st:0 2nd:0 3rd:0 Ran:1
1998 Turf 0-1: (10f) (frm)
Leggy, currently very poor gelding - 6th of 6 to Connoisseur Bay (29 May Bath 10f frm RF 1565). **D Burchell [0-1] Lyn Phillips.*

TOMMY TEMPEST BHB 25f27a RR 15f 27a 3647[8]
9 ch g Northern Tempest (USA) 6.1f **(41)** - Silently Yours (USA) (Silent Screen (USA)) 8.6f **(65)**
Form - 008008
Record 1998 - 1st:0 2nd:0 3rd:0 Ran:4
Pre1998 - 1st:4 2nd:6 3rd:5 Ran:76
Win Prizemoney £11,409 *Total Prizemoney* £17,543
Wins * 1997 Jly Windso (G-F) H 5f 35 42
* *1995 Jly Lingfi (STD) C 5f 48* <
1994 Jly Wolver (STD) H 5f 32 32
1998 Turf 0-3: (5f 3) (gd 2, hrd) 1998 AW 0-1: (6f) (Fibr)
Little account gelding, effective 5f, acts on frm, often wears blinkers. Turf high 15 (began Jly).
**R E Peacock [2-38] R E Peacock (from A Bailey [1-17] Feb 1995).*

TOMMY TORTOISE BHB 70f RR 72f 5081[P]
4 b g Rock Hopper 10.6f **(54)** - Wish You Well (Sadler's Wells (USA)) 10f **(76)**
Form - 7P
Record 1998 - 1st:0 2nd:0 3rd:0 Ran:2
Pre1998 - 1st:2 2nd:2 3rd:1 Ran:10
Win Prizemoney £6,060 *Total Prizemoney* £8,126
Wins 1997 Oct Newcas (G-F) H 16.1f 70 72 <
1997 Jun Bright (FRM) 11.9f 64
1998 Turf 0-1: (16f) (gd) 1998 AW 0-1: (12f) (Fibr)
Scopey, above-average gelding, effective 12 to 16f, acted on g-f to frm, best on g-f. (DEAD)
**R A Fahey [0-2] Tommy Staunton (from Miss Gay Kelleway [2-7] Oct 1997).*

TOMOE GOZEN (IRE) BHB 73f RR 72f 3736[10]
2 b f Brief Truce (USA) 9.1f **(73)** - Deelish (IRE) (Caerleon (USA)) 8.6f **(71)**
Form - 260
Record 1998 - 1st:0 2nd:1 3rd:0 Ran:3
Win Prizemoney £0 *Total Prizemoney* £1,391
1998 Turf 0-3: (6f 2, 7f) (gd, g-f, frm)
Currently above-average filly. Turf high 72 (1st run) - 2nd of 7 getting 5lb from Black Amber (19 Jun Newmarket 6f g-f RF 2125). Made a promising debut in a maiden on the July Course, but was last in a listed race there next time.
**S P C Woods [0-3] Michael Simpson.*

TOM PADDINGTON BHB 74f RR 82f 5008[1]
3 b g Rock Hopper 10.6f **(54)** - Mayfair Minx (St Columbus) 11.7f **(82)**
Form - 025441
Record 1998 - 1st:1 2nd:1 3rd:0 Ran:6
Win Prizemoney £3,582 *Total Prizemoney* £5,413
Wins * **1998** Oct Bath (HVY) 11.7f 79 <
1998 Turf 1-6: (10f, 11f, 12f 1-3, 14f) (sft 1-1, g-s, gd 2, g-f 2)
Neat, decent gelding, effective 12f, acts on sft to g-s. Turf high 82 - 2nd of 8 to Vrin (12 Jun York 12f g-s RF 1951) - also 1st of 13 from Mane Frame (27 Oct Bath RF 5008).
**H Morrison [1-6] M S Wilson Mrs Wilson (Camp Farm Racing).*

TOM PLADDEY BHB 26f22a RR 23f 22a 214[9]
4 ch c Clantime 6.6f **(57)** - Croft Original (Crofthall) 6.3f **(59)**
Form - 00
Record 1998 - 1st:0 2nd:0 3rd:0 Ran:2
Pre1998 - 1st:0 2nd:0 3rd:1 Ran:12
Win Prizemoney £0 *Total Prizemoney* £359
1998 AW 0-2: (7f, 8f) (Fibr 2)
Little account colt, has worn blinkers.
**R Bastiman [0-14] A D Bastiman.*

TOM TAILOR (GER) RR 62f 4747[13]
4 b g Beldale Flutter (USA) 10.2f **(62)** - Thoughtful (Northfields (USA)) 9f **(72)**
Form - 00
Record 1998 - 1st:0 2nd:0 3rd:0 Ran:2
Pre1998 - 1st:1 2nd:1 3rd:1 Ran:10
Win Prizemoney £3,030 *Total Prizemoney* £5,506
Wins * 1997 May Windso (SFT) 10f 74 <
1998 Turf 0-2: (14f, 17f) (gd, g-f)
Scopey, average gelding, effective 10 to 11f, acts on gd to frm, favours tight tracks. Turf high 56 (began Spt). Consistent.
**D R C Elsworth [3-19] The A A Partnership.*

TOM TOM (IRE) BHB 56a RR 82f 56a 509[9]
6 b g Dancing Dissident (USA) 6.8f **(65)** -Ashanti Yankee Gold)7.6f **(55)**
Form - 560
Record 1998 - 1st:0 2nd:0 3rd:0 Ran:3
Pre1998 - 1st:1 2nd:0 3rd:1 Ran:8
Win Prizemoney £3,596 *Total Prizemoney* £3,888
Wins 1997 Jly Dundal (GD) H 7.8f 83 82 <
1998 AW 0-3: (5f, 7f 2) (Equi, Fibr 2)
Decent gelding, effective 8f, acts on gd, has worn blinkers, likes left handed tracks. AW high 56. Becoming disappointing.
**Noel Chance [0-3] J J Mullan (from J P Kavanagh in IRE [0-1] Jly 1997).*

TOM TUN BHB 54f53a RR 52f 53a 4811[6]
3 b g Bold Arrangement 8.7f **(57)** - B Grade (Lucky Wednesday) 8f **(50)**
Form - 008155176
Record 1998 - 1st:2 2nd:0 3rd:0 Ran:9
Win Prizemoney £5,751 *Total Prizemoney* £5,751

Wins *** 1998** Spt Newcas (GD) H 6f 49 50 <
*** 1998** *Jly Southw (STD) H 6f 42 44*
1998 Turf 1-6: (5f, 6f 1-3, 7f 2) (gd 4, frm 1-2) 1998 AW 1-3: (5f, 6f 1-2) (Fibr 1-3)
Workmanlike, fair gelding, effective 6f, acts on frm - acts on Fibr. Turf high 52 - also 1st of 20 getting 12lb from Chinaider (8 Spt Newcastle RF 4153). AW high 46 (began Jly) - also 1st of 11 getting 5lb from Amington Girl (9 Jly Southwell RF 2656).
**Miss J F Craze [2-9] Mrs O Tunstall.*

TONGARIRO (USA) RR 38f 5137[12]

2 ch c Trempolino (USA) 11.9f **(77)** - Air de Noblesse (USA) (Vaguely Noble) 10.1f **(72)**
Form - 00
Record 1998 - 1st:0 2nd:0 3rd:0 Ran:2
1998 Turf 0-2: (7f, 8f) (gd 2)
Currently very moderate colt. Turf high 38 (began Oct).
**H R A Cecil [0-2] H R H Prince Fahd Salman.*

TONG ROAD BHB 45f RR 31f 4937[16]

2 gr g Petong 7.6f **(58)** - Wayzgoose (USA) (Diesis) 9.3f **(69)**
Form - 000
Record 1998 - 1st:0 2nd:0 3rd:0 Ran:3
1998 Turf 0-3: (5f 2, 6f) (gd 3)
Currently very moderate gelding. Turf high 31 (began Aug).
**B R Cambidge [0-3] B R Cambidge.*

TONIC RR 76f 5057[2]

2 b c Robellino (USA) 9.5f **(68)** - Alyara (USA) (Alydar (USA)) 9.1f **(76)**
Form - 32
Record 1998 - 1st:0 2nd:1 3rd:1 Ran:2
Win Prizemoney £0 *Total Prizemoney* £1,259
1998 Turf 0-2: (8f 2) (sft, g-f)
Currently above-average colt. Turf high 76 (began Spt) - 2nd of 6 getting 4lb from Spree Vision (30 Oct Newcastle 8f sft RF 5057).
**M Johnston [0-2] Robinson (Wigan).*

TONIGHT'S PRIZE (IRE) BHB 88f RR 88f 4848[27]

4 b g Night Shift (USA) 8.1f **(73)** - Bestow (Shirley Heights) 10.3f **(74)**
Form - 083515300
Record 1998 - 1st:1 2nd:0 3rd:2 Ran:9
Pre1998 - 1st:1 2nd:4 3rd:0 Ran:7
Win Prizemoney £11,202 *Total Prizemoney* £19,342
Wins *** 1998** Aug Pontef (G-F) H 8f 82 87 <
* 1997 Oct Pontef (G-F) 8f 72
1998 Turf 1-9: (8f 1-4, 9f 4, 10f) (gd 5, g-f 3, frm 1-1)
Neat, useful gelding, effective 8 to 10f, best at 8f, acts on gd to hrd, prefers tight tracks, excels at Newbury and Pontefract. Turf high 88 - 3rd of 20 giving 17lb to Indium (19 Spt Newbury 8f g-f RF 4381) - also 1st of 19 getting 2lb from Abajany (16 Aug Pontefract RF 3673). He won at Pontefract on his final start of 1997, and returned to winning form on the same track in July. He ideally needs ten furlongs or a very stiff mile to be seen at his best.
**C F Wall [2-16] Shunya Seki.*

TONNERRE BHB 55f54a RR 58f 54a 2936[6]

6 b g Unfuwain (USA) 11.4f **(74)** - Supper Time (Shantung) 9.8f **(64)**
Form - 6001346
Record 1998 - 1st:1 2nd:0 3rd:1 Ran:7
Pre1998 - 1st:2 2nd:1 3rd:1 Ran:18
Win Prizemoney £10,860 *Total Prizemoney* £13,759
Wins *** 1998** Jun Ripon (SFT) H 10f 51 58
* 1997 Jun Nottin (SFT) H 10f 52 59
1995 Jun Haydoc (G-S) 14f 75 <
1998 Turf 1-7: (10f 1-3, 11f 2, 12f 2) (gd 1-1, g-f 4, frm 2)
Fair gelding, effective 10 to 14f, best at 10f, acts on sft to frm, likes tight tracks. Turf high 58 - 1st of 6 getting 26lb from Mr Bombastique (17 Jun Ripon RF 2073). Inconsistent. Give him ten furlongs on soft ground, and he is a much-improved horse. It was under precisely those conditions that he scored at Ripon in June.
**B A McMahon [2-19] Ian Guise (from C W Fairhurst [1-6] Oct 1995).*

TONRIN BHB 20a RR 20a 273[8]

6 b g General Wade 5.5f **(40)** - Hot Tramp (Country Retreat)
Form - 000088
Record 1998 - 1st:0 2nd:0 3rd:0 Ran:4
Pre1998 - 1st:0 2nd:0 3rd:0 Ran:2
1998 AW 0-4: (10f 2, 12f, 16f) (Equi 4)
Very poor gelding. AW high 7. **J J Bridger [0-9] J J Bridger.*

TONY'S MIST BHB 24f52a RR 26f 52a 2928[15]

8 b g Digamist (USA) 8.8f **(56)** - Tinas Image (He Loves Me) 7.9f **(55)**
Form - 8005700
Record 1998 - 1st:0 2nd:0 3rd:0 Ran:7
Pre1998 - 1st:3 2nd:4 3rd:2 Ran:33
Win Prizemoney £9,334 *Total Prizemoney* £14,173
1998 Turf 0-7: (8f 5, 10f, 11f) (gd, g-f 3, frm 3)
Above-average gelding, has worn blinkers. Turf high 31.
**J M Bradley [1-48] Robert Bailey (from R Hannon [3-16] Nov 1993).*

TONY TIE BHB 84f RR 89f 5143[6]

2 b c Ardkinglass 5f **(64)** - Queen of the Quorn **(51df 45a)** (Governor General)
Form - 1043106
Record 1998 - 1st:2 2nd:0 3rd:1 Ran:7
Win Prizemoney £9,765 *Total Prizemoney* £10,424
Wins *** 1998** Aug Cheste (G-S) H 7f 87 89 <
*** 1998** May Salisb (G-S) 5f 79
1998 Turf 2-7: (5f 1-1, 6f, 7f 1-3, 8f 2) (gd 2-4, g-f, frm 2)
Useful colt, effective 5 to 7f, acts on gd. Turf high 89 - 1st of 12 giving 19lb to Prideway (22 Aug Chester RF 3803). Looked to need further than the minimum trip when making a winning debut, and was outclassed in the Coventry next time. Returned to winning ways on soft ground at Chester, where the seven furlongs and soft ground suited. **W G M Turner [2-7] Frank Brady.*

TOO BLUE BY FAR RR 36f 5080[13]

2 br f Pharly (FR) 11.5f **(64)** - Blue Rag (Ragusa) 10.7f **(51)**
Form - 660
Record 1998 - 1st:0 2nd:0 3rd:0 Ran:3
1998 Turf 0-2: (6f 2) (g-s, g-f) 1998 AW 0-1: (6f) (Fibr)
Currently very moderate filly. Turf high 36 (began Oct).
**J L Spearing [0-3] T N Bailey.*

TOPACIO RR 12f 4989[10]

2 b c Saddlers' Hall (IRE) 10.5f **(65)** - Teresa (SPA) (Rheffissimo (FR))
Form - 0
Record 1998 - 1st:0 2nd:0 3rd:0 Ran:1
1998 Turf 0-1: (8f) (sft)
Currently poor colt. **S C Williams [0-1] Livingston Trading Ltd.*

TOP ACT BHB 55f RR 69f 4709[19]

2 b c Inchinor 8.9f **(64)** - Actress (Known Fact (USA)) 7.4f **(67)**
Form - 6080
Record 1998 - 1st:0 2nd:0 3rd:0 Ran:4
1998 Turf 0-4: (6f 2, 8f 2) (gd, frm 3)
Average colt. Turf high 69.
**N Tinkler [0-2] D Drewery, P Drewery & W Burton (from G R Oldroyd [0-2] Jly 1998).*

TOPATORI (IRE) BHB 76f RR 78f 5126[3]

4 ch f Topanoora 8.3f **(67)** - Partygoer (General Assembly (USA)) 10f **(68)**
Form - 155030600033
Record 1998 - 1st:1 2nd:0 3rd:3 Ran:12
Pre1998 - 1st:2 2nd:2 3rd:2 Ran:12
Win Prizemoney £11,046 *Total Prizemoney* £19,119
Wins *** 1998** Apr Leices (SFT) H 8f 76 84+ <
* 1997 Oct Haydoc (SFT) H 10.5f 71 75
* 1997 Jun Yarmou (FRM) 7f 66
1998 Turf 1-12: (8f 1-4, 9f 4, 10f 4) (hvy, sft 1-2, g-s 2, gd 6, g-f)
Light-framed, above-average filly, effective 8 to 10f, best at 8f, acts on sft to gd, best on gd, likes tight tracks. Turf high 86 - also 1st of 13 giving 21lb to Queen's Insignia (2 Apr Leicester RF 0542). Won first time out in soft ground, but has faced some stiff tasks since.
**M H Tompkins [3-24] M P Bowring.*

TOPAZ BHB 45f RR 42f 4801[9]

3 b c Alhijaz 7.7f **(57)** - Daisy Topper (Top Ville) 11.7f **(68)**
Form - 6060000
Record 1998 - 1st:0 2nd:0 3rd:0 Ran:7
Pre1998 - 1st:0 2nd:0 3rd:0 Ran:1
1998 Turf 0-7: (9f, 10f 3, 12f 3) (sft, g-s, gd 2, g-f, frm 2)
Workmanlike, moderate colt. Turf high 61. Consistent.

**H J Collingridge [0-4] The Topaz Partnership (from J W Hills [0-4] Jun 1998).*

TOP BANANA BHB 71f **RR 75f** 4308[9]
7 ch g Pharly (FR) 11.5f **(64)** - Oxslip (Owen Dudley) 8.3f **(61)**
Form - 3704670
Record 1998 - 1st:0 2nd:0 3rd:1 Ran:7
Pre1998 - 1st:4 2nd:4 3rd:4 Ran:29
Win Prizemoney £19,435 *Total Prizemoney* £52,396
Wins * 1996 Jun Newmar (G-F) H 5f 91 95 <
* 1995 Jly Newbur (GD) H 5.2f 84 88
* 1995 Jun Newbur (FRM) H 5.2f 79 84
* 1995 Jun Warwic (GD) 6f 83+
1998 Turf 0-7: (6f 5, 7f 2) (gd 2, g-f 4, frm)
Above-average gelding, effective 6 to 7f, acts on g-f to frm, has worn blinkers. Turf high 80 (1st run) - 3rd of 17 giving 22lb to Gay Breeze (4 May Doncaster 6f g-f RF 1011). A useful sprint handicapper at his best, he is on a long losing run.
**H Candy [4-36] Henry Candy.*

TOP CEES BHB 98f **RR 98f** 3674[1]
8 b g Shirley Heights 12.1f **(76)** - Sing Softly (Luthier) 9.8f **(71)**
Form - 302121
Record 1998 - 1st:2 2nd:2 3rd:1 Ran:6
Pre1998 - 1st:5 2nd:5 3rd:1 Ran:29
Win Prizemoney £100,586 *Total Prizemoney* £151,608
Wins * **1998** Aug Pontef (G-F) H 12f 96 98 <
* **1998** Jun Ayr (G-F) H 15f 93 96+
* 1997 Spt Ayr (GD) H 13.1f 90 97
* 1997 May Cheste (SFT) H 18.7f 87 98 <
* 1996 Jly Newmar (G-F) H 14.8f 82 88+
* 1995 May Cheste (G-F) H 18.7f 72 81+
1998 Turf 2-6: (12f 1-2, 14f, 15f 1-1, 19f 2) (sft, g-s, g-f 1-3, frm 1-1)
Very useful gelding, effective 12 to 19f, acts on g-s to frm, prefers left handed tracks, likes tight tracks, and excels at Ayr. Turf high 98 - 1st of 7 giving 22lb to Brave Noble (16 Aug Pontefract RF 3674) - also 1st of 4 giving 1lb to Motet (20 Jun Ayr RF 2145). Consistent. The winner of two Chester Cups, this marvellous dual-purpose horse suffered a terrible passage in the same race this year. He later won at Ayr and over twelve furlongs Pontefract. He is due to join Ian Balding now Lynda Ramsden has retired.
**Mrs J R Ramsden [9-39] Charlton Bloodstock Ltd (from P W Harris [1-12] Oct 1994).*

TOP FIT BHB 56f **RR 58f** 5094[2]
2 b c Thatching 7.8f **(69)** - Diplomatist **(55f)** (Dominion) 8.5f **(63)**
Form - 80042
Record 1998 - 1st:0 2nd:1 3rd:0 Ran:5
Win Prizemoney £0 *Total Prizemoney* £930
1998 Turf 0-5: (5f 3, 7f, 8f) (g-s, gd, frm 3)
Fair colt, has worn blinkers. Turf high 58 (began Aug) - 2nd of 22 getting 16lb from Seren Hill (2 Nov Redcar 8f gd RF 5094).
**W J Haggas [0-5] K H Fung.*

TOP FLOOR (IRE) BHB 51f49a **RR 57f 49a** 4920[2]
3 ch g Waajib 8.9f **(67)** - Keen Note (Sharpo) 7.7f **(59)**
Form - 805310855742
Record 1998 - 1st:1 2nd:1 3rd:1 Ran:12
Pre1998 - 1st:0 2nd:0 3rd:0 Ran:6
Win Prizemoney £2,220 *Total Prizemoney* £2,950
Wins 1998 Mar Hamilt (HVY) S 8.3f 52 <
1998 Turf 1-8: (7f 2, 8f 1-6) (sft 1-1, g-s 3, gd 2, frm 2) 1998 AW 0-4: (6f 2, 7f 2) (Fibr 4)
Workmanlike, fair gelding, likes tight tracks. Turf high 57. AW high 55. Inconsistent.
**J L Spearing [0-2] J Spearing (from N Tinkler [1-16] Aug 1998).*

TOP GEAR (IRE) BHB 56f **RR 59f** 683[15]
3 ch c Case Law 6f **(64)** - Fleur-de-Luce (Tumble Wind (USA)) 7.5f **(57)**
Form - 00
Record 1998 - 1st:0 2nd:0 3rd:0 Ran:2
Pre1998 - 1st:0 2nd:0 3rd:0 Ran:2
1998 Turf 0-2: (6f, 7f) (gd 2)
Fair colt. Turf high 39. (DEAD) **P Howling [0-4] Liam Sheridan.*

TOP JEM BHB 61f60a **RR 71f 60a** 4776[11]
4 b f Damister (USA) 9.1f **(66)** - Sharp Top (Sharpo) 7.7f **(59)**
Form - 7864003680
Record 1998 - 1st:0 2nd:0 3rd:1 Ran:10
Pre1998 - 1st:2 2nd:3 3rd:1 Ran:10
Win Prizemoney £10,599 *Total Prizemoney* £16,054
Wins * 1997 Jun Newcas (HVY) H 10.1f 67 79 <
* 1997 Jun Yarmou (FRM) H 10.1f 65 65
1998 Turf 0-7: (10f 7) (sft, g-s 3, gd 2, g-f) 1998 AW 0-3: (10f, 11f, 12f) (Equi, Fibr 2)
Leggy, above-average filly, effective 10 to 11f, best at 10f, acts on sft to frm, prefers left handed tracks, excels at Yarmouth. Turf high 75 (1st run) - 4th of 12 getting 4lb from Largesse (31 Mar Nottingham 10f g-s RF 0520). AW high 62.
**M J Ryan [2-20] Norcroft Park Stud.*

TOP MAITE BHB 34f **RR 44f** 4535[13]
3 ch c Komaite (USA) 6.9f **(61)** - Top Yard (Teekay)
Form - 0577004060
Record 1998 - 1st:0 2nd:0 3rd:0 Ran:10
Pre1998 - 1st:0 2nd:0 3rd:0 Ran:3
1998 Turf 0-10: (7f 2, 8f 6, 10f, 11f) (hvy, g-s, gd 3, g-f, frm 4)
Leggy, moderate colt, has worn blinkers. Turf high 44. Becoming disappointing.
**G F H Charles-Jones [0-7] The Top Maite Partnership (from E A Wheeler [0-3] May 1998).*

TOP OF THE CHARTS BHB 55f **RR 56f** 4984[7]
2 b c Salse (USA) 10.9f **(71)** - Celebrity (Troy) 10.4f **(68)**
Form - 007
Record 1998 - 1st:0 2nd:0 3rd:0 Ran:3
1998 Turf 0-3: (7f 3) (g-s, gd 2)
Currently fair colt. Turf high 56 (began Oct).
**J Noseda [0-3] P D Savill.*

TOP OF THE FORM (IRE) BHB 53f **RR 56f** 4837[5]
4 ch f Masterclass (USA) 5.9f **(63)** - Haraabah (USA) (Topsider (USA)) 8.3f **(71)**
Form - 0604578565
Record 1998 - 1st:0 2nd:0 3rd:0 Ran:10
Pre1998 - 1st:4 2nd:0 3rd:3 Ran:15
Win Prizemoney £12,984 *Total Prizemoney* £15,696
Wins 1997 Aug Pontef (G-F) C 5f 77
1997 Jly Catter (G-F) C 6f 55
1996 Jly York (GD) H 5f 81 <
1996 Jun Mussel (FRM) 5f 80+
1998 Turf 0-10: (5f 8, 6f 2) (g-s, gd 3, g-f 2, frm 4)
Unfurnished, fair filly, effective 5f, acts on frm, has worn blinkers, likes left handed tracks, likes tight tracks. Turf high 56.
**K A Ryan [0-10] Swan at Whalley Premier Partnership (from R A Fahey [1-6] Nov 1997).*

TOP OF THE GREEN (IRE) BHB 46f **RR 43f** 1805[15]
4 b g Common Grounds 8.1f **(66)** - Grayfoot (Grundy) 10.3f **(65)**
Form - 00
Record 1998 - 1st:0 2nd:0 3rd:0 Ran:2
Pre1998 - 1st:0 2nd:0 3rd:0 Ran:4
1998 Turf 0-2: (8f, 10f) (gd, frm)
Leggy, moderate gelding. Turf high 26.
**P J Makin [0-6] Terence Molossi.*

TOP OF THE MORNING BHB 57f **RR 62f** 4878[5]
2 b f Keen 11.1f **(58)** - Kelimutu (Top Ville) 11.7f **(68)**
Form - 07045
Record 1998 - 1st:0 2nd:0 3rd:0 Ran:5
1998 Turf 0-4: (6f 2, 7f, 8f) (gd, g-f 2, frm) 1998 AW 0-1: (7f) (Fibr)
Average filly. Turf high 62 (began Aug) - 4th of 16 to Helen's Stardust (25 Spt Folkestone 6f g-f RF 4473).
**J Pearce [0-5] Mrs Jennie Furlong.*

TOP ORDER (USA) BHB 83f **RR 76f** 2970[6]
2 b br f Dayjur (USA) 6.8f **(79)** - Victoria Cross (USA) (Spectacular Bid (USA)) 11.2f **(76)**
Form - 54106
Record 1998 - 1st:1 2nd:0 3rd:0 Ran:5
Win Prizemoney £3,559 *Total Prizemoney* £3,852
Wins * **1998** Jun Warwic (SFT) 5f 76 <
1998 Turf 1-5: (5f 1-5) (g-s, gd 1-4)
Above-average filly. Turf high 76 - 1st of 9 from Key (8 Jun

Warwick RF 1815). She won a poor-looking soft-ground Warwick maiden by a street, but has been well held otherwise.
**P F I Cole [1-5] H R H Prince Fahd Salman.*

TOP PRIZE BHB 23f27a **RR 23f 27a** 1065[11]

10 b g High Top 11f **(60)** - Raffle (Balidar) 7.9f **(63)**
Form - 6588660
Record 1998 - 1st:0 2nd:0 3rd:0 Ran:7
Pre1998 - 1st:5 2nd:3 3rd:2 Ran:48
Win Prizemoney £13,117 *Total Prizemoney* £16,823
Wins * 1996 *May Southw (STD) H 16f 28 35*
* 1995 Aug Beverl (G-F) SH 16.2f 34 46 <
* 1995 Aug Nottin (G-F) SH 14.1f 30 36
* 1994 *Spt Southw (STD) H 16f 30 34*
* 1994 Aug Redcar (G-F) SH 14.1f 27 33
1998 Turf 0-4: (16f 3, 22f) (g-s, gd 3) 1998 AW 0-3: (16f 3) (Fibr 3)
Little account gelding, effective 16f, - acts on Fibr, often wears blinkers, likes left handed tracks. Turf high 30. AW high 25. Inconsistent. **M Brittain [6-58] Mel Brittain.*

TOP SHELF BHB 30f39a **RR 31f 39a** 4143[10]

4 b f Warning 8.1f **(77)** - Troy Moon (Troy) 10.4f **(68)**
Form - 00077320
Record 1998 - 1st:0 2nd:1 3rd:1 Ran:8
Pre1998 - 1st:1 2nd:0 3rd:2 Ran:11
Win Prizemoney £3,562 *Total Prizemoney* £5,682
Wins *1997 Feb Lingfi (STD) H 8f 66 70* <
1998 Turf 0-7: (8f, 10f 5, 12f) (gd, g-f, frm 5) 1998 AW 0-1: (10f) (Equi)
Workmanlike, very moderate filly, effective 8f, - acted on Equi, had worn blinkers, liked left handed tracks. Turf high 31. (DEAD)
**P D Evans [0-4] V Loizou (from P J Bevan [1-9] Jly 1998).*

TOP STAR (IRE) **RR 72f** 4967[6]

2 b c Thatching 7.8f **(69)** - Decadence Star (IRE) (High Estate)
Form - 406
Record 1998 - 1st:0 2nd:0 3rd:0 Ran:3
Win Prizemoney £0 *Total Prizemoney* £325
1998 Turf 0-3: (6f 3) (sft, gd, g-f)
Currently above-average colt. Turf high 72 (began Spt).
**M R Channon [0-3] Stephen Crown.*

TOP TARN (IRE) BHB 54f **RR 56f** 4122[12]

2 b f Royal Academy (USA) 7.8f **(77)** - Laugharne (Known Fact (USA)) 7.4f **(67)**
Form - 000
Record 1998 - 1st:0 2nd:0 3rd:0 Ran:3
1998 Turf 0-3: (5f 2, 6f) (gd, frm 2)
Currently fair filly. Turf high 56 (began Jly).
**C F Wall [0-3] Sir Stanley and Lady Grinstead.*

TOPTON (IRE) BHB 63f69a **RR 55f 69a** 5079[2]

4 b g Royal Academy (USA) 7.8f **(77)** - Circo (High Top) 10.2f **(67)**
Form - 0026156380000072
Record 1998 - 1st:1 2nd:2 3rd:1 Ran:16
Pre1998 - 1st:1 2nd:3 3rd:1 Ran:8
Win Prizemoney £7,628 *Total Prizemoney* £15,810
Wins * **1998** Jun Doncas (GD) H 7f 69 74 <
1997 Oct Folkes (GD) 6f 74 <
1998 Turf 1-16: (6f 3, 7f 1-11, 8f 2) (sft, g-s 2, gd 3, g-f 1-6, frm 3, hrd)
Scopey, average gelding, effective 6 to 7f, best at 7f, acts on gd to frm, mostly wears blinkers (effectively), likes left handed tracks, likes tight tracks. Turf high 74 - 1st of 20 giving 7lb to Smokey From Caplaw (6 Jun Doncaster RF 1770). Mixed form last year, beating a big field in a Doncaster handicap.
**P Howling [1-16] Liam Sheridan (from I A Balding [1-8] Oct 1997).*

TORCH VERT (IRE) BHB 67f **RR 70f** 2015[P]

6 b g Law Society (USA) 11.6f **(71)** - Arctic Winter (CAN) (Briartic (CAN)) 9.5f **(84)**
Form - 41P
Record 1998 - 1st:1 2nd:0 3rd:0 Ran:3
Pre1998 - 1st:2 2nd:1 3rd:1 Ran:13
Win Prizemoney £13,833 *Total Prizemoney* £17,834
Wins * **1998** May Warwic (G-F) H 14.9f 65 70+
1995 Spt Ayr (GD) H 13.1f 73 83 <
1995 Jun Beverl (G-F) 12f 68
1998 Turf 1-3: (15f 1-1, 17f, 20f) (gd, frm 1-2)
Above-average gelding, had worn blinkers. Turf high 70. (DEAD)
**M C Pipe [4-9] Paul Green (from N J H Walker [0-6] Nov 1996).*

TOREERO **RR 37f** 2348[8]

3 b c Cadeaux Genereux 7.9f **(76)** - Free City (USA) (Danzig (USA)) 8.4f **(76)**
Form - 8
Record 1998 - 1st:0 2nd:0 3rd:0 Ran:1
1998 Turf 0-1: (8f) (sft)
Currently very moderate colt.
**J H M Gosden [0-1] Sheikh Ahmed Al Maktoum.*

TORIANNA (USA) BHB 51f **RR 55f** 3250[9]

3 b f Hermitage (USA) 8.6f **(84)** -The High Dancer (High Line) 10.3f **(70)**
Form - 7503060
Record 1998 - 1st:0 2nd:0 3rd:1 Ran:7
Pre1998 - 1st:0 2nd:1 3rd:0 Ran:2
Win Prizemoney £0 *Total Prizemoney* £1,185
1998 Turf 0-7: (6f 3, 7f, 8f 2, 12f) (g-s, gd 2, g-f 3, frm)
Scopey, fair filly, effective 5 to 8f, acts on gd to g-f. Turf high 55 - 3rd of 7 to Miss Bussell (17 Jun Hamilton 8f gd RF 2059).
**Martyn Wane [0-7] Darren & Annaley Yates (from D Nicholls [0-1] Aug 1997).*

TORNADO PRINCE (IRE) BHB 62f **RR 69?f** 3692[6]

3 ch c Caerleon (USA) 10.9f **(79)** - Welsh Flame (Welsh Pageant) 10f **(65)**
Form - 07136
Record 1998 - 1st:1 2nd:0 3rd:1 Ran:5
Pre1998 - 1st:0 2nd:0 3rd:0 Ran:3
Win Prizemoney £3,492 *Total Prizemoney* £3,883
Wins * **1998** Jly Folkes (G-F) H 9.7f 62 69+ <
1998 Turf 1-5: (8f, 10f 1-3, 12f) (gd, g-f 2, frm 1-2)
Workmanlike, average colt, effective 10f, acts on g-f to frm, prefers tight tracks. Turf high 69 - 1st of 5 giving 2lb to Nisaba (27 Jly Folkestone RF 3136). He showed very little before getting off the mark in a small five-runner event at Folkestone in July.
**N A Callaghan [1-8] M Tabor & Mrs John Magnier.*

TORPEDO RAY (IRE) BHB 45f **RR 38f** 4548[7]

2 b f Up and At 'em - Empress Kim (Formidable (USA)) 9.2f **(63)**
Form - 02007
Record 1998 - 1st:0 2nd:1 3rd:0 Ran:5
Win Prizemoney £0 *Total Prizemoney* £521
1998 Turf 0-3: (5f, 6f, 7f) (gd 2, g-f) 1998 AW 0-2: (6f, 7f) (Fibr 2)
Moderate filly. Turf high 38 (began Jly). AW high 49 (began Jly).
**J Berry [0-5] The Viking Partnership.*

TORRENT BHB 77f **RR 76f** 4872[10]

3 ch g Prince Sabo 6.6f **(64)** - Maiden Pool (Sharpen Up) 8.3f **(67)**
Form - 16106700
Record 1998 - 1st:2 2nd:0 3rd:0 Ran:8
Pre1998 - 1st:0 2nd:0 3rd:1 Ran:4
Win Prizemoney £11,112 *Total Prizemoney* £12,272
Wins * **1998** May Thirsk (G-F) H 5f 78 83 <
* **1998** Apr Catter (GD) 6f 79
1998 Turf 2-8: (5f 1-4, 6f 1-4) (g-s, gd 1-3, g-f 1-4)
Scopey, above-average gelding, effective 5 to 6f, best at 6f, acts on gd to g-f, best on g-f. Turf high 83 - 1st of 13 getting 10lb from Night Shot (16 May Thirsk RF 1272) - also 1st of 11 giving 5lb to Lindesberg (1 Apr Catterick RF 0533). Consistent. Got off the mark when winning a Catterick maiden on his reappearance by a wide margin, and has shown mixed form since, though he did win at Thirsk. Hung away from the whip when in front in a warm York handicap in June, and clearly has his quirks.
**T D Barron [2-8] Mrs J Hazell (from P F I Cole [0-4] Oct 1997).*

TORRY LOON BHB 49f **RR 48f** 5116[7]

2 b c Deploy 11.4f **(67)** - Gay Hostess (FR) (Direct Flight) 13.1f **(51)**
Form - 087
Record 1998 - 1st:0 2nd:0 3rd:0 Ran:3
1998 Turf 0-3: (6f 2, 8f) (g-s, gd, g-f)
Currently moderate colt. Turf high 48 (began Spt).
**J L Eyre [0-3] B A Kidd.*

TORSO BHB 68f **RR 73f** 2000[2]

3 b g Rudimentary (USA) 8.2f **(66)** - Tosara (Main Reef) 9.6f **(57)**

Form - 1062
Record 1998 - 1st:1 2nd:1 3rd:0 Ran:4
Pre1998 - 1st:0 2nd:0 3rd:0 Ran:3
Win Prizemoney £2,320 *Total Prizemoney* £3,902
Wins * **1998** Apr Thirsk (G-S) 7f 66 <
1998 Turf 1-4: (7f 1-1, 8f 2, 10f) (g-s 1-2, gd, frm)
Workmanlike, above-average gelding, effective 7 to 10f, acts on g-s, has worn blinkers. Turf high 73 - 2nd of 6 giving 11lb to Chlo-Jo (15 Jun Pontefract 10f g-s RF 2000) - also 1st of 10 giving 3lb to Dry Lightning (18 Apr Thirsk RF 0754). Came with a late rattle to land an ordinary race at Thirsk. Never got going until too late in a big field next time, and benefited from the step up to ten furlongs when runner-up at Pontefract in June.
**Mrs J R Ramsden [1-4] Lord Swaythling (from J W Watts [0-3] Spt 1997).*

TORY BOY BHB 66f RR 76f 3466[4]

3 b c Deploy 11.4f **(67)** - Mukhayyalah (Dancing Brave (USA)) 8.4f **(76)**
Form - 71574
Record 1998 - 1st:1 2nd:0 3rd:0 Ran:5
Win Prizemoney £3,235 *Total Prizemoney* £3,483
Wins * **1998** Jun Warwic (SFT) 10.8f 76 <
1998 Turf 1-5: (11f 1-2, 12f, 14f 2) (gd 1-4, g-f)
Lengthy, above-average colt. Turf high 76 - 1st of 7 from Tai Tam Warrior (8 Jun Warwick RF 1813). Won a Warwick maiden on his second start but looks moderate.
**Ian Williams [1-5] Mrs Nichola Mathias.*

TOSHIBA TALK (IRE) BHB 48f RR 48f 5061[1]

6 ch g Horage 11.4f **(58)** - Court Ballet (Barrons Court) 10.1f **(40)**
Form - 451
Record 1998 - 1st:1 2nd:0 3rd:0 Ran:3
Pre1998 - 1st:1 2nd:0 3rd:1 Ran:11
Win Prizemoney £7,148 *Total Prizemoney* £8,269
Wins * **1998** Oct Newcas (SFT) H 10.1f 41 48 <
* 1995 May Redcar (FRM) H 10f 49 48 <
1998 Turf 1-3: (10f 1-2, 11f) (sft 1-2, gd)
Moderate gelding. Turf high 48 - 1st of 12 getting 1lb from Es Go (30 Oct Newcastle RF 5061). **B Ellison [5-35] Toshiba (UK) Ltd.*

TOSHIBA TIMES RR 47f 5093[9]

2 b g Persian Bold 10f **(69)** - Kirkby Belle (Bay Express) 7.1f **(60)**
Form - 0
Record 1998 - 1st:0 2nd:0 3rd:0 Ran:1
1998 Turf 0-1: (7f) (gd)
Currently moderate gelding. **B Ellison [0-1] Toshiba (UK) Ltd.*

TOTAL DELIGHT RR 59f 5093[5]

2 b c Mtoto 11.5f **(71)** - Shesadelight (Shirley Heights) 10.3f **(74)**
Form - 5
Record 1998 - 1st:0 2nd:0 3rd:0 Ran:1
1998 Turf 0-1: (7f) (gd)
Currently fair colt. **Lady Herries [0-1] Hesmonds Stud.*

TOTAL TROPIX BHB 40f RR 50f 1546[4]

3 b f Saddlers' Hall (IRE) 10.5f **(65)** - Ivana (IRE) (Taufan (USA)) 7f **(57)**
Form - 44
Record 1998 - 1st:0 2nd:0 3rd:0 Ran:2
Pre1998 - 1st:0 2nd:0 3rd:0 Ran:4
1998 Turf 0-2: (10f, 12f) (g-f 2)
Light-framed, fair filly, effective 10f, acts on g-f. Turf high 44 - 4th of 9 getting 13lb from Prophits Pride (28 May Ayr 10f g-f RF 1546).
**Mrs S C Bradburne [0-1] J G Bradburne (from B J Meehan [0-1] May 1998).*

TOTEM DANCER BHB 81f71a RR 82f 71a 5151[6]

5 b m Mtoto 11.5f **(71)** - Ballad Opera (Sadler's Wells (USA)) 10f **(76)**
Form - 43542312246
Record 1998 - 1st:1 2nd:3 3rd:2 Ran:11
Pre1998 - 1st:2 2nd:4 3rd:2 Ran:15
Win Prizemoney £12,076 *Total Prizemoney* £28,537
Wins * **1998** Aug Cheste (GD) H 12.3f 75 79 <
* 1997 Spt Hamilt (GD) H 12.1f 69 76
* 1996 Oct Nottin (GD) 14.1f 76
1998 Turf 1-10: (12f 1-5, 13f 2, 14f 3) (sft 3, g-s 2, gd 1-4, frm) 1998 AW 0-1: (14f) (Fibr)
Decent filly, effective 12 to 14f, best at 14f, acts on sft to frm, prefers left handed tracks, excels at York. Turf high 82 - 2nd of 7 getting 8lb from Raise A Prince (19 Spt Ayr 13f sft RF 4369) - also 1st of 8 giving 5lb to Master Beveled (21 Aug Chester RF 3787). Consistent. Ran well last term, landing an amateurs' event at Chester in August and performing with credit afterwards. Suited by a strongly-run race at twelve furlongs.
**J L Eyre [3-26] Diamond Racing Ltd.*

TO THE LAST MAN BHB 65f RR 74f 5005[4]

2 b c Warrshan (USA) 9.7f **(59)** - Shirley's Touch (Touching Wood (USA)) 8.2f **(55)**
Form - 2642004
Record 1998 - 1st:0 2nd:2 3rd:0 Ran:7
Win Prizemoney £0 *Total Prizemoney* £1,662
1998 Turf 0-5: (7f 4, 8f) (sft, gd, g-f, frm 2) 1998 AW 0-2: (5f 2) (Fibr 2)
Above-average colt, effective 7f, acts on g-f. Turf high 74 - 2nd of 17 getting 4lb from Bathwick (3 Jly Warwick 7f g-f RF 2512). AW high 47. **M D I Usher [0-7] Trevor Barker.*

TO THE ROOF (IRE) BHB 105f RR 106f 4741[15]

6 b g Thatching 7.8f **(69)** -Christine Daae(Sadler's Wells (USA))10f **(76)**
Form - 32405210
Record 1998 - 1st:1 2nd:2 3rd:1 Ran:8
Pre1998 - 1st:4 2nd:7 3rd:2 Ran:28
Win Prizemoney £65,651 *Total Prizemoney* £92,910
Wins * **1998** Spt Ascot (SFT) H 5f 102 106 <
* 1996 Jun Epsom (G-F) LH 5f 90 92
* 1996 May Thirsk (G-F) H 6f 84 90
* 1996 May Bath (G-F) H 5.1f 79 87
* 1996 Apr Mussel (GD) H 5f 67 69
1998 Turf 1-8: (5f 1-4, 6f 4) (g-s, gd 1-4, g-f 3)
Pattern-class gelding, effective 5 to 6f, best at 5f, acts on gd to g-f, best on g-f. Turf high 106 - 1st of 9 getting 3lb from Repertory (27 Spt Ascot RF 4516). Consistent. He receives precious little help from the Handicapper, and was winning his first race for over two years when reeling in Repertory at Ascot in September. He invariably looks well and seems best when racing up with the pace over five furlongs. **P W Harris [5-36] Mrs P W Harris.*

TOTO CAELO RR 77f 4541[6]

2 b c Mtoto 11.5f **(71)** - Octavia Girl (Octavo (USA)) 14.4f **(54)**
Form - 66
Record 1998 - 1st:0 2nd:0 3rd:0 Ran:2
1998 Turf 0-2: (7f, 8f) (frm 2)
Currently above-average colt. Turf high 77 (began Jly).
**B W Hills [0-2] John Leat.*

TOTOM BHB 64f RR 56f 5070[18]

3 b f Mtoto 11.5f **(71)** - A Lyph (USA) (Lypheor) 12f **(71)**
Form - 32400
Record 1998 - 1st:0 2nd:1 3rd:1 Ran:5
Pre1998 - 1st:0 2nd:1 3rd:0 Ran:1
Win Prizemoney £0 *Total Prizemoney* £6,215
1998 Turf 0-5: (8f 3, 9f, 10f) (gd, g-f 3, frm)
Average filly, effective 8f, acts on g-f. Turf high 73 (1st run) - 3rd of 17 getting 5lb from Temeraire (22 Jun Windsor 8f g-f RF 2184).
**Lord Huntingdon [0-6] Chris van Hoorn.*

TOUCHANOVA BHB 43f48a RR 40f 48a 3931[12]

3 gr f Touch of Grey 8.1f **(47)** - Mazurkanova (Song) 7.2f **(61)**
Form - 0717270506060
Record 1998 - 1st:0 2nd:1 3rd:0 Ran:10
Pre1998 - 1st:1 2nd:0 3rd:0 Ran:8
Win Prizemoney £2,294 *Total Prizemoney* £2,879
Wins 1997 *Dec Wolver (STD) C 6f 52 <*
1998 Turf 0-5: (6f, 7f 2, 8f 2) (gd 2, g-f, frm 2) 1998 AW 0-5: (6f 2, 7f 2, 8f) (Fibr 5)
Light-framed, moderate filly, effective 6f, - acts on Fibr, has worn blinkers, likes left handed tracks. Turf high 40. AW high 49. She was very much favoured by running against the inside rail when winning a Wolverhampton claimer in December, as there was a strong bias towards the inside at that particular meeting. Very modest form otherwise.
**P W D'Arcy[0-8]Mrs Jean Mitchell(from G G Margarson[1-5]Jan 1998).*

TOUCHEZ DU BOIS (IRE) BHB 70f RR 63df 4355[12]

3 ch c Cadeaux Genereux 7.9f **(76)** - Fire Flash (Bustino) 10.4f **(64)**

Form - 15660
Record 1998 - 1st:1 2nd:0 3rd:0 Ran:5
Win Prizemoney £3,403 *Total Prizemoney* £3,549
Wins * **1998** Apr Hamilt (HVY) 11.1f 70 <
1998 Turf 1-5: (11f 1-1, 12f, 13f, 14f, 17f) (sft 1-2, gd 2, frm)
Scopey, average colt. Turf high 70 (1st run) - 1st of 7 from All Made Up (4 Apr Hamilton RF 0561). Made a successful debut in a Hamilton maiden on very soft ground. It was not a great race, and he has been found out since. **M Johnston [1-5] R W Huggins.*

TOUCH GOLD (USA) RR 5168a8

4 b c Deputy Minister (CAN) 9.2f **(71)** - Passing Mood (USA) (Buckpasser) 10.8f **(80)**
Form - 8
1998 AW 0-1: (10f) (Dirt)
Currently very high-class colt. Denied Silver Charm the American Triple Crown when coming late to win the Belmont Stakes in 1997, but he ran most disappointingly when last in the Breeders' Cup Classic. He failed to make an impression in the same race in 1998.
**P Byrne in USA [0-1] F Stronach & Stonerside Stable (from D Hofmans in USA [1-2] Nov 1997).*

TOUCH'N'GO BHB 60f60a RR 53f 60a 38293

4 b g Rainbow Quest (USA) 11.2f **(81)** - Mary Martin (Be My Guest (USA)) 9.3f **(67)**
Form - 03
Record 1998 - 1st:0 2nd:0 3rd:1 Ran:2
Pre1998 - 1st:2 2nd:1 3rd:1 Ran:8
Win Prizemoney £5,046 *Total Prizemoney* £6,811
Wins 1997 *Mar Lingfi (STD) H 10f 60 70* <
1997 *Feb Southw (STD) H 8f 51 55*
1998 AW 0-2: (9f, 11f) (Fibr 2)
Neat, fair gelding, effective 10 to 11f, - acts on AW. AW high 57 (began Jly). Consistent.
**G Woodward [0-2] Wetherby Racing Bureau 36 (from M Johnston [2-8] Jun 1997).*

TOUCH OF LOVE RR 74f 48239

2 b c Pursuit of Love 9.5f **(69)** - Nitouche (Scottish Reel) 7f **(61)**
Form - 00
Record 1998 - 1st:0 2nd:0 3rd:0 Ran:2
1998 Turf 0-2: (7f, 8f) (gd, frm)
Currently above-average colt. Turf high 74 (began Oct).
**J Noseda [0-2] Harvey Rosenblatt & Norman Mandell.*

TOUCH UP (IRE) BHB 77f RR 75f 2417a20

2 ch c Up and At 'em - Fingers (Lord Gayle (USA)) 8.8f **(62)**
Form - 4150
Record 1998 - 1st:1 2nd:0 3rd:0 Ran:4
Win Prizemoney £3,016 *Total Prizemoney* £3,382
Wins * **1998** *Apr Lingfi (STD) 5f 71+* <
1998 Turf 0-3: (5f 2, 6f) (g-s, gd, frm) 1998 AW 1-1: (5f 1-1) (Equi 1-1)
Above-average colt. Turf high 75 - 5th of 9 giving 6lb to Westminster City (8 May Lingfield 5f frm RF 1103). (1st run) - 1st of 4 giving 5lb to Mayfair Ballerina (3 Apr Lingfield RF 0553). Missed the break on his debut in the Brocklesby, but ran on to finish a highly-promising fourth, and went on to get off the mark in a four-runner maiden on the Lingfield Equitrack despite not getting the clearest of runs. Finished last of 20 in Ireland on his final start.
**Miss Gay Kelleway [1-4] Sheet & Roll Convertors Ltd.*

TOUGH ACT BHB 85f RR 82f 485021

4 b g Be My Chief (USA) 10.2f **(62)** - Forelino (USA) (Trempolino (USA)) 12f **(71)**
Form - 1623150
Record 1998 - 1st:2 2nd:1 3rd:1 Ran:7
Pre1998 - 1st:0 2nd:4 3rd:0 Ran:7
Win Prizemoney £7,939 *Total Prizemoney* £18,728
Wins * **1998** Spt Goodwo (G-S) 12f 79+ <
* **1998** Jun Goodwo (G-F) 12f 76
1998 Turf 2-7: (11f, 12f 2-2, 13f, 14f 2, 18f) (gd 1-4, g-f 1-3)
Neat, decent gelding, effective 11 to 14f, best at 14f, acts on gd to g-f, best on gd, prefers right handed tracks, prefers tight tracks. Turf high 82 - also 1st of 8 giving 2lb to Livius (11 Spt Goodwood RF 4236). He made a winning reappearance on the Flat at Goodwood in June, and followed up on the same track in the autumn.
**Mrs A J Perrett [4-19] Mrs R Doel (from G Harwood [0-4] Oct 1996).*

TOUGH GUY (IRE) RR 92f 49692

2 b c Namaqualand (USA) - Supreme Crown (USA) (Chief's Crown (USA)) 9.8f **(72)**
Form - 4U161052
Record 1998 - 1st:2 2nd:1 3rd:0 Ran:8
Win Prizemoney £8,851 *Total Prizemoney* £10,621
Wins * **1998** Aug Newmar (G-F) 7f 92 <
* **1998** Jun Kempto (SFT) 6f 88
1998 Turf 2-8: (6f 1-4, 7f 1-3, 8f) (sft, g-s 2, gd 1-1, frm 1-4)
Useful colt, effective 6 to 7f, best at 7f, acts on g-s to frm. Turf high 92 - 2nd of 10 giving 25lb to Boogy Woogy (24 Oct Doncaster 7f g-s RF 4969) - also 1st of 5 giving 8lb to Kuwait Dawn (1 Aug Newmarket RF 3273). Inconsistent. He looked a moody customer when getting rid of his pilot at Yarmouth on his second start, but was on his best behaviour at Kempton when seeming to appreciate the very testing ground. Used his stamina to good effect when winning at Newmarket, and ran well in decent nurseries on his last two starts. **M A Jarvis [2-8] Sqdn Ldr Milsom.*

TOUGH LEADER BHB 96f95a RR 97f 95a 438016

4 b c Lead on Time (USA) 7.5f **(69)** - Al Guswa (Shernazar) 10.2f **(73)**
Form - 71413134162340
Record 1998 - 1st:4 2nd:1 3rd:3 Ran:14
Pre1998 - 1st:1 2nd:1 3rd:1 Ran:7
Win Prizemoney £23,017 *Total Prizemoney* £38,745
Wins * **1998** Jly York (G-F) H 11.9f 91 95 <
* **1998** May Sandow (GD) H 10f 78 82
* **1998** *Mar Southw (STD) H 12f 77 80*
* **1998** *Feb Wolver (STD) H 9.4f 75 77*
* 1996 Jun Thirsk (FRM) 7f 66
1998 Turf 2-10: (10f 1-4, 12f 1-4, 13f, 14f) (g-s, gd 2, g-f 1-5, frm 1-2)
1998 AW 2-4: (8f, 9f 1-1, 10f, 12f 1-1) (Equi 2, Fibr 2-2)
Strong, very useful colt, effective 10 to 14f, best at 12f, acts on gd to frm, best on gd, excels at Epsom. Turf high 97 - 2nd of 9 giving 6lb to Rokeby Bowl (9 Aug Epsom 12f gd RF 3482) - also 1st of 7 giving 15lb to Blueprint (10 Jly York RF 2699). AW high 80. Consistent. Lightly-raced in previous seasons, he showed much-improved form when tried on Fibresand during the winter, winning twice, and continued the improvement on to turf. He won twice, at Sandown and a good handicap at York, as well as running fine races at Epsom and Ascot. **B Hanbury [5-21] G G Grayson.*

TOUJOURS RIVIERA BHB 71f77a RR 79f 77a 507822

8 ch g Rainbow Quest (USA) 11.2f **(81)** - Miss Beaulieu (Northfields (USA)) 9f **(72)**
Form - 531724003402480
Record 1998 - 1st:1 2nd:2 3rd:1 Ran:13
Pre1998 - 1st:7 2nd:4 3rd:7 Ran:51
Win Prizemoney £47,765 *Total Prizemoney* £66,460
Wins * **1998** *Jan Lingfi (STD) H 12f 73 77*
* 1997 Spt Bright (FRM) H 8f 74 81
* 1997 Aug Hamilt (G-F) H 8.3f 71 74
* 1995 Jly Yarmou (G-F) H 8f 84 89 <
* 1994 Oct Newmar (G-F) H 8f 79 82
* 1994 Oct Ascot (G-F) H 8f 73 77
* 1994 Aug Sandow (GD) H 8.1f 66 70
* 1994 Jun Folkes (GD) 6.9f 61
1998 Turf 0-9: (7f, 8f 7, 10f) (sft, gd, g-f 4, frm 3) 1998 AW 1-4: (11f, 12f 1-3) (Equi 1-2, Fibr 2)
Above-average gelding, effective 8 to 12f, best at 8f, acts on gd to frm - acts on Equi, best on frm, excels at Brighton, does well at Newmarket. Turf high 79 - 3rd of 20 giving 5lb to Mount Holly (7 Jly Newmarket 8f frm RF 2579). AW high 77 (1st run) - 1st of 11 giving 11lb to Quiet Arch (3 Jan Lingfield RF 0020). Won on the Lingfield Equitrack in January, and ran one of his best races of the year on turf when staying on strongly into third at the July Meeting. Rather hard to win with.
**J Pearce [8-61] Jeff Pearce (from G Wragg [0-4] Oct 1993).*

TOULSTON LADY (IRE) BHB 22f32a RR 21f 32a 39444

6 b m Handsome Sailor 6.6f **(53)** - Rainbow Lady (Jaazeiro (USA)) 9.2f **(54)**
Form - 2500004
Record 1998 - 1st:0 2nd:1 3rd:0 Ran:7
Pre1998 - 1st:0 2nd:0 3rd:3 Ran:10
Win Prizemoney £0 *Total Prizemoney* £1,892
1998 Turf 0-4: (10f, 12f 2, 14f) (sft, g-f, frm, hrd) 1998 AW 0-3: (12f 2, 16f) (Fibr 3)

Very moderate mare, effective 12f, - acts on Fibr, often wears blinkers (very effectively), likes left handed tracks, favours tight tracks. Turf high 21. AW high 35 (1st run) - 2nd of 10 getting 16lb from Misty Rain (19 Jan Southwell 12f Fibr RF 0118).
**J Wharton [1-19] Hickling and Squires Ltd (from M J Camacho [0-5] Aug 1996).*

TOUS LES JOURS (USA) BHB 72f **RR 74f** 4767[3]
2 b f Dayjur (USA) 6.8f **(79)** -Humility (USA)(Cox's Ridge (USA)) 8f **(68)**
Form - 34841033
Record 1998 - 1st:1 2nd:0 3rd:3 Ran:8
Win Prizemoney £3,455 *Total Prizemoney* £5,920
Wins * 1998 Aug Beverl (G-F) H 7.5f 67 74 <
1998 Turf 1-8: (5f 3, 6f, 7f 1-1, 8f 3) (sft 2, g-s, g-f 2, frm 1-2, hrd)
Above-average filly, effective 5 to 7f, acts on frm. Turf high 74 - 1st of 10 getting 15lb from Ringside Jack (13 Aug Beverley RF 3601). She looked to have some temperament in her early races, but got off the mark in a Beverley nursery over the extended seven furlongs. **M Johnston [1-8] J S Morrison.*

TOWNVILLE CEE CEE BHB 41f **RR 45f** 5059[15]
3 b f Anshan 8.2f **(63)** - Holy Day (Sallust) 8.4f **(63)**
Form - 70600400
Record 1998 - 1st:0 2nd:0 3rd:0 Ran:8
Pre1998 - 1st:0 2nd:0 3rd:0 Ran:7
Win Prizemoney £0 *Total Prizemoney* £281
1998 Turf 0-8: (6f 2, 7f 2, 8f 4) (sft, g-s, gd, g-f, frm 3, hrd)
Scopey, moderate filly. Turf high 45.
**G Woodward [0-1] Townville C C Racing Club (from J S Wainwright [0-14] Aug 1998).*

TOY BOX (IRE) BHB 56f **RR 63df** 4883[12]
3 b f Salse (USA) 10.9f **(71)** - Belle Enfant (Beldale Flutter (USA)) 9.7f **(71)**
Form - 07500
Record 1998 - 1st:0 2nd:0 3rd:0 Ran:5
1998 Turf 0-5: (8f, 10f 2, 12f 2) (g-s, gd, frm 3)
Leggy, average filly. Turf high 63. **G C Bravery [0-5] D B Clark.*

TOY TRADER BHB 59f **RR 70f** 4569[5]
2 b g High Estate 10.5f **(66)** - Fairy Magic (IRE) (Fairy King (USA)) 7.7f **(59)**
Form - 8573665
Record 1998 - 1st:0 2nd:0 3rd:1 Ran:7
Win Prizemoney £0 *Total Prizemoney* £464
1998 Turf 0-7: (5f 4, 6f 2, 7f) (gd, g-f 6)
Above-average gelding, has worn blinkers. Turf high 70.
**A P Jarvis [0-7] Grant & Bowman Ltd.*

TRACKING BHB 109f **RR 109f** 4361[1]
3 ch c Machiavellian (USA) 9.8f **(83)** - Black Fighter (USA) (Secretariat (USA)) 9f **(79)**
Form - 0431
Record 1998 - 1st:1 2nd:0 3rd:1 Ran:4
Pre1998 - 1st:2 2nd:2 3rd:0 Ran:5
Win Prizemoney £18,320 *Total Prizemoney* £29,620
Wins * 1998 Spt Newbur (gd) 9f 109 <
* 1997 Jly York (GD) 7f 82
* 1997 Jun Nottin (GD) 6.1f 79+
1998 Turf 1-4: (7f 2, 8f, 9f 1-1) (sft, gd, g-f, frm 1-1)
Pattern-class colt, effective 7 to 9f, acts on gd to frm. Turf high 109 - 1st of 5 from Haami (18 Spt Newbury RF 4361). He was entered for the sales in the autumn, but was granted a reprieve after beating Haami at Newbury in September. That form looks useful in light of Haami's revival and, still lightly raced, this colt could yet win a Pattern event. **H R A Cecil [3-9] Buckram Oak Holdings.*

TRAGIC DANCER BHB 65f **RR 73?f** 4663[10]
2 b c Tragic Role (USA) 9.4f **(63)** - Chantallee's Pride (Mansooj)
Form - 08030
Record 1998 - 1st:0 2nd:0 3rd:1 Ran:5
Win Prizemoney £0 *Total Prizemoney* £480
1998 Turf 0-4: (6f, 7f, 10f 2) (g-s, g-f 2, frm) 1998 AW 0-1: (7f) (Fibr)
Above-average colt. Turf high 73 - 3rd of 11 to Bergamo (28 Spt Bath 10f g-f RF 4526). **K McAuliffe [0-5] Treadwell, Chung & Butler.*

TRAILBLAZER BHB 57f70a **RR 60f 70a** 4536[5]
4 b g Efisio 7.7f **(69)** -Flicker Toa Flame(USA)(Empery (USA))11.2f **(69)**
Form - 0531425
Record 1998 - 1st:1 2nd:1 3rd:1 Ran:7
Pre1998 - 1st:1 2nd:0 3rd:1 Ran:8
Win Prizemoney £5,329 *Total Prizemoney* £9,120
Wins * 1998 *Aug Wolver (STD) S 9.4f 68 <*
** 1996 Nov Wolver (STD) 6f 66*
1998 Turf 0-6: (7f, 8f 2, 9f 2, 10f) (g-s 2, gd 3, g-f) 1998 AW 1-1: (9f 1-1) (Fibr 1-1)
Above-average gelding, effective 8 to 9f, acts on gd - acts on Fibr, likes tight tracks. Turf high 60 - 2nd of 10 getting 26lb from Wuxi Venture (7 Spt Hamilton 8f gd RF 4132). (1st run) - 1st of 13 giving 7lb to Mandhar (22 Aug Wolverhampton RF 3829). Took a Wolverhampton seller quite comfortably in August, and may well be able to win slightly better races on that surface.
**C W Thornton [2-15] Guy Reed.*

TRAIT DE GENIE (FR) **RR 112f** 5155a[1]
6 ch g Diamond Prospect (USA) 8f **(62)** -Garmeritte(FR)(Garde Royale)
Form - 211
1998 Turf 2-2: (12f 2-2) (hvy 1-1, gd 1-1)
Group-class gelding, effective 12f, acts on hvy to gd. Turf high 112 (began Spt) - 1st of 11 giving 16lb to Aka Lady (2 Nov Nantes RF 5155a) - also 1st of 9 from Galtee (27 Spt Dielsdorf RF 4605a). He is tough and genuine and always to be respected in Listed events.
**A Lyon in FR [3-3] J Bouchara (from J Bouchara in FR [1-1] Spt 1998).*

TRAKELOR BHB 37f35a **RR 49?f 35a** 4922[10]
3 b f Most Welcome 8.6f **(66)** - French Cooking (Royal And Regal (USA)) 9.5f **(60)**
Form - 0476501820
Record 1998 - 1st:1 2nd:1 3rd:0 Ran:8
Pre1998 - 1st:0 2nd:0 3rd:0 Ran:2
Win Prizemoney £2,385 *Total Prizemoney* £3,009
Wins * 1998 Apr Pontef (G-S) S 12f 49 <
1998 Turf 1-4: (8f, 12f 1-1, 14f, 16f) (g-s 1-3, frm) 1998 AW 0-4: (11f 2, 12f 2) (Fibr 4)
Workmanlike, moderate filly, effective 12f, acts on g-s, has worn blinkers. Turf high 49 - 1st of 7 getting 5lb from King's Hussar (27 Apr Pontefract RF 0879). AW high 26.
**R Hollinshead [1-10] L A Morgan.*

TRAMLINE BHB 55f49a **RR 57f 49a** 5150[9]
5 b h Shirley Heights 12.1f **(76)** - Trampship (High Line) 10.3f **(70)**
Form - 77730
Record 1998 - 1st:0 2nd:0 3rd:1 Ran:5
Pre1998 - 1st:1 2nd:0 3rd:0 Ran:7
Win Prizemoney £3,557 *Total Prizemoney* £4,176
Wins * 1997 Jun Newmar (G-S) 14.8f 82 <
1998 Turf 0-3: (12f, 14f, 17f) (g-s 2, gd) 1998 AW 0-2: (13f, 16f) (Equi, Fibr)
Fair colt, effective 15f, acts on gd. Turf high 57 (began Oct). AW high 52. Consistent. **M Blanshard [1-12] H C Promotions Ltd.*

TRANQUIL LIFE (USA) **RR 77+f** 4937[1]
2 b f Dayjur (USA) 6.8f **(79)** - Sanctuary (Welsh Pageant) 10f **(65)**
Form - 1
Record 1998 - 1st:1 2nd:0 3rd:0 Ran:1
Win Prizemoney £3,781 *Total Prizemoney* £3,781
Wins * 1998 Oct Nottin () 5.1f 77+ <
1998 Turf 1-1: (5f 1-1) (gd 1-1)
Currently above-average filly. (1st run) - 1st of 18 getting 5lb from Get Stuck In (22 Oct Nottingham RF 4937). Has plenty of speed in her pedigree, being closely related to Sheikh Albadou.
**D R Loder [1-1] Maktoum Al Maktoum.*

TRANS ISLAND BHB 111f **RR 110f** 1227a[8]
3 b c Selkirk (USA) 7.9f **(76)** - Khubza (Green Desert (USA)) 8.6f **(78)**
Form - 228
Record 1998 - 1st:0 2nd:2 3rd:0 Ran:3
Pre1998 - 1st:3 2nd:2 3rd:0 Ran:5
Win Prizemoney £29,918 *Total Prizemoney* £65,688
Wins * 1997 Aug Deauvi (SFT) L 7f 91+
* 1997 Jly Newbur (G-F) 7f 93 <
* 1997 Jun Newbur (G-F) 6f 86
1998 Turf 0-3: (7f, 8f 2) (sft, gd 2)

Scopey, Group-class colt, effective 7 to 8f, best at 8f, acts on sft to gd, best on gd, excels at Newbury. Turf high 110 - 2nd of 13 to Crisos Il Monaco (26 Apr Capannelle 8f gd RF 0947a). He ran out a clear cut winner of the Premio Parioli (Italian 2000 Guineas), but was disqualified for causing interference inside the final furlong. Pat Eddery reported that he found the ground too fast in the German equivalent, and one can only presume he was correct as we did not see this useful colt again.

**I A Balding [3-8] Al Muallim Partnership.*

TRANSYLVANIA BHB 78f **RR 80f** 5078[20]

3 b f Wolfhound (USA) 7.3f **(71)** - Slava (USA) (Diesis) 9.3f **(69)**

Form - 422312100

Record				
1998 -	1st:2	2nd:3	3rd:1	Ran:9
Pre1998 -	1st:0	2nd:0	3rd:0	Ran:1

Win Prizemoney £6,807 *Total Prizemoney* £11,750

Wins				
* **1998** Spt	Mussel (GD)	8f	80	<
* **1998** Aug	Chepst (G-F)	7.1f	75	

1998Turf 2-9:(7f 1-2, 8f 1-3, 9f 2, 10f 2)(sft 2, g-s, gd 4, g-f 1-1, frm 1-1)

Unfurnished, decent filly, effective 7 to 10f, acts on sft to frm, best on gd, excels at Chepstow. Turf high 80 - 2nd of 15 giving 1lb to Pay On Red (5 Spt Epsom 9f gd RF 4101) - also 1st of 5 from Night Flyer (27 Spt Musselburgh RF 4522). She won nicely at Chepstow and Musselburgh, and though neither event was particularly competitive, she could win a handicap or two next season.

**J L Dunlop [2-10] Capt J Macdonald-Buchanan.*

TRAPPER NORMAN BHB 32f27a **RR 38f 27a** 3562[4]

6 b g Mazilier (USA) 8.5f **(56)** - Free Skip (Free State) 8.7f **(61)**

Form - 4

Record				
1998 -	1st:0	2nd:0	3rd:0	Ran:1
Pre1998 -	1st:0	2nd:0	3rd:0	Ran:10

1998 Turf 0-1: (8f) (g-f)

Very moderate gelding.

**C Smith [0-4] Brian Culley (from R Ingram [0-10] Jan 1997).*

Form - 380

Record				
1998 -	1st:0	2nd:0	3rd:1	Ran:3
Pre1998 -	1st:0	2nd:0	3rd:0	Ran:1

Win Prizemoney £0 *Total Prizemoney* £490

1998 Turf 0-3: (12f, 14f 2) (g-s, gd, frm)

Lengthy, fair colt. Turf high 52. **B A McMahon [0-4] R L Bedding.*

TRAVELMATE BHB 96f **RR 93f** 4537[1]

4 b g Persian Bold 10f **(69)** - Ustka (Lomond (USA)) 8.8f **(65)**

Form - 516161

Record				
1998 -	1st:3	2nd:0	3rd:0	Ran:6
Pre1998 -	1st:2	2nd:1	3rd:0	Ran:6

Win Prizemoney £29,543 *Total Prizemoney* £30,651

Wins						
* **1998** Spt	Newmar (GD)	H	12f	91	93	<
* **1998** Aug	Newmar (G-F)	H	14.8f	81	84+	
* **1998** Jun	Newmar (GD)	H	12f	76	79	
* 1997 Jun	Newmar (G-S)	H	12f	73	74	
* 1997 May	Nottin (GD)	H	10f	66	74+	

1998 Turf 3-6: (12f 2-4, 15f 1-2) (gd 3, g-f 1-1, frm 2-2)

Leggy, useful gelding, effective 12 to 15f, best at 15f, acts on gd to frm, best on frm, excels at Newmarket. Turf high 93 - 1st of 11 giving 10lb to Rainbow High (29 Spt Newmarket RF 4537) - also 1st of 12 giving 11lb to Highwayman (28 Aug Newmarket RF 3930). He won twice early in 1997, but was absent from the track after winning at Newmarket in June. He won the same race on his second run back last term, but may have run again too soon when beaten next time. Very easy winner when stepped up in trip to an extended fourteen furlongs in August, and won cleverly on his final start.

**J R Fanshawe [5-12] Barford Bloodstock II.*

TRAWLING **RR 74f** 4575[2]

2 b f Mtoto 11.5f **(71)** - Ghost Tree (IRE) (Caerleon (USA)) 8.6f **(71)**

Form - 22

Record				
1998 -	1st:0	2nd:2	3rd:0	Ran:2

Win Prizemoney £0 *Total Prizemoney* £1,446

Travelmate has a very impressive record at Newmarket

TRAVELLING CLOCK BHB 55f **RR 52f** 1759[9]

3 ch c Deploy 11.4f **(67)** - Travel Mystery (Godswalk (USA)) 7.3f **(58)**

1998 Turf 0-2: (7f 2) (g-f, frm)

Currently above-average filly. Turf high 74 (began Spt) - 2nd of 13

to Come What May (30 Spt Newcastle 7f g-f RF 4575).
**B W Hills [0-2] Mrs H Theodorou.*

TREAD SOFTLY (IRE) BHB 73f **RR 81f** 5144^{9}

2 b f Roi Danzig (USA) 10.5f **(62)** -Albenita (IRE)(Alzao (USA)) 7.1f **(68)**
Form - 210
Record 1998 - 1st:1 2nd:1 3rd:0 Ran:3
Win Prizemoney £2,442 *Total Prizemoney* £3,224
Wins * **1998** Oct Pontef (SFT) 6f 71 <
1998 Turf 1-3: (5f 2, 6f 1-1) (gd 1-3)
Currently decent filly. Turf high 81 (1st run) (began Spt) - 2nd of 17 giving 7lb to Oriel Star (1 Spt Ripon 5f gd RF 4009).
**R A Fahey [1-3] Capt C M Ryan.*

TREASURE CHEST (IRE) RR 82f 4841^{6}

3 b g Last Tycoon 9.4f **(73)** - Sought Out (IRE) (Rainbow Quest (USA)) 10.4f **(75)**
Form - 538226
Record 1998 - 1st:0 2nd:2 3rd:1 Ran:6
Pre1998 - 1st:0 2nd:0 3rd:1 Ran:3
Win Prizemoney £0 *Total Prizemoney* £3,908
1998 Turf 0-6: (10f, 14f 3, 16f, 18f) (g-s 2, g-f 2, frm 2)
Scopey, decent gelding, effective 10 to 18f, acts on g-f to frm, best on frm, has worn blinkers, favours tight tracks. Turf high 82 - 2nd of 5 getting 12lb from Etterby Park (17 Spt Yarmouth 18f frm RF 4335). Has joined Martin Pipe.
**M P Tregoning [0-6] Lord Weinstock (from Major W R Hern [0-3] Spt 1997).*

TREASURE DOME (IRE) BHB 42f **RR 32f** 4931^{9}

4 b g Treasure Kay 6.5f **(53)** -Royal Saint (USA)(Crimson Satan) 8f **(67)**
Form - 00
Record 1998 - 1st:0 2nd:0 3rd:0 Ran:2
Pre1998 - 1st:0 2nd:0 3rd:0 Ran:10
1998 Turf 0-2: (10f, 12f) (g-s, g-f)
Very moderate gelding, has worn blinkers. Turf high 32 (began Jly). Inconsistent.
**C Weedon [0-2] David Cross Leisure Ltd (from N Meade in IRE [1-17] Jly 1998).*

TREASURE ISLAND BHB 50f49a **RR 46f 49a** 2762^{10}

3 b f Rainbow Quest (USA) 11.2f **(81)** - Cockatoo Island (High Top) 10.2f **(67)**
Form - 87160
Record 1998 - 1st:1 2nd:0 3rd:0 Ran:4
Pre1998 - 1st:0 2nd:0 3rd:0 Ran:3
Win Prizemoney £2,836 *Total Prizemoney* £2,836
Wins * **1998** Jun Hamilt (G-S) H 11.1f 43 46 <
1998 Turf 1-3:(10f, 11f 1-1, 14f) (gd 2, g-f 1-1) 1998 AW 0-1: (12f) (Fibr)
Light-framed, moderate filly, effective 11f, acts on g-f, likes tight tracks. Turf high 46 (1st run) - 1st of 11 getting 10lb from Forty Love (24 Jun Hamilton RF 2246). **Sir Mark Prescott [1-7] Lord Derby.*

TREASURE TOUCH (IRE) BHB 61f76a **RR 52f 76a** 3567^{9}

4 b g Treasure Kay 6.5f **(53)** - Bally Pourri (IRE) (Law Society (USA)) 9.9f **(70)**
Form - 80000600
Record 1998 - 1st:0 2nd:0 3rd:0 Ran:8
Pre1998 - 1st:5 2nd:1 3rd:3 Ran:18
Win Prizemoney £22,384 *Total Prizemoney* £24,599
Wins * 1997 May Thirsk (GD) H 5f 85 85+
* 1997 Apr Newmar (G-F) H 6f 72 86 <
* 1997 Apr Nottin (G-F) H 6.1f 63 78+
* 1997 Mar Nottin (G-F) H 6.1f 63 71+
1997 *Feb Southw (STD) 6f 69+*
1998 Turf 0-8: (5f 5, 6f 3) (g-s 2, gd 2, g-f 4)
Scopey, average gelding, effective 5 to 6f, best at 5f, acts on g-s to frm, excels at Nottingham. Turf high 70. He rose dramatically in the handicap as a result of a successful 1997, and has found life tougher since.
**D Nicholls [4-19] N Honeyman (from G M Moore [1-6] Feb 1997).*

TREASURY RR 70f 5148^{15}

2 ch f Generous (IRE) 11.5f **(82)** - Atlantic Flyer (USA) (Storm Bird (CAN)) 10.3f **(74)**
Form - 7000
Record 1998 - 1st:0 2nd:0 3rd:0 Ran:4
1998 Turf 0-4: (7f 4) (gd 2, frm 2)
Above-average filly. Turf high 70 (began Spt).
**Sir Mark Prescott [0-4] Cheveley Park Stud.*

TREAT ME BOLD BHB 30f **RR 39f** 3980^{8}

6 b g Bold Owl 9.7f **(47)** - Sodina (Saulingo) 6.2f **(53)**
Form - 608
Record 1998 - 1st:0 2nd:0 3rd:0 Ran:3
1998 Turf 0-3: (8f, 11f, 12f) (g-f, frm 2)
Very moderate gelding. Turf high 39 (began Jly).
**P Bowen [0-11] Dewi Evans.*

TREBIZOND (IRE) RR 91f $5108a^{5}$

2 b c Sadler's Wells (USA) 11.3f **(87)** - Karri Valley (USA) (Storm Bird (CAN)) 10.3f **(74)**
Form - 325
1998 Turf 0-3: (7f, 8f, 9f) (g-s, gd 2)
Currently useful colt. Turf high 91 (began Aug) - 2nd of 18 giving 5lb to Maid Of Killeen (10 Oct Cork 9f g-s RF 4787a).
**C O'Brien in IRE [0-3] Dr M V O'Brien.*

TREBLE TERM BHB 66f65a **RR 65f 65a** 518^{16}

3 ch f Lion Cavern (USA) 7.5f **(74)** - Treble Hook (IRE) (Ballad Rock) 7.8f **(63)**
Form - 6220
Record 1998 - 1st:0 2nd:2 3rd:0 Ran:3
Pre1998 - 1st:0 2nd:0 3rd:0 Ran:3
Win Prizemoney £0 *Total Prizemoney* £1,809
1998 Turf 0-1: (6f) (g-s) 1998 AW 0-2: (6f 2) (Equi 2)
Workmanlike, average filly, effective 6f, - acts on Equi. AW high 66 (1st run) - 2nd of 4 giving 2lb to Legal Lark (8 Jan Lingfield 6f Equi RF 0050). **P J Makin [0-6] Mrs P J Makin.*

TREMENDISTO BHB 42f30a **RR 26f 30a** 338^{8}

8 b g Petoski 10.4f **(56)** - Misty Halo (High Top) 10.2f **(67)**
Form - 8
Record 1998 - 1st:0 2nd:0 3rd:0 Ran:1
Pre1998 - 1st:0 2nd:5 3rd:3 Ran:29
Win Prizemoney £0 *Total Prizemoney* £6,323
1998 AW 0-1: (16f) (Fibr)
Little account gelding.
**D McCain [0-5] L A Morgan (from Capt J Wilson [1-34] Jan 1997).*

TREMONNOW BHB 40f **RR 45f** 3644^{10}

3 b f Reprimand 8.2f **(63)** - Tree Mallow (Malicious) 8.7f **(50)**
Form - 02868400
Record 1998 - 1st:0 2nd:1 3rd:0 Ran:8
Pre1998 - 1st:0 2nd:0 3rd:1 Ran:7
Win Prizemoney £0 *Total Prizemoney* £1,173
1998 Turf 0-8: (6f 5, 7f 2, 8f) (gd 2, g-f 4, frm 2)
Light-framed, moderate filly, effective 6f, acts on gd to frm, has worn blinkers. Turf high 45.
**J M Bradley [0-15] Overmonnow Racing Club.*

TREMPLIN (USA) BHB 64f62a **RR 64f 62a** 4470^{6}

6 b g Trempolino (USA) 11.9f **(77)** - Stresa (Mill Reef (USA)) 10.5f **(78)**
Form - 066
Record 1998 - 1st:0 2nd:0 3rd:0 Ran:2
Pre1998 - 1st:0 2nd:0 3rd:0 Ran:11
Win Prizemoney £0 *Total Prizemoney* £397
1998 Turf 0-2: (8f, 10f) (gd, frm)
Average gelding, has worn blinkers. Turf high 64 (began Spt). Consistent. Formerly a fair sort in France at three, he has shown a glimmer of ability since coming to this country but looks one to be wary of.
**N A Callaghan [0-12] M Tabor (from A Fabre in FR [0-1] Apr 1995).*

TRENDY INDIAN (IRE) RR 71f 1613^{5}

3 ch f Indian Ridge 7.6f **(74)** - Moving Trend (IRE) (Be My Guest (USA)) 9.3f **(67)**
Form - 5
Record 1998 - 1st:0 2nd:0 3rd:0 Ran:1
1998 Turf 0-1: (8f) (g-f)
Workmanlike, currently above-average filly.
**J H M Gosden [0-1] Sheikh Ahmed Al Maktoum.*

TRENT MAYFLY BHB 33f33a **RR 25f 33a** 3396[10]
4 b f Flockton's Own 7f **(42)** - Trent Lane (Park Lane)
Form - 005800
Record 1998 - 1st:0 2nd:0 3rd:0 Ran:6
1998 Turf 0-5: (6f, 7f, 8f, 10f 2) (gd 2, g-f, frm 2) 1998 AW 0-1: (6f) (Fibr)
Little account filly. Turf high 25. *°C Smith [0-6] J Payne.*

TRES HEUREUX (GER) RR 110f 4829a[1]
8 b h Konigsstuhl (GER) 9f **(115)** - Tres Magnifique
Form - 1
1998 Turf 1-1: (9f 1-1) (hvy 1-1)
Group-class horse. (1st run) - 1st of 11 giving 6lb to Page's King (11 Oct Dusseldorf RF 4829a). He retains all his ability at eight and splashed through Dusseldorf mud to win a Group Three in October. *°Frau E Mader in GER [2-7] Stall Mucos.*

TRESORIERE (USA) RR 110f 4954a[2]
4 f b Lyphard (USA) 10.6f **(75)** - Time Deposit (USA) (Halo (USA)) 10.6f **(75)**
Form - 2
1998 Turf 0-1: (10f) (frm)
Currently Group-class. (1st run) - 2nd of 8 giving 5lb to Zomaradah (18 Oct Woodbine 10f frm RF 4954a). *°C Clement in USA [0-1].*

TRIANO (GER) RR 109f 3054a[2]
5 ch h Zampano (GER) - Twist Love (GER) (Surumu (GER)) 10f **(83)**
Form - 2
1998 Turf 0-1: (10f) (g-f)
Currently Pattern-class colt. (1st run) - 2nd of 12 giving 12lb to Aboard (19 Jly Frankfurt 10f g-f RF 3054a). Touched off at Frankfurt in July, he is a useful horse at around a mile and a quarter. *°H Remmert in GER [0-1] Frau H Harzheim.*

TRIBAL MOON (IRE) BHB 45f **RR 58f** 3638[14]
5 b g Ela-Mana-Mou 12.7f **(72)** - Silk Blend (Busted) 10.2f **(61)**
Form - 60
Record 1998 - 1st:0 2nd:0 3rd:0 Ran:2
Pre1998 - 1st:0 2nd:0 3rd:0 Ran:5
1998 AW 0-2: (12f, 14f) (Fibr 2)
Fair gelding. (began Jly).
°J G Portman [0-2] J G B Portman (from Lady Herries [0-5] Jly 1997).

TRIBAL PEACE (IRE) BHB 49f57a **RR 55f 57a** 4933[9]
6 ch g Red Sunset 9f **(57)** - Mirabiliary (USA) (Crow (FR)) 7.4f **(75)**
Form - 34804480
Record 1998 - 1st:0 2nd:0 3rd:1 Ran:8
Pre1998 - 1st:5 2nd:5 3rd:3 Ran:34
Win Prizemoney £21,403 *Total Prizemoney* £31,368
Wins ° 1997 Jly Goodwo (G-F) H 9f 60 64
° *1997 Jan Lingfi (STD) H 10f 65 70*
° *1996 Jan Lingfi (STD) C 10f 67*
° 1995 Spt Goodwo (G-S) H 9f 65 71 <
° *1995 Feb Lingfi (STD) 10f 60*
1998 Turf 0-6: (8f 2, 9f 3, 10f) (g-s, gd 2, g-f, frm, hrd) 1998 AW 0-2: (10f 2) (Equi 2)
Average gelding, effective 9 to 10f, best at 9f, acts on gd to g-f - acts on Equi, best on gd, likes right handed tracks, favours tight tracks. Turf high 55. AW high 64.
°B Gubby [5-40] Brian Gubby Ltd (from B J Meehan [0-2] Spt 1994).

TRICKS (IRE) RR 35f 4146[15]
2 b f First Trump - Party Line **(57f 60a)** (Never so Bold) 6.3f **(66)**
Form - 0
Record 1998 - 1st:0 2nd:0 3rd:0 Ran:1
1998 Turf 0-1: (6f) (g-f)
Currently fair filly. *°Lord Huntingdon [0-1] Miss Holmes a' Court.*

TRICOLORE RR 73f 4959[3]
2 b f Sadler's Wells (USA) 11.3f **(87)** - Tricorne **(72f)** (Green Desert (USA)) 8.6f **(78)**
Form - 3
Record 1998 - 1st:0 2nd:0 3rd:1 Ran:1
Win Prizemoney £0 *Total Prizemoney* £680
1998 Turf 0-1: (7f) (frm)
Currently above-average filly. *°J L Dunlop [0-1] Michael Page.*

TRIDENT (USA) BHB 103f **RR 106f** 4843[7]
3 b c Red Ransom (USA) 8.6f **(83)** - Lady di Pomadora (USA) (Danzig Connection (USA)) 8f **(68)**
Form - 5317
Record 1998 - 1st:1 2nd:0 3rd:1 Ran:4
Pre1998 - 1st:1 2nd:0 3rd:1 Ran:2
Win Prizemoney £8,546 *Total Prizemoney* £13,537
Wins ° **1998** Oct Ascot (SFT) 8f 106 <
° 1997 Jly Sandow (G-F) 7.1f 85+
1998 Turf 1-4: (8f 1-1, 9f 2, 10f) (g-s 1-1, gd, g-f 2)
Well made, Pattern-class colt, effective 8f, acts on g-s. Turf high 106 - 1st of 5 getting 3lb from Ghalib (9 Oct Ascot RF 4736). He is hard to quantify, but managed to win an uncompetitive conditions race at Ascot in October. He made 50,000 guineas at the Tattersalls Autumn Horses In Training Sales and will be trained by California-based Jim Cassidy.
°Sir Michael Stoute [2-6] Highclere Thoroughbred Racing Ltd.

TRIENNIUM (USA) BHB 44f **RR 15f** 1546[8]
9 ch g Vaguely Noble 10.6f **(68)** - Triple Tipple (USA) (Raise A Cup (USA)) 7.6f **(74)**
Form - 8
Record 1998 - 1st:0 2nd:0 3rd:0 Ran:1
Pre1998 - 1st:0 2nd:1 3rd:2 Ran:6
Win Prizemoney £0 *Total Prizemoney* £1,655
1998 Turf 0-1: (10f) (g-f)
Poor gelding.
°P Monteith [3-14] M C Boyd (from R Allan [0-1] Oct 1993).

TRIENTA MIL BHB 23a **RR 46f 23a** 370[10]
4 b g Prince Sabo 6.6f **(64)**-Burmese Ruby(Good Times (ITY)) 6.6f **(54)**
Form - 43000
Record 1998 - 1st:0 2nd:0 3rd:1 Ran:5
Pre1998 - 1st:0 2nd:0 3rd:0 Ran:2
Win Prizemoney £0 *Total Prizemoney* £285
1998 AW 0-5: (8f, 11f 2, 12f 2) (Fibr 5)
Workmanlike, moderate gelding, has worn blinkers. AW high 40.
°P T Dalton [0-10] Mrs Jeffrey Robinson.

TRIGGER HAPPY (IRE) BHB 102f **RR 97f** 3776[7]
3 ch f Ela-Mana-Mou 12.7f **(72)** - Happy Tidings (Hello Gorgeous (USA)) 9.7f **(63)**
Form - 27
Record 1998 - 1st:0 2nd:1 3rd:0 Ran:2
Pre1998 - 1st:1 2nd:0 3rd:0 Ran:2
Win Prizemoney £9,035 *Total Prizemoney* £13,615
Wins ° 1997 Nov Newmar (G-F) L 10f 85 <
1998 Turf 0-2: (11f, 12f) (g-f, frm)
Leggy, very useful filly. Turf high 97 (1st run) - 2nd of 6 giving 3lb to Bristol Channel (9 May Lingfield 11f g-f RF 1124). A sister to the stable's ill-fated Eldorado, she won the ten-furlong Zetland Stakes at two and was beaten narrowly in the Lingfield Oaks Trial first time out in 1998. Off the track until finishing well beaten in a listed race in August. *°M Johnston [1-4] R W Huggins.*

TRIMILKI (IRE) RR 43f 4575[9]
2 b f Lahib (USA) 8f **(69)** -Timissara (USA)(Shahrastani (USA))8.8f **(72)**
Form - 0
Record 1998 - 1st:0 2nd:0 3rd:0 Ran:1
1998 Turf 0-1: (7f) (g-f)
Currently moderate filly. *°T J Etherington [0-1] Callers And Clerks.*

TRINA'S PET BHB 57f65a **RR 59f 65a** 4863[5]
2 ch f Efisio 7.7f **(69)** - Lindy Belle **(35f)** (Alleging (USA))
Form - 704131005
Record 1998 - 1st:2 2nd:0 3rd:1 Ran:9
Win Prizemoney £3,887 *Total Prizemoney* £4,199
Wins **1998** *Jly Southw (STD) S 5f 72* <
1998 *Jun Southw (STD) S 5f 72* <
1998 Turf 0-5:(5f 2, 6f 3) (gd 2, frm 3) 1998 AW 2-4:(5f 2-3, 6f)(Fibr 2-4)
Above-average filly, effective 5f, - acts on Fibr. Turf high 59. AW high 72 - 1st of 4 from Super Strides (29 Jun Southwell RF 2385) - also 1st of 10 giving 5lb to Bevelena (9 Jly Southwell RF 2658).
°J Balding [0-3] Mrs J Coghlan-Everitt (from B J Meehan [2-6] Jly 1998).

TRINITY (IRE) RR **88?f** 4699^{4}
2 b c College Chapel - Kaskazi (Dancing Brave (USA)) 8.4f **(76)**
Form - 462532284
Record 1998 - 1st:0 2nd:3 3rd:1 Ran:9
Win Prizemoney £0 *Total Prizemoney* £11,010
1998 Turf 0-9: (5f 4, 6f 5) (g-s, gd 3, g-f 3, frm 2)
Useful colt, effective 5 to 6f, best at 5f, acts on gd to frm, best on gd. Turf high 88 - 5th of 19 to Flanders (18 Jly Newbury 5f gd RF 2910). **M Brittain [0-9] Miss Debi Woods.*

TRINITY REEF BHB 74f **RR 76f** 4815^{4}
3 b f Bustino 11f **(64)** - Triple Reef (Mill Reef (USA)) 10.5f **(78)**
Form - 14604
Record 1998 - 1st:1 2nd:0 3rd:0 Ran:5
Pre1998 - 1st:0 2nd:0 3rd:0 Ran:3
Win Prizemoney £3,028 *Total Prizemoney* £3,614
Wins * 1998 Apr Folkes (GD) H 12f 65 75++ <
1998 Turf 1-5: (12f 1-4, 16f) (gd 1-2, g-f, frm 2)
Light-framed, above-average filly, effective 12f, acts on gd to frm, best on gd. Turf high 76 - 4th of 14 giving 21lb to Sing And Dance (15 Oct Catterick 12f gd RF 4815) - also 1st of 11 giving 8lb to Last Knight (1 Apr Folkestone RF 0539). Showed little at two, but won a Folkestone handicap on her reappearance. She looks to be well suited by middle distances. **J L Dunlop [1-8] Hesmonds Stud.*

TRIO RR **78f** 5143^{3}
2 b c Cyrano de Bergerac 7.3f **(58)** - May Light **(60df)** (Midyan (USA)) 6f **(60)**
Form - 35603143
Record 1998 - 1st:1 2nd:0 3rd:3 Ran:8
Win Prizemoney £19,737 *Total Prizemoney* £23,083
Wins * 1998 Spt Doncas (GD) H 8f 72 78 <
1998 Turf 1-8: (6f 2, 7f 3, 8f 1-3) (gd 1-4, g-f 3, frm)
Above-average colt, effective 6 to 8f, best at 8f, acts on gd to g-f, best on g-f. Turf high 78 - 4th of 6 to Boatman (18 Spt Newbury 8f g-f RF 4359) - also 1st of 16 from Fiori (10 Spt Doncaster RF 4204). **G Lewis [1-8] City Industrial Supplies Ltd.*

TRIPLE DASH RR **96f** 5074^{2}
2 ch c Nashwan (USA) 10.3f **(79)**-Triple Joy **(104f 98a)**(Most Welcome)
Form - 12
Record 1998 - 1st:1 2nd:1 3rd:0 Ran:2
Win Prizemoney £3,468 *Total Prizemoney* £5,409
Wins * 1998 Oct Newcas (SFT) 6f 74+ <
1998 Turf 1-2: (6f 1-2) (g-s 1-2)
Currently very useful colt. Turf high 96 (began Oct) - 2nd of 9 getting 14lb from Gorse (31 Oct Newmarket 6f g-s RF 5074). Won on his debut, despite looking in need of the race, then gave the year-older Gorse a good race on his only subsequent start.
**Sir Mark Prescott [1-2] Hesmonds Stud.*

TRIPLE HAY BHB 96f **RR 98f** 4055^{18}
4 ch c Safawan 6.6f **(60)** - Davinia (Gold Form) 5.6f **(55)**
Form - 104040
Record 1998 - 1st:1 2nd:0 3rd:0 Ran:6
Pre1998 - 1st:2 2nd:1 3rd:0 Ran:10
Win Prizemoney £14,679 *Total Prizemoney* £18,700
Wins * 1998 May Goodwo (G-F) H 6f 93 94 <
* 1997 Jun Windso (G-F) 6f 93
* 1996 Oct Leices (GD) 6f 90
1998 Turf 1-6: (6f 1-6) (gd 3, g-f 1-2, frm)
Scopey, very useful colt, effective 6 to 7f, best at 6f, acts on gd to frm, best on gd, does well at Goodwood. Turf high 98 - 4th of 15 getting 1lb from Brave Edge (12 Jly Newbury 6f gd RF 2749) - also 1st of 7 giving 11lb to Silvering (20 May Goodwood RF 1355). Had managed to win a race in his first two seasons, and won an ordinary Goodwood handicap first time out in 1998 following a wind operation. He showed mixed form in competitive sprints afterwards, and fetched just 1,000 gns at Tattersalls in October.
**R Hannon [3-16] The Broadgate Partnership.*

TRIPLE HIGH BHB 55f **RR 55f** 2835^{9}
4 b f Reprimand 8.2f **(63)** - Rambadale (Vaigly Great) 7f **(58)**
Form - 5070
Record 1998 - 1st:0 2nd:0 3rd:0 Ran:4
1998 Turf 0-4: (8f 2, 10f, 11f) (gd, g-f, frm 2)
Leggy, fair filly. Turf high 55. **C F Wall [0-4] The Triple S Partnership.*

TRIPLE RAISE (GER) BHB 65f **RR 66f** 4261^{17}
2 b f Wolfhound (USA) 7.3f **(71)** - Timely Raise (USA) (Raise A Man (USA)) 7.8f **(78)**
Form - 8360
Record 1998 - 1st:0 2nd:0 3rd:1 Ran:4
Win Prizemoney £0 *Total Prizemoney* £535
1998 Turf 0-4: (5f, 6f 2, 7f) (gd 2, g-f, frm)
Average filly. Turf high 66 - 3rd of 9 to Shoogle (11 Jly Salisbury 7f frm RF 2716). **R Hannon [0-4] J C Smith.*

TRIPLE TIME $5160a^{5}$
2 f
Form - 5
Record 1998 - 1st:0 2nd:0 3rd:0 Ran:1
1998 Turf 0-1: (9f) (hvy)
Currently very poor filly - 5th of 9 getting 3lb from River Hill (7 Nov San Siro 9f hvy RF 5160a). **L M Cumani [0-1].*

TRIPLE TREASURE (USA) RR **86f** 701^{3}
3 b f Gone West (USA) 7.8f **(82)** - Lemhi Go (USA) (Lemhi Gold (USA))
Form - 3
Record 1998 - 1st:0 2nd:0 3rd:1 Ran:1
Win Prizemoney £0 *Total Prizemoney* £826
1998 Turf 0-1: (8f) (sft)
Scopey, currently useful filly. (1st run) - 3rd of 19 to The Sandfly (15 Apr Newmarket 8f sft RF 0701). Stayed on nicely into third in the Wood Ditton, but was not seen again.
**H R A Cecil [0-1] The Thoroughbred Corporation.*

TROIS ELLES RR 5146^{12}
2 b c Elmaamul (USA) 8.1f **(70)** - Ca Ira (IRE) **(24f)** (Dancing Dissident (USA))
Form - 0
Record 1998 - 1st:0 2nd:0 3rd:0 Ran:1
1998 Turf 0-1: (8f) (gd)
Currently very poor colt. **R C Spicer [0-1] John Purcell.*

TROJAN GIRL (IRE) BHB 51f59a **RR 49f 59a** 5080^{2}
2 b f Up and At 'em - Lady-Mumtaz (Martin John) 13.1f **(62)**
Form - 22486302
Record 1998 - 1st:0 2nd:3 3rd:1 Ran:8
Win Prizemoney £0 *Total Prizemoney* £2,268
1998 Turf 0-3: (5f 2, 6f) (sft, gd, frm) 1998 AW 0-5: (5f 4, 6f) (Fibr 5)
Fair filly, effective 5 to 6f, best at 5f, - acts on Fibr, prefers left handed tracks. Turf high 49 (began Jly). AW high 58 - 2nd of 13 getting 5lb from Moon Shot (31 Oct Wolverhampton 6f Fibr RF 5080). She has shown a bit of ability on Fibresand and can probably win a small race on that surface.
**N P Littmoden [0-8] Trojan Racing.*

TROJAN HERO (SAF) BHB 66a **RR 61f** 5097^{10}
7 ch g Raise A Man (USA) 7.3f **(63)** - Helleness (SAF) (Northfields (USA)) 9f **(72)**
Form - 31234522174880270
Record 1998 - 1st:1 2nd:3 3rd:1 Ran:14
Pre1998 - 1st:2 2nd:2 3rd:2 Ran:11
Win Prizemoney £7,470 *Total Prizemoney* £14,058
Wins * 1998 Jun Warwic (GD) 7f 64
* 1997 *Nov Wolver (STD) H 7f 54 59+*
1997 Jun Leices (G-F) C 8f 70+ <
1998 Turf 1-9: (5f 2, 6f, 7f 1-6) (g-s, gd 1-6, frm 2) 1998 AW 0-5: (6f, 7f 2, 8f 2) (Fibr 5)
Above-average gelding, effective 6 to 8f, acts on gd - acts on AW, best on Fibr, excels at Wolverhampton, likes Southwell. Turf high 64 (1st run) - 1st of 14 giving 3lb to Bold Tina (3 Jun Warwick RF 1708). AW high 70 - 2nd of 12 giving 22lb to Rude Awakening (13 Feb Southwell 6f Fibr RF 0284). Formerly trained in South Africa, where he had won six times, he was in good form on sand during the winter. Won at Warwick in June on his return to Turf but was held afterwards.
**Mrs M Reveley [2-24] C C Buckley (from B W Hills [1-1] Jun 1997).*

TROJAN RISK BHB 66f70a **RR 65f 70a** 2526^{4}
5 ch g Risk Me (FR) 8f **(53)** - Troyes (Troy) 10.4f **(68)**
Form - 724
Record 1998 - 1st:0 2nd:1 3rd:0 Ran:3
Pre1998 - 1st:2 2nd:6 3rd:1 Ran:21

Win Prizemoney £18,140 *Total Prizemoney* £33,822

Wins 1997 Jly Sandow (G-S) H 10f 71 76 <
1996 May Kempto (G-F) H 9f 72 71

1998 Turf 0-3: (10f 2, 12f) (g-s 2, frm)

Average gelding, effective 10f, acts on gd, has worn blinkers, favours tight tracks. Turf high 65. Consistent.

**Mrs M Reveley [0-6] Andy Peake & David Jackson (from G Lewis [2-21] Oct 1997).*

TROJAN WOLF BHB 68f **RR 73df** 4753[4]

3 ch c Wolfhound (USA) 7.3f **(71)** - Trojan Lady (USA) (Irish River (FR)) 8.6f **(78)**

Form - 0464444

Record 1998 - 1st:0 2nd:0 3rd:0 Ran:7
Pre1998 - 1st:0 2nd:0 3rd:0 Ran:1

Win Prizemoney £0 *Total Prizemoney* £1,486

1998 Turf 0-7: (8f 2, 9f 2, 10f 2, 11f) (sft, g-s, gd, frm 4)

Tall, above-average colt, effective 9 to 10f, acts on frm, has worn blinkers. Turf high 77 - 4th of 10 to Moratorium (17 May Ripon 9f frm RF 1290). **M H Tompkins [0-8] Kenneth MacPherson.*

TROPHY CENTRE BHB 18f **RR** 4304[18]

3 b f Paris House 5.9f **(64)** - Kentucky Tears (USA) (Cougar (CHI)) 12.6f **(64)**

Form - 0080

Record 1998 - 1st:0 2nd:0 3rd:0 Ran:4

1998 Turf 0-4: (5f 2, 6f 2) (gd 3, g-f)

Leggy, very poor filly. **Miss L A Perratt [0-4] Cree Lodge Racing Club.*

TROPHY WIFE (FR) **RR 81f** 1747[8]

3 b f Double Bed (FR) 13.9f **(54)** - Hornblower Girl (Faraway Times (USA)) 7.4f **(52)**

Form - 38

Record 1998 - 1st:0 2nd:0 3rd:1 Ran:2
Pre1998 - 1st:0 2nd:0 3rd:1 Ran:1

Win Prizemoney £0 *Total Prizemoney* £3,636

1998 Turf 0-2: (12f 2) (sft, gd)

Currently decent filly. Turf high 81 (1st run) - 3rd of 9 to Pharatta (24 Apr Longchamp 12f sft RF 0945a). She was purchased to act as a pacemaker for Midnight Line in the Oaks. How good she is in her own right is difficult to gauge though she was no world-beater when racing in France.

**H R A Cecil [0-1] H R H Prince Fahd Salman (from FR [0-2] Apr 1998).*

TROPICAL BEACH BHB 46f65a **RR 48f 65a** 4867[1]

5 b g Lugana Beach 7f **(63)** - Hitravelscene (Mansingh (USA)) 7.4f **(55)**

Form - 07557402601

Record 1998 - 1st:1 2nd:1 3rd:0 Ran:11
Pre1998 - 1st:5 2nd:2 3rd:5 Ran:40

Win Prizemoney £18,394 *Total Prizemoney* £24,164

Wins * **1998** *Oct Wolver (STD) H 8.5f 55 58*
1997 Jly Carlis (GD) H 5f 55 61
1996 Aug Hamilt (G-F) H 5f 57 62 <
1996 Aug Thirsk (G-F) SH 6f 57 61
1996 Jun Hamilt (GD) H 5f 53 56
1995 Apr Mussel (GD) 5f 51t

1998 Turf 0-10: (5f 3, 6f 2, 7f 4, 8f) (gd 4, g-f 3, frm 2, hrd) 1998 AW 1-1: (8f 1-1) (Fibr 1-1)

Average gelding, effective 5 to 8f, best at 5f, acts on gd to frm - acts on Fibr, has worn blinkers. Turf high 48. (1st run) - 1st of 13 getting 1lb from Arc (17 Oct Wolverhampton RF 4867). He was on a long losing run before winning a small handicap on the Wolverhampton Fibresand in October. He seems to have been suited by being stepped up in trip.

**J Pearce [1-12] A J Thompson (from J Berry [5-39] Spt 1997).*

TROPICAL FOREST (IRE) BHB 41f **RR 54f** 4808[8]

2 ch f Forest Wind (USA) - Tropical Desert (IRE) (King Persian)

Form - 0850808

Record 1998 - 1st:0 2nd:0 3rd:0 Ran:7

1998 Turf 0-6: (5f 2, 7f 3, 10f) (gd 3, g-f 3) 1998 AW 0-1: (7f) (Fibr)

Fair filly, often wears blinkers. Turf high 47.

**D J S ffrenchDavis [0-1] A Rybak (from M Kettle [0-4] Aug 1998).*

TROPICOOL (USA) **RR** 551a[7]

5 b h Carr de Naskra (USA) 10.4f **(76)** - Mended Heart (UAE) (Le Febuleux (UAE))

Form - 37

1998 AW 0-2: (10f 2) (Dirt 2)

High-class colt, has worn blinkers. AW high 107. He could not match strides with decent handicappers in Dubai.

**D J Selvaratnam in UAE [1-4] Sheikh Ahmed Al Maktoum.*

TROPPA FRESKA (USA) **RR 93f** 3060a[2]

3 f Silver Hawk (USA) 11.2f **(85)** - Goodnight Moon (Ela-Mana-Mou) 10.1f **(70)**

Form - 02

1998 Turf 0-2: (8f, 11f) (sft, g-f)

Currently useful filly. Turf high 93 - 2nd of 9 giving 7lb to Sces (19 Jly San Siro 11f g-f RF 3060a).

**A Tortorella in ITY [0-1] (from P Guarsegnati in ITY [0-1] Apr 1998).*

TRUANT (USA) **RR 92f** 4950a[4]

2 b c Alleged (USA) 11.8f **(81)** - Top Roberto (USA) (Topsider (USA)) 8.3f **(71)**

Form - 334

Record 1998 - 1st:0 2nd:0 3rd:2 Ran:3

Win Prizemoney £0 *Total Prizemoney* £10,014

1998 Turf 0-3: (7f, 8f 2) (sft, g-f, frm)

Currently useful colt. Turf high 92 (began Aug) - 4th of 9 giving 3lb to Noble Pearl (18 Oct San Siro 8f sft RF 4950a). Third of five in a listed race on his debut and was fourth in an Italian Group One on his final start. Sure to win races, probably at ten furlongs plus.

**W Jarvis [0-3].*

TRUDIES TRYST BHB 51f **RR 51f** 5042[8]

2 ch f Rudimentary (USA) 8.2f **(66)** - Trevorsninepoints **(57df)** (Jester)

Form - 0008

Record 1998 - 1st:0 2nd:0 3rd:0 Ran:4

1998 Turf 0-4: (5f, 6f, 7f 2) (sft, gd 3)

Fair filly. Turf high 51 (began Spt). **G G Margarson [0-4] T S Child.*

TRUE FLYER **RR 46f** 4856[14]

2 b f Midyan (USA) 9.9f **(64)** -Surf Bird(Shareef Dancer (USA)) 9.9f **(73)**

Form - 0

Record 1998 - 1st:0 2nd:0 3rd:0 Ran:1

1998 Turf 0-1: (7f) (sft)

Currently moderate filly. **J D Bethell [0-1] T R Lock.*

TRUE LOVE WAYS BHB 47f **RR 49f** 5117[5]

2 ch f Anshan 8.2f **(63)** - Halimah (Be My Guest (USA)) 9.3f **(67)**

Form - 03570030645

Record 1998 - 1st:0 2nd:0 3rd:2 Ran:11

Win Prizemoney £0 *Total Prizemoney* £754

1998 Turf 0-10: (5f 8, 6f 2) (hvy, sft 2, gd 4, g-f 2, frm) 1998 AW 0-1: (5f) (Fibr)

Moderate filly, has worn blinkers. Turf high 54.

**W G M Turner [0-11] Mascalls Stud.*

TRUEWIN (IRE) BHB 58f **RR 57f** 3895[15]

3 b g Brief Truce (USA) 9.1f **(73)** - Wasmette (IRE) (Wassl) 9.7f **(62)**

Form - 36600

Record 1998 - 1st:0 2nd:0 3rd:1 Ran:5

Win Prizemoney £0 *Total Prizemoney* £455

1998 Turf 0-4: (7f, 8f 2, 10f) (sft, g-s, frm 2) 1998 AW 0-1: (7f) (Equi)

Small, fair gelding, has worn blinkers. Turf high 70.

**R W Armstrong [0-2] Sunny Yam (from B Hanbury [0-3] May 1998).*

TRUFFLE (IRE) BHB 82f **RR 75f** 4110[1]

2 b f Ezzoud (IRE) - Queen Cake (Sandhurst Prince) 7.9f **(63)**

Form - 31

Record 1998 - 1st:1 2nd:0 3rd:1 Ran:2

Win Prizemoney £2,512 *Total Prizemoney* £2,842

Wins * **1998** Spt Thirsk (GD) 7f 75 <

1998 Turf 1-2: (7f 1-2) (frm 1-2)

Currently above-average filly. Turf high 75 (began Jly) - 1st of 12 giving 4lb to Highly Fancied (5 Spt Thirsk RF 4110).

**J R Fanshawe [1-2] D I Russell.*

TRULY BEWITCHED (USA) **RR 88+f** 4853[10]

2 ch f Affirmed (USA) 10.3f **(75)** - Fabulous Fairy (USA) **(68f)** (Alydar (USA)) 9.1f **(76)**

Form - 10

Record 1998 - 1st:1 2nd:0 3rd:0 Ran:2

Win Prizemoney £3,574 *Total Prizemoney* £3,574
Wins * **1998** Spt Redcar (G-F) 6f 88+ <
1998 Turf 1-2: (6f 1-1, 7f) (gd, frm 1-1)
Currently useful filly. Turf high 88 (1st run) (began Spt) - 1st of 10 from Desdemona (25 Spt Redcar RF 4489).
**J Noseda [1-2] W L Armitage.*

TRUMPET BLUES (USA) RR 74f 4611[2]
2 br c Dayjur (USA) 6.8f **(79)** - Iosifa (Top Ville) 11.7f **(68)**
Form - 02
Record 1998 - 1st:0 2nd:1 3rd:0 Ran:2
Win Prizemoney £0 *Total Prizemoney* £1,440
1998 Turf 0-2: (6f 2) (g-s, gd)
Currently above-average colt. Turf high 74 (began Spt) - 2nd of 17 to Voracious (2 Oct Lingfield 6f g-s RF 4611).
**J L Dunlop [0-2] Bob Lalemant.*

TRUMP STREET BHB 85f RR 79f 4489[4]
2 b f First Trump - Pepeke (Mummy's Pet) 7.7f **(60)**
Form - 424
Record 1998 - 1st:0 2nd:1 3rd:0 Ran:3
Win Prizemoney £0 *Total Prizemoney* £1,493
1998 Turf 0-3: (6f 2, 7f) (g-f 2, frm)
Currently above-average filly. Turf high 79 (began Aug) - 2nd of 10 to Alabaq (8 Spt Lingfield 7f g-f RF 4144).
**N A Graham [0-3] Paul Jacobs.*

TRUSCOTT (IRE) BHB 78f RR 74f 1984[3]
3 ch c Thatching 7.8f **(69)** - Remember Mulvilla (Ballad Rock) 7.8f **(63)**
Form - 07533
Record 1998 - 1st:0 2nd:0 3rd:2 Ran:5
Win Prizemoney £0 *Total Prizemoney* £1,585
1998 Turf 0-5: (7f, 8f 4) (g-s, gd 3, frm)
Above-average colt, has worn blinkers. Turf high 78.
**G Wragg [0-5] Mollers Racing.*

TRUTH SEEKER RR 86+f 4333[6]
2 b c Wolfhound (USA) 7.3f **(71)** - Swame (USA) (Jade Hunter (USA))
Form - 16
Record 1998 - 1st:1 2nd:0 3rd:0 Ran:2
Win Prizemoney £3,680 *Total Prizemoney* £3,730
Wins * **1998** Spt Haydoc (GD) 5f 86+ <
1998 Turf 1-2: (5f 1-1, 6f) (frm 1-2)
Currently useful colt. Turf high 86 (1st run) (began Spt) - 1st of 17 giving 5lb to Acicula (4 Spt Haydock RF 4088). Reported to have finished lame on his second run. **P J Makin [1-2] Brian Kan.*

TRY AGAIN (IRE) RR 30f 4086[6]
3 b f Mujadil (USA) 7.7f **(70)** - Fast Bay (Bay Express) 7.1f **(60)**
Form - 86
Record 1998 - 1st:0 2nd:0 3rd:0 Ran:2
1998 Turf 0-2: (6f, 9f) (gd, frm)
Workmanlike, currently very moderate filly. Turf high 30 (began Aug). **S Dow [0-2] A F Merritt.*

TRYARDIA-ON-AGAIN (IRE) BHB 61f RR 64df 2261[4]
2 ch f Petardia 8.2f **(58)** - Trysinger (IRE) (Try My Best (USA)) 7.6f **(67)**
Form - 5844
Record 1998 - 1st:0 2nd:0 3rd:0 Ran:4
Win Prizemoney £0 *Total Prizemoney* £198
1998 Turf 0-4: (5f 3, 6f) (gd 3, frm)
Average filly. Turf high 64. **P D Evans [0-4] Men Behaving Badly.*

TSUNAMI BHB 70f RR 70f 4998[4]
2 b f Beveled (USA) 6.9f **(64)** - Alvecote Lady (Touching Wood (USA)) 8.2f **(55)**
Form - 0004
Record 1998 - 1st:0 2nd:0 3rd:0 Ran:4
Win Prizemoney £0 *Total Prizemoney* £235
1998 Turf 0-4: (7f 4) (sft, g-f 2, frm)
Above-average filly. Turf high 70 (began Jly) - 4th of 10 to City of Gold (26 Oct Lingfield 7f sft RF 4998).
**D R C Elsworth [0-3] Miss Juliet Reed (from N Tinkler [0-1] Jly 1998).*

TUDOR HALL (IRE) BHB 84f RR 79f 5072[3]
2 ch f Thatching 7.8f **(69)** - Confidence Boost (USA) (Trempolino (USA)) 12f **(71)**
Form - 53243
Record 1998 - 1st:0 2nd:1 3rd:2 Ran:5
Win Prizemoney £0 *Total Prizemoney* £2,569
1998 Turf 0-5: (6f, 7f 3, 8f) (gd 3, g-f, frm)
Above-average filly. Turf high 79 (began Aug) - 3rd of 16 to Eden (31 Oct Newmarket 7f gd RF 5072). **B W Hills [0-5] Sceptre Racing.*

TUDOR ROMANCE BHB 30f RR 9f 1990[9]
13 b g Aragon 7.7f **(58)** - Dovey (Welsh Pageant) 10f **(65)**
Form - 80
Record 1998 - 1st:0 2nd:0 3rd:0 Ran:2
Pre1998 - 1st:1 2nd:0 3rd:0 Ran:2
Win Prizemoney £2,616 *Total Prizemoney* £2,616
1998 Turf 0-2: (7f, 10f) (gd 2)
Very poor gelding. Turf high 9.
**L A Dace [0-2] T J Arnold (from M W Eckley [1-4] Apr 1990).*

TUFTY STAR BHB 26f RR 31f 4890[13]
3 b f Sirgame - Raffles Virginia (Whistling Deer) 16.4f **(48)**
Form - 045080000
Record 1998 - 1st:0 2nd:0 3rd:0 Ran:9
Win Prizemoney £0 *Total Prizemoney* £247
1998 Turf 0-9: (8f, 10f 2, 11f, 12f 3, 16f 2) (sft, g-s, g-f 3, frm 4)
Light-framed, very moderate filly, effective 12f, acts on sft. Turf high 48 - 4th of 6 to Winsa (7 Apr Folkestone 12f sft RF 0583).
**J Pearce [0-9] G H Tufts.*

TUI BHB 51f46a RR 56f 46a 4270[12]
3 b f Tina's Pet 7.4f **(56)** - Curious Feeling (Nishapour (FR)) 9.1f **(61)**
Form - 770322155156000
Record 1998 - 1st:2 2nd:2 3rd:1 Ran:15
Pre1998 - 1st:0 2nd:0 3rd:0 Ran:4
Win Prizemoney £7,755 *Total Prizemoney* £9,629
Wins * **1998** Aug Newmar (G-F) H 12f 51 56 <
* **1998** Jly Beverl (GD) H 9.9f 42 47
1998 Turf 2-14: (8f 2, 10f 1-9, 12f 1-3) (gd 4, g-f 1-6, frm 1-4) 1998 AW 0-1: (6f) (Fibr)
Light-framed, fair filly, effective 8 to 12f, acts on gd to frm, best on frm, prefers right handed tracks. Turf high 56 - 1st of 17 giving 3lb to Hetra Heights (1 Aug Newmarket RF 3275) - also 1st of 9 from Second Term (3 Jly Beverley RF 2486). She was kept busy in 1998, but she has given connections plenty of fun and has improved as she has gone up in trip.
**P Bowen [2-15] David Evans (from K McAuliffe [0-4] Aug 1997).*

TUIGAMALA BHB 25f52a RR 14f 52a 1481[11]
7 b g Welsh Captain 7.2f **(54)** - Nelliellamay (Super Splash (USA)) 7.3f **(54)**
Form - 0
Record 1998 - 1st:0 2nd:0 3rd:0 Ran:1
Pre1998 - 1st:3 2nd:1 3rd:1 Ran:33
Win Prizemoney £8,145 *Total Prizemoney* £10,258
Wins * 1996 *Feb Lingfi (STD) H 8f 55 58* <
* 1995 *Nov Lingfi (STD) 7f 57*
* 1995 Aug Bright (FRM) H 7f 37 31
1998 Turf 0-1: (8f) (gd)
Fair gelding, effective 7 to 8f, - acts on Equi, likes left handed tracks. Becoming disappointing.
**R Ingram [3-34] Up and Downer Partnership.*

TULLICH REFRAIN BHB 50f57a RR 60f 57a 3846[14]
3 b f Petardia 8.2f **(58)** - Norfolk Serenade (Blakeney) 10.5f **(64)**
Form - 000
Record 1998 - 1st:0 2nd:0 3rd:0 Ran:3
Pre1998 - 1st:0 2nd:0 3rd:1 Ran:6
Win Prizemoney £0 *Total Prizemoney* £820
1998 Turf 0-3: (6f 2, 8f) (frm 3)
Light-framed, average filly, effective 5f, acts on frm. Turf high 30. Becoming disappointing. **W R Muir [0-9] J Jannaway.*

TULLYNESSLE RR 35f 3159[16]
2 ch f King's Signet (USA) 7f **(51)** - Miss Klew (Never so Bold) 6.3f **(66)**
Form - 660
Record 1998 - 1st:0 2nd:0 3rd:0 Ran:3
1998 Turf 0-3: (5f 3) (g-s, gd 2)
Currently very moderate filly. Turf high 35.
**M W Easterby [0-3] Brig Racing Club.*

TULSA (IRE) BHB 35f **RR 51f** 4931[7]
4 b g Priolo (USA) 10.9f **(71)** - Lagrion (USA) (Diesis) 9.3f **(69)**
Form - 466007
Record 1998 - 1st:0 2nd:0 3rd:0 Ran:6
Pre1998 - 1st:0 2nd:1 3rd:2 Ran:16
Win Prizemoney £0 *Total Prizemoney* £2,173
1998 Turf 0-6: (8f 2, 10f 3, 12f) (g-s, gd 2, g-f, frm, hrd)
Fair gelding, effective 8 to 10f, best at 8f, acts on g-s to g-f, best on gd, has worn blinkers, prefers right handed tracks. Turf high 51 - 6th of 12 getting 30lb from Brandon Jack (8 Jun Windsor 10f g-f RF 1820). Becoming disappointing. **B Gubby [0-22] Brian Gubby Ltd.*

TUMBLEWEED GLEN (IRE) BHB 82f **RR 79f** 4732[7]
2 ch c Mukaddamah (USA) 7.6f **(74)** - Mistic Glen (IRE) (Mister Majestic)
Form - 0835517
Record 1998 - 1st:1 2nd:0 3rd:1 Ran:7
Win Prizemoney £7,635 *Total Prizemoney* £8,063
Wins *** 1998** Spt Warwic (G-F) H 8f 75 75 <
1998 Turf 1-7: (6f, 7f 4, 8f 1-2) (g-s, gd 3, g-f 2, frm 1-1)
Above-average colt, effective 7 to 8f, best at 8f, acts on gd to frm, best on gd. Turf high 79 - also 1st of 10 giving 10lb to Melody Queen (22 Spt Warwick RF 4414).
**B J Meehan [1-7] The Fifth Tumbleweed Partnership.*

TUMBLEWEED HERO BHB 78f **RR 79f** 4935[2]
3 b c Alzao (USA) 9.8f **(73)** - Julip (Track Spare) 8.8f **(62)**
Form - 0302
Record 1998 - 1st:0 2nd:1 3rd:1 Ran:4
Pre1998 - 1st:0 2nd:2 3rd:0 Ran:3
Win Prizemoney £0 *Total Prizemoney* £5,417
1998 Turf 0-4: (7f, 8f 2, 10f) (gd 3, frm)
Well made, above-average colt, effective 6 to 8f, best at 7f, acts on gd to g-f, best on gd. Turf high 79 - 3rd of 21 getting 9lb from Jila (14 Apr Newmarket 7f gd RF 0682).
**B J Meehan [0-7] The Third Tumbleweed Partnership.*

TUMBLEWEED QUARTET (USA) BHB 100f **RR 93f** 4972[6]
2 b c Manila (USA) 10f **(81)** - Peggy's String (USA) (Highland Park (USA))
Form - 1336
Record 1998 - 1st:1 2nd:0 3rd:2 Ran:4
Win Prizemoney £6,257 *Total Prizemoney* £17,824
Wins *** 1998** Jun Newbur (SFT) 6f 71+ <
1998 Turf 1-4: (6f 1-1, 7f 2, 8f) (sft, g-s 1-1, gd, g-f)
Useful colt. Turf high 93 - 3rd of 8 to Auction House (11 Spt Doncaster 7f g-f RF 4225). Looked a decent prospect on his debut in soft ground but ran only respectably under his penalty on a fast surface. Stayed on really well into third in the Champagne Stakes next time, but was a flop in the Racing Post Trophy, dropping away in the heavy ground after racing prominently.
**B J Meehan [1-4] The Tumbleweed Partnership.*

TUMBLEWEED RIDGE BHB 105f91a **RR 109f 91a** 4695a[4]
5 ch h Indian Ridge 7.6f **(74)** - Billie Blue (Ballad Rock) 7.8f **(63)**
Form - 16170004
Record 1998 - 1st:2 2nd:0 3rd:0 Ran:8
Pre1998 - 1st:3 2nd:5 3rd:3 Ran:23
Win Prizemoney £77,232 *Total Prizemoney* £125,970

Wins	*** 1998**	Jun	Leopar (SFT)	G3	7f		109	<
	*** 1998**	Apr	Newmar (SFT)	H	7f	101	106	
	* 1997	Jly	Newmar (G-F)	H	7f	94	101	
	* 1995	Oct	Newbur (G-S)	G3	7.3f		103	
	* 1995	Jly	Lingfi (G-F)		5f		84+	

1998 Turf 2-8: (7f 2-8) (hvy, sft 2-2, gd 2, g-f 3)
Pattern-class colt, effective 7f, acts on sft to frm, best on sft, often wears blinkers. Turf high 109 - 1st of 5 getting 7lb from Wizard King (10 Jun Leopardstown RF 2036a) - also 1st of 16 giving 9lb to Gulf Shaadi (15 Apr Newmarket RF 0695). Becoming disappointing. Connections could write a book on him entitled `trials and tribulations', but everything slotted into place when he pinched a lead and won the Group Three Ballycorus Stakes at Leopardstown in June. From that moment on, however, his season fell to pieces.
**B J Meehan [5-31] The Tumbleweed Partnership.*

TUMBLEWEED RIVER (IRE) **RR 83f** 4743[2]
2 ch c Thatching 7.8f **(69)** - Daphne Indica (IRE) (Ballad Rock) 7.8f **(63)**
Form - 2
Record 1998 - 1st:0 2nd:1 3rd:0 Ran:1
Win Prizemoney £0 *Total Prizemoney* £2,058
1998 Turf 0-1: (7f) (g-s)
Currently decent colt.
**B J Meehan [0-1] The Fourth Tumbleweed Partnership.*

TUMBLWEED PROSPECT BHB 79f **RR 83f** 1044[12]
3 ch g Lion Cavern (USA) 7.5f **(74)** - Ring of Pearl (Auction Ring (USA)) 8.6f **(65)**
Form - 0
Record 1998 - 1st:0 2nd:0 3rd:0 Ran:1
Pre1998 - 1st:0 2nd:2 3rd:0 Ran:4
Win Prizemoney £0 *Total Prizemoney* £2,512
1998 Turf 0-1: (8f) (g-f)
Leggy, decent gelding.
**B J Meehan [0-5] The Second Tumbleweed Partnership.*

Tuning, the first filly to win the Ebor for forty years

TUNING BHB 110f **RR 107f** 4186[7]
3 ch f Rainbow Quest (USA) 11.2f **(81)** - Discomatic (USA) (Roberto (USA)) 10f **(76)**
Form - 212217
Record 1998 - 1st:2 2nd:3 3rd:0 Ran:6
Pre1998 - 1st:0 2nd:1 3rd:0 Ran:1
Win Prizemoney £109,837 *Total Prizemoney* £126,700

Wins	*** 1998**	Aug	York (G-F)	H	13.9f	102	107	<
	*** 1998**	Jun	Yarmou (GD)		14.1f		85+	

1998 Turf 2-6: (12f 2, 14f 2-3, 15f) (gd 2, g-f 1-1, frm 1-3)
Scopey, Pattern-class filly, effective 12 to 14f, best at 14f, acts on gd to frm, best on frm. Turf high 107 - 1st of 21 getting 16lb from Sheer Danzig (19 Aug York RF 3754). She ended a 40-year hoodoo for fillies when winning the Tote Ebor at York, where the lightning-fast ground suited her admirably. Caught out by a rain-softened surface at Doncaster in September, she is capable of winning a Group race under suitable conditions. **H R A Cecil [2-7] K Abdulla.*

TUNNEL BRIDGE BHB 64f **RR 59f** 4352[7]
2 b g Merdon Melody 6.8f **(56)** - Tripolitaine (FR) (Nonoalco (USA)) 8.5f **(66)**
Form - 0547
Record 1998 - 1st:0 2nd:0 3rd:0 Ran:4
Win Prizemoney £0 *Total Prizemoney* £252
1998 Turf 0-4: (6f 3, 8f) (sft, g-s, gd, frm)
Fair gelding. Turf high 59 (began Jly).
**K A Ryan [0-4] J J Stephenson.*

TURAATH (IRE) RR 84f 4773[3]
2 b c Sadler's Wells (USA) 11.3f **(87)** - Diamond Field (USA) (Mr Prospector (USA)) 8.8f **(78)**
Form - 43
Record 1998 - 1st:0 2nd:0 3rd:1 Ran:2
Win Prizemoney £0 *Total Prizemoney* £1,422
1998 Turf 0-2: (7f 2) (gd 2)
Currently decent colt. Turf high 84 (began Oct) - 3rd of 7 to Conflict (13 Oct Leicester 7f gd RF 4773). Sure to win a race or two at middle distances. **B W Hills [0-2] Hamdan Al Maktoum.*

TURBO DRIVE RR 95f 4470h[5]
4
Form - 5
1998 Turf 0-1: (10f) (gd)
Currently very useful. (1st run) - 5th of 9 to Oxalagu (20 Spt Frankfurt 10f gd RF 4470h). He is not Group class.
**B Schutz in GER [0-3].*

TURF MOOR (IRE) BHB 39f44a **RR 37f 44a** 4877[7]
3 b f Mac's Imp (USA) 5.6f **(54)** - Tuft Hill (Grundy) 10.3f **(65)**
Form - 000408000057
Record 1998 - 1st:0 2nd:0 3rd:0 Ran:12
Pre1998 - 1st:0 2nd:1 3rd:1 Ran:7
Win Prizemoney £0 *Total Prizemoney* £2,015
1998 Turf 0-10: (5f 3, 6f 4, 7f, 8f 2) (sft, g-s 2, gd 4, g-f 2, frm) 1998 AW 0-2: (5f, 6f) (Fibr 2)
Light-framed, very moderate filly, effective 5f, acts on gd, has worn blinkers. Turf high 38. AW high 23. Bits and pieces of placed form in varied company, but she spurned more chances than Burnley.
**E J Alston [0-6] Valley Paddocks Racing Ltd (from J J O'Neill [0-13] Jun 1998).*

TURGENEV (IRE) BHB 67f64a **RR 68f 64a** 5150[14]
9 b g Sadler's Wells (USA) 11.3f **(87)** - Tilia (ITY) (Dschingis Khan) 11.3f **(75)**
Form - 75521748200
Record 1998 - 1st:1 2nd:2 3rd:0 Ran:11
Pre1998 - 1st:7 2nd:5 3rd:2 Ran:38
Win Prizemoney £54,459 *Total Prizemoney* £73,428
Wins * **1998** Jun Sandow (SFT) H 14f 60 68
* 1997 Aug Sandow (GD) H 14f 64 70
* 1997 Jly Haydoc (GD) H 14f 60 65
* 1997 May Haydoc (SFT) H 14f 63 69
* 1996 Jun Haydoc (G-S) H 14f 58 66
1998 Turf 1-11: (14f 1-8, 15f, 17f 2) (g-s 1-2, gd 8, frm)
Average gelding, effective 14 to 16f, best at 14f, acts on sft to gd, best on gd, has worn blinkers, excels at Sandown and does well at York. Turf high 68. Inconsistent.
**R Bastiman [5-33] Mrs Bridget Tranmer (from J H M Gosden [3-16] Aug 1993).*

TURNOFACARD RR 58f 5072[9]
2 ch f First Trump - Barbary Court (Grundy) 10.3f **(65)**
Form - 0
Record 1998 - 1st:0 2nd:0 3rd:0 Ran:1
1998 Turf 0-1: (7f) (gd)
Currently fair filly. **P J Makin [0-1] A W Schiff.*

TURNPOLE (IRE) BHB 84f **RR 89df** 3288[4]
7 br g Satco (FR) 14.2f **(57)** - Mountain Chase (Mount Hagen (FR)) 8.4f **(70)**
Form - 1274
Record 1998 - 1st:1 2nd:1 3rd:0 Ran:4
Pre1998 - 1st:4 2nd:5 3rd:0 Ran:15
Win Prizemoney £94,787 *Total Prizemoney* £114,574
Wins * **1998** Mar Doncas (GD) H 18f 82 87 <
* 1997 Oct Newmar (GD) H 18f 74 82
* 1997 May York (GD) H 13.9f 70 78
* 1997 Apr Hamilt (G-S) 12.1f 69
* 1995 Aug Redcar (FRM) H 11f 63 66
1998 Turf 1-4: (18f 1-1, 19f 2, 20f) (gd 1-2, g-f 2)
Useful gelding, effective 18 to 19f, best at 18f, acts on gd to g-f, best on gd. Turf high 89 - 2nd of 18 getting 3lb from Silence in Court (6 May Chester 19f g-f RF 1059) - also 1st of 13 giving 17lb to Fabillion (27 Mar Doncaster RF 0478). Had a rewarding season on the level in 1997, winning the Cesarewitch. After a light hurdling campaign, he was a game winner back on the Flat at Doncaster before running a good second in the Chester Cup. Not disgraced at Ascot, he will continue to be a threat in marathon races.
**Mrs M Reveley [8-28] & Mrs W J Williams.*

TURNTABLE (IRE) RR 55f 4761[13]
2 b f Dolphin Street (FR) - Sharp Circle (IRE) (Sure Blade (USA)) 11.3f **(67)**
Form - 0
Record 1998 - 1st:0 2nd:0 3rd:0 Ran:1
1998 Turf 0-1: (7f) (gd)
Currently fair filly. **G Wragg [0-1] Cheveley Park Stud.*

TURN TO STONE (IRE) BHB 37f **RR 32f** 1926[13]
4 b g West China - Marronzina (IRE) (Burslem) 8.8f **(53)**
Form - 0640
Record 1998 - 1st:0 2nd:0 3rd:0 Ran:4
Pre1998 - 1st:0 2nd:0 3rd:0 Ran:4
1998 Turf 0-4: (6f 2, 8f, 11f) (gd, g-f 2, frm)
Very moderate gelding, has worn blinkers. Turf high 32.
**J Neville [0-5] George Moore & Peter Corrigan (from Michael Flynn in IRE [0-3] May 1997).*

TURRILL HOUSE BHB 25f20a **RR 24f 20a** 1690[5]
6 b m Charmer 9f **(59)** - Megabucks (Buckskin (FR))
Form - 65
Record 1998 - 1st:0 2nd:0 3rd:0 Ran:1
Pre1998 - 1st:0 2nd:0 3rd:1 Ran:8
Win Prizemoney £0 *Total Prizemoney* £293
1998 Turf 0-1: (16f) (gd)
Little account mare.
**W J Musson [3-23] J R Hawksley & C H Pettigrew.*

TURTLE BHB 71f **RR 78f** 4376[16]
2 b c Turtle Island (IRE) - Kate Marie (USA) (Bering) 7.4f **(61)**
Form - 50330
Record 1998 - 1st:0 2nd:0 3rd:2 Ran:5
Win Prizemoney £0 *Total Prizemoney* £1,032
1998 Turf 0-5: (5f 2, 6f 2, 7f) (g-s, gd, g-f, frm 2)
Above-average colt. Turf high 78 (began Jly) - 3rd of 7 to Billy McCaw (9 Aug Epsom 6f gd RF 3480).
**M Johnston [0-5] M J Pilkington.*

TURTLE'S RISING (IRE) BHB 84f **RR 78f** 4405[4]
2 b f Turtle Island (IRE) - Zabeta (Diesis) 9.3f **(69)**
Form - 315404
Record 1998 - 1st:1 2nd:0 3rd:1 Ran:6
Win Prizemoney £3,566 *Total Prizemoney* £4,754
Wins * **1998** Jly Sandow (G-F) 5f 78 <
1998 Turf 1-6: (5f 1-6) (gd, g-f 3, frm 1-2)
Above-average filly, effective 5f, acts on g-f to frm. Turf high 78 (began Jly) - 4th of 14 getting 3lb from Open Secret (22 Spt Beverley 5f g-f RF 4405) - also 1st of 10 getting 7lb from Sports Road (23 Jly Sandown RF 3043).
**B J Meehan [1-6] Total (Bloodstock) Ltd.*

TURTLE VALLEY (IRE) BHB 72f **RR 72df** 4519[4]
2 b c Turtle Island (IRE) - Primrose Valley (Mill Reef (USA)) 10.5f **(78)**
Form - 062764
Record 1998 - 1st:0 2nd:1 3rd:0 Ran:6
Win Prizemoney £0 *Total Prizemoney* £1,452
1998 Turf 0-6: (6f 2, 7f 3, 8f) (gd 2, g-f, frm 2, hrd)
Above-average colt, effective 7f, acts on gd, has worn blinkers. Turf high 72 - 2nd of 7 to Mixsterthetrixster (25 Jun Newcastle 7f gd RF 2268). Ordinary maiden form, giving the impression that he requires at least a mile. **J L Dunlop [0-6] Hesmonds Stud.*

TUSCAN DAWN BHB 63f72a **RR 67df 72a** 2886[8]
8 ch g Clantime 6.6f **(57)** - Excavator Lady (Most Secret) 7.1f **(58)**
Form - 8
Record 1998 - 1st:0 2nd:0 3rd:0 Ran:1
Pre1998 - 1st:5 2nd:12 3rd:5 Ran:54
Win Prizemoney £18,535 *Total Prizemoney* £47,540
Wins * 1996 Spt Epsom (G-F) H 5f 74 75
* 1996 May Thirsk (G-F) H 5f 74 74
1998 Turf 0-1: (5f) (frm)
Average gelding, effective 5f, acts on gd to frm.
**J Berry [5-55] Chris & Antonia Deuters.*

TUSCAN DREAM BHB 57f **RR 69f** 4757[8]
3 b g Clantime 6.6f **(57)** - Excavator Lady (Most Secret) 7.1f **(58)**
Form - 2302688
Record 1998 - 1st:0 2nd:2 3rd:1 Ran:7
Win Prizemoney £0 *Total Prizemoney* £2,030
1998 Turf 0-6: (5f 4, 6f 2) (sft, gd, g-f 2, frm 2) 1998 AW 0-1: (5f) (Fibr)
Tall, average gelding, effective 5f, acts on g-f, has worn blinkers. Turf high 69 (began Jly) - 2nd of 9 giving 5lb to Bollin Ann (15 Aug Ripon 5f g-f RF 3657). In the frame in sprint maidens.
**J Berry [0-7] Chris & Antonia Deuters.*

TUSSLE BHB 98f **RR 100?f** 5074[7]
3 b c Salse (USA) 10.9f **(71)** -Crime Ofthecentury(Pharly (FR)) 9.8f **(68)**
Form - 487
Record 1998 - 1st:0 2nd:0 3rd:0 Ran:3
Pre1998 - 1st:1 2nd:1 3rd:0 Ran:2
Win Prizemoney £4,077 *Total Prizemoney* £6,537
Wins * 1997 Oct Newmar (G-F) 6f 95+ <
1998 Turf 0-3: (6f 3) (g-s 2, g-f)
Scopey, very useful colt. Turf high 100 (began Spt) - 8th of 16 to Bold Edge (16 Oct Newmarket 6f g-f RF 4844). Michael Bell holds this colt in high regard, but he has been difficult to train and made just three appearances in 1998. Far from disgraced on any of those outings, he could prove himself an above-average sprinter in 1999. **M Bell [1-5] Lordship Stud.*

TUULI (IRE) BHB 44f **RR 56f** 4300[14]
2 b g Forest Wind (USA) - Rifaya (IRE) (Lashkari) 9.8f **(67)**
Form - 5040000
Record 1998 - 1st:0 2nd:0 3rd:0 Ran:7
1998 Turf 0-7: (5f, 6f 3, 7f 3) (gd 2, g-f 2, frm 2, hrd)
Fair gelding. Turf high 56. **B S Rothwell [0-7] Mrs H M Carr.*

TUXEDO JUNCTION (USA) RR 5166a[6]
5 b m Black Tie Affair 10.5f **(64)** - Hidden Trail (USA) (Gleaming (USA)) 11.5f **(75)**
Form - 6
1998 AW 0-1: (9f) (Dirt)
Currently very useful filly, always wears blinkers.
**J Hollendorfer in USA [0-1] Edward Taylor & George Todaro.*

TWENTY FIRST RR 50f 4846[18]
2 ch f Inchinor 8.9f **(64)** - Picnicing (Good Times (ITY)) 6.6f **(54)**
Form - 0
Record 1998 - 1st:0 2nd:0 3rd:0 Ran:1
1998 Turf 0-1: (6f) (g-f)
Currently fair filly. **G Wragg [0-1] Bloomsbury Stud.*

TWICE AS SHARP BHB 85f **RR 84f** 5096[2]
6 ch h Sharpo 7.5f **(68)** - Shadiliya (Red Alert) 7.6f **(66)**
Form - 002
Record 1998 - 1st:0 2nd:1 3rd:0 Ran:3
Pre1998 - 1st:4 2nd:4 3rd:5 Ran:33
Win Prizemoney £37,275 *Total Prizemoney* £51,100
Wins * 1997 May York (GD) H 5f 83 86
* 1996 Jun Newcas (FRM) H 5f 84 88 <
* 1995 Spt Newcas (GD) H 5f 81 84
* 1995 May Pontef (GD) 6f 77
1998 Turf 0-3: (5f, 6f 2) (gd 3)
Decent horse, effective 5 to 6f, best at 5f, acts on gd to frm, best on g-f, does well at York and Newmarket. Turf high 84 - 2nd of 19 getting 7lb from Classy Cleo (2 Nov Redcar 6f gd RF 5096). Consistent. **P W Harris [4-36] Formula Twelve.*

TWICKERS RR 62f 3525[4]
2 b f Primo Dominie 7.2f **(67)** - Songstead (Song) 7.2f **(61)**
Form - 4
Record 1998 - 1st:0 2nd:0 3rd:0 Ran:1
Win Prizemoney £0 *Total Prizemoney* £228
1998 Turf 0-1: (5f) (frm)
Currently average filly. **R Guest [0-1] J W Hill.*

TWIN CREEKS BHB 58f84a **RR 64f 84a** 3839[13]
7 b g Alzao (USA) 9.8f **(73)** - Double River (USA) (Irish River (FR)) 8.6f **(78)**
Form - 26250424427730
Record 1998 - 1st:0 2nd:2 3rd:1 Ran:11
Pre1998 - 1st:8 2nd:5 3rd:7 Ran:52
Win Prizemoney £25,881 *Total Prizemoney* £38,065
Wins * 1997 *Nov Lingfi (STD) H 7f 74 77* <
* 1997 Jun Warwic (FRM) 7f 56
* 1997 *Jan Lingfi (STD) H 7f 70 73*
* 1996 *Nov Lingfi (STD) H 7f 65 67*
* 1996 *Oct Lingfi (STD) 7f 62*
1996 *Feb Southw (STD) H 8f 52 54*
1995 Jly Hamilt (FRM) H 9.2f 47 52
1995 *Feb Southw (STD) 7f 53*
1998 Turf 0-9: (7f 4, 8f 5) (g-s, gd, g-f 5, frm 2) 1998 AW 0-2: (7f 2) (Equi, Fibr)
Useful gelding, effective 7 to 8f, best at 8f, - acts on Equi, likes left handed tracks, favours tight tracks. Turf high 64. AW high 72. Generally ran well in 1998 without getting his head in front.
**V Soane [5-37] The Armchair Jockeys (from M D Hammond [3-19] Apr 1996).*

TWIN ENGINES (USA) RR 62f 4745[6]
2 b c Lear Fan (USA) 10.4f **(80)** - Dixie Duo (USA) (Dixieland Band (USA)) 7f **(74)**
Form - 06
Record 1998 - 1st:0 2nd:0 3rd:0 Ran:2
1998 Turf 0-2: (7f, 8f) (gd, frm)
Currently average colt. Turf high 62 (began Aug).
**N A Graham [0-2] The Thoroughbred Corporation.*

TWIN TIME BHB 65a **RR 63f** 4270[13]
4 b f Syrtos 8.1f **(57)** - Carramba (CZE) (Tumble Wind (USA)) 7.5f **(57)**
Form - 35256170
Record 1998 - 1st:1 2nd:1 3rd:1 Ran:8
Pre1998 - 1st:0 2nd:2 3rd:1 Ran:7
Win Prizemoney £2,739 *Total Prizemoney* £6,089
Wins * **1998** Aug Bath (GD) H 10.2f 63 60 <
1998 Turf 1-8: (8f, 9f 2, 10f 1-4, 12f) (gd 2, g-f 1-3, frm 3)
Workmanlike, average filly, effective 8 to 10f, best at 8f, acts on gd to frm, best on frm, prefers left handed tracks, prefers tight tracks, excels at Bath. Turf high 65 (1st run) - 3rd of 18 giving 11lb to Questan (18 May Bath 8f frm RF 1292) - also 1st of 7 getting 17lb from Livius (4 Aug Bath RF 3326).
**J S King [1-10] Dajam Ltd (from M J Heaton-Ellis [0-6] Aug 1997).*

TWIZZLE (IRE) RR 100f 5019a[2]
2 ch f Arazi (USA) 9.2f **(74)** - Twyla (Habitat) 9.4f **(70)**
Form - 632
1998 Turf 0-3: (6f, 8f 2) (hvy, gd, frm)
Currently very useful filly. Turf high 100 - 2nd of 17 to Pink Coral (21 Oct Navan 8f hvy RF 5019a).
**J Oxx in IRE [0-3] Sheikh Mohammed.*

TWO CLUBS BHB 100f **RR 97f** 4974[1]
2 br f First Trump - Miss Cindy (Mansingh (USA)) 7.4f **(55)**
Form - 1141
Record 1998 - 1st:3 2nd:0 3rd:0 Ran:4
Win Prizemoney £18,255 *Total Prizemoney* £24,282
Wins * **1998** Oct Doncas (HVY) L 6f 97 <
* **1998** Spt Yarmou (G-S) 6f 85
* **1998** Jly Newcas (G-F) 6f 74+
1998 Turf 3-4: (6f 3-4) (sft 1-2, gd 1-1, frm 1-1)
Very useful filly. Turf high 97 (began Jly) - 1st of 7 getting 5lb from Perugino Bay (24 Oct Doncaster RF 4974). Created a most favourable impression at Yarmouth, having previously won at Newcastle. She was unable to give her trainer a big win before retirement in the sales race at Redcar, but was able to finish the

season on a winning note in a Doncaster listed event. She represents a useful tool for her new trainer.
**Mrs J Cecil [3-4] Stephen Hobson.*

TWOFORTEN BHB 43f **RR 47f** 4574[11]
3 b g Robellino (USA) 9.5f **(68)** - Grown At Rowan (Gabitat) 5f **(44)**
Form - 00057300
Record 1998 - 1st:0 2nd:0 3rd:1 Ran:8
Pre1998 - 1st:0 2nd:0 3rd:0 Ran:3
Win Prizemoney £0 *Total Prizemoney* £412
1998 Turf 0-8: (6f 2, 7f, 8f, 9f, 10f 2, 12f) (gd 4, g-f, frm 3)
Workmanlike, moderate gelding, has worn blinkers. Turf high 47.
**M Madgwick [0-11] T G N Burrage.*

TWO ON THE BRIDGE BHB 46f **RR 49f** 4256[8]
4 b g Chilibang 7f **(55)** - Constant Companion (Pas de Seul) 9.1f **(67)**
Form - 0808
Record 1998 - 1st:0 2nd:0 3rd:0 Ran:4
Pre1998 - 1st:0 2nd:4 3rd:3 Ran:16
Win Prizemoney £0 *Total Prizemoney* £5,341
1998 Turf 0-4: (6f, 7f 2, 8f) (gd, frm 3)
Leggy, moderate gelding, effective 6 to 7f, best at 6f, acts on g-s to frm, has worn blinkers, excels at Thirsk. Turf high 49 (began Aug).
**Denys Smith [0-20] Denys Smith.*

TWO PACK RR 42f 4818[18]
2 b c Diesis 9f **(80)** - Zonda (Fabulous Dancer (USA)) 9.4f **(70)**
Form - 0
Record 1998 - 1st:0 2nd:0 3rd:0 Ran:1
1998 Turf 0-1: (7f) (frm)
Currently moderate colt.
**B A Pearce [0-1] Richard J Gray & Stanley Selby.*

TWO SOCKS BHB 71f56a **RR 70f 56a** 2553[2]
5 ch g Phountzi (USA) 9.6f **(60)** -Mrs Feathers (Pyjama Hunt) 11.1f **(38)**
Form - 132
Record 1998 - 1st:1 2nd:1 3rd:1 Ran:3
Pre1998 - 1st:1 2nd:6 3rd:1 Ran:26
Win Prizemoney £6,844 *Total Prizemoney* £15,165
Wins * **1998** Jun Warwic (GD) H 10.8f 66 67 <
1996 Jly Lingfi (FRM) H 11.5f 57 59
1998 Turf 1-3: (11f 1-2, 12f) (gd 1-2, g-f)
Above-average gelding, effective 11 to 12f, best at 11f, acts on gd to hrd, best on gd, has worn blinkers. Turf high 70 - 2nd of 10 giving 16lb to Warning Reef (4 Jly Sandown 11f gd RF 2553) - also 1st of 6 giving 17lb to U K Magic (3 Jun Warwick RF 1711). Consistent.
**J S King [1-10] Mrs Satu Marks (from P Burgoyne [0-2] Oct 1996).*

TWO TOO MUCH BHB 30f **RR 3f** 4387[11]
2 b f Clantime 6.6f **(57)** - Lightning Belle **(54f)** (Belfort (FR)) 6.8f **(63)**
Form - 600
Record 1998 - 1st:0 2nd:0 3rd:0 Ran:3
1998 Turf 0-1: (7f) (frm) 1998 AW 0-2: (5f, 7f) (Fibr 2)
Currently poor filly. AW high 16.
**M Waring [0-3] Dunstall Park Centre Ltd.*

TWO-TWENTY-TWO (IRE) RR 109+f 4695a[1]
3 b c Fairy King (USA) 7.7f **(75)** - Easy to Copy (USA) (Affirmed (USA)) 9.3f **(79)**
Form - 11164421
1998 Turf 4-8: (7f 3-4, 8f 1-2, 9f, 10f) (hvy 1-1, sft 3-3, gd 4)
Pattern-class colt, effective 7 to 10f, acts on hvy to gd, has worn blinkers, likes Curragh. Turf high 114 - 1st of 5 from Chateau Royal (19 Apr Leopardstown RF 0805a) - also 1st of 6 giving 7lb to Hasanat (4 Oct Tipperary RF 4695a). Consistent. He had a super season, winning in Listed and Group Three company. Probably at his best on an easy surface, he will surely be placed to advantage by his shrewd trainer next season.
**D K Weld in IRE [5-10] Moyglare Stud Farm.*

TWO WILLIAMS BHB 53f **RR 52f** 4921[5]
3 b g Polar Falcon (USA) 9f **(74)** - Long View (Persian Bold) 9.3f **(66)**
Form - 03005
Record 1998 - 1st:0 2nd:0 3rd:1 Ran:5
Pre1998 - 1st:1 2nd:1 3rd:1 Ran:11
Win Prizemoney £3,673 *Total Prizemoney* £5,819
Wins * 1997 Jly Beverl (HVY) 5f 76+ <
1998 Turf 0-5: (5f 3, 6f 2) (g-s 3, gd 2)
Strong, fair gelding, effective 5 to 7f, acts on sft to g-f. Turf high 52. Given an enterprising ride to win a maiden at two but has not shown a great deal since, although he ran better in testing ground at Ripon in June. **M W Easterby [1-16] W L Caley.*

TYCOON GIRL (IRE) BHB 63f **RR 61f** 1270[9]
4 b f Last Tycoon 9.4f **(73)** - Forest Berries (IRE) (Thatching) 8f **(66)**
Form - 580
Record 1998 - 1st:0 2nd:0 3rd:0 Ran:3
Pre1998 - 1st:1 2nd:0 3rd:1 Ran:10
Win Prizemoney £3,834 *Total Prizemoney* £4,324
Wins * 1996 Oct Redcar (G-F) 6f 73 <
1998 Turf 0-3: (7f 3) (g-s, gd, frm)
Light-framed, average filly, effective 7f, acts on g-f, has worn blinkers. Turf high 61. Inconsistent. **B J Meehan [1-13] F C T Wilson.*

TYCOON'S DOLCE (IRE) RR 102f 5130a[4]
2 b f Rainbows For Life (CAN) 9.3f **(64)** - Tycoon's Drama (IRE) (Last Tycoon) 8.5f **(62)**
Form - 33724
1998 Turf 0-5: (7f 2, 8f 3) (hvy 2, sft 2, gd)
Very useful filly. Turf high 102 (began Aug) - 2nd of 6 to Comillas (20 Oct Deauville 8f hvy RF 5051a). She was heavily campaigned for a classy juvenile filly, but never let the side down, although often seeming slightly out of her depth. She deserves to find a Listed race. **R Collet in FR [0-5] R C Strauss.*

TYCOON TED RR 14f 1716[6]
5 b g Starch Reduced 5.9f **(46)** - Royal Tycoon (Tycoon II) 8.7f **(47)**
Form - 6
Record 1998 - 1st:0 2nd:0 3rd:0 Ran:1
Pre1998 - 1st:0 2nd:0 3rd:0 Ran:1
1998 Turf 0-1: (12f) (gd)
Poor gelding, has worn blinkers. **W M Brisbourne [0-6] D Slingsby.*

TYCOON TINA BHB 47f41a **RR 51f 41a** 5119[16]
4 b f Tina's Pet 7.4f **(56)** - Royal Tycoon (Tycoon II) 8.7f **(47)**
Form - 4021716205565380
Record 1998 - 1st:2 2nd:2 3rd:1 Ran:14
Pre1998 - 1st:1 2nd:3 3rd:0 Ran:14
Win Prizemoney £8,232 *Total Prizemoney* £13,071
Wins * **1998** Apr Beverl (SFT) H 9.9f 53 58 <
* **1998** Mar Hamilt (HVY) H 12.1f 49 52
* 1997 May Mussel (G-S) H 8f 46 51
1998 Turf 2-12: (10f 1-3, 12f 1-6, 13f 3) (sft 1-3, g-s 1-4, gd 4, g-f) 1998 AW 0-2: (12f 2) (Fibr 2)
Leggy, fair filly, effective 8 to 13f, acts on sft to frm, prefers right handed tracks, excels at Musselburgh, does well at Hamilton. Turf high 58 - 1st of 15 giving 12lb to Cabcharge Blue (23 Apr Beverley RF 0828) - also 1st of 11 giving 3lb to Classical Dance (30 Mar Hamilton RF 0504). AW high 50. No world-beater but she wins her share. Twice successful in 1998, she is ideally suited by middle-distances and soft ground. **W M Brisbourne [3-28] Brooke Rankin.*

TYKEYVOR (IRE) BHB 72f **RR 76f** 4731[5]
8 b g Last Tycoon 9.4f **(73)** - Ivoronica (Targowice (USA)) 11.4f **(70)**
Form - 6003638355
Record 1998 - 1st:0 2nd:0 3rd:3 Ran:10
Pre1998 - 1st:6 2nd:2 3rd:4 Ran:31
Win Prizemoney £50,225 *Total Prizemoney* £59,481
Wins * 1997 Jly Ascot (SFT) H 12f 86 94 <
* 1996 Jun Ascot (G-F) H 12f 82 87
* 1996 Jun Beverl (G-F) H 12f 77 83
* 1995 Aug Sandow (G-F) H 10f 75 80
* 1995 May Salisb (GD) 10f 70
1998 Turf 0-10: (10f 3, 12f 7) (g-s 2, gd 2, g-f 2, frm 3, hrd)
Above-average gelding, effective 12f, acts on gd to frm, has worn blinkers. Turf high 76. A one-time useful middle-distance handicapper, he is on the downgrade nowadays. Reportedly suffers from problems with his joints and can't act on fast ground.
**Lady Herries [5-30] Seymour Bloodstock (UK) Ltd (from M H Tompkins [1-14] Oct 1994).*

TYLER'S TOAST RR 79f 4892[3]
2 ch c Grand Lodge (USA) - Catawba (Mill Reef (USA)) 10.5f **(78)**
Form - 3

Record 1998 - 1st:0 2nd:0 3rd:1 Ran:1
Win Prizemoney £0 *Total Prizemoney* £506
1998 Turf 0-1: (7f) (gd)
Currently above-average colt.
**W Jarvis [0-1] Lady Howard de Walden.*

TYPHOON EIGHT (IRE) BHB 56f RR 52f 4112[9]

6 b g High Estate 10.5f **(66)** - Dance Date (IRE) (Sadler's Wells (USA)) 10f **(76)**
Form - 6600
Record 1998 - 1st:0 2nd:0 3rd:0 Ran:4
Pre1998 - 1st:1 2nd:1 3rd:2 Ran:20
Win Prizemoney £4,662 *Total Prizemoney* £8,137
Wins 1996 Oct Catter (GD) H 12f 66 71 <
1998 Turf 0-4: (8f 2, 10f, 12f) (gd 2, frm 2)
Fair gelding, effective 10 to 11f, best at 10f, acts on gd to frm, best on gd, has worn blinkers, prefers right handed tracks. Turf high 52. Becoming disappointing.
**D Nicholls [0-4] Cairnford Ltd (from R W Armstrong [0-5] Aug 1997).*

TYPHOON GINGER (IRE) BHB 60f RR 57f 4961[3]

3 ch f Archway (IRE) 8.5f **(60)** - Pallas Viking (Viking (USA)) 6.7f **(65)**
Form - 26403
Record 1998 - 1st:0 2nd:1 3rd:1 Ran:5
Win Prizemoney £0 *Total Prizemoney* £1,908
1998 Turf 0-5: (5f, 6f 2, 7f 2) (gd, g-f, frm 3)
Scopey, fair filly. Turf high 65 (1st run) - 2nd of 10 to Tattinger (25 May Redcar 6f gd RF 1459). Placed form in sprint maidens, looking likely to be suited by at least seven furlongs.
**G Woodward [0-5] Andrew Lloyd.*

TYPHOON LAD BHB 40f35a RR 42f 35a 4654[9]

5 ch h Risk Me (FR) 8f **(53)** - Muninga 00
Form - 0005400
Record 1998 - 1st:0 2nd:0 3rd:0 Ran:7
Pre1998 - 1st:0 2nd:1 3rd:0 Ran:7
Win Prizemoney £0 *Total Prizemoney* £1,591
1998 Turf 0-5:(8f, 10f 3, 12f)(gd, g-f 3, frm) 1998 AW 0-2:(10f 2)(Equi 2)
Moderate colt. Turf high 42. AW high 39 (began Jly). An ex-Irish maiden, he has embarked on a hurdling career.
**S Dow [0-12] P McCarthy (from M Halford in IRE [0-3] Apr 1996).*

TYROLEAN DANCER (IRE) BHB 31f RR 13f 3414a[6]

4 b f Tirol 8.1f **(64)** - Waffling (Lomond (USA)) 8.8f **(65)**
Form - 8006
Record 1998 - 1st:0 2nd:0 3rd:0 Ran:4
Pre1998 - 1st:0 2nd:0 3rd:0 Ran:5
Win Prizemoney £0 *Total Prizemoney* £227
1998 Turf 0-3: (10f, 12f, 17f) (gd, g-f, frm) 1998 AW 0-1: (8f) (Equi)
Scopey, poor filly.
**A J Chamberlain [0-8] (from S P C Woods [0-5] Jly 1997).*

TYROLEAN DREAM (IRE) BHB 66f RR 66f 4372[6]

4 b g Tirol 8.1f **(64)** - Heavenly Hope (Glenstal (USA)) 10.1f **(64)**
Form - 086
Record 1998 - 1st:0 2nd:0 3rd:0 Ran:3
Pre1998 - 1st:1 2nd:1 3rd:0 Ran:6
Win Prizemoney £3,468 *Total Prizemoney* £4,328
Wins * 1997 Spt Hamilt (GD) 9.2f 51 <
1998 Turf 0-3: (10f, 12f 2) (sft, gd, frm)
Strong, average gelding, likes tight tracks. Turf high 65.
**M H Tompkins [2-13] P Heath.*

TYROLEAN LOVE (IRE) RR 43f 5072[12]

2 b f Tirol 8.1f **(64)** - Paradise Forum (Prince Sabo) 7.2f **(62)**
Form - 00
Record 1998 - 1st:0 2nd:0 3rd:0 Ran:2
1998 Turf 0-2: (7f 2) (g-s, gd)
Currently moderate filly. Turf high 43 (began Oct).
**C A Horgan [0-2] Mrs B Sumner.*

U K MAGIC (IRE) BHB 58f RR 62f 3501[4]

3 b g Alzao (USA) 9.8f **(73)** - Lightino (Bustino) 10.4f **(64)**
Form - 62704
Record 1998 - 1st:0 2nd:1 3rd:0 Ran:5
Pre1998 - 1st:0 2nd:0 3rd:0 Ran:2
Win Prizemoney £0 *Total Prizemoney* £1,342
1998 Turf 0-5: (7f, 10f, 11f, 12f 2) (gd 2, g-f, frm 2)
Neat, average gelding, effective 10 to 11f, acts on gd to frm, has worn blinkers. Turf high 62 - 2nd of 6 getting 17lb from Two Socks (3 Jun Warwick 11f gd RF 1711).
**J E Banks [0-7] UK Packaging Supplies Ltd.*

UKRAINE VENTURE BHB 94f RR 96f 658[2]

4 b f Slip Anchor 12.7f **(75)** - Sherkraine (Shergar) 10.4f **(66)**
Form - 2
Record 1998 - 1st:0 2nd:1 3rd:0 Ran:1
Pre1998 - 1st:1 2nd:0 3rd:1 Ran:6
Win Prizemoney £3,993 *Total Prizemoney* £10,878
Wins * 1997 Apr Sandow (G-F) 10f 88++ <
1998 Turf 0-1: (10f) (hvy)
Scopey, very useful filly, effective 10f, acts on gd to frm. Fair effort on her '98 bow but failed to reappear.
**S P C Woods [1-7] Dr Frank Chao.*

ULTIMATE SMOOTHIE BHB 82f RR 78?f 2830[P]

6 b g Highest Honor (FR) 10.9f **(72)** - Baino Charm (USA) (Diesis) 9.3f **(69)**
Form - 311P
Record 1998 - 1st:2 2nd:0 3rd:1 Ran:4
Pre1998 - 1st:1 2nd:0 3rd:0 Ran:5
Win Prizemoney £10,530 *Total Prizemoney* £10,998
Wins * 1998 Jly Warwic (GD) H 14.9f 67 78+ <
*** 1998** Jun Warwic (G-S) H 14.9f 67 76+
* 1997 Jly Salisb (FRM) 14f 68+
1998 Turf 2-4: (14f 2, 15f 2-2) (gd, g-f 2-3)
Above-average gelding, effective 14 to 15f, best at 15f, acted on g-f. Turf high 78 - 1st of 8 giving 12lb to Woody's Boy (3 Jly Warwick RF 2514) - also 1st of 9 getting 10lb from Silently (24 Jun Warwick RF 2259). A decent hurdler, he won a couple of very modest handicaps at Warwick this season with a lot in hand, but unfortunately pulled up lame in July. (DEAD) **M C Pipe [9-22] Isca Bloodstock.*

ULTRA BEET BHB 54f55a RR 56f 55a 5003[7]

6 b g Puissance 7.1f **(60)** - Cassiar (Connaught) 7.7f **(63)**
Form - 6823822276377507
Record 1998 - 1st:0 2nd:3 3rd:2 Ran:13
Pre1998 - 1st:9 2nd:5 3rd:7 Ran:47
Win Prizemoney £26,285 *Total Prizemoney* £35,703

Wins								
1997	*Jan*	*Wolver*	*(STD)*	*C*	*6f*		*72*	
1997	*Jan*	*Lingfi*	*(STD)*	*H*	*6f*	*65*	*68*	
1996	*Aug*	*Wolver*	*(STD)*	*S*	*6f*		*57*	
1995	Jun	Hamilt	(FRM)	H	6f	66	73	
1995	*Mar*	*Wolver*	*(STD)*	*C*	*5f*		*75*	
1995	*Feb*	*Lingfi*	*(STD)*	*H*	*5f*	*76*	*79*	<
1995	*Jan*	*Lingfi*	*(STD)*	*C*	*5f*		*68*	
1995	*Jan*	*Wolver*	*(STD)*	*C*	*5f*		*71*	
1995	*Jan*	*Lingfi*	*(STD)*		*5f*		*71*	

1998 Turf 0-5: (6f 3, 7f 2) (gd 2, g-f 3) 1998 AW 0-8: (6f 7, 7f) (Equi 5, Fibr 3)
Fair gelding, effective 6f, - acts on AW, best on Equi, has worn blinkers, likes left handed tracks, likes tight tracks. Turf high 56. AW high 57. Though running the odd good race, his form looks to be on a downward curve, as he has been beaten in sellers.
**R M Flower [0-7] The Forging Ahead Partnership (from P C Haslam [9-53] Feb 1998).*

ULTRA CALM (IRE) BHB 54f RR 56f 2935[9]

2 ch g Doubletour (USA) 12f **(46)** - Shyonn (IRE) (Shy Groom (USA)) 10f **(66)**
Form - 000
Record 1998 - 1st:0 2nd:0 3rd:0 Ran:3
1998 Turf 0-3: (5f 2, 6f) (g-s, g-f, hrd)
Currently fair gelding. Turf high 56.
**P C Haslam [0-3] Pet Express (W&R) Ltd.*

ULTRA NEAT BHB 41f RR 29f 2726[6]

2 b c Puissance 7.1f **(60)** - Cassiar (Connaught) 7.7f **(63)**
Form - 046
Record 1998 - 1st:0 2nd:0 3rd:0 Ran:3
1998 Turf 0-2: (5f, 6f) (gd, g-f) 1998 AW 0-1: (6f) (Fibr)
Currently little account colt. Turf high 29.
**P D Evans [0-3] John Pugh.*

UMBRIAN GOLD (IRE) RR 83f 5041[2]
2 b f Perugino (USA)- Golden Sunlight(Ile de Bourbon (USA)) 10.1f **(67)**
Form - 2
Record 1998 - 1st:0 2nd:1 3rd:0 Ran:1
Win Prizemoney £0 *Total Prizemoney* £939
1998 Turf 0-1: (7f) (sft)
Currently decent filly. No match for impressive Ballet Master on her debut at Yarmouth. **J A R Toller [0-1] Mrs R W Gore-Andrews.*

UNA KASALA (GER) RR 92f 1093a[4]
3 f
Form - 4
1998 Turf 0-1: (8f) (sft)
Currently useful filly. **A Lowe in GER [0-1].*

UNCHAINED MELODY BHB 21f **RR 18f** 3628[5]
3 ch f Vague Shot 11f **(53)** - My Sweet Melody (Music Boy) 6.8f **(57)**
Form - 060075
Record 1998 - 1st:0 2nd:0 3rd:0 Ran:6
1998 Turf 0-6: (6f 2, 8f, 12f 2, 16f) (sft, g-s, g-f, frm 2, hrd)
Unfurnished, poor filly. Turf high 18.
**John Berry [0-6] Samantha Paxton And Partner.*

UNCHAIN MY HEART BHB 69f **RR 66f** 4868[3]
2 b f Pursuit of Love 9.5f **(69)** - Addicted to Love **(66f)** (Touching Wood (USA)) 8.2f **(55)**
Form - 003
Record 1998 - 1st:0 2nd:0 3rd:1 Ran:3
Win Prizemoney £0 *Total Prizemoney* £336
1998 Turf 0-3: (6f 2, 7f) (gd 2, g-f)
Currently average filly. Turf high 66 (began Oct) - 3rd of 18 to Tread Softly (19 Oct Pontefract 6f gd RF 4868).
**B J Meehan [0-3] Mascalls Stud.*

UNCHANGED BHB 66f **RR 66f** 2259[3]
6 b m Unfuwain (USA) 11.4f **(74)** - Favorable Exchange (USA) (Exceller (USA)) 12.5f **(74)**
Form - 66103
Record 1998 - 1st:1 2nd:0 3rd:1 Ran:5
Pre1998 - 1st:3 2nd:3 3rd:1 Ran:20
Win Prizemoney £18,173 *Total Prizemoney* £28,649
Wins * **1998** May Thirsk (GD) H 16f 60 66
1997 Spt Folkes (FRM) H 15.4f 60 64
1995 Spt Cheste (G-S) H 15.9f 66 74 <
1995 Spt Folkes (G-F) H 15.4f 62 69
1998 Turf 1-5: (14f 2, 15f, 16f 1-1, 20f) (sft, g-s, gd 1-2, g-f)
Average mare, effective 15 to 18f, acts on gd to frm, has worn blinkers, favours tight tracks. Turf high 66 - 1st of 9 getting 4lb from Noufari (15 May Thirsk RF 1255). This doughty stayer was an easy winner at Thirsk in May and ran respectably in the Ascot Stakes next time.
**John Harris [1-5] Mrs Tracey Martin (from C E Brittain [3-20] Spt 1997).*

UNCLE DOUG BHB 58f53a **RR 59f 53a** 1788[25]
7 b g Common Grounds 8.1f **(66)** - Taqa (Blakeney) 10.5f **(64)**
Form - 6540
Record 1998 - 1st:0 2nd:0 3rd:0 Ran:4
Pre1998 - 1st:3 2nd:5 3rd:2 Ran:29
Win Prizemoney £11,120 *Total Prizemoney* £19,416
Wins 1996 Aug Ripon (HVY) H 16f 55 60 <
1996 May Thirsk (G-F) H 16f 49 56
1994 Oct Newcas (G-S) H 16.1f 48 54
1998 Turf 0-3: (12f, 14f, 16f) (gd 2, hrd) 1998 AW 0-1: (16f) (Fibr)
Fair gelding, effective 14 to 16f, best at 14f, acts on g-s to gd, best on gd. Turf high 59 (1st run) - 5th of 13 giving 25lb to Dally Boy (6 May Musselburgh 16f gd RF 1065).
**J L Eyre [0-6] D D Saul (from Mrs M Reveley [6-39] Oct 1997).*

UNCLE DUNCAN RR 28f 4473[12]
2 ch c Ardkinglass 5f **(64)** - Angel's Sing (Mansingh (USA)) 7.4f **(55)**
Form - 0
Record 1998 - 1st:0 2nd:0 3rd:0 Ran:1
1998 Turf 0-1: (6f) (g-f)
Currently little account colt. **J S Moore [0-1] J S Moore.*

UNCLE OBERON RR 54f 5137[20]
2 b c Distant Relative 7f **(69)** - Fairy Story (IRE) **(75f 64a)** (Persian Bold) 9.3f **(66)**
Form - 00
Record 1998 - 1st:0 2nd:0 3rd:0 Ran:2
1998 Turf 0-2: (6f, 7f) (gd, g-f)
Currently fair colt. Turf high 54 (began Oct).
**G A Butler [0-2] The Fairy Story Partnership.*

UNDERSTUDY BHB 50f37a **RR 51f 37a** 87[8]
4 b f In The Wings 11.2f **(77)** - Pipina (USA) (Sir Gaylord) 10.6f **(64)**
Form - 0048
Record 1998 - 1st:0 2nd:0 3rd:0 Ran:3
Pre1998 - 1st:0 2nd:1 3rd:1 Ran:6
Win Prizemoney £0 *Total Prizemoney* £1,607
1998 AW 0-3: (12f, 15f, 16f) (Fibr 3)
Fair filly. AW high 37. Inconsistent.
**R Hollinshead [0-9] R Hollinshead.*

UNDETERRED BHB 100f **RR 99f** 4746[1]
2 ch c Zafonic (USA) 9f **(83)** - Mint Crisp (IRE) (Green Desert (USA)) 8.6f **(78)**
Form - 4141
Record 1998 - 1st:2 2nd:0 3rd:0 Ran:4
Win Prizemoney £13,814 *Total Prizemoney* £14,384
Wins * **1998** Oct York (GD) L 6f 99 <
* **1998** Aug Yarmou (FRM) 6f 69
1998 Turf 2-4: (6f 2-4) (gd 1-1, frm 1-3)
Very useful colt. Turf high 99 (began Jly) - 1st of 11 from Indiana Legend (10 Oct York RF 4746). He got off the mark by dead-heating in a Yarmouth maiden, and won a listed race at York in October, having appeared to have had his limitations exposed by the useful Two Clubs in between. He looks capable of progressing further in 1999, and may stay further. **C F Wall [2-4] S Fustok.*

UNGARO (GER) RR 118f 4951a[3]
4 b c Goofalik (USA) 15.4f **(66)** - Ustina (GER) (Star Appeal) 9.6f **(65)**
Form - 3711243
1998 Turf 2-7: (8f 1-1, 11f, 12f 1-5) (sft 3, gd 1-3, g-f 1-1)
High-class colt, effective 8 to 14f, best at 12f, acts on sft to g-f, best on gd, and excels at Cologne. Turf high 118 - 1st of 7 giving 14lb to Tiger Hill (26 Jly San Siro RF 3227a) - also 1st of 10 from Santillana (21 Jun San Siro RF 2293a). Consistent. A useful German-trained colt, he won Group Ones in his native country and in Italy during the summer, but was unable to cope with British opposition in his last three starts. **H Blume in GER [4-12].*

UNICAMP BHB 90f **RR 82f** 3688[2]
2 ch f Royal Academy (USA) 7.8f **(77)** - Honeyspike (IRE) **(64f)** (Chief's Crown (USA)) 9.8f **(72)**
Form - 1452
Record 1998 - 1st:1 2nd:1 3rd:0 Ran:4
Win Prizemoney £3,492 *Total Prizemoney* £5,195
Wins * **1998** May Nottin (FRM) 6.1f 67+ <
1998 Turf 1-4: (5f, 6f 1-3) (gd 2, frm 1-2)
Decent filly. Turf high 82 - 2nd of 7 getting 3lb from Dramatize (18 Aug Brighton 5f frm RF 3688). There was plenty to like about her debut victory at Nottingham, and she has looked to require seven furlongs in a couple of listed races since.
**E A L Dunlop [1-4] Coutinho Nogueira.*

UNIFORM BHB 52f **RR 54f** 4861[3]
3 ch f Unfuwain (USA) 11.4f **(74)** - Trachelium **(44df)** (Formidable (USA)) 9.2f **(63)**
Form - 04631303
Record 1998 - 1st:1 2nd:0 3rd:3 Ran:8
Pre1998 - 1st:0 2nd:0 3rd:0 Ran:3
Win Prizemoney £2,500 *Total Prizemoney* £4,088
Wins * **1998** Spt Hamilt (SFT) H 12.1f 51 54 <
1998 Turf 1-8: (8f, 10f 2, 12f 1-2, 14f, 16f, 17f) (sft 2, g-s, gd 1-2, g-f 2, hrd)
Scopey, fair filly, effective 12 to 14f, best at 12f, acts on g-s to g-f, prefers tight tracks. Turf high 54 - 1st of 18 giving 9lb to Fatehalkhair (7 Spt Hamilton RF 4134). **Miss S E Hall [1-11] C Platts.*

UNINHIBITED (IRE) RR 100f 3421a[8]
3 b f Lahib (USA) 8f **(69)** - Etiquette (Law Society (USA)) 9.9f **(70)**

Form - 28
1998 Turf 0-2: (7f, 8f) (hvy, gd)
Very useful filly. Turf high 100 (1st run) - 2nd of 7 to Cortona (10 Apr Maisons-laffitte 7f hvy RF 0725a). She was being considered for the 1,000 Guineas in the spring, but proved nowhere near that standard. **A Fabre in FR [0-2] G Biszantz.*

UNITUS (IRE) BHB 52f RR 53f 4704[20]

5 b h Soviet Star (USA) 8.6f **(74)** - Unite (Kris) 9.5f **(73)**
Form - 000054040
Record 1998 - 1st:0 2nd:0 3rd:0 Ran:9
Pre1998 - 1st:1 2nd:1 3rd:0 Ran:6
Win Prizemoney £3,753 *Total Prizemoney* £5,730
Wins 1996 Jly Windso (G-F) 10f 78+ <
1998 Turf 0-9: (7f, 8f, 9f, 10f 4, 12f, 18f) (gd, g-f 3, frm 4, hrd)
Fair colt. Turf high 65.
**M C Chapman [0-9] Barry Brown (from Sir Michael Stoute [1-6] May 1997).*

UNMASKED RR 25f 2897[8]

2 ch f Safawan 6.6f **(60)** - Unveiled **(54f 48a)** (Sayf El Arab (USA)) 7.1f **(54)**
Form - 48
Record 1998 - 1st:0 2nd:0 3rd:0 Ran:2
Win Prizemoney £0 *Total Prizemoney* £183
1998 Turf 0-1: (5f) (g-f) 1998 AW 0-1: (6f) (Fibr)
Currently little account filly. **J Berry [0-2] William Burns.*

U-NO-HARRY (IRE) BHB 44f56a RR 41f 56a 4867[11]

5 b h Mansooj 10.6f **(53)** -Lady Roberta (USA) (Roberto (USA)) 10f **(76)**
Form - 825761237825345537310
Record 1998 - 1st:2 2nd:2 3rd:4 Ran:19
Pre1998 - 1st:5 2nd:5 3rd:6 Ran:47
Win Prizemoney £22,180 *Total Prizemoney* £32,260
Wins * **1998** *Aug Southw (STD) C* *7f* *59*
* **1998** *Feb Southw (STD) S* *7f* *55*
* 1996 Jly Cheste (G-F) H 5.1f 68 69 <
* 1996 Jun Lingfi (FRM) H 6f 57 65
* 1996 Jun Thirsk (FRM) H 6f 57 52
* 1995 Jly Catter (G-F) S 5f 66
* 1995 May Leices (G-F) C 6f 66
1998 Turf 0-2: (6f, 7f) (gd, frm) 1998 AW 2-17: (6f 2, 7f 2-10, 8f 5) (Fibr 2-17)
Moderate colt, effective 5 to 7f, acts on g-f to frm - acts on Fibr, has worn blinkers, prefers left handed tracks, likes tight tracks, and likes Southwell. Turf high 40. AW high 63 - 2nd of 6 getting 4lb from Italian Symphony (25 Feb Wolverhampton 7f Fibr RF 0358) - also 1st of 11 getting 10lb from Italian Symphony (14 Aug Southwell RF 3637). Consistent. He is certainly kept busy but has a moderate strike rate. **R Hollinshead [7-66] D Coppenhall.*

UNSHAKEN BHB 66f49a RR 67f 49a 4918[17]

4 b c Environment Friend 7.5f **(67)** - Reel Foyle (USA) (Irish River (FR)) 8.6f **(78)**
Form - 33521361237250
Record 1998 - 1st:2 2nd:3 3rd:4 Ran:14
Pre1998 - 1st:1 2nd:0 3rd:0 Ran:11
Win Prizemoney £7,801 *Total Prizemoney* £19,178
Wins * **1998** Jun Hamilt (G-S) 6f 67
* **1998** May Carlis (G-S) H 5.9f 46 56
1996 Oct Folkes (G-S) 5f 86 <
1998 Turf 2-12: (5f 2, 6f 2-10) (sft, g-s 2, gd 2-6, g-f, frm 2) 1998 AW 0-2: (6f 2) (Fibr 2)
Scopey, average colt, effective 5 to 6f, best at 6f, acts on gd to frm, best on frm, has worn blinkers. Turf high 67 - 1st of 7 giving 10lb to Piccolo Cativo (30 Jun Hamilton RF 2402). AW high 47.
**E J Alston [2-18] G G Sanderson & M Twentyman & A J Picton (from J R Fanshawe [1-7] Jly 1997).*

UNTOLD RICHES (USA) BHB 69f RR 61f 4542[22]

2 b f Red Ransom(USA) 8.6f **(83)** -Asdaf (USA)**(57f)**(Forty Niner (USA))
Form - 000
Record 1998 - 1st:0 2nd:0 3rd:0 Ran:3
1998 Turf 0-3: (7f 3) (g-f, frm 2)
Currently average filly. Turf high 61 (began Aug).
**J H M Gosden [0-3] Hamad Saeed.*

UP AND ABOUT RR 71f 4505[6]

2 b f Barathea (IRE) - Upend (Main Reef) 9.6f **(57)**
Form - 6
Record 1998 - 1st:0 2nd:0 3rd:0 Ran:1
1998 Turf 0-1: (8f) (gd)
Currently above-average filly. **D R Loder [0-1] S Frisby.*

UP AT THE TOP (IRE) BHB 81f RR 86f 4966[12]

3 b f Waajib 8.9f **(67)** - Down The Line (Brigadier Gerard) 9.3f **(58)**
Form - 48124000
Record 1998 - 1st:1 2nd:1 3rd:0 Ran:8
Pre1998 - 1st:1 2nd:0 3rd:1 Ran:3
Win Prizemoney £9,684 *Total Prizemoney* £12,730
Wins * **1998** Aug Haydoc (G-S) H 10.5f 81 82 <
* 1997 Spt Folkes (GD) 6f 64+
1998 Turf 1-8: (7f 2, 9f, 10f 4, 11f 1-1) (sft, gd 2, g-f 1-3, frm 2)
Scopey, useful filly, effective 10 to 11f, acts on gd to g-f, likes left handed tracks. Turf high 86 - 2nd of 8 getting 8lb from Brave Reward (21 Aug Chester 10f gd RF 3792) - also 1st of 9 getting 1lb from Gatecrasher (6 Aug Haydock RF 3407).
**B W Hills [2-11] Mrs E Roberts.*

UP IN FLAMES (IRE) BHB 47f50a RR 50f 50a 4995[4]

7 br g Nashamaa 8.1f **(58)** - Bella Lucia (Camden Town) 9.3f **(53)**
Form - 75124150026084
Record 1998 - 1st:1 2nd:1 3rd:0 Ran:10
Pre1998 - 1st:4 2nd:4 3rd:3 Ran:41
Win Prizemoney £25,525 *Total Prizemoney* £32,738
Wins * **1998** *Jan Southw (STD) H* *8f* *47* *55*
* 1997 *Dec Wolver (STD) H* *9.4f* *41* *46*
* 1997 Nov Nottin (GD) H 8.2f 43 46
1995 Jun Epsom (G-F) H 8.5f 70 75 <
1995 May Haydoc (GD) H 8.1f 63 71+
1998 Turf 0-6: (8f 5, 9f) (sft, gd 3, g-f 2) 1998 AW 1-4: (8f 1-1, 9f, 11f, 12f) (Fibr 1-4)
Fair gelding, effective 8f, acts on gd - acts on Fibr, likes left handed tracks, likes tight tracks. Turf high 50 - 2nd of 16 to Miskin Heights (3 Jun Warwick 8f gd RF 1709). AW high 55 - 1st of 12 getting 6lb from Live Project (30 Jan Southwell RF 0190).
**S R Bowring [3-25] Mark Kilner (from M D Hammond [2-23] Aug 1996).*

UPLIFTING BHB 64f RR 55f 5007[14]

3 b f Magic Ring (IRE) 6.5f **(64)** - Strapless (Bustino) 10.4f **(64)**
Form - 22510000
Record 1998 - 1st:1 2nd:2 3rd:0 Ran:8
Pre1998 - 1st:0 2nd:1 3rd:1 Ran:3
Win Prizemoney £2,448 *Total Prizemoney* £6,476
Wins * **1998** Jly Leices (GD) 5f 74+ <
1998 Turf 1-8: (5f 1-5, 6f 3) (sft, g-s 2, gd 3, frm 1-2)
Small, fair filly, effective 5 to 6f, best at 6f, acts on gd to frm, best on gd, has worn blinkers. Turf high 77 - 2nd of 12 to Moon Tango (13 Jun Lingfield 6f gd RF 1967) - also 1st of 9 getting 5lb from Doberman (22 Jly Leicester RF 3030). Becoming disappointing. She always looked to have ability, but made hard work of winning a weak Leicester maiden and was well beaten afterwards.
**L G Cottrell [1-11] Gerry Albertini.*

UPPER CHAMBER BHB 66f RR 71f 3747[7]

2 b c Presidium 7.5f **(56)** - Vanishing Trick (Silly Season) 9.7f **(56)**
Form - 346627
Record 1998 - 1st:0 2nd:1 3rd:1 Ran:6
Win Prizemoney £0 *Total Prizemoney* £1,642
1998 Turf 0-6: (5f 6) (gd 2, g-f 3, frm)
Above-average colt, effective 5f, acts on g-f to frm. Turf high 71 (1st run) - 3rd of 14 to Light Fingered (11 Jun Carlisle 5f g-f RF 1889). **J G FitzGerald [0-6] N H T Wrigley.*

UP THE CLARETS (IRE) BHB 44f54a RR 52f 54a 4939[11]

3 b g Petardia 8.2f **(58)** - Madeira Lady (On Your Mark) 7.7f **(58)**
Form - 5736860
Record 1998 - 1st:0 2nd:0 3rd:1 Ran:6
Pre1998 - 1st:0 2nd:0 3rd:1 Ran:9
Win Prizemoney £0 *Total Prizemoney* £737
1998 Turf 0-6: (7f 3, 8f 2, 10f) (gd 3, g-f, frm 2)
Leggy, fair gelding, has worn blinkers. Turf high 52.
**J J O'Neill [2-20] Valley Paddocks Racing Ltd.*

UP THE WALL BHB 48f **RR 47f** 2477^{13}
3 b c Aragon 7.7f **(58)** - Ridalia (Ridan (USA)) 8.3f **(65)**
Form - 800
Record 1998 - 1st:0 2nd:0 3rd:0 Ran:3
Pre1998 - 1st:0 2nd:1 3rd:1 Ran:8
Win Prizemoney £0 *Total Prizemoney* £1,585
1998 Turf 0-2: (8f 2) (g-f, hrd) 1998 AW 0-1: (8f) (Fibr)
Leggy, moderate colt, effective 7f, acted on frm. Turf high 40. (DEAD)
**K G Wingrove [0-1] The Up The Wall Partnership (from John Berry [0-7] May 1998).*

URBAN LILY RR 14f 2841^{8}
8 ch m Town And Country 8.5f **(47)** - Laval (Cheval) 17.1f **(39)**
Form - 8
Record 1998 - 1st:0 2nd:0 3rd:0 Ran:1
Pre1998 - 1st:0 2nd:0 3rd:0 Ran:1
1998 Turf 0-1: (12f) (gd)
Poor mare, always wears blinkers. **R J Hodges [4-36] Mrs C J Cole.*

URBAN OCEAN (FR) RR 93f $4909a^{7}$
2 ch c Bering 9.6f **(80)** -Urban Sea (USA) **(119f)**(Miswaki (USA)) 9f **(81)**
Form - 1387
1998 Turf 1-4: (8f 1-4) (g-s, gd 1-3)
Useful colt. Turf high 93 (began Jly) - 3rd of 10 giving 6lb to Athlumney Lady (26 Aug Tralee 8f gd RF 4024a). Won his maiden at Naas and has been beaten in nurseries since.
**A P O'Brien in IRE [1-4] David Tsui.*

URGENT REPLY (USA) BHB 48f **RR 53?f** 4777^{9}
5 b g Green Dancer (USA) 11.9f **(77)** - Bowl of Honey (USA) (Lyphard (USA)) 9.9f **(72)**
Form - 65011176080
Record 1998 - 1st:3 2nd:0 3rd:0 Ran:11
Pre1998 - 1st:2 2nd:2 3rd:0 Ran:14
Win Prizemoney £13,062 *Total Prizemoney* £15,088
Wins * **1998** Jly Chepst (GD) H 12.1f 44 51
* **1998** Jun Mussel (SFT) H 16f 44 49
* **1998** Jun Hamilt (SFT) H 13f 40 44
* 1997 Aug Catter (G-F) C 12f 51
* 1997 Jly Hamilt (G-F) C 12.1f 52 <
1998 Turf 3-11: (12f 1-8, 13f 1-1, 14f, 16f 1-1) (sft, g-s 2, gd 2-5, g-f 1-2, frm)
Fair gelding, effective 12 to 14f, acts on gd to g-f, has worn blinkers, favours tight tracks, excels at Musselburgh, likes Hamilton. Turf high 53. **C A Dwyer [5-30] The Select Newmarket Partnership.*

URGENT SWIFT BHB 65f **RR 59f** 1804^{9}
5 ch g Beveled (USA) 6.9f **(64)** - Good Natured (Troy) 10.4f **(68)**
Form - 8050
Record 1998 - 1st:0 2nd:0 3rd:0 Ran:4
Pre1998 - 1st:1 2nd:5 3rd:3 Ran:21
Win Prizemoney £4,159 *Total Prizemoney* £15,334
Wins 1996 Spt Redcar (FRM) H 10f 67 71 <
1998 Turf 0-4: (12f, 14f 2, 16f) (hvy, sft, gd, g-f)
Fair gelding, has broken blood-vessels, effective 12 to 14f, best at 12f, acts on gd to frm, best on gd, has worn blinkers. Turf high 59. Inconsistent.
**M Pitman [0-8] A L R Morton (from A P Jarvis [1-21] Spt 1997).*

URSA MAJOR BHB 67f82a **RR 50f 82a** 4854^{21}
4 b g Warning 8.1f **(77)** - Double Entendre (Dominion) 8.5f **(63)**
Form - 081411144000
Record 1998 - 1st:4 2nd:0 3rd:0 Ran:10
Pre1998 - 1st:1 2nd:1 3rd:0 Ran:12
Win Prizemoney £13,709 *Total Prizemoney* £16,077
Wins * **1998** *Feb Lingfi (SLW) H 8f 82 87+* <
* **1998** *Jan Lingfi (STD) H 8f 70 87+* <
1998 *Jan Southw (STD) C 8f 82+*
1998 *Jan Southw (STD) C 8f 69*
1996 *Dec Lingfi (STD) 6f 70+*
1998Turf 0-2:(7f, 8f)(gd, g-f)1998 AW 4-8:(7f, 8f 4-7)(Equi 2-4, Fibr 2-4)
Decent gelding, effective 7 to 8f, best at 8f, - acts on AW, best on Equi, prefers left handed tracks, prefers tight tracks. Turf high 50. AW high 87 - 1st of 6 getting 3lb from Plan For Profit (7 Feb Lingfield RF 0243) - also 1st of 10 giving 12lb to Shontaine (29 Jan Lingfield RF 0180). Becoming disappointing. Was in brilliant form at the beginning of '98, winning four times in fine style on both Fibresand and Equitrack, before his form started to tail off a little. He is very difficult to catch when able to dominate.
**C N Allen [2-7] Newmarket Connections Ltd (from A Kelleway [2-5] Jan 1998).*

USCADO (GER) RR 95f $835a^{2}$
3 ch c Zampano (GER) - Una Spezia (GER) (Sparkler) 8.4f **(55)**
Form - 2
1998 Turf 0-1: (7f) (sft)
Currently very useful colt. (1st run) - 2nd of 5 giving 6lb to Minaccia (19 Apr Krefeld 7f sft RF 0835a).
**H Steinmetz in GER [0-1] H-J Biber.*

UTAH (IRE) BHB 55f **RR 52?f** 1901^{8}
4 b g High Estate 10.5f **(66)** - Easy Romance (USA) (Northern Jove (CAN)) 9.7f **(66)**
Form - 8
Record 1998 - 1st:0 2nd:0 3rd:0 Ran:1
Pre1998 - 1st:0 2nd:0 3rd:0 Ran:4
1998 Turf 0-1: (10f) (g-s)
Fair gelding.
**B Gubby [0-3] Brian Gubby Ltd (from L MontagueHall [0-2] Oct 1996).*

UTHER PENDRAGON (IRE) BHB 25f **RR 12f** 1469^{12}
3 b g Petardia 8.2f **(58)** -Mountain Stage (IRE) (Pennine Walk) 8.5f **(61)**
Form - 780
Record 1998 - 1st:0 2nd:0 3rd:0 Ran:3
Pre1998 - 1st:0 2nd:0 3rd:0 Ran:2
1998 Turf 0-1: (8f) (g-f) 1998 AW 0-2: (5f, 8f) (Equi 2)
Leggy, very moderate gelding, has worn blinkers. AW high 30.
**M Bradstock [0-1] Miss J C Blackwell (from J A Bennett [0-4] Jan 1998).*

UTMOST ZEAL (USA) BHB 50f52a **RR 49f 52a** 4385^{10}
5 b g Cozzene (USA) 10.1f **(87)** - Zealous Lady (USA) (Highland Blade (USA)) 6.9f **(67)**
Form - 000
Record 1998 - 1st:0 2nd:0 3rd:0 Ran:3
Pre1998 - 1st:1 2nd:1 3rd:2 Ran:18
Win Prizemoney £3,309 *Total Prizemoney* £5,501
Wins 1996 Aug Folkes (G-F) H 6.9f 50 58+ <
1998 Turf 0-1: (5f) (gd) 1998 AW 0-2: (6f, 8f) (Fibr 2)
Moderate gelding, has worn blinkers. AW high 38. Consistent.
**J L Spearing [0-3] Dancersend Racing (from P W Harris [1-18] Jun 1997).*

UZY RR 75f 5122^{2}
2 ch c Common Grounds 8.1f **(66)** - Loch Clair (IRE) (Lomond (USA)) 8.8f **(65)**
Form - 02
Record 1998 - 1st:0 2nd:1 3rd:0 Ran:2
Win Prizemoney £0 *Total Prizemoney* £895
1998 Turf 0-2: (6f 2) (sft, g-s)
Currently above-average colt. Turf high 75 (began Oct) - 2nd of 9 to Full Egalite (5 Nov Brighton 6f g-s RF 5122).
**I A Balding [0-2] Stamford Bridge Partnership.*

VAGABOND CHANTEUSE BHB 85f **RR 94f** 3752^{9}
4 ch f Sanglamore (USA) 12.9f **(67)** - Eclipsing (IRE) (Baillamont (USA)) 7f **(78)**
Form - 3630080
Record 1998 - 1st:0 2nd:0 3rd:2 Ran:7
Pre1998 - 1st:1 2nd:1 3rd:4 Ran:12
Win Prizemoney £3,317 *Total Prizemoney* £28,182
Wins * 1996 Aug Thirsk (GD) 7f 77 <
1998 Turf 0-7: (7f, 8f, 10f 4, 12f) (gd 3, g-f, frm 3)
Rangy, useful filly, effective 10 to 12f, best at 12f, acts on gd to g-f, best on gd, has worn blinkers. Turf high 94 - 3rd of 6 getting 5lb from Redbridge (13 Jun Leicester 12f gd RF 1961). Inconsistent. Proved hard to place last season, but ran a fair third in a listed race in June. **T J Etherington [1-19] W R Green.*

VAGRANT (FR) RR 96f $3856a^{3}$
3 ch c Nashwan (USA) 10.3f **(79)** - Valdera (USA) 00
Form - 22133
1998 Turf 1-5: (11f 1-1, 12f 3, 13f) (sft, gd 2, g-f 1-2)

Very useful colt, often wears blinkers. Turf high 100 (1st run) - 2nd of 11 giving 5lb to Hazarama (29 May Wexford 13f gd RF 1661a). He ran consistently in reasonable company, and made 26,000 guineas at the Tattersalls Autumn Horses In Training Sales.
**D K Weld in IRE [1-5] Mrs A J F O'Reilly.*

VALAGALORE BHB 67f **RR 70f** 4500[4]

4 b f Generous (IRE) 11.5f **(82)** - Victoria Cross (USA) (Spectacular Bid (USA)) 11.2f **(76)**
Form - 085404
Record 1998 - 1st:0 2nd:0 3rd:0 Ran:6
Pre1998 - 1st:2 2nd:0 3rd:1 Ran:8
Win Prizemoney £7,409 *Total Prizemoney* £10,182
Wins * 1997 Aug Haydoc (G-F) H 14f 78 85 <
* 1997 Jly Catter (G-F) 13.8f 75
1998 Turf 0-6: (12f 2, 14f, 15f, 16f 2) (hvy, g-f, frm 4)
Tall, above-average filly, effective 14f, acts on gd to frm, likes left handed tracks, likes tight tracks. Turf high 70. Showed progressive form in '97, but has yet to recapture his best.
**B W Hills [2-14] Mrs A D Bourne.*

VALANTINE ANNA BHB 48f **RR 51f** 4643[10]

2 b f Perpendicular - Fool's Errand (Milford) 9f **(61)**
Form - 0070
Record 1998 - 1st:0 2nd:0 3rd:0 Ran:4
1998 Turf 0-4: (5f, 6f, 7f, 8f) (g-f 2, frm 2)
Fair filly. Turf high 51 (began Jly). **D HaydnJones [0-4] Trio Racing.*

VALDINI (IRE) BHB 83f **RR 73f** 4144[3]

2 b f Common Grounds 8.1f **(66)** - Windini (Windjammer (USA)) 7f **(59)**
Form - 703
Record 1998 - 1st:0 2nd:0 3rd:1 Ran:3
Win Prizemoney £0 *Total Prizemoney* £469
1998 Turf 0-3: (7f 3) (g-f, frm 2)
Currently above-average filly. Turf high 73 (began Aug).
**P W Harris [0-3] Spirits In Common.*

VALENTINE GIRL **RR 100f** 4725a[9]

2 b f Alzao (USA) 9.8f **(73)** -Set Fair (USA)**(89f)**(Alleged (USA)) 10f **(76)**
Form - 100
Record 1998 - 1st:1 2nd:0 3rd:0 Ran:3
Win Prizemoney £9,436 *Total Prizemoney* £9,436
Wins * **1998** Aug Newbur (G-F) L 7f 80+ <
1998 Turf 1-3: (7f 1-1, 8f 2) (sft, gd, g-f 1-1)
Currently very useful filly. Turf high 100 (began Aug) - 9th of 11 to Juvenia (4 Oct Longchamp 8f sft RF 4725a). She made the perfect start to her career in a Listed event at Newbury in August, but was never seen with a chance in two Group races. Big and scopey, she will improve over the winter but may fall short of her trainer's expectations. **B W Hills [1-3] K Abdulla.*

VALENTINE WALTZ (IRE) BHB 100f **RR 100f** 4853[2]

2 b f Be My Guest (USA) 10.2f **(66)** - Save Me The Waltz (Kings Lake (USA)) 10.8f **(67)**
Form - 4334132
Record 1998 - 1st:1 2nd:1 3rd:3 Ran:7
Win Prizemoney £3,566 *Total Prizemoney* £16,643
Wins * **1998** Spt Bright (GD) 7f 84+ <
1998 Turf 1-7: (5f 3, 6f 2, 7f 1-2) (hvy, sft, gd 4, g-f 1-1)
Very useful filly, effective 7f, acts on gd. Turf high 100 - 2nd of 14 to Hula Angel (17 Oct Newmarket 7f gd RF 4853). She proved a shade frustrating for Aidan O'Brien, but improved markedly after gaining a confidence-boosting win at Brighton on her first start for John Gosden. A staying-on second in the Group Two Rockfel Stakes at Newmarket in October, she is just the sort to do well on the continent as a three-year-old.
**J H M Gosden [1-3] Kirby Maher Syndicate (from A P O'Brien in IRE [0-4] Jun 1998).*

VALE OF LEVEN (IRE) BHB 63f **RR 56f** 5012[1]

2 b g Fayruz 6.6f **(63)** - Speedy Action (Horage) 10.3f **(61)**
Form - 808421
Record 1998 - 1st:1 2nd:1 3rd:0 Ran:6
Win Prizemoney £3,141 *Total Prizemoney* £3,725
Wins * **1998** Oct Redcar (SFT) H 6f 51 56 <
1998 Turf 1-5: (6f 1-3, 7f, 8f) (g-s, gd 1-2, g-f, frm) 1998 AW 0-1: (7f) (Fibr)
Average gelding, effective 6 to 7f, acts on gd - acts on Fibr. Turf high 56 (began Aug) - 1st of 14 getting 23lb from The Haulier (27 Oct Redcar RF 5012). (1st run) - 2nd of 16 to Sounds Solo (19 Oct Southwell 7f Fibr RF 4878).
**K A Ryan [1-6] Clayton Bigley Partnership Ltd.*

VALES ALES BHB 19f **RR 8f** 125[9]

5 b g Dominion Royale 7.8f **(63)** - Keep Mum (Mummy's Pet) 7.7f **(60)**
Form - 0
Record 1998 - 1st:0 2nd:0 3rd:0 Ran:1
Pre1998 - 1st:0 2nd:0 3rd:1 Ran:8
Win Prizemoney £0 *Total Prizemoney* £502
1998 AW 0-1: (8f) (Fibr)
Very poor gelding. **R M McKellar [0-10] Waygateshaw Racing Club.*

VALIANT CHARGE (IRE) BHB 33f **RR 24f** 1452[5]

2 ch f Forest Wind (USA) - Popcorn **(50df)** (Pharly (FR)) 9.8f **(68)**
Form - 8465
Record 1998 - 1st:0 2nd:0 3rd:0 Ran:4
1998 Turf 0-3: (5f 2, 6f) (gd, g-f, frm) 1998 AW 0-1: (5f) (Fibr)
Little account filly. Turf high 24. **J S Moore [0-4] Chris Bradbury.*

VANADIUM ORE BHB 58f **RR 52f** 5061[12]

5 b g Precious Metal 9.3f **(42)** - Rockefillee (Tycoon II) 8.7f **(47)**
Form - 66011152750
Record 1998 - 1st:3 2nd:1 3rd:0 Ran:11
Pre1998 - 1st:1 2nd:2 3rd:0 Ran:9
Win Prizemoney £12,155 *Total Prizemoney* £15,550
Wins * **1998** Jun Newcas (GD) H 10.1f 52 60 <
* **1998** Jun Ayr (G-F) H 10.9f 52 56
* **1998** Jun Cheste (GD) H 10.3f 50 53
* 1997 Oct Newcas (G-F) H 10.1f 48 52
1998 Turf 3-11: (10f 2-8, 11f 1-1, 12f 2) (sft 2, gd 2-4, g-f 1-1, frm 4)
Fair gelding, effective 10 to 12f, best at 12f, acts on gd to frm, best on gd, has worn blinkers, favours left handed tracks, excels at Newcastle. Turf high 60 - 1st of 7 giving 17lb to Beau Roberto (26 Jun Newcastle RF 2306) - also 1st of 14 getting 4lb from Superpride (20 Jun Ayr RF 2147). Consistent. Completed a hat-trick in minor handicaps in June. Has a useful turn of foot, and is best coming from behind off a strong pace.
**W McKeown [4-16] Garth Ormond (from J L Eyre [0-7] Dec 1996).*

VANBOROUGH LAD BHB 44f40a **RR 44f 40a** 3144[1]

9 b g Precocious 7.2f **(54)** - Lustrous (Golden Act (USA)) 8.8f **(67)**
Form - 4504200561
Record 1998 - 1st:1 2nd:1 3rd:0 Ran:10
Pre1998 - 1st:5 2nd:9 3rd:8 Ran:66
Win Prizemoney £17,752 *Total Prizemoney* £34,637
Wins * **1998** Jly Windso (G-F) H 10f 42 44
* 1997 May Bath (GD) H 8f 37 39
* 1995 May Bath (G-F) H 8f 52 48
* 1994 May Bath (GD) H 8f 51 54
1998 Turf 1-10: (7f, 8f 7, 10f 1-2) (gd 5, g-f 2, frm 1-3)
Moderate gelding, effective 8 to 10f, best at 8f, acts on g-s to hrd, best on frm, has worn blinkers, likes left handed tracks, favours tight tracks, excels at Bath, likes Windsor. Turf high 45 (1st run) - 4th of 18 getting 7lb from Questan (18 May Bath 8f frm RF 1292) - also 1st of 13 getting 23lb from Contentment (27 Jly Windsor RF 3144). His only victories since 1991 had been three wins in the same race at Bath during May. He ran well in it again this year but was probably inconvenienced by not having had a previous run. He was running consistently well after, and broke the trend by scoring at Windsor in the summer.
**M J Bolton [4-48] Mrs S P Elphick (from M J Haynes [2-34] Spt 1993).*

VAN GURP BHB 53f83a **RR 55f 83a** 4955[11]

5 ch g Generous (IRE) 11.5f **(82)** - Atlantic Flyer (USA) (Storm Bird (CAN)) 10.3f **(74)**
Form - 5800
Record 1998 - 1st:0 2nd:0 3rd:0 Ran:4
Pre1998 - 1st:1 2nd:1 3rd:3 Ran:18
Win Prizemoney £6,108 *Total Prizemoney* £10,975
Wins 1996 Spt York (GD) 7.9f 87 <
1998 Turf 0-4: (7f 3, 8f) (g-s, g-f, frm 2)
Fair gelding, effective 7f, acts on g-f, has worn blinkers, likes left handed tracks, likes tight tracks. Turf high 55 (began Jly). Inconsistent.
**H Alexander [0-7] R V Jackson (from B A McMahon [1-18] Oct 1997).*

VANTAGE POINT BHB 53f **RR 42f** 5146[8]
2 b c Casteddu 7.4f **(54)** - Rosie Dickins (Blue Cashmere) 6.4f **(54)**
Form - 088
Record 1998 - 1st:0 2nd:0 3rd:0 Ran:3
1998 Turf 0-3: (6f, 8f 2) (sft, gd 2)
Currently moderate colt. Turf high 42 (began Jly).
**K McAuliffe [0-3] The Hare and Hounds Partnership.*

VARNISHING DAY (IRE) BHB 55f **RR 57f** 2878[8]
6 b g Royal Academy (USA) 7.8f **(77)** -Red Letter Day (Crepello) 9f **(65)**
Form - 08
Record 1998 - 1st:0 2nd:0 3rd:0 Ran:1
Pre1998 - 1st:1 2nd:0 3rd:1 Ran:8
Win Prizemoney £4,077 *Total Prizemoney* £5,240
Wins 1994 Aug Newbur (GD) 7f 88+
1998 Turf 0-1: (8f) (frm)
Fair gelding, has worn blinkers. Inconsistent.
**Miss Z C Davison [0-1] Mrs J Irvine (from P W Chapple-Hyam [1-8] Nov 1997).*

VARYKINO RR 57f 791[4]
3 b f Soviet Star (USA) 8.6f **(74)** - Wantage Park (Pas de Seul) 9.1f **(67)**
Form - 4
Record 1998 - 1st:0 2nd:0 3rd:0 Ran:1
Win Prizemoney £0 *Total Prizemoney* £242
1998 Turf 0-1: (6f) (g-s)
Scopey, currently fair filly. **J R Fanshawe [0-1] T & J Vestey.*

VASARI (IRE) BHB 74f **RR 76f** 4360[4]
4 ch g Imperial Frontier (USA) 7f **(65)** - Why Not Glow (IRE) (Glow (USA)) 6.7f **(71)**
Form - 6646034
Record 1998 - 1st:0 2nd:0 3rd:1 Ran:7
Pre1998 - 1st:1 2nd:1 3rd:2 Ran:9
Win Prizemoney £7,112 *Total Prizemoney* £13,263
Wins * 1996 May Cheste (GD) 5.1f 83+ <
1998 Turf 0-7: (5f 2, 6f 3, 7f 2) (gd 3, g-f 2, frm 2)
Scopey, above-average gelding, effective 6f, acts on gd to g-f, best on g-f. Turf high 76 (began Jly) - 6th of 22 getting 6lb from Cadeaux Cher (15 Aug Ripon 6f g-f RF 3661). Consistent. Has shown mixed form, running well when a close sixth in a hotly contested handicap at Ripon in August and when stepping up to seven furlongs at Haydock in September. Has joined Willie Musson. **M R Channon [1-16] Alec Tuckerman.*

VAX RAPIDE BHB 66f **RR 52f** 3215[5]
3 ch f Sharpo 7.5f **(68)** - Vax Lady (Millfontaine)
Form - 5805
Record 1998 - 1st:0 2nd:0 3rd:0 Ran:4
Pre1998 - 1st:1 2nd:0 3rd:0 Ran:2
Win Prizemoney £3,044 *Total Prizemoney* £3,183
Wins 1997 Mar Warwic (G-F) 5f 80 <
1998 Turf 0-4: (5f 2, 6f 2) (sft, g-s, g-f 2)
Light-framed, fair filly, effective 5f, acts on frm. Turf high 75.
**Ian Williams [0-1] A J & Mrs L Brazier (from J L Spearing [1-5] May 1998).*

VEGA NEUTRAL BHB 42f **RR 40f** 3686[10]
2 ch f King's Signet (USA) 7f **(51)** - Factuelle (Known Fact (USA)) 7.4f **(67)**
Form - 00
Record 1998 - 1st:0 2nd:0 3rd:0 Ran:2
1998 Turf 0-2: (5f, 6f) (frm, hrd)
Currently moderate filly. Turf high 40.
**P Shakespeare [0-2] Jamie Donovan.*

VELLUM RR 78f 4802[10]
3 b f Warning 8.1f **(77)** - Avowal (Kris) 9.5f **(73)**
Form - 310
Record 1998 - 1st:1 2nd:0 3rd:1 Ran:3
Win Prizemoney £4,012 *Total Prizemoney* £4,572
Wins * **1998** Spt Folkes (G-F) 9.7f 78 <
1998 Turf 1-3: (8f, 10f 1-1, 11f) (sft, g-f 1-1, hrd)
Workmanlike, currently above-average filly. Turf high 78 (began Aug) - 1st of 9 getting 6lb from Marozia (25 Spt Folkestone RF 4477). **H R A Cecil [1-3] K Abdulla.*

VELVET JONES BHB 39f55a **RR 45f 55a** 4529[10]
5 b gr g Sharrood (USA) 11.1f **(67)** - Cradle of Love (USA) (Roberto (USA)) 10f **(76)**
Form - 0506400
Record 1998 - 1st:0 2nd:0 3rd:0 Ran:7
Pre1998 - 1st:0 2nd:4 3rd:4 Ran:31
Win Prizemoney £0 *Total Prizemoney* £5,105
1998 Turf 0-7: (6f 2, 7f 2, 8f 3) (gd 3, g-f 3, frm)
Moderate gelding, effective 7 to 8f, acts on frm, has worn blinkers, likes left handed tracks, likes tight tracks. Turf high 45 - 4th of 18 getting 3lb from Polonaise Prince (11 Aug Bath 8f frm RF 3524).
**G F H Charles-Jones [0-34] Mrs Jessica Charles-Jones (from P F I Cole [0-6] Spt 1995).*

VELVET STORY BHB 43f38a **RR 23f 38a** 1720[16]
3 ch g Aragon 7.7f **(58)** - Lucy Manette (Final Straw) 7.9f **(64)**
Form - 887000
Record 1998 - 1st:0 2nd:0 3rd:0 Ran:5
Pre1998 - 1st:0 2nd:1 3rd:0 Ran:5
Win Prizemoney £0 *Total Prizemoney* £607
1998 Turf 0-3: (6f, 8f 2) (g-f 2, frm) 1998 AW 0-2: (7f 2) (Equi, Fibr)
Neat, little account gelding, effective 5f, acts on hrd, has worn blinkers. Turf high 23. AW high 21.
**P D Evans [0-7] Diamond Racing Ltd (from N Tinkler [0-3] Jun 1997).*

VENETIAN PEARL (IRE) RR 55f 4846[13]
2 ch f Generous (IRE) 11.5f **(82)** - Veronica (Persian Bold) 9.3f **(66)**
Form - 0
Record 1998 - 1st:0 2nd:0 3rd:0 Ran:1
1998 Turf 0-1: (6f) (g-f)
Currently fair filly. **G Wragg [0-1] Baron G Von Ullmann.*

VENETIAN SCENE BHB 66f **RR 67f** 1627[12]
4 ch f Night Shift (USA) 8.1f **(73)** - Revisit (Busted) 10.2f **(61)**
Form - 57520
Record 1998 - 1st:0 2nd:1 3rd:0 Ran:5
Pre1998 - 1st:1 2nd:0 3rd:1 Ran:4
Win Prizemoney £5,677 *Total Prizemoney* £8,247
Wins 1997 Apr Leices (G-S) H 11.8f 64 69 <
1998 Turf 0-5: (12f 3, 14f, 16f) (hvy, sft, frm 3)
Unfurnished, average filly, effective 12f, acts on gd to frm, best on frm. Turf high 67 - 5th of 15 giving 13lb to Veronica Franco (14 May Salisbury 12f frm RF 1218). Consistent. Daughter of a doughty stayer in Revisit, she only ran once in 1997, winning at Leicester in April. She ran creditably in the Queen's Prize early in 1998, but did not really build on that subsequently.
**M C Pipe [0-8] Richard Green (Fine Paintings) (from P F I Cole [1-4] Apr 1997).*

VENICE BEACH BHB 44f48a **RR 58df 48a** 9[9]
6 b g Shirley Heights 12.1f **(76)** - Bold and Beautiful (Bold Lad (IRE)) 8.4f **(68)**
Form - 0
Record 1998 - 1st:0 2nd:0 3rd:0 Ran:1
Pre1998 - 1st:0 2nd:2 3rd:1 Ran:9
Win Prizemoney £0 *Total Prizemoney* £3,531
1998 AW 0-1: (8f) (Fibr)
Fair gelding.
**R Simpson [0-1] Ms K Churchill (from C P E Brooks [0-5] Apr 1997).*

VENTURE CAPITALIST BHB 90f **RR 92f** 4534[7]
9 ch g Never so Bold 7.1f **(62)** - Brave Advance (USA) (Bold Laddie (USA)) 5.6f **(69)**
Form - 74004241507
Record 1998 - 1st:1 2nd:1 3rd:0 Ran:11
Pre1998 - 1st:7 2nd:11 3rd:10 Ran:68
Win Prizemoney £112,037 *Total Prizemoney* £175,061
Wins * **1998** Jly Doncas (G-F) 6f 92
* 1996 May York (G-F) G3 6f 106 <
* 1995 May York (G-F) H 6f 100 104
* 1995 Apr Thirsk (GD) 6f 99
1994 Jun Ascot (G-F) H 6f 91 91
1998 Turf 1-11: (5f 3, 6f 1-8) (g-s 2, gd 3, g-f 1-3, frm 3)
Useful gelding, effective 5 to 6f, best at 6f, acts on gd to frm, best on g-f, has worn blinkers (extremely effectively), does well at Doncaster, likes York. Turf high 95 - 4th of 6 to Bolshoi (9 May Beverley 5f frm RF 1118) - also 1st of 4 giving 5lb to Iceband (29

Jly Doncaster RF 3193). **Inconsistent. This grand veteran sprinter gained his first win for a long time in a minor event in July 1998, having been just touched off a couple of runs previously. He can win again, although he can be opposed with confidence if he runs over seven furlongs because he does not stay it.**
**D Nicholls [4-46] W G Swiers (from R Hannon [4-33] Oct 1994).*

VENTURE ISLAND (IRE) BHB 44f **RR 49f** 4300[11]

2 br f Petardia 8.2f **(58)** - Island Adventure (Touching Wood (USA)) 8.2f **(55)**
Form - 08400

Record		1st	2nd	3rd	Ran
	1998 -	1st:0	2nd:0	3rd:0	Ran:5

1998 Turf 0-5: (6f, 7f 4) (g-f 3, frm 2)
Moderate filly. Turf high 49. **W J Musson [0-5] The Square Table.*

VERASICA BHB 24f **RR 24f** 4768[17]

4 b f Handsome Sailor 6.6f **(53)** - Vera Musica (USA) (Stop The Music (USA)) 9.2f **(71)**
Form - 00

Record		1st	2nd	3rd	Ran
	1998 -	1st:0	2nd:0	3rd:0	Ran:2
	Pre1998 -	1st:0	2nd:0	3rd:0	Ran:2

1998 Turf 0-2: (6f, 9f) (sft, frm)
Workmanlike, little account filly. Turf high 24 (began Spt).
**J Berry [0-2] R Leah (from R Hollinshead [0-2] Jun 1997).*

VERDANT EXPRESS BHB 35f40a **RR 32f 40a** 4885[11]

3 b f Greensmith - Ballynora (Ballacashtal (CAN)) 5.3f **(50)**
Form - 380000

Record		1st	2nd	3rd	Ran
	1998 -	1st:0	2nd:0	3rd:1	Ran:6
	Pre1998 -	1st:0	2nd:1	3rd:0	Ran:5

Win Prizemoney £0 *Total Prizemoney* £855
1998 Turf 0-6: (5f 4, 6f, 7f) (g-s, gd, g-f, frm 3)
Light-framed, very moderate filly, effective 5f, acts on gd. Turf high 36. **W G M Turner [0-11] Vale Racing.*

Form - 1
1998 Turf 1-1: (9f 1-1) (gd 1-1)
Currently Group-class gelding. (1st run) - 1st of 10 giving 1lb to Tangazi (18 Oct Belmont Park RF 4945a).
**M Hennig in USA [1-1] December Hill Farm.*

VEROCITY (FR) BHB 52f55a **RR 52f 55a** 2376[14]

3 b g Groom Dancer (USA) 9.5f **(75)** - Villella (Sadler's Wells (USA)) 10f **(76)**
Form - 3060

Record		1st	2nd	3rd	Ran
	1998 -	1st:0	2nd:0	3rd:1	Ran:4
	Pre1998 -	1st:0	2nd:0	3rd:0	Ran:1

Win Prizemoney £0 *Total Prizemoney* £363
1998 Turf 0-3: (10f, 12f 2) (gd, frm 2) 1998 AW 0-1: (10f) (Equi)
Light-framed, fair gelding, has worn blinkers. Turf high 52.
**G Wragg [0-5] John Newton.*

VERONICA FRANCO BHB 84f48a **RR 86f 48a** 5151[12]

5 b m Darshaan 11.9f **(81)** - Maiden Eileen (Stradavinsky) 12.5f **(64)**
Form - 11153132150

Record		1st	2nd	3rd	Ran
	1998 -	1st:5	2nd:1	3rd:2	Ran:11
	Pre1998 -	1st:2	2nd:1	3rd:2	Ran:20

Win Prizemoney £43,594 *Total Prizemoney* £49,582

Wins								
	*** 1998**	Spt	Newbur (GD)	H	13.3f	74	80	<
	*** 1998**	Jly	Ascot (G-F)	H	12f	67	68	
	*** 1998**	Jun	Goodwo (GD)	H	16f	64	66+	
	*** 1998**	May	Sandow (G-S)	H	14f	59	63	
	*** 1998**	May	Salisb (FRM)	H	12f	54	60	
	* 1997	Spt	Sandow (G-F)	H	14f	49	52	
	* 1997	Aug	Folkes (G-F)	H	12f	45	49	

1998 Turf 5-11: (12f 2-5, 13f 1-1, 14f 1-4, 16f 1-1) (gd 2-5, g-f 2-4, frm 1-2)
Useful filly, effective 12 to 13f, acts on g-f to frm, has worn blinkers, likes right handed tracks. Turf high 86 - 5th of 13 giving 5lb to Rainbow Ways (15 Oct Newmarket 12f frm RF 4824) - also 1st of 20 getting 5lb from Pairumani Star (19 Spt Newbury RF 4380). Did well in the latter part of 1997 and continued on the upgrade, com-

Veronica Franco likes to come with a late run.

VERGENNES (USA) **RR 114f** 4945a[1]

3 b g Dynaformer (USA) 12f **(82)** - Shareefa (USA) (Fabuleux Dancer (USA))

pleting a hat-trick, and adding further victories at Ascot and Newbury (Autumn Cup). Does not find a great deal off the bridle, and is usually produced very late, but struck the front a lot earlier when impressive at Newbury.
**P R Hedger [7-17] J J Whelan (from R Ingram [0-4] Jly 1997).*

VERPOSEN (IRE) BHB 59f **RR 64f** 4929[12]
2 b c Posen (USA) 8.6f **(59)** - Jet Set Bunny (USA) (Northjet) 10.3f **(74)**
Form - 3026500
Record 1998 - 1st:0 2nd:1 3rd:1 Ran:7
Win Prizemoney £0 *Total Prizemoney* £1,085
1998 Turf 0-7: (6f 2, 7f 4, 8f) (g-s 3, g-f 2, frm 2)
Average colt, effective 7f, acts on g-s to frm, has worn blinkers. Turf high 64 (began Aug) - 2nd of 11 getting 4lb from Archie Babe (5 Spt Thirsk 7f frm RF 4115). **J Pearce [0-7] Chris Marsh.*

VERRO (USA) BHB 15f20a **RR 10f 20a** 5128[10]
11 ch g Irish River (FR) 9f **(77)** -Royal Rafale(USA) (Reneged) 5.5f **(44)**
Form - 000
Record 1998 - 1st:0 2nd:0 3rd:0 Ran:3
Pre1998 - 1st:2 2nd:0 3rd:4 Ran:72
Win Prizemoney £5,328 *Total Prizemoney* £6,941
1998 Turf 0-3: (6f 2, 7f) (g-s, g-f 2)
Poor gelding, has broken blood-vessels, often wears blinkers. Turf high 10. **P D Purdy [0-6] P D Purdy (from K Bishop [0-31] May 1997).*

VERVE (IRE) BHB 65f **RR 67f** 5062[4]
3 b f Saddlers' Hall (IRE) 10.5f **(65)** -Arousal (Rousillon (USA)) 8.2f **(74)**
Form - 734754
Record 1998 - 1st:0 2nd:0 3rd:1 Ran:6
Win Prizemoney £0 *Total Prizemoney* £1,116
1998 Turf 0-6: (10f 3, 12f 3) (sft 2, g-s, gd, frm 2)
Workmanlike, average filly, effective 10f, acts on sft to gd. Turf high 71 - 4th of 8 to Rajaiyma (1 Jly Kempton 10f gd RF 2443). Rather one-paced middle-distance maiden, but should find a small race. **R Charlton [0-6] Lord Weinstock.*

VERY MUCH SO RR 25f 2079[4]
2 ch c Wolfhound (USA) 7.3f **(71)** - Desert Girl (Green Desert (USA)) 8.6f **(78)**
Form - 04
Record 1998 - 1st:0 2nd:0 3rd:0 Ran:2
Win Prizemoney £0 *Total Prizemoney* £204
1998 Turf 0-1: (6f) (g-f) 1998 AW 0-1: (6f) (Fibr)
Very moderate colt. (DEAD)
**Dr J D Scargill [0-2] Premier Bloodhorse Partners.*

VET'S DECEIT (IRE) BHB 31f **RR 32f** 2399[12]
3 ch g Statoblest 6.4f **(63)** - Maniusha (Sallust) 8.4f **(63)**
Form - 00
Record 1998 - 1st:0 2nd:0 3rd:0 Ran:2
Pre1998 - 1st:0 2nd:0 3rd:0 Ran:2
1998 Turf 0-2: (5f, 6f) (sft, gd)
Light-framed, very moderate gelding.
**Ronald Thompson [0-4] Ronald Thompson.*

VEZING (FR) RR 107f 1737a[7]
3 b/ c Bering 9.6f **(80)** - Marie de Vez (FR) (Crystal Palace (FR)) 12.5f **(76)**
Form - 37
1998 Turf 0-2: (12f 2) (gd 2)
Currently Pattern-class colt. Turf high 107 (1st run) - 3rd of 7 to Dream Well (14 May Longchamp 12f gd RF 1374a). He could not hold a light to Dream Well in a Group Three, and was even further adrift when thrown into the Classic cauldron at Chantilly in May. A doctor would prescribe a drop in class. **P Demercastel in FR [0-2].*

VIALLI (IRE) RR 114f 839a[2]
7 ch h Niniski (USA) 13.2f **(67)** - Vaison la Romaine (Arctic Tern (USA)) 8.9f **(69)**
Form - 2
1998 Turf 0-1: (10f) (g-f)
Currently Group-class horse. (1st run) - 2nd of 11 giving 5lb to Oriental Express (19 Apr Sha Tin 10f g-f RF 0839a). A typically tough Kiwi, he was inched out in the Queen Elizabeth II Cup in Sha Tin. **D & P O'Sullivan in NZ [0-3].*

VIBRANCE (IRE) RR 77+f 972[4]
2 b c College Chapel - Shalara (Dancers Image (USA)) 9.3f **(71)**
Form - 4
Record 1998 - 1st:0 2nd:0 3rd:0 Ran:1
Win Prizemoney £0 *Total Prizemoney* £339
1998 Turf 0-1: (5f) (gd)
Currently above-average colt. **J Noseda [0-1] M Olden.*

VICE PRESIDENTIAL BHB 62f65a **RR 77f 65a** 4751[22]
3 ch g Presidium 7.5f **(56)** - Steelock (Lochnager) 6f **(59)**
Form - 0501135057000
Record 1998 - 1st:2 2nd:0 3rd:1 Ran:13
Pre1998 - 1st:1 2nd:0 3rd:1 Ran:7
Win Prizemoney £7,884 *Total Prizemoney* £9,050

Wins						
1998	Jun	Mussel	(SFT)	C	7.1f	62+
1998	Jun	Warwic	(SFT)	C	7f	77
1997	May	Hamilt	(SFT)		5f	93+ <

1998 Turf 2-10: (6f 4, 7f 2-6) (g-s 2, gd 2-5, g-f 2, frm) 1998 AW 0-3: (6f, 7f 2) (Equi, Fibr 2)
Scopey, above-average gelding, effective 5 to 7f, acts on gd, likes tight tracks. Turf high 77. AW high 65. He is a totally different horse on soft ground, conditions under which he easily won two claimers in June.
**M P Bielby [0-7] A Clarke (from T J Etherington [3-13] Jun 1998).*

VICIOUS CIRCLE BHB 88f **RR 97?f** 5126[16]
4 b g Lahib (USA) 8f **(69)** - Tight Spin (High Top) 10.2f **(67)**
Form - 4210
Record 1998 - 1st:1 2nd:1 3rd:0 Ran:4
Pre1998 - 1st:0 2nd:0 3rd:1 Ran:1
Win Prizemoney £3,496 *Total Prizemoney* £5,356
Wins * **1998** Oct Ayr (HVY) 10f 97+ <
1998 Turf 1-4: (8f, 10f 1-3) (sft 1-1, g-s, g-f, hrd)
Lengthy, very useful gelding. Turf high 97 (began Aug) - 1st of 5 giving 10lb to Blow Me A Kiss (13 Oct Ayr RF 4770). Showed promise on his seasonal debut, having been off for a year. He got off the mark when encountering heavy ground, which really seemed to suit, but was disappointing when favourite for a handicap at Brighton on his last start. **L M Cumani [1-5] S K S C Racing.*

VICKY JAZZ BHB 30f **RR 28f** 3365[11]
3 ch f Alhijaz 7.7f **(57)** - Kinkajoo (Precocious) 8.6f **(62)**
Form - 000
Record 1998 - 1st:0 2nd:0 3rd:0 Ran:3
Pre1998 - 1st:0 2nd:0 3rd:0 Ran:3
1998 Turf 0-3: (10f 2, 12f) (g-f 2, frm)
Light-framed, little account filly. Turf high 17.
**J S Moore [0-6] S M Boddy.*

VICTOR BLUM (USA) BHB 23f **RR 35f** 2325[11]
5 b g Dr Blum (USA) - Victoria Elena (USA) (Gold Stage (USA))
Form - 00
Record 1998 - 1st:0 2nd:0 3rd:0 Ran:2
Pre1998 - 1st:0 2nd:0 3rd:1 Ran:9
Win Prizemoney £0 *Total Prizemoney* £466
1998 Turf 0-2: (16f, 17f) (gd 2)
Very moderate gelding, often wears blinkers. Turf high 13.
**C A Horgan [0-11] R Del Rosario.*

VICTORIA DAY BHB 24f26a **RR 29f 26a** 111[8]
6 b m Reference Point 12f **(66)** - Victoress (USA) (Conquistador Cielo (USA)) 8.8f **(69)**
Form - 008
Record 1998 - 1st:0 2nd:0 3rd:0 Ran:3
Pre1998 - 1st:0 2nd:0 3rd:0 Ran:10
Win Prizemoney £0 *Total Prizemoney* £284
1998 AW 0-3: (8f, 12f, 16f) (Fibr 3)
Little account mare, has worn blinkers. AW high 4. Becoming disappointing.
**D Shaw [0-3] Paul Murphy (from B A McMahon [0-5] Oct 1996).*

VICTORIA HOUSE (IRE) BHB 20f **RR 24f** 223[9]
4 b f River Falls 8.2f **(56)** - Double Grange (IRE) (Double Schwartz) 7.9f **(55)**
Form - 00
Record 1998 - 1st:0 2nd:0 3rd:0 Ran:2
Pre1998 - 1st:0 2nd:0 3rd:0 Ran:4

1998 AW 0-2: (7f, 12f) (Equi 2)
Light-framed, little account filly, has worn blinkers.
**B A Pearce [0-2] Gerry Boyer (from M J Heaton-Ellis [0-4] Oct 1997).*

VICTORIAN GUIDE (ITY) RR 101f — 947a4

3 c
Form - 4
1998 Turf 0-1: (8f) (gd)
Currently very useful colt. He is useful, but looked out of his depth in Group Two company. **F Camici in ITY [0-1].*

VICTORIOUS RR 66f — 46414

2 ch c Formidable (USA) 7.8f **(60)** - Careful Dancer (Gorytus (USA)) 7.8f **(60)**
Form - 004

Record	**1998 -**	1st:0	2nd:0	3rd:0	Ran:3

Win Prizemoney £0 — *Total Prizemoney* £211
1998 Turf 0-3: (6f 3) (gd, g-f 2)
Currently average colt. Turf high 66 (began Aug).
**B A McMahon [0-3] Mrs J McMahon.*

VICTOR LASZLO BHB 31f37a RR 22f 37a — 62910

6 b g Ilium 11.7f **(46)** - Report 'em (USA) (Staff Writer (USA)) 10f **(54)**
Form - 50

Record	**1998 -**	1st:0	2nd:0	3rd:0	Ran:2
	Pre1998 -	1st:1	2nd:0	3rd:1	Ran:10

Win Prizemoney £3,252 — *Total Prizemoney* £3,772

Wins	* 1996	May	Hamilt	(G-F)	H	13f	36	41	<

1998 Turf 0-2: (12f, 16f) (sft, gd)
Little account gelding, has worn blinkers. Turf high 22.
**R Allan [1-13] Ian Dalgleish (from J D Bethell [0-4] Nov 1995).*

Victory Note made a winning reappearance at Newbury

VICTORY GALLOP (CAN) RR 122f — 5168a4

3 b c Cryptoclearance (USA) - Victorious Lil (CAN) (Vice Regent (CAN)) 8.7f **(74)**
Form - 2214
1998 Turf 0-1: (10f) (frm) 1998 AW 1-3: (10f 2, 12f 1-1) (Dirt 1-3)
High-calibre colt. (1st run) - 2nd of 15 to Real Quiet (2 May Churchill Downs 10f frm RF 1090a). AW high 131 - 4th of 10 to Awesome Again (7 Nov Churchill Downs 10f Dirt RF 5168a) - also 1st of 11 from Real Quiet (6 Jun Belmont Park RF 1913a). Denied Real Quiet the Triple Crown when collaring him in the Belmont Stakes and continued to show high-class form, coming from out of the clouds to finish fourth in the Breeders' Cup Classic. That run was all the more meritorious as he had been off for 70 days following surgery on a breathing problem.
**W E Walden in USA [1-4] Prestonwood Farm Inc.*

VICTORY NOTE (USA) BHB 120f RR 119df — 48498

3 b c Fairy King (USA) 7.7f **(75)** -Three Piece (Jaazeiro (USA)) 9.2f **(54)**
Form - 11408

Record	**1998 -**	1st:2	2nd:0	3rd:0	Ran:5
	Pre1998 -	1st:1	2nd:1	3rd:1	Ran:4

Win Prizemoney £130,722 — *Total Prizemoney* £148,492

Wins	* **1998**	May	Longch	(GD)	G1	8f	119	<
	* **1998**	Apr	Newbur	(HVY)	G3	7f	109	
	* 1997	Jly	Newbur	(G-F)	L	6f	103+	

1998 Turf 2-5: (7f 1-2, 8f 1-3) (sft 1-1, gd 1-4)
Workmanlike, high-class colt, effective 7 to 8f, acts on sft to gd. Turf high 119 - 1st of 12 from Muhtathir (10 May Longchamp RF 1230a). After holding on well to win the Greenham in heavy ground on his reappearance, he took the French Guineas in game style. Bypassing the Irish Guineas, his connections preferring to rely on Second Empire, he was supplemented for the St James's Palace Stakes but could finish only fourth on ground too soft for him. He ran very poorly in his final two outings in the Sussex and the Challenge Stakes. Reported to have been retired.
**P W Chapple-Hyam [3-9] Mrs J Magnier & R E Sangster.*

VICTORY SPIN RR 95f — 37602

2 ch c Beveled (USA) 6.9f **(64)** - Victoria Mill (Free State) 8.7f **(61)**
Form - 2

Record	**1998 -**	1st:0	2nd:1	3rd:0	Ran:1

Win Prizemoney £0 — *Total Prizemoney* £1,142
1998 Turf 0-1: (6f) (g-f)
Currently very useful colt. (1st run) - 2nd of 14 getting 2lb from Island Sands (20 Aug Salisbury 6f g-f RF 3760). Made an encouraging debut in August on his only appearance, and should be capable of winning races. **L M Cumani [0-1] M J Dawson.*

VICTORY TEAM (IRE) BHB 60f70a RR 66f 70a — 48867

6 b g Danehill (USA) 9.1f **(79)** - Hogan's Sister (USA) (Speak John) 10.7f **(72)**
Form - 06680004007

Record	**1998 -**	1st:0	2nd:0	3rd:0	Ran:9
	Pre1998 -	1st:5	2nd:5	3rd:3	Ran:31

Win Prizemoney £16,336 — *Total Prizemoney* £24,039

Wins	1997	Oct	Newbur	(GD)	H	7f	75	81	<
	1997	Spt	Folkes	(GD)	H	6.9f	72	76	
	1997	Apr	Folkes	(G-F)		6.9f		67	
	1996	*Mar*	*Lingfi*	*(STD)*	*H*	*8f*	*64*	*72*	
	1996	*Mar*	*Lingfi*	*(STD)*	*H*	*8f*	*64*	*63*	

1998 Turf 0-8: (6f 2, 7f 6) (sft, g-s, gd 2, g-f, frm 3) 1998 AW 0-1: (7f) (Equi)
Average gelding, effective 7 to 8f, best at 7f, acts on gd to g-f, best on g-f, has worn blinkers, likes right handed tracks, likes tight tracks, excels at Folkestone. Turf high 66. He won three times on Turf in '97, appearing to go particularly well after a break. Did not sparkle this term.
**Miss E C Lavelle [0-2] R J Lavelle (from G B Balding [5-34] Jly 1998).*

VIDAME (FR) RR 64f — 50085

3 b g Kaldoun (FR) 9.9f **(84)** -Vallee Normande (FR)(Bellypha) 9.8f **(73)**
Form - 05

Record	**1998 -**	1st:0	2nd:0	3rd:0	Ran:2

1998 Turf 0-2: (10f, 12f) (sft 2)
Leggy, currently average gelding. Turf high 64 (began Oct).
**R M Flower [0-2] M G Rogers.*

VIGNETTE (USA) RR 95f — 27007

3 b f Diesis 9f **(80)** - Be Exclusive (Be My Guest (USA)) 9.3f **(67)**
Form - 37

Record	**1998 -**	1st:0	2nd:0	3rd:1	Ran:2
	Pre1998 -	1st:1	2nd:0	3rd:0	Ran:2

Win Prizemoney £3,493 — *Total Prizemoney* £4,394

Wins	* 1997	Aug	Haydoc	(G-F)	6f	82+	<

1998 Turf 0-2: (6f 2) (g-f, frm)
Leggy, very useful filly. Turf high 95 (1st run) - 3rd of 5 to Qilin (26 Jun Newmarket 6f g-f RF 2317). Improved from her debut to score very easily on her second start of 1997 at Haydock. Swished her tail on her belated reappearance and found nothing when asked

on her only other appearance. She obviously had her problems and her attitude was questionable. Connections may well have decided not to persevere. **J H M Gosden [1-4] George Strawbridge.*

VILLAGE HOP (IRE) BHB 69f **RR 65f** 4465[9]

2 b c Shalford (IRE) 7.8f **(63)** - Fille Dansante (IRE) (Dancing Dissident (USA))
Form - 000
Record 1998 - 1st:0 2nd:0 3rd:0 Ran:3
1998 Turf 0-3: (6f 3) (frm 3)
Currently average colt. Turf high 65 (began Jly).
**C F Wall [0-3] K K Lau.*

VILLAGE NATIVE (FR) BHB 66f60a **RR 62f 60a** 4635[10]

5 ch g Village Star (FR) 5.7f **(61)** - Zedative (FR) (Zeddaan) 9f **(76)**
Form - 713635467757100165710
Record 1998 - 1st:3 2nd:0 3rd:1 Ran:17
Pre1998 - 1st:3 2nd:2 3rd:2 Ran:27
Win Prizemoney £16,535 *Total Prizemoney* £20,237
Wins * **1998** *Spt Wolver (STD) H 6f 56 59*
* **1998** Jly Bath (GD) C 5.1f 61
* **1998** May Sandow (G-S) C 8.1f 52
* 1997 *Nov Wolver (STD) H 5f 54 57*
* 1997 *Aug Wolver (STD) H 5f 52 59*
* 1995 Nov Folkes (G-F) 6f 76 <
1998 Turf 2-9: (5f 1-2, 6f, 7f 3, 8f 1-3) (sft, g-s, gd 2-3, g-f 2, frm 2) 1998 AW 1-8: (5f 2, 6f 1-3, 7f 3) (Equi 2, Fibr 1-6)
Average gelding, effective 5 to 8f, best at 5f, acts on sft to frm - acts on Fibr, often wears blinkers. Turf high 62 - 6th of 16 giving 9lb to Maladerie (3 Aug Windsor 5f frm RF 3319) - also 1st of 12 giving 4lb to Henry The Proud (16 Jly Bath RF 2844). AW high 60 - 4th of 9 giving 2lb to Mr Frosty (17 Mar Southwell 7f Fibr RF 0434) - also 1st of 13 getting 14lb from Dancing Mystery (19 Spt Wolverhampton RF 4385). Consistent. Effective on Turf and Fibresand, he won over a mile at Sandown in May, but is better known as a sprinter, and reverted to shorter distances to record two further victories. **K O Cunningham-Brown [6-44] A J Richards.*

VILLAGE PUB (FR) BHB 35f24a **RR 33f 24a** 2669[13]

4 ch g Village Star (FR) 5.7f **(61)** - Sloe Berry (Sharpo) 7.7f **(59)**
Form - 0880660
Record 1998 - 1st:0 2nd:0 3rd:0 Ran:4
Pre1998 - 1st:0 2nd:0 3rd:1 Ran:19
Win Prizemoney £0 *Total Prizemoney* £1,553
1998 Turf 0-2: (6f, 8f) (gd, g-f) 1998 AW 0-2: (6f 2) (Equi, Fibr)
Light-framed, very moderate gelding, effective 5f, acts on g-f, often wears blinkers. Turf high 33. AW high 17.
**B J Llewellyn [0-2] Alan Williams (from K O Cunningham-Brown [0-21] Feb 1998).*

VILLA WANDA **RR 42f** 5072[13]

2 ch f Grand Lodge (USA) - Gisarne (USA) (Diesis) 9.3f **(69)**
Form - 0
Record 1998 - 1st:0 2nd:0 3rd:0 Ran:1
1998 Turf 0-1: (7f) (gd)
Currently moderate filly. **W Jarvis [0-1] Lord Howard de Walden.*

VINCENT BHB 40f47a **RR 50f 47a** 1799[9]

3 b c Anshan 8.2f **(63)** -Top-Anna (IRE) **(52f)**(Ela-Mana-Mou) 10.1f **(70)**
Form - 52000
Record 1998 - 1st:0 2nd:1 3rd:0 Ran:5
Pre1998 - 1st:0 2nd:0 3rd:0 Ran:2
Win Prizemoney £0 *Total Prizemoney* £922
1998 Turf 0-3: (10f, 12f 2) (sft, gd, frm) 1998 AW 0-2: (12f, 15f) (Fibr 2)
Leggy, fair colt, effective 12f, - acts on Fibr, has worn blinkers, likes tight tracks. Turf high 50. AW high 53 (1st run) - 2nd of 6 giving 13lb to Silver Hope (30 Apr Wolverhampton 12f Fibr RF 0942).
**J L Harris [0-7] P Caplan.*

VINDALOO BHB 78f65a **RR 60?f 65a** 117[8]

6 ch g Indian Ridge 7.6f **(74)** -Lovely Lagoon(Mill Reef (USA))10.5f **(78)**
Form - 08
Record 1998 - 1st:0 2nd:0 3rd:0 Ran:1
Pre1998 - 1st:11 2nd:4 3rd:4 Ran:42
Win Prizemoney £42,455 *Total Prizemoney* £58,468
Wins 1995 *Jly Lingfi (STD) H 12f 60 64*
1995 *Jly Wolver (STD) H 9.4f 60 65*
1995 Jly Leices (GD) H 11.8f 78 81 <
1995 Jly Carlis (FRM) H 12f 71 76
1995 Jun Redcar (FRM) H 10f 64 64
1995 Jun Warwic (G-F) H 10.8f 57 59+
1995 Jun Nottin (G-F) 10f 63
1995 Jun Yarmou (GD) H 10.1f 48 60
1995 May Leices (G-F) C 8f 53
1995 May Newcas (GD) H 8f 45 48
1995 Apr Mussel (GD) SH 7.1f 42 44
1998 AW 0-1: (12f) (Fibr)
Average gelding. Becoming disappointing.
**M Johnston [0-15] David Abell (from J L Harris [11-30] Spt 1996).*

VINKA (USA) **RR 97f** 4691a[4]

3 ch f Strawberry Road (AUS) 14.5f **(57)** - Cockney Lass (Camden Town) 9.3f **(53)**
Form - 614
1998 Turf 1-3: (8f 1-2, 10f) (g-s, gd 1-1, g-f)
Currently very useful filly. Turf high 97 - 4th of 9 to Darina (3 Oct Curragh 10f g-s RF 4691a). She won a small race at Listowel, and ran fourth in a listed event on her only other run.
**D K Weld in IRE [1-3] Allen Paulson.*

VINO VERITAS (USA) **RR 58f** 3132[11]

2 br f Chief's Crown (USA) 10.2f **(75)** - Wild Vintage (USA) (Alysheba (USA)) 9f **(84)**
Form - 40
Record 1998 - 1st:0 2nd:0 3rd:0 Ran:2
Win Prizemoney £0 *Total Prizemoney* £229
1998 Turf 0-2: (7f 2) (gd 2)
Currently fair filly. Turf high 58.
**J R Fanshawe [0-2] Car Colston Hall Stud.*

VINTAGE PRIDE (IRE) BHB 77f **RR 74f** 5123[1]

2 ch f Pips Pride 6.7f **(70)** - Vieux Carre (Pas de Seul) 9.1f **(67)**
Form - 737000621
Record 1998 - 1st:1 2nd:1 3rd:1 Ran:9
Win Prizemoney £2,965 *Total Prizemoney* £4,065
Wins * **1998** Nov Bright (SFT) 6f 74 <
1998 Turf 1-9: (5f 5, 6f 1-3, 7f) (g-s 1-2, gd 6, g-f)
Above-average filly, effective 5 to 6f, best at 5f, acts on g-s to gd, best on g-s, often wears blinkers (extremely effectively). Turf high 74 - 1st of 10 getting 5lb from Bartholomew (5 Nov Brighton RF 5123). **R Hannon [1-9] R Hannon.*

VINTAGE TAITTINGER (IRE) BHB 25f47a **RR 11f 47a** 3504[9]

6 b g Nordico (USA) 8.2f **(59)** - Kalonji (Red Alert) 7.6f **(66)**
Form - 70
Record 1998 - 1st:0 2nd:0 3rd:0 Ran:2
Pre1998 - 1st:2 2nd:1 3rd:1 Ran:15
Win Prizemoney £4,938 *Total Prizemoney* £5,961
Wins * 1997 Jun Mussel (G-S) H 16f 27 32
1995 *Apr Wolver (STD) H 12f 40 42* <
1998 Turf 0-2: (16f 2) (gd, frm)
Moderate gelding, effective 16f, acts on gd to frm. Turf high 11.
**J S Goldie [5-19] Die-Hard Racing Club (from T Dyer [0-9] May 1996).*

VIOLET (IRE) BHB 70f **RR 67f** 4928[4]

2 b f Mukaddamah (USA) 7.6f **(74)** - Scanno's Choice (IRE) (Pennine Walk) 8.5f **(61)**
Form - 054
Record 1998 - 1st:0 2nd:0 3rd:0 Ran:3
Win Prizemoney £0 *Total Prizemoney* £144
1998 Turf 0-3: (7f 3) (g-s, gd, frm)
Currently average filly. Turf high 67 (began Spt) - 4th of 14 getting 5lb from Pagan King (22 Oct Brighton 7f g-s RF 4928).
**Lord Huntingdon [0-3] Anglia Bloodstock Syndicate 1997.*

VIOLETTE SABO BHB 35f40a **RR 28f 40a** 5114[10]

4 b f Prince Sabo 6.6f **(64)** - Kajetana (FR) (Caro) 9.3f **(74)**
Form - 35000
Record 1998 - 1st:0 2nd:0 3rd:0 Ran:4
Pre1998 - 1st:0 2nd:0 3rd:1 Ran:3
Win Prizemoney £0 *Total Prizemoney* £314
1998 Turf 0-4: (7f, 8f 3) (g-s 3, gd)
Strong, very moderate filly. Turf high 45.
**T J Etherington [0-7] R V Hughes and Partners.*

V I P CHARLIE BHB 43f52a **RR 46f 52a** 4234[15]
4 b c Risk Me (FR) 8f **(53)** - Important Guest (Be My Guest (USA)) 9.3f **(67)**
Form - 0080000
Record 1998 - 1st:0 2nd:0 3rd:0 Ran:7
Pre1998 - 1st:2 2nd:0 3rd:1 Ran:12
Win Prizemoney £5,111 *Total Prizemoney* £5,832
Wins * 1997 *Feb Lingfi (STD) H 6f 60 71+*
* 1997 *Feb Southw (STD) H 6f 60 74+* <
1998 Turf 0-4: (8f, 9f, 10f 2) (gd, g-f 2, frm) 1998 AW 0-3: (7f 3) (Equi 2, Fibr)
Scopey, moderate colt, effective 6f, - acts on AW, likes left handed tracks, likes tight tracks. Turf high 42. AW high 29.
**J R Jenkins [2-17] Andy Taylor (from K G Wingrove [0-2] Jan 1998).*

VIRBIUS (IRE) RR 53f 4823[23]
2 ch c Wolfhound (USA) 7.3f **(71)** - Virelai (Kris) 9.5f **(73)**
Form - 60
Record 1998 - 1st:0 2nd:0 3rd:0 Ran:2
1998 Turf 0-2: (8f 2) (g-f, frm)
Currently fair colt. Turf high 53 (began Spt).
**C E Brittain [0-2] Saeed Manana.*

VIRGIN SOLDIER (IRE) RR 65f 4860[6]
2 ch g Waajib 8.9f **(67)** - Never Been Chaste (Posse (USA)) 8.9f **(61)**
Form - 036
Record 1998 - 1st:0 2nd:0 3rd:1 Ran:3
Win Prizemoney £0 *Total Prizemoney* £556
1998 Turf 0-3: (6f, 8f, 10f) (sft, gd, frm)
Currently average gelding. Turf high 65 (began Spt).
**T J Etherington [0-3] David Abell.*

VIRKON VENTURE (IRE) BHB 55f42a **RR 61df 42a** 442[12]
10 b g Auction Ring (USA) 8.4f **(62)** - Madame Fair (Monseigneur (USA)) 7.7f **(63)**
Form - 00
Record 1998 - 1st:0 2nd:0 3rd:0 Ran:2
Pre1998 - 1st:4 2nd:0 3rd:2 Ran:23
Win Prizemoney £24,186 *Total Prizemoney* £26,597
Wins 1994 May Hamilt (SFT) H 13f 55 63
1994 Apr Ascot (G-S) H 12f 55 60
1998 AW 0-2: (7f, 8f) (Equi, Fibr)
Average gelding. AW high 47. Inconsistent.
**R Guest [0-2] A B Coogan (from M H Tompkins [4-35] Mar 1995).*

VIRTUAL REALITY BHB 87f **RR 88f** 4631[26]
7 b g Diamond Shoal 9.8f **(79)** - Warning Bell (Bustino) 10.4f **(64)**
Form - 160120
Record 1998 - 1st:2 2nd:1 3rd:0 Ran:6
Pre1998 - 1st:2 2nd:6 3rd:2 Ran:26
Win Prizemoney £20,256 *Total Prizemoney* £41,968
Wins * **1998** Aug Salisb (G-F) H 8f 78 84 <
* **1998** May Bath (GD) H 8f 75 78
1994 Jun Newmar (G-F) H 10f 68 72+
1994 May Bright (G-F) 10f 59+
1998 Turf 2-6: (7f, 8f 2-4, 9f) (gd, g-f 2, frm 2-3)
Useful gelding, effective 8 to 10f, best at 8f, acts on gd to frm, best on frm, has worn blinkers, prefers tight tracks. Turf high 88 - 2nd of 8 giving 10lb to Pedro (28 Aug Thirsk 8f frm RF 3935) - also 1st of 5 giving 21lb to Bomb Alaska (7 Aug Salisbury RF 3446). Inconsistent. Goes well when fresh, and recorded his first win for four years at Bath in May 1998. Continued to run well in the summer, scoring at Salisbury.
**J A R Toller [2-13] Ash Partnership (from A Hide [2-19] Oct 1995).*

VIRTUOUS BHB 96f **RR 92f** 1124[3]
3 b f Exit To Nowhere (USA) 8.7f **(77)** - Exclusive Virtue (USA) (Shadeed (USA)) 8.2f **(70)**
Form - 73
Record 1998 - 1st:0 2nd:0 3rd:1 Ran:2
Pre1998 - 1st:1 2nd:0 3rd:1 Ran:4
Win Prizemoney £4,597 *Total Prizemoney* £8,502
Wins * 1997 Oct Nottin (G-F) 8.2f 75+ <
1998 Turf 0-2: (10f, 11f) (gd, g-f)
Scopey, useful filly, effective 11f, acts on g-f. Turf high 92 - 3rd of 6 to Bristol Channel (9 May Lingfield 11f g-f RF 1124). Has had her limitations exposed in Pattern company, although she did not run badly in Lingfield's Oaks Trial. Lacks a turn of foot.
**Sir Michael Stoute [1-6] Cheveley Park Stud.*

VISCOUMTESS BRAVE (IRE) RR 94f 741[11]
4 b or br f Law Society (USA) 11.6f **(71)** - Vadrouille (USA) (Foolish Pleasure (USA)) 8.9f **(72)**
Form - 460
Record 1998 - 1st:0 2nd:0 3rd:0 Ran:2
Pre1998 - 1st:3 2nd:1 3rd:1 Ran:7
Win Prizemoney £27,811 *Total Prizemoney* £47,899
Wins * 1997 Oct San Si (G-F) 10f 94+ <
* 1996 Nov Capann (HVY) 7f
* 1996 Oct San Si (G-S) 7.5f ?
1998 Turf 0-2: (12f 2) (sft 2)
Useful filly, effective 10 to 12f, best at 10f, acts on sft to g-f. Turf high 15. **Lord Huntingdon [3-9] Pietro Somaini.*

VISION OF NIGHT BHB 100f **RR 102f** 4593[3]
2 b c Night Shift (USA) 8.1f **(73)** - Dreamawhile (Known Fact (USA)) 7.4f **(67)**
Form - 2113
Record 1998 - 1st:2 2nd:1 3rd:1 Ran:4
Win Prizemoney £9,467 *Total Prizemoney* £22,927
Wins * **1998** Spt Doncas (GD) 6f 93+ <
* **1998** Aug Ripon (G-F) 6f 89+
1998 Turf 2-4: (6f 2-4) (gd, g-f 2-2, frm)
Very useful colt. Turf high 102 (began Aug) - also 1st of 6 from Chomper (12 Spt Doncaster RF 4237). He is not the best looking colt in the world, but handsome is as handsome does and he can certainly gallop. An easy winner at Ripon and Doncaster, he was thrown in at the deep end in the Group One Middle Park Stakes, but enhanced his reputation by finishing third. He seems likely to stay further than his full-brother Struggler, and is worth a try over seven furlongs or a mile. **J L Dunlop [2-4] Hesmonds Stud.*

VISION OF SPIRIT (USA) RR 99f 279a[2]
4 ch c Chief's Crown (USA) 10.2f **(75)** - Viendra (USA) (Raise A Native) 11.2f **(69)**
Form - 2
1998 Turf 0-1: (8f) (gd)
Currently very useful colt. (1st run) - 2nd of 8 getting 3lb from Desert Track (8 Feb Saint-moritz 8f gd RF 0279a).
**U Suter in SWI [0-1] (from H Jentzsch in GER [0-2] May 1997).*

VISTA ALEGRE BHB 61f85a **RR 56f 85a** 3742[18]
3 b g Petong 7.6f **(58)** - Duxyana (IRE) (Cyrano de Bergerac) 6f **(68)**
Form - 2162000
Record 1998 - 1st:1 2nd:1 3rd:0 Ran:6
Pre1998 - 1st:0 2nd:1 3rd:0 Ran:5
Win Prizemoney £3,387 *Total Prizemoney* £5,287
Wins * **1998** *Jan Lingfi (STD) 6f 59+* <
1998 Turf 0-3: (5f 2, 6f) (g-f, frm 2) 1998 AW 1-3: (5f, 6f 1-2) (Equi 1-2, Fibr)
Scopey, useful gelding, effective 5f, - acts on Equi. Turf high 56. AW high 86 - 2nd of 5 giving 25lb to Miss Bananas (21 Feb Lingfield 5f Equi RF 0332). **P J Makin [1-11] D M Ahier.*

VOGUE RR 50f 4524[7]
2 b f Clantime 6.6f **(57)** - Slipperose (Persepolis (FR)) 6.4f **(67)**
Form - 07
Record 1998 - 1st:0 2nd:0 3rd:0 Ran:2
1998 Turf 0-2: (6f 2) (g-f, frm)
Currently fair filly. Turf high 50 (began Jly).
**J S Moore [0-2] Western Solvents Ltd.*

VOGUE IMPERIAL (IRE) BHB 35f **RR 26f** 2656[11]
3 b g Imperial Frontier (USA) 7f **(65)** - Classic Choice (Patch) 11.5f **(51)**
Form - 00
Record 1998 - 1st:0 2nd:0 3rd:0 Ran:2
Pre1998 - 1st:0 2nd:0 3rd:0 Ran:4
1998 Turf 0-1: (6f) (gd) 1998 AW 0-1: (6f) (Fibr)
Workmanlike, very moderate gelding, has worn blinkers.
**D W Chapman [0-2] David Chapman (from P C Haslam [0-4] Jly 1997).*

VOILA PREMIERE (IRE) BHB 64f **RR 64f** 4987[5]
6 b g Roi Danzig (USA) 10.5f **(62)** - Salustrina (Sallust) 8.4f **(63)**

Form - 7551715
Record 1998 - 1st:2 2nd:0 3rd:0 Ran:7
Pre1998 - 1st:2 2nd:4 3rd:4 Ran:22
Win Prizemoney £20,865 *Total Prizemoney* £28,307
Wins * **1998** Spt Hamilt (SFT) H 12.1f 61 64
* **1998** Aug Hamilt (SFT) H 13f 59 62
1996 Oct York (GD) H 11.9f 66 76 <
1995 May Hamilt (G-F) 8.3f 60
1998 Turf 2-7: (12f 1-4, 13f 1-2, 14f) (sft, g-s 1-2, gd 1-3, frm)
Average gelding, effective 10 to 13f, acts on g-s to frm, has worn blinkers, likes right handed tracks, prefers tight tracks. Turf high 64 - 1st of 17 giving 1lb to Rossel (28 Spt Hamilton RF 4532) - also 1st of 6 giving 17lb to Lord Advocate (12 Aug Hamilton RF 3578).
**Lady Herries [2-6] B W Gaule (from P G Murphy [0-8] Mar 1998).*

VOLA VIA (USA) BHB 85f **RR 84f** 4646[3]
5 b br g Known Fact (USA) 8.3f **(72)** - Pinking Shears (USA) (Sharpen Up) 8.3f **(67)**
Form - 000264676151013
Record 1998 - 1st:3 2nd:1 3rd:1 Ran:15
Pre1998 - 1st:3 2nd:4 3rd:4 Ran:27
Win Prizemoney £25,189 *Total Prizemoney* £37,441
Wins * **1998** Spt Pontef (G-F) H 10f 80 84 <
* **1998** Aug Goodwo (G-F) H 9f 75 80+
* **1998** Aug Lingfi (G-F) H 10f 69 66+
* 1997 Jun Goodwo (G-S) 10f 84 <
* 1997 May Kempto (G-F) H 9f 79 83
* 1995 Jly Bath (HRD) 5.7f 75
1998Turf 3-15:(9f 1-4, 10f 2-9, 11f, 12f)(sft, g-s 2, gd 3, g-f 1-5, frm 2-4)
Decent gelding, effective 9 to 11f, best at 10f, acts on gd to frm, best on gd, has worn blinkers, likes right handed tracks, prefers tight tracks, excels at Kempton and likes Warwick. Turf high 84 - 1st of 11 getting 2lb from Free Option (24 Spt Pontefract RF 4467) - also 1st of 10 giving 5lb to River's Source (29 Aug Goodwood RF 3950). Often ridden by inexperienced jockeys, he did not get off the mark last season until Lingfield in August, having been given some chance by the Handicapper. Added an amateurs' race at Goodwood, and the blinkers have clearly worked. Sold for 25,000 guineas at Tattersalls in October. **I A Balding [6-42] G M Smart.*

VOLCANIC STAR BHB 57f **RR 57f** 4613[16]
2 ch f Primo Dominie 7.2f **(67)** - Lava Star (IRE) (Salse (USA)) 7.5f **(66)**
Form - 026500
Record 1998 - 1st:0 2nd:1 3rd:0 Ran:6
Win Prizemoney £0 *Total Prizemoney* £1,055
1998 Turf 0-6: (5f 3, 7f 3) (g-s 2, gd 3, g-f)
Fair filly, effective 5 to 7f, acts on gd to g-f. Turf high 57 - 5th of 11 getting 17lb from Asley (14 Aug Folkestone 7f g-f RF 3626).
**M Bell [0-6] Deln Ltd.*

VOLLEY (IRE) **RR 80f** 4360[18]
5 b m Al Hareb (USA) 9.4f **(53)** - Highdrive (Ballymore) 7.3f **(64)**
Form - 450570
Record 1998 - 1st:0 2nd:0 3rd:0 Ran:6
Pre1998 - 1st:1 2nd:1 3rd:3 Ran:11
Win Prizemoney £4,003 *Total Prizemoney* £12,491
Wins 1996 Oct Redcar (G-F) 6f 81 <
1998 Turf 0-6: (7f 3, 8f 3) (gd, g-f 3, frm 2)
Decent filly, effective 7 to 8f, best at 7f, acts on g-f to frm, best on g-f, likes tight tracks. Turf high 87 (1st run) - 4th of 12 giving 5lb to China Red (19 May Goodwood 8f g-f RF 1326). Inconsistent.
**Major D N Chappell [0-14] R C C Villers (from J Berry [1-3] Nov 1996).*

VOLONTIERS (FR) BHB 93f **RR 101f** 4617[8]
3 b c Common Grounds 8.1f **(66)** - Senlis (USA) (Sensitive Prince (USA)) 9.1f **(60)**
Form - 421100038
Record 1998 - 1st:2 2nd:1 3rd:1 Ran:9
Pre1998 - 1st:0 2nd:1 3rd:0 Ran:1
Win Prizemoney £24,913 *Total Prizemoney* £29,246
Wins * **1998** Jun Epsom (GD) L 7f 101 <
* **1998** May Haydoc (G-S) 7.1f 95
1998 Turf 2-9: (6f, 7f 2-7, 8f) (hvy, g-s, gd 1-3, g-f 1-2, frm 2)
Strong, very useful colt, effective 7f, acts on gd to g-f. Turf high 101 - 1st of 9 getting 6lb from Merlin's Ring (6 Jun Epsom RF 1779) - also 1st of 8 giving 5lb to Hebony (23 May Haydock RF 1420). Described as `the best horse in the yard' by his trainer, he bullied the opposition when winning at Haydock and Epsom, but seemed to lose his way in the second half of the season. He starts 1999 on a reasonable mark and is one to watch out for in handicaps.
**P W Harris [2-10] The Commoners.*

VONISPET **RR** 4765[19]
3 ch f Cotation - Cawkwell Queen (Mummy's Pet) 7.7f **(60)**
Form - 0
Record 1998 - 1st:0 2nd:0 3rd:0 Ran:1
1998 Turf 0-1: (7f) (gd)
Unfurnished, currently very poor filly - 19th of 19 to Oare Kite (12 Oct Leicester 7f gd RF 4765). **R F Marvin [0-1] G S Alcock.*

VOODOO LOUNGE (GER) **RR 91f** 1093a[5]
3 f
Form - 5
1998 Turf 0-1: (8f) (sft)
Currently useful filly. **R Suerland in GER [0-1].*

VORACIOUS BHB 85f **RR 83f** 4891[4]
2 b c Cadeaux Genereux 7.9f **(76)** - Victoriana (USA) (Storm Bird (CAN)) 10.3f **(74)**
Form - 214
Record 1998 - 1st:1 2nd:1 3rd:0 Ran:3
Win Prizemoney £4,792 *Total Prizemoney* £6,590
Wins * **1998** Oct Lingfi (SFT) 6f 82 <
1998 Turf 1-3: (6f 1-3) (g-s 1-1, gd 2)
Currently decent colt. Turf high 83 (began Spt) - also 1st of 17 from Trumpet Blues (2 Oct Lingfield RF 4611).
**H R A Cecil [1-3] K Abdulla.*

VOSBURGH BHB 57f **RR 58f** 3486[6]
2 br g Petong 7.6f **(58)** - Pour Moi (Bay Express) 7.1f **(60)**
Form - 030246
Record 1998 - 1st:0 2nd:1 3rd:1 Ran:6
Win Prizemoney £0 *Total Prizemoney* £1,509
1998 Turf 0-6: (5f 2, 6f 4) (g-s, gd 3, g-f, frm)
Fair gelding, effective 6f, acts on gd, has worn blinkers. Turf high 58 - 2nd of 6 getting 18lb from Perigeux (18 Jly Ayr 6f gd RF 2904).
**P Calver [0-6] Mrs Janis MacPherson.*

VRENNAN BHB 55f62a **RR 47f 62a** 4839[4]
4 ch f Suave Dancer(USA)10.7f **(68)**-Advie Bridge(High Line) 10.3f **(70)**
Form - 42146077834
Record 1998 - 1st:0 2nd:0 3rd:1 Ran:7
Pre1998 - 1st:1 2nd:3 3rd:1 Ran:9
Win Prizemoney £1,998 *Total Prizemoney* £5,756
Wins 1997 *Dec Lingfi (G-S) H 12f 65 69* <
1998 Turf 0-3: (14f 2, 16f) (hvy, g-s 2) 1998 AW 0-4: (11f, 12f 3) (Equi 3, Fibr)
Lengthy, average filly, effective 12 to 15f, best at 12f, acts on gd - acts on AW, best on Equi, has worn blinkers. Turf high 47. AW high 63. Inconsistent.
**W Jarvis [0-8] Canisbay Bloodstock Ltd (from J R Fanshawe [1-8] Dec 1997).*

VRIN (IRE) BHB 81f **RR 83f** 1951[1]
3 b c Mukaddamah (USA) 7.6f **(74)** - Traumerei (GER) (Surumu (GER)) 10f **(83)**
Form - 81
Record 1998 - 1st:1 2nd:0 3rd:0 Ran:2
Win Prizemoney £4,425 *Total Prizemoney* £4,425
Wins * **1998** Jun York (G-S) 11.9f 83 <
1998 Turf 1-2: (10f, 12f 1-1) (g-s 1-1, g-f)
Scopey, currently decent colt. Turf high 83 - 1st of 8 from Tom Paddington (12 Jun York RF 1951). Won with a bit in hand at York and should progress further as he accumulates experience.
**L M Cumani [1-2] J Camuda.*

WAABL (IRE) **RR 75+f** 5037[2]
2 b c Caerleon (USA) 10.9f **(79)** - Amandine (IRE) (Darshaan) 9.9f **(84)**
Form - 2
Record 1998 - 1st:0 2nd:1 3rd:0 Ran:1
Win Prizemoney £0 *Total Prizemoney* £948
1998 Turf 0-1: (7f) (g-s)
Currently above-average colt. (1st run) - 2nd of 11 to Jahaam (28 Oct Yarmouth 7f g-s RF 5037). Beat all bar the highly-regarded Jahaam on his debut. **J H M Gosden [0-1] Hamdan Al Maktoum.*

WAASEF BHB 43f48a **RR 41f 48a** 3404[6]
5 b g Warning 8.1f **(77)** - Thubut (USA) (Tank's Prospect (USA))
Form - 0826
Record 1998 - 1st:0 2nd:1 3rd:0 Ran:4
Pre1998 - 1st:0 2nd:0 3rd:0 Ran:5
Win Prizemoney £0 *Total Prizemoney* £595
1998 Turf 0-3: (7f, 8f, 10f) (gd, g-f, frm) 1998 AW 0-1: (10f) (Equi)
Moderate gelding, effective 10f, - acts on Equi, likes tight tracks. Turf high 41 (began Jly). (1st run) - 2nd of 9 to Coalminersdaughter (25 Jly Lingfield 10f Equi RF 3107).
**Miss Gay Kelleway [0-9] Another Seventh Heaven Partnership.*

WADADA BHB 42f34a **RR 46f 34a** 156[4]
7 b or br g Adbass (USA) 12.2f **(45)** - No Rejection (Mummy's Pet) 7.7f **(60)**
Form - 4
Record 1998 - 1st:0 2nd:0 3rd:0 Ran:1
Pre1998 - 1st:1 2nd:0 3rd:1 Ran:14
Win Prizemoney £2,810 *Total Prizemoney* £3,627
Wins * 1996 Jun Bath (FRM) SH 17.2f 40 46 <
1998 AW 0-1: (12f) (Fibr)
Moderate gelding, had worn blinkers. (DEAD)
**D Burchell [4-21] Mrs Ruth Burchell (from S W Campion [0-11] Apr 1995).*

WADERS DREAM (IRE) BHB 34f33a **RR 35f 33a** 352[8]
9 b g Doulab (USA) 7.4f **(61)** - Sea Mistress (Habitat) 9.4f **(70)**
Form - 0736458
Record 1998 - 1st:0 2nd:0 3rd:1 Ran:6
Pre1998 - 1st:2 2nd:2 3rd:5 Ran:65
Win Prizemoney £4,969 *Total Prizemoney* £9,851
Wins * 1996 Aug Folkes (G-F) 6f 53
1998 AW 0-6: (6f, 7f 2, 8f 3) (Equi 6)
Moderate gelding, effective 7f, - acts on Equi, mostly wears blinkers, likes left handed tracks, likes tight tracks. AW high 46 - 3rd of 14 to Paint It Black (8 Jan Lingfield 7f Equi RF 0046).
**Pat Mitchell [1-36] Mrs Anna Sanders (from P Mitchell [0-23] Feb 1995).*

WADI BHB 82f **RR 81f** 3028[6]
3 b c Green Desert (USA) 7.8f **(78)** - Eternal (Kris) 9.5f **(73)**
Form - 016
Record 1998 - 1st:1 2nd:0 3rd:0 Ran:3
Pre1998 - 1st:0 2nd:0 3rd:2 Ran:2
Win Prizemoney £3,631 *Total Prizemoney* £4,806
Wins * **1998** Jly Pontef (G-F) 10f 79 <
1998 Turf 1-3: (10f 1-2, 12f) (g-f, frm 1-2)
Workmanlike, decent colt. Turf high 79 - 1st of 12 giving 5lb to Moulin Rouge (7 Jly Pontefract RF 2587).
**H R A Cecil [1-5] K Abdulla.*

WAFF'S FOLLY BHB 55f **RR 51f** 4961[6]
3 b f Handsome Sailor 6.6f **(53)** - Shirl (Shirley Heights) 10.3f **(74)**
Form - 176006
Record 1998 - 1st:1 2nd:0 3rd:0 Ran:6
Pre1998 - 1st:0 2nd:0 3rd:0 Ran:2
Win Prizemoney £2,070 *Total Prizemoney* £2,070
Wins * **1998** Apr Folkes (GD) 6f 65 <
1998 Turf 1-6: (6f 1-4, 7f 2) (gd 1-2, g-f 2, frm 2)
Unfurnished, fair filly, effective 6f, acts on gd. Turf high 65 (1st run) - 1st of 9 getting 5lb from Kennet (1 Apr Folkestone RF 0538). Consistent. **G F H Charles-Jones [1-8] P H Wafford.*

WAFIR (IRE) BHB 79f **RR 79f** 3674[7]
6 b h Scenic 10.6f **(66)** - Taniokey (Grundy) 10.3f **(65)**
Form - 55444317
Record 1998 - 1st:1 2nd:0 3rd:1 Ran:8
Pre1998 - 1st:2 2nd:2 3rd:2 Ran:20
Win Prizemoney £15,913 *Total Prizemoney* £30,243
Wins * **1998** Aug Newcas (GD) 12.4f 79
* 1997 May Ayr (G-F) H 10f 80 83+ <
* 1996 Aug Ripon (HVY) H 10f 80 83
1998 Turf 1-8: (10f 4, 12f 1-4) (g-s, gd 3, g-f 1-2, frm 2)
Above-average horse, effective 10 to 12f, best at 10f, acts on g-s to frm, best on g-f, likes left handed tracks, likes tight tracks, excels at Redcar and likes Newcastle. Turf high 83 - 5th of 13 getting 12lb from Largesse (12 May York 12f gd RF 1164) - also 1st of 5 giving 14lb to Mole Creek (2 Aug Newcastle RF 3295). Consistent. An ex-Irish colt, he does not win often, but has faced some very stiff tasks and usually does his best. He needs things to go his way, as was the case when he landed a Newcastle classified stakes in August. **P Calver [3-28] Kenneth MacPherson.*

WAGGA MOON (IRE) BHB 35f **RR 36f** 2934[13]
4 b g Mac's Imp (USA) 5.6f **(54)** - Faapette (Runnett) 7f **(59)**
Form - 540065750
Record 1998 - 1st:0 2nd:0 3rd:0 Ran:9
Pre1998 - 1st:0 2nd:0 3rd:3 Ran:14
Win Prizemoney £0 *Total Prizemoney* £1,773
1998 Turf 0-8:(8f 7, 9f) (hvy, gd 3, g-f 2, frm 2) 1998 AW 0-1:(12f) (Fibr)
Unfurnished, very moderate gelding, effective 7f, acts on frm, has worn blinkers. Turf high 45.
**M Brittain [0-9] Mel Brittain (from J J O'Neill [0-14] Aug 1997).*

WAGON LIMIT (USA) **RR** 4827a[1]
4 ch c Conquistador Cielo (USA) 9.8f **(67)** - Darlin Lady (USA) (Cox's Ridge (USA)) 8f **(68)**
Form - 1
1998 AW 1-1: (10f 1-1) (Dirt 1-1)
Currently top-class colt. (1st run) - 1st of 6 from Gentlemen (10 Oct Belmont Park RF 4827a). Sprung a big surprise to take some notable scalps in a gruelling renewal of the Jockey Club Gold Cup.
**H A Jerkens in USA [1-1] J Shields Jnr.*

WAHJ (IRE) **RR 103+f** 3978[1]
3 ch c Indian Ridge 7.6f **(74)** - Sabaah (USA) (Nureyev (USA)) 8.7f **(78)**
Form - 11
Record 1998 - 1st:2 2nd:0 3rd:0 Ran:2
Win Prizemoney £9,162 *Total Prizemoney* £9,162
Wins * **1998** Aug Chepst (G-F) 7.1f 103 <
* **1998** Aug Windso (G-F) 8.3f 91++
1998 Turf 2-2: (7f 1-1, 8f 1-1) (gd 1-1, frm 1-1)
Scopey, currently very useful colt. Turf high 103 (began Aug) - 1st of 4 giving 4lb to Headhunter (31 Aug Chepstow RF 3978). A half-brother to the dual Classic winner Desert King, he justified good home reports when making an impressive debut at Windsor in August. A cosy winner from Headhunter and Wizard King at Chepstow later that month, he looked a hot prospect, but did not run again. He is obviously not the easiest to train, but will surely prove up to Pattern class if all is well.
**Sir Michael Stoute [2-2] Hamdan Al Maktoum.*

WAHOO **RR 90f** 4715a[4]
2 br c Warning 8.1f **(77)** - Jubilee Trail (Shareef Dancer (USA)) 9.9f **(73)**
Form - 144
Record 1998 - 1st:1 2nd:0 3rd:0 Ran:3
Win Prizemoney £5,049 *Total Prizemoney* £7,835
Wins * **1998** Aug Newmar (FRM) 7f 86+ <
1998 Turf 1-3: (7f 1-2, 9f) (sft, gd, frm 1-1)
Currently useful colt. Turf high 90 (began Aug) - also 1st of 12 from Adnaan (7 Aug Newmarket RF 3440). He got into all sorts of trouble on his Newmarket debut, but showed a decent turn of foot to get up and score by the minimum margin. Fourth to Desaru in a moderately-run race next time, he filled the same position in a Longchamp Group Three, failing to handle the sticky ground.
**J H M Gosden [1-3] K Abdulla.*

WAIKIKI BEACH (USA) BHB 43f62a **RR 45f 62a** 4234[16]
7 ch g Fighting Fit (USA) 7.9f **(70)** - Running Melody (Rheingold) 10.4f **(62)**
Form - 35100203000
Record 1998 - 1st:1 2nd:1 3rd:2 Ran:11
Pre1998 - 1st:5 2nd:6 3rd:2 Ran:35
Win Prizemoney £28,793 *Total Prizemoney* £38,019
Wins * **1998** *Apr Southw (STD) H 8f 56 61*
* 1996 *Dec Lingfi (STD) C 10f 69*
* 1996 *Jun Lingfi (STD) 8f 80+*
* 1996 *Apr Wolver (STD) 8.5f 65*
* 1994 Aug Baden (GD) 8f 92 <
* 1994 Jly Chepst (FRM) 7.1f 74
1998 Turf 0-5: (8f 3, 10f 2) (gd 2, frm 3) 1998 AW 1-6: (8f 1-6) (Equi 2, Fibr 1-4)
Fair gelding, effective 8f, acts on g-f - acts on Fibr, has worn blinkers. Turf high 45. AW high 61. Inconsistent. A winner of a Listed Race in Germany in 1994, he wins his share on the All-Weather,

though he sometimes steers an erratic course due to him suffering from claustrophobia. **G L Moore [6-46] Mrs J Moore.*

WAIT FOR THE WILL (USA) RR 76f
4526[5]

2 ch c Seeking the Gold (USA) 7.4f **(80)** - You'd Be Surprised (USA) (Blushing Groom (FR)) 10.3f **(76)**

Form - 55

Record 1998 - 1st:0 2nd:0 3rd:0 Ran:2

Win Prizemoney £0 *Total Prizemoney* £160

1998 Turf 0-2: (8f, 10f) (gd, g-f)

Currently above-average colt. Turf high 76 (1st run) (began Spt) - 5th of 7 getting 3lb from Bathwick (15 Spt Sandown 8f gd RF 4266). **I A Balding [0-2] Paul Mellon.*

WAITING KNIGHT (USA) BHB 70f RR 66f
4052[4]

3 b br c St Jovite (USA) 11.8f **(75)** - Phydilla (FR) (Lyphard (USA)) 9.9f **(72)**

Form - 2000230284

Record 1998 - 1st:0 2nd:3 3rd:1 Ran:10

Win Prizemoney £0 *Total Prizemoney* £4,201

1998 Turf 0-10: (7f 3, 8f 4, 9f 2, 10f) (sft, gd 4, g-f, frm 4)

Rangy, average colt, effective 7f, acts on gd. Turf high 87 (1st run) - 2nd of 13 to Chattan (27 Mar Doncaster 7f gd RF 0481). Placed in maidens, but he looks a disappointing sort.

**B Hanbury [0-10] Abdullah Ali.*

WAIT'N'SEE BHB 56f50a RR 58f 50a
4874[10]

3 b g Komaite (USA) 6.9f **(61)** - Kakisa (Forlorn River) 7.3f **(54)**

Form - 27506480300

Record 1998 - 1st:0 2nd:1 3rd:1 Ran:11
Pre1998 - 1st:1 2nd:0 3rd:0 Ran:7

Win Prizemoney £2,947 *Total Prizemoney* £4,119

Wins * 1997 Jun Carlis (FRM) 5f 77 <

1998 Turf 0-8: (5f, 6f 4, 7f 3) (gd 3, g-f 4, frm) 1998 AW 0-3: (6f 2, 8f) (Fibr 3)

Light-framed, fair gelding, effective 5 to 6f, acts on gd to frm, has worn blinkers. Turf high 68 (1st run) - 2nd of 20 getting 1lb from Mohawk (4 May Newcastle 6f gd RF 1021). AW high 49 (began Spt).

**M W Easterby [1-18] M W Easterby.*

WAJORI (USA) BHB 79f RR 79f
3428[3]

3 b c Diesis 9f **(80)** - Wajna (USA) (Nureyev (USA)) 8.7f **(78)**

Form - 02323

Record 1998 - 1st:0 2nd:2 3rd:2 Ran:5

Win Prizemoney £0 *Total Prizemoney* £3,584

1998 Turf 0-5: (7f 5) (g-s, gd, g-f, frm 2)

Scopey, above-average colt. Turf high 79 - 2nd of 9 to Shadow Creek (24 Jly Thirsk 7f frm RF 3086). Placed in four seven-furlong maidens, he is one-paced. **J H M Gosden [0-5] Sheikh Mohammed.*

WAKEEL (USA) BHB 85f RR 86f
1357[5]

6 b g Gulch(USA) 9.6f **(79)** -Raahia(CAN)(Vice Regent (CAN)) 8.7f **(74)**

Form - 205

Record 1998 - 1st:0 2nd:1 3rd:0 Ran:3
Pre1998 - 1st:3 2nd:4 3rd:4 Ran:33

Win Prizemoney £21,219 *Total Prizemoney* £39,814

Wins 1997 Jly Bright (FRM) H 11.9f 74 78
1996 Jan Cagnes (HVY) 8f 77
1994 Aug Newmar (G-F) 7f 80

1998 Turf 0-3: (12f, 14f, 19f) (sft, g-f 2)

Useful gelding, effective 8 to 19f, best at 12f, acts on sft to g-f, best on g-f, has worn blinkers, prefers left handed tracks, prefers tight tracks. Turf high 86 (1st run) - 2nd of 11 giving 9lb to Assured Gamble (22 Apr Epsom 12f sft RF 0813). After a spell of hurdling, he ran well to finish runner-up in the Great Metropolitan Handicap at Epsom. **M Pitman [1-6] M Chavoush (from S Dow [2-26] Spt 1997).*

WAKY NAO RR 116f
5165a[13]

5 b h Alzao (USA) 9.8f **(73)** - Waky Na (GER) (Ahonoora) 8.1f **(73)**

Form - 4111510

1998 Turf 4-6: (8f 4-6) (sft 1-1, g-s 1-1, gd 2-3, frm)

High-class colt, effective 6 to 8f, best at 8f, acts on sft to gd, best on gd, excels at Baden-Baden and San Siro. Turf high 116 - 1st of 11 giving 11lb to Lend A Hand (12 Jly Hoppegarten RF 2863a) - also 1st of 8 from Kierkegaard (11 Oct San Siro RF 4833a). German-trained, he made hay in German Group Twos and Threes, and also landed his first Group One when winning in Italy in October. However, he found the competition in the Jacques le Marois and the Breeders' Cup Mile too much for him.

**A Schutz in GER [4-6] H von Finck (from B Schutz in GER [1-3] Nov 1997).*

WALES BHB 99f RR 99f
4798[2]

3 ch c Caerleon (USA) 10.9f **(79)** - Knight's Baroness (Rainbow Quest (USA)) 10.4f **(75)**

Form - 426502

Record 1998 - 1st:0 2nd:2 3rd:0 Ran:6
Pre1998 - 1st:1 2nd:0 3rd:2 Ran:4

Win Prizemoney £4,207 *Total Prizemoney* £12,050

Wins * 1997 Spt Goodwo (GD) 8f 82 <

1998 Turf 0-6: (12f 4, 15f, 16f) (sft, gd 2, frm 3)

Light-framed, very useful colt, effective 12 to 16f, acts on sft to frm, has worn blinkers. Turf high 99 - 2nd of 6 getting 2lb from Alcazar (14 Oct Haydock 12f sft RF 4798). He did not run up to expectations in 1998, seeming to lack pace. His best run was his last, and he may do better next term.

**P F I Cole [1-10] H R H Prince Fahd Salman.*

WALK ON BY BHB 60f RR 63f
582[6]

4 gr g Terimon 8.7f **(58)** - Try G's (Hotfoot) 10.5f **(59)**

Form - 6

Record 1998 - 1st:0 2nd:0 3rd:0 Ran:1
Pre1998 - 1st:0 2nd:0 3rd:1 Ran:7

Win Prizemoney £0 *Total Prizemoney* £356

1998 Turf 0-1: (15f) (sft)

Scopey, average gelding, effective 10f, acts on frm. Consistent.

**J S King [0-5] Mrs R M Hill (from R Hannon [0-7] Jly 1997).*

WALK THE BEAT BHB 51f60a RR 50f 60a
4093[9]

8 b g Interrex (CAN) 7.7f **(51)** - Plaits (Thatching) 8f **(66)**

Form - 06008570

Record 1998 - 1st:0 2nd:0 3rd:0 Ran:6
Pre1998 - 1st:11 2nd:6 3rd:5 Ran:58

Win Prizemoney £28,021 *Total Prizemoney* £37,813

Wins * 1997 Aug Lingfi (GD) H 6f 59 63
* 1997 *Mar Wolver (STD) C 6f 56*
* 1997 *Mar Southw (STD) C 7f 65*
* 1997 *Jan Southw (STD) H 6f 65 68* <
* 1996 *Oct Wolver (STD) H 6f 60 63*
* 1996 Jly Bath (G-F) H 5.1f 61 61
* 1996 Jun Lingfi (FRM) H 5f 59 61
* 1995 *May Wolver (STD) C 6f 56*
1994 *Nov Southw (STD) C 6f 53*

1998 Turf 0-6: (5f 2, 6f 4) (sft, gd, frm 4)

Fair gelding, effective 6 to 7f, best at 7f, acts on frm - acts on Fibr, has worn blinkers, likes left handed tracks, likes tight tracks. Turf high 50.

**M Meade [8-43] Ladyswood Racing Club (from R Simpson [3-21] Mar 1995).*

WALLACE BHB 95f RR 88+f
4182[5]

2 b c Royal Academy (USA) 7.8f **(77)** - Masskana (IRE) (Darshaan) 9.9f **(84)**

Form - 3435

Record 1998 - 1st:0 2nd:0 3rd:2 Ran:4

Win Prizemoney £0 *Total Prizemoney* £3,040

1998 Turf 0-4: (7f 4) (gd 2, g-f, frm)

Useful colt. Turf high 88 (1st run) (began Jly) - 3rd of 11 to Enrique (31 Jly Goodwood 7f gd RF 3233). Has done nothing wrong so far in decent company and an ordinary maiden should be a formality. **R Hannon [0-4] J A Lazzari.*

WALTER PLINGE RR
5073[17]

2 b g Theatrical Charmer 10.9f **(63)** - Carousel Zingira (Reesh)

Form - 0

Record 1998 - 1st:0 2nd:0 3rd:0 Ran:1

1998 Turf 0-1: (8f) (gd)

Currently very poor gelding. **S C Williams [0-1] Stuart Williams.*

WALTHAM BLACKBIRD BHB 43f RR 45f
4334[19]

3 b f Tigani - Heemee (On Your Mark) 7.7f **(58)**

Form - 8750

Record 1998 - 1st:0 2nd:0 3rd:0 Ran:4

1998 Turf 0-4: (5f 3, 6f) (g-f, frm 3)

Scopey, moderate filly. Turf high 45 (began Jly) - 5th of 12 getting 7lb from Most Respectful (29 Aug Beverley 5f frm RF 3940).
**K A Morgan [0-4] D & M Cased Hole.*

WALTHAM SKYLARK BHB 41f **RR 45f** 4624[9]

3 b f Puissance 7.1f **(60)** - Pear Drop (Bustino) 10.4f **(64)**
Form - 0500
Record 1998 - 1st:0 2nd:0 3rd:0 Ran:4
1998 Turf 0-4: (5f 3, 6f) (g-f 3, frm)
Lengthy, moderate filly. Turf high 45 (began Jly).
**K A Morgan [0-4] D & M Cased Hole.*

WALTZING MATILDA BHB 51f **RR 53f** 4315[7]

3 b f Mujtahid (USA)7.4f **(69)** -Where's the Dance(Alzao (USA))7.1f **(68)**
Form - 007
Record 1998 - 1st:0 2nd:0 3rd:0 Ran:3
1998 Turf 0-3: (6f 2, 8f) (gd, frm 2)
Currently fair filly. Turf high 53 (began Aug).
**C E Brittain [0-3] Mrs J Costelloe.*

WALTZ TIME BHB 32f **RR 49f** 4838[13]

4 b f Rambo Dancer (CAN) 8.4f **(59)** - Kiveton Komet (Precocious) 8.6f **(62)**
Form - 0100407070
Record 1998 - 1st:1 2nd:0 3rd:0 Ran:10
Pre1998 - 1st:0 2nd:0 3rd:0 Ran:4
Win Prizemoney £2,652 *Total Prizemoney* £2,652
Wins * 1998 Jly Mussel (GD) SH 8f 46 49 <
1998 Turf 1-10: (7f 2, 8f 1-2, 9f 4, 10f, 12f) (sft, g-s 3, gd 3, frm 1-3)
Moderate filly, effective 8f, acts on frm. Turf high 49 - 1st of 14 giving 7lb to Doctor Bravious (6 Jly Musselburgh RF 2561). Inconsistent.
**I Semple [1-10] Andy Dickie (from Miss L A Perratt [0-4] Nov 1996).*

Record 1998 - 1st:0 2nd:0 3rd:0 Ran:2
Pre1998 - 1st:0 2nd:0 3rd:0 Ran:3
1998 Turf 0-1: (8f) (gd) 1998 AW 0-1: (7f) (Fibr)
Leggy, moderate gelding, had worn blinkers. (DEAD)
**M Dods [0-5] Vernon Spinks.*

WANDERING WOLF BHB 77f **RR 69f** 1028[15]

3 ch c Wolfhound (USA) 7.3f **(71)** - Circle of Chalk (FR) (Kris) 9.5f **(73)**
Form - 50
Record 1998 - 1st:0 2nd:0 3rd:0 Ran:2
Pre1998 - 1st:0 2nd:0 3rd:0 Ran:3
Win Prizemoney £0 *Total Prizemoney* £486
1998 Turf 0-2: (7f 2) (g-s, g-f)
Average colt. Turf high 58. Beat one home in the Windsor Castle on his debut.
**R Hannon [0-5] Lucayan Stud.*

WANNABE GRAND (IRE) BHB 100f **RR 104f** 4539[1]

2 b f Danehill (USA) 9.1f **(79)** - Wannabe (Shirley Heights) 10.3f **(74)**
Form - 42114241
Record 1998 - 1st:3 2nd:2 3rd:0 Ran:8
Win Prizemoney £124,563 *Total Prizemoney* £149,858
Wins * 1998 Spt Newmar (GD) G1 6f 104 <
*** 1998** Jly Newmar (G-F) G2 6f 103
*** 1998** Jun Newmar (GD) L 6f 74
1998 Turf 3-8: (6f 3-7, 7f) (gd 1-2, g-f 2, frm 2-3, hrd)
Very useful filly, effective 6 to 7f, best at 6f, acts on gd to frm, best on frm. Turf high 104 - 1st of 9 from Imperial Beauty (29 Spt Newmarket RF 4539) - also 1st of 10 from Pipalong (7 Jly Newmarket RF 2580). Inconsistent. Every young trainer needs a flagship, and this smashing filly did a fine job for Jeremy Noseda. Successful in a Listed race and the Group Two Cherry Hinton Stakes at Newmarket during the summer, she ran well although defeated on her next three starts, seeming not to stay seven furlongs in the Moyglare Stud Stakes at the Curragh. It was a different story back at six furlongs in the Cheveley Park Stakes in October, where, looking better than ever, she quickened at the

Wannabe Grand (right) takes the Cheveley Park for Noseda

WALWORTH WIZARD BHB 51f **RR 48f** 632[P]

3 b g Presidium 7.5f **(56)** - Mrs Magic (Magic Mirror)
Form - 0P

two-furlong pole and held off a late challenge from Imperial Beauty. Her trainer described that Group One victory as this filly's Classic, and hinted that she might not stay a mile as a three-year-old. She is game and a credit to her connections.
**J Noseda [3-8] B McAllister.*

WANSFORD LADY **RR 24f** 4808^{11}

2 b f Michelozzo (USA) - Marnie's Girl (Crooner) 9.9f **(49)**
Form - 0
Record 1998 - 1st:0 2nd:0 3rd:0 Ran:1
1998 Turf 0-1: (10f) (gd)
Currently little account filly. **C N Kellett [0-1] Mrs V Robson.*

WANSTEAD (IRE) BHB 38f **RR 33f** 2260^{10}

6 ch g Be My Native (USA) 11.2f **(62)** - All The Same (Cajun) 5.2f **(54)**
Form - 0
Record 1998 - 1st:0 2nd:0 3rd:0 Ran:1
Pre1998 - 1st:0 2nd:0 3rd:0 Ran:1
1998 Turf 0-1: (13f) (g-f)
Very moderate gelding, has broken blood-vessels, always wears blinkers. **J R Jenkins [0-24] T H Ounsley.*

WARDARA BHB 72f75a **RR 104f 75a** $1731a^{6}$

6 ch m Sharpo 7.5f **(68)** - Ward One (Mr Fluorocarbon) 6f **(55)**
Form - 46
1998 Turf 0-2: (5f, 6f) (g-s, gd)
Very useful mare, effective 5 to 6f, best at 5f, acts on g-s to gd, best on g-s, mostly wears blinkers (effectively). Turf high 104 (1st run) - 4th of 5 to Spelunar (20 Apr Chantilly 6f g-s RF 0943a). Formerly trained by Chris Dwyer, she has done well in France but is not Group class. **F Bellenger in FR [0-6].*

WAR DECLARATION (IRE) **RR 109f** $4951a^{4}$

4 br c Persian Bold 10f **(69)** - Lutoviska (Glenstal (USA)) 10.1f **(64)**
Form - 217144
1998 Turf 2-6: (8f, 10f, 11f 1-1, 12f 1-3) (sft 1-2, g-s 2, g-f 1-2)
Pattern-class colt, effective 10 to 12f, best at 12f, acts on sft to g-f, best on g-f. Turf high 109 - also 1st of 5 giving 4lb to Special Star (6 Spt San Siro RF 4221a). Consistent. He is a tough campaigner and probably ran his best race yet when finishing a close fourth behind Silver Patriarch in a Group One during October. He will win another big prize when the Brits stay at home.
**B Grizzetti in ITY [3-10].*

WARNINGFORD BHB 105f **RR 104f** 4849^{10}

4 b c Warning 8.1f **(77)** - Barford Lady (Stanford) 7.9f **(56)**
Form - 0260251861030
Record 1998 - 1st:2 2nd:2 3rd:1 Ran:13
Pre1998 - 1st:1 2nd:0 3rd:0 Ran:5
Win Prizemoney £20,276 *Total Prizemoney* £27,395
Wins * **1998** Spt Goodwo (SFT) H 7f 99 104 <
* **1998** Jly Yarmou (G-F) H 7f 97 99
* 1997 Jun Sandow (G-F) 7.1f 90
1998 Turf 2-13: (6f, 7f 2-11, 8f) (sft, g-s 1-1, gd 6, g-f 1-3, frm 2)
Scopey, very useful colt, effective 7f, acts on g-s to frm, often wears blinkers (extremely effectively). Turf high 104 - 1st of 9 giving 5lb to Al Muallim (12 Spt Goodwood RF 4244) - also 1st of 6 giving 22lb to Free Option (15 Jly Yarmouth RF 2838). This seven-furlong specialist held his form well through a busy campaign, winning twice. Connections were chancing their arm when popping him in a Group Two at Newmarket in October, but he would not be a forlorn hope in Listed company.
**J R Fanshawe [3-18] Barford Bloodstock.*

WARNING REEF BHB 64f65a **RR 65f 65a** 4973^{7}

5 b g Warning 8.1f **(77)** - Horseshoe Reef (Mill Reef (USA)) 10.5f **(78)**
Form - 527632112125337
Record 1998 - 1st:3 2nd:4 3rd:3 Ran:15
Pre1998 - 1st:0 2nd:3 3rd:2 Ran:20
Win Prizemoney £25,820 *Total Prizemoney* £42,274
Wins * **1998** Aug Ascot (G-F) H 12f 57 60 <
* **1998** Jly Sandow (GD) H 11.4f 53 54
* **1998** Jun Carlis (G-S) H 12f 49 51
1998 Turf 3-13: (8f, 9f, 10f 2, 11f 1-1, 12f 2-8) (sft 3, g-s, gd 2-3, g-f 1-4, frm 2) 1998 AW 0-2: (9f, 11f) (Fibr 2)
Average gelding, has worn blinkers, prefers right handed tracks. Turf high 65. AW high 51. Consistent. In fine form in 1998, landing his third win from four starts at Ascot in August. Still at the right end of the handicap.
**E J Alston [3-15] Valley Paddocks Racing Ltd (from P Eccles [0-7] Aug 1997).*

WARP DRIVE (IRE) BHB 30a **RR 30a** 35^{8}

4 ch g Bluebird (USA) 7.9f **(71)** - Red Roman (Solinus) 9f **(71)**
Form - 0808
Record 1998 - 1st:0 2nd:0 3rd:0 Ran:1
Pre1998 - 1st:0 2nd:1 3rd:0 Ran:9
Win Prizemoney £0 *Total Prizemoney* £644
1998 AW 0-1: (8f) (Equi)
Scopey, very moderate gelding, has worn blinkers. Inconsistent.
**W R Muir [0-10] Mrs Danita Winstanly.*

WARREN KNIGHT BHB 46f **RR 47f** 2280^{12}

5 b g Weldnaas (USA) 8.4f **(55)** - Trigamy (Tribal Chief) 8.5f **(61)**
Form - 40
Record 1998 - 1st:0 2nd:0 3rd:0 Ran:2
Pre1998 - 1st:0 2nd:0 3rd:0 Ran:9
Win Prizemoney £0 *Total Prizemoney* £390
1998 Turf 0-2: (8f, 10f) (gd, g-f)
Moderate gelding. Turf high 47. Inconsistent.
**C A Horgan [0-11] Mrs B Sumner.*

WARRING BHB 55f49a **RR 60f 49a** 4807^{16}

4 b g Warrshan (USA) 9.7f **(59)** - Emerald Ring (Auction Ring (USA)) 8.6f **(65)**
Form - 05214210400
Record 1998 - 1st:2 2nd:2 3rd:0 Ran:11
Pre1998 - 1st:0 2nd:1 3rd:0 Ran:12
Win Prizemoney £10,552 *Total Prizemoney* £15,661
Wins * **1998** Aug Windso (G-F) H 8.3f 54 60 <
* **1998** Jly Windso (G-F) H 8.3f 46 54
1998 Turf 2-11: (8f 2-10, 9f) (gd 5, g-f 1-4, frm, hrd 1-1)
Average gelding, effective 7 to 8f, best at 8f, acts on gd to hrd, best on hrd, likes tight tracks, and excels at Windsor. Turf high 60 - 1st of 15 getting 1lb from Daintree (10 Aug Windsor RF 3515) - also 1st of 18 getting 16lb from Twin Creeks (6 Jly Windsor RF 2574).
**M S Saunders [2-19] Chris Scott (from M R Channon [0-4] Oct 1996).*

WARRING KINGDOM **RR 22f** 4881^{11}

2 b c Warrshan (USA) 9.7f **(59)** - Rise and Fall (Mill Reef (USA)) 10.5f **(78)**
Form - 0
Record 1998 - 1st:0 2nd:0 3rd:0 Ran:1
1998 Turf 0-1: (5f) (g-s)
Currently little account colt. **John Berry [0-1] The 1997 Partnership.*

WARRIOR KING (IRE) BHB 37f **RR 42f** 2510^{11}

4 b g Fairy King (USA) 7.7f **(75)** - It's All Academic (IRE) (Mazaad) 7.1f **(45)**
Form - 006400
Record 1998 - 1st:0 2nd:0 3rd:0 Ran:6
Pre1998 - 1st:1 2nd:3 3rd:1 Ran:19
Win Prizemoney £3,241 *Total Prizemoney* £5,740
Wins 1997 Aug Mussel (GD) H 7.1f 47 53 <
1998 Turf 0-6: (6f 2, 7f 2, 8f 2) (gd 4, g-f 2)
Moderate gelding, effective 7 to 12f, best at 8f, acts on gd to frm, best on frm, has worn blinkers. Turf high 42.
**J E Banks [0-6] North End Partnership (from C A Dwyer [1-8] Oct 1997).*

WARWICK (GER) **RR 101f** $1919a^{7}$

3 c
Form - 77
1998 Turf 0-2: (8f, 10f) (g-s, gd)
Currently very useful colt. Turf high 101. He was way off the pace in Group Two events. **H Blume in GER [0-2].*

WATCHING BRIEF (IRE) **RR** 4138^{16}

3 b f Brief Truce (USA) 9.1f **(73)** - Lady's Bridge (USA) (Sir Ivor) 10.2f **(70)**
Form - 50
Record 1998 - 1st:0 2nd:0 3rd:0 Ran:2
1998 Turf 0-2: (10f, 12f) (gd, g-f)

Workmanlike, currently very poor filly. **B Hanbury [0-2] J Shack.*

WATER FORCE BHB 56f RR 59f 4653^{10}

3 b g River Falls 8.2f **(56)** -Quelle Chemise (Night Shift (USA)) 7.2f **(69)**
Form - 0080144840
Record 1998 - 1st:1 2nd:0 3rd:0 Ran:10
Pre1998 - 1st:0 2nd:0 3rd:0 Ran:7
Win Prizemoney £3,680 *Total Prizemoney* £4,398
Wins * 1998 Jly Epsom (G-F) H 8.5f 53 59 <
1998 Turf 1-10: (6f, 7f, 8f 4, 9f 1-3, 10f) (gd 2, g-f 1-4, frm 4)
Neat, fair gelding, effective 8 to 9f, acts on g-f to frm. Turf high 59 - 1st of 12 giving 10lb to Magical Dancer (29 Jly Epsom RF 3202).
**G B Balding [1-17] B T Attenborough.*

WATERFORD SPIRIT (IRE) BHB 81f RR 81f 4836^{2}

2 ch c Shalford (IRE) 7.8f **(63)** - Rebecca's Girl (IRE) (Nashamaa) 7.1f **(66)**
Form - 5522
Record 1998 - 1st:0 2nd:2 3rd:0 Ran:4
Win Prizemoney £0 *Total Prizemoney* £2,214
1998 Turf 0-4: (5f 3, 6f) (g-s, gd, g-f 2)
Decent colt. Turf high 81 (began Spt) - 2nd of 5 to Ptarmigan Ridge (16 Oct Catterick 5f g-s RF 4836). **T D Barron [0-4] P D Savill.*

WATERFRONT (IRE) RR 76f 2578^{7}

2 b c Turtle Island (IRE) - Rising Tide (Red Alert) 7.6f **(66)**
Form - 7
Record 1998 - 1st:0 2nd:0 3rd:0 Ran:1
1998 Turf 0-1: (7f) (frm)
Currently above-average colt. Showed plenty of speed in a warm maiden on his debut. Might be interesting over six furlongs.
**P W Chapple-Hyam [0-1] R E Sangster & A K Collins.*

WATER LOUP RR 54f 4880^{6}

2 b f Wolfhound (USA) 7.3f **(71)** - Heavenly Waters (Celestial Storm (USA))
Form - 56
Record 1998 - 1st:0 2nd:0 3rd:0 Ran:2
1998 Turf 0-2: (6f, 7f) (g-s, g-f)
Currently fair filly. Turf high 54 (began Oct). **W R Muir [0-2] J Haim.*

WATHIK (USA) RR $551a^{6}$

8 ch h Ogygian (USA) 6.6f **(65)** - Copper Creek (Habitat) 9.4f **(70)**
Form - 16
1998 AW 1-2: (8f 1-1, 10f) (Dirt 1-2)
Group-class horse, has worn blinkers (extremely effectively). AW high 113 (1st run) - 1st of 7 from Fly To The Stars (22 Jan Nad Al Sheba RF 0228a). He seems to have been around forever, but looked as fresh as paint when beating Fly To The Stars in Dubai during January.
**P L Rudkin in UAE [1-6] Saeed Al Ghandi (from H ThomsonJones [2-9] Spt 1993).*

WATKINS BHB 46f RR 28f 1957^{7}

3 ch g King's Signet (USA) 7f **(51)** - Windbound Lass (Crofter (USA)) 8.4f **(56)**
Form - 200067
Record 1998 - 1st:0 2nd:1 3rd:0 Ran:6
Pre1998 - 1st:0 2nd:0 3rd:0 Ran:5
Win Prizemoney £0 *Total Prizemoney* £850
1998 Turf 0-4: (8f, 10f, 12f 2) (gd 2, frm 2) 1998 AW 0-2: (8f 2) (Equi 2)
Fair gelding, has worn blinkers. Turf high 28. AW high 52. Becoming disappointing.
**M A Buckley [0-6] R W Savery (from F Murphy [0-5] Spt 1997).*

WAVE OF OPTIMISM BHB 72f RR 80f 4809^{1}

3 ch g Elmaamul (USA) 8.1f **(70)** - Ballerina Bay **(68f 63a)** (Myjinski (USA)) 9.5f **(54)**
Form - 3221
Record 1998 - 1st:1 2nd:2 3rd:1 Ran:4
Win Prizemoney £4,045 *Total Prizemoney* £6,108
Wins * 1998 Oct Nottin (SFT) 14.1f 80 <
1998 Turf 1-4: (11f 2, 12f, 14f 1-1) (gd 1-1, g-f 3)
Light-framed, decent gelding. Turf high 80 (began Aug) - 1st of 7 giving 5lb to Moon Masquerade (14 Oct Nottingham RF 4809).
**J Pearce [1-4] Wave of Optimism Partnership.*

WAVE RACER RR 11f 1877^{11}

3 b c Royal Academy (USA) 7.8f **(77)** - Upend (Main Reef) 9.6f **(57)**
Form - 00
Record 1998 - 1st:0 2nd:0 3rd:0 Ran:2
1998 Turf 0-2: (8f, 12f) (g-s, gd)
Currently poor colt. Turf high 11. **B Hanbury [0-2] Khalifa Sultan.*

WAVE ROCK BHB 85f RR 88f 2913^{7}

3 br g Tragic Role (USA) 9.4f **(63)** - Moonscape (Ribero) 9.3f **(56)**
Form - 1547
Record 1998 - 1st:1 2nd:0 3rd:0 Ran:4
Pre1998 - 1st:1 2nd:0 3rd:0 Ran:4
Win Prizemoney £7,999 *Total Prizemoney* £9,074
Wins * 1998 May Salisb (G-S) H 9.9f 85 88 <
* 1997 Oct Nottin (SFT) 10f 82
1998 Turf 1-4: (10f 1-1, 12f 2, 13f) (g-s, gd 1-2, frm)
Lengthy, useful gelding, effective 10f, acts on gd, has worn blinkers. Turf high 88 (1st run) - 1st of 5 giving 3lb to Raffaello (3 May Salisbury RF 1000). **J L Dunlop [2-8] The Earl Cadogan.*

WAY BACK (IRE) BHB 60f RR 63f 4053^{11}

2 b c Toca Madera - My Robin (IRE) (Cyrano de Bergerac) 6f **(68)**
Form - 3770
Record 1998 - 1st:0 2nd:0 3rd:1 Ran:4
Win Prizemoney £0 *Total Prizemoney* £307
1998 Turf 0-4: (6f, 7f 2, 8f) (frm 4)
Average colt. Turf high 63. **B S Rothwell [0-4] Mrs G M Z Spink.*

WAYNE LUKAS BHB 62f RR 71f 4648^{15}

3 b c Don't Forget Me 9.5f **(66)** - Modern Dance (USA) (Nureyev (USA)) 8.7f **(78)**
Form - 65180
Record 1998 - 1st:1 2nd:0 3rd:0 Ran:5
Pre1998 - 1st:0 2nd:0 3rd:0 Ran:1
Win Prizemoney £2,736 *Total Prizemoney* £2,736
Wins 1998 Aug Kempto (G-F) C 9f 58 <
1998 Turf 1-5: (8f 2, 9f 1-2, 10f) (gd, g-f 2, frm 1-2)
Scopey, above-average colt. Turf high 71.
**P R Hedger [0-3] J J Whelan (from H R A Cecil [1-4] Aug 1998).*

WAY OF LIGHT (USA) RR 106f $4830a^{1}$

2 br c Woodman (USA) 9.7f **(77)** - Salchow (Nijinsky (CAN)) 10.3f **(77)**
Form - 21
1998 Turf 1-2: (8f 1-2) (hvy, g-s 1-1)
Currently Pattern-class colt. Turf high 106 (began Spt) - 1st of 7 from Red Sea (11 Oct Longchamp RF 4830a). He looked unlucky when beaten by Grazalema at Longchamp in September, and proved that assessment correct when winning the Grand Criterium the following month, where his old rival was ten lengths back in fifth. Cash Asmussen, who is never afraid to use a hundred words when one will do, rates him the best juvenile he has ridden since the explosive filly Coup de Genie, and he certainly showed plenty of speed in appalling conditions when gaining his Group One success. A line through Red Sea and Glamis suggests he has something to find with the very best of his generation, but he has bags of scope and will take plenty of beating in the French 2000 next spring. **P Bary in FR [1-2] Niarchos Family.*

WAY OUT YONDER BHB 74f RR 88f 4354^{17}

3 b c Shirley Heights 12.1f **(76)** - Patsy Western (Precocious) 8.6f **(62)**
Form - 472231080
Record 1998 - 1st:1 2nd:2 3rd:1 Ran:9
Pre1998 - 1st:0 2nd:1 3rd:1 Ran:2
Win Prizemoney £3,590 *Total Prizemoney* £9,773
Wins * 1998 Jly Lingfi (G-F) 14f 80+ <
1998 Turf 1-9: (7f, 10f 3, 12f 2, 14f 1-2, 16f) (sft, g-s, gd 4, g-f, frm 1-2)
Scopey, useful colt, effective 6 to 12f, acts on g-s to g-f, has worn blinkers. Turf high 91 (1st run) - 4th of 18 to Greek Dance (14 Apr Newmarket 10f gd RF 0685). Becoming disappointing. Often placed before getting off the mark in a modest Lingfield maiden over fourteen furlongs, he was beaten out of sight over the same trip at Goodwood. Dropped back to seven furlongs on his final start, and was sold cheaply soon after.
**B W Hills [1-11] Maktoum Al Maktoum.*

WEALTHY STAR (IRE) RR 92f 2174^{1}

3 b c Soviet Star (USA) 8.6f **(74)** - Catalonda (African Sky) 7.9f **(63)**

Form - 61
Record 1998 - 1st:1 2nd:0 3rd:0 Ran:2
Win Prizemoney £4,467 *Total Prizemoney* £4,467
Wins * **1998** Jun Nottin (GD) 8.2f 92 <
1998 Turf 1-2: (8f 1-2) (gd 1-1, g-f)
Well made, currently useful colt. Turf high 92 - 1st of 11 from Cadette (22 Jun Nottingham RF 2174). Progressed from his debut to win a Nottingham maiden in June, and probably has a bit more improvement in him. **B Hanbury [1-2] Ahmed Ali.*

WEAVER OF WORDS BHB 82f RR 79f 4538[2]

2 b f Danehill (USA) 9.1f **(79)** - Canadian Mill (USA) (Mill Reef (USA)) 10.5f **(78)**
Form - 5222
Record 1998 - 1st:0 2nd:3 3rd:0 Ran:4
Win Prizemoney £0 *Total Prizemoney* £8,760
1998 Turf 0-4: (6f, 7f 3) (gd, g-f, frm 2)
Above-average filly. Turf high 79 (began Aug) - 2nd of 13 giving 12lb to Melody Queen (29 Spt Newmarket 7f frm RF 4538). Sure to win a race or two, probably over a mile.
**B W Hills [0-4] Maktoum Al Maktoum.*

WEDDING BAND BHB 44f RR 45f 4375[13]

3 b f Saddlers' Hall (IRE) 10.5f **(65)** - Priceless Bond (USA) (Blushing Groom (FR)) 10.3f **(76)**
Form - 000160662320
Record 1998 - 1st:1 2nd:2 3rd:1 Ran:12
Pre1998 - 1st:0 2nd:1 3rd:0 Ran:4
Win Prizemoney £2,301 *Total Prizemoney* £4,678
Wins 1998 May Warwic (G-F) C 10.8f 45 <
1998 Turf 1-11: (7f, 8f, 10f 3, 11f 1-1, 12f, 16f 3, 17f) (sft, gd 2, g-f 5, frm 1-3) 1998 AW 0-1: (11f) (Fibr)
Scopey, moderate filly, effective 7 to 17f, acts on g-f to frm, best on frm, often wears blinkers, likes left handed tracks, prefers tight tracks. Turf high 45 - 1st of 7 getting 2lb from Senor Hurst (23 May Warwick RF 1438). Inconsistent.
**S C Williams [0-4] Mrs Celia Miller (from N Tinkler [0-1] Jun 1998).*

WEE CHRISTY (IRE) BHB 31f28a RR 30f 28a 2693[5]

3 gr c Contract Law (USA) 8.9f **(54)** - Eternal Optimist (Relko) 9.9f **(59)**
Form - 03880405
Record 1998 - 1st:0 2nd:0 3rd:1 Ran:8
Pre1998 - 1st:0 2nd:0 3rd:0 Ran:8
Win Prizemoney £0 *Total Prizemoney* £317
1998 Turf 0-7: (7f, 8f, 12f 4, 14f) (hvy, gd 2, g-f 3, frm) 1998 AW 0-1: (9f) (Fibr)
Leggy, very moderate colt, effective 12f, acts on g-f, has worn blinkers, likes tight tracks. Turf high 41 - 3rd of 5 giving 8lb to Ludere (1 May Musselburgh 12f g-f RF 0954). Inconsistent.
**W McKeown [0-16] Christy Golfing Society.*

WEE JIMMY BHB 62f RR 71f 4142[12]

2 b c Lugana Beach 7f **(63)** - Cutlass Princess (USA) (Cutlass (USA)) 8.5f **(76)**
Form - 440
Record 1998 - 1st:0 2nd:0 3rd:0 Ran:3
Win Prizemoney £0 *Total Prizemoney* £589
1998 Turf 0-3: (5f, 6f, 7f) (gd 2, g-f)
Currently above-average colt. Turf high 71.
**B A McMahon [0-3] J D Graham.*

WEET-A-MINUTE (IRE) BHB 95f90a RR 106f 90a 4986[2]

5 ro h Nabeel Dancer (USA) 6.1f **(65)** - Ludovica (Bustino) 10.4f **(64)**
Form - 3422535283002
Record 1998 - 1st:0 2nd:4 3rd:3 Ran:13
Pre1998 - 1st:3 2nd:3 3rd:5 Ran:26
Win Prizemoney £23,244 *Total Prizemoney* £63,442
Wins * 1995 Oct Pontef (FRM) L 8f 101 <
* 1995 Oct York (G-F) H 7.9f 84 94
* 1995 Spt Beverl (GD) 7.5f 78
1998 Turf 0-13: (8f 8, 9f 2, 10f 2, 11f) (sft, gd 4, g-f 5, frm 3)
Pattern-class colt, effective 8 to 11f, best at 9f, acts on sft to frm, likes left handed tracks, and excels at York. Turf high 106 - 3rd of 10 giving 1lb to Great Dane (3 Spt York 9f g-f RF 4068). He has an appalling wins-to-runs ratio for one of his ability and is always one to oppose. A mile and a furlong seems to be the limit of his stamina. **R Hollinshead [3-39] Ed Weetman (Haulage & Storage) Ltd.*

WEET FOR ME BHB 83f RR 79f 5143[2]

2 b c Warning 8.1f **(77)** - Naswara (USA) (Al Nasr (FR)) 9.3f **(68)**
Form - 422
Record 1998 - 1st:0 2nd:2 3rd:0 Ran:3
Win Prizemoney £0 *Total Prizemoney* £2,868
1998 Turf 0-3: (8f 3) (sft, gd, g-f)
Currently above-average colt. Turf high 79 (began Spt) - 2nd of 6 getting 2lb from Bring Sweets (6 Nov Doncaster 8f gd RF 5143).
**R Hollinshead [0-3] Ed Weetman (Haulage & Storage) Ltd.*

WEETMAN'S WEIGH (IRE) BHB 76f82a RR 77f 82a 5147[19]

5 b h Archway (IRE) 8.5f **(60)** -Indian Sand(Indian King (USA)) 7.4f **(64)**
Form - 174600731502610
Record 1998 - 1st:3 2nd:1 3rd:1 Ran:15
Pre1998 - 1st:7 2nd:7 3rd:4 Ran:30
Win Prizemoney £44,248 *Total Prizemoney* £60,138
Wins * **1998** Oct Newmar (SFT) H 7f 72 77
* **1998** Aug Newcas (GD) H 7f 67 72
* **1998** *Feb Wolver (STD) H 7f 79 84* <
* 1997 Jun Thirsk (FRM) 7f 81
* 1997 May Redcar (G-F) 7f 81
* 1997 May Thirsk (G-F) H 7f 73 76
* 1996 Mar Leices (SFT) H 6f 68 75
* 1996 *Jan Wolver (STD) H 6f 74 74*
* 1996 *Jan Southw (STD) H 6f 64 65*
* 1995 Jly Carlis (FRM) 5f 66
1998 Turf 2-12: (7f 2-8, 8f 4) (sft 1-1, gd 1-6, g-f 2, frm 2, hrd) 1998 AW 1-3: (7f 1-1, 8f 2) (Fibr 1-3)
Decent colt, effective 7 to 8f, best at 7f, acts on sft to frm - acts on Fibr, likes left handed tracks, likes tight tracks, excels at Wolverhampton and Thirsk, likes Newcastle. Turf high 77 - 1st of 26 giving 13lb to Topton (31 Oct Newmarket RF 5079). AW high 84 (1st run) - 1st of 9 giving 13lb to Trojan Hero (18 Feb Wolverhampton RF 0309). He is a capable performer on sand, coming back to win a good handicap at Wolverhampton in February, but has looked not to stay a mile since. He is much better suited by seven furlongs, the trip over which he scored at Newcastle in August, and Newmarket in October.
**R Hollinshead [10-45] Ed Weetman (Haulage & Storage) Ltd.*

WEET U THERE (IRE) BHB 66f RR 70f 5144[16]

2 b c Forest Wind (USA) - Lady Aladdin (Persian Bold) 9.3f **(66)**
Form - 6055300
Record 1998 - 1st:0 2nd:0 3rd:1 Ran:7
Win Prizemoney £0 *Total Prizemoney* £260
1998 Turf 0-5: (5f 2, 7f, 8f 2)(gd 2, g-f, frm 2)1998 AW 0-2: (6f 2)(Fibr 2)
Above-average colt, effective 7f, acts on g-f. Turf high 70 (began Aug). AW high 55.
**R Hollinshead [0-7] Ed Weetman (Haulage & Storage) Ltd.*

WELCOME HEIGHTS BHB 58f62a RR 59f 62a 5126[12]

4 b g Most Welcome 8.6f **(66)** - Mount Ida (USA) (Conquistador Cielo (USA)) 8.8f **(69)**
Form - 21361008356700
Record 1998 - 1st:1 2nd:0 3rd:2 Ran:12
Pre1998 - 1st:3 2nd:3 3rd:2 Ran:15
Win Prizemoney £14,155 *Total Prizemoney* £18,698
Wins * **1998** May Leices (GD) H 8f 55 64 <
* 1997 *Dec Lingfi (STD) H 10f 57 60*
* 1997 Jly Doncas (GD) H 7f 48 55
* 1997 Jly Chepst (G-S) H 6.1f 38 44
1998 Turf 1-10: (8f 1-8, 9f, 10f) (g-s, gd 4, g-f 1-4, hrd) 1998 AW 0-2: (8f, 10f) (Equi 2)
Strong, average gelding, effective 7 to 10f, acts on gd to g-f - acts on Equi, excels at Chepstow, does well at Lingfield. Turf high 65 - 3rd of 12 getting 22lb from Supreme Sound (18 Jly Newbury 9f gd RF 2914) - also 1st of 12 getting 5lb from Zimiri (25 May Leicester RF 1450). AW high 63 (1st run) - 3rd of 10 giving 26lb to Sakharov (3 Apr Lingfield 10f Equi RF 0558). Consistent. Best coming off a strong pace.
**M J Fetherston-Godley [4-27] The Most Welcome Partnership.*

WELCOME LU BHB 26f32a RR 22f 32a 2383[8]

5 ch m Most Welcome 8.6f **(66)** -Odile (Green Dancer (USA)) 10.3f **(74)**
Form - 1304407738
Record 1998 - 1st:1 2nd:0 3rd:2 Ran:10
Pre1998 - 1st:2 2nd:0 3rd:2 Ran:22
Win Prizemoney £8,657 *Total Prizemoney* £10,595

Wins * **1998** *Feb Southw (STD) H 8f 28 40+*
* 1996 Aug Catter (G-F) H 7f 31 43 <
* 1996 Aug Bright (FRM) H 7f 31 41+
1998 Turf 0-2: (7f, 11f) (gd, frm) 1998 AW 1-8: (7f, 8f 1-3, 9f, 10f, 12f 2) (Equi, Fibr 1-7)
Moderate filly, effective 7 to 12f, - acts on Fibr, has worn blinkers, favours left handed tracks, favours tight tracks. Turf high 21. AW high 40 (1st run) - 1st of 7 getting 20lb from Molly Music (16 Feb Southwell RF 0300).
**J L Harris [3-25] M F Hyman (from P S Felgate [0-7] Jun 1996).*

WELCOME SUNSET BHB 70f RR 74f 3956[15]

3 b c Most Welcome 8.6f **(66)** - Deanta in Eirinn (Red Sunset) 8.2f **(63)**
Form - 4230
Record 1998 - 1st:0 2nd:1 3rd:1 Ran:4
Pre1998 - 1st:1 2nd:0 3rd:1 Ran:5
Win Prizemoney £2,277 *Total Prizemoney* £4,952
Wins * 1997 Jly Nottin (SFT) 5.1f 74 <
1998 Turf 0-4: (7f, 8f 3) (g-f, frm 3)
Leggy, above-average colt, effective 5 to 8f, acts on gd to frm, best on gd, has worn blinkers. Turf high 74 (began Jly) - 2nd of 14 getting 7lb from Sunstreak (1 Aug Newmarket 8f frm RF 3278). Inconsistent. Just touched off by Sunstreak on his second run back, but has disappointed since. **J Wharton [1-9] John Goddard.*

WELLAKI (USA) BHB 68f RR 70f 4350[2]

4 ch g Miswaki (USA) 8.1f **(81)** - Wellomond (FR) (Lomond (USA)) 8.8f **(65)**
Form - 70033002
Record 1998 - 1st:0 2nd:1 3rd:2 Ran:8
Pre1998 - 1st:1 2nd:0 3rd:0 Ran:4
Win Prizemoney £3,582 *Total Prizemoney* £6,518
Wins * 1996 Nov Mussel (G-S) 8.1f 80 <
1998 Turf 0-8: (8f 3, 9f 2, 10f 3) (sft 2, gd 3, g-f 2, frm)
Scopey, above-average gelding, effective 8 to 9f, acts on sft to g-f, has worn blinkers (extremely effectively), prefers tight tracks. Turf high 75. **J H M Gosden [1-12] C T S Racing Partnership.*

WELL DRAWN BHB 41f62a RR 46f 62a 5098[8]

5 b g Dowsing (USA) 7f **(61)** - Classic Design (Busted) 10.2f **(61)**
Form - 06558
Record 1998 - 1st:0 2nd:0 3rd:0 Ran:5
Pre1998 - 1st:1 2nd:0 3rd:1 Ran:7
Win Prizemoney £3,866 *Total Prizemoney* £4,304
Wins * 1996 *Jan Lingfi (STD) 8f 64* <
1998 Turf 0-5: (8f 2, 10f 3) (gd 2, g-f, frm 2)
Average gelding. Turf high 46 (began Jly).
**H Candy [1-12] Mrs David Blackburn.*

WELODY RR 41f 5137[11]

2 ch c Weldnaas (USA) 8.4f **(55)** - The Boozy News (USA) (L'Emigrant (USA)) 10.5f **(62)**
Form - 0
Record 1998 - 1st:0 2nd:0 3rd:0 Ran:1
1998 Turf 0-1: (7f) (gd)
Currently moderate colt. **K Mahdi [0-1] Hamad Al-Mutawa.*

WELSH ASSEMBLY BHB 43f53a RR 47f 53a 4762[16]

2 ch c Presidium 7.5f **(56)** - Celtic Chimes (Celtic Cone) 9.8f **(43)**
Form - 33681000
Record 1998 - 1st:1 2nd:0 3rd:2 Ran:8
Win Prizemoney £1,917 *Total Prizemoney* £2,417
Wins * **1998** *Jly Southw (STD) S 6f 51* <
1998 Turf 0-3: (5f, 6f, 10f) (gd 2, frm) 1998 AW 1-5: (5f 2, 6f 1-2, 7f) (Fibr 1-5)
Fair colt, effective 6f, - acts on Fibr, likes tight tracks. Turf high 47. AW high 51 - 1st of 7 from Grey Strike (11 Jly Southwell RF 2726).
**G P Enright [1-8] Chris Wall.*

WELSH AUTUMN RR 108f 1382a[4]

3 b f Tenby 10.4f **(76)** - Autumn Tint (USA) (Roberto (USA)) 10f **(76)**
Form - 124
1998 Turf 1-3: (8f 1-1, 10f, 11f) (hvy, g-s 1-1, gd)
Currently Pattern-class filly. Turf high 108 - 4th of 9 to Zainta (17 May Longchamp 10f gd RF 1382a). She is a sweet filly, who ran well in smart company during the spring. **M Zilber in FR [1-3].*

WELSH FAIRING RR 49f 4882[14]

2 b f King's Signet (USA) 7f **(51)** - Princess Fair (Crowned Prince (USA)) 10.1f **(67)**
Form - 00
Record 1998 - 1st:0 2nd:0 3rd:0 Ran:2
1998 Turf 0-2: (5f, 6f) (g-s 2)
Currently moderate filly. Turf high 49 (began Oct).
**M Blanshard [0-2] J G Charlton.*

WELSH MOUNTAIN BHB 39f RR 39f 4416[13]

5 b g Welsh Captain 7.2f **(54)** - Miss Nelski (Most Secret) 7.1f **(58)**
Form - 458170
Record 1998 - 1st:1 2nd:0 3rd:0 Ran:6
Pre1998 - 1st:2 2nd:2 3rd:2 Ran:21
Win Prizemoney £8,765 *Total Prizemoney* £11,768
Wins * **1998** Aug Carlis (G-S) H 8f 36 39
1997 Aug Yarmou (G-F) SH 8f 38 43
1995 Jly Folkes (G-F) H 5f 75 <
1998 Turf 1-6: (8f 1-2, 10f 3, 11f) (gd 1-1, g-f, frm 4)
Very moderate gelding, effective 8f, acts on gd to frm, has worn blinkers. Turf high 39 - 1st of 12 giving 14lb to Get A Life (3 Aug Carlisle RF 3303).
**K A Morgan [1-9] Mrs P A L Butler (from M J Heaton-Ellis [2-20] Aug 1997).*

WELSH WARRIOR RR 31f 2069[18]

5 b g Librate 10.4f **(37)** - Mayo Melody (Highland Melody) 6.3f **(55)**
Form - 0000
Record 1998 - 1st:0 2nd:0 3rd:0 Ran:4
1998 Turf 0-3: (7f, 10f 2) (gd, frm 2) 1998 AW 0-1: (7f) (Equi)
Very moderate gelding. Turf high 31. **J M Bradley [0-4] E A Hayward.*

WELTON ARSENAL BHB 77f RR 84f 4985[9]

6 b g Statoblest 6.4f **(63)** - Miller's Gait (Mill Reef (USA)) 10.5f **(78)**
Form - 00623400
Record 1998 - 1st:0 2nd:1 3rd:1 Ran:8
Pre1998 - 1st:3 2nd:4 3rd:3 Ran:32
Win Prizemoney £17,070 *Total Prizemoney* £38,403
Wins * 1997 May Newmar (GD) H 7f 88 93 <
1996 Apr Warwic (GD) 7f 91
1994 Jly Salisb (FRM) 6f 79+
1998 Turf 0-8: (6f, 7f 3, 8f 4) (g-s 2, gd 3, g-f 2, frm)
Decent gelding, effective 6 to 8f, acts on gd to g-f, best on gd, has worn blinkers. Turf high 84 - 2nd of 8 giving 3lb to White Heart (10 Jly Chepstow 6f g-f RF 2672). He has so much ability, but only produces when he feels like it. Ran two fine races in quick succession in July, however. A fast-run seven furlongs is ideal.
**K Bishop [2-22] Paulton Bloodstock (from M R Channon [2-25] Nov 1996).*

WELVILLE BHB 72f RR 56f 4854[27]

5 b g Most Welcome 8.6f **(66)** -Miss Top Ville (FR) (Top Ville) 11.7f **(68)**
Form - 000
Record 1998 - 1st:0 2nd:0 3rd:0 Ran:3
Pre1998 - 1st:1 2nd:2 3rd:0 Ran:5
Win Prizemoney £5,166 *Total Prizemoney* £8,955
Wins * 1995 Spt Goodwo (GD) 6f 87 <
1998 Turf 0-3: (6f, 7f 2) (gd 3)
Fair gelding. Turf high 55. Becoming disappointing.
**P J Makin [1-8] T G Warner.*

WENDA (IRE) BHB 88f RR 91f 4620[6]

3 ch f Priolo (USA) 10.9f **(71)** - Pennine Drive (IRE) (Pennine Walk) 8.5f **(61)**
Form - 2030206
Record 1998 - 1st:0 2nd:2 3rd:1 Ran:7
Pre1998 - 1st:1 2nd:0 3rd:0 Ran:3
Win Prizemoney £11,964 *Total Prizemoney* £23,477
Wins * 1997 Spt Ascot (G-F) 6f 86 <
1998 Turf 0-7: (6f, 7f 2, 8f 2, 9f, 11f) (sft, gd 3, g-f 3)
Scopey, useful filly, effective 6 to 11f, acts on gd to g-f, best on g-f. Turf high 95. Well beaten in the Rockfel, but ran an encouraging race to finish runner-up in the Fred Darling on her reappearance. She was well held after. **C E Brittain [1-10] B H Voak.*

WEND'S DAY (IRE) BHB 65f RR 64f 2752[5]

3 br g Brief Truce(USA) 9.1f **(73)** -Iswara (USA)(Alleged (USA)) 10f **(76)**

Form - 045
Record 1998 - 1st:0 2nd:0 3rd:0 Ran:3
Win Prizemoney £0 *Total Prizemoney* £251
1998 Turf 0-3: (10f 2, 12f) (gd 2, g-f)
Workmanlike, currently average gelding. Turf high 64.
**S E H Sherwood [0-1] Uplands Bloodstock (from S E Sherwood [0-2] Jun 1998).*

WENTBRIDGE LAD (IRE) BHB 38f43a **RR 37f 43a** 5114[8]

8 b g Coquelin (USA) 9.7f **(55)** - Cathryn's Song (Prince Tenderfoot (USA)) 9f **(61)**
Form - 00768338062546408
Record 1998 - 1st:0 2nd:1 3rd:2 Ran:16
Pre1998 - 1st:10 2nd:11 3rd:10 Ran:84
Win Prizemoney £33,657 *Total Prizemoney* £56,952

Wins									
	1997	Aug	Bright	(FRM)	H	10f	47	60	
	1997	Aug	Haydoc	(G-F)	H	10.5f	48	55	
	1995	Jly	Cheste	(G-F)	H	7.6f	56	67	
	1995	*Jly*	*Wolver*	*(STD)*	*C*	*8.5f*		*76*	<
	1995	*Jun*	*Wolver*	*(STD)*	*C*	*7f*		*76*	<
	1994	*Nov*	*Wolver*	*(STD)*	*H*	*8.5f*	*74*	*75*	
	1994	*Jly*	*Wolver*	*(STD)*	*H*	*9.4f*	*69*	*71*	
	1994	*Jun*	*Wolver*	*(STD)*	*H*	*9.4f*	*62*	*63*	
	1994	*May*	*Wolver*	*(STD)*	*H*	*7f*	*56*	*55*	

1998 Turf 0-16: (8f 4, 9f 3, 10f 5, 11f 2, 12f 2) (sft, g-s 3, gd 4, g-f 5, frm 3)
Fair gelding, effective 10 to 11f, best at 10f, acts on g-s to frm, mostly wears blinkers, likes left handed tracks, favours tight tracks. Turf high 56 - 3rd of 8 to I Can't Remember (24 Jun Chester 10f gd RF 2231).
**W M Brisbourne [0-16] Dennis Newton (from A Bailey [2-11] Dec 1997).*

WESLEY'S LAD (IRE) BHB 44f49a **RR 54f 49a** 4417[5]

4 b br g Classic Secret (USA) 8.8f **(56)** -Galouga (FR)(Lou Piguet (FR))
Form - 5
Record 1998 - 1st:0 2nd:0 3rd:0 Ran:1
Pre1998 - 1st:0 2nd:0 3rd:2 Ran:9
Win Prizemoney £0 *Total Prizemoney* £799
1998 Turf 0-1: (16f) (frm)
Fair gelding.
**D Burchell [2-9] Brian Williams (from J Neville [0-8] Jly 1997).*

WESTCOURT MAGIC BHB 77f **RR 78f** 5142[14]

5 b g Emarati (USA) 6.6f **(63)** -Magic Milly (Simply Great (FR)) 8.2f **(65)**
Form - 510176407401870000
Record 1998 - 1st:3 2nd:0 3rd:0 Ran:18
Pre1998 - 1st:7 2nd:3 3rd:1 Ran:30
Win Prizemoney £66,946 *Total Prizemoney* £86,753

Wins									
	* **1998**	Aug	Cheste	(G-S)	H	5.1f	83	87	
	* **1998**	May	Cheste	(G-F)	H	5.1f	87	89	
	* **1998**	Mar	Newcas	(G-S)	H	5f	80	85	
	* 1997	Aug	Cheste	(SFT)	H	5.1f	80	88	
	* 1996	Apr	Haydoc	(GD)	L	5f		103	
	* 1995	Spt	Ayr	(GD)	L	5f		104	<
	* 1995	Aug	Thirsk	(G-F)	H	6f	77	88+	
	* 1995	Aug	Sandow	(G-F)	H	5f	66	88+	
	* 1995	Aug	Beverl	(G-F)	H	5f	66	68	
	* 1995	Jly	Newcas	(G-F)	S	5f		63+	

1998 Turf 3-18: (5f 3-13, 6f 5) (sft 2, g-s 2, gd 2-9, g-f 1-2, frm 3)
Above-average gelding, effective 5 to 6f, best at 5f, acts on sft to g-f, excels at Chester and Newcastle. Turf high 89 - 1st of 8 giving 1lb to Ziggy's Dancer (7 May Chester RF 1072) - also 1st of 11 giving 29lb to Palacegate Jack (22 Aug Chester RF 3805). Becoming disappointing. A very useful sprint handicapper, he is a difficult horse to pass if able to dominate. He goes particularly well at Chester. **M W Easterby [10-48] K Hodgson & Mrs J Hodgson.*

WESTCOURT RUBY BHB 42f **RR 34f** 3281[13]

3 b f Petong 7.6f **(58)** - Red Rosein (Red Sunset) 8.2f **(63)**
Form - 00
Record 1998 - 1st:0 2nd:0 3rd:0 Ran:2
Pre1998 - 1st:0 2nd:0 3rd:0 Ran:3
1998 Turf 0-2: (6f 2) (g-f 2)
Scopey, very moderate filly. Turf high 23 (began Jly).
**M W Easterby [0-5] K Hodgson & Mrs J Hodgson.*

WESTENDER (FR) **RR 41f** 5137[10]

2 b c In The Wings 11.2f **(77)** -Trude (GER)(Windwurf (GER)) 12.7f **(72)**
Form - 0
Record 1998 - 1st:0 2nd:0 3rd:0 Ran:1
1998 Turf 0-1: (7f) (gd)
Currently moderate colt. **W J Haggas [0-1] Khalifa Dasmal.*

WESTERN FOLLY (USA) BHB 89f **RR 79f** 4584[2]

2 ch c Gone West (USA) 7.8f **(82)** -Nimble Folly(USA) (Cyane) 8.8f **(67)**
Form - 622
Record 1998 - 1st:0 2nd:2 3rd:0 Ran:3
Win Prizemoney £0 *Total Prizemoney* £2,144
1998 Turf 0-3: (7f, 8f 2) (gd, g-f, frm)
Currently above-average colt. Turf high 79 (began Jly) - 2nd of 10 to Lucido (30 Spt Salisbury 8f gd RF 4584).
**H R A Cecil [0-3] K Abdulla.*

WESTERN SONATA (IRE) BHB 67f62a **RR 67f 62a** 307[2]

5 b m Alzao (USA) 9.8f **(73)** - Musique Classique (USA) (Exclusive Native (USA)) 9.1f **(81)**
Form - 2
Record 1998 - 1st:0 2nd:1 3rd:0 Ran:1
Pre1998 - 1st:0 2nd:2 3rd:1 Ran:6
Win Prizemoney £0 *Total Prizemoney* £3,747
1998 AW 0-1: (9f) (Fibr)
Average filly. **Lord Huntingdon [0-7] Ken Nishikawa.*

WESTERN VENTURE (IRE) BHB 29f29a **RR 39f 29a** 4768[16]

5 ch g Two Timing (USA) 7.1f **(58)** - Star Gazing (IRE) (Caerleon (USA)) 8.6f **(71)**
Form - 6050
Record 1998 - 1st:0 2nd:0 3rd:0 Ran:4
Pre1998 - 1st:2 2nd:2 3rd:3 Ran:23
Win Prizemoney £6,599 *Total Prizemoney* £9,488

Wins									
	* 1997	Aug	Hamilt	(G-F)	SH	9.2f	27	31	
	1995	Aug	Folkes	(FRM)		5f		68	<

1998 Turf 0-4: (9f 3, 10f) (sft, g-s, gd 2)
Very moderate gelding, effective 9f, acts on gd to frm, has worn blinkers, likes right handed tracks, favours tight tracks. Turf high 39 (began Aug) - 5th of 11 giving 5lb to Portite Sophie (7 Spt Hamilton 9f gd RF 4133). Inconsistent.
**Martyn Wane [1-11] William Graham (from R M McKellar [0-14] Jun 1997).*

WEST ESCAPE BHB 79f **RR 80f** 5124[2]

2 ch f Gone West (USA) 7.8f **(82)** -Sans Escale (USA) (Diesis) 9.3f **(69)**
Form - 64342
Record 1998 - 1st:0 2nd:1 3rd:1 Ran:5
Win Prizemoney £0 *Total Prizemoney* £2,078
1998 Turf 0-5: (6f 2, 7f 2, 8f) (sft, g-s, frm 3)
Decent filly. Turf high 80 (began Aug) - 2nd of 9 to Spitzbergen (5 Nov Brighton 8f g-s RF 5124).
**M A Jarvis [0-5] Mohammed Bin Hendi.*

WESTMINSTER (IRE) BHB 63f **RR 76f** 3513[3]

6 ch g Nashamaa 8.1f **(58)** -Our Galadrial(Salmon Leap (USA)) 11f **(61)**
Form - 127153253
Record 1998 - 1st:2 2nd:2 3rd:2 Ran:9
Pre1998 - 1st:3 2nd:3 3rd:2 Ran:26
Win Prizemoney £13,823 *Total Prizemoney* £21,454

Wins									
	* **1998**	Jun	Carlis	(G-S)		12f		76	<
	* **1998**	Jun	Windso	(G-F)	H	11.6f	55	63	
	* 1997	Jun	Ayr	(GD)	H	10.9f	60	68	
	* 1996	Jun	Windso	(G-F)	C	11.6f		66	
	* 1995	May	Hamilt	(G-F)		12.1f		65	

1998 Turf 2-9: (10f 2, 12f 2-6, 13f) (g-s, gd 1-4, g-f 1-2, frm, hrd)
Above-average gelding, effective 11 to 13f, best at 12f, acts on gd to hrd, best on gd, mostly wears blinkers (effectively), favours tight tracks. Turf high 76 - 1st of 8 from Polar Champ (24 Jun Carlisle RF 2230). He is useful in claiming company, but is no better than that. **M H Tompkins [5-37] Michael Jenkins.*

WESTMINSTER CITY (USA) BHB 85f **RR 95f** 5065[7]

2 b c Alleged (USA) 11.8f **(81)** - Promanade Fan (USA) (Timeless Moment (USA)) 6f **(72)**
Form - 1737
Record 1998 - 1st:1 2nd:0 3rd:1 Ran:4

Win Prizemoney £3,187 *Total Prizemoney* £4,287
Wins * **1998** May Lingfi (GD) 5f 76 <
1998 Turf 1-4: (5f 1-1, 6f, 7f, 8f) (g-s, g-f, frm 1-2)
Very useful colt. Turf high 95 - 3rd of 3 to Haafiz (25 Aug Pontefract 6f frm RF 3851). This lightly-made colt won on his debut, but never really progressed in three subsequent runs.
**C E Brittain [1-4] A J Richards.*

WESTSIDE FLYER BHB 61f55a **RR 59f 55a** 4570[13]
2 ch f Risk Me (FR) 8f **(53)** -Celtic River(IRE)(Caerleon (USA)) 8.6f **(71)**
Form - 756635460
Record 1998 - 1st:0 2nd:0 3rd:1 Ran:9
Win Prizemoney £0 *Total Prizemoney* £649
1998 Turf 0-7: (5f 3, 6f 2, 7f 2) (sft, gd, g-f 3, frm, hrd) 1998 AW 0-2: (7f, 8f) (Fibr 2)
Fair filly, effective 7f, acts on g-f, has worn blinkers. Turf high 59 - 4th of 11 getting 20lb from Asley (14 Aug Folkestone 7f g-f RF 3626). AW high 40 (began Jly). Inconsistent.
**A Kelleway [0-9] Kevin Hudson.*

WEST STREET BLUES BHB 48f **RR 34f** 4882[13]
2 ch f Then Again 7.4f **(52)** - Calametta (Oats) 8.9f **(46)**
Form - 0000
Record 1998 - 1st:0 2nd:0 3rd:0 Ran:4
1998 Turf 0-4: (5f 2, 6f 2) (g-s, g-f, frm 2)
Very moderate filly. Turf high 34.
**T D McCarthy [0-4] Epsom Sporting Proposals Ltd.*

WESTWOOD VIEW BHB 60f **RR 65f** 4812[5]
2 b f Puissance 7.1f **(60)** - Long View (Persian Bold) 9.3f **(66)**
Form - 30005
Record 1998 - 1st:0 2nd:0 3rd:1 Ran:5
Win Prizemoney £0 *Total Prizemoney* £544
1998 Turf 0-5: (5f 3, 6f, 7f) (sft, g-s, gd 2, frm)
Average filly. Turf high 74 (1st run) - 3rd of 11 getting 6lb from Kastaway (17 Apr Thirsk 5f g-s RF 0737).
**J J Quinn [0-5] The Westwood Partnership.*

WHACKER-DO (IRE) BHB 39f32a **RR 46f 32a** 4877[6]
3 ch c Archway (IRE) 8.5f **(60)** - Denowski (Malinowski (USA)) 10f **(56)**
Form - 0070550200736
Record 1998 - 1st:0 2nd:1 3rd:1 Ran:13
Pre1998 - 1st:0 2nd:0 3rd:0 Ran:8
Win Prizemoney £0 *Total Prizemoney* £1,050
1998 Turf 0-10: (5f, 6f 4, 8f 5) (g-s, gd 4, frm 5) 1998 AW 0-3: (6f 2, 8f) (Fibr 3)
Small, moderate colt. Turf high 48. AW high 47.
**R Hollinshead [0-21] Clayton Bigley Partnership Ltd.*

WHATEVER'S RIGHT (IRE) BHB 62f46a **RR 61f 46a** 4475[2]
9 b g Doulab (USA) 7.4f **(61)** - Souveniers (Relko) 9.9f **(59)**
Form - 47675061472
Record 1998 - 1st:1 2nd:1 3rd:0 Ran:11
Pre1998 - 1st:9 2nd:4 3rd:6 Ran:53
Win Prizemoney £31,954 *Total Prizemoney* £41,037

Wins								
* **1998**	Aug	Salisb	(G-F)	H	7f	55	60	
* 1997	Jly	Windso	(GD)	H	8.3f	63	67	<
* 1996	*Jly*	*Lingfi*	*(STD)*		*7f*		*64*	
* 1996	Jly	Warwic	(FRM)	H	7f	60	63	
* 1995	Jun	Warwic	(GD)		7f		67	<
* 1995	*May*	*Lingfi*	*(STD)*	*H*	*8f*	*57*	*59*	
* 1994	Spt	Leices	(G-F)	H	7f	58	60	
* 1994	Jly	Lingfi	(GF)	H	7.6f	52	54	
* 1994	Jun	Nottin	(G-F)	H	8.2f	46	51	
* 1994	*Feb*	*Lingfi*	*(STD)*		*8f*		*56*	

1998 Turf 1-9: (7f 1-3, 8f 5, 10f) (gd 2, g-f 4, frm 1-3) 1998 AW 0-2: (8f, 10f) (Equi 2)
Average gelding, effective 7 to 10f, acts on gd to frm, has worn blinkers, excels at Windsor. Turf high 61 - 2nd of 16 giving 7lb to Mutabassir (25 Spt Folkestone 7f gd RF 4475) - also 1st of 15 getting 15lb from Big Ben (7 Aug Salisbury RF 3448). AW high 40. He does not win very often, and his Salisbury victory came in an apprentice event. **M D I Usher [10-66] M S C Thurgood.*

WHATTA MADAM BHB 64f **RR 67f** 3400[2]
2 gr f Whittingham (IRE) - Sylvan Song (Song) 7.2f **(61)**
Form - 02342
Record 1998 - 1st:0 2nd:2 3rd:1 Ran:5
Win Prizemoney £0 *Total Prizemoney* £1,381
1998 Turf 0-5: (5f, 6f 4) (gd, g-f 2, frm 2)
Average filly. Turf high 67 - 2nd of 10 to En Grisaille (6 Aug Folkestone 6f frm RF 3400). **G L Moore [0-5] C F Sparrowhawk.*

WHAT THE DEVIL BHB 32f **RR 32f** 1761[6]
5 ch m Devil to Play - Whats Yours Called (Windjammer (USA)) 7f **(59)**
Form - 646
Record 1998 - 1st:0 2nd:0 3rd:0 Ran:3
Win Prizemoney £0 *Total Prizemoney* £237
1998 Turf 0-1: (14f) (frm) 1998 AW 0-2: (12f 2) (Fibr 2)
Very moderate filly. AW high 34.
**J P Smith [0-10] Mrs Frances Draper.*

WHEELS OF STEEL BHB 54f50a **RR 50f 50a** 4639[7]
2 ch g Chilibang 7f **(55)** - Magic Tower (Tower Walk) 10f **(62)**
Form - 007
Record 1998 - 1st:0 2nd:0 3rd:0 Ran:3
1998 Turf 0-2: (5f 2) (gd, g-f) 1998 AW 0-1: (5f) (Fibr)
Currently fair gelding. Turf high 50 (began Spt).
**J P Leigh [0-3] The Country Stayers.*

WHEN (IRE) RR 1156[6]
2 br f Petardia 8.2f **(58)** - Eternal Optimist (Relko) 9.9f **(59)**
Form - 46
Record 1998 - 1st:0 2nd:0 3rd:0 Ran:2
1998 AW 0-2: (5f 2) (Fibr 2)
Currently moderate filly. AW high 41.
**D J S Cosgrove [0-2] D J S Cosgrove.*

WHERE'S ALBERT BHB 29f **RR 9f** 1818[14]
3 ch g Out of Hand - Stellajoe (Le Dauphin)
Form - 080
Record 1998 - 1st:0 2nd:0 3rd:0 Ran:3
1998 Turf 0-3: (8f, 10f, 12f) (g-f 2, frm)
Workmanlike, currently very poor gelding. Turf high 9.
**Derrick Morris [0-3] J Daniels.*

WHIRLWIND BHB 52f **RR 52f** 4919[11]
3 b g Puissance 7.1f **(60)** - Yours Or Mine (IRE) (Exhibitioner) 8.7f **(61)**
Form - 005100
Record 1998 - 1st:1 2nd:0 3rd:0 Ran:6
Win Prizemoney £2,948 *Total Prizemoney* £2,948
Wins * 1998 Jly Ayr (GD) H 7f 49 52 <
1998 Turf 1-5: (6f, 7f 1-2, 8f 2) (g-s, gd 1-3, frm) 1998 AW 0-1: (6f) (Fibr)
Light-framed, fair gelding, effective 7f, acts on gd. Turf high 52 - 1st of 11 getting 7lb from Technician (13 Jly Ayr RF 2758). Found a poor race on his handicap debut. **C W Thornton [1-6] Guy Reed.*

WHISPER LOW (IRE) BHB 40f28a **RR 42f 28a** 1964[8]
4 ch f Shalford (IRE) 7.8f **(63)** - Idle Gossip (Runnett) 7f **(59)**
Form - 07708
Record 1998 - 1st:0 2nd:0 3rd:0 Ran:5
Pre1998 - 1st:0 2nd:0 3rd:1 Ran:13
Win Prizemoney £0 *Total Prizemoney* £639
1998 Turf 0-2: (6f, 7f) (gd, frm) 1998 AW 0-3: (6f, 7f 2) (Fibr 3)
Strong, moderate filly. Turf high 42. AW high 4.
**R Hollinshead [0-18] D Lowe.*

WHISTLE TEST BHB 55f **RR 57f** 4108[11]
3 gr g Kris 10f **(75)** - Cut Velvet (USA) (Northern Dancer) 9.6f **(80)**
Form - 607680
Record 1998 - 1st:0 2nd:0 3rd:0 Ran:6
1998 Turf 0-6: (8f 3, 10f, 11f 2) (sft, g-f 3, frm 2)
Workmanlike, fair gelding, has worn blinkers. Turf high 82.
**S P C Woods [0-6] D Sullivan.*

WHISTLING DIXIE (IRE) BHB 78f **RR 74f** 4463[9]
2 ch g Forest Wind (USA) - Camden's Gift (Camden Town) 9.3f **(53)**
Form - 04820
Record 1998 - 1st:0 2nd:1 3rd:0 Ran:5
Win Prizemoney £0 *Total Prizemoney* £1,554
1998 Turf 0-5: (6f 3, 7f, 8f) (gd 2, g-f 2, frm)
Above-average gelding. Turf high 74 - 2nd of 13 giving 4lb to Hoh Steamer (15 Aug Newbury 7f g-f RF 3655).

**M R Channon [0-5] Mrs P D Savill.*

WHISTLING JACK (IRE) BHB 69f **RR 75f** 4808[1]

2 b g Roi Danzig (USA) 10.5f **(62)** - Candy's Sister (Great Nephew) 9.9f **(64)**
Form - 6631
Record 1998 - 1st:1 2nd:0 3rd:1 Ran:4
Win Prizemoney £2,532 *Total Prizemoney* £2,918
Wins * 1998 Oct Nottin (SFT) 10f 68 <
1998 Turf 1-3: (7f 2, 10f 1-1) (gd 1-1, frm 2) 1998 AW 0-1: (8f) (Fibr)
Above-average gelding. Turf high 75 (began Aug) - also 1st of 13 giving 5lb to Quilt (14 Oct Nottingham RF 4808). He showed ability before winning a soft-ground maiden over ten furlongs at Nottingham, though it was not a great race.
**B J Meehan [1-4] Michael Peart.*

WHITECHAPEL (USA) BHB 81f80a **RR 86f 80a** 4963[13]

10 br g Arctic Tern (USA) 12.2f **(71)** - Christchurch (FR) (So Blessed) 8.7f **(67)**
Form - 5160020
Record 1998 - 1st:1 2nd:1 3rd:0 Ran:7
Pre1998 - 1st:9 2nd:3 3rd:7 Ran:43
Win Prizemoney £107,405 *Total Prizemoney* £160,184
Wins * 1998 Jun York (G-S) H 11.9f 81 86
* 1997 Oct Newbur (GD) H 16f 79 82
* 1997 May Newbur (G-S) H 12f 80 89
* 1995 Spt Newbur (G-S) H 13.3f 80 90
* 1994 Spt Ascot (GS) H 12f 84 92 <
1998 Turf 1-7: (12f 1-2, 13f, 16f 4) (sft 2, g-s 1-2, gd 2, g-f)
Useful gelding, effective 12 to 16f, best at 12f, acts on g-s to gd, best on g-s. Turf high 86 - 1st of 13 giving 7lb to Pekay (13 Jun York RF 1982). Inconsistent. He looked in need of his reappearance, but won a valuable ladies' event next time. Modest efforts most starts since. **Lord Huntingdon [10-50] The Queen.*

WHITE EMIR BHB 73f **RR 75f** 5142[6]

5 b g Emarati (USA) 6.6f **(63)** - White African (Carwhite) 7.2f **(61)**
Form - 22880633036
Record 1998 - 1st:0 2nd:2 3rd:3 Ran:11
Pre1998 - 1st:4 2nd:7 3rd:2 Ran:36
Win Prizemoney £14,009 *Total Prizemoney* £47,365
Wins 1997 Jun Salisb (G-S) H 5f 80 80 <
1997 Jun Sandow (G-F) C 5f 80 <
1995 Spt Sandow (G-S) H 5f 80 80 <
1995 May Redcar (GD) 5f 60+
1998 Turf 0-11: (5f 7, 6f 4) (sft, g-s, gd 3, g-f 2, frm 4)
Above-average gelding, effective 5 to 6f, best at 5f, acts on sft to frm, best on g-f, has worn blinkers, excels at Bath. Turf high 80 - 2nd of 16 getting 20lb from Selhurstpark Flyer (6 Jun Epsom 6f g-f RF 1781). Consistent. He seems to appreciate being held up for a late run, but can sometimes wander under pressure.
**B R Millman [0-11] The Three Bears Racing (from B J Meehan [3-31] Oct 1997).*

WHITEGATE'S SON BHB 34f **RR 37f** 4408[11]

4 ch g Minster Son 10.9f **(56)** -Whitegates Lady(Le Coq d'Or) 13.3f **(55)**
Form - 0
Record 1998 - 1st:0 2nd:0 3rd:0 Ran:1
Pre1998 - 1st:0 2nd:0 3rd:0 Ran:4
1998 Turf 0-1: (10f) (g-f)
Unfurnished, very moderate gelding.
**B Ellison [1-9] Brian Ellison Racing Club.*

WHITE HEART BHB 100f **RR 97f** 4494[1]

3 b g Green Desert (USA) 7.8f **(78)** - Barari (USA) (Blushing Groom (FR)) 10.3f **(76)**
Form - 11241
Record 1998 - 1st:3 2nd:1 3rd:0 Ran:5
Win Prizemoney £60,752 *Total Prizemoney* £66,107
Wins * 1998 Spt Ascot (GD) H 7f 95 97 <
*** 1998** Jly Chepst (GD) 6.1f 88+
*** 1998** Mar Newcas (G-S) 7f 86+
1998 Turf 3-5: (6f 1-2, 7f 2-3) (sft, gd 2-3, g-f 1-1)
Scopey, very useful gelding, has worn blinkers. Turf high 97 - 1st of 25 getting 5lb from Sugarfoot (26 Spt Ascot RF 4494) - also 1st of 8 getting 3lb from Welton Arsenal (10 Jly Chepstow RF 2672). A gelded brother to Green Barries, he was unraced as a two-year-old, but won his first two starts, including beating some established sprinters at Chepstow. He lost nothing in defeat when runner-up in a classified stakes at Glorious Goodwood, but did not look at all an easy ride there. He ran a very strange race in the Ayr Gold Cup in first-time blinkers, coming home in great style to finish fourth after a tardy start, and once again the steering looked dodgy. However, given a positive ride, he gained a brave victory in the Festival Handicap at Ascot, despite wandering about in the closing stages. Despite his quirks, there is no reason why he should not be worth a try in Pattern company.
**M Johnston [3-5] Maktoum Al Maktoum.*

WHITE PLAINS (IRE) BHB 79f89a **RR 69f 89a** 431[6]

5 b g Nordico (USA) 8.2f **(59)** - Flying Diva (Chief Singer) 8.9f **(66)**
Form - 21132126
Record 1998 - 1st:1 2nd:2 3rd:0 Ran:4
Pre1998 - 1st:9 2nd:3 3rd:4 Ran:33
Win Prizemoney £33,213 *Total Prizemoney* £42,251
Wins * 1998 *Feb Southw (STD) 12f 84*
* 1997 *Dec Lingfi (STD) H 10f 72 90+* <
* 1997 *Dec Lingfi (STD) H 10f 69 75+*
* 1997 Jly Hamilt (G-S) C 9.2f 81
1997 Apr Nottin (G-F) H 10f 75 80
1996 Spt Lingfi (FRM) H 10f 70 74
1996 Spt Leices (FRM) H 10f 71 75+
1996 Aug Newcas (G-F) 9f 72
1996 Jun Lingfi (FRM) H 10f 68 74
1995 Nov Folkes (G-F) 6f 70
1998 AW 1-4: (8f, 10f 2, 12f 1-1) (Equi 2, Fibr 1-2)
Useful gelding, effective 8 to 12f, best at 10f, acts on gd to g-f - acts on AW, best on Equi, likes left handed tracks, favours tight tracks, does well at Lingfield. AW high 89 - 6th of 13 giving 9lb to Fayik (14 Mar Wolverhampton 8f Fibr RF 0431) - also 1st of 4 giving 12lb to Tycoon Tina (20 Feb Southwell RF 0325). Consistent. He hit form on the Lingfield Equitrack in December, winning twice over ten furlongs, which looks to be his trip despite his win in a non-event over twelve furlongs at Southwell. He lost nothing in defeat when outpointed by the useful sand performer Steamroller Stanly at Lingfield in February, but patently found a mile too sharp at Wolverhampton in March.
**K R Burke [4-17] Nigel Shields (from M C Pipe [1-9] Jun 1997).*

WHITE SETTLER BHB 66f57a **RR 68f 57a** 4201[1]

5 b g Polish Patriot (USA) 7.8f **(70)** - Oasis (Valiyar) 8.5f **(73)**
Form - 10230021
Record 1998 - 1st:2 2nd:2 3rd:1 Ran:8
Pre1998 - 1st:1 2nd:1 3rd:4 Ran:19
Win Prizemoney £8,648 *Total Prizemoney* £13,703
Wins * 1998 Spt Chepst (G-S) S 8.1f 56+
1998 Apr Leices (SFT) S 7f 63
1996 Jly Chepst (G-F) H 7.1f 64 67 <
1998 Turf 2-7: (6f, 7f 1-3, 8f 1-3) (sft 1-2, g-s, gd 1-1, g-f, frm 2) 1998 AW 0-1: (7f) (Fibr)
Average gelding, effective 6 to 8f, best at 7f, acts on sft to frm, best on frm, has worn blinkers, excels at Chepstow, likes Salisbury. Turf high 68 - 2nd of 13 to Salty Behaviour (13 Aug Chepstow 7f frm RF 3609) - also 1st of 14 from Birchwood Sun (9 Apr Leicester RF 0616).
**Miss S J Wilton [1-7] John Pointon and Sons (from R J Hodges [2-17] Apr 1998).*

WHITE VALLEY (IRE) RR 47f 1283[8]

3 b br f Tirol 8.1f **(64)** - Royal Wolff (Prince Tenderfoot (USA)) 9f **(61)**
Form - 8
Record 1998 - 1st:0 2nd:0 3rd:0 Ran:1
1998 Turf 0-1: (7f) (g-f)
Currently moderate filly. **S Dow [0-1] I P Blance.*

WHITEWATER BOY RR 79f 4999[2]

2 b g Emarati (USA) 6.6f **(63)** - Chacewater (Electric) 10.1f **(61)**
Form - 2
Record 1998 - 1st:0 2nd:1 3rd:0 Ran:1
Win Prizemoney £0 *Total Prizemoney* £1,040
1998 Turf 0-1: (7f) (sft)
Currently above-average gelding. (1st run) - 2nd of 9 to Highest Peak (26 Oct Lingfield 7f sft RF 4999).
**B J Meehan [0-1] Lime Street Racing Syndicate.*

WHITLEY GRANGE BOY BHB 55f65a **RR 56f 65a** 4627[19]
5 b g Hubbly Bubbly (USA) 9.5f **(43)** - Choir (High Top) 10.2f **(67)**
Form - 133156470
Record 1998 - 1st:1 2nd:0 3rd:0 Ran:6
Pre1998 - 1st:2 2nd:0 3rd:3 Ran:18
Win Prizemoney £8,086 *Total Prizemoney* £9,382
Wins * **1998** *Jan Southw (STD) H 16f 61 64 <*
* 1997 *Nov Southw (STD) H 14f 56 60*
* 1997 Oct Catter (SFT) H 12f 46 55
1998 Turf 0-4: (13f, 14f, 16f, 18f) (g-s, gd, g-f, frm) 1998 AW 1-2: (16f 1-2) (Fibr 1-2)
Average gelding, effective 12 to 16f, best at 16f, acts on g-s - acts on Fibr, likes left handed tracks, prefers tight tracks, excels at Southwell. Turf high 56. AW high 64 (1st run) - 1st of 11 giving 1lb to Mondragon (9 Jan Southwell RF 0054). He is a talented and consistent stayer on the Fibresand. **J L Eyre [3-24] Mrs Carole Sykes.*

WHITS END RR 4650[9]
2 b g Whittingham (IRE) - Mybella Ann (Anfield) 8.5f **(59)**
Form - 0
Record 1998 - 1st:0 2nd:0 3rd:0 Ran:1
1998 Turf 0-1: (6f) (g-f)
Very poor gelding. (DEAD) **W G M Turner [0-1] Paul De Weck.*

WHO DEALT BHB 23f19a **RR 25tf 19a** 1765[8]
4 ch f Nalchik (USA) 12.6f **(44)** - Lana's Secret (Most Secret) 7.1f **(58)**
Form - 54067008
Record 1998 - 1st:0 2nd:0 3rd:0 Ran:8
Pre1998 - 1st:0 2nd:0 3rd:0 Ran:5
1998 Turf 0-2: (10f 2) (frm 2) 1998 AW 0-6: (8f, 11f, 12f 4) (Fibr 6)
Rangy, very moderate filly, effective 11f, - acts on Fibr. Turf high 39. AW high 33 (1st run) - 5th of 10 getting 3lb from Cruz Santa (5 Jan Southwell 11f Fibr RF 0024).
**R Hollinshead [0-13] Brian Rogerson.*

WHO GOES THERE RR 42f 3760[11]
2 ch f Wolfhound (USA) 7.3f **(71)** - Challanging (Mill Reef (USA)) 10.5f **(78)**
Form - 080
Record 1998 - 1st:0 2nd:0 3rd:0 Ran:3
1998 Turf 0-3: (6f 2, 7f) (g-f 2, frm)
Currently moderate filly. Turf high 42 (began Jly).
**T M Jones [0-3] The Rest Hill Partnership.*

WHOOPS RR 61f 4812[6]
2 b f Shernazar 11.8f **(71)** - Ten to Six (Night Shift (USA)) 7.2f **(69)**
Form - 06
Record 1998 - 1st:0 2nd:0 3rd:0 Ran:2
1998 Turf 0-2: (7f 2) (gd, frm)
Currently average filly. Turf high 61 (began Spt).
**E Weymes [0-2] E G Moorey.*

WHO'S MILETRIAN (IRE) BHB 52f **RR 51f** 4264[14]
2 br c Up and At 'em - Crimson Crest (Pampapaul) 10.9f **(63)**
Form - 350
Record 1998 - 1st:0 2nd:0 3rd:1 Ran:3
Win Prizemoney £0 *Total Prizemoney* £515
1998 Turf 0-3: (5f 2, 6f) (g-s, gd 2)
Currently fair colt. Turf high 51. **M R Channon [0-3] Miletrian Plc.*

WHO'S NOBLE RR 15f 2516[15]
2 b g Noble Patriarch 12.2f **(43)** - Who's That Lady (Nordance (USA)) 7.5f **(52)**
Form - 0
Record 1998 - 1st:0 2nd:0 3rd:0 Ran:1
1998 Turf 0-1: (7f) (g-f)
Currently poor gelding. **T D Easterby [0-1] M H Easterby.*

WHO'S THAT MAN BHB 49f40a **RR 37f 40a** 575[7]
4 gr g Mystiko (USA) 7.7f **(59)** - Milne's Way (The Noble Player (USA)) 6.5f **(67)**
Form - 06707
Record 1998 - 1st:0 2nd:0 3rd:0 Ran:4
Pre1998 - 1st:2 2nd:0 3rd:1 Ran:14
Win Prizemoney £4,999 *Total Prizemoney* £5,382
Wins 1997 Jly Bright (FRM) H 10f 57 60 <
1997 Jun Redcar (FRM) H 10f 54 53
1998 Turf 0-1: (10f) (gd) 1998 AW 0-3: (8f, 10f, 12f) (Equi, Fibr 2)
Lengthy, moderate gelding, effective 8 to 10f, best at 10f, acts on g-f to frm, best on frm, has worn blinkers, likes tight tracks. AW high 46. **J L Eyre [0-1] J E Wilson (from S C Williams [2-17] Mar 1998).*

WHY WORRY NOW (IRE) RR 68f 4991[2]
2 ch f College Chapel - Pretext (Polish Precedent (USA)) 10.2f **(60)**
Form - 00862
Record 1998 - 1st:0 2nd:1 3rd:0 Ran:5
Win Prizemoney £0 *Total Prizemoney* £2,320
1998 Turf 0-5: (5f, 6f 2, 7f 2) (sft 2, g-f, frm 2)
Average filly. Turf high 68 - 2nd of 10 giving 9lb to Rex Is Okay (26 Oct Leicester 7f sft RF 4991). **R Hannon [0-5] N Hayes.*

WICHITA RR 2686[7]
3 ch f Gabitat 8.5f **(44)** - Gabibti (IRE) (Dara Monarch) 8.8f **(59)**
Form - 7
Record 1998 - 1st:0 2nd:0 3rd:0 Ran:1
1998 AW 0-1: (5f) (Equi)
Neat, currently poor filly. **B Gubby [0-1] Brian Gubby Ltd.*

WICKHAM RR 13f 4668[17]
2 b f Thowra (FR) 11.2f **(47)** - Lizzy Cantle (Homing) 7.8f **(59)**
Form - 0
Record 1998 - 1st:0 2nd:0 3rd:0 Ran:1
1998 Turf 0-1: (6f) (gd)
Currently poor filly. **R Simpson [0-1] Brian Cantle.*

WIGGING BHB 88f **RR 94f** 4461[8]
3 b f Warning 8.1f **(77)** - Pushy (Sharpen Up) 8.3f **(67)**
Form - 22158
Record 1998 - 1st:1 2nd:2 3rd:0 Ran:5
Pre1998 - 1st:0 2nd:0 3rd:1 Ran:2
Win Prizemoney £4,003 *Total Prizemoney* £6,873
Wins * **1998** Aug Thirsk (GD) 7f 54+ <
1998 Turf 1-5: (7f 1-5) (gd 2, g-f 1-1, frm 2)
Workmanlike, useful filly, effective 7f, acts on gd. Turf high 94 - 5th of 14 getting 3lb from Ashraakat (10 Spt Doncaster 7f gd RF 4208). A half-sister to Bluebook and Myself, she secured her stud value with a maiden win and ran well in a listed race next time.
**N A Graham [1-7] Bloomsbury Stud.*

WILCUMA BHB 90f **RR 91f** 2738[16]
7 b g Most Welcome 8.6f **(66)** -Miss Top Ville (FR) (Top Ville) 11.7f **(68)**
Form - 050
Record 1998 - 1st:0 2nd:0 3rd:0 Ran:3
Pre1998 - 1st:7 2nd:2 3rd:5 Ran:34
Win Prizemoney £102,964 *Total Prizemoney* £119,656
Wins * 1996 Dec Evry (HLD) L 10f 109 <
* 1996 Oct Newbur (SFT) H 9f 100 107
* 1996 Jly York (GD) H 10.4f 89 97
* 1995 Spt Haydoc (GD) H 8.1f 80 86
* 1994 Spt Sandow (G-S) H 8.1f 78 80
* 1994 Spt Kempto (GD) H 8f 75 79
* 1994 Aug Leices (G-F) H 8f 71 70
1998 Turf 0-3: (8f, 10f 2) (gd, g-f, frm)
Useful gelding, effective 10f, acts on frm, has worn blinkers (very effectively), likes right handed tracks. Turf high 91. Inconsistent. The 1996 Magnet Cup winner, he has been out of form for some time, but showed definite signs of a revival at Sandown in July. Never got into it in this year's John Smith's Cup, however, and that was that for the season. *P J Makin [7-37] T G Warner.*

WILD BROOK (IRE) RR 5060[12]
8 b g Mandalus - My Lily (Levanter)
Form - 0
Record 1998 - 1st:0 2nd:0 3rd:0 Ran:1
1998 Turf 0-1: (8f) (sft)
Formerly very poor gelding. **B Ellison [1-15] Fred Hayne.*

WILD CANARY BHB 60f60a **RR 65f 60a** 5081[4]
3 ch f Groom Dancer (USA) 9.5f **(75)** - Nest (Sharpo) 7.7f **(59)**
Form - 8150404
Record 1998 - 1st:1 2nd:0 3rd:0 Ran:6
Pre1998 - 1st:0 2nd:0 3rd:0 Ran:1

Win Prizemoney £2,085 *Total Prizemoney* £2,310
Wins **1998** *Feb Southw (STD) 11f 67* <
1998 Turf 0-4: (10f 2, 11f, 13f) (gd, g-f 2, frm) 1998 AW 1-2: (11f 1-1, 12f) (Fibr 1-2)
Lengthy, average filly, effective 11f, acts on g-f - acts on Fibr, mostly wears blinkers (extremely effectively). Turf high 65. AW high 67 (1st run) - 1st of 6 getting 5lb from Miracle Island (6 Feb Southwell RF 0236).
**D Marks [0-2] C R Buttery (from Lord Huntingdon [1-5] Jun 1998).*

WILD CITY (USA) BHB 23f23a **RR 39f 23a** 4113[10]
4 b br g Wild Again (USA) 10.7f **(69)** - Garvin's Gal (USA) (Seattle Slew (USA)) 9.4f **(76)**
Form - 0000800000
Record 1998 - 1st:0 2nd:0 3rd:0 Ran:10
Pre1998 - 1st:0 2nd:0 3rd:0 Ran:2
1998 Turf 0-4: (6f 2, 8f, 10f) (g-f, frm 2, hrd) 1998 AW 0-6: (5f, 6f, 7f 2, 8f, 11f) (Fibr 6)
Strong, very moderate gelding, has worn blinkers. Turf high 39 (began Jly). AW high 25.
**R F Marvin [0-10] P J Cronin (from B Hanbury [0-2] Apr 1997).*

WILD COLONIAL BOY (IRE) BHB 54f **RR 63f** 4817[4]
3 b c Warning 8.1f **(77)** - Loch Clair (IRE) (Lomond (USA)) 8.8f **(65)**
Form - 870536023238544
Record 1998 - 1st:0 2nd:2 3rd:3 Ran:15
Win Prizemoney £0 *Total Prizemoney* £3,717
1998 Turf 0-15:(7f 2, 8f 3, 10f 3, 12f 2, 13f, 14f, 16f 3)(gd 6, g-f 3, frm 6)
Scopey, average colt, effective 7 to 12f, best at 12f, acts on gd to frm, best on frm, has worn blinkers, likes left handed tracks, prefers tight tracks. Turf high 63. Consistent. He has a long name but appears not to be long on talent.
**R Hannon [0-15] G Howard-Spink.*

WILD EAGLE BHB 85a **RR 69f 85a** 179[1]
3 ch c Lion Cavern (USA) 7.5f **(74)** - Krameria (Kris) 9.5f **(73)**
Form - 21
Record 1998 - 1st:1 2nd:1 3rd:0 Ran:2
Pre1998 - 1st:0 2nd:0 3rd:0 Ran:1
Win Prizemoney £3,387 *Total Prizemoney* £4,432
Wins * **1998** *Jan Lingfi (STD) 8f 77+* <
1998 AW 1-2: (7f, 8f 1-1) (Equi 1-2)
Currently above-average colt. AW high 77 - 1st of 6 getting 20lb from Castle Ashby Jack (29 Jan Lingfield RF 0179). He finished runner-up on his first outing on the Lingfield Equitrack in January, but made no mistake when beating a poor field at the same track next time when long odds-on. He did not reappear afterwards.
**J Noseda [1-2] Mrs J M Ryan (from J S Bolger in IRE [0-1] Oct 1997).*

WILDER JAGER (GER) **RR 106f** 4470h[3]
5 b h Mulberry (FR) - Wild Bidder (USA) (Bold Bidder) 8.8f **(67)**
Form - 3
1998 Turf 0-1: (10f) (gd)
Currently Pattern-class colt. (1st run) - 3rd of 9 to Oxalagu (20 Spt Frankfurt 10f gd RF 4470h). He stayed on well over a mile and a quarter at Frankfurt in September and will go further.
**P Rau in GER [0-1].*

WILDFIRE (SWI) BHB 41f47a **RR 34f 47a** 54[7]
7 br g Beldale Flutter (USA) 10.2f **(62)** - Little White Star (Mill Reef (USA)) 10.5f **(78)**
Form - 467
Record 1998 - 1st:0 2nd:0 3rd:0 Ran:1
Pre1998 - 1st:3 2nd:2 3rd:5 Ran:34
Win Prizemoney £9,218 *Total Prizemoney* £13,426
Wins 1997 *Feb Southw (STD)* H *11f 42 50*
1995 *Dec Southw (STD)* H *11f 42 48*
1994 May Chepst (SFT) H 12.1f 64 55 <
1998 AW 0-1: (16f) (Fibr)
Moderate gelding, effective 9 to 12f, best at 9f, - acts on Fibr, favours left handed tracks. Consistent. Has been campaigned mainly on the All-Weather in recent seasons, but had only a limited campaign in '98. Not the most reliable of characters.
**J Akehurst [0-3] Canisbay Bloodstock Ltd (from R Akehurst [3-32] Spt 1997).*

WILD HADEER BHB 28a **RR 38f 28a** 394[9]
4 ch g Hadeer 8.9f **(58)** - Wild Moon (USA) (Arctic Tern (USA)) 8.9f **(69)**
Form - 06440
Record 1998 - 1st:0 2nd:0 3rd:0 Ran:5
Pre1998 - 1st:0 2nd:0 3rd:0 Ran:2
1998 AW 0-5: (7f, 12f 2, 13f, 16f) (Equi 3, Fibr 2)
Workmanlike, very moderate gelding. AW high 30.
**John Upson [0-5] The Fourways Partnership (from W J Haggas [0-2] Oct 1996).*

WILD HEAVEN (IRE) **RR 93f** 5026a[1]
2 bb f Darshaan 11.9f **(81)** - Mild Intrigue (USA) (Sir Ivor) 10.2f **(70)**
Form - 6611
1998 Turf 2-4: (7f, 8f 1-2, 9f 1-1) (hvy 1-1, g-s 1-1, gd, frm)
Useful filly. Turf high 93 (began Aug) - 1st of 8 giving 12lb to Kasota (24 Oct Leopardstown RF 5026a).
**C O'Brien in IRE [2-4] Dr Anne Heffernan.*

WILD LILLY BHB 37f30a **RR 21f 30a** 5121[F]
3 b f Elmaamul (USA) 8.1f **(70)** - Chrisanthy (So Blessed) 8.7f **(67)**
Form - 0000F
Record 1998 - 1st:0 2nd:0 3rd:0 Ran:5
Pre1998 - 1st:0 2nd:0 3rd:0 Ran:5
1998 Turf 0-5: (6f 2, 7f 3) (g-s 4, gd)
Light-framed, little account filly, has worn blinkers. Turf high 35. Inconsistent. **M J Ryan [0-10] Mrs A M Byrne.*

WILD NETTLE BHB 30f34a **RR 44f 34a** 5127[8]
4 ch f Beveled (USA) 6.9f **(64)** - Pink Pumpkin (Tickled Pink) 6.5f **(59)**
Form - 202303408486488
Record 1998 - 1st:0 2nd:1 3rd:2 Ran:13
Pre1998 - 1st:0 2nd:1 3rd:0 Ran:14
Win Prizemoney £0 *Total Prizemoney* £2,113
1998 Turf 0-8: (6f, 7f, 8f 6) (sft, g-s, gd 2, g-f 3, frm) 1998 AW 0-5: (6f 5) (Equi 5)
Workmanlike, moderate filly. Turf high 50. AW high 32.
**J C Fox [0-27] Mrs J A Cleary.*

WILD PALM BHB 58f58a **RR 60df 58a** 2392[12]
6 b g Darshaan 11.9f **(81)** - Tarasova (USA) (Green Forest (USA)) 9.9f **(68)**
Form - 6400
Record 1998 - 1st:0 2nd:0 3rd:0 Ran:4
Pre1998 - 1st:3 2nd:1 3rd:2 Ran:28
Win Prizemoney £11,493 *Total Prizemoney* £16,051
Wins 1996 Jly Yarmou (FRM) H 8f 64 68
1996 Jun Newmar (G-F) H 7f 64 72 <
1995 Spt Nottin (G-S) 8.2f 64
1998 Turf 0-4: (8f 2, 10f 2) (gd, g-f 2, frm)
Average gelding, effective 8 to 10f, acts on gd to frm, often wears blinkers (very effectively). Turf high 62 (1st run) - 6th of 24 getting 1lb from Carlys Quest (1 May Newmarket 10f gd RF 0962).
**Mrs A E Johnson [0-4] S Fustok (from W A O'Gorman [3-28] Spt 1997).*

WILD RICE BHB 83f80a **RR 92df 80a** 447[7]
6 b g Green Desert (USA) 7.8f **(78)** -On Show (Welsh Pageant) 10f **(65)**
Form - 7
Record 1998 - 1st:0 2nd:0 3rd:0 Ran:1
Pre1998 - 1st:4 2nd:0 3rd:2 Ran:14
Win Prizemoney £21,000 *Total Prizemoney* £23,370
Wins 1995 Aug Cheste (G-F) H 7f 87 87 <
1995 Aug Kempto (G-F) H 7f 79 85+
1995 *Feb Lingfi (STD) 10f 76+*
1995 *Feb Lingfi (STD) 7f 57++*
1998 AW 0-1: (10f) (Equi)
Useful gelding, has worn blinkers. Inconsistent.
**P Winkworth [0-1] N A Dunger (from G Wragg [4-14] Jun 1997).*

WILD RITA BHB 74f **RR 78f** 3930[11]
6 ch m Risk Me (FR) 8f **(53)** - Ma Pierrette (Cawston's Clown) 8f **(60)**
Form - 050
Record 1998 - 1st:0 2nd:0 3rd:0 Ran:3
Pre1998 - 1st:3 2nd:5 3rd:4 Ran:21
Win Prizemoney £12,681 *Total Prizemoney* £24,590
Wins * 1997 Jly Leices (GD) H 11.8f 79 83 <
* 1996 Aug Windso (G-F) H 11.6f 71 70

* 1995	Spt	Bright	(GD)	11.9f	69+

1998 Turf 0-3: (13f, 14f, 15f) (gd, g-f, frm)
Above-average mare, effective 12 to 15f, best at 12f, acts on gd to frm. Turf high 78 (1st run) (began Jly) - 9th of 15 getting 1lb from Seignorial (28 Jly Goodwood 14f gd RF 3163). Consistent.
**W R Muir [3-26] Perspicacious Punters Racing Club.*

WILD RUSH (USA) RR 5164a[14]
4 b c Wild Again (USA) 10.7f **(69)** - Rose Park (USA) (Plugged Nickle (USA))
Form - 0
1998 AW 0-1: (6f) (Dirt)
Currently Pattern-class colt, always wears blinkers.
**P Byrne in USA [0-1] Stronach Stables.*

WILD SKY (IRE) BHB 81f RR 84f 4848[3]
4 br g Warning 8.1f **(77)** - Erwinna (USA) (Lyphard (USA)) 9.9f **(72)**
Form - 202286053
Record 1998 - 1st:0 2nd:3 3rd:1 Ran:9
Pre1998 - 1st:1 2nd:2 3rd:2 Ran:11
Win Prizemoney £5,361 *Total Prizemoney* £26,094
Wins * 1997 Nov Newmar (G-F) H 7f 72 76 <
1998 Turf 0-9: (8f 8, 9f) (gd 2, g-f 5, frm 2)
Scopey, decent gelding, effective 7 to 9f, best at 8f, acts on gd to frm, has worn blinkers, excels at Newmarket. Turf high 84 - 2nd of 20 giving 8lb to Mount Holly (7 Jly Newmarket 8f frm RF 2579). Very consistent, he has produced some decent efforts in the last two seasons but has found it hard to win, apart from scoring at Newmarket at the end of 1997. He has made the frame in some very competitive handicaps and deserves a decent prize. Suited by a strong pace and a straight track.
**M J Heaton-Ellis [1-20] The Gold Partnership.*

WILD THING RR 13f 4382[21]
2 b c Never so Bold 7.1f **(62)** -Tame Duchess(Saritamer(USA))9.5f **(63)**
Form - 0
Record 1998 - 1st:0 2nd:0 3rd:0 Ran:1
1998 Turf 0-1: (6f) (g-f)
Currently poor colt. *R Hannon [0-1] B T Stewart-Brown.*

WILD TIMES RR 22f 2716[9]
2 b c Emarati (USA) 6.6f **(63)** - Pink Pumpkin (Tickled Pink) 6.5f **(59)**
Form - 000
Record 1998 - 1st:0 2nd:0 3rd:0 Ran:3
1998 Turf 0-3: (5f, 6f, 7f) (gd, g-f, frm)
Currently little account colt. Turf high 22.
**E A Wheeler [0-3] Mrs J A Cleary.*

WILD WILLIE-D (IRE) RR 3451[4]
3 b g Balla Cove - Fine Print (IRE) (Taufan (USA)) 7f **(57)**
Form - 4
Record 1998 - 1st:0 2nd:0 3rd:0 Ran:1
1998 AW 0-1: (9f) (Fibr)
Workmanlike, currently fair gelding.
**T T Clement [0-1] Sackville House Racing.*

WILLA WOOSTER BHB 45f RR 51f 1938[14]
3 b f Sure Blade (USA) 10.6f **(66)** - Bertrade (Homeboy) 6.6f **(55)**
Form - 000
Record 1998 - 1st:0 2nd:0 3rd:0 Ran:3
Pre1998 - 1st:0 2nd:0 3rd:0 Ran:1
1998 Turf 0-3: (8f 2, 11f) (gd, g-f, frm)
Workmanlike, fair filly. Turf high 51.
**P G Murphy [0-4] Miss Amanda Rawding.*

WILLIAMSHAKESPEARE (IRE) RR 73+f 5065[6]
2 b c Slip Anchor 12.7f **(75)** - Rostova (Blakeney) 10.5f **(64)**
Form - 6
Record 1998 - 1st:0 2nd:0 3rd:0 Ran:1
Win Prizemoney £0 *Total Prizemoney* £77
1998 Turf 0-1: (8f) (g-f)
Currently above-average colt. **B W Hills [0-1] W J Gredley.*

WILLIAM'S WELL BHB 52f50a RR 55f 50a 4469[3]
4 ch g Superpower 6.6f **(58)** - Catherines Well (Junius (USA)) 7.7f **(65)**
Form - 45337450423
Record 1998 - 1st:0 2nd:1 3rd:3 Ran:11
Pre1998 - 1st:2 2nd:3 3rd:3 Ran:26
Win Prizemoney £5,783 *Total Prizemoney* £13,089
Wins * 1997 Jun Mussel (GD) H 5f 51 53 <
* 1997 Jun Catter (GD) H 5f 43 44
1998 Turf 0-10: (5f 9, 6f) (gd 2, g-f 3, frm 5) 1998 AW 0-1: (5f) (Fibr)
Scopey, fair gelding, effective 5 to 6f, best at 5f, acts on sft to hrd, mostly wears blinkers (extremely effectively), likes Catterick and Thirsk. Turf high 56 - 5th of 18 getting 15lb from Mungo Park (9 May Beverley 5f frm RF 1119). Consistent.
**M W Easterby [2-37] K Hodgson & Mrs J Hodgson.*

WILLIE CONQUER BHB 80f RR 80f 3106[9]
6 ch g Master Willie 9.2f **(67)** - Maryland Cookie (USA) (Bold Hour) 10f **(81)**
Form - 0030
Record 1998 - 1st:0 2nd:0 3rd:1 Ran:4
Pre1998 - 1st:3 2nd:2 3rd:2 Ran:19
Win Prizemoney £18,530 *Total Prizemoney* £31,643
Wins 1996 Oct Newmar (G-F) H 12f 84 92 <
1996 Spt Goodwo (G-F) 12f 82
1996 Aug Newbur (GD) 12f 80
1998 Turf 0-4: (12f 4) (gd 2, g-f 2)
Decent gelding, effective 12 to 14f, best at 12f, acts on g-f to frm, best on g-f, likes right handed tracks. Turf high 80. Inconsistent. Out of sorts in '98 and is not easy to place.
**Miss Gay Kelleway [0-4] Raymond Tooth (from R Akehurst [3-17] Nov 1997).*

WILLOW DALE (IRE) BHB 84f RR 83f 3656[7]
5 b m Danehill (USA) 9.1f **(79)** - Miss Willow Bend (USA) (Willow Hour (USA)) 5.6f **(71)**
Form - 38837
Record 1998 - 1st:0 2nd:0 3rd:2 Ran:5
Pre1998 - 1st:5 2nd:4 3rd:4 Ran:32
Win Prizemoney £22,071 *Total Prizemoney* £31,177
Wins * 1997 Aug Newbur (G-F) H 5.2f 77 81
* 1997 Jun Windso (SFT) H 6f 68 74
* 1995 Spt Newbur (G-S) H 5.2f 79 84 <
* 1995 Spt Kempto (G-F) H 6f 74 78
* 1995 Jun Salisb (FRM) 5f 74
1998 Turf 0-5: (5f 4, 6f) (gd 2, g-f, frm 2)
Decent filly, effective 5 to 6f, best at 5f, acts on gd to frm, best on g-f, has worn blinkers. Turf high 83 - 3rd of 9 giving 30lb to Apple Sauce (4 Aug Bath 5f g-f RF 3323). A useful sprint handicapper on her day, she ran a blinder on her Salisbury reappearance in June considering she had been off the track for ten months, but did not really do any better in her subsequent starts.
**D R C Elsworth [5-37] Michael Jackson Bloodstock Ltd.*

WILL TO WIN BHB 38f44a RR 43f 44a 4401[16]
4 b f Mazilier (USA) 8.5f **(56)** - Adana (FR) (Green Dancer (USA)) 10.3f **(74)**
Form - 000764006600
Record 1998 - 1st:0 2nd:0 3rd:0 Ran:12
Pre1998 - 1st:2 2nd:3 3rd:6 Ran:28
Win Prizemoney £6,664 *Total Prizemoney* £12,212
Wins * 1997 *Mar Wolver (STD) S 6f 58* <
* 1997 *Feb Wolver (STD) S 5f 54*
1998 Turf 0-10: (5f 3, 6f 6, 7f) (g-s 2, gd, g-f 2, frm 5) 1998 AW 0-2: (7f 2) (Fibr 2)
Light-framed, moderate filly, effective 5 to 6f, best at 5f, acts on gd to g-f - acts on Fibr, has worn blinkers, does well at Windsor, likes Wolverhampton. Turf high 43. AW high 30.
**P G Murphy [2-40] Mrs Pat Wyatt.*

WILLY WILLY RR 85f 4893[10]
5 ch g Master Willie 9.2f **(67)** - Monsoon (Royal Palace) 9f **(56)**
Form - 15740
Record 1998 - 1st:1 2nd:0 3rd:0 Ran:5
Win Prizemoney £3,915 *Total Prizemoney* £4,577
Wins * **1998** Jly Lingfi (G-F) 9f 85 <
1998 Turf 1-5: (9f 1-1, 10f 3, 12f) (gd, g-f 2, frm 1-2)
Useful gelding. Turf high 85 (1st run) (began Jly) - 1st of 6 giving 10lb to Banker Dwerry (11 Jly Lingfield RF 2715). He won a bad Lingfield maiden on his debut, but was well beaten in a hot classified stakes at Newbury next time. Little promise in handicaps.
**H Candy [1-5] Mrs George Tricks.*

WILTON BHB 70f74a **RR 71f 74a** 5120[2]
3 ch c Sharpo 7.5f **(68)** - Poyle Amber (Sharrood (USA)) 10.5f **(72)**
Form - 180024315162
Record **1998** - 1st:2 2nd:2 3rd:1 Ran:11
Pre1998 - 1st:1 2nd:0 3rd:0 Ran:3
Win Prizemoney £14,976 *Total Prizemoney* £17,858
Wins * **1998** Oct Redcar (HVY) H 8f 62 70 <
* **1998** Oct Pontef (G-S) H 8f 52 60
* 1997 *Nov Southw (STD) 6f 68*
1998 Turf 2-10: (5f, 6f 2, 7f 2, 8f 2-5) (sft 1-3, g-s, gd 1-4, g-f, frm) 1998 AW 0-1: (7f) (Fibr)
Unfurnished, above-average colt, effective 6 to 8f, best at 8f, acts on sft to gd - acts on Fibr, prefers tight tracks. Turf high 71 - 2nd of 12 giving 14lb to Holy Smoke (4 Nov Musselburgh 8f gd RF 5120) - also 1st of 8 getting 4lb from Band on the Run (17 Oct Redcar RF 4859). (1st run) - 2nd of 12 getting 13lb from Diamond Drill (5 Spt Wolverhampton 7f Fibr RF 4118). He did not show his best form until the autumn, including winning handicaps at Pontefract and Redcar. A mile on soft ground look to be his ideal conditions. **J Hetherton [3-14] George Moore.*

WINCE BHB 100f **RR 98+f** 4853[7]
2 b f Selkirk (USA) 7.9f **(76)** - Flit (USA) (Lyphard (USA)) 9.9f **(72)**
Form - 312157
Record **1998** - 1st:2 2nd:1 3rd:1 Ran:6
Win Prizemoney £10,614 *Total Prizemoney* £14,179
Wins * **1998** Aug Cheste (GD) 6.1f 92 <
* **1998** Jly Kempto (G-S) 7f 75+
1998 Turf 2-6: (5f, 6f 1-1, 7f 1-4) (gd 2-3, g-f, frm 2)
Very useful filly, effective 6 to 7f, best at 7f, acts on gd to frm. Turf high 98 - 5th of 10 to Smittenby (3 Oct Newmarket 7f g-f RF 4628) - also 1st of 6 from Dipple (21 Aug Chester RF 3788). This filly progressed steadily with experience, but her limitations appeared to be exposed in Pattern company at the end of the term.
**H R A Cecil [2-6] K Abdulla.*

WINDANCE RR 56[9]
3 br f Nomination 7.3f **(57)** - Northern Swinger (Northern State (USA))
Form - 0
Record **1998** - 1st:0 2nd:0 3rd:0 Ran:1
1998 AW 0-1: (7f) (Fibr)
Leggy, currently very poor filly. **N P Littmoden [0-1] Philip Harvey.*

WINDBORN BHB 35f41a **RR 36f 41a** 2477[P]
4 b f Superpower 6.6f **(58)** - Chablisse (Radetzky) 9.8f **(56)**
Form - 6P
Record **1998** - 1st:0 2nd:0 3rd:0 Ran:2
Pre1998 - 1st:0 2nd:3 3rd:8 Ran:23
Win Prizemoney £0 *Total Prizemoney* £4,701
1998 Turf 0-2: (8f 2) (gd, hrd)
Unfurnished, moderate filly, effective 7f, - acts on Equi, has worn blinkers, likes left handed tracks, likes tight tracks. Turf high 33. Inconsistent.
**C N Allen [0-16] C N Allen (from K McAuliffe [0-9] Spt 1996).*

WIND CHEETAH (USA) BHB 104f **RR 107f** 680[7]
4 b br c Storm Cat (USA) 7f **(86)** - Won't She Tell (USA) (Banner Sport (USA)) 8.6f **(93)**
Form - 7
Record **1998** - 1st:0 2nd:0 3rd:0 Ran:1
Pre1998 - 1st:1 2nd:0 3rd:1 Ran:6
Win Prizemoney £3,570 *Total Prizemoney* £7,960
Wins * 1996 Oct Lingfi (GD) 6f 88+ <
1998 Turf 0-1: (6f) (gd)
Pattern-class colt. **Sir Michael Stoute [1-7] Cheveley Park Stud.*

WIND IN WINNIPEG (IRE) BHB 68f **RR 72f** 4820[12]
2 b f Midhish - Tara View (IRE) (Wassl) 9.7f **(62)**
Form - 85430221720
Record **1998** - 1st:1 2nd:3 3rd:1 Ran:11
Win Prizemoney £3,452 *Total Prizemoney* £8,330
Wins * **1998** Spt Hamilt (SFT) H 5f 58 66 <
1998 Turf 1-11: (5f 1-7, 6f 4) (sft, g-s, gd 1-4, frm 5)
Above-average filly, effective 5 to 6f, best at 5f, acts on g-s to frm. Turf high 72 - 2nd of 13 to Red Amazon (28 Spt Hamilton 6f g-s RF 4533) - also 1st of 7 getting 4lb from Ladycake (7 Spt Hamilton RF 4129). **J S Wainwright [1-11] Rosaly Racing.*

WIND OF CHANCE (GER) RR 90f 3918a[3]
5
Form - 3
1998 Turf 0-1: (9f) (gd)
Useful. **M Weiss in SWI [0-1] (from B Schutz in GER [0-3] Spt 1996).*

WINDRUSH BOY BHB 43f39a **RR 52f 39a** 4004[3]
8 br g Dowsing (USA) 7f **(61)** -Bridge Street Lady (Decoy Boy) 6.7f **(56)**
Form - 816804063
Record **1998** - 1st:1 2nd:0 3rd:1 Ran:9
Pre1998 - 1st:3 2nd:5 3rd:2 Ran:48
Win Prizemoney £12,716 *Total Prizemoney* £18,353
Wins * **1998** Jun Lingfi (GD) H 5f 38 41
1996 Aug Warwic (GD) C 5f 57 <
1995 Aug Leices (G-F) H 5f 62 54
1994 Aug Windso (G-F) H 5f 56 53
1998 Turf 1-9: (5f 1-9) (g-f 2, frm 1-6, hrd)
Fair gelding, effective 5f, acts on g-f to frm, likes left handed tracks. Turf high 52 - 3rd of 14 getting 3lb from Broadway Melody (31 Aug Warwick 5f frm RF 4004).
**M R Bosley [1-17] Miss Cynthia Commons (from J R Bosley [3-33] Jan 1997).*

WINDSHIFT (IRE) BHB 51f **RR 53f** 4984[10]
2 b g Forest Wind (USA)-Beautyofthepeace (IRE)(Exactly Sharp (USA))
Form - 470
Record **1998** - 1st:0 2nd:0 3rd:0 Ran:3
Win Prizemoney £0 *Total Prizemoney* £263
1998 Turf 0-3: (7f, 10f 2) (g-s, gd 2)
Currently fair gelding. Turf high 53 (began Oct).
**D Shaw [0-3] G E Griffiths.*

WINDSOR CASTLE BHB 113f **RR 116f** 2345[11]
4 b c Generous (IRE) 11.5f **(82)** - One Way Street (Habitat) 9.4f **(70)**
Form - 4300
Record **1998** - 1st:0 2nd:0 3rd:1 Ran:4
Pre1998 - 1st:4 2nd:1 3rd:1 Ran:8
Win Prizemoney £113,437 *Total Prizemoney* £133,317
Wins * 1997 Jun Newcas (HVY) H 16.1f 96 112 <
* 1997 Jun Ascot (G-F) G3 16.2f 101
* 1996 Oct Leices (G-F) 10f 101
* 1996 Spt Redcar (FRM) 9f 63+
1998 Turf 0-4: (16f 3, 20f) (sft, g-s, gd 2)
Workmanlike, high-class colt, effective 15 to 16f, best at 16f, acts on sft to g-f, best on gd, often wears blinkers (extremely effectively). Turf high 115 (1st run) - 4th of 10 getting 3lb from Persian Punch (1 May Newmarket 16f gd RF 0964). A game and useful stayer in 1997, winner of the Queen's Vase and Northumberland Plate, he struggled in Pattern company last term. He was not seen out after July. **P F I Cole [4-12] H R H Prince Fahd Salman.*

WINDSTORM (IRE) BHB 33f **RR 31f** 4569[10]
2 b f Forest Wind (USA) - Kaya (GER) (Young Generation) 7.7f **(63)**
Form - 00000
Record **1998** - 1st:0 2nd:0 3rd:0 Ran:5
1998 Turf 0-5: (5f 2, 6f 2, 8f) (g-f 3, frm 2)
Very moderate filly. Turf high 31. **H Morrison [0-5] The Forest Club.*

WINDY GULCH (USA) BHB 63f68a **RR 71f 68a** 4883[3]
3 b f Gulch (USA) 9.6f **(79)** - Wyndalia (USA) (Seattle Slew (USA)) 9.4f **(76)**
Form - 536506263
Record **1998** - 1st:0 2nd:1 3rd:2 Ran:9
Win Prizemoney £0 *Total Prizemoney* £2,581
1998 Turf 0-8: (8f 3, 10f 4, 12f) (g-s, gd 2, g-f 3, frm 2) 1998 AW 0-1: (9f) (Fibr)
Scopey, above-average filly, effective 9 to 10f, best at 10f, acts on gd to g-f - acts on Fibr, has worn blinkers. Turf high 71 (1st run) (began Jly) - 5th of 8 to Rajaiyma (1 Jly Kempton 10f gd RF 2443). (1st run) - 2nd of 13 giving 4lb to Sparkling Harry (3 Oct Wolverhampton 9f Fibr RF 4640). Consistent.
**P F I Cole [0-9] Lord Lloyd-Webber.*

WINGED GREYBIRD RR 41f 4990[14]
4 gr f Batshoof 9.5f **(66)** - To Oneiro (Absalom) 7.2f **(58)**
Form - 00
Record **1998** - 1st:0 2nd:0 3rd:0 Ran:2

1998 Turf 0-2: (8f, 10f) (sft, g-f)
Currently moderate filly. Turf high 41 (began Spt).
**Miss A M Newton-Smith [0-2] Miss Patricia Pratt.*

WINGED HUSSAR RR 97f 4688a[12]

5 b g In The Wings 11.2f **(77)** - Akila 00
Form - 61320
1998 Turf 1-4: (12f 1-3, 16f) (hvy, g-s, gd 1-2)
Very useful gelding, effective 12 to 16f, best at 12f, acts on hvy to gd, best on gd, has worn blinkers, prefers right handed tracks. Turf high 97 (1st run) - 1st of 11 getting 2lb from Kayaara (24 May Curragh RF 1514a). A pretty useful Irish staying handicapper, he has shown good form over slightly shorter distances too, including finishing a good third in the Bessborough, if beaten a fair way by the first two. **J Oxx in IRE [2-10] Dundalk Racing Club.*

WING OF A PRAYER BHB 49f37a RR 49f 37a 166[10]

4 b g Statoblest 6.4f **(63)** - Queen Angel (Anfield) 8.5f **(59)**
Form - 6660
Record 1998 - 1st:0 2nd:0 3rd:0 Ran:4
Pre1998 - 1st:0 2nd:0 3rd:1 Ran:6
Win Prizemoney £0 *Total Prizemoney* £821
1998 AW 0-4: (7f, 8f, 10f 2) (Equi 4)
Leggy, moderate gelding. AW high 37. Inconsistent.
**P Mitchell [0-5] Thurloe Thoroughbreds (from W Jarvis [0-6] Jun 1997).*

WINGS AWARDED BHB 62f62a RR 62f 62a 5070[8]

3 b f Shareef Dancer (USA) 10.1f **(67)** - Ruda (FR) (Free Round (USA)) 11.7f **(70)**
Form - 70156521252552238
Record 1998 - 1st:2 2nd:5 3rd:1 Ran:17
Win Prizemoney £5,596 *Total Prizemoney* £10,228
Wins * **1998** Jly Folkes (G-F) H 12f 56 60+ <
* **1998** May Windso (G-F) C 8.3f 60
1998 Turf 2-16: (8f 1-1, 9f 2, 10f 5, 11f 2, 12f 1-6) (g-s 2, gd 6, g-f 1-5, frm 1-3) 1998 AW 0-1: (12f) (Fibr)
Leggy, average filly, effective 8 to 12f, best at 12f, acts on g-s to frm, best on gd, favours tight tracks, excels at Nottingham. Turf high 68 - 2nd of 8 giving 2lb to On Call (14 Jly Brighton 12f gd RF 2781) - also 1st of 18 getting 2lb from Theatre of Dreams (11 May Windsor RF 1158). Consistent. Fast ground and middle distances seem to suit her admirably if her Folkestone victory is anything to go by. **M R Channon [2-17] The Crews Missile Syndicate.*

WINKIE (IRE) BHB 34f RR 41f 3396[13]

4 b f Fools Holme (USA) 10.3f **(64)** -Pas du Tout (Pas de Seul) 9.1f **(67)**
Form - 00500
Record 1998 - 1st:0 2nd:0 3rd:0 Ran:5
1998 Turf 0-5: (6f, 8f 2, 9f, 10f) (gd 2, g-f, frm 2)
Workmanlike, moderate filly. Turf high 41.
**J Akehurst [0-5] Hefin Jones.*

WINLEAH RR 37f 5063[15]

2 gr c Petong 7.6f **(58)** - Tower Glades (Tower Walk) 10f **(62)**
Form - 00
Record 1998 - 1st:0 2nd:0 3rd:0 Ran:2
1998 Turf 0-2: (5f, 6f) (g-s, g-f)
Currently very moderate colt. Turf high 34 (began Oct).
**A G Newcombe [0-2] Advanced Marketing Services Ltd.*

WINNING SAINT (IRE) BHB 64f RR 77df 4987[11]

3 ch g St Jovite (USA) 11.8f **(75)** - Winning Heart (Horage) 10.3f **(61)**
Form - 0240
Record 1998 - 1st:0 2nd:1 3rd:0 Ran:4
Win Prizemoney £0 *Total Prizemoney* £1,308
1998 Turf 0-4: (10f, 12f, 14f 2) (sft, g-f, frm 2)
Workmanlike, above-average gelding. Turf high 77 - 2nd of 4 to Way Out Yonder (11 Jly Lingfield 14f frm RF 2714).
**M H Tompkins [0-4] Michael Keogh.*

WINNING SMILE (FR) RR 109f 943a[3]

8 br h Never so Bold 7.1f **(62)** - Funny Reef (FR) (Mill Reef (USA)) 10.5f **(78)**
Form - 13
1998 Turf 0-1: (6f) (g-s)
Pattern-class horse, has worn blinkers. (1st run) - 3rd of 5 giving 3lb to Spelunar (20 Apr Chantilly 6f g-s RF 0943a). He is genuine, but not up to Group class. **T Clout in FR [2-7] Yoshio Asakawa.*

WINNING TOWN RR 759[5]

5 ch g Jester 8.5f **(43)** - Lurex Girl (Camden Town) 9.3f **(53)**
Form - 5
Record 1998 - 1st:0 2nd:0 3rd:0 Ran:1
1998 AW 0-1: (12f) (Fibr)
Moderate gelding. **Paddy Farrell [0-4] B R G Racers.*

WINNOWER RR 52f 1688[7]

2 b f Robellino (USA) 9.5f **(68)** - Corn Circle (IRE) (Thatching) 8f **(66)**
Form - 07
Record 1998 - 1st:0 2nd:0 3rd:0 Ran:2
1998 Turf 0-2: (6f 2) (g-f, frm)
Currently fair filly. Turf high 52.
**J L Dunlop [0-2] Aylesfield Farms Ltd.*

WINONA (IRE) RR 117+f 4343a[9]

3 b f Alzao (USA) 9.8f **(73)** -My Potters (USA)(Irish River (FR)) 8.6f **(78)**
Form - 4310
1998 Turf 1-4: (8f 2, 12f 1-2) (hvy, gd 1-3)
High-class filly, effective 12f, acts on gd. Turf high 117 - 1st of 9 from Kitza (12 Jly Curragh RF 2805a). She ran a fine race to finish fourth in the Irish 1000 Guineas on her return, and ran right up to that form when third in the Coronation Stakes, on both occasions looking likely to appreciate further. This was proved to be the case when she landed the Irish Oaks by an impressive seven lengths, but unfortunately she did not match that form afterwards, finishing down the field in the Vermeille and in America in the Yellow Ribbon. Johnny Murtagh was the Winona rider.
**J Oxx in IRE [2-8] Lady Clague.*

WINSA (USA) BHB 79f RR 83f 1289[6]

3 b f Riverman (USA) 9.7f **(78)** - Wasnah (USA) (Nijinsky (CAN)) 10.3f **(77)**
Form - 16
Record 1998 - 1st:1 2nd:0 3rd:0 Ran:2
Pre1998 - 1st:0 2nd:1 3rd:2 Ran:4
Win Prizemoney £3,817 *Total Prizemoney* £6,168
Wins * **1998** Apr Folkes (SFT) 12f 55 <
1998 Turf 1-2: (12f 1-2) (sft 1-1, frm)
Lengthy, decent filly, effective 7 to 8f, acts on g-f. Turf high 60. A sister to Bahri and half-sister to Bahhare, she secured her paddock value with a maiden win first time in 1998.
**J L Dunlop [1-6] Hamdan Al Maktoum.*

WINSOME GEORGE BHB 74f RR 83f 4487[7]

3 b g Marju (IRE) 9.2f **(76)** - June Moon (IRE) (Sadler's Wells (USA)) 10f **(76)**
Form - 5611233250767
Record 1998 - 1st:2 2nd:2 3rd:2 Ran:13
Pre1998 - 1st:1 2nd:1 3rd:2 Ran:10
Win Prizemoney £10,819 *Total Prizemoney* £17,529
Wins * **1998** May Redcar (G-F) H 11f 70 82 <
* **1998** May Beverl (GD) H 12f 70 76
* 1997 Jun Ayr (GD) 7f 77
1998 Turf 2-13: (10f, 11f 1-2, 12f 1-4, 14f 4, 15f, 16f) (gd 1-5, g-f 3, frm 1-5)
Workmanlike, decent gelding, effective 6 to 14f, acts on gd to hrd, best on gd, often wears blinkers (very effectively), likes left handed tracks, likes tight tracks, and excels at Redcar and York. Turf high 83 - 2nd of 5 giving 7lb to In The Sun (23 Jly Sandown 14f frm RF 3047) - also 1st of 9 giving 3lb to Fantasy Night (25 May Redcar RF 1457). Generally ran well last term after acquiring a visor. Usually held up. **C W Fairhurst [3-23] C D Barber-Lomax.*

WINSTON BHB 39f50a RR 49df 50a 5017[9]

5 b g Safawan 6.6f **(60)** - Lady Leman (Pitskelly) 8.5f **(53)**
Form - 4050072430
Record 1998 - 1st:0 2nd:1 3rd:1 Ran:10
Pre1998 - 1st:2 2nd:1 3rd:4 Ran:26
Win Prizemoney £6,957 *Total Prizemoney* £13,175
Wins * 1996 May Newcas (GD) H 8f 60 62 <
* 1996 Apr Nottin (G-F) H 8.2f 56 52
1998 Turf 0-10: (7f 2, 8f 8) (g-s 3, gd 2, g-f 4, frm)
Moderate gelding, effective 8f, acts on g-s to g-f, best on g-f, has worn blinkers, likes right handed tracks, likes tight tracks. Turf

Winona took the leading role in the Irish Oaks

high 49. *J D Bethell [2-36] Mrs J E Vickers.

WINTER GARDEN BHB 104f **RR 97f** 4063[3]
4 ch g Old Vic 12.8f **(72)** - Winter Queen (Welsh Pageant) 10f **(65)**
Form - 43
Record 1998 - 1st:0 2nd:0 3rd:1 Ran:2
Pre1998 - 1st:2 2nd:2 3rd:0 Ran:8
Win Prizemoney £8,522 *Total Prizemoney* £20,905
Wins * 1997 Jun Salisb (G-F) 14f 90 <
* 1997 May Thirsk (G-F) 12f 80+
1998 Turf 0-2: (13f, 14f) (gd 2)
Scopey, very useful gelding, effective 12 to 16f, acts on g-s to frm, excels at Salisbury. Turf high 97 (began Aug) - 3rd of 3 to Sadian (3 Spt Salisbury 14f gd RF 4063). Consistent. A half-brother to Safety In Numbers, he was not at his best in 1998 after a 13-month absence and a gelding operation. Has joined Noel Meade.
*L M Cumani [2-10] Sheikh Mohammed.

WINTER PAGEANT BHB 65f **RR 64f** 4861[7]
3 ch f Polish Precedent (USA) 9f **(73)** - Winter Queen (Welsh Pageant) 10f **(65)**
Form - 8437
Record 1998 - 1st:0 2nd:0 3rd:1 Ran:4
Win Prizemoney £0 *Total Prizemoney* £776
1998 Turf 0-4: (10f, 12f 2, 14f) (g-s, gd, frm 2)
Scopey, average filly. Turf high 64.
*L M Cumani [0-4] Aston House Stud.

WINTER RIVAL RR 120[9]
3 b f Prince Daniel (USA) 11.4f **(46)** - Playtex (Be Friendly) 9.3f **(53)**
Form - 00
Record 1998 - 1st:0 2nd:0 3rd:0 Ran:2
1998 AW 0-2: (8f 2) (Equi 2)
Light-framed, currently very poor filly. AW high 3.
*G L Moore [0-2] C J Pennick.

WINTER ROMANCE BHB 110f **RR 111f** 4718a[10]
5 ch h Cadeaux Genereux 7.9f **(76)** - Island Wedding (USA) (Blushing Groom (FR)) 10.3f **(76)**
Form - 6281540
Record 1998 - 1st:1 2nd:1 3rd:0 Ran:7
Pre1998 - 1st:3 2nd:3 3rd:3 Ran:17
Win Prizemoney £81,050 *Total Prizemoney* £103,541
Wins * **1998** Jly Ayr (SFT) G3 10f 111 <
* 1997 Spt York (SFT) L 8.9f 107
* 1997 Jun Ascot (SFT) H 10f 100 108
* 1996 May Haydoc (G-S) H 8.1f 90 99
1998 Turf 1-7: (10f 1-6, 11f) (hvy, sft, g-s, gd 1-3, g-f)
Group-class colt, effective 9 to 11f, best at 10f, acts on sft to g-f, best on gd, likes left handed tracks, likes tight tracks, excels at Ayr, likes Ascot. Turf high 111 - 1st of 8 giving 10lb to Rabi (20 Jly Ayr RF 2949). Inconsistent. He had perfect conditions when winning the Group Three Scottish Classic at Ayr in July; soft ground, soft rivals and a strong jockey. Life got progressively more difficult thereafter. *E A L Dunlop [4-24] Sheikh Mohammed Al Maktoum.

WINTER SCOUT (USA) BHB 39f **RR 45f** 3958[9]
10 ch g It's Freezing (USA) 6.6f **(73)** - His Squaw (USA) (Tom Rolfe) 9.4f **(75)**
Form - 300840400
Record 1998 - 1st:0 2nd:0 3rd:1 Ran:9
Pre1998 - 1st:6 2nd:1 3rd:3 Ran:31
Win Prizemoney £16,603 *Total Prizemoney* £19,352
Wins * 1997 Jun Carlis (FRM) H 6.9f 57 61 <
* 1997 Jun Carlis (FRM) C 5.9f 60
1996 Jun Carlis (FRM) C 5.9f 60
1995 Aug Newcas (GD) C 6f 57
1994 Aug Newcas (G-F) C 6f 53
1994 Jun Carlis (G-F) S 5.9f 50
1998 Turf 0-9: (6f, 7f 5, 8f, 9f, 10f) (gd 3, g-f 3, frm 3)
Moderate gelding, effective 6 to 7f, best at 7f, acts on gd to frm, best on frm, has worn blinkers, prefers right handed tracks, likes tight tracks. Turf high 52 (1st run) - 3rd of 11 getting 8lb from Monica's Choice (8 May Carlisle 7f gd RF 1096). Appreciates the stiff track at Carlisle, but none too consistent.
R A Fahey [2-18] Mrs S M Russell (from C P E Brooks [1-10] Spt 1996).

WINTERTIME BHB 73f **RR 71f** 4138[6]
3 b g Robellino (USA) 9.5f **(68)** - Naturally Fresh (Thatching) 8f **(66)**
Form - 6
Record 1998 - 1st:0 2nd:0 3rd:0 Ran:1
Pre1998 - 1st:0 2nd:0 3rd:0 Ran:3
1998 Turf 0-1: (10f) (g-f)
Scopey, above-average gelding.
**Miss E C Lavelle [0-1] R J Lavelle (from G Lewis [0-3] Oct 1997).*

WISCALINA (GER) RR 100f 2481a[3]
3 b f Linamix (FR) 8.2f **(64)** - Wiscaria (GER) (Ashmore (FR)) 8.5f **(65)**
Form - 3
1998 Turf 0-1: (11f) (gd)
Currently very useful filly. (1st run) - 3rd of 11 getting 13lb from Saperlipoupette (27 Jun Hamburg 11f gd RF 2481a).
**A Schutz in GER [0-1] (from B Schutz in GER [0-1] Jly 1997).*

WISHAH (USA) RR 87+f 4148[1]
2 b f Red Ransom (USA) 8.6f **(83)** - Ninja Gold (USA) (Nijinsky (CAN)) 10.3f **(77)**
Form - 1
Record 1998 - 1st:1 2nd:0 3rd:0 Ran:1
Win Prizemoney £3,306 *Total Prizemoney* £3,306
Wins * 1998 Spt Lingfi (G-S) 7f 87+ <
1998 Turf 1-1: (7f 1-1) (g-f 1-1)
Currently useful filly. (1st run) - 1st of 9 from Beryl (8 Spt Lingfield RF 4148). Made a big impression in a Lingfield maiden on her debut, though the opposition did not amount to much.
**J H M Gosden [1-1] Hamdan Al Maktoum.*

WISHBONE ALLEY (IRE) BHB 60f **RR 57f** 5142[16]
3 b g Common Grounds 8.1f **(66)** - Dul Dul (USA) (Shadeed (USA)) 8.2f **(70)**
Form - 23026251030060
Record 1998 - 1st:1 2nd:3 3rd:2 Ran:14
Pre1998 - 1st:0 2nd:0 3rd:1 Ran:6
Win Prizemoney £4,597 *Total Prizemoney* £8,421
Wins * 1998 Aug Thirsk (G-F) H 5f 59 63 <
1998 Turf 1-14: (5f 1-7, 6f 7) (sft, g-s, gd 6, g-f 2, frm 1-4)
Workmanlike, fair gelding, effective 5 to 6f, best at 5f, acts on gd to frm, best on frm, excels at Thirsk. Turf high 64 - 3rd of 15 getting 2lb from Pleasure Time (28 Aug Thirsk 5f frm RF 3938) - also 1st of 11 getting 2lb from Tancred Times (10 Aug Thirsk RF 3506). He took a long time in getting off the mark, but managed it in a Thirsk handicap in August when well drawn. **M Dods [1-20] Doug Graham.*

WISHING (USA) BHB 70f **RR 58f** 3210[P]
7 b g Lyphard's Wish (FR) 9.3f **(75)** - Vivre Libre (USA) (Honest Pleasure (USA)) 10.4f **(73)**
Form - 0P
Record 1998 - 1st:0 2nd:0 3rd:0 Ran:2
Pre1998 - 1st:4 2nd:3 3rd:3 Ran:21
Win Prizemoney £23,859 *Total Prizemoney* £39,933
Wins 1995 Jun York (G-F) H 13.9f 92 99 <
1995 Apr Kempto (G-F) H 12f 85 91
1994 Apr Salisb (G-F) 10f 93
1998 Turf 0-2: (16f, 17f) (gd, g-f)
Fair gelding. Turf high 58. (DEAD)
**T D McCarthy [0-6] A D Spence (from R Akehurst [2-8] Spt 1995).*

WITCHFINDER (USA) BHB 62f80a **RR 62f 80a** 1215[15]
6 b g Diesis 9f **(80)** - Colonial Witch (USA) (Pleasant Colony (USA)) 7f **(70)**
Form - 3311114560
Record 1998 - 1st:3 2nd:0 3rd:0 Ran:7
Pre1998 - 1st:1 2nd:0 3rd:2 Ran:8
Win Prizemoney £13,242 *Total Prizemoney* £14,599
Wins * 1998 *Feb Lingfi (SLW) H 7f 70 80+* <
*** 1998** *Jan Lingfi (STD) H 7f 62 71*
*** 1998** *Jan Lingfi (STD) H 7f 55 63*
* 1997 *Dec Lingfi (STD) 7f 60*
1998 Turf 0-2: (7f 2) (gd, frm) 1998 AW 3-5: (6f, 7f 3-4) (Equi 3-5)
Decent gelding, effective 7f, - acts on Equi, often wears blinkers (extremely effectively), prefers left handed tracks, prefers tight tracks. Turf high 62. AW high 80 - 1st of 7 giving 29lb to Axeman (7 Feb Lingfield RF 0244) - also 1st of 9 giving 11lb to Mustang (31 Jan Lingfield RF 0198). He had already shown some ability in a couple of events on the Lingfield Equitrack, before storming away with a maiden over seven furlongs there in December. He went on to win three handicaps over the same course and distance after, but seemed to lose his form after February.
**Mrs L Stubbs [4-13] Maurice Parker (from J H M Gosden [0-2] Spt 1995).*

WITCHING HOUR (IRE) BHB 90f **RR 95f** 658[5]
4 b f Alzao (USA) 9.8f **(73)** - Itching (IRE) (Thatching) 8f **(66)**
Form - 535
Record 1998 - 1st:0 2nd:0 3rd:1 Ran:3
Pre1998 - 1st:1 2nd:1 3rd:0 Ran:3
Win Prizemoney £3,489 *Total Prizemoney* £8,303
Wins * 1996 May Salisb (SFT) 6f 84+ <
1998 Turf 0-3: (8f 2, 10f) (hvy, sft, gd)
Workmanlike, very useful filly. Turf high 95 - 3rd of 8 getting 5lb from Hornbeam (26 Mar Doncaster 8f gd RF 0473).
**Mrs J Cecil [1-6] Greenbay Stables Ltd.*

WITH A WILL BHB 62f **RR 62f** 3222[20]
4 b g Rambo Dancer(CAN) 8.4f **(59)** -Henceforth(Full of Hope) 8.5f **(64)**
Form - 7361140
Record 1998 - 1st:2 2nd:0 3rd:1 Ran:7
Pre1998 - 1st:1 2nd:0 3rd:1 Ran:10
Win Prizemoney £9,964 *Total Prizemoney* £11,515
Wins * 1998 Jun Lingfi (GD) H 9f 58 62
*** 1998** May Kempto (GD) H 9f 56 59
* 1997 Jly Chepst (G-F) H 8.1f 61 66 <
1998 Turf 2-7: (8f 3, 9f 2-3, 10f) (g-s, gd 1-4, frm 1-2)
Unfurnished, average gelding, effective 7 to 10f, acts on gd to frm. Turf high 62 - 1st of 13 giving 12lb to Hawksbill Henry (20 Jun Lingfield RF 2152) - also 1st of 12 getting 19lb from Vola Via (30 May Kempton RF 1590). He is no world-beater, but gained two victories over nine furlongs last season. Sarah Jackson has been successful on him twice during the past two seasons.
**H Candy [3-17] Henry Candy.*

WITHOUT FRIENDS (IRE) BHB 41f62a **RR 43f 62a** 3949[19]
4 b g Thatching 7.8f **(69)** - Soha (USA) (Dancing Brave (USA)) 8.4f **(76)**
Form - 523411318003700
Record 1998 - 1st:3 2nd:0 3rd:2 Ran:12
Pre1998 - 1st:4 2nd:2 3rd:3 Ran:21
Win Prizemoney £15,944 *Total Prizemoney* £18,560
Wins * 1998 *Mar Lingfi (SLW) 8f 66*
*** 1998** *Feb Lingfi (SLW) SH 8f 50 64*
*** 1998** *Feb Lingfi (SLW) S 8f 61*
1997 Mar Newcas (GD) S 6f 56
1996 Jly Chepst (G-F) C 6.1f 71 <
1996 May Goodwo (GD) C 6f 63
1996 Apr Folkes (FRM) S 5f 63
1998 Turf 0-5: (8f 3, 10f 2) (gd 3, g-f, frm) 1998 AW 3-7: (8f 3-6, 10f) (Equi 3-7)
Neat, average gelding, effective 6 to 8f, best at 8f, acts on frm - acts on Equi, has worn blinkers. Turf high 43. AW high 66 - 1st of 8 giving 4lb to Amico (3 Mar Lingfield RF 0395) - also 1st of 9 giving 21lb to Great Chief (21 Feb Lingfield RF 0330). He is fairly useful, if exposed, in sellers and claimers, but had a very productive time over a mile on the Lingfield Equitrack early in the year, winning three modest events.
**J Ffitch-Heyes [3-26] Mrs D R Hunnisett (from W Storey [1-2] Apr 1997).*

WITH THE FLOW (USA) RR 114f 1230a[9]
3 ch c Irish River (USA) - Principle (CAN) (Viceregal (CAN)) 6.8f **(64)**
Form - 10
1998 Turf 1-2: (8f 1-2) (hvy 1-1, gd)
Currently Group-class colt, always wears blinkers. Turf high 114 (1st run) - 1st of 7 from Loudeac (19 Apr Longchamp RF 0837a). Rated a hot prospect after running away with a listed heat on his reappearance, he looked in a foul mood before the Poule d'Essai des Poulains (French 2,000 Guineas) and ran accordingly. Whether we have seen the best of him remains to be seen.
**Mme C Head in FR [1-2].*

WITNEY-DE-BERGERAC (IRE) BHB 65f60a **RR 65f 60a** 3811[13]
6 b g Cyrano de Bergerac 7.3f **(58)** - Spy Girl (Tanfirion) 7f **(61)**

Form - 10155740
Record 1998 - 1st:2 2nd:0 3rd:0 Ran:8
Pre1998 - 1st:2 2nd:1 3rd:3 Ran:32
Win Prizemoney £15,896 *Total Prizemoney* £21,058
Wins * **1998** Jun Bath (G-S) H 17.2f 58 63
* **1998** May Bath (GD) H 17.2f 55 61
* 1995 Spt Newbur (G-S) H 12f 57 63
* 1994 Jun Bath (GD) 5.1f 67
1998 Turf 2-7: (16f 4, 17f 2-2, 20f) (gd 1-4, g-f 2, frm 1-1) 1998 AW 0-1: (16f) (Equi)
Average gelding, has broken blood-vessels, effective 16 to 20f, acts on gd to frm, best on gd, has worn blinkers. Turf high 65 - 4th of 8 giving 3lb to Noufari (5 Aug Newcastle 16f g-f RF 3382) - also 1st of 9 getting 15lb from Star Rage (13 Jun Bath RF 1955). Was having his first run for eighteen months when scoring at Bath in May. Suited by coming late off a fast pace, he added another victory at Bath before finishing a good fifth under a penalty in the Ascot Stakes. **J S Moore [4-45] Ernie Houghton.*

WITNEY WEAVER (IRE) RR 596[5]

2 ch g Imp Society (USA) 7.1f **(63)** - Rose 'n Reason (IRE) (Reasonable (FR))
Form - 065
Record 1998 - 1st:0 2nd:0 3rd:0 Ran:3
1998 Turf 0-1: (5f) (gd) 1998 AW 0-2: (5f 2) (Equi, Fibr)
Currently little account gelding, has worn blinkers. AW high 25.
**J S Moore [0-3] Ernie Houghton.*

WIXIM (USA) BHB 110f RR 119?f 4992[2]

5 ch h Diesis 9f **(80)** - River Lullaby (USA) (Riverman (USA)) 9.1f **(76)**
Form - 32
Record 1998 - 1st:0 2nd:1 3rd:0 Ran:1
Pre1998 - 1st:3 2nd:3 3rd:3 Ran:11
Win Prizemoney £44,689 *Total Prizemoney* £153,868
Wins * 1997 Apr Sandow (G-F) G2 8.1f 115 <
* 1996 May Doncas (G-F) 8f 99+
* 1996 Apr Ripon (G-F) 8f 83+
1998 Turf 0-1: (7f) (sft)
High-class colt, effective 8 to 9f, best at 9f, acts on sft to frm. Consistent. He did not make his reappearance until October and, though a well-beaten second, was entitled to need it. However, he does not look the same horse that won a Group Two at Sandown in 1997. **R Charlton [3-12] K Abdulla.*

WIZARD KING BHB 119f RR 121df 3978[3]

7 b h Shaadi (USA) 8.1f **(75)** - Broomstick Cottage (Habitat) 9.4f **(70)**
Form - 4423
Record 1998 - 1st:0 2nd:1 3rd:1 Ran:2
Pre1998 - 1st:18 2nd:7 3rd:5 Ran:39
Win Prizemoney £249,895 *Total Prizemoney* £321,128
Wins * 1997 Oct Tipper (GD) G3 7f 121 <
* 1997 Spt Currag (SFT) G3 7f 121 <
* 1997 Jly Newcas (GD) G3 7f 121 <
* 1997 Jun Leopar (SFT) G3 7f 113+
* 1997 Apr Leices (G-S) L 7f 118
* 1996 Nov Leopar (G-S) L 7f 113
* 1996 Oct Tipper (G-S) G3 7f 107+
* 1996 Aug Chepst (GD) 7.1f 113
* 1996 Aug Salisb (GD) 7f 111
* 1996 Aug Cheste (G-F) 7f 98
* 1995 Spt Currag (GD) L 7f 113
* 1995 Aug Fairyh (FRM) L 8f 105
* 1994 Spt Ascot (GD) H 7f 87 102
* 1994 Aug Cheste (GD) H 7f 87 93+
* 1994 Jun Ascot (G-F) H 8f 72 83+
* 1994 Jun Lingfi (G-F) H 7f 72 71+
* 1994 Apr Newmar (G-S) H 7f 60 64
1998 Turf 0-2: (7f 2) (sft, gd)
Very high-class horse, effective 7f, acts on hvy to g-f, likes Leopardstown. Turf high 114 (1st run) - 2nd of 5 giving 7lb to Tumbleweed Ridge (10 Jun Leopardstown 7f sft RF 2036a). Consistent. He had a wonderful time in 1997 with five victories, but was limited to just two outings last term, finishing runner-up at Leopardstown on his belated reappearance and a well beaten third of five in a minor event at Chepstow. He has been retired to stud.
**Sir Mark Prescott [18-41] Sheikh Ahmed bin Saeed Al Maktoum.*

WOLFHUNT BHB 72f95a RR 73f 95a 4923[16]

3 b c Wolfhound (USA) 7.3f **(71)** - Vayavaig (Damister (USA)) 9f **(73)**
Form - 121400060
Record 1998 - 1st:1 2nd:0 3rd:0 Ran:7
Pre1998 - 1st:1 2nd:2 3rd:0 Ran:6
Win Prizemoney £6,606 *Total Prizemoney* £9,936
Wins * **1998** *Jan Wolver (STD) 6f 97* <
* 1997 *Dec Wolver (STD) 6f 89*
1998 Turf 0-5: (6f 2, 7f 2, 8f) (sft, g-s, gd 2, g-f) 1998 AW 1-2: (6f 1-2) (Fibr 1-2)
Very useful colt, effective 6f, - acts on AW, best on Fibr, has worn blinkers. Turf high 78. AW high 97 (1st run) - 1st of 7 getting 16lb from Musafi (21 Jan Wolverhampton RF 0128).
**P J Makin [2-13] Mrs Eileen Queally.*

WOLF TOOTH BHB 85f RR 86+f 4266[3]

2 ch c Wolfhound (USA) 7.3f **(71)** - Collide (High Line) 10.3f **(70)**
Form - 066443
Record 1998 - 1st:0 2nd:0 3rd:1 Ran:6
Win Prizemoney £0 *Total Prizemoney* £1,517
1998 Turf 0-6: (5f, 6f, 7f 3, 8f) (gd, g-f, frm 4)
Useful colt, effective 6 to 8f, acts on gd to g-f. Turf high 86 - 6th of 10 to Agreeable (30 May Newmarket 6f g-f RF 1609). Likely to need seven furlongs plus. **D R C Elsworth [0-6] Raymond Tooth.*

WONDERBOY (IRE) BHB 40f36a RR 54f 36a 1690[12]

4 ch g Arazi (USA) 9.2f **(74)** - Alsaaybah (USA) (Diesis) 9.3f **(69)**
Form - 770
Record 1998 - 1st:0 2nd:0 3rd:0 Ran:3
Pre1998 - 1st:0 2nd:0 3rd:0 Ran:5
1998 Turf 0-1: (16f) (gd) 1998 AW 0-2: (12f 2) (Equi 2)
Light-framed, fair gelding. AW high 32. Becoming disappointing.
**Derrick Morris [0-5] J Daniels (from R Akehurst [0-5] Aug 1997).*

WONDERFUL MAN BHB 57f RR 53f 5139[11]

2 ch c Magical Wonder (USA) 7.2f **(60)** - Gleeful (Sayf El Arab (USA)) 7.1f **(54)**
Form - 500
Record 1998 - 1st:0 2nd:0 3rd:0 Ran:3
1998 Turf 0-3: (6f 3) (g-s, gd, g-f)
Currently fair colt. Turf high 53 (began Aug).
**M J Heaton-Ellis [0-3] F J Sainsbury.*

WONTCOSTALOTBUT BHB 47f45a RR 39?f 45a 3437[8]

4 b f Nicholas Bill 9.8f **(56)** - Brave Maiden (Three Legs) 11.1f **(54)**
Form - 8
Record 1998 - 1st:0 2nd:0 3rd:0 Ran:1
Pre1998 - 1st:0 2nd:0 3rd:0 Ran:5
1998 Turf 0-1: (16f) (frm)
Neat, moderate filly. **M J Wilkinson [1-15] Wontcostalot Partnership.*

WON'T FORGET ME (IRE) BHB 41f55a RR 52f 55a 5081[9]

3 br g Don't Forget Me 9.5f **(66)** - Lucky Realm (Realm) 8.1f **(65)**
Form - 0064520450
Record 1998 - 1st:0 2nd:1 3rd:0 Ran:9
Pre1998 - 1st:2 2nd:1 3rd:0 Ran:9
Win Prizemoney £3,969 *Total Prizemoney* £6,119
Wins 1997 Spt Bright (G-F) S 7f 62 <
1997 Aug Folkes (G-F) S 6.9f 59
1998 Turf 0-8: (9f, 10f, 11f 4, 12f 2) (sft, gd 4, g-f 2, frm) 1998 AW 0-1: (12f) (Fibr)
Lengthy, fair gelding, effective 7f, acts on g-f to frm, best on g-f, has worn blinkers. Turf high 52. Inconsistent.
**I Semple [0-10] Ian Crawford (from M H Tompkins [2-8] Oct 1997).*

WOODCUT (IRE) RR 30f 4259[11]

2 ch g Woods of Windsor (USA) - Lady of State (IRE) (Petong) 6.6f **(58)**
Form - 000
Record 1998 - 1st:0 2nd:0 3rd:0 Ran:3
1998 Turf 0-3: (6f 3) (gd, g-f, frm)
Currently very moderate gelding. Turf high 34.
**P S Felgate [0-3] Yorkshire Racing Club Owners Group 1990.*

WOODETTO (IRE) BHB 35f37a RR 41f 37a 3579[12]

4 b g Maledetto (IRE) - Wood Kay (IRE) (Treasure Kay)
Form - 00
Record 1998 - 1st:0 2nd:0 3rd:0 Ran:2

Pre1998 - 1st:0 2nd:1 3rd:0 Ran:7
Win Prizemoney £0 *Total Prizemoney* £938
1998 Turf 0-2: (7f, 9f) (gd 2)
Moderate gelding. (began Aug). Becoming disappointing.
**E Weymes [0-9] Mrs P M Weymes.*

WOODLAND MELODY (USA) BHB 110f **RR 94f** 1749[7]
3 b f Woodman (USA) 9.7f **(77)** - Eloquent Minister (USA) (Deputy Minister (CAN)) 7.4f **(80)**
Form - 7
Record **1998** - 1st:0 2nd:0 3rd:0 Ran:1
Pre1998 - 1st:3 2nd:0 3rd:0 Ran:3
Win Prizemoney £37,477 *Total Prizemoney* £37,477
Wins 1997 Aug Deauvi (SFT) G3 7f 94 <
1997 Jly Sandow (G-F) L 7.1f 94 <
1997 Jly Haydoc (GD) 6f 83
1998 Turf 0-1: (9f) (gd)
Lengthy, useful filly. She won all three of her starts in 1997, including a Group Three in soft ground at Deauville on her final start. Having moved to Godolphin, she was very disappointing in an Epsom Listed event on her reappearance, and was not seen again.
**S bin Suroor [0-1] Godolphin (from P W Chapple-Hyam [3-3] Aug 1997).*

WOODLAND NYMPH BHB 50a **RR 40f** 2534[8]
4 gr f Norton Challenger 10f **(41)** - Royal Meeting (Dara Monarch) 8.8f **(59)**
Form - 58
Record **1998** - 1st:0 2nd:0 3rd:0 Ran:2
Pre1998 - 1st:0 2nd:1 3rd:1 Ran:9
Win Prizemoney £0 *Total Prizemoney* £1,350
1998 Turf 0-2: (15f, 18f) (gd, g-f)
Scopey, moderate filly, effective 14f, acts on g-f, has worn blinkers, favours tight tracks. Turf high 40. Inconsistent.
**D J G MurraySmith [0-14] The Woodland Partners.*

WOODLANDS PRIDE (IRE) BHB 24f **RR 18f** 2457[12]
3 ch f Petardia 8.2f **(58)** - Valediction (Town Crier) 10.2f **(55)**
Form - 86080006000
Record **1998** - 1st:0 2nd:0 3rd:0 Ran:11
Pre1998 - 1st:0 2nd:0 3rd:0 Ran:3
1998 Turf 0-5: (7f, 8f, 10f 3) (g-s 2, gd, frm 2) 1998 AW 0-6: (6f 3, 7f 2, 8f) (Fibr 6)
Leggy, poor filly. Turf high 25. AW high 11.
**M C Chapman [0-14] Eric Knowles.*

WOOD POUND (USA) **RR 66+f** 5039[5]
2 b c Woodman (USA) 9.7f **(77)** - Poundzig (USA) (Danzig (USA)) 8.4f **(76)**
Form - 5
Record **1998** - 1st:0 2nd:0 3rd:0 Ran:1
1998 Turf 0-1: (8f) (g-s)
Currently average colt. **Sir Michael Stoute [0-1] Peter Wetzel.*

WOODWIN (IRE) **RR 100f** 2426a[5]
3 ch f Woodman (USA) 9.7f **(77)** - Klarifi (Habitat) 9.4f **(70)**
Form - 3215
1998 Turf 1-4: (7f 2, 8f 1-2) (sft 2, gd 1-2)
Very useful filly, effective 7 to 8f, acts on sft to gd, has worn blinkers. Turf high 100 (1st run) - 3rd of 5 to Idle Rich (19 Apr Leopardstown 7f sft RF 0807a) - also 1st of 10 getting 5lb from Pirro (6 Jun Cork RF 1860a). Placed in a listed race on her reappearance, she won her maiden but proved a shade disappointing later in the campaign. Her future seems to lie in handicaps.
**J Oxx in IRE [1-6] Gerald Jennings.*

WOODY'S BOY (IRE) BHB 65f **RR 65f** 3437[1]
4 gr g Roi Danzig (USA) 10.5f **(62)** - Smashing Gale (Lord Gayle (USA)) 8.8f **(62)**
Form - 15231
Record **1998** - 1st:2 2nd:1 3rd:1 Ran:5
Pre1998 - 1st:0 2nd:1 3rd:1 Ran:8
Win Prizemoney £10,338 *Total Prizemoney* £13,441
Wins * **1998** Aug Newmar (FRM) H 16.1f 60 65 <
* **1998** May Newmar (G-F) H 14f 58 61
1998 Turf 2-5: (14f 1-1, 15f, 16f 1-1, 17f 2) (gd 2, g-f, frm 2-2)
Average gelding, effective 12 to 17f, acts on gd to frm, and excels at Newmarket and Windsor. Turf high 65 - 1st of 8 getting 7lb from Grimshaw (7 Aug Newmarket RF 3437) - also 1st of 8 giving 4lb to Zermatt (16 May Newmarket RF 1266). He is a pretty fair staying handicapper who scored twice at Newmarket last term. Seems particularly suited by fast ground.
**M J Heaton-Ellis [2-16] Vic Woodason.*

WOOLLY WINSOME BHB 65f **RR 66f** 4880[9]
2 br g Lugana Beach 7f **(63)** - Gay Ming (Gay Meadow)
Form - 250
Record **1998** - 1st:0 2nd:1 3rd:0 Ran:3
Win Prizemoney £0 *Total Prizemoney* £930
1998 Turf 0-3: (7f 2, 8f) (g-s 2, frm)
Currently average gelding. Turf high 66 (began Spt).
**B Smart [0-3] W Clifford.*

WOORE LASS (IRE) BHB 74f **RR 70f** 4538[9]
2 ch f Persian Bold 10f **(69)** - Miss Ballylea (Junius (USA)) 7.7f **(65)**
Form - 84152000
Record **1998** - 1st:1 2nd:1 3rd:0 Ran:8
Win Prizemoney £2,510 *Total Prizemoney* £4,241
Wins * **1998** Jun Salisb (G-S) 6f 64 <
1998 Turf 1-8: (5f, 6f 1-2, 7f 5) (gd 1-2, g-f 2, frm 4)
Above-average filly, effective 6 to 7f, acts on gd to frm. Turf high 70 - 2nd of 10 giving 9lb to Catch Me (11 Jly Chester 7f frm RF 2704) - also 1st of 13 giving 7lb to Brenda Dee (9 Jun Salisbury RF 1830). She put her experience to good use in order to get off the mark in a Salisbury maiden auction event, but she is only modest.
**R Hannon [1-8] Jimm Racing.*

WORLD ALERT (IRE) **RR 86f** 4541[4]
2 b c Alzao (USA) 9.8f **(73)** - Steady The Buffs (Balidar) 7.9f **(63)**
Form - 54
Record **1998** - 1st:0 2nd:0 3rd:0 Ran:2
Win Prizemoney £0 *Total Prizemoney* £374
1998 Turf 0-2: (6f, 8f) (g-f, frm)
Currently useful colt. Turf high 86 (began Jly) - 4th of 19 to Timahs (29 Spt Newmarket 8f frm RF 4541). A brother to the useful Aldbourne, he was easy in the market and pulled too hard in the race on his Ascot debut. Fair effort in a useful maiden next time.
**P W Chapple-Hyam [0-2] R E Sangster & A K Collins.*

WORLD EXPRESS (IRE) BHB 50f56a **RR 50f 56a** 1567[4]
8 b g Jareer (USA) 10.2f **(54)** - Eight Mile Rock (Dominion) 8.5f **(63)**
Form - 64
Record **1998** - 1st:0 2nd:0 3rd:0 Ran:2
Pre1998 - 1st:4 2nd:0 3rd:1 Ran:23
Win Prizemoney £14,425 *Total Prizemoney* £15,032
Wins * 1996 May Sandow (G-S) H 14f 53 59
* 1994 Spt Chepst (G-S) H 10.2f 60 62
* 1994 Jun Chepst (SFT) H 10.2f 56 61
1998 Turf 0-2: (16f, 17f) (frm 2)
Fair gelding, has worn blinkers (effectively). Turf high 50 - 4th of 9 getting 1lb from Tasik Chini (29 May Bath 17f frm RF 1567). Consistent. **B R Millman [7-42] The Dragisic Partnership.*

WORLD PREMIER BHB 100f **RR 101f** 2107[28]
5 b g Shareef Dancer (USA) 10.1f **(67)** - Abuzz (Absalom) 7.2f **(58)**
Form - 130
Record **1998** - 1st:1 2nd:0 3rd:1 Ran:3
Pre1998 - 1st:2 2nd:3 3rd:5 Ran:25
Win Prizemoney £40,214 *Total Prizemoney* £70,247
Wins * **1998** May York (GD) H 6f 96 100 <
* 1995 Jun Ascot (G-F) L 6f 97
* 1995 Mar Doncas (GD) 5f 77t
1998 Turf 1-3: (6f 1-3) (gd 1-2, g-f)
Very useful gelding, effective 6 to 7f, best at 6f, acted on gd to g-f, best on gd. Turf high 101 - also 1st of 13 giving 2lb to Sheltering Sky (12 May York RF 1167). Consistent. He bounced back to form when winning a hot handicap at York in May. Third in a listed event on his next start, he was never going the pace in the Wokingham at Royal Ascot and sadly had to be put down in October. (DEAD) **C E Brittain [3-28] Mrs C E Brittain.*

WORTH A TURN **RR 38f** 5000[8]
2 ch f Chaddleworth (IRE) - Taciturn (USA) (Tasso (USA))
Form - 8

Record 1998 - 1st:0 2nd:0 3rd:0 Ran:1
1998 Turf 0-1: (7f) (sft)
Currently very moderate filly. **R Rowe [0-1] Winterfields Farm Ltd.*

WORTH THE EFFORT BHB 58f **RR 73f** 4759[16]

3 b f Beveled (USA) 6.9f **(64)** - Haiti Mill (Free State) 8.7f **(61)**
Form - 23355R87030

Record	**1998 -**	1st:0	2nd:1	3rd:3	Ran:11
	Pre1998 -	1st:0	2nd:0	3rd:0	Ran:1

Win Prizemoney £0 *Total Prizemoney* £2,696
1998 Turf 0-11: (7f 4, 8f 6, 9f) (g-s, gd 5, g-f 2, frm 2, hrd)
Light-framed, above-average filly, effective 7 to 8f, acts on gd to hrd, has worn blinkers. Turf high 73 - 3rd of 14 giving 8lb to Yulara (6 Jun Newmarket 7f hrd RF 1791). Inconsistent. She has shown some ability in maiden and handicap company, but refused to race at Ripon in July and may be one to treat with caution.
**M H Tompkins [0-12] Adrienne and Michael Barnett.*

WOSAITA BHB 74f **RR 72f** 2076[3]

3 b f Generous (IRE) 11.5f **(82)** - Eljazzi (Artaius (USA)) 9f **(69)**
Form - 53

Record	**1998 -**	1st:0	2nd:0	3rd:1	Ran:2
	Pre1998 -	1st:0	2nd:0	3rd:0	Ran:1

Win Prizemoney £0 *Total Prizemoney* £520
1998 Turf 0-2: (9f, 12f) (gd 2)
Scopey, currently above-average filly. Turf high 72.
**J L Dunlop [0-3] Prince A A Faisal.*

WOTTASHAMBLES BHB 39f60a **RR 37f 60a** 93[P]

7 b or br g Arrasas (USA) 14.4f **(37)** - Manawa (Mandamus) 12.6f **(56)**
Form - 0P

Record	**1998 -**	1st:0	2nd:0	3rd:0	Ran:2
	Pre1998 -	1st:6	2nd:6	3rd:5	Ran:42

Win Prizemoney £15,105 *Total Prizemoney* £22,918

Wins	* 1997	*Feb*	*Lingfi*	*(STD)*	*H*	*13f*	*57*	*63*	<
	* 1996	*Dec*	*Lingfi*	*(STD)*	*H*	*16f*	*47*	*52*	
	* 1996	*Dec*	*Lingfi*	*(STD)*	*H*	*16f*	*40*	*45*	
	* 1996	*Jan*	*Lingfi*	*(STD)*	*H*	*16f*	*33*	*38*	
	* 1995	Jly	Chepst	(G-F)	H	12.1f	37	42	
	1994	*Dec*	*Lingfi*	*(STD)*	*H*	*13f*	*37*	*39*	

1998 AW 0-2: (12f, 16f) (Equi 2)
Average gelding, effective 13 to 16f, best at 16f, - acts on Equi, has worn blinkers. Becoming disappointing.
**L MontagueHall [8-36] Dream On Racing Partnership (from G Lewis [1-17] Mar 1995).*

WREN (IRE) RR 104f 2637[2]

3 ch f Bob Back (USA) 11.5f **(71)** - In the Rigging (USA) (Topsider (USA)) 8.3f **(71)**
Form - 2

Record	**1998 -**	1st:0	2nd:1	3rd:0	Ran:1
	Pre1998 -	1st:3	2nd:0	3rd:0	Ran:3

Win Prizemoney £57,619 *Total Prizemoney* £70,319

Wins	* 1997	Oct	San Si	(G-F)	G3	8f	100+	<
	* 1997	Aug	Bordea	(G-F)	L	6f	?	
	* 1997	Jly	San Si	(GD)		6f		

1998 Turf 0-1: (8f) (frm)
Very useful filly. (1st run) - 2nd of 13 to Lovers Knot (8 Jly Newmarket 8f frm RF 2637). She won three times on the continent as a juvenile, and ran encouragingly to finish second in the Group Two Falmouth Stakes on her reappearance. She did not run again, but is obviously a smart filly.
**Lord Huntingdon [3-4] Anglia Bloodstock Syndicate 1996.*

WRN PRINCESS BHB 28f **RR 26f** 223[10]

4 ch f Handsome Sailor6.6f **(53)** -Sovereign Rose(Sharpen Up)8.3f **(67)**
Form - 00

Record	**1998 -**	1st:0	2nd:0	3rd:0	Ran:2
	Pre1998 -	1st:0	2nd:0	3rd:0	Ran:6

1998 AW 0-2: (6f, 7f) (Equi 2)
Little account filly.
**J R Poulton [0-2] Come Racing Ltd (from B J Meehan [0-6] Jly 1997).*

WROUGHT IRON (USA) BHB 69f69a **RR 62f 69a** 592[4]

3 b br f Dayjur (USA) 6.8f **(79)** - Pris de Fer (USA) (Sir Ivor) 10.2f **(70)**
Form - 314

Record	**1998 -**	1st:1	2nd:0	3rd:1	Ran:3
	Pre1998 -	1st:0	2nd:0	3rd:0	Ran:2

Win Prizemoney £2,788 *Total Prizemoney* £3,194

Wins	*** 1998**	*Feb*	*Wolver*	*(STD)*	*9.4f*	*60*	<

1998 AW 1-3: (9f 1-3) (Fibr 1-3)
Average filly. AW high 62 (1st run) - 3rd of 11 getting 5lb from Prince Ashleigh (24 Jan Wolverhampton 9f Fibr RF 0152) - also 1st of 8 getting 5lb from Naked Oat (7 Feb Wolverhampton RF 0248). Showed nothing on turf but improved when tried on Fibresand at the start of 1998, including a clear-cut victory in a maiden on the Wolverhampton Fibresand in February.
**M Bell [1-5] Nasser Abdullah.*

WRY ARDOUR BHB 55f **RR 64f** 4928[10]

2 b g Pursuit of Love 9.5f **(69)** - Wryneck (Niniski (USA)) 10.6f **(65)**
Form - 000
Record 1998 - 1st:0 2nd:0 3rd:0 Ran:3
1998 Turf 0-3: (6f, 7f 2) (g-s, frm 2)
Currently average gelding. Turf high 61 (began Spt).
**A G Newcombe [0-3] Advanced Marketing Services Ltd.*

WUXI VENTURE BHB 90f **RR 95f** 4621[2]

3 b g Wolfhound (USA) 7.3f **(71)** - Push a Button (Bold Lad (IRE)) 8.4f **(68)**
Form - 1252238815102

Record	**1998 -**	1st:3	2nd:4	3rd:1	Ran:13
	Pre1998 -	1st:0	2nd:1	3rd:3	Ran:6

Win Prizemoney £15,900 *Total Prizemoney* £33,745

Wins	*** 1998**	Spt	Hamilt	(SFT)	H	8.3f	88	91	<
	*** 1998**	Aug	Haydoc	(GD)	H	8.1f	85	88	
	*** 1998**	Apr	Ripon	(SFT)		8f		86	

1998 Turf 3-13: (8f 3-9, 9f 2, 10f 2) (sft 1-3, g-s, gd 2-7, g-f 2)
Very useful gelding, effective 8 to 10f, best at 8f, acts on sft to g-f, best on gd, has worn blinkers, likes right handed tracks, likes tight tracks, does well at Sandown. Turf high 95 - 2nd of 5 giving 7lb to Keld (2 Oct Newmarket 8f gd RF 4621) - also 1st of 10 giving 26lb to Trailblazer (7 Spt Hamilton RF 4132). He seems to need the ground no faster than good. **S P C Woods [3-19] Dr Frank Chao.*

WYCHWOOD TIMES RR 57f 2513[11]

3 b f Timeless Times (USA) 6.1f **(56)** - Lanzamar **(27f)** (Buzzards Bay)
Form - 70
Record 1998 - 1st:0 2nd:0 3rd:0 Ran:2
1998 Turf 0-2: (5f, 6f) (g-f 2)
Scopey, currently fair filly. Turf high 57.
**H J Collingridge [0-2] R H Coombes.*

WYN BHB 51f51a **RR 66f 51a** 4338[7]

3 b f Gildoran 11.6f **(58)** - Its A Romp (Hotfoot) 10.5f **(59)**
Form - 0276067
Record 1998 - 1st:0 2nd:1 3rd:0 Ran:7
Win Prizemoney £0 *Total Prizemoney* £852
1998 Turf 0-6: (5f, 6f, 7f 3, 8f) (gd 2, g-f 2, frm 2) 1998 AW 0-1: (8f) (Fibr)
Neat, average filly. Turf high 66. **C A Dwyer [0-7] A J Owen.*

WYNBURY WARRIOR RR 3831[16]

2 b c Then Again 7.4f **(52)** - Fair Attempt (IRE) (Try My Best (USA)) 7.6f **(67)**
Form - 0
Record 1998 - 1st:0 2nd:0 3rd:0 Ran:1
1998 Turf 0-1: (5f) (g-f)
Currently very poor colt.
**F Murphy [0-1] The Bakers Dozen Partnership.*

XAAR RR 127?f 4294a[3]

3 b c Zafonic (USA) 9f **(83)** - Monroe (USA) (Sir Ivor) 10.2f **(70)**
Form - 1423
1998 Turf 1-4: (8f 1-2, 10f 2) (gd 1-4)
Top-class colt, effective 7 to 10f, acts on gd, excels at Newmarket. Turf high 124 (1st run) - 1st of 6 giving 3lb to Gulland (16 Apr Newmarket RF 0710). Champion juvenile of 1997, he was sent to Newmarket for the Craven for his reappearance, and scored in fine style after having looked outpaced at one stage. He never appeared to be going in the 2000 Guineas, and could only struggle on into fourth. He was well ahead of his generation at two, but the gap seemed to have disappeared. Came back from a break to finish a close second at Deauville, and ran arguably his best race of

Xaar will run in the Godolphin Blue next season

the season when third in the Irish Champion Stakes. He will race for Godolphin in 1999. **A Fabre in FR [4-8] K Abdullah.*

XANADU RR 16f 5011^{5}

2 ch g Casteddu 7.4f **(54)** - Bellatrix (Persian Bold) 9.3f **(66)**
Form - 05
Record 1998 - 1st:0 2nd:0 3rd:0 Ran:2
1998 Turf 0-2: (5f, 7f) (sft, gd)
Currently poor gelding. Turf high 16 (began Oct).
**Miss L A Perratt [0-2] T P Finch.*

XENOPHON OF CUNAXA (IRE) BHB 55f50a RR 28f 50a 339^{P}

5 b g Cyrano de Bergerac 7.3f **(58)** - Annais Nin (Dominion) 8.5f **(63)**
Form - 345P
Record 1998 - 1st:0 2nd:0 3rd:0 Ran:3
Pre1998 - 1st:2 2nd:1 3rd:2 Ran:21
Win Prizemoney £7,787 *Total Prizemoney* £9,915
Wins 1996 May Newbur (SFT) 7.3f 80 <
1995 Aug Bath (HRD) 5.7f 80 <
1998 AW 0-3: (9f 2, 10f) (Equi, Fibr 2)
Moderate gelding, effective 6 to 9f, acted on frm - acted on Equi to Fibr, had worn blinkers, liked left handed tracks, preferred tight tracks. AW high 46. (DEAD)
**B J Llewellyn [0-6] Alan Williams (from M J Fetherston-Godley [2-20] Oct 1997).*

XSYNNA BHB 68f RR 79f 4613^{14}

2 b c Cyrano de Bergerac 7.3f **(58)** - Rose Ciel (IRE) (Red Sunset) 8.2f **(63)**
Form - 07273570
Record 1998 - 1st:0 2nd:1 3rd:1 Ran:8
Win Prizemoney £0 *Total Prizemoney* £1,818
1998 Turf 0-8: (5f 3, 6f 4, 7f) (g-s, gd, g-f 3, frm 3)
Above-average colt, effective 5 to 6f, acts on g-f to frm, has worn blinkers. Turf high 79 - 3rd of 7 giving 3lb to Miss Rimex (5 Aug Kempton 6f frm RF 3370). **S C Williams [0-8] Chris Wright.*

XYLEM (USA) BHB 51f46a RR 63f 46a 4545^{12}

7 ch g Woodman (USA) 9.7f **(77)** - Careful (USA) (Tampa Trouble (USA)) 8f **(87)**
Form - 0053634000
Record 1998 - 1st:0 2nd:0 3rd:2 Ran:10
Pre1998 - 1st:2 2nd:0 3rd:1 Ran:13
Win Prizemoney £6,554 *Total Prizemoney* £10,297
Wins 1997 Oct Newcas (G-F) H 8f 69 70
1998 Turf 0-9: (8f 4, 10f 5) (sft, g-s, g-f, frm 6) 1998 AW 0-1: (11f) (Fibr)
Average gelding, effective 8 to 10f, best at 8f, acts on gd to frm, has worn blinkers, likes left handed tracks. Turf high 64 - 5th of 20 giving 14lb to Ellopassoff (23 May Warwick 8f frm RF 1436).
**J H M Gosden [1-17] Christopher Ranson (from L M Cumani [1-6] Nov 1997).*

YA-AIN RR 83f 4772^{2}

2 b c Warning 8.1f **(77)** - Ahbab (IRE) (Ajdal (USA)) 9.2f **(89)**
Form - 02
Record 1998 - 1st:0 2nd:1 3rd:0 Ran:2
Win Prizemoney £0 *Total Prizemoney* £996
1998 Turf 0-2: (6f, 7f) (g-s, gd)
Currently decent colt. Turf high 83 (began Oct) - 2nd of 17 to Senure (13 Oct Leicester 7f gd RF 4772).
**P T Walwyn [0-2] Hamdan Al Maktoum.*

YABINT EL SHAM BHB 85f RR 90f 4183^{6}

2 b f Sizzling Melody 6.3f **(49)** - Dalby Dancer (Bustiki) 8.7f **(78)**
Form - 5106
Record 1998 - 1st:1 2nd:0 3rd:0 Ran:4
Win Prizemoney £3,496 *Total Prizemoney* £3,496
Wins * 1998 Aug Leices (GD) 5f 85 <
1998 Turf 1-4: (5f 1-1, 6f 2, 7f) (gd 2, frm 1-2)
Useful filly. Turf high 85 (began Jly) - 1st of 9 from Dangerous

Dancer (5 Aug Leicester RF 3374). A half-sister to Yabint El Sultan, she too has ability judging by her Leicester win, but has been too highly tried otherwise and, like her relative, may come to herself more as she gets older. **B A McMahon [1-4] G S D Imports Ltd.*

YABINT EL SULTAN BHB 92f **RR 97f** 4733[4]

4 ch f Safawan 6.6f **(60)** - Dalby Dancer (Bustiki) 8.7f **(78)**
Form - 114800804

Record		1st	2nd	3rd	Ran
1998 -		1st:2	2nd:0	3rd:0	Ran:9
Pre1998 -		1st:2	2nd:2	3rd:4	Ran:14

Win Prizemoney £39,026 *Total Prizemoney* £48,145

Wins								
*** 1998**	May	Newmar	(G-S)	L	9f		100	<
*** 1998**	Apr	Newbur	(HVY)	H	8f	83	90	
* 1997	Aug	Cheste	(G-S)	H	10.3f	74	87	
* 1997	Jly	Cheste	(G-F)		7.6f		59	

1998 Turf 2-9: (8f 1-4, 9f 1-3, 10f 2) (sft 1-1, g-s, gd 1-3, g-f 3, frm)
Scopey, very useful filly, effective 8 to 9f, acts on sft to gd, likes left handed tracks. Turf high 100 - 1st of 8 getting 3lb from Supercal (1 May Newmarket RF 0963). She improved from three to four and won a listed race at Newmarket in May. A shade below par through the summer, she ran well at Ascot in October and goes well on soft ground. She made 80,000 guineas at the Tattersalls Autumn Horses In Training Sale and will continue her career in the Middle East. **B A McMahon [4-23] G S D Imports Ltd.*

YAGLI (USA) **RR 123f** 5167a[2]

5 ch h Jade Hunter (USA) 10.4f **(72)** - Nijinsky's Best (USA) (Nijinsky (CAN))
Form - 2
1998 Turf 0-1: (12f) (frm)
Currently very high-class colt. (1st run) - 2nd of 13 to Buck's Boy (7 Nov Churchill Downs 12f frm RF 5167a). He was the only horse to present a serious challenge to Buck's Boy in the 1998 Breeders' Cup Turf. **W Mott in USA [0-1] Allen Paulson.*

YAJREE (IRE) **RR 40f** 4071[6]

3 b c Selkirk (USA) 7.9f **(76)** - Ustka (Lomond (USA)) 8.8f **(65)**
Form - 6

Record	1st	2nd	3rd	Ran
1998 -	1st:0	2nd:0	3rd:0	Ran:1

1998 Turf 0-1: (8f) (g-f)
Leggy, currently moderate colt.
**A C Stewart [0-1] Sheikh Ahmed Al Maktoum.*

YAJTAHED (IRE) BHB 61f **RR 62f** 5006[1]

3 ch g Mujtahid (USA) 7.4f **(69)** - Rainstone (Rainbow Quest (USA)) 10.4f **(75)**
Form - 06001

Record	1st	2nd	3rd	Ran
1998 -	1st:1	2nd:0	3rd:0	Ran:5
Pre1998 -	1st:0	2nd:0	3rd:0	Ran:1

Win Prizemoney £2,584 *Total Prizemoney* £2,584

Wins								
*** 1998**	Oct	Bath	(SFT)	H	8f	56	62	<

1998 Turf 1-5: (6f, 8f 1-1, 10f 2, 12f) (sft 1-1, g-s, gd, g-f, frm)
Workmanlike, average gelding, effective 8f, acts on sft, has worn blinkers. Turf high 62 (began Spt) - 1st of 17 giving 6lb to Ra Ra Rasputin (27 Oct Bath RF 5006).
**G L Moore [1-5] Nick Clark (from J H M Gosden [0-1] May 1997).*

YAK ALFARAJ BHB 40f **RR 48f** 4458[8]

4 b g Sadler's Wells (USA) 11.3f **(87)** - Clara Bow (USA) (Coastal (USA)) 11.5f **(72)**
Form - 606608

Record	1st	2nd	3rd	Ran
1998 -	1st:0	2nd:0	3rd:0	Ran:6
Pre1998 -	1st:0	2nd:1	3rd:1	Ran:6

Win Prizemoney £0 *Total Prizemoney* £1,818
1998 Turf 0-6: (14f, 16f 3, 17f, 18f) (gd 3, g-f 2, frm)
Scopey, moderate gelding, effective 16f, acts on g-f to frm, best on g-f, has worn blinkers, prefers left handed tracks, prefers tight tracks. Turf high 61. Inconsistent.
**P G Murphy [0-9] Miss J Collison (from Sir Michael Stoute [0-6] Aug 1997).*

YAKAREEM (IRE) **RR 81f** 5138[3]

2 b c Rainbows For Life (CAN) 9.3f **(64)** -Brandywell (Skyliner) 7.3f **(53)**
Form - 23

Record	1st	2nd	3rd	Ran
1998 -	1st:0	2nd:1	3rd:1	Ran:2

Win Prizemoney £0 *Total Prizemoney* £1,547
1998 Turf 0-2: (7f 2) (sft, gd)
Currently decent colt. Turf high 81 (1st run) (began Oct) - 2nd of 10 to Bound For Pleasure (26 Oct Lingfield 7f sft RF 4997). Placed in two maidens at the back end, he has ability but looked a thoroughly awkward ride on the second occasion.
**K Mahdi [0-2] Hamad Al-Mutawa.*

YALTA (IRE) BHB 83f **RR 82f** 2251[7]

5 b g Soviet Star (USA) 8.6f **(74)** - Gay Hellene (Ela-Mana-Mou) 10.1f **(70)**
Form - 237

Record	1st	2nd	3rd	Ran
1998 -	1st:0	2nd:1	3rd:1	Ran:3
Pre1998 -	1st:3	2nd:2	3rd:1	Ran:12

Win Prizemoney £13,217 *Total Prizemoney* £20,327

Wins								
* 1997	Spt	Kempto	(GD)	H	8f	78	82	
* 1997	Jly	Sandow	(G-F)	C	8.1f		84	<
* 1996	Jly	Sandow	(G-F)		8.1f		83	

1998 Turf 0-3: (7f, 8f 2) (gd, frm 2)
Decent gelding, has broken blood-vessels, effective 8f, acts on gd to frm, best on frm, often wears blinkers (extremely effectively). Turf high 82 (1st run) - 2nd of 17 getting 1lb from Young Precedent (22 May Haydock 8f gd RF 1392). **R Charlton [3-15] Lord Weinstock.*

YA MALAK BHB 106f **RR 108f** 4404[6]

7 b g Fairy King (USA) 7.7f **(75)** - La Tuerta (Hot Spark) 7.6f **(62)**
Form - 8507356

Record	1st	2nd	3rd	Ran
1998 -	1st:0	2nd:0	3rd:1	Ran:7
Pre1998 -	1st:10	2nd:7	3rd:3	Ran:42

Win Prizemoney £136,602 *Total Prizemoney* £189,055

Wins								
* 1997	Aug	York	(GD)	G1	5f		115	<
* 1997	Jly	Sandow	(G-S)	L	5f		111	
* 1997	Jun	Epsom	(GD)	LH	5f	104	114+	
* 1997	May	Beverl	(G-S)		5f		86	
1995	Jun	Kempto	(GD)	L	5f		101	
1994	Jly	Cheste	(G-F)		5.1f		98	
1994	Jun	Nottin	(G-F)		5.1f		98	
1994	May	Beverl	(G-F)		5f		93	

1998 Turf 0-7: (5f 7) (gd 2, g-f 2, frm 3)
Pattern-class gelding, effective 5f, acts on gd to frm, best on gd, has worn blinkers. Turf high 112. He looked well last season, but never threatened to repeat his thrilling dead-heat with Coastal Bluff in the 1997 Nunthorpe Stakes. If anyone can turn back time it is his shrewd handler.
**D Nicholls [4-16] Contrac Promotions,I Blakey, V Greaves (from I A Balding [0-2] Oct 1996).*

YANABI (USA) BHB 80f **RR 83f** 4737[4]

3 b f Silver Hawk (USA) 11.2f **(85)** - Halholah (USA) (Secreto (USA)) 8.7f **(72)**
Form - 313245814

Record	1st	2nd	3rd	Ran
1998 -	1st:2	2nd:1	3rd:2	Ran:9
Pre1998 -	1st:0	2nd:1	3rd:2	Ran:4

Win Prizemoney £13,302 *Total Prizemoney* £20,875

Wins								
*** 1998**	Spt	Ayr	(G-S)	H	15f	80	83	<
*** 1998**	May	Bath	(GD)		8f		75	

1998 Turf 2-9: (8f 1-2, 10f, 12f 4, 15f 1-1, 16f) (g-s 2, gd 1-2, g-f 2, frm 1-3)
Strong, decent filly, effective 6 to 16f, best at 12f, acts on g-s to frm, likes tight tracks. Turf high 83 - 1st of 7 giving 10lb to Lady Rachel (17 Spt Ayr RF 4324) - also 1st of 8 from Sweet Pea (10 May Bath RF 1129). Consistent. She made the frame in decent maiden company prior to her victory at Bath. Has run respectably in middle-distance handicaps since, and scored again on easy ground at the Western meeting. **P T Walwyn [2-13] Hamdan Al Maktoum.*

YANOMAMI (USA) BHB 57f **RR 37f** 5142[19]

3 ch f Slew O' Gold (USA) 10.2f **(73)** - Sunerta (USA) (Roberto (USA)) 10f **(76)**
Form - 28080

Record	1st	2nd	3rd	Ran
1998 -	1st:0	2nd:1	3rd:0	Ran:5
Pre1998 -	1st:0	2nd:1	3rd:1	Ran:2

Win Prizemoney £0 *Total Prizemoney* £2,724
1998 Turf 0-5: (5f 2, 6f 2, 7f) (g-s, gd 3, g-f)
Neat, moderate filly, effective 5f, acts on g-s. Turf high 78 (1st run) - 2nd of 10 getting 5lb from Easter Ogil (23 Apr Beverley 5f g-s RF 0824). She only narrowly failed to make a winning reappearance at Beverley. Well beaten since.
**J Berry [0-5] T G & Mrs M E Holdcroft (from J H M Gosden [0-2] Spt 1997).*

YANSHAN BHB 47f47a **RR 38f 47a** 3638[2]
3 b g Anshan 8.2f **(63)** - Joy of Freedom **(51f)** (Damister (USA)) 9f **(73)**
Form - 0852

Record					
	1998 -	1st:0	2nd:1	3rd:0	Ran:4
	Pre1998 -	1st:0	2nd:0	3rd:0	Ran:3

Win Prizemoney £0 *Total Prizemoney* £768
1998 Turf 0-3: (12f 2, 16f) (g-s, gd, frm) 1998 AW 0-1: (14f) (Fibr)
Workmanlike, moderate gelding. Turf high 38.
**Bob Jones [0-7] Mrs S Osborne.*

YAROB (IRE) BHB 84f84a **RR 80f 84a** 431[13]
5 ch h Unfuwain (USA) 11.4f **(74)** - Azyaa (Kris) 9.5f **(73)**
Form - 420

Record					
	1998 -	1st:0	2nd:1	3rd:0	Ran:3
	Pre1998 -	1st:1	2nd:2	3rd:0	Ran:11

Win Prizemoney £4,455 *Total Prizemoney* £16,116

Wins							
1995	Jly	Lingfi	(G-F)		6f	82+	<

1998 AW 0-3: (8f, 9f, 11f) (Fibr 3)
Decent colt. AW high 80. Inconsistent. He ran pretty well on Fibresand at the start of the year apart from flopping in the Lincoln Trial. **D R Loder [0-3] Lucayan Stud (from R Akehurst [0-2] Oct 1997).*

YAVANA'S PACE (IRE) BHB 112f **RR 114f** 5151[1]
6 ch g Accordion 11.3f **(75)** - Lady in Pace (Burslem) 8.8f **(53)**
Form - 531142223121

Record					
	1998 -	1st:4	2nd:4	3rd:2	Ran:11
	Pre1998 -	1st:1	2nd:1	3rd:2	Ran:14

Win Prizemoney £103,137 *Total Prizemoney* £164,281

Wins								
* **1998**	Nov	Doncas	(SFT)	H	12f	105	114	<
* **1998**	Spt	Galway	(HVY)	L	12f		98+	
* **1998**	Jly	Sandow	(GD)	H	10f	88	92	
* **1998**	May	Ayr	(GD)	H	10f	83	87	
1996	Jun	Leopar	(GD)	H	7f	90	75	

1998 Turf 4-11: (8f, 10f 2-4, 12f 2-5, 14f) (hvy 1-1, g-s 1-1, gd 2-5, g-f, frm 3)
Group-class gelding, effective 12f, acts on gd. Turf high 114 - 1st of 23 giving 26lb to Carlys Quest (7 Nov Doncaster RF 5151). An ex-Irish gelding, he proved an admirably tough and consistent middle-distance handicapper last year. Landed the very valuable Hong Kong Trophy at Sandown under oriental ace Eddie Lai, and ran three times in six days at the end of July, at Ascot and twice at Glorious Goodwood, finishing second each time. Again in the frame in the Ebor and in a valuable Ascot handicap, he ended the season looking better than ever when running away with the November Handicap. Plans to run him over hurdles have been shelved, and he looks set to make his mark in listed company in 1999.
**M Johnston [4-11] Mrs Joan Keaney (from M Cunningham in IRE [0-13] Nov 1997).*

YAVERLAND (IRE) BHB 28f44a **RR 28f 44a** 4879[2]
6 b g Astronef 7.9f **(59)** - Lautreamont (Auction Ring (USA)) 8.6f **(65)**
Form - 732508302

Record					
	1998 -	1st:0	2nd:2	3rd:2	Ran:8
	Pre1998 -	1st:0	2nd:0	3rd:1	Ran:13

Win Prizemoney £0 *Total Prizemoney* £2,645
1998 Turf 0-3:(11f, 12f, 14f) (g-f 2, frm) 1998 AW 0-5:(12f 4, 14f)(Fibr 5)
Average gelding, effective 12f, - acts on Fibr. Turf high 28. AW high 63 - 2nd of 9 giving 8lb to Bathe In Light (11 Feb Wolverhampton 12f Fibr RF 0264). Inconsistent. He has shown some ability on Fibresand but is proving expensive to follow.
**John Berry [0-12] Mrs B A Blackwell (from C A Dwyer [0-6] Spt 1996).*

YEAST BHB 76f **RR 83f** 4822[3]
6 b g Salse (USA) 10.9f **(71)** - Orient (Bay Express) 7.1f **(60)**
Form - 065404673

Record					
	1998 -	1st:0	2nd:0	3rd:1	Ran:9
	Pre1998 -	1st:5	2nd:3	3rd:1	Ran:15

Win Prizemoney £107,318 *Total Prizemoney* £115,912

Wins								
* 1996	Oct	Newmar	(G-F)	L	8f		108	<
* 1996	Jly	Ascot	(G-F)	H	8f	97	107	
* 1996	Jun	Ascot	(G-F)	H	8f	87	102	
* 1996	May	Ascot	(G-F)	H	7f	80	87	
* 1996	Mar	Newcas	(G-S)		8f		83	

1998 Turf 0-9: (7f 3, 8f 2, 10f 3, 12f) (g-s, gd 2, g-f 3, frm 3)
Decent gelding, effective 8f, acts on gd. Turf high 89. A one-time very useful handicapper, and a winner in listed company, he has been below his best for some time now. He has slipped down the handicap as a result and ran his best race for a while when third at Newmarket in October, though whether he can build on that is anyone's guess. Ideally suited by forcing tactics.
**W J Haggas [5-24] B Haggas.*

YELLOW RIBBON (IRE) BHB 69f **RR 70f** 3987[7]
2 b f Hamas (IRE) 8f **(72)** - Busker (Bustino) 10.4f **(64)**
Form - 377

Record					
	1998 -	1st:0	2nd:0	3rd:1	Ran:3

Win Prizemoney £0 *Total Prizemoney* £600
1998 Turf 0-3: (5f, 6f, 7f) (sft, gd, g-f)
Currently above-average filly. Turf high 70. Promising debut at the Craven Meeting, but did not progress from that.
**B W Hills [0-3] A N Foster.*

YEOMAN OLIVER BHB 73f62a **RR 73f 62a** 5147[2]
5 b g Precocious 7.2f **(54)** - Impala Lass (Kampala) 8.5f **(56)**
Form - 62223244863632261112

Record					
	1998 -	1st:2	2nd:6	3rd:3	Ran:17
	Pre1998 -	1st:4	2nd:8	3rd:3	Ran:32

Win Prizemoney £16,896 *Total Prizemoney* £30,588

Wins								
* **1998**	Oct	Nottin	(SFT)	C	8.2f		72	<
* **1998**	Spt	Ripon	(SFT)	C	8f		64	
* 1997	*Jan*	*Southw*	*(STD)*	*H*	*8f*	*64*	*67*	
* 1996	Aug	*Wolver*	*(STD)*	*C*	*9.4f*		*64*	
* 1996	*May*	*Southw*	*(STD)*	*H*	*8f*	*66*	*66*	
* 1996	*Feb*	*Wolver*	*(STD)*		*8.5f*		*58*	

1998 Turf 2-4: (8f 2-4) (g-s 1-2, gd 1-2) 1998 AW 0-13: (7f 2, 8f 8, 9f 3) (Fibr 13)
Above-average gelding, effective 7 to 8f, best at 8f, acts on g-s to gd - acts on Fibr, best on gd, often wears blinkers (extremely effectively), and likes Southwell. Turf high 73 - 2nd of 24 giving 8lb to Band on the Run (7 Nov Doncaster 8f gd RF 5147) - also 1st of 17 from Sharp Rebuff (14 Oct Nottingham RF 4804). AW high 70 - 2nd of 11 giving 10lb to Theatre Magic (5 Jan Southwell 7f Fibr RF 0023). His wins to runs ratio is not very good these days. Even when he did manage to get his head in front at Southwell in February, the Stewards took the race away from him. He finally got his act together on turf with two victories in soft ground in the autumn. **B A McMahon [6-49] Michael Stokes.*

YES KEEMO SABEE BHB 62f58a **RR 64f 58a** 2332[8]
3 b g Arazi (USA) 9.2f **(74)** - Nazeera (FR) (Lashkari) 9.8f **(67)**
Form - 458

Record					
	1998 -	1st:0	2nd:0	3rd:0	Ran:3

Win Prizemoney £0 *Total Prizemoney* £243
1998 Turf 0-3: (10f, 12f, 14f) (gd 2, frm)
Light-framed, currently average gelding. Turf high 64.
**B A McMahon [0-3] Ian Guise.*

YET AGAIN BHB 60f60a **RR 63f 60a** 2763[3]
6 ch g Weldnaas (USA) 8.4f **(55)** - Brightelmstone (Prince Regent (FR)) 9.8f **(54)**
Form - 2141523

Record					
	1998 -	1st:2	2nd:2	3rd:1	Ran:7
	Pre1998 -	1st:7	2nd:3	3rd:2	Ran:29

Win Prizemoney £23,723 *Total Prizemoney* £31,207

Wins								
* **1998**	Jun	Bright	(FRM)	H	11.9f	55	57	
* **1998**	*Jan*	*Lingfi*	*(STD)*	*H*	*12f*	*56*	*58*	
* 1997	Aug	Chepst	(G-F)	H	12.1f	50	54	
* 1997	Apr	Bright	(FRM)	H	11.9f	40	50	
* 1997	*Jan*	*Lingfi*	*(STD)*	*H*	*13f*	*40*	*52*	
* 1997	*Jan*	*Lingfi*	*(STD)*	*H*	*12f*	*40*	*53+*	
* 1996	*Dec*	*Lingfi*	*(STD)*	*H*	*12f*	*40*	*50+*	
1996	Jun	Warwic	(FRM)	S	10.8f		43	
1995	Jun	Bright	(G-F)		11.9f		69	<

1998 Turf 1-5: (12f 1-5) (gd 3, g-f 1-1, frm) 1998 AW 1-2: (12f 1-2) (Equi 1-2)
Average gelding, effective 12f, acts on gd to frm - acts on Equi, has worn blinkers, prefers left handed tracks, favours tight tracks, and excels at Lingfield. Turf high 63 - 2nd of 9 getting 16lb from Montecristo (1 Jly Brighton 12f frm RF 2439) - also 1st of 9 getting 5lb from Be True (2 Jun Brighton RF 1642). AW high 58 - 1st of 7 from Time Can Tell (10 Jan Lingfield RF 0059). Consistent. A winner on the Flat and over hurdles, he has been equally successful over middle distances on turf and sand in recent years.
**Miss Gay Kelleway[10-27] A P Griffin(from B Hanbury [2-16] Jly 1996).*

YO-MATE BHB 23f33a **RR 13f 33a** 2958[13]

7 b g Komaite (USA) 6.9f **(61)** - Silent Sun (Blakeney) 10.5f **(64)**

Form - 0

Record	**1998 -**	1st:0	2nd:0	3rd:0	Ran:1
	Pre1998 -	1st:0	2nd:0	3rd:0	Ran:5

1998 Turf 0-1: (12f) (frm)

Very moderate gelding.

**R Simpson [0-1] Miss L A Elliott (from T Hind [0-1] Jun 1997).*

YORBA LINDA (IRE) **RR 94f** 3863a[3]

3 ch f Night Shift (USA) 8.1f **(73)** - Allepolina (USA) 00

Form - 7282633

1998 Turf 0-7: (5f 4, 6f 2, 7f) (hvy, g-s, gd 2, g-f 2, frm)

Useful filly, effective 5 to 6f, best at 5f, acts on gd to g-f, best on gd, has worn blinkers. Turf high 94.

**J S Bolger in IRE [1-9] T F Brennan.*

YORKIES BOY BHB 112f **RR 116f** 5152[2]

3 ro c Clantime 6.6f **(57)** - Slipperose (Persepolis (FR)) 6.4f **(67)**

Form - 1180002

Record	**1998 -**	1st:2	2nd:1	3rd:0	Ran:7
	Pre1998 -	1st:1	2nd:2	3rd:0	Ran:12

Win Prizemoney £34,651 *Total Prizemoney* £50,371

Wins	* **1998**	May Newmar (G-S)	G3	5f	113	<
	* **1998**	Apr Newmar (SFT)	L	5f	109	
	* 1997	Jun Cheste (G-F)		5.1f	76+	

1998 Turf 2-7: (5f 2-5, 6f 2) (gd 2-3, g-f, frm 3)

Scopey, high-class colt, effective 5 to 6f, best at 5f, acts on gd. Turf high 116 - 2nd of 12 giving 6lb to Gorse (7 Nov Doncaster 6f gd RF 5152) - also 1st of 13 getting 9lb from My Best Valentine (2 May Newmarket RF 0975). Inconsistent. Made a fine start to this season by winning his first two starts at Newmarket, the second of which was the Palace House Stakes. The fast ground was against him on his next couple of starts and he quickly retreated into the wings. He proved his liking for a soft surface at Doncaster on the last day of the Flat season, when he finished runner-up in a Listed race behind Gorse. **B A McMahon [3-19] Mrs M Beddis.*

	Pre1998 -	1st:1	2nd:2	3rd:1	Ran:7

Win Prizemoney £15,512 *Total Prizemoney* £58,005

Wins	* **1998**	May Newbur (G-F)	L	13.3f	107	<
	* 1996	Oct Salisb (G-S)		8f	97+	

1998 Turf 1-6: (12f, 13f 1-1, 14f, 16f 2, 22f) (sft, gd 3, frm 1-2)

Unfurnished, Group-class gelding, effective 12 to 16f, best at 16f, acts on sft to frm, best on gd, prefers left handed tracks, excels at Newbury. Turf high 112 - 5th of 24 giving 3lb to Jezabeel (3 Nov Flemington 16f gd RF 5153a) - also 1st of 8 from Ferny Hill (16 May Newbury RF 1259). Consistent. Unlike his namesakes, he has not always been noted for a terrier-like will-to-win. However, he is capable of excellent form and repaid his connections' faith when finishing an honourable fifth in the Foster's Melbourne Cup. Australian jockey Danny Nikolic believes he is a ready-made winner of that great race and he will probably be back for round two next year. **P F I Cole [2-13] H R H Prince Fahd Salman.*

YORKSHIRE GRIT BHB 57f **RR 60f** 4253[16]

2 ch f Ardkinglass 5f **(64)** - Jarrettelle (All Systems Go)

Form - 8601730

Record	**1998 -**	1st:1	2nd:0	3rd:1	Ran:7

Win Prizemoney £1,884 *Total Prizemoney* £2,254

Wins	* **1998**	Jly Catter (GD)	S	5f	60	<

1998 Turf 1-6: (5f 1-6) (gd 2, g-f, frm 1-3) 1998 AW 0-1: (5f) (Fibr)

Average filly, effective 5f, acts on g-f to frm. Turf high 60 - 1st of 6 getting 5lb from Ladycake (2 Jly Catterick RF 2461).

**R M Whitaker [1-7] Michael Wilson.*

YOUNG ANNABEL (USA) BHB 60f56a **RR 60f 56a** 234[5]

5 ch m Cahill Road (USA) 8.5f **(82)** - Only for Eve (USA) (Barachois (CAN)) 8.3f **(63)**

Form - 05

Record	**1998 -**	1st:0	2nd:0	3rd:0	Ran:2
	Pre1998 -	1st:1	2nd:1	3rd:1	Ran:10

Win Prizemoney £3,534 *Total Prizemoney* £4,706

Wins	1996	*Jly Southw (STD)*	*H*	*7f*	*58 63*	<

1998 AW 0-2: (8f 2) (Fibr 2)

Yorkshire did not quite rise to the occasion at Ascot

YORKSHIRE (IRE) BHB 110f **RR 112f** 5153a[5]

4 ch g Generous (IRE) 11.5f **(82)** - Ausherra (USA) (Diesis) 9.3f **(69)**

Form - 172655

Record	**1998 -**	1st:1	2nd:1	3rd:0	Ran:6

Average filly. AW high 27.

**D Morris [0-2] Baker Street Partnership (from C A Dwyer [1-10] May 1997).*

YOUNG BEN (IRE) BHB 43f32a **RR 42f 32a** 3309[16]
6 ch g Fayruz 6.6f **(63)** - Jive (Ahonoora) 8.1f **(73)**
Form - 3603250200
Record 1998 - 1st:0 2nd:2 3rd:2 Ran:10
Pre1998 - 1st:1 2nd:1 3rd:5 Ran:31
Win Prizemoney £3,731 *Total Prizemoney* £9,461
Wins * 1997 Jly Beverl (G-F) H 5f 36 43 <
1998 Turf 0-7: (5f 7) (gd 4, g-f, frm 2) 1998 AW 0-3: (5f, 6f 2) (Fibr 3)
Moderate gelding, effective 5f, acts on gd to frm, best on frm, mostly wears blinkers (effectively). Turf high 44. AW high 37. Inconsistent. **J S Wainwright [1-41] S Pedersen.*

YOUNG BENSON BHB 52f39a **RR 58f 39a** 4402[15]
6 b g Zalazl (USA) 10f **(55)** - Impala Lass (Kampala) 8.5f **(56)**
Form - 0808208300
Record 1998 - 1st:0 2nd:1 3rd:1 Ran:10
Pre1998 - 1st:2 2nd:1 3rd:5 Ran:27
Win Prizemoney £4,788 *Total Prizemoney* £9,844
Wins 1996 *Apr Wolver (STD) H 7f 47 64* <
1996 Apr Thirsk (G-F) 7f 61
1998 Turf 0-5: (7f, 8f 4) (gd 3, g-f, frm) 1998 AW 0-5: (6f, 7f 2, 8f, 9f) (Fibr 5)
Fair gelding, effective 8f, acts on gd, has worn blinkers, likes tight tracks. Turf high 58 (1st run) - 2nd of 14 giving 10lb to Nkapen Rocks (30 May Musselburgh 8f gd RF 1607). AW high 39.
**T Wall [0-19] E A Lee (from B A McMahon [2-23] May 1996).*

YOUNG BIGWIG (IRE) BHB 66f70a **RR 76f 70a** 4771[7]
4 b g Anita's Prince 6f **(62)** - Humble Mission (Shack (USA)) 5.8f **(53)**
Form - 070170124503360007
Record 1998 - 1st:2 2nd:1 3rd:2 Ran:17
Pre1998 - 1st:2 2nd:3 3rd:2 Ran:18
Win Prizemoney £18,592 *Total Prizemoney* £50,136
Wins * **1998** Jun Hamilt (SFT) H 5f 73 76
* **1998** May Thirsk (GD) H 5f 70 75
1996 Jly Goodwo (G-F) H 6f 96 <
1996 *May Wolver (STD) 5f 65*
1998 Turf 2-16: (5f 2-8, 6f 8) (sft, g-s 2, gd 2-7, g-f, frm 5) 1998 AW 0-1: (6f) (Fibr)
Neat, above-average gelding, effective 6f, acts on gd, has worn blinkers. Turf high 76. He looked progressive at two, but was disappointing last season. He has changed stables for this season, and has rewarded his new trainer with victories at Thirsk and Hamilton. Some excellent efforts in hot handicaps since.
**D W Chapman [2-19] Miss N F Thesiger (from J Berry [2-16] Oct 1997).*

YOUNG DABBER RR 12f 2543[9]
2 ch c King's Signet (USA) 7f **(51)** - Indian Flower (Mansingh (USA)) 7.4f **(55)**
Form - 50
Record 1998 - 1st:0 2nd:0 3rd:0 Ran:2
1998 Turf 0-2: (5f 2) (gd, g-f)
Currently poor colt. Turf high 12.
**J A Pickering [0-2] George Patching.*

YOUNG DALESMAN BHB 37f **RR 39f** 2229[4]
5 br g Teenoso (USA) 10.5f **(62)** -Fabulous Molly (Whitstead) 11.5f **(63)**
Form - 564
Record 1998 - 1st:0 2nd:0 3rd:0 Ran:3
Pre1998 - 1st:0 2nd:0 3rd:0 Ran:5
1998 Turf 0-3: (14f, 17f, 18f) (g-s, gd 2)
Very moderate gelding. Turf high 39. **A Streeter [2-14] B J Garrett.*

YOUNG IBNR (IRE) BHB 54f55a **RR 68f 55a** 4757[6]
3 b g Imperial Frontier (USA) 7f **(65)** - Zalatia (Music Boy) 6.8f **(57)**
Form - 47722743750340606
Record 1998 - 1st:0 2nd:2 3rd:2 Ran:17
Pre1998 - 1st:1 2nd:1 3rd:0 Ran:6
Win Prizemoney £2,879 *Total Prizemoney* £6,373
Wins * 1997 Apr Pontef (G-F) 5f 82 <
1998 Turf 0-11: (5f 11) (sft, g-s, gd 2, g-f 3, frm 4) 1998 AW 0-6: (5f 4, 6f 2) (Equi, Fibr 5)
Light-framed, average gelding, effective 5f, acts on gd to frm, has worn blinkers. Turf high 68. AW high 64.
**P D Evans [1-23] Mrs C A Torkington.*

YOUNG JOSH BHB 90f **RR 92f** 1746[17]
3 b c Warning 8.1f **(77)** - Title Roll (IRE) (Tate Gallery (USA)) 7.4f **(67)**
Form - 020
Record 1998 - 1st:0 2nd:1 3rd:0 Ran:3
Pre1998 - 1st:1 2nd:0 3rd:0 Ran:3
Win Prizemoney £4,199 *Total Prizemoney* £6,499
Wins * 1997 Spt Goodwo (GD) 6f 83 <
1998 Turf 0-3: (7f 3) (gd 2, g-f)
Useful colt, effective 6 to 7f, acts on g-f. Turf high 92 - 2nd of 10 giving 4lb to Adjutant (19 May Goodwood 7f g-f RF 1324). He obviously likes Goodwood, as he won there as a juvenile and was demoted after 'winning' a handicap at the same track on his second start at three. Moderate efforts otherwise.
**J H M Gosden [1-6] D H Armitage.*

YOUNG MAZAAD (IRE) BHB 57f66a **RR 47f 66a** 2824[6]
5 b g Mazaad 8.5f **(53)** - Lucky Charm (IRE) (Pennine Walk) 8.5f **(61)**
Form - 3876
Record 1998 - 1st:0 2nd:0 3rd:1 Ran:4
Pre1998 - 1st:1 2nd:6 3rd:0 Ran:13
Win Prizemoney £2,381 *Total Prizemoney* £7,779
Wins * 1996 May Folkes (GD) 6.9f 57 <
1998 Turf 0-4: (6f, 7f 2, 8f) (g-f, frm 3)
Average gelding, has worn blinkers. Turf high 56.
**D C O'Brien [1-16] Mrs S Harris (from R Curtis [0-2] Spt 1995).*

YOUNG NINER (USA) RR 42f 4192[5]
2 b c Forty Niner (USA) 8.8f **(73)** - Testy Trestle (USA) (Private Account (USA)) 8.5f **(74)**
Form - 5
Record 1998 - 1st:0 2nd:0 3rd:0 Ran:1
Win Prizemoney £0 *Total Prizemoney* £159
1998 Turf 0-1: (7f) (gd)
Currently moderate colt. **P W Chapple-Hyam [0-1] R Barnett.*

YOUNG PRECEDENT BHB 91f **RR 92f** 5078[18]
4 b c Polish Precedent(USA) 9f **(73)** -Guyum(Rousillon (USA)) 8.2f **(74)**
Form - 0315414636410
Record 1998 - 1st:3 2nd:0 3rd:2 Ran:13
Pre1998 - 1st:2 2nd:1 3rd:0 Ran:7
Win Prizemoney £43,971 *Total Prizemoney* £50,536
Wins * **1998** Oct Leices (SFT) H 7f 86 92 <
* **1998** Jly York (G-F) H 7.9f 85 88
* **1998** May Haydoc (GD) H 8.1f 83 85
* 1997 Aug Newbur (G-F) H 7.3f 81 82
* 1997 May Thirsk (G-F) 7f 71
1998 Turf 3-13: (7f 1-2, 8f 2-9, 9f 2) (sft, g-s 1-1, gd 1-4, g-f 3, frm 1-4)
Leggy, useful colt, effective 7 to 9f, best at 8f, acts on g-s to frm, best on frm, prefers left handed tracks, excels at York. Turf high 92 - 1st of 20 giving 2lb to Smooth Sailing (25 Oct Leicester RF 4985) - also 1st of 12 giving 2lb to High Spirits (10 Jly York RF 2701). Consistent. He was awarded a race at Haydock in May, but needed no assistance from that quarter when making all at York in July or winning again at Leicester in October. Lacks a turn of foot, so forcing tactics are ideal. **P W Harris [5-20] Pendley Knights.*

YOUNG ROSEIN BHB 54f **RR 61f** 4994[5]
2 b f Distant Relative 7f **(69)** - Red Rosein (Red Sunset) 8.2f **(63)**
Form - 605
Record 1998 - 1st:0 2nd:0 3rd:0 Ran:3
1998 Turf 0-3: (6f 3) (sft, gd, g-f)
Currently average filly. Turf high 61 (began Oct).
**Mrs G S Rees [0-3] J W Gittins.*

YOUNG-UN BHB 59f **RR 66f** 4614[16]
3 b c Efisio 7.7f **(69)** - Stardyn (Star Appeal) 9.6f **(65)**
Form - 0787570
Record 1998 - 1st:0 2nd:0 3rd:0 Ran:7
1998 Turf 0-7: (6f, 7f 5, 8f) (g-s, gd 2, g-f, frm 3)
Neat, average colt. Turf high 67. **S Dow [0-7] M F Kentish.*

YOUNICO BHB 65f55a **RR 68f 55a** 4384[5]
3 b g Nordico (USA) 8.2f **(59)** - Young Wilkie (Callernish) 12.6f **(58)**
Form - 7236124385
Record 1998 - 1st:1 2nd:2 3rd:2 Ran:9
Pre1998 - 1st:0 2nd:0 3rd:0 Ran:1
Win Prizemoney £2,206 *Total Prizemoney* £4,978

Wins * **1998** Jly Catter (GD) 13.8f 55 <
1998 Turf 1-5: (12f, 14f 1-3, 17f) (gd, frm 1-4) 1998 AW 0-4: (10f 2, 12f, 15f) (Equi 3, Fibr)
Average gelding, effective 10 to 14f, best at 14f, acts on gd to frm - acts on Equi, best on frm, often wears blinkers, and excels at Catterick. Turf high 68 (began Jly) - 2nd of 7 getting 5lb from Adeste Fideles (15 Jly Catterick 12f frm RF 2813). AW high 59 - 3rd of 9 getting 21lb from Dick Turpin (27 Jan Lingfield 10f Equi RF 0168). **M Johnston [1-10] C H Greensit.*

YOURS IN SPORT BHB 50f50a **RR 54f 50a** 883[8]
4 b g Slip Anchor 12.7f **(75)** -Birthdays' Child (Caerleon (USA)) 8.6f **(71)**
Form - 08
Record 1998 - 1st:0 2nd:0 3rd:0 Ran:2
Pre1998 - 1st:0 2nd:0 3rd:0 Ran:5
1998 Turf 0-1: (10f) (g-s) 1998 AW 0-1: (8f) (Fibr)
Scopey, fair gelding.
**D Nicholls [0-2] Bryan Robson (from J W Watts [0-5] Spt 1997).*

YOUR THE LIMIT (IRE) BHB 23f **RR 20f** 3309[19]
5 b g Don't Forget Me 9.5f **(66)** - Excruciating (CAN) (Bold Forbes (USA)) 8.9f **(59)**
Form - 6000
Record 1998 - 1st:0 2nd:0 3rd:0 Ran:3
Pre1998 - 1st:0 2nd:0 3rd:1 Ran:12
Win Prizemoney £0 *Total Prizemoney* £195
1998 Turf 0-2: (5f, 7f) (gd, g-f) 1998 AW 0-1: (8f) (Fibr)
Little account gelding, has worn blinkers. Turf high 2 (began Jly).
**J Parkes [0-7] Mrs B Cooney (from P J Flynn in IRE [0-11] Jly 1997).*

YUAN (USA) **RR 97f** 4793a[9]
3 ch c Miswaki (USA) 8.1f **(81)** - Northern Trick (USA) (Northern Dancer) 9.6f **(80)**
Form - 351210
1998 Turf 2-6: (9f, 10f 1-2, 11f, 12f 1-2) (g-s 2, gd 2-4)
Very useful colt, effective 9 to 12f, acts on gd. Turf high 97 - 2nd of 8 giving 5lb to Balla Sola (12 Spt Leopardstown 9f gd RF 4297a) - also 1st of 7 giving 5lb to Dee-One-O-One (6 Spt Curragh RF 4181a). Out of the very useful Northern Trick, this colt managed a couple of wins, and can progress further.
**A P O'Brien in IRE [2-6] Patrick Biancone.*

YULARA (IRE) BHB 90f **RR 99f** 4602a[12]
3 b f Night Shift (USA) 8.1f **(73)** - Fifth Quarter (Cure The Blues (USA)) 9.5f **(63)**
Form - 801610630
Record 1998 - 1st:2 2nd:0 3rd:1 Ran:9
Pre1998 - 1st:0 2nd:0 3rd:0 Ran:6
Win Prizemoney £11,810 *Total Prizemoney* £15,848
Wins * **1998** Jly Warwic (G-F) H 7f 70 76 <
* **1998** Jun Newmar (GD) H 7f 65 70
1998 Turf 2-9: (7f 2-7, 8f 2) (sft 3, gd, frm 1-4, hrd 1-1)
Very useful filly, effective 7f, acts on sft. Turf high 99 - 3rd of 4 getting 6lb from Alamo Bay (19 Spt Longchamp 7f sft RF 4470g). Inconsistent. She suddenly struck form with a game victory in a Newmarket handicap in June, and won again at Warwick two runs later. Not easy to catch right.
**B J Meehan [2-9] (from G M Lyons in IRE [0-6] Oct 1997).*

YVECRIQUE (FR) **RR 109f** 1226a[3]
4 f
Form - 13
1998 Turf 0-1: (11f) (g-s)
Currently Pattern-class filly. (1st run) - 3rd of 9 giving 7lb to Lexa (8 May Lyon Parilly 11f g-s RF 1226a).
**J-P Gauvin in FR [1-3] Mme Pierrette Fargier.*

ZAAHIR (IRE) BHB 32f36a **RR 41f 36a** 4536[10]
4 b g Marju (IRE) 9.2f **(76)** - Abhaaj (Kris) 9.5f **(73)**
Form - 00405000500
Record 1998 - 1st:0 2nd:0 3rd:0 Ran:11
Pre1998 - 1st:0 2nd:0 3rd:1 Ran:6
Win Prizemoney £0 *Total Prizemoney* £1,067
1998 Turf 0-10: (5f, 6f 3, 7f 2, 8f 3, 10f) (g-s 2, gd 3, g-f 2, frm 3) 1998 AW 0-1: (6f) (Fibr)
Workmanlike, moderate gelding, effective 8f, acts on gd, has worn blinkers, likes left handed tracks. Turf high 41.

**W Storey [0-14] D C Batey (from B W Hills [0-5] Jun 1997).*

ZAAJER (USA) **RR 97f** 4743[1]
2 ch c Silver Hawk (USA) 11.2f **(85)** - Crown Quest (USA) (Chief's Crown (USA)) 9.8f **(72)**
Form - 21
Record 1998 - 1st:1 2nd:1 3rd:0 Ran:2
Win Prizemoney £7,387 *Total Prizemoney* £12,039
Wins * **1998** Oct Ascot (SFT) 7f 97 <
1998 Turf 1-2: (7f 1-2) (g-s 1-1, gd)
Currently very useful colt. Turf high 97 (began Spt) - 1st of 7 getting 4lb from Queensland Star (10 Oct Ascot RF 4743). This American-bred cost $430,000 as a yearling, and made a promising debut at Ascot. He got off the mark a fortnight later on the same course when long odds on, and looks to have a future.
**E A L Dunlop [1-2] Hamdan Al Maktoum.*

ZAALEFF (USA) BHB 33f50a **RR 39f 50a** 1037[5]
6 ch h Zilzal (USA) 8.5f **(79)** - Continual (USA) (Damascus (USA)) 8.9f **(71)**
Form - 8755
Record 1998 - 1st:0 2nd:0 3rd:0 Ran:4
Pre1998 - 1st:0 2nd:1 3rd:1 Ran:15
Win Prizemoney £0 *Total Prizemoney* £1,666
1998 Turf 0-4: (8f, 12f 3) (sft 2, g-s, gd)
Fair horse, often wears blinkers. Turf high 39.
**K Mahdi [0-6] Hamad Al-Mutawa (from B Hanbury [0-11] Jly 1996).*

ZABAAD (USA) BHB 75f **RR 77f** 4148[3]
2 b f Kingmambo (USA) 10.9f **(85)** - Skeeb (USA) (Topsider (USA)) 8.3f **(71)**
Form - 553
Record 1998 - 1st:0 2nd:0 3rd:1 Ran:3
Win Prizemoney £0 *Total Prizemoney* £469
1998 Turf 0-3: (6f, 7f 2) (gd, g-f 2)
Currently above-average filly. Turf high 77 (began Jly).
**M P Tregoning [0-3] Hamdan Al Maktoum.*

ZABRISKIE BHB 46f **RR 35?f** 5128[13]
4 b g Polish Precedent (USA) 9f **(73)** - Somfas (USA) (What A Pleasure (USA)) 8.4f **(61)**
Form - 000
Record 1998 - 1st:0 2nd:0 3rd:0 Ran:3
Pre1998 - 1st:0 2nd:1 3rd:0 Ran:5
Win Prizemoney £0 *Total Prizemoney* £1,610
1998 Turf 0-3: (6f, 7f, 8f) (g-s, g-f, frm)
Lengthy, very moderate gelding, effective 7f, acts on frm, has worn blinkers. (began Oct). Becoming disappointing.
**G L Moore [0-5] R Kiernan (from Sir Michael Stoute [0-3] Jun 1997).*

ZADA BHB 42f54a **RR 42df 54a** 4574[20]
3 b g Distant Relative 7f **(69)** - Handy Dancer (Green God) 9.6f **(68)**
Form - 52300
Record 1998 - 1st:0 2nd:0 3rd:1 Ran:3
Pre1998 - 1st:0 2nd:1 3rd:0 Ran:6
Win Prizemoney £0 *Total Prizemoney* £1,184
1998 Turf 0-2: (8f, 10f) (g-f, frm) 1998 AW 0-1: (10f) (Equi)
Scopey, average gelding, effective 10f, - acts on Equi, likes tight tracks. (began Spt). Inconsistent. **G L Moore [0-9] Bryan Pennick.*

ZAHA (IRE) BHB 60f **RR 63f** 3088[3]
3 b c Lahib (USA) 8f **(69)** - Mayaasa (USA) (Lyphard (USA)) 9.9f **(72)**
Form - 8803
Record 1998 - 1st:0 2nd:0 3rd:1 Ran:4
Win Prizemoney £0 *Total Prizemoney* £610
1998 Turf 0-4: (10f 3, 12f) (gd 2, frm 2)
Workmanlike, average colt. Turf high 63.
**R W Armstrong [0-4] Hamdan Al Maktoum.*

ZAHARAN BHB 58f **RR 48f** 2437[4]
2 b g Mazaad 8.5f **(53)** - Green Pool (Whistlefield) 5f **(55)**
Form - 874
Record 1998 - 1st:0 2nd:0 3rd:0 Ran:3
1998 Turf 0-3: (6f, 7f 2) (g-s, frm 2)
Currently moderate gelding, has worn blinkers. Turf high 44.
**R Hannon [0-3] Mrs Jenny Reglar.*

ZAHRAN (IRE) BHB 39f37a **RR 44f 37a** 4920[11]
7 b h Groom Dancer (USA) 9.5f **(75)** - Welsh Berry (USA) (Sir Ivor) 10.2f **(70)**
Form - 0200000202002200
Record 1998 - 1st:0 2nd:5 3rd:0 Ran:16
Pre1998 - 1st:4 2nd:7 3rd:10 Ran:66
Win Prizemoney £11,598 *Total Prizemoney* £25,464
Wins * 1996 *Nov Lingfi (STD) H 8f 39 44*
* 1995 Aug Hamilt (FRM) SH 9.2f 43 50
* 1995 *Mar Lingfi (STD) H 8f 53 55*
1994 Jun Beverl (G-F) 7.5f 73 <
1998 Turf 0-15: (7f, 8f 10, 10f 4) (g-s, gd 5, g-f 2, frm 7) 1998 AW 0-1: (8f) (Fibr)
Fair horse, effective 7 to 8f, best at 8f, acts on gd to frm, best on gd, has worn blinkers. Turf high 49 (1st run) - 2nd of 20 to Gymcrak Premiere (17 May Ripon 8f frm RF 1285).
**J M Bradley [3-79] Smith (Saul) (from H R A Cecil [1-4] Jun 1994).*

ZAHRAT DUBAI RR 72+f 4595[6]
2 b f Unfuwain(USA) 11.4f **(74)** -WalesianaGER)(Star Appeal) 9.6f **(65)**
Form - 6
Record 1998 - 1st:0 2nd:0 3rd:0 Ran:1
1998 Turf 0-1: (7f) (gd)
Currently above-average filly.
**D R Loder [0-1] Sheikh Ahmed Al Maktoum.*

ZAIDAAN RR 38f 4395[11]
2 b c Ezzoud (IRE) - River Maiden (USA) (Riverman (USA)) 9.1f **(76)**
Form - 80
Record 1998 - 1st:0 2nd:0 3rd:0 Ran:2
1998 Turf 0-2: (5f, 8f) (gd, frm)
Currently very moderate colt. Turf high 38.
**C J Benstead [0-2] Hamdan Al Maktoum.*

ZAIN DANCER BHB 37f46a **RR 38f 46a** 72[9]
6 ch g Nabeel Dancer (USA) 6.1f **(65)** - Trojan Lady (USA) (Irish River (FR)) 8.6f **(78)**
Form - 00
Record 1998 - 1st:0 2nd:0 3rd:0 Ran:1
Pre1998 - 1st:1 2nd:3 3rd:3 Ran:27
Win Prizemoney £2,277 *Total Prizemoney* £6,861
Wins * 1997 *Jly Southw (STD) H 6f 42 46 <*
1998 AW 0-1: (7f) (Fibr)
Moderate gelding, effective 6 to 7f, - acts on Fibr, has worn blinkers, prefers left handed tracks, prefers tight tracks. Becoming disappointing. **D Nicholls [1-22] S Aitken (from A A Scott [0-6] Aug 1994).*

ZAINTA (IRE) RR 115f 4727a[13]
3 b f Kahyasi 12.9f **(74)** - Zaila (IRE) (Darshaan) 9.9f **(84)**
Form - 111130
1998 Turf 4-6: (10f 2-2, 11f 1-1, 12f 1-3) (hvy, sft 3-4, gd 1-1)
High-class filly, effective 10 to 12f, acts on hvy to gd. Turf high 115 - 3rd of 11 to Leggera (13 Spt Longchamp 12f hvy RF 4343a) - also 1st of 11 from Abbatiale (7 Jun Chantilly RF 1918a). She won the Prix Vanteaux and the Prix Saint-Alary in the spring before showing commendable courage to scramble home in the Prix de Diane. Returned from a break to win at Deauville, but lost her unbeaten record in soft ground in the Vermeille, and ran moderately in the Arc. She has been retired. **A deRoyerDupre in FR [4-6] Aga Khan.*

ZAKUSKA BHB 90f **RR 94f** 2849[2]
3 b f Zafonic (USA) 9f **(83)** - Connecting Link (USA) (Linkage (USA)) 9.1f **(82)**
Form - 412
Record 1998 - 1st:1 2nd:1 3rd:0 Ran:3
Win Prizemoney £3,915 *Total Prizemoney* £6,364
Wins * **1998** Jun Doncas (GD) 10.3f 84 <
1998 Turf 1-3: (8f, 10f 1-2) (gd 1-1, frm 2)
Workmanlike, currently useful filly. Turf high 94 - 2nd of 8 giving 2lb to Naskhi (16 Jly Doncaster 10f frm RF 2849).
**H R A Cecil [1-3] Clark Industrial Services Partnership.*

ZALAIYKA (FR) RR 113f 4217a[4]
3 b f Royal Academy (USA) 7.8f **(77)** - Zanadiyka (FR) (Akarad (FR)) 9f **(76)**
Form - 1124
1998 Turf 2-4: (8f 2-4) (hvy 1-1, sft, gd 1-2)
Group-class filly. Turf high 113 - 1st of 14 from Cortona (10 May Longchamp RF 1229a) - also 1st of 5 from Miss Berbere (19 Apr Longchamp RF 0838a). She broke the Longchamp course record when running away with the Poule d'Essai des Pouliches (French 1000 Guineas) and was duly sent off a short-priced favourite for the Coronation Stakes at Royal Ascot. However, the combination of a lengthy journey (she came by horse-box rather than plane) and slow ground did not help her chance, and she could not match the finishing burst of Exclusive. Reported to have suffered a setback during August, she could only manage fourth in the Prix du Moulin, where the soft ground was again against her. In retrospect, she did not beat a great field when winning her Classic and may have been overrated. She has been retired.
**A deRoyerDupre in FR [3-5] Aga Khan.*

ZALAL (IRE) BHB 93f **RR 86+f** 4705[1]
3 b c Darshaan 11.9f **(81)** - Zallaka (IRE) (Shardari) 11f **(46)**
Form - 651081
Record 1998 - 1st:2 2nd:0 3rd:0 Ran:6
Win Prizemoney £11,883 *Total Prizemoney* £11,883
Wins * **1998** Oct York (GD) 11.9f 86+ <
* **1998** Jly Bath (GD) 10.2f 69+
1998 Turf 2-6: (10f 1-3, 12f 1-3) (gd 2, g-f 1-2, frm 1-2)
Workmanlike, useful colt, effective 12f, acts on frm. Turf high 86 - 1st of 4 from Buzz (8 Oct York RF 4705). Gradually improving, he got off the mark in a Bath maiden despite not having the clearest of runs. Beaten favourite in a mile and a half handicap at Glorious Goodwood, possibly found out by the trip, but bounced back with an easy win at York. **L M Cumani [2-6] H H Aga Khan.*

ZALOTTO (IRE) BHB 47f48a **RR 37df 48a** 2964[12]
4 b g Polish Patriot (USA) 7.8f **(70)** - Honest Penny (USA) (Honest Pleasure (USA)) 10.4f **(73)**
Form - 232312660450
Record 1998 - 1st:1 2nd:1 3rd:1 Ran:9
Pre1998 - 1st:0 2nd:5 3rd:2 Ran:14
Win Prizemoney £2,085 *Total Prizemoney* £6,617
Wins 1998 *Jan Southw (STD) 7f 57 <*
1998 AW 1-9: (7f 1-5, 8f 3, 9f) (Equi, Fibr 1-8)
Rangy, average gelding, effective 6 to 8f, best at 8f, - acts on Fibr, mostly wears blinkers (extremely effectively), prefers left handed tracks, prefers tight tracks, excels at Southwell. AW high 62 - 2nd of 6 getting 2lb from Kingchip Boy (16 Feb Southwell 7f Fibr RF 0296) - also 1st of 11 from Pow Wow (23 Jan Southwell RF 0142). Not the easiest of rides, it took him a long time to get off the mark, but he managed to win a modest maiden in January, despite not looking all that keen.
**M P Bielby [0-3] K H Benson (from T J Etherington [1-20] Apr 1998).*

ZAMALEK (USA) BHB 50f40a **RR 50f 40a** 390[4]
6 b g Northern Baby (CAN) 10.2f **(74)** - Chellingoua (USA) (Sharpen Up) 8.3f **(67)**
Form - 654
Record 1998 - 1st:0 2nd:0 3rd:0 Ran:3
Pre1998 - 1st:4 2nd:3 3rd:1 Ran:28
Win Prizemoney £13,921 *Total Prizemoney* £19,434
Wins * 1997 Jly Sandow (G-F) H 10f 42 45
* 1997 Jun Lingfi (G-F) H 10f 40 43
* 1997 *Jan Lingfi (STD) H 10f 38 44*
1994 Aug York (G-F) 7f 84
1998 AW 0-3: (10f 2, 13f) (Equi 3)
Fair gelding, effective 8 to 12f, acts on g-f to frm - acts on Equi, best on g-f, has worn blinkers, likes right handed tracks, favours tight tracks, and does well at Sandown. AW high 36.
**R M Flower [3-18] Miss Victoria Markowiak (from G L Moore [0-8] Spt 1996).*

ZAMAN RR 82+f 5041[5]
2 b c Caerleon (USA) 10.9f **(79)** - Zafadola (IRE) (Darshaan) 9.9f **(84)**
Form - 5
Record 1998 - 1st:0 2nd:0 3rd:0 Ran:1
1998 Turf 0-1: (7f) (sft)
Currently decent colt. A half-brother to Zelanda, he caught the eye on his debut and looks a ready-made future winner.
**Sir Michael Stoute [0-1] Sheikh Mohammed.*

ZAMHAREER (USA) BHB 27f **RR 32df** 3382[8]
7 b g Lear Fan (USA) 10.4f **(80)** - Awenita (Rarity) 10.1f **(60)**

Form - 708
Record **1998 -** 1st:0 2nd:0 3rd:0 Ran:3
Pre1998 - 1st:2 2nd:2 3rd:2 Ran:26
Win Prizemoney £7,191 *Total Prizemoney* £11,880
Wins * 1996 May Ripon (GD) H 16f 42 56 <
* 1996 May Newcas (GD) H 16.1f 42 51
1998 Turf 0-3: (16f 3) (gd, g-f, frm)
Very moderate gelding, effective 16f, acts on sft to g-f, has worn blinkers, likes tight tracks. Turf high 32.
W Storey [4-38] Richard Thompson (from N A Callaghan [0-5] Jun 1994).

ZANABAY BHB 38f34a **RR 35f 34a** 13[11]
4 b f Unfuwain (USA) 11.4f **(74)** - Chrisanthy (So Blessed) 8.7f **(67)**
Form - 00
Record 1998 - 1st:0 2nd:0 3rd:0 Ran:1
Pre1998 - 1st:0 2nd:0 3rd:0 Ran:10
1998 AW 0-1: (11f) (Fibr)
Neat, very moderate filly. Becoming disappointing.
G Fierro [0-4] Pete Daykin (from W Storey [0-3] Jly 1997).

ZANAY BHB 78f **RR 79f** 4984[2]
2 b c Forzando 7.2f **(63)** - Nineteenth of May (Homing) 7.8f **(59)**
Form - 422
Record 1998 - 1st:0 2nd:2 3rd:0 Ran:3
Win Prizemoney £0 *Total Prizemoney* £2,255
1998 Turf 0-3: (7f 3) (sft, g-s, g-f)
Currently above-average colt. Turf high 79 (began Spt).
R T Phillips [0-3] Sanford Racing.

ZANTE BHB 106f **RR 107f** 3589[1]
3 b f Zafonic(USA) 9f **(83)** -Danthonia (USA)(Northern Dancer) 9.6f **(80)**
Form - 1251
Record 1998 - 1st:2 2nd:1 3rd:0 Ran:4
Win Prizemoney £13,009 *Total Prizemoney* £17,764
Wins * **1998** Aug Salisb (G-F) L 9.9f 103 <
* **1998** May Kempto (G-F) 8f 80
1998 Turf 2-4: (8f 1-1, 10f 1-3) (g-s, gd 2-3)
Scopey, Pattern-class filly. Turf high 107 - 5th of 9 getting 3lb from Alborada (1 Aug Goodwood 10f gd RF 3256) - also 1st of 8 from Innuendo (12 Aug Salisbury RF 3589). She was given a moderate ride when held-up off a slow pace in the Nassau Stakes, and set about her work with greater zest when making all to win a Listed event at Salisbury. A filly who lengthens rather than quickens, she has bags of scope and could win a Group race on the continent as a four-year-old. *H R A Cecil [2-4] K Abdulla.*

ZANY LADY BHB 46f **RR 45f** 5006[13]
3 gr f Arzanni - Lady Antonia (Owen Anthony)
Form - 5406040
Record 1998 - 1st:0 2nd:0 3rd:0 Ran:7
Pre1998 - 1st:0 2nd:0 3rd:0 Ran:1
Win Prizemoney £0 *Total Prizemoney* £513
1998 Turf 0-7: (7f, 8f 3, 10f 3) (sft, gd, g-f 2, frm 3)
Moderate filly. Turf high 61. Inconsistent.
R J Hodges [0-8] Shirley Barraclough and Partners.

ZARAGOSSA BHB 77f **RR 76f** 4813[5]
2 gr f Paris House 5.9f **(64)** - Antonia's Folly **(53f 53a)** (Music Boy) 6.8f **(57)**
Form - 175
Record 1998 - 1st:1 2nd:0 3rd:0 Ran:3
Win Prizemoney £3,821 *Total Prizemoney* £3,821
Wins * **1998** Aug Thirsk (GD) 5f 73+ <
1998 Turf 1-3: (5f 1-3) (gd 2, g-f 1-1)
Currently above-average filly. Turf high 76 (began Aug) - 5th of 11 giving 1lb to Northern Svengali (15 Oct Catterick 5f gd RF 4813) - also 1st of 7 getting 5lb from Get Stuck In (1 Aug Thirsk RF 3279).
J Berry [1-3] Slatch Farm Stud.

ZARFOOT RR 85f 5063[3]
2 br c Zafonic (USA) 9f **(83)** -Harefoot(Rainbow Quest (USA)) 10.4f **(75)**
Form - 3
Record 1998 - 1st:0 2nd:0 3rd:1 Ran:1
Win Prizemoney £0 *Total Prizemoney* £525
1998 Turf 0-1: (6f) (g-f)
Currently useful colt. *L M Cumani [0-1] D Hinojosa.*

ZARIFA BHB 38f25a **RR 26f 25a** 3809[9]
3 gr f Touch of Grey 8.1f **(47)** - Snow Huntress (Shirley Heights) 10.3f **(74)**
Form - 68780U000800
Record 1998 - 1st:0 2nd:0 3rd:0 Ran:12
1998 Turf 0-9: (5f 2, 6f, 7f 4, 8f 2) (gd, g-f 4, frm 3, hrd) 1998 AW 0-3: (7f 2, 8f) (Equi 3)
Neat, little account filly, has worn blinkers. Turf high 51. AW high 16. *R M Flower [0-12] Rare Stakes Partnership.*

ZARILIYA (IRE) RR 62f 4806[3]
2 b f Darshaan 11.9f **(81)** - Zariya (USA) (Blushing Groom (FR)) 10.3f **(76)**
Form - 3
Record 1998 - 1st:0 2nd:0 3rd:1 Ran:1
Win Prizemoney £0 *Total Prizemoney* £535
1998 Turf 0-1: (8f) (gd)
Currently average filly. *Sir Michael Stoute [0-1] H H Aga Khan.*

ZAYA RR 99f 3761[2]
3 ch c Zafonic (USA) 9f **(83)** - Ayah (USA) (Secreto (USA)) 8.7f **(72)**
Form - 82
Record 1998 - 1st:0 2nd:1 3rd:0 Ran:2
Pre1998 - 1st:1 2nd:0 3rd:0 Ran:1
Win Prizemoney £4,243 *Total Prizemoney* £6,049
Wins * 1997 Oct Doncas (GD) 7f 89++ <
1998 Turf 0-2: (8f 2) (gd, g-f)
Tall, currently very useful colt. Turf high 99 - 2nd of 3 getting 11lb from Soviet Bureau (20 Aug Salisbury 8f g-f RF 3761). Very impressive winner of his maiden in 1997, he never fulfilled the promise of that run in just two outings. However, he must have been well thought of, as his first run was in the French 2000 Guineas.
S bin Suroor [1-3] Godolphin.

ZECHARIAH BHB 66f55a **RR 65f 55a** 4835[10]
2 b c Kasakov - Runfawit Pet (Welsh Saint) 7.6f **(64)**
Form - 53075250
Record 1998 - 1st:0 2nd:1 3rd:1 Ran:8
Win Prizemoney £0 *Total Prizemoney* £1,166
1998 Turf 0-5: (6f, 7f 4) (g-s, gd, frm 3) 1998 AW 0-3: (5f 3) (Fibr 3)
Average colt, effective 7f, acts on frm, likes left handed tracks, likes tight tracks. Turf high 65 (began Aug). AW high 46.
J L Eyre [0-8] John Ashcroft.

ZEENEH BHB 64f **RR 69f** 2587[10]
3 b f Machiavellian (USA) 9.8f **(83)** - Possessive Dancer (Shareef Dancer (USA)) 9.9f **(73)**
Form - 600
Record 1998 - 1st:0 2nd:0 3rd:0 Ran:3
1998 Turf 0-3: (10f 3) (g-f, frm, hrd)
Lengthy, currently average filly. Turf high 69.
M A Jarvis [0-3] Sheikh Ahmed Al Maktoum.

ZEITZ (FR) RR 85+f 4344a[3]
2 b c Zieten (USA) - Zarzaya (USA) (Caro) 9.3f **(74)**
Form - 13
Record 1998 - 1st:1 2nd:0 3rd:1 Ran:2
Win Prizemoney £3,704 *Total Prizemoney* £7,744
Wins * **1998** Aug Beverl (G-F) 7.5f 85+ <
1998 Turf 1-2: (7f 1-1, 8f) (hvy, g-f 1-1)
Currently useful colt. Turf high 85 (1st run) (began Aug) - 1st of 10 giving 5lb to Salestria (12 Aug Beverley RF 3566). Despite looking backward, he made a winning debut in a Beverley maiden in August, but was a bit disappointing in a French Group Three on his only other start. *M Johnston [1-2] B Yeardley Contin Ltd.*

ZELAH (IRE) RR 74df 4933[7]
3 b f Alzao (USA) 9.8f **(73)** -Marie Noelle(FR)(Brigadier Gerard)9.3f **(58)**
Form - 16407
Record 1998 - 1st:1 2nd:0 3rd:0 Ran:5
Pre1998 - 1st:0 2nd:0 3rd:0 Ran:1
Win Prizemoney £4,045 *Total Prizemoney* £4,755
Wins * **1998** May Lingfi (G-F) 7f 91 <
1998 Turf 1-5: (7f 1-1, 8f 3, 10f) (g-s, gd 3, frm 1-1)
Neat, above-average filly, effective 7f, acts on frm. Turf high 91 (1st run) - 1st of 7 getting 9lb from Ring Dancer (13 May Lingfield RF 1201). *B Smart [1-6] John Hawker.*

ZELANDA (IRE) BHB 108f **RR 110f** 4330[7]
3 gr f Night Shift (USA) 8.1f **(73)** - Zafadola (IRE) (Darshaan) 9.9f **(84)**
Form - 051117
Record 1998 - 1st:3 2nd:0 3rd:0 Ran:6
Pre1998 - 1st:1 2nd:1 3rd:1 Ran:4
Win Prizemoney £28,191 *Total Prizemoney* £31,578
Wins * **1998** Aug Pontef (G-F) L 6f 108+
* **1998** Jly Newmar (G-F) 6f 110+ <
* **1998** Jly Newmar (G-F) 5f 100+
* 1997 Aug Haydoc (G-F) 6f 85+
1998 Turf 3-6: (5f 1-2, 6f 2-4) (gd, g-f, frm 3-4)
Scopey, Group-class filly, effective 5 to 6f, best at 6f, acts on frm. Turf high 110 - 1st of 6 giving 6lb to Ffestiniog (31 Jly Newmarket RF 3239) - also 1st of 7 from Bayleaf (16 Aug Pontefract RF 3672). A fairly useful juvenile in 1997, she was well beaten in softish ground on her seasonal debut but ran better on faster ground at Newmarket. She then hit a rich vein of form, completing a fine hat-trick on fast ground, but did not last long when going for a four-timer. **J H M Gosden [4-10] Sheikh Mohammed.*

ZELDA ZONK BHB 55f **RR 54f** 2630[17]
6 b m Law Society (USA) 11.6f **(71)** - Massive Powder (Caerleon (USA)) 8.6f **(71)**
Form - 0800
Record 1998 - 1st:0 2nd:0 3rd:0 Ran:4
Pre1998 - 1st:2 2nd:1 3rd:7 Ran:26
Win Prizemoney £7,189 *Total Prizemoney* £14,092
Wins * 1996 Jun Kempto (GD) H 7f 68 71 <
* 1996 May Redcar (G-F) H 7f 66 69
1998 Turf 0-4: (7f 4) (gd, g-f 2, frm)
Fair mare, effective 7f, acts on g-f to frm, best on frm, prefers right handed tracks. Turf high 54. Inconsistent.
**B J Meehan [2-30] Mrs Christine Painting.*

ZELDING (IRE) RR 109?f 4726a[4]
3 b f Warning 8.1f **(77)** - Zelda (IRE) (Caerleon (USA)) 8.6f **(71)**
Form - 23014
1998 Turf 1-5: (5f 1-3, 6f 2) (sft, g-s 2, gd 1-2)
Pattern-class filly, effective 5 to 6f, best at 5f, acts on sft to gd. Turf high 106 - 1st of 8 getting 3lb from Monday Night (1 Aug Deauville RF 3418a). She was blown away in the Cork And Orrery Stakes at Royal Ascot, but ran well on most of her other starts, notably when finishing fourth in the Group One Prix de l'Abbaye de Longchamp. There has never been much strength in depth in French sprinting and she should pick up another Group race.
**R Collet in FR [2-10] R C Strauss.*

ZEPPO (IRE) BHB 59f **RR 64f** 4390[20]
3 ch c Fayruz 6.6f **(63)** -Chase Paperchase (Malinowski (USA)) 10f **(56)**
Form - 0261566240
Record 1998 - 1st:1 2nd:2 3rd:0 Ran:10
Pre1998 - 1st:0 2nd:0 3rd:0 Ran:3
Win Prizemoney £7,385 *Total Prizemoney* £9,449
Wins * **1998** Jun Lingfi (G-F) H 6f 60 62 <
1998 Turf 1-10: (5f 4, 6f 1-6) (g-s, gd 2, g-f 1-4, frm 2, hrd)
Strong, average colt, effective 5 to 6f, best at 5f, acts on gd to hrd, best on g-f. Turf high 64 - 2nd of 12 giving 2lb to Sky Red (17 Aug Windsor 5f hrd RF 3687) - also 1st of 11 getting 20lb from Easter Ogil (23 Jun Lingfield RF 2201).
**B R Millman [1-10] The Plyform Syndicate (from M J Heaton-Ellis [0-3] Spt 1997).*

ZEPTEPI (IRE) BHB 25f **RR 14f** 941[13]
3 b f Astronef 7.9f **(59)** - Tangle Thorn (Thatching) 8f **(66)**
Form - 0
Record 1998 - 1st:0 2nd:0 3rd:0 Ran:1
Pre1998 - 1st:0 2nd:0 3rd:0 Ran:3
1998 AW 0-1: (9f) (Fibr)
Strong, poor filly.
**R Simpson [0-2] Kings Cross Racing (from T E Powell [0-2] Spt 1997).*

ZERMATT (IRE) BHB 50f49a **RR 56f 49a** 4589[9]
8 b h Sadler's Wells (USA) 11.3f **(87)** - Chamonis (USA) (Affirmed (USA)) 9.3f **(79)**
Form - 806445245242505107450
Record 1998 - 1st:1 2nd:3 3rd:0 Ran:17
Pre1998 - 1st:4 2nd:5 3rd:3 Ran:53
Win Prizemoney £21,601 *Total Prizemoney* £35,860
Wins * **1998** Jly Nottin (G-F) H 10f 50 56
* 1997 Jly Chepst (G-S) H 8.1f 50 51
* 1996 May Kempto (G-S) H 10f 67 74
* 1995 Jun Bath (G-F) H 8f 66 69
* 1994 May Chepst (SFT) 8.1f 79 <
1998 Turf 1-12: (8f, 10f 1-4, 12f 4, 14f 2, 16f) (sft, gd 1-5, g-f 3, frm 3)
1998 AW 0-5: (12f 2, 16f 3) (Equi, Fibr 4)
Fair horse, effective 8 to 14f, best at 9f, acts on sft to frm - acts on Fibr, has worn blinkers (extremely effectively), likes left handed tracks, excels at Wolverhampton. Turf high 56 - 2nd of 8 getting 4lb from Woody's Boy (16 May Newmarket 14f frm RF 1266) - also 1st of 15 getting 10lb from Include Me Out (18 Jly Nottingham RF 2924). AW high 53 - 5th of 7 giving 13lb to Shanghai Lil (21 Mar Wolverhampton 12f Fibr RF 0458).
**M D I Usher [5-70] Mrs M P Pearson.*

ZESTI BHB 37f35a **RR 39f 35a** 249[5]
6 br g Charmer 9f **(59)** - Lutine Royal (Formidable (USA)) 9.2f **(63)**
Form - 6245
Record 1998 - 1st:0 2nd:1 3rd:0 Ran:4
Pre1998 - 1st:0 2nd:1 3rd:3 Ran:11
Win Prizemoney £0 *Total Prizemoney* £2,429
1998 AW 0-4: (12f 2, 16f 2) (Fibr 4)
Moderate gelding. AW high 45. (DEAD)
**P Howling [0-6] Mrs J Lewis (from T T Clement [0-11] Nov 1996).*

ZIBAK (USA) BHB 39f **RR 42f** 4771[19]
4 b br g Capote (USA) 9.1f **(84)** - Minifah (USA) (Nureyev (USA)) 8.7f **(78)**
Form - 800727600
Record 1998 - 1st:0 2nd:1 3rd:0 Ran:9
Pre1998 - 1st:0 2nd:0 3rd:0 Ran:2
Win Prizemoney £0 *Total Prizemoney* £725
1998 Turf 0-8: (6f 2, 7f 3, 8f 2, 11f) (sft, gd, g-f 2, frm 4) 1998 AW 0-1: (10f) (Equi)
Scopey, moderate gelding. Turf high 42.
**J S Goldie [0-8] Mrs Lisa Olley (from B J McMath [0-3] Apr 1998).*

ZIBETH BHB 50f **RR 52f** 4451[5]
4 b f Rainbow Quest (USA) 11.2f **(81)** - Tiger Flower (Sadler's Wells (USA)) 10f **(76)**
Form - 008003312105
Record 1998 - 1st:2 2nd:1 3rd:2 Ran:12
Pre1998 - 1st:1 2nd:0 3rd:1 Ran:5
Win Prizemoney £9,196 *Total Prizemoney* £11,727
Wins * **1998** Aug Chepst (G-F) H 12.1f 47 52
* **1998** Jly Chepst (GD) H 12.1f 35 38
* 1997 Spt Goodwo (G-F) H 12f 54 59 <
1998 Turf 2-12: (9f, 10f, 12f 2-8, 14f 2) (g-s, gd 3, g-f 1-3, frm 1-5)
Workmanlike, fair filly, effective 12f, acts on frm, likes left handed tracks, favours tight tracks. Turf high 52 - 1st of 8 getting 1lb from Ronquista d'Or (13 Aug Chepstow RF 3611). A game and genuine filly, she runs from the front.
**S Dow [3-14] N Boyle (from L M Cumani [0-3] May 1997).*

ZIDAC BHB 64f63a **RR 63f 63a** 4670[6]
6 b or br g Statoblest 6.4f **(63)** - Sule Skerry (Scottish Rifle) 10f **(55)**
Form - 00316
Record 1998 - 1st:1 2nd:0 3rd:1 Ran:5
Pre1998 - 1st:2 2nd:2 3rd:1 Ran:22
Win Prizemoney £9,454 *Total Prizemoney* £13,279
Wins * **1998** Spt Warwic (G-F) CH 10.8f 59 63
* 1996 May Lingfi (G-F) H 10f 70 74 <
* 1996 Apr Leices (GD) H 10f 64 72
1998 Turf 1-5: (8f, 9f, 10f 2, 11f 1-1) (g-s, frm 1-4)
Average gelding, effective 8 to 11f, best at 10f, acts on gd to frm, best on gd, likes left handed tracks, favours tight tracks. Turf high 63. **P J Makin [3-30] Brian Brackpool.*

ZIELANA GORA BHB 35f **RR 11f** 2963[17]
3 b f Polish Precedent (USA) 9f **(73)** - La Lutine (My Swallow) 9.2f **(71)**
Form - 4000
Record 1998 - 1st:0 2nd:0 3rd:0 Ran:4
Pre1998 - 1st:0 2nd:0 3rd:0 Ran:2
Win Prizemoney £0 *Total Prizemoney* £237
1998 Turf 0-4: (6f, 7f, 8f, 10f) (gd, g-f, frm 2)
Unfurnished, poor filly. Turf high 56.

**C A Dwyer [0-4] Skeltools Ltd (from J G Smyth-Osborne [0-1] Spt 1997).*

ZIGERE RR 54f 1895^{5}
2 ch c Lycius (USA) 8.8f **(71)** - Zia (USA) (Shareef Dancer (USA)) 9.9f **(73)**
Form - 5
Record 1998 - 1st:0 2nd:0 3rd:0 Ran:1
1998 Turf 0-1: (6f) (g-s)
Currently fair colt. **C E Brittain [0-1] Sheikh Marwan Al Maktoum.*

ZIGGY'S DANCER (USA) BHB 89f72a **RR 95f 72a** 4821^{6}
7 b h Ziggy's Boy (USA) 6.1f **(61)** - My Shy Dancer (USA) (Northjet) 10.3f **(74)**
Form - 05153202200434563046
Record 1998 - 1st:1 2nd:3 3rd:3 Ran:20
Pre1998 - 1st:7 2nd:10 3rd:8 Ran:72
Win Prizemoney £39,366 *Total Prizemoney* £92,899

Wins							
* **1998**	*Feb Southw*	*(STD)*	*C*	*6f*		*76+*	
* 1997	Jun Cheste	(G-F)	H	5.1f	81	82	
* 1995	*Dec Lingfi*	*(STD)*	*H*	*5f*	*80*	*76*	
* 1995	Jly Cheste	(GD)		5.1f		94	<
* 1995	May Beverl	(G-F)		5f		94?	
* 1995	Apr Carlis	(GD)	H	5.9f	64	70+	
* 1995	*Mar Wolver*	*(STD)*	*H*	*6f*	*66*	*69*	
* 1995	*Feb Wolver*	*(STD)*	*H*	*7f*	*50*	*60+*	

1998 Turf 0-13: (5f 8, 6f 5) (sft, g-s, gd 5, g-f 4, frm 2) 1998 AW 1-7: (6f 1-4, 7f 3) (Fibr 1-7)
Very useful horse, effective 5 to 7f, best at 5f, acts on gd to frm - acts on Fibr, likes left handed tracks, likes tight tracks, excels at Chester. Turf high 95. AW high 76. He found an opportunity on the Southwell Fibresand in February, making all to win a claimer with the utmost ease. He failed to win in a further 17 outings, but was placed on six occasions and deserves another win.
**E J Alston [8-81] J Connor (from R W Armstrong [0-11] Oct 1994).*

ZIGGY STARDUST (IRE) BHB 44f35a **RR 45f 35a** 5002^{8}
3 b g Roi Danzig (USA) 10.5f **(62)** - Si Princess (Coquelin (USA)) 8.4f **(58)**
Form - 675230248
Record 1998 - 1st:0 2nd:2 3rd:1 Ran:9
Pre1998 - 1st:0 2nd:0 3rd:0 Ran:2
Win Prizemoney £0 *Total Prizemoney* £2,122
1998 Turf 0-6: (10f, 11f, 12f 4) (g-s, gd, g-f 3, frm) 1998 AW 0-3: (8f, 11f, 12f) (Equi 2, Fibr)
Unfurnished, moderate gelding, effective 10 to 12f, best at 12f, acts on gd to frm, best on g-f, favours tight tracks. Turf high 45 - 2nd of 10 getting 21lb from Royal Legend (13 Jun Lingfield 10f gd RF 1969). AW high 34. **Mrs A J Bowlby [0-11] Joe Cool Partnership.*

ZIGGY'S VIOLA (IRE) BHB 47f **RR 52f** 4252^{16}
4 b f Roi Danzig (USA) 10.5f **(62)** - Olivia Jane (IRE) (Ela-Mana-Mou) 10.1f **(70)**
Form - 00
Record 1998 - 1st:0 2nd:0 3rd:0 Ran:2
Pre1998 - 1st:1 2nd:1 3rd:1 Ran:12
Win Prizemoney £2,197 *Total Prizemoney* £3,159
Wins 1997 Spt Catter (G-F) S 13.8f 52 <
1998 Turf 0-1: (12f) (frm) 1998 AW 0-1: (12f) (Fibr)
Rangy, fair filly, effective 12 to 16f, best at 14f, acts on g-s to frm, prefers left handed tracks, favours tight tracks.
**Mrs A M Naughton [0-2] Mrs C T Woodley (from Mrs M Reveley [1-12] Oct 1997).*

ZIHAAM (USA) BHB 85f **RR 89+f** 1887^{1}
3 gr ro c Dayjur (USA) 6.8f **(79)** - Asl (USA) (Caro) 9.3f **(74)**
Form - 621
Record 1998 - 1st:1 2nd:1 3rd:0 Ran:3
Win Prizemoney £3,805 *Total Prizemoney* £4,980
Wins * **1998** Jun Salisb (G-S) 7f 89+ <
1998 Turf 1-3: (6f 2, 7f 1-1) (gd 1-2, frm)
Scopey, currently useful colt. Turf high 89 - 1st of 10 from Gleaming Hill (10 Jun Salisbury RF 1887). Likely to stay further than the seven furlongs over which he won his maiden. Withdrawn at the start after becoming upset in the stalls next time.
**J L Dunlop [1-3] Hamdan Al Maktoum.*

ZILLION (IRE) BHB 28f **RR 20f** 3134^{4}
3 b g Priolo (USA) 10.9f **(71)** - Arab Scimetar (IRE) (Sure Blade (USA)) 11.3f **(67)**
Form - 0044
Record 1998 - 1st:0 2nd:0 3rd:0 Ran:4
Pre1998 - 1st:0 2nd:0 3rd:0 Ran:4
Win Prizemoney £0 *Total Prizemoney* £376
1998 Turf 0-4: (8f, 10f, 12f, 15f) (g-s, gd, frm 2)
Workmanlike, moderate gelding, has worn blinkers. Turf high 20.
**J W Payne [0-8] Marwan Tabsh.*

ZILVA BHB 50f **RR 64f** 4961^{16}
3 b f Mazilier (USA) 8.5f **(56)** - Thulium (Mansingh (USA)) 7.4f **(55)**
Form - 0500
Record 1998 - 1st:0 2nd:0 3rd:0 Ran:4
1998 Turf 0-4: (7f, 8f 3) (g-s, gd, g-f, frm)
Workmanlike, average filly. Turf high 64.
**P J Makin [0-4] T G Warner.*

ZIMIRI BHB 60f80a **RR 59f 80a** 2972^{13}
4 ch c Keen 11.1f **(58)** - Annabrianna (Night Shift (USA)) 7.2f **(69)**
Form - 12380
Record 1998 - 1st:1 2nd:1 3rd:1 Ran:5
Pre1998 - 1st:1 2nd:0 3rd:0 Ran:6
Win Prizemoney £10,007 *Total Prizemoney* £12,009
Wins * **1998** *May Lingfi (STD) H 8f 74 79* <
* 1996 *Dec Lingfi (STD) 8f 74*
1998 Turf 0-3: (7f, 8f 2) (gd, g-f, frm) 1998 AW 1-2: (8f 1-2) (Equi 1-1, Fibr)
Scopey, above-average colt, effective 8f, - acts on AW, likes tight tracks. Turf high 59. AW high 79 (1st run) - 1st of 12 giving 2lb to Sweet Wilhelmina (8 May Lingfield RF 1105). Inconsistent. He has been fairly lightly raced in his career, and has looked a much better performer on Equitrack.
**J A R Toller [2-11] Rannerdale, D G & N A Fraser.*

ZINDABAD (FR) RR 97+f 4950a[2]
2 b c Shirley Heights 12.1f **(76)** - Miznah (IRE) (Sadler's Wells (USA)) 10f **(76)**
Form - 212
Record 1998 - 1st:1 2nd:2 3rd:0 Ran:3
Win Prizemoney £3,347 *Total Prizemoney* £32,222
Wins * **1998** Spt Pontef (G-F) 8f 97+ <
1998 Turf 1-3: (8f 1-3) (sft, g-s, frm 1-1)
Currently very useful colt. Turf high 97 (began Spt) - 2nd of 9 giving 3lb to Noble Pearl (18 Oct San Siro 8f sft RF 4950a) - also 1st of 9 from Fort Sumter (24 Spt Pontefract RF 4468). After a promising debut, this colt took a small race at Pontefract in easy fashion. He then ran second in the Gran Criterium in Milan and, although that race was not really Group One standard, he can win more Pattern races abroad. **B Hanbury [1-3].*

ZINEDINE RR 90f 4950a[5]
2 b c Zafonic (USA) 9f **(83)** - New Europe (Sharpo) 7.7f **(59)**
Form - 415
1998 Turf 1-3: (7f, 8f 1-2) (sft 1-2, gd)
Currently useful colt, often wears blinkers. Turf high 90 (began Spt). Comfortable winner of his maiden before finishing fifth in an Italian Group One. **A P O'Brien in IRE [1-3].*

ZIPPERGATE RR 87f 5064^{1}
2 b c Mystiko (USA) 7.7f **(59)** - Branitska (Mummy's Pet) 7.7f **(60)**
Form - 71
Record 1998 - 1st:1 2nd:0 3rd:0 Ran:2
Win Prizemoney £3,655 *Total Prizemoney* £3,655
Wins * **1998** Oct Newmar (G-S) 6f 87 <
1998 Turf 1-2: (6f 1-2) (g-f 1-2)
Currently useful colt. Turf high 87 (began Oct) - 1st of 16 from Candleriggs (30 Oct Newmarket RF 5064). Looked a potential Starr at Newmarket, and will do even better once stepped up in Tripp.
**B W Hills [1-2] W J Gredley.*

ZIRCON (IRE) RR 64f 4047^{2}
2 ch g Perugino (USA) - Tinktura (Pampapaul) 10.9f **(63)**
Form - 3036552
Record 1998 - 1st:0 2nd:1 3rd:2 Ran:7
Win Prizemoney £0 *Total Prizemoney* £1,562

1998 Turf 0-7: (5f 3, 6f, 7f 3) (hvy, gd 2, g-f, frm 3)
Average gelding, effective 7f, acts on gd to frm. Turf high 64 - 2nd of 9 to Divine Lady (2 Spt Brighton 7f frm RF 4047). He looks as though he will come into his element over longer trips, and when he tackles a mile he will be interesting.
**M R Channon [0-7] Mrs M J Vincent.*

ZIRCONI (FR) **RR 99f** 5130a[3]
2 b c Zieten (USA) - Muirfield (Crystal Glitters (USA)) 11.3f **(79)**
Form - 236323
1998 Turf 0-6: (5f, 6f 2, 7f 3) (hvy, sft 3, gd 2)
Very useful colt, effective 5 to 7f, acts on sft to gd, best on gd. Turf high 99 (began Jly) - 2nd of 7 giving 3lb to Stella Berine (7 Oct Saint-cloud 7f sft RF 4825a). This colt ran in most of the top two-year-old races in France and, although placed, failed to win one. Deserves to find a good race in 1999.
**Mme C Head in FR [0-6] P D Savill.*

ZIZI (IRE) BHB 84f **RR 84f** 2582[3]
3 b f Imp Society (USA) 7.1f **(63)** - Timinala (Mansingh (USA)) 7.4f **(55)**
Form - 03
Record 1998 - 1st:0 2nd:0 3rd:1 Ran:2
Pre1998 - 1st:1 2nd:0 3rd:4 Ran:6
Win Prizemoney £3,358 *Total Prizemoney* £9,888
Wins * 1997 Jly Ripon (G-F) 5f 76 <
1998 Turf 0-2: (6f, 7f) (g-s, frm)
Strong, decent filly, effective 5 to 7f, best at 6f, acts on g-f to frm, best on frm, has worn blinkers. Turf high 84 - 3rd of 15 getting 9lb from Misbah (7 Jly Newmarket 6f frm RF 2582).
**K R Burke [1-8] Nigel Shields.*

ZMILE BHB 80f **RR 75f** 4969[3]
2 b c Ezzoud (IRE) - Mountain Bluebird (USA) (Clever Trick (USA)) 6.6f **(77)**
Form - 4203
Record 1998 - 1st:0 2nd:1 3rd:1 Ran:4
Win Prizemoney £0 *Total Prizemoney* £2,157
1998 Turf 0-4: (5f, 6f 2, 7f) (g-s, g-f 2, frm)
Above-average colt. Turf high 75 - 3rd of 10 giving 14lb to Boogy Woogy (24 Oct Doncaster 7f g-s RF 4969).
**B W Hills [0-4] W J Gredley.*

ZOBAIDA (IRE) BHB 64f74a **RR 63+f 74a** 4677[15]
3 b f Green Desert (USA) 7.8f **(78)** - Charmante (USA) (Alydar (USA)) 9.1f **(76)**
Form - 67143000
Record 1998 - 1st:1 2nd:0 3rd:1 Ran:8
Pre1998 - 1st:0 2nd:0 3rd:0 Ran:2
Win Prizemoney £2,070 *Total Prizemoney* £2,847
Wins * **1998** *May Wolver (STD) H 7f 64 70++* <
1998 Turf 0-4: (7f 3, 8f) (gd 3, g-f) 1998 AW 1-4: (7f 1-3, 8f) (Fibr 1-4)
Workmanlike, above-average filly, effective 7f, - acts on Fibr, has worn blinkers, likes tight tracks. Turf high 63. AW high 73 - also 1st of 12 giving 11lb to River Ensign (29 May Wolverhampton RF 1582). Inconsistent. The race she won on her sand debut at Wolverhampton in May was very modest, and she has been quite comfortably held since. **M A Jarvis [1-10] Sheikh Ahmed Al Maktoum.*

ZOLA (IRE) BHB 57f **RR 63f** 4762[4]
2 ch c Indian Ridge 7.6f **(74)** - Fluella (Welsh Pageant) 10f **(65)**
Form - 0084
Record 1998 - 1st:0 2nd:0 3rd:0 Ran:4
1998 Turf 0-4: (7f, 8f, 10f 2) (gd 3, g-f)
Average colt. Turf high 63 (began Aug).
**M Quinn [0-2] & Mrs Gary Pinchen (from M R Channon [0-2] Spt 1998).*

ZOLA POWER BHB 60f57a **RR 66f 57a** 4876[8]
2 ch f Efisio 7.7f **(69)** - Caroline Connors (Fairy King (USA)) 7.7f **(59)**
Form - 624644038
Record 1998 - 1st:0 2nd:1 3rd:1 Ran:9
Win Prizemoney £0 *Total Prizemoney* £1,643
1998 Turf 0-8: (5f 6, 6f 2) (gd 2, g-f 4, frm 2) 1998 AW 0-1: (6f) (Fibr)
Average filly, effective 5f, acts on gd to g-f. Turf high 66 - 4th of 12 getting 7lb from Saafend Rock (23 Jun Lingfield 5f g-f RF 2200).
**G L Moore [0-9] Miss Nadia Benjamin.*

ZOMARADAH BHB 112f **RR 113f** 4954a[1]
3 b f Deploy 11.4f **(67)** - Jawaher (IRE) (Dancing Brave (USA)) 8.4f **(76)**
Form - 11851
Record 1998 - 1st:3 2nd:0 3rd:0 Ran:5
Pre1998 - 1st:0 2nd:0 3rd:0 Ran:1
Win Prizemoney £214,144 *Total Prizemoney* £215,225
Wins * **1998** Oct Woodbi (FRM) 10f 113 <
* **1998** May San Si (HVY) G1 11f 103+
* **1998** Apr Bright (GD) 10f 66+
1998 Turf 3-5: (10f 2-2, 11f 1-2, 12f) (hvy 1-1, g-s, gd 1-1, g-f, frm 1-1)
Scopey, Group-class filly, effective 10 to 11f, best at 11f, acts on hvy to frm. Turf high 113 - 1st of 8 getting 5lb from Tresoriere (18 Oct Woodbine RF 4954a). She put up an authoritative display to win the Oaks d'Italia, but ran poorly in the Ribblesdale Stakes at Royal Ascot and went on a three-month sabbatical. Unplaced on her return, she roared back to top form when winning the E P Taylor Stakes in Woodbine, where the silky-smooth Gary Stevens gave her a typically astute ride. She has looked a top-class filly when playing away and it would be nice if she could improve her record at home in 1999.
**L M Cumani [3-6] Darley Stud Management LTD.*

ZOOL **RR 39f** 3675[9]
3 ch c Wolfhound (USA) 7.3f **(71)** - Tisza (Kris) 9.5f **(73)**
Form - 00
Record 1998 - 1st:0 2nd:0 3rd:0 Ran:2
1998 Turf 0-2: (8f, 11f) (g-f, frm)
Lengthy, currently very moderate colt. Turf high 39 (began Aug).
**B Hanbury [0-2] Ahmed Ali.*

ZOOM UP (IRE) BHB 60f **RR 65f** 4893[12]
4 ch g Bluebird (USA) 7.9f **(71)** - Senane (Vitiges (FR)) 8.2f **(59)**
Form - 8086040
Record 1998 - 1st:0 2nd:0 3rd:0 Ran:7
Pre1998 - 1st:1 2nd:1 3rd:1 Ran:9
Win Prizemoney £3,318 *Total Prizemoney* £7,855
Wins * 1997 May Warwic (GD) 8f 82 <
1998 Turf 0-7: (10f 6, 12f) (g-s, gd, g-f 4, frm)
Lengthy, average gelding, effective 8 to 10f, best at 8f, acts on gd to frm, has worn blinkers. Turf high 70. Consistent. Ran some fair races in handicaps after winning at Warwick in May '97.
**M J Heaton-Ellis [1-16] K Maeda.*

ZORBA BHB 62f48a **RR 63f 48a** 1305[1]
4 b g Shareef Dancer(USA) 10.1f **(67)** -Zabelina(USA) (Diesis) 9.3f **(69)**
Form - 0733612621
Record 1998 - 1st:2 2nd:2 3rd:2 Ran:9
Pre1998 - 1st:3 2nd:4 3rd:7 Ran:28
Win Prizemoney £13,428 *Total Prizemoney* £22,889
Wins * **1998** *May Southw (STD) C 11f 54*
* **1998** Mar Hamilt (HVY) C 9.2f 47
* 1997 Oct Ayr (SFT) H 9f 60 64
1997 Jun Redcar (GD) C 10f 69 <
1997 Jun Hamilt (GD) S 9.2f 64
1998 Turf 1-4: (8f 2, 9f 1-1, 10f) (hvy, sft 1-2, g-s) 1998 AW 1-5: (8f 3, 10f, 11f 1-1) (Equi, Fibr 1-4)
Scopey, average gelding, effective 8 to 10f, best at 10f, acts on sft to frm - acts on Fibr, has worn blinkers, favours tight tracks, excels at Redcar and does well at Hamilton. Turf high 63 - 2nd of 16 giving 8lb to Mr Fortywinks (20 Apr Nottingham 10f sft RF 0775). AW high 54.
**J Hetherton [3-21] C D Barber-Lomax (from C W Thornton [2-16] Jun 1997).*

ZORRO BHB 52f50a **RR 51f 50a** 1204[4]
4 gr gTouch of Grey 8.1f 47) -Snow Huntress(Shirley Heights)10.3f **(74)**
Form - 062224
Record 1998 - 1st:0 2nd:3 3rd:0 Ran:5
Pre1998 - 1st:1 2nd:0 3rd:2 Ran:11
Win Prizemoney £2,168 *Total Prizemoney* £5,392
Wins * 1997 Jun Yarmou (FRM) H 10.1f 51 57 <
1998 AW 0-5: (10f 2, 12f 3) (Equi 5)
Workmanlike, fair gelding, effective 10 to 12f, best at 10f, acts on frm - acts on Equi, prefers left handed tracks, favours tight tracks. AW high 55 - 2nd of 11 getting 4lb from Chingachgook (17 Feb Lingfield 12f Equi RF 0306). Failed to make his mark in 1998, despite some good runs on the Equitrack.
**R M Flower [1-16] Mrs G M Temmerman.*

ZUCCHERO RR 62f 4006[12]
2 br c Dilum (USA) 7.1f **(56)** - Legal Sound (Legal Eagle) 7.3f **(54)**
Form - 000
Record 1998 - 1st:0 2nd:0 3rd:0 Ran:3
1998 Turf 0-3: (6f 2, 7f) (frm 3)
Currently average colt. Turf high 62 (began Jly).
**D W P Arbuthnot [0-3] Philip Banfield.*

ZUGUDI BHB 77f **RR 80f** 3276[8]
4 b c Night Shift (USA) 8.1f **(73)** - Overdrive (Shirley Heights) 10.3f **(74)**
Form - 006004058
Record 1998 - 1st:0 2nd:0 3rd:0 Ran:9
Pre1998 - 1st:2 2nd:1 3rd:2 Ran:19
Win Prizemoney £7,263 *Total Prizemoney* £15,498
Wins * 1997 Jun Yarmou (FRM) H 6f 70 73 <
1996 Jly Yarmou (FRM) 6f 63
1998 Turf 0-9: (7f, 8f 2, 10f 4, 12f 2) (hvy, sft, gd 5, g-f, frm)
Scopey, decent colt, effective 10f, acts on gd, has worn blinkers. Turf high 82. Inconsistent.
**K Mahdi [1-22] Sheik Ahmad Yousuf Al Sabah (from B Hanbury [1-6] Oct 1996).*

ZUHAIR BHB 70f80a **RR 82f 80a** 4864[4]
5 ch g Mujtahid (USA) 7.4f **(69)** - Ghzaalh (USA) (Northern Dancer) 9.6f **(80)**
Form - 076400520004
Record 1998 - 1st:0 2nd:1 3rd:0 Ran:12
Pre1998 - 1st:2 2nd:3 3rd:3 Ran:18
Win Prizemoney £5,864 *Total Prizemoney* £18,202
Wins * 1997 *May Wolver (STD) C 6f 66*
1995 Jun Newmar (G-F) 6f 85+ <
1998 Turf 0-10: (5f, 6f 8, 7f) (g-s, gd 5, frm 4) 1998 AW 0-2: (5f, 6f) (Fibr 2)
Decent gelding, effective 6f, acts on gd, has worn blinkers. Turf high 83. AW high 77. Capable of winning a six-furlong handicap or two, but does seem a shade high in the weights. Sold for 11,000 gns in October.
**D McCain [1-27] Clayton Bigley Partnership Ltd (from Major W R Hern [1-3] Jly 1995).*

ZULAL (USA) BHB 71f **RR 63+f** 5093[4]
2 ch c Zilzal (USA) 8.5f **(79)** - My Shafy (Rousillon (USA)) 8.2f **(74)**
Form - 004
Record 1998 - 1st:0 2nd:0 3rd:0 Ran:3
Win Prizemoney £0 *Total Prizemoney* £243
1998 Turf 0-3: (7f 3) (gd 2, frm)
Currently average colt. Turf high 63 (began Oct).
**E A L Dunlop [0-3] Hilal Salem.*

ZULU DAWN (USA) RR 73f 2909[5]
2 b c El Gran Senor (USA) 8.9f **(85)** - Celtic Loot (USA) (Irish River (FR)) 8.6f **(78)**
Form - 5
Record 1998 - 1st:0 2nd:0 3rd:0 Ran:1
Win Prizemoney £0 *Total Prizemoney* £265
1998 Turf 0-1: (7f) (gd)
Currently above-average colt.
**J W Hills [0-1] The Jampot Partnership.*

ZURS (IRE) BHB 69f75a **RR 67df 75a** 5125[4]
5 b g Tirol 8.1f **(64)** - Needy (High Top) 10.2f **(67)**
Form - 00254353313730154
Record 1998 - 1st:2 2nd:1 3rd:5 Ran:16
Pre1998 - 1st:3 2nd:2 3rd:4 Ran:24
Win Prizemoney £13,919 *Total Prizemoney* £25,911
Wins * **1998** Spt Salisb (HVY) H 9.9f 67 67 <
* **1998** Aug Sandow (G-F) H 8.1f 64 66
* 1997 Spt Folkes (FRM) H 6.9f 52 65
* 1997 Spt Leices (G-F) 8f 58
1997 *Feb Lingfi (STD) 8f 56+*
1998 Turf 2-16: (7f 2, 8f 1-9, 9f, 10f 1-3, 12f) (sft 2, g-s, gd 1-5, g-f 4, frm 1-3, hrd)
Above-average gelding, has worn blinkers, likes right handed tracks, likes tight tracks. Turf high 67.
**J R Poulton [4-24] Chris Steward (from Miss Gay Kelleway [1-16] Aug 1997).*

ZURYAF (IRE) BHB 43f60a **RR 51f 60a** 3692[5]
3 b g Fayruz 6.6f **(63)** - The Way She Moves (North Stoke) 10.4f **(55)**
Form - 00456382015
Record 1998 - 1st:1 2nd:1 3rd:1 Ran:11
Pre1998 - 1st:0 2nd:1 3rd:0 Ran:5
Win Prizemoney £1,856 *Total Prizemoney* £4,125
Wins 1998 Jly Windso (GD) S 11.6f 46 <
1998 Turf 1-10: (7f, 8f 2, 9f, 10f 4, 12f 1-2) (sft 2, gd 3, g-f 1-3, frm 2)
1998 AW 0-1: (11f) (Fibr)
Workmanlike, average gelding, effective 7 to 11f, acts on gd - acts on Fibr, often wears blinkers (very effectively). Turf high 55. (1st run) - 2nd of 7 to Heathyards Sheik (29 Jun Southwell 11f Fibr RF 2382).
**S Dow [0-1] Cazanove Clear Height Racing (from B J Meehan [1-15] Jly 1998).*

ZYDECHO QUEEN BHB 36f **RR 18f** 2565[7]
4 b f Then Again 7.4f **(52)** - Royal Resort (King of Spain) 7.8f **(52)**
Form - 7
Record 1998 - 1st:0 2nd:0 3rd:0 Ran:1
Pre1998 - 1st:0 2nd:0 3rd:0 Ran:3
1998 Turf 0-1: (12f) (frm)
Workmanlike, poor filly.
**J S Haldane [0-1] J S Haldane (from P Calver [0-3] Aug 1996).*

ZYDECO (IRE) BHB 92f **RR 92f** 1625[4]
3 b c Darshaan 11.9f **(81)** - Cajun Melody (Cajun) 5.2f **(54)**
Form - 24
Record 1998 - 1st:0 2nd:1 3rd:0 Ran:2
Pre1998 - 1st:0 2nd:2 3rd:0 Ran:3
Win Prizemoney £0 *Total Prizemoney* £3,281
1998 Turf 0-2: (10f, 12f) (g-s, frm)
Scopey, useful colt. Turf high 92 (1st run) - 2nd of 11 to Peak Path (28 Apr Bath 10f g-s RF 0890). He has put up some fine efforts in maiden company, but keeps finding one too good, though he has been narrowly beaten on two occasions.
**M C Pipe [0-3] James Hartnett (from J L Dunlop [0-2] Aug 1997).*

ZYGO (USA) BHB 52f **RR 60f** 4867[5]
6 b g Diesis 9f **(80)** - La Papagena (Habitat) 9.4f **(70)**
Form - 56005
Record 1998 - 1st:0 2nd:0 3rd:0 Ran:5
Pre1998 - 1st:0 2nd:2 3rd:1 Ran:9
Win Prizemoney £0 *Total Prizemoney* £3,487
1998 Turf 0-4: (7f 3, 8f) (gd 2, frm 2) 1998 AW 0-1: (8f) (Fibr)
Average gelding. Turf high 60.
**R T Phillips [0-8] The Beechdowners (from W Jarvis [0-7] Aug 1996).*

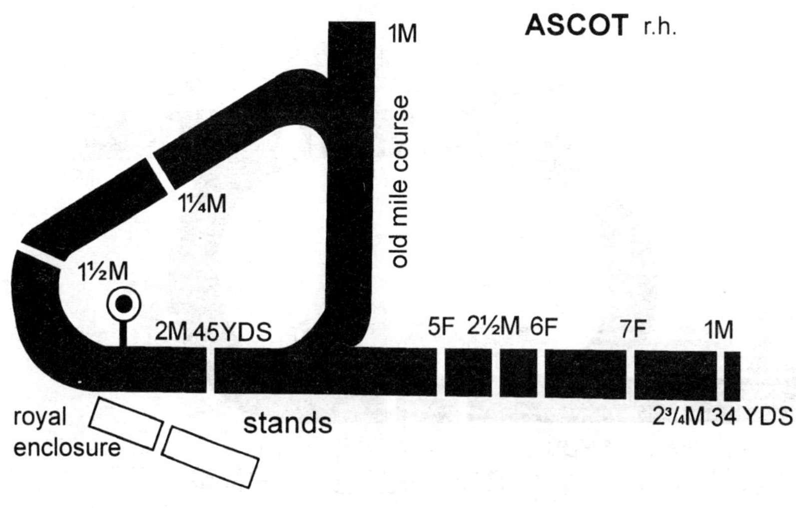

ASCOT

Address: Ascot Racecourse, Ascot, Berkshire SL5 7JN Tel: (01344) 622211
Fax: (01344) 624978
E-mail: AscotatITL.Net **Internet:** http://www.sportinglife.co.uk/ascot/
A triangular course of 1m 6f 34y. The course goes downhill from the mile and a half start for three furlongs into Swinley Bottom (the lowest part of the track): it soon joins the Old Mile (which starts on a chute) and is then uphill with a straight run-in of two and a half furlongs, the last 100y being level. The straight mile (Royal Hunt Cup Course) is downhill from the start, rises to the five furlong gate and then falls slightly to the junction of the courses. The whole course is of a galloping nature with easy turns but is nevertheless a testing one, especially on soft going.
Clerk of the Course: Mr N. Cheyne, Ascot Racecourse, Ascot, Berkshire SL5 7JN. Tel: (01344) 874567.
Racecourse Manager: Mr D. Erskine-Crum
Going Reports: (01344) 874567/ (0585) 505407 (Mobile)
Free stabling: shavings, straw or paper Tel: 01344 25630
By Car: West of the town on the A329. Easy access from the M3 (Junc 3) and the M4 (Junc 6). Car parking adjoining the course and Ascot Heath. Contact the Secretary, Ascot Authority. Tel: (01344) 876456.
By Rail: Regular service from Waterloo to Ascot (500y from the racecourse).
By Air: Helicopter landing facility at the course. London (Heathrow) Airport 15 miles, White Waltam Airfield 12 miles.

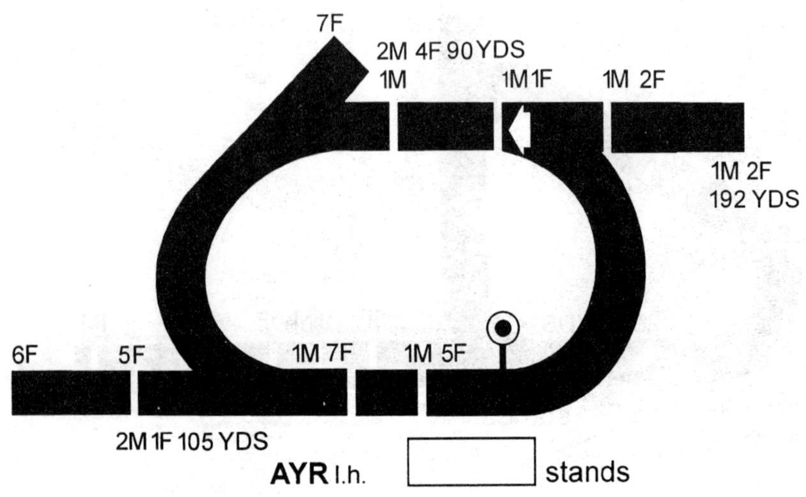

AYR

Address: Ayr Racecourse, Whitletts Road, Ayr KA8 0JE Tel: (01292) 264179
Fax: (01292) 610140
Internet: www.ayr-racecourse.com
A wide, relatively flat oval track of just over 1m 4f. An extension to the back straight provides a 1m 3f course with a sweeping turn at the top of the track tojoin the straight course four furlongs from the winning post. The straight six furlongs falls slightly for some three and a half furlongs and then rises slightly. In general, this is a very fair galloping course.
Clerk of the Course and Manager: Mr Mark Kershaw, Racecourse Office, 2 Whitletts Road, Ayr. Tel: (01292) 264179. Mobile: (0850) 464258.
Free stabling and accommodation for lads and lasses. Tel: (01292) 264179.
By Car: East of the town on the A758. Free parking for buses and cars.
By Rail: Ayr Station (trains on the half hour from Glasgow Central). Journey time 55 minutes. Buses and taxis also to the course.
By Air: Prestwick International Airport (10 minutes by car). Glasgow Airport (1hour).

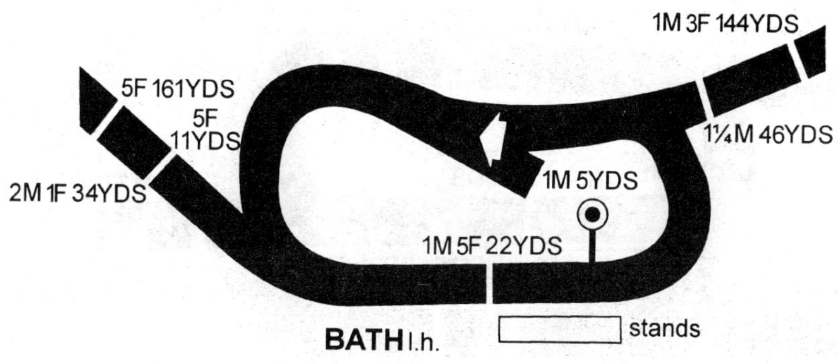

BATH

Address: The Racecourse, Lansdown, Bath Tel: Office (01291) 622260 Racedays (01225) 424609

An oval track of 1m 4f 25y with 1m 3f 144y, 1m 2f 46y and 1m 5y starts set on chutes from the back straight and an uphill run-in of four furlongs, which bends to the left. There is no straight course but an extension provides for races of five furlongs and of 5f 167y, which run generally uphill and left-handed to a distinct left-handed curve about a furlong from the winning post.

Clerk of the Course: Mr R. D. Farrant, Tylers Farm, Gravel Hill Road, Yate, Bristol BS37 7BN. Tel: (01454) 313186 Mobile (0850) 888380

Secretary: Miss S.J. Wilcox, Hopkins Farm, Lower Tysoe, Warwick, CV35 0BN Tel/Fax: (01295) 688030

Free stabling and accommodation for lads and lasses. Tel: (01225) 444274

By Car: 2 miles North-West of the City (M4 Junc 18) at Lansdown. Unlimited free car and coach parking space immediately behind the stands. Special bus services operate from Bath to the racecourse.

By Rail: Bath Station (from Paddington), regular bus service from Bath to the course (3 miles).

By Air: Bristol or Colerne Airports. (no landing facilities at the course).

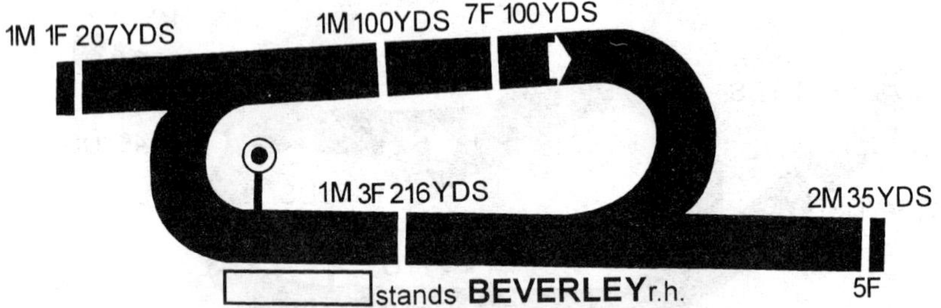

BEVERLEY

Address: Beverley Race Co. Ltd., York Road, Beverley, E.Yorkshire HU17 9QZ
Tel: (01482) 867488/882645 **Fax:** (01482) 863892
An oval course of 1m 3f set on two levels. A chute to the back straight provides a mile and a quarter course, which has a straight run of some five furlongs to a steep downhill bend into the home turn and an uphill run-in of two and a half furlongs. The five furlong course, which rises throughout with a distinct jink after a furlong and a slight bend to the right at halfway, provides a severe test for juveniles at the start of the season. The downhill turn into the straight and the short run-in prevent this from being an entirely galloping track.
Clerk of the Course and Manager: Mr J. G. Cleverly, F.R.I.C.S., Glebe House, Settrington, York. Tel: (01944) 768203 (evenings), (01482) 867488/882645 (Course Office).
Course foreman - Home (01430) 888907, Mobile (0585 678186).
Free stabling.
By Car: 7 miles from the M62 (Junc 38) off the A1035. Free car parking opposite the course. Owners and Trainers use a separate enclosure.
By Rail: Beverley Station (Hull-Scarborough line). Occasional bus service to the course (1 mile).
By Air: Helicopter landings by prior arrangement. Light aircraft landing facilities at Linley Hill, Leven airport.

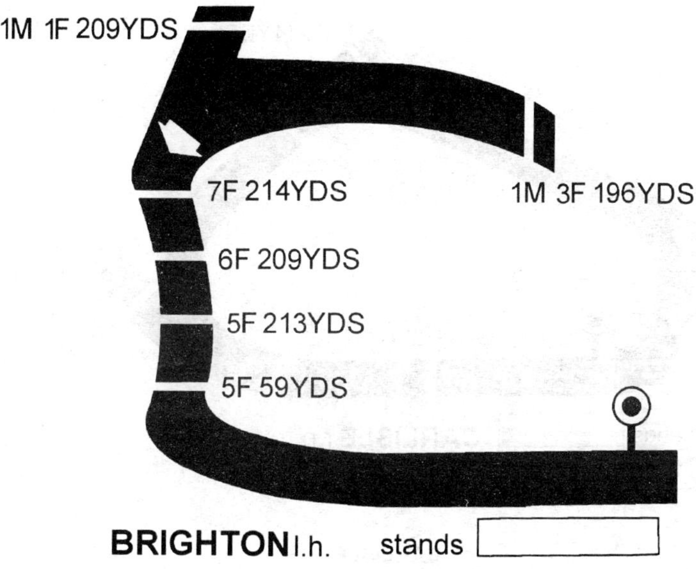

BRIGHTON

Address: Brighton Racecourse, Freshfield Road, Brighton, Sussex BN2 2XZ
Tel: (01273) 603580 **Fax:** (01273) 673267 **E-mail:** 1016111.141@compuserve.com
The course forms a horseshoe of 1m 4f round with easy turns and a run-in of three and a half furlongs. The first three furlongs are slightly uphill. Then there is a gentle descent and rise to about four furlongs from home. From there the ground falls steeply until about two furlongs out; then a sharp rise with the last 100y level. This sharp track, reminiscent of Epsom with its pronounced gradients, is unsuitable for big, long-striding animals, but it suits sharp sorts and is something of a specialists' course.
Clerk of the Course: Mr Jeremy Martin Tel. (0411) 739103 (mobile)
Stabling and accommodation available on request. Tel: (01273) 682912
By Car: East of the town on the A27 (Lewes Road). There is a car park adjoining the course.
By Rail: Brighton Station (from Victoria on the hour, London Bridge or Portsmouth). Special bus service to the course from the station (approx 2 miles) and to the sea front.
By Air: No racecourse facilities.

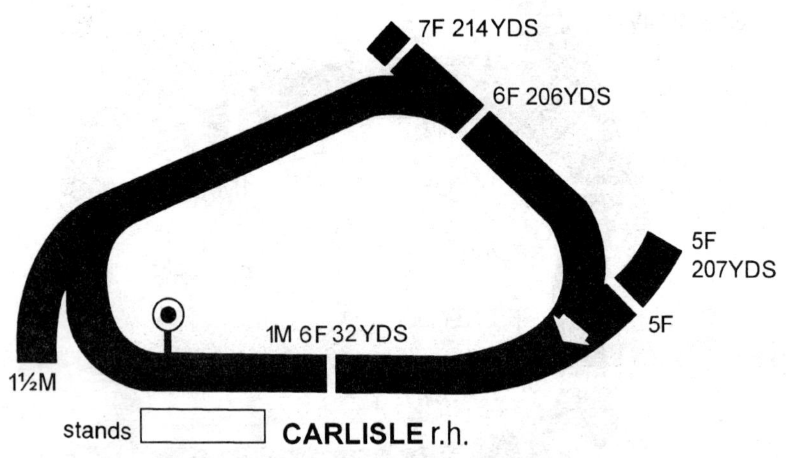

CARLISLE

Address: Carlisle Racecourse, Durdar Road, Carlisle CA2 4TS
Tel: (01228) 522973 **Fax:** Office (01228) 591827 Weighing room (01228) 523751
A pear-shaped, undulating course of 1m 5f with an extension for a mile and a half start and a straight uphill run-in of three and a half furlongs. The six furlong course (which includes the five furlong) starts on a chute, bears right for the first furlong and a half and again at the turn into the straight. The rise to the winning post, although it begins to level out from `the distance', makes it a stiff test of stamina.
Clerk of the Course: Mr J. E. Fenwicke-Clennell Tel: (01228) 522504 Mobile: (0860) 737729.
General Manager: I. R. Duff Esq, Grandstand Office, Carlisle Racecourse, Durdar Road, Carlisle, Cumbria CA2 4TS. Tel: (01228) 522973 Fax: (01228) 591827.
Club Secretary: Mrs Ann Bliss, Brackenridge, Brackenthwaite, Wigton, Cumbria, CA7 8AS. Tel: (01228) 522973.
Stabling and accommodation available on request. Please phone Head Groundsman on (01228) 546188, or Stable Office on (01228) 549489 by 5pm day before racing.
By Car: 2 miles south of the town (Durdar Road). Easy access from the M6 (Junc 42). The car park is free (adjacent to the course). Trackside car parking £3 (except Saturdays & Bank Holidays £5).
By Rail: Carlisle Station (2 miles from the course).
By Air: Helicopter landing facility by prior arrangement.

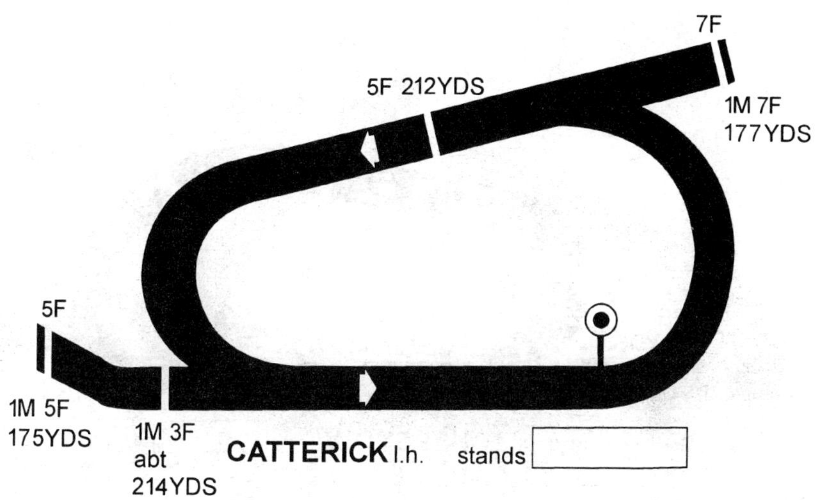

CATTERICK

Address: The Racecourse, Catterick Bridge, Richmond, North Yorkshire DL10 7PE Tel: (01748) 811478 **Fax:** (01748) 811082
An oval, undulating course of 1m 180y with two chutes, one for seven furlong and another for five furlong starts, and a straight run-in of three furlongs. The five furlong course is downhill throughout, sharply at first, and jinks left-handed at the junction of the courses. The seven furlong track joins the round course at the six furlong gate and is slightly downhill to the home turn. This sharp track is entirely unsuitable for long-striding gallopers and is often a specialists' track for both horse and jockey.
Clerk of the Course: (Flat) Mr James Sanderson, c/o The Racecourse, Catterick Bridge, Richmond, North Yorkshire DL10 7PE Tel: Mobile (0850) 058019
Secretary: International Racecourse Management Ltd., c/o The Racecourse, Catterick Bridge, Richmond, North Yorkshire DL10 7PE. Tel: (01748) 811478. Fax: (01748) 811082.
Boxes are allotted on arrival. Contact Mr Adrian Swingler, Racecourse Lodge, Catterick. Tel: (01748) 811478.
By Car: The course is adjacent to the A1, 1 mile North-West of the town on the A6136. There is a free car park.
By Rail: Darlington Station (special buses to course - 14 mile journey).

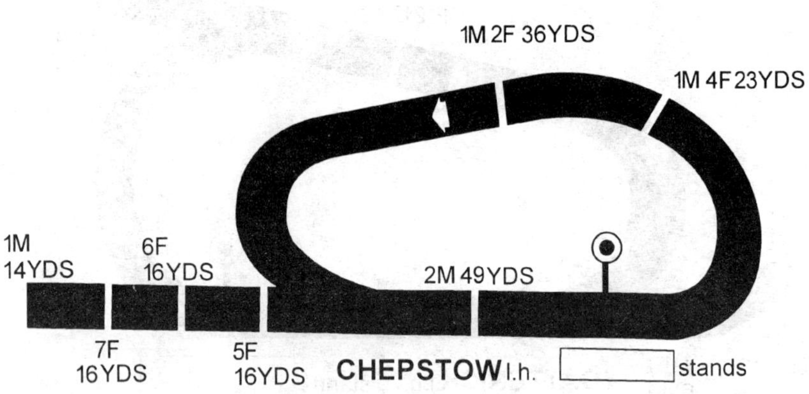

CHEPSTOW

Address: Chepstow Racecourse, Chepstow, Gwent NP6 5YH Tel: (01291) 622260 **Fax:** (01291) 625550

An oval, undulating course, about 2m in circumference with a straight run-in of five furlongs, which extends to make a straight mile. All races of up to a mile are run on the latter, which is downhill to the five furlong start and then rises sharply for two and a half furlongs before levelling out to the winning post. The changing gradients prevent this from being a really galloping track.

Clerk of the Course and Manager: Mr R. Farrant, Tylers Farm, Gravel Hill Road, Yate, nr Bristol BS37 7BN. Tel: Office (01291) 622260 Home (01454) 313186 Mobile (0850) 888380

Managing Director: Mr G. C. Francis, 17 Welsh Street, Chepstow, Gwent NP6 5YH.

Stabling: 109 boxes, allotted on arrival. Limited accommodation for lads and lasses. Apply: (01291) 623414.

By Car: 1 mile North-West of the town on the A466. (1 mile from Junc 22 of the M4 (Severn Bridge)). There is a Free public car park opposite the Stands entrance.

By Rail: Chepstow Station (from Paddington, change at Gloucester or Newport). The course is 1 mile from station.

By Air: Helicopter landing facility in the centre of the course.

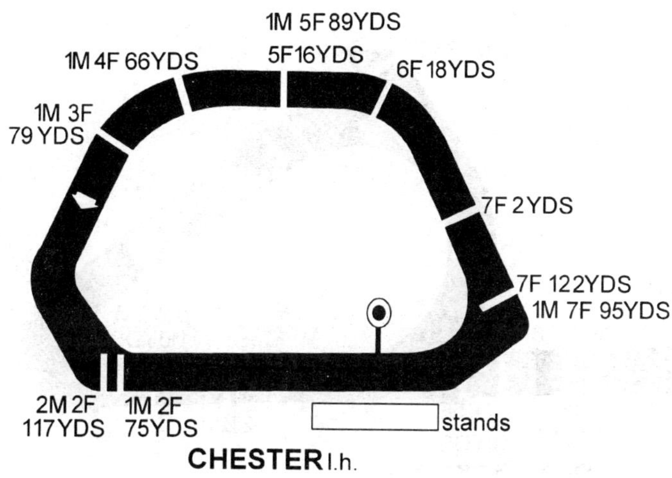

CHESTER

Address: The Racecourse, Chester CH1 2LY Tel: (01244) 323170 **Fax:** (01244) 344971

A perfectly flat, circular course, 1m 73y in circumference, with a sharp bend to a straight run-in of 230y. Long distance events are an extreme test of stamina, but for middle-distance races and sprints, the course greatly favours a sharp-actioned horse. Horses with previous winning form on this track are worthy of note.

Clerk of the Course: Mr C. H. Barnett, Aintree Racecourse, Aintree, Liverpool L9 5AS. Tel: (0151) 523 2600 or (01244) 323170 (racedays).

Racecourse Manager: Mr R. Walls Tel. (01244) 327171

Secretaries: Messrs Kidsons Impey, Steam Mill, Chester. CH3 5AN Tel: (01244) 327171.

Free stabling (175 boxes) and accommodation.

By Car: The course is near the centre of the city on the A548 (Queensferry Road). The Owners and Trainers car park is adjacent to the County Stand. There is a public car park in the centre of the course.

By Rail: Chester Station (3/4 mile from the course). Services from Euston, Paddington and Northgate.

By Air: Hawarden Airport (2 miles).

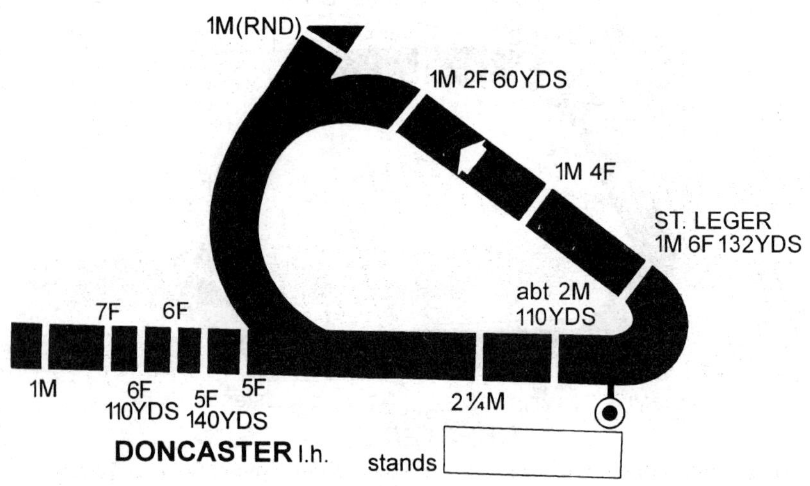

DONCASTER

Address: Doncaster Racecourse, Grand Stand, Leger Way, Doncaster DN2 6BB
Tel: (01302) 320066 **Fax:** (01302) 323271 **E-mail:** info@britishracing.com
Internet: www.britishracing.com
A pear-shaped track, about 1m 7f 110y in circumference with a distinct rise and fall to the mile marker. There is a level run-in of four and a half furlongs, extending to a straight mile, which tapers from a width of 88ft at the five-furlong pole to 60ft at the winning post. A round mile joins the straight course at a tangent. This good galloping track is suitable for strongly-built stayers and calls for stamina and courage.
Chief Executive & Clerk of Course (Flat): Mr J. Sanderson, International Racecourse Management Ltd., Grandstand, Leger Way, Doncaster DN2 6BB. Tel: (01302) 320066. Fax: Office (01673) 843434
Free stabling and accommodation Tel: (01302) 349337
By Car: East of the town, off the A638 (M18 Junc 3 & 4). Club members car park reserved. Large public car park free and adjacent to the course.
By Rail: Doncaster Central Station (from King's Cross). Special bus service from the station (1 mile).
By Air: Helicopter landing facility by prior arrangement only.

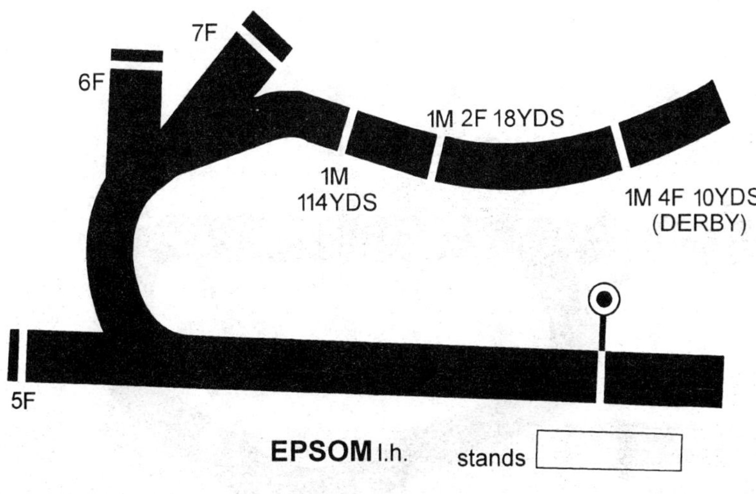

EPSOM

Address: United Racecourses Ltd., The Racecourse, Epsom Downs, Surrey KT18 5LQ Tel: (01372) 726311 **Fax:** (01372) 748253

From the Derby start at the top of the Downs, the course climbs steadily for the first gently-bending four furlongs, then levels out for nearly two furlongs before falling sharply round the bend to Tattenham Corner and into the straight. This is of less than four furlongs and ends with a fairish rise of just over a furlong to the winning post. The City and Suburban course and the Epsom Mile are, respectively, the last 1m 2f 15y and the last 1m 110y of the Derby course. The five furlong course (Egmont Course) is perfectly straight and, running sharply downhill to the junction with the round course, is the fastest in the world. The Derby course is a unique test for the thoroughbred, the frequently fast early pace demanding stamina, and the bends and gradients calling for a faultless action. Well-balanced, medium-sized, handy sorts seem to do best over five furlongs.

Clerk of the Course: Mr A. J. Cooper, The Grandstand, Epsom Downs, Surrey KT18 5LQ. Tel: (01372) 726311, Mobile (0374) 230850

General Manager: Mr Stephen Wallis Tel. (01372) 463072

Free stabling and accommodation Tel: (01372) 725794

By Car: 2 miles South of the town on the B290 (M25 Junc 8 & 9). For full car park particulars apply to: The Club Secretary, The Racecourse, Epsom Downs, Surrey KT18 5LQ. Tel: (01372) 726311.

By Rail: Epsom, Epsom Downs or Tattenham Corner Stations (trains from London Bridge, Waterloo, Victoria). Regular bus services run to the course from Epsom and Morden Underground Station.

By Air: London (Heathrow) and London (Gatwick) are both within 20 miles of the course. Heliport (Derby Meeting only) apply to Hascombe Aviation Tel: (01279) 680291.

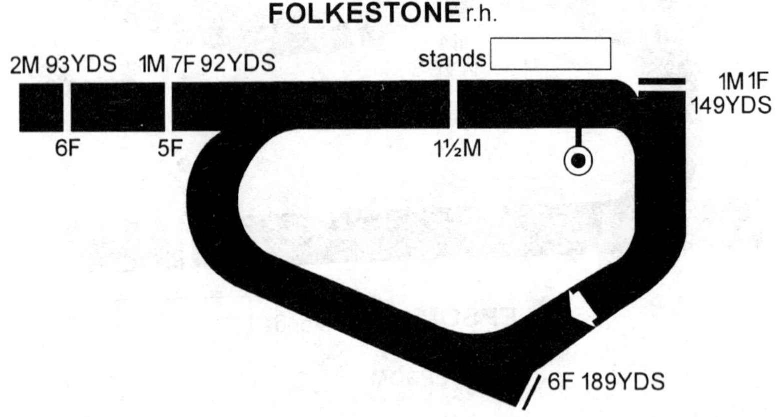

FOLKESTONE

Address: Folkestone Racecourse, Westenhanger, Hythe, Kent CT21 4HX
Tel: (01303) 266407 **Fax:** (01303) 260185 **E-mail:** 1016111.141@compuserve.com
A circuit of 1m 3f, somewhat undulating, with a straight run-in of two and a half furlongs. Five and six furlong races start on an extension which joins the round course about three furlongs from the line and has a slight rise over the final furlong. Despite its gentle turns and its width, Folkestone can not be described as a galloping track.
Director of Racing: Mr G. R. Stickels, Lingfield Park (1991) Ltd., Lingfield, Surrey RH7 6PQ. Tel: (01342) 834800 Home (01303) 873114 Mobile (0973) 737006 or (01303) 266407 (racedays).
Clerk of the Course: Mr P. D. Deacon, Lingfield Park 1991 Ltd., Lingfield, Surrey.
Stabling: 84 boxes allotted in rotation. Advance notice required for overnight accommodation, before 12 noon on the day prior to racing Tel: 01303 268449
By Car: 6 miles West of town at Westenhanger. Easy access from Junc 11 of the M20. Car park adjoins stands. (Free, except course enclosure £4).
By Rail: Westenhanger Station adjoins course. Trains from Charing Cross.
By Air: Helicopter landing facility by prior arrangement.

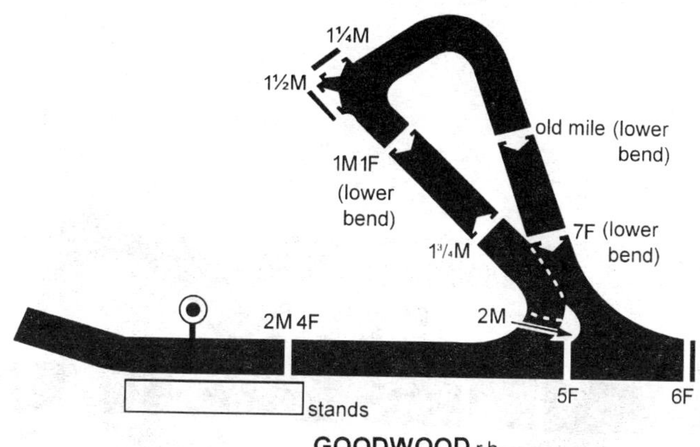

GOODWOOD r.h.

GOODWOOD

Address: Goodwood Racecourse Ltd., Goodwood, Chichester, West Sussex PO18 0PX Tel: (01243) 755022 **Fax:** (01243) 755025
Internet: http://www.demon.co.uk/racenews/goodwood
Set on the edge of the Downs, a straight six furlongs with a triangular loop on one side provides a variety of courses with the possibility of re-entering just above or below the five furlong gate. The Cup Course of about two and a half miles starts on a chute adjacent to the five furlong start and, running the reverse way of the course, turns left after about four furlongs and returns to the straight five furlong run-in by the top bend. The Stakes Course is the last 2m 3f, the Bentinck Course the last 1m 6f and the Gratwicke Course the last 1m 4f of the Cup Course. The Craven Course is 1m 2f, starting in almost the same spot as the Gratwicke Course but running in the reverse direction and returning to the five furlong run-in by the top bend. The Old Mile and seven furlong courses start on the Cup Course and join the five furlong course on the lower bend. The five and six furlong (Stewards' Cup) courses are perfectly straight, the first furlong of the latter being uphill and then slightly undulating to the finish. The sharp bends and downhill gradients suit the handy, well-balanced, neat-actioned sort over middle-distances and are against the big, long-striding horse.
Clerk of the Course and General Manager: Mr R. N. Fabricius, Goodwood Racecourse Limited, Chichester, Sussex. Tel: (01243) 755021 or (0374) 100223
Free stabling and accommodation for runners (110 well equipped boxes at Goodwood House). Subsidised canteen and recreational facilities.Tel: (01243) 774157 or 774107
By Car: 6 miles North of Chichester between the A286 & A285. There is a car park adjacent to the course. Ample free car and coach parking.
By Rail: Chichester Station (from Victoria or London Bridge). Regular bus service to the course (6 miles).
By Air: Helicopter landing facility by prior arrangement with Stephenson Aviation. Tel: (01243) 779222. Goodwood Airport 2 miles (taxi to the course).

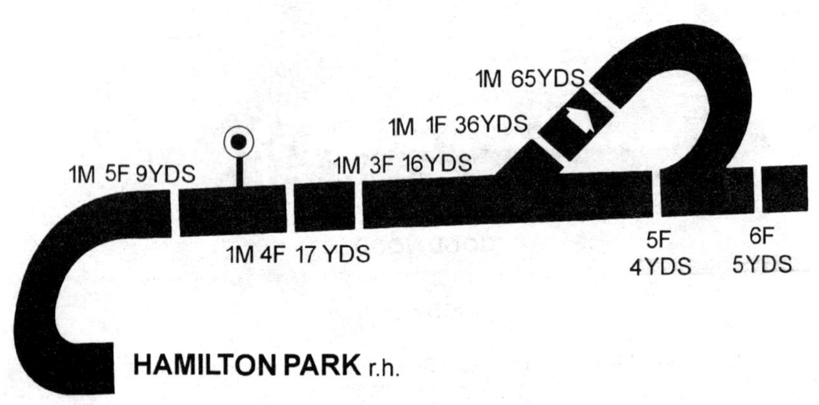

HAMILTON

Address: Hamilton Park Racecourse, Bothwell Road, Hamilton, Lanarkshire ML3 0DW Tel: (01698) 283806 **Fax:** (01698) 286621
A straight six furlongs with a pear-shaped loop course of 1m 5f from a start in front of the stands and a run-in of five and a half furlongs. The turns are easy on the loop. The track is undulating with a dip (which can be very testing in wet weather) about three furlongs out and then rises to level out for the last 150y. A course where judgement and experience can make a considerable difference. Races are usually run at a true gallop here and form can be relied upon.
Clerk of the Course: Mr W. G. Farnsworth, The Racecourse, Bothwell Road, Hamilton ML3 0DW Tel: (01698) 283806 Mobile (0410) 536134
Chief Executive: Miss H. Dudgeon, The Racecourse, Bothwell Road, Hamilton ML3 0DW. Tel: (01698) 283806. Fax: (01698) 286621.
Going details Tel: (0850) 609037 Head Groundsman.
Free stabling (120 boxes) and accommodation on request. Tel: (01698) 284892.
By Car: Off the A74 on the B7071 (Hamilton-Bothwell road). (M74 Junc 5). Free parking for cars and buses.
By Rail: Hamilton West Station (1 mile).
By Air: Glasgow Airport (20 miles).

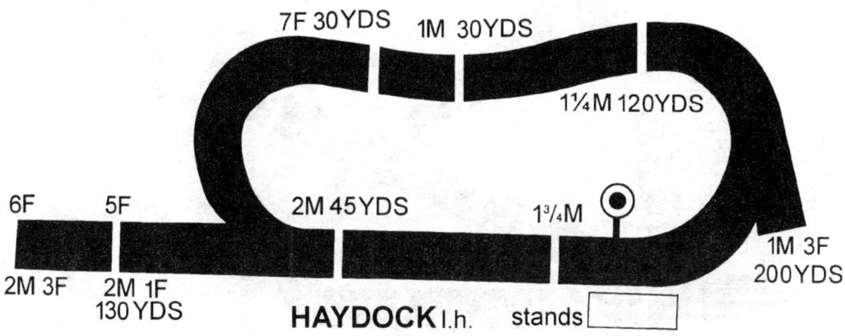

HAYDOCK

Address: Haydock Park Racecourse, Newton-le-Willows, Merseyside WA12 0HQ
Tel: (01942) 725963 **Fax:** (01942) 270879
An almost flat, oval track, 1m 5f round, with a run-in of four and a half furlongs and a straight six furlong course. The 1m 4f gate is set on a short chute. This course, which is of a galloping nature, suits the long-striding horse. On rain-affected turf, the going down the stands' rail in the straight is often faster and horses have often won races by being brought over to that side.
Clerk of the Course: Major P. W. F. Arkwright, Shirley Farm, Little Wolford, Shipston-on-Stour, Warwickshire. Tel: (01608) 684460.
Managing Director: Mr R. G. Thomas, Haydock Park Racecourse, Newton-le-Willows, Merseyside WA12 0HQ. Tel: (01942) 725963.
Applications to be made to the Racecourse for stabling (140 boxes) and accommodation for lads/girls.
By Car: The course is on the A49 near Junc 23 of the M6.
By Rail: Newton-le-Willows Station (Manchester-Liverpool line) is 21/2 miles from the course. Earlstown 3 miles from the course. Warrington Bank Quay and Wigan are on the London to Carlisle/ Glasgow line.
By Air: Landing facilities in the centre of the course for helicopters and planes not exceeding 10,000lbs laden weight. Apply to the Sales Office

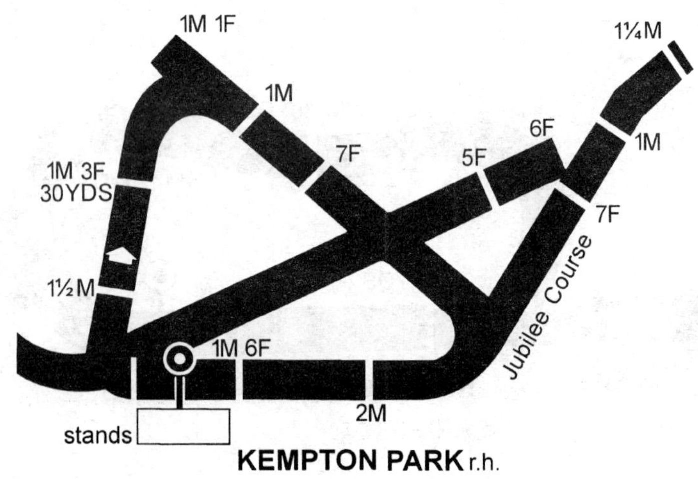

KEMPTON

Address: Kempton Park Racecourse, Sunbury-on-Thames, Middlesex TW16 5AQ
Tel: (01932) 782292 **Fax:** (01932) 782044 **Raceday Fax:** (01932) 779525
Internet: http://www.demon.co.uk/.racenews/rht
A 1m 5f triangular course with a three and a half furlong straight run-in. The 1m 2f Jubilee Course starts on an extension to the round course and sprint races are run over a separate diagonal course. Kempton is a perfectly flat track which can not be described as either sharp or galloping.
Clerk of the Course: Mr A. J. Cooper, Kempton Park, Sunbury-on-Thames. Tel: (01932) 782292.
General Manager: Mr J. M. Thick, Kempton Park, Sunbury-on-Thames. Tel: (01932) 782292.
Stabling allocated on arrival (99 boxes). Prior booking required for overnight stay Tel: (01932) 783334
By Car: On the A308 near Junc 1 of the M3. Main car park £2, Silver Ring and centre car park free.
By Rail: Kempton Park Station (from Waterloo).
By Air: London (Heathrow) Airport 6 miles.

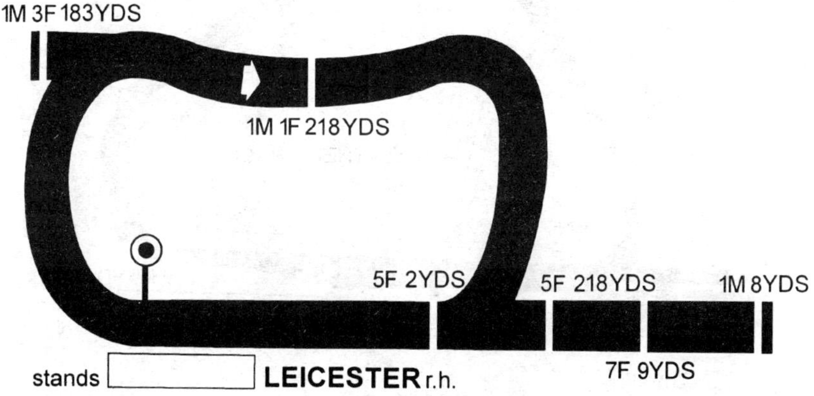

LEICESTER

Address: Leicester Racecourse, Oadby, Leicester LE2 3QH Tel: (01162) 2716515
An oval track of approximately 1m 5f with a straight run-in of five furlongs. Races of a mile and less are run on a dead straight course which joins the round course five furlongs from the finish, the first half being downhill, followed by an ascent gradually levelling off to the winning post. The bends into the straight and after the winning post have been cambered to make a more galloping track.
Clerk of the Course: Captain N. E. S. Lees, Westfield House, The Links, Newmarket, Suffolk CB8 0TG. Tel: (01162) 2716515 Newmarket (01638) 663482 or Home (01284) 386651.
Manager: Mr D. C. Henson, Leicester Racecourse Co. Ltd., The Racecourse, Leicester. Tel: (0116) 2716515 or (01604) 30757.
Going details Tel: (01374) 497281 Head Groundsman
109 boxes allocated on arrival. Accommodation for one attendant per horse only Tel: (01162) 712115 Canteen opens at 7.30a.m.
By Car: The course is 21/2 miles South-East of the City on the A6 (M1, Junc 21). The car park is free.
By Rail: Leicester Station (from St Pancras) is 21/2 miles.
By Air: Helicopter landing facility in the centre of the course.

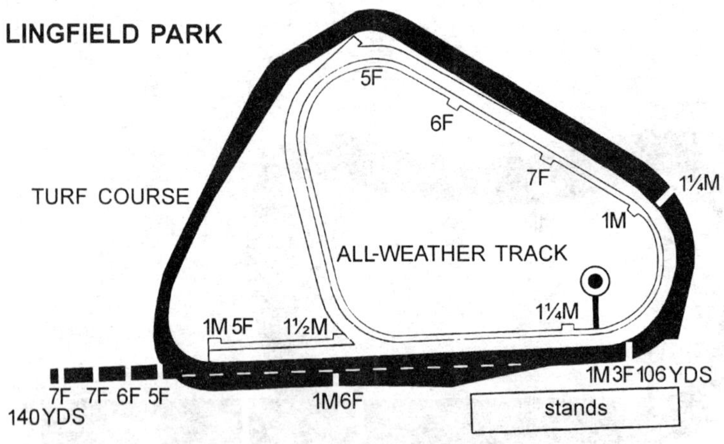

LINGFIELD

Address: Lingfield Park Racecourse, Lingfield, Surrey RH7 6PQ

Tel: (01342) 834800 **Fax:** (01342) 832833 **E-mail:** 1016111.141@compuserve.com

A 7f 140y straight course with a downhill gradient for about five furlongs, a slight rise and then a gradual fall to the winning post. The round turf course joins the straight at the four furlong post and then follows round the outside of the All-Weather tracks to the summit of a slight hill before turning downhill into the straight. The Derby Trial Course (1m 3f 106y) is very similar to the Epsom Derby Course and provides a good test for the Classic. The re-alignment of the turf course to accomodate the All-Weather tracks has made the turn out of the back straight much less pronounced. However, most of the characteristics remain. The Equitrack course favours the keen, free-running, sharp-actioned horse, particularly so in sprints, which are run on the turn.

Director of Racing: Mr G. R. Stickels, Lingfield Park Racecourse, Surrey RH7 6PQ (01342) 834800 Mobile (0973) 737006.

Clerks of the Course: Mr P. D. Deacon & Mr F. I. W. Cameron (address as above), 180 boxes available. For details of accommodation apply to the Manager, Mr W. Sutton (01342) 834800. Advance notice for overnight accommodation required before 12 noon on the day before racing.

By Car: South-East of the town off the A22 (M25 Junc 6). Ample free parking. Reserved car park £3.

By Rail: Lingfield Station (regular services from London Bridge and Victoria). 1/2m walk to the course.

By Air: London (Gatwick) Airport 10 miles. Helicopter landing facility south of windsock.

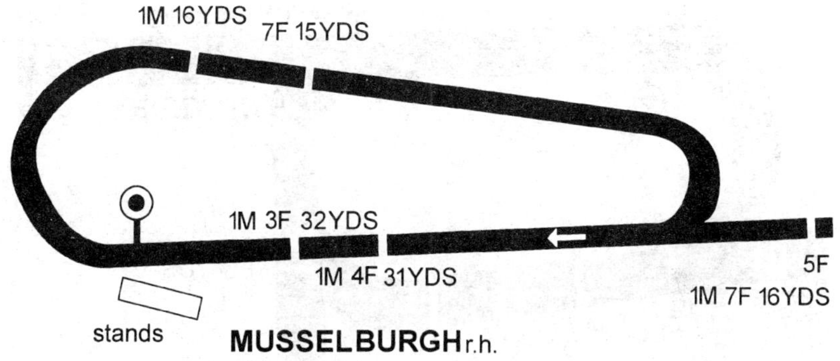

MUSSELBURGH

Address: Musselburgh Racecourse, Linkfield Road, Musselburgh, East Lothian
Tel: (0131) 665 2859 Racecourse (01292) 264179 **Fax:** (0131) 653 2083
An oval of 1m 2f, with sharp bends and a straight, slightly undulating run-in of four furlongs. An extension provides a five furlong course, which bears slightly left and makes a distinct right-hand inclination after a furlong. Musselburgh is virtually flat but, with the turns being very sharp, handiness and manoeuvrability are at a premium.
Clerk of the Course & Manager: Mr M. Kershaw, Racecourse Office, 2 Whitletts Road, Ayr. Tel: Office (01292) 264179 Racedays (0131) 6652859 Mobile (0850) 464258 Fax: (01292) 610140.
Free stabling Tel: (0131) 665 4955. Report to the main Security Office at Goose Green Stables. Accommodation for one night in B & B provided.
By Car: Musselburgh, 5 miles East of Edinburgh on the A1. Car park adjoining course, free for buses and cars.
By Rail: Waverley Station (Edinburgh). Local Rail service to Musselburgh.
By Air: Edinburgh (Turnhouse) Airport 30 minutes by car.

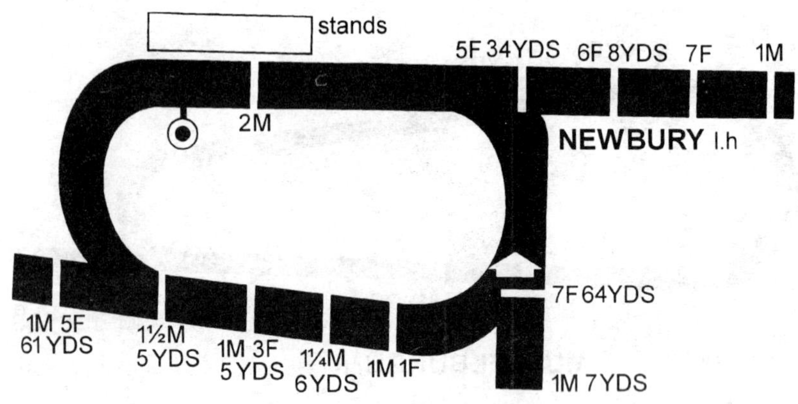

NEWBURY

Address: The Racecourse, Newbury, Berkshire RG14 7NZ
Tel: (01635) 40015 or 550354 **Fax:** (01635) 528354
Internet: http://www.raceweb.com/newbury **E-mail:** newbury@raceweb.com
An oval track of about 1m 7f, 80 feet wide with a slightly undulating straight mile. The round mile and 7f 60y starts are set on a chute from the round course and both join the straight about five furlongs from the finish. Newbury is a good, galloping track, which is efficiently watered during dry periods.
Clerk of the Course: R. N. J. Pridham, 109 Greenham Road, Newbury, Berkshire RG14 7JE. Tel: (01635) 49511 or Racecourse Office (01635) 40015.
Chief Executive, Secretary and Club Secretary: Major General J. D. G. Pank, C.B. Tel: (01635) 40015.
Free stabling (127 boxes) and accommodation for lads and lasses.
By Car: East of the town off the A34 (M4, Junc 12 or 13). Car park, adjoining enclosures, free, except Southmead £2
By Rail: Newbury Racecourse Station, adjoins course.
By Air: Light Aircraft landing strip East/West. 830 metres by 30 metres wide. Helicopter landing facilities.

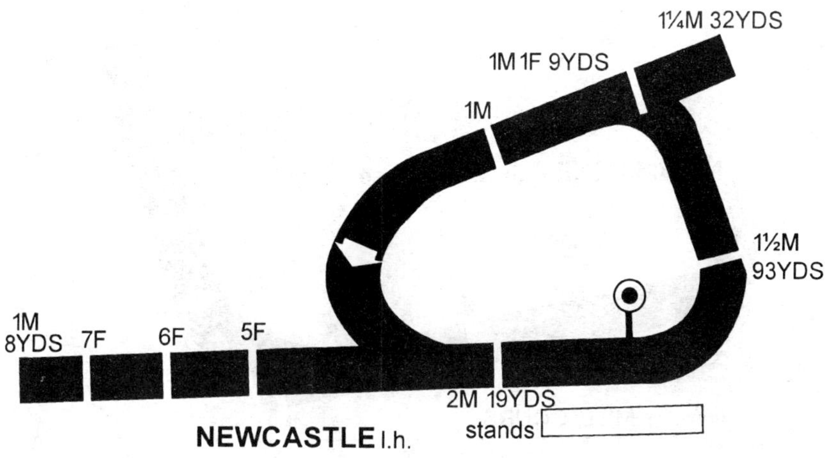

NEWCASTLE

Address: High Gosforth Park, Newcastle-Upon-Tyne NE3 5HP Tel: (0191) 236 2020 **Fax:** (0191) 236 7761

An oval course of 1m 6f with a chute to provide a 1m 2f start and a straight run-in of four furlongs, gradually rising until levelling off in the final 100y. The run-in extends to allow a straight mile, which is against the collar all the way. Newcastle is a galloping track with the final climb making it a test of stamina and is not one for short runners.

Clerk of the Course: David McAllister c/o High Gosforth Park Ltd, High Gosforth Park, Newcastle-upon-Tyne. NE3 5HP. Tel: (0191) 236 2020 Mobile (0860) 286003.

Chairman: Mr S. W. Clarke C.B.E. Tel. (0191) 2362020

Free stabling (120 boxes). It is essential to book accommodation in advance. Apply to the Manager. Tel: (0191) 217 0060 the day before racing, or the Racecourse Office otherwise.

By Car: 4 miles North of the city on the A6125 (near the A1). Car and coach park free.

By Rail: Newcastle Central Station (from King's Cross), a free bus service operates from South Gosforth and Regent Centre Metro Station.

By Air: Helicopter landing facility by prior arrangement. The Airport is 4 miles from the course.

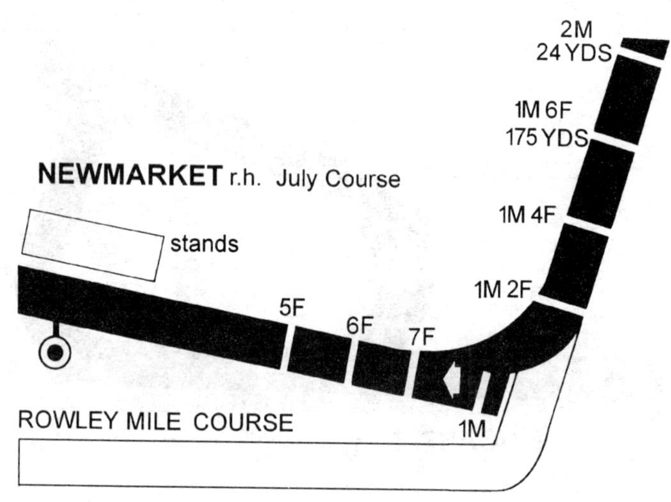

NEWMARKET - July Course

Address: Newmarket Racecourse, Newmarket, Suffolk CB8 0TG
Tel: Main Office (01638) 663482 Rowley (01638) 662524 July (01638) 662752
Fax: (01638) 663044
(July Course) - All races up to a mile inclusive are run on the straight Bunbury Mile, which has a steadily increasing downhill gradient after two furlongs, the final furlong being uphill. Races further than a mile start on the Cesarewitch course and turn right into the straight mile. Like the Rowley Mile course, this is a wide, galloping track.
Clerk of the Course: Captain N. E. S. Lees, Westfield House, The Links, Newmarket. Tel: (01638) 663482 or (01284) 386651 (home).
Manager: Mr C. R. Kennedy Tel: (01638) 663482
100 boxes and free accommodation available at the Links Stables Tel: (01638) 662200
By Car: South-West of the town on the A1304 London Road (M11 Junc 9). Free car parking at the rear of the enclosure. Members car park £1 all days; Free courtesy bus service from Newmarket Station, Bus Station and High Street, commencing 90 minutes prior to the first race, and return trips up to 60 minutes after the last race.
By Rail: Infrequent rail service to Newmarket Station from Cambridge (Liverpool Street) or direct bus service from Cambridge (13 mile journey).
By Air: Landing facilities for light aircraft and helicopters on racedays at both racecourses. See Flight Guide. Cambridge Airport 11 miles.

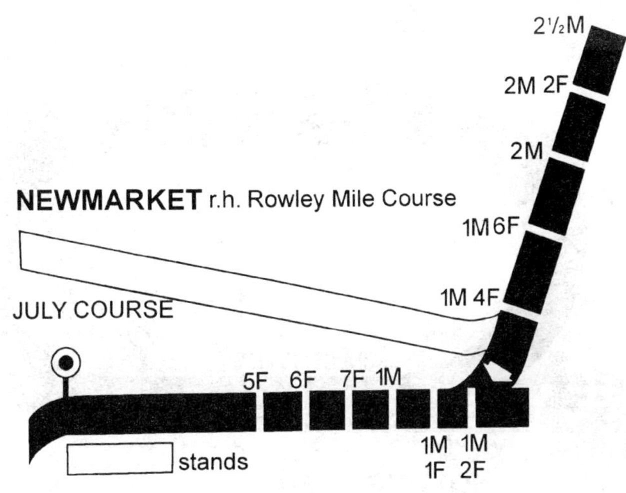

NEWMARKET - Rowley Mile

Address: Newmarket Racecourse, Newmarket, Suffolk CB8 0TG
Tel: Main Office (01638) 663482 Rowley (01638) 662524 July (01638) 662752
Fax: (01638) 663044
(Rowley Mile Course) - There is a straight course of ten furlongs with slight undulations as far as 'The Bushes', about two furlongs from the finish. From that point it is downhill for a furlong to 'The Dip', the final furlong being uphill. The Cesarewitch course starts on the Beacon Course, which turns right into the straight. The ten furlong straight is a wide, galloping track ideal for long-striding horses.
Clerk of the Course: Captain N. E. S. Lees, Westfield House, The Links, Newmarket. Tel: (01638) 663482 or (01284) 386651 (home).
Manager: Mr C.R. Kennedy Tel: (01638) 663482.
100 boxes and free accommodation available at the Links Stables Tel: (01638) 662200
By Car: South-West of the town on the A1304 London Road (M11 Junc 9). Free car parking at the rear of the enclosure. Members car park £1 all days; Free courtesy bus service from Newmarket Station, Bus Station and High Street, commencing 90 minutes prior to the first race, and return trips up to 60 minutes after the last race.
By Rail: Infrequent rail service to Newmarket Station from Cambridge (Liverpool Street) or direct bus service from Cambridge (13 mile journey).
By Air: Landing facilities for light aircraft and helicopters on racedays at both racecourses. See Flight Guide. Cambridge Airport 11 miles.

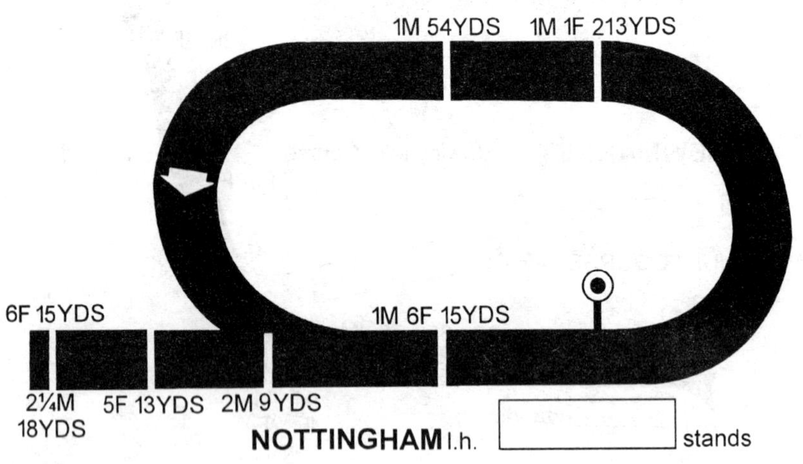

NOTTINGHAM

Address: Nottingham Racecourse, Colwick Park, Nottingham NG2 4BE
Tel: (0115) 958 0620 **Fax:** (0115) 958 4515
A galloping oval track with a straight run-in of about five furlongs, from which a chute provides a straight six furlongs. The turns on this flat course are easy.
Clerk of the Course: Major C. Moore, Hamilton House, Toft-next-Newton, Market Rasen, Lincolnshire LN8 3NE. Tel: (01673) 843434 (office) (01673) 878575 (home).
Manager: Mrs Jan Lloyd, The Racecourse Office, Colwick Park, Nottingham NG2 4BE Tel: (0115) 958 0620
Free stabling. 120 boxes allotted on arrival. New hostel for lads and lasses Tel: (0115) 950 1198
By Car: 2 miles East of the City on the B686. The car park is free. Silver Ring Picnic Car Park £12 (admits car and four occupants).
By Rail: Nottingham (Midland) Station. Regular bus service to course (2 miles).
By Air: Helicopter landing facility in the centre of the course.

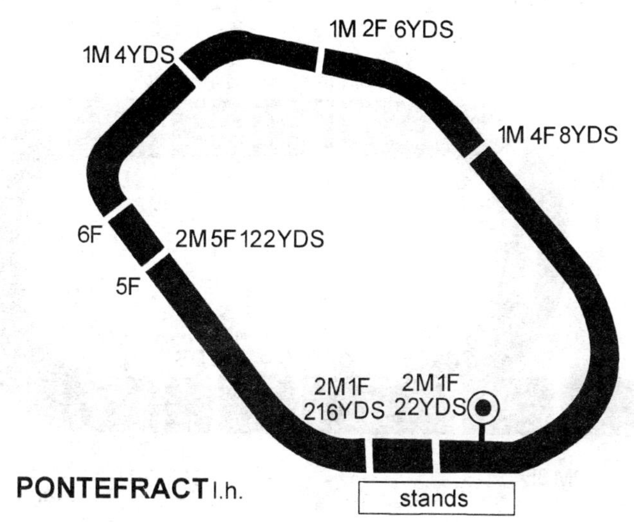

PONTEFRACT

Address: Pontefract Park Race Co. Ltd., The Park, Pontefract, West Yorkshire
Tel: Admin Office (01977) 703224 Racedays (01977) 702210
Fax: Admin Office (01977) 600577 Racedays (01977) 702210
An oval, undulating course of 2m 133y with two sharp bends and a straight run-in of only two furlongs. There is a steep ascent over the last three furlongs. The undulations make it unsuitable for a long-striding horse, although a degree of stamina is called for. There have been a number of course specialists at Pontefract.
Clerk of the Course and Secretary: Mr J. N. Gundill, 33 Ropergate, Pontefract, West Yorkshire. WF8 1LE Tel: Office (01977) 703224 Home (01977) 620649 Racedays (01977) 702210.
116 boxes available. Stabling and accommodation must be reserved. They will be allocated on a first come-first served basis. Tel: (01977 702323)
By Car: 1 mile North of the town on the A639. Junc 32 of M62. Free car park adjacent to the course.
By Rail: Pontefract Station (Baghill), 11/2 miles from the course. Regular bus service from Leeds.
By Air: Helicopters by arrangement only. (Nearest airfield: Doncaster, Sherburn-in-Elmet, Yeadon (Leeds/Bradford).

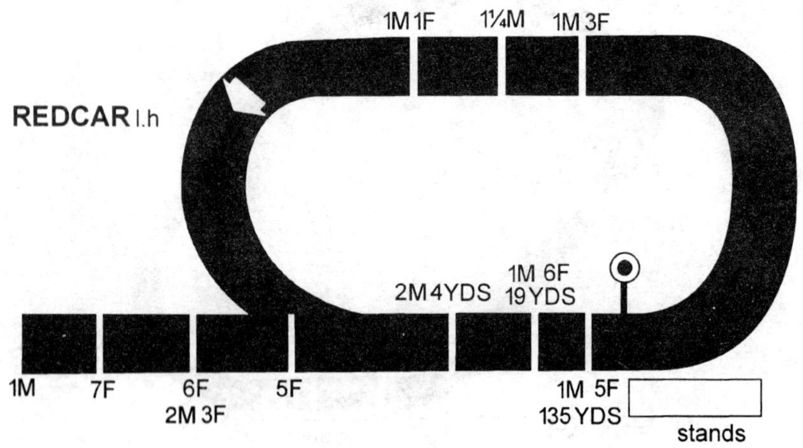

REDCAR

Address: Redcar Racecourse, Redcar, Cleveland TS10 2BY Tel: (01642) 484068
Fax: (01642) 488272
A perfectly flat, narrow, oval course of two miles with a straight run-in of five furlongs, which extends backwards to make a straight mile. Despite two very tight bends into and out of the back straight, Redcar is an excellent galloping course.
Clerk of the Course & General Manager: Mr J. Gundill, Racecourse Office, The Racecourse, Redcar, Cleveland TS10 2BY. Tel: (01642) 484068 or (01482) 867488 Mobile (0370) 613049.
Groundsman: Mr J. Berry, The Racecourse, Redcar, Cleveland. Tel: (01642) 489861
Stables Tel: (on racedays only) (01642) 484254.
By Car: In town off the A1085. Free parking adjoining the course for buses and cars.
By Rail: Redcar Station (1/4 mile from the course).
By Air: Landing facilities at Turners Arms Farm (600y runway) Yearby, Cleveland. 2 miles South of the racecourse - transport available. Teeside airport (18 miles west of Redcar).

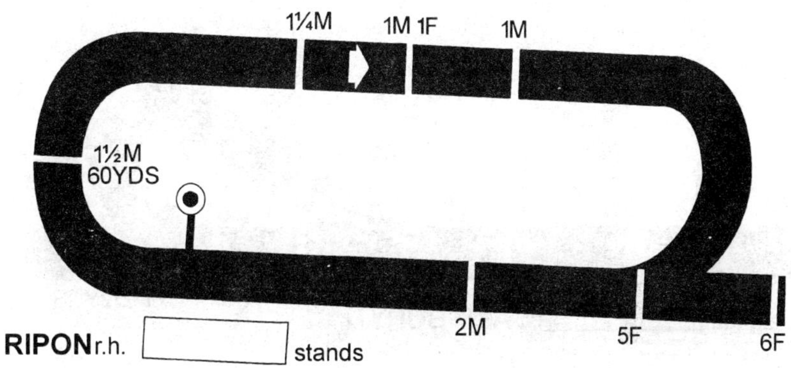

RIPON

Address: Ripon Racecourse, Boroughbridge Road, Ripon, North Yorkshire HG4 3UG Tel: (01765) 602156 **Fax:** (01765) 690018
E-mail: mail@hutchbuch.demon.co.uk
An oval course of 1m 5f, joined to a straight six furlongs by a tightish bend at the five furlong point. The straight course is slightly on the ascent except for a shallow dip at the 'distance' and, in general, this is a rather sharp track, a course where experience can be decisive.
Clerk of the Course: Mr J. M. Hutchinson, 77 North Street, Ripon HG4 1DS. Tel: (01765) 602156 Evenings (01845) 567378 Mobile (0860) 679904.
Non-racedays: Admin Office, 77, North Street, Ripon HG4 1DS. Tel: (01765) 602156. Fax (01765) 690018. Racedays: The Racecourse, Boroughbridge Road, Ripon HG4 3UG. Tel: (01765) 603696.
Trainers requiring stabling (104 boxes available) are requested to contact Mr P. Bateson, The Racecourse, Ripon prior to 11a.m. the day before racing. Tel: (01765) 603696.
By Car: The course is situated 2 miles South-East of the city, on the B6265. There is ample free parking for cars and coaches. For reservations apply to the Secretary.
By Rail: Harrogate Station (11 miles), or Thirsk (15 miles). Bus services to Ripon.
By Air: Helicopters only on the course. Otherwise Leeds/Bradford airport.

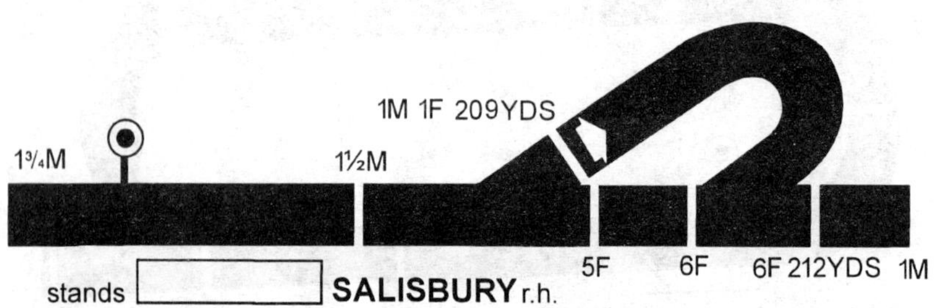

SALISBURY

Address: Salisbury Racecourse, Netherhampton, Salisbury, Wiltshire SP2 8PN
Tel: (01722) 326461 **Fax:** (01722) 412710
The course consists of a loop with an arm of about four furlongs for the finish of all races. Contests of up to a mile are almost straight except for a slight right-hand bend at halfway. On the 1m 6f course, horses start opposite the stands, turn to the left around the loop and re-enter the straight at the seven furlong starting gate. The last half-mile is uphill, providing a stiff test of stamina.
Clerk of the Course: Mr R. I. Renton, Salisbury Racecourse, Netherhampton, Salisbury, Wiltshire SP2 8PN. Tel: (01722) 326461 Mobile (0836) 784543.
Secretary: The Bibury Club, Salisbury Racecourse, Netherhampton, Salisbury, Wiltshire. Tel: (01722) 326461.
Free stabling (112 boxes) and accommodation for lads and lasses, apply to the Stabling Manager Tel: (01722) 327327.
By Car: 3 miles South-West of the city on the A3094 at Netherhampton. Free car park adjoins the course.
By Rail: Salisbury Station is 31/2 miles (from Waterloo). Bus service to the course.
By Air: Helicopter landing facility near the ten furlong start.

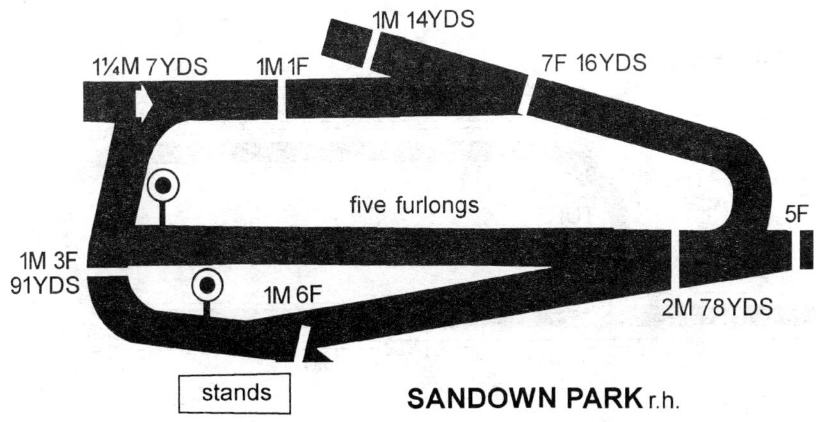

SANDOWN

Address: Sandown Park Racecourse, Esher, Surrey KT10 9AJ
Tel: (01372) 463072 **Fax:** (01372) 470427
An oval course of 1m 5f with a straight run-in of four furlongs. The ground is almost level until entering the straight, where it rises to the winning post. Five furlong contests are run on a separate straight course which cuts diagonally across the inside of the main circuit and is uphill all the way. The track suits long-striding horses and is a real test of stamina.
Clerk of the Course: Mr A. J. Cooper, Sandown Park, Esher, Surrey. Tel: (01372) 463072 Mobile (0374) 230850.
Managing Director: Mrs S. C. Ellen (address & tel as above).
Going Line Tel: (01372) 461212
108 boxes available. Free stabling and accommodation for lads and lasses Tel: (01372) 463511.
By Car: 4 miles South-West of Kingston-on-Thames, on the A307 (M25 Junc 10). The members' car park in More Lane £2. All other car parking is free.
By Rail: Esher Station (from Waterloo) adjoins the course.
By Air: London (Heathrow) Airport 12 miles.

SOUTHWELL

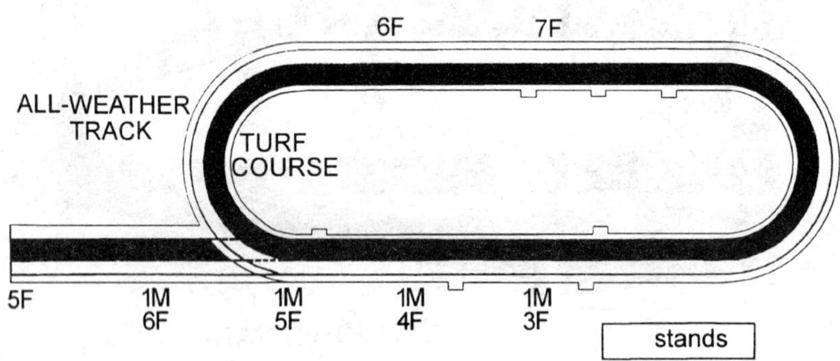

SOUTHWELL

Address: Southwell Racecourse, Rolleston, Newark, Nottinghamshire NG25 0TS
Tel: (01636) 814481 **Fax:** (01636) 812271
The All-Weather Fibresand track consists of an oval circuit, 1m 2f in circumference, with a three furlong straight and a spur to provide a five furlong straight All-Weather track. The turf tracks are on the inside of the All-Weather track. A sharp, flat circuit, Southwell suits the keen, front-running sort.
Clerk of the Course: Mr M. Prosser, Wolverhampton Racecourse Tel. (01902) 421421, Mobile (07971) 531162, Fax (01902) 421621
Going details Tel: (0468) 053391 Head Groundsman
110 boxes at the course. Applications for staff and horse accommodation to be booked by noon the day before racing on (01636) 814481
By Car: The course is situated at Rolleston, 3 miles South of Southwell, 5 miles from Newark.
By Rail: Rolleston Station (Nottingham-Newark line) adjoins the course.

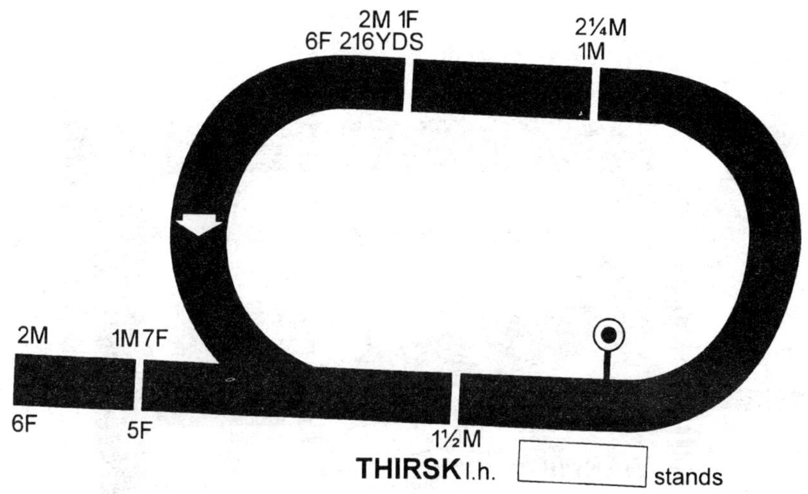

THIRSK

Address: Thirsk Racecourse, Station Road, Thirsk, North Yorkshire YO7 1QL
Tel: (01845) 522276 **Fax:** (01845) 525353
An oval track of 1m 2f, with fairly tight turns and an undulating run-in of four furlongs. Races of five and six furlongs start on a straight, more undulating two furlong extension of the run-in. Though the turns on the round course are comparatively easy, the track is somewhat sharp. The going seldom rides heavy.
Managing Director & Clerk of the Course: Mr Christopher Tetley, The Racecourse, Station Road, Thirsk, North Yorkshire YO7 1QL. Tel: (01845) 522276.
Club Secretary: Mr D. Whitehead, Thirsk Racecourse Limited, The Racecourse, Station Road, Thirsk, North Yorkshire YO7 1QL. Tel: (01845) 522276 Fax: (01845) 525353.
112 boxes available. For stabling and accommodation apply to, The Racecourse, Station Road, Thirsk, North Yorkshire. Tel: (01845) 522276 Racedays (01845) 522096.
By Car: West of the town on the A61. Free car park adjacent to the course for buses and cars.
By Rail: Thirsk Station (from King's Cross). 1/2 mile from the course.
By Air: Helicopters only, landing on the hockey pitch. Prior arrangement required.Tel: Racecourse (01845) 522276. Fixed wing aircraft can land at RAF Leeming. Tel: (01677) 423041. Light aircraft at Bagby. Tel: (01845) 597385 or (01845) 537555.

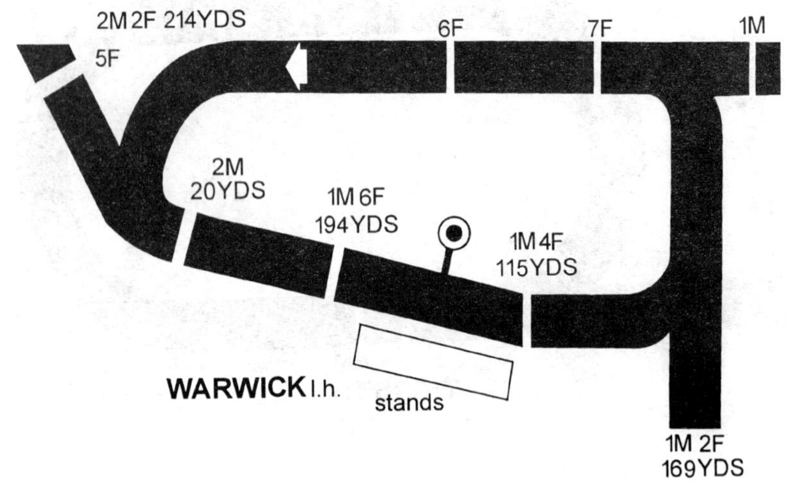

WARWICK

Address: Warwick Racecourse, Hampton Street, Warwick CV34 6HN
Tel: (01926) 491553 **Fax:** (01926) 403223
A nearly circular track, 1m 6f 32y in circumference, with a distinct rise and fall levelling off a mile from home, and a run-in of about two and a half furlongs. The five furlong course has a left-hand elbow at the junction with the round course. The mile course, straight for the first five furlongs, then turns into the home straight. This sharp track favours handiness and speed rather than staying power.
Clerk of the Course & Racecourse Manager: Miss Lisa Rowe, Warwick Racecourse, Hampton Street, Warwick CV34 6HN. Tel: (01926) 491553. Fax (01926) 403223.
Raceday Clerk of the Course: Mr Adam Waterworth, Warwick Racecourse, Hampton Street, Warwick CV34 6HN. Tel: Racedays (01926) 491553.
112 boxes allocated on arrival or by reservation Tel: (01526) 493803.
By Car: West of the town on the B4095 adjacent to Junc 15 of the M40. Free parking (except the Members' Car Park, £5 to Daily Club Members).
By Rail: Warwick or Leamington Spa Station.

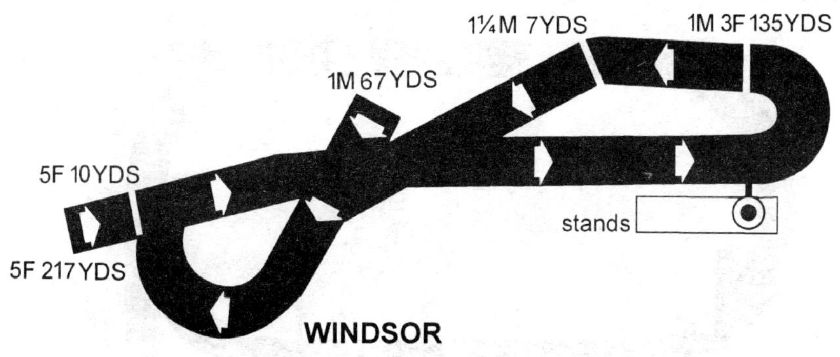

WINDSOR

Address: Royal Windsor Racecourse, Maidenhead Road, Windsor, Berkshire SL4 5JJ Tel: (01753) 864076/865234/864726 **Fax:** (01753) 830156

In the form of a figure eight, Windsor has a circuit of 1m 4f 110y. Although both left and right-hand turns are met in races of a mile and a half, only right-hand turns occur in races up to 1m 70y. The five furlong course bends slightly to the right approaching halfway but is otherwise straight. The track is perfectly flat and its sharpness is largely offset by the long run-in.

Clerk of the Course (to 31/12/98): Hugo Bevan, The Old House, Little Everdon, Daventry, Northamptonshire. Tel: (01327) 361266

Clerk of the Course (from 1/1/99): Mr F. Garrity Tel. (01753) 864076

Racecourse Manager: Mrs S. Dingle, The Racecourse, Windsor, Berkshire. Tel: (01753) 865234 or (01753) 864726 Stables (01753) 865350.

Reservation required for overnight stay and accommodation only. Tel: (01753) 865234.

By Car: North of the town on the A308 (M4 Junc 6). Car parks adjoin the course (£1, £1.50, £2).

By Rail: Windsor Central Station (from Paddington) or Windsor & Eton Riverside Station (from Waterloo).

By Air: London (Heathrow) Airport 15 minutes by car via the M4. Also White Waltham Airport (West London Aero Club) 15 minutes.

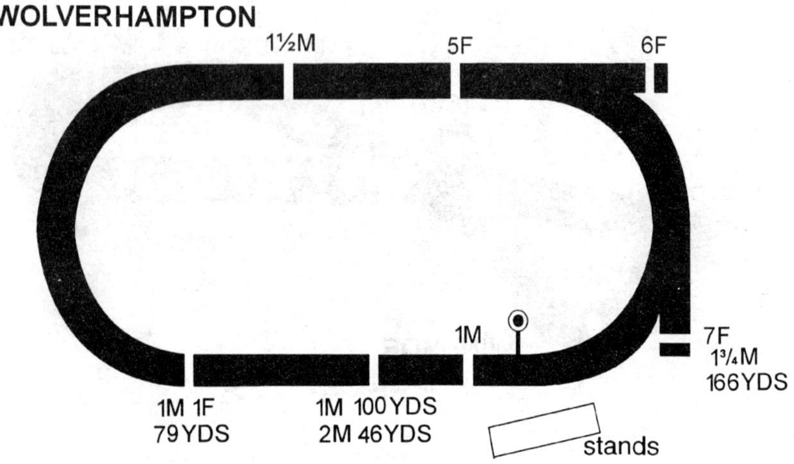

WOLVERHAMPTON

Address: Wolverhampton Racecourse, Dunstall Park, Gorsebrook Road, Wolverhampton WV6 0PE Tel: (01902) 421421 **Fax:** (01902) 716626
An oval circuit, a mile in circumference with a run-in of 380y. The Fibresand surface consists of a blended mixture of silica sand and synthetic fibres set in a re-enforced sub-base.A turf track for hurdles and chases is situated on the outside of the All-Weather track.
Clerk of the Course: Mr M. Prosser, Wolverhampton Racecourse Tel. (01902) 421421, Mobile (07971) 531162, Fax (01902) 421621
74 boxes allotted on arrival. Applications for lads and lasses, and overnight stables must be made to Racecourse by noon on the day before racing. Tel: (01902) 421421. Fax: (01902) 716626
By Car: 1 mile North of town on the A449 (M54 Junc 2 or M6 Junc 12). Car parking free of charge.
By Rail: Wolverhampton Station (from Euston) 1 mile.
By Air: Halfpenny Green Airport 8 miles.

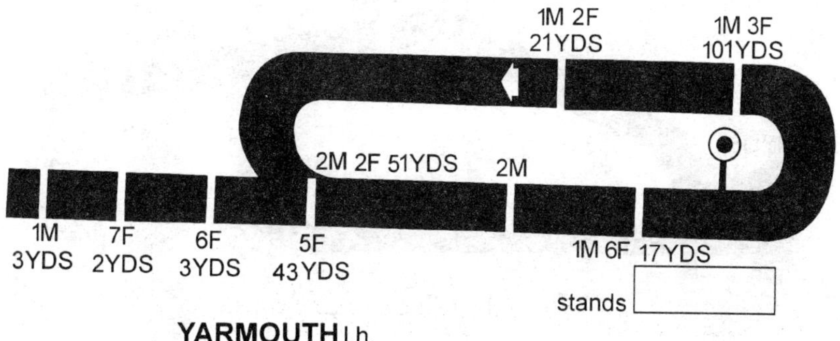

YARMOUTH

Address: The Racecourse, Jellicoe Road, Great Yarmouth, Norfolk NR30 4AU
Tel: (01493) 842527 **Fax:** (01493) 843254
An oblong course of about 1m 4f with a slight fall to a run-in of five furlongs. The straight mile joins the round course at the run-in and is perfectly level. The five, six and seven furlong courses form part of the straight mile.
Clerk of the Course: Mr D. C. Henson, F.R.I.C.S., 2 Lower Mounts, Northampton NN1 3DE. Tel: (01604) 630757. Fax: (01604) 630758.
Manager: Mr David Thompson, The Racecourse, Jellicoe Road, Great Yarmouth, Norfolk NR30 4AU. Tel: (01493) 842527 Fax: (01493) 843254.
Stabling allocated on arrival. Tel: (01493) 855651.
By Car: 1 mile East of town centre (well sign-posted from A47 & A12). Large car park adjoining course £1.
By Rail: Great Yarmouth Station (1 mile). Bus service to the course.
By Air: Helicopter landing facilities available 300y from the course at North Denes Airfield. Tel: (01493) 851500. Fixed wing aircraft landing facilities are available at a private airfield in Ludham. Prior permission is required through Mr R. Collins. Tel: (01493) 843211. Fax: (01493) 859555.

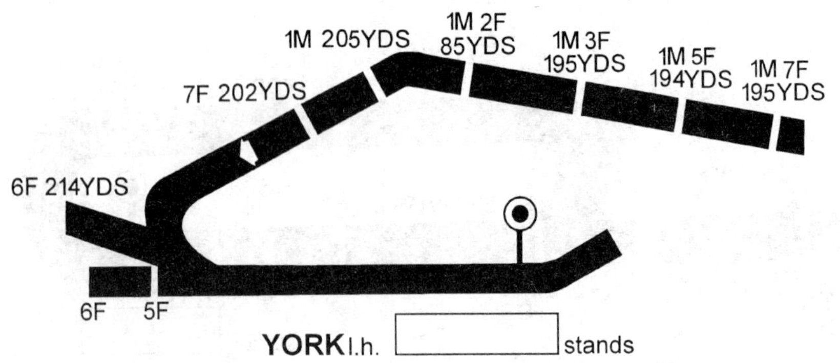

YORK

Address: The Racecourse, York YO23 1EX Tel: (01904) 620911
Fax: (01904) 611071
From the two mile start at the bottom of the Knavesmire, this wide, U-shaped course runs parallel with the Tadcaster Road for five furlongs before bending left to pass under Knavesmire Wood and join the straight six furlongs round a sweeping turn in front of the five furlong gate. A new two furlong extension, set at a tangent, also joins the round course here and caters for seven furlong events. A fair, galloping course which calls for stamina and courage, especially in the wet weather when the going can be very testing. Because of the watering system, when the going is soft, much better ground can be found by racing wide in the back straight.
Manager, Clerk of the Course and Secretary: Mr J. L. Smith F.C.A., The Racecourse, York YO2 1EX. Tel: (01904) 620911 Home (01759) 368455. Fax: (01904) 611071.
Free stabling (200 boxes) Tel: Racedays (01904) 706317.
By Car: 1 mile South-East of the city on the A1036. Car parking bookings can be made prior to race meetings (except August) for reserved car park (£2 (inc. VAT) per day). All other parking is free.
By Rail: 1 1/2 miles York Station (from King's Cross). Special bus service from station to the course.
By Air: Light aircraft and helicopter landing facilities available at Rufforth aerodrome (5,000ft tarmac runway). £20 landing fee-transport arranged to course. Leeds/Bradford airport (25 miles).

LEADING JOCKEYS AT ASCOT

(SINCE 1994)

	Total W-R	Per cent	£1 Level stake
L. Dettori	50-261	19.0	+ **42.27**
Pat Eddery	29-264	10.0	- 102.45
M. J. Kinane	29-199	14.0	- 14.46
J. Reid	28-248	11.0	+ **22.33**
T. Quinn	25-211	11.0	- 51.28
R. Hills	23-155	14.0	+ **33.67**
K. Fallon	16-130	12.0	- 35.64
M. Hills	12-155	7.0	- 41.67
O. Peslier	11-76	14.0	+ **76.33**
J. Weaver	9-94	9.0	- 38.13
D. Holland	9-75	12.0	+ **34.75**
K. Darley	8-108	7.0	- 12.13
W. R. Swinburn	8-123	6.0	- 79.01
M. Roberts	7-135	5.0	- 49.50
R. Hughes	6-96	6.0	+ **5.75**
R. Cochrane	6-116	5.0	- 61.00
T. Sprake	5-48	10.0	+ **28.00**
S. Sanders	4-75	5.0	- 26.00
G. Duffield	4-21	19.0	+ **4.63**
Paul Eddery	4-73	5.0	- 47.00
Gary Stevens	3-13	23.0	+ **9.50**
Dane O'Neill	3-56	5.0	- 1.75
J. P. Murtagh	3-20	15.0	- 2.50
A. Whelan	3-27	11.0	+ **30.00**
B. Doyle	3-71	4.0	+ **24.00**

LEADING JOCKEYS AT AYR

(SINCE 1994)

	Total W-R	Per cent	£1 Level stake
J. Weaver	30-174	17.0	- 49.85
K. Darley	29-185	15.0	- 25.64
J. Fortune	22-155	14.0	+ **4.90**
K. Fallon	21-134	15.0	- 26.80
D. Holland	20-113	17.0	- 18.92
J. Carroll	13-183	7.0	- 115.31
A. Culhane	12-85	14.0	+ **75.00**
Dean McKeown	10-107	9.0	- 37.01
L. Charnock	9-93	9.0	+ **2.00**
N. Kennedy	9-107	8.0	- 12.00
Darren Moffatt	7-57	12.0	- 14.50
G. Carter	7-60	11.0	- 24.95
M. Hills	6-31	19.0	- 15.69
L. Dettori	6-29	20.0	- 9.15
J. Lowe	6-45	13.0	+ **24.50**
J. F. Egan	5-50	10.0	+ **39.50**
S. Maloney	5-38	13.0	- 11.25
D. Wright	5-81	6.0	- 57.50
G. Duffield	5-69	7.0	- 45.38
A. Mackay	5-87	5.0	- 49.00
W. Supple	4-32	12.0	+ **23.00**
F. Lynch	4-15	26.0	+ **15.33**
Paul Eddery	4-22	18.0	- 14.56
J. Tate	4-31	12.0	+ **5.25**
R. Havlin	4-37	10.0	- 15.55

LEADING JOCKEYS AT BATH

(SINCE 1994)

	Total W-R	Per cent	£1 Level stake
Pat Eddery	28-112	25.0	- 8.07
T. Quinn	20-135	14.0	- 31.62
J. Reid	19-128	14.0	- 10.05
R. Hughes	15-103	14.0	+ **3.07**
Martin Dwyer	13-78	16.0	+ **18.00**
R. Cochrane	13-80	16.0	- 8.27
T. Sprake	13-146	8.0	- 16.75
L. Dettori	12-53	22.0	+ **14.66**
M. Hills	12-54	22.0	+ **22.99**
M. Henry	11-58	18.0	+ **28.95**
S. Sanders	11-103	10.0	- 6.17
S. Whitworth	11-83	13.0	- 22.06
B. Thomson	11-47	23.0	+ **40.75**
Paul Eddery	11-85	12.0	- 46.89
P. P. Murphy	8-62	12.0	+ **5.95**
S. Drowne	8-148	5.0	- 31.13
C. Rutter	8-72	11.0	- 20.01
Dane O'Neill	7-83	8.0	- 26.75
J. Carroll	7-33	21.0	+ **14.39**
B. Doyle	6-57	10.0	+ **15.00**
K. Fallon	6-31	19.0	+ **0.40**
J. Weaver	6-21	28.0	+ **7.63**
R. Ffrench	5-46	10.0	+ **16.38**
M. Roberts	5-54	9.0	- 5.25
C. Lowther	4-22	18.0	+ **16.88**

LEADING JOCKEYS AT BEVERLEY

(SINCE 1994)

	Total W-R	Per cent	£1 Level stake
K. Darley	50-254	19.0	- 34.89
K. Fallon	26-173	15.0	- 59.17
J. Weaver	22-166	13.0	- 54.28
J. Carroll	18-142	12.0	- 57.25
J. Fortune	17-154	11.0	- 65.06
A. Culhane	16-156	10.0	- 53.00
L. Charnock	15-204	7.0	- 91.98
M. Fenton	14-83	16.0	+ **16.33**
D. Holland	11-77	14.0	- 12.07
W. Ryan	11-50	22.0	- 18.76
L. Dettori	11-47	23.0	- 0.41
R. Cochrane	10-51	19.0	+ **4.63**
Dean McKeown	10-152	6.0	- 52.00
G. Carter	8-76	10.0	- 27.80
C. Lowther	7-39	17.0	+ **11.50**
J. Quinn	7-87	8.0	- 17.75
J. Lowe	7-78	8.0	- 42.00
T. Williams	6-84	7.0	- 32.88
Alex Greaves	6-54	11.0	- 21.38
N. Connorton	6-41	14.0	+ **4.83**
R. Ffrench	5-8	62.0	+ **22.75**
F. Lynch	5-63	7.0	- 25.10
D. Harrison	5-42	11.0	- 16.38
G. Bardwell	5-51	9.0	- 11.75
J. Fanning	5-60	8.0	- 24.25

LEADING JOCKEYS AT BRIGHTON
(SINCE 1994)

	Total W-R	Per cent	£1 Level stake
T. Quinn	53-215	24.0	+ **27.18**
Dane O'Neill	30-188	15.0	+ **2.33**
S. Sanders	24-150	16.0	+ **7.78**
J. Reid	19-104	18.0	- 1.65
R. Hughes	17-116	14.0	+ **3.98**
M. Roberts	16-89	17.0	- 5.70
S. Whitworth	16-135	11.0	- 22.75
Martin Dwyer	15-88	17.0	- 7.40
G. Duffield	15-99	15.0	- 4.84
B. Doyle	14-82	17.0	+ **2.71**
R. Ffrench	12-82	14.0	+ **7.67**
J. Quinn	11-130	8.0	- 15.47
D. Sweeney	10-70	14.0	+ **24.46**
Pat Eddery	10-47	21.0	- 10.40
A. Clark	10-134	7.0	- 44.71
Paul Eddery	9-94	9.0	- 47.37
D. Harrison	9-72	12.0	- 20.25
N. Pollard	8-33	24.0	+ **37.38**
M. Fenton	8-62	12.0	- 13.75
T. Sprake	8-94	8.0	- 12.50
Stephen Davies	8-31	25.0	+ **16.38**
W. Woods	8-43	18.0	- 3.88
D. Biggs	8-75	10.0	- 30.45
A. Daly	8-94	8.0	+ **7.75**
M. Henry	7-55	12.0	+ **0.25**

LEADING JOCKEYS AT CATTERICK
(SINCE 1994)

	Total W-R	Per cent	£1 Level stake
K. Darley	31-160	19.0	- 27.62
J. Fortune	23-140	16.0	- 29.60
J. Carroll	19-150	12.0	- 53.44
L. Charnock	14-178	7.0	- 36.45
J. Weaver	14-82	17.0	- 22.62
T. Williams	10-117	8.0	- 48.25
K. Fallon	10-45	22.0	+ **6.88**
A. Culhane	10-143	6.0	- 66.25
P. Fessey	8-92	8.0	- 38.13
G. Duffield	8-73	10.0	- 31.28
F. Lynch	7-37	18.0	+ **3.51**
J. F. Egan	7-50	14.0	- 7.75
J. Lowe	7-59	11.0	+ **17.91**
D. Holland	6-28	21.0	+ **7.75**
G. Carter	6-35	17.0	- 14.35
Dale Gibson	6-90	6.0	- 52.38
Alex Greaves	6-49	12.0	- 28.28
C. Lowther	5-41	12.0	+ **40.75**
R. Mullen	5-16	31.0	+ **20.24**
J. Quinn	5-38	13.0	+ **25.13**
Dean McKeown	5-117	4.0	- 86.50
R. Lappin	5-50	10.0	- 8.75
M. Hills	4-6	66.0	+ **13.95**
S. Copp	4-12	33.0	+ **2.08**
G. Parkin	4-56	7.0	- 23.25

LEADING JOCKEYS AT CARLISLE
(SINCE 1994)

	Total W-R	Per cent	£1 Level stake
K. Darley	25-126	19.0	- 13.32
J. Fortune	19-130	14.0	- 33.49
K. Fallon	13-71	18.0	+ **6.58**
J. Weaver	13-81	16.0	+ **1.50**
J. Carroll	11-129	8.0	- 35.89
A. Culhane	10-76	13.0	- 13.25
G. Duffield	9-74	12.0	- 41.01
J. Fanning	7-65	10.0	- 25.00
R. Winston	6-41	14.0	- 13.50
Dean McKeown	6-88	6.0	- 5.67
P. Robinson	6-24	25.0	+ **2.50**
R. Hughes	5-8	62.0	+ **4.54**
T. Williams	5-55	9.0	- 16.81
J. Stack	5-30	16.0	- 5.79
C. Lowther	4-22	18.0	- 7.40
P. Fessey	4-59	6.0	- 30.25
A. Nicholls	3-12	25.0	+ **18.00**
W. Supple	3-23	13.0	+ **7.00**
R. Lappin	3-32	9.0	- 1.25
F. Norton	3-15	20.0	+ **2.00**
S. Maloney	3-28	10.0	- 18.20
L. Charnock	3-86	3.0	- 71.90
M. Fenton	2-17	11.0	- 10.83
G. Hind	2-7	28.0	- 2.56
C. Teague	2-20	10.0	+ **9.50**

LEADING JOCKEYS AT CHEPSTOW
(SINCE 1994)

	Total W-R	Per cent	£1 Level stake
J. Reid	16-90	17.0	- 22.95
S. Drowne	12-111	10.0	- 34.00
T. Sprake	11-87	12.0	+ **18.50**
S. Whitworth	10-67	14.0	- 1.63
T. Quinn	10-86	11.0	- 53.46
L. Dettori	9-29	31.0	- 2.21
Pat Eddery	8-40	20.0	- 14.51
S. Sanders	7-75	9.0	- 47.04
R. Hughes	7-50	14.0	- 3.42
R. Ffrench	6-25	24.0	+ **9.08**
W. Ryan	6-40	15.0	+ **12.30**
G. Duffield	6-43	13.0	- 20.70
R. Havlin	5-36	13.0	- 6.25
R. Hills	5-31	16.0	- 0.75
J. Williams	5-39	12.0	+ **2.25**
J. D. Smith	4-19	21.0	- 0.25
Dane O'Neill	4-57	7.0	- 28.50
W. R. Swinburn	4-8	50.0	+ **5.17**
R. Cochrane	4-29	13.0	+ **7.80**
D. Harrison	4-36	11.0	+ **12.00**
C. Rutter	4-55	7.0	- 32.67
R. Price	4-31	12.0	- 1.50
A. Mackay	4-35	11.0	+ **15.00**
N. Adams	4-93	4.0	- 49.00
K. Fallon	3-12	25.0	+ **5.80**

LEADING JOCKEYS AT CHESTER (SINCE 1994)

	Total W-R	Per cent	£1 Level stake
K. Darley	17-102	16.0	+ **14.53**
K. Fallon	16-120	13.0	- 32.85
J. F. Egan	13-90	14.0	+ **17.75**
D. Holland	13-56	23.0	+ **15.63**
J. Reid	11-54	20.0	+ **1.55**
J. Fortune	10-91	10.0	- 38.09
M. Hills	10-85	11.0	- 43.15
L. Dettori	10-71	14.0	- 30.21
Pat Eddery	9-61	14.0	- 17.80
Paul Eddery	8-48	16.0	- 17.58
W. R. Swinburn	8-32	25.0	- 5.22
J. Carroll	8-78	10.0	- 49.38
R. Cochrane	7-63	11.0	- 21.34
D. Wright	7-59	11.0	- 16.67
M. Roberts	7-45	15.0	- 7.27
S. Sanders	6-24	25.0	+ **10.50**
R. Hills	6-29	20.0	- 9.83
W. Ryan	6-41	14.0	- 12.73
T. Quinn	6-73	8.0	- 49.79
J. Quinn	6-55	10.0	- 7.00
A. Culhane	5-32	15.0	- 5.75
R. Hughes	5-23	21.0	+ **3.83**
J. Weaver	5-50	10.0	- 25.00
A. Mackay	4-26	15.0	+ **14.50**
G. Bardwell	4-22	18.0	+ **10.50**

LEADING JOCKEYS AT EPSOM (SINCE 1994)

	Total W-R	Per cent	£1 Level stake
Pat Eddery	17-92	18.0	- 13.52
S. Sanders	13-80	16.0	- 7.21
L. Dettori	13-76	17.0	- 19.18
K. Fallon	10-44	22.0	+ **9.87**
M. Roberts	10-79	12.0	+ **6.73**
T. Quinn	9-123	7.0	- 86.49
R. Cochrane	9-71	12.0	- 3.00
Dane O'Neill	8-81	9.0	- 55.42
G. Carter	8-37	21.0	+ **39.75**
J. Reid	8-87	9.0	- 44.46
W. Ryan	6-39	15.0	+ **5.88**
J. Weaver	5-27	18.0	- 3.75
M. Hills	5-36	13.0	- 12.43
C. Lowther	4-13	30.0	+ **16.83**
M. Henry	4-32	12.0	+ **6.50**
A. Daly	4-26	15.0	+ **1.91**
J. Quinn	4-45	8.0	- 18.00
R. Hughes	4-47	8.0	- 34.25
S. Whitworth	4-46	8.0	- 28.92
B. Doyle	4-18	22.0	+ **20.83**
T. Sprake	4-24	16.0	+ **39.00**
D. Harrison	4-20	20.0	+ **40.00**
M. J. Kinane	4-29	13.0	+ **4.00**
D. Holland	4-45	8.0	- 25.92
D. Sweeney	3-11	27.0	+ **4.00**

LEADING JOCKEYS AT DONCASTER (SINCE 1994)

	Total W-R	Per cent	£1 Level stake
K. Fallon	34-237	14.0	- 70.49
K. Darley	33-294	11.0	- 44.14
M. Hills	32-191	16.0	- 4.45
L. Dettori	31-196	15.0	- 37.91
Pat Eddery	25-172	14.0	- 10.79
J. Fortune	20-219	9.0	- 77.01
R. Hills	18-105	17.0	- 4.24
W. Ryan	17-132	12.0	- 42.51
R. Cochrane	17-148	11.0	+ **7.88**
D. Holland	16-82	19.0	+ **23.88**
T. Quinn	15-140	10.0	- 34.15
J. Reid	14-185	7.0	- 127.93
J. Weaver	14-182	7.0	- 53.30
J. Carroll	14-147	9.0	- 35.13
G. Carter	13-117	11.0	- 36.29
G. Hind	13-87	14.0	- 0.50
W. R. Swinburn	13-78	16.0	- 18.11
M. Roberts	10-94	10.0	- 4.81
R. Hughes	9-63	14.0	+ **14.00**
D. Harrison	9-95	9.0	- 43.50
A. Mackay	8-59	13.0	+ **36.00**
T. Sprake	7-65	10.0	- 8.17
A. Culhane	7-113	6.0	- 19.00
J. Quinn	7-128	5.0	- 81.04
R. Winston	6-42	14.0	+ **23.00**

LEADING JOCKEYS AT FOLKESTONE (SINCE 1994)

	Total W-R	Per cent	£1 Level stake
T. Quinn	22-154	14.0	- 13.63
Dane O'Neill	19-123	15.0	+ **46.60**
Paul Eddery	19-113	16.0	- 11.59
S. Sanders	17-137	12.0	- 19.93
T. Sprake	13-96	13.0	- 34.75
G. Duffield	13-88	14.0	- 32.79
A. Whelan	11-77	14.0	- 8.84
M. Hills	11-31	35.0	+ **36.41**
J. Quinn	11-157	7.0	- 44.01
S. Drowne	10-78	12.0	- 8.38
A. Clark	9-120	7.0	- 78.78
Martin Dwyer	8-61	13.0	+ **18.00**
D. Harrison	8-55	14.0	+ **28.73**
R. Hughes	8-54	14.0	- 29.08
C. Rutter	8-68	11.0	+ **1.96**
M. Fenton	7-70	10.0	+ **1.75**
S. Whitworth	7-75	9.0	- 37.40
K. Fallon	6-29	20.0	+ **3.60**
M. Rimmer	6-39	15.0	+ **5.42**
K. Darley	6-23	26.0	+ **26.63**
W. Ryan	6-37	16.0	- 1.47
D. Biggs	6-55	10.0	- 4.13
P. Robinson	6-63	9.0	- 32.15
R. Cochrane	6-96	6.0	- 67.92
G. Bardwell	6-109	5.0	- 77.00

LEADING JOCKEYS AT GOODWOOD
(SINCE 1994)

	Total W-R	Per cent	£1 Level stake
T. Quinn	47-318	14.0	- 50.01
L. Dettori	46-211	21.0	**+ 3.46**
J. Reid	41-294	13.0	- 97.49
Pat Eddery	36-221	16.0	- 56.74
K. Fallon	20-107	18.0	- 7.08
R. Hills	20-130	15.0	**+ 0.59**
M. Hills	19-139	13.0	**+ 37.66**
Dane O'Neill	18-153	11.0	**+ 32.87**
R. Cochrane	18-150	12.0	**+ 4.37**
M. Roberts	15-145	10.0	- 41.96
K. Darley	14-110	12.0	**+ 5.57**
W. R. Swinburn	12-73	16.0	- 1.58
W. Ryan	12-102	11.0	- 46.02
J. Quinn	11-110	10.0	- 35.95
R. Hughes	11-123	8.0	- 7.13
J. Weaver	11-77	14.0	**+ 13.19**
Paul Eddery	9-169	5.0	- 120.25
M. J. Kinane	8-42	19.0	**+ 10.35**
G. Carter	8-95	8.0	- 29.42
T. Sprake	8-95	8.0	- 34.13
R. Ffrench	7-46	15.0	**+ 3.13**
S. Sanders	7-129	5.0	- 75.75
A. Clark	7-115	6.0	- 41.09
M. Henry	7-69	10.0	**+ 17.25**
O. Peslier	7-23	30.0	**+ 30.75**

LEADING JOCKEYS AT HAYDOCK
(SINCE 1994)

	Total W-R	Per cent	£1 Level stake
Pat Eddery	32-104	30.0	**+ 51.20**
W. Ryan	25-101	24.0	**+ 20.33**
K. Darley	24-201	11.0	- 68.07
K. Fallon	20-139	14.0	- 22.20
J. Weaver	20-131	15.0	- 6.32
L. Dettori	19-116	16.0	- 45.00
J. Reid	18-103	17.0	- 16.80
R. Hills	18-102	17.0	- 6.81
J. Carroll	18-214	8.0	- 100.63
M. Hills	15-53	28.0	**+ 60.33**
T. Sprake	15-79	18.0	**+ 56.58**
J. Fortune	14-136	10.0	- 52.17
G. Carter	13-108	12.0	- 0.38
Paul Eddery	12-65	18.0	**+ 2.24**
T. Quinn	11-53	20.0	**+ 11.30**
G. Hind	10-91	10.0	- 36.38
D. Harrison	10-48	20.0	**+ 12.96**
J. F. Egan	9-91	9.0	**+ 2.88**
A. Culhane	8-87	9.0	- 19.00
D. Holland	8-74	10.0	- 31.76
W. R. Swinburn	8-44	18.0	- 11.72
M. Roberts	7-63	11.0	- 20.44
Dean McKeown	6-109	5.0	- 44.50
J. Quinn	6-86	6.0	- 33.30
Dane O'Neill	5-46	10.0	- 26.50

LEADING JOCKEYS AT HAMILTON
(SINCE 1994)

	Total W-R	Per cent	£1 Level stake
J. Weaver	46-173	26.0	**+ 39.48**
K. Darley	35-211	16.0	- 43.86
J. Fortune	27-147	18.0	- 14.47
J. Carroll	25-228	10.0	- 71.38
A. Mackay	24-126	19.0	**+ 2.25**
K. Fallon	19-127	14.0	- 36.79
N. Kennedy	15-103	14.0	**+ 42.75**
T. Williams	14-122	11.0	- 46.38
G. Duffield	14-91	15.0	- 13.00
L. Charnock	13-122	10.0	- 29.00
A. Culhane	12-87	13.0	- 31.25
Dean McKeown	11-162	6.0	- 111.25
P. Robinson	10-32	31.0	**+ 9.33**
O. Pears	7-47	14.0	- 10.40
R. Lappin	7-52	13.0	- 7.38
D. Wright	7-45	15.0	- 13.75
P. Fessey	6-101	5.0	- 60.25
J. Fanning	6-105	5.0	- 38.00
Dale Gibson	6-99	6.0	- 16.13
Darren Moffatt	6-88	6.0	- 16.50
S. Whitworth	5-14	35.0	**+ 4.13**
T. Quinn	4-7	57.0	**+ 0.54**
J. D. Smith	4-5	80.0	**+ 14.91**
K. Sked	4-55	7.0	- 25.50
S. Drowne	4-19	21.0	**+ 22.75**

LEADING JOCKEYS AT KEMPTON
(SINCE 1994)

	Total W-R	Per cent	£1 Level stake
Pat Eddery	42-208	20.0	- 2.59
J. Reid	29-170	17.0	- 4.42
T. Quinn	29-246	11.0	- 46.03
L. Dettori	21-117	17.0	- 26.05
R. Hughes	18-98	18.0	**+ 105.71**
R. Cochrane	17-134	12.0	**+ 6.82**
T. Sprake	12-75	16.0	**+ 26.62**
R. Hills	12-101	11.0	**+ 1.54**
M. Hills	11-103	10.0	- 31.42
W. Ryan	11-104	10.0	- 25.75
S. Sanders	9-115	7.0	- 61.50
W. R. Swinburn	9-66	13.0	- 11.63
K. Fallon	8-40	20.0	- 1.95
Dane O'Neill	8-106	7.0	- 57.25
D. Harrison	7-94	7.0	- 39.25
N. Pollard	6-21	28.0	**+ 33.25**
G. Hind	5-69	7.0	- 22.75
S. Whitworth	5-71	7.0	**+ 0.75**
J. Quinn	5-68	7.0	- 12.00
B. Thomson	5-52	9.0	- 9.75
A. Clark	5-119	4.0	- 33.00
M. Roberts	5-70	7.0	- 41.00
Paul Eddery	5-91	5.0	- 68.59
R. Perham	4-56	7.0	**+ 21.00**
W. Newnes	4-42	9.0	**+ 7.00**

LEADING JOCKEYS AT LEICESTER (SINCE 1994)

	Total W-R	Per cent	£1 Level stake
L. Dettori	40-160	25.0	+ **14.87**
Pat Eddery	39-162	24.0	- 14.64
K. Fallon	22-129	17.0	- 2.40
T. Quinn	17-156	10.0	- 41.30
J. Reid	17-133	12.0	- 48.32
G. Carter	16-150	10.0	- 33.38
M. Roberts	16-88	18.0	+ **39.06**
R. Cochrane	15-139	10.0	- 25.52
Dane O'Neill	14-109	12.0	- 20.00
T. Sprake	13-136	9.0	- 45.18
G. Duffield	13-119	10.0	- 50.33
W. Ryan	13-118	11.0	- 56.31
J. Weaver	12-79	15.0	+ **36.75**
R. Hills	12-99	12.0	- 5.84
M. Hills	11-132	8.0	- 50.50
C. Rutter	8-102	7.0	- 20.00
J. Fortune	8-76	10.0	- 22.42
F. Lynch	7-75	9.0	- 16.00
W. R. Swinburn	7-49	14.0	- 15.75
K. Darley	7-99	7.0	- 63.30
D. Holland	7-72	9.0	- 7.42
A. Clark	7-94	7.0	- 42.42
A. Mackay	7-76	9.0	- 24.00
R. Perham	7-68	10.0	- 2.25
J. Stack	6-38	15.0	+ **7.66**

LEADING JOCKEYS AT LINGFIELD All Weather (SINCE 1994)

	Total W-R	Per cent	£1 Level stake
J. Weaver	76-334	22.0	+ **14.14**
A. Clark	64-484	13.0	- 49.15
L. Dettori	57-235	24.0	- 11.02
S. Sanders	53-458	11.0	- 93.61
R. Cochrane	51-300	17.0	- 31.52
S. Whitworth	45-269	16.0	- 61.20
D. Holland	42-181	23.0	+ **21.71**
D. Harrison	35-250	14.0	- 42.77
J. Quinn	32-571	5.0	- 325.80
D. Biggs	30-306	9.0	- 118.16
W. Ryan	26-127	20.0	+ **11.26**
Dean McKeown	23-132	17.0	+ **2.48**
Candy Morris	21-212	9.0	- 20.25
G. Duffield	20-143	13.0	- 52.46
G. Carter	19-148	12.0	- 55.40
T. Williams	19-177	10.0	- 28.44
Dane O'Neill	17-207	8.0	- 110.46
C. Rutter	17-186	9.0	- 16.50
D. Sweeney	16-96	16.0	- 5.82
D. R. McCabe	16-130	12.0	- 38.51
Martin Dwyer	15-177	8.0	- 95.09
A. Whelan	15-181	8.0	- 105.04
W. Woods	15-124	12.0	- 29.97
B. Doyle	15-91	16.0	- 22.22
M. Wigham	15-129	11.0	- 50.28

LEADING JOCKEYS AT LINGFIELD- Turf (SINCE 1994)

	Total W-R	Per cent	£1 Level stake
J. Reid	22-130	16.0	- 23.27
Pat Eddery	18-75	24.0	- 9.55
R. Hills	17-71	23.0	+ **5.76**
R. Cochrane	17-99	17.0	+ **49.25**
S. Sanders	15-130	11.0	- 30.46
T. Quinn	15-126	11.0	- 39.38
K. Fallon	14-42	33.0	+ **25.06**
L. Dettori	14-78	17.0	- 40.50
Dane O'Neill	12-128	9.0	- 31.13
R. Perham	12-96	12.0	+ **67.50**
A. McGlone	10-72	13.0	- 30.71
Martin Dwyer	9-75	12.0	+ **21.00**
C. Rutter	9-78	11.0	+ **13.13**
B. Doyle	9-55	16.0	+ **6.14**
G. Hind	9-66	13.0	- 2.20
T. Sprake	9-91	9.0	- 25.15
G. Carter	9-69	13.0	- 28.04
A. Clark	9-147	6.0	- 54.38
W. Ryan	8-88	9.0	- 20.07
W. Woods	8-29	27.0	+ **2.26**
M. Tebbutt	8-65	12.0	- 3.50
M. Hills	8-45	17.0	- 8.79
M. Roberts	8-83	9.0	- 11.00
J. Stack	7-37	18.0	+ **19.50**
R. Hughes	7-81	8.0	- 49.92

LEADING JOCKEYS AT MUSSELBURGH (SINCE 1994)

	Total W-R	Per cent	£1 Level stake
K. Darley	38-185	20.0	+ **15.52**
J. Weaver	23-125	18.0	- 32.92
J. Carroll	22-180	12.0	+ **1.73**
A. Culhane	21-129	16.0	+ **10.88**
K. Fallon	21-108	19.0	- 20.23
J. Fortune	19-172	11.0	- 76.54
L. Charnock	17-137	12.0	- 0.34
J. F. Egan	12-81	14.0	- 34.43
P. Fessey	11-106	10.0	- 51.76
R. Winston	10-49	20.0	+ **25.00**
D. Holland	9-26	34.0	+ **22.38**
T. Williams	9-126	7.0	- 20.63
R. Lappin	9-63	14.0	+ **49.50**
G. Carter	8-32	25.0	+ **1.23**
M. Fenton	8-27	29.0	+ **57.20**
C. Lowther	6-31	19.0	- 0.00
G. Duffield	6-47	12.0	- 16.31
J. Quinn	5-47	10.0	+ **5.00**
J. Stack	5-47	10.0	- 27.38
Dean McKeown	5-110	4.0	- 88.38
D. Wright	5-41	12.0	+ **15.00**
Darren Moffatt	5-48	10.0	+ **34.50**
N. Connorton	5-44	11.0	+ **64.00**
J. Fanning	5-110	4.0	- 43.56
J. Bramhill	4-36	11.0	- 13.75

LEADING JOCKEYS AT NEWBURY (SINCE 1994)

	Total W-R	Per cent	£1 Level stake
L. Dettori	48-246	19.0	+ **22.23**
J. Reid	47-305	15.0	+ **13.69**
T. Quinn	37-290	12.0	+ **45.40**
Pat Eddery	32-309	10.0	- 136.11
K. Fallon	24-126	19.0	- 8.99
M. Hills	20-213	9.0	- 47.47
R. Hills	18-126	14.0	- 14.94
R. Cochrane	17-158	10.0	+ **18.83**
W. Ryan	17-97	17.0	+ **33.48**
S. Sanders	12-122	9.0	- 17.70
W. R. Swinburn	12-107	11.0	- 30.63
D. Harrison	11-131	8.0	- 0.50
M. Roberts	10-139	7.0	- 59.00
Dane O'Neill	8-155	5.0	- 73.25
R. Hughes	8-136	5.0	- 14.25
J. Quinn	8-89	8.0	- 24.25
K. Darley	7-82	8.0	- 48.52
Paul Eddery	7-97	7.0	- 49.92
J. Weaver	6-55	10.0	+ **21.63**
G. Hind	6-37	16.0	+ **6.25**
S. Whitworth	6-74	8.0	- 25.50
A. Clark	5-68	7.0	- 10.00
B. Doyle	5-110	4.0	- 65.00
D. Holland	5-57	8.0	+ **20.00**
R. Perham	4-82	4.0	- 4.50

LEADING JOCKEYS AT NEWCASTLE (SINCE 1994)

	Total W-R	Per cent	£1 Level stake
K. Darley	34-237	14.0	- 78.01
J. Weaver	28-169	16.0	+ **15.75**
K. Fallon	22-136	16.0	- 16.32
J. Carroll	22-202	10.0	- 45.83
J. Fortune	21-179	11.0	- 52.28
G. Duffield	16-113	14.0	+ **2.50**
D. Holland	15-78	19.0	- 12.17
L. Charnock	13-161	8.0	- 43.50
L. Dettori	11-47	23.0	- 3.91
Dean McKeown	9-139	6.0	- 73.00
R. Hills	8-35	22.0	+ **1.25**
M. Fenton	8-44	18.0	+ **0.33**
G. Carter	7-56	12.0	- 20.63
T. Williams	7-88	7.0	- 20.50
W. Ryan	7-40	17.0	- 16.55
G. Hind	7-44	15.0	+ **20.50**
J. Quinn	7-76	9.0	- 3.17
R. Lappin	6-51	11.0	+ **38.50**
A. Culhane	6-132	4.0	- 84.25
T. Quinn	6-43	13.0	- 20.33
M. Hills	5-21	23.0	- 3.40
N. Connorton	5-44	11.0	- 22.65
Dale Gibson	5-86	5.0	- 42.00
R. Winston	4-31	12.0	+ **10.00**
G. Bardwell	4-19	21.0	+ **10.50**

LEADING JOCKEYS AT NEWMARKET- Rowley (SINCE 1994)

	Total W-R	Per cent	£1 Level stake
L. Dettori	65-387	16.0	- 103.96
Pat Eddery	48-317	15.0	- 76.92
K. Fallon	39-233	16.0	- 27.63
R. Hills	33-237	13.0	- 0.36
M. Hills	29-304	9.0	- 48.73
J. Reid	25-299	8.0	- 110.86
T. Quinn	21-302	6.0	- 174.75
M. J. Kinane	20-124	16.0	+ **10.65**
W. R. Swinburn	16-140	11.0	- 8.25
J. Weaver	14-135	10.0	- 39.52
W. Ryan	14-135	10.0	- 28.13
M. Roberts	12-183	6.0	- 67.00
K. Darley	11-163	6.0	- 69.25
R. Cochrane	11-168	6.0	- 74.63
S. Sanders	9-103	8.0	- 28.00
R. Hughes	9-99	9.0	- 35.52
M. Fenton	8-82	9.0	- 26.02
G. Carter	8-124	6.0	- 21.25
D. Harrison	8-110	7.0	+ **29.75**
Dane O'Neill	7-125	5.0	- 33.50
G. Duffield	7-66	10.0	- 28.25
R. Ffrench	6-68	8.0	- 5.00
O. Peslier	6-48	12.0	- 15.56
A. Clark	6-79	7.0	+ **56.57**
B. Doyle	5-95	5.0	- 60.67

LEADING JOCKEYS AT NEWMARKET- July (SINCE 1994)

	Total W-R	Per cent	£1 Level stake
L. Dettori	42-197	21.0	- 36.37
Pat Eddery	37-205	18.0	- 73.05
R. Hills	28-137	20.0	+ **2.87**
K. Fallon	21-89	23.0	- 1.91
J. Reid	16-114	14.0	+ **20.00**
W. Ryan	14-143	9.0	- 72.26
M. Hills	14-140	10.0	+ **10.08**
W. R. Swinburn	12-88	13.0	+ **4.33**
T. Quinn	11-122	9.0	- 42.92
J. Quinn	11-62	17.0	+ **1.92**
D. Harrison	10-63	15.0	+ **5.13**
P. Robinson	10-130	7.0	- 56.25
R. Cochrane	9-103	8.0	- 29.50
D. R. McCabe	9-50	18.0	+ **57.33**
R. Hughes	8-85	9.0	- 6.13
S. Sanders	8-55	14.0	+ **48.50**
M. J. Kinane	8-62	12.0	- 25.57
J. Weaver	8-77	10.0	- 31.72
M. Roberts	8-99	8.0	- 47.38
Dane O'Neill	7-55	12.0	+ **14.25**
M. Fenton	7-90	7.0	- 33.90
G. Carter	7-82	8.0	- 22.13
R. Ffrench	6-57	10.0	+ **23.23**
T. Sprake	6-41	14.0	- 2.17
K. Darley	6-62	9.0	- 23.02

LEADING JOCKEYS AT NOTTINGHAM (SINCE 1994)

	Total W-R	Per cent	£1 Level stake
K. Fallon	36-195	18.0	- 23.56
T. Sprake	22-186	11.0	+ **46.60**
Pat Eddery	20-87	22.0	- 13.67
L. Dettori	20-108	18.0	- 17.80
G. Duffield	19-127	14.0	- 6.06
T. Quinn	17-126	13.0	- 23.67
R. Hills	16-94	17.0	- 8.84
J. Quinn	16-189	8.0	+ **7.50**
W. Ryan	16-115	13.0	- 34.05
J. Fortune	15-127	11.0	- 16.67
J. Reid	14-108	12.0	- 13.50
D. Holland	13-80	16.0	+ **45.25**
M. Fenton	12-113	10.0	- 16.72
D. Harrison	11-91	12.0	+ **2.33**
J. Weaver	11-108	10.0	- 26.70
P. Robinson	10-86	11.0	+ **63.33**
G. Carter	10-205	4.0	- 135.43
M. Roberts	10-107	9.0	- 23.25
A. Clark	9-96	9.0	- 36.83
M. Hills	9-62	14.0	- 24.63
S. Drowne	9-138	6.0	- 26.50
Dean McKeown	9-115	7.0	- 61.75
K. Darley	9-126	7.0	- 69.13
R. Cochrane	9-102	8.0	- 54.00
A. Culhane	8-97	8.0	- 51.09

LEADING JOCKEYS AT REDCAR (SINCE 1994)

	Total W-R	Per cent	£1 Level stake
K. Darley	48-270	17.0	- 15.77
J. Weaver	23-141	16.0	- 32.81
J. Carroll	21-161	13.0	+ **42.36**
K. Fallon	20-114	17.0	- 31.48
L. Charnock	19-209	9.0	+ **58.50**
J. Fortune	19-212	8.0	- 90.73
G. Carter	18-90	20.0	- 9.23
A. Culhane	15-173	8.0	- 69.14
G. Duffield	12-91	13.0	- 38.01
W. Ryan	12-75	16.0	- 27.72
Dean McKeown	12-152	7.0	- 65.25
G. Hind	11-52	21.0	+ **11.50**
L. Dettori	10-46	21.0	- 16.19
D. Holland	10-52	19.0	+ **7.04**
M. Fenton	9-79	11.0	+ **1.75**
Dale Gibson	8-129	6.0	- 52.63
G. Parkin	7-85	8.0	- 23.25
R. Hills	7-44	15.0	- 16.50
R. Cochrane	6-30	20.0	+ **22.60**
P. Fessey	6-70	8.0	- 21.00
S. Maloney	6-51	11.0	- 13.67
Kim Tinkler	6-137	4.0	- 28.00
J. Stack	6-62	9.0	- 33.70
S. Copp	5-44	11.0	- 18.46
D. Harrison	5-37	13.0	- 3.00

LEADING JOCKEYS AT PONTEFRACT (SINCE 1994)

	Total W-R	Per cent	£1 Level stake
K. Fallon	38-190	20.0	+ **60.00**
K. Darley	31-238	13.0	- 24.84
J. Fortune	23-201	11.0	- 28.39
L. Dettori	23-101	22.0	+ **20.88**
Pat Eddery	17-46	36.0	+ **26.16**
J. Carroll	14-153	9.0	- 28.90
J. Weaver	13-131	9.0	- 50.40
W. Ryan	12-71	16.0	- 30.98
A. Culhane	11-128	8.0	+ **13.08**
M. Hills	8-39	20.0	- 6.11
L. Charnock	7-125	5.0	- 50.50
R. Hills	7-74	9.0	- 60.18
Dean McKeown	7-157	4.0	- 43.40
F. Lynch	6-73	8.0	- 28.00
G. Duffield	6-86	6.0	- 54.27
D. Holland	6-64	9.0	- 21.38
R. Winston	5-37	13.0	+ **12.75**
G. Carter	5-77	6.0	- 34.50
T. Quinn	4-20	20.0	+ **8.44**
A. McGlone	4-23	17.0	- 1.67
Paul Eddery	4-39	10.0	- 28.00
G. Bardwell	4-43	9.0	- 19.00
R. Cochrane	4-42	9.0	- 7.14
S. Sanders	4-46	8.0	- 7.83
F. Norton	4-49	8.0	+ **3.00**

LEADING JOCKEYS AT RIPON (SINCE 1994)

	Total W-R	Per cent	£1 Level stake
K. Darley	42-163	25.0	+ **71.73**
K. Fallon	22-115	19.0	+ **11.82**
J. Weaver	20-118	16.0	+ **2.73**
W. Ryan	16-55	29.0	+ **1.35**
J. Carroll	15-160	9.0	- 63.38
R. Cochrane	12-64	18.0	- 10.65
L. Dettori	12-32	37.0	+ **12.06**
J. Fortune	11-157	7.0	- 93.21
G. Carter	11-68	16.0	+ **2.10**
L. Charnock	10-140	7.0	- 82.63
D. Holland	10-48	20.0	+ **10.39**
G. Hind	10-55	18.0	- 13.73
Dean McKeown	8-121	6.0	- 48.63
R. Hills	8-27	29.0	- 2.33
A. Culhane	7-127	5.0	- 48.50
R. Ffrench	5-24	20.0	+ **5.88**
O. Urbina	5-23	21.0	- 7.85
S. Sanders	5-16	31.0	+ **8.11**
J. Fanning	5-98	5.0	- 35.00
D. Harrison	5-38	13.0	- 15.88
A. McGlone	4-22	18.0	- 8.50
T. Williams	4-103	3.0	- 58.00
C. Teague	4-28	14.0	+ **9.00**
N. Connorton	4-73	5.0	- 40.75
J. Quinn	4-55	7.0	- 22.75

LEADING JOCKEYS AT SALISBURY

(SINCE 1994)

	Total W-R	Per cent	£1 Level stake
L. Dettori	26-98	26.0	+ **13.30**
T. Quinn	25-159	15.0	- 39.78
Pat Eddery	25-123	20.0	- 17.99
J. Reid	24-183	13.0	- 49.29
R. Hughes	18-123	14.0	- 27.80
Dane O'Neill	18-159	11.0	- 66.17
T. Sprake	14-179	7.0	- 94.76
B. Doyle	11-60	18.0	+ **60.61**
K. Fallon	10-37	27.0	+ **40.20**
G. Duffield	10-42	23.0	+ **18.75**
S. Drowne	9-137	6.0	- 34.00
D. Harrison	9-98	9.0	- 29.90
R. Hills	9-57	15.0	- 0.90
C. Rutter	8-100	8.0	- 16.68
A. Clark	8-129	6.0	- 57.50
S. Sanders	7-106	6.0	- 70.38
M. Henry	7-58	12.0	- 4.06
D. Holland	7-39	17.0	+ **7.50**
M. Roberts	7-60	11.0	+ **4.58**
N. Varley	6-40	15.0	+ **50.00**
G. Carter	6-47	12.0	- 10.50
R. Cochrane	6-90	6.0	- 34.50
M. Hills	6-60	10.0	- 1.17
W. Ryan	6-38	15.0	- 15.32
D. Sweeney	5-23	21.0	+ **79.50**

LEADING JOCKEYS AT SOUTHWELL

(SINCE 1994)

	Total W-R	Per cent	£1 Level stake
J. Weaver	45-275	16.0	+ **8.93**
J. Quinn	35-511	6.0	- 278.35
G. Duffield	33-244	13.0	- 96.56
L. Charnock	33-389	8.0	- 186.07
C. Teague	30-291	10.0	- 62.87
D. Holland	29-143	20.0	+ **41.78**
Dean McKeown	27-346	7.0	- 208.92
A. Culhane	25-262	9.0	- 72.09
K. Fallon	25-128	19.0	+ **34.35**
D. Harrison	25-130	19.0	+ **23.13**
L. Dettori	25-131	19.0	- 39.40
F. Lynch	24-187	12.0	- 12.17
S. Sanders	20-179	11.0	+ **10.13**
R. Cochrane	20-161	12.0	- 28.38
Emma O'Gorman	19-76	25.0	+ **21.16**
A. Clark	19-219	8.0	- 97.36
G. Carter	18-239	7.0	- 131.51
T. Williams	18-270	6.0	- 81.30
P. McCabe	17-136	12.0	+ **52.05**
F. Norton	16-151	10.0	+ **4.00**
Alex Greaves	16-137	11.0	- 66.40
A. McCarthy	15-152	9.0	- 84.83
D. Sweeney	15-105	14.0	- 6.83
M. Fenton	15-142	10.0	- 42.15
C. Lowther	14-112	12.0	- 0.88

LEADING JOCKEYS AT SANDOWN

(SINCE 1994)

	Total W-R	Per cent	£1 Level stake
Pat Eddery	62-285	21.0	- 4.92
L. Dettori	56-252	22.0	- 26.20
J. Reid	30-236	12.0	- 84.86
T. Quinn	24-186	12.0	- 54.14
M. Hills	18-140	12.0	- 6.55
M. Roberts	17-148	11.0	- 48.09
Dane O'Neill	16-140	11.0	- 30.00
K. Fallon	15-99	15.0	+ **1.99**
R. Hills	15-128	11.0	- 49.27
W. R. Swinburn	12-84	14.0	- 11.19
J. Weaver	12-71	16.0	+ **14.83**
R. Cochrane	12-127	9.0	- 35.92
G. Carter	11-76	14.0	+ **9.96**
M. J. Kinane	11-64	17.0	+ **7.85**
D. Harrison	10-96	10.0	- 3.05
W. Ryan	10-108	9.0	- 54.18
S. Sanders	9-136	6.0	- 70.50
Paul Eddery	9-125	7.0	- 37.84
B. Doyle	8-142	5.0	- 55.50
T. Sprake	7-75	9.0	+ **4.55**
G. Duffield	7-58	12.0	- 19.17
C. Rutter	7-73	9.0	+ **44.00**
R. Hughes	6-75	8.0	- 22.77
J. Tate	6-24	25.0	+ **17.88**
D. Holland	6-66	9.0	- 12.17

LEADING JOCKEYS AT THIRSK

(SINCE 1994)

	Total W-R	Per cent	£1 Level stake
J. Weaver	26-115	22.0	+ **26.44**
J. Fortune	24-153	15.0	- 5.30
K. Darley	23-137	16.0	- 34.17
J. Carroll	19-168	11.0	- 65.18
G. Duffield	16-92	17.0	- 2.21
A. Culhane	16-145	11.0	- 28.02
K. Fallon	13-64	20.0	+ **4.07**
L. Charnock	12-170	7.0	- 75.52
D. Holland	10-46	21.0	+ **15.40**
W. Ryan	10-36	27.0	+ **19.78**
G. Carter	10-83	12.0	- 28.17
Alex Greaves	9-78	11.0	- 8.15
J. F. Egan	8-53	15.0	+ **7.50**
R. Hills	8-40	20.0	- 8.94
D. Harrison	6-34	17.0	+ **0.66**
Paul Eddery	6-25	24.0	- 6.30
Dean McKeown	6-81	7.0	- 31.17
F. Lynch	5-33	15.0	- 12.50
S. Sanders	5-24	20.0	+ **29.50**
J. Stack	5-54	9.0	- 33.63
T. Williams	4-88	4.0	- 37.00
A. McGlone	4-22	18.0	- 10.38
Dale Gibson	4-96	4.0	- 53.00
G. Hind	4-48	8.0	- 22.75
S. Whitworth	4-14	28.0	+ **27.50**

LEADING JOCKEYS AT WARWICK (SINCE 1994)

	Total W-R	Per cent	£1 Level stake
J. Reid	18-90	20.0	+ **2.37**
T. Quinn	15-91	16.0	- 1.54
T. Sprake	15-117	12.0	- 1.56
Pat Eddery	14-37	37.0	+ **17.35**
G. Carter	12-90	13.0	- 25.98
D. Harrison	11-67	16.0	+ **22.50**
R. Hughes	10-49	20.0	- 3.33
G. Bardwell	10-63	15.0	+ **16.50**
M. Hills	9-44	20.0	- 7.00
G. Duffield	9-57	15.0	+ **15.00**
A. Clark	9-63	14.0	+ **33.25**
S. Drowne	8-106	7.0	- 53.00
R. Cochrane	8-49	16.0	- 9.75
Paul Eddery	8-56	14.0	- 14.08
P. Robinson	8-52	15.0	+ **13.00**
Martin Dwyer	7-51	13.0	- 18.38
S. Sanders	7-64	10.0	+ **13.16**
C. Rutter	7-100	7.0	- 48.50
M. Rimmer	6-37	16.0	+ **5.50**
F. Norton	6-73	8.0	- 26.25
M. Fenton	6-77	7.0	- 14.00
N. Adams	6-90	6.0	- 28.30
R. Havlin	5-43	11.0	+ **0.83**
S. Whitworth	5-45	11.0	+ **31.75**
K. Fallon	5-29	17.0	- 9.47

LEADING JOCKEYS AT WOLVERHAMPTON (SINCE 1994)

	Total W-R	Per cent	£1 Level stake
J. Weaver	61-294	20.0	+ **43.06**
S. Sanders	49-370	13.0	- 26.08
G. Duffield	36-228	15.0	- 39.46
D. Holland	35-164	21.0	+ **2.57**
Dean McKeown	34-291	11.0	- 87.93
G. Carter	32-231	13.0	- 47.20
L. Dettori	32-147	21.0	- 26.92
J. Quinn	30-467	6.0	- 168.75
F. Lynch	28-293	9.0	- 114.54
K. Darley	26-104	25.0	+ **31.44**
A. Clark	24-237	10.0	- 0.47
T. Williams	24-241	9.0	- 116.22
D. Wright	23-255	9.0	- 21.90
J. F. Egan	22-150	14.0	+ **66.30**
R. Cochrane	22-127	17.0	- 25.50
S. Whitworth	21-209	10.0	- 109.27
D. Harrison	21-164	12.0	- 32.13
A. McCarthy	20-152	13.0	+ **3.00**
A. Mackay	20-267	7.0	- 125.38
A. Culhane	19-205	9.0	+ **0.50**
S. Drowne	19-252	7.0	- 65.63
L. Charnock	19-201	9.0	- 49.88
T. Sprake	18-168	10.0	- 16.20
K. Fallon	18-115	15.0	- 36.87
C. Lowther	17-122	13.0	- 35.88

LEADING JOCKEYS AT WINDSOR (SINCE 1994)

	Total W-R	Per cent	£1 Level stake
Pat Eddery	41-207	19.0	- 45.95
L. Dettori	37-141	26.0	+ **2.74**
J. Reid	30-189	15.0	- 23.10
T. Quinn	19-162	11.0	- 16.95
Martin Dwyer	12-87	13.0	+ **18.83**
S. Sanders	12-129	9.0	- 8.25
Paul Eddery	12-131	9.0	- 43.42
R. Cochrane	10-99	10.0	- 22.50
M. Roberts	10-94	10.0	- 22.91
W. R. Swinburn	9-25	36.0	+ **25.44**
T. Sprake	8-105	7.0	- 16.42
D. Harrison	8-102	7.0	- 34.50
D. Holland	8-69	11.0	- 8.13
B. Doyle	8-92	8.0	- 10.00
R. Hughes	7-83	8.0	- 27.34
Dane O'Neill	7-138	5.0	- 53.50
S. Drowne	7-103	6.0	- 41.75
K. Fallon	6-47	12.0	- 11.25
W. Ryan	6-57	10.0	- 25.84
M. Fenton	5-49	10.0	- 1.00
J. Quinn	5-98	5.0	- 55.00
W. Newnes	5-29	17.0	+ **21.50**
M. Hills	5-75	6.0	- 33.25
C. Rutter	5-107	4.0	- 66.50
A. McGlone	5-70	7.0	- 46.75

LEADING JOCKEYS AT YARMOUTH (SINCE 1994)

	Total W-R	Per cent	£1 Level stake
L. Dettori	43-145	29.0	- 11.93
R. Hills	34-160	21.0	+ **11.50**
M. Hills	27-177	15.0	+ **11.74**
K. Fallon	19-96	19.0	- 14.24
W. Ryan	19-147	12.0	- 68.04
Pat Eddery	18-81	22.0	- 26.58
M. Roberts	16-98	16.0	+ **59.45**
K. Darley	14-61	22.0	+ **11.80**
R. Cochrane	11-96	11.0	- 47.20
B. Doyle	11-71	15.0	- 5.00
G. Carter	11-84	13.0	- 22.81
D. Holland	10-46	21.0	+ **12.71**
J. Reid	9-58	15.0	- 11.50
A. McGlone	9-68	13.0	- 24.52
D. Harrison	9-66	13.0	- 20.50
G. Bardwell	9-102	8.0	- 16.50
G. Duffield	8-72	11.0	- 13.03
A. Clark	8-53	15.0	+ **37.25**
J. Stack	7-41	17.0	+ **3.25**
G. Hind	7-84	8.0	- 42.31
J. Quinn	7-116	6.0	- 48.00
M. Fenton	7-77	9.0	- 36.92
P. Robinson	7-91	7.0	- 1.25
W. R. Swinburn	7-52	13.0	- 23.90
S. Sanders	6-56	10.0	8.61

LEADING JOCKEYS AT

YORK (SINCE 1994)

	Total W-R	Per cent	£1 Level stake
L. Dettori	49-223	21.0	**+ 31.40**
K. Fallon	30-216	13.0	- 37.98
Pat Eddery	30-211	14.0	- 26.32
M. J. Kinane	21-124	16.0	- 10.49
J. Reid	21-157	13.0	- 44.06
T. Quinn	21-192	10.0	- 75.87
K. Darley	20-201	9.0	- 32.59
M. Hills	17-177	9.0	- 31.87
D. Holland	14-73	19.0	**+ 54.25**
W. R. Swinburn	13-79	16.0	- 12.00
J. Fortune	12-125	9.0	- 44.76
W. Ryan	12-91	13.0	- 19.51
J. Weaver	11-177	6.0	- 31.63
R. Hills	10-112	8.0	- 32.00
M. Roberts	9-92	9.0	- 46.42
R. Cochrane	8-120	6.0	- 60.00
G. Duffield	7-60	11.0	- 5.17
L. Charnock	5-101	4.0	- 67.00
O. Peslier	4-29	13.0	- 12.79
M. Fenton	4-55	7.0	- 32.00
T. Sprake	4-30	13.0	**+ 1.25**
P. Robinson	4-51	7.0	- 19.00
A. Culhane	4-59	6.0	- 22.50
G. Carter	4-66	6.0	- 32.70
G. Parkin	3-26	11.0	- 6.00

LEADING FLAT TRAINERS AT ASCOT (SINCE 1994)

	Total W-R	2yo Stks	3yo Stks	Other Stks	2yo H'caps	3yo H'caps	Other H'caps	App'ce	Amateurs	Per cent	£1 Level stake
J. L. Dunlop	29-165	6-29	2-17	9-37	1-4	2-17	9-60	0-1	0-0	17.6	**+ 63.46**
S bin Suroor	22-80	5-13	1-18	15-42	0-0	0-3	1-4	0-0	0-0	27.5	**+ 54.73**
Sir Michael Stoute	22-189	3-37	6-34	6-54	0-1	2-21	5-41	0-0	0-1	11.6	- 52.42
J. H. M. Gosden	21-139	4-20	4-32	4-28	0-1	4-18	5-39	0-1	0-0	15.1	- 15.29
P. F. I. Cole	20-138	10-41	2-11	2-22	0-3	2-21	4-38	0-2	0-0	14.5	**+ 22.80**
H. R. A. Cecil	18-104	5-17	6-31	5-36	0-0	1-11	1-9	0-0	0-0	17.3	- 18.08
R. Hannon	16-209	7-69	1-19	0-25	4-12	1-25	3-56	0-3	0-0	7.7	- 43.92
M. Johnston	13-115	2-18	1-6	3-23	0-2	4-14	3-52	0-0	0-0	11.3	**+ 40.38**
L. M. Cumani	13-77	4-10	0-13	4-24	0-2	2-9	3-18	0-1	0-0	16.9	**+ 8.71**
D. R. Loder	11-81	7-26	3-12	1-18	0-1	0-10	0-14	0-0	0-0	13.6	**+ 4.48**
B. W. Hills	11-118	7-40	2-19	2-20	0-5	0-11	0-23	0-0	0-0	9.3	- 53.05
Lady Herries	10-62	1-1	0-1	1-6	0-0	0-3	7-49	1-1	0-1	16.1	**+ 26.38**
J. Berry	8-53	2-22	0-1	1-9	0-0	0-1	5-20	0-0	0-0	15.1	**+ 45.50**
I. A. Balding	8-113	4-15	0-9	1-12	0-2	2-12	1-60	0-2	0-1	7.1	- 59.54
C. E. Brittain	7-137	2-28	2-22	2-29	1-1	0-8	0-48	0-1	0-0	5.1	**+ 21.00**
G. Wragg	7-50	0-6	2-10	5-17	0-0	0-5	0-10	0-2	0-0	14.0	**+ 38.33**

LEADING FLAT TRAINERS AT AYR (SINCE 1994)

	Total W-R	2yo Stks	3yo Stks	Other Stks	2yo H'caps	3yo H'caps	Other H'caps	App'ce	Amateurs	Per cent	£1 Level stake
M. Johnston	24-193	10-68	1-4	1-12	2-20	3-17	7-70	0-1	0-1	12.4	- 81.21
B. W. Hills	23-75	9-24	3-6	6-15	2-7	0-6	3-15	0-0	0-2	30.7	**+ 9.83**
Mrs M. Reveley	14-93	0-7	0-1	8-23	0-0	0-3	5-51	0-0	1-8	15.1	- 24.45
A. Bailey	14-116	2-9	1-4	0-14	0-6	2-10	9-66	0-3	0-4	12.1	- 38.59
Mrs J. R. Ramsden	14-82	4-17	0-1	1-2	1-10	0-4	7-44	0-0	1-4	17.1	- 12.91
Miss L. A. Perratt	12-222	2-44	0-4	0-15	0-8	1-20	8-119	0-6	1-6	5.4	- 104.00
J. L. Dunlop	11-46	4-13	1-2	3-8	1-7	0-0	2-15	0-0	0-1	23.9	- 5.54
J. Berry	11-224	3-66	2-4	0-17	1-13	3-14	2-108	0-1	0-1	4.9	- 162.13
J. S. Goldie	10-133	1-8	0-2	0-14	1-8	0-9	7-80	1-2	0-10	7.5	- 58.75
M. R. Channon	10-59	4-21	1-3	1-3	2-4	0-7	2-19	0-2	0-0	17.0	- 1.75
S. E. Kettlewell	10-45	0-0	1-1	0-6	0-0	1-4	8-28	0-1	0-5	22.2	**+ 40.25**
Sir Michael Stoute	9-26	0-4	1-1	6-13	1-1	0-0	1-7	0-0	0-0	34.6	- 1.47
D. Moffatt	8-53	2-11	0-5	1-14	1-3	1-5	2-14	1-1	0-0	15.1	**+ 14.25**
P. Calver	8-30	0-2	0-0	0-1	0-2	1-2	7-22	0-0	0-1	26.7	**+ 30.25**
N. Bycroft	7-94	1-11	0-1	0-2	0-1	0-13	6-61	0-2	0-3	7.5	- 50.13
P. W. Chapple-Hyam	7-37	3-13	0-1	4-9	0-2	0-3	0-9	0-0	0-0	18.9	- 22.18

LEADING FLAT TRAINERS AT BATH (SINCE 1994)

	Total W-R	2yo Stks	3yo Stks	Other Stks	2yo H'caps	3yo H'caps	Other H'caps	App'ce	Amateurs	Per cent	£1 Level stake
I. A. Balding	20-106	4-19	3-13	4-20	0-2	5-11	4-37	0-4	0-0	18.9	- 9.50
R. Charlton	19-62	5-14	2-11	11-22	0-3	0-4	1-6	0-2	0-0	30.7	**+ 10.79**
M. R. Channon	18-141	6-42	4-22	5-20	0-6	2-15	1-35	0-1	0-0	12.8	- 22.25
P. F. I. Cole	15-86	2-16	3-15	3-12	2-6	0-10	5-23	0-4	0-0	17.4	- 13.59
J. Berry	13-62	6-23	0-5	3-12	1-2	1-4	2-15	0-1	0-0	21.0	**+ 28.54**
W. R. Muir	12-81	0-15	1-7	2-8	1-3	0-3	6-39	2-6	0-0	14.8	**+ 10.50**
B. W. Hills	12-68	4-19	3-16	2-16	0-0	0-4	3-12	0-1	0-0	17.7	- 18.33
R. Hannon	12-135	6-49	1-17	3-27	2-8	0-10	0-23	0-1	0-0	8.9	- 60.95
J. W. Hills	11-72	1-13	3-13	2-9	0-1	1-7	4-28	0-1	0-0	15.3	**+ 11.33**
D. R. C. Elsworth	9-61	3-13	3-11	2-12	0-2	0-2	1-21	0-0	0-0	14.8	**+ 13.25**
R. J. Hodges	9-131	0-13	0-9	4-32	0-1	0-3	5-68	0-5	0-0	6.9	- 54.55
J. L. Dunlop	8-41	0-6	3-11	0-3	0-4	1-5	4-12	0-0	0-0	19.5	- 19.37
M. D. I. Usher	8-79	0-8	0-6	1-12	0-0	0-1	4-44	3-8	0-0	10.1	- 23.00
J. A. R. Toller	7-33	2-8	1-5	1-7	0-0	1-2	2-10	0-1	0-0	21.2	**+ 13.60**
J. S. King	7-38	0-0	0-3	0-2	0-0	0-0	6-31	1-2	0-0	18.4	**+ 5.00**
Sir Michael Stoute	7-29	1-2	2-13	2-10	0-0	0-1	2-3	0-0	0-0	24.1	- 4.52

LEADING FLAT TRAINERS AT BEVERLEY (SINCE 1994)

	Total W-R	2yo Stks	3yo Stks	Other Stks	2yo H'caps	3yo H'caps	Other H'caps	App'ce	Amateurs	Per cent	£1 Level stake
M. Johnston	33-142	11-42	3-9	1-7	3-5	2-20	13-57	0-2	0-0	23.2	**+ 36.40**
J. Berry	24-157	14-78	2-15	4-25	2-12	0-3	2-20	0-2	0-2	15.3	- 31.74
Mrs J. R. Ramsden	22-135	3-28	1-2	0-6	0-4	6-26	11-60	1-3	0-6	16.3	- 15.84
D. R. Loder	19-38	10-18	2-4	4-6	0-0	3-6	0-4	0-0	0-0	50.0	**+ 5.63**
T. D. Easterby	15-134	5-33	0-4	1-9	0-5	3-18	4-57	2-6	0-2	11.2	- 34.08
H. R. A. Cecil	15-29	6-11	1-4	7-10	0-0	0-2	1-2	0-0	0-0	51.7	**+ 3.32**
Mrs M. Reveley	15-119	0-8	0-6	3-16	0-1	0-9	12-77	0-1	0-1	12.6	- 43.55
J. L. Eyre	14-133	2-18	0-3	0-9	0-2	2-15	9-77	0-6	1-3	10.5	- 43.00
M. W. Easterby	13-237	4-109	0-4	0-7	2-12	4-24	3-67	0-14	0-0	5.5	- 155.50
J. L. Dunlop	12-55	1-19	2-6	0-4	0-1	4-12	5-13	0-0	0-0	21.8	- 15.18
L. M. Cumani	11-26	1-2	3-6	5-9	0-0	1-3	1-6	0-0	0-0	42.3	**+ 12.66**
A. C. Stewart	8-24	2-6	0-2	3-7	0-0	1-3	2-6	0-0	0-0	33.3	**+ 6.13**
N. Tinkler	8-88	2-28	0-7	3-12	0-3	1-5	2-31	0-2	0-0	9.1	- 34.25
D. Nicholls	8-96	0-3	0-4	2-16	0-2	0-7	5-59	1-4	0-1	8.3	- 29.38
J. G. FitzGerald	7-52	0-14	0-2	1-9	2-2	0-8	4-15	0-2	0-0	13.5	**+ 13.75**
M. Bell	7-36	4-11	0-4	1-2	0-1	0-4	2-11	0-3	0-0	19.4	**+ 1.33**

LEADING FLAT TRAINERS AT BRIGHTON (SINCE 1994)

	Total W-R	2yo Stks	3yo Stks	Other Stks	2yo H'caps	3yo H'caps	Other H'caps	App'ce	Amateurs	Per cent	£1 Level stake
R. Hannon	41-256	16-67	8-37	3-39	3-23	3-24	7-63	1-3	0-0	16.0	- 27.81
G. L. Moore	37-276	1-31	2-16	12-62	2-8	1-17	15-122	3-15	1-5	13.4	- 54.26
S. Dow	23-170	4-18	4-15	2-28	0-6	5-19	7-80	1-3	0-1	13.5	- 16.65
Miss Gay Kelleway	19-97	2-10	1-6	5-27	0-4	0-8	10-37	1-5	0-0	19.6	**+ 29.84**
B. J. Meehan	19-132	13-55	2-11	0-9	0-14	4-16	0-26	0-0	0-1	14.4	- 22.04
M. R. Channon	19-142	6-42	3-15	0-17	0-11	3-12	5-41	2-4	0-0	13.4	- 24.64
R. M. Flower	14-115	0-2	0-7	1-17	0-0	3-7	8-72	2-8	0-2	12.2	**+ 11.00**
Sir Mark Prescott	13-51	0-14	2-4	3-11	3-8	2-9	3-5	0-0	0-0	25.5	**+ 1.91**
W. R. Muir	13-62	3-14	1-10	6-12	0-3	1-4	2-19	0-0	0-0	21.0	**+ 25.75**
J. L. Dunlop	13-47	5-13	2-5	1-6	2-3	1-6	2-13	0-0	0-1	27.7	**+ 8.64**
P. F. I. Cole	13-96	3-19	1-14	5-20	0-6	1-17	3-18	0-2	0-0	13.5	- 49.22
L. M. Cumani	12-39	0-6	4-12	5-9	0-0	3-5	0-7	0-0	0-0	30.8	- 5.57
R. J. O'Sullivan	10-72	0-0	0-3	4-12	0-0	1-3	5-53	0-1	0-0	13.9	- 6.00
T. G. Mills	9-52	2-6	0-2	1-7	2-3	1-9	3-24	0-1	0-0	17.3	**+ 24.25**
K. T. Ivory	9-49	3-8	0-1	0-4	0-0	2-9	4-27	0-0	0-0	18.4	**+ 29.00**
J. Pearce	8-60	0-3	0-2	3-13	0-3	0-3	5-28	0-4	0-4	13.3	**+ 29.00**

LEADING FLAT TRAINERS AT CARLISLE (SINCE 1994)

	Total W-R	2yo Stks	3yo Stks	Other Stks	2yo H'caps	3yo H'caps	Other H'caps	App'ce	Amateurs	Per cent	£1 Level stake
Mrs M. Reveley	16-75	1-6	1-2	7-19	0-0	1-9	6-34	0-3	0-2	21.3	**+ 16.13**
M. R. Channon	15-34	6-8	1-3	7-12	0-0	1-7	0-4	0-0	0-0	44.1	**+ 16.81**
J. Berry	15-125	4-36	2-10	7-35	0-0	0-11	2-30	0-3	0-0	12.0	- 62.73
M. Johnston	14-81	1-22	1-5	2-11	0-0	3-16	7-26	0-1	0-0	17.3	**+ 9.08**
Mrs J. R. Ramsden	13-60	3-11	0-2	3-7	0-0	3-16	4-24	0-0	0-0	21.7	**+ 2.43**
M. Dods	11-61	0-6	0-1	2-17	0-0	0-3	7-28	2-6	0-0	18.0	**+ 36.50**
M. H. Tompkins	10-36	2-5	1-4	2-12	0-0	3-7	1-7	0-0	1-1	27.8	**+ 19.35**
J. L. Eyre	9-67	0-3	0-3	0-15	0-0	2-5	6-35	1-5	0-1	13.4	**+ 8.25**
Sir Mark Prescott	8-27	2-6	1-2	3-11	0-0	0-4	2-4	0-0	0-0	29.6	- 0.76
T. D. Easterby	7-65	3-13	1-4	1-7	0-0	0-15	1-24	1-2	0-0	10.8	- 30.23
R. A. Fahey	7-40	0-7	0-1	4-10	0-0	1-6	2-16	0-0	0-0	17.5	**+ 22.50**
E. Weymes	7-34	3-8	2-3	0-11	0-0	0-2	2-8	0-2	0-0	20.6	**+ 26.75**
J. J. O'Neill	5-64	0-11	0-0	2-23	0-0	0-9	2-19	1-2	0-0	7.8	- 27.50
E. J. Alston	5-55	0-2	0-0	0-13	0-0	0-6	5-31	0-3	0-0	9.1	- 4.00
G. M. Moore	5-22	0-5	0-0	2-8	0-0	0-1	2-7	0-0	1-1	22.7	**+ 14.25**
Don Enrico Incisa	4-32	0-0	0-0	1-6	0-0	2-8	1-18	0-0	0-0	12.5	**+ 9.00**

LEADING FLAT TRAINERS AT CATTERICK (SINCE 1994)

	Total W-R	2yo Stks	3yo Stks	Other Stks	2yo H'caps	3yo H'caps	Other H'caps	App'ce	Amateurs	Per cent	£1 Level stake
J. Berry	35-206	13-70	1-17	11-36	1-21	4-24	4-29	1-9	0-0	17.0	- 4.09
B. W. Hills	21-64	5-11	7-12	6-13	0-3	1-5	2-16	0-3	0-1	32.8	+ 17.12
Mrs M. Reveley	19-108	1-6	4-9	6-26	0-1	0-10	6-50	2-5	0-1	17.6	+ 31.37
M. Johnston	16-104	6-31	1-6	3-9	0-10	3-18	1-26	2-4	0-0	15.4	- 18.23
J. L. Eyre	16-139	1-15	2-7	1-27	0-9	1-9	10-61	1-10	0-1	11.5	+ 28.00
M. W. Easterby	15-140	2-27	0-2	1-4	2-25	3-26	7-55	0-1	0-0	10.7	- 28.75
T. D. Barron	14-63	4-10	0-3	4-10	2-6	0-4	3-29	1-1	0-0	22.2	+ 99.23
M. R. Channon	14-68	6-22	3-7	0-5	0-10	1-5	3-17	1-2	0-0	20.6	- 13.41
D. Nicholls	10-100	0-5	0-3	6-33	0-1	0-5	3-48	1-5	0-0	10.0	- 60.38
T. D. Easterby	9-76	1-16	1-4	2-10	0-9	3-14	0-18	2-5	0-0	11.8	+ 17.38
J. Pearce	8-33	0-1	1-3	0-6	1-2	0-1	3-12	1-4	2-4	24.2	+ 34.82
D. W. Barker	7-41	1-4	0-1	1-8	1-4	1-3	2-19	0-1	1-1	17.1	- 5.00
W. Jarvis	7-20	1-4	0-2	2-3	1-2	0-1	1-5	2-3	0-0	35.0	+ 10.50
P. D. Evans	7-86	3-19	0-2	2-21	2-10	0-9	0-19	0-4	0-2	8.1	- 42.75
Sir Michael Stoute	7-19	2-6	4-8	1-2	0-1	0-1	0-0	0-1	0-0	36.8	- 5.10
N. Tinkler	6-44	1-6	0-0	0-13	0-3	3-9	2-9	0-4	0-0	13.6	+ 10.80

LEADING FLAT TRAINERS AT CHEPSTOW (SINCE 1994)

	Total W-R	2yo Stks	3yo Stks	Other Stks	2yo H'caps	3yo H'caps	Other H'caps	App'ce	Amateurs	Per cent	£1 Level stake
P. W. Chapple-Hyam	13-48	6-19	4-8	3-10	0-3	0-4	0-4	0-0	0-0	27.1	+ 15.94
R. Hannon	13-133	5-44	1-8	4-15	1-9	1-13	1-41	0-2	0-1	9.8	- 73.18
Sir Michael Stoute	12-30	6-10	3-6	2-9	0-0	0-3	1-2	0-0	0-0	40.0	+ 5.12
L. M. Cumani	11-17	2-4	2-4	3-3	0-0	2-4	1-1	1-1	0-0	64.7	+ 18.07
D. W. P. Arbuthnot	11-52	2-11	0-0	0-2	1-4	0-4	5-26	0-0	3-5	21.2	+ 42.50
J. M. Bradley	10-108	0-7	1-6	0-8	0-1	0-6	8-68	0-0	1-12	9.3	- 41.50
L. MontagueHall	7-7	0-0	0-0	0-0	0-0	0-0	4-4	3-3	0-0	100	+ 32.75
J. L. Dunlop	7-53	4-24	0-4	1-5	0-2	2-7	0-10	0-0	0-1	13.2	- 23.20
B. Palling	7-58	5-15	1-5	1-9	0-6	0-1	0-20	0-0	0-2	12.1	+ 2.50
H. Candy	7-39	0-4	1-6	3-9	0-0	1-3	2-16	0-0	0-1	18.0	+ 27.00
B. W. Hills	6-33	2-12	2-6	1-2	0-1	0-5	1-6	0-0	0-1	18.2	- 5.88
Sir Mark Prescott	6-25	3-11	0-0	1-5	1-1	1-3	0-5	0-0	0-0	24.0	- 13.49
J. Berry	6-30	1-8	1-2	1-7	0-3	0-1	2-7	1-1	0-1	20.0	+ 22.00
W. R. Muir	6-53	1-4	0-2	0-5	0-3	0-3	5-31	0-2	0-3	11.3	- 13.75
P. F. I. Cole	6-67	1-24	1-11	2-12	0-1	2-10	0-9	0-0	0-0	9.0	- 27.62
B. R. Millman	6-48	0-7	0-2	0-5	0-1	1-3	5-27	0-1	0-2	12.5	+ 6.50

LEADING FLAT TRAINERS AT CHESTER (SINCE 1994)

	Total W-R	2yo Stks	3yo Stks	Other Stks	2yo H'caps	3yo H'caps	Other H'caps	App'ce	Amateurs	Per cent	£1 Level stake
Sir Michael Stoute	21-76	5-14	3-18	4-15	0-2	5-14	4-13	0-0	0-0	27.6	+ 19.70
A. Bailey	20-163	2-23	1-12	1-7	0-4	2-15	11-89	3-13	0-0	12.3	- 57.92
J. Berry	16-154	10-43	1-8	1-12	0-7	1-24	3-56	0-4	0-0	10.4	- 64.13
P. D. Evans	15-135	0-26	0-4	1-4	4-17	3-15	6-61	1-8	0-0	11.1	+ 5.50
B. W. Hills	15-87	4-14	4-29	2-15	0-4	2-11	3-14	0-0	0-0	17.2	- 1.61
B. A. McMahon	12-75	4-18	1-7	4-9	0-2	2-10	1-27	0-2	0-0	16.0	+ 11.71
E. J. Alston	11-113	2-18	0-1	3-13	0-4	1-6	5-67	0-4	0-0	9.7	- 34.13
P. W. Chapple-Hyam	10-47	2-9	5-18	1-2	0-0	1-10	1-7	0-1	0-0	21.3	+ 1.58
J. H. M. Gosden	10-42	0-2	4-15	4-11	0-1	2-8	0-5	0-0	0-0	23.8	+ 3.38
R. Hannon	10-63	8-24	0-5	0-4	0-10	2-15	0-5	0-0	0-0	15.9	- 13.34
H. R. A. Cecil	9-38	3-5	3-12	3-13	0-0	0-1	0-7	0-0	0-0	23.7	- 16.48
P. F. I. Cole	9-49	3-11	2-10	1-8	1-4	0-9	2-7	0-0	0-0	18.4	- 16.49
J. L. Dunlop	8-29	3-7	0-6	2-3	0-0	0-2	3-11	0-0	0-0	27.6	- 2.63
M. W. Easterby	7-30	0-2	0-0	0-0	1-7	0-3	5-17	1-1	0-0	23.3	+ 6.25
M. C. Pipe	6-23	0-0	0-0	3-6	1-1	0-1	2-14	0-1	0-0	26.1	- 3.87
M. Johnston	6-56	1-7	1-3	0-2	0-3	1-9	3-32	0-0	0-0	10.7	- 24.50

LEADING FLAT TRAINERS AT DONCASTER (SINCE 1994)

	Total W-R	2yo Stks	3yo Stks	Other Stks	2yo H'caps	3yo H'caps	Other H'caps	App'ce	Amateurs	Per cent	£1 Level stake
B. W. Hills	44-247	12-74	10-47	14-46	3-24	1-7	4-45	0-3	0-1	17.8	**+ 54.70**
J. H. M. Gosden	34-158	10-49	4-20	12-47	1-5	2-6	5-30	0-1	0-0	21.5	**+ 27.71**
J. L. Dunlop	31-160	12-61	2-17	8-25	4-13	1-12	4-32	0-0	0-0	19.4	**+ 1.47**
H. R. A. Cecil	25-101	8-22	4-20	11-46	0-0	0-3	2-10	0-0	0-0	24.8	- 1.29
Mrs J. R. Ramsden	23-236	3-24	0-7	1-7	3-31	3-27	11-124	1-14	1-2	9.8	- 81.26
M. Johnston	20-180	3-39	2-11	5-31	1-22	4-18	5-59	0-0	0-0	11.1	- 79.18
Sir Michael Stoute	19-94	6-35	1-11	8-29	0-3	1-2	2-13	1-1	0-0	20.2	**+ 14.53**
S bin Suroor	13-40	6-13	5-10	2-12	0-2	0-1	0-2	0-0	0-0	32.5	**+ 18.27**
M. R. Channon	12-103	7-35	0-16	3-5	0-8	0-9	2-27	0-3	0-0	11.7	- 10.25
J. L. Eyre	11-150	0-12	0-2	0-5	1-5	3-15	7-94	0-14	0-3	7.3	- 42.00
R. W. Armstrong	11-42	4-10	1-6	4-13	0-1	1-2	1-10	0-0	0-0	26.2	**+ 10.23**
I. A. Balding	11-91	3-23	1-6	1-11	1-8	1-3	4-38	0-2	0-0	12.1	- 15.75
Miss Gay Kelleway	11-65	0-8	1-4	2-9	0-0	0-4	6-33	2-7	0-0	16.9	**+ 31.00**
J. Berry	11-149	6-42	0-6	3-21	0-10	0-13	2-53	0-4	0-0	7.4	- 80.88
R. Hannon	11-205	4-45	2-16	2-38	1-37	0-17	2-45	0-7	0-0	5.4	- 85.75
D. R. Loder	10-56	5-24	1-9	2-12	0-2	1-2	1-7	0-0	0-0	17.9	- 9.85

LEADING FLAT TRAINERS AT EPSOM (SINCE 1994)

	Total W-R	2yo Stks	3yo Stks	Other Stks	2yo H'caps	3yo H'caps	Other H'caps	App'ce	Amateurs	Per cent	£1 Level stake
R. Hannon	17-142	10-42	2-19	3-13	1-7	1-20	0-38	0-2	0-1	12.0	- 79.08
Lord Huntingdon	12-34	1-4	2-4	0-1	1-1	0-2	7-20	0-1	1-1	35.3	**+ 22.47**
J. L. Dunlop	12-46	2-7	2-9	5-10	0-0	1-7	2-13	0-0	0-0	26.1	- 2.62
P. F. I. Cole	12-77	2-15	3-19	3-10	0-1	1-7	2-22	1-3	0-0	15.6	- 17.34
M. Johnston	10-46	5-14	0-5	0-1	1-1	0-7	4-18	0-0	0-0	21.7	**+ 6.33**
Sir Michael Stoute	8-59	0-0	2-20	4-19	0-1	0-9	2-9	0-0	0-1	13.6	- 27.17
J. Berry	8-40	2-7	0-2	1-5	1-2	0-2	4-22	0-0	0-0	20.0	**+ 32.50**
S. Dow	7-96	0-15	0-5	0-7	0-3	1-5	3-55	3-6	0-0	7.3	- 26.68
P. W. Harris	6-35	0-1	2-4	0-2	0-1	0-2	4-25	0-0	0-0	17.1	**+ 11.00**
D. R. C. Elsworth	6-34	1-3	1-7	2-5	0-1	1-2	1-14	0-1	0-1	17.7	**+ 13.38**
M. A. Jarvis	5-22	0-5	0-2	1-3	0-1	4-6	0-5	0-0	0-0	22.7	**+ 21.50**
H. R. A. Cecil	5-23	0-0	4-12	1-5	0-0	0-2	0-4	0-0	0-0	21.7	- 7.96
I. A. Balding	5-67	0-5	2-11	1-8	0-2	0-6	2-34	0-1	0-0	7.5	- 43.97
G. L. Moore	5-81	0-8	0-5	1-8	0-2	0-11	4-42	0-4	0-1	6.2	- 44.00
G. Lewis	5-85	2-25	1-7	0-7	1-5	0-10	1-30	0-1	0-0	5.9	- 60.38
G. B. Balding	4-7	0-0	0-0	0-0	0-0	1-2	2-4	1-1	0-0	57.1	**+ 34.00**

LEADING FLAT TRAINERS AT FOLKESTONE (SINCE 1994)

	Total W-R	2yo Stks	3yo Stks	Other Stks	2yo H'caps	3yo H'caps	Other H'caps	App'ce	Amateurs	Per cent	£1 Level stake
R. Hannon	19-152	7-63	5-16	4-20	1-9	0-10	2-29	0-5	0-0	12.5	- 20.71
J. Pearce	15-85	0-8	0-0	5-18	0-0	1-4	5-45	1-5	3-5	17.7	**+ 20.00**
G. L. Moore	15-123	3-25	2-6	0-21	0-3	1-8	7-49	2-5	0-6	12.2	- 40.07
J. L. Dunlop	13-52	5-17	1-8	4-10	0-2	1-10	2-4	0-1	0-0	25.0	- 4.38
M. R. Channon	12-106	6-41	4-15	0-11	1-5	0-11	1-15	0-7	0-1	11.3	- 55.38
Sir Mark Prescott	11-49	5-27	0-1	3-6	0-4	1-4	1-5	0-1	1-1	22.5	- 9.10
C. E. Brittain	10-83	1-14	2-7	0-13	1-3	1-10	5-32	0-1	0-3	12.1	**+ 46.50**
S. C. Williams	10-51	1-10	1-7	3-6	0-2	2-8	3-14	0-4	0-0	19.6	**+ 31.74**
N. A. Callaghan	9-34	2-9	0-0	1-6	1-4	2-8	2-6	1-1	0-0	26.5	**+ 26.54**
W. R. Muir	9-55	3-16	1-7	4-10	0-3	0-5	1-13	0-1	0-0	16.4	- 0.54
D. W. P. Arbuthnot	9-39	2-8	0-0	0-2	1-1	2-5	4-19	0-0	0-4	23.1	**+ 26.33**
Lady Herries	9-45	0-1	0-2	2-12	0-0	1-5	5-20	0-3	1-2	20.0	- 5.09
Miss Gay Kelleway	9-56	2-7	0-1	5-17	0-2	0-2	1-24	0-2	1-1	16.1	- 1.50
M. Bell	9-63	4-17	1-9	2-8	0-2	1-11	1-11	0-5	0-0	14.3	- 22.75
S. Dow	9-139	2-16	0-12	3-26	0-5	2-12	1-56	1-8	0-4	6.5	- 57.17
C. A. Horgan	8-39	0-4	0-2	1-6	0-0	0-2	7-23	0-1	0-1	20.5	**+ 1.00**

LEADING FLAT TRAINERS AT GOODWOOD (SINCE 1994)

	Total W-R	2yo Stks	3yo Stks	Other Stks	2yo H'caps	3yo H'caps	Other H'caps	App'ce	Amateurs	Per cent	£1 Level stake
R. Hannon	36-373	15-105	5-44	4-45	2-27	3-47	7-101	0-1	0-3	9.7	- 126.38
P. F. I. Cole	33-158	13-52	6-24	5-20	2-8	5-25	2-29	0-0	0-0	20.9	**+ 16.01**
Sir Michael Stoute	28-105	3-12	6-24	8-29	1-1	4-19	6-20	0-0	0-0	26.7	**+ 30.27**
J. H. M. Gosden	28-154	7-32	6-30	5-35	0-0	1-18	9-36	0-1	0-2	18.2	**+ 10.03**
J. L. Dunlop	26-221	5-64	6-30	5-36	0-9	1-34	9-48	0-0	0-0	11.8	- 94.44
H. R. A. Cecil	26-114	11-25	5-24	5-34	0-0	2-12	3-19	0-0	0-0	22.8	- 18.17
I. A. Balding	18-146	0-22	0-14	6-17	3-4	2-16	7-70	0-3	0-0	12.3	- 15.97
M. R. Channon	16-153	6-46	4-14	1-9	0-14	1-12	3-49	0-8	1-1	10.5	- 7.50
S bin Suroor	15-43	2-7	10-12	3-22	0-0	0-1	0-1	0-0	0-0	34.9	**+ 10.70**
L. M. Cumani	15-113	5-17	4-23	0-15	0-3	3-26	3-29	0-0	0-0	13.3	- 32.31
E. A. L. Dunlop	13-55	2-9	3-14	2-6	1-1	1-9	3-15	1-1	0-0	23.6	**+ 32.26**
D. R. C. Elsworth	13-96	1-14	3-21	2-18	0-1	0-4	5-34	2-4	0-0	13.5	- 10.65
P. W. Chapple-Hyam	12-87	10-37	0-11	0-17	0-2	1-8	1-12	0-0	0-0	13.8	- 25.83
Lady Herries	12-84	0-4	0-9	3-11	0-0	3-8	6-49	0-3	0-0	14.3	**+ 98.00**
B. J. Meehan	11-100	5-30	1-7	0-8	1-12	2-14	2-27	0-1	0-1	11.0	**+ 2.00**
G. L. Moore	11-123	1-11	0-6	0-9	0-5	1-9	9-74	0-4	0-5	8.9	- 11.50

LEADING FLAT TRAINERS AT HAMILTON (SINCE 1994)

	Total W-R	2yo Stks	3yo Stks	Other Stks	2yo H'caps	3yo H'caps	Other H'caps	App'ce	Amateurs	Per cent	£1 Level stake
M. Johnston	39-197	14-72	1-8	8-19	2-7	2-12	12-75	0-4	0-0	19.8	- 45.15
J. Berry	39-272	19-99	5-19	5-32	1-11	2-16	5-72	1-15	1-8	14.3	- 49.35
Miss L. A. Perratt	27-344	4-31	0-9	5-40	2-7	1-12	11-186	2-36	2-23	7.9	- 44.50
P. C. Haslam	22-118	2-14	2-7	3-10	0-3	1-9	13-60	1-11	0-4	18.6	- 13.08
Mrs M. Reveley	18-135	1-9	2-8	6-26	0-0	0-3	9-85	0-3	0-1	13.3	- 53.53
D. HaydnJones	14-78	1-8	0-0	2-5	0-3	2-4	9-49	0-6	0-3	18.0	- 21.75
M. H. Tompkins	13-34	3-6	3-5	2-6	0-0	4-8	1-9	0-0	0-0	38.2	**+ 0.52**
M. R. Channon	12-69	5-23	2-14	0-7	0-0	1-6	3-16	1-3	0-0	17.4	**+ 8.38**
C. W. Thornton	12-97	2-15	1-7	2-12	0-1	1-4	6-55	0-1	0-2	12.4	- 34.75
R. M. McKellar	11-161	0-6	1-3	0-17	0-2	0-4	7-94	2-21	1-14	6.8	- 35.50
S. E. Kettlewell	11-63	0-1	0-2	4-16	0-0	0-0	5-33	0-6	2-5	17.5	- 2.50
S. C. Williams	11-23	2-2	4-9	2-2	0-3	0-2	3-5	0-0	0-0	47.8	**+ 33.75**
Sir Mark Prescott	10-38	3-14	1-3	2-4	0-1	2-6	1-8	1-1	0-1	26.3	- 4.30
D. W. Chapman	10-76	0-1	0-0	0-3	0-2	0-0	6-52	1-8	3-10	13.2	**+ 17.75**
J. L. Eyre	10-88	0-4	0-2	3-16	0-1	1-3	5-53	1-4	0-5	11.4	- 29.25
D. A. Nolan	10-217	0-3	0-2	0-31	0-0	0-1	8-134	1-24	1-22	4.6	- 136.75

LEADING FLAT TRAINERS AT HAYDOCK (SINCE 1994)

	Total W-R	2yo Stks	3yo Stks	Other Stks	2yo H'caps	3yo H'caps	Other H'caps	App'ce	Amateurs	Per cent	£1 Level stake
J. L. Dunlop	33-128	13-35	3-13	5-20	1-1	5-26	6-32	0-0	0-1	25.8	**+ 12.50**
B. W. Hills	27-105	10-31	4-13	7-20	0-4	2-18	4-19	0-0	0-0	25.7	**+ 33.62**
J. H. M. Gosden	24-123	5-21	7-30	5-29	0-0	2-14	5-27	0-0	0-2	19.5	- 9.89
H. R. A. Cecil	23-61	6-10	3-13	12-22	0-0	1-8	1-8	0-0	0-0	37.7	**+ 16.80**
J. Berry	18-217	5-79	3-14	4-19	0-21	2-18	3-61	1-5	0-0	8.3	- 85.88
Mrs M. Reveley	16-102	0-9	0-4	2-12	0-2	1-9	12-59	1-6	0-1	15.7	- 11.80
P. W. Chapple-Hyam	14-56	6-18	5-17	1-10	0-0	1-5	1-5	0-1	0-0	25.0	- 8.48
R. Hannon	13-140	8-45	1-16	1-24	0-6	1-23	2-26	0-0	0-0	9.3	- 83.38
L. M. Cumani	12-63	1-4	3-13	2-16	0-0	1-12	4-15	1-3	0-0	19.1	- 11.58
Sir Michael Stoute	11-65	6-19	3-14	0-10	0-0	0-10	2-12	0-0	0-0	16.9	- 27.16
M. Johnston	11-118	5-36	0-7	2-13	0-4	2-20	2-36	0-2	0-0	9.3	- 50.07
B. J. Meehan	9-41	2-14	1-3	1-4	1-3	3-9	1-7	0-0	0-1	22.0	**+ 2.74**
P. D. Evans	9-142	2-38	0-5	2-9	2-14	0-9	3-57	0-5	0-5	6.3	- 70.13
P. F. I. Cole	9-76	4-19	0-7	1-12	0-1	2-18	2-19	0-0	0-0	11.8	- 17.70
R. Charlton	9-53	1-5	4-9	3-15	0-1	0-9	1-14	0-0	0-0	17.0	- 13.32
P. W. Harris	8-54	2-11	1-4	2-6	0-0	0-10	3-23	0-0	0-0	14.8	- 8.13

LEADING FLAT TRAINERS AT KEMPTON (SINCE 1994)

	Total W-R	2yo Stks	3yo Stks	Other Stks	2yo H'caps	3yo H'caps	Other H'caps	App'ce	Amateurs	Per cent	£1 Level stake
R. Hannon	36-290	12-82	9-49	4-33	0-9	4-28	5-76	2-13	0-0	12.4	- 23.65
Sir Michael Stoute	17-104	3-28	8-33	4-24	0-0	0-5	2-14	0-0	0-0	16.4	- 21.59
J. L. Dunlop	16-124	2-36	6-36	3-13	1-1	0-13	4-25	0-0	0-0	12.9	- 32.47
H. R. A. Cecil	15-68	1-9	11-34	2-17	0-0	0-1	1-7	0-0	0-0	22.1	- 7.53
R. Charlton	14-71	5-20	3-24	0-8	0-0	1-6	5-13	0-0	0-0	19.7	**+ 14.87**
P. F. I. Cole	13-110	5-28	1-27	3-19	0-1	0-9	4-25	0-1	0-0	11.8	- 15.85
I. A. Balding	11-88	3-20	3-25	1-8	0-1	0-4	3-26	1-4	0-0	12.5	- 23.75
D. R. C. Elsworth	11-88	1-20	1-25	1-7	2-3	1-3	5-27	0-3	0-0	12.5	**+ 13.25**
J. R. Fanshawe	11-71	2-9	5-27	2-10	0-0	0-4	2-21	0-0	0-0	15.5	**+ 27.74**
P. W. Harris	9-84	2-20	2-20	1-8	0-0	1-4	2-30	1-2	0-0	10.7	**+ 26.58**
B. J. Meehan	9-102	3-38	2-10	0-6	1-5	1-12	2-30	0-1	0-0	8.8	- 44.27
W. J. Musson	8-52	0-2	0-2	0-1	0-1	0-0	6-40	2-6	0-0	15.4	**+ 19.50**
G. Wragg	8-40	2-5	1-16	2-9	0-0	1-2	2-8	0-0	0-0	20.0	**+ 0.74**
M. R. Channon	8-90	2-24	2-15	1-9	0-4	2-7	1-27	0-4	0-0	8.9	**+ 12.88**
L. M. Cumani	7-36	3-6	2-15	1-11	0-0	0-2	1-2	0-0	0-0	19.4	**+ 6.75**
P. W. Chapple-Hyam	7-29	1-10	4-13	2-6	0-0	0-0	0-0	0-0	0-0	24.1	**+ 10.00**

LEADING FLAT TRAINERS AT LEICESTER (SINCE 1994)

	Total W-R	2yo Stks	3yo Stks	Other Stks	2yo H'caps	3yo H'caps	Other H'caps	App'ce	Amateurs	Per cent	£1 Level stake
R. Hannon	34-195	12-60	9-31	3-25	4-22	3-19	3-34	0-4	0-0	17.4	**+ 70.35**
J. L. Dunlop	30-152	12-71	5-22	4-21	0-5	5-19	4-14	0-0	0-0	19.7	**+ 43.34**
H. R. A. Cecil	21-81	11-36	5-16	5-22	0-0	0-2	0-5	0-0	0-0	25.9	- 4.93
Sir Michael Stoute	16-74	7-39	3-9	6-18	0-0	0-2	0-5	0-1	0-0	21.6	- 8.53
P. F. I. Cole	16-134	7-57	3-25	1-15	1-10	3-13	1-11	0-3	0-0	11.9	- 52.11
J. H. M. Gosden	13-86	1-29	4-14	7-22	0-2	0-5	1-8	0-6	0-0	15.1	- 26.28
B. W. Hills	12-80	7-43	1-10	3-7	1-5	0-9	0-5	0-1	0-0	15.0	- 22.77
L. M. Cumani	11-48	3-19	3-9	1-7	0-0	0-4	3-7	1-2	0-0	22.9	- 14.28
D. R. Loder	11-31	8-20	3-6	0-4	0-0	0-1	0-0	0-0	0-0	35.5	- 0.11
J. L. Harris	10-75	0-6	1-8	2-19	1-2	0-2	4-30	2-8	0-0	13.3	**+ 37.00**
R. Hollinshead	10-140	4-28	1-25	1-25	0-5	1-13	3-40	0-4	0-0	7.1	- 68.50
Sir Mark Prescott	10-54	2-22	1-7	2-8	2-3	1-5	2-6	0-2	0-1	18.5	- 5.71
M. J. Ryan	10-100	1-19	1-5	0-9	0-4	0-11	8-48	0-4	0-0	10.0	**+ 17.83**
H. Candy	8-57	1-17	1-7	1-5	0-0	1-7	4-20	0-1	0-0	14.0	**+ 43.88**
P. J. Makin	8-43	1-11	2-6	0-3	0-0	1-8	4-15	0-0	0-0	18.6	**+ 14.50**
B. Hanbury	8-36	1-8	2-7	3-11	1-1	0-2	0-5	1-2	0-0	22.2	- 1.75

LEADING FLAT TRAINERS AT LINGFIELD- Turf (SINCE 1994)

	Total W-R	2yo Stks	3yo Stks	Other Stks	2yo H'caps	3yo H'caps	Other H'caps	App'ce	Amateurs	Per cent	£1 Level stake
R. Hannon	24-226	14-92	1-16	3-39	1-14	3-29	2-35	0-1	0-0	10.6	- 95.05
Sir Michael Stoute	15-67	6-22	3-11	5-23	0-0	1-5	0-6	0-0	0-0	22.4	**+ 16.91**
B. J. Meehan	14-92	9-41	1-6	0-4	1-4	2-18	1-17	0-0	0-2	15.2	- 10.79
J. L. Dunlop	13-99	5-52	3-7	2-11	0-4	2-13	1-11	0-0	0-1	13.1	- 70.08
J. Berry	13-61	11-32	0-1	2-8	0-0	0-7	0-13	0-0	0-0	21.3	**+ 8.83**
H. R. A. Cecil	12-40	4-9	3-10	5-19	0-0	0-2	0-0	0-0	0-0	30.0	- 13.32
G. L. Moore	11-148	4-31	1-11	0-19	0-1	3-16	2-57	1-11	0-2	7.4	- 67.68
J. H. M. Gosden	10-60	3-19	0-4	5-25	1-1	0-4	1-7	0-0	0-0	16.7	- 25.78
C. F. Wall	10-36	1-4	1-2	0-3	0-2	1-7	4-13	2-4	1-1	27.8	**+ 8.83**
L. M. Cumani	9-37	1-9	3-7	2-12	0-1	2-4	0-2	1-2	0-0	24.3	- 2.96
B. Hanbury	9-38	2-9	1-3	1-11	0-1	1-4	4-10	0-0	0-0	23.7	**+ 12.75**
P. T. Walwyn	9-51	0-15	2-5	2-7	0-5	2-7	2-10	0-0	1-2	17.7	**+ 8.58**
B. W. Hills	9-46	3-18	1-7	3-7	0-2	1-6	1-4	0-1	0-1	19.6	**+ 3.84**
M. Bell	9-74	3-26	0-2	1-10	0-6	2-15	2-10	1-5	0-0	12.2	- 40.37
M. R. Channon	9-93	3-36	1-3	2-11	0-7	1-13	2-23	0-0	0-0	9.7	- 3.50
Sir Mark Prescott	8-45	2-21	1-4	0-1	1-3	2-7	2-9	0-0	0-0	17.8	- 15.86

LEADING FLAT TRAINERS AT LINGFIELD- All Weather (SINCE 1994)

	Total W-R	2yo Stks	3yo Stks	Other Stks	2yo H'caps	3yo H'caps	Other H'caps	App'ce	Amateurs	Per cent	£1 Level stake
G. L. Moore	85-607	4-21	5-40	21-141	3-17	10-45	34-284	3-31	5-28	14.0	- 76.35
M. Johnston	50-265	2-15	11-32	8-42	4-15	10-55	13-100	2-6	0-0	18.9	- 14.14
Lord Huntingdon	41-196	1-9	10-33	12-51	1-2	2-10	12-79	3-12	0-0	20.9	- 25.71
R. J. O'Sullivan	37-272	0-1	0-5	13-61	0-0	0-4	22-181	0-12	2-8	13.6	- 65.63
S. Dow	35-341	0-11	3-23	4-53	0-7	7-31	17-176	0-20	4-20	10.3	- 81.50
Miss Gay Kelleway	34-212	1-6	2-8	11-65	0-4	1-7	16-104	2-12	1-6	16.0	- 85.24
A. Moore	34-373	0-10	1-16	10-112	1-4	0-2	19-195	2-11	1-23	9.1	- 55.75
C. A. Cyzer	31-214	0-3	1-11	9-58	0-2	3-9	16-117	2-8	0-6	14.5	- 24.12
T. J. Naughton	30-242	2-19	7-34	10-49	1-8	3-22	6-94	0-10	1-6	12.4	- 81.71
R. Hannon	29-180	6-30	4-24	4-36	4-20	7-27	2-34	2-6	0-3	16.1	- 33.73
R. Ingram	27-205	0-6	2-13	11-60	0-3	0-10	13-102	0-7	1-4	13.2	- 7.22
W. R. Muir	25-222	1-15	2-32	7-60	0-8	6-17	8-75	1-10	0-5	11.3	- 73.50
C. E. Brittain	24-145	1-9	3-16	6-27	0-1	4-18	10-71	0-1	0-2	16.6	- 10.84
J. Berry	23-114	10-22	3-14	3-30	2-6	1-10	3-29	1-2	0-1	20.2	- 7.17
J. J. Bridger	23-322	1-18	1-27	5-103	1-8	1-13	12-128	1-9	1-16	7.1	- 48.25
P. C. Haslam	21-112	1-1	7-18	0-14	0-1	8-32	5-41	0-4	0-1	18.8	- 11.89

LEADING FLAT TRAINERS AT MUSSELBURGH (SINCE 1994)

	Total W-R	2yo Stks	3yo Stks	Other Stks	2yo H'caps	3yo H'caps	Other H'caps	App'ce	Amateurs	Per cent	£1 Level stake
J. Berry	43-207	22-77	0-6	6-26	1-20	1-14	13-55	0-6	0-3	20.8	**+ 58.28**
Mrs M. Reveley	18-108	0-9	2-7	8-18	0-2	0-1	8-67	0-4	0-0	16.7	- 28.64
M. Johnston	17-120	6-30	1-4	2-11	2-4	2-13	4-56	0-2	0-0	14.2	- 62.46
J. S. Goldie	11-105	0-3	0-1	1-4	1-3	1-5	7-78	1-9	0-2	10.5	- 18.75
M. R. Channon	11-44	3-14	0-2	2-9	2-3	0-4	4-12	0-0	0-0	25.0	**+ 6.79**
T. D. Barron	10-49	2-9	1-1	2-7	1-4	2-5	2-21	0-1	0-1	20.4	**+ 26.16**
J. L. Eyre	10-110	0-10	0-5	2-7	0-3	0-5	8-74	0-4	0-2	9.1	- 9.00
P. D. Evans	9-74	5-24	0-0	0-5	1-8	0-6	2-28	1-2	0-1	12.2	- 39.28
N. Tinkler	9-46	2-10	0-2	3-5	0-1	0-4	4-24	0-0	0-0	19.6	- 7.49
Denys Smith	9-79	1-13	0-1	0-5	1-2	0-12	7-42	0-4	0-0	11.4	- 10.38
D. W. Chapman	9-67	0-1	0-0	1-5	0-0	0-1	5-50	1-5	2-5	13.4	- 13.00
M. W. Easterby	8-41	3-12	0-0	0-2	0-5	1-2	4-18	0-2	0-0	19.5	**+ 17.75**
M. H. Tompkins	8-26	3-6	0-3	3-6	0-1	0-2	2-8	0-0	0-0	30.8	**+ 10.03**
S. C. Williams	8-41	0-2	2-7	1-5	0-2	0-8	5-16	0-1	0-0	19.5	- 8.38
D. Nicholls	8-65	0-6	0-1	1-8	0-3	3-8	3-37	1-1	0-1	12.3	- 24.50
M. Bell	7-17	0-2	2-3	0-1	0-0	1-2	4-9	0-0	0-0	41.2	**+ 25.70**

LEADING FLAT TRAINERS AT NEWBURY (SINCE 1994)

	Total W-R	2yo Stks	3yo Stks	Other Stks	2yo H'caps	3yo H'caps	Other H'caps	App'ce	Amateurs	Per cent	£1 Level stake
J. H. M. Gosden	35-140	10-33	9-46	11-30	0-1	3-9	2-21	0-0	0-0	25.0	**+ 73.95**
P. W. Chapple-Hyam	34-168	24-70	6-40	2-18	0-4	1-12	1-20	0-4	0-0	20.2	- 8.93
R. Hannon	25-443	7-161	7-69	3-40	1-27	2-26	5-107	0-13	0-0	5.6	- 235.95
P. F. I. Cole	24-212	5-61	5-34	6-34	2-10	4-26	2-43	0-4	0-0	11.3	**+ 15.05**
H. R. A. Cecil	20-106	3-15	7-43	6-28	0-0	1-6	3-14	0-0	0-0	18.9	**+ 7.26**
J. L. Dunlop	19-193	2-71	6-32	4-24	0-12	4-20	3-34	0-0	0-0	9.8	- 98.50
I. A. Balding	18-218	8-64	2-42	4-19	0-2	1-20	3-67	0-4	0-0	8.3	- 101.74
B. W. Hills	15-211	9-92	1-37	2-23	0-5	0-14	3-39	0-1	0-0	7.1	- 103.63
L. M. Cumani	14-58	2-7	5-21	1-11	1-1	0-6	4-11	1-1	0-0	24.1	- 4.43
R. Charlton	14-120	3-29	5-42	2-14	0-2	1-8	3-21	0-4	0-0	11.7	- 43.04
Lord Huntingdon	13-138	1-23	1-24	3-16	0-2	0-4	8-62	0-7	0-0	9.4	- 21.50
B. J. Meehan	12-174	3-70	4-26	1-10	2-24	1-8	1-32	0-4	0-0	6.9	- 27.00
M. R. Channon	12-177	4-60	1-27	0-4	3-20	0-6	4-53	0-7	0-0	6.8	- 75.40
Sir Michael Stoute	11-102	2-20	2-23	5-31	0-2	1-11	1-14	0-1	0-0	10.8	- 19.17
Lady Herries	10-81	0-1	4-15	1-18	0-0	0-1	5-44	0-2	0-0	12.4	- 3.47
G. Lewis	9-65	1-23	0-10	1-2	1-5	2-6	3-17	1-2	0-0	13.9	**+ 44.50**

LEADING FLAT TRAINERS AT NEWCASTLE (SINCE 1994)

	Total W-R	2yo Stks	3yo Stks	Other Stks	2yo H'caps	3yo H'caps	Other H'caps	App'ce	Amateurs	Per cent	£1 Level stake
M. Johnston	29-184	9-64	0-4	5-20	1-10	2-20	12-64	0-2	0-0	15.8	- 20.43
J. Berry	25-175	12-60	1-7	6-27	2-7	0-12	4-55	0-6	0-1	14.3	- 44.04
Mrs J. R. Ramsden	18-160	1-21	3-7	0-4	0-10	3-20	10-92	1-3	0-3	11.3	- 55.90
Sir Michael Stoute	15-62	7-17	2-6	2-10	0-0	1-7	3-22	0-0	0-0	24.2	- 18.38
J. L. Dunlop	14-58	4-13	2-7	3-8	0-4	2-7	3-19	0-0	0-0	24.1	- 15.91
H. R. A. Cecil	14-35	2-5	2-5	8-13	0-0	0-1	2-11	0-0	0-0	40.0	**+ 12.38**
M. Bell	13-50	2-11	3-6	1-9	2-3	3-8	1-12	1-1	0-0	26.0	**+ 8.81**
Mrs M. Reveley	12-171	0-19	0-4	3-27	0-7	2-14	5-89	2-9	0-2	7.0	- 92.00
Sir Mark Prescott	11-41	4-14	0-3	3-9	0-3	2-4	1-6	0-1	1-1	26.8	**+ 10.00**
T. D. Easterby	9-96	2-24	0-2	0-3	1-9	1-17	5-41	0-0	0-0	9.4	- 37.67
M. W. Easterby	9-137	3-36	0-2	0-5	0-10	2-22	4-60	0-1	0-1	6.6	- 65.90
D. R. Loder	7-22	4-10	1-2	1-5	0-0	0-0	1-5	0-0	0-0	31.8	- 2.88
J. L. Eyre	7-97	0-17	0-2	2-9	0-3	0-8	5-53	0-3	0-2	7.2	- 16.00
T. D. Barron	7-57	1-9	0-0	0-3	0-2	0-8	6-34	0-1	0-0	12.3	**+ 3.00**
Martyn Wane	6-37	0-1	0-0	2-10	0-0	1-3	2-20	1-3	0-0	16.2	**+ 10.50**
J. H. M. Gosden	6-32	1-9	2-6	3-10	0-0	0-3	0-4	0-0	0-0	18.8	- 6.50

LEADING FLAT TRAINERS AT NEWMARKET- Rowley (SINCE 1994)

	Total W-R	2yo Stks	3yo Stks	Other Stks	2yo H'caps	3yo H'caps	Other H'caps	App'ce	Amateurs	Per cent	£1 Level stake
H. R. A. Cecil	45-200	10-36	27-102	6-35	0-0	0-4	2-23	0-0	0-0	22.5	**+ 17.12**
B. W. Hills	28-287	10-89	4-69	4-32	2-16	2-24	6-57	0-0	0-0	9.8	- 82.53
J. H. M. Gosden	24-200	6-56	9-71	5-28	0-3	0-9	4-31	0-2	0-0	12.0	- 71.84
D. R. Loder	23-104	14-48	3-16	4-22	1-4	1-4	0-10	0-0	0-0	22.1	**+ 7.75**
L. M. Cumani	22-168	4-45	3-54	7-21	0-3	4-18	4-26	0-1	0-0	13.1	- 59.36
J. L. Dunlop	22-230	7-59	5-51	5-38	0-9	0-19	5-54	0-0	0-0	9.6	- 57.79
S bin Suroor	20-77	8-22	8-26	4-25	0-1	0-0	0-3	0-0	0-0	26.0	**+ 29.40**
Sir Michael Stoute	20-228	5-62	7-71	6-48	0-4	1-16	1-27	0-0	0-0	8.8	- 112.04
R. Hannon	19-319	6-87	3-42	2-41	1-34	4-44	3-68	0-3	0-0	6.0	- 149.95
P. F. I. Cole	15-144	9-51	0-24	5-20	1-9	0-16	0-24	0-0	0-0	10.4	- 70.89
C. E. Brittain	14-194	1-39	7-54	4-34	0-8	0-14	2-44	0-1	0-0	7.2	- 43.29
P. W. Chapple-Hyam	13-104	5-35	5-36	3-15	0-4	0-11	0-1	0-2	0-0	12.5	- 23.11
M. Johnston	11-116	2-18	1-10	2-20	3-14	0-16	3-36	0-2	0-0	9.5	**+ 3.75**
M. Bell	11-140	4-45	1-22	1-15	1-9	3-25	1-21	0-3	0-0	7.9	- 50.52
I. A. Balding	10-103	3-20	1-15	4-13	0-3	1-12	1-38	0-2	0-0	9.7	**+ 9.25**
J. R. Fanshawe	10-114	0-21	0-16	3-23	2-6	0-6	5-40	0-2	0-0	8.8	- 41.88

LEADING FLAT TRAINERS AT NEWMARKET- July (SINCE 1994)

	Total W-R	2yo Stks	3yo Stks	Other Stks	2yo H'caps	3yo H'caps	Other H'caps	App'ce	Amateurs	Per cent	£1 Level stake
H. R. A. Cecil	28-110	11-26	7-30	4-32	0-0	3-11	3-11	0-0	0-0	25.5	- 25.28
J. H. M. Gosden	25-151	5-55	7-26	10-37	0-0	1-20	2-13	0-0	0-0	16.6	- 38.13
J. L. Dunlop	23-144	9-70	2-11	4-20	1-5	3-14	4-24	0-0	0-0	16.0	- 30.17
R. Hannon	20-218	4-66	2-21	8-30	2-23	4-42	0-31	0-4	0-1	9.2	- 112.97
L. M. Cumani	19-134	6-43	3-28	3-22	0-0	3-15	4-25	0-1	0-0	14.2	- 40.02
D. R. Loder	14-78	12-42	0-2	0-13	0-3	0-11	2-7	0-0	0-0	18.0	- 34.10
B. Hanbury	13-89	5-25	1-10	4-12	0-2	1-9	2-29	0-0	0-2	14.6	**+ 8.66**
Sir Michael Stoute	12-108	5-41	1-15	3-23	0-0	1-13	2-16	0-0	0-0	11.1	- 51.79
B. W. Hills	10-101	4-51	1-11	1-9	0-3	1-10	2-16	1-1	0-0	9.9	- 22.75
P. F. I. Cole	9-85	6-30	0-12	1-11	1-9	1-15	0-8	0-0	0-0	10.6	- 20.42
G. Wragg	9-64	5-24	1-8	1-14	0-0	1-7	1-10	0-1	0-0	14.1	**+ 6.96**
R. W. Armstrong	9-73	4-30	0-3	2-9	0-1	1-12	2-17	0-1	0-0	12.3	- 8.65
B. J. Meehan	9-82	1-22	1-10	0-9	1-8	2-15	4-16	0-1	0-1	11.0	- 5.90
Mrs J. R. Ramsden	8-40	0-3	1-2	1-1	1-11	0-2	5-20	0-1	0-0	20.0	**+ 10.00**
R. Charlton	8-57	1-16	3-11	3-13	0-1	1-8	0-8	0-0	0-0	14.0	- 19.50
E. A. L. Dunlop	7-59	1-20	1-6	1-9	0-0	0-4	4-20	0-0	0-0	11.9	- 1.50

LEADING FLAT TRAINERS AT NOTTINGHAM (SINCE 1994)

	Total W-R	2yo Stks	3yo Stks	Other Stks	2yo H'caps	3yo H'caps	Other H'caps	App'ce	Amateurs	Per cent	£1 Level stake
J. L. Dunlop	23-149	7-53	3-20	3-19	0-4	6-27	4-26	0-0	0-0	15.4	- 48.49
H. R. A. Cecil	18-70	10-31	4-16	4-19	0-0	0-3	0-1	0-0	0-0	25.7	- 18.88
Mrs J. R. Ramsden	14-99	1-20	2-5	0-5	0-3	2-23	9-39	0-3	0-1	14.1	- 1.25
M. Bell	13-89	8-29	0-10	2-8	0-4	2-15	0-20	1-3	0-0	14.6	- 14.89
J. R. Fanshawe	11-58	1-9	3-14	2-11	1-1	2-5	2-18	0-0	0-0	19.0	**+ 39.83**
B. A. McMahon	11-161	1-35	2-15	4-32	0-2	1-13	3-58	0-6	0-0	6.8	- 53.50
Sir Mark Prescott	11-49	3-17	3-8	2-6	1-1	2-5	0-10	0-2	0-0	22.5	**+ 19.28**
B. J. Meehan	10-80	4-27	2-12	2-6	0-5	2-18	0-11	0-1	0-0	12.5	**+ 15.36**
R. Hollinshead	10-144	1-25	0-18	0-15	0-5	2-27	6-48	1-6	0-0	6.9	- 72.00
Mrs M. Reveley	9-88	0-3	0-2	4-17	0-2	0-9	5-48	0-5	0-2	10.2	- 51.47
J. H. M. Gosden	9-56	5-24	2-10	1-11	0-1	1-4	0-6	0-0	0-0	16.1	- 17.05
P. F. I. Cole	9-68	3-29	3-10	1-5	0-4	2-12	0-7	0-1	0-0	13.2	- 6.65
M. Johnston	9-86	4-28	0-4	3-11	0-7	1-18	1-16	0-2	0-0	10.5	- 50.09
M. R. Channon	9-89	5-28	2-8	1-11	0-8	1-14	0-17	0-3	0-0	10.1	- 24.13
M. A. Jarvis	8-43	5-17	1-7	1-4	1-1	0-6	0-7	0-1	0-0	18.6	**+ 38.88**
P. J. Makin	8-61	0-8	1-4	2-15	0-1	2-14	2-14	1-4	0-1	13.1	**+ 3.50**

LEADING FLAT TRAINERS AT PONTEFRACT (SINCE 1994)

	Total W-R	2yo Stks	3yo Stks	Other Stks	2yo H'caps	3yo H'caps	Other H'caps	App'ce	Amateurs	Per cent	£1 Level stake
Mrs J. R. Ramsden	42-229	5-36	0-6	4-14	6-19	6-28	19-116	1-7	1-3	18.3	**+ 23.90**
J. L. Eyre	17-174	1-17	1-6	0-14	0-9	2-17	12-97	1-13	0-1	9.8	- 12.75
H. R. A. Cecil	14-37	3-4	1-7	10-20	0-0	0-2	0-4	0-0	0-0	37.8	**+ 15.90**
J. L. Dunlop	14-55	3-9	1-5	7-17	0-6	1-7	2-9	0-2	0-0	25.5	**+ 1.71**
Mrs M. Reveley	14-136	0-6	1-10	5-30	0-8	1-5	6-71	0-5	1-1	10.3	- 60.48
I. A. Balding	13-63	3-10	4-16	0-6	0-2	2-6	3-19	1-3	0-1	20.6	**+ 12.65**
M. Johnston	12-119	5-37	0-6	2-11	3-16	1-17	1-31	0-1	0-0	10.1	- 42.77
J. Berry	11-127	1-52	3-15	2-16	0-6	2-4	2-30	1-4	0-0	8.7	- 60.50
J. H. M. Gosden	9-39	1-4	2-13	5-13	0-0	0-3	1-6	0-0	0-0	23.1	- 5.43
R. Hollinshead	9-161	2-31	3-28	1-22	0-12	0-13	3-49	0-6	0-0	5.6	- 73.00
B. W. Hills	8-41	2-6	1-8	2-10	0-4	1-3	2-10	0-0	0-0	19.5	**+ 11.50**
R. A. Fahey	8-47	4-14	2-5	0-5	2-6	0-4	0-12	0-1	0-0	17.0	**+ 18.50**
A. C. Stewart	8-28	0-0	2-9	1-8	0-1	0-0	4-9	0-0	1-1	28.6	- 1.73
L. M. Cumani	8-41	1-4	1-10	5-18	0-0	0-1	1-5	0-3	0-0	19.5	- 10.03
R. Hannon	7-46	3-17	4-11	0-3	0-4	0-5	0-6	0-0	0-0	15.2	- 5.97
Sir Mark Prescott	7-25	1-8	2-3	0-6	0-0	0-1	2-5	2-2	0-0	28.0	**+ 5.69**

LEADING FLAT TRAINERS AT REDCAR (SINCE 1994)

	Total W-R	2yo Stks	3yo Stks	Other Stks	2yo H'caps	3yo H'caps	Other H'caps	App'ce	Amateurs	Per cent	£1 Level stake
Mrs M. Reveley	38-346	0-31	2-17	10-52	0-15	3-24	20-182	1-11	2-14	11.0	- 17.76
J. H. M. Gosden	23-66	4-17	1-7	8-17	0-0	6-11	4-13	0-1	0-0	34.9	**+ 36.75**
Mrs J. R. Ramsden	18-118	3-24	0-0	1-6	1-5	2-19	6-54	3-7	2-3	15.3	**+ 0.83**
M. Johnston	18-151	7-62	1-4	3-11	0-7	2-15	5-50	0-2	0-0	11.9	- 34.88
J. Berry	18-162	9-60	2-13	2-24	0-13	2-12	2-33	1-4	0-3	11.1	- 43.50
J. L. Eyre	16-136	2-16	0-3	1-16	1-6	0-11	10-71	0-7	2-6	11.8	- 29.06
J. L. Dunlop	16-62	6-19	0-2	3-5	2-5	0-9	5-22	0-0	0-0	25.8	**+ 5.68**
M. W. Easterby	14-160	3-47	0-0	0-4	3-30	1-22	6-45	1-5	0-7	8.8	- 58.00
Sir Mark Prescott	13-40	5-17	2-3	1-3	1-3	1-5	3-8	0-0	0-1	32.5	**+ 10.24**
T. D. Barron	11-100	4-23	0-1	0-5	0-6	4-11	2-44	1-5	0-5	11.0	- 14.13
D. R. Loder	10-29	7-20	1-2	2-3	0-0	0-1	0-3	0-0	0-0	34.5	**+ 7.31**
E. A. L. Dunlop	9-29	2-6	0-1	3-8	0-1	4-5	0-8	0-0	0-0	31.0	- 1.57
T. D. Easterby	8-103	4-34	0-4	0-3	0-6	1-16	3-32	0-3	0-5	7.8	- 16.00
C. A. Dwyer	7-26	0-5	0-1	1-2	0-2	2-7	3-7	1-1	0-1	26.9	**+ 10.25**
H. R. A. Cecil	7-37	3-13	1-8	1-3	0-0	0-4	2-9	0-0	0-0	18.9	- 15.20
M. Bell	7-51	2-14	0-2	3-9	0-2	2-15	0-7	0-1	0-1	13.7	- 15.69

LEADING FLAT TRAINERS AT RIPON (SINCE 1994)

	Total W-R	2yo Stks	3yo Stks	Other Stks	2yo H'caps	3yo H'caps	Other H'caps	App'ce	Amateurs	Per cent	£1 Level stake
M. Johnston	23-125	4-31	2-10	3-12	1-2	1-23	12-46	0-1	0-0	18.4	**+ 23.74**
T. D. Easterby	17-126	5-30	0-6	1-8	0-2	3-29	7-46	1-5	0-0	13.5	- 46.78
H. R. A. Cecil	16-38	0-0	4-9	10-18	0-0	0-4	2-7	0-0	0-0	42.1	**+ 0.18**
J. Berry	16-141	9-70	0-2	2-13	0-4	0-15	4-32	1-5	0-0	11.4	- 64.99
L. M. Cumani	12-47	3-5	3-11	3-14	0-0	0-6	3-11	0-0	0-0	25.5	- 11.15
J. L. Dunlop	11-46	5-6	1-8	0-2	0-0	3-16	2-14	0-0	0-0	23.9	**+ 8.10**
J. H. M. Gosden	11-57	0-2	3-17	6-31	0-0	1-4	1-3	0-0	0-0	19.3	- 25.17
M. W. Easterby	11-174	1-48	0-7	0-11	0-6	4-31	5-59	1-12	0-0	6.3	- 98.25
Sir Michael Stoute	9-42	0-2	4-14	1-10	0-0	2-6	2-10	0-0	0-0	21.4	- 3.16
Mrs M. Reveley	9-101	0-7	0-3	3-16	0-0	2-13	4-57	0-5	0-0	8.9	- 48.54
B. W. Hills	9-45	1-7	2-10	3-14	0-0	0-7	3-7	0-0	0-0	20.0	- 5.63
D. R. Loder	7-16	1-3	1-5	2-2	1-1	1-3	1-2	0-0	0-0	43.8	**+ 8.87**
J. Pearce	7-31	0-1	0-2	0-5	0-0	0-1	6-19	1-3	0-0	22.6	**+ 24.25**
M. R. Channon	7-46	2-19	1-2	0-0	0-0	3-12	1-11	0-2	0-0	15.2	- 4.75
Miss S. E. Hall	7-65	1-21	0-5	0-8	0-0	3-13	2-17	1-1	0-0	10.8	- 33.67
J. R. Fanshawe	7-23	2-4	1-5	2-5	0-0	0-2	2-7	0-0	0-0	30.4	**+ 9.33**

LEADING FLAT TRAINERS AT SALISBURY (SINCE 1994)

	Total W-R	2yo Stks	3yo Stks	Other Stks	2yo H'caps	3yo H'caps	Other H'caps	App'ce	Amateurs	Per cent	£1 Level stake
R. Hannon	40-369	16-152	11-42	4-39	0-0	3-37	5-86	1-9	0-4	10.8	- 133.03
J. L. Dunlop	25-131	10-60	2-16	4-19	0-0	4-16	5-20	0-0	0-0	19.1	- 32.40
P. F. I. Cole	15-100	7-38	3-20	2-9	0-0	0-13	3-17	0-3	0-0	15.0	- 32.78
Lord Huntingdon	15-72	3-13	0-12	1-8	0-0	2-8	7-24	1-4	1-3	20.8	**+ 34.42**
I. A. Balding	15-141	2-42	4-30	3-19	0-0	1-15	5-28	0-5	0-2	10.6	- 55.06
P. T. Walwyn	13-73	4-28	1-7	1-6	0-0	2-8	3-21	0-0	2-3	17.8	**+ 5.88**
R. Charlton	13-79	7-36	1-12	1-12	0-0	3-7	1-12	0-0	0-0	16.5	- 24.40
J. H. M. Gosden	13-58	4-18	3-17	3-8	0-0	0-2	3-11	0-2	0-0	22.4	**+ 9.17**
M. R. Channon	11-174	4-57	1-21	0-10	0-0	1-16	4-59	1-8	0-3	6.3	- 96.93
D. R. C. Elsworth	10-129	5-31	1-27	1-13	0-0	0-11	3-43	0-1	0-3	7.8	- 77.08
L. M. Cumani	9-34	0-5	5-10	2-10	0-0	0-3	2-6	0-0	0-0	26.5	- 10.59
P. W. Chapple-Hyam	9-43	4-18	3-11	2-8	0-0	0-4	0-2	0-0	0-0	20.9	- 6.35
B. J. Meehan	9-105	4-48	0-7	1-4	0-0	1-12	3-28	0-0	0-6	8.6	- 34.50
Miss Gay Kelleway	9-80	2-13	0-12	3-10	0-0	1-5	3-37	0-3	0-0	11.3	**+ 18.63**
S. Dow	9-90	2-14	0-10	1-4	0-0	2-11	1-41	1-3	2-7	10.0	- 4.75
H. R. A. Cecil	8-32	1-3	4-16	3-9	0-0	0-1	0-3	0-0	0-0	25.0	- 13.49

LEADING FLAT TRAINERS AT SANDOWN (SINCE 1994)

	Total W-R	2yo Stks	3yo Stks	Other Stks	2yo H'caps	3yo H'caps	Other H'caps	App'ce	Amateurs	Per cent	£1 Level stake
R. Hannon	32-332	14-102	3-23	4-42	2-12	4-69	5-72	0-10	0-2	9.6	- 100.02
Sir Michael Stoute	30-150	8-28	4-22	10-50	0-1	3-20	5-28	0-0	0-1	20.0	- 7.13
J. L. Dunlop	22-137	9-35	2-10	2-25	0-1	3-28	6-37	0-0	0-1	16.1	- 24.72
J. H. M. Gosden	20-125	3-21	6-28	5-46	0-1	4-19	2-10	0-0	0-0	16.0	- 36.16
H. R. A. Cecil	17-83	5-18	2-20	5-32	0-0	3-6	2-7	0-0	0-0	20.5	- 16.03
I. A. Balding	16-102	3-25	0-10	5-16	0-0	4-19	4-31	0-1	0-0	15.7	- 20.70
B. J. Meehan	15-136	7-49	1-10	2-14	1-12	1-21	3-29	0-0	0-1	11.0	**+ 1.76**
J. R. Fanshawe	13-68	1-7	4-11	4-13	0-0	1-12	3-25	0-0	0-0	19.1	**+ 51.95**
P. F. I. Cole	13-98	6-32	3-17	1-12	0-1	2-17	1-17	0-2	0-0	13.3	- 8.17
D. R. C. Elsworth	12-94	4-17	3-16	2-24	0-0	0-4	3-31	0-2	0-0	12.8	- 8.00
M. Johnston	11-61	1-11	0-0	3-15	0-4	4-12	3-18	0-0	0-1	18.0	**+ 47.58**
S bin Suroor	10-22	4-6	1-1	4-14	0-0	1-1	0-0	0-0	0-0	45.5	**+ 10.98**
J. Berry	9-41	1-12	0-0	8-20	0-5	0-1	0-3	0-0	0-0	22.0	**+ 8.78**
G. Wragg	9-39	0-0	1-11	5-22	0-0	0-3	1-1	1-1	1-1	23.1	**+ 49.33**
G. Lewis	9-86	4-37	0-4	1-6	0-7	1-15	3-16	0-1	0-0	10.5	**+ 30.38**
D. R. Loder	8-48	5-14	0-6	2-19	0-0	1-3	0-6	0-0	0-0	16.7	- 17.47

LEADING FLAT TRAINERS AT SOUTHWELL (SINCE 1994)

	Total W-R	2yo Stks	3yo Stks	Other Stks	2yo H'caps	3yo H'caps	Other H'caps	App'ce	Amateurs	Per cent	£1 Level stake
S. R. Bowring	48-412	1-12	0-27	4-59	1-4	8-33	29-238	4-29	1-10	11.7	- 89.20
J. L. Eyre	47-327	1-16	0-18	12-58	0-4	2-11	24-172	3-13	5-35	14.4	- 68.31
M. Johnston	47-239	5-37	8-28	6-34	2-13	10-47	14-70	2-6	0-4	19.7	**+ 36.78**
D. W. Chapman	45-495	0-9	0-7	14-104	0-5	0-12	23-292	2-30	6-36	9.1	- 109.45
R. Hollinshead	40-426	2-29	4-56	17-106	0-9	3-38	11-166	3-20	0-2	9.4	- 180.21
D. Nicholls	36-250	0-9	0-13	16-72	0-4	0-19	14-112	4-15	2-6	14.4	- 52.36
Mrs N. Macauley	33-338	0-20	6-31	11-92	0-2	3-18	13-158	0-12	0-5	9.8	- 34.92
J. Berry	29-244	14-70	2-25	8-61	0-13	2-21	2-45	1-8	0-1	11.9	- 109.39
Mrs M. Reveley	28-124	0-3	2-3	7-28	0-1	3-7	14-71	1-3	1-8	22.6	**+ 17.65**
Sir Mark Prescott	26-89	4-29	1-6	4-11	2-4	5-15	7-21	0-0	3-3	29.2	**+ 4.73**
M. J. Ryan	26-159	0-8	0-2	4-26	0-1	1-9	19-98	0-2	2-13	16.4	**+ 6.48**
T. D. Barron	25-159	1-11	5-12	3-30	1-3	2-20	12-76	1-5	0-2	15.7	- 6.29
P. C. Haslam	22-132	2-19	3-15	1-11	1-11	11-31	4-34	0-8	0-3	16.7	- 19.34
W. A. O'Gorman	19-80	3-15	2-10	8-18	0-4	1-4	5-29	0-0	0-0	23.8	**+ 17.24**
Lord Huntingdon	19-77	0-3	5-11	4-15	0-0	2-9	6-34	2-5	0-0	24.7	**+ 27.19**
J. A. Glover	17-112	1-2	2-7	3-22	0-1	1-10	9-66	1-4	0-0	15.2	**+ 4.80**

LEADING FLAT TRAINERS AT THIRSK (SINCE 1994)

	Total W-R	2yo Stks	3yo Stks	Other Stks	2yo H'caps	3yo H'caps	Other H'caps	App'ce	Amateurs	Per cent	£1 Level stake
M. Johnston	18-97	6-28	2-8	0-9	0-2	2-13	8-37	0-0	0-0	18.6	- 3.77
D. Nicholls	18-142	0-11	0-4	5-17	0-2	1-13	9-90	3-5	0-0	12.7	- 25.90
J. L. Eyre	16-154	1-20	1-5	2-27	0-3	1-10	10-84	1-5	0-0	10.4	- 28.25
J. Berry	16-144	10-62	1-9	2-15	0-6	1-16	2-34	0-2	0-0	11.1	- 45.40
Mrs J. R. Ramsden	15-110	2-23	0-3	2-7	1-4	1-14	9-57	0-2	0-0	13.6	- 23.03
Sir Michael Stoute	13-38	1-4	8-16	4-12	0-0	0-1	0-5	0-0	0-0	34.2	**+ 9.10**
T. D. Barron	12-109	1-14	0-5	0-8	1-5	3-9	7-66	0-2	0-0	11.0	- 18.75
J. L. Dunlop	11-32	1-8	5-10	2-5	0-0	1-2	2-7	0-0	0-0	34.4	**+ 1.49**
M. W. Easterby	10-195	3-88	0-4	0-10	1-6	1-14	5-69	0-4	0-0	5.1	- 127.40
T. D. Easterby	8-124	2-37	0-4	0-12	1-4	1-13	3-50	1-4	0-0	6.5	- 98.95
B. W. Hills	8-23	2-4	3-10	1-5	0-0	0-1	2-3	0-0	0-0	34.8	**+ 2.03**
H. R. A. Cecil	8-20	1-1	3-11	3-7	0-0	0-0	1-1	0-0	0-0	40.0	**+ 5.90**
Sir Mark Prescott	8-25	4-10	1-3	1-5	0-0	0-0	2-6	0-1	0-0	32.0	**+ 2.04**
J. M. Bradley	7-42	0-1	0-0	0-1	0-0	1-5	5-27	1-8	0-0	16.7	**+ 10.83**
J. R. Fanshawe	7-30	3-7	1-5	1-7	0-0	1-3	1-8	0-0	0-0	23.3	**+ 14.41**
P. D. Evans	7-56	3-16	0-0	0-3	2-4	0-4	2-25	0-4	0-0	12.5	- 14.50

LEADING FLAT TRAINERS AT WARWICK (SINCE 1994)

	Total W-R	2yo Stks	3yo Stks	Other Stks	2yo H'caps	3yo H'caps	Other H'caps	App'ce	Amateurs	Per cent	£1 Level stake
M. C. Pipe	14-48	2-6	0-1	2-7	0-0	0-3	9-28	1-2	0-1	29.2	**+ 11.24**
B. J. Meehan	12-87	3-33	3-6	1-10	1-5	2-19	1-11	1-1	0-2	13.8	**+ 16.42**
P. F. I. Cole	12-86	3-21	2-8	2-13	3-10	1-9	1-19	0-6	0-0	14.0	- 28.49
J. Berry	11-69	6-22	0-3	5-21	0-4	0-1	0-15	0-3	0-0	15.9	- 18.72
R. Hannon	10-94	7-40	1-7	1-12	1-7	0-10	0-15	0-3	0-0	10.6	- 50.32
B. A. McMahon	10-65	0-9	0-2	1-20	0-1	2-3	5-27	2-3	0-0	15.4	**+ 25.75**
B. W. Hills	9-54	2-12	1-3	4-16	0-5	1-4	0-12	1-2	0-0	16.7	- 7.70
J. L. Dunlop	9-46	1-11	0-0	2-6	1-4	1-12	4-12	0-1	0-0	19.6	**+ 4.97**
J. M. Bradley	8-109	0-5	0-1	1-22	0-1	0-2	5-59	1-15	1-4	7.3	- 30.75
Miss Gay Kelleway	7-30	0-5	1-1	2-8	0-0	1-5	3-10	0-1	0-0	23.3	**+ 11.75**
P. W. Chapple-Hyam	7-40	2-13	0-0	4-12	0-4	1-5	0-4	0-2	0-0	17.5	- 12.10
P. J. Makin	7-41	0-8	1-4	1-9	0-1	0-3	5-15	0-1	0-0	17.1	**+ 0.50**
R. Charlton	7-17	1-3	1-2	2-6	0-0	1-2	2-4	0-0	0-0	41.2	**+ 18.88**
J. Pearce	7-42	0-1	0-0	3-7	0-1	0-2	4-26	0-3	0-2	16.7	**+ 25.63**
M. Bell	7-57	2-12	1-5	4-16	0-1	0-13	0-10	0-0	0-0	12.3	- 28.97
J. W. Hills	6-36	3-13	1-2	2-9	0-0	0-5	0-5	0-2	0-0	16.7	- 10.80

LEADING FLAT TRAINERS AT WINDSOR (SINCE 1994)

	Total W-R	2yo Stks	3yo Stks	Other Stks	2yo H'caps	3yo H'caps	Other H'caps	App'ce	Amateurs	Per cent	£1 Level stake
R. Hannon	37-271	22-115	1-13	4-37	2-7	5-46	3-51	0-2	0-0	13.7	- 92.22
Sir Michael Stoute	14-58	0-8	5-17	5-22	0-0	1-3	3-8	0-0	0-0	24.1	**+ 2.80**
P. F. I. Cole	12-98	2-27	0-14	4-18	0-2	3-17	2-19	1-1	0-0	12.2	- 16.88
J. H. M. Gosden	11-69	1-6	2-24	5-25	0-0	2-8	1-6	0-0	0-0	15.9	- 24.66
C. F. Wall	10-69	2-11	0-6	0-7	0-0	4-24	4-21	0-0	0-0	14.5	- 3.50
I. A. Balding	10-74	0-15	1-14	2-16	0-0	3-8	4-17	0-2	0-2	13.5	- 18.72
W. R. Muir	10-99	1-26	0-8	5-18	0-2	1-14	3-30	0-1	0-0	10.1	- 21.86
H. R. A. Cecil	10-34	0-1	6-11	4-20	0-0	0-0	0-2	0-0	0-0	29.4	**+ 9.72**
B. J. Meehan	10-126	6-57	0-8	4-9	0-8	0-29	0-14	0-1	0-0	7.9	- 79.76
H. Candy	8-46	1-9	1-10	1-5	1-1	1-4	2-16	1-1	0-0	17.4	**+ 21.50**
Lord Huntingdon	8-56	2-13	2-13	1-13	0-0	1-5	2-11	0-1	0-0	14.3	**+ 0.13**
K. T. Ivory	8-85	2-19	0-1	1-8	0-4	3-16	2-35	0-2	0-0	9.4	- 15.50
M. J. Ryan	7-56	1-7	0-1	2-10	0-2	1-8	3-27	0-1	0-0	12.5	- 18.40
P. J. Makin	7-59	2-15	0-7	2-11	0-0	0-10	3-15	0-1	0-0	11.9	- 3.25
G. Lewis	7-69	2-29	1-5	0-4	0-1	2-12	2-17	0-1	0-0	10.1	- 28.40
S bin Suroor	6-8	0-0	2-2	4-6	0-0	0-0	0-0	0-0	0-0	75.0	**+ 6.50**

LEADING FLAT TRAINERS AT WOLVERHAMPTON (SINCE 1994)

	Total W-R	2yo Stks	3yo Stks	Other Stks	2yo H'caps	3yo H'caps	Other H'caps	App'ce	Amateurs	Per cent	£1 Level stake
R. Hollinshead	69-679	3-73	9-87	12-141	0-11	9-56	36-291	0-15	0-5	10.2	- 246.66
M. Johnston	59-271	13-42	7-21	7-34	1-12	7-47	24-112	0-3	0-0	21.8	**+ 26.46**
J. Berry	53-357	23-109	6-35	10-73	3-12	7-37	2-80	1-6	1-5	14.9	- 123.65
P. C. Haslam	45-245	6-57	9-22	8-24	1-11	7-39	9-77	3-11	2-4	18.4	**+ 4.79**
P. D. Evans	39-423	6-69	0-26	15-99	0-11	0-27	16-166	0-7	2-18	9.2	- 91.30
A. Bailey	34-311	4-23	1-27	13-63	0-4	7-28	9-155	0-3	0-8	10.9	- 90.90
Sir Mark Prescott	33-134	12-45	3-18	8-20	0-4	3-15	7-32	0-0	0-0	24.6	- 12.49
N. P. Littmoden	30-302	10-60	1-31	8-64	0-6	1-20	8-103	2-10	0-8	9.9	- 84.84
B. A. McMahon	29-270	4-46	6-16	3-58	0-2	1-21	15-122	0-4	0-1	10.7	- 25.22
J. L. Eyre	28-182	0-10	3-9	2-32	2-2	3-14	15-99	1-4	2-12	15.4	**+ 2.82**
Lord Huntingdon	24-101	5-9	6-26	5-22	0-1	4-9	4-32	0-2	0-0	23.8	**+ 0.57**
D. HaydnJones	21-220	1-14	0-7	2-31	0-0	0-2	17-161	1-5	0-0	9.6	- 29.50
J. Pearce	20-98	0-0	0-1	5-25	0-0	0-4	11-52	2-3	2-13	20.4	**+ 74.62**
D. W. Chapman	20-224	0-2	0-7	5-45	0-0	0-2	13-139	0-6	2-23	8.9	- 62.09
Mrs N. Macauley	18-205	1-11	0-15	5-44	0-1	1-17	11-110	0-4	0-3	8.8	- 46.50
M. Bell	17-80	3-11	1-11	5-14	0-1	5-18	3-23	0-2	0-0	21.3	**+ 4.53**

LEADING FLAT TRAINERS AT YARMOUTH (SINCE 1994)

	Total W-R	2yo Stks	3yo Stks	Other Stks	2yo H'caps	3yo H'caps	Other H'caps	App'ce	Amateurs	Per cent	£1 Level stake
H. R. A. Cecil	27-107	9-35	6-22	8-39	0-0	1-4	3-7	0-0	0-0	25.2	- 38.89
C. E. Brittain	23-173	2-30	4-22	5-30	2-8	4-16	6-63	0-4	0-0	13.3	**+ 5.78**
M. Bell	18-105	6-23	1-3	2-9	1-7	2-16	4-39	2-8	0-0	17.1	**+ 9.16**
D. R. Loder	16-56	11-33	2-7	2-8	0-2	0-3	1-3	0-0	0-0	28.6	- 3.14
J. H. M. Gosden	16-110	4-25	5-29	4-29	1-4	0-5	2-17	0-1	0-0	14.6	- 38.40
L. M. Cumani	15-71	2-17	4-15	4-16	2-4	0-1	3-18	0-0	0-0	21.1	- 9.45
J. R. Fanshawe	13-89	2-26	4-13	3-17	0-0	1-5	3-28	0-0	0-0	14.6	- 22.00
C. A. Dwyer	12-96	5-27	0-6	1-8	2-7	0-10	4-37	0-1	0-0	12.5	- 45.33
Sir Michael Stoute	12-96	3-43	2-12	3-13	1-5	0-7	3-16	0-0	0-0	12.5	- 49.61
M. R. Channon	11-59	4-17	0-3	1-5	0-7	2-6	4-20	0-1	0-0	18.6	**+ 7.75**
E. A. L. Dunlop	10-50	4-22	0-7	3-9	1-2	1-2	1-7	0-1	0-0	20.0	- 10.47
B. Hanbury	10-68	3-9	1-13	2-12	0-2	0-5	4-27	0-0	0-0	14.7	- 10.50
N. A. Callaghan	10-59	1-10	0-7	1-4	1-7	1-4	6-25	0-2	0-0	17.0	- 8.20
J. Pearce	10-92	0-1	1-7	2-16	1-4	0-3	6-54	0-7	0-0	10.9	**+ 8.00**
M. J. Ryan	10-96	0-17	0-7	2-6	0-5	4-9	3-47	1-5	0-0	10.4	- 27.00
S bin Suroor	9-20	3-10	2-2	3-7	0-0	1-1	0-0	0-0	0-0	45.0	**+ 12.21**

LEADING FLAT TRAINERS AT YORK (SINCE 1994)

	Total W-R	2yo Stks	3yo Stks	Other Stks	2yo H'caps	3yo H'caps	Other H'caps	App'ce	Amateurs	Per cent	£1 Level stake
Sir Michael Stoute	28-144	2-20	12-27	6-36	1-4	4-19	3-38	0-0	0-0	19.4	**+ 0.14**
H. R. A. Cecil	25-103	7-17	7-26	6-32	0-0	1-7	4-21	0-0	0-0	24.3	- 6.40
M. Johnston	18-163	6-36	1-6	3-22	3-11	1-16	4-71	0-1	0-0	11.0	- 30.01
P. F. I. Cole	17-131	12-45	3-18	1-11	0-4	1-16	0-34	0-3	0-0	13.0	- 54.15
L. M. Cumani	16-93	4-11	1-12	9-24	0-2	1-18	1-25	0-1	0-0	17.2	- 19.50
B. W. Hills	16-152	8-45	0-22	3-19	1-6	2-23	2-37	0-0	0-0	10.5	- 47.23
D. R. Loder	15-55	6-17	0-9	3-9	1-2	2-3	3-15	0-0	0-0	27.3	**+ 5.65**
J. L. Dunlop	14-106	9-23	1-14	1-17	0-4	0-11	3-37	0-0	0-0	13.2	- 59.74
J. H. M. Gosden	13-92	2-17	7-25	3-14	0-2	0-6	1-28	0-0	0-0	14.1	- 39.80
R. Hannon	12-131	6-46	1-5	1-13	1-12	1-21	2-34	0-0	0-0	9.2	- 46.25
I. A. Balding	11-95	3-11	0-6	2-11	1-1	2-23	3-43	0-0	0-0	11.6	- 27.30
S bin Suroor	10-36	0-6	4-9	6-18	0-0	0-0	0-3	0-0	0-0	27.8	**+ 3.03**
T. D. Barron	10-65	0-1	0-0	2-2	0-6	1-7	6-43	1-6	0-0	15.4	**+ 40.00**
J. L. Eyre	9-94	0-6	0-0	1-6	1-6	1-5	5-64	1-7	0-0	9.6	**+ 6.50**
Mrs J. R. Ramsden	9-130	2-17	0-0	1-5	2-17	0-9	4-78	0-4	0-0	6.9	- 48.00
P. W. Harris	8-72	0-6	0-5	1-5	0-1	1-6	6-48	0-1	0-0	11.1	- 9.92

FOUR-SEASON DRAW ANALYSIS FOR BRITISH FLAT TRACKS

The following table shows the record of draw position categories over various distances on each track from January 1st 1995 to November 7th 1998. For example, a winner would be added to the 'Low' category if it was drawn in the lowest third of the field, irrespective of the number of runners, i.e. drawn between 1 and 6 in an 18-runner field. Distances which have not had at least ten races run over them during the period are not shown.

ASCOT

Distance : *Flat 5f*

Draw Category	Winners	% Winners/Races
Low	16	37
Middle	12	28
High	15	35

Distance : *Flat 6f*

Draw Category	Winners	% Winners/Races
Low	14	32
Middle	15	34
High	15	34

Distance : *Flat 7f*

Draw Category	Winners	% Winners/Races
Low	14	33
Middle	17	40
High	11	26

Distance : *Str 1m*

Draw Category	Winners	% Winners/Races
Low	15	38
Middle	13	33
High	11	28

Distance : *Rnd 1m*

Draw Category	Winners	% Winners/Races
Low	12	26
Middle	21	46
High	13	28

Distance : *Flat 1m 2f*

Draw Category	Winners	% Winners/Races
Low	9	32
Middle	10	36
High	9	32

Distance : *Flat 1m 4f*

Draw Category	Winners	% Winners/Races
Low	20	31
Middle	27	42
High	17	27

Distance : *Flat 2m 45y*

Draw Category	Winners	% Winners/Races
Low	8	32
Middle	10	40
High	7	28

AYR

Distance : *Flat 5f*

Draw Category	Winners	% Winners/Races
Low	15	29
Middle	22	43
High	14	27

Distance : *Flat 6f*

Draw Category	Winners	% Winners/Races
Low	17	29
Middle	25	42
High	17	29

Distance : *Flat 7f*

Draw Category	Winners	% Winners/Races
Low	14	23
Middle	31	51
High	16	26

Distance : *Flat 1m*

Draw Category	Winners	% Winners/Races
Low	17	35
Middle	24	49
High	8	16

Distance : *Flat 1m 2f*

Draw Category	Winners	% Winners/Races
Low	8	19
Middle	19	45
High	15	36

Distance : *Flat 1m 2f 192y*

Draw Category	Winners	% Winners/Races
Low	5	24
Middle	12	57
High	4	19

Distance : *Flat 1m 5f 13y*

Draw Category	Winners	% Winners/Races
Low	7	29
Middle	11	46
High	6	25

Distance : *Flat 1m 7f*

Draw Category	Winners	% Winners/Races
Low	3	23
Middle	6	46
High	4	31

BATH

Distance : *Flat 5f 11y*

Draw Category	Winners	% Winners/Races
Low	26	32
Middle	27	33
High	29	35

Distance : *Flat 5f 161y*

Draw Category	Winners	% Winners/Races
Low	19	35
Middle	19	35
High	16	30

Distance : *Flat 1m 5y*

Draw Category	Winners	% Winners/Races
Low	27	36
Middle	28	37
High	21	28

Distance : *Flat 1m 2f 46y*

Draw Category	Winners	% Winners/Races
Low	14	26
Middle	25	47
High	14	26

Distance : *Flat 1m 3f 144y*

Draw Category	Winners	% Winners/Races
Low	7	22
Middle	17	53
High	8	25

Distance : *Flat 1m 5f 22y*

Draw Category	Winners	% Winners/Races
Low	4	36
Middle	3	27
High	4	36

Distance : *Flat 2m 1f 34y*

Draw Category	Winners	% Winners/Races
Low	14	39
Middle	14	39
High	8	22

BEVERLEY

Distance : *Flat 5f*

Draw Category	Winners	% Winners/Races
Low	24	20
Middle	39	32
High	58	48

Distance : *Flat 7f 100y*

Draw Category	Winners	% Winners/Races
Low	27	25
Middle	49	45
High	33	30

Distance : *Flat 1m 100y*

Draw Category	Winners	% Winners/Races
Low	10	16
Middle	26	43
High	25	41

Distance : *Flat 1m 1f 207y*

Draw Category	Winners	% Winners/Races
Low	22	29
Middle	23	30
High	32	42

Distance : *Flat 1m 3f 216y*

Draw Category	Winners	% Winners/Races
Low	19	33
Middle	25	44
High	13	23

Distance : *Flat 2m 35y*

Draw Category	Winners	% Winners/Races
Low	5	16
Middle	10	31
High	17	53

BRIGHTON

Distance : *Flat 5f 59y*

Draw Category	Winners	% Winners/Races
Low	21	36
Middle	18	31
High	20	34

Distance : *Flat 5f 213y*

Draw Category	Winners	% Winners/Races
Low	32	37
Middle	32	37
High	23	26

Distance : *Flat 6f 209y*

Draw Category	Winners	% Winners/Races
Low	35	33
Middle	43	40
High	29	27

Distance : *Flat 7f 214y*

Draw Category	Winners	% Winners/Races
Low	20	22
Middle	36	40
High	35	38

Distance : *Flat 1m 1f 209y*

Draw Category	Winners	% Winners/Races
Low	17	28
Middle	28	47
High	15	25

Distance : *Flat 1m 3f 196y*

Draw Category	Winners	% Winners/Races
Low	20	26
Middle	38	49
High	20	26

CARLISLE

Distance : *Flat 5f*

Draw Category	Winners	% Winners/Races
Low	8	16
Middle	26	53
High	15	31

Distance : *Flat 5f 207y*

Draw Category	Winners	% Winners/Races
Low	8	17
Middle	25	54
High	13	28

Distance : *Flat 6f 206y*

Draw Category	Winners	% Winners/Races
Low	10	26
Middle	21	54
High	8	21

Distance : *Flat 7f 214y*

Draw Category	Winners	% Winners/Races
Low	9	21
Middle	17	40
High	17	40

Distance : *Flat 1m 4f*

Draw Category	Winners	% Winners/Races
Low	9	29
Middle	12	39
High	10	32

CATTERICK

Distance : *Flat 5f*

Draw Category	Winners	% Winners/Races
Low	18	25
Middle	33	46
High	24	34

Distance : *Flat 5f 212y*

Draw Category	Winners	% Winners/Races
Low	19	33
Middle	16	28
High	22	39

Distance : *Flat 7f*

Draw Category	Winners	% Winners/Races
Low	36	34
Middle	48	45
High	27	25

Distance : *Flat 1m 3f 214y*

Draw Category	Winners	% Winners/Races
Low	18	33
Middle	20	36
High	19	35

Distance : *Flat 1m 5f 175y*

Draw Category	Winners	% Winners/Races
Low	8	24
Middle	17	52
High	10	30

Distance : *Flat 1m 7f 177y*

Draw Category	Winners	% Winners/Races
Low	10	37
Middle	9	33
High	8	30

CHEPSTOW

Distance : *Flat 5f 16y*

Draw Category	Winners	% Winners/Races
Low	8	32
Middle	16	64
High	1	4

Distance : *Flat 6f 16y*

Draw Category	Winners	% Winners/Races
Low	17	40
Middle	14	33
High	11	26

Distance : *Flat 7f 16y*

Draw Category	Winners	% Winners/Races
Low	14	33
Middle	11	26
High	18	42

Distance : *Flat 1m 14y*

Draw Category	Winners	% Winners/Races
Low	15	31
Middle	19	40
High	14	29

Distance : *Flat 1m 2f 36y*

Draw Category	Winners	% Winners/Races
Low	12	33
Middle	13	36
High	11	31

Distance : *Flat 1m 4f 23y*

Draw Category	Winners	% Winners/Races
Low	13	38
Middle	15	44
High	6	18

CHESTER

Distance : *Flat 5f 16y*

Draw Category	Winners	% Winners/Races
Low	24	46
Middle	21	40
High	7	13

Distance : *Flat 6f 18y*

Draw Category	Winners	% Winners/Races
Low	16	53
Middle	12	40
High	2	7

Distance : *Flat 7f 2y*

Draw Category	Winners	% Winners/Races
Low	18	41
Middle	16	36
High	10	23

Distance : *Flat 7f 122y*

Draw Category	Winners	% Winners/Races
Low	10	34
Middle	16	55
High	3	10

Distance : *Flat 1m 2f 75y*

Draw Category	Winners	% Winners/Races
Low	15	44
Middle	8	24
High	11	32

Distance : *Flat 1m 4f 66y*

Draw Category	Winners	% Winners/Races
Low	12	33
Middle	19	53
High	5	14

Distance : *Flat 1m 5f 89y*

Draw Category	Winners	% Winners/Races
Low	7	47
Middle	4	27
High	4	27

Distance : *Flat 1m 7f 195y*

Draw Category	Winners	% Winners/Races
Low	6	50
Middle	4	33
High	2	17

DONCASTER

Distance : *Flat 5f*

Draw Category	Winners	% Winners/Races
Low	26	33
Middle	28	35
High	25	32

Distance : *Flat 6f*

Draw Category	Winners	% Winners/Races
Low	18	23
Middle	35	44
High	26	33

Distance : *Flat 7f*

Draw Category	Winners	% Winners/Races
Low	32	35
Middle	34	37
High	26	28

Distance : *Str 1m*

Draw Category	Winners	% Winners/Races
Low	18	38
Middle	18	38
High	12	25

Distance : *Rnd 1m*

Draw Category	Winners	% Winners/Races
Low	15	28
Middle	21	39
High	18	33

Distance : *Flat 1m 2f 60y*

Draw Category	Winners	% Winners/Races
Low	21	31
Middle	34	50
High	13	19

Distance : *Flat 1m 4f*

Draw Category	Winners	% Winners/Races
Low	16	34
Middle	18	38
High	13	28

Distance : *Flat 1m 6f 132y*

Draw Category	Winners	% Winners/Races
Low	11	37
Middle	11	37
High	8	27

Distance : *Flat 2m 110y*

Draw Category	Winners	% Winners/Races
Low	5	38
Middle	3	23
High	5	38

EPSOM

Distance : *Flat 5f*

Draw Category	Winners	% Winners/Races
Low	5	31
Middle	7	44
High	4	25

Distance : *Flat 6f*

Draw Category	Winners	% Winners/Races
Low	12	28
Middle	22	51
High	9	21

Distance : *Flat 7f*

Draw Category	Winners	% Winners/Races
Low	12	30
Middle	18	45
High	10	25

Distance : *Flat 1m 114y*

Draw Category	Winners	% Winners/Races
Low	21	45
Middle	13	28
High	13	28

Distance : *Flat 1m 2f 18y*

Draw Category	Winners	% Winners/Races
Low	7	19
Middle	16	43
High	14	38

Distance : *Flat 1m 4f 10y*

Draw Category	Winners	% Winners/Races
Low	16	34
Middle	22	47
High	9	19

FOLKESTONE

Distance : *Flat 5f*

Draw Category	Winners	% Winners/Races
Low	21	31
Middle	29	43
High	18	26

Distance : *Flat 6f*

Draw Category	Winners	% Winners/Races
Low	30	38
Middle	21	26
High	29	36

Distance : *Rnd 6f 189y*

Draw Category	Winners	% Winners/Races
Low	19	27
Middle	26	37
High	26	37

Distance : *Str 7f*

Draw Category	Winners	% Winners/Races
Low	4	20
Middle	7	35
High	9	45

Distance : *Flat 1m 1f 149y*

Draw Category	Winners	% Winners/Races
Low	18	34
Middle	18	34
High	17	32

Distance : *Flat 1m 4f*

Draw Category	Winners	% Winners/Races
Low	15	25
Middle	29	48
High	16	27

Distance : *Flat 1m 7f 92y*

Draw Category	Winners	% Winners/Races
Low	3	19
Middle	7	44
High	6	38

Distance : *Flat 2m 93y*

Draw Category	Winners	% Winners/Races
Low	3	25
Middle	4	33
High	5	42

GOODWOOD

Distance : *Flat 5f*

Draw Category	Winners	% Winners/Races
Low	16	37
Middle	15	35
High	12	28

Distance : *Flat 6f*

Draw Category	Winners	% Winners/Races
Low	32	33
Middle	36	37
High	30	31

Distance : *Flat 7f*

Draw Category	Winners	% Winners/Races
Low	25	26
Middle	33	35
High	37	39

Distance : *Flat 1m*

Draw Category	Winners	% Winners/Races
Low	18	22
Middle	28	35
High	35	43

Distance : *Flat 1m 1f*

Draw Category	Winners	% Winners/Races
Low	9	21
Middle	19	45
High	14	33

Distance : *Flat 1m 1f 192y*

Draw Category	Winners	% Winners/Races
Low	4	21
Middle	6	32
High	9	47

Distance : *Flat 1m 2f*

Draw Category	Winners	% Winners/Races
Low	13	25
Middle	21	40
High	19	36

Distance : *Flat 1m 4f*

Draw Category	Winners	% Winners/Races
Low	9	20
Middle	15	33
High	22	48

Distance : *Flat 1m 6f*

Draw Category	Winners	% Winners/Races
Low	7	39
Middle	4	22
High	7	39

Distance : *Flat 2m*

Draw Category	Winners	% Winners/Races
Low	7	39
Middle	9	50
High	2	11

HAMILTON

Distance : *Flat 5f 4y*

Draw Category	Winners	% Winners/Races
Low	17	20
Middle	36	43
High	30	36

Distance : *Flat 6f 5y*

Draw Category	Winners	% Winners/Races
Low	22	26
Middle	24	28
High	40	47

Distance : *Flat 1m 65y*

Draw Category	Winners	% Winners/Races
Low	13	17
Middle	38	49
High	27	35

Distance : *Flat 1m 1f 36y*

Draw Category	Winners	% Winners/Races
Low	8	15
Middle	27	51
High	18	34

Distance : *Flat 1m 3f 16y*

Draw Category	Winners	% Winners/Races
Low	13	30
Middle	15	35
High	15	35

Distance : *Flat 1m 4f 17y*

Draw Category	Winners	% Winners/Races
Low	9	24
Middle	15	39
High	14	37

Distance : *Flat 1m 5f 9y*

Draw Category	Winners	% Winners/Races
Low	9	24
Middle	16	43
High	12	32

HAYDOCK

Distance : *Flat 5f*

Draw Category	Winners	% Winners/Races
Low	13	18
Middle	24	33
High	35	49

Distance : *Flat 6f*

Draw Category	Winners	% Winners/Races
Low	22	24
Middle	36	39
High	35	38

Distance : *Flat 7f 30y*

Draw Category	Winners	% Winners/Races
Low	25	33
Middle	28	37
High	23	30

Distance : *Flat 1m 30y*

Draw Category	Winners	% Winners/Races
Low	18	28
Middle	21	32
High	26	40

Distance : *Flat 1m 2f 120y*

Draw Category	Winners	% Winners/Races
Low	17	25
Middle	18	27
High	32	48

Distance : *Flat 1m 3f 200y*

Draw Category	Winners	% Winners/Races
Low	15	23
Middle	29	45
High	20	31

Distance : *Flat 1m 6f*

Draw Category	Winners	% Winners/Races
Low	11	24
Middle	21	47
High	13	29

KEMPTON

Distance : *Flat 5f*

Draw Category	Winners	% Winners/Races
Low	6	40
Middle	5	33
High	4	27

Distance : *Flat 6f*

Draw Category	Winners	% Winners/Races
Low	16	26
Middle	20	32
High	26	42

Distance : *Jub 7f*

Draw Category	Winners	% Winners/Races
Low	14	26
Middle	24	45
High	15	28

Distance : *Rnd 7f*

Draw Category	Winners	% Winners/Races
Low	3	25
Middle	4	33
High	5	42

Distance : *Jub 1m*

Draw Category	Winners	% Winners/Races
Low	15	33
Middle	22	48
High	9	20

Distance : *Rnd 1m 1f*

Draw Category	Winners	% Winners/Races
Low	8	40
Middle	5	25
High	7	35

Distance : *Jub 1m 2f*

Draw Category	Winners	% Winners/Races
Low	14	38
Middle	13	35
High	10	27

Distance : *Flat 1m 4f*

Draw Category	Winners	% Winners/Races
Low	14	34
Middle	17	41
High	10	24

Distance : *Flat 1m 6f 92y*

Draw Category	Winners	% Winners/Races
Low	4	36
Middle	5	45
High	2	18

LEICESTER

Distance : *Flat 5f 2y*

Draw Category	Winners	% Winners/Races
Low	14	31
Middle	20	44
High	11	24

Distance : *Flat 5f 218y*

Draw Category	Winners	% Winners/Races
Low	23	28
Middle	41	49
High	19	23

Distance : *Flat 7f 9y*

Draw Category	Winners	% Winners/Races
Low	34	30
Middle	44	39
High	36	32

Distance : *Flat 1m 8y*

Draw Category	Winners	% Winners/Races
Low	26	29
Middle	33	37
High	30	34

Distance : *Flat 1m 1f 218y*

Draw Category	Winners	% Winners/Races
Low	20	27
Middle	26	35
High	28	38

Distance : *Flat 1m 3f 183y*

Draw Category	Winners	% Winners/Races
Low	20	30
Middle	34	51
High	13	19

LINGFIELD

Distance : *Flat 5f*

Draw Category	Winners	% Winners/Races
Low	21	30
Middle	29	42
High	19	28

Distance : *Flat 6f*

Draw Category	Winners	% Winners/Races
Low	16	19
Middle	30	35
High	40	47

Distance : *Flat 7f*

Draw Category	Winners	% Winners/Races
Low	25	27
Middle	34	36
High	35	37

Distance : *Flat 7f 140y*

Draw Category	Winners	% Winners/Races
Low	8	16
Middle	25	50
High	17	34

Distance : *Flat 1m 1f*

Draw Category	Winners	% Winners/Races
Low	7	33
Middle	9	43
High	5	24

Distance : *Flat 1m 2f*

Draw Category	Winners	% Winners/Races
Low	14	32
Middle	21	48
High	9	20

Distance : *Flat 1m 3f 106y*

Draw Category	Winners	% Winners/Races
Low	19	40
Middle	19	40
High	10	21

Distance : *Flat 1m 6f*

Draw Category	Winners	% Winners/Races
Low	4	25
Middle	7	44
High	5	31

Distance : *Equi 5f*

Draw Category	Winners	% Winners/Races
Low	31	27
Middle	48	42
High	35	31

Distance : *Equi 6f*

Draw Category	Winners	% Winners/Races
Low	44	30
Middle	56	38
High	48	32

Distance : *Equi 7f*

Draw Category	Winners	% Winners/Races
Low	45	22
Middle	88	43
High	73	35

Distance : *Equi 1m*

Draw Category	Winners	% Winners/Races
Low	68	30
Middle	88	38
High	73	32

Distance : *Equi 1m 2f*

Draw Category	Winners	% Winners/Races
Low	73	30
Middle	108	44
High	65	26

Distance : *Equi 1m 4f*

Draw Category	Winners	% Winners/Races
Low	31	28
Middle	40	37
High	38	35

Distance : *Equi 1m 5f*

Draw Category	Winners	% Winners/Races
Low	14	26
Middle	20	38
High	19	36

Distance : *Equi 2m*

Draw Category	Winners	% Winners/Races
Low	18	25
Middle	34	47
High	20	28

MUSSELBURGH

Distance : *Flat 5f*

Draw Category	Winners	% Winners/Races
Low	35	35
Middle	40	40
High	25	25

Distance : *Flat 7f 30y*

Draw Category	Winners	% Winners/Races
Low	14	22
Middle	26	41
High	23	37

Distance : *Flat 1m 16y*

Draw Category	Winners	% Winners/Races
Low	23	37
Middle	25	40
High	15	24

Distance : *Flat 1m 3f 32y*

Draw Category	Winners	% Winners/Races
Low	4	17
Middle	10	43
High	9	39

Distance : *Flat 1m 4f 31y*

Draw Category	Winners	% Winners/Races
Low	8	16
Middle	32	64
High	10	20

Distance : *Flat 1m 7f 16y*

Draw Category	Winners	% Winners/Races
Low	2	17
Middle	6	50
High	4	33

Distance : *Flat 2m*

Draw Category	Winners	% Winners/Races
Low	5	26
Middle	11	58
High	3	16

NEWBURY

Distance : *Flat 5f 34y*

Draw Category	Winners	% Winners/Races
Low	10	21
Middle	23	48
High	15	31

Distance : *Flat 6f 8y*

Draw Category	Winners	% Winners/Races
Low	16	21
Middle	30	40
High	29	39

Distance : *Str 7f*

Draw Category	Winners	% Winners/Races
Low	10	23
Middle	19	44
High	14	33

Distance : *Rnd 7f 64y*

Draw Category	Winners	% Winners/Races
Low	19	33
Middle	20	35
High	18	32

Distance : *Str 1m*

Draw Category	Winners	% Winners/Races
Low	5	13
Middle	21	55
High	12	32

Distance : *Rnd 1m 7y*

Draw Category	Winners	% Winners/Races
Low	4	36
Middle	5	45
High	2	18

Distance : *Flat 1m 1f*

Draw Category	Winners	% Winners/Races
Low	4	31
Middle	4	31
High	5	38

Distance : *Flat 1m 2f 6y*

Draw Category	Winners	% Winners/Races
Low	18	30
Middle	25	41
High	18	30

Distance : *Flat 1m 4f 5y*

Draw Category	Winners	% Winners/Races
Low	12	31
Middle	12	31
High	15	38

Distance : *Flat 1m 5f 61y*

Draw Category	Winners	% Winners/Races
Low	6	26
Middle	8	35
High	9	39

Distance : *Flat 2m*

Draw Category	Winners	% Winners/Races
Low	6	29
Middle	10	48
High	5	24

NEWCASTLE

Distance : *Flat 5f*

Draw Category	Winners	% Winners/Races
Low	27	41
Middle	20	30
High	23	35

Distance : *Flat 6f*

Draw Category	Winners	% Winners/Races
Low	23	35
Middle	23	35
High	21	32

Distance : *Flat 7f*

Draw Category	Winners	% Winners/Races
Low	24	34
Middle	30	42
High	17	24

Distance : *Rnd 1m*

Draw Category	Winners	% Winners/Races
Low	8	19
Middle	21	50
High	13	31

Distance : *Str 1m 3y*

Draw Category	Winners	% Winners/Races
Low	3	16
Middle	5	26
High	11	58

Distance : *Flat 1m 2f 32y*

Draw Category	Winners	% Winners/Races
Low	12	27
Middle	22	49
High	15	33

Distance : *Flat 1m 4f 93y*

Draw Category	Winners	% Winners/Races
Low	7	23
Middle	17	57
High	6	20

Distance : *Flat 2m 19y*

Draw Category	Winners	% Winners/Races
Low	9	38
Middle	10	42
High	7	29

NEWMARKET

Distance : *Rwly 5f*

Draw Category	Winners	% Winners/Races
Low	13	28
Middle	19	40
High	15	32

Distance : *Rwly 6f*

Draw Category	Winners	% Winners/Races
Low	23	30
Middle	27	35
High	27	35

Distance : *Rwly 7f*

Draw Category	Winners	% Winners/Races
Low	27	23
Middle	57	50
High	31	27

Distance : *Rwly 1m*

Draw Category	Winners	% Winners/Races
Low	23	28
Middle	29	35
High	30	37

Distance : *Rwly 1m 1f*

Draw Category	Winners	% Winners/Races
Low	7	32
Middle	11	50
High	4	18

Distance : *Rwly 1m 2f*

Draw Category	Winners	% Winners/Races
Low	15	27
Middle	23	41
High	18	32

Distance : *Rwly 1m 4f*

Draw Category	Winners	% Winners/Races
Low	10	22
Middle	16	36
High	19	42

Distance : *Rwly 1m 6f*

Draw Category	Winners	% Winners/Races
Low	5	31
Middle	7	44
High	4	25

Distance : *Jly 5f*

Draw Category	Winners	% Winners/Races
Low	9	43
Middle	7	33
High	5	24

Distance : *Jly 6f*

Draw Category	Winners	% Winners/Races
Low	32	30
Middle	43	41
High	31	29

Distance : *Jly 7f*

Draw Category	Winners	% Winners/Races
Low	23	23
Middle	46	46
High	31	31

Distance : *Jly 1m*

Draw Category	Winners	% Winners/Races
Low	16	23
Middle	31	45
High	22	32

Distance : *Jly 1m 2f*

Draw Category	Winners	% Winners/Races
Low	16	31
Middle	20	39
High	15	29

Distance : *Jly 1m 4f*

Draw Category	Winners	% Winners/Races
Low	19	42
Middle	19	42
High	7	16

Distance : *Jly 1m 6f 175y*

Draw Category	Winners	% Winners/Races
Low	3	23
Middle	4	31
High	6	46

NOTTINGHAM

Distance : *Flat 5f 13y*

Draw Category	Winners	% Winners/Races
Low	24	35
Middle	24	35
High	20	29

Distance : *Flat 6f 15y*

Draw Category	Winners	% Winners/Races
Low	34	27
Middle	40	31
High	54	42

Distance : *Flat 1m 54y*

Draw Category	Winners	% Winners/Races
Low	49	32
Middle	57	37
High	48	31

Distance : *Flat 1m 1f 213y*

Draw Category	Winners	% Winners/Races
Low	45	39
Middle	35	31
High	34	30

Distance : *Flat 1m 6f 15y*

Draw Category	Winners	% Winners/Races
Low	21	33
Middle	21	33
High	22	34

Distance : *Flat 2m 9y*

Draw Category	Winners	% Winners/Races
Low	11	41
Middle	13	48
High	3	11

PONTEFRACT

Distance : *Flat 5f*

Draw Category	Winners	% Winners/Races
Low	11	20
Middle	18	33
High	25	46

Distance : *Flat 6f*

Draw Category	Winners	% Winners/Races
Low	33	30
Middle	44	40
High	33	30

Distance : *Flat 1m*

Draw Category	Winners	% Winners/Races
Low	28	33
Middle	35	41
High	23	27

Distance : *Flat 1m 2f 6y*

Draw Category	Winners	% Winners/Races
Low	26	28
Middle	32	34
High	36	38

Distance : *Flat 1m 4f 8y*

Draw Category	Winners	% Winners/Races
Low	15	38
Middle	15	38
High	10	25

Distance : *Flat 2m 1f 22y*

Draw Category	Winners	% Winners/Races
Low	3	21
Middle	7	50
High	4	29

Distance : *Flat 2m 1f 216y*

Draw Category	Winners	% Winners/Races
Low	3	25
Middle	5	42
High	4	33

REDCAR

Distance : *Flat 5f*

Draw Category	Winners	% Winners/Races
Low	14	26
Middle	21	39
High	19	35

Distance : *Flat 6f*

Draw Category	Winners	% Winners/Races
Low	27	32
Middle	28	33
High	29	35

Distance : *Flat 7f*

Draw Category	Winners	% Winners/Races
Low	36	37
Middle	37	38
High	25	26

Distance : *Flat 1m*

Draw Category	Winners	% Winners/Races
Low	7	14
Middle	25	49
High	19	37

Distance : *Flat 1m 1f*

Draw Category	Winners	% Winners/Races
Low	6	23
Middle	9	35
High	11	42

Distance : *Flat 1m 2f*

Draw Category	Winners	% Winners/Races
Low	17	30
Middle	23	40
High	17	30

Distance : *Flat 1m 3f*

Draw Category	Winners	% Winners/Races
Low	10	26
Middle	12	31
High	17	44

Distance : *Flat 1m 6f 19y*

Draw Category	Winners	% Winners/Races
Low	9	21
Middle	21	49
High	13	30

Distance : *Flat 2m 4y*

Draw Category	Winners	% Winners/Races
Low	6	43
Middle	5	36
High	3	21

RIPON

Distance : *Flat 5f*

Draw Category	Winners	% Winners/Races
Low	22	35
Middle	20	32
High	21	33

Distance : *Flat 6f*

Draw Category	Winners	% Winners/Races
Low	23	32
Middle	25	34
High	25	34

Distance : *Flat 1m*

Draw Category	Winners	% Winners/Races
Low	13	21
Middle	30	48
High	20	32

Distance : *Flat 1m 1f*

Draw Category	Winners	% Winners/Races
Low	6	30
Middle	7	35
High	7	35

Distance : *Flat 1m 2f*

Draw Category	Winners	% Winners/Races
Low	14	22
Middle	26	41
High	24	38

Distance : *Flat 1m 4f 60y*

Draw Category	Winners	% Winners/Races
Low	15	27
Middle	25	45
High	15	27

Distance : *Flat 2m*

Draw Category	Winners	% Winners/Races
Low	4	33
Middle	3	25
High	5	42

SALISBURY

Distance : *Flat 5f*

Draw Category	Winners	% Winners/Races
Low	8	25
Middle	12	38
High	12	38

Distance : *Flat 6f*

Draw Category	Winners	% Winners/Races
Low	22	28
Middle	29	36
High	29	36

Distance : *Flat 6f 212y*

Draw Category	Winners	% Winners/Races
Low	20	23
Middle	36	41
High	31	36

Distance : *Flat 1m*

Draw Category	Winners	% Winners/Races
Low	22	34
Middle	21	32
High	22	34

Distance : *Flat 1m 1f 209y*

Draw Category	Winners	% Winners/Races
Low	7	29
Middle	8	33
High	9	38

Distance : *Flat 1m 4f*

Draw Category	Winners	% Winners/Races
Low	13	34
Middle	16	42
High	9	24

Distance : *Flat 1m 6f*

Draw Category	Winners	% Winners/Races
Low	5	19
Middle	11	41
High	11	41

SANDOWN

Distance : *Flat 5f 6y*

Draw Category	Winners	% Winners/Races
Low	27	23
Middle	40	34
High	51	43

Distance : *Flat 7f 16y*

Draw Category	Winners	% Winners/Races
Low	24	30
Middle	30	38
High	25	32

Distance : *Flat 1m 14y*

Draw Category	Winners	% Winners/Races
Low	28	31
Middle	35	39
High	27	30

Distance : *Flat 1m 2f 7y*

Draw Category	Winners	% Winners/Races
Low	20	25
Middle	32	40
High	28	35

Distance : *Flat 1m 3f 91y*

Draw Category	Winners	% Winners/Races
Low	6	32
Middle	10	53
High	3	16

Distance : *Flat 1m 6f*

Draw Category	Winners	% Winners/Races
Low	7	19
Middle	20	54
High	10	27

Distance : *Flat 2m 78y*

Draw Category	Winners	% Winners/Races
Low	4	25
Middle	7	44
High	5	31

SOUTHWELL

Distance : *Fibr 5f*

Draw Category	Winners	% Winners/Races
Low	22	25
Middle	42	48
High	24	27

Distance : *Fibr 6f*

Draw Category	Winners	% Winners/Races
Low	60	31
Middle	81	42
High	52	27

Distance : *Fibr 7f*

Draw Category	Winners	% Winners/Races
Low	57	28
Middle	78	38
High	68	33

Distance : *Fibr 1m*

Draw Category	Winners	% Winners/Races
Low	62	24
Middle	106	41
High	91	35

Distance : *Fibr 1m 3f*

Draw Category	Winners	% Winners/Races
Low	42	33
Middle	49	39
High	36	28

Distance : *Fibr 1m 4f*

Draw Category	Winners	% Winners/Races
Low	18	15
Middle	55	45
High	48	40

Distance : *Fibr 1m 6f*

Draw Category	Winners	% Winners/Races
Low	13	28
Middle	22	47
High	12	26

Distance : *Fibr 2m*

Draw Category	Winners	% Winners/Races
Low	10	24
Middle	22	52
High	10	24

THIRSK

Distance : *Flat 5f*

Draw Category	Winners	% Winners/Races
Low	12	18
Middle	31	46
High	24	36

Distance : *Flat 6f*

Draw Category	Winners	% Winners/Races
Low	14	22
Middle	19	30
High	31	48

Distance : *Flat 7f*

Draw Category	Winners	% Winners/Races
Low	30	41
Middle	28	38
High	16	22

Distance : *Flat 1m*

Draw Category	Winners	% Winners/Races
Low	19	23
Middle	39	48
High	24	29

Distance : *Flat 1m 4f*

Draw Category	Winners	% Winners/Races
Low	10	22
Middle	20	44
High	15	33

Distance : *Flat 2m*

Draw Category	Winners	% Winners/Races
Low	3	25
Middle	7	58
High	2	17

WARWICK

Distance : *Flat 5f*

Draw Category	Winners	% Winners/Races
Low	24	46
Middle	12	23
High	16	31

Distance : *Flat 6f*

Draw Category	Winners	% Winners/Races
Low	12	40
Middle	12	40
High	6	20

Distance : *Flat 7f*

Draw Category	Winners	% Winners/Races
Low	19	27
Middle	32	46
High	19	27

Distance : *Flat 1m*

Draw Category	Winners	% Winners/Races
Low	16	28
Middle	19	33
High	23	40

Distance : *Flat 1m 2f 169y*

Draw Category	Winners	% Winners/Races
Low	23	36
Middle	21	33
High	20	31

Distance : *Flat 1m 4f 115y*

Draw Category	Winners	% Winners/Races
Low	10	36
Middle	13	46
High	5	18

Distance : *Flat 1m 6f 194y*

Draw Category	Winners	% Winners/Races
Low	6	32
Middle	8	42
High	5	26

Distance : *Flat 2m 20y*

Draw Category	Winners	% Winners/Races
Low	2	17
Middle	6	50
High	4	33

WINDSOR

Distance : *Flat 5f 10y*

Draw Category	Winners	% Winners/Races
Low	14	24
Middle	20	34
High	25	42

Distance : *Flat 5f 217y*

Draw Category	Winners	% Winners/Races
Low	32	37
Middle	26	30
High	28	33

Distance : *Flat 1m 67y*

Draw Category	Winners	% Winners/Races
Low	25	32
Middle	27	35
High	26	33

Distance : *Flat 1m 2f 7y*

Draw Category	Winners	% Winners/Races
Low	15	19
Middle	36	47
High	26	34

Distance : *Flat 1m 3f 135y*

Draw Category	Winners	% Winners/Races
Low	18	31
Middle	26	45
High	14	24

WOLVERHAMPTON

Distance : *Fibr 5f*

Draw Category	Winners	% Winners/Races
Low	32	23
Middle	54	38
High	55	39

Distance : *Fibr 6f*

Draw Category	Winners	% Winners/Races
Low	53	24
Middle	83	38
High	82	38

Distance : *Fibr 7f*

Draw Category	Winners	% Winners/Races
Low	60	31
Middle	65	34
High	68	35

Distance : *Fibr 1m 100y*

Draw Category	Winners	% Winners/Races
Low	32	19
Middle	75	44
High	64	37

Distance : *Fibr 1m 1f 79y*

Draw Category	Winners	% Winners/Races
Low	36	23
Middle	55	35
High	68	43

Distance : *Fibr 1m 4f*

Draw Category	Winners	% Winners/Races
Low	32	21
Middle	54	35
High	67	44

Distance : *Fibr 1m 6f 166y*

Draw Category	Winners	% Winners/Races
Low	16	28
Middle	19	33
High	23	40

Distance : *Fibr 2m 46y*

Draw Category	Winners	% Winners/Races
Low	3	13
Middle	9	39
High	11	48

YARMOUTH

Distance : *Flat 5f 43y*

Draw Category	Winners	% Winners/Races
Low	8	28
Middle	10	34
High	11	38

Distance : *Flat 6f 3y*

Draw Category	Winners	% Winners/Races
Low	19	20
Middle	42	44
High	34	36

Distance : *Flat 7f 3y*

Draw Category	Winners	% Winners/Races
Low	29	27
Middle	38	36
High	40	37

Distance : *Flat 1m 3y*

Draw Category	Winners	% Winners/Races
Low	15	23
Middle	32	48
High	19	29

Distance : *Flat 1m 2f 21y*

Draw Category	Winners	% Winners/Races
Low	25	39
Middle	27	42
High	12	19

Distance : *Flat 1m 3f 101y*

Draw Category	Winners	% Winners/Races
Low	12	41
Middle	7	24
High	10	34

Distance : *Flat 1m 6f 17y*

Draw Category	Winners	% Winners/Races
Low	6	18
Middle	20	59
High	8	24

YORK

Distance : *Flat 5f*

Draw Category	Winners	% Winners/Races
Low	8	21
Middle	20	53
High	10	26

Distance : *Flat 6f*

Draw Category	Winners	% Winners/Races
Low	26	27
Middle	37	39
High	33	34

Distance : *Flat 6f 214y*

Draw Category	Winners	% Winners/Races
Low	11	23
Middle	14	29
High	23	48

Distance : *Flat 7f 202y*

Draw Category	Winners	% Winners/Races
Low	22	40
Middle	17	31
High	16	29

Distance : *Flat 1m 205y*

Draw Category	Winners	% Winners/Races
Low	9	56
Middle	2	13
High	5	31

Distance : *Flat 1m 2f 85y*

Draw Category	Winners	% Winners/Races
Low	23	38
Middle	25	41
High	13	21

Distance : *Flat 1m 3f 195y*

Draw Category	Winners	% Winners/Races
Low	19	40
Middle	21	44
High	8	17

Distance : *Flat 1m 5f 194y*

Draw Category	Winners	% Winners/Races
Low	14	38
Middle	11	30
High	12	32

FOUR-SEASON FRONT-RUNNERS ANALYSIS FOR BRITISH FLAT TRACKS

The following table shows the record of front runners over various distances on each track from January 1st 1995 to November 7th 1998. In order to qualify for inclusion in the Winners column, the horse has earned the Raceform comment 'Made All', 'Made Virtually All' or 'Made Most'. Distances which have not had at least ten races run over them during the period are not shown.

ASCOT

Distance	Winners	Races	% Winners/Races
5f	4	43	9
6f	9	44	20
7f	4	42	10
1m Str	6	39	15
1m Rnd	4	46	9
1m 2f	3	28	11
1m 4f	5	64	8
2m 45y	3	25	12

AYR

Distance	Winners	Races	% Winners/Races
5f	11	51	22
6f	9	59	15
7f	9	61	15
1m	11	49	22
1m 2f	7	42	17
1m 2f 192y	0	21	0
1m 5f 13y	8	24	33
1m 7f	4	13	31

BATH

Distance	Winners	Races	% Winners/Races
5f 11y	18	82	22
5f 161y	8	54	15
1m 5y	9	76	12
1m 2f 46y	16	53	30
1m 3f 144y	5	32	16
1m 5f 22y	3	11	27
2m 1f 34y	4	36	11

BEVERLEY

Distance	Winners	Races	% Winners/Races
5f	33	121	27
7f 100y	22	109	20
1m 100y	12	61	20
1m 1f 207y	9	77	12
1m 3f 216y	6	57	11
2m 35y	1	32	3

BRIGHTON

Distance	Winners	Races	% Winners/Races
5f 59y	14	59	24
5f 213y	18	87	21
6f 209y	18	107	17
7f 214y	21	91	23
1m 1f 209y	11	60	18
1m 3f 196y	14	78	18

CARLISLE

Distance	Winners	Races	% Winners/Races
5f	12	49	24
5f 207y	7	46	15
6f 206y	6	39	15
7f 214y	6	43	14
1m 4f	4	31	13

CATTERICK

Distance	Winners	Races	% Winners/Races
5f	16	71	23
5f 212y	15	57	26
7f	14	107	13
1m 3f 214y	7	55	13
1m 5f 175y	5	33	15
1m 7f 177y	2	27	7

CHEPSTOW

Distance	Winners	Races	% Winners/Races
5f 16y	6	25	24
6f 16y	12	42	29
7f 16y	7	43	16
1m 14y	14	48	29
1m 2f 36y	3	36	8
1m 4f 23y	6	34	18

CHESTER

Distance	Winners	Races	% Winners/Races
5f 16y	17	52	33
6f 18y	10	30	33
7f 2y	10	44	23
7f 122y	4	29	14
1m 2f 75y	4	34	12
1m 4f 66y	10	36	28
1m 5f 89y	4	15	27
1m 7f 195y	2	12	17

DONCASTER

Distance	Winners	Races	% Winners/Races
5f	14	79	18
6f	15	80	19
7f	16	93	17
1m Str	5	51	10
1m Rnd	6	54	11
1m 2f 60y	7	68	10
1m 4f	7	49	14
1m 6f 132y	4	30	13
2m 110y	0	14	0

EPSOM

Distance	Winners	Races	% Winners/Races
5f	2	16	13
6f	8	43	19
7f	7	40	18
1m 114y	7	47	15
1m 2f 18y	8	37	22
1m 4f 10y	4	47	9

FOLKESTONE

Distance	Winners	Races	% Winners/Races
5f	18	68	26
6f	16	80	20
6f 189y Rnd	9	71	13
7f Str	6	20	30
1m 1f 149y	5	53	9
1m 4f	9	60	15
1m 7f 92y	3	16	19
2m 93y	3	12	25

GOODWOOD

Distance	Winners	Races	% Winners/Races
5f	8	43	19
6f	13	98	13
7f	15	95	16
1m	11	81	14
1m 1f	5	42	12
1m 1f 192y	4	19	21
1m 2f	11	53	21
1m 4f	2	46	4
1m 6f	7	18	39
2m	5	18	28

HAMILTON

Distance	Winners	Races	% Winners/Races
5f 4y	22	83	27
6f 5y	18	86	21
1m 65y	10	78	13
1m 1f 36y	14	53	26
1m 3f 16y	11	43	26
1m 4f 17y	7	38	18
1m 5f 9y	6	37	16

HAYDOCK

Distance	Winners	Races	% Winners/Races
5f	21	72	29
6f	20	93	22
7f 30y	22	76	29
1m 30y	13	65	20
1m 2f 120y	12	67	18
1m 3f 200y	7	64	11
1m 6f	7	45	16

KEMPTON

Distance	Winners	Races	% Winners/Races
5f	1	15	7
6f	6	62	10
7f Jub	10	53	19
7f Rnd	1	12	8
1m Jub	2	46	4
1m 1f	1	20	5
1m 2f	5	37	14
1m 4f	3	41	7
1m 6f 92y	4	11	36

LEICESTER

Distance	Winners	Races	% Winners/Races
5f 2y	2	45	4
5f 218y	10	83	12
7f 9y	19	114	17
1m 8y	9	89	10
1m 1f 218y	8	74	11
1m 3f 183y	6	67	9

LINGFIELD TURF

Distance	Winners	Races	% Winners/Races
5f	25	69	36
6f	12	86	14
7f	20	94	21
7f 140y	8	50	16
1m 1f	6	21	29
1m 2f	8	44	18
1m 3f 106y	10	48	21
1m 6f	5	16	31

LINGFIELD AW

Distance	Winners	Races	% Winners/Races
5f	21	114	18
6f	23	148	16
7f	26	206	13
1m	23	229	10

1m 2f	30	246	12
1m 4f	5	109	5
1m 5f	4	53	8
2m	5	72	7

MUSSELBURGH

Distance	Winners	Races	% Winners/Races
5f	30	100	30
7f 30y	13	63	21
1m 16y	10	63	16
1m 3f 32y	2	23	9
1m 4f 31y	7	50	14
1m 7f 16y	0	12	0
2m	0	19	0

NEWBURY

Distance	Winners	Races	% Winners/Races
5f 34y	6	48	13
6f 8y	7	75	9
7f	3	43	7
7f 64y	8	57	14
1m Str	2	38	5
1m 7y Rnd	1	11	9
1m 1f	4	13	31
1m 2f 6y	8	61	13
1m 4f 5y	4	39	10
1m 5f 61y	4	23	17
2m	3	21	14

NEWCASTLE

Distance	Winners	Races	% Winners/Races
5f	16	66	24
6f	15	65	23
7f	11	71	15
1m Rnd	2	42	5
1m 3y Str	4	19	21
1m 2f 32y	10	45	22
1m 4f 93y	3	30	10
2m 19y	1	24	4

NEWMARKET ROWLEY

Distance	Winners	Races	% Winners/Races
5f	9	47	19
6f	10	77	13
7f	14	115	12
1m	9	82	11
1m 1f	3	22	14
1m 2f	8	56	14
1m 4f	4	45	9
1m 6f	1	16	6

NEWMARKET JULY

Distance	Winners	Races	% Winners/Races
5f	2	21	10
6f	20	106	19
7f	12	100	12
1m	5	69	7
1m 2f	1	51	2
1m 4f	7	45	16
1m 6f 175y	1	13	8

NOTTINGHAM

Distance	Winners	Races	% Winners/Races
5f 13y	14	68	21
6f 15y	25	128	20
1m 54y	16	154	10
1m 1f 213y	6	114	5
1m 6f 15y	2	64	3
2m 9y	3	27	11

PONTEFRACT

Distance	Winners	Races	% Winners/Races
5f	9	54	17
6f	24	110	22
1m 4y	10	86	12
1m 2f 6y	15	94	16
1m 4f 8y	7	40	18
2m 1f 22y	1	14	7
2m 1f 216y	0	12	0

REDCAR

Distance	Winners	Races	% Winners/Races
5f	15	54	28
6f	7	84	8
7f	8	98	8
1m	4	51	8
1m 1f	2	26	8
1m 2f	5	57	9
1m 3f	2	39	5
1m 6f 19y	4	43	9
2m 4y	1	14	7

RIPON

Distance	Winners	Races	% Winners/Races
5f	23	63	37
6f	19	73	26
1m	11	63	17
1m 1f	4	20	20
1m 2f	12	64	19
1m 4f 60y	5	55	9
2m	1	12	8

SALISBURY

Distance	Winners	Races	% Winners/Races
5f	9	32	28
6f	14	80	18
6f 212y	10	87	11
1m	4	65	6
1m 1f 209y	1	24	4
1m 4f	8	38	21
1m 6f	5	27	19

SANDOWN

Distance	Winners	Races	% Winners/Races
5f 6y	26	118	22
7f 16y	12	79	15
1m 14y	14	90	16
1m 2f 7y	9	80	11
1m 3f 91y	2	19	11
1m 6f	4	37	11
2m 78y	2	16	13

SOUTHWELL

Distance	Winners	Races	% Winners/Races
5f	21	88	24
6f	32	193	17
7f	32	203	16
1m	29	259	11
1m 3f	17	127	13
1m 4f	18	121	15
1m 6f	4	47	9

THIRSK

Distance	Winners	Races	% Winners/Races
5f	17	67	25
6f	17	64	27
7f	13	74	18
1m	14	82	17
1m 4f	6	45	13
2m	6	12	50

WARWICK

Distance	Winners	Races	% Winners/Races
5f	9	52	17
6f	5	30	17
7f	17	70	24
1m	8	58	14
1m 2f 169y	4	64	6
1m 4f 115y	6	28	21
1m 6f 194y	1	19	5
2m 20y	1	12	8

WINDSOR

Distance	Winners	Races	% Winners/Races
5f 10y	13	59	22
5f 217y	13	86	15
1m 67y	14	78	18
1m 2f 7y	11	77	14
1m 3f 135y	8	58	14

WOLVERHAMPTON

Distance	Winners	Races	% Winners/Races
5f	28	141	20
6f	38	218	17
7f	34	193	18
1m 100y	16	171	9
1m 1f 79y	19	159	12
1m 4f	15	153	10
1m 6f 166y	4	58	7
2m 46y	3	23	13

YARMOUTH

Distance	Winners	Races	% Winners/Races
5f 43y	6	29	21
6f 3y	27	95	28
7f 3y	24	107	22
1m 3y	11	66	17
1m 2f 21y	6	64	9
1m 3f 101y	4	29	14
1m 6f 17y	2	34	6

YORK

Distance	Winners	Races	% Winners/Races
5f	7	38	18
6f	18	96	19
6f 214y	4	48	8
7f 202y	8	55	15
1m 205y	1	16	6
1m 2f 85y	8	61	13
1m 3f 195y	4	48	8
1m 5f 194y	2	37	5

RACEFORM STANDARD TIMES 1999

ASCOT

5f 1m 00.2
6f 1m 14.0
7f 1m 27.0
1m (Rnd) 1m 40.0
1m (Str) 1m 39.0
1m 2f 2m 05.3
1m 4f 2m 30.0
2m 45y 3m 26.5
2m 4f 4m 17.0
2m 6f 34y 4m 50.0

AYR

5f ....56.8 secs
6f 1m 09.8
7f 1m 25.0
1m 1m 37.4
1m 1f 1m 49.0
1m 2f 2m 05.3
1m 2f 192y 2m 15.0
1m 5f 13y 2m 46.0
1m 7f 3m 10.7
2m 1f 105y 3m 40.5

BATH

5f 11y 1m 00.5
5f 161y 1m 09.5
1m 5y 1m 37.8
1m 2f 46y 2m 06.5
1m 3f 144y 2m 26.9
1m 5f 22y 2m 45.0
2m 1f 34y 3m 41.4

BEVERLEY

5f 1m 01.8
7f 100y 1m 31.1
1m 100y 1m 43.5
1m 1f 207y 2m 02.2
1m 3f 216y 2m 31.8
2m 35y 3m 30.5

BRIGHTON

5f 59y 1m 00.0
5f 213y 1m 07.2
6f 209y 1m 20.0
7f 214y 1m 31.5
1m 1f 209y 1m 58.3
1m 3f 196y 2m 26.7

CARLISLE

5f 59.7secs
5f 207y 1m 11.6
6f 206y 1m 24.6
7f 214y 1m 37.0
1m 1f 61y 1m 53.0
1m 4f 2m 28.7
1m 6f 32y 3m 00.2
2m 1f 52y 3m 37.0

CATTERICK

5f ....57.5 secs
5f 212y 1m 10.9
7f 1m 23.6
1m 3f 214y 2m 32.0
1m 4f 44y 2m 34.0
1m 5f 175y 2m 56.0
1m 7f 177y 3m 22.0

CHEPSTOW

5f 16y ....56.8 secs
6f 16y 1m 09.0
7f 16y 1m 19.3
1m 14y 1m 31.2
1m 2f 36y 2m 05.0
1m 4f 23y 2m 31.5
2m 49y 3m 28.0
2m 2f 3m 49.0
2m 2f 33y 3m 52.0

CHESTER

5f 16y 1m 00.2
6f 18y 1m 13.3
7f 2y 1m 25.2
7f 122y 1m 31.0
1m 1f 70y 2m 08.7
1m 2f 75y 2m 08.7
1m 3f 79y 2m 23.6
1m 4f 66y 2m 36.2
1m 5f 89y 2m 51.5
1m 7f 195y 3m 22.9
2m 2f 147y 4m 02.0

DONCASTER

5f ....58.9 secs
5f 140y 1m 06.6
6f 1m 12.1
6f 110y 1m 18.3
7f 1m 24.5
1m (Str) 1m 38.2
1m (Rnd) 1m 38.0
1m 2f 60y 2m 07.8
1m 4f 2m 30.0
1m 6f 132y 3m 05.0
2m 110y 3m 31.5
2m 2f 3m 54.0

EPSOM

5f ....54.5 secs
6f 1m 07.8
7f 1m 20.3
1m 114y 1m 42.0
1m 2f 18y 2m 05.0
1m 4f 10y 2m 34.5

FOLKESTONE

5f ....57.9 secs
6f 1m 10.2
6f 189y 1m 21.4
7f (Str) 1m 23.0
1m 1f 149y 1m 57.7
1m 4f 2m 31.2
1m 7f 92y 3m 16.5
2m 93y 3m 29.0

GOODWOOD

5f ....56.7 secs
6f 1m 09.8
7f 1m 24.8
1m 1m 36.5
1m 1f 1m 51.8
1m 2f 2m 06.5
1m 4f 2m 33.2
1m 6f 2m 58.0
2m 3m 21.5
2m 4f 4m 11.0

HAMILTON

5f 4y ....57.5 secs
6f 5y 1m 08.7
1m 65y 1m 42.6
1m 1f 36y 1m 51.5
1m 3f 16y 2m 16.2
1m 4f 17y 2m 28.5
1m 5f 9y 2m 42.5

HAYDOCK

5f ....59.4 secs
6f 1m 11.7
7f 30y 1m 28.0
1m 30y 1m 40.6
1m 2f 120y 2m 11.0
1m 3f 200y 2m 29.4
1m 6f 2m 57.5
2m 45y 3m 27.2

KEMPTON

5f ....59.1 secs
6f 1m 11.2
7f (Rnd) 1m 23.5
7f (Jub) 1m 24.5
1m (Jub) 1m 37.7
1m (Rnd) 1m 36.4
1m 1f (Rnd) 1m 50.6
1m 2f (Jub) 2m 03.5
1m 3f 30y 2m 18.8
1m 4f 2m 29.4
1m 6f 92y 3m 02.0
2m 3m 24.6

LEICESTER

5f 2y ....58.3 secs
5f 218y 1m 10.0
7f 9y 1m 22.6
1m 8y 1m 34.4
1m 1f 218y 2m 02.4
1m 3f 183y 2m 28.0

LINGFIELD (TURF)

5f ....56.8 secs
6f 1m 09.0
7f 1m 21.2
7f 140y 1m 28.8
1m 1f 1m 51.0
1m 2f 2m 05.0
1m 3f 106y 2m 24.7
1m 6f 2m 59.0
2m 3m 24.0

LINGFIELD (AWT)

5f ....58.4 secs
6f 1m 11.5
7f 1m 24.2
1m 1m 37.4
1m 2f 2m 04.5
1m 4f 2m 30.0
1m 5f 2m 42.5
2m 3m 22.5

MUSSELBURGH

5f ....57.5 secs
7f 30y 1m 26.0
1m 16y 1m 37.5
1m 3f 32y 2m 19.0
1m 4f 31y 2m 31.5
1m 6f 2m 56.6
2m 3m 22.0

NEWBURY

5f 34y 1m 00.5
6f 8y 1m 11.8
7f (Str) 1m 24.1
7f 64y (Rnd)....................1m 27.6
1m (Str) 1m 37.5
1m 7y (Rnd) 1m 35.5
1m 1f 1m 50.3
1m 2f 6y 2m 04.0
1m 3f 5y 2m 18.0
1m 4f 5y 2m 30.0
1m 5f 61y 2m 45.5
2m 3m 24.2

NEWCASTLE

5f ....59.2 secs
6f 1m 12.5
7f 1m 24.7
1m (Rnd) 1m 39.4
1m 3y (Str)....................1m 38.6
1m 1f 9y 1m 52.3
1m 2f 32y 2m 06.2
1m 4f 93y 2m 36.0
2m 19y 3m 25.5

NEWMARKET (ROWLEY MILE COURSE)

5f ....58.7 secs
6f 1m 11.8
7f 1m 24.5
1m 1m 37.3
1m 1f 1m 50.5
1m 2f 2m 04.0
1m 4f 2m 30.0
1m 6f 2m 56.0
2m 3m 24.0
2m 2f 3m 50.4

Group One Races

1000 GUINEAS

1998 Cape Verdi (IRE)
1997 Sleepytime (IRE)
1996 Bosra Sham (USA)
1995 Harayir (USA)
1994 Las Meninas (IRE)
1993 Sayyedati
1992 Hatoof (USA)
1991 Shadayid (USA)
1990 Salsabil
1989 Musical Bliss (USA)

2000 GUINEAS

1998 King Of Kings (IRE)
1997 Entrepreneur
1996 Mark of Esteem (IRE)
1995 Pennekamp (USA)
1994 Mister Baileys
1993 Zafonic (USA)
1992 Rodrigo de Triano (USA)
1991 Mystiko (USA)
1990 Tirol
1989 Nashwan (USA)

DERBY

1998 High-Rise (IRE)
1997 Benny The Dip (USA)
1996 Shaamit (IRE)
1995 Lammtarra (USA)
1994 Erhaab (USA)
1993 Commander in Chief
1992 Dr Devious (IRE)
1991 Generous (IRE)
1990 Quest for Fame
1989 Nashwan (USA)

CORONATION CUP

1998 Silver Patriarch (IRE)
1997 Singspiel (IRE)
1996 Swain (IRE)
1995 Sunshack
1994 Apple Tree (FR)
1993 Opera House
1992 Saddlers' Hall (IRE)
1991 In the Groove
1990 In the Wings
1989 Sheriff's Star

ST JAMES'S PALACE STAKES

1998 Dr Fong (USA)
1997 Starborough
1996 Bijou d'Inde
1995 Bahri (USA)
1994 Grand Lodge (USA)
1993 Kingmambo (USA)
1992 Brief Truce (USA)
1991 Marju (IRE)
1990 Shavian
1989 Shaadi (USA)

CORONATION STAKES

1998 Exclusive
1997 Rebecca Sharp
1996 Shake the Yoke
1995 Ridgewood Pe[illegible]
1994 Kissing Co[illegible]n (IRE)
1993 Gold Sp[illegible]sh (USA)
1992 Mar[illegible]g (IRE)
1991 K[illegible]yonga (IRE)
1990 Chimes of Freedom (USA)
1989 Golden Opinion (USA)

OAKS

1998 Shahtoush (IRE)
1997 Reams of Verse (USA)
1996 Lady Carla
1995 Moonshell (IRE)
1994 Balanchine (USA)
1993 Intrepidity
1992 User Friendly
1991 Jet Ski Lady (USA)
1990 Salsabil
1989 Snow Bride (USA) (Aliysa disq)

CORAL-ECLIPSE STAKES

1998 Daylami (IRE)
1997 Pilsudski (IRE)
1996 Halling (USA)
1995 Halling (USA)
1994 Ezzoud (IRE)
1993 Opera House
1992 Kooyonga (IRE)
1991 Environment Friend
1990 Elmaamul (USA)
1989 Nashwan (USA)

JULY CUP

1998 Elnadim (USA)
1997 Compton Place
1996 Anabaa (USA)
1995 Lake Coniston (IRE)
1994 Owington
1993 Hamas (IRE)
1992 Mr Brooks
1991 Polish Patriot (USA)
1990 Royal Academy (USA)
1989 Cadeaux Genereux

GOLD CUP

1998 Kayf Tara
1997 Celeric
1996 Classic Cliche (IRE)
1995 Double Trigger (IRE)
1994 Arcadian Heights
1993 Drum Taps (USA)
1992 Drum Taps (USA)
1991 Indian Queen
1990 Ashal
1989 Sadeem (USA)

JUDDMONTE INTERNATIONAL STAKES

1998 One So Wonderful
1997 Singspiel (IRE)
1996 Halling (USA)
1995 Halling (USA)
1994 Ezzoud (IRE)
1993 Ezzoud (IRE)
1992 Rodrigo de Triano (USA)
1991 Terimon
1990 In the Groove
1989 Ile de Chypre

ASTON UPTHORPE YORKSHIRE OAKS

1998 Catchascatchcan
1997 My Emma
1996 Key Change (IRE)
1995 Pure Grain
1994 Only Royale (IRE)
1993 Only Royale (IRE)
1992 User Friendly
1991 Magnificent Star (USA)
1990 Hellenic
1989 Roseate Tern

KING GEORGE VI & QUEEN ELIZABETH DIAMOND STAKES

1998 Swain (IRE)
1997 Swain (IRE)
1996 Pentire
1995 Lammtarra (USA)
1994 King's Theatre (IRE)
1993 Opera House
1992 St Jovite (USA)
1991 Generous (IRE)
1990 Belmez (USA)
1989 Nashwan (USA)

SUSSEX STAKES

1998 Among Men (USA)
1997 Ali-Royal (IRE)
1996 First Island (IRE)
1995 Sayyedati
1994 Distant View (USA)
1993 Bigstone (IRE)
1992 Marling (IRE)
1991 Second Set (IRE)
1990 Distant Relative
1989 Zilzal (USA)

QUEEN ELIZABETH II STAKES

1998 Desert Prince (IRE)
1997 Air Express (IRE)
1996 Mark of Esteem (IRE)
1995 Bahri (USA)
1994 Maroof (USA)
1993 Bigstone (IRE)
1992 Lahib (USA)
1991 Selkirk (USA)
1990 Markofdistinction
1989 Zilzal (USA)

NUNTHORPE STAKES

1998 Lochangel
1997 Coastal Bluff & Ya Malak (dead heat)
1996 Pivotal
1995 So Factual (USA)
1994 Piccolo (Blue Siren disq)
1993 Lochsong
1992 Lyric Fantasy (IRE)
1991 Sheikh Albadou
1990 Dayjur (USA)
1989 Cadeaux Genereux

HAYDOCK PARK SPRINT CUP

1998 Tamarisk (IRE)
1997 Royal Applause
1996 Iktamal (USA)
1995 Cherokee Rose (IRE)
1994 Lavinia Fontana (IRE)
1993 Wolfhound (USA)
1992 Sheikh Albadou
1991 Polar Falcon (USA)
1990 Dayjur (USA)
1989 Danehill (USA)

DUBAI CHAMPION STAKES

1998 Alborada
1997 Pilsudski (IRE)
1996 Bosra Sham (USA)
1995 Spectrum (IRE)
1994 Dernier Empereur (USA)
1993 Hatoof (USA)
1992 Rodrigo de Triano (USA)
1991 Tel Quel (FR)
1990 In the Groove
1989 Legal Case

ST LEGER

1998 Nedawi
1997 Silver Patriarch (IRE)
1996 Shantou (USA)
1995 Classic Cliche (IRE)
1994 Moonax (IRE)
1993 Bob's Return (IRE)
1992 User Friendly
1991 Toulon
1990 Snurge
1989 Michelozzo (USA) (at Ayr)

LOCKINGE

1998 Cape Cross (IRE)
1997 First Island (IRE)
1996 Soviet Line (IRE)
1995 Soviet Line (IRE)
1994 Emperor Jones (USA)
1993 Swing Low
1992 Selkirk (USA)
1991 Polar Falcon (USA)
1990 Safawan
1989 Most Welcome

Group Two Races

DANTE

1998 Saratoga Springs (CAN)
1997 Benny The Dip (USA)
1996 Glory of Dancer
1995 Classic Cliche (IRE)
1994 Erhaab (USA)
1993 Tenby
1992 Alnasr Alwasheek
1991 Environment Friend
1990 Sanglamore (USA)
1989 Torjoun (USA)

YORKSHIRE CUP

1998 Busy Flight
1997 Celeric
1996 Classic Cliche (IRE)
1995 Moonax (IRE)
1994 Key to My Heart (IRE)
1993 Assessor (IRE)
1992 Rock Hopper
1991 Arzanni
1990 Braashee
1989 Mountain Kingdom (USA)

QUEEN ANNE STAKES

1998 Intikhab (USA)
1997 Allied Forces (USA)
1996 Charnwood Forest (IRE)
1995 Nicolotte
1994 Barathea (IRE)
1993 Alflora (IRE)
1992 Lahib (USA)
1991 Sikeston (USA)
1990 Markofdistinction
1989 Warning

PRINCE OF WALES'S STAKES

1998 Faithful Son (USA)
1997 Bosra Sham (USA)
1996 First Island (IRE)
1995 Muhtarram (USA)
1994 Muhtarram (USA)
1993 Placerville (USA)
1992 Perpendicular
1991 Stagecraft
1990 Batshoof
1989 Two Timing (USA)

SANDOWN MILE

1998 Almushtarak (IRE)
1997 Wixim (USA)
1996 Gabr
1995 Missed Flight
1994 Penny Drops
1993 Alhijaz
1992 Rudimentary (USA)
1991 In the Groove
1990 Markofdistinction
1989 Reprimand

JOCKEY CLUB STAKES

1998 Romanov (IRE)
1997 Time Allowed
1996 Riyadian
1995 Only Royale (IRE)
1994 Silver Wisp (USA)
1993 Zinaad
1992 Sapience
1991 Rock Hopper
1990 Roseate Tern
1989 Unfuwain (USA)

RIBBLESDALE

1998 Bahr
1997 Yashmak (USA)
1996 Tulipa (USA)
1995 Phantom Gold
1994 Bolas
1993 Thawakib (IRE)
1992 Armarama
1991 Third Watch
1990 Hellenic
1989 Alydaress (USA)

HARDWICKE

1998 Posidonas
1997 Predappio
1996 Oscar Schindler (IRE)
1995 Beauchamp Hero
1994 Bobzao (IRE)
1993 Jeune
1992 Rock Hopper
1991 Rock Hopper (Topanoora disq.)
1990 Assatis (USA)
1989 Assatis (USA)

KING'S STAND

1998 Bolshoi (IRE)
1997 Don't Worry Me (IRE)
1996 Pivotal
1995 Piccolo
1994 Lochsong
1993 Elbio
1992 Sheikh Albadou
1991 Elbio
1990 Dayjur (USA)
1989 Indian Ridge

KING EDWARD VII

1998 Royal Anthem (USA)
1997 Kingfisher Mill (USA)
1996 Amfortas (IRE)
1995 Pentire
1994 Foyer
1993 Beneficial
1992 Beyton (USA)
1991 Saddlers' Hall
1990 Private Tender
1989 Cacoethes (USA)

PRINCESS OF WALES

1998 Fruits of Love (USA)
1997 Shantou (USA)
1996 Posidonas
1995 Beauchamp Hero
1994 Wagon Master (FR)
1993 Desert Team (USA)
1992 Saddlers' Hall (IRE)
1991 Rock Hopper
1990 Sapience
1989 Carroll House

NASSAU

1998 Alborada
1997 Ryafan (USA)
1996 Last Second (IRE)
1995 Caramba
1994 Hawajiss
1993 Lyphard's Delta (USA)
1992 Ruby Tiger
1991 Ruby Tiger
1990 Kartajana
1989 Mamaluna (USA)

CHALLENGE STAKES

1998 Decorated Hero
1997 Kahal
1996 Charnwood Forest (IRE)
1995 Harayir (USA)
1994 Zieten (USA)
1993 Catrail (USA)
1992 Selkirk (USA)
1991 Mystiko (USA)
1990 Sally Rous
1989 Distant Relative

GOODWOOD CUP

1998 Double Trigger (IRE)
1997 Double Trigger (IRE)
1996 Grey Shot
1995 Double Trigger (IRE)
1994 Tioman Island
1993 Sonus (IRE)
1992 Further Flight
1991 Further Flight
1990 Lucky Moon
1989 Mazzacano

GREAT VOLTIGEUR

1998 Sea Wave (IRE)
1997 Stowaway
1996 Dushyantor (USA)
1995 Pentire
1994 Sacrament
1993 Bob's Return (IRE)
1992 Bonny Scot (IRE)
1991 Corrupt (USA)
1990 Belmez (USA)
1989 Zalazl (USA)

FALMOUTH

1998 Lovers Knot
1997 Ryafan (USA)
1996 Sensation
1995 Caramba
1994 Lemon Souffle
1993 Niche
1992 Gussy Marlowe
1991 Only Yours
1990 Chimes of Freedom (USA)
1989 Magic Gleam (USA)

CELEBRATION MILE STAKES

1998 Muhtathir
1997 Among Men (USA) (Cape Cross disq.)
1996 Mark of Esteem (IRE)
1995 Harayir (USA)
1994 Mehthaaf (USA)
1993 Swing Low
1992 Selkirk (USA)
1991 Bold Russian
1990 Shavian
1989 Distant Relative

DIADEM

1998 Bianconi (USA)
1997 Elnadim (USA)
1996 Diffident (FR)
1995 Cool Jazz
1994 Lake Coniston (IRE)
1993 Catrail (USA)
1992 Wolfhound (USA)
1991 Shalford (IRE)
1990 Ron's Victory (USA)
1989 Chummy's Favourite

SUN CHARIOT

1998 Kissogram
1997 One So Wonderful
1996 Last Second (IRE)
1995 Warning Shadows (IRE)
1994 La Confederation
1993 Talented
1992 Red Slippers (USA)
1991 Ristna
1990 Kartajana
1989 Braiswick

GEOFFREY FREER

1998 Multicoloured (IRE)
1997 Dushyantor (USA)
1996 Phantom Gold
1995 Presenting
1994 Red Route
1993 Azzilfi
1992 Shambo
1991 Drum Taps (USA)
1990 Charmer
1989 Ibn Bey

TEMPLE STAKES

1998 Bolshoi (IRE)
1997 Croft Pool
1996 Mind Games
1995 Mind Games
1994 Lochsong
1993 Paris House
1992 Snaadee (USA)
1991 Elbio
1990 Dayjur (USA)
1989 Dancing Dissident (USA)

Top Two-Year-Old Races

MIDDLE PARK STAKES

1998 Lujain (USA)
1997 Hayil (USA)
1996 Bahamian Bounty
1995 Royal Applause
1994 Fard (IRE)
1993 First Trump
1992 Zieten (USA)
1991 Rodrigo de Triano (USA)
1990 Lycius (USA)
1989 Balla Cove

DEWHURST STAKES

1998 Mujahid (USA)
1997 Xaar
1996 In Command (IRE)
1995 Alhaarth (IRE)
1994 Pennekamp (USA)
1993 Grand Lodge (USA)
1992 Zafonic (USA)
1991 Dr Devious (IRE)
1990 Generous (IRE)
1989 Dashing Blade

FILLIES' MILE

1998 Sunspangled (IRE)
1997 Glorosia (FR)
1996 Reams of Verse (USA)
1995 Bosra Sham (USA)
1994 Aqaarid (USA)
1993 Fairy Heights (IRE)
1992 Ivanka (IRE)
1991 Culture Vulture (USA)
1990 Shamshir
1989 Silk Slippers (USA)

RACING POST TROPHY

1998 Commander Collins (IRE)
1997 Saratoga Springs (CAN)
1996 Medaaly
1995 Beauchamp King
1994 Celtic Swing
1993 King's Theatre (IRE)
1992 Armiger
1991 Seattle Rhyme (USA)
1990 Peter Davies (USA)
1989 Be My Chief (USA) (at Newcastle)

CHEVELEY PARK STAKES

1998 Wannabe Grand (IRE)
1997 Embassy
1996 Pas De Reponse (USA)
1995 Blue Duster (USA)
1994 Gay Gallanta (USA)
1993 Prophecy (IRE)
1992 Sayyedati
1991 Marling (IRE)
1990 Capricciosa (IRE)
1989 Dead Certain

COVENTRY STAKES

1998 Red Sea
1997 Harbour Master (FR)
1996 Verglas (IRE)
1995 Royal Applause
1994 Sri Pekan (USA)
1993 Stonehatch (USA)
1992 Petardia
1991 Dilum (USA)
1990 Mac's Imp (USA)
1989 Rock City

GIMCRACK

1998 Josr Algarhoud (IRE)
1997 Carrowkeel (IRE)
1996 Abou Zouz (USA)
1995 Royal Applause
1994 Chilly Billy
1993 Turtle Island (IRE)
1992 Splendent (USA)
1991 River Falls
1990 Mujtahid (USA)
1989 Rock City

SOLARIO

1998 Raise A Grand (IRE)
1997 Little Indian
1996 Brave Act
1995 Alhaarth (IRE)
1994 Lovely Millie (IRE)
1993 Island Magic
1992 White Crown (USA)
1991 Chicmond (IRE)
1990 Radwell
1989 Be My Chief (USA)

QUEEN MARY

1998 Bint Allayl
1997 Nadwah (USA)
1996 Dance Parade (USA)
1995 Blue Duster (USA)
1994 Gay Gallanta (USA)
1993 Risky
1992 Lyric Fantasy (IRE)
1991 Marling (IRE)
1990 On Tiptoes
1989 Dead Certain

NORFOLK

1998 Rosselli (USA)
1997 Tippitt Boy
1996 Tipsy Creek (USA)
1995 Lucky Lionel (USA)
1994 Mind Games
1993 Turtle Island (IRE)
1992 Niche
1991 Magic Ring (IRE)
1990 Line Engaged (USA)
1989 Petillante

CHERRY HINTON

1998 Wannabe Grand (IRE)
1997 Asfurah (USA)
1996 Dazzle
1995 Applaud (USA)
1994 Red Carnival (USA)
1993 Lemon Souffle
1992 Sayyedati
1991 Musicale (USA)
1990 Chicarica (USA)
1989 Chimes of Freedom (USA)

CHAMPAGNE VINTAGE

1998 Aljabr (USA)
1997 Central Park (IRE)
1996 Putra (USA)
1995 Alhaarth (IRE)
1994 Eltish (USA)
1993 Mister Baileys
1992 Maroof (USA)
1991 Dr Devious (IRE)
1990 Mukaddamah (USA)
1989 Be My Chief (USA)

ROYAL LODGE

1998 Mutaahab (CAN)
1997 Teapot Row (IRE)
1996 Benny The Dip (USA)
1995 Mons
1994 Eltish (USA)
1993 Mister Baileys
1992 Desert Secret (IRE)
1991 Made of Gold (USA)
1990 Mujaazif (USA)
1989 Digression (USA)

RICHMOND

1998 Muqtarib (USA)
1997 Daggers Drawn (USA)
1996 Easycall
1995 Polaris Flight (USA)
1994 Sri Pekan (USA)
1993 First Trump
1992 Son Pardo
1991 Dilum (USA)
1990 Mac's Imp (USA)
1989 Contract Law (USA)

MILL REEF

1998 Golden Silca
1997 Arkadian Hero (USA)
1996 Indian Rocket
1995 Kahir Almaydan (IRE)
1994 Princely Hush (IRE)
1993 Polish Laughter (USA)
1992 Forest Wind (USA)
1991 Showbrook (IRE)
1990 Time Gentlemen
1989 Welney

LOWTHER

1998 Bint Allayl
1997 Cape Verdi (IRE)
1996 Bianca Nera
1995 Dance Sequence (USA)
1994 Harayir (USA)
1993 Velvet Moon (IRE)
1992 Niche
1991 Culture Vulture (USA)
1990 Only Yours
1989 Dead Certain

FLYING CHILDERS

1998 Sheer Viking (IRE)
1997 Land of Dreams
1996 Easycall
1995 Cayman Kai (IRE)
1994 Raah Algharb (USA)
1993 Imperial Bailiwick (IRE)
1992 Poker Chip
1991 Paris House
1990 Distinctly North (USA)
1989 ABANDONED

CHAMPAGNE STAKES

1998 Auction House (USA)
1997 Daggers Drawn (USA)
1996 Bahhare (USA)
1995 Alhaarth (IRE)
1994 Sri Pekan
1993 Unblest
1992 Petardia
1991 Rodrigo de Triano (USA)
1990 Bog Trotter (USA)
1989 ABANDONED

Major Handicaps

LINCOLN

1998 Hunters of Brora (IRE)
1997 Kuala Lipis (USA)
1996 Stone Ridge (IRE)
1995 Roving Minstrel
1994 Our Rita
1993 High Premium
1992 High Low (USA)
1991 Amenable
1990 Evichstar
1989 Fact Finder

EBOR

1998 Tuning
1997 Far Ahead
1996 Clerkenwell (USA)
1995 Sanmartino (IRE)
1994 Hasten to Add (USA)
1993 Sarawat
1992 Quick Ransom
1991 Deposki
1990 Further Flight
1989 Sapience

AYR GOLD CUP

1998 Always Alight
1997 Wildwood Flower
1996 Coastal Bluff
1995 Royale Figurine (IRE)
1994 Daring Destiny
1993 Hard to Figure
1992 Lochsong
1991 Sarcita
1990 Final Shot
1989 Joveworth

CAMBRIDGESHIRE

1998 Lear Spear (USA)
1997 Pasternak
1996 Clifton Fox
1995 Cap Juluca (IRE)
1994 Halling (USA)
1993 Penny Drops
1992 Rambo's Hall
1991 Mellottie
1990 Risen Moon
1989 Rambo's Hall

CESAREWITCH

1998 Spirit of Love (USA)
1997 Turnpole (IRE)
1996 Inchcailloch (IRE)
1995 Old Red (IRE)
1994 Captain's Guest
1993 Aahsaylad
1992 Vintage Crop
1991 Go South
1990 Trainglot
1989 Double Dutch

ROYAL HUNT CUP

1998 Refuse To Lose
1997 Red Robbo (CAN)
1996 Yeast
1995 Realities (USA)
1994 Face North (IRE)
1993 Imperial Ballet (IRE)
1992 Colour Sergeant
1991 Eurolink the Lad
1990 Pontenuovo
1989 True Panache (USA)

WOKINGHAM

1998 Selhurstpark Flyer (IRE)
1997 Selhurstpark Flyer (IRE)
1996 Emerging Market
1995 Astrac (IRE)
1994 Venture Capitalist
1993 Nagida
1992 Red Rosein
1991 Amigo Menor
1990 Knight of Mercy
1989 Mac's Fighter

HONG KONG TROPHY

1998 Yavana's Pace
1997 Hawksley Hill (IRE)
1996 Sheer Danzig (IRE)
1995 Yoush (IRE)
1994 Knowth (IRE)
1993 Smarginato (IRE)
1992 Fire Top
1991 You Know the Rules
1990 Bold Fox
1989 Unknown Quantity

STEWARDS' CUP

1998 Superior Premium
1997 Danetime (IRE)
1996 Coastal Bluff
1995 Shikari's Son
1994 For the Present
1993 King's Signet (USA)
1992 Lochsong
1991 Notley
1990 Knight of Mercy
1989 Very Adjacent

NORTHUMBERLAND PLATE

1998 Cyrian (IRE)
1997 Windsor Castle
1996 Celeric
1995 Bold Gait
1994 Quick Ransom
1993 Highflying
1992 Witness Box (USA)
1991 Tamarpour (USA)
1990 Al Maheb (USA)
1989 Orpheus (USA)

WILLIAM HILL MILE

1998 For Your Eyes Only
1997 Fly To The Stars
1996 Moscow Mist (IRE)
1995 Khayrapour (IRE)
1994 Fraam
1993 Philidor
1992 Little Bean
1991 Sky Cloud
1990 March Bird
1989 Safawan

JOHN SMITH'S CUP

1998 Porto Foricos (USA)
1997 Pasternak
1996 Wilcuma
1995 Naked Welcome
1994 Cezanne
1993 Baron Ferdinand
1992 Mr Confusion (IRE)
1991 Halkopous
1990 Eradicate
1989 Icona (USA)

STAMINA OF SIRES' PROGENY

The following table gives the average distance in furlongs of races won at three-year-old and upwards by the progeny of the stallions named for the period 1990-1998. The mean average distance is the figure shown immediately after the stallion's name. The following two figures are the shortest and longest distances at which a sire's progeny were successful during the period 9/11/97 - 7/11/98.

A

Absalom	7.1f	6.0	8.2
Accordion	10f	10.0	13.1
Affirmed (USA)	10.3f	9.2	12.0
Akarad (FR)	9.9f	7.6	10.2
Al Hareb (USA)	9.4f	7.0	9.0
Al Nasr (FR)	9.8f	5.0	11.9
Alhijaz	7.5f	6.0	10.1
Alleged (USA)	11.7f	8.0	16.0
Alleging (USA)	8.8f	6.0	16.2
Alnasr Alwasheek	9.4f	7.0	12.1
Alwasmi (USA)	12.8f	14.1	14.1
Always Fair (USA)	14f	6.5	6.5
Alydeed (CAN)	8f	8.0	8.0
Alzao (USA)	9.7f	6.0	16.5
Anita's Prince	6f	5.0	8.1
Anshan	8.3f	5.0	16.2
Apalachee	8.8f	9.0	9.0
Aragon	7.7f	5.0	12.1
Arazi (USA)	9.2f	7.0	14.0
Arcane (USA)	11.5f	12.0	12.0
Archway (IRE)	8.7f	7.0	12.0
Arctic Tern (USA)	12.2f	11.9	12.0
Ardar	9.5f	10.0	12.0
Ardkinglass	5f	5.0	5.0
Ardross	12.5f	12.0	12.0
Arkan	9.7f	12.4	12.4
Astronef	8.3f	5.0	6.1

B

Bairn (USA)	9.4f	7.0	8.5
Balidar	6.6f	6.1	6.1
Ballad Rock	7.1f	5.0	10.0
Batshoof	9.2f	6.0	17.1
Bay Express	7.1f	9.4	10.0
Be My Chief (USA)	10.2f	6.0	16.0
Be My Guest (USA)	10.2f	8.0	14.0
Be My Native (USA)	11.1f	9.5	16.0
Beldale Flutter (USA)	10.2f	16.0	16.4
Belmez (USA)	11.5f	9.9	10.0
Bering	9.7f	7.1	12.0
Beveled (USA)	6.8f	5.0	12.3
Big Shuffle (USA)	6.3f	6.0	6.5
Bikala	12.1f	12.0	12.0
Black Tie Affair	10.5f	10.0	10.0
Blakeney	11.9f	12.0	13.8
Bluebird (USA)	7.9f	5.9	14.6
Blushing Groom (FR)	10.2f	11.9	16.0
Blushing John (USA)	8.9f	6.0	13.0
Bob Back (USA)	11.5f	8.0	8.0
Bold Arrangement	8.7f	5.0	14.1
Bold Owl	9.7f	8.0	8.0
Brief Truce (USA)	9.1f	5.0	14.1
Broken Hearted	10.1f	6.0	10.0
Burslem	9.4f	10.0	10.0
Bustino	11f	12.0	14.0
Buzzards Bay	8.9f	6.1	6.1

C

Cadeaux Genereux	7.9f	5.0	12.0
Caerleon (USA)	10.9f	7.0	16.4
Cahill Road (USA)	7f	10.0	10.0
Cannonade (USA)	9.9f	10.0	10.0
Capote (USA)	8.9f	7.0	12.3
Carmelite House (USA)	8.2f	10.0	10.0
Case Law	6f	6.0	6.0
Casteddu	7.1f	5.1	11.0
Charmer	9f	9.0	14.0
Chief Singer	8.6f	5.0	5.0
Chief's Crown (USA)	10.2f	8.0	14.0
Chilibang	7f	5.7	16.0
Clantime	6.5f	5.0	12.0
Classic Music (USA)	7.2f	5.0	6.0
Classic Secret (USA)	8.8f	6.0	9.2
Clever Trick (USA)	7.5f	7.0	8.3
Colmore Row	8f	12.0	12.0
Commanche Run	10.3f	16.0	16.0
Common Grounds	8.2f	5.0	12.0
Conquering Hero (USA)	10.3f	10.0	13.0
Conquistador Cielo	9.8f	10.0	10.0
Contract Law (USA)	8.8f	5.0	16.0
Cozzene (USA)	10.1f	10.0	10.0
Cree Song	6.9f	8.0	8.1
Cricket Ball (USA)	7.9f	5.0	6.0
Crowning Honors (CAN)	10.1f	9.0	10.1
Crystal Glitters (USA)	8f	17.2	17.2
Cyrano de Bergerac	7.3f	5.0	17.2

D

Damister (USA)	9.1f	6.0	12.1
Dance of Life (USA)	9.3f	12.0	12.0
Dancing Brave (USA)	10.4f	8.0	8.0
Dancing Dissident (USA)	6.9f	5.0	7.0
Danehill (USA)	8.8f	6.0	16.2
Danzatore (CAN)	9f	6.0	6.0
Danzig (USA)	8.2f	5.0	10.0
Danzig Connection (USA)	8.2f	10.0	10.0
Daring March	9f	6.0	6.0
Darshaan	11.7f	8.5	17.2
Dashing Blade	7.9f	8.0	10.0
Dayjur (USA)	6.9f	5.0	9.4
Deploy	11.4f	6.9	12.3
Deputy Minister (CAN)	9.2f	10.0	12.0
Desse Zenny (USA)	12f	12.1	12.1
Devil's Bag (USA)	9.3f	7.0	8.0
Diamond Prospect (USA)	8f	8.0	12.4
Diamond Shoal	10f	8.0	10.5
Diesis	9f	7.0	12.0
Digamist (USA)	8.8f	7.0	10.0
Dilum (USA)	7.1f	7.1	7.1
Distant Relative	7f	5.0	10.1
Distinctive Pro (USA)	8f	8.0	8.0
Distinctly North (USA)	7.5f	7.0	10.0
Dixieland Band (USA)	10.1f	6.5	10.0
Dominion	8.9f	5.0	10.8

Dominion Royale	7.8f	5.0	16.0
Domynsky	8f	5.0	12.3
Don't Forget Me	9.6f	5.0	14.1
Double Bed	13.9f	8.0	8.0
Double Schwartz	7f	6.0	7.0
Doulab (USA)	7.4f	5.0	11.7
Dowsing (USA)	7f	5.0	10.0
Doyoun	10.7f	9.4	12.0
Dr Devious (IRE)	9.9f	9.9	9.9
Drumalis	8.8f	12.0	12.0
Dunbeath (USA)	9.8f	10.1	14.0
Durandal	6f	6.0	6.0
Durgam (USA)	12.3f	6.0	16.0
Dynaformer (USA)	10f	9.0	16.0

E

Efisio	7.6f	5.0	17.1
El Gran Senor (USA)	9f	7.0	10.4
Ela-Mana-Mou	12.6f	9.4	18.0
Elbio	9f	8.0	10.0
Elmaamul (USA)	8.2f	5.0	14.1
Emarati (USA)	6.7f	5.0	12.0
Emperor Fountain	9.9f	10.0	10.0
Environment Friend	7.3f	5.9	8.0
Eskimo (USA)	8.2f	8.0	8.0
Exactly Sharp (USA)	8.5f	7.0	8.0
Executive Man	8.6f	10.0	10.0
Exit To Nowhere (USA)	8.7f	8.0	10.1

F

Fairy King (USA)	7.7f	5.0	16.0
Faustus (USA)	9.1f	7.0	17.2
Fayruz	6.6f	5.0	13.0
Fighting Fit (USA)	7.9f	8.0	8.0
Flockton's Own	7f	7.0	7.0
Flying Tyke	6.3f	10.0	10.0
Fools Holme (USA)	10.3f	7.0	12.0
Formidable (USA)	7.8f	6.0	14.0
Forzando	7.3f	5.0	8.0

G

Gabitat	8.5f	10.0	10.0
Geiger Counter (USA)	7.9f	5.0	8.0
General Holme (USA)	5.7f	15.5	15.5
Generous (IRE)	11.4f	8.0	15.0
Gilded Time (USA)	7f	6.0	8.0
Glenstal (USA)	10f	10.0	10.0
Glow (USA)	10.2f	11.0	12.0
Gold Legend (USA)	8f	8.0	8.0
Golden Heights	7.1f	8.0	8.3
Gone West (USA)	7.9f	6.0	16.0
Good Thyne (USA)	11.8f	11.8	11.8
Goofalik (USA)	16f	12.0	16.0
Governor General	6.8f	5.0	5.0
Great Commotion (USA)	8.7f	8.0	12.0
Green Dancer (USA)	11.9f	8.0	16.0
Green Desert (USA)	7.9f	5.0	12.0
Green Forest (USA)	7.5f	6.0	9.9
Green Ruby (USA)	6.9f	5.0	6.0
Grey Dawn II	6.8f	6.0	7.0
Grey Desire	9.4f	6.0	7.9
Groom Dancer (USA)	9.5f	7.0	12.0
Gulch (USA)	9.7f	7.1	9.9
Gunner B	11.2f	11.0	12.1

H

Hadeer	8.9f	6.0	14.0
Hallgate	6.8f	12.0	12.0
Handsome Sailor	6.6f	6.0	6.1
Hansel (USA)	12.6f	12.0	12.0
Hard Fought	8.8f	8.0	12.1
Hector Protector (USA)	9f	9.0	12.0
Heights of Gold	11.2f	10.0	10.0
Henbit (USA)	10.2f	11.5	11.5
Heraldiste (USA)	8.9f	10.0	10.0
Hermitage (USA)	9f	7.0	8.0
Hero's Honor (USA)	9f	10.0	10.0
High Estate	10.6f	5.9	14.9
High Kicker (USA)	8.4f	7.0	8.0
High Top	11f	12.0	12.0
Highest Honor	10.9f	7.0	14.9
Horage	11.4f	7.0	16.2
Houmayoun (FR)	7.1f	7.0	7.1
Housebuster (USA)	7f	7.0	8.0
Hubbly Bubbly (USA)	9.5f	8.0	16.0

I

Imp Society (USA)	7.1f	5.0	11.0
Imperial Falcon (CAN)	9.1f	9.4	12.0
Imperial Frontier (USA)	7f	5.0	10.8
In The Wings	11.3f	7.0	14.4
Inca Chief (USA)	5.6f	8.5	8.5
Inchinor	6.9f	6.0	17.5
Indian Ridge	7.7f	5.0	12.0
Interrex (CAN)	7.8f	5.0	14.1
Irish River (FR)	8.9f	8.0	11.9
Irish Tower (USA)	7.3f	10.0	10.0

J

Jade Hunter (USA)	9f	10.0	13.3
Jalmood (USA)	11.1f	8.0	8.0
Java Gold (USA)	9.1f	10.0	10.8
Joli Wasfi (USA)	12f	11.5	12.0
Jupiter Island	10.3f	9.4	16.2

K

K-Battery	12.4f	14.0	16.0
Kahyasi	12.8f	8.0	16.1
Kala Shikari	6.1f	5.0	5.0
Kalaglow	11.2f	8.0	16.0
Kaldoun (FR)	9.9f	8.0	11.0
Keen	10.8f	7.0	17.2
Kefaah (USA)	11.2f	10.0	16.0
Kendor	12.2f	8.0	14.0
Kenmare (FR)	9.7f	5.0	12.3
Kind of Hush	9.6f	11.0	14.0
King of Clubs	9.3f	9.7	12.0
King's Signet (USA)	7f	7.0	8.0
Kingmambo (USA)	9.5f	7.1	14.0
Known Fact (USA)	8.2f	7.0	10.1
Komaite (USA)	6.9f	5.0	10.0
Konigsstuhl	9f	8.5	14.0
Kris	10f	5.0	13.0
Kris S (USA)	9.3f	8.0	10.0
Kylian (USA)	8.2f	6.1	10.2

L

Lahib (USA)	7.9f	7.0	10.0
Lashkari	13.1f	16.2	16.2
Last Tycoon	9.5f	6.0	12.0
Latest Model	5.4f	5.1	5.1

Law Society (USA)	11.7f	7.0	21.6
Lead on Time (USA)	7.5f	6.0	12.0
Lear Fan (USA)	10.5f	8.0	15.5
Legend of France (USA)	11.4f	14.1	14.1
Lesotho (USA)	6f	6.0	6.0
Liboi (USA)	11.7f	10.0	10.0
Librate	10.4f	8.0	10.2
Lighter	9.5f	10.0	10.0
Linamix (FR)	8.2f	8.2	12.0
Lion Cavern (USA)	7.4f	7.0	8.1
Lochnager	6.9f	6.0	7.0
Lomond (USA)	9.8f	16.0	16.0
Longleat (USA)	7.2f	5.1	6.0
Lord At War (ARG)	6.1f	8.1	8.1
Lord Bud	8.2f	11.0	11.0
Lugana Beach	6.9f	6.0	8.5
Lycius (USA)	9f	5.0	13.0
Lyphard (USA)	10.6f	8.5	14.0

M

Mac's Imp (USA)	5.6f	5.0	6.0
Machiavellian (USA)	9.6f	7.0	20.0
Maelstrom Lake	8.9f	8.0	8.5
Magic Ring (IRE)	6.6f	5.0	8.1
Magical Wonder (USA)	7.1f	8.0	8.0
Man Among Men (IRE)	8f	8.0	8.0
Manila (USA)	10f	8.0	8.0
Mansooj	11f	7.0	7.0
Marching On	5.7f	5.0	5.0
Marju (IRE)	9.4f	7.0	16.2
Master Willie	9.2f	7.5	9.0
Masterclass (USA)	6f	5.0	7.0
Mazaad	8.5f	5.0	8.1
Mazilier (USA)	8.6f	6.9	12.0
Midyan (USA)	9.9f	5.0	16.0
Mining (USA)	7.8f	7.0	12.0
Minshaanshu Amad (USA)	11.5f	10.0	10.0
Minster Son	10.9f	10.0	10.0
Mister Majestic	10f	9.2	9.2
Miswaki (USA)	8.1f	7.0	10.0
Moment of Hope (USA)	6.9f	6.0	7.0
Mon Tresor	7.6f	6.0	16.0
Most Welcome	8.5f	5.0	16.0
Mr Prospector (USA)	8.5f	9.0	12.0
Mt Livermore (USA)	7.7f	6.0	6.0
Mtoto	11.5f	7.0	16.0
Mujadil (USA)	7.3f	5.0	12.4
Mujtahid (USA)	7.4f	5.0	8.0
Mukaddamah (USA)	8f	5.0	11.9
Music Boy	6.5f	10.0	10.0
Mystiko (USA)	7.6f	5.0	10.0

N

Nabeel Dancer (USA)	6.1f	5.5	6.0
Naevus (USA)	7.2f	7.0	7.0
Nashamaa	8f	8.0	12.0
Nashwan (USA)	10.1f	7.0	18.7
Neshad (USA)	5.5f	5.0	5.0
Never So Bold	7f	5.0	10.0
New Express	6.8f	7.0	8.0
Nicholas (USA)	6.1f	5.0	6.1
Night Shift (USA)	8.2f	5.0	16.0
Niniski (USA)	13f	10.0	20.0
Nishapour (FR)	11.1f	7.1	7.1
Noble Patriarch	11.3f	7.0	15.8
Nomination	7.3f	5.0	11.0
Nordance (USA)	7.4f	9.2	9.2
Nordico (USA)	8.1f	6.0	13.8
North Briton	8.2f	7.0	8.2
Northern Park (USA)	10f	10.0	10.0
Northern State (USA)	12.3f	18.0	18.0
Northiam (USA)	6f	6.0	6.0
Northjet	14.1f	12.1	16.0
Nureyev (USA)	8.3f	7.0	12.5

O

Ogygian (USA)	6.6f	8.0	8.0
Old Vic	12.9f	10.0	16.1
Orchestra	7.4f	8.0	10.5

P

Paris House	5.9f	5.0	7.0
Pennine Walk	8.9f	8.1	12.0
Persian Bold	9.9f	7.0	16.4
Persian Heights	10.4f	7.1	16.4
Petardia	7.3f	5.0	12.0
Petong	7.6f	5.0	12.0
Petorius	7.9f	5.0	12.1
Petoski	10.4f	8.0	14.8
Pharly (FR)	11.5f	8.0	14.1
Phone Trick (USA)	7f	7.0	7.0
Phountzi (USA)	9.6f	8.0	10.8
Picea	12.7f	8.0	8.0
Pips Pride	6.6f	5.0	10.0
Pleasant Colony (USA)	12.4f	14.0	14.0
Plugged Nickle (USA)	7.4f	8.0	8.0
Polar Falcon (USA)	9f	6.0	12.0
Polish Patriot (USA)	7.7f	5.0	12.0
Polish Precedent (USA)	9f	6.0	12.0
Posen (USA)	8.6f	8.0	8.1
Precious Metal	9.3f	10.1	10.9
Precocious	7.2f	6.0	10.0
Presidium	7.5f	5.0	16.2
Primo Dominie	7.2f	5.0	10.8
Prince Daniel (USA)	11f	9.0	16.2
Prince Rupert (FR)	10.6f	8.0	8.0
Prince Sabo	6.6f	5.0	12.0
Priolo (USA)	10.4f	10.0	15.4
Private Account (USA)	10.1f	10.0	12.5
Project Manager	7.2f	7.0	7.0
Puissance	7.1f	6.0	12.0
Pursuit of Love	9.5f	5.0	15.8

Q

Quiet American		7.5	10.0

R

Rahy (USA)	9.5f	6.0	16.2
Rainbow Quest (USA)	11.2f	7.0	16.0
Rainbows For Life (CAN)	9.8f	6.0	14.0
Raise A Man (USA)	7.3f	7.0	7.0
Rambo Dancer (CAN)	8.4f	5.7	14.1
Rare Performer (USA)	7.6f	8.0	8.0
Red Ransom (USA)	8.6f	7.0	12.0
Red Sunset	9f	6.9	8.3
Relief Pitcher	8f	7.0	8.0
Reprimand	8.1f	6.0	16.0
Respect	6f	5.0	6.0
Rich Charlie	5.9f	6.0	8.0
Risk Me (FR)	8.1f	5.0	12.0
River Falls	8.1f	6.0	10.0
River God (USA)	6f	6.0	6.1
Riverman (USA)	9.7f	6.0	12.0
Robellino (USA)	9.5f	5.0	12.5
Robin Des Pins (USA)	8f	8.0	8.0
Rock City	8.9f	5.0	12.5
Rock Hopper	10.3f	8.0	15.0

Rocky Marriage (USA)	6.6f	6.0	6.0
Roi Danzig (USA)	10.3f	6.0	16.1
Rolfe (USA)	10.6f	10.0	13.8
Ron's Victory (USA)	9.3f	7.9	12.5
Rousillon (USA)	10.4f	8.0	16.0
Rubiano (USA)	7.1f	7.0	7.0
Rudimentary (USA)	7.8f	5.0	12.0
Runaway Groom (CAN)	8.3f	5.0	6.0
Rusticaro (FR)	11.3f	8.0	11.0
Rymer	7.1f	7.0	7.0

S

Sabrehill (USA)	8.3f	7.0	10.2
Saddlers' Hall (IRE)	10.4f	6.0	12.5
Sadler's Wells (USA)	11.3f	8.0	20.0
Safawan	6.4f	5.0	15.8
Salse (USA)	10.8f	6.0	16.1
Salt Dome (USA)	6.5f	5.0	8.5
Sanglamore (USA)	13.1f	9.9	16.0
Saratoga Six (USA)	8.5f	9.2	9.2
Satco (FR)	14.2f	18.0	18.0
Saumarez	15.1f	10.0	13.4
Savahra Sound	7.9f	7.1	7.1
Sayf El Arab (USA)	8.2f	7.0	12.0
Scallywag	15f	12.0	16.2
Scenic	10.3f	8.0	14.0
Second Set (IRE)	8f	6.0	12.1
Secreto (USA)	9.9f	11.5	11.9
Seeking the Gold (USA)	7.4f	6.0	6.5
Selkirk (USA)	7.9f	5.0	12.4
Seymour Hicks (FR)	9.6f	12.0	12.0
Shaadi (USA)	8.1f	6.0	12.0
Shadeed (USA)	7.6f	6.0	10.0
Shalford	7.6f	5.1	14.8
Shardari	12.1f	8.0	8.0
Shareef Dancer (USA)	10.1f	6.0	17.2
Sharp Victor (USA)	10f	8.0	14.0
Sharpo	7.5f	5.0	9.0
Sharrood (USA)	10.9f	6.0	18.0
Shavian	7.7f	5.0	14.1
Sheikh Albadou	8.8f	8.0	12.4
Shernazar	11.9f	8.2	16.2
Shirley Heights	12.1f	6.0	15.0
Shy Groom (USA)	8.2f	8.5	8.5
Siberian Express (USA)	9f	5.0	5.0
Silly Prices	6.8f	8.3	8.3
Silver Hawk (USA)	10.9f	8.0	18.2
Silver Kite (USA)	10.2f	8.0	12.0
Simply Great (FR)	11.9f	6.0	12.1
Simply Majestic (USA)	7.8f	7.6	7.6
Sizzling Melody	6.3f	6.0	8.0
Slew O' Gold (USA)	10f	10.0	12.0
Slip Anchor	12.7f	8.0	18.0
Smile (USA)	9.8f	8.0	8.0
Song	6.4f	8.0	8.0
Songlines (FR)	5f	5.0	5.0
Sovereign Dancer (USA)	9.6f	8.0	8.0
Soviet Lad (USA)	9.3f	6.1	11.5
Soviet Star (USA)	8.7f	7.0	10.4
St Jovite (USA)	11.8f	11.9	17.2
Stalwart (USA)	11.8f	16.0	16.0
Star de Naskra (USA)	8.8f	9.0	9.0
Starry Night (USA)	5.2f	5.0	5.0
Statoblest	6.3f	5.0	10.8
Storm Bird (CAN)	8.5f	8.0	15.4
Storm Cat (USA)	7f	6.1	8.5
Strawberry Road (AUS)	14.5f	9.0	9.0
Suave Dancer (USA)	10.3f	6.0	14.6
Sunshine Forever (USA)	12.7f	12.0	18.0
Superlative	8.8f	5.0	13.8
Superpower	6.6f	5.0	9.3
Supreme Leader	10.9f	12.0	16.0
Sure Blade (USA)	10.6f	9.7	14.1
Sword Dance	9.4f	8.0	10.0
Sylvan Express	9.6f	13.0	13.0
Syrtos	6f	6.0	10.2

T

Tate Gallery (USA)	8.2f	12.0	12.0
Taufan (USA)	8.3f	6.0	16.0
Teamster	10.8f	12.0	12.0
Teenoso (USA)	10.5f	12.0	12.0
Tejano (USA)	6.5f	6.0	12.0
Tenby	9.5f	8.0	12.0
Terimon	8.9f	8.0	16.2
Thatching	7.8f	5.0	11.6
Theatrical	11.4f	9.0	12.0
Theatrical Charmer	10.9f	9.0	12.3
Then Again	7.4f	7.0	12.0
Thethingaboutitis (USA)	16.2f	15.9	16.2
Thowra (FR)	11.2f	8.0	8.0
Timeless Times (USA)	6.1f	5.0	7.0
Tina's Pet	7.3f	5.0	12.1
Tirol	8f	6.0	14.1
Top Ville	11f	12.0	12.0
Topanoora	8.3f	8.0	8.0
Touch of Grey	7.9f	5.0	12.0
Tragic Role (USA)	9.5f	5.9	11.9
Treasure Kay	6.5f	6.0	7.0
Trempolino (USA)	11.6f	10.0	18.0
Try My Best (USA)	7.8f	5.0	10.0

U

Uncle Pokey	9.6f	14.0	16.0
Unfuwain (USA)	11.4f	6.0	22.2

V

Village Star (FR)	5.7f	5.0	8.1
Vin St Benet	11.4f	12.3	12.3
Vision (USA)	10.4f	12.0	13.0

W

Waajib	8.9f	7.1	10.5
Warning	8.1f	5.0	12.5
Warrshan (USA)	9.7f	6.0	14.8
Weldnaas (USA)	8.5f	5.0	12.0
Well Decorated (USA)	6.3f	5.0	5.0
Welsh Captain	7.2f	8.0	8.0
With Approval (CAN)	8.9f	7.0	9.0
Wolfhound (USA)	7.5f	6.0	8.3
Woodman (USA)	9.7f	7.0	13.0

Y

Young Senor (USA)	8f	8.0	8.0

Z

Zafonic (USA)	9f	7.0	11.5
Ziggy's Boy (USA)	6.1f	6.0	6.0
Zilzal (USA)	8.6f	7.0	10.0

Computer Raceform

The Official Computer Form-Book

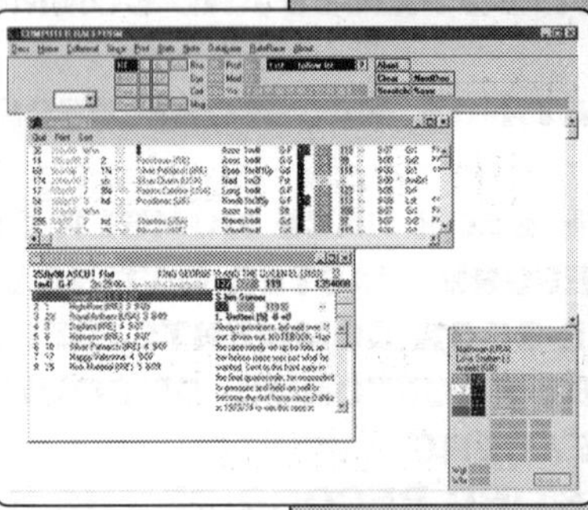

- **Clear, Concise Screens**
- **The Best Race Comments**
- **Easy-to-Use Point and Click Simplicity**
- **Quality Raceform Ratings**
- **Race Analysis and Profile Against Each horse in a Race**
- **Database and Systems Analyser**
- **Full Irish results**

No wonder the professionals all use Computer Raceform!

Ring now for our brochure and/or demonstration disk

(24-hour answering)

01635 578080

Taking you into the future with confidence

Compton, Newbury, Berkshire, RG20 6NL, UK
Tel: 01635 578080 Fax: 01635 578101